Who's Who in America®

Who's Who in America®

2020

MARQUIS Who's Who®

350 RXR Plaza, Uniondale, New York 11556
www.marquiswhoswho.com

Who's Who in America®

Table of Contents

Preface...VI

Key to Information..VII

In Memoriam VIII

Distinguished Listees 1

Acclaimed Listees 1431

Esteemed Listees..1635

Alphabetical Index 2635

Preface

"Who's Who in America shall endeavor to list those individuals who are of current national interest and inquiry either because of meritorious achievement or because of the positions they hold." — 1899

Albert Nelson Marquis
Founder

Marquis Who's Who is proud to present the 73rd edition of Who's Who in America. This 2020 compilation features over 6,100 profiles of prominent individuals representing virtually every major field of endeavor.

On the pages that follow, you will find Nobel and Pulitzer Prize winners, legendary athletes, best-selling authors, university presidents, accomplished artists, renowned entertainers, entrepreneurs and corporate executives, government and religious leaders, innovators/inventors, as well as professionals in the fields of education, law, medicine, broadcasting, publishing, information technology, and more.

As in all Marquis Who's Who biographical volumes, the individuals profiled in Who's Who in America are selected on the basis of current reference value. Factors such as position, noteworthy accomplishments, visibility, and prominence in a field are all taken into account.

Among those listed in the 73rd edition include:

- **José Andrés**, Chef and Founder of the World Central Kitchen

- **Tiffani Ashley Bell**, Founder and Executive Director of The Human Utility, Inc.

- **Safra Catz**, Chief Executive Officer of Oracle

- **George Floyd Jr.**, Security Guard whose death sparked protests and demonstrations in all 50 states and globally against police brutality and lack of social justice caused by the intersectionality of race, class and gender

- **Greta Thunberg**, Swedish Environment Activist who has gained international recognition for shedding light on the crisis arising from climate change

In an effort to further illuminate our biographical coverage we asked many of our listees to tell us in narrative form about the attributes that contributed to their success, why they chose the profession they did, and what they consider to be the highlight of their career. The result is thousands of biographies that go beyond the facts of their lives to shed additional light on what makes these inspiring individuals tick.

While the vast majority of the individuals profiled are American, also included are the biographies of select individuals from around the world whose lives have had considerable impact and influence in America.

Biographical information is gathered in a variety of manners. In most cases, we invite our biographees to submit their biographical details. In some cases, though, the information is collected by our research and editorial staffs, which use a wide assortment of tools to gather the most complete, accurate and up-to-date information available.

While the Marquis Who's Who editors exercise the utmost care in preparing each biographical sketch for publication, it is inevitable in a publication involving so many profiles that occasional errors will appear. Users of this publication are urged to notify the publisher of any issues so that adjustments can be made, which will be reflected not only in all subsequent editions but which will also be immediately displayed via Marquis Biographies Online.

All of the profiles in Who's Who in America are available on Marquis Biographies Online through a subscription. At the present time, subscribers to Marquis Biographies Online have access to all the names included in all of the Marquis Who's Who publications, as well as many new biographies that will appear in upcoming publications.

We sincerely hope that this volume will be an indispensible reference tool for you. We are always looking for ways to better serve you and welcome your ideas for improvements. In addition, we continue to welcome your Marquis Who's Who nominations.

Key to Information

DOE, JOHN ANDERSON JR., T: President **I:** Manufacturing **CN:** Doe Widget Company **DOB:** 01/01/1930 **PB:** Syracuse **SC:** NY/USA **YOP:** 2018 **PT:** John Anderson Doe Sr.; Josephine Doe **MS:** Married **SPN:** Jane (Richards) Doe (September 23, 1952) **CH:** Jeremy; Robert; Annabelle **ED:** JD, Yale University (1987); MS in Physical Science, Massachusetts Institute of Technology (1968); BA in Physics, Yale University (1950) **CT:** Certification in Widget Manufacturing, National Widget Certification Board **C:** President, Doe Widget Company (1999-2017); Vice President of Production, Roe Manufacturing, Inc. (1980-1998); Production Manager, Roe Manufacturing, Inc. (1972-1980); Postgraduate Researcher, Massachusetts Institute of Technology (1968-1972) **CR:** Vice Chairman, Syracuse Chamber of Commerce (1990-2003) **CIV:** Volunteer, American Red Cross; Fundraiser, National Audubon Society **MIL:** Lieutenant, U.S. Army (1957-1965) **CW:** "Essentials of Widget Manufacturing" (1991) **AW:** Lifetime Achievement Award, Syracuse Chamber of Commerce (2014) **MEM:** National Audubon Society; American Widget Association **BAR:** American Bar Association; New York State Bar Association **MH:** Albert Nelson Marquis Lifetime Achievement Award (2017) **AS:** He attributes his success to his father, who taught him everything he knew. **BI:** He became involved in his profession after attending a widget-making seminar in college. **HC:** A highlight of his career was overseeing the production of WIDGITEX, a revolutionary widget designing software program. **AV:** Birdwatching; Watching sports; Spending time with his family **PA:** Independent **RE:** Presbyterian **URL:** http://www.johndoewidgets.com **THT:** "Life is for living. It's better to regret something you have done than to regret something you haven't."

Key

T:	Title	**MIL:**	Military Service
I:	Industry	**CW:**	Creative Works
CN:	Company Name	**AW:**	Awards
DOB:	Date of Birth	**MEM:**	Memberships
PB:	Place of Birth	**BAR:**	Bar Admissions
SC:	State/Country of Origin	**MH:**	Marquis Who's Who Honors
YOP:	Year of Passing	**AS:**	Attribute Your Success
PT:	Parents	**BI:**	Became Involved in Your Profession
MS:	Marital Status	**HC:**	Highlight of Your Career
SPN:	Spouse Name	**AV:**	Avocations
CH:	Children	**PA:**	Political Affiliations
ED:	Education	**RE:**	Religion
CT:	Certifications	**URL:**	Website
C:	Career	**THT:**	Thoughts on Life
CR:	Career Related		
CIV:	Civic		

In Memoriam

Marquis Who's Who

dedicates this registry to the memory of the following listees:

Raymond Acker	John Gavrity	Ewell Pendergrass
Alex Alston	Ruth Bader Ginsburg	John Peterson
Lucille Arking	John Goodyear	Frances Robbins
Joan Bartolomei	William Graff	Linnea Rounds
Rudy Behlmer	Stephen Gullo	Donald Royston
Chadwick Boseman	William Hayes	Brunilda Ruiz
Frank Boyer Salisbury	George Hickenlooper	Jacob Schneps
William Brown	Katherine Hoover	Jag Singh
Kobe Bryant	Jane Hutchison	Catherine Spalding
Richard Bucy	Joseph Immel	Maria Stycos
N. Gordon Carper	William Jackson	Paul Tedesco
Ronnie Chalif	Daniel Kelly	Ival Thornton
Chia-Hwa "Lydia" Chang	Richard Lagow	Gary Trunk
Joan Chatfield	Wil Lepkowski	Frederick Wallenberger
Carl Degler	John Lewis	Thomas Ward
Brian Dennehy	Verna Linzey	Nelson Warren
Michael DiTeresa	Marvin Litvak	Warren Nelson
Ibrahim Elbarbary	Lynn Markley	Dolores Whitelaw
James Emmett	William Martin	William Wiebenga
Robert Field	Alfred Morgan	Raymond Wilder
Richard Friedman	John Morris	John Wilson
Ugo Gagliardi	John Oates	
Bernard Gauthier	Marie Otto	

DISTINGUISHED LISTEES

73rd Edition

Dawn Abell

Title: Elementary and Secondary School Educator, Administrator (Retired) **Industry:** Education/Educational Services **Date of Birth:** 09/23/1947 **Place of Birth:** Detroit **State/ Country of Origin:** MI/USA **Education:** Coursework, Converse College (2006); Coursework, Winthrop University (2004); Master of Education in School Administration and Supervision, Winthrop University, Rock Hill, SC (1980-1982); Bachelor of Arts in Art Education, Eastern Michigan University, Ypsilanti, MI (1965-1969) **Certifications:** Certification in Elementary Education, Middle Tennessee State University (1998); Certification as a Vocational Center Director, University of South Carolina (1990); Certification in Secondary Administration and Supervision, University of South Carolina, Aiken, SC (1989); Certification as a Specialist in Reading, Winthrop University (1982-1983); Educator Certificate, South Carolina State Board of Education, Certification in Elementary Education, Eastern Michigan University (1972-1978) **Career:** Retired (2009); Adult Education Instructor, Chester County School District, Chester, SC (2008-2009); Computer Lab Manager, York School District One, York, SC (2006-2008); Substitute Teacher, K - High School (2007-2008); Substitute Teacher, K - High School (2004-2005); Assistant Principal, Charlotte-Mecklenburg Schools, Sedgefield Middle School, Charlotte, NC (2001-2003); Assistant Principal for Instruction, Starmount Elementary (2000-2001); Assistant Principal, Midwood High School (1998-2000); Special Advisor to Vocational Education, Wilson County Schools (1997-1998); Administrative Assistant, Assistant Principal, Union County Schools, Monroe, SC (1996-1997); Teacher of Art, Gaston County Schools, Monroe, NC (1994-1996); Technical Preparatory Director, Teacher of Art, Gaston County Schools, Gastonia, NC (1993-1994); Curriculum Supervisor, Beaufort-Jasper Career Education Center, Ridgeland, SC (1992-1993); Vocational Coordinator, Richland County School District 1, Columbia, SC (1990-1992); Adjunct Professor, University of South Carolina, Columbia, SC (1990); Assistant Director, South Carolina Council on Vocational and Technical Education, Columbia, SC (1989-1990); District Vocational Coordinator, Aiken County Public Schools, South Carolina (1987-1989); Teacher, Cherokee County School District I, Gaffney, SC (1985-1987); Teacher of Art, Remedial Reading and Writing, Clover School District 2, South Carolina (1979-1984); Teacher First Grade Learning Improvement Center, Melvindale Northern-Allen Park, MI (1969-1979); Teacher of First Grade, Art and Learning Improvement Center, Melvindale Northern-Allen Park, MI (1969-1979) **Career Related:** Teacher, Gaston College of Interior Design (2004); Facilitator, National Career Development Teleconferencing Workshop, Dallas, NC (1994); Member, Engineering Technology Advisory Committee, Gaston College, Dallas, NC (1993); Business and Education Partnership, Gastonia, NC (1993); Member, SACS Evaluation Team, Lancaster High School and Vocational Center, Lancaster, SC (1992); Member, Five Year SACS Review Committee, Lancaster, SC (1992); Chairperson, Legislative Committee for South Carolina Vocational Special Needs Division, Columbia, SC (1991-1992); Department Chair, Eau Claire High School, Columbia, SC (1990-1992) **Creative Works:** Organizer, Creator, Focus: Special Populations 2000 Conference (1990); Author, "Noted Educator Advocated Restructure to Meet Societal and Industrial Change", National Dropout Prevention (1991); Co-author, "Job Seeking and Job Keeping", Aiken County Economic Classes; Author, "Special Needs Populations in Vocational Education", South Carolina Council on Vocational and Technical Education; Author, "An American Tragedy Unfolding: Our Educational System"; Contributor, Articles to Professional Journals **Awards:** Who's Who in American Education (1997); Who's Who in Governmental Services (1990); Certification of Appreciation, South Carolina Commission on Women **Memberships:** South Carolina Vocational Association; National Dropout Prevention Network; National Business Education Association; Marketing Education Association; Association for Supervision and Curriculum Development; South Carolina Network for Women Administrators in Education; National Association of Secondary Supervisors and Principals; International Technical Education Association; American Vocational Association; South Carolina Vocational Director's Association; National Tech Prep Network; SC Vocational Special Needs Division; South Carolina Technical Education Association **Marquis Who's Who Honors:** Albert Nelson Marquis Lifetime Achievement Award; Marquis Who's Who Top Professional **To what do you attribute your success:** Ms. Abell credits her success on her honesty, as well as her propensity for treating every children as though they were special. **Why did you become involved in your profession or industry:** Ms. Abell initially studied art while attending college, and began to teach the subject after entering the field of education. **Avocations:** Horseback riding; Painting

Richard Bender Abell, JD

Title: Federal Judiciary (Retired) **Industry:** Law and Legal Services **Date of Birth:** 12/2/1943 **Place of Birth:** Philadelphia **State/Country of Origin:** PA/USA **Parents:** Lon Edward Welch Jr.; Charlotte Amelia Bender **Marital Status:** Married **Spouse Name:** Lucia del Carmen Lombana-Cadavid (12/2/1968) **Children:** David; Christian; Rachel **Education:** JD, George Washington University Law School, Washington, DC (1974); BA in International Affairs, George Washington University, Washington, DC (1966); Conestoga High School, Berwyn, PA **Career:** Special Trial Judge/Special Master, U.S. Court Federal Claims, Washington, DC (1991-2010); Appointed, Confirmed, Assistant Attorney General, U.S. Department of Justice by President Reagan (1986-1990); Deputy Assistant Attorney General, Office Justice Programs, U.S. Department of Justice, Washington, DC (1983-1986); Director, Office of Program Development, Peace Corps, Washington, DC (1981-1983); Staff Member, U.S. Sen. Richard Schweiker, U.S. Senate, Washington, DC (1979-1980); Associate, Reilly & Fogwell, West Chester, PA (1974-1980); Assistant District Attorney, Chester County, PA (1974-1979); Deputy Sheriff, Chester County, PA (1976-1978) **Career Related:** YR Alumni Network, Inc. (2009-Present); Board of Directors, Federal Prison Industries, Inc. (Now UNICOR) (1985-1991); Co-chairman, Advisory Committee, National Center for State and Local Law Enforcement Training (1987-1990); Chairman, National Crime Prevention Council (1986-1990); Advisory Board, National Institute of Corrections (1986-1990); National Drug Policy Board, Enforcement Coordinating Group, The White House, Washington, DC (1988-1989); National Drug Policy Board Coordinating Group for Drug Abuse, Prevention and Health, The White House, Washington, DC (1988-1989); Vice Chairman, Research and Development Review Board, U.S. Department of Justice (1987-1989); Adjunct Faculty, Delaware Law School, Widener University, Wilmington, DE (1975-1977); Adjunct Faculty, West Chester University (1976) **Civic:** Commissioner, President's Commission on Agricultural Workers (1988-1993); Coordinating Council on Juvenile Justice and Delinquency Prevention (1986-1990); President's Task Force on Adoption (1987-1988); Board of Directors, Young Americans for Freedom, Young America's Foundation (1979-1983); Chairman, Young Republicans National Federation (YRNF), Washington, DC (1979-1981); Executive Committee, Republican National Committee (RNC) (1979-1981); Volunteer, Peace Corps, Colombia (1967-1969) **Military Service:** U.S. Army (1969-1971) **Creative Works:** Editor, "Sojourns of a Patriot: Field and Prison Papers of An Unreconstructed Confederate" (1998); Author, "Peter Smith of Westmoreland County, Virginia (Died 1741) and Some Descendants" (1996) **Awards:** Jefferson Davis Historical Gold Medal, United Daughters of the Confederacy (2000); Decorated Purple Heart, U.S. Army (1970); Commendation Medal for Heroism, U.S. Army (1970); Air Medal, U.S. Army (1970); Combat Infantryman's Badge, U.S. Army (1970) **Memberships:** Knight, Most Venerable Order of Hospital St. John, Jerusalem, Israel (Now Order of St. John); Order of the Indian Wars of the United States; General Society of Colonial Wars; Society of the Cincinnati; General Society Sons of the Revolution; Aztec Club of 1847; General Society of the War of 1812 **Bar Admissions:** Pennsylvania (1974) **Marquis Who's Who Honors:** Albert Nelson Marquis Lifetime Achievement Award; Marquis Who's Who Top Professional; Marquis Who's Who Humanitarian Award **To what do you attribute your success:** Mr. Abell attributes his success to his faith in God. **Why did you become involved in your profession or industry:** Mr. Abell became involved in his profession because it presented itself. He wasn't thinking about it and it happened. **Avocations:** History; Genealogy; Reading; Hunting **Religion:** Anglican Catholic **Thoughts on Life:** More than a half-century ago, Mr. Abell was a member of the Boy Scouts. What was taught to him then has stayed with him. Their words of wisdom have always rung in his ears – Pro Deo et Patria – "For God and Country." There can be no higher definition of our national purpose. He has tried to let this phrase guide him during these past six decades since being a Boy Scout – both parts – for God and for country. They go together. Our nation has been blessed by Divine Providence because of our faith. When we lose that faith, we will lose our country and the principles that have made us the great nation that we still are. Further, it is not happenstance that "God" is placed before "country" in this phrase. Additionally, it behooves him to mention that he has also always been guided by the words of one of our truly greatest men, Robert E. Lee - "Do your duty in all things. You cannot do more, you should never wish to do less."

Clarence A. Abramson

Marquis Who's Who
18 98
Biographee

Title: Pharmaceutical Company Executive, Lawyer **Date of Birth:** 10/15/1937 **Place of Birth:** Fort Worth **State/Country of Origin:** TX/USA **Parents:** Samuel; Katherine (Berg) Abramson **Marital Status:** Married **Spouse Name:** Maureen L. Foley **Children:** Steven; Eric; Katherine **Education:** JD, University of Texas (1954); BBA, University of Texas (1952) **Bar Admissions:** Pennsylvania (1974); New Jersey (1972); New York (1963); Texas (1954) **Career:** Retired, President, HCDI Bio Tech Consulting Company; President, Health Care Ventures International, Inc., Scotch Plains, NJ (1994-Present); Director, founder, Poly Pharm Inc., New York, NY (1993-Present); Co-founder, Managing Director, Gulf Stream Pharms., LLC, Boca Raton, FL (1995); Vice President, Secretary, Merck & Co., Inc., Rahway, NJ (1991-1993); Secretary, Chief Counsel, Merck & Co., Inc., Rahway, NJ (1989-1990); Associate General Counsel, Merck & Co., Inc., Rahway, NJ (1986-1989); International General Counsel, Merck & Co., Inc., Rahway, NJ (1970-1986); Of Counsel, Mobil Oil Corp., New York, The Hague and London (1962-1969); Attorney, Securities and Exchange Commission, Washington (1961-1962); Partner, Wynne & Wynne, Dallas (1954-1961) **Career Related:** Board of Directors, Handy & Herman, Inc.; Board of Directors, Polypharm, Inc.; Board of Directors, Acorda Therapeutics, Inc.; Board of Directors, Gliamed, Inc.; Board of Directors, N'Gene Pharma Inc.; Board of Directors, Chairman of the Board, Gulfstream Pharma LLC; Advisory Board Member, Institute for Circadian Physiology, Cambridge, MA; Adjunct Professor of Legal Studies, Montclair State University **Civic:** Trustee, Community Health Law Project; Member, S.C.O.R.E. (Service Corps of Retired Executives) **Memberships:** Bar Affiliations, American Bar Association; Texas Bar Association; New Jersey Bar Association; Pennsylvania Bar Association; New York State Bar Association **Marquis Who's Who Honors:** Albert Nelson Marquis Lifetime Achievement Award **Why did you become involved in your profession or industry:** Mr. Abramson became involved in his profession because he was 16 years old when he started college and he thought he wanted to be a doctor. He did a few organic chemistry classes and realized he did not want to do that. His second choice was to become a lawyer. His mother, Katherine Abramson, named him after a famous lawyer by the name of Clarence Darrow, who was involved in the Scopes Monkey Trial in Tennessee. That intrigued him and the more he looked into it he felt that's what he wanted to do so he switched his major and ended up going to law school. He always had a passion to get into academia but law is where he found satisfaction. **Avocations:** Golf; Tennis; Squash; Gardening; Travel

Ali F. AbuRahma, MD

Title: Professor of Surgery **Industry:** Medicine & Health Care **Company Name:** West Virginia University - Charleston Division **Date of Birth:** 04/22/1946 **State/Country of Origin:** Jordan **Spouse Name:** Marion AbuRahma **Children:** Zachary AbuRahma, DO; Chelsea AbuRahma-Maxwell; Joseph AbuRahma, MD **Education:** Intern, Alexandria University Hospitals, Alexandria, Egypt (1970-1971); Bachelor of Medicine, Bachelor of Surgery, Alexandria University School of Medicine, Alexandria, Egypt, Summa Cum Laude (1970); Graduate, Pre-Medicine, Alexandria University, Alexandria, Egypt (1965) **Certifications:** Registered Physician Vascular Interpretation (RPVI), American Registry of Diagnostic Medical Sonographers (2006); Registered Vascular Technologist (RVT), American Registry of Diagnostic Medical Sonographers (1997); Certificate, Vascular Surgery Board, American Board of Surgery (1984); Certificate, American Board of Surgery (1978); Licensed, Arizona (1977); Licensed, Michigan (1977); Licensed, West Virginia (1975) **Career:** Director, Integrated Vascular Surgery Residency Program, Charleston Area Medical Center, West Virginia University (2012-Present); Director, Vascular Surgery Fellowship Program, Charleston Area Medical Center, West Virginia University (2009-Present); Professor and Chief of Vascular Surgery, Robert C. Byrd Health Sciences Center, West Virginia University (1991-Present); Director of Surgery Research, Robert C. Byrd Health Sciences Center, West Virginia University (1991-Present); Surgery Grand Rounds Coordinator, Robert C. Byrd Health Sciences Center, West Virginia University (1989-2008); Professor of Surgery, West Virginia University Health Sciences Center (1986-1990); Clinical Associate Professor of Surgery, West Virginia University Health Sciences Center (1982-1985); Clinical Assistant Professor of Surgery, West Virginia University Health Sciences Center (1979-1982); Clinical Instructor of Surgery, West Virginia University Health Sciences Center (1978-1979); Fellow, Vascular Surgery, Arizona Heart Institute (1977-1978); Resident in Surgery, State University of New York (1973-1974); House Officer, Dhahran Health Center, American Hospital of Arab American Oil Company (ARAMCO), Dhahran, Saudi Arabia (1971-1973); Medical Director, Diagnostic Medical Sonography Advisory Board, Bridge Valley Community & Technical College **Career Related:** Co-Director, Vascular Center of Excellence, Charleston Area Medical Center (2002-Present); Chief, Vascular Surgery, Charleston Area Medical Center (1987-Present); Active Member, Staff, Charleston Area Medical Center (1978-Present); President, Medical Staff, St. Francis Hospital (1988-1989); Vice President, President-Elect, Medical Staff, St. Francis Hospital (1988, 1987); Chief, Department of Surgery, Charleston Area Medical Center (1986, 1985); Member, Courtesy Staff, Thomas Memorial Hospital (1981); Presented, Over 500 National/International Meetings **Creative Works:** Member, Editorial Board, Journal of Vascular Surgery (2010-Present); Journal of Vascular Surgery: Cases & Innovative Techniques (2016-Present); Reviewer, American Surgeon (2012-Present); Associate Editor, Vascular (2006-Present); Vascular & Endovascular Surgery (2002-Present); Annals of Vascular Surgery (1999-Present); Journal of Endovascular Therapy (1997-Present); Archives of Surgery (1991-Present), American Journal of Surgery (1990-Present); Stroke (1990-Present); Journal of Diabetes and Its Complications (1990-Present); Associate Editor, Book, "Rutherford's Vascular Surgery and Endovascular Therapy" (2014, 2018); Editor, Associate Editor, Book "Noninvasive Vascular Diagnosis: A Practical Guide to Therapy" 1st-4th Eds. (2000, 2007, 2013, 2017); Dataset Papers in Medicine (2012-2013); Vascular Specialist (2005-2013); Vascular (2004) **Awards:** SVS Presidential Citation Award, SVS Foundation Development Committee (2016); Vincent Von Kern Award, Charleston Division, West Virginia University Health Sciences Center (2002); Benedum Distinguished Scholar Award in Biosciences and Health Sciences, West Virginia University (1999-2000); First Recipient of the Steven J. Jubelirer Research Award, Charleston Area Medical Center/ Robert C. Byrd Health Sciences Center, West Virginia University (1999); Clinician of the Year Award, Voted Outstanding Teacher of the Year, Class of 1994 Medical Students, Charleston Division, West Virginia University (1994); Vincent Von Kern Award, Charleston Division, West Virginia University Health Sciences Center (1986) **Memberships:** American Surgical Association; Distinguished Fellow, Treasurer, Vice President, President-Elect, Society for Vascular Surgery; American Association of Vascular Surgery; Southern Association for Vascular Surgery; Eastern Vascular Society; Society for Clinical Vascular Surgery; The American Venous Forum; American College of Angiology; Allegheny Vascular Society; Southern Surgical Association; Royal College of Surgeons of Canada; American College of Surgeons; Southeastern Surgical Congress; Central Surgical Association; International Federation of Surgical Colleges; International College of Surgeons; West Virginia Medical Association; American College of Surgeons-West Virginia Chapter; Kanawha Valley Medical Society **Marquis Who's Who Honors:** Albert Nelson Marquis Lifetime Achievement Award

Raymond A. Acker

Title: Minister, Army Chaplain (Retired) **Industry:** Religious **Date of Birth:** 01/04/1932 **Place of Birth:** Hartford **State/Country of Origin:** CT/USA **Parents:** Abijah Acker; Mary Esther (Willys) Acker **Marital Status:** Married **Spouse Name:** D. Jean Rineer (09/03/1960); Anne Hamm (06/14/1958, Deceased 09/1959) **Children:** Thomas R. Acker; Douglas B. Acker **Education:** Master of Science in Guidance and Counseling, Long Island University Brooklyn (1973); Master of Theology, Dallas Theological Seminary (1964); Master of Divinity, Reformed Episcopal Seminary (1962); Bachelor of Science in Bible Studies, Philadelphia Biblical University (1959) **Certifications:** Ordained to Ministry, Reinhart Bible Church, Dallas, TX (1964) **Career:** Director, World Wide Bible Institutes, South Gibson, PA (1990-1995); Assistant to General Director, Biblical Ministries Worldwide, Lawrenceville, GA (1984-1989); Director, Alumni Affairs, Philadelphia Biblical University, Langhorne, PA (1983-1984) **Career Related:** Member, Various Corporations (1996-Present); Member, Personnel Policy Committee, Calvary Fellowship Homes, Lancaster, PA (2000); Secretary, Treasurer, Mid-Atlantic Pastors Fellowship and Bible Conference (1995-2001); Vice President, Delmarva Regional Interfaith Council For Action Indiana (1981-1983); Member, Chaplains Commission (1977-1992); Member, Interfaith Council For Action (1960-1992) **Civic:** Member, Centennial Committee, Reformed Episcopal Seminary (1983-1987); Committee Member, Boy Scouts of America, Copperas Cove, TX (1976-1979); President, Parent Teacher Association, Giessen, Germany (1975-1976); President, Parent Teacher Association, Aberdeen, MD (1971-1972) **Military Service:** Retired, U.S. Army (1983); Advanced through Grades to Lieutenant Colonel, U.S. Army (1978); Chaplain, U.S. Army (1964-1983); Commissioned Second Lieutenant, U.S. Army (1963); Enlisted, U.S. Army (1953-1955) **Creative Works:** Author, "History of the Theological Seminary of the Reformed Episcopal Church" (1965) **Awards:** North America Missionary of Year Award, Association North America Missions (1994); Decorated Bronze Star **Memberships:** Chairman, Northeast Region, Association North America Missions (1997-1998, 1991-1995); Life Member, National Association for Uniformed Services; Life Member, Military Officers Association; Life Member, Military Chaplains Association; Life Member, Blinded Veterans Association; Life Member, American Legion; Life Member, Disabled American Veterans **Marquis Who's Who Honors:** Albert Nelson Marquis Lifetime Achievement Award; Marquis Who's Who Top Professional; Marquis Who's Who Humanitarian Award **Why did you become involved in your profession or industry:** Chaplain Acker became involved in his profession after enlisting in the Army and seeing the opportunities chaplains had. His knowledge of scripture also encouraged him to make the decision. **Political Affiliations:** Republican **Religion:** Protestant

Lillian Ackerman, PhD

Title: Anthropologist **Industry:** Education/Educational Services **Company Name:** Washington State University **Date of Birth:** 4/14/1928 **Place of Birth:** Detroit **State/Country of Origin:** MI/USA **Parents:** John Hanjian; Marie (Eurenjian) Hanjian **Marital Status:** Married **Spouse Name:** Robert Edwin Ackerman (3/30/1952) **Children:** Laura Lynn; Gail Ellen; James Eric **Education:** PhD in Anthropology, Washington State University (1982); MA in Anthropology, University of Michigan (1951); BA in Anthropology, University of Michigan (1950) **Career:** Adjunct Professor, Washington State University (2001); Adjunct Associate Professor, Washington State University, Pullman, WA (1994-2001); Instructor of Anthropology, Wenatchee Valley College, Nespelem, WA (1979); Researcher Associate, Department of Anthropology, Washington State University, Pullman, WA (1967-1975); Instructor of Anthropology, Washington State University, Pullman, WA (1963-1965); Russian Translator, Arctic Institute North America, Toronto, ON, Canada (1960-1962); Social Case Worker, Traveler's Aid Society, San Antonio, TX (1956); Social Case Worker, Wayne County Bureau of Social Aid, Detroit, MI (1951-1956) **Career Related:** Consultant in Anthropology, Pullman, WA (1982-Present); Expert Witness, Case for Wenatchi Tribe, Portland, OR (2007-2009); Invited Speaker, Honors Presentation, College of Liberal Arts (2005); Expert Witness, Child Custody Case, Colville Indian Reservation Tribal Court (2004); Chairperson of Master's Thesis, Washington State University (2003); Consultant, Pleasant Company, Middleton, WI (1998-2002); Consultant, Visual Education Corporation, Princeton, NJ (1999-2000); Invited Guest Speaker, First Annual Native American Studies Conference, Boise, ID (1998); Researcher, Consultant, U.S. Census, Washington (1989-1990); Woodrow Wilson Fellowship (1979); Fellowship, American Association of University Women (1979); Fellow, American Anthropological Association; Fellow, Society for Applied Anthropology **Civic:** Former Chairperson of Developmental Disabilities Board, Whitman County, Washington (1969-1984) **Creative Works:** Author, "A Necessary Balance: Gender and Power Among Indians of The Columbia Plateau" (2003); Author, "A Song to The Creator: Traditional Arts of Native American Women of The Plateau" (1996); Author, "Ethnographic Overview and Assessment of Federal and Tribal Lands in The Lake Roosevelt Area Concerning The Confederated Tribes of The Colville Indian Reservation" (1996); Author, with Laura F. Klein, "Women and Power In Native North America" (1995); Contributor, 25 Peer-Reviewed Articles; Contributor, Four Books; Contributor, Articles to Professional Journals **Awards:** Grantee, Phillips Fund of American Philosophical Society (1988); Grantee, Phillips Fund of American Philosophical Society (1979) **Memberships:** Grantee, Sigma Xi (1978); American Ethnological Society; Alaska Anthropological Association; Society for American Archaeology **Marquis Who's Who Honors:** Albert Nelson Marquis Lifetime Achievement Award; Marquis Who's Who Top Professional **Why did you become involved in your profession or industry:** When Dr. Ackerman entered her profession because when she was in Detroit, she was raised in a Armenian community. She was always interested in how Americans lived.Dr. Ackerman also had a friend who was in anthropology. She was reading her book, and realized that anthropology explained a lot about her questions between Armenian culture and American culture. That is when she switched from general studies to anthropology. **Avocations:** Reading **Political Affiliations:** Democrat **Thoughts on Life:** Dr. Ackerman was able to work with a number of tribes and that was achievement enough. She also did some work with Nez Perce to develop the Nez Perce doll, called "the American Girl Doll." In 2002, after the Nez Perce doll came out, she was invited to the Nez Perce tribe. She and the others were divided that worked on it. She did writings involved with that. She also did a census job in research.

Nels John Ackerson

Title: Former Chairman/Founder, Lawyer (Retired) **Industry:** Law and Legal Services **Company Name:** Ackerson Kauffman Fex **Date of Birth:** 04/12/1944 **Place of Birth:** Indianapolis **State/Country of Origin:** IN/USA **Parents:** Ralph D. Ackerson; Mariel F. (Maze) Ackerson **Marital Status:** Widowed **Spouse Name:** Sharon Carroll Ackerson (06/11/1983, Deceased 02/2020) **Children:** Betsy Virginia; Peter Nels; Stacia Carroll Loveall (Stepdaughter); Joshua Michael (Stepson) **Education:** Honorary PhD, Purdue University (2006); JD, Harvard Law School, Cum Laude (1971); MA in Public Policy, Harvard University (1971); BS, Purdue University, with Distinction (1967) **Certifications:** United States Court of Appeals for the Fourth Circuit (1999); United States Court of Appeals for the Sixth Circuit (1996); United States Court of International Trade (1991); Supreme Court of the United States (1989); United States Court of Appeals for the District of Columbia Circuit (1985); Washington, DC (1985); Indiana (1971); United States District Court for the Southern District of Indiana (1971); United States Court of Appeals for the Seventh Circuit (1971) **Career:** Former Founder/Chairman, Ackerson Kauffman Fex, Washington, DC (2004-Present); Chairman, Class Corridor LLC (2001-Present); Retired, Partner, Director, Sommer Barnard Ackerson PC (2002-2004); Chairman, Ackerson & Bishop Chartered, The Ackerson Group, Chartered, Washington, DC (1991); Partner, Sidley & Austin (Now Sidley Austin LLP), Cairo, Washington, DC (1982-1991); Partner, Sidley, Austin & Naguib (Now Sidley Austin LLP), Cairo, Washington, DC (1982-1984); Partner, Campbell, Kyle & Proffitt, Noblesville, IN (1979-1982); Chief Counsel, Executive Director, United States Senate Subcommittee on Constitution, Washington, DC (1977-1979); Chief Counsel, United States Senate Subcommittee, Constitutional Amendments, Washington, DC (1976-1977); Associate, Barnes, Hickam, Pantzer & Boyd, Indianapolis, IN (1971-1976); Advisor, Harvard Advisory Mission to Republic of Colombia (1970) **Career Related:** Class Counsel, Harvard Advisory Mission to Republic of Colombia; Advisor, Communications Environmental and Land Use Law Report; Class Counsel, AT&T Fiber Optic Litigation Board **Civic:** Liberal Arts Advisory Council, Purdue University (1997-2000); Democratic Nominee for United States Congress, Fifth District, State of Indiana (1980) **Creative Works:** Board of Editors, "Harvard Law Review" (1968-1971) **Memberships:** President, American Chamber of Commerce in Egypt (1984); Litigation Section, ABA; Business and Banking Section, ABA; International Law Section, ABA; Administrative Law Section, ABA; American Agricultural Law Association; Center for National Policy; Food and Agriculture Committee, National Policy Association; Association of Trial Lawyers of America **Marquis Who's Who Honors:** Albert Nelson Marquis Lifetime Achievement Award; Marquis Who's Who Top Professional **Avocations:** Singing; Traveling **Political Affiliations:** Democrat **Religion:** Presbyterian

Loren Adams

Title: Visionary Artist, Writer, Publisher **Company Name:** The Loren Adams Collection **Date of Birth:** 09/28/1945 **Place of Birth:** Linton **State/Country of Origin:** IN/USA **Parents:** Sergeant Major Loren Dean (Ace) Adams; Norma Lee (Hunter) Adams **Marital Status:** Married **Spouse Name:** Patricia U. Adams **Children:** David Wayne; Jeremy Brian **Education:** BA in Entrepreneurship, American Public University (2020) **Certifications:** Certificate of Fine Arts, University of Hawai'i, With Honors (2013) **Career:** The Loren Adams Collection (2019-Present); Founder, Loren Adams Studio & Museum of Fine Art, Makawao, Hawaii (1987-Present) **Civic:** High Priest, Elders Quorum, Kahului Hawai'i Stake of the Church of Jesus Christ of Latter-Day Saints (1985-2020); Choir Director, Kahului Hawai'i Stake of the Church of Jesus Christ of Latter-Day Saints (1985-2020); Mission Leader, Ward Counsel, Kahului Hawai'i Stake of the Church of Jesus Christ of Latter-Day Saints (1985-2020) **Military Service:** Army Junior ROTC, Pacific High School; Commanding Officer, Color Guard (1964) **Creative Works:** Permanent Collection, R.W. Norton Art Gallery (1979-Present); Permanent Collection, Vancouver Maritime Museum; Permanent Collection, Balmoral Castle Library, Aberdeenshire, Scotland **Awards:** Artist of the Year, Covington Who's Who (2014); Professional of the Year, Covington Who's Who (2013) **Memberships:** Resident Artist, Fundraiser, The Hui O Wa'a Kaulua (2010-2020); Maui Choral Arts Association; Maui Chamber Orchestra **Marquis Who's Who Honors:** Albert Nelson Marquis Lifetime Achievement Award **To what do you attribute your success:** Mr. Adams' attributes his success to his desire to create and make beautiful things, as well as his natural talent and hand-eye coordination. **Why did you become involved in your profession or industry:** Mr. Adams became involved in his profession because he has been painting since he was a child. **Avocations:** Playing classical piano and accordion; Singing; Public speaking; Multitrack recording **Political Affiliations:** Liberal **Religion:** Church of Jesus Christ of Latter-Day Saints

Susan Silliman Addiss, MPH, MUrS

Title: Public Health Administrator (Retired) **Industry:** Medicine & Health Care **Date of Birth:** 04/03/1931 **Place of Birth:** New Haven, **State/Country of Origin:** CT/USA **Parents:** Thomas North Tracy (Deceased 1996); Susan Silliman (Bennett); Tracy Pearson (Deceased 1987) **Marital Status:** Divorced **Spouse Name:** James M. Addiss, (04/21/1956, Divorced 07/1967) **Children:** Justus; Susan **Education:** MPH, MUrS in Urban Studies, Yale University (1969); BA, Smith College (1951); Phi Beta Kappa **Career:** Retired (1995); Health Commissioner, Connecticut State Department of Public Health, Hartford, CT (1991-1995); Health Director, Quinnipiack Valley Health District, Hamden, CT (1985-1991); Health Planning Bureau Chief, Connecticut Department of Health Services, Hartford, CT (1976-1985); Health Director, Naugatuck Valley Health District, Ansonia, CT (1972-1976); Health Educator, New Haven Health Department (1969-1972) **Career Related:** Assistant Clinical Professor, Yale School of Nursing (1988-Present); Lecturer, University of Connecticut Health Center, Farmington, CT (1978-Present); Lecturer, Department of Epidemiology & Public Health, Yale University (1970-1995); Singer, Capella Cordina **Civic:** Board, Watershed Fund (1999-Present); Board, Environment and Human Health Incorporated (1997-Present); Advisory Board, Community Fund for Women & Girls, New Haven, CT (2012-2018); Board, CT Health Foundation (1999-2008) **Creative Works:** Author, "Some Ironies at the Interface of Medicine and Public Health," Yale Medicine (1993); Co-author, "Economics of Community Health: Dealing with the Realities," Economics of Health Care and Nursing, American Academy of Nursing (1985); Author, Annual Meeting of the American Public Health Association, American Journal of Public Health (1985); Author, Presidential Address, "Setting Goals and Priorities" (1984); Author, "Area Health Planning," Church and Society Magazine (1984); Author, "Data Deterioration and Public Health Policy," Journal of Public Health Policy (1983); Author, "Primary Health Care: A Responsibility of Local Health Departments?," Connecticut Public Health Association (1981); Author, "Administration of a National Health Service: The Planner's Viewpoint," Annual Meeting of the American Public Health Association (1977); Author, "Women and Health Careers," Westover Alumnae Magazine, Hall (1975); Guest Editor, "Leave the 'Local' Alone!," Environmental News Digest (1973); Author, "Pediatric Health Care Patterns in a Low Middle-Income Population" (1969); Co-author, "Analysis of Marionville" (1968) **Awards:** C.E.A. Winslow Award (1994); Distinguished Alumna Award, Association of Yale Alumni in Public Health (1994); Smith College Medal (1981) **Memberships:** Board Chair, Planned Parenthood of CT (1999-2002); President, Quota International New Haven (1996-1997); President, Connecticut Public Health Association (1985-1987); President, American Public Health Association (1984); Life Member, Board of Governors, Westover School; Founding Member, Smith College Chamber Singers **Marquis Who's Who Honors:** Albert Nelson Marquis Lifetime Achievement Award **Why did you become involved in your profession or industry:** As a young mother living in a time when men were going to college and women would stay and maintain the home, Ms. Addiss would make money proof-reading the work of students. Ms. Addiss ended up making friends with another couple. The husband was a public health physician and a sports doctor. His wife was a nurse and Ms. Addiss would frequently have lunch or dinner with them. When her marriage fell apart, the husband of the couple, Bill Kissick suggested that she should take up a career in public health, even though she was a music & singing major in college. He then proceeded to elaborate on the proper channels to take to do so. He also wrote her a letter of recommendation that got her into the Yale school of Public Health. Ms. Addiss was interviewed and accepted into the program where she received 2 degrees. Her degrees were in public health and a master's degree in Urban Studies. Bill continued to be a mentor to Ms. Addiss for her entire career. **Avocations:** Tennis; Cooking; Needle-crafts; Music; Art appreciation **Political Affiliations:** Democratic

Avi Adri

Title: Concept Creator **Industry:** Food & Restaurant Services **Company Name:** Don't Tell Supper Club **Marital Status:** Married **Spouse Name:** Veronica **Children:** Ariel; Eliam; Neiv **Career:** Owner/Concept Creator, Don't Tell Supper Club (2017-Present); Owner, Levu Nightclub (2012-2017); Owner, Aura Lounge (2008-2011); Owner, Rockin Taco **Civic:** Events to raise money, Genesis Women's Shelter Outreach **To what do you attribute your success:** Mr. Adri attributes his success in the field to his propensity for empathy and constructing a happy place for people. **Why did you become involved in your profession or industry:** Mr. Adri first became involved in the nightclub industry at a young age, attending a teenage nightclub in Dallas at the age of 16. He was often approached to help set up the venue during certain nights, which set him on the path to pursuing this field professionally. **Avocations:** Surfing; Traveling

Ali Ahmed, MD

Industry: Medicine & Health Care **Date of Birth:** 07/10/1934 **Place of Birth:** Hyderabad **State/Country of Origin:** India **Parents:** Mohammed Abdul; Yaseen Rahim **Marital Status:** Married **Spouse Name:** Sabiha Ahmed **Education:** MB, BS, Dow Medical College, Karachi, Pakistan (1963); BSc, Dayaram Jethamal Sindh Government Science College, Karachi, Pakistan (1957) **Career:** Attending Psychiatrist, Edgewater Psychiatric Center, Harrisburg, PA (1989-Present); Attending Psychiatrist, Holy Spirit Hospital, Camp Hill, PA (1987-Present); Attending Psychiatrist, Harrisburg Hospital, Harrisburg, PA (1983-1987); Superintendent, Fulton State Hospital, Fulton, MO (1983); Assistant Professor, Department of Psychiatry, University of Missouri, Columbia, MO (1980-1983); Chief of Staff, Fulton State Hospital, Fulton, MO (1980-1982); Resident, University of Missouri, Columbia, MO **Career Related:** Consultant Psychiatrist, Tevens Mental Health Center, Carlisle, PA (1987-Present) **Memberships:** American Medical Association; American Psychiatric Association; Pakistan Psychiatric Society **Marquis Who's Who Honors:** Albert Nelson Marquis Lifetime Achievement Award **Thoughts on Life:** Dr. Ahmed was an active participant in British politics with the liberal party when he was practicing in the United Kingdom. Here in the United States, he continues to support and work for the Democratic Party.

S. Basheer Ahmed, PhD

Title: Research Company Executive, Educator **Industry:** Education/Educational Services **Company Name:** Pearce Consultant Services **Date of Birth:** 01/01/1934 **Place of Birth:** Kurnool, Andhra **State/Country of Origin:** India **Parents:** S.M. Hussain; K.A. (Bee) Hussain **Marital Status:** Married **Spouse Name:** Alice Cordelia Pearce (09/21/1968) **Children:** Ivy Amina **Education:** PhD, Texas A&M University (1966); MS, Texas A&M University (1963); MA, Osmania University, Hyderabad, India (1957); BA, Osmania College, Kurnool (1955) **Career:** President, Pearce Consulting (2000-Present); Professor Emeritus, Pace University (1993-2003); President, Princeton Economic Research, Inc. (1980-1999); Professor of Management Sciences, Lubin Graduate School Business, Pace University (1982-1992); Director, Doctoral Program, Pace University (1982-1992); Visiting Fellow, Princeton University, New Jersey (1977-1978); Professor, Western Kentucky University (1970-1980); Assistant Professor, Ohio University, Athens (1968-1970); Assistant Professor, Tennessee Technical University, Cookeville (1966-1968) **Career Related:** Consultant, Honeywell International Inc. (1985); Consultant, Institute for Energy Analysis, Oak Ridge, Tennessee (1975); Consultant, Oak Ridge National Laboratory (1969-1977) **Civic:** Member, Rotary Club, Bowling Green, Kentucky (2012-Present); Member, Board of Directors, The Kennedy Center (1997-2000); Golden Circles Board, The Kennedy Center for the Performing Arts, Washington, DC (1994-1999); Rotary, Bowling Green, KY (1975-1985) **Creative Works:** Author, "Technology, International Stability, and Growth" (1984); Editor, "Technology, International Stability, and Growth" (1984); Author, "Nuclear Fuel and Energy Policy" (1979); Author, "Quantitative Methods for Business" (1974) **Awards:** Millennium Medal (2000); Centennial Medal, IEEE (1983); Achievement Award, Oak Ridge National Laboratory (1977) **Memberships:** President, Systems, Man, and Cybernetics Society, IEEE (1980-1982); Fellow, American Association for the Advancement of Science **Marquis Who's Who Honors:** Albert Nelson Marquis Lifetime Achievement Award (2018-2019) **Why did you become involved in your profession or industry:** He first wanted to be a medical doctor, and then a physicist, but he became an economist. Education gave him the opportunity to see and do what he wanted to do. **Avocations:** Travel; Health and fitness **Political Affiliations:** Republican **Religion:** Muslim

Elizabeth Franz Albert

Title: Investor, Environmentalist **Industry:** Fine Art **Place of Birth:** Chicago **State/Country of Origin:** IL/USA **Parents:** Herbert George Franz; Louise Anders Franz **Marital Status:** Married **Spouse Name:** Henry Burton Albert **Education:** Coursework, Chevy Chase Junior College **Career:** Investor; Stock Market; Real Estate; Environmentalist **Career Related:** Trainer, Several Champion Miniature Poodles **Civic:** Former Member, Landmarks Preservation Council of Chicago **Creative Works:** Exhibitor, Portraits; Exhibitor, Still Life Paintings; Contributor, Biology Textbook; Editor, Biology Textbook **Memberships:** American Farmland Trust; National Trust for Historical Preservation; Founding Member, Cousteau Society; Natural Resources Defense Council; Osprey Society, Environmental Defense Fund; Charter Member, National Museum Women in the Arts; Chicago Symphony Orchestra Society; Lifetime Member, Art Institute of Chicago **Marquis Who's Who Honors:** Albert Nelson Marquis Lifetime Achievement Award **Why did you become involved in your profession or industry:** While coming of age, Ms. Albert developed Brucellosis by drinking unpasteurized milk. The illness was treated like a chronic disease, and the experience changed her life considerably. Though she had originally aspired to become a ballet dancer or to study medicine, she eventually resolved to become a painter. **Avocations:** Music; Renovating houses; Antiques; Gardening; Reading **Political Affiliations:** Republican **Religion:** Episcopalian **Thoughts on Life:** Ms. Albert feels that there is a moral obligation to protect the environment. Likewise, she does all that she can to be as helpful as she can in whatever way is possible.

Jean M. Alberti, PhD

Title: Clinical Psychologist **Industry:** Medicine & Health Care **Company Name:** Alberti Psychological Services **Place of Birth:** Buffalo **State/Country of Origin:** NY/USA **Parents:** Anthony & Mary Alberti **Education:** Master of Science, George Williams College, Downers Grove, IL; Doctor of Medicine, Master of Education, State University of New York at Buffalo; Bachelor of Science, D'Youville College, Buffalo, NY **Certifications:** Clinical Psychologist, Illinois; Elementary Principal and Supervisor Teacher, New York **Career:** Owner, Clinical Psychologist, Alberti Psychological Services, Glen Ellyn, IL (1981-Present); National Institutes of Health Grant, Director of Evaluation, Northwestern University Medical School Arthritis Center (1984-1988); National Institutes of Health Grant, Chicago Heart Association, Heart Health Curriculum Project (1981-1984); Chair, Associate Professor, Department of Health Sciences Education, University of Health Sciences, The Chicago Medical School (1975-1980); Assistant Professor, Medical Education, University of Illinois Medical School, Chicago, IL (1972-1975); Director, University Research Office, State University of New York at Buffalo (1968-1972); Teacher, Elementary, NY **Career Related:** Founder, Dr. Jean M. Alberti Center for the Prevention of Bullying Abuse and School Violence, State University of New York at Buffalo Graduate School of Education (2010); Consultant, National Institutes of Health Grant Reviewer, Washington, DC (1977-1980) **Creative Works:** Presenter, "Three Steps to Ending School Violence," Pi Lambda Theta Biennial Conference (2001); Co-Author, Eight Manuscripts & Six Abstracts in Eight Professional Journals (1977-1986); Presenter, 23 Topics to 16 Professional Associations (1970-1988); 26 Psychological Topics to 38 Community Groups **Awards:** Dean's Service Award, Graduate School of Education, University at Buffalo (2013); Distinguished Alumni Award, University at Buffalo Graduate School of Education (2010); Scepter & Key Award, Pi Lambda Theta (2003); Distinguished Pi Lambda Thetan (1991); Woman of Achievement, Women in Management, Oak Brook, IL (1983); International Directory of Distinguished Leadership (1989); Charlotte Danstrom Award, Woman of Achievement/Academia, Women in Management, National Award (1981); Chicago Woman of Leadership Award, International Organization of Women Executives (1977); Outstanding Young Women of America Award (1965) **Memberships:** International President, Pi Lambda Theta (1977-1981); International First Vice President, Pi Lambda Theta (1973-1977); Vice President, Pi Lambda Theta (1969-1973); American Psychological Association **Marquis Who's Who Honors:** Albert Nelson Marquis Lifetime Achievement Award **To what do you attribute your success:** Dr. Alberti attributes her success to the influence of her parents, her philosophy and Pi Lambda Theta. **Why did you become involved in your profession or industry:** Dr. Alberti initially became involved in her career path because there were typically two options for college-bound women; becoming a nurse, or teaching. She chose the latter. Through Pi Lambda Theta, she was able to transition toward medical education. Following this accomplishment, she became a licensed clinical psychologist. **Thoughts on Life:** "Whatever happens, you have to make it work for you."

Sonja L. Alcon

Title: Medical Social Worker (Retired) **Industry:** Medicine & Health Care **Company Name:** Hanover Hospital **Date of Birth:** 08/02/1937 **Place of Birth:** Orange City, IA/USA **State/Country of Origin:** IA/USA **Parents:** A. Lee Gerard; Clarice V (Brown) deBey **Marital Status:** M **Spouse Name:** David E. Alcon; (07/20/1985); George Ryan, (12/28/2019); Richard Gebhardt, (06/06/2019) **Children:** Russell L Ryan; Cheryl L Dherit; Maj Gen Kurt J Ryan (all nee Gebhardt) **Education:** MSW, Univ of MD School of SW (1973); BA, Western MD College (1959) **Certifications:** ACSW **Career:** Director, SW Dept. Hanover Hosp. PA (1966-1996); Caseworker, Springfield State Hosp. Sykesville, MD (1959-1961) **Career Related:** Clinical Assoc Prof, U of MD SSW (1987-1992); Chm Prof, Advisory Comm, Visiting Nurses Assoc Hanover and Spring Grove (1986-1989); SW Advisory Council, WMC; (1984-1986, 1979-1981); Cons to 4 agencies; WMC Field Instructor (1967-1996) **Civic:** National Association of Social Workers; (early 1970's-present); Academy of Certified Social Workers (1973-present); Elected Rep, Eisenlohr Apts. Retirement Living Residents Assoc, Masonic Villages (2018-2020); Vestry, church choir, soloist, All Saints Episcopal Church (1997, 1983-1986, 1976-1979, 1973-1974); Active, YWCA (1996-1998, 1979-1984); Community Advisory Committee, Health South Rehabilitation Hosp of York (1995-1996); Volunteer, Hanover Hosp; Case Management Network, South Central PA (1994-1996); South Central PA Coalition on Organ and Tissue Donation (1994-1996); Altar Guild, All Saints Episcopal Church (1992-1993); Active, Community Needs Coalition (1990-1996); Co-facilitator, \"I Can Cope\" Classes, American Cancer Society (1989-1992); Advisory Bd, United Cerebral Palsy of South Central PA (1989-1990); Administrator, Special Needs Fund, Hanover General Hosp (1986-1996); Advisory Council, Parents Anonymous (1985-1992, 1976-1979); Vice President, Human Services Organization (1985-1986); Co-organizer, Adams-Hanover Chapter, Compassionate Friends (1983); Secretary, Hanover Community Players (1982); Advisory Council, Hanover Hospice (1982-1985); President, Human Services Organization (1980); Bd of Directors, Hospice of York (1980-1982); Diocesan Delegate, All Saints Episcopal Church, Central PA (1980-1986, 1978); Initiator, Co-trustee, Children's Cardiac Fund (1979-1982); Organizer, Local Chapters, Make Today Count and Preemie Parent Support Group (1979); Treasurer, Church Women, All Saints Episcopal Church (1979-1983); Bd of Directors, Episcopal Home, Shippensburg PA (1979-1985); Advisory Group, Institute of Pastoral Care (1976-1977); Treasurer, Hanover Community Progress Council (1976-1980); Bd of Directors, Hanover Chapter, American Red Cross (1976-1979); Vestry Secretary, All Saints Episcopal Church (1975); Bd of Directors, Hanover Community Players (1974-1977); Volunteer, Hanover Area Council Churches, Bd of Directors, Adams-Hanover Mental Health (1973-76); Member, Adams-Hanover Sheltered Workshop Committee (1968-1970); Altar Guild, All Saints Episcopal Church (1968-1986); Bd of Directors, Western MD College Alumni Association (1983); Bd of Directors, Eastern Star Home, Warminster, PA (1986-1989) **Awards:** Companion Temple Award, Grand Encampment, Knights Templar (1999); Finalist, YWCA Salute to Women (1986, 87); York Daily Record Exceptional Citizen Award (1979) **Memberships:** Elizabethtown Chapter, #407, plural, (2017-Present), (Worthy Matron, 2019-2021); Ozemb Temple #52, Daughters of Nile; (1996-present); Supreme Finance Committee, Supreme Assembly, Social Order of Beauceant, (2016-2022, Chairman, 2019-2021); Grand Representative, Order of the Amaranth, North Carolina (2019-2021); Kansas (2016-2017); Queensland, Australia (2015-2016); Washington (2014-2015); California (2013-2014); Royal Matron, Dr. J.M. Hyson Memorial Court #106, OOA (2011-2012); GR, OOA Florida (2010-2011); Life Member, York Chapter No. 169, primary Chapter, OES, (Worthy Matron, 2014-2015; Hanover Chapter No. 378, OES Star, (2009-2010, 1985-1986); Worthy President, Elizabethtown Assembly No. 265, SOOB (2020,2021, 2001,2000); Westminster Assembly #245, (2006, 1999); Supreme Worthy Pres, Supreme Assembly, SOOB (2006-2007); GR, OOA, Iowa (2005-2006); Supreme Assembly, SOOB (2003-2004); GR, England, (2002-2003); President, PA White Shrine Club (2002-2003); G. Standard Bearer, OOA (2001-2002); Royal Patron, OOA (2001-2002); GR, Ont. Canada (2000-2001); Charter Worthy President, Elizabethtown Assembly, SOOB (2000-2001); Royal Matron, Harmony Court #146, OOA (1999-2000); Supreme Worthy Herald, Supreme Shrine, Order White Shrine of Jerusalem (1999-2000); Watchman of Shepherds (1999-2000); G. Historian, OOA (1998-1999); GR, OOA, Maine (1997-1998); Grand Representative, OOA, Maryland (1996-1997); Royal Matron, Harmony Court #146, OOA (1995-1996); Grand Representative, OOA, Wisconsin (1994-1995); Worthy High Priestess, Samaria Shrine. OWSJ (1994-1995); Westminster Assembly #245, SOOB, (Worthy President 1996); Royal Patron, Harmony Court #146; Order of Amaranth (1988-1989, 1987) **Marquis Who's Who Honors:** Albert Nelson Marquis LA Award; Humanitarian Award; **To what do you attribute your success:** A good gene pool, Education, Motivation, Wide variety interests, Dedication. **Why did you become involved in your profession or industry:** She felt that she was called to Social Work because of her family history in the "helping professions". **Avocations:** Reading; Masonically affiliated orders; Traveling; Volunteering **Political Affiliations:** Republican **Religion:** Anglican

Marthanne Payne Alemán, PhD

Title: Environmental Scientist, Consultant **Industry:** Sciences **Date of Birth:** 12/03/1938 **Place of Birth:** Houston **State/Country of Origin:** TX/USA **Parents:** Charles Franklin Payne; Evelyn Inez (Dudley) Payne **Marital Status:** Married **Spouse Name:** Samuel Garza Alemán (07/05/1968) **Education:** PhD in Urban and Regional Science, Texas A&M University (1995); MS in Interdisciplinary Studies, Texas Tech University (1989); BS in Landscape Architecture, Texas A&M University, Magna Cum Laude (1988) **Career:** Consultant, Rio Verde Land & Investment Corp., Calvert, TX (1995-Present); Research Assistant, Texas A&M University, College Station, TX (1993-1994); Research Assistant, Texas Tech University, Lubbock, TX (1988-1991); Entrepreneur, Rio Verde Farm, San Benito, TX (1972-1983); Engineering Aide, Bryant-Curington Engineers, Austin, TX (1969-1972); Engineering Aide, Austin, TX (1966-1969) **Career Related:** Secretary, Treasurer, Board of Directors Texas Avocado Growers Association, Weslaco, TX (1979-1983) **Civic:** Active Participant, Robertson County Historical Commission (1980-1983) **Creative Works:** Author, "Export-Driven Development of Soil and Water Resources: Barrier to Sustainable Development and Inducement to Desertification" (1995); Author, "Soil Salinity in the Texas Lower Rio Grande Valley: Cause for Concern" (1987) **Awards:** Presidential Scholar, US Federal Register (1993;) National Collegiate Architectural and Design Award, US Achievement Academy, Lexington, KY (1989) **Memberships:** American Planning Association; Soil and Water Conservation Society of America **Marquis Who's Who Honors:** Albert Nelson Marquis Lifetime Achievement Award; Marquis Who's Who Top Professional **Why did you become involved in your profession or industry:** Ms. Alemán chose her career after spending 10 years working on an avocado farm. She wanted to make a change after seeing resources deteriorate because her team was not able to raise a full compliment of crops. **Avocations:** Collie breeding

Lori Alessandrini

Title: Medical Spa Owner **Industry:** Medicine & Health Care **Company Name:** Essential Aesthetics and Laser **Marital Status:** Married **Children:** Three Children; Two Stepchildren **Certifications:** Licensed Esthetician, Esthetics, Miller-Motte College, Wilmington, NC (2013); Certified Medical Assistant, Allied Health and Medical Assisting Services, Concorde Career Institute-Jacksonville **Career:** Owner, Essential Aesthetics and Laser (2014-Present); Surgical Assistant, Atlantic Oral, Implant and Facial Surgery (2006-2011); Surgical Assistant, Charlotte Oral Surgery (2001-2005) **Awards:** Face of Esthetics, Charlotte Magazine (2018-2017) **To what do you attribute your success:** Ms. Alessandrini attributes her success to a propensity for hard work, as well as the support system that exists in her family. Likewise, she is grateful for the strength she finds in her Christian faith. **Avocations:** Traveling

Kim D. Alexander, EdD

Title: Chancellor; President **Industry:** Education/Educational Services **Company Name:** Collegiate Edu-Nation; Alexander Ag **Date of Birth:** 07/18/1955 **Place of Birth:** Sweetwater **State/Country of Origin:** TX/USA **Marital Status:** Married **Spouse Name:** Marsha **Children:** Roddy; Kari Suzanne **Education:** EdD, Texas A&M University, College Station, TX/Texas Tech University, Lubbock, TX (2007); MA in Education Administration, Abilene Christian University, Abilene, TX (1985); BS in Education, Angelo State University, San Angelo, TX (1976) **Certifications:** Accredited Land Consultant **Career:** Chancellor, Collegiate Edu-Nation (2019-Present); President, Self-Employed Production Agriculturalist, Alexander Ag (1977-Present); Superintendent, Roscoe Independent School District (now Roscoe Collegiate ISD) (2003-2019); High School Principal, Roscoe Independent School District (2000-2003); Grant Writer, Roscoe Independent School District (1999-2000); Instructor of English Language Arts/Kinesiology, Roscoe Independent School District (1988-1999); Instructor of English Language Arts/Kinesiology, Sweetwater Independent School District (1987-1988) **Career Related:** Chancellor, Collegiate Edu-Nation: A P-20 System Model for 21st Century School Transformation **Civic:** 501c3 Nonprofit Organization **Creative Works:** Co-Author, "Texas Economy Depends on Educational Climate Change," Public Education Section, Perspectives on Texas, The Texas Tribune (2018); Co-Author, "Small Schools Perspective, Boldness Required: An Invitation to Action for Rural Schools," Texas Association of School Administrators Professional Journal: INSIGHT (2018); Co-Author, "A View from A Rural Superintendent's Perspective," Texas Association of School Administrators Professional Journal: INSIGHT (2017) **Awards:** Partnership Award in Excellence, Texas A&M System (2018); Man of the Year in Texas Agriculture Award for District 7, Texas County Agriculture Agents Association (2016); Dr. Grover C. Morlan Educator of the Year Award, Abilene Christian University (2015); John Hoyle Texas School District Excellence in Education Award, Texas A&M University (2014); Agricultural Education and Communications Outstanding Distance Education Student, Texas Tech University (2008); Influence of Creative Problem Solving Upon Ninth-Grade Student Achievement and Satisfaction (2008); Agricultural Leadership, Education, and Communications Outstanding Joint EdD Student, Texas A&M University (2007) **Memberships:** Texas Association of School Administrators; Texas Association of Professional Educators; American Association of School Administrators; American Cotton Growers Association; Red Angus Association of America; Realtors Land Institute; Phi Kappa Phi **Marquis Who's Who Honors:** Marquis Who's Who Top Professional **To what do you attribute your success:** Dr. Alexander attributes his success to surrounding himself with good people. Any success he has enjoyed has been a collaborative effort. **Why did you become involved in your profession or industry:** Dr. Alexander became involved in his profession because he always had an interest in education and a desire to improve the world. **Religion:** Church of Christ **Thoughts on Life:** We don't care where you come from...we just care about where you are wanting to go.

David Henry Allard

Title: Judge **Industry:** Government Administration/Government Relations/ Government Services **Date of Birth:** 01/10/1929 **Place of Birth:** Snohomish **State/Country of Origin:** Washington **Parents:** Clayton Frederick Allard; Ruth Elizabeth (Winston) Allard **Marital Status:** Widower **Spouse Name:** Married Hildred McClelland (6/19/2003, Deceased) **Children:** John M. Allard; Rev. Clayton F. Allard **Education:** LLB, Duke University School of Law (1956); AB, Whitman College (1951) **Career:** Retired (1998); Regional Chief Administrative Law Judge, Social Security Administration, Boston, MA (1992-1997); Administrative Law Judge, Office of Hearings and Appeals, Social Security Administration (1986-1998); Administrative Chief Law Judge, Department of Health and Human Services, Tucson, AZ (1986-1992); Chief Administrative Law Judge, Interstate Commerce Commission (1980-1986); Administrative Law Judge, Interstate Commerce Commission (1967-1972, 1973-1980); Administrative Law Judge, Federal Trade Commission (1972-1973); Member, Staff, Interstate Commerce Commission, Washington (1958-1967) **Career Related:** Special Master, United States Court of Appeals for the First Circuit (1992) **Civic:** Establishing Scholarships **Military Service:** U.S. Army, Korean War (1951-1953) **Creative Works:** Editor-in-Chief, Journal, Federal Bar Association (1972); Law Reporter, Presidential Task Force on Career Advancement (1967); Member, Commercial Panel, American Arbitration Association; Author, "Uncle Clayton- A Soldiers Life In Letters"; Editor, Federal Bar News, Federal Bar Association **Awards:** Achievement Award, Young Lawyers Section, ABA (1965) **Memberships:** Chairman, Education Board, Federal Bar Association (1976-1982); President, Federal Bar Association (1974); American Bar Association; Federal Administrative Law Judges Conference; Delta Tau Delta **Bar Admissions:** Washington State; Supreme Court of the United States **Marquis Who's Who Honors:** Albert Nelson Marquis Lifetime Achievement Award **Why did you become involved in your profession or industry:** Mr. Henry wanted to be a lawyer for as long as he can remember. He was probably in the 3rd or 4th grade when it started. **Avocations:** Golf

Edward Charles "Ed" Allard

Title: College Official, Industrial Education Educator **Industry:** Education/Educational Services **Date of Birth:** 07/22/1936 **Place of Birth:** Wyandotte **State/Country of Origin:** MI/USA **Parents:** Emile Fredrick Allard; Mary Ann (Fecho) Allard **Marital Status:** Widowed **Spouse Name:** Judith Kay McKitrick **Children:** Douglas Edward; Susan Kathleen **Education:** MS in Industrial Education, Wayne State University (1968); BS in Industrial Education, Wayne State University (1962); Coursework, University of Detroit (1954-1955) **Certifications:** Secondary Permanent Teacher, Permanent Vocational Teacher, Michigan **Career:** Director, Trade and Apprentice Education, Henry Ford C.C. (1973-2000); Training Supervisor, Henry Ford C.C. (1969-1973); Instructor, Industrial Education, Henry Ford C.C. (1967-1969); Teacher, Dearborn Public Schools (1965-1967); Teacher, Melvindale-North Allen Park Public Schools (1962-1965); Layout Detailer-Designer, Various Engineering Companies (1958-1962) **Career Related:** Director, UAW-Ford Motor Co. Career Services & Reemployment Assistance Center (1983-1984); Treasurer, Michigan Apprenticeship Steering Committee, Inc. (1976-1990); Part-Time Industrial Drafting, Henry Ford Community College (1969-2000) **Civic:** Secretary, Rotary (1987-1991); Kiwanis (1963-1965) **Military Service:** Michigan Air National Guard (1954-1962) **Awards:** Certificate of Meritorious Service, The United States Department of Labor (2000); Rotarian of the Year, Dearborn Sunshine Rotary Club (1992); Senior Member Award; Meritorious Service Award, United States Power Squadrons **Memberships:** Commander, Grosse Ile Power Squadron (2001); Treasurer, Henry Ford Chamber of Commerce Administrators Association (1981-1985); Secretary, President, Michigan Educators Apprenticeship and Training Association (1972-1986) **Marquis Who's Who Honors:** Albert Nelson Marquis Lifetime Achievement Award; Marquis Who's Who Top Professional **Avocations:** Wood carving; Guitar playing; Weekly sing-a-long at Atria Kinghaven **Political Affiliations:** Democrat **Religion:** Lutheran

David Allen

Title: Owner **Industry:** Agriculture **Company Name:** GreenBird LLC **Date of Birth:** 07/16/1948 **Place of Birth:** Washington Court House **State/Country of Origin:** OH/USA **Marital Status:** Married **Spouse Name:** Dan Schwandner **Children:** Eleise Foley; Tessa Braun **Education:** BFA in Illustration, Minor in Advertising, Columbus College of Art & Design (1971) **Career:** Owner, GreenBird LLC (2008-Present); Vice President, Creative Director, Jap-Orr Company, Cincinnati, Ohio (1998-2012); Owner, Allen + Associates, Waynesville, Ohio (1989-1998); Vice President, Creative Director, McNally Communications, Dayton Ohio (1986-1989); Art Director, Applied Communications Services, Inc., Dayton, Ohio (1981-1986); Art Director, Production Manager, Weir McBride Advertising, Dayton, Ohio (1981-1984); Corporate Art Director, Super Food Services, Inc., Dayton, Ohio (1977-1981) **Civic:** Volunteer, Voice of Hope, American Cancer Society, Inc. **Awards:** Best of Cincinnati Award, Business and Efforts to Impact the Environment (2019) **Memberships:** Past President, Rotary International; Past President, Jaycee; Past President, Chambers of Commerce **To what do you attribute your success:** Mr. Allen attributes his success to always enjoying his work. He has never had a job he disliked, as he likes to see the effect his actions can have on the world surrounding him. **Why did you become involved in your profession or industry:** One day, as Mr. Allen was walking into his former job at an advertising agency, he had a thought about disposable paper birdhouses. It was an "ah-ha" moment; he went to his office and began researching the idea. He found a great deal of supportive evidence for his theory. He then designed the birdhouse. As his birdhouses picked up recognition, he began to design other "green" products, which was the start of GreenBird. Though his financial success was not initially what he needed, through his work, he met great people and felt like he was doing something good. In high school, he got involved in design after a program was implemented at his school wherein students could study for half the day and work for the other half. With that, he found a viable talent in design. He proceeded to attend the Columbus College of Art & Design.

Wayne Kendall Aller, PhD

Title: Psychologist, Educator, Computer Company Executive, Philanthropist **Industry:** Education/Educational Services **Date of Birth:** 02/20/1933 **Place of Birth:** Sylvia **State/Country of Origin:** KS/USA **Parents:** Alvin Ray Aller; Florence Dorothy (Snowbarger) Aller **Marital Status:** Married **Spouse Name:** Sharon Cecelia (Forray) Aller (08/21/1962, Divorced); Sonia Y. Konialian (04/08/1969) **Children:** Jay Ramzi; Joyce Amal **Education:** Visiting Scholar, UCLA (1983); PhD in Psychology, University of Washington (1964); MS in Psychology, University of Washington (1960); BA in Physics, Northwest Nazarene College (Now Northwest Nazarene University), Nampa, ID (1955) **Career:** President, Learning Unlimited (1983-1987); President, CompuLearn (1983-1987); Acting Chair, Psychology Department, Indiana State University, Terre Haute, IN (1982); Professor, Indiana State University, Terre Haute, IN (1969-1982); Associate Professor, Indiana State University, Terre Haute, IN (1968-1985); Associate Professor, Mankato State College, Minnesota (1967-1968); Founder, Conductor, Chorale, Beirut College for Women (1966-1967); Assistant Professor, Chairman, Division of Behavioral Science, Beirut College for Women (1964-1967); Assistant Professor of Psychology, Pacific Lutheran University (1962-1964) **Career Related:** Chair, Organizing America, North San Fernando Valley (2009); Adjunct Professor of Psychology, California State University, Northridge (1984-2003); Visiting Scholar, Psychology Department, University of California, Los Angeles (1982-1983); Consultant, English as a Foreign Language, Vietnamese Affairs Center, Terre Haute, IN (1976-1978); Ministry Planning, Republic of Lebanon, Beirut (1974-1975); American University of Beirut (1974-1975); Senior Research Associate, Center for Behavioral Research; Speaker in the Field; Senior, Research Advisory Center, Educational Research and Development **Civic:** Member, Industries Advisory Committee, Southern California Goodwill (2019); Lay Leader, Santa Barbara District United Methodist Church (2011); Founder, Director, Greater Granada Hills Organizing for America (2009-2011); Secretary, Earth Stewardship Ministry, Knollwood United Methodist Church (2009); Chair, Greater Granada Hills Organizing for America (2009); Member, Leadership Team, United Methodist Church of California, Pacific Annual Conferences, Methodist Federation for Social Action (2008-2010); Chairman, LA County Sunshine Canyon Landfill Community Advisory Committee (2008-2009); Chairman, Church Council, Knollwood United Methodist Church (2007-2010); Advisory Board, Community Integration Services (2007-2009); Member, Cantori Domina (2007); Chairman, Board of Trustees, Knollwood United Methodist Church (2006-2009); Advisory Board, United Campus Ministries, California State University, Northridge (2005-2007); Member, LA County Sunshine Canyon Landfill Community Advisory Committee (2002-2009); City of LA Sunshine Canyon Landfill Citizens Advisory Committee (2002-2009); Secretary, City of LA Sunshine Canyon Landfill Citizens Advisory Committee (2002-2009); President, Knollwood Property Owners Association (2002-2007); Board of Directors, Granada Hills North Neighborhood Council (2002-2006); Member, Technical Advisory Committee **Creative Works:** Author, "Readings and Experiments in General Psychology, Revised Edition" (1971); Author, "Readings and Experiments in General Psychology" (1970) **Awards:** LA Pearl Award, Outstanding Senior Citizen (2007); Grantee, Ford Foundation (1974-1975) **Memberships:** President, Speech and Hearing (1981-1982); Western Psychological Association; New York Academy of Science; Society for Computers in Psychology (SCiP); Computer Users in Speech and Hearing; Apple Buyers Club, Wabash Valley (Terre Haute); Los Angeles Astronomical Society; Sigma Xi, Psi Chi; Sigma Phi Iota **Marquis Who's Who Honors:** Albert Nelson Marquis Lifetime Achievement Award; Marquis Who's Who Top Professional; Marquis Who's Who Humanitarian Award **Why did you become involved in your profession or industry:** Dr. Aller became involved in his profession because his father was the chair of the division of natural science and mathematics at Northwest Nazarene University; he was additionally a botanist. His mother held a PhD in educational psychology; in fact, she founded the home economics department at Northwest Nazarene University. She was also the first resident of the state of Idaho to earn a doctoral degree. Dr. Aller grew up around hard working individuals, so it was only natural for him to also be a hard worker. **Avocations:** Alpine skiing; Wilderness backpacking; Choral singing; Astronomy **Political Affiliations:** Progressive **Religion:** Methodist **Thoughts on Life:** Dr. Aller set up several scholarships to support the education of the future. There were two at Northwest Nazarene University, two at Southern Nazarene University, one American College fund, and one at the Lebanese American University Center for Women's Studies. He also put together the first science fair in Idaho in 1955. Additionally, Dr. Aller volunteers at North Valley Caring Services. Lastly, he just finished grinding a six-inch Cassegrain telescope.

Paul R. Alter, Esq.

Title: Real Estate Consultant, Lawyer **Industry:** Real Estate **Date of Birth:** 6/22/1941 **Place of Birth:** New York **State/Country of Origin:** NY/USA **Marital Status:** Widowed **Children:** Scott; Alexandra **Education:** JD, Cornell Law School, Cornell University, Ithaca, NY (1965); AB, Columbia College, Columbia University, New York, NY (1962) **Career:** Consultant, Real Estate (2015-Present); Partner, Management Shareholder, Greenberg Traurig, LLP, New York, NY (1994-2015); Founder, Real Estate Department, New York Office, Greenberg Traurig, LLP, New York, NY (1994-2006); Co-Head, Real Estate Department, Jones Day, New York, NY (1989-1994); Founder, Partner, Real Estate Department, Kronish Lieb (Now Cooley LLP) (1971-1989) **Career Related:** General Counsel, Citizens Budget Commission (2004-2012); Founder, Chair, Real Estate Specialists, Lawyers Division, UJA-Federation of New York (1988-2004) **Civic:** Executive Committee, Young Men's Division, Albert Einstein College of Medicine (1978-1988); Trustee, Citizens Budget Commission; Director, President, New York Association for New Americans, Inc.; Director, UJA-Federation of New York; Council of Overseers, UJA-Federation of New York; Chair, Young Leadership Division, UJA-Federation of New York; Board Member, Anti-Defamation League; National Young Leadership Cabinet, The Jewish Federations of North America; Executive Committee, Lawyers Division, UJA-Federation of New York; Class Agent, Columbia College, Columbia University; Class Agent, Cornell Law School, Cornell University; Board of Trustees, HIAS **Awards:** Guest of Honor, Annual Dinner, Real Estate Specialists, Lawyers Division, UJA-Federation of New York (1990); International Award for Leadership, Jewish Federations of North America (1975) **Memberships:** Board of Governors, Secretary, City Athletic Club; Association of the Bar of the City of New York; Real Property, Trust and Estate Law Section, American Bar Association; Committee on New Developments in Real Estate Law and Practice; American Land Title Association; New York State Bar Association **Bar Admissions:** State of New York (1965) **Marquis Who's Who Honors:** Albert Nelson Marquis Lifetime Achievement Award; Marquis Who's Who Top Professional **To what do you attribute your success:** Mr. Alter attributes his success to hard work and self-reliance. He held many jobs while paying his way through two Ivy League schools, spending time as a waiter, chef, taxi driver and postal clerk. He also gives praise to his mentors including the late Neil Underberg, an influential lawyer. **Why did you become involved in your profession or industry:** With encouragement from his mother, Mr. Alter became involved in his profession by seizing the opportunities in front of him. He attended Columbia initially as a pre-medical student before deciding law suited him best. He specialized his career by applying his passion for transactional law to realty. Mr. Alter's first legal job was at a boutique real estate law firm and throughout his career, he has headed the real estate departments of three major law firms. **Avocations:** Golfing; Tennis; Theater; Concerts; Traveling; Race car driving; Collecting vintage cars **Religion:** Jewish **Thoughts on Life:** As a teenager at Bayside High School in Queens, New York, Mr. Alter was the only student ever elected student body president twice. In that position, he was able to persuade legendary disc jockey Alan Freed to perform for Bayside students; this was the only public high school concert of Freed's career. He also negotiated with the City of New York in order to secure baseball and football fields for the school, benefiting future generations of Bayside students.

Sally L. Altman

Title: Educator (Retired) **Company Name:** Eureka Union School District **Date of Birth:** 03/28/1934 **Place of Birth:** Berkeley/CA **State/Country of Origin:** California/USA **Parents:** Daughter of E. Allen and Helen Lucile (Struthers) Phillips **Marital Status:** Widow **Spouse Name:** Arthur Lewis Altman, 12/27/1983 (Deceased 2008); Married Gerald C. Angove 03/25/1956 (Div. 1981) **Children:** Jay (Deceased); Douglas; Bill; **Education:** PE Workshop, Cal Poly, San Luis Obispo (1989-1994); MA, Stanford University (1957); BA, Stanford University (1956) **Certifications:** Certified Teacher, California **Career:** Retired (1996); Substitute Teacher (1996); Teacher, Coach, Cavitt Junior High, Granite Bay, CA (1982-1996); Teacher, Coach, Eureka School, Roseville, CA (1978-1982); Teacher, Physical Education, Placer High School, Auburn, CA (1978-1979); Coach, Placer High School, Auburn, CA (1975-1979); Teacher, Modesto High School (1968-1975); Coach, Modesto High School (1968-1975) Teacher, College of Sequois Evening School, Visalia, CA (1957-1968); Teacher, Mount Whitney High School, Visalia, CA (1962-1968); Teacher, Divisadero Junior High School, Visalia, CA (1960-1961); Instructor, College of the Sequoias, Visalia, CA (1957-1960) **Career Related:** Presenter, Various Workshops, National Evaluation Systems (1996-2001); Counselor, Tech Trek Camps, Stanford, UC Davis; Co-Director, Stanford Camp Hopper; Co-chairman, Tech Trek Committee; Secretary, Roseville-South Placer Branch, American Association of University Women; Chairman, Eureka Retired Faculty Staff Group; Chairman, American Association of University Women Neighborhood Group **Civic:** Instructor/Trainer, American Red Cross, Sacramento-Auburn (1988-2018); Member, Health Services Committee, Auburn (1989-1996); Active Valley Springs Presbyterian Church; VP, Physical Education for Professional Organizations **Military Service:** Armed Forces (1955) **Awards:** Inducted, Synchronized Swimming Hall of Fame (2018); National Synchronized Swimming Champion (1954); Pan American Games, Synchronized Swimming Gold Medal **Memberships:** Member American Association of University Women, AARP, California Association Health, Physical Education, Recreation and Dance (Retiree Section Chair (1997-1999), State, Vice President, Elect Physical education (1991-1992) Vice President (1992-1993), North, District president (1988-1990), North, District Rep. (1993-1996), Unit President (1986-1988), North, District Honor Award, 1991), Eureka Retired Staff Organization (Co-chair 2000-2010, Chair 2010-2018), Eureka Union Faculty Organization, Meals on Wheels. **Marquis Who's Who Honors:** Albert Nelson Marquis Lifetime Achievement Award **To what do you attribute your success:** Mrs. Altman attributes her success to her ambition and competitiveness, as well as her not being able to turn down a task when asked to complete it. **Why did you become involved in your profession or industry:** Mrs. Altman became involved in her profession because she loved swimming and teaching. She decided being a physical education teacher would fit those needs, and she is interested in staying healthy so she minored in that field. **Avocations:** Swimming; Skiing: Traveling; Reading; Bridging; Walking **Political Affiliations:** Republican **Religion:** Presbyterian **Thoughts on Life:** "I love the life I live and hope to keep on enjoying it until I turn 100+ years old." She has had a beautiful life, including all of her traveling, currently she is on a bus, on a tour of Archer's National Park in Canon Ranch Land, beautiful sights, headed toward a dinosaur museum. After her husband died, she started traveling with a tour group out of Sacramento, with other widows. Her sons are married, her youngest son has the two girls. Her oldest grandchild, is the one whose father passed away, her other son is married, but no children. Her second husband had four children, they are all married, of those there is a step-grand daughter who had a baby boy, so she has a step-great-grand son.

Maad al-Zikry

Title: Video Journalist **Industry:** Other **Company Name:** Associated Press **Career:** Video Journalist, Associated Press **Creative Works:** Contributor, Articles, Associated Press, The Washington Post, Fox News, USA Today, El Pais, Yahoo India, SFGate, ABC NewsOne, PBS NewsHour, Toronto Star Newspapers Ltd., The Seattle Times **Awards:** Pulitzer Prize in International Reporting (2019)

Kate Amend

Title: Film Editor, Educator **Industry:** Media & Entertainment **Place of Birth:** San Francisco **State/Country of Origin:** CA/USA **Parents:** Carroll Conrad Amend; Mary Florence (Saller) Amend **Education:** Honorary Doctorate, Academy of Art University, San Francisco, CA (2016); MA, California State University, San Francisco (1973); BA, University of California, Berkeley (1969) **Career:** Film Editor, Los Angeles, CA (1982-Present); Researcher, Administrator, Judy Chicago's "The Dinner Party", Santa Monica, CA (1978-1981); Administrator, Through the Flower Corp., Santa Monica, CA (1978-1981); Instructor, Humanities and Women's Studies, Diablo Valley College (1973-1978); Instructor, Humanities, City College of San Francisco (1973-1978) **Career Related:** Adjunct Professor, University of Southern California School of Cinematic Arts (1992-Present) **Creative Works:** Editor, "Visible: Out on Television" Apple Plus TV Series (2020); Editor, "Foster" (2018); Editor, "Feminists: What Were They Thinking?" (2018); Editor, "The Keepers" (2017); Editor, "Serena" (2016); Editor, "The Case Against 8" (2014); Editor, "Birth Story: Ina May Gaskin and the Farm Midwives" (2012); Editor, "Crazy Wisdom: The Life & Times of Chogyam Trungpa Rinpoche" (2011); Editor, "First Position" (2011); Editor, "Man from Plains" (2007); Editor, "Cowboy del Amor" (2005); Editor, "Beah: A Black Woman Speaks" (2004); Editor, "Pandemic: Facing AIDS" (2002); Editor, "Into the Arms of Strangers: Stories of the Kindertransport" (2001); Editor, "Tobacco Blues" (1997); Editor, "Some Nudity Required" (1998); Editor, "The Long Way Home" (1997); Editor, "Arrested Development in the House" (1995); Editor, "Spread the Word: The Persuasions Sing Acapella" (1994); Editor, "Skinheads USA: Soldiers of the Race War" (1993); Editor, Films **Awards:** Best Editing Award, "Dave Grusin: Not Enough Time," Beverly Hills Film Festival (2020); Co-nominee, Emmy Award, "The Case Against 8," Academy of Television Arts & Sciences (2014); Outstanding Achievement in Editing Award, International Documentary Association (2005); Co-recipient, Peabody Award, "Beah: A Black Woman Speaks" (2004); Co-recipient, Academy Award, "Into the Arms of Strangers," Academy of Motion Picture Arts and Sciences; Eddie Award, American Cinema Editors (2001); Co-recipient, Academy Award, "The Long Way Home," Academy of Motion Picture Arts and Sciences (1997) **Memberships:** Advisor, Documentary Edit and Story Lab, Sundance Institute (2004-2019); Governor, Documentary Branch, Academy of Motion Picture Arts and Sciences; International Documentary Association; American Cinema Editors **Marquis Who's Who Honors:** Albert Nelson Marquis Lifetime Achievement Award; Marquis Who's Who Top Professional **To what do you attribute your success:** Ms. Amend attributes her success to her decision to move to Los Angeles to work with Judy Chicago on the monumental feminist art work, "The Dinner Party." Working with Chicago, she learned the value of creating a meaningful career in the arts. It was there that she met director and editor, Johanna Demetrakas, who was filming her documentary, "Right Out of History: The Making of Judy Chicago's Dinner Party." That was the first documentary Ms. Amend worked on (as an assistant editor), and Demetrakas became a mentor, a professional colleague, and a lifelong friend and inspiration. **Why did you become involved in your profession or industry:** Ms. Amend became involved in her industry with inspiration from the women's movement, crediting an influential wave of women filmmakers and documentary makers in the 1970s. At the time, Ms. Amend was teaching at the City College of San Francisco, where she began taking film classes. She fell in love with editing in particular, and ultimately decided to pursue documentary editing as a career. **Avocations:** Gardening; Playing tennis; Cooking; Jazz **Political Affiliations:** Democrat **Thoughts on Life:** Ms. Amend is the editor of the Academy Award-winning documentary films "The Long Way Home" (1998) and "Into the Arms of Strangers: Stories of the Kindertransport" (2001). For the latter, she won the American Cinema Editors' prestigious Eddie Award. Ms. Amend has also edited the Oscar-nominated documentary short "On Tiptoe: Gentle Steps to Freedom," and the Peabody Award-winning "Beah: A Black Woman Speaks". In 2005, she received the inaugural Outstanding Achievement in Editing Award from the International Documentary Association. Ms. Amend is a member of the American Cinema Editors' Board of Directors and represents the Documentary Branch on the Board of Governors of the Academy of Motion Picture Arts and Sciences. She is an advisor for the Sundance Institute's Documentary Storytelling Lab and the National Association of Latino Independent Producers' Academy. She teaches documentary editing courses at the USC. In 2016, she received an honorary doctorate from the Academy of Art University. Her film, "Dave Grusin: Not Enough Time," received the Best Editing Award at the 2020 Beverly Hills Film Festival. Currently, Ms. Amend is editing "Viva Maestro!," a documentary on Gustavo Dudamel, renowned Venezuelan conductor of the Los Angeles Philharmonic.

Albert Jay Ammerman, PhD

Title: Research Professor, Archaeologist, Humanities Educator **Industry:** Education/Educational Services **Company Name:** Colgate University **Date of Birth:** 07/07/1942 **Place of Birth:** Detroit **State/Country of Origin:** MI/USA **Parents:** Albert Merlin Ammerman; Ruth Lennox Ammerman **Marital Status:** Married **Spouse Name:** Rebecca Lynne Miller (7/16/1983) **Children:** Richard Albert; Dora Q. **Education:** Fellowship, Origins of Rome, American Council of Learned Societies (2003-2004); Kress Senior Fellow, Reconstructing Ancient Rome, Center for Advanced Study in the Visual Arts, National Gallery of Art (1995-1996); Guggenheim Foundation Fellowship, Environmental Studies in Ancient Rome, John Simon Guggenheim Memorial Foundation (1990-1991); Mellon Fellowship in Classical Studies, Early Rome, American Academy in Rome (1987-1988); Research Fellowship, Vico's Anthropology, National Endowment for the Humanities (1984); PhD, UCL Institute of Archaeology (1972); BA in Honors English Literature, University of Michigan (1964) **Career:** Research Professor, Colgate University, Hamilton, NY (2011-Present); O'Connor Visiting Professor of Humanities, Colgate University (2007-2009); Senior Research Associate, Colgate University (1986-2003); Visiting Professor, University of Trento, Italy (1994-1999); Visiting Professor, Università di Parma, Italy (1982-1993); Assistant Professor, Binghamton University State University of New York, Binghamton, NY (1978-1983); Senior Research Associate, Lecturer in Human Biology, Stanford University, Palo Alto, CA (1972-1977); Research Professor, Archaeologist, Humanities Educator **Career Related:** Director, Venice Study Group, Colgate University, Hamilton, NY (1999-2013); Director, Archaeology Summer School, American Academy in Rome (2001); Director, Inside Archaeology LLC **Creative Works:** Co-Author, "New Light on the Temple of Athena: Re-shaping the Landscape" (2019); Editor, "Island Archaeology and the Origins of Seafaring in the Eastern Mediterranean" (2013-2014); Editor, "The Widening Harvest" (2003); Editor, "Venice Before San Marco" (2001); Author, "The Acconia Survey: Neolithic Settlement and the Obsidian Trade" (1985); Co-Author, "The Neolithic Transition and the Genetics of Populations in Europe" (1984); Contributor, Articles, Professional Journals; Guest Speaker, Invited Lectures; Contributor, Antiquity; Contributor, Science; Contributor, Journal of Roman Archaeology; Contributor, American Journal of Archaeology; Contributor, Journal of Field Archaeology; Contributor, World Archaeology **Awards:** Lifetime Foreign Member, Istituto Veneto, Italy (2020); Grantee, Gladys Krieble Delmas Foundation (1990-2018); Grantee, Institute for Aegean Prehistory (INSTAP) (2004-2012); Grantee, National Geographic Society (1985-2002); the National Science Foundation (1979, 1982); Writing Awards, University of Michigan (1964) **Memberships:** Managing Committee, American School of Classical Studies of Athens (1990-Present); International Strategic Committee, Université Nice Sophia Antipolis (2016-2019); Science Committee, Archaeological Institute of America (1992-1998) **Marquis Who's Who Honors:** Albert Nelson Marquis Lifetime Achievement Award; Marquis Who's Who Top Professional **To what do you attribute your success:** Dr. Ammerman attributes his success to developing new lines of interdisciplinary studies. He brings together two fields that were essentially separate ones previously. Some call it transdisciplinary research today. He was, for instance, a senior research associate and lecturer in human biology at Stanford University in Palo Alto, California, from 1972 through 1977. Working in collaboration with Lucca Cavalli-Sforza in the Department of Genetics at Stanford University, he pioneered a new field of research that brought archaeology and human genetics for the first time. In Rome, Dr. Ammerman then conduced 23 years of archaeological fieldwork and environmental studies at many sites in the ancient city, including the Forum, the Capitoline Hill and the east bank of the Tiber. In each case, he documented that there was the purposeful transformation of the landscape in the time before the Republic. In Venice, he also carried out 14 years of interdisciplinary investigations at a number of sites in the city and the lagoon, which shed new light on the origins of Saint Mark's Square and how the city began. He and his wife, Rebecca Miller Ammerman, are now working on the temple of Athena at Paestum, a Greek city-state in southern Italy. He and others have recently created Inside Archaeology LLC in New York state, whose purpose is to lead people on trips to raise money for archaeological research. For much of his career, he has divided his time between the United States and Italy. **Avocations:** Winemaking, Rowing **Thoughts on Life:** Dr. Ammerman believes that the earth will witness the active growth of cities in the 21st century and, in turn, there will be the need to reshape and transform them. Transformations of this kind have deep time roots, as his research has shown. In the case of three leading civic centers in world history – the Forum in Rome, the Agora of ancient Athens and Saint Mark's Square in Venice – each of them began its life as a marginal place on the landscape.

Barbara Louise Anderson

Title: County Librarian, Retired **Industry:** Library Management/Library Services **Company Name:** San Bernardino County Library **Date of Birth:** 01/05/1933 **Place of Birth:** San Diego **State/Country of Origin:** CA/USA **Parents:** Lorenzo Anderson; Louise (Morgan) Anderson **Marital Status:** Single **Children:** Sean Allen (Deceased) **Education:** MLS, Kansas State Teachers College (1955); BS, San Diego State University (1954) **Career:** Retired (1994-Present); County Librarian, San Bernardino County Library (1974-1994); Head of Readers Services, Riverside City and County Public Library (1972-1974); Coordinator, Serra Reference Project, Serra Regional Library System, San Diego, CA (1969-1971); Librarian, U.S. Army, Europe (1964-1969); Branch Library, Reference, Young Adult Library, San Diego Public Library (1959-1964); Branch Library, Los Angeles Public Library (1956-1959) **Career Related:** Delegate, White House Conference on Libraries and Information Services (1979) **Civic:** Riverside County Library Advisory Board (1997-Present); Riverside County Archives Commission (1996-Present); Lake Elsinore Womens Club (1997); Citizens Advisory Board, San Bernardino YWCA (1988-1989); Board of Directors, Inland Empire Symphony (1982-1984); Riverside Mental Health Association (1975-1979) **Creative Works:** Contributor, Articles, Professional Journals **Memberships:** Business and Professional Women of San Bernardino (1975-Present); California County Librarians Association (1974-Present); California Library Association (1956-Present); Congress of Public Library Systems (1956-Present); OCLC Users Council, California Society of Libraries (1984-1988); President, Congress of Public Library Systems (1984); President, Riverside Branch, American Association of University Women (1976-1977); President, California Society of Libraries (1974-1975); National Association For The Advancement Of Colored People; Black Caucus California Library Association; American Library Association **Marquis Who's Who Honors:** Albert Nelson Marquis Lifetime Achievement Award **Why did you become involved in your profession or industry:** While Ms. Anderson was in college working part-time, she didn't drive or have much money. Her mother encouraged her to go to college, but her father thought that she should get a job with the local telephone company. She went to college, among the jobs that she had, and worked in a library. By her junior year of college, she began to wonder what she would do with a degree. She knew that she didn't want to teach and was no good at science. She began looking around the library speaking to the librarians and thought the librarians look happy with their jobs, even though they don't make much money. She then figured that money isn't the most important thing when choosing a career, as long as she could sustain herself and buy the things that she liked. After she completed her undergraduate program, she had choices between University of California Berkeley and University of Southern California (USC); Berkeley was always filled and USC was too expensive. She then began to apply to other schools throughout the Midwest, writing letter after letter. Eventually, she was met with two options - University of Oklahoma or Kansas State University. She chose Kansas State, even though it was a smaller school. She has no regrets about her choice. Her first semester, because she had to pay out-of-state tuition, she received a job at a local hospital that supplied her meals everyday. She eventually received a scholarship to the school, alleviating her financial burdens until her completion. **Avocations:** Traveling; Reading; Volunteering **Political Affiliations:** Democrat **Religion:** Baptist **Thoughts on Life:** Ms. Anderson was the first minority county librarian in the state, as well as the first minority department head in the county. Although she is glad to have that title, she feels that the first should have been appointed 100 years prior. Ms. Anderson's mother grew up in Newbury, South Carolina, at a time when education for African Americans was very limited. She grew up in a family of 10. Her father was a blacksmith, farmer, a truck driver and car salesman, and her mother took care of the children. There were no colleges in the area, nor would she be able to attend college as a black woman. There were academies available that were comparable to the community college level although very small. Her mother attended and received a teaching degree, and eventually taught in rural South Carolina. Ms. Anderson has come from quite a remarkable family. Despite the odds stacked against them in the south, they were able to overcome and be successful.

Bill Maxwell Anderson

Title: Owner **Industry:** Fine Art **Company Name:** Bill Anderson Art Gallery **Date of Birth:** 07/31/1941 **Place of Birth:** Mankato **State/Country of Origin:** MN/USA **Parents:** Robert Arthur Anderson; June Arlene Anderson **Marital Status:** Married **Spouse Name:** Ausma Edite Leipins Anderson (08/05/1962) **Children:** Kerri; Craig **Education:** Graduate Coursework, Minnesota State University, Mankato, MN (1974); Graduate Coursework, University of California, Irvine, CA (1969); Graduate Coursework, California State University, Long Beach, CA (1964-1968); BS, Minnesota State University, Mankato, MN (1963) **Career:** Owner, Bill Anderson Art Gallery (1994-Present); Art Teacher, Muralist, East Los Angeles College (2001-2002); Art Teacher, Orange County School of the Arts (1985-1996); Art Teacher, Los Alamitos Unified School District, California (1980-2001); Art Teacher, Anaheim Union High School District (1973-1980); Art Teacher, Appleton West High School, Appleton, WI (1969-1973); Art Teacher, Long Beach Unified School District (1963-1969) **Civic:** President, Allied Arts Board, City of Huntington Beach, CA (1989-1991); Member, Allied Arts Board, City of Huntington Beach, CA (1979-1991) **Creative Works:** Author, "Huntington Beach, Surf City" (2018); Author, "Sunset Beach, Through the Eyes of Artist Bill Anderson" (2017); Author, "Huntington Beach: Through the Eyes of Artist Bill Anderson" (2016); Author, "Baseball, Great American Pastime Through the Eyes of Artist Bill Anderson" (2016); Author, "The Female Form: Through the Eyes of Artist Bill Anderson" (2016); Author, "The Fantastic Horse: Through the Eyes of Artist Bill Anderson" (2016); Author, "Greece: Through the Eyes of Artist Bill Anderson" (2014); Author, "The Heritage Series: U.S. Military Joint Forces Training Base" (2014); Exhibitor, One-Man Show, Chaffey Community Museum of Art, Rancho Cucamonga, CA, Joint Forces Training Base, Los Alamitos, CA (2007); Exhibitor, Ontario Museum, Ontario, California (2004-2005); Millard Sheets Art Center, Pomona, CA (2004); Painter, Murals (2001-2002); Exhibitor, Vincent Price Art Museum (2000); Exhibitor, Luckman Fine Arts Complex, California State University, Los Angeles, CA (1995); Exhibitor, Museo Nacional de la Acuarela, Mexico (1994); Author, "The Work of Bill Anderson" (1984); Exhibitor, Group Exhibit, "Olympic International Artist Exchange," Huntington Beach Art Center (1984); Exhibitor, Group Exhibit, "IV Taller Invierno 1983," Museum of Modern Art, Guadalajara, Mexico (1983); Exhibitor, One-Man Show, University of California, Los Angeles, CA (1981); Exhibitor, One-Man Show, Galleria Coyoacan, Mexico City, Mexico (1981); Illustrator, "The Rebel Reverend"; Illustrator, "Ulysses S. Grant"; Illustrator, "Gold Rush Glimpses III"; Illustrator, "Old West Wow!"; Illustrator, "Old West Christmas: Tales With A Twist"; Exhibitor, Numerous Exhibitions **Awards:** First Outstanding Artist of the Year, Huntington Beach, CA (1986); Outstanding Teacher of the Year, Anaheim Union High School District (1977, 1975) **Marquis Who's Who Honors:** Albert Nelson Marquis Lifetime Achievement Award **To what do you attribute your success:** Mr. Anderson attributes his success to his wife, Ausma Edite Liepins Anderson. **Why did you become involved in your profession or industry:** Mr. Anderson was inspired to pursue a career in art because his grandfather, Oscar H. Anderson, was an artist. **Avocations:** Art **Religion:** Lutheran

Gordon Wood Anderson

Title: Research Physicist **Industry:** Engineering **Date of Birth:** 03/08/1936 **Place of Birth:** Evanston **State/Country of Origin:** IL/USA **Parents:** Gordon Hilmer; Avis Elizabeth (Hillman) Anderson **Marital Status:** Partner **Spouse Name:** Sharron Walther Kaplan **Education:** Doctor of Philosophy in Physics, University of Illinois at Urbana-Champaign (1969); Master of Science in Physics, University of Illinois at Urbana-Champaign (1961); Master of Engineering, Cornell University, Ithaca, NY (1959); Bachelor of Electrical Engineering, Cornell University, Ithaca, NY (1959) **Career:** General Engineer, Office of the Secretary of Defense, Defense Technology Security Administration (1998-2008); Technology Advisor, Office of Naval Research (1991-1997); Consultant, Planning & Human Systems, Washington (1978-1979); Research Physicist, United States Naval Research Laboratory (1969-1998); Instructor, Tougaloo College, Mississippi (1965); Research Assistant, University of Illinois (1960-1969) **Career Related:** Adjunct Professor, City University of New York (2009-Present); Consultant, Institute for Defense Analysis (2008-Present); Agency Advisor, Planning & Human Systems, Incorporated, Washington (1978-1979); Postdoctoral Research Associate, National Research Council (1969-1970); Office of Naval Research, Naval Systems Commands, Advanced Research Projects **Civic:** Affiliate Honorary Board Director, Epilepsy Foundation of America (1989-Present); Treasurer, DC Center for Independent Living (1992-1993); President, DC Center for Independent Living (1990-1992); Treasurer, DC Center for Independent Living (1989-1990); Board of Directors, Capitol Hill Restoration Society (1988-1989); Vice President, DC Center for Independent Living (1982-1983); Board of Directors, Founding Member, DC Center for Independent Living (1981-1993); National Board Director, Epilepsy Foundation of America (1979-1985); Member Affiliate, Professional Advisory Board, Epilepsy Foundation of America (1978-1992); Affiliate President, Epilepsy Foundation of America (1976-1978); Affiliate Board Director, Epilepsy Foundation of America (1974-1986); Board of Directors, Secretary-Treasurer, Colonial Singers & Players (1973-1998); Secretary Affiliate, Professional Advisory Board, Epilepsy Foundation of America (1972-1976); Member Affiliate, Professional Advisory Board, Epilepsy Foundation of America (1972-1976); Founding Member, Affiliate Board Director, Epilepsy Foundation of America (1972-1973) **Creative Works:** Contributor, Articles to Professional Journals, Chapters to Books **Awards:** Exceptional Civil Services Award, Office of the Secretary Defense, Defense Technology Security Administration (2008); Grantee, National Science Foundation (1963); Fellow, Ford Foundation (1959-1961); Williams College Book Award (1957); Numerous Naval Research Laboratory Awards **Marquis Who's Who Honors:** Albert Nelson Marquis Lifetime Achievement Award; Marquis Who's Who Top Professional; Marquis Who's Who Humanitarian Award **Why did you become involved in your profession or industry:** Mr. Anderson became involved in his profession due to the influence of his grandfather, Wayne W. Hillman Grant, as well as his great uncle and cousins, who were civil engineers with the railroad. He spent much of his youth traveling on and watching trains until he became fascinated with them. **Political Affiliations:** Democrat **Religion:** Episcopalian

Marilyn Echols Anderson

Title: Partner **Industry:** Architecture & Construction **Company Name:** Anderson Enterprises **Date of Birth:** 03/03/1937 **Place of Birth:** McRae **State/Country of Origin:** GA/USA **Parents:** Marion Ishmael; Ruth Evelyn (Lord) Echols **Marital Status:** Married **Spouse Name:** William Harvey Anderson **Children:** William David Anderson (Deceased); William Alan Anderson; Alicia Dawn Anderson **Education:** Degree, Business School (1955) **Career:** Business Partner, Developer, W. Harvey Anderson Construction Company (1992-Present); Real Estate Developer, W. Harvey Anderson Construction Company Inc. (1963-Present); Draftsman Partner, W. Harvey Anderson Construction Company (1963-1992) **Career Related:** Partnership, Anderson Enterprises **Civic:** Member, Saltwater Licensing Committee, GA; Member, President Jimmy Carter Presidential Campaign **Creative Works:** Author, "Recipes & Inspirations" (2000) **Awards:** Top Angler Award (1993-1995); Top Lady Angler Award (1992) **Memberships:** Captain, Northeast Florida Marlin Association (1995-2000); President, Golden Isles Sport Fishing Club (1990-1991) **Marquis Who's Who Honors:** Albert Nelson Marquis Lifetime Achievement Award **To what do you attribute your success:** Ms. Anderson attributes her success to her motivation and ambition. **Why did you become involved in your profession or industry:** Ms. Anderson became involved in her profession because of her studies upon graduating high school. One opportunity led to another and allowed her to do what she does today. **Avocations:** Painting; Traveling; Saltwater fishing; Gourmet cooking; Interior decorating **Political Affiliations:** Democrat **Religion:** Methodist **Thoughts on Life:** Ms. Anderson states, "Embrace every moment and surround yourself with the ones you love."

Merlyn D. Anderson

Title: Lawyer **Industry:** Law and Legal Services **Company Name:** Law Office of Merlyn Anderson **Date of Birth:** 12/24/1941 **Place of Birth:** Slayton **State/Country of Origin:** MN/USA **Parents:** Minard Anderson; Ethel (Vihlen) Anderson **Education:** JD, University of South Dakota (1972); MA in Educational Psychology, University of South Dakota (1965); BA, Yankton College (1964) **Career:** Solo Practice, Slayton, MN (1979-Present); City Attorney, Cities of Avoca, Hadley, Iona, Lake Wilson, Slayton, MN (1974-Present); County Attorney, Murray County, MN (1979-1995); Lawyer, Roy K. Rietz Law Office, Slayton, MN (1973-1979); Lawyer, Frank Vladyka Law Office, Tyndall, SD (1972); Social Worker, South Dakota Department of Welfare, Yankton, SD (1969); Guidance Counselor, Freeman Public Schools (1966) **Career Related:** Bank Attorney, Murray County State Bank, Slayton, MN (1979-2014); Personnel Board, New Dawn, Incorporated, Slayton, MN (1973-1977) **Civic:** Secretary, Lesterville Volunteer Fire Department (1972-1978); Mayor, Council Member, Town of Lesterville (1972-1978); Council Member, Town of Lesterville (1970-1972); Volunteer Fireman, Lesterville Volunteer Fire Department (1969-1978) **Military Service:** United States Army Reserves (USAR) (1991-2005); South Dakota Army National Guard Military Band (1968-1972); Active Duty. U.S. Army (1966-1967) **Awards:** Featured Listee, Outstanding Young Men of America (1976); Featured Listee, Who's Who in America; Featured Listee, International Register of Profiles; Featured Listee, Who's Who in Executives and Professionals; Featured Listee, Who's Who in the Midwest; Featured Listee, Who's Who in American Law; Featured Listee, Who's Who in the World **Memberships:** Adjudant, American Legion (2008-Present); Secretary-Treasurer, 13th Minnesota District Bar Association (1982); Treasurer, Kiwanis (1974-1988); American Bar Association; Minnesota Bar Association; Lions **Bar Admissions:** Minnesota (1972); South Dakota (1972); Iowa (1972) **Marquis Who's Who Honors:** Albert Nelson Marquis Lifetime Achievement Award; Distinguished Humanitarian **Why did you become involved in your profession or industry:** During his time in college, Mr. Anderson found an interest in the field of law. Influenced by his friends also studying law, he enrolled in law school and consequently graduated with a Juris Doctor. Ever since then, he has been a successful lawyer. **Avocations:** Reading; Attending sporting events

José Ramón "José Andrés" Andrés Puerta

Title: Chef; Founder **Industry:** Food & Restaurant Services **Company Name:** World Central Kitchen **Date of Birth:** 07/13/1969 **Place of Birth:** Mieres **State/Country of Origin:** Asturias/Spain **Marital Status:** Married **Spouse Name:** Patricia Fernandez de la Cruz **Children:** Three Children **Education:** Coursework, Escola de Restauracio i Hostalatge de Barcelona (1990) **Career:** Executive Chef, Partner, Jaleo, Crystal City, VA (2004-Present); Executive Chef, Partner, Oyamel Cocina Mexicana (2004-Present); Executive Chef, Partner, Zaytinya (2002-Present); Executive Chef, Partner, Jaleo, Washington, DC (1993-Present); Chef, El Dorado Petit, New York, NY (1990-1993); Executive Chef, Café Atlantico; Executive Chef, Partner, Jaleo, Bethesda, MD; Owner, Minibar by José Andrés; Chef, The Quilted Giraffe; Owner/Co-Owner, America Eats Tavern; Owner/Co-Owner, barmini by José Andrés; Owner/Co-Owner, Bazaar; Owner/Co-Owner, Meat by José Andrés; Owner/Co-Owner, Butterfly Tacos y Tortas; Owner/Co-Owner, Chilcano; Owner/Co-Owner, Poblano; Owner/Co-Owner, Fish; Owner/Co-Owner, Mercado Little Spain; Owner/Co-Owner, Ovations by America Eats; Owner/Co-Owner, Pepe and Tres by José Andrés **Career Related:** Founder, ThinkFoodTank, ThinkFoodGroup (2004-Present); Instructor, The George Washington University (2012); Dean, Spanish Studies, The International Culinary Center (2012); Co-instructor, Culinary Physics, Harvard University (2010); Apprentice, El Bullí (1985-1988) **Civic:** Founder, World Central Kitchen (2010-Present); Chef, Partner of Distinction, DC Central Kitchen (2001); Chair, Board, DC Central Kitchen **Military Service:** Cook, Military Service, Spain **Creative Works:** Author, "We Fed an Island: The True Story of Rebuilding Puerto Rico, One Meal at a Time" (2018); Appearance, Television Series, "Anthony Bourdain: Parts Unknown" (2018); Appearance, Television Series, "American Masters" (2017); Culinary Consultant, Television Series, "Hannibal" (2013-2015); Guest Judge, Television Series, "The Taste" (2013); Guest Judge, Television Series, "Top Chef" (2010); Host, Television Series, "Made in Spain" (2008); Appearance, Television Series, "Anthony Bourdain: No Reservations" (2008); Author, "Los Fogones de José Andrés" (2008); Co-author, "Made in Spain: Spanish Dishes for the American Kitchen" (2008); Appearance, Television Series, "Iron Chef America" (2007); Author, "Vamos a Cocinar" (2007); Host, Producer, Television Series, "Vamos a Cocinar" (2005-2007); Contributor, "How to Cook Everything: Bittman Takes on America's Chefs" (2005); Co-Author, "Tapas: A Taste of Spain in America"; Contributing Editor, Food Arts; Featured, Gourmet Magazine, "Sunday Morning News with Chris Wallace," Food Network, USA Today **Awards:** Humanitarian of the Year, James Beard Foundation (2018); Lifetime Achievement Award, International Association of Culinary Professionals (2017); National Humanities Medal, National Endowment for the Humanities (2015); Named, One of the 100 Most Influential People in the World, Time Magazine (2012); Outstanding Chef Award, James Beard Foundation (2011); Order of Arts and Letters Medallion, Spain (2010); Vilcek Prize in Culinary Arts, Vilcek Foundation (2010); Chef of the Year, GQ Magazine (2009); Chef of the Year, RAMW (2006); Listee, Saveur 100 List, Saveur Magazine (2004); Chef of the Year, Bon Appetit (2004); Named, One of the 35 Under 35 Tastemakers List, Food & Wine Magazine (2004); Best Chef of the Mid-Atlantic Region, James Beard Foundation (2003); Named, One of the Rising Stars of American Cuisine, Wine Spectator Magazine (1999)

William F. Andrews

Title: Manufacturing Company and Private Equity Firm Executive (Retired) **Industry:** Financial Services **Company Name:** Kohlberg & Company, Corrections Corporation of America **Date of Birth:** 10/07/1931 **Place of Birth:** Easton **State/Country of Origin:** PA/USA **Parents:** William Frederick; Lydia Nielson (Cross) Andrews **Marital Status:** Married **Spouse Name:** Lin Howard **Children:** William Frederick III; Whitney; Carter; Clayton; Sloane **Education:** Master of Business Administration in Marketing, Seton Hall University, South Orange, NJ (1961); Bachelor of Science in Business Administration, University of Maryland (1953) **Certifications:** Kohlberg & Company, Corrections Corporation of America **Career:** Retired (2014); Partner, Kohlberg & Company (1997-2014); Principal, Kohlberg & Company (1992-2014); Chief Executive Officer, Chairman, Board of Directors, Amdura Corporation, Connecticut (1992-1994); President, Chief Executive Officer, UNR Industries Incorporated (1990-1992); President, Chief Executive Officer, Chairman, Massey Investment Company (1989-1990); Chairman, President, Chief Executive Officer, Singer Sewing Machine Company (1986-1989); Chairman, President, Chief Executive Officer, Scovill Manufacturing Company (1981-1986); President, Scovill Manufacturing Company, Waterbury, CT (1979-1981); Group Vice President, Scovill Manufacturing Company, Nashville, TN (1973-1979); Vice President, General Manager, Scovill Manufacturing Company, Raleigh, NC (1968-1973); Product Manager, Scovill Manufacturing Company, Waterbury, CT (1965-1968) **Career Related:** Chairperson, Board of Directors, Katy Industries, Incorporated (2001-Present); Chairperson, Board of Directors, Thomas Nelson Publications (2010-2012); Chairperson, Executive Committee, Corrections Corporation of America (2008-2014); Chairperson, Board of Directors, Central Parking (2007-2012); Chairperson, Board of Directors, Singer Sewing Company (2004-2012); Board of Directors, O'Charleys Incorporated (2004-2012); Chairperson, Board of Directors, Corrections Corporation of America (2000-2008); Chairperson, Board of Directors, Allied Aerospace Industries, Incorporated (2000-2006); Board of Directors, Trex Company Incorporated (1999-2013); Chairperson, Board of Directors, Northwestern Steel & Wire Company (1998-2001); Chairperson, Board of Directors, Schrader Bridgeport (1995-1998); Board of Directors, Black Box Incorporated (1992-2013); Chairperson, Board of Directors, Utica Corporation (1992-1994); Board of Directors, Corrections Corporation of America (1986-1998); Board of Directors, First Bank **Civic:** Board Member, First Bank (2017-Present); Chairperson, Red Cross; Chairperson, Easter Seals; Chairperson, Cheekwood Botanical Gardens & Art Museum; Chairperson, Waterbury Chamber of Commerce; Chairperson, National Fluid Power Association **Military Service:** Captain, United States Air Force (1953-1956) **Awards:** Named, ODX Director of Year (2011); Silver Beaver Award, Boy Scouts of America, Significant Sig Award (2000) **Memberships:** Snake River Sporting Club, Jackson, WY; Shooting Star Country Club; International Polo Club, Wellington, FL; Old Natchez Country Club, Nashville, TN; Belle Meade Country Club, Nashville, TN; Wanderers Club, Wellington, FL; Golf Club, Tennessee; Tennessee University Club, New York); Chicago Club; Master of Hounds, Middlebury, Litchfield, CT **Marquis Who's Who Honors:** Albert Nelson Marquis Lifetime Achievement Award **To what do you attribute your success:** Mr. Andrews attributes his success to a propensity for hard work, persistence and collaboration with others. **Avocations:** Horseback riding; Swimming; Skiing; Tennis; Golf **Political Affiliations:** Republican **Religion:** Episcopalian

Peter Gregory Angelo, PhD

Title: Professor Emeritus **Industry:** Education/Educational Services **Company Name:** Stony Brook University **Date of Birth:** 7/1/1947 **Place of Birth:** New York **State/Country of Origin:** NY/USA **Parents:** Vincent Peter Angelo; Stella Elizabeth (Galasso) Angelo **Education:** PhD in English, Stony Brook University (1978); MA in English, Stony Brook University (1972); BA in Psychology & Biology/Pre-Med, Stony Brook University (1969) **Certifications:** Instructor Training and CPR (1972) **Career:** Professor Emeritus, Stony Brook University, (2017-Present); Director of Adapted Aquatics and Emergency Response Programs, School of Health Technology and Management, Health Sciences Center, Stony Brook University, Stony Brook, NY (1978-2017); Coordinator, Recreational Swimming Programs, Catholic Child Care Society (1969-1987); Assistant Professor, English Department, Stony Brook University (1973-1978); Fellowship, Endowment for the Humanities, Stony Brook University (1969-1973); Director, Aquatics, New York Association for Brain Injured Children, Suffolk County, New York (1971-1972); Director, Aquatics, Catholic Child Care Center, Shoreham, NY (1968-1969) **Career Related:** Director, Fitness and Aquatics, New York Institute of Technology, Central Islip, NY (1988-1990); Instructor, Trainer, Water Safety, Northport Veterans Hospital (1980-1988); Adjunct Professor, C.W. Post College, Long Island University, Brentwood, NY (1984); Assistant Professor, English Department, Hofstra University, Hempstead, NY (1979-1980); Full Professor, C.W. Post College, Long Island University, Brentwood, NY **Civic:** Instructor, Scripture and Theology, Archdiocese of New York (1998-Present); Chairman, Adapted Aquatics, Suffolk County Chapter, American Red Cross (1984-Present); Instructor, Scripture and Theology, Roman Catholic Diocese, Rockville Centre, NY (1982-Present); Instructor, Trainer, American Red Cross, Suffolk County, NY (1968-Present); Co-Founder, Steering Committee Hartsell Cancer Fund, Hauppauge, NY (1984-1986) **Creative Works:** Editor, Emergency Response Text Book (2005); Author, "Fall to Glory: Theological Reflections on Milton's Epics" (1988) **Awards:** New York State Chancellor's Award for Excellence in Teaching (1998); President's Award for Excellence in Teaching, Stony Brook University **Marquis Who's Who Honors:** Albert Nelson Marquis Lifetime Achievement Award **To what do you attribute your success:** There were several people who were very important in Dr. Angelo's life; there was Archbishop Fulton J. Sheen, who is up for sainthood right now, Auxiliary Bishop of New York Joseph Perniconi, who was the priest in his childhood parish, and his alter boy moderator Father Nicholas Milazzo. **Why did you become involved in your profession or industry:** During Dr. Angelo's graduate studies, he was preparing for the Olympic trials for the Munich games. He was great swimmer and might've ended up going, but several things happened: one was the terrorist attack on the Israeli athletes, and the other was that he was approached about founding the adaptive aquatics program. He was very excited about the opportunity because his grandmother had been disabled. She suffered a stroke when he was younger and because of medical practices of the time, there was very little for her in the way of rehabilitation of recreation. Her only recreational activity was sitting at the window and watching the streets below. He wanted to ensure that no other disabled person would ever have to live like that. **Avocations:** Art; Swimming; Theater; Films; Photography; Botany **Religion:** Roman Catholic **Thoughts on Life:** Dr. Angelo's PhD program had three areas of concentration, including the English Renaissance, and the printing and publication of the King James Bible. This makes him a biblical expert. He was the first person in the history of the university to receive a doctorate in a theological area. The other two areas of expertise are Shakespeare and Milton, and the history of theater from the Greeks to the Renaissance.

Jennifer Joanna Aniston

Title: Actress, Producer **Industry:** Media & Entertainment **Company Name:** Echo Films **Date of Birth:** 02/11/1969 **Place of Birth:** Sherman Oaks **State/Country of Origin:** CA/USA **Parents:** John Aniston; Nancy Maryanne Dow **Marital Status:** Divorced **Spouse Name:** Justin Theroux (08/05/2015, Divorced 2017); Brad Pitt (07/29/2000, Divorced 10/02/2005) **Education:** Diplomate, Fiorello H. LaGuardia High School of Music & Art and Performing Arts, NY **Career:** Co-founder, Echo Films (2008-Present); Co-founder, Co-owner, Plan B Entertainment Holdings, LLC (2001-2005) **Civic:** Fundraiser, St. Jude Children's Research Hospital (2008-Present); Benefactor, The Ricky Martin Foundation (2017); Benefactor, The American National Red Cross (2017); Supporter, Comic Relief Inc. (2015); Ambassador, Saks Fifth Avenue Key to the Cure Campaign, Entertainment Industry Foundation (EIF) (2013); Supporter, Friends of El Faro (2010); Fundraiser, "Hope for Haiti Now: A Global Benefit for Earthquake Relief" (2010); Benefactor, Doctors Without Borders (2010); Benefactor, Partners in Health (2010); Benefactor, Americares (2010); Host, "Stand Up to Cancer," Entertainment Industry Foundation (EIF) (2008); Supporter, Clothes Off Our Back Foundation; Supporter, Feeding America; Supporter, EB Medical Research Foundation (EBMRF); Supporter, Project ALS; Supporter, OmniPeace Foundation; Supporter, RAINN **Creative Works:** Actress, Executive Producer, "The Morning Show" (2019-2020); Actress, Executive Producer, "Murder Mystery" (2019); Actress, Executive Producer, "Dumplin'" (2018); Actress, Executive Producer, "The Yellow Birds" (2017); Contributor, "For the Record," HuffPost Women, Verizon Media (2016); Actress, "Office Christmas Party" (2016); Voice Actress, "Storks" (2016); Actress, "Mother's Day" (2016); Actress, "Horrible Bosses 2" (2014); Actress, Executive Producer, "Cake" (2014); Actress, "She's Funny That Way" (2014); Actress, Executive Producer, "Life of Crime" (2013); Actress, "We're the Millers" (2013); Executive Producer, "Call Me Crazy: A Five Film" (2013); Executive Producer, "Icizzle Presents Dog IDS" (2013); Actress, "Burning Love" (2012); Actress, "Wanderlust" (2012); Actress, "Horrible Bosses" (2011); Actress, "Just Go with It" (2011); Executive Producer, Director, "Five" (2011); Actress, "Cougar Town" (2010); Actress, Executive Producer, "The Switch" (2010); Actress, "The Bounty Hunter" (2010); Actress, "Love Happens" (2009); Actress, "He's Just Not That Into You" (2009); Executive Producer, "Becoming Icizzle" (2009); Actress, "Marley & Me" (2008); Actress, "30 Rock" (2008); Actress, Executive Producer, "Management" (2008); Director, "It Can't Wait" (2008); Actress, "Dirt" (2007); Actress, "The Break-Up" (2006); Actress, "Friends with Money" (2006); Director, "Room 10" (2006); Actress, "Rumor Has It..." (2005); Actress, "Derailed" (2005); Actress, "Friends" (1994-2004); Actress, "Along Came Polly" (2004); Actress, "Freedom: A History of Us" (2003); Actress, "Bruce Almighty" (2003); Voice Actress, "King of the Hill" (2003); Actress, "The Good Girl" (2002); Actress, "Rock Star" (2001); Voice Actress, "The Iron Giant" (1999); Voice Actress, "South Park" (1999); Actress, "Office Space" (1999); Voice Actress, "Hercules" (1998); Actress, "The Thin Pink Line" (1998); Actress, "The Object of My Affection" (1998); Actress, "'Til There Was You" (1997); Actress, "Picture Perfect" (1997); Actress, "She's the One" (1996); Actress, Numerous Films and Television Shows **Awards:** Screen Actors Guild Award for Outstanding Performance by a Female Actor in a Drama Series, SAG-AFTRA (2020); Artists Inspiration Award, Patron of the Artists Awards, SAG-AFTRA Foundation (2019); Named People's Icon of the Year, People's Choice Awards, E! Entertainment Television, LLC (2019); Honoree, Variety Power of Women, Variety Media, LLC (2019); Experience Award, Giffoni International Film Festival, Ente Autonomo Giffoni Experience (2016); Montecito Award, Santa Barbara International Film Festival (2015); Capri-Hollywood International Film Festival Award for Best Actress, Capri World (2014); People Magazine Award for Movie Performance of the Year – Female, Meredith Corporation (2014); Named One of the 100 Most Powerful Actresses in Hollywood, Forbes Media LLC (2013); People's Choice Award for Favorite Comedic Movie Actress, CBS Interactive (2013); Gracie Allen Award for Outstanding Drama, Alliance for Women in Media and Foundation (2012); Recipient, Star, Hollywood Walk of Fame (2012); Women's Image Network Award for Outstanding Show Produced by a Woman, Women's Image Network (2012); Named Woman of the Year, Elle Women in Hollywood Awards, Hearst Magazine Media, Inc. (2011); Teen Choice Award for Choice Movie – Chemistry, Fox Media LLC (2006, 2011); Crystal Award, Women in Film (2009); Award for Best Short Film, CineVegas International Film Festival (2007); Vanguard Award, GLAAD Media Awards, GLAAD (2007); Named GQ Woman of the Year, Condé Nast (2005); Award for Female Star of the Year, ShoWest Convention, National Association of Theatre Owners (2005); Teen Choice Award for Choice TV Actress – Comedy, Fox Media LLC (2002-2004); People's Choice Award for Favorite Female Television Performer, CBS Interactive (2001-2004); Golden Globe Award for Best Actress – Television Series Musical or Comedy, Hollywood Foreign Press Association (2003); Recipient, Numerous Awards **Avocations:** Yoga; Budokan karate **Political Affiliations:** Democrat

Cyrus Ansary

Title: President **Industry:** Financial Services **Company Name:** Investment Services International Company LLC **Date of Birth:** 11/20/1933 **Place of Birth:** Shiraz **State/Country of Origin:** Iran **Parents:** A. Russell Ansary; Jamali (Mostmand) Ansary **Marital Status:** Married **Spouse Name:** Janet C. Hodges (8/1/1970) **Children:** Douglas C.; Pary Ann; Jeffrey C.; Bradley C. **Education:** JD, Columbia University (1958); BS, American University (1955) **Certifications:** Certified in French Civilization, University of Paris (1966) **Career:** President, Investment Services International Company LLC, Washington, DC (1973-Present); Chairman, MACO Bancorp, Washington, DC (1988-1995); Chairman of the Board, John L. Lindstrom and Associates, Incorporated, Washington, DC (1962-1986); Chairman board, IK Investment A.G., Zurich, Switzerland (1974-1979); Chairman of the Board, Campbell Music Company, Washington, DC (1968-1972); Chairman of the Board, Financial Dynamics Corporation, Washington, DC (1967-1972); Lecturer, School Business Administration, American University (1967-1971); Organizer, Woodland National Bank, Alexandria, Virginia (1963-1967); First Chairman of the Board, Woodland National Bank, Alexandria, Virginia (1963-1967); President, Woodland National Bank, Alexandria, Virginia (1963-1967); Chairman of the Board, Industry Reports, Inc., Washington, DC (1960-1972); Senior Partner, Ansary, Kirkpatrick and Rosse (1964-1972); Lawyer, Private Practice, Washington, DC (1959-1972) **Career Related:** Chairman, Fort Knox National Company; Chairman, American Funds Tax-Exempt Series I, JPMorgan Chase & Company; Chairman, Value Opportunities Fund, Washington Mutual Investors Fund; Emeritus Director, Washington Mutual Investors Fund **Civic:** Member, Woodrow Wilson Council, Washington, DC (2000-Present) President, Ansary Foundation, Washington, DC (1983-Present); Trustee, American University (1968-1996); Chairman of the Board, American University (1982-1991); Trustee, Washington Opera Society (1982-1989); Trustee, International Law Institute (1976-1988); Trustee, Wolf Trap Foundation, Vienna, Virginia (1977-1982); Trustee, Fried. Krupp Foundation, Essen, Germany (1977-1979) **Military Service:** United States Marine Corps Reserve (1959-1964) **Awards:** Established The Cyrus A. Ansary Prize for Courage and Character (2014); Honoree, The Cyrus A. Ansary Medal, established by American University in (1989) **Memberships:** Leadership Council, Pennsylvania Cardiovascular Institute, Penn Medicine, University of Pennsylvania; CFA Institute; The National Economics Club, Incorporated; Washington Association of Money Managers; The National Press Club; The Economic Club of Washington, D.C.; The Economic Club of New York; Life Guard Society, Mount Vernon; Congressional Country Club; Chevy Chase Country Club; The Metropolitan Club of the City of Washington; Rotary International **Bar Admissions:** Virginia State Bar (1961); The District of Columbia Bar (1960); Maryland State Bar Association, Incorporated (1959) **Marquis Who's Who Honors:** Albert Nelson Marquis Lifetime Achievement Award **Avocations:** Skiing; Walking; Swimming

Leslie Peter Antalffy

Title: Mechanical Engineer **Industry:** Engineering **Company Name:** Fluor Enterprises **Date of Birth:** 10/31/1942 **Place of Birth:** Budapest **State/Country of Origin:** Hungary **Parents:** Vilmos Leslie Antalffy; Margo (Simay) Antalffy **Marital Status:** Married **Spouse Name:** Barbara Ann Clark (01/19/1970) **Children:** Julie; Michael; Nicole **Education:** MBA, Sam Houston State University (1980); Bachelor's Degree in Mechanical Engineering, University of Adelaide, Adelaide, South Australia (1970) **Certifications:** Registered Professional Engineer, State of Texas; Chartered Professional Engineer, Australia; APEC Engineer International PE, Australia **Career:** Retired; Executive Director of Process Technology and Engineering, Fluor Enterprises, Houston, TX (2008-Present); Senior Fellow, Senior Mechanical Engineering Director, Fluor Enterprises, Houston, TX (1995-Present); Mechanical Engineering Director, Fluor Enterprises, Houston, TX (1989-1995); Supervising Mechanical Engineer, Fluor Enterprises, Houston, TX (1980-1989); Principal Engineer, Fluor Enterprises, Houston, TX (1975-1980); Senior Vessel Engineer, Fluor Enterprises, Houston, TX (1973-1975); Senior Vessel Engineer, Lummus Company, Toronto, ON, Canada (1972-1973); Vessel Engineer, A.G. McKee & Company, Toronto, ON, Canada (1972); Vessel Engineer, Lummus Company, Toronto, ON, Canada (1970-1971); Mechanical Engineer, T. O'Connor & Sons, Adelaide, South Australia, Australia (1968-1969) **Career Related:** Life Fellow, The American Society of Mechanical Engineers **Creative Works:** Contributor, Articles, Professional Journals; Presenter, Technical Papers, International Conferences **Awards:** Lifetime Achievement Award, Hydrocarbon Processing Journal, Awards Banquet Dinner, Vienna, Austria (2017) **Memberships:** Numerous Technological Committees, The American Society of Mechanical Engineers **Marquis Who's Who Honors:** Albert Nelson Marquis Lifetime Achievement Award; Marquis Who's Who Top Professional; Marquis Who's Who Humanitarian Award **Why did you become involved in your profession or industry:** As a young man Mr. Antalffy was always working on cars. His parents influenced him to get a proper education. When Mr. Antalffy first came to Canada, the first job that he had in North America is what is he doing now. He has been doing the same thing for 50 years, working on pressure equipment. **Political Affiliations:** Republican **Religion:** Roman Catholic

John Simmons Antrobus, PhD

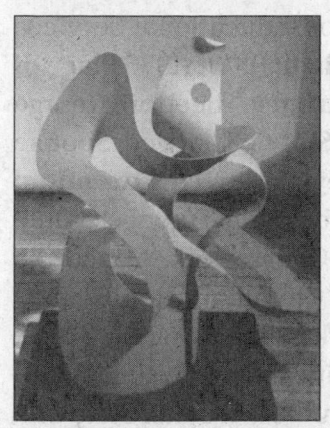

Title: Professor (Retired) **Industry:** Education/Educational Services **Date of Birth:** 08/07/1932 **Place of Birth:** Peace River **State/Country of Origin:** Alberta/Canada **Parents:** Fred Antrobus; Margaret Ida (Simmons) Antrobus **Marital Status:** Married **Spouse Name:** Dr. Suzanne Salzinger (06/10/1988) **Children:** Natalia; Nadia; Leslie; Alison; Meryl; John **Education:** PhD, Columbia University, New York, NY (1963); BA, University of British Columbia, Vancouver, Canada (1954) **Certifications:** Licensed Psychologist, New York **Career:** Emeritus Head, PhD Program in Cognitive Neuroscience, The City University of New York (CUNY), New York, NY (2005-Present); Associate to Full Professor, The City College of New York, New York, NY (1967-2005); Research Associate, The City University of New York (CUNY), New York, NY (1967-1970) **Creative Works:** Editor, Book, "The Neuropsychology of Sleep and Dreaming" (1992); Co-Editor, Book, "The Mind in Sleep: Psychology and Psychophysiology" (1991); Author, Book, "Cognition and Affect" (1970) **Memberships:** American Psychological Association; American Association for the Advancement of Science; American Psychological Society; International Neurological Network Society (Now International Neural Network Society); Eastern Psychological Society (Now Eastern Psychological Association) **Marquis Who's Who Honors:** Albert Nelson Marquis Lifetime Achievement Award **Why did you become involved in your profession or industry:** Dr. Antrobus became involved in his profession because he grew up in an extremely religious family. Everyone was either a preacher or a missionary. He had his doubts about it all and it compelled him to become a scientist to find the evidence of things and question everything. He was influenced by Dr. Kenny, one of his professors at UBC, from whom he really got into experimental methods in a strong way and who helped push him toward the sciences. **Thoughts on Life:** Dr. Antrobus said, "The past 60 years of cognitive neuroscience has revolutionized our understanding of the mind-brain. I'm forever grateful to the many people that supported my participation in this exciting research endeavor. First, Doug Kenny, my undergraduate UBC experimental Psychology professor, later became the President of UBC, who introduced me to the empirical methods of science by which my models and theories could be confidently evaluated. Then, Joseph Barmack, our CCNY Psychology Chair who pulled Psychology out of the Philosophy Dept., who strongly favored empirical research over psychoanalytic belief systems, and the study of normal behavior as a basis for understanding psychopathology, advised that a good theory is one that provides the basis for empirical research that produces a superior theory. If it can't do that in three or four years, it's not a good theory! Now the lag is only three or four months! Then, my mentor and colleague, Jerome L. Singer, initiated research on the positive functions of spontaneous thought and imagery, and persuaded NIMH to support this effort, recently described in an Oxford Handbook, K. Fox and K. Christoff, Ed's. And then Bill Dement, who not only persuaded NIMH to study the brain processes that create mental experience and funded our first sleep lab, but inspired an international collaborative cognitive neuroscience research community, especially Mario Bertini and Cristiano Violani. All of my research was possible only with the dedicated support of many students, now colleagues, especially, George Fein, Erin Wamsley, Debbie Sewitch, Ruth Reinsel and Miriam Wollman. In my current research on the collaborative interaction of top-down, frontal cortex conceptual activation with bottom-up lexical word recognition, the support of Bala Sundaram, George Sperling and Wolfgang Pauli has been invaluable."

Mark Leonard Appold

Title: Pastor, Religion Educator **Industry:** Education/Educational Services **Company Name:** Truman State University **Date of Birth:** 08/08/1936 **Place of Birth:** Chicago **State/Country of Origin:** IL/USA **Parents:** Theodore George Appold; Hertha Mina (Guettler) Appold **Marital Status:** Married **Spouse Name:** Rosemarie **Children:** Kenneth; Martin; Kevin; Kirsten **Education:** ThD in New Testament Studies, Eberhard Karls Universität Tübingen; One-Year Vicarage, Concordia Theological Seminary; Coursework, Concordia University Wisconsin **Career:** St. Paul Lutheran Church, Memphis, MO (2002-Present); Pastor, Faith Lutheran Church, Kirksville, MO (1967-2002); Student Pastor, Campus Ministry, Cologne University, Germany (1965-1966) **Career Related:** Associate Professor of Religious Studies, Truman State University, Kirksville, MO (1976-2018); LSTC (1986); Christ Seminary, St. Louis, MO (1982); Visiting Professor, The University of Iowa (1976-1977); Visiting Professor, Concordia Theological Seminary **Civic:** Chairman, Kirksville Hospital Chaplaincy, Inc., Kirksville; Board of Directors, Kirksville Osteopathic Medical Center; President, Kirksville Interchurch Ministries; Co-Director, Bethsaida Excavations Project, Israel **Creative Works:** Author, "The Oneness Motif in the Fourth Gospel: Motif Analysis and Exegetical Probe into the Theology of John" (1976); Author, "Bethsaida in Archaeology, History and Ancient Culture"; Author, Articles **Awards:** Grantee, Lutheran World Federation, Geneva (1962, 1965-1966); Retirement Award, Truman State University; Scholarship for Language Study, German Academic Exchange Service, Germany **Memberships:** Society of Biblical Literature; American Academy of Religion; The Park Ridge Center for the Study of Health, Faith, and Ethic **Marquis Who's Who Honors:** Albert Nelson Marquis Lifetime Achievement Award **To what do you attribute your success:** Dr. Appold attributes his success to his patience, family support, studying and his faith. **Why did you become involved in your profession or industry:** Dr. Appold became involved in his profession because of the family in which he was raised. Four of his relatives were Lutheran pastors and his grandfathers were both Lutheran school teachers. **Political Affiliations:** Independent **Religion:** Lutheran

Nick Aragonesi

Title: Owner **Industry:** Retail/Sales **Company Name:** CBD Superstore **Marital Status:** Married **Children:** Two Children **Education:** Master of Business Administration, Long Island University, Brookville, NY (2008); Bachelor of Business Administration, Hofstra University, Hempstead, NY (2006) **Career:** Owner, CBD Superstore (2015-Present); Real Estate Broker (2013-Present); Owner, Construction Company (1999-Present); Owner, Vape Shop (2013-2015) **Civic:** Vice President, Whitestone Merchant Association; Member, We Love Whitestone Civic Association; Volunteer, The Malba Field & Marine Crew **Marquis Who's Who Honors:** Marquis Who's Who Top Professional **To what do you attribute your success:** Mr. Aragonesi attributes his success to dedication, hard work, doing research, and being ahead of the market. **Why did you become involved in your profession or industry:** Mr. Aragonesi opened his vape shop to help people quit smoking. At that time, there was nothing like it in his neighborhood. He saw the opportunity and seized it; as a real estate broker, he knew there was an empty store around the corner from his office. He ordered some products to start, and the business took off. In fact, it became so successful that he had to put his real estate business on hold. After two or three successful years, the vape shop expanded its horizons to sell CBD products. Mr. Aragonesi brought in a few CBD products to test how receptive his customers would be. They worked so well and brought so much success to the store that Mr. Aragonesi made the executive decision to rebrand, rename and now only sell CBD products.

Byron Halevy Arison, PhD

Title: Chemist, Researcher (Retired) **Industry:** Research **Date of Birth:** 02/20/1923 **Place of Birth:** New York **State/Country of Origin:** NY/USA **Parents:** Theodore Arison; Bertha Moselle Arison **Marital Status:** Widow **Spouse Name:** Arlene Cacoso Peterson (11/19/2006, Deceased 2016); Ritsu Nakashima (1956, Deceased 2005) **Education:** PhD in Organic Chemistry, New York University Tandon School of Engineering, Brooklyn, NY (1967); MS in Organic Chemistry, New York University Tandon School of Engineering, Brooklyn, NY (1951); BS in Chemistry, University of Michigan, Ann Arbor, MI (1944) **Career:** Research Chemist, Merck & Co., Inc., Rahway, NJ (1947-2004); Chemist, Hanford Site, University of Chicago, Chicago, IL, Washington (1944-1945); Chemist, Manhattan Project, DuPont, Hanford, WA (1944); Director, Department of Metabolism, Merck & Co., Inc. **Career Related:** Consultant, Nuclear Magnetic Resonance Facility (2004-Present); Speaker, "My Personal Experiences on the Manhattan Project: The Making of the Atomic Bomb," Old Guard of Summit (2015); Speaker, Nuclear Magnetic Resonance Spectroscopy, Fellowship Residence Village, Kiwanis Club; Consultant, Steraloids Inc. **Military Service:** U.S. Army (1945-1946) **Creative Works:** Contributor, 214 Articles to Professional Journals **Memberships:** Board of Trustees, New Jersey Festival Orchestra (2008-Present); American Chemical Society **Marquis Who's Who Honors:** Marquis Who's Who Top Professional; Marquis Who's Who Humanitarian Award **To what do you attribute your success:** Dr. Arison attributes his success to avoiding scientific jargon while delivering speeches regarding his experiences with the Manhattan Project, which helps him connect with his audience. **Why did you become involved in your profession or industry:** After earning a Bachelor of Science in chemistry during the Second World War, Dr. Arison was invited by DuPont to work on the Manhattan Project. Fully briefed on the subject of the project, he was part of a group in Hanford, Washington, that loaded one of the reactors with uranium. Throughout his involvement with the project, he had to maintain strict secrecy, but has delivered five talks before audiences on the subject since then. **Avocations:** Music; Theater; Photography; Travel **Thoughts on Life:** Dr. Arison, formerly director of Merck's Department of Metabolism, spoke to the Old Guard of Summit, New Jersey, at a 2015 meeting. His subject was "My Personal Experiences on the Manhattan Project: the Making of the Atomic Bomb." He will also be giving talks on the subject of nuclear magnetic resonance spectroscopy to his local Kiwanis Club and at an independent living facility in upcoming months.

Mary B. Armstrong

Title: Director, Consultant **Industry:** Education/Educational Services **Company Name:** University of Texas **Date of Birth:** 01/25/1935 **Place of Birth:** Longview **State/Country of Origin:** TX/US **Parents:** Acey Frank Johnson; Lois (Winchester) Johnson **Marital Status:** Married **Spouse Name:** John D. Armstrong **Children:** Richard Kevin Steel; Randal Kirk Steel; Pamela Lee Pancroft **Education:** Certified Supervisor, Our Lady of the Lake University (1987); MA, University of Texas, San Antonio, TX (1986); BS, Texas Women's University, Denton, TX (1956) **Career:** Director, Consultant; Director of Certificates, University of Texas (1994-1998); Faculty, University of Texas (1993-1994); Consultant, Scott Foresman Public Company (1991-1993); Teaching Associate, Our Lady of the Lake University (1991-1992); Supervisor of Social Studies, Kindergarten, Northside Independent School District, San Antonio, TX (1986-1992); Teacher, K-2, Northside Independent School District, San Antonio, TX (1966-1986) **Career Related:** Board of Directors, Institute of Texan Cultures, San Antonio, TX (1996-1998); Lecturer in Field **Civic:** Standing Committee on Teacher Education, University of Texas, San Antonio, TX (1994-1998); Division of Education, Consortium of Local Districts, University of Texas (1994-1998) **Creative Works:** Contributor, Articles, Professional Journals **Awards:** Outstanding Teaching Award, University of Texas, San Antonio, TX (1992); Trinity Prize For Outstanding Educator (1983); Award for Distinguished Teacher, Northside Independent School District (1983); Northside Teacher of the Year, Northside Teachers Association (1976) **Memberships:** National Association for Education of Young Children; International Association of Childhood; Phi Delta Kappa **Marquis Who's Who Honors:** Albert Nelson Marquis Lifetime Achievement Award; Marquis Who's Who Top Professional **Why did you become involved in your profession or industry:** Ms. Armstrong loved working with small children growing up. She loves the little ones. This motivated her to go into kindergarten. When she first went into teaching, there was no kindergarten in public schools in Texas. She taught first and second grade until kindergarten came to public schools. A friend of hers got into this, and she observed her and went to visit at the university and it became something she wanted to do. She worked in church with young children, which added to it. She always loved working with young children. **Avocations:** Gardening; Art; Music; Antiques; Crafts **Political Affiliations:** Republican **Religion:** Presbyterian

P A Arnold

Title: Special Education Educator **Industry:** Education/Educational Services **Place of Birth:** Toledo **State/Country of Origin:** OH/USA **Parents:** Mattie Spear **Marital Status:** Married **Spouse Name:** Earl E. Arnold **Children:** Diane; Zona **Education:** MS, Nova University (1986); MA, Wayne State University (1962); BA, BS, David Lipscomb College (1960) **Certifications:** Certified in Bible, Special Education, Psychology, Speech, Mental Retardation, Emotional Disturbance, State of Florida, Formerly in States of Tennessee, Michigan, Arkansas, New Mexico **Career:** Teacher of Dactyology, Interpreter for Deaf (1960-Present); Teacher, Hobbs Municipal Schools (1981-1982); County Advocate for the Deaf Director, Four-County Center for the Handicapped, Arkansas (1977-1981); Director, RSVP Pilot Program, Widely Replicated, On Intergenerational Learning (1977-1981); Teacher of Special Education, City Systems, Rockford and Warren, MI (1960-1967) **Career Related:** Director, Model Project ACTION; Director, RSVP Model Program, Intergenerational Learning; Project TREE Technical Resources In Exceptional Education; Conference Presenter In Fields **Civic:** Exceptional Education, Department of Education (2000); Board of Directors, Deaf Advisor, Hearing Society of Volusia County; Project TREE; Florida State University Center for Educational Technology **Creative Works:** Author, "Trapezoid of Children" (1999); Author, "Little Red Schoolhouse" (1998); Author, "Ol' Time Preacher Man" (1995); Author, "Instructor," "Light for Deaf" (1992); Author, "Love Story in Academia" **Awards:** Grantee, Public Welfare; Multiple FUTURES Grantee, National Gardening Association; County Education Science Award in Special Gardening **Memberships:** National Education Association; American Red Cross; Association for Supervision and Curriculum Development; Volusia Educational Association; Florida Education Association; Council for Exceptional Children; American Association on Mental Deficiency; National Association for the Deaf; National, State and County Associations for the Mentally Retarded; National Gardening Association; FUTURES; Newspapers in Education **Marquis Who's Who Honors:** Albert Nelson Marquis Lifetime Achievement Award **To what do you attribute your success:** Ms. Arnold's mother valued education highly and was a lifelong learner. We were exposed to a great work ethic - if you want it, you work for it, earn it and get it. Then, there have been great professional field colleagues; her first superintendent retired to Florida and she looked them up when she arrived there. He postponed going to his Kiwanis meeting to take her to the local school superintendent's office, crashing past his receptionist, pushing her forward and saying, "Don't let her get away." **Why did you become involved in your profession or industry:** Ms. Arnold attributes her inspiration in her profession to good teachers. Her mother, Mattie Spear, was a teacher; she would teach and would work alongside her in the classroom, earning the Teacher-Volunteer Team of the Year Award from Volusia Public Schools in 1985. As a child, after being her teacher all day, a teacher would often come over to swap recipes with her grandmother. Her best friends, when they were no longer her teacher, became her friends and have also been her mentors. **Avocations:** Hydroponic and other growing; Gardening **Political Affiliations:** Independent **Religion:** Christian **Thoughts on Life:** The book "Ol' Time Preacher Man" was based around Ms. Arnold's husband, Earl E. Arnold, an evangelist for more than 65 years after an acting chaplain aboard the LST647 in the Pacific in World War II - a blessing to have shared this walk towards eternity with him.

Mark A. Ary

Title: President, Chief Executive Officer **Industry:** Consumer Goods and Services **Company Name:** Ary Co A/C & Heat LLC **Date of Birth:** 01/25/1982 **Place of Birth:** Fort Worth **State/Country of Origin:** TX/USA **Parents:** Aboud Ary; Cindy Ary **Marital Status:** Married **Spouse Name:** Karis **Children:** Kailey Claire; Gemma Claire **Education:** High School Diploma (2000) **Certifications:** Certified, Railroad Commission; Universal EPA Certification; HVAC License, Class A Texas Department **Career:** Owner, Ary Co. A/C & Heat LLC (1997-Present) **Career Related:** Zoning Board of Adjustment, Decatur, TX **Civic:** United Way; Chamber of Commerce; Decatur Forward **Creative Works:** Operator, Social Media Platform; Host, Social Media Podcast; Home Builder **Awards:** Top 40 Under 40, Air Conditioning, Heating & Refrigeration News (2018); Listee, Top 40 Under 40 in the United States in the HVAC Industry; "Best of Wise," The Reader's Choice, Wise County Messenger; First Place, Decatur Readers Choice **Memberships:** Chamber of Commerce; TAB; National Business Association; Better Business Bureau; Greater Decatur Chamber of Commerce; Bridgeport Chamber of Commerce; Wise County Chamber of Commerce **To what do you attribute your success:** Mr. Ary attributes his success to a self-driven and highly-motivated desired to succeed. He studied materials and found an interest that he knows will make a difference. He enjoys contributing his time to charities, political causes, and any other types of work in which he believes. **Avocations:** Public speaking; Fishing; Spending time with family; Motor cross; Outdoors; Camping **Political Affiliations:** Republican **Religion:** Christian

William James Ash, PhD

Title: Professor Emeritus **Industry:** Sciences **Company Name:** Stony Brook University **Date of Birth:** 11/03/1931 **Place of Birth:** Brooklyn **State/Country of Origin:** NY/USA **Parents:** William Ash; Anna Albertina Marie (Ruegg) Ash **Marital Status:** Widowed **Spouse Name:** Gwendolyn E. Rose (Companion) (Deceased 05/25/2016); Gertrude Louise Kehm Ash (Deceased 06/6/2001) **Children:** Annalee Marie; Barbara Ann (Deceased); William James Jr.; James Joseph; Lydia Ann **Education:** PhD in Animal Genetics, Pathology, Endocrinology, Cornell University (1960); MS in Animal Genetics and Endocrinology, Cornell University (1958); BS in Animal and Zoological Sciences, Cornell University (1953); NYS Regents Diploma, Brooklyn Technical High School, NY (1949); Diploma, Saint Elizabeth Roman Catholic School, Ozone Park, NY (1945) **Career:** Professor Emeritus of Biochemistry and Cell Biology, Stony Brook University, NY (1991-Present); Professor of Ecology and Evolution, Biochemistry and Cell Biology, Stony Brook University, NY (1985-1991); Senior Staff, U.S. Representation, U.S.-Saudi Joint Commission, U.S. Department of the Treasury, Riyadh, Saudi Arabia (1982-1983); U.S. Delegate, Indo-U.S. Subcommission on Science and Technology, New Delhi, India (1980); President, Advisory Associates International, Westhampton, NY (1979-1995); Program Officer, Africa-Asia Section, Division of International Programs, National Science Foundation, Washington, DC (1979-1981); Professor of Developmental Genetics, Department of Zoology, Faculty of Sciences, Kuwait University, Arabian Gulf (1976-1978); Professor, Associate Professor of Genetics and Embryology, St. Lawrence University, NY (1966-1981); Assistant Professor, Departments of Biology and Animal and Veterinary Science, West Virginia University, Morgantown, WV (1965-1966); Director of Research, Crescent Corporation, Aquebogue, NY (1964-1965); Research Geneticist, Eastport, NY Laboratory, Cornell University (1959-1963); Graduate Research Assistant, Cornell University (1955-1959) **Career Related:** Visiting Scientist, Pune, India (1980); Visiting Scientist, Deutsches Democratic Republic (DDR) (1963) **Civic:** Commander, Peconic Bay Power Squad, NY (1986-1988); Appleton Arena Announcer, Division 1 Ice Hockey, St. Lawrence University (1974-1976); Coach, U.S. Amateur Ice Hockey Association, Canton, NY (1970-1976); Cubmaster, Boy Scouts of America (1967-1969); President Emeritus, New Bern Alpenverein and New Bern Genealogical Society **Military Service:** Honorable Discharge, United States Army (1965); USAR, QM Research and Engineering Command, Natick, MA, Climatology, Southeast Asia, (1961-1962); Captain, QMC (1959); With, United States Army Reserve (1955-1965); First Lieutenant, QMC (1954); War Dog Training Officer, 7717 USAREUR QM School, Lenggries, Germany (1953-1955); Staff and Faculty, 36th QM Composite Battalion, QM School, Fort Lee, VA (1953); Company Officer Course, Fort Lee, VA (1953); Second Lieutenant, QM, United States Army, Ithaca, NY (1953) **Creative Works:** Author, Raising of Commercial Waterfowl, USDA Farmer's Bulletin; Author, Scientific Papers on Avian Genetics, Reproductive Physiology, Virology, Bacteriology, Pathology and Human Dermatoglyphics, Pathology and Genetics; Author, 150 Short Stories, Fiction, Plus Fact on Nautical Education for USSPS **Awards:** Travel Grantee, National Science Foundation, Pune, India (1983); Grantee, Assignment to Division of International Programs, National Science Foundation (1979-1981); Grantee, Faculty Research, St. Lawrence University, National Science Foundation (1970-1972); Travel Award, XI International Congress of Genetics, Den Hauge, The Netherlands and DDR (East Germany), Cornell University (1963); Named to Sigma Xi, Scabbard and Blade, and Ho Nun De Kah **Memberships:** Cape Lookout Sail and P.S. (1995- Present); United States Sail and Power Squadrons (1961-Present); Senior Navigator, Board of Directors, Emeritus; Sigma Xi; Knights of Columbus (Fourth Degree) **Marquis Who's Who Honors:** Albert Nelson Marquis Lifetime Achievement Award; Marquis Who's Who Top Professional **To what do you attribute your success:** Dr. Ash attributes his success to attending Brooklyn Technical High School and learning the importance of academic discipline. This provided the foundation for earning university degrees. **Why did you become involved in your profession or industry:** Dr. Ash became involved in his profession to make the world a better place, mold young minds, and enable his students, colleagues and friends to view the human race in wholesome and meaningful ways. **Avocations:** Sailing; Gardening; Travel; Amateur radio; Genealogy; Celestial navigation **Political Affiliations:** Republican **Religion:** Roman Catholic **Thoughts on Life:** Life is an ascending spiral staircase; for each step upward one views a new and widening horizon with which to work. I hope I have satisfied those ascending requirements of Professors Sam Leonard (endocrinologist supreme), R.K. Cole (geneticist, as tough as they come) and Charles Rickard (a pathologist who made a difficult subject read like a novel) in my upward climb. I could not have had a more understanding, loving wife, Trudy, who left too soon. Our loving children, while not following in my footsteps, excelled in their works. My companion, Gwen, a god-send who helped beyond belief during my darkest days, also left too soon. Life rolls the dice and you do the very best with what comes up!

Bernard F. Ashe, Esq.

Title: Lawyer, Arbitrator **Industry:** Law and Legal Services **Date of Birth:** 03/08/1936 **Place of Birth:** Baltimore **State/Country of Origin:** MD/USA **Parents:** Victor Joseph Ashe (Deceased, 1974); Frances Cecelia (Johnson) Flemming (Deceased, 1988) **Marital Status:** Married **Spouse Name:** Grace Nannette Pegram Ashe (03/23/1963) **Children:** Walter J. Ashe; David B. Ashe **Education:** JD, Howard University, Washington, DC (1961); BA, Howard University, Washington, DC (1956) **Career:** Retired (1996); Labor Arbitrator, Mediator, Albany, NY (1971-2016); General Counsel, New York State United Teachers, Albany, NY (1971-1996); Assistant General Counsel, United Auto Workers, Detroit, MI (1963-1971); Attorney, National Labor Relations Board, Washington, DC (1961-1963); Teacher, Baltimore City Public Schools (1956-1958) **Career Related:** Adjunct Faculty, Fordham University School of Law (1996-1998); Adjunct Faculty, Roger Williams University School of Law (1996-1998); Adjunct Faculty, Cornell School of Industrial and Labor Relations, Albany Division (1987, 1981) **Civic:** Trustee, Adelphi University, Garden City, NY (1997-2005); Trustee, New York State Lawyers Fund for Client Protection (1981-2008); First Vice President, Urban League of Albany (1981-1985); Board of Directors, Urban League of Albany (1979-1985) **Creative Works:** Journal Editorial Board, American Bar Association (ABA) (2003-2007); Bernard F. Ashe Collection, Schomburg Center for Research in Black Culture, The New York Public Library, NY; Contributor, Articles on Labor and Constitutional Law, Professional Journals **Awards:** Arvid Anderson Public Employment Lawyer of the Year Award, Section of Labor and Employment, American Bar Association (2017); National Weinberg Award, Wayne State University, Detroit, MI (2001); Thurgood Marshall Justice Award, National Association for the Advancement of Colored People, Albany, NY Chapter (2000); American Arbitration Whitney North Seymour Senior Medal (1989) **Memberships:** ABA (1961-Present); Advisory Commission on Judiciary in 21st Century, ABA (2002-2003); Standing Committee on Client Protection, ABA (1998-2001); Chair, Drafting Committee, ABA (1998-2000); Standing Committee on Group and Prepaid Legal Services, ABA (1996-1997); Chairman, Standing Committee on Group and Prepaid Legal Services, ABA (1996-1997); Senior Lawyers Division Council, ABA (1994-2000); Accreditation Committee, Section of Legal Education and Admission to the Bar, ABA (1994-1998); Executive Committee, ABA (1993-1994); Board of Governors, ABA (1991-1994); Nominating Committee, ABA (1988-1991); Commission on Public Understanding about the Law, ABA (1987-1991); House of Delegates, ABA (1985-1996); Board of Directors, American Arbitration Association (1982-1998); Chairman, Section of Labor and Employment Law, ABA (1982-1983); Consortium on Legal Services and the Public, ABA (1979-1984); Fellow, American Bar Foundation; Life Member, Emeritus Member, The College of Labor and Employment Lawyers Inc.; New York State Bar Association; Albany County Bar Association; Life Member, The American Law Institute **Bar Admissions:** New York State Bar Association (1971); State Bar of Michigan (1964); The District of Columbia Bar (1963); Virginia State Bar (1961) **Marquis Who's Who Honors:** Albert Nelson Marquis Lifetime Achievement Award; Marquis Who's Who Top Professional **To what do you attribute your success:** Mr. Ashe attributes his success to opportunity, and professional mentoring along the path. **Avocations:** Reading; Travel **Thoughts on Life:** Mr. Ashe believes that failure is only a rock on the path to success.

John F. Asmus

Title: Research Physicist **Industry:** Sciences **Company Name:** University of California San Diego **Date of Birth:** 01/20/1937 **Place of Birth:** Pasadena **State/Country of Origin:** CA/USA **Parents:** William F. Asmus; Eleanor E. (Kocher) Asmus **Marital Status:** Married **Spouse Name:** Barbara Ann Flaherty (2/23/1963) **Children:** Joanne M. Barron; Rosemary H. Johnson **Education:** PhDEE in Physics, Quantum Physics, Electrical Engineering and Physics, California Institute of Technology (1965); MSEE, California Institute of Technology (1959); BSEE, California Institute of Technology (1958); Degree in Physical Sciences Aid, US Naval Ordinance Laboratory (1954-1960) **Career:** Research Physicist, Co-Founder, Art And Science Center, University Of California San Diego (1973-Present); Lecturer, University Of California San Diego, Davis, CA (1974); Vice President, Board Member, Science Applications, Inc., Albuquerque, NM (1971-1973); Research Staff, Institute of Defense Analyses, Arlington, VA (1969-1971); Head, Laser Department, Gulf General Atomic, San Diego, CA (1964-1969); Head, Optical Systems Department, Aero Geo Astro Corp., Alexandria, VA (1960-1964); Physical Science Aid, US Naval Ordnance Laboratory, Corona, CA (1954-1960) **Career Related:** Keynote Speaker, US National Park Service Convention, San Francisco, CA (2014); Consultant in Field; Editorial Board, Elsevier Pub., Springer Verlag, Wiley-VCH; Co-Director, JASON National Laser Program, Office of the President of the United States **Creative Works:** Editorial Board, Journal Cultural Heritage (2004-Present); Contributor, Scientific Papers, Professional Journals **Awards:** John Asmus Award (2010); Rank Prize Mentor (2004); Explorers Club Fellow (1997); George Eastman Lecturer, Optical Society of America (1994); Rolex Laureate for Enterprise Award for Restoration Xian Terra Cotta Warriors, Montes Rolex SA (1990); Fellow, Oberlin College (1990); Winner, IBM Supercomputing Competition for Image Enhancement for Mona Lisa (1989); Getty Fellow (1989); Best Scholarly Article Award, Society Tech. Committee (1988); Tektronix Fellow (1960-1961); Schlumberger Fellow (1959-1960); Decorated Knight, Holy Sepulchre of Jerusalem **Memberships:** Faculty Advisor, University of California San Diego Student Alumni Book Club (2009-Present); Editorial Board Member, Society of Photo-Optical Instrumentation Engineers (2002-Present); Past Member, IEEE; Venice Society; National Trust Historical Preservation; American Institute of Conservation; International Institute for the Conservation of Historical and Artistic Works; Science Board Member, Honorary President, Lasers Conservation Artworks; Bay Area Art Conservation Guild; Sigma Xi; Tau Beta Pi **Marquis Who's Who Honors:** Albert Nelson Marquis Lifetime Achievement Award; Marquis Who's Who Top Professional **Why did you become involved in your profession or industry:** Dr. Asmus became involved in his profession because his father was an electrical engineer; it seemed natural that he would do the same. His science teachers in high school had connections with the Navy. Because of their connections, he got his first job with the Navy Ordnance Laboratory. **Avocations:** Art history; Gardening; Travel; Writing; Public speaking **Political Affiliations:** Progressive **Religion:** Roman Catholic

Robert S. Attiyeh

Title: Biotechnology Executive (Retired) **Industry:** Biotechnology **Date of Birth:** 06/10/1934 **Place of Birth:** Oak Park **State/Country of Origin:** IL/USA **Parents:** Semeer M.; Dorothy Lydia Attiyeh **Marital Status:** Married **Spouse Name:** Linda Helen Harden (07/20/1963) **Children:** Robert; Jenny **Education:** Master of Business Administration, Harvard University (1961); Bachelor of Science in Electrical Engineering, Cornell University (1956) **Career:** Senior Vice President, Finance & Corporate Development, Chief Financial Officer, Amgen Inc., Thousand Oaks, CA (1994-1998); Director, McKinsey & Co., Los Angeles, CA (1967-1994); General Manager, TRW Electronics, El Segundo, CA (1961-1967) **Civic:** Director, Federal Reserve Bank of San Francisco (1997- Present); President, Chairman, Board, Los Angeles Philharmonic Association (1994-1999); Chairman, Board, House Ear Institute (1991-1996); President, Chairman, Board, Natural History Museum, Los Angeles, CA (1990-1996); **Military Service:** US Navy (1956-1959); Served on a Destroyer, USS Barry DD 933, Atlantic Fleet and 6th Fleet. **Creative Works:** Contributor, Numerous Articles to Professional Journals **Memberships:** California Club; L.A. Club **Marquis Who's Who Honors:** Albert Nelson Marquis Lifetime Achievement Award **Why did you become involved in your profession or industry:** Mr. Attiyeh became involved in his profession after graduating from the Harvard Business School. Though he initially aspired to enlist in the U.S. Navy and serve on a nuclear submarine, he joined a friend of his in the aerospace industry. He had served in multiple fields, including space electronics and biotechnology. Throughout this time, he has learned the importance of fact-based analysis of any given situation. **Avocations:** Ranching; Restoring and preserving historical properties and open space; Reading; Good movies

W. Gerald Austen, MD

Title: Churchill Distinguished Professor, Harvard, Surgeon in Chief Emeritus, MGH **Industry:** Medicine & Health Care **Company Name:** Massachusetts General Hospital, MGH **Date of Birth:** 01/20/1930 **Place of Birth:** Akron **State/Country of Origin:** OH/USA **Parents:** Karl Arnstein; Bertl (Jehle) Arnstein **Marital Status:** Married **Spouse Name:** Patricia Ramsdell (1/28/1961) **Children:** Karl Ramsdell; William Gerald Jr.; Christopher Marshall; Elizabeth A. Lawson **Education:** Intern Then Resident in General Surgery & Cardiothoracic Surgery, Massachusetts General Hospital, Boston, MA (1955-1961); MD, Harvard Medical School (1955); BS in Mechanical Engineering, Massachusetts Institute of Technology (1951) **Certifications:** Diplomate, The American Board of Thoracic Surgery; Diplomate, American Board of Surgery, Inc. **Career:** Honorary Trustee, Chairman Emeritus, Massachusetts General Physicians Organization, Boston, MA (2000-Present); Surgeon-in-Chief Emeritus, Massachusetts General Hospital, Boston, MA (1997-Present); Honorary Trustee, Massachusetts General Hospital, Boston MA (1999-Present); Co-chair, Philanthropy Program, Massachusetts General Hospital, Boston MA (1980-Present); Trustee, Massachusetts General Hospital, Boston MA (1994-1999); Chief Executive Officer, Massachusetts General Physicians Organization, Boston, MA (1994-1999); President, Massachusetts General Physicians Organization, Boston, MA (1994-1999); Surgeon-in-Chief, Massachusetts General Hospital, Boston, MA (1989-1997); Chief of Surgical Services, Massachusetts General Hospital, Boston, MA (1969-1997); Chief, Surgical Cardiovascular Research Unit, Massachusetts General Hospital, Boston, MA (1963-1969); Chief of Cardiac Surgery, Massachusetts General Hospital (1965-1969); Surgeon, Clinic Surgery, National Heart Institute, Bethesda, MD (1961-1962); Chairman, Chief's Council, Massachusetts General Hospital, Boston, MA (1992-Present) **Career Related:** Edward D. Churchill Distinguished Professor, Harvard Medical School (2011-Present); Edward D. Churchill Professor of Surgery, Harvard Medical School (1974-2011); Member, Residency Review Committee, Surgery Accreditation Council, Graduate Medical Education (Now ACGME) (1988-1993); Professor of Surgery, Harvard Medical School (1966-1974); Associate Professor, Surgery (1965-1966); Instructor in Surgery (1963-1965) **Civic:** Member, President Advisory Council, The University of Akron (2014-Present); Chairman Emeritus, John S. and James L. Knight Foundation (2010-Present); Life Member Emeritus, The MIT Corporation (2005-Present); Honorary Trustee, Akron Art Museum (2004-Present); Honorary Trustee, Massachusetts General Hospital (1999-Present); Trustee, Dana-Farber/Partners Cancer Care (1999-2016); Trustee, North Shore Medical Center (2001-2013); Trustee, Massachusetts Taxpayers Foundation (2000-2013); Chairman, John S. and James L. Knight Foundation (1996-2010); Trustee, John S. and James L. Knight Foundation (1986-2010); Trustee, Massachusetts Eye and Ear Infirmary (1991-2010); Life Member, The MIT Corporation (1982-2005); Member, The MIT Corporation (1972-2005); Board of Directors, Foundation for Biomedical Research (1988-2000); Trustee, Massachusetts General Hospital (1994-1999); Member, Executive Committee, The MIT Corporation (1986-1998); Founding Trustee, Partners HealthCare System Inc. (Now Mass General Brigham) (1994-1997); Vice Chairman, John S. and James L. Knight Foundation (1991-1996) **Creative Works:** Editor, Medical Textbooks; Contributor, Articles, Professional Journals **Awards:** W. Gerald Austen, MD Building, Massachusetts General Hospital (2019); National Physician of the Year Lifetime Achievement Award, Castle Connolly Medical (2016); W. Gerald Austen Inpatient Care Pavilion, Massachusetts General Hospital (2010); W. Gerald Austen Chair, Polymer Science & Polymer Engineering, The University of Akron (2016); Nathan Smith Distinguished Service Award, New England Surgical Society (2002); Massachusetts General Hospital Trustees Gold Medal (1997); W. Gerald Austen Professor of Surgery at Harvard Medical School (1997); Honorary Fellow, The Royal College of Surgeons of England (1986); Paul Dudley White Medal, American Heart Association, Inc. (1981); Gold Heart Award, American Heart Association, Inc. (1980); Markle Scholar (1963-1968) Honorary DSc, Northeast Ohio Medical University (1996); Honorary DSc, University of Massachusetts (1985); Honorary DSc, University of Athens (1981); Honorary HHD, The University of Akron (1980); Member of Institute of Medicine (Now National Academy of Medicine) (1974); Fellow of the American Academy of Arts and Sciences (1974); President, Society of University of Surgeons (1972-1973) **Memberships:** Senior Member, American Board of Surgery, Inc. (1974-2005); President, American College of Surgeons (1992-1993); Regent, American College of Surgeons (1982-1991); Chairman, Board of Regents, American College of Surgeons (1989-1991); Board of Directors, The American Board of Thoracic Surgery (1984-1990); President, American Association for Thoracic Surgery (1988-1989); Vice President, American Association for Thoracic Surgery (1987-1988); President, American Surgical Association (1985-1986); Secretary, American Surgical Association (1979-1984); President, American Heart Association, Inc. (1977-1978); President, Massachusetts Chapter, American Heart Association, Inc. (1972-1974) **Marquis Who's Who Honors:** Albert Nelson Marquis Lifetime Achievement Award

J. Max Austin Jr., MD

Title: Professor Emeritus **Industry:** Education/Educational Services **Company Name:** University of Alabama at Birmingham Medical Center **Date of Birth:** 04/28/1941 **Place of Birth:** Mobile **State/Country of Origin:** AL/USA **Marital Status:** Married **Spouse Name:** Nancy Jane Musgrove **Children:** Lindsey Austin Trammell; J. Max III **Education:** MD, Medical College of Alabama (1967); BA, Chemistry, Emory University (1963); Associate Degree, Emory at Oxford, Emory University (1961); Graduate Coursework, Wetumpka Secondary Public School (1959) **Certifications:** Medical License, State of Alabama (1968-Present); Certificate of Special Competence, Gynecology-Oncology, American Board of Obstetrics and Gynecology (1977); Diplomate, American Board of Obstetrics and Gynecology (1973) **Career:** Professor Emeritus, Gynecologic Oncology, University of Alabama (2013-Present); Margaret Spain Chair in Obstetrics and Gynecology, University of Alabama (2008-2013); Professor, Division of Gynecologic Oncology, University of Alabama (2000-2013); Professor of Clinical Obstetrics and Gynecology, Division of Gynecologic Oncology, University of Alabama Medical Center (1990-2000); President, Founder, Managing Partner, Southern GYN Oncology, P.C., Birmingham, AL (1977-2000); Gynecologic Fellowship, Norway (1974); Assistant Professor, Obstetrics and Gynecology, Division of Gynecologic Oncology, University of Alabama Medical Center (1973-1977); Gynecologic Oncology Fellowship, Department of Obstetrics and Gynecology, University of Alabama Medical Center (1973-1975); Instructor, Chief Resident, Obstetrics and Gynecology, Medical College of Alabama (1970-1971); Senior Resident, Obstetrics and Gynecology, Medical College of Alabama (1969-1970); Junior Assistant Resident, Obstetrics and Gynecology, Grady Memorial Hospital, Emory University (1968-1969); Internship, Mobile General Hospital (1967-1968) **Career Related:** Retired, Director of Philanthropic Initiatives, Department of Obstetrics and Gynecology, University of Alabama (2013-2019); Staff, University Hospital, Birmingham, AL (1973-2013) **Civic:** Board Member, Oxford College, Emory University **Military Service:** Chief, Obstetrics and Gynecology, Homestead Air Force Base, Florida (1972-1973); Major, U.S. Air Force (1971-1973); Department of OB/GYN, U.S. Air Force Hospital, Homestead Air Force Base, Florida (1971-1972) **Creative Works:** Contributor, Over 75 Publications and Abstracts **Awards:** Distinguished Alumnus Award, Medical Alumni Association, University of Alabama at Birmingham Medical Center (2019); Inductee, Alabama Legend in Obstetrics and Gynecology, Alabama Section, American Congress of Obstetrics and Gynecology (2015); Significant Sig, Sigma Chi (2012); Paul W. Burleson Award, Medical Association of the State of Alabama (2010); Carl Chandler Alumnus Award, Oxford College of Emory University Board of Counselors (2008); Argus Best Faculty Teacher, Department of Obstetrics and Gynecology, University of Alabama School of Medicine (2007); Health Care Hero, Physician and Provider, Birmingham Business Journal (2006); Nominee, Argus Teaching Award for Best Faculty Teacher, Department of Obstetrics and Gynecology, University of Alabama School of Medicine (2005-2006); Nominee, Best Faculty Teacher, Department of Obstetrics and Gynecology, University of Alabama School of Medicine (2005-2006); Outstanding Excellence in Teaching Award, Association of Professors in Obstetrics and Gynecology (2003-2005); Excellence in Medical Student Education Award, University of Alabama School of Medicine (2001-2008) **Memberships:** Elected Permanent Member, Board of Counselors, Emory at Oxford College (1996-Present); Society of 1906, Southern Medical Association (1992-Present); Charter Member, Alabama Society of Clinical Oncology (1979-Present); South Central Obstetrical and Gynecological Society (1979-Present); Fellow, American College of Surgeons (1978-Present); Charles E. Flowers Society (1977-Present); American Society for Colposcopy and Colpomicroscopy (1974-Present); American Medical Association (1974-Present); Jefferson County Medical Society (1974-Present); Medical Association of the State of Alabama (1974-Present); Alabama Association of Obstetrics and Gynecology (1973-Present); Fellow, American College of Obstetricians and Gynecologists (1973-Present); Greater Birmingham Obstetrical and Gynecological Society (1973-Present); Chairman, Subcommittee on GYN Oncology, American College of Obstetricians and Gynecologists (1994-1995); Subcommittee on GYN Oncology, Committee on Gynecologic Practice, Representative to the Society of Gynecologic Oncologists, American College of Obstetricians and Gynecologists (1993-1995); President, South Central Obstetrical and Gynecological Society (1992-1993); President, Jefferson County Medical Society (1986-1987); Board of Censors, Jefferson County Medical Society (1978-1987); Vice President, Chairman of the Board, Board of Counselors, Emory at Oxford College (1984-1986); President, Alabama Association of Obstetrics and Gynecology (1984-1985); Vice President, Jefferson County Medical Society (1984-1985); Secretary-Treasurer, Jefferson County Medical Society (1983-1985); Vice President, President-Elect, Alabama Association of Obstetrics and Gynecology (1983-1984); Quality Assurance Committee, Alabama Medical Review (1978-1980); Birmingham Academy of Medicine (1977-1980); First President, Charles E. Flowers Society (1977-1978); Charter Member, Charles E. Flowers Society (1977); Sigma Chi (1961-1963) **Marquis Who's Who Honors:** Marquis Who's Who Top Professional **To what do you attribute your success:** Dr. Austin attributes his success to the support of his parents and his work ethic. **Why did you become involved in your profession or industry:** Dr. Austin became involved in his profession because of his family's support and his medical education, which exposed him to people who also had careers in medicine. He also wanted to teach young people. **Religion:** Baptist **Thoughts on Life:** Dr. Austin and his wife, Nancy, take great pride in their two children, Lindsey and Max, and in their five grandchildren. His daughter is a registered nurse and his son is in the real estate industry. Dr. Austin remains grounded by spending time at his timber farm in Elmore County, Alabama. As said in his nomination letter, "Dr. Austin epitomizes the ultimate as a physician servant and as a gentleman doctor." He was nominated by colleagues Dr. Pink Folmar and Dr. Ed Partr.

Stephen Avery

Title: Freelance Reporter **Industry:** Media & Entertainment **Date of Birth:** 03/20/1955 **Place of Birth:** Hot Springs **State/Country of Origin:** AR/USA **Parents:** Leo A. Avery; Dedette Carol (Miles) Sullivan **Marital Status:** Married **Spouse Name:** Kathleen Annette Twin Avery (09/07/1979) **Career:** Freelance Reporter, Writer, The Sentinel-Record, Hot Springs, AR (1970-1973); Freelance Reporter, New Era, Hot Springs, AR (1970-1973) **Civic:** Founding Sponsor, National Museum of American Jewish History (2009-Present); Founding Sponsor, Flight 93 National Memorial (2006-Present); Founding Sponsor, Martin Luther King Jr. National Memorial (2005-Present); President's Council, World Jewish Congress (2005-Present); Scholarship Committee, American Indian Education Fund, Partnership with Native Americans (2005-Present); Ameri-Cares (2004-Present); Active Member, National Republican Congressional Committee (2004-Present); International Rescue Committee (2004-Present); Founders Circle, Vada Sheid Community Development Center, Arkansas State University, Mountain Home (2002-Present); Founding Member, The National Campaign for Tolerance (2002-Present); Active Member, United States Holocaust Memorial Museum (2001-Present); Founding Sponsor, Statue of Liberty Museum, Ellis Island (2018); Leadership Council, Southern Poverty Law Center (2002-2015); Delegate, Republican, Senatorial Election Platform Committee (2012); Friends of Sesame Workshop (2005-2008); Active Member, Simon Wiesenthal Center (2002-2006); Honorary Co-Chair, President's Dinner for George W. Bush (2004, 2005); Active Member, Beil Hashoah Museum of Tolerance (2003-2006); Active Member, American Jewish Committee (2003-2005) **Military Service:** U.S. Navy (1973-1977) **Creative Works:** Production Partner, "Viva la Causa," Southern Poverty Law Center Documentary (2008); Production Partner, "Ever Again," Moriah Films Documentary (2005); Author, "Burning Bridges" (1999); Author, "Insidious" (1992); Author, "Because" (1991); Author, "Hungry: Three Plays" (1991) **Awards:** Inclusion, Smithsonian National Air and Space Museum Wall of Honor (2018); World Jewish Congress Medallion of Commitment (2013); Gateway Award, Save Ellis Island, Inc. (2012); Leadership Award, World Jewish Congress Foundation (2011); Nahum Goldmann Leadership Award, World Jewish Congress Foundation (2007); Republican Senatorial American Spirit Medal (2007); Congressional Order of Merit (2006, 2007); Inclusion, Republican Presidential Honor Roll by Order of the Executive Committee, National Republican Congressional Committee (2005) **Memberships:** Inaugural Member, The Write Stuff Society of the Dramatists Guild Foundation (2019); American Film Institute (2019); Kennedy Center National Patron (2019); Charter Member, George W. Bush Presidential Center; Drama League; Theater Communications Group; Authors League of America (Now Authors Guild); Dramatists Guild of America, Inc.; Charter Member, World Trade Center Memorial Foundation (Now National September 11th Museum); Americans for the Arts Action Fund; Save Ellis Island, Inc.; National Museum of the American Indian, Smithsonian Institution; National D-Day Museum (Now National World War II Museum); National Museum for Women in the Arts; National Trust for Historic Preservation; Habitat for Humanity International; National Campaign for Tolerance **Marquis Who's Who Honors:** Albert Nelson Marquis Lifetime Achievement Award **To what do you attribute your success:** Mr. Avery attributes his success to dedication, perseverance, the right luck, and a patient wife. **Why did you become involved in your profession or industry:** Mr. Avery became involved in his profession because of his desire to live a life of contribution and significance. **Avocations:** Museum and gallery exhibitions

Anne Louise Ayers

Title: Small Business Owner, Counselor, administrator **Industry:** Business Management/ Business Services **Date of Birth:** 10/22/1948 **Place of Birth:** Albuquerque **State/Country of Origin:** NM/USA **Parents:** F. Ernest Ayers; Gladys Marguerite (Miles) Ayers **Marital Status:** Single **Education:** Civilian Graduate, Transportation Officer Basic Program, United States Army (1978); MEd in Counseling/Guidance Psychology and Educational Administration, Seattle Pacific University (1971); BA in Research Psychology, Speech Pathology and Audiology, The University of Kansas (1970); PhD-Level Coursework, Research and Planning, Educational Administration, Counseling Guidance/Psychology, Policy Studies, Virginia Polytechnic Institute and State University; Coursework, Psychology Courses, Doctoral Program, William and Mary; Graduate Coursework, Therapy Skills Course, American University; Business Law Coursework, Hampton University; Undergrad Physics Coursework, University of Washington; Counselor/Speech Pathologist Internship; Counselor Intern, Seattle Central Community College **Certifications:** Court-Appointed Estate Administrator, Washington, California (2008-Present); Court-Appointed Estate Administrator, Maryland (2010-2019); **Career:** Probate Estate Administrator, States of WA and CA (2008-Present); Appalachian Love Arts President, Manufacturer, Seller of Patented Items (1981-Present); Probate Estate Administrator, State of MD (2010-2019); Education Services Specialist, Program Managers of NASA Headquarters Teacher Resource Center Network, and of Space Science Student Involvement (1989-1996); Education Specialist, National Mine Health and Safety Academy, Beckley, WV (1979-1989); Education Specialist, U.S. Army Transportation School, Fort Eustis, VA (1977-1979); Education Service Specialist, General Educational Development Center, Fort Monroe, VA (1975-1977); Evening Instructors of Psychology for Hampton (1975-1979), and for Chapman Universities (1973-1975); Director, Aerospace Defense Command Resident Education Centers for ND and MT, Chapman University (1972-1974); Staff Consultant in Student Development, Central Washington University (1971-1972) **Career Related:** Substitute Counselor, Berkeley County, West Virginia (1997-2013) **Civic:** Social Chairman, Church Youth Group (1965-1966); Faith Chairman, Church Youth Group (1965-1966); Volunteer, Methodist Church; Church Camp Counselor, Seattle First United Methodist Church, Seattle, WA **Creative Works:** Photographer, Published Over Six Photographs, International Library of Photography (1992-2010); Featured Actor, Mine Safety Color Video (1988); Author, "Educational Feasibility Study of Computer Uses in MSHA" (1987); Author, "Developing Criterion-Referenced Instruction Based on Valid Job Performance Analysis," International Symposium for the Prevention of Risks in the Mining Industry in Conjunction with United States Department of State, Mine Safety and Health Administration and United States Department of Labor (1981); Author, "Educational Cost-Effectiveness of Two Methods of U.S. Army Training" (1979); Author, Ganzfeld Research Psychology Publication, Psychomotor and Perceptual Skills (1973); Featured Actor, Newspaper and Television Ads, Chapman University (1972-1974); Author, 29 On-the-Job Mine Safety Books; Author, National Institute for Occupational and Safety Health Pneumonoconiosis Booklet **Awards:** Alumnus of Growing Vision for the Century in Education Award, Seattle Pacific University (1991); Runner-Up, Theme Song Contest, WCIR Radio (1988); Expert in Criterion Referenced Training on the Bureau of Mines Contracting Board (1988); Honoree, Transportation Section, National Directory of Women Administrators in Vocational Education (1979); Toastmaster's Trophy for Best Speech, Virginia Group, Toastmasters International (1979); United States Army Training Board (1978-1979): Leadership Scholarship, Humble Oil and Refining Co. (Now Exxon Mobile Corporation) (1972); Church Scholarships (1966-1968); Excellence in Oboe Solo Award, State of Washington (1963-1965); First Place, Aerospace Pure Science, Boeing (1963); First Place, Encyclopedia Britannica (1963); First Place for "Sending Sound Over a Beam of Light," King County Science Fair (1963); Boeing Pure Science Award from Wernher Von Braun; Growing Vision for the Century in Education Award **Memberships:** National Society of Inventors; National Association of Women Deans, Administrators, and Counselors (Now National Association of Students Personal Administration); International Photography Association; International Platform Association; Mayflower Society **Marquis Who's Who Honors:** Albert Nelson Marquis Lifetime Achievement Award; Marquis Who's Who Top Professional; Marquis Who's Who Humanitarian Award **To what do you attribute your success:** Ms. Ayers attributes her success to the saying, "Anything worth doing at all, is worth doing well." **Why did you become involved in your profession or industry:** Ms. Ayers became involved in her profession to make a difference in people's lives. **Avocations:** Coin collecting/numismatics; Mining gems; Design settings & selling jewelry on eBay Inc.; Playing clarinet and oboe; Playing games; Rock garden; Supervising outdoor work; Auto repair; Artistic activities; Designing things of beauty; Gardening; Genealogy; Crocheting **Political Affiliations:** Independent **Religion:** Methodist

Harry Brandt Ayers

Title: Editor, Publisher, Columnist **Industry:** Writing and Editing **Date of Birth:** 04/08/1935 **Place of Birth:** Anniston **State/Country of Origin:** AL/USA **Parents:** Harry Mell Ayers; Edel Olga (Ytterboe) Ayers **Marital Status:** Married **Spouse Name:** Josephine Ehringhaus **Children:** Margaret **Education:** LittD, The University of Alabama at Birmingham, AL (2004); Honorary LHD, The University of Alabama at Birmingham, AL (1994); BA in History, The University of Alabama, Tuscaloosa, AL (1959) **Career:** Publisher, The Anniston Star, (1969-2018); Editor, The Anniston Star (1969-2013); Managing Editor, The Anniston Star (1963-1969); Correspondent, Bascom Timmons Bureau, Washington, DC (1961-1963); Political Writer, The Raleigh Times (1959-1961) **Career Related:** Chair, Consolidated Publication Co. (1976-2018); Commentator, "Morning Edition," NPR **Civic:** American Committee, International Press Institute, Vienna, Austria (1985-Present); Council on Foreign Relations, New York, NY (1983-Present); Board of Directors, Southern Center for International Studies, Atlanta, GA (1979-Present); Board of Directors, Inter American Press Association, Miami, FL (2003, 1992-1993); Chairman, U.N. Day, AL (2000); Wooster School, Danbury, CT (1989-1990); The Century Foundation (1985-2005); Center for Excellence in Government (1985-1988); Board of Foreign Scholarships, Washington, DC (1981-1984); Trustee, Talladega College (1972-1989); Co-founder, LQC Lamar Society (1970); Advisory Board, The American Ditchley Foundation, London, England, United Kingdom **Military Service:** With, United States Navy (1956-1958) **Creative Works:** Contributor, "Loving Dixie, Cussing Dixie" (2016); Author, "In Love with Defeat" (2013); Author, "The 2013 BCS National Championship" (2012); Co-author, "Dixie Dateline" (1983); Advisory Board, "Inside Story," Public Broadcasting System, New York, NY (1981-1985); Co-author, Inaugural Book, President Carter (1977); Co-author, "A Bicentennial Portrait of the American People," U.S. News Books (1976); Co-editor, "You Can't Eat Magnolias" (1972); Contributor, International, Newspapers; Contributor, National Newspapers **Awards:** Editorial Leadership Award, Society of Newspaper Editors (2003); Lifetime Achievement Award, Alabama Press Association (2003); Julia Tutwiler Distinguished Service Award (2002); Inductee, Hall of Fame, The University of Alabama School of Communication and Information Sciences (2000); Alabama Academy Honor (1991); Senior Fellow, Gannett Center, Columbia University (1989); Green Eyeshade Award, Society of Professional Journalists (1985); Human Relations Award, American Jewish Committee (1977); Fellow, Nieman Foundation, Harvard University (1968); Distinguished Journalism Graduate, The University of Alabama (1967); Distinguished Alumni Award, The Wooster School **Memberships:** Director, Southern Newspaper Publishers Association (1981-1984); Founding President, Alabama Press Journalism Foundation (1969); American Society of Newspaper Editors; The Century Association, New York, NY; The Metropolitan Club of the City of Washington, Washington, DC **Marquis Who's Who Honors:** Albert Nelson Marquis Lifetime Achievement Award **Why did you become involved in your profession or industry:** Mr. Ayers was born into his profession. He made his way in the ruthless struggle of life with the small talents of nepotism and monopoly. His father was the founder and owned The Anniston Star that was a combination of two existing papers that merged together. His mother wrote a small book, "The Old Maine," which was about the main building at Northfield College. **Political Affiliations:** Democrat **Religion:** Episcopalian

Alex Michael Azar II

Title: United States Secretary of Health and Human Services **Industry:** Government Administration/Government Relations/Government Services **Date of Birth:** 6/17/1967 **Place of Birth:** Jonestown **State/Country of Origin:** PA/USA **Parents:** Alex Azar; Lynda (Zarisky) Azar **Marital Status:** Married **Spouse Name:** Jennifer Azar **Children:** Two Children **Education:** JD, Yale Law School (1991); AB in Government and Economics, Dartmouth College, with Highest Honors, Summa Cum Laude (1988) **Career:** United States Secretary of Health and Human Services, United States Department of Health and Human Services, Washington, DC (2018-Present); President, Eli Lilly USA, Eli Lilly & Company, Indianapolis, IN (2012-2017); Vice President, U.S. Managed Care Services & Puerto Rico, Eli Lilly & Company, Indianapolis, IN (2009-2011); Senior Vice President, Corporate Affairs & Communications, Eli Lilly & Company, Indianapolis, IN (2007-2009); Deputy Secretary, United States Department of Health and Human Services, Washington, DC (2005-2007); General Counsel, United States Department of Health and Human Services, Washington, DC (2001-2005); Partner, Wiley, Rein & Fielding LLP (Now Wiley Rein LLP), Washington, DC (1996-2001); Associate Independent Counsel, Whitewater Investigation, Washington, DC (1994-1996); Associate, Kirkland & Ellis LLP, Washington, DC (1993-1994); Law Clerk to Associate Justice Antonin Scalia, Supreme Court of the United States, Washington, DC (1992-1993); Law Clerk to Honorable J. Michael Luttig, United Sates Court Appeals for the Fourth Circuit (1991-1992) **Civic:** Board, HMS Holdings; Board, American Council on Germany; Chairman, Strategic Planning Committee, American Council on Germany; Board, Indianapolis Symphony Orchestra **Creative Works:** Executive Committee, Yale Law Journal **Memberships:** Worldwide Speakers Group; Kappa Kappa Kappa **Bar Admissions:** The District of Columbia Bar (1995); Maryland State Bar Association (1993) **Political Affiliations:** Republican

Daniel L. Azarnoff, MD

Title: Pharmaceutical Executive **Industry:** Education/Educational Services **Company Name:** DL Azarnoff Associates **Date of Birth:** 08/04/1926 **Parents:** Samuel J. Azarnoff; Kate Azarnoff **Marital Status:** Married **Spouse Name:** Joanne Stokes (12/26/1951) **Children:** Rachel; Richard; Martin **Education:** Resident, National Heart Institute Research Fellow, The University of Kansas School of Medicine (1956-1958); Intern, The University of Kansas School of Medicine(1955-1956); MD, University of Kansas (1955); Research Fellow, University of Kansas Medical School (1950-1952); MS, Rutgers, The State University of New Jersey (1948); BS, Rutgers, The State University of New Jersey (1947) **Career:** President, DL Azarnoff Associates, Southern San Francisco, CA (1987-Present); Senior Vice President, Clinical Development and Pharmacology, Congentus Pharmaceuticals (2006-2007); Senior Vice President, Clinical Regulatory Affairs, Cellegy Pharmaceuticals, San Francisco, CA (1998-2003); Clinical Medical Professor, Stanford University School of Medicine (1998-2002); Professor of Medicine, The University of Kansas School of Medicine (1997-2007); Chairman, Board of Directors, Alpha RX Corp., Southern San Francisco, CA (1992-1994); President, Azarnoff Associates, Inc., Evanston, IL (1986-1987); Commissioner, National Commission on Orphan Diseases (1985-1987); Clinical Professor of Medicine, The University of Kansas School of Medicine (1982-1996); President, Searle R&D, Skokie, IL (1979-1985); Professor of Pathology, Clinical Professor of Pharmacology, Northwestern University Medical School (1978-1985); Senior Vice President, Worldwide R&D, G.D. Searle & Co., Skokie, IL (1978); Distinguished Professor, The University of Kansas School of Medicine(1973-1978); President, Sigma Xi Club, The University of Kansas School of Medicine (1968-1969); Professor of Medicine and Pharmacology, The University of Kansas School of Medicine (1968); Director, Clinical Pharmacology-Toxicology Center, The University of Kansas School of Medicine (1967-1978); Associate Professor of Pharmacology, The University of Kansas School of Medicine (1965-1968); Professor of Medicine, The University of Kansas School of Medicine (1965-1967); Director, Clinical Pharmacology Study Unit, The University of Kansas School of Medicine (1964-1968); Associate Professor, The University of Kansas School of Medicine (1964-1968); Assistant Professor of Medicine, The University of Kansas School of Medicine (1962-1954); Assistant Professor of Medicine, St. Louis University School of Medicine (1960-1962); Special Trainee, National Institute of Neurological Diseases and Blindness, Washington University School of Medicine (1958-1960); Assistant Instructor of Anatomy, The University of Kansas School of Medicine (1949-1950) **Career Related:** Chief Executive Officer, Vitalsensor, Inc. (2004-2005); Chairman, Board of Directors, Vitalsensor, Inc. (2004-2005); Chairman, Board of Directors, Oread, Inc., Lawrence, KS (1998-1999); Chairman, Board of Directors, Cibus Pharmaceutical Inc. (1996-1997); Chief Executive Officer, Cibus Pharmaceutical Inc., Burlingame, CA (1996-1997); Professorial Lecturer, The University of Chicago (1978-1986); Chairman, Committee on Problems of Drug Safety NRC-NAS (1972-1976); Director, Second Workshop on Principals Drug Evaluation in Man (1970) **Military Service:** U.S. Army (1945-1946) **Creative Works:** Editorial Board, Clinical Drug Investigation (1989-Present); Series Editor, Monographs in Clinical Pharmacology (1977-1984); Editor, Yearbook of Drug Therapy (1977-1979); Editor, Development of Drug Interactions (1974-1977) **Awards:** Nathanial T. Kwit Memorial Distinguished Service Award, American College of Clinical Pharmacology (2002); Distinguished Medical Alumnus, University of Kansas College of Health Science (1995); Research Achievement Award in Clinical Sciences, American Association of Pharmaceutical Scientists (1995); Oscar B. Hunter Memorial Award, American Society of Clinical Pharmacology and Therapeutics (1995); 7th Sir Henry Hallett Dale Lecturer, John Hopkins University Medical School (1978); Bruce Hall Memorial Lecturer, St. Vincent's Hospital, Sydney (1976); William N. Creasy Visiting Professor of Clinical Pharmacology, Medical College of Virginia (1975); Fulbright Scholar, Karolinska Institute, Stockholm (1968) **Memberships:** Chairman, Pharmaceutical Division, American Association for the Advancement of Science (2002-2003); Chairman Elect, Pharmaceutical Section, American Association for the Advancement of Science (2001); Blue Ribbon Committee on Generic Medicine, GPIA (1990); Executive Committee, American Society of Pharmacology and Experimental Therapeutics (1978-1981); Secretary, Clinical Pharmacology Section, International Union of Pharmacologists (1975-1981); International Advisory Committee, Paris Congress, International Union of Pharmacologists (1978); Councillor, Society for Experimental Biology and Medicine (1976-1980); Delegate, American Society of Pharmacology and Experimental Therapeutics (1975-1978); Executive Committee, American Society of Pharmacology and Experimental Therapeutics **Marquis Who's Who Honors:** Albert Nelson Marquis Lifetime Achievement Award **Avocations:** Camping; Traveling

Maria Baan

Title: Set Nurse, Actress, Author **Industry:** Health, Wellness and Fitness **Company Name:** Bona-Fide Services **Certifications:** Licensed Nurse; Licensed Professional Set Nurse; Licensed Esthetician **Career:** Set Nurse, Medical Consultant, Film, "The Breaks," Breaks LLC, VH1 (2016); Guest Host, Numerous Positions, Radio Shows, LifeStyle Radio, ABC RADIO (2014-2015); Co-Host, Commercial, LifeStyle Radio, "Beauty Expert"; Set Nurse, Medic, Tombstone Productions LLC, "A Walk Among the Tombstone"; Medical Spokesperson, MSN, "Rapid Response"; Actress, Mom/Lead, Music Video, Scott Franklin Productions, "DNA," Ultraviolent; Actress, Mom/Lead, Music Video, Scott Franklin Productions, "Big City Life," Mattafix; Lead Actress, Clinical Instructor, Centocor, "Remicade"; Role, Dove, Real Women Beautiful Skin; Dr. Summersbond, Raphael Rizzo, "Time of My Life Dr. (Soap)"; CPR Demonstrator, Aide, Tutor, Film, "Bringing Out the Dead," Directed by Martin Scorsese; Set Nurse, Medic, Film, "A Walk Among the Tombstone," Tombstone Productions; Actress, "The Sopranos," Directed by Tim Van Patten; Actress, "Moral Dilemma," Punched in the Head Productions; Nurse, Medical Consultant, "Blue Bloods," Blue Bloods LLC; Nurse, Medical Consultant, "Golden Boy," Golden Boy Productions; CPR Consultant, Nurse, "Royal Pains," Open 4 Business; Set Nurse, Medic, "Rescue Me," Rescue Me Productions; Set Nurse, Medical Consultant, "Fringe," John Galontis; Writer, Lead Actress, "Finding Lou," Bonafide Productions **Career Related:** Author **Creative Works:** Author, "Are Miracles for Real? You Be the Judge" (2019); Author, "Making Every Moment Count," MSN **Awards:** Semifinalist, Amazing Nurse of the Year, Johnson & Johnson **Memberships:** SAG-AFTRA; Local 52 **Marquis Who's Who Honors:** Marquis Who's Who Top Professional **To what do you attribute your success:** Ms. Baan attributes her success to her faith in God. **Why did you become involved in your profession or industry:** Ms. Baan became involved in her profession because early on, she was working three jobs at once; she was a private duty nurse, a surgical nurse, and an actress. One night in between jobs, one of her friends mentioned to Ms. Baan that she had noticed she was great with people and had already gotten her foot in the door of the entertainment industry. This friend suggested she pursue a set nurse position. At first, Ms. Baan was reluctant, but she eventually applied. It worked out because she is now a very successful nurse on movie sets. As a nurse, from a very young age, she always had her heart set on helping people. She always had a desire to help people, and she sees this in her daughter and granddaughter. But, with the nursing, she sees when people are helpless, in need of help, or that someone needs to be a voice for them, especially when there is injustice and her heart goes out to them to help. As an actress, she began at the age of 28. After sneaking past the security of a casting agent, she managed to secure the part of an unnamed hostage on "Nighthawks" in 1981. She later played the role of Fran in an episode of "The Sopranos" in 2004. In addition, as far as the acting, even when she was in nursing school and they did skits, they told her she was in the wrong profession and that she might be a great nurse, but would be a better actress. However, she always had the desire to get into different characters, it was something she enjoyed. She kind of grew into it, but as she got older, she was typecast in some roles, such as being a therapist, like on "Time of My Life," an upcoming soap opera. In this particular role, the dialogue was made up of things she would say to her patients and to people in real life.

Antonino F. Badalamenti, PhD

Title: Adjunct Assistant Professor **Industry:** Education/Educational Services **Company Name:** John Jay College of Criminal Justice **Date of Birth:** 05/02/1960 **Place of Birth:** New York **State/Country of Origin:** NY/USA **Parents:** Antonino Badalamenti; Teresa Cima **Education:** PhD in Andrgogy in Mathematics and Post-Adult Education, University of California, Berkeley; PhD in Andragogy in Mathematics and Post-Adult Education, University of Minnesota Twin Cities, Minneapolis, MN; MS in Education and Mathematical Instruction, Iona College, New Rochelle, NY; BA in Mathematics and Science, Marymount Manhattan College, New York, NY; Associate of Science in Liberal Arts, Borough of Manhattan Community College, New York, NY **Certifications:** Education Inner City Students; Working with LGBT+ Students; Identifying and Assisting "At Risk" Students **Career:** Adjunct Lecturer Professor, Department of Mathematics, Borough of Manhattan Community College, New York, NY; Adjunct Associate Professor, Department of Mathematics and Technology, John Jay College of Criminal Justice, New York, NY; Substitute Professor, Marymount Manhattan College, New York, NY; New York Public Schools, New York, NY **Career Related:** Research and Program Development Assistant, Dr. Lillian Nash, Inc., New York, NY (1978-2008); Research Assistant, Web-Based and Statistical Research for "Preserving New York: Winning the Rights to Protect a City's Landmarks," New York Preservation Archive Project **Civic:** Benefactor and Co-Founder, The First Church of Saint Pio; Volunteer, Church of Padre Pio, Archive Project New York, Archdiocese New York, Saint Josephs Indian School, Visiting Nurse Service, Womens Zionist Service **Creative Works:** Author, Study Guide, "Quantitative Reasoning" (2014); Author, Book, "You Got the Vibe" (2008); Statistical Researcher, Publication, "Preserving New York: Winning the Rights to Protect a City's Landmarks"(2007); Contributing Author, Local Publications, including "East Side Express" and "Our Town" **Awards:** Philanthropic Work Award for Helping Students with Accessibility Problems and Handicaps (2019) **Memberships:** New York Mathematics Association; The John Calandra Italian American institute of the City University of New York; New York Archive Project; Our Lady of Good Counsel Outreach and All Night Vigil, Archdiocese of New York **Marquis Who's Who Honors:** Albert Nelson Marquis Lifetime Achievement Award; Marquis Who's Who Top Professional **To what do you attribute your success:** Dr. Badalamenti attributes his success to God, his parents, and his spouse. **Why did you become involved in your profession or industry:** Dr. Badalamenti became involved in his profession because his passion is to help and educate others. He believes that "if you give a person a fish, they will have been fed but once, [but] when you teach them how to fish, they can be fed forever." **Religion:** Roman Catholic/Episcopal **Thoughts on Life:** Dr. Badalamenti said, "Being born LGBTQ+ and Italian American on the Upper East Side of Manhattan and growing during the 1960s and 1970s, I was subjected to physical and psychological abuse. With God's great blessings, I was able to not only overcome this discrimination but turn it to my advantage by becoming more resilient. Trained as a professional gemologist, I also became a collector. Being called to serve others, I decided to devote myself to teaching and acquired my graduate and post-graduate degrees. That began my three decades of teaching in the CUNY system. During that period, I have taught generations of students, many being the first in their family to attend college. Beyond the classroom, I am also active in my church, founding and leading a First-Friday all-night prayer vigil. Like so many others, I have been inspired by Pope Benedict and his welcoming of diversity within the Church."

Najat Badriyeh

Title: Founder/CEO **Industry:** Business Management/Business Services **Company Name:** Naprotek, Inc **State/Country of Origin:** Lebanon **Marital Status:** Married **Spouse Name:** Khalil (05/27/1978) **Children:** Fida; Adel; Wafa **Education:** Coursework completed **Career:** Chief Executive Officer, President, Naprotek, Inc. (1995-Present) **Awards:** Founder of the Week Award (2018); CEO of the Year, Today USA Magazine (2018); CEO of the Year, Acquisition International (2018); Excellence Award; Top 10 Fastest Growing Business in Silicon Valley; Top 500 Fastest-Growing Women in the United States; Top 100 in California **Memberships:** CEO's of Silicon Valley **Marquis Who's Who Honors:** Marquis Who's Who Top Professional **To what do you attribute your success:** Ms. Badriyeh attributes her success to strong leadership skills and being an understanding human. She cares a lot about other individuals and is very giving; she has been throughout her entire life. **Why did you become involved in your profession or industry:** Ms. Badriyeh became involved in her profession because she had a passion for the electronics industry for as long as she can remember. Hoping to start her own business, she surrounded herself with electronics as a child. All throughout her life, she was consistently motivated to succeed by her passion.

Marvin O. Bagby, LHD (Hon.)

Title: Chemist **Industry:** Sciences **Date of Birth:** 09/27/1932 **Place of Birth:** Macomb **State/Country of Origin:** IL/USA **Parents:** Byron Orville Bagby; Geneva Floriene (Filbert) Bagby **Marital Status:** Married **Spouse Name:** Mary Jean Jennings, (8/31/1957) **Children:** Gary Lee; Gordon Eugene **Education:** Honorary LHD, Western Illinois University (1992); MS in Organic Chemistry, Western Illinois State College (1957); BS in Chemistry and Education, Western Illinois State College (1957) **Career:** Retired (1996); Research Leader, Oil Chemical Research, National Center for Agricultural Utilization Research (1985-1996); Manager, Northern Agricultural Energy Center (1980-1985); Research Leader, Hydrocarbon Plants and Biomass Research, Northern Agricultural Energy Center (1980-1982); Research Leader, Hydrocarbon Plants and Biomass Research (1979-1981); Research Leader, Fibrous Products Research Unit, Northern Regional Research Center, U.S. Department of Agriculture, Agricultural Research Service, Peoria, IL (1974-1979); Chemist, Research Chemist, Senior Research Chemist (1957-1974); With, Northern Regional Research Center, U.S. Department of Agriculture, Agricultural Research Service, Peoria, IL (1957-1996) **Career Related:** Panel Manager, U.S. Department of Agriculture, Cooperative State Research Education and Extension Service, Funds for Rural America, Value Added/New Uses (1997-1999); Consultant, Numerous Special Assignments and Government Projects Team Leader Developing Process for Making Newsprint **Civic:** President, Home Owners Association; Board Member, Cornville/Page Springs Community Association; Planning and Zoning Committee **Military Service:** U.S. Army (1953-1955) **Creative Works:** Contributor, More than 200 Publications; Five Patents **Awards:** Honorary Life Membership Award, American Soybean Association (1993); Distinguished Service Award, U.S. Department Agriculture (1992); Award for Excellence in Technology Transfer, Federal Laboratory Consortium (1991); ARS Technology Transfer Award (1990); Domestic Marketing Award, American Soybean Association (1990); Research and Development 100 Award (1988); Certificate of Merit for Exceptional Performance (1988); Certificate of Merit for Outstanding Performance, Northern Agricultural Energy Center (1981); Alumni Achievement Award, Western Illinois University (1980); Various Agency Performance Awards **Memberships:** American Association for the Advancement of Science; Technical Association of Pulp and Paper Industry; American Chemical Society; American Oil Chemists Society; New York Academy Science; American Society Agricultural Engineers; Association for the Advancement Industrial Crop; Fellow, American Institute of Chemists **Marquis Who's Who Honors:** Albert Nelson Marquis Lifetime Achievement Award **Why did you become involved in your profession or industry:** Mr. Bagby became involved in his profession because when he was a high school junior he took a chemistry class which he thoroughly enjoyed and also a book keeping class which he also enjoyed. He considered majoring in business, but by the end of his college freshman year he decided he was going to major in chemistry. He had an excellent high school chemistry teacher whose name was Mr. Fesler. **Religion:** Protestant

Patricia P. Bailey

Title: Lawyer; Former Government Official **Date of Birth:** 06/20/1937 **Place of Birth:** Forth Smith **State/Country of Origin:** AR/USA **Parents:** Margaret; John (Pat) Price **Marital Status:** Widowed **Spouse Name:** Douglas L. Bailey **Children:** Edward; Katherine Bailey **Education:** JD, American University, Washington, DC, Summa Cum Laude (1976); MA in International Affairs, Tufts University The Fletcher School of Law and Diplomacy (1960); BA in History, Lindenwood College (Now Lindenwood University), Cum Laude (1959) **Career:** Partner, Squire, Sanders & Dempsey (Now Squire Patton Boggs), Washington, DC (1989-Present); Commissioner, Federal Trade Commission, Washington, DC (1979-1988); Executive Assistant to General Counsel, U.S. Merit Systems Protection Board (1979); Special Assistant to Assistant Attorney General, United States Department of Justice (1977-1979); Legal Assistant, Office of Counsel to President in White House (1976); Advisor of Foreign Affairs, Representative F. Bradford Morse (1967-1968); Executive Assistant, Bureau for Latin America, Then Assistant to Deputy Coordinator, Alliance for Progress, Agency for Internationally Development (1961-1966); Editor, Research Analyst, Bureau of Intelligence and Research, U.S. Department of State (1960-1961) **Career Related:** Advisory Committee, Impact of Women in Public Office, Eagleton Institute of Politics, Rutgers, The State University of New Jersey; Board of Directors, Trustee, Avdel PLC; Board of Directors, Arbella Mutual Insurance Company **Civic:** Member, Special Commission to Review the Honor System and Honor Code at West Point (1988); Board of Directors, The Washington Center (1987-1989); Board of Directors, Women's Legal Defense Fund (1982-1983); Member, Dean's Advisory Council, American University Washington College of Law; Board of Directors, Foundation for Women's Resources; Board of Directors, Lindenwood College (Now Lindenwood University) **Creative Works:** Contributor, Articles to Professional Journals **Awards:** Named Woman Lawyer of the Year, Women's Bar Association of the District of Columbia and WBA Foundation (1988); Special Recognition Award, National Association of Attorneys General (NAAG) (1987); Philip Hart Public Service Award, Consumer Federation of America (1985) **Memberships:** Board of Directors, Women's Bar Association Foundation (Now WBA Foundation) (1981-1985); Board of Directors, Women's Bar Association of the District of Columbia (1981-1983) **Bar Admissions:** District of Columbia; United States Court Appeals for the District of Columbia Circuit; United States Court of Appeals for the Eighth Circuit; Supreme Court of the United States **Marquis Who's Who Honors:** Albert Nelson Marquis Lifetime Achievement Award **Why did you become involved in your profession or industry:** Mrs. Bailey didn't go to law school until she already had children. Her youngest child was 4 years old when she began law school. She recalled that she had always wanted to go and finally enrolled 16 years after she completed her master's degree. **Political Affiliations:** Democrat **Religion:** Episcopalian **Thoughts on Life:** Mrs. Bailey succeeded Elizabeth Dole, the wife of Senator Bob Dole, as the commissioner for the Federal Trade Commission. Mrs. Bailey was the third woman elected for the position after Mrs. Dole. Prior to Mrs. Dole holding the position, the only other woman was appointed in 1913. Despite graduating with her JD 16 years after receiving her master's degree, Mrs. Bailey managed to finish first in her class upon graduation.

Barbara Jean Baker

Title: Restaurant Owner **Industry:** Food & Restaurant Services **Company Name:** Donatelli's Bistro **Date of Birth:** 06/28/1964 **Place of Birth:** Effingham **State/Country of Origin:** IL/USA **Parents:** Jack West; Mary West **Marital Status:** Married **Spouse Name:** Don Baker **Children:** Nicholas Giganti; Zachary Giganti; Brandon Giganti; Gary Baker (Stepson); Stephanie Simpson (Stepdaughter) **Education:** Associate Degree in Business **Career:** Owner, Donatelli's Bistro, Lake St. Louis, MO (2011-Present); Assistant Manager, Panera Bread, Lake St. Louis, MO; Independent Contractor, Creative Memories; Executive Secretary, Edison Brothers **Career Related:** Booking Live Entertainment; Party Planning; Consumer Relations; Stay at Home Mother (20 Years) **Creative Works:** Party Planning; Scrapbooking; Designing; Decorating **To what do you attribute your success:** Ms. Baker attributes her success to her husband and partner, Don. She additionally credits the work ethic instilled in her by her parents. **Why did you become involved in your profession or industry:** Ms. Baker became involved in her field because of how much she enjoys it. No day is ever the same. She enjoys working with people. **Avocations:** Photography; Scrapbooking; Exercising; Golfing; Vacationing; Sports; Spending time with family and grandchildren

Brent H. Baker

Title: Foundation Executive, Blogger **Industry:** Media & Entertainment **Company Name:** Media Research Center **Date of Birth:** 03/15/1963 **Place of Birth:** Pittsburgh **State/Country of Origin:** PA/USA **Parents:** Burnham H.; Florence E. (French) Baker **Marital Status:** Single **Education:** Bachelor of Arts in Political Science, George Washington University, with Special Honors (1985) **Career:** Editor-at-Large, NewsBusters.org, Media Research Center, Reston, VA (2005-Present); Editor, CyberAlert Email Report, Media Research Center, Alexandria, VA (1996-2015); Editor, Newswatch, National Conservative Foundation, Alexandria, VA (1985-1987); Steven P.J. Wood Senior Fellow and Vice President, Research Publications, Media Research Center, Alexandria and Reston, VA **Career Related:** Lead Content Producer, DisHonors Awards (1999-2017) **Creative Works:** Editor, "Campaign 2000 Media Reality Check" (2000); Author, "How to Identify, Expose and Correct Liberal Media Bias" (1994); Co-editor, "And That's The Way It Isn't: A Reference Guide to Media Bias" (1990); Editor, "Notable Quotables Newsletter" (1988-2015); Editor, "MediaWatch" (1988-1999); Editor, "CyberAlert" (1996-2015); Contributor, Articles to New York Post, Wall Street Journal, Investor's Business Daily, Washington Times, Colorado Springs Gazette-Telegraph, Etc **Memberships:** National Stuttering Association; Presidents Club of the Young Americas Foundation **Marquis Who's Who Honors:** Albert Nelson Marquis Lifetime Achievement Award; Marquis Who's Who Top Professional **To what do you attribute your success:** Mr. Baker credits his success on the hard work and good luck, as well as his ability to network with other professionals. **Why did you become involved in your profession or industry:** Mr. Baker first became interested in his profession due to his passion for politics and the news media. **Avocations:** Washington Capitals hockey team; Cruises **Political Affiliations:** Republican

James Dale Ball, MD

Title: Associate Professor Emeritus **Industry:** Education/Educational Services **Company Name:** Wake Forest Baptist Health, Medical Center **Date of Birth:** 03/04/1942 **Place of Birth:** Yale **State/Country of Origin:** MI/USA **Parents:** B. Dale Ball; Francis M. Ball **Children:** Victoria Hook; Christopher Ball **Education:** MD, Feinberg School of Medicine, Northwestern University (1969); BA, Michigan State University (1965) **Certifications:** Diplomate, American Board of Radiology; Diplomate, American Board of Nuclear Medicine **Career:** Associate Professor Emeritus, Wake Forest Baptist Health, Medical Center (2015-Present); Fellow, Wake Forest Baptist Health, Medical Center (1975); Head of Nuclear Medicine, College of Medicine, University of Florida (1975) **Military Service:** Major, US Air Force **Awards:** Quinn Award for Teaching Excellence (2007) **Memberships:** Society of Nuclear Medicine & Molecular Imaging; American College of Nuclear Medicine; American Medical Association **Marquis Who's Who Honors:** Albert Nelson Marquis Lifetime Achievement Award; Marquis Who's Who Top Professional **To what do you attribute your success:** Dr. Ball attributes his success to being mentored by Dr. Douglas Maynard. **Why did you become involved in your profession or industry:** Dr. Ball became involved in his profession because he wanted to help people and felt that nuclear medicine was a good way to go about doing that. **Avocations:** Dog obedience; Photography **Political Affiliations:** Republican **Religion:** Christian

Linda Irene Balthaser

Title: Faculty Academic Administrator (Retired) **Date of Birth:** 05/25/1939 **Place of Birth:** Kokomo **State/Country of Origin:** IN/USA **Parents:** Earl Isaac Showalter; Evelyn Pauline (Troyer) Showalter **Marital Status:** Widowed **Spouse Name:** Kenneth James Balthaser (06/01/1963, Deceased 2009) **Education:** Master of Science, Indiana University (1962); Bachelor of Science, University of Indianapolis, Magna Cum Laude (1961) **Career:** Assistant Dean Emerita, Indiana University-Purdue University Fort Wayne (2002-Present); Assistant Dean of Arts and Sciences, Indiana University-Purdue University Fort Wayne (1987-2002); Assistant Dean of Arts and Letters, Indiana University-Purdue University Fort Wayne (1986-1987); Assistant to Dean of Arts and Letters, Indiana University-Purdue University Fort Wayne (1970-1986); With, Indiana University-Purdue University Fort Wayne (1969-2002); Administrative Secretary, Office of the President, Indiana University, Bloomington, IN (1963-1966); Teacher of Business Education, Southport High School, Indianapolis, IN (1962-1963) **Career Related:** Board of Directors, Associated Churches of Fort Wayne and Allen County (1980); Founding Co-Director, Weekend College, Indiana University-Purdue University Fort Wayne (1979-1980); Indiana Conference North, Evangelical United Brethren Church Scholar (1957-1961); Member, Indiana Committee, National Museum of Women in the Arts **Civic:** Assistant Moderator, Plymouth Congregational Church of Fort Wayne, United Church of Christ (2007); Moderator, Plymouth Congregational Church of Fort Wayne, United Church of Christ (2005-2006); Assistant Moderator, Plymouth Congregational Church of Fort Wayne, United Church of Christ (2004); Council Member, Plymouth Congregational Church of Fort Wayne, United Church of Christ (2000-2007); Trustee, Plymouth Congregational Church of Fort Wayne, United Church of Christ (1994-1997); Volunteer, Indiana University-Purdue University Fort Wayne; Active Member, Plymouth Congregational Church of Fort Wayne, United Church of Christ **Awards:** Recipient, Lifetime Achievement Award (2019); Recipient, Women of Achievement Award, YWCA of Northeast Indiana (1990); Recipient, Scholarship, Indiana North Conference of the Evangelical United Brethren Church (1957) **Memberships:** Committee, Association of Indiana University-Purdue University Fort Wayne Women (2004); Co-Chair of Steering Committee, Association of Indiana University-Purdue University Fort Wayne Women (2003-2004); College and University Representative, American Association of University Women (2000-2002); Secretary, Steering Committee, Association of Indiana University-Purdue University Fort Wayne Women (1999-2003); Co-Chair of Steering Committee, Association of Indiana University-Purdue University Fort Wayne Women (1998-1999); Trustee, American Association of University Women (1995-1997); National Grantee, Fort Wayne Branch, American Association of University Women (1995); President, Association of Indiana University-Purdue University Fort Wayne Women (1967-1968); Association of Indiana University-Purdue University Fort Wayne Women; Former Member, Fort Wayne Zoological Society; Fort Wayne Museum of Art; Embassy Theater Foundation Inc.; Allen County-Fort Wayne Historical Society; American Mensa Limited; Phi Kappa Phi; Alpha Chi; Phi Alpha Epsilon; Delta Pi Epsilon **Marquis Who's Who Honors:** Albert Nelson Marquis Lifetime Achievement Award **To what do you attribute your success:** In accounting for her success, Ms. Balthaser credits the influence of her parents, whose optimism was an inspiration. Likewise, she benefited from the tutelage of several mentors and colleagues. **Why did you become involved in your profession or industry:** Ms. Balthaser entered her profession because she always loved school. She was the first member of her family to attend college, and her life has been changed by the influence of higher education. **Avocations:** Reading; Knitting; Sewing; Quilting; Choral singing **Religion:** Christian

Maria Lourdes Geraldine Banaad-Omiotek, MD

Title: Medical Doctor **Industry:** Medicine & Health Care **Company Name:** Swedish Covenant Hospital/Northshore **Children:** Two boys **Education:** Chief Resident in Family Medicine, Swedish Covenant Hospital, Chicago, IL (2003-2004); Resident in Family Medicine, Swedish Covenant Hospital, Chicago, IL (2001-2004); Chief Resident, Cardinal Santos Medical Center (1997); Resident in Internal Medicine, Cardinal Santos Medical Center (1995-1997); Postgraduate Intern, Cardinal Santos Medical Center, San Juan, Philippines (1994); MD, UER-MMMCI (University of the East Ramon Magsaysay Memorial Medical Center), Quezon City, Philippines (1993); BS in Biology, Ateneo de Manila University, Quezon City, Philippines (1989) **Certifications:** Certified in Family Medicine, The American Board of Family Medicine, Inc. (2004-Present); Diplomate, Philippine College of Physicians (1998-Present); Diplomate, Educational Commission for Foreign Medical Graduates (1995-Present); Licensed to Practice Medicine, State of Illinois **Career:** Attending Physician, Family Doctor-Family Healthcare, Presence Health, Chicago, IL (2004); Research Assistant, Department of Hepatology, Rush University Medical Center (1999-2001); Doctor, G.D. Banaad Clinic, Quezon City, Philippines (1998); Medical Doctor, Swedish Covenant Hospital (now Northshore University HealthSystems) **Career Related:** Director, Scholarship Program, Ateneo Alumni Association of North America, Inc. (2017-Present) **Civic:** Director, Scholarship Program, Ateneo de Manila University (2017-Present) **Creative Works:** Co-Author, "Current liver biopsy practices for suspected parenchymal liver diseases in the United States: The evolving role of radiologists," American Journal of Gastroenterology (2002); Co-Author, "Adult Living Donor Liver Transplantation: Preferences About Donation Outside the Medical Community," Liver Transplantation (2001); Co-Author, "Patient's Values for Health States Associated With Hepatitis C and Physicians' Estimates of Those Values," American Journal of Gastroenterology (2001); Co-Author, "Liver biopsy practices in the United States," American College of Gastroenterology (2001); Co-Author, "Universal precaution practices of gastrointestinal endoscopy personnel," American College of Gatroenterology (2001); Co-Author, "Differing attitudes towards virtual and conventional colonoscopy for colorectal cancer screening: Surveys among primary care physicians and potential patients," American Journal of Gastroenterology (2001) **Awards:** Honoree, Via Times Hall of Fame for Excellence in Medicine, CPRTV Channel, Via Times (2017); Honoree, Most Outstanding Resident, Swedish Covenant Hospital, Chicago, IL (2003-2004) **Memberships:** Director, Scholarship Program, Ateneans USA (2017-Present); Shodan, World Seido Karate Organization (2009-Present); American Academy of Family Physicians; American Board of Family Medicine; Chicago Medical Society; Illinois Academy of Family Physicians; Philippine College of Physicians **Marquis Who's Who Honors:** Albert Nelson Marquis Lifetime Achievement Award; Marquis Who's Who Top Professional; Distinguished Humanitarian **To what do you attribute your success:** Dr. Banaad-Omiotek attributes her success to the encouragement that she received from her parents. She was good at science, so they encouraged her to go into the medical field. **Why did you become involved in your profession or industry:** Dr. Banaad-Omiotek became involved in her profession because it was something that was generally suggested by her parents. They didn't force it, but she knew that's what they wanted. Dr. Banaad-Omiotek's uncle was a physician, so she was exposed to the industry as a child. She liked the sciences and completed a residency program in the Philippines in internal medicine. When she came to the United States, Dr. Banaad-Omiotek applied to internal medicine. She was matched to a family practice residency, which became the perfect fit. **Avocations:** Family; Travel; Children's activities; Martial arts

Leor Barak

Title: Owner **Industry:** Food & Restaurant Services **Company Name:** The New York Grilled Cheese Company **State/Country of Origin:** Canada **Children:** Mia Sara Barak **Education:** Coursework in Hotel Restaurant Management, Hospitality, George Brown College (1999); Coursework in Health and Nutrition, Ryerson University, Toronto, ON **Career:** Owner, Founder, New York Grilled Cheese Company (2013-Present); Owner, Chief Executive Officer, Nuts About Yogurt (2011-2014); Director and Operations Manager, Barak Logistics Corporation, Concord, Ontario, Canada (2006-2009); Logistics Manager, Karnak Transport Incorporated, Concord, Ontario, Canada (1999-2006) **Civic:** Volunteer, Baycrest, Ontario, Canada; Economic Development Task Force, Wilton Manor, FL **Awards:** Small Business of the Year Award **Memberships:** Fort Lauderdale Chamber of Commerce; Florida Restaurant Association **To what do you attribute your success:** Mr. Barak feels that his product simply speaks for itself, as it is a unique take on an already well-loved product. The local community is very supportive of his business as well. Further, he always had a very strong understanding of social media marketing and tapping into his client base effectively, to which he attributes much of his success. **Why did you become involved in your profession or industry:** Mr. Barak is originally from Canada. He decided to move to the United States for a business opportunity. His first venture in the states was a frozen yogurt shop, back when frozen yogurt was seemingly lucrative and popular. Unfortunately, the market became tight and over-saturated, causing Mr. Barak to seek a new opportunity. He has a culinary background, graduating from a French culinary school in Canada. He decided to add menu items to sell yogurt as well. With some clever thinking, he made some modifications to the store and began to sell unique grilled cheeses. He began to notice that they were selling very well, though the frozen yogurt was failing. He then decided to convert an entire area dedicated to dining. From there, the business continued to take off; it gained a cult-following overnight. Along with his culinary background, Mr. Barak also has a background in nutrition, which he made use of by teaching nutrition. In addition, Mr. Barak's one and only inspiration in life was his grandmother, Esfir. Ever since he was a young boy, she raised him. She was of European heritage and made every meal from scratch. He loved to watch her cook. It brought so much comfort to him that he fell in love with the whole concept of bringing people together through food.

Jack D. Barchas, MD

Title: Professor and DeWitt Wallace Distinguished Scholar (Retired) **Industry:** Medicine & Health Care **Company Name:** New York-Presbyterian/Weill Cornell Medical Center **Date of Birth:** 11/02/1935 **Place of Birth:** Los Angeles **State/Country of Origin:** CA/USA **Parents:** Samuel Barchas; Cecile Barchas **Marital Status:** Married **Spouse Name:** Rosemary Anne Stevens (08/09/1994); Patricia Ruth Corbitt (02/09/1957, Deceased) **Children:** Isaac Doherty; Carey T. Stevens (Stepchild); Richard N. Stevens (Stepchild) **Education:** Resident in Psychiatry, Stanford Medical School (Now Stanford Medicine), Palo Alto, CA (1964-1967); Medical Intern, Pritzker School of Medicine, University of Chicago, Chicago, IL (1961-1962); MD, Yale Medical School (Now Yale School of Medicine) (1961); BA, Pomona College (1956) **Certifications:** Licensed Psychiatrist, State of New York (1994) **Career:** DeWitt Wallace Distinguished Scholar, Psychiatry, Weill Cornell Medical College (2018-2019); Chair of Psychiatry and Psychiatrist-in-Chief, New York-Presbyterian/Weill Cornell Medical Center (1993-2018); Barklie McKee Henry Professor, Weill Cornell Medical College, NY (1993-2018); Dean, Neurosciences and Research Development, Professor Above Scale, Psychiatry, University of California, Los Angeles David Geffen School of Medicine (1990-1993); Nancy Friend Pritzker Professor and Director, Nancy Pritzker Laboratory of Behavioral Neurochemistry, Stanford Medical School (now Stanford Medicine) (1976-1989); Associate Professor (1971-1976) and Assistant Professor (1967-1971) Psychiatry, Stanford Medical School (now Stanford Medicine), Palo Alto, CA ; Director, Laboratory for Behavioral Neurochemistry, Department of Psychiatry, Stanford Medical School (now Stanford Medicine) (1964-1976); Research Associate, National Institute of Health, Bethesda, MD (1962-1964) **Career Related:** Co-Director, Weill Cornell Node of Pritzker Consortium (1996-Present); Chair, Committee of Review and Promotions, Weill Cornell Medical College (Now Weill Cornell Medicine) (2015-2018); Executive Director, Pritzker Network on Mental Disorders, NY (1996-2010); Co-Founder, Co-chair Science Advisory Board, Board of Directors, NEUREX Corporation, Menlo Park, CA (1984-1990); First Director, MacArthur Foundation Depression Network, John D. and Catherine T. MacArthur Foundation; Chaired Institute of Medicine Committee responding to a request from the White House dealing with opportunities and needs for research in mental health, drug and alcohol abuse, which resulted in a doubling of funding for research in those fields; Conceived and chaired for its 25 year history annual prizes by the Robert and Claire Pasarow Foundation of Los Angeles for exceptional contributions in cancer, cardiovascular and neuropsychiatric diseases. Six of this outstanding group have so far, subsequently received a Nobel Prize **Civic:** Board of Trustees, Shirley & Stefan Hatos Neuroscience Research Foundation, Los Angeles, CA (1993-Present); Science Advisory Board, National Alliance for Research on Schizophrenia and Depression (Now The Brain and Behavior Research Foundation) (1987-Present) **Military Service:** Lieutenant Commander, U.S. Public Health Service (1962-1964) **Creative Works:** A psychiatrist-neuroscientist, Dr. Barchas is interested in the mix of science and types of knowledge that expand understanding in psychiatry. He has been involved in basic, transitional and clinical research, as well as educational programs, provision of services, and health policies. A major focus has been neurotransmitters and their intersections with behavior. Publications include information about the formation and metabolism of neurotransmitters to the first demonstration that behaviors/stress can differentially change neurotransmitters in the brain. They include finding that melatonin is capable of changing sleep. Other activities and publications deal with clinical topics such as a time study of medical teaching rounds and privacy issues. He served as editor of "Archives Of General Psychiatry" American Medical Association (1994 to 2001) and co-editor of "Psychopharmacology From Theory To Practice," and 300 other publications. He is grateful to the wonderful mentors, trainees and donors he has had throughout his career. His programs attracted colleagues and trainees whose further development and success have given him great pleasure. **Awards:** Rhoda and Bernard Sarnat International Prize in Mental Health, Institute of Medicine (Now Health and Medicine Division), National Academy of Sciences (2006); Thomas William Salmon Medal, The New York Academy of Medicine; Daniel H. Efron Research Award, American College of Neuropsychopharmacology; A.E. Bennett Research Award and Lifetime Achievement Award, Society of Biological Psychiatry; Grantee: National Science Foundation, NASA, Office of Naval Research, and National Institutes of Health for Mental Illness, Drug Abuse, and Alcohol Abuse; Greenberg Award, NewYork–Presbyterian Hospital; Honorary Alumni Award, Weill Cornell Medicine **Memberships:** Chair, Board of Biobehavioral Sciences and Mental Disorders, Institute of Medicine (Now Health and Medicine Division), National Academy of Sciences (1982-1994); Lifetime Member, American Psychiatric Association; Honorary Member, American Psychoanalytic Association **Marquis Who's Who Honors:** Albert Nelson Marquis Lifetime Achievement Award; Marquis Who's Who Top Professional; Marquis Who's Who Humanitarian Award

Robert G. Barcus

Title: Educational Association Administrator (Ret.) **Industry:** Education/Educational Services **Date of Birth:** 10/22/1937 **Parents:** Harold Eugene; Marjorie Irene (Dilling) B. **Education:** Postgraduate, Purdue University (1967); Superintendents License, Butler University (1967); Postgraduate, Indiana University (1966); MA, Ball State University (1963); BPE, Purdue University (1959) **Career:** Retired, Indiana State Teachers Association (2003); Associate Executive Director, Labor Relations and Administration, Indiana State Teachers Association, Indianapolis, IN (1993-2002); Assistant Executive Director, Labor Relations and Administration, Indiana State Teachers Association, Indianapolis, IN (1985-1993); Assistant Executive Director Administration, Personnel and Governance, Indiana State Teachers Association, Indianapolis, IN (1982-1985); Assistant Executive Director, Special Services and Teacher Rights, Indiana State Teachers Association, Indianapolis, IN (1973-1982); Administrative Assistant, Indiana State Teachers Association, Indianapolis, IN (1972-1973); Executive Assistant, Indiana State Teachers Association, Indianapolis, IN (1971-1972); Director, Special Services, Indiana State Teachers Association, Indianapolis, IN (1968-1970); Assistant Director Research, Indiana State Teachers Association, Indianapolis, IN (1967-1968); Salary Consultant, Indiana State Teachers Association, Indianapolis, IN (1965-1967); Teacher, Coach, North Central High School, Indianapolis, IN (1964-1965); Teacher, Coach, Wabash High School (1963-1964); Teacher, Coach, Wabash (Indiana) Junior High School (1959-1963) **Civic:** President, Indiana State Library and Historical Board (2010-Present); Indiana State Library Foundation (2012-2013); Finance Secretary, Church of the Brethren (2000-2008, 2010); Vice President, Indiana State Library and Historical Board (2006); Trustee, Manchester University (2004); Indiana State Library and Historical Board (2000); Chairman, Church of the Brethren (1979-1983, 1987, 1992-1999); Clerk, Church of the Brethren (1966-1974) **Awards:** Sagamore of the Wabash Award, State of Indiana (2002); Benefit Pioneer Award, National Education Association (1991); Alumni Scholar, Purdue University (1959) **Memberships:** President, Indiana State Teachers Association (2009-Present); Board Director, Indiana State Teachers Association (2004-2010); Greater Indianapolis Retired Chapter Treasurer, Indiana State Teachers Association (2008-2009); National Education Association; Past President, Wabash City Teacher Association; Past President, Washington Township Teacher Association; Indianapolis Press Club; National Education Association; Phi Delta Kappa; Greater Indianapolis Retired Teachers **Marquis Who's Who Honors:** Albert Nelson Marquis Lifetime Achievement Award; Marquis Who's Who Top Professional **Why did you become involved in your profession or industry:** Mr. Barcus fell in love with his first grade teacher and from then on, he wanted to be a teacher. She made a great impact on him and he patterned most of his activities as a professor on things that she did. **Avocations:** Stamps; Coin collecting

Bishop Dr. Edward "Bishop Barnett" Barnett

Title: Bishop, Mental Health (Behavior Specialist) **Industry:** Health, Wellness and Fitness **Company Name:** Greater Grace Family Ministries Inc. **Date of Birth:** 04/13/1962 **Place of Birth:** Washington **State/Country of Origin:** DC/USA **Parents:** Edward Barnett, Sr. (Deceased); Mary Helen (Brooks) Barnett **Marital Status:** Married **Spouse Name:** Adrienne H. Barnett **Children:** Donnell; Emmanuel; Gabrielle **Education:** Doctor of Divinity, (2015); Doctor of Humanities, (2014); Master's Degree in Professional Counseling, (2008); Bachelor of Science in Management, (2002) Anger Management Specialist, (2006) **Certifications:** Certified Substance Counselor, (2013); Certified Anger Management (2006); Pastoral & Family Counseling; Certified Mental Health Consulting; Mental Health Behavioral Specialist **Career:** Pastor, Bishop, Quality Improvement & Recruitment Director, Community Support Services, Mental Health (2019-2020); Chief Executive Officer, Founder, E. Barnett & Associates Community Development Corporation (2008-Present); Pastor, Founder, Greater Grace Family Ministries Church (1991-Present); Chairman, Founder, Little Upperroom Prayer Ministries (1987-Present); Director of Residential Services, Nonprofit D C Mental Health (2009-2019); Supervisor, Maryland Department of Health and Mental Hygiene (2002-2008); Conflict Resolution Instructor, Department of Juvenile Services, Cheltenham Youth Detention Center (1998-2002) **Career Related:** Youth Mentoring and Educational Services, Leadership Enhancement Institute, Mental Health Consulting, Nonprofit Establishment, Men Modeling Excellence **Civic:** Advisor, Counselor-treasurer, D.C. Kenya Exchange Program, Washington, DC (1990-1991) **Creative Works:** Author, "Living Wittingly," Thomas Nelson Publishing (2015); Author, Podcast, weekly Mental Health Radio Program, "Help for the Hurting Mental Health in the Community," Washington, DC & MD (2014-2017) **Awards:** Bishop Dr. Edward Barnett Recognition Resolution of 2017, Washington, DC City Counsel, Washington, DC (2017); Listed, International Top 100 Business Magazine, Special Edition (2014); Ambassador of Peace, Universal Peace Federation; Caregiver of the Year Award **To what do you attribute your success:** Dr Barnett attributes all his success to the overpowering love and intelligence of God through educational pathology that has awakened his internal competence to self-maximizing and developing skill-sets that develop those around him. He learned that he grows as he help others to grow. **Why did you become involved in your profession or industry:** Dr. Barnett was inspired to get involved in this profession because he had a very deep sense of calling from God for helping people. He was a teenager when he felt this calling. At nineteen, he had a son and was a single parent until his son was 5 years old. Having his son catapulted him into being focused concerning truly fulfilling his life purpose from God. He started volunteering and spending more time at his church and was trained as a Youth Leader. Then began to volunteer in community with teens, then recruited to work with adjudicated youth in Md. In 1987, he was asked to go to an organization that housed young juvenile males that were separated from their families because of drugs or other bad situations or choices. They were detained, but for their own safety. They needed counselors, therapy and specialist to talk with. He was a young effective minister at the time, so he was asked to come talk about family dynamics and focus on the youth. He continued for about seven years; the first three years were voluntary, then they brought him on full time and he became a supervisor. He was recruited by the Juvenile Justice System for the State of Maryland, where he worked as a conflict resolution instructor. From there, he went to the Maryland Department of Health and Mental Hygiene, where he worked for about seven years as a supervisor for mental health counselors. **Avocations:** Family and Mental Health **Religion:** Christian (Nondenominational) **Thoughts on Life:** We must yield ourselves to God who is over us, so we don't have to fall to things and those beneath us! Work everyday to be the best you, you can be!

Kara Silber Barnett

Title: Executive Director; Theater Producer **Industry:** Media & Entertainment **Company Name:** American Ballet Theatre **Date of Birth:** 09/26/1978 **Place of Birth:** Durham **State/Country of Origin:** NC/USA **Parents:** Jeffrey Roy Medoff, MD; Debra Fran Silber **Marital Status:** Married **Spouse Name:** Dov Mayer Barnett (08/20/2006) **Children:** Three Children **Education:** MBA, Harvard Business School (2007); BA in English, Duke University, Summa Cum Laude (2000); Coursework in Shakespeare, West End Theatre, London, United Kingdom; Intern, Emanuel Azenberg, NY; Coursework, School of Greensboro Ballet **Career:** Executive Director, American Ballet Theatre, Ballet Theatre Foundation, Inc. (2016-Present); Managing Director, Lincoln Center International (2012-2016); Senior Director, Capital Campaign, Lincoln Center (2007-2012); Director of Strategy and Business Development, Lincoln Center (2007-2010); Fellowship, HBS Leadership Fellows Program, Lincoln Center for the Performing Arts (2007) **Career Related:** Panelist, Town & Country's Philanthropy Summit (2018); Panelist, Blackstone Women's Initiative's Leading with Purpose (2018); Founding Producer, Board Member, Ars Nova **Civic:** Advisory Committee, American Theatre Wing; Member, Leadership Committee, Centennial Leadership Committee, Manhattan School of Music **Creative Works:** Associate Producer, "Long Day's Journey into Night" (2003); Producer, "Modern Orthodox" (2003); Producer, Theatre, Off-Broadway and Broadway, NY **Awards:** Named to the Class of 2015 Henry Crown Fellows, The Aspen Institute (2015); Named One of the 40 Under 40, Crain's New York Business (2014); Tony Award for Best Revival of a Play (2003); Trinity Scholarship, Duke University **Memberships:** Term Member, Council on Foreign Relations **Religion:** Jewish

Robert Charles "Bob" Baron

Title: Publishing Executive **Industry:** Writing and Editing **Company Name:** Fulcrum Publishing Inc. **Date of Birth:** 01/26/1934 **Place of Birth:** Los Angeles **State/Country of Origin:** CA/USA **Parents:** Leo Francis Baron; Marietta (Schulze) Baron **Marital Status:** Married **Spouse Name:** Charlotte Foehner Baron **Children:** Brett Foehner; Kristen Foehner **Education:** BS in Physics, St. Joseph's University, Philadelphia, PA (1956) **Certifications:** Registered Professional Engineer, Massachusetts **Career:** Founder, Chairman, Publishing Executive, Fulcrum Publishing Inc., Golden, CO (1984-Present); Private Practice, Boston, MA (1976-1983); Founder, President, Chief Executive Officer, Prime Computer (1971-1975); Worldwide Systems Manager, Honeywell Minicomputer (1970-1971); Engineering Manager, Computer Control Company (1965-1969); Program Manager, Mariner II and IV Space Computers, Computer Control Company (1961-1965); Engineer, Computer Control Company, Framingham, MA (1959-1961); Engineer, RCA, Camden, NJ (1955-1957) **Career Related:** Board of Directors, Fulcrum Group; Board of Directors, Golden; Board of Directors, Fulcrum Publications **Civic:** Founder, International League Conservation Writers (2010-Present); Chairman Emeritus, WILD Foundation (2008-Present); Annual Robert C. Baron Lectures, American Antiquarian Society (2004-Present); Founded, Third: Educational Programs for Older Americans (2014); Overseer, Massachusetts Historical Society (2009-2012); President, Denver Public Library Friends Foundation (1994-1996); Board of Directors, Denver Public Library Friends Foundation (1989-1996); Board of Directors, Rocky Mountain Women's Institute, Denver, CO (1987-1990); Trustee, Lincoln Filene Center, Tufts University, Medford, MA (1982-1984); Vice-Chairman, Board of Directors, Massachusetts Audubon Society, Lincoln, MA (1980-1985); Founder, Films by Fulcrum; Organized, John Adams/Thomas Jefferson Conference **Military Service:** U.S. Army **Creative Works:** Author, "The Light Shines from the West: A Western Perspective on the Growth of America" (2018); Author, "Forbidden Carols of Christmas" (2018); Author, "Four Children From Baden" (2015); Author, "Screenplay Wilderness in America" (2014); Author, "The Libraries, Leadership and Legacy of John Adams and Thomas Jefferson" (2010); Author, "Heaven and Nature Sing" (2009); Author, "John Adams: In His Own Words" (2009); Author, "Thomas Jefferson: In His Own Words" (2009); Author, "Journey To the Mountaintop" (2007); Author, "Hudson: The Story of a River" (2004); Author, "Pioneers and Plodders: The American Entrepreneurial Spirit" (2004); Author, "What Was It Like Orville: The Early Space Program" (2002); Author, "Footsteps on the Sands of Time" (1999); Author, "20th Century America: Key Events in History" (1996); Editor, "Thomas Hornsby Ferrill and the American West" (1996); Author, "America in the Twentieth Century" (1995); Editor, "Colorado Rockies: The Inaugural Season" (1993); Editor, "Soul of America: Documenting Our Past (1492-1974)" (1989); Editor, "The Garden and Farm Books of Thomas Jefferson" (1987); Author, "Micropower Electronics" (1970); Author, "Digital Logic and Computer Operations" (1966) **Awards:** Best Book in American History, The Independent Press Association (2019) **Memberships:** Board of Directors, American Antiquarian Society (1993-2003); Board of Directors, International Wilderness Leadership Foundation (1990-2008); Hakluyt Society; Fellow, Massachusetts Historical Society; Thoreau Society; Cactus Club; Literary Club; Explorer's Club; Grolier Club **Marquis Who's Who Honors:** Albert Nelson Marquis Lifetime Achievement Award; Marquis Who's Who Top Professional **To what do you attribute your success:** Mr. Baron attributes his success to working with creative and caring people, as well as continually learning. **Why did you become involved in your profession or industry:** When Mr. Baron turned 50, he decided he wanted to take a different career path from his that of his previous career. He decided to start a book publishing company as a result of his desire to be around creative people. **Avocations:** Writing; Reading; Sports; Gardening; Collecting clocks; Fly fishing; Bird watching

Mary Ann Bartels

Title: Head of the Research Investment Committee and ETF **Industry:** Financial Services **Company Name:** Bank of America-Merrill Lynch **Children:** George Ross Grappotte; Lorraine Grappotte; **Education:** MS, Economics, Fordham University; BS, Economics, Fordham University **Career:** Head, Research Investment Committee and ETF, Bank of America-Merrill Lynch (1999-Present); Portfolio Manager, Batterymarch Portfolio Manager, Avatar Associates; Portfolio Manager, Zweig Associates, NY; Kennelman & Beard JC Bradford; Manufacturers Bank and Trust; **Civic:** Presidents Council, Fordham University; **Awards:** Listed, Institutional Investor All American Research Team (2001-2006) **Marquis Who's Who Honors:** Marquis Who's Who Top Professional **To what do you attribute your success:** Ms. Bartel attributes her success to communicating and connecting to clients. **Why did you become involved in your profession or industry:** Ms. Bartel's aunt, Bernadette Bartels Murphy, was one of the first women to graze Wall Street. She was her inspiration. In addition, her Aunt came to Wall street in 1956 and she was her mentor showing her that women could be successful on Wall Street. She didn't really realize what she was getting herself into because she was just trying to emulate her Aunt Bernadette. The family loves her. They call her Aunt B. and Ms. Bartels would not know where she would be now if it was not for her aunt. Her aunt worked until she was 80 and is now enjoying life. **Avocations:** Gardening; Walking; Spending time with family; Knitting; Ping pong; Maintaining brain and body health

William Frederick Barthel Jr.

Title: Engineer, Electronics Company Executive (Retired) **Industry:** Engineering **Company Name:** Gables Engineering, Inc. **Date of Birth:** 07/14/1940 **Place of Birth:** Washington **State/Country of Origin:** DC/USA **Parents:** William Frederick; Eva Barthel **Marital Status:** Married **Spouse Name:** Barbara Joan Adams (11/18/1961) **Children:** William Frederick, III **Education:** BS, McNeese State University (1972) **Certifications:** First Class Radio Operator with Ship Radar Endorsement **Career:** Retired (2008); Vice President of Operations, Gables Engineering, Inc., Coral Gables, FL (1993-2008); Director of Quality, Gables Engineering, Inc., Coral Gables, FL (1991-1993); Engineering Manager, Performance Assurance, Digital Equipment Corporation, Andover, MA (1987-1991); Engineering Manager, Process Reliability, Digital Equipment Corporation, Andover, MA (1981-1987); Senior Engineering Scientist, Process Control Development, Rockwell International, Cedar Rapids, Iowa (1980-1981); Manager of Quality Assurance, Rockwell International, Cedar Rapids, Iowa (1979); Engineer of Quality Control, Rockwell International, Cedar Rapids, Iowa (1974-1979); Shop Manager, Electronics Unlimited, Lake Charles, LA (1968) **Military Service:** With, United States Air Force (1958-1962) **Memberships:** American Institute of Chemists; American Chemical Society **Marquis Who's Who Honors:** Albert Nelson Marquis Lifetime Achievement Award **To what do you attribute your success:** Mr. Barthel attributes his success to working in emerging fields. **Why did you become involved in your profession or industry:** Mr. Barthel became involved in his field because in the early part of his career he was a quality engineer. He was also one of the early ones who was a part of quality assurance as opposed to quality control. So, he worked in many fields. As a result, he was able to do different things such as making radios, instruments and controls, then finally into process controls and later using lasers for manufacturing processes. **Avocations:** Sailing **Political Affiliations:** Republican

Katherine Bartol

Title: Mezzo Soprano, Choral Conductor, Music Educator, Pianist/Keyboardist **Industry:** Media & Entertainment **Date of Birth:** 12/06/1959 **Place of Birth:** Indianapolis **State/Country of Origin:** IN/USA **Parents:** Clarence Joseph (1930-1989); Sophia Martha Bartol (1936) **Marital Status:** Married **Spouse Name:** Gary Richard Beveridge (12/23/1994) **Children:** Christa Lisette (1996); Heather Katherine (2000) **Education:** MusM, West Chester University (1989); BS in Music Education, West Chester University (1981); Postgraduate Coursework, University of Minnesota, Indiana University, University of Pennsylvania, Pennsylvania State University; Westminster Choir College, University of the Arts **Certifications:** Certified, Instructional Music K-12, Kodaly, Orff-Schulwerk **Career:** Private Voice and Piano Instructor (2016-Present); Conductor, Director, Choral Music, Department Chair, Selinsgrove High School (1997-2016); Director, Show Choir, Susquehanna University, Selinsgrove, PA (1988-1989); Music Instructor, Chorus Director, Selinsgrove Middle School (1983-1997); Private Piano and Voice Instructor, Selinsgrove, PA (1981-1989); Music Instructor, Chorus Director, Selinsgrove Elementary Schools (1981-1983); Performing Musician **Career Related:** Cooperating Teacher, Pennsylvania State University, Susquehanna University; Professional Singer, Studio Recordings, Dance/Rock Bands; Guest Artists, Symphonic Concerts, Pennsylvania, New York **Civic:** Volunteer Musician, Local Area Nursing Homes; Volunteer Musician, Saint Monica Church, Sunbury, PA; Volunteer, American Heart Association **Awards:** Exemplary Choral Performance, Pennsylvania Middle School Association (1994); Exemplary Choral Performance, Pennsylvania Music Educators Association (1993) **Memberships:** National Education Association; Pennsylvania State Education Association; Pennsylvania Middle School Association; American Choral Directors Association; Kodaly Educators of Eastern Pennsylvania; Pennsylvania Music Educators Association; National Association for Music Education **Marquis Who's Who Honors:** Albert Nelson Marquis Lifetime Achievement Award **Why did you become involved in your profession or industry:** Ms. Bartol grew up in a musical family and always had a love for music. She also had a very successful cousin in the music industry who inspired her to succeed. She became more heavily involved in music in high school as a result of the successes she was beginning to have. When the time came for her to choose a career, she realized that music was not only what she loved, but also what she was the best at. She decided that music education was the best fit for her. Through music, she felt that she is able to not only pass down skill but also pass the joy of playing to students. **Avocations:** Skiing; Snorkeling; Bicycling; Painting; Travel **Religion:** Roman Catholic

Kit Smyth Basquin, PhD

Title: Writer, Art Historian (Retired) **Industry:** Fine Art **Date of Birth:** 07/03/1941 **Place of Birth:** New York **State/Country of Origin:** NY/USA **Parents:** Joseph Percy; Virginia Sandford (Gibbs) Smyth **Marital Status:** Divorced **Spouse Name:** Maurice Hanson Basquin, (2/4/1967, Divorced 02/1984) **Children:** Susan; Peter Lee; William **Education:** PhD, Union Institute and University, Cincinnati, OH (2009); MA, Indiana University (1970); BA, Goucher College, Baltimore, MD (1963) **Career:** Writer, Art Historian (Retired); Associate, Print Study Room, Metropolitan Museum of Art, New York, NY (2000-2014); Research Associate, Brooklyn Museum of Art (2000); Exhibition Manager, William Doyle New York Galleries, New York, NY (2000); Marketing, William Doyle Galleries, New York, NY (1999); Curator, Marvin Lowe Retrospective, Indiana University Art Museum (1998); Director, Outreach Milwaukee, Wisconsin Humanities Council (1995-1998); Curator, Education, Haggerty Museum of Art, Marquette University, Milwaukee, WI (1988-1995); Director, Kit Basquin Gallery, Milwaukee, WI (1981-1983); Director, Washington Gallery, Indianapolis, IN (1977-1979); Director, Washington Gallery, Frankfort, IN (1972-1979); Assistant Director, Public Relations, Indianapolis Museum of Art (1971-1972) **Career Related:** Secretary, Board of Directors, Manhattan Graphics Center (2020-Present); Member, Master Voices (2015-Present); Member, Collegiate Chorale (2013-2015); Advisory Board, Gordon Peaks Gallery, Metropolitan State University, Minneapolis, MN (2012-2013); Guest Curator, Wording The Image, Sherman Gallery, School Visual Arts, Boston University (2010-2011); Guest Curator, Gallery of College States Island, City University of New York (2009-2010); President, Print Forum (1996-1997); Instructor, Marquette University, Gaza (1996); Member, Program Committee, Midwest Museum Conference, Milwaukee, WI (1992); Prints and Drawings Subcommittee, Milwaukee Art Museum (1991-1999); Instructor, Art History, Concordia University, Mequon, WI (1991); President, Contemporary Art Society, Milwaukee Art Museum (1986-1987); Teacher, Art History, Addis Ababa, Ethiopia (1967-1968) **Civic:** Singer, MasterVoices (Formerly Collegiate Chorale) (2013-Present); Choir, St. BArts Singers (1999-Present); Member, Alumnae Board, Spence School, New York (2005-2018); Member, Advisory Board, Ten Chimneys Foundation (2000-2001); Trustee, Ten Chimneys Foundation, Genesee Depot, WI (1997-1999) **Creative Works:** Member, St. Barts Singers (1999-Present); Author, "Biography of Mary Ellen Bute: Pioneer Animator" (2020); Wisconsin Editor, New Art Examiner (1980-1981); Contributor, Articles, Professional Journals; Singer, Master Voices (including Art in Print) (Mary Ellen Bute, 1906-1983) **Memberships:** Special Events Committee, University Club of New York (2016-Present); Library & Art Committee, University Club of New York (2011-2016); James Joyce Society; MasterVoices **Marquis Who's Who Honors:** Albert Nelson Marquis Lifetime Achievement Award; Marquis Who's Who Top Professional **Why did you become involved in your profession or industry:** In high school, at The Spence School, Margaret Scolari, wife of then-director of The Museum of Modern Art, Alfred Barr, taught her art history for two years. Her enthusiasm, energy, and expertise converted Ms. Basquin and many of her students to art history. **Avocations:** Singing; Walking; Swimming **Religion:** Episcopalian **Thoughts on Life:** Life is uncertain. Learn to be flexible.

Samantha Bass

Title: Worldwide Top Model **Industry:** Apparel & Fashion **Company Name:** Samantha's Modeling **Date of Birth:** 07/03/1972 **Place of Birth:** Hartford **State/Country of Origin:** CT/USA **Parents:** Rose Wright Bass **Marital Status:** Single **Children:** Tyler A. Wortham (Stepson); Connor C. Wortham (Daughter); Hailey J. Wortham (Daughter) **Education:** Diploma, John Casablancas (2009) **Certifications:** Insurance License, State of Connecticut **Career:** Instructor, John Casablancas (2011-2013); Founder, Owner, Samantha's Modeling; Account Manager, MassMutual; Life, Accident and Health Insurance Agent, Licensed Insurance Producer, Connecticut **Career Related:** Model; Actress, Films, Television; Public Speaker **Civic:** Former Chairperson, ALL Hartford, ALL Ladies League (2015-2016) **Awards:** Featured, Cover Story, Magic Image Hollywood Magazine (2020); Featured, Cover Story, Stardom101 Magazine (2017); Grand Finalist, Top Model Worldwide International Model Search, London, England (2016); Iconic Innovator, New Delhi, India (2016) **Memberships:** Lifetime Member, ALL Ladies League **Marquis Who's Who Honors:** Albert Nelson Marquis Lifetime Achievement Award **To what do you attribute your success:** Ms. Bass attributes her success to her mother, Rose Wright Bass, as well as her ancestors. **Why did you become involved in your profession or industry:** Ms. Bass became involved in her profession because modeling felt natural. At just 7 years old, she attended her first fashion show and has been enthralled ever since. Being a model is more than a job; it is who she is. She loves what she does. **Avocations:** Spending time with her mother and children; Traveling; Listening to smooth jazz and live bands; Networking **Political Affiliations:** Democrat **Religion:** Christian

John Batzer

Title: Senior Staff Scientist (Retired) **Industry:** Sciences **Date of Birth:** 02/21/1946 **Place of Birth:** Elizabeth **State/Country of Origin:** NJ/USA **Parents:** R. Kirk Batzer; Marjorie W. (White) Batzer **Marital Status:** Married **Spouse Name:** Elizabeth Ashe (Cranmer) Batzer **Children:** John; Jessica; Bobby (Deceased); Lisa; Michael; **Education:** MBA in Computer-Aided Information Systems, New York University, New York, NY (1975); BS in Engineering Physics, Lehigh University, Bethlehem, PA (1973) **Career:** Retired (2014); Independent Consultant, Global Wireless Technologies, LLC, New Jersey (2013-2014); Senior Staff Scientist, ITT Exelis Space Systems Division, New Jersey (2011-2013); Staff Scientist, ITT Electronic Systems (2008-2011); Senior Technical Consultant, ITTT Avionics (2004-2007); Senior Scientist, ITT A/CD (1989-2004); Senior Staff Scientist, ITT Corporation (1978) **Civic:** Treasurer, St. Andrew's Church, New Providence, NJ (2011-Present); Vestry, St. Andrew's Church, New Providence, NJ (1994-Present); Board of Trustees, Treasurer, St. Andrew's Nursery School, New Providence, NJ (1996-1997); President, New Providence Music Boosters (1991-1996) **Military Service:** U.S. Army (1969-1972) **Creative Works:** Patentee in Field **Awards:** Recipient, Commendation Medal, U.S. Army **Memberships:** Senior Lifetime Member, IEEE **Marquis Who's Who Honors:** Albert Nelson Marquis Lifetime Achievement Award; Marquis Who's Who Top Professional **To what do you attribute your success:** Mr. Batzer attributes his success to his determination to rise through the corporate ladder. He additionally credits his patents and his community service experience. **Why did you become involved in your profession or industry:** When Mr. Batzer was a child, he was always interested in science and received the grand prize at a science fair in ninth grade. His project was about the repulsion coil. He still has the project in his basement today as a reminder of where he came from. **Avocations:** Working with his Church; Traveling; Spending time family; Playing bridge **Religion:** Episcopalian

Jack Beary

Title: Journalist; Educator; County Official; City Official **Industry:** Education/Educational Services **Company Name:** St. Petersburg College **Date of Birth:** 06/10/1951 **Place of Birth:** Chicago **State/Country of Origin:** IL/USA **Parents:** John Thomas Beary; Kathleen Mary Beary (Reardon) **Marital Status:** Single **Education:** MA in Political Science, University of Illinois at Chicago (2003); MA in Public Affairs Reporting, University of Illinois Springfield (1974); BA in Political Science, Benedictine University (1973) **Career:** Adjunct Instructor, St. Petersburg College, FL (2006-Present); Adjunct Instructor, Pasco-Hernando State College, Spring Hill, FL (2005-2006); Adjunct Instructor, St. Petersburg College, FL (2004-2005); Public Information Officer, City of Chicago, IL (2002-2004); Press Secretary, President's Office, Cook County Board, Chicago, IL (1997-2002); Public Information Officer, Cook County Government, Chicago, IL (1996-1997); Reporter, United Press International, Inc., Chicago, IL (1985-1990); Assignment Editor, WBBM-TV, CBS Broadcasting, Inc., Chicago, IL (1982-1985) **Career Related:** Delegate Member, Model UN, United Nations Foundation, New York, NY (1972-1973) **Awards:** Peter Lisagor Award for Exemplary Journalism for Team Coverage on Education and Education Funding (1994); Award, Chicago Headline Club (1994) **Marquis Who's Who Honors:** Albert Nelson Marquis Lifetime Achievement Award **To what do you attribute your success:** Mr. Beary attributes his success to a great family and a great education. **Why did you become involved in your profession or industry:** Mr. Beary had always wanted to be a journalist. He started out at that profession, thinking that if he could actually make it in the news business, there were two places he wanted to work, United Press International and CBS. He had a chance to work for both of them. **Avocations:** Beach Volleyball; Beachgoing; Bike riding **Political Affiliations:** Independent **Religion:** Roman Catholic

Diana Scott Beattie, PhD

Title: Biochemistry Professor **Industry:** Education/Educational Services **Date of Birth:** 08/11/1934 **Place of Birth:** Cranston **State/Country of Origin:** RI/USA **Parents:** Kenneth Allen Scott; Lillian Francis (Barton) Scott **Marital Status:** Married **Spouse Name:** Robert Nathan Stuchell; Benjamin Howard Beattie (06/30/1956, Divorced 1975) **Children:** Elizabeth; Sara; Rachel; Ruth **Education:** PhD, University of Pittsburgh, Pittsburgh, PA (1961); MS, University of Pittsburgh, Pittsburgh, PA (1958); BA, Swarthmore College, Swarthmore, PA (1956) **Career:** Dean, Premedical and Pharmacy Programs, Oman Medical College (2006-2014, Retired); Chairman, Department of Biochemistry and Molecular Pharmacology, West Virginia University School of Medicine, Morgantown, WV (2001-2006); Professor, Chairman, Department of Biochemistry, West Virginia University School of Medicine, Morgantown, WV (1985-2001); Professor, Biochemistry, Mount Sinai School of Medicine (Now The Icahn School of Medicine at Mount Sinai) New York, NY (1976-1985); Faculty, Mount School of Medicine (Now The Icahn School of Medicine at Mount Sinai), New York, NY (1968-1985); Research Associate, VA Hospital, Pittsburgh, PA (1967-1968); Research Associate, University of Pittsburgh, Pittsburgh, PA (1961-1967) **Career Related:** Shandong University, China (2000); University of Nairobi, Kenya (1993); Graduate Faculty, Biochemistry, West Virginia University School of Medicine, Morgantown, WV (1985-2006); Visiting Professor, The Université Catholique de Louvain, Belgium (1982); Physical Biochemistry, Study Section, National Institutes of Health (1993-1997, 1981-1985); Chairman, Physical Biochemistry, Study Section, Institutes of Health (1995-1997, 1983-1985); Basic Science Merit Review Panel (1989-1992); Metabolic Biology Panel, National Science Foundation (1986-1989); Ad Hoc Biochemistry, Study Section, National Institutes of Health (1979-1981, 1976-1977); Biology, City University of New York (1974-1985); Biochemistry, City University of New York (1971-1985); Graduate Faculty, Biomedical Science, City University of New York (1968-1986); NIH Study Section **Creative Works:** Journal of Bioenergetics (1975-Present); Editorial Board, Archives of Biochemistry and Biophysics (1985-2000, 1975-1978); Contributor, Articles, Professional Journals **Awards:** Grantee, National Science Foundation (1997-2001, 1970-1992); Fulbright Fellow (1993); Fogarty International Fellow (1982); Award Metropolitan New York Chapter, Association for Women in Science (1979); National Institutes of Health (1966-2004) **Memberships:** Advisory Committee for Medical School Programs, Association of American Medical Colleges (2003-2006); Cell Biology Test Committee, Association of American Medical Colleges (1998-2001); Chair, Association of American Medical Colleges (1998); President, Association of Medical and Graduate Departments of Biochemistry (1996); President-Elect, Association of Medical and Graduate Departments of Biochemistry (1995); Administrative Board, Association of American Medical Colleges (1994-1999); Chair, National Board of Medical Examiners (1994-1995); Vice-Chair, National Caucus of Basic Biomedical Science Chairs (1991-2006); Biochemistry Test Committee, National Board of Medical Examiners (1991-1993); Council of Academy Societies, Association of American Medical Colleges (1989-2001); Executive Committee, Association of Medical and Graduate Departments of Biochemistry (1989-1992); Membership Committee, American Society of Biological Chemists (1987-1989); American Society for Cell Biology; Biophysics Society **Marquis Who's Who Honors:** Albert Nelson Marquis Lifetime Achievement Award; Marquis Who's Who Top Professional; Distinguished Humanitarian **Why did you become involved in your profession or industry:** Dr. Beattie learned how to be a leader during her time in private school. Her family encouraged her to further her education by going to college. Deciding to attend Swarthmore College, she found biology and unearthed a passion for the field. **Avocations:** Reading; Hiking; Skiing; Book Clubs; Taking Ali courses

Maureen "Mo" Beck

Title: Sales Coordinator, Paraclimbing Athlete **Industry:** Athletics **Company Name:** Eldorado Climbing Walls **Marital Status:** Married **Education:** Bachelor of Science in Forestry, The University of Vermont Rubenstein School of Environment and Natural Resources (2009) **Career:** Sales Coordinator, Eldorado Climbing Walls, Boulder, CO (2016-Present); AP Specialist, Assistant Staff Accountant, ZOLL Medical Corporation, Broomfield, CO (2014-2016); Treasurer, Board Member, Paradox Sports, Boulder, CO (2013-2016); Staff II Accountant, Master Accounts & Commercial Lease, Vail Resorts, Broomfield, CO (2012-2014); Treasurer, CRAG-VT, Richmond, VT (2008-2013); Department Manager, Cash Accounting, Stowe Mountain Resort, Stowe, VT (2010-2012); Supervisor, Telluride Ski Resort (2009-2010); Store Guide, Eastern Mountain Sports, Burlington, VT (2006-2010); LANDS Intern, Student Conservation Association, Burlington, VT (2008); Supervisor, Patrick Gymnasium and Field House Facility, The University of Vermont (2005-2007) **Civic:** Chair, USAC Paraclimbing Committee **Creative Works:** Featured, "Stumped" **Awards:** National Geographic Adventurer of the Year (2019); Third Place - Female Upper Limb, IFSC Paraclimbing World Championship, Innsbruck, Austria (2018); First Place - Female Upper Limb, USA Paraclimbing National Championships, Columbus, Ohio (2018); First Place - Female Upper Limb, USA Paraclimbing National Championships, Boston, MA (2017); First Place in Combined RP1, RP2, IFSC Paraclimbing World Cup, Edinburgh, Scotland (2017); First Place - Female Upper Limb, USA Paraclimbing National Championships, Atlanta, GA (2016); First Place - Female Upper Limb, Female Overall, USA Climbing Adaptive Bouldering Championships, Madison, WI (2016); Gold Medal, Women's Upper Limb, IFSC Paraclimbing World Championship, Spain and France (2014, 2016); Third Place - Female Upper Limb, IFSC World Cup, Sheffield, England (2015); First Place - Female Upper Limb, USA Paraclimbing Championships, Atlanta, GA (2015); Five National Paraclimbing Titles

David Robert Joseph Beckham, OBE

Title: President, Co-Owner, Former Professional Soccer Player **Industry:** Athletics **Company Name:** Inter Miami CF **Date of Birth:** 05/02/1975 **Place of Birth:** Leytonstone **State/Country of Origin:** London/England **Parents:** David Edward Alan Beckham; Sandra Georgina (West) Beckham **Marital Status:** Married **Spouse Name:** Victoria (Adams) Beckham (07/04/1999) **Children:** Brooklyn Joseph; Romeo James; Cruz David; Harper Seven **Career:** Co-Owner, Director, Salford City, England (2019-Present); President, Co-Owner, Inter Miami CF, Major League Soccer (2014-Present); Professional Soccer Player, Paris Saint-German, France (2013); Professional Soccer Player, AC Milan, Italy (2009-2010); Professional Soccer Player, LA Galaxy, Major League Soccer, Los Angeles, CA (2007-2012); Professional Soccer Player, Real Madrid, Spain (2003-2007); Professional Soccer Player, Preston North End, England (1994-1995); Professional Soccer Player, Manchester United, England (1993-2003) **Career Related:** Founder, David Beckham Academy (2005-2009); England National Team (1996-2009); Creator, Fragrance (2007); Captain, England National Team (2000-2006) **Civic:** 7: The David Beckham UNICEF Fund (2015-Present); Founding Member, Malaria No More UK (2009-Present); Goodwill Ambassador, UNICEF (2005-Present); Supporter, Help for Heroes; Former Patron, Elton John AIDS Foundation; Benefactor, Unite for Children, Unite Against AIDS **Creative Works:** Appearance, "King Arthur: Legend of the Sword" (2017); Appearance, "The Man from U.N.C.L.E." (2015); Appearance, "Goal III: Taking on the World" (2009); Appearance, "Goal II: Living the Dream" (2007); Appearance, "Goal!" (2005); Co-Author, "Both Feet on the Ground: An Autobiography" (2003); Author, "David Beckham: My Side" (2002); Co-Author, "Beckham: My World" (2001); Model, Numerous Publications **Awards:** EFA President's Award (2018); Sexiest Man Alive, People Magazine (2015); Choice Male Athlete, Teen Choice Awards (2006, 2008-2010, 2012, 2013); MLS Cup with LA Galaxy (2011, 2012); ESPY Award for Best MLS Player, ESPN (2008, 2012); MLS Comeback Player of the Year (2011); BBC Sports Personality of Year Lifetime Achievement Award (2010); Named, One of the 100 Most Influential People, Time Magazine (2008); Named to English Football Hall of Fame (2008); Named, One of the 100 Most Powerful Celebrities, Forbes.com (2008); Named, One of the Most Influential People in the World of Sports, Business Week (Now Bloomberg Businessweek) (2007); Man of the Match, FIFA World Cup (2006); Real Madrid Player of the Year (2005); ESPY Award for Best Male Soccer Player, ESPN (2004); Named, One of the FIFA 100 (2004); Decorated Most Excellent Order of the British Empire (OBE) by Queen Elizabeth II (2003); PFA Players' Player of the Year Award (2003); Supercopa de Espana with Real Madrid (2003); Sportsman of the Year, Sports Press Association (2001); BBC Sports Personality of the Year (2001); Intercontinental Cup with Manchester United (1999); PFA Players' Young Player of the Year Award (1997); Inductee, AC Milan Hall of Fame; Named One of the IFFHS Legends; Numerous Club Awards

John Barry Beemer, Esq.

Title: Lawyer **Industry:** Law and Legal Services **Date of Birth:** 09/4/1941 **Place of Birth:** Scranton **State/Country of Origin:** PA/USA **Parents:** Ellis T. Beemer; Rose Mary (Costello) Beemer **Spouse Name:** Diane Montgomery Fletcher (07/18/1964, Deceased 07/1999) **Children:** David; Bruce **Education:** LLB, George Washington University (1966); BS, University of Scranton (1963) **Certifications:** State of Pennsylvania (1966); Supreme Court of the United States (1980); Certified Civil Trial Advocate, National Board of Trial Advocacy **Career:** Partner, Beemer & Beemer, Scranton, PA (1984-Present); President, Beemer, Rinaldi, Fendrick & Mellody, Professional Corporation, Scranton, PA (1977-1983); Partner, Beemer, Brier, Rinaldi & Fendrick (1972-1977); Associate, Warren, Hill, Henkelman & McMenamin, Scranton, PA (1968-1972); Clerk to Judge, U.S. District Court for the Middle District of Pennsylvania (1967-1968); Law Clerk, U.S. Court of Claims (1966-1967) **Career Related:** Lecturer in Law, University of Scranton (1969-1970) **Civic:** Chairman, Professional Division, American Cancer Society Drive, Lackawanna County, Pennsylvania (1976); National Chairman, University of Scranton Alumni Fund Drive (1972); Chairman, Committee on the Constitution and Bylaws Revision, Lackawanna County, Pennsylvania, United Fund (1971) **Memberships:** Board of Directors, Lackawanna Bar Association (1984); American Bar Association; Pennsylvania Bar Association; Association of Trial Lawyers of America; Pennsylvania Trial Lawyers Association; Phi Delta Phi **Marquis Who's Who Honors:** Albert Nelson Marquis Lifetime Achievement Award **Why did you become involved in your profession or industry:** In high school, Mr. Beemer found out he had a talent for the written and spoken word, so his natural inclination was to become a lawyer. He had a great uncle that was a lawyer.

Daniel Beffa Jr.

Title: Owner **Industry:** Manufacturing **Company Name:** Dansha Farms **Date of Birth:** 02/16/1953 **Place of Birth:** Providence **State/Country of Origin:** RI/USA **Parents:** Daniel Beffa; Isabel Beffa **Marital Status:** Married **Spouse Name:** Sharon **Children:** Daniella **Education:** National Aviation Academy (1973); Coursework in Leadership, Dale Carnegie & Associates, Inc. **Certifications:** Federal Airframe and Power Plant License (1975); Private Pilot License; Certification in Air Conditioning and Refrigeration **Career:** Owner, Dansha Farms (2007-Present); Owner, All Phase Marine Electric, Inc. (1985-2002) **Civic:** Communication Volunteer, Madison Amateur Radio **Military Service:** Armed Escort, Secret Service, Air National Guard **Awards:** First Place, Best Milker on the Market **Memberships:** Amateur Radio Emergency Service **To what do you attribute your success:** Mr. Beffa attributes his success to perseverance. Whenever he gets knocked down, he gets right back up and tries again. **Why did you become involved in your profession or industry:** Mr. Beffa became involved in his profession due to his lifelong interest in aviation. Though he pursued other lines of work for a few years, he returned to field and grew within it until he opened his own business. **Avocations:** Fractal wood burning **Political Affiliations:** Independent

Robert J. Begiebing

Title: Emeritus Professor of English **Industry:** Education/Educational Services **Company Name:** Southern New Hampshire University **Date of Birth:** 11/18/1946 **Place of Birth:** Adams **State/Country of Origin:** MA/USA **Marital Status:** Married **Spouse Name:** Linda Adams (06/05/1968) **Children:** Brie Adams; Kate Adams **Education:** PhD in English, University of New Hampshire (1977); MA in English, Boston College (1970); BA, Norwich University, with High Honors (1968) **Career:** English Professor, Director of Creative Writing, Southern New Hampshire University (2003); Humanities and English Coordinator, New Hampshire College (1994-1996); English Professor, New Hampshire College (1993-1996); Associate Professor, Assistant Professor, New Hampshire College (1977-1984); Dissertation Fellowship, New Hampshire College (1976-1977); Teaching Assistant, University of New Hampshire (1972-1976); Instructor, Fort Knox Center, University of Kentucky (1971) **Career Related:** Founder, Head, MFA Program in Fiction and Non-Fiction, Southern New Hampshire University (2006-2011); Finalist Judge, Langume Prize in Historical Fiction (2009-2010); Board of Advisers, McIninch Gallery, Southern New Hampshire University (2008-2011); State Councilor, New Hampshire State Council on the Arts(2007-2011); Member, Board of Trustees, The Norman Mailer Society, Provincetown, MA (2005-2008); Editorial Board, Manor Review, University of South Florida (2005-2008); Consultant, Manuscript Review Service, New Hampshire Writer's Project (2000-2004); Member, Board of Trustees, New Hampshire Writers' Project (2002-2003); Visiting Fellow for Creative Artists and Writers, American Antiquarian Society (1996) Manuscript Reviewer, The University of Alabama Press; Manuscript Reviewer, University Press of New England; Teacher, Summer Workshop, The Norman Mailer Society, Provincetown, MA **Civic:** Volunteer, Recycling Program, Newfields, NH (1989-1995); Vice President, Exeter High School Parents' Association (1993-1994); Volunteer, School Improvement Team, Newfields, NH (1986-1987) **Military Service:** 1st Lieutenant, US Army Reserve (1970-1972) **Creative Works:** Author, "The Territory Around Us: Collected Literary and Political Journalism, 1982-2015." (2015); Author, "A Berkshire Boyhood Confessions and Reflections of a Baby Boomer" (2014); Author, "The Turner Erotica: A Biographical Novel" (2013); Author, "Rebecca Wentworth's Distraction" (2003); Author, "The Strange Death of Mistress Coffin" (1991); Author, "Toward a New Synthesis: John Fowles, John Gardner, Norman Mailer (Challenging the Literary Canon)" (1990); Author, "The Literature of Nature: The British and American Traditions" (1990); Acts of Regeneration: Allegory and Archetype in the Works of Norman Mailer (1981); Published, Numerous Poems, Connecticut Quarterly, Country Journal, Boston Arts, Noon Feather **Awards:** Langume Prize for Historical Fiction (2003); Excellence in Teaching Award (1979, 1981, 1996-1997); Visiting Fellowship for Creative and Performing Artists (1996); Artist Opportunity Grant, New Hampshire Council on the Arts (1994); University Dissertation Fellowship (1976-1977); Fellowship, Southern New Hampshire University (1974-1976); Academic Scholarship, Norwich University (1964-1968); Senior English Scholar Medal, Academic Honor Society; Who's Who In American Colleges and Universities **Memberships:** Modern Language Association; Authors Guild; American Studies Association; New England American Studies Association **Marquis Who's Who Honors:** Albert Nelson Marquis Lifetime Achievement Award **To what do you attribute your success:** Dr. Begiebing attributes his success to outstanding mentors, including Dr. Loring Hart, former president of the Norwich University, Wesley McNair, a colleague and poet, Professor Bob Lucid of the University of Pennsylvania, and Professor Michael Lennon of Wilkes University. **Why did you become involved in your profession or industry:** Dr. Begiebing became involved in his profession because of his love of reading and his ability to interpret literary text. **Avocations:** Jogging; Bicycling; Kayaking; Hiking; Swimming; Organic gardening

David A. Bego

Title: Owner, Chief Executive Officer **Industry:** Business Management/Business Services **Company Name:** Executive Management Services, Inc. **Marital Status:** Married **Spouse Name:** Barb **Children:** Three Children **Education:** MS in Microbiology, Ball State University (1975); BS in Biology, Tri-State University (1975) **Certifications:** Cleaning Industry Management Standard, with Honors **Career:** President, Chief Executive Officer, Executive Management Services, Inc. (1989-Present); Owner, Maple Creek Country Club; Owner, Barrett Supplies & Equipment; Owner, Delta Security Services; Owner, The EAS Group; Owner, Moorfeed **Civic:** Fundraiser, Riley Hospital for Children **Creative Works:** Author, "The Devil at My Doorstep" (2012); Author, "The Devil at Our Doorstep" **Awards:** Elite American Executive (2015) **Memberships:** Building Services Cleaning Association International **To what do you attribute your success:** Mr. Bego attributes his success mostly to the way his parents raised him. They taught him many positive lessons about working hard and being successful. All of the friends he has made, as well as his wife, have additionally played a key role in moving Mr. Bego in the right direction. Additionally, he is proud of his ability to build relationships at all levels with customers, employees and vendors. **Why did you become involved in your profession or industry:** Mr. Bego took a job with a janitorial company, which inspired him to start his own company. **Avocations:** Basketball; Golf; Reading; Flying; Skiing; Spending time with grandchildren

William Stephen "Bill" Belichick

Title: Professional Football Coach **Industry:** Athletics **Company Name:** New England Patriots **Date of Birth:** 04/16/1952 **Place of Birth:** Nashville **State/Country of Origin:** TN/USA **Parents:** Stephen Belichick; Jeannette (Munn) Belichick **Marital Status:** Divorced **Spouse Name:** Debby Clarke (04/30/1977-2006) **Children:** Amanda; Stephen; Brian **Education:** Honorary LHD, Wesleyan University (2005); Honorary LHD, New England Institute of Technology (2004); Honorary LHD, Boston University (2004); BS in Economics, Wesleyan University (1975) **Career:** Head Coach, New England Patriots, Foxborough, MA (2000-Present); Assistant Head Coach, Defensive Coordinator, New York Jets (1997-2000); Assistant Head Coach, Defensive Backs Coach, New England Patriots, Foxborough, MA (1996-1997); Head Coach, Cleveland Browns (1991-1996); Defensive Coordinator, New York Giants (1985-1990); Special Teams Coordinator, Linebackers Coach, New York Giants (1979-1984); Assistant Special Teams Coach, Defensive Assistant, Detroit Lions (1978); Assistant Special Teams Coach, Tight Ends and Receivers Coach, Detroit Lions (1976-1977); Assistant to Head Coach, Baltimore Colts (1975) **Creative Works:** Appearance, "Before the Kick: The Brian Kinchen Story" (2020); Subject, "Belichick & Saban: The Art of Coaching" (2019); Subject, "A Football Life" (2012-2018); Appearance, "Timeless Rivals" (2017); Appearance, "Jack" (2017); Actor, "Rescue Me" (2006) **Awards:** 100th Anniversary All-Time Team, NFL (2019); Inductee, Athletics Hall of Honor, Phillips Academy (2011); 2000s All-Decade Team, NFL (2010); NFL Coach of the Year, Associated Press (2003, 2007, 2010); Inductee, Athletics Hall of Fame, Wesleyan University (2008); TIME 100, TIME USA, LLC. (2004); Baldwin Medal, Wesleyan University (2002) **Memberships:** Chi Psi

James Bell

Title: Pastor **Industry:** Religious **Company Name:** Greater Saint John Baptist Church **Career:** Pastor, Greater Saint John Baptist Church (2006-Present) **Civic:** Volunteer, Community Service with Children; Volunteer, Boys and Girls Club **Awards:** Top Ten Most Giving Church (Two Years) **Memberships:** Baptist General Commission of Texas; Greater Baptist Association **Marquis Who's Who Honors:** Marquis Who's Who Top Professional **To what do you attribute your success:** Pastor Bell credits his success on following the tenets of his Christian faith. **Why did you become involved in your profession or industry:** Pastor Bell was inspired to enter his profession due to his sister, who became sick with thyroid cancer. This experience led him to discover the comfort of prayer; to this day, his sister is healthy and well.

Daniel Lawrence "Dan" Ben-Asher

Title: Legislative Staff Member (Retired) **Industry:** Government Administration/Government Relations/Government Services **Company Name:** New Jersey State Legislature **Date of Birth:** 04/15/1946 **Place of Birth:** Newark **State/Country of Origin:** NJ/USA **Parents:** Jerry Ben-Asher; Florence (Tasoff) Ben-Asher **Marital Status:** Married **Spouse Name:** Michele Lauren Cohn (07/16/1978) **Children:** Sarah; Joshua **Education:** MA, University of Minnesota (1970); AB, Rutgers College (Now Rutgers, The State University of New Jersey (1968); Diploma, Livingston High School (1964) **Career:** Freelance Photojournalist, NJ (2005-2007); Retired Legislative Staff Member, Office of Legislative Services, (OLS), New Jersey State Legislature, Trenton, NJ (2003); Senior Research Analyst, Nonpartisan Office of Legislative Services, (OLS), New Jersey State Legislature, Trenton, NJ (1999-2003); Senior Research Associate, Office of Legislative Services, (OLS), New Jersey State Legislature, Trenton, NJ (1987-1998); Research Associate, Office of Legislative Services, (OLS), New Jersey State Legislature, Trenton, NJ (1976-1987); Research Assistant, Office of Legislative Services, (OLS), New Jersey State Legislature, Trenton, NJ (1971-1976); Plant Personnel Administrator, Tanatex Chemical Company, Division of Sybron Corp., Lyndhurst, NJ (1970-1971) **Career Related:** Member, New Jersey Tobacco Age-of-Sale Enforcement Task Force (1994-1996); Staff, Assembly Housing Committee (1995); With, Assembly Drug and Alcohol Abuse Policy Committee (1990-1991); Member, Politics and Government Judges Panel, Best in America Special Edition, U.S. News & World Report (1990); With, Assembly Commerce and Industry Committee (1981-1982); With, New Jersey Employer-Employee Relations Study Commission (1976); With, New Jersey Assembly Labor Committee (1974-1981) **Civic:** Chairman, Mason Gross (Presidential) Memorial, Class of 1968, Rutgers, The State University of New Jersey, New Brunswick, NJ (1992-Present); Township Chairman, "Guide to Lawrenceville's Historical Landmarks" (1991-1993); Financial Coordinator, Lawrence Township Historical Preservation Advisory Committee, NJ (1985-1992); Member, Ewing Township Rent Control Board, NJ (1976-1977); Alumni Admissions Representative, Rutgers, The State University of New Jersey, New Brunswick, NJ (1994-2001); Member, National Alumni Advisory Committee of Admissions, Rutgers, The State University of New Jersey, New Brunswick, NJ **Creative Works:** Editor, Photographer, "Guide to Lawrenceville's Historical Landmarks, Second Edition" (2009); **Awards:** Podmore-Dwyer Historic Award, Lawrence Township, NJ (2010); Loyal Son Award for Extraordinary Service to Alma Mater, Rutgers Alumni Association (1996) **Marquis Who's Who Honors:** Albert Nelson Marquis Lifetime Achievement Award; Marquis Who's Who Top Professional; Marquis Who's Who Humanitarian Award **Why did you become involved in your profession or industry:** Mr. Ben-Asher worked in the private sector first; when an opportunity to work at a professional level in the public sector arrived, he jumped at it. **Avocations:** Travel; Photography; Family **Political Affiliations:** Independent

Raymond C. "Ray" Benn, PE

Title: Materials Engineer, PE **Industry:** Engineering **Company Name:** Pratt & Whitney **Date of Birth:** 10/20/1946 **Place of Birth:** London **State/Country of Origin:** England **Parents:** Frank Abraham Benn; Eileen Mabel (Ashford) Benn **Marital Status:** Widower **Spouse Name:** Pamela W. Benn (4/1/1952) **Children:** Briana Benn-Mirandi; Britanny Buckley **Education:** EMBA, University of New Haven, CT (1995); BSc in Metallurgy, Surrey University, England (1970); Chemical Engineering Coursework, University of London (1965-1966) **Certifications:** Professional Engineer, Connecticut; Chartered Engineer, United Kingdom **Career:** Staff Engineer, Pratt & Whitney, East Hartford, CT (2005-2013); Principal Scientist, United Technologies Research Center, East Hartford, CT (2000-2005); Chief Technologist, Wyman-Gordon Groton, CT (1995-2000); Staff Engineer, Allied Signal Engines (Textron-Lycoming), Stratford, CT (1989-1995); Group Leader and Senior Metallurgist, Inco Alloys International, Inc. (Now Special Metals Corp.), Huntington, WV (1984-1989); Principal Metallurgist, Inco Alloy Products Company Research Center (Now Special Metals Corp.), Suffern, NY (1982-1984); Section Manager, Inco Alloy Products Company Research Center (Now Special Metals Corp.), Suffern, NY (1977-1982); Senior Research Metallurgist, Inco Alloys Ltd. (Now Special Metals Corp.), Hereford, England (1974-1977); Development Metallurgist, Delta Materials Research (1970-1974) **Creative Works:** Contributor, More than 50 Articles, Professional Publications; Co-author, 27 US Patents; Co-author, Two Books **Awards:** Bachelor Honoris Causa, University of Surrey (2011); Co-recipient, Innovative P/M Award, European Powder Metallurgy Association (1992); Chapter Chairman Award (1987, 1884); Co-recipient, IR-100 Award (1980) **Memberships:** Chairman, Specialty Materials Division, ASM (1988-1992); Fellow ASM International, ASM; Chairman, West Virginia Chapter, ASM (1986-1987); Chairman, Hudson Valley Chapter, ASM (1983-1984); Chairman, Heat Resistant Materials Group ASM (1983-1988); Fellow, Institute of Materials, Minerals and Mining; Member TMS-AIME; Chapter Chairman Sigma Xi **Marquis Who's Who Honors:** Albert Nelson Marquis Lifetime Achievement Award **To what do you attribute your success:** Mr. Benn attributes his success to his avid interest in metallurgy/materials science and engineering, diligence in all aspects of his profession, interest in pursuing advanced and new materials and respect and friendship with his peers. **Why did you become involved in your profession or industry:** He became involved in his profession because he has a passionate interest in the science and engineering of metallurgy. **Avocations:** Model ship building; Boating; Rowing; Archery **Political Affiliations:** Democrat **Religion:** Universal Unitarism **Thoughts on Life:** "Follow your dreams"

Dorothy Spurlock Benner

Title: Elementary School Educator **Industry:** Education/Educational Services **Date of Birth:** 12/17/1938 **Place of Birth:** Greeley **State/Country of Origin:** CO/USA **Parents:** Lloyd Elsworth (Deceased); Helen Rosalee (Pierce) Spurlock (Deceased) **Marital Status:** Married **Spouse Name:** Jerry Benner **Children:** Shey; Craig **Education:** Education Specialist Degree, University of Northern Colorado (1978); Master of Arts in Special Education and Emotional Behavior Disorders, Colorado State College (1968); Bachelor of Arts, Colorado State College (1962) **Certifications:** Certified Teacher of Elementary and Business Education, Special Education and School Psychology **Career:** Substitute Teacher (2002-Present); Retired, Elementary School Educator (2002); Teacher, School District 6, Greeley, CO (1968-2002); Substitute Teacher, School District 6 and Outlying Districts, Greeley, CO (1962-1967); Secretary, Connecticut Mutual Life, Greeley, CO (1960-1961); Telephone Operator, Mountain Bell, Greeley, CO (1957) **Career Related:** Teacher, Night School, Aims Community College (1989-1993) **Civic:** Committee to Raise Money for 9/11 First Responders **Awards:** Commendations from Greeley Police Department and Greeley Fire Department (2002); Lion Award From Greeley Education Association; Innovative Educator from Colorado Department of Education; Recognition Article in Woman's World Magazine for a School Adopt-An-Officer Program; Teacher Who Makes A Difference Award, Channel 4 News Center and The Rocky Mountain News **Memberships:** President, Greeley Education Association (1993-1996); Vice President, Greeley Education Association (1991-1992); Secretary, Greeley Education Association (1985-1991); Negotiation Team, Greeley Education Association (1981-2000); Lifetime Member, National Education Association; Chairperson, UniServ; Lifetime Member, Colorado Education Association; Kappa Delta Pi; Delta Kappa Gamma; Officer, Greeley Education Association **Marquis Who's Who Honors:** Albert Nelson Marquis Lifetime Achievement Award **Why did you become involved in your profession or industry:** Ms. Benner entered the field of education because she always enjoyed a good rapport with both students and parents. **Avocations:** Piano playing; Reading; Sewing; Substitute teaching; Musicals; TV; Genealogy scrapbooks **Political Affiliations:** Republican **Religion:** Christian

Robert Martin Bennett

Title: Professor Emeritus (Medicine) **Industry:** Education/Educational Services **Company Name:** Oregon Health and Science University **Date of Birth:** 11/30/1940 **Place of Birth:** Berkhamsted **State/Country of Origin:** England **Parents:** Leonard; Gladys May (Young) **Marital Status:** Married **Spouse Name:** Sharon Clark (8/29/1989); Jennifer Delmira Montagu (6/26/1964, Divorced 1986) **Children:** Emma; Jeremy; Katrina **Education:** Doctor of Medicine, University of London (1964); Bachelor of Medicine, Bachelor of Surgery, University of London (1964); Berkhamsted School, Hertfordshire, England, UK **Certifications:** Diplomate, American Board of Internal Medicine; Diplomate, American Board of Rheumatology **Career:** Professor Emeritus, Oregon Health and Science University, Portland, OR (2018-Present); Professor of Medicine, Oregon Health & Sciences University, Portland, OR (1980-2018); Associate Professor of Medicine, Oregon Health & Sciences University, Portland, OR (1976-1980); Assistant Professor of Medicine, University of Chicago (1973-1976); Instructor of Medicine, University of Chicago (1972-1973); Tutor, Royal Postgraduate, Medical School, London (1970-1972) **Career Related:** Founder, Fibromyalgia Information Foundation (1996); Chairman and Founder, Division of Arthritis & Rheumatic Diseases, Oregon Health & Sciences University (1976-2000) **Civic:** Editorial Board, Pain, Arthritis and Rheumatism; Editorial Board, Journal of Musculoskeletal Pain; Past President, American College of Rheumatology, Western Region; Past President, International Myopain Society **Military Service:** Flight Lieutenant, Royal Air Force (1964-1970) **Creative Works:** Contributor, Over 300 Peer Reviewed Publications; Contributor, 68 Book Chapters **Awards:** Master, American College of Rheumatology (2007) **Memberships:** President, International Myopain Society (2001-2004); Fellow, American College of Physicians; Fellow, Royal College of Physicians; Master, American College of Rheumatology **Marquis Who's Who Honors:** Albert Nelson Marquis Lifetime Achievement Award; Marquis Who's Who Top Professional **Avocations:** History of science; Gardening; Skiing; Mountaineering **Political Affiliations:** Democrat

Sebastien I. Bensidoun

Title: Owner **Industry:** Business Management/Business Services **Company Name:** Bensidoun USA Inc.; French Market of Chicago LLC **Date of Birth:** 05/16/1974 **State/Country of Origin:** Paris/France **Parents:** Rolland Bensidoun; Simone Bensidoun **Marital Status:** Married **Spouse Name:** Jennifer Bensidoun **Children:** Ava; Levana **Career:** Owner, Chicago French Market LLC (2009-Present); Executive Vice-President, Bensidoun USA, Inc. (1996-Present) **Civic:** Board Member, Comité Paris-Chicago Sister City **Awards:** Best Business Award, French in Chicago Community Awards (2010); Best Redevelopment of The Year, Chicago Commercial Real Estate Awards (2010); Les 50 Français qui Comptent aux Etats-Unis, France-Amerique **Memberships:** Association France-Amériques; Fondation Louis Vuitton; French-American Foundation; Kids of Courage Cedarhurst; MoMA Museum; Simon Wiesenthal Center; St. Jude Children's Research Hospital; The Jewish Museum NY; The Metropolitan Museum of Art; UJA-Federation of New York; Yad Vashem Circle of Friends **Why did you become involved in your profession or industry:** Mr. Bensidoun is a fourth-generation market operator and developer, guiding this family business forward and into the 21st century. His apprenticeship began when he was just 19 years old; his love, dedication, and commitment to the enduring tradition of the public marketplace has only grown over the course of time. The hallmark and the appeal of the public marketplaces remain as it was in the beginning; the establishment and the nurturing of local food and retail hubs, connecting communities directly with food growers, producers, and retailers and supporting an ecosystem of geographically connected consumers and suppliers. Currently, Mr. Bensidoun's operations include a total of 95 markets, including 40 markets in Paris and additional markets throughout France, as well as in the United States. Expansion into the United States began in 1997 with an initial market opening in the Chicago suburb of Wheaton, Illinois. That first market continues to thrive with over 75 producers and local start-up retailers participating. He is proud to have thousands of customers served each market day; over the past few decades, their United States footprint has grown to 14 markets, including the famous Chicago French Market, which is located in the Ogilvie Transportation Center in Chicago West Loop.

Milan Beres, MD, FACS

Title: Surgeon (Retired) **Industry:** Medicine & Health Care **Date of Birth:** 01/13/1936 **Place of Birth:** Trebisov **State/Country of Origin:** Slovak Republic **Parents:** Juraj Beres; Barbara (Hrinova) Beres **Marital Status:** Married **Spouse Name:** Terezia Marcinova (11/17/1962) **Children:** Stephen; Milan Jr. **Education:** MD, P.J. Safarik University, Slovak Republic (1959); Graduate Coursework, Slovak University (1955) **Career:** Retired (2000); Chief, Otolaryngology, Bridgeport Hospital (1987-1996); Resident Physician, Otolaryngology, Facial, Plastic and Reconstructive Surgery, University of Connecticut Health Center, Farmington, CT (1971-1974); Fellow, Otolaryngology, Cleveland Clinical Educational Foundation (1970-1971); Otolaryngologist, University Hospital, Kosice, Slovak Republic (1962-1968) **Career Related:** Clinical Assistant, Otolaryngology Division, School of Medicine, University of Connecticut, Farmington, CT (1974-2000); Fellow, American College of Surgeons (1974) **Civic:** President, Slovak-American Cultural Center, New York, NY (1991-1994); Vice President, New England States Slovak League of America **Creative Works:** Author and Co-author, Articles, Peer-Reviewed Medical Journals **Awards:** Presidential Medal of Recognition of Services Rendered to Slovakia, President of the Slovak Republic (1998); First Prize, Best Picture, Michalovce County Amateur Photography Competition (1961); Several Physician's Recognition Awards, American Medical Association **Memberships:** American Medical Association; Connecticut Medical Association; Fairfield County Medical Association; Greater Bridgeport Medical Association; American Academy of Otolaryngology; American College of Surgeons; International Corresponding Society of Ophthalmologists and Otolaryngologists; New England Otolaryngology Society; Pan American Association of Oto-rhino-laryngology, Head and Neck Surgery **Marquis Who's Who Honors:** Albert Nelson Marquis Lifetime Achievement Award **To what do you attribute your success:** Dr. Beres let his faith in God shape his life philosophy and he tried hard to act accordingly. That includes, but it is not limited to, his decision to leave the then-Socialist Czechoslovak Republic in 1968, when it was militarily invaded by Soviet Union Red Army, and to apply for the political asylum in the United States of America. **Why did you become involved in your profession or industry:** Dr. Beres grew up with a sick mother and he often cared for her. This sparked his fascination with medicine. He began his work as a pediatrician and eventually transferred to otolaryngology. He enjoys it because he likes to work with his hands as a surgeon. **Religion:** Roman Catholic

Micah Berg

Title: Chief Executive Officer **Industry:** Leisure, Travel & Tourism **Company Name:** RealJoy Vacations **Marital Status:** Married **Spouse Name:** Elyse **Children:** Ethan; Isbael **Education:** High School Diploma **Career:** Chief Executive Officer, RealJoy Vacations; Chief Executive Officer, Vacation Rental University **Military Service:** U.S. Marine Corps (2002-2006) **Awards:** Impact Company of the Year, DotCom Magazine (2019); Listee, Top 100 Entrepreneurs in Real Estate (2018); Listee, Inc. 5000 List (2018) **To what do you attribute your success:** Mr. Berg attributes his success to his focus on his clients to ensure they get what they need, as well as his business partners, Jakob Dwyer and Bryan Olin, who have been instrumental in his success. **Why did you become involved in your profession or industry:** Mr. Berg became involved in his profession because he felt like no one treated properties like they were true financial assets. He saw that there was a need and the opportunity really spoke to him.

Diane Bergmanson

Title: Director, Access & Technology Center (Retired) **Industry:** Technology **Company Name:** Hunter College **Date of Birth:** 11/11/1943 **Place of Birth:** New York **State/Country of Origin:** NY/USA **Parents:** Carl Bergmanson; Mary Hishadag Kambourian **Marital Status:** Widowed **Education:** MA in Counseling, New York University, New York, NY (1995); MBA, Bernard M. Baruch College, New York, NY (1977); BBA, Bernard M. Baruch College, New York, NY (1968) **Certifications:** Ordained Minister, Registered, State of New York (2001-Present); Certified Notary Republic **Career:** Retired (2004-Present); Director, Access & Technology Center, Hunter College, New York, NY (2000-2004); Counselor, Student with Disabilities, Hunter College, New York, NY (2000-2004); Global Accountant Manager, Xerox Corporation, New York, NY (1990-1999); National Accountant Manager, Xerox Corporation, New York, NY (1980-1990); Accountant Specialist, Xerox Corp., New York, NY (1973-1980); Executive Assistant to Chief Executive Officer, President, U.S. Building Management, New York, NY (1964-1973) **Career Related:** Educational Improvement, Hunter College, New York, NY (2005-Present); Astrologer, Woodstock, NY (2004-Present); Exam Proctor, Princeton Testing Center, Princeton, NJ (2002-Present); Co-op Board Member, 300 East 74th Corporation, New York, NY (2000-Present) **Civic:** Poll Watcher, New York State (2004, 2016, 2017, 2019); State President, Business & Professional Women's Club Association, New York, NY (1987-1988); District Director, Business & Professional Women's Club Association, New York, NY (1982-1984) **Awards:** Outstanding Achievement Award, Xerox Corporation (1972-2004); Outstanding Women's Achievement Award, Business and Professional Women's Club (1983); Outstanding Businesswomen's Award, Business and Professional Women's Club of America **Memberships:** Jung Institute; National Council of Geographic Research; Business and Professional Women's Club **Marquis Who's Who Honors:** Albert Nelson Marquis Lifetime Achievement Award; Marquis Who's Who Top Professional **Why did you become involved in your profession or industry:** Ms. Bergmanson was interested in sales and they were just opening it up to women; Xerox was at the forefront of that. Her friend told her about it and she applied. When she went to Xerox, she knew it was a big company and she wanted to be free of any authority over her. She wanted to be her own person. She took the sales path rather than the management path, and even though she eventually became an international account manager, she was her own boss. Working as a director for students with disabilities was the most rewarding. She is still in close contact with several of her students. **Avocations:** Esoteric arts to include the study of the Akashic records; Bridge; Piano **Political Affiliations:** Democrat

C. Fred Bergsten, LHD, PhD

Title: Senior Fellow, Director Emeritus **Industry:** Education/Educational Services **Company Name:** Peterson Institute for International Economics **Date of Birth:** 04/23/1941 **Place of Birth:** Brooklyn **State/Country of Origin:** NY/USA **Parents:** Carl Alfred Bergsten; Lois Halkaline (Kirk) Bergsten **Marital Status:** Married **Spouse Name:** Virginia Lee Wood Bergsten (06/16/1962) **Children:** Mark **Education:** LHD, Central Methodist College, Fayette, MO (1995); PhD, Fletcher School Law and Diplomacy, Medford, MA (1969); MA in Law and Diplomacy, Fletcher School Law and Diplomacy, Medford, MA (1963); MA, Fletcher School Law and Diplomacy, Medford, MA (1962); BA, Central Methodist University, Fayette, MO, Magna Cum Laude (1961) **Career:** Senior Fellow, Director Emeritus, Founding Director, Peterson Institute for International Economics (1981-2012); Senior Associate, Carnegie Endowment of International Peace (1981); Assistant Secretary, Treasury for International Affairs (1977-1981); Senior Fellow, Brookings Institution (1971-1976); Assistant, International Economic Affairs, National Security Council (1969-1971); Visiting Fellow, Council on Foreign Relations (1967-1968); International Economist, Department of State (1963-1967) **Career Related:** Vice Chairman, Advisory Committee, Foreign Economic Policy, Department of State (1996-Present); Bretton Wood Committee (1989-Present); Advisory Committee, Trade Policy and Negotiations, President Donald Trump (2018); Advisory Committee, Trade Policy and Negotiations, President Barack Obama (2010, 2014); Chairman, Task Force on Foreign Ownership and Control (1991-1997); Competitiveness Policy Council (1991-1997); Chairman, APEC Eminent Persons Group (1993-1995) **Creative Works:** Author, Short Publication, "China and the United States: Trade Conflict and Systemic Competition" (2018); Author, Short Publication, "Trade Balances and the NAFTA Renegotiation" (2017); Author, "A Path Forward for NAFTA" (2017); Co-Author, "Currency Conflict and Trade Policy: A New Strategy for the United States" (2017); Co-Author, "International Monetary Cooperation: Lessons from the Plaza Accord After Thirty Years" (2016); Author, Short Publication, "TPP and Exchange Rates" (2016); Author, Short Publication, "India's Rise: A Strategy for Trade-Led Growth" (2015); Author, "Bridging the Pacific: Toward Free Trade and Investment Between China and the United States" (2014); Author, Short Publication, "Addressing Currency Manipulation Through Trade Agreements" (2014); Author, Short Publication, "The Coming Resolution of the European Crisis" (2012) **Awards:** First Class of the Order of Diplomatic Service Merit, Gwanghwa Medal of the Government of Korea (2016); Swedish American of the Year (2014); Officer's Cross of the Order of Merit of the Federal Republic of Germany (2014); World Trade Award of the national Foreign Trade Council (2013); The Royal Order of the Polar Star, Government of Sweden (2013); Distinguished Leadership Award, The Fletcher School (2010); Listee, The Power Elite: The 100 Most Influential People in Private Washington, Regardies (1990); French Legion of Honor (1987); Legion d'Honneur from the Government of France (1985) **Memberships:** Trilateral Commission, Executive Committee (1991-Present); Board of Curators, Central Methodist College (1982-1990); Board of Directors, U.S.-Israel Binational Industrial Research and Development Foundation (1997-1980); Board of Directors, Consumers Union of United States, Inc. (1976); Rapporteurs, Task Force on International Institutions (1975-1976); Board of Directors, Overseas Development Council (1974-1976); Editorial Board, Foreign Affairs (1973-1976); Faculty Member, Salzburg Seminar in American Studies (1972); Council on Foreign Relations; American Economic Association **Marquis Who's Who Honors:** Albert Nelson Marquis Lifetime Achievement Award; Marquis Who's Who Top Professional **Why did you become involved in your profession or industry:** Dr. Bergsten became involved in his profession because his father, Carl Alfred Bergsten, was a Methodist minister. When he was 10 years old, his father had an exchange pastorate in England and their family spent the summer there. It was his first international exposure at a time when not many people traveled internationally. That event triggered an interest in international affairs and global affairs. That stuck with him for the rest of his life and oriented him to national affairs. He attended Fletcher School of Law and Diplomacy; he was there just at the time when globalization began to get under way and he was particularly inspired by a couple of his professors there. He focused on international economic affairs within the broader foreign policy and the international relations universe. He specialized in that area and he decided to pursue a career in that field. **Avocations:** Swimming; Snorkeling; Playing and watching basketball; Reading science fiction and counterfactual history; Movies; Photography; Travel **Political Affiliations:** Independent **Religion:** Methodist

Paul D. Berk, MD, FACP, FAASLD, AGAF, FTOS

Title: Internist; Research Scientist; Educator **Industry:** Health, Wellness and Fitness **Company Name:** Columbia University **Date of Birth:** 04/03/1938 **Place of Birth:** Brooklyn **State/Country of Origin:** NY/USA **Parents:** Charles Berk; Helen (Goell) Berk **Marital Status:** Married **Spouse Name:** Nicole Polak (1991); Aviva Ancona (07/04/1965, Divorced 08/1990) **Children:** Claire; Philip; Edward; David **Education:** Fellow, Hematology, Columbia-Presbyterian Medical Center, New York, NY (1969-1970); Resident, Columbia-Presbyterian Medical Center, New York, NY (1965-1966); Intern, Columbia-Presbyterian Medical Center, New York, NY (1964-1965); MD, Columbia University, New York, NY (1964); Honorary BA in Chemistry, Swarthmore College, Swarthmore, PA (1959) **Certifications:** Diplomate, American Board of Hematology (1972); Diplomate, American Board of Internal Medicine (1971); Qualifying Certificate, American Board of Internal Medicine (1970); Diplomate, National Board of Medical Examiners (1965); Certification, University of St. Andrews, Scotland (1960) **Career:** Professor, Department of Medicine, Columbia University College of Physicians and Surgeons, New York, NY (2004-Present); Henry and Lillian Stratton Professor of Molecular Medicine, Mount Sinai School of Medicine, New York, NY (1989-2004); Chief, Division of Liver Disease, Mount Sinai School of Medicine, New York, NY (1989-2001); Acting Chief, Mount Sinai School of Medicine, New York, NY (1989-1990); Professor of Biochemistry, Mount Sinai School of Medicine, New York, NY (1987-1999); Albert and Vera List Professor of Medicine, Mount Sinai School of Medicine, New York, NY (1980-1989); Professor of Medicine, Mount Sinai School of Medicine, New York, NY (1977-2004); Chief, Division of Hematology, Mount Sinai School of Medicine, New York, NY (1977-1989); Clinical Associate Professor, Georgetown University, Washington, DC (1975-1977); Chief, Section on Diseases of the Liver, National Institute Arthritis, Metabolism and Digestive Diseases, National Institutes of Health, Bethesda, MD (1973-1977); Clinical Assistant Professor of Medicine, Georgetown University, Washington, DC (1971-1975); Senior Investigator, National Cancer Institute, Bethesda, MD (1970-1973); Clinical Associate, Metabolism Branch, National Cancer Institute, Bethesda, MD (1966-1969) **Career Related:** Professor, Biochemistry and Molecular Biology, Mount Sinai School Medicine (1999-2004); Member, Advisory Council, National Institute of Diabetes and Digestive and Kidney Diseases (1990-1994); Adjunct Professor, Rockefeller University (1987-1989); Consultant in Liver Disease, National Institutes of Health (1977-1980) **Civic:** Senior Surgeon, United States Public Health Service (1966-1969, 1975-1977) **Military Service:** Commissioned Officer, United States Public Health Service (1975-1977, 1966-1969) **Creative Works:** Editor-in-chief, Seminars in Liver Disease (1996-Present); Contributing Editor, "Polcythemia Vera" (1994); Contributing Editor, "Hepatic Transport and Bile Secretion" (1993); Contributing Editor, "Hans Popper: A Tribute" (1992); Editor-in-chief, "Hepatology" (1991-1996); Contributing Editor, "Myelofibrosis and the Biology of Connective Tissue" (1984); Editor-in-chief, Seminars in Liver Disease (1981-1990); Contributing Editor, "Frontiers in Liver Disease" (1981); Member, Editorial Board, "Liver" (1980-1993); Member, Editorial Board, "Artificial Organs" (1979-1992); Contributing Editor, "Chemistry and Physiology of the Bile Pigments" (1977); Contributor, Articles to Professional Journals **Awards:** George Jamieson Humanitarian Award, American Liver Foundation (2004); Distinguished Service Award, American Association for the Study of Liver Disease (2003); Special Award, Columbia University College of Physicians and Surgeons (1992); Merck Award, Columbia University College of Physicians and Surgeons (1964); Mosby Book Award, Columbia University College of Physicians and Surgeons (1963); Fulbright Scholar, Department of Applied Mathematics, University of St. Andrews, Scotland (1959-1960); Ivy Medal, Swarthmore College (1959); Honorable Mention, Westinghouse Scientific Talent Search (1955); Columbia University College of Physicians and Surgeons; George Jamieson Humanitarian Award **Memberships:** Chairman, Board of Directors, American Liver Foundation (2000-2004); Councilor, Society for Experimental Biological Medicine (1993-1996); President, American Association Study of Liver Disease (1989); Councilor, International Association Study of Liver (1988-1991); Vice President, American Association Study of Liver Disease (1988); Councilor, American Association Study of Liver Disease (1985-1993); President, New York Society Study of Blood (1982-1983); Vice Chairman, National Polycythemia Vera Study Group (1978-1995); Sigma Xi; Phi Beta Kappa; Alpha Omega Alpha; American Physiology Society; American Society for Clinical Investigation; Association of American Physicians; Fellow, American College of Physicians; Fellow, American College of Gastroenterology; American Society for Hematology; American Clinical and Climatological Association; Fellow, The Obesity Society; Research Society on Alcohol; The Harvey Society **Marquis Who's Who Honors:** Albert Nelson Marquis Lifetime Achievement Award; Marquis Who's Who Top Professional

Eugene Bertram "Bert" Berkley, LHD

Title: Chairman of the Board **Industry:** Business Management/Business Services **Company Name:** Tension Corporation **Date of Birth:** 05/08/1923 **Place of Birth:** Kansas City **State/Country of Origin:** MO/USA **Parents:** Eugene Bertram Berkowitz; Caroline Newman (Newburger) Berkowitz **Marital Status:** Widowed **Spouse Name:** Joan Meinrath (09/01/1948) **Children:** Janet Lynn (Berkley) Dubrava; William "Bill" Spencer Berkley; Jane Ellen (Berkley) Levitt **Education:** Honorary LHD, Missouri Valley College, Marshall, MO (2010); MBA, Harvard Business School, Harvard University (1950); BA, Duke University (1948) **Career:** Chairman of the Board, Tension Corporation, Kansas City, MO (1967-Present); President, Tension Corporation, Kansas City, MO (1962-1988); Chief Executive Officer, Tension Corporation, Kansas City, MO (1962-1988) **Career Related:** Chairman, Global Envelope Alliance (2005-2011); President, Envelope Manufacturers Association (1983-1985); Executive Committee, Envelope Manufacturers Association (1981-1983); Vice Chairman, Executive Committee, Envelope Manufacturer's Association (1981-1983); Executive Committee, Envelope Manufacturer's Association (1976-1979); Executive Committee, Envelope Manufacturer's Association (1967-1970); Executive Committee, Envelope Manufacturers Association (1960-1963) **Civic:** Council of Champions, National Grade Level Reading Effort (2018-Present); Member, Advisory Council, Smithsonian National Postal Museum (2016-Present); Director, Turn the Page KC (2012-Present); Board of Directors, Institute for Educational Leadership, Washington, DC (2000-Present); Founder, Chairman, Board Member, Local Investment Commission, Investing in Children and Families (1992-Present); Chair, Jewish Community Relations Bureau, American Jewish Committee (2009); Board of Directors, Centerpoint for Leaders, Washington, DC (2001-2004); Director, Missouri Family and Community Trust, MO (1999-2012); Board of Directors, National Youth Information Network (1997-2004); Director, Biodiversity Institute & Natural History Museum University of Kansas (1994-2000); Member, Advisory Board, National Council for Economic Education (1993-1995); Chairman, Board of Directors, Center for Workforce Preparation, United States Chamber of Commerce (1991-2002); Board of Directors, Ewing Marion Kaussman Foundation Center for Entrepreneurial Leadership (1990-2002); Business Round Table, Department of Social Services, State of Missouri (1989-1999); Board of Directors, National Minority Supplier Development Council (1989-1998); Member, Kitchen Cabinet, Kansas City Public Schools (1990-1992); Chairman, The Center for Business Innovation (1987-1989); Member, Advisory Board, National Parks Conservation Association (1986-2006); Chairman, Board of Directors, National Minority Supplier Development Council (1986-1988); Chairman, Board of Directors, Human Services Testing and Retesting Council (1983-1990) **Military Service:** First Lieutenant, Infantry, United States Army **Creative Works:** Co-author, "Giving Back: Connecting You, Business and Community" (2009) **Awards:** Janet Miller Community Involvement Award, The Kansas City Friends of Alvin Ailey (2020); 70 over 70 Honored for Lifetime Achievement, The Shepard Center (2019); Community Guardian Award, AdHoc Group Against Crime (2017); Lauriat, Jr. Achievement Business Hall of Fame (2016); Hugh J. Zimmer Award for Excellence in Urban Education, University of Missouri-Kansas City (2016); Adele Hall Spirit of Caring Award, United Way of Greater Kansas City (2015); Kansas City Globe Newspaper Lifetime Honoree, Society of Influentials Award (2015); Robert H. Meneilly Stand Up Speak Out Award from Mainstream Coalition (2014); Legacy Award, MidAmerica Minority Supplier Development Council, Kansas City, MO (2013); Award, The Pembroke Hill School (2011); Mayor of Independence, MO Award (2010); Harold L. Holliday Senior Civil Rights Award, NAACP (2009); Founder's Award, Envelope Manufacturer's Association (EMA) (2009); Proclamation from Mayor & City Council, Kansas City, MO (2008); Distinguished Service to State Government Award, National Governors Association (2000); Honorary Star, STOP Violence Coalition (1999); Human Relations Award, Jewish Community Relations Bureau, American Jewish Committee (1997); CEO Advocate of the Year Award, Mid-America Minority Supplier Development Council (1991); Chancellor's Medal, University of Missouri-Kansas City (1989); Chairman's Award, EMA (1988); Distinguished Service Award, Friends of Johnson County Library (1982); Mr. Kansas City Award, Chamber of Commerce of Greater Kansas City (1972); Brotherhood Award, National Conference of Christians and Jews (1968); Named Leader, Kansas Citian Magazine, Chamber of Commerce (1967); Young Leadership Award, Jewish Federation & Council of Greater Kansas City (1960); Bronze Star; Combat Infantry Badge **Memberships:** Leadership Council, Graduate School of Education, Harvard University (2011-2014); Ewing Marion Kauffman Foundation, Center for Entrepreneurial Leadership (1990-2002); Board of Directors, Flexographic Technology Association (1993-1997); Director, Council for Economic Education (1993-1995) **Marquis Who's Who Honors:** Albert Nelson Marquis Lifetime Achievement Award; Marquis Who's Who Top Professional **To what do you attribute your success:** Mr. Berkley attributes his success to the cooperation of others. **Why did you become involved in your profession or industry:** Mr. Berkley was fortunate to be able to join a family business **Avocations:** Fly fishing; Camping; Whitewater rafting

David William Bernstein

Title: Counsel **Industry:** Law and Legal Services **Company Name:** Goodwin Procter LLP **Date of Birth:** 02/13/1938 **Place of Birth:** Brooklyn **State/Country of Origin:** NY/USA **Parents:** Sidney Abraham Bernstein; Carol Elsa Silverman Bernstein **Marital Status:** Married **Spouse Name:** Melissa Lewis (3/7/1980); Carol Ellen Lamberg (6/16/1959, Divorced 1977) **Children:** Andrew; Donna; Lauren **Education:** Bachelor of Laws, Harvard University, Magna Cum Laude (1962); Bachelor of Arts, Harvard University, Magna Cum Laude (1959) **Career:** Counsel, Goodwin Procter, LLP (2015-Present); Partner, K & L Gates LLP, New York, NY (2009-2015); Chairman, Corporate Department, Rogers & Wells, New York, NY (1989-1997); Partner, Clifford Chance Rogers & Wells (1967-2009); Associate Attorney, Rogers & Wells, New York, NY (1962-1967) **Civic:** Board of Directors, International Preschools (1966-Present); New York City Ballet; Donor, Harvard University **Creative Works:** Contributor, More than 40 Articles to International Financial Law Review (1996-Present) **Memberships:** Board Governor, Inwood Country Club (2003-Present); Board Governor, Inwood Country Club (1982-1991); American Bar Association; Harvard Club of New York City **Bar Admissions:** New York (1962) **Marquis Who's Who Honors:** Albert Nelson Marquis Lifetime Achievement Award; Marquis Who's Who Top Professional **Why did you become involved in your profession or industry:** During the fourth grade, Mr. Bernstein's class had a moot court competition and the teacher told him that he would make a very good lawyer, which inspired him to become involved in the profession. **Avocations:** Golf **Political Affiliations:** Republican **Religion:** Jewish

James Edwin Berrian

Title: Field Entomologist (Retired) **Industry:** Sciences **Date of Birth:** 01/04/1951 **Place of Birth:** Pasadena **State/Country of Origin:** CA/USA **Parents:** James Henry Berrian; Bette Jo (Durant) Berrian **Marital Status:** Married **Spouse Name:** Robyn M. Garcia (11/11/1989) **Children:** Nathaniel; James **Education:** Certified Teacher, National University, San Diego (1984); Postgraduate Degree, San Diego State University (1979-1983); Bachelor of Science in Zoology, San Diego State University (1978); Associate of Arts in Zoology, Southwestern College, with Honors (1976) **Career:** Field Entomologist, Associate in Herpetology and Entomology, San Diego Natural History Museum (1997-Present); Science Teacher, El Cajon Valley High School (1993-Present); Curatorial Assistant, Research Assistant, Field Associate in Herpetology, San Diego Natural History Museum (1993); Science Teacher, Bonita Vista High School, Chula Vista (1985-1992); Science Teacher, Montgomery Middle School, El Cajon, CA (1984-1985); Science Teacher, Emerald Junior High School, El Cajon, CA (1984); Curatorial Assistant, Research Assistant, Field Associate in Herpetology, San Diego Natural History Museum (1981-1983); Agricultural Technician Aide, San Diego County Department of Agriculture (1980-1981); Senior Veterinary Technician, Chula Vista Veterinary Clinic, CA (1978-1979); Chair, Department of Science, El Cajon Valley High School **Career Related:** Presenter of Workshops and Seminars in Field **Civic:** Initiator, School-wide Community Paper Recycling and Water Conservation Projects; Guest Speaker to Various Community Groups **Military Service:** Hospital Corpsman, U.S. Navy (1970-1974) **Creative Works:** Contributor, Articles to Professional Publications in Herpetology and Arachnology **Memberships:** National Center for Science Education; American Arachnological Society; U.S. Naval Institute **Marquis Who's Who Honors:** Albert Nelson Marquis Lifetime Achievement Award **Why did you become involved in your profession or industry:** Mr. Berrian first became involved in his profession due to his exposure to science at a young age; his father held a doctorate in embryology, and his earliest memories are of helping in the laboratory. **Avocations:** Camping; Reading; Travel; Study of spiders; Nature photography **Political Affiliations:** Liberal

Adam M. Betz

Title: Owner **Industry:** Business Management/Business Services **Company Name:** Family Golf and Learning Center **Education:** Student, University of Missouri—St. Louis; Student, Spring Hill College **Certifications:** Certified Golf Professional, PGA of America (2018) **Career:** Owner, Family Golf and Learning Center (2018-Present); Golf Professional, Meadowbrook Country Club (2011-2018); Golf Instructor, Big Bend Golf Center (2010-2011); Touring Golf Professional, Birdie Hunter, LLC (2006-2010); Outside Operations/Assistant Caddy Master, Lost Tree Club (2007-2010); Assistant Golf Professional, Burnt Pine Golf Club (2003-2005) **Civic:** Board Member, Golf Foundation of Missouri; Volunteer, Yearly Golf Camp; Member, Teaching and Coaching Committee, PGA of America **Awards:** Awarded 2018 Top 50 Stand Alone Range, Golf Range Association of America (2018) **Memberships:** PGA Class A Member **To what do you attribute your success:** Mr. Betz attributes his success to his unwavering commitment to working hard; his work ethic has always been good. The ability to build relationships has been the biggest key. **Why did you become involved in your profession or industry:** Mr. Betz became involved in his profession because he started golfing when he was 7. By 10, he told his parents that he wanted to be a golf pro. He went to college but never finished because he knew he wanted to get into the golf business. He moved down to Destin, Florida, and played in all the local golf courses. After he was done playing, he would apply for a job at every course. In eight days, he applied to 10 golf courses. His father called him for his birthday and said that he would pay for a round of golf for his birthday. When he was asked where he would like to play, he said, "Without a doubt Burnt Pines." It was too much money for him to pay for on his own. Mr. Betz showed up for the 9 a.m. tee time his father set up, and the women there said it was nice speaking to his father he was such a nice man. His father had told her that he was looking for a job at a golf course, so she said to him he could have her job; she had just been promoted. She set up an interview with John Ward, the director of golf, for later in the afternoon. He was hired and started working the next day. While working, he stayed very active in playing. In the winter of 2006, he played on the Grey Goose Gateway Tour. After three years of doing tours, he was really good and the plan was for him to go to PGA qualifying school. He came very close, he got through pre qualifying and first stage, but during the second stage on the fourth day he fell short. He moved back to St. Louis where he was from and started working at Meadowbrook Country Club, and during his time there, he found a passion for teaching. His position there evolved into a full time teacher, he was the director of instruction by the time he left. Mr. Betz got married and shortly after that got very sick. After spending two weeks in the hospital, when he was released, he told his wife he didn't want to go back to Meadowbrook; he couldn't reach as many people as he wanted to. That is when they started to research driving ranges and practice ranges. St. Louis was lacking a quality range. After much research, they found the Family Golf and Learning Center, which is where he learned how to play. It really became a full circle.

Annette Beyer-Mears

Title: Fellow of the Royal Society of Medicine **Industry:** Medicine & Health Care **Company Name:** University of Medicine and Dentistry of New Jersey **Date of Birth:** 05/26/1941 **Place of Birth:** Madison **State/Country of Origin:** WI/USA **Parents:** Karl Beyer; Annette (Weiss) Beyer **Children:** Carl **Education:** Doctor of Philosophy, University of Medicine and Dentistry of New Jersey (1977); Master of Science, Fairleigh Dickinson University (1973); Bachelor of Arts, Vassar College (1963) **Career:** Associate Professor, Department of Ophthalmology, University of Medicine and Dentistry of New Jersey, Rutgers New Jersey Medical School (1986-2014); Associate Professor, Department of Physiology, University of Medicine and Dentistry of New Jersey, Rutgers New Jersey Medical School (1986-2014); Assistant Professor, Department of Physiology, University of Medicine and Dentistry of New Jersey, Rutgers New Jersey Medical School (1980-1985); Assistant Professor, Department of Ophthalmology, University of Medicine and Dentistry of New Jersey, Rutgers New Jersey Medical School (1979-1985); Fellow, National Institutes of Health, Department of Ophthalmology, University of Medicine and Dentistry of New Jersey, Rutgers New Jersey Medical School (1978-1980); Teaching Assistant, Department of Physiology, University of Medicine and Dentistry of New Jersey, Rutgers New Jersey Medical School (1974-1977); Instructor of Physiology, Springside Chestnut Hill Academy, Philadelphia, PA (1967-1971); Fellow, National Institutes of Health, Weill Cornell Medicine, Cornell University (1963-1965) **Career Related:** Visiting Associate Professor, Department of Ophthalmology and Vision Science, University of Wisconsin–Madison (1995-2014); Consultant, Novartis AG **Civic:** Vestry, Christ Church, Ridgewood, NJ (1994-1995); Long Range Planning Committee, Christ Church, Ridgewood, NJ (1985-1987); Fundraising Chairman, Saint Bartholomew Episcopal Church (1978-1979); Member, Minister Search Committee, Saint Bartholomew Episcopal Church (1978); Delegate, Episcopalian Diocesan Convention (1977-1978); Chairman of Admissions, Vassar College (1974-1979); Retired Trustee, National Foundation of Eye Research **Creative Works:** Contributor, Articles in Diabetic Lens & Kidney Therapy, Professional Journals **Awards:** Wright Spirit Award, Frank Lloyd Wright Building Conservancy (2007); Grant, Pfizer Inc (1993-2000); Grant, Pfizer Inc (1985-1989); Grant, JDRF (1985-1987); NEI Grantee, National Institutes of Health (1980-1995); Research Award, Foundation for the University of Medicine and Dentistry of New Jersey, Rutgers New Jersey Medical School (1980); National Research Service Award, National Institutes of Health (1978-1980) **Memberships:** Fellow, Royal Society of Medicine (1992); The American Physiological Society; The Physiological Society; The American Society for Pharmacology and Experimental Therapeutics; The Association for Research in Vision and Ophthalmology; International Society for Eye Research; American Association for the Advancement of Science; International Diabetes Federation; American Diabetes Association; Retired Trustee, National Foundation for Eye Research; Aircraft Owners and Pilots Association; Sigma Xi **Marquis Who's Who Honors:** Albert Nelson Marquis Lifetime Achievement Award; Marquis Who's Who Top Professional **To what do you attribute your success:** Dr. Beyer-Mears attributes her success to an abiding passion for her work. **Avocations:** Listening to international news; Piloting

Annmarie Bhola

Title: Chief Executive Officer **Industry:** Business Management/Business Services **Company Name:** Enhanced Building Solutions LLC **Place of Birth:** Brooklyn **State/Country of Origin:** NY/USA **Parents:** Narish Bhola (Deceased); Lakshmi Bhola **Education:** BS in Plant Facilities Engineering, State University of New York Maritime College (SUNY Maritime College), Bronx, NY (1998) **Certifications:** Minority & Women-owned Business Enterprise (M/WBE), NYC Department of Small Business Services (2017-2022); Minority Women-Owned Business Enterprise, The Port Authority of New York & New Jersey (2017-2020); Certificate in Human Resources, Pace University (2016); BPI Multifamily Building Operator Professional Certified, Building Performance Institute, Incorporated; Construction Project Management Certificate; Licensed BPI Multifamily Building Operator Professional; USCG Third Assistant Engineers License, Unlimited Steam HP **Career:** Chief Executive Officer, Enhanced Building Solutions LLC (EBS), New York, NY (2016-Present); Part-Time Instructor, Multifamily Building Operator Course, 32BJ SEIU (2015-2016); Senior Business Development Manager, LogCheck (2015-2016); Construction Project Manager, Related Management Company (2013-2014); AVP/Director of Mechanical Commissioning, Related Management Company (2006-2012); Assistant Manager, Technical Services, Aramark Engineering & Asset Solutions, Madison, CT (2003-2006); Production Technician, Taylor Made, Fort Lauderdale, FL (2003); HVAC Instructor, ATI Career Training Center- Fort Lauderdale, FL (2001-2003); Instructor, Fundamentals of Air Conditioning and Refrigeration & Basic Electricity, ATI Career Training Center (2001-2003); Associate Field Engineer, Dome Tech Engineering, Edison, NJ (2000-2001); Third Assistant Engineer-3A/E, Mobil Oil (1999-2000); Account Executive, Sales Engineer, Carrier Corporation (1998-1999) **Career Related:** Training Videos for Building Operations Staff, Mount Sinai Hospital (2019); Subcontractor, Asset Management Data Integration Project (2019); Training Videos for Operations Staff, Memorial Sloan Kettering Cancer Center (2018-2019); Commissioning Services, Aramark, NYU Tisch, NYU Skirball, Kings County Hospital, SUNY Downstate, University of Pittsburgh, Albert Einstein College of Medicine, Metropolitan Museum of Art, MoMa, Rubin Museum of Art, NYS Psychiatric Facilities (2003-2006); Ship Familiarization Video for Compliance and Training Purposes, Liberty Maritime Corporation **Civic:** Board Member, Seaport South Condo Board (2016-Present); Board Member, Fort Schulyer Maritime Alumni Association (2013-Present) **Creative Works:** Host, Podcast, Discussing Engineering to Operations, "Annmarie's Breaking Ground Podcast" **Memberships:** Women's International Shipping & Trading Association (WISTA); American Society of Heating and Air-Conditioning Engineers (ASHRAE); Association of Energy Engineers (AEE); Fort Schuyler Maritime Alumni Association; Seaport South Condominium Association **Marquis Who's Who Honors:** Marquis Who's Who Top Professional **To what do you attribute your success:** Ms. Bhola attributes her success to hard work. Her parents would give her chores to do around the house from as early as age six. Most of the chores involved cleaning around the house. Ms. Bhola believes that this is part of the reason she is so great at coming into situations and cleaning them up is because of the sense of responsibility her chores gave her at an early age. **Why did you become involved in your profession or industry:** Ms. Bhola's father was an HVAC technician. Her mother would send her and her siblings with him to work from time to time. When they would accompany him, he would put them to work as well. From that experience, she learned a lot about different tools, and her earliest experience of working with machinery. She admired her father and his career. He unfortunately passed when she was only 15 years old. She believes that most of her decisions and where her career has led her was based off of carrying out her father's legacy. **Thoughts on Life:** Let's leave it a little bit better than we found it.

Nadia Judith Bijaoui, DHEd, PHD, MAP

Industry: Research **Company Name:** Bio Health Education **Parents:** Annie Boukris; Rémy Bijaoui **Children:** David Jacob Ohayon; Joshua Simon Ohayon; Natacha Esther Ohayon; Guido Boccara (Great-graddaughter) **Education:** DHEd, A.T. Still University of Health Sciences; PhD in Psychology, Southern California Psychoanalytic Institute; Master Degree in Psycho-Educational Counseling, Anitoch University, Los Angeles, CA; Bachelor of Science in Health Promotion and Disease Prevention, Preventive Medicine Department, Keck School of Medicine, University of Southern California, Los Angeles, CA; Graduate from the University of Southern California Neuroscience Department; Bachelor of Art in French Literature, University of Southern California, Los Angeles, CA. **Certifications:** Certified Research Psychoanalyst, Medical Board of California **Career:** Director of Bio Health Education, Independent Researcher, Consultant, System Designer (2005-Present); Online Instructional Designer, Health Science Faculty, United States University, Chula Vista, CA (2009-2014); Psychological Assistant, Dr. MacLeay Psychological Services (2003-2005) **Career Related:** Creator, Bio Health Education (BHE); Creator, "Discover Your Nightlife! Dream Mysteries Decoded"; Creator, Video, BHE Anti-Stress Tips; Creator, "Viva La Difference! In Prevention & Reduction of Bullyism"; **Civic:** Conservator, Mentor, Down-Syndrome Adult; Tutor, No Child Left Behind, Los Angeles Unified School District, Professional Tutors of America, Brea, CA; Volunteer Therapist, Individuals in Need; Volunteer, Theater Groups, Non-Profit Organizations; Fundraiser, Children with Leukemia; Volunteer, Senior Citizens. **Creative Works:** Author, "From Silent Spring to Silent Cemetery" (2017 & 2020); Principal Contributor: "Can Dream Science Be Used to Elicit Healthy Behaviors?," The International Journal of Dream Research (2019); Principal Contributor: "Can Dream Science Be Used to Elicit Healthy Behaviors?" (2018); Author, "The Other Side of the Curtain: Recovering from Deep Coma" (2017); Author, "Hate is a disease"; Author, "Hate is a contagious disease"; Author, "Hate is a virus" **Awards:** Bio Health Education's Wish Upon A Star" (2019); Most Questionable Health News (2018); Inductee, Association of Interdisciplinary Doctors of Health Science (2014); Certificate of Academic Excellence, A.T. Still University, School of Health Management (2012); Inductee, National Society of Collegiate Scholars, University of Southern California (2000); Certified Renaissance Scholar Recognition Award, University of Southern California (1999-2000); McNair Scholarship, University of Southern California (1999); Dean's List, University of Southern California (1997-1999) **Memberships:** Pi Phi Delta Society, University of Southern California; Association of Interdisciplinary Doctorate of Health Science **To what do you attribute your success:** Dr. Bijaoui attributes her success to her intuition, her ability to foresee and strategize and to her determination while staying flexible. **Why did you become involved in your profession or industry:** Dr. Bijaoui was in a tragic accident in 1969, in France. While rebuilding herself physically and mentally in the United States, her accident inspired her to help others. Even before her accident, she was fascinated by the interactions of the body and the mind. She also was drawn to prevention and to neuroscience. Therefore, she interconnected mind, body, and brain in her research and practice. Presently, she is designing self-help and self-development projects within the online educational system she created, Bio Health Education. **Religion:** Jewish **Thoughts on Life:** Dr. Bijaoui thoughts on life are to find balance between heart and brain. Since COVID-19, her thoughts on life are also Aragon's words (translated in English): "Nothing is ever granted to Man, not his strength, not his weakness, not his heart..."- Protection is in learning because knowledge brings freedom from anxiety.

Irwin Morton Birnbaum

Title: Educational Consultant, Lawyer **Industry:** Education/Educational Services **Company Name:** Yale School of Medicine **Date of Birth:** 07/15/1935 **Place of Birth:** Brooklyn **State/Country of Origin:** NY/USA **Parents:** Sol N. Birnbaum; Rose (Cohen) Birnbaum **Marital Status:** Married **Spouse Name:** Arlene R. Burrows (06/08/1957) **Children:** Bruce J.; Leslie R. Birnbaum Kline; Amy G. Birnbaum Heath **Education:** JD, New York University (1961); BS in Accounting, Brooklyn College (1956) **Career:** Senior Adviser, Robert Wood Johnson Clinical Scholars Program, Yale School of Medicine (2005-Present); Senior Adviser to the Dean, Yale School of Medicine (2004-2005); Chief Operating Officer, Yale School of Medicine, New Haven, CT (1997-2004); Partner, Proskauer & Rose LLP, New York, NY (1989-1997); Counsel, Proskauer & Rose LLP, New York, NY (1986-1989); Vice President, Montefiore Medical Center (1970-1986); Chief Financial Officer, Montefiore Medical Center (1970-1986); Budget Officer, Montefiore Medical Center, Bronx, NY (1962-1970) **Career Related:** Mediator, Arbitrator, Alternative Dispute Resolution Service, American Health Lawyers Association (2008-Present); Chairman, Board of Directors, FOJP Service Corporation (2006-2011); Board of Directors, FFH Insurance Company (1998-2006); Member, Executive Committee, MCIC Vermont (1997-2005); Chair, Financial Committee, MCIC Vermont (1997-2005); Adjunct Professor, Yale School of Medicine; Lecturer, Public Health and Health Policy Administration, Yale School of Medicine **Civic:** Trustee, South County Health Systems, South Kingston, RI (2007-Present); Trustee, Hospital Association of Rhode Island, Cranston, RI (2007-Present); Trustee, Malmonides Medical Center, Brooklyn, NY (1988-Present); Treasurer, Malmonides Medical Center, Brooklyn, NY (1988-Present); Member, Executive Committee, Malmonides Medical Center, Brooklyn, NY (1988-Present); Trustee, Cross Mills Public Library, Charlestown, RI (2011); Board of Directors, Jewish Home for the Aged, New Haven, CT (2003-2007); Secretary-Treasurer, Hospital Trustees of New York State (1990-1997); Executive Committee, Hospital Trustees of New York State (1990-1997) **Creative Works:** Editor, "Health Care Law Treatise" (1990); Editor, "Montefiore Medical Center and the Loeb Center Experience: A Hospital's Fiscal Perspective"; Editor, "Medicare and Extended Care" **Memberships:** Secretary, Health Law Committee, Association of the Bar of the City of New York (1995-1996); Secretary, Committee on Medicine and Law, Association of the Bar of the City of New York (1989-1990); Fellow, The New York Academy of Medicine; Special Committee on Healthcare Systems, American Academy of Hospital Attorneys (Now American Health Lawyers Association) **Bar Admissions:** New York (1962) **Marquis Who's Who Honors:** Albert Nelson Marquis Lifetime Achievement Award; Marquis Who's Who Top Professional **To what do you attribute your success:** Mr. Birnbaum attributes his success to the fact that he likes people and forming special bonds. **Avocations:** Sailing; Playing tennis; Reading; Traveling

Deborah Leah Birx

Title: Coronavirus Response Coordinator **Industry:** Government Administration/Government Relations/Government Services **Company Name:** The White House **Date of Birth:** 04/04/1956 **State/Country of Origin:** PA/USA **Parents:** Donald Birx; Adele Sparks Birx **Marital Status:** Married **Spouse Name:** Paige Reffe **Children:** Two children **Education:** Residency in Internal Medicine, Walter Reed Army Medical Center (1981-1983); Internship in Categorical Medicine, Walter Reed Army Medical Center (1980-1981); MD, Penn State College of Medicine (1980); BS, Houghton College (1976) **Career:** Ambassador-at-Large, Coordinator, U.S. Government Global HIV/AIDS Activities, U.S. Department of State (2014-Present); Director, Centers for Disease Control and Prevention, U.S. Department of Health & Human Services, Atlanta, GA (2005-2014); Director, U.S. Military HIV Research Program, Walter Reed Army Institute of Research (1996-2005); Laboratory Director, HIV-1 Vaccine Development, Walter Reed Army Institute of Research (1995-1996); Chief, Department of Retroviral Research, Walter Reed Army Institute of Research (1994-1995); Assistant Chief, Department of Retroviral Research, Walter Reed Army Institute of Research (1989-1994); Investigator, Cellular Immunology, National Institutes Of Health (1986-1989); Assistant Chief, Allergy Immunology Service, Walter Reed Army Medical Center (1985-1989); Fellowship in Diagnostic and Clinical Immunology, Walter Reed Army Medical Center (1985-1986); Fellowship in Allergy and Clinical Immunology, Walter Reed Army Medical Center (1983-1985) **Career Related:** Adjunct Professor, University of North Carolina (2012-Present); Consultant, Walter Reed Army Medical Center (1989-Present); Assistant Professor, Uniformed Services University of the Health Sciences (1985-Present) **Civic:** Coronavirus Response Coordinator, Coronavirus Task Force, The White House (2020-Present) **Awards:** Lifetime Achievement Award, African Society for Laboratory Medicine (2011); Outstanding Manager, Federal Executive Boards (2008); Decorated Legion of Merit; U.S. Meritorious Service Medal

Paul Edward Bishop, PhD, MS

Title: Microbiologist (Retired) **Industry:** Sciences **Date of Birth:** 02/12/1940 **Place of Birth:** Portland **State/Country of Origin:** OR/USA **Parents:** Paul Emory; Elizabeth Ann (Burnett) **Marital Status:** Married **Spouse Name:** Lola Germania Montesdeoca (06/16/68) **Children:** Paul Emory II (Deceased) **Education:** PhD, Oregon State University (1973); MS, Oregon State University (1970); BS, Washington State University (1964) **Career:** Microbiologist, USDA Agricultural Research Service, Food Science Research Unit, Department of Food, Bioprocessing & Nutrition Sciences, NC State University (1977-1984, 1985-Present); Research Microbiologist, USDA Agricultural Research Service, University of Sussex (1984-1985); Research Associate, University of Wisconsin-Madison (1975-1977); Research Associate, Oregon State University (1973-1975); Technician, School of Medicine, University of Washington (1966-1967); Volunteer, Peace Corps, Panama (1964-1966) **Creative Works:** Contributor, Articles, Professional Journals **Awards:** Grant, U.S. Department of Agriculture (1978, 1981, 1984, 1986, 1988, 1990, 1992, 1994, 1996);Scientist of Year Award, U.S. Department of Agriculture (1982) **Memberships:** The American Society for Microbiology; The Honor Society of Phi Kappa Phi **Marquis Who's Who Honors:** Albert Nelson Marquis Lifetime Achievement Award **To what do you attribute your success:** Dr. Bishop attributes his success to perseverance. **Avocations:** Camping; Taking photos; Reading Spanish; Weightlifting; Playing trumpet; Performing **Political Affiliations:** Democrat **Religion:** Methodist

Michael G. Bissell, MD, PhD, MPH

Title: Professor Emeritus **Industry:** Education/Educational Services **Company Name:** Ohio State University College of Medicine **Date of Birth:** 03/05/1947 **Place of Birth:** Ridgecrest **State/Country of Origin:** CA/USA **Parents:** Henry Robert Benefiel (Deceased, 2000); Margaret Alberta (Encell) Benefiel (Deceased, 2000) **Marital Status:** Married **Spouse Name:** Mary Bissell (03/17/2010); Lita A. Hill (11/29/1991, Deceased); Sherrie L. Lyons (03/27/1977, Divorced 1990) **Children:** Grahame (1983); Cassandra (1978) **Education:** Master of Public Health, University of California Berkeley (1978); PhD in Neurobiology, Stanford University (1977); MD, Stanford University (1975); BS in Mathematics, University of Arizona (1969); BS in Chemistry, University of Arizona (1969) **Certifications:** MRO Certification, American Association of Medical Review Officers (AAMRO) (2005-Present); License, Physician and Surgeon, Ohio (1997-Present); Diplomate in Clinical Pathology, American Board of Pathology (1981-Present); Certification, American Board of Pathology (1996-2007); Licensed Physician and Surgeon, Numerous States **Career:** Retired (2014); Director, Laboratory Medical, Vice-Chair, Pathology, Associate Dean, Applied Research, Ohio State University, Columbus, OH (2000-2014); Director, Clinical Pathology, Allegheny General Hospital, Pittsburgh, PA (1998-2000); Director, Laboratory Medicine, Associate Professor, Pathology, University of Texas (1993-1997); Vice President, Medical Director, Nichols Institute, Reference Laboratory, San Juan Capistrano, CA (1991-1993); Director, Clinical Pathology, City of Hope National Medical Center, Duarte, CA (1988-1991); Assistant Professor, Pathology, University of Chicago Medical Center (1984-1988); Research Fellow, National Institute of Mental Health, Bethesda, MD (1981-1984); Resident, Martinez VA Medical Center, University of California Davis (1978-1981) **Career Related:** Speaker in the Field (1985-2013); Presenter, 67 National and International Presentations **Civic:** Former Senior Warden, St. Alban's Episcopal Church, Bexley, OH; Board of Directors, Partners-in-Ministry-in-Liberia (PIMIL) **Creative Works:** Author, "Toxicology Testing, An Issue of Clinics in Laboratory Medicine - E-Book (The Clinics: Internal Medicine) 1st Edition, Kindle Edition" (2012); Author, "Laboratory-Related Measures of Patient Outcomes: An Introduction 1st Edition by Michael G. Bissell" (2000); Author/Editor, "Automated Integration of Clinical Laboratories: A Reference Paperback" (1998); Four Patents; Contributor, Articles, Professional Journals; Author, 138 Papers and 16 Book Chapters **Awards:** Fellow, National Academy of Clinical Biochemistry (2000-Present); Ohio State University College of Medicine Excellence in Teaching Award for Pathology (2007-2008); Ohio State University Pathology, Clinical Pathology Residency Program Teacher of the Year (2007-2008); Teacher of the Year, Ohio State University Clinical Pathology Program (2001-2002); Outstanding Volunteer, St. Vincent's Free Clinic, Galveston, TX (1997); Sterling Service Award, Clinical Laboratory Management Association (1996); Citation, Outstanding Contribution, Clinical Laboratory Management Association (1992) **Memberships:** Fellow, College of American Pathologists; American Society of Clinical Pathologists; National Committee Clinical Laboratory Standards; American Association Clinical Chemistry; Treasurer, Clinical Laboratory Management Association; Activist, Lecturer, Physicians for National Health Program; Lifetime Member, Sierra Club; Lifetime Member, Sigma Xi **Marquis Who's Who Honors:** Albert Nelson Marquis Lifetime Achievement Award **To what do you attribute your success:** Dr. Bissell attributes his success to perseverance. **Avocations:** Painting; Stamp collecting (philately); Drawing; Writing; Genealogy; Playing the harp **Political Affiliations:** Democrat **Religion:** Episcopalian

Brad James Bittenbender

Title: Safety Engineer **Industry:** Engineering **Date of Birth:** 12/04/1948 **Place of Birth:** Kalamazoo **State/Country of Origin:** MI/USA **Parents:** Don J. Bittenbender; Thelma Lula (Bacon) Bittenbender **Marital Status:** Married **Spouse Name:** Margaret Stahl Hubbell **Children:** Scott Hubbell; Susan Hubbell; David Hubbell **Education:** Certificate in Environmental Auditing, California State University, Long Beach (1992); Certificate in Hazardous Material Management, University of California, Irvine (1987); BS, Western Michigan University (1972) **Certifications:** National Board Certified, Safety Professional of the Americas (CSP); National Board Certified, Hazardous Materials Manager (CHMM); Authorized Outreach Trainer, United States Department of Labor, Occupational Safety and Health Administration; Licensed Hoist Engineer, Massachusetts State Department of Public Safety **Career:** Senior Safety Specialist, Jacobs Engineering Group Inc., General Electric Aviation, Lynn, MA (2000-Present); Manager, Safety, Health and Environmental Department, Cytec Fiberite-California Division (1998-1999); Director, Environmental Safety and Health Department, Culver City Composites Corporation (1996-1998); Manager, Environmental, Safety, Industrial Hygiene Department, Structural Polymer Systems, Inc., Montedison, CA (1991-1995); Manager, Environmental, Safety, Industrial Hygiene Department, Composites Division, Ferro Corporation, Los Angeles, CA (1988-1991); Senior Environmental Engineer, Ferro Corporation, Los Angeles, CA (1980-1987); Environmental Administrator, Productol Chemical Division, Ferro Corporation, Santa Fe Springs, CA (1979-1980); Supervisor, Manufacturing, Productol Chemical Division, Ferro Corporation, Santa Fe Springs, CA (1977-1979) **Career Related:** Participant, Conference, Best Practices, Occupational Health Aspects of Advanced Composite Technology, Aerospace Industry, United States Air Force (1989); Mediated Rule Making Advisory Committee, Workplace Exposure to Methylenedianiline, Federal OSHA (1988); Member, Advisory Board, University of California-Irvine Extension Program, Industrial Health and Safety Education (1985-1991); Member, Suppliers of Advance Composites Material Association, Health and Safety Committee **Civic:** Founding Sponsor, Challenger Center, Boston Athenaeum (2015-Present); Region-9 Instructor, Occupational Safety and Health Administration, On-Boarding Candidate Special Government Employees (2019); Occupational Safety and Health Administration, Voluntary Protection Program Participant Association, Washington DC Legislative Out-Reach Team (2018); Delegation Member, People to People International, Cambodia, Vietnam (2012); Delegation Member, American Society Safety Engineers, China, Brazil and India (2010-2013); Advisory Committee, Hazardous Materials Community Right-To-Know, Culver City, CA (1987-1991); Museum of Contemporary Art, Los Angeles, CA (1985-2000); California Museum Foundation, Los Angeles, CA (1985-1990); United States Department of Labor Special Government Employee, Federal Occupational Safety and Health Administration, Voluntary Protection Program Administration; Volunteer, Board Member, Upkeep of the Church **Creative Works:** Contributor, Pamphlet, "Safe Handling of Advance Composite Materials," SACMA Second Edition (1991) **Awards:** Named Region-1 Special Government Employee of the Year, United States Department of Labor, Occupational Safety and Health Administration (2018) **Memberships:** People to People International (2010-Present); Environmental Health and Safety Committee, Suppliers Advanced Composites Materials Association (1989-1992); American Society of Safety Professionals; Alliance of Hazardous Materials Professionals; National Fire Protection Association; Society of Fire Protection Engineers; Engineers Without Borders of the United States; The Society of the Cincinnati; General Society of Mayflower Descendants; Board Member, Massachusetts Society of the Sons of the American Revolution; Board Member, Properties Wellesley Village Church **Why did you become involved in your profession or industry:** Mr. Bittenbender became interested in engineering when he was a freshman in college. He wanted to be able to do something that was meaningful and rewarding; engineering gave him the ability to make a difference in civil society. **Avocations:** Family genealogy; Revolutionary war re-enacting; Hobby farm **Political Affiliations:** Independent **Religion:** Congregational United Church of Christ

Arthur G. "Art" Black

Title: Electrical Engineer **Industry:** Technology **Company Name:** Fairchild Semiconductor **Date of Birth:** 01/17/1948 **Place of Birth:** Kansas City **State/Country of Origin:** MO/USA **Parents:** Wilbur Charles Black; Frances (Nichols) Black **Marital Status:** Widower **Spouse Name:** Lorraine K. Yamashita (09/06/1998); Patricia Mae Smith (01/01/1979, Divorced 1989) **Children:** Kristina R. Black **Education:** Master of Science in Electrical Engineering, University of Michigan, Ann Arbor, MI (1972); Bachelor of Science in Electrical Engineering, University of Kansas, Lawrence, KS (1971) **Career:** Retired (2014); Manager, Discrete Applications Department, Fairchild Semiconductor (2004-2014); Manager, Power Conversion Department, Sun Microsystems, Menlo Park, CA (1996-2004); Head, Power Management Applications Group, National Semiconductor, Santa Clara, CA (1993-1996); Advisory Engineer, IBM, Kingston, NY (1984-1993); Associate, Senior Associate, Staff Engineer, IBM, Boulder, CO (1977-1984); Member, Technical Staff, Bell Telephone Laboratories, Holmdel, NJ (1972-1977) **Career Related:** Panelist, Applied Power Electronics Conference and Exposition (2005) **Civic:** Member, Board of Trustees, Local Church (2014-2019); Scoutmaster, Boy Scouts of America (1982-1984) **Creative Works:** Workshop Panelist, High Frequency Power Conversion Conference (1993); Guest Lecturer, Ulster County Community College Course on Analog Circuit Design (1986); Invited Reviewer for APEC Papers; Author, Numerous Papers Delivered at Internal IBM Technical Conferences; Patentee in the Field **Memberships:** Institute of Electrical and Electronic Engineers; Tau Beta Pi; Eau Kappa Nu **Marquis Who's Who Honors:** Albert Nelson Marquis Lifetime Achievement Award; Marquis Who's Who Top Professional **To what do you attribute your success:** Mr. Black attributes his success to the guidance and passion of his college instructors. He also credits his ability to learn from his failures, as well as his successes. **Why did you become involved in your profession or industry:** In becoming involved with his profession, Mr. Black drew inspiration from the example of his father, who distinguished himself as a civil engineer. **Avocations:** Ballroom dancing; Hiking and backpacking; Baking; Photography **Political Affiliations:** Democrat **Religion:** Methodist

Alan Ralph Blackford

Title: Vocal Teacher **Industry:** Education/Educational Services **Company Name:** Waterford Township School District **Date of Birth:** 05/20/1957 **Place of Birth:** Camden **State/Country of Origin:** NJ/USA **Parents:** Ralph Kurtz Blackford; Jean Mabel Blackford **Marital Status:** Married **Spouse Name:** Susan C. Banyai **Children:** Bryan (Stepson); Meghan (Stepdaughter); Sarah J. (Stepdaughter) **Education:** MusM, Philadelphia College of Performing Arts, Philadelphia, PA (1982); MusB in Music Education, Philadelphia College of Performing Arts, Philadelphia, PA (1980) **Certifications:** Teacher of Music, Grades K-12, State of New Jersey, Commonwealth of Pennsylvania **Career:** Vocal Teacher, Waterford Township School District, Atco, NJ (1985-2017) **Career Related:** Accompanist, Associate Director, Director, Cinnaminson Community Chorus, Cinnaminson, NJ (1972-Present); Organist, Choir Director, Trinity Episcopal Church, Delran, NJ (1974-2016) **Creative Works:** Composer, "Sanctus" **Awards:** Teacher Recognition Award, New Jersey Governor (1988); Philadelphia College of Performing Arts Alumni Graduation Award, Philadelphia College of Performing Arts Alumni Association (1980); Scholar, Ezerman Piano Scholarship, Philadelphia College of Performing Arts (1977) **Memberships:** New Jersey Education Association **Marquis Who's Who Honors:** Albert Nelson Marquis Lifetime Achievement Award; Marquis Who's Who Top Professional **Why did you become involved in your profession or industry:** Mr. Blackford's grandfather was not a musician by trade, but he was an amateur drummer with a jazz band back in the 1920s. He was part of Mr. Blackford's inspiration to go into music; the other was going back to the phonograph. He was a very young child, but he was not mechanical at all. One of the first things that he learned how to operate was the record player that they had in his home. He would sit in front of it for hours; he was not all that interested in the television. Mr. Blackford was fascinated by the record player and the music that came out of it. His grandparents had a piano, and he would go to their house and just tinker around on the piano. He had basically no idea what he was doing, but he was happy to try it. Later, his parents noticed his gift and enrolled him in lessons, which led to his enrollment at the Philadelphia Musical Academy, now known as the College of Performing Arts/University of the Arts in Philadelphia, Pennsylvania. Mr. Blackford was accepted. In the years that followed, he established himself as a musician. **Avocations:** Rare and unusual recordings; Collecting vintage wristwatches, radios, and phonographs

Sara Treleaven Blakely

Title: Founder, Chief Executive Officer **Industry:** Business Management/Business Services **Company Name:** Spanx, Inc. **Date of Birth:** 02/27/1971 **Place of Birth:** Clearwater **State/Country of Origin:** FL/USA **Parents:** John Blakely; Ellen (Ford) Blakely **Marital Status:** Married **Spouse Name:** Jesse Itzler (2008) **Children:** Lazer Blake **Education:** BA in Legal Communications, Florida State University (1993) **Career:** Founder, Chief Executive Officer, Spanx, Inc., Atlanta, GA (2000-Present); Saleswoman, Danka (Now Konica Minolta Business Solutions U.S.A., Inc.), FL (1993-2000); Employee, Walt Disney World, Orlando, FL (1993); Co-Owner, Atlanta Hawks **Career Related:** Speaker in Field **Civic:** Founder, Sara Blakely Foundation (2006-Present) **Awards:** Named, One of the 100 Most Powerful Women, Forbes Magazine (2013-2014); Named, One of the 100 Most Influential People in the World, Time Magazine (2012); Entrepreneur of the Year, Ernst & Young; Listee, Oprah Winfrey's Favorite Things List, "The Oprah Winfrey Show" (2000) **Memberships:** Delta Delta Delta Fraternity **Religion:** Jewish

Michael A. Blakney, CPA, CMA

Title: Senior Level Finance Manager **Industry:** Financial Services **Date of Birth:** 11/15/1972 **Place of Birth:** Windsor **State/Country of Origin:** Canada **Education:** Bachelor's Degree in Commerce, University of Windsor (1995) **Certifications:** Certified Management Accountant (2000) **Career:** Senior Level Finance Manager, KaVo North America,; Financial Manager, KaVo Kerr; Senior Manager, Operations and Finance, KaVo Kerr **Awards:** Named, Outstanding Professional of the Year; Named, VIP of the Year; Distinguished Humanitarian Award; Listee, Elite American Executives; Featured, Live 365 Radio Network; Featured, Front Cover of Pro-Files Magazine **Memberships:** American Institute of Certified Public Accountants **Marquis Who's Who Honors:** Albert Nelson Marquis Lifetime Achievement Award; Marquis Who's Who Top Professional **To what do you attribute your success:** Mr. Blakney attributes his success to hard work and strong organizational skills. He is eager to learn, flexible and a team player. **Why did you become involved in your profession or industry:** Mr. Blakney became involved in his profession because he has always been good with numbers and found that this was an appropriate position for someone with his personality and skills. **Avocations:** Golfing; Music; Cars

William Gilbert Grover Blakney, MS

Title: Associate Professor Emeritus **Industry:** Education/Educational Services **Company Name:** Auburn University **Date of Birth:** 04/04/1926 **Place of Birth:** Moncton **State/Country of Origin:** New Brunswick/Canada **Parents:** Donald Mariner Blakney; Ruth M. (Keans) Blakney **Marital Status:** Widowed **Spouse Name:** L. Marie Woodman (10/20/1951, Deceased 2018) **Children:** Dawn Marie; Carol Lynn **Education:** MS in Photogrammetry, The Ohio State University (1955); BS in Mining, Nova Scotia Technical College (Now Dalhousie University) (1949); Diploma in Engineering, Dalhousie University, Halifax, Nova Scotia, Canada (1947) **Career:** Associate Professor Emeritus, Auburn University, Alabama (1990-Present); Associate Professor of Industrial Engineering, Auburn University, AL (1983-1990); Associate Professor of Technology Services, Auburn University, AL (1981-1983); Associate Professor of Civil Engineering, Auburn University, AL (1958-1981); Topographic Engineer, Mines and Technology Surveys, Ottawa, Ontario, Canada (1950-1958) **Civic:** Carter Center, Atlanta, GA; Public Citizen **Awards:** Recipient, Various Awards **Memberships:** Secretary, Danforth Associates (1990-Present); President, Alabama Society of Professional Land Surveyors (1980); Fellow, American Congress on Surveying and Mapping; Lifetime Member, American Society for Photogrammetry and Remote Sensing (ASPRS); Lifetime Member, Canadian Institute of Quantity Surveyors; Lifetime Member, Alabama Society of Professional Land Surveyors; American Society for Engineering Education (ASEE) **Marquis Who's Who Honors:** Albert Nelson Marquis Lifetime Achievement Award; Marquis Who's Who Top Professional **Why did you become involved in your profession or industry:** Mr. Blakney entered his profession because it was a family ambition. He was the first one in his family to even think about going to university, and his father was a self-educated engineer. Everyone in his family encouraged him to follow the engineering path. **Avocations:** Politics **Political Affiliations:** Democrat

Arthur M. Blank

Title: Owner; Co-Founder **Industry:** Athletics **Company Name:** Alanta Falcons Football Club, Atlanta United **Date of Birth:** 09/27/1942 **Place of Birth:** Queens **State/Country of Origin:** NY/USA **Parents:** Max Blank; Molly Blank **Marital Status:** Divorced **Spouse Name:** Angela Macuga (06/2016, Divorced 2019); Stephanie V. Blank (1995, Divorced 2014); Diana Blank (Divorced 1993) **Children:** Joshua Blank; Max Blank; Kylie Blank; Kenny Blank; Dena Blank Kimball; Danielle Blank Thomsen **Education:** Honorary LLD, Babson College (1998); MBA, Harvard Business School; BS, Babson College **Career:** Owner, Chief Executive Officer, Atlanta United, MLS (2017-Present); Owner, Chief Executive Officer, Atlanta Falcons Football Club, NFL (2002-Present); Chairman, President, Chief Executive Officer, AMB Group LLC, The Blank Family of Businesses (2001-Present); Chairman, Arthur M. Blank Family Foundation (1995-Present); Co-Chairman, Home Depot Inc., Atlanta, GA (2000-2001); President, Chief Executive Officer, Home Depot Inc., Atlanta, GA (1997-2000); President, Chief Operating Officer, Home Depot Inc., Atlanta, GA (1978-1997); Co-Founder, Home Depot Inc., Atlanta, GA (1978); Vice President, Treasurer, Handy Dan Home Improvement Centers, Inc., Los Angeles, CA (1974-1978); President, Elliott's Drug Stores/Stripe Discount Stores, Daylin Inc., Los Angeles, CA (1967-1974); Senior Accountant, Arthur Young & Company (Now Ernst & Young), New York, NY (1963-1967) **Career Related:** Distinguished Executive in Residence, Emory University Goizueta Business School (2001); Board of Directors, Staples, Inc.; Board of Directors, Cox Enterprises, Inc.; Owner, Mountain Sky Guest Ranch and West Creek Ranch, Emigrant, MT; Owner, Several PGA TOUR Superstores **Civic:** Board Member, North Carolina Outward Bound School; Trustee, The Cooper Institute; Trustee, Emory University; Trustee, The Carter Center; Participant, The Giving Pledge **Awards:** Named, One of Forbes 400: Richest Americans (2006-Present); MLS Cup Champion (as Owner of Atlanta United) (2018); NFL NFC Champion (as Owner of Atlanta Falcons) (2016); Freeing Voices, Changing Lives Award, American Institute for Stuttering (2011); Inductee, Junior Achievement U.S. Business Hall of Fame (2006); Named, One of the 50 Most Generous Philanthropists, BusinessWeek (Now Bloomberg Businessweek) (2005); Georgia's Most Respected CEO, Georgia Trend Magazine (2001, 2003); Inductee, Business Hall of Fame, Georgia State University (2002); Junior Achievement Award, Atlanta, GA (2001); Co-Recipient, Abe Goldstein Human Relations Award, Anti-Defamation League (2001); Georgia Philanthropist of the Year, National Society of Fundraising Executives (2000); Named to the Academy of Distinguished Entrepreneurs, Babson College (1995); Brotherhood/Sisterhood Award, National Conference of Christians & Jews (NCCJ) (1994) **Memberships:** The Commerce Club

Richard F. Blewitt

Title: Management Consultant **Industry:** Business Management/Business Services **Date of Birth:** 03/26/1947 **Place of Birth:** Scranton **State/Country of Origin:** PA/USA **Parents:** Frank Joseph Blewitt; Margaret (Kearney) Blewitt **Marital Status:** Married **Spouse Name:** Elizabeth Reinhardt **Children:** MarLynn Morabito; Carrie Blewitt; Shane Blewitt **Education:** Postgraduate Coursework, Harvard Business School (1992-1994); MBA, University of Chicago (1981); BS in Government and Politics, University of Maryland (1973) **Career:** Advisor to the Chairman, UMUC Ventures (2016-Present); Senior Advisor to the President, University of Maryland University College (2011-Present); Managing Partner, R&B Associates (2008-Present); President, Co-founder, Rowan & Blewitt Incorporated (1984-2007); Vice President, Corporate Affairs, Velsicol Chemical LLC, Chicago, IL (1978-1984); Manager, Public Relations, FMC Corp. Chemical Group, Philadelphia, PA (1975-1978); Manager, Press Relations, Manufacturing Chemists Association, Washington (1972-1975); Press Relations Assistant, American Trucking Associations, Washington (1970-1972); Staff Writer, Scranton Times (1966-1968) **Career Related:** Founder, Pillars of Strength Scholarship Program, The Blewitt Foundation **Military Service:** U.S. Navy (1968-1970) **Creative Works:** Contributing Editor, "World Book Encyclopedia" (1973-1983) **Marquis Who's Who Honors:** Albert Nelson Marquis Lifetime Achievement Award **Why did you become involved in your profession or industry:** At 11 years old, Mr. Blewitt began working with his father, the general manager of a local newspaper. Mr. Blewitt loved pedaling newspapers because he felt like it was in his blood. He eventually advanced to become a young reporter with his father's newspaper and became attracted to the communications side of the business. With this background, he decided to go into public relations, with the hope of owning his own company one day. He went on to start his own firm after a few corporate positions. He specialized in issue and crisis management for major corporations for more than 25 years. **Religion:** Roman Catholic **Thoughts on Life:** Mr. Blewitt wants others to stay motivated and know that anything can be accomplished.

Evelyn Blount

Title: Executive Director/Treasurer (Retired) **Industry:** Religious **Company Name:** Woman's Missionary Union Auxiliary South Carolina Baptist Convention **Date of Birth:** 11/20/1942 **Place of Birth:** Winder **State/Country of Origin:** GA/USA **Parents:** Willie Brown; Ouida (Pool) B. **Marital Status:** Single **Education:** Master of Religious Education, Southern Baptist Theological Seminary (1969); Bachelor of Science in Education, Woman's College of Georgia (1964) **Career:** Retired (2008); Executive Director and Treasurer, Woman's Missionary Union Auxiliary to the South Carolina Baptist Convention, Columbia, SC (1985-2008); Youth Department Supervisor, Field Services Director, National Enlargement Plan Director, Program Design Specialist, Woman's Missionary Union Auxiliary Southern Baptist Convention, Birmingham, AL (1973-1985); Acting Director, Woman's Missionary Union, Auxiliary Georgia Baptist Convention, Atlanta, GA (1970-1973); Minister of Education, First Baptist Church, Auburn, AL (1969-1970); Group Leader, Baptist Center, Louisville, KY (1967-1969); Teacher, Berkmar High School, Gwinnette County, GA (1966-1967); Teacher, Blue Mountain College (1964-1966) **Career Related:** Member, Hold Out the Lifeline: Prenatal & Family Ministries; Member, State Steering Committee, South Carolina Department of Health and Environmental Control; Member, Governor's Council on Mentoring **Civic:** Church and Appalachian Association Woman's Missionary Union Director; Leadership Service, Barrow County Detention Center **Creative Works:** Co-author, "No Longer Forgotten: The Remarkable Story of the Christian Women's Job Corps" (1998); Author, "Youth Ministry Missions Projects" (1978); Author, "Code E and Teachers Guide for Code E" (1973) **Awards:** Named, Honorary Lifetime Member, U.S. Air Force Air Defense (1959) **Memberships:** National Association of Female Executives; Board of Directors, Barrow County Cooperative Benevolence Ministries **Marquis Who's Who Honors:** Albert Nelson Marquis Lifetime Achievement Award; Marquis Who's Who Top Professional **To what do you attribute your success:** Ms. Blount attributes her success to the call of her Christian faith. **Why did you become involved in your profession or industry:** Having grown up in the missions organization, Ms. Blount felt a calling to continue that work, and drew inspiration from the example of her mother. **Avocations:** Wood carving; Camping; Music **Religion:** Southern Baptist

Barry William Boehm, PhD, ScD

Title: Distinguished Professor, Engineer, Researcher **Industry:** Technology **Company Name:** University of Southern California **Date of Birth:** 05/16/1935 **Place of Birth:** Santa Monica **State/Country of Origin:** CA/USA **Parents:** Edward G. Boehm; Kathryn G. (Kane) Boehm **Marital Status:** Married **Spouse Name:** Sharla Perrine (07/01/1961) **Children:** Romney Ann; Tenley Lynn **Education:** Honorary ScD, Computer Science and Software Engineer, Institute of Software, Chinese Academy of Sciences (2011); Honorary ScD, Computer Science, University of Massachusetts (2000); PhD, Mathematics, University of California, Los Angeles (1964); MS in Mathematics, University of California, Los Angeles (1961); BA, Mathematics, Harvard University (1957) **Career:** Director, Research, Chief Scientist, Department of Defense Systems, Engineer Research Center (2009-Present); Distinguished Professor, TRW Professor, Software Engineering, Director, Center for Software Engineering, University of Southern California (1992-Present); Honorary Chair Professor, Hanglow Dianzi University (2018); Director, Software and Computer Technology Office, Director, Defense Research and Engineering, Department of Defense, Arlington, VA (1992); Director, Information Science and Technology Office, Defense Advanced Research Agency, Department of Defense, Arlington, VA (1989-1992); Research Leader, Chief Engineer, Scientist, TRW Defense Systems Group, Redondo Beach, CA (1973-1989); Programmer to Head of the Computer Science Department, Information Science Department, Rand Corp., Federal Research Center, Santa Monica, CA (1959-1973); Programmer, Analyst, General Dynamics, San Diego, CA (1955-1959); Distinguished Professor, Engineer, Researcher **Career Related:** Chairman, Board of Visitors, Carnegie Mellon University Software Engineering Institute (1997-Present); Visiting Professor, Chinese Academy of Science (2005); Chairman, Army/DARPA Future Combat Systems Software Steering Committee (2001); Chairman, USAF-Science Advisory Board, Information Technology Panel (1994-1997); Chairman, DOD Software Technology Plan WG, Arlington, VA (1990-1992); Co-chairman, Federal Coordinating Council of Science, Engineering and Technology High-Performance Computing WG, Washington DC (1989-1991); NASA G & C/Infosystems Advisory Committee, Washington DC (1973-1976); Guest Lecturer, USSR Academy of Science (1970) **Civic:** Chair, The Research Council of the Defense Department, Research Center **Creative Works:** Co-Editor, "Disciplinary Convergence in Systems Engineering Research" (2017); Co-Editor, "Software Engineering" (2007); Co-Author, "Software Engineering, Barry W. Boehm's Contributions" (2007); Co-Editor, "Foundations of Empirical Software Engineering" (2005); Co-Editor, "Value-Based Software Engineering" (2005); Co-Editor, "Unifying The Software Process Spectrum" (2005); Co-author, "Balancing Agility and Discipline" (2004); Co-Author, "Software Cost Estimation with COCOMO II" (2000); Co-Author, "Software Risk Management" (1989); Author, "Software Engineering Economics" (1981); Co-Author, "Characteristics of Software Quality" (1978); Co-Editor, "Planning Community Information Utilities" (1972); Author, "ROCKET" (1964); Author, Over 500 Papers and Books **Awards:** Named Professor of the Year, International Association of Top Professionals (2019); Nancy Mead Lifetime Achievement Award in Software Engineering Education (2015); Stevens Software Engineering Lifetime Achievement Award (2011); Simon Ramo Systems Engineering Medal, IEEE (2010); H.D. Mills Award, IEEE (2000); Distinguished Research Award in Software Engineering, Association for Computing Machinery (1997); American Society for Quality Control Lifetime Achievement Award (1994); Award for Excellence, Office of the Secretary of Defense (1992); Freiman Award, International Society of Parametric Analysts (1988); Warnier Prize, Society Software Analysts (1984); Information Systems Award, American Institute of Aeronautics and Astronautics (1979); Recipient, Research Grants, 30 Industrial Organizations **Memberships:** Governor Board, Computer Science, IEEE (1986-1987, 1981-1982); Chair, TC Computers, American Institute of Aeronautics and Astronautics (1968-1970); Fellow, International Council on Systems Engineering; Fellow, Association for Computing Machinery; NAE **Marquis Who's Who Honors:** Albert Nelson Marquis Lifetime Achievement Award; Marquis Who's Who Top Professional **Why did you become involved in your profession or industry:** Dr. Boehm became involved in his profession because he was a mathematics major, though he was never quite sure what he could do as a career. At the time, he considered becoming an insurance company actuary or a statistician. After his sophomore year at Harvard University, he got an internship at General Dynamics. There, he was introduced to digital mathematics, which led him to computer programming. While he had no prior experience, Dr. Boehm quickly discovered that he had a passion for the work. **Avocations:** Tennis

Philip F. Boelter

Title: Executive Vice President / Chief Operating Officer **Industry:** Architecture & Construction **Company Name:** Kraus-Anderson Companies, Inc **Date of Birth:** 03/25/1943 **Place of Birth:** Independence **State/Country of Origin:** IA/USA **Parents:** Floyd Joseph Boelter; Eileen R. (Wilson) Boelter **Marital Status:** Married **Spouse Name:** Linda Lee Franck, (6/7/1964) **Children:** Carrie Lynn; John Philip **Education:** JD, University of Iowa (1968); BS, Industrial Engineering, Iowa State University (1965) **Career:** Executive Vice President, Chief Operating Officer, Kraus-Anderson, Minneapolis (2002-Present); Partner, Dorsey & Whitney, Minneapolis, (1968-2002) **Civic:** Board of Directors, Junior Achievement of the Upper Midwest (2003-2004); Trustee, Gustavus Adolphus College (1996-2005) **Awards:** Minnesota Icon Award (2019); Recognized in the Best Lawyers in America; Recognized in Super Lawyers in the State of Minnesota **Memberships:** Member, Minneapolis Athletic Club (Treasurer 1992, Secretary 1993, Vice President 1994, President 1995); Edina Country Club **Bar Admissions:** State of Minnesota; State of Iowa **Marquis Who's Who Honors:** Albert Nelson Marquis Lifetime Achievement Award **To what do you attribute your success:** Mr. Boelter attributes his success to preparation, hard work, great mentors, humility, wonderful opportunities, talented and capable colleagues, empathy, gratitude and thankfulness. **Why did you become involved in your profession or industry:** Mr. Boelter became involved in his profession when he was an undergraduate and decided after his sophomore year that he wanted to get an advanced degree. Through his interviewing of local executives that were very helpful, he learned that a number of senior executives had law degrees. He didn't even know a lawyer. He wanted to know what it would be like to go to law school. He went to law school solely for the idea of going into business. **Avocations:** Landscape gardening; Alpine skiing; Golfing; Reading **Religion:** Lutheran **Thoughts on Life:** Mr. Boelter believes in the idea: "Love your wife, children and grandchildren for they will sustain and comfort you in times of difficulty and reward you in with great happiness. Never surrender your integrity and hold yourself to high standards of character and morality and sound principles."

Lawrence William "Larry" Boes, JD

Title: Lawyer **Industry:** Law and Legal Services **Company Name:** Law Office of Lawrence W. Boes **Date of Birth:** 08/03/1935 **Place of Birth:** Brooklyn **State/Country of Origin:** NY/USA **Year of Passing:** 1965 **Parents:** Lawrence Boes; Lissi (Schaefer) Boes **Marital Status:** Widower **Spouse Name:** Joan Mary Elward (10/02/1965, Deceased 08/07/2018) **Children:** Lawrence E.; Siobhan; Thomas **Education:** Doctor of Jurisprudence, Columbia University (1964); Bachelor of Arts, Columbia College (1961) **Career:** Attorney, Law Office of Lawrence W. Boes (2001-Present); Retired Partner, Norton Rose Fulbright LLP, New York, NY (2001-Present); Partner, Norton Rose Fulbright & Jaworski LLP, New York, NY (1989-2000); Partner, Reavis & McGrath (1971-1988); Associate, Reavis & McGrath, New York, NY (1965-1971); Law Clerk to Judge, U.S. Court Appeals for the Second Circuit (1964-1965) **Civic:** Trustee, Westbury Memorial Public Library (2002-2007); Member, Code Review Commission, Village of Westbury, NY (1983-2015) **Military Service:** Corporal, Company Clerk, US Army (1958-1960) **Creative Works:** Reviews Editor, Columbia Law Review (1963-1964) **Awards:** National Scholar, Columbia University (1962); Pulitzer Scholar, New York City Board of Education (1954) **Memberships:** Society of American Baseball Research (1991-Present); President, Local Chapter, Rotary (2004-2005); Committee on Standards of Attorney Conduct, New York State Bar Association (1999-2002); Secretary, University Glee Club, New York (1998-2004); Chairperson, Nassau County Bar Association (1998-2000); Empire State Counsel; American Bar Association **Bar Admissions:** U.S. Court of Appeals for the Third Circuit (1988); U.S. Court of Appeals for the Ninth Circuit (1982); Supreme Court of the United States (1974); U.S. Court of Appeals for the Eighth Circuit (1974); U.S. Court Appeals for the Second Circuit (1971); U.S. District Court for the Eastern District of New York (1968); U.S. District Court for the Southern District of New York (1968); New York (1965) **Marquis Who's Who Honors:** Albert Nelson Marquis Lifetime Achievement Award; Marquis Who's Who Top Professional **To what do you attribute your success:** Mr. Boes credits his success on the influence of his mother, who taught him to appreciate reading books and newspapers, as well as his father, who taught him in elementary mathematics before he was 5 years old. **Why did you become involved in your profession or industry:** Mr. Boes became involved in his profession due to support of his parents, who encouraged him to pursue the study of constitutional law at Columbia College. As a result of his military service as a law clerk, he was often asked by officers to write formal letters, and he participated in special courts martial, which spurred his interest in the legal process. **Avocations:** Gardening; Baseball; Choral singing **Political Affiliations:** Democrat **Religion:** Christian

Dan Calvin Boger, PhD

Title: Science Professor, Consultant **Industry:** Military & Defense Services **Company Name:** Naval Postgraduate School **Date of Birth:** 07/09/1946 **Place of Birth:** Salisbury **State/Country of Origin:** NC/USA **Parents:** Brady Cashwell Boger (Jr.); Gertrude Virginia (Hamilton) Boger **Marital Status:** Married **Spouse Name:** Gail Lorraine Zivna (6/23/1973) **Children:** Gretchen; Gregory **Education:** PhD in Economics, University of California Berkeley (1979); MA in Statistics, University of California Berkeley (1977); MS in Management Science, Naval Postgraduate School, Monterey, CA (1969); BS in Management Science, University of Rochester (1968) **Certifications:** Certified Professional Estimator, Certified Cost Analyst **Career:** Acting Dean, Graduate School of Operational and Information Sciences (2020-Present); Professor, Naval Postgraduate School, Monterey, CA (1992-Present); Chairman, Cyber Academic Group (2017-2019); Executive Director, National Security Institute (2008-2012); Dean Research (2006-2009);Founding Chairman, Department of Information Sciences, Naval Postgraduate School, Monterey, CA (2002-2020); Dean, Division of Computer and Information Sciences, Operations, Naval Postgraduate School, Monterey, CA (1997-2001); Chairman, Department of Information Warfare, Naval Postgraduate School, Monterey, CA (1997-2001); Chairman, Department of Computer Science, Naval Postgraduate School, Monterey, CA (1997-2001); Chairman, Department of Command, Control, and Communications, Naval Postgraduate School, Monterey, CA (1995-2001); Associate Professor, Naval Postgraduate School, Monterey, CA (1985-1992); Assistant Professor, Economics, Naval Postgraduate School, Monterey, CA (1979-1985); Research Assistant, University of California Berkeley (1975-1979) **Career Related:** Consultant, Economics and Statistical Legal Matters (1977-Present); Board of Directors, Evan-Moor Corp. (1990-1995); CSX Corp. **Civic:** California Alumni Association of the Monterey Peninsula **Military Service:** Lieutenant, U.S. Navy (1968-1975) **Creative Works:** Associate Editor, Journal Cost Analysis (1989-1992); Editorial Review Board, Journal of Transportation Research Forum (1987-1991); Associate Editor, Logistics and Transportation Review (1981-1985); Contributor, Articles, Professional Journals **Awards:** Dissertation, Research Grantee, A.P. Sloan Foundation (1978-1979); Flood Fellow, Department of Economics, University of California Berkeley (1975-1976) **Memberships:** Secretary-Treasurer, Military Applications Society, Institute for Operations Research and Management Science (1987-1991); American Economic Association; American Institute of Aeronautics and Astronautics; American Statistical Association; Association for Computing Machinery; IEEE Communications Society; IEEE Computer Society **To what do you attribute your success:** For Dr. Boger, perseverance is absolutely essential in life, and especially in the working world. As Edison said, "Success is one percent inspiration and ninety-nine percent perspiration." **Why did you become involved in your profession or industry:** Dr. Boger became interested in academics as a result of the opportunity he earned to do research. Over the years, he became interested in all aspects of decision making, especially in the military. He later found teaching to be remarkably stimulating, which is what inspired him to pursue a career in the field. **Avocations:** Golfing **Religion:** Protestant **Thoughts on Life:** Dr. Boger believes a loving spouse and family are the important things in life, though both require perseverance.

Edra Charlotte Bogle, PhD

Title: Literature Educator **Industry:** Education/Educational Services **Date of Birth:** 1/4/1934 **Place of Birth:** Des Moines **State/Country of Origin:** IA/USA **Parents:** John Paul Bogle; Mary Mildred (Hastings) Bogle **Marital Status:** Married **Spouse Name:** Thomas M. Cain **Education:** PhD in Comparative Literature, University of Southern California, Los Angeles, CA (1968); MLS, Columbia University (1957); BA, University of Northern Iowa (1956) **Career:** Retired (2004); Coordinator, Women's Studies, North Texas State University (Now University of North Texas), Denton, TX (1992-1994); Associate Professor, North Texas State University (Now University of North Texas), Denton, TX (1968-1994); Associate Librarian for Public Services, University of Southern California (1964-1968); Education Librarian, University of Southern California, Los Angeles, CA (1960-1964); Assistant Librarian, Frostburg State University (Now Frostburg State Teachers College), Frostburg, MD (1959-1960); Assistant Librarian, Western Oregon University (Now Oregon College of Education), Monmouth, OR (1957-1959); Literature Educator; Secretary, Faculty Senate **Career Related:** Indexer, Annual Bibliography of English Language and Literature (1972-1984); Associate Editor, "Halkett & Laing's Dictionary of Anonymous and Pseudonymous Works," Third Edition (1980) **Civic:** Democratic Candidate, State Board of Education District (2006); Denton County Democratic Chair (2003-2006); County Chair, Jesse Jackson Campaign, Denton, TX (1988); Co-Chair, Lesbian/Gay Democrats of Texas (1986-1987) **Creative Works:** Publisher, Booklet (2004); Contributor, Article **Awards:** Michael Lynch Service Medal, Gay/Lesbian Caucus for Modern Language, Modern Language Association (1991) **Memberships:** Treasurer, Science Fiction Research Association (1991-1992); Chair, 22nd Conference, Science Fiction Research Association (1991); Delegate of the Assembly Modern Language Association (1986-1988); Editor, Modern Language Association **Marquis Who's Who Honors:** Albert Nelson Marquis Lifetime Achievement Award; Marquis Who's Who Top Professional **Why did you become involved in your profession or industry:** Dr. Bogle realized ever since the third grade that she was like LGBT people. In addition, she would sometimes read a story about it or her mother's journals, and when she got older, she was reading some of the books by other people about it. It was actually back then in junior high school in a town of 2,700 and surprisingly enough, their bookstore helped her find science fiction. She received allowance and sold night crawlers in the summertime for more money to buy science fiction books, and she noticed books on LGBTQ topics, which taught her a great deal. Dr. Bogle would also like to add that she was very fortunate to be in Denton, Texas, because they had a black population. A few years before that, some of the prominent women in town decided that the African American people were not being treated properly, and had gone out to their churches and other groups, such as the Chambers of Commerce, to at least include one African American person in some sort of prominent position such as the board of directors. Denton was not completely a southern town, but it did help a lot. **Avocations:** Slogan buttons; Antiques and collectibles; Art; Music; Cats **Political Affiliations:** Democrat **Religion:** Agnostic

Therese A. Boisvert, MSEd

Title: Credentialing Compliance Coordinator **Industry:** Medicine & Health Care **Company Name:** Logistics Health Incorporated (LHI) **Date of Birth:** 04/22/2001 **Place of Birth:** LaCrosse **State/Country of Origin:** WI/USA **Parents:** Walter; Joanne (McKee) Boisvert **Education:** Claims Up Skilling, LHI (2019); MS in Education and Library Sciences, University of Wisconsin-La Crosse (1985); BS in Pre-Law Studies and Political Science, Minor in Sociology, University of Wisconsin-La Crosse (1982) **Career:** Credentialing Compliance Coordinator, Logistics Health Incorporated (2017-Present); Assistant, Vicar, The Roman Catholic Diocese of La Crosse (2011-2017); Occupational Health Department Specialist, Gundersen Lutheran (1989-2011) **Civic:** Catholic Daughters of America (2019-Present); Liaison to the Diocese, La Crosse Council of Catholic Women; Secretary, La Crosse Deanery Parish Council of Catholic Women; Secretary, Cathedral Council of Catholic Women; Former Chairperson, Aquinas Education Commission; Education Committee, The Cathedral of St. Joseph the Workman; Volunteer, Church **Awards:** Named, Professional Woman of the Year, National Association of Professional Women; Listee, Sterling Registry of Outstanding Professionals; Listee, Continental Who's Who Registry of National Business Leaders; Listee, Stanford Who's Who; Listee, Presidential Who's Who **Memberships:** Policy Committee, Cathedral Parish Council of Catholic Women; National Association of Professional Women **Marquis Who's Who Honors:** Albert Nelson Marquis Lifetime Achievement Award; Marquis Who's Who Top Professional; Marquis Who's Who Humanitarian Award **To what do you attribute your success:** Ms. Boisvert attributes her success to the support she receives from her parents and older brother. **Why did you become involved in your profession or industry:** Ms. Boisvert became involved in her profession after working in the medical field for more than 26 years. **Avocations:** Needlepoint; Ice skating; Reading **Religion:** Catholic

Gary Dean Boldt

Title: Farmer **Industry:** Agriculture **Date of Birth:** 07/13/1941 **Place of Birth:** Wichita **State/Country of Origin:** KS/USA **Parents:** Earl Boldt; Dorothy Boldt **Marital Status:** Single **Education:** Bachelor of Arts in Botany and Mathematics, University of Kansas (1963) **Career:** Farmer, Self-Employed, Ulysses, KS (1974-Present) **Career Related:** Cimarron Regional Advisory Committee, State of Kansas Water Office, (Present) **Civic:** Former Secretary and President, Ulysses Lions Club **Military Service:** United States Peace Corps, East Pakistan (1963-1965) **Memberships:** Member of Cimarron Regional Advisory Committee, Kansas Water Office; Member, Grant County Conservation District Board **Marquis Who's Who Honors:** Albert Nelson Marquis Lifetime Achievement Award **Why did you become involved in your profession or industry:** Mr. Boldt grew up on a family farm and has helped his father and mother, Earl and Dorothy Boldt, since he was a young man in school. In high school, he became interested in botany and mathematics and decided to study those subjects at University of Kansas. Mr. Boldt chose botany and mathematics because it was needed at the time when the Soviet Union had launched a space probe and America needed more scientists. His inspiration in farming came from his father's hard work on the farm and his passion to help others within the community. **Avocations:** Walking; Trying to satisfy his curiosity **Political Affiliations:** Republican **Religion:** Methodist

Tommy Rocky Bolduc

Title: Owner **Industry:** Business Management/Business Services **Company Name:** Optiline Enterprises, LLC **Date of Birth:** 11/18/1986 **Place of Birth:** Quebec **State/Country of Origin:** Canada **Parents:** Roger Bolduc; Linda Beaudoin **Marital Status:** Married **Spouse Name:** Mylene Drouin **Children:** One Daughter; Two Sons **Career:** Owner, Optiline Enterprises, LLC (2006-Present); Loyal Storage LLC **Civic:** Wish Granter, Make-a-Wish Foundation (2017-Present); Toys for Tots; Nashua Soup Kitchen; Rally Organizer, Mission 22; Advocate, Veteran Suicide Awareness; Salvation Army; Boys & Girls Clubs of America **Creative Works:** Featured, "Keeping Quality in Line: Optiline Enterprises Equals Optimum Performance"; Featured, "Construction Students Go Above and Beyond" **Awards:** Entrepreneur of the Year Award (2018); Diamond Award for a Safe Worksite, America's Builder Committee (2017); DeWaltt Power Drive Challenge Winner, Speed With a Drill **Memberships:** America's Builders Committee, New Hampshire; America's Builders Committee, Massachusetts **Marquis Who's Who Honors:** Marquis Who's Who Top Professional **To what do you attribute your success:** Mr. Bolduc attributes his success to the support of his wife. He has always balanced his family life and his work life, and he believes that his wife has helped him get to his current level of success. He also attributes his success to the morals that his parents taught him; they taught him to be kind to others, and, now, he treats each of his clients with the highest level of dedication. Lastly, he attributes much of his success to the decision to team up with his cousin, Mick Bolduc, in business. **Why did you become involved in your profession or industry:** Mr. Bolduc became involved in his profession because he worked in construction from a very young age, and his passion for the profession grew from there. His father had his own business and taught him what he knew. Mr. Bolduc decided he would start his own business as well. He was inspired by the cash flow in the business and also enjoyed creating an impact on other employees. **Avocations:** Motorsports

Jean Shinoda Bolen, MD

Title: Psychiatrist, Jungian Analyst, Author, Women's Activist **Industry:** Medicine & Health Care **Date of Birth:** 06/29/1936 **Place of Birth:** Los Angeles **State/Country of Origin:** CA/USA **Parents:** Joseph Shinoda; Megumi Yamaguchi Shinoda, MD **Marital Status:** Single **Spouse Name:** James Bolen (Divorced 1987) **Children:** Melody Jean Bolen; Andre Joseph Bolen **Education:** Residency, Langley Porter Psychiatric Hospital and Clinics (1963-1966); Internship, Los Angeles General Hospital, University of Southern California (1962-1963); School of Medicine, UCSF (1958-1962); MD, University of California, Berkeley (1958); BA, Pomona College (1957); UCLA (1954-1955) **Certifications:** Licensed Physician and Surgeon, State of California (1963-2022); Diploma, International Association for Analytical Psychology (1974); Certified, American Board of Psychiatry and Neurology, Inc. (1971) **Career:** Private Practice in Jungian Analysis (1974-Present); Private Practice in Psychiatry (1967-Present); Clinical Professor, UCSF Health (1967-2010); Teaching Faculty, Certifying Board, C.G. Jung Institute of San Francisco **Career Related:** Council on Psychiatric Services, American Psychiatric Association (1983-1986); Chair, Council on National Affairs, American Psychiatric Association (1982-1983); Member, Council on National Affairs, American Psychiatric Association (1973-1983); Board of Trustees, International Transpersonal Association; Board of Trustees, American Orthopsychiatric Association **Civic:** Millionth Circle (2002-Present); Women's World Summit Foundation (2016-2018); NGO Delegate Representative, United Nations Commission on the Status of Women (2002-2015); Delegate to Parliament of World Religions, Women Economic Forum **Creative Works:** Author, "Artemis: The Indomitable Spirit in Everywoman" (2014); Author, "Moving Toward the Millionth Circle: Energizing the Global Women's Movement" (2013); Author, "Like a Tree: How Trees, Women, and Tree People Can Save the Planet" (2011); Author, "Close to the Bone: Life-Threatening Illness as a Soul Journey" (1996, 2007); Author, "Urgent Message from Mother: Gather the Women, Save the World" (2005); Author, "Crones Don't Whine: Concentrated Wisdom for Juicy Women" (2003); Author, "Goddesses in Older Women: Archetypes in Women over Fifty" (2001); Author, "The Millionth Circle: How to Change Ourselves and The World–The Essential Guide to Women's Circles" (1999); Author, "Ring of Power: Symbols and Themes Love Vs. Power in Wagner's Ring Cycle and in Us- A Jungian-Feminist Perspective" (1992, 1999); Author, "Crossing to Avalon: A Woman's Midlife Quest for the Sacred Feminine" (1994); Author, "Gods in Everyman: Archetypes That Shape Men's Lives" (1989); Author, "Goddesses in Everywoman: Powerful Archetypes in Women's Lives" (1984); Author, "The Tao of Psychology: Synchronicity and the Self" (1979) **Awards:** Top Doctor of the Year in Psychology, IAOTP (2020); Demeter Award, The Association for the Study of Women and Mythology (2014); Distinguished Lifetime Fellow, American Psychiatric Association (2003); Award, Institute for Health & Healing (2002) **Memberships:** C.G. Jung Institute of San Francisco (1997-Present); International Association for Analytical Psychology (1997-Present); Fellow, The American Academy of Psychodynamic Psychiatry and Psychoanalysis; Northern California Psychiatric Society **Marquis Who's Who Honors:** Albert Nelson Marquis Lifetime Achievement Award (2020) **To what do you attribute your success:** Dr. Bolen attributes her success to a lifetime of experiences, lessons in humility, her willingness to speak up and learn, and doing what she loves. **Avocations:** Walking in Muir Woods and on Muir Beach in Marin County; Tending flowers; Writing; Reading; Painting **Political Affiliations:** Democrat **Religion:** Protestant **Thoughts on Life:** It is Summer 2020, I turned 84. The global pandemic is ongoing. I am doing my psychiatric-Jungian analysis office sessions virtually from home and busier than ever. Saying 'yes!' to invitations to participate in conferences, talks, interviews, doing online teaching. I'm responding because it feels like this is my "assignment." I call it the dandelion effect: it is like blowing on the dandelion flower when its fluffy white and has turned to seed. My words can go out on Internet winds, and aided by synchronicity–meaningful coincidence, will land on fertile soil.

August Constantino Bolino, PhD

Industry: Education/Educational Services **Date of Birth:** 09/30/1922 **Place of Birth:** Boston **State/Country of Origin:** MA/USA **Parents:** Nicholas Bolino; Rose (Capozzi) Bolino **Marital Status:** Married **Spouse Name:** Thora Johnson (09/15/1951) **Children:** Bradlee; Douglas; Jacquelyn; Gregory **Education:** PhD in Economics, St. Louis University (1957); Postgraduate, University of Washington (1950-1952); MBA, University of Michigan (1949); BBA, University of Michigan (1948) **Career:** Professor, Catholic University, Washington (1970-Present); Associate Professor, Catholic University, Washington (1966-1969); Chief, Division of Economic Analysis Of Automation, Office of Manpower Automation And Training, U.S. Department of Labor, Washington (1962-1964); Assistant To Associate Professor of Economics, St. Louis University (1955-1962); Instructor, Business And Economic, Idaho State University, Pocatello, ID (1952-1955); Instructor of Statistics, University of Washington, Seattle, WA (1950-1951) **Career Related:** Lecturer, University of Maryland, College Park (1963, 1970-1976); Adjunct Professor, Economics, American University, Washington (1964-1966); Director, Evaluation Of Manpower Development And Utilization Of Programs Branch, U.S. Department of Health, Education And Welfare (1964-1966); Assistant To U.S. Commissioner Of Education (1964-1966); Consultant In Field **Civic:** Vice President of Research, Ellis Island Restoration Commission (1978-Present); ETO **Military Service:** Lieutenant, U.S. Air Force (1942-1945) **Creative Works:** Author, "The Kid and the Clipper" (2006); Author, "Brother Brigham's Trial" (2002); Author, "Thomas Angel, American" (2001); Author, "A Century of Human Capital by Education and Training" (1989); Author, "The Watchmakers of Massachusetts" (1987); Author, "The Ellis Island Source Book" (1985); Author, "Career Education: Contributions to Economic Growth" (1973); Author, "Manpower and the City" (1969); Author, "The Development of the American Economy" (1961); Contributor, Articles, Professional Journals **Awards:** Award, D.C. Community Humanities Council (1983); U.S. Manpower Administration (1971-1972); Research Grantee, American Philosophical Society (1969); Distinguished Service Award, Alpha Kappa Psi (1949, 1960); Ford Foundation Grantee, University of Minnesota (1957); Research Fellow, University of Michigan (1949) **Memberships:** Alpha Kappa Psi **Marquis Who's Who Honors:** Albert Nelson Marquis Lifetime Achievement Award **Why did you become involved in your profession or industry:** When Dr. Bolino was in high school, his father insisted that he get a trade so that he could work with his hands. He went to a school called Boston Tech and he graduated in 1939, and as soon as he graduated, he got a job in a machine shop and worked there for four years. He joined the Army Air Corps because he was drafted to join, and he wound up in England and became a member of a flying fortress crew. When he was discharged in 1945, he had five years of the GI Bill, which was free, and in the first four years, he received a Master of Business Administration and decided he wanted to be a teacher. He started a PhD program, but was not making any progress until he got married. His wife said to him that if he wanted to be a professor, he needed to get a PhD, which he thought he could not afford. She said that he should sign up for it and she would take care of everything else. What started him teaching was when he earned his PhD in 1957. The dean came to him and asked if he could teach a class of American economic development. He became a teacher and the dean then asked him if he could write a book on that subject, and it was a great success, to the point they asked him to write a second edition, which he did, and it sold several thousand more copies. **Avocations:** Watch collecting; Coin collecting/numismatics **Political Affiliations:** Democrat **Religion:** Roman Catholic

Bernard Saturnin Bonbon

Title: Associate Professor, Researcher, Specialist in Mathematical Problems of Visual Space **Industry:** Education/Educational Services **Company Name:** Ministère de l'Enseignement Supérieur et de la Recherche **Date of Birth:** 11/29/1941 **Place of Birth:** Terre-de-Haut **State/Country of Origin:** France **Marital Status:** Married **Spouse Name:** Gwendal Bernard Morgan Bonbon **Children:** Maéva Claudie Mélodie; Fabrice Yann Hervé; Laurent Stève Wilhem **Education:** Doctorate, Honoris Causa, International Acadèmy for Contemporani Art (1992); DFA in Mathematics, Arts, Université Paris 8 (1981); DSc, École des Hautes Études en Sciences Sociales (1976); Coursework, National School of Fine Arts; Coursework, School of Applied Arts; Coursework, Gerville Reaache High School, Basse-Terre, France; PhD in Information Sciences and Communication; PhD in Fine Arts; BA, DEA in Education Sciences, Agrégation en Arts Plastics **Career:** Associate Professor, Domaine Universitaire de Saint-Martin d'Hères; Lecturer, Domaine Universitaire de Saint-Martin d'Hères; Specialist in Mathematics of Visual Space, Domaine Universitaire de Saint-Martin d'Hères; Associate Professor, Collège Jean Jaurès, Saint-Ouen; Professor of Technical Education, Lycée d'Enseignement Professionnel; Professor of Design, Collège d'Enseignement Technique de dessin Industriel; Professor, University of Grenoble Alpes **Career Related:** Senior Lecturer, Fine Arts; Researcher, Art Sciences **Creative Works:** Author, "Geometry of Visual Relief or Binocular Perspective" (1990); Author, "Sloping Perspectives - Perspectives of Shadows and Reflections" (1989); Author, "Three-dimensional Spherical Geometry" (1985); Author, "The Modern Perspective - Normed Networks Method (MRN)" (1983); Author, "The Scientific and Artistic Perspective" (1972); Author, "Mathematical and Computer Art - Trigono-Plastic Art"; Contributor, "Art Theorem" Catalog; Producer, Large Format Paintings; Author, Books, Italian, German **Awards:** Golden Years Award (1985-1987); Reconnaissance, Nationale Chevalier dans L'Ordre National du Merite; Award, Ministerial Commission of Books; Acclaim, French and Foreign Scientific Universities; International Art Awards, Paintings; Grand Prix, French and Foreign Distinctions, Belgium, Montreux, Rome, Italy, Nice, Cannes, Strasbourg, Haute-Savoie, Sélestat, Caen, Alençon, Lisieux, Metz, Mâcon, Bédarieux; Cup of the City of Paris; Grand Prix, Academic Institute of the Golden Hand; Ambassador, Arts, Letters; Commander, Academic Gold Palms; Golden Tie with Rosette; International Prize for Applied Sciences **Marquis Who's Who Honors:** Albert Nelson Marquis Lifetime Achievement Award **Avocations:** Collecting books; Collecting paintings; Collecting bronze sculptures; Oil painting; Visiting historical monuments **Religion:** Catholic

Lauren F. Book

Title: Senator **Industry:** Government Administration/Government Relations/Government Services **Company Name:** The Florida Senate **Date of Birth:** 10/12/1984 **Place of Birth:** Hollywood **State/Country of Origin:** FL/USA **Parents:** Ron Book; Patricia Book **Marital Status:** Married **Spouse Name:** Blair Byrnes **Children:** Two children **Education:** MS in Education, University of Miami, Coral Gables, FL (2012); BA in Elementary Education and Creative Writing, University of Miami, Coral Gables, FL (2008) **Career:** Senator, District 32, Florida State Legislature (2016-Present); Founder, Chief Executive Officer, Lauren's Kids, Aventura, FL (2007-Present); Co-Teacher, Henry S. West Laboratory School, Miami, FL (2007-2008); Former Senate Democratic Leader Pro Tempore, Broward County, FL **Career Related:** Board Member, Past Vice President, Florida Network of Children's Advocacy Centers; Advocate, Childhood Survivors of Sexual Assault **Creative Works:** Speaker, TED Talks, "Find Your X, but First, Find Your (wh) Y?" Oxford, England (2016); Speaker, Keynote Address, Georgia Sheriff's Association Training Academy, Savannah, GA (2016); Guest Lecturer, Impact of Sexual Violence, Department of Social Sciences, University of Oxford, Oxford, England (2016); Author, Children's Book, "Lauren's Kingdom" (2015); Presenter, "Safer, Smarter Kids" Abuse Prevention Curriculum, College of Central Florida (2015); Speaker, Keynote Address, National Rapporteur's Symposium on Sexual Violence Against Children, The Hague, Netherlands (2014); Panel Speaker, Child Sexual Abuse Prevention in Communities, Crime Stoppers International Conference, Cape Town, South Africa (2014); Speaker, Keynote Address, Prevention and Effects of Child Sexual Abuse, Break the Silence Conference, UNICEF, Barbados (2014); Speaker, Keynote Address, Prevention and Effects of Child Sexual Abuse, Crime Stoppers International Conference, Barbados (2013); Speaker, Keynote Address, Preventing Child Sexual Abuse and Supporting Survivors, Children's Treatment Centre Celebrity Walk (2013); Author, Memoir, "It's OK to Tell: A Story of Hope and Recovery" (2011); Published, Newsweek Magazine, FOX News, Cosmopolitan Magazine, Huffington Post, NPR, USA Today, New York Daily News, Numerous Local Papers **Awards:** Change Maker Award, Child Mind Institute (2019); Heroes Among Us Award, Glamour Magazine Women of the Year Summit (2018); Emmy Award, Producer, Television Program, "Child Sexual Abuse: Prevention Through Education" (2018); Emmy Award, Producer, Television Program, "Lauren's Kingdom" (2018); Breaking the Silence Award, Goodman Jewish Family Services (2017); Emmy Award, Producer, Television Program, "What if I Told You" (2016); ADDY Award for Content Direction, "Safer, Smarter Kids" Curriculum (2016); Legacy Award, The Ancient Spanish Monastery Foundation (2016); Care for Kids Award, ChildNet (2016); Lollipop Award, Amigos for Kids (2015); Impact Award, Gainesville Home Magazine (2015); KIND Causes Winner, KIND Snacks (2015); Citizen of the Year, Biscayne Bay Kiwanis Club (2014); Daily Points of Light Award, Points of Light (2014); Gracie Award, Producer, "Intimate Crimes" Television Special (2014); National Woman of Worth, The National L'Oreal Paris (2013); ADDY Award for Content Direction, "Safer, Smarter Kids" Curriculum Kit (2013); Lewis Hine Award, National Child Labor Committee (2012); Emmy Award, Storytelling, Television Special, "Out of Darkness, Into Light" (2012); Congressional Medal of Merit, Senator Bill Nelson (2011) **Memberships:** Florida Children and Youth Cabinet; Marjory Stoneman Douglas High School Public Safety Commission; Broward Crime Stoppers **Marquis Who's Who Honors:** Marquis Who's Who Top Professional; Marquis Who's Who Humanitarian Award **To what do you attribute your success:** Senator Book attributes her success to the fear of failure, along with the feeling of constantly wanting to push herself to continue to be a better version of herself everyday, as well as be an example to her children. **Why did you become involved in your profession or industry:** Senator Book became involved in her profession because she is a survivor of childhood sexual abuse. From the ages of 11 to 16, she was the victim of sexual abuse from her family nanny. Senator Book recalls that she had trouble finding a coping method after revealing the abuse to her family; she would only go to school and then come home to cry. Eventually, Senator Book's mother revealed to her that she too had been sexually assaulted. She said that these were "regular occurrences" for women, and that they simply had to get over their trauma and live their life. From that moment on, Senator Book decided she would do everything in her power to be stronger. She now challenges herself every day to help young survivors. She learned at an early age that working through legislature and shaping the laws that protect those who are vulnerable can be an effective way to make change. **Religion:** Jewish **Thoughts on Life:** Senator Book believes, "You don't choose your circumstances, but you can choose how you overcome them." Additionally, she states "sexual abuse can color your life, but you choose what color to paint it."

Donald Eugene Boomershine

Title: Municipal Official (Retired) **Industry:** Business Management/Business Services **Date of Birth:** 10/05/1931 **Place of Birth:** Brookville **State/Country of Origin:** OH/USA **Parents:** Harold Everett Boomershine; Elsie (Rhoads) Boomershine **Marital Status:** Married **Spouse Name:** Patti Watson (05/29/1985); Marilyn Sullivan (8/29/1953, Deceased) **Children:** Jeffrey Alan; Andrew Raine (Stepson) **Education:** Postgraduate Coursework, University of Oklahoma, National Senior Commercial Lending School (1974); Graduate Diploma, Bank Management, ABA Stonier Graduate School of Banking (1969-1972); Graduate Coursework, Bank Marketing Graduate School, Northwestern University (1965); Bachelor of Science, Bowling Green State University, Ohio (1953) **Career:** President, Chief Executive Officer, Better Business Bureau, Central Alabama, Birmingham, AL (1982-2007); Chief Executive Officer, Better Business Bureau, Central Alabama, Birmingham, AL (1982-2007); Vice President, Sales Manager, Circle S. Division, Metropolitan Development Board (1980-1982); Vice President, Community Development, Metropolitan Development Board (1980-1982); Vice President, Birmingham Trust National Bank (1978-1980); Vice President, National Division, Birmingham Trust National Bank (1965-1978); Business Development Representative, Exchange Security Bank, Birmingham, AL (1961-1965); Assistant Cashier, Exchange Security Bank, Birmingham, AL (1961-1965); Senior Sales Representative, IBM, Birmingham, AL (1957-1961); Junior Executive Program, Frigidaire Division, General Motors Corporation, Dayton, OH (1955-1957) **Career Related:** Business Advisory Council, Sorrell College of Business, Troy University (1991-Present); Interim Executive Director, Alabama Public Television (2012); Chairman, Atlanta-Birmingham Branch, Federal Reserve Board (1996, 1993); Atlanta-Birmingham Branch, Federal Reserve Board (1990-1997); Chairman, Business Tomorrow Conference, University of South Alabama (1976); Educational Chairman, Associated Industries of Alabama (1975-1977) **Civic:** Founder, Board of Directors, Jump$tart Coalition for Personal Financial Literacy (2002); Designated Information Officer, U.S. Naval Academy (1982-2004); Board of Directors, Downtown YMCA, Metropolitan YMCA (1992-1997); Alumnus, Leadership Birmingham (1991); Steering Committee, University of Mobile (1987-1990); Board of Directors, Second Vice President, Better Business Bureau, Council of Better Business Bureaus, Inc., Birmingham, AL (1980-1982); Advisory Board, Alabama State Board of Education (1976-1978); Chairman, American Cancer Crusade (1976); Advisory Board, University of South Alabama (1975-1978); Board of Directors, Birmingham Children's Theatre (1974-1975); Corporation Director, U.S. Youth Games (1973); Blue and Gold Board, U.S. Naval Academy (1972-2011); Vice President, National Veterans' Day, U.S. Naval Academy (1972-2011); Board of Directors, Birmingham Zoological Society (1972-1976); Trustee, YWCA Central Alabama, Birmingham, AL (1972-1975); With, American National Red Cross (1968-2018); Board of Directors, The American National Red Cross (1968-1980); Board of Trustees, Alabama Association of Independent Colleges and Universities (1967) **Military Service:** Advisory Board, U.S. Service Academy (1991-2018); Retired Colonel, U.S. Marine Corps Reserve (1984); Second Lieutenant, U.S. Marine Corps (1953); Senior Air Director, Combat Air Operations Center, Airborne Interceptors; Senior Officer for Air Marine/Navy Services; Airborne Qualified Aviation and Senior Umpire for Air, Navy/Marine Amphibious Exercises **Awards:** Named, Military Veterans of Influence, Birmingham Business Journal (2019); Golden Falcon Award (2015); Community Alliance Church Youth Leadership Award (2011); Yacht Leadership Development Program Award (2011); Significant Sig Award, Sigma Chi Fraternity (2011); Diamond Level, Kiwanis International, Birmingham, AL (2011); Tablet of Honor, Kiwanis International, Birmingham, AL (2010); Lifetime Achievement Award, Federal Reserve Bank of Atlanta (2009); Legion Honor Award, Kiwanis International, Birmingham, AL (2006); Named, Birmingham Better Business Bureau Hall of Fame (2006); Inductee, Alabama Senior Citizen Hall of Fame (2005); Alumni Community Service Award, Bowling Green State University (2001); Commandant's Director Award (1999); Outstanding Broadcasters Cooperation Award, Alabama Broadcasters Association (1998); Commandant Award, United States Naval Academy (1994); Named, Alumni Hall of Fame, Brookville High School (1991); Eponym, Donald E. Boomershine Day (1985); Eponym, Reserve Day, Birmingham, AL (1983) **Memberships:** Lifetime Member, Marine Corps League (2013-Present); Founding Member, Marine Corps League (2013-Present); Board Member, Sigma Chi Fraternity (1971-Present); Interim Executive Director, Alabama Public Television (2012); Founding Member, Board of Directors, Summit Club (2004); Diamond Leuch Hixson Fellowship, Kiwanis International, Birmingham, AL (2003); Vice President, Sigma Chi Fraternity (1988-2011); National Tournament Sponsor Committee, Ladies Professional Golf Association (1979); National Director, Marine Corps Reserve Officers Association (1974-1976); Founder, Chairman, Diplomats of Birmingham (1973); Chairman, Alabama Native Sons and Daughters (1971-1972); **Marquis Who's Who Honors:** Albert Nelson Marquis Lifetime Achievement Award

Carol Marie Booth

Title: Writer, Songwriter, Advocate **Industry:** Media & Entertainment **Company Name:** Carol Marie's Music (and Enterprises) **Place of Birth:** Knoxville **State/Country of Origin:** TN/USA **Parents:** James Luther McCoy; Carrie Marie McCoy **Marital Status:** Divorced **Spouse Name:** Darwin Albritton (Divorced 10/30/1970) (Deceased) **Children:** Rhonda Beheler; Sheila Rogerson; Sandra Lee **Education:** Coursework in English and Literature, Louisiana Tech University, Ruston, LA; Union Parish High School, Farmerville, LA **Career:** Talent Manager, Tim McGraw, Nashville, TN (1991, 1988-1989); Songwriter, Publisher, Carol Marie's Music (1985-1989); Coordinator, Public Relations, McDonald's, Houston, TX (1978-1985); Marketing, Advertising Manager, The Vindicator, Liberty, TX (1970-1977) **Civic:** Advocate for Child Abuse Victims **Creative Works:** Freelance Feature Writer (1965-Present); Author, "Atonement Child: a True Story of Surviving Childhood Abuse" (2013); Co-Author, "Storm at Midnight" (1978) **Memberships:** Past Member, Country Music Association Inc; Louisiana Public Broadcasting, Louisiana Educational Television Authority; National League of American Pen Women; Broadcast Music Inc. **Marquis Who's Who Honors:** Albert Nelson Marquis Lifetime Achievement Award **To what do you attribute your success:** Ms. Booth attributes her success to escaping from abuse as a child and the subsequent transformation of her life. She was inspired by the beauty of the world beyond her four walls, and used writing as a creative vessel and therapeutic tool. **Why did you become involved in your profession or industry:** Ms. Booth became involved in her profession because, in spite of a childhood filled with abuse, she was determined from a young age to be a high achiever. She fondly remembers a sixth-grade teacher who told her she was a gifted writer beyond her years and advised her to never give up in her pursuit of a happy, productive life.What inspired Ms. Booth to work on books for children was that she sees what a troubled world we have now and how many things are being taught to children that are wrong. **Avocations:** Producing songs; Reading; Dancing; Poetry; Interviewing celebrities; Publishing stories and articles; Inspiring people to reach great goals; Learning and caring about people **Political Affiliations:** Republican **Religion:** Baptist

Herbert Boothroyd

Title: Insurance Company Executive (Retired) **Industry:** Insurance **Date of Birth:** 12/23/1928 **Place of Birth:** Mason City **State/Country of Origin:** IA/USA **Parents:** Herbert L. Boothroyd; Clara (Schmitt) Boothroyd **Marital Status:** Married **Spouse Name:** Barbara Elizabeth Dunne (02/09/1962) **Children:** Diane Lea; John Herbert **Education:** MA, University of Michigan (1953); BA in Mathematics, University of Michigan, With Honors (1952) **Certifications:** Enrolled Actuary (1976); Massachusetts Institute of Technology (1971); Certified in Executive Management Programs, Columbia (1964) **Career:** Executive Vice President, Group Operations, New England Mutual Life Insurance Company (1983-1987); President, Director, New England General Life (1983-1985); President, New England Pension and Annuity Company (1981-1987); Director, New England Pension and Annuity Company (1980-1987); Senior Vice President, Pension Operations, New England Mutual Life Insurance Company (1977-1982);Vice President, New England Mutual Life Insurance Company (1967-1977); With, New England Mutual Life Insurance Company, Boston, MA (1957-1987); With, Massachusetts Mutual Life Insurance Company (1953-1957) **Career Related:** Director, New England Mutual Life Insurance Company (1984-1987); Director, New England Variable Life Insurance Company (1984-1987) **Civic:** Overseer, Handel and Haydn Society (1994-2003); Secretary, Handel and Haydn Society (1986-1994); Vice Chairman, Member, Executive Committee, Better Business Bureau, Eastern Massachusetts (1985-1988); Board of Governors, Handel and Haydn Society (1984-1994); Member, National Campaign Committee, University of Michigan (1983-1990); Board of Directors, Better Business Bureau, Eastern Massachusetts (1980-1988); Board of Directors New England Chapter, American Diabetes Association (1979-1984) **Military Service:** U.S. Army (1946-1947) **Creative Works:** Co-Author, "Cockrill Families of Northern Virginia" (2002); Co-Author, "Hammett Families" (1983); Co-Author, "Life and Health Insurance Handbook" (1973) **Memberships:** Chair, National Clubs Council, Michigan Alumni Association (1999-2000); National Board of Directors, Michigan Alumni Association (1997-2000); President, University of Michigan Alumni Association (1991-1993); Vice President, 1st District, University of Michigan Alumni Association (1989-1991); Fellow, Society of Actuaries (SOA); Sons of the American Revolution; American Academy of Actuaries; International Congress of Actuaries; New England Historic Genealogical Society; Kentucky Historical Society; Society of Colonial Wars in Massachusetts; Phi Beta Kappa, Theta Delta Chi **Marquis Who's Who Honors:** Albert Nelson Marquis Lifetime Achievement Award **Avocations:** Genealogy; Music; Skiing; Traveling; Playing piano

Deborah Borda

Title: President, Chief Executive Officer **Industry:** Media & Entertainment **Company Name:** New York Philharmonic **Date of Birth:** 7/15/1949 **Place of Birth:** New York **State/Country of Origin:** NY/USA **Parents:** William Borda; Helene (Malloy) Borda **Education:** Honorary MusD, Curtis Institute of Music; Diploma, Royal College of Music, London, England (1972-1973); BA, Bennington College (1971) **Career:** President, Chief Executive Officer, New York Philharmonic (2017-Present); President, Chief Executive Officer, Los Angeles Philharmonic (2003-2017); Executive Vice President, Managing Director, Los Angeles Philharmonic (2000-2003); Executive Director, New York Philharmonic, New York, NY (1991-1999); President, Minnesota Orchestra, Minneapolis, MN (1990-1991); Executive Director, Detroit Symphony Orchestra (1988-1990); President, St. Paul Chamber Orchestra (1986-1988); General Manager, San Francisco Symphony (1979-1986); General Manager, Handel And Haydn Society, Boston, MA (1977-1979); Manager, Boston Musica Viva, Boston, MA (1976-1977); Program Director, Massachusetts Council on Arts and the Humanities, Boston, MA (1974-1976) **Civic:** Leader-in-Residence, Harvard Kennedy School's Center for Public Leadership (2015) **Awards:** John C. Argue Dickens Medal of Honor; Charles Flint Kellogg Award in Arts and Letters **Memberships:** David C. Bohnett Presidential Chair, Los Angeles Philharmonic Association

Walter Borenstein

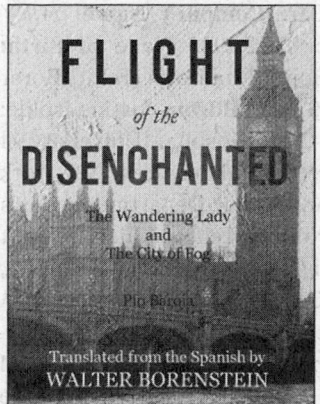

Title: Professor **Industry:** Education/Educational Services **Company Name:** State University of New York at New Paltz **Date of Birth:** 03/31/1927 **Place of Birth:** Brooklyn **State/Country of Origin:** NY/USA **Parents:** Morris Joseph; Lillian (Ross) B. **Marital Status:** Married **Spouse Name:** Audrey M. Farrell **Children:** Jeffrey T.; Shari R **Education:** PhD, University of Illinois (1954); MA, University of Illinois (1949); BA, University of Illinois (1947); Coursework, City College of New York (1942-1945) **Career:** Professor Emeritus, State University of New York at New Paltz (1992-Present); Professor, State University of New York at New Paltz (1971-1992);Coordinator, Spanish, State University of New York, at New Paltz (1980-1992); Chairman, State University of New York at New Paltz (1970-1980);Associate Professor, Spanish, State University of New York at New Paltz (1971-1992); Associate Professor, Cornell College, Mount Vernon, IA (1964-1969); Associate Professor, Louisiana State University, Baton Rouge, LA (1961-1964); Assistant Professor, Louisiana State University, Baton Rouge, LA (1957-1961); Instructor, Louisiana State University, Baton Rouge, LA (1954-1957) **Career Related:** Student Advisor (1954-Present) **Civic:** American Legion **Military Service:** United States Navy (1945-1946) **Creative Works:** Editor, "North America Review," (1965-1968); Author, "Flight of the Deschanted"; Author, "The Wandering Lady"; Author, "The City of Fog"; Author, "Two Novels of Pio Baroja"; Contributor, Articles on 20th Century Spanish Literature, Professional Journals; Translator, 8 Spanish Novels, Short Stories; Author, Short Stories, Professional Magazines **Awards:** Ford Foundation Fellow (1967); Honorable Mention for Short Story (1967) **Memberships:** Modern Language Association; American Association of Teachers of Spanish and Portuguese; American Association of University Professors **Marquis Who's Who Honors:** Albert Nelson Marquis Lifetime Achievement Award; Marquis Who's Who Top Professional **To what do you attribute your success:** Dr. Borenstein credits his professor, John Van Horne, with inspiring him to become a Spanish language professor. He has always sought to become just as successful as Mr. Van Horne. **Why did you become involved in your profession or industry:** After the war, Dr. Borenstien attended the University of Illinois. It was here that he met his favorite professor, John Van Horne. He was very famous in his career through his work in Spanish plays, which inspired Dr. Borenstein. **Political Affiliations:** Democrat **Religion:** Jewish

Jeffrey Stephen Borer, MD

Title: Professor of Medicine **Industry:** Medicine & Health Care **Company Name:** SUNY Downstate University of the Health Sciences **Date of Birth:** 02/22/1945 **Place of Birth:** Deland **State/Country of Origin:** FL/USA **Parents:** Lee Norton Borer; Rita Doris (Feldt) Borer **Marital Status:** Married **Spouse Name:** Brondi Beth Topchik (1978) **Children:** Justine Isolde; Jon Andrew **Education:** Visiting Fellow, Cardiac Department, Guy's Hospital, University of London, London, England (1974-1975); Glorney-Raisbeck Fellow, Medical Sciences, New York Academy of Medicine (1974-1975); Senior Fulbright-Hays Scholar, Cardiac Department, Guy's Hospital, University of London, London, England (1974-1975); Cardiology Fellow, Chief Resident Physician, National Heart, Lung and Blood Institute, National Institutes of Health, Bethesda, MD (1971-1974); Assistant Resident, Medicine, Massachusetts General Hospital, Boston, MA (1970-1971); Clinical Fellow, Medicine, Harvard University, Cambridge, MA, Boston, MA (1969-1971); Intern, Medicine, Massachusetts General Hospital, Boston, MA (1969-1970); MD, Weill Cornell Medicine, Cornell University (1969); BA, Government, Harvard College, Cum Laude (1965); Diploma, Wingate High School (1961) **Certifications:** Diplomate, Certification Board of Nuclear Cardiology (1996); Diplomate, Subspecialty Board of Cardiovascular Disease (1975); Diplomate, American Board of Internal Medicine (1973); Medical License, New York; Medical License, Washington, DC **Career:** Professor, Public Health, SUNY Downstate Medical University (2016-Present); Professor, Surgery, SUNY Downstate Medical University (2009-Present); Professor, Cell Biology, SUNY Downstate Medical University (2009-Present); Professor, Radiology, SUNY Downstate Medical University (2009-Present); Professor, Medicine, SUNY Downstate Medical University (2009-Present); Adjunct Professor, Cardiovascular Medicine in Cardiothoracic Surgery, Weill Cornell Medicine, Cornell University (2008-Present); Chairman, Schiavonne Cardiovascular Translational Research Institute, SUNY Downstate Medical University (2008-Present); Chairman, Howard Gilman Institute for Heart Valve Disease, SUNY Downstate Medical University (2008-Present); Chairman, Department of Medicine, SUNY Downstate Medical University (2009-2013); Chief, Division of Cardiovascular Medicine, SUNY Downstate Medical University (2008-2015); Director, Howard Gilman Institute for Heart Valve Disease, Weill Cornell Medicine, Cornell University (2000-2008); Chief, Cardiovascular Pathophysiology Division, Weill Cornell Medicine, Cornell University (1996-2008); Professor, Cardiovascular Medicine in Cardiothoracic Surgery, Weill Cornell Medicine (1996-2008); Chief, Division of Cardiovascular Pathophysiology, Department of Medicine, New York-Presbyterian/Weill Cornell Medical Center (1996-2007); Professor, Cardiovascular Medicine in Radiology, Weill Cornell Medicine (1990-2008) **Career Related:** Chairman, Cardiovascular Devices Subcommittee of the International Standardization Organization (2016-Present); Fellow, International Academy of Cardiovascular Sciences (2011-Present); Ad Hoc Member, Cardiovascular Devices Advisory Panel, Division of Devices and Radiological Health, United States Food and Drug Administration (2009-Present); United States Valve Experts Committee, Association for the Advancement of Medical Instrumentation (2007-Present); Consultant, Circulatory Devices Advisory Committee (2004-Present) **Civic:** Chairman, Committee on Restoration and Building Preservation, Brooklyn Jewish Center (2009-Present); President, Board of Trustees, Corlette Glorney Foundation, Inc. (2000-Present); Trustee, The Glorney Foundation, New York, NY (1999-Present); Committee for the Dance Collection, The New York Public Library (1999-Present) **Military Service:** Senior Surgeon 05, U.S. Public Health Service (1976-1979); Surgeon 04, U.S. Public Health Service (1975-1976); Surgeon 04, U.S. Public Health Service (1971-1974) **Creative Works:** Editorial Board, European Heart Journal (2008-Present); Editor-in-Chief, Cardiology (2005-2015); Editor-in-Chief, "Advances in Cardiology" (2001-Present) **Awards:** Doctor of the Decade (2020); Doctor of the Year (2019); Kanu Chatterjee Lifetime Achievement Award for Contributions to Cardiovascular Medicine (2018); Award for Lifetime Achievement in Heart Valve Diseases, The Heart Valve Society of America, Society for Heart Valves Disease, London, England (2014); Legend of Cardiology Award, 10th Annual Global Summit (2014); Diversity in Cardiology Award, Association of Black Cardiologists (2013); Transforming Lives through Research Award, SUNY Downstate Medical Center (2009) **Memberships:** Board of Trustees, The Heart Valve Society (2015-Present); President, The Heart Valve Society of America (2004-2014); Chairman, Due Process and Appeals Committee, Certification Board of Nuclear Cardiology (2002-2004) **Marquis Who's Who Honors:** Marquis Who's Who Top Professional (2019); Marquis Who's Who Humanitarian Award (2019); Albert Nelson Marquis Lifetime Achievement Award (2018) **Avocations:** Sports; Theater; Opera; Calligraphy; History **Religion:** Jewish

Allen Born

Title: Chairman, Chief Executive Officer **Industry:** Financial Services **Company Name:** Born Investments LLC **Date of Birth:** 07/04/1933 **Place of Birth:** Durango **State/Country of Origin:** CO/USA **Parents:** C. S. Born; Bertha G. (Tausch) Born **Marital Status:** Married **Spouse Name:** Patricia Beaubien (03/23/1953) **Children:** Michael; Scott (Deceased); Brett **Education:** Honorary Doctorate in Engineering, Colorado School of Mines (1992); Bachelor of Science in Metallurgy and Geology, The University of Texas at El Paso (1958) **Career:** Chairman, Alumax Incorporated, New York, NY (1993-1998); Chief Executive Officer, Chairman, AMAX Inc., New York, NY (1986-2004); President, Chairman, Chief Executive Officer, Board of Directors, Placer Development Limited, Vancouver, British Columbia, Canada (1981-1985); President, AMAX of Canada Limited (1977-1981); President, Chief Executive Officer, Canada Tungsten Mining Corp. Limited (1976-1981); Chief Metallurgist and Superintendent, Manager, AMAX Inc., New York, NY (1967-1976); Assistant Superintendent, MolyCorp (1964-1967); General Foreman, Pima Mining (1962-1964); Metallurgist, Vanadium Corporation of America (1960-1962); Exploration Geologist, El Paso Natural Gas, Texas (1958-1960); Chairman, Cyprus-Amax **Career Related:** Chairman, Board, Chief Executive Officer, Alumax Incorporated (1996); Consultant, Investor in Field; Board of Directors, AMAX Gold Incorporated; International Primary Aluminum Institute; AK Steel Holding Corporation; Past Chairman, Aluminum Association; Co-Chairman, Board, Cyprus Amax Minerals Company **Civic:** Board of Trustees, Robert W. Woodruff Arts Center **Military Service:** Far East Command, United States Army (1952-1955) **Creative Works:** Contributor, Numerous Articles, Mining Journals **Awards:** Bronze Award, Financial World (1987-1989); Golden Nugget Award, College of Science, University of Texas at El Paso (1987); Chief Executive Officer of the Year in Mining Industry (1986-1992); Silver Award, All Industry Finance World Magazine (1986) **Memberships:** American Institute of Mining; National Mining Association; Sky Club of New York City; Vancouver Club; Atlanta Athletic Club; Boulders Club, Carefree, AZ **Marquis Who's Who Honors:** Albert Nelson Marquis Lifetime Achievement Award; Marquis Who's Who Top Professional **Why did you become involved in your profession or industry:** Mr. Born became involved in his profession because he wanted to discover and produce oil and gas. He was also very interested in metallurgy, because his grandfather and father were both in the mining business many years ago. He became very interested in how mines were discovered, how they were put to use, how to process what is found out of the mines and what to do with it. **Political Affiliations:** Independent **Religion:** Episcopal **Thoughts on Life:** Mr. Born lives by the philosophy, "Fix it, sell it, or shoot it."

Terry Bos

Title: President, Chief Executive Officer **Industry:** Business Management/Business Services **Company Name:** Sault Ste. Marie Airport Development Corporation **Parents:** Bernie Bos; Donna Bos **Marital Status:** Married **Spouse Name:** Kerri Bos **Children:** Stephen; Isabella **Education:** BBA in Business Administration, Algoma University, Sault Ste. Marie, Ontario, Canada (1997) **Certifications:** Accredited Airport Executive, International Association of Airport Executives Canada (IAAE Canada) (2014) **Career:** President, Chief Executive Officer, Accountable Executive, Airport Manager, Finance Manager, Sault Ste. Marie Airport Development Corporation, Ontario, Canada (1999-Present); General Labourer, Algoma Steel Inc., Sault Ste. Marie, Ontario, Canada (1997-1998) **Career Related:** Chair, International Association of Airport Executives Canada (IAAE Canada) (2019); Vice-Chair, International Association of Airport Executives Canada (IAAE Canada) (2017); Board of Directors, International Association of Airport Executives Canada (IAAE Canada) (2016); President, Airport Management Council of Ontario (AMCO) (2010); Chair, Board of Directors, Airport Management Council of Ontario (AMCO) (2010); Treasurer, Airport Management Council of Ontario (AMCO) **Awards:** Distinguished Alumni Award, Algoma University, Sault Ste. Marie, Ontario, Canada **Memberships:** International Association of Airport Executives Canada (IAAE Canada) (2006) **Marquis Who's Who Honors:** Marquis Who's Who Top Professional **To what do you attribute your success:** Mr. Bos attributes his success to dedication and hard work, as well as continually learning and listening and putting that into practice and development. **Why did you become involved in your profession or industry:** Mr. Bos became involved in his profession because he initially came to the airport to help them write their business plan. As he had the BBA and marketing background, he helped them write their business plan and they were impressed with his work and kept him at the airport. He has successfully moved up the ranks; he was in a marketing position, then became a finance manager and eventually airport manager, which worked into what he is today. He still kept the finance position because that was his background and he is good with numbers. **Thoughts on Life:** Terry Bos joined the Sault Ste. Marie Airport Development Corporation on February 28, 1999, less than one year after the transfer of the airport to a private not-for-profit corporation from the federal government. Terry was brought in on a one year contract to assist the corporation in completing their first business and land use master plan to guide them through their new airport ownership. Holding a Bachelor of Business Administration from Algoma University the business experience was an essential ingredient in the position. Following the completion of the Business and Land Use Master Plan the Corporation determined that Terry was an asset and retained him in a marketing position. On November 1, 2002 Terry was promoted to Finance Manager, on July 1, 2004 Terry was promoted to Airport Manager, on January 22, 2008 Terry was appointed Accountable Executive, on July 27, 2010 Terry was named CEO, and effective May 26, 2015 Terry was appointed as the President/CEO and Accountable Executive. During Terry's tenure as CEO the corporation has seen record passenger levels at the Sault Ste. Marie Airport increasing from a low of 121,991 in 2010 to 212,831 in 2017. Terry joined AMCO (Airport Management Council of Ontario) in the position of President at the Annual General Meeting election in 2010, and became the first and so far only President to serve a maximum four year term limit, then sat as Past President of AMCO effective November 1, 2014 to November 1, 2016 when he took on the position of AMCO treasurer. He was re-elected for a second term as treasurer, effective November 1, 2018. Terry has been a member of IAAE Canada (International Association of Airport Executives Canada) since 2006 and achieved the Accredited Airport Executive designation in October 2014. Terry joined the Board of Directors for IAAE Canada in June 2016. After joining the board Terry took on the role of Chair of the Accreditation Committee and Chair of the Board of Examiners and in 2017 IAAE Canada achieved their highest number of newly certified members since inception. In 2017 Terry also took on the position of Vice-Chair for IAAE Canada, and after serving as Vice-Chair of IAAE Canada for two years, Terry took on the role of Chair for IAAE Canada in 2019.

George "Bill" Bouffioux

Title: Owner, Manager **Industry:** Agriculture **Company Name:** XY Bison Ranch, Ltd. **Date of Birth:** 06/21/1942 **Place of Birth:** Fort St. John **State/Country of Origin:** BC/Canada **Marital Status:** Married **Spouse Name:** Fayette (06/25/1963) **Children:** Sandra Lee Bunche; Cynthia Ann Donnelly **Education:** Associate Degree in Farm Mechanics, SAIT, Calgary, Alberta, Canada, with Honors (1963) **Career:** Owner, Manager, XY Bison Ranch, Ltd. (1989-Present) **Career Related:** Executive, President, Canadian Bison Association; President, British Columbia Bison Association **Creative Works:** Winner, International Bison Conference Poster Contest (2000); Featured, Cover Photo, North American Livestock Journal **Awards:** Bareback Trophy, Northwest Pro Rodeo Association (1963); 15 Grand Champion Trophies; Various XY Ranch Awards **Memberships:** British Columbia Bison Association; Canadian Bison Association **Marquis Who's Who Honors:** Albert Nelson Marquis Lifetime Achievement Award **To what do you attribute your success:** Mr. Bouffioux attributes his success for excellent females, replacement bulls, and proper feeding. Additionally, he attributes it to all the family help. He remembers going to a future farmers meeting in Vancouver when he was in 11th grade - that was the first time he ever saw registered cattle, and he thought that was the way to go. That is how he got into cattle, but he would eventually switch to bison because of the workload. Bison can graze all winter long. If they are given sufficient space, they do not even need to be fed during the winter time, as they are largely self-sufficient. Mr. Bouffioux went to a few livestock shows and noticed that his bison were just as high quality as the ones shown. He started showing his bison and has been very successful with that. **Why did you become involved in your profession or industry:** Mr. Bouffioux became involved in his profession because it was one-fifth the work of cattle for three times the money. Bison are very self-sufficient with virtually no calving problems and can withstand the most severe winter without shelters. He also grew up on a farm. He and his wife bought a ranch, which had Hartford cattle for years but it got to be so much work for the family. They start calving in early March and they have to be put in the barn and watched for six weeks; it was a lot of work. They are also susceptible to more diseases, such as pink eye and foot rot. He started talking to a bison producer and found that the bison are much harder animals. They were able to cut the work load down to a tenth of what they had to do with the cattle. **Avocations:** Deep-sea fishing; Watching and participating in rodeos

Brenda Lee Bowens, CNOR, RN

Title: First Assistant **Industry:** Medicine & Health Care **Company Name:** Bronson Healthcare Systems, Battle Creek **Date of Birth:** 8/11/1954 **Place of Birth:** Flint **State/Country of Origin:** MI/USA **Parents:** James Mohn; Erma Lee (Sexton) Mohn **Marital Status:** Married **Spouse Name:** Bill Bowens (2010) **Children:** Travis; Jessica; Meighan; Danielle **Education:** BSN, University of Michigan (1990); AAS, Kellogg Community College, Battle Creek, MI (1974) **Certifications:** CNOR **Career:** First Assistant, RNFA Operating Room, Bronson Healthcare Systems, Battle Creek, MI (1992-Present); Operating Room Nurse, Battle Creek Health Systems (1992-Present); Staff Nurse, CSRU, CSU Borgess Medical Center, Kalamazoo, MI (1987-1992); Staff Nurse, Operating Room, Battle Creek Health Systems (1974-1987) **Career Related:** Clinical Instructor, Kalamazoo Community Valley College (1990-1991) **Awards:** Service Award **Memberships:** Former Member, American Association of Critical Care Nurses; Former Member, American Nurses Association; Association of Operating Room Nurses (AORN) **Marquis Who's Who Honors:** Albert Nelson Marquis Lifetime Achievement Award; Marquis Who's Who Top Professional **To what do you attribute your success:** Ms. Bowens attributes her success to her mentor Joan Miller. She was the educator in the operating room. She was passionate and dedicated to nursing in general, but especially in the OR. She was the type of person who you wanted to emulate. Her enthusiasm helped me decide that this was my chosen career path. **Why did you become involved in your profession or industry:** Ms. Bowens became involved in her profession because she was always interested in nursing and health care, and that's where she decided to pursue her career. There weren't many career choices for women at that time. It was either nursing or teaching, and she was not interested in teaching. In addition, It was the cool hats and the scrubs that the nurses wore. There weren't a lot of career choices then. Nursing has become so diverse today and it offers many more opportunities. **Thoughts on Life:** If you stay focused, you can achieve anything.

Maurice Donald "Bugs" Bower

Title: Record Company President, Producer, Composer, Arranger, Teacher **Industry:** Media & Entertainment **Company Name:** Dr. Maurice "Bugs" Bower **Date of Birth:** 07/16/1922 **Place of Birth:** Atlantic City **State/Country of Origin:** NJ/USA **Parents:** Fred Bower; Rhea Bower **Marital Status:** Partner **Spouse Name:** Kathryn Stanley Podwall **Children:** Nancy Coker (Deceased 08/01/2019); Lizz Larsen **Education:** MusD, Five Towns College, Dix Hills, NY (1980); Coursework, Julliard School of Music **Civic:** Volunteer, Veterans Hospitals & Music Schools **Military Service:** 89th Infantry Division, U.S. Army (1942-1946) **Creative Works:** Author, Over 30 Music Books Including "Chords and Progressions and Rhythms"; Producer, "Hollywood Swinging," "Jungle Boogie," "Celebration," "Itsy-Bitsy-Teeny Weeny Yellow Polka Dot Bikini," "Walk Hand in Hand With Me," "The Mission of St. Augustine," "Aerobic Dancing," "Aerobic Shape Up," "Tijuana Christmas," Others; Author, "Nice Stories About Nice People" **Awards:** Paul Harris Fellow Award, Rotary International; Inductee, Nassau County Veteran's Wall of Honor; U.S. Holocaust Memorial Consul Award for Opening Camp Ohrdruf, Germany; 12 Gold Record Million Seller Awards; Grammy Award for Best Children's Recording of the Year, "The Little Prince"; Grammy Award for Best Spoken Word Recording of the Year, "Everything You Always Wanted to Know About Home Computers" **Memberships:** Rotary International **Marquis Who's Who Honors:** Marquis Who's Who Top Professional **To what do you attribute your success:** Mr. Bower's father, Fred Bower, was a music arranger and he learned to compose, arrange and publish music from him. **Why did you become involved in your profession or industry:** Mr. Bower grew up in Atlantic City, New Jersey. He aspired to be like the famous trumpeter, Harry James. His father decided to send him to New York to study because New York had the best music teachers. After graduating high school, he worked for the Miss America Beauty Pageant in the local convention hall. Then, he proceeded to Long Island, New York.

Grant C. Boyd, JD

Title: Attorney **Industry:** Law and Legal Services **Company Name:** O'Brien Law Firm **Date of Birth:** 05/13/1988 **Place of Birth:** St. Louis **State/Country of Origin:** MO/USA **Parents:** Larry Boyd; Lisa Friedman-Boyd **Marital Status:** Single **Education:** JD, Saint Louis University School of Law (2014); BA in Psychology and Legal Studies, Saint Louis University (2010) **Career:** Attorney, O'Brien Law Firm, (2020-Present); Junior Partner, Sindel Noble, St. Louis, MO (2014-2020) **Civic:** United Way; Tiny Super Heroes; St. Louis Junior Blues Hockey Organization **Awards:** Super Lawyers Rising Star (2020); Missouri Lawyers Awards Legal Champion (2020); Super Lawyers Rising Star (2019); Missouri Lawyers Top Settlements Award (2018); Super Lawyers Rising Star (2018); Top 10 out of 40 Attorneys Award, National Association of Collegiate Directors of Athletics (2017); Super Lawyers Rising Star (2017); Top 10 Attorneys Under 40 (2017); 30 Under 30, St. Louis Business Journal (2016); Milton F. Napier Award for Excellence in Trial Skills, Lawyer's Association of St. Louis (2014) **Memberships:** National Crime Victim Bar Association; American Association for Justice; Bar Association of Metropolitan St. Louis; Missouri Association of Trial Attorneys **Bar Admissions:** United States District Court for the Western District of Missouri; United States District Court for the Eastern District of Missouri; United States District Court for the Southern District of Illinois **Marquis Who's Who Honors:** Marquis Who's Who Top Professional **To what do you attribute your success:** Mr. Boyd attributes his success to the many mentors who taught him how to "get his hands dirty." **Why did you become involved in your profession or industry:** Mr. Boyd became involved in his profession after leaving his undergraduate pre-med program and switching to law. Mr. Boyd interned at local public defender's offices and was eventually hired by Sindel Noble as a law clerk and then an attorney. **Avocations:** Ice hockey; Cooking

Arnie Rolf Braafladt

Title: Deputy Chief Counsel (Retired) **Industry:** Law and Legal Services **Company Name:** California School Employees Association **Date of Birth:** 10/17/1951 **Place of Birth:** Moorehead **State/Country of Origin:** MN/USA **Parents:** Halvor John Braafladt; Arlene Olga (Johnson) Lumley **Marital Status:** Divorced **Spouse Name:** Nancy Jeanne Holmes (08/1976, Divorced 1990) **Children:** Nicole Yvonne Farrell; Sarah Arlene Shaffer **Education:** JD, Willamette University (1978); MA in Urban Studies, Occidental College (1976); AB in Political Science and Journalism, Humboldt State University, Magna Cum Laude (1974) **Certifications:** Licensed, States of Oregon, Washington and California **Career:** Retired (2017); Deputy Chief Counsel, California School Employees Association (2007-2017); Senior Staff Counsel, California School Employees Association (2001-2006); Staff Attorney, California School Employees Association (1993-2001); Lawyer and Labor Relations Manager, Oregon Executive Department (1992); Deputy Legislative Counsel, Oregon Legislature (1991); Associate, Howser & Munsell, Ashland, OR (1989-1990); Partner, Shields & Braafladt, Eureka, CA (1982-1988); Deputy Legislative Counsel, Oregon Legislature, Salem, OR (1980-1982); Law Clerk to Presiding Justice, Washington Supreme Court, Olympia, WA (1979-1980) **Career Related:** Lecturer of Media Law, Humboldt State University, Arcata, CA (1983); Legal Counsel, Student Newspaper, The Lumberjack (1984) **Civic:** Board of Directors, Redwood Community Action Agency (1985-1986); Chairman, Vice Chairman, Humboldt County Democratic Central Committee, CA (1974); Active, Various Political Campaigns (1972-1978) **Creative Works:** Associate Editor, Willamette Law Journal (1977-1978); Contributor, Articles to Professional Journals **Awards:** Bill Farr Freedom of Press Award, California Society of Newspaper Editors and Freedom Information Committee (1987); Freedom of Information Award, Northern California Chapter, Society of Professional Journalists (1987); Named Outstanding Associate Editor, Willamette Law Journal (1978); Fellow, Coro Foundation (1974-1975) **Memberships:** Advisor, Executive Committee, Labor and Employment Law Section, State Bar of California (2012-2016); Executive Committee, Labor and Employment Law Section, State Bar of California (2007-2012); President, Humboldt State University Alumni Association (1987-1988); Vice President, Humboldt State University Alumni Association (1986-1987); Board of Directors, Humboldt State University Alumni Association (1985-1987); California Bar Association; Oregon Bar Association; Washington State Bar Association; Association of Trial Lawyers of America (Now American Association for Justice); California Trial Lawyers Association; Green Key Society; Golden Key International Honour Society; American Constitution Society **Bar Admissions:** United States District Court for the District of Oregon (1987); United States Court of Appeals for the Ninth Circuit (1984); United States District Court for the Northern District of California (1984); Washington (1981); California (1980); Oregon (1978) **Marquis Who's Who Honors:** Albert Nelson Marquis Lifetime Achievement Award; Marquis Who's Who Top Professional **To what do you attribute your success:** Mr. Braafladt attributes his success to his dedication, tenacity, resilience, scholarship, writing and advocacy skills, and his passion for and devotion to fairness and justice. **Why did you become involved in your profession or industry:** Mr. Braafladt always thought he would go to law school eventually; he spent the years after Humboldt with a public affair fellowship in San Francisco, which was a really great experience for him coming from a rural area like Humboldt county. Spending a year in San Francisco was a great exposure to an urban environment and he never expected that he would live so many years there. San Jose is a very large city and very diverse. It's been beneficial. **Avocations:** Camping; Hiking; Travel **Political Affiliations:** Democrat **Religion:** Lutheran

Everette Arnold Braden, JD

Title: Lawyer, Judge **Industry:** Law and Legal Services **Company Name:** Everette A. Braden, Attorney at Law **Date of Birth:** 11/03/1932 **Place of Birth:** Chicago **State/Country of Origin:** IL/USA **Parents:** Zedrick Thomas Braden; Bernice (Beckwith) Braden **Marital Status:** Married **Spouse Name:** Mary Jeanette Hemphill (09/26/1964) **Children:** Marilynne **Education:** JD, John Marshall Law School, Chicago, IL (1961); BS, Northwestern University, Evanston, IL (1954); LLB, John Marshall Law School, Chicago, IL **Certifications:** Supreme Court of the United States (1990); United States District Court for the Northern District of Illinois (1969) **Career:** Associate Judge, Office of the Clerk of the Circuit Court of Cook County, Chicago, IL (1977-1987); Supervising Trial Attorney, Law Office of the Cook County Public Defender, Chicago, IL (1976-1977); Trial Attorney, Law Office of the Cook County Public Defender, Chicago, IL (1969-1976); Property and Insurance Consultant, Cook County Sheriff's Office, Chicago, IL (1961-1969); Lawyer, Everette A. Braden Attorneys **Civic:** Board of Directors, LAF (1977); Vice President, Southeast CDC; President, South Shore Valley Community Organization; President, Board of Trustees, Illinois Bar Foundation; Secretary, Board of Trustees, St. Mark's United Methodist Church; NAACP; Illinois Congress of Parents and Teachers; Board of Directors, DuSable High School Alumni Coalition for Action; Board of Commissioners, Cook County, IL; Supervising Judge, Child Support Enforcement Court, Cook County, IL; Justice, Illinois Appellate Court **Awards:** Chairman Emeritus and Lifetime Achievement Award, Illinois Judicial Council Foundation (2017); Man of the Year, St. Mark's United Methodist Church (2012); Court of Honor, Chicago Volunteer Legal Services (2000); Meritorious Service Award, Cook County Bar Association; Award of Merit, Illinois Judges Association; Distinguished Service Award, The John Marshall Law School; Community Service Award, MRT Scholarship Foundation; 33rd Degree Grand Inspector General, Prince Hall Mason; Award in Recognition of Outstanding Accomplishments and Dedicated Service to the Legal Community, The Black Law Students Association; Chairperson's Award for Outstanding Leadership, Illinois Judicial Council; Award for Outstanding Community Service, Geneva Scott Outreach Services; Inductee, Hall of Fame, Cook County Bar Association; Mary Merrick Lifetime Achievement Award; Action Award for Distinguished Achievement in the Legal and Judicial System and Continuing Dedication to DuSable High School and the Alumni Coalition; Honoree, Senior Counselor, Cook County Bar Association; Trailblazer Award, Troop 534, Boy Scouts of America; Award for Service to Freemasonry, Masons; Founder's Award, Illinois Judicial Council; Certificate of Excellence, Board of Directors, The Mary Herrick Scholarship Fund; Recognized as One of the 100 Top Lawyers in the Country; **Memberships:** President, John Marshall Law School Alumni Association (1990-1991); Second Vice President, John Marshall Law School Alumni Association (1988-1990); Board of Directors, Illinois Judges Association (1985-1991); Chairman, Illinois Judicial Council (1985-1986); Secretary, Illinois Judicial Council (1982-1984); Treasurer, Illinois Judges Association (1980-1981); Chairman, General Practice Section, Illinois State Bar Association (1979-1980); President, Cook County Bar Association (1975-1976); Illinois Bar Foundation; Lions Club International; The Chicago Assembly; Kappa Alpha Psi Fraternity, Inc.; Board of Directors, Phi Alpha Delta Law Fraternity, International; Northwestern University Alumni Association; Honorary Life Member, Prince Hall Masons; Board of Directors, Mary Merrick Scholarship Fund; National Bar Association **Bar Admissions:** Illinois State Bar Association (1969) **Marquis Who's Who Honors:** Albert Nelson Marquis Lifetime Achievement Award; Marquis Who's Who Top Professional **To what do you attribute your success:** Mr. Braden attributes his success to his helpful nature and passion for the work he does. **Why did you become involved in your profession or industry:** Mr. Braden became involved in his profession because of his father, who was an attorney. He was additionally inspired by his brother, who was also an attorney. His brother has two sons who are lawyers, and his sister has a son who is a lawyer. It was a natural progression given his family history. Another inspiration came from Col. Charles Cain. When he left the army, he was interviewed by him, and he said to him "the main purpose in life is to help someone else, beginning with your family." He told him that when he comes to Chicago, IL, he wants to hear that he is one of the best lawyers. His father had a saying "where ever men congregate there should be a lawyer there".

David G. Bradley

Title: Owner, Publishing Executive **Industry:** Publishing **Company Name:** Atlantic Media **Place of Birth:** Washington, DC **State/Country of Origin:** DC/USA **Marital Status:** Married **Spouse Name:** Katherine Brittain Bradley **Education:** JD, Georgetown University Law Center (1983); MBA, Harvard Business School; BA, Swarthmore College **Career:** Owner, The Atlantic Monthly, Washington, DC (2005-Present); Owner, National Journal Group (1997-Present); Owner, Quartz (2012-2018); Owner, The Atlantic Monthly, Boston, MA (1999-2005); Chairman, Owner, Atlantic Media, Washington, DC **Career Related:** Professor, University of the City of Manila **Civic:** Founder, The Corporate Executive Board Company (Now Gartner), Washington, DC (1997); Founder, The Advisory Board Company (Advisory Board Acquired by Optum) (1976); Board Member, Council on Foreign Relations; Board Member, New America; Board Member, KIPP DC Public Charter School; Board Member, Bridges of Understanding; Board Member, Child Protection Network, Philippine General Hospital, Manila **Awards:** Named, One of the 50 Most Powerful People in DC, GQ Magazine (2007); Fulbright Scholar **Political Affiliations:** Centrist

Richard Eugene Bradshaw

Title: Chief Executive Officer **Industry:** Oil & Energy **Company Name:** Atlas Energy Technologies Inc. **Date of Birth:** 01/15/1950 **Place of Birth:** Rocky Mount **State/Country of Origin:** NC/USA **Parents:** Harvey Edmond Bradshaw; Grace Darling (Cowley) Bradshaw **Marital Status:** Married **Spouse Name:** Pamela A. Lacey (06/03/1989) **Children:** Douglas E. N. Bradshaw **Education:** Postgraduate Work, University of South Carolina (1977-1978); Master of Arts in International Relations, East Carolina University, Summa Cum Laude (1977); Bachelor of Arts in Political Science and History, The University of North Carolina at Chapel Hill (1974) **Career:** Chief Executive Officer, Atlas Energy Technologies Inc., Washington, DC (2012-Present); Principal, Stirling Strategic Services LLC, Washington, DC (2001-2012); Special Assistant to the Secretary of Energy, U.S. Department of Energy, Washington, DC (1997-2000); Staff Adviser, International Monetary Fund, Washington, DC (1995-1996); Principal, North Atlantic Research Inc., Washington, DC (1993-1995); Program Director, International Division, National Science Foundation, Washington, DC (1987-1993); Assistant Professor, George Mason University, Fairfax, VA (1987-1993); Foreign Service Officer, U.S. Department of State, Washington, DC (1978-1983); Foreign Service Officer, U.S. Department of State, Paris, France (1978-1983); Director, Center for the Study of International Technology Transfer, George Mason University, Fairfax, VA; Consultant, North American Telecommunications Association; Consultant, Washington Nichibei Consultant **Career Related:** Liaison, Personal Adviser, Energy & Water Appropriations Subcommittee, U.S. Department of Energy (2000); Visiting Fellow, George Mason University, Arlington, VA (1996-1998); Volunteer Staff Member, Finance Committee, Clinton Re-election Campaign (1996); Adviser, Bill Clinton for President Campaign (1992); Committee on European Integration in Science & Technology, National Science Foundation **Civic:** Presidential Inauguration Financial Committee Staff, Clinton/Gore (1997); Campaign Staff, Clinton/Gore (1996); Policy Coordinator for Sciences and Technology Issues, Bill Clinton for Presidency Campaign (1992) **Military Service:** With, U.S. Army (1972-1973) **Creative Works:** Co-author, "Technology for America's Economic Growth, A New Direction to Build Economic Strength" (1992); Author, "Technology: The Engine of Economic Growth" (1992); Contributor, "The Politics of North Korea" (1978); Contributor, "Journal of Maritime Law and Commerce, Vol. 10"; Author, "S&T Integration in Europe and Influences on U.S.-European Cooperation," National Science Foundation; Author, "White Paper on European Community S&T," Executive Office of the President; Contributor, Articles and Reports, Professional Journals **Awards:** Several Awards, U.S. Department of Energy **Memberships:** American Council on Renewable Energy (2001-Present); Pi Sigma Alpha **Marquis Who's Who Honors:** Albert Nelson Marquis Lifetime Achievement Award **Why did you become involved in your profession or industry:** During Mr. Bradshaw's undergraduate years at the the University of North Carolina at Chapel Hill, he decided he wanted a career in the foreign service. His goal was to serve his country by helping resolve conflicts peacefully and by assisting foreigners in better understanding the U.S. better. At that time, it was exceedingly difficult to get into the foreign service; candidates had to take a series of written and oral examinations. It took Mr. Bradshaw a couple of tries before he was offered an appointment. **Avocations:** Golf; Fitness; Sailing; Coaching Little League baseball **Political Affiliations:** Democrat **Religion:** Episcopalian

P. James "Jim" Brady, CPA

Title: Vice Chair **Industry:** Financial Services **Company Name:** alliantgroup, LP **Parents:** Patrick James Brady Junior (Deceased 2016) **Marital Status:** Married **Spouse Name:** Barbara (1996) **Children:** Alex (22); Chris (20) **Education:** BSBA in Business Administration, Bryant University, Summa Cum Laude; **Certifications:** Certified Public Accountant, NSABA **Career:** Vice Chair, alliantgroup, LP (2019-Present); Chief Operating Officer, U.S. Grant Thornton, LLP (2015-2019); Partner, Deloitte & Touche, LLP (1988-2015); Certified Public Accountant, Deloitte; Chief Operating Officer, Grant Thornton **Civic:** Board Member, Networked (2019-Present); Advisory Board, Bridgei2i Analytics; Board Member, Board of Trustee, Chair, Chautauqua Institution; Board Member, VisionSpring; Chairman, Deans Council, Business School **Awards:** Lifetime Achievement Alumni Award, Bryant University **Marquis Who's Who Honors:** Marquis Who's Who Top Professional **To what do you attribute your success:** Mr. Brady attributes his success to his overseas assignments in Moscow from 1995 to 1998, as well as 10 years later in India from 2008 to 2012. He lived aboard twice. **Why did you become involved in your profession or industry:** Mr. Brady's college Professor Michael Lynch inspired him to go into his profession.In addition, he chose the career path growing up as a teenager and looking up to his grandfather and father being business people. They were both in consumer electronics. **Avocations:** Tennis; Boating

Rev. Stephen Jon Brandow, MDiv

Title: Staff Chaplain-Alexandria VA Healthcare System/Catholic Priest **Industry:** Religious **Company Name:** The Diocese of Alexandria **Date of Birth:** 12/25/1960 **Place of Birth:** Olean **State/Country of Origin:** NY/USA **Parents:** David Arden Brandow; Jacqueline Delores (Johns) Brandow **Education:** MDiv, Notre Dame Seminary Graduate School of Theology (1996); BA in Social Work, Northwestern State University (1985); BA, Northwestern State University (1983) **Certifications:** Ordained to Ministry, Catholic Church (1996) **Career:** Staff Chaplain, US Department of Veterans Affairs, Alexandria, LA (2000-Present); Associate Pastor, Immaculate Heart of Mary Parish, Tioga, LA (1997-2000); Associate Pastor, St. Rita Parish, Alexandria, LA (1996-1997); Medical Clerk, Alexandria VA Health Care System, US Department of Veterans Affairs (1986-1991); Social Worker, Woodview Regional Hospital, Pineville, LA (1986) **Career Related:** Chaplain, Alexandria VA Health Care System, U.S. Department of Veterans Affairs (1998-Present); Committee Member, Continuing Formation of Clergy (1996-Present); Appointed Chaplain, VISN 16 (Chapter Area) (2019); Chaplain, CHRISTUS St. Frances Cabrini Hospital, Alexandria, LA (1997-2001); Chaplain, Central Louisiana State Hospital, Louisiana State Department of Health (1997-2000); Secretary, Diocese of Alexandria, Louisiana (1996-1997) **Civic:** Member, Community Advisory Board, Louisiana Purchase Council, Boy Scouts of America (2003-Present); Member, National Catholic Committee on Scouting (1997-Present); Board of Directors, Council of Central Louisiana, Girl Scouts of the United States of America (2001-2002); Vice President, Louisiana Purchase Council, Boy Scouts of America **Awards:** Bronze Pelican, National Catholic Committee on Scouting (2003); Whitney M. Young Jr. Service Award, Boy Scouts of America (2002); James E. West Fellowship (2002) **Memberships:** Board of Directors, Louisiana Chaplains Association, Inc. (1999-2002); American Association of Christian Counselors; National Conference of Veterans Affairs Catholic Chaplains; Chairman of the Board, NAVAC; National Association of Catholic Chaplains **Marquis Who's Who Honors:** Albert Nelson Marquis Lifetime Achievement Award; Marquis Who's Who Top Professional; Marquis Who's Who Humanitarian Award **Avocations:** Yoga

Richard Charles Nicholas Branson

Title: Entrepreneur, Philanthropist **Industry:** Business Management/Business Services **Company Name:** Virgin **Date of Birth:** 07/18/1950 **Place of Birth:** London **State/Country of Origin:** United Kingdom **Parents:** Edward James Branson; Eve (Huntley Flindt) Branson **Marital Status:** Married **Spouse Name:** Joan Templeman (12/20/1989); Kristen Tomassi (07/22/1972, Divorced 1979) **Children:** Sam; Holly; Clare **Education:** Honorary Doctor, Honoris Causa, Kaunas Technology University, Kaunas, Lithuania (2013); Honorary Doctor of Technology, Loughborough University (1993) **Career:** Founder, Chairman, Virgin Group Ltd. (1986-Present); Founder, Virgin Comics (2006); Founder, Virgin Mobile (Sold to NTL: Telewest) (1999-2006); Founder, V2 Records (1996); Founder, Virgin Trains (1993); Founder, Virgin Atlantic Airways (1984); Founder, Virgin Records (Sold to EMI) (1972-1992); Founder, Virgin Mail Order Company (1970); Founder, Virgin Express, Virgin Megastores, Virgin Books, Virgin Galactic, Others **Career Related:** Founder, Virgin Health Bank, London, United Kingdom (2007-Present); President, UK 2000 (1988-Present); Founder, Branson School of Entrepreneurship (2006); Director, Intourist Moscow Ltd. (1988-1990); Chairman, UK 2000 (1986-1988) **Civic:** Commissioner, Broadband Commission for Digital Development (2010-Present); Co-founder, The Elders (2007-Present); Co-founder, Virgin Unite (2004-Present); Founding Sponsor, The International Centre for Missing and Exploited Children (1999); Trustee, Virgin Healthcare Foundation; Signatory, Global Zero **Creative Works:** Author, "The Virgin Way: Everything I Know About Leadership" (2014); Author, "Reach for the Skies: Ballooning, Birdmen and Blasting into Space" (2011); Author, "Screw Business as Usual" (2011); Author, "Business Stripped Bare: Adventures of a Global Entrepreneur" (2010); Appearance, TV Series, "Entourage" (2010); Author, "Screw It, Let's Do It: Lessons in Life" (2006); Appearance, Film, "Superman Returns" (2006); Executive Producer, TV Series, "The Rebel Billionaire: Branson's Quest for the Best" (2004); Actor, "Around the World in 80 Days" (2004); Author, "Losing My Virginity: How I've Survived, Had Fun, and Made a Fortune Doing Business My Way" (1998); Appearance, TV Series, "Friends" (1998); Founder, Student Magazine (1966) **Awards:** Named One of the World's Richest People, Forbes Magazine (1999-Present); Named Citizen of the Year, UNCA (2007); Named One of the World's Most Influential People, Time Magazine (2007); Named to 50 Who Matter Now, Business 2.0, CNNMoney.com (2006); Named Knight Commander for Services to Entrepreneurship, Most Excellent Order of the British Empire, Her Majesty Queen Elizabeth II (1999)

W. Robert Brazelton, PhD

Title: Professor Emeritus **Industry:** Education/ Educational Services **Company Name:** University of Missouri-Kansas City **State/Country of Origin:** OK/USA **Parents:** Arthur Davis Brazelton; Lela Dorothy (Sautbine) Brazelton **Marital Status:** Single **Education:** PhD, Economics and Finance, Oklahoma University (1961); MA, Economic, Oklahoma University (1960); BA, Economics, Dartmouth College (1956) **Career:** Professor Emeritus (1999-Present); Professor, University of Missouri-Kansas City (1963-1999); Assistant Professor, Kansas State University (1961-1963); Instructor, University of Wisconsin-Milwaukee (1961) **Career Related:** Editor, Southwestern Journal of Economic Abstracts (1979-1989); Editorial Review Board Chairman, Journal of Economics (1988) **Civic:** Board of Directors, Omicron Delta Epsilon Fraternity in Economics **Creative Works:** Author, "U.S. Economic Policy: An Analytical Biography of Leon H. Keyserling," Wiley Press (2001); Author, "Alternate Paradigm in Economic" (1987); Contributor, Articles, Professional Journals; Contributor, Chapter, "Economica" **Memberships:** President, Missouri Valley Economic Association (1986); President, Central Slavic Association (1985); American Economic Association; Midwest Economic Association; Southwest Economic Association; Association for Comparative Economics **Marquis Who's Who Honors:** Albert Nelson Marquis Lifetime Achievement Award; Marquis Who's Who Top Professional **Why did you become involved in your profession or industry:** Mr. Brazelton became involved in his profession because of his interest in public affairs and economic affairs. **Avocations:** Travel

Allen Eugene Brennecke, Esq.

Title: Attorney at Law **Industry:** Law and Legal Services **Company Name:** Moore, McKibben, Goodman & Lorenz, LLP **Date of Birth:** 01/08/1937 **Place of Birth:** Marshalltown **State/Country of Origin:** IA/USA **Parents:** Arthur Lynn Brennecke; Julia Alice (Allen) Brennecke **Marital Status:** Married **Spouse Name:** Billie Jean Johnstone (1958) **Children:** Scott; Stephen; Beth; Gregory; Kristen **Education:** JD, College of Law, University of Iowa (1961); BBA, University of Iowa (1959) **Career:** Counsel, Moore, McKibben, Goodman & Lorenz, LLP., Marshalltown, IA (2000); Partner, Moore, McKibben, Goodman & Lorenz, LLP., Marshalltown, IA (1966-2000); Associate, Moore, McKibben, Goodman & Lorenz, LLP., Marshalltown, IA (1962-1966); Law Clerk, United States District Judge, Des Moines, IA (1961-1962) **Career Related:** Fellow, American Bar Association **Civic:** First United Methodist Church, Marshalltown, IA (1978-1981, 1987-1989); Board of Trustees, Iowa Law School Foundation (1973-1986); Finance Chairman, Republican Party, Fourth Congressional District, Iowa (1970-1973); Marshall County Republican Party, Iowa (1967-1970); Board of Directors, Marshalltown YMCA (1966-1971) **Creative Works:** Contributor, Articles, Professional Journals **Awards:** Award of Merit, Iowa State Bar Association (1987) **Memberships:** President, Iowa State Bar Association (1990-1991); Chairman, House of Delegates, ABA (1984-1986); Board of Directors, National Judicial College, ABA (1982-1988); Board of Governors, ABA (1982-1986); American College of Trust and Estate Counsel; American College of Tax Counsel; American Bar Foundation; Mason; Promise Keepers **Bar Admissions:** State of Iowa (1961) **Marquis Who's Who Honors:** Albert Nelson Marquis Lifetime Achievement Award; Marquis Who's Who Top Professional **To what do you attribute your success:** Mr. Brennecke attributes his success to being blessed with a wonderful wife, five children and their spouses, 19 grandchildren, three great-grandchildren, good friends, and gifts from the Lord. **Why did you become involved in your profession or industry:** Mr. Brennecke became involved in his profession upon earning a juris doctor degree, which was a great and respected degree to have for business. He was influenced by friends in college. **Avocations:** Golf; Travel; Sports **Political Affiliations:** Republican **Religion:** Methodist

Allen Brings, DMA

Title: Musician, Professor Emeritus **Industry:** Education/Educational Services **Date of Birth:** 02/24/1934 **Place of Birth:** New York **State/Country of Origin:** NY/USA **Parents:** Adam Brings; Elfrieda (Kruse) Brings **Marital Status:** Married **Spouse Name:** Genevieve Chinn (08/29/1959) **Children:** Keira **Education:** DMA in Music, Boston University, Boston, MA (1964); Postgraduate Coursework, Princeton University, Princeton, NJ (1962-1963); MA, Columbia University, New York, NY (1957); BA, Queens College, City University of New York, Queens, NY (1955) **Career:** Professor Emeritus, Queens College, City University of New York, Queens, NY (2001-Present); Teacher, Associate Director, Weston Music Center and School of the Performing Arts, Weston, CT (1960-Present); Professor of Music, Aaron Copland School of Music, Queens College, City University of New York, Queens, NY (1963-2001); Teaching Fellow, Boston University, Boston, MA (1960-1962); Instructor of Music, Bard College, Annandale-on-Hudson, New York (1959-1960) **Career Related:** Coordinator, Theory and Ear Training Program, Aaron Copland School of Music at Queens College, City University of New York, Queens, NY **Civic:** Catholic Commission on Intellectual and Cultural Affairs **Military Service:** Active Service, Second Armored Cavalry Regiment, West Germany (1957-1959) **Creative Works:** Composer, "Sinfonia da Camera" (1990); Composer, "Symphony" (1984); Composer, "Trio" (1984); Composer, "Five Pieces for Piano" (1980); Composer, "Tre Sonetti" (1975); Composer, 242 Works **Awards:** Artist Grant, Connecticut Commission on the Arts (1988); John Castellini Silver Jubilee Award, Choral Society, Queens College of the City University of New York (1983) **Memberships:** American Society of Composers, Authors & Publishers (1975-Present); Chairman, Region II, Society of Composers (1968-1971); National Association of Composers/USA; College Music Society; Vice President, Connecticut Composers; Long Island Composers Alliance; Society for Catholic Liturgy; Christian Fellowship of Art Music Composers; Phi Beta Kappa **Marquis Who's Who Honors:** Albert Nelson Marquis Lifetime Achievement Award; Marquis Who's Who Top Professional; Marquis Who's Who Humanitarian Award **Why did you become involved in your profession or industry:** As a child of immigrants from Germany, Dr. Brings was especially guided by his father, who, although he became a tool and die maker, had not only learned to play musical instruments before he came to America, but had attended live performances by some of the greatest classical singers of his time. Dr. Brings greatest influence as a child was to listen to the 78 rpm recordings he brought home from which he learned what great art is. **Avocations:** Tennis; Ballroom dancing

Gerald F. Brommer, DLitt

Title: Artist, Writer **Industry:** Writing and Editing **Date of Birth:** 01/08/1927 **Place of Birth:** Berkeley **State/Country of Origin:** CA/USA **Parents:** Edgar C. Brommer: Helen (Wall) Brommer **Marital Status:** Married **Spouse Name:** Georgia Elizabeth Pratt (12/19/1948) **Education:** DLitt, Concordia University (1985); Master of Arts, University of Nebraska (1955); Bachelor of Science in Education, Concordia College (1948); Postgraduate Coursework, Chouinard Art Institute; Postgraduate Coursework, Otis Art Institute;Postgraduate Coursework, University of Southern California; Postgraduate Coursework, University of California Los Angeles **Career:** Instructor, Lutheran High School, Los Angeles, CA (1955-1976); Instructor, Saint Paul's School, North Hollywood, CA (1948-1955) **Career Related:** Associate Artist Workshops; Tour Agy; Springmaid Watercolor Workshops; Hudson River Valley Art Workshops; Art in the Mountains Workshops; International Artists Workshops **Creative Works:** Editor, "Insight to Arts" Series (1977-Present); Author, "Discovering Art History," Fourth Edition" (2006); Author, "Emotional Content" (2003); Author, "Careers in Art," Second Edition (2001); Author, "Collage Techniques" (1994); Author, "Understanding Transparent Watercolor" (1993); Author, "Exploring Drawing" (1990); Author, "Exploring Painting" (1989); Author, "Watercolor and Collage Workshop" (1986); Author, "Careers in Art" (1984); Author, "Discovering Art History" (1981); Author, "The Art of Collage" (1978); Author, "Drawing" (1978); Author, "Landscapes" (1977); Author, "Art in your World" (1977); Author, "Art: Your Visual Environment" (1977); Author, "Movement and Rhythm" (1975); Editor, "The Design Concept Series, 10 Volumes" (1974-1975); Author, "Space" (1974); Author, "Transparent Watercolor" (1973); Author, "Relief Printmaking" (1970); Author, "Wire Sculpture" (1968); Artist, Group Exhibition, American Watercolor Society; Artist, Group Exhibition, National Watercolor Society; Artist, Group Exhibition, National Academy of Design; Artist, Group Exhibition, Royal Watercolor Society of London; Artist, One Man Exhibitions, Various Locations Artist, Permanent Collections, Various Hilton Hotels Throughout the United States; Artist, Permanent Collection, Claremont College; Artist, Permanent Collection, Pacific Telesis; Artist, Permanent Collection, Epcot Center; Artist, Permanent Collection, Harvey Mudd College; Artist, Permanent Collection, Laguna Beach Museum of Art; Artist, Permanent Collection, Springfield Art Museum, Missouri; Artist, Permanent Collection, TRW; Artist, Permanent Collection, Coca Cola Co., Kentucky; Artist, Permanent Collection, Concordia University; Artist, Permanent Collection, Utah State University; Author, 12 Video Art Presentations, Crystal Productions Inc.; Author, Set of 14 Design Posters for Schools and 10 Watercolor Posters for Schools, Crystal Productions Inc. **Awards:** Art Prize, California State Fair (1975); Art Prize, L.A. City Art Festival (1975); Art Prize, American Watercolor Society (1971); Art Prize, Watercolor USA (1973, 1970); Art Prize, L.A. City Art Festival (1970); Art Prize, American Watercolor Society (1968, 1965) **Memberships:** Treasurer, Vice President, National Watercolor Society; West Coast Watercolor Society; West Coast Watercolor Society, National Arts Club; Rocky Mountain National Watermedia Society; Watercolor USA; National Art Education Association; National Arts - New York; Philadelphia Water Color Club; Louisiana Watercolor Society; Honorary President, International Society of Acrylic Painters **Marquis Who's Who Honors:** Albert Nelson Marquis Lifetime Achievement Award **Why did you become involved in your profession or industry:** Despite encountering resistance to the idea, Mr. Brommer aspired to become an artist since coming of age, and eventually found a career where he could pursue his dreams. **Political Affiliations:** Republican **Religion:** Lutheran

Forest Clyde "Forrie" Brooks

Title: Civil Engineer, Project Manager **Industry:** Engineering **Company Name:** U.S. Army Corps of Engineers **Date of Birth:** 09/13/1947 **Place of Birth:** Seattle **State/Country of Origin:** WA/USA **Parents:** Clyde N. Brooks; Angela Teresa (Kennedy) Brooks **Marital Status:** Married **Spouse Name:** Catherine Susan (Burns) Brooks (10/15/1977) **Education:** BS in Civil Engineering, Seattle University, Seattle, WA (1970) **Certifications:** Water Resources Planner Certified, Board of Engineers for Rivers and Harbors, Fort Belvoir, VA (1980) **Career:** Project Manager, Civil Engineer, Unites States Army (GS 13), AK (2000-2012); Project Manager, Civil Engineer, Unites States Army (GS 12), Seattle, WA (1984-2000); Study Manager, Civil Engineer, Unites States Army, Seattle, WA (1973-1984); Study Manager Assistant, Civil Engineer, United States Army (GS 11), Seattle, WA (1972-1973); Hydraulic Engineer, Civil Engineer, United States Army (GS 9), Seattle, WA (1969-2012); Engineer Trainee, Civil Engineer, United States Army, Seattle, WA (1969-1971); Survey Crew Member, Civil Engineer, United States Army, Eureka, MT (1969) **Career Related:** Board of Directors, Alaska Veterans Museum (2001-2008); Board of Directors, Veterans Memorial Museum, Centralia, WA (1998-2000) **Civic:** Contributor, Athletic Program, Immaculate Conception Academy, Post Falls, Idaho (2016-Present); Participant, U.S. Masters Swimming (1985-Present); Member, Unlimiteds Unanimous, Unlimited Hydroplane Hobby Club (1968-Present); Volunteer, Track and Swimming, National Veterans Wheelchair Games, Veterans Administration, Anchorage, Alaska (2006); Volunteer, Computer Center, Iditarod Trail Sled Dog Race, Anchorage, Alaska (2000-2014); Coach, Babe Ruth Baseball, Eureka and Libby, MT (1969-1970); Volunteer, Course and Survey, Program, and Pit Tour Committees, Seattle Seafair Unlimited Hydroplane Races (1966-2000); Contributor, Athletic Program, Seattle University (1965-2000); Coach, Athletic Program, Seattle Preparatory School (1965-2000); Coach, Catholic Youth Organization, St. Edward's Parish Elementary School (Now Saint Edward Parish School), Seattle, WA (1965-1975) **Creative Works:** Designer, Retirement Home (2015-2016); Co-author, Seattle Seafair Race Program (1982-1989); Co-editor, Author, Monthly Newsletter, Unlimited News Journal (1981-1988) **Awards:** Bronze Order of the De Fleury Medal, Army Engineer Association (2012); Superior Civilian Service Award, Pacific Ocean Division, U.S. Army Corps of Engineers (2012); Board Member of the Year Award, Alaska Veterans Museum (2003, 2008); St. Ignatius Award for 35 Years Service, Seattle Prep Athletics (2000); Superior Civilian Service Award for 31 Years Exemplary Service, Northwestern Division, U.S. Army Corps of Engineers (2000); Named Federal Employee "Star", Federal Executive Board (1999); Two-time Recipient, Commander's Teamwork Award, Seattle District (1995); Quarter Century of Service Award, Seattle Preparatory School (1992); Named Engineer of the Year, Seattle District (1992); Civil Project Manager of the Year, Seattle District, U.S. Army Corps of Engineers (1989); Outstanding Achievement and Contribution Award for 20 Years of Service to Seattle University Athletics (1985) **Memberships:** Society of American Military Engineers (SAME); Alaska Veterans Museum, Veterans Memorial Museum; Motts Military Museum, Inc.; The Steamship Historical Society of America; National Building Museum; National Maritime Historical Society; Alaska Association of Masters Swimmers (Now Alaska U.S. Masters Swimming (AKMS)); The Tau Beta Pi Association, Inc.; Pi Mu Epsilon; Alpha Sigma Nu **Marquis Who's Who Honors:** Marquis Lifetime Achievement Award; Marquis Who's Who Top Professional, Who's Who in the West/America/World **To what do you attribute your success:** Mr. Brooks attributes his success to his Catholic faith trusting in Jesus Christ coupled with a long marriage to a wonderful wife. **Why did you become involved in your profession or industry:** Mr. Brooks became involved in his profession because he was always interested in civil engineering. When he was a kid, his family camped in mountain woods. While his parents were setting up camp and fixing food, he would run off to the nearest creek and play in nature's sandbox, building roads. In school days during his homework time, he would be doodling or sketching layouts of cities or homes. It was an interest he had, so when he graduated from high school, he pursued civil engineering in college. **Avocations:** Photography; Swimming; History **Political Affiliations:** Republican **Religion:** Roman Catholic **Thoughts on Life:** Mr. Brooks' motto is "pray, hope, don't worry, and trust in Jesus."

B. Thomas Brown, MD, MBA

Title: Urologist **Industry:** Medicine & Health Care **Date of Birth:** 09/30/1948 **Place of Birth:** Beckley **State/Country of Origin:** WV/USA **Parents:** Benjamin Porter Junior; Nancy Jo (Ballengee) Brown **Marital Status:** Divorced **Children:** Elizabeth Timbrook Brown, MD; J. Schuyler Brown, JD **Education:** Master of Business Administration, University of South Florida, Tampa, FL (1997); Doctor of Medicine, School of Medicine, West Virginia University, Morgantown, WV (1973); Coursework, John Hopkins University (1966-1969) **Certifications:** Diplomate, American Board of Urology (1980); Licensure, Certification, West Virginia; Licensure, Certification, Florida **Career:** Atlantic Urological Associates, Daytona Beach, FL (1990-2014); Chief of Staff, Memorial Hospital, Ormond Beach, FL (1986-1987); Chief of Urology, Halifax Medical Center, Daytona Beach, FL (1982-1984); Chief of Surgery, Memorial Hospital, Ormond Beach, FL (1980-1982); Private Practice, Daytona Beach, FL (1978-2016); Daytona Beach Urology Clinic, Daytona Beach, FL (1978-1990); Resident in Urology, University of Miami, Florida (1975-1978); Resident in Medicine, West Virginia University, Morgantown, WV (1974-1975); Surgical Intern, West Virginia University, Morgantown, WV (1973-1974) **Career Related:** Clinical Assistant Professor, Family Practice, University of South Florida, Tampa, FL (1979-Present); Surveyor, American Association for Ambulatory Health Care Realtor **Civic:** President, Board of Directors, Volusia County Cooperative Health Group (1998-Present); Chairman, Subcommittee on Prostate Cancer (2001-2004); Member, Subcommittee on Prostate Cancer (1998-2001); President, Unit Board of Directors, American Cancer Society (1998-1999); President-Elect, Unit Board of Directors, American Cancer Society (1997-1998); Board of Directors, Florida Division, American College of Surgeons (1996-2005); Vice President, Board of Directors, Partners for Community Health Group (1996-1997); Chairman, Board of Directors, Volusia County Cooperative Health Group (1994-1997); Second Vice President, Unit Board of Directors, American Cancer Society (1994-1997); Vice Chairman, Volusia County Cooperative Health Group (1993-1994); Pastor, Member, Pastor-Parish Relations Committee (1990-1994); Vice Chairman, Administrative Board, United Methodist Church (1990-1991); President, I-Care, Child Abuse, Daytona Beach, FL (1988); Past President and Board Member, Ormond Memorial Art Museum; Treasurer, President, Southeastern Section of American Urological Association; Board of Directors, American Urological Association **Creative Works:** Co-Author, "Urinary Retention in Patients with BPH Treated with Finasteride or Placebo Over 4 Years," European Urology (2000); Co-Author, "Outpatient Transurethral Resections of the Prostate with Vaporization Assistance: A Two Year Experience in a Free Standing Ambulatory Surgery Center," Journal of Urology (1997); Co-Author, "Guanethidine Sulphate in the Treatment of Autonomic Hyperreflexia," Journal of Urology (1979); Co-Author, "Bee Sting Anaphylaxis," West Virginia Medical Journal (1975); Contributor, Articles to Professional Journals **Awards:** Best Guest Feature by a Physician, Second Place, 21st Annual FMA County Medical Society Publications Contest (1998); West Virginia 4-H All Star, Milton Copeland Pyelogram Hour, Urological Association First Place (1977) **Memberships:** Chairman, Committee on Applicants, Central Florida, American College of Surgeons (1998-Present); Board of Directors, Southeastern Section, American Urological Association (1994-Present); President, Florida Urological Society (1999-2000); President, Tiger Bay Club (1998-2000); Chairman, Board of Governors, Volusia County Medical Society (1997-1998,); Second Vice President, Tiger Bay Club (1995-1997); Membership Committee, Florida Urological Society (1994-1996); Chairman, Board of Governors, Volusia County Medical Society (1994-1995); Chairman, Bylaws Committee, Florida Urological Society (1992-1994); President, Board of Governors, Volusia County Medical Society (1992-1993); Executive Committee, Florida Urological Society (1990-2001); Florida Medical Association (1990-1996); Secretary, Board of Governors, Volusia County Medical Society (1990-1991); Team Physician, Daytona Beach Quarterback Club (1987); University Club of Volusia County (1986-1989); Masons; Rotary **Marquis Who's Who Honors:** Albert Nelson Marquis Lifetime Achievement Award **Avocations:** Studying the ocean; Reading; Civic activities; Traveling to South America **Political Affiliations:** Republican **Religion:** Methodist

Brandon Scott Brown, Master HVAC, Universal CFC Mast

Title: Owner **Industry:** Architecture & Construction **Company Name:** Browns Heating & Air **Marital Status:** Married **Spouse Name:** Dara Brown (2011) **Children:** Parker; Dawson **Education:** AA in Career Studies, Heating and Air, Community College **Certifications:** Master HVAC; Universal CFC **Career:** Owner, Browns Heating & Air, Timberlake, VA (2006-Present) **Civic:** Volunteer, Challenge Sports Exchange **Awards:** Central VA Business Coalition 2019 Service Provider of the Year (2019); Named, 2018 Lynchburg Business Young Business Owner of the Year (2018); Named, Best HVAC Company, Lynchburg Living and Lynchburg Business Magazine **Memberships:** Connect (Local Networking Group) **Marquis Who's Who Honors:** Marquis Who's Who Top Professional **To what do you attribute your success:** Mr. Brown attributes his success to his faith in God and the way he was raised. He was raised in a Christian Baptist Church and was always taught to do right and give first. **Why did you become involved in your profession or industry:** Mr. Brown became involved in his profession because he came from a big family. After high school, he got an offer from a company saying if he worked for them, they would pay for him to go to community college. The longer Mr. Brown was in the business, the more he learned about the company and felt it wasn't right for him. He then decided to open his own company that treated customers with respect and kindness but still provided a high-quality job.

Lee Brown

Title: Chairman, Chief Executive Officer **Industry:** Law and Legal Services **Company Name:** Brown Group International **Date of Birth:** 10/04/1937 **Place of Birth:** Wewoka **State/Country of Origin:** OK/USA **Parents:** Andrew Brown; Zelma (Edwards) Brown **Marital Status:** Married **Spouse Name:** Frances M. Young (12/29/1995); Yvonne Carolyn Streets (07/14/1958, Deceased) **Children:** Patrick; Torri; Robyn: Jenna; Farrah (Step-Child); Ava Keitta Renya (Step-Child) **Education:** PhD in Criminology, University of California Berkeley (1970); MS in Criminology, University of California Berkeley (1968); MA in Sociology, San Jose State University (1964); BS in Criminology, Fresno State University (1960) **Career:** Chairman, Chief Executive Officer, Brown Group International (2005-Present); Herbert Autry Visiting Scholar, School of Social Sciences, Rice University (2004-2005); Mayor, City of Houston (1998-2004); Radoslav A. Tsanoff Professor of Public Affairs in the Department of Sociology and Senior Scholar in the James A. Baker III Institute for Public Policy, Rice University (1996-1997); Director, White House Office of National Drug Control Policy and Member of the President's Cabinet, United States Government (1993-1995); Distinguished University Professor, Texas Southern University (1992-1993); Police Commissioner, New York City Police Department (1990-1992); Chief of Police, Houston Police Department, Houston, TX (1982-1990); Public Safety Commissioner, Atlanta, GA (1978-1982); Director, Department of Justice Services, Multnomah County, OR (1976-1978); Sheriff, Sheriff's Department, Multnomah County, OR (1975-1976); Associate Director, Institute for Urban Affairs and Research, Professor of Public Administration and Director of Criminal Justice Programs, Howard University (1972-1974); Chairman and Professor, Department of Administration of Justice, Portland State University (1968-1972); Assistant Professor, Department of Administration of Justice, San Jose State University (1967-1968); Police Official, San Jose, California Police Department (1960-1968) **Career Related:** Research Fellow, Kennedy School of Government, Harvard University; United Nations Program for the Prevention of Crime and Treatment of Offenders, United States National Correspondent; National Research Council, Committee on Research on Law Enforcement and Criminal Justice; Member, Chairman, Education and Training Committee, National Commission on Criminal Justice Standards and Goals; National Commission on Drug-Free Schools; National Minority Advisory Council on Criminal Justice; Chairman, National Center for the Assessment of the Juvenile Justice System; Board Member, Academy of Criminal Justice Sciences; Founding Member, Chairman, Commission on Accreditation of Law Enforcement Agencies; National Commission on Higher Education for the Police; President, International Association of Chiefs of Police; Founding Member, National Association of Black Law Enforcement Executives; Founding Member, Police Executive Research Forum; Board Member, Police Foundation; Advisory Board, United States Conference of Mayors **Civic:** Past President, Executive Board, International Association of Chiefs of Police; Honorary Chairman of Board, U.S. Fund for UNICEF, Southwest Region; Board of Directors, Rock and Wrap It Up; American Leadership Forum; Board of Directors, Houston Museum of African American Culture; Board of Trustees, National Law Enforcement Museum **Creative Works:** Editor, "Policing in The 21st Century: Community Policing" (2013); Editor, "Growing UP to be Mayor" (2013); Co-Author, "Police and Society" (1981); Editor, "Neighborhood Team Policing" (1976); Editor, "Violent Crime" (1981); Co-Author, "Attitudes of Black Police Officers" (1976); Author, Numerous Articles, Book Chapters **Awards:** Silicon Valley Black Legend Award (2015); Alumnus of the Year, University of California at Berkley (2004); Honorary Doctorate, Paul Quinn College (2002); Honorary LLD, The College at Brockport, State University of New York (1995); Honorary LHD, Fresno State University (1994); Honorary HHD, Portland State University (1990); Honorary LLD, John Jay College (1985); Honorary Doctor of Public Affairs, Florida International University (1982) **Memberships:** Board of Directors, Forum Club of Houston (1987-Present); Vice President, National Organization of Black Law Enforcement Executives (1985); Past President, International Association Chiefs of Police; Police Executive Research Forum; International Narcotic Enforcement Officers Association; National Forum for Black Public Administrators; New York Police Chiefs Association; Texas Police Association; Texas Criminal Justice Task Force; National Police Athletic League; Michigan State University; National Research Council **Marquis Who's Who Honors:** Albert Nelson Marquis Lifetime Achievement Award **To what do you attribute your success:** Dr. Brown attributes his success to his upbringing, which was largely influenced by his mother, as his father passed away when he was young. **Why did you become involved in your profession or industry:** Dr. Brown wanted to be a juvenile detention probation officer, which required three years of college. However, he only completed two years of college, which was just enough to be a police officer. **Avocations:** Travel; Reading; Writing **Political Affiliations:** Democrat

Stephen Brown

Title: Superior Court Judge (Retired) **Industry:** Law and Legal Services **Date of Birth:** 06/29/1941 **Place of Birth:** Birmingham **State/Country of Origin:** AL/USA **Parents:** William P.; Milledge (Anderson) Brown **Marital Status:** Married **Spouse Name:** Dorothy Louise Ogden (08/6/1967) **Children:** Katherine; Phillip; Stephen **Education:** Bachelor of Laws, Walter F. George School Law (1967); Coursework in Civil Engineering Studies, Cooperative Education Program, Auburn University; Coursework, Working Cooperative Program, Civil Engineering Office of Southern Railway, Engineering Department **Career:** Retired (2018); Judge, Superior Court of Macon, Judicial Circuit (1996-2016); Partner, Brown, Katz, Flatau & Hasty, Macon, GA (1969-1995); Attorney, Regional Counsel, IRS, New York, NY (1967-1969); Attorney, Anderson, Walker and Reichert, Macon, GA **Civic:** Representative, Georgia House of Representatives, Atlanta, GA (1971-1974) **Military Service:** U. S. Army Reserves (1960-1965) **Creative Works:** Author, Work-in-Progress Book on the Nature of Religion **Awards:** Continental Pinnacle Professional Member, Top 100 Registry (2019); Top Attorneys of North America, Roundtable Magazine (2019); Man of the Year, Life Time Member Continental Who's Who Life Time (2019); Diamond Award (2018); Top Attorneys of North America, Roundtable Magazine (2018); Top Attorneys of North America (2017-2018); Top Attorneys of North America, Roundtable Magazine (2017); Top Professional as Honorary Judge; Certificate of Achievement, Continental Who's Who **Bar Admissions:** Georgia (1967); U.S. District Court for the Middle District of Georgia (1967); U.S. Court of Appeals for the 11th Circuit of Georgia (1967); Supreme Court of the United States (1967) **Marquis Who's Who Honors:** Albert Nelson Marquis Lifetime Achievement Award; Marquis Who's Who Top Professional **Why did you become involved in your profession or industry:** Mr. Brown became involved in his profession due to the influence of his father, Amos Milledge Anderson, who was a superior court judge. **Avocations:** Organic gardening; Reading; Writing

Timothy Charles Brown

Title: International Affair Specialist **Industry:** Government Administration/ Government Relations/Government Services **Date of Birth:** 06/09/1938 **Parents:** Gilbert Edgar Brown; Frances G. (Shaw) Milum (Deceased) **Marital Status:** Married **Spouse Name:** Leda Moraima Zuniga Fernandez (9/11/1958) **Children:** Barbara; Rebecca; Tamara; Timothy Patrick **Education:** PhD, New Mexico State University (1997); MA in International Trade and Economics, Foreign Service Institute, US Department of State (1974); BA in International Relations, University of Nevada, Reno, NV (1965) **Career:** Research Fellow, Hoover Institution on War, Revolution and Peace, Stanford University, Stanford, CA (1994-Present); Freelance Writer, Hoover Institution on War, Revolution and Peace, Stanford University, Stanford, CA (1994); Independent Scholar, Trade Consultant, International and National Lecturer (1992-1997); Senior Fellow, Border Research Institute, New Mexico State University, Las Cruces, NM (1990-1992); Senior Liaison, Central America, UN Observer Force in Central America (1989-1990); Senior Liaison, Central America, Organization of American States International Commission Cease-Fire Verification and Assistance (1989-1990); Senior Liaison, Central America, Nicaraguan Democratic Resistance, Tegucigalpa, Honduras (1987-1990); U.S. Consul General, French Caribbean Departments, Martinique, France (1983-1987); Deputy Coordinator, Cuban Affairs, U.S. Department of State, Washington, DC (1981-1983); Coordinator, Cuban Embargo and Radio Marti, Washington, DC (1981-1983); Desk, Organization for Economic Cooperative & Development (1980-1981); Foreign Service Officer, U.S. Department of State (1965-1992) **Career Related:** Presenter; Lecturer **Military Service:** Sergeant, United States Marine Corps (1954-1964) **Creative Works:** Author, Book, "Diplomarine: Terrorism, Turf Wars, Cocktail Parties and Other Painful Joys" (2014); Author, "The Real Contra War: Highlander Peasant Resistance in Nicaragua" (2001); Author, "The Causes of Continuing Conflict in Nicaragua: A View from the Radical Middle" (1995); Author, "When the AK-47s Fall Silent: Revolutionaries, Guerillas, and the Dangers of Peace" (2000); Author, "A Guide to Thailand" (1962); Contributing Author, Wall Street Journal; Contributing Author, Professional Journals; Author, Various Academic Articles **Awards:** Superior Honor Medal (1990); National Award for Human Intelligence (1990); Director Generals' Reporting Awards (1989); Meritorious Honor Awards (1982); Meritorious Honor Awards (1978); Commendation, State Department, Thailand (1963); Distinguished Service Award, Vietnam (1967); Commendation, Marine Corps, Nicaragua (1959); Editor's Pick Award; Book of the Year Award; Foreign Legion Award, Honorary Member, The Third French Foreign Legion **Memberships:** Rotary Club; Marine Corps Association; The Third French Foreign Legion **Marquis Who's Who Honors:** Albert Nelson Marquis Lifetime Achievement Award **Why did you become involved in your profession or industry:** Dr. Brown became involved in his career as a diplomarine because of his prior experience in the military and civic fields. When he was 16 years old, Dr. Brown served in the Marine Corp, and later, when he was 17, he became the youngest corporal in the Marine Corp. He wanted to become an embassy guard, and although he qualified, he did not meet the age requirement as a 17 year old. Dr. Brown's sergeant put him through anyway, and he excelled as an embassy guard in Nicaragua. **Avocations:** History; Literature; Music; Social dancing; Golf **Thoughts on Life:** Dr. Brown's son, Timothy Patrick, followed in his footsteps and became an even higher-ranked diplomat than he was, formerly serving as a consul general in Monterrey and currently serving as director for the U.S. in Cuba.

Kobe Bean Bryant

Title: Professional Basketball Player (Retired) **Date of Birth:** 08/23/1978 **Place of Birth:** Philadelphia **State/Country of Origin:** PA/USA **Year of Passing:** 2020 **Parents:** Joe Bryant; Pamela (Cox) Bryant **Marital Status:** Married **Spouse Name:** Vanessa Laine **Children:** Natalia Diamante; Bianka Bella; Capri Kobe; Gianna Maria-Onore (Deceased) **Education:** Diplomate, Lower Merion High School, Ardmore, PA (1996) **Career:** Founder, Coach, Mamba Sports Academy (2018-2020); Shooting Guard, Los Angeles Lakers, NBA (1996-2016) **Career Related:** Co-founder, Bryant Stibel (2016); Founder, Kobe Inc. (2014); Founder, Granity Studios (2013); Member, United States Men's National Basketball Team (2007, 2008, 2012) **Civic:** Founder, Kobe Bryant China Fund (2009); Co-founder, Kobe and Vanessa Bryant Family Foundation; Founding Donor, National Museum of African American History and Culture; Supporter, Make-A-Wish Foundation of America; Ambassador, ASAS **Creative Works:** Co-author, "The Wizenard Series (2019-Present); Co-author, "Geese are Never Swans" (2020); Co-author, "Epoca: The Tree of Ecrof" (2019); Author, "The Mamba Mentality: How I Play" (2018); Subject, "Kobe Doin' Work" (2009) **Awards:** Emmy Governors Award for Philanthropy, Los Angeles Area Emmy Awards (2020); Academy Award for Best Animated Short Film, Academy of Motion Picture Arts and Sciences (2018); Western Conference All-Star (1998, 2000-2016); All-NBA First Team (2002-2004, 2006-2013); Listee, 35 Greatest Mc-Donald's All-Americans (2012); NBA All-Star Game MVP (2002, 2007, 2009, 2011); NBA All-Defensive First Team (2000, 2003, 2004, 2006-2011); NBA Athlete of the Decade, 2000s, Sporting News (2010); NBA Finals MVP (2009, 2010); NBA MVP (2008); NBA Slam Dunk Contest Champion (1997); Naismith Prep Player of the Year Award, Atlanta Tipoff Club (1996); First-Team All-American, Parade Magazine (1996); McDonald's All-American (1996); All-USA First Team, USA Today (1996); Men's National Basketball Player of the Year, Gatorade (1996) **Religion:** Catholic

Elizabeth Spoon Buchanan, PhD

Title: Assistant Principal, Language Educator **Industry:** Education/Educational Services **Company Name:** Tabernacle Elementary School **Date of Birth:** 06/07/1942 **Place of Birth:** Ashboro **State/Country of Origin:** NC/USA **Parents:** Ernest Clyde Spoon; Ada Roanna Spoon **Marital Status:** Divorced **Children:** Amy Louise Buchanan-Feinberg **Education:** EdM in Administration and Supervision, George Mason University, Fairfax, VA (1990); PhD in Applied Linguistics, Georgetown University, Washington, DC (1984); MA in French, University of South Carolina, Columbia, SC (1973); BA in History, Winthrop University, Rock Hill, SC (1962) **Certifications:** Teacher; Administration & Supervision **Career:** Teacher, English as Second Language, Tabernacle Elementary School (1998-Present); Program Director, English as a Second Language, Rutherford County Schools (2006-2011); Instructor, Randolph Community College, Asheboro, NC (1999-2006); Teacher, Fairfax County Schools, Reston, VA (1978-1998); Teacher, Wake County Schools, Raleigh, VA (1968-1972); Teacher, Charleston County Schools, SC (1962-1968) **Career Related:** Bilingual Interpreter, Randolph Hospital, Asheboro, NC (1999-2006) **Civic:** Treasurer, Gamecock Alumni Club of Triad, High Point, NC (2000-Present); Undergraduate Admissions Board, Asheboro, NC (1999-Present); Secretary-Treasurer, Randolph Historical Society, Asheboro, NC (1998-Present) **Creative Works:** Author, "Death of an American Dream" (1996); Author, Poetry **Awards:** Fulbright Scholar, Scotland (2003); Distinguished Educator Award, Randolph County Schools (2002); Distinguished Educator Award, Randolph County Schools (2001); Golden Eagle Award, Fairfax County Schools (1996); Fulbright Scholar, Mexico (1992); Fulbright Scholar, Argentina (1986) **Memberships:** Association for Supervision and Curriculum Development; North Carolina Association for Principals and Assistant Principals **Marquis Who's Who Honors:** Albert Nelson Marquis Lifetime Achievement Award; Marquis Who's Who Top Professional **Why did you become involved in your profession or industry:** Dr. Buchanan became involved in her profession because of family circumstances. When Dr. Buchanan was 9, her mother passed away and she was sent to live with her oldest sister, who was the principal of First Baptist School in Charleston, South Carolina. In the 1960s, the only career choices women had were nursing, education, and secretarial work, so Dr. Buchanan followed the family tradition and went into teaching. A trip she took to Canada with her family when she was 16 inspired her to teach French because the language excited her. **Avocations:** Pottery; Quilting; Travel; Theater **Religion:** Baptist

Jacqueline Chase Buchin, PsyD

Title: Research Clinician **Industry:** Medicine & Health Care **Company Name:** Massachusetts General Hospital **Date of Birth:** 11/27/1935 **Place of Birth:** Providence **State/Country of Origin:** RI/USA **Parents:** Leslie Thurber Chase; Mary Hillyer (Lyon) Chase **Marital Status:** Married **Spouse Name:** Stanley Ira Buchin (09/14/1957) **Children:** Linda Chase Sullivan; David Lyon; Gordon Tomlinson **Education:** PsyD, Massachusetts School of Professional Psychology (Now William James College), Newton, MA (1990); Psychology Intern, Behavior Associates, Boston, MA (1986-1990); Psychology Intern, Solomon Carter Fuller Hospital (Now Dr. Solomon Carter Fuller Mental Health Center), Boston, MA (1985-1986); Psychology Intern, Arbour Hospital, Boston, MA (1984-1985); Family Therapy Intern, Framingham Youth Guidance (Now Metro West Youth Guidance Center), Masterclasses (1982-1984); Family Therapy Intern, Newton Guidance Clinic (1981-1982); MEd in Counseling Psychology, Antioch University (1979); BA, Wellesley College (1957) **Certifications:** Licensed Clinical Psychologist, Commonwealth of Massachusetts **Career:** Research Clinician, Massachusetts General Hospital, The General Hospital Corporation, Partners HealthCare, Boston, MA (1995-Present); Clinical Associate, Massachusetts General Hospital, The General Hospital Corporation, Partners HealthCare, Boston, MA (1995-Present); Staff Psychologist, Biobehavioral Treatment Center, Brookline, MA (1990-Present); Assistant Professor, Department of Psychiatry, Tufts University School of Medicine, Boston, MA (2007-2011); Clinical Associate of Department of Psychology, Center for Anxiety and Related Disorders, Boston University (2005-2008); Fellow in Clinical Cognitive Therapy Program, Massachusetts General Hospital, The General Hospital Corporation, Partners HealthCare, Boston, MA (1993-1995); Director, Coordinator, Emergency Housing Program, Multi-Service Center, Newton, MA (1978-1981) **Career Related:** Clinical Associate, Psychology Department, Harvard Medical School, Boston, MA (1995-Present); Founding Member, Academy of Cognitive Therapy (2000); Faculty Member, Institute of Cognitive Therapy, Massachusetts General Hospital, The General Hospital Corporation, Boston, MA (1996-1999) **Civic:** Trustee, Massachusetts School of Professional Psychology (Now William James College) (1991-2007); Board of Directors, Wellesley Community Child Care (Now Wellesley Community Children's Center) (1976); Member, Board of Directors, The Junior League of Boston, Inc. (1975-1977); Board of Directors, Wellesley Friendly Associate (Now Wellesley Friendly Aid Association) (1972-1973); Board of Directors, Wellesley Community Chest and Council (1972-1973); President, Wellesley Junior Service League (1972-1973); Board of Directors, Family Counseling Region West (1969); Board of Directors, Human Relations Service, Massachusetts School of Professional Psychology (Now William James College); Board of Directors, Wellesley Chapter, The American National Red Cross **Memberships:** Association for the Advancement of Cognitive Behavior Therapy; International OCD Foundation **Marquis Who's Who Honors:** Albert Nelson Marquis Lifetime Achievement Award **Religion:** Episcopalian

Stanley Ira Buchin, DBA

Title: Marketing and Finance Educator **Company Name:** Boston University and Lasell College **Date of Birth:** 09/07/1931 **Place of Birth:** New York **State/Country of Origin:** NY/USA **Parents:** K. Buchin; Bertha (Handman) Buchin **Marital Status:** Married **Spouse Name:** Jacqueline C. Thurber, PsyD (Chase) (09/14/1957) **Children:** Linda C.; David L.; Gordon T. **Education:** Doctor of Business Administration, Harvard University (1962); Master of Business Administration, with Distinction, Harvard University(1956); Bachelor of Science, Massachusetts Institute of Technology (1952) **Career:** Adjunct Lecturer, Lasell College (2014-Present); Hospitality Industry Advisory Board, Lasell College (2014-Present); Professor of Practice Emeritus, Boston University (2014-Present); Visiting Lecturer, University of Paris (2013-Present); Professor of Practice, Boston University (2012-2014); Associate Professor, Boston University (1997-2012); With, General Ship Cruising Corp. (1994-1997); President, Boston-Bermuda Cruising Ltd. (1992-1997); Visiting Lecturer, Templeton College, Oxford University (1991-1993); Senior Vice President, Oliver Wyman, Lexington, MA (1978-1990); President, Founder, Management Consultant, Applied Decision Systems, Wellesley, MA (1969-1978); Associate Professor, Harvard Business School, Harvard University (1966-1969); Assistant Professor, Harvard Business School, Harvard University (1962-1966); Lecturer, Harvard Business School, Harvard University (1961-1962); Instructor, Harvard Business School, Harvard University (1960-1961); Research Associate, Harvard Business School, Harvard University (1959-1960); Research Assistant, Harvard Business School, Harvard University (1958-1959); Assistant to Treasurer, Bay State Abrasives (1956-1958); Faculty Chair, Boston University School of Hospitality Administration; Member, University Faculty Council Executive Committee, Boston University; Vice Chairman, University Student Life Committee, Boston University **Career Related:** Board of Directors, Electrolyzer Corp; Board of Directors, Multicomp Computing Corp; Board of Directors, Diamond Machining Technology **Civic:** Executive Committee, Resident Advisory Council, Lasell Village; Chair, Finance Committee, Lasell Village; Trustee, Long-Range Planning Committee, Massachusetts School of Professional Psychology; Chairman, Long-Range Planning Committee, Massachusetts School of Professional Psychology; Treasurer, Human Relations Service, Wellesley and Weston, MA; Governor's Advisory Commission on Mental Health; Trustee Emeritus, Massachusetts School of Professional Psychology; Chairman, Board of Deacons, Wellesley Congregational Church **Military Service:** Captain, US Army (1956); Lieutenant, Chemical Corps, US Army (1952-1960) **Creative Works:** Author, "Hospitality Revenue Management Without Tears, Re-Published" (2019); Author, "Statistics Without Tears for Business Management" (2017); Author, "Statistics Without Tears for Hospitality Management (2017); Author, "Product Life Cycle: Moving From Theory to Practice," Boston Hospitality Review (2015); Author, "E-Book About Marketing" (2001); Author, "E-Book About Business Strategy" (2000); Author, "AT&T Business Services Management Simulation Simulation Exercise" (1984); Author, "HIHOST Hotel Management Simulation Exercise" (1982); Author, "Exponentially-Weighted Regression Analysis" (1976); Author, "WISE Worldwide Management Simulation Exercise" (1974); Author, "ADSIM Computer Simulation Language" (1973); Author, "ADDATA Data Management Language" (1973); Author, "NUPROD New Product Introduction Model" (1972); Author, "Army Heavy Lift Helicopter Program Management Simulation Exercise" (1970); Author, "Ford-Fulkerson Linear Programming Code" (1970); Author, "DOT Highway Management Simulation Exercise" (1970); Author, "OEO Community Action Agency Management Simulation Exercise" (1969); Author, "SIMPAK Computer Simulation Language" (1966); Author, "Harbets Simulation Exercise and Management Control, Management Controls: New Directions in Basic Research" (1964); Author, "Harbus 2 Model of the Firm" (1962); Contributor, Numerous Articles and Speeches; Author, "Statistics Without Tears: Quantitative Analysis and Forecasting in Hospitality & Tourism" **Awards:** Recipient, IBM Fellowship, Harvard University (1962-1963); Recipient, George F. Baker Scholarship (1956) **Memberships:** Tau Beta Pi, Massachusetts Institute of Technology (1951); Kappa Kappa Sigma (1951); Class Secretary-Treasurer, Massachusetts Institute of Technology (1949-1957); American Marketing Association; Institute of Management Sciences; Financial Management Association; Harvard Club of Boston **Marquis Who's Who Honors:** Albert Nelson Marquis Lifetime Achievement Award **Political Affiliations:** Independent **Religion:** Congregationalist

Peter J. Buckley

Title: Psychiatrist **Industry:** Medicine & Health Care **Date of Birth:** 04/02/1943 **Place of Birth:** Dunedin **State/Country of Origin:** New Zealand **Parents:** William Charles Buckley; Anne Agnes (Campbell) Buckley **Marital Status:** Married **Spouse Name:** Maxine Joan Antell (07/07/1977); Denise Joan Almao (12/11/1968, Divorced 1977) **Children:** Eric **Education:** Fellow, Child and Adolescent Psychiatry, Albert Einstein College of Medicine, New York (1970-1972); Resident, Psychiatry, Albert Einstein College of Medicine, New York (1968-1970); Intern, Dunedin Public Hospital, New Zealand (1967); MD, University of Otago, Dunedin, New Zealand (1966) **Certifications:** Diplomate, American Board of Psychiatry and Neurology **Career:** Professor Emeritus (2018); Professor, Psychiatry, Albert Einstein College of Medicine, New York (1987-2017); Associate Professor, Psychiatry, Albert Einstein College of Medicine, New York (1980-1987); Director, Psychiatry Out-Patient Services, Jacobi, New York (1976-1993) **Career Related:** Professor Emeritus, Albert Einstein College of Medicine, (2017-Present); Training and Supervisor Psychoanalyst, Columbia University Center for Psychoanalytic Training and Research, New York (1996-2015); Director, Residency Training in Psychiatry, Albert Einstein College of Medicine, New York (1993-2014) **Creative Works:** Co-Author, The Psychiatric Interview in Clinical Practice (2016); Author, Essential Papers on Psychosis, New York University Press (1988); Editor, Essential Papers on Object Relations (1986); Author, 50 Papers, Peer-Reviewed Journals **Awards:** Distinguished Life Fellow, American Psychiatric Association (2010) **Memberships:** Fellow, American Psychiatric Association; American Psychoanalytic Association **Marquis Who's Who Honors:** Albert Nelson Marquis Lifetime Achievement Award; Marquis Who's Who Top Professional **Why did you become involved in your profession or industry:** Dr. Buckley always had a general interest in psychiatry. It was an easy decision to go to medical school and pursue his career path. **Avocations:** Art history

Ernest D. Buff

Title: Chair, Managing Partner **Industry:** Law and Legal Services **Company Name:** Ernest D. Buff & Associates, LLC **Marital Status:** Married **Spouse Name:** Elizabeth Logan Buff **Children:** Two Children **Education:** JD, Boston University School of Law (1969); BS in Engineering, Syracuse University (1966) **Career:** Chair, Managing Partner, Ernest D. Buff & Associates (2004-Present); Attorney, Riker Danzig Scherer Hyland & Perretti LLP; Ally Chemical (now Honeywell) **Civic:** Member, President's Advisory Council for Small Business (2003-Present) **Awards:** Attorney of the Month Award, National Firm (2019); William Berry Award; Chicago Tribune Silver Medal Award, ROTC **Memberships:** American Bar Association; Morris County Bar Association; The District of Columbia Bar Association; Massachusetts Bar Association; New Jersey Bar Association; Patent Bar Association **Bar Admissions:** New Jersey; Massachusetts; District of Columbia; Patent Bar; CAFC; U.S. Court of Claims; Supreme Court of the United States **Marquis Who's Who Honors:** Albert Nelson Marquis Lifetime Achievement Award; Marquis Who's Who Top Professional **To what do you attribute your success:** The love that he has for what he does, the interest he has for the projects he is engaged in. The support and cooperation he has from his family. They understand that he loves it and they all pull together, it is a very good environment. **Why did you become involved in your profession or industry:** Mr. Buff had a joy of reading and writing and wanted to write about improvements in the state of the arts prevalent in the country. This would advance the state of science and the useful arts and help protect projects based on those improvements while, at the same time, educating everyone on what those improvements are so we can progress collectively and understand how technology is working to help all of us. In addition, his father-in-law, an admiral in the Navy at the time, told him that because he loves to write and won awards at writing, and is good in engineering, that he should consider patent law, and Mr. Buff wondered what that was. So he thought about it after his father-in-law told him that he would be writing about inventions, helping to advance the state of the arts, and he should consider it. Mr. Buff took his father-in-law's advice, and the very first day that he attended law school he knew that he loved it and never looked back. Engineering is an excellent background to study law, although most people don't do that. They either go on for business administration or advanced engineering. Mr. Buff worked for Polaroid while he was in law school, At that time, Polaroid's Patent Department had an excellent reputation and was preeminent. Camera users wanted instant realization, which the Polaroid process provided; and Polaroid's patents for a rapid-picture development process covered instant picture realization. Mr. Buff worked at Polaroid for a while and, in doing so, developed a strong propensity for patent law. **Avocations:** Tennis; Piano; French horn; Symphonies that he plays along with; Golf

Delores Buford

Title: Education Educator, Researcher **Industry:** Education/Educational Services **Date of Birth:** 12/18/1933 **Place of Birth:** Dallas **State/Country of Origin:** TX/USA **Parents:** George Jefferson; Louisa May (Daniel) Phife **Marital Status:** Married **Spouse Name:** Thomas Oliver Buford (12/27/1954, Deceased 2018) **Children:** Russell Warren; Robert Carl (Deceased); Anna Louise **Education:** Doctor of Education, Nova University (1982); Master of Arts, Furman University (1974); Postgraduate, Boston University (1958-1960); Bachelor of Arts, North Texas State University (1954) **Career:** Retired (2000); Instructor of Educational Research, Office of Installation Planning and Research, Furman University (1977-2000); Research Associate, Office of Installation Planning and Research, Furman University, Greenville, SC (1974); Member, Steering Committee, Junior Great Books Program, Greenville County Public Schools, South Carolina (1968-1972); Teacher, Fort Worth Public School District, Texas (1955-1958); Teacher, Dallas Public School District, Texas (1954-1955) **Career Related:** Secretary, Education Communications (1991-1993); Board of Directors, Education Communications (1988-1994); Member, Education Communications (1986-1992); Member, Mental Health Association of Greenville County (1984); Member, Greenville Fine Arts Festival Committee (1975); President, Eastside High School Parent Teacher Association (1976) **Civic:** Former Member, Chairperson, Various Committees, Local Church; Former Deacon, Local Church; Former Chairperson, Local Church **Awards:** Recipient, Service Award, Mental Health America (1993); Best Paper Award, Southern Association for Institutional Research (1985); Recipient, Service Award, Mental Health America (1977) **Memberships:** State Secretary, South Carolina, American Association of University Women (1994-Present); Chairperson, Nominating Committee, North Carolina Association for Installation Research (1993-Present); Executive, Board of Directors, South Carolina, American Association of University Women (1991-Present); Board Director, Greenville Branch, American Association of University Women (1969-Present); Chairperson, Philanthropic Educational Organization (1993-1995); President, Greenville Branch, American Association of University Women (1991-1993); Chairperson, Roundtables (1991-1992); Trustee, Program for Continuing Education, Philanthropic Educational Organization (1989-1995); Chairperson, Philanthropic Educational Organization (1989-1991); President, North Carolina Association for Installation Research (1989-1990); President, Association for Installation Research, Furman Campus Club (1988-1989); Chairperson, Awards Committee, Southern Association for Institutional Research (1988); Executive, Board of Directors, North Carolina Association for Installation Research (1987-1991); Nominating Committee, International Chapter, Philanthropic Educational Organization (1987-1989); President, Past President Club, Philanthropic Educational Organization (1987-1988); Secretary, North Carolina Association for Installation Research (1987-1988); Chairperson, Best Paper Award Committee, Southern Association for Institutional Research (1986); President, Philanthropic Educational Organization (1985-1986); Chairperson, Contributed Papers Committee, Southern Association for Institutional Research (1985); State Executive Board, Philanthropic Educational Organization (1980-1986) **Marquis Who's Who Honors:** Albert Nelson Marquis Lifetime Achievement Award; Marquis Who's Who Top Professional **Why did you become involved in your profession or industry:** Dr. Buford became involved in her profession due to her curious nature, having always enjoying analyzing details and aspiring to help others. Her propensity for leadership began in high school, having won all but one debate tournaments and serving, with distinction, on the debate team. **Avocations:** Needlecrafts; Reading; Dance; Skydiving **Political Affiliations:** Democrat **Religion:** Baptist

Renee Bundi

Title: Art Director, Graphic Designer, App Designer **Industry:** Fine Art **Company Name:** Left Handed Art **Date of Birth:** 04/20/1962 **Place of Birth:** Elmont **State/Country of Origin:** NY/USA **Parents:** Anthony Joseph Bundi; Marion Rose (Graziano) Bundi **Education:** Coursework, St. John's University (1980-1984); Coursework, School of Visual Arts (1985-1987) **Career:** Freelance App Designer, Left Handed Art (2019-Present); Digital Production Manager, Meredith Corp. (Time Inc.) (2010-2019); Art Director, MetroSource Magazine (2008-2010); Production Designer, Suede Magazine, Time, Inc. (2003-2005); Program Director, Gibbs Design and Animation Center (2002-2003); Chair, Web Design, Digital Media and Animation, Program Director, The Gibbs School, Design and Animation Center (2001-2002); Instructor, Graphic Design and Media Arts, The Gibbs School (2000-2001); Senior Art Director, Information Week Magazine (1994-2000); Associate Art Director, VarBusiness CMP Publication (1991-1994); Assistant Art Director, CMP Public/VarBusiness Computer Systems News, Manhasset, NY (1989-1991); Senior Production Editor, CMP Public/VarBusiness Computer Systems News, Manhasset, NY (1987-1989); Art and Production Coordinator, Cahner's Publishing Co./Datamation Magazine, New York, NY (1986-1987); Creative Director, Coastal Communications, New York, NY (1985-1986) **Creative Works:** Exhibitor, Fine Art Show, "After The Dance" and "Waiting", HerStory: Honoring The Women in Our Lives and In History (2020); Exhibitor, Fine Art Show, Barnes Gallery, Garden City, NY (2019); Exhibitor, Fine Art Show, Garden City Public Library, Garden City, NY (2019) **Awards:** Excellence in Design Award, Society of Publication Designers (1987-1989, 1992-1994, 1999); Print Design Award, Print Magazine (1988, 1991-1995, 1998-2000); Ozzie Design Award, Magazine Design and Production (1988-1991, 1998-2000); Excellence of Design, ASBPE (1997-2000); Best Spot Illustration, Society of Illustrators **Memberships:** Graphic Artist Guild; Society of Publication Designers; ASBPE; MacIntosh User's Group; Society of Illustrators **Marquis Who's Who Honors:** Albert Nelson Marquis Lifetime Achievement Award; Marquis Who's Who Top Professional **Why did you become involved in your profession or industry:** Ms. Bundi started working on her high school newspaper. She always wanted to be an artist, but her father was very practical and asked how she would make money doing that. So she went into graphic design, where she could still dabble in the arts and be creative. She has seen the industry completely change, publishing is a very tough field. There has been a lot of change in the publishing field, especially newspaper and magazine publishing. She has had to reinvent herself a number of times to stay in the field. She went from print to digital, then to apps for phones and tablets. **Avocations:** painting; photography **Religion:** Roman Catholic

Paul Frederick Burmeister

Title: Owner/Farmer **Industry:** Agriculture **Company Name:** Paul Burmeister Farm **Date of Birth:** 06/11/1938 **Place of Birth:** Great Bend **State/Country of Origin:** KS/USA **Parents:** Ferdinand Frederick Adam Burmeister; Gertrude Nellie (Hanson) Burmeister **Marital Status:** Single **Education:** Coursework, "Can Man Survive?," Fort Hays State University (1971); Postgraduate Coursework, University of Kansas (1961); BA in Chemistry and Agriculture, Fort Hays State University (1960) **Career:** Farmer, Claflin, KS (1952-Present) **Career Related:** Natural Resources Defense Council, New York, NY (1975-Present); Kansas Natural Resource Council, Topeka, KS (1975-Present); Farmer Advisory Committee, Sunshine Farm Project, The Land Institute (1995-2001); Guest Speaker, Rapid City, SD (1993); Kansas Rural Center, Whiting, KS (1991-1992); Panel Member, Kansas Sustainable Agriculture Conference (1991-1992); National Low-Level Radioactive Waste Management Strategy Review Workshop (1981); Office Radiation Programs, Environmental Protection Agency (1978); Participant, University Akron National Energy Forum (1976); Farmer, Cooperative Kansas Agricultural Experiment Station, Fort Hays Branch Station, Hays, KS (1970) **Civic:** The Menninger Foundation, Topeka, KS (1989-Present); Environmental Action (1982-Present); Renew Am., Washington (1980-Present); Board of Directors, Kansas-Oklahoma Conference Foundation (2008-2014); Board of Trustees, Clara Barton Hospital Foundation, Hoisington, KS (2005-2010); Network Environmental and Economic Responsibility Delegate, 23rd General Synod Meeting, United Church Of Christ, Kansas City, MO (2001); Kansas-Oklahoma Conference Council, United Church Christ (1999-2003); Commission on Outreach, Kansas-Oklahoma Conference (1988-1999); Kansas Citizens Forum Committee for Humanities, Topeka, KS (1987); Lay Member, Ad Hoc Task Force on Ecology, Christian Lifestyle United Church Of Christ (1977-1978); Lobbyist, Environmental Protection and Conservation Issues, Topeka, KS (1976-1980); Volunteer, American Peace Corps, Ludhiana, India (1961-1963); Local Organizer, Campaign Union of Concerned Scientists, Cambridge, MA **Military Service:** U.S. National Guard (1963-1969) **Creative Works:** Contributor, Articles, Environmental and Agricultural Journals **Awards:** Bankers Award, Banks of Barton County, Kansas and U.S. Soil Conservation Service (1990) **Memberships:** Midwest Renewable Energy Association (1998-Present); National Audubon Society (2017); Secretary, Scholar, Tau Kappa Epsilon (1958-1959); Historian, Phi Eta Sigma (1958-1959); Life Member, National Wildlife Federation; National Council of Returned Peace Corps Volunteers; Charter Member, National Arbor Day Foundation, World Wildlife Fund; American Wind Energy Association; Life Member, American Solar Energy Society; Heartland Renewable Energy Society; Kansas Association of Wheat Growers; Life Member, Kansas Farmers Union; Friends of the Earth; Founding Member, Cousteau Society; Life Member, Kansas State Historical Society; Kansas Wildlife Federation; Life Member, Sierra Club; Native Forest Council; Ducks Unltd. Inc.; Environmental Defense; Wilderness Society; Friends of India; Rainforest Alliance; National Parks Conservation Association; Ocean Conservancy; Nature Conservancy; Phi Kappa Phi; Delta Epsilon **Marquis Who's Who Honors:** Albert Nelson Marquis Lifetime Achievement Award **Why did you become involved in your profession or industry:** Mr. Burmeister became involved in his profession because he was raised on the farm and grew up helping his parents maintain it. He would ride along on the tractor when his father was doing fieldwork and observe his mother carry out various farming and weather tasks. He never lost interest in agricultural work, as he knows it is one of the most important industries. **Avocations:** Photography; Hiking **Political Affiliations:** Republican **Religion:** United Church of Christ

T.D. Burns

Title: Small Business Owner **Industry:** Business Management/Business Services **Date of Birth:** 04/22/1926 **Place of Birth:** Winston-Salem **State/Country of Origin:** NC/USA **Parents:** Charles Harvey Burns; Ruth (Graves) Burns **Marital Status:** Widowed **Spouse Name:** Jean Whisnant (08/09/1947, Deceased 2014) **Education:** Extensively Self-Educated in the Fields of Astronomy (With Home Observatory), Geology, Mineralogy, Chemistry, Atomic Structure, and Earth Sciences, Among Other Subjects **Career:** Small Business Owner;Co-Founder, President, Science Educational Products, Inc., Inventor/Developer of 24 Science-Related Products for Retail Sales, Matthews, NC (1989-2003); Co-Founder, President, Science and Nature Distributors, Inc., First All Science Retail Products Distributor in America, Matthews, NC (1983-1989); Co-Founder, President, Science Hobbies, Inc., First Retail All-Science Hobby Store in America, Charlotte, NC (1961-1983) **Career Related:** Designer, Patentee, Manufacturer, Marketed Teacher, Model Atom (1973-1983) **Military Service:** U.S. Navy (1944-1946) **Creative Works:** Author, Illustrator, Book, "A Matter of the Heart" (2004); Author, Illustrator, Book, "Rocks and Minerals Coloring Book" (1995); Author, Illustrator, Unpublished Manuscripts and Booklets, "Exploring Atomic Structure By Building Model Atoms," "3-D Photography With A Single Lens Camera," "Establishing America's First All-Science Hobby Shop With Only $500.00," and "Naval Jargon - WWII, etc."; Photographed, Wrote, and Narrated 14 Multimedia Slide Programs Consisting of Travelogues, Science and Historical Documentaries Recorded with a Computerized Dissolve Unit Utilizing 4-Slide Projectors and Shown to More Than 100 Civic, Church, Historical, and Science Organizations in Three States; Inventor in the Field; Author, Illustrator, Three Published Books; Author, Producer, Photographer, Slide Documentaries; Photographer, Designer, Posters; Author, Illustrator, Coloring and Activity Books **Awards:** Named, Paul Harris Fellow, Rotary International (2016); Nominated for North Carolina's Top Scientist of 2016 Award, Anson County's Planetarium & Science Center's Officials and Several Others (2016); Recognized and Honored by the Local Planetarium & Science Center with Large Trophy Engraved with "Anson County's Most Famous Scientist & Philanthropist" (2016) **Marquis Who's Who Honors:** Albert Nelson Marquis Lifetime Achievement Award; Marquis Who's Who Top Professional **To what do you attribute your success:** Mr. Burns attributes his success to learning and acquiring as much knowledge as possible about things that interest him. **Why did you become involved in your profession or industry:** Mr. Burns became involved in his profession because the day he graduated high school, at the peak of World War II, he boarded the bus to begin his service in the U.S. Navy. When he finished his active duty and returned home, there was very little to no opportunity for him to receive a job. He only had a high school education, and due to the nature of the war in the Pacific, he had no time to learn a real trade while enlisted. Mr. Burns had always been interested in collecting rocks and minerals. Eventually he set up a laboratory in his basement to conduct experiments with his findings and with chemistry as well. He also built his own telescope and eventually he began to study these subjects in depth at his own leisure. As his knowledge expanded, he pursued his dream of opening his own science hobby store. Eventually, Mr. Burns and his wife put together $500 and opened the store. In addition, he developed an interest in science since the first time that he got into mineralogy and then expanded to everything. He just could not find a stopping point still today he is just as interested today. No matter how much he studies because there is so much there will be some that he will never know or understand. That is what makes it so intriguing, he thinks. He has studied all phases of science. What attracted him to his career goes back to the 1950s when he read an article in a science magazine about the uranium boom that was going on out west. The government was giving bonuses to those who discovered new radio activity and he knew nothing about that at the time. However, the following weekend he took his wife on a fishing trip down to his home town. Walking among the railroad tracks he saw a green stone among the dark cedars. He picked it up and skipped across the water, later stuck it in his pocket. That stone changed his life forever. It is totally responsible for him being interested in all phases of science. However, he later learned that the stone was not radioactive, but florescent and made of glass. **Avocations:** Astronomy; Collecting minerals and fossils; Nature photography **Thoughts on Life:** During World War II, Mr. Burns served in the Pacific as RDM-2c (Petty Officer 2C Radar Man, Aboard Amphibious Landing Ship).

Richard Marshall Burr

Title: Municipal Government Administrator (Retired) **Industry:** Government Administration/Government Relations/Government Services **Company Name:** Borough of Westville, NJ **Date of Birth:** 04/22/1943 **Place of Birth:** Woodbury **State/Country of Origin:** NJ/USA **Parents:** Samuel Marshall; Erna Louise (Fierke) Burr **Marital Status:** Married **Spouse Name:** Janet Eileen Enzman **Children:** Sarah Elizabeth Burr; Richard Marshall Burr **Education:** Postgraduate Studies, Utah State University (1968-1973); Postgraduate Studies, University of Montana (1968-1969); MS, University of Delaware (1968); BS, Philadelphia College Pharmacy (University of the Sciences in Philadelphia) (1966) **Certifications:** Certified Municipal Financial Officer, New Jersey; Registered Municipal Clerk, Registrar of Vital Statistics **Career:** Treasurer (Retired), Westville Board of Education (1977-Present); Westville Board of Education, Custodian School Funds (2018); Chief Financial Officer (1989-2006); Borough Administrator (1983-1986); Registrar Vital Statistics (1980-2006); Borough Clerk (1980-2006); Municipal Government Administrator (Retired), Treasurer, Borough of Westville, NJ (1976-1989); Senior Publications Chairman, New Jersey Chapter **Civic:** Vice-Chairman, Westville Emergency Management Council (1990-Present); Active, Westville Emergency Management Council (1987-Present); Commissioner, Westville Emergency Management Council (1987-Present); Assistant Librarian, Genealogy Branch Library, Cherry Hill, NJ (1983-Present); Coordinator, United Way (1983-Present); Chairman, Salvation Army (1980-Present); Charter Member, Descendants of the Templar Knights, (2018); Children of American Revolution (1988-1990); Secretary, Westville Environmental Commission (1987); Member, Vocational Education Advisory Committee (1984); Member, Westville Plan Board (1979); Westville Board of Education; TRICO JIF Chairman and Secretary; Member, American Royal Descent; Member, Sons Colonial Wars; Board Member, Registrar, Sons of American Colonists **Military Service:** ROTC **Creative Works:** National Wildlife Conference Paper, Cited in 25 Different Articles in Canada, US, Japan, China, Netherlands (1968); Contributor, Articles, Professional Journals **Awards:** Distinguished Service Medal, South Jersey Chapter, Sons of the American Revolution (2019); Citation of Merit, New Jersey Mayors Association (1989); Research Fellow, University Montana (1968-1969); Research Fellow, University of Delaware (1966-1968); Delegate to NJ Boys State (1960); Samuel Victor Constant Fellow (Society of Colonial Wars); Presidential Lifetime Achievement Award for Volunteerism **Memberships:** Executive Board, New Jersey Chapter, Government Finance Officers Association (GFOA) (1989-Present); Treasurer, Westville Republican Club (1978-Present); Treasurer, Clerk, Chief Financial Officer, Westville Planning Board (Present); Gloucester County Historical Society (2015-2016); President, South Jersey Chapter, Sons of the American Revolution (1985-1987); Vice President, South Jersey Chapter, Sons of the American Revolution (1983-1984); Vice President, Tri-County Association Tax Collectors and Treasurers (1981-1982); Environmental Committee, Westville Concerned Citizens; Genealogy Society of Pennsylvania; New Jersey Municipal Managers Association; New Jersey Police Office of Emergency Management; International Institute of Municipal Clerks; Gloucester County Municipal Clerks Association; Municipal Clerks' Association of New Jersey; Descendants of Founders of New Jersey; Society of the Descendants of the Founders of Hartford, CT; Order of the Crown Charlemagne; Trustee, Former Vice President, The Baronial Order of the Magna Charta; Flagon and Trencher (Descendants of Colonial Tavern Keepers); Wyckoff Family Association; Townsend Family Association; New Jersey Municipal Finance Officers Association; Rotary; Alpha Phi Omega; Alpha Zeta; Magna Charta Research Foundation Board; Descendants of Washington's Army at Valley Forge; National Society Sons and Daughters of the Pilgrims; President, Vice President, General Assistant Historian, Assistant Registrar, Society of the War of 1812 in New Jersey; Historian, Board Member, New Jersey Society "Sons of the Revolution"; Vice President, Treasurer, Francis Hopkinson Chapter, Sons of the Revolution; Board Member, Military Order of The Crusades (MOC); New Jersey Membership Committee, Society of the Cincinnati; Commander, J.E.B. Stuart Camp 1506, Sons of Confederate Veterans; Philadelphia Museum of Art; Philadelphia Zoo; National Audubon Society; Delmarva Ornithological Society; American Ornithologist Union; American Society of Mammalogists; Sierra Club, National Wildlife Federation; Colonial Williamsburg Foundation; The Camden Aquarium; Founding Member, Museum of the American Revolution; Presidential Advisory Board, Friends of Indian King Tavern **Marquis Who's Who Honors:** Albert Nelson Marquis Lifetime Achievement Award **Avocations:** Family history; Environmental science **Political Affiliations:** Republican **Religion:** Mormon **Thoughts on Life:** One of Mr. Burr's ancestors was the governor of Bermuda back in 1644. They had a chair there made in 1643 and every governor was able to sit in it and call government to order. So, he went to the Senate Chamber and asked about it; they took him up and he later wrote an article about it.

R. Anthony Burrows

Title: Owner **Industry:** Medicine & Health Care **Company Name:** Desert Springs Family Dentistry **Marital Status:** Married **Children:** Four Children **Education:** Residency in General Practice, Denver General Hospital (1992-1993); DDS, University of Colorado (1992); BS in Biology and Chemistry, Northern Arizona University (1986) **Career:** Team Leader, Dental Net (1993-1997); Dentist, Owner, Desert Spring Family Dentistry **Civic:** Dental Director, Alternative Mission; Women's Health Organization; MOM, Phoenix; Hopefest, Tucson, AZ **Awards:** Top Dentist, Tuscon Lifestyle Magazine (2012-Present); Number 1 Dentist, Outstanding Dentist in Tuscon, Tuscon Business, Tuscon Local Media **Memberships:** American Dental Association; Alpha Omega; Arizona Dental Association; Southern Arizona Dental Association; Academy of General Dentistry **To what do you attribute your success:** Dr. Burrows attributes his success to a blessing from God. Likewise, he credits his wife with many of his accomplishments, as she is a constant inspiration. **Why did you become involved in your profession or industry:** Dr. Burrows always wanted to be a doctor. However, he quickly found that he desired a career outside of general medicine. When he found dentistry, he knew it was the perfect industry for him. **Avocations:** Gardening; Travel; Golf; Hanging out with friends; Playing with grandkids; Barbecuing **Thoughts on Life:** Dr. Burrows' motto is, "Treat others better than you would like to be treated."

Richard Roderick Burton, PhD

Title: Computer Scientist **Industry:** Sciences **Date of Birth:** 10/07/1948 **Place of Birth:** Oakland **State/Country of Origin:** CA/USA **Parents:** Charles Roderick Burton; Lulu Faye (Urbach) Burton **Marital Status:** Married **Spouse Name:** Lauren Ann Sargeant (11/09/1997); Laura Jean DeYoung (09/20/1992); Katherine Krase (06/14/1970-06/30/1973) **Children:** John Charles Burton **Education:** PhD in Information and Computer Science, University of California, Irvine (1976); BS in Mathematics, California Institute of Technology (1970) **Career:** Senior Scientist, Acuitus, Sunnyvale, CA (2004-Present); Area Manager, Computer Sciences Laboratory, Palo Alto Research Center Incorporated, Palo Alto, CA (1996-2004); President, Windrose Consulting Group, Palo Alto, CA (1989-1995); Area Manager of User Systems Research, Xerox Palo Alto Research Center, (Now Palo Alto Research Center Incorporated), Palo Alto, CA (1986-1988); Research Staff, Xerox Palo Alto Research Center, (Now Palo Alto Research Center Incorporated), Palo Alto, CA (1978-1986); Research Staff, Bolt Beranek and Newman Inc. (Now Raytheon Company), Cambridge, MA (1973-1978) **Creative Works:** Co-Author, "Reactive Learning Environments for Teaching Electronic Troubleshooting," Advances in Man-Machine Systems Research (1987); Author, "Diagnosing Bugs in a Simple Procedural Skill" (1982); Co-Author, "An investigation of Computer Coaching for Informal Learning Activities: (1982); Co-Author, "Diagnostic Models for Procedural Bugs in Basic Mathematical Skills" (1978) **Awards:** Inductee, ICS Hall of Fame (2017); Charter Fellow, Software System Award, ACM, Inc. (1992) **Memberships:** ACM, Inc. **Marquis Who's Who Honors:** Albert Nelson Marquis Lifetime Achievement Award **To what do you attribute your success:** Dr. Burton attributes his success to hard work, persistence, curiosity and willingness to work on the boundaries between different disciplines. **Why did you become involved in your profession or industry:** Dr. Burton became involved in his profession because of his experiences in high school. He felt that it wasn't an effective learning experience for him. After the advent of the computer, he noticed the importance of its role in education and began to pursue a career in computer science. At the University of California, Irvine, Dr. Burton focused on computer science in his quest to address the education problems and continued developing computer systems to this end into the early 1990s. He worked alongside linguists, cognitive psychologists, sociologists, educators and fellow computer scientists in a profound effort, but after a number of years, he decided he could not move forward with education as the focal point of his career. At that time, Mr. Burton, a natural problem-solver, moved into the consulting field with the ambition to help others. Currently, having returned to the field of education at the birth of his son, he is developing an educational system that teaches network troubleshooting. **Avocations:** Sailing; Playing soccer and volleyball

William Read Bush, PhD, JD

Title: Computer Scientist **Industry:** Technology **Date of Birth:** 02/08/1950 **Place of Birth:** San Francisco **State/Country of Origin:** CA/USA **Parents:** Walter Nelson Bush; Sarah Lillian (Lewis) Bush **Marital Status:** Partner **Spouse Name:** Ellen Peel **Children:** Elizabeth Loea Bush-Peel **Education:** PhD, University of California Berkeley (1992); MS, University of California Berkeley (1985); JD, Boston University (1977); AB, Harvard College (1972) **Career:** Consulting Computer Scientist, D'Crypt PTE ltd, Singapore (2013-Present); Director of Engineering, Movious, Palo Alto, CA (2009-2013); Senior Scientist, Kestrel Technology, Mountain View, CA (2006-2008); Senior Scientist, Sun Microsystems, Palo Alto, CA (1997-2006); Founder, Principal Scientist, Intrinsa Corp., Palo Alto, CA (1994-Present); Computer Scientist, University of California Berkeley (1991-1993); Postgraduate Researcher, University of California Berkeley (1986-1990); Research Assistant, University of California Berkeley (1983-1984); Teaching Assistant, University of California Berkeley (1982-1983); Member, Technology Staff, Computer Corp. of America, Cambridge, MA (1973-1977); Senior Programmer, Harvard University, Cambridge, MA (1977-1982) **Career Related:** Principal Investigator, AKM Associates, San Mateo, CA (1989-1991, 1993-1994); Consultant Computer Scientist, AKM Associates, San Mateo, CA (1986-1989) **Creative Works:** Contributor, Articles, Professional Journals **Memberships:** IEEE; Association for Computing Machinery; The Philharmonia Baroque Orchestra **Marquis Who's Who Honors:** Albert Nelson Marquis Lifetime Achievement Award; Marquis Who's Who Top Professional **Why did you become involved in your profession or industry:** Mr. Bush became involved in his profession because he was interested in science and almost went into physics in college. He spent a summer in a sponsored NSF program in physics and was being considered by Cornell but he realized he was not sure he wanted to do that. He went into computers instead because of the practical side of it. It was sort of immediate and it was a combination of things and it was also easy for him to do. He liked making stuff. **Avocations:** Music; Literature; Sports

Roderick Paul Bushnell

Title: Owner **Industry:** Law and Legal Services **Company Name:** Law Offices of Roderick P. Bushnell **Date of Birth:** 03/06/1944 **Place of Birth:** Buffalo **State/Country of Origin:** NY/USA **Parents:** Paul Hazen Bushnell; Martha Atlee Bushnell **Marital Status:** Married **Spouse Name:** Suzanne Bushnell (1967) **Children:** Arlo Bushnell **Education:** JD, Georgetown University Law Center, Georgetown University, Washington, DC (1969); BA in History, Rutgers, The State University of New Jersey (1966) **Certifications:** Board Certified, Civil Trial Law Advocate, National Board of Trial Advocacy (1998); Board Certificate, Civil Trial Advocate, California State Bar (1998) **Career:** Owner, Law Offices of Roderick P. Bushnell (2016-Present); Partner, Bushnell & Caplan (2012-2016); Partner, Bushnell, Caplan Fielding, San Francisco, CA (1971-2012); Attorney, Department of Water Resources, Sacramento, CA (1969-1971) **Career Related:** Contributor, Seminars on Employment and Labor Law, Practicing Law Institute, San Francisco Bar Association, California Employment Lawyers Association **Civic:** Former Board Member, California Lawyers for the Arts; Former Board Member, Former Chairman of the Board, Bread and Roses **Creative Works:** Contributor, Articles, Professional Journals **Awards:** Named, Northern California Super Lawyer, Law and Politics (2006-2014) **Memberships:** Labor & Employment Section, American Association for Justice; Labor and Employment Section, International Law Section, American Bar Association; Arbitrator, Labor and Employment Sections, San Francisco Bar Association; Arbitrator, San Francisco Superior Court; Early Neutral Evaluator, United States District Court; Labor and Employment Sections, California Bar Association; Labor and Employment Sections, Consumer Attorneys of California; San Francisco Trial Lawyers Association; National Employment Lawyers Association; California Employment Lawyers Association **Bar Admissions:** U.S. Court of Appeals for the Federal Circuit (1984); Supreme Court of the United States (1980); U.S. Court of Appeals for the Ninth Circuit (1973); U.S. District Court for the Northern District of California (1971); California (1970) **Marquis Who's Who Honors:** Albert Nelson Marquis Lifetime Achievement Award; Marquis Who's Who Top Professional **To what do you attribute your success:** Mr. Bushnell attributes his success to his mentors. He has been married for 51 years, and he is thankful for the ceaseless support of his wife. **Why did you become involved in your profession or industry:** Mr. Bushnell became involved in his profession because, when he graduated from college in 1966, the Vietnam War was in full force. If he didn't go to graduate school, he would have been drafted. While in graduate school, he chose to pursue law. **Avocations:** Skiing

Alexander Porter Butterfield

Title: Military Officer; Presidential Appointee; Aviation Executive **Industry:** Military & Defense Services **Date of Birth:** 04/06/1926 **Place of Birth:** Pensacola **State/Country of Origin:** FL/USA **Parents:** Horace Bushnell Butterfield; Susan A. (Alexander) Butterfield **Marital Status:** Single **Spouse Name:** Charlotte Mary Maguire (09/09/1949, Divorced 01/1985) **Children:** Leslie Carter (Deceased); Alexander Porter Jr.; Susan Carter-Hol **Education:** PhD Candidate in Clemency and Presidential Pardons, University of California (2005-Present); MA in American History, University of California (2005); Honorary PhD, Embry-Riddle Aeronautical University (1973); MS in International Affairs, George Washington University (1967); Coursework, National War College (1966-1967); BS in Political Science, University of Maryland (1956); Diploma, St. John's Military Academy, Cum Laude (1944) **Career:** Retired (1995); Founder, Consulting Firm, Armistead and Alexander, Inc., Los Angeles, CA (1983); President, Director, Chief Operating Officer, California Life Corporation (1979-1980); Director, Executive Vice President, Chief Operating Officer, International Air Service Company Ltd. (1977-1979); Lecturer, Ethics in Government, American Program Bureau, Inc. (1975-1976); Administrator, Federal Aviation Administration (FAA) (1973-1975); Deputy White House Chief of Staff to President Nixon, Secretary to Cabinet, The White House (1969-1973); Deputy Chief of Staff and Chief Administrative Officer, White House Staff (1969); Military and Special Assistant for White House Matters, Immediate Office of the Secretary of Defense, United States Department of Defense (1965-1966); Assistant Professor, United States Air Force Academy (1957-1959) **Career Related:** Vice President, Chairman, Board of Directors, Dr. Seuss Enterprises, LP (2014-2017); Guest Lecturer, Eccles Centre for American Studies (2015); Guest Lecturer, University College of London (2015); Guest Lecturer, University of Warwick (2015); Guest Lecturer, University of Oxford (2014-2015); Guest Lecturer, University of Bristol (2014); Guest Lecturer, University of California, Berkeley, Harvard University and Princeton University **Civic:** Chairman, Board of Directors, The Brain Observatory (2013-Present); Vice President, Board of Trustees, Dr. Seuss Foundation (2015-2017); Chairman, Dr. Seuss Foundation (2014-2017); Board of Directors, Dr. Seuss Enterprises LP (2013-2017); Chairman, Chancellor's Associates, University of California, San Diego (2004-2006); Board of Directors, Natural History Museum of Los Angeles County (1981-1985); Board of Directors, Aloha Airlines, Inc. (1979-1980); Board of Directors, Flight Safety Foundation (1976-1981); Key Witness, Deliberations of Impeachment of President Richard Nixon, U.S. House Committee on the Judiciary (1974); Key Witness at Hearings, Watergate, Select Committee on Presidential Campaign Activities (1973) **Military Service:** Senior U.S. Military Officer, Representative of the Commander-in-chief, Pacific, Commonwealth of Australia (1967-1969); Colonel, United States Air Force (USAF) (1966); Tactical Air Warfare Policy Planner, USAF Headquarters (1964-1965); Accrued, 98 Combat Sorties in Southeast Asia (1964); Commander, Tactical Reconnaissance Task Forces, Southeast Asia (1963-1964); Commander, Fighter Squadron, Japan (1962-1964); Senior Aide to Commander-in-chief, Pacific Air Forces (1959-1962); Operations Officer, Interceptor Squadron (1955-1956); Aide to Commander, Fourth Allied Tactical Air Force, NATO (1954-1955); Right Wing, Deputy Lead, Jet Aerobatic Team "Skyblazers" (1950); Command Pilot, Parachutist, Skyblazers, USAF, NV (1949-1953); Pilot, P-51 Mustang, USAF (1949-1950); Commissioned Second Lieutenant, USAF (1949); Colonel, United States Air Force (1948-1969); Flight Instructor, USAF Weapons School, United States Air Force, NV; Weapons Officer, 86th Fighter Group, Germany **Creative Works:** Subject, "The Last of the President's Men" by Bob Woodward (2015); Consultant, Screenplay, Oliver Stone, "Nixon" (1995); Editorial Board, Terra, Natural History Museum of Los Angeles County (1983-1986); Author, "Fighter-Gunnery Training Manual," First 12th Air Force and USAF, Europe; Contributor, Articles, Professional Journals and National Magazines; Body Double; Voice Actor; Writer, Scenes, Paul Newman **Awards:** Archibald Cox Uncommon Heroes of Watergate Award, Common Cause (2013); Decorated, Legion of Merit, Admiral John McCain, Commander-in-chief of Pacific Command (1969); Decorated, Distinguished Flying Cross; Decorated, Air Medal with Three Bronze Oak Leaf Clusters; Decorated, Four Air Medals; Decorated, Bronze Star **Marquis Who's Who Honors:** Albert Nelson Marquis Lifetime Achievement Award; Marquis Who's Who Top Professional; Marquis Who's Who Humanitarian Award **Why did you become involved in your profession or industry:** Mr. Butterfield entered the field because he wanted to follow in his father's footsteps as a career U.S. Navy aviator. He failed the physical exam to enter San Diego Boyden Naval Academy, just one of two of the 13 boys from San Diego Boyden Naval Academy Prep. School who failed. Though he qualified for West Point Academy, he declined entry. Ultimately, he joined the United States Naval Air Reserve in 1948 in the aftermath of WWII. **Avocations:** Reading; Writing

Amity P. Buxton, PhD

Title: Founder, Educator **Company Name:** Straight Spouse Network **Date of Birth:** 02/20/1929 **Place of Birth:** Medford **State/Country of Origin:** MA/USA **Parents:** Alfred Pierce; Nancy Walsh Pierce **Marital Status:** Married **Spouse Name:** Robert Steen Strand (06/27/1991); John William Buxton (06/27/1958, Divorced) **Children:** Pierce Alfred; Felicity Loring **Education:** PhD, Columbia University Teachers College, NY (1962) **Certifications:** Certified in Administrative Services, State of California (1980); General Teaching Credential, State of California (1973); General Teaching Credential, State of Michigan (1952-1954); General Teaching Credential, State of New York **Career:** Founder, Straight Spouse Network, Mahwah, NJ (1991-Present); Executive Director, Straight Spouse Network, El Cerrito, CA (2001-2007); Staff Development Coordinator, Oakland Unified School District (1980-1986); Director, Teachers' Center, Oakland, CA (1974-1986); Extension Faculty, California State University, Hayward, CA (1974-1980); Extension Instructor, University of California, San Diego (1974-1975); Adjunct Faculty, San Francisco State University (1973-1974); Adjunct Faculty, Mills College, Oakland, CA (1973); Director, Teachers' Active Learning Center, San Francisco, CA (1969-1974); College Assistant Professor, San Francisco State College University (1966-1971); Teacher, St. David's School, NY (1957-1958) **Career Related:** Presenter, Professional Conference, American Psychological Association (1994-2012); Presenter, Professional Conference, Association of Family and Conciliation Courts, Madison, WI (1994-2010); Presenter, Professional Conference, Bisexuality Network, San Diego, CA (1992-2006) **Civic:** Board of Directors, Family Equality Council (2010-Present); Board of Directors, Straight Spouse Network (2008-Present); Member, Junior League of San Francisco (1953-Present); Board of Directors, Family Equality Council, Boston, MA (1996-2002); Board of Directors, United Way, San Francisco, CA (1959-1963); Board of Directors, Catholic Association of Lesbian and Gay Ministry, Berkeley, CA; Parish Council Member, St. Leo the Great, Oakland, CA **Creative Works:** Author, "The Other Side of the Closet: The Coming-Out Crisis for Straight Spouses and Families"; Author, "Supporting the Learning Teacher"; Author, "Building a Teachers' Center"; Author, "Portraits of High Schools: A Report on Secondary Education in America"; Author, "The Scientific Basis of Child Custody Decisions"; Author, "Home Fronts: Controversies in Nontraditional Parenting"; Author, "Facts and Fictions: Experiencing Male Bisexuality"; Author, "Current Research in Bisexuality"; Author, "Interventions with Families of Gay, Lesbian, Bisexual, and Transgender People: From the Inside Out"; Author, "Unseen-Unheard: Straight Spouses"; Author, Books; Contributor, Articles, Professional Journals **Awards:** Evelyn Hooker Award for Distinguished Contribution, American Psychological Association **Memberships:** American Psychological Association **Marquis Who's Who Honors:** Albert Nelson Marquis Lifetime Achievement Award **Why did you become involved in your profession or industry:** Dr. Buxton became involved in Straight Spouse Network, because when her husband came out in 1983, there were several support groups that she went to. When it happened she thought she was the only one; it had affected her sexuality, confidence, her morals, everything. When she got through it, she heard of an organization called P-Flag (Parents, Family, Lesbians, and Gays) and the founder of that organization turned it over to her. They were support groups and she decided it should become a network like her center and that is what got her started. In addition, she got her PhD so that she could become a professor and began volunteering. She was doing nonprofit work in San Francisco during the time that lead up to desegregating schools. Furthermore, Dr. Buxton was inspired because she initially wanted to become a writer, but she did not have enough money to do so. She decided to become a teacher. While in Detroit, Labor Day, there was a rally for labor unions and as she listened to the speakers, it opened her eyes. That is what got her started on wanting to be able to reach every individual so that they could do his or her highest and to teach kids to learn about life and to be an educated person. This all lead her to open the center, which became a network of professors. When she was five, she had a series of medical issues but the doctor saved her life so she realized that God must have made her live so that she could do something; that is what she had in the back of her mind, a mission in life. Her father was very supportive with a sense of humor and her mother was very beautiful. She is not sure where it all came from, but her two children are very supportive as well, along with her current partner. It is all team work. **Avocations:** Walking; Painting; Travel; Theater; Music; Poetry; Sketching; Playing piano **Political Affiliations:** Liberal

Terrell Bynum

Title: Distinguished Connecticut State University Professor **Industry:** Education/Educational Services **Company Name:** Southern Connecticut State University **Parents:** Terrell Waltham; Elizabeth Bynum **Marital Status:** Married **Spouse Name:** Aline **Children:** Timothy, Andrew **Education:** PhD in Philosophy, City University of New York, New York, NY (1986); MPhil, City University of New York, New York, NY (1984); MA in Philosophy, Princeton University, NJ (1966); BA in Philosophy, University of Delaware, with Honors and Distinction, Newark, DE (1963); BS in Chemistry, University of Delaware, with Honors and Distinction, Newark, DE (1963) **Career:** Distinguished Professor, Southern Connecticut State University (2016-Present); Professor, Philosophy, Southern Connecticut State University, New Haven, CT (1989-2016); Associate Professor, Philosophy, Southern Connecticut State University, New Haven, CT (1987-1989); Associate Professor, Philosophy, Dutchess College of State University of New York (1978-1987); Assistant Professor, Philosophy, Dutchess College of State University of New York, Poughkeepsie, NY (1975-1978); Assistant Professor, Philosophy, Ramapo College, Mah Wah, NJ (1974-1975); Assistant Professor, Philosophy, State University of New York, Albany, NY (1968-1974); Assistant Professor, Philosophy, American University, Washington, DC (1967-1968) **Career Related:** Co-Director, Research Center on Values in Emerging Science and Technology, Southern Connecticut State University, New Haven, CT (2016-2017); Director, Research Center on Computing & Society, Southern Connecticut State University, New Haven, CT (1987-2016); Organizer, International Conferences on Computer Ethics; Chair, Committee on Philosophy and Computing, American Philosophical Association, Newark, NJ (1994-1997); Chair, Committee on Professional Ethics, Association for Computing Machinery, New York, NY (1993-1996); President, American Association of Philosophy Teachers (1990-1992); Organizer, Co-Director, National Conference on Computing and Values, New Haven, CT (1988-1992); Executive Director, American Association of Philosophy (1980-1982); Founder, American Association of Philosophy (1978-1980) **Creative Works:** Translator, Biographer, Author, Editor: Gottlob Frege, Conceptual Notation and Related Articles, Oxford University Press Scholarly Classic (1972, 2000); Founder, Editor-in-Chief, Metaphilosophy (1968-1993); Co-editor, Author, Computer Ethics and Professional Responsibility; Co-editor, Cyberphilosophy: The Intersection of Philosophy and Computing, The Digital Phoenix: How Computers Are Changing Philosophy; Host, Associate Producer, Video Series What Is Computer Ethics?; Contributor, Articles, Professional Journals on Developmental Psychology, Education, Philosophy, Philosophy of Mathematics, Philosophy of Physics **Awards:** Preston Covey Lifetime Achievement Award, International Association Computing & Philosophy (2011); INSEIT-Weizenbaum Award, International Society Ethics Information Technology (2009); Barwise Prize Winner, American Philosophical Association (2008); Dartmouth College Humanities Research Fellowship (1998); Grantee, Computer Ethics Research, National Science Foundation (1993, 1992, 1991, 1989); Fellow, Andrew Mellon Foundation (1982-1983); Fellow, Danforth Foundation (1963-1967); Fellow, Woodrow Wilson Foundation (1963-1965); Fulbright Fellow in England, US Government (1963-1964) **Memberships:** Board Member, International Association for Computing and Philosophy (2001); International Society for Ethics and Information Technology; Association for Computing Machinery; American Philosophical Association; Life Member, American Association of Philosophy Teachers; Life Member, Computer Professionals for Social Responsibility **Marquis Who's Who Honors:** Albert Nelson Marquis Lifetime Achievement Award; Marquis Who's Who Top Professional; Marquis Who's Who Humanitarian Award **To what do you attribute your success:** Dr. Bynum attributes his success to his wife Aline, his parents Elizabeth and Terrell Bynum, high school mentors Dr. Leah Jordan and Dr. James DeRose, university mentor Professor Bernard H. Baumrin, professional colleagues Professors James A. Thomas, James H. Moor, Simon Rogerson, Ken Gatzke, Donald Gotterbarn, and Krystyna Gorniak-Kocikowska. **Why did you become involved in your profession or industry:** Dr. Bynum knew since high school that he wanted to go into education, because he had some high school teachers that were inspirational. **Avocations:** Travel; Walking; Reading; Writing; Birdwatching

Jeffrey E. Byrne, PhD

Title: Pharmacology Researcher, Educator, Consultant **Industry:** Research **Date of Birth:** 07/15/1939 **Place of Birth:** Minneapolis **State/Country of Origin:** MN/USA **Parents:** Maurice Charles Byrne; Edna F. (Kinney) Byrne **Marital Status:** Married **Spouse Name:** Margaret Ann Kaiser (6/17/1978); Janice Grove (2/1/1960, Deceased 1976) **Children:** Jason; Christopher; Maura **Education:** PhD, University of South Dakota (1966); MA, University of South Dakota (1964); BA, University of North Dakota (1962) **Career:** Consultant (1994-2014); Developer, Programmer, Database Applications (1995-2000); Programmer, Software (1995-2000); Senior Research Scientist II, Bristol-Myers Squibb Company, Wallingford, CT and Princeton, NJ (1987-1994); Principal Research Scientist, Bristol, Myers and Company (Now Bristol-Myers Squibb Company), Evansville, IN (1981-1987); Senior Research Associate, Bristol, Myers and Company (Now Bristol-Myers Squibb Company), Evansville, IN (1969-1981); Animal Research, Bristol-Myers Squibb Company, Princeton, NJ **Career Related:** Adjunct Faculty, School of Medicine, Indiana University, Evansville, IN (1972-1981); Adjunct Faculty, School of Nursing, University of Evansville (1972-1981) **Civic:** Volunteer, Local Church; Volunteer, Habitat for Humanity® International **Creative Works:** Contributor, Articles, Professional Journals **Memberships:** President, Warrick County Museum, Inc. (2016-Present) **Marquis Who's Who Honors:** Albert Nelson Marquis Lifetime Achievement Award **Why did you become involved in your profession or industry:** Dr. Byrne became involved in his profession by changing fields and pursuing a degree in pharmacology. His initial ambition was to become a doctor, but he realized he preferred research, particularly in heart diseases, to patient care. **Avocations:** Reading; Playing guitar **Political Affiliations:** Republican **Religion:** Lutheran **Thoughts on Life:** Dr. Byrne's career achievements include the discovery of Encainide, an antiarrhythmic drug.

Courtney Lynn Caldwell, JD, MA

Title: Lawyer, Real Estate Consultant **Industry:** Real Estate **Date of Birth:** 03/05/1948 **State/Country of Origin:** WA/USA **Parents:** Joseph Morton Caldwell; Moselle (Smith) Caldwell **Marital Status:** Divorced **Education:** JD, George Washington University, with Highest Honors (1982); MA in History of Religion, University of California, Santa Barbara, CA (1975); BA, University of California, Santa Barbara, CA (1970); Coursework, University of California, Berkeley (1967-1969); Coursework, Duke University (1966-1968) **Career:** Independent Consultant, Orange County, California (1998-2017); Senior Vice President, Education Real Estate Service, Inc., Irvine, CA (1991-1998); Director, Western Operations, Education Real Estate Service, Inc., Irvine, CA (1988-1991); Associate, Perkins Coie, Seattle (1985-1988); Associate, Arnold and Porter, Washington, DC (1983-1985); Judicial Clerk, United States Court of Appeals for 9th Circuit, Seattle, WA (1982-1983) **Civic:** Board Director, University Town Center Association (1994); Chair, Legal Committee (1994); Board Director, Habitat for Humanity, Orange County (1993-1994) **Creative Works:** Commercial Project Development, Washington Real Estate Deskbook (1986); National Commercial Finance Association, Compendium of Commercial Finance Law, Washington Opinions, Usury, Secret Liens (1986); Martindale-Hubbell Washington State Law Summaries, Brokers, Deeds, Notaries, Uniform Commercial Code (1986); 49 George Washington Law Review 339 (1981) **Awards:** Named, National Law Center Law Review Scholar (1981-1982) **Memberships:** California Bar Association **Bar Admissions:** States of California (1989); Washington (1986); District of Columbia (1984) **Marquis Who's Who Honors:** Albert Nelson Marquis Lifetime Achievement Award **Why did you become involved in your profession or industry:** Ms. Caldwell became involved in her profession because her father's half sister was an attorney. She worked for the justice department and the chief justice said she was the most eloquent lawyer he met, which inspired Ms. Caldwell. **Avocations:** Gardening **Political Affiliations:** Democrat

Mary Callahan Erdoes

Title: Chief Executive Officer **Industry:** Financial Services **Company Name:** JPMorgan Chase & Co. **Date of Birth:** 08/13/1967 **Parents:** Patrick Joseph Callahan; Patricia Ann (Henebry) Callahan **Marital Status:** Married **Spouse Name:** Philip Erdoes **Children:** Mia; Morgan; Mason **Education:** MBA, Harvard Business School (1993); BS in Mathematics, Georgetown University (1989) **Career:** Chief Executive Officer, J.P. Morgan Asset Management, JPMorgan Chase & Co., New York, NY (2009-Present); Chief Executive Officer, J.P. Morgan Private Bank, JPMorgan Chase & Co. (2005-2009); Managing Director, Global Head of Investments for Private Banking Clients, JPMorgan Chase & Co. (2000-2005); Head of Investment Management and Alternative Solutions, Private Banking, JPMorgan Chase & Co. (1999); Head, Fixed Income Group, JPMorgan Chase & Co., New York, NY (1996-1999); Portfolio Manager, Managing Director, Meredith, Martin & Kaye (1993-1996); Analyst, Bankers Trust (1989-1991) **Civic:** Board of Directors, UNICEF USA (2005-Present) **Awards:** Named, 50 Most Powerful Women in Business, Fortune Magazine (2010-2015); Named, 50 Most Influential People in Global Finance, Bloomberg Markets (2012-2014); Named, 25 Most Powerful Women in Finance, American Banker (2012-2014); Named, 100 Most Powerful Women, Forbes Magazine (2005, 2009-2014); Named, 50 Most Powerful Women in New York, Crain's New York Business (2011); Named, 25 Most Powerful Women in Banking, American Banker (2007, 2009-2011); Named, 100 Most Influential Women in New York City Business (2007); Named, 40 Under 40 (2002) **Religion:** Catholic

Catherine Bejerana Camacho

Title: Lawyer **Industry:** Law and Legal Services **Company Name:** Law Office of Catherine Bejerana Camacho, Esq. **Date of Birth:** 08/13/1974 **Place of Birth:** Philippines **State/Country of Origin:** Cebu **Parents:** Alix Ollada Bejerana; Nena Maningo Bejerana **Marital Status:** Married **Children:** Anica Bejerana Camacho; Zetta Bejerana Camacho **Education:** JD, University of Hawai'i at Manoa William S. Richardson School of Law, Cum Laude; BA in American Studies, Minor in Philosophy and International Business, Mount Saint Mary's University, Los Angeles, CA, Summa Cum Laude; High School Diploma, Academy of Our Lady of Guam; Middle School Diploma, Santa Barbara School **Career:** Lawyer/Owner, Law Office of Catherine Bejerana Camacho, Esq. (2008-Present); Associate Attorney, Berman O'Connor & Mann (2003-2008); Law Clerk to Honorable Chief Justice F. Philip Carbullido, Supreme Court of Guam (2001-2003) **Creative Works:** Co-host, Radio Show, "Damdaming Pinoy," Station KTKB 101.9 FM (2012-Present); Author, Newspaper Monthly Column, "Immigration Matters," Guam Pacific Daily News (2010-Present); Featured and Contributor, "Cooking A La Diva Cookbook" (2012); Author, "Capitalist Manifesto: The Inadequacy of Antitrust Laws in Preventing the Cannibalism of Competition," Asian-Pacific Law & Policy Journal (2001) **Awards:** Named One of the Top 64 Filipinos on Guam, Filipino Community of Guam (2018); Named One of the 10 Influential Filipinos, Marianas Variety Publication (2010); Named One of the 12 Outstanding Filipinos on Guam, University of the Philippines Alumni-Guam (2009); Named in Who's Who in Among Students in American Universities & Colleges; Named in Who's Who in American Law Students; Named Valedictorian, Academy of Our Lady of Guam and Santa Barbara School **Memberships:** American Immigration Lawyers Association; Guam Chambers of Commerce **Bar Admissions:** Supreme Court of California; Supreme Court of Guam; United States Court of Appeals for the Ninth Circuit; United States Tax Court; United States Court of Appeals for the Federal Circuit; United States District Court for the District of Guam; United States Court of International Trade **To what do you attribute your success:** Any success Mrs. Bejerana Camacho has achieved in life can only be attributed to the blessings of God. Her parents, daughters, and she are devout Catholics and followers of the Santo Nino of Cebu. Additionally, her parents have been her greatest supporters throughout her whole life. They have supported her in all of her educational, professional, and personal endeavors. Her two daughters, Anica and Zetta, are her greatest inspiration. Everything she does is dedicated to these two girls. **Why did you become involved in your profession or industry:** When Mrs. Bejerana Camachowas in high school, she was on the debate team and she always wanted to become a lawyer. Thus, going to law school was something she needed to cross off her bucket list. She had two brilliant uncles, who always dreamed of becoming lawyers, but they never fulfilled their dream. These two uncles almost appeared to live vicariously through her when it came to being a lawyer. In the end, it does not matter whether you end up failing or succeeding, so long as you do not have any regrets. Failing and having gone through the experience is ultimately better, than regretting and wondering, "what if?" **Avocations:** Church; Exercise; Cooking for her girls and family **Political Affiliations:** Republican **Religion:** Roman Catholic **Thoughts on Life:** Mrs. Bejerana Camacho specializes in immigration corporate, real property, and family law. She and her daughters live with the motto, "in it to win it." Whether they ultimately win or lose is not the dispositive factor. Whenever they participate in a task, an activity or a competition, they must give it their best and ensure they bring it to its completion. In a competition, they must fight like there's no tomorrow, but accept the ultimate will of God.

Richard Douglas "Trooper Dick" Cameron, MG USA (Ret.)

Title: Major General **Industry:** Military & Defense Services **Date of Birth:** 02/16/1937 **Place of Birth:** Philadelphia **State/Country of Origin:** PA/USA **Parents:** Richard Ray Cameron; Ellen Irene (Jones) Cameron **Marital Status:** Married **Spouse Name:** Kay Anette Christie (02/27/1960) **Children:** Douglas; Shannon; Morgan **Education:** MHA, Baylor University (1974); Resident, Letterman General Hospital, San Francisco (1966-1969); Rotating Internship, Brooke Army Medical Center, Fort Sam Houston, San Antonio, TX (1965-1966); MD, Iowa State University, Iowa City, IA (1965); BS, State University of Iowa, Iowa City, IA (1961); Student, Command & General Staff School, Industrial College of the Armed Forces, Senior Management in Government, Harvard University, Advance Management, Yale University; Rotating Internship, Brooke Army Medical Center, Fort Sam Houston, San Antonio, TX **Certifications:** Distinguished Fellow, The American College of Physician Executives (1996); Certification, American Board of Psychiatry & Neurology (1973) **Career:** Executive Director, Senior Member, Mercy Health Plans Inc., Fort Smith (1995-2000) **Civic:** James E. West Fellow Designee, Boy Scouts of America; District Chairman, Butterfield Trails District; President, Western Area Council **Military Service:** Deputy Commanding General, U.S. Army Medical Command, Fort Sam Houston, San Antonio, TX (1994-1995); Commanding General, U.S. Army Health Services Command, Fort Sam Houston, San Antonio, TX (1992-1994); Commanding General, Walter Reed Army Medical Center, Washington, DC (1989-1992); Advanced Through Grades to Major General, U.S. Army (1989); Appointed Deputy Assistant Secretary of Defense, Washington, DC (1988-1989); Deputy Assistant Secretary of Defense for Medical Readiness, Office of the Secretary of Defense, Washington, DC (1988-1989); Commanding General, William Beaumont Army Medical Center, Fort Bliss, TX (1986-1988); Commander of Hospital, Darnall Army Hospital, III Corps Surgeon, Fort Hood, TX (1983-1986); Deputy Chief of Staff for Operations, Health Services Command, Fort Sam Houston, San Antonio, TX (1980-1983); Chief, Medical Team, Saudi Arabian National Guard Modernization Program, Riyadh, Saudi Arabia (1980); Commander, 56th General Hospital, Baumholder, Federal Republic of Germany (1977-1979); Surgeon, 3rd Armored Division, Frankfurt, Federal Republic of Germany (1976-1977); Chief of Psychiatry, 2nd General Hospital, Landstuhl, Federal Republic of Germany (1975-1976); Chief, Department of Psychiatry, Fort Bliss, TX (1974-1975); Resident, Health Care Administration, Fort Sam Houston, San Antonio, TX (1973-1974); Psychiatrist, Behavioral Science Division, Fort Sam Houston, San Antonio, TX (1972); Instructor, Alcohol, Drug, Office Deputy Chief of Staff Personnel, Washington, DC (1971-1972); Division Psychiatrist, 1st Cavalry Division, Vietnam (1970); Commanding Officer, 98th Medical Detachment, Vietnam (1969-1970); Commissioned 2nd Lieutenant, U.S. Army (1964); Forces, JFK School of Government, Harvard University, Advanced Management, Yale University **Awards:** Distinguished Alumni Award for Service to the Nation, University of Iowa College of Medicine (2000); John D. Chase Award for Physician Executive Excellence, U.S. Department of Defense (1994); Distinguished Service Medal; Legion of Merit with Three Oak Leaf Clusters; Bronze Star Medal; Meritorious Service Medal with One Oak Leaf Cluster; Air Medal; Army Commendation Medal with Four Oak Leaf Clusters; Vietnam Service Medal; Vietnam Campaign Medal; National Defense Service Medal with Service Star; Expert Field Medical Badge; Parachutist Badge **Memberships:** Distinguished Fellow, American College of Physician Executives; Association of the U.S. Army Interagency Institute for Federal Healthcare Executives; Federal Institute Health Care Executives; Regent, the American Board of Medical Management; Diplomate, American Board of Psychiatry and Neurology; Association of Military Surgeons; Society of Medical Consultants to the Armed Forces **Marquis Who's Who Honors:** Albert Nelson Marquis Lifetime Achievement Award **Why did you become involved in your profession or industry:** Dr. Cameron became involved in his profession because he grew up in an Army family. his father was a flight surgeon in the Army Air Corps during World War II and retired as a colonel in the U.S. Air Force. He was a man he greatly admired. He believes he set him on his path. As an undergraduate, he was interested in anthropology and zoology. Medical school was exciting for him. **Avocations:** Hunting; Fishing; Shooting; Sports; Cowboy action shooting **Political Affiliations:** Republican **Religion:** Episcopalian

Barbara Campagna

Title: Bank Vice President; College Corporate Relations; Sales Marketing & Promotional Products; Community Volunteer **Industry:** Financial Services **Date of Birth:** 07/01/1941 **Place of Birth:** Buffalo **State/Country of Origin:** NY/USA **Parents:** Vincent Joseph Campagna; Philomena Marie (Pepe) Campagna **Marital Status:** Single **Education:** Certificate, State University at Buffalo, The State University of New York (1985); Certificate, University of Wisconsin (1982); Diploma, American Institute of Banking (1968); BS in Business, D'Youville College (1963) **Career:** Sales Manager, Proforma Total Business (2011-2016); Sales Manager, Globe Advertising (1997-2016); Director, Corporate Relations and Planned Giving, D'Youville College, Buffalo, NY (1994-1996); Advanced to Vice President, Team Leader, Marine Midland (Now HSBC Bank USA) Buffalo, NY (1963-1994) **Civic:** Member, Buffalo Women's Golf League (2006-Present); Treasurer, Bistro Bookers, Buffalo, NY (1995-Present); Active Member, Working for Downtown, Buffalo, NY (1989-Present); Committee Member, Hickory Hill Estates Condominium Development (2005-2018); Board Member, Executive Women's Golf Association (Now LPGA Amateur Golf Association) (2005); Member, Committee, United Way of Buffalo and Erie County (1996-1999, 2004); Member, Marketing Committee, YWCA (2004); Vice President, Hickory Hill Estates Condominium Development (1997-2002); Member, Development Committee, Buffalo and Erie County Historical Society (1997-2001); Treasurer, Hickory Hill Estates Condominium Development (1995-1997); Member, Board of Managers, Hickory Hill Estates Condominium Development (1994-2002); Secretary, Hickory Hill Estates Condominium Development (1994-1995); Member, Board of Directors, Committee Chairman, Buffalo Urban League (1991-2001); Treasurer, Working for Downtown, Buffalo, NY (1991-1992); Member, Board of Directors, Committee Chairman, Kenmore Mercy Foundation (1988-1991); Member, Board of Directors, Sisters of St. Mary of Namur (1985-2004); Eucharistic Minister, St. Gregory the Great Church **Awards:** Certificate of Appreciation "for Active and Cooperative Service as Chair of the Finance Committee," Rotary Club of Buffalo (2005-2006, 2006-2007); Exceptional Contributions and Dedication to the D'Youville College Community Award (2006); Alumni Service Award, D'Youville College (1998); D'Youville College Alumni Recognition for Service, D'Youville College Alumni Association Board of Directors (1994); Community Person of the Day Award, Station WBFO, Buffalo, NY (1989); Key Club Salesperson Award, Buffalo Area Chamber of Commerce & Tourism (1982); Three-time Recipient, Paul Harris Award, Rotary Club of Buffalo **Memberships:** Sunshine Day Committee (1996-Present); Board of Directors, Treasurer, Rotary Club (1999-2001, 2005-2007); Board of Directors, Tan Tara 9 Hole Golf League (1994-1998); Secretary, Tan Tara 9 Hole Golf League (1994-1997); Board of Directors, Treasurer, Secretary, D'Youville College Alumni Association (1989-1994); D'Youville College Alumni Association; St. Mary's Seminary Alumni Association **Marquis Who's Who Honors:** Albert Nelson Marquis Lifetime Achievement Award **Why did you become involved in your profession or industry:** Ms. Campagna became involved in her profession because when she graduated from D'Youville College, she took the summer off to look for a job but her father did not approve. He told her banks were a good place to work so he sent her to a bank where one of his friends worked. There was a long history of bankers in her family. Her grandfather owned a private bank before the 1930s and then they started another bank by the name of Niagara National Bank of Buffalo. It grew to the point where M&T bank bought them out. So banking turned out to be a good fit for her; she started in the accounting department. She spent five years in the cost accounting department and while doing that, she went around in all the various departments and did cost studies including the mail room. She eventually got tired of that and decided to apply for the management training program. She was the first woman to go through and complete the program in 1968. **Avocations:** Golfing; Bicycling; Traveling; Reading; Cultural activities; Skiing; Playing tennis **Political Affiliations:** Republican **Religion:** Roman Catholic

Arthur Waldron Campbell

Title: Lawyer, Author, Educator **Industry:** Law and Legal Services **Date of Birth:** 03/29/1944 **Place of Birth:** Brooklyn **State/Country of Origin:** NY/USA **Parents:** Wilburn Camrock Campbell; Janet Louise (Jobson) Campbell **Marital Status:** Widowed **Spouse Name:** Drusilla Campbell (Deceased 2014) **Children:** Wilburn C. Campbell; Matthew P. Campbell **Education:** Master's Degree in Criminal Justice, Georgetown University (1975); Doctor of Jurisprudence, West Virginia University (1971); Bachelor of Arts, Harvard University (1966) **Career:** Law Professor, California Western School of Law, San Diego, CA (1976 to 2021); Clinical Instructor, Deputy Director, DC Consortium of Law Schools (1973-1976); Special Assistant U.S. Attorney, U.S. Justice Department, Washington, DC (1971-1973) **Career Related:** Board of Director, San Diego Writers' Ink (2012-2013); Neighborhood Legal Services, San Diego, CA (1982); Chief Executive Officer, Trudar Productions Inc., San Diego, CA (1981-1990); Chairman, Virginia Section, National Association of Criminal Defense Lawyers Strike Force on Grand Jury Abuse (1975-1976); Private Practice (1976); DC Bar Landlord and Tenant Committee (1975); Member, American Bar Association, Committee on Privacy, Washington, DC (1974); Consultant, West Virginia State Legislature Committee to Rewrite Criminal Code (1972-1973); Member, Center for Creative Problem Solving **Civic:** President, Peace Store, San Diego, CA (1986) **Military Service:** Second Lieutenant, U.S. Air Force Air National Guard (1968-1974) **Creative Works:** Author, "Trial & Error: The Education of a Freedom Lawyer," Three Volumes (2007-2012); Author, "Law of Sentencing" Third Edition (2004); Author, "Entertainment Law," First through Fifth Editions (1991-1998); Author, "Entertainment Law," First through Fifth Editions (1991-1998); Author, Poetry, Published Nationally and Internationally, Winning Over A Dozen Prizes **Awards:** Middleweight Boxing Champion, Harvard University (1964-1965); National Honor Society Award (1962); Eagle Scout Award (1957) **Memberships:** Member, Board of Directors, Federal Defenders **Bar Admissions:** California (1974); West Virginia (1971); District of Columbia (1971) **Marquis Who's Who Honors:** Albert Nelson Marquis Lifetime Achievement Award **To what do you attribute your success:** Mr. Campbell credits his success on perseverance and a great amount of good luck. **Why did you become involved in your profession or industry:** Mr. Campbell entered the field of law because of his father, a Bishop in the Episcopalian church, who ruled his family in an authoritarian manner. Mr. Campbell decided he wanted to go into a field that would speak truth to power, defend the powerless, and resolve disputes with facts and rationality. **Avocations:** Polo; Running; Camping **Political Affiliations:** Independent **Religion:** Zen practitioner

Fred Campbell

Title: President, Owner **Company Name:** Creative Masonry, Inc. **Date of Birth:** 09/13/1971 **Place of Birth:** Johnson City **State/Country of Origin:** TN/USA **Marital Status:** Married **Spouse Name:** Sharon (10/14/1989) **Children:** Kayla; Krista; Kendra; Kylie; Lacie; Braylon **Education:** Coursework, Vocational School **Certifications:** MCCR **Career:** President, Owner, Creative Masonry, Inc. **Awards:** Named World's Best Bricklayer, Spec Mix Bricklayer 500 Competition (2013, 2015) **Why did you become involved in your profession or industry:** Mr. Campbell's dad taught him masonry work at a very early age. He took over his company at the age of 18. He does all types of masonry work and all different sized jobs. He has about 40+ employees, some who have been with him from the start 23 years ago. **Thoughts on Life:** Mr. Campbell's motto is "hard work always pays off."

Steven J. Cann

Title: Political Science Professor **Industry:** Education/Educational Services **Company Name:** Washburn University **Date of Birth:** 10/30/1944 **Place of Birth:** Faribault **State/Country of Origin:** MN/USA **Parents:** Katherine Cann (Deceased 1995); Stanley Cann (Deceased 1989) **Marital Status:** Married **Spouse Name:** Rita Cann (07/13/1989) **Children:** Brian Cann; Brent; Thomas; James; Brian **Education:** PhD in Political Science, Purdue University (1977); MA in Social Science, North Dakota State University (1972); BS in Social Science, North Dakota State University (1970) **Career:** Professor of Political Science, Washburn University, Topeka, KS (1985-2019); Associate Professor, Idaho State University (1983-1985); Assistant Professor, Idaho State University, Pocatello, ID (1977-1983) **Career Related:** Former President, Kansas Chapter, American Association for Public Administration; Former Faculty Representative, Board of Regents, Washburn University **Civic:** Past Kansas Mediator Volunteer, Topeka Victim Offender Mediation Project, Parent-Adolescent Mediation Project **Military Service:** U.S. Navy (1966-1968) **Creative Works:** Author, "Administrative Law, Fourth Edition" (2006); Author, "Politics in Brown and White: Resegregation in America," Volume 88 #2, Judicature (2004); Contributor, Articles, Professional Journals **Awards:** Award, Heartland Mediators Association (2014); Listee, Montclair's Who's Who in College Faculty (2011-2012); Listee, Who's Who Among American Teachers (1996, 1998); President's Award for Significant Contributions to the Promotion of Mediation and for Increasing Public Awareness of Conflict Resolution **Memberships:** Mortar Board (2009-Present); Former Member, Board of Directors, Past President, Kansas Chapter, American Society for Public Administration **Marquis Who's Who Honors:** Albert Nelson Marquis Lifetime Achievement Award **Why did you become involved in your profession or industry:** Dr. Cann became involved in his profession because he had to go into the Navy in 1966, which he was not happy about, so he decided to major in political science to see if he could discover what happened to himself. **Avocations:** Playing billiards; Reading; Researching **Political Affiliations:** Democrat **Religion:** Episcopalian

Bonnie Mae Capehart

Title: English Educator (Retired) **Industry:** Education/Educational Services **Company Name:** Bonita Vista Middle School **Parents:** Kenneth James; Marion June Hawkins **Marital Status:** Married **Spouse Name:** David Harold Capehart (08/22/1992); Eugene Thomas Smithers (Deceased); Donn Robert Holmer (Divorced) **Children:** Robert James Holmer **Education:** Master's in Teaching, National University, San Diego, CA (2005);BA in Applied Arts and Sciences, San Diego State University (1987) **Certifications:** Certified Teacher, California **Career:** Retired (2011); English Teacher, Bonita Vista Middle School, Chula Vista, CA (2006-2011); English Teacher, Southwest Middle School (1999-2006); AVID Coordinator, Southwest Middle School, San Diego, CA (1999-2006) **Career Related:** Mathematics Support Teacher, Bonita Vista Middle School (2008-2010); AVID Coordinator (2007); Newspaper Adviser (2006-2010) **Memberships:** National Education Association; California Teachers Association; NCTE; Tennessee Genealogical Society; San Diego Genealogical Society **Marquis Who's Who Honors:** Albert Nelson Marquis Lifetime Achievement Award; Marquis Who's Who Top Professional **To what do you attribute your success:** Ms. Capehart attributes her success to personal determination and great mentors. **Why did you become involved in your profession or industry:** Ms. Capehart became involved in her profession because she wanted to work with children in order to encourage them to strive for their best. **Avocations:** Genealogy; Reading; Gardening; Taking photographs; Used to go surfing

Peter Mallison Carney, MD, FAANS

Title: Neurosurgeon **Industry:** Medicine & Health Care **Company Name:** Peter M. Carney, M.D. **Date of Birth:** 03/14/1936 **Place of Birth:** Cleveland **State/Country of Origin:** OH/USA **Parents:** Richard Birchnal Westnedge; Dorothy (Mallison) Carney **Marital Status:** Married **Spouse Name:** Gloria Smith (4/11/1970) **Education:** Resident in Neurosurgery, Yale New Haven Hospital (1965-1968); Resident in General Surgery, Yale New Haven Hospital (1964); Resident in Neurosurgery, Yale New Haven Hospital (1963); Intern in Surgery, Yale New Haven Hospital (1962-1963); MD, Case Western Reserve University (1962); BA, Williams College (1958) **Certifications:** Diplomate, American Board of Neurological Surgeons (1971) **Career:** Active Staff, Community Hospital of Bremen (2006-Present); Private Practice in Neurosurgery and Pain Medicine, (1985-Present); Courtesy Staff, Elkhart General Hospital (2006-2017); Director, Pain Management Clinic, Northern Indiana VA Health Care System (2002-2004); Neurosurgeon, Active Staff, Elkhart General Hospital (1985-2005); Mellon Fellow, Program in Science, Technology, and Society, Massachusetts Institute of Technology, Cambridge, MA (1984-1985); Chairman, Department of Surgery, King Faisal Specialist Hospital & Research Center, Riyadh, Saudi Arabia (1980-1983); Chief, Division of Neurosurgery, King Faisal Specialist Hospital & Research Center (1977-1983); Neurosurgeon, King Faisal Specialist Hospital & Research Center (1977-1978); Active Staff-Chief, Neurosurgery, Cape Cod Hospital, Hyannis, MA (1971-1977); Private Practice in Neurosurgery (1971-1977); Acting Neurosurgeon in Chief, New England Medical Center Hospital (1970-1971) **Career Related:** Chairman, Bioethics Committee, Elkhart General Hospital (1997-1999); Secretary-Treasurer, Elkhart General Hospital (1996); Member-at-Large, Executive Committee, Elkhart General Hospital (1994-1995); Chairman, Department of Surgery, King Faisal Specialist Hospital (1980-1983); Consulting Staff, Neurosurgery, Falmouth Hospital, Nantucket Hospital, Martha's Vineyard Hospital, Barnstable County Hospital, Tobey Hospital (1971-1977); Instructor in Neurosurgery, Tufts Medical School (1968-1971); Instructor in Neurosurgery, Yale Medical School (1967-1968); Fellow, American Association of Neurological Surgeons **Military Service:** Captain, U.S. Army Reserves (1963-1969) **Creative Works:** Contributor,"An Effective Treatment for Painful Peripheral Neuropathy Exists today" Pain Medicine (2020). "The New Three R's to Treat Neuropathy," Nociceptor (2019); Contributor, "Conflicts from the Past; Lessons for the Present" (2011); Contributor, "Decompressive Craniectomies and Dural Grafting in the Treatment of Coma Secondary to Acute Subdural Hematoma," Journal of Neurosurgery (1996); Deputy Executive Editor, King Faisal Specialist Hospital & Research Center Medical Journal (1980-1983); Contributor, Over 25 Articles, Professional Journals; Contributor, "The New 3 R's for Treating Neurology," Midwest Pain Society; Presenter, Over 104 Presentations in Medical Care **Awards:** Blue Ribbon Award, Best Poster Presentation, 25th Annual Meeting, American Academy of Pain Management (2014) **Memberships:** American Medical Association; American Association of Neurological Surgeons; American Society of Law, Medicine, and Ethics; Congress of Neurologic Surgeons; International Association of the Study of Traumatic Brain Injuries; Indiana State Medical Association; Congress of Neurological Surgeons; International Association for the Study of Neuropathic Pain SIG; Yale Surgical Society; American Academy of Pain Medicine **Marquis Who's Who Honors:** Albert Nelson Marquis Lifetime Achievement Award; Marquis Who's Who Top Professional **To what do you attribute your success:** Dr. Carney attributes his success to great parents and great teachers, who instilled in him a commitment to honesty, integrity, and compassion. **Why did you become involved in your profession or industry:** Dr. Carney became involved in his profession because the art of medicine represents the greatest endeavor ever created by the mind of human beings. Its a privilege you get to help people. It is his basic philosophy. It is an incredible privilege to be a doctor. **Avocations:** Travel; Antiques; Chess; Music; History **Religion:** Mennonite

Dick H. Caro, MBA

Title: Marketing and Technology Consultant **Industry:** Technology **Company Name:** CMC Associates **Date of Birth:** 09/30/1936 **Place of Birth:** New York **State/Country of Origin:** NY/USA **Parents:** Marshall H. Caro; Mildred (Miller) Caro **Marital Status:** Married **Spouse Name:** Jeanne Marie Harrington (07/19/2018); Kathy Lynn Schaefer (09/25/1982, Divorced 2001); Patricia McCallum (08/03/1958, Divorced 1978) **Children:** Alexander John; James Richard; Annette Louise; Debora Lynn; Christopher Marshall **Education:** MBA, Alexander Hamilton Institute, New York, NY (1972); MS, Louisiana State University (1964); BS, University of Florida (1957) **Certifications:** Certified Automation Professional, International Society of Automation (2004) **Career:** Chief Executive Officer, CMC Associates (2001-Present); Vice President, Automation Research Corporation, Dedham, MA (1997-2001); Senior Manager, Arthur D. Little, Inc., Cambridge, MA (1988-1997); President, ControlMaster Corp., Coral Springs, FL (1985-1988); Vice President of Marketing, Autech Data Systems, Inc., Pompano Beach, FL (1981-1985); Director of Process Marketing, Modular Computer Systems, Fort Lauderdale, FL (1978-1981); Director of Advanced Development, The Foxboro Co., Foxboro, MA (1970-1978); Senior Engineer, Union Camp Corp., Savannah, GA (1962-1970); Process Engineer, Ethyl Corp., Baton Rouge, LA (1957-1962) **Career Related:** Vice President of Planning, Purdue Workshop on Industrial Control, Lafayette, IN (1976-1980); Chairman of International Electrotechnology Committee SC65C/WG6, Fieldbus Standards **Awards:** Standards Award, International Society of Automation (1991, 1996, 2000) **Memberships:** Chairman, SP50, Fieldbus Standards Committee, International Society of Automation (1993-Present); Florida Goldcoast Chapter President, International Society of Automation (1986-1988); Fellow, Industrial Computer Society; Fellow, International Society of Automation; Senior Member, International Society of Automation; International Society of Automation **Marquis Who's Who Honors:** Albert Nelson Marquis Lifetime Achievement Award **To what do you attribute your success:** Mr. Caro attributes his success to constant learning and becoming an expert from the things he's learned. The internet has opened the door for research. It's constant learning. Everything he has done with a very small exception is something that he learned after graduating from college. Mr. Caro became an expert, not from schooling, but from a ferocious appetite for reading. **Why did you become involved in your profession or industry:** Mr. Caro started off in chemical engineering. What he's doing now is not remotely related to that. Mr. Caro is still in a technical field even though the title is chief executive officer. He does consulting for a company. **Avocations:** Reading murder mysteries; Keeping up with changes in the automation field

C. Donald Carpenter Jr.

Title: Land Surveyor, Title Researcher (Retired) **Industry:** Engineering **Date of Birth:** 11/09/1933 **Place of Birth:** Ballston Spa **State/Country of Origin:** NY/USA **Parents:** C. Donald Carpenter; Carolyn (Male) Carpenter **Marital Status:** Widower **Children:** Ann M.; Arthur D.; Marilyn J.; Catherine M.; Duane D.; John T.; Scott C. **Education:** Coursework, Rensselaer Polytechnic Institute (1951-1958) **Certifications:** Certified Engineering Technician; Licensed Land Surveyor **Career:** President, Carpenter Associates, PC, Galway, NY (1984-Retired); Principal, C. Donald Carpenter, Galway, NY (1973-1984); Deputy Director, Saratoga County Real Property Tax, Ballston Spa, NY (1971-1973); Deputy Director, Saratoga County Planning Board, Ballston Spa, NY (1966-1971); Office Manager, Coulter McCormack Surveyors, Saratoga Springs, NY (1964-1966); Computer Programmer, Rist-Frost Associates, Glen Falls, NY (1962-1964); Highway Designer, J. Clarkeson Consultant Engineer, Albany, NY (1957-1962); Designer, Medium Motors Department, General Electric Co., Schenectady, NY (1955-1957) **Career Related:** Consultant, Ancient Land Title and Municipal Boundary Matters; Expert Witness, Land Patent and Boundary Disputes; Self-taught Historian **Civic:** Committeeman, Galway Conservative Party (1978); Active, Greenfield Environmental Commission (1972-1976); Early American Industries Association **Military Service:** R.O.T.C.; U.S. Army Reserve **Creative Works:** Reconstructor, Land Patent Maps from Original Survey Records, The Mosher Furance of Galway, New York (2010); Author, "Kayaderosseras Allotment Maps" (1964); Author, "A Comprehensive History of Kayaderosseras Patent" **Awards:** Award of Merit, Federation Historical Services (1988); 1st Place, Map Competition, New York State Association of Professional Land Surveyors **Memberships:** New York State Association of Professional Land Surveyors; Past Board of Directors, Eastern New York Society of Professional Land Surveyors; Lodges: Lions; Schenectady County Historical Society; Galway Preservation Society; Butternut Valley Tractor Club; Tri-State Antique Tractor Club **Marquis Who's Who Honors:** Albert Nelson Marquis Lifetime Achievement Award; Marquis Who's Who Top Professional **Why did you become involved in your profession or industry:** Mr. Carpenter always had an interest in engineering. He grew up in the country, there were people in his church who ran an engineering and land surveying business. They liked to hire engineering students for summer help, and they hired him. Although he tried many different fields, Mr. Carpenter always returned back to land surveying. He worked for General Electric in 1957 and he was able to work on the Nautilus and the Atomic Submarine. He was eventually laid off from General Electric and he went back to land surveying and he stayed in that field his whole career. **Avocations:** Hunting; Farming; Music; Writing; Antique books **Religion:** Methodist

N. Gordon Carper, PhD

Title: Historian, Educator **Industry:** Education/Educational Services **Date of Birth:** 05/10/1935 **Place of Birth:** Bettsville **State/Country of Origin:** OH/USA **Parents:** Glenn Carper; Cal Carper **Spouse Name:** Selma Joyce Carper **Children:** Noel; Todd **Education:** Postdoctoral Studies, Harvard University (1969); PhD, Florida State University (1964); MA, Florida State University (1961); BA, Heidelberg College, Tiffin, OH (1960) **Career:** Dana Professor of History, Berry College, Mount Berry, GA (1975-Present); Coordinator, History Department, Berry College, Mount Berry, GA (1999-2001); Dana Professor of History, Chairman, Social Sciences Department, Berry College, Mount Berry, GA (1969-1975);Professor of History, Chairman, Social Sciences Department, Berry College, Mount Berry, GA (1967-1969);Associate Professor of History, Berry College, Mount Berry, GA (1965-1967); Assistant Professor of History, Muskingum College, New Concord, OH (1963-1965) **Career Related:** Consultant, Georgia Endowment for Humanities; Consultant, Southern Regional Education Board, Atlanta, GA; Consultant, National Endowment of the Humanities; Consultant, Georgia Governor's Honors' Program **Civic:** Chairman, Georgia Committee, National Endowment of the Humanities, Atlanta, GA (1978-1980); Chairman, Georgia Committee, National Endowment of the Humanities, Athens, Greece (1978-1980); Co-Director, March of Dimes, Rome, GA; Board of Directors, Rome YMCA; Reading Committee, Georgia State Committee for National Endowment for the Humanities; Chairman, Bi-Centennial Committee, Georgia Committee for the Humanities **Military Service:** Specialist, 5th Class, U.S. Army (1954-1957) **Creative Works:** Co-Author (With Selma Joyce Carper), "The Meaning of History: A Dictionary of Quotations" (1990); Contributor, Chapters, Books; Contributor, Dozens of Lectures and Papers, Southeast **Awards:** Lifetime Achievement Award, College Bowl, Inc. (2002); Leadership Award, Georgia House of Representatives (2000); Vulcan Teaching Excellence Award (2000); Lifetime Achievement Award, Academy Competition Federation (1999); Governor's Awards in the Humanities, Governor of Georgia (1994); Governor's Award in the Humanities, Governor Zell Miller (1994); Inductee, College Bowl Hall of Fame (1984); Honoree, Georgia Endowment for the Humanities (1982); Elected Faculty Member of the Year, Berry College (1975); Fellowship, National Defense Education Act (1960-1963); Listee, Directory of American Scholars; Listee, Who's Who Among Social Scientists in the Southeast; Listee, Personalities of the South; Listee, Community Leaders of America **Memberships:** Southern Historical Association; American Historical Association; Organization of American Historians; Phi Kappa Phi; Phi Alpha Theta; Pi Sigma Alpha; Honor Society of Heidelberg College; Friends of the Humanities **Marquis Who's Who Honors:** Albert Nelson Marquis Lifetime Achievement Award **Why did you become involved in your profession or industry:** Dr. Carper became involved in his profession because he always had a passion for history. **Avocations:** Reading; Traveling; Playing golf

Barry Lynn Carr, Sr.

Title: President, Chief Executive Officer **Industry:** Media & Entertainment **Company Name:** TeleVideo Production Co. Inc. **Date of Birth:** 04/04/1953 **Place of Birth:** York **State/Country of Origin:** PA/USA **Parents:** Harold Leonard Sr.; Nancy (Castleman) Carr. **Marital Status:** Married **Spouse Name:** Yvette Marie (Chambers) Carr **Children:** Barry Carr Jr.; Brandon Lee Carr **Education:** Coursework, William Penn Senior High School; Coursework, Pennsylvania State University; Coursework, York College of Pennsylvania; Coursework, Harrisburg Area Community College; Cadet, Pennsylvania State Police Academy **Certifications:** Qualified Video Producer, Department of Defense; FCC Radio Broadcasting License; Lethal Weapons Certification, Pennsylvania **Career:** Trooper, Pennsylvania State Police (1978- 2003); With, Bureau of York City Police (1975- 1978); Freelancer Artist & Illustrator (1972-1975) **Career Related:** President, Chairman, TeleVideo Production Co. Inc.; Webmaster, PaStateTrooper.com (2019-Present); Webmaster, Pennsylvania State Police-Oral History in Association (2005-Present); Webmaster, TeleVideo Music (1999-Present); Webmaster, free2explore.com (1998-Present) **Civic:** Fund Raising Chairman, Parents Advocates for Children (2016); Member, National Federation of Independent Business (2016); Committee Member, Parents Advocates for Children (2015); The York County Chamber of Commerce (1994); York, Pennsylvania Minority Business Association Past President (1993); Mentor, Star Up Business Owners (1993); Committee Member, York City Planning Commission (1993); Committee Member, Small MBE Business Loan Development Fund (1993); Past President, South York Lions Club, Lions Clubs International (1991); Editor, PSP-Historical, Educational, Memorial Center (Museum) Newsletter **Creative Works:** Composer, Over 1,000 Music Compositions (1999-Present); Writer, Producer, Director, "Evolution of Women in Law Enforcement" (2015); Writer, Producer, Director, Theatrical Play "Then and Now" (2005); Contributing Writer, "An Artist a Day Almanac," (2012); Composer, Producer, "The First and Finest" (1986); Writer, Producer, Director: "Our Nations First State Constabulary" (1985) **Awards:** Selectee, Best of York Awards for Music Producer, York Awards Program (2018); Recipient, Best of 2018 Music Producer Award for Television Production Co. (2018); Small CAP Award for Best Multi-media Business Service, Corp America-News (2016); Best of Business Award for Business Services, York Awards Program (2016); Pennsylvania State Police Commissioners Award for Excellence (2000, 2002, 2003); Award, School Bus Safety Education from the Pennsylvania Department of Transportation (2002); Award for Public Relations Video, American Association of Motor Vehicle Administrators (2000); Award, Best Director Award from the Municipal Police Officers' Education & Training Commission (1997); Pennsylvania Municipal Police Standardized Training Award, PA Municipal Police (1997); Business of the Year Award, MBA -Business Association (1992); Knights of Columbus Council No. 1530 for Outstanding Public Service (1977); Commendation for Excellent Performance of Duty, The City of York, Pennsylvania Bureau of Police (1975); Commendation, York City Director of Public Safety (1975); The National Scholastic Art & Writing Achievement Award, Scholastic Inc. (1971); 2 "Gold Key" Art Awards, Harrisburg, PA (1970) **Memberships:** MBA Business Association of York; York County Chamber of Commerce; National Federation of Independent Business **Marquis Who's Who Honors:** Albert Nelson Marquis Lifetime Achievement Award; Marquis Who's Who Top Professional; Who's Who in the East **To what do you attribute your success:** Mr. Carr credits his success on his propensity for drive, self-reliance, willpower, patience, integrity, passion, optimism and ambition. **Why did you become involved in your profession or industry:** Mr. Carr first became involved in his profession out of a drive to pursue a career that spoke to his strengths. **Avocations:** Reading; Writing; Art; Science; Astrophysics; Music **Political Affiliations:** Independent **Religion:** Presbyterian

Tracy Carson

Title: Chief Executive Officer **Industry:** Consulting **Company Name:** Carson Consulting Corp. **Parents:** Michelle Childs **Children:** One Son; One Daughter **Career:** Chief Executive Officer, Carson Consulting Corp. (2016-Present); Business Development Manager, Staffing and Recruiting (2015-2016); Sales Manager, Outside Sales (2011-2015); Account Executive, Valley Yellow Pages (2009-2011) **Civic:** Volunteer, Coach, Union City Baseball League; Volunteer, Coach, Union City Colts Football League; Volunteer, Coach, Union City Colts Cheerleading **Marquis Who's Who Honors:** Marquis Who's Who Top Professional **To what do you attribute your success:** Ms. Carson believes her genuine drive to help people is where she gained the most success from. She also acknowledged that whenever she makes a mistake, she isn't afraid to admit to her error and repair it as quickly as possible. **Why did you become involved in your profession or industry:** Ms. Carson initially wanted to work in sales, preferably as an account manager. She saw how people's lives were changed from sales, both positively and negatively. She hated watching people be depleted down to a number, but she did appreciate when people came back and told her how the opportunity they gained from her help changed their life. Ms. Carson was eventually promoted to a branch manager, and that is when she found her true calling. She didn't like seeing how poorly most employees were treated. Ms. Carson took that as a message to open her own business; her goal was to make individuals happy in their job. If this could be achieved, they would be happier with their life as a whole, and the company would prosper. **Thoughts on Life:** The additional exposure that Ms. Carson will gain from this biography is important to her. She wants to be able to help as many people as possible. This business is not run by Ms. Carson alone; she has help from her son, cousin and daughter-in-law each day.

Annette Carter

Title: Former State Legislator, House of Representatives **Industry:** Government Administration/Government Relations/Government Services **Date of Birth:** 05/24/1941 **Marital Status:** Divorced **Children:** Junetta Mitchell; Cynthia Tucker; Sheila Robinson; Donna Ward; Fretta Davis **Education:** Diploma, Alabama State College (Now Alabama State University); Coursework, Rensselaer Polytechnic Institute; Coursework, Hartford Community Trainers; Coursework, Manchester Community College **Certifications:** University of Hartford (1981); Certified Moderator, State of Connecticut (1980) **Career:** Member, Connecticut House of Representatives, Hartford, CT (1988-2008); Assistant Majority Whip and Vice Chairperson of Appropriations; Housing Adviser, Capitol Region Conference of Churches; Assembly District Seven Representative, Connecticut House of Representatives, Hartford, CT; Assistant Majority Leader, Member, Black Caucus, Connecticut House of Representatives, Hartford, CT; Vice Chairman, Appropriations Committee, Connecticut House of Representatives, Hartford, CT; Member, Public Safety, Community and Exportation Committees, Connecticut House of Representatives, Hartford, CT **Career Related:** Speaker in the Field **Civic:** Advocacy Work, Funding for Programs Including Dial-A-Ride, Community Health Services, Blue Hills Hospital and Mt. Sinai Rehabilitation Center, Various Teen Pregnancy Prevention Programs in the City of Hartford, Research Efforts on African Trade in Connecticut; Blue Hills Civic Association; Sojourner Network of Democratic Women; Sponsor, Delta Sigma Theta Sorority Inc.; Urban League of Greater Hartford; Supporter, Friends of Keney Park; Rehabilitation of Rawson School; Advisory Board, Channel, 3 Kids Country Camp **Creative Works:** Featured, Segment, "Highlights of Accomplishments" and Impact of Her Work in her Community, "NBC Nightly News," Tom Brokaw **Awards:** Certificate of Honor and Marble Apple Award, College Board of New England, Episcopal Church Women of St. Monica's Episcopal Church (2002); Award, Greater Hartford Community College (Now Capital Community College) (2001); 2000 Presidential Forum for Freedom Award (2001); Award, National Association for the Advancement of Colored People (NAACP) (1993); Connecticut State Black Democratic Award (1992); Crispus Attucks Award (1991); Outstanding Accomplishments Award, Hope Seventh-day Adventist Church (1990); Award, National Council Negro Women, Inc., Connecticut Chapter; Channel 3 Kids Camp Dedicated Service Award; Certificate of Appreciation, United States Dept. of Commerce Bureau of the Census **Memberships:** National Association for the Advancement of Colored People (NAACP); Greater Hartford Black Democratic Club; Sojourner Network of Democratic Women; Professional Democratic Black Women of Greater Hartford; African American Parade Committee; The Hartford Larrabee Corporation **Marquis Who's Who Honors:** Albert Nelson Marquis Lifetime Achievement Award **Why did you become involved in your profession or industry:** Ms. Carter became involved in her profession because when she came to Hartford, Connecticut, she felt she needed to get involved in something. Her mother and father, J.D. Wheeler and Jewel Wheeler, were always involved in community activities and functions and so she thought it was something to do so that her children would see her giving back to the community. So she had been doing that ever since. **Political Affiliations:** Democrat **Religion:** Episcopalian

Thomas Allen Carter

Title: Engineering Executive (Retired) **Industry:** Engineering **Date of Birth:** 07/12/1935 **Place of Birth:** Cincinnati **State/Country of Origin:** OH/USA **Parents:** Fernando Albert Carter; Mary Gladys (Gover) Carter **Marital Status:** Married **Spouse Name:** Janet Tucker (10/14/1956) **Children:** Barry Everett; Duane Allen; Sarita Anne **Education:** BBA, Jones College, Cum Laude (1982); AB, Jones College (1980) **Certifications:** Certified Construction Inspector **Career:** Engineering Executive (Retired); Estimator, Independent Mechanical Design Co., Inc. (1996-2005); Chief Engineer, D.A.M.S., Inc., Orlando, FL (1984-1991); Secretary, Blacando Development Corp., Orlando, FL (1980-1984); Private Practice, Orlando, FL (1978-1980); Contract Administrator, Red Lobster Restaurants, Orlando, FL (1976-1978) **Career Related:** Consultant in Field **Military Service:** Master Chief, U.S. Navy (1954-1976) **Memberships:** Fleet Reserve Association; Armed Forces Top Enlisted Association; RAFMAN (Retired Air Force Marine Army Navy), Club Orlando, (1976); American Legion; Disabled American Veterans; National Pinochle Association; Navy SeaBee Veterans of America **Marquis Who's Who Honors:** Albert Nelson Marquis Lifetime Achievement Award; Marquis Who's Who Top Professional **Avocations:** Bowling; Tennis; Travel **Political Affiliations:** Democrat **Religion:** Methodist

L. Curtis Cary, MD

Title: Program Director, Medical Educator **Industry:** Medicine & Health Care **Date of Birth:** 10/15/1978 **Place of Birth:** Louisville **State/Country of Origin:** KY/USA **Parents:** Larry Burr Cary; Mary Ann McCool **Marital Status:** Married **Spouse Name:** Patricia (2007) **Education:** MD, University of Kentucky (2004); BS, Western Kentucky University (2000) **Certifications:** Certified, American Board of Internal Medicine; Certified, American Board of Pediatrics **Career:** Internal Medicine Residency Program Director, University of Tennessee College of Medicine Chattanooga (2018-Present); Associate Professor, Internal Medicine and Pediatrics, Erlanger Health System, University of Tennessee College of Medicine Chattanooga (2017-Present); Medical Director, Polk Dalton Clinic (2016-2017); Associate Professor, Internal Medicine and Pediatrics, University of Kentucky College of Medicine, UK Healthcare (2015-2017); MedPeds Residency Program Director, University of Kentucky College of Medicine, UK Healthcare (2011- 2016); Assistant Professor, Internal Medicine and Pediatrics, University of Kentucky College of Medicine, UK Healthcare (2009-2015) **Career Related:** Governor's Council, Kentucky Chapter of the American College of Physicians (2009-2017) **Awards:** Eagle Scout Award, Boy Scouts America; William R. Willard Teaching Award, University Kentucky Department Of Pediatrics; Abraham Flexner Master Educator Award, Office Excellence Medical Education University Kentucky College Medicine **Memberships:** Fellow, American Academy of Pediatrics; Fellow, American College of Physicians; Member, American Medical Association; Society of General Internal Medicine; Infectious Diseases Society of America; Society of Hospital Medicine **Marquis Who's Who Honors:** Albert Nelson Marquis Lifetime Achievement Award; Marquis Who's Who Top Professional **To what do you attribute your success:** Dr. Cary attributes his success to hard work and perseverance. **Why did you become involved in your profession or industry:** Dr. Cary had interactions as a child with the medical community. He was inspired, as he thought that through his work, he could give back to his community. **Avocations:** Movies; Travel; History **Political Affiliations:** Democrat **Religion:** Methodist **Thoughts on Life:** Dr. L. Curtis Cary specializes in pediatrics and internal medicine. In addition to his clinical focus, he also serves the health system in a teaching capacity through the UT College of Medicine Chattanooga. He has served in a variety of medical and teaching positions and has numerous accreditations and published research in the areas of medical education and health policy. Prior to joining Erlanger, Dr. Cary served as the residency program director for the Internal Medicine and Pediatrics Residency Program at the University of Kentucky, medical director of Polk Dalton Clinic in downtown Lexington, Kentucky, and a pediatric hospitalist at Kentucky Children's Hospital.

Lawrence Edward "Larry" Castle, Esq.

Industry: Law and Legal Services **Company Name:** Castle Lantz Maricle, LLC (Pan American Legal Services, LLC, Member) **Date of Birth:** 06/18/1953 **Place of Birth:** Summit **State/Country of Origin:** NJ/USA **Parents:** Wesley G. Castle; Eleanor A. Castle **Marital Status:** Married **Spouse Name:** Caren Jacobs Castle, Esq. **Children:** Associate Judge Sarah A. Castle; Wesley L. Castle - Professional Chef; Ethan P. Castle - Golf Professional **Education:** LLM in Taxation, New York University School of Law (1981); JD, Southwestern University School of Law, Cum Laude (1980); BA, Colorado State University (1976) **Career:** Member, Castle Lantz Maricle, LLC (2019-Present); Founding Member, Pan American Legal Services, LLC (2017-Present); CMS Consulting Services Corp., S.A., Panama City, Panama (2009-2014); Member, Law Firms Operating in Arizona, Nevada, New Mexico, Utah, Wyoming (2007-2014); Founding Member, Castle Law Group, LLC; Castle Barrett Daffin & Frappier, LLC; Castle & Castle, LLC; Castle Meinhold Stawiarski, LLC; and Castle Stawiarski, LLC (1990 -2014); Associate, Partner, Hopper, Kanouff, Smith, Peryam, Terry and Duncan (1984-1990) **Awards:** AV Preeminent Peer Review Rating, Martindale-Hubbell **Memberships:** Tax Law Section and Real Estate Section Council, Colorado Bar Association (2001-2007); American Bar Association; Real Estate Law Section, Colorado Bar Association; Business Law Section, Colorado Bar Association; Legislative Committee, Colorado Mortgage Lenders Association; Hispanic Chamber of Commerce; Colorado Association of Commerce & Industry; Rocky Mountain Home Association; VISTAGE International, Inc. **Bar Admissions:** Licensed in Colorado, California, New Jersey; United States District Court for the District of Colorado; United States District Court for the District of Central California; United States Tax Court **Marquis Who's Who Honors:** Albert Nelson Marquis Lifetime Achievement Award; Marquis Who's Who Top Professional **To what do you attribute your success:** Mr. Castle attributes his success to his understanding of business, which helps him provide clients with practical approaches and solutions for their business needs. **Why did you become involved in your profession or industry:** Mr. Castle became involved in his profession due to the influence of his father. **Avocations:** Cooking

James Newton Cather, PhD

Title: Embryologist, Educator **Industry:** Education/Educational Services **Date of Birth:** 03/17/1931 **Place of Birth:** Carthage **State/Country of Origin:** MO/USA **Parents:** John Ward Cather; Liza Jane (Webb) Cather **Marital Status:** Married **Spouse Name:** Jane Ruth Julian (07/21/1951) **Children:** Alicia Ruth; Craig Julian **Education:** PhD in Radiation Effects on Cell Division, Emory University (1958); MS in Embryology, Southern Methodist University (1955); BS in Embryology, Southern Methodist University (1954) **Career:** Professor Emeritus (1996-Present); Professor, University of Michigan, Ann Arbor, MI (1958-1995); Director, Office of International Programs, University of Michigan, Ann Arbor, MI (1982-1992); Associate Dean of College of Literature, Science and the Arts, University of Michigan, Ann Arbor, MI (1982-1988); Associate Chairman, Division on Biological Sciences, University of Michigan, Ann Arbor, MI (1976-1981); Associate Professor, University of Michigan, Ann Arbor, MI (1965-1973); Assistant Professor of Biological Sciences, University of Michigan, Ann Arbor, MI (1960-1965); Instructor, University of Michigan, Ann Arbor, MI (1958-1960) **Career Related:** Bermuda Biological Station (1972-1976); Visiting Professor, Oregon Institute of Marine Biology (1974); Visiting Professor, Oregon Institute of Marine Biology (1969); Staff, Embryology Course, Marine Biological Laboratory, Woods Hole, MA (1966-1967); Upjohn Faculty Fellowship (1965) **Military Service:** U.S. Marine Corps Reserve (1948-1958); Active Duty, U.S. Marine Corps (1950-1952) **Awards:** Award for Outstanding Undergraduate Teaching, University of Michigan Class (1964) **Memberships:** International Society of Development Biologists; Society for Developmental Biology; American Society of Zoologists; Malacological Society of London **Marquis Who's Who Honors:** Albert Nelson Marquis Lifetime Achievement Award; Marquis Who's Who Top Professional **Why did you become involved in your profession or industry:** Dr. Cather spent a lot of time outdoors as a child and got interested in the critters that lived there, and decided to study embryology. He saw the critters in their development stages and decided to study in embryology.

Safra Ada Catz

Title: Chief Executive Officer **Company Name:** Oracle Corporation **Date of Birth:** 12/01/1961 **Place of Birth:** Holon **State/Country of Origin:** Israel **Parents:** Leonard Catz; Judith Catz **Marital Status:** Married **Spouse Name:** Gal Tirosh **Children:** Two Children **Education:** JD, University of Pennsylvania Law School (1986); BA, The Wharton School, The University of Pennsylvania, Philadelphia, PA (1983) **Career:** Chief Executive Officer, Oracle Corporation, Redwood City, CA (2019-Present); Co-Chief Executive Officer, Oracle Corporation, Redwood City, CA (2014-2019); President, Chief Financial Officer, Oracle Corporation, Redwood City, CA (2011-2014); President, Chief Financial Officer, Oracle Corporation, Redwood City, CA (2005-2008); President, Oracle Corporation, Redwood City, CA (2004-2005, 2008-2011); Executive Vice President, Oracle Corporation, Redwood City, CA (1999-2004); Senior Vice President, Oracle Corporation, Redwood City, CA (1999); Managing Director, Donaldson, Lufkin & Jenrette (1997-1999); Senior Vice President, Donaldson, Lufkin & Jenrette (1994-1997); Various Investment Banking Positions, Donaldson, Lufkin & Jenrette (1986-1994) **Career Related:** Board of Directors, The Walt Disney Company (2018-Present); Board of Directors, HSBC Holdings PLC (2008-Present); Board of Directors, Hyperion Solutions Corporation (2007-Present); Board of Directors, Oracle Corporation (2001-Present); Board of Directors, Stellent Inc. (2006-2007); Lecturer in Accounting, Stanford University Graduate School of Business **Awards:** Named, One of the 100 Most Powerful Women, Forbes Magazine (2005-2009, 2011-2014); Named, One of the 10 Most Powerful Women in Silicon Valley, San Jose Mercury News (2011); Named, One of the Most Influential Women in Technology, Fast Company Magazine (2009); Named, One of the 50 Most Powerful Women in Business, Fortune Magazine (2008-2015); Named, One of the 50 Women to Watch, The Wall Street Journal (2005, 2008) **Religion:** Jewish

Joseph Cawley, PhD

Title: Educator Emeritus **Industry:** Education/Educational Services **Date of Birth:** 12/12/1929 **Place of Birth:** Savannah **State/Country of Origin:** GA/USA **Parents:** Henry Hughes; Bertha (Platt) Cawley **Marital Status:** Married **Spouse Name:** Jacqueline Boss (05/22/1987); Grace Ashliman (06/21/1951) **Children:** Lorraine Cawley Gaufin; Carolyn (Genie) Nielsen **Education:** PhD, University of Utah (1970); MS, University of Utah (1961); BS, Brigham Young University (1954) **Certifications:** Certified Elementary Teacher, Utah, Georgia **Career:** Professor Emeritus, MSU Denver (2001-Present);Professor, Chairman, Reading Department, MSU Denver; Assistant Professor, Education, Adams State College, Alamosa, CO;Teacher, Salt Lake City School District; Teacher, DeKalb County School District **Creative Works:** Author, "From Ballymoran to South Carolina Colonel Robert Stewart 1755-1820 British Officer and Merchant" (2008); Author, "From Virginia to Georgia Captain Henry Hughes 1756-1814, Patriot of the Continental Line" (2006); Author, "From Mounthill to Georgia Lieutenant Colonel Matthew Lyle 1748-1831, Loyalist, Militiaman" (2005); Author, "From Lampertheim to South Carolina Captain Daniel Strobel 1735-1806 Patriot, Civic Leader And Some of His Children and Grandchildren" (2004); Author, "From Herrstein to South Carolina, John Nicholas Martin 1724-1795 Pastor, Patriot" (2003); Author, "From Alsace to South Carolina: Jonas Beard, 1730-1796, patriot, statesman" (2002); Author, "Handbook for Experiential Education" (1988) **Awards:** Outstanding Counselor Award, Kappa Delta Pi; President Award, CCIRA **Memberships:** Past President, CCIRA; Society of the Cincinnati in the State of Georgia; Kappa Delta Pi; Phi Delta Kappa **Marquis Who's Who Honors:** Albert Nelson Marquis Lifetime Achievement Award; Marquis Who's Who Top Professional **To what do you attribute your success:** Dr. Cawley attributes his success to the research that he found and the experience that he had of his own contributed to it because he learned from the students. He learned what their needs were, so it was kind of individualized. **Why did you become involved in your profession or industry:** Dr. Cawley became involved in his profession because when he went for his bachelor's degree, he majored in science and English. He also got married and had two kids by the time he graduated. There were no jobs in political science so he had to stay an extra year and get a teaching certificate. After he did that, he then signed up to teach at Salt Lake City. He decided to make education a career although he had not planned on being a teacher. However, he enjoyed it so much and was thrilled to work with the young students and see them grow. He earned his master's degree and his consultant from the University of Utah was so impressed with him that she encouraged him to go for his doctorate. **Avocations:** Family history research **Political Affiliations:** Republican **Religion:** Church of Jesus Christ of Latter-Day Saints

Warren A. Cebulko

Title: Supervisor **Industry:** Medicine & Health Care **Company Name:** Advocate Aurora Health Care **Place of Birth:** Canton **State/Country of Origin:** OH/USA **Parents:** Fred Cebulko; Rose Marie Cebulko **Marital Status:** Married **Spouse Name:** Lizhu **Education:** MBA, DePaul University (1995); BS in Accounting, DePaul University (1974) **Certifications:** CCS-P **Career:** Supervisor, Coding Education and Compliance, Advocate Health Care **Civic:** Supporter, American Heart Association, Inc.; Blood Donor, American Heart Association, Inc.; Supporter, March of Dimes; Volunteer, Local Church **Memberships:** American Health Information Management Association; Institute of Management Accountants **Marquis Who's Who Honors:** Marquis Who's Who Top Professional **To what do you attribute your success:** Mr. Cebulko attributes his success to his education and driven nature. **Why did you become involved in your profession or industry:** Mr. Cebulko became involved in his profession through his accounting and finance background. He became involve because of his wife, who was a physician, and he saw it as a growth opportunity. He felt confident that he could segue the work into his background. **Avocations:** Traveling; Golf

Frank Celico

Title: Owner **Industry:** Food & Restaurant Services **Company Name:** Warehouse Beer-Wine-Liquor LLC, DBA The Wine Store **Marital Status:** Married **Spouse Name:** Donna (1964) **Children:** Franklin; Amy; Timothy; Daniel (Deceased) **Career:** Owner, Warehouse Beer-Wine-Liquor LLC, DBA The Wine Store (1985-Present) **Awards:** Retailer of the Year Award, Beverage Dynamics (2017-2018) **Memberships:** Past President, Rotary; Chamber of Commerce **Why did you become involved in your profession or industry:** Mr. Celico is a native of Wesley, Rhode Island, and has been in various businesses throughout his life. He had an opportunity to buy the store from a friend who was looking to retire. At that time, it was in a little shopping center, but he bought a piece or property and built a new store. In Rhode Island, the class A liquor license is limited by population.

Joseph Cerny III, PhD

Title: Chemistry Professor, Dean, Director **Industry:** Education/Educational Services **Company Name:** University of California Berkeley **Date of Birth:** 04/24/1936 **Place of Birth:** Montgomery **State/Country of Origin:** AL/USA **Parents:** Joseph Cerny (Deceased); Olaette Genette (Jury) Cerny **Marital Status:** Married **Spouse Name:** Susan Dinkelspiel Stern (11/12/1983); Barbara Ann Nedelka (06/13/1959-1982) **Children:** Keith Joseph; Mark; Evan **Education:** Honorary PhD in Physics, University of Jyväskylä, Finland (1990); PhD in Nuclear Chemistry, University of California, Berkeley (1961); Postgraduate Coursework, The University of Manchester, United Kingdom (1957-1958); BSChemE, The University of Mississippi, Oxford, MS (1957) **Career:** Professor, Chemistry, University of California Berkeley (2000-2013); Vice Chancellor, Research Division, University of California Berkeley (1994-2000); Provost, Research Division, University of California Berkeley (1986-1994); Dean, Graduate Division, University of California Berkeley (1985-2000); Associate Director, Lawrence Berkeley National Laboratory, University of California Berkeley (1979-1984); Head, Nuclear Science Division, University of California Berkeley (1979-1984); Chairman, Department of Chemistry, University of California Berkeley (1975-1979); Associate Professor, University of California Berkeley (1967-1971); Assistant Professor, Chemistry, University of California Berkeley (1961-1967) **Career Related:** Chairman, Subcommittee on Education, Nuclear Science Advisory Committee, U.S. Department of Energy (2003-2004); Study of Research Doctorates, National Research Council, National Academy of Sciences (1992-1995); Advisory Council, University Relations Task Force, National Aeronautics and Space Administration (1991-1993); Chair, Nuclear Physics Panel, Physics Commission, National Academy of Sciences (1983-1986) **Military Service:** U.S. Army (1962-1963) **Creative Works:** Editor, Four Volumes, "Nuclear Reactions and Spectroscopy" (1974); Contributor, Articles, Professional Journals **Awards:** Inductee, Alumni Hall of Fame, The University of Mississippi (1988); Humboldt Research Award (1985); Glenn T. Seaborg Award for Nuclear Chemistry, American Chemical Society (1984); Ernest Orlando Lawrence Award, United States Atomic Energy Commission (1974); Fulbright Scholar, The University of Manchester, United Kingdom (1957-1958) **Memberships:** Vice President, Council of Graduate Schools (1992-1994); President, Council of Graduate Schools (1992-1994); American Physical Society; American Chemical Society; Fellow, American Association for the Advancement of Science **Marquis Who's Who Honors:** Albert Nelson Marquis Lifetime Achievement Award **Avocations:** Traveling; Hiking **Political Affiliations:** Democrat

George Chakoian

Title: Aerospace Engineer **Industry:** Engineering **Date of Birth:** 6/14/1924 **Place of Birth:** Providence **State/Country of Origin:** RI/USA **Parents:** Daniel Chakoian; Margaret (Derderian) Chakoian **Marital Status:** Married **Spouse Name:** Marion Mahdesian (8/29/1948) **Children:** Janis; Cynthia; Laura **Education:** BS in Mechanical Engineering, Tri-State University (1950); BS in Machine Design, Rhode Island School of Design (1949); Technical Coursework, Massachusetts Institute of Technology, Cambridge, MA; Coursework, Northeastern University, Boston, MA; Coursework, Pennsylvania State University **Certifications:** Registered Professional Engineer, Rhode Island and Massachusetts **Career:** Supervisory Aerospace Engineer, U.S. Army Natick Research, Development and Engineering Center, Natick, MA (1981-1990); Aerospace Engineer, U.S. Army Natick Research, Development and Engineering Center, Natick, MA (1966-1981); Assistant Technical Director, Supervisory Mechanical Engineer, U.S. Naval Aircraft Torpedo Unit, U.S. Naval Air Station, Quonset Point, RI (1958-1966); Mechanical Engineer, U.S. Naval Air Station, Quonset Point, RI (1956-1958); Mechanical Engineer, R. M. Hallam Consulting Engineers, U.S. Naval Underwater Ordnance Station, Newport, RI (1955-1956); Engineer, B.I.F. Industries, Inc., Providence, RI (1950-1955) **Civic:** Secretary, Diocese of Armenian Church America (1999-2001); Diocesan Delegate, St. Sahag and St. Mesrob Armenian Apostolic Church (1975-1983, 1987-2001); Assistant Treasurer, Diocesan Council, Diocese of Armenian Church America (1997-1999); Chairman, Church Building Committee, St. Sahag and St. Mesrob Armenian Apostolic Church (1987-1996); Chairman, School Building Committee, Lincoln, RI (1968-1975); Parish Council, St. Sahag and St. Mesrob Armenian Apostolic Church (1967-1974) **Military Service:** Radio Operator/Mechanic/Gunner, B-24 Bomber Aircraft, 46 Combat Missions, 416 Combat Hours, U.S. Army Air Force (1943-1945) **Creative Works:** Author or Co-Author, 26 Technical Reports, U.S. Navy, Quonset Point, RI; Author or Co-Author, Technical Reports on Airdrop Systems, U.S. Army Natick Research, Development and Engineering Center, Natick, MA; Contributor, Articles, Professional Journals; Patents in Field **Awards:** Nominee, Ellis Island Medal of Honor (2019); St. Nerses Shnorhali Medal, Catholicos of All Armenians Karekin II (2001); Knight of the Year, Knights of Vartan (1994); Past Achievement Award, Knights of Vartan (1989); Science Award, Armenian Students Association (1975); Air Medals with Four Oak Leaf Clusters; Four Battle Stars; Two Presidential Unit Citations **Memberships:** Trustee, Armenian Historical Association of Rhode Island (1997-Present); Trustee, Armenian Students Association (1989-Present); Chairman, Board of Trustees, Armenian Students Association (2000-2005); Vice President of Trustees, Armenian Students Association (1998-2000); General Chairman, Aerodynamic Deceleration International Conference, American Institute of Aeronautics and Astronautics (1989); New York Academy of Sciences; Knights of Vartan; Armenian General Benevolent Union **Marquis Who's Who Honors:** Albert Nelson Marquis Lifetime Achievement Award. **Why did you become involved in your profession or industry:** Mr. Chakoian became involved in his profession because his parents wanted him to go to college. He made up his mind that he wanted to study architecture or engineering. However, World War II intervened and he volunteered to enter the service as an aviation cadet in the U.S. Army Air Force. When he got out of the service after the war, he applied to Brown University and took an aptitude test, which he passed. They asked him what would he like to do, and he said he would like to be either an architect or an engineer. They told him he could study engineering at Brown University, but to study architecture, he would have to go to the Rhode Island School of Design (RISD). He went to RISD and got a degree in machine design. While at RISD, he met a professor from Brown University teaching physics. He said that if he had a son and he wanted him to be an engineer, he would send him to Tri-State College in Angola, Indiana. He and four of his classmates went to Tri-State College and received degrees in engineering. He studied engineering because he was interested in mathematics, construction and engineering subjects, so he believed he made the right choice. **Avocations:** Music

Carol Ziegler Champagne

Title: Retired **Industry:** Financial Services **Company Name:** H&R Block **Date of Birth:** 05/09/1941 **Place of Birth:** Chicago **State/Country of Origin:** IL/USA **Parents:** George Elliott Ziegler; Ruth (Thomas) Ziegler **Marital Status:** Widow **Spouse Name:** Robert D. Champagne (2/19/1966, Deceased) **Children:** Thomas Elliott (1974); Corrin Marie (1975) **Education:** MEd in Secondary Education, Bridgewater State University, Bridgewater, MA (1971); BA in Mathematics, Carleton College, Northfield, MN (1963) **Certifications:** Enrolled Agent (2008) **Career:** Retired (2019); Tax Preparer, H&R Block, MA (1999-2019); Administrative Assistant, American Baptist Church of Massachusetts (1996-2006); Administrative Assistant, Reebok, Randolph, MA (1992-1996); With Sales Administration, High Vacuum Equipment Corporation, Hingham, MA (1989-1990); Legal Secretary, Driscoll and Davis, Marshfield, MA (1988-1989); Administrative Assistant, The Talbots, Inc., Hingham, MA (1987-1988); Mathematician, Programmer, Peoplesmith, Inc., Scituate, MA (1985-1986); Freelancer Writer, Mariner Newspaper (1985-1986); Consultant, Scituate, MA (1984-1989); Tax Preparer, H&R Block, MA (1979-1985); Research Mathematician, Liaison, Factory Mutual Research Corporation, Norwood, MA (1966-1974); Mathematician, Programmer, Brockton Taunton Gas & Electric Light Company, Boston, MA (1963-1966) **Career Related:** Inventor, Patentee **Civic:** Executive Board Member, Massachusetts Hockey (1985-2015); Board of Directors, Cohasset Community Theater, MA (1975-1976); Board of Directors, League of Women Voters, Scituate, MA (1982-1984); Administrative Advisory Committee, Scituate Public Schools, MA (1981-1983); School Advisory Committee, Scituate Public Schools, MA (1980-1982); Board of Directors, Cohasset Community Theater, MA (1975-1976); Board of Directors, Curtain Call Theatre, Weymouth, MA (1964-1974); Lifetime Board Member, Massachusetts Hockey **Creative Works:** Patentee, Patent in Fire Protection **Awards:** Inductee, Massachusetts Hockey Hall of Fame (2013) **Memberships:** Lifetime Member, Director-at-large, Massachusetts Hockey; Mensa International Limited **Marquis Who's Who Honors:** Albert Nelson Marquis Lifetime Achievement Award **Why did you become involved in your profession or industry:** Mrs. Champagne became a teacher to provide herself with a career in case something happened to her husband. She had been a math tutor already, so she went back to school to get a master's degree. **Avocations:** Victorian home restoration; Spending time with children and grandchildren

Priscilla Chan, MD

Title: Pediatrician; Co-founder, Co-chief Executive Officer; Philanthropist **Industry:** Nonprofit & Philanthropy **Company Name:** Chan Zuckerberg Initiative **Date of Birth:** 02/24/1985 **Place of Birth:** Braintree **State/Country of Origin:** MA/USA **Marital Status:** Married **Spouse Name:** Mark Zuckerberg (05/19/2012) **Children:** August; Maxima Chan **Career:** Co-founder, Co-Chief Executive Officer, Chan Zuckerberg Initiative (2015-Present) **Awards:** Time 100 Most Influential (2016)

Josh Chandler

Title: Chief Executive Officer, Partner **Industry:** Architecture & Construction **Company Name:** Chandler Cabinets **Parents:** Buster Chandler **Children:** Josh; Jett; Victoria **Education:** Coursework, Tarleton State University (1995-1997) **Certifications:** Kitchen and Bath Certification **Career:** Chief Executive Officer, Chandler Cabinets (2014-Present); Chief, Designer and Business Developments, Chandler Cabinets (2004-2013); Draftsman and Installation Manager, Chandler Cabinets (1997-2003) **Civic:** Maingate Organization; Pat & Emmitt Smith Charity **Awards:** Named Best Library over 5000; Named Best Kitchen over 5000; Named Best Closet over 5000 **Memberships:** Cabinet Makers Association; Home Builders Association (Now National Association of Home Builders); National Kitchen and Bath Association **Marquis Who's Who Honors:** Marquis Who's Who Top Professional **To what do you attribute your success:** Mr. Chandler attributes his success to the knowledge his dad gave him, as well as his innovation. The biggest asset he brought to the company was his ability to draw cabinets on the computer rather than by hand like his father has done, which he believes helped their growth. **Why did you become involved in your profession or industry:** Two years into college, Mr. Chandler worked summers in the family business and he saw the potential. He learned drafting in college and he took that knowledge and applied it to the business; the business blossomed from 10 employees to 250 employees and it is one of the largest cabinet companies in Texas. **Avocations:** Charity events; Real estate

Choongseok Chang

Title: Managing Principal Physicist **Industry:** Sciences **Date of Birth:** 11/12/1951 **Place of Birth:** Yechon **State/Country of Origin:** Republic of Korea **Parents:** Ki-oh Chang; Oh-Young Kim **Spouse Name:** Inja Chang Tong **Children:** Andrew; Seleme **Education:** PhD in Physics, University of Texas at Austin (1979); BS in Physics, Seoul National University (1974) **Career:** Plasma Physics Member, Picscie, Princeton University (2019-Present); Managing Principal Research Physicist, Princeton University Plasma Physics Laboratory (2011-Present); Research Professor, Courant Institute of Mathematical Sciences, New York University (1988-2011); Professor, Korea Advanced Institute of Science and Technology (1986-2011);Staff Scientist, Applied Microwave Plasma Concepts (1984-1986); Senior Scientist, General Atomics (1979-1984) **Career Related:** ITER Science Fellow (2019-Present); International Executive Committee, International Conference on Data Drive Driven Plasma Sciences (2018-Present); International Organizing Committee, Asia-Pacific Conference on Plasma Physics (2018-Present); PI, Aurora Exascale XGC Early Science Project, Argonne Leadership Class Facility Co-Head for Science, ECP High-Fidelity Whole Device Modeling (2016-Present); U.S. Organizer, Annual U.S.-Japan Exascale Computing Workshops (2015-Present); Head, SciDAC-4 Partnership Center for High-Fidelity Boundary Plasma Simulation (HBPS) (2016-Present); U.S. Representative for Theory, IAEA-FEC Program Committee (2018); Chair, DOE FES/ASCR Exascale Requirement Review (2016); Head, SciDAC-3 Center for Edge Plasma Simulation (EPSi) (2011-2016); Head, SciDAC-3 Center for Edge Plasma Simulation (CPES) (2005-2011); U.S. Department of Energy, Fusion Theory Coordinating Committee; Executive Committee, U.S. Transport Task Force Council; Chair, U.S. Burning Plasma Organization; Head, Korean Plasma Physics Society; KSTAR Physics Design Team; Chair, KSTAR Research Council; Founding Committee, Asia Pacific Plasma Theory Conference **Awards:** Recipient, Numerous ALCC Awards, U.S. Department Energy; Recipient, Numerous INCITE Awards, Oak Ridge National Laboratory; Awarded, Argonne National Laboratory **Memberships:** Fellow, American Physical Society; Executive Committee, Transport Task Force; Council Member, U.S. Burning Plasma Organization; International Traffic in Arms Regulations **Marquis Who's Who Honors:** Albert Nelson Marquis Lifetime Achievement Award **Why did you become involved in your profession or industry:** When Dr. Chang was in high school, he knew he wanted to be a scientist and that he would be involved in physics. He is currently researching the peaceful use of nuclear energy, which would solve the energy problem for billions of years.

Robert "Bob" Chapek

Title: Chief Executive Officer **Industry:** Business Management/Business Services **Company Name:** The Walt Disney Company **Marital Status:** Married **Spouse Name:** Cynthia Ann Ford **Children:** Three Children **Education:** MBA, Michigan State University (1984); BS in Microbiology, Indiana University Bloomington (1981) **Career:** Chief Executive Officer, The Walt Disney Company (2020-Present); President, Disney Consumer Products, The Walt Disney Company (2011-2015); President of Distribution, Walt Disney Studios, The Walt Disney Company (2009-2011); President, Worldwide Home Video Arm, Buena Vista Home Entertainment, The Walt Disney Company (2006-2009); President, Digital Entertainment Group, The Walt Disney Company (2002-2007); President, Buena Vista Home Entertainment, The Walt Disney Company (2000-2006); Senior Vice President of Marketing, North America, Buena Vista Home Entertainment, The Walt Disney Company (1998-2000); Director of Marketing, Vice President of Brand Marketing, Sell-through Products, Buena Vista Home Entertainment Affiliate, The Walt Disney Company, Burbank, CA (1993-1998); H.J. Heinz Company (Now Kraft-Heinz, Inc.); Various Advertising Positions, J. Walter Thompson **Civic:** Board of Directors, The Walt Disney Company (2020-Present); Chairman, Walt Disney Parks and Resorts, The Walt Disney Company (2015-2020); Chairman, Digital Entertainment Group, The Walt Disney Company (2007-2020)

Richard Alexander Chapman

Title: Research Scientist **Industry:** Sciences **Company Name:** University of Texas at Dallas **Date of Birth:** 09/24/1932 **Place of Birth:** Teague **State/Country of Origin:** TX/USA **Parents:** Richard Franklin Chapman; Hazel Irene (Stevens) Chapman **Marital Status:** Married **Spouse Name:** Barbara Madden (06/08/1954) **Children:** Carol Faldet; Janet McCormack; Laura Owens; Richard Madden Chapman **Education:** PhD in Nuclear Physics, Rice University (1957); MA, Rice University (1955); BA in Physics, Rice University (1954) **Career:** Research Scientist, University of Texas, Dallas (2008-Present); Consultant, Texas Instruments, Inc., Dallas, TX (1998-2007); Senior Fellow, Texas Instruments, Inc., Dallas, TX (1994-1998); Fellow, Texas Instruments, Inc., Dallas, TX (1987-1994); Member of Technical Staff, Branch Manager, Senior Member of Technical Staff, Texas Instruments, Inc., Dallas, TX (1959-1987); Technical Staff, General Electric Vallecitos, California (1957-1959) **Career Related:** Governor, Advisor, Rice University Board of Governors, Houston, TX (2008-Present); General Chairman, Very Large Scale Integration Technology Symposium Program (1995-Present); Chairman, Very Large Scale Integration Technology Symposium Program (1993-1994) **Creative Works:** Contributor, 154 Articles, Professional Journals; Patentee, 42 U.S. Patents; Patentee, 8 Foreign Patents in Field **Awards:** Rice University Distinguished Alumnus (2017); Rice University Athletic Hall of Fame (1997); IEEE Jack A. Morton Award (1987) **Memberships:** Visiting Committee, Electrical Engineering Department, University of Texas at Austin (1990-1993); Board of Directors, Cotton Bowl Athletic Association, Dallas, TX (1977-1987); Fellow, American Physical Society; Fellow, IEEE **Marquis Who's Who Honors:** Albert Nelson Marquis Lifetime Achievement Award; Marquis Who's Who Top Professional **Why did you become involved in your profession or industry:** Dr. Chapman believes that his father's interest in astronomy is what initially pushed him into his field. **Avocations:** Reading; Listening to classical music **Religion:** Presbyterian

Guy J. Chartrand

Title: President, Chief Executive Officer **Industry:** Business Management/Business Services **Company Name:** Freightworld Logistics Inc. **Date of Birth:** 02/23/1953 **Place of Birth:** Winsor **State/Country of Origin:** Ontario/Canada **Parents:** Danielle Chartrand **Marital Status:** Married **Spouse Name:** Marlene M. Chartrand **Children:** Charlene Ouellette; Paul Guy Chartrand (Deceased, 09/20/1989) **Certifications:** Two-Year Certificate, C.I.T.T, Ryerson University, Toronto, Ontario, Canada (1974); Certificate, International Standers Organization **Career:** President, Chief Executive Officer, Freightworld Logistics Inc. (1994-Present); Vice President, Traffic and Business Development; Traffic Manager **Awards:** Recognized, Professional of the Year, Strathmore Publication (2019-2020); Canadian Business Awards, Best Multimodal Transportation Company, Corporate Vision Magazine (2019); Ontario's Top 100 Entrepreneurs Award (1996, 1995) **Marquis Who's Who Honors:** Marquis Who's Who Top Professional **To what do you attribute your success:** Mr. Chartrand attributes his success to his corporate policy, which is to provide each one of his distinguished clients an unsurpassed service that is dedicated to quality and economics in a worldwide market. They will employ the necessary resources to solve any service required within and beyond the realm of common reach. Their services will lend credence to the existence and will be supported by using the highest standard of ethics and credibility. Enclosing this will be done by a confident team of highly motivated individuals who will make a change and take responsibility for leadership in quality assurance, productivity, and excellence. **Why did you become involved in your profession or industry:** Mr. Chartrand had been working in logistics for a long time prior to opening up his own company. He got involved in the business in 1970 while in high school; he then dedicated himself part-time to practicing after school and later decided he was going to stick with it. He continued to stick with it because of his determination, finding that he quite liked the business. **Thoughts on Life:** Mr. Chartrand's motto is, "Anywhere, anytime, on time, every time!"What was the big break that lead you into the field?Mr. Chartrand had been doing logistics for a long time and prior to opening up his own company. He got into the business around 1970 while in high school he started doing it part time after school, and then decided he was going to stick with it. He didn't have a career ahead of him, but he liked this kinds of work. He continued to stick with it because of determination and he liked the business he was in. What has been a crowning professional achievement?The achievement in itself was starting his own business back in 1994. Because he had been in the business from 1970 to 1994, that is 24 years. He figured he spend 24 years in the business and had seen all kinds of levels of management and businesses and had worked for several large based companies in a corporate position, and he figured he knew how the business ran so he took a big leap and started his own business 26 years ago. He says in his corporate mission statement "Our corporate policy is to provide each of our distinguished clients with unsurpassed service dedicated to quality and economics in a worldwide market. We will employ the necessary resources to solve any service requirement within and beyond the realm of common reach. Our services will be supported by using the highest standards of ethics and accountability. This would be delivered by a competent team of highly motivated individuals who embrace change and take responsibility for leadership in quality assurance, productivity, innovation, and excellence." He had the tenacity over the years, and the determination and the unrelenting efforts, and the energy to get something going and make something of it, and he did. What has been a personal achievement?Recognized as a professional of the year in 2019 and 2020 by Strathmore publication.https://www.pr.com/press-release/798239 If you had to summarize your life's work in a single word or phrase what would it be?Phenomenal, Awesome. He has faith. Who was a personal inspiration for you?He believes in himself and his partner who is his wife, and his daughter who is also working with them, and Frank who is the VP of sales and marketing. These are the people who are his inspiration and he is theirs because they work as a team. At the end of the day it all works out in their best interest because they work as a team and they all support each other.What lessons would you pass onto the next generation?If someone wants to get into business they have to have the tenacity, they have to have the determination, the motivation. They have to have all of the things that make a person a leader, and if you're a leader then you can't go wrong, because followers is not the philosophy here, leadership is the philosophy. By being a follower you won't go anywhere in life because you will only go as far as the person your following, and when they stop you stopped dead in your tracks. You need to have your own determination, your own beliefs, your own dream, and you have to have a passion in your heart to want to have a big break, no one is going to do it for you. Wife, Marlene partner;Daughter, Charlene Corporate Director of Sales;Frank is a seasoned sales professional, he is the VP of sales of marketing.

Jeanette Knapp Chase

Title: Music Educator (Retired) **Industry:** Education/Educational Services **Place of Birth:** New Orleans **State/Country of Origin:** LA/USA **Parents:** Roger Seaman Knapp; Jean Louise Sinclair **Marital Status:** Married **Spouse Name:** William Raymond Chase (08/03/1957) **Children:** William Edward II; Beverly Ann **Education:** Postgraduate Studies, 30 Hours in Choral Conducting and Vocal Pedagogy (1984-1988); MA in Fine Arts Education, University of Houston-Clear Lake (1982); BM in Vocal Performance, University of Houston (1976); AA in Vocal Performance, San Jacinto College Central, Pasadena, TX (1972);Diploma in Nursing, Methodist Hospital School of Nursing, Houston TX (1958) **Certifications:** Registered Nurse, Texas (1958) **Career:** Director of Music Emerita, Webster Presbyterian Church (2001-Present); Synchronized Swimming-Competitor, Coach, Teacher, Official, Judge (1956-Present); Member, Houston Grand Opera Chorus (2016-2017); Voice Teacher, Lee College, Baytown, TX (1992-2004); Private Voice Teacher, El Lago, TX (1977-2019);Voice Teacher, Choral Director, San Jacinto College Central, Pasadena, CA (1977-1993); Director of Music, Webster Presbyterian Church (1972-2001); Staff Nurse, Pasadena Bayshore Hospital, Texas (1965-1969); Staff Nurse, Southeast Baptist Hospital, Houston, TX (1963-1964); Staff Nurse, Gulfway General Hospital, Houston, TX (1962-1963); Staff Nurse, St. Agnus Hospital, Baltimore, MD (1960-1961); Staff Nurse, Columbia Hospital, Pittsburgh, PA (1959-1960); Office Nurse, Lab Technician, Office of Dr. Terry Vincent, Houston, TX (1958-1959); Staff Nurse, Methodist Hospital, Houston, TX (1957-1959); Music Educator (Retired) **Career Related:** Vocalist Temple Beth Israel, Houston, TX (1975-1981) **Civic:** US Synchronized Swimming (USSS) Colorado Springs (1977-Present); Treasurer, Gulf Association USSS Administration (1977-Present); USSS South Zone (1977-Present); Deacon, Elder, Webster Presbyterian Church, (1972-Present); Board of Governors, Judge, Level 4R, Coach Cert. Level III, Audit Committee (2007-2011); Chairman, Gulf Association USSS Administration (1977-2010); Coach, Director, Aquanauts (1965); Coach, Director, KTRK Kittens (1960-1961); (Shamrock Hilton) Corkettes **Awards:** 2017 USSS Lillian MacKellar Distinguished Service Award In Recognition Of Selfless Service And Dedication To The Enrichment Of Those Encountered (2017); Named 2016 South Zone Contributor Of Year (2016); BAC Continuing Musical Excellence Award (1992); Outstanding High School Voice Teacher, Baylor University (1990); Named To Outstanding Young Women Of America (1973); Texas All State Choir Award, Texas Music Educators Association (1954) **Memberships:** Correspondent, Bay Area Chorus (1972-Present); Delegate, National Convention Synchronized Swimming (1962-Present); Contributor, President, Bay Area Youth Singers (2008-2012); Founding Board Member, Bay Area Youth Singers (2007-2013); Board of Governors, National Amateur Athletic Union (1965-1977); Life Member, Gulf Association (USSS) (1962-1977); Life Member, Amateur Athletic Union of the United States, Inc. Bay Area Youth Singers; Correspondent, Texas Choral Directors Association; Correspondent, American Choral Directors Association; Greater Houston Chapter, National Association Teachers Singing (NATS) **Marquis Who's Who Honors:** Albert Nelson Marquis Lifetime Achievement Award; Marquis Who's Who Top Professional **Why did you become involved in your profession or industry:** Ms. Chase became involved in her profession because in high school, she taught swimming for Red Cross and enjoyed going to Esther Williams movies; she thought she would like to do that so she picked up a book at the YMCA about synchronized swimming. She read up on it and made a show team with some of her friends in Corpus Christi, Texas where she grew it. She had a friend in Houston, where she was going to nursing school where they had a team that competed. She presented herself at the Shamrock Hilton Hotel. Later in life she found herself judging shows and set down. In addition, Mrs. Chase was told she could not make a living doing synchronize swimming, so she went into nursing school, where she directed a choir at the hospital. She volunteered and directed kid's choirs at churches. She was told she did not know anything because she did not have an education is music. So she quit her job at the hospital and went back to school. She was a registered nurse for major of her career. After obtaining her associates degree in music, she became a director of music at a local church. She continued to received her bachelor's degree. She was asked to teach voice, she was director there. She continued to get her masters degree and continued schooling after that. **Avocations:** Synchronized swimming; Singing; Traveling **Political Affiliations:** Republican **Religion:** Presbyterian **Thoughts on Life:** Ms. Chase's son and daughter both did water shows until the age of 30.

Joan Chatfield, MM

Title: Church Administrator **Industry:** Religious **Date of Birth:** 10/07/1932 **Place of Birth:** Elizabeth **State/Country of Origin:** NJ/USA **Parents:** Henry Summers Chatfield; Angela Dorothea (McCahill) Chatfield **Marital Status:** Single **Education:** Doctor of Philosophy, Graduate Theological Union, University of California, Berkeley, CA (1983); Master of Arts, University of San Francisco (1968); Bachelor of Arts, Manhattanville College (1956) **Career:** Dean, School of Humanities and Fine Arts, Chaminade University of Honolulu (1990-1998); Chair, Ecumenical Commission, Roman Catholic Diocese of Honolulu (1983-1990); Ecumenical Officer, Roman Catholic Diocese of Honolulu (1983-1990); Executive Director, Institute for Religion and Social Change, Honolulu, HI (1980-2016); Director, Maryknoll Mission Institute (1974-1978); Secondary School Teacher, Catholic School Department, Hawaii (1956-1972) **Career Related:** President, Hawaii Institute for Theological Studies, Honolulu, HI (1980-Present); Vice President, Western Fellowship for Professors of Mission, California (1989-1992); Board of Directors, Interfaith Ministries of Hawaii, Honolulu, HI (1985) **Civic:** President, Project Realize, Effective Support Programs for the Elderly, Honolulu, HI (1983-Present); Board of Directors, Honolulu Theater for Youth (1991-1994, 1983-1988); Vice Chair, City & County Status of Women, Honolulu, HI (1981-1986) **Creative Works:** Contributor, Articles, Professional Journals **Awards:** Presidents Award, International Association for Mission Studies (1988); Women of Note, Honolulu Status of Women Commission (1982); Teacher of Year, Finance Factors, Honolulu, HI (1964); Living Treasure of Hawaii **Memberships:** President, Rotary International, East Honolulu, HI (1999-2000); Chair, Educational Foundation Program, American Association of University Women (1986-1988); President, Educational Foundation Program, American Association of University Women (1986-1988); Rotary International (1985-2010); President, American Society of Missiology (1984-1986) **Marquis Who's Who Honors:** Albert Nelson Marquis Lifetime Achievement Award **Why did you become involved in your profession or industry:** Sister Joan decided that she wanted to teach when she was 17 years old. When she arrived in Honolulu to teach science, she knew that she wanted to teach there for the rest of her career. **Avocations:** Stained glass **Political Affiliations:** Democrat **Religion:** Roman Catholic

Richard Douglas Chatham

Title: Associate Professor **Industry:** Education/Educational Services **Company Name:** Morehead State University **Date of Birth:** 06/05/1968 **Place of Birth:** Statesville **State/Country of Origin:** NC/USA **Parents:** Ricky Morgan Chatham; Geraldine Moose Chatham **Marital Status:** Single **Education:** University of Tennessee, Knoxville (1992-2000); Undergraduate, Wake Forest University (1990) **Career:** Associate Professor, Morehead State University (2007-Present); Assistant Professor, Morehead State University (2001-2007); Visiting Assistant Professor, Wake Forest University (2000-2001) **Career Related:** Interim Chair, Department of Mathematics and Physics, Morehead State University (2015-2016); Chair, Faculty Senate, Morehead State University (2012-2013) **Civic:** Member, Advisory Board, Morehead State Public Radio Community (2019-Present) **Creative Works:** Host, Numerous Episodes, Comedy Music Program, "Odd Numbers," Morehead State Public Radio, WMKY 90.3 FM, Morehead, KY **Memberships:** Kentucky Academy of Science (2005); Mathematical Association of America (2002); American Mathematical Society (2002) **To what do you attribute your success:** Mr. Chatham attributes his success to having been blessed with talent and intelligence, got a lot of help from professors and loved mathematics and the academic environment. **Why did you become involved in your profession or industry:** Mr. Chatham became involved in his profession because he had a very good high school mathematics teacher, whose name was Ruth Rufty. She was his inspiration to get more involved in mathematics. He also had as an undergrad at Wake Forest, Elmer Hayashi who was also an inspiration because he taught with passion. **Avocations:** Reading; Comedy; Science; Science fiction; Computer programming **Political Affiliations:** Democrat

Willie Mae Chatman, BS, BA

Title: Division Head of Business/Law **Industry:** Education/Educational Services **Company Name:** Northern High School **Date of Birth:** 11/01/1945 **Place of Birth:** St. Louis **State/Country of Origin:** MO/USA **Parents:** James Henry Artis (Deceased 1994); Mosella (Reed) Artis (Deceased 1982) **Marital Status:** Divorced **Spouse Name:** Lindbergh Chatman (08/17/1966, Divorced 1979) **Education:** Postgraduate Coursework, Wayne State University, Detroit, MI (1981); MA, Western Michigan University, Kalamazoo, MI (1973); BS, Western Michigan University, Kalamazoo, MI (1970); Coursework, Jackson Community College (1967); Coursework, Jackson Community College (1964); Postgraduate Coursework, University of Michigan, Central Michigan; BA, 30+ Hours of Administration Certification **Certifications:** Seminars, Detroit Public Schools, Management Academy (1983); Certification in Secondary Continuing Vocational and Competency Based Education (1983); Administrative Certification, Wayne State University; Certification in Management Based Education, Michigan in Management Level (1981) **Career:** Head, Department of Business and Vocational Education, Northern High School, Detroit, MI (1979-2007); Teacher, Business Education, Northern High School, Detroit, MI (1971-1979); Secretary, Kalamazoo National Bank (1969-1970); Secretary to Director of Information, Western Michigan University (1968-1969); Clerk-typist, Michigan Employment Securities Commission (1966-1968); Junior Stenographer, Consumers Power Co., Jackson, MI (1964-1966); Consultant, North Central Steering Committee; Evaluator, Metro Detroit Typing-shorthand Annual Contest **Career Related:** Adjunct Professor, Henry Ford College; Educational Consultant, Newsweek Magazine **Civic:** Leadership Person for Various Events; Speaker for Breast Cancer Awareness **Awards:** Certificate of Recognition, Detroit Public Schools (1974, 1977, 1979); Vocational Education and Career Development Award, Michigan Department of Education (1979) **Memberships:** Friends of the Smithsonian Honor Roll (2020); Association Black School Educators, Detroit, MI; Business Education Association, Detroit, MI; Organization of School Administrators and Supervisors (OSAS); Michigan Business Education Association; Business Office Education Club; NAACP National Museum of African American History & Culture; Culture Friends of Smithsonian **Marquis Who's Who Honors:** Albert Nelson Marquis Lifetime Achievement Award **Why did you become involved in your profession or industry:** Ms. Chatman became involved in her profession because of encouragement from her parents at a young age to value education. They were not high school graduates, and indicated to Ms. Chatman and her siblings that education was most important in life. Therefore, she strived to excel in learning, and the support and assistance of her parents helped her through her entire career path. **Avocations:** Collecting crystal; Photography; Gardening; Traveling; Collecting coins; Landscaping; Word search enthusiast **Political Affiliations:** Democrat **Religion:** Non-denominational Christian **Thoughts on Life:** Ms. Chatman wants to continue to be an inspiration to her family and friends. She has a lot of nieces and nephews, and she adopted a great-niece at age 7. She has served as a mentor to many people within her community.

Julia Taylor Cheek

Title: Chief Executive Officer and Founder **Industry:** Health, Wellness and Fitness **Company Name:** EverlyWell **Education:** Master of Business Administration, Harvard Business School (2011); Bachelor of Arts, Vanderbilt University (2002-2005) **Career:** Venture Partner, NextGen Venture Partners (2016-Present); Chief Executive Officer, Founder, EverlyWell (2015-Present); Vice President, Moneygram International (2013-2015); Director, Strategy and Operations, George W. Bush Presidential Center (2011-2013)

Wen-Hsiung Chen, PhD

Title: Engineering Executive, Educator **Industry:** Engineering **Date of Birth:** 12/8/1938 **Place of Birth:** Hsin-chu **State/Country of Origin:** Taiwan **Parents:** Toh-huang Chen; Mei-mei Tzen **Marital Status:** Married **Spouse Name:** Lung-yu Hong **Children:** Dr. Caren H.; Dr. Christina H.; Colleen Y., Esq. **Education:** PhD, University of Southern California, Los Angeles, CA (1973); MS, Kansas State University, Manhattan, KS (1966); BS, National Taiwan University, Taipei, Taiwan (1962) **Career:** Cisco Fellow, Cisco Systems, Inc., San Jose, CA (2000-2015); Founder, CTO, Komodo Technology, Inc. (Acquired by Cisco), San Jose, CA (1999-2000); Founder, Chairman, CEO, V-Bits, Inc. (Acquired by Cisco), San Jose, CA (1997-1999); Executive Vice President, Chief Scientist, Compression Laboratories, Incorporated, San Jose, CA (1977-1998); Adjunct Professor, California State University, San Jose, CA (1982-1997); Senior Engineering Specialist, Ford Aerospace & Communications Corporation, Palo Alto, CA (1973-1977); Research Associate, University of Southern California, Los Angeles, CA (1970-1973); Instructor, University of Southern California, Los Angeles, CA (1968-1970); Electrical Engineer, Allis-Chalmers Company, Harvey, IL (1966-1968) **Career Related:** Visiting Professor, Beijing Broadcasting Institute, Tianjin University, China (1994-Present); Honorary Professor, Nanjing University Posts & Telecommunications, China (1994-Present); Fellow, IEEE (Institute of Electrical and Electronic Engineers (1995); Advisory Professor, Beijing University Posts & Telecommunications (1994); Life Fellow, IEEE **Civic:** Technical Board Member, Chief Technical Adviser, Vovile Systems Incorporated, VisualOn **Creative Works:** Contributor, Numerous Papers (1972-2009) **Awards:** CIE/USA Engineer of the Year Award (2006); IMTC Leadership Award (2005); CLI President Awards, CLI (1981, 1985); Achievement Award, Tokyo, Japan (1977); Best Algorithm Award in Coding Color Images (1976); Best Color Image Coding Award (1973); Best Monochrome Image Coding Award (1973); Top Placement, Electrical Engineering Department, University of Southern California (1971); Chao Yu-chu Scholarship Award, National Taiwan University, Taipei, Taiwan (1962) **Memberships:** Honorary Board Member, CINA (Chinese Information Networking Association); Life Member, NATEA (North America Taiwanese Engineers' Association); Former Member, San Jose State University EE Department Advisory Council; Former Member, AVS (Audio Video Coding Standard) Advisory Board of China; Vobile Advisory Board; VisualOn Advisory Board; ITRI Technical Advisory Committee **Marquis Who's Who Honors:** Albert Nelson Marquis Lifetime Achievement Award **Why did you become involved in your profession or industry:** Dr. Chen became involved in his profession because after he graduated college in Taiwan, his only options were to work for an electrical company, be a teacher or move to the United States to further his education. 90% of his graduating class chose to move to the United States, so he decided he would do the same. When he got to the United States, he enrolled and graduated from Kansas State University with a specialization in image processing. After working for some time in Chicago, he decided again to further his schooling and enrolled at University of Southern California to specialize, and become a pioneer in the "field of the future" called digital image compression.

Theresa Cheng, MD

Title: Neurosurgeon **Industry:** Medicine & Health Care **Parents:** Wayne Cheng; Florence Cheng **Education:** MBA, Johns Hopkins University Carey Business School (2016); Postdoctoral Fellowship in Molecular Genetics, Mayo Clinic, Rochester, MN (1992-1993); Neurological Surgery Residency, Mayo Clinic, Rochester, MN (1989-1995); MD, Medical College of Wisconsin, Milwaukee, WI (1989); PhD in Molecular Biological Neurosciences, Medical College of Wisconsin, Milwaukee, WI (1987); Diploma in Biomedical Engineering, Marquette University (1982) **Certifications:** Advanced Trauma Life Support, American College of Surgeons (1996); Certified Advanced Cardiac Life Support, American Heart Association (1989); Certified Instructor for Stephen Covey's "7 Habits of Highly Effective People" Course; Eucharistic Ministry Catholic Church (1980) **Career:** Director of Medical Operations, Affinity Health Systems, Oshkosh, WI (2007-Present); Chief of Neurosurgery, Affinity Health Systems, Oshkosh, WI (2002-Present); Started and Developed, Neurosurgery Program, Mercy Medical Center, Affinity Health Systems, Oshkosh, WI (2002-Present); Chairman, Department of Neurosurgery, Luther Midelfort (Now Mayo Clinic Health System), Eau Claire, WI (2000-2002); Consultant, Neurosurgery, Luther Midelfort (Now Mayo Clinic Health System), Eau Claire, WI (1995-2002); Special Fellow in Neurosurgery, Mayo Clinic, Rochester, MN (1998-1999); Postdoctoral Fellow in Molecular Genetics, Mayo Clinic, Rochester, WI (1992-1993); Adjunct Instructor, Medical Neuroanatomy, Department of Anatomy and Cellular Biology, Medical College of Wisconsin, Milwaukee, WI (1987-1989); Teaching Assistant, Medical Neuroanatomy, Department of Anatomy and Cellular Biology, Medical College of Wisconsin, Milwaukee, WI (1984-1987); Research Assistant, Department of Neurology, Medical College of Wisconsin, Milwaukee, WI (1984); Research Assistant, Department of Medicine and Endocrinology, Medical College of Wisconsin, Milwaukee, WI (1984); Teaching Assistant, Medical Gross Anatomy, Department of Anatomy and Cellular Biology, Medical College of Wisconsin, Milwaukee, WI (1983-1984); Teaching Assistant, Engineering Level, Mathematics and Physics, Marquette University, Milwaukee, WI (1979-1982) **Civic:** Establishment of Theresa M. Cheng, MD, PhD Endowment for Medical Missionary Work and Medical Excellence, Mercy Medical Foundation, Ascension Mercy Medical System, Oshkosh, WI (2006-Present); Board of Directors, Gold Cross Ambulance Service, Inc., Fox Valley Area, WI (2002-Present); Elected to Medical Executive Committee, Luther Midelfort (Now Mayo Clinic Health System), Eau Claire, WI (2001-2002); Co-director of Neuro-peds-trauma Intensive Care Unit, Luther Midelfort (Now Mayo Clinic Health System), Eau Claire, WI (2001-2002); Medical Director, ThinkFirst Foundation, Eau Claire, WI (2000-2002); Board of Directors, Dunn-Eau Claire-Pepin County Medical Society (Now Wisconsin Medical Society) (1999-2002); President-elect, Board of Directors, Professional Advisory Board, Epilepsy Foundation of Western Wisconsin, Eau Claire, WI (1999-2002); Eucharistic Minister, Catholic Church (1980-2008); Board of Directors, Mercy Medical Foundation, Ascension Mercy Medical System, Oshkosh, WI; Board of Directors, Making the Ride Happen, Lutheran Social Services, Fox Cities, WI; Board of Directors, Missions at New Life Community Church **Creative Works:** Author, Multiple Articles, Numerous Peer-reviewed Professional Journals **Awards:** Numerous Awards for Medical Excellence While at Luther Midelfort Mayo Health System and Affinity Health System (1995-Present); Grantee, Mayo Clinic (1992); Lemmon Award for Outstanding Medical Student in Surgery (1989); Second Place Award, Wisconsin State Fair (1985); Summer Research Fellow in Three Different Disciplines, Medical College of Wisconsin, Milwaukee, WI (1983); Scholar, Nicolet Medical Clinic (1979, 1980); Scholar, American Association of University Women (AAUW) (1979); Winner as a Freshman College Student, University-Wide Essay Contest, Marquette University (1979); Scholar, The American Legion (1979); Named #1 Spine Surgery Program Based upon Quality Metrics, WI; Regional United States Philanthropy Award, St. Louis, MO **Memberships:** Honorary Master, Epilepsy Foundation of Western Wisconsin; American Association for the Advancement of Science; American Association for Cancer Research; Wisconsin Medical Society; Am. Association of Neurological Surgeons; Congress of Neurological Surgeons; Doctors Mayo Society; Caduceus Society; Samaritan Club; Alpha Epsilon Delta; The Tau Beta Pi Association, Inc. **Marquis Who's Who Honors:** Albert Nelson Marquis Lifetime Achievement Award **Why did you become involved in your profession or industry:** Dr. Cheng became involved in her profession because she loved to work with her hands and was fascinated with the brain and spinal cord. She always wanted to help people. **Avocations:** Outdoor activities; Sports and recreation; Music including the violin and basic piano; Creative writing; Reading; Mastering technology

Chwan-Hwa Peter Chiang

Title: Director **Industry:** Technology **Company Name:** Foxconn International Co. **Place of Birth:** Taiwan **Parents:** King-Hai Chiang; Yu-Chuan Chiang **Marital Status:** Married **Spouse Name:** Ellen Xia **Children:** David; Bella **Education:** Doctor of Philosophy in Polymer Science and Engineering, Case Western Reserve University (1981); Master of Science in Chemistry, University of Texas at El Paso (1977); Bachelor of Science in Chemistry, Tamkang University, Taiwan (1971) **Career:** Retired (2018); Director, Foxconn International Co. (2007-2018); Senior Scientist, Sherwin Williams (1980-2007) **Civic:** Chairperson, Chinese Professional and Academic Association of Midwest, USA **Military Service:** Marine Corps, Taiwan (Two Years) **Creative Works:** Invention of iPhone shining Logo for iPhone 3; Invention of camouflage aircraft coating; Ceramic coating **Awards:** Best R&D Achievement Award, Sherwin Williams (1988) **Memberships:** American Chemical Society; Coating Technology Association **Marquis Who's Who Honors:** Marquis Who's Who Top Professional **To what do you attribute your success:** Mr. Chiang credits his success on his propensity for details and problem solving. **Why did you become involved in your profession or industry:** Mr. Chiang became involved in his profession because he had an interest in chemistry. **Political Affiliations:** Republican

Sara E. Chiarilli

Title: Owner, Designer **Industry:** Fine Art **Company Name:** Artful Conceptions **Parents:** Frederick Frankel **Marital Status:** Married **Spouse Name:** Gregory Chiarilli **Children:** Aaron; Aiden; Elliana **Education:** BA in Studio Art, University of South Florida (2003) **Career:** Owner, Designer, Artful Conceptions (2009-Present); Senior Designer, Norwalk Furniture & Design (2003-2009) **Creative Works:** Author, Book, "Artfully Curated" (2019); Author, Book, "Designing You" (2018); Contributor, Articles, Apollo Beach Magazine; Quoted and Featured, Realtor.com, U.S. News & World Report, Bed Bath and Beyond, Sears; Featured, Podcasts, Radio Shows, Daytime NBC, Extreme Living HGTV, Comic Con Booth, NYC Comic Con, CBS; Speaker, Weekly Guest, ABC Morning Blend, Women Groups, Business Networking Chapters/Organizations **Awards:** Named Top Interior Designer, Expertise (2017, 2018); Named to Best of Houzz, Houzz (2015, 2018); Named to Best of Apollo Beach, Best Businesses (2014, 2015, 2016); Named Woman of the Year, National Association of Professional Women (2014) **Memberships:** American Society of Interior Designers; International Furnishings and Design Association **To what do you attribute your success:** Mrs. Chiarilli attributes her success to her vision, drive and attitude that nothing else is acceptable expect for moving forward. She had very supportive people in her life. **Why did you become involved in your profession or industry:** Mrs. Chiarilli originally started working in the industry right out of college. As a child, she remembers she was constantly moving furniture around in her room and in her house. Also, her grandmother taught her how to draw at the age of 4. She would draw buildings. She believes this is what she had set in her mind at any early age. In addition, her aunt is an interior designer, and she was surrounded by art and design in her youth.

Jai H. Cho, MD

Title: Chief Medical Officer **Industry:** Health, Wellness and Fitness **Company Name:** veriMED IPA, LLC **Date of Birth:** 5/1/1942 **Place of Birth:** Busan **State/Country of Origin:** Republic of Korea **Parents:** Neung Whan Cho; Heo Jai (Min) Cho **Marital Status:** Married **Spouse Name:** Jawon Nam (10/8/1971) **Children:** Karen; Austin **Education:** MD, Catholic Medical College, Seoul, Republic of Korea (1968) **Certifications:** Diplomate, American Board of Internal Medicine **Career:** Principal, Chief Medical Officer, veriMed IPA, LLC (2011-Present); Private Practice, Internal Medicine and Hematology, Tampa, FL (1979-2011); Fellow in Hematology and Oncology, University of South Florida Medical College, Tampa, FL (1977-1979); Fellow in Hematology, Winthrop University Hospital, Mineola, NY (1976-1977); Resident in Internal Medicine, Winthrop University Hospital, Mineola, NY (1973-1976); Intern, White Plains Hospital, New York (1972-1973) **Career Related:** Clinical Assistant Professor of Medicine, University of South Florida College of Medicine (1985-1992); Co-Founder, InterMed LLC, PrimeCare LLC and veriMED IPA LLC **Military Service:** Medical Officer, Korean Army (1968-1971) **Memberships:** American College of Physicians **Marquis Who's Who Honors:** Albert Nelson Marquis Lifetime Achievement Award; Marquis Who's Who Top Professional **To what do you attribute your success:** When a business opportunity came, Dr. Cho took it with confidence when others passed away **Why did you become involved in your profession or industry:** Dr. Cho has always liked science; there is no other physician in his family at all. His family did not want him to go to medical school; they wanted him to attend business school, but he proceeded to attend medical school. He is a very curious person. He became a doctor because he enjoys taking care of people. He came back to the business side later in life. He enjoys what he does, which is teaching the young doctors how to practice. **Avocations:** Art; Architecture; Interior design; Landscaping; Cars **Political Affiliations:** Republican **Religion:** Methodist **Thoughts on Life:** Always look at life with a positive way.

Title: Chief Executive Officer; Software Engineer **Industry:** Information Technology and Services **Company Name:** Block Party; Project Include **Education:** Master of Science in Computer Science, Stanford University (2010); Intern Rocket Scientist, Rocket Fuel Inc. (2009); Software Development Intern, Facebook (2008); Associate Technology Manager Intern, Google (2007); Summer Engineering Intern, Winbond (2006); Bachelor of Science in Electrical Engineering, Stanford University (2009); Coursework, Bing Overseas Studies Program, Peking University (2008) **Career:** Chief Executive Officer, Block Party (2018-Present); Co-founder, Founding Advisor, The Arena (2016-Present); Co-founder, Founding Advisor, Project Include (2015-Present); LD11 Cohort Member, Entrepreneur First (2018); Founder, Y Combinator (2017); Advisor, Homebrew (2014-2018); Consultant, United States Digital Service (2015-2016); Software Engineer, Pintrest (2011-2016); Software Engineer, Quora (2010-2011); CS107 Teaching Assistant, Stanford University (2007) **Career Related:** Speaker in Field **Civic:** Co-founder, Founding Advisor, #MovingForward (2018-Present); Mentor, Hackbright Academy (2012, 2013); Member, Finalist Selection Panel, Girls Who Code (2013); Mentor, Code 2040 (2012-2016); Application Grader, Code 2040 (2012) **Awards:** Edmund Hillary Fellow (2018); Named, One of the 35 Innovators Under 35, MIT Technology Review (2017); Crunchie Award (2017); Named, One of the Women in Tech, Elle Magazine (2015); Named, One of the Most Creative People in Business, Fast Company (2015); Named, One of the Tech 30 Under 30, Forbes Magazine (2014); Named, One of the 30 Under 30, Refinery29 San Francisco's Rising Stars (2013); Mayfield Fellow (2009); Terman Scholar, Stanford University (2009) **Memberships:** Tau Beta Pi; Phi Beta Kappa

James Thomas Christy

Title: Wealth Advisor, Lawyer **Industry:** Financial Services **Company Name:** Northwest Financial Services **Date of Birth:** 11/02/1947 **Place of Birth:** Cincinnati **State/Country of Origin:** OH/USA **Parents:** Thomas Perry Christy; Mary (Vatsures) Christy **Marital Status:** Married **Spouse Name:** Grace Thunborg (05/10/1975) **Children:** James; Diane; Caroline; Elizabeth; John; Catherine **Education:** JD, University of Cincinnati (1972); BBA, University of Cincinnati (1969) **Career:** Wealth Advisor, Northwest Financial Services (2003-Present); Senior Vice President, Pharmaceutical Research and Manufacturers of America (2000-2001); Vice President, Government Relations, TRW Inc., Arlington, VA (1993-1999); Director of Federal Relations, Air Products & Chemicals Inc., Washington, DC (1988-1993); Deputy Director of Federal Relations, Air Products & Chemicals Inc., Washington, DC (1986-1988); Manager of Federal Relations, Air Products & Chemicals Inc., Washington, DC (1985-1986); Legislative Counsel, U.S. Department of Interior, Washington, DC (1984-1985); Counsel, U.S. House of Representatives, Committee on Energy and Commerce, Washington, DC (1981-1984); Private Practice Attorney, Milford, Ohio (1976-1981); Administrative Assistant, U.S. House of Representatives, Washington, DC (1975-1976); Legislature Assistant, U.S. House of Representatives, Washington, DC (1973-1975) **Civic:** Candidate, Sixth Congressional District, United States Congress, Ohio (1980); Chairman, Board of Governors, Bryce Harlow Foundation; Board of Visitors, University of Cincinnati College of Law **Military Service:** Retired Captain, United States Army Reserve **Awards:** Named Five Star Wealth Manager (2015-2019) **Memberships:** Past Chairman, Bryce Harlow Foundation (1995-1996); Public Affairs Steering Committee, National Association of Manufacturers (1989-1999); Business-Government Relations Council; Founder, The Ohio Forum; University of Cincinnati College of Law Alumni Association; Board of Directors, U.S. Capitol Historical Society; **Marquis Who's Who Honors:** Albert Nelson Marquis Lifetime Achievement Award; Marquis Who's Who Top Professional **Why did you become involved in your profession or industry:** For Mr. Christy, practicing law was an opportunity to do public service. Initially, after graduating from law school and his army service, he came to the US House of Representatives and worked in Congress. It was part of his desire to be involved in public policy and serve the citizens of Ohio. He had two uncles who were lawyers, who he admired greatly.

Joseph John Cipfl, PhD

Title: President, Chief Executive Officer Emeritus **Industry:** Education/Educational Services **Company Name:** Illinois Community College Board **Date of Birth:** 01/23/1945 **Place of Birth:** East St. Louis **State/Country of Origin:** IL/USA **Parents:** Joseph J. Cipfl; Marguerite E. Cipfl **Marital Status:** Married **Spouse Name:** Linda Louise Cipfl **Children:** Joseph J. III; Jennifer C. Filyaw **Education:** PHD, St. Louis University; EdS, Southern Illinois University; MS, Southern Illinois University; BS, Illinois State University; Honorary Associate Degree, Elgin College; Honorary Associate Degree, Morraine Valley College; Diploma, Cathedral High School **Certifications:** Illinois Superintendent; Illinois Principal; Illinois K-12 Teacher **Career:** Chairperson, School of Education, Dean, Graduate School, McKendree University (2004-2017); President, Chief Executive Officer, Illinois Community College Board, (1997-2004); President, Southwestern Illinois College (1988-1997); Superintendent, Belleville School District 118 (1976-1988); Regional Director, Abraham Lincoln, Dewey and Mount Pleasant Schools, Belleville School District 118 (1973-1976); Principal, Abraham Lincoln School, Belleville School District 118 (1970-1973); Sixth Grade Teacher, Abraham Lincoln School, Belleville School District 118 (1968-1970); Middle School Teacher, East St. Louis School District 189 (1967-1968) **Career Related:** Instructor, St. Louis University; Instructor, Southern Illinois University; Consultant, Illinois Administrators Academy **Civic:** President, Belleville Area Chamber of Commerce; President, United Way Illinois; President, Belleville Optimist Club; President, Boy Scouts of America, Okaw Valley; President, Racial Harmony Organization, St. Clair County, Illinois; Board of Directors, Southwestern Illinois Women's Crisis Center; Board of Directors, Belleville YMCA; Board of Directors, Belleville Economic Progress; Board of Directors, United Way of Greater St. Louis; Board of Directors, O'Fallon, Illinois Rotary **Awards:** College of Education Hall of Fame, Illinois State University; Shirley B. Gordon Outstanding Community College President Award, Phi Theta Kappa; Distinguished Citizen Award, Boy Scouts of America; Outstanding Educator, National PTA; Carroll E. Kimmel Community Service Award, Southern Illinois University; Presidents Award for impact upon adult education, Illinois Adult and Continuing Educators Association; Meritorious Service Award for outstanding service to Illinois community colleges, Illinois Community College Trustees Association; Outstanding Educator Award, National PTA; Educator of the 90s Award, U.S. Congress; School Superintendent Excellence Award, Illinois State Board of Education; Optimist of Year Award, Optimists International; Outstanding Volunteer Award, United Way Greater St. Louis; Distinguished Citizen Award, Boy Scouts of America; Extraordinary Leader Impacting Today's Environment Award, Racial Harmony Organization, St. Clair County, Illinois; Outstanding Citizen Award, Belleville Chamber of Commerce; Distinguished Citizen Award, Belleville Chamber of Commerce; Outstanding Educator Award, Belleville Chamber of Commerce Award; Outstanding Young Person State of Illinois, Illinois Chamber of Commerce **Memberships:** American Association of Community Colleges; Illinois Council of Community College Presidents; American Association of School Administrators; National PTA; Illinois PTA; Phi Theta Kappa; Phi Delta Kappa **Marquis Who's Who Honors:** Albert Nelson Marquis Lifetime Achievement Award; Marquis Who's Who Top Professional; Marquis Who's Who Humanitarian Award **To what do you attribute your success:** Dr. Cipfl's parents, Joseph Sr. and Marguerite, were extraordinary examples of kindness, goodwill and accomplishment. They instilled upon him the need and responsibility to achieve and give back. His wife, Linda, has been his partner and motivator in every aspect of his professional life. Her knowledge, warmth and personality helped enable them to build the necessary and strategic relationships that were so essential. **Why did you become involved in your profession or industry:** During his high school days, while reflecting upon and considering the factors that his parents had instilled within him regarding the need and responsibility to make a positive difference, he determined that he must teach. Then upon experiencing teaching, he determined that he could provide successful leadership. He was fortunate to achieve success and each leadership position led to another, principal, regional director, superintendent, college president, and president and CEO of a state-wide system. **Avocations:** Avid water enthusiast; Family gatherings and activities; Extensive baseball memorabilia collector with particular emphasis upon St. Louis Cardinals; Model railroading including locomotives, train cars, signalling, bridges, houses, buildings, vehicles and lights; Extensive collection of books within personal library **Religion:** Roman Catholic

Michael V. Ciresi, JD

Title: Lawyer **Industry:** Law and Legal Services **Company Name:** Ciresi Conlin LLP, Robins Kaplan LLP **Date of Birth:** 04/18/1946 **Place of Birth:** St. Paul **State/Country of Origin:** MN/USA **Parents:** Samuel Vincent Ciresi; Selena Marie (Bloom) Ciresi **Marital Status:** Married **Spouse Name:** Ann Ciresi **Children:** Caroline; Dominic; Adam **Education:** Honorary LLD, Southwestern University (2001); JD, University of Minnesota (1971); BBA, University of St. Thomas, Minnesota (1968) **Career:** Founding Partner, Ciresi Conlin LLP (2015-Present); Chairman, Executive Board, Robins Kaplan, LLP, Minneapolis, MN (1995-Present); Partner, Robins Kaplan, LLP, Minneapolis, MN (1978-2015); Executive Board, Robins Kaplan, LLP, Minneapolis, MN (1983-2008); Associate, Robins Kaplan, LLP, Minneapolis, MN (1971-1978) **Civic:** Member, Board of Directors, Parent Aware (2010-Present); Former Member, Board of Directors, Saint Paul Public Schools Foundation (2009-2012); Member, Board of Directors, Minnesota Early Learning Foundation (2009-2012); Former Member, Board of Directors, Guthrie Theater (2005); Former Member, Board of Directors, Public Justice Foundation (1997-2005); Candidate, United States Senate (2000); Former Member, Board of Directors, Children's Minnesota; Former Member, Board of Directors, Regions Hospital; Former Member, Board of Directors, Equal Justice Works; Former Co-Chair, Hennepin County Office to End Homelessness **Awards:** Top 100 Trial Lawyers in America, Benchmark Litigation (2015); Top 10 Attorneys in Minnesota, Minneapolis St. Paul Magazine (2015); Food and Beverage MVP, Law360 (2014); Opus Sancti Thomae Award, Saint Thomas Academy (2014); Lawyer of the Year in Bet-The-Company Litigation, Best Lawyers (2012, 2014); 500 Leading Lawyers in America (2010-2014); 100 Most Influential Lawyers in America, The National Law Journal (1997, 2000, 2006-2007); Ellis Island Medal of Honor, National Ethnic Coalition of Organizations (Now Ellis Island Honors Society) (2002); Outstanding Achievement Award, University of Minnesota (1999); Distinguished Alumnus Award, University of St. Thomas (1999); Lifetime Achievement Award, Minnesota Association for Justice (1998); Top 10 Trial Lawyers in American (1989, 1993); Best Lawyer, Minneapolis, MN; Litigation Lawyer of the Year; Trial Lawyer of the Year; Product Liability Lawyer of the Year; Inductee, Litigation Hall of Fame; 500 Leading Lawyers in America, Lawdragon Inc. **Memberships:** American Association for Justice; American Bar Association; Warren E. Burger Society, National Center for State Courts; American College of Trial Lawyers; The International Academy of Trial Lawyers; Public Justice; The Inner Circle of Advocates; International Bar Association; American Board of Trial Advocates; Ramsey County Bar Association; Hennepin County Bar Association; Minnesota State Bar Association **Bar Admissions:** United States Court of Appeals for the Fifth Circuit (1999); United States Court of Appeals for the Federal Circuit (1998); New York State Bar Association (1995); Tenth Circuit Court of Appeals (1990); United States Court of Appeals for the Ninth Circuit (1987); United States Court of Appeals for the Second Circuit (1986); Supreme Court of the United States (1981); United States District Court for the District of Minnesota (1974); United States Court of Appeals for the Eighth Circuit (1971); Minnesota State Bar Association (1971) **Marquis Who's Who Honors:** Albert Nelson Marquis Lifetime Achievement Award **Why did you become involved in your profession or industry:** Mr. Ciresi became involved in his profession so he could level the legal playing field. After 43 years of practicing law, and working on some of the highest profile cases in the country, he has never accepted that our system of justice should only benefit those with the greatest resources or who dance in the shadows of the ambiguity of the law. **Avocations:** Playing and watching sports; Studying U.S. history **Religion:** Roman Catholic

Max Citrin

Title: Chief Executive Officer, President, Owner **Industry:** Medicine & Health Care **Company Name:** Citrin Medical **Education:** Traditional Rotating Internship with an Orthopedic Focus, University Hospitals Regional Hospitals, Richmond Heights, OH (2013-2014); Degree in Medicine, Nova Southeastern University College of Osteopathic Medicine (2013); Doctor of Osteopathic Medicine, Davidson College, Davidson NC (2005); BS in Biology, Tampa Preparatory School, Cum Laude, Tampa, FL (2001) **Certifications:** Certified Strength and Conditioning Specialist, National Strength and Conditioning Association (2005-Present); Certified Personal Trainer, National Strength and Conditioning Association (2001-2013) **Career:** Chief Executive Officer, President, Owner, Citrin Medical Corporation, Florida (2015-Present); Attending Physician, MDNow Urgent Care, Fort Lauderdale, FL (2014-Present); Urgent Care of Fort Lauderdale, Fort Lauderdale, FL (2014); Orthopedic Research Assistant, Holy Cross Hospital, Fort Lauderdale, FL (2014) **Civic:** Volunteer, Weinberg Assisted Living Facilities, Tampa, FL (2010); Volunteer, Shands Pediatric Lipids Clinic, University of Florida, Gainesville, FL (2007-2009); YMCA Volunteer, Exercise Instruction for Mentally Disabled Teens, Davidson, NC (2004); Volunteer Strength and Conditioning Coach Intern, Davidson College (2002-2004); Volunteer Strength and Conditioning Coach Intern, Wake Forest University (2002) **Creative Works:** Contributor, Articles, Professional Journals **Awards:** Nominee, Student of the Year, Nova Southeastern University College of Osteopathic Medicine (2010); Carolyn L. Kuckein Student Research Fellowship Award, Alpha Omega Alpha (2006); Inductee, Beta Beta Beta Biology Honor Society, Davidson College (2002-2005); Inductee, Alpha Epsilon Delta Premed Honor Society, Davidson College (2002-2005); National Residence Hall Honor, Davidson College (2001) **Memberships:** Founding Fellow, American Association of Stem Cell Physicians; American Academy of Lifestyle Medicine; Florida Osteopathic Medical Association; Florida Medical Association; American Academy of Anti-Aging Medicine **Marquis Who's Who Honors:** Marquis Who's Who Top Professional **To what do you attribute your success:** Dr. Citrin attributes his success to hard work and perseverance. **Why did you become involved in your profession or industry:** Dr. Citrin didn't always know he was going to pursue osteopathic medicine. He had an interest in the muscular skeleton structure, which encouraged him to help an art professor who was no longer able to paint due to extensive pain in his arm. Through this experience, Dr. Citrin found his calling.

Rosemary Christine Ciullo, PsyD

Title: Clinical Psychologist **Industry:** Medicine & Health Care **Place of Birth:** Chicago **State/Country of Origin:** IL/USA **Parents:** Leonard Ciullo (Deceased 1998); Anna Auriemma Ciullo (Deceased 1991) **Education:** Coursework in Child and Adolescent Psychology, International College of Professional Psychology (2005); Doctorate in Psychology, The School of Professional Psychology at Forest Institute, with High Distinction (1986); MA, Governors State University, University Park, IL (1977); BA, University of Illinois at Chicago (1974) **Career:** Psychologist, Private Practice, Illinois (1995-2000); Henry Horner Children's Center (1987-1993); Ada McKinley Foster Care (1974-1977); St. Ann's Hospital (1969-1980) **Civic:** Cursillo Group; Former Volunteer, Women's Choice Services; St. Jude Children's Research Hospital; Shriners Hospital for Children; Ann & Robert H. Lurie Children's Hospital of Chicago; Ronald McDonald House Charities; Anti-Cruelty Cause; People for the Ethical Treatment of Animals (PETA) **Creative Works:** Co-Author, Article, "Small Group Interaction and Behavior in Latency-Age Children," Sage Publications, Inc. (1988); Co-Founder, Graphic Newsletter; Co-Author, "Difference in Behavior In Latency Age Children"; **Awards:** Named, Outstanding Student, The School of Professional Psychology at Forest Institute **Memberships:** American Psychological Association; Former Member, Prescribing Psychologists Register; American Association of Suicidology; Association for Psychological Science; American Orthopsychiatry Association; Former Member, Illinois Psychological Association; The American Psychological Society **Marquis Who's Who Honors:** Albert Nelson Marquis Lifetime Achievement Award; Marquis Who's Who Top Professional **To what do you attribute your success:** Dr. Ciullo attributes her success to Dr. Carmen Pofner, her supervisor when she first got started, who became her mentor. She was her supervisor during her internship at the same place where she wound up getting a job. Dr. Ciullo still continues to be inspired by her. **Why did you become involved in your profession or industry:** Dr. Ciullo became involved in her profession because she was initially going to go to medical school. She studied nursing, and something hit her while working as a nursing assistant. She was working at a hospital with a nurse, a little lady, and one of the doctors threw a chart at her. She was very angry but the nurse handled it very well. She told him, "Don't you ever do that to me again." The next day the doctor came in and apologized to the nurse, but Dr. Ciullo just decided that she was not going to become a nurse because she refused to put up with nonsense from doctors. She had also been walking with crutches since 1980 and thought she would not be strong enough to stand for rotations and surgeries. Dr. Ciullo had to be realistic. So, she looked around and took some psychology classes. She fell in love with the subject. Then, Dr. Ciullo decided she wanted to help children, so she went into child psychology. She got a job at a state mental hospital for children. Dr. Ciullo loved it and stayed with it until budget cuts forced the closing of these hospitals. After she left, she had a lot of surgical procedures on her hips. Dr. Ciullo was in a lot of pain but did some volunteering. She opened a private practice in her home. **Avocations:** Reading; Workshops in continuing education; Volunteering; Writing; Working with the church **Religion:** Catholic **Thoughts on Life:** Dr. Ciullo believes if you have you treat people with dignity and respect, then you will receive dignity and respect back.

C. Clair Claiborne, PhD

Title: Polymer Materials Scientist **Industry:** Consulting **Company Name:** Claiborne Consulting LLC **Date of Birth:** 05/30/1952 **Place of Birth:** Fredonia **State/Country of Origin:** KS/USA **Parents:** Sylvester Oty Claiborne; Edna Claire (Cummings) Claiborne **Marital Status:** Married **Spouse Name:** Patricia Claiborne **Education:** PhD in Materials Science and Engineering, Northwestern University (1984); BA in Chemistry, The University of Kansas (1973) **Career:** Polymer Materials Scientist, Claiborne Consulting LLC, Apex, NC (2017-Present); Principal Consulting R&D Scientist, ABB Inc., Raleigh, NC (2002-2017); United States Environmental Specialist, ABB Inc., Raleigh, NC (2000-2011); Fellow Scientist, ABB Inc., Raleigh, NC (1997-2002); Senior Scientist, Westinghouse Electric (Now ABB Power T&D Company Inc.), Raleigh, NC (1991-1997); Senior Scientist, Westinghouse Electric (Now ABB Power T&D Company Inc.), Sharon, PA (1984-1991); Research Chemist, Phillips Petroleum, Bartlesville, OK (1980-1984); Research Assistant, Northwestern University (1976-1980); Engineer, Janes Manufacturing Inc., Fort Scott, KS (1975-1976); Chemotechnician, Sued Chemie A.G., Moosburg, Germany (1973-1975) **Career Related:** Convenor, IEC PT62975, Natural Ester Use and Maintenance (2014-Present); Chairman, ASTM D27, Electrical Insulating Liquids and Gases (2008-2013); Fellowship, College of Scientists Foundation (1980); Fellow, American Society for Testing and Materials **Creative Works:** Author, "Working with Metals" (1981); Author, "Working with Non-Metals" (1981); Contributor, Over 75 Articles, Professional Journals **Awards:** Named Material Scientist of the Year, IAOTP (2019); Elected Alternate Councilor, American Chemical Society and Central Carolina Society (2015); Regional Innovation Award for the Invention of BIOTEMP, American Chemical Society (2002); Co-recipient, IR Award for the Invention of BIOTEMP (2000) **Memberships:** Senior Member, IEEE (2012-Present); Senior Member, Society of Plastics Engineers (2000-Present); American Chemical Society; International Electrotechnical Commission (IEC); International Council on Large Electric Systems; Alpha Kappa Lambda **Marquis Who's Who Honors:** Albert Nelson Marquis Lifetime Achievement Award; Marquis Who's Who Top Professional **Why did you become involved in your profession or industry:** Dr. Claiborne wanted to be a chemist, and he then decided that he wanted to be a material scientist after he worked for a German company. He decided to attend school for it. **Avocations:** Piano; Amateur radio **Political Affiliations:** Democrat **Religion:** Methodist

Barbara Ann Clark

Title: Counseling Administrator (Retired) Licensed Professional Counselor **Date of Birth:** 07/18/1937 **Place of Birth:** Macon **State/Country of Origin:** GA/USA **Parents:** LeRoy Dumas Randall; Lillian Evelyn Battle **Marital Status:** Widowed **Spouse Name:** Carl Oliver Clark (Deceased 8/8/2017) **Children:** Carl Robert; Angela Teresa **Education:** MEd, South Carolina State University (1976); BS in Chemistry-Mathematics, Morgan State University (1959); Post-graduate Coursework **Certifications:** Certified Public Notary (1987) **Career:** School Counselor, Nix Elementary School, Orangeburg, SC (1990-2000); School Counselor, Marshal Elementary School, Orangeburg, SC (1990-1993); Counselor, Coordinator, Editor, Public Relations, Orangeburg School District 1 (1986-1990); Math-Science Teacher, Norway Junior High School, South Carolina (1984-1986); Administrator, Instructor, Claflin University, Orangeburg, SC (1977-1984); In-school Suspension Director, Counselor, Belleville Junior High School, Orangeburg, SC (1976-1977); Testing Evaluator, Orangeburg School District 5 (1975-1976); Chemistry Instructor, South Carolina State University, Orangeburg, SC (1966-1967); Research Chemist, National Institutes Health/City Hospitals, Baltimore, MD (1959-1966) **Career Related:** Mentor, Nix Elementary School, Orangeburg, SC (1990-2020) **Civic:** Vice Chairman, Board of Directors, The CROWN Group; President, Author, Board of Directors, Tutor, Orangeburg Literary Council (2001-Present); Volunteer, Meals on Wheels, County Council on Aging, Orangeburg, SC (2002-2011); Board Chair, Orangeburg Disabilities Special Needs Foundation (1992-2008); Board of Directors, Edisto Habitat for Humanity (2005-2008); Committee Member, Community of Character (2005); Board of Directors, Volunteer, Habitat for Humanity; Committee Member, Friends of South Carolina State University Museum **Creative Works:** Author, "Trailblazer" (2014); Author, "Snippets" (2013); Author, "If You Can Read" (2011); Author, "Jump Start" Dealing with Teaching 12 Character Traits to Children (Ages 4-12) (2007); Author, "K.I.D.S. (Kids Practicing Character In Daily Stuff)(2005); Co-Author, "Soul" (2004); Author, "Beams and Bits" (2000); Author, "Alabama Angel" (1997); Author, "Getting Ready to Fly" (1997); Author, "Booker T." (1996); Author, "Masks!" (1993); Author, "Impressions" (1988); Author, "Pieces" (1985); Author, "Reflections" (1982) **Awards:** Named, South Carolina Counselor of the Year (1993); One of the 75 Delta Diamonds Honoree, Delta Sigma Theta Sorority, Inc.(1988) **Memberships:** Emeritus Member, Licensed Professional Counselor, South Carolina Counselors Association; Founder, Orangeburg Red Hatters; Lifetime Member, Communications Chair, Editor, Past Vice President, Past President, Past Treasurer, Past Journalist, Orangeburg Alumnae Chapter, Delta Sigma Theta, Sorority, Inc. **Marquis Who's Who Honors:** Albert Nelson Marquis Lifetime Achievement Award **To what do you attribute your success:** Ms. Clark attributed her success to perseverance, gratefulness and blessings. Her intellectual hunger has been fed from the vast sea of knowledge to nourish her mind for personal enrichment. She learned to love herself and not agonize over flaws suggested by others' notions of beauty but to focus on spiritual beauty and never stay in the pain of injustice. Realizing that the nature of her thinking is advanced or limited by her experiences, Ms. Clark sought to be a well-grounded, compassionate being, capable of listening, learning, sharing and growing. **Why did you become involved in your profession or industry:** Ms. Clark became involved in her profession to lift others and to learn. **Avocations:** Writing; Sewing; Reading; Traveling **Political Affiliations:** Democrat **Religion:** Roman Catholic **Thoughts on Life:** Ms. Clark and her twin brother Glenn Mason Randall learned to read before the age of three. They are constant friends and always played together. "Bury only my faults, any weaknesses I may have had and any prejudices against my fellow man. If, by chance, you wish to remember me, do it with a kind word or deed to someone who needs you - then I will live forever."

Benjamin King Clarke

Title: Anesthesiologist (Retired), State Representative, State Legislator **Industry:** Government Administration/Government Relations/Government Services **Date of Birth:** 04/23/1928 **Place of Birth:** Columbus **State/Country of Origin:** OH/USA **Parents:** Benjamin King Clarke; Harriett Lucinda (Russ) Wilson **Marital Status:** Married **Spouse Name:** Mavis Moreen Hooper (07/09/1956) **Children:** Benjamin Clarke III; Edgar Dumas (Stepchild) **Education:** Doctor of Medicine, University of Colorado, Boulder, CO (1959); Bachelor of Science in Chemistry, University of Denver, Denver, CO (1950) **Career:** State Representative, State Legislature (1994-2000); Chief Anesthesiologist, Porter & Swedish Hospital, Denver, CO (1980-1993); Director, Porter & Swedish Hospital, Denver, CO (1980-1981); Member, Staff, Porter & Swedish Hospital, Denver, CO (1971-1980); Member, Staff, General Rose & Mercy Hospital, Denver, CO (1969-1970); Member, Staff, Roosevelt Hospital, New York, NY (1968-1969); Member, Staff, Harlem Hospital, New York, NY (1966-1968); Chief, Whitestone, Queens, NY (1964-1966); Member, Staff, Maimonides Hospital, Brooklyn, NY (1962-1964) **Civic:** Founder, Minority-Based Chess Club in Elementary Schools; Became Involved in Desegregation in Elementary Schools in New Jersey in the 1960s **Creative Works:** Featured in Denver Post and on the Tom Brokaw Show **Awards:** Best Politician (1997); Award Westword News, Denver, CO **Memberships:** President, Mile High Medical Society (1978-1979); American Medical Association; American Society of Anesthesiologists; Colorado Medical Society **Marquis Who's Who Honors:** Albert Nelson Marquis Lifetime Achievement Award; Marquis Who's Who Top Professional **Why did you become involved in your profession or industry:** Dr. Clarke became involved in his profession because, as a chemist, he could not see himself supporting a family in the position so he decided to go back to school. **Avocations:** Tennis; Travel **Political Affiliations:** Democrat **Religion:** Episcopalian

Robert Reside Clarke

Title: Biochemist, Researcher **Industry:** Sciences **Date of Birth:** 03/03/1956 **Place of Birth:** Londonderry, Northern Ireland **State/Country of Origin:** United Kingdom **Parents:** Thomas Clarke; Eileen (Mateer) Clarke **Marital Status:** Married **Spouse Name:** Leena Anikki Hilakivi-Clarke, PhD (09/24/1989) **Children:** Tomas Nikolai Clarke; Johan Alexander Clarke; Robin Clarke **Education:** DSc, Queen's University Belfast (1999); PhD, Queen's University Belfast (1986); MSc in Biochemistry, Queen's University Belfast (1982); BSc in Biological Sciences, Ulster University (1980) **Certifications:** Chartered Biologist; Chartered Chemist **Career:** Co-leader, Breast Cancer Program, Lombardi Comprehensive Cancer Center, Georgetown University (2006-Present); Professor, Department of Oncology, Georgetown University (1999-Present); Member, Lombardi Comprehensive Cancer Center, Georgetown University (1988-Present); Dean for Research, Georgetown University Medical Center (2011-2019); Director, Georgetown University Center for Cancer Systems Biology (2010-2016); Interim Associate Vice President, Georgetown University Medical Center (2007-2019); Interim Director, Biomedical Graduate Research Organization, Georgetown University Medical Center (2007-2019); Co-chair, Division of Molecular Endocrinology, Nutrition, and Obesity, Department of Oncology, Georgetown University (2004-2008); Professor, Department of Physiology and Biophysics, Georgetown University (1999-2010); Associate Professor, Department of Physiology and Biophysics, Georgetown University (1995-1999); Adjunct Graduate Professor, Department of Genetics and Human Genetics, Howard University (1994-2001); Assistant Professor, Department of Physiology and Biophysics, Georgetown University (1991-1995); Director, Animal Model Shared Resource, Georgetown Lombardi Comprehensive Cancer Center (1989-2006); Research Assistant Professor, Department of Physiology and Biophysics, Georgetown University (1988-1991); Breast Cancer Study Group Fellow, Breast Cancer Section, Medicine Branch, National Cancer Institute, National Institutes of Health (1987-1988); Research Fellow, Department of Biochemistry, Queen's University Belfast (1986) **Career Related:** Contributor, Multiple Internal Pilot Grant Peer Review Panels (2011-Present); Interim Director, Biomedical Graduate Research Organization, Georgetown University Medical Center (2007-Present); With, National Institutes of Health (1996-Present); With, U.S. Department of Defense, Frederick, MD (1995-Present); With, Cancer Research Foundation of America (1995-Present); United States-Ireland Consultant, American Institute of Cancer Research (1990-Present); Chair, Co-director, Division of Molecular Endocrinology, Obesity and Nutrition (2006-2009); Leader, Georgetown University's caBIG Team (2004-2012); Secretary/Treasurer, Georgetown University Faculty Senate (2004-2007); Vice President, Academic Outreach Biolink USA-Ireland (2003-2008); Chair, Lombardi Comprehensive Cancer Center Bioinformatics Task Force (2002-2004); Chair, Co-chair, Panel Member, Numerous Study Sections and Grant Reviews; Chair, Numerous Sessions, International Research Conferences; Lecturer, Numerous Laboratory- and Lecture-Based Training Workshops **Civic:** Computational Core Advisory Committee, Georgetown University (2004-Present); Working Group to Establish Venture Philanthropy Fund for Georgetown (2018-2019); Georgetown University Campaign Council (2018-2019); Chair, Selection Committee, Fifth Annual AACR Outstanding Investigator for Breast Cancer Research, Funded by Susan G. Komen for the Cure (2012); Selection Committee for the InBev-Baillet Latour Fund Health Prize (2012); Executive Committee, Biomedical Graduate Research Organization (GUMC), Georgetown University (2007-2011); Selection Committee, George J. Mitchell Scholarship Program (2006, 2007); Chair, Selection Committee for the BioLink USA-Ireland Life Science Awards (2005-2007); Member, Scientific Advisors to the Northern Ireland Bureau (2005-2007); Animal Research Resource Scientific and Oversight Committee (LCCC), Georgetown University (1989-2006) **Creative Works:** Associate Editor, Endocrine Related Cancer (2012-Present); Senior Editor, Cancer Research (2007-Present); Managing Editor, Frontiers in Bioscience (2004-Present); Editor, Book, "The Unfolded Protein Response in Cancer" (2019); Co-editor, Book, "Cancer Gene Networks" (2017); Guest Editor, Journal of Mammary Gland Biology and Neoplasia (2000); Member, Numerous Editorial Boards Including Cells, Anticancer Research and ROS (Reactive Oxygen Species); Manuscript Reviewer, Numerous Journals Including Science, Cancer Cell and Nature Cell Biology; Contributor, More Than 300 Articles, Professional Journals; Contributor, Chapters, Books; Speaker, Numerous Podium Presentations, Seminars, International Workshops, and Panels **Awards:** Grantee, U.S. Department of Defense (1996-Present); Grantee, National Institutes of Health (1989-Present) **Memberships:** Fellow, Member, Royal Society of Biology, Royal Society of Medicine and Royal Society of Chemistry; American Association for the Advancement of Science; American Association for Cancer Research; American Chemical Society; Biochemical Society; Endocrine Society; The New York Academy of Sciences; Society for Endocrinology; Sigma Xi **Marquis Who's Who Honors:** Albert Nelson Marquis Lifetime Achievement Award **Avocations:** Sailing; Music

Herbert Clay

Title: Design Engineer (Retired) **Industry:** Engineering **Company Name:** Aerovironment **Marital Status:** Married **Spouse Name:** Wynema Ligons (1964) **Children:** Herbert Jr.; Sylvia; Carl; Stacy; Bonnie; Menzah **Education:** Undergraduate Coursework, West Coast University, Irvine, CA; Undergraduate Coursework, Wichita State University, Wichita, KS **Certifications:** Teaching Credential, Abram Freidman College (1981) **Career:** Adjunct Professor, Santa Monica Community College (1984-2004); With, Northrop Grumman (1984-2004); With, G&H Technology, Santa Monica, CA (1979-1984); Project Engineer, Ancra Divisions (1977-1979); Project Engineer, Hardman Aerospace (1967-1977); With, Boeing; Design Engineer, Numerous Companies, including Rotonics, Pentadine, and AeroVironment (Seven Years) **Civic:** Volunteer, Rotonics **Creative Works:** Patented designs; Flywheel housing; Cooling systems; Solid works drafting software **Marquis Who's Who Honors:** Marquis Who's Who Top Professional **To what do you attribute your success:** Mr. Clay attributes his success to hardwork, and tenacity. He also prides himself on his lack of animosity towards anyone. **Why did you become involved in your profession or industry:** Mr. Clay became involved in his profession because math was always an easy subject for him. After attending Wichita State University, which was known for its aerospace and aeronautics programs, he secured a position with Boeing working on the new 747 aircraft. **Avocations:** Church activities; Yard work; Cars **Religion:** Christian

Gilles Clement

Title: Interior Designer **Industry:** Fine Art **Company Name:** Gilles Clement Designs **Marital Status:** Married **Spouse Name:** Aida Clements **Education:** Bachelor of Arts in Interior Design, Fairfield University (2003) **Career:** Owner, Gilles Clement Designs (2009-Present); Producer, Promoter (1988-2003) **Awards:** Connecticut Cottages and Garden Innovation Design Award (2007) **To what do you attribute your success:** Mr. Clement attributes his success to not only his talent but his work ethic as well. He has been extremely devoted to his work and works seven days a week. He vacations rarely and is fully dedicated to his businesses. His wife is also a part of the business and has been a great help. **Why did you become involved in your profession or industry:** Mr. Clement became involved in his profession due to the influence of his parents, who owned an art studio. Much of his artistic abilities and desires stem from that time. He began his career in the music business as a producer and promoter between 1988 and 2003. When he attended Fairfield College, he took a course in interior design and fell in love with the subject.

Hillary Diane Clinton

Title: Former U.S. Secretary; Former U.S. Senator from New York; Former First Lady **Industry:** Government Administration/Government Relations/Government Services **Company Name:** U.S. Department of State **Date of Birth:** 10/26/1947 **Place of Birth:** Chicago **State/Country of Origin:** IL/USA **Parents:** Hugh Ellsworth Rodham; Dorothy (Howell) Rodham **Marital Status:** Married **Spouse Name:** William Jefferson Clinton (10/11/1975) **Children:** Chelsea Victoria **Education:** Honorary LLD, University of St. Andrews (2013); Honorary LLD, Yale University (2009); Honorary LLD, Marymount Manhattan College (2005); Honorary LLD, Rensselaer Polytechnic Institute (RPI) (2005); Honorary LLD, Ulster University (2004); Honorary DHL, Manhattanville College (2004); Honorary DHL, Pace University (2003); Honorary DHL, Ohio University (1997); Honorary DHL, Drew University (1996); Honorary Doctorate in Public Service, University of Maryland, College Park, MD (1996); Honorary LLD, University of Minnesota (1995); Honorary LLD, San Francisco State University (1995); Honorary Doctorate in Public Service, George Washington University (1994); Honorary LLD, University of Illinois (1994); Honorary LLD, The University of Sunderland (1993); Honorary LLD, University of Pennsylvania (1993); Honorary LLD, University of Michigan (1993); Honorary LLD, Hendrix College (1992); Honorary LLD, Arkansas University (1988); JD, Yale Law School (1973); BA in Political Science, Wellesley College, with High Honors (1969) **Career:** Founder, Onward Together (2017-Present); Secretary, U.S. Department of State, Washington, DC (2009-2013); Member, U.S. Senate Committee on Armed Services (2003-2011); Member, U.S. Senate Committee on Health, Education, Labor and Pensions (2001-2011); Member, U.S. Senate Committee on Environment and Public Works (2001-2011); U.S. Senator, State of New York (2001-2009); Member, U.S. Senate Budget Committee (2001-2002); First Lady of the United States, Washington, DC (1993-2001); Chair, Presidential Task Force on National Health Care Reform (1993); First Lady of Arkansas (1979-1981, 1983-1992); Assistant Professor of Law, University of Arkansas School of Law (1979-1980); Partner, Rose Law Firm, Little Rock, AR (1977-1992); Assistant Professor of Law, Director, Legal Aid Clinic, University of Arkansas School of Law (1974-1977); Counsel, Impeachment Inquiry Staff, U.S. House Judiciary Committee, Washington, DC (1974); Legal Consultant, Carnegie Council on Children, New Haven, CT (1973-1974); Attorney, Children's Defense Fund, Cambridge, MA and Washington, DC (1973-1974) **Career Related:** Presidential Candidate, Democratic Party Nominee, 2016 Presidential Election (2016); Candidate for Democratic Party Nomination, 2008 Presidential Election (2008) **Civic:** Honorary Member, Pen + Brush (1996-Present); Honorary Chair, The New York Academy of Sciences Annual Gala (2005); Board of Directors, Public/Private Ventures (1990-1992); Board of Directors, La5arge (1990-1992); Board of Directors, Sesame Workshop (1989-1992); Board of Directors, Arkansas Children's Hospital (1988-1992); Board of Directors, Roosevelt Institute (1988-1992); Member, Advisory Board, HIPPY USA (1988-1992); Board of Directors, NCEE (1987-1992); Board of Directors, Child Care Action Campaign (1986-1992); Board of Directors, Walmart Inc. (1986-1992); Board of Directors, TCBY (1986-1992); Chair, Children's Defense Fund (1986-1991); Member, Commission on Quality Education, Southern Regional Education Board (SREB) (1984-1992); Chairman, Arkansas Education Standards Committee (1983-1984); Board of Directors, New World Foundation (1982-1988); Chair, Legal Services Corporation (1978-1980); Member, Numerous Committees/Organizations **Creative Works:** Author, "Hard Choices" (2014); Author, Autobiography, "Living History" (2003); Author, "An Invitation to the White House: At Home with History" (2000); Author, "Dear Socks, Dear Buddy: Kids' Letters to the First Pets" (1998); Author, "It Takes a Village: And Other Lessons Children Teach Us" (1996); Author, Syndicated Columnist, "Talking it Over" (1995-2000); Author, "Handbook on Legal Rights for Arkansas Women" (1977, 1987); Contributor, Articles to Professional Journals **Awards:** Named One of the 100 Most Influential People in the World, TIME Magazine (2004, 2006-2012, 2014); Named the Most Fascinating Person, Barbara Walters' Special (2012, 2013); Medal for Distinguished Public Service, U.S. Department of Defense (2013); Liberty Medal, National Constitution Center (2013); Award of Merit, Yale Law School (2013); Champion of Peace Award, Women for Women International (2013); Named One of the 50 Most Powerful People in DC, GQ Magazine (2007, 2009, 2012); Named One of the 100 Most Powerful Women in DC, Washingtonian Magazine (2009, 2011); Named One of the 10 Most Powerful Women in Washington, Fortune Magazine (2009, 2010); Recipient, Numerous Awards **Memberships:** Chair, Commission on Women in the Profession, ABA (1987-1991); Fellow, American Academy of Arts & Sciences; Fellow, American Bar Foundation; ABA; American Association for Justice; Pulaski County Bar Association; AAWL; Arkansas Trial Lawyers Association; Arkansas Bar Association **Bar Admissions:** Supreme Court of the United States (1975); State of Arkansas (1973); United States District Court for the Eastern District of Arkansas (1973); United States District Court for the Western District of Arkansas (1973); United States Court of Appeals for the Eighth Circuit (1973) **Political Affiliations:** Democrat **Religion:** Methodist

Wes Coates, MBA

Title: General Manager **Industry:** Leisure, Travel & Tourism **Company Name:** Delaware & Ulster Railroad **Date of Birth:** 01/28/1954 **Marital Status:** Married **Spouse Name:** Katherine Coates (07/01/2000) **Education:** MBA, Operations Management and Supervision (2002); Coursework, Sage College of Albany (2002); BA in Managerial Economics, Lycoming College (1976) **Career:** General Manager, Delaware & Ulster Railroad (2017-Present); Consultant, HNTB Corporation (2014-Present); Sector Manager, Operations Analysis & Planning, SYSTRA (2013-2014); Railroad Planning and Operations, URS Corp. (2002-2013); General Manager, Empire Corridor, Amtrak (1995-2001) **Career Related:** Speaker/Presenter in Field **Civic:** Volunteer, Delaware and Ulster Railroad **Creative Works:** Presenter, New York Society of Professional Engineers (2019); Electronic Trains to Reading Terminal (1991) **Awards:** Tourism Achievement Award, Delaware Chamber of Commerce, New York State (2018); Distinguished Service Award, National Park Service (2001); President Achievement Award, Empire State Passenger Association (1997) **Memberships:** American Association of Railroad Superintendents; Lexington Group and Transportation History; National Railroad Historical Society; Railroad and Locomotive Historical Society; Heritage Rail Alliance **Marquis Who's Who Honors:** Albert Nelson Marquis Lifetime Achievement Award **To what do you attribute your success:** Mr. Coates attributes his success to his passion for excellence, his passion for accomplishing things and always making sure the railroad does the right thing. It is about people and your place in the community, that has always been his approach. **Why did you become involved in your profession or industry:** Mr. Coates is the fourth member of his family to work for the railroad. He has had a lifelong love of trains, and has grown up with them. His first job out of college was with the water authority, but he didn't like it as much has he liked working with the railroad. Working with the railroad, he worked in the office, outside, and with people, and he felt that he was truly accomplishing something.

Rowena Noelani Cobb

Title: Real Estate Broker **Industry:** Real Estate **Date of Birth:** 05/01/1939 **Place of Birth:** Kauai **State/Country of Origin:** HI/USA **Parents:** Bernard K. Blake; Hattie Kanui Yuen **Marital Status:** Married **Spouse Name:** James Jackson Cobb (12/22/1962) **Children:** Shelly Ranelle Noelani; Bret Kimo Jackson **Education:** Broker's License, Vitousek School Real Estate, Honolulu, HI (1981); Bachelor of Science in Education, Bob Jones University (1961) **Certifications:** Certified Residential Specialist (1995-Present); Licensed Real Estate Broker, Honolulu, HI **Career:** Principal Broker, Cobb Realty, Lihue, HI (1983-Present); Chairperson, MLS Hawaii Inc., Honolulu, HI (1988-1990); Vice Chairperson, Neighbor Island MLS Service, Honolulu, HI (1987-1988); Secretary, Neighbor Island MLS Service, Honolulu, HI (1985-1987); Business Manager, Micronesian Occupational Center, Koror Palau, HI (1968-1970); Medical Supervisor, Hawaii Medical Service Association (1964-1965, 1966-1968) **Civic:** Member, Hoi'Ke Public TV (1998-Present); Director, Koloa Community Association (2005-2007); Board Director, Kauai United Way (2005-2006); Chairman, Kauai Center Arts, Education and Technology (2005); Chairman, Kauai Center Arts, Education and Technology (2004); President, Hoi'Ke Public TV (2003-2004); Board Director, Kauai United Way (2003-2004); Chairman, Kauai Center Arts, Education and Technology (2003); Board Director, Koloa Community Association (2002-2004); Vice President, Hoi'Ke Public TV (2002); President, Hoi'Ke Public TV (2000-2002); Member, Advisory Board, KKCR Radio (2000); President, Kauai Schools Advisory Council (2000); Board Director, Kekahu Foundation (1999-2001); Treasurer, Hoi'Ke Public TV (1999); Vice Chair, Kauai Schools Advisory Council (1995-1998); President, Koloa Community Association (1989); Secretary, Koloa Community Association (1981-1998) **Creative Works:** Associate Editor, Journal of Entymology (1965-1966) **Memberships:** Treasurer, Kauai Board of Realtors (2007-Present); Director, Hawaii Association of Realtors (2004-2006); Treasurer, Kauai Board of Realtors (1999); Board of Directors, Kauai Board of Realtors (1995-1997); Director, Hawaii Association of Realtors (1995-1996); Treasurer, Soroptimists (1989); Board Director, Lihue Chapter, Soroptimists (1986-1989); Realtor Associate of the Year Award Kauai Board of Realtors (1986); President, Kauai Board of Realtors (1985); Vice President, Hawaii Association of Realtors (1985); Vice President, Kauai Board of Realtors (1984); State Board Director, Hawaii Association of Realtors (1984); Realtor Associate of the Year Award Kauai Board of Realtors (1983); National Association Realtors **Marquis Who's Who Honors:** Albert Nelson Marquis Lifetime Achievement Award **Why did you become involved in your profession or industry:** Ms. Cobb became involved in her profession due to being asked by one of her friends, who was running to become a state senator, to be her aid in Honolulu. Throughout the course of her experiences in government, she was persuaded to obtain her broker's license, and start her own company. **Avocations:** Reading; Music; Travel

Sandra Signorelli Coelho

Title: Elementary and Secondary School Educator, Consultant **Industry:** Education/Educational Services **Date of Birth:** 11/19/1940 **Place of Birth:** Torrington **State/Country of Origin:** CT/USA **Parents:** Ernest J. (Deceased); Linda M. (Zanolli) Signorelli (Deceased) **Marital Status:** Married **Spouse Name:** Walter S. Coelho (7/11/1964, Deceased) **Education:** Doctor of Philosophy, Richmond University (2006); Master of Science, Central Connecticut State University (1969); Bachelor of Science, Central Connecticut State University (1962) **Certifications:** Certified, Intermediate Administration, Central Connecticut State (1980) **Career:** Retired (2008); K-12 Technical and Mathematics Coordinator, East Windsor Board of Education, Connecticut (2007-2008); Advisor, Presidential Advisory Committee, Addison-Wasley Connect Mathematics Services (2008); Associate Director of Mathematics, PIMMS Wesleyan University (2004-2008); Consultant, PIMMS (2004-2008); Consultant, Connecticut Academy (2003-2004); Consultant, Enfield Town Hall (2002); K-12 Technical and Mathematics Coordinator, East Windsor Board Education, Connecticut (1965-2002); Teacher, Torrington Board Education, Connecticut (1962-1965) **Career Related:** President, Advisory Board, Addison Wesley Connect Metal (2008); Past President, CCLM (2008); Assistive Technical Task Force, State of Connecticut; Presenter, C.A.B.E.; Consultant, Town of Enfield, CT; Educational Reviewer, Corwin Press **Civic:** Chairperson, Town-wide Curriculum Committee, East Windsor, CT; Chairperson, East Windsor Technical Committee (1990) **Awards:** Nominee, Golden Apple Award (1998); Apple Computer Scholar (1996); Best Mentor-Assessor (1995); PIMMS (Project to Improve Mastery in Mathematics and Science) Fellow, Wesleyan University (1980s) **Memberships:** Past President, East Windsor Education Association (1993-1996); Past Vice President, Rho Chapter, Delta Kappa Gamma (1980s-1990s); National Education Association; Connecticut Education Association; Advisor, Connecticut Educators Computing Association; President, Connecticut Council Leaders Mathematics; Council for Leaders of Math; Pi Lambda Theta; Executive Board, Phi Delta Kappa **Marquis Who's Who Honors:** Albert Nelson Marquis Lifetime Achievement Award; Marquis Who's Who Top Professional **Why did you become involved in your profession or industry:** Ms. Coelho originally aspired to become a nun, but eventually decided to enter the field of education due to the influence of her parents, as well as her past experience as a babysitter.

Frederick R. Cohen, PhD

Title: Professor of Mathematics **Industry:** Sciences **Company Name:** University of Rochester **Date of Birth:** 08/23/1945 **Place of Birth:** Chicago **State/Country of Origin:** IL/USA **Parents:** Harry Cohen; Helen Nora (Malman) Cohen **Marital Status:** Married **Spouse Name:** Kathleen Marie Whalen (06/26/1976) **Children:** Helen Beatrice; Sarah Frances **Education:** Doctor of Philosophy, The University of Chicago (1972); Bachelor of Arts in Mathematics, Brandeis University, Magna Cum Laude (1967) **Career:** Professor, University of Rochester, New York (1989-Present); Institute for Advanced Study, Princeton, NJ (2005-2006, 2010-2011); Associate Professor, Professor, University of Kentucky, Lexington, KY (1979-1988); Institute for Advanced Study, Princeton, NJ (1975-1977); Assistant Professor, Associate Professor, Northern Illinois University, DeKalb, IL (1972-1979) **Career Related:** Visiting Lecturer, Moscow State University (2010); Visiting Lecturer, National Academy of Sciences, Mexico City (2006); Distinguished Visiting Lecturer, Pacific Institute of Mathematics (2005); Visiting Lecturer, Max Planck Institute for Mathematics (2001); Visiting Lecturer, Centre de Recerca Matematica, Barcelona, Spain (1998); Visiting Lecturer, Fields Institute of Mathematics, Toronto (1996); Visiting Lecturer, Institut Mittag-Leffler, Stockholm, Sweden (1992); Visiting Lecturer, Nankai University, Tianjin, China (1992); Visiting Lecturer, Gottingen University (1987) **Creative Works:** Editorial Board, Journal of Homotopy Theory and Related Structures (2014-Present); Editorial Board, Algebraic and Geometric Topology (2001-2020); Editorial Board, Forum Mathematicum, Walter Degruyter Co. (1988-1996); Editorial Board, Proceedings of the American Mathematical Society (1988-1991); Author, Various Scientific Publications **Awards:** Goergen Award for Distinguished Achievement and Artistry in Undergraduate Education, University of Rochester (2008); Honoree, 60th Birthday Conference, The University of Tokyo, Tokyo, Japan (2005); Grantee, National Science Foundation (1975-1996); Fellowship, A.P. Sloan Foundation (1979-1983); Grantee, DARPA; Fellowship, American Mathematical Society **Memberships:** Fellow, American Mathematical Society (2012); Member, American Mathematical Society **Marquis Who's Who Honors:** Albert Nelson Marquis Lifetime Achievement Award; Marquis Who's Who Top Professional **Why did you become involved in your profession or industry:** Dr. Cohen first became interested in mathematics when his father gave him a geometry book by H.S. M. Coxeter, who proved an elegant theorem known as Morley's Theorem.

Irving David Cohen

Title: Science Administrator **Industry:** Sciences **Company Name:** Enviro-Sciences, Inc. **Date of Birth:** 05/12/1945 **Place of Birth:** Brooklyn **State/Country of Origin:** NY/USA **Parents:** Harry Cohen; Fay (Minchenberg) Cohen **Marital Status:** Married **Spouse Name:** Dorothy Ann Joseph (08/21/1966) **Children:** Miriam Susan Cohen; Esther Heidi Cohen; Daniel Marc Cohen; Aaron Michael Cohen **Education:** Postgraduate Coursework, Environmental Safety and Health, New York University (1970-Present); MSChemE, New York University (1970); BSChemE, The City College of New York (1967) **Certifications:** Certified Environmental Inspector (1989); National Association of Environmental Professionals; Certified Environmental Specialist, National Association of Environmental Professionals (1989); Certified Environmental Professional, Academy of Board Certified Environmental Professionals (1981); Licensed Subsurface Evaluation and Closure, State of New Jersey **Career:** Chief Executive Officer, Board Chairman, Enviro-Sciences, Inc., Mount Arlington, NJ (1975-Present); Senior Project Manager, Woodward-Envicon, Inc., Clifton, NJ (1972-1975); Associate Chemical Engineer, Hoffmann-LaRoche, Nutley, NJ (1971-1972); Senior Process Engineer, Crawford & Russell, Inc., Stamford, CT (1967-1971) **Career Related:** Board Chairman, Art International Inc. (1988-2004); Board Chairman, Ecra Laboratories, Inc. (Sold) (1986-1992); Board Chairman, Aero Instrumentation Resources, Inc. (Closed) (1978-2004) **Civic:** Active Board Member, National Association of Environmental Professionals (2009-Present); Active Board Member, Council of Engineering Specialty Boards (2007-Present); Active Board Member, Academy of Board Certified Environmental Professionals (2001-Present); **Creative Works:** Author, "Environmental Impact Reports for Energy Related Projects and Environmental Liability Audits" (1973) **Memberships:** American Institute of Chemical Engineers; American Industrial Hygiene Association (AIHA); Worldwide Pollution Control Association; Scientists Committee for Publication Information; Air Pollution Control Association; The New York Academy of Sciences; Academy of Board Certified Environmental Professionals; Board Member, Council of Engineering and Scientific Society Executives; Board, Air & Waste Management Association, Pennsylvania and New Jersey Chapter; Fellow, American College of Forensic Examiners Institute **Marquis Who's Who Honors:** Albert Nelson Marquis Lifetime Achievement Award **Why did you become involved in your profession or industry:** Mr. Cohen joined his profession out of his desire to keep and preserve the Earth in an ever-changing world of progress. **Religion:** Jewish **Thoughts on Life:** http://www.linkedin.com/in/irving-cohen-3322767/

Robert Stephan Cohen

Title: Lawyer **Industry:** Law and Legal Services **Company Name:** Cohen Clair Lans Greifer Thorpe & Rottenstreich LLP **Date of Birth:** 1/14/1939 **Place of Birth:** New York **State/Country of Origin:** NY/USA **Parents:** Abraham Cohen; Florence Cohen **Marital Status:** Married **Spouse Name:** Stephanie J. Stiefel **Children:** Christopher; Ian; Joshua; Nicholas **Education:** LLB, Fordham University (1962); BA, Alfred University (1959) **Career:** Judicial Screening Committee, First Judicial Department (2011-Present); Senior Partner, Cohen Clair Lans Greifer & Thorpe LLP (1968) **Career Related:** Adjunct Professor, Law, University of Pennsylvania Law School (2003-Present); Fellow, American College of Family Trial Lawyers **Military Service:** First Lieutenant, Judge Advocate General, U.S. Army Reserve (1965-1967) **Creative Works:** Author, "Reconcilable Differences," Simon & Schuster (2004); Editor, Law Review, New York State Bar Association (1963); Contributor, Various Articles, Legal Journals **Memberships:** American Bar Association; New York State Bar Association; Association of the Bar of the City of New York; New York American Academy of Matrimonial Lawyers; International Academy of Matrimonial Lawyers **Bar Admissions:** U.S. Court of Appeals for the Second Circuit (1965); U.S. District Court, Southern and Eastern Districts, State of New York (1964) **Marquis Who's Who Honors:** Albert Nelson Marquis Lifetime Achievement Award

D. Jackson Coleman, MD

Title: Ophthalmologist; Professor of Ophthalmology **Industry:** Medicine & Health Care **Date of Birth:** 12/01/1934 **Place of Birth:** Waverly **State/Country of Origin:** NY/USA **Parents:** Max Elliot Coleman; Frances Agnes (Henton) Coleman **Marital Status:** Married **Spouse Name:** Jane Marie Holmes (07/06/1963) **Children:** Jeffrey; Jonathan; Jeremy **Education:** Honorary Doctor of Medical Science, University of Ferrara; Resident in Ophthalmology, Edward S. Harkness Eye Institute, NewYork-Presbyterian/Columbia University Medical Center, New York, NY (1964-1967); Intern, Columbia Medical Division, Bellevue Hospital, New York, NY (1960-1961); MD, University at Buffalo, with Thesis Honor (1960); BS, Union College (1956) **Certifications:** Board Certified in Ophthalmology **Career:** Chairman Emeritus, NewYork Hospital-Weill Cornell Medical Center (2006-Present); John Milton McLean Professor, Cornell University Medical College, Weill Cornell Medicine, New York, NY (1979-2012); Ophthalmologist-in-chief, NewYork Hospital-Weill Cornell Medical Center (1979-2006); Chairman, Department of Ophthalmology, NewYork Hospital- Weill Cornell Medical Center (1979-2006); Member Faculty, Staff, Edward S. Harkness Eye Institute, NewYork-Presbyterian/Columbia University Medical Center, New York, NY (1967-1979);Lieutenant Commander, Bureau of State Services, Heart Disease Control Program, US Public Health Service, Washington, DC (1961-1964); Professor of Ophthalmology, Columbia University Valegos College of Physicians and Surgeons **Career Related:** Research in Ultrasonography of the Eye Mechanism of Accommodation of the Eye **Creative Works:** Senior Author, "Ultrasonography of Eye and Orbit, Second Edition" (2006); Senior Author, "Ultrasonography of Eye and Orbit" (1977); Contributor, Over 250 Articles to Medical Journals **Awards:** Weisenfeld Award, The Association for Research in Vision and Opthalmology (1996); Lucien Howe Medal (1988); Wacker Award, Club Jules Gonin, International Retina Society (1976); National Institutes of Health Grantee **Memberships:** Executive Committee, Club Jules Gonin (1992-Present); Board of Governors, American Society Ophthalmic Ultrasound (1976-Present); President, Club Jules Gonin (1998-2004); Vice President, Club Jules Gonin (1993-1998); President, American Retina Society (1991-1993); Vice President, American Retina Society (1989-1991); Science Advisor, American Intraocular Lens Society (1976-1979); Executive Board, World Federation Ultrasound Medicine and Biology (WFUMB) (1973-1982); Secretary-treasurer, World Federation Ultrasound Medicine and Biology (WFUMB) (1973-1977); Treasurer, World Federation Ultrasound Medicine and Biology (WFUMB) (1977-1982); Executive Board, Societas Internationalis de Diagnostic Ultrasonica in Ophthalmology (1971-1981); Board of Governors, American Institute of Ultrasound in Medicine (1970-1973); Fellow, American College of Surgeons; Fellow, American Academy of Ophthalmology; American Ophthamological Society; The Association for Research in Vision and Opthalmology; American Medical Association; New York County Medical Society; American Eye Study Club **Marquis Who's Who Honors:** Albert Nelson Marquis Lifetime Achievement Award; Marquis Who's Who Top Professional **Why did you become involved in your profession or industry:** Dr. Coleman became interested in ophthalmology because he was interested in the physics of optics. **Avocations:** Fishing; Sailing **Political Affiliations:** Republican **Religion:** Methodist

Stephen R. Coleman

Title: Professor of Psychology Emeritus **Industry:** Education/Educational Services **Company Name:** Cleveland State University **Date of Birth:** 09/06/1942 **Place of Birth:** Medford **State/Country of Origin:** MA/USA **Parents:** Gerard Joseph Coleman; Alice Irene (Ryan) Coleman **Marital Status:** Widowed **Spouse Name:** Katherine Ann Brase (12/30/1967, Deceased, 2017) **Children:** Jason G.; David F. **Education:** PhD in Psychology, Department of Psychology, University of Iowa, Iowa City, IA (1972); MA in Psychology, Department of Psychology, University of Iowa, Iowa City, IA (1970); Graduate Study in Psychology, Department of Psychology, Indiana University (1965-1966); BA in Psychology, University of Massachusetts, Amherst, MA, Magna Cum Laude (1965) **Career:** Retired (2009), Professor, Psychology, Cleveland State University, Cleveland, OH (1989-2009); Associate Professor, Psychology, Cleveland State University, Cleveland, OH (1978-1989); Assistant Professor, Psychology, Cleveland State University, Cleveland, OH (1972-1978); Instructor in Psychology, Cleveland State University, Cleveland, OH (1971-1972); Teaching-Research Fellow, University of Iowa, Iowa City, IA (1968-1971); NSF Predoctoral Fellow, University of Iowa, Iowa City, IA (1966-1968); NSF Predoctoral Fellow, Indiana University Bloomington, Bloomington, IN (1965-1966) **Civic:** Team Manager, Suburban Hockey League, Cleveland Heights, OH (1988-1992); Secretary, Board of Trustees, Neighborhood Counseling Service, Cleveland, OH (1986-1988) **Creative Works:** Regular Reviewer, Psychological Reports (2005-2008); Occasional Reviewer of Book Manuscripts (1985-2004); Consulting Editor, Behavior and Philosophy (1987-1997); Reviewer, B.F. Skinner Special Issue, I.P. Pavlov Special Issue, American Psychologist (1997, 1992); Occasional Reviewer, Journal Manuscripts in History of Psychology and Psychology of Learning (1988-1990); Contributor, Numerous Articles, Professional Journals; Speaker, Presenter, Numerous Convention Papers, Presentations **Awards:** Volunteer of the Year, Neighborhood Counseling Service (1988); Pre-Doctoral Fellow, National Science Foundation (1965-1968); Woodrow Wilson Fellow (1965) **Memberships:** Cheiron Inc.; International Society for the History of the Behavioral and Social Sciences; Phi Beta Kappa; Phi Kappa Phi **Marquis Who's Who Honors:** Albert Nelson Marquis Lifetime Achievement Award **To what do you attribute your success:** Dr. Coleman was fortunate to be raised by capable, kind parents of substantial intelligence and hard-working nature. He developed constructive work-life attitudes and skills, which provided him with the opportunity to attain success in both his personal and career endeavors. **Why did you become involved in your profession or industry:** As a teenager, Dr. Coleman was often puzzled by why others behaved the way they did. This interest led him to pursue psychology in college, eventually leading him to acquire a background in laboratory research. He later became involved in the history of psychology, which is now his career-topic of study and what he primarily investigates. **Avocations:** Photography; Gardening; Landscaping; Carpentry; Listening to classical music **Political Affiliations:** Democrat

Donald Bruce Colhour

Title: Producer, Director; Clergyman, Theologian **Industry:** Religious **Date of Birth:** 05/28/1946 **Place of Birth:** Ellsworth **State/Country of Origin:** KS/USA **Parents:** Bruce; Ruth (Williams) C. **Spouse Name:** Terrence John Dyck **Education:** MPhil in Theology and Ethics of Communications, The University of Edinburgh, Scotland, United Kingdom (1997); ThM/MPhil, The University of Edinburgh, Scotland, United Kingdom (1995); BS in Journalism, The University of Kansas (1969); Diploma, Russell High School (1964) **Certifications:** Ordained Congregational Minister **Career:** Founder, Chief Executive Officer, Luftschloss Projects (2014-Present); Senior Minister, Wilshire Christian Church, Disciples of Christ (1998-2012); Executive Producer, Special Projects, ABC Entertainment, Los Angeles, CA (1987-1989); Director, Special Projects, ABC Entertainment, CA (1983-1987); Manager, Special Projects, ABC Entertainment, CA (1980-1983); Unit Production Manager, ABC, Inc., CA (1969-1980) **Career Related:** Consultant, Claremont School of Theology (1986-Present); President, Chief Executive Officer, HMC Entertainment, Hollywood, CA (1989); Chairman, Founder, American Pilgrim Chorus (1988); Sponsor, American-Soviet Film Initiative (1988); Chairman, Commonwealth Theatre, Los Angeles, CA (1987-1989); Executive Producer, LA Bach Festival, CA (1985-1989) **Civic:** Executive Producer, Director, YWCA Leader's Luncheon (1989-Present); Chairman, Ecumenical Council on Drama & Arts, Los Angeles, CA (1989-Present); Member, U.S. Project Literacy (Project Literacy U.S. (PLUS)) (1987-Present); Founder, President, L.A. Project Literacy (1987-Present); Communicator on Ministry, National Association of Congregation Christian Churches (NACCC), Los Angeles, CA (1986-Present); Founder, Chairman, American Pilgrim Chorus (1989); National Conference of Christians and Jews (1984, 1986, 1988); ABC-TV West Coast Representative Sponsor, American-Soviet Film Initiative (1988); National Center for Hyperactive Children (1988); Entertainment Industries Council on Drug Abuse (Now Entertainment Industries Council, Inc.) (1986); Producer, AIDS Project, Los Angeles, CA (1985); Beverly Hills B'nai B'rith (1985); United Jewish Fund (1984); Boys Club of America (1984); American Jewish Committee (AJC) (1984); United Cerebral Palsy Tennis Festival (1983-1988); Devereux Foundation (1983-1985); Lay Minister, First Congregational Church of Los Angeles; Associate Minister, The Church of Scotland, United Kingdom **Creative Works:** Writer, Producer, "Voyage to Freedom II" (1991); Producer, Puget Sound Freedom Tour (1991); Founder, American Women Awards (1990); Producer, American Pilgrim Chorus European Freedom Tour (1989); Writer, Producer, "A Canticle of Freedom" (1989); Producer, Director, George Burns and the Pointer Sisters (1989); Producer, Director, Tribute to Neil Simon (1988); Creator, Producer, National Literacy Honor Honoring Barbara Bush (1988); Creator, Star Spangled Celebration to Promote Literacy in America, St. Louis, MO (1987-1988); Executive Producer and Director, Tribute to George Gershwin (1987); Theatrical Reviewer, "You'll Love It" (1986); Producer, Theatrical Concert, Dionne Warwick (1984); Producer, Theatrical Concert, Dudley Moore (1983); Producer, Theatrical Concert, John Denver (1983); Producer, Theatrical Concert, Wayne Newton (1983); Producer, Theatrical Concert, Perry Como (1982) **Awards:** Leadership in Literacy Award, Laubach Literacy Action (1987) **Memberships:** Hollywood Radio and TV Society (HRTS); Academy of Television Arts & Sciences; Lodges: Masons **Marquis Who's Who Honors:** Albert Nelson Marquis Lifetime Achievement Award **Why did you become involved in your profession or industry:** Mr. Colhour as a young man was a very good pianist and organist; he could sing and was involved in everything all the time. He worked at a local music store and demonstrated Baldwin theater organs at the fairs. When he was not at the fairs, he was working at the music store after school on weekends. He also worked with a woman who knew his mother, as it was a small town. One day, a fellow walked in with his mother and Helen Zimmerman, who was his mother's friend, told him if he wants to go into television, he should go and attend to that man. He responded by saying, "Wow, who's that?" She said he was their classmate and that he was vice president of ABC television. So Mr. Colhour went over and attended to him and he bought a television for his mother, who was a friend of the family. As he paid the bill, Mr. Colhour told Mr. Mills that he was very interested in television and Mr. Mills told him to get in touch with him after he got his degree if he was still interested. Mr. Colhour went off to the University of Kansas, where he was majoring in religion, but he was also in the KU band and doing theological training, as well as musical training. He was very active in the antiwar movement and dropped out of ROTC because he thought the events in Vietnam was unjust; he was very involved in politics at the university. He discovered who he really was and that was when he came out. When he was growing up, he had a loving church and was never judged by anyone whom he grew up with his whole life. He did get the job at ABC and flew out to California and went to see Mr. Mills who gave him a contract. Mr. Colhour went back home and graduated. His father fixed his car for him and he returned to California and never went back. **Avocations:** Religion; Arts; Music **Political Affiliations:** Democrat **Religion:** Christian/Congregational

Brandi Compass

Title: Teacher **Industry:** Education/Educational Services **Company Name:** Cape Girardeau Public Schools **Date of Birth:** 01/20/1985 **Place of Birth:** Cape Girardeau **State/Country of Origin:** MO/USA **Parents:** Larry Compass; Kim Compass **Education:** MA in Elementary Education, Southeast Missouri State; BS in Elementary Education with Math Concentration, Lindenwood University **Certifications:** Certified K-12 Math Teacher **Career:** Softball Coach; Volleyball Coach; Part-Time Adjunct Professor, College Level; Teacher, Public Schools, Ten Years; Kindergarten Teacher **Career Related:** Volunteer, Limited Resource Teacher Training (LRTT) **Memberships:** Missouri State Teachers Association; National Council of Teachers of Mathematics **To what do you attribute your success:** Ms. Compass has always been very driven. Throughout her journey to success, she has set goals for herself, all of which have been achieved by perseverance. She always wants to be better than the day before. **Why did you become involved in your profession or industry:** Ms. Compass became a teacher because she wanted to positively impact the lives of her students. Throughout her career, she has always strived to teach her students to be the best versions of themselves.

246 • Distinguished Listees   Who's Who in America

Gary O. Concoff

Title: Partner **Industry:** Law and Legal Services **Company Name:** Rufus-Isaacs, Acland & Grantham LLP **Date of Birth:** 6/28/1936 **Place of Birth:** Los Angeles **State/Country of Origin:** CA/USA **Marital Status:** Married **Spouse Name:** Jean F. Concoff (06/23/1963) **Children:** Cory N.; Andrew L. **Education:** LLB, Harvard Law School, Harvard University (1962); BSBA in Accounting, University of California Los Angeles (1958) **Career:** Partner, Rufus-Isaacs, Acland & Grantham LLP, Beverly Hills, CA (2018-Present); Attorney, Troy Gould Attorneys (1996-Present); Partner, Mitchell Silberberg (Now Mitchell Silberberg & Knupp LLP) (1988-1995); Partner, Sidley Austin LLP (1981-1988); Partner, Kaplan, Livingston et al, Beverly Hills, CA (1965-1981); Associate, Kaplan, Livingston et al, Beverly Hills, CA (1965-1981); Associate, O'Melveny & Myers LLP (1962-1965) **Career Related:** Adjunct Professor, Law Lecturer, University of California Los Angeles (1980-1982); Founder, Entertainment Symposium, University of California Los Angeles (1976-1978); Co-chair, Entertainment Symposium, University of California Los Angeles (1976-1978) **Military Service:** Second Lieutenant, U.S. Army (1958) **Creative Works:** Speaker, Moderator, Organizer and Co-chair, Several Programs, Cannes Film Festival (2009-2014); Contributor, Articles, Professional Journals **Awards:** Outstanding Practitioner of the Year, UCLA Anderson School of Management **Memberships:** Former Board of Directors, British Academy of Film and Television Arts (2001-2002); Chairman, Forum Committee, Motion Picture and Television Division, ABA (1987-1992); Los Angeles County Bar Association (1963); ABA; Board of Trustees, Los Angeles Copyright Society; State Bar of California **Bar Admissions:** State of California (1963) **Marquis Who's Who Honors:** Albert Nelson Marquis Lifetime Achievement Award; Marquis Who's Who Top Professional **Why did you become involved in your profession or industry:** Early in Mr. Concoff's career, a superior said he was born to be a motion picture lawyer.

Branden C. Cook

Title: President **Industry:** Architecture & Construction **Company Name:** Homeland Construction **Parents:** Jim Bob Cook **Marital Status:** Marreid **Spouse Name:** Lindsay **Children:** Emery (6); Parker (3); **Education:** High School Diploma **Career:** President, Owner, Operator, Homeland Construction (2011-Present) **Civic:** Sponsorship, Local Schools, Football Teams, Race Cars **Marquis Who's Who Honors:** Marquis Who's Who Top Professional **To what do you attribute your success:** Mr. Cook attributes his success to God. He gave him the mathematical mindset/skill set that he has on his strong faith. **Why did you become involved in your profession or industry:** Mr. Cook worked for a really great home building company. He has a strong construction background. His father was a builder and not only did his father build but he did rock masonry and framing. He worked with Lewis Jones, who really changed his life. He owns Custom Homes. He gave him the confidence to see where his skill sets were. In addition, he grew up around high quality builders. He has always enjoyed stepping back and looking at something that he has made that will stand time. Also as a builder, leaving his mark. **Avocations:** Fishing; Family time; Guitar; Writing songs

Joseph V. Cook Jr., MD

Title: Physician and Medical Director **Industry:** Medicine & Health Care **Date of Birth:** 09/07/1935 **Place of Birth:** Brigham City **State/Country of Origin:** UT/USA **Parents:** Joseph Vernon Cook; Berniece (Kimball) Cook **Marital Status:** Married **Spouse Name:** Nancy Carlson Cook (7/7/1958) **Children:** Joseph David; John Carlson; Paul Carlson **Education:** Medical Intern, University Of Oklahoma (1963); MD, University of Utah (1962); BS, Utah State University (1959) **Certifications:** Diplomate, American Board of Family Practice (1970-2026) **Career:** Physician, Utah State Developmental Center (2017-Present); Chairman, Quality and Financial Assurance Committee DMBA, The Church of Jesus Christ of Latter-day Saints (2005-Present); Medical Director, Utah State Developmental Center (2007-2016); Consultant, Health Plans, Utah, California, Texas (2004-2007); Medical Director, Medicare Northwest, Portland, OR (2005); Chief Medical Officer, Health Plan of the Redwoods, Santa Rosa, CA (1998-2001); Vice President, Medical Affairs, Medspan Incorporated Hartford, CT (1993-1998); Medical Director, Aetna Health Plans (1991-1993); Senior Vice President, Medical Director, Bay Pacific Health Plan, San Bruno, CA (1989-1991); Chairman, Family Medical Clinics of San Mateo (1982-1989); Private Practice (1967-1989) **Career Related:** Clinical Professor (1990-1993, 1999-2003); Clinical Faculty, University of California San Francisco (1971-1993, 1999-2003) **Civic:** Mission President, Pennsylvania Philadelphia Mission Church of Jesus Christ of Latter-day Saints (2001-2004) **Military Service:** Lieutenant, United States Navy (1963-1967) **Creative Works:** Contributor, Articles, Professional Journals; Contributor, Letters to the Editor, Peer-Reviewed Professional Journals: Speaker, Extensive Oral Medical Presentations, United States, South Africa **Awards:** Nominated, Kaiser Award for Excellence in Teaching (1980, 1983); Selected, United States Navy Senior Student Program (1961-1962); Blue Key Award, Utah State University (1955); Continuous Certification, American Board of Family Medicine **Memberships:** Rotary Club, San Mateo, CA (1975-1993); Phi Kappa Phi (1959) **Marquis Who's Who Honors:** Albert Nelson Marquis Lifetime Achievement Award **Why did you become involved in your profession or industry:** From a young age, Dr. Cook knew he wanted to become a doctor. Seeking to pursue an interesting and important career, he enrolled in medical school when the time was right. **Avocations:** Reading; Public speaking **Political Affiliations:** Republican **Religion:** The Church of Jesus Christ of Latter-Day Saints

Morreece "Elaine" Cook, LCSW (Retired)

Title: Clinical Social Work **Industry:** Medicine & Health Care **Date of Birth:** 06/17/1946 **Place of Birth:** Owosso **State/Country of Origin:** MI/USA **Parents:** Charles M.; Freda Belle Saunders. **Education:** Doctoral Coursework, Wayne State University (1988); Master of Social Work, Wayne State University, Detroit, MI (1985); Bachelor of Arts in Psychology, Mercy College, Detroit, MI (1971) **Certifications:** Certified Social Worker, Michigan; Diplomate in Clinical Social Work **Career:** Senior Social Worker, Community Hospice (2002-2004); Manager, Social Work: Henry Ford-Wyandotte Hospital & Medical Center (1999-2002); Project Manager, Human Performance Technologist, General Motors Corporation and Kmart Corporation (1996-1999); Manager of Education, Wayne State University Medical School (1991-1996); Senior Social Worker, Sinai Hospital of Detroit, MI (1972-1991) **Career Related:** Member, Greater Detroit Area Health Education Council Secretary, Downriver Human Services Forum (1993-1994); Member, Faculty Wayne State University School Social Work; Speaker at Professional Organization Meetings **Creative Works:** Master's Thesis: "Paradigm for Achieving Self-Enablement: A Problem-Solving Model for Implementing Personal Health Care Goals **Awards:** National Academy of Certified Social Workers **Memberships:** Board of Directors, Michigan Society for Hospital Social Work Directors (1993-1994); Vice President, Social Workers Club of Detroit (1979); Secretary, Medical Council, National Association of Social Workers (1979); President, Social Workers Club of Detroit (1978); National Association of Oncology Social Workers; National Society for Hospital Social Work Directors; American Public Health Association; Michigan Public Health Association: Michigan Society of Clinical Social Workers; International Society for Performance Improvement; American Society for Training and Development; National Hospice Association **Marquis Who's Who Honors:** Albert Nelson Marquis Lifetime Achievement Award; Marquis Who's Who Top Professional **Why did you become involved in your profession or industry:** Ms. Cook cannot recall a time in her life, that she didn't get pleasure from helping others. She decided on the medical field right after high school, when she needed two major surgeries. She eventually became more comfortable in the medical field and decided she could combine her desire to help others and work in the medical field. **Avocations:** Nature experiences; Stained glass creations; Music; Art; Travel **Religion:** Roman Catholic

Patrick Louis Cooney

Title: Writer **Industry:** Writing and Editing **Date of Birth:** 04/07/1947 **Place of Birth:** Bellflower **State/Country of Origin:** CA/USA **Parents:** Jack W. Cooney (Deceased); Lauretta (Jenkins) Cooney (Deceased) **Marital Status:** Married **Spouse Name:** Rosemary Santana Cooney (09/10/1967) **Children:** Carl **Education:** MBA in Sociology, Fordham University, Bronx, NY (1979); PhD in Sociology, The University of Texas at Austin, Texas (1976); MA in Sociology, The University of Texas at Austin, Texas (1972); BA in Sociology, Florida State University, Tallahassee, FL (1969) **Certifications:** Certified in Field Botany, New York Botanical Garden, Bronx, NY (1993) **Career:** Marketing Executive, Publishing Firms (1980-1989); Assistant Professor of Sociology, College of Mount Saint Vincent, Bronx, NY (1975-1977) **Career Related:** Speaker, Westchester Martin Luther King, Jr. Institute for Nonviolence, Westchester, NY (1994); Writer **Civic:** Civil Rights Activist **Military Service:** With, Army National Guard (1966-1973) **Creative Works:** Editor, Book, "Witness to Civil Rights History: The Essays and Autobiography of Henry W. Powell" (2001); Co-author, Book, "The Life and Times of the Prophet Vernon Johns: Father of the Civil Rights Movement" (1998); Author, Book, "The Role of Multiculturalism in Establishing a New Period of Separate but Equal Segregation in the United States: A Comparison of the Periods After and First and Second Civil Wars" (1997); Author, Book, "Seeing the United States as the South and the World Community of the North: Using the Approach of Martin Luther King, Jr. to Invigorate the Next Civil Rights Movement" (1994); Author, Book, "Discovering the Mid-Atlantic: Historical Tours" (1991) **Awards:** Dissertation Fellow, Swedish Institute, New York, NY (1973-1974) **Memberships:** Chairperson, Field Committee, Torrey Botanical Club; The Phi Beta Kappa Society; Society of Friends **Marquis Who's Who Honors:** Albert Nelson Marquis Lifetime Achievement Award **Why did you become involved in your profession or industry:** Dr. Clooney became involved in his profession because as a young man, he couldn't help but notice that Black people were treated differently than white people. He studied sociology to better understand why this occurred. **Avocations:** Travel; Historical research **Political Affiliations:** Democrat **Religion:** Religious Society of Friends

Dr. Delberta "Debbie" Hollaway Coonrod-Vannoy

Title: Educator (Retired), Consultant **Industry:** Education/Educational Services **Date of Birth:** 10/21/1937 **Place of Birth:** Eldon **State/Country of Origin:** MO/USA **Parents:** Delbert Leland Hollaway; Zealoth (Stevens) Hollaway **Marital Status:** Married **Spouse Name:** Charles Richard Vannoy (10/05/2015); Charles Ralph Coonrod (08/26/1961, Deceased 2013) **Children:** Charles Leland Coonrod (1962); Marcia Renee Coonrod (1970) **Education:** EdD in Education, Indiana University (1977); MS in Education, Indiana University (1972); BS in Education, The University of Kansas (1961); Postgraduate Coursework, Texas Woman's University; Postgraduate Coursework, The University of Texas **Certifications:** English as a Second Language, State of Texas (1986); Certified Elementary Teacher, States of Kansas, Nebraska, Indiana, and Texas **Career:** Writer, Reporter, Shelby County Herald, Shelbyville, MO (2003-2007); Retired (2002); Associate Professor, Director, Teacher Education, Culver-Stockton College, Canton, MO (2001-2002); Classroom Teacher, Fort Wayne Independent School District, Texas (1985-2001); Private Practice Consultant, Bloomington, IN (1981-1985); President, Debcon, Inc., Bloomington, IN (1979-1981); Assistant Professor, Indiana State University, Terre Haute, IN (1975-1976); Associate Instructor, Visiting Assistant Professor, Indiana University Bloomington (1972-1979); Classroom Teacher, South Bend Community School Corporation (1967-1972); Classroom Teacher, Lincoln Public Schools (1964-1966); Classroom Teacher, Emporia Public Schools (1961-1962); Classroom Teacher, Hood School and Heizer Elementary, Barton County, KS (1957-1960) **Career Related:** Visiting Adjunct Assistant Professor, Binh Duong University, Vinh Duong Province, Vietnam (2016); Member, Advisory Committee, Fort Wayne Independent School District, Texas (1996-1998); Instructor, Weatherford College (1996-1997); Instructor, Edison State Community College, Piqua, Ohio (1994); Instructor, Tarrant County College (1992-1994); Adjunct Professor, Texas Christian University (1991-1992); Consultant, Fort Hays State University (1990); Adjunct Assistant Professor, Texas Woman's University (1987-2000); Administrative Project Director, Monroe County School Corporation, Bloomington, IN (1983-1985); National Approved Trainer, Head Start (1982-1985); Head Administrator, Hoosier Courts Nursery School, Indiana University Bloomington (1978-1979); Kindergarten Consultant, P-H-M School Corporation, Mishawaka, IN (1970-1971) **Civic:** County Exit Chairman, Shelby County Outreach and Extension Council (2010-Present); Director, NECAC (2008-Present); Media Chair, Relay for Life, Shelby County, MO (2004-Present); Chapter Member, P.E.O. Sisterhood (2003-Present); Member, Policy Board, Shelby County Economic Development Council, Media (2007); Member, Policy Board, RSVP, Hannibal, MO (2006-2008); Member, Policy Board, Douglass Community Services, Hannibal, MO (2006-2008); Member, Numerous Organizations **Creative Works:** Editor, GRIT, Delta Theta Tau National Sorority (2007-Present); Reporter, Shelby County Herald, Shelbyville, MO (2003-2008); Contributor, Articles, Professional Journals **Awards:** Named to Extension Leaders Honor Roll, University of Missouri (2004); Named NYL Care Health Plans Chair, Teaching Excellence in Early Childhood Education (1997-1998); Honoree, Early Childhood Promising Practices Inclusion Model, Texas Education Agency (1993-1994); Named Dillard Teacher of Week (1992-1993); International Recognition Award, Outstanding Pi Lambda Thetan (1992); Recipient, Numerous Awards **Memberships:** International First Vice President, Pi Lambda Theta (2003); Education Endowment Board, Pi Lambda Theta (1996-2002); Public Advisory Board, Pi Lambda Theta (1995-1997); President, Great Lakes Region II, Pi Lambda Theta (1993-1997); National Vice President, Pi Lambda Theta (1985-1989); Member, Numerous Organizations **Marquis Who's Who Honors:** Albert Nelson Marquis Lifetime Achievement Award **To what do you attribute your success:** Dr. Coonrod-Vannoy attributes much of her success to her supportive parents, who understood and encouraged her dreams. **Why did you become involved in your profession or industry:** Dr. Vannoy has dreamed of teaching since she was 2 years old; back then, her father would pretend to be her student. She was inspired by her mother, who was a teacher. Dr. Coonrod-Vannoy would often sit in on her classes. When she attended the University of Kansas, her father encouraged her by making sure she had all the materials she needed. He also attended every one of her graduations. After a long career doing what she loved in Fort Worth, Texas, Dr. Coonrod-Vannoy decided to move to Missouri. She became the director of teacher education at Culver-Stockton College and was looking for some additional work. Based on her prior experience writing a weekly article for the South Bend Tribune in Indiana, she went down to the local newspaper, the Shelby County Herald, and saw they were looking for a reporter. She interviewed, got the position, and held the role for several years. **Avocations:** Poetry; Piano; Photography; Public speaking; Journalism **Political Affiliations:** Republican **Religion:** Baptist

Fred W. Cooper, PhD

Title: Chief Executive Officer, Founder **Industry:** Consumer Goods and Services **Company Name:** ARIIX **Date of Birth:** 01/12/1963 **Place of Birth:** Sacramento **State/Country of Origin:** CA/USA **Parents:** A. Edward Cooper; Janeal Y. Cooper **Marital Status:** Married **Spouse Name:** Jennifer L. Cooper **Children:** Cameron Stihl; Brady Danger; Austin Wild; Andrew Trouble **Education:** Doctor of Philosophy in Business Administration, University of Utah, David Eccles School of Business (1994); Bachelor of Science in Finance, University of Utah (1988); Bachelor of Science in Psychology, University of Utah (1988) **Career:** Chief Executive Officer, Founder, ARIIX LLC, Bountiful, UT (2011–Present); Owner, Founder, Campus Park Housing, Twin Falls, ID (2006–Present); Proprietor, Wasatch Investment Management, SLC, UT (1992–Present); Commodity Trade Advisor, Selected Private Accounts (1992–Present); President, USANA Health Sciences (2008–2011); Board Chairman/Founder, iCentris Incorporated, SLC, UT (1999–2003); Chief Operating Officer, USANA Health Sciences (1998–2011); Corporate Network Operations, Aetna, SLC, UT (1996–1998); Director Marketing Research, Human Affairs International, SLC, UT (1994–1996); Board of Directors, Chief Operating Officer, Synecor Corporation, Costa Mesa, CA (1992–1993); Adjunct Professor, University of Utah (1988-2005); President, Chief Executive Officer, Fashion Academy, Costa Mesa, CA (1988–1993) **Career Related:** Consultant, Toyota, Franklin Quest, Union Carbide, Morton Thiokol, Gloria Natalia, Your True Colors, Ohio Gas, Bioform, Spa Destinations, American Petroleum Promotions, Krieger Industries, Autoliv, Iomega, Numerous Other Companies, Direct Selling Industry; Honorary Professor, University of International Business and Economics, Beijing, China **Civic:** Boy Scouts of America; ARIIX Foundation for Human Potential **Creative Works:** Co-Author, "Familial Advanced Sleep-Phased Syndrome; A Short-Period Circadian Rhythm Variant in Humans," (1999); Co-Author, "The Effects of Forecasting Error Measures and Autocorrelation on Operations Total Cost," (1993) **Awards:** Gold, Most Innovative Company of the Year, Stevie American Business Awards (2019); Silver, 2018 Management Team Achievements, Stevie American Business Awards (2019); Bronze, 2018 Fastest-Growing Company of the Year, Stevie American Business Awards (2019); Gold, CEO Achievers Transformation Leader of the Year, CEO World Awards (2019); Silver, Most Innovative Company of the Year, CEO World Awards (2019); Bronze, Management Team of the Year, Stevie International Business Awards (2019); Silver, Company of the Year, Golden Bridge Awards (2019); Gold, Company of the Year, One Planet Awards (2019); Gold, Innovator of the Year, One Planet Awards (2019); Grand Trophy Award, One Planet Awards (2019). Gold, CEO Achievement of the Year, CEO World Awards (2018); Silver, Management Team of the Year, Stevie American Business Awards (2018); Silver, Management Team of the Year, Stevie American Business Awards (2017); Bronze, Most Innovative Company of the Year, Stevie American Business Awards (2017); Gold, Executive Team of the Year, One Planet Awards (2017); Silver, Company of the Year, One Planet Awards (2017); Gold, Best Overall Company of the Year, CEO World Awards (2017); Gold, Management Team of the Year, CEO World Awards (2017); Gold, CEO of the Year, CEO World Awards (2017); Silver, Most Innovative Company of the Year, CEO World Awards (2017); Top 5 CEOs in Direct Selling, Business for Home (2016); Gold, Executive Team of the Year, One Planet Awards (2016); Silver, CEO of the Year, One Planet Awards (2016); Silver, Fastest-Growing Company of the Year, One Planet Awards (2016); Visionary Award, Direct Selling Management Association (2015) **Memberships:** Chinese Academy of International Trade and Economic Cooperation; Society for Quality Control; Decision Sciences Institute **To what do you attribute your success:** Dr. Cooper attributes his success to diligence. He believes there's no "try," only success or failure. With failure not being an option, he chooses to consistently put in the effort using many alternatives until success is attained. **Why did you become involved in your profession or industry:** Originally interested in corporate law, Dr. Cooper did not initially plan on working in direct sales. One of his MBA students was working for the auditing firm of USANA, evaluating their compensation plan. However, the accounting firm could not find anyone capable of solving USANA's commission payout problem. Dr. Cooper's student made the introduction to USANA as one who could resolve the problem. After determining and resolving the statistical and mathematical commission problem, his career in the direct selling industry began. **Religion:** Church of Jesus Christ of Latter-Day Saints

James Cooper-Jones

Title: Chief Executive Officer **Industry:** Agriculture **Company Name:** CropLogic **Children:** 2 Boys; 1 Girl **Education:** Bachelor of Arts in Financial Accounting and Asian Studies, University of New England **Career:** Chief Executive Officer, CropLogic (2018-Present); Non-Executive Director, Covocate (2016-Present); Chief Financial Officer and Company Secretary, CropLogic (2017-2018); Capital Markets Advisor, CropLogic (2016-2017); Managing Director, Sohdan, Capital (2016-2017); Company Secretary, Chief Financial Officer, Impact Minerals Limited (2010-2016); Company Secretary, Chief Financial Officer, Invictus Gold Limited (2010-2014); Corporate Advisor, Idochine Mining Limited (2009-2010); Founder, Company Secretary, Ignite Golf Pty Ltd (2007-2010); Company Secretary, Chief Financial Officer, Outback Metals Limited (2007-2009); Company Accountant, Cooper Resources Corporation (2006-2007) **Civic:** Assistant Instructor, Karrinyup Little Athletics **Awards:** Innovative Chief Executive Officer (2019); Perth Fellow, Institute of Public Accountants **Memberships:** FINFIA **To what do you attribute your success:** Mr. Cooper-Jones attributes his success to good mentors. **Why did you become involved in your profession or industry:** In becoming involved in his profession, Mr. Cooper-Jones saw an opportunity and seized upon it. He has been grateful for the companies he has worked for, and passionately applies his experience toward great management practices.

Francis Coppola

Title: Film Producer, Director, Screenwriter **Industry:** Media & Entertainment **Date of Birth:** 04/07/1939 **Place of Birth:** Detroit **State/Country of Origin:** MI/USA **Parents:** Carmine Coppola; Italia Coppola **Marital Status:** Married **Spouse Name:** Eleanor Neil **Children:** Gian-Carlo (Deceased); Roman; Sofia **Education:** Master of Fine Arts, University of California Los Angeles (1968); Bachelor of Arts, Hofstra University (1958) **Career:** Founder, Blancaneaux Turtle Inn (2000-Present); Founder, Zoetrope All-Story (1997-Present); Owner, Niebaum Coppola Estate Winery, Napa Valley (1995-Present); Founder, American Zoetrope, Ltd., San Francisco (1968-Present); Publisher, City Magazine, San Francisco (1975-1976) **Creative Works:** Director, Producer, Writer, "Distant Vision" (2015); Executive Producer, "On the Road" (2012); Director, Producer, Writer, "Twixt" (2011); Executive Producer, "Somewhere" (2010); Director, Producer, Writer, "Tetro" (2009); Executive Producer, "The 4400" (2007); Director, Writer, "Youth Without Youth" (2007); Executive Producer, "Marie Antoinette" (2006); Executive Producer, "The Good Shepherd" (2006); Executive Producer, "Kinsey" (2004); Executive Producer, "Jeepers Creepers II" (2003); Executive Producer, "Platinum" (2003); Executive Producer, "Lost in Translation" (2003); Executive Producer, "Pumpkin" (2002); Executive Producer, "Assassination Tango" (2002); Executive Producer, "In My Life" (2002); Executive Producer, "CQ" (2001); Executive Producer, "No Such Thing" (2001); Executive Producer, "Jeepers Creepers" (2001); Executive Producer, "Suriyothai" (2001); Executive Producer, "Dr. Jekyll and Mr Hyde" (1999); Executive Producer, "The Virgin Suicides" (1999); Executive Producer, "The Third Miracles" (1999); Executive Producer, "Goosed" (1999); Producer, "The Florentine" (1999); Executive Producer, "Sleepy Hollow" (1999); Executive Producer, "Outrage" (1998); Executive Producer, "Moby Dick" (1998); Executive Producer, "First Wave" (1998); Producer, "Lanai-Loa" (1998); Director, Writer, "The Rainmaker" (1997); Executive Producer, "Survival on the Mountain" (1997); Executive Producer, "The Odyssey" (1997); Executive Producer, "Buddy" (1997); Executive Producer, "Dark Angel" (1996); Director, Producer, "Jack" (1996); Executive Producer, "White Dwarf" (1995); Executive Producer, "Tecumseh: The Last Warrior" (1995); Executive Producer, "Kidnapped" (1995); Executive Producer, "My Family" (1995); Executive Producer, "Haunted" (1995); Producer, "Don Juan DeMarco" (1995); Producer, "Frankenstein" (1994); Producer, "The Junky's Christmas" (1993); Executive Producer, "The Secret Garden" (1993); Executive Producer, "Wind" (1992); Director, Producer, "Bram Stoker's Dracula" (1992); Appeared, "Hearts of Darkness: A Filmmaker's Apocalypse" (1991); Executive Producer, "The Outsiders" (1990); Director, Producer, Writer, "The Godfather: Part III" (1990); Executive Producer, "Wait Until Spring, Bandini" (1989); Director, "Tucker: The Man and His Dream" (1988); Executive Producer, "Lionheart" (1987); Executive Producer, "Tough Guys Don't Dance" (1987); Director, Producer, "Gardens of Stone" (1987); Director, Writer, "Captain EO" (1986); Director, "Peggy Sue Got Married" (1986); Executive Producer, "Mishima: A Life in Four Chapters" (1985); Director, "The Cotton Club" (1984); Director, "The Outsiders" (1983); Director, Executive Producer, Writer, "Rumble Fish" (1983); Executive Producer, "The Escape Artist" (1982); Executive Producer, "Kagemusha" (1980); Executive Producer, "The Black Stallion" (1979); Director, Producer, Writer, "Apocalypse Now" (1979); Director, Producer, Writer, "The Godfather: Part II" (1974); Producer, "American Graffiti" (1973); Director, Writer, "The Godfather" (1972); Executive Producer, "THX 1138" (1971); Screenplay Author, "Patton" (1970); Director, Writer, "The Rain People" (1969); Director, "Finian's Rainbow" (1968); Director, Writer, "You're a Big Boy Now" (1966); Director, Producer, "The Terror" (1963); Director, Writer, "Dementia 13" (1963); Director, Producer, Writer, "Tonight for Sure" (1962); Director, "The Bellboy and the Playgirls" (1962); Director, "Nebo Zovyot" (1960) **Awards:** Mary Pickford Award (2001); Lifetime Achievement Award, Directors Guild of America (1998); Bill Wilder Award, National Board Review (1997); Career Golden Lion award, Venice Film Festival (1992); British Academy of Film and Television Arts Award for Best Director (1979); Golden Palm Award, Cannes Film Festival (1979); Golden Globe Award for Best Director, Hollywood Foreign Press (1979); Academy Award for Best Picture (1975); Academy Award for Best Adapted Screenplay (1975); Award for Best Director, National Society of Film Critics (1975); Award for Best Screenplay, Writer Guild of America (1975); Golden Palm Award, Cannes Film Festival (1974); National Board Review Award for Best Director (1974); Academy Award for Best Adapted Screenplay (1973); Golden Globe Award for Best Director, Hollywood Foreign Press (1973); Golden Globe Award for Best Screenplay, Hollywood Foreign Press (1973); Writer Guild America Award for Best Screenplay (1973); Academy Award for Best Original Screenplay (1971) **Memberships:** Directors Guild of America

Anthony S. Coppolella

Title: Poet, Songwriter, Author **Industry:** Writing and Editing **Company Name:** Hilltop Records **Date of Birth:** 12/02/1947 **Place of Birth:** Easton **State/Country of Origin:** PA/USA **Parents:** Anthony Coppolella (12/1906); Grace (Sabatino) Coppolella (08/1906) **Children:** Marlo Lynn (07/02/1971); Anthony Christopher (11/03/1976); Angelica Christa (12/1978) **Education:** Diploma, Bangor High School, Pennsylvania (1966) **Career:** Songwriter, Rainbow Records, Hollywood, CA (1994-Present); Songwriter, Hilltop Records, Hollywood, CA (1994-Present); Quality Control, Fanatics (1998) **Creative Works:** Contributor, "Best Poems of 1995" (1995); Contributor, "Outstanding Poets of 1994" (1994); Contributor, "Wind in the Night Sky" (1993) **Awards:** Aaronic Priesthood, Latter Day Saints Church (1991); Editor's Choice Award (1995); Sales Award, The Eastern Express (1964) **Memberships:** Lifetime Member, Consulting-Advisor, International Society of Poets (1994-Present); National Writers Association; National Library of Poetry **Marquis Who's Who Honors:** Albert Nelson Marquis Lifetime Achievement Award **Why did you become involved in your profession or industry:** Mr. Coppolella never thought that he would be a writer because he was more into sports. He has written 30 songs, 15 of which are contracted out. **Avocations:** Art; Writing; Sports; Dance; Cooking **Political Affiliations:** Democrat **Religion:** Mormon **Thoughts on Life:** If it is something you want to do, do it. Don't be afraid. Do it.

Daniel Robert Coquillette

Title: Lawyer, Educator **Industry:** Law and Legal Services **Date of Birth:** 05/23/1944 **Place of Birth:** Boston **State/Country of Origin:** MA/USA **Parents:** Robert McTavish Coquillette; Dagmar Alvida (Bistrup) Coquillette **Marital Status:** Married **Spouse Name:** Judith Courtney Rogers, (07/05/1969) **Children:** Anna; Sophia; Julia **Education:** JD, Harvard University (1971); MA in Jurisprudence, University College, Oxford University, England (1969); AB, Williams College (1966) **Career:** Charles Warren Visiting Professor of American Legal History, Harvard Law School (2008-Present); J. Donald Monan S.S. Professor, Boston College of Law (1996-Present); Professor, Boston College of Law (1993-1996); Dean, Professor, Boston College of Law (1985-1993); Partner, Palmer & Dodge, Boston, MA (1980-1985); Associate Professor of Law, Boston University (1975-1978); Associate, Palmer & Dodge, Boston, MA (1973-1975); To Chief Justice Warren E. Burger, Supreme Court of the United States (1972-1973); Law Clerk, Massachusetts Supreme Court (1971-1972) **Career Related:** Charles Warren Visiting Professor, American Legal History (2008-Present); Overseers Committee, Lester Kissel Visiting Professor (2001-2007); Visiting Professor of Law, Harvard University (1978-1979, 1984-1985, 1994-2001); Reporter, Committee on Rules And Procedures, Judicial Conference, U.S. Member of Task Force On Rules Of Attorney Conduct, Supreme Judicial Court Of Massachusetts (1996-1997); Visiting Associate Professor of Law, Cornell University, Ithaca, NY (1977-1978, 1984) **Civic:** Board of Overseers, Visiting Committee, Harvard Law School (1993-2003); Trustee, Secretary-Treasurer Ames Foundation; Proprietor, Trustee Emeritus, Boston Athenaeum **Creative Works:** Board of Directors, New England Quarterly (1986-Present); Editor, "Real Ethics for Real Lawyer" (2012, 2016); Co-Editor, "On the Battlefield of Merit: Harvard Law School, The First Century" (2015); Co-Editor, "Lawyer & Fundamental Moral Responsibility" (2010); Co-Editor, "Portrait of a Patriot, The Quincy Papers" (2007); Editor, "The Law Commonplace" (2007); Co-Author, "The Southern Journal of Josiah Quincy" (2007); Author, "The Law Commonplace of Josiah Quincy" (2007); Author, "Real Ethics for Real Lawyers" (2005); Co-Author, "Portrait of a Patriot, Political and Legal Papers of Josiah Quincy" (2005); Editor, "Anglo-American Legal Heritage" (2004); Author, "The Anglo-American Legal Heritage" (1999, 2004); Co-Author, "Federal Law of Attorney Conduct" (2001); Co-Author, "Lex Mercatoria and Legal Pluralism" (1999); Author, "Working Papers on Rules Governing Attorney Conduct" (1997); Editor, "Moore's Federal Practice," Third Edition (1997); Author, "Lawyers and Fundamental Moral Responsibility" (1995); Author, "Francis Bacon" (1993); Author, "The Civilian Writers of Doctors Commons," London, England (1988); Editor, "Law in Colonial Massachusetts" (1985); Contributor, Articles, Professional Journals **Awards:** Peter Dobkin Hall Prize, Association For Research On Nonprofit Organization, Arnova (2017); Distinguished Service Medal, Boston College Law School (2007); Fulbright Scholar (1966-1968); Hutchins Scholar (1966-1967); Kaufman Prize In English Williams College (1966); Sentinel Of The Republic Prize In Political Science Williams College (1965) **Memberships:** Committee On Professional Ethics, American Bar Association (1990-1993); Board of Directors, Massachusetts Society of Continuing Legal Education (1985-1989); Board of Directors, American Society of Legal History (1985-1989); American Law Institute; Task Force On Model Rules Of Professional Conduct, Massachusetts Bar Association; Boston Bar Association; State Correspondent, Selden Society; Vice President, Council Member, Colonial Society of Massachusetts; Board of Directors, Anglo-American Cathedral Society; Massachusetts Historical Society; American Antiquarian Society; Phi Beta Kappa **Bar Admissions:** Massachusetts (1974); U.S. District Court, State of Massachusetts (1974); U.S. Court of Appeals for the First Circuit (1974) **Marquis Who's Who Honors:** Albert Nelson Marquis Lifetime Achievement Award; Marquis Who's Who Top Professional **To what do you attribute your success:** Mr. Coquillette attributes his success to his mentors. **Why did you become involved in your profession or industry:** What impacted Mr. Coquillette was his high school teacher in history, Mr. Gibson at Lexton High School; he was a terrific history teacher, and that got him interested both in history and law. **Avocations:** Collecting early law books and early books on literature, Vermont and hiking **Political Affiliations:** Democrat **Religion:** Society of Friends

James R. Couch Jr., MD, PhD, FAAN, FANA, FAHS

Title: Professor and Chair **Industry:** Education/Educational Services **Company Name:** The University of Oklahoma Health Sciences Center **Date of Birth:** 10/25/1939 **Place of Birth:** Bryan **State/Country of Origin:** TX/USA **Parents:** James Russell Couch; Vilma E. (Holland) Couch **Marital Status:** Married **Spouse Name:** Pamela Elizabeth Durre (04/04/1964) **Children:** James Russell; Patrick **Education:** Postgraduate Coursework, National Institute of Neurological Disorders and Stroke (NINDS) (1969-1972); Resident in Neurology, Washington University in St. Louis (1969-1972); Fellow, Laboratory of Neuropharmacology, National Institute of Mental Health (NIMH) (1967-1969); Intern, Barnes-Jewish Hospital (1966-1967); PhD in Physiology, Baylor University (1966); MD, Baylor University (1965); BS in Zoology, Texas A&M University (1961) **Certifications:** Certified in Headache Medicine, United Council for Neurologic Subspecialties (2006); Re-certified, Diplomate in Clinical Neurophysiology, American Board of Psychiatry and Neurology, Inc. (2002); Diplomate in Clinical Neurophysiology, American Board of Psychiatry and Neurology, Inc. (1992); Licensed Physician, State of Oklahoma (1992); Licensed Physician, State of Illinois (1979); Licensed Physician, State of Kansas (1972); Licensed Physician, State of Maryland (1968); Licensed Physician, State of Missouri (1966); Licensed Physician, State of Texas **Career:** Professor of Neurology, The University of Oklahoma Health Sciences Center (2006-Present); Chairman of Department of Neurology, The University of Oklahoma Health Sciences Center (1992-2006); Acting Chairman, Department of Medicine, Southern Illinois University School of Medicine (1988-1989); Director of EEG Laboratory, Memorial Health System (1979-1992); Director of Muscular Dystrophy Clinic, Memorial Health System (1979-1992); Consultant of Speech and Hearing Laboratory, Memorial Health System (1979-1992); Chief, Division of Neurology, Southern Illinois University School of Medicine (1979-1992); Professor of Neurology, Southern Illinois University School of Medicine (1979-1992); Associate Professor, The University of Kansas Medical Center (1976-1979); Assistant Professor, Division of Neurology, The University of Kansas Medical Center (1972-1976) **Career Related:** Examiner, American Board of Psychiatry and Neurology, Inc. (2008); Committee Member, Southern Illinois University School of Medicine (2006); Visiting Professor of Neurology, Albert Einstein College of Medicine (2006); Examiner, American Board of Psychiatry and Neurology, Inc. (2005); Committee Member, Saint Louis University School of Medicine (2004); Committee Member, Southern Illinois University School of Medicine (2003-2004) **Civic:** Executive Board, Chairman of Education Committee, American Society of Neurorehabilitation (1990-1995); Medical Advisory Board, Lincoln Land Epilepsy Association (1980-1992) **Creative Works:** Section Editor, "Headache Current Treatment Options Neurology" (2003-Present); Editorial Board Member, "Journal of Stroke & Cerebrovascular Disease" (1995-2008); Editorial Board Member, "Headache" (1979-1992); Reviewer, Medical Journals; Contributor, Over 100 Scientific Articles, Professional Journals; Presenter, Papers, National and International Meetings **Awards:** Recipient, Numerous Grants for Neurology Research (1969-Present); Lifetime Achievement Award, Headache Cooperative of New England (2018); Fellow, National Institute of Mental Health (1967-1969); Fellow, National Heart Institute (Now National Heart, Lung, and Blood Institute), National Institute of Health (1965-1966) **Memberships:** Clinical Action Team, American Headache Society (2008-Present); Publications Committee, American Headache Society (1986-Present); Chair, Headache Section, American Academy of Neurology (2003-2005); Program Director, Consortium of Neurology Program, American Academy of Neurology (2003-2005); Chairman, Section of Headache and Facial Pain, American Academy of Neurology (2003-2005); Nominating Committee, American Headache Society (2001-2008); President, American Headache Society (1998-2000); Chairman, VAMC Committee, AAUP (1997-2001); Chair, Education Committee, American Headache Society (1996-1998); President-Elect, American Headache Society (1996-1998) **Marquis Who's Who Honors:** Albert Nelson Marquis Lifetime Achievement Award; Marquis Who's Who Top Professional; Marquis Who's Who Humanitarian Award **To what do you attribute your success:** Dr. Couch attributes his success to the support of his wife, Pamela, and his family throughout his career. **Why did you become involved in your profession or industry:** Dr. Couch entered his profession because his father pushed him in that direction. His father wanted to be a doctor, but was busy with the war. He always liked biology. **Avocations:** Tennis; Racquetball; Bicycling; Collecting old medicine bottles

Robert Barnard "Bob" Couch, MD, (Retired)

Title: Professor Emeritus **Industry:** Medicine & Health Care **Company Name:** The University of Texas Medical Branch **Date of Birth:** 09/25/1930 **Place of Birth:** Guntersville **State/Country of Origin:** AL/USA **Parents:** Ezekiel Harvey; Frances Jane (Barnard) C. **Marital Status:** Widower **Spouse Name:** Katherine Frances Klein (04/23/1955, Deceased 2006) **Children:** Robert Steven; Leslie Ann; Colleen Frances; Elizabeth Lee **Education:** Doctor of Medicine, Vanderbilt University (1956); Bachelor of Arts, Vanderbilt University (1952) **Certifications:** Diplomate, American Board of Internal Medicine **Career:** Professor Emeritus, Baylor College of Medicine (2012-Present); Adjunct Professor, Internal Medicine, University Texas Medical Branch, Galveston, TX (2013-2019); Professor of Molecular Virology, Microbiology and Medicine, Baylor College Medicine, Houston, TX (2000-2012); Director, Center for Infection and Immunity Research, Baylor College Medicine, Houston, TX (1999-2012); Director, Respiratory Pathogens Research Unit, Baylor College Medicine, Houston, TX (1996-2012); Distinguished Professor, Baylor College Medicine, Houston, TX (1995-2012); Director, Acute Viral Respiratory Diseases Unit, Baylor College Medicine, Houston, TX (1991-1996); Chairman, Department of Microbiology and Immunology, Baylor College of Medicine, Houston, TX (1989-2000); Head of Infectious Diseases, Section of Medicine, Baylor College Medicine, Houston, TX (1987-1992); Director, Influenza Research Center, Baylor College of Medicine (1974-1991); Professor Microbiology, Immunology And Medicine, Baylor College Medicine, Houston, TX (1971-2000); Associate Professor, Baylor College Medicine, Houston, TX (1966-1971); Head of Clinical Virology Section, National Institutes of Allergy and Infectious Diseases, Washington, DC (1965-1966); Senior Investigator, National Institutes of Allergy and Infectious Diseases, Washington, DC (1961-1965); Chief Resident Physician, Vanderbilt University Hospital, Nashville, TN (1960-1961); Resident Physician, Vanderbilt University Hospital, Nashville, TN (1959-1960); Intern, Vanderbilt University Hospital, Nashville, TN (1956-1957); Clinical Associate, National Cancer Institute, Washington, DC (1957-1959) **Career Related:** Research Advisory Panels on Infectious Diseases, Consultant, National Institutes of Health, Department of Defense, Food and Drug Administration **Civic:** Served to Senior Surgeon, U.S. Public Health Service (1957-1966) **Creative Works:** Contributor, Articles to Professional Journals **Awards:** Dr. Charles Merieux Award, National Foundation for Infectious Diseases (2011) **Memberships:** Alpha Omega Alpha; American College of Physicians; American Association for the Advancement of Science; Society for Experimental Biology and Medicine; American Society for Microbiology; Infectious Diseases Society of America; American Association of Immunologists; American Federation for Clinical Research; American Society of Clinical Investigation; Southern Society of Clinical Investigation; American Association of Physicians; American Society of Epidemiology; American Society of Virology **Marquis Who's Who Honors:** Albert Nelson Marquis Lifetime Achievement Recipient **To what do you attribute your success:** Dr. Couch attributes his success to the good opportunities he received due to his hard work and intelligence. He used to work up to 70+ hours a week, and his wife was very tolerant and patient of his long hours. **Why did you become involved in your profession or industry:** Particularly interested in science since attending high school, Dr. Couch benefited from the tutelage of several wonderful mentors, including his sister, who suggested that he attend Vanderbilt University.

Paul Henry Couture, CLU, ChFC, CEP

Title: President **Industry:** Financial Services **Company Name:** Couture Financial Services **Date of Birth:** 06/19/1954 **Place of Birth:** Northbridge **State/Country of Origin:** MA/USA **Parents:** Damase Couture; Henrietta A. (Provost) Couture **Marital Status:** Married **Spouse Name:** Katy **Children:** Paul H, Couture, Jr (PJ); Carissa Couture **Education:** Coursework in Psychology, Assumption College, Worcester, MA; Coursework, The American College; Coursework, The Liberty Institute **Certifications:** The Charted Life Underwriter (1989); Charted Financial Consultant; Certified Estate Planner **Career:** President/ Founder, Couture Financial Services (2008-Present) **Career Related:** New England Financial Insurance and Investment Planning (1976-2008) **Civic:** Notary Public **Awards:** Vanguard Award (1989); Life Member, Million Dollar Roundtable; Qualifier, U.S. Mid Amateur/U.S. Senior Amateur Championship (Golf); 5 Star Professional, Boston Magazine; Best of Worcester; Best Finical Planner **Memberships:** Past President, The Estate and Business Planning Council of Worcester County; Builders Association of Central Massachusetts; Society of Seniors; Executive Committee, New England Leaders Association **Marquis Who's Who Honors:** Marquis Who's Who Top Professional **To what do you attribute your success:** Mr. Couture always does his best for his clients by giving them the best product available. **Why did you become involved in your profession or industry:** Mr. Couture was inspired by someone he knew in the industry. **Avocations:** Hockey; Golf **Thoughts on Life:** Motto: We work for You.

Dennis Cox, DMA

Title: Music Educator, Conductor **Industry:** Education/Educational Services **Date of Birth:** 03/11/1943 **Place of Birth:** Ord **State/Country of Origin:** NE/USA **Parents:** George Harvey Cox; Muriel Jane Bartz Cox **Marital Status:** Married **Spouse Name:** Elizabeth Anne Downing (08/29/1992) **Children:** Amy; Katherine; Kirk **Education:** DMA, University of Missouri-Kansas City Conservatory of Music and Dance (1978); MA, West Virginia University, Morgantown, WV (1974); MusM, University of Colorado Boulder, CO (1969); BME, University of Nebraska, Lincoln, NE (1965) **Career:** Professor Emeritus (2014-Present); Professor of Music, Graduate Coordinator, University of Maine, Orono, ME (1978-2014); Assistant Professor, Music, Salem University, West Virginia (1968-1975); Instructor, Vocal Music, Casey Middle School, Boulder, CO (1967-1968); Instructor, Vocal Music, Superior High School, Superior, NE (1965-1967) **Career Related:** Freelance Guest Conductor, United States, Europe, Canada (1978-Present); Judge, Heritage Festivals, Salt Lake City, Utah (1982-2014) **Military Service:** With, ROTC (1961-1963) **Creative Works:** Contributor, Articles, Journals Including Choral Journal, Main Music Educators Association (MMEA) and The American Choral Review **Awards:** Black Bear Award, University of Maine Alumni Association (2001); Vincent Hartgen Award, University of Maine Patrons of the Arts (2000); Outstanding Educators of America Award (1974) **Memberships:** National Association of Teachers of Singing, Inc.; American Choral Directors Association; National Association for Music Education **Marquis Who's Who Honors:** Albert Nelson Marquis Lifetime Achievement Award **Why did you become involved in your profession or industry:** Dr. Cox always loved music, and started piano lessons as a child. Dr. Cox began his college career studying medicine at the University of Nebraska, but eventually found that he was more passionate about music. He is happy about his decision to pursue music, and feels he has a achieved a rewarding career. **Avocations:** Fishing; Travel; Boston sports **Political Affiliations:** Democrat **Religion:** Agnostic

Jerry J. Cox

Title: Lawyer **Industry:** Law and Legal Services **Company Name:** Law Offices of Jerry J Cox, PSC **Marital Status:** Married **Spouse Name:** Ticki (8/20/1966) **Education:** Doctor of Jurisprudence, University of Kentucky (1968); Bachelor of Arts in History and Political Science, Berea College (1965) **Certifications:** Certified, Criminal Specialist, National Board of Trial Advocacy **Career:** Sole Practitioner, Criminal Defense Law, PSC (1973-Present) **Career Related:** Chairman, Public Advocacy Commission (2010-Present); Examiner, National Board of Trial Advocacy (2004); Member, Public Advocacy Commission (1999); Drug Strategy Committee, Kentucky Criminal Justice Council (1999); Faculty Member, Department of Public Advocacy Practice Institute; Lecturer in Field **Civic:** Former Chairman, Various District Health Departments; Former Swimming Coach **Military Service:** U.S. Army, Vietnam (1969-1970) **Creative Works:** Contributor, Articles, Professional Publications **Awards:** President's Commendation, National Association of Criminal Defense Lawyers (2009); President's Special Award, Kentucky Bar Association (2004); Nelson Mandela Lifetime Achievement Award, Department of Public Advocacy (2002); President's Award, Kentucky Association of Criminal Defense Lawyers (1995) **Memberships:** Trustee, Foundation for Criminal Justice (2009-Present); President, National Association of Criminal Defense Lawyers (2013-2014); Prescription Drug Abuse Task Force, Kentucky Bar Association (2003); President, Kentucky Bar Foundation (2002-2003); Board of Directors, National Association of Criminal Defense Lawyers (2000-2006); Legislative Committee, Kentucky Bar Association (1999-2005); Board of Directors, Kentucky Bar Foundation (1995-2004); Chair, Criminal Law Section, Kentucky Bar Association (1994); Unauthorized Practice of Law Committee, Kentucky Bar Association (1993-2007); Foundation for Criminal Justice; Kentucky Bar Foundation; Kentucky Association of Criminal Defense Lawyers; Kentucky Bar Association; American Bar Association; National Association of Criminal Defense Lawyers; Chairman, Audit Committee, National Association of Criminal Defense Lawyers **Marquis Who's Who Honors:** Albert Nelson Marquis Lifetime Achievement Award; Marquis Who's Who Top Professional **Avocations:** Running marathons in every state, with only three states to go; Kayaking

Richard Crawford

Title: Musicology Educator **Industry:** Education/Educational Services **Date of Birth:** 05/12/1935 **Place of Birth:** Detroit **State/Country of Origin:** MI/USA **Parents:** Arthur Richard Crawford; Mary Elizabeth Crawford **Marital Status:** Married **Spouse Name:** Penelope Marie Ball; Sophie Shambes (Divorced) **Children:** Amy Elizabeth; Lynn; William; Anne **Education:** PhD, University of Michigan (1965); MusM, University of Michigan (1959); MusB, University of Michigan (1958) **Career:** Hans T. David Distinguished University Professor Emeritus, University of Michigan (2004-Present); Professor, University of Michigan, Ann Arbor, MI (1975-2003); Associate Professor, University of Michigan, Ann Arbor, MI (1969-1975); Assistant Professor, University of Michigan, Ann Arbor, MI (1966-1969); Instructor, Musicology, University of Michigan, Ann Arbor, MI (1962-1966) **Career Related:** Founding Editor-in-Chief, Music of the United States of America (1993); Visiting Ernest Bloch Professor, University of California Berkeley (1985); Visiting Professor, Brooklyn College, City University of New York (1973-1974) **Civic:** Consultant, National Endowment of the Humanities **Creative Works:** Author, "Summertime: George Gershwin's Life in Music" (2019); Author, "America's Musical Life: A History" (2005); Author, "America's Musical Life: A History" (2001); Author, "An Introduction to America's Music" (2001); Author, "The American Musical Landscape" (1993); Author, "American Sacred Music Imprints, 1698-1810: A Bibliography" (1990); Author, "A Celebration of American Music" (1990); Co-Editor, "The Core Repertory of Early American Psalmody" (1984); Author, "American Studies and American Musicology" (1975); Co-Author, "William Billings of Boston: 18th-century Composer" (1975); Author, "Andrew Law, American Psalmodist" (1968); Contributor, Articles, Reviews, Professional Journals; Editor, Various PhD Dissertations **Awards:** Fellow, National Endowment for Humanities (1993-1994); Guggenheim Fellow (1977-1978); Senior Research Fellow, Institute for Studies in American Music, New York, NY (1973-1974); Postdoctoral Fellow, University of Michigan Rackham (1969-1970); Postdoctoral Fellow, Rackham Graduate School, University of Michigan (1967) **Memberships:** American Musicological Society (1984-Present); American Antiquarian Society (1972-Present); President, American Musicological Society (1982-1984); Editorial Board, New World Records, New York, NY (1975-1978); Fellow, American Antiquarian Society, Worcester, MA (1973); Fellow, American Antiquarian Society, Worcester, MA (1972); Society of American Music; American Academy of Arts and Sciences **Marquis Who's Who Honors:** Albert Nelson Marquis Lifetime Achievement Award **To what do you attribute your success:** Mr. Crawford attributes his success to Hans David, a professor at the University of Michigan. He was an excellent advisor when it came to Mr. Crawford's writing. Another mentor was H. Wiley Hitchcock, a well-respected professor and friend, who Mr. Crawford met at the University of Michigan. **Why did you become involved in your profession or industry:** Mr. Crawford's interest in music was cultivated by the extensive music programs available in the Detroit public schools he attended. He took an interest in learning to play the piano and saxophone, as well as studying jazz music. Initially, his field of study was engineering, but he switched to the study of early American music in the 1960s. The various musicology programs available in his hometown of Michigan were beneficial in preparing him for his career in music. **Thoughts on Life:** Mr. Crawford enjoys learning and continues to contribute to the field of musicology.

Clinton F. Cross

Title: Lawyer (Retired) **Industry:** Law and Legal Services **Date of Birth:** 03/02/1939 **Place of Birth:** Waco **State/Country of Origin:** TX/USA **Parents:** Clinton Janes Heath; Mary Augusta Cross **Marital Status:** Single **Spouse Name:** Nellie Cross (1973, Divorced 1976) **Children:** Joyce; Roberta **Education:** LLB, The University of Texas at Austin School of Law, Texas (1968); BA, Pomona College (1962) **Career:** Assistant County Attorney, Office of the El Paso County Attorney (1986, 1996-2015); Associate, Gage, Gage and Kern LLP (1993-1996); Lawyer, Private Practice (1986-1993); Director, Texas Legal Services Center (1977-1985); Assistant Attorney General, Attorney General of Texas (1973-1976); Staff Attorney, El Paso Legal Assistance Society (1969-1973) **Career Related:** Instructor, El Paso Community College (1974-1976, 1989-1992) **Civic:** Secretary, President, Sutton Place One Condominium Association, AtHomeNet, Inc. (2014-2017); Member, President, Sutton Place One Condominium Association, AtHomeNet, Inc. (2006-2014); Member, National Legal Aid & Defender Association (1980-1983); Board of Directors, El Paso Legal Assistance Society (1973-1976) **Military Service:** With, United States Marine Corps Reserve (1962-1968) **Creative Works:** Co-author with Colbert Nathaniel Coldwell, "The Saga of Judge Colbert Coldwell" (2020); Author, "Overcoming Great Odds: The Life of William Tillett Watt (And Overlook Ghosts)" (2017); Author, "James Sampson Ferguson" (2011); Editor, El Paso Bar Journal (2008-2016); Associate Editor, El Paso Bar Journal (2006-2008); Author, "Eliza Sims and Two Libraries" (2006); Contributor, Articles to Professional Publications **Awards:** Albert Armendariz Senior Award (2015); Lifetime Achievement Award, El Paso Bar Association (2015); President's Award, El Paso Bar Association (2011, 2013-2014); County Attorney Award (2010); Outstanding Senior Lawyer, El Paso Young Lawyer's Bar Association (2010); Honoree, Community Adviser of the Year, Office of the El Paso County Attorney (2005) **Memberships:** Boards of Directors, Texas Appleseed (2010-2017); El Paso Bar Association (2004-2007); Chairman, Legal Aid Lawyer Referral Committee, El Paso Bar Association (1993-1994); Chairman, Consumer Law Committee, El Paso Bar Association (1991-1992); Consumer Law Section Council, State Bar of Texas (1973-1987); Ad Hoc Committee for Creation of Texas Lawyers Care, State Bar of Texas (1982-1985); National Legal Aid and Defender Association (1980-1983); Chairman, Committee on Legal Services to Indigent in Civil Matters, State Bar of Texas (1977-1980); El Paso Legal Assistance Society (1973-1976) **Bar Admissions:** United States District Court for the Western District of Texas (1987); United States Court of Appeals for the Fifth Circuit (1986); United States District Court for the Northern District of Texas (1972); State Bar of Texas (1968) **Marquis Who's Who Honors:** Albert Nelson Marquis Lifetime Achievement Award; Marquis Who's Who Top Professional **To what do you attribute your success:** Mr. Cross attributes his success to being persistent and fortunate. He quoted Confucius in that "It does not matter how slowly you go so long as you do not stop." He considered himself a slow walker. When he confronted failure, he kept walking. He has also been in the right place at the right time. In politics, timing is almost everything, he noted. **Why did you become involved in your profession or industry:** Mr. Cross became involved in his profession because of his grandfather, who served as his first role model. He was a farmer, part-time lawyer, and politician who crusaded against the Ku Klux Klan in Waco, Texas, in the 1920s. **Avocations:** Chess **Political Affiliations:** Democrat **Thoughts on Life:** Mr. Cross's thoughts on life are "Success, meaningful success, lies in helping others, not in acquiring money, power or awards." He hopes he has helped more people than he has disappointed.

Joshua Crossney

Title: Chief Executive Officer **Industry:** Business Management/Business Services **Company Name:** Cannabis Science Conference **Education:** AS in Business, Management, Marketing, Related Support, Anne Arundel Community College (2006) **Career:** Advisory Board Member, Cannakids (2017-Present); Contributing Writer, 1000 Watts Publications, Medical Jane (2016-Present); President, Chief Executive Officer, Founder, CSC Events, LLC (2015-Present); Founding President, jCannna, Inc. (2014-Present); Host, Personality, The Medical Cannabis Report (2016-2017); National Events Director, Women Grow (2016-2017) **Creative Works:** Contributing Editor, Cannabis Science & Technology Magazine (2018-Present) **Awards:** Global Health and Pharma Medical Marijuana Awards (2019); 40 under 40, Marijuana Ventures; Best Annual Cannabis Science Event **Marquis Who's Who Honors:** Marquis Who's Who Top Professional **Why did you become involved in your profession or industry:** Mr. Crossney saw the boom of marijuana out in the west coast moving east. He connected with Tracey Ryan, the chief executive officer of a cannabis organization called Cannakids, where she told him the story of her first born having a rare Optic Pathway Glaucoma brain tumor, and was told to do chemotherapy. She researched and was told to try cannabis to help her 8 month old child. He's inspired by the patients and the families and the people that are struggling and the people that did not look at this as an option and still don't. "We work with a lot of celebrity sponsors which is great."

June Crow

Title: Chief Financial Officer **Company Name:** Boys and Girls Clubs of the Mississippi Delta **Date of Birth:** 08/15/1953 **Place of Birth:** Philadelphia **State/Country of Origin:** MS/USA **Parents:** Julian Preston; Sula Kate Ferguson **Marital Status:** Married **Spouse Name:** John C Crow **Children:** Heather Ryan; Sarah Ryan; Joshua Ryan; John C. Crow Jr.; Mandy Crow; Mollie Crow; Katie Crow; Six Grandchildren **Career:** Chief Financial Officer, Boys & Girls Clubs of the Mississippi Delta (2014-Present); Program Director, Boys & Girls Clubs of the Mississippi Delta (2006-2014); Book Keeper, Local Pharmacy; Owner, CPA Practice **Civic:** Board Member, Martha Coker Green Houses; Board Member, Chamber of Commerce **Awards:** Southeast Regions Recognition Award for Administrative Staff Member of the Year for Enhancing the Profession of Boys and Girls Clubs work through Dedication, Leadership, and Vision (2018); Boys and Girls Clubs of America National Conference in San Diego, CA (2018); Mississippi Professional of the Year (2017); National Service to Youth Award, Boys and Girls Clubs of America (2015); National Professional Service Award, Boys and Girls Clubs of America (2011) **Memberships:** Lifetime Member, National Association of Junior Auxiliaries Inc. **Marquis Who's Who Honors:** Albert Nelson Marquis Lifetime Achievement Award; Marquis Who's Who Humanitarian Award **To what do you attribute your success:** Ms. Crow credits her success on her Christian faith, as well as her drive to help those less fortunate than herself, especially children. **Why did you become involved in your profession or industry:** Ms. Crow became involved in her profession after joining her daughter's organization, the Boys & Girls Clubs of the Mississippi Delta. After the group secured a grant, she became a program manager. **Thoughts on Life:** When you put others first, you will have a very rich life.

Logan Crow

Title: Founder **Industry:** Media & Entertainment **Company Name:** The Frida Cinema **Education:** Graduate, The Emerging Leaders Program, Leadership Institute, The Nonprofit Partnership **Certifications:** Licensed Real Estate Agent **Career:** Founder, Executive Director, The Frida Cinema (2014-Present); Founder, President, Long Beach Zombie Walk (2009-2014); Founder, CEO, MondoCelluloid.com (2008-2013); Freelance Writer; Mortgage Broker **Career Related:** Speaker in Field **Civic:** Co-Founder, Cultural Alliance of Long Beach; Former Member, Board, Downtown Long Beach **Awards:** People of OC, OC Weekly Magazine (2016); Reader's Choice Award, Best Indie Movie Theater in Orange County, OC Weekly Magazine (2014); Long Beach 40 under 40, Long Beach Post (2012); Top 100 Independent Businesses in the Country, Yelp Inc.; Five-Time Winner, Best Independent Theater in Orange County, OC Weekly Magazine; Two-Time Winner, Best Theater in Orange County **Memberships:** Art House Convergence **Why did you become involved in your profession or industry:** Mr. Crow became involved in his profession because of a profound vision and desire to fill an empty space in his neighborhood. In bringing together creativity, cinema and the community, he has, in one space, built a local hub, movie theater and mission-driven cultural center. Mr. Crow goes above and beyond just film; his cinema hosts art shows every two months and always celebrates diversity and the arts.

Mart Crowley

Title: Playwright **Industry:** Media & Entertainment **Date of Birth:** 08/21/1935 **Place of Birth:** Vicksburg **State/Country of Origin:** MI/USA **Education:** Diploma, The Catholic University of America, Washington, DC (1957) **Career Related:** Assistant to Natalie Wood **Creative Works:** Guest Appearance, "Making the Boys" (2011); Guest Appearance, "Dominick Dunne: After the Party" (2007); Writer, Reunion Special, "Hart to Hart" (1996); Guest Appearance, "The Celluloid Closet" (1995); Scriptwriter, "People Like Us" (1990); Scriptwriter, "Bluegrass" (1988); Scriptwriter, "There Must Be a Pony" (1986); Executive Script Editor, Producer, "Hart to Hart (1979-1980); Playwright, "The Boys in the Band" (1968); Playwright, "The Men from the Boys"; Writer, Producer, "Remote Asylum"; Writer, Producer, "A Breeze from the Gulf" **Awards:** Tony Award, Best Revival of a Play (2018); Audience Choice Awards for Favorite Play Revival, Broadway.com (2018)

Barbara Ann Croyle

Title: Executive Director **Industry:** Health, Wellness and Fitness **Company Name:** Jenner's Pond Continuing Care Retirement Community **Date of Birth:** 10/22/1949 **Place of Birth:** Knoxville **State/Country of Origin:** TN/USA **Parents:** Charles Evans Croyle; Myrtle Elizabeth (Kellam) Croyle **Marital Status:** Married **Spouse Name:** Jeffery Volpe **Education:** MS, Gerontology, St. Joseph's University (2012); MBA, University of Denver (1983); Certificate, Program Management Development, Colorado Women's College (1980); JD, University of Colorado (1975); Certificate, Corporate Tax and Securities Law, Institute of Paralegal Training (1971); BA, Sociology, College of William and Mary, Cum Laude (1971) **Certifications:** Nursing Home Administrator; Lecturer **Career:** Executive Director, Jenner's Pond Retirement Community (2017-Present); Executive Director, Stratford House Retirement Community, Danville, VA (2014-Present); Executive Director, Lutheran Senior Services of Southern Chester Company (2010-2013); Executive Vice President, Peninsula United Methodist Homes, Inc., Hockessin, DE (2003-2010); Executive Director, Swedish American Center for Complementary Medicine, Rockford, IL (2000-2002); Vice President, Ambulatory Care Services, Compliance Officer, Franciscan Medical Center, Dayton, OH (1994-2000); COO, Vice President, D.T. Watson Rehabilitation Hospital (1992-1993); Managing Director, Benefit Resource Management Group (Subsidiary of Blue Cross of Western Pennsylvania) (1987-1992); Manager of Strategic Planning, Westinghouse, Transportation Division, Denver, CO (1985-1987); Manager of Acquisitions/Lands, Petro-Lewis Corporation, Denver, CO (1977-1985); Associate of the Firm, Shaw Spangler & Roth, Denver, CO (1976-1977); Law Clerk, Colorado Court of Appeals, Denver, CO (1976); Paralegal, Holland and Hart, Denver, CO (1972-1973) **Career Related:** Teacher, Oil and Gas Law, Colorado Paralegal Institute (1978-1979); Arbitrator, American Arbitration Association **Memberships:** American Bar Association **Bar Admissions:** State of Pennsylvania (1990); State of Colorado (1976) **Marquis Who's Who Honors:** Albert Nelson Marquis Lifetime Achievement Award; Marquis Who's Who Top Professional **To what do you attribute your success:** Ms. Croyle attributes her success to the influence of good parents and a good education. She additionally credits a passion for learning and a curiosity for new adventures, as well as her resilient spirit and optimistic outlook. **Why did you become involved in your profession or industry:** Ms. Croyle got involved in senior living because it is a positive working environment where she can give and receive love. **Thoughts on Life:** To Ms. Croyle, the meaning of life is to have a purpose and recognize the importance of freedom to think for oneself.

Judith "Judy" A. Beekman Cruz, RN, BSN, MS

Title: Nursing Administrator **Company Name:** BCBSMA **Date of Birth:** 02/27/1938 **Place of Birth:** Utica **State/Country of Origin:** NY/USA **Parents:** Leon G. Beekman; Anne Marie (McGillis) Beekman **Marital Status:** Single **Children:** Sharon Ann **Education:** MS in Health Care Administration, Salve Regina University, Newport, RI (1990); BS in Nursing, Salve Regina University, Newport, RI (1986); Diploma, Elizabeth General Hospital, Elizabeth, NJ (1961) **Certifications:** Certified Emergency Nurse, Emergency Nurses Association (1980-Present) **Career:** On Site Case Manager (1992-2003); Positions for BCBSMA Insurance Co. Emergency Clinician Utilization Review (1992); Independent Medical Legal consultant for law firms (1991-1992); Coordinator Project Management & Operations (1990-1991); Various Positions, Rhode Island Hospital, Providence, RI (1961-1991); Director, Emergency Nursing, Rhode Island Hospital, Providence, RI (1986-1990); Assistant Director of Emergency Nursing, Rhode Island Hospital, Providence, RI (1978-1986); Nurse Leader of the Emergency Department, Rhode Island Hospital, Providence, RI (1970-1978); Assistant Head Nurse, Rhode Island Hospital, Providence, RI (1964-1970); Staff Nurse, Day Shift, Rhode Island Hospital, Providence, RI (1964); Charge Staff Nurse, Night Shift, Rhode Island Hospital, Providence, RI (1962-1964); Charge Staff Nurse, Rhode Island Hospital, Providence, RI (1961-1962) **Career Related:** National ENA Trauma Nursing Care Instructor (1987-1991); Basic Cardiac Life Support Instructor, American Heart Association (1979-1987); Advanced Life Support Instructor, American Heart Association (1979-1987); Management and Clinical Consultant, St. Luke's Emergency Department, New Bedford, MA (1985); Nursing Faculty, Continuing Education, Rhode Island Junior College (Now Community College of Rhode Island) (1979); A.C.L.S. Instructor, for Guadalajara Medical School, Mexico **Civic:** Member, Rhode Island Hospital Association; Member, Rhode Island Nursing Executive; Member, Emergency Services Advisory; Member, Collaborative Practice; Member, Emergency Information Committee; Member, Occupational Health Steering Committee; Member, Disaster Committee; Member, Emergency Department Staff Advisory; Member, Emergency Department Equipment Committee; Member, Planning Committee for New England ENA Symposium; Member, Hospitality Committee; Member, Quality Assurance Committee **Creative Works:** Speaker, ENA New England Symposium, "Cost Effective Customer Relations" (1990); Speaker, ENA New England Symposium, "Trauma" and "Customer Relations" (1987); Numerous Lectures and Presentations Concerning Emergency Nursing Topics, Including Advanced Triaging, Multiple Trauma, Arterial Blood Gases, Anatomy and Physiology of Cardiac Conduction System, Disaster, Radiation Disaster, DKA, Epidemiology, Trauma Scores, and Legal Aspects of Nursing and Customer Relations **Memberships:** Society for Ambulatory Care Professionals; American Nurses Association; Association for Female Executives; Emergency Nurses Association; United States Achievement Academy **Marquis Who's Who Honors:** Albert Nelson Marquis Lifetime Achievement Award **To what do you attribute your success:** God's blessings and gift of good parents. Faith and family. **Why did you become involved in your profession or industry:** Ms. Cruz became involved in her profession because she started out as a school teacher and her sister was a nurse. She was in college and was going to be a kindergarten teacher and attended a teacher's college in New Jersey. She was very unhappy at the college. She transitioned from a private school and did not like it, then the student nurses visited one day and she sat and had lunch with them and listened to them talk about nursing. It was at that point that a light went on in her head and from that moment she knew that this was what she wanted to do. Her father was not pleased, as he wanted her to be a teacher. Her mother was pleased, as she herself wanted to be a nurse. However, her father agreed and sent her to the same nursing school as her sister. **Avocations:** Lay Religious-Franciscan Tertiary of the Immaculate-Presenting Days of Prayer" A Day with Mary," different parish churches 2004-2018 **Religion:** Roman Catholic **Thoughts on Life:** "Believe that you have a mission in life to complete. Forge ahead and never give up."

Kenneth Thomas Cuccinelli II

Title: Acting Deputy Secretary of Homeland Security **Industry:** Government Administration/ Government Relations/Government Services **Company Name:** U.S. Department of Homeland Security **Date of Birth:** 07/30/1968 **Place of Birth:** Edison **State/Country of Origin:** NJ/USA **Parents:** Kenneth Thomas Cuccinelli; Maribeth (Reilly) Cuccinelli **Marital Status:** Married **Spouse Name:** Teiro Davis **Children:** Two Sons; Five Daughters **Education:** MA in International Commerce Policy, George Mason University (2000); JD, George Mason University School of Law, Arlington, VA (1995); BS in Mechanical Engineering, University of Virginia (1990) **Career:** Acting U.S. Deputy Secretary of Homeland Security (2019-Present); President, Senate Conservatives Fund (2014-Present); Acting Director, U.S. Citizenship and Immigration Services (2019-2020); Attorney General, Commonwealth of Virginia, Richmond, VA (2010-2014); Member, District 37, Virginia State Senate, Richmond, VA (2002-2010); Partner, Cuccinelli & Day PLLC, Fairfax, VA; Patent Attorney, Oblon Spivak, VA **Civic:** Board of Directors, Families Inc. (1998-2000); Advisory Committee, Virginia Juvenile Justice & Delinquency Protection (1994-1999) **Creative Works:** Co-author, "The Last Line of Defense: The New Fight for American Liberty" (2013) **Memberships:** Fairfax Bar Association; Virginia State Bar **Avocations:** Spending time with family; Reading; Shooting; Watching college basketball **Political Affiliations:** Republican **Religion:** Roman Catholic

Elijah Eugene Cummings

Title: Former U.S. Representative from Maryland **Industry:** Government Administration/Government Relations/Government Services **Date of Birth:** 01/18/1951 **Place of Birth:** Baltimore **State/Country of Origin:** MD/USA **Year of Passing:** 2019 **Parents:** Robert Cummings; Ruth Elma (Cochran) Cummings **Marital Status:** Married **Spouse Name:** Maya Rockeymoore Cummings (2009); Joyce Matthews (Divorced 1982) **Children:** Jennifer J. Cummings; Adia Cummings; One Son **Education:** JD, University of Maryland Francis King Carey School of Law (1976); BS, Howard University (1973) **Career:** Ranking Democrat, U.S. House Select Committee on Events Surrounding the 2012 Terrorist Attack in Benghazi (2014-2019); Ranking Member, U.S. House Committee on Oversight and Government Reform, Washington, DC (2011-2019); Member, U.S. House of Representatives from Maryland's Seventh Congressional District, United States Congress, Washington, DC (1996-2019); Chairman, Congressional Black Caucus, Washington, DC (2003-2005); Chairman, Committee on Economic Development, Maryland House of Delegates, Annapolis, MD (1996); Speaker Pro Tempore, Maryland House of Delegates, Annapolis, MD (1995-1996); Vice Chairman, House of Economic Matters Committee, Maryland House of Delegates, Annapolis, MD (1994-1996); Vice Chairman, Constitutional and Administrative Law Committee, Maryland House of Delegates, Annapolis, MD (1987-1996); Maryland House of Delegates, Annapolis, MD (1983-1996); Attorney, Maryland General Assembly (1982); Private Law Practice (1980-1996) **Civic:** Chairman, Congressional Black Caucus Foundation, Inc. (2003-2019); Chairman, Governor's Commission on Black Males (1990-2019); First Vice Chairman, Board of Directors, Congressional Black Caucus Foundation, Inc. (1998); Chairman, Legislative Black Caucus of Maryland; President, Bancroft Literary Society **Awards:** Named, 10 Members to Watch in the 112th Congress, Roll Call (2011); Named, Power 150, Ebony Magazine (2008); Named, Most Influential Black Americans, Ebony Magazine (2006); Outstanding U.S. Student Government Leader, Royal Arts Society of London (RSA) **Memberships:** Maryland State Bar Association **Bar Admissions:** State of Maryland (1976) **Political Affiliations:** Democrat **Religion:** Baptist

Jerome John "Jerry" Cuomo, PhD

Title: Materials Scientist **Industry:** Technology **Company Name:** IBM, North Carolina State University **Date of Birth:** 09/30/1936 **Place of Birth:** New York **State/Country of Origin:** NC/USA **Parents:** Gennaro (Jerry); Rose Cuomo **Marital Status:** Widower **Spouse Name:** Rita Cossa (06/20/1959, Deceased 2016) **Children:** Stephanie Rose; Gennaro Anthony (Jerry); Andrea Marie. **Education:** Doctor of Philosophy in Physics, University of Southern Denmark (1979); Master of Science in Physical Chemistry, St. Johns University (1960); Bachelor of Science in Chemistry, Manhattan College (1958) **Career:** Distinguished Research Professor of Materials Science & Engineering, North Carolina State University, Raleigh, NC (1993-Present); Senior Manager of Materials Laboratory, Central Scientific Services, IBM, Yorktown Heights, NY (1975-1993); Manager, Materials Processing Group, Central Scientific Services, IBM, Yorktown Heights, NY (1968-1975); Staff Member, Processing Group, Central Scientific Services, IBM, Yorktown Heights, NY (1963-1968); Chief Chemist, Secon Metal (1960-1963) **Career Related:** Affiliate Professor, Department of Materials Science and Engineering, Cornell University (1983-Present); Organizer, Co-Chairman, First Topical Symposium On Energetic Condensation, American Vacuum Society (1992); Adjunct Professor, Electrical Engineering Department, Michigan State University (1990); Member, Advisory Board, Materials Research Laboratory on Diamonds, Case Western Reserve University, Cleveland, OH (1990); Organizer, Chairman, Symposium On Silicon Nitride Electrochemical Society (1966); Elected Member, Japanese and U.S. Workshop on Diamond Technology; Adjunct Professor, Colorado State University; Co-Founder, Kyma Technologies; Co-Founder, Premitec; Co-Founder, Tribofilm Research; Co-Founder, Atmospheric Plasma Solutions **Creative Works:** Co-editor, "Handbook of Ion Beam Processing Technology," with S. Rossnagel and H. Kaufman (1989); Co-editor, "Handbook of Plasma Processing Technology, with S. Rossnagel and W. Westwood (1989); Contributor, More than 300 Articles and Papers to Professional Journals **Awards:** National Medal of Technology (1995); Morris N. Liebman Field Award, Institute of Electrical and Electronics Engineers (1992); Outstanding Paper Award, American Society of Metals (1985); Industrial Research IR-100 Award (1975, 1974) **Memberships:** National Academy of Inventors (2014); Fellow of World Innovation Foundation (2004); New York Academy of Sciences (1995); Organizer, Chairperson, Sputtering Topical Symposium, American Vacuum Society (1986); Program Committee Thin Film Division, American Vacuum Society (1983-1984); Board Directors, American Vacuum Society (1981-1982); Program Chairperson, Program Committee Thin Film Division, American Vacuum Society (1982, 1977); Steering Committee, American Vacuum Society (1973-1979); National Academy of Engineering; European Academy of Sciences; Life Fellow, Institute of Electrical and Electronics Engineers; **Marquis Who's Who Honors:** Albert Nelson Marquis Lifetime Achievement Award; Marquis Who's Who Top Professional **To what do you attribute your success:** Dr. Cuomo credits his success on his parents, who imbued him with a focus on education. Likewise, he is glad for the influence of his many mentors and colleagues. **Why did you become involved in your profession or industry:** Dr. Jerome became interested in his profession while attending secondary school and college. He eventually specialized in chemistry, physics and mathematics, and built a chemistry laboratory in his home while in college. He subsequently worked for IBM for three decades, during which time he was exposed to the highest level of science and technology, which is the foundation for his career. **Avocations:** Constitutional research **Political Affiliations:** Conservative **Religion:** Roman Catholic

Lizbeth Jane Curme Stevens, PhD, CCC-SLP

Title: Speech-Language Pathologist, Special Education Educator, Researcher **Industry:** Education/Educational Services **Company Name:** Eastern Michigan University **Date of Birth:** 10/31/1949 **Place of Birth:** Angola **State/Country of Origin:** IN/USA **Parents:** Gilbert Emmett Curme; Billie Jean Bassett **Marital Status:** Married **Spouse Name:** John Alden Stevens (2/11/1947) **Children:** Kimberly Jean Steiner; Joshua Alexander; Miranda Christine **Education:** PhD, Wayne State University, Detroit, MI (1992); MS, University of Michigan, Ann Arbor, MI (1976); BA, University of Michigan, Ann Arbor, MI (1974) **Certifications:** Michigan 30-Hour Continuing Teaching Certificate in Speech and Language Impairment, K-12, Psychology (1979); Certified, Clinical Competence in Speech-Language Pathology, American Speech-Language-Hearing Association (1977) **Career:** Fellow, American Speech-Language-Hearing Foundation (2016-Present); Professor Emerita, College of Education, Eastern Michigan University, Ypsilanti, MI (2019); Professor, Department of Special Education, College of Education, Eastern Michigan University, Ypsilanti, MI (1998-2019); Fellow, American Speech-Language-Hearing Association (2007); Speech-Language Pathologist, Daly's Speech & Language Center, Farmington, MI (2002); Speech-Language Pathologist, Warren Woods Public Schools, Warren, MI (1978-1998); Speech-Language Pathologist, Northville Public Schools, Northville, MI (1976-1978) **Career Related:** Site Visitor, Council on Academic Accreditation, Audiology, Speech-Language Pathology (2011-Present); Adjunct Instructor, Wayne State University, Detroit, MI (1997-1998); Adjunct Instructor, Marygrove College, Detroit, MI (1990-1995) **Civic:** University Giving Ambassador, American Speech-Language-Hearing Foundation (2016-Present); Vice-Chair, Michigan Board of Speech-Language Pathology (2012); Appointment to Michigan Board of Speech-Language Pathology (2009-2012); President, Council of State Association Presidents (CSAP) (2008); President, Board of Directors, Michigan Speech-Language-Hearing Foundation (2006-2007) **Creative Works:** Contributor, Articles, Issues in Augmentative & Alternative Communication (2012); Contributor, Articles, ASHA Perspectives on Issues in Higher Education (2002, 2009); Contributor, Articles, Journal of Speech, Language, and Hearing Research (1954); Author, Book Chapters **Awards:** Awards for Continuing Education, American Speech-Language-Hearing Association (1983-2020); Distinguished Woman in Higher Education Leadership, Eastern Michigan University (2019); Dale Rice Award for Academic Innovation in AS-L and Community Engagement, Eastern Michigan University (2011); Honors, Michigan Speech-Language Hearing Association (2008); Delta Kappa Gamma (2006); Clara B. Stoddard Award, Wayne State University, Detroit, MI (1987); James B. Angell Scholar, University of Michigan, (1975); Kothe-Hildner Prize (German), University of Michigan (1967) **Memberships:** Advisory Council, American Speech-Language-Hearing Association (2008); President, Michigan Speech-Language-Hearing Association (2006); ASHA State Education Advocacy Leaders (SEALs), American Speech-Language-Hearing Association (2000-2004); Vice-President for Public Schools, Michigan Speech-Language-Hearing Association (2000-2003); Legislative Councilor, American Speech-Language-Hearing Association (1995-2000) **Marquis Who's Who Honors:** Albert Nelson Marquis Lifetime Achievement Award **Why did you become involved in your profession or industry:** Growing up, Dr. Stevens had a cousin with Down syndrome. She always brought gifts for her when she visited and her cousin always loved them. Ever since then, she has wanted to help people who have challenges with communication. **Avocations:** Cooking; Gardening; Piano; Reading; Travel **Political Affiliations:** Democrat **Religion:** Methodist

Peter William Curreri, MD

Title: Health Facility Administrator (Retired) **Industry:** Medicine & Health Care **Company Name:** Strategem of Alabama Inc. **Date of Birth:** 09/02/1936 **Place of Birth:** Milwaukee **State/Country of Origin:** WI/USA **Parents:** Anthony Rudolph Curreri; Dorothea Christiana (Heubsch) Curreri **Marital Status:** Single **Spouse Name:** Patricia Ann Egry (08/14/1958, Divorced 1975) **Children:** Charles Anthony; James Bradley; Regina Dawn **Education:** Resident, Surgery, Hospital of the University of Pennsylvania (1963-1968); Intern, Hospital of the University of Pennsylvania (1962-1963); MD, University of Pennsylvania (1962); BA, Swarthmore College (1958) **Certifications:** Certified Health Facility Administrator (Retired) **Career:** Health Facility Administrator (Retired), Chairman, Strategem of Alabama, Inc. (1988-Present); Professor, College of Medicine, USA Health,University of South Alabama (1981-1988); Chairman, Surgery, USA Health, College of Medicine, University of South Alabama (1981-1988); Professor of Surgery, Weill Cornell Medical College, Cornell University (1977-1981); Associate Professor of Surgery, University of Washington School of Medicine (1974-1977); Assistant Professor of Surgery, University of Texas Southwestern Medical Center (1971-1974) **Career Related:** Member, Medicare Payment Advisory Commission (MedPAC) (1997-1999); Commissioner, Physician Payment Review Commission (PPRC) (1988-1997); Chairman, Surgery, Anesthesiology and Trauma Study Section, National Institutes of Health (NIH) (1986-1988); Member, Surgery, Anesthesiology and Trauma Study Section, National Institutes of Health (NIH) (1980-1984) **Military Service:** Lieutenant Colonel, U.S. Army (1968-1971) **Creative Works:** Contributor, Articles, Professional Journals **Awards:** Curtis P. Artz Award, American Trauma Society (1989); Research Career Development Award, National Institutes Of Health (NIH) (1972); Meritorious Service Medal **Memberships:** President, American Association for the Surgery of Trauma (1989-1990); President, The Halsted Society (1988-1989); Secretary, Board of Governors, American College of Surgeons (1987-1989); American Burn Association (1983-1984); President, Society of University Surgeons (SUS) (1980-1981); Recorder, Association for Academic Surgery (AAS) (1972-1974) **Marquis Who's Who Honors:** Albert Nelson Marquis Lifetime Achievement Award; Marquis Who's Who Top Professional **Why did you become involved in your profession or industry:** Dr. Curreri became involved in his profession because he was stimulated by his father, who was a surgeon and a professor at the University of Wisconsin. He always admired his work and eventually realized he wanted to follow in his footsteps as he went through medical school. While in college, Dr. Curreri initially didn't know what he wanted to do. As he went through his education, he became interested in science and knew he wanted to pursue some kind of scientific career. He went to medical school and decided surgery was right for him—from there, it was a natural progression. **Avocations:** Playing golf; Walking **Thoughts on Life:** Dr. Curreri's personal definition of success is admiration from colleagues and friends around the country as well as satisfaction with one's career.

Thomas Arthur Currey, MD

Title: Ophthalmologist (Retired) **Industry:** Medicine & Health Care **Company Name:** Ophthalmologist Retired Eye Specialists Assoc. PC **Date of Birth:** 07/09/1933 **Place of Birth:** Itawamba County **State/Country of Origin:** MS/USA **Parents:** Charles Edward Currey; Anna L. (Williams) Currey **Marital Status:** Married **Spouse Name:** Carol Ann Clabough (11/07/1959) **Children:** Thomas A. Junior; C. Russell **Education:** Resident in Ophthalmology, University of Tennessee, Memphis (1962-1965); Basic Medical Skills, John A. Murphy Clinic (1959-1962); Internship, John Gaston Hospital, University of Tennessee, Memphis (1958-1959); MD, University of Tennessee (1958); BS in Pre-medicine, University of Mississippi (1955) **Certifications:** Diplomate, American Board of Ophthalmology **Career:** Retired Ophthalmologist, Eye Specialists Assoc. PC (2010); President, Medical Staff, St. Francis Hospital (1985-1986); President, Medical Staff, St. Joseph's Hospital, Tennessee (1970-1971); Private Practice, Memphis, TN (1965-2010); Ophthalmologist, St. Joseph Hospital (1965-1970) **Career Related:** Associate Instructor, Family Practice, Ophthalmology Department (1990-Present); Assistant Clinical Instructor, Ophthalmology, University of Tennessee (1965-Present) **Creative Works:** Author, Paper, American Journal of Ophthalmology **Memberships:** Vice President, Tennessee Medical Association (1987); President, Tennessee Academy Ophthalmology (1975); Fellow, American College of Surgeons; Vice President, Secretary, Head of Business Bureau, Treasurer, Memphis & Shelby County Medical Society **Marquis Who's Who Honors:** Albert Nelson Marquis Lifetime Achievement Award; Marquis Who's Who Top Professional **Why did you become involved in your profession or industry:** In the late 1950s, Dr. Currey interned at John Gaston Hospital in Memphis and did a month in ophthalmology among the other fields. He found that he liked it immensely, seeing how happy and satisfied all the staff there was, and appreciating how interesting the work was. When he was growing up the nearest ophthalmologist was about 100 miles away and any one with eye problems would have to travel 100 miles to get to the ophthalmologist. His mother would carry them once and twice a year to see the doctor and it would take all day. He saw a need for an ophthalmologist in the area where he lived so that motivated him to pursue his field. He was 10 years old when he was inspired to do so. **Avocations:** Photography; Travel; Sports **Religion:** Christian

David Philip Curtis

Title: Artist, Educator **Industry:** Fine Art **Date of Birth:** 04/24/1950 **Place of Birth:** Brookline **State/Country of Origin:** MA/USA **Parents:** Roger William Curtis; Winifred Joan (Fountain) Curtis **Marital Status:** Married **Spouse Name:** Judith Anne Revell (12/27/1986) **Children:** Noah Gordon; Samuel Richmond **Education:** Coursework, R. H. Ives Gammell (1968-1972); Coursework, Vesper George School of Art (1968); Coursework, Boston Museum School (1968); Coursework, Robert Douglas Hunter **Career:** Sight & Insight Workshops, Lorwen C. Nagle PhD (2018-Present); Art Instructor, Curtis Plein Air, Gloucester, MA (1992-Present); Art Instructor, North Yorkshire County Council, Harrogate, England (1991-1992); Gallery Manager, The Guild of Boston Artists (1986-1991); Proprietor, Wind 'N' Water Art Gallery, Gloucester, MA (1972-1974) **Military Service:** National Guard (1970-1976) **Creative Works:** Author, "The Collected Letters of David P. Curtis" (2019); Author, "Field Notes: A Revised Guide to Oil Painting Outdoors" (2019); Author, "Highlights & Accents: En Plein Air" (2000-2019); Sight & Insight Podcast; Author, "Field Notes: A Practical Guide to Oil Painting Outdoors" (1999-2018); Exhibition, Francesca Anderson Gallery, Boston, MA (1988, 1987); Ruthven Gallery, Lancaster, OH (1988); Exhibition, St. Botolph Club, Boston, MA (1987); Exhibition, Hammer Galleries, New York, NY (1986); National Trust, Brimham Rocks, North Yorkshire, England; Workshop Instructor, Rockport Art Association & Museum, "Copying the Masters" **Awards:** Arline W. Manning Memorial Award, North Shore Arts Association (2016); Helen Van Wyk Memorial Medal (2016); Charles Movalli Memorial Award, Rockport Art Association & Museum (2016); North Shore Arts Association Award (2013); Ruth Anderson Memorial Award, North Shore Arts Association (2011); R. H. Ives Gammell Award, The Guild of Boston Artists (2011); Genevieve Wilhelm Memorial Award (2010); Lydia & Chester Roberts Award (2010); Rockport Art Association; Virginia Karl Memorial Award (2008); Frank S. Raphael Award (1993); Guild of Boston Artists Award (1993); Garie and Kenneth Perry Award (1993); Roger W. Clark Popular Award (1993); Beverly DeMont Memorial Award (1991); People's Choice Award, Manchester Arts Gala (1990); Gordon Grant Award (1990); Robb Sagendorph Memorial Award (1990); Copley Artist Award (1990); Copley Master Award (1990); Best in Show Award, Copley Society of Boston (1988); Ruth L. Anderson Memorial Award (1986); Emile Gruppe Memorial Award (1986); Meriden Women's Club Award (1986); American Artists Professional League Award (1985); A. T. Hibbard Memorial Award (1985); Annie I. McCarthy Memorial Award (1984, 1882); American Artists Professional League Award (1983); Best in Oil Award, Annisquam Art Association (1983); First Prize, Arts and Crafts Association of Meriden (1983, 1982); Maurice Goldberg Memorial Award (1981); New Member Award, Rockport Art Association (1979); A. T. Hibbard Memorial Award (1976); President Award, American Artists Professional League (1975); Ruth Nettleton Memorial Award (1974); Lazare Barth Memorial Award (1972) **Memberships:** Guild of Boston Artists (1993-Present); Chairman, Arts and Exhibitions Committee (1985); North Shore Arts Association, Gloucester, MA; Rockport Art Association & Museum, Rockport, MA **Marquis Who's Who Honors:** Albert Nelson Marquis Lifetime Achievement Award **To what do you attribute your success:** Mr. Curtis has always taken an open-minded approach to the arts. An artist should always be willing to learn more, especially from the older masters in the field. He attributes his success to this mindset. **Why did you become involved in your profession or industry:** Mr. Curtis was brought up in an artistic family, so painting and teaching seemed to be a logical and satisfying way of life. The arts are an important part of the culture and the emotional well-being of society, particularly in times of trial. This is why Mr. Curtis has remained involved in his field. **Avocations:** Reading; Art history **Religion:** Episcopalian

Denise Ann Da Moude, MA

Title: Passport Clerk (Retired) **Industry:** Government Administration/Government Relations/Government Services **Date of Birth:** 10/27/1953 **Place of Birth:** West Point **State/Country of Origin:** NE/USA **Parents:** Dean Welch; Ella Marie (Knobel) Da Moude **Marital Status:** Single **Education:** Master of Arts in Community Mental Health, Regent University (1996); Bachelor of Science in Education, Chadron State College (1976) **Certifications:** Certified, Critical Incident Stress Management (2003); EMT Certification, Emergency Medical Technician (1982); Certified Teacher, Nebraska and South Dakota **Career:** Passport Clerk, United States Postal Service, Portsmouth, VA (2003-2010); City Carrier, United States Postal Service, Portsmouth, VA (1993-2003); Clerk, United States Postal Service, Chadron, NB (1983-1992); City Carrier, United States Postal Service, Chadron, NB (1981-1983); Dorm Supervisor and Counselor, United States Forest Service, Chadron, NB (1980-1981); Teacher, Physical Education and Health, Coach, Pine Ridge Middle School, South Dakota (1977-1979) **Career Related:** Women's Program Committee United States Postal Service, North Platte, NB (1986-1990); Mental Health Counselor Facilitator for Boundaries, Divorce Care and Sexual Brokeness Groups **Civic:** Trustee, Kempsville Presbyterian Church (2019-Present); Project Lifesaver (2015-Present); Just Older Youth Ministry (2010-Present); Ordained Deacon, Kempsville Presbyterian Church (2014-2016); Clothing Closet, Chairman for Food Pantry, Kempsville Presbyterian Church (2004-2006); Chairman, Food Pantry, Kempsville Presbyterian Church (2001-2003); Ordained Deacon, Kempsville Presbyterian Church (2000-2006); Board of Directors, Guiding Star Council, Girl Scouts United States America, Ogallala, NB (1990-1992); Superintendent, Christian Education Committee, Chadron Community Church (1988-1991); Co-Chairman, Christian Education Committee, Chadron Community Church (1987-1988); Committee, Fellowship of Christian Adult Singles, West Nebraska (1986-1992); Singles Move (1985-1992); Active with College Students and Single Parent Households, Chadron Community College (1983-1992); Board of Directors, Guiding Star Council, Girl Scouts United States America, Ogallala, NB (1981-1983); Day Camp Director, Chadron Community College (1978); Senior Troop Leader, Chadron Council (1977-1979); International Missionary Work; Virginia Beach Volunteer Police Chaplain; Community Chorus, Chadron **Awards:** Girl Scout Appreciation Award (1990) **Memberships:** American Association of Christian Counselors (1996-Present); Chairmen of Trustees, Kempsville Presbyterian Church, KPC (2020); National Association of Female Executives (1996-2001); Christian Association for Psychological Studies (1994-2000); Board of Directors, Secretary, Natural Food Cooperative Chadron Northeast (1984-1986); Cardinal Key; Sigma Delta Nu; Girl Scouts of America **Marquis Who's Who Honors:** Albert Nelson Marquis Lifetime Achievement Award **Why did you become involved in your profession or industry:** While Ms. Da Moude began her career as a teacher, she eventually elected to change professions and joined the United States Forest Service, where she remained for a year, after which she entered the United States Postal Service. She drew inspiration from her brother, who is a police chief in Nebraska. **Avocations:** Gardening; Travel; Swimming; Reading; Walking **Political Affiliations:** Republican **Religion:** Protestant

Edward Dabrowski

Title: Television Engineering Technical Director **Industry:** Media & Entertainment **Company Name:** NBCUniversal, Chicago **Date of Birth:** 11/16/1957 **Place of Birth:** Chicago **State/Country of Origin:** IL/USA **Parents:** Edward J. Dabrowski; Justina J. (Grilc) Dabrowski **Marital Status:** Single **Education:** BS in Electrical Engineering, Illinois Institute of Technology, Chicago, IL (1979) **Career:** Technical Director of Engineering Development Group, NBCUniversal, Chicago, IL (1976-Present); Engineering-in-charge, "The Jenny Jones Show" (1995); Technical Director, Station WMAQ-TV, Chicago, IL (1983-1996); Engineer, Station WMAQ-TV, Chicago, IL (1976-1983) **Creative Works:** Technical Director, "Chicago Sisslin" (1993); Technical Director, "Fast Break to Glory: Dusable Panthers," WMAQ-TV (1988); Technical Director, "The Sixth Street Kids," NBC (1984) **Awards:** Emmy Award, Academy of Television Arts & Sciences (2003, 2000, 1999); Millennium Special Coverage Award, Technology Award, Chicago Marathon (2002); Emmy Nomination, Chicago Chapter, National Academy of Television Arts & Sciences (1998) **Memberships:** Recording Secretary of Lodge 449, President of Chicago District, Slovene National Benefit Society (2003-Present); Steward and Executive Board Member, Chicago Local 41, American Federation of Labor and Congress of Industrial Organizations (AFL-CIO) (1999-Present); Mobilization Coordinator, National Association of Broadcast Employees and Technicians (NABET-CWA), Chicago, IL (1994-1995); Steward, Chicago Chapter, National Association of Broadcast Employees and Technicians (NABET-CWA) (1981-1987); National Association of Broadcast Employees and Technicians (NABET-CWA); Broadcasting and Cable Television Workers Sector, of the Communications Workers of America; Lifetime Member, American Radio Relay League (ARRL); Chicago Suburban Radio Association; Charter Member, Museum of Broadcast Communications; American Fraternal Union; IEEE; Society of Broadcast Engineers, Inc.; National Academy of Television Arts & Sciences **Marquis Who's Who Honors:** Albert Nelson Marquis Lifetime Achievement Award; Marquis Who's Who Top Professional **Why did you become involved in your profession or industry:** Mr. Dabrowski got into his profession because he enjoyed playing with old radios as a child. He would take them apart and put them back together. **Avocations:** Amateur radio; Photography **Political Affiliations:** Democrat **Religion:** Roman Catholic

Per Fridtjof Dahl

Title: Physicist **Industry:** Sciences **Date of Birth:** 08/01/1932 **Place of Birth:** Washington **State/Country of Origin:** DC/USA **Parents:** Odd Dahl; Anna Augusta (Mathiesen) Dahl **Marital Status:** Married **Spouse Name:** Eleanor Carman (10/15/1966) **Children:** Erik Johan; Thomas **Education:** Doctor of Philosophy, University of Wisconsin (1960); Master of Science, University of Wisconsin (1957); Bachelor of Science, University of Wisconsin (1956) **Career:** With, Department of Energy, Routhersburg, MD (1994-1986); Physicist, Superconducting Super Collider Laboratory, Dallas, TX (1989-1994); Physicist, Brookhaven National Laboratory, Upton, NY (1970-1989); Associate Physicist, Brookhaven National Laboratory, Upton, NY (1965-1970); Assistant Physicist, Brookhaven National Laboratory, Upton, NY (1963-1965); Project Scientist, Air Force Weapons Laboratory, Albuquerque, AZ (1962-1963); Research Grantee Ford Foundation, Niels Bohr Institute, Copenhagen, Denmark (1960-1962) **Career Related:** Superconducting Super Collider Central Design Group, Berkeley, CA (1986-1989); Visiting Scientist, National Laboratory for High Energy Physics, Tsuituba, Japan (1974) **Military Service:** With U.S. Army (1949-1952) **Memberships:** American Association for the Advancement of Science; American Physical Society; History of Science Society **Marquis Who's Who Honors:** Albert Nelson Marquis Lifetime Achievement Award

David J. Dahlberg

Title: Forestry Technician (Prevention) **Industry:** Government Administration/Government Relations/Government Services **Company Name:** Los Padres National Forest **Parents:** James "Bo" Dahlberg Jr.; Diane Sleeter **Marital Status:** Fiance **Spouse Name:** Lauren W. Flatley (Fiance) **Children:** Owen J. Dahlberg **Education:** AS in Fire Technology, Columbia Junior College, California (2009) **Certifications:** Certified EMT; California State Firefighter I; NREMT-B; CPR, AED and Basic First Aid; Fire Control III Structural Fire Fighting; Auto Extrication; Swift Water Awareness; WPGA Propane Emergencies; Driver Operator 1A & 1B; Commercial Driver License; Confined Space Rescue Awareness; Hazardous Materials Awareness; Hazardous Materials Operations; Low Angle Rope Rescue; Rappelling and Tower Rescue; Wildland Firefighter Specialist; PEPP; Forest Service Basic 32; Fire Protection Officer; EVOT/CEVO; SUBE; Numerous Others **Career:** Forestry Technician, Prevention, Forest Protection Officer, Patrol Officer, Fire Technician, U.S. Forest Service (2014-Present); Apprentice to Senior Firefighter, Fire Technician, U.S. Forest Service (2011-2014); Assistant Forest Protection Officer, Fire Technician, U.S. Forest Service (2008-2010); Intern Firefighter, City of Sonora Fire Department (2007-2008); Forestry Technician, U.S. Forest Service (2004-2006) **To what do you attribute your success:** Mr. Dahlberg attributes his success to his personality, his desire and genuine enjoyment helping others, even if it's one person at a time. **Why did you become involved in your profession or industry:** In high school, Mr. Dahlberg had an uncle that worked for the fire department and he had the opportunity to go on a ride along with him. He got a firsthand look at what firefighters do on a daily basis, and he was immediately hooked. Helping people and making the world a better place is where he felt he fit in the best. In addition, before his fire fighting days he was a lifeguard so the public service kind of attracted him. It felt like his calling even as a lifeguard.

Elaine Damschen

Title: President **Industry:** Utilities **Company Name:** Mainstream Electric Heating Cooling & Plumbing **Date of Birth:** 08/14/1969 **Place of Birth:** Spokane **State/Country of Origin:** WA/USA **Parents:** Jack Heston; Ton (Nguyen) Heston **Marital Status:** Married **Spouse Name:** Todd **Children:** Hunter; Rhett; Emily **Education:** Executive Master of Business Administration, Boise State University, Boise, ID (2011); Bachelor of Arts in Elementary Education, Boise State University, Boise, ID (1992) **Career:** President, Co-Owner, Mainstream Electric Heating Cooling & Plumbing, Spokane Valley, WA (2000-Present); Teller, Bank of America, Idaho (1999-2002); Teacher of Sixth Grade, Emmett Middle School, Emmett, ID (1992-1999) **Civic:** Board of Directors, Nexstar Network (2017-Present); Board Member, Nexstar Network (2016-Present); Blazen Divaz (2015-Present); Board Member, Better Business Bureau Northwest and Pacific (2014-Present); Host, Annual Golf Tournament, Troops to Trades (2019, 2018); Marketing and Dance Troupe, Cherry Blossom Parade (2017); Representative of Idaho, Pearl Harbor Parade (2016); Hollywood Christmas Parade (2015); Red Hot Mamas (2014); Leadership Team and Dance Troop, Macy's Thanksgiving Day Parade (2014); Board Member, Bookkeeper, Kids Helping Kids Fix Broken Hearts (2010-2018); President Bush's First Inaugural Parade (2001); Board of Directors, Mainstream Electric, Heating, Cooling, & Plumbing **Awards:** Named, Number 429 of 1000 Financial Times The Americas' Fastest Growing Companies (2020); Named, Number 3,680 of the 5,000 Fastest-Growing Companies Inc. Magazine (2019); Named, Number 3,937 of the 5,000 Fastest-Growing Companies Inc. Magazine (2018); Featured, Women in Business Leadership, Spokane Coeur D'alene Magazine (2018) **Marquis Who's Who Honors:** Albert Nelson Marquis Lifetime Achievement Award **To what do you attribute your success:** Ms. Damschen achieved success through small, incremental actions and decisions, as well as faith in that her decisions would lead her closer to her vision. **Why did you become involved in your profession or industry:** Ms. Damschen entered her profession because her husband is an electrician, and when he started the business, he needed help on the business side, and it was a natural, organic process for her from that point onward. **Avocations:** Family time at her cabin on the St. Joe River in the mountains of Northern Idaho; Traveling; Outreach

Arlie V. Daniel, PhD

Title: Professor Emeritus **Industry:** Education/Educational Services **Company Name:** East Central University **Date of Birth:** 05/15/1943 **Place of Birth:** Spencer **State/Country of Origin:** IA/USA **Parents:** Arlie Verl Daniel; Eleanor Marie (Grover) Daniel **Children:** Lam Dinh **Education:** PhD, University of Nebraska (1981); MA, University of Iowa (1978); BA, Morningside College (1965); AA, Iowa Lakes Community College (1963) **Career:** Professor Emeritus, East Central University (2010-Present); Linscheid Distinguished Professor, East Central University, Ada, OK (2006-2010); Director, Speech Education, East Central University, Ada, OK (1981-2010); High School Teacher, Clinton Public Schools (1971-1978); High School Teacher, Missouri Valley Public Schools (1965-1968) **Civic:** Rotary; Visitor, Assisted Living Facilities **Military Service:** 1st Lieutenant, U.S. Army (1968-1971) **Creative Works:** Contributing Author, "Creating Competent Communicators: Activities for Teaching, Speaking, Listening and Media Literacy in the K-12 Classroom" (2003); Co-Author, Chapter, "Basic Communication Course Annual" (1994); Contributor, Chapter, "Teaching and Directing the Basic Communication Course" (1993); Editor, "Activities Integrating Oral Communication Skills for Students in Grades K-8" (1992); Co-Author, "Project Text for Public Speaking" (1991) **Awards:** Inductee, Hall of Fame, Central States Communications Association (2010); Linscheid Distinguished Teaching Professor (2006); Teaching Excellence Award, East Central University (1995) **Memberships:** Past District Governor, Rotary District 5770, Rotary International (2017-2018); Assistant District Governor, Rotary International (2013-2015); Vice President, Ada Rotary Club (2004-2005); Rotary Chair, Rotary International (2003-2013); President, Ada Rotary Club (2003-2004); President, Central States Communications Association (1999-2000); Vice President, Central States Communication Association (1997-1998); Executive Director, Central States Communications Association (1994-1997); President, Oklahoma Speech Theatre Communications Association (1986-1987); American Association of University Professors; Association of Teacher Educators; International Communications Association; Oklahoma Speech Theatre Communications Association; Central States Communications Association; National Communications Association; Rotary International; Pi Kappa Delta **Marquis Who's Who Honors:** Albert Nelson Marquis Lifetime Achievement Award **To what do you attribute your success:** Mr. Daniel attributes his success to hard work and always staying true to his word. **Why did you become involved in your profession or industry:** Mr. Daniel became involved in the communication field because he took speech classes as a child. Initially, Mr. Daniel protested his guidance counselor's insistence that he take the class, but his parents required him to go through with it. The class ended up changing his life, and now Mr. Daniel does so much more than just his job. He has taken on leadership roles and participated in a number of communication associations.Mr. Daniel, being the jack of all trades that he is, doesn't just work in communications. He also made wine for several years, which was a fun hobby. **Avocations:** Golf; Bowling; Winemaking **Political Affiliations:** Democrat **Religion:** Methodist

James R. "Jim" Daniel

Title: Vice Chairman **Industry:** Financial Services **Company Name:** BancFirst Corporation **Date of Birth:** 01/05/1940 **Place of Birth:** Oklahoma City **State/Country of Origin:** OK/USA **Parents:** Reverend John T. Daniel (Deceased); Winifred (Banta) Daniel (Deceased) **Marital Status:** Married **Spouse Name:** Lajuana Gail Jones (07/03/1965) **Education:** BBA in Finance and Economics, Baylor University, Waco, TX (1962); Diploma, Southwestern Graduate School of Banking, Southern Methodist University, Dallas, TX; Diploma, Northwest Classen High School, Oklahoma City, OK **Career:** From Assistant Vice President to President, Chief Executive Officer, Friendly Bank of Oklahoma City (1964-1972); Management Trainee, Central National Bank, Oklahoma City, OK (1962-1964); Chief Executive Officer, Friendly Bank of Oklahoma City; Chairman, Chief Executive Officer, Bank One Corporation, Oklahoma; Vice Chairman, BancFirst Corporation, Oklahoma **Career Related:** Director of Executive Committee, Friendly Bank (1972-Present); Director of Executive Committee, Central Bank, Oklahoma City, OK (1970-Present); Director, Secretary, Baptist Medical Center, Oklahoma City, OK (1993); Director, Consumer Bankers Association (1993); Chairman, Consumer Bankers Association (1991); Chairman, Baptist Medical Center, Oklahoma City, OK (1988-1990); Chairman, President, Chief Executive Officer, Bank One, Oklahoma City, OK; Board of Directors, Oklahoma Retailers Foundation **Civic:** Past Chairman, Integris Health of Oklahoma; Member, Integris Health Physicians' Board; Past Officer, Member, Executive Committee, Southern Baptist Convention, Nashville, TN; Treasurer, Director, Research Institute for Economic Development; Lifetime Director, South Oklahoma City Chamber of Commerce; Lifetime Director, Southwest Homebuilders Association; Former Board Member, Past Chairman, The Foundation for Oklahoma City Public Schools Foundation; Business Boosters Tip Club; Past Chairman, Audit Committee, Oklahoma City Community Foundation; Former Member, Oklahoma State Pension Board; Former President, Member, Economic Club of Oklahoma; Past President, Baylor Lettermen's Association; Old Main Society, Baylor University; Board Member, Treasurer, Fellowship of Christian Athletes of Oklahoma (Now Oklahoma FCA); Men's Dinner Club; Oklahoma Venture Forum; Oklahoma City Golf and Country Club; Member, Teacher, Singles Department, Quail Springs Baptist Church; Member, Past Chairman, Committee of One Hundred; Past Board Member, Francis Tuttle Foundation; Appointed, Professional Responsibility Tribunal for the State of Oklahoma; President, Baylor University Chamber of Commerce; Past President, Baylor Letterman's Association; Sunday School Teacher, Single Adults (12 Years); Member, First Southern Baptist Church of Del City, Oklahoma City, OK (31 Years); Past Chairman, Deacon, First Southern Baptist Church of Del City, Oklahoma City, OK **Awards:** Named, Distinguished Alumni, Baylor University (2013); Recognition, Oklahoma Bankers Association for 50-Years in Banking (2011); Listee, Wall of Fame, Oklahoma City Public Schools Foundation (2009); Eponym, Jim Daniel Day, Governor Frank Keating, Oklahoma (2001); Named, Man of the Year, Fellowship of Christian Athletes (Now Oklahoma FCA), Oklahoma (1974); Winner, State Championship for Baseball, Northwest Classen High School (1957); Anton H. Classen Award, Northwest Classen High School; Runner-Up, Outstanding Athlete Award; Named, Citizen of the Year, South Oklahoma City Chamber of Commerce; Circle of Excellence Award, Integris Healthcare System; Inductee, Letterman's Wall of Honor; Inductee, Alumni Wall of Fame **Memberships:** Past Director, Oklahoma City Chamber of Commerce; Former Director, Southern Baptist Convention Foundation, Nashville, TN; Past President, Economic Club of Oklahoma; Past Director, Petroleum Club of Oklahoma City; Past President, Rotary Club 29, Oklahoma City; Past President, Rotary Foundation of Oklahoma City; Past Chairman, Consumer Bankers Association, Washington, DC; Former Board of Directors, Baylor Alumni Council; Past Chairman, Hillcrest Health Center; Former Commissioner, Oklahoma City Housing Authority; Previous Chairman, Oklahoma City Housing Authority; Past Member, Appointee, State of Oklahoma Futures Committee; Former Board Member, United Way; Former Board Member, Salvation Army; Former Trustee, Oklahoma City Community College **Marquis Who's Who Honors:** Albert Nelson Marquis Lifetime Achievement Award **Why did you become involved in your profession or industry:** Mr. Daniel became involved in his profession because his father was a Baptist minister and his mother was the daughter of a banker who was one of the discoverers of the purple creek mine. He started working at the bank after he graduated from high school and would work there in the summer and Christmas vacation and had several jobs when he got out of high school. Mr. James decided to go back to the bank after a couple of years and, as it turned out, they wanted him to stay. They opened a new bank and, at age 32, they made him the youngest bank president in Oklahoma and that was because he had five outstanding mentors.

Hal Daub

Title: Senior Counsel **Industry:** Law and Legal Services **Company Name:** Husch Blackwell LLP **Parents:** Harold C. Daub **Spouse Name:** Mary Mernin **Children:** Three Children **Education:** JD, College of Law, University of Nebraska-Lincoln (1966); BS, Washington University in St. Louis (1963) **Career:** Of Senior Counsel, Husch Blackwell LLP (2001-Present); Mayor; Congressman **Career Related:** Chairman, Presidentially Appointed, Social Security Advisory Board; Senate, Social Security Advisory Board; Elected Regent, University of Nebraska-Lincoln; Mentor, Rotary Club of Omaha, ClubRunner; Mentor, Optimist International **Civic:** Affiliate, Capitol Campaign, Madonna School; Affiliate, Various Charitable Events **Creative Works:** Contributor, Articles **Awards:** Hope is Help Award, Autism Action Partnership (2017); Distinguished Eagle Scout, Mid-America Council, Boy Scouts of America; Silver Beaver Awards in Scouting, Mid-America Council, Boy Scouts of America; Citizen of the Year, Mid-America Council, Boy Scouts of America; Inductee, Omaha Chamber of Commerce Business Hall of Fame; Humanitarian Award, Grand Lodge AF & AM of Nebraska; Toastmasters International; Named, 33rd Degree Mason **Memberships:** Chairman, "Be a Hero" Luncheon, Salvation Army; Chairman, Tree of Lights, Salvation Army; Board Member, Boy Scouts, Mid-America Council; Board Member, Salvation Army; Board Member, Autism Actions Partnership; Board Member, Wounded Warrior Family Support and Fatherhood Family Initiative; VFW Post 2503; Post 112, American Legion; "40 & 8," The American Legion; Reserve Officers Association of the United States **Marquis Who's Who Honors:** Albert Nelson Marquis Lifetime Achievement Award **To what do you attribute your success:** Mr. Daub attributes his success to learning from his family about hard work and saving money. His family really didn't have much money while he was growing up. His father was a blacksmith with great work ethic, and he saved his money and eventually became a millionaire. **Why did you become involved in your profession or industry:** Mr. Daub became involved in his profession when he was a freshman in high school, during which he absolutely loved his minister and wanted to be a Presbyterian minister. The minister was charismatic and somewhat evangelical. He enjoyed speech, debate and drama, and loved his church youth group activities. By the time he was a sophomore, because he loved his ROTC, with all the maneuvers in the woods after school, he decided that he wanted to go to West Point, New York. By the time he was a junior in high school, he was watching "Perry Mason," and was fascinated by how he and Della Street worked together, Mason's persuasive ideas, and how he worked with a judge and jury, which led him to decide that he wanted to be a lawyer. In addition, Mr. Daub had the ability to challenge and persuade; that is why he was able to become an attorney. However, he got into commercial after he got back from the military infantry in Korea. Thus, he did a lot of work there, but it was not what he enjoyed. In three years, he realized he liked the business side of the law. **Avocations:** Travel; Collecting U.S. stamps and coins; Piano **Political Affiliations:** Republican

Evelyne Monique Davidson, MD

Title: Internist; Principal Investigator **Industry:** Medicine & Health Care **Company Name:** Smoky Mountain Home Health & Hospice; New Phase Research and Development **Date of Birth:** 04/05/1961 **Place of Birth:** Knoxville **State/Country of Origin:** TN/USA **Parents:** Elvyn Verone Davidson; Esther J. (Johnson) Davidson **Education:** Resident in Internal Medicine, New Hanover Memorial Hospital (Now New Hanover Regional Medical Center), Wilmington, NC (1988-1990); Intern, New Hanover Memorial Hospital (Now New Hanover Regional Medical Center), Wilmington, NC (1987-1988); MD, East Tennessee State University Quillen College of Medicine (1987); BS in Biomedical Engineering, Vanderbilt University School of Engineering (1983) **Career:** Principal Investigator, New Phase Research and Development (2013-Present); Medical Director, Smoky Mountain Home Health & Hospice, Knoxville, TN (2011-Present); Retired, Private Practice (2009); Physician, Premier Medical Associates (1998-2009); Physician, Baptist Primary Care System (1994-1998); Private Practice, Knoxville, TN (1990-1994) **Career Related:** Co- author, "Bimodal Release Ondansetron Improves Stool Consistence and Symptomatology in Diarrhea-Predominant Irritable Bowel Syndrome: A Randomized, Double-Blind, Parallel-Group Trial," American Journal of Gastroenterology **Civic:** Tutor and Mentor, Elementary to High School Children, The Links, Incorporated **Memberships:** American College of Physicians; American Medical Association; National Medical Association; Tennessee Medical Association; Knoxville Academy of Medicine **Marquis Who's Who Honors:** Albert Nelson Marquis Lifetime Achievement Award **To what do you attribute your success:** Dr. Davidson attributes her success to perseverance, not letting barriers interfere with where she wants to go and who she wants to be. **Why did you become involved in your profession or industry:** Dr. Davidson's mother was a nurse and her father was a doctor. She had been exposed to the medical field for as long as she could remember. Dr. Davidson also received a job dealing with clinical drug trails from responding to an ad she came across in the newspaper. **Avocations:** Spending time with her family; Traveling; Reading; Shopping **Thoughts on Life:** Dr. Davidson tries to be a role model, especially for African American females, and to help them understand that no matter where you are from, it is possible to attain higher education and become a professional. Dr. Davidson also believes that "To whom much is given, much is expected." She tried her best to come back to the community she is from and give back to the people.

C. Dean Davis, JD

Title: Lawyer, Consultant (Retired) **Industry:** Law and Legal Services **Date of Birth:** 09/12/1932 **Place of Birth:** Abilene **State/Country of Origin:** TX/USA **Parents:** Emmett Dean Davis; Marye (Creswell) Davis **Marital Status:** Married **Spouse Name:** Mollie Veret (1958) **Children:** Addison Dean; Kevin Tucker **Education:** JD, University of Texas (1958); BA, Political Science, Economics, University of North Texas, With Honors (1953) **Career:** Senior, Managing Partner, Davis & Davis, Professional Corporation, Austin, TX (1961-Present); Assistant Attorney General, State of Texas, Austin, TX (1958-1961) **Career Related:** Director, Texas Junior Bar Conference (1964-1965); Co-Founder, First President, Texas Bar Health Law Section **Civic:** Adjunct Professor, Hospital Law, Trinity University, San Antonio, TX (1967-1990); Chairman, Hospital Law, Trinity University, San Antonio, TX (1988); University of North Texas Board of Regents (1967-1988); Chairman, Board of Regents, University of North Texas Health and Science System (1967-1988); Adjunct Professor of Pharmacy, Jurisprudence, University of Texas (1969-1975) **Military Service:** NATO Courier, U.S. Army, Germany (1954-1956) **Creative Works:** Author, Texas Legal and Consent Manual for Texas Hospitals (1967-1990); Articles, Professional Journals **Awards:** Award, Texas Hospital Association (1990); Distinguished Alumni Award, University of North Texas (1980); Outstanding Service Award, Texas Association of Child Care Facilities; Distinguished Service Award, Texas Pharmaceutical Association; Outstanding Achievement Award, Texas Association of Life Underwriters **Bar Admissions:** State of Texas (1958); 911 Texas Federal District Courts; Texas Supreme Court; Supreme Court of the United States **Marquis Who's Who Honors:** Albert Nelson Marquis Lifetime Achievement Award; Marquis Who's Who Top Professional **To what do you attribute your success:** Mr. Davis' uncle, Dudley Davis, was a great inspiration to him and encouraged him to pursue a career in law. The Attorney General of Texas, Will Wilson, was also an important mentor. Capt. Richards was another great mentor. **Why did you become involved in your profession or industry:** Mr. Davis' spent his childhood summers at his paternal grandmother's home in Center, Texas. His father's youngest brother, Dudley Davis, was the district attorney at that time. He spent a lot of those summers in his office and in the courtroom watching him, and he was very instrumental in helping and encouraging him in his career. **Avocations:** Cattle ranching; Travel **Political Affiliations:** Independent **Religion:** Episcopalian

Clive Jay Davis

Title: Chief Creative Officer **Industry:** Media & Entertainment **Company Name:** Sony Music Entertainment **Date of Birth:** 04/04/1932 **Place of Birth:** Brooklyn **State/Country of Origin:** NY/USA **Parents:** Herman Davis; Florence Davis **Marital Status:** Divorced **Spouse Name:** Janet Adelberg (1965, Divorced 1985); Helen Cohen (1956, Divorced 1965) **Children:** Fred; Lauren; Mitchell; Doug **Education:** Diploma, Harvard Law School (1956); Diploma in Political Science, New York University College of Arts & Science, Magna Cum Laude (1953) **Career:** Chief Creative Officer, Sony Music Entertainment (2018-Present); President, Chief Executive Officer, Chair, RCA Music Group (2002-2008); Founder, Chief Executive Officer, Chair, J Records (2000); Founder, Arista Records, Sony Music Entertainment (1975-2000); Former President, Columbia-CBS Group (1967-1973); Chief Executive Officer, Chair, BMG North America **Career Related:** Head, Music Operations, Columbia-CBS Group (1966-1967); Administrative Vice President and General Manager, Columbia Records Group (1965-1966); Assistant Counsel to General Counsel, CBS Records; With, Rosenman, Colin, Kaye, Petschek, and Freund **Civic:** Board of Advisers, Harvard Law School; Benefactor, New York University **Creative Works:** Author, "The Soundtrack of My Life" (2013); Author, "Clive: Inside the Record Business" (1975) **Awards:** Honoree, The New Jewish Home's Eight Over Eighty Gala (2018); Named One of 31 Icons of the LGBT History Month, Equality Forum (2015); Grammy Award for Best R&B Album, "Jennifer Hudson," The Recording Academy (2009); President's Merit Award, Grammy Awards, The Recording Academy (2009); Grammy Award for Best Pop Vocal Album, "Breakaway," The Recording Academy (2006); Grammy Award for Album of the Year, "Supernatural," The Recording Academy (2000); Grammy Award for Best Rock Album, "Supernatural," The Recording Academy (2000); Grammy Trustees Award, The Recording Academy (2000); Inductee, Rock and Roll Hall of Fame (2000) **Memberships:** The Phi Beta Kappa Society

Jack C. Davis, Esq.

Title: Lawyer **Industry:** Law and Legal Services **Company Name:** Loomis Law Firm **Marital Status:** Married **Spouse Name:** Sue **Education:** LLB, Harvard University (1964); BS in History, University of Wisconsin-Madison (1960) **Career:** Senior Partner, Lawyer, Loomis Law Firm (1966-Present); Lawyer, Kirkland & Ellis LLP, Chicago, IL **Civic:** President, Lansing Regional Chamber of Commerce; Chair, Regional Board, The Eli and Edythe Broad Art Museum; Board of Directors, H.O.P.E. Scholarship; Board of Directors, Lansing Promise; Founder, Former Trustee, Lansing Community College Foundation; Founder, Former Trustee, Okemos Education Foundation; Founder, Former Trustee, Opera Company of Mid-Michigan; Founder, Former Trustee, Legal Aid of Central Michigan; Boys and Girls Club **Creative Works:** Author, "The Purposive Approach to Interpretation of Sales Tax Statutes," Ohio State Law Journal (1966); Program Presenter, Ingham County Bar Association; Program Presenter, The Institute of Continuing Legal Education; Program Presenter, Various Business and Professional Groups on Tax Matters and Estate Planning **Awards:** Best Lawyers in America (2020); AV-Preeminent Rating, Martindale-Hubbell (2019); Lawyer of Distinction for Real Estate and Property Law (2019); Power Lawyer, Lawyers of Distinction, New York Times (2019); Top 10 Estate Planning Attorneys in Michigan, American Jurist Institute (2019); Premier Lawyer in Estate Planning and Probate, Premier Lawyers of America (2019); Real Estate and Property Law Award, Lawyers of Distinction (2019); One of Ten Best Estate Planning Attorneys, American Institute of Legal Counsel (2018, 2019); Top 10 Estate Planning Attorneys, Attorney and Practice Magazine (2018); Marquis Who's Who (2017-2018); Community Service Pioneer Award, Lansing Regional Chamber of Commerce (2017); Leading Lawyers (2015-2019); Leo A. Farhat Outstanding Attorney Award, Ingham County Bar Association (2014) **Memberships:** Delegation Sent to Other Former Eastern Bloc Countries (1990); Delegation Sent to Former USSR (1989); Delegation Sent to China (1987); Chair, Regional Art Museum; State Bar of Michigan; American Bar Association; Ingham County Bar Association; Fellow, Michigan State Bar Foundation; Chair, Executive Committee, Lansing Economic Area Partnership; Director, Former Chair, Boys & Girls Club of Lansing; Chair, Regional Blue Ribbon Panel on Retention, General Motors; Former Member, Chair, Board of Education, Lansing Public Schools; Lansing Mayor's Blue Ribbon Panel on Lansing Public Schools and the "Ready to Succeed" Initiative; Past Chair, Board of Directors, Impression Five Museum; Michigan Bar Association; Fellow, Michigan State Bar Foundation **Bar Admissions:** State Bar of Michigan **Marquis Who's Who Honors:** Albert Nelson Marquis Lifetime Achievement Award; Marquis Who's Who Top Professional **To what do you attribute your success:** Mr. Davis attributes his success to giving solid advice to his clients whether positive or negative. **Why did you become involved in your profession or industry:** Mr. Davis became involved in his profession because he did not want to get into any kind of internal politics that came from academia. After going into the ROTC, he entered the military and served for six months before returning and being admitted to Harvard Law. **Avocations:** Traveling

Paul Joseph Davis, MD

Title: Endocrinologist **Industry:** Medicine & Health Care **Company Name:** Albany Medical Center **Date of Birth:** 10/28/1937 **Place of Birth:** Chicago **State/Country of Origin:** IL/USA **Parents:** Paul Albert Davis; Maxine Lydia (Mason) Davis **Marital Status:** Married **Spouse Name:** Faith Ainsworth Baker (12/08/1962) Deceased **Children:** Matthew; John; Sarah **Education:** Resident in Medicine, Bronx Municipal Hospital Center (Now NYC Health + Hospitals/Jacobi, The City of New York) (1964-1967); Intern, Bronx Municipal Hospital Center (Now NYC Health + Hospitals/Jacobi, The City of New York) (1963-1964); MD, Harvard University, Cum Laude (1963); BA, Westminster College, Magna Cum Laude (1959) **Career:** Senior Associate Dean for Clinical Research, Albany Medical College, Albany Medical Center (1998-Present); Professor, Albany Medical College, Albany Medical Center (1990-1999); Chairman, Department of Medicine, Albany Medical College, Albany Medical Center (1990-1999); Chief of Medical Service, VA Western New York Healthcare System, U.S. Department of Veterans Affairs (1980-1990); Professor of Medicine, University at Buffalo (1975-1990); Head, Endocrinology Division, University at Buffalo (1975-1990); Head, Endocrinology Division, Baltimore City Hospitals (1970-1975); Senior Staff Associate, National Institutes of Health (1969-1970); Clinical Associate, National Institutes of Health, Bethesda, MD (1967-1969); Vice Chairman, Department of Medicine, School of Medicine, University at Buffalo **Career Related:** External Reviewer Panel, Chernobyl Tissue Bank, European Union (2010-Present); National Advisory Council, Health Sciences Center, West Virginia University (2007-Present); Ordway Signal Transduction, Inc. (2011); Director, Ordway Research Institute, Albany, NY (1999-2011); Merit Review Board of Endocrinology, American Board of Internal Medicine; Merit Review Board of Oncology, American Board of Internal Medicine; VA Board of Directors, American Board of Internal Medicine; National Advisory Council, Health Sciences Center, West Virginia University; Board of Directors, Hauptman Woodward Medical Research Institute, Buffalo, NY **Civic:** Trustee, Westminster College, Fulton, MO (2000-Present) **Creative Works:** Secretary Editor, "Current Opinion in Endocrinology, Diabetes, Obesity" (2004-Present); Editor-in-Chief, "Immunology, Endocrine and Metabolic Agents in Medicinal Chemistry" (2007-2011); Editorial Board Member, "Hormones Cancer" **Awards:** Distinguished Service Award, American Thyroid Association (2003) **Memberships:** President, American Thyroid Association (1997-1998); Governor, Upstate New York Region, American College of Physicians; President, New York Chapter, American College of Physicians; The Gerontological Society of America; American Federation for Medical Research; American Society for Biochemistry and Molecular Biology; Board of Directors, American Thyroid Association; Endocrine Society; Board of Science Counselors, National Institute on Aging, National Institutes of Health **Marquis Who's Who Honors:** Albert Nelson Marquis Lifetime Achievement Award; Marquis Who's Who Top Professional

Mark L. Davison, PhD

Title: John P. Yackel and American Guidance Service Professor of Educational Assessment and Measurement **Industry:** Education/Educational Services **Company Name:** University of Minnesota **Date of Birth:** 12/07/1947 **Place of Birth:** Manastee **State/Country of Origin:** MI/USA **Parents:** Rexford J. Davison; Helen L. (Plumb) Davison **Marital Status:** Married **Spouse Name:** Leslie J. Danuser (06/10/1978) **Children:** John M. Froiland; Andrew M. **Education:** PhD, University of Illinois at Urbana-Champaign (1974); MA, University of Illinois at Urbana-Champaign (1972); AB, Augustana College Illinois, Rock Island, IL (1970) **Career:** Program Coordinator, Quantitative Methods in Education, University of Minnesota (2012-Present); John P. Yackel & American Guidance Service Incorporated Professor of Educational Assessment and Measurement, University of Minnesota (2004-Present); Director, Minnesota Interdisciplinary Training Educational Research, University of Minnesota (2005-2012); Director, Office of Educational Accountability, University of Minnesota (1998-2005); Chair, Department of Educational Psychology, University of Minnesota (1990-1996) **Career Related:** Journal Editor, "Applied Psychological Measurement" (2007-2012) **Creative Works:** Author, "Multidimensional Scaling"; Contributor, Articles to Professional Journals **Awards:** Distinguished Teaching Award, University of Minnesota (2018); Grant, United States Department of Education (2005-2012); Fellowship, Minnesota Department of Education (1997-2005); Fellowship, United States Navy (1989); Fellowship, Spencer Foundation (1979-1982) **Memberships:** Chair, Committee on Psychological Testing and Assessment (1996-1997); President, Division Five, American Psychological Association (1995-1996); American Educational Research Association; Psychometric Society; National Council on Measurement in Education; Fellow, American Psychological Association **Marquis Who's Who Honors:** Albert Nelson Marquis Lifetime Achievement Award; Marquis Who's Who Top Professional **To what do you attribute your success:** Dr. Davison attributes his success from those who know him best and respect him most. **Why did you become involved in your profession or industry:** Dr. Davison became involved in his profession because as an undergraduate, he was hired by a professor doing work, using testing in college selection. After working with this professor for a while, Dr. Davison's interests in measuring academic talent began. He became convinced that identifying and preparing talent is critical to progress in society and the success of future generations. This is what led Dr. Davison to pursue education and assessment for the identification of talent. **Avocations:** Jogging; Swimming; Sailing; Reading historical biographies **Religion:** Christian

Judith Elizabeth Day, PhD

Title: Educator, Author, State Representative (Retired) **Industry:** Other **Date of Birth:** 12/26/1948 **Place of Birth:** Salem **State/Country of Origin:** MA/USA **Parents:** Esther Day; Robert Day **Marital Status:** Married **Spouse Name:** R. Laurence Miller Jr. **Education:** PhD in Education Curriculum, University of New Hampshire; MEd in Special Education, University of Southern Maine; BA in English, University of Southern Maine **Certifications:** Assessment Specialist **Career:** Member, Education Committee, Rockingham District 13, New Hampshire House of Representatives (2006-2010); Member, Student Support Services Office, University of New Hampshire (1988); Special Education Teacher, Hampton, NH (1978-1988); State Legislator **Career Related:** Member, Planning Board, Town of North Hampton (2002-2007); Student Supervisor, Wesleyan College; Member, Americans With Disabilities Act Office, University of New Hampshire **Civic:** Member, Board of Trustees, North Hampton Public Library and Cultural Center **Creative Works:** Author, "The Good Wizard's Castle" **Marquis Who's Who Honors:** Albert Nelson Marquis Lifetime Achievement Award; Marquis Who's Who Top Professional; Marquis Who's Who Humanitarian Award **Why did you become involved in your profession or industry:** Ms. Day became involved in her profession because her family valued education, which inspired her to pursue a career in the field. **Avocations:** Reading; Politics **Political Affiliations:** Democrat

Bertrand Lambert de Frondeville

Industry: Engineering **Date of Birth:** 09/18/1934 **Place of Birth:** Marseille **State/Country of Origin:** France **Parents:** Maurice Lambert de Frondeville; Anne-Marie (D'Alauzier) de Frondeville **Marital Status:** Married **Spouse Name:** Barbara de Frondeville (1960) **Children:** Tristan; Eric; Alexis **Education:** Postgraduate Studies, School of Business, University of Columbia (1978); MS in Nuclear Engineering, University of California Berkeley (1959); MS in Naval Architecture, ENSGM (1958); MS in Ecole Polytechnique (1955); Bachelor's Degree in Mathematics and Science, Lycee Chasseloup-Laubat (Now Le Quy Don High School) (1950) **Certifications:** Executive Management Program, Columbia Business School, Columbia University (1978) **Career:** Managing Director, BDF International Co. (1975-1992, 1997-Present); Vice President and Senior Engineer, Technology Services Group, Deutsche Bank A.G., New York, NY and Frankfurt, Germany (1992-1997); Vice President of Projects and Engineering, Burmah Oil Tankers Ltd. (1972-1975); Senior Staff Member, Arthur D. Little (1967-1972); President, American Technigaz, Inc. (1965-1967); Director, Metallurgical Research and Quality Assurance, Indret, France (1963-1965); Senior Engineer, French Naval Architect Corps, Indret, France (1959-1963) **Career Related:** Instructor of Ethics Seminars Columbia Business School, Columbia University (1990-Retired); Adjunct Professor of International Business, Pace University (1990-1992); Senior Advisor BNP, San Paolo Bank (1986-1992) **Civic:** Citizen Financial Advisory Committee, Rye, NY (1991-Present); Union of Concerned Scientists (1975-Present); Commander, French Naval Reserve (1975-Present); Founder, Instructor, Manchester Sailing Association (1967-Present); Citizen Advisory Committee to New York State Senators, Westchester, NY (1982); Committee Member, National Academy of Sciences (1976-1980) **Military Service:** French Naval Architecture Corps Reserves (1965); French Naval Architecture Corps (Genie Maritime) (1955-1965) **Creative Works:** Author, "Fighting for The World Bank Environmental Guidelines in an OECD Country" (1998); Author, "Managing Technical Risks of Advanced Power Projects" (1997); Author, "Advanced Gas Turbines, Technology Risk Management, Lenders Viewpoints" (1997); Presenter, Keynote Address on Risk Management in Financing Gasification Plants (1997); Reviewer, Commentator, "Financing Energy Projects in Emerging Economies" (1996); Author, "Financing Gasification Plants for Power" (IGCC) or Chemicals" (1995); Co-Author, "Safety Aspects of LNG in the Marine Environment; Reviewer, "Hazardous Materials Transportation Committee Report" (1985); Author, "The Canadian Arctic LNG Pilot Project: A Broad Technology Frontier" (1980); Author, "Reliability and Safety of LNG Shipping: Lessons from Experience" (1977); Author, "Some Highlights of Foreign Experience in Deep Water Port Development" (1975); Author, "Reflections on Port Planning in the Seventies, Milwaukee WI" (1973); Co-Author, "Editor, Foreign Deep Water Ports, Lessons for America" (1972); Author, "Bending Fatigue Properties of 304L Stainless Steel Sheet Metal at 20° and -196°C." (1967); Author, "Land Storage of LNG using the Technigaz Waffled Membrane developed for Shipboard Integrated Tanks." (1967); Author, "Contribution to the study of Electroslag Welding" (1962); Co-Author, "A Nuclear Reactor with Integrated Superheat" (1959) **Awards:** Certificate in Appreciation, U.S. Holocaust Memorial Museum (2018) **Memberships:** Environmental Section, New York Academy of Sciences; American Yacht Club **Marquis Who's Who Honors:** Albert Nelson Marquis Lifetime Achievement Award **Why did you become involved in your profession or industry:** Mr. de Frondeville became involved in his profession because he was a Navy brat and his father was a naval architecture commander. His father was in charge of the Casa Blanca Naval Base during World War II. His father was then sent to Vietnam and he followed him from 1948 to 1949.Mr. de Frondeville believed these experiences showed him the importance of representation in developing countries. He was then able to establish local relations that he still has contacts with today. At first, he refused to become a citizen of the U.S., but then he wanted to help the U.S. get out of Vietnam and he did just that. **Avocations:** Music; Backpacking; Wind surfing; Offshore sailing; Mountain and desert trekking; Horseback riding; Teaching Tai Chi **Political Affiliations:** Independent **Religion:** Catholic **Thoughts on Life:** Mr. de Frondeville did something rather unusual with liquefied natural gas. He had seven liquefied natural gas carriers at a cost of about $1 billion with the construction built in the United States. He also had under contract vessels placed in Japan and Indonesia. After 25 years, those vessels have been retired from five terminals in Japan and two terminals in Indonesia.

David John de Harter, MD

Title: Radiation Oncologist (Retired) **Industry:** Medicine & Health Care **Company Name:** Mid-Florida Radiation Oncology Associates **Date of Birth:** 04/12/1942 **Place of Birth:** Milwaukee **State/Country of Origin:** WI/USA **Parents:** George Herbert Harter; Marion Bertha née Kahl **Marital Status:** Widowed **Spouse Name:** Diane Leigh (Kuebler) de Harter **Children:** Renée; Andrew; Susannah Lee **Education:** Resident in Radiation Oncology, The University of Texas MD Anderson Cancer Center (1972-1975), Rotating Internship, U.S. Naval Hospital Bethesda (1968-1969); MD, School of Medicine and Public Health, University of Wisconsin (1964-1968) **Certifications:** License to Practice Medicine, State of Florida (1996); Certified in Therapeutic Radiology and Radiation Oncology, American Board of Radiology (1975) **Career:** Partner, Assistant Medical Director, Mid-Florida Radiation Oncology Associates (1999-2009); Head of Operations, Radiation Oncology, Treasure Coast Radiation Oncology, Port St. Lucie, FL (1996-2010); Cancer Center of Northern Arizona, Northern Arizona Health Care (1994-1996); Director of Radiation Oncology, Flagstaff Medical Center (1994-1996); Director of Radiation Oncology, CHI Health Immanuel (1978-1994); Director of Radiation Oncology, Bishop Clarkson Memorial Hospital, Omaha, NE (1977-1980); Attending Radiation Oncologist, St. Joseph, Wheaton Franciscan Healthcare (1976-1977); Director of Radiation Oncology, Columbia St. Mary's Hospital (1976-1977); Attending Radiation Oncologist, Carilion Roanoke Memorial Hospital (1975-1976); Attending Radiation Oncologist, LewisGale Medical Center (1975-1976) **Career Related:** Director, Panasiatic Corp., Seattle, WA (1988-Present); President, Harter Land and Lumber Company, Green County, VA (1986-Present); Consultant, W.L. Gore, Inc., Flagstaff, AZ (1994-1999); Clinical Lecturer, Department of Radiation Oncology, University of Arizona College of Medicine (1994-1998), Assistant Clinical Radiology Professor, University of Nebraska Medical Center, Omaha, NE (1978-1994) **Civic:** Member, Cancer Committee, St. Lucie Medical Center (1996-Present); Chair, Parks and Recreation Committee, Founding Chair, Art in Public Places Committee, and Trustee, Public Library (Omaha, 1984-1994); Board of Directors, and President, American Cancer Society, Nebraska Division, and Member, Research Committee, ACS Florida Division; Board of Trustees, Millicent Rogers Museum, Taos, NM (1988); Major Contributor, CHI Health Immanuel, Omaha, NE; Co-Founder, Carson Cancer Center, Norfolk, NE; St. Mary's Episcopal Church, Stuart, FL; Phoenix Fund, MD Anderson Cancer Center; The Harter Prize for Excellence in Clinical Training Research, MD Anderson Cancer Center; Gilbert H. Fletcher Memorial Distinguished Chair, MDACC, David J. and Diane L. de Harter/Alpha Omega Alpha Visiting Professorship; Jesuit Order; University of Florida School of Engineering **Military Service:** Staff General Medical Officer in Orthopedics, Charleston Naval Hospital, U.S. Navy, Charleston, SC (1970-1971); Assistant Chief Medical Officer, Naval Health Clinic Charleston, Charleston, SC (1969-1970); Staff Medical Officer, Atlantic Fleet, Destroyer Division 42, U.S. Navy, Charleston, SC; Lieutenant Commander, U.S. Navy **Creative Works:** Portrait, Figurative, Abstract Sculpture in Steel, Clay, Bronze, and Stone **Awards:** Middleton Fellow, School of Medicine and Public Health, University of Wisconsin (2012); Chancellor's Club, University of Nebraska (1985), First Prize for Research, The University of Texas MD Anderson Cancer Center and School of Medicine and Public Health (1974); Lewis E. and Edith Phillips Scholarship (1968); Evan S. and Marion Helfaer Scholarship (1967) **Memberships:** Piper's Landing Yacht & Country Club; Central Arizona Masonic Lodge **Marquis Who's Who Honors:** Albert Nelson Marquis Lifetime Achievement Award; Marquis Who's Who Top Professional **To what do you attribute your success:** He attributes his success to good fortune. **Why did you become involved in your profession or industry:** He pursued medicine after he became ill. **Avocations:** Sculpture **Political Affiliations:** Republican **Religion:** Episcopalian **Thoughts on Life:** Twenty-first century Americans swim in a sea of facts, and ride great ships of knowledge, but wisdom is as inaccessible as ever, lodged high in the mountains of the interior.

Christine Elizabeth De Zeeuw

Title: Electrical Engineer **Industry:** Engineering **Company Name:** SeaLandAire Technologies **Date of Birth:** 04/04/1994 **Place of Birth:** Ann Arbor **State/Country of Origin:** MI/USA **Parents:** Darren De Zeeuw; Susan De Zeeuw **Marital Status:** Single **Education:** BA, Calvin College, Grand Rapids, MI **Career:** Electrical Engineer, SeaLandAire Technologies (2016-2020) **Career Related:** Designer, Tester, Circuit Boards for Defense Applications for Marine/Research; Designer, Tester, Sonobuoys **Civic:** Church Member; Praise Team, Church; Singer, Church **Marquis Who's Who Honors:** Marquis Who's Who Top Professional **To what do you attribute your success:** Ms. De Zeeuw attributes her success to determination, wanting to get the work done and having the drive to do it without someone having to tell her. She also attributes it to her problem-solving and creative thinking skills, which have helped her work around and troubleshoot issues. She has had to think outside the zone many times throughout her career. **Why did you become involved in your profession or industry:** Ms. De Zeeuw became involved in her profession because of inspiration from her family. Her father is an aerospace engineer, her mother is a math teacher, and she has aunts and uncles who are also engineers, so she came from a long line of logical thinkers and problem solvers. She decided to pursue her field in college and see if it was a good fit for her, and it was. **Avocations:** Cross-stitch; Watching movies; Reading books; Being with friends; Making and playing music; Singing **Religion:** Christian

Amanda Mayhew Dealey

Title: Community Volunteer and Activist **Date of Birth:** 07/17/1950 **Place of Birth:** Dallas **State/Country of Origin:** TX/USA **Parents:** Charles Milton Mayhew; Audrey (Overton) Mayhew **Marital Status:** Divorced **Spouse Name:** Lawrence W. Speck (10/03/1992, Divorced 2005); Joe M. Dealey Jr. (11/4/1972, Divorced 1978) **Children:** Christopher Charles **Education:** Master's in Public Affairs, The University of Texas at Austin (2003); BA in Art History, The University of Texas at Austin (1972) **Civic:** Chair, KMFA Classical Radio (2014-Present); Member, Advisory Council, Harry Ransom Center, The University of Texas at Austin (2009-Present); Member, Board of Directors, James Dick Foundation (1978-Present); Member, Board of Directors, Planned Parenthood Foundation (2008-2011); Member, Board of Directors, Planned Parenthood Action Fund, Inc. (2006-2009); Member, Board of Directors, Planned Parenthood Federation of America Inc. (2005-2011); Secretary, Austin Community Foundation (2003-2008); Secretary-Treasurer, Texas Association for Symphony Orchestras (1988-1989); Member, Advisory Council, University of Texas at Austin School of Nursing (1987-1994); Member, Board of Directors, Mid-American Arts Alliance, Kansas City, MO (1987-1990); Founding Vice President, Lyric Opera (1986-1991); Vice Chairman, Texas Arts Alliance (1986-1989); Member, Executive Committee, Austin Symphony Orchestra (1983-1986); Board Secretary, Treasurer, Director, Creekmore and Adele Fath Charitable Fund; Chair, City of Austin Planning Commission; Member, Board of Trustees, Austin Museum **Awards:** Tom and Robbie Ausley Leadership Award, Planned Parenthood of Greater Texas, Inc. **Memberships:** Chair, The Texas Lyceum (1996); Vice President, Mental Health Association in Texas (Mental Health America of Texas) (1995-1998); President, The Texas Lyceum (1995); President, Austin Mental Health Association; Vice Chair, Texas Mental Health Association; Philosophical Society of Texas; Foundation for Women's Resources, Texas State Historical Association (TSHA) (Formerly the Texas Foundation for Women's Resources); The Honor Society of Phi Kappa Phi **Why did you become involved in your profession or industry:** Ms. Dealey became involved in her profession because her parents were both active community volunteers. **Avocations:** Traveling **Thoughts on Life:** Ms. Dealey was the former foundation administrator, a position she held for two different foundations, one professionally and the other as a volunteer. Professionally, it was for the Foundation for Women's Resources in Texas and it entailed running leadership for Texas, which was a leadership program that Ann Richards and Sarah Weddington and others started in the early 1990s as a way to help women become better leaders. It was also a way to help them establish a network throughout the state of Texas. She enjoyed doing that. Additionally, in her volunteer position, she was the secretary/treasurer and director of the Creekmore and Adele Fath Charitable Foundation, which was a philanthropic foundation.

Margaret Genevieve Dean, Esq.

Title: Lawyer; Commentator **Company Name:** Private Practice; Station 960 WELI, iHeartMedia, Inc. **Date of Birth:** 12/30/1943 **Place of Birth:** Brooklyn **State/Country of Origin:** NY/USA **Parents:** Richard Gerard Dean (1916-1988); Pearl Dorothy (Olson) Dean (1918-2004) **Marital Status:** Married **Spouse Name:** Norman Dean (04/03/1966) **Children:** Peter Richard Dean **Education:** JD, University of Connecticut (1980); BA, Hunter College (1967) **Certifications:** State Court Mediator, North Carolina State Bar (1994); Board Certified, Dispute Resolution Board, North Carolina State Bar **Career:** Commentator, Station 960 WELI, iHeartMedia, Inc. (1976-2014); Employment Rights and Labor Lawyer, Private Practice (1980-2013); Op-editorial Column Writer, New Haven Register (1983-1985); Associate, Hartford, CT (1978-1981); Women's Advisory Panel, Station-WTNH-TV, New Haven, CT (1975-1978); Research Assistant, Department of Internal Medicine, Yale University Medical School (1974); Research Assistant, Department of Pediatrics Psychiatry, Brooklyn Jewish Medical Center (1965-1966) **Career Related:** State Court Mediator, North Carolina Courts **Civic:** National Insurance Task Force, National Organization for Women (1976-1977); Citizens' Advisory Board, Connecticut State Police and Sex Crimes Advisory Board (1974-1975); Public Education Committee, Connecticut Division, American Cancer Society, Inc. (1973-1974); Founder, New Haven Chapter, National Organization for Women (1973); Co-founder, Arizona Women's Political Caucus (1972); Employment Task Force, National Organization for Women, Tucson, AZ (1970-1971); Orange Democratic Town Committee, State of Connecticut; Executive Board, American Lung Association of Connecticut; Board of Directors, Chairman, Legislative and By-laws Committee, Griffin Hospital Auxiliary, Derby, CT **Memberships:** Connecticut Bar Association; Former Member, New Haven Bar Association; North Carolina Association of Women Attorneys; Former Member, North Carolina Bar Association **Bar Admissions:** North Carolina State Bar (1994); Connecticut Bar Association (1980) **Marquis Who's Who Honors:** Albert Nelson Marquis Lifetime Achievement Award; Marquis Who's Who Top Professional **Why did you become involved in your profession or industry:** Mrs. Dean was a chemistry major in college and worked in the department of pediatric psychiatry doing research on Down Syndrome and DNA, which was in its infancy stage. When her husband was drafted into the Vietnam War, they moved to Alabama. When the war was over, they moved to Arizona, where Mrs. Dean struggled to find a permanent position. She applied for jobs at places known for rejecting female applicants, and a couple of people wanted her to sue for sex discrimination. When they moved to Connecticut, she decided to go to law school to make a difference, and today, she is an active feminist in the legal field. **Avocations:** Knitting; Reading; Swimming **Political Affiliations:** Democrat **Religion:** Roman Catholic

Colleen DeCourcy

Title: Co-President, Chief Creative Officer **Industry:** Business Management/Business Services **Company Name:** Wieden + Kennedy **Education:** Diploma in English and Journalism, Western University, London, Canada (1985) **Career:** Co-President, Chief Executive Officer, Wieden + Kennedy, Portland, OR (2018-Present); Global Executive Creative Director, Wieden + Kennedy, Portland, OR (2013-Present); Chief Executive Officer, Socialistic (2011-2013); Chief Digital Officer, TBWA, New York, NY (2007-2011); Chief Experience Officer, JWT (2006-2007); Chief Experience Officer, Organic, New York, NY (2000-2006); Executive Creative Director, Organic, New York, NY (2004-2005); Director of Creative Strategy, Integrated Communications and Entertainment, New York, NY (1998-2000); Chief Creative Officer, Spaxfax/Aspen PLC, London, England; Receptionist, Saffer Cravit & Freedman **Career Related:** Founder, Socialistic (2010) **Awards:** Creative Leader of the Decade, Adweek (2019); U.S. Agency of the Year, Adweek (2018, 2019); Global Agency of the Year (2017) **Memberships:** Agency Advisory Board, Interactive Advertising Bureau (IAB)

Carl Neumann Degler, PhD

Title: Professor Emeritus **Industry:** Education/Educational Services **Company Name:** Stanford University **Date of Birth:** 02/06/1921 **Place of Birth:** Orange **State/Country of Origin:** NJ/USA **Parents:** Casper Degler; Jewell (Neumann) Degler **Marital Status:** Married **Spouse Name:** "Tessa" Therese Baker-Degler (10/27/2000); Catherine Grady (11/19/1948, Deceased 1998) **Children:** Paul Grady; Suzanne Catherine **Education:** LLD, Colgate University, Hamilton, NY (19780); LLD, Ripon College, Ripon, WI (1976); MA, University of Oxford, Oxford, England (1973); PhD, Columbia University, New York, NY (1952); MA, Columbia University, New York, NY (1947); LHD, Upsala College, East Orange, NJ (1969); AB, Upsala College, East Orange, NJ (1942) **Career:** Professor Emeritus, Stanford University, Stanford, CA (1990-1998); Retired, Margaret Byrne Professor, American History, Stanford University, Stanford, CA (1972-1990); Professor, American History, Stanford University, Stanford, CA (1968-1998); Chairman, Department, Vassar College, Poughkeepsie, NY (1966-1968); Professor, History, Vassar College, Poughkeepsie, NY (1962-1968); Member, Faculty, Vassar College, Poughkeepsie, NY (1952-1968); Adjunct Professor, City College of New York, New York, NY (1952); Adjunct Professor, Adelphi University, Garden City, NY (1950-1951); Adjunct Professor, New York University, New York, NY (1947-1949); Adjunct Professor, Hunter College, New York, NY (1947-1948) **Career Related:** Visiting Fellow, St Catherine's College, University of Oxford (1989); Assessor, International Committee of Historical Sciences/Comité international des Sciences historiques (ICHS/CISH) (1985-1990); Fellow, Humanities Center, Stanford University, Stanford, CA (1983-1984); Member, California Council for Humanities (1979-1985); Fellow, Center for Advanced Study in the Behavioral Sciences (1979-1980); Harmsworth Professor Oxford University, Oxford, England (1973-1974); Visiting Professor, Stanford University, Summer (1964); Visiting Professor, Graduate School of Arts and Sciences, Columbia University, New York, NY (1963-1964) **Military Service:** U.S. Army, India (1942-1945); U.S. Army Air Forces During World War II **Creative Works:** Featured in Article, "A New Americanism: Why a Nation Needs a National Story," Foreign Affairs (2019); Author, "In Search of Human Nature: The Decline and Revival of Darwinism in American Social Thought" (1991); Author, Book, "Out of Our Past" (1983); Author, Book, "At Odds: Women and the Family in America from the Revolution to the Present" (1980); Member, Editorial Board, Plantation Society (1979-1998); Revisionist, Journal of Family History (JFH) (1977-1988); Author, Book, "Place Over Time: The Continuity of Southern Distinctiveness" (1977); Author, Book, "Affluence and Anxiety" (1975); Author, Book, "The Other South: Southern Dissenters in the Nineteenth Century" (1974); Member, Editorial Board, Signs: Women in Culture and Society (1974-1985); Author, Book, "Neither Black nor White: Slavery and Race Relations in Brazil and the United States" (1971); Editor, "The New Deal" (1970); Member, Board of Editors, American Quarterly (1967-1970); Editor, "Women and Economics" (1970); Author, Book, "Age of Economic Revolution" (1967) **Awards:** Ralph Walde Emerson Prize, Phi Beta Kappa (1991); Named, Outstanding Scholar, LaGuardia Archives (1991); National Endowment of the Humanities Fellow (1976-1977, 1983-1984); Guggenheim Fellow (1972-1973); American Council Learned Societies Fellow (1964-1965); Scholar, American Philosophical Society **Memberships:** Assessor, International Committee of Historical Sciences (1985-1990); President, Southern Historical Association (1985-1986); President, American Historical Association (1985-1986); President, Organization of American Historians (OAH) (1979-1980); President, Pacific Coast Branch, American Historical Association (1974-1975); American Association of University Professors; American Academy of Arts and Sciences; American Philosophical Society; Antiquarian Society; American Studies Association **Marquis Who's Who Honors:** Albert Nelson Marquis Lifetime Achievement Award; Marquis Who's Who Top Professional **To what do you attribute your success:** Dr. Degler attributed his success to his propensity for leading small group discussions as opposed to lecturing, as he did not believe that was the best way to teach his students. **Why did you become involved in your profession or industry:** Dr. Degler became involved in his profession because he was drafted in 1942 and served in the Army Air Forces after traveling in the military as a weather observer. He received the GI Bill and was not sure what he wanted to do. He came from a very blue collar family – his father was a fireman in Newark, New Jersey – but wanted to be a historian. He thought he would go to Rutgers University but wanted to utilize the GI Bill so he decided to go across the river and attend Columbia University.

John J. "Jack" Degnan III, PhD

Title: Physicist, Technical Consultant **Industry:** Consulting **Company Name:** Self-Employed **Date of Birth:** 12/10/1945 **Place of Birth:** Philadelphia **State/Country of Origin:** PA/USA **Parents:** John James Jr.; Ruth Dolores (Vece) **Marital Status:** Divorced **Spouse Name:** Adele Susan Henry (06/27/1969) **Children:** Adam John; Andrew Paul **Education:** PhD Physics, University of Maryland, College Park (1979); MS in Physics, University of Maryland, College Park (1970); BS in Physics, Drexel University, Philadelphia, PA (1968) **Career:** Technical Consultant (2019-Present); Chief Scientist, Sigma Space Corporation, Lanham, MD (2003-2018); Head, Geoscience Technology Office, Goddard Space Flight Center, NASA, Greenbelt, MD (1996-2003); Head of Space Geodesy, Altimetry Projects Office, Goddard Space Flight Center, NASA (1993-1996); Deputy Manager, Crustal Dynamics Project, Goddard Space Flight Center, NASA (1989-1993); Section Head, Goddard Space Flight Center, NASA (1979-1989); Senior Physicist, Goddard Space Flight Center, NASA (1972-1979); Physicist, Goddard Space Flight Center, NASA (1968-1972); Student Trainee, Goddard Space Flight Center, NASA (1964-1967) **Career Related:** Traveling Lecturer Program, OSA (2017-Present); Invited Lecturer, SLR School, Germany (2019); Chairman, Governing Board, International Laser Ranging Service (1998-2002); Technology Board, Wegener (1992-2000); Chairman, CSTG SLR/LLR Subcommittee, International Laser Ranging Service (1992-1998); Distinguished Adjunct Professor of Physics, American University, Washington, DC (1988-1993); Associate Member, Advanced Group (1980-1985); Physics Instructor, Drexel University (1967-1968) **Civic:** Director, Performer, 60 Productions, Maryland Community Theater (1982-Present); Bowie Community Theatre (2017-2018); Vice President, Treasurer, Pasadena Theatre Company (1982-1984); Treasurer, MAD Productions **Creative Works:** Patentee, Internal Optical Scanner (2012); Patentee, 3D Imaging Lidar (2007); Patentee, Microaltimeter (2002); Contributor, 230 Articles, Professional Journals and Conference Papers **Awards:** SLR Pioneer Award, International Laser Ranging Service (2014); Alumni Circle of Distinction Award, Drexel University (2005); Space Act Award, NASA (2003); Tsiolkovsky Medal, Russian Space Agency (2002); William T. Pecora Group Award to Topex/Poseidon Team, NASA (1998); Group Achievement Award for Topex/Poseidon Mission Design, NASA (1993); Group Achievement Award for Lageos 2 Iris Mission Support, Italian Space Agency/NASA (1993); Marple-Newtown School District Hall of Fame Award (1989); Moe I. Schneebaum Memorial Award for Engineering, Goddard Space Flight Center, NASA (1987); Group Achievement Award, Crustal Dynamics Project, NASA (1986); Who's Who in Lasers and Quantum Electronics, Society for Optical and Quantum Electronics (1982); Scholar, Board of Trustees, Drexel University (1963) **Memberships:** Steering Committee Member, American Geophysical Union (1998-2002); International Laser Ranging Society; Senior Member, American Physical Society; Senior Member, IEEE; Fellow, The Optical Society; Fellow, International Association of Geodesy; Sigma Pi Sigma-The Physics Honor Society; SPIE; The Planetary Society; Union of Concerned Scientists; National Space Club & Foundation; American Civil Liberties Union; American Volkssport Association; Sierra Club; Sigma Pi Fraternity; Common Cause; Executive Board, CSTG **Marquis Who's Who Honors:** Albert Nelson Marquis Lifetime Achievement Award **To what do you attribute your success:** Dr. Degnan attributes his success to his outstanding teachers, supervisors, co-workers and international colleagues. **Why did you become involved in your profession or industry:** Dr. Degnan became involved in his profession because he was intrigued by how physics permeated the other sciences and depended heavily on mathematics. **Avocations:** Hiking; Performing in community theater; Playing guitar; Traveling internationally **Political Affiliations:** Democrat **Religion:** Roman Catholic

D. Gregory "Greg" Deitch

Title: Meteorologist (Retired) **Industry:** Civil Service **Company Name:** U.S. Government/USAF **Date of Birth:** 08/22/1953 **Place of Birth:** Gettysburg **State/Country of Origin:** PA/USA **Parents:** Druid Cassatt Deitch and Betty Jane (Ridinger) Deitch **Marital Status:** Married **Spouse Name:** Judith Deitch (9/1/1990) **Education:** Master of Science in Meteorology, University of Utah (1981); Bachelor of Science in Meteorology, University of Utah (1978); Bachelor of Science in Astronomy, Villanova University (1975) **Career:** Meteorologist, Air Force Technical Applications Center, Patrick Air Force Base, Florida (1998-2014); Meteorologist in Climatology, Air Force Combat Climatology Center, Asheville, NC (1990-1998); Operational and Ballistics Meteorologist, U.S. Army Atmospheric Sciences Laboratory, White Sands Missile Range, New Mexico (1982-1990); Meteorologist, Amundsen-Scott South Pole Station, ITT Antarctic Services (1981-1982); Meteorologist Intern, National Earth Satellite Service, Honolulu, HI (1980); Meteorologist Intern, National Earth Satellite Service, Anchorage, AK (1979) **Career Related:** Team Chief, Fort Huachuca Meteorological Team, Arizona (1985) **Awards:** Eagle Scout Award (1971); Numerous Meteorology Awards **Memberships:** Former Member, American Meteorological Society **Marquis Who's Who Honors:** Albert Nelson Marquis Lifetime Achievement Award **To what do you attribute your success:** Mr. Deitch credits his standout success on the influence of his parents, family and various educational opportunities he had enjoyed. **Why did you become involved in your profession or industry:** Mr. Deitch became involved in his profession after receiving a Bachelor of Science in astronomy. However, he found that field too difficult to enter, and switched to meteorology. **Avocations:** Physical fitness; Photography; Numismatics; Traveling and singing with Brevard Community Chorus **Political Affiliations:** Republican **Religion:** Protestant

Joseph Paul Delaney

Title: Managing Director **Industry:** Consulting **Company Name:** Deloitte **Marital Status:** Married **Spouse Name:** Nancy (09/11/1971) **Children:** Tracey; Joseph **Education:** BA in Humanities, Seton Hall University (1967) **Career:** Partner, Managing Director, Deloitte LLP (1969-2010); Director, New York Practice Administrative Services; Director, Tri-State Audit Scheduling, Director Northeast Alumni Relations **Civic:** Chairman, Board of Directors, Catholic Charities of Staten Island (2016-Present); Executive Director, Notre Dame Club of Staten Island- Bread of Life Food Drive (1992-Present); Director, Notre Dame Club, Christmas Toy Drive; Leader Project Warmth Coat Drive, Notre Dame Club; Board of Directors, Bernikow Jewish Community Center of Staten Island; Board Member, Project Hospitality; National Board Member, Virtual Enterprises International **Awards:** Subway Alum of the Year Award, University of Notre Dame (2018); Volunteer of the Year Award, University of Notre Dame Alumni (2012, 2018); U.S. Marine Corps Reserve Award (2011-2015); Volunteer of the Year, Staten Island (2011-2015); Excellence in Community Service Award, Bernikow Jewish Community Center of Staten Island (2013); Legion of Honor, Chapel of the 4 Chaplains Foundation (2012); Community Service Award, Staten Island Catholic Youth Organization (2010); Staten Island Knights of Columbus Award (2009); DAVOS Award, Deloitte Global Organization (2007); Silva Award, Virtual Enterprises International (2006); American Legion, Richmond County's Citizen of the Year (2005); Greater NY Board, March of Dimes Volunteer of the Year (2004); Top Walker, March of Dimes, New York (1997-2004); Man of the Year, Cross Road Foundation (2004); Outstanding Community Service Volunteer, Deloitte Global Organization (2002-2003); Father Putz Award, Notre Dame Alumni Association (2002); Young Democrats' Hubert H. Humphrey Community Service Award (2001); R.S.V.P. Volunteer of the Year (1994); Hero of Staten Island, Assemblyman Robert Straniere (1999); Robert Parker Community Service Award, North Shore Democratic Club (1998); Volunteer of the Year, March of Dimes (1998); Service Volunteer Award, Battery Dance Company (1998); Notre Dame Cornelius O'Reagan Award (1995); Appreciation Award, Staten Island Saints Football Team (1994); Service Award, Boy's League Football Parents (1991) **Memberships:** Board of Directors, University of Notre Dame Alumni Association; (2018-2020); President, University of Notre Dame Alumni Club of Staten Island (1996-2006); Board of Directors, Bernikow Jewish Community Center of Staten Island; Chairman of the Board, Catholic Charities of Staten Island; Project Hospitality; Virtual Enterprises International; Board Member, The Archbishop Fulton Sheen Foundation; Board Member, Jewish Community Center of Staten Island **Marquis Who's Who Honors:** Marquis Who's Who Top Professional **To what do you attribute your success:** Mr. Delaney attributes his success to the support and love of his wife and family. He was encouraged by them to keep at his work, and having that support inspired him to appreciate their time together more. **Why did you become involved in your profession or industry:** Deloitte's service component is what made Mr. Delaney want to join the firm. He feels he would have been unable to work in any other environment besides professional service. Every day at Deloitte was different. Mr. Delaney always had an agenda of what needed to get done; however, he could always count on something unexpected coming up. He thrived on helping clients. As soon as he started his career with Deloitte, Mr. Delaney knew he would never want to work anywhere else. He loved how Deloitte encouraged its staff and Partners to give back to the community. Mr. Delaney found it challenging and rewarding to look at a problem and offer a solution and move on to the next problem. He loved to work in an environment where he could put his integrity to practice. **Avocations:** Directing the annual Notre Dame Bread of Life Food Drive; Sharing and enjoying volunteer opportunities with his wife; Traveling to visit family in London; Reading American history; Practicing his Catholic faith

Robin Kay DeMark

Title: Consultant **Industry:** Consulting **Date of Birth:** 10/05/1961 **Place of Birth:** Elmira **State/Country of Origin:** NY/USA **Parents:** John DeMark; Betty DeMark **Education:** MLS in Library and Information Science, East Carolina University, Greenville, NC (1993); BA in Psychology, East Carolina University, Greenville, NC (1984) **Certifications:** Certified Beekeeper, State of North Carolina (2014-Present); Certificate, Leadership Development Seminar, United States Office of Personnel Management (2009); Public Affairs Officer Qualification, Defense Information School, Fort Meade, Maryland (2003); Certified in Services Marketing Management, HQ Air Combat Command (2001); Library Quality Assurance Evaluator, HQ Air Force Services Agency (1998); Certified Public Librarian, State of North Carolina (1994); Certificate, FEMA Emergency Management Institute **Career:** Bee School Education Director, Board of Directors, Beekeepers of the Neuse, North Carolina State Beekeepers Association (2016-Present); Vice President, Board of Directors, Duplin County Beekepers Association, Kenansville, NC (2015-2016); Public Affairs Officer, Veterans Affairs Medical Center, Fayetteville, NC (2011-2014); Chief of Community Relations, Emergency Response Manager, Fourth Fighter Wing Public Affairs, Seymour Johnson Air Force Base, North Carolina (2001-2011); Marketing Director, Fourth Services Squadron, Seymour Johnson Air Force Base, North Carolina (1999-2001); Library Director, Pope Air Force Base Library, Pope Air Force Base, North Carolina (1996-1999); Reference Librarian, Pope Air Force Base Library, Fort Bragg, North Carolina (1995-1996); Reference/Business Librarian, Wayne County Public Library, Goldsboro, NC (1993-1995); Graduate Student Library Instructor, Part-Time Reference Staff, East Carolina University Joyner Library, Greenville, NC (1991-1993) **Career Related:** Librarian, Public Affairs, Event Consultant **Civic:** Beekeepers of the Neuse, Wayne County (2016-Present); Board Member, Education Director, North Carolina State Beekeeping Association (2014-2018); Duplin County Beekeepers Association, Duplin County (2014-2016); North Carolina Women Veterans Committee (2011-2012); Board of Directors, North Carolina Community Federal Credit Union (2007-2008); Marketing Vice President, Wayne County United Way (2001-2004); Executive Board of Directors, Wayne County United Way (2000-2004) **Military Service:** Civil Service, U.S. Air Force, U.S. Army, Veterans Affairs; Public Affairs Officer, U.S. Air Force **Creative Works:** Writer, Editor, "North Carolina Beekeepers Association 100th Anniversary Yellow Book" (2017); Featured, "Duplin Times" (2016); Author, Writer, Photographer, "North Carolina Bee Buzz Magazine" (2014-2016); Story Author, Photographer, "North Carolina State Magazine" (2014); Featured, "Health Coaching for Veterans," Veterans Affairs National Magazine (2012); Book Contributor, "My Enemy, My Friend" (2009); Author, Manual, "An Introduction to Computerized Resources and Database Searching in an Academic Library" (1993); Author, Master's Thesis, "Research Using Subject-Based Electronic Databases in a College Library,"East Carolina University; Contributor, "Mayor Scott B. Berkeley and Seymour Johnson Air Force Base: An Analysis of One Man's Efforts to Save a Base," Wayne County Library Special Collections **Awards:** Mentorship Certification Award, Veterans Administration (2013); Named, Senior Civilian of the Quarter, Fourth Fighter Wing Staff Agency (2010); Named, Air Combat Command Superior Performer, Unit Compliance Inspection (2008); Named, Senior Civilian of the Year, Fourth Fighter Wing Staff Agency (2004); Named, Third Runner Up, Miss Fayetteville Scholarship Pageant, Fayetteville, NC (1980); Recipient, Public Affairs Recognition, United States Air Force Thunderbirds, United States Navy Blue Angels **Marquis Who's Who Honors:** Albert Nelson Marquis Lifetime Achievement Award; Marquis Who's Who Top Professional **Why did you become involved in your profession or industry:** Ms. DeMark became involved in her profession because she started doing event planning and DJ planning as a way to support herself through college. Over the year, it grew and became a small company. Ms. DeMark got involved with bees because when she retired from the federal government a friend of hers introduced her to beekeeping by taking her to a local club meeting. From there, she got into beekeeping and selling honey on the side. **Avocations:** Consulting; Event planning; Beekeeping **Political Affiliations:** Independent **Religion:** Roman Catholic

C. David DePriest

Title: Engineering Executive, Military Officer (Retired) **Industry:** Engineering **Date of Birth:** 10/18/1938 **Place of Birth:** Mount Pleasant **State/Country of Origin:** PA/USA **Parents:** Dr. Charles Leonard DePriest; Elizabeth Carolyn (Hoover) DePriest **Marital Status:** Widowed **Spouse Name:** Marlena J. Brechtel (2000, Deceased 2001); Blanquita Reinoso Rivas (07/01/1960, Divorced 1991) **Children:** Lisa Lynn Nees; Diane Cokerdem DePriest; David Eric DePriest **Education:** Master of Science in Electro-optics, Air Force Institute of Technology, Wright-Patterson Air Force Base, OH (1975); Bachelor of Arts in Electrical Engineering, Air Force Institute Technology, Wright-Patterson Air Force Base, OH, With Distinction (1974) **Certifications:** Certified Professional Logistician (CPL), Society of Logistics Engineers **Career:** President, DePriest Associates Inc., Warner Robins, GA (1997-2015); Manager, Warner Robins Applications Department, and Site Manager, The Analytic Sciences Corporation Inc., Warner Robins, GA (1992-1997); Director, Plans and Operations, Electronic Combat Office, U.S. Air Force, Wright-Patterson Air Force Base, Greene County, OH (1988-1991); Director, Intercommand Electronic Warfare, Wright-Patterson Air Force Base, Greene County, OH (1986-1988); Chief, Engineering Division, Warner Robins Air Logistics Complex, Warner Robins, GA (1984-1986); Program Element Monitor, Deputy Division Chief, Avionics and Armament Division, Air Staff, Headquarters Air Force, Washington, DC (1979-1983); Program Manager, GPS Missile Guidance Program, Chief, Missile Guidance Branch, U.S. Air Force Armament Lab, Eglin Air Force Base, Florida (1975-1979); B-52 Stanboard Radar Navigator, Wright-Patterson Air Force Base, Greene County, OH (1968-1972); B-52 Stanboard Navigator, Beale Air Force Base, Marysville, CA (1964-1968) **Military Service:** Advanced through Grades to Colonel, U.S. Air Force, (1959-1984, Retired 1991) **Awards:** Decorated Meritorious Service Medal with Two Bronze Oak Leaf Clusters; Air Medal with silver oak leaf cluster; Distinguished Flying Cross; Legion of Merit **Memberships:** Senior Member, Institute of Electrical and Electronics Engineers (IEEE); Society Of Logistics Engineers; Air Force Association; Mensa International; Rotary International; Association of Old Crows; American Contract Bridge League; Tau Beta Pi **Marquis Who's Who Honors:** Albert Nelson Marquis Lifetime Achievement Award; Marquis Who's Who Top Professional; Marquis Who's Who Humanitarian Award **Why did you become involved in your profession or industry:** Mr. DePriest became involved in his profession because he always wanted to fly. **Avocations:** Duplicate bridge **Religion:** Christian

Nellie Louise Derise, PhD

Title: Nutritionist, Educator, Researcher **Industry:** Education/Educational Services **Date of Birth:** 08/09/1930 **Place of Birth:** Jeanerette **State/Country of Origin:** LA/USA **Parents:** O'Niell Paul Derise ; Anita (Savoy) Derise **Marital Status:** Single **Education:** PhD, Virginia Polytechnic Institute (1973); MS, University of Alabama (1964);BS, University of Southwestern Louisiana (1962) **Career:** Retired, Nutritionist, Educator, Researcher (1994); Professor, Home Economics, University of Southwestern Louisiana, Lafayette, LA (1981-1994); Associate Professor, University of Southwestern Louisiana, Lafayette, LA (1973-1981); Assistant Professor, Iowa State University, Ames, IA (1968-1970); Assistant Professor, University of Southwestern Louisiana, Lafayette, LA (1964-1968); Graduate Assistant, University of Alabama, Tuscaloosa, AL (1962-1964) **Career Related:** Chairman, Louisiana State Nutrition Council (1977-1978) **Civic:** Jeanerette Museum Board; Vice President, Catholic Daughters of the Americas; The Legion of Mary **Creative Works:** Contributor, Articles, Professional Journals **Awards:** Jeanerette Chamber of Commerce Outstanding Citizen of the Year (2015); Certificate of Merit for Service to the Community, The Retired and Senior Volunteer Program of The U.S.A. (2008); AARP Citizen of Month (1999) **Memberships:** Board of Directors, Louisiana Dietetic Association (1982-1986); Board of Directors, Louisiana Home Economics Association (1973-1975); American Home Economics Association; American Dietetic Association; U.S. Metric Association; Society of Nutrition Education; Institute Food Technology; Sigma Xi **Marquis Who's Who Honors:** Albert Nelson Marquis Lifetime Achievement Award; Marquis Who's Who Top Professional **Why did you become involved in your profession or industry:** Dr. Nellie Derise always liked to learn new things, she was very curious, she always thought learning was exciting. She grew up in a rural area and attended a small country school. When Dr. Derise went to high school, the school would encourage the girls to go into home economics but Dr. Derise enjoyed science so she took chemistry and physics. She eventually decided on home economics but not in education. Dr. Derise decided to take extra science classes in college and from there she went for her master's degree. With the encouragement from her parents and her professors, she applied and received several fellowships and scholarships to help pay for her education so she could move on to receive her PhD from Virginia Polytechnic Institute. Her father, did not have the opportunity as a child to really get the education he would have liked. He had to quit school because his parents had difficulty and problems. But he kept reading and learning and teaching himself. As she was growing up, he always pushed education, he would say you can't learn enough in this world, today you need that knowledge to go forward and he was the one who really inspired her to keep trying no matter what. **Avocations:** Painting with water colors; Sewing; Walking; Line dancing **Political Affiliations:** Democrat **Religion:** Roman Catholic

Ruslan Desyatnikov

Title: Founder, Chief Executive Officer **Industry:** Information Technology and Services **Company Name:** QA Mentor, Inc. **Date of Birth:** 02/01/1976 **Place of Birth:** Kishinev **State/Country of Origin:** Moldova **Parents:** Greta Desyatt; Michael Desyatnikov **Marital Status:** Married **Spouse Name:** Lyudmila Elgort **Children:** Brielle Desyatnikov **Education:** Certificate Program - Mastering Growth, Entrepreneurship/Entrepreneurial Studies, Harvard University (2020); Certificate Program - Entrepreneurship/Entrepreneurial Studies, The Wharton School, The University of Pennsylvania (2019); MBA in Technology Management, University of Phoenix (2005); Associate Certificate in Project Management, The George Washington University (2004); BA in Computer Information Systems, Baruch College (1998) **Certifications:** Professional Certification for NeoLoad, Neotys; Professional Certification for Software Testing, Brainbench **Career:** Co-founder, Chief Executive Officer, Occygen (2016-Present); Chief Executive Officer, QA Mentor, Inc. (2010-Present); Global Head of Testing, Worldlink Technology, Citigroup, Inc. (2014-2015); Senior Global Program Test Manager/Senior Management Consultant, Citigroup, Inc. (2012-2015); Director/Vice President, Global Quality Assurance & Testing, Sterling Info-systems, Inc. (2006-2012); Global Test Manager, HSBC Bank USA (2002-2006); Quality Assurance Consultant and Advisor, Digital Edge Ventures, Inc. (2002-2006); Senior Lead QA Analyst, Solbright Digital Solutions (Now Operative) (2000-2002); Analyst, UnicastCo (1998-1999) **Civic:** Supporter/Contributor, Various Organizations Around the World **Creative Works:** Contributor, Articles to Many Popular Magazines Including Forbes, CIOReview, Outsourcing Gazette, Tea-Time with Testers, Mirror Review, Stickyminds, LinkedIn, and Multiple QA Blogs **Awards:** Named One of the World's Best QA Testing & Solution Providers (2020); Named One of the Industry Leaders in QA and Testing to Watch Out for (2020); Named One of the 10 Most Advanced QA Companies, Mirror Review Magazine (2019); Named One of the Fastest Growing Companies in United States, The Technology Headlines Magazine (2019); Named One of the 10 Most Promising Software Testing Services in Consulting/Services Companies, CIOReview Magazine (2018); Named Company of the Year, CIOReview Magazine (2018); Named the CIOReview Magazine Cover Story and One of the 20 Most Promising Testing Solution Providers (2018); Named One of the 30 Most Daring CEOs in Business, Insight Success Magazine (2018); Named One of the 10 Best QA and Testing Solution Providers, Mirror Review Magazine, 2018; Named One of the Top 10 Automation Testing Solution Providers, CIO Applications Magazine (2018); Named One of the 10 Best Performing Software Testing Solution Providers of 2018, Insight Success Magazine (2018); Named One of the 30 Most Creative CEOs, Mirror Review Magazine (2018); CEO Today USA Award, CEO Today Magazine (2017); European Leading Vendor Award, The European Testing Awards (2017); Leading Vendor Award, European Software Testing Awards (2017); Named One of the TOP 10 QA Testing Companies, Technology Widgets Magazine (2017); Named One of the 10 Best CEOs of 2017, Industry Era Magazine (2017); **Marquis Who's Who Honors:** Marquis Who's Who Albert Nelson Marquis Lifetime Achievement Award (2019); Marquis Who's Who Top Professional **To what do you attribute your success:** Mr. Desyatnikov attributes his success to hard work, motivation, and discipline. His motto is to follow your dreams, don't give up; if you fall you have to stand up and keep going. Don't look backwards, keep looking forward. **Why did you become involved in your profession or industry:** After Mr. Desyatnikov graduated, he wasn't able to find a job. He founded a start up company, and took a job as a junior tester. He hasn't regret that since; he is happy he ended up in quality assurance. He has moved up the ladder at many companies, and then was ready to start his own company and offer his services. Right now they support 380 clients in 27 different countries around the world, and 280 employees globally. **Avocations:** Chess; Soccer; Stamp collector; Traveling around the world with family; Learning new cultures and customs; tennis **Thoughts on Life:** Mr. Desyatnikov brings 23 years of quality assurance, quality control, process improvement and software testing experience. Mr. Desyatnikov is the founder and chief executive officer of QA Mentor, Inc., a multi-award winning, leading software testing company headquartered in NY. Prior to expanding operations at QA Mentor, Inc., he worked at CitiBank for three years as the Global Head of Testing of Worldlink Technology. Prior to working at Citi, he was with Sterling InfoSystems. During his six years tenure, he was responsible for testing functions, process improvements, and quality strategic directions across the entire organization. On a larger scale, Mr. Desyatnikov performed similar duties for four years at HSBC bank. There, he established a Testing Center of Excellence and managed eight Global QA teams in seven different countries with 150+ testers worldwide. Mr. Desyatnikov holds a number of quality assurance/testing and project management certifications and is an active board member of multiple QA organizations in the U.S. and Europe. He has also developed a number of e-learning QA courses and training materials, which has taught over 10,000 students worldwide. Under his guidance and leadership, QA Mentor, Inc. has won over 60 global awards and recognitions and achieved CMMI Level 3 appraisal with three ISO certificates.

Robert G. Dettmer

Title: Beverage Company Executive (Retired) **Industry:** Food & Restaurant Services **Date of Birth:** 09/11/1931 **Place of Birth:** Parson **State/Country of Origin:** KS/USA **Parents:** Ira Gerhart Dettmer; Dema (Hinze) Dettmer **Marital Status:** Married **Spouse Name:** Patricia Isabel York (08/20/1955) **Children:** Stephanie; Constance; Robert Brantley **Education:** Honorary DHL, Manhattanville College; MBA, Harvard University (1957); BS in Business and Engineering Administration, Massachusetts Institute of Technology (1955); Coursework, United States Naval Academy (1949-1952) **Career:** Retired (2003); Board of Directors, Valero Marketing and Supply Company (1996-2003); Executive Vice President, Chief Financial Officer, PepsiCo, Purchase, NY (1986-1996); President, Pepsi Cola Bottling Group Subsidiary, PepsiCo, Purchase, NY (1979-1986); Vice President, Finance Management and Planning, PepsiCo, Purchase, NY (1976-1979); President, North America Van Lines, Inc. Subsidiary, PepsiCo Fort Wayne, IN (1973-1976); President, Division A-T-O, George J. Meyer Manufacturing, Milwaukee, WI (1970-1972); President, Division A-T-O, Scott Aviation, Inc., Lancaster, NY (1968-1970); Vice President of Operations, Tasa Corporation, Pittsburgh, PA (1966-1968); Proprietor, Robert G. Dettmer, Investment Management, Cleveland, Ohio (1964-1966);Associate, Booz Allen Hamilton, Inc., Cleveland, Ohio (1960-1964); Engineer, The Lincoln Electric Company, Cleveland, Ohio (1957-1960) **Career Related: Civic:** Chairman, Board of Trustees, Manhattanville College (1988-1992); Trustee, Manhattanville College (1986-1989); Trustee, Miss Porter's School (1978-1984); Chairman, Board, American Movers Conference, American Moving & Storage (1974-1976) **Memberships:** Chairman, Board, Harvard Business School, Greater New York (1982-1983); Chairman, Board, Harvard Business School, Westchester-Fairfield County (1977-1980); Delta Tau Delta; The Tau Beta Pi Association, Inc. **Marquis Who's Who Honors:** Albert Nelson Marquis Lifetime Achievement Award; Marquis Who's Who Humanitarian Award **Why did you become involved in your profession or industry:** Mr. Dettmer's parents were educated, and both college graduates. His father was the manager of an electrical utility area in Kansas and his mother a teacher, who graduated from college the same day that Mr. Dettmer graduated from MIT. After college, Mr. Dettmer started out as an engineer for the Lincoln Electric Company in 1957 and he managed to keep receiving positions that kept him moving up in various companies until he became the executive vice president and chief financial officer of PepsiCo in 1986. **Avocations:** Boating; Traveling; Tennis; Swimming

Richard A. Devall

Title: Air Force Lieutenant Colonel (Retired) **Industry:** Military & Defense Services **Date of Birth:** 03/11/1947 **Place of Birth:** Jennings **State/Country of Origin:** LA/USA **Parents:** John Tabor; Florence Rosannah (Minnix) Devall **Marital Status:** Married **Spouse Name:** Rose Mary (2009) **Children:** Suzanne; Miriam; Ralph **Education:** Master of Arts, Louisiana State University (2001); Master of Science, Midwestern University (1975); Bachelor of Science, University of Louisiana at Lafayette (1969); Residency, Squadron Officer School and Air Command and Staff College, Air War College; National Security Management by Correspondence; Completed, Religious Studies Institute of the Diocese of Baton Rouge **Career:** Retired (1991); Director, Medical Resource Management, Keesler Technical Training Center Medical Center, Keesler Air Force Base, MS (1985-1991); Director, Medical Resource Management, U.S. Air Force Hospital, Osan Air Force Base, Republic of Korea (1984-1985); Health Systems Analyst, Air Force Medical Service Center, Brooks Air Force Base, TX (1978-1984); Health Systems Analyst, Office of the Air Force Surgeon General, Washington (1976-1978); Training Evaluation Officer, School of Health Care Sciences U.S. Air Force, Sheppard Air Force Base, TX (1971-1976); Student Squadron Commander, School Health Care Sciences U.S. Air Force, Sheppard Air Force Base, TX (1971); Commissioned Second Lieutenant, U.S. Air Force (1971); Clerk, Medical Resource Management, U.S. Air Force Hospital Altus, Altus Air Force Base, OK (1970-1971) **Career Related:** Instructor, Continuing Medical Readiness Training, Keesler Technology Training Center Medical Center, Keesler Air Force Base (1985-1988) **Civic:** Eucharistic Minister, Our Lady Help of Christians Catholic Church, Jennings, LA (2006-2009); Eucharistic Minister, Saint Jean Vianney Catholic Church (1994-2006); Fourth Degree, Delegate to Louisiana State Knights of Columbus Convention (1994); Chairperson, Catholic Chaplain Fund Council, Keesler Air Force Base, MS (1989-1991); Member, Catholic Chaplain Fund Council, Keesler Air Force Base, MS (1988-1991); Eucharistic Minister, Keesler Air Force Base, MS (1988-1991); Member, Catholic Chaplain Fund Council, Osan Air Base, Korea (1984-1985); Eucharistic Minister, Osan Air Base, Korea (1984-1985); Eucharistic Minister, Brooks Air Force Base Catholic Chapel (1983-1984); Key Worker, Air Force Assistant and Fund Campaign, Brooks Air Force Base, Texas (1983); Vice President, Council of Catholic Men Sheppard Air Force Base (1971-1972) **Military Service:** Advanced through Grades to Lieutenant Colonel, U.S. Air Force **Awards:** National Defense Service Medal, with 1 Device, Air Force Commendation Medal; Good Conduct Medal; Two Air Force Meritorious Service Medals with One Device; Air Force Commendation Medal; Humanitarian Service Medal **Memberships:** Faithful Navigator, Knights of Columbus (1996-1998); Treasurer, Knights of Columbus (1995-1996); Grand Knight Councilor, Knights of Columbus (1994-1996); Lifetime Member, Air Force Association; International Order of Alhambra; Lifetime Member, Veterans of Foreign Wars; American Legion; Military Officer Association of America **Marquis Who's Who Honors:** Albert Nelson Marquis Lifetime Achievement Award **To what do you attribute your success:** He was very detail oriented. Mr. Devall credits his standout success on his detail-oriented nature. **Why did you become involved in your profession or industry:** Having always wanted to be involved in the Air Force, Mr. Devall joined the military shortly after graduating from college. He continued to serve even after his tour of duty elapsed. **Avocations:** Travel; Golf **Political Affiliations:** Republican **Religion:** Roman Catholic

Jeannette DeVaris

Title: Psychologist **Industry:** Social Work **Date of Birth:** 01/07/1947 **Place of Birth:** Burbank **State/Country of Origin:** CA/USA **Parents:** Nicholas Propper Klein Schaeffe; Elizabeth (Von Lichtenberg) Schaeffe **Marital Status:** Divorced **Children:** Brendon Blake **Education:** Doctor of Philosophy in Clinical Psychology, Seton Hall University (1987); Master of Arts in Clinical Psychology, Fairleigh Dickinson University (1977); Bachelor of Arts, Psychology, Adelphi University (1968) **Certifications:** Licensed Psychologist, New Jersey **Career:** Private Practice, Summit, NJ (2006-Present); Private Practice, South Orange, NJ (1990-2006); Senior Psychologist, R. Hall Community Mental Health Center, Bridgewater, NJ (1979-1990); Psychologist, Greystone Psychiatric Hospital, Greystone Park, NJ (1979); Psychological Intern, New Jersey State Intern Program, Trenton, NJ (1977-1978); Alcohol and Drug Rehabilitation Counselor, U.S. Army, Fort Monmouth, NJ (1972-1976); Caseworker, New York City Welfare Department (1968-1972) **Civic:** Impact 100 **Creative Works:** Contributor to Professional Journal; Contributor, Several Articles, Frontier Academia **Awards:** Named, Top Doctors of New Jersey (2014-2018); Distinguished Achievement Award, New Jersey Psychological Association **Memberships:** American Psychological Association; New Jersey Psychological Association; Essex Union County Psychological Association **Marquis Who's Who Honors:** Albert Nelson Marquis Lifetime Achievement Award; Marquis Who's Who Top Professional **Why did you become involved in your profession or industry:** Dr. DeVaris became inspired to enter her profession due to the influence of her mother, who studied psychology herself. **Avocations:** Travel; Reading

Marlene Ruth DeVoe, PhD

Title: Professor Emeritus, Department of Psychology **Industry:** Education/Educational Services **Company Name:** St. Cloud State University **Date of Birth:** 12/13/1942 **Place of Birth:** Chicago **State/Country of Origin:** IL/USA **Parents:** John Joseph Persik; Marjorie Lucille (Hoffman) Glazier **Marital Status:** Married **Spouse Name:** Phillip Christian Schloss (8/17/2002); Peter DeVoe, (3/3/1962, Divorced 1985) **Children:** Deborah Fehrenbach; Kathie DeVoe **Education:** PhD in Psychology, Wayne State University (1990); MA in Psychology, Wayne State University (1988); BS in Psychology and Health Sciences, Grand Valley State University, Cum Laude (1982) **Certifications:** Licensed Nurse Practitioner, Michigan (1967) **Career:** Professor Emeritus, St. Cloud State University (2017); Professor, St. Cloud State University (1992-2001); Research Scientist, Philadelphia Geriatric Center (1989-1992); Graduate Research Assistant, Wayne State University, Detroit, MI (1985-1989); Graduate Research Assistant, Lafayette Clinic, Detroit, MI (1983-1984) **Career Related:** Temple University, Philadelphia, PA (1991); Adjunct Assistant Professor, Drexel University, Philadelphia, PA (1990-1992); Instructor, Community College of Philadelphia (1990-1992); Ad Hoc Reviewer, Psychology and Aging (1990-1991); Eastern Michigan University (1989) **Civic:** Director, Q-7 New Venture Grant, State University System of Minnesota (1993-1997); President, Phi Kappa Phi, St. Cloud State University (1993-1997); Co-Host, Television Series on Death and Dying, KTVC (1992) **Creative Works:** "Memory performance in individuals with primary degenerative dementia: Its similarity to diazepam-induced impairments," Experimental Aging Research (2015); "The Effects of Study Abroad" (2015); Speaker, Lecture Series, International American University (2006); Speaker, "External Control of Boys and Boys Self Regulation," Oxford Round Table (2003); Speaker, "Cohort Attitudes Toward War on Terrorism," 17th Annual Adult Development Symposium (2002); Speaker, "The importance of intrinsic work characteristics in predicting older worker job satisfaction" (1993); Speaker, "John and Mary Meet Aristotle and Think Critically in a Rhetorical Scene" (1992); Speaker, "Video-Taped expressions of affect in Nursing Home Residents: Do attributions match self-ratings?" Annual Meeting, Gerontological Society of America, Washington, DC (1992); Co-Author, "Relationship of events and affect in the Daily Life of an Elderly Population. Psychology and Aging" (1991); "Emotional regulation in adulthood: A developmental perspective," Annual Review of Gerontology and Geriatrics: Vol. 11. (1989); "Speaking about feelings: Conceptions of emotions across the life span. Psychology and Aging" (1989); Speaker, "An adult developmental analysis of causes of emotions," Annual Meeting, American Psychological Association, Boston, MA (1988); "Emotions and self-regulation: A life-span view. Human Development" (1985); "Clinical ratings: Relationship to objective psychometric assessment in individuals with dementia. Psychological Reports" (1985); Poster, "Smiles and expressivity: Relationship to age and measures of psychological development," Gerontological Society of America, San Francisco, CA **Awards:** Postdoctoral Fellow, National Research Award National Institute of Mental Health, Philadelphia Geriatric Center, Philadelphia PA (1990-1992); National Institute of Mental Health Graduate Fellow (1987-1988); Thomas C. Rumble University Graduate Fellow, Wayne State University (1984-1985); Distinguished Psychology Graduate, Grand Valley State College (1982); Inductee, The Honor Society of Phi Kappa Phi, Grand Valley State College (1982); Merit Scholarship, Grand Valley State University (1980-1982); Summer Fellow, The Brookdale Foundation/National Institute on Aging **Memberships:** American Psychological Association; American Psychological Society; Gerontological Society of America; Phi Kappa Phi; The Delta Kappa Gamma Society International **To what do you attribute your success:** Dr. DeVoe attributes her success to her mother and every advisor with whom she has worked. She also credits her perseverance, curiosity, and intelligence. **Why did you become involved in your profession or industry:** Dr. DeVoe has always had a pure love for psychology and learning. **Avocations:** Ballroom dancing; Photography; Gardening; Watercolor and oil painting **Thoughts on Life:** Dr. DeVoe believes a pebble cast causes ripples in mysterious and far-reaching ways.

T. Jay DiBacco

Title: Financial Planner **Industry:** Financial Services **Company Name:** Wealthmaker$ **Date of Birth:** 06/08/1954 **Place of Birth:** Casper **State/Country of Origin:** WY/USA **Parents:** Albert Joseph DiBacco; Evelyn DiBacco **Marital Status:** Married **Spouse Name:** Nadine **Education:** MBA, Almeda College (2003); Diploma, U.S. Army Command and General Staff College, Fort Leavenworth, KS (1994); Bachelor of Music, Certificate in Education, University of Wyoming (1976) **Certifications:** Life Underwriter Training Council Fellow, National Association of Insurance and Financial Advisors (1987); Registered Principal, FINRA **Career:** President, Wealthmaker$, Omaha, NE (2009-Present); Regional Vice President, Ohio National Financial Services, Inc. (2005-2009); President, Chief Executive Officer, DiBacco & Associates - Wealth-Makers, Scottsbluff, NE (1999-2005); Senior Associate, Hi-Plains Financial Services Inc., Scottsbluff, NE (1985-1999); Advanced Underwriter, Security Mutual Life Nebraska, Scotts-bluff, NE (1981-1999); Sales Associate, Panhandle Co-Op System, Scottsbluff, NE (1980-1981); Instrumental Music Teacher, Gering Public Schools (1977-1979); Music Teacher, St. Agnes Academy, Alliance, NE (1976-1977) **Career Related:** General Agent, Ohio National Financial Services, Inc. (2009-Present, 2000-2005); Registered Principal, The O.N. Equity Sales Company (1999-Present); Circle of Wealth, Private Reserve Strategy; Wealth Building Cornerstones, LLC **Civic:** Chairman, Co-Chairman, Presidential Business Round Table, NE (2002-2005); Active Licensed Operator, Amateur Radio Emergency Service, Scottsbluff, NE (1990-2005); Advisory Board, Regional West Foundation (1989-2005); MBA, Catalyst Group, University of Nebraska Panhandle Station, Scottsbluff, NE (1990-1992); Founding President, Panhandle Estate Planning Council, Scottsbluff, NE (1982-1992); Adjunct Faculty, Western Nebraska Community College, Scottsbluff, NE (1989-1990); District Commissioner, Longs Peak Council, Boy Scouts of America (1980-1983); Diplomat Chairman, Scottsbluff/Gering United Chamber of Commerce **Military Service:** US National Guard (1975-2004); Lieutenant Colonel (Retired) **Creative Works:** Writer, Local Newspaper Column (2000-2005); Contributor, Articles, Professional Journals **Awards:** International Management Award, General Aviation Manufacturers Association (GAMA) (2015-Present); National Manager Award, National Association of Insurance and Financial Advisors (NAIFA) (2005); Regional Service Award, The Society for Creative Anachronism, Inc. (1995); Agent of the Year, National Association of Insurance and Financial Advisors (NAIFA) (1991); Achievement Award, Nebraska Association of Health Under-writers (1988); Local President (1986-1987); National Rookie of the Year, Security Mutual Life Nebraska (1981); Longs Peak Council, Boy Scouts of America; Scouter's Key Award, Boy Scouts of America; Religious Award, Boy Scouts of America; Dec-orated Meritorious Service Medal; Army Commendation Medal with Oak Leaf Clusters; American Spirit Honor Medal; U.S. Army Chief of Staff Supply Excellence Award **Memberships:** President, Valley Vintner (2002-2006); Regional Safety Officer, The Society of Creative Anachronism, Inc. (1995-1999); GAMA International; NAIFA; Barbershop Harmony Society; Pathfinder Chorus; Military Officers Association of America; National Eagle Scout Association; The National Guard Association of the United States **Marquis Who's Who Honors:** Albert Nelson Marquis Lifetime Achievement Award; Marquis Who's Who Top Professional **To what do you attribute your success:** Mr. DiBacco attributes his success to his belief in God, his faith in his family, his confidence in himself and his perseverance. Additionally, he was inspired by several caring mentors - a benefit he hopes to pass on to others - continued education and having a "glass that is refillable" attitude. Whether it is half empty or half full, it doesn't matter; it's refillable! **Why did you become involved in your profession or industry:** Mr. DiBacco became involved in his profession because he was inspired by his father, a builder. During a shift in political power, he entered the insurance business with a long-time friend and helped many people. As a young man, he remembers having their bills covered at several restaurants due to his father's stellar customer service. Throughout his career, he has striven to earn similar respect from his own clients. **Avocations:** Music; History; Traveling; Photography; Vintner **Thoughts on Life:** "Where there is hatred, let me sow love; Where there is injury, pardon: Where there is doubt, faith; Where there is despair, hope; Where there is darkness, light: Where there is sadness, joy. Grant that I may not so much seek to be consoled as to console; to be understood as to understand; to be loved as to love. For it is in giving that we receive; In pardoning that we are pardoned; And in dying that we are born to Eternal Life." - St. Francis of Assisi

Matthew D. DiBrino

Title: Chief Executive Officer **Industry:** Law and Legal Services **Company Name:** HQM Loans **Children:** Stevie Jo **Education:** JD, Rutgers Law School (2002); BA in English, Montclair State University (1999) **Certifications:** Licensed Mortgage Broker, State of New Jersey (2014) **Career:** Founder, Owner, HQM Loans (2015-Present); Managing Member, The Law Offices of Matthew D. DiBrino (2005-Present); Municipal Prosecutor, Borough of Totowa, NJ (2011); Adjunct Professor, Berkeley College (2008); Attorney, The Law Office of Weiner & Mazzei (2005); Attorney, Bastarrika, Soto, Gonzalez & Somohano, L.L.P. (2003-2005); Legal Intern, Fusco (2001-2002); Clinic Participant, Child Advocacy Clinic, Rutgers, The State University of New Jersey; Founder, MoonChild Properties **Civic:** The Sunshine Group **Awards:** Nominee, Five-Star Professional, New Jersey Magazine **To what do you attribute your success:** Mr. DiBrino attributes his success to his helping others make the biggest purchases of their lives. **Why did you become involved in your profession or industry:** Mr. DiBrino became involved in his profession after having an argument with an English teacher. After numerous school absences, the teacher wanted to drop his grade despite the excellence he displayed in the class. He had a conversation with the English teacher, as well as the dean, and advocated for a passing grade so that he wouldn't need to repeat the class. The dean agreed to his request and encouraged him to go to law school. **Avocations:** Spending time with his wife and daughter; Coaching youth athletics; Reading; Traveling **Thoughts on Life:** Mr. DiBrino believes "where you get your mortgage from matters."

Daniel Francis DiFonzo

Title: President **Industry:** Corporate Communications & Public Relations **Company Name:** Planar Communications Corporation **Date of Birth:** 10/10/1940 **Place of Birth:** West Chester **State/Country of Origin:** PA/USA **Parents:** Donato DiFonzo; Anna Rose (DiObilda) DiFonzo **Marital Status:** Married **Spouse Name:** Sharon Lee Cowgill (10/20/1962) **Children:** Daniel F.; David C.; Michael J. **Education:** MS in Engineering, California State University, Northridge (1972); BEE, Villanova University (1962) **Career:** President, Planar Communications Corporation (1989-Present); Vice President, General Manager, Communications Satellite Corporation Systems Division (1987-1989); Vice President, COMSAT Technology Services, Communications Satellite Corporation, Clarksburg, MD (1986); Vice President, Assistant Director, COMSAT Laboratories (1985-1986); Senior Director of Corporate Development, Communications Satellite Corporation, Washington, DC (1984-1985); Associate Director of Microwave Technology Division, COMSAT Laboratories (1983-1984); Director of Antenna and Propagation Laboratory, COMSAT Laboratories (1981-1983); Manager of Antennas, COMSAT Laboratories (1977-1981); Technical Staff, COMSAT Laboratories, Clarksburg, MD (1969-1977); Senior Engineer, Bunker-Ramo Corporation, Canoga Park, CA (1966-1969); Development Engineer, American Electronic Laboratories, Colmar, PA (1962-1966) **Career Related:** Board of Directors, COMSAT Retirees Association (2015-Present); National Research Council Panel Assessment, National Institute of Standards and Technology Programs (1987-1993); Consultant in Field **Civic:** Alternate Representative, Industrial Research Institute (1985-1989); Treasurer, Troop 493, Boy Scouts of America, Rockville, MD (1973-1977); Vice President, Rock Creek Valley Elementary School PTA (1973-1974); Cubmaster, Pack 1327 **Creative Works:** Contributor, Scientific Papers; Contributor, Chapters, Books; Contributor, Short Courses **Awards:** Innovation Award, COMSAT **Memberships:** Communications and Information Policy Committee, IEEE (1987-1990); Chairman of Washington Chapter, Antennas and Propagation Society (1981-1982); Microwave Theory and Techniques Society; Senior Member, American Institute of Aeronautics and Astronautics **Marquis Who's Who Honors:** Albert Nelson Marquis Lifetime Achievement Award **Why did you become involved in your profession or industry:** Since Mr. DiFonzo was a child, he was always interested in electronics. **Avocations:** Photography; Golf **Religion:** Roman Catholic

Antonetta Anna DiGiustini

Title: Highly Experienced, Consummate Nonprofit and Public Sector Professional; Dedicated, Accomplished Master Educator **Industry:** Education/Educational Services **Company Name:** The Commonwealth of Massachusetts, House of Representatives, Office of House Counsel; Milton Academy **Date of Birth:** 07/10/1961 **Place of Birth:** Boston **State/Country of Origin:** MA/USA **Parents:** Luigi DiGiustini; Elisa Carolina (Castrucci) DiGiustini **Marital Status:** Single **Education:** AB in History, (Concentration in Modern European History), Harvard College, Cambridge, MA, Dean's List (1997); Mount Saint Joseph Academy, Brighton, MA, Valedictorian, President of Student Council **Career:** Clerk of the House Committee on Bills in the Third Reading, Office of House Counsel, House of Representatives, The Commonwealth of Massachusetts, Boston, MA (2008-Present); Writing Tutor, Private Practice, Boston, MA (2005-Present); Master Teacher, Faculty Member, The Saturday Course, Milton Academy, Milton, MA (2000-Present); Research Analyst, Joint Committee on Mental Health and Substance Abuse, House of Representatives, The Commonwealth of Massachusetts, Boston, MA (2007-2008); Co-Founder, Director, Teacher: Co-Founder, Director, and Teacher, LearningBOSTON, The Advent School, Boston, MA (1999-2007); Teacher, LearningBOSTON, The Advent School, Boston, MA (1999-2007); Long-Term Substitute Teacher, The Advent School, Boston, MA, The Winsor School, Boston, MA, and Brimmer and May School, Chestnut Hill, MA (2001-2006); Account Manager, Loaned Executive Program, Fundraising, United Way of Massachusetts Bay (UWMB), Boston, MA (2004-2005); Stewardship Coordinator, Radcliffe Development Office, Radcliffe Institute for Advanced Study, Harvard University, Cambridge, MA (1998-2003); Staff Assistant, Development Information Services, Radcliffe Institute for Advanced Study, Harvard University, Cambridge, MA (1995-1998); Assistant Director of Public Programs and Education, The Bostonian Society, Old State House Museum, Boston, MA (1991-1993); Teacher, Coordinator of Scholarship Program, Counselor-in-Training, and CRCAP Alumna, Charles River Creative Arts Program (CRCAP), Charles River School, Dover, MA (1977-1992) **Career Related:** Crossroads Anti-Racism Training Workshop: Understanding and Analyzing Systemic Racism. Presented by Crossroads Anti-Racism Organizing and Training, Chicago, IL (2017); We'll Never Turn Back: Voices of the Civil Rights Movement: A Conference for Teachers of History, John F. Kennedy Presidential Library and Museum, Boston, MA (2013); Reading, Writing, and History: A Conference for Teachers of History, John F. Kennedy Presidential Library and Museum, Boston, MA (2008); Seminars on the Massachusetts Legislative Process and the Budget Process (2007-2008); The National Conference of State Legislatures (NCSL) Annual Meeting, Boston, MA (2007) **Civic:** Anti-Racism Team, Trinity Church, Boston, MA (2017-Present); PBHA Public Service Alumna Mentor (2015-Present); Harvard Center for Public Interest Careers (CPIC), CPIC Public Service Alumna Mentor, Harvard University, Cambridge, MA (2012-Present); Alumna Leader, Presenter, and Mentor, Harvard's Annual Public Interested, Public Service Conference (2012-Present); PBHA Class of 1983 Representative (2008-Present); Co-Chair, Harvard Class of 1983 Reunion Memorial Services (2008-Present); Leadership Member, Class of 1983 Reunion Planning Committees (2008-Present); Alumna Commencement Marshal, Harvard Commencements (2003-Present); Harvard Alumni Association (HAA), Class of 1983 Class Leader; Dedicated HAA Volunteer, Harvard University, Cambridge, MA (1983-Present); Phillips Brooks House Association (PBHA), Harvard University, Cambridge, MA (1979-Present); Vice President, Founding Member, Board of Directors, PBHA Alumni Association, (2015-2019) **Creative Works:** Author, Poetry, Various Literary Anthologies (1976-Present); Author, Senior Thesis in History, "Centro-sinistra: Italy's Opening to the Left of 1962: The Case of Continued Christian Democratic Rule or Real Opening to a Christian Democratic-Socialist Coalition" **Awards:** Harvard Faculty Scholarship (1996-1997); Radcliffe College Scholarships (1979-1983); Harvard University Endorsement for Rhodes Scholarship (1982); Rotary Club Fellowship Candidate, Boston Finalist (1982); National Italian American Foundation Scholarship (1982); Radcliffe Club of Boston Scholar (1979); National Council of Teachers of English Award (1978); Westinghouse Science Talent Search Honors Group (1978); Massachusetts State Science Fair, First Prize (1977-1978) **Memberships:** National Association for Gifted Children, Washington, DC (2012-Present); Organization of American Historians Bloomington, IN (2002-Present); American Historical Association and the Society for History Education, Washington, DC (2000-Present); Dedicated HAA Volunteer, Harvard University, Cambridge, MA (1983-Present) **Marquis Who's Who Honors:** Albert Nelson Marquis Lifetime Achievement Award (2019-Present) **Why did you become involved in your profession or industry:** Ms. DiGiustini's parents and teachers all professed the importance of service to others and giving back to society, as well as the importance of education. As a first-generation American and as the daughter of Italian immigrants of the World War II generation, Ms. DiGiustini was raised by her mother and father with a deep appreciation for education, history, democracy, and service to others, as well as with the importance of respecting the dignity of every human being, regardless of race, ethnicity, gender, or creed. **What do you consider to be the highlight of your career?:** The highlight of Ms. DiGiustini's career has been the teaching and mentoring in people's lives. She has tried to foster their growth and potential to the fullest. Another highlight for her was returning to Harvard to complete her college education after a long battle with illness. **Thoughts on Life:** Ms. DiGiustini has had a lifelong love of learning and a quest for knowledge since her childhood. She has additionally always cared deeply about making a difference. She has never envisioned her love of learning and education as an end in itself; rather, she has envisioned and embraced her education as ways in which she could make a difference, as ways in which she could contribute and serve. She has devoted her career and lifework to public service, to "the call of service." **Avocations:** Poetry; Photography; Reading; History; Art; Classical music; Nature; Walking **Political Affiliations:** Democrat **Religion:** Christian

Mary Dillon

Title: Chief Executive Officer **Industry:** Cosmetics **Company Name:** Ulta Salon Cosmetics & Fragrance **Place of Birth:** Chicago **State/Country of Origin:** IL/USA **Education:** Bachelor's Degree in Marketing and Asian Studies, University of Illinois at Chicago (1983) **Career:** Chief Executive Officer, Ulta Salon Cosmetics & Fragrance (2013-Present); Chief Executive Officer, Ulta Beauty Inc. (2013-Present); President, Chief Executive Officer, U.S. Cellular, Telephone & Data Systems Inc. (2010-2013): President, Chief Executive Officer, U.S. Cellular Corporation (2010-2013): Executive Vice President, Global Chief Marketing Officer, McDonald's Corporation (2005-2010); President, Quaker Foods, PepsiCo Inc. (2004-2005): Vice President, Marketing, Quaker Oats Company (2002-2004): Vice President, Marketing, PepsiCo Inc. (2000-2002): Senior Vice President, Marketing, Gardenburger Inc. (1996-2000); Director, Product Offerings, Snapple Beverage Corporation (1995-1996) **Career Related:** Non-Executive Director, Starbucks **Civic:** Trustee, Save the Children Federation (2016) **Awards:** Named, Barron's Best CEO (2019); Sandra Taub Humanitarian Award for Philanthropic Leadership (2018)

Michael A. DiTeresa, MD

Title: Physician, Internist **Industry:** Medicine & Health Care **Year of Passing:** 2020 **Company Name:** Tomball Adult Internal Medicine **Education:** MD in Internal Medicine, University of Texas Southwestern Medical Center, Dallas, TX (2000); Bachelor's Degree, Rice University, Magna Cum laude (1996); Residency in Internal Medicine, Baylor Health Care System **Career:** Physician, Tomball Adult Internal Medicine **Civic:** Mentor, MS Society **Awards:** On-Time Doctor Award (2014); Recipient, Compassionate Doctor Award (2013); Compassionate Doctor Recognition (2009-2013); On-Time Doctor Award (2008); Patients' Choice Award (2008) **Marquis Who's Who Honors:** Albert Nelson Marquis Lifetime Achievement Award; Marquis Who's Who Top Professional **To what do you attribute your success:** Dr. DiTeresa attributes his success to always focusing on his patients' care and remaining as humble as he can possibly be. **Why did you become involved in your profession or industry:** Dr. DiTeresa became involved in this profession simply because his seventh grade biology teacher inspired him and sparked his interest in medicine and health care. **Avocations:** Reading; Working on antique cars; Traveling

Judy Sue Dixson

Title: Retired Elementary School Educator **Industry:** Education/Educational Services **Company Name:** Manchester G.A.T.E. **Date of Birth:** 12/30/1944 **Place of Birth:** Bell **State/Country of Origin:** CA/USA **Parents:** Jack C. Parsons; Arlyne J. (Priddy) Parsons **Marital Status:** Married **Spouse Name:** Michael Dennis Dixson (08/21/1965) **Children:** Tiffany Anne; Michael Bradley (Deceased 1999) **Education:** BA in Biology, Fresno State University, California (1966) **Certifications:** Certified Teacher, California **Career:** Teacher, Manchester Gifted And Talented Education Elementary School, (Manchester G.A.T.E.), Fresno, CA (1983-2002); Teacher, Grades 3-5, Fresno Unified School District (1966-2002); Teacher Leader, California Elementary Mathematics Initiative, Sacramento, CA (1994-1995); Lead Teacher, California Science Implementation Network, Fresno, CA (1993-1994); Mentor Teacher, Fresno Unified School District (1985-1986) **Career Related:** Tutor and Volunteer (2002-Present); Master Teacher, National Teacher Training Institute, Fresno, CA (1994-1995); San Joaquin Valley Mathematics Project, Fresno, CA (1992); Tutor, Samaritan Women **Civic:** Secretary, Prayer Team, New Covenant Community Church (2015-Present); Prayer Team, New Covenant Community Church (2003-Present); Deacon, New Covenant Community Church, Fresno, CA (2013-2017) **Creative Works:** Writer, Educational Materials **Memberships:** California Retired Teachers Association **Marquis Who's Who Honors:** Albert Nelson Marquis Lifetime Achievement Award; Marquis Who's Who Top Professional **To what do you attribute your success:** Ms. Dixson attributes her success to God. She always knew that God put kids in her class to learn lessons. It is her faith. She learned so many lessons as a teachers aide because the kids helped her to be a better teacher. **Why did you become involved in your profession or industry:** Ms. Dixson got into teaching because she enjoys working with children. She was one of the first teacher's aides in Fresno County and went on to teach in the county. In addition, Ms. Dixson wanted to teach children. **Avocations:** Square dancing; Round and line dancing; Sewing; Camping; Knitting; Traveling

Constance N. Dodge Knight, PhD

Title: Independent Geologist **Industry:** Oil & Energy **Company Name:** Constance Knight, Independent Geologist **Place of Birth:** Scottsbluff **State/Country of Origin:** NE/USA **Parents:** Daniel Nuss (Deceased); Wilma Nuss (Deceased) **Marital Status:** Married **Spouse Name:** Roger E. Knight **Children:** Nathan W. Dodge; Elisa A. Landreth **Education:** Doctor of Philosophy in Geology, Colorado School of Mines (1999); Professional Degree in Hydrogeology, Colorado School of Mines (1993); Master of Science in Geology, University of Arizona (1973); Bachelor of Science in Geology, Western Colorado University (1970) **Certifications:** Registered Professional Geologist in Wyoming; Licensed Professional Geologist in Utah **Career:** Independent Contractor (2008-2020); Vice President of Exploration, Three Start-Up Companies (2000-2008); Consultant (1995-2000); Senior Principal Environmental Engineer, EG&G Rocky Flats, Golden, CO (1991-1995); Independent Contractor (1978-1991); Senior Petroleum Geologist, AMOCO Standard Oil of Indiana (1973-1978); Sole Owner, Geo-Educational Services, Founder, New Geologic Teaching Product **Career Related:** Chairman, Denver Chapter, Society of Independent Professional Earth Sciences (2016-2018); Selected, One of 100 Professionals for "Who's Who in Energy" and One of the "Top 40 Women in Energy," Denver Business Journal (2017); Chief Technical Editor, Book, "Application of Structural Methods to Rocky Mountain Hydrocarbon Exploration and Development," American Association of Petroleum Geologists (2013); Member, Board of Directors, Rocky Mountain Association of Geologists (2009, 2010); Member, Speaker, Oral and Visual Presentations, Posters, Short Courses, American Association of Petroleum Geologists, Department of Energy, Geologic Society of America, Rocky Mountain Association of Geologists, Society of Independent Professional Earth Scientists, Society of Petroleum Engineers, U.S. Geological Survey, Wyoming Geological Association; Credited with Gas Well Discovery During the First Two Years of AMOCO Employment **Civic:** Organizer, More Than 100 Presentations in Local Schools, Speakers Bureau, Rocky Mountain Association of Geologists Volunteers **Creative Works:** Author, 44-Page Teacher's Guide and Copy Masters for 11 Activities; Author, Contributor, Numerous Published Works **Awards:** 2011 Distinguished Public Service to the Earth Science Award, Rocky Mountain Association of Geologists (2011); Featured in the publication "Who's Who Among Students in American Universities and Colleges (1970, 1969) **Memberships:** House of Delegates, American Association of Petroleum Geologists; Society of Independent Professional Earth Scientists; Rocky Mountain Association of Geologists; Wyoming Geological Association Denver Well Log Society **Marquis Who's Who Honors:** Albert Nelson Marquis Lifetime Achievement Award; Marquis Who's Who Top Professional **To what do you attribute your success:** Dr. Knight, formerly known as Constance Dodge, attributes her success to growing up in a family of German-Russian immigrants. In her family, hard work and tenacity were pivotal. Much of her success has stemmed from that example. Her grandfather, William Stoll, taught her that she could do anything that boys do. **Why did you become involved in your profession or industry:** Dr. Knight became involved in her profession due to her passion for geology since coming of age. She is still developing and marketing exploration and development energy prospects in the Rocky Mountain region. **Avocations:** Traveling; Nature **Political Affiliations:** Independent **Religion:** Baha'i Faith

Sheperd S. "Shep" Doeleman, PhD

Title: Astrophysicist, Assistant Director **Industry:** Education/Educational Services **Company Name:** Harvard University **Place of Birth:** Wilsele **State/Country of Origin:** Belgium **Parents:** Nels Doeleman (Adoptive Stepfather) **Education:** Doctor of Philosophy in Astrophysics, Massachusetts Institute of Technology (1995); Bachelor of Arts, Reed College (1986) **Career:** Assistant Director, Haystack Observatory, Black Hole Initiative, Harvard University; Director, Event Horizon Telescope, Harvard University **Career Related:** Guggenheim Fellow (2012); With, Max Planck Institute for Radio Astronomy, Bonn, Germany (1995) **Creative Works:** Contributor, "Jet-Launching Structure Resolved Near the Supermassive Black Hole in M87," Science (2012); Contributor, "Detecting Flaring Structures in Sagittarius A* with High-Frequency VLBI," Astrophysics Journal (2009); Contributor, "Event-horizon-scale Structure in the Supermassive Black Hole Candidate at the Galactic Centre," Nature (2008); Author, Dissertation, "Imaging Active Galactic Nuclei with 3mm-VLBI" (1995)

Hellmut Hans Doelling, PhD

Title: Geologist **Industry:** Sciences **Date of Birth:** 07/25/1930 **Place of Birth:** New York **State/Country of Origin:** NY/USA **Parents:** Otto Johannes Doelling (Deceased); Emma Camilla (Hartmann) Doelling (Deceased) **Marital Status:** Married **Spouse Name:** Gerda Anna Scherwinski (05/25/1960) **Children:** David; Barbara; Jedediah; Doris; Peggy; Teresa; Matthew **Education:** PhD, University of Utah (1964); BS, University of Utah (1956) **Career:** Independent Mapping Geologist, Manti, Utah (2004-Present); Senior Mapping Geologist, Utah Geological and Mineral Survey (UGMS), Salt Lake City Utah (1996-2003); Section Chief and Senior Mapping Geologist, Utah Geological and Mineral Survey (UGMS), Salt Lake City, Utah (1983-1995); Economic Geologist, Utah Geological and Mineral Survey (UGMS), Salt Lake City, Utah (1966-1973); Assistant Professor of Geology, Midwestern State University, Wichita Falls, Texas (1964-1966); Staff Geologist, Utah Geological and Mineral Survey (UGMS), Salt Lake City, Utah (1959-1964) **Military Service:** Corporal, United States Army (1951-1953) **Creative Works:** Author, "Geological Map of Smoky Mountain" (2006); Author, "Geological Map of Kanab" (2004); Author, "Geological Map of San Rafael Desert" (2002); Author, "Geological Map of LaSal" (1999); Author, "Geological Map of Escalante" (1998); Author, "30'x 06' Maps: Moab" (1993); Author, Bulletins of Utah County Studies (1975, 1980, 1989); Author, "County Geologic Studies: Kane County, Utah" (1989); Author, "Geological Map of Antelope Island, SP" (1988); Author, "Geological Map of Arches NO" (1985); Author, "Geological Map of Grand Staircase N.M." (1977); Author, "County Geologic Studies: Box Elder County, Utah" (1980); Author, "Methane Content of Utah Coals" (1979); Author, "County Geologic Studies: Garfield County, Utah" (1975); Author, "Coal in Utah" (1972) **Awards:** Distinguished Service Award, Utah Department of Natural Resources (2018); Lehi Hintze Award for Outstanding Contributions to the Geology of Utah, Utah Geological Association (2004); Utah Governor's Medal for Science and Technology (1993) **Memberships:** President, Utah Geological Association (1990); American Association for the Advancement of Science; Society Economic Geologists; Utah Geological Association; Sigma Xi, the Scientific Research Honor Society; Society of Economic Geologists, Inc.; Utah Geological Association **Marquis Who's Who Honors:** Albert Nelson Marquis Lifetime Achievement Award **Why did you become involved in your profession or industry:** Dr. Doelling originally wanted to become a doctor but was unable to follow through with that goal. While enlisted in the United States Army, he would "crawl around on infiltration courses" in El Paso, Texas and noticed "interesting rocks," which began his curiosity with geology. When he finished his time with the Army, he decided to enroll in the University of Utah and received his degree in geology. **Avocations:** Music; Genealogy; Playing the piano **Political Affiliations:** Independent **Religion:** Latter-day Saints Church

Marshall J. Doke Jr., LLB

Title: Partner **Industry:** Law and Legal Services **Company Name:** Gardere Wynne Sewell LLP **Date of Birth:** 06/09/1934 **Place of Birth:** Wichita Falls **State/Country of Origin:** TX/USA **Parents:** Marshall J. Doke; Mary Jane (Johnson) Doke **Marital Status:** Married **Spouse Name:** Betty Marie Orsini (6/2/1956) **Children:** Gregory J.; Michael J.; Laetitia Marie **Education:** LLB, Southern Methodist University, Magna Cum Laude (1959); BA, Hardin-Simmons University, Magna Cum Laude (1956) **Career:** Partner, Gardere, Dallas, TX (1996-Present); Partner, McKenna & Cuneo (1993-1996); Founding Partner, Doke & Riley, Dallas, TX (1987-1992); Founding Partner, Rain Harrell Emery Young & Doke, Dallas, TX (1965-1987); Associate, Thompson, Knight, Wright & Simmons (Now Thompson & Knight), Dallas, TX (1959, 1962-1965) **Career Related:** Member, Advisory Council, U.S. Court of Federal Claims (1982-Present); Member, Federal Acquisitions Advisory Panel, United States Office of Management and Budget (2005-2006); General Counsel, Texas Republican Party (1976-1977) **Civic:** Chairman, Texas Historical Foundation (2004-Present); Director, Texas Historical Foundation (1993-Present); Member, McDonald Observatory, The University of Texas at Austin (1990-Present); President, Texas Historical Foundation (2000-2004); Chair, Judicial Nominating Commission, Dallas, TX (2000-2005); Member, Judicial Nominating Commission, Dallas, TX (1997-2005); President, Hope Cottage Foundation (1998-2002); Member, Hope Cottage Foundation (1997-2002); Vice Chair, Judicial Nominating Commission, Dallas, TX (1998-2000); Vice President, Texas Historical Foundation (1996-1998); Chairman, Board of Directors, The International Trade Association of the Dallas Fort Worth Area (1993-1994); Secretary, Board of Directors, Mayor's International Committee, City of Dallas (1984-1987); President, Board of Directors, Dallas-Fort Worth Section, World Trade Association (1979-1980); Law Committee, Board of Trustees, Southern Methodist University (1977-1978); President, Hope Cottage-Children's Bureau, Inc. (1969-1970); Member, Board of Visitors, School of Law, Southern Methodist University (1966-1969) **Military Service:** First Lieutenant, U.S. Army (1959-1962); Judge Advocate, General Corps, U.S. Army (1959-1962) **Creative Works:** Editor-in-Chief, "Southwestern Law Journal" (1958-1959); Author, "Annual Procurement Review"; Author, "Government Contractor Briefing Papers"; Author, "Contract Changes"; Author, "Federal Contract Management"; Contributor, Articles, Professional Journal **Awards:** J. Woodall Rodgers Award; Honoree, Distinguished Military Graduate; Featured Listee, The Best Lawyers in America **Memberships:** Section Chairman, The America Bar Association; Advisory Committee, US Court of Federal Claims Bar Association (2006-Present); Member, Board of Governors, Boards of Contract Appeals Bar Association, Inc. (1988-Present); National Board of Advisers, National Contract Management Association (1983-Present); Standing Committee on Audit, ABA (2003); House of Delegates, ABA (1970-1972, 1974-2003); Chairman Conference Section Delegates, ABA (1991-2003); Nominating Committee, ABA (1988-1991, 2000-2003); Board of Governors, U.S. Court of Federal Claims Bar Association (1987-2001); President, Board of Governors, U.S. Court of Federal Claims Bar Association (1996); President, Boards of Contract Appeals Bar Association, Inc. (1988-1990); Co-chairman, National Conference Of Lawyers And Certified Public Accountants (1983-1985); President, Board of Directors, American Bar Retirement Association (1982-1984); Trustee, Board of Directors, American Bar Retirement Association (1980-1984); Chairman, International Committee, Dallas Regional Chamber (1979-1983); Board of Governors, ABA (1980-1982); Chairman, Section on Public Contract Law, ABA (1969-1970); Fellow, American Bar Foundation; Fellow, Texas Bar Foundation **Bar Admissions:** State of Texas (1959); U.S. Court of Federal Claims; United States Court of Appeals for the Federal Circuit; Supreme Court of the United States **Marquis Who's Who Honors:** Albert Nelson Marquis Lifetime Achievement Award **Why did you become involved in your profession or industry:** It started in the seventh grade. He knew from that day he wanted to become a lawyer, his Sunday school teacher was a WWII hero, and also the district attorney in the county where he lived. This teacher was his hero and he would go down and watch him try cases and give him books that he treasured. He knew from that time that he wanted to be a lawyer and never deviated from it.

Charles L. Donahue Jr.

Title: Healthcare Consultant **Industry:** Medicine & Health Care **Date of Birth:** 03/31/1943 **Place of Birth:** Norwood **State/Country of Origin:** MA/USA **Parents:** Charles Donahue; Katherine (Gallagher) Donahue **Marital Status:** Married **Spouse Name:** Nancy Turner (08/15/1971) **Children:** Jessica; Charles; Morgan; Caroline; Matthew **Education:** MA, Cornell University, Ithaca, NY (1973); AB, Brown University, Providence, RI (1965) **Career:** Senior Health Care Adviser to the Governor, Rhode Island (2004-2007); President, Co-Founder, HealthCare VALUE Management, Norwood, MA (1990-2004); Executive Director, Health Planning Council for Greater Boston, Inc., Boston, MA (1981-1989); Public Health Adviser, Regional Program Consultant, Health Planning Unit, Public Health Service, Department of Health and Human Services, John F. Kennedy Federal Building, Boston, MA (1980-1981); Director, Health Plan Development, Boston University Center for Health Planning, Boston University Health Policy Center, Boston, MA (1976-1980); Co-Director, Massachusetts Maternity and Newborn Regionalization Project, Massachusetts Health Research Institute, Boston, MA (1975-1976); Planner, Massachusetts Maternity and Newborn Regionalization Project, Massachusetts Health Research Institute, Boston, MA (1974-1975); Planner, Director, Region 6, Health Planning Council for Greater Boston, Inc., Boston, MA (1973-1974) **Career Related:** Member, Dean's Advisory Council, Boston University School of Public Health, Boston, MA (2014-Present); Invited Speaker, Harvard School of Public Health, Boston University School of Management, Boston University School of Public Health, Harvard Business School, Boston College School of Management, Simmons College, Labor Guild School for Industrial and Labor Relations, American Arbitration Association (1983-Present); Adjunct Assistant Professor of Health Services, Boston University School of Public Health, Boston, MA (1991-2003) **Civic:** Board of Directors, Irish American Partnership (2012-Present); Board of Directors, Francis Ouimet Scholarship Fund (2011-Present); Board of Directors, Boston Irish Business Association (2010-Present); Board Member, Brown University Sports Foudnation (2006-Present); Board Member Emeritus, Vice President, New England Employee Benefit Council (2004-Present); Board of Directors, New England Employee Benefit Council (2000-Present); Board of Directors, Vice President, New England Employee Benefits Council (2002-2011); President, Westwood Youth Hockey (2002-2003); Volunteer, U.S. Peace Corps, Trengganu, Malaysia (1967-1968) **Creative Works:** Co-Author, Peer-Reviewed Article, "Variations in Pediatric Pneumonia and Bronchitis/Asthma Admission Rates," Archives of Pediatrics and Adolescent Medicine (1995); Co-Author, Peer-Reviewed Article, "Variations in Hysterectomy Rates Across small geographic areas of Massachusetts," American Journal of Obstetrics and Gynecology (1993); Lecturer, "Reducing Health Insurance Costs," A Program of the Massachusetts Teachers Association (1991); Lecturer, "Causes and Solutions to the Health Cost Problem in Massachusetts," Management Forum on Health Cost Containment (1989); Co-Author, Article, "Identifying Problems of Access to Health Care for Massachusetts Children," Mothers, Infants and Children at Risk (1989); Lecturer, "Analysis of Physician Practice Patterns as a Tool for Implementation of Quality of Care in Massachusetts," community Health Planning Section of the American Public Health Association (1988); Co-Author, Peer-Reviewed Article, "Cesarean Birth Rate: Small Geographic Area Analysis," American Journal of Obstetrics and Gynecology (1988) **Awards:** Citizen of the Year Award, Friends of St. Nick, Norwood, MA (2008); Community Service Award of the Massachusetts League of Community Health Centers (1989); Richard H. Schlesinger Achievement Award in Community Health Planning, Community Health Planning Section of the American Public Health Association and the American Health Planning Association (1988); Superior Performance Award, Public Health Service, Department of Health and Human Services (1980); Financial Award, Cornell University Center for International Studies Research Grants Committee (1972); Financial Award for Research on the British National Health Service, Cornell Research Grants Committee (1970); Financial Award for Research with the Study Group on Comparative Health Systems, Program of Structural Chance and Modernizations, Cornell University (1969) **Memberships:** Chairman, New England Chapter, Ireland Chamber of Commerce - United States (2004); Westwood Massachusetts; School Committee Chair Irish American Partnership Board; Dean's Advisory Council, Boston "University School of Public Health; Board member, Brown Sports Foundation; Board member, Irish international immigrant center **Why did you become involved in your profession or industry:** Mr. Donahue became involved in his profession because he served two years in the Peace Corps in Malaysia in a tuberculosis control program. It was his giving back and thanking the country that inspired him to go into the health field. **Avocations:** Coaching youth hockey; Golf; Teaching history

David Donaldson

Title: Consultant Chemical Pathologist (Retired) **Industry:** Sciences **Date of Birth:** 02/13/1936 **Place of Birth:** Birmingham **State/Country of Origin:** United Kingdom **Parents:** Henry Donaldson; Esther Donaldson **Education:** MB, ChB, University of Birmingham (1959) **Certifications:** EurClinChem (Registered European Clinical Chemist) **Career:** Consultant, Chemical Pathology, Gatwick Park Bupa Health Centre, Bupa (1984-2006); Consultant, Chemical Pathology, Crawley Hospital, Surrey and Sussex Healthcare NHS Trust, Crawley, West Sussex, United Kingdom (1970-2001); Consultant, Chemical Pathology, East Surrey Hospital, Surrey and Sussex Healthcare NHS Trust, Redhill, Surrey, United Kingdom (1970-2001); Clinical Director, Pathology, East Surrey Hospital, Surrey and Sussex Healthcare NHS Trust, Redhill, Surrey, United Kingdom (1991-1994); Lecturer, Honorary Senior Registrar, Chemical Pathology, Institute of Neurology (Now UCL Queen Square Institute of Neurology), National Hospital for Neurology and Neurosurgery, University College London Hospitals NHS Foundation Trust (1964-1970); Registrar, General Medicine, Keighley and District Victoria Hospital, Keighley, West Yorkshire, United Kingdom (1963-1964); Assistant Resident Medical Officer, Leeds General Infirmary, The Leeds Teaching Hospitals, Leeds, West Yorkshire, United Kingdom (1961-1962); Registrar, General Medicine, Leeds General Infirmary, The Leeds Teaching Hospitals, Leeds, West Yorkshire, United Kingdom (1961-1962); Senior House Officer, Clinical Pathology, Queen Elizabeth Hospital, Birmingham, West Midlands, United Kingdom (1960-1961); House Surgeon, Birmingham Women's and Children's, Birmingham, West Midlands, United Kingdom (1960); House Physician, Selly Oak Hospital, Birmingham, West Midlands, United Kingdom (1959-1960) **Career Related:** Lecturer, Clinical Biochemistry, London South Bank University (1997-2011); Chairman, Chemical Pathology Advisory Sub-Committee, South West Thames Regional Health Authority (1995-2000); Vice Chairman, Medical Sub-Committee, Marie Curie Memorial Foundation, Marie Curie (1978-1983); Lecturer, Chemical Pathology **Civic:** Piano Player, Standen House and Garden, National Trust **Creative Works:** Deputy Honorary Editor, Editorial Board Member, "Journal of the Royal Society for the Promotion of Health" (1997-2004); Author, "Psychiatric Disorders with a Biochemical Basis" (1998); Co-Author, "Diagnostic Function Tests in Chemical Pathology" (1989); Co-Author, "Essential Diagnostic Tests in Biochemistry and Hematology" (1971); Contributor, Chapters, Books; Contributor, Articles, Over 100 Professional Journals **Awards:** Five-Year Voluntary Long Service Award, Standen House and Garden, National Trust (2017); Prof. M. Mori Felicitation Award, International College of Human Nutrition and Functional Medicine (2002) **Memberships:** Guild of Freemen of the City of London (2002); Fellow, Royal Society of Biology (2001); Fellow, Royal Society of Chemistry (2001); Fellow, Royal College of Physicians (1999); Chairman, East Surrey District, South Eastern Branch, BMA (1992-1993); Fellow, The Royal College of Pathologists (1981); Member, The Royal College of Pathologists, (1969); Member, Royal College of Physicians (1963); Fellow, The Hunterian Society; Fellow, The Medical Society of London; Life Fellow, International College of Human Nutrition and Functional Medicine; The Royal Society of Medicine; Royal Society for Public Health; Royal Geographical Society; British Association for the Advancement of Science (Now British Science Association); HEART UK; The Association for Clinical Biochemistry and Laboratory Medicine; Harveian Society of London; American Association for the Advancement of Science, (AAAS); The New York Academy of Sciences; American Society for Clinical Pathology; Faculty, History, The Worshipful Society of Apothecaries; Faculty, Philosophy of Medicine and Pharmacy, The Worshipful Society of Apothecaries **Marquis Who's Who Honors:** Albert Nelson Marquis Lifetime Achievement Award; Marquis Who's Who Top Professional; Marquis Who's Who Humanitarian Award **To what do you attribute your success:** Dr. Donaldson has always believed that everything is interesting, so long as you can find the interest in it. He attributes his success to identifying and developing his own interests. **Why did you become involved in your profession or industry:** Dr. Donaldson became involved in his profession while he was a student at King Edward's School in Birmingham. There, he developed an interest in and passion for chemistry, biology and physics. Fittingly, Dr. Donaldson's father worked as a chemist, and exposed his son to the wonders of chemistry from an early age. **Avocations:** Playing piano; Music; Studying the history of medicine

Brian "KAWS" Donnelly

Title: Artist **Industry:** Fine Art **Date of Birth:** 11/4/1974 **Place of Birth:** Jersey City **State/Country of Origin:** NJ/USA **Education:** Bachelor of Fine Arts in Illustration, School of Visual Arts (1996) **Career:** Freelance Animator, Jumbo Pictures, New York, NY **Career Related:** Graffiti Artist, New York, NY **Creative Works:** Collaborator, Clothing and Soft Toys, Sesame Street And Uniglo (2018); Collaborator, Sneakers, Jordan Brand (2017); Collaborator, KAWS Companion Action Figure Collection, Museum Of Modern Art (2017); Collaborator, Uniqlo (2016); Designer, Girl By Commes Des Garçons And Pharrell Williams (2014); Artist, Redesign, MTV Moonman Trophy (2013); Solo Show, "Beautiful Losers" (2012); Guest Judge, "Work Of Art: The Next Great Artist" (2011); Collaborator, Guitar Picks, John Mayer (2008); Album Cover Artist, "808s & Heartbreak" (2008); Album Cover Artist, "'Till The Casket Drops" (2008); Collaborator, Billboard, Undefeated Brand (2004); Sculpture, "Companion" (1999); Collaborator, Vinyl Toy, Bounty Hunter (1999); Collaborator, Vinyl Toy, Nigo For A Bathing Ape (Bape); Collaborator, Vinyl Toy, Medicom Toy; Collaborator, Vinyl Toy, Santastic!; Collaborator, Vinyl Toy, Undercover, Kung Fax; Collaborator, Burton; Collaborator, Sneakers, Vans; Collaborator, Clothing, Supreme; Collaborator, Shoes, DC Shoes; Collaborator, Glass Bottle, Dos Equis; Collaborator, Glass Bottle, Hennessy; Collaborator, Rugs, Gallery 1950; Collaborator, Cosmetics, Kiel's Cosmetics; Artist, "The Kimpsons"; Permanent Collection, "Where The End Starts"; Permanent Collection, "Along The Way," Brooklyn Museum, Brooklyn, NY; Permanent Collection, Museum Of Contemporary Art San Diego, San Diego, CA; Permanent Collection, "Waiting," One Campus Martius, Detroit, MI

Jennifer Anne Doudna

Title: Biochemist **Industry:** Sciences **Date of Birth:** 02/19/1964 **Place of Birth:** Washington **State/Country of Origin:** DC/USA **Marital Status:** Married **Spouse Name:** Jamie Cate **Children:** One Son **Education:** Honorary DSc, University of Oxford (2019); Honorary DSc, York University, Toronto, ON, Canada (2019); Honorary DSc, University of Southern California (2018); Honorary DSc, University of Hong Kong (2017); Honorary DSc, Yale University, New Haven, CT (2016); PhD in Biological Chemistry and Molecular Pharmacology, Harvard University, Cambridge, MA (1989); BA in Biochemistry, Pomona College, Claremont, CA (1985) **Career:** Professor of Biochemistry and Molecular Biology, University of California Berkeley (2002-Present); Henry Ford II Professor, Molecular Biophysics and Biochemistry, Yale University, New Haven, CT (1999-2002); Assistant to Associate Professor, Yale University, New Haven, CT (1994-1998); Postdoctoral Research Fellow, Biomedical Science, University of Colorado (1991-1994); Postdoctoral Research Fellow, Molecular Biology, Massachusetts General Hospital/Harvard Medical School, Boston, MA (1989-1991) **Career Related:** Fellow, American Academy of Inventors (2014); R.B. Woodward Visiting Professor, Harvard University, Cambridge, MA (2000-2001); Investigator, Howard Hughes Medical Institute, Chevy Chase, MD; Faculty Scientist, Physical Biosciences Division, Lawerence Berkeley National Laboratory, Berkeley, CA **Creative Works:** Contributor, Articles, Professional Journals **Awards:** Co-Recipient, Wolf Prize in Medicine (2020); Nierenberg Prize (2019); Lui Che Woo Prize (2019); Co-Recipient, Harvey Prize (2018); Co-Recipient, Medal of Honor, American Cancer Society (2018); Pearl Meister Grrengard Prize, Rockefeller University (2018); Croonian Medal and Lecture, Royal Society (2018); Named, Forbes' America's Top 50 Women in Tech (2018); Johnson Foundation Prize for Innovative Research (1996, 2018); Dickson Prize in Science, Carnegie Mellon University (2018); Carl Sagan Prize for Science Popularization (2017); Co-Recipient, Albany Medical Center Prize (2017); F. Albert Cotton Medal (2017); Co-Recipient, Japan Prize (2017); L'Oréal-UNESCO Award for Women in Science (2016); Co-Recipient, BBVA Foundation Frontiers of Knowledge Award (2016); Co-Recipient, HFSP Nakasone Award (2016); Co-Recipient, Tang Prize (2016); Heineken Prize for Biochemistry and Biophysics (2016); Co-Recipient, Paul Ehrlich and Ludwig Darmstaedter Prize (2016); Co-Recipient, Warren Alpert Foundation Prize (2016); Co-Recipient, Canada Gairdner International Award (2016); Co-Recipient, Gruber Prize in Genetics (2015); Co-Recipient, Princess of Asturias Awards (2015); 100 Most Influential People in the World, "TIME" (2015); Co-Recipient, Massry Prize (2015); Co-Recipient, Breakthrough Prize in Life Sciences (2015); Co-Recipient, Dr. Paul Janssen Award for Biomedical Research (2014); Lurie Prize in Biomedical Sciences from the Foundation for the National Institutes of Health (2014); Co-Recipient, Jacob Heskel Gabbay Award (2014); Mildred Cohn Award in Biological Chemistry, American Society for Biochemistry and Molecular Biology (2013); Eli Lilly Award in Biological Chemistry, American Chemical Society (2013); Kaval Prize in Nanoscience; Eli Lilly Award in Biological Chemistry, American Chemical Society (2001); Alan T. Waterman Award, National Science Foundation (2000); Alan T. Waterman Award (2000); NAS Award for Initiatives in Research (1999); Beckman Young Investigators Award (1996); David & Lucile Packard Foundation Fellow Award (1996); Beckman Young Investigator Award, Arnold & Mabel Beckman Foundation (1996); Searle Scholar Award (1996); Lucille P. Markey Scholar Award in Biomedical Science (1991); National Research Service Award in Biomedical Science (1986) **Memberships:** Foreign Member, Royal Society (2016); National Academy of Medicine (2010); National Academy of Arts and Sciences (2003); National Academy of Sciences (2002); Board of Trustees, Pomona College, Claremont, CA

Kirk Douglas

Title: Actor, Film Producer, Director **Industry:** Media & Entertainment **Date of Birth:** 12/9/1916 **Place of Birth:** Amsterdam **State/Country of Origin:** Netherlands **Year of Passing:** 2020 **Parents:** Herschel Danielovitch; Bryna Danielovitch **Marital Status:** Married **Spouse Name:** Anne Buydens; Diana Dill (Divorced) **Children:** Michael; Joel; Peter; Anthony; Eric (Deceased) **Education:** Honorary Doctor of Fine Arts, St. Lawrence University, Canton, NY (1958); Coursework, American Academy of Dramatic Arts (1939-1941); Bachelor of Arts, St. Lawrence University, Canton, NY (1938) **Career:** Actor; Film Producer; Director **Civic:** Goodwill Ambassador, U.S. Information Agency; Donor, Harry's Haven; Founder, The Anne Douglas Center for Homeless Women, Los Angeles Mission; Donor, The Kirk Douglas Theater at the Aish Center; Donor, Children's Hospital Los Angeles **Military Service:** Serviceman, U.S. Navy (1941-1944) **Creative Works:** Actor, "Empire State Building Murders" (2008); Actor, "Illusion" (2004); Actor, "It Runs in the Family" (2003); Actor, "Touched by an Angel" (2000); Actor, "Diamonds" (1999); Actor, "Xena: Warrior Princess" (1997); Actor, "The Simpsons" (1996); Actor, "Take Me Home Again" (1994); Actor, "Greedy" (1994); Actor, "A Century of Cinema" (1994); Actor, "The Secret" (1992); Actor, "Tales From The Crypt" (1991); Actor, "Veraz/Welcome to Veraz" (1991); Actor, "Oscar" (1991); Actor, "Oscar" (1991); Actor, "Inherit the Wind" (1988); Actor, "Queenie" (1987); Actor, "Tough Guys; Actor, Film Amos" (1985); Actor, "Hollywood Greats" (1984); Actor, "Draw!" (1984); Actor, "Eddie Macon's Run" (1983); Actor, "Remembrance of Love" (1982); Actor, The Man from Snowy River" (1982); Actor, "The Final Countdown" (1980); Actor, "Home Movies" (1980); Actor, "Saturn 3" (1980); Actor, "The Villain" (1979); Actor, "The Fury" (1978); Actor, "Holocaust 2000" (1977); Actor, "Victory at Entebbe" (1976); Actor, "Once is Not Enough" (1975); Actor, "Posse" (1975); Actor, "Mousey" (1974); Actor, "Dr. Jekyll and Mr. Hyde" (1973); Actor, "Scalawag" (1973); Actor, "The Master Touch" (1972); Actor, "A Gunfight" (1971); Actor, "The Light at the Edge of the World" (1971); Actor, "To Catch a Spy" (1971); Actor, "The Johnny Cash Show" (1970); Actor, "There Was a Crooked Man…" (1970); Actor, "The Arrangement" (1969); Actor, "The Brotherhood" (1968); Actor, "A Lovely Way to Die" (1968); Actor, "Once Upon a Wheel" (1968); Actor, "The War Wagon" (1967); Actor, "The Way West" (1967); Actor, "Is Paris Burning?" (1966); Actor, "Cast a Giant Shadow" (1966); Actor, "The Heroes of Telemark" (1965); Actor, "In Harm's Way" (1965); Actor, "Seven Days in May" (1964); Actor, "For Love or Money" (1963); Actor, "The List of Adrian Messenger" (1963); Actor, "The Hook" (1963); Actor, Two Weeks in Another Town" (1962); Actor, Lonely Are the Brave" (1962); Actor, "Lonely Are the Brave" (1962); Actor, "The Last Sunset" (1961); Actor, "Town Without Pity" (1961); Actor, "Spartacus" (1960); Actor, "The Devil's Disciple" (1959); Actor, "Last Train from Gun Hill" (1959); Actor, "The Vikings" (1958); Actor, "Paths of Glory" (1957); Actor, "Gunfight at the O.K. Corral" (1957); Actor, "Top Secret Affair" (1957); Actor, "Lust for Life" (1956); Actor, "The Indian Fighter" (1955); Actor, "Man Without a Star" (1955); Actor, "Ulysses" (1955); Actor, "The Racers" (1955); Actor, "20,000 Leagues Under the Sea" (1954); Actor, "The Jack Benny Show" (1954); Actor, "Act of Love" (1953); Actor, "The Juggler" (1953); Actor, "The Bad and the Beautiful" (1952); Actor, Film The Big Sky" (1952); Actor, "The Big Trees" (1952); Actor, "Along the Great Divide" (1951); Actor, "The Glass Menagerie" (1950); Actor, "Young Man with a Horn" (1950); Actor, "Champion" (1949); Actor, "A Letter to Three Wives" (1949); Actor, "My Dear Secretary" (1948); Actor, "The Walls of Jericho" (1948); Actor, "Out of the Past" (1947); Actor, "The Strange Love of Martha Ivers" (1946); Author, "The Ragman's Son"; Author, "Dance with the Devil"; Author, "The Gift"; Author, "Last Tango in Brooklyn"; Author, "The Broken Mirror: A Novella"; Author, "Young Heroes of the Bible"; Author, "Climbing the Mountain: My Search for Meaning"; Author, "My Stroke of Luck"; Author, "Let's Face It: 90 Years of Living, Loving and Learning" **Awards:** Excellence in Film, Santa Barbara International Film Festival (2006); National Medal of Arts (2002); Golden Bear Award, Berlin Film Festival (2001); Lifetime Achievement Jerusalem Film Festival (2000); Spencer Tracy Award Outstanding Achievement in Drama (1999); Lifetime Achievement Award, Screen Actors Guild (1999); Meltze Award for Breaking Blacklist, Writers Guild of America (1999); Lifetime Achievement, Honorary Oscar (1996); Kennedy Center Honors (1994); Lifetime Achievement Award, American Film Institute (1991); Officer de la Legion d'Honneur (1990); Chevalier de la Legion d'Honneur (1985); Decorated Legion of Honor, France (1985); Inductee, Cowboy Hall of Fame (1984); S. Roger Horchow Award for Greatest Public Service by a Private Citizen, Jefferson Awards (1983); Presidential Medal of Freedom (1981); Cecil B. DeMille Award for Contributions in the Entertainment Field (1967); Named, Congressional Record for service as Goodwill Ambassador (1964); Splendid American Award of Merit, Washington Carver Memorial Foundation (1957); Nominee, Academy Award (1949, 1952, 1956) **Avocations:** Blogging **Religion:** Jewish

Stephen B. Douglas

Title: Publishing Company Executive **Industry:** Publishing **Date of Birth:** 04/20/1954 **Place of Birth:** Glendale **State/Country of Origin:** CA/USA **Career:** Founder, President, Redheads International, Corona del Mar, CA (1981-Present); Executive Director, Producer, USA Petites, Productions, Inc. **Creative Works:** Author, "The Redhead Dynasty" (1986) **Avocations:** Writing **Political Affiliations:** Democrat

James L. Dozier

Title: Security Consultant (Retired); Military Officer (Retired) **Industry:** Military & Defense Services **Date of Birth:** 04/10/1931 **Place of Birth:** Arcadia **State/Country of Origin:** FL/USA **Parents:** Joseph B.; Leota (Caruthers) D. **Marital Status:** Married **Spouse Name:** Sharlene Hamel (12/01/2006) **Children:** Cheryl Lyn; Scott Lee **Education:** MS in Aerospace Engineering, The University of Arizona (1964); BS, United States Military Academy (1956) **Career:** Retired Security Consultant (2004); Owner, JCS Group, Fort Myers, FL (1993-2004); General Manager, David C. Brown Enterprises (1988-1993); President, Sun Coast Media Group, Venice, FL (1987); President, Golden Grove Management Corp., Arcadia, FL (1985-1987); Retired Military Officer (1985) **Career Related:** Lecturer, Conductor, Seminars on Kidnapping Experience, Various Military Organizations **Civic:** Board Chair, Good Wheels; Board Member, Lee County Electric Coop (LCEC); Board Member, Disabled Veterans Insurance Careers; Former President, Small Business Political Action Committee, Lee County, FL; Board Member, Organization that Provides Low Income Housing for Veterans; Advisor, Military Museum, Cape Coral, FL; Serves, Nominating Committee for Congressman for Service Academy **Military Service:** Retired, United States Army (1985); Deputy Commanding General, III Corps and Fort Hood, United States Army, Fort Hood, Texas (1983-1985); Advanced through Grades to Major General, United States Army (1984); Assistant Commandant, Armor School, United States Army, Fort Knox, KY (1982-1983); Deputy Chief of Staff Logistics and Administration, Allied Land Forces Southern Europe, United States Army, Verona, Italy (1980-1982); Chief of Staff, III Corps and Fort Hood, United States Army, Fort Hood, Texas (1979-1980); Chief of Staff, Second Armored Division, United States Army, Fort Hood, Texas (1978-1979); Commander, Second Brigade, Second Armored Division, United States Army, Fort Hood, Texas (1976-1978); Military Assistant to Assistant Secretary of Army, United States Army, Washington, DC (1974-1976); Staff Officer, Office of Deputy Chief of Staff for Research, Development and Acquisition, United States Army, Washington, DC (1974-1976); Commander, First Squadron, First Cavalry, First Armored Division, United States Army, Germany (1971-1973); Commissioned Second Lieutenant, United States Army (1956) **Creative Works:** Contributing Author, "Winter of Fire" (1990); Author, Autobiography, "Pole Star"; Contributor, Articles to Military Journals **Awards:** Decorated Silver Star; Legion of Merit; Bronze Star with V Device; Two Oak Leaf Clusters; Air Medals; Purple Heart **Marquis Who's Who Honors:** Albert Nelson Marquis Lifetime Achievement Award; Marquis Who's Who Top Professional **Why did you become involved in your profession or industry:** General Dozier did not start out to seek a military career, but the social thing to do in his high school class was to join the Florida National Guard. He did along with others, but he did this three weeks before the North Koreans invaded South Korea. His National Guard unit was federalized. He liked the military life, so he applied for a National Guard appointment to West Point, and was accepted, and that started it. After he was commissioned, he was in an armored cavalry regiment that controlled the iron curtain in Germany. **Avocations:** Fishing; Boating; Woodworking (building shelves); Tropical plants; Sitting on Boards and not-for-profits

James Francis Drane

Title: Philosophy Educator **Industry:** Education/Educational Services **Date of Birth:** 04/06/1930 **Place of Birth:** Chester **State/Country of Origin:** PA/USA **Parents:** James Drane; Anna (King) Drane **Marital Status:** Single **Education:** Postgraduate Coursework, Georgetown University School of Medicine (1981); Postgraduate Coursework, Menninger School of Psychiatry (1976-1977); Postgraduate Coursework, Yale University (1967-1969); Postgraduate Coursework, Union Theological Seminary (1966); Postgraduate Coursework, Georgetown University (1965); PhD in Philosophy/Ethics, University of Madrid (1964); MA in Romance Languages, Middlebury College (1961); BD in Theology, Pontifical Gregorian University (1953); AB in Philosophy, Little Rock College (Not University of Arkansas at Little Rock) (1951) **Career:** Professor Emeritus, Edinboro University, PA (1992-Present); Russell B. Roth Professor of Clinical Medical Ethics, Edinboro University, PA (1987-1992); Teacher of Philosophy, Religion, Medical Ethics, Edinboro University, PA (1969-1992); Psychiatric Residency, Faculty and Staff Education, Warren State Hospital (1978-1984); Teacher of Religious Studies, Summers, Webster University (1967-1969); Teacher of Philosophy and Romance Languages, University of Arkansas at Little Rock (1956-1967) **Career Related:** Visiting Associate, University of Pittsburgh Center of Medical Ethics, Pittsburgh, PA (1991-1993); Fellow, Kennedy Institute for Ethics, Georgetown University (1990); First Resident Bioethicist, Pan America Division, World Health Organization (1990); Member, Faculty of Medicine, University of Madrid (1987); Visiting Scholar, Ortega y Gasset University Research Institute, University of Madrid (1985); Visiting Scholar, Researcher, The University of Tennessee School of Medicine (1982); Visiting Scholar, The University of Tennessee College of Medicine (1982); Visiting Scholar, Kennedy Institute for Bioethics, Georgetown University (1981); Visiting Professor, Menninger School of Psychiatry, Topeka, KS (1976-1977); Special Consultant to Spanish Hierarchy on Religious Liberty (1963); Consultant, Pennsylvania Catholic Conference, American Association of Nurse Anesthetists; Ethics Advisor, Education Consultant, Pennsylvania Healthcare Institutions; Multiple Courses Developed for Schools and Institutions **Civic:** Commonwealth Speaker, Pennsylvania Humanities Council (1988, 1990, 1992, 1993); Associate, Danforth Foundation, St. Louis, MO (1973); Member, U.S. Commission on Civil Rights (1965) **Creative Works:** Author, "Medicine Ethics Religion" (2018); Author, "A Liberal Catholic Bioethics" (2010); Author, "Finding Relief from Suffering and Depression" (2010); Author, "Sufrimiento y Depresion" (2009); Author, "Medicina Mas Humana" (2006); Author, "Bioethica, Medicina e Technologia: Desafios Eticlos Na Fornteira Do Conhecimiente Humano" (2005); Author, "More Humane Medicine: A Liberal Catholic Bioethics" (2003); Editor, Book, "Bioethical Perspectives from Ibero-America" (1996); Editor, "The Journal of Medicine and Philosophy: A Forum for Bioethics and Philosophy of Medicine" (1996); Contributor, Television and Radio Programs (1975-2005); Member, Editorial Boards, Health Progress, Quiron, Cuadernos del Programa Regional de Bioetica, and Humanitas Journal of Medicine and Humanities; Author, Books; Contributor, Articles to Professional Journals and Newspapers; Contributor, Chapters to Books **Awards:** Inductee, Saint James Catholic High School Wall of Honor (2015); Named Outstanding Book of the Year, Best Health Book, "More Humane Medicine: A Liberal Catholic Bioethics", Independent Publisher Book Awards (2004); Martin Luther King Jr. Award (2002); Grantee, DeFrees Foundation (1985-1990, 1992-1993); Grantee, Institute for Humanities and Medicine (1988-1989); Named Distinguished Educator, Erie-Chautauqua Magazine (1988); Grantee, U.S.-Spanish Joint Committee for Cultural and Educational Cooperative, Fulbright Commission (1986); Grantee, St. Mary's Foundation (1983, 1984); Grantee, National Endowment of the Humanities (1982); Grantee, Pennsylvania State College Educational Trust Fund (1976-1977); Grantee, Pennsylvania Department of Education (1976-1977); Named Distinguished Teaching Chair of Pennsylvania, Secretary of Education, PA (1976); Excellence in Teaching Award (1975) **Memberships:** President, St. John's Alumni Association (1966-1967); Society for Christian Ethics; Society for Health and Human Values; America Society of Law, Medicine and Ethics (ASLME); Society for Bioethics Consultation (Now American Society for Bioethics and Humanities); The Catholic Health Association of the United States **Marquis Who's Who Honors:** Albert Nelson Marquis Lifetime Achievement Award **Why did you become involved in your profession or industry:** Dr. Drane was inspired by the obligations associated with the priesthood. He studied in Rome with the priesthood theology and that was the beginning of contact with a world of academic realities. It was not just theology, it was linked to all kind of realities in other nations that was the immersion into broader intellectual prospective. **Religion:** Catholic

Hannah Dreier

Title: National Reporter **Industry:** Other **Company Name:** The Washington Post **Education:** Ochberg Fellowship, Dart Center for Journalism & Trauma, Columbia Journalism School (2018); Poynter Fellowship in Journalism, Yale University; Seminars for Business Journalists, The Wharton School, The University of Pennsylvania; Kiplinger Fellowship for Public Affairs Journalism, The Ohio State University; H.F. Guggenheim Foundation Journalism Fellowship for Reporting on Violence, John Jay College of Criminal Justice; BA, Wesleyan University **Career:** National Reporter, The Washington Post (2019-Present); Reporter, Pro Publica Inc. (2017-2019); Venezuela Correspondent, Associated Press (2014-2017); Gambling Correspondent, Associated Press (2013-2014); Politics Reporter, Associated Press (2012-2013); Metro Reporter, The Mercury News (2010-2012) **Creative Works:** Contributor, "Best American Magazine Writing," Columbia University Press (2019); Author, "MS-13 on Long Island," Pro Publica Inc. (2018); Author, "Venezuela Undone," Associated Press (2017) **Awards:** Pulitzer Prize for Feature Writing (2019); Robert F. Kennedy Journalism Award (2019); Fred M. Hechinger Grand Prize, Education Writers Association (2019); Hillman Prize for Magazine Journalism (2019); Finalist, Livingston Awards for Young Journalists (2019); The Molly National Journalism Prize (2019); Ethics in Journalism Award, Society of Professional Journalists (2019); John Bartlow Martin Award for Public Interest Magazine Journalism (2019); Finalist, National Magazine Award (2019); Finalist, Peabody Awards (2019); Daniel Schorr Journalism Prize for Public Radio Reporting (2019); John Jay/Harry Frank Guggenheim Award for Excellence in Criminal Justice Journalism (2019); Sidney Award for Journalism (2018); Feature Category, Online Journalism Awards (2018); Feature Category, Education Writers Association (2018); Overseas Press Club Hal Boyle Award (2017); Finalist, The Michael Kelly Awards, Atlantic Media (2017); Gerald Loeb Award for International Reporting (2017); James Foley Medill Medal for Courage in Journalism (2017); Ethics in Journalism Award, Society of Professional Journalists (2017); Ancil Payne Award for Ethics in Journalism, University of Oregon (2017); Finalist, Deborah Howell Award for Writing Excellence, American Society of News Editors Awards (2016); Finalist, Livingston Awards for Young Journalists (2016); Large Feature, Best in Business, Society for Advancing Business Editing and Writing (2016); Finalist, Livingston Awards for Young Journalists (2013); National Headliner Award for Beat Coverage (2013); James Madison Freedom of Information Award, Society of Professional Journalists (2013); Latino Journalists of California Ruben Salazar Award (2012)

David M. Dressler, MD

Title: Psychiatrist and Jungian Analyst **Industry:** Medicine & Health Care **Date of Birth:** 05/09/1939 **Place of Birth:** Chicago **State/Country of Origin:** IL/USA **Marital Status:** Engaged **Spouse Name:** Susan **Children:** One Son; One Daughter **Education:** Graduate, C.G. Jung Institute of New York (1992); Fellowship, Yale University, New Haven, CT (1968-1969); Residency, Strong Memorial Hospital, Rochester, NY (1965-1968); Internship, San Francisco General Hospital (1964-1965); MD, University of Chicago (1964); BA, Reed College (1960) **Certifications:** Diplomate, American Board of Psychiatry and Neurology **Career:** Private Practice, Roxbury, CT (1992-Present); Chief, Psychiatry, New Britain General Hospital (1973-1992); Associate Professor, Psychiatry, University of Connecticut School of Medicine (1973-1992); Assistant Professor, Psychiatry, Yale University, New Haven, CT (1969-1973) **Career Related:** Distinguished Life Fellow, American Psychiatric Association **Creative Works:** Author, Pamphlet, "Guidelines for a Productive, Meaningful and Fulfilling Life: Practical Wisdom gained from 50 years of clinical practice and 80 years of life experience and self reflection" (2019) **Awards:** Top Psychiatrist in Connecticut, Top Docs (2019) **Memberships:** American Psychiatric Association; Connecticut State Medical Society **Marquis Who's Who Honors:** Albert Nelson Marquis Lifetime Achievement Award; Marquis Who's Who Top Professional **To what do you attribute your success:** Dr. Dressler attributes his success to personal integrity, emotional relatedness, commitment and perseverance. **Why did you become involved in your profession or industry:** Dr. Dressler became involved in his profession because as a senior in college, he did not want to go to graduate school in chemistry. A dream informed him that he would become a psychiatrist. He is currently in his 51st year of practice. **Avocations:** Music; Reading history, biography and fiction books; Exercising and fitness; Golfing; Fine dining; Traveling **Thoughts on Life:** Dr. Dressler decided to be a union analyst; he was 40 when he made that decision. He read a book by Carl Young called "Modern Man in Search of a Soul." After reading that book, he knew that was the right path for him because Carl Young was a spiritual teacher, which he is today, and it resonated with him. Dr. Dressler does not live in a box, he is always free in any moment in time to make a choice. He's not programmed in any way. Most people are programmed, meaning there's an earlier experience that shapes what they do and as a general rule, they have a hard time behaving differently.

Lawrence Michael DuBuske, MD

Title: Clinical Professor of Medicine, Immunologist, Allergist **Industry:** Medicine & Health Care **Company Name:** The George Washington University School of Medicine and Health Sciences **Date of Birth:** 10/16/1954 **Place of Birth:** Jersey City **State/Country of Origin:** NJ/USA **Parents:** Stanley DuBuske (1920- 2018)Josephine DuBuske (1919-2017) **Marital Status:** Married **Spouse Name:** Dr. Ilona DuBuske, DO **Children:** Robert DuBuske (1982); Barbara DuBuske Lynch (1980) **Education:** Fellow, Allergy, Rheum and Res Immunology, Brigham and Women's Hospital, Harvard Med School, Boston (1981-1984); Internal Medicine Residency, Barnes Hospital, Asso in Med, Washington University in St. Louis (1978-1981); MD, Northwestern University, Chicago, IL, With Distinction (1978); BS, Northwestern University, Evanston, IL, With Distinction (1976) **Certifications:** Diplomate, Rheumatology (Sub-Spec Cert), American Board of Internal Medicine (ABIM) (1991-2001); Diplomate, American Board of Allergy and Immunology (1984); Diplomate, American Board of Internal Medicine (ABIM) (1981) **Career:** Clinical Professor of Medicine, Division of Allergy and Immunology, Department of Internal Medicine, George Washington University, Washington, DC (2010-Present); President, Medical Education and Research Management Services of New England (2005-Present); Director, Immunology Research Institute of New England, Gardner, MA (1990-Present); Director, Allergy and Arthritis Family Treatment Center, Gardner, MA (1984-Present); Founder, Boston Allergy Group, Newton Center, MA (2020); Director of Immunology, New England Educational Institute (1999-2005); Clinical Instructor in Medicine, Harvard Medical School (1984-2010); Consult Physician, Brigham and Women's Hospital, Boston, MA (1984-2010) **Career Related:** Consult, Allergy Therapeutics (2004-Present); Consult, Abionic, Switzerland (2019-2020); Consult, ALK Pharma (2018-2020); Consult, Regeneron (2018-2020); Consult, Sanofi Genzyme (2018-2020); Consult, Astra Zenenca (2017-2019); President, Interasma (Global Asthma Association (2017-2019); Consult, Genentech (2002-2008); Consult, Sanofi-Aventis (2002-2003); Consult, Novartis (2002); Consult, Upjohn(1997); Consult, Hycor (1995-1997); Consult, Hoeschst Marion Roussel (1995-1997); Consult- Advisory Board, Hycor (1995-1997); Consult, Schering Plough, NJ (1994-2009); Past Consult, Merck, Meda, Mylan, Teva, Phadia; Visiting Professor, Uniwersytet Medyczny w Bialymstoku, Bialystok, Poland (2010); Member, Visiting Faculty, Belarusian Allergy Society, Minsk, Belarus (2010); Honorary Professor, Institute of Immunology, Ministry of Health, Russia (2002); Honorary Professor, Crimea State Medical University (2001); Co-Director, Allergy Fellow, Training Program, Brigham and Women's Hospital, Boston, MA (1994-1998); Distinguished Fellow, Former Regent and Speaker, House of Delegates, American College of Allergy, Asthma, and Immunology; Past President, American Association of Certified Allergists (AACA) **Civic:** Speaker, 400 Invited Lectures, CME **Creative Works:** Member, Editorial Board, Balkan Allergy Journal (2002-Present); Contributing Editor, American Journal of Respiratory and Critical Care Medicine (2001-Present); Contributing Editor, Asthma and Allergy Proceedings (1994-Present); Contributing Editor, International Journal of Rehabilitation Research (1998); Contributing Editor, Journal of Allergy and Clinical Immunology (1996-1997); Member, Editorial Boards, Allergy & Asthma Proceedings, Journal of Allergy and Clinical Immunology **Awards:** Top Doc Allergy, Castle Connolly (2012); Distinct Diploma, Ukrainian Society of Allergy and Clinical Immunology (2010); Award, American College of Allergy, Asthma and Immunology, Phoenix, AZ (2010); American College of Allergy, Asthma, and Immunology Distinguished Fellow Award (2004); Honorary Diploma, Polish Society of Allergology (2007) **Memberships:** Chairman, Practice and Therapeutics Committee, American Academy Of Allergy, Asthma & Immunology (1996-2000); President, Northwestern Chapter, Alpha Omega Alpha Chapter (1977-1978); American Thoracic Society; European Academy of Allergy and Clinical Immunology; European Respiratory Society; Clinical Immunology Society; American Society for Microbiology; New England Society of Allergy; Greater Washington Allergy Society; Western Society of Allergy, Asthma and Immunology; Allergists for Israel; Lifetime Member, New York Academy of Science; Board Member, Kosciusko Foundation;Fellow, American College of Clinical Pharmacy; Fellow, American College of Allergy, Asthma & Immunology; Fellow, American College of Physicians; Fellow, American College of Chest Physicians; Fellow, American College of Rheumatology; Fellow, American Academy Of Allergy, Asthma & Immunology; Case Review, Physicians Network; Consult, Coleman Research **Marquis Who's Who Honors:** Albert Nelson Marquis Lifetime Achievement Award **To what do you attribute your success:** Dr. DuBuske attributes his success to his determination to achieve the best for himself and all those with whom he collaborated. **Why did you become involved in your profession or industry:** Dr. DuBuske became involved in his profession as a fourth-year medical student who had a strong allergist mentor, Professor Roy Patterson. **Avocations:** Watching football and baseball; Jazz music **Thoughts on Life:** Dr. DuBuske is married to Dr. Ilona DuBuske, DO, an accomplished physician.

Joseph D. Duffey

Title: Academic Administrator **Industry:** Education/Educational Services **Date of Birth:** 07/01/1932 **Place of Birth:** Huntington **State/Country of Origin:** WV/USA **Parents:** Joseph Ivan Duffey; Ruth (Wilson) Duffey **Marital Status:** Widowed **Spouse Name:** Anne Wexler (1974) **Children:** Michael; David (Deceased 2019) **Education:** Honorary LittD, Ritsuimaneu University, Kyoto, Japan (1993); LHD, University of Massachusetts Amherst, Amherst, MA (1991); LittD, Monmouth College, IL (1980); LittD, Dickinson College, Carlisle, PA (1978); LittD, Gonzaga University, Spoken, WA (1980); LHD, City University of New York, New York, NY (1978); LittD, Centre College, Danville, KY (1977); PhD, Hartford Seminary Foundation (Now Hartford Seminary), Hartford, CT (1970); STM, Yale University, New Haven, CT (1959); BD, Andover Newton Theological School, Newton, MA (1957); BA, Marshall University, Huntington, WV (1954); LittD, Adelphi University, Central Florida; LittD, Alderson Broaddus University, Philippi, WV; LLD, Austin College, Sherman, TX; LLD, Bethany College, Bethany, WV; LLD, Amherst College, Amherst, MA; LittD, City College of New York, New York, NY **Career:** Senior Executive, Chairman International University Project, Sylvan Learning Systems, Washington, DC (1999-Present); Director, United States Information Agency, Washington, DC (1993-1998); President, American University, Washington, DC (1991-1993); President, University of Massachusetts (1990-1991); Chancellor, University of Massachusetts Amherst, Amherst, MA (1982-1991); Chairman, National Endowment of the Humanities (1978-1981); Assistant Secretary for Educational and Cultural Affairs, U.S. Department of State (1977); Executive Officer, American Association of University Professors (1974-1977); Adjunct Professor, Fellow, Calhoun College, Yale University, New Haven, CT (1971-1973); Fellow, John F. Kennedy School of Government, Harvard University, Cambridge, MA (1971); Associate Professor, Director, Center for Urban Studies (1965-1970); Hartford Seminary, Hartford, CT (1960-1963) **Career Related:** U.S. Department, 20th and 21st General Conferences, United Nations Educational, Scientific and Cultural Organization, United Nations Educational, Scientific and Cultural Organization (1978, 1980); Board of Directors, Bay Bank Valley Trust Company, Springfield, MA; Executive Committee, National Council of Competitiveness **Civic:** Board of Directors, Springfield Symphony; Board of Directors, Library of The Jewish Theological Seminary; Board of Directors, Westmass Area Development Corporation (Westmass); Board of Directors, East-West Center; Board of Directors, Woodrow Wilson International Center for Scholars; Trustee Emeritus, John F. Kennedy Center for the Performing Arts; Trustee, Milton S. Eisenhower Foundation; Trustee, Center for the Study of the Presidency and Congress **Creative Works:** Speaker, Appearance, 23 Videos, C-SPAN Video Library (1999-Present); Contributor, Numerous Articles, Professional Journals **Awards:** Tree of Life Award, National Jewish Fund (1987); Scholar, Rockefeller Foundation (1966-1968) **Memberships:** Council on Foreign Relations (1979-Present); Century Association; Cosmos Club **Why did you become involved in your profession or industry:** Dr. Duffey became involved in his profession because he was raised in West Virginia. He was eagerly ambitious to pursue school, though he never imagined he would earn a degree from Yale University. He never let his goals escape from his sight. **Thoughts on Life:** "Dr. Duffey has served as senior presidential appointee under three US presidents: Assistant Secretary of State for Educational and Cultural Affairs and Chairman of the National Endowment for the Humanities under Presidents Jimmy Carter and Ronald Reagan, and Director of the US Information Agency with Cabinet Status under President Bill Clinton. He served as President of American University in Washington, DC and previously Chancellor and President of the University of Massachusetts and as a member of the faculty at Yale University and a Fellow of the JFK School of Government at Harvard University.Dr. Duffey holds 14 honorary degrees from American colleges and universities and in 1993 was awarded the honorary Doctor of Letter by Ritsemaken University in Japan. In 1980 he was named Commander of the Order of the Crown by the King of Belgium. He has been a member of the Council on Foreign Relations since 1979. A native of West Virginia and a graduate of Marshall University, Dr. Duffey received graduate degrees from Yale University, Andover Newton Theological School and the Hartford Seminary Foundation. He has published widely on themes relating to higher education and social and economic issues. Dr. Duffey has been Stern lecturer at Syracuse University, Lund lecturer at Northwestern University, Sparkman Lecturer at the University of Alabama, and Lesser lecturer at the University of Southern California."

Paul Stephen Duffey, PhD

Title: Microbiologist **Industry:** Sciences **Date of Birth:** 11/24/1939 **Place of Birth:** Oakland **State/Country of Origin:** CA/USA **Parents:** Norman David Duffey; Saphrona Carol (Korkus) Duffey **Marital Status:** Widowed **Spouse Name:** Dixon Anita Herrick (06/24/1988, Deceased 2014); Marlen Gregory (01/17/1962, Deceased 1975) **Education:** PhD, University of Michigan (1974); Postgraduate Coursework, University of California (1968); BA, San José State University (1963) **Certifications:** Certified Public Health Microbiologist, State of California **Career:** Research Scientist, California Department of Health Care Services, Berkeley, CA (1981-2018); Assistant Professor of Microbiology, University of Texas Health Science Center, San Antonio, TX (1976-1981); Assistant Professor of Research, University of Michigan Medical School, Ann Arbor, MI (1974-1976) **Career Related:** Governors Task Force on Biotechnology, Sacramento, CA (1985-2018) **Memberships:** The New York Academy of Sciences; American Association of Immunologists; American Society for Microbiology; Northern California Chapter, American Society of Microbiology; Northern California Public Health Microbiologists Association **Marquis Who's Who Honors:** Albert Nelson Marquis Lifetime Achievement Award; Marquis Who's Who Top Professional; Distinguished Humanitarian **Why did you become involved in your profession or industry:** Dr. Duffey found a love for biology in college. That is when he started to learn about how people get blood disease, what causes it, how to find it, and how to treat it. **Avocations:** Computer assembly; Software writing **Political Affiliations:** Democrat **Religion:** Catholic

John Duffy

Title: Latin Teacher, Chairman of English & Foreign Languages (Retired) **Industry:** Education/ Educational Services **Date of Birth:** 10/06/1934 **Place of Birth:** Whittemore **State/Country of Origin:** IA/USA **Parents:** Lewis A. Duffy; Dorothy (Bestenlehner) Duffy **Marital Status:** Married **Spouse Name:** Anne O'Brien (07/19/1958) **Children:** Jane; Dr. Paul; Sarah; Steven **Education:** Coursework, University of Minnesota, Minneapolis, MN (1967); MS in Education, Creighton University, Omaha, NE (1961); BA, Loras College, Dubuque, IA (1956) **Career:** Latin Teacher, Chairman of English & Foreign Languages (Retired 1996);Chairman, English and Reading Division, Larkin High School, Elgin, IL (1977-1996); Teacher, Latin, Larkin High School, Elgin, IL (1962-1996); Chairman, English and Foreign Languages, Larkin High School, Elgin, IL (1970-1977); Students' Council Advisor, Larkin High School, Elgin, IL (1965-1971); Teaching Assistant, University of Iowa, Iowa City, IA (1961-1962); High School Teacher, Clear Lake Community Schools, Iowa (1958-1961); Teacher, Junior and Senior High School, Coach, Presentation Academy, Whittemore, IA (1957-1958) **Career Related:** Teacher, Preparatory Courses for ACT, PSAT and SAT Elgin YWCA and Larkin High School, Elgin, IL (1977-1996) **Civic:** Elected Trustee, Elgin Community College Board of trustee (ECC), Elgin, IL (1975-Present); Chairman, Board, Policies Review, Elgin Community College (ECC), Elgin, IL (1979, 1997, 2007); Chairman, President, Search Committee, Elgin Community College (ECC), Elgin, IL (1981, 1998, 2006); Chairman, Board, Elgin Community College (ECC), Elgin, IL (1997-1999, 1985-1987, 1980-1981); Vice Chairman, Board, Elgin Community College (ECC), Elgin, IL (1994-1995, 1981-1984); President, Elgin Area Catholic Social Services (1986-1988); Board of Directors, Elgin Area Catholic Social Services (1981-1990); Member, St. Laurence Parish Board (1974-1979); Chairman, Education Commission (1974-1979); Member, Education Commission (1972-1979); State Adviser, Iowa Junior Classical League (1960-1961) **Creative Works:** Summer Chef's Assistant, The Frugal Gourmet, WTTW-TV, Chicago, IL (1983); Contributor, Textbook; Co-Wrote, Article on Teachers Aides, Reading Department; Contributor, HS English Book **Awards:** Trustee of the Year Award, State Trustee Association, ; Central Region Trustee of the Year Award (2002, 1991); Named Kane County Distinguished Educator of Year (1982); Outstanding Young Men in America (1970); Outstanding Young Educator Award, Elgin Jaycees (1969) **Memberships:** Board of Directors, American Association of Community Colleges (1990-1993); Association of Community College Trustees (1981-2008); Illinois Community College Trustees Association (1981-2004); Chairman, Ad Hoc Committee on Teacher Tenure, Illinois Education Association (1972-1973); Legislator, Chairman, Northeastern Division, Illinois Education Association (1969-1971); President, Elgin Teachers Association (1966-1967); Welfare Chairman, Chief Negotiator, Elgin Teachers Association (1963-1965); American Association of Community Colleges; Illinois Council of Teachers of English; National Council of Teachers of English; Illinois Classical League; American Classical League; Association of Elgin School Administrators **Marquis Who's Who Honors:** Albert Nelson Marquis Lifetime Achievement Award **Why did you become involved in your profession or industry:** Mr. Duffy became involved in his profession because early on when he was a teacher he took to heart the words of John F. Kennedy who said 'Ask not what your country can do for you, but what you can do for your country'. So he was very active in the local teachers organization but when he got to Illinois in 1962 he had Five years of teaching already behind him and the first thing he did was to become active in the Elgin teachers association. In the second year he was there the incoming president asked him if he would be the welfare chairman and chief negotiator. He accepted and continued doing that for two years. Mr. Duffy became involved in teaching Latin because he had a couple of really good Latin teachers in HS at The Presentation Academy, with the sisters. So when he got into college he took Latin and more Latin until he decided he wanted to teach English and Latin. **Avocations:** Traveling; Reading; Spending time with his family; Politics; Walking

Carol McCarthy Duhme, DHL (Hon.)

Title: Civic Leader (Retired) **Industry:** Civil Service **Date of Birth:** 04/13/1917 **Place of Birth:** St. Louis **State/Country of Origin:** MO/USA **Parents:** Eugene Ross McCarthy; Louise (Roblee) McCarthy **Marital Status:** Married **Spouse Name:** H. Richard Duhme Jr. (04/09/1947); Sheldon Ware (06/12/1941, Deceased 1944) **Children:** David; Benton **Education:** Honorary DHL, Eden Theological Seminary (2002); AB, Vassar College (1939) **Career:** Board of Deacons, St. Louis Association Congressional Church (1992-1995); Member, Church Council, St. Louis Association Congressional Church (1987-1989); Chairman Board, Christian Education, St. Louis Association Congressional Church (1987-1988); Member, Church Council, St. Louis Association Congressional Church (1984-1985); Board of Deacons, St. Louis Association Congressional Church (1982-1985); Board of Deaconesses, St. Louis Association Congressional Church (1978-1981); Member, Church Council, St. Louis Association Congressional Church (1974-1975); Trustee, First Congregational Church (1964-1966); Moderator, St. Louis Association Congressional Churches (1959-1962); Teacher, Elementary School (1942-1944); Teacher, Elementary School (1939-1941) **Career Related:** Member, Advisory Council to the Board (1987-Present); Chairman, Annual Fund, YWCA, St. Louis, MO (1989-1990); Board of Directors, YWCA, St. Louis, MO (1973-1976); Board of Directors, Chautauqua Institution, NY (1971-1979); Board of Directors, North Side Team Ministry (1968-1984); Former Board of Directors, Community Music Schools, St. Louis, MO; Former Board of Directors, Community School; Former Board of Directors, Church Women United; Former Board of Directors, John Burroughs School; Former Board of Directors, St. Louis Bicentennial Women's Committee; President, St. Louis Junior League; President, St. Louis Vassar Club **Civic:** Member, Local Council, School of Social Work, Washington University in St. Louis (1987-Present); Trustee, Joseph H. and Florence A. Roblee Foundation, St. Louis, MO (1984-Present); President, Board of Directors, Joseph H. and Florence A. Roblee Foundation, St. Louis, MO (2002); Chairman, 150th Annual Committee, Eden Theological Seminary (1996-2000); Member, UNA-USA National Council (1995-2001); National Council, United Nations Association, St. Louis, MO (1995-2001); Council of Advisors, United Nations Association, St. Louis, MO (1993-2010); Presidential Search Committee, Eden Theological Seminary (1992-1993); Vice President, Board of Directors, Eden Theological Seminary (1991); Presidential Search Committee, Eden Theological Seminary (1986-1987); President, Joseph H. and Florence A. Roblee Foundation, St. Louis, MO (1984-1990); Member, Executive Committee, Board of Directors, Eden Theological Seminary (1981-1995); Member, Chancellor's Long Range Planning Committee, Washington University in St. Louis (1980-1981); Member, Corporate Assembly, Blue Cross Hospital Service of Missouri (1978-1986); President, Board of Directors, Family and Children's Service of Greater St. Louis (1977-1979); Secretary, Board of Directors, United Nations Association, St. Louis, MO (1976-1984); Member, Advisory Council, Missouri Baptist Hospital (1973-1989); Chairman, Chautauqua Bell Tower Scholar Fund (1961-2014); Board of Directors, St. Louis Mercantile Library; Board of Directors, National Inland Waterways Library; Chairman, Benton Roblee Duhme Scholar Fund **Awards:** Dean's Medal, Washington University in St. Louis School of Social Work (2015); Lifetime Achievement Award, Women's Foundation, Greater St. Louis (2011); Humanitarian Award, Planned Parenthood, St. Louis, MO (2000); Outstanding Alumna Award, John Burroughs School (1992); Outstanding Lay Women Nomination, Missouri United Church Of Christ (1991); Woman of Achievement Award, St. Louis Globe Democrat (1980); Volunteer of the Year Award, YWCA (1976); Mary Alice Messerley Award for Volunteerism, Health And Welfare Council, St. Louis, MO (1971) **Marquis Who's Who Honors:** Albert Nelson Marquis Lifetime Achievement Award; Marquis Who's Who Top Professional; Marquis Who's Who Humanitarian Award **Thoughts on Life:** Even though Ms. Duhme is retired, she remains active in her community.

Phyllis Mckinney Duke

Title: School Administrator, Business Management **Industry:** Education/Educational Services **Company Name:** Oakwood Academy, Duke Properties **Date of Birth:** 05/03/1932 **Place of Birth:** Mason City **State/Country of Origin:** IA/USA **Parents:** Wilbur Rhode Kellogg; Dorothy Margaret (Bauer) Kellogg **Marital Status:** Widow **Children:** Curtis Henry; Cathy McWilliams; David Henry **Education:** MA in Supervision and Administration, California State University Los Angeles (1968); BA in Elementary Education, California State University Los Angeles (1963); AA in Elementary Teaching, University of Northern Iowa (1953) **Certifications:** Certified Credentialed School Administrator, Reading Specialist, Elementary Teacher **Career:** School Administrator, Oakwood Academy, Long Beach, CA (1975-2019); Consultant, Orange County Department of Education, Santa Ana, CA (1970-1975); Consultant, Reading, State Department of California, Sacramento, CA (1969-1970); Teacher, Supervisor, ABC School District, Cerritos, CA (1963-1969); Teacher, St. Louis Park Public School, Minnesota (1953-1955); Teacher, Arlington Public School, Iowa (1951-1952) **Career Related:** Chairman, Board of Directors, New City Bank, Orange, CA; Business Management, Duke Properties **Civic:** Conference Coordinator, State Department of Education, Sacramento, Santa Barbara, CA (1970) **Creative Works:** Author, "Destined to Live 9 Lives" (2005); Author, "Song of Sounds, 3rd Edition" (2002); Author, "Beginnings for Christian Schools" (1976); Author, "Striving for Success in Life" **Awards:** Outstanding Leadership Award, State Department of Education (1970) **Memberships:** Director, Seminars, National Independent Private School (1983); Vice President, National Independent Private School (1982-1983); Legislative Chair, Pre-School Association, California (1978-1984); President, Reading Specialists, California (1970-1973) **Marquis Who's Who Honors:** Albert Nelson Marquis Lifetime Achievement Award **To what do you attribute your success:** Insight into the big picture; wanting to see all the issues and attempting to fix them. On a personal level, the ability to lead is also a factor in her success. **Avocations:** Skiing; Scuba diving; Painting; Photography; Travel; Enjoys competing in square dancing festivals **Political Affiliations:** Republican **Religion:** Christian

Wolcott Balestier Dunham Jr., Esq.

Title: Of Counsel **Industry:** Law and Legal Services **Company Name:** Debevoise & Plimpton LLP **Date of Birth:** 09/14/1943 **Place of Birth:** New York **State/Country of Origin:** NY/USA **Parents:** Wolcott Balestier Dunham; Isabel Caroline (Bosworth) Dunham **Marital Status:** Married **Spouse Name:** Joan Scott Findlay (01/26/1974) **Children:** Mary Findlay Dunham; James Wolcott Dunham **Education:** LLB, Harvard University, Cum Laude (1968); AB in Economics, Harvard University, Magna Cum Laude (1965) **Career:** Of Counsel, Debevoise & Plimpton LLP and Predecessor Debevoise, Plimpton, Lyons & Gates (2011-Present); Partner, Debevoise & Plimpton LLP and Predecessor Debevoise, Plimpton, Lyons & Gates, New York, NY (1977-2010); Associate, Debevoise & Plimpton LLP and Predecessor Debevoise, Plimpton, Lyons & Gates, New York, NY (1969-1976) **Career Related:** Preeminent Insurance Industry Lawyer; Chair for Programs at Practising Law Institute **Civic:** Chair, Board of Trustees, Union Theological Seminary, New York, NY (2012-Present); Trustee, Union Theological Seminary, New York, NY (2011-Present); Board of Directors, Dutchess Land Conservancy (1996-Present); President, Fund for Astrophysical Research (1984-Present); Board of Directors, Neighborhood Coalition for Shelter, Inc. (1983-Present); Treasurer, Trustee, Fund for Astrophysical Research, New York, NY (1970-Present); Senior Warden, St. James' Church (2012-2018); Trustee, Episcopal Diocese of New York (2009-2017); Members Committee, Terrafirma RRG LLC (2011-2014); Board of Directors, Episcopal Charities (2005-2012); Chancellor, St. James' Church (1994-2012); President, Board of Directors, Eastside Community Center, Inc. (1988-2010); New York State Commission to Modernize the Regulation of Financial Services (2007-2009); Board of Managers, Shekomeko Valley Farm Association, LLC (Now Shekomeko Farms LLC) (1996-2003); Advisory Council, United Nations Association, United Nations Foundation (1992-2000); Senior Warden, St. James' Church (1994-1995); Vestry Member, St. James' Church, New York, NY (1987-1995); Junior Warden, St. James' Church (1993-1994); Clerk, St. James' Church (1988-1993); Secretary, Fund for Astrophysical Research (1970-1984); Vice Chairman, United Nations Association of New York (1975-1979); Board of Directors, United Nations Association, United Nations Foundation, New York, NY (1973-1979); Executive Director, New York State Executive Advisory Commission on Insurance Industry Regulatory Reform (1972); VISTA Volunteer (Volunteers in Service to America) (1968-1969) **Creative Works:** Co-Author, "Insurance M&A" (1997-Present); General Editor and Chapter Author, "New York Insurance Law, Second Edition" (2009); General Editor and Chapter Author, "New York Insurance Law" (1991); General Editor and Author, Annual Supplements; Contributor, Articles to Professional Journals **Awards:** Bishop's Cross, Episcopal Bishop of New York (2015); Buist M. Anderson Distinguished Service Award, Association of Life Insurance Counsel (2012); Servant of Justice Award, Episcopal Diocese of New York (2011); Family of New York Award for Helping Establish a Community Shelter for Homeless Women, Presented by New York Governor Mario Cuomo (1983) **Memberships:** Board of Governors, Association of Life Insurance Counsel (2008-2012); Chairman Committee, Association of the Bar of the City of New York (1984-1987); Committee on Insurance, Association of the Bar of the City of New York (1981-1987); Chairman, Committee on Insurance Section, Administrative Law, ABA (1979-1983); Director, Harvard Law School Association of New York City (1978-1981); ABA; Union Internationale des Avocats; The American Society of International Law **Bar Admissions:** New York State Bar Association (1969) **Marquis Who's Who Honors:** Albert Nelson Marquis Lifetime Achievement Award **To what do you attribute your success:** Mr. Dunham attributes his success to the public service example of his parents and his education that served as strong foundations of his accomplishments. **Why did you become involved in your profession or industry:** Mr. Dunham became involved in his profession because during his time at Harvard Law School, he was able to sit in on classes and found them fascinating and enjoyed his experience as manager of the Harvard radio station, which needed to be run as a business. He found all his courses were challenging and wonderful professors were drawn to the business and management issues that came up in his courses. He was also drawn to public service and student organization, such as Civil Liberties Law Review, and gained a great deal by spending a year as a VISTA volunteer living in Cleveland, helping a local nonprofit organization develop a shopping center to offer low-income housing and retail space. **Religion:** Episcopalian

Jeff Davis Duty Jr.

Title: President, Chief Executive Officer **Industry:** Law and Legal Services **Company Name:** Duty and Duty Attorneys at Law and Social Security Advocates **Date of Birth:** 12/20/1934 **Place of Birth:** Rogers **State/Country of Origin:** AR/USA **Parents:** Jeff Duty, Sr.; Lois Duty **Marital Status:** Married **Spouse Name:** Barbara (05/26/1993) **Children:** Diana Lynn West; John Ellis Duty; Snow Hendryx **Education:** JD, University of Arkansas, Fayetteville, AR (1960); BA in Political Science, University of Arkansas, Fayetteville, AR, Magna Cum Laude (1958) **Career:** Attorney, Duty & Duty, Attorneys at Law (1984-Present); Appointed, Administrative Law Judge with the United States Social Security Administration (1975-1984); Attorney, Anti-Trust Division, Department of Justice, Washington, DC (1960-1975) **Career Related:** Elected Positions, City Attorney and Municipal Judge of Rogers, Arkansas; Faculty, Principles of Ethics and Professionalism, Arkansas Supreme Court Practicum; Lecturer, Continuing Legal Education; National Organization of Social Security Claimants' Representatives; Dean's Circle, University of Arkansas School of Law **Creative Works:** Author, "A Family Called Duty 100 Generations"; Author, "In the Line of Duty" **Awards:** Fulbright Scholar, International Law, London School of Economics, England (1957-1958); AV Preeminent, Martindale-Hubbell **Memberships:** Phi Delta Theta; Phi Beta Kappa; Omicron Delta Kappa; Phi Alpha Delta; Scottish Clans: McDonald of the Isles; American Bar Association; Arkansas Bar Association; Arkansas Trial Lawyers Association; The American Association of Visually Impaired Attorneys **Bar Admissions:** Western and Eastern Federal District Courts of Arkansas; Northern and Eastern Federal District Courts of Oklahoma; Arkansas Supreme Court; U.S. Supreme Court **Marquis Who's Who Honors:** Albert Nelson Marquis Lifetime Achievement Award; Marquis Who's Who Top Professional **To what do you attribute your success:** Long term adherence to ones principles and morality and an effort to leave the world a better place than he found it. **Why did you become involved in your profession or industry:** Mr. Duty became involved in his profession because he never had a choice; it was expected of him from the day he was born. His father was a lawyer, prosecuting attorney, and assistant state attorney general who practiced until his death in February 1998, and his mother was a career school teacher. **Avocations:** Bagpiper; Genealogy; Chess **Political Affiliations:** Democrat **Religion:** Episcopalian **Thoughts on Life:** Mr. Duty's grandfather started out as a general practitioner and corporate counsel for the Frisco Railroad back in the early 1900s. He then went onto general practice. His father was an Arkansas state assistant Attorney General and an elected prosecuting attorney for three terms. Mr. Duty is the first one who came across the area of Social Security Disability. He started out practicing with the Department of Justice in Washington, DC in the Antitrust Division. After that, he became an administrative law judge with the Social Security Administration. After 10 years, he decided to return to private practice to help those seeking Social Security Disability, which he is still doing today. Mr. Duty said, "During the summer before my senior year in high school, I applied for a seeing eye guide dog from the Seeing Eye school in Morristown, New Jersey (the first and oldest school founded to train service dogs to guide people with visual impairments) and, in June 1952, I traveled to Morristown to be trained with my first dog, a female German Shepherd named Binney. In total, I have been blessed with nine canine companions– seven German Shepherds and two retrievers. Currently I am one of the oldest, if not the oldest, active guide dog user in the world."

Joy Ann Dyer-Raffler

Title: Special Education Diagnostician (Retired), Art Teacher (Retired), Athlete **Date of Birth:** 08/10/1935 **Place of Birth:** Stiltner **State/Country of Origin:** WV/USA **Parents:** Ralph William Dyer; Hazel (Terry) Dyer **Marital Status:** Widowed **Spouse Name:** John William Raffler Sr. (01/01/1993, Deceased) **Children:** Keith Brian DeArmond **Education:** MEd in Special Education, The University of Arizona, Tucson (1976); MEd in Secondary Education, The University of Arizona, Tucson (1974); BA, The University of North Carolina at Chapel Hill (1969) **Certifications:** Certified in Special Education, Learning Disabilities, Emotional Handicaps and Art Education **Career:** Retired (2005); Teacher, Exceptional Education, Tucson Unified School District, Tucson, AZ (2003-2005); Diagnostician, Special Education, Tucson Unified School District (1989-2003); Teacher, Special Education, Tucson Unified School District (1975-1989); Art Educator, Tucson Unified School District (1970-1975) **Career Related:** Model **Civic:** Den Mother, Cub Scouts of America, Raleigh, NC (1968-1969) **Awards:** Grantee, Tucson Unified School District (1977) **Memberships:** Arizona Education Association **Marquis Who's Who Honors:** Albert Nelson Marquis Lifetime Achievement Award; Marquis Who's Who Top Professional; Marquis Who's Who Humanitarian Award **Why did you become involved in your profession or industry:** Mrs. Dyer-Faffler was aware of what her father was doing and she saw that he really enjoyed his career very much. She feels she was influenced in that way. Her family is very much into education, her brother graduated from the university when he was 19. He was a huge influence; he was a very good example of many things. When she got divorced, her father encouraged her to get into either education or nursing, and she decided on education. **Avocations:** Painting; Skiing; Birdwatching; Weightlifting; Tennis; Running

Robert Dzioba

Title: Professor of Orthopedic Surgery **Industry:** Medicine & Health Care **Company Name:** University of Arizona **Date of Birth:** 08/10/1941 **State/Country of Origin:** Ukraine **Parents:** Raisa Dzioba; Marian Dzioba **Marital Status:** Widower **Spouse Name:** Martha (1970, Deceased 2016) **Education:** Attending Staff, University of Toronto, Toronto Western Hospital (1976-1981); Orthopedic Residency, University of Toronto Hospitals (1970-1976); MD, University of Western Ontario Schulich School of Medicine & Dentistry, London, ON (1970); BA in Sciences, University Of Western Ontario, Cum Laude (1966) **Certifications:** Medical License, Texas (1978); Medical License, Arizona (1978) Certified, Ontario College Physicians and Surgeons (1971) **Career:** Professor of Orthopedic Surgery;Chief Executive Officer, Motion Preservation Technologies, Inc., Tucson, AZ (2017- Present); Chief, Orthopedic Surgery, University Medical Center Corporation (2006-2011); Chair, Credential Committee, University Medical Center (1992-1996); Chief, Section of Orthopedic Surgery, University of Arizona College of Medicine (1992-1993); Chair, University of Arizona College of Medicine (1992-1993); Surgical Director, Arizona Arthritis Center (1992-1993); Chief of Staff, University Medical Center (1991-1992); Chief, Operations Room Committee, University Medical Center (1990); Associate Professor, University of Arizona College of Medicine (1987-2011); Head, Spinal Surgery Division, University Medical Center (1986-2006); Assistant Professor, University of Arizona Medical School (1981); Chief of Orthopedic Residency, Kino Community Hospital (1981); Team Physician, Surgeon, Toronto Argonaut Football, Canadian Football League (1975-1981) **Career Related:** Dr. Ruth Jackson Visiting Professorship, Orthopedic Surgery, Dallas, TX (1986); Prosecutor, Arizona Board of Medical Examiners, Arizona Attorney General's Office, Phoenix, AZ; Visiting Professor, Lecturer, Speaker in Field; Speaker, Various National Television Appearances **Civic:** Rotary, Tuscon, AZ; The Eradication of Polio Annual Event, University of Arizona **Creative Works:** Author, "The Classification and Treatment of Acute Articular Cartilage Lesions" (1988); Contributor, Articles, Professional Journals **Awards:** Elected, Chief of Staff, University Medical Center, University of Arizona (1991-1992); Elected, Orthopedic Guild (1985); Listee, Best Doctors in America **Memberships:** North American Spine Society (NASS); American Orthopedic Society for Sports Medicine (AOSSM); Orthopedic Research Society **Marquis Who's Who Honors:** Albert Nelson Marquis Lifetime Achievement Award **To what do you attribute your success:** Dr. Dzioba attributes his success to consistent motivation. He has always focused on the job at hand, and he credits many of his accomplishments to his belief in a higher power. **Why did you become involved in your profession or industry:** Though Dr. Dzioba initially pursued civil engineering, he quickly realized he desired a profession that was more exciting. He discovered orthopedics after becoming more involved in biomechanics. He chose to pursue the field, as it directly involved his love of mathematics and physics. Ever since then, he has been successful. **Avocations:** Tennis; Skiing; Golf

Ola May Earnest

Title: Historian, Genealogist **Industry:** Research **Company Name:** Linn County Historical Museum and Library **Date of Birth:** 04/05/1934 **Place of Birth:** Montrose **State/Country of Origin:** MI/USA **Parents:** Marion Leslie Callahan; Vianna Elizabeth Wallace **Marital Status:** Widowed **Spouse Name:** Jesse E. Earnest (12/06/1950) **Children:** Jesse L.; Linda K.; Billy J.; Rodney G.; Diana L. **Education:** Coursework in Genealogy, Pittsburgh State University, Kansas (1974); Coursework in Genealogy, Fort Scott Community College (1974); GED, Pleasanton High School **Career:** President, Curator, Linn County Historical Society Museum and Genealogy Library, Pleasanton, SC (1980-Present); President, Linn County Genealogical Society (1978-1979); Vice President, Linn County Genealogical Society, Pleasanton, KS (1975-1978) **Civic:** Treasurer, Potosi Township, Linn County, Kansas (1992-Present); Treasurer, South East Kansas Tourism, Kansas (1990-2000); Member, Linn County Republican Women, Linn County, Kansas **Creative Works:** Editor and Designer, Bleeding Kansas (2003); Author, 100 Cemetaries - Linn County, Kansas (1987); Researcher, Three Volumes of Family History; Co-author, Three Volumes, "Pioneering to Present, Civil War Soldiers of Linn Co. KS" **Awards:** Recipient Commitment to History Award, Kansas, (2005); Community Service Award, Beta Pi Sorority (1989); Named Woman of Year, Iota Phi Sorority (1985) **Memberships:** National Society Washington Family Descendants (1987); Territorial Kansas Heritage Alliance (1980); National Society Daughters Americans Revolution (1980); Kansas State Historical Society (1975) **Marquis Who's Who Honors:** Marquis Lifetime Achievement Award **Why did you become involved in your profession or industry:** Earnest Ola became involved in her profession of curator due to researching her own genealogy and realizing what is needed to document it. She also does for the love of her family. **Avocations:** Genealogy; Gardening; Reenactments **Political Affiliations:** Republican **Religion:** Methodist **Thoughts on Life:** Mrs. Earnest initiated the start up of the genealogy library part of the museum in 1975. She has been active there ever since and has compiled many records for the library, including the census records from 1860 up to present day. She had even walked and cataloged every cemetery in the county, which the society published a book on the 100 cemeteries in Linn County. Mrs. Ola has been a volunteer there and has volunteered all her work to society ever since. She has also conducted tours through the county in regards to historical sites and furnished information to local students and colleges when requested.

Douglas C. Eaton, PhD

Title: Distinguished Professor **Industry:** Education/Educational Services **Company Name:** Emory University **Date of Birth:** 01/31/1945 **Place of Birth:** Sioux Falls **State/Country of Origin:** SD/USA **Parents:** Charles Barker Eaton; Dorothy Helen Eaton **Marital Status:** Married **Spouse Name:** Emma Jane Fenn **Children:** Eric Fenn; Amity Fenn Eaton **Education:** Doctor of Philosophy in Neuroscience, University of California, San Diego, CA (1971); Master of Science in Marine Biology, Scripps Institute of Oceanography, University of California, San Diego, CA (1969); Bachelor of Science in Chemistry and Biology, California Institute of Technology, Pasadena, CA **Career:** Emeritus Professor, Department of Physiology, Emory School of Medicine, Atlanta, GA (2018-Present); Distinguished Professor, Department of Medicine, Emory School of Medicine, Atlanta, GA (2018-Present); Director, Fellowships in Research and Science Teaching (FIRST) Program, Emory University Medical School, Atlanta, GA (2005-Present); Director, Investigator, Research Center for Cell and Molecular Signaling, Emory School of Medicine (1995-Present); Chair, Department of Physiology, Emory School of Medicine, Atlanta, GA (2008-2016); Interim Chair, Department of Physiology, Emory School of Medicine, Atlanta, GA (2007-2008); Distinguished Professor, Department of Physiology, Emory School of Medicine, Atlanta, GA (2002-2018); Director of Graduate Studies in Cell and Developmental Biology, Emory University Graduate School of Arts and Sciences, Atlanta, GA (1996-1999); Deputy Chair, Department of Physiology, Emory School of Medicine, Atlanta, GA (1987-2007); Professor, Department of Physiology, Emory School of Medicine, Atlanta, GA (1986-2002); Professor, Department of Physiology and Biophysics, University of Texas Medical Branch at Galveston, Texas (1985-1986); Associate Professor, Department of Physiology and Biophysics, University of Texas Medical Branch at Galveston, Texas (1978-1985); Assistant Professor, Department of Physiology and Biophysics, University of Texas Medical Branch at Galveston, Texas (1973-1978) **Career Related:** Emeritus Professor, Department of Pediatrics, Emory School of Medicine, Atlanta, GA (2018-Present); Consultant, Scientific Advisory Board, Sucampo Pharmaceuticals Inc. (2007-2016); Consultant, Scientific Advisory Board, Takeda Pharmaceutical Company Limited, Chicago, IL (2006-2015); Professor, Department of Pediatrics, Emory School of Medicine, Atlanta, GA (1990-2018); Director of Graduate Studies in Cell and Developmental Biology, Emory University Graduate School of Arts and Sciences, Atlanta, GA (1988-1992); Acting Chairman, Department of Physiology, Emory School of Medicine, Atlanta, GA (1988); Director, Department of Physiology and Biophysics Graduate Program, University of Texas Medical Branch at Galveston, Texas (1985-1986); Presenter in Field, Lectureships, Seminar Invitations, Symposia, Visiting Professorships, National and International Conferences **Military Service:** Airborne Medical Technician, U.S. Air Force Reserve (1974-1984); Unit Administrator, U.S. Marine Corps Reserve (1972-1973); LN2/LO2 Plant Operator, U.S. Marine Corps (1971-1972) **Creative Works:** Associate Editor, American Journal of Physiology: Physiology Selects (2018-Present); Editor, Frontiers in Physiology: Renal and Epithelial Physiology (2009-Present); Editorial Board, American Journal of Physiology: Physiology Selects (2016-2018); Associate Editor, Journal of Physiological Science (2013-2015); Editorial Board, American Journal Physiology: Renal Physiology, Fluid and Electrolytes (2007-2017); Associate Editor, Journal of Physiological Science (2007-2011); Associate Editor, Channels (2007-2010); Editorial Board, Nanomedicine (2005–2010); Editorial Board, Journal of Biological Chemistry (2003–2008); Author, 202 Scientific Peer-reviewed Publications; Contributor, 18 Book Chapters; Author, Eight Books **Awards:** Fellow, American Physiological Society (2016); Robert W. Berliner Award for Excellence in Renal Physiology, American Physiological Society (2012); Bodil Schmitt-Neilson Distinguished Mentor and Scientist Award, American Physiological Society (2011); Hugh Davson Distinguished Lecturer of the Cell and Molecular Section, American Physiological Society (2008); Fellow, American Association of Nanomedicine (2005); Fellow, American Society of Nephrology (2003); Merit Award, NIDDK (2001); Grantee, Numerous Grants **Memberships:** American Physiological Society Daggs Award Committee (2010-2015); Committee on Faculty Diversity and Retention (2010); External Advisor, National Center for Biomimetic Nanotechnology (2006-2011); President's Advisory Committee (2005-2008); Charter Member, American Academy of Nanomedicine (2005); President-elect, President, Past President, American Physiological Society (2004-2007); Council Member, American Physiological Society (2000-2003); National Institutes of General Medical Sciences (2000); American Heart Association (2000-2002); Councilor, American Physiological Society (1999-2003); Executive Committee, Renal Section, American Physiological Society (1996-1999) **To what do you attribute your success:** Dr. Eaton attributes his success to his mentors, Dr. Felix Strumwasser and Dr. Susumu Hagiwara, his undergraduate adviser and thesis adviser, respectively. **Why did you become involved in your profession or industry:** Dr. Eaton became involved in his profession because he has always been interested in the properties of cell membranes and ion channels and how they communicate with the environment. **Avocations:** Scuba Diving

Ala Ebaid

Title: Hematology/Oncology Fellow **Industry:** Medicine & Health Care **Company Name:** University of New Mexico Comprehensive Cancer Center **Date of Birth:** 10/06/1983 **Place of Birth:** Amman **State/Country of Origin:** Jordan **Parents:** Edward Ebaid; Ibtisam Ebaid **Marital Status:** Married **Spouse Name:** Lisa **Children:** One Son **Education:** MD, University of Jordan (2007) **Certifications:** Board Certified in Internal Medicine; Clinical Research, University of Mexico **Career:** Hematology/Oncology Fellow, University of New Mexico Comprehensive Cancer Center (2017-Present); Internal Medicine Specialist, Private Practice (2013); Residency in Internal Medicine, University of New Mexico (2010-2013); Residency, Jordan (2007-2010) **Awards:** Resident of the Year, University of New Mexico (2013) **Memberships:** American Society for Clinical Oncology; American Society of Hematology; American College of Physicians; American Association for the Advancement of Science **To what do you attribute your success:** Dr. Ebaid attributes his success to his parents, who never forced him to do anything he didn't want to do. His father set an excellent example of what hard work could achieve. His mother was another inspiration. Later, after coming to the United States, Dr. Ebaid met his wife. She provided endless emotional and physical support, as did his mentors at the University of Mexico, Dr. Rabinowitz and Dr. Lower. Dr. Ebaid is happy to be a doctor and help each of his patients. **Why did you become involved in your profession or industry:** Dr. Ebaid wanted to study medicine because his mother was very sick when he was a teenager; he thought he was going to lose her. This, combined with his lifelong interest in the human body and how it works, brought him to study biology. At 26, Dr. Ebaid immigrated to the United States to study medicine. He ended up in New Mexico, where he acquired a fellowship working with cancer patients. He loves his work. **Religion:** Catholic

Harry Allen Ecker

Title: Telecommunications Company Executive (Retired) **Company Name:** CISCO **Date of Birth:** 10/22/1935 **Place of Birth:** Athens **State/Country of Origin:** GA/USA **Marital Status:** Married **Spouse Name:** Sandra **Children:** Stephen (Deceased); Sharon; Michael **Education:** PhD in Electrical Engineering, The Ohio State University (1965); MSEE, Georgia Institute of Technology (1957); BSEE, Georgia Institute of Technology (1958) **Career:** Executive Vice President, Scientific-Atlanta, Inc. (Now CISCO) (1998- 2008); Senior Vice President/Chief Technical Officer, Scientific-Atlanta, Inc. (Now CISCO) (1988-1998); Vice President, Group Executive of Telecommunications, Scientific-Atlanta, Inc. (Now CISCO) (1982-1988); Vice President, Research and Development, Scientific-Atlanta, Inc. (Now CISCO) (1979-1982); Director, Research and Development, General Manager of Electro-Products, Scientific-Atlanta, Inc. (Now CISCO) (1977-1979); Director, Research and Development, Scientific-Atlanta, Inc. (Now CISCO) (1976-1977); Director, Applied Engineering, Georgia Institute of Technology, Atlanta, GA (1975 -1976); Chief, Radar Division, Georgia Institute of Technology (1972-1975); Head, Radar Branch, Georgia Institute of Technology (1969-1972) **Career Related:** Board of Trustees, Georgia Tech Foundation; External Advisory Board, Georgia Institute of Technology School of Electrical and Computer Engineering; Advisory Board, Georgia Institute of Technology Arts at Tech; Advisory Board, Georgia Institute of Technology Scheller College of Business; EXEL Program Co-Chair, Class of 1957 40th and 50th Reunion Committees, Georgia Institute of Technology; Member, Georgia Institute of Technology Alexander-Tharpe Fund; Board Member, Georgia Tech Alumni Association; Board Member, Advisory Board, Georgia Tech Research Institute (GTRI) **Civic:** Active Member, Board of Trustees, Marcus Autism Center; Chair, Innovation and Commercialization Committee, Marcus Autism Center; Member, Boards of Trustees, Haygood Memorial United Methodist Church; Member, Center of Innovation for Information Technology, Georgia Department of Economic Development; Policy Council Chairman, Georgia Radio Communication Committee; Chairman, Board, Georgia Center for Advanced Telecommunications Technology (GCATT) **Military Service:** Retired Captain, United States Air Force (1966); Advanced through Grades to Captain, United States Air Force (1959-1966) **Creative Works:** Co-author, Antenna Design Chapter, "The Electronic Communications Handbook"; Co-author, Chapter, "Biological Effects of Electromagnetics"; Contributor, Over 75 Articles to Professional Journals **Awards:** Inductee, National Cable & Telecommunications Association (Now The Internet & Television Association) (NCTA) Hall of Fame (2010); Lifetime Achievement Award for Innovation, Atlanta Telecom Professionals (2005); Award for Leadership in Interactive Television, National Cable & Telecommunications Association (Now The Internet & Television Association) (NCTA) (2004); Inductee, Technology Hall of Fame of Georgia (1999); Named Innovator of the Year, Southeastern Cable Television Association (1995); Recognition for Contributions in Technology and Economic Development, Georgia State Legislature in House Resolution HR 1124; Inductee, Georgia Institute of Technology Engineering Hall of Fame; Inductee, Georgia Institute of Technology Athletic Hall of Fame; Joseph Mayo Petit Distinguished Service Award, Georgia Institute of Technology; Fellow, Institute of Electrical and Electronic Engineers (IEEE) **Memberships:** Trustee, Georgia Tech Alumni Association (1989-Present); Fellow, IEEE; Executive Committee, Dodd's Boys Georgia Tech Letterwinners Club; Electronic Industries Association; Sigma Xi, the Scientific Research Honor Society; Eta Kappa Nu; The Tau Beta Pi Association, Inc.; The Honor Society of Phi Kappa Phi; Omicron Delta Kappa **Marquis Who's Who Honors:** Albert Nelson Marquis Lifetime Achievement Award **Why did you become involved in your profession or industry:** Dr. Ecker became involved in his profession because while he was in the Air Force, he had the opportunity to be in the research development command and was able to do quite a bit of work on radar and counter measures so that was one of the factors in deciding what profession he should choose. Also, he was aware that scientific lab companies were started by people from Georgia Tech and he saw it as a potential for how they got started in the areas in the market they were in as a real opportunity. **Avocations:** Tennis; Skiing; Football **Religion:** Methodist

Charles J. Egan Jr., LLB

Title: Lawyer, Foundation Trustee **Industry:** Law and Legal Services **Date of Birth:** 08/11/1932 **Place of Birth:** Cambridge **State/Country of Origin:** MA/USA **Parents:** Charles Joseph Egan; Alice Claire (Ball) Egan **Marital Status:** Married **Spouse Name:** Mary Bowersox (8/6/1955) **Children:** Timothy; Sean; Peter; James **Education:** LLB, Columbia University (1959); AB, Harvard University (1954) **Career:** Vice President, General Counsel, Hallmark Cards, Inc., Kansas City, MO (1972-2004); Vice President, General Counsel, Thomson & McKinnon Securities, New York, NY (1969-1970); Partner, Hall, McNicol, Marett & Hamilton, New York, NY (1962-1968); Associate, Donovan, Leisure, Newton & Irvine, New York, NY (1959-1962) **Career Related:** Board of Directors, American Multi Cinema, Inc., Kansas City, MO (1986-2004) **Civic:** Trustee, Kansas City Art Institute (1995-Present); Member, Dean's Council, Columbia Law School (1991-Present); Co-Chairman, Harvard College Fund (2000-2003); Vice Chairman, Harvard College Fund (1994-1999); Trustee, Pembroke Country Day School, Kansas City, MO (1976-1982); Board of Directors, Kansas City YMCA (1976-1980); Trustee, Notre Dame de Sion Schools of Kansas City, Missouri (1973-1977); Co-Trustee, Stanley H. Durwood Foundation **Military Service:** First Lieutenant, U.S. Marine Corps (1954-1956) **Memberships:** President, Harvard Alumni Association (1989-1990); Executive Committee, Harvard Alumni Association (1987-2003); President, Harvard Club of Kansas City (1985-1987); Missouri Bar Association; Kansas City Lawyers Association; Century Association; Somerset Club; Harvard Club of New York **Bar Admissions:** Missouri (1973); New York (1960) **Marquis Who's Who Honors:** Albert Nelson Marquis Lifetime Achievement Award; Marquis Who's Who Top Professional **Why did you become involved in your profession or industry:** What attracted Mr. Egan in his career was his experience in the Marine Corps. He was trying court martial cases. **Religion:** Roman Catholic

William Albert Ehlers

Title: Psychiatrist **Industry:** Health, Wellness and Fitness **Date of Birth:** 02/02/1942 **Place of Birth:** Marshall **State/Country of Origin:** MN/USA **Parents:** Millard Earl Ehler; Doris Sylva (Wall) Ehler **Marital Status:** Married **Spouse Name:** Jeanne **Children:** William Z.; Albert; Andrew; Sarah **Education:** MD, University of Chicago (1968); BA, St. Olaf College, Cum Laude (1964) **Certifications:** Board Certified, American College of Forensic Examiners **Career:** Staff Psychiatrist, Western State Hospital, Fort Steilacoom, WA (1986-Present); Private Practice, Portland, OR (1975-1986); Resident in Psychiatry, University of Oregon Medical School, Portland, OR (1972-1975); Resident in Psychiatry, University of British Columbia Medical School, Vancouver, Canada (1971-1972); Rotating Intern, University of Oregon Medical School, Portland, OR (1968-1969) **Career Related:** Research Assistant, Minneapolis Veterans Admin Hospital (1961); Past Consultant, Mental Health Center; Fellowship Residencies, General Psychiatry, Child Psychiatry; Psychiatric Consultant, Indian Health Services **Civic:** Member, Chirch Council, Trinity Lutheran Church, Tacoma, WA (1989-1991); Bible Camp Counselor, Trinity Lutheran Church **Military Service:** U.S. Army, Medical Corps (1969-1970) **Awards:** Bronze Star, U.S. Army; Valedictorian, High School **Memberships:** American Association for the Advancement of Science; American Psychiatric Association; American Academy of Child Psychiatry; Audubon Society; Tacoma Astronomical Society; Cornell Laboratory Ornithology; Vice President, Mensa; Wright Park Conservatory; C.G.Young Society; Oregon Psychoanalytical Association; Boy Scouts of America **Marquis Who's Who Honors:** Albert Nelson Marquis Lifetime Achievement Award; Marquis Who's Who Top Professional **Why did you become involved in your profession or industry:** Dr. Ehlers was inspired by one of his college roommates to pursue medicine. He wanted to do something besides lab work as a scientist, and he figured medicine would be the perfect field. **Avocations:** Ornithology; Astronomy; Construction; Camping; Canoeing; Hockey; Airplanes; Archaeology; Birds; Paleontology **Religion:** Lutheran

Charles A. Ehren Jr., JD

Title: Professor of Law Emeritus **Industry:** Education/Educational Services **Company Name:** School of Law, Valparaiso University **Date of Birth:** 12/13/1932 **Place of Birth:** New York **State/Country of Origin:** NY/USA **Parents:** Charles Alexander Ehren; Alma Elise (Holmstrom) Ehren **Marital Status:** Married **Spouse Name:** Joan Anne Bansemer (9/4/1954) **Education:** JD, Columbia Law School, Columbia University (1956); AB, Columbia College (1954) **Career:** Professor Emeritus, Law, Valparaiso University (1996-Present); Professor, School of Law, Valparaiso University (1977-1996); Dean, School of Law, Valparaiso University (1977-1982); Visiting Scholar, Columbia Law School, Columbia University (1976-1977); Dean, Professor, Elisabeth Haub School of Law at Pace University (1975-1976); Professor, Strum College of Law, University of Denver (1974-1975); Associate Professor, Law, University of Denver (1970-1974); Director, Curriculum, National Institute for Education in Law and Poverty, Northwestern University Pritzker School of Law (1968-1970); Associate, LeBoeuf, Lamb & Leiby, New York, NY (1958-1967) **Career Related:** Trustee, Indiana Continuing Legal Education Foundation-ICLEF (1977-1982); Board of Directors, Westchester Legal Services (Now Legal Services of the Hudson Valley) (1975-1977); Board of Directors, Legal Aid Society of Westchester, White Plains, NY (1975); Reginald Heber Smith Community Lawyer Fellowship, Legal Aid Society of Westchester, University of Pennsylvania Carey Law School, White Plains, NY (1967-1968) **Military Service:** U.S. Army (1956-1958) **Creative Works:** Co-Author, "Electricity and the Environment—The Reform of Legal Institutions: Report of the Association of the Bar of the City of New York; Special Committee on Electric Power and the Environment" (1972) **Memberships:** Indiana State Bar Association (1977-1982); Executive Director, Special Committee on Electric Power and Environment, Association of the Bar of the City of New York (1971-1973); American Bar Association; New York State Bar Association; EBA; Society of American Law Teachers **Bar Admissions:** State of New York (1956) **Marquis Who's Who Honors:** Albert Nelson Marquis Lifetime Achievement Award **To what do you attribute your success:** Mr. Ehren credits his success to good luck and hard work, as well as a group of influential teachers at Columbia University. **Why did you become involved in your profession or industry:** Mr. Ehren became involved in his profession because of his enduring interests in public affairs and the operations of a democratic society. **Avocations:** Appreciating music; Residential architecture; Collecting automobile memorabilia **Political Affiliations:** Democrat **Religion:** Lutheran **Thoughts on Life:** Among many career achievements, Mr. Ehren has drafted and lobbied to Congress a comprehensive model legislation for reorganizing the federal government's regulatory system for electric energy; increased the size of faculty and faculty salaries, raised school standards and managed long-range planning processes as dean and professor at Valparaiso University School of Law; recruited and incorporated staff for Westchester Legal Services, Inc.; conducted a nationwide training program for lawyers in the Legal Services Corporation; and, after retirement, led an ad hoc citizens activist group in an effort to refurbish a nature preserve in East Hampton, New York.

David John Eicher

Title: Editor-in-Chief **Industry:** Writing and Editing **Date of Birth:** 08/07/1961 **Place of Birth:** Oxford **State/Country of Origin:** OH/USA **Parents:** John Harold Eicher; Susan Ann (Arne) Eicher **Marital Status:** Married **Spouse Name:** Lynda Ann Tortomasi Eicher **Children:** Christopher David **Education:** Student, Miami University, Oxford, OH (1979-1982) **Career:** Editor-In-Chief, Astronomy Magazine (2002–Present); Managing Editor, Astronomy Magazine (1996-2002); Senior Editor, Astronomy Magazine (1996); Astronomy Books Editor, Kalmbach Publishing Co., Waukesha, WI (1991-1996); Associate Editor, Astronomy Magazine, Kalmbach Publishing Co., Waukesha, WI (1990-1996); Editor-In-Chief Deep Sky Magazine, Astromedia Corp., Milwaukee, WI (1982-1992); Assistant Editor, Astronomy Magazine, Astromedia Corp., Milwaukee, WI (1982-1989); Founder, Editor, Deep Sky Monthly, Inc., Oxford (1977-1982) **Creative Works:** Author, "Galaxies, Inside the Universe's Star Cities" (2020); Co-Author, "Cosmic Clouds 3-D" (2020); Author, "Astronomy Backstage Pass: Northern Arizona" (2019); Co-Author, "Mission Moon 3-D" (2019); Author, "Astronomy Backstage Pass: Chicago" (2018); Author, "Starmus: Discovering the Universe" (2016); Author, "The New Cosmos, Answering Astronomy's Big Questions" (2015); Author, "Starmus: 50 Years of Man in Space" (2014); Author, "COMETS! Visitors from Deep Space" (2013); Author, "Astronomy Magazine: The Complete Collection" (2011); Author, "Lincoln the Liberal Strategist" (2011); Author, "A New Birth of Freedom: Abraham Lincoln's Bicentennial" (2009); Author, "50 Greatest Mysteries of the Universe" (2007); Author, "Dixie Betrayed, How the Confederacy Really Lost the Civil War" (2006); Author, "Beginner's Guide to Astronomy" (2003); Author, "Gettysburg Battlefield, The Definitive Photographic History" (2003); Author, "The Longest Night, A Military History of the Civil War" (2001); Co-Author, "Civil War High Commands" (2001); Author, "Mystic Chords of Memory, Civil War Battlefields and Historic Sites Recaptured" (1998); Author, "Robert E. Lee, A Life Portrait" (1997); Author, "The Civil War in Books: An Analytical Bibliography" (1997); Author, "Civil War Battlefields, A Touring Guide" (1995); Author, "Beginner's Guide to Amateur Astronomy" (1993); Author, "The New Cosmos: The Astronomy of Our Galaxy and Beyond" (1992); Author, "Galaxies and the Universe, An Observing Guide from Deep Sky Magazine" (1992); Author, "Stars and Galaxies, Astronomy's Guide to Observing the Cosmos" (1992); Author, "Beyond the Solar System" (100 Best Deep-Sky Objects for Amateur Astronomers" (1992); Author, "Civil War Journeys Calendar" (1990–2000); Author, "Deep-Sky Observing with Small Telescopes" (1989); Author, "The Universe from Your Backyard" (1988) **Awards:** Eponym, Asteroid 3617 Eicher, International Astronomical Union, Cambridge, MA (1990); Herschel Award, Western Amateur Astronomers, Los Angeles, CA (1987); Lone Stargazer Award, Texas Star Party, Fort Davis, TX (1987) **Memberships:** American Astronomical Society; National Association of Science Writers; Abraham Lincoln Association; U.S. Grant Association; Milwaukee Civil War Round Table **Marquis Who's Who Honors:** Albert Nelson Marquis Lifetime Achievement Award **Why did you become involved in your profession or industry:** Mr. Eicher became involved in his profession because his father, John Harold Eicher, was a chemistry professor, so he grew up around a scientific background and a chemistry lab. He became interested in the sciences. He was interested in becoming a physician, but one night, he went to a star party and saw Saturn through a telescope, which electrified him and got him instantly interested in astronomy. He was always a writer early on and the local astronomy club chose him to write for their newsletter, which started him writing about space. He soon founded his own publication, Deep Sky Monthly, at age 15, which became popular as it spread through the community of amateur astronomers. That publication rose to a circulation of 1,000 and introduced him to the editors of the larger magazines, where he brought his title, recast as a quarterly. He then also became a young editor at Astronomy Magazine, the world's largest title on the subject. That was in 1982, and he has worked continuously on the magazines and on many book and associated projects since that time. **Avocations:** American and ancient history; Mineralogy; Music; Reading; Collecting documents; Artifacts; Coins

Michael Leonard Einhorn

Title: State Auditor **Industry:** Government Administration/Government Relations/Government Services **Date of Birth:** 12/08/1952 **Place of Birth:** Detroit **State/Country of Origin:** MI/USA **Parents:** Carl M.; Ruth A. (Hollander) E. **Education:** Master of Business Administration, Monmouth College, West Long Branch, NJ (1982); Bachelor of Science in Accounting, Quinnipiac College, Hamden, CT (1974) **Career:** Retired (2015); Auditor II, Taxation, State of New Jersey, Trenton (1988-2015); Taxation Auditor III, State of New Jersey, Trenton (1981-1988); Accounting Assistant, State of New Jersey, Trenton (1976-1981) **Career Related:** Auditor 1 Taxation, Trenton, NJ (1998-2015); Auditor 2, Taxation, Trenton, NJ (1997) **Civic:** Member, East Brunswick, NJ Recycling Committee (1983-1984) **Memberships:** Knights of Pythias (1989-Present); Assistant Membership Chairperson, Trenton Chapter, Association of Government Accountants (1985-1986) **Marquis Who's Who Honors:** Albert Nelson Marquis Lifetime Achievement Award; Marquis Who's Who Top Professional

Christopher Ludwig Eisgruber

Marquis Who's Who
18 98
Biographee

Title: President **Industry:** Education/Educational Services **Company Name:** Princeton University **Date of Birth:** 09/24/1961 **Place of Birth:** West Lafayette **State/Country of Origin:** IN/USA **Parents:** Ludwig Maria Eisgruber; Eva R. Eisgruber **Marital Status:** Married **Spouse Name:** Lori A. Martin (6/14/1987) **Children:** Danny **Education:** JD, University of Chicago (1988); MLitt in Politics, Oxford University (1987); AB in Physics, Princeton University (1983) **Career:** President, Princeton University (2013-Present); Laurance S. Rockefeller Professor of Public Affairs, Woodrow Wilson School of Public Affairs, University Center For Human Values, Princeton University (2004-2013); Provost, Princeton University (2004-2013); Director, Law & Public Affairs Program, Princeton University (2001-2004); Professor of Law, New York University School of Law, New York, NY (1995-2004); Associate Professor, New York University School of Law, New York, NY (1993-1995); Assistant Professor, New York University School of Law, New York, NY (1990-1993); Law Clerk, Justice John Paul Stevens, U.S. Supreme Court, Washington, DC (1989-1990); Law Clerk To Hon. Patrick Higginbotham, U.S. Court of Appeals for the Fifth Circuit, Dallas, TX (1988-1989) **Creative Works:** Co-Author, "Religious Freedom and the Constitution" (2007); Author, "The Next Justice: Repairing the Supreme Court Appointments Process" (2007); Co-Author, "Global Justice and the Bulwarks of Globalism: Human Rights in Campus" (2005); Author, "Constitutional Self Government" (2001); Co-Convenor, Colloquium in Constitutional Theory (1993-1997); Editor-in-Chief, University of Chicago Law Review (1987-1988) **Awards:** Rhodes Scholar (1983) **Memberships:** American Law Institute

Mohamed El Sayed Nasser El Deeb

Title: Professor Emeritus **Industry:** Education/Educational Services **Company Name:** Division of Oral and Maxillofacial Surgery, University of Minnesota School of Dentistry **Date of Birth:** 05/19/1950 **Place of Birth:** Cairo **State/Country of Origin:** Egypt **Parents:** El Sayed Nasser El Deeb; Olaft Mohamed Riad **Marital Status:** Married **Spouse Name:** Marwa Sallam; Margaret Mary El Deeb (06/30/1983) **Children:** Shereen; Nadine; Ahmed; Youssef **Education:** MS in Dentistry, University of Minnesota School of Dentistry (1979); Residency Training Program, Division of Oral and Maxillofacial Surgery, University of Minnesota School of Dentistry (1979); Diploma, Cairo University School of Dentistry (1972) **Career:** Professor, Department of Oral and Maxillofacial Surgery, University of Minnesota, Minneapolis, MN (1991-Present); International Consultant, World Hospital, Cairo, Egypt (2014-2016); Vice President, American Cleft Palate and Craniofacial Deformities Association (ACPA) (1990-1991); Director, Dental Implant Program, University of Minnesota School of Dentistry (1989-1991); Associate Professor, Director of Research, Department Oral and Maxillofacial Surgery, University of Minnesota, Minneapolis, MN (1985-1990); President, American Society of Dental Anaesthesiologists (ASDA), Upper Midwest (1985-1989); Director, Union Gospel Mission Dental Clinic, St. Paul, MN (1982-1996); Assistant Professor, Department Oral and Maxillofacial Surgery, University of Minnesota, Minneapolis, MN (1980-1985); Instructor in Oral Surgery, Al-Azhar University, Cairo, Egypt (1973-1976) **Career Related:** Staff, University of Minnesota Hospital (M Health Fairview University of Minnesota Medical Center), Fairview Hospital (Fairview Health Services), Fairview University Hospital (Fairview Health Services), Cook Clinic (Cook Hospital), United Hospital, Allina Health, M Health Fairview Southdale, North Memorial Hospital (North Memorial Health) and Abbot Northwestern Hospital, Allina Health **Civic:** Board of Directors, Union Gospel Mission Dental Clinic, St. Paul, MN (1983-Present); Instructor, Trainer, Basic and Advanced Cardiac Life Support, American Heart Association, Inc., Minneapolis, MN (1981-Present); Chairman, National Meeting **Creative Works:** Author, 4-5 Educational Papers, Topics Include the Future of Dentistry in Egypt (2019); Editorial Board, Cleft Palate Journal; Editorial Board, Saudi Medical Journal; Author, Over 100 Research Papers, Professional Journals and Science Publications; Contributor, Abstracts, Textbook Chapters **Awards:** Union Gospel Mission Dental Clinic Service Award (1986, 1991); Certification as Diplomat, International Congress of Oral Implantologists (ICOI) (1991); Certification as Diplomat, American of Osseointegration (1991); Fellow, International Congress of Oral Implantologists (ICOI) (1990); Fellow, American Dental Society of Anesthesiology (ADSA) (1987); Fellow, American College of Dentists (1985); Life Fellow, International Association of Oral and Maxillofacial Surgeons (1984); Fellow, American Association of Hospital Dentists (1984); Fellow, International College of Dentists (1984) **Memberships:** President, Upper Midwest Section, American Dental Society of Anesthesiology (ADSA) (1986-1989); Fellow, American Association of Hospital Dentists; Fellow, American College of Dentists; Fellow, The American College of Oral and Maxillofacial Surgeons (ACOMS); Fellow, International College of Dentists; Fellow, American Dental Society of Anesthesiology (ADSA); Fellow, American Cleft Palate Association (ACPA); American Dental Association; American Association of Dental Schools; American Association of Oral and Maxillofacial Surgeons (AAOMS); International Association of Oral and Maxillofacial Surgeons; Egyptian Dental Association; International Congress of Oral Implantologists (ICOI); Minnesota Dental Association; Minnesota Society of Oral and Maxillofacial Surgeons; Midwestern Society of Oral & Maxillofacial Surgery; Omicron Kappa Epsilon; Beta Beta Beta; Fellow, Director, Minnesota Section, Global Institute for Dental Education (gIDE); Director, Study Club, Minnesota Section, Global Institute for Dental Education (gIDE) **Marquis Who's Who Honors:** Albert Nelson Marquis Lifetime Achievement Award **Why did you become involved in your profession or industry:** Dr. El Deeb's boss, Daniel T. Waites, was visiting Egypt at the time when Dr. El Deeb was first entering the work force. They struck up a friendship over tennis, and Mr. Waites convinced him to apply at the University of Minnesota. **Avocations:** Riding and training horses; Reading **Political Affiliations:** Independent **Religion:** Muslim

Dr. Ibrahim Abdel Tawab Elbarbary, PhD

Title: Chemist **Industry:** Sciences **Company Name:** Bureau of Engraving & Printing, U.S. Treasury **Date of Birth:** 01/17/1933 **Place of Birth:** Alexandria **State/Country of Origin:** Arab Republic of Egypt **Year of Passing:** 1999 **Parents:** Sheikh Abdel Tawab Ali Elbarbary; Tafida Ibrahim Basuni **Marital Status:** Married **Spouse Name:** Fatma Oweiss Elbarbary (9/17/1972 **Children:** Meeral, Mohamed; Raney; Ibrahim (Grandson) **Education:** PhD in Chemistry, Binghamton University State University of New York (1977); PhD in Environmental Sciences, Air and Water Pollution, Binghamton University State University of New York (1974); MS in Chemistry, Cairo University, Cairo, Arab Republic of Egypt (1968); BS in Chemistry and Zoology, Faculty of Science, Alexandria University, Arab Republic of Egypt (1956) **Career:** Chief, Office of Material Technology at the Bureau of Engraving & Printing, U.S. Treasury; Project Manager, Bureau Engraving & Printing, U.S. Treasury, Washington, DC (1986-Present); United States Environmental Protection Agency USEPA, in Cooperation with Howard University and Georgia Tech University (1975-1985); Head, Environmental Studies, King Abdul Aziz University, Jeddah, Saudi Arabia (1985); Associate Professor, The Georgia Institute of Technology, Atlanta, GA (1981-1983); Teaching Fellow, Binghamton University State University of New York (1976-1985); Chief Chemist, Belmont Smelting and Refining Works, Brooklyn, NY (1970-1976); Laboratories Director, Chemistry Department, Ministry of Industry, Cairo, Egypt (1957-1970) **Career Related:** Consultant, Water Programs, The U.S. Agency for International Development, Washington, DC (1979-Present); Consultant, The United Nations Development Programme, New York, NY (1982-1983); Chairman, Department of Environmental Studies King Abdul Aziz University, Jeddah, Saudi Arabia (1981-1983) **Military Service:** Egyptian Army (1957-1958) **Creative Works:** Author, 27 Papers and Reports **Awards:** Postgraduate Study Award, Egyptian Government, Max Planck Institute for Iron Research, Dusseldorf, Federal Republic of Germany (1961-1963); Delegated by The United Nations to work in the TOKTEN Program **Memberships:** Fellow, The American Institute of Chemists; American Society for Metals; American Chemical Society; Secretary, Association of Egyptian American Scholars. **Marquis Who's Who Honors:** Albert Nelson Marquis Lifetime Achievement Award **Avocations:** Traveler; Collector; Artist; Avid stamp collector **Religion:** Muslim

Hector Elizondo

Title: Actor **Industry:** Media & Entertainment **Date of Birth:** 12/22/1936 **Place of Birth:** New York **State/Country of Origin:** NY/USA **Parents:** Martin Echevarria Elizondo; Carmen Medina (Reyes) Elizondo **Marital Status:** Married **Spouse Name:** Carolee Campbell (4/13/1969) **Children:** Rodd **Education:** Coursework, The City College of New York (1955-1956); Coursework, Ballet Arts Company of Carnegie Hall **Creative Works:** Actor, "Last Man Standing," ABC (2011-Present); Author, "Cane" (2007-Present); Actor, "Valentine's Day" (2010); Actor, "Music Within" (2007); Actor, "Love in the Time of Cholera" (2006); Actor, "sequel" (2004); Actor, "The Princess Diaries 2: The Royal Engagements" (2004); Actor, "Celestine Prophecies" (2004); Actor, "Century City" (2003-2004); Actor, "Miracles" (2003); Actor, "Without a Trace" (2003); Actor, "The West Wing" (2002); Actor, "Kate Brasher" (2001); Actor, "Tortilla Soup" (2001); Actor, "How High" (2001); Actor, "The Princess Diaries" (2001); Actor, "The Other Sister" (1998); Actor, "Runaway Bride" (1998-1999); Actor, "Borrowed Hearts" (1997); Actor, "Safe House" (1996); Actor, "Turbulence" (1996); Actor, "Dear God" (1996); Actor, "Romy & Michelle" (1996); Actor, "The Impatient Heart" (1994-2000); Actor, "All in the Family" (1994-2000); Actor, "Chicago Hope" (1994-2000); Actor, "Exit to Eden" (1993); Actor, "Getting Even with Dad" (1993); Actor, "Beverly Hills Cop III" (1993); Actor, "Mrs. Cage" (1992); Actor, "Being Human" (1992); Actor, "The Burden of Proof" (1992); Actor, "Chains of Gold" (1991); Actor, "Paydirt" (1991); Actor, "Necessary Roughness" (1991); Actor, "Frankie and Johnny" (1991); Actor, "The Amnesty File" (1990); Actor, "Leviathan, Pretty Woman" (1990); Actor, "Your Mother Wears Combat Boots" (1989); Actor, "Natica Jackson" (1987); Actor, "Great Performances," WCET (1987); Actor, "Courage" (1986); Actor, "Freebie and the Bean, Foley Square" (1985); Actor, "Nothing in Common" (1985); Actor, "Out of the Darkness" (1985); Actor, "The Flamingo Kid" (1984); Actor, "Casablanca" (1983); Actor, "Young Doctors in Love" (1983); Actor, "Medal of Honor Rag" (1982); Actor, "Honey Boy" (1982); Actor, "American Gigolo" (1979); Actor, "The Fan" (1979); Actor, "The Dain Curse" (1978); Actor, "Cuba" (1978); Actor, "The Great White Hope" (1977); Actor, "Popi" (1976); Actor, "Report to the Commissioner" (1975); Actor, "The Taking of Pelham-1-2-3" (1975); Actor, "Prisoner of Second Avenue" (1974); Actor, "The Price, Drums in the Night" (1970); Actor, "Steambath" (1970); Actor, "The American Experience Discovery"; Actor, "American Playhouse"; Actor, "Sly Fox"; Actor, "Medal of Honor Rag" **Awards:** Lifetime Achievement IMPACT Award (2002); Best Actor in Drama Series (2000); Latin Legends Award, New York, NY (2000); Best Actor, American Latino Media Arts Award (1998); Lifetime Achievement Image Award (1997) **Memberships:** Amnesty International; The Creative Coalition **Marquis Who's Who Honors:** Albert Nelson Marquis Lifetime Achievement Award **Why did you become involved in your profession or industry:** Growing up in the generation that came from the Great Depression, Mr. Elizondo has always valued the importance of hard work. Mr. Elizondo built his reputation by working hard and staying humble in each job he's had over the years. His passion for acting comes from a desire to leave something behind for others to enjoy. **Religion:** Roman Catholic

Miriam Charlotte Elkin

Title: Nurse **Industry:** Medicine & Health Care **Date of Birth:** 08/30/1932 **Place of Birth:** Millbrook **State/Country of Origin:** AL/USA **Parents:** Alton Kimbrough; Edna Lee (Cheves) Helton **Marital Status:** Widowed **Spouse Name:** Oran Gerald Carpenter (01/23/1970); Thomas Elkin (02/12/2000) **Children:** Nanette Weimer; Jenna Ormsbee; Joey Culbreth **Education:** EdD, Texas Women's University (1997); MS, East Texas State University (1985); BSN, The University of Texas (1982); BS, East Texas State University (1979); AA, College of the Mainland (1977) **Certifications:** Board Certified Drug and Alcohol Counselor, State of Texas (1999); Licensed Nursing Home Administrator, State of Oklahoma (1998); Licensed Chemical Dependency Counselor, State of Texas (1998); Registered Nurse; Certified Criminal Justice Specialist, Master Addiction Counselor, National Association of Forensic Counselors; Certified Criminal Reformation Clinician in Forensic Counseling **Career:** Retired (1996); Psychiatric Nurse, Program Therapist, Arbor Creek-Turning Point of Paris (1992-1996); Nursing Instructor, Paris Junior College (1992-1996); Assistant Director, Paris Outreach Center (1989-1992); Nursing Director, Leisure Lodge (1988-1989); Director of Quality Assurance, Infection Control Nurse, Choctaw Memorial Hospital (1986-1987); Nursing Director, Delta Home Health Care (1985-1986); House Supervisor, Quality Assurance Coordinator, Sam Rayburn Memorial Veterans Center(1984-1985); Director of Hospital-Wide Quality Assurance, St. Joseph Hospital (1980-1984); House Supervisor, Nurse Training Coordinator, St. Joseph Hospital (1977-1979); Internal Medicine Patient Care Coordinator, The University of Texas Medical Branch at Galveston (1976-1977); Registered Nurse Case Manager, Northeast Texas Council On Alcohol and Drug Abuse Inc.; Operating Room Supervisor, Choctaw Memorial Hospital **Career Related:** Member, President's Club, Paris Junior College (1999); Drug and Alcohol Counselor Intern, Texas Commission on Alcohol and Drug Abuse (1999); Nursing Home Training Instructor, Paris Junior College (1992); Health Occupations Committee, Paris Junior College (1988); Member, Board of Directors, Medical Plaza Home Health, Paris, TX (1984-1985) **Civic:** Appointed Member, Board of Chance Inc. (1999-Present); Volunteer, St. Joseph Hospital (1982-1987); Member, Church Choir **Awards:** Notable Women of Texas (1984) **Memberships:** Secretary, Treasurer, Texas Chapter, Lions International (1990-1991); Texas Industrial Vocational Association; Texas Exes; Alumni Association, East Texas State University; Alumni Association, Texas Woman's University; Kappa Delta Phi; Phi Theta Kappa Honor Society **Marquis Who's Who Honors:** Albert Nelson Marquis Lifetime Achievement Award **Why did you become involved in your profession or industry:** Ms. Elkin became involved in her profession because of her extracurricular activities in high school. **Avocations:** Reading; Studying **Political Affiliations:** Democrat **Religion:** Methodist

Alfred Elkins

Title: Insurance Company Executive (Retired) **Industry:** Insurance **Date of Birth:** 09/16/1946 **Place of Birth:** New York **State/Country of Origin:** NY/USA **Parents:** Nathaniel Elkins; Emily Elkins **Marital Status:** Widower **Spouse Name:** Ethel (Lehman) Elkins (09/24/1978, Deceased 2017) **Education:** AB, Herbert H. Lehman College, Bronx, NY (1969) **Career:** Computer Operator, Filling Department (2011-2012); Documents File Administrator, Mutual of America (1996-2011); Corporate Proofreader, Mutual of America, New York, NY (1985-1996) **Career Related:** Poet Laureate, Mutual of America, New York **Creative Works:** Author, 50 Anthologies **Awards:** Editor's Choice Award, International Library of Poetry (2004); Editor's Choice Award, National Library of Poetry (1994); Golden Poet Trophy, World of Poetry (1991) **Memberships:** Academy of American Poets; American Historical Association; Smithsonian Institution **Marquis Who's Who Honors:** Albert Nelson Marquis Lifetime Achievement Award **Why did you become involved in your profession or industry:** Mr. Alfred Elkins, has always written poetry. Although he was a poet by nature, he attended Lehman College and graduated with a Bachelor of Arts degree. He went to work for Mutual of America in 1985 as a corporate proofreader and worked his way up to work as a Documents file administrator in 1996. Mr. Elkins had an opportunity to utilize his love for poetry, within Mutual of America. He became the Poet Laureate, and he would compose poems for special occasions within the company. **Avocations:** Reading; Writing; Poetry; Music

Bruce Robert Ellig

Title: Human Resource Executive (Retired), Author **Industry:** Human Resources **Date of Birth:** 10/15/1936 **Place of Birth:** Manitowoc **State/Country of Origin:** WI/USA **Parents:** Robert Louis Ellig; Lucille Marie (Westphal) Ellig **Marital Status:** Married **Spouse Name:** Janice Reals **Children:** Brett **Education:** MBA, University of Wisconsin (1960); BBA, University of Wisconsin (1959) **Career:** Retired Human Resource Executive (1996-Present); Pfizer, Inc., New York, NY (1960-1996); Vice President, Personnel, Pfizer, Inc., New York, NY (1985-1995); Vice President, Employee Relations, Pfizer, Inc., New York, NY (1983-1985); Vice President, Compensation and Benefits, Pfizer, Inc., New York, NY (1978-1983); Corporate Director, Compensation and Benefits, Pfizer, Inc., New York, NY (1970-1978); Manager, Compensation and Personnel Research, Pfizer, Inc., New York, NY (1968-1970); Vice President, Employee Resources, Pfizer, Inc., New York, NY; Author **Career Related:** Advisory Panel, Career Central (2001-2003); Consultant, Organization Resources Counselors Inc. (1996-2001); Corporate Advisory Council (1996-2001); Savings and Investment, Retirement Plan Assets, Retirement Plan, Employee Compensation & Management Development Standing Committees, Pfizer (1985-1996); Speaker in Field; Aresty Fellow, Wharton Business School; Fellow, Employer Benefits Research Institute; Fellow, National Academy of Human Resources **Civic:** CalPERS Panel Discussion (2014); Dean's Advisory Board, School of Business, University of Wisconsin (2004-2008); Center for Advanced Human Resource Studies, Cornell University (1985-1995); Advisory Board, Global Remuneration Organization (1987-1990); Advisory Board, Kentucky Educational TV (1987-1990); Chairman, Mayor's Advisory Pay Commission, New York, NY (1980); Sector Staff, Council for Wage and Price Stability (1979-1980); Merit Pay Task Force, U.S. Civil Service Commission (1979); Mayor's Advisory Pay Commission, New York, NY (1977-1978); Presidential Quadrennial Pay Commission (1976) **Creative Works:** Author, "American History Impact on Employee Pay and Benefits - 3rd Edition" (2017); Author, "The Complete Guide to Executive Compensation - 3rd Edition" (2014); Contributing Author, "Compensation Handbook" (2008); Author, "The Evolution of Employee Pay in the United States" (2005); Contributing Author, "The Future of Human Resource Management" (2005); Advisory Board, Executive Compensation Reports (1999-2002); Author, "Future Focus: Human Resources in the 21st Century" (1998); Contributing Author, "Tomorrow's Human Resources Management" (1997); Consultant Editor, Compensation and Benefits Review (1984-1996); Member, Advisory Board, Journal of Compensation and Benefits (1984-1996); Contributing Author, "Handbook for Professional Managers" (1985); Author, "Compensation and Benefits: Design and Analysis" (1985); Contributing Author, "Handbook of Business Administration" (1984); Author, "Executive Compensation, A Total Pay Perspective" (1982); Author, "Compensation and Benefits: Analytical Strategies" (1978); Contributing Author, "Encyclopedia of Professional Management" (1978); Contributor, Over 100 Articles, Professional Journals; Contributor, Over 400 Presentations, Radio and Television **Awards:** Distinguished Business Alumnus Award, University of Wisconsin School of Business (2007); Keystone Award, American Compensation's (1999); Lifetime Achievement Award, Society for Human Resource Management (1999); Human Resources Executive of the Year, Human Resource Executive Magazine (1995); Person of the Year, University of Wisconsin Alumni Club of New York (1995); Wall of Fame Award, American Management Association **Memberships:** Chairman, Board of Directors, Society of Human Resource Management (1996); Senior Executives Forum; Human Resources Roundtable Group; Advisory Council, Human Resource Management, Business Roundtable Conference Board; Life Member, Personnel Round Table; American Compensation Association; Life Member, Society of Human Resource Management; Past President, New York Personnel Management Association; New York Chamber of Commerce; Charter President, New York Association of Compensation Administrators; Board of Directors Emeritus, University of Wisconsin Business School Alumni; Advisory Board Emeritus, University of Southern California Center for Effective Organizations; Past Partner, University of Illinois Center for Human Resource Management; Wharton/Spencer Stuart Director Institute; Phi Beta Kappa; Phi Eta Sigma; Beta Gamma Sigma **Marquis Who's Who Honors:** Albert Nelson Marquis Lifetime Achievement Award; Marquis Who's Who Top Professional **To what do you attribute your success:** Mr. Ellig attributes his success to his passion for finding incentives for employees to do a better job. **Why did you become involved in your profession or industry:** Mr. Ellig's father wanted him to become either a doctor or a lawyer. He attempted pre-law, but he found that it wasn't for him, so he transferred to business school, and found that he was interested in the wage and salary administration course. He decided to pursue a master's degree in Wisconsin. He was hired by Pfizer in 1960 and retired in 1996 after a successful career.

Janice Ellinwood, MFA, BS

Title: Professor Emerita of Fashion Design and Merchandising, Author, Artist, Illustrator **Industry:** Education/Educational Services **Company Name:** Marymount University **Date of Birth:** 07/04/1952 **Place of Birth:** Hartford **State/Country of Origin:** CT/USA **Parents:** Bennett Greenberg; Hilda Rose (Podnetsky) Greenberg **Marital Status:** Single **Spouse Name:** Edward Scott Rosenthal (11/12/1978, Divorced 1991) **Children:** Amy Dawn; Lindsey Jean; Samantha Robyn **Education:** MFA, George Washington University, Washington, DC (1986); BS, Skidmore College, Saratoga Springs, NY (1974); Postgraduate Coursework, University of Massachusetts; Postgraduate, Syracuse University **Career:** Professor Emerita, Fashion Design and Merchandising, Marymount University (2018-Present); Chair, Fashion Design, Fashion Merchandising, Marymount University, Arlington, VA (1987-Present); Lecturer to Professor, Department Chairmen, Fine and Applied Arts, Marymount University, Arlington, VA (1980-Present); Instructor in Business, Bay Path College (Now Bay Path University), Longmeadow, MA (1977-1978); Buyer, Visual Presentation Director, Blake's Department Stores, Springfield, MA (1974-1977) **Career Related:** Faculty Advisor, Air France International Design Competition (1992-1994); Faculty Advisor, Lifestyles '90 Competition, Dupont Inc., Underfashions Club (1990); Faculty Advisor, American Dress Design Competition, Lord & Taylor (1989-1995); Juror, Elementary School, High School, Art Competition, Catholic Daughters of America (1989-1994); Fashion Illustrator, Nordstrom, Tysons Corner, VA (1988) **Creative Works:** International Colored Pencil Exhibition, Colored Pencil Society of America (1993); Exhibited, Drawings (1992-1994); Exhibited, Drawings (1989); United States Geological Survey, Fine Arts Media Exhibition; American Drawing Biannual Three **Awards:** Honorary Mention Award, American Home Economics Association Exhibition (1986) **Memberships:** American Artists Registry; College Art Association; Colored Pencil Society; Costume Society of America; Fashion Group International; Foundation in Art Theory and Education; International Textile and Apparel Association **Marquis Who's Who Honors:** Albert Nelson Marquis Lifetime Achievement Award **Why did you become involved in your profession or industry:** Ms. Ellinwood became involved in her profession after graduating from the University of Massachusetts. She found a mentor to teach her fashion design. **Avocations:** Horseback riding

Carolyn J. Else

Title: Library Director (Retired) **Industry:** Library Management/Library Services **Company Name:** Pierce County Library District **Date of Birth:** 01/31/1934 **Place of Birth:** Minneapolis **State/Country of Origin:** MN/USA **Parents:** Elmer Oscar Wahlberg; Irma Carolyn (Seibert) Wahlberg **Marital Status:** Divorced **Spouse Name:** Floyd Warren Else (1962, Divorced 1968) **Children:** Stephen Alexander; Catherine Elizabeth **Education:** MLS, University of Washington (1957); BS, Stanford University (1956) **Certifications:** Certified Professional Librarian, Washington **Career:** Retired Library Director (1994); Director, Pierce County Library District, Tacoma, WA (1965-1994); Branch Librarian, Pierce County Library, Tacoma, WA (1963-1965); Information Librarian, Bennett Martin Library, Lincoln, NE (1962-1963); Librarian, U.S. Army Special Services, France, Germany (1959-1962); Librarian, Queens Borough Public Librarian, New York, NY (1957-1959) **Career Related:** Wellness Consultant, Nikken, Inc. (1994-Present) **Civic:** Advisory Committee, Tacoma Community College (2007-2009); Distribution Committee, Greater Tacoma Community Foundation (2005-2011); Board of Directors, Tacoma Philharmonic (2005-2012); Board of Directors, Community Health Care (1997-2003); Higher Education Council, South Puget Sound (1988-1992); Study Commission, Washington State Local Governance (1985-1988); Board of Directors, Campfire, Tacoma, WA (1984-1992) **Memberships:** Board of Directors, Tacoma Condominium Association (2010-Present); Board of Directors, Tacoma Rotary #8 Club (2008-Present); Secretary, Pacific Northwest Library Association (1969-1971); Vice President, Washington Library Association (1969-1971); American Library Association; Rotary Club; City Club **Marquis Who's Who Honors:** Albert Nelson Marquis Lifetime Achievement Award **Why did you become involved in your profession or industry:** Ms. Else graduated from Stanford University with a degree in psychology, though she did not see a future in that profession. She always loved libraries while growing up, which drew her to the profession. **Avocations:** Reading

David Lee Elson

Title: Oncologist, Educator (Retired) **Industry:** Medicine & Health Care **Date of Birth:** 10/31/1950 **Place of Birth:** Leon **State/Country of Origin:** IA/ USA **Parents:** Charles Lee Elson; Nancy Ann Elson **Marital Status:** Married **Spouse Name:** Julie Ann **Children:** Andrew Charles; Michael David **Education:** Doctor of Medicine, University of Iowa, Iowa City, IA (1975); Bachelor of Arts in Biology and Chemistry, Cornell College, Mount Vernon, NY, Cum Laude (1972) **Certifications:** Diplomate, National Board Medical Examiners; Iowa Board Examiners in Basic Sciences, American Board of Internal Medicine; Internal Medicine and Medical Oncology **Career:** Chairman, Cancer Committee, Sioux Valley Hospital, Sioux Falls, SD (1982-1983); Chief, Medical Oncology Section, Department of Internal Medicine, University of South Dakota Sanford School of Medicine, Sioux Falls, SD (1980-2016); Chief, Oncology Service, R.C.Johnson Virginia Hospital, Sioux Falls, SD (1980-1990); Resident in Medical Oncology, University of Texas Health Science Center at San Antonio, San Antonio, TX (1978-1980); Resident in Internal Medicine, University of Texas Health Science Center at San Antonio, San Antonio, TX (1976-1978); Intern, University of Texas Health Science Center at San Antonio, San Antonio, TX (1975-1976) **Career Related:** Professor Emeritus, Internal Medicine, University of South Dakota Sanford School of Medicine (2016-Present); Professor, Internal Medicine, University of South Dakota Sanford School of Medicine (2013-2016); Governor, South Dakota Chapter, American College of Physicians (2004-2008); Associate Professor, Internal Medicine, University of South Dakota Sanford School of Medicine (1986-2013); Assistant Professor, Internal Medicine, University of South Dakota Sanford School of Medicine (1980-1986) **Civic:** President, South Dakota Division, American Cancer Society (1985-1987, 1994-1995); Chairman, Professional Education Committee, American Cancer Society (1980-1985, 1990-1991); Del. Director, National Board of Directors, American Cancer Society (1989) **Creative Works:** Contributor, Numerous Articles to Professional Journals and Chapters to Books **Awards:** Laureate Award, South Dakota Chapter, American College of Physicians (2010); V.W. and Cornelia R. Scarbrough Foundation Fellow, Texas Division, American Cancer Society (1977-1989) **Memberships:** Fellow, American College of Physicians; Emeritus Member, South Dakota State Medical Association; South Dakota Chapter Alpha Omega Alpha **Marquis Who's Who Honors:** Albert Nelson Marquis Lifetime Achievement Award; Marquis Who's Who Top Professional; Marquis Who's Who Humanitarian Award **Why did you become involved in your profession or industry:** Dr. Elson became involved in his profession because, when he started his career at Cornell College as a music major, he found himself impressed with the results of the hospital's cancer program. Following a year in the music program, he decided to switch to pre-med after taking a biology course. **Avocations:** Biking; Boating; Pickleball; Choral music and church choir **Political Affiliations:** South Dakota Republican Party **Religion:** Roman Catholic

Carlos Embry Jr.

Title: State Legislator **Industry:** Government Administration/Government Relations/Government Services **Date of Birth:** 06/29/1941 **Place of Birth:** Louisville, **State/Country of Origin:** KY/USA **Parents:** Carlos Brogdon Embry; Zora Romans Embry **Marital Status:** Married **Spouse Name:** Wanda Lou Ralph (1962) **Children:** Laura Ann; Barbara Ann; Carlos Brogdon III **Career:** State Senator (2015); Kentucky State Representative, District 17 (2003-2014); General Manager, Hughes & Coleman, Plc (1996-2000); Organization Chairman, Hopkins Governor Campaign (1991); Executive, Ohio County (1982-1989); Director, Ohio County Comprehensive Employment & Training Act, United States Department of Labor (1978-1981); General Manager, Embry Newspapers, Incorporated (1978-1989); Chairman, Ohio County Republican Committee, Kentucky (1975-1977); Chairman, 1st District Republican Committee (1975-1978); National Committeeman, Kentucky Young Republicans (1975-1977); Co-Owner, Embry's Valley Shopping Center, Beaver Dam, KY (1974-1995); Judge, Ohio County (1974-1977); Judge, Ohio County, Kentucky (1974-1977); Mayor, Beaver Dam, KY (1970-1973); Former Treasurer, Kentucky Republican Party; Former Co-chairman, Local & State Programs, Young Republican National Federation; Teacher, Horse Branch Junior High (1969-1970); Teacher, Pleasant Ridge Elementary School (1964-1965); General Manager, Embry Newspapers, Incorporated (1963-1973) **Creative Works:** Contributor, Articles; Author, Book, "How To Add Years To Your Life" (1979); Author, "Down the Beaver Trail"; Author, "Melody of Death (A collection of Kentucky short-stories)" **Awards:** Named, Ohio County Citizen of the Year, Ohio County Chamber of Commerce (1982); Outstanding Young Republican National; National Young Republicans; Outstanding Young Republican Kentucky; Kentucky Young Republican Federation (1973-1974); Beaver Dam's Outstanding Young Man; Beaver Dam Jaycees (1973, 1969); George Washington Honorary Medal; National Freedoms Foundation (1970); Outstanding Community Leader, Butler County **Memberships:** F&AM; Louisville Scottish Rite; Fellow, Christian Athletics; Butler/Edmonson Gideons; Former Vice Chairman, Kentucky Republican Judge-Executive's Association; Board Director, Former Chairman, Green River Area Development District; Former President, Ohio County Historical Society; Promise Keepers; Kosair Temple Shriners; Louisville Scottish Rite; Fellow, Christian Athletics; Butler/Edmonson Gideons; Former Vice Chairman, Kentucky Republican Judge-Executive's Association; Board Director, Former Chairman, Green River Area Development District; Former President, Ohio County Historical Society; Promise Keepers; Kosair Temple Shriners; Honorary Order of Kentucky Colonels **Marquis Who's Who Honors:** Albert Nelson Marquis Lifetime Achievement Award; Marquis Who's Who Top Professional **Why did you become involved in your profession or industry:** What attracted Senator C. B. Embry to his career in state legislation was his upbringing and family history. Mr. Embry's parents were both very active in public service. It was a great example to him and made him want to do similar endeavors. His father was a state senator when he was about 4 years old, as well as being a former newspaper owner. He was a writer of several books and articles. His mother was very active in civic related endeavors all throughout the state of Kentucky as well as in church. **Political Affiliations:** Republican **Religion:** Baptist

Margaret Burke Emmett

Title: Computer Consultant, Mathematician **Industry:** Consulting **Company Name:** The Oak Ridge National Laboratory **Date of Birth:** 07/13/1939 **Place of Birth:** Warrenton **State/Country of Origin:** VA/USA **Parents:** Walter Edgar Burke; Rachael Louise (Keathley) Boyer **Marital Status:** Married **Spouse Name:** Raymond Lee McDonough (08/09/2008); John McCue Emmett (09/13/1959, Deceased 1990); John Wells Wachter **Children:** Brian Keathley; Gregory Allyn **Education:** Postgraduate Coursework, University of Tennessee (1965-1970); BS in Mathematics, Tennessee Technological University (1960) **Career:** Section Head, Nuclear Code Development, Oak Ridge National Laboratory (1987-2001); Computing Consultant, Affirmative Action Representative, Oak Ridge National Laboratory (1980-1999); Mathematician, Computer Specialist, Oak Ridge National Laboratory (1960-1980) **Career Related:** Delegate, American Nuclear Community Leaders, USSR (1986); Delegate, American Nuclear Community Leaders, Hungary, (1986); Delegate, American Nuclear Community Leaders, Czechoslovakia (1986) **Civic:** Fountain City Town Hall, Knoxville, TN (1973-Present); Tennessee Leadership (1991) **Creative Works:** Editor, The Tennessean (1985-1987); Author, Poetry; Contributor, Articles, Professional Journals **Awards:** American Association of University Women (1991-Present); Golden Poet Award (1988); Margaret Emmett Educational Grant (2019) **Memberships:** Securities and Exchange Commission, Regional Director (1997-1999); Chair, Radiation Protection and Shielding Division (1992-1993); President Tennessee (1991-1994); Executive Board, Chairman, Oak Ridge-Knoxville Section; Fellow (2001), American Nuclear Society (1991); Branch President, American Association of University Women (1982-1984); Phi Kappa Phi; Kappa Mu Epsilon; Association of Women in Science **Marquis Who's Who Honors:** Albert Nelson Marquis Lifetime Achievement Award **To what do you attribute your success:** Ms. Emmett attributes her success to being highly motivated to excel within her field. **Why did you become involved in your profession or industry:** Ms. Emmet became involved in her profession because she studied mathematics and physics at Tennessee Tech. Ms. Emmet was hired at the Oak Ridge Nuclear Laboratory after she graduated because of her mathematics skills. **Avocations:** Reading; Computers; Ballroom Dancing; Sports **Religion:** Christian

Anthony Endieveri

Title: Trial Lawyer **Industry:** Law and Legal Services **Date of Birth:** 05/21/1939 **Place of Birth:** Syracuse **State/Country of Origin:** NY/USA **Parents:** Santo Endieveri; Rose (Zeolla) Endieveri **Marital Status:** Married **Spouse Name:** Arlen Rita McDonald (05/20/1967) **Children:** Anne C.; Steven A. **Education:** JD, Syracuse University (1968); LLB, Syracuse University (1965); BA in Liberal Arts, Syracuse University (1961) **Certifications:** Certified Civil Trial Lawyer, National Board of Legal Specialty **Career:** Retired (2016); Attorney, Anthony F. Endieveri, Attorney at Law, Camillus, NY (1968-2016); Assistant Corporate Counsel, City of Syracuse, NY (1970-1974); Hiscock Legal Aid, New York State (1968-1970) **Career Related:** Lecturer, Melvin Belli Seminar, San Francisco, CA (1987, 1993); Lecturer, San Diego, CA (1990); Lecturer, Boston, MA (1989); Lecturer, Kansas City, MO (1988); Participant, National College Advocacy Group (NCAG, Inc.) (1981-1983, 1986); Speaker in Field **Civic:** Member, Ministry Program, Syracuse Diocese Pre-Deacon Study (1980-1982); Volunteer, Eucharistic Minister, VA Hospital **Military Service:** Retired Major, Untied States Marine Corps Reserve (1999); Major, United States Marine Corps Reserve (1972-1988) **Awards:** Ranked Number One, Syracuse University Football Team (1959); Hall of Fame Award, American Biographical Institute; Lifetime Achievement Award, International Biographical Center; Named to Top Trial Lawyers in U.S.A.; Million Dollar Award and Multi-Million Dollar Award; Named to Top One Percent of the Nation in Income; Named to Top Trial Lawyer in America; Named to Top 19, U.S.A. Winning Awards **Memberships:** Brain Injury Association of New York (BIANYS); National Brain Injury Association; American Trial Lawyers Association (Now American Association for Justice; New York State Trial Lawyers Association (NYSTLA); New York State Bar Association; Onondaga County Bar Association; Syracuse University Football Team **Bar Admissions:** Supreme Court of the Untied States (1970); United States Court of Appeals for the Second Circuit (1969); New York (1967); United States District Court for the Northern District of New York **Marquis Who's Who Honors:** Albert Nelson Marquis Lifetime Achievement Award; Marquis Who's Who Top Professional **Why did you become involved in your profession or industry:** Mr. Endieveri got a job out of Syracuse University selling for Colgate Palmolive and they sent him to the west coast. This guy who was known to have a bad temper asked him to leave his store. He said to himself he wasn't cut out to be a salesman because he was offended that he didn't treat him professionally. Some of his friends were going to law school, so he decided to go, too It was a profession where he could help more people, serve more people and he felt he could make a change in somebody's life. **Avocations:** Golf; Sports; Sports cars; Jaguars

Mazi Enti

Title: Owner, General Manager **Industry:** Food & Restaurant Services **Company Name:** Scuzzi's Italian Restaurant **Education:** MA in Software Engineering/Computers, Azad University, Iran (2002); BA in Mathematics, Motahari University (2000) **Career:** Owner, General Manager, Two Locations, Scuzzi's Italian Restaurant, San Antonio TX (2008-Present); Dishwasher, Busboy, Salsalito Cantina Mexican Restaurant (2003-2008) **Awards:** Featured, San Antonio Magazine; Featured, Dominion Magazine; Open Table, Yelp, Urban Spoon; Nine Year Talk of the Town on Customer Service **To what do you attribute your success:** His passion to learn, and learning from those he worked with. **Why did you become involved in your profession or industry:** From 2003-2008, Mr. Enti worked at multiple restaurant locations, Mexican cuisine, Chinese cuisine, everything was high volume and fast. He wanted to open a restaurant that was slow and calming and where people could open a bottle of wine and relax. Also, Mr. Enti lived in Naples before coming to the United States.

Gerard E. Evans, Esq.

Title: Lobbyist **Industry:** Government Administration/Government Relations/Government Services **Company Name:** Evans & Associates **Marital Status:** Married **Children:** Five Children **Education:** JD, University of Baltimore (1985); Master of Public Policy, University of Maryland; BS, University of Maryland **Career:** Lobbyist, Evans & Associates (1987-Present) **Civic:** Pro Bono Professor, University of Maryland School of Public Policy (1999-Present); Founding Board of Leadership, Cambridge University, England; Board Member, Next One Up; Board Member, Christmas in April; Former Volunteer, Boy Scouts of America; Former Board of Visitors Member, University of Maryland; Former Dean, Advisory Counsel, University of Baltimore Law School **Awards:** Top 40 under 40 (1999); Distinguish Alumni Award, University of Baltimore Law School; Several Governors Citations; Legislative Citations for Community Activities **Why did you become involved in your profession or industry:** Mr. Evans became involved in his profession because of an internship he had in 1976 at the University of Maryland. He interned with a senator, and at the time he was the only staff member. He answered the phones, did the typing drafted bills, he was only a sophomore in college. They formed a friendship and he became then the longest serving senate president in the history of our country. He worked for him off and on for years, until he started his private practice. **Avocations:** Reading; Spending time with family **Thoughts on Life:** You have to have a servants heart to be in politics, and if you don't you don't belong here. We serve our clients and then in turn it serves the public interest. Lobbyist are people you hire to protect you from people that you elect.

Mark I. Evans, MD

Title: Obstetrician, Geneticist **Industry:** Medicine & Health Care **Company Name:** Comprehensive Genetics **Date of Birth:** 05/14/1952 **Place of Birth:** Brooklyn **State/Country of Origin:** NY/USA **Parents:** Robert Bernard Evans; Sonia Beatrice Evans **Marital Status:** Married **Spouse Name:** Robyn Searles (05/17/2014) **Children:** Shara M. Evans **Education:** Medical Genetics Fellow, National Institutes of Health, Bethesda, MD (1982-1984); Resident in Obstetrics-Gynecology, University of Chicago (1978-1982); MD, SUNY Downstate Health Sciences University, Brooklyn, NY (1978); BS in Psychology, Tufts University (1973) **Certifications:** Diplomate, American Board of Obstetrics and Gynecology; Diplomate, American Board of Medical Genetics and Genomics **Career:** Professor, Obstetrics and Gynecology, Mount Sinai School of Medicine (2005-Present); President, Fetal Medicine Foundation of America (2001-Present); President, International Fetal Medicine and Surgery Society Foundation (1996-Present); Director of Institute Genetics and Fetal Medicine, Columbia University College of Physicians and Surgeons, New York, NY (2002-2004); Professor of Obstetrics and Gynecology, St. Lukes Roosevelt Hospital Center, Columbia University (2002-2004); Professor, Chairman of Obstetrics and Gynecology, Professor of Human Genetics, Director of Fetal Therapy, Hahnemann Hospital, Philadelphia, PA (2001-2002); Director of Fetal Therapy Program, MCP Hahnemann University (2000-2002); Distinguished Professor, Hutzel Hospital, Wayne State University, Detroit, MI (2000); Chairman, Chief, Hutzel Hospital, Wayne State University, Detroit, MI (1998-1999); Director of Human Genetics Program, Wayne State University, Detroit, MI (1996-2001); Charlotte B. Failing Professor of Obstetrics-Gynecology and Human Genetics, Center for Molecular Medicine/Pathology, Wayne State University (1991-2001); Director, Center for Fetal Diagnosis and Therapy, Hutzel Hospital, Wayne State University, Detroit, MI (1985-2001); Director of Reproductive Genetics, Wayne State University, Detroit, MI (1984-2001) **Career Related:** Director, Science Advisory Board, Manhattan Professional Laboratories (2008-2011); International Organizer, Nobel Foundation Symposium (1998); Advisory Board, Corning Metpath, Quest Diagnostics (1988-2000); Member of Ethics Committee, American College of Obstetricians and Gynecologists (1987-1990); Advisory Board, Ehlers-Danlos Society (1986-2004); Committee on Molecular Medicine and Genetics, Wayne State University **Civic:** Pro Bono Work **Creative Works:** Co-Editor, "Prenatal Diagnosis, Chinese Edition" (2010); Co-Editor, "High Risk Obstetrics" (2009); Co-Editor, "Prenatal Diagnosis" (2006); Co-Editor, "New Genetics for the Clinician" (2002); Co-Editor, "The Genetic Revolution and Obstetrics and Gynecology" (2002); Author, "The Unborn Patient" (2001); Co-Author, "Ultrasound and Fetal Therapy" (2000); Co-Author, "Fetal Therapy" (2000); Co-Author, "Pretest: Obstetrics and Gynecology, Ninth Edition" (Author, "Principles and Practice of Medical Therapy in Pregnancy" (1998); Author, "Invasive Outpatient Procedures in Reproductive Medicine" (1997); Author, "Maternal Genetic Disease" (1996); Author, "Reproductive Risks and Prenatal Diagnosis" (1992); Author, Co-Author, "Fetal Diagnosis Therapy: Science, Ethics and the Law" (1989); Author, "Intrauterine Growth Retardation" (1984); Contributor, Articles to Professional Journals **Awards:** Visionary Award, Central Association of Obstetricians and Gynecologists (2009); Presidents Award, Society for Reproductive Investigation (1999); Awards, Planned Parenthood, National Organization of Women **Memberships:** President, Central Association of Obstetricians and Gynecologists (2007); Vice President, Central Association Obstetrics and Gynecologists (2004); Board of Directors, Central Association of Obstetricians and Gynecologists (1998-2000); Course Coordination Committee, American College of Obstetricians and Gynecologists (1996-1999); President, International Fetal Medicine Surgery Society (1996-1997); National Ultrasound Task Force, American Medical Association (1990-1991); President, International Fetal Medicine Surgery Society (1986-1987); American Society of Human Genetics; Society for Gynecologic Investigation; Society of Perinatal Obstetricians; American Gynecological and Obstetrics Society; Fellow, American College of Obstetricians and Gynecologists; Founder, American College of Medical Genetics **Marquis Who's Who Honors:** Albert Nelson Marquis Lifetime Achievement Award; Marquis Who's Who Top Professional; Marquis Who's Who Humanitarian Award **Why did you become involved in your profession or industry:** Dr. Evans has been interested in genetics since high school. He became an obstetrician as opposed to a pediatrician because he wanted to prevent birth defects. **Religion:** Jewish

Nancy J. Evans

Title: Nursing Educator **Industry:** Medicine & Health Care **Date of Birth:** 06/17/1937 **Place of Birth:** Canton **State/Country of Origin:** OH/USA **Parents:** Alfred; Kathleen P. (McWilliams) Davies **Marital Status:** Married **Spouse Name:** Donald Evans (02/14/1959, Deceased) **Children:** Jean Ann Evans Childress; Donna Jane Evans McCoy **Education:** Postgraduate Studies, University of Akron (1988); Master of Education, Kent State University, Summa Cum Laude (1983); Bachelor of Science, Mount Union College, Summa Cum Laude, Alliance, OH (1978); Diploma, Aultman Hospital School Of Nursing, Canton, OH (1958) **Certifications:** Registered Nurse, Ohio; Certified Instructor on Diversified Health Occupations, Cooperative Health Occupations and CPR **Career:** Nursing Educator; Instructor of Health Occupations, Canton Local Schools; Clinical Supervisor, Medical-Surgical Units, Aultman Hospital; Staff, Float Nurse, Mercy Medical Center, Canton, OH; Coordinator of Diversified Cooperative Health Occupations, Canton Local School District **Awards:** Grantee, College Club **Memberships:** American Nurses Association; National Education Association; Ohio Education Association; Canton Local Education Association; Voting Delegate, Stark-Carroll District Nurses Association; Grantee, Ohio Vocational Association; College Club **Marquis Who's Who Honors:** Albert Nelson Marquis Lifetime Achievement Award; Marquis Who's Who Top Professional **Why did you become involved in your profession or industry:** Ms. Evans initially became involved in the educational profession due to her experiences as a surgical nurse. Additionally, she was inspired by her upbringing and family, having come of age in England. She drew a great deal of inspiration from the stories she heard of the London Bombing during the Second World War, and the exemplary feats in nursing that took place during that time. **Avocations:** Reading; Knitting; Church choirs; Mission work; Meals for deceased church families **Political Affiliations:** Independent **Religion:** Baptist

Parker Evatt

Title: Commissioner, State Legislator (Retired) **Industry:** Government Administration/ Government Relations/Government Services **Company Name:** South Carolina **Date of Birth:** 08/27/1935 **Place of Birth:** Greenville **State/Country of Origin:** SC/USA **Parents:** H.D. Evatt; Ruby (Parker) Evatt **Marital Status:** Married **Spouse Name:** Jane Mangum (09/02/1960) **Children:** Katherine; Alan **Education:** Master's Degree in Criminal Justice, University of South Carolina (1978); LLD, Presbyterian College (1977); BS in Mechanical Engineering, University of South Carolina (1958) **Career:** Senior Vice President, Just Care, Inc. (1996-2000); Director, Commissioner, South Carolina Department of Corrections (1987-1995); Member, South Carolina House of Representatives, District 71, Richland County, SC (1974-1987); Executive Director, Alston Wilkes Society, Columbia, SC (1966-1987); Mechanical Engineer, South Carolina State Highway Department (1960-1966); Commissioner, State Legislator (Retired) **Civic:** Delegate to Jurisdiction Conferences (1972, 1976, 1980, 1984); Member, Administrative Board, Virginia Wingard Memorial, United Methodist Church, Delegate to General Conference (1972); Past Lay Leader, Columbia Methodist District **Military Service:** Commander (Retired), U.S. Naval Reserve (1986-Present); Officer in Charge, Naval Recruiting Assistance Council (1974-1986); Commanding Officer, Three Divisions (1960-1974); Served, U.S. Navy (1958-1960) **Creative Works:** University of South Carolina Advisory Board, "The South Carolina Forum," Quarterly Magazine, Institute of Public Affairs (1990-Present); Author, "Security Classification: Both... and Not either...Or," Corrections Today (1989); Author, "Turning Around the Dangerous Juvenile Offender," Portfolio of State Issues (1987); Author, "Children Don't Belong in Jail," Engage Social Action (1983); Author, "Volunteer Named Bob," VIP News (1977); Author, "Second Careers," S.C. United Methodist Advocate (1971); Author, "Alston Wilkes Society," Baptist Courier (1967) **Awards:** Algernon Sydney Sullivan Award, My Carolina (2014); E.R. Cass Award, American Correctional Association (1994); State Representatives Achievement Award, Southern States Correctional Association (1991, 1992); Named Citizen of the Year, South Carolina Chapter, National Association of Social Workers (1978); Named Legislator of the Year, Ten Different Groups; Numerous Awards and Citations from Civic, Religious and Professional Organizations **Memberships:** Legislative Committee, American Correctional Association (1995-Present); Host Committee, Southern States Correctional Association (1992-Present); Delegate Assembly, American Correctional Association (1987-Present); Southern States Correctional Association (1987-Present); Rotary Club of Five Points (1972-Present); American Correctional Association (1966-Present); 125th Anniversary Committee, American Correctional Association (1994); State-Federal Committee, Association of State Correctional Administrators (1994); Advisory Board, College of Humanities and Social Sciences, University of South Carolina (1994); Executive Committee Representing Southern Correctional Administrators, Association of State Correctional Administrators (1988-1990, 1993-1994); President, Southern Correctional Administrators Association (1988-1990, 1993-1994); Representative for Southern Correctional Administrators Association to Association of State Correctional Administrators, Executive Committee (1988-1990, 1993-1994); United States Attorney, District of South Carolina, Executive Board, Law Enforcement Coordinating Council (1993-1994); Chairman, Southern States Correctional Association (1993); Panel Member, Governor's South Carolina Education Goals (1992-1994); Executive Board, Appointed by U.S. Attorney/District of South Carolina, Law Enforcement Coordinating Committee (1992-1994); Chairman, Committee on Resolutions & Policy Development, American Correctional Association (1988-1994, 1992-1993); Legislative Committee, Association of State Correctional Administrators (1992-1993); Community Corrections Committee, American Correctional Association (1991-1993); Substance Abuse Committee, American Correctional Association (1991-1992); Chairman, Committee on Victims, American Correctional Association (1991-1992); Vice Chairman, South Carolina Human Services Coordinating Council (1991); Chairman, Substance Abuse Committee, Association of State Correctional Administrators (1990-1992); Chairman, Task Force on Substance Abuse, American Correctional Association (1990); Board of Directors, United Way of South Carolina, South Carolina Partnership (1990); S.C. Partnership, Board of Directors, United Way of South Carolina (1990); South Carolina Sentencing Guidelines Commission (1989-1994); South Carolina State Representative, Southern States Correctional Association (1989-1994); Trustee, United Way of the Midlands (1989-1991); Chairman, Corrections Committee, South Carolina Law Enforcement Officers Association (1989-1990); Chairman, Policy & Resolutions Committee, Association of State Correctional Administrators (1989); Board of Advisors, Volunteers in Prevention, Probation & Prisons, Inc. (1988-1994); Chairman, Governor's Strategic Council on Drug Education, Enforcement and Treatment (1987-1994) **Marquis Who's Who Honors:** Albert Nelson Marquis Lifetime Achievement Award; Marquis Who's Who Humanitarian Award **Why did you become involved in your profession or industry:** Dr. Evatt became involved in his profession because he always wanted to help others. **Avocations:** Golf **Religion:** United Methodist

Jack Robert Ewing

Title: Certified Public Accountant (Retired) **Industry:** Financial Services **Date of Birth:** 02/14/1947 **Place of Birth:** San Francisco **State/Country of Origin:** CA/USA **Parents:** Son of Robert Maxwell and Blanche Julia (Diak) E. **Education:** Bachelor of Science, University Missouri, St. Louis (1969) **Certifications:** Certified Public Accountant, Retired **Career:** Owner, Jack R. Ewing, CPA (1993-2007); Stockholder, Owner, Hunt, Spillman & Ewing, Professional Corporation, Fort Collins, CO (1982-1993); Audit Manager, Erickson, Hunt & Spillman, PC, Fort Collins, CO (1979-1982); Supervisor Auditor, Fox & Co., St. Louis, MO (1974-1979); Internal Auditor, Air Force Audit Agency, Francis E. Warren Air Force Base (1972-1974); Radio Station Operator, US Air Force, Mountain Home Air Force Base (1970-1972); Staff Accountant, Fox & Co., St. Louis, MO (1969-1970) **Career Related:** Lecturer and writer on mental illness and suicide prevention (1986-Present) **Civic:** Member Steering Committee, Mental Health and Substance Abuse Partnership (1997-2012); Member, Suicide Resource Center of Larimer County, Fort Collins (1992-2008); President, Suicide Resource Center of Larimer County, Fort Collins (1998-2003); Member, State of Colorado Mental Health Planning Council (1993-2000); Member, Indicators and Outcomes Committee, State of Colorado (1998-2000); Member, Governor's Citizen Panel on Suicide Prevention (1998-2000); President, Advisory Board, Board of Mental Health, Larimer County (1992-1999); Vice President, Colorado Behavioral Healthcare Council (1995-1997); Member Mental Health Pro Bono Project (1996-1997); Member, Board of Directors, One West Contemporary Art Center (1989-1997); Member State of Colorado Suicide Prevention Coalition (1993-1996); Director Treasurer, Center for Diversity in Work Place (1991-1996); Member, Leadership Fort Collins (1992); Member, Entrepreneur of the Year Selection Committee, Fort Collins, CO (1989-1992); President, Parental Advisory Board, Beattie Elementary School (1986-1987); Member, Parental Advisory Board, Beattie Elementary School (1982-1983); President, Alpha Phi Omega (1967-1969); Member, Alpha Phi Omega (1966-1969); Member, Board of Directors, Suicide Resource Center of Larimer County, Fort Collins, CO **Military Service:** U.S. Air Force (1970-1974) **Awards:** Everyday Heroes and Heroines Award, Colorado Society of Certified Public Accountants (2006) **Memberships:** Member, American Institute of Certified Public Accountants; Member, Colorado Society of Certified Public Accountants **Marquis Who's Who Honors:** Albert Nelson Marquis Lifetime Achievement Award **Avocations:** Writing; Hiking; Traveling

Michael J. Eyre

Title: Attorney **Industry:** Law and Legal Services **Company Name:** Law Offices of Michael J. Eyre **Date of Birth:** 04/10/1960 **Place of Birth:** Inglewood **State/Country of Origin:** CA/USA **Parents:** James Eyre; Jo-Ann Eyre **Marital Status:** Single **Children:** Joseph; Katherine **Education:** JD, Western State College of Law (1987); Postgraduate Studies in Political Science, California State University Long Beach (1983); BA in English Literature, University of California at Irvine (1982) **Career:** Principal, Owner, Law Offices of Michael J. Eyre, Long Beach and Lakewood, CA (2009-Present); Associate Attorney, Law Office of Rice & Rothenberg/The Law Firm of Marc S. Rothenberg, Long Beach, CA (2000-2009); Associate Attorney, Hollins, Schechter, Feinstein & Condas (1999-2000); Associate Attorney, Veatch, Carlson, Grogan & Nelson (Now Veatch Carlson Attorneys at Law), Los Angeles, CA (1997-1999); Associate Attorney, Cone, Chairez & Kassel/Law Offices of Joseph L. Chairez (1996-1997); Associate Attorney, Kaiser, DeBiaso, Palmer & Lopez (1988-1996) **Civic:** Community Volunteer, Shortstop Program, Long Beach Bar Foundation, Inc. (2010-Present); Instructor, Shortstop Program, Long Beach Bar Foundation, Inc. (2008-Present); Advisory Board, Paralegal Department, Mt. San Antonio College (2008-Present); Volunteer Mock Trial Coach, Mt. San Antonio College (2009-2012); Boy Scouts of America **Awards:** Silver Client Champion Award, Martindale-Hubbell (2017); Instructor of the Year, SHORTSTOP (2017); Honoree, One of the Top Temporary Judges in the Superior Court of California, County of Los Angeles (2014-2018); Honoree, Southern California Top Attorney, Super Lawyers (2013-2016); Client Distinction Award, Martindale-Hubbell (2013-2016); Honoree, PRR AV Preeminent Attorney, Lawyers.com (2011-2017); Honoree, AV Preeminent Attorney, Martindale-Hubbell (2011-2015); Honoree, PRR BV Distinguished Attorney, American Registry (2010); 10.0 Superb Rating, Avvo Inc. **Memberships:** The State Bar of California; Orange County Bar Association; ABA; Long Beach Bar Association; Consumer Attorneys Association of Los Angeles **Bar Admissions:** California; United States District Court for the Central District of California; United States Court of Appeals for the Ninth Circuit; Supreme Court of the United States **Marquis Who's Who Honors:** Albert Nelson Marquis Lifetime Achievement Award; Marquis Who's Who Top Professional; Marquis Who's Who Humanitarian Award **To what do you attribute your success:** Mr. Ford attributes his success to being passionate about the field, as well as understanding the business of law and not just the practice of it. He also credits his focus on being productive and not just keeping busy. **Why did you become involved in your profession or industry:** Mr. Eyre became involved in his profession because he knew at the age of 14 that he wanted to be an attorney. His uncle, Donald M. Pach, was a lawyer and after watching him in court, he knew he wanted to be an attorney. **Avocations:** Camping; Hiking; Backpacking; Cycling; Water sports **Political Affiliations:** Libertarian

Anne R. Fabbri

Title: Critic, Curator (Retired) **Industry:** Fine Art **Place of Birth:** Norristown **State/Country of Origin:** PA/USA **Parents:** Remo; Anna Wild (Butterworth) F. **Marital Status:** Divorced **Spouse Name:** Joseph Henry Butera **Children:** Virginia; Remo; Joseph F. (Jay) **Education:** Master of Arts in Art History, Bryn Mawr College (1971); Bachelor of Arts, Harvard University, Cum Laude **Career:** Art Critic, Broad Street Review (2006-Present); Art Critic, Art in America (2002-Present); Art Critic, The Art Newspaper (2000-Present); Art Critic, Philadelphia Daily News (1999-Present); Art Critic, American Artist (1998-Present); Art Critic, Art Matters (1996-Present); Art Critic, Philadelphia Style Magazine (2003-2005); Lecturer of Humanities, Rosemont College (2001-2003); Lecturer of Arts Administration, Rosemont College (2000-2003); Director, Paley Design Center, Philadelphia University (1991-2001); Director, The Noyes Museum, Oceanville, NJ (1982-1991); Director, Alfred O. Deshong Museum, Widener University, Chester, PA (1980-1982); Art Critic, The Bulletin, Philadelphia, PA (1978-1980); Art Critic, Art Editor, The Drummer, Philadelphia, PA (1976-1979); Art Lecturer, Drexel University, Philadelphia, PA (1974-1976); Art Lecturer, Villanova University, Pennsylvania, PA (1971-1973) **Career Related:** Board of Directors, Philadelphia Volunteer Lawyers for the Arts (2001-2003); Member, Advisory Committee, Main Line Art Center (1999-2009); Chair, New Visions, Philadelphia Furniture Exhibition (1998-2004) **Civic:** Chair, Advisory Committee, Art in City Hall (1999-2010) **Awards:** John Cotton Dana Award, New Jersey Association of Museums (1991); Visiting Fellow, National Endowment of the Humanities, Princeton University (1981); Visiting Fellow, National Endowment of the Humanities, University of California Berkeley (1980) **Memberships:** American Association of Museums **Marquis Who's Who Honors:** Albert Nelson Marquis Lifetime Achievement Award **Why did you become involved in your profession or industry:** Ms. Fabbri initially entered her profession as a philosophy and economics major while studying in college. Throughout the course of her studies, she discovered the subject of art history and became fascinated with it. **Avocations:** Travel **Political Affiliations:** Democrat

Tasheema L. Fair, MD, FACOG

Title: OBGYN/Health and Wellness Coach **Industry:** Health, Wellness and Fitness **Company Name:** Herbalife Nutrition **Date of Birth:** 03/18/1978 **Place of Birth:** Brooklyn **State/Country of Origin:** NY/USA **Education:** MD, The University of Tennessee Health Science Center (2005) **Certifications:** Board Certified in Obstetrics and Gynecology **Career:** Owner, OBGYN/Physician/Health and Wellness Coaching, Obstetrics and Gynecology, Herbalife Nutrition, (Ladydoc); OBGYN, All Women's Care (2014-2019) **Career Related:** Doctor, St. Vincent Anderson Regional Hospital, Indiana; Doctor, Shift Work, Martin TN **Military Service:** Army Reserves **Awards:** Army Commendation Medal; Army Achievement Medal **Marquis Who's Who Honors:** Albert Nelson Marquis Lifetime Achievement Award; Marquis Who's Who Top Professional; Marquis Who's Who Humanitarian Award **To what do you attribute your success:** She attributes her success to God and working hard and doing what she needed to do to be where she is now. In addition, if it was not for God she would not be able to do what she does. **Why did you become involved in your profession or industry:** She joined the Army because of her father (he was in the Army) and as a way to pay for medical school. She has always wanted to be a doctor (since she was 4 years old). Dr. Fair became a doctor because she never wanted to be anything else. At the young age of 4 she said that she wanted to be a doctor. Her grandfather was in the military, as well. **Avocations:** Shopping; Traveling; Reading; Running; Exercising **Religion:** Non-demoninational **Thoughts on Life:** Previously worked at All Women's Care PLLC for 4 1/2 years as an OB/GYN

Jonathan Leo Fairbanks

Title: Emeritus Director, Senior Research Associate, Museum Executive, Museum Curator, Artist **Industry:** Museums & Institutions **Company Name:** Fuller Craft Museum **Date of Birth:** 02/19/1933 **Place of Birth:** Ann Arbor **State/Country of Origin:** MI/USA **Parents:** Avard T. Fairbanks; Beatrice Maude (Fox) Fairbanks **Marital Status:** Married **Spouse Name:** Louise Ann Eckenbrecht (02/12/1954) **Children:** Theresa Louise Fairbanks Harris; Hilary-Ann Fairbanks Burtons **Education:** MA, University of Delaware (1961); MFA, University of Pennsylvania (1957); Coursework, Pennsylvania Academy of the Fine Arts (1956-1957); BFA, The University of Utah (1953) **Career:** Senior Research Associate, Emeritus Director, Fuller Craft Museum (2018-Present); Vice President of Research, Artfact (2005-Present); Director, Fuller Craft Museum (2014-2018); Founder, Department of American Decorative Arts and Sculpture, Museum of Fine Arts, Boston (1971-1999); Curatorial Assistant, Associate Curator, Winterthur Museum, Garden & Library (1961-1971); Katharine Lane Weems Senior Curator of American Decorative Arts and Sculpture, Museum of Fine Arts, Boston **Career Related:** Adjunct Lecturer, University of Delaware; Instructor, Utah State University Extension, Brigham Young University, West Virginia University; Adjunct Professor, American & New England Studies Program, Boston University; Trustee, Texas Pioneer Arts Foundation; Foundation Trustee, Incorporator, Dublin Seminar for New England Folklife, Department of Art History, Boston University; Honorary Chairman, Board of Directors, The Decorative Arts Trust **Civic:** Member, Board of Directors, The Paul Revere House; Member, Board of Directors, The Fairbanks House, Dedham, MA; Member, Board of Directors, The Charles J. Connick Stained Glass Foundation; Member, Board of Directors, The Shirley-Eustis House; Former Member, Committee for the Preservation of the White House; Former President, The Decorative Arts Trust; Former Trustee, Forest Hills Cemetery; Former Trustee, The Wayside Inn Foundation **Military Service:** Commander, Cruiser Division Four, Atlantic Fleet, US Navy (1953-1955) **Creative Works:** One-Man Exhibition, Washington County Museum of Fine Arts (2004); Curator, Exhibitions and Catalogues, "Paul Revere's Boston: 1735-1818," "New England Begins: The Seventeenth Century, "Glass Today," U.S. Department of State (2003); Exhibition, Haley and Steele Gallery and Framing (2001, 2002); Co-Author, "American Furniture: 1620 To the Present" (1981); Mural, Hall of Earth History, The Academy of Natural Sciences of Drexel University (1957) **Awards:** Luminaries Award, Fuller Craft Museum (2009); Iris Award, Bard Graduate Center (2006); Award of Distinction, The Furniture Society (2003); Ellen Banning Ayer Award (1999); Medal, Society of Arts & Crafts (1997); Robert H. Lord Award for Excellence in History Studies, Emmanuel College (1983); Distinguished Service Award, Antiques Monthly (1983); C.F. Montgomery Award, Decorative Arts Society (1983); Winterthur Fellowship (1959-1961) **Memberships:** President, Westwood Historical Society (1978-1981); Vice President, Decorative Arts Society (1978-1979); Fellow, American Institute for Conservation; Honorary Fellow, American Craft Council; Former Vice President, Victorian Society in America; The International Institute for Conservation of Historic and Artistic Works; American Alliance of Museums; Society of Architectural Historians; National Trust for Historic Preservation; American Society of Interior Designers; Massachusetts Historical Society; American Antiquarian Society; Walpole Society; St. Botolph Club **Marquis Who's Who Honors:** Albert Nelson Marquis Lifetime Achievement Award **Why did you become involved in your profession or industry:** Mr. Fairbanks became involved in his profession because of the studio life he had with his father, a famous sculptor. The arts were a long tradition in his family. In addition to his father, Mr. Fairbanks' grandfather was a painter who went to Paris, France, to learn landscape painting in 1890. **Avocations:** Collecting Americana books **Political Affiliations:** Democrat **Religion:** Mormon

O. Joe Faires

Title: Concert Promoter (Retired) **Industry:** Media & Entertainment **Company Name:** JF Productions **Date of Birth:** 11/11/1931 **Place of Birth:** Corinth **State/Country of Origin:** MS/USA **Parents:** Son of Con Franklin; Maude (Frink) F **Marital Status:** Widower **Spouse Name:** Pauline Faires (04/03/1954, Deceased 2017) **Children:** Vivian Lea; O. Joe Junior **Education:** Bachelor of College Studies in Accounting, Southeastern University (1957); Bachelor of Laws, Blackstone College (1954) **Certifications:** Police Instructor on Fingerprinting, General Management and Hostage Negotiations, Federal Bureau of Investigation **Career:** Retired (2005); Concert Promoter, JF Productions, Herndon, VA (1986-2005); Supervisory Special Agent, Federal Bureau of Investigation, Washington, DC (1979-1986); Special Agent, Federal Bureau of Investigation, Mobile, AL (1973-1979); Police Instructor (1975); President, Oklahoma Plastic Container Corp., Oklahoma City (1966-1972); Special Agent, Federal Bureau of Investigation, Oklahoma City, OK (1961-1966); Special Agent, Federal Bureau of Investigation (1957-1966); Special Agent, Federal Bureau of Investigation, New York, NY (1959-1961); Special Agent, FBI, Cincinnati, OH (1958-1959); Fingerprint Technician, Federal Bureau of Investigation, Washington, DC (1950-1951, 1955-1957) **Military Service:** With, U.S. Air Force (1951-1954) **Awards:** Numerous Letters of Commendation from the Director, Federal Bureau of Investigation **Memberships:** Country Music Association; Society of Former Special Agents of the Federal Bureau of Investigation; American Legion **Marquis Who's Who Honors:** Albert Nelson Marquis Lifetime Achievement Award **To what do you attribute your success:** Mr. Faires credits his success on his propensity for dedication and a desire to reach certain goals. **Why did you become involved in your profession or industry:** Mr. Faires became involved in his profession due to a friend, who recommended he apply to join the Federal Bureau of Investigation. Following his service, he went into country music production due to another friend of his, James Brady, who invited him to Nashville for Fanfare. During that trip, he realized that the country music scene was very popular in Washington, DC, and decided to enter the field. **Avocations:** Golf; Tennis; Bowling; Fishing **Political Affiliations:** Republican **Religion:** Baptist

Maria J. Falco, PhD

Title: Academic Administrator, Political Scientist (Retired) **Industry:** Education/Educational Services **Company Name:** DePauw University **Date of Birth:** 07/07/1932 **Place of Birth:** Wildwood **State/Country of Origin:** NJ/USA **Education:** Student Management Program, Carnegie-Mellon University, Pittsburgh, PA (1993); Postdoctoral Research Fellow, Yale University (1965-1966); PhD in Political Science, Bryn Mawr College, Pennsylvania (1963); MA, Fordham University (1958); Fulbright Scholar, University of Florence, Italy (1954-1955); AB, Immaculata College, Pennsylvania (1954) **Career:** Professor Emerita, DePauw University, Greencastle, IN (1993-Present); Professor, Political Science, DePauw University, Greencastle, IN (1988-1993); Academic Vice President, DePauw University, Greencastle, IN (1986-1988); Professor, Political Science, Loyola University, New Orleans, LA (1985-1986); Dean, College Arts and Sciences, Loyola University, New Orleans, LA (1979-1985); Chair, Faculty, Social and Behavioral Sciences, University of Tulsa, OK (1976-1979); Professor, Political Science, Stockton State College, Pomona, NJ (1973-1976); Chair, Department of Political Science, Le Moyne College, Syracuse, NY (1967-1973); Assistant Professor to Associate Professor, Political Science, Le Moyne College, Syracuse, NY (1966-1973); Research Assistant to Genevieve Blatt (1964-1965); Assistant Professor, Political Science, Washington College, Chestertown, MD (1963-1964); Instructor to Assistant Professor, History and Political Science, Immaculata College, Pennsylvania (1957-1963) **Civic:** Chairperson, New Parishioners Committee, St. An Church, Metairie, LA (2007-Present); Extraordinary Minister of Communion, St. An Church, Metairie, LA (2004-Present); President, Business and Professional Women, Jefferson Parish (2004-2005); 1st Vice President, Business and Professional Women, Jefferson Parish (2002-2004); President, Business and Professional Women's Association (2000-2004); Member, President's Council, Urban Partners, Institute of Human Relations, Loyola University, New Orleans, LA (1997-2000); President, Indiana Political Science Association (1992-1993); Chair, Indiana Political Science Association (1992-1993); Chair, Board of Directors, Personnel Management Committee, Institute for Human Understanding, New Orleans, LA (1985-1986); Board of Directors, Urban Partners, Institute of Human Relations, Loyola University, New Orleans, LA (1984-1986); Board of Directors, Committee for the Enhancement and Support of Liberal Arts, American Conference of Academic Deans (1984-1985); Member, Mayor's Task Force on the Future of New Orleans (1983-1985); Vice President, Le Moyne College Chapter, American Association of University Professors (1971-1972); President, Syracuse Chapter, New Democratic Coalition (1970-1971) **Awards:** Louisiana American Italian Woman of the Year Award, AIRF Sports Hall of Fame Banquet (2016); Panzeca Scholarship Presentation, Loyola, MD (2015); Named Mentor of Distinction, Women's Caucus for Political Science (1989); Grantee, Summer Research Grant National Science Foundation (1968); Faculty Fellow in State and Local Politics, National Center for Education in Politics (1964); Fulbright Scholar, University of Florence, Italy (1954-1955) **Memberships:** Member, Advisory Committee, Women's Opera Guild (2013-Present); Board of Directors, Country Club Estates Civic Association (2008-Present); Webmaster, Country Club Estates Civic Association (2008-Present); Corresponding Secretary, American Italian Federation of the Southeast (2007-Present); Secretary, Women for a Better Louisiana (2007-Present); Recording Secretary, East Jefferson Italian-American Society (2005-Present); Women and Politics Research Section, American Political Science Association (1987-Present); Member, Advisory Council, New Orleans Opera Association (2010-2016); President, Women for a Better Louisiana (2012-2013); Webmaster, East Jefferson Italian-American Society (2008); Woman of the Year, East Jefferson Italian-American Society (2008); President, Jefferson Parish League of Women Voters (2001-2004); Board of Directors, Jefferson Parish League of Women Voters (1999-2004); Computer Users Section, American Political Science Association (1987-1993); Foundations Political Theory Group, American Political Science Association (1973-1993); Chair, Committee for Outstanding Convention Paper Award, American Political Science Association (1990-1991); Dean's Council, Common Cause, Great Lakes College Association (1986-1988); Dean's Council, Association of Jesuit Colleges and Universities (1979-1985); Outstanding Convention Paper Committee, Southwest Political Science Association (1979-1980); Professional Ethics, American Political Science Association (1977-1980); Academy Freedom Committee, American Political Science Association (1977-1980); President, Women's Caucus for Political Science (1976-1977); Benjamin Evans Lippincott Award Committee, American Political Science Association (1976); Vice President, Women's Caucus for Political Science (1975-1976); Chair, Program Committee, Women's Caucus for Political Science (1975-1976); Program Chair, Epistemology and Methodology Section, American Political Science Association (1975); Program Section Chair, American Political Science Association (1975); **Religion:** Roman Catholic

Diane M. Falk

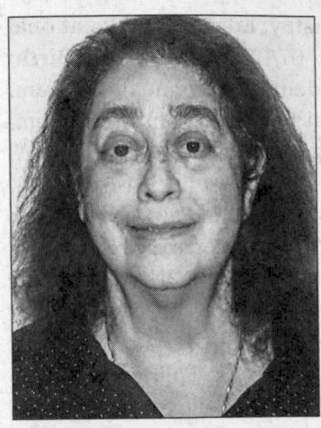

Title: Writer, Editor, Educator Research Information Specialist **Industry:** Writing and Editing **Company Name:** The World & I Magazine (The Washington Times) **Date of Birth:** 5/22/1947 **Place of Birth:** New York **State/Country of Origin:** NY/USA **Parents:** Leon H.E. Falk; J. Constance M. (Lilienthal) Falk **Marital Status:** Married **Spouse Name:** William Patrick Fitzpatrick (5/9/2006) **Children:** Rondi J. Silva **Education:** MLS in Interdisciplinary Research Studies and Journalism, Columbia University (1979); BA in English and International Literature, Columbia University (1973) **Career:** Director, Research Department, The World and I: The Magazine for Lifelong Learners (Now The World and I Online), Washington, DC (1986-2004); Head Librarian, The World and I: The Magazine for Lifelong Learners (Now The World and I Online), Washington, DC (1986-2004); Editorial Research Specialist, The World and I: The Magazine for Lifelong Learners (Now The World and I Online), Washington, DC (1986-2004); Website Education Program Associate, The World and I: The Magazine for Lifelong Learners (Now The World and I Online), Washington, DC (1986-2004); Text Editor, Bibliographical Enhancement, New York Times Information Service, Inc., New York, NY (1980-1986); Research Information Specialist and Writer, News World Communications, Inc. and The New-York Tribune, New York, NY (1985); Research Librarian and Writer/Journalist, News World Communications, Inc., New York, NY (1985); Research Information Specialist, Harkavy Information Service, New York, NY (1983-1984); Bibliographical Organization, The Rockefeller Foundation, New York, NY (1983); Indexer, H. W. Wilson & Company (Now EBSCO Industries, Inc.), Bronx, NY (1982); Fact-Checker, H. W. Wilson & Company (Now EBSCO Industries, Inc.), Bronx, NY (1982); Cataloger, Exxon Education Foundation (Now ExxonMobil Foundation, Exxon Mobil Corporation), New York, NY (1982); Project Coordinator, Legal Department, GAF Corporation, New York, NY (1981-1982); Research Librarian, Atlantis Energy and Minerals (Now Atlantis Energy), New York, NY (1980-1981); Documents Analyst, Atlantis Energy and Minerals (Now Atlantis Energy), New York, NY (1980-1981); Document Analyst, United Nations Certified Transnational Corps. (1979); Features Writer, News World Communications, Inc., New York, NY (1977-1978); Participant and Contributor, Numerous International Services and Education Projects; Educational Program Associate, Worldandl.com; Researcher Writer, Articles and Book Reviews, Worldandl.com; Editor, Worldandl.com; Freelance Research Specialist/Consultant **Career Related:** Copy Editor, HSA-UWC, New York, NY and Washington, DC (1986); Research Manager, HSA-UWC, New York, NY and Washington, DC (1986); Reference Assistant, Lehman Social Sciences Library, Columbia University, New York, NY (1978); Copy Editor, HSA-UWC, New York, NY and Washington, DC (1974-1975); Research Manager, HSA-UWC, New York, NY and Washington, DC (1974-1975); Research Librarian, Lehman Social Sciences Library, Columbia University, New York, NY **Civic:** Volunteer, Ambassadors for Peace Seminars, Universal Peace Foundation (2001-Present); Literary, Business, Legal and Political Groups and Issues (1991-Present); Sponsor, Service for Peace (2002); English Professor, Howard University, Washington, DC (1992-1994); Volunteer Staff, Ukraine (CIS) (1992) **Creative Works:** Website Articles about Family and Accomplishments, School of General Studies, Columbia University (2013); Writer, Tribute Book, HSA-UWC, FFWPU (2010-2011); Writer, "Best Practices for Government Libraries" (2010); Contributing Author, "Best Practices for Government Libraries" (2010); Writer, New World Encyclopedia (2007); Editor/Writer, Newsletter, Prosperity Council (1991); Editor-in-Chief, Focus (1979-1980) **Awards:** Award, International Seminars, Universal Peace Federation (2012-2014); Award, International Federal for World Peace (Now Universal Peace Federation) (2013); Award, International Federal for World Peace (Now Universal Peace Federation) (2011); Recognition Ceremony, HSA-UWC, FFWPU (2010-2011); HSA-UWC Recognition Ceremony, FFWPU (2007); Award, Inter Religious and International Federation for World Peace and Inter Religious International Peace Council (2006) **Memberships:** Conference Coordinator, Women's Federation for World Peace (2007-Present); Secretary, DC Chapter, Women's Federation for World Peace (1993-Present); Acting Secretary, International Federation for World Peace (1993-Present); Staff Volunteer, International Leadership Seminars (1991-Present); Volunteer, International Federation for World Peace (1990-Present) **Marquis Who's Who Honors:** Albert Nelson Marquis Lifetime Achievement Award; Marquis Who's Who Top Professional **To what do you attribute your success:** Ms. Falk attributes her success to her mentors including encouraging educators, family and friends, and the great spiritual leaders of various faith traditions. **Why did you become involved in your profession or industry:** Ms. Falk became involved in her profession because she feels that research and writing are essential to record legacy and perspective, and the constructive ideas and accomplishments of our time. **Political Affiliations:** Independent

Shih-fang Fan

Title: Professor **Industry:** Education/Educational Services **Date of Birth:** 10/19/1929 **Place of Birth:** Shanghai **State/Country of Origin:** China **Parents:** Donald Tin-jiu Fan; Elliot Zhe-fun (Chou) Fan **Marital Status:** Married **Spouse Name:** Chen-yu Yang (04/20/1962) **Children:** Chao-hui **Education:** Diploma, Department of Physics, National Chao Tung University, Shanghai, China (1950) **Career:** Visiting Professor, Albert Einstein College of Medicine, NY (1989-1993); Visiting Scientist, Brookhaven National Laboratory, Upton, NY (1985-1990); Visiting Professor then Research Professor, Stony Brook University, NY (1980-2007); Research Associate to Assistant Professor to Associate Professor to Professor, Shanghai Institute of Physiology, Chinese Academy of Sciences (1950-1989) **Career Related:** Consultant, Department of Pharmacology, Health Sciences Center at Brooklyn, State University of New York (Now SUNY Downstate Health Sciences University) (1987-1992) **Creative Works:** Contributor, Articles to Professional Journals **Awards:** Recipient, Science Prizes, Chinese Academy of Sciences (1986); Recipient, Science Prizes, Department of Public Health, China (1980); Recipient, Science Prizes, Shanxi Province, China (1979); Recipient, Science Prizes, Institute of Physiology, Chinese Academy of Sciences (1956) **Memberships:** Biophysical Society of China; Chinese Physical Society; Chinese Society for Physiological Sciences; Chinese Biochemistry Society; Biophysical Society, United States; Society for Neuroscience, United States **Marquis Who's Who Honors:** Albert Nelson Marquis Lifetime Achievement Award **Why did you become involved in your profession or industry:** Mr. Fan became involved in his profession because his parents was a professor and, both his parents, Donald Tin-jiu and Elliot Zhe-fun (Chou) Fan, got their degree from the University of Chicago in 1928. They both encouraged him to go into the academic field. **Avocations:** Playing piano

Richard Claborn "Dick" Farr

Title: Corporate Executive, Private Investor **Industry:** Financial Services **Company Name:** Farr Investments **Date of Birth:** 11/02/1928 **Place of Birth:** Wynne **State/Country of Origin:** AR/USA **Parents:** Jesse William Farr; Francis Adele (Hooper) Farr **Marital Status:** Married **Spouse Name:** Marcille Mullikin (12/25/1950) **Children:** Denise Farr Isaac; Richardson Lloyd Farr; David Randall Farr **Education:** Bachelor of Arts in Philosophy and Religion, Hendrix College, Conway, AR (1952); Postgraduate Coursework, Southern Methodist University; Postgraduate Coursework, Stanford University **Certifications:** Certified Master Carpenter; Licensed Owner of Thoroughbred Race Horses, Including Graded Stakes I Championship Winners **Career:** Founder, Chairman, Chief Executive Officer, Farr Investments (1980-Present); Executive Vice President, Crown Zellerbach Corporation, San Francisco, CA (1979-1983); Corporate Vice President, Heublein, Incorporated, Farmington, CT (1971-1979); Managing Director, Lehman Brothers, Inc., New York, NY (1970-1971); Senior Vice President, Continental Grain Company, New York, NY and Paris, France (1965-1970); Executive Position, Procter & Gamble Company, Numerous Locations (1952-1965) **Career Related:** Member, Board of Directors, Consumer Financial Institute (1984-2014); Member, Board of Directors, Bouton Inc. (1982-2015); Member, Board of Directors, Toyon Associates Inc. (1956-2002); Chairman of the Board, Bituminous Coal Corporation, Incorporated; Chairman, Chief Executive Officer, Lincoln Logs Limited; Chairman of the Board, Palladium Industries Inc.; Trustee, Scottish Widows International Fund, Advantage Mutual Bond Fund, Federated Investors; Member, Board of Directors, Archimedes Systems Inc.; Member, Board of Directors, Hunter Environmental Services Inc.; Member, Board of Directors, First Federal of Arkansas; Member, Board of Directors, Air Florida Systems; Lead Director, Seal Incorporated **Civic:** Trustee, Hendrix College (1988-2000); Numerous Directorships, Trusteeships, Officer Positions, Numerous Civic and Religious Organizations; Significant Contributor, Charitable and Religious Organizations **Military Service:** U.S. Naval Academy (1948); Regular Army of the United States (1946-1948); Veteran of World War II **Creative Works:** Lecturer, Numerous Lectures, "Christian Ethics in Business" **Awards:** Recognized as One of 10 Such Listees Selected as "Most Distinguished," Wall Street Journal (2020); Distinguished Alumni Award, Hendrix College (1986); Fulbright Scholar (1952); Eagle Scout, Several Palm Awards, Boy Scouts of America (1944) **Memberships:** President, Hartford Golf Club; Ventana Canyon Golf and Country; The Ford Plantation Club; Ogeechee Golf Club; Burlingame Country Club; Junior, Senior, Golfing Society of Connecticut; Oyster Harbors Club; Brookhaven Golf and Country Club; The Lake Club; The University Club, New York, NY **Marquis Who's Who Honors:** Albert Nelson Marquis Lifetime Achievement Award (2019); Marquis Who's Who Top Professional **To what do you attribute your success:** Mr. Farr attributes his success to the blessing of being born and raised in rural Arkansas in a modest economic situation during the Great Depression. In his family, there was abundant love, respect and generosity for others. **Why did you become involved in your profession or industry:** Mr. Farr became involved in his profession because of his strong religious background, which was influenced by wonderful ministers during his early life; he felt there was a place for lay ministry for a person who has the religious faith but does not want a career in the ministries. He wanted to develop a sufficient academic background, so he could translate the wisdom of the Bible in a business world. That was the path he chose to follow. He was very fortunate to get a job with Procter & Gamble Company, which, at that time, was only hiring people with master's degrees. They were impressed enough with him that, even though he did not have a master's degree, they hired him anyway. to Continental Grain was attracted to Mr. Farr through an executive search. The company was impressed with him being an effective organizational manager and making things work on the business side. They were a private worldwide organization and appreciated Mr. Farr's ethics and his ability to organize multi-faceted businesses. **Avocations:** Numerous competitive athletic activities; Fine woodworking; Photography; Gardening; Serious conversation; Homemaking **Political Affiliations:** Independent **Religion:** Christian **Thoughts on Life:** Mr. Farr's motto is, "Self confidence is a prerequisite to successful undertaking."

Manu Farrarons

Title: Owner/Artist **Industry:** Fine Art **Company Name:** Mana'o Tattoo Los Angeles LLC **Education:** Bachelor of Science in Geography and History, Ecole Normale Mixte de Polynésie Française (1989) **Career:** Owner, Mana'o Tattoo Los Angeles LLC, Los Angeles, CA (2018-Present); Tattoo Artist, Royal Heritage Tattoo, Venice, CA (2016-2017); Tattoo Artist, Zulu Tattoo, Los Angeles, CA (2015); Owner, Tattoo Artist, Mana'o Tattoo Studio, Pape'ete, Tahiti, French Polynesia (2003-2015); Tattoo Artist, Jordi's Tattoo Shop, Pape'ete, Tahiti, French Polynesia (1991-2003); Teacher, Ministère de l'Éducation Nationale et de la Jeunesse, Pape'ete, Tahiti, French Polynesia (1986-2003) **Creative Works:** Appearance, Main Speaker, French TV Documentary, "Tatau, la culture d'un art" (2014) **Awards:** Air Tahiti Nui Cultural Ambassador (2015-Present); Mana'o Tattoo Los Angeles Awarded Best Tattoo Studio in Studio City, CA (2019), Best of Day, New Zealand Tattoo & Art Festival, Taranaki, NZ (2016); Best Tribal Artist, Art Gathering LA, Long Beach, CA (2016); Best Tribal Artist, Ink N Iron, Long Beach, CA (2015); President of the Jury, Polynesia Tatau Convention, Tahiti (2014); Best Tattoo Artist, Open Category, Polynesia Tatau Festival, Tahiti (2013); Best Tribal Artist, Ink N Iron, Long Beach, CA (2011); Runner-up, Best Polynesian (Male), Sydney Tattoo Expo, Sydney, AU (2010); Runner-up, Best Polynesian (Female), Sydney Tattoo Expo, Sydney, AU (2010); Best Tribal Artist, Ink N Iron, Long Beach, CA (2008); Best of Day, Festival Tattoonesia, Mo'orea, French Polynesia (2005) **To what do you attribute your success:** Mr. Farrarons' knowledge and specialization in Polynesian symbols and traditional tattoos is what has brought him his success. He has created various styles now used by thousands of tattoo artists all over the world, especially the modern Polynesian style for women, which has became a reference internationally. **Why did you become involved in your profession or industry:** As a child, Mr. Farrarons was inspired and later mentored by his father, a tattoo artist. Involved in tattooing from an early age, he pursued his own professional practice beginning in 1991.

John David "Jack" Fassett

Title: Utility Executive (Retired), Consultant **Industry:** Utilities **Date of Birth:** 01/30/1926 **Place of Birth:** East Hampton **State/Country of Origin:** NY/USA **Parents:** Howard J. (Deceased 1971); Irene (Darby) F. (Deceased 1973) **Marital Status:** Widowed **Spouse Name:** Betty Jean Conrad (08/04/1947, Deceased 2013) **Children:** Ellen Joy Fassett Mermin (1948); John D. (1951); Lora Jean Fassett Mason (1963) **Education:** Honorary LHD, North Carolina Central University (2016); Honorary LLD, Kentucky Wesleyan College (1999); JD, Yale Law School, Cum Laude (1953); BA, University of Rochester, Cum Laude (1948) **Career:** Chairman of the Board, United Illuminating Co. (Now Avangrid), New Haven, CT (1985-1987); Chief Executive Officer, United Illuminating Co. (Now Avangrid), New Haven, CT (1976-1984); President, United Illuminating Co. (Now Avangrid), New Haven, CT (1974-1975); Vice President, General Counsel, United Illuminating Co. (Now Avangrid), New Haven, CT (1973); Partner, Wiggin and Dana LLP, New Haven, CT (1958-1973); Associate, Wiggin and Dana LLP, New Haven, CT (1954-1958); Law Clerk to Associate Justice Stanley F. Reed, Supreme Court of the United States, Washington, DC (1953-1954) **Career Related:** Chairman, NEPOOL (1955-1959); Faculty, Political Science, Yale University (1957-1958); Director, New Haven Savings Bank; Director, Barnes Group Inc.; Director, Register Publishing Co. (Now Hearst Media Services) **Civic:** Chairman, Greater New Haven Chamber of Commerce; Chairman, Connecticut Public Expenditure Council **Military Service:** First Lieutenant, Legal Officer, Transportation Corps, Fort Eustis, VA (1950-1951); Sergeant, U.S. Air Force (1943-1946) **Creative Works:** Contributor, "Clerking for Stanley F. Reed," "Of Courtier and Kings: More Stories of Supreme Court Law Clerks and Their Justices," University of Virginia Press (2015); Author, "Jack Fassett, A Memoir of Essays, Volume II," Chapel Hill Press (2015); Author, "Jack Fassett, A Memoir of Essays," Chapel Hill Press (2013); Author, "Betty: Chronicle of a Moving Life," Chapel Hill Press (2008); Author, "The Shaping Years: A Memoir of My Youth and Education" (2000); Author, "New Deal Justice: The Life of Stanley Reed of Kentucky" (1994); Author, "UI: History of an Electric Company, A Saga of Problems, Personalities and Power Politics" (1991) **Memberships:** PSI Upsilon Fraternity **Marquis Who's Who Honors:** Albert Nelson Marquis Lifetime Achievement Award **Why did you become involved in your profession or industry:** Mr. Fassett became involved in his career because of his longstanding interest in law, and attended law school following several years of military service. He was particularly challenged by the idea of participating in lawsuits. **Avocations:** Playing tennis; Reading; Writing **Political Affiliations:** Republican

Anthony Stephen Fauci

Title: Director **Industry:** Medicine & Health Care **Company Name:** National Institute of Allergy and Infectious Diseases (NIAID) **Date of Birth:** 12/24/1940 **Place of Birth:** Brooklyn **State/Country of Origin:** NY/USA **Parents:** Stephen A. Fauci; Eugenia Abys Fauci **Marital Status:** Married **Spouse Name:** Christine Grady (1985) **Children:** Three Children **Education:** Honorary DSc, Duke University (1995); Honorary DSc, University of Connecticut Health Center (1994); Honorary DSc, State University of New York at Farmingdale (1994); Honorary DSc, Bates College (1993); Honorary DSc, Bard College (1993); Honorary DSc, Medical College of Wisconsin (1993); Honorary DSc, Long Island University (1992); Honorary DSc, St. John's University (1991); Honorary DSc, Universita di Roma (1990); Honorary DSc, Mount Sinai School of Medicine (1990); Honorary DSc, Hahnemann University (1990); Honorary DSc, Georgetown University (1990); Honorary DSc, College of the Holy Cross (1987); MD, Cornell University Medical College, New York, NY (1966); AB, College of the Holy Cross, Worcester, MA (1962) **Certifications:** Diplomate, American Board of Infectious Diseases; Diplomate, American Board of Allergy & Immunology; Diplomate, American Board of Internal Medicine **Career:** Director, National Institute of Allergy & Infectious Diseases (NIAID) (1984-Present); Chief, Immunoregulation Laboratory, National Institute of Allergy & Infectious Diseases (NIAID) (1980-Present); Associate Director To Director, National Institutes Of Health Office for AIDS Research, Bethesda, MD (1988-1994); Deputy Clinical Director, National Institutes Of Health (1977-1980); Head, Clinical Physiology Section, National Institutes Of Health (1974-1980); Senior Investigator, National Institutes Of Health (1972-1974); Chief Resident, Department of Medicine, New York Hospital-Cornell Medical Center (1971-1972); Senior Staff Fellow, National Institutes Of Health (1970-1971); Clinical Associate, National Institute of Allergy & Infectious Diseases (NIAID), Bethesda, MD (1968-1970); Assistant Resident, Department of Medicine, New York Hospital-Cornell Medical Center (1967-1968); Intern, New York Hospital-Cornell Medical Center (1966-1967) **Career Related:** Consultant, Naval Medical Center, Bethesda, MD (1972-Present); Lecturer in Field **Civic:** Trustee, Doris Duke Charitable Foundation **Creative Works:** Editor, "Harrison's Principles of Internal Medicine"; Contributor, Numerous Articles, Professional Journals **Awards:** Robert Koch Prize (2013); Presidential Medal Of Freedom, White House (2008); Named, 25 Greatest Public Servants Over Past 25 Years, Council on Excellence In Government (2008); Named, America's Best Leaders, U.S. News & World Report (2008); Mary Woodard Lasker Award For Public Service, Albert & Mary Lasker Foundation (2007); National Science Medal, National Science Foundation (2007); 10th Most-Cited HIV/AIDS Researcher, Institute for Science Information (1996-2006); Named, Scientist Of the Year, R&D Magazine (2005); Lifetime Achievement Award, American Association of Immunologists (2005); Honorary Extraordinary Accomplishments Award, New York Academy of Medicine (2004); Ellis Island Family Heritage Award, Statue Of Liberty-Ellis Island Foundation (2003); Named, Top 50 Science Leaders, Science America (2003); Ninth Most Cited Scientist In Immunology (1993-2003); 13th Most Cited Scientist Amongst Public Journal Articles (1983-2002); Frank Annunzio Humanitarian Award, Christopher Columbus Fellowship Foundation (2001); Named, America's Best In Science & Medicine, CNN/TIME Magazine (2001); Frank Brown Berry Prize, U.S. Medical & Delta Dental Plan, California (1999); Thomas J. D'Alesandro Junior Award, Association of Italian American Charities (1997); Maryland Governor's Citation (1997); John Phillips Memorial Award, American College of Physicians (1997); Honorary John P. McGovern Award, American Medical Writers Association (1997); Ellen Browning Scripps Medal, Scripps Federation of Medicine & Research (1996); David Rumbough Science Award, Juvenile Diabetes Federation International (1996); Theobald Smith Award, Albany Medical College (1995); Richard & Hinda Rosenthal Award, American College of Physicians (1995); Cartwright Prize, Columbia University College of Physicians & Surgeons (1993); Humanitarian Award, Tiro A. Segno Federation (1993); Outstanding Achievement Award, Howard University (1992) **Memberships:** Councillor, Association of American Physicians (1993-Present); Recorder, Association of American Physicians (1988-1993); Kober Lecturer, American Association of Immunologists (1988); Progressive Chairman, American Association of Immunologists (1982-1985); President, American Federation of Clinical Research (1980-1981); Master, American Association for the Advancement of Science; Fellow, American College of Physicians; American Academy of Microbiology; New York Academy of Medicine; American Academy of Arts & Sciences; Honorary Member, American Academy of Allergy, Asthma & Immunology; American Medical Writers Association; National Academy of Sciences; American Philosophical Society; Royal Academy of Medicine, Spain; Royal Danish Academy of Science & Letters; Council Member, Institute of Medicine; American Society of Clinical Investigation; Infectious Diseases Society of America; International AIDS Society; American Society of Cell Biology; American Society of Virology **Avocations:** Running; Tennis **Religion:** Roman Catholic

Marian L. Faupel

Title: Of Counsel **Industry:** Law and Legal Services **Company Name:** Faupel Musser Love PC **Date of Birth:** 07/30/1943 **Place of Birth:** Detroit **State/Country of Origin:** MI/USA **Parents:** William Barrett; Jay Elizabeth Locke **Marital Status:** Married **Spouse Name:** Kirk Arthur Faupel (03/27/1965) **Children:** Corey Barrett **Education:** Doctor of Jurisprudence, Wayne State University Law School (1983); Bachelor of Arts in English, Minor in Latin and Psychology, University of Michigan (1965) **Career:** Of Counsel, Faupel Musser Love PC, Ann Arbor, MI (2019-Present); Sole Shareholder, Faupel & Associates, Ann Arbor, MI (1990-Present); Adjunct Professor, Family Law, Wayne University Law School (2003-2018); Of Counsel, Schlussel, Lifton, Simon, Rands, Galvin & Jackier, Professional Corporation, Ann Arbor, MI (1988-1990); Associate, Burnham, Connolly, Oesterle & Henry, Ann Arbor, MI (1986-1988); Associate, Hill, Lewis, Adams, Goodrich & Tait, Ann Arbor, MI (1984-1986); Associate, Smith, Hirsch, Brody & Weingarden, Detroit, MI (1983-1984); Journalist, Saline Reporter, Saline, MI (1971-1974); Teacher, English, Latin, Communication Arts (1965-1970) **Career Related:** Litigation Experience, Various Cities and Courts of Claims; Presenter in the Field **Civic:** Trustee, Saline Area Board of Education (1978-1990); Chairman, Industrial Development Commission (1970-1980); Vice President, United Fund (1970-1980); Past Director, Washtenaw School Officers Association; Public Relations Consultant, Saline Community Hospital; American Red Cross; Saline Area Schools **Military Service:** Personnel Specialist, U.S. Army Signal School, Fort Monmouth, NJ (1967-1968) **Creative Works:** Editor, Washtenaw County Bar Association Magazine, Res Ipsa Loquitur (1985-1995); Review of Legal Issues (1983-1984); Survey Editor, Wayne Law Review (1982-1983); Author, 15 Published Articles in the Wayne Review; Appeared, Numerous Seminars; Presenter, Numerous Presentations in the Field; Contributor, Numerous Articles to Professional Journals **Awards:** Fifth Annual William Barber Distinguished Alumni Award, Wayne Law Review (2008); Michiganian of the Year, Detroit News (1994); Certificate of Achievement, Washtenaw County Bar Association (1986); William D. Traitel Scholarship, Wayne State University Law School (1982-1983); Distinguished Service Award, Woman of the Year, Saline Area Jaycees, Saline, MI **Memberships:** Twice-Elected Member, Representative Assembly of Michigan Bar Association; Washtenaw County Bar Association; Kappa Tau Alpha **Bar Admissions:** Michigan; Michigan Court of Appeals; Indiana (Pro Hac Vice); Florida (Pro Hac Vice); U.S. District Court for the Eastern District of Michigan; Supreme Court of the United States; 14th Judicial District Court **Marquis Who's Who Honors:** Albert Nelson Marquis Lifetime Achievement Award **Why did you become involved in your profession or industry:** Ms. Faupel became involved in her profession due to her lifelong interest and dedication toward public education. She began at the board of education in order to make a more substantial impact on her field, and kept getting reelected. After more than a decade, she decided to return to the the traditional workforce and became an attorney. **Avocations:** Couture sewing; Writing; Mentoring **Religion:** Episcopalian

Thomas Fortune Fay

Title: Lawyer, Founder **Industry:** Law and Legal Services **Company Name:** Fay Law **Education:** JD, Rutgers, The State University of New Jersey (1965); BA in Political Science, University of Notre Dame (1961) **Awards:** Washington D.C. Super Lawyers (2010); Special Commendation, Civil Justice Foundation (2002); Trial Lawyer of the Year Award (2001); Cash Prize for Excellence in Anti-Terrorism **Bar Admissions:** The District of Columbia; State of Maryland **Marquis Who's Who Honors:** Marquis Who's Who Top Professional **To what do you attribute your success:** Mr. Fay attributes his success to his hard work and perseverance. **Why did you become involved in your profession or industry:** Mr. Fay became involved in his profession because he had always wanted to be a lawyer. In addition, he has always enjoyed the prospect of professional debates. **Avocations:** Reading historical books **Thoughts on Life:** Mr. Fay was motivated to become an attorney after listening to the speech of Senator Taft in the early 1950s. He has won many verdicts and settled more than 100 cases, resulting in multimillion-dollar awards for his clients. He is admitted to practice in the U.S. Court of Appeals for the Fourth and Ninth Circuits.

Michael Faynzilberg

Title: Owner **Industry:** Medicine & Health Care **Company Name:** Whiting Dental Arts **State/Country of Origin:** Ukraine **Education:** DMD, Henry M. Goldman School of Dental Medicine, Boston University, Cum Laude (2013) **Career:** Owner, Whiting Dental Arts (2017-Present); Associate Dentist, Boston (2002-2017); North Shore Dental Associates **Career Related:** Clinical Professor, Department of General Dentistry, Boston University (2013-Present); Lecturer, Dentsply Sirona; Lecturer, Institut Straumann AG **Civic:** Volunteer Dentist for Children, Boston University; Volunteer Dentist, Mission Trips **Awards:** Top Cosmetic Dentist in Boston, Boston Magazine (2018-2019); Outstanding Patient and Practice Management Award, Boston University (2013); Mentorship Award, APEX Program, Henry M. Goldman School of Dental Medicine, Boston University **Memberships:** American Dental Association; Massachusetts Dental Society **Marquis Who's Who Honors:** Marquis Who's Who Top Professional **Why did you become involved in your profession or industry:** Dr. Faynzilberg became involved in his profession because of several family members that are practicing dentists. During his adolescence, he was lucky enough to be mentored by them, so he received opportunities in the field at an early age.

Bruce A. Featherstone

Title: Managing Member **Industry:** Law and Legal Services **Date of Birth:** 03/02/1953 **Place of Birth:** Detroit **State/Country of Origin:** MI/USA **Parents:** Ronald A. Featherstone; Lois R. (Bosshart) Featherstone **Marital Status:** Married **Spouse Name:** Sabrina Saunders **Children:** Leigh Allison; Edward Alan; Rex Saunders **Education:** JD, University of Michigan, Magna Cum Laude (1977); BA in Economics, Yale University, Cum Laude, With Distinction (1974) **Career:** Managing Member, Featherstone DeSisto LLC (2013-Present); Managing Partner, Featherstone, Petrie, DeSisto LLP (2006-2013); Managing Partner, Featherstone DeSisto LLP, Denver, CO (1999-2006); Managing Partner, Featherstone & Shea, LLP, Denver, CO (1996-1999); Partner, Kirkland & Ellis, Denver, CO (1983-1996); Associate, Kirkland & Ellis, Denver, CO (1977-1983) **Civic:** Dean's Alumni Relations and Development Committee, Michigan Law School (2009) **Creative Works:** Articles Editor, University of Michigan Law Review (1976-1977) **Awards:** Martindale Hubbell AV Rating; Listed, Colorado Super Lawyers **Memberships:** Litigation Section, Tort and Insurance Practice Section, Professor Liability Section, Antitrust Section, American Bar Association; Association of Trial Lawyers of America; Colorado Bar Association; Colorado Trial Lawyers Association; Denver Bar Association; Order of the Coif **Bar Admissions:** U.S. Court of Appeals for the Ninth Circuit (1990); Supreme Court of the United States (1984); U.S. Court of Appeals for the Federal Circuit (1984); State of Colorado (1983); U.S. Court of Appeals for the 10th Circuit (1983); U.S. District Court, State of Colorado (1983); U.S. Court of Appeals for the Seventh Circuit (1981); U.S. Court of Appeals for the Fifth Circuit (1980); State of Illinois (1977); U.S. District Court, Northern District, State of Illinois (1977) **Marquis Who's Who Honors:** Albert Nelson Marquis Lifetime Achievement Award; Marquis Who's Who Top Professional **Why did you become involved in your profession or industry:** Mr. Featherstone became involved in his profession because the competitor to going to law school was journalism. He had spent time with Detroit News and another paper in the Detroit area, and enjoyed covering the courts and political beats. The role of reporter was one of observer and not of participant, and back in the 70s, that was the view he had. He wanted to be more of a participant and that made him oriented into going into one direction than in the other. The other thing was as a litigator, he was getting the diversity of experiences he had with industries, different people, different clients and different parts of the country. Litigating the cases and learning the facts were things he experienced and fortunate to have had in his career.

Alejandra Febre

Title: Franchise Owner **Industry:** Education/Educational Services **Company Name:** School of Rock Cypress **Marital Status:** Married **Children:** Dominique; Santiago; Michelle **Education:** AA in Music, Lone Star College, Tomball (2019); BS in Chemical Engineering, Tecologico de Monterrey (1996) **Career:** Franchise Owner/General Manager, School of Rock, Cypress (2015-Present); Owner/Manager, Blue Music Box (2015-Present); Chemistry Teacher, Research Abilities Teacher, Environmental Resources Teacher, Universidad de Monterrey, Mexico (2007-2009); Research Assistant, INSEAD, France (1999-2001) **Civic:** Treasurer, Troop 156, Boy Scouts of America (2018-Present); Team Leader, Parents Social Committee at The Woodlands Preparatory School (2014-2015); Former Co-Chair, Parent Teacher Association, Philanthropic Projects, The Woodlands Preparatory School **Creative Works:** Author, "Nitrogen's Role in Industrial Systems," Journal of Industrial Ecology (2001) **Awards:** Best of Music Studio and Lessons, Living Magazine, Cyprus (2015-Present) **To what do you attribute your success:** Ms. Febre has great ambition. She always has her eyes on the end goal; having this mental orientation opened up a wide variety of paths towards achieving her dreams. She excels in inspiring her team members to think the same way. She doesn't consider herself to be a boss; however, she does consider herself an inspiration. **Why did you become involved in your profession or industry:** Ms. Febre started her career as a chemical engineer. After having children, she retired to raise them. Her children became very involved in music, and after a few years, she decided to open her own studio. She called it the School of Rock, Cyprus. Her father was in a famous rock band in Mexico, which was a positive influence. When she founded the School of Rock, she found that playing music is not just based on the act of the adult teaching the child, but more about performance and the band environment. That is where children really thrive and become musicians. Ms. Febre is passionate about providing musical education for the children who have the talent, the will, and the desire to become musicians. Additionally, in her youth, Ms. Febre worked as a professional model. This taught her about both the marketing and photography industries. She believes that her professional background makes her a well-rounded candidate to teach children exactly how to have stage presence and a personality behind a camera. She truly loves her job.

Michael Dennis Feit, PhD

Title: Physicist **Industry:** Sciences **Company Name:** Lawrence Livermore National Laboratory **Date of Birth:** 11/15/1942 **Place of Birth:** Easton **State/ Country of Origin:** PA/USA **Parents:** Joel E. Feit; Kathryn T. (Bracken) Feit **Marital Status:** Married **Spouse Name:** Mary Kay Kalson (2/11/2006); Lorraine R. Mauriel (12/30/1967, Deceased) **Children:** Sean M.; Kathryn R. **Education:** Doctor of Philosophy in Physics, Rensselaer Polytechnic Institute (1969); Bachelor of Arts in Physics, Lehigh University, with Honors and Special Honors (1964) **Career:** Physicist, Visiting Scientist of Professionals Program, Lawrence Livermore National Laboratory (2013-Present); Leader of Laser Damage Modeling Group, National Ignition Facility, Lawrence Livermore National Laboratory (1997-2005); Leader for Theoretical Optics, Short Pulse Lasers, Applications and Technology, Lawrence Livermore National Laboratory (1996-2003); Leader of Optical Physics Group, Physics & Space Technology, Lawrence Livermore National Laboratory (1992-1996); Adjunct Faculty, Department of Applied Science, Lawrence Livermore National Laboratory, University of California, Davis (1984-1990); Physicist, Lawrence Livermore Laboratory (1972-2013); Research Associate, Department of Physics, University of Illinois (1969-1972); Research and Teaching Assistant, Rensselaer Polytechnic Institute (1964-1969) **Career Related:** Co-Director, Summer School on Chaos in Physical Systems, Lawrence Livermore National Laboratory (1992); Research Project Leader, Undergraduate Summer Institute, Lawrence Livermore National Laboratory (1987-1997); Organizing Committee, International Conference on the Physics of Chaos and Systems Far from Equilibrium (1987); Physics Committee, Associateship Program, National Research Council (1984, 1982) **Creative Works:** Scientific Editor, Inertial Confinement Fusion Quarterly (1998); Associate Editor, OSA Optics Express (1997-2003); Contributing Author, Articles, More than 250 Publications **Awards:** Recipient, Research and Design 100 Award (2014); Recipient, Physical and Life Sciences Award, Lawrence Livermore National Laboratory (2014); Recipient, Photon Science Award, National Ignition Facility, Lawrence Livermore National Laboratory (2013); Honoree, Ranked 21 of 50 Most Cited Articles Since 1962, Applied Optics (2012); Recipient, Directorate Award, National Ignition Facility, Lawrence Livermore National Laboratory (2010); Honoree, Most Cited Article, Journal of Non-Crystalline Solids (2006-2010); Recipient, Directorate Award, National Ignition Facility, Lawrence Livermore National Laboratory (2005-2007); Recipient, Chemistry and Materials Science Associate Director Award, Lawrence Livermore National Laboratory (2004); Recipient, Programs Award, National Ignition Facility, Lawrence Livermore National Laboratory (2003); Recipient, Performance Award, National Ignition Facility, Lawrence Livermore National Laboratory (2002); Recipient, Research and Design 100 Award (1997); Recipient, Physics Distinguished Achievement Award, Lawrence Livermore National Laboratory (1995); Recipient, Fellowship, Optical Society of America (1992); Recipient, Physics Distinguished Achievement Award, Lawrence Livermore National Laboratory (1990); Recipient, Fellowship, American Physical Society (1988) **Memberships:** American Physical Society; American Association for the Advancement of Science; Optical Society of America; The Phi Beta Kappa Society; Sigma Xi; Sigma Xi, The Scientific Research Honor Society **Marquis Who's Who Honors:** Albert Nelson Marquis Lifetime Achievement Award **Why did you become involved in your profession or industry:** Dr. Feit became involved in his profession because he enjoyed the subject of physics while attending college. **Avocations:** Painting

Daniel A. Felicetti

Title: Academic Administrator, Educator **Industry:** Education/Educational Services **Date of Birth:** 04/25/1942 **Place of Birth:** New York **State/Country of Origin:** NY/USA **Parents:** Ernest Felicetti (1917-1966); Rose (DiAdamo) Felicetti (1917-10/21/1995) **Marital Status:** Married **Spouse Name:** Barbara D'Antonio Felicetti (07/13/1969, Deceased 2019) **Education:** Honorary Doctor of Humane Letters, Marian College (Now Marian University) (1999); PhD in Political Science, New York University (1971); MA in Political Science, New York University (1966); BA in Political Science, Hunter College (1963) **Career:** Founder, Higher Education Leadership Projects Consulting Service (2001-2015); President, Capital University, Columbus, OH (1999-2001); President, Marian College, Indianapolis, IN (1989-1999); Vice President of Academic Affairs, University of Detroit (Now University of Detroit Mercy) (1984-1989); Senior Vice President for Academic Affairs, Southeastern University, Washington, DC (1982-1984); Senior Vice President for Academic Affairs, The College of New Rochelle (Now Mercy College) (1980-1981); Academic Vice President, Academic Dean, Wheeling College (Now Wheeling University), West Virginia (1977-1980); Special Assistant to President, Fairfield University, Connecticut (1977); Intern, ACE Fellows Program, American Council on Education, Washington, DC (1976-1977); Visiting Faculty Fellow, Guest Lecturer, Thematic Summer Term Program, Yale University, New Haven, CT (1975); Chair, Department of Politics, Fairfield University (1973-1976); Assistant to Associate Professor, Instructor of American Politics for Undergraduate and Graduate Programs, Fairfield University (1967-1977) **Career Related:** Board Member, National Association of Independent Colleges (Now National Association of Independent Colleges and Universities) (1999-2001); Indiana Conference for Higher Education (1996-1999); Indiana Campus Compact (1995-1999); Elected Member, Board of Directors, The Council of Independent Colleges, Washington, DC (1995-1998); National Advisory Council, National Commission on Higher Education Issues (Now National Commission on Higher Education Attainment) (1981); Visiting Associate, Program for National Leaders in Higher Education, Institute for Educational Management, Graduate School of Education, Harvard University, Cambridge, MA (1981) **Civic:** Presidents' Summit for America's Future; Trustee, Board of Directors, Michigan and Indiana Chapters, American Heart Association, Inc.; Rotary International; Indiana Mental Health Association of Marion County; The Economic Club of Indiana, Indianapolis, IN; Mental Health and Substance Abuse Committee, New Detroit; Greater Indianapolis Progress Committee, Indy Chamber; United Way of Central Ohio; Columbus Council on World Affairs **Creative Works:** Author, "Flies Off the Wall: Text/Toons to Uplift Campus Mood," Maple Creek Media, Maryland (2016); Author, Two Books and 10 Published Professional Articles (1977-1997); Author, "Mental Health and Retardation Politics: The Mind Lobbies in Congress," Praeger, NY (1976) **Awards:** Certificate of Recognition, Senator Richard Lugar, State of Indiana (1994); Named, The Sagamore of the Wabash, Governor Evan Bayh, State of Indiana (1990); Inductee, Hunter Hall of Fame, Alumni Association of Hunter College (1986); Paul Harris Fellow, Rotary International; Founders' Day Certificate, New York University **Memberships:** Former Member, Indianapolis Athletic Club; Former Member, Public Relations Committee, Columbus Chamber of Commerce, Ohio; Former Member, Rotary International; Honorary Former Member, Alpha Sigma Nu; Honorary Former Member, Beta Gamma Sigma **Marquis Who's Who Honors:** Albert Nelson Marquis Lifetime Achievement Award **To what do you attribute your success:** Dr. Felicetti attributes his success to his extraordinary and loving wife and family, as well as many excellent teachers, professors, mentors, close friends and colleagues. **Why did you become involved in your profession or industry:** Dr. Felicetti became involved in his profession to maximize learning and mentoring opportunities for students. **Avocations:** Playing baseball; Reading; Antiquing; Traveling **Political Affiliations:** Independent Democrat **Religion:** Roman Catholic

Timothy Roy Felthouse, ChD

Title: Technical Fellow **Industry:** Technology **Company Name:** DuPont Clean Technologies, MECS, Inc. **Date of Birth:** 09/25/1951 **Place of Birth:** Berkeley **State/Country of Origin:** CA/USA **Parents:** James Whitman Felthouse; Patricia Mae (Avrit) Felthouse **Marital Status:** Married **Spouse Name:** Janine Marie (Tillinger) Felthouse (07/13/1996) **Children:** Karin Marie Messmer; Gilbert Esteban Singh **Education:** Postdoctoral Coursework, Inorganic Chemistry, Texas A&M University (1978-1980); ChD, University of Illinois at Urbana-Champaign (1978); BS, Chemistry, University of the Pacific, Stockton, CA, Magna Cum Laude (1973) **Career:** Technical Fellow, Catalyst, DuPont Clean Technologies, MECS, Inc., St. Louis, MO (2016-Present); Technical Fellow, Catalyst, DuPont Sustainable Solutions, MECS, Inc., St. Louis, MO (2011-2015); Fellow, MECS, Inc., St. Louis, MO (2005-2010); Fellow, Monsanto Co., St. Louis, MO (2003-2005); Catalyst Research Scientist, Monsanto Co., St. Louis, MO (2001-2003); Senior Research Associate, Huntsman Corp., Austin, TX (1996-2001); Fellow, Huntsman Specialty Chemicals Corp., St. Louis, MO (1994-1996); Fellow, Monsanto Co., St. Louis, MO (1992-1993); Associate Fellow, Monsanto Co., St. Louis, MO (1988-1992); Senior Research Specialist, Monsanto Co., St. Louis, MO (1987-1988); Research Specialist, Monsanto Co., St. Louis, MO (1983-1987); Senior Research Chemist, Monsanto Co., St. Louis, MO (1980-1983); Research Associate, Texas A&M University, College Station, TX (1978-1980); Grad. Teaching Research Assistant, University of Illinois-Urbana-Champaign, Champaign County, IL (1973-1978); Research Assistant, University of the Pacific, Stockton, CA (1973); National Science Foundation Research Participant, Washington State University, Pullman, WA (1972) **Creative Works:** Contributor, Articles and Reviews on Chemistry and Chemical Technology, Professional Journals and Books; 10 U.S. Patents and International Patentee in Field; Journal Reviewer, American Chemical Society, Journal of Catalysis, Applied Catalysis, Catalysis Letters; Proposal Reviewer, National Science Foundation, U. S. Department of Energy **Awards:** California State Scholarship (1969-1973); Analytical Division Undergraduate Award (1972); Governor's Scholar (1969) **Memberships:** Finance Committee Chairman, American Chemical Society (1995); Science Fairs Chairman, American Chemical Society (1991); Chairman, Monsanto Catalysis Club (1982-1983); News Editor, American Chemical Society (1981-1982); American Institute of Chemists; New York Academy of Sciences; Phi Kappa Phi; Sigma Xi; Phi Lambda Upsilon **Marquis Who's Who Honors:** Albert Nelson Marquis Lifetime Achievement Award; Marquis Who's Who Top Professional **Why did you become involved in your profession or industry:** Dr. Felthouse had a knack for doing chemistry in high school and did well in undergraduate work as well. He learned from both organic and inorganic professors. His organic chemistry class was extremely competitive and filled with pre-medical students. When working in the organic chemistry laboratory, he found that he produced better results than almost all of the pre-medical students. When he attended the University of Illinois, the university then was the largest annual producer of PhD-level chemists. While in graduate school, there were more than 500 students. Upon graduation, he pursued a postdoctoral appointment that strengthened and broadened his expertise in inorganic chemistry. In addition, the educational system and Dr. Felthouse's upbringing had something to do with his chosen profession. **Religion:** Methodist

Patrick Felvey

Title: President, Owner **Industry:** Real Estate **Company Name:** HF Appraisal Ltd. **Marital Status:** Married **Spouse Name:** Georgeann **Children:** Two Children **Education:** AA in Business Administration, Elgin Community College, IL **Certifications:** Accredited Senior Appraiser **Career:** Owner, National Director of Business Development, Accurity Valuation LLC, IL (2018-Present); President, HF Appraisal Ltd., IL (1993-Present) **Civic:** President, Goodfellows of Genoa-Kingston, IL; President, Illinois Coalition of Appraisal Professionals **Awards:** Award for Outstanding Service and Contributions, Illinois Coalition of Appraisal Professionals **Memberships:** Illinois Coalition of Appraisal Professionals **To what do you attribute your success:** Mr. Felvey attributes his success to hard work and dedication. Also he believes that respecting people will get you much further in life. **Why did you become involved in your profession or industry:** Mr. Felvey had a friend who was an appraiser and worked for a small company. They offered him a position as a marketer for their business. After three years, the owners wanted to leave the business to Mr. Felvey and his partner. When the owners brought their daughter into the business, she decided that she wanted to be an appraiser, and Mr. Felvey realized his plans of running the company were over.

John William Fenker

Title: Energy Company and Museum Executive **Industry:** Engineering **Date of Birth:** 11/16/1926 **Place of Birth:** Lakewood **State/Country of Origin:** OH/USA **Marital Status:** Widowed **Spouse Name:** Martha Monahan (06/06/1959) **Children:** Steven M.; Bridget A.; Lisabeth J. **Education:** Graduate, Advanced Management Program, Harvard Business School (1983); Master of Business Administration, Case Western Reserve University (1964); Bachelor of Science in Electrical Engineering, Cleveland State University (1955); Graduate, Rocky River High School (1944) **Certifications:** Registered Professional Engineer, Ohio **Career:** President, Cleveland Health Education Museum (1988-Present); Senior Vice President, Engineering and Operations, Cleveland Electric Illuminating Company (1986-1988); Vice President, Power Supply, Cleveland Electric Illuminating Company (1980-1986); Vice President, Administrative Services, Cleveland Electric Illuminating Company (1977-1980) **Military Service:** U.S. Navy (1944-1946); Flew off U.S.S. Midway as Aviation Radioman Gunner in SB2C Dive Bomber in WWII **Memberships:** Cleveland Engineering Society; National Society Professional Engineers; Rotary, Clevelander Club; Omega Delta Epsilon; United Way; Sigma Chi **Marquis Who's Who Honors:** Albert Nelson Marquis Lifetime Achievement Award; Marquis Who's Who Top Professional **Why did you become involved in your profession or industry:** Mr. Fenker initially entered his profression out of a desire to fully explore the field of electrical engineering, seeing this as a challenge worthy of his time. **Avocations:** Duplicate bridge; Golf **Political Affiliations:** American

Hugh M. Ferguson, MBA, CPA

Title: Independent Management Consultant **Industry:** Consulting **Date of Birth:** 11/11/1934 **Place of Birth:** Tacoma **State/Country of Origin:** WA/USA **Parents:** Robert Woods Ferguson; Charlotte Evelyn (Hemmings) Ferguson **Marital Status:** Married **Spouse Name:** Rose Marie (Deceased 07/23/2019) **Children:** Kathleen M.; Karen M.; Robert M. **Education:** MBA, The George Washington University (1963); BS, Seattle University (1956) **Certifications:** Deep Sea Diving Certification, US Navy (1960); Certified in Naval Communications (1959); Certified Data Processing Auditor; Certified Data Processor; Certified Public Accountant, State of California **Career:** President, Director, Amicon Corporation (1980-2000); Management Consultant, Ernst & Whinney (Now EY) (1970-1980); Manager of Systems and Programming, Western Pacific Railroad, San Francisco (1964-1970); Data Systems Consultant, Technical Operations Research Company, Washington (1963-1964); Data Systems Consultant, CEIR, Arlington, VA (1961-1963) **Civic:** Member, Finance Management Advisory Board, San Francisco Unified School District (1977-1978) **Awards:** Golfer of the Year (2010); Inductee, Alpha Sigma Nu (1956) **Memberships:** American Institute of Certified Public Accountants; California Society of CPAs; Association for Systems Management; Society of Mayflower Descendants; Naval Reserve Association; Reserve Officers Association; U.S. Navy League; Presidio Golf Club; San Francisco Commercial Club **Marquis Who's Who Honors:** Albert Nelson Marquis Lifetime Achievement Award; Marquis Who's Who Top Professional **Why did you become involved in your profession or industry:** In high school, Mr. Ferguson was assigned to take many technical classes because of his Seattle Prep School background. He didn't dislike all of them, but he knew he could be spending his time better elsewhere. Mr. Ferguson went to his principal and explained that he was interested in business. The principal transferred him into an accounting and bookkeeping class, which in hindsight turned out to be an excellent choice. Mr. Ferguson ended up majoring in accounting at Seattle University and eventually pursuing his career based off those interests. **Avocations:** Golfing **Political Affiliations:** Republican **Religion:** Roman Catholic

Jennifer Lee Berry Ferguson, EdD

Title: Retired Professor in Kinesiology, English Specialist **Industry:** Education/Educational Services **Date of Birth:** 02/04/1946 **Place of Birth:** Houston **State/Country of Origin:** TX/ USA **Parents:** Carnie Delton Berry; Martha June (McAlexander) Berry **Marital Status:** Married **Spouse Name:** Jerry Duane Ferguson (12/12/1981); David Eugene Wilson Jr. (05/31/1968, Divorced 1978) **Children:** Shawn Berry Benton Ferguson; Claire Katherine Lee Ferguson (Grandchild); Chloe Jane Ferguson (Grandchild); Case Benjamin Ferguson (Grandchild) **Education:** EdD, University of Houston (1994); MEd, Stephen F. Austin University (1979); BA, Houston Baptist University (1968) **Certifications:** Teacher, State of Texas; Certified, English-as-a-Second Language, 6-12; Trained Language Arts Teacher Specialist; Laying the Foundation Certification 6-12; Trained Pre-AP Writing Judge Texas **Career:** Retired (2015); English Specialist, KFHS Klein Independent School District (2012-2015); English Specialist, Houston Independent School District (2005-2011); Teacher of English, Pre-AP Grady JH Houston Independent School District (2003-2005); Teacher of Senior English, Cheer Coach, Houston Christian High School (2001-2003); Professor, Coach, Volleyball, Houston Baptist University (1986-2003); Teacher, English, Coach, Memorial High School, Spring Branch Independent School District (1979-1986); Graduate Assistant, Stephen F. Austin State University (1978-1979); Teacher, Dance Team Coach, Spring Woods High School, Spring Branch Independent School District, Houston (1975-1978); Teacher, Houston, TX (1968-1975); Teacher, Coach, Stovall Junior High Dance Team **Career Related:** English Specialist, Trainer of Teachers, Laying the Foundation (2005-2015); Presenter in Kinesiology (1986-2003); Interpreter, Texas STAAR Test; Speaker, Seminars; Advisor, Phi Mu Fraternity Collegians, University of Houston; Alumnae Coordinator West Region, Phi Mu **Civic:** Fundraiser, Houston Public Library (2018-2020); Chair, Fall Coffee (2019); Ladies Reading Club; Chair, Silver Tea (2018); Chair, Museum Day Luncheon, Houston Baptist University (2017); Choreographer, Music Productions, Second Baptist Church, Houston, TX (1990-1995); Executive Council, District IV National Association of Intercollegiate Athletics (1987-1990); Supporter, American Museum Society; The Guild, Houston Baptist University; Houston Heritage Society **Creative Works:** Curriculum Development, Catalog Creation, Kinesiology Majors at Houston Baptist University; Developer, Over 200 Lessons and Teaching Tools for the English Classroom, "Laying the Foundation" Standards **Awards:** Meritorious Alumni Award, Houston Baptist University (1996); Faculty Woman of the Year, Houston Baptist University (1992); Memorial High School Teacher of the Year (1985) **Memberships:** Texas Association of Physical Education, Recreation, and Dance; Kappa Delta Pi; Delta Psi Kappa; Texas Retired Teachers; American Museum Society; Houston Baptist University Retired Teachers Association, Phi Mu Fraternity **Marquis Who's Who Honors:** Albert Nelson Marquis Lifetime Achievement Award **To what do you attribute your success:** Dr. Ferguson attributes her success to her committed, driven dedication to the success of everyone with whom she was trusted to teach and guide. She sets realistic but high expectations, planning to ensure academic achievement, informing and posting expected outcomes, physically organizing the classroom to aid in achieving expectations, and most importantly structuring lessons so students can see how they are going to reach the end product. She has a strong classroom culture, consisting of an entry routine, seat signals, and tight transitions to the next activity. These strategies used consistently in any job or profession will render favorable outcomes that can lead to success, according to Dr. Ferguson. **Why did you become involved in your profession or industry:** Dr. Ferguson has a deep love for learning and passing along her knowledge. She loves to see a student experience success and understand the importance of perseverance. Teaching yields visible results. **Avocations:** Interior decorating; Sewing; Cooking; Gardening; Tutor in writing and English **Political Affiliations:** Bipartisan **Religion:** Baptist **Thoughts on Life:** Dr. Ferguson looks at life with the glass half full. She stands firm on her core values, accepts her faults, and takes responsibility for knowing her worth.

Joanne Fern

Title: Business Owner **Industry:** Business Management/Business Services **Company Name:** J&S Operated Equipment Rentals **Marital Status:** Married **Spouse Name:** Scott **Children:** Three Children; Four Step-Children **Education:** Diploma, High School (1978) **Career:** Business Owner, J&S Operated Equipment Rentals, Palmdale, CA (1993-Present); Bindery and Press Person, Reseda Printing (1989-1993) **Civic:** Member, Angels Against Hunger; Member, Various Charitable Organizations **Memberships:** Council of Better Business Bureaus; Contractors Register, Inc.; Air Resources Board **Marquis Who's Who Honors:** Albert Nelson Marquis Lifetime Achievement Award; Marquis Who's Who Top Professional; Marquis Who's Who Humanitarian Award **To what do you attribute your success:** Ms. Fern attributes her success to her perseverance, hard work and ability to keep the customers happy. **Why did you become involved in your profession or industry:** Ms. Fern became involved in her profession because her husband was a heavy equipment operator. He was working with a woman who needed more owners and operators and she told him she would help so she could get a contract. **Avocations:** Watching NASCAR

Waldo Fernandez

Title: Founder, Interior Designer **Industry:** Architecture & Construction **Company Name:** Waldo's Designs **Place of Birth:** Havana **State/Country of Origin:** Cuba **Education:** Coursework in Architecture and Design, University of California Los Angeles **Career:** Founder, Interior Designer, Waldo's Designs **Creative Works:** Designer, Wolfgang Puck's Spago, Beverly Hills, CA; Designer, CUT; Designer, Four Seasons Bahrain Bay; Designer, Live Nation Executive Offices, Westwood, CA; Designer, Nobu Ryokan Hotel, Malibu, CA; Designer, The Forum, Inglewood, CA **Awards:** Listee, AD100, Architectural Digest (2019)

Gary B. Ferngren

Title: Emeritus Professor of History **Industry:** Education/Educational Services **Date of Birth:** 04/14/1942 **Place of Birth:** Bellingham **State/Country of Origin:** WA/USA **Parents:** Al B. (Deceased, 1975); Wilma E. (Edberg) F. (Deceased, 1988) **Marital Status:** Widower **Spouse Name:** Agnes Loewen, (Deceased, 2006) **Children:** Suzanne Mancus; Anne-Marie Nakhla; Heather Morton **Education:** PhD, University of British Columbia (1973); MA, University of British Columbia (1967); BA, Western Washington College (1964) **Career:** Emeritus Professor of History, Oregon State University (2020-Present); Professor of History, Oregon State University (1984-2020); Associate Professor of History, Oregon State University (1978-1984); Assistant Professor of History, Oregon State University (1970-1978) **Career Related:** Professor, First Moscow State Medical University (2014-2017); Sandy and Elva Sanders Eminent Professor, University Honors College, Oregon State University (2012) **Creative Works:** Author, Essential Readings in Medicine and Religion, with Ekaterina Lomperis (2017); Medicine and Religion, A Historical Introduction (2014); Medicine and Health Care in Early Christianity (2009); Editor, Science and Religion, A Historical Introduction (2002), Second Edition, (2017); General Editor, The History of Science and Religion in the Western Tradition, An Encyclopedia (2000); Co-Editor, From Athens to Jerusalem, Medicine in Hellenized Jewish Lore and in Early Christian Literature (2000); Contributor, Professional Journals, Chapters to books **Awards:** Fellow, National Endowment of the Humanities (1990-1991); Fellow, College Physicians of Philadelphia (1981); Fellow, Oregon Committee for Humanities (1985, 1989, 1995) **Memberships:** Fellow, International Society of Religion and Science (2019-Present); International Society of the History of Medicine (Vice President, 1996-1998); U.S. Delegate, Council member (1992-2016); Associate General Secretary, 2002-2005); American Association for the History of Medicine; American Osler Society **Marquis Who's Who Honors:** Albert Nelson Marquis Lifetime Achievement Award **Why did you become involved in your profession or industry:** As a boy, Dr. Ferngren became interested in the classical world. He began to read widely in Roman history and archeology, and decided by the time he was in high school that he wanted to teach ancient history at the university level. **Avocations:** Reading; Playing classical music; Traveling **Religion:** Evangelical Christian

Thomas Torrence Fetters

Title: Research Executive (Retired), Author **Industry:** Research **Date of Birth:** 01/07/1938 **Place of Birth:** Neenah **State/Country of Origin:** WI/USA **Parents:** James Louthan Fetters; Constance Louise (Torrence) Fetters **Marital Status:** Married **Spouse Name:** Gloria Renisann Beckway Fetters (05/11/1968) **Children:** Jean Leann Fetters Conner **Education:** BS in Chemical Engineering, Clemson University (1961) **Career:** Director of Packing Research, Crown Cork and Seal (White Cap Company and Continental Can Company) Alsip, IL (1995-1999); Manager of Crown Research, Crown Cork and Seal, Alsip, IL (1991-1995); Manager of Gasketing, White Cap Company, Downers Grove, IL (1980-1991); Researcher, Science, Continental Can Company, Chicago, IL (1961-1980) **Civic:** Founder, Lustron Research, Lombard, IL (1987-Present); Past President, Board of Directors, Lombard Historical Society (Six Years) **Creative Works:** Host, Writer, Director, PBS Video, "Logs Bogs and Cabbagestocks" (1995); Author, "Logging Railroads of South Carolina" (1991); Author, "Palmetto Traction" (1978); Author, "Piedmont and Northern" (1974); Author, "Lustron Home, the History of a Post-War Prefabricated Housing Experiment"; Author, "Bare Balls and Sidewinders, Timber Times & Press"; Author, Video Script, "Logs, Bogs and Cabbage Stocks"; Author, "Charleston-Hamburg Railroad"; Author, "Logging Railroads of the Blue Ridge and Smoky Mountains, Volume 1 and Volume 2"; Author, "Phosphate Mining in South Carolina"; Author, "Railroads of Colleton County, South Carolina"; Author, "Pickens Railroad; Greenville & Northern Railroad of South Carolina"; Author, "History of the Alcolu Railroad" **Awards:** South Carolina House of Representatives Commendation, Columbia, SC (1985); American Merit Scholarship (1956) **Memberships:** Mensa International (1962); Former Member, DuPage County Genealogical Society; Former Member, Electric Railroaders Association Inc.; Former Member, Central Electric Railfans' Association; Retired Member, Society of Soft Drink Technology; American Society of Brewing Chemists; International Society of Beverage Technologists **Marquis Who's Who Honors:** Albert Nelson Marquis Lifetime Achievement Award; Marquis Who's Who Top Professional **Why did you become involved in your profession or industry:** Mr. Fetters became involved in his profession because his mother wanted him to go to a military academy in Charleston, but he wasn't very interested in that and ended up at Clemson University instead, where he earned a Bachelor of Science in Chemical Engineering, a field full of utility that could speak to many other kinds of science and applications. **Avocations:** Lustron research; Carolina railroading history; Genealogy; Old radio show history; Dirigible history; Traveling to many countries, including Canada, Mexico, Venezuela, Guyana, Trinidad, Barbados, Brazil, Argentina, Peru, Belgium, the Netherlands, France, Germany, Italy, Liechtenstein, and Switzerland **Thoughts on Life:** While in high school, Mr. Fetters won the American Merit Scholarship in 1956. Since 2004, he has served as the Village of Lombard Commissioner on the Preservation Commission.

Robert Earl Fidoten, PhD

Title: Consultant, Information and Communication Educator **Industry:** Education/Educational Services **Date of Birth:** 10/21/1927 **Place of Birth:** New York **State/Country of Origin:** NY/USA **Parents:** Herman Fidoten; Martha (Pomerantz) Fidoten **Marital Status:** Married **Spouse Name:** Marsha A. Fidoten (04/21/1948) **Children:** Douglas Sinclair; Eric Bradford **Education:** PhD in Information Science, University of Pittsburgh (1970); Coursework, Harvard University Graduate School of Education (1950-1952); BLS, Pratt Institute (1950); BA, New York University (1949) **Career:** Retired (2007); Project Manager, Digital Magic, Inc., Pittsburgh, PA (1992); President, Founder, REF Associates, Pittsburgh, PA (1989-1997); Associate Professor, Slippery Rock University, Pennsylvania (1989-2007); Director of Information Systems, PPG Industries Glass Group, Pittsburgh, PA (1971-1989); Engineering Index (1969); Manager of Research and Staff Services, PPG Industries Glass Research, Pittsburgh, PA (1964-1971); Chief Librarian, Republic Aviation Corp., Farmingdale, NY (1956-1964); Brandeis University (1951-1952); Emerson College (1950-1951) **Career Related:** Board of Visitors, Slippery Rock University College of Information, Science & Business Administration (1988-1991); Consultant, Vernante Pennitalia SPA, Genoa, Italy (1985-1988); Consultant, Boussois, S.A., Paris, France (1985-1988) **Civic:** Board Member, Pittsburgh Chapter, National Society of Arts & Letters (2012-2017); Committee Member, Sierra Club of Allegheny County, Pittsburgh, PA (1991); Civil Service Commissioner, O'Hara Township, Pennsylvania (1979-1982); President of School Board, Plainview-Old Bethpage, New York (1962-1964) **Military Service:** U.S Army Air Corps (1946-1947); Information & Education Specialist **Creative Works:** Doctoral Research (1969) **Awards:** Named, Distinguished Alumnus, University of Pittsburgh School of Library of Information Science (1981); Presidential Citation, American Ceramic Society (1980) **Memberships:** Vice President of Professional Studies, Office Systems Research Association (1993-1995); President, Pittsburgh Chapter, American Society of Information Science (1991-1992); Vice President of Membership Committee, Office Systems Research Association (1991-1992); President, Office Systems Research Association (1988-1989); Co-Chair of Curriculum Revision Committee, Office Systems Research Association; International Interactive Communications Association of Pennsylvania; Chairman of Congress, International Commission on Glass; Broadcast Education Association **Marquis Who's Who Honors:** Albert Nelson Marquis Lifetime Achievement Award; Marquis Who's Who Top Professional **To what do you attribute your success:** Dr. Fidoten attributes his success to his experience in establishing and maintaining relationships with his colleagues and coworkers. **Why did you become involved in your profession or industry:** Dr. Fidoten started his career in library science and initially worked at two academic institutions at the very beginning of his career. Then, he moved into the aerospace industry. Dr. Fidoten then transitioned out of the military defense industry into the commercial industry and launched a 25-year career at PPG Industries. He worked in what was then the glass division of the company at the research laboratory, as well as the corporate headquarters. During that period, he worked on and earned a doctoral degree.

Helen Fioratti

Title: Artist; Designer; Antique Dealer; Author; Lecturer **Industry:** Fine Art **Date of Birth:** 03/16/1931 **Place of Birth:** New York **State/Country of Origin:** NY/USA **Parents:** Arturo; Ruth (Teschner) Costantino **Marital Status:** Widow **Spouse Name:** Nereo Fioratti **Children:** Arianna **Education:** BS, Parsons School of Design, The New School **Career:** President, L'Antiquaire and the Connoisseur, Incorporated, New York, NY (1988-Present); Vice President Connoisseur (1963-1982); President, L'Antiquaire (1963-1982); Jewelry Designer; Furniture Designer **Career Related:** Artist, One-woman Shows of Paintings; Illustrator **Creative Works:** Author, "How to Know French Antiques"; Author, "Playing Games"; Author, "Please Be Seated"; Author, "Illuminating Their World"; Author, "Tempting Pandora"; Author, "Il Mobile Italiano" **Awards:** Award for 25-Years, Accademia Italiana della Cucina **Memberships:** Board Member, Art and Antique Dealers League of America, Inc. (Present); Italian American Society; Accademia Italiana della Cucina **Marquis Who's Who Honors:** Albert Nelson Marquis Lifetime Achievement Award **Why did you become involved in your profession or industry:** Mrs. Fioratti was inspired by her mother, Ruth. She was the first female fine arts dealer in antiques in the United States. She attended Parsons School of Design so she could follow in her mother's footsteps. **Avocations:** Cooking; Baking **Religion:** Catholic

Pamela Fiori

Title: Publishing Executive, Writer **Industry:** Writing and Editing **Date of Birth:** 02/26/1944 **Place of Birth:** Newark **State/Country of Origin:** NJ/USA **Parents:** Edward Fiori; Rita (Rascati) Fiori **Marital Status:** Married **Spouse Name:** Colton Givner **Education:** BA, Jersey City State College, Cum Laude (1966) **Career:** Editor-at-Large, Town & Country, New York, NY (2010-Present); Editor-in-Chief, Town & Country TRAVEL, New York, NY (2003-Present); Editor-in-Chief, Town & Country, New York, NY (1993-2010); Editorial Director, Executive Vice President, Travel & Leisure/Food & Wine, American Express Publishing Corp., New York, NY (1989-1993); Editor-in-Chief, Executive Vice President, Travel & Leisure/Food & Wine, American Express Publishing Corp., New York, NY (1980-1989); Editor-in-Chief, Travel & Leisure Magazine, New York, NY (1975-1980); Senior Editor, Travel & Leisure Magazine, New York, NY (1974-1975); Associate Editor, Travel & Leisure Magazine, New York, NY (1971-1974); Associate Editor, Holiday Magazine, New York, NY (1968-1971); Teacher, English, Governor Livingston High School, Berkeley Heights, NJ (1966-1967) **Civic:** Board of Trustees, U.S. Fund for UNICEF; Founding Chairman, UNICEF Snowflake Project **Creative Works:** Columnist, Town & Country (1993-2010); Columnist, Travel & Leisure (1976-1989); Author, Seven Books on Travel & Food Subjects, Capri, St. Barths, Palm Beach (Asseulena); A Table at Le Arque and Holiday (both by Rizzoli), Ronny Jagnes (Glittereli); Contributor, Articles, Periodicals **Awards:** Matrix Award, Women in Communications, Inc. (2007); Gem Award, Jewelry Information Council (2006); Audrey Hepburn Humanitarian Award, UNICEF (2005); Fashion Oracle of Year, Council of Fashion Designers (2004); Fashion Icon Award, Council of Fashion Designers (2004); Business Award, National Italian American Foundation (1996); Outstanding Woman of the 90s Award, Foundation for Neurosurgery Research (1994); Melva C. Pederson Award for Distinguished Travel Journalism, American Society of Travel Agents (1992); Chevalier de l'Ordre du Merite (1985) **Marquis Who's Who Honors:** Albert Nelson Marquis Lifetime Achievement Award **Why did you become involved in your profession or industry:** Ms. Fiori became involved in her profession as she had left her first year in teaching because she thought she was too young and wanted to see more of what was out there. She ended up spending a few months in Italy on her own and that taught her a great deal about independence. When she returned she was not ready to go back to teaching and she wanted a job in New York but was not quite sure how to find it. Just as she was about to give up and go back to teaching she saw an ad in The New York Times. It was for a research associate at a magazine which she applied for and it turned out to be a fact checking job, which was great because she loved research. She started in 1968 and that was the beginning of everything. It felt like a place she wanted to be at and she got along with her co-workers.

Myrna Leah Fischman, PhD, CPA

Title: Professor Emerita, Accountant, Director (Retired) **Industry:** Education/Educational Services **Company Name:** LIU Brooklyn **Parents:** Isidore Fischman; Sally (Goldstein) Fischman **Education:** PhD, New York University (1976); MS, Baruch College, New York, NY (1964); BS, Baruch College, New York, NY (1960) **Certifications:** CPA (Certified Public Accountant), State of New York (1964) **Career:** Self-Employed Accountant, New York, NY (1960-Present); Professor Emerita, Finance, Law, Accounting, Taxation Department, LIU Brooklyn (2019); Director, Center for Accounting & Tax Education, LIU Brooklyn (1986-2019); Director, School of Professional Accountancy, LIU Brooklyn (1984-2019); Coordinator, Graduate Capstone Courses, Long Island University (1982-1986); Professor, Accounting, Taxation, Law, LIU Brooklyn (1979-2019); Advisor, Professor, Long Island University (1970-1979); Community Fellowship Coordinator, Queens District Attorney's Office (1970-1971); Chief Accountant Investigator, Queens District Attorney's Office (1969-1970); Instructor, Accounting, Borough of Manhattan Community College, New York, NY (1963-1966); Vice-Advisor, Center Commercial High School, New York, NY (1963-1966); Teacher, Accounting, Center Commercial High School, New York, NY (1960-1963); Chief Accountant Investigator, Queens District Attorney (1954-1970); Chairman, Department of Accounting, Long Island University; Assistant to Controller, Sam Goody, Inc., New York, NY **Career Related:** Lecturer, Tax Seminar (2017); Special Trustee, Professor Leo Schloss Excellence in Accounting Scholarship; Advisor, Accounting Society, Long Island University; Developer, BS/MS Accounting Program, Long Island University **Civic:** Business Education Advisory Council, Accounting Department Advisory Board, Borough of Manhattan Community College (1997-Present); New York City Department of Education (1992-2000); Subcommittee on Business Education, Economic Development and Marketing Committee, Brooklyn Chamber of Commerce (1984-2015); Chairman, Supervisory Committee, LOMTO Federal Credit Union #1532, New York, NY (1983-2016); Chairman, Consumer Council, Astoria Medical Center (1980-1992); Legislative Advisory Board, New York State Assemblyman Dennis Butler (1979-1997); Chancellor, Committee Against Discrimination in Education (1976-1997); Educational Task Force, The Atlanta Journal-Constitution (AJC) (1972-1995); Steering Committee, Youth Division, New York County Democratic Committee (1967-1968); Representative, Women's Activities Committee, Young Democrats of America (1967); Delegate, National Convention, Young Democrats of America (1967); Treasurer, Breakfree Inc., Lower East Side Preparatory School; Accountant, Institute for the Advancement of Criminal Justice; Advisor, Institute for the Advancement of Criminal Justice; Accountant-Consultant, Coalition Development Corporation; Accountant-Consultant, Interracial Council for Business Opportunities; Research Consultant, Pre-Technology Program, New York City Board of Education **Creative Works:** Editor, "Eastern Business Educators Journal" (1988) **Awards:** Special Award for 40 Years of Service to the Volunteer Income Tax Assistance Program, Internal Revenue Service, (2014); Lifetime Achievement Award, Soroptimist International, Brooklyn, NY (1997) **Memberships:** Public Relations Committee, New York State Society of Certified Public Accountants (1992-Present); Director, Brooklyn Chapter, Tax & Accounting Institute, Long Island University (1984-Present); Director, New York Chapter, Institute of Management Accountants (1983-Present); Board of Directors, New York State Society of Certified Public Accountants (2005-2010); President, Brooklyn Chapter, New York State Society of Certified Public Accountants (2001-2002); Board of Directors, New York Chapter, American Accounting Association (1994-1996); Director of University Relations, New York Chapter, Institute of Management Accountants (1993-1994); General Committee on Education in Colleges and Universities, New York State Society of Certified Public Accountants (1991-1997); Auditing Committee, New York State Society of Certified Public Accountants (1991-1993); Director of Manuscripts, New York Chapter, Institute of Management Accountants (1991-1992); President, New York Chapter, Association of Government Accountants (1990-1991); President, New York Chapter, American Accounting Association (1990-1991); National Education Association; American Association of University Professors; Association of International Certified Professional Accountants; Young Alumni Association; American Association of Junior Colleges; Financial Executives Institute; Jewish Guild for the Blind; JBI International; Community Welfare Committee Association; Friends of the Metropolitan Museum of Art **Marquis Who's Who Honors:** Albert Nelson Marquis Lifetime Achievement Award; Marquis Who's Who Top Professional; Marquis Who's Who Humanitarian Award **To what do you attribute your success:** Dr. Fischman attributes her success to having great parents. **Why did you become involved in your profession or industry:** Dr. Fischman became involved in her profession because she loved the ambiance of the world of business. **Avocations:** Dancing **Political Affiliations:** Democrat **Religion:** Jewish

George Fish

Title: Writer, Poet **Industry:** Writing and Editing **Date of Birth:** 12/27/1946 **Place of Birth:** St. Louis **State/Country of Origin:** MO/USA **Parents:** George Thomas Fish; Geraldine Ann (Sasek) Fish **Marital Status:** Single **Education:** AB in Economics, Indiana University (Now Indiana University Bloomington), Bloomington, IN (1977) **Certifications:** Certified in Chinese, Washington University, St. Louis, MO (1970); Certified Paralegal **Career:** Freelance Writer (1981); Blue Collar Worker, Grocery Store; Temp Work (14 Years) **Career Related:** Freelance, Paralegal, and Legal Writer and Researcher (1988-Present) **Civic:** Member, Indianapolis Peace and Justice Center **Creative Works:** Author, 24 Published Poems (2007-Present); Contributor, Articles, Publications, Including "The Guardian," "In These Times," "Monthly Revised," "Living Blues," "Blues Access," "Skeptical Inquirer," "NUVO," "Bloomington Voice," "Socialism and Democracy," "Science and Society," "New Politics," "Against the Current," "Flying Island Journal," "Tipton Poetry Journal"; Contributor, Articles, Professional Journals **Awards:** First National Merit Finalist in his High School's History **Memberships:** South Central Indiana Blues Society; Democratic Socialists of America; Committees of Correspondence for Democracy and Socialism; Central Indiana Democratic Socialists of America; Freedom From Religion Foundation **Marquis Who's Who Honors:** Albert Nelson Marquis Lifetime Achievement Award; Marquis Who's Who Top Professional **Why did you become involved in your profession or industry:** Mr. Fish became involved in his profession because he was always an active reader, starting from when he was a child and adolescent. At an early age, he was always impressed by the written word and decided to pursue that professionally. He got off to a late start, but once he started, he became a regular freelance writer at several publications and found a ready market for his writing and just kept pursuing it. **Avocations:** Performing Lenny Bruce/George Carlin-inspired stand-up comedy **Political Affiliations:** Democratic Socialist **Religion:** Atheist (Former Catholic) **Thoughts on Life:** In addition to attending Indiana University, Mr. Fish also studied at Michigan State University in East Lansing, Michigan, from 1965 to 1972. Mr. Fish's published articles can be found at: http://sdonline.org/; https://solidarity-us.org/atc/current/; http://inthesetimes.com

Charles John Fisk

Title: Meteorologist, Researcher, Consultant **Industry:** Sciences **Company Name:** Naval Base Ventura County **Place of Birth:** Minneapolis **State/Country of Origin:** MN/USA **Parents:** Everett Vincent Fisk; Florence Linnea Carlson Fisk **Education:** Master of Science in Meteorology, University of Wisconsin (1984) **Career:** Meteorologist, Naval Base Ventura County, Point Mugu, CA (1986-Present); Climatologist, Naval Base Ventura County, Point Mugu, CA (1986-Present) **Career Related:** Consultant, Long-Range Forecasting of Southern California Temperatures and Precipitation (1996-Present) **Creative Works:** Author, "The First Fifty Years of Continuous Recorded Weather History In Minnesota (1820-1869) - A Narrative Chronology"; (2010); Contributor, 27 Articles to Professional Journals; Author, Various Proceedings **Memberships:** American Statistical Association; American Meteorological Society **Marquis Who's Who Honors:** Marquis Who's Who Top Professional **Avocations:** Reading; Travel; Web publishing; Genealogy; Genetic genealogy; Gym

Ira J. Fistell

Title: Newspaper Editor, Educator, Radio and Television Personality, Lecturer, Writer **Place of Birth:** Chicago **State/Country of Origin:** IL/USA **Parents:** Harry Fistell; Marion Fistell **Marital Status:** Separated **Education:** MA, U.S./American History, University Wisconsin-Madison, Madison, WI (1967); JD, University of Chicago, Chicago, IL (1964); AB, University of Chicago, with Honors (1962) **Certifications:** Illinois Bar Association (1964) **Career:** Radio Personality, Station KABC-AM, Los Angeles, CA (2001-2006); National Radio Personality, TalkAmerica Radio Network (1998-2001); Editor, LA Jewish News (1995-1996); National Radio Personality, ABC Talkradio Network, Los Angeles, CA (1982-1988); TV Personality, USA & ESPN Cable Networks (1980-1984); Radio Personality, Station KABC-AM, Los Angles, CA (1977-1995); Radio Personality, Station WEMP-AM, Milwaukee, WI (1971-1977); Radio Personality, Station WKOW-AM, Madison, WI (1968-1971) **Career Related:** Instructor, English and U.S. History, Concord Prep High School, Santa Monica, CA (1998-2000); Faculty Member, University of Phoenix, Los Angeles, CA (1998) **Creative Works:** Author, "The Hidden Holmes: A Sherlock Holmes Companion" (2020); Author, "Encounters with Mark Twain" (1995); Author, "Oddball America" (1986); Author, "America By Train" (1982); Writer, Monthly Journal, "Topics" (Now in its 33rd Year of Regular Monthly Publication) **Awards:** Golden Spike Award for Service to Rail Passengers, NARRP, Anaheim, CA (1987) **Memberships:** Screen Actors Guild - American Federation of Television and Radio Artists (SAG-AFTRA) **Marquis Who's Who Honors:** Albert Nelson Marquis Lifetime Achievement Award **Why did you become involved in your profession or industry:** Mr. Fistell became involved in his profession because he was always interested in radio since childhood, and eventually made a career out of broadcasting. Naturally, his passion for reading and radio expanded into writing and education as well. **Avocations:** Music; Reading; White Sox baseball; Traveling; Spending time with his daughter and grandchildren

Mary Elizabeth Flanagan, MLS

Title: Elementary School Educator (Retired) **Industry:** Education/Educational Services **Company Name:** Westview Elementary School **Date of Birth:** 12/26/1936 **Place of Birth:** Zanesville **State/Country of Origin:** OH/USA **Parents:** John Walter; Martha Elizabeth (Nosker) Combs **Marital Status:** Widow **Spouse Name:** Oliver Louis Flanagan (06/18/1976, Deceased 2005); Robert Lee Snyder (09/09/1955, Divorced 05/1973) **Children:** Robyn L. Kimble (Deceased); Mark A. Snyder; Libby Rebecca E. Hardwick Musking **Education:** Postgraduate Coursework, Ohio University (1986-2000); MLS, Ohio University (1985); BS in Elementary Education, Muskingum College (1957) **Certifications:** Elementary Teacher **Career:** Retired (2001); Teacher, 2nd Grade, Westview Elementary School, Zanesville, OH (1973-2001); Teacher, Kindergarten, Munson Elementary School, Zanesville, OH (1971-1974); Teacher, 2nd Grade for the Hearing Impaired, Pioneer Elementary School, Zanesville, OH (1964-1965); Teacher, Kindergarten, Madison Elementary School, Zanesville, OH (1963-1964); Teacher, Kindergarten, Munson Elementary School, Zanesville, OH (1957-1960) **Career Related:** Co-Developer, Partners In Literacy Program **Civic:** Deacon, Trinity United Presbyterian Church (2012-2019); Volunteer, Salvation Army Auxiliary, Partners in Literacy Program (2001-2005); Inclusion Teacher, Zanesville City Schools, Partners in Literacy Program, Teacher's Committee (1994-2004); Muskingum College Teacher Education Committee, New Concord, OH (1991-1999); President, Forest Ave Presbyterian Church Women's Association, Zanesville, OH (1969); American Association of University Women, Pioneer and Historical Society Life Time, Cultural Interest in AAUW Group; President, Tots to Teens Child Conservation League, Zanesville, OH **Awards:** Co-Recipient, Family Partnership Award, Ohio Department of Education (2001); Ohio's Best Practice Award, Ohio Department Education (1999); Partners In Literacy Program Award, Southeastern School Board Association in Ohio, Department of Education (1998); Martha Holdren Jennings Scholar (1985); Ohio Reads Grant for Partners in Literacy Program; State Award, Partners In Literacy Program **Memberships:** National Education Association; American Association of University Women; Ohio Retired Teacher Association; Ohio Education Association; Ohio Pioneer Historical Society; Epsilon Sigma Alpha **Marquis Who's Who Honors:** Albert Nelson Marquis Lifetime Achievement Award **Why did you become involved in your profession or industry:** Mrs. Flanagan was inspired to become a teacher because she always had a love for the education system. **Avocations:** Reading; Travel; Dollhouses; Collecting Shawnee pottery: Stamp collecting/philately; Animals; Music **Political Affiliations:** Republican **Religion:** Presbyterian

Mickie Flanigan

Title: Architect, Construction Executive **Industry:** Architecture & Construction **Date of Birth:** 03/21/1944 **Place of Birth:** Chicago **State/Country of Origin:** IL/USA **Parents:** Howard Edward Flanigan; May (Babcock) Flanigan **Marital Status:** Single **Spouse Name:** John Louis Malec (10/27/1975, Divorced 06/1987) **Children:** Erin Flanigan; Brendan Christopher **Education:** MArch, Illinois Institute of Technology, Chicago, IL (1990); MBA, University of Pittsburgh (1970); BA, Duquesne University, Pittsburgh, PA (1966) **Career:** Architecture (1986-2000); Private Practice, Chicago, IL (1983-1986); President, Chief Executive Officer, Analytica, Inc., Barrington, IL (1979-1983); Founding Member, Director, Information Resources Inc. (1977-1983); Marketing Director, Management Decision Systems, Boston, MA (1977-1978); Vice President, NPD Research, Schaumburg, IL (1973-1977); Worked in Business (1966-1985) **Civic:** Computer Technician, President Obama Campaign (2008, 2012); National Assistant Secretary, Young Representatives (1969-1971) **Memberships:** National Organization of Women (1976-Present) **Marquis Who's Who Honors:** Albert Nelson Marquis Lifetime Achievement Award **Why did you become involved in your profession or industry:** What attracted Ms. Flanigan to her profession is that she has been an outsider her whole life. She moved to Mobile, Alabama where everyone called her an angry person, and she worked herself through college. She was a writer. She asked if she could write on the business end, but she was told that "[we] don't let girls do that." This surprised her, and she went to the University of Pittsburgh and signed up for the MBA program, where they didn't care if she was a female, only that her scores and entrance tests were excellent. Her first course in business school was a computer course and she asked the instructor if he knew someone who would hire a woman, because no one would hire her as a women, and he said that he worked for a professor C. Miller, who didn't pay much, but would hire anybody. She ended up working for him running their data processing and computer processing department. Then she started a new business division. She worked 60 hours a week, and earned more because she worked more. When she finished her MBA she decided to go kick butt, so she applied to a large company's macroeconomic modeling division. She called the company to follow up and was hung up on. The company informed her that they didn't hire women. All Ms. Flanigan could think was that was the stupidest thing that she had ever heard. So, since she couldn't get a job in Pittsburgh she went to Washington DC and one of the places that she visited was one office, and her excellent resume led her to three job offers. She could be secretary of the media department, or the hiring manager's personal secretary, or the manager of all of the secretaries. These positions all had their upsides, but she did not want to become a secretary. She found another division within the company that would test her as an engineer and compare her test scores with the other engineers in the company. Impressed by her results, they gave her an excellent offer. **Avocations:** Tennis; Reading; Skiing; Animals; Travel **Religion:** Roman Catholic

Sander Allen Flaum

Title: Founder, Principal **Industry:** Business Management/Business Services **Date of Birth:** 04/05/1937 **Parents:** Joseph Flaum; Rose (Deutsch) Flaum **Marital Status:** Widowed **Spouse Name:** Mechele Plotkin Flaum (04/25/1990) **Children:** Pamela; Jonathan **Education:** MBA, Fairleigh Dickinson University, Teaneck, NJ, Magna Cum Laude (1970); BA, Ohio State University, Columbus, OH (1958) **Career:** Founder, Principal, Chairman, Fordham Leadership Forum, Fordham University (1999-Present); Founder, Flaum Navigators, Inc. (2004); Chairman, Euro RSCG Life (2001-2003); Chairman, Chief Executive Officer, Robert A. Becker, Euro RSCG (1988-1998); Executive Vice President, Klemtner Advertising (1984-1988); Marketing Director, Division, American Cyanamid Company, Lederle Laboratories, Wayne, NJ (1974-1982); Chief Executive Officer, Flaum Partners, Inc.; Numerous Positions, Including Task Force Chairman, Lederle Generic Products Division, Lederle Laboratories **Career Related:** Board of Directors, VIASYS Healthcare Inc. (2003); Board of Directors, Eagle Pharmaceuticals; Adjunct Professor, Management Fordham Graduate School of Business; Executive-in-Residence, Board Member, Fisher College of Business, Ohio State University **Civic:** Board Member, Edge4Vets (2015-Present) **Military Service:** U.S. Army (1959-1961) **Creative Works:** Co-Author, "Boost Your Career: How to Make an Impact, Get Recognized, and Build the Career you Want" (2017); Co-Author, "The Best Thing That Could Ever Happen to You: How a Career Reversal Can Reinvigorate Your Life" (2013); Author, "Big Shoes: How Successful Leaders Grow Into New Roles" (2009); Author, "The 100-Mile Walk: A Father and Son on a Quest to Find the Essence of Leadership" (2006); Author, "The Shortest Road to Success"; Author, "Focusing Is for Tough Guys"; Author, "The Leader's Edge"; Author, "There's a Little Consumer in Every M.D."; Author, "Great Is Better than Good"; Author, "Hocus Focus"; Author, "Survival of Fastest, Focus on the Future Direction: Outward"; Columnist, Monthly Column on the Pharmaceutical Industry, Medical Marketing & Media; Contributor, Weekly Radio Show, Public Service Radio, The Leader's Edge **Awards:** Lifetime Achievement Award, PM360 Magazine **Memberships:** American Marketing Association **Marquis Who's Who Honors:** Albert Nelson Marquis Lifetime Achievement Award **Why did you become involved in your profession or industry:** Mr. Flaum became involved in his profession because while in high school, he had a very bad speech impediment, a stutter, and was advised by his mother, Rose Flaum, that he needed to be smarter and work harder than everybody else. He now has a foundation named after her to help those who don't have the funds to receive help with their speech impediments. **Avocations:** Running; Playing golf **Political Affiliations:** Independent **Religion:** Jewish

Paul D. Fleming III

Title: Professor **Industry:** Education/Educational Services **Company Name:** Western Michigan University **Date of Birth:** 06/01/1943 **Place of Birth:** Tampa **State/Country of Origin:** FL/USA **Parents:** Paul Daniel Fleming Jr.; Margie Elaine (Bowman) Fleming **Marital Status:** Married **Spouse Name:** Mary Ellen Fleming (09/02/1967) **Children:** Paul IV; Meredith; Mark **Education:** Doctor of Philosophy in Chemical Physics (1970); Master of Arts in Physics Harvard University, Cambridge, MA (1966) ; Bachelor of Science in Physics, Ohio State University, Columbus, OH (1964) **Career:** Professor of Chemical and Paper Engineering, Western Michigan University (2006-Present); Associate Professor, Kalamazoo, MI (1996-2006) Group Leader, GenCorp, Akron, OH (1986-1996); Senior Research Specialist, Phillips Petroleum, Bartlesville, OK (1974-1986); Postdoctoral Research Associate, Brown University, Providence, RI (1971-1974); Postdoctoral Research Associate, Columbia University, New York, NY (1970-1971); **Creative Works:** Co-Author, Peer-Reviewed Article, "Lateral Paper Web Position During Commercial Heat Set Web Offset Printing" (2018); Co-Author, Peer-Reviewed Article, "Graphene Inks for Printed Electronics" (2012); Co-Author, Peer-Reviewed Article, "The Study of Ink Pigment Dispersion Parameters" (2006); Co-Author, Peer-Reviewed Article, "Color Management and ICC Profiles: Can't Live Without It So Learn to Live With It!" (2002); Co-Author, Peer-Reviewed Article, "A New Attempt to Reconcile the Statistical and Phenomenological Theories of Rubber Elasticity" (1997); Co-Author, Peer-Reviewed Article, "Toward a Molecular Equation of State for Real Materials" (1987); Co-Author, Peer-Reviewed Article, "Spinning Drop Interfacial Viscometer" (1980); Author, Peer-Reviewed Article, "The Hard Sphere Glass Transition" (1976); Co-Author, Peer-Reviewed Article, "Resonant Transport Coefficients of Polyatomic Gases in Oscillating Magnetic Fields" (1972); Contributor, More Than 350 Publications **Memberships:** Technical Editor, Society of Petroleum Engineers (1974-1993); American Physical Society; Technical Association of the Graphic Arts; Information Systems & Technology **Marquis Who's Who Honors:** Albert Nelson Marquis Lifetime Achievement Award; Marquis Who's Who Top Professional **Why did you become involved in your profession or industry:** Dr. Fleming first became interested in his profession while attending middle school, during which time he learned a great deal of astronomy and planets. He started to read about atomic energy, and aspired for a time to become a nuclear physicist. In time, he began to major in molecular atomic physics. **Avocations:** Working in the yard; Watching sports

Joe Flickinger, PhD

Title: Professor Emeritus **Industry:** Education/Educational Services **Date of Birth:** 02/04/1949 **Place of Birth:** Cadilac, Michigan **State/Country of Origin:** MI/USA **Parents:** Arden Henry Flickinger; Stella Frances (Hurst) Flickinger **Marital Status:** Married **Spouse Name:** Judith Marie (Gardner) Flickinger (09/18/1971) **Children:** Jan Elsa Allnutt; Jill Kimberly Brown **Education:** PhD, University of Oregon (1993); AS, Clatsop Community College (1985); MA, University of Southern California (1975); BA, Kalamazoo College, Michigan (1971) **Career:** Professor Emeritus, Radford University (2016-Present); Professor, School of Communication, Radford University; Visiting Professor, Communication, American University of Bulgaria, Blagoevgrad, Bulgaria (2007); Chair, Media Studies Department, Radford University (1998-2006); Director, Graduate Program, Corporate and Professional Communication, Radford University (1996-1998); Visiting Assistant Professor, Lewis and Clark College, Portland, OR (1991-1992); Senior Marketing Consultant, RKM Corporation, Vancouver, WA (1990-1993); Graduate Teaching Fellow, Telecommunications, University of Oregon, Eugene, OR (1988-1990); Studio Operator, Instructor, Clatsop Community College, Astoria, OR (1975-1988); Station Engineer, Station KAST-AM-FM, Astoria, OR (1974-1975); Assistant Chief Engineer, Station KUSC-FM, LA (1972-1974) **Career Related:** Session Organizer, High Definition TV, Northcon (1989); Session Organizer, IEEE and ERA Technical Conference (1989) **Civic:** President, Board of Directors, Station KMUN-FM Tillicum Foundation, Astoria, OR (1983-1984); Canvasser, Friends of College, Astoria, OR (1982); Director, TV Muscular Dystrophy Telethon, Astoria Jaycees (1980-1981) **Memberships:** Region Chair, District 24-E, Radford Host Lions Club (1999-2002); Secretary, Sunset Empire Amateur Radio Club (1978-1981); Life Member IEEE; IEEE Computer Society; IEEE Communications Society; Life Member, American Radio Relay League; Pacific Telecommunications Council; Northcom Inner Circle; New York Academy Sciences; National Model R.R. Association **Marquis Who's Who Honors:** Albert Nelson Marquis Lifetime Achievement Award; Marquis Who's Who Top Professional **Why did you become involved in your profession or industry:** Dr. Flickinger says all things happened strangely. He began as a chemist and physicist. He decided that he did not like his work, so he changed his career to theater arts. From there, his wife had taken a required speech class and when the class concluded, a teacher made an announcement that the chief engineer of the radio class will be leaving for the Alaskan pipeline and was in need of a replacement. Dr. Flickinger applied and got hired. In that process, he discovered how much he loved teaching. He tied together his physics and engineering background to his teaching. At a later point, he thought to himself, "If you're going to teach in a four-year institution, you need a PhD," which he eventually completed. **Avocations:** Amateur radio; Golf; Fishing; Astronomy; Cooking **Thoughts on Life:** Dr. Flickinger wants people to go where your heart is and things will follow. It is more important to like your job than to get a lot of money for it. Sometimes the best opportunities aren't the best in the long run. Take life as its presented to you.

Joseph James "Joe" Floyd

Title: Owner **Industry:** Agriculture **Company Name:** Impact Landscape & Irrigation **Date of Birth:** 04/04/1958 **Place of Birth:** West Palm Beach **State/Country of Origin:** FL/USA **Parents:** George Floyd; Margeret Floyd **Marital Status:** Married **Spouse Name:** Nicole **Children:** Joe Jr.; Natasja; Danielle; Kailyn; Keira; Lareina; Elijah **Education:** BS in Ornamental Horticulture, School of Agriculture, University of Florida (1981) **Certifications:** Florida State Irrigation License **Career:** Owner, Impact Landscaping (2007-Present); Sod, Landscape, and Irrigation Division, DiVosta Homes (1984-2007) **Civic:** Volunteer, First Familes **Awards:** Top 100 List, Lawn and Landcaping Magazine (2017-2018) **Memberships:** Florida Nursery; Growers and Landscape Association **Marquis Who's Who Honors:** Albert Nelson Marquis Lifetime Achievement Award **To what do you attribute your success:** Mr. Floyd attributes his success to being very family orientated. He is fair with his employees and treats them like family, which builds a positive work environment. **Why did you become involved in your profession or industry:** When Mr. Floyd was growing up, his father maintained estates in Palm Beach. Some of these estates were so big they had a full-time house staff. When he was about 12, his mother told him that he was old enough to start mowing the lawn for his father. One day, he was mowing the grass on a big estate and met Colonel Leon Mandel, who told him to "always be happy at what you do, It will help you live a long life. Always take care of yourself because your health is more important than your wealth." As Mr. Floyd grew up, he pursued college, Mr. Mandel's advice sticking with him all the while. Mr. Floyd studied landscaping and the environment, proceeding to receive a degree in ornamental horticulture. This enabled him to start his own business. **Political Affiliations:** Republican **Religion:** Catholic

Robert Lopez Flynn

Title: Author **Industry:** Writing and Editing **Date of Birth:** 04/12/1932 **Place of Birth:** Wilbargar County **State/Country of Origin:** TX/USA **Parents:** James Emmett Flynn; Gladys Lopez (Wilkinson) Flynn **Marital Status:** Married **Spouse Name:** Norma Jean Sorrels (Deceased 2013) **Children:** Deirdre Siobhan (Deceased); Flynn-Bass; Brigid Erin (Deceased) **Education:** MA, Baylor University (1956); BA, Baylor University (1954) **Career:** Novelist in Residence, Trinity University, San Antonio, TX (1963-2001); Professor, Baylor University, Waco, TX (1959-1963); Professor, Gardner-Webb College, Boiling Springs, NC (1957-1959) **Military Service:** United States Marine Corps (1950-1952) **Creative Works:** Author, Story Collections, "Living with the Hyenas" (1996); Author, "The Last Klick" (1994); Author, Memoir, "Personal War in Vietnam" (1989); Author, "Wanderer Springs" (1987); Author, Story Collections, "Seasonal Rain" (1984); Author, "Sounds of Rescue, Signs of Hope" (1970); Author, "In the House of the Lord" (1969); Author, "North to Yesterday" (1967) **Awards:** Wrangler Award (1967, 1996); Spur Award (1987); Southwest Booksellers Award (1970); National Cowboy Hall of Fame; Texas Literary Hall of Fame **Memberships:** President, Texas Institute of Letters (1990-1992); PEN; Associate Marine Combat Correspondence; Fellow, Texas Institute Letters **Marquis Who's Who Honors:** Albert Nelson Marquis Lifetime Achievement Award; Marquis Who's Who Top Professional **Why did you become involved in your profession or industry:** Mr. Flynn's father, James Emmett was a World War I veteran and constantly kept a journal. His father encouraged him to do the same and Flynn became infatuated with writing and made it a career. **Religion:** Baptist

Rev. Dr. Thomas R. Flynn

Title: Priest, Philosopher, Educator **Industry:** Education/Educational Services **Company Name:** Emory University **Date of Birth:** 06/02/1936 **Place of Birth:** Spokane **State/Country of Origin:** WA/USA **Parents:** Thomas J. Flynn; Bernice E. (Colliton) Flynn **Marital Status:** Single **Education:** LHD (Honorary), Carroll College, Helena, MT (2006); PhD, Columbia University, New York, NY (1970); STL, Gregorian University, Rome, Italy (1962); BA, Carroll College, Helena, MT (1958) **Certifications:** Ordained, Catholic Priest (1961) **Career:** Samuel Candler Dobbs Professor of Philosophy, Emory University, Atlanta, GA (1987-2020); Professor (1985-1987); Associate Professor (1981-1985); Assistant Professor (1978-1981); Assistant Professor, Catholic University of America, Washington, DC (1971-1975); Instructor, Philosophy, Carroll College, Helena, MT (1962-1966) **Creative Works:** Author, "Sartre: A Philosophical Biography" (2014); Author, "Existentialism: A Very Short Introduction" (2006); Co-Editor, "Über Sartre" (2005); Author, "Sartre, Foucault and Historical Reason, Vol. 2" (2004); Co-Editor, "Ethics of History" (2004); Author, "Sartre, Foucault and Historical Reason, Vol. 1" (1997); Co-Editor, "Dialectic and Narrative" (1992); Author, "Sartre and Marxist Existentialism" (1984); Author, Over 100 Essays, Various Journals **Awards:** Fellow, Fox Center for Humanistic Inquiry, Emory University (2005-2006); Fellow, Institute for Advanced Study, Princeton (1998-1999); Fellow, National Humanities Center, Research Triangle Park, North Carolina (1991-1992); Emory Williams Distinguished Teaching Award in Humanities (1990); United Methodist Church Award for University Scholar-Teacher (1986); Senior Fellow, American Council of Learned Societies (1983-1984); Emory Williams Distinguished Teaching Award (1981); Grantee, Danforth Foundation (1966-1968) **Memberships:** Senior Faculty Fellow, Fox Center for Humanistic Inquiry, Emory University (2005-2006); Institute for Advanced Study, Princeton University (1998-2019); President, American Catholic Philosophical Association (1993-1994); Andrew W. Mellon Fellow, National Humanities Center, North Carolina (1991-1992); Executive Committee, International Association for Philosophy and Literature (1988-1992); Executive Director, Sartre Society North America (1988-1991); Board of Directors, American Philosophical Association (1988-1991); Executive Committee, Society for Phenomenology and Existential Philosophy (SPEP) (1985-1987) **Marquis Who's Who Honors:** Albert Nelson Marquis Lifetime Achievement Award **To what do you attribute your success:** Mr. Flynn attributes his success to valuing a spirit of cooperation and mutual respect in addition to hard work. **Why did you become involved in your profession or industry:** Though he was a talented musician, Mr. Flynn wanted to do something purposeful with his life. This is why he became a priest. **Avocations:** Music; Voice; Piano; Organ; Travel; Fine arts; Debate; Swimming; Camping; Boy Scouts of America **Political Affiliations:** Independent **Religion:** Roman Catholic **Thoughts on Life:** Mr. Flynn believes that life is a gift and it should not be taken for granted.

Jonathan Foley

Title: Environmentalist **Industry:** Environmental Services **Career:** Executive Director, Project Drawdown (2018-Present); Executive Director, California Academy of Sciences (2014-2018); Founding Director, Institute on the Environment, University of Minnesota (2008-2014); McKnight Presidential Chair, Global Environment and Sustainability, University of Minnesota (2008-2014); University of Wisconsin (1993-2008) **Career Related:** Founder, Climate, People and Environment Program (CPEP); Founder, Center for Sustainability and the Global Environment (SAGE); Gaylord Nelson Distinguished Professor of Environmental Studies; Instructor, Various Universities; Fellow, Aldo Leopold Leadership **Creative Works:** Author, 130 Peer-Reviewed Scientific Articles; Author, Articles, National Geographic, The New York Times, The Guardian, Scientific American **Awards:** Highly Cited Researcher, Thomson Reuters (2014); Heinz Award for the Environment (2014); Presidential Early Career Award for Scientists and Engineers; 21st Century Science Award, J.S. McDonnell Foundation; Sustainability Science Award, Ecological Society of America; Early Career Development Award, National Science Foundation

William Harper Forman Jr., JD

Title: Attorney at Law **Industry:** Law and Legal Services **Date of Birth:** 08/13/1936 **Place of Birth:** Houston **State/Country of Origin:** TX/USA **Parents:** William Harper Forman; Ermaleen (Lukas) Forman **Marital Status:** Married **Spouse Name:** Olive Goodwill Roberts (06/17/1967) **Children:** William Harper III **Education:** Graduate, Air War College Correspondence Program (1986); Master of Arts in Government, Louisiana State University, National Defense Education Act Fellow (1970); Postgraduate Coursework in Criminology, The College of William & Mary, Williamsburg, VA (1965); JD, Tulane University, New Orleans, LA (1961); Bachelor of Arts, Tulane University, New Orleans, LA (1958) **Certifications:** Notary Public, Orleans Parish, Louisiana (1975) **Career:** Professor, Naval War College (2000-2011); Adjunct Professor, Departments of History and Political Science, Tulane University (1995-1999); Member, Law Offices Of Inabnett, Suthon, Forman and Justrabo (1989-1995); Of Counsel, Law Office of Robert C. Evans (1986-1988); Private Practice (1977-1995); Counsel, Downtown Development District, New Orleans, LA (1975-1981); Attorney, City of New Orleans, Louisiana Community Improvement Agency (1972-1979); Attorney, Federal Trade Commission, New Orleans, LA (1969-1972) **Career Related:** Lecturer, International Law of War, Military Criminal Law, Tulane University (1978-1985); Lecturer, Military Criminal Law, Tulane University, University of New Orleans (1972-1991) **Civic:** Incorporator, Preservation Resource Center of New Orleans (1974); Vestry, Christ Church Cathedral (2009-2012); Senior Warden, Christ Church Cathedral (2003-2004); Vestry, Christ Church Cathedral (2000-2004); President, George Washington Chapter, Sons of the American Revolution (1995-1996); Vice President, George Washington Chapter, Sons of the American Revolution (1994-1995); Chapter Chairman, ROTC Awards Committee, George Washington Chapter, Louisiana Sons of the American Revolution (1987-2010); President, Louisiana Association, The Society of Cincinnati (1987-1989); Vice President, Louisiana Association, The Society of Cincinnati (1985-1987); Treasurer, Louisiana Association, The Society of Cincinnati (1983-1985); Vice President, Louisiana Sons of the American Revolution (1981-1987); Trustee, Louisiana Landmarks Society (1981-1983); Corresponding Secretary, Louisiana Landmarks Society (1979-1981); Trustee, Louisiana Landmarks Society (1978-1979); Chairman, ROTC Awards Committee, Louisiana Sons of the American Revolution (1975-1987); Louisiana State Consumer Advisory Board (1975-1981); President, Jefferson City Improvement Association, New Orleans, LA (1975-1979); Treasurer, Louisiana Landmarks Society (1974-1976); Treasurer, Preservation Resource Center of New Orleans (1974-1976); President, Louisiana Consumers' League (1972-1973); Director, Louisiana Consumers' League (1970-1975) **Military Service:** U.S. Air Force Reserve Duty, Lieutenant Colonel, Judge Advocate, International Law Division, U.S. Air Force Headquarters, Washington, DC (1984-1989); Lieutenant Colonel, Judge Advocate, U.S. Air Force Reserve, Keesler Air Force Base, Mississippi (1981-1984); Captain and Major, Judge Advocate, U.S. Air Force Reserve, Keesler Air Force Base, Mississippi (1968-1981); U.S. Air Force Active Duty, Captain, Staff Judge Advocate, U.S. Air Force, Bossier Air Force Base, Louisiana (1963-1967); Commissioned 1st Lieutenant Judge Advocate (Legal Officer), U.S. Air Force, Clark Air Force Base, Philippines (1961-1963) **Creative Works:** Author, "Notes on Contemporary Christianity, United States Policy & Torture," Sewanee Theological Review (2008); Author, "The Case Against Torture," The Officer (2007); Author, Texts, Louisiana State Historical Markers, Calumet Plantation and Jefferson City in New Orleans; Author, "Briefing Paper on the Law of Armed Conflict: Strategic Air War Planning & Operations by the U.S. Army Air Forces & U.S. Air Force," Washington, DC; Contributor, Articles, Professional Journals **Awards:** AV Preeminent Rating, Martindale-Hubbell (1986-Present); Meritorious Service Medal, U.S. Air Force Headquarters, Washington, DC **Bar Admissions:** U.S. Court of Military Appeals (1989); U.S. District Court for the Eastern District of Louisiana (1982); State of Louisiana (1961) **Marquis Who's Who Honors:** Albert Nelson Marquis Lifetime Achievement Award; Marquis Who's Who Top Professional **Why did you become involved in your profession or industry:** Mr. Forman became involved in his profession because he comes from a long line of lawyers. **Avocations:** Distance walking; Photography; Traveling **Political Affiliations:** Republican **Religion:** Episcopalian

Virginia Ann Foxx

Title: U.S. Representative from North Carolina; Ranking Member of the House Committee on Education and Labor **Industry:** Government Administration/Government Relations/Government Services **Date of Birth:** 06/29/1943 **Place of Birth:** Bronx **State/Country of Origin:** NY/USA **Parents:** Nunzio John Palmieri; Dollie (Garrison) Palmieri **Marital Status:** Married **Spouse Name:** Thomas A. Foxx **Children:** One Child **Education:** EdD in Curriculum and Teaching/Higher Education, University of North Carolina at Greensboro (1985); MA in College Teaching, University of North Carolina at Chapel Hill (1972); AB in English, University of North Carolina at Chapel Hill (1968) **Career:** Chairwoman, House Committee on Education and Labor (2017-Present); Secretary, U.S. House Republican Conference, Washington, DC (2013-Present); Member, U.S. House of Representatives from North Carolina's Fifth Congressional District, United States Congress, Washington, DC (2005-Present); Member, North Carolina State Senate, Raleigh, NC (1995-2004); President, Consultant, Mayland Community College, Spruce Pine, NC (1987-1994); Owner, Operator, Grandfather Nursery, Banner Elk, NC; Department Secretary, Management, North Carolina Department of Administration; Assistant Dean, General College, Appalachian State University; Professor, Sociology, Appalachian State University, Boone, NC; Professor, Caldwell Community College and Technical Institute, Hudson, NC; Secretary, Research Assistant, University of North Carolina at Chapel Hill **Civic:** Member, Watauga County Board of Education (1976-1988) **Awards:** Reagan Award, National Republican Congressional Committee (NRCC) (2010); Contributions to Sociology Award, North Carolina Sociological Association (2002); Alan Keith-Lucas Friend of Children Award, NC Licensed Child Care Association (2002); Guardian of Small Business Award, National Federation of Independent Business (2000); North Carolina Carpathian Award (1994); Distinguished Fundraising Award, YMCA (1993); Award, The Order of the Long Leaf Pine Society, North Carolina Governor Jim Martin (1992); North Carolina Distinguished Women's Award (1990); Award for Outstanding Citizenship and Exceptional Public Service, Watauga County League of Women Voters (1988); Outstanding Public Official Award, NC Christmas Tree Association **Memberships:** National Foundation for Women Legislators; American Legislative Exchange Council; NCCBI; NCCPPR; Women's Forum of North Carolina **Avocations:** Reading; Gardening **Political Affiliations:** Republican

Sylvan L. "Syl" Franklin

Title: Commercial Bank Executive **Industry:** Financial Services **Company Name:** Retired **Date of Birth:** 09/26/1934 **Place of Birth:** Sailor Springs **State/Country of Origin:** IL/USA **Parents:** Henry Franklin; Hilda I. (Thomann) Franklin **Marital Status:** Married **Spouse Name:** Jacqueline R. Benge (08/22/1954) **Children:** Kristy; Tracy; Deborah; Vicki; Rebecca; Parker (Grandchild); Harrison (Grandchild); Spencer (Grandchild); Graham (Grandchild); Madeliene (Grandchild) **Education:** Coursework, Graduate School of Banking, University of Wisconsin (1969-1971); BS in Commerce and Law, University of Illinois (1957) **Career:** Retired (2000); President, Chief Executive Officer, Board Of Directors, Herget National Bank, Pekin, IL (1987-2000); President, Chief Executive Officer, Board of Directors, First National Bank, Lincoln, IL (1975-1987); Senior Vice President, Board of Directors, First National Bank, Waukesha, WI (1973-1975); Vice President, Continental Illinois National Bank, Chicago, IL (1959-1973) **Career Related:** Board of Directors Tazewell Machine Works, Inc., Pekin, IL; Board of Directors, Pekin Insurance Companies, Pekin, IL **Civic:** Chairman, Pekin Economic Development Commission (1991-1992); Board of Directors, Peoria Area Economic Development Community (1990-1992); Peoria Civic Opera Board (1990-1991); Board of Directors, Lincoln Economic Development Corp. (1989); Lincoln Area Chamber of Commerce (1979-1985); Board of Directors, Everett M. Dirksen Congressional Research Foundation **Military Service:** First Lieutenant, U.S. Army (1957-1959); 122nd Ordnance BN, Germany **Awards:** Distinguished Service Award, Lincoln Area Chamber of Commerce (1985); Meritorious Service Award, University of Illinois Alumni Association (1981) **Memberships:** President, Pekin Country Club (1990-1991); Robert Morris Associates; Board of Directors, Pekin Community Concert Association; Indiana Order of Odd Fellows; Elks; Rotary International **Marquis Who's Who Honors:** Albert Nelson Marquis Lifetime Achievement Award; Marquis Who's Who Top Professional **To what do you attribute your success:** Mr. Franklin attributes his success to his management skills, as well as his talents for interviewing and selecting good co-workers. **Why did you become involved in your profession or industry:** Mr. Franklin became involved in his profession because of his interest in finance and banking. **Avocations:** Reading; Fishing; Travel **Religion:** United Methodist **Thoughts on Life:** Mr. Franklin feels he has been fortunate in life.

Herschel P. Franks

Title: Judge (Retired) **Industry:** Law and Legal Services **Company Name:** Tennessee Court of Appeals **Date of Birth:** 05/28/1930 **Place of Birth:** Savannah **State/Country of Origin:** TN/USA **Parents:** Herschel R. Franks; Pickens Vada Franks **Marital Status:** Married **Spouse Name:** Judy Black **Children:** Ramona **Education:** Diploma, The University of Tennessee, Knoxville; JD, The University of Tennessee, Knoxville; Coursework, University of Maryland; Physician Assistant Program, The University of Tennessee **Career:** Judge, Tennessee Court of Appeals (1978-Present); Presiding Judge, Tennessee Court of Appeals (2004-2012); Chancellor, Third Chancery Division, Hamilton County, TN (1970-1978); Partner, Harris, Moon, Meacham & Franks, Chattanooga, TN (1959-1970); Claims Attorney, United States Fidelity and Guaranty Company, Knoxville, TN (1958) **Career Related:** Special Justice, Tennessee Supreme Court (1979, 1986-1987, 2002-2004); With, Commission to Study Appellate Courts, Tennessee Court of Criminal Appeals (1990-1992); Special Judge, Tennessee Court of Criminal Appeals (1990-1992); Presiding Judge, Hamilton County Trial Courts (1977-1978) **Military Service:** With, United States Air Force (1950-1954); With, United States Air National Guard (1949-1950) **Awards:** Justice Francis F. Drowota III Award, Tennessee Bar Association (2009); Foundations of Freedom Award, Chattanooga Bar Association (1986); Community Service Award, Optimist International (1971); Merit Award, Tennessee Bar Association (1968-1969); Merit Award, American Bar Association (ABA) **Memberships:** President, Chattanooga Bar Association (1968-1969); Optimist International (1965-1966); American Bar Association (ABA); Institute Judicial Administration; Chattanooga Bar Foundation; Tennessee Bar Foundation; Mountain City Club; City Farmers Club; Phi Alpha Delta **Marquis Who's Who Honors:** Albert Nelson Marquis Lifetime Achievement Award **Why did you become involved in your profession or industry:** What attracted Hon. Franks to his career was neither his upbringing nor family, but his experience in the Air Force; he was involved in observing and participating in various court-martial instances and that sparked his interest in the law. It was then that he decided he wanted to go to law school. **Religion:** United Church of Christ **Thoughts on Life:** Hon. Franks served as a Tennessee judge for 42 years, which is one of the longest serving terms in the state's history.

Jane Fraser

Title: Chief Executive Officer **Industry:** Financial Services **Company Name:** Citi Latin America, Citigroup Inc. **Date of Birth:** 07/13/1967 **Place of Birth:** St Andrews **State/Country of Origin:** United Kingdom **Marital Status:** Married **Spouse Name:** Francisco Aristeguieta **Children:** Two Children **Education:** MBA, Harvard Business School (1994); MA in Economics, University of Cambridge (1988) **Career:** Chief Executive Officer, Citi Latin America, Citigroup Inc., Miami, FL (2015-Present); Chief Executive Officer, U.S. Consumer & Commercial Banking, CitiMortgage, Citigroup Inc. (2014-2015); Chief Executive Officer, CitiMortgage, Citigroup Inc. (2013-2014); Managing Director, Global Chief Executive Officer, Citi Private Bank, Citigroup Inc. (2009-2013); Global Head Strategy, Mergers & Acquisition, Citigroup Inc. (2007-2009); Head, Client Strategy & Management, Global Banking Division, Citigroup Inc., London, United Kingdom (2004-2007); Partner, McKinsey & Company, New York, NY and London, United Kingdom (1994-2004); Associate, Asesores Bursátiles, Spain (1990-1992); Analyst Mergers & Acquisition Department, Goldman Sachs, London, United Kingdom (1988-1990) **Civic:** Board of Directors, TouchFoundation (2006-Present) **Creative Works:** Author, "Race for the World" (1999); Contributor, Articles, Professional Journals **Awards:** Named, 50 Most Powerful Women in Business, Fortune Magazine (2014-2015); Named, 25 Women to Watch, American Banker (2013-2014); Named, 25 Most Powerful Women in Banking (2011-2012); Named, 25 Women to Watch, U.S. Banker (2009) **Memberships:** Council on Foreign Relations

Richard Fredricks

Title: Baritone **Industry:** Media & Entertainment **Date of Birth:** 08/15/1933 **Place of Birth:** Los Angeles **State/Country of Origin:** CA/USA **Parents:** Shannan Leigh; Stephanie Brooke; Sean Richard **Marital Status:** Divorced **Children:** Shannan Leigh; Stephanie Brooke; Sean Richard **Education:** Coursework, Voice Scholarship, University of Denver (1956-1957); Coursework in Pre-Engineering, El Camino Junior College (1954-1956) **Certifications:** Private Pilot's License, Single and Multi-Engine, Land and Sea; Aerobatics Proficient **Career:** Lab Engineer, Airesearch Manufacturing Company, El Segundo, CA (1955-1956); Major Voice Teacher, Master Classes **Career Related:** Instructor, Five Opera Videos; Performer, Live from Lincoln Center: The Ballad of Baby Doe, La Traviata, Manon, Roberto Devereux, Lizzie Borden; Performer, Eleven Performances in the Hollywood Bowl; Two-Time Performer, National Anthem **Military Service:** Honorable Discharge (1954); U S Navy (1951-1954); 105 Howitzer Battalion (1950); Submarine Duty, USS Tiru; Submarine Duty, USS Bergall; Submarine Duty, USS Irex; U.S. Marine Corps Reserve **Creative Works:** Principal Baritone, Metropolitan Opera (1975-1985); Principal Baritone, San Francisco Opera (1961-1966); Principal Baritone, The New York City Opera (1960-1981); Principal Baritone, Various Opera Companies; Leading Role, Rigoletto; Leading Role, La Forza Del Destino; Leading Role, Thais; Leading Role, La Gioconda; Leading Role, Don Giovanni; Leading Role, Trovatore; Leading Role, Don Carlo; Leading Role, Il Barbiere Di Siviglia; Leading Role, Il Puritani; Leading Role, Lucia; Leading Role, Un Ballo In Maschera; Leading Role, Tosca; Soloist, Philadelphia Orchestra; Soloist, Chicago Symphony; Soloist, San Francisco Symphony; Soloist, Cleveland Orchestra; Soloist, Boston Symphony; Soloist, Boston Pops; Soloist, New York Philharmonic; Soloist, L.A. Philharmonic; Santiago Opera; Israel Philharmonic; Hamburg Staatsoper; Frankfurt Staatsoper; La Fenice, Venice; Starred, Belshazzar's Feast; Starred, Carmina Burana; Starred, Cantata Misericorium; Starred, Kennedy Center, New York, NY; Guest Starred, "The Odd Couple"; Guest Starred, "Quincey"; Guest Starred, "Tonight Show"; Guest Starred, "Merv Griffin Show"; Guest Starred, "Mike Douglas Show"; Guest Starred, "Dinah Shore Show" **Memberships:** Bohemian, San Francisco, CA; Lotos, New York, NY; Players, New York, NY **Marquis Who's Who Honors:** Albert Nelson Marquis Lifetime Achievement Award; Marquis Who's Who Top Professional **Why did you become involved in your profession or industry:** When Mr. Fredricks left the submarine service, his superiors told him that they wanted to recommend him to officer candidate school. However, he had already decided to become an engineer. He moved back to Los Angeles and enrolled at El Camino Junior College as a pre-engineering student. Shortly after enrolling, he went into the choral office, hoping to sing. He found himself performing for the choral director, who was highly impressed. In the years that followed, Mr. Fredericks pursued a career in singing and performing. He has been a voice teacher of note since 1962. Later, while at the Metropolitan Opera, in 1983, he participated in an International Symposium of Voice. At the Alice Tully Hall, he was asked to speak briefly on the subject of starting voice lessons with a student. At that presentation, all 145 of Mr. Fredericks' former students filled the room. The session went swimmingly, and afterward, he was asked to join the faculty at Alice Truly Hall. Mr. Fredricks' performance schedule rendered the offer unfeasible, at the time. In 2001, he joined the faculty at the University of Southern California in Los Angeles. **Political Affiliations:** Conservative **Thoughts on Life:** When Mr. Fredricks left Los Angeles, he came to New York City as a leading baritone in the opera. His friend, J. Reuben Hawking, asked if he could perform in "The Caller," to which Mr. Fredericks said yes. He proceeded to audition and consequently earned a leading role. Throughout his life, Mr. Fredericks was responsible for bringing back many great singers who had stopped performing. He said, "In Howard [Keel]'s case, he hadn't sung higher than a middle C for seven years. I brought him back to full Howard...in one week and he went on two record three Gold Records in England and sing on 'Love Boat,' which revived his career. Pat [Boone] hadn't sung in 14 years ... I brought his voice back in two weeks. He's singing at the Grand Ole Opry house next week .. at the ripe old age of 86! Andy Williams was canceling his 17 week season in Branson...I brought him back, twice in two years, with six-ten sessions. I prepared Renata Scotto for her final concert at the Paris Opera ... fixed the wobble and her consistent 'break' between high B flat and C...ultimately adding 18 years to her career. I'm still making professional singers outta people who didn't know the 'the voice is a wind instrument!' and I showed them how it works!"

Bryant C. Freeman

Title: Foreign Language Educator **Industry:** Education/Educational Services **Date of Birth:** 06/26/1931 **Place of Birth:** Richmond **State/Country of Origin:** VA/USA **Parents:** Loomin Oscar Freeman, Jr.; Virginia Bourke (Oliver) Freeman **Marital Status:** Married **Spouse Name:** Stephanie L. Freeman (1986) **Children:** Timothy Oliver Freeman **Education:** PhD, Yale University, New Haven, CT (1961); MA, Yale University, New Haven, CT (1954); BA, University of Virginia, Charlottesville, VA (1953) **Career:** Founder and Director, Institute of Haitian Studies (1992-2006); Professor, University of Kansas, Lawrence, KS (1989-2006); Professor, French, University of Kansas, Lawrence, KS (1971-2006); United Nations Observer, Haiti (1993-1994); Chairman, Department of French, Francophone & Italian Studies, University of Kansas, Lawrence, KS (1971-1976); Associate Professor, French, University of Virginia, Charlottesville, VA (1966-1971); Assistant Professor, French, University of Virginia, Charlottesville, VA (1961-1966); Instructor, French, Yale University, New Haven, CT (1955-1959) **Career Related:** Consultant on Haitian Creole, Indiana University Bloomington, Bloomington, IN (1991-Present); Lecturer, Kansas Committee on the Humanities (1991-Present); Consultant on Haiti, U.S. Department of Justice (1988-Present); Consultant on Haiti, U.S. Immigration and Naturalization Service (1991-1992) **Military Service:** Major-General, U.S. and U.N. Peace-Keeping Forces, Haiti; Instructor, U.S. Peace Corps Volunteers **Creative Works:** Author, Book, "Foklo Peyi Dayiti Liv 2: Haitian Folktales in Haitian Language" (2002); Author, Book, "Survival Haitian" (1999); Author, Book, "Third-World Folk Beliefs and Practices: Haitian Medical Anthropology" (1998); Author, "Haitian-English Medical Phraseology" (1997); Author, Book, "Haitian-English Dictionary" (1996); Author, Book, "Toussaint's Consitution (1801)" (1994); Author, Book, "Haitian Creole Medical Dictionary with Glossary of Food and Drink" (1992); Author, Book, "Survival Creole" (1992); Author, Book, "Chita Pa Bay: Elementary Readings in Haitian Creole" (1984); Author, Book, "Concordances Du Theatre Et Des Poesies De Jean Racine" (1968); Editor, Collection of the Works of Carrié Paultre; Leading Haitian Novelist **Awards:** Fulbright Scholar, Paris, France (1959-1961); Woodrow Wilson Fellow, Yale University (1953-1955); Lifetime Achievement Award for Service to the Haitian People; U.S. Department of Justice Special Service Award; Numerous Kansas Humanities Council and Kansas French Educator of the Year Awards; Lifetime Achievement Award, American Embassy, Haiti; Award for Service, Haitian Community, Miami, FL **Memberships:** Life Member, Modern Language Association (MLA); Life Member, American Association of Teachers of French; Board of Directors, Haitian Studies Association; Society for Caribbean Linguistics; Lawrence Symphony Orchestra; Alvamar Country Club; Phi Beta Kappa **Marquis Who's Who Honors:** Albert Nelson Marquis Lifetime Achievement Award **Why did you become involved in your profession or industry:** Mr. Freeman became involved in his profession because his mother was of French heritage. She encouraged him to study French, which he fell in love with in high school. **Avocations:** Music (contrabassoon); Dogs

Melanie L. Freese, MLS

Title: Associate Professor of Library Services **Industry:** Library Management/Library Services **Company Name:** Hofstra University **Date of Birth:** 05/12/1945 **Place of Birth:** Mineola **State/Country of Origin:** NY/USA **Parents:** Dr. Walter C. Freese; Agnes (Jensen) Freese **Marital Status:** Married **Spouse Name:** Lisa Beth Gundermann **Education:** MLS, Long Island University Post (1977); EdM in Elementary Education, Hofstra University (1969); EdB in Elementary Education, Minor in History, Hofstra University (1967) **Certifications:** Certified Public Librarian (1977); Certified Teacher, Nursery to Sixth Grade, State of New York (1969) **Career:** Assistant Dean, Chairwoman of Technical Services, Joan and Donald E. Axinn Library, Hofstra University (1999-2001); Senior Catalog Librarian, Hofstra University (1984-1999); Assistant to Social Work Librarian, Assistant to Acquisitions Librarian and Biographical Searcher, Reserve Librarian, Circulation Assistant, Swirbul Library, Adelphi University, Garden City, NY (1972-1983); Elementary School Teacher, Roosevelt and Massapequa, NY (1967-1971); Grace Episcopal Day School, Massapequa, NY (1959-1970) **Career Related:** Establishing Library Resident, Wayside Home School for Girls (1993); Library Founder, St Peter's Lutheran Church, Baldwin, NY (1975) **Civic:** President, Board of Advisers, Business and Professional Woman of Nassau County Inc. (1990-2010); Board of Advisers, Business and Professional Woman of Nassau County Inc. (1985-2010); Professional Women of Nassau County (1984-2008); Board of Directors, Academic and Special Libraries Division, Nassau County Library Association (1984-2005); Chair, Institutional Services Committee, Nassau County Library Association (1992-1996); President, Academic and Special Libraries Division of Nassau County Library Association (1984-1986, Board, 1983-1993); Sunday School Teacher, Librarian, Lector, St. Peter's Lutheran Church, Baldwin, NY; Story Teller, Leader, Vacation Bible School; Baldwin Life Stitches **Creative Works:** Author, "Fostering Communication and Understanding at Hofstra University's Axinn Library," PNLA Quarterly (2002); Author, "Charles Leonard Woolley, 1880-1960," Pierian Press, Ann Arbor, MI (1989); Author, "Missing Links: Smart barcodes and inventory analysis at Hofstra University's Axinn Library," Library and Archival Security (1989); Reviewer, Libraries Alive! Lutheran Libraries; Reviewer, Public Services Quarterly, Taylor and Francis **Awards:** Woman of the Year, Business and Professional Women of Nassau County, Inc. (1994); Twentieth Century Award for Achievement, International Biographical Centre, Cambridge, England (1994); Distinguished Service Award, St. Peter's Lutheran Church, Baldwin, NY (1993); International Order of Merit, International Biographical Centre, Cambridge, England (1980) **Memberships:** Vice President, Woman's Advance Club, Baldwin, NY (2019-Present); Woman's Advance Club, Baldwin, NY (2012-Present); Baldwin Civic Association, Inc.; OLAC; NCLA; American Library Association; Kappa Delta Pi; International Honor Society in Education; Beta Phi Mu; Women's Advanced Club of Baldwin **Marquis Who's Who Honors:** Marquis Who's Who Top Professional **To what do you attribute your success:** Ms. Freese attributes her success to her education and work ethic. **Why did you become involved in your profession or industry:** Ms. Freese became involved in her profession after gaining experience as a support staff member at the academic library at Adelphi University. **Avocations:** Knitting; Needlework; Crocheting; Piano **Thoughts on Life:** Ms. Freese has presented numerous training workshops on various aspects of cataloging and classification to faculty and staff in both technical and public services. She also reviews materials for "Libraries Alive," a publication of the National Church Library Association. She authored a chapter titled, "Smart Barcodes and Inventory Analysis," which appeared in the ninth volume of Library and Archival Security in 1989, and in the 66th volume of PNLA Quarterly. Libraries and librarians are still needed in this 21st century technological world. Librarians are information specialists who can help users navigate the ever-expanding informational universe. Google can never replace libraries or librarians. Librarians, as trained information specialists, can provide patrons with search strategies and tools to successfully complete research and find what they are looking for effectively and efficiently. Libraries are increasingly becoming digital repositories for information. Libraries are becoming more virtual as they become increasingly digitized. As long as people read and seek information there will be a need for libraries, librarians and especially books, either traditional books or electronic. Ms. Freese sees herself as an educator as well as an information specialist. She shares her knowledge gained over a 40-year career with others in her field and also the students she interacts with. Currently she is mentoring a younger colleague who is learning to catalog materials for the Music Library at Hofstra University. Mentoring is a vital part of any profession. Library schools teach the theoretical principles of librarianship, but she can give the pragmatic and practical applications beyond the theoretical that are so necessary for the librarian in the field.

Robert C. Frere

Title: Clinical Associate Professor **Industry:** Education/Educational Services **Company Name:** Brody School of Medicine, East Carolina University **Date of Birth:** 11/24/1953 **Place of Birth:** Cleveland **State/Country of Origin:** OH/USA **Parents:** Ralph Emil Frere; Katherine (Gilbo) Frere **Marital Status:** Divorced **Spouse Name:** Susan Cramer Gilliam, (10/17/1981) **Children:** Elizabeth; Garrett; Zachary; Olivia **Education:** Clinical Neurophysiology Fellowship, Mayo Clinic, Rochester, MN (1988-1989); Neurology Resident, Barnes Hospital, St. Louis, MO (1985-1988); Intern in Internal Medicine, Ohio State University Hospitals (1984-1985); MD, The Ohio State University (1984); MS, Neuroscience, University of Michigan (1981); BS, The Ohio State University (1975) **Certifications:** Diplomate, National Board Medical Examiners; Diplomate, American Board Psychiatry and Neurology; Diplomate, American Board Clinical Neurophysiology; Diplomate, American Board Electrodiagnostic Medicine **Career:** Clinical Associate Professor, Neuroogy, Brody School of Medicine, East Carolina University (2013-Present); Staff Neurologist, East Carolina Neurology, East Carolina University, (2000-2013); Staff Neurologist, Department of Medicine, St. John's Mercy Medical Center, St. Louis, MO (1989-2000); Research Assistant, Department of Neurology, University of Michigan Medical School (1979-1981); Quality Control Analyst, The Harshaw Chemical Co., Elyria, OH (1978-1979); Secondary Science Teacher in French, The Peace Corps, Zaire, Africa (1975-1977) **Career Related:** Medical Director, Hunter ALS Clinic, Greenville, NC (2007-Present); Member, Professional Advisory Board, Epilepsy Foundation of St. Louis (1995-2000) **Memberships:** Fellow, American Electroencephalographic Society; American Academy of Neurology; Mayo Alumni Association; American Epilepsy Society; St. Louis Society of Neurological Sciences; American Association of Electrodiagnostic Medicine **Marquis Who's Who Honors:** Albert Nelson Marquis Lifetime Achievement Award; Marquis Who's Who Top Professional **Why did you become involved in your profession or industry:** Dr. Frere became involved in his profession because he had an interest in science and the brain. It seemed to be a natural sub-specialty he would go into when he attended medical school. **Avocations:** Biking; Tennis; Hiking; Travel **Political Affiliations:** Independent **Religion:** Christian

Peter J. Freyd, PhD

Title: Professor **Industry:** Education/Educational Services **Company Name:** University of Pennsylvania **Date of Birth:** 02/05/1936 **Place of Birth:** Evanston **State/Country of Origin:** IL/USA **Parents:** Paul Robert Freyd; Pauline Margaret (Pattinson) Freyd **Marital Status:** Married **Spouse Name:** Pamela Parker (01/01/1957) **Children:** Jennifer Joy; Gwendolyn Ann **Education:** PhD, Princeton University (1960); MA, Woodrow Wilson Fellow, Princeton University (1959); AB, Brown University, Magna Cum Laude (1958) **Career:** Director, Laboratory for Logic and Computation (1993-Present); Professor of Computer Information Science, University of Pennsylvania (1987-Present); Professor of Mathematics, University of Pennsylvania (1968-Present); Faculty, University of Pennsylvania (1962-Present); Chairman, Graduate Group on Mathematics, University of Pennsylvania (1982-1987); Teacher in Dramatics, American School, Shiraz, Iran (1968); J.F. Ritt Instructor in Mathematics, Columbia University, New York, NY (1960-1962); Instructor, Academy Potential Project, Brown University, Providence, RI (1960); Assistant Instructor in Mathematics, Princeton University (1959-1960); Instructor in Mathematics, National Science Foundation Program, Brown University, Providence, RI (1958-1959); Assistant Instructor of Mathematics, Brown University, Providence, RI (1957); Instructor in Statistics, Batton, Barton, Durstine and Osborn, New York, NY (1956); Teacher in Carpentry, Camp Cragged Mountain Farm, Freedom, NH (1954); Teacher in Art, Conti Art School, Providence, RI (1952-1954) **Career Related:** Visiting Professor in Computer Science, Carnegie Mellon University (1988-1989); Visiting Researcher, University of Parma (1990); Visiting Researcher, University of Milan (1986); Visiting Researcher, University of Sydney (1985); Visiting Professor, University of Louvain, Belgium (1981); Fellow, St. John's College, Cambridge University, England (1980-1981); Visiting Professor, University of Chicago (1980); Visiting Researcher, University of Mexico (1975); Lecturer, Canadian National Research Seminar (1974); Visiting Researcher, Swiss Federal Institute of Technology, Zurich, Switzerland (1969); Adviser, Pahlavi University, Shiraz, Iran (1968) **Creative Works:** Editor, Journal of Knot Theory and Its Ramifications (1991-Present); International Journal of Algebra and Computation (1990-Present); Editor, Mathematical Structures in Computer Science (1989-Present); Editor, Theoretical Computer Science (1988-Present); Co-Author, "Categories, Allegories" (1990); Founder, Journal of Pure and Applied Algebra (1970); Author, "Abelian Categories" (1964) **Awards:** Fulbright Scholar, Australia (1971) **Memberships:** Isaac Newton Institute (1995); Phi Beta Kappa; Sigma Xi **Marquis Who's Who Honors:** Albert Nelson Marquis Lifetime Achievement Award; Marquis Who's Who Top Professional **Why did you become involved in your profession or industry:** He became involved in his profession because he loves to do mathematics, and he was able to find a culture that would pay him to do what he loved.

Jeffrey M. Friedman

Title: Top Scientist **Industry:** Sciences **Date of Birth:** 07/20/1954 **Place of Birth:** Orlando **State/Country of Origin:** FL/USA **Marital Status:** Married **Spouse Name:** Lily **Children:** Alexandra; Nathalie **Education:** Postgraduate Fellow, Weill Cornell Medicine (1980-1981); Medical Residency, Albany Medical College (1980); PhD, Rockefeller University (1986); MD, Albany Medical Center (1977); BS, Rensselaer Polytechnic Institute (1973); Diploma, Hewlett High School (1971) **Career:** Marilyn M. Simpson Professorship, Howard Hughes Medical Institute, The Rockefeller University (1998); Investigator, Howard Hughes Medical Institute, The Rockefeller University (1996-1998); Associate Investigator, Howard Hughes Medical Institute, The Rockefeller University (1991-1996); Assistant Investigator, Howard Hughes Medical Institute, The Rockefeller University (1986-1991) **Creative Works:** Contributor, 150 Publications, 10 Book Chapters **Awards:** Breakthrough Prize in Life Sciences (2020); Wolf Prize in Medicine (2019); King Faisal International Prize in Medicine (2013); Co-Recipient, Frontiers of Knowledge Award in Biomedicine, BBVA Foundation (2012); UCL Prize Lecture in Clinical Science, University College London (2012); 11th Endocrine Regulation Prize, Foundation Ipsen (2012); Albert Lasker Basic Medical Research Award (2010); Robert J. and Claire Passano Foundation Award (2010); Citation Laureate, Thomson Reuters (2010); Hamdan Award for Medical Research Excellence (2009); Shaw Prize for Life Sciences and Medicine (2009); Keio Medical Science Prize (2009); Danone International Prize (2007); Jessie Stevenson Kovalenko Medal (2006); Gairdner International Award, Gairdner Foundation (2005); Passano Award, The Passano Foundation, Inc. (2005); Award for Distinguished Achievement in Metabolic Research, Bristol-Myers Squibb (2001); Rolf Luft Award, Karolinska University Hospital (2000); Endocrinology Transatlantic Medal (2000); Steven C. Beering Award (1999); Jacobaeus Prize (1997); Heinrich Wieland Prize (1996); Best of Science, TIME (1994, 1996); Best of Science Award, Popular Science (1995) **Memberships:** American Academy of Arts & Sciences (2013); Foreign Member, The Royal Swedish Academy of Sciences (2005); National Academy of Sciences (2001)

Richard Charles Friedman, MD

Title: 1) Psychiatrist 2) Adjunct Research Professor of Psychology 3) Clinical Professor **Industry:** Medicine & Health Care **Company Name:** 1) New York Hospital 2) Derner Institute of Advanced Psychological Studies, Adelphi University 3) Cornell University Medical College **Date of Birth:** 01/20/1941 **Place of Birth:** New York **State/Country of Origin:** NY/USA **Parents:** William Friedman; Henrietta Friedman **Marital Status:** Married **Spouse Name:** Susan Matorin (11/24/1979) **Children:** Jeremiah Simon **Education:** Graduate Coursework, Columbia University (1978); Chief Resident, New York State Psychiatric Institute (1969-1970); Chief Resident, Department of Psychiatry, Columbia Presbyterian Medical Center, New York, NY (1969-1970); Resident in Psychiatry, New York State Psychiatric Institute (1967-1969); Resident in Psychiatry, Columbia Presbyterian Medical Center (1967-1969); MD, University of Rochester, NY (1966); BA, Bard College, Annandale-on-Hudson, NY (1961) **Certifications:** Diplomate, American Board of Psychiatry and Neurology, New York (1973) **Career:** Psychiatrist, New York Hospital (1996-Present); Clinical Professor, Cornell University Medical College (1996-Present); Lecturer in Psychiatry, Columbia University (1994-Present); Adjunct Research Professor of Psychology, Derner Institute of Advanced Psychological Studies, Adelphi University, NY (1989-Present); Associate Clinical Professor of Psychiatry, Columbia University (1986-1994); Associate Psychiatrist, St. Luke's-Roosevelt Hospital Center, New York, NY (1986-1994); Clinical Associate Professor of Psychiatry, Cornell University Medical College (1983-1986); Associate Psychiatrist, New York Hospital-Cornell Medical Center, White Plains, NY (1981-1986); Associate Professor of Clinical Psychiatry, Cornell University Medical College (1981-1983); Assistant Professor of Clinical Psychiatry, Cornell University Medical College, New York, NY (1977-1981); Adjunct Assistant Professor, School of Public Health, Columbia University (1977-1979); Assistant Professor, of Clinical Psychiatry, Columbia University (1977); Associate Psychiatrist, Presbyterian Hospital (1976-1981); Instructor of Clinical Psychiatry, College of Physicians and Surgeons, Columbia University (1973-1976); Assistant Psychiatrist, Presbyterian Hospital, NY, NY (1972-1976); Chief of In-Patient Psychiatry, William Beaumont General Hospital, El Paso, TX (1970-1971) **Career Related:** Associate Editor (2003-Present); Editorial Board Member, Archives of Sexual Behavior (1998-Present); Consultant (1997-Present); Editor-in-Chief, Psychodynamic Psychiatry (2012); Co-Leader, Group for the Advancement of Psychiatry, Dallas, TX (2004); President, American College of Psychoanalysts, Dallas, TX (1997-1998); Assistant Editor, Journal of The American Academy of Psychoanalysis and Dynamic Psychiatry (1989-2002); International Journal of Sex Research; Psychodynamic Psychiatry: The Official Journal of the American Academy of Psychoanalysis and Dynamic Psychiatry; Member, Consultant, Joint Committee of the American Psychoanalytic Association, New York, NY; American Academy of Psychoanalysis and Dynamic Psychiatry **Military Service:** Major, Medical Corps, U.S. Army (1970-1972); Major, William Beaumont General Hospital; Captain, U.S. Army **Creative Works:** Editor, "Psychonynamm Psychiatry Sturnol" (2012); Author, "Male Homosexuality: A Contemporary Psychoanalytic Perspective"; Editor, "Behavior and the Menstrual Cycle"; Co-Author, "Sexual Orientation and Psychoanalysis: Sexual Science and Clinical Practice"; Co-Editor, "Masculinity and Sexuality: Selected Topics in the Psychology of Men"; Co-Editor, "Sexuality: New Perspectives"; Co-Editor, "Sex Differences in Behavior"; Speaker, Invited Lecturer, Psychoanalysis, Psychotherapy, Sexual Orientation, Gender Role Behavior, Homosexuality, Historical Issues and Homophobia from a Psychoanalytic Perspective; Contributor, Articles, Professional Journals; Co-Leader, Human Sexuality Committee **Awards:** Recipient, Best Doctors in America Award, Castle Connolly Medical Ltd. (2006-Present); Recipient, John and Samuel Bard Award, Bard College (2011); Recipient, Presidential Award, Academy of Psychoanalysis and Dynamic Psychiatry (2009); Recipient, Mary S. Sigourney Award, International Psychoanalytic Association and The Sigourney Trust (2009); Recipient, American Henry and M. Page Laughlin Distinguished Teaching Award, American College of Psychoanalysts (2002); Recipient, Henry P. Laughlin Award (2002); Honoree, Teacher of the Year, Cornell University Medical College (1998); Recipient, Laughlin Award, Columbia University (1970) **Memberships:** American Psychiatric Association; International Psychoanalytic Association; Group for the Advancement of Psychiatry; American Psychoanalytic Association; Association for Psychoanalytic Medicine; American Association for the Advancement of Science; International Academy of Sex Research **Avocations:** Piano; Playing Scrabble; Walking; History; Literature; Reading

Oris D. Friesen, PhD

Title: Software Engineer; Historian **Industry:** Information Technology and Services **Company Name:** Future Information Technologies **Date of Birth:** 01/4/1940 **Place of Birth:** York **State/Country of Origin:** AZ/USA **Parents:** Harry H. Friesen; Malita Wanda (Ratzlaff) Friesen **Marital Status:** Married **Spouse Name:** Carey Lea (Burbank) Friesen (5/28/1964) **Children:** Isabelle Anne; Aric Alan (Deceased 2018) **Education:** PhD, Arizona State University, Tempe, AZ (1982); MA, University of Arizona, Tucson, AZ (1966); BS, University of Arizona, Tucson, AZ (1964) **Career:** Consultant, Field (2002-Present); President, Future Information Technology (2000-Present); Co-Founder, Ontopilot (2008-2019); Research Professor, Computer Science and Engineering, Arizona State University, Tempe, AZ (1999-2001); Engineering Fellow, Database Management, Bull Worldwide Information Systems, Phoenix, AZ (1990-1999); Engineering Fellow, Database Management, Honeywell Information Systems, Phoenix, AZ (1984-1990); Database System Designer, Honeywell Information Systems, Phoenix, AZ (1970-1984); Computer System Designer, General Electric, Phoenix, AZ (1969-1970); Computer System Analyst, Computer Sciences Corporation, Richland, WA (1967-1969) **Career Related:** Board of Directors, GAZeL Greater Arizona E-Learning Association (2000-Present); Vice Chair, Arizona Learning Tech. Partnership (1996-Present); Charter Member and Officer, Steering Committee, Arizona Telecommunications and Information Council Foundation Group of Arizona Governor's Strategic Partnership for Economic Development (1994-Present); International Council on Systems Engineers (2018); Founder, Chairman, Organizer, XPRIZE Think Tank, Phoenix, AZ (2015-2017); Director, eLearning Systems for Arizona Teachers and Students (2006-2010); Adjunct Faculty, Information Assurance, Cyber Forensics, Software Quality Engineering, Digital Visual Literacy, Mesa Community College, Mesa, AZ (2002-2009); Chairman, Manager, Wireless Fidelity Security, for First Responders Project, Arizona Telecommunications and Information Council (1999-2006); Research Professor, Computer Science, Arizona State University, Tempe, AZ (1999-2001); Treasurer, Steering Committee for International Conference on Deductive and Object-Oriented Databases, Scottsdale, AZ (1997-2000); Adjunct Professor, Engineering, Arizona State University, Tempe, AZ (1984-1999); Member, Industrial Council, College of Engineering, Northern Arizona University, Flagstaff, AZ (1995-1999); Board of Directors, ACTC Technologies, Calgary, Alberta, Canada (1996-1998); General Chairman, International Conference on Deductive and Object-Oriented Databases, Scottsdale, AZ (1991-1994); Vice Chairman, Database Standards, American National Standards Institute, Washington (1980-1985); Rapporteur, Database Standards, International Standards Organizations, Geneva (1984-1985); Arizona Representative, North American Free Trade Association **Civic:** Arizona Precinct Committeeman, Democratic Party (2017-Present); Officer, Steering Committee for Arizona Telecommunications and Information Council, Foundation of Arizona Governor's Strategic Partnership for Economic Development (1994-Present); Phoenix Futures Forum (1988-1991); Officer, North Tatum Community Homeowners Association, Phoenix, AZ (1985-1988) **Military Service:** U.S. Marine Corps Reserves (1957-1965) **Creative Works:** Author, "Software Integrity Assessment: A Guide for Software Maintenance and Development" (2020); Author, "China Reporting: An Oral History of American Journalism in the 1930's & 1940's" (1987); Editor, "Proceedings of Phoenix Conference on Computers and Communications" (1987); Contributor, Articles; Contributor, Professional Journals **Awards:** Honeywell's H. W. Sweatt Award for Engineers/Scientists (1978) **Memberships:** International Council on Systems Engineering (2018-Present); Vice Chairman, Globecom 97 Conference, IEEE, (1995-1997); General Chairman, Phoenix Conference on Computers and Communications, IEEE (1990-1991); Association for Computing Machinery; Association for Asian Studies; American Historical Association; Organization of American Historians **Marquis Who's Who Honors:** Albert Nelson Marquis Lifetime Achievement Award **To what do you attribute your success:** Dr. Friesen was mentored by Charles W. Bachman in database technology and Stephen R. MacKinnion in Chinese history. **Why did you become involved in your profession or industry:** Dr. Friesen became involved in his profession because he was originally a math major. When he was in school in the 1960s, there was no such thing as computer science. As technology evolved, he used his background in mathematics to experiment with computer programming, then database management and software engineering. When he was completing a bachelor's degree, he became interested in Chinese language, and eventually went on to earn a degree in Asian literature and languages. **Avocations:** Chinese language; Genealogy **Political Affiliations:** Democrat

Kenneth Fuchs

Title: Composer **Industry:** Other **Date of Birth:** 07/01/1956 **Marital Status:** Married **Spouse Name:** Chris von Rosenvinge (4/28/2009) **Career:** Composer, Naxos Digital Services Ltd. **Career Related:** Professor of Music Composition, University of Connecticut; London Symphony Orchestra; American String Quartet **Awards:** Grammy Award for Best Classical Compendium (2018)

John Cronin Fullam

Title: Clarinetist **Industry:** Media & Entertainment **Date of Birth:** 12/19/1951 **Place of Birth:** New York **State/Country of Origin:** NY/USA **Parents:** Francis A. Fullam Jr.; Helen (Cronin) Fullam **Marital Status:** Married **Spouse Name:** Lois Robinson **Children:** Matthew; Janice **Education:** Diploma, Orchestral Studies, Mozateum Academy, Salzburg, Austria (1976); MusM, Julliard School (1975); MusB, Julliard School (1974) **Career:** Principal Clarinetist, Buffalo Philharmonic (1992-Present); Professor of Clarinet, State University Of New York, Buffalo, NY (1993-Present); Associate Principal Clarinetist, Portland Symphony (1990-1992); Professor of Clarinet, Director Chamber Music, Boston Conservatory (1989-1992); Principal Clarinetist, Boston-Philharmonic (1988-1992); Professor of Clarinet, Thayer Conservatory (1988-1992); Professor of Clarinet, Worcester Polytechnic Institute (1988-1989); Professor of Clarinet, Utah University (1987-1988); Associate Principal Clarinetist, Utah Symphony Orchestra, Salt Lake City, UT (1986-1988); Principal Clarinetist, Central Massachusetts Symphony, Worcester, MA (1986-1988); Principal Clarinetist, Municipal Symphony, Caracas, Venezuela (1984-1985); Principal Clarinetist, Caracas Philharmonic (1980-1984); Associate Principal Clarinetist, National Orchestral Association Orchestra, New York, NY (1978-1980); Principal Clarinetist, International Symphony Venice, Italy (1976-1977) **Career Related:** Professor, Clarinet, Fredonia University (1997-Present); Raycroft Festival Chamber Players (1996-Present); Buffalo Wind Quintet (1994-Present); Guest Professor, Clarinet, Studio-Eastman School (1994-1995); Marlboro Music Festival Professor, Philharmonic Conservatory, Caracas, Venezuela (1980-1985); Soloist, Avery Fisher Hall, Lincoln Center, Carnegie Hall, New York, NY **Creative Works:** Recording Artist, Marlboro, Pro Arte, Masters, Pickwick and Mode Labels, Venezuelan National TV and Radio, Radio Hong Kong **Awards:** C.D. Jackson Master Award (1977); Grantee, Berkshire Music Center, Tanglewood, NY (1977); Award, National Arts Club, New York, NY (1973); Diploma D'Honore, Government of Italy (1971) **Memberships:** American Federation of Musicians; Florida Local 427-721; Florida Gulf Coast Musicians Association **Marquis Who's Who Honors:** Albert Nelson Marquis Lifetime Achievement Award; Marquis Who's Who Top Professional **Avocations:** Photography; Physical fitness; Nautilus; Jogging; Swimming; Biking; traveling; His dog; Chamber ensembles; Arrangements

Blake Fuller

Title: Operator **Industry:** Food & Restaurant Services **Company Name:** Chicken Salad Chick **Certifications:** High School Diploma **Career:** Operator, Chicken Salad Chick (2015) **Awards:** Recognized as the Number One Sales Volume Store (2018); Named Best New Business (2018) **To what do you attribute your success:** Mr. Fuller attributes his success to his faith in God and he is grateful for the many blessings he has received. **Why did you become involved in your profession or industry:** Mr. Fuller became involved in his profession because initially his dad, David Fuller, was a business owner and he came from a broken and poor home. He decided that he did not want the same for his family and was determined to be successful. Seeing his dad and knowing his story gave him the drive and influenced him to go into business on his own. Mr. Fuller was a food broker for about five years and loved to work in kitchens. He then got the opportunity to meet the founders of Chicken Salad Chick, Stacey and then husband, Kevin, when he was pitching his sales calls. He learned a little about their story and saw the success they were having. He got the opportunity to go into business and be a franchisee with his wife and a couple partners in 2015. He and his wife signed a bill to do multiple units in multiple locations. They own and operate two businesses now and hope to do more.

Karen E. Gable, EdD

Title: Health Sciences Educator **Industry:** Education/Educational Services **Company Name:** Indiana University, Indianapolis Campus **Date of Birth:** 11/12/1939 **Place of Birth:** Des Moines **State/Country of Origin:** IA/USA **Parents:** John Emmitt Clay; Mabel Irene (Davis) Clay **Marital Status:** Married **Spouse Name:** Robert W. Gable, Junior (02/04/61) **Children:** Susan Kay; Barbara Lynne; Robert John Kent **Education:** EdD, Indiana University (1985); MS in Education, Indiana University (1979); BS in Education, Indiana University (1976); AS in Dental Hygiene, Indiana University, School of Dentistry (1969) **Certifications:** Registered Dental Hygienist, Indiana University (1969); Certified Dental Assistant, Indiana University **Career:** Professor Emerita, Indiana University, Indianapolis (2006-Present); Retired (2006); Chair, Department of Health Science, Indiana University (2002-2006); Program Director, Indiana University (1994-2006); Associate Professor, School of Health and Rehabilitation Sciences, Indiana University (1994-2006); Clinical Instructor, Dental Hygiene Program, School of Dentistry, Indiana University (1976-1994) **Civic:** Secretary, Avon Community Schools Building Corporation **Creative Works:** Contributor, Articles, Professional Journals; Speaker, Multiple National and International Presentations **Awards:** Distinguished Dental Hygiene Alumna Award, Indiana University School of Dentistry; Outstanding Service Award, Health Occupations Education Division, American Vocational Association; Award for Dedication and Service as President, Association of Health Occupations Teacher Educators; Dedication to Students of Avon Community Schools, Avon Community School Corporation; Teaching Award, Indiana University Trustees; Excellence in Teaching Award, Indiana University School of Medicine; Excellence in Service Award, Indiana University School of Health Sciences; Outstanding Career and Technical Educator of the Year, Indiana Association of Career and Technical Education **Memberships:** Policy Board, Association for Career and Technical Education/Health Occupations Education (2002-Present); Indiana Career and Technical Education Association; Secretary, Indiana Dental Hygienists Association; President-Elect, President, Indiana Health Careers Association; Treasurer, President, Indiana Health Occupations, Supervisors, and Teacher Educators Council; Sigma Phi Alpha; Director Emeritus, Avon Education Foundation **Marquis Who's Who Honors:** Albert Nelson Marquis Lifetime Achievement Award **To what do you attribute your success:** Dr. Gable attributes her success to the support and mentorship of her family, friends, and colleagues. **Why did you become involved in your profession or industry:** After establishing herself as a dental hygenist, Dr. Gable knew she wanted to further her education to become a teacher and educate future hygienists. **Avocations:** Gardening plants and flowers; Family genealogy **Religion:** United Methodist **Thoughts on Life:** Dr. Gable believes determination and perseverance are critical to success in life.

Joyce Ann Gaetano

Title: Chemical Engineer, Business Manager (Retired) **Industry:** Engineering **Date of Birth:** 04/04/1956 **Place of Birth:** Pittsburgh **State/Country of Origin:** PA/USA **Parents:** Samuel Salvatore Gaetano; Elizabeth Ann (Brandy) Gaetano **Marital Status:** Single **Education:** BS in Chemical Engineering, University of Pittsburgh, With Honors (1978); 25 Credits, Continuing Education in Leadership, Negotiations and Business Management **Career:** Industry Manager for Raw Materials, Bayer AG, Pittsburgh, PA (2002-2003); Marketing Manager for Elastomer Textile Backings, Bayer AG, Pittsburgh, PA (1995-2000); Manager of New Markets Development, Bayer AG, Pittsburgh, PA (1993-1995); Supervisor of Specialty Transportation Polymers, Bayer Material Science LLC (1986-1992); Technical Marketing Specialist for Reaction Injection Molding, Mobay Chemical Corporation (1983-1985); Product Manager, Mobay Chemical Corporation (1981-1983); Technical Product Representative, Mobay Chemical Corporation (1979-1981); Apprentice Chemical Engineer, Nuclear Research and Development Group, Westinghouse Electric Corporation (1978); Apprentice Chemical Engineer in Dam Water Analysis, US Army Corps of Engineers (1976) **Civic:** Active Member, Progressive Politics; National Organization for Women; Volunteer, Youth Mentoring Programs **Creative Works:** Contributor, Articles, Various Publications; Contributor, White Papers, Symposia **Awards:** Marketing Excellence Award, Bayer AG; Leadership Award, SPI; Multiple Presidential Achievement Awards, Bayer AG **Memberships:** Chairman, Polyurethane Committee, Plastics Industry Association (1979-1986); ESWP; SAE International; NAFE **Marquis Who's Who Honors:** Albert Nelson Marquis Lifetime Achievement Award; Marquis Who's Who Top Professional **To what do you attribute your success:** Ms. Gaetano attributes her success to a solid education, a high school chemistry teacher who pointed to her aptitude in chemistry and mathematics, the positive encouragement of her family, belief in herself when doubt is cast, determination, sacrifice, and finally, the opportunities she was provided by employers. **Why did you become involved in your profession or industry:** Ms. Gaetano became involved in her profession after meeting college recruiters during her senior year of high school. During a conversation with a female recruiter, she was encouraged to pursue a career in engineering. **Avocations:** Swimming; Reading; Listening to music; Volunteering **Political Affiliations:** Progressive **Religion:** Christian; Eastern philosophies

Ugo Oscar Gagliardi

Title: Application Developer **Industry:** Education/Educational Services **Company Name:** Harvard University **Date of Birth:** 07/23/1931 **Place of Birth:** Naples **State/Country of Origin:** Italy **Parents:** Edgardo Gagliardi; Lina (Valenzuela) Gagliardi **Spouse Name:** Anna Josephine Italiano (1954-1972) **Children:** Oscar Marco; Alex Piero **Education:** DEng in Electrical Engineering, Università degli Studi di Napoli Federico II, Naples, Italy (1954); Diploma in Mathematics and Physics, Università degli Studi di Napoli Federico II, Naples, Italy (1951) **Career:** Visiting Professor, Harvard University Graduate School of Design (2000-Present); Gordon McKay Professor of the Practice of Computer Engineering, Harvard University, Cambridge, MA (1983-2000); Chairman, Software Technology, Inc. (1982-1999); President, General Systems Group, Salem, NH (1975-Present); Professor of Practice of Computer Engineering, Harvard University, Cambridge, MA (1974-1983); Director of Engineering, Honeywell Information Systems, Waltham, MA (1970-1975); Vice President of Tech. Operations, Interactive Sciences Corporation, Braintree, MA (1968-1970); Lecturer, Harvard University, Cambridge, MA (1967-1974); Research Fellow, Harvard University, Cambridge, MA (1966-1967); Chief Scientist, U.S. Air Force, Hanscom Air Force Base, MA (1965-1966) **Awards:** Fulbright Scholar, Columbia University (1955-1956)

Gail T. Galasko

Title: Pharmacologist, Educator **Company Name:** Florida State University **Date of Birth:** 05/28/1942 **Place of Birth:** Johannesburg **State/Country of Origin:** South Africa **Parents:** David I. Galasko; Rose Shames Galasko **Education:** PhD, Queen Mary University of London (1970); MSc, University of the Witwatersrand, Johannesburg (1965); BSc, University of the Witwatersrand, Johannesburg (1963); Postdoctoral Fellow, California Institute of Technology **Certifications:** Fellow, Gemmological Association of Great Britain; Natural Scientist **Career:** Professor, Florida State University College of Medicine (2005-Present); Year 2 Director, Florida State University College of Medicine (2008-2010); Associate Professor, Section Head, Pharmacology, SIU School of Dental Medicine (1994-2005); Research Associate Professor, University of Virginia (1989-1994); Lecturer, Senior Lecturer, Associate Chair, University of the Witwatersrand, Johannesburg (1972-1989) **Career Related:** Visiting Scientist, Weizmann Institute of Science (1985); Visiting Research Associate Professor, University of Virginia (1981); Visiting Professor, West Virginia University (1972-1973) **Civic:** Board Member, Secretary, President, Board of Directors, Temple Israel, Godfrey; Member, South African Women's Bureau, Chairman, Women and the Sciences Committee **Creative Works:** Contributor, Articles to Professional Publications **Memberships:** President, Council Number 1 of the South Africa Region, ITC (1979-1980); President, Johannesburg Toastmistress Club (1976); Life Member, Hadassah; Fellow, Gemmological Association of Great Britain; Gemmological Association of South Africa; President, Johannesburg Toastmistress Club; President, Tamarisk ITC Club; Editor, SA Toastmistress; Zonta International; President, Vice President, Second Vice President, Zonta Club of Alton-Wood River **Why did you become involved in your profession or industry:** Dr. Galasko became involved in her profession when she heard of receptors. At that time research on receptors were done in pharmacology departments, so, after completing her postdoctoral studies, she looked for an academic position in a department of pharmacology, although she knew nothing about pharmacology. She had gone back to South Africa after completing her post-doctoral studies because she had been in the USA on an exchange visa, and was required to leave the United States. She got a position in the Department of Experimental and Clinical Pharmcology at the University of the Witwatersrand, her alma mater, and has spent her entire teaching career in pharmacology. **Avocations:** Reading; Traveling; Calligraphy; Dogs

Gus A. Galatianos

Title: Computer Company Executive, Consultant, Real Estate Developer, Educator **Industry:** Education/Educational Services **Date of Birth:** 01/18/1947 **Place of Birth:** Hermoupolis **State/Country of Origin:** Siros/Greece **Parents:** Athanassios Constantine Galatianos; Despina Athanassios (Stefanou) Galatianos **Marital Status:** Married **Spouse Name:** Katerina E. Saridis, (09/29/1974) **Children:** Athanassios; Deborah **Education:** PhD in Computer Science, Polytechnic University, New York, NY (1986); MS in Computer Science, Stevens Institute Technology (1977); MS in Systems Engineering, Columbia University (1977); BSEE, New York Institute Technology (1974); Degree from the Greek Air Force, Greece; Degree in Electronic Engineering, Greece **Career:** Professor Emeritus, State University of New York (2001-Present); Professor, Chairman, Department of Computer Science, State University of New York (1993-2000); President, ACCI Properties, Inc., New York, NY (1988-Present); President, Advanced Computer Consultant International, New York, NY (1988-2004); Manager, Finance Systems, Singer/Electronic Systems Division, Little Falls, NJ (1984-1987); Associate Professor, Chairman, Department of Computer Science, State University of New York, Old Westbury, NY (1979-1993); Technical Director, Computer Dynamics Corp., New York, NY (1977-1979); Computer Consultant, University of Computer Centers, New York, NY (1973-1977); Manager, Operations, Solomos Business Machines, Athens, Greece (1970-1973) **Career Related:** Consultant in Field; Owner, Chief Executor, Multi-Family Property in New York and Properties in New Jersey **Civic:** Police Athletic League, New York, NY (2010-Present); Representative Presidential Task Force, Washington DC (1984-Present); Greater Whitestone Taxpayers Civic Association, New York, NY (1984-Present) **Military Service:** Greek Air Force (1968-1970) **Creative Works:** Author, "Principles of Software Engineering" (1986); Author, "Principles of Database Systems" (1986); Contributor, Articles, Professional Journals **Marquis Who's Who Honors:** Albert Nelson Marquis Lifetime Achievement Award **Avocations:** Music; Hunting; Travel; Reading **Political Affiliations:** Republican **Religion:** Greek Orthodox

Timothy Galfas II

Title: President, Director **Date of Birth:** 09/28/1943 **Place of Birth:** Atlanta **State/Country of Origin:** GA/USA **Parents:** Timothy Galfas; Louise (Cooledge) Galfas **Marital Status:** Married **Spouse Name:** Jytte Holst Malling (060/1/1974) **Children:** Kara Erika; Vikki Luise; Erin Kristiana **Education:** Coursework, Columbia University, New York, NY (1961); Coursework, French Institute of Athens, Greece (1959-1960) **Career:** President, Center for Business Regeneration, Atlanta, GA (1991-Present); Director, Center for Business Regeneration, Atlanta, GA (1991-Present); Executive Vice President of Sales & Marketing, Sortimo of North America, Inc. (2007-2012); Chief Operating Officer, Board of Directors, Insular Corp., Baltimore, MD (2006-2010); Chief Operating Officer, Board of Directors, ASAP Walls, Baltimore, MD (2006-2009); Chief Executive Officer, Automotive Resources International, Inc., Houston, TX (2005); Board Chairman, Automotive Resources International, Inc., Houston, TX (2005); Chief Executive Officer, Board of Directors, Restcon Development Ltd., Atlanta, GA (2003-2005); President, Maximum Recon, Inc., Atlanta, GA (2002); Chief Executive Officer, Maximum Recon, Inc., Atlanta, GA (2002); Chief Operating Officer, Isthmos, Inc., Atlanta, GA (2001-2002); President, Franchise Operations Division, Aero Colours, Inc., Atlanta, GA (1999-2001); Vice President of Franchise Development, Philly Franchising Co., Atlanta, GA (1998-1999); President, Colors in Europe, Inc., Norcross, GA (1997-1998); Chief Executive Officer, Colors in Europe, Inc., Norcross, GA (1997-1998); Chairman, Board of Directors, Colors in Europe, Inc., Norcross, GA (1997-1998); President, Total Car Franchising Corp., Norcross, GA (1994-1998); Chief Executive Officer, Total Car Franchising Corp., Norcross, GA (1994-1998); Vice President, Total Car Franchising Corp., Atlanta, GA (1991-1994); Director, Total Car Franchising Corp., Atlanta, GA (1991-1994); Director of Franchise Operations, Mighty Distributing Systems, Inc., Atlanta, GA (1982-1991); President, Delamotte-Turner International, Atlanta, GA (1978-1982); Writer, Galfas Productions, Inc., Allendale, NJ (1977-1978); Producer, Galfas Productions, Inc., Allendale, NJ (1977-1978); Professor, Gilead College, New York, NY (1967-1977); Editor, Galfas Productions, Inc., New York, NY (1961-1971); Producer, Galfas Productions, Inc., New York, NY (1961-1971) **Career Related:** Board of Directors, Simcik, Inc., Vineyard Haven, MA (2010-Present); Board of Directors, JVG Civil Engineering, Inc., Atlanta, GA (2009-Present); Board of Directors, Carworks Inc., Atlanta, GA (2002-Present); President, Board of Directors, Ultimate Appearance Franchising Inc., Atlanta, GA (2002) **Civic:** Active Member, Immigrants and Refugees, East & French West Africa Across United States Jehovah's Witnesses (2001-Present); Active Member, Haitian Earthquake Victim Relief, Atlanta, GA (2010) **Creative Works:** Author, "The Unrepentant Idealist" (2018); Author, "The Nefertiti Love Songs" (2018); Author, "Corporate Takeovers and Assorted Love Songs" (2018); Author, 365 Radio Scripts, "Galfas Notes" (2012); Author, "What Every Business Owner Better Know" (2006); Author, "To Touch the Leper, Review Edition" (2005); Author, "To Touch the Leper" (2002); Author, "Akhnaton Waits Alone" (2000); Author, "Regenerating the Franchise System" (1993); Author, "Corporate Takeovers and Assorted Love Songs" (1991); Author, "Creating and Managing a Distributing System" (1990); Author, "Take a Brave New Look at Your Business" (1990); Publisher, Newsletter, "Regenerator" **Awards:** Franchiser of Year, American Association Franchises & Dealers (2006); Trailblazer Award (2005); Franchiser of Year, Southeast Franchise Forum and Kennesaw State University (1998); Achievement of Vision Award, Colors on Parade Franchise Advisory Council (1995); Named, Best Director, Peachtree Players, Atlanta, GA (1980, 1983); Best Editing of TV Commercial Award, New York Art Directors Club (1967) **Marquis Who's Who Honors:** Albert Nelson Marquis Lifetime Achievement Award **Why did you become involved in your profession or industry:** Mr. Galfas is the oldest of nine children and just automatically fell into the role of a caretaker. He finds that he easily reaches out to people because he's a caretaker and it's what made him what he is. He asks himself, "Can I help somebody? Can I make someone's life better?" Mr. Galfas loves franchising because he can make people independent of being fired, and teach them how to earn a good living for their families and for themselves. It's really wonderful for him now because he helped a grandfather get the business running and now the third-generation of the family is running that business. It's not only a way for people to make money, but also contribute to the society where they live. **Avocations:** Legos; Concert; Violin; Poetry; Soccer **Thoughts on Life:** Mr. Galfas speaks the following languages: Amharic, Pidgins and Creoles, French-based Danish, English, French, Greek, Italian, Latin, Portuguese and Spanish.

Gay Galleher, PhD

Title: Clinical Psychologist, Artist **Industry:** Fine Art **Company Name:** Gay Galleher Art **Date of Birth:** 11/03/1946 **Place of Birth:** Delaware **State/Country of Origin:** OH/USA **Parents:** Richard Adair Galleher; Ellen Jean Huntsberger **Marital Status:** Divorced **Education:** PhD in Psychology, School of Graduate Psychology, Pacific University (1987); MS in Psychology, School of Graduate Psychology, Pacific University (1983); MS in Learning Disabilities, Pacific University (1976) **Certifications:** Board Certified Clinical Psychologist; Licensed Psychologist, State of Maine; Board Certified Diplomate in Clinical Psychology, American Board of Professional Psychology **Career:** Artist; Private Practice Clinical Psychologist, Gay Galleher PhD, Maine (2001-2018); Private Practice Clinical Psychologist, Gay Galleher PhD, ABPP, West Bath (2004-2012); Civilian Contract Clinical Psychologist, USAG, Baumholder, Germany (2009-2010); Civilian Contract Clinical Psychologist, U.S. Air Force, Lakenheath, England (2001) **Military Service:** Civil Contract Clinical Psychologist, U.S. Air Force (2009-2010); Civilian Contractor, 48th Medical Group, U.S. Air Force (2001-2002) **Creative Works:** Contributor, Articles, Professional Journals; Various Original Artworks **Memberships:** American Board of Professional Psychology; National Register of Health Service Psychologists; San Francisco Psychotherapy Research Group; Associate Member, American Watercolor Society **Marquis Who's Who Honors:** Albert Nelson Marquis Lifetime Achievement Award; Marquis Who's Who Top Professional **To what do you attribute your success:** Dr. Galleher attributes her success to the support of her father. **Avocations:** Painting; Gardening; Interior decorating; Renovating old homes **Political Affiliations:** Democrat **Religion:** Congregationalist **Website:** https://www.gaygalleherart.com/

Isabela Amie Garcia, Esq.

Title: Founder and Managing Attorney **Industry:** Law and Legal Services **Company Name:** Garcia-Windsor, P.C. **Education:** JD, Dedman School of Law, Southern Methodist University (2011); Coursework, International Tax Law and European Union Law, Oxford Law School (2008); PhB, Minor in Business, University of Texas at Austin, Cum Laude (2007) **Career:** Founder and Managing Attorney, Family Law Litigation Attorney, Garcia-Windsor, P.C., Dallas, TX (2013-Present); Legal Research Assistant, Clouse Dunn LLP, Dallas, TX (2011); Legal Intern, Genesco Sports Enterprises, Inc., Dallas, TX (2010-2011); Legal Research Assistant, Marc I. Steinberg, Senior Associate Dean for Research, Professor of Law, Dallas, TX (2010); Judicial Intern, Hon. Sam A. Lindsay of U.S. District Court in the Northern District of Texas, Dallas, TX (2008); Judicial Intern, Hon. Carl Ginsberg, 193rd Civil District Court, Dallas, TX (2008); Public Information and Assistance Division Intern, Office of the Texas Attorney General, Austin, TX (2005); Legal Intern, Law Office of Mark R. Lee, Austin, TX (2005) **Career Related:** Advisor, Uptmoor Enterprises, LLC, Dallas, TX (2011-Present); Univision Possible Summit Speaker (2018); Tennis Professional, Director of the Junior Program, The Hills Club Corp Country Club, Austin, TX (2001-2003); Tennis Professional, Director of the Junior Program, The Hills Club Corp Country Club, Austin, TX (1999); Women's Tennis Association Professional Athlete, International Tennis Federation, London, England (1995-1998); Lecturer, Community Outreach Law-Related Education, Dedman School of Law, Southern Methodist University; Leader, Speaker, Unity, Diversity and Development Board Conference **Civic:** Organizer, Moderator, Top NFL Agent and Lawyer Symposium, Dedman School of Law, Southern Methodist University (2010); Sponsor, Texas Offender Reentry Program; Pro Bono, Family Court Orders for Juveniles Facing Deportation; Mentor, Students With Educational Troubles; President, Isabela Amie Garcia Foundation; Sponsor, Texas Offenders Reentry Initiative **Awards:** Empire Builder Award Quality and Excellence Award, Greater Dallas Hispanic Chamber of Commerce, Dallas, TX (2019); Young Entrepreneur of the Year, Association of Mexican Entrepreneurs, Dallas, TX (2019); Named, America's Top Latino Lawyers, Latino Leander's Magazine, Dallas, TX (2019); Lawyer of Distinction Award, Family Law, Orlando, FL (2019); Named, Top 10 Family Law Attorney Under 40 in Northern Texas, National Academy of Family Law Attorneys, Dallas, TX (2018); Named, Top 10 Family Law Firms in Texas, Attorney and Practice Magazine, American Institute of Family Law Attorneys, Dallas, TX (2017-2019); AVVO Client's Choice Award, AVVO Lawyer Directory, Dallas, TX (2017-2018); Appreciation Award **Memberships:** Mock Trial Academy, Dedman School of Law, Southern Methodist University (2008); Board of Directors, Mexican American Bar Association of Dallas; Officer, SMU Sports and Entertainment Law Association, Dedman School of Law, Southern Methodist University; Phi Theta Kappa International Honor Society; Gamma Beta Phi; National Scholars Honor Society; President, Founder, Women's Pre-Law Academic Society; Dallas Family Law Bar Association; State Bar of Texas Family Law Section; Dallas Hispanic Bar Association; Hispanic Chamber of Commerce; Dallas Women's Lawyers Association; Association of Mexican Entrepreneurs (AEM) **Marquis Who's Who Honors:** Marquis Who's Who Top Professional **To what do you attribute your success:** Ms. Garcia attributes her success to her clients; everything else falls second after that. **Why did you become involved in your profession or industry:** When Ms. Garcia was studying for the bar exam, her ex-husband divorced her; it was traumatic. At the time, a friend of hers was a prestigious family attorney. He extended his firm and represented her throughout the divorce. At that moment, she knew she wanted to provide the same help to others in the future. **Avocations:** Going out for dinner; Sports; Church **Thoughts on Life:** Ms. Garcia's motto is "Be honest and work hard."

Minerva A. Garcia

Title: 1) Associate Director of Microbiology 2) General Supervisor, Microbiology Lab **Industry:** Sciences **Company Name:** 1) Jacobi Medical Center 2) Wyckoff Heights Medical Center **Date of Birth:** 11/01/1959 **Place of Birth:** Santiago **State/Country of Origin:** Dominican Republic **Parents:** Lydia E. Frias; Seferino Frias **Marital Status:** Married **Spouse Name:** Jose N. Garcia (08/25/1985) **Children:** James S. Garcia **Education:** Pursuing Masters in Medical Microbiology, Long Island University; BS in Biology, St. Francis College (1984); Coursework, City University of New York; Postgraduate Coursework, Wagner College **Certifications:** Certified Clinical Laboratory Technologist; Board of Regents, Department of Education, State of New York; American Society Clinical of Pathologists; Certified Medical Spanish Interpreter, New York University **Career:** Jacobi Medical Center (2013-Present); Wycoff Heights Medical Center (2013-Present); Bacteriologist, Staten Island, NY **Career Related:** Clinical Laboratory Scientist **Creative Works:** Poet, "The Journey of a Rainbow," Book of Collected Poetry (2018); Poet, Anthologies (1994); Contributor, Newspapers and Magazines; Poet, "In the Microbiology Lab"; Poet, "The Role Of Poet"; Poet, "The Love Of A Flower"; Poet, "Paper Frog" **Awards:** Dr. Ellen Jo Baron and Dr. Sydney M. Finegold Anaerobic Bacteriology Award (1992); Mayor's Scholarship Award (1978); Excellence in Written Oral Spanish and Portuguese (1978); New York City Honor Citation Award (1975) **Memberships:** American Association of University Women; Alliance for Prudent Use of Antibiotics; American Chemical Society; New York Academy of Sciences; American Society of Microbiology; New York Mycological Society; Clinical Laboratory Management Association **Marquis Who's Who Honors:** Albert Nelson Marquis Lifetime Achievement Award; Marquis Who's Who Top Professional **Why did you become involved in your profession or industry:** Ms. Garcia became a candy striper at age 12, and a gynecologist at the hospital saw how hard she worked. He offered her a job as his medical assistant when she was 14. She always excelled in the laboratory, and her talents in teaching and research became evident when she was working at Beth Israel Medical Center. She is a published scientist, as well as a published poet. **Avocations:** Poetry; Stained glass; Meditation; Music; Art; Running; Dancing; Travelling; Tai Chi; Singing **Religion:** Catholic

Nancy Garfield-Woodbridge

Title: Children's Book Author **Industry:** Writing and Editing **Place of Birth:** New York **State/Country of Origin:** NY/USA **Parents:** Solomon Silbowitz; Betty Silbowitz **Marital Status:** Married **Spouse Name:** George Charles Woodbridge (04/20/1980) **Children:** Maurice; Joshua **Education:** Postgraduate Coursework, Hofstra University (1973); Master of Education, Hofstra University (1972); Bachelor of Arts in Literature, Bennington College (1955) **Certifications:** Certified Teacher in Grades K-8, State of New York; Certified Teacher in English in Grades 7-9, State of New York **Career:** Author, Children's Books (2000-Present); Director of Special Projects, Girl Scouts of the United States of America, New York, NY (1973-2000); Research Associate to Vice President and Editor, New York Institute of Technology, Westbury, NY (1972-1973); Vice President, Information Retrieval Systems, Great Neck, NY (1958-1972); Editor-in-Chief, The Gifted Child Magazine, New York, NY (1957-1958); Picture Editor, Forbes Magazine, New York, NY (1955-1956); Editorial Assistant, Wenner-Gren Foundation for Anthropological Research, New York, NY (1952-1955) **Career Related:** Presenter, Education Commission for the States, Denver, CO (1979); With, Vice President's Task Force on Youth Employment, Little Rock, AR (1979); Speaker, Governor's Conference on Juvenile Justice, Baton Rouge, LA **Civic:** Appointed, New York State Board of Education Commission on Education, Albany, NY; Volunteer, Biafran Refugee Campaign, New York to London (1967); Volunteer, Kennedy Kenya Airlift Program, New York, NY (1962); Fundraiser, Sara's Center Very Special Arts Festival, Long Island to Washington **Creative Works:** Author, "Suns of Darkness," (2020); Author, "The Honey Hunt" (2018); Author, "Arctic Butterfly" (2016); Author, "The Islanders" (2016); Author, "Poems in Exile" (2012); Author, "A Bouquet of Fairy Tales" (2012); Author, "Hilary and the Secret Skulls" (2012); Author, "Journey" (2012); Author, "If I Had $1500 I Would Clean My Karma" (2012); Author, "Stories from Around the World" (2012); Author, "More Stories from Around the World" (2012); Author, "Juvenile Justice" (1981); Author, "The Dancing Monkey" (1970); Author, "The Tuesday Elephant" (1968); Contributor, "Directory of Anthropological Institutions," Wenner-Gren Foundation for Anthropological Research (1952-1955); Contributor, "Man's Role in Changing the Face of Earth," Wenner-Gren Foundation for Anthropological Research (1952-1955); Author, "RainBird"; Author, "Shanti Means Peace"; Author, "The Magic Paint Brush"; Author, "MoonBeam Flowers"; Author, "Gideon's Dream"; Contributor, Articles to Professional Journals and Magazines **Awards:** Dr. John C. Sevier Award For Service to Youth With Disabilities, YMCA of the USA (1989); Scholarship, Breadloaf Writers Conference, Vermont (1967) **Memberships:** Academy of American Poets; Authors Guild; Milford Fine Arts Council; Society of Children's Book Writers and Illustrators **Marquis Who's Who Honors:** Albert Nelson Marquis Lifetime Achievement Award; Marquis Who's Who Humanitarian Award **Why did you become involved in your profession or industry:** Ms. Garfield-Woodbridge became involved in her profession because she worked in anthropology and performed research on man's role in changing the face of the earth. In this fashion, she developed a sense for how incredibly diverse the world is. She felt it was important for children to develop a working knowledge of different cultures. **Avocations:** Travel; Reading; Opera; Painting; Photography; Sociology; Biography; Poetry; Music **Thoughts on Life:** Ms. Garfield-Woodbridge is interested in writing books that deal with diversity due to current events. She believes that if children are given a chance to feel safe with people who are different from themselves, they'll be more likely to empathize with others.

Lloyd Robert Garrison

Title: Marketing and Sales Professional **Industry:** Advertising & Marketing **Date of Birth:** 03/10/1942 **Place of Birth:** Buffalo **State/Country of Origin:** NY/USA **Parents:** Lloyd Garrison; Lois Garrison **Marital Status:** Married **Spouse Name:** Marion (03/17/1979) **Education:** Postgraduate Coursework, Clairmont Graduate School (1977-1979); MA in Political Science-Economics California State University (1977); BA in Political Science, California State University (1975); MBA Coursework in International Marketing, Clairmont Graduate School **Career:** Technical Manager, Pacific Division, Brenntag, Specialty Chemical (2010); Technical Manager, Brenntag, Western Division (2002-2008); International Business Manager, Hampshire Chemical Corporation, Lexington, MA (1993-2001); Senior Sales Engineer, W.R. Grace & Company, Lexington, MA (1985-1993); Senior Sales Engineer, Ferro Corporation, Cleveland (1980-1985); Laboratory Technician, Bell & Howell (1969-1974); Laboratory Technician, Wyandotte Chemical Corporation, Detroit (1966-1969); Laboratory Technician, Spencer Kellogg, Buffalo, NY (1963-1966) **Civic:** Lecturer, California State University-Osher Institute **Creative Works:** Patentee, Fire Retardant Urethane (1963) **Memberships:** Board of Directors, San Bernardino Symphony Orchestra (2010-Present); Society of Plastics Engineers; The Applied Pulp Paper Institute; Los Angeles Society for World Affairs; Osher Lifelong Learning Institute at California State University-Fullerton; Upland Chamber of Commerce **Marquis Who's Who Honors:** Albert Nelson Marquis Lifetime Achievement Award; Marquis Who's Who Top Professional; Distinguished Humanitarian **To what do you attribute your success:** Mr. Garrison attributes his success to his wife, Marion Garrison. **Why did you become involved in your profession or industry:** Mr. Garrison first worked for an individual named John Roker, who inspired him to be very thorough and inspired a curiosity about Palmer R&D. He then became involved with the organo-metallic electric chemical properties of magnetic phenomena. At that time, he was giving lectures on special magnetic phenomena for ultra stem cells for Bell and Howell. As he was finishing his first degree, he encountered a professor at Wayne State University in Detroit who had a phenomenal influence on him. Because of her, Mr. Garrison's thinking changed in regard to political and social phenomena. He stayed in the field of polymers and coatings until he retired. In the years after his retirement, he pursued his second love, which was social sciences in political economics. This became his second career as a lecturer at California State University, Fullerton. **Avocations:** Classical music; Reading; Skiing; Tennis **Political Affiliations:** Democrat **Thoughts on Life:** Mr. Garrison believes life is organic and always changing. Mankind should aspire to influence that change for the betterment of all people.

Mark Garver

Title: Chief Executive Officer **Industry:** Information Technology and Services **Company Name:** agri-space, llc **Education:** Student, Computer Engineering, Case Western Reserve University; Student, Military Strategic Intelligence, American Military University Student MIT Sloan/CSAIL AI Implications on Business Strategy **Certifications:** Diplomate, American Board for Certification in Homeland Security (2003-Present); Executive Certification, AI in Business Strategy MIT Sloan/CSAIL (2019); Certified National Threat Analyst (CNTA), American Board for Certification in Homeland Security (2016); Certified in Homeland Security Emergency Medical Response, American Board for Certification in Homeland Security (2016); Certified in Disaster Preparedness (CDP-I), American Board for Certification in Homeland Security (2016); Certification in Dignitary and Executive Protection (CDEP), American Board for Certification in Homeland Security (2015); Certification in Homeland Security Level 1-5 (CHS-V), American Board for Certification in Homeland Security (2003) **Career:** Founder and Chief Executive Officer, agri-space, llc (2019-Present) Former Chief Executive Officer, GEOS Response LLC (2008-2019); Chief Operating Officer, Guidry Group (2008-2009); Senior Project Manager, Wells Fargo (2007-2008); Founder and Chairman, Specialty Intelligence Group (2006-2017); Senior Project Manager, U.S. Bank (2006-2007); CHS-V and Instructor, American Board for Certification in Homeland Security (2003-2017); Chief Executive Officer, Transparence Inc. (2002-2006); Vice President, Internet Solutions, BSDi (2000-2002); Chief Executive Officer, NEtOps (1999-2000); General Manager, Ascend Communications (1996-2000); Vice President, Sales and Marketing, Netstar (1995-1996); General Manager, Dell (1994-1995); Vice President, Tricord Systems (1989-1994) **Civic:** Official Member, Houston Business Journal Leadership Trust (2019-Present); Founding Board Member, Candidate Evaluation Committee, American Board for Certification in Dignitary and Executive Protection (2011-Present); Board Member, American Board for Intelligence Analysis Certification (2012-2018); Board Member, Springhill School (2006-2008); Volunteer, Big Brothers, Donator, Four Oceans, St. Josephs School, Saint Judes Hospital, USO **Creative Works:** Contributor, "How To Endure Anything: Tap into your mental fortitude with these strategies," Men's Health Magazine (2011); Contributor, Article, "Leadership and Guidance Art The Issue," Albuquerque Business Journal (2005) **Awards:** CEO of the Year - Transformational CEO (2019) **Memberships:** Protective Security Council; International Association of Healthcare Safety and Security (IAHSS); National Emergency Number Association; National Search and Rescue Committee (NSARC); Overseas Security Advisory Council; Military Intelligence Corps Association; International Association for Conterterrorism and Security Professionals; National Association for Search and Rescue (NASAR); European Emergency Number Association **To what do you attribute your success:** Mr. Garver attributes his success to surrounding himself with exceptional people, and not being afraid to surround himself with smart people who challenge him and others on the team. He is a good listener. **Why did you become involved in your profession or industry:** Possessed of a thirst for knowledge, Mr. Garver pursued a career in technological development. He greatly enjoys innovating and examining the market in different ways. Likewise, he was fortunate to be mentored by several wonderful CEOs, who saw in him a great strategic mind. **Thoughts on Life:** Don't dream your life, live your dream!

Stephen E. Gasper

Title: President **Industry:** Engineering **Company Name:** Gasper Engineering, Inc. **Date of Birth:** 10/01/1967 **Place of Birth:** Columbus **State/Country of Origin:** IN/USA **Children:** Braden; Derek; Megan; Blakley (Grandchild) **Education:** BA in Electrical Technology, Purdue University (1990); AS in Electrical Engineering Technology, Purdue University (1986) **Career:** President, Gasper Engineering, Inc. (1999-Present); Owner, Steve Gasper Real Estate LLC; Owner, Steve Gasper Industrial Real Estate LLC; Owner, Millers Tavern MV LLC **Awards:** Corporate Livewire Innovation and Excellence (2019) **Memberships:** Board Member, CASA for Children; Board Member, RMC **To what do you attribute your success:** Mr. Gasper attributes his success to honesty and hard work, which always grants him customer satisfaction. **Why did you become involved in your profession or industry:** When Mr. Gasper was a child, he always wanted to know what happened when someone turned on a light switch. This is what led him to the field of engineering. **Thoughts on Life:** Mr. Gasper's motto is, "If you're not happy we're not done; If you can dream it we can build it."

Larry Wayne Gatlin

Title: President **Industry:** Engineering **Company Name:** LWG Services LLC **Date of Birth:** 03/16/1945 **Place of Birth:** Paragould **State/Country of Origin:** AR/USA **Parents:** Louie M. Gatlin; Helen L. Gatlin **Marital Status:** Married **Spouse Name:** Alma Rosa Salinas **Children:** Tammy Lee Hilligeist; Timothy Eric Gatlin; Joe Patrick Gatlin **Education:** Coursework, Hazardous Waste Management, Texas A&M Engineering Extension Service (1990); Bachelor of Science in Chemistry, Louisiana State University, Monroe, LA (1969); Coursework, Louisiana State University at Alexandria, Alexandria, LA (1968); Coursework, Louisiana Polytechnic Institute, Ruston, LA (1965); Diploma, Lecompte High School, Lecompte, LA (1963); Coursework in Corrosion Control, Continuing Engineering Education, The University of Oklahoma, Norman, OK **Certifications:** ISO 9001 Certification for Alpha Intermediates (1996); National Certification of Corrosion Engineers; Certification for Weatherford Downhole Foaming Agents for low pressure natural gas wells. **Career:** Owner, LWG Service LLC (2007-Present); Vice President of Research and Development, Refinery Specialties Inc. **Career Related:** Research Chemist, Manager of Technical Services, Manager of Research and Product Development, Champion Chemicals Inc., Champion Northwestern Chemicals Ltd. (1969-1978); Teaching Assistant, Research Assistant, Louisiana State University at Alexandria, Alexandria, LA (1966-1967); Camco Inc. (1965-1968); Consultant in Oilfield (1978); Fincher Engineering; V. P. of Chemical Manufacturing Exchange, Latexo, Tx, 1978 -1984; Director of Research and Plant Operations, Alpha Intermediates, 1982-2000; Research and plant Operations for Clearwater-Weatherford International, 2000-2006; Director of Research for CST, Conroe, Tx 2006-2014. **Creative Works:** Author, "Evaluation of Inhibitors for Wet Sour Gas Gathering Systems", Materials Performance (1978); Author, "Fluorimetric Monitoring of Corrosion Inhibitor Residual" (1977); Author, "Corrosion from Wet Gas Controlled," Oil and Gas Journal (1975); 17 Canadian patents; 40 US patents; 18 Great Britain patents; 15 Australian patents **Memberships:** American Association for the Advancement of Science; American Association of Chemists; Society of Petroleum Engineers; Sustaining Fellow, American Institute of Chemists; Past Member, National Association of Corrosion Engineers; American Chemical Society; Member of Honor Guard, Disabled American Veterans; AARP of Texas; National Wildlife Federation: Alberta Sulphur Research Ltd., Calgary, Alberta **Marquis Who's Who Honors:** Marquis Who's Who Top Professional **To what do you attribute your success:** Mr. Gatlin attributes his success to the time that he put in to the profession. He believes in the following sentiment: "If you don't learn to think in school, you won't be able to outside of school." In his career life, Mr. Gatlin had several influential people who taught him different aspects of the oil field operations and associated chemistry, naming Ben Davis, Stewart Cooper, Barry Hugghins, C. B Trial, Dan Dostie, Glen Walden, and Mickey Tucker, but also to his brother Richard and his oldest son Timothy Eric. **Why did you become involved in your profession or industry:** Having hailed from a poor family, Mr. Gatlin had to work diligently through work. Following his graduation, he worked off shore for an oil well service company that a family friend of his owned. It was an interesting business, so when returned to school at Louisiana State University, he ended up working for a professor that wanted him to do undergraduate research. **Avocations:** Ancestry; Environmental chemistry **Political Affiliations:** Republican **Religion:** Protestant

Roberta Elisabeth Gausas, MD

Title: Surgeon **Industry:** Medicine & Health Care **Company Name:** University of Pennsylvania Medical School **Date of Birth:** 01/06/1964 **Place of Birth:** Chicago **State/Country of Origin:** IL/USA **Parents:** Anthony Gausas; Margaretha Gausas **Marital Status:** Married **Spouse Name:** Allen J. Model (1/11/2003) **Children:** Thea Jordan **Education:** Doctor of Medicine, Feinberg School of Medicine, Northwestern University, Chicago, IL (1989); Bachelor of Arts in Science, Northwestern University, Chicago, IL (1987) **Certifications:** Diplomate, American Board of Ophthalmology (1996) **Career:** Associate Professor, Department of Ophthalmology, Perelman School of Medicine, University of Pennsylvania, Philadelphia, PA (1996-2016); Director of Oculoplastic and Orbital Surgery Service, Perelman School of Medicine, University of Pennsylvania, Philadelphia, PA (1996-2015); Instructor, University of Wisconsin, Madison Hospital and Clinics (1995-1996); Fellow in Orbital Surgery, Moorfields Eye Hospital, London, England (1994-1995); Fellow in Oculoplastic Surgery, University of Wisconsin, Madison (1993-1994); Resident, University of Wisconsin, Madison Hospital and Clinics (1990-1993); Intern, McGaw Hospital, Chicago, IL (1989-1990) **Career Related:** Fellow, American Society of Ophthalmic, Plastic and Reconstructive Surgery **Civic:** Board of Overseers, Children's Hospital of Philadelphia Foundation (2018-Present); Chair, American Society of Ophthalmic, Plastic, and Reconstructive Surgery Foundation (2016-2018); Trustee, American Society of Ophthalmic, Plastic and Reconstructive Surgery Foundation (2011-2018) **Creative Works:** Lecturer in Field, National and International; Contributor, Book Chapters, Professional Journals **Awards:** Top Doctor Award, Philadelphia Magazine (2002); Achievement Award, American Academy of Ophthalmology (2001); Top Doctor Award, Philadelphia Magazine (2000); Merrill Reeh Pathology Award, American Society of Ophthalmic, Plastic, and Reconstructive Surgery (1999); Scholar, German Academic Exchange Service (1985); Listee, Best Doctors; Senior Achievement Award, American Academy of Ophthalmology; American of Ophthalmology Achievement Award **Memberships:** Program Chairman, Annual Spring Science Symposium, American Society of Ophthalmic, Plastic and Reconstructive Surgery (2003); Executive Committee, American Society of Ophthalmic, Plastic and Reconstructive Surgery (2002-2004); Program Chairman, Annual Science Symposium, American Society of Ophthalmic, Plastic and Reconstructive Surgery (2002); American Academy of Ophthalmology **Marquis Who's Who Honors:** Marquis Who's Who Top Professional **To what do you attribute your success:** Dr. Gausas attributes her success to her mentors, Dr. Richard Dortzbach and Mr. John Wright. Mr. Wright is now retired, but practiced in London, England, where he was internationally recognized. **Why did you become involved in your profession or industry:** Dr. Gausas' interest in her profession started during an early stage of her life. The two areas she was most passionate about were science and art. She was able to combine these interests in medicine, particularly in the surgical field, which she ended up sub-specializing in. She did not realize that she would focus on oculoplastic surgery, but she is now doing reconstructive surgery recreating patients' faces after trauma or cancer as a form of rehabilitation. **Avocations:** Travel; Conservation; Art; Photography

Bernard Gauthier, MBBS, FRACP

Title: Chief Emeritus **Industry:** Health, Wellness and Fitness **Company Name:** Long Island Jewish Health Systems **Date of Birth:** 05/02/1934 **Place of Birth:** Paris **State/Country of Origin:** France **Parents:** Gustave Gauthier; Odette (Bernadoy) Gauthier **Marital Status:** Married **Spouse Name:** Jellie Bosma **Children:** Philippe; Jean-Paul **Education:** Fellow, Pediatric Nephrology, SUNY Downstate Medical Center (1970-1972); Resident, Prince of Wales Children's Hospital, Sydney, Australia (1965-1968); Intern, Pediatrics, Royal Alexandra Hospital for Children, Sydney, Australia (1964); Intern, Bankstown District Hospital, Sydney, Australia (1962-1963); Bachelor of Medicine, Bachelor of Surgery, University of Sydney, Australia (1962) **Certifications:** Diplomate, American Board of Pediatrics; Diplomate, American Board of Pediatric Nephrology **Career:** Chief Emeritus, Division of Nephrology, Schneider Children's Hospital (2000-2004); Professor, Pediatrics, Albert Einstein College of Medicine, Bronx, NY (1995-2004); Pediatric Nephrologist, Schneider Children's Hospital, North Shore Long Island Jewish Health Systems, New Hyde Park, NY (1995-2004); Associate Professor, Pediatrics, Albert Einstein College of Medicine, Bronx, NY (1990-1995); Assistant Professor, Pediatrics, Albert Einstein College of Medicine, Bronx, NY (1989-1990); Chief, Pediatric Nephrology, Schneider Children's Hospital, North Shore Long Island Jewish Health Systems, New Hyde Park, NY (1975-1994); Assistant Professor, Health Sciences Center, Stony Brook University (1975-1989); Assistant Professor, Pediatrics, SUNY Downstate Medical Center (1973-1975); Chief, Pediatric Nephrology, SUNY Downstate Medical Center (1973-1975); Nephrologist, SUNY Downstate Medical Center (1972-1973); Staff Pediatrician, Prince of Wales Children's Hospital, Sydney, Australia (1968-1970) **Career Related:** New York-New Jersey Pediatric Nephrology Study Group (1988-2004); Consultant, Institutional Review Board of New York, New York, NY (1992-1997); Director, Quality Assurance, Schneider Children's Hospital (1990-1992); Chairman, Participant, National Study Group on Growth Failure in Children with Renal Diseases **Creative Works:** Co-author, "Efficacy of mycophenolate mofetil in pediatric patients with steroid-dependent nephrotic syndrome," Pediatric Nephrology (2005); Co-author, "Is Antibiotic Prophylaxis Indicated for a Voiding Cystourethrogram?," Pediatric Nephrology (2004); Co-author, "Cardiac disease in children with primary glomerular disorders – role of focal segmental glomerulosclerosis," Pediatric Nephrology (2004); Co-author, "Outcome after renal transplantation in children: Results of follow-up by nephrologists in a primary referral center," Pediatric Transplantation (2003); Co-author, "Urinary tract infection, VUR and autosomal dominant polycystic kidney disease," Pediatric Nephrology (2003); Co-author, "Long versus standard initial steroid therapy for children with the nephrotic syndrome, A report from the Southwest Pediatric Nephrology Study Group," Pediatric Nephrology (2003); Co-author, "Angiotensin converting enzyme inhibitor therapy in children with Alport syndrome: effect on urinary albumin, TGF-beta, and nitrite excretion," BMC Nephrology (2002); Co-author, "Bartter syndrome and focal segmental glomerulosclerosis: a possible link between the two diseases," Pediatric Nephrology (2000); Co-author, "Vitamin E treatment of focal segmental glomerulosclerosis: results of an open-label study," Pediatric Nephrology (1999); Co-author, "Pharmacological Treatment of the Nephrotic Syndrome," Drugs of Today (1999); Co-author, "Magnetic resonance imaging in acute pyelonephritis," Pediatric Nephrology (1998); Co-author, "Acute interstitial nephritis associated with IgA nephropathy in children," Pediatric Nephrology (1997); Co-author, "Short-acting Nifedipine," Pediatric Nephrology (1997); Co-author, "Textbook of Nephrology, 3rd Edition," Pediatric Nephrology (1996) **Memberships:** Fellow, Royal Australasian College of Physicians; American Society of Nephrology; American Society of Pediatric Nephrology; International Society of Nephrology International Pediatric Nephrology Association; New York Society of Nephrology; New York Pediatric Society; Pediatric Society of Queens; Nassau Pediatric Society; New York–New Jersey Pediatric Nephrology Group **Marquis Who's Who Honors:** Albert Nelson Marquis Lifetime Achievement Award; Marquis Who's Who Top Professional **Why did you become involved in your profession or industry:** Mr. Gauthier became involved in his profession because he decided he was going to be a doctor when he was 11 years old. He has always been interested in scientific subjects. In France, the only science they had access to was related to the human body and personal hygiene and such other things. They didn't get physics and chemistry until later. He was the first health care provider in the family. **Avocations:** Reading; Traveling; Skiing; Sailing; Windsurfing; Running; Playing the cello

Linda R. Gay

Title: Human Resources Director (Retired) **Industry:** Human Resources **Date of Birth:** 01/24/1952 **Place of Birth:** New York **State/Country of Origin:** NY/USA **Parents:** Ramon Perez; Virginia Mary (McCall) Perez **Marital Status:** Widowed **Spouse Name:** Peter A. Gay (Deceased) **Children:** Larissa L. Gay **Education:** Coursework, Fitchburg State College, Andover, MA (1975-1976) **Career:** Director of Human Resources, Cablevision, Hudson, MA (1987-1996); Recruiter, Zayre Corporation, Framingham, MA (1986-1987); Senior Human Resources Representative, Wang Laboratories, Incorporated, Lowell, MA (1980-1985); Assistant Manager of Affirmative Action, Raytheon Company, Andover, MA (1974-1980) **Career Related:** Vice President, Massachusetts 9/11 Fund Board (2005-2016); Substitute Teacher **Civic:** Volunteer, Tewksbury Senior Center; Administrator Leader Trainee, Leader, Girls Scouts of America; Former President and Treasurer, Parent Teacher Organization **Memberships:** Secretary, Boston Chapter, Women in Cable (1988-1989); Northeast Human Resource Association; Minority Human Resource Association **Marquis Who's Who Honors:** Albert Nelson Marquis Lifetime Achievement Award; Marquis Who's Who Top Professional **To what do you attribute your success:** Ms. Gay attributes her success to her determination to be the best at what she's doing. **Why did you become involved in your profession or industry:** Ms. Gay entered her profession because she is a good listener and a good problem solver. She can come up with a solution that works for both sides. These skills helped with representing companies and employees. **Avocations:** Scuba diving; Sailing; Water sports **Political Affiliations:** Independent **Religion:** Roman Catholic **Thoughts on Life:** Ms. Gay would like to honor the memory of her husband, Peter A. Gay, who was murdered on September 11th, 2001, on American Airlines Flight 11.

David Lawrence Geffen

Title: Music Executive **Industry:** Media & Entertainment **Date of Birth:** 02/21/1943 **Place of Birth:** Brooklyn **State/Country of Origin:** NY/USA **Parents:** Abraham Geffen; Batya (Volovskaya) Geffen **Education:** Coursework, University of Texas (1961-1963); Diploma, New Utrecht High School (1960); Coursework, Brooklyn College; Coursework, Santa Monica College **Career:** Co-Chairman, Dreamworks SKG, Glendale, CA (2006-2008); Co-Founder, Dreamworks SKG, Universal City, CA (1994-2008); Chairman, Dreamworks SKG, Universal City, CA (1994-2006); Founder, President, David Geffen Co. (1990-1995); Founder, President, Chairman, Geffen Records & Geffen Film Co., LA (1980-1989); President, Elektra-Asylum Records (1973-1976); Vice-Chairman & Chief Assistant to Chairman, Warner Brothers Pictures (1974-1975); President, Asylum Records (1970-1973); President, Geffen-Roberts Inc. (1970-1971); Executive Vice President, Agent, Creative Management Associates (1969); Ashley Famous Agency (1968); William Morris Agency, New York, NY (1964-1968); Founder and President, Tuna Fish Public Co. **Career Related:** Appointed Regent, University of California, Government of California (1980-1987); Faculty, Yale University (1978); Board of Councilors, University of Southern California School of Cinema-TV **Civic:** Donor, David Geffen Hall, Lincoln Center for the Performing Arts (2015); Donor, School of Medicine, University of California Los Angeles (2002); Donor, Geffen Playhouse, University of California Los Angeles (1995); Board of Directors, Los Angeles County Art Museum **Awards:** Named, World's Richest People, Forbes Magazine (2001-Present); Named, Forbes 400: Richest Americans (1999-Present); President's Merit Award, National Academy of Recording Arts and Sciences (2011); Ahmet Ertegun Award, Rock and Roll Hall of Fame (2010); Named, Top 200 Collectors, ARTnews Magazine (2004-2008); Named, 50 Most Powerful People in Hollywood, Premiere Magazine (2005-2006) **Avocations:** Collecting modern and contemporary art **Political Affiliations:** Democrat

Peter David Geldner, MD

Title: Plastic Surgeon, President **Industry:** Health, Wellness and Fitness **Company Name:** The Geldner Center **Date of Birth:** 02/22/1957 **Place of Birth:** Warsaw **State/Country of Origin:** Poland **Parents:** Michael M. Geldner; Barbara Geldner **Marital Status:** Married **Spouse Name:** Juliann Youngerman (10/14/1990) **Children:** Nathan B.; Aaron G. **Education:** Plastic Surgery Residency, University of Texas Medical Branch, Galveston, TX (1988-1990); Plastic Surgery Residency, Wayne State University, Detroit, MI (1987-1988); General Surgery Residency, University of Chicago, Chicago, IL (1983-1987); MD, University of Wisconsin (1983); BA, Johns Hopkins University (1979) **Certifications:** American Board of Plastic Surgery (1993) **Career:** Clinical Associate, University of Chicago (2003-Present); Private Practice, The Geldner Center (2003-Present); Attending Surgeon in Plastic Surgery, Illinois Masonic Hospital, Chicago, IL (1993-Present); Assistant Clinical Professor, University of Illinois, Chicago, IL (1990-Present); Private Practice, New Dimensions Center For Cosmetic Surgery, Chicago, IL (1990-2003); Deputy Chief, Division of Plastic Surgery, Michael Reese Hospital, Chicago, IL (1990-2001) **Career Related:** Delegate, Illinois State Medical Society (2013); Vice President, President, Chicago Society of Plastic Surgery (1999-2004); Chief, Bio-Ethics Committee, Michael Reese Hospital (1995-2001); Membership Coordinator, Treasurer, Secretary, Fee Mediation Committee Member, Chicago Medical Society (1994-1997); Director, Wound Care Clinic, Michael Reese Hospital (1993-2001); Consultant Committee, Michael Reese Hospital (1992-2001) **Awards:** Listee, Best Doctors in America (2011-Present); Listee, Top Doctors: Chicago Metro Area, Castle Connolly (2005-Present); Listee, Americas Cosmetic Doctors and Dentists, Castle Connolly (2003-Present); Americas Top Plastic Surgeons. Consumers Research Council of America (2002-Present); Talk of the Town Chicago Award (2011-2015); Novo Award, National Council of Leaders in Breast Aesthetics (2007); Listee, How to Find the Best Doctors, Chicago, Castle Connolly (1999); Listee, Outstanding Young Men of America (1998); Listee, Who's Who in Medicine and Healthcare (1997) **Memberships:** American Medical Association; Illinois Medical Society; Chicago Medical Society; American Society Plastic Surgeons; Chicago Society of Plastic Surgery; Illinois Society of Plastic Surgery; American Society of Aesthetic Plastic Surgery **Marquis Who's Who Honors:** Albert Nelson Marquis Lifetime Achievement Award; Marquis Who's Who Top Professional **Avocations:** Alpine skiing; Boating; Motorcycle riding; Krav Maga; Scuba Diving **Religion:** Jewish

James M. Gelwicks

Title: Emeritus Assistant Professor **Industry:** Education/Educational Services **Company Name:** Western Colorado University **Date of Birth:** 11/14/1949 **Place of Birth:** Boulder **State/Country of Origin:** CO/USA **Parents:** Melvin Gelwicks Jr.; Maryjoel Gelwicks **Education:** Master of Arts in Communication Theory and Research, Northern Illinois University (1977); All But Dissertation, Communication Theory and Research, Florida State University (1973-1982); Bachelor of Arts, University of Colorado (1972) **Career:** Mayor, Gunnison, CO (2017-Present); Emeritus Assistant Professor, Western Colorado University (2005-Present); Mayor, Gunnison, CO (1993-1995); Assistant Professor, Western Colorado University (1981-2004); Adjunct Professor, Florida State University (1980); Research Consultant, Tallahassee, FL (1975-1981); Decontamination Trainee, The Dow Chemical Company, Rocky Flats, CO (1969) **Career Related:** Department Chair, Communication Arts and Sociology, Western Colorado University (1992-1999); General Manager, KWSB-FM, Western State Colorado University (1987-2001); Delegate, People to People Speech Communications Leaders, People's Republic of China, Union of Soviet Socialist Republics (1984); Fellow, Corporation for Public Broadcasting (1973-1974) **Civic:** Mayor, Gunnison, CO (2017-Present); Speaker, Consulado General de Mexico, Mexican Independence Day, Denver, CO (2019); President, Gunnison Chapter, AARP (2008-2010); Vice Chair, Colorado Fund for Children and Public Education (2001-2006); Chair, Environmental Health Board, Gunnison County, CO (2000-2003); Chair, Colorado Advisory Commission on Intergovernmental Relations (1995); President, Colorado Municipal League (1994-1995); Chair, Gunnison County Emergency Telephone Service Authority (1993-1997); Chair, Colorado Education Association Legislative Commission (1988-1990); City Council, Gunnison, CO (1987-1997); Chair, Gunnison County Democratic Party (1985-1987); Democratic State Committeeman, Leon County, FL (1980-1981); Co-Chair, WFSU-TV Auction, Tallahassee, FL (1979); Eagle Scout, Boy Scouts of America (1967) **Creative Works:** Contributing Author, Articles, Professional Journals; Panelist International, National, Regional Conferences **Awards:** Nominee, Sam Mamet Good Governance Award, Colorado Municipal League (2020); Honoree, Member of the Year, Sons of the American Legion (2005); Lion Award, Colorado Education Association (2002); Honoree, Broadcast Citizen of the Year, Colorado Broadcasters Association (1994); Nominee, Tallahassee Volunteer of the Year, FL (1980, 1979); Honoree, Outstanding Senior Debater, Colorado-Wyoming Forensics Association (1971) **Memberships:** President, Gunnison Valley Forever Buffs University of Colorado Boulder Alumni Chapter (2000-Present); Detachment Financial Officer, Sons of the American Legion (2008-2020); Member, North American Mayors Summit, Los Cabos, Mexico (2019); Signatory, International Sister Cities, Gunnison, CO and Majhkali, India (2018); National Executive Committeeman, Sons of the American Legion (2011-2016); National Executive Committeeman, Sons of the American Legion (2011-2015); National Vice Commander, Sons of the American Legion (2009-2010); National Executive Committeeman, Sons of the American Legion (2007-2009); Detachment Commander, Sons of the American Legion (2004-2005); Chair, Public Broadcast Committee, Colorado Broadcasters Association (1992-1994); Lifetime Member, National Communication Association; Lifetime Member, Western States Communication Association; BPO Elks **Marquis Who's Who Honors:** Albert Nelson Marquis Lifetime Achievement Award **To what do you attribute your success:** In accounting for his standout success, Mr. Gelwicks credits his propensity for determination and ability to learn from his mistakes. **Why did you become involved in your profession or industry:** Mr. Gelwicks drew heavily from the influence of Emerson Wilson, Bob Skorkowsky and Ted Clevenger. **Avocations:** Fly fishing; Hiking; Philately (stamp collecting)

Roger L. Gentry, PhD

Title: Research Wildlife Biologist (Retired) **Industry:** Sciences **Company Name:** NOAA **Date of Birth:** 03/19/1938 **Place of Birth:** Bakersfield **State/Country of Origin:** CA/USA **Parents:** Roger Howard Gentry; Harriette Viola (Childs) Gentry **Marital Status:** Single **Children:** Melissa O'Brien; Erin Neville Gentry; Alison Childs Gentry **Education:** Postdoctoral Fellowship, University of Adelaide Mawson Institute for Antarctic Research, Australia (1970-1971); PhD, University of California Santa Cruz (1970); MA, San Francisco State University (1966); BA, San Francisco State University (1962) **Career:** First Seal Research and Acoustics, NOAA Acoustics Program, NOAA (1998-2005); Retired Research Wildlife Biologist, National Marine Mammal Laboratory, NOAA, Seattle, WA (1998); Research Wildlife Biologist, National Marine Mammal Laboratory, National Oceanographic and Atmospheric Administration (NOAA), Seattle, WA (1974-1998); Research Faculty, University of California Santa Cruz (1971-1974) **Career Related:** U.S. Delegate, Standing Science Committee, Interim Convention on North Pacific Fur Seals, Moscow, Russia (1980, 1984); Participant, Food and Agriculture Organization Consultation, Marine Mammals, Bergen, Norway (1976); Researcher and Presenter in Field **Military Service:** Medic, Petty Officer, Second Class, United States Coast Guard (1958-1960) **Creative Works:** Co-author, "Behavior and Ecology of the Northern Fur Seal" (1996); Co-author, "The Status, Biology and Ecology of Fur Seals" (1987); Co-author, "Fur Seals: Maternal Strategies on Land and at Sea" (1986); Contributor, 51 Articles, Professional Journals; Speaker, 50 Talks, Conferences **Awards:** Grantee, National Geological Society (1985-1991, 2015); Grantee, National Aeronautics and Space Administration (NASA) (1973-1974) **Memberships:** American Association for the Advancement of Science; The American Society of Mammalogists; Animal Behavior Society; The Society for Marine Mammalogy; The Oceanography Society **Marquis Who's Who Honors:** Albert Nelson Marquis Lifetime Achievement Award **To what do you attribute your success:** Dr. Gentry attributes his success to Burney J. LeBoeuf, his major professor in his doctorate program. **Why did you become involved in your profession or industry:** Dr. Gentry was inspired by his father, who was mostly an uneducated oil worker. Dr. Gentry recalls him as a "very rough man," who had the ability to attract animals to him unlike he has ever seen before. The way that animals reacted to his father is what inspired him to pursue his career as a wildlife research biologist. He was largely focused on individual behaviors of animals, aside from the normal study of group interactions. He became interested in working with seals while studying echolocation in bats. He recalls reading a book called "Listening in the Dark" by Don Griffin, and how intrigued he was to think about how animals use high-pitched sounds to get through life. He read an article sometime later detailing how seals also use echolocation. The laboratory that published the article happened to only be 25 miles from the school he was attending. He met the director and was offered a job on the spot doing research at his laboratory. **Avocations:** Building furniture; Restoring houses **Political Affiliations:** Democrat **Thoughts on Life:** Dr. Gentry always tried to gather people together in a symposium setting to share their information on the species they were working on so that the group could have a better understanding of that group of animals. He really has enjoyed that process. He was one of the organizers of the Monocle Conference of the Marine Mammal Society. It was one of his favorite events in his career because it brought people from all across the world to discuss what they knew about the northern fur seal family. From 2005 until 2018, Dr. Gentry advised oil and gas companies on research they should fund relative to the effects of industry sound on marine mammals.

Louis "Lou" Gerber

Title: Legislative Director (Retired) **Industry:** Government Administration/ Government Relations/Government Services **Date of Birth:** 05/22/1944 **Place of Birth:** Washington, DC **State/Country of Origin:** DC/USA **Parents:** William Gerber; Sylvia (Wigdor) Gerber **Marital Status:** Married **Spouse Name:** Dolores T. Gerber **Children:** Jonathan Brown; Meagan Bratton **Education:** MA, University of Maryland, College Park, MD (1969); BA, University of Pennsylvania, Philadelphia, PA (1966) **Career:** Senior Fellow, Food Research & Action Center (2010-2020); Registered Lobbyist, Legislative Director, Communications Workers of America, AFL-CIO, Washington, DC (1972-2010); Legislative Consultant, Joint Committee on Congressional Operations, United States Congress, Washington, DC (1971); Legislative Assistant, United States Senator Stephen M. Young, United States Congress, Washington, DC (1970) **Career Related:** Member, Administrative Committee on Legislation, AFL-CIO (1972-2010) **Civic:** Former Appointed Member, Northern Virginia Workforce Investment Board; Big Brother, Big Brother Program, Big Brothers Big Sisters, National Capital Area, Washington, DC **Creative Works:** Author, Chapters in Two Books **Awards:** Special Recognition Award for Anti-Hunger Work, Food Research and Action Center (2004) **Memberships:** Council on Foreign Relations; Board of Directors, Congressional Hunger Center; Board of Directors, Americans for Democratic Action (ADA); Executive Board, Jewish Labor Committee **Marquis Who's Who Honors:** Albert Nelson Marquis Lifetime Achievement Award **To what do you attribute your success:** Mr. Gerber attributes his success to persistence and determination, as well as playing to strengths. **Why did you become involved in your profession or industry:** Mr. Gerber became involved in his profession because he grew up in Washington, DC, and at the time, the city was the classic example of taxation without representation. There was no representation in Congress or no election of a mayor and he thought that was an outrage. Mr. Gerber majored in political science and was always interested in politics and legislation, therefore, in order for there to be change, he decided to do that through law as opposed to doing it through individual behavior. He had also read in an article that congressional staff influenced the development of legislation and public policy, which he thought was a good article so he tore out the page and kept it because he found it interesting. Mr. Gerber wanted to make a difference in the lives of as many people as he could. It always felt to him that doing something in a legislative process where you can help make laws that have national or big impact is better than trying to be dealing with individual cases, not that individual cases don't have merit. However, in order to really effectuate change, working to help achieve progress through national laws is a great way to do it. Mr. Gerber likes the free flow that went with Congress. He likes the collaboration. Congress was more bipartisan than it is today; there was more courage and statesmanship in times of crisis. He likes the idea of trying to help make a difference and always thought the labor movement had an important role to play. Not only in serving as a voice for its own members, but more importantly, serving as a voice for people who didn't belong to an organization which could speak on their behalf to public officials. **Avocations:** Reading; Watching sports **Political Affiliations:** Democrat **Religion:** Jewish **Thoughts on Life:** Mr. Gerber said the following: "I'm a work in progress, rather than a finished product. Learning to be persistent without being relentless is especially challenging. Live in the moment as much as you can. Appreciating people for who they are is rewarding." Mr. Gerber has authored chapters in two books, one dealing with the future of organized labor and the other addressing organized labor's role in international telecommunications.

John Louis Gerin, PhD

Title: Virologist, Educator **Industry:** Education/Educational Services **Date of Birth:** 09/28/1937 **Place of Birth:** St. Paul **State/Country of Origin:** MN/USA **Parents:** Marcel Raymond Gerin; Mary (Olesen) Gerin **Spouse Name:** Suzanne Nott (08/27/1960, Deceased) **Children:** Kathleen Marcelle **Education:** PhD in Physiology, University of Tennessee (1964); MS in Physiology, University of Tennessee (1961); BS in Biology, Georgetown University (1959) **Career:** Professor, Department of Microbiology and Immunology, Georgetown University School of Medicine, Washington, DC (1979-2005); Director, Molecular Anatomy Program, Rockville, MD (1969-1978); Director, Molecular Anatomy, Infectious Diseases Program, Oak Ridge National Laboratory (1967-1979); Research Scientist, Oak Ridge National Laboratories (1967-1968); Group Leader, Abbott Laboratories, Inc., North Chicago, IL (1966-1967); Research Scientist, Abbott Laboratories, Inc., North Chicago, IL (1965-1966); Professor Emeritus, Georgetown University; Director, Division of Molecular Virology & Immunology, Georgetown University Medical Center, Rockville, MD **Career Related:** Scientific Advisory Board, New York Blood Center, New York, NY; Advisory Committee, University of California San Francisco; National Institutes of Health, Bethesda, MD **Civic:** Election Judge, Montgomery County, MD **Creative Works:** Co-Editor, Genotype-Specific Complementation of Hepatitis Delta Virus RNA Replication by Hepatitis Delta Antigen (1990, 1987); Contributor, Over 350 Articles, Professional Journals **Awards:** Co-Recipient, King Faisal Foundation International Prize for Medicine (1998) **Memberships:** American Association of Immunology; Infectious Diseases Society of America; American Society of Microbiology; American Association of Virology; American Association for Advancement of Science; Sigma Xi **Marquis Who's Who Honors:** Albert Nelson Marquis Lifetime Achievement Award; Marquis Who's Who Top Professional **Why did you become involved in your profession or industry:** Dr. Gerin became involved in his profession because he was trained in physiology and specialized in instrumentation that had been developed in the Oak Ridge National Laboratory. This technology was in high demand by the pharmaceutical companies for making vaccines, so he was hired to run the program at Abbott Laboratories. He then became interested in virology. Oak Ridge called him and asked if he would work on this new activity with the National Institutes of Health in the Bethesda area. He agreed and, by chance, breakthroughs were coming from the field of hepatitis B at the time, which led to its vaccinations. **Political Affiliations:** Independent **Religion:** Roman Catholic

Dr. Timothy J. Giardino

Title: Vice President of Human Resources **Industry:** Technology **Company Name:** BMC Software **Date of Birth:** 07/23/1977 **Place of Birth:** Rome **State/Country of Origin:** NY/USA **Parents:** Paul Giardino/Theresia Giardino **Marital Status:** Widow **Children:** Alessandra Giardino/Isabella Giardino **Education:** DBA, Walden University, Minneapolis, MN, Magna Cum Laude (2016); MBA, Baker College, Flint, MI, Magna Cum Laude; BS, Embry-Riddle Aeronautical University, Daytona Beach, FL **Certifications:** Senior Certified Professional in Human Resources, IPMA-HR; Workforce Planning and Analytics Certification, Institute for Human Resources; Integrated Talent Management Certification, Institute for Human Resources; Certified Six Sigma Black Belt, International Six Sigma Institute; Project Management Qualified, Management and Strategy Institute; Building a Better Response (International Humanitarian Coordination System), Harvard Business School; Executive Leadership Course, U.S. Army; Staff Planning Course, U.S. Army **Career:** Vice President of Human Resources, BMC Software (2020-Present); Meta Healthcare IT Solutions (2018-2020); Vice President of Human Resources, Cantata Health (2017-2020); Director, Workforce Management and Support, Texas Department of Family and Protective Services (2015-2017); Program Liaison Officer, U.S. Army (2013-2015); Global Human Resources Business Partner, U.S. Army (2008-2013) **Civic:** Volunteer, MicroMentor to Small-Business Owners, Mercy Corps (2013-2016); Carpenter, General Laborer, Committee Leader, Donations Manager, Ministry of Education, Afghanistan (2005); Habitat for Humanity International (2003) **Military Service:** U.S. Army (1995-2015) **Memberships:** Forbes Human Resource Council (2018-Present); National D.B.A. Society; Cheeky Scientist Association; Society for Human Resources Management (SHRM); International Public Management Association for Human Resources **Marquis Who's Who Honors:** Marquis Who's Who Top Professional **To what do you attribute your success:** Dr. Giardino attributes his success to a combination of formal education, practical experiences, and invaluable mentors. His drive and ambition are primarily fueled by both providing and being an example for his teenage daughters, Alessandra and Isabella. **Why did you become involved in your profession or industry:** Dr. Giardino became involved in his field as a direct result of his natural affinity for business and leadership. Though it was a challenge, he found that he was gifted in these fields and subsequently devoted his life's work to them.

Ernest Henry "Ernie" Gilmour

Title: Professor Emeritus; Paleontology Researcher **Industry:** Education/Educational Services **Company Name:** Eastern Washington University **Date of Birth:** 08/17/1936 **Place of Birth:** Adin **State/Country of Origin:** CA/USA **Parents:** Harold J. Gilmour; Velma Nettie (Helgerson) Gilmour **Marital Status:** Married **Spouse Name:** Venera A. Karimova (12/2000); Peggy June Keller (12/22/1982, Divorced 10/1999); Marie Jeanne Melton (06/27/1957, Divorced 09/1980) **Children:** Ernest Henry Jr. (Deceased); William Bryce (Deceased); Nadine Marie: Laura Lee **Education:** PhD, University of Montana (1967); MS, University of Montana (1964); BS, University of Southern California (1960) **Certifications:** Registered Professional Geologist, Idaho **Career:** Professor Emeritus, Eastern Washington University, Cheney, WA (2010-Present); Professor of Geology, Eastern Washington University (1967-2010); Senior Vice President, Provost, Eastern Washington University (1989-1991); Consultant to Archaeological Services Group, Eastern Washington University (1983-1991); Vice Provost for Graduate Studies and Research, Eastern Washington University (1987-1989); Department Chairman, Eastern Washington University (1976-1987); Assistant Professor, Montana College of Mineral Science and Technology (Now Montana Technological University), Butte, MT (1965-1967); Mineral Fuels Geologist, Montana Bureau of Mines and Geology, Montana Technological University (1965-1967); Field Geologist, U.S. Geological Survey (USGS), Great Falls, MT (1964-1965); Instructor, University of Montana, Missoula, MT (1964); Engineering Geologist, Department of Water Resources, State of California (1956-1961) **Career Related:** Paleontology Researcher (2010-present); Vice President, IGAL, Incorporated, Cheney, WA (1984-1985); Consultant, Senior Geologist, Salisbury and Dietz, Inc., Spokane, WA (1978-1984); Director, Strategic Minerals Analysis Project, United States Bureau of Mines (1975-1981); Director, Mineral Industry Locations Project (1975-1980); Director, Domestic Mining Fellowship Program, U.S. Department of Health & Human Services (1975-1980); Consultant, Vanguard Exploration Co., Spokane, WA (1969-1971); Consultant Micropaleontologist, Goudkoff and Hughes, Los Angeles, CA (1967); Teaching Assistant, University of Southern California (1960-1961); Reviewer, Grant Proposals, Division of Earth Sciences, National Science Foundation and Others **Creative Works:** Northwest Regional Editor, Paleontological Research Institute Newsletter (1980-1985); Member, Editorial Advisory Board, Northwest Geology (1975-1985); Contributor, Numerous Articles to Professional Journals **Awards:** Grantee, U.S. Department of Education (1987-Present); Grantee, Eastern Washington State University (1975, 1986-1987); Grantee, Smithsonian Institution (1986-1987); Fulbright Scholar, Pakistan (1980-1981); Trustee's Medal, Eastern Washington University (1978); Grantee, U.S. Department of Health & Human Services (1975-1980); Grantee, National Science Foundation (1974, 1975); Grantee, United States Bureau of Mines (1974-1980); Named Engineer of Year, Spokane Section, American Institute of Mining, Metallurgical, and Petroleum Engineers (1974); Grantee, Montana Bureau of Mines and Geology (1968); Fellow, National Defense Education Act (1961-1964); Summer Fellow, National Science Foundation (1961); Academic Scholar, University of Southern California (1954); Recipient, Numerous Grants **Memberships:** Secretary, Rocky Mountain Section, The Paleontological Society (1985-1991, 1995-Present); President, Pacific Section, The Paleontological Society (1979-1980, 1988-1989); Trustee, Northwest Mining Association (NWMA) (1971-1974, 1981-1984); President, Northwest Science Association (1975-1976); Fellow, The Geological Society of America, Inc.; American Association for the Advancement of Science; Life Member, Paleontological Research Institution; American Association of Petroleum Geologists (AAPG); International Bryozoology Association (IBA); National Association of Geology Teachers; International Paleontological Union; Honorary Life Member, Northwest Mining Association (NWMA); Western Society of Naturalists; Life Member, Trustee, Sigma Xi, the Scientific Research Honor Society; Sigma Gamma Epsilon; Phi Sigma; The Honor Society of Phi Kappa Phi **Marquis Who's Who Honors:** Albert Nelson Marquis Lifetime Achievement Award; Marquis Who's Who Top Professional **Why did you become involved in your profession or industry:** Dr. Gilmour was first studying journalism at the University of Southern California when he was challenged by one of his professors, Prof. William Easton. Prof. Easton inspired him to pursue a career in geology and especially paleontology. Also, Prof. Richard Stone was a great influence in his teaching career. He went to USC on a journalism scholarship, but after a year he switched his major to geology and paleontology. **Avocations:** Watercolor painting; Writing poetry; Pickleball; Pool **Political Affiliations:** Independent **Religion:** Humanist

Joan "Ruth" Bader Ginsburg

Title: Associate Justice **Industry:** Law and Legal Services **Company Name:** Supreme Court of the United States **Date of Birth:** 2/15/1933 **Place of Birth:** Brooklyn **State/Country of Origin:** NY/USA **Year of Passing:** 2020 **Parents:** Nathan Bader; Celia (Amster) Bader **Marital Status:** Widowed **Spouse Name:** Martin D. Ginsburg (06/23/1954, Deceased 06/27/2010) **Children:** Jane Carol; James Steven **Education:** Honorary Doctor of Laws, Harvard University (2011); Honorary Doctor of Laws, Princeton University (2010); Honorary Doctor of Laws, Willamette University (2009); Honorary Doctor of Laws, University of Pennsylvania (2007); Honorary Doctor of Laws, The George Washington University Law School (1997); Honorary Doctor of Laws, The Jewish Theological Seminary (1997); Honorary Doctor of Laws, Wheaton College (1997); Honorary Doctor of Laws, Brandeis University (1996); Honorary Doctor of Laws, University of Illinois (1995); Honorary Doctor of Laws, Long Island University (1994); Honorary Doctor of Laws, Smith College (1994); Honorary Doctor of Laws, Columbia University (1994); Honorary Doctor of Laws, New York University (1994); Honorary Doctor of Laws, Radcliffe College (Now Radcliffe Institute for Advanced Study), Harvard University (1994); Honorary Doctor of Laws, Lewis & Clark College (1992); Honorary Doctor of Laws, Rutgers, The State University of New Jersey (1991); Honorary Doctor of Laws, Amherst College (1991); Honorary Doctor of Humane Letters, Hebrew Union College - Jewish Institute of Religion (1988); Honorary Doctor of Laws, Brooklyn Law School (1987); Honorary Doctor of Laws, DePaul University (1985); Honorary Doctor of Laws, Georgetown University (1985); Honorary Doctor of Laws, Vermont Law School (1984); Honorary Doctor of Laws, American University (1981); Honorary Doctor of Laws, Lund University, Sweden (1969); Bachelor of Laws, Columbia Law School, NY (1959); Bachelor of Arts, Cornell University, Ithaca, NY (1954) **Career:** Associate Justice, Supreme Court of the United States, Washington, DC (1993-Present); Judge, United States Court of Appeals for the District of Columbia Circuit, Washington, DC (1980-1993); Professor, Columbia Law School (1972-1980); Professor, Rutgers Law School, Newark, NJ (1969-1972); Associate Professor, Rutgers Law School, Newark, NJ (1966-1969); Assistant Professor, Rutgers Law School, Newark, NJ (1963-1966); Associate Director, Project International Procedure, Columbia Law School (1962-1963); Research Associate, Columbia Law School (1961-1962); Law Clerk to Honorable Edmund L. Palmieri, United States District Court for the Southern District of New York (1959-1961) **Career Related:** Visiting Faculty, The Aspen Institute, CO (1990); Visiting Faculty, Salzburg Seminar of American Studies, Austria (1984); Board of Directors, American Civil Liberties Union (1974-1980); General Counsel, American Civil Liberties Union (1973-1980); Visiting Faculty, New York University School of Law (1978); Fellow, Center for Advanced Study in the Behavioral Sciences, Stanford University, CA (1977-1978); Visiting Faculty, University of Strasbourg (1975); Visiting Faculty, University of Amsterdam (1975); Founder, Director, American Civil Liberties Union Women's Rights Project (1972); Visiting Faculty, Harvard Law School (1971) **Creative Works:** Co-author, "My Own Words" (2016); Co-author, with H.H. Kay and K. M. Davidson, "Text, Cases and Materials on Sex-based Discrimination" (1974); Author, "Swedish Code of Judicial Procedure" (1968); Co-author, with Anders Bruzelius, "Civil Procedure in Sweden" (1965); Contributor, Numerous Articles to Books, Legal Texts and Professional Journals **Awards:** Berggruen Prize for Philosophy and Culture, Berggruen Institute (2019); Named One of the Women of the Year, Glamour Magazine (2012); Named One of Washington's Most Influential Women Lawyers, The National Law Journal (2010); Named One of the 100 Most Powerful Women in DC, Washingtonian Magazine (2009); Named One of the 100 Most Powerful Women, Forbes Magazine (2004, 2005, 2007-2010); Named to the National Women's Hall of Fame (2002); Fordham-Stein Ethics Prize, Fordham University (2001) **Memberships:** Council Member, The American Law Institute (1978-1993); Board of Directors, American Bar Foundation (1979-1989); Fellow, Honorary Life Member, Federal Bar Association; Fellow, American Academy of Arts & Sciences; Fellow, American Bar Foundation; Fellow, Honorary Member, American College of Trial Lawyers; American Bar Association; American Association for the Advancement of Science; Council on Foreign Relations; The American Law Institute **Bar Admissions:** The District of Columbia (1975); Supreme Court of the United States (1967); State of New York (1959) **Avocations:** Opera; Reading mysteries; Watching old movies; Horseback riding; Water-skiing; Golf **Religion:** Jewish

Simon Aaron Ginzburg, PhD

Title: Electrical Engineer (Retired) **Industry:** Research **Company Name:** The MITRE Corporation **Date of Birth:** 11/20/1937 **Place of Birth:** Moscow **State/Country of Origin:** Russia **Parents:** Broha Moisha (Obrant) Ginzburg (1910-2007); Aaron Samuel Ginzburg (1900-1984) **Marital Status:** Divorced **Children:** Irina; Natasha; Michael **Education:** PhD, Kotelnikov Institute of Radioengineering and Electronics (1969); MS, Kotelnikov Institute of Radioengineering and Electronics (1961) **Career:** Retired (2007); Lead Engineer, The MITRE Corporation, Bedford, MA (1997-2007); Senior Member, Technical Staff, Racal-Datacom, Inc., Boxborough, MA (1992-1997); Principal Engineer, Digital Equipment Corporation, Littleton, MA (1985-1992); Principal Engineer, Wang Laboratories, Lowell, MA (1980-1985); Engineer, Senior Engineer, Principal Engineer, Central Research Institute of Communication, Moscow, Russia (1969-1980) **Creative Works:** Author, "System of Information Transmission over Optical Cable" (1980); Author, "Lightwave Transmission Systems" (1980); Editor, "Waveguides for Communications" (1980); Author, "Statistical Communication" (1979); Author, "Statistical Communication" (1977); Author, "Waveguides with Discrete Correction" (1975) **Marquis Who's Who Honors:** Albert Nelson Marquis Lifetime Achievement Award **To what do you attribute your success:** Dr. Ginzburg attributes his success to perseverance. **Why did you become involved in your profession or industry:** Dr. Ginzburg became involved in his profession because he used to build AM radio receivers as a child. Due to his lifelong interest, he pursued studies in radio engineering at the collegiate level. **Avocations:** Cross-country skiing; Long-distance biking; Running; Swimming; Hiking **Political Affiliations:** Republican **Thoughts on Life:** Dr. Ginzburg said, "Trust God in difficult situations."

James N. Girardi

Title: Co-Founder, Chief Operating Officer **Industry:** Business Management/Business Services **Company Name:** Forcewave **Marital Status:** Married **Children:** Two Daughters **Education:** MBA, George Mason University School of Business; BA, William & Mary University; Residency, International Business, European Markets and Economics, University of Oxford; Residency, International Business, European Markets and Economics, University of Oxford **Certifications:** Agile Coach Certification (ICP-ACC); Certified Scrum Professional, Product Owner (CSP-PO); Certified Scrum Professional, ScrumMaster (CSP-SM); Certified Scrum Product Owner (CSPO); Certified ScrumMaster (CSM); ITIL v3; PMI Agile Certified Practitioner (PMI-ACP); Project Management Professional (PMP); CMMI-SVC; Apple Hardware **Career:** Chief Technology Officer, Director, We Rock Cancer (2019-Present); Vice President, Nova Labs (2018-Present); Co-Founder, Chief Operating Officer, Forcewave (2016-Present); Treasurer, Nova Labs (2017-2018); Senior Consultant, Knight Point Systems, LLC (2013-2016); Senior Consultant, Englity Corporation (2010-2013); Technical Specialist, Apple Inc. (2008-2010); Founder, Executive Director, Ambient Foundation (2006-2009); Operations Lead, Conceptual Vision Corporation (2006-2008); Consultant, Saitama Board of Education (2003-2006); Operations Lead, Management Applications Program (1996-2001) **Awards:** Leadership Award, Apple Inc. **Memberships:** American Mensa; IVY Mensa; International National Contract Management Association; Nova Labs; Project Management Institute; Scrum Alliance **To what do you attribute your success:** Mr. Girardi attributes his success to learning from his mistakes, as well as those of other people. He believes that success comes from failure. He comes from a family of entrepreneurs, which was a positive environment in which to grow up. **Why did you become involved in your profession or industry:** In the early 1990s, the internet was the next frontier. The internet helped businesses equal out the playing field, and while it didn't necessarily work out that way, it gave Mr. Girardi an opportunity to get into markets that were so closely held by other companies. Mr. Girardi thought technology was the most interesting ticket for him to do something meaningful.

Susan Aurelia Gitelson, PhD

Title: President and CEO **Industry:** International Affairs/International Business **Company Name:** MTIIC Corporation **Place of Birth:** New York **State/Country of Origin:** NY/USA **Parents:** Moses Leo Gitelson; Miriam Evelyn (Silverman) Gitelson **Education:** Honorary Degree, Hebrew University of Jerusalem (2004); Degree, University of California Berkeley; PhD, Columbia University; Master of International Affairs, Columbia SIPA; BA, Barnard College **Career:** President, MTIIC Corporation; President, International Consultants, Inc.; Director of International Affairs and the Third World, World Jewish Congress; Research Associate, Columbia University; Assistant Professor of International Relations, Hebrew University of Jerusalem; Trainee, Rockefeller Foundation **Civic:** Vice President, American Friends of the Hebrew University; Board of Directors, American Friends of the Hebrew University; Board of Overseers, Harry S. Truman Research Institute for the Advancement of Peace, Hebrew University of Jerusalem; Sponsor, Gitelson Peace Papers and Publications; Sponsor, Gitelson Peace Prize, Harry S. Truman Research Institute for the Advancement of Peace, Hebrew University of Jerusalem; Sponsor, Gitelson Lecture on Human Rights and U.S. Foreign Policy, Columbia University; President, Dr. Susan Aurelia Gitelson Foundation, Inc.; Sponsor, Dr. Susan Aurelia Gitelson Fund for Innovative Programs, Columbia School of International and Public Affairs; Co-Chair, Dean's Council, Columbia School of International and Public Affairs; Sponsor, Gitelson Essay Awards Center for Study of the Presidency; Sponsor, Gitelson Award, Columbia School of International and Public Affairs; Sponsor, Gitelson Policy Forum, Columbia School of International and Public Affairs; Sponsor, Dr. Susan Aurelia Gitelson Fund for Innovative Programs, Faculty of Arts and Sciences, Columbia University; Board of Advisors, National Committee on American Foreign Policy; Sponsor, Gitelson-Meyerowitz Distinguished Service Award, Sutton Place Synagogue; Trustee, Sutton Place Synagogue; Board of Overseers, Museum of Jewish Heritage—A Living Memorial to the Holocaust; International Board of Governors, Hebrew University of Jerusalem **Creative Works:** Author, "Giving Is Not Just For The Very Rich: A How-to Guide for Giving and Philanthropy," On-Demand Publishing, LLC (2012); Co-Editor, "Israel in the Third World," Transaction Publishers (1976); Author, "Multilateral Aid for National Development and Self-Reliance: A Case Study of the UNDP in Uganda and Tanzania" (1975); Contributor, Articles, Professional Journals; Editorial Committee, Jerusalem Papers on Peace Problems **Awards:** Alumni Medal for Distinguished Service, Columbia University; Outstanding Service Award, Columbia School of International and Public Affairs **Memberships:** President, Columbia School of International and Public Affairs Branch, Columbia Alumni Association, Columbia University (1980-1984); National Institute of Social Sciences; Columbia University Seminars, Columbia University; Executive Committee, Columbia Alumni Association, Columbia University; Carnegie Council; Columbia University Club; Einstein Visionaries Society; Network 2020; National Committee on American Foreign Policy; Center for the Study of the Presidency **Marquis Who's Who Honors:** Albert Nelson Marquis Lifetime Achievement Award; Distinguished Humanitarian Award **To what do you attribute your success:** Dr. Gitelson attributes her success to adaptability and the fact that she has always wanted to learn. She also likes interacting with people from many different fields and countries. These skills have enabled her to succeed in academia, entrepreneurial businesses and cultural organizations. **Why did you become involved in your profession or industry:** Dr. Gitelson chose her profession because she has always been internationally minded and all of her careers have been international with the same outlook. It is not enough to think only of oneself, family, community, etc., but it is marvelous to learn about other people. Other people seem to appreciate it when you show concern for them. She has been able to build relationships with many people by creating trust. **Thoughts on Life:** Dr. Gitelson is most proud that she established the Gitelson Award for Human Values and International Affairs at the Columbia School of International and Public Affairs in 1979, and later founded the Gitelson Peace Prize at the Truman Institute in Israel in 1989. These awards demonstrate her concern with human values and peace.

Stephen Michael Gleason

Title: Former Professional Football Player **Industry:** Leisure, Travel & Tourism **Company Name:** New Orleans Saints **Date of Birth:** 03/19/1977 **Place of Birth:** Spokane **State/Country of Origin:** WA/USA **Marital Status:** Married **Spouse Name:** Michel Rae Varisco **Children:** Rivers; Gray **Education:** Diplomate, Washington State University, Pullman, WA (1995); Diplomate, Gonzaga Preparatory School, Spokane, WA **Career:** Professional Football Player, New Orleans Saints, NFL (2000-2006); Professional Football Player, Indianapolis Colts, NFL (2000); Football Player, Washington State University, Pullman, WA **Civic:** Contributor, ALS Awareness, The ALS Association **Creative Works:** Co-collaborator, "Gleason" (2016); Guest Appearance, "A Football Life," NFL Network (2013) **Awards:** Congressional Gold Medal (2019); George Halas Award, Pro Football Writers Association (2015); Recipient, Key to the City of New Orleans (2011); Super Bowl Ring (2011)

Francis S. "Bo" Godbold

Title: Investment Banker, Security Firm Executive **Company Name:** Raymond James Financial, Inc. **Place of Birth:** Charleston **State/Country of Origin:** SC/USA **Parents:** Francis Stanley Godbold; Ula Leigh (Waddey) Godbold **Marital Status:** Married **Spouse Name:** Lelia Elizabeth Harman (09/24/1966) **Children:** John A.; Laura H. Blair **Education:** MBA, Harvard University (1969); BS, Industrial Engineering, Georgia Institute of Technology, With Honors (1965) **Career:** Vice-Chairman, Raymond James Financial, Inc. (2002-Present); Executive Vice President, Raymond, James & Associates, Inc., St. Petersburg, FL (1978-Present); President, Raymond James Financial, Inc. (1987-2002); Senior Vice President, Raymond, James & Associates, Inc., St. Petersburg, FL (1974-1978); Vice President, Raymond, James & Associates, Inc., St. Petersburg, FL (1969-1974) **Career Related:** Director, Raymond James Financial (1977-Present); Regional Firms Advisory Committee, New York Stock Exchange (1990-1993); Board of Directors, Raymond James Bank, Raymond James Financial **Civic:** Trustee, Georgia Technical Foundation, Inc. (2003-Present); Leadership St. Petersburg (1974-Present); Chairman, Investments Committee, Georgia Technical Foundation (2007-2009); Georgia Technical Foundation Executive Committee (2007); Board of Directors, Academy Preparatory (1999-2007); President, Elk River Properties Owners Association (2004-2006); Chairman, Finance Committee, Elk River Properties Owners Association (2003-2004); Director, Georgia Technical Industrial and Systems Engineering Alumni Award (1997); Tampa Bay Area Regional Development Council (1995); Lakewood High School Parent Action Committee (1984-1990); President, Lakewood High School Parent Action Committee (1987-1988); President, Baypoint Middle School Parent Action Committee (1982-1983); Bay Vista Parent Action Committee (1979-1980); Scoutmaster, Boy Scouts of America (1966-1967); Finance Committee, Elk River Club; Board Director, Banner Elk Heritage Foundation **Military Service:** Captain, U.S. Army (1965-1967) **Awards:** Inductee, Georgia Tech Engineering Hall of Fame (2020); Joseph Mayo Pettit Distinguished Service Award, Georgia Institute of Technology (2016); Georgia Tech Distinguished Engineering Alumni (1997); Real Estate Investment Performance Award, Raymond James (1981); Raymond James Man of the Year (1978); Raymond James Image Maker Award (1972); Eagle Scout (1956) **Memberships:** Trustee, Georgia Technical Alumni Association (2002-2005); Regional Firms Committee, Securities Industry Association (1995-1999); Chairman, Regional Firms Committee, Securities Industry Association (1998); Nominating Committee, Securities Industry Association (1997); National Director, Securities Industry Association (1995-1997); Tax Policy Committee, Securities Industry Association (1995-1997); Executive Committee, Securities Industry Association (1988-1996); Chairman, Securities Industry Association (1987); Treasurer, Securities Industry Association (1986); Treasurer, Harvard Business School Club (1984); Vice Chairman, Southern District, Securities Industry Association (1980); President, Harvard Club Of West Coast Florida (1973-1974); Vice President, Harvard Club Of West Coast Florida (1972-1973); Secretary-Treasurer, Harvard Club Of West Coast Florida (1971-1972); St. Petersburg Country Club; Elk River Club; Diamond Creek Golf Club; Tau Beta Pi; Phi Kappa Phi; Alpha Pi Mu; Phi Delta Theta **Avocations:** Golf **Political Affiliations:** Republican **Religion:** Protestant **Thoughts on Life:** Mr. Godbold is analytical, inquisitive, conservative, outspoken, and tough, but he is fair.

Lillian Gohlke

Title: School Librarian (Retired) **Industry:** Library Management/Library Services **Date of Birth:** 02/02/1937 **Place of Birth:** Nada **State/Country of Origin:** TX/USA **Parents:** Fred Joe Kubesch; Frieda (Meismer) Kubesch **Marital Status:** Married **Spouse Name:** Roddy Hobbs (10/19/2018); William Carlton Gohlke (08/01/1964, Deceased 10/28/2012) **Children:** David; Kristi **Education:** MA, Sam Houston State University (1963); BA, Sam Houston State University (1959); AA, Wharton County Junior College (1957) **Certifications:** Library Certificate (1961) **Career:** School Librarian (Retired); Public Library Volunteer, Sheridan Memorial Library (1992-2002); School Librarian, Rice High School, Altair, TX (1981-1992); Teacher, English, Rice High School, Altair, TX (1970-1981); Teacher, English/Spanish, Sheridan High School (1959-1970) **Career Related:** Future Teacher Advisor (1971-1992); Universal Interscholastic League Coordinator, Rice High School, Altair, TX (1970-1992); National Defense Education Act Fellow, English, University of Texas (1962); National Defense Education Act Fellow, Spanish University of Texas (1960) **Civic:** Board of Directors, San Bernard Electric Cooperative, Bellville, TX (1980-Present); Instrumental in Initiation of STEP for Libraries Senior Texan Employment Program, Waco, TX (1993-2003); Summer Swimming Instructor, Sheridan Swimming Pool (1960-1980) **Creative Works:** Author, Texas Outlook Magazine (1964) **Awards:** John H. Lovelady Lifetime for Youth Award, Future Teachers America (1992) **Memberships:** Texas State Teachers Association; Texas Library Association; Texas Association of Family and Community Education; Catholic Daughters of America; Delta Zeta; Texas Retired Teachers; National Education Association **Marquis Who's Who Honors:** Albert Nelson Marquis Lifetime Achievement Award; Marquis Who's Who Top Professional **Why did you become involved in your profession or industry:** Ms. Gohlke played fictional "school" as a child. She was always the teacher and her siblings loved every second of it. As she grew up, she began getting the best grades in her English classroom; this led her to major in English. Next, when she had to take a foreign language class, she chose Spanish and found that it came easily to her. Thus, the choice to begin teaching was easily made. The most satisfying part of her life as a teacher is that she is fulfilling a dream her mother had, but never carried out. **Avocations:** Reading; Travel; Working with plants; Walking; Jogging **Political Affiliations:** Republican **Religion:** Roman Catholic

Stanley Irwin Goldberg

Title: Real Estate Company Executive **Industry:** Real Estate **Company Name:** Mutual Realty Corp **Date of Birth:** 05/13/1934 **Place of Birth:** Newport News **State/Country of Origin:** VA/USA **Parents:** David Goldberg; Sara (Levy) Goldberg **Marital Status:** Widower **Spouse Name:** Marilyn Levin (11/22/1963, Deceased 10/1970) **Children:** Andrew Garfield **Education:** Coursework, University of Virginia (1954-1955); Coursework, College of William and Mary (1952-1954) **Certifications:** Licensed Real Estate Broker, Virginia **Career:** President, Mutual Realty Corp, Newport News, VA (1973-Present); Managing Partner, Goldkress Investment Co, Newport News, VA (1970-2015); Board of Directors, Goldkress Investment Co, Newport News, VA (1970-2015); President, Bedding Supply Co, Newport News, VA (1962-1970); Executive Vice President, Bedding Supply Co, Newport News, VA (1960-1961); Vice President, Bedding Supply Co., Inc., Newport News, VA (1956-1959) **Civic:** Trustee, Temple Sinai; Trustee, Newport News **Military Service:** U.S. Air Force (1957-1958) **Memberships:** National Association of Realtors; Virginia Association of Realtors; Virginia Peninsula Association of Realtors; Virginia Elks Lodge Youth Camp **Marquis Who's Who Honors:** Albert Nelson Marquis Lifetime Achievement Award **To what do you attribute your success:** Mr. Goldberg attributes his success to the time he spent at the University of Virginia, which changed his life. **Why did you become involved in your profession or industry:** Mr. Goldberg became involved in real estate because his father started their family company, which was involved in the war effort by putting mattresses on the ships before they went out. This is how the family became associated with Who's Who. **Avocations:** Sports; Sports memorabilia; Billiards; Playing cards; Jazz music

Jeffrey A. Golds, PhD

Title: Fellow Software Engineer **Industry:** Engineering **Company Name:** AMD, Inc. **Date of Birth:** 6/4/1969 **Place of Birth:** Dearborn **State/Country of Origin:** MI/USA **Marital Status:** Married **Spouse Name:** Kathleen (2000) **Children:** Alexander; Sebastian **Education:** PhD in Mathematics, Ohio State University (1998); BA in Mathematics, College of Wooster (1991) **Career:** Fellow, Software Development Engineer, Advanced Micro Devices, Inc. (AMD) (2015–Present); Principal Member of Technical Staff, Advanced Micro Devices, Inc. (AMD) (2011–2015); Lead for the OpenCL Driver Performance Team, Senior Member Technical Staff, Advanced Micro Devices, Inc. (AMD) (2006–2011); Software Engineer, S3 Graphics (1999–2011); Staff Engineer, ATI (2005–2006); Senior Software Engineer, ATI (2002–2005); Senior Software Engineer, Resilience (2001–2002); Contractor, Silicon Graphics (1998–1999) **Creative Works:** Author, Dissertation (1999) **To what do you attribute your success:** Dr. Golds attributes his success to his problem solving abilities. Because of his years of experience, others come to him for answers. He started his career in tech support and it was not what he wanted to do, but he needed a job before he could find something he was interested in. **Why did you become involved in your profession or industry:** Dr. Golds became involved in his profession as a software engineer, but currently works in hardware engineering. His biggest competition is Intel and Nvidia, so he tries to understand their methods and compare his strengths to theirs. **Avocations:** Astronomy; Chess; Skiing **Thoughts on Life:** Looking toward the future, Dr. Golds sees a lot of changes to his industry. Machine learning is going to change everything, from self-driving cars to self-identifying diseases. He fears this will lead to job losses. His work is focused on GPU architecture and competitive analysis.

Duncan Goldthwaite

Title: Petroleum Geologist, Consultant **Industry:** Oil & Energy **Date of Birth:** 03/31/1927 **Place of Birth:** New York **State/Country of Origin:** NY/USA **Parents:** George Edgar Goldthwaite; Emily Jack (Duncan) Goldthwaite **Marital Status:** Married **Spouse Name:** Margaret Turner Temple (2/4/1956) **Children:** Madelyn; Virginia; Mary Catherine; Martha Nell **Education:** MA, Harvard University (1952); BA, Oberlin College (1950) **Career:** Consultant, Petroleum Geologist, Metairie, LA (1985-Present); Exploration Geologist, Oil, Cas and Minerals, Various Locations, Chevron U.S.A. (1952-1985) **Career Related:** Teacher, Subsurface Mapping, Atwater Consultant Ltd., New Orleans, LA (1986) **Civic:** Member, City Council, City of Gulf Breeze, Florida (1962-1964); Captain, Gulf Breeze Volunteer Fire Department (1960-1965) **Military Service:** Served with U.S. Navy, Aviation Radio now Third Cross (1945-1946) **Creative Works:** Co-author, Subsurface Mapping Course (1994); Editor, Contributing Author, "Introduction to Central Gulf Coast Geology" (1991) **Awards:** Distinguished Service Award, Gulf Coast Association of Geological Societies (1995) **Memberships:** President, New Orleans Geological Society (1982-1983); Fellow, Geological Society America; American Association of Petroleum Geologists; Honorary Life Member, New Orleans Geological Society **Marquis Who's Who Honors:** Albert Nelson Marquis Lifetime Achievement Award **Why did you become involved in your profession or industry:** Mr. Goldthwaite became involved in his profession because he was interested in science since he was a small kid. His father was an electrical engineer and so that was what got him started early and the interest remained. **Avocations:** Reading history and science; Mountain climbing **Religion:** Congregationalist

Bridgette L. Gomillion-Williams, PhD

Title: Senior Silicone Chemist **Industry:** Sciences **Company Name:** Quanex Building Products **Date of Birth:** 07/19/1966 **Place of Birth:** Augusta **State/Country of Origin:** GA/USA **Marital Status:** Married **Spouse Name:** Robert **Children:** Catherine **Education:** PhD in Polymer Science, School of Material Science and Engineering, Clemson University (2000); BS in Polymer Chemistry, Georgia Institute of Technology (1990) **Career:** Senior Silicone Chemist, Quanex Building Products Corporation (2017-Present); Technical Research Specialist, Saint-Gobain Performance Plastics (2009-2017); Product Development Specialist, The Dow Chemical Company (2003-2009); Senior Research Engineer, The Dow Chemical Company (2000-2003); Extrusion Plant Chemical Engineer, Shaw Industries (1990-1992) **Civic:** United Way **Awards:** Featured Member, Calendar Series (2017); Named, Professional of the Year (2017); Named, Industry Expert Honoree (2017); Inductee, Top Female Executives (2016-2017); Featured Member, Pro-Files Magazine (2016); Inductee, Elite Women Worldwide (2016); Recipient, Worldwide Lifetime Achievement Award (2015-2017); Inductee, Elite American Executives (2015-2016); Named, Professional of the Year (2014-2015); Inductee, Top Female Executives (2012-2014); Featured Member, Pro-Files Magazine (2012-2013); Named, Professional of the Year (2011-2012); Recipient, Worldwide Lifetime Achievement (2011); Inductee, Elite American Executives (2011) **Memberships:** American Institute of Chemical Engineers; American Fiber Society; American Chemical Society; Society of Plastics Engineers **Marquis Who's Who Honors:** Albert Nelson Marquis Lifetime Achievement Award; Marquis Who's Who Top Professional **To what do you attribute your success:** Dr. Gomillion-Williams attributes her success to her natural curiosity. **Why did you become involved in your profession or industry:** Dr. Gomillion-Williams became involved in her profession after majoring in chemical engineering and working with The Dow Chemical Company. **Avocations:** Golfing; Reading; Piano; Flute

Martin G. Gonzales

Title: Owner/Chief Executive Officer **Industry:** Food & Restaurant Services **Company Name:** La Milpa, Real Mexican Food & Market **Marital Status:** Single **Children:** One Son **Education:** Degree in Architecture **Career:** Owner, La Milpa Restaurant & Market (2000-Present); **Career Related:** Teacher, Art, Local School **Civic:** Supplier, Market and Restaurant, Community and Local Farmers **Awards:** Nominated, Elvis Award for Best Restaurant **Thoughts on Life:** Inspire your community.

Jesse Gonzalez

Title: Founder, Chief Managing Member, Lawyer **Industry:** Law and Legal Services **Company Name:** The J. Gonzalez Injury Attorneys P.L.L.C. **Date of Birth:** 07/11/1968 **Place of Birth:** McAllen **State/Country of Origin:** TX/USA **Education:** JD, St. Mary's School of Law (2000); MEd, University of Texas – Pan American (1995); BIS, University of Texas–Pan American (1992) **Career:** Owner, Attorney, J. Gonzalez Law Firm (2000-Present); Teacher, 12th Grade English; Elementary Teacher **Awards:** Martindale-Hubbell Client's Champion Platinum (2020, 2019); List of the Best Car Accident Lawyers in McAllen, Expertise (2019); Avvo Client's Choice (2019); Best of Thervo (2019); ThreeBestRated® Certificate of Excellence (2019); Elite Advocate (2018); Lawyer of the Year (2013, 2015, 2016, 2018); Listee, Top 3 Personal Injury Attorneys in McAllen; Listee, Million Dollar Advocates Forum; Listee, Best of the Best Attorneys; Lifetime Charter Member, Best Attorneys in America; ListaLegal's Latinos' Choice; Listee, Premier Lawyers of America **Memberships:** State Bar of Texas (2001) **Bar Admissions:** Texas (2001) **Marquis Who's Who Honors:** Marquis Who's Who Top Professional **To what do you attribute your success:** Mr. Gonzalez attributes his success to client feedback. He has represented thousands of clients in various cases, all of which provided him with valuable career insights. **Why did you become involved in your profession or industry:** Mr. Gonzalez was working as an elementary school teacher and then moved on to teaching 12th-grade literature. Later in life, he decided he wanted to become a principal; he went back to school to get a master's degree, and eventually took a class on educational law. It was there that he found his passion. He then went to St. Mary's School of Law School to earn a Juris Doctor. Prior to becoming a lawyer, Mr. Gonzalez was passionate about helping people. He felt frustrated that he couldn't do more when he saw loved ones in need of legal aid, which inspired his career choice. **Thoughts on Life:** Mr. Gonzalez's motto is, "This is your life. Follow your heart, follow your passion, and be careful with some of the advice that people will give you because it may limit your potential."

Hector R. Gonzalez-Romanace

Title: Bank Director and Telecommunications Executive (Retired), Private Investor **Industry:** Telecommunications **Company Name:** Ventek Group Inc. **Date of Birth:** 12/13/1933 **Place of Birth:** Ponce **State/Country of Origin:** Puerto Rico **Parents:** Carlos Gonzalez; Jacqueline (Romanace Porrata-Doria) Gonzalez **Marital Status:** Married **Spouse Name:** Provita Torres **Children:** Leticia; Hector Orestes; Miguel Eduardo **Education:** Postgraduate Coursework, Columbia University (1955-1956); Bachelor's Degree in Economics, College of the Holy Cross, Worcester, MA (1955) **Career:** President, Chief Executive Officer, Ventek Group, Inc. (1997-Present); Board of Directors, Banco Popular/Popular Inc. (1991-2004); President, Chief Executive Officer, TPC Communications of PR Inc., and Subsidiary of Teleponce Cable TV Inc. (1978-2001); Trustee, Finance and Executive Committee, Damas Foundation and Hospital, Ponce, PR (1975-2000); Board of Directors, Banco De Ponce, Puerto Rico and New York (1973-1991); President, Gonzalez & Co., Family Firm Involved in Real Estate, Travel Agencies, Wholesale Drugs (1972-1983) **Military Service:** U.S. Army (1958-1960) **Awards:** Honorary Consul, France (1969); Youth Development Program Award, Vice President of the United States (1966) **Memberships:** President, Ponce Chapter, Rotary Club (1963); National Cable TV Association; Club Deportivo; Yacht Club; Bankers **Marquis Who's Who Honors:** Albert Nelson Marquis Lifetime Achievement Award; Marquis Who's Who Top Professional **To what do you attribute your success:** Mr. Gonzalez-Romanace attributes his success to his father and mentor, and his determination. **Why did you become involved in your profession or industry:** The cable television business was a novel industry with enormous possibilities. **Avocations:** Travel **Political Affiliations:** Independent **Religion:** Roman Catholic **Thoughts on Life:** Life is beautiful and with lots of opportunities to enjoy it.

Jane Goodall

Title: Primatologist, Anthropologist **Industry:** Sciences **Date of Birth:** 04/03/1934 **Place of Birth:** London **State/Country of Origin:** United Kingdom **Parents:** Mortimer Herbert Morris-Goodall; Vanne (Joseph) Morris-Goodall **Marital Status:** Widowed **Spouse Name:** Derek Bryceson (1975, Deceased 1980); Hugo Van Lawick (1964, Divorced 1974) **Children:** Hugo Eric Louis **Education:** Honorary Degree, Hasselt University (2020); Honorary Degree, National Tsing Hua University, Taiwan (2012); Honorary Degree, University of Toronto (2008); Honorary Degree, Rutgers, the State University of New Jersey (2005); Honorary Degree, Syracuse University, NY (2005); Honorary Degree, University of Pécs, Hungary (2005); Honorary Degree, University of Central Lancashire, England, United Kingdom (2003); Honorary Degree, Sweet Briar College, VA (2002); Honorary Degree, Elon University, NC (2002); Honorary Degree, Providence University, Taiwan (2001); Honorary Degree, Ryerson University, Canada (2001); Honorary Degree, University at Buffalo (2001); Honorary Degree, University of Minnesota (2001); Honorary Degree, Wesleyan College, Macon, GA (2000); PhD in Ethology, University of Cambridge (1965); Numerous Other Honorary Degrees **Career:** Researcher in Animal Behavior, Scientific Director, Gombe Stream Research Centre, Tanzania (1960-2003); Assistant, Secretary to Dr. Louis S.B. Leakey, Coryndon Memorial Museum, National History, Olduvai Gorge, Tanzania **Career Related:** Messenger, Peace UN (2002-Present); Honorary Visiting Professor, Zoology, University of Dar es Salaam, Tanzania (1973-Present); Andrew D. White Professor-at-large, Cornell University (1996-2002); Associate, Cleveland Museum of Natural History (1990); Distinguished Adjunct Professor, Occupational Therapy and Anthropology, University of Southern California (1990); Adjunct Professor, Department of Environmental Studies, Tufts University Cummings School of Veterinary Medicine (1987-1988); Visiting Professor, Psychiatry, Human Biology, Stanford University (1971-1975); Lecturer, Yale University (1973); Speaker, "20/20," "Nightline," "Good Morning America"; Honorary Fellow, Royal Anthropological Institute **Civic:** Advisory Board, Friends of Africa International, Inc. (2005-Present); Advisory Council, Cincinnati Zoo & Botanical Garden (2005-Present); Advisory Board, Initiative for Animals and Ethics, Harvard University (2004-Present); International Advisory Board, Teachers Without Borders (2001-Present); Advisory Board, Laboratory Primate Advocacy Group (2001-Present); Advisory Board, Stitching Fred Foundation, The Netherlands (1996-Present); Advisory Board, Dolphin Project International and Dolphin Project Europe (1995-Present); Advisory Board, Trees for Life, Scotland, United Kingdom (1994-Present); Trustee, Jane Goodall Institute, Canada (1993-Present); Advisory Board, Albert Schweitzer Institute for the Humanities (1991-Present); Advisory Board, Advocates for Animals, Ltd., Scotland, United Kingdom (1990-Present); Trustee, The Jane Goodall Institute, England, United Kingdom (1988-Present); International Director, ChimpanZoo: Research, Education and Enrichment (1984-Present); Scientific Governor, Chicago Academy of Sciences (1981-Present); Founder, The Jane Goodall Institute (1977-Present) **Creative Works:** Co-author, "Seeds of Hope: Wisdom and Wonder from the World of Plants" (2013); Author, "Hope for Animals and Their World: How Endangered Species Are Being Rescued from the Brink" (2009); Co-author, "Harvest for Hope: A Guide to Mindful Eating" (2005); Co-author, "Rickie and Henri: A True Story" (2004); Co-author, "The Ten Trusts: What We Must Do to Care for the Animals We Love" (2002); Author, "Jane Goodall's Wild Chimpanzees" (2002); Author, "Chimpanzees I Love: Saving Their World and Ours" (2001); Author, "Chimps R Us" (2001); Author, "Beyond Innocence: An Autobiography in Letters" (2001); Author, "The Eagle and the Wren" (2000); Author, "Africa in My Blood: An Autobiography in Letters" (2000); Author, "Dr. White" (1999); Author, "40 Years at Gombe" (1999); Author, "Jane Goodall: Reason for Hope" (1999); Author, "Brutal Kinship" (1999); Author, "Jane Goodall: With Love" (1994); Author, "Visions of Caliban" (1993); Author, Books; Contributor, Numerous Articles, Professional Journals **Awards:** Named One of the Women of Discovery (2007): International Patron, Immortal Chaplains Foundation (Now Four Chaplains Memorial Foundation) (2006); Lifetime Achievement Award, Jules Verne Adventures (2006); Gold Medal Award, United Nations Educational (2006); Pax Natura Award (2005); President's Medal for Exemplary Achievement, Westminster College (2005); European Heroes Award, Time Magazine (2004); Nierenberg Prize for Science in the Public Interest (2004); Prince of Asturias Award (2003); Benjamin Franklin Medal in Life Science (2003); Huxley Memorial Medal, Royal Anthropological Institute (2001-2002); Gandhi/King Award for Nonviolence (2001); John Hay Award, Orion Society (1998); Public Service Award, National Scientific Board (1998); Recipient, Numerous Awards **Memberships:** Academia Scientiarium Et Artium Europaea Austria; Deutsche Akademie Der Naturforscher Leopoldina; Society of Women Geographers; The American Philosophical Society; Foreign Member, Research Center for Human Ethology; Honorary Foreign Member, American Academy of Arts & Sciences; The Explorer's Club

Roger Stokoe Goodell

Title: Commissioner **Industry:** Athletics **Company Name:** National Football League (NFL) **Date of Birth:** 02/19/1959 **Place of Birth:** Jamestown **State/Country of Origin:** NY/USA **Parents:** Charles Ellsworth Goodell; Jean (Rice) Goodell **Marital Status:** Married **Spouse Name:** Jane Skinner (10/25/1997) **Children:** Two Children **Education:** Intern, NFL, New York, NY (1982-1983); BA in Economics, Washington & Jefferson College (1981) **Career:** Commissioner, National Football League (NFL), New York, NY (2006-Present); Executive Vice President, Chief Operating Officer, NFL, New York, NY (2001-2006); Executive Vice President of Business, Properties and Club Services, NFL, New York, NY (2000-2001); Executive Vice President, Football Development, NFL, New York, NY (1997-2000); Senior Vice President, League and Football Development, NFL, New York, NY (1995-1997); Vice President, International Operations, Business Development, NFL, New York, NY (1992-1995); Executive Director, Club Relations and International Development, NFL, New York, NY (1991-1992); Director, Club Administration and International Development, NFL, New York, NY (1990-1991); Assistant to President, American Football Conference (AFC) (1987-1990); Public Relations Assistant, NFL, New York, NY (1984-1987); Member, Public Relations, Administration, New York Jets, NFL (1983-1984) **Civic:** Member, Board, Big Brothers Big Sisters of America, New York City Chapter, NY **Awards:** Named One of the 50 Most Powerful People in Sports, Sports Illustrated (2013); Named One of the Most Influential People in the World of Sports, Business Week (Now Bloomberg Businessweek) (2007, 2008); Named One of the 50 Most Influential People in Sports Business, Street & Smith's SportsBusiness Journal (2007-2009)

John Bannister Goodenough

Title: Scientist, Physicist, Professor **Industry:** Education/Educational Services **Company Name:** The University of Texas at Austin **Date of Birth:** 07/25/1922 **Place of Birth:** Jena **State/Country of Origin:** Germany **Parents:** Erwin Ramsdell Goodenough; Helen Meriam (Lewis) Goodenough **Marital Status:** Married **Spouse Name:** Irene Johnston Wiseman (06/16/1951) **Education:** Honorary Doctorate, Universidade de Santiago de Compostela (2002); Honorary MA, University of Oxford (1976); Honorary Doctorate, Université de Bordeaux (1967); PhD, The University of Chicago (1952); MS, The University of Chicago (1951); BA, Yale University (1943) **Certifications:** Registered Professional Engineer **Career:** Virginia H. Cockrell Centennial Chair, The University of Texas at Austin (1986-Present); Professor of Engineering, The University of Texas at Austin (1986-Present); Professor, University of Oxford (1976-1986); Head of Inorganic Chemical Laboratory, University of Oxford (1976-1986); Research Scientist, Massachusetts Institute of Technology (1952-1976); Group Leader, Massachusetts Institute of Technology (1952-1976); Lincoln Laboratory, Massachusetts Institute of Technology (1952-1976); Research Engineer, Westinghouse Research Corporation (1951-1952) **Career Related:** Honorary Professor, Northwestern University (1996); Honorary Professor, Jilin University (1996); Visiting Raman Professor, Indian Institute of Science (1983); Centenary Lecturer, Royal Society of Chemistry (1976); Trustee, Neuroscience Research Program (1962-1976); Fellow, Neuroscience Research Program (1962-1976); Fellow, American Association for the Advancement of Science **Military Service:** Captain, U.S. Air Force (1942-1948) **Creative Works:** Associate Editor, Journal of Materials Chemistry (1991-Present); Associate Editor, "Solid State Ionics" (1980-Present); Author, "Witness to Grace" (2008); Associate Editor, "Structure and Bonding" (1977-2001); Associate Editor, Journal of Solid State Chemistry (1968-2001); Associate Editor, European Journal of Inorganic Chemistry (1992); Associate Editor, "Chemistry of Materials" (1989-1992); Editorial Board Member, Journal of Applied Electrochemistry (1982-1989); Associate Editor, Superconductor Science and Technology (1987); Associate Editor, Materials Research Bulletin (1966-1980); Author, "Les Oxydes des Métaux de Transition" (1973); Author, "Magnetism and the Chemical Bond" (1963); Co-Author, "Solid Oxide Fuel Cell Technology: Principles, Performance and Operations"; Contributor, Articles, Professional Journals; Contributor, Chapters, Books **Awards:** Nobel Prize in Chemistry (2019); Charles Stark Draper Prize, National Academy of Engineering, National Academy of Sciences (2014); Lifetime Achievement Award, NAATBatt International (2012); Medal, National Academy of Sciences (2012); Medal for Environmental and Safety Technologies, IEEE (2012); Distinguished Alumni Award, Department of Mechanical Engineering, Cockrell School of Engineering, The University of Texas at Austin (2012); National Medal of Science (2011); Inventor of The Year Award, Office of Technology Commercialization, The University of Texas at Austin (2011); Foreign Membership, The Royal Society (2010); Enrico Fermi Award, U.S. Department of Energy (2009); Honorary Member, The World Innovation Foundation (2002); Hocott Award, Department of Mechanical Engineering, Cockrell School of Engineering, The University of Texas at Austin (2001-2002); Japan Prize, The Japan Prize Foundation (2001); Olin Palladium Award, The Electrochemical Society (1999); John Bardeen Award, MetSoc of CIM (1997); Von Hippel Award, Materials Research Society (1989); Solid State Chemistry Prize, Royal Society of Chemistry (1980) **Memberships:** The Royal Society; Royal Society of Chemistry; American Physical Society; Foreign Associate, Indian Academy of Sciences, Bengaluru; National Academy of Engineering, National Academy of Sciences; Foreign Associate, French Académie des Sciences; Honorary Member, Materials Research Society; Foreign Associate, Real Academia de Ciencias; American Chemical Society; The Physical Society of Japan; Ashmolean Club, University of Oxford; Skull and Bones; The Phi Beta Kappa Society; Sigma Xi, The Scientific Research Honor Society **Marquis Who's Who Honors:** Albert Nelson Marquis Lifetime Achievement Award **Why did you become involved in your profession or industry:** Dr. Goodenough became involved in his profession because of a series of opportunities with which he was presented. **Thoughts on Life:** Dr. Goodenough dedicates the award to his late wife, Irene.

Major M. Goodman

Title: Botanical Sciences Educator **Industry:** Education/Educational Services **Date of Birth:** 09/13/1938 **State/Country of Origin:** IA/USA **Parents:** Jarrett Wilson (Deceased 1947); Mable Ollie (Michael) (Deceased 1978) **Marital Status:** Married **Spouse Name:** Sheila Goodman (08/08/1970) **Children:** Sean Balfour Dail; Andrew Scot Dail **Education:** PhD, NC State University (1965); MS, NC State University (1963); BS, Iowa State University of Science and Technology (1960) **Career:** William Neal Reynolds Distinguished Professor, NC State University, Raleigh, NC (1988-Present); Professor of Crop Science, Statistics, Genetics and Botany, NC State University, Raleigh, NC (1976-1988); Associate Professor, NC State University, Raleigh, NC (1970-1976); Assistant Professor, NC State University, Raleigh, NC (1968-1970); Visiting Assistant Professor, NC State University, Raleigh, NC (1967-1968); Postdoctoral Fellow, Escola Superior de Agricultura, Institute of Genetics, National Science Foundation (1965-1967); Cooperative Fellow, National Science Foundation, NC State University, Raleigh, NC (1961-1965); Research Assistant, NC State University, Raleigh, NC (1960-1961) **Creative Works:** Co-Author, "Races of Maize in Brazil and Adjacent Areas" (1977); Author, Technical Articles **Awards:** Research Award, Crop Science Society of America (2005); Holladay Medal, NC State University (2003); Frank N. Meyer Medal for Plant Genetic Resources, Crop Science Society of America (2000); O. Max Gardner Award (1987); Research Awards, Sigma Xi (1973); Award, National Association of Plant Breeders **Memberships:** The Society for Economic Botany; National Academy of Sciences **Marquis Who's Who Honors:** Albert Nelson Marquis Lifetime Achievement Award **Why did you become involved in your profession or industry:** Dr. Goodman became involved in his profession because of his experiences working for the Pioneer Hybrid Corn Company, which encouraged him to pursue higher education in the field. **Avocations:** Reading

J. Max Goodson, DDS, PhD

Title: Senior Member of the Staff Emeritus **Industry:** Education/Educational Services **Company Name:** The Forsyth Institute **Parents:** Bob Frank; Nina Mae **Marital Status:** Married **Spouse Name:** Stevanka Goodson **Children:** Eric; Christopher **Education:** PhD in Pharmacology, University of Rochester (1970); MSc in Dental Research, University of Rochester (1969); DDS, University of Texas Health Sciences Center (1962); BA in Chemistry, Texas Tech University, Lubbock, TX (1962) **Career:** Senior Member of the Staff Emeritus, The Forsyth Institute, (1976-Present); Associate Clinical Professor, Harvard School of Dental Medicine (1976-Present); Professor, University of California San Francisco (1969-1976) **Creative Works:** Author, Abstract, "Life on a string: development of the tetracycline fiber delivery system," Technology and Health Care (1996) **Awards:** IADR Distinguished Scientist Award **Memberships:** International Association for Dental Research (IADR) (1962) **To what do you attribute your success:** Dr. Goodson attributes his success to everything that he learned from his life on the ranch. Hard work makes it work, nobody owes you a living, and you have to do it yourself. That is what carried him through. **Why did you become involved in your profession or industry:** Dr. Goodson became involved in his profession because his father served in the U.S. Navy during World War II, during which time he had a roommate who was a dentist; he felt like it was one of the most honorable professions in the world. "All they do is make jewelry," his father would say and laugh. As a child, growing up on a ranch in Texas, Dr. Goodson didn't know too many options to choose from as a profession. Truman became president and he was the one that established NIDR, The National Institute of Dental Research and that funded research that gave Mr. Goodson a PhD, he received his PhD with no cost just because he was a good student and they wanted to create a science condray they went out to get people like him and changed the profession and become scientists he didn't regret it because its been a terrific area the mouth is in many ways where everything starts **Avocations:** Travel; Performance arts (The Metropolitan Opera); Museums particularly art museums

John L. Goodyear

Title: Artist, Professor Emeritus **Industry:** Education/Educational Services **Company Name:** Rutgers, The State University of New Jersey **Date of Birth:** 10/22/1930 **Place of Birth:** South Gate **State/Country of Origin:** CA/USA **Year of Passing:** 2019 **Parents:** Ronald R. Goodyear; Lillian Lake Goodyear **Marital Status:** Married **Spouse Name:** Anne Dixon (12/12/1953) **Children:** Sarah Goodyear-La Grange; Amy Goodyear **Education:** Master's Degree in Design, University of Michigan (1954); Bachelor's Degree in Design, University of Michigan (1952) **Career:** Professor Emeritus, Artist, Mason Gross School of Visual Art, Rutgers, The State University of New Jersey, New Brunswick, NJ (1997-Present); Professor to Chairman of Art Department, Mason Gross School of Visual Art, Rutgers, The State University of New Jersey, New Brunswick, NJ (1964-1997); Instructor, University of Massachusetts Amherst (1962-1964); Instructor, University of Michigan, Ann Arbor, MI (1956-1962) **Career Related:** Co-Curator, "Dada Country," Hunterdon Museum of Art, Clifton, NJ (2000); Fellowship, Center for Advanced Visual Studies, Massachusetts Institute of Technology, Cambridge, MA **Military Service:** United States Army, Japan (1954-1956) **Creative Works:** Exhibited, RCM Gallery, France; Exhibited, Berry Campbell Gallery, New York, NY (2018); Exhibited, Berry Campbell Gallery, New York, NY (2015-2016); Exhibited, David Richard Gallery, Santa Fe, NM (2015); Exhibited, 10 Ways, RCM Galerie, Paris, France (2015); Exhibited, Solo Show, Berry Campbell Gallery, New York, NY (2015); Exhibited, Group Show, New Jersey State Museum, Trenton, NJ (2013); Exhibited, Group Show, Hunterdon Art Museum, Clifton, NJ (2013); Exhibited, Solo Show, David Hall Fine Art, Wellesley, MA (2012); Exhibited, Solo Show, Visual Art Center of New Jersey (2012); Exhibited, Group Show, Zimmerli Art Museum, New Brunswick, NJ (2011); Exhibited, Group Show, Hostetter Gallery, Martinsville, NJ (2011); Exhibited, Group Show, David Richards Gallery, Santa Fe, NM (2010); Exhibited, Group Show, Rupert Ravens Contemporary, Newark, NJ (2008); Exhibited, Group Show, Mason Gross Galleries, New Brunswick, NJ (2008); Exhibited, Group Show, Francis M. Naumann Fine Art, New York, NY (2007); Exhibited, Solo Show, Gallery at Rider University, Lawrenceville, NJ (2005); Exhibited, Solo Show, Hunterdon Museum of Art, Clifton, NJ (2005); Exhibited, Group Show, Jack S. Blanton Museum of Art, Austin, TX (2004); Exhibited, Group Show, Rosenwald-Wolf Gallery (2004); Exhibited, Group Show, Gary Snyder Fine Art, New York, NY (2002); Artist, Public Commission, "The Four Arts," Rutgers University, NK (2002); Exhibited, Group Show, Gallery Bristol-Myers Squibb, Lawrenceville, NJ (2001); Exhibited, Solo Show, Ben Shahn Galleries at Paterson University, Wayne, NJ (2001); Exhibited, Solo Show, Ericson Gallery, Philadelphia, PA (2000); Exhibited, Solo Show, Michener Museum, Doylestown, PA (2000); Exhibited, Group Show, New Jersey State Museum, Trenton, NJ (1996); Exhibited, Solo Show, Frank Martin Gallery, Allentown, PA (1995); Exhibited, Group Show, Art Gallery of Hamilton, Canada (1994); Exhibited, Group Show, Horodner-Romley Gallery, New York, NY (1992); Exhibited, Solo Show, Snyder Fine Art (1992); Artist, Public Commission, "The Dawn of Law," State House, Trenton, NJ (1991); Exhibited, Group Show, Amerikahaus, Cologne, Germany (1990); Exhibited, Group Show, Henri Gallery, Washington, DC (1989); Exhibited, Solo Show, Pyramid Gallery, New York, NY (1989); Exhibited, Group Show, Kunsthalle, Karlsruhe, Germany (1988); Exhibited, Group Show, Macedonian Center for Contemporary Art, Thessalonika, Greece (1987); Exhibited, Solo Show, Princeton Gallery of Fine Arts (1987); Exhibited, Group Show, Atrium Gallery, Schenectady, NY (1985); Artist, Public Commission, "Drawn from the Water," The Jewish Center, Princeton, NJ (1984); Artist, Public Commission, "Chiron," University College of Medicine and Dentistry, Piscataway, NJ (1983); Artist, Public Commission, "Taking Flight," Triangle Park, Raleigh, NC (1981); Exhibited, Solo Show, New Jersey State Museum, Trenton, NJ (1981); Artist, Public Commission, "The Test," Princeton, NJ (1980); Exhibited, Group Show, Neuberger Museum, Purchase, NY (1980); Exhibited, Solo Show, Massachusetts Institute of Technology, Cambridge, MA (1976); Exhibited, Group Show, Massachusetts Institute of Technology (1973); Exhibited, Group Show, Museum of Modern Art, New York, NY (1972) **Awards:** Recipient, Major Retrospective, Michener Museum, Doylestown, PA (2000); Grantee, Graham Foundation (1962) **Memberships:** American Abstract Artists (1976-Present) **Marquis Who's Who Honors:** Albert Nelson Marquis Lifetime Achievement Award **Why did you become involved in your profession or industry:** Mr. Goodyear knew he wanted to go into art since he was a child. It was something that he enjoyed doing. Mr. Goodyear felt the calling to pursue art from as far back as he can remember.

David A. Gooray, MD, FACC

Title: Cardiologist **Industry:** Medicine & Health Care **Company Name:** Prince George's Hospital Center **Date of Birth:** 06/29/1949 **Place of Birth:** Henrietta **State/Country of Origin:** Guyana **Children:** Three Children **Education:** Chief Medical Resident, District of Columbia General Hospital, Washington, DC (1982-1983); Resident, District of Columbia General Hospital, Washington, DC (1981-1983); Intern in Internal Medicine, Medical Division, Howard University, District of Columbia General Hospital, Washington, DC (1980-1981); Doctor of Medicine, College of Medicine, Howard University, Washington, DC (1980); Bachelor of Science in Chemistry, District of Columbia Teachers College, Washington, DC (1974); Resident in Internal Medicine, Medical Division, Howard University **Certifications:** Medical License, State of Maryland (1982); Medical License, District of Columbia (1981); Diplomate, National Board of Medical Examiners; Diplomate, American Board of Internal Medicine; Diplomate, American Board of Internal Medicine and Cardiovascular Disease **Career:** Chairman, Research Committee, Prince George's Hospital Center, Cheverly, MD (2013-Present); Faculty, Internal Medicine Residency Program, Prince George's Hospital Center, Cheverly, MD (1990-Present); Chief of Cardiology, Prince George's Hospital Center, Cheverly, MD (2003-2013); Instructor in Medicine, Howard University Medical Services, District of Columbia General Hospital, Washington, DC (1986-2000); Medical Officer, Alcoholic Detoxification Unit, Department of Human Resources, Washington, DC (1982-1984); Research Associate, College of Medicine, Howard University, Washington, DC (1974-1976) **Career Related:** Fellow, Cardiovascular Medicine, Medical Division, Howard University, District of Columbia General Hospital, Washington, DC (1983-1985); Fellow, American College of Cardiology; Fellow, American College of Chest Physicians **Civic:** Board of Directors, United Therapeutic Corporation (1999-2002); Advisory Board, Heart Failure Disease, Novartis; Advisory Board, Ischemic Heart Disease, Gilead; Speaker's Bureau, Boehringer Ingelheim, Arbor/Takeda, Novartis, Gilead, and Lilly Pharmaceuticals; Advisory Board, Consensus Statements, Calcium Channel Blockers; U.S. Perindopril Advisory Group; Vascular Biology Working Group **Creative Works:** Presenter, "The Metabolism of 8-Methoxy Psoralen by Liver Mixed Function Oxidases," College of Medicine, Howard University (1979); Presenter, "Syntheses of Hydroxy Metabolites of 8-MOP," College of Medicine, Howard University (1978); Co-Author, "Determination of 8MOP in Plasma by Scanning Fluorometry After Thin Layer Chromatography," Clinical Chemistry (1978); Co-Author, "A Spectrophotometric Method for Methaxalen," Clinical Chemistry (1977); Presenter, "Purification of Keratohyalin Proteins of Epidermis," European Society of Investigational Dermatology, Amsterdam, Netherlands (1975) **Awards:** Outstanding Physician Award, Prince George's Hospital Center, Cheverly, MD (2012); Outstanding Resident Award, College of Medicine, Howard University, Washington, DC (1981-1982); National Summer Research Fellowship Grant (1978); Outstanding Student Research Award (1977) **Memberships:** President, Howard University Hospital Medical Alumni Association (2014-Present); Participant, Annual Medical Conferences, GME, Howard University (1992-Present); FDA Review Committee on Cardiovascular Devices (1996-1998); Principal Investigator, AFFIRM and PEACE, National Institutes of Health Trials **Marquis Who's Who Honors:** Albert Nelson Marquis Lifetime Achievement Award; Marquis Who's Who Top Professional **Why did you become involved in your profession or industry:** Dr. Gooray was fascinated with the molecular biology of humans and linking the science with the basic functionality of the body. **Avocations:** Sending time with his family

Lee Alice Goscin, MD, PhD

Title: Endocrinologist, Educator **Industry:** Medicine & Health Care **Company Name:** Lee Pletts Goscin, MD, PhD, PA **Parents:** Donald Cole Pletts; Janet Garwood Pletts **Marital Status:** Single **Children:** Christopher Paul, MD **Education:** MD, University of Miami (1986); PhD in Biochemistry, Duke University (1973); BS in Chemistry, University of Florida (1968) **Certifications:** Diplomate, Endocrinology, Diabetes and Metabolism, American Board of Internal Medicine (1995); Diplomate, American Board of Internal Medicine (1991) **Career:** Endocrinologist, Largo, FL (2016-Present); Endocrinologist, McAlester, OK (2012-2016); CCOM Endocrinologist, Muskogee, OK (2011-2012); Palm Beach Diabetes and Endocrine Specialists (2010-2011); Clinical Associate Professor, University of Miami, Florida (2000-2004); Clinical Instructor, University of Miami, Florida (1991-1999); Fellow in Endocrinology, Diabetes and Metabolism, University of Miami-Jackson Memorial Hospital, Florida (1989-1991); Resident in Internal Medicine, Natick Medical Center, Framingham, MA (1987-1989); Intern, Mount Sinai Medical Center, Miami Beach, FL **Civic:** Political Advisor, President, Alpha Phi Omega Sorority **Creative Works:** Contributor, Multiple Publications (2018); Participant, 14 Years Study, "Undertreatment of Subclinical Hypothyroidism Increases Miscarriages and Lowers Baby's IQ," American Thyroid Association Annual Meeting **Awards:** Outstanding Chronology Award, Las Vegas, NV (2018); Winner, Fourth Flight Florida State Golf Tournament (2006); Outstanding Math High School Student, National Honor Society, University of Florida **Memberships:** Toastmasters (2013); Florida Medical Association; Endocrine Society; American College of Endocrinology; American Association of Clinical Endocrinologists; American Diabetes Association; President, Alpha Phi Omega **Marquis Who's Who Honors:** Albert Nelson Marquis Lifetime Achievement Award; Marquis Who's Who Top Professional **Why did you become involved in your profession or industry:** Dr. Goscin is the first of three children to very smart parents and her son is fifth generation medical doctor from her father's side. Her father got in to medical school after World War II, but there was a two-year waiting list. His father and grandfather were the town physicians in Maine. Her mother was in Mensa. She and her son were both bought up by generational doctors. She wanted to be a doctor because it runs in her family. Nurses and doctors save people's lives and they have to work really hard. She has a very strong parental and grandparental influence. **Avocations:** Golf **Political Affiliations:** Republican **Religion:** Methodist

Robert Pike "Bob" Goss Jr.

Title: Assistant Professor, Assistant Dean (Retired) **Industry:** Education/Educational Services **Company Name:** Brigham Young University **Date of Birth:** 07/29/1943 **Place of Birth:** Queens **State/Country of Origin:** NY/USA **Parents:** Robert Pike (Deceased); Alvor F. Goss (Deceased) **Marital Status:** Married **Spouse Name:** Connie Kitchen Goss **Children:** Susan; Robert Pike III; Rebecca; Colleen; Aaron; Brendan; Janelle; Jonathan **Education:** PhD in Public Administration, University of Colorado Denver (1997); JD, Georgetown University Law Center (1977); MS, Brigham Young University (1969); BA, Brigham Young University (1967); Diploma, North Shore High School (1961) **Certifications:** Certified Financial Planner, Colorado (1987) **Career:** President, Chief Executive Officer, Certified Financial Planner Board of Standards, Inc., Denver, CO; Executive Director, Institute of Certified Financial Planners, Inc., Denver, CO; Executive Director, Certified Financial Planner Board of Standards, Inc.; Lawyer and President, Dominion Financial Planning Services (Now Dominion Financial Consultants), Stafford VA; Washington Director & Counsel, State-Federal Relations, National Conference of State Legislatures, Washington, DC; Executive Director, Governor's Office of Manpower and Human Development, Springfield IL; Special Assistant to Assistant Secretary, Intergovernmental Relations Officer, U.S. Department of Transportation, Washington, DC; Director, State-Federal Relations, Employment & Vocational Training Program, Special Assistant to Deputy Secretary, Governor of New York, Washington Office; Assistant Director, Emergency Employment Program, New York State Department of Labor; Senior Administrative Analyst, Executive Assistant to Industrial Commissioner, New York Department of Labor; Public Administration Intern, New York State Department of Civil Service **Career Related:** Assistant Dean, Brigham Young University College of Family Home and Social Sciences; Assistant Professor, Associate Director, Master's in Public Policy Degree, Brigham Young University; Member, Board of Directors, Financial Planners Professional Liability Insurance Co., VT; Member, Board of Directors, Academy of Financial Services; Counsel, American Traffic Safety Services Association, VA; Chairman, Board of Directors, State Services Organization, Inc., Washington, DC; Member, Board of Directors, Potomac Financial Group, VA; Member, Financial & Estate Planning Advisory Board, Commerce Clearing House (CCH Incorporated) **Civic:** Troop Chairman, Boy Scouts of America **Creative Works:** Author, Doctoral Dissertation, "Norms and Values for a Public Administration Ethics," University of Colorado School of Public Affairs (1997); Author, Master's Thesis, "A Study of Metropolitan County Provisions of Urban Services Including a Case of Salt Lake County, Utah" (1969); Staff, Law & Policy in International Business, Georgetown University Law Center; Associate Editor, The Tax Lawyer; Columnist, Journal of Financial Planning, Articles & Information; Board of Directors, Journal of the American Society of Chartered Life Underwriters **Awards:** Scholarship, Brigham Young University (1965-1967) **Memberships:** Chair, Committee on Ethics and Malpractice, American Bar Association (ABA) (1992-1995); President, Denver Chapter, BYU Management Society (1990-1992); Task Force on Legal Financial Planning, ABA (1989-1991); Academy of Financial Services; ABA (1989-1991); Vice President, Washington Chapter, BYU Management Society (1987-1988); National Association of Estate Planners & Councils (NAEPC); Colorado Bar Association; The Virginia Bar Association; The American Society for Public Administration **Bar Admissions:** Supreme Court of the United States (1994); Colorado Bar Association (1988); Virginia State Bar (1977) **Marquis Who's Who Honors:** Albert Nelson Marquis Lifetime Achievement Award 2020 **To what do you attribute your success:** Dr. Goss attributes his success to melding the need to support a family of eight children, with his wife Connie. **Why did you become involved in your profession or industry:** After Dr. Goss received a Masters Degree in Public Administration, he became involved in government and non-for-profit organizations. While in Albany, he pursued a doctorate in public administration at the Graduate School of Public Affairs, State of NY at Albany in 1970-1971. While still in the NYS Department of Labor, he decided that he didn't want to finish the doctorate program because he wanted to go to law school instead and enrolled at Georgetown University Law Center while he worked full-time for four years. Sometime after he completed law school, he opened his own law practice in Stafford, VA. While working in DC, he observed what was going on in the federal government with the appalling events happening with President Nixon and others, and then found a passion to make a contribution on behalf of the people with integrity. **Avocations:** Family history; Genealogy **Religion:** The Church of Jesus Christ of Latter-day Saints **Thoughts on Life:** One significant thought is that Dr. Goss was born in this wonderful nation, with ancestors who migrated to the US during the colonial years before 1776.

Harry E. Gould Jr.

Title: Paper Company Executive **Industry:** Business Management/Business Services **Company Name:** Gould Paper Corporation **Date of Birth:** 09/24/1938 **Place of Birth:** New York **State/Country of Origin:** NY/USA **Parents:** Harry Edward (Deceased 1971); Lucille (Quartucy) Gould (Deceased 2005) **Marital Status:** Married **Spouse Name:** Barbara Clement (4/26/1975, Deceased 2018) **Children:** Harry Edward III; Alexandra Scott; Katharine Elizabeth (Deceased 2004) **Education:** MBA, Columbia University (1964); Coursework, Harvard Business School, (1960, 1961); BA, Colgate University, Magna Cum Laude (1960); Coursework, Oxford University (1958) **Career:** Retired from Gould Paper Corp.; Chairman, Price & Pierce Finland Oy, Helsinki, Finland (2004-Present); Chairman, Price & Pierce International, Inc., New York, NY (2004-Present); Chairman, President of the Holding Company, Chief Executive Officer, Signature Communications Ltd., Los Angeles and New York (1986-Present); Chairman, President, Chief Executive Officer, Owner, Gould Paper Corp., New York, NY (1969-Retired); Chairman, Price & Pierce; Chairman of the Board, Legion Paper West Corp., Commerce, CA (1997-2003); Chairman of the Board, Lewis & Gould Paper Co., Inc., Northfield, IL (1975-1978); Chairman of the Board, Director, Vrisimo Manufacturing, Inc. (Now Weiss McNair), Chico, CA (1974-1985); President, Chairman, Board of Directors, Gould Paper Corp., New York, NY; Vice President, Administration and Finance, Universal American Corp. (1968-1969); Member, Executive Committee, Vice President, Secretary-Treasurer, Daybrook-Ottawa Corp., Bowling Green, OH (1967-1969); Board of Directors, Young Spring & Wire Corp., Detroit, MI; Executive Vice President, Chief Operating Officer, Young Spring & Wire Corp., Detroit, MI (1967-1969); Director, Member, Executive Committee, American Medical Insurance Co., New York, NY (1966-1974); Secretary, Treasurer, Young Spring & Wire Corp., Detroit, MI (1965-1967); Executive Assistant to Senior Vice President, Operations, Universal America, New York, NY (1964-1965); Associate, Corporate Finance Department, Goldman, Sachs & Co., New York, NY (1961-1962) **Career Related:** Owner, Operating Company, Denmaur Paper Media, United Kingdom (2019-Present); Chairman, Board of Directors, Weiss/McNair/Ramacher, Inc., Chico, CA (1974-Present); Board of Directors, Member, Environmental and Health and Safety Committee, Domtar, Inc., Montreal, Canada (1995-2003); Chairman, Executive Committee, Board of Directors, Richard Lewis Paper Corp., Northfield, IL (1992-1997); Chairman, Board of Directors, Ingalls Manufacturing, Inc., Ceres (1974-1999); Ltd. Partner, Hardy & Co., New York, NY (1973-1978); Chairman, Board of Directors, Samuel Porritt & Co., East Peoria, IL (1970-1986); Chairman, Board of Directors, Hawthorne Paper Co., Kalamazoo, MI (1970-1975) **Civic:** Member, Board of Overseers, Columbia Business School (2014-Present); Vice Chairman, Residential Mortgage Insurance Corp. (2013-Present); Trustee Emeritus, Colgate University (2012-President); Board Member, Roundabout Theatre Company, New York (2011-Present); Board of Directors, Residential Mortgage Insurance Corp. (1992-Present); Vice Chairman, Housing New York Corp. (1987-Present); Board of Directors, Housing New York Corp. (1986-Present); Member, Executive Branch, Academy Motion Picture Arts and Sciences (1985-Present); Vice Chairman, Governance Committee, New York City Housing Development Corp. (HDC) (1977-Present); Vice Chairman, Residential Mortgage Insurance Corp. (2013); Member, Board of Directors, Roundabout Theatre Co. (2011); Member, Board of Governors, Actors, Studio Drama School, New School University (1995-2005); Trustee, Riverdale Country School (1990-1998); Chairman, President, Cinema Group, Inc., Los Angeles, CA (1982-1986); Board of Directors, United Service Organizations of Metropolitan New York (1981-2008); Board of Directors, Chairman, Executive Committee, Cinema Group, Inc., Los Angeles, CA (1979-1986); Member, Executive Committee, Chairman, Export Expansion Subcommittee, Member, Export Promotion Subcommittee, Vice Chairman, U.S. President's Export Council (1979-1982); National Trustee, Member, Executive Committee, National Symphony Orchestra, Washington DC (1978-1999); Board of Directors, National Multiple Sclerosis Society (1977-2008); Board of Directors, United Cerebral Palsy Research and Educational Foundation (1976-1997); Treasurer, New York State Democratic Committee (1976-1977) **Memberships:** Trustee, Audit Committee, American Management Association (1997-2000); Chairman, Paper Distribution Council (1993-1994); Director, Member, Printing Paper Committee, National Paper Trade Alliance (1973-1974): Director, Paper Merchants Association New York (1972-1984); Young President Organization; G100; Les Ambassadeurs (London); Harvard Club; Harvard Business School Club; Phi Kappa Tau **Marquis Who's Who Honors:** Albert Nelson Marquis Lifetime Achievement Award **Why did you become involved in your profession or industry:** Mr. Gould thought about becoming a professor in literature. He wanted to go to Yale but you had to be fluent in Latin or Greek and he wasn't ready for another language. So he started at Goldman, Sachs & Co. He got about a 15 year education and learned all the facets of business. His father Harry handed his business to Mr. Gould and helped it grow. **Avocations:** Playing with his Maltese named Ms. Lucy

Elena Jane "Ellie" Goulding

Title: Singer **Industry:** Media & Entertainment **Date of Birth:** 12/30/1986 **Place of Birth:** Hereford **State/Country of Origin:** United Kingdom **Marital Status:** Married **Spouse Name:** Caspar Jopling (08/31/2019) **Education:** Coursework in Drama and Theatre Studies, University of Kent; Diploma, Lady Hawkins' High School, Kington, England, United Kingdom **Career:** Singer (2009-Present) **Career Related:** Endorser, Pantene Pro-V (2016-Present); Spokesmodel, Womanism Campaign, Marks and Spencer's (2013); Contributing Singer, John Lewis (2010) **Civic:** Goodwill Ambassador, UNEP (2018); Volunteer, The Marylebone Project (2015); Performer, Streets of London, Royal Albert Hall (2014-2018); Performer, Band Aid 30 (2014); Participant, Nike Women's Half Marathon, Washington, DC (2013); Performer, Chime for Change, Gucci (2013); Partner, Pandora Radio (Now Pandora Media, LLC) and Free the Children (Now WE Charity) (2012); Participant, She Runs LA, Students Run LA (2011); Participant, Bupa Great North Run, British Heart Foundation (2010); BBC Children in Need; Vote Remain **Creative Works:** Featured Musician, "Worry About Me" (2020); Featured Musician, "Times Like These" (2020); Musician, "River" (2019); Featured Musician, "Hate Me" (2019); Musician, "Sixteen" (2019); Featured Musician, "Return to Love" (2019); Featured Musician, "Mama" (2019); Musician, "Flux" (2019); Guest Appearance, "Sesame Street" (2018); Featured Musician, "Close to Me" (2018); Musician, "Vincent" (2018); Musician, "O Holy Night" (2017); Featured Musician, "First Time" (2017); Musician, "Still Falling for You" (2016); Musician, "Delirium" (2015); Musician, "Love Me Like You Do" (2015); Featured Musician, "Powerful" (2015); Advisor, "The Voice" (2015); Musician, "Beating Heart" (2014); Featured Musician, "Do They Know It's Christmas?" (2014); Featured Musician, "Outside" (2014); Featured Musician, "Flashlight" (2014); Musician, "Halcyon Days: The Remixes" (2014); Musician, "Halcyon Days" (2013); Guest Appearance, "The Sound Change Live" (2013); Actress, Short Film, "Tom & Issy" (2013); Featured Artist, "Who is...?" (2013); Featured Musician, "I Need Your Love" (2013); Musician, "Halcyon" (2012); Musician, "Bright Lights" (2010); Musician, "Lights" (2010); Musician, EP, "Run into the Light" (2010); Featured Musician, "Wonderman" (2010); Musician, EP, "An Introduction to Ellie Goulding" (2009) **Awards:** Choice Electronic/Dance Song, Teen Choice Awards (2019); Global Leadership Award, United Nations Foundation (2017); International Modern Pop-Rock Album of the Year, Hungarian Music Awards (2016); Named Favorite Song of the Year, People's Choice Awards (2016); Award Winning Song, BMI London Awards (2015); Best International Song, Best International Act, Los Premios 40 Principales (2015); Le Prix de la Révélation Internationale de l'Année, NRJ Music Awards (2015); Best Tormentone, MTV Italian Music Awards (2015); Named Musician of the Year, Harper's Bazaar Women of the Year Awards (2015); Cointreau Solo Artist Award, Glamour Awards (2015); Three Pop Awards, BMI London Awards (2014); Named Best Female – International, Jimmy Awards (2014); Named Best Female Solo Artist, Brit Awards (2014); Named Best Solo Artist, Q Awards (2013); Named Ultimate Music Star, Cosmopolitan's Ultimate Women of the Year Awards (2013); Named Pandora Breakthrough Artist, Glamour Awards (2011); Named Sound of 2010, BBC Sound of... (2010); Named Critics' Choice, Brit Awards (2010) **Political Affiliations:** Labour Party

Peter Francis Goyer Jr., MD

Title: Medical Doctor; Researcher Teacher **Date of Birth:** 06/21/1943 **Place of Birth:** Urbana **State/Country of Origin:** IL/USA **Parents:** Peter Goyer; Evelyn Goyer **Marital Status:** Married **Spouse Name:** Christine Krebs (06/08/1965) **Children:** Maraya; Peter; Kathryn **Education:** Research Fellowship, National Institute of Mental Health (1977-1978); Resident in Psychiatry, National Naval Medical Center (Now Walter Reed National Military Medical Center) (1975-1977); Intern, Walter Reed National Military Medical Center (1974-1975); MD, Johns Hopkins School of Medicine (1974); MS in Biophysics, University of Delaware (1968); BS in Physics, University of Notre Dame, with Honors (1965) **Certifications:** Diplomate, American Board of Nuclear Medicine (1987); Diplomate, American Board of Psychiatry and Neurology (1980); Board Certification in Psychiatry and in Nuclear Medicine; Private Pilots License **Career:** Director of Mental Health for Five VA Hospitals and 20 VA Outpatient Facilities, VISN 10, Ohio (2008-2013); Co-chief of Staff, Cleveland VA Medical Center (1992-2008); Associate Professor of Psychiatry and Radiology, Director of Neuropsychiatric Brain Imaging Research, Case Western Medical School and University Hospitals, Cleveland, Ohio (1989-2013); Chairman, Department of Psychiatry, Walter Reed National Military Medical Center (1988-1989); Joint Staff in Nuclear Medicine and in Psychiatry, Walter Reed National Military Medical Center (1987-1989); Consultant Staff in Psychiatry, Walter Reed National Military Medical Center (1985-1987); Fellowship in Nuclear Medicine, Walter Reed National Military Medical Center (1985-1987); Fellowship in Positron Emission Tomography, National Institutes of Health (1985-1987); Assistant Chairman, Department of Psychiatry, Portsmouth Naval Hospital (Now Naval Medical Center Portsmouth), VA (1984-1985); Director, Inpatient Psychiatry, Naval Medical Center Portsmouth (1983-1984); Director, Outpatient Psychiatry, Naval Medical Center Portsmouth (1980-1982); Staff Psychiatrist, Naval Medical Center Portsmouth (1978-1979) **Career Related:** Teacher of Math and Nuclear Reactor Physics, United States Naval Nuclear Power School, Bainbridge, MD (1965-1970) **Military Service:** With, United States Navy (1965-1989): Retired Captain, United States Navy (0-6) **Creative Works:** Author, Numerous Articles, Peer-reviewed Medical Journals and Medical Book Chapters in Nuclear Medicine and Psychiatry; Presenter, Numerous Invited Oral Presentations, National Medical Meetings, Nuclear Medicine and Psychiatry **Awards:** Nuclear Medicine Fellowship, National Naval Medical Center (1985-1987); Research Fellowship, National Institute of Mental Health (1977-1978) **Memberships:** American Psychiatric Society; Society of Biological Psychiatry; American Medical Association; Society of Nuclear Medicine and Molecular Imaging **Marquis Who's Who Honors:** Marquis Who's Who in America (2020); Marquis Who's Who Top Professional: Doctors (2020); Marquis Who's Who in America (2019); Albert Nelson Marquis Lifetime Achievement Award (2018); Marquis Who's Who in the East (1990) **To what do you attribute your success:** Dr. Goyer attributes his success to determination, education, and hard work. **Why did you become involved in your profession or industry:** In high school, Dr. Goyer's main career goal was to obtain a PhD in physics. Based on various high school achievements, the United States Navy offered him a full scholarship to obtain a BS in physics, contingent on his acceptance to a school of his choice, which was the University of Notre Dame. In his sophomore year, he decided that he wanted to go to medical school and become a psychiatrist. Due to his navy commitment to obtain a physics degree, he took his pre-med courses as electives while continuing his physics major. In 1965, he graduated with cum laude honors in physics and then completed five years teaching math and nuclear reactor physics at the Naval Nuclear Power School. Finally, after completing his navy commitment in 1970, he began his medical career as a student at Johns Hopkins Medical School. His naval career continued concomitant with his medical career; as the 10 years of his medical training, which included medical school and two post graduate residencies/fellowships, were funded by naval scholarships and he continued on active duty during those 10 years. His subsequent naval commitment for the medical training, plus his five years teaching at the Nuclear Power School completed his 24 year naval career. **Avocations:** Eagle Scout; Scouting Order of the Arrow; First solo single engine airplane flight; High school varsity track and football; Flying single engine airplanes **Thoughts on Life:** Peter Goyer and Christine Krebs were married in the Log Chapel on the Notre Dame campus on 06/08/1965. They celebrated their 55th wedding anniversary in June 2020. They have eight grandchildren, Sarah, William, Emma, Gabrielle, Sydney, Fiona, Primo and Vincenzo.Dr. Goyer has a board certification in psychiatry and in nuclear medicine which facilitated his brain imaging research using Positron Emission Tomography (PET).

William Pancsovai Graff

Title: Architect **Industry:** Architecture & Construction **Date of Birth:** 06/19/1925 **Place of Birth:** Budapest **State/Country of Origin:** Hungary **Parents:** William Graff II; Clara (Pejtsik) Graff **Marital Status:** Married **Spouse Name:** Clara Lenke Marot (12/19/1959) **Children:** Marcella; Carlo; Guido; Mattias **Education:** MArch, Royal Jozsef Nador Technical University, Budapest, Hungary (1949) **Career:** Consultant, U.S. Department of State (1990-1994); Private Practice Consultant (1987-1990); President, Graff & Associates, American Institute of Architects, Washington DC (1983-1989); Consultant, U.S. Department of State, American Embassy, Budapest, Hungary (1983-1988); Partner, Holle and Graff, Washington DC (1967-1982); Vice President, International Modular Systems, Limited, Washington DC (1975-1980); Generale Immobiliare, Rome, Italy, Washington DC (1962-1967); The Architects Collaborative, Rome, Italy (1959-1962); Hugh Stubbins, Cambridge, MA (1956-1959); Maguolo & Quick, Baltimore, MA (1954-1956); John B. Parkin, Toronto, Ontario, Canada (1953-1954); Marani & Morris (Now Marani, Lawson & Morris) Toronto, Ontario, Canada (1951-1953) **Creative Works:** American International School of Budapest (1988); Vista Hotel (Now The Westin) Washington DC (1984); Porto Vecchio Apartments, Alexandria, VA (1983); Montebello Apartments, Alexandria, VA (1982); The Rotonda Condominiums, McLean, VA (1980); Watergate at Landmark, Alexandria, VA (1975); 1801 K Street NW, Washington DC (1971) Jefferson Plaza, Alexandria, VA (1971); International Club of DC Inc., Washington DC (1971); Watergate Apartments, Washington DC (1963-1966); Port Royal Apartments, Montreal, Quebec, Canada (1963); Place Victoria, Montreal, Quebec, Canada (1962); University of Baghdad, Iraq (1960); 330 Beacon Street, Boston, MA (1958) **Awards:** Finest For Family Living Award, Metropolitan Washington Builders Association (1976); Gold Medal, National Spa and Pool Institute (1976) **Memberships:** Knights of Malta (1972-Present); American Institute of Architects **Marquis Who's Who Honors:** Albert Nelson Marquis Lifetime Achievement Award; Marquis Who's Who Top Professional **Why did you become involved in your profession or industry:** Mr. Graff became involved in his profession because he was always passionate about buildings. As a child, he spent time in Rome, Italy. His mother loved the architectural design of the city. Her appreciation for the aesthetic of the buildings inspired him to go into architecture.

David Bolden Graham

Title: Food Products Executive **Industry:** Food & Restaurant Services **Date of Birth:** 02/10/1927 **Place of Birth:** Miami Beach **State/Country of Origin:** FL/ USA **Parents:** Robert Cable Graham; Bertha Eugenia (Hack) Graham **Marital Status:** Married **Spouse Name:** Stuart Hill Smith (09/01/1956, Deceased) **Children:** Bird; Ellen; Darnall; Lamar; Lyle; Gerard; Barbara; David **Education:** Postgraduate Coursework; BS, Georgetown University (1949); Coursework, Colegio de san Bartolome, Bogota, Colombia (1946) **Certifications:** Coast Guard Auxiliary Licensed Master; Federal Communications Commission Marine Radio Licensed, Great Lakes or Inland Waters **Career:** Secretary, Bal Harbour Shops, Florida (1956-1957); Chairman, Graham Cheese Corp., Washington, IN (1950-1999); Chairman, Graham Farms, Inc., Washington, IN (1950-1999); Secretary, Graham Brothers, Inc., Washington, IN (1950-1972) **Career Related:** Chairman, Peoples National Bank; Director, Community National Bank, Bal Harbour, FL; Director, German American Bank **Civic:** Member, Olympic Yachting Staff (1996); Past President, Washington Planning Commission; Past President, Regional Planning Commission; Past Board of Directors, Historical Landmarks Foundation; Independent Member, Revolving Fund Committee, Historical Landmarks Foundation; Member, Rural Preservation Committee, Historical Landmarks Foundation; Past Member, Independent; Past Member, Agricultural Advisory Council; Past Member, Advisory Council, Bureau of Water and Mineral Resources; Director, Natural Resources Commission Member, Various Methodist Awareness Committees; Vice President, Independent Regional Highway Coalition; Past President, I-69 Mid-Continent Highway Coalition; Member, National Turkey Federation **Military Service:** 445th Bomb Squadron Adjutant; Aide de Camp, General 813 Air Division; Lt. Colonel U.S. Air Force Reserve **Creative Works:** Author, "The Secret Spy, Mission Moscow; The Princess and The Crown" (2014); Author, "The Hockey Puck" (2013); Author, "Showdown at the Grotto" (2013); Author, "Taco Tales" (2012); Author, "Rusty Scuppers"; Contributor, Articles on Agriculture, Transportation and Early Fur Traders, Various Publications; Contributor, Terrorists in the Panama Jungle, Terrorists in Cuba, Terrorists on The Chesapeake, Terrorists in Everglades, Miss Sarah and Princess Elizabeth; Contributor, Jesus, A Boy of Nazareth **Memberships:** Columbia Club, Indianapolis, IN; Honorary Member, Past President, Paul Harris Fellow, Rotary; Atlantic Cruising Club; Inland Yacht Club; Elks; Society of Children's Book Writers; Life Member, North America Fishing Club; Florida Writers Association; Villages Polo **Marquis Who's Who Honors:** Albert Nelson Marquis Lifetime Achievement Award **Why did you become involved in your profession or industry:** Mr. David Graham's father was an entrepreneur and an Industrialist, and he passed the legacy of running a business and building foundations to his sons. Mr. Graham was in business with his brothers and and they had a factory and they made cheese for Kraft. They made turkeys for the Armour company and made flour for Girl Scout cookies. **Avocations:** Author, Children's Books **Political Affiliations:** Republican **Religion:** Roman Catholic

Judy Kay Gray

Title: Chief Executive Officer, Founder **Industry:** Manufacturing **Company Name:** North American Herb and Spice **Place of Birth:** Kansas City **State/ Country of Origin:** MO/USA **Parents:** John Madison Gleason; Dorthy Gay (Maltsbarger) Gleason **Marital Status:** Married **Spouse Name:** William Conner Gray (5/28/1966) **Education:** MSE, University of Central Missouri, Warrensburg (1968); BSE, University of Central Missouri, Warrensburg (1967) **Career:** Owner, JK Gray Antiques, Lake Forest, IL (2007-Present); Chief Executive Officer, Founder, North American Herb and Spice LLC (1999-Present); Chief Executive Officer, President, American Institute of Curative Medicine (1990-1998); Clinic Administrator, Physician's Clinic, Arlington Heights, IL (1987-1990); Director of Nutrition, Cancer Treatment Centers of America, Zion, IL (1984-1987); Marketing Specialist, Specialized Marketing, Dallas, TX (1982-1984); Professional Writer, Central Texas College, Killeen, TX (1980-1982); Instructor, Temple University (1974-1979); Instructor, University of Maryland (1974-1979); Instructor, Central Texas College, Germany (1974-1979); Instructor, Big Bend College, Germany (1974-1979); Instructor, Department of the Army, Fort Leonard Wood, MO (1971-1973); Dietician Applicant, Independence Sanitarium and Hospital (1969-1970) **Career Related:** Past Board of Directors, Nutrition for Optimal Health, Winnetka, IL, Past Speaker, Mid-American Health Organization; Speaker, We Can, United States Army; Consultant, Blue Cross Blue Shield; Chicago Host, Nutrition And Cooking Segment, Strength and Fitness, National Cable TV Show; Host, Nutrition Review, 150 Radio Stations, Social Media Channels; Consultant in Field **Civic:** Contributor, The National Tiger Sanctuary, Branson, MO (2010-Present); Contributor, NAHS Foundation School Limited, Uganda (2020); Contributor, Heifer; Contributor, Covenant House; Contributor, Catholic Charities; Contributor, A Greater Good Foundation; Built Schools, Kenya, Turkey; Built Factories, Turkey; Built Wells, Turkey; Contributor, School, Orphanage, Nigeria; Planter, 10,000 Trees, Ontario; Contributor, Numerous Animal Charities; Donor, Blankets, Food, Chicago; Volunteer, Contributor, Wikipedia **Creative Works:** Co-Author, "The Handbook of Nutrition Quizzes" (1993); Co-Author, "Eat Right or Die Young" (1990); Contributor, Articles, Professional Journals; Author, Book, "Kids Need Care"; Author, Book, "Greatest Treasure of All"; Artist, Oil paintings, Landscapes, Still lives, Portraits **Awards:** Lifetime Award for Quality (2019); Platinum Award, Best Immune/Oregano (2019); National Nutrition Award, Best Herb, Oregano (2018); Nikon Photography Award, Dallas, TX (1984); Crisco Award, High School **Memberships:** National Association of Female Executives; International Association Clinical Nutritionists; American Association Clinical Nutritionists; National Health Federation; National Nutrition Foods Association; Officer's Wives; Toastmaster's Club; Organic Consumer Association; Lake Forest Chamber of Commerce **Marquis Who's Who Honors:** Distinguished Humanitarian; Marquis Top Professional; Albert Nelson Marquis Lifetime Achievement Award **To what do you attribute your success:** Ms. Gray attributes her success to being grateful to a higher being, persistence, and determination. **Why did you become involved in your profession or industry:** During Ms. Gray's sophomore year of high school, her family moved to a small town. At her new school, she was editor of the newspaper, president of the home economics society, and president of the senior class. Though she was initially hesitant, the move was essential to her growth. She was the first person in her family to go to college. She furthered her education with a bachelor's and a master's degree in nutrition. She later started working for the Department of Defense and taught in Germany. She was one of the main teachers for Project Transition 100,000, which was a wonderful experience. She has traveled around the world researching why some societies live longer, better, and healthier than others, and also examining those who are less fortunate. Ms. Gray has always loved nutrition. **Avocations:** Writing; Traveling throughout the world; Making the world a better place through nutrition **Thoughts on Life:** Ms. Gray believes unexpected events are part of the process for growth.

Marybeth Gray

Title: Senior Vice President of Health & Welfare Consulting **Industry:** Consulting **Company Name:** Trion Group **Children:** Nicholas; Louis **Education:** BS in Health Policy and Administration, The Pennsylvania State University (1989) **Certifications:** License in Accident, Health, Life and Fixed Annuities, 32 States **Career:** Senior Consultant, Senior Vice President of Health and Welfare Consulting, Trion Group (2000-Present); Vice President, Aon Plc (1999-2000); National Account Manager, Aetna Inc. (1989-1999) **Career Related:** Guest Lecturer in Health Policy and Administration, The Pennsylvania State University; Speaker, Various Annual Domestic Conferences **Civic:** Board of Corporators, UPMC; Alumni Association, The Pennsylvania State University; Keynote Speaker, University Conference Services; Academic Partner, UNC Kenan Flagler Business School; RMHC; Volunteer, Community Events **Awards:** Tip Consultant Award, Trion Group (2016-2017, 2019); Most Influential Women in Benefits Advising, Employee Benefit Adviser (2017) **Memberships:** Business Group on Health, Washington, DC; Founding Member, GROW Initiative, Marsh & McLennan **Marquis Who's Who Honors:** Albert Nelson Marquis Lifetime Achievement Award **To what do you attribute your success:** Ms. Gray attributes her success to her amazing team of professionals and subject matter experts at Marsh. **Why did you become involved in your profession or industry:** Ms. Gray became involved in her profession because of her desire to make health care more affordable.

Karen Ina Green

Title: Licensed Psychologist **Industry:** Medicine & Health Care **Company Name:** Green Associates **Date of Birth:** 01/27/1939 **Place of Birth:** New York **State/Country of Origin:** NY/USA **Parents:** Irwin Margulies; Roberta Rose (Goodbinder) Margulies-Varon **Marital Status:** Divorced **Spouse Name:** L.R. Green, (12/22/1961, Divorced 6/1981) **Children:** Garth Lorin; Allison Dawne (Deceased) **Education:** MA in Literature, American University (1973); Postgraduate Coursework, Boston University (1960-1963); MA, Boston University (1960); BA in Psychology, Duke University, with Distinction (1959) **Certifications:** License Psychologist, Washington, DC **Career:** Professor, Literature, University of the District of Columbia, Washington, DC (1991-Present); Private Practice, Clinical Psychologist, Washington DC (1972-Present); Psychologist Consultant, Associated Health Practitioners, Washington, DC (1987-1990); Psychologist Consultant, Behavioral Factors, Inc., Washington, DC (1986-1989); Consultant Psychologist, Hood College, Frederick, MD (1985); Consultant Psychologist, New Ventures, Inc., Bowie, MD (1984); Consultant Psychologist, Providence Hospital, Washington DC (1981-1982); English Teacher, Maryland School of Art & Design, Wheaton, MD (1980); Licensed Psychologist, Private Practice, Psychotherapy, Green Associates, Washington, DC (1968-2019) **Career Related:** Research Psychologist, President's Commission on Obscenity and Pornography, Washington, DC (1968-1970); Consultant, Psychologist, Public Defender Service, Washington, DC (1968-1970); School Psychologist, Public Schools, Washington, DC (1967-1968); Adjunct Professor, Literature, University of the District of Columbia, Washington, DC **Creative Works:** Author, Short Story, "Late Night Blossoms" (2001); Author, Short Story, "Repetition" (1990); Director, Play, "Where Has Love Gone" (1985); Director, Play, "Songs We've Never Sung" (1984); Playwright, "These Dead Ladies Are My Friends" (1983); Publisher, "Bloodlines, by Karen Margulies Green"; Contributor, Articles, Professional Journals; Contributor, Poetry, Anthologies; Contributor, Short Stories, Anthologies **Awards:** Winner, Playwriting Contest (1983) **Memberships:** Academy of American Poets, Washington, DC (2019); Associate Member, American Psychological Association; International Council of Psychologists; D.C. Psychological Association; National Register of Health Service Providers; Phi Beta Kappa **Marquis Who's Who Honors:** Albert Nelson Marquis Lifetime Achievement Award; Marquis Who's Who Top Professional **Why did you become involved in your profession or industry:** Ms. Green became involved in her profession because her mother was a philosopher and a feminist who talked about philosophers like Freud and others all the time. So she listened to what she had to say and fought the same fight. **Avocations:** Flamenco dancing; Writing; Acting; Swimming; Jazz; Greek oriental dancing; Arts; Music; Theatre & poetry; Support for Women's Achievements **Political Affiliations:** Democrat

Charles Hirsch Greenbaum, MD, FACP

Title: Dermatologist, Educator **Industry:** Medicine & Health Care **Company Name:** Holy Redeemer Hospital **Date of Birth:** 02/22/1925 **Place of Birth:** Philadelphia **State/Country of Origin:** PA/USA **Parents:** Sigmund Samuel Greenbaum, MD; Rae Shirley (Refowich) Greenbaum **Marital Status:** Widowed **Spouse Name:** Julia Heimowitz (07/03/1955) **Children:** Steven Samuel Greenbaum, MD; Lynne Carol; Robert David **Education:** Resident, Hospital of the University of Pennsylvania (1957-1958); Resident, Pennsylvania Hospital (1956-1957); Intern, Philadelphia General Hospital (1954-1955); MD, Jefferson Medical College (1954); AB, University of Pennsylvania (1948); AB, Central High School, Philadelphia, PA **Certifications:** Diplomate, American Board of Dermatology (1960) **Career:** Emeritus Staff, Holy Redeemer Hospital, Meadowbrook, PA (1995-Present); Attending Physician, Chief of Dermatology, Holy Redeemer Hospital, Meadowbrook, PA (1958-1995); Private Practice, Medicine, Dermatology, Philadelphia, PA (1958-1995) **Career Related:** Honorary Professor of Dermatology, Jefferson Medical College, Philadelphia, PA (1995-Present); Clinical Professor, Jefferson Medical College, Philadelphia, PA (1981-1995); Medical Adviser, Pennsylvania Blue Cross (1973-1995); Clinical Associate Professor, Jefferson Medical College, Philadelphia, PA (1972-1981); Instructor in Dermatology, Jefferson Medical College, Philadelphia, PA (1958-1972); Instructor in Dermatology, Graduate School of Medicine, University of Pennsylvania (1958-1970); Fellow, American College of Physicians **Civic:** American Academy of Dermatology (1968-1972); Board of Trustees, Dermatology Foundation; Board of Directors, Holy Redeemer Hospital **Military Service:** U.S. Marine Corps (1943-1946) **Creative Works:** Contributor, Articles, Professional Journals **Memberships:** Chairman, Audit Committee, American Academy of Dermatology (1991-1993); Chairman, Committee on Evaluation, American Academy of Dermatology (1979-1982); President, Solomon Solis-Cohen Medical Literary Society (1978); Section on Dermatology, American Medical Association (1978); Director, Philadelphia County Medical Society (1977); Chairman, Advisory Board Council, American Academy of Dermatology (1977); President, Philadelphia Dermatological Society (1976-1977); President, Pennsylvania Academy of Dermatology (1976-1977); Board of Directors, North Branch, Philadelphia County Medical Society (1976); Pennsylvania Medical Society; College of Physicians of Philadelphia; Society of Investigative Dermatology; American Dermatological Association; American Academy of Dermatology **Marquis Who's Who Honors:** Albert Nelson Marquis Lifetime Achievement Award; Marquis Who's Who Top Professional **To what do you attribute your success:** Dr. Greenbaum's late wife, Julia, had an enormous impact on his life and was very supportive. **Why did you become involved in your profession or industry:** Dr. Greenbaum wanted to be a doctor since he was 5 years old. Dr. Greenbaum comes from a long line of physicians, including his father, the founder of the Society of Investigative Dermatology. **Avocations:** Sculpture; Painting; Reading; Theater; Travel

Philip Alan Greenberg

Title: Family Attorney, Civil Litigation **Date of Birth:** 08/02/1948 **Place of Birth:** Brooklyn **State/Country of Origin:** NY/USA **Parents:** Harry Greenberg; Jeannette (Nataf) Greenberg **Marital Status:** Married **Spouse Name:** Cheryl Rosenberg Greenberg **Education:** JD, New York University Law School (1973); BA in Political Science/Sociology, Brooklyn College, Cum Laude (1970) **Career:** Partner, Private Practice, Philip A. Greenberg, P.C., New York, NY (2000-Present); Partner, Wallman Greenberg Gasman & McKnight, New York, NY (1995-2000); Managing Partner, Bizar & Martin, New York, NY (1993-1995); Managing Partner, Segal & Greenberg, New York, NY (1987-1993); Managing Partner, Segal, Greenberg & McDonald, New York, NY (1986-1987); Managing Partner, Segal, Greenberg, McDonald & Maher, New York, NY (1985-1986); Managing Partner, Segal, Post, DeMott & Crow, New York, NY (1985); Partner, Segal & Greenberg, New York, NY (1984); Partner, Segal, Liling & Greenberg, New York, NY (1982-1984); Partner, Segal, Liling, Erlitz & Greenberg, New York, NY (1982); Partner, Kamerman & Kamerman, New York, NY (1978-1982); Associate, Kamerman & Kamerman, New York, NY (1973-1978) **Career Related:** Lecturer, National Business Institute (2010-Present); Lecturer, Sobelsohn Paralegal School, New York, NY (1988-2000) **Civic:** Trustee, Congregation Emunath Israel (1984-1999) **Creative Works:** Co-author, "Divorce Incites: Conversations with America's Leading Divorce Professionals" (2019) **Awards:** Named to Super Lawyers (2009-2011); AV Rating, Martindale-Hubbell (1985-Present) **Memberships:** President, Masters and Wardens Association (2003-2005); Secretary, Masters and Wardens Association (2000-2003); President, 6th Manhattan, Masters and Wardens Association (1990-1991); American Bar Association (ABA); New York State Bar Association; Association of the Bar of the City of New York; Masons; Maimonides-Marshall #739, Masons; Master Mason; Masters and Wardens Association; International Associate Tribune; Phi Alpha Delta **Bar Admissions:** New Jersey State Bar (1988); Bar of the Supreme Court of the United States (1977); United States Tax Court (1975); United States District Court for the Southern District of New York (1975); United States District Court for the Eastern District of New York (1975); United States Federal Courts (1975); New York State Bar (1974) **Marquis Who's Who Honors:** Albert Nelson Marquis Lifetime Achievement Award; Marquis Who's Who Top Professional; Marquis Who's Who Humanitarian Award **Why did you become involved in your profession or industry:** Mr. Greenberg wanted to be an entertainer when he was younger, but his mother told him that he'd starve if he did that. As a heavy-set young man, starving didn't sound like something he wanted to do. So, because Abraham Lincoln was his idol, he decided to go into law and politics. He didn't stick with politics, but has been practicing law for a long time now.

Steven Morey Greenberg

Title: Lawyer **Industry:** Law and Legal Services **Company Name:** Greenberg & Lanz, LLC **Date of Birth:** 04/09/1949 **State/Country of Origin:** NJ/USA **Parents:** Joseph Greenberg; Rhoda (Weisenfeld) Greenberg **Education:** JD, University of Pennsylvania Law School, Philadelphia, PA (1974); AB in Political Science, Syracuse University, Cum Laude, Syracuse, NY (1971) **Career:** Partner, Greenberg & Lanz, LLC, Hackensack, NJ (1997-Present); Attorney, Bergenfield, New Jersey Rent Leveling Board (1985-1989, 1992-1993, 1999); Partner, Greenberg & Marmorstein, Esqs., Hackensack, NJ (1994-1997); Attorney, Bergenfield, New Jersey Planning Board (1993-1996); Sole Practice, Hackensack, NJ (1979-1994); Associate, Cole Berman & Belsky, Rochelle Park, NJ (1977-1979); Associate, Carpenter, Bennett & Morrissey, Newark, NJ (1974-1977) **Civic:** Board of Directors, Jewish Home Family (2007-Present); Vice President, Jewish Home at Rockleigh (2003-Present); Board of Directors, Jewish Home at Rockleigh (1999-Present); Executive Committee, Jewish Home at Rockleigh (1999-Present); Director, Community Advocacy Program, Jewish Federation of Northern New Jersey (1995-Present); Board of Directors, Jewish Home Foundation of North Jersey (2003-Present); Secretary, Jewish Home Assisted Living (2014-2019); Board of Directors, Jewish Home Assisted Living (2011-2019); Governing Committee, Jewish Home Assisted Living (2019-Present); President, Teaneck Jewish Memorial Association (1992-Present); Member, Community Resource Council (2010-Present); Board of Directors, Adler Aphasia Center (2012-Present); Honorary Trustee, Jewish Association for Developmental Disabilities (2008-Present); Board of Trustees, Endowment Foundation (2003-2019); Board of Trustees, Jewish Center of Teaneck (1978-2015); Board of Trustees, Jewish Federation of Northern New Jersey (1997-2015); New Jersey Regional Advisory Board, Anti-Defamation League (1989-2014); Board of Directors, The Jewish Institute of Bioethics (1998-2014); President, Jewish Home Foundation of North Jersey (2009-2012); Board of Trustees, Jewish Family Services, Inc. (1986-1996, 2005-2011); Vice President, Jewish Family Services, Inc. (1992-1996, 2007-2009); Jewish Community Relations Council, Jewish Federation of Northern New Jersey (1986-1993, 1999-2007); Vice President, Jewish Federation of Northern New Jersey (2001-2003, 2005-2007); Board of Trustees, American Society for the Protection of Nature in Israel (2006-2007); Board of Trustees, Bergen County High School of Jewish Studies (2000-2005); Treasurer, Jewish Federation of Northern New Jersey (2003-2005); Annual Campaign Chair, Jewish Federation of Northern New Jersey (2004-2005); President, The Jewish Institute of Bioethics (1998-2004); New Jersey Leadership Think Tank, The Allen and Joan Bildner Center for the Study of Jewish Life, Rutgers, the State University of New Jersey (2001-2004); Vice President, Jewish Home & Rehabilitation Center (1990-2003); Board of Directors, Jewish Home & Rehabilitation Center (1986-2003); Board of Trustees, Association of Jewish Federations of New Jersey (2002-2003); Chairman, Planning and Allocations Committee, Jewish Federation of Northern New Jersey (2000-2002); Board of Trustees, Bergenfield Museum Society (1989-1999); Director, Union for Traditional Judaism (1993-1997); President, Jewish Center of Teaneck (1994-1997); Board of Directors, Sam Gorovoy Group Care Home for Senior Adults (1983-1996); Vice President, Jewish Center of Teaneck (1992-1994); Director, JH & RC Senior Housing, Inc. (1991-1994); Vice President, JH & RC Senior Housing, Inc. (1991-1994); Jewish Community Council of Teaneck (1989-1993); Treasurer, Jewish Family Services, Inc. (1990-1992); Vice President, Teaneck Jewish Memorial Association (1990-1992); President, Sam Gorovoy Group Care Home for Senior Adults (1986-1990); Board of Trustees, Solomen Schechter Day School of Bergen County (1986-1987); Advisory Board of Directors, Jewish Home & Rehabilitation Center (1982-1986) **Awards:** Highest Rating in Legal Ability and Ethical Standards, Martindale-Hubbell (1980-Present); Guest of Honor, Bnos Menachem Yeshiva for Young Women Annual Gala Dinner (2016); Dr. Harry Brandeis Memorial Community Service Award, Community Resource Council (2010); Gates of Jerusalem Award, Boys Town Jerusalem (2004); Americanism Award, Anti-Defamation League (2003); Award, Ma'Ayanot Yeshiva High School Girls (2001); Second Century Award, Jewish Theological Seminary of America (1998); Award, Jewish Center of Teaneck (1997); Community Service Award, Friends of Lubavitch (1997) **Memberships:** American Bar Association; New York State Bar Association; Bergen County Bar Association; New Jersey Bar Association; Pi Sigma Alpha; Phi Kappa Phi **Bar Admissions:** United States Court of Federal Claims (1989); United States Court of Appeals for the Third Circuit (1987); United States District Court for the Eastern District of New York (1986); United States District Court for the Southern District of New York (1986); New York (1980); United States District Court for the District of New Jersey (1974); New Jersey (1974) **Marquis Who's Who Honors:** Albert Nelson Marquis Lifetime Achievement Award

Edward F. Greene

Title: Senior Counsel **Industry:** Law and Legal Services **Company Name:** Cleary Gottlieb Steen & Hamilton LLP **Date of Birth:** 10/18/1941 **Place of Birth:** New York **State/Country of Origin:** NY/USA **Parents:** Foster Comings; Marjorie (Brier) Greene **Marital Status:** Married **Spouse Name:** Diana Barton Harding (08/05/1967) **Children:** Anna Tucker; Mary Barclay **Education:** LLB, Harvard Law School (1966); BA, Amherst College (1963) **Career:** Senior Counsel, Cleary Gottlieb Steen & Hamilton LLP, Washington, DC, Tokyo, Japan, London, England, United Kingdom and New York, NY (2009-Present); General Counsel, Institutional Clients Group, Citigroup, Inc., New York, NY (2004-2008); Partner, Cleary Gottlieb Steen & Hamilton LLP, Washington, DC, Tokyo, Japan, London, England, United Kingdom and New York, NY (1982-2004); General Counsel, U.S. Securities and Exchange Commission, Washington, DC (1981-1982); Director, Corporate Finance Division, U.S. Securities and Exchange Commission, Washington, DC (1979-1981); Deputy Director, Corporate Finance Division, U.S. Securities and Exchange Commission, Washington, DC (1978-1979); Partner, Willkie Farr & Gallagher, LLP, New York, NY (1972-1978); Associate, Willkie Farr & Gallagher, LLP, New York, NY (1968-1971); Assistant professor, Wayne State University Law School, Detroit, MI (1967-1968) **Career Related:** Senior Lecturer of Law, Columbia Law School (2012-Present); Adjunct Professor of Law, University of Tokyo (1989-Present); Adjunct Professor of Law, University of Pennsylvania, Philadelphia, PA (1984-1987); Adjunct Professor of Law, Georgetown University, Washington, DC (1982-1984) **Creative Works:** Contributor, Articles to Professional Journals **Awards:** Teaching Fellow, Boston College Law School (1966-1967); Named One of the Best Capital Markets Lawyers, Chambers Global **Memberships:** Executive Member, Federal Securities Committee, Federal Bar Association (1983-Present); Executive Committee, University of California Securities Regulation Institute (1983-Present); Executive Committee, Institute of U.S. Securities and Exchange Commission and Financial Reporting (1983-Present); The American Law Institute; Founding Member, Lawyers Alliance for New York **Bar Admissions:** New York (1971); District of Columbia; United States District Court for the Southern District of New York **Marquis Who's Who Honors:** Albert Nelson Marquis Lifetime Achievement Award; Marquis Who's Who Top Professional **Why did you become involved in your profession or industry:** When Mr. Greene graduated from college, initially he was unsure of what he wanted to do with his career. Law seemed to provide "quite a bit of flexibility" according to Greene. Also influenced by a group of close students of his graduating class, a majority of them decided to take on law as their next step together. Mr. Greene always had an interest in public service, so when the opportunity presented itself to join the U.S. Securities Exchange Commission, Mr. Greene took advantage of the opportunity and says it was the best decision he's made for his career. **Avocations:** Reading; Crossword puzzles **Political Affiliations:** Democrat **Thoughts on Life:** Mr. Greene is the author of a number of leading books and law review articles, including "U.S. Regulation of the International Securities and Derivatives Markets" and "The Sarbanes-Oxley Act: Analysis and Practice," both of which were co-authored with several partners at Cleary Gottlieb and are widely used as essential sources of practical advice. Mr. Greene has been recognized as one of the best capital markets lawyers by Chambers Global. His practice focuses on securities, corporate governance, regulatory and financial services reform, and other corporate law matters.

Sarah C. Greenfield, PhD

Title: Counselor (Retired) **Industry:** Health, Wellness and Fitness **Date of Birth:** 07/07/1937 **Place of Birth:** Rochester **State/Country of Origin:** NY/USA **Parents:** George Stoner Curtice; Margaret (Sidebotham) Curtice **Marital Status:** Married **Spouse Name:** James Dwight Greenfield **Education:** PhD in Adult Education, Arizona State University, Tempe, AZ (1975); Administrative Intern in Adult Education, Office of University Extension and Summer Sessions, Arizona State University, Tempe, AZ (1972); Counseling Practicum, Counselor Training Center, Arizona State University, Tempe, AZ (1969-1970); MA in Counseling, Arizona State University, Tempe, AZ (1970); MEd, Arizona State University, Tempe, AZ (1968); BA in General Science, University of Rochester, Rochester, NY (1959) **Career:** School Counselor, Chinle Junior High School, Chinle Unified School District #24 (1977-2001); Counselor/Tutor, Title IV Program, Alum Rock School District, San Jose, CA (1977); Adult Education Consultant, Designing and Developing a Masters Program in Adult Education, Fort Wright College, Spokane, WA (Now Heritage University) (1976); Instructor in Adult Education, Fort Wright College (1976); Biochemical Laboratory Technician, Pabst Biochemical Laboratory, Milwaukee, WI (1962-1963); Biochemical Laboratory Technician, Strong Memorial Hospital, Rochester, NY (1959-1961) **Career Related:** Data Analyst, Far West Laboratory for Educational Research and Development, San Francisco, CA (1975); Marketing Research Interviewer, Behavior Research Center, Phoenix, AZ (1974-1975); Fellow, The Rockefeller Foundation (1972); Marketing Research Interviewer, Behavior Research Center, Phoenix, AZ (1971-1972); Research Biochemical Laboratory Technician, Pabst Biochemical Laboratories, Milwaukee, WI (1962-1963); Research Biochemical Laboratory Technician, Department of Experimental Radiology, Strong Memorial Hospital, University of Rochester School of Medicine and Dentistry, Rochester, NY (1959-1961) **Civic:** Volunteer, Heard Museum (2001-Present); Executive Board, Heard Museum Shop (2005-2006); Volunteer Crisis Worker, ADABI, Chinle, AZ (1989-1999); Member, Executive Board, Interfaith Counseling Northwest, Phoenix, AZ (1970-1971); Counseling Volunteer, Psychiatric Ward, St. Luke's Hospital, Phoenix, AZ; Executive Board, Heard Museum Shop (1969-1970); Publicity Committee, Heard Museum Indian Fair & Market, Heard Museum and Heard Museum Guild (1967); Heard Committee, Heard Museum Indian Fair & Market, Heard Museum and Heard Museum Guild (1967); Volunteer, Heard Museum Guild, Heard Museum of Anthropology and Primitive Art, Phoenix, AZ (1965-1973); Volunteer, Phoenix Little Theater (Now The Phoenix Theatre Company), Phoenix, AZ (1965-1969) **Creative Works:** Nonverbal Communication Abstracter (1980); Nonverbal Communication Abstracter, Journal Articles (1980); Contributor, "Body Movement & Nonverbal Communication: An Annotated Bibliography," Institute for Nonverbal Communication Research (1971-1980) **Awards:** Fellowship, The Rockefeller Foundation (1972) **Memberships:** Counseling and Development Section, American School Counselor Association; Arizona Counseling Association; Chinle Education Association; Arizona Education Association; National Education Association; Laban/Bartenieff Institute of Movement Studies; Pi Lambda Theta **Marquis Who's Who Honors:** Albert Nelson Marquis Lifetime Achievement Award; Marquis Who's Who Humanitarian Award **Why did you become involved in your profession or industry:** Dr. Greenfield became involved in her profession after working for Strong Memorial Hospital as a unit clerk who filled in when employees went on vacation. After graduation, Dr. Greenfield had trouble finding her desired position, so she applied to Strong Memorial Hospital again and was hired as a lab technician. When Dr. Greenfield first moved to Phoenix, AZ, she was a housewife who did volunteer work for various places, such as Phoenix Little Theater and the Heard Museum. She decided she wanted to do something more, but wasn't quite sure as to what that would be. Dr. Greenfield planned on going back to school to study psychology, but she encountered a meeting about counseling by chance, and signed up for that instead. Dr. Greenfield had prior training in both counseling and student teaching and ended up becoming a public school counselor because both forms of training were a requirement for the role. **Avocations:** Photography; Traveling; Reading; Writing **Religion:** Presbyterian

Charles August Greenhall, PhD

Title: Mathematician **Industry:** Sciences **Company Name:** Jet Propulsion Laboratory **Date of Birth:** 05/05/1939 **Place of Birth:** New York **State/Country of Origin:** NY/USA **Parents:** A. Frank Greenhall; Miriam Housman **Education:** PhD, California Institute of Technology, Pasadena, CA (1966); BA, Pomona College, Claremont, CA (1961) **Career:** Senior Member, Technical Staff, Jet Propulsion Laboratory, Pasadena, CA (1977-Present); Assistant Professor, Mathematics, University of Southern California, Los Angeles, CA (1968-1973) **Creative Works:** Contributor, Articles, Professional Journals **Memberships:** Life Senior Member, IEEE; Mathematics Association of America **Marquis Who's Who Honors:** Albert Nelson Marquis Lifetime Achievement Award **Avocations:** Running **Political Affiliations:** Republican

James Paul Gregory

Title: Lawyer **Industry:** Law and Legal Services **Date of Birth:** 11/07/1949 **Place of Birth:** Detroit **State/Country of Origin:** MI/USA **Parents:** James Gregory; Betty Jean (Kinsler) Gregory **Marital Status:** Married **Spouse Name:** Ranelle Leftridge (12/11/1987); Carol L. Geis (08/12/1972, Divorced 1987) **Children:** Sarah E; Jessen L.; J. Nicholas; Laurence Thompson; Angela Smith **Education:** LLM, New York University (1976); JD, Wayne State University (1974); BA, University of Michigan (1971) **Career:** Attorney, Ruddy Gregory (2017-Present); Attorney, Gregory & Gregory (2010-2017); Attorney, Sterling, Gregory & Plotkin (2002-2010); Attorney, Gelt, Fleishman & Sterling, Professional Corporation, Denver (1994-2002); Attorney, Haligman and Lottner, Professional Corporation, Denver, CO (1976-1994) **Civic:** Treasurer, Opera Colorado, Denver, CO (1997, 1998); Director, Opera Colorado, Denver, CO (1995) **Memberships:** American Bar Association.; Colorado Bar Association; Denver Bar Association; The District of Columbia Bar **Bar Admissions:** District of Columbia (2001); U.S. Tax Court (1980); Colorado (1976); U.S. Court of Appeals for the 10th Circuit (1976); Michigan (1974) **Marquis Who's Who Honors:** Albert Nelson Marquis Lifetime Achievement Award; Marquis Who's Who Top Professional **Why did you become involved in your profession or industry:** Mr. Gregory became involved in his profession because of a friend of his parents. He was a lawyer and he thought that had a very interesting life and had a amazing quality of life which appealed to him. As did the law course he took throughout his academic career. He added to those by taking accounting classes during a gap year between law school and getting his master's degree. He was interested in a friend of his parents' quality of life and his parents' admiration of him and felt it was something he wanted to aspire to. **Avocations:** Italian cooking; Reading; Following international affairs; Playing golf

Vicki L. Gregory

Title: Library and Information **Industry:** Education/Educational Services **Company Name:** University of South Florida **Date of Birth:** 02/13/1950 **Place of Birth:** Chattanooga **State/Country of Origin:** TN/USA **Parents:** John Allen Lovelady; Mary (Carter) Lovelady **Marital Status:** Married **Spouse Name:** William Stanley Gregory (08/15/1970) **Education:** PhD, Rutgers University, the State University of New Jersey (1987); MLS, University of Alabama (1974); MA, University of Alabama (1973); AB, University of Alabama (1971) **Career:** Assistant Professor, Associate Professor, Professor, University of South Florida, Tampa, FL (1988-Present); Audio-Visual Librarian, Head of Department System and Operations, Auburn University, Montgomery, AL (1976-1988) **Creative Works:** "Introduction to Collection Development and Management for 21st Century Libraries," First Edition (2011); "Selecting and Managing Electronic Resources (2006); Author, Editor, "The State and the Academic Library" (1993); Editor, "A Dynamic Tradition: A History of Alabama Academic Libraries" (1991); Contributor, Articles, Professional Journals **Awards:** Watson Davis Award, Association for Information Science & Technology (2014); Dissertation Fellowship, Association of College Research Libraries Doctoral (1985) **Memberships:** Executive Board, Southeastern Library Association (1986-2020); President, Treasurer, Beta Phi Mu Library and Information Science Honorary Society (2017-2019); Secretary, Treasurer, Library Research Roundtable (1994-1996); Executive Council, Alabama Library Association (1988-1989); American Library Association; Association of College & Research Libraries; Association of Library and Information Science Educators; Florida Library Association **Marquis Who's Who Honors:** Albert Nelson Marquis Lifetime Achievement Award; Marquis Who's Who Top Professional **Why did you become involved in your profession or industry:** In college, Professor Gregory studied history. Being that it was such a wide field, she spent a lot of time in the library. She then earned a graduate student position in the library, which led her to pursue a career in library information education. **Avocations:** Reading; Flute/piccolo in the community band

Karan Grewal

Title: Financial Reporting Manager **Industry:** Financial Services **Company Name:** Center for Strategic and International Studies **Date of Birth:** 12/12/1985 **State/Country of Origin:** India **Education:** BS in Accounting, Virginia Polytechnic Institute and State University, Blacksburg, VA (2007) **Certifications:** Certified Public Accountant, Virginia Board of Accountancy **Career:** Financial Reporting Manager, Center for Strategic and International Studies (CSIS), Washington, DC (2012-Present); Staff Accountant II, Aronson, LLC, Rockville, MD (2011-2012); Staff Accountant, Charles Coker, CPA, LLC (2009-2010); Audit Senior Assistant, Deloitte (2007-2009); Intern, Freddie Mac (2006) **Awards:** Business Student of the Year, High School **Marquis Who's Who Honors:** Albert Nelson Marquis Lifetime Achievement Award; Marquis Who's Who Top Professional **Why did you become involved in your profession or industry:** Mr. Grewal became involved in his profession because he wanted to do something with business since high school. He took accounting because it seemed like an area that was growing. In 2007, it was one of the hottest professions to get into. He took Accounting 101 and was hooked. Like most accounting graduates, Mr. Grewal started out working for a big public accounting firm, specifically Deloitte; while he was there, he had multiple industry clients. He was in financial services and nonprofits, the latter of which stuck with him because it was unique and it was not one kind of revenue stream. Thus, when the opportunity for the Center for Strategic and International Studies opened, he made his move there. **Thoughts on Life:** Mr. Grewal started out as a junior accountant, a role in which he learned the complexities of the field, and now he manages a staff of five, running day-to-day accounting functions.

Agnes M. Griffen, MLS

Title: Library Administrator (Retired) **Industry:** Library Management/Library Services **Company Name:** Tucson Pima County Public Library **Date of Birth:** 08/25/1935 **Place of Birth:** Fort Dauphin **State/Country of Origin:** Madagascar **Parents:** Frederick Stang; Alvilde Margrethe (Torvik) Hallanger **Marital Status:** Divorced **Spouse Name:** Thomas Michael Griffen (Divorced 11/1969) **Children:** Shaun Helen Griffen; Christopher Patrick; Adam Andrew **Education:** Postgraduate Coursework, Harvard University (1993); Urban Executive Certified, Massachusetts Institute of Technology (1976); MLS, University of Washington (1965); BA in English, Pacific Lutheran University, Cum Laude (1957) **Certifications:** Certified Librarian, Maryland (1981); Certified Librarian, Arizona (1974); Certified Librarian, Washington, DC (1965) **Career:** Retired (2003); Library Director, Tucson-Pima Public Library (1997-2003); Director, Montgomery County Department of Public Libraries, Rockville, MD (1980-1996); Deputy Library Director, Tucson Public Library (1974-1980); Deputy Librarian, Staff and Program Development, King County Library Systems, Seattle, OR (1971-1974); Coordinator, Institutional Libraries, King County Library Systems, Seattle, OR (1968-1971); Area Children's Librarian, King County Library Systems, Seattle, OR (1965-1968) **Career Related:** Visiting Lecturer, School Librarianship, University of Washington, Seattle, OR (1983); Lecturer, Graduate Library School, University of Arizona, Tucson, AZ (1979); Lecturer, Graduate Library School, University of Arizona, Tucson, AZ (1976-1977) **Civic:** Arizona Statewide Library Development Commission (2000-2002); Advisory Council, Arizona State Librarians (1998); President of the Board, National Capital Area Public Access Network (1993-1994); Council, National Capital Area Public Access Network (1992-1994); Maryland Humanities Council, Baltimore, MD (1986-1992); Charter Member, Executive Women's Council of Southern Arizona, Tucson, AZ (1979-1980); Arizona Humanities Council, Phoenix, AZ (1977-1980) **Creative Works:** Contributor, Articles, Library Periodicals, Professional Journals **Awards:** Helping Hand Award, Maryland Association of the Deaf (1985); Certified Recognition, Montgomery County Hispanic Employees Association (1985); Henry Scholar, University of Washington School Librarianship (1965) **Memberships:** Legislative Committee, Arizona State Library Association (1997-Present); Legislative Committee, American Library Association (1998-2002); Chairman, Committee on Program Evaluation and Support, American Library Association (1987-1988); Councilor-at-Large, American Library Association (1986-1993); Executive Board, American Library Association (1983-1993); Division President, Public Library Association Board, American Library Association (1981-1982); Councilor-at-Large, American Library Association (1972-1976); Maryland Library Association **Marquis Who's Who Honors:** Albert Nelson Marquis Lifetime Achievement Award **Why did you become involved in your profession or industry:** Ms. Griffen wanted to become an author since she was a little girl; the impulse to write was always in her. **Avocations:** Reading; Supporting independent book stores **Political Affiliations:** Democrat

Jane E. Grigger

Title: Teacher **Industry:** Education/Educational Services **Company Name:** Princeton Day School **Date of Birth:** 06/07/1947 **Place of Birth:** Philadelphia **State/Country of Origin:** PA/USA **Parents:** John Casimer Grigger; Rozanne Marie (Peters) Grigger **Marital Status:** Single **Education:** MEd in Earth Science Education, Temple University (1971); BS in Geology, Bucknell University (1969) **Certifications:** Certified Science Teacher of Grades K-12, State of New Jersey; Certified Secondary Teacher of Grades 7-12, Commonwealth of Pennsylvania **Career:** Teacher of Middle School Earth Science and Physical Science, Princeton Day School (1975-Present); Teacher of Secondary Science, Princeton Regional Schools, New Jersey (1972-1975); Teacher of Secondary Science, Bensalem Township School District, Cornwells Heights, PA (1970-1972) **Career Related:** Teacher, Partners in Education Geology Program, Princeton University (1985); Photographer, Journals; Sports Photographer, Princeton Day School **Civic:** Troop Adviser, Southeast Pennsylvania Council, Girl Scouts of the United States of America (1969-Present); Photographer, International Event, Girl Scouts of the United States of America (1975-1976) **Creative Works:** Co-Author, "Make the Rafters Ring: Remembering Camp Hagan," Brown Acorn Press (2015) **Awards:** Citizenship Award, Camp Hagan (2014) **Memberships:** Philadelphia Geological Society; Field Conference of Pennsylvania Geologists; New Jersey Science Teachers Association (NJSTA); Association for Women Geoscientists; New Jersey Earth Science Teachers Association (NJESTA); National Association of Geology Teachers (NAGT); National Science Teaching Association; Plainsboro Historical Society; Bucknell University Alumni Association; Temple University Alumni Association; International Sand Collectors Society **Marquis Who's Who Honors:** Albert Nelson Marquis Lifetime Achievement Award **Avocations:** Playing guitar; Playing flute; Collecting postcards; Collecting rocks and minerals; Singing; Reading; Civil War studies; Traveling; Spending time with family; Genealogy **Political Affiliations:** Democrat **Religion:** Episcopalian

Richard Louis Grill

Title: Music Educator **Industry:** Education/Educational Services **Date of Birth:** 10/09/1943 **Place of Birth:** Chicago **State/Country of Origin:** IL/USA **Parents:** Emil Joseph Grill; Rose Jean (Retel) Grill **Marital Status:** Widower **Spouse Name:** Mary Bernadette Moran (12/30/1967, Deceased 12/22/2012) **Children:** Rick **Education:** MusM in Organ Performance, Cleveland Institute of Music (1970); MusB, DePaul University, Chicago, IL (1965) **Certifications:** Licensed Teacher, State of Indiana **Career:** Organist, Grace Lutheran Church, Missouri Synod (2015-Present); Director of Music and Liturgy, St. Mary Church, Muncie, IN (1972-2009); Director of Music, Our Lady of Angels Church, Cleveland, OH (1966-1972); Director of Music, St. Denis Church, Chicago, IL (1964-1966); Director of Music, St. Paul Church, Chicago, IL (1962-1964) **Career Related:** Board Member, East Central Indiana Chamber Orchestra (2015-Present); Advisor, Muncie Symphony Children's Concerts (1994-Present); Music Textbook Reviewer, Indiana Department of Education (2005); Delegate to Hungary, Poland, Czech Republic, People to People, Seattle, WA (1998); Organ Concert, St. John Evangelist Church, Hartford City, IN (1987-1988); Music Commission, Diocese Lafayette-in-Indiana (1980-1990); Conductor, Beethoven Mass in C, Our Lady of Angels Catholic Church, Cleveland, OH (1972); Music Commission, Diocese of Cleveland (1969-1972); Conductor, Dubois Seven Last Words (1966-1972) **Civic:** Boys Choir, The Shamrockers, St. Mary School (1991); Choir, St. Mary Church, Muncie, IN (1973) **Creative Works:** Conductor, "Seven Last Words," East Central Indiana Chamber (2015); Conductor, "Vivaldi: Gloria," East Central Indiana Chamber Orchestra" (2014); Contributor, Articles on Liturgy Explanation of the Catholic Mass, Voice of St. Mary (2000-2009) **Memberships:** Conductor, Planet Earth Singers (2013-Present); Treasurer, Harvest Soup Kitchen (2013-2018); Colleague, American Guild Organists (1984); Treasurer, Dean, American Guild Organists (1986-1990) **Marquis Who's Who Honors:** Albert Nelson Marquis Lifetime Achievement Award **Why did you become involved in your profession or industry:** Mr. Grill decided on his profession at a young age. When was a child, his mother sang in the church choir and he used to watch her. Standing near the organ, Mr. Grill became fascinated with how the organist would move her hands and feet at the same time, which inspired him to pursue music. His great grandfather was a church organist back in Solvenia. **Avocations:** Harpsichord building; Photography; Travel **Religion:** Roman Catholic

Meyer Stewart Grinberg

Title: Financial Planner **Industry:** Financial Services **Date of Birth:** 08/31/1944 **Place of Birth:** New Brunswick **State/Country of Origin:** NJ/USA **Parents:** Allen Lewis Grinberg; Edith (Bart) Grinberg **Marital Status:** Married **Spouse Name:** Mary F. Grinberg **Children:** David; Lee; Benjamin **Education:** Master of Business Administration, George Washington University (1973); Doctor of Jurisprudence, University of Pennsylvania (1968); Bachelor of Arts, Franklin and Marshall College (1965) **Certifications:** Certified Public Accountant, State of Pennsylvania **Career:** Financial Advisor, Luttner Financial Group (2004-Present); Executive Director, Jewish Education Institute Pittsburgh, PA (1991-2004); Vice President, Co-Owner, Buy-Wise, Incorporated, Pittsburgh, PA (1977-1991); Tax Accountant, Arthur Andersen & Company, Pittsburgh, PA (1973-1977) **Civic:** Vice President, School of Advanced Studies, Pittsburgh, PA; President, Community Day School; President, Western Pennsylvania Region, United Synagogues American, Pittsburgh, PA; Executive Vice President, Congressional B'nai Israel, Pittsburgh, PA; Board of Directors, Yeshiva Schools of Pittsburgh; Board of Directors, Jewish Federation of Greater Pittsburgh; Board of Directors, Secretary, Jewish Cemetery and Burial Association; Chairman, Invitational Maccabi Youth Games; Past Vice President, Board of Directors, Solomon Schechter National Day School Association; Board of Directors, Forward-Shady Housing Project, United Synagogue of Conservative Judaism-Israel Affairs Committee; Chairman, Pittsburgh Delegation, Maccabi Games; Board Member, Jewish National Fund; Jewish Committee Center; Coach, Little League; Chairman, Health and Physical Education Committee, Jewish Community Center; North America Youth Maccabi Games Committee; Board of Directors, Hebrew Institute of Pittsburgh; Make-A-Wish Foundation; Chairman, National Maccabi Culture and Education Committee; Melanoma Action Coalition; Melanoma Research Alliance; Chairman, Partnership2gether; President, Pittsburgh Three Rivers Marathon; Chairman, Community Relations Council; President, Jewish Assistance Fund; Board of Directors, Bair Find Foundation; Chair, Repair the World Advisory Committee; Vice Chair, Jewish Council of Public Affairs **Military Service:** Active Duty Judge Advocate General Officer, U.S. Coast Guard (1968-1973) **Awards:** Zionist Organization of America Israel Service Award (2018); Jewish National Fund, Guardian of Israel Award (2016); Volunteer of the Year Award, Jewish Federation of Greater Pittsburgh (2015); Levinson Community Service Award, Community Relations Council (2015); Humanitarian Award, Western Pennsylvania Jewish Sports Hall of Fame (2013); Community Day School Leadership Award (2011); Honoree, Community Day School (1991); New Leadership Award, Jewish Welfare Board (1990); Rogal-Ruslander Leadership Award, Jewish Community Center (1990); Outstanding Citizen of Pittsburgh, Station WQEX, Pittsburgh Post-Gazette (1989); Latterman Volunteer Mitzvah Award (1988) **Memberships:** American Institute of Certified Public Accountants; Pennsylvania Institute of Certified Public Accountants; Pennsylvania Bar Association; Kiwanis **Bar Admissions:** State of Pennsylvania; United States Court Claims; United States Customs Court; United States Court International Trade; United States Court Military Appeals; United States Supreme Court **Marquis Who's Who Honors:** Albert Nelson Marquis Lifetime Achievement Award; Marquis Who's Who Top Professional; Marquis Who's Who Humanitarian Award **To what do you attribute your success:** Mr. Grinberg's success can be attributed to maintaining a goal tied to his concern for people, as well as his individual traits of integrity, humility, listening and hard work. **Avocations:** Jogging; Photography **Political Affiliations:** Democrat **Religion:** Jewish

Bernard I. Grosser

Title: Psychiatrist, Educator (Retired) **Industry:** Medicine & Health Care **Date of Birth:** 04/19/1929 **Place of Birth:** Boston **State/Country of Origin:** MA/USA **Parents:** John Grosser; Katherine Grosser **Marital Status:** Married **Spouse Name:** Karen McArthur, RN, MS, MBA **Children:** Steven Grosser, MD; Mark Grosser, MBA; Minda Grosser Levin, MBA **Education:** Residency in Psychiatry, The University of Utah (1960-1965); Internship, The University of Utah (1959-1960); MD, Case Western Reserve University, Cleveland, OH (1959); MS, University of Michigan (1953); BA, University of Massachusetts Amherst (1950) **Certifications:** Diplomate, American Board of Psychiatry and Neurology, Inc. (1965-2012) **Career:** Chairman, Department of Psychiatry, University of Utah School of Medicine (1978-2007); Professor, University of Utah School of Medicine (1975-2012); Associate Professor, University of Utah School of Medicine (1971-1975); Assistant Professor of Psychiatry, University of Utah School of Medicine (1967-1971) **Career Related:** Member, Review Panel, Extramural LRP (2008-2010); Ad Hoc Member, Special Emphasis Panel, National Institute of Mental Health (NIMH) (2000-2006); Ad Hoc Member, Review Committee, Mental Health Clinical Research Center, National Institute of Mental Health (NIMH) (1997); Senior Science Adviser, SAMHA (Substance Abuse and Mental Health Services Administration) (1987-1988); Member, Intramural Science Advisory Board, National Institute of Mental Health (NIMH) (1984-1988); Member, Pre-Clinical and Clinical Psychopharmacology Review Committee, National Institute of Mental Health (NIMH) (1974-1979, 1980-1984) **Military Service:** Captain, U.S. Air Force (1965-1967) **Creative Works:** Contributor, Book Chapters; Contributor, Articles, Professional Journals **Awards:** Best Doctors in America (2009-2010); Exemplary Psychiatrist Award, National Alliance on Mental Illness (1997); Grantee, U.S. Food and Drug Administration (1985-1988); Research Career Development Award (1963-1965, 1967-1975); Grantee, National Institute of Mental Health (1959-1984); Listed, Third Edition, Who's Who Among Human Services Professionals; Listed, 24 Editions, Who's Who in America; Listed, Two Editions, Who's Who in American Education; Listed, Eight Editions, Who's Who in Medicine and Healthcare; Listed, Two Editions, Who's Who in Science and Engineering; Listed, Eighteen Editions, Who's Who in the West; Listed, Eleven Editions, Who's Who in the World **Memberships:** Secretary, Treasurer, American Psychiatric Association (2005-2006); Council Member, American Psychiatric Association (1997-2005); President, Psychiatric Research Society (1986-1987); Chairman, American Psychiatric Association (1978-2007); Treasurer, International Society of Psychoneuroendocrinology (1974-1988); American Psychiatric Association (1965-2012); Society for Neuroscience; The New York Academy of Sciences **Marquis Who's Who Honors:** Albert Nelson Marquis Lifetime Achievement Award **Why did you become involved in your profession or industry:** Dr. Grosser became involved in his profession because of his lifelong interest in behavior and science. His early research on steroids while at the University of Michigan led to his specific interest in the brain. **Avocations:** Traveling nationally and internationally; Reading; Swimming **Political Affiliations:** Republican **Religion:** Jewish

Robert Grossman, MD

Title: Professor of Neurosurgery **Industry:** Education/Educational Services **Company Name:** Houston Methodist Hospital **Date of Birth:** 01/24/1933 **Place of Birth:** New York **State/Country of Origin:** NY/USA **Parents:** Ferenc Grossman; Vivian (Isenberg) Grossman **Marital Status:** Married **Spouse Name:** Elin Grossman **Children:** Amy; Kate; Jennifer **Education:** Resident, Presbyterian Hospital, Columbia University, New York, NY (1960-1963); Intern, Strong Memorial Hospital, University of Rochester, Rochester, NY (1957-1958); Doctor of Medicine, College of Physicians and Surgeons, Columbia University (1957); Bachelor of Arts, Swarthmore College (1953) **Certifications:** Diplomate, American Board of Neurological Surgery (1966); Diplomate, National Board of Medical Examiners (1958) **Career:** Academic Practice on Medicine Specializing in Neurological Surgery, Houston, TX (1963-Present); Director, Neurological Institute, Chairman, Department of Neurosurgery, Professor of Neurosurgery, Houston Methodist Hospital, Houston, TX (2005-2013); Associate Dean, Clinical Affairs, Baylor College of Medicine (2002-2005); Professor, Chair, Department of Neurosurgery, Baylor College of Medicine (1980-2005); Professor, Chairman, Division on Neurological Surgery, University of Texas Medical Branch at Galveston (1973-1980); From Associate Professor to Professor of Neurological Surgery, Albert Einstein College of Medicine (1969-1973); From Instructor to Associate Professor of Neurological Surgery, University of Texas Southwest Medical School (1963-1968) **Career Related:** Member, Board of Science Counselors, National Institute of Neurological Disorders and Stroke, National Institutes of Health (1993-1996); Chairman, Neurology, B Study Section, United States Public Health Service, National Institutes of Health (1972-1974) **Military Service:** With, U.S. Army (1958-1960); With, Walter Reed Army Institute of Research **Creative Works:** Chairman of Editorial Board, Journal of Neurosurgery (1987); Author, with W. D. Willis, "Medical Neurobiology, Third Edition" (1981) **Awards:** Recipient, Cushing Medal, American Association of Neurological Surgeons (2007); Recipient, Albert and Ellen Grass Foundation Prize and Medal, The Society of Neurological Surgeons **Memberships:** President, Society of Neurological Surgeons (1995); Chairman of Board of Directors, American Board of Neurological Surgery (1989-1990); President, American Epilepsy Society (1982); President, Society of University Neurosurgeons (1980); American College of Surgeons; Vice President, American Academy of Neurological Surgery; American Association of Neurological Surgeons **Marquis Who's Who Honors:** Albert Nelson Marquis Lifetime Achievement Award; Marquis Who's Who Top Professional **Why did you become involved in your profession or industry:** Dr. Grossman initially entered his profession due to a family history in medicine. Additionally, he was quite interested in working with the brain.

Robert Martin Gruninger Sr.

Title: Civil Engineer **Industry:** Engineering **Date of Birth:** 08/20/1937 **Place of Birth:** Paterson **State/Country of Origin:** NJ/ USA **Parents:** Martin A. Gruninger; Henrietta (Van Decker) Gruninger **Marital Status:** Married **Spouse Name:** Margaret M. Cooke (08/29/1959, Deceased 09/20/2019) **Children:** Robert M.; John M. **Education:** MS in Civil Engineering, New Jersey Institute Technology (1968); BS in Civil Engineering, New Jersey Institute Technology (1960) **Career:** Civil Engineer; Vice President, Gannett Fleming Inc., Baltimore, MD (1991-1992); Vice President, Lewis & Zimmerman Associates, Inc., Rockville, MD (1990-1991); Vice President, Community College Johnson & Malhotra, Professional Corporation, Silver Spring, MD (1979-1990); Project Manager, Malcolm Pirnie, Incorporated, Paramus, NJ (1968-1979); Engineer, Project Engineer, Malcolm Pirnie, Incorporated, White Plains, NY (1966-1968); Engineer, New York Telephone Company, Bronx, NY (1960-1966) **Career Related:** Chairman, Engineering Foundation Conference on Solid Waste Management, New York, NY (1983) **Civic:** Member, Gideon's International **Creative Works:** Editorial Director, Industrial Water Engineering (1980-1985) **Memberships:** Committee Chair, Maryland and District of Columbia, AAEE (1986-Present); President, Bergen County Society Professional Engineers (1975-1976); American Society of Civil Engineers; American Water Works Association; Water Environmental Federation **Marquis Who's Who Honors:** Albert Nelson Marquis Lifetime Achievement Award; Marquis Who's Who Top Professional **Why did you become involved in your profession or industry:** Mr. Gruninger's had always been into architecture and building. As he got into college, he gravitated toward the environmental side of civil engineering. He graduated with a general civil engineering degree in 1960. Shortly after, he received a job with a telephone company but ultimately was not happy with his position. He then decided to pursue his master's degree with a focus on environmental civil engineering. After graduating, he made his transition from the phone company to his desired focus on environmental civil engineering with Malcolm Pirnie Incorporated.

Kenneth Allen Guenther

Title: President, Chief Executive Officer (Retired) **Industry:** Financial Services **Company Name:** Independent Community Bankers Association of America **Date of Birth:** 12/01/1935 **Place of Birth:** Rochester **State/Country of Origin:** NY/USA **Parents:** Walter K. Guenther; Erna (Ahrenz) Guenther **Marital Status:** Married **Spouse Name:** Lilly Hoesli (01/11/1964) **Children:** Christine (Stineli) **Education:** Postgraduate Coursework (PhD candidate), Yale University, New Haven, CT (1959-1960); Postgraduate Coursework, Rangoon-Hopkins Center for Southeast Asian Studies, Rangoon, Burma (1958-1959); Postgraduate Coursework, Johns Hopkins School of Advanced International Studies (1957-1958); Bachelor of Arts, University of Rochester, Rochester, NY, Cum Laude (1957) **Career:** Consultant (2004-2012); President, Chief Executive Officer, Independent Community Bankers of America, Washington, DC (2001-2004); Executive Vice President, Director, Independent Community Bankers of America, Washington, DC (1985-2001); Executive Director, Independent Community Bankers of America, Washington, DC (1982-1985); Associate Director, Independent Community Bankers of America, Washington, DC (1980-1982); Assistant to the Board of Governors, Federal Reserve Systems (1975-1979) under FED Chairmen Arthur F. Burns, G. William Miller and Paul A. Volcker; Acting Deputy Special Trade Representative, the White House, Washington, DC (1974-1975); Presidential Appointment, U.S. Alternate Executive Director, Inter-American Development Bank, Washington, DC (1973-1974) Special Assistant to Senator Jacob K. Javits, U.S. Senate, Washington, DC (1969-1973); Foreign Service Officer, U.S. Department of State, Washington, DC (1965, 1968-1969); Foreign Service Officer, Assistant Labor Attache, American Embassy, U.S. Department of State, Santiago, Chile (1966-1968); International Economist, U.S. Department of Commerce, Washington, DC (1962-1965); Economist, U.S. Department of Commerce, Washington, DC (1960-1961) **Career Related:** Board of Directors, IBAA-ICBA Services Corp (1983-2004); Board of Directors, IBAA-ICBA Bancard Inc. (1982-2004); Board of Directors, Independent Community Bankers of America, Washington, DC (1979-2004) **Civic:** Chairman, Homeownership Alliance (2003-2004); Board of Directors, Washington Campus (2002-2004); Board of Directors, Chairman Homeownership Alliance Alliance (2001-2004); Chairman, Vice Chairman, Washington Campus (2001-2004); Member, Advisory Committee, The Golden Dollar, U.S. Mint (1999-2000); Member, Advisory Council, Small Business Administration (1994-2000); Board of Directors, CERTEGY Inc.; Board of Directors, CLARK CONSULTING Inc.; Member, Bush-Cheney Transition Advisory Committee, U.S. Department of the Treasury **Military Service:** U.S. Army Reserve (1961-1966) **Creative Works:** Contributor, Op Ed Articles, Numerous Publications **Awards:** Hero Award, Homeownership Alliance (2004); Electronic Funds Transfer Achievement Award, U.S. Department of the Treasury (1995); Presidential Pen (1980); Special Achievement Award for Work on Historic Depository Institutions Deregulation and Monetary Control Act, Federal Reserve Systems (1977) **Memberships:** Board of Directors, Social Compact (1994-1999); Board of Overseers, Russian American Committee; Exchequer Club; Kenwood Golf and Country Club **Marquis Who's Who Honors:** Albert Nelson Marquis Lifetime Achievement Award; Marquis Who's Who Top Professional **To what do you attribute your success:** Mr. Guenther attributes his success to dedicated parents, superior teachers and gifted mentors. **Why did you become involved in your profession or industry:** Mr. Guenther became involved in his professions by being in the right place at the right time. **Avocations:** Golf; Tennis; Hiking; Swimming **Political Affiliations:** Republican; Independent **Religion:** Protestant

Jim Reid Gulnick

Title: Vice President, Director of Operations **Industry:** Business Management/Business Services **Company Name:** McGrory Glass **Date of Birth:** 06/25/1964 **State/Country of Origin:** NJ/USA **Marital Status:** Married **Spouse Name:** Lisett Guevara (08/26/2011) **Children:** Alfredo; Jessica; Irene **Education:** BS in Innovation of Products and Services, Massachusetts Institute of Technology (2016); PhD in Industrial and Organizational Psychology, Grand Canyon University (2016); MBA in Marketing, The University of Kansas (2002); BSEE in Electrical Engineering, Fairleigh Dickinson University (1987) **Career:** Vice President, Director of Operations, McGrory Glass, Philadelphia, PA (2011-Present); Consultant, Author, Radio Host, 90 Day Solutions (2010-Present); Sales Manager, Underwriter, DriveTime (2009-2011); Operations Manager, Engineering, Project and Financial Management, AGC Fabrication (2008-2009); Branch Manager, AGC Fabrication (2007-2009); Operations Manager, AFG Industries (2007-2009); Sales Manager, Tamglass, Limited (2005-2007); Electrotechnology Processing Expert, UtiliCorp United, Kansas City, MO (1995-1998); Vice President, Sales, Technical Sales Engineering, Glass Industry Experience (1991-2005); Regional Sales Manager, Casso-Solar, Pomona, NY (1991-1995) **Civic:** Ayuda Venezuela, Inc. (AyudaVen.org) **Creative Works:** Author, Book, "E6 Excellence: Employee Selection and Coaching" (2018); Author, Book, "Write Now!" (2017); Author, Book, "The 90 Day Challenge" (2014); Author, Book, "90 Day Soulmate" (2011); Author, Publication, National Glass Association (2006); Creator, Video, "Introduction to Heat Processing for Tempering"; Instructor, Workshop, "Quality & Business Profitability Solutions" **Marquis Who's Who Honors:** Marquis Who's Who Top Professional; Marquis Who's Who Humanitarian Award **To what do you attribute your success:** Mr. Gulnick attributes his success to his ADHD, he laughs. He also attributes it to being with good people who see the value in what he does and vice versa. He additionally credits his willingness to continue to learn new things and get better at what he does. He says, "It's better to invest in tools rather than time..." **Why did you become involved in your profession or industry:** Mr. Gulnick became involved in his profession because he began his career working with and processing glass in 1991. He worked with electro-technologies in the heat processing of materials in all industries, from food, textiles, glass and many others. He eventually began working in the equipment portion of the industry as a sales engineer. Eventually, through his work, he became a part owner in a joint venture of the company, bringing in polishing equipment for glass from Italy. In three years, Mr. Gulnick built a company that once consisted of only himself to one with 14 employees. After many years of becoming more involved in the selling, tempering and bending systems of glass, he was then asked to become a branch operations manager at a large glass fabricating facility. It was the first time he had run such a large facility with 114 employees. They hired him because of his experience in all aspects of the glass industry from the manufacturing to the marketing. What was most attractive about the industry was that it was small, and he saw it as an opportunity to have impact, meet a lot of people, and enjoy many years of being involved. **Thoughts on Life:** Mr. Gulnick runs a charity that is nationally recognized by the government with his wife, Lisett. Lisett Guevara Gulnick was born in Valencia, Venezuela. The mission of the charity is to offer support to orphan children living in an orphanage.

Evalyn Hartung Gurney

Title: Secondary School Educator (Retired) **Industry:** Education/Educational Services **Date of Birth:** 10/19/1931 **Place of Birth:** Jersey City **State/Country of Origin:** NJ/USA **Parents:** Arthur Bullivant Hartung; Eva May (Ennis) Hartung **Marital Status:** Married **Spouse Name:** Charles William Gurney (06/22/1957) **Children:** Judith Gurney Hooper; Pamela Gurney Mullican; Susan Gurney Martin; William Charles **Education:** MA, University at Albany, State University of New York (1973); BA, Montclair State University, Upper Montclair, NJ (1951) **Certifications:** Certified Preschool and Elementary English, Social Studies, Reading and Remedial English Teacher, State of New York **Career:** Retired (1991); English Teacher, Shenendehowa Central School District, Clifton Park, NY (1970-1991); Elementary Teacher, Mary C. Howse Elementary School, Exton, PA (1965-1970); Organizer, Principal Migrant School, Brigham City, UT (1960-1965); Elementary Teacher, Verona Public Schools, New Jersey (1951-1954, 1955-1958); Elementary Teacher, Pine Hill Union School, Cheektowaga, NY (1954-1955) **Career Related:** Adviser, Senior High Girls' Bowling Team (1987-1991); Ninth Grade Dean; Adviser, Newspaper Club; Adviser, Builders Club; Adviser, Junior High Yearbook; Adviser, Focus Alternative Education Group **Civic:** Director, Bible School, Downingtown, PA (1964-1965); Active Member, Community Organizations **Awards:** Facilitator, Capital District World of Difference Campaign; Excellence in Education Award, Shenendehowa Central School District **Memberships:** ASCD; NCTE; New York State United Teachers; Shenendehowa Teachers Association; Kiwanis International; Wagonmaster, Holiday Rambler Recreational Vehicle Club **Marquis Who's Who Honors:** Albert Nelson Marquis Lifetime Achievement Award; Marquis Who's Who Humanitarian Award **To what do you attribute your success:** Ms. Gurney attributes her success to her immeasurable patience. **Why did you become involved in your profession or industry:** Ms. Gurney became involved in her profession because of her father. He was not a teacher, but he was a steadfast proponent of education. She was the first female in the family to get a college degree. **Avocations:** Bowling; Putting together puzzles

Jan-Ake Gustafsson

Title: Professor **Industry:** Research **Company Name:** University of Houston **Date of Birth:** 08/04/1943 **Place of Birth:** Stockholm **State/Country of Origin:** Sweden **Parents:** Ake Gustafsson; Ingegerd Gustafsson **Marital Status:** Married **Spouse Name:** Margaret Warner **Children:** Jan **Education:** Honorary Doctor of Medicine, University of Athens, Athens, Greece (2014); Honorary Doctor in Medicine, University of Turku, Turku, Finland (2011); Honorary Doctor of Medicine, University of Milan, Milan, Italy (2008); Doctor of Medicine, Karolinska Institute, Sweden (1971); Doctor of Philosophy, Karolinska Institute, Sweden (1968) **Career:** Founding Director, Center for Nuclear Receptors and Cell Signaling, University of Houston (2009-Present); Robert A. Welch Professor, University of Houston **Awards:** Named, Distinguished Professor of Dalian Medical University, China (2015); Recipient, Honorary Fellowship, South Australian Health and Medical Research Institute, Adelaide, Australia (2014); Recipient, Grand Silver Medal, Karolinska Institute (2011); Recipient, Award of Merit, Princess Takamatsu Cancer Research Fund (2009); Recipient, Grand Nordic Fernstrom Prize, University of Lund (2009); The Soderberg Prize in Medicine (2008); The Anders Jahre Prize, Oslo, Norway (2002); Foreign Member of the US National Academy of Sciences (2002); Fred Konrad Koch Award (2002) **Marquis Who's Who Honors:** Albert Nelson Marquis Lifetime Achievement Award; Marquis Who's Who Top Professional **To what do you attribute your success:** Energy, competitiveness, luckDr. Gustafsson attributes his success to energy, competitiveness and a good deal of luck. **Religion:** Christian

Jon Sheldon Guttman

Title: Magazine Editor, Historian **Industry:** Publishing **Company Name:** Historynet **Date of Birth:** 01/03/1951 **Place of Birth:** Flushing **State/Country of Origin:** NY/USA **Parents:** Paul Dennis Gutman; Lee Ann (Sterling) Gutman **Marital Status:** Single **Education:** MA in European History, State University of New York at Albany, Albany, NY (1975); BA in History, State University of New York at Albany (1973) **Career:** Research Director, Writer, Photographer, "World War II," "Aviation History," "Vietnam," "MHQ," "America's Civil War," "Wild West," Historynet, Vienna, VA (1988-Present); Editor, "Military History," Weider Publications, Leesburg, VA (1994-2007); Recruiter, New York Army National Guard, Valhalla, NY (1986-1988); Art Director, Custombook, Inc., Tappan, NY (1985-1986); Cook, Rick's Club American, Congers, NY (1985); Security Guard, Titan Security Systems, Inc., West Nyack, NY (1985); Artist, Dynamic Graphics, Nanuet, NY (1983-1984, 1981); Sales Representative, Sales Manager, First Investors Corp., Hartsdale, NY (1982-1983); Artist, Divisional Ad Comp, Northvale, NJ (1975-1981); Freelance Writer, Freelance Copy Editor **Career Related:** Flieger Revue X, Bergkirchen, Germany (2013-Present); Foundation, Pensacola, FL (2007-Present); Writer, Albatross Productions, Ltd., Berkhamsted, Herts, England (1989-Present); Esprit de Corps., Ottawa, Ontario, Canada (2013-2018); Writer, Sea Classic International, Windsock International, Hemel Hempstead, Hertfordshire, England (1987); Contributor, Numerous Periodicals **Military Service:** Master Sergeant, Virginia Army National Guard (1988-2005); Master Sergeant, New York Army National Guard (1984-1988) **Creative Works:** Author, "Zeppelin vs British Home Defence 1915-1918" (2018); "Grim Reapers: French Escadrille 94 in World War I" (2016); "Fighter Aircraft Combat Debuts" (2014); "Reconnaissance and Bomber Aces of World War I" (2014); "Sopwith Camel" (2013); "Naval Aces of World War I, Part II" (2012); Editor, Co-Author, "War in the Pacific" (2011); Author, "Naval Aces of World War I, Part I" (2011); Editor, Co-Author, "World War II in Color" (2010); Editor, Co-Author, "Spad Two-Seat Fighters of World War I" (2010); Author, SE 5a vs Albatros D V" (2009); "The Origin of the Fighter Aircraft" (2009); "Pusher Aces of World War I" (2009); Author, "SPAD XIII vs "Fokker D VII" (2009); "USAS 1st Pursuit Group" (2008); "Sopwith Camel vs Fokker Dr I" (2008); "Bristol F2 Fighter Aces of World War I" (2007); "Nieuport Flyers of the Lafayette" (2006); "Balloon Busting Aces of World War I" (2005); Author, "Salmson 2A2" (2005); Author, "Groupe de Combat 12 Les Cigognes" (2004); "N.124 Lafayette Escadrille" (2004); "American DH4" (2004); "Caudron G.4" (2002); "Caudron G.3" (2002); SPAD XII/XIII Aces of World War I" (2002); Author, "SPAD VII Aces of World War I" (2001); "Fighting Firsts" (2000); Editor, Co-Author, "Great Commanders in Action" (1996); Contributing Writer, "Best of the Wild West" (1996); Contributing Writer, "Salmson Aircraft of World War I" (2001); Author, "James V. Martin K. III Kitten" (1996); "Defiance at Sea" (1995); Editor, Co-Author, "Desert Storm" (1992); Author, "Nieuport 28"; Television Appearances, "Clouds of Death," The History Channel; "The American Century," WABC; "The Daily Show," Comedy Central; "Dogfights," The History Channel; Film, "War of the Worlds" **Awards:** Thornton D. Hooper Award (2016, 2008, 1991, 1988); Two Army Commendation Medals; Three Army Achievement Medals; NATO Medal; Virginia Emergency Service Ribbon; New York State Recruiter's Medal; Listee, Who's Who in American Colleges and Universities; Listee, Who's Who in the Southeastern United States **Memberships:** League of World War I Aviation Historians; Cross & Cockade International; Western Front Association; Vice President, Loudon County Civil War Roundtable; American Fighter Aces Association; National Honor Society **Marquis Who's Who Honors:** Albert Nelson Marquis Lifetime Achievement Award **To what do you attribute your success:** Mr. Guttman attributes his success to a persistent focus on his job at hand. He additionally credits his writing and organizational skills. **Why did you become involved in your profession or industry:** As a child, Mr. Guttman made models of World War I airplanes. He loved to meet the people that flew them, as well as interviewing and writing articles about said individuals. This led him to his career. **Avocations:** History; Chess; Travel; Model building **Political Affiliations:** Democrat **Religion:** Jewish

Mary "Dolly" Gwinn, D.D.G., I.O.M., L.F.I.BA.

Title: American Philosopher, Organizational Theorist, Business Developer, International Speaker, Lecturer, Management Consultant, Artist, Author, Originator, Original Thinker **Industry:** Business Management/Business Services **Parents:** Epifanio Cruz; Carolina (Lopez) Cruz **Marital Status:** Married **Spouse Name:** James Monroe Gwinn (10/23/1965) **Children:** Larry Allen **Education:** Self-Study in Neurosciences, Specifically the Brain and its Functions (1983-1984); Alumni, Graduate, Dale Carnegie Course, Dale Carnegie Sales Course, Dale Carnegie Management Course (1978-1979); Attended, Monterey Peninsula College (1965) **Career:** Founder, President, GWINN GENIUS Institute, Arizona's Innovative Business Development Center (1995-Present); Founder, President, International Institute for Conceptual Education (1991-Present); Founder, President, STRATEGIC INTEGRATIONS (1985-Present); Affiliated, The Buzan Centre of Chicago (1997-1998); Manager, KTAR News and Radio (1982); Technical Recruiter, Len Annuzzi, Technical Recruiters (1980-1981); Salesperson, Dale Carnegie & Associates (1978-1979); Retail Store Manager, Consumers Distribution Division, May Company (1973-1978) **Career Related:** Chosen to be on the Smithsonian Institute website (2020); Chairperson, Lecturer, "MIND OF GENIUS", ABI/IBC International Congress (2000); Invited to lecture to Government/University audiences, India (2000); Speaker, Antelope Valley College (1998); Player, Industrial Ecology Prototype Prosperity Games, Scandia Laboratories (1998); Invited to sponsor CNN 2nd National Memory Championships, New York, NY, United States; World Championships, London, England (1998); Chairperson, IBC/ABI International Congress on Arts and Communications, University of Oxford (1997); "Management in the 21st Century", Inc. Magazine (1996); Invited exhibitor, speaker, publisher, China (1996); GWINN GENIUS INSTITUE invited to establish center, Gulf Counties (1995); DESTINATION SUCCESS wants to publish GWINN GENIUS INSITUTE audio albums (1995); Guest of the Harvard Club (1993); Seminar Speaker, University of Cambridge (1992); Speaking at Commission of Women in Science, Technology, and Medicine, Sopron, Hungary and the Vienna Technical Museum, Austria (1992); Featured, PANACHE Magazine (1992); Commissioned to create and conduct a corporate seminar, "Whole Brain Business Theory: A View for the Corporate Mind" for Advantest America, Inc. (1991); Profundities praised by the Guru of Fujitsu, Global 500 company; Meeting with corporate staff and toured factory of Advantest Japan, Inc., Fukushima, Japan (1991); Interviewed Raymond G, Rottas, Treasurer of the State of Arizona at the Capital (1988); Members of Arizona House of Representatives give resounding standing ovation (1988); Political Strategist, Candice Nagel, Member, Arizona House of Representatives (1988); Meetings with Herbert K. Cummings, President, Herbert K. Cummings Foundation, Board of Trustees, Nathaniel Cummings Foundation (1985-1997); Creator, Marketing Brochure Dale Carnegie recommend to all franchisees worldwide (1978); Created "active" store model for Consumers Distributing, Division, May Company to raise capital and expand to 200 stores nationwide (1973-1979) **Civic:** Judge, Arizona International Pageants (2018) **Creative Works:** Author, "Genius Leadership Secrets from the Past for the 21st Century" (1996); GWINNGENIUS SHOWCASE (1992); Founded the scientific fields of Geniustics and NeuroBusiness (1989); Whole Brain Business Theory Case Study (1989); The Business Portfolio and Business Portfolio Chief Executive Officer Companion Guide and Strategic Planner (1989); Interactive Whole Brain Business Management System (1989); GWINNGENIUSBUSINESS THEATER WORKSHOP (1988) Playwright, Producer, "SEASONS OF A WOMANS LIFE" (1988); Profiling "The Thought of Genius" (1987); Whole Brain Business Modeling Process (1987); Whole Brain Business Theory Case Study (1986); Whole Brain Communication Model (1986); Whole Brain Business Theory Process and Practice (1985); Profiling "The Thought Process of Genius" (1985); Creator, "Whole Brain Business Theory" **Awards:** The Coveted and Prestigious Dr. Earnest Kay Congress Award (2000); Nominated for the Ernst & Young LLP, Entrepreneur, Educator - Supporter Award, United States (1997); International Order of Merit, Authorized Citation, For Services to Businessand Profiling the Thought of Genius, IBC Cambridge, England (1993); 20th Century Award in Recognition for Outstanding Achievements in the Field of Business, Education and Science" IBC Cambridge (1993); World Intellectual in the Field of Business and for ProfilingThe Thought Process of Genius IBC Cambridge (1993); Dale Carnegie Salesperson of the Month Award (1978) **Memberships:** Akademie (M.I.D.I.) (1994); Maison Internationale des Intellectuels (M.I.D.I.), Germany **Marquis Who's Who Honors:** Marquis Who's Who in the World (2020); Marquis Who's Who, A Lifetime Achievement of Achievement Vol. II Book (2019); Albert Nelson Marquis Lifetime Achievement Award (2017-2018) **Political Affiliations:** Republican **Religion:** Christian

Katherine Gyékényesi Gatto, PhD

Title: Modern Languages and Literature Educator **Industry:** Education/Educational Services **Date of Birth:** 11/27/1945 **Place of Birth:** Braunau **State/Country of Origin:** Austria **Parents:** Gorgy Laszlo Gyékényesi; Katalin (Korcsmor) Gyékényesi **Marital Status:** Widowed **Spouse Name:** Gregory Francis Gatto (08/10/1968, Deceased 2001) **Children:** Gregory; Georgina; Peter; Stephen **Education:** Doctor of Philosophy, Case Western Reserve University, Cleveland, OH (1975); Master of Arts, Case Western Reserve University, Cleveland, OH (1971); Bachelor of Arts, John Carroll University, University Heights, OH, Magna Cum Laude (1967) **Career:** Founding Director, Women's and Gender Studies, John Carroll University, Cleveland, OH (2012-Present); Professor of Spanish, John Carroll University, Cleveland, OH (1992-Present); Part-time Coordinator, Department of Classical and Modern Languages & Cultures, John Carroll University, Cleveland, OH (1997-1999); Chairman, Department of Classical and Modern Languages & Cultures, John Carroll University, Cleveland, OH (1990-1997); Associate Professor of Spanish, John Carroll University, Cleveland, OH (1980-1992); Assistant Professor of Spanish, John Carroll University, Cleveland, OH (1977-1980); Visiting Assistant Professor of Spanish, John Carroll University, Cleveland, OH (1975-1977) **Career Related:** Acting Director, University Honors Program (1988-1989); Director of Language Laboratory (1980-1981); Spanish Teacher, Hathaway Brown School, Shaker Heights, OH (1973-1974); Lecturer, Cleveland State University, Cleveland, OH (1971); Member, Adjunct Faculty, Cuyahoga Community College, Cleveland, OH **Creative Works:** Author, Editor, Book, "Spain's Literary Legacy: Studies in Spanish Literature and Culture from the Middle Ages to the Nineteenth Century" (2005); Co-Editor, Co-Translator, Book, "The Lapidary of King Alfonso X, the Learned" (1997); Editor, Translator, "Treasury of Hungarian Love Poems: Quotations and Proverbs in Hungarian and English" (1996); Co-Author, Book, "Of Kings and Poets: Cancionero Poetry of the the Trastámara Courts" (1992); Co-Author, Book, "Manual Terapeutico para el Adulto Con Dificultades Del Habla y Lenguaje: Una Seleccion de Materiales de Estimulo" (1985); Author, Contributor, Numerous Articles, Essays, and Translations; Author, Contributor, Numerous Book Reviews; Contributor, Presenter, Numerous Papers and Presentations **Awards:** Influential Alumni Award, John Adams High School (2017); Lucrezia Culicchia Awards for Teaching Excellence in the College of Arts and Sciences (2001); Nominee, Lucrezia Culiccia Award for Teaching Excellence in the College of Arts and Sciences (2000); Outstanding Young Woman of 1978 Award (1978); Spanish Award, John Carroll University (1967); Von Steuben Medal for German **Memberships:** Executive Board of Hungarian Literature Discussion Group, Modern Language Association (1999-Present); Vice President, Program Chairman, Fulbright Association (1996-1998); Board of Directors, Northeast Ohio Chapter, Fulbright Association (1994-1999); President, American Hungarian Educators Association (1992-1994); Executive Board of Hungarian Literature Discussion Group, Modern Language Association (1982-1988); American Association for the Advancement of Slavic Studies; Hungarian Academy of Sciences; Writers and Artists Abroad; Ohio Foreign Language Association; American Association of Teachers of Spanish and Portuguese; Medieval Association of the Midwest; Midwest Modern Language Association; National Women's Studies Association **Marquis Who's Who Honors:** Albert Nelson Marquis Lifetime Achievement Award **Why did you become involved in your profession or industry:** Dr. Gatto became involved in her profession after learning Spanish while studying in college. She also drew a wealth of inspiration from her mentors at Case Western Reserve University, as well as John Carroll University. For her excellent performance, she received many scholarships, including a Fulbright scholarship to Spain. **Avocations:** Opera; Folklore; Travel; Theater; Hiking; Tennis; Swimming; Camping

Raymond M. Hakim, MD, PhD

Title: Professor **Industry:** Education/Educational Services **Company Name:** Vanderbilt University Medical Center **Marital Status:** Married **Education:** Research and Clinical Fellow in Medicine, Nephrology, Brigham and Women's Hospital, Harvard Medical School (1981); Internship and Residency in Internal Medicine, Royal Victoria Hospital, Montreal, Quebec, Canada (1976-1979); MD, McGill University, Montreal, Quebec, Canada (1976); PhD in Engineering, Massachusetts Institute of Technology, Cambridge, MA (1967); MS in Engineering, Rensselaer Polytechnic Institute, Troy, NY (1965) **Certifications:** Tennessee Medical Licensure (1987); Board Certified in Nephrology, United States (1982); Diplomate, American Board of Internal Medicine (1980); Certification of Specialist in Internal Medicine, Quebec, Canada (1980); Massachusetts Medical Licensure (1979); Quebec Medical Licensure (1977) **Career:** Clinical Professor of Medicine, Nephrology, Vanderbilt University, Nashville, TN (2012-Present); Attending Physician, Vanderbilt University Medical Center, Nashville, TN (2012-Present); Co-founder, Fresenius Medical Care (1995-Present); Professor of Medicine, Division of Nephrology, Vanderbilt University School of Medicine (1987-Present); Director, Clinical Services in Nephrology, Vanderbilt University School of Medicine (1987-Present); Chief Medical Officer, Fresenius Medical Care, Nashville, TN (2009-2012); Chief Medical Officer, Clinical & Scientific Affairs, Fresenius Medical Care, Nashville, TN (2010-2011); Senior Executive Vice President, Clinical & Scientific Affairs, Fresenius Medical Care, Nashville, TN (2010-2011); Adjunct Clinical Professor of Medicine, Vanderbilt University, Nashville, TN (1996-2011); Senior Executive Vice President, Clinical & Scientific Affairs, Fresenius Medical Care, Nashville, TN (2006-2009); Chief Medical Officer, Fresenius Medical Care (1995-2007); Executive Vice President, University Division, Renal Care Group, Inc., Nashville, TN (1996-2006); Chief Medical Officer, University Division, Fresenius Medical Care, Nashville, TN (1996-2006); Director, University Division, Fresenius Medical Care, Nashville, TN (1996-2006); Medical Director, Inpatient and Outpatient Dialysis Services, Vanderbilt Dialysis Unit, Nashville, TN (1987-1999); Professor of Medicine, Vanderbilt University, Nashville, TN (1991-1996); Attending on the Renal Consult, Dialysis and Transplantation Services, Vanderbilt University Medical Center, Nashville, TN (1987-1996); Director, Clinical Nephrology, Vanderbilt University Medical Center, Nashville, TN (1987-1991); Associate Professor of Medicine, Vanderbilt University, Nashville, TN (1987-1991); Associate Professor of Medicine, Harvard Medical School, Boston, MA (1986-1987); Attending on the Renal Consult, Dialysis and Transplantation Services and Chronic Renal Failure Clinic, Brigham and Women's Hospital, Boston, MA (1982-1987); Associate Physician, Brigham and Women's Hospital, Boston, MA (1982-1986); Assistant Professor of Medicine, Harvard Medical School, Boston, MA (1981-1986); Attending Physician, The Kidney Center, Boston, MA (1981-1986); Assistant Physician, Brigham and Women's Hospital, Boston, MA (1981-1982); Consultant, Hydro-Quebec, Montreal, Quebec, Canada (1972-1976); Research Scientist, Hydro-Quebec, Montreal, Quebec, Canada (1968-1972) **Creative Works:** Co-editor, "Clinical Nephrology, Dialysis and Transplantation" (1999); Guest Co-editor, "25 Years of the ESRD Program, Part 1 & 2," Seminars in Nephrology (1997); Guest Editor, "Seminars in Nephrology" (1994); Author, Co-author, Articles, Journals; Author, Book Chapters, Books; Editorial Board Member, American Journal of Kidney Diseases; Editorial Board Member, Seminars in Dialysis; Editorial Board, Kidney International **Awards:** Belding H. Scribner Award, American Society of Nephrology (2017); Medal of Excellence Award, American Association of Kidney Patients (2011); Joel D. Kopple Award, National Kidney Foundation (2009); Award for Excellence in Teaching, Internal Medicine Housestaff, Vanderbilt University Medical Center, Nashville, TN (1982); J. Francis Williams Prize in Medicine and Clinical Medicine, McGill University (1976); Campbell Howard Prize in Clinical Medicine, McGill University (1976) **Marquis Who's Who Honors:** Albert Nelson Marquis Lifetime Achievement Award; Marquis Who's Who Top Professional; Marquis Who's Who Humanitarian Award **To what do you attribute your success:** Dr. Hakim attributes his success to having been mentored by Dr. Ed Lowrie, Dr. Barry Brenner, Dr. Douglas Fearon, and Dr. Harry Jacobson. He also credits his coworkers for the team effort in applying the principles of "Continuous Quality Improvement." His strategy is summed up by the question he often poses to himself and those he works with: "How can we do better for patients entrusted to our care?" **Why did you become involved in your profession or industry:** Dr. Hakim became involved in his profession to improve the health of others and make a positive difference in people's lives **Thoughts on Life:** we can always do better, and we need to work hard to do so.

Adel F. Halasa, PhD

Title: Chemist **Industry:** Sciences **Date of Birth:** 12/24/1933 **Place of Birth:** Madaba **State/Country of Origin:** Jordan **Parents:** Farhan Halasa; Kathrin Halasa **Marital Status:** Married **Spouse Name:** Ofelia Vinlauan (2/2/1955) **Children:** Malu; Marni; Whitney; Brianna; Nathan **Education:** PhD, Purdue University (1964); MS, Butler University (1958); BSc, Oklahoma University (1955) **Career:** Research and Development Fellow, The Goodyear Tire and Rubber Company, Akron, OH (1984-2009); Director, Material & Petro-Chemical, KISR (Kuwait Institute of Science and Research) (1979-1984); Senior Research Associate, The Firestone Tire and Rubber Company (1974-1979); Associate Scientist, The Firestone Tire and Rubber Company, Akron, OH (1968-1974); Group Leader, The Firestone Tire and Rubber Company, Akron, OH (1965-1968) **Career Related:** InternationalPolymerconsultant.com (2009-Present) **Civic:** Area Director, Akron Anti Discrimination Council (1989) **Creative Works:** Contributor, Articles, Technical Publications; 340 United States Patents; 185 United States Patent The Good Year; 155 United States Patent to First; Author, 150 United States Publications, Scientific Journals **Awards:** Charles Goodyear Medal, Rubber Division, American Chemical Society (1997); Local Section Service Award, American Chemical Society (1995); The Charles Goodyear Medal, Rubber Division, ACS; Purdue University Distinguished Alumni **Memberships:** Chairman, APLG, American Chemical Society (1968); Chairman, Akron Section, American Chemical Society (1967); Fellow, America Institute of Chemists, New York Academy Sciences; American Association for the Advancement of Science; Sigma Xi **Marquis Who's Who Honors:** Albert Nelson Marquis Lifetime Achievement Award; Marquis Who's Who Top Professional **To what do you attribute your success:** Dr. Halasa's philosophy is age is irrelevant. He maintains good health, a healthy mind and a passion for science, to keep him going. **Why did you become involved in your profession or industry:** Dr. Halasa was born in the country of Jordan. After graduating high school, his options were to either join the military or to do something else. An English teacher thought it would be a wise decision to go to the United States to pursue higher education. Dr. Halasa was accepted into Greenville College, in Greenville, Illinois. He spent one year at Greenville before transferring to the University of Oklahoma. He was very fortunate to meet wonderful people throughout his career to assist him along his academic and professional journey. **Avocations:** Marathon runner **Religion:** Eastern Orthodox

John Haldon

Title: Historian and Archaeologist **Industry:** Education/Educational Services **Company Name:** Princeton University **Date of Birth:** 10/23/1948 **Place of Birth:** New Castle on Tyne **State/Country of Origin:** United Kingdom **Marital Status:** Married **Spouse Name:** Valerie **Children:** Three Children **Education:** PhD, University of Birmingham, United Kingdom (1975); MA in Byzantine Studies, University of Birmingham, United Kingdom (1971); BA in Ancient and Medieval History, University of Birmingham, United Kingdom (1970) **Career:** Shelby Cullom Davis '30 Professor Emeritus of European History, Department of History, Princeton University, Princeton, NJ (2012-2018); Professor of Byzantine History and Hellenic Studies, Princeton University, Princeton, NJ (2005-2018); Head of School of Historical Studies, University of Birmingham, United Kingdom (2000-2004); Director, Centre for Byzantine, Ottoman, and Modern Greek Studies, University of Birmingham, United Kingdom (1996-2004); Personal Chair in Byzantine History, University of Birmingham, United Kingdom (1996); Reader in Byzantine Studies, University of Birmingham, United Kingdom (1993-1996); British Academy/East German Academy of Sciences Exchange Fellow (1990); Visiting Professor, Max Planck Institute for European Legal History, Frankfurt am Main, Germany (1987-1988); Senior Alexander von Humboldt Fellow, University of Munich, Germany (1984); Lecturer in Byzantine Language and Literature, Centre for Byzantine, Ottoman, and Modern Greek Studies, University of Birmingham, United Kingdom (1980-1983); Alexander von-Humboldt Fellow, Ludwig Maximilian University of Munich, Munich, Germany (1976-1979) **Career Related:** President, Association Internationale des Etudes Byzantines; Corresponding Member, Austrian Academy of Sciences **Creative Works:** Editor, Editorial Board, Birmingham Byzantine and Ottoman Studies (1988-Present); Co-author, Book, "Archaeology and Urban Settlement in Late Roman and Byzantine Anatolia" (2019); Author, Book, "A Tale of Two Saints: The Martyrdoms and Miracles of Saints Theodore 'the Recruit' and 'the General'" (2016); Author, Book, "The Empire That Would Not Die: The Paradox of Eastern Roman Survival, 640-740" (2016); Co-author, "Byzantium in the Iconoclast Era, c. 680-850: A History" (2015); Co-author, Book, "The Oxford Handbook of Byzantine Studies" (2009); Author, Book, "Byzantine Wars" (2008); Author, Book, "The Social History of Byzantium" (2008); Author, Book, "Byzantium: A History" (2005); Co-author, Book, "The Byzantine and Early Islamic Near East: Elites Old and New" (2004); Author, Book, "Byzantium at War" (2002); Author, Book, "Warfare, State And Society in the Byzantine World 565-1204" (1999); Editor, Editorial Board, Byzantine and Modern Greek Studies (1984-2005); Author, Numerous Monographs (1979-2016); Author, Co-author, More Than 25 Books; Author, Contributor, Numerous Articles in Refereed Journals; Member, Editorial Advisory Committee, Historical Materialism; Member, Editorial Board, Jahrbuch der Österreichischen Byzantinistik; Member, Editorial Board, Byzantinische Zeitschrift; Member, Advisory Board, Sociedades Precapitalistas; Member, Editorial Board, Medieval Worlds - Comparative and Interdisciplinary Studies; Member, Editorial Board, Tusculum-Lexikon Byzantinischer Autoren; Editorial Board, Various Scholarly Journals, Europe and the United States **Awards:** Greek National Research Foundation (IKY) and British Council Graduate Scholarship (1972-1974) **Memberships:** Governing Board Member, Trustee, British Institute of Archaeology in Ankara (Now BIAA) (2010-2016); Senior Fellow, Dumbarton Oaks Center for Byzantine Studies, Washington, DC (2007-2013); Corresponding Member, Austrian Academy of Sciences; Advisory Board, WissenschaftsCampus Mainz; Advisory Board, Centre for Mediterranean Studies, Haifa University, Israel; American Byzantine Studies Association (Now Byzantine Studies Association of North America, Inc. (BSANA)); American Institute of Archaeology; Society for the Promotion of Byzantine Studies (SPBS) **Marquis Who's Who Honors:** Marquis Who's Who Top Professional **Why did you become involved in your profession or industry:** Dr. Haddon became involved in his profession because of his passion for history. When he was 8 years old, his father gave him a world history book, which he read cover-to-cover about 10 times. In high school, he studied Latin and history, and in college, he studied medieval history and archaeology. **Thoughts on Life:** Dr. Haldon's greatest legacy, besides his grandchildren, has been introducing comparative sociological theory into his field, which had traditionally involved more old-fashioned approaches. He was part of the first generation in his field to combine archaeology with environmental science, anthropology, and sociology. This kind of work has helped to broaden the horizons of thought in his field.

Alan C. Hall

Title: Library Director Emeritus **Industry:** Library Management/Library Services **Date of Birth:** 03/09/1954 **Place of Birth:** Marietta **State/Country of Origin:** OH/USA **Parents:** Harry Edward Hall; Flossie June (Heddleston) Hall **Marital Status:** Married **Spouse Name:** Barbara Ann Metzger Hall **Children:** Shawn Alan Hall **Education:** MLS, Case Western University (1977); BS in Education, West Virginia University (1976) **Certifications:** Public Librarian Certification, Ohio Library Council (2006-2018) **Career:** Director, Public Library of Steubenville and Jefferson County (1983-2018); Director, Delphos Public Library (1977-1983); With, Government Documents Department, Freiberger Library, Cleveland, OH (1976-1977); With, Circulation Department, Washington County Public Library, Marietta, OH (1970-1975) **Career Related:** Member, State Library of Ohio Board (2019-Present); Historic Interpreter, Fort Steuben Project (2000-Present); President, Board of Directors, SOLO Regional Library Systems, Ohio (2002-2003); Committee Review Board Structure, Ohio Library Council, Columbus, OH (1999); Co-chair, Ohio Statewide Resource Sharing Committee (1998-1999); Consultant, Reed Memorial Library, Ravenna, OH (1997-1998); Chair, Ohio Library Council, Columbus, OH (1994); Consultant, Morgan County Library, McConnellsville, OH (1992-1993); Consultant, Barnesville Public Library (1991) **Civic:** Assistant Governor, Rotary District 6650 (2019-Present); Clerk Session, Two Ridges Presbyterian Church (2003-Present); Vice President, Community Foundation Jefferson County (2000-Present); President, Steubenville OH Rotary Club (2017-2018); Board Member, Secretary, Historical Fort Steuben (2006-2013); Member, Bicentennial Committee, Two Ridges Presbyterian Church (2002); Member, Community Foundation Jefferson County (1999-2003); Ruling Elder, Starkdale Presbyterian Church (1985-1988, 1994-1996, 1998-2000); Chairman, Pastor Nominating Committee, Starkdale Presbyterian Church (1996-1997); Chairperson, Ohio Humanities Council, Steubenville, OH (1991); President, Retired Senior Volunteer Program, Steubenville, OH (1989-1990) **Creative Works:** Contributor, Public Libraries in Ohio, State Library of Ohio (2020); Contributor, The Nathan Stern Archives (2018); Contributor, School Newspaper for Ludlow High School (2012); Contributor, History of the Hub Department Store, Steubenville, OH (2008); Co-author, "Steubenville: Images of America" (2005); Contributor, History of Ohio's Public Libraries (2003); Author, "The Mary Thompson Collection" (1997); Editor, "Steubenville Bicentennial History Book" (1996-1997); Editor, "Richmond, Ohio Cemetery Book" (1995); Author, "Marietta's Innkeeper" (1991); Editor, "Abandoned Underground Coal Mines of Jefferson County" (1991); Compiler, "Historic Pages Series" (1975-1976); Editor, "The Papers of A.T. Nye" (1975); Contributor, The Bloomfield Miniature 1929-1962; Contributor, Articles, Professional Publications **Awards:** Hall of Fame Librarian, Ohio Library Council (2019); Outstanding Contribution Award, Historic Fort Steuben (2012); Librarian of the Year, Ohio Library Association (1989) **Memberships:** President, Ohio Library Association (1992-1993); President, Steubenville Lions Club (1986-1987); American Library Association; National Association of Road Passengers; Jefferson County Historical Society; Steubenville Rotary Sons of the American Revolution; Life Member, Ohio Library Council **Marquis Who's Who Honors:** Albert Nelson Marquis Lifetime Achievement Award **To what do you attribute your success:** A lot of it was that everything fell into place at the right time. So many things happened when he hoped it would happen. Just like being appointed to the state library board just as he is retiring. Now he has the time and can do that and he will still be contributing to the library world. **Why did you become involved in your profession or industry:** When Mr. Hall was in high school his second grade teacher and moved to the high school to be the librarian. She asked him to come help her out in the library and he found that he enjoyed it. His mother had wanted to be a librarian but she grew up during the depression and couldn't afford college. She was extremely supportive. **Avocations:** Railroading; Genealogy **Religion:** Presbyterian

J. Robert Hall

Title: Chief Executive Officer **Industry:** Consumer Goods and Services **Company Name:** Ole Smoky Distillery **Date of Birth:** 08/14/1952 **Place of Birth:** Tadcaster **State/Country of Origin:** Yorkshire/England **Marital Status:** Married **Spouse Name:** Elizabeth Hall **Children:** Emma; Alistair; Duncan **Education:** MBA, Wharton School, University of Pennsylvania, Philadelphia, PA (1976); BA in Natural Sciences, Oxford University, England (1974) **Career:** Chief Executive Officer, Ole Smoky Distillery LLC (2016-Present); Managing Director, Centerview Capital (2014-2015); Chief Executive Officer, Ardale Enterprises, Mendham, NJ (1998-2013); President, Lenox Brands, Lawrenceville, NJ (1996-1998); President, Specialty Products Company, Nabisco, Parsippany, NJ (1993-1996); President, Christie Brown & Co., Toronto, ON, Canada (1992-1993); Vice President, Strategy, Cheese, Kraft U.S.A., Glenview, IL (1992); Vice President, Business Unit Manager, Kraft General Foods, Toronto, ON, Canada (1989-1992); Vice President, Business Unit Manager, Cheese, Kraft Ltd., Montreal, Quebec, Canada (1986-1989); Director, Strategic Planning and Business Development, Kraft Ltd., Montreal, Quebec, Canada (1985-1986); Business Director, Nestle, White Plains, NY (1983-1985); Group Product Manager, Nestle, White Plains, NY (1981-1983); Product Manager, Nestle, White Plains, NY (1977-1980); Sales Representative, Nestle, Philadelphia, PA (1977); Brand Assistant, Nestle, White Plains, NY (1976-1977) **Career Related:** Chairman, Nominating & Governance Committee, Glatfelter (2012-Present); Public Board Member, Glatfelter (2002-Present); Lead Director, Glatfelter (2014-2015); Chairman, Audit Committee, Glatfelter (2006-2012); Public Board Member, Ault Foods, Canada (1994-1997); Private Board Member, Frozen Specialties; Private Board Member, Custom Food Products; Private Board Member, Chungs Gourmet Foods; Private Board Member, Chairman, Wise Foods; Private Board Member, Taco Bueno Restaurants; Private Board Member, Chief Executive Officer, Castro Cheese; Private Board Member, Belmay; Private Board Member, Yucatan Foods **Civic:** Board Member, Boys & Girls Club of the Smoky Mountains (2019-Present) **Awards:** Hot Brand Award (2017-2019); Thouron Scholarship, University of Pennsylvania (1974-1976) **Memberships:** Board Member, Distilled Spirits Council of the US (2019-Present); Tennessee Distillers' Guild Legislative Committee (2019-Present); National Tabletop Association (1997-1998); Chairman, Marketing Council, Grocery Products Manufacturers of Canada (1992); International Cheese Council of Canada (1987-1989) **Marquis Who's Who Honors:** Albert Nelson Marquis Lifetime Achievement Award **To what do you attribute your success:** He has analytical ability and can relate to people. He works hard to get to the bottom of a situation, and he follows through to make sure a solution is implemented successfully. The ability to develop a strategy and then identify the actions that will execute that strategy with excellence. **Why did you become involved in your profession or industry:** While Mr. J. Robert Hall attended Oxford University, he decided that he wanted to have an impact on the world during his life, and although he was studying science and mathematics, he decided he wanted to get into business and grow to become the CEO of a significant enterprise, impacting many peoples' lives. In order to achieve that, early in his career he focused on growing in the marketing area of a consumer product focused on business. After High School and before attending University, he came to the United States and worked for Procter & Gamble in Cincinnati, OH and then he went back to England to earn his undergraduate degree at Oxford. From there, he returned to the United States to receive his MBA at the University of Pennsylvania. After attending college, Mr. Hall worked for Nestle for over nine years in the marketing area on coffee, cheese and new products before moving on to Kraft. **Avocations:** Sports; Investing

Stanley Eckler Hall

Title: International Financial Consultant (Retired) **Industry:** Financial Services **Date of Birth:** 01/10/1934 **Place of Birth:** Cooperstown **State/Country of Origin:** NY/USA **Parents:** Wesley Claude; Cynthia Helen (Eckler) Hall **Marital Status:** Married **Spouse Name:** Jewel Irene Breiner (08/10/1957) **Children:** Brian Vernon; Sandra Jewel; Nancy Jane Cynthia **Education:** MS, Clarkson University, 1970; BSEE, Purdue University (1959); MEd, St. Lawrence University (1967); BS, St. Lawrence University (1955) **Career:** President, Chief Executive Officer, Leatherstocking Consultants, Cooperstown, NY (1991-1995); President, Brakeley Recruiting, Stamford, CT (1989-1991); Senior Vice President, Brakeley, John Price Jones, Inc., Stamford, CT (1988-1991); Vice President of Public Affairs, Colgate University, Hamilton, NY (1978-1988); Vice President of Planning and Development, Hartwick College, Oneonta, NY (1974-1978); Vice President of University Development, Purdue University, West Lafayette, IN (1972-1974); Vice President of Development, Hiram College, Ohio (1970-1972); Director of Development, St. Lawrence University, Canton, NY (1965-1970); Director of Operation Enterprise, American Management Association, Hamilton, NY (1964-1965); Supervisor of Sales Training, General Electric, Schenectady, NY (1962-1964); Sales Engineer, General Electric, Schenectady, NY (1959-1962) **Career Related:** Development Consultant, International College, Beirut, Lebanon (1990-1993); International Development Consultant, Bermuda Cathedral (1989) **Civic:** Board of Directors, Adirondack Mountain Club (1998-2000); Sayre House Restoration, Milford, NY (1992-Present); Hyde Hall Restoration, Cooperstown, NY (1991-1993); Bassett Hospital Foundation (1985-1991); Catskill Mountain Educational Center, Stamford, NY (1974-1978); Vice President, Board of Directors, Purdue Research Foundation, West Lafayette, NY (1972-1974); Trustee, Purdue Foundation (1972-1974); State Chairman, New York Crusade, American Cancer Society, Inc., Syracuse, NY (1970) **Military Service:** First Lieutenant, Military Police Corps, United States Army; Company Commander, 6016th Military Police Company and Commander, Post Prison, Yuma Test Station **Awards:** Recipient, Distinguished Alumni Citation, St. Lawrence University, Canton, NY (1990); Best Speaker Award, "Effective Presentation of Business Ideas," General Electric (1960) **Memberships:** Executive Council, St. Lawrence Alumni Association (1991-1993); Rotary International (1972-1978); Native Sons of Cooperstown; Adirondack Mountain Club; Life Member, Sigma Chi Fraternity **Marquis Who's Who Honors:** Albert Nelson Marquis Lifetime Achievement Award; Marquis Who's Who Top Professional **Why did you become involved in your profession or industry:** Mr. Hall became involved in his profession because at St. Lawrence University he earned his bachelor degree and he loved being there. After a few years in the business world, he decided to take on a job there. After five years of higher education, he went into consulting. He was a consultant to the board in Beirut. **Avocations:** Backpacking; Canoeing; Climbing Adirondack High Peaks; Cross-country skiing; Fishing; Photography; Sailing **Political Affiliations:** Republican

John O. Hallquist, PhD

Title: Founder, President **Industry:** Engineering **Company Name:** Livermore Software Technology Corporation **Education:** PhD in Mechanical Engineering and Engineering Mechanics, Michigan Technological University (1974); MS in Engineering Mechanics, Michigan Technological University (1972); BS in Industrial Engineering, Western Michigan University, Magna Cum Laude (1970) **Career:** Founder, President, Livermore Software Technology Corporation, California (1987-Present); Employee, Weapons Laboratory, Lawrence Livermore National Laboratory (1974-1987) **Awards:** Applied Mechanics Division Award, The American Society of Mechanical Engineers (2003); Significant Contributions to the Nuclear Weapons Progression, US Department of Energy (1986) **Memberships:** National Academy of Engineering (NAE) **Marquis Who's Who Honors:** Albert Nelson Marquis Lifetime Achievement Award; Marquis Who's Who Top Professional **Why did you become involved in your profession or industry:** Dr. Hallquist became involved in his profession because he always had an interest in the field of engineering. He also enjoyed programming. This, coupled with the fact that he wanted to secure a position straight out of college, encouraged him to pursue that industry. **Avocations:** Bicycling

Charles J. Hamilton Jr.

Title: Attorney **Industry:** Law and Legal Services **Company Name:** Windels Marx Lane & Mittendorf, LLP **Date of Birth:** 10/16/1947 **Place of Birth:** Pittsburgh **State/Country of Origin:** PA **Parents:** Charles J Hamilton, Sr.; Geraldine Alma (Taylor) Hamilton **Spouse Name:** Pamela G. Carlton (1979) **Children:** Charles J Hamilton III; Samuel Aaron Hamilton **Education:** JD, Harvard Law School (1975); Master of City Planning, Massachusetts Institute of Technology, with Honors (1975); Bachelor of Arts, Harvard College, Cum Laude (1969) **Awards:** SuperLawyers Metro New York (2014); Real Estate for Business and for Nonprofits (2008-2009); Paul Hastings Janofsky & Walker, LLP and Robert P. Hastings Partnership Award for Firm Leadership in Community Service (2006); Outstanding Leadership, NUL Trustee and Service as Outside General Counsel, National Urban League, Inc. Collins Award (2006); America's Top Black Lawyers, Black Enterprise Magazine, November (2003); W.E.B. DuBois Medal for Academic Leadership, Harvard University (2000); New York's Most Powerful Lawyers, New York Magazine (1999); Top Attorneys in the New York Metro Area Badge **To what do you attribute your success:** He attributes his success to the fact that he tries to understand clients needs and interests. He has excellent relationship building skills and builds rapport with clientele. **Why did you become involved in your profession or industry:** He became involved in his profession because he always had an interest in law. He enjoys working with and counseling clients, and also enjoys advocating on their behalf. **Avocations:** Traveling; Reading; Skiing

Richard Hamilton, PhD

Title: Professor **Industry:** Education/Educational Services **Company Name:** The Ohio State University **Date of Birth:** 01/18/1930 **Place of Birth:** Kenmore **State/Country of Origin:** NY/USA **Parents:** Delmer Vernon Hamilton; Ethelwyn Gertrude (Stevenson) Hamilton **Marital Status:** Married **Spouse Name:** Irene Maria Elisabeth Wagner (08/12/1957) **Children:** Carl Thomas; Tilman Michael **Education:** PhD, Columbia University (1963); MA, Columbia University (1953); AB, The University of Chicago (1950); Coursework, University of Michigan (1947-1948) **Career:** Retired Professor, The Ohio State University, Columbus, Ohio (1986-Present); Professor, McGill University, Montreal, Quebec, Canada (1970-1986); Associate Professor, Professor, University of Wisconsin-Madison (1966-1970); Assistant Professor, Princeton University (1964-1966); Instructor, Binghamton University Harpur College of Arts and Sciences, NY (1959-1964); Instructor, Skidmore College, Saratoga Springs, NY (1957-1959) **Civic:** Council, Inter-University Consortium for Political and Social Research (1975-1979) **Military Service:** Served, Army of the United States (1954-1956) **Creative Works:** Author, "The Bourgeois Epoch" (1991); Co-author, "The State of the Masses" (1986); Author, "Who Voted for Hitler?" (1982); "Restraining Myths" (1975); Author, "Class and Politics in the United States" (1972); Author, "Affluence and the French Worker in the Fourth Republic" (1967); Contributor, 15 Books **Awards:** Various Awards, Mershon Center (2006); Distinguished Scholar Award, The Ohio State University (1993); Grantee, Seed Grant, The Ohio State University (1988); Grantee, Social Science and Humanities Research Council of Canada (1983-1986); Research Leave Grant, Social Science and Humanities Research Council of Canada (1981-1982); Canada Council Grant (1974-1978); Grantee, Social Science and Humanities Research Council of Canada (1971); Grantee, McGill University (1970-1974); Grantee, National Science Foundation (1969-1971); Faculty Research Grantee, Social Science Research Council (1968); Research Committee Grantee, University of Wisconsin (1967-1968); Faculty Research Grantee, Social Science Research Council (1966); Grantee, Center of International Studies, Princeton University (1964-1965); Committee on Research Grantee, Princeton University (1964-1965); Grantee, Research Foundation, State University of New York (1960-1963); Grantee, Columbia University (1953); The University of Chicago Scholarship (1950); New York State Scholarship (1947) **Memberships:** Steering Committee, Council for European Studies (1975-1978) **Marquis Who's Who Honors:** Albert Nelson Marquis Lifetime Achievement Award; Marquis Who's Who Top Professional

Benjamin F. Hammond, PhD, DDS

Title: Retired Professor of Medicine **Industry:** Education/Educational Services **Date of Birth:** 02/28/1934 **Place of Birth:** Austin **State/Country of Origin:** TX/USA **Parents:** Dr. Virgil Thomas Hammond; Helen Marguerite (Smith) Hammond **Education:** PhD, University of Pennsylvania (1962); DDS, Meharry Medical College (1958); BA, University of Kansas (1954) **Career:** Director, Oral Microbiology Testing Service Laboratory, Medical College of Pennsylvania (1995-Present); Director, Periodontal Microbiology Laboratory, University of Pennsylvania (1985-Present); Professor of Microbiology, School of Dental Medicine, University of Pennsylvania, Philadelphia, PA (1970-Present); Faculty, School of Dental Medicine, University of Pennsylvania, Philadelphia, PA (1958-Present); Research Professor, Periodontology, Temple University, Philadelphia, PA (1998-2009); Professor of Medicine, Medical College of Pennsylvania (1995-2000); Department Chairman, School Dental Medicine, University of Pennsylvania, Philadelphia, PA (1972-1985); Associate Dean of Academy Affairs, University of Pennsylvania (1984); President's Lecturer, University of Pennsylvania (1981) **Career Related:** Distinguished Lecturer, Paul Sabatier University, Toulouse, France (1991); Ralph Metcalf Distinguished Visiting Professor, Marquette University (1986) **Civic:** Trustee, Brandywine Conservancy, Pennsylvania **Creative Works:** Contributor, Over 100 Articles, Professional Journals **Awards:** Award, Alumni, University of Pennsylvania Dental School (2017); Grantee, National Institutes of Health (1981-1986); Silver Medal City of Paris (1978); Lindback Award, University of Pennsylvania (1969); Research Career Development Award, U.S. Public Health Service (1965); E.H. Hatton Award, International Association of Dental Research (1959) **Memberships:** National Advisory, Dental Research Council (1975-Present); Oral Biology and Medicine Study Section, National Institutes of Health (1995-1999); President, American Association of Dental Research (1978-1980); Oral Biology and Medicine Study Section, National Institutes of Health (1972-1975); American Society of Microbiology; International Association of Dental Research; College Physicians of Philadelphia; Trustee, Philadelphia Museum of Art; Philadelphia Club; Sunny Brook Golf Club **Marquis Who's Who Honors:** Albert Nelson Marquis Lifetime Achievement Award **Why did you become involved in your profession or industry:** Dr. Hammond became involved in his profession because his father was a dentist and many of his cousins were medical doctors. **Avocations:** Classical music; Art

Sam F. Hamra, LLB

Title: Lawyer, Restauranter, Philanthropist **Industry:** Law and Legal Services **Company Name:** Hamra Enterprises **Date of Birth:** 01/21/1932 **Place of Birth:** Steele **State/Country of Origin:** MO/USA **Parents:** Sam Farris Hamra; Victoria (Homra) Hamra **Marital Status:** Married **Spouse Name:** June Samaha (4/1/1956) **Children:** Sam F., III; Karen E.; Michael K.; Jacqueline K. **Education:** LLB, University of Missouri (1959); BSBA, University of Missouri (1954); Diploma, Gulf Coast Military Academy **Career:** Lawyer, Restauranter, Philanthropist; Founder, Boston Bread, LLC, Hamra Enterprises (2001-Present); Chairman, Boston Bread, LLC, Hamra Enterprises (2001-Present); Founder, Chicago Bread, LLC, Hamra Enterprises (1998-Present); Chairman, Chicago Bread, LLC, Hamra Enterprises (1998-Present); Private Practice, The Law Offices of Sam F. Hamra, P.C., Springfield, MO (1976-Present); Founder, Wendy's of Missouri, Inc., Hamra Enterprises (1975-Present); Chairman, Wendy's of Missouri, Inc., Hamra Enterprises (1975-Present); Founder, Hamra Enterprises (1975-Present); Chairman, Hamra Enterprises (1975-Present); Organizer, OakStar Bank (2005); Founding Member, OakStar Bank (2005); Partner, Hamra & Crow, Springfield, MO (1971-1975); Private Practice, The Law Offices of Sam F. Hamra, P.C., Springfield, MO (1966-1971); Junior Partner, Miller, Fairman & Sanford, Springfield, MO (1959-1965) **Career Related:** Board of Directors, Landmark Bancshares, Inc. (1980-1991); Landmark Bank, Springfield, MO (1980-1981); Chairman, Law Day, U.S.A. (1960) **Civic:** Emeritus Board Member, CoxHealth (2010-Present); Board of Directors, OTC Foundation, Ozarks Technical Community College (2008-Present); Member, Advisory Board, Missouri Sports Hall of Fame (2005-Present); Board of Directors, ALSAC, St. Jude Children's Research Hospital, Memphis, TN (1985-Present); Lay Reader, St. James Episcopal Church (1959-Present); Member, Board of Directors, CoxHealth (1986-2010); Member, Board of Directors, Smith-Glynn-Callaway Medical Foundation (1997-2009); President, Missouri Sports Hall of Fame (1994-2005); Chairman, Jefferson Club Board of Trustees, University of Missouri (1988-1992) **Military Service:** U.S. Civilian Aide to the Secretary of the U.S. Army, Missouri (1997-2003); First Lieutenant, U.S. Army (1956); Second Armored Cavalry Regiment, Fort Meade, MD (1955-1956); Second Armored Cavalry Regiment, Bamberg, Germany (1955); 70th U.S. Field Artillery Battalion, Nuremberg, Germany (1954-1955); Second Lieutenant, U.S. Army Field Artillery, University of Missouri (1954) **Awards:** Annual Springfieldian of the Year Award for Outstanding Community Service, Excellence in Field and Long-time Dedication to Improve the Quality of Life for Springfield and Its Citizens, Springfield Area Chamber of Commerce (2018); Hamra Enterprises, Philanthropic Business of the Year, Springfield Business Journal, Economic Impact Awards Dinner (2017); Recognized as a Legend, July 2017 Issue, Springfield Business Journal (2017); President's Award, Missouri Sports Hall of Fame (2014); President's Award, Springfield Missouri Bar Association (2013); Hall of Fame Award, Wendy's International, Inc. (2013); Distinguished Tiger Award, Greater Ozarks Chapter, University of Missouri Alumni Association (2012); Eponym, Sam F. Hamra Center for Justice (2012); Charter Class of the Man of the Year Award, Springfield Business Journal (2011); Original Class, 20 Men of the Year in Springfield and Southwest Missouri, Springfield Business Journal (2011); Excellence In Business Award, Ozarks Technical Community College (2010); Lifetime Achievement in Business Award, Springfield Business Journal (2010); Wendy's International Dave Thomas Founders Award for Outstanding Franchise of the Year (2009); Elected, Missouri Academy of Squires (2004); Citation of Merit Award, School of Law University of Missouri (2003); Distinguished Service Award, University of Missouri (2003); Missourian Award, American Heart Association, Inc. (2001) **Memberships:** Founder, Rotary Club of Springfield Southeast (1967-Present); Charter President, Rotary Club of Springfield Southeast (1967-Present); Member, Hickory Hills Country Club (1961-Present); ABA (1959-Present); The Missouri Bar (1959-Present); Board Member, Truman Library Institute (2003-2012); Board of Directors, Bear's Paw Country Club, Naples, FL (2009-2011); President, Bear's Paw Country Club, Naples, FL (2010); President, Southern Federation of Syrian Lebanese American Clubs, Inc. (1984-1985); Chairman, Board, Southern Federation of Syrian Lebanese American Clubs, Inc. (1981-1982); Charter President, Board of Directors, Legal Aid Association, Greene County, MO (1976-1978); Board of Directors, Springfield Area Chamber of Commerce (1971-1977); Charter Chairman, Legal Internship Program, Greene County Bar Association (1969) **Bar Admissions:** Missouri (1959) **Marquis Who's Who Honors:** Albert Nelson Marquis Lifetime Achievement Award; Marquis Who's Who Top Professional; Marquis Who's Who Humanitarian Award **To what do you attribute your success:** Mr. Hamra attributes his success to being hardworking, and fair to all those who work with him. **Why did you become involved in your profession or industry:** Mr. Hamra was encouraged to become an attorney by his father and by former Federal Judge Roy Harper, who, at age 14, started working for Mr. Hamra's father in his clothing store. **Avocations:** Golf; Spending time with family; Collecting art; Donating art **Political Affiliations:** Democrat

John Fredrick Brown Haney

Title: Psychiatrist **Industry:** Medicine & Health Care **Date of Birth:** 06/07/1938 **Place of Birth:** Hempstead **State/Country of Origin:** NY/USA **Parents:** John Budd Haney; Evelyn Mae (Brown) Haney **Marital Status:** Married **Spouse Name:** Judith Lynn Fredrick (12/26/1986); Sara Jane Davidson (06/21/1961, Divorced 1983) **Children:** Bethany; Timothy; Andrew; John; Jeffrey **Education:** Residency in Psychiatry, Yale University School of Medicine (1965-1968); Internship, Medicine, University of Colorado (1964-1965); MD, Yale University (1964); BS in Chemistry, Yale University (1959) **Certifications:** Licensed Physician, Connecticut (1965); Diplomate, American Board of Psychiatry and Neurology; Certificate, 100 Young Eagles **Career:** Private Practice, Mansfield Center, CT (1993-Present); Medical Director, Natchaug Hospital (1997-2003); Attending Psychiatrist, Natchaug Hospital (1993-2003); Director of Treatment, Connecticut Valley Hospital (1990-1992); Director of Staff Growth And Development, Connecticut Valley Hospital, Middletown, CT (1986-1992); Psychiatrist, University of Connecticut, Storrs, CT (1970-1986); Chief of Psychiatry, U.S. Naval Submarine Base Hospital, Groton, CT (1968-1970); Resident In Psychiatry, Yale University School of Medicine, New Haven, CT (1965-1968); Intern In Internal Medicine, University of Colorado, Denver, CO (1964-1965) **Career Related:** Chairman, Board of Directors, Perception Programs, Inc. (1972-Present); Consultant Psychiatrist, Youth Service Bureau, Mansfield, CT (1972-Present); Associate Professor, University of Connecticut, Farmington, CT (1970); Fellow, American Psychiatric Association **Civic:** Medical Director, Chairman of Board of Directors, Perception Programs, Inc. **Military Service:** U.S. Naval Reserves (1970-1995); Active Duty, U.S. Navy, Naval Submarine Base, New London, CT (1968-1970); Captain, Medical Corps **Awards:** Distinguished Life Fellow, American Psychiatric Association **Memberships:** American Medical Association; American Group Psychotherapy Association; ASEL; ASES; IFR; President, EAA Chapter 1035, Danielson, CT **Marquis Who's Who Honors:** Albert Nelson Marquis Lifetime Achievement Award **Why did you become involved in your profession or industry:** Mr. Haney became involved in his profession because he did not want to be boxed into in a lab. He loved chemistry, but wanted something that left him working with people every day. Psychiatry was good that way, and medicine became kind of a formula and sort of the right thing to do. He found psychiatry more interesting. His father was a warm and a general person, and loved counseling his students. He was a professor of literature, and could recite poetry at long length and an interesting philosopher. **Avocations:** Aviation **Political Affiliations:** Republican

Peter Michael Haney, MD, PhD

Title: Neonatologist **Industry:** Medicine & Health Care **Date of Birth:** 08/30/1958 **Place of Birth:** Brooklyn **State/Country of Origin:** NY/USA **Parents:** Thomas Haney (1928-1998); Eileen Haney (1931-2015) **Marital Status:** Married **Spouse Name:** Helen Marie Haney (08/07/1982) **Children:** Eileen (1986); Ann Marie (1989); Karen (1991); Maria (1994); Teresa (1996); Thomas (1999); Elizabeth (2003) **Education:** Fellowship in Newborn Medicine, Department of Pediatrics, Washington University School of Medicine, St. Louis, MO (1989-1992); Residency in Pediatrics, Johns Hopkins Medicine, The Johns Hopkins University, Baltimore, MD (1987-1989); Internship in Pediatrics, Johns Hopkins Medicine, The Johns Hopkins University, Baltimore, MD (1986-1987); MD, Case Western Reserve University (1986); PhD, Case Western Reserve University (1984); BS, The University of Scranton (1979); Coursework, Universität Konstanz, Konstanz, Germany (1977-1978) **Certifications:** Diplomate, The American Board of Pediatrics (1993-Present); Certification, Neonatal-Perinatal Medicine, The American Board of Pediatrics (1993-Present) **Career:** Chairman, Ethics Committee, The Woman's Hospital of Texas, C-HCA, Inc. (2016-Present); Staff Neonatologist, The Woman's Hospital of Texas, MEDNAX Services, Inc. (Now C-HCA, Inc.) (2009-Present); Staff Neonatologist, Houston Neonatal - Perinatal Physicians (2006-2009); Assistant Professor, Pediatrics, Baylor College of Medicine, Houston, Texas (1997-2006); Assistant Professor, Department of Cell Biology & Physiology, Washington University School of Medicine, St. Louis, MO (1995-1997); Assistant Professor, Department of Pediatrics, Washington University School of Medicine, St. Louis, MO (1993-1997); Instructor, Department of Pediatrics, Washington University School of Medicine, St. Louis, MO (1992-1993) **Career Related:** Director, Neonatal-Perinatal Medicine Fellowship Program, Washington University School of Medicine (1993-1997) **Creative Works:** Contributor, Articles, Professional Journals **Awards:** First Award, National Institutes of Health, U.S. Department of Health & Human Services (1998-2003); New Investigator Award, Breast Cancer Research Program, U.S. Department of Defense, CDMRP (1996-1999); National Research Service Award, National Institutes of Health, U.S. Department of Health & Human Services (1992-1994) **Memberships:** Fellow, American Academy of Pediatrics (1989); Society for Pediatric Research **Marquis Who's Who Honors:** Albert Nelson Marquis Lifetime Achievement Award; Marquis Who's Who Top Professional **Why did you become involved in your profession or industry:** Dr. Haney became involved in his profession with inspiration from his mother, who was a nurse, and he knew from an early age that he wanted to be a doctor. He enjoyed science and biology as a student, and applied these interests to health care, ultimately pursuing a PhD in biochemistry and an MD degree. Dr. Haney chose neonatology because of its emphasis on taking care of the patient as a whole, as opposed to just one specialized area. **Avocations:** Running marathons **Religion:** Roman Catholic

Mazen Hanna, PhD

Title: Pharmaceutical Executive, President **Industry:** Pharmaceuticals **Company Name:** TransGenex Nanobiotech Inc. **Marital Status:** Married **Education:** PhD in Pharmacy, University of Bradford, England (1995); BS in Chemistry, University of Baghdad (1981) **Career:** President, TransGenex Nanobiotech Inc. (2017-Present); Chief Scientific Officer, Thar Pharma Ltd., Bradford, United Kingdom (2006-2016); Pharmaceutical Applications Consultant, Thar Technologies Inc., Pittsburgh, PA (2003-2006); Principal Scientist, Bradford Particle Design, Nektar Therapeutics, San Carlos, CA (2000-2003); Scientific Director, Bradford Particle Design, United Kingdom (1996-2000) **Career Related:** Research and Development Experience in Pharmaceutical Industry in General and Supercritical Fluid Technology, Molecular Design and its Application to Create New Drug Forms, Improve Existing on the Market IV Cancer Drugs through Enhancing Their Solubility, Permeability, and Subsequent Oral Bioavailability (More Than 25 Years); Industrial Experience in Technology Transfer from Lab to cGMP Manufacturing Including Manufacturing of Dosage Forms Used in Preclinical and Clinical Trials (Phases I-III) (More Than 15 Years); Research Work Experience in Supercritical Fluid Extraction and Chromatography of Natural Products (5 Years); Major Technical Input in Transferring the SEDS Technology from BPD to Several Major Pharmaceutical Companies; Transferring Cocrystal Platform Technology from Thar to Contract Manufacturers to Produce cGMP T121 Drug Substance for Clinical and Subsequent Commercial Use; Enhancement of Permeability of Poorly Permeable Drugs to Allow IV to Oral Switch; Expanding the Applicability of the Base SEDS and Cocrystal Technologies Through Conception and Implementation of New Ideas to Widen Company's Patent Portfolio; Supervising Production of cGMP Batches of Pharmaceutical Particulate Materials Designed by SEDS, cGMP Cocrystallization of Drug Substance for Clinical Trials; Extensive Knowledge of Patents and Literature of Supercritical Fluid Particle Formation, Bisphosphonates Landscape such as Zoledronic Acid and Technical Patent Knowledge, Competitive IP Landscape; Hands-on Experience of Solid State Characterization Methods such as X-ray Powder Diffraction (XRD), Differential Scanning Calorimetry (DSC), Thermal Gravimetry (TGA), Scanning Electron Microscopy (SEM), Dry and Wet Particle Size Analysis (PSA) with Theoretical and Practical Knowledge of Analytical Techniques such as Gas, Liquid and Supercritical Fluid Chromatography; Practical Experience of Design and Construction of Nozzles Suitable for Atomization of Liquids by Supercritical Carbon Dioxide and Substantial Knowledge of Materials and Material Properties Suitable for High Pressure Applications such as Supercritical Fluid Extraction **Creative Works:** Primary Author, More than 55 US and World Patents; Contributor to Tens of Publications in Professional Journals, Conferences and Meetings; Inventor, Novel SEDS TM Process for Manufacturing Micro and Nano Particles of Pharmaceutical Materials, and Cocrystallisation from Supercritical Fluids **Awards:** SBIR Phase II Award, National Institutes of Health (2017); SPUR Award, Department of Trade and Industry, United Kingdom (1997); Small Manufacturing Award for Research and Technology (1997); **Memberships:** American Association of Pharmaceutical Scientists; American Society of Clinical Oncology (ASCO) **Marquis Who's Who Honors:** Albert Nelson Marquis Lifetime Achievement Award **Avocations:** Photography; Scuba diving; Languages; Chess

Larry Lee Hansen, BS

Title: Executive Vice President **Industry:** Technology **Company Name:** Varian Associates **Date of Birth:** 08/19/1928 **Place of Birth:** Ephraim **State/Country of Origin:** UT/USA **Parents:** Lester J Hansen (deceased); Ethel Mary (Larson) Hansen (Deceased) **Marital Status:** Married **Spouse Name:** Barbara Louise Jones (11/26/1964, Deceased 2017) **Children:** Jana Lee; Lizbeth Ann; Bradley L; Karen Lynne **Education:** BS in Electrical Engineering, Utah State University (1958) **Certifications:** Business Management University of Utah **Career:** Retired; Corporate Executive, Industrial Equipment Group, Eimac Division, Varian Associates, Palo Alto, CA (1975-Present); Vice President, Industrial Equipment Group, Eimac Division, Varian Associates, Palo Alto, CA (1975-Present); President, Industrial Equipment Group, Eimac Division, Varian Associates, Palo Alto, CA (1975-Present); Plant Manager, Varian Associates, Eimac Division, Salt Lake City, UT (1964-1970); **Career Related:** Chairman, Advisory Committee, Semiconductor Manufacturing Equipment, Department of Commerce (1975); Board of Directors, Five Public Companies; Board of Directors, Three Private Companies **Military Service:** U.S. Air Force (1950-1954) **Memberships:** President, Semiconductor Equipment and Material Institute (1980); Chairman Board, Semiconductor Equipment and Material Institute (1980); Director, Semiconductor Equipment and Material Institute (1975) **Marquis Who's Who Honors:** Albert Nelson Marquis Lifetime Achievement Award; Marquis Who's Who Top Professional **Why did you become involved in your profession or industry:** Mr. Hansen became involved in his profession through the discovery of his love for electronics while serving in the Air Force. Mr. Hansen didn't want to have to hurt anyone, so rather than allowing himself to be drafted, he decided to go into the Air Force. Mr. Hansen went to electronic school and radar school there, which proved to be very valuable educations. Mr. Hansen spent four years serving the Air Force, and later went to Europe for three years, which turned out to be a turning point in his life: He knew then that he wanted to go into engineering, so he went to Engineering school. **Religion:** LDS Church

Laurene "Laurie" Hansen

Title: Realtor **Industry:** Real Estate **Company Name:** Intero **Marital Status:** Married **Children:** Two daughters **Education:** BA in History and Government, Minor in Psychology, College of Arts & Sciences, Boston University (1965) **Certifications:** Licensed Real Estate Agent (1979) **Career:** Realtor, Intero (2009-Present); Realtor, Century 21 Real Estate LLC (1998-2003); Realtor, Gibson Properties, Better Homes and Gardens® Real Estate LLC (1981-1998); Realtor, Windermere Services Company **Awards:** Top Listing Agent (1983-Present); Top Sales Agent (1983-Present) **Memberships:** Santa Clara County Realtors; California Association of Realtors; National Association of Realtors **To what do you attribute your success:** Ms. Hansen attributes her success to consistency. For example, since 1980, she has mailed newsletters and postcards on a monthly basis to keep in touch with her community. Much of Ms. Hansen's business success depends on referrals, and she prioritizes marketing herself along with her services. **Why did you become involved in your profession or industry:** Ms. Hansen became involved in her profession because of her fascination with real estate and the construction process. Unfortunately, Ms. Hansen's interest in investment real estate was cut short due to a change in tax laws; in 1984, she began focusing on single family real estate. She quickly grew to enjoy making families' dreams come true, and found it personally rewarding to help buyers and sellers achieve their goals.

Arnold C. Harberger

Title: Economist, Educator **Industry:** Education/Educational Services **Date of Birth:** 07/27/1924 **Place of Birth:** Newark **State/Country of Origin:** NJ/USA **Parents:** Ferdinand C. Harberger; Martha (Bucher) Harberger **Marital Status:** Widowed **Spouse Name:** Ana Beatriz Valjalo (03/15/1958, Deceased 2011) **Children:** Paul Vincent; Carl David **Education:** Doctorate (Honorary), Universidad del Desarollo (Chile) (2017); Doctorate (Honorary), University Americana (2006); Doctorate (Honorary), Instituto Tecnológico Autónomo de México (2006);Doctorate (Honorary), Francisco Marroquín University (2004);Doctorate (Honorary), Central American Technological University (1989); Doctorate (Honorary), Pontifical Catholic University of Chile (UC) (1988); Doctorate (Honorary), National University of Tucumán (1979); PhD, University of Chicago (1950); MA, University of Chicago (1947); Student, Johns Hopkins University (1941-1943) **Career:** Professor Emeritus, UCLA (2015-Present); Professor Emeritus, University of Chicago (1991-Present);Distinguished Professor (1992-2014); Professor of Economics, UCLA (1984-1992); Gustavus F. and Ann M. Swift Distinguished Service Professor, University of Chicago (1977-1991); Director, Center for Latin American Studies, University of Chicago (1965-1991);Chairman, Department, University of Chicago (1964-1971, 1975-1980);Professor, University of Chicago (1959-1991);Associate Professor of Economics, University of Chicago (1953-1959); Assistant Professor of Political Economy, Johns Hopkins University (1949-1953) **Career Related:** Visiting Professor, University of Paris (1986); Visiting Professor, UCLA (1983, 1984); Visiting Professor, Princeton University (1973-1974); Visiting Professor, Harvard University (1971-1972); Visiting Professor, Economic Development Institute, International Bank for Reconstruction and Development (1965); Consultant, Pan-American Union (1962-1976); Consultant, Committee Economic Development (1961-1978); Consultant, U.S. Treasury Department (1961-1975); Consultant, Planning Commission, India (1961-1962, 1973); Visiting Professor, MIT Center for International Studies, New Delhi (1961-1962); Consultant, U.S. President's Materials Policy Commission (1951-1952); Consultant, International Monetary Fund (1950, 1989, 2002-2006) **Civic:** U.S. Army (1943-1946) **Creative Works:** Co-Author, "Sense and Economics: An Oral History" (2016); Co-Author, "On the Process of Growth and Economic Policy in Developing Countries" (2005); Co-Author, "Cost-Benefit Analysis" (2002); Author, "World Economic Growth" (1985); Author, "Taxation and Welfare" (1974); Author, "Project Evaluation" (1972); Contributor, Science Papers, Professional Journals **Awards:** Life for Freedom Award, Caminos de la Libertad Foundation, Mexico (2016); Bradley Prize (2009); Holland Medal, National Tax Association (2001); Faculty Research Fellow, Ford Foundation (1968-1969); Guggenheim Fellow; Fulbright Scholar; Faculty Research Fellow, Social Science Research Council **Memberships:** Fellow, Econometric Society; American Academy of Arts and Sciences; American Economic Association; Western Economic Association; Royal Economic Society; National Tax Association; Society for Benefit-Cost Analysis; National Academy of Sciences; Phi Beta Kappa **Marquis Who's Who Honors:** Albert Nelson Marquis Lifetime Achievement Award; Marquis Who's Who Top Professional; Marquis Who's Who Humanitarian Award **Why did you become involved in your profession or industry:** Mr. Harberger became involved in his profession because all through his career he was inspired and helped by key figures. His start in economics began when he first went to John Hopkins at the age of 17. The inspiration came from a teacher named Clarence Long, who was the father of another Clarence Long who became his colleague at John Hopkins in the 1950s and later became a congressman for Baltimore County, Maryland.

Jo-Ann D. Harkleroad

Title: Educational Diagnostician; Author **Industry:** Education/Educational Services **Date of Birth:** 10/22/1936 **Place of Birth:** Wilkes-Barre **State/Country of Origin:** PA/USA **Parents:** Leon Joseph Decker Sr.; Beatrice Catherine (Wright) Decker **Marital Status:** Married **Spouse Name:** A. Dwayne Harkleroad **Children:** Dr. Leon W. Harkleroad; Franny (Harkleroad) Neil **Education:** Postgraduate Coursework, George Washington University (1997-1999); MA in Special Education and Educational Diagnosis and Prescription, George Washington University (1969); BS in Health, Physical Education and Recreation, George Washington University (1968); AS, George Washington University (1960) **Career:** Director, Special Education, Highland County Schools, Monterey, VA (1987-1990); Writer, Editor, Station WNVT-TV, Fairfax, VA (1980-1982); Supervisor Title I, Prince William County Schools, Manassas, VA (1971-1972); Educational Diagnostician, Prince William County Schools, Manassas, VA (1969-1971); Teacher, Bush Hill Day School, Franconia, VA (1961-1963); Instructor, The Catholic University of America, Washington, DC (1960-1961) **Career Related:** Reviewer, Writers Readers **Civic:** President, Vice President, Secretary, Bath-Highland Retired Educators Association (1995-Present); Ruling Elder, Presbyterian Church, McDowell, VA; Member, Faith in Action Hunger Committee, Shenandoah Presbytery, Clifton, VA; Director, McDowell Presbyterian Church Choir; Rotating Director and Director, Highland County Community Choir; Past President, Highland County Public Library Board; Lifetime Member, Presbyterian Women; Member, Valley Christian Fellowship, Panguitch, Utah; Member, Highland Baptist Church, Monterey, VA **Creative Works:** Author, "Freezeout" (2008); Author, "Swep Culhane" (2007); Author, "Ketch Colt" (2005); Author, "Blood Atonement" (2004); Author, "Horse Thief Trail," Third Edition (1986); Author, "Horse Thief Trail" (1981); With, Wyoming Valley Philharmonic Symphony Orchestra (1953-1954); Columnist, Op-ed Page, The Recorder; Radio Broadcaster, Station WVMR, Frost, WV **Awards:** Meritorious Service Medal, President's Committee on Employment of People with Disabilities (1988); Appreciation Certificate, Fairfax County Police Department, VA (1987); Virginia State Championship, Women's Rifle Team, George Washington University (1960); National Intercollegiate Rifle Team Championship, George Washington University (1960); Meritorious Citizenship Award (1953); Citizenship Award, Fairfax County, VA; Honoree, City of Clifton, VA; Senior Academic Award, Department of Health, Physical Education and Recreation, George Washington University **Memberships:** Past President, Stonewall Women's Club (1990-1992); International Women's Leadership Association; National Association Professional Women; Women Writing the West; Western Writers of America; Life Member, Presbyterian Women; Pi Lamda Theta **Avocations:** Hiking; Camping; Rifleshooting; Reading; Gardening **Political Affiliations:** Independent **Religion:** Christian

Robert Allen Harling

Title: Oil Industry Executive (Retired) **Industry:** Oil & Energy **Date of Birth:** 02/06/1930 **Place of Birth:** Woodland **State/Country of Origin:** CA/USA **Parents:** Robert Douglas Harling; Elizabeth (Allen) Harling **Marital Status:** Married **Spouse Name:** MarJeanne Louise Borg (06/13/1953) **Children:** Jayne Katherine Bremer; Allyn Elizabeth Testroet; Robert Warren **Education:** Certificate, University of Arizona (1979); BSBA, University of Omaha (1955) **Career:** Manager, Warehouse and Supply, Phillips Petroleum Company, Bartlesville, OK (1985-1986); District Manager, Phillips Petroleum Company, St. Louis, MO (1980-1985); District Manager, Phillips Petroleum Company, Minneapolis, MN (1977-1980); Assistant to Sales Manager, Phillips Petroleum Company, Raleigh, NC (1973-1977); District Manager, Phillips Petroleum Company, Madison, NJ (1962-1973); Marketing Representative, Phillips Petroleum Company, Raleigh, NC (1955-1961); Warehouse Clerk, Phillips Petroleum Company, Omaha, NE (1949-1951) **Career Related:** Board of Directors, Political Action Committee, Phillips Petroleum Company **Civic:** Elected Member, Tri-County Regional Vocational Technical Board of Education (1992-Present); Board of Directors, Adoption Center of Northeast Oklahoma (1987-Present); President, Adoption Center of Northeast Oklahoma (1991-1992); Elder, Presbyterian Church **Military Service:** Corporal, U.S. Army (1951-1953) **Awards:** Cornerstone Award, United Way (2019); District Service Award, Sales and Marketing Executives (1993) **Memberships:** President-Elect, Board of Directors, Rotary International (1995-Present); Board of Directors, Hillcrest Country Club (1991-Present); Board of Directors, St. Louis Chapter, Sales and Marketing Executives (1992-1993); Board of Directors, Bartlesville Area Chamber of Commerce (1987-1989); Bartlesville Chapter, Rotary International (1987-1988); Vice President, Ballwin, Missouri Chapter, Rotary International (1983-1985); Board of Directors, Madison Chapter, Rotary International (1970-1973); Secretary, Rotary International (1970-1973); Sales and Marketing Executives; Bartlesville Council of Social Services; Bartlesville Area Chamber of Commerce; Hillcrest Country Club; Rotary International **Marquis Who's Who Honors:** Albert Nelson Marquis Lifetime Achievement Award; Marquis Who's Who Humanitarian Award **Avocations:** Playing bridge; Volunteering; Reading; Foreign and domestic travel **Political Affiliations:** Republican **Religion:** Presbyterian

Theodore Carter "Ted" Harman, MS

Title: Physicist, Researcher (Retired) **Industry:** Sciences **Company Name:** Lincoln Laboratory **Date of Birth:** 07/22/1929 **Place of Birth:** Warsaw **State/Country of Origin:** Poland **Parents:** Seward W. Harman; Bernice E. (Irvine) Harman **Marital Status:** Widower **Spouse Name:** Marilyn Irene Axline (08/03/1957, Deceased 11/03/18) **Children:** Elizabeth; Janet; Kathryn; Thomas **Education:** MS in Physics, Purdue University (1953); AB in Physics, Chemistry, and Math, Manchester College (1951) **Career:** Lincoln Laboratory, Massachusetts Institute of Technology, Lexington, MA (1987-2009); Senior Staff Member, Lincoln Laboratory, Massachusetts Institute of Technology, Lexington, MA (1978-1987); Assistant Group Leader, Lincoln Laboratory, Massachusetts Institute of Technology, Lexington, MA (1959-1978); Program Manager, Defense Project, Research Agency, U.S. Department of Defense, Washington, DC (1965-1966); Project Leader, Battelle Memorial Institute, Columbus, OH (1953-1958) **Creative Works:** Co-Author, "Narrow Gap Semiconductors" (1974); Editor, "Journal of Electronic Materials" (1972-2006); Co-Author, "Thermoelectric and Thermomagnetic Effects" (1967); Co-Author, "Physics and Chemistry of II-VI Compounds" (1967); Contributor, Articles, Professional Journals; Patentee in Field **Marquis Who's Who Honors:** Albert Nelson Marquis Lifetime Achievement Award; Marquis Who's Who Top Professional **To what do you attribute your success:** Mr. Harman was inspired by his hero, Albert Einstein. He attributes his success to hard work. **Avocations:** Jogging; Walking; Bocce; Astronomy club; Harvard astrophysics lectures **Political Affiliations:** Republican **Religion:** United Methodist

Kamala Devi Harris

Title: Vice President-Elect of the United States **Industry:** Government Administration/Government Relations/Government Services **Date of Birth:** 10/20/1964 **Place of Birth:** Oakland **State/Country of Origin:** CA/USA **Parents:** Donald Harris; Shyamala (Gopalan) Harris **Marital Status:** Married **Spouse Name:** Douglas Emhoff (08/22/2014) **Children:** Two Stepchildren **Education:** JD, University of California Hastings College of the Law San Francisco (1989); BA, Howard University, Washington, DC (1986) **Certifications:** The State Bar of California (1990) **Career:** Vice Presidential Running Mate, Biden-Harris Campaign, 2020 Presidential Election (2020); U.S. Senator, State of California (2017-Present); Presidential Candidate, Democratic Nominee, 2020 Presidential Election (2018-2019); Attorney General, State of California, Sacramento, CA (2011-2017); District Attorney, Office of the District Attorney, San Francisco, CA (2004-2010); Head, City Attorney's Division on Families and Children, Office of the District Attorney, San Francisco, CA (2000-2004); Managing Attorney, Career Criminal Unit, Office of the District Attorney, San Francisco, CA (1998-2000); Deputy District Attorney, Office of the District Attorney, Alameda County, CA (1990-1998) **Civic:** Founder, Coalition to End Exploitation of Kids; Founder, Mentoring Program, San Francisco Museum of Modern Art; President, Board of Directors, Partners Ending Domestic Abuse; Co-chair, Lawyers' Committee for Civil Rights **Creative Works:** Author, "Superheroes are Everywhere," Penguin Young Readers Group (2019); Author, "The Truths We Hold: An American Journey," Diversified Publishing (2019); Author, "Smart on Crime: A Career Prosecutor's Plan to Make Us Safer," Chronicle Books (2009) **Awards:** Named One of the 100 Most Influential People in the World, Time Magazine (2013); Named to the Power 150, Ebony Magazine (2008); Thurgood Marshall Award, National Black Prosecutors Association (2005); Named Child Advocate of the Year, San Francisco Child Abuse Prevention Council (2004); Named One of the Top 20 Young Lawyers of California, Daily Journal (1998) **Political Affiliations:** Democrat

Cecil W. J. Hart, MA, MB, BCh, BAO (TCD); FACS

Title: Otolaryngologist, Surgeon **Industry:** Medicine & Health Care **Date of Birth:** 05/27/1931 **Place of Birth:** Bath **State/Country of Origin:** Somerset/ England **Parents:** William Theodore Hart; Paulina Olive (Adams) Gilmer **Marital Status:** Married **Spouse Name:** Brigid Frances Molloy (6/15/1957, Deceased 1984); Doris C **Children:** Geoffrey Arthur; Paula Mary; John Adams **Education:** MA in Liberal Arts, Trinity College, Dublin, Ireland (1958); Bachelor of Medicine, Bachelor of Surgery, Bachelor of Obstetrics, Trinity College, Dublin, Ireland (1955); Bachelor of Arts in Liberal Arts, Trinity College, Dublin, Ireland (1952) **Certifications:** Diplomate, American Board of Otolaryngology **Career:** Medical Practitioner Specializing in Otolaryngology, Chicago, IL (1958-Present); Staff Member, Loyola University Medical Center (1997-2002); Retired (1997); Staff Member, LaGrange Community Memorial Hospital, Illinois (1977-1994); Staff Member, Little Company of Mary Hospital (1977-1994); Staff Member, Children's Memorial Hospital (1972-1997); Staff Member, Northwestern Memorial Hospital (1972-1997); Staff Member, Rehabilitation Institute Chicago, IL (1965-1997); Assistant Professor, University of Chicago Medical School (1964-1965); Instructor, University of Chicago Medical School (1962-1964); Resident in Otolaryngology, University of Chicago Hospital and Clinic (1959-1962); Staff Member, Little Company Mary Hospital, Evergreen Park, IL (1958-1959); Intern, Little Company Mary Hospital, Evergreen Park, IL (1957); Intern, Dr. Steevens Hospital, Dublin, Ireland (1956) **Career Related:** Professor Emeritus (1997-Present); Professor of Otolaryngology, Head and Neck Surgery (1997-2001); Professor (1992-1997); Medical Advisory Board, Southern Hearing and Speech Foundation, National Institute of Deafness and Other Communicative Disorders (1989-1995); Associate Professor, Department of Otolaryngology-Head and Neck Surgery, Northwestern University Medical School (1975-1992); Lecturer, Department of Otorhinolaryngology, Loyola University (1972); Director of Otolaryngology, Northwestern University Medical School (1969-1992); Teaching Associate, Cleft Palate Institute (1968); Assistant Professor, Department of Otolaryngology-Head and Neck Surgery, Northwestern University Medical School (1965-1975) **Creative Works:** Producer, Movies and Videos; Contributor, Numerous Articles to Professional Journals and Magazines; Guest Appearances, Various Radio and Television Talk Shows **Memberships:** Computer Committee, American Academy of Otolaryngology – Head and Neck Surgery (1987-1990); Chairman, Subcommittee on Equilibrium, American Academy of Otolaryngology – Head and Neck Surgery (1980-1986); Constitution and Bylaws Committee, American Neurotology Society (1979-1997); President, Northwestern Clinical Faculty Medical Association (1979-1981); Chairman, Editorial Review & Publication Committee, American Neurotology Society (1978-1979); Vice Chairman, Northwestern Clinical Faculty Medical Association (1976-1978); Vice President, Chicago Laryngological and Otological Society (1975-1976); President, American Neurotology Society (1974-1975); Fellow, American College of Surgeons (American Board of Otolaryngology); Fellow, American Neurotology Society; American College of Surgeons; Institute of Medicine of Chicago; Society for Ear, Nose and Throat Advances in Children; American Medical Association; British Medical Association; Illinois State Medical Society; Chicago Medical Society; American Cleft Palate Association; American Council of Otolaryngology; American Otological Society; Barany Society; Royal Society of Medicine; Irish Otolaryngological Society; Medical Advisory Board, Southern Hearing and Speech Foundation; President, Chicago Hearing and Balance Association; Sigma Xi **Marquis Who's Who Honors:** Albert Nelson Marquis Lifetime Achievement Award; Marquis Who's Who Top Professional **Why did you become involved in your profession or industry:** Possessed of many interests in the field of medicine, Dr. Hart originally aspired to become a neurologist. However, he initially began his career as an otolaryngologist. **Avocations:** Travel; Baroque music; Symphony; Opera; Tennis

Alan C. Hartford, MD, PhD, FACR

Title: Associate Professor **Industry:** Education/Educational Services **Company Name:** Dartmouth-Hitchcock Medical Center **Date of Birth:** 01/06/1962 **Place of Birth:** Berkeley **State/Country of Origin:** CA/USA **Parents:** John Jewell Hartford; Heidi Marie (Fröning) Hartford **Marital Status:** Divorced **Spouse Name:** Arianna Vora (Divorced) **Children:** Anya Hartford **Education:** PhD in Political Economy and Government, Harvard University (1997); MD, Harvard Medical School (1992); MA in Philosophy, Stanford University (1983); BS in Biological Sciences, Stanford University, with Distinction (1983) **Certifications:** Diplomate, American Board of Radiology (2019, 2009, 1999); Medical License, State of Vermont (2007); Medical License, State of New Hampshire (2004); Medical License, Commonwealth of Massachusetts (1996) **Career:** Program Director, Radiation Oncology Residency, Dartmouth-Hitchcock Medical Center (2016-Present); Associate Professor of Medicine, Dartmouth Geisel School of Medicine (2010-Present); Interim Chief, Section of Radiation Oncology, Dartmouth-Hitchcock Medical Center (2006-2016); Assistant Professor of Medicine, Dartmouth Geisel School of Medicine (2004-2010); Fellow in Radiation Oncology, Massachusetts General Hospital, Boston, MA (1998-1999); Residency in Radiation Oncology, Massachusetts General Hospital, Boston, MA (1993-1998); Internship, Beth Israel Deaconess Hospital, Boston, MA (1992-1993) **Career Related:** President-elect, Council of Associated Regional Radiation Oncology Societies, American College of Radiology (2020-Present); Genitourinary Cancer Core Committee, NRG Oncology Clinical Trials Group (2016-Present); Commission on Cancer, American College of Surgeons (2015-Present); Chair of Cancer Clinical Research Quality Improvement Committee, Norris Cotton Cancer Center, Dartmouth-Hitchcock Medical Center (2015-Present); Grand Rounds Course Director, Norris Cotton Cancer Center at Dartmouth-Hitchcock Medical Center (2009-Present); Principal Investigator, NRG-RTOG Clinical Trials Group, Dartmouth-Hitchcock Medical Center (2006-Present); More than 20 NIH-NCI Scientific Study Sections and Panels (2004-Present); Scores of Courses and Lectures for Medical Students, Residents and Fellows, Dartmouth Geisel School of Medicine (2004-Present); Chair, Committee on Practice Parameters and Technical Standards in Radiation Oncology, American College of Radiology (2012-2019); Vice-Chair, Committee on Practice Parameters and Technical Standards in Radiation Oncology, American College of Radiology (2010-2012); Executive Committee, Norris Cotton Cancer Center at Dartmouth-Hitchcock Medical Center (2006-2016); Scientific Program Committee for Radiation Oncology, Radiological Society of North America (2003-2009); Professionalism Committee, Radiological Society of North America (2003-2008); Scores of Courses and Lectures for Medical Students, Residents and Fellows, Harvard Medical School (1998-2004); Admissions Committee, Harvard Medical School (1996-2004); Council on Ethical & Judicial Affairs, American Medical Association (1995-1998); Council on Medical Service, American Medical Association (1990-1991); Board of Trustees, American Medical Association (1989-1990); Council on Long Range Planning & Development, American Medical Association (1987-1989) **Civic:** Cast, Band Member, Up With People (1983-1984); Support Through Financial Contributions and Organizational Activities, Christian Ministries, Educational Institutions, Charitable Groups **Creative Works:** Co-Author, Numerous Original Articles, Scientific Reviews, Medical Journals (1992-Present); Author (Pen Name, Alan Fröning), "First Days of August," Archway Publishing (2015) **Awards:** Top Doctor, International Association of Top Professionals (2020); Excellence in Teaching Award, Department of Medicine, Dartmouth Geisel School of Medicine (2019); New Hampshire's Top Doctors, New Hampshire Magazine (2017-2020); Fellow, American College of Radiology (2015); America's Top Cancer Doctors, Newsweek Magazine (2015); New Hampshire's Top Doctors, New Hampshire Magazine (2014); Excellence in Teaching Award, Department of Medicine, Dartmouth Geisel School of Medicine (2014); Continuing Medical Education Faculty Director Award, Dartmouth Geisel School of Medicine (2013); America's Top Doctors, Castle Connolly Medical Ltd. (2012-2020); New Hampshire's Top Doctors, New Hampshire Magazine (2012); AACR-AFLAC Scholar in Cancer Research Award (2000); Graduate Research Fellowship, MacArthur Foundation (1996); Graduate Fellowship, Program in Ethics and the Professions, Harvard University (1991); Nominee, Rhodes Scholarship, Stanford University (1983); The Phi Beta Kappa Society (1981) **Memberships:** American Society for Radiation Oncology; American College of Radiology; American Medical Association; Radiological Society of North America; New Hampshire Medical Society; Vermont Medical Society; Massachusetts Medical Society **Marquis Who's Who Honors:** Albert Nelson Marquis Lifetime Achievement Award **To what do you attribute your success:** Dr. Hartford attributes his success to the grace of God, tended by the love of two wonderful parents and manifested through the care of cherished friends and colleagues. **Why did you become involved in your profession or industry:** Dr. Hartford became involved in his profession because, to him, there is no greater joy than to nurture the development, growth, and healing of others. Science is a romantic quest for knowledge, and its application in medicine is a true art. Creative work in medicine, literature, music, or any art keeps life fresh. **Avocations:** Jazz piano; Creative writing **Political Affiliations:** Independent **Religion:** Presbyterian

Marjorie I. Hartog-Vander Aarde

Title: Bureau Chief, Nursing Administrator, Educator, Chief Executive Officer **Industry:** Government Administration/Government Relations/Government Services **Company Name:** State of Montana Department of Certification **Date of Birth:** 11/12/1938 **Place of Birth:** Orange City **State/Country of Origin:** IA/USA **Parents:** John Hartog; Gertrude Marie (Hofland) Hartog **Marital Status:** Married **Spouse Name:** Robert Leon Vander Aarde (06/18/1960) **Children:** Tamela Vander Aarde Scholten, MD; Liesl Renae Vander Aarde **Education:** MS in Health Care Administration, University of Colorado (1990); MSN, Texas Women's University (1982); BSN, Montana State University (1975); Diploma, Swedish Covenant Hospital, Chicago, IL (1960) **Certifications:** Registered Nurse, Montana, Michigan, Illinois **Career:** Director, Human Resources, Montana Deaconess Medical Center, Great Falls, MT (1993-1997); Vice President, Human Services, Montana Deaconess Medical Center, Great Falls, MT (1990-1993); Assistant Vice President, Montana Deaconess Medical Center, Great Falls, MT; Assistant Director, Education, Montana Deaconess Medical Center, Great Falls, MT; Critical Care Education Coordinator, Montana Deaconess Medical Center, Great Falls, MT; Head, Nurse Critical Care Units, Montana Deaconess Medical Center, Great Falls, MT; Staff Educator, Montana Deaconess Medical Center, Great Falls, MT; From Staff to Charge Nurse, Montana Deaconess Medical Center, Great Falls, MT; Consultant, American Mission Hospital, Kuwait; Staff Nurse, Operating Room, Emergency Department, Holland City Hospital **Career Related:** Fellow, American College of Healthcare Executives (2008-Present); Bureau Chief of Certification of Quality Assurance Division, Department of Public Health, Montana (2000, 2006); Chief Executive Officer, Coalinga Regional Medical Center, Coalinga, CA (2000); Chief Operating Officer, Coalinga Regional Medical Center, Coalinga, CA (1997); Instructor, Montana State University School of Nursing, Great Falls, MT **Civic:** Executive Board Advisor, Women's Guild Christ Church on the Hill; R.C.A., Worship; Education and Music Committee Board of Directors, United Way of Cascade County; Personnel, Executive Committee; Chair, Nominating Committee **Awards:** Distinguished Alumni Award "for Service to Humankind," Northwestern College, Iowa (2015); Certificate of Appreciation, Montana Department Health and Environmental Science **Memberships:** American Association of Critical-Care Nurses (AACN); Nominee, American College of Healthcare Executives; Phi Kappa Phi; Sigma Theta Tau **Marquis Who's Who Honors:** Albert Nelson Marquis Lifetime Achievement Award; Marquis Who's Who Top Professional **Why did you become involved in your profession or industry:** Ms. Hartog-Vander Aarde became involved in her profession because when she was in college, she really wanted to become a doctor. At that time, she tried to be part of a premed group, but wasn't allowed to sit in on a meeting because it was only for men. Her brother-in-law suggested that she should go into nursing. She never did go back to trying to be a doctor. She loved nursing and found that she could do a lot more that was satisfying to her. In addition, she came to her position as a consultant for American Mission Hospital in Kuwait because it was interesting work; she worked in surgery at the time and was there for eight years. **Avocations:** Reading; Sewing **Political Affiliations:** Independent

Irene Janofsky Hartzell, PhD

Title: Educational Consultant, Psychologist, Author, Mediator **Industry:** Medicine & Health Care **Parents:** Leonard S. Janofsky; Annelies Janofsky **Children:** One Child **Education:** Intern, Human Resources Committee, Oregon Legislature (1974-1975); PhD in Counseling Psychology, Minor in Elementary Education, University of Oregon, Eugene, OR (1970); MA in Education, University of California Berkeley (1965); BA in Psychology, University of California Berkeley (1963); Diploma in Psychology, Ludwig Maximilian University, Muenchen, Germany (1961) **Certifications:** Certified Mediator, Pierce County Dispute Resolution Center, Tacoma, WA (2010); Advanced Paralegal Certificate, Edmonds Community College, WA (2010) **Career:** Founder, Kids Like Learning, LLC (2015-Present); Small Claims Court Mediator, Riverside County, CA (2008-Present); Small Claims Court Mediator, Pierce County, WA (2008-Present); Clinical Psychologist, Kaiser Permanente, Woodland Hills, CA (1979-1994); Clinical Instructor, Pediatrics, College of Medicine, University of California, Irvine, CA (1975-1978); Director, Parent Education, Children's Hospital, Orange, CA (1975-1978); Staff Psychologist, VA Medical Center, Long Beach, CA (1973-1974); School Psychologist, Lake Washington School District, Kirkland, WA (1971-1972); Staff Psychologist, VA Medical Center, Seattle, WA (1970-1971) **Civic:** King County Human Resources Commission (2006) **Creative Works:** Publisher, "A Wizard's Guide to Study Skills" (2017); Author, "The Study Skills Advantage"; Contributor, Articles, Professional Journals **Awards:** Fellowship, United States Vocational Rehabilitation Administration, University of Oregon (1969); Fellowship, United States Vocational Rehabilitation Administration, University of Oregon (1966-1967) **Marquis Who's Who Honors:** Albert Nelson Marquis Lifetime Achievement Award

Javad K. Hasan

Title: Founder, Chairman **Industry:** Technology **Company Name:** NeST Group, SFO Technologies **State/Country of Origin:** India **Marital Status:** Single **Education:** Honorary PhD, New Jersey Institute of Technology, Newark, NJ; MS in Material Science, Engineering, University of Bridgeport, Bridgeport, CT; BS, Columbia University, New York, NY; BS in Mechanical Engineering, University of Kerala, India **Career:** Entrepreneur Founder, Chairman, NeST Group (1998-Present); Head, IBM Semi-Conductor and Development Operations (1978-Present); President, Global Interconnects & System Business (1988-1998); Corporate Head, Engineering and Technology, IBM World Headquarters (1988); Engineer, Semi-Conductor Operations, IBM, Fishkill, NY (1968-1978) **Civic:** Board of Directors, Sibley Hospital, Washington, DC; The JKH Foundation **Creative Works:** Patentee, Over 20 Patents **Awards:** Fellow, Institute of Electrical and Electronics Engineers **Memberships:** Honoree Fellow, Institute of Electrical and Electronics Engineers (IEEE) **Marquis Who's Who Honors:** Albert Nelson Marquis Lifetime Achievement Award **To what do you attribute your success:** Dr. Hasan attributes his success to innovation and creativity, which he believes are the fundamentals of human life. He said, "If one does not innovate, one will disappear."

Charles John William Hass

Title: Criminal Justice Program Coordinator **Industry:** Government Administration/Government Relations/Government Services **Date of Birth:** 08/19/1934 **Place of Birth:** Fond du Lac **State/Country of Origin:** WI/USA **Parents:** Bernard Albert Andrew Haas; M. Elizabeth (Diener) Haas **Marital Status:** Married **Spouse Name:** Glenda Gwenelle Strickland (08/04/1974); Barbara Jane Demyen (12/24/1964, Divorced 02/1973) **Children:** Albert Andrew Anthony **Education:** MBA, University of West Florida (1982); Postgraduate Coursework, University of Oklahoma (1979-1980); Bachelor's Degree, University of Southern Florida (1977); BBA, University of Wisconsin (1959) **Career:** Senior Officer, Administrator, Community Corrections Division, Pensacola, FL (1983-1998); Administrator, Business/Employment Development, Escambia County Board of County Commissioners, Pensacola, FL (1975-1983); Sales Executive, Cuccia Oldsmobile-Cadillac Co., Annapolis, MD (1973-1975); President, Chairman, Chief Executive Officer, Hass Instrument Corp. (1963-1973); Secretary, Director, C. & K. Enterprises, Washington, DC (1961-1962); Vice President, Secretary, Hass Instrument Corp., Washington, DC (1959-1962); Assistant to President, Hass Instrument Corp., Washington, DC (1956-1959); Engineering Assistant, Giddings & Lewis, Inc., Fond du Lac (1953-1954) **Civic:** First Elder, University Parkway Seventh-day Adventist Church, Pensacola, FL (1980-1988, 1992-Present); Board of Directors, Secretary, Hearthstone Owners Mutual Endeavor, Inc., Pensacola, FL (1976-1986, 1991-2012); Trustee, Southern Union Conference Seventh-day Adventists, Atlanta, GA (1991-2002); Trustee, Executive Committee, Gulf State Conference/Association Seventh-day Adventists, Montgomery, AL (1985-1990); Board of Directors, Florida Council on Crime/Delinquency (1983-2015); Board of Directors, Chairman, Kiddie Korral Daycare Center, Pensacola, FL (1983); Campaign Coordinator, United Way of Escambia County, Pensacola, FL (1975-1998) **Military Service:** With U.S. Army (1954-1956) **Awards:** Paul Harris Fellow Award, Pensacola Suburban West Chapter, Rotary (1995, 1998); Paul Harris Award, Pensacola Suburban West Chapter, Rotary (1985) **Memberships:** President, Southern Prince Georges Chapter, Rotary (1974-1975); Air Force Association; Life Member, Society of Manufacturing Engineers; Life Member, Alpha Kappa Psi **Marquis Who's Who Honors:** Albert Nelson Marquis Lifetime Achievement Award **To what do you attribute your success:** He attributes his success to a variety of things, educational levels, and the U.S. Army. **Why did you become involved in your profession or industry:** Mr. Haas was in engineering to begin with, when he went in the U.S. Army. They sent him to Army Administration School. The rest of the time he was head of the finance section. As a result, he was eligible for a GI bill, so he went back and finished his bachelor's degree in business but also in mechanical engineering. By that time, the company's instrument business had grown to the point where they needed some more administrative experience. He had both the administrative and engineering background so he fit right in. When his brother was killed in a plane crash in 1963, he became president and chief executive officer for the next 10 years. All of that experience helped him in this role. In 1940, he built an instrument for temperature and gravity for Air Force **Avocations:** Photography **Political Affiliations:** Republican **Religion:** Seventh Day Adventist

Vera Hauptfeld-Dolejsek, PhD, D.(ABHI), CSc

Title: Medicine Professor, Director Histocompatibility Lab **Industry:** Education/Educational Services **Company Name:** University of Alabama at Birmingham **Date of Birth:** 04/13/1944 **State/Country of Origin:** Czech Republic **Parents:** Vaclav (1895-1945); Vera (1914-2000) **Marital Status:** Divorced **Children:** Rikard; Katerina **Education:** CSc, Institute of Molecular Genetics, Czech Academy of Sciences, Prague, Czech Republic (1996); RNDr in Experimental Zoology and Embryology, Charles University, Prague, Czechoslovakia (1968); Coursework, Faculty of Natural Sciences and Institute of Experimental Biology and Genetics, Charles University, Prague, Czechoslovakia (1966-1968); MS in Biology and Experimental Zoology, Charles University, Prague, Czechoslovakia (1966); Coursework, Faculty of Natural Sciences, Charles University, Prague, Czechoslovakia (1961-1966) **Certifications:** American Board of Histocompatibility and Immunogenetics (1995) **Career:** Professor, Department of Surgery, University of Alabama at Birmingham (UAB)(2018-Present); Director, Clinical Consultant, Histocompatibility and Immunogenetics Laboratory at UAB (2005-Present); Associate Professor, Department of Surgery, UAB (2005-2018); Director of Histocompatibility Laboratory, Associate Professor of Pathology, University of Massachusetts Memorial Health Care, Worcester, MA (2000-2005); Scientific Director, Human Leukocyte Antigen Typing Laboratory, and Associate Director of Molecular Genetics Program at Center for Cancer Treatment and Research, Palmetto Richland Memorial Hospital, South Carolina (1999-2000); Research Professor, Department of Medicine, University of South Carolina (1998-2000); Research Associate Professor, Department of Surgery, Associate Director of Human Leukocyte Antigen Typing Laboratory, Saint Louis University, Saint Louis, MO (1993-1997); Research Biologist, Immunogenetics Laboratory, Veteran's Administration, Saint Louis, MO (1993-1997); Research Assistant Professor, Washington University Department of Genetics, School of Medicine, Saint Louis, MO (1977-1992); Research Associate, Department of Microbiology, University of Texas, Southwestern Medical School, Dallas, TX (1974-1976); Research Assistant, Department of Microbiology, University of Texas, SW School, Dallas, TX (1973-1974); Research Scholar, Department of Microbiology, University of Texas, Southwestern Medical School, Dallas, TX (1974-1975); Research Scholar, Department of Human Genetics, University of Michigan, Ann Arbor, MI (1972-1973); Research Assistant, Institute of Experimental Biology and Genetics, Czech Academy of Sciences, Prague, Czechoslovakia (1966-1969) **Career Related:** Commissioner, Accreditation Review Board, American Society of Histocompatibility and Immunogenetics (ASHI) (2017-Present); Member, Bylaws Committee, ASHI (2013-Present); Invited Speaker, One Lambda Annual Clinical Histocompatibility Antibody Workshops (2009-Present); Member, Abstract Review Committee, ASHI (2007-Present); Advisory Board Committee OPO AL (2006-Present); Lecturer on Histocompatibility to Residents (2005-Present); ASHI Accreditation Laboratory Inspector; (2001-Present); Member, Accreditation Review Board, American Board of Histocompatibility and Immunogenetics: Vice President (2008-2010), President (2011-2013); Past President (2014-2015). Member, Examination Committee; Member, Proficiency Testing Committee, American Board of Histocompatibility and Immunogenetics (2004-2013); Ombudsman; Co-Chair, Session on Tolerance, Fifth Congress of the International Pancreas and Islet Transplant Association, Miami, FL (1995); Member, Interviewing Committee for Graduate and MST Programs, Washington University, Saint Louis, MO (1989-1992); Faculty Representative of the Department of Genetics Animal Facility, Washington University (1987-1992); Dissertation Committee Member, Several PhD Thesis Defenses **Creative Works:** Author and Co-author, Over 60 Publications in Peer-Reviewed Scientific Journals, Books, and Numerous Abstracts **Awards:** Postgraduate Scholarship, Institute of Cancerology and Immunogenetics, Hospital Paul Bruce, Paris-Villejuif, France (1969-1970) **Memberships:** American Society for Histocompatibility and Immunogenetics (ASHI); Laboratory Director, American Board for Histocompatibility and Immunogenetics (ABHI); American Society of Transplantation (AST) **To what do you attribute your success:** Dr. Hauptfeld-Dolejsek's father was her role model. He was a nuclear scientist who was taken away by a German Gestapo when she was only 9 months old. Her mother successfully kept his memory alive and his country dedicated a memorial to his accomplishments. He was a Nobel Prize nominee, an underground resistance supporter and a truly dedicated human being. She is aware that we can thank to people like her father for our freedom today and that we have an obligation to all fallen soldiers to keep our country free. **Why did you become involved in your profession or industry:** Dr. Hauptfeld-Dolejsek had always been interested in science. Her father was a nuclear scientist, and her mother a pharmacist. Education was an integral part of her upbringing. In high school, she fell in love with biology. She did her dissertation on transplant immunology, and it was a very advanced field in 1965. From then on she continued her career in that direction, in research with mice and discovered class II histocompatibility antigens. **Political Affiliations:** Democrat

Michael George Hauser

Title: Astronomer Emeritus **Industry:** Sciences **Company Name:** Space Telescope Science Institute **Date of Birth:** 12/03/1939 **Place of Birth:** Chicago **State/Country of Origin:** IL/USA **Parents:** Julius Hauser; Sylvia Ann (Gross) Hauser **Marital Status:** Married **Spouse Name:** Deanna S. Hauser (05/08/1981); Miriam Freedman (09/11/1960, Divorced 1977) **Children:** Karen C. Hauser (Deceased); Gerald P. Hauser; Amy Lynn Canby; Elizabeth Grove; Lisa Greening **Education:** PhD in Physics, California Institute of Technology, Pasadena, CA (1967); Bachelor in Engineering Physics, Cornell University, Ithaca, NY (1962) **Career:** Astronomer Emeritus, Space Telescope Science Institute, Baltimore, MD (2011-Present); Adjunct Professor, Physics & Astronomy, Johns Hopkins University, Baltimore, MD (1997-2017); Retired, Astronomer, Space Telescope Science Institute, Baltimore, MD (2009-2010); Visiting Associate Professor, Physics, California Institute of Technology, Pasadena, CA (2009-2010); Deputy Director, Space Telescope Science Institute, Baltimore, MD (1995-2009); Chief, Solar Physics and Astronomy Laboratory, Goddard Space Flight Center, Greenbelt, MD (1988-1995); Adjunct Professor, Astronomy, University of Maryland, College Park (1987-1995); Head, Infrared Astrophysics Branch, Astronomy and Solar Physics Laboratory, Goddard Space Flight Center, Greenbelt, MD (1987); Head, Infrared Astrophysics Branch, Extraterrestrial Physics Laboratory, Goddard Space Flight Center, Prince Greenbelt, MD (1985-1987); Head, Infrared Astrophysics Section, Extraterrestrial Physics Laboratory, Goddard Space Flight Center, Greenbelt, MD (1977-1985); Head, Infrared Astronomy Group, Laboratory for High Energy Astrophysics, Goddard Space Flight Center, Greenbelt, MD (1974-1977); Senior Research Fellow in Physics, California Institute of Technology, Pasadena, CA (1972-1974); Assistant Professor, Physics, Princeton University, Princeton, NJ (1970-1972); Instructor, Princeton University, Princeton, NJ (1967-1970) **Career Related:** Spitzer Science Center Oversight Committee (2001-2018); COSPAR Working Group on the Future of Space Astronomy (2010-2011); Scientific Organizing Committee, Sixth Ann. Irvine Cosmology Workshop (2010); Program Prioritization Panel, Electromagnetic Observations from Space, National Research Council (2010); Decadal Survey on Astronomy and Astrophysics (2009-2010); National Research Council Panel Rev. (2005); Stratospheric Observatory for Infrared Astronomy Science Council, University of Space Research Association (2002-2004); Two Micron All Sky Survey External Review Board (1995-2003); NASA Research and Analysis Program Senior Rev. Board (2001); NASA Astrophysics Senior Rev. Board (2000); NASA Astrophysics Senior Consultant, NASA Mars Climate Orbiter Mishap Investigation Board (1999-2000); Panel, Astronomy Education and Policy, Astronomy and Astrophysics Survey Committee, National Research Council (1999-2000); Chairman, NASA Astrophysics Senior Review Board (1998); NASA Space Science Advisory Committee (1994-1997); NASA and Associate University Research Astronomy Committee HST & Beyond (1994-1996); NASA Management, Operations Working Group for Infrared, Submillimeter, and Radio Astronomy (1992-1994); Vice President, Light the Night Sky, International Astronomical Union Commission (1991-1994); Chairman, Science Organizing Committee, Infrared and Submillimeter Astronomy, Committee on Space Research (1992); NASA Management, Operations Working Group, Space Astronomy (1981-1984); Infrared Detector Subpanel, NASA Management, Operations Working Group, Airborne Astronomy (1978-1979) **Civic:** Vice President, John & Jane Mather Foundation for Science & the Arts (2007-2019); Executive Board, Parent-Teacher Association, Kensington Junior High School, South Kensington, MD (1978-1979); Vice President, Parent-Teacher Association, Kensington Junior High School, South Kensington, MD (1977-1978) **Creative Works:** Numerous Refereed, Non-Refereed Publications, High Energy Physics, Technology, Astronomy, Astrophysics, Cosmology **Awards:** Van Biesbroeck Prize, American Astronomical Society (2014); Life-Long Cosmology Prize, Gruber Foundation (2006); AURA Science Award, Association Universities for Research In Astronomy (1998) **Memberships:** Fellow, American Physical Society; American Association for the Advancement of Science; American Astronomical Society; International Astronomical Union; Sigma Xi **Marquis Who's Who Honors:** Albert Nelson Marquis Lifetime Achievement Award **Why did you become involved in your profession or industry:** Growing up, Dr. Hauser's father was a chemist, which piqued his interest in the field. Throughout school, he gravitated towards mathematics as a result of his natural abilities. By the time he was at Cornell University, he decided to pursue the five-year engineering and physics curriculum. This was a good decision and proved useful when Dr. Hauser attended graduate school at Princeton University. There, he began working with the Penn Princeton Accelerator, which inspired him to study astrophysics. **Avocations:** Tennis; Music; Reading

Margaret Daly Hayes, PhD

Title: Political Scientist, Latin American Security Issues **Industry:** Education/Educational Services **Company Name:** Georgetown University **Date of Birth:** 07/10/1943 **Place of Birth:** Washington, DC **State/Country of Origin:** DC/USA **Parents:** Thomas Reed Daly; Mary Gertrude (Tubbs) Daly **Marital Status:** Married **Spouse Name:** Richard Edward Hayes (09/06/1969) **Children:** Michael Thomas Hayes **Education:** PhD in Political Science, Indiana University (1975); MA in Political Science, Indiana University (1970); MA in Spanish Literature, New York University, Madrid, Spain (1966); BS in Journalism, Northwestern University (1965) **Certifications:** Black Belt, Tae Kwan Do; Certified, Scuba Instructor **Career:** Adjunct Professor, Latin American Security Studies, Georgetown University (2004-2017); Director, Center for Hemispheric Defense Studies, National Defense University (1997-2004); Visiting Fellow, Center for Naval Analysis (1992); Director of External Affairs, Inter-American Development Bank, Washington, DC (1988-1992); Director, Council of the Americas, Washington Office (1984-1988); Senior Professional Staff Member, Western Hemisphere, U.S. Senate Foreign Relations Committee, Washington, DC (1981-1984); Associate Director, Center of Brazilian Studies, Johns Hopkins University School Advanced International Studies, Washington, DC (1977-1980); Senior Associate Policy Sciences Division, CACI, Inc., Arlington, VA (1974-1977); Senior Analyst, Evidence Based Research Inc. **Career Related:** National Advisory Committee, Hubert H. Humphrey International Fellowship Program, Washington, DC (1985); Consultant, U.S. Information Agency, Washington, DC (1977-1979); Foreign Service Institute, Bipartisan National Commission on Central America; Board of Directors, International Development Conference, Washington; Lecturer in Field **Civic:** Assistant Advisor, Explorer Scout Post 860, Boy Scouts of America **Creative Works:** Author, "Latin America and the United States National Interest" (1984); Contributor, Articles, Professional Journals; Contributor, Chapters, Books **Awards:** Indiana University (1972); Fulbright Hays Grantee (1971-1972); Fellow, National Defense Foreign Language Title VI (1967-1970) **Memberships:** President, Capital Divers Association (1986-1987); President, Capital Divers Association (1981-1983); President, Inter-American Council, Washington DC (1981-1982); Council on Foreign Relations, Inc., Latin American Studies Association; International Studies Association **Marquis Who's Who Honors:** Albert Nelson Marquis Lifetime Achievement Award **Why did you become involved in your profession or industry:** Dr. Hayes became involved in her profession because of the time she spent in Spain during her junior year of college. It was at a time when they were transitioning from Francisco Franco's leadership to a democratic government, which got her interested in political science. She then applied for a national defense graduate study fellowship that would assist in her study of Spanish to understand Latin America. **Avocations:** Scuba diving; Traveling; Theater; Symphony; Reading

Patricia Thornton Hayes

Title: Music Educator, Director (Choral and Orchestra) **Industry:** Media & Entertainment **Date of Birth:** 07/16/1934 **Place of Birth:** Chesapeake **State/Country of Origin:** WV/USA **Marital Status:** Married **Spouse Name:** Raymond S. Hayes Jr. (11/28/1959) **Children:** Rhett S.; Amber **Education:** MEd, Special Education, Old Dominion University (1970); MusB, West Virginia University Institute of Technology (1956) **Career:** Retired (2005-Present); Specialist of Music, Portsmouth Diagnostic Center (1993-2005); Director of Choral and Orchestra, Portsmouth City Schools, Virginia (1973-1996); Director of Music, Meadowbrooke & Lakeview Elementary, Norfolk, VA (1972-1973); Teacher of Music and Special Education, Mount Zion Elementary School, Suffolk, VA (1970-1971); Director of Music, Bayview Elementary School, Norfolk, VA (1959-1960); Director of Music, Suburban Park Elementary School, Norfolk, VA (1958-1960); Director of Music, Campostella Heights Elementary, Norfolk, VA (1958-1959); Director of Music, Shelton Park Elementary School, Virginia Beach, VA (1957-1958); Choral Director of Music, Clendenin High School, Kanawha County Schools, Charleston, WV (1956-1957) **Career Related:** Judge, Doris Sahr Memorial Piano Competition; Helper for Doris Sahr, Chesapeake Little Theater, Chesapeake, VA; Director of School Theatre Productions; Organist, Churches, Weddings and Receptions **Civic:** Historic St. Luke's Church (2006-Present); Volunteer, Beazley Foundation, Inc., Portsmouth, VA (2003-Present); Affiliate, Portsmouth Police (1996-2001); Charleston Symphony Youth Orchestra (1957); All State College Chorus and Orchestra, West Virginia University Institute of Technology (1956); Charleston Light Opera Guild; Active Member, Neat Summit, Neat Method; Portsmouth Concert Association; Tidewater Community Band **Creative Works:** Accompany, The Singing Beaz (2007-Present); Composer, "We're Supporting You All The Way" (1991); Choral Director, Mayor's Breakfast; Choral Director, Seawall Festival; Choral Director, Manor High School Award Banquet; Choral Director, NAVSEA; All-State Performer, Orchestra; All-State Performer, Chorus **Awards:** Outstanding Music Award, Portsmouth City School Board, Virginia (1992); Proclamation Award, Fine Arts Commission, Chesapeake, VA (1981-1989); Listed, Who's Who Amongst Students in American Universities and Colleges (1956); Grand Cross of Color, International Order of the Rainbow for Girls (1950) **Memberships:** National Association for Music Education (1956); Virginia Music Educators Association (1956); Order of the Eastern Star (1953); Virginia Education Association; American String Teachers Association; Virginia PTA; West Virginia University Institute of Technology; Virginia Retired Teachers Association; Alpha Psi Omega; Delta Sigma Lambda; Phi Mu Gamma; Portsmouth Retired Teachers Association; Music Education National Conference **Marquis Who's Who Honors:** Albert Nelson Marquis Lifetime Achievement Award; Marquis Who's Who Top Professional; Marquis Who's Who Humanitarian Award **Why did you become involved in your profession or industry:** Ms. Hayes started playing when she was a little girl, playing anything she wanted to. As she grew up, she wanted to continue with her music. She is thankful to have been able to share her music with children and adults. **Thoughts on Life:** Ms. Hayes believes that music is used throughout the world. Instead of cutting music programs from the school system, arts should be included in the education of every school. It's important for the children to learn because they use music in every aspect of life. No matter what form of music is taught, it's just as important as sports and it is worth having in the school system. Ms. Hayes taught general music to all children and she tried to motivate them to love music no matter what was taught. She would hold programs/performances at every school, in which she taught, whether it was on a stage or just in the hallway. She would try to incorporate all kinds of music, not just classical music.

Richard Webb Riemenschneider "Dick" Haymaker, PhD

Title: Emeritus Professor **Industry:** Education/Educational Services **Company Name:** Louisiana State University **Date of Birth:** 02/13/1940 **Place of Birth:** San Francisco **State/Country of Origin:** CA/USA **Parents:** Evelyn (Anderson) Haymaker (Deceased 1986); Webb Edward Haymaker (Deceased 1985) **Marital Status:** Married **Spouse Name:** Holley Galland Haymaker (11/01/1970) **Children:** Elizabeth; Webb **Education:** PhD in Physics, University of California, Berkeley, (1967); BA in Physics, Carleton College, Northfield, MN (1961) **Career:** Professor Emeritus, Louisiana State University, Baton Rouge, LA (2003-Present); Professor, Louisiana State University, Baton Rouge, LA (1982-2003); Associate Professor, Louisiana State University, Baton Rouge, LA (1976-1982); Assistant Professor, Louisiana State University, Baton Rouge, LA (1971-1976); Acting Assistant Professor, Cornell University (1970-1971); Research Associate, Instructor, Cornell University (1969-1970); Research Associate, Instructor, UC Santa Barbara (1967-1969) **Career Related:** Visiting Scientist, Tata Institute of Fundamental Research, India (1986); Visiting Scientist, KEK Accelerator Laboratory, Japan (1985); Interviewer, Physics Project, Southeast Asia (1983); Visiting Staff Member, Los Alamos National Laboratory (1977-1978); Referee for Submissions, Physical Review, Physical Review Letters, American Journal of Physics **Civic:** President, Baton Rouge Council on Human Relations (2003-2006) **Creative Works:** Contributor, Articles, Professional Journals **Awards:** Powell-Renznikoff Humanitarian Award, Baton Rouge Council on Human Relations (2013); Distinguished Research Professor in Theoretical Physics, Louisiana State University (2003); Grant, Louisiana State University, U.S. Department of Energy (1976-2003); Brij Mohan Distinguished Professor Award, Louisiana State University (2001); Wade Mackie Peacemaker Award, Bienville House Center for Peace and Justice (1994); Visitor, Aspen Institute of Physics (1973) **Memberships:** American Physical Society; The Phi Beta Kappa Society; Sigma Xi **Marquis Who's Who Honors:** Albert Nelson Marquis Lifetime Achievement Award **Why did you become involved in your profession or industry:** Dr. Haymaker became involved in his profession because of his interest in physics in high school. **Avocations:** Woodworking; Bicycling; Reading **Political Affiliations:** Democrat **Religion:** Unitarian Universalist

Jack R. Haynes, PhD

Title: Psychology Educator **Industry:** Education/Educational Services **Date of Birth:** 06/14/1932 **Place of Birth:** Daingerfield **State/Country of Origin:** TX/USA **Parents:** Jack E.; Mary B. (Read) H. **Marital Status:** Married **Spouse Name:** Tempie Kyla Newton (11/23/1960) **Children:** Kyla; Kenneth; Dennis **Education:** PhD, Texas Christian University (1964); MA, North Texas State University (Now University of North Texas) (1958); BA, North Texas State University (Now University of North Texas) (1957) **Certifications:** Certified and Licensed Psychologist, State of Texas **Career:** Chairman, Department of Psychology, North Texas State University (Now University of North Texas), Denton, Texas (1981-1989); Professor, North Texas State University (Now University of North Texas), Denton, Texas (1974-1981); Associate Professor, North Texas State University (Now University of North Texas), Denton, Texas (1967-1974); Assistant Professor of Psychology, North Texas State University (Now University of North Texas), Denton, Texas (1964-1967) **Career Related:** Consultant in Field **Creative Works:** Contributor, Articles to Professional Journals **Memberships:** American Psychological Association; International Neuropsychological Association; American Educational Research Association; Southwestern Psychological Association; Texas Psychological Association **Marquis Who's Who Honors:** Albert Nelson Marquis Lifetime Achievement Award **Why did you become involved in your profession or industry:** Dr. Haynes isn't exactly sure why he chose his career path. All that he knew is that he had an interest in psychology. **Avocations:** Avocations: Golf; Travel **Religion:** Presbyterian

James Fred Hays

Title: Geologist, Educator **Industry:** Education/Educational Services **Date of Birth:** 07/10/1933 **Place of Birth:** Little Rock **State/Country of Origin:** AR/USA **Parents:** Orren Lee Hays; Virginia (Russell) Hays **Marital Status:** Married **Spouse Name:** Diane Lee Huntoon (12/22/1956) **Children:** Lee Hays Romano **Education:** PhD, Harvard University (1966); MS, California Institute Technology (1961); AB, Columbia University (1954) **Career:** Director, Earth Sciences Division, National Science Foundation (1991-1995); Senior Science Advisor, National Science Foundation (1987-1991); Director, Division of Earth Sciences, National Science Foundation (1982-1987); Chairman, Department of Geological Sciences, Harvard University (1981-1982); Professor, Harvard University (1972-1984); Associate Professor, Harvard University (1969-1972); Assistant Professor, Geology, Harvard University (1966-1969); Guest Investigator, Geophysical Laboratory, Carnegie Institution of Washington (1965); Society of Fellows Junior Fellow, Harvard University (1963-1966); Geologist, United States Geological Survey (1961) **Career Related:** Visiting Scholar, University of Arizona (1997-Present); Member, National Research Council Committee on Research Opportunities and Priorities for EPA (1995-1997); Member, Space Grant Review Panel, NASA (1992-1995); Executive Secretary, President's Committee on National Medal Science (1987-1991); Member, Science Advisory Board, Mount St. Helens National Volcanic Monument (1983-1987); Member, Advisory Committee on Mining and Minerals Research, Department of the Interior (1983-1985); Member, Working Group, United States-Peoples' Republic of China Agreement for Cooperation in Earth Sciences (1982-1987); Chairman, Lunar and Planetary Review Panel (1978-1981); Visiting Professor, Chemistry and Geology, Arizona State University (1978-1979); Administrative Board, Harvard and Radcliffe Colleges (1976-1978); Member, NASA Lunar Sample Analysis Planning Team (1973-1976); Principal Investigator, Apollo Lunar Sample Program (1971-1982); Member, Harvard Center for Earth and Planetary Physics (1970-1984); Member, Faculty Council, Faculty of Arts and Sciences, Harvard University (1970-1973); Consultant, NASA Astronaut Training Program (1969-1973) **Civic:** Volunteer, Tuscon Audubon Society; Volunteer, Arizona Geological Society **Military Service:** Served to Captain, U.S. Naval Reserve (1954-1993); Naval Aviator **Creative Works:** Associate Editor, Journal Geophysical Research (1978-1980, 1983-1985); Associate Editor, Nature of the Solid Earth (1970) **Awards:** Presidential Rank Award, United States Government (1994); National Science Foundation Grantee (1974-1982); NASA Grantee (1971-1982) **Memberships:** Councilor, Geological Society of Arizona (2004-2007); Councilor, American Association for the Advancement of Science (1989-1992); Councilor, Geological Society of America (1988-1991); Fellow, American Association for the Advancement of Science; American Ornithological Society; Naval Reserve Association; Harvard Club; Cosmos Club; Phi Beta Kappa; Sigma Xi; National Science Foundation Fellow; Mineralogical Society America; American Geophysical Union **Marquis Who's Who Honors:** Albert Nelson Marquis Lifetime Achievement Award **Why did you become involved in your profession or industry:** Mr. Hays had always been interested in the sciences. He also loved hiking, mountain climbing and other outdoor activities. As he grew older, he realized becoming a geologist was a great way to combine those interests. Through school, he had excellent geology instructors, so it seemed the natural way to go.

Winston Haythe

Title: Chief Counsel (Retired) **Industry:** Law and Legal Services **Company Name:** National Enforcement Training Institute **Date of Birth:** 10/10/1940 **Place of Birth:** Reidsville **State/Country of Origin:** NC/USA **Parents:** McDonald Swann Haythe; Henrietta Elizabeth (East) Haythe **Spouse Name:** Glenann Leigh Rogers (8/17/1963, Divorced 1977) **Children:** Sheila Elaine; Rhonda Leigh; Kevin McDonald (Deceased) **Education:** Graduate Coursework, National Defense University (1984); Graduate Coursework, Command and General Staff School, Fort Leavenworth, KS (1982); LLM, The Judge Advocate General's Legal Center & School (1976); Postgraduate Coursework, University of Virginia (1968-1969); JD, William & Mary (1967); BS, Missouri State University (1963) **Career:** Chief Counsel, National Enforcement Training Institute (2005-2009); Senior Counsel, Office of Criminal Enforcement, Forensics and Training (2001-2005); Senior Legal Counsel, U.S. Environmental Protection Agency, Washington DC (1996-2001); Assistant Director, U.S. Environmental Protection Agency, Washington, DC (1994-1996); Senior Attorney, National Enforcement Training Institute, U.S. Environmental Protection Agency, Washington DC (1991-1994); Senior Attorney for Enforcement Policy, U.S. Environmental Protection Agency, Washington, DC (1985-1991); Staff Director, Legal Office, U.S. Environmental Protection Agency, Washington, DC (1982-1983); Assistant General Counsel, Senior Attorney, Consumer Produce Safety Commission, Washington, DC (1973-1982); Senior Trial Attorney, Atomic Energy Commission, Washington, DC (1972-1973); Associate, Rhyne & Rhyne, Washington, DC (1969-1972) **Career Related:** Board of Directors, Foundation of the Federal Bar Association (2012-Present); Adjunct Professor of Law, The George Washington University Law School (2002-Present); Consultant, Barrister Entertainment, Washington, DC (1978-Present); Member, Federal Dispute Resolution Conference Advisory Board (2004-2009); National Advocacy Center, U.S. Department of Justice, Columbia, SC (1999-2009); Member, Strayer University, Business Administrative Program Advisory Council (2003-2005); Guest Lecturer, The George Washington University Law School (1999-2002); Elected Member, Undergraduate Programs Advisory Council, University of Maryland (1993-1995); Advisory Council, Paralegal Studies, University of Maryland (1980-1995); Law Faculty, The Judge Advocate General's Legal Center & School, Charlottesville, VA (1969-1994); Legislative Fellow, United States Senate, Washington, DC (1983-1985) **Civic:** Clerk of Session, Georgetown Presbyterian Church (2003-2007); Elder, Member of Session, Georgetown Presbyterian Church (2000-2003); President of Trustees, Georgetown Presbyterian Church (1997-1998); Trustee, Georgetown Presbyterian Church (1995-1998); Vice President of Trustees, Georgetown Presbyterian Church (1996) **Military Service:** Colonel Judge Advocate, General Corps, U.S. Army Reserve (1967-1994) **Memberships:** Council Member, Foundation of the Federal Bar Association (2003-2012); National Council, Federal Bar Association (1998-2009); Board of Directors, William & Mary Law School Association (1988-1995); Federal Career Services Division, Federal Bar Association (1974-1990); Lifetime Fellow, Foundation of the Federal Bar Association; WETA Leadership Circle; The Phillips Collection; Victorian Society, Washington, DC; St. Andrews Society, Washington DC; Kappa Mu Epsilon; Cosmos Club; English Speaking Union; Knights Templar; The Social List of Washington **Bar Admissions:** The District of Columbia Bar (1969); Virginia State Bar (1967) **Marquis Who's Who Honors:** Albert Nelson Marquis Lifetime Achievement Award; Marquis Who's Who Top Professional; Marquis Who's Who Humanitarian Award **Avocations:** Playing organ and piano; Theater; Concerts; Reading **Religion:** Presbyterian

Linda Ann Hazelip

Title: Musician, Small Business Owner, Senior Administrative Assistant **Industry:** Education/Educational Services **Date of Birth:** 10/20/1952 **Place of Birth:** El Campo **State/Country of Origin:** TX/USA **Parents:** Daughter of Al Gareth and Annabelle (Black) Braswell; **Marital Status:** Divorced **Spouse Name:** Richard Chris Hazelip (07/28/1972-08/30/1984) **Education:** Diploma in Computer Programming and Data Processing, Massey Business College (1972) **Certifications:** Certified Teacher, Progressive Series, Intermediate Level Piano, St. Louis Conservatory of Music (1971) **Career:** Community Partnerships Administration (2018-Present); Teacher, Voice, Organ, Piano (2000-Present); Business Owner, Organist, Choirmaster, Pianist, Vocalist, Sacred Occasions and Select Secular Special Occasions, Southeast and Houston, TX (1986-Present); Senior Administrative Assistant, The University of Texas MD Anderson Cancer Center (2016-2018); Secretary, Administrator, Management Assistant, Halliburton, Houston, TX (1991-1996); Executive Secretary, InterFirst Bank, Post Oak, Houston, TX (1986); Director, Executive Secretary, Exponet Trading Co., Houston, TX (1983-1986); Secretary, St. Andrew's United Methodist Church, Houston, TX (1975-1979); Bookkeeper, Millar Instruments, Houston, TX (1973-1974); Teacher, Basic Music and Piano (1971-1979); **Career Related:** Organist for Traditional Worship, Southminster Presbyterian Church, Missouri City, TX (2017- Present); Choir Director, Covenant United Methodist Church, Houston, TX (1985-1986); Choir Director, Vocalist, Reid Memorial United Methodist Church, Houston, TX (1985); Organist, Choir Director, Vocalist, Parker Memorial United Methodist Church, Houston, TX (1984-1985); Organist, Vocalist, St. Stephen's United Methodist Church, Houston, TX (1983-1985); Organist, Vocalist, Music Director, St. John's United Methodist Church, Baytown, TX (1980-1984); Organist, Vocalist, Children's Music Director, Old River Terrace UMC, Channelview, TX (1978-1980); Organist, Vocalist, Pianist, Children's Music Director, Faith United Methodist Church, Houston, TX (1972-1977) **Civic:** First United Methodist Church, Houston, TX (1986-Present); Vocalist, Pianist, Open Door Mission, Houston, TX (1997-2014) AW: Woman of the Year, Skyscraper Chapter, American Business Women's Association Management LLC (1993-1994) **Awards:** Woman of the Year, Skyscraper Chapter, ABWA Management LLC (1993-1994) **Memberships:** Mu Alpha Theta; National Honor Society; American Guild of Organists; ABWA Management LLC; Choristers Guild **Marquis Who's Who Honors:** Albert Nelson Marquis Lifetime Achievement Award **To what do you attribute your success:** Ms. Hazelip attributes her success to her Lord and Savior, as well as to her many wonderful mentors and supportive friends. **Why did you become involved in your profession or industry:** Ms. Hazelip became involved in her profession because of talent for and enjoyment of providing administrative support to executives and upperlevel management in the business sector. Just as well, she is driven by her desire to use her God-given musical talents. **Avocations:** Holy Land study tours **Political Affiliations:** Republican **Religion:** Methodist **Thoughts on Life:** Ms. Hazelip shares it is only by God's grace that she lives a normal life developing and using the talents given her. Born with a dislocated hip, a team of doctors from around the world selected her to try to help. She learned to walk three times before the age of 5. At age 3, Jesus came to her in a dream and told her three times one night that she could walk. With childlike faith, she did walk while continuing her rehabilitation; a miracle in medical history. Ms. Hazelip's continual prayer is for her life to be a living testimony of what is possible with God if we only believe.

Howard R. Hechtman

Title: Financial Analyst (Retired) **Industry:** Infrastructure **Company Name:** NYC Transit Authority **Place of Birth:** New York **State/Country of Origin:** NY/USA **Parents:** Charles Hechtman; Pauline (Barmatz) Hechtman **Marital Status:** Single **Spouse Name:** Marsha Louise Garwin (12/19/1976, Divorced 1984) **Education:** Master of Business Administration in Management, Adelphi University, with distinction (1972); Master of Science in Physics, Adelphi University (1970); Bachelor of Science, Brooklyn Polytechnic University (1968) **Certifications:** Advanced Certification in Labor Relations, Cornell University (2000); Certified in Labor Relations, Cornell University (1999) **Career:** Retired (2016); Assistant and Associate Financial Analyst, New York City Transit Authority (1973-2016); Graduate Teaching Assistant, Physics Computer Center, Adelphi University, Garden City, NY (1970-1972) **Career Related:** Committee Member, Delegate, Civil Service Technical Guild Local 375; Delegate, Civil Service Technical Guild Local 375 **Military Service:** Captain, New York National Guard, New York State Division of Military and Naval Affairs **Awards:** Certificate of Merit, Republican National Committee (1990); Patron of the Arts, Society of Theater Arts Resources (1989-1990) **Memberships:** Life Director, Polytechnic University Alumni Association (1996-Present); Delegate, Civil Service Technical Guild (1994-Present); Alumni Board of Directors, Polytechnic University Alumni Association (1978-Present); Gold Circle, Veterans of Foreign Wars (2010); Society of American Military Engineers; Polytechnic University Alumni Association; Civil Service Technical Guild Local 375; **Marquis Who's Who Honors:** Albert Nelson Marquis Lifetime Achievement Award; Marquis Who's Who Top Professional **To what do you attribute your success:** Mr. Hechtman attributes his success to God's wondrous handiwork of the universe. **Avocations:** Volunteering at senior centers

Herbert "Bert" Heger, PhD

Title: Professor Emeritus **Industry:** Education/Educational Services **Company Name:** The University of Texas at El Paso **Date of Birth:** 06/15/1937 **Place of Birth:** Cincinnati **State/Country of Origin:** OH/USA **Parents:** J. Herbert Heger; Leona (Krueger) Heger **Marital Status:** Married **Spouse Name:** Thyra Cleek **Children:** Kelly Ramey; William Stacklind **Education:** PhD, The Ohio State University (1969); MEd, Miami University (1965); BS in Education, Miami University (1962); AS, Ohio Mechanics Institute (1956) **Career:** Professor Emeritus, The University of Texas at El Paso, Texas (1999-Present); Professor of Education, The University of Texas at El Paso, Texas (1982-1999); Associate Professor of Education, Whitworth University, Spokane, WA (1978-1982); Dean, Graduate School, Whitworth University, Spokane, WA (1979-1982); Chairman, Whitworth University, Spokane, WA (1978-1979); Coordinator, Curriculum and Instruction, The University of Texas at San Antonio, Texas (1977-1978); Visiting Professor, Pepperdine University School of Professional Studies (1975-1978); Assistant Professor, Division of Education, The University of Texas at San Antonio (1975-1978); Director of Student Teaching, The University of Texas at San Antonio, Texas (1975-1977); Associate Director, Louisville Urban Education Center (1971-1975); Assistant Professor, University of Kentucky (1969-1975); Graduate Assistant, Graduate Associate, Miami University (1966-1969); Graduate Assistant, Graduate Associate, The Ohio State University (1966-1969); Teacher of Mathematics, Mt. Healthy Jr/Sr High School, Ohio (1963-1966); Teacher, Marshall Middle School, Pomona, CA (1962-1963) **Career Related:** Consultant in the Field **Civic:** Las Cruces Chapter, Hearing Loss Association of America; Member, Church of Christ **Creative Works:** Editor, "Ethical Leadership" (1998-Present); Editor, Alumni Newsletter (1998-Present); Author; The Journal of Men's Studies (1996); Author, "The Clearing House" (1992); Author, "Teacher Education and Practice" (1990-1991); Author, "Students at Risk Workshop: The UTEP PDK Research Procedure" (1990); Author, "Implications of the UTEP PDK Students at Risk Study" (1990); Author, "The Impact of Testing on the Supply of Minority Teachers" (1989); Author, "The Texas Academic Skills Program: Excellence or Folly?" (1989); Author, "A Prescription for Academic Success: The U.T. El Paso Academic Advancement Center" (1989); Author, "Designing a Response to a State Mandated Basic Skills Test Requirement" (1987); Author, "An Initial Estimate of the Likely Effect of the Texas Rising Junior Test on Enrollment at The University of Texas at El Paso" (1987); Author, "Basic Skill Weaknesses Among Teacher Candidates" (1987); Co-author, "Career Choice and Role Equity: Monitoring The University of Texas at El Paso Teacher Candidate Screening and Advising Program" (1987); Author, "Accelerated Professional Teacher Education Programs: Alternatives to Alternative Teacher Education" (1986); Author, "An Analysis by Ethnic Group of Specific Mathematics Skill Strengths and Weaknesses Among Prospective Teacher Education Students" (1986); Author, "PPST Related Enrollment Trends at The University of Texas at El Paso" (1986); Co-author, "Reading and Mathematics Skill Analysis of Prospective Teacher Candidates" (1986); Contributor, "The PPST Guide: A Practice Book for College Level Standardized Achievement Tests in Reading, Mathematics and Writing" (1986); Author, College Student Journal Author, Journal of Teacher Education (1985); Author, Journal of Educational Studies, Volume Four (1985); Author, "Coping with Change in Texas: Implications of House Bill 72" (1985); Author, "Screening and Advising Teacher Education Prospects" (1985); Co-author, "The University of Texas at El Paso Basic Skills Assessment Instruments" (1985); Author, "Helping Students Prepare for Pre-service Teacher Examinations" (1985); Author, "Supporting Excellence through Teacher Expectations" (1985); Author, "Community College Student Performance on the Salinger-Burns Pre Basic Skills Test (PBST), Form A, Compared with Their Performance on the Nelson Denny Reading Achievement Test, Form D and the Wide-Range Achievement Test" (1985); Author, "The Salinger-Burns Pre Basic Skills Tests (PBST) as Predictors of Student Performance on the Pre-Professional Skills Tests" (1985); Author, "Texas Teacher Education Forum" (1985); Author, "The Progress Report on the UTEP Testing Program" (1985); Contributor, Books, Articles to Professional Journals **Memberships:** American Educational Research Association; National Society for the Study of Education (PDK International); Phi Delta Kappa; **Marquis Who's Who Honors:** Albert Nelson Marquis Lifetime Achievement Award; Marquis Who's Who Top Professional **Why did you become involved in your profession or industry:** Dr. Heger graduated high school when he was too young to attend most universities. He did an associate's degree and worked in a county park district for three years. Dr. Heger decided he wanted to become a teacher and went back to college. Dr. Heger had many mentors and people who helped him make decisions. Dr. Heger became a math teacher and then went on to teach at various universities. **Avocations:** Ancestry research; reading history **Political Affiliations:** Republican **Religion:** Church of Christ

Richard William Hemingway, Esq.

Title: Law Educator **Industry:** Education/Educational Services **Company Name:** University of Oklahoma **Date of Birth:** 11/24/1927 **Place of Birth:** Detroit **State/Country of Origin:** MI/USA **Parents:** William Oswald Hemingway; Iva Catherine (Wildfang) Hemingway **Marital Status:** Married **Spouse Name:** Vera Cecilia Eck (09/12/1947) **Children:** Margaret Catherine (Deceased); Carol Elizabeth; Richard Albert **Education:** LLM, University of Michigan (1969); JD, Southern Methodist University, Magna Cum Laude (1955); BBA in Business, University of Colorado (1950) **Career:** Eugene Kuntz Professor Emeritus, University of Oklahoma, Norman, OK (1992-Present); Eugene Kuntz Professor of Oil, Gas and Natural Resources Law, University of Oklahoma, Norman, OK (1983-1992); Professor of Law, University of Oklahoma, Norman, OK (1981-1983); Dean Ad Interim, Texas Tech University Law School, Lubbock, TX (1980-1981); Acting Dean, Texas Tech University Law School, Lubbock, TX (1974-1975); Paul W. Horn Professor, Texas Tech University Law School, Lubbock, TX (1972-1981); Professor of Law, Texas Tech University Law School, Lubbock, TX (1968-1971); Visiting Associate Professor, Southern Methodist University Law School (1965-1968); Associate Professor of Law, Baylor University Law School, Waco, TX (1960-1965); Lecturer, Bates School of Law, University of Houston (1960); Associate, Fulbright, Crooker, Freeman, Bates & Jaworski, Houston, TX (1955-1960) **Career Related:** William S. Cook Fellow (1968) **Military Service:** U.S. Army Air Force (1945-1947) **Creative Works:** Author, "West's Texas Forms (Mines and Minerals)" (1977); Author, "The Law of Oil and Gas" (1971); Contributing Editor, Various Law Reports, Cases and Materials **Awards:** Outstanding Professor, University of Oklahoma (1992); Horn Professor, Texas Tech University (1972); J. Woodall Rogers Senior Gold Medal (1955) **Memberships:** Texas Bar Association; Scribes; Order of the Coif; Beta Gamma Sigma **Bar Admissions:** Oklahoma State Bar (1981); Texas State Bar (1955) **Marquis Who's Who Honors:** Albert Nelson Marquis Lifetime Achievement Award; Marquis Who's Who Top Professional **Why did you become involved in your profession or industry:** Mr. Hemingway was going to school and was going to be a doctor, but taking chemical engineering courses. His wife asked him to take an aptitude test, and he found out he didn't have much aptitude for chemistry and more for business. He switched to the business school in Colorado, and business law was taught by a law professor. He caught his attention and after he got out, he came down to Dallas, Texas. Before Mr. Hemingway was in law, he spoke to a co-worker of his who was taking law classes at night while working full-time. He went home and told his wife that he wanted to do that as well. Mr. Hemingway first practiced in a law firm in Houston, Texas for five years. Then, the dean of the University of Houston Law School asked him if he wanted to teach law classes, and he accepted the offer. **Avocations:** Amateur radio **Political Affiliations:** Republican **Religion:** Lutheran

Allen Polk Hemphill

Title: Management Consultant **Industry:** Consulting **Date of Birth:** 08/22/1933 **Place of Birth:** Montgomery **State/Country of Origin:** AL/USA **Parents:** Alan Polk Hemphill; Elizabeth Evans (Orr) Hemphill **Marital Status:** Married **Spouse Name:** Jean Tilden Baker (06/08/1957) **Children:** Elizabeth; Alan; Laurie **Education:** MA in Management, National University (1987); BS, United States Naval Academy, Annapolis, MD (1957); Coursework, Officer's Submarine School, CT **Certifications:** License in Real Estate **Career:** Professor of Computer Science, National University, CA (1984-1997); President, Community Business Consultant, CA (1984-1985); Chairman, Board of Directors, Oak Broadcasting Systems, CA (1983-1984); President, Chief Executive Officer Station, KBSC-TV, CA (1982-1983); Founder, Orion Business Systems, CA (1980-1982); Manager, Prestige Properties, CA (1977-1980); Computer Programmer, Electronics Laboratory, CA (1967); Various Assignments, CA (1957-1977); Project Director, Integrated Flagship Data System, Electronics Laboratory, CA; Systems Analyst, Integrated Flagship Data System, Electronics Laboratory, CA **Career Related:** Executive Director, The Community Foundation of North San Diego County (1996-1997); Senior Vice President, Orion Network Solutions (1990-1991); Panelist, TV Series, "On Edge" (1986-1988); Board of Directors, Community Business Consultant, CA (1984); Consultant, Oak Industries, CA (1984); Trustee, Station KBSC-TV, Stock of Oak Industries, CA (1982-1984); Founder, Hidden Meadows Community Foundation **Civic:** President, Board of Directors, North County Board of Junior Achievement (1979); President, Chairman of Board, Green Valley Civic Association, CA (1974-1975) **Military Service:** Lieutenant Commander, United States Navy (1977); Commissioned Ensign, United States Navy (1957) **Creative Works:** Contributor, More than 2,000 Articles and Columns to Professional Journals; Contributor, Community News Network, Inc., Pomerado Press; Contributor, Chapters to Books **Awards:** Lifetime Achievement Award, Hidden Meadows **Memberships:** Director of Alumni, National University Alumni Association (1992-1994); President, National University Alumni Association (1991-1992); President, Rancho Bernardo Chapter, Kiwanis Club (1980-1981) **Marquis Who's Who Honors:** Albert Nelson Marquis Lifetime Achievement Award; Marquis Who's Who Top Professional; Marquis Who's Who Humanitarian Award **Why did you become involved in your profession or industry:** Mr. Hemphill was orphaned by age 5 and spent six years in military schools, aspiring to graduate from the naval academy because he was a poor, orphaned boy who often had nothing. His grandmother told him that he would never be able to afford to go to college so he had to work his way through if he wanted to get a college education. Mr. Hemphill joined the Navy at age 17 and was in the Korean War. He entered the naval academy in 1953, graduated in 1957 and spent 23 years in the military, primarily in submarines. Strangely enough, he lucked into things. Although he would like to take credit for them, the truth is he was in the right place at the right time. Mr. Hemphill never applied for a job and was asked to do each and everything that he did; he was invited to take positions, even as president at a television station in Los Angeles, CA. He did not aspire to those things, as he did not apply for nor did he expect them. But, someone came along and said to him, "How would you like to...?," and because of that, he was fortunate enough to never have to fill out a job application, which was very liberating. **Avocations:** Blogging **Political Affiliations:** Libertarian **Thoughts on Life:** Mr. Hemphill and his wife have been married 61 years and never an unkind word has passed them in all that time because she is a saint. He believes a hand to hold never gets cold. They have absolute love. Upon first meeting his wife, she turned down a blind date nine times during their college days. He believes that he is the luckiest man alive. They are joined at the hip and she was an active member of the union. He heard that 90% of your pain and 90% of your pleasure comes from your spouse, but 0% of the pain and 100% of his pleasure came from his wife.

Josephine Gattuso Hendin, PhD

Title: Language Educator, Writer **Industry:** Education/Educational Services **Company Name:** Department of English, New York University **Place of Birth:** New York **State/Country of Origin:** NY/USA **Parents:** Charles; Florence G. **Marital Status:** Married **Spouse Name:** Herbert Hendin (06/07/1968) **Children:** Neil; Erik **Education:** PhD, Columbia University (1968); MA, Columbia University (1965); BA, City College of New York (1964) **Career:** Professor, New York University (1979-Present); Tiro A. Segno Professor, Italian American Studies, New York University (2001-Present); Adjunct Professor, New School for Social Research, New York (1969-1979); Assistant Professor, Yale University, New Haven, CT (1968-1969) **Career Related:** President, Executive Committee, Italian American Studies Association **Civic:** Chair, Department of English, New York University (1995-1999); Director, Expository Writing Program, New York University (1983) **Creative Works:** Author, "Heartbreakers: Women and Violence in Contemporary Culture and Literature" (2004); Editor, "Concise Companion to Postwar American Literature and Culture" (2004); Author, "Vulnerable People: A View of American Fiction Since 1945" (1978); Author, "The World of Flannery O'Connor" (1970); Author, "The Right Thing to Do"; Contributor, "The Bostonians"; Contributor, Articles, Professional Journals **Awards:** American Book Award, Before Columbus Foundation (1989); Elena Lucrezia Cornaro Award, National Order Sons And Daughters Columbus (1983-1984); Fellow John Simon Guggenheim Fellowship, John Simon Guggenheim Foundation (1975-1976); President's Fellowship, Columbia University (1967-1968); Vera B. David Fellowship (1965-1966); Woodrow Wilson Fellowship, Woodrow Wilson Foundation (1964-1966) **Memberships:** Former President, Executive Board, American Italian Historical Association (2001); Modern Language Association of America; National Book Critics Circle; National Italian American Foundation **Marquis Who's Who Honors:** Albert Nelson Marquis Lifetime Achievement Award; Marquis Who's Who Top Professional **To what do you attribute your success:** Dr. Hendin attributes her success to a passion for reading and writing. **Why did you become involved in your profession or industry:** Dr. Hendin became involved in her profession because she had a love for literature and spent most of her time at the local library. She loved that reading took her places she could only dream of. **Avocations:** Speed walking; Traveling; Reading **Religion:** Catholic

Kathy Henkel

Title: Composer **Industry:** Media & Entertainment **Company Name:** Sign of the Silver Birch Music **Date of Birth:** 11/20/1942 **Place of Birth:** Los Angeles **State/Country of Origin:** CA/USA **Parents:** Norman Nicholas Henkel; Lila Rhea (Lee) Henkel **Marital Status:** Divorced **Spouse Name:** Michael Eric Manes (Divorced) **Education:** MusM, California State University, Northridge (1982); MusB, California State University, Northridge (1976); BA in History, University of California Los Angeles (1965) **Career:** Composer, Owner, Sign of the Silver Birch Music, Los Angeles, CA (2004-Present); Education Consultant, Los Angeles Chamber Orchestra (1998-Present); Liner Note Writer, Pro Piano Records, New York, NY (1994-2003); Program Annotator, Los Angeles Chamber Orchestra (1988-1998); Program Annotator, Education Consultant, Chamber Music/LA Festival (1987-1995); Visiting In-school Classroom Speaker, On-stage Host, Music Outreach Program, Chamber Music/LA Festival Program (1990-1993); Scriptwriter, Producer, KUSC-FM, Los Angeles, CA (1984-1989); Music Researcher, Paramount Pictures, Los Angeles, CA (1978-1981); Music Reviewer, Los Angeles Times (1979); Administrative Staff, Los Angeles Philharmonic Orchestra **Career Related:** Advisory Board, Los Angeles City College Music Department (1994-Present) **Civic:** National Association of Recording Artists and Sciences (NARAS); Grammy's **Creative Works:** Composer, "NightHawks" (2018); Participant, Dana School New Music Festival; Composer, Chamber Music, Song Cycles **Awards:** Commission for Music Award, State of Alaska (1994) **Memberships:** Recording Academy; American Federation of Musicians Local 47; Phi Beta Kappa Alumni; Phi Beta Women's Professional Fraternity; Delta Omicron; National Association of Composers/USA **Marquis Who's Who Honors:** Albert Nelson Marquis Lifetime Achievement Award; Marquis Who's Who Top Professional **Avocations:** Traveling; Gardening; Astronomy; Hiking the Cornwall coastal path **Thoughts on Life:** Ms. Henkel is a composer. She self-publishes and takes her music out there to the people. Composers have to decide how to distribute music. As a person who mostly writes for individual instruments, she focuses on chamber music. She decided she wanted to go out and meet the people. She has two vices, which are music and traveling. She has now combined them. Her father would never leave Los Angeles and she is a "travel freak." The first traveling she did was going overseas after college. Now, her music is performed at art festivals in England, Austria, Canada, Mexico and the United States. In order to spend more time composing, she recently retired from freelance work as program annotator and pre-concert lecturer for various chamber music groups, and duties as docent trainer for the Los Angeles Chamber Orchestra's "Meet the Music" elementary school outreach program. Her publishing company consists of her copyist and a logo designer. The three of them are very important. There is very little room for mistakes and it is very labor intensive.

Carl Arthur Henlein, Esq.

Title: Attorney-at-Law **Industry:** Law and Legal Services **Company Name:** Carl Arthur Henlein, Esq. **Marital Status:** Married **Spouse Name:** Barbara Osprey Henlein **Children:** Emily; Susan; Elizabeth; Tam **Education:** Doctor of Jurisprudence, Louis D. Brandeis School of Law, University of Louisville, KY (1964); Honorary Doctor of Letters, Georgetown College, Georgetown, TN; Bachelor of Arts in Business Administration and English, Georgetown College, Georgetown, TN; Coursework, Kentucky Military Institute **Career:** Attorney-at-Law, Brown University, Todd & Haver (Retired 2013) **Civic:** Chairperson, Board of Trustees, Georgetown College Foundation **Creative Works:** Author, "A Nation of Lawyers, Not Laws" **Awards:** Listed, "America's Leading Lawyers for Business," Chambers USA (2008-2009); Listed, International Who's Who of Product Liability Lawyers (2008); Listed, "Guide to the World's Leading Product Liability Lawyers," Second Edition; Martindale-Hubbell AV Preeminent Rated; Distinguished Alumni Award, University of Louisville Louis D. Brandeis School of Law **Memberships:** Section Member, Defense Research Institute; Complex Litigation, Defense Research Institute; Mass Tort Task Force, Defense Research Institute; Center for Public Resources; Legal Liability Working Group, U.S. Chamber Institute for Legal Reform **Bar Admissions:** Florida; Kentucky **To what do you attribute your success:** Mr. Henlein has many amazing mentors to whom he attributes his success, including O'Grant Brutton, Charles Metalton Jr., General Kirbin and Albert Wrightlinger. **Why did you become involved in your profession or industry:** Mr. Henlein knew he wanted to build his career as a lawyer after receiving strong mentoring at a small but powerful law firm located in Louisville, Kentucky. His time there allowed him to practice in a unique setting, which fostered life-long principles of law practice, entrepreneurship and hands-on client engagement. Some of his early clients were U.S. Steel, Firestone, Chevron, P. Lorillard, Brown and Williamson, the Southern, K&I and C&O railroads, International Harvester and LG&E Energy. It was only three weeks after passing the bar exam in both Kentucky and Florida that Mr. Henlein began jury trial work. **Thoughts on Life:** Mr. Henlein's motto is, "When in doubt, sit back and look out the window. The answer will come to you."

Darl Henley

Title: Librarian, Educator **Industry:** Education/Educational Services **Date of Birth:** 12/23/1944 **Place of Birth:** Dyersburg **State/Country of Origin:** TN/USA **Parents:** Hobert Valentine Heathcott; Martha Erle (McClearn) Heathcott **Marital Status:** Married **Spouse Name:** James Robert Henley (2/20/1988); Paul N. Herron, III (06/06/1964, Divorced 09/1987) **Children:** Dawn Michele Dunn; Mark Heathcott Herron **Education:** Postgraduate Coursework, University of Kentucky (1970-1971); BS in Elementary Education and Library Science, Murray State University, Kentucky (1966) **Certifications:** Certified, K-12 Teacher Librarian; Certified, K-8 Teacher **Career:** Elementary Librarian, Crittenden County Elementary School, Marion, KY (1984-2001); Sixth Grade Teacher, Crittenden County Elementary School, Marion, KY (1980-1984); Sixth Grade Teacher, Marion Elementary (1980-1981); Librarian, Remedial Teacher, Henderson City High School (1971-1973); Substitute Teacher, Henderson City Schools (1970); Sixth Grade Teacher, Weaverton Elementary School, Henderson, KY (1966-1968) **Civic:** State President, Kappa Kappa Iota National Teachers Sorority; Democratic Executive Chairman, District Area Agency for Aging; Donor, St. Jude's Children's Hospital; Volunteer, Relay for Life **Awards:** First Place, Management and Safety, "Ought to Be a Law Contest"; First Place, Nutrition, State Homemaker Contest **Memberships:** Cumberland Presbyterian Women Fellowship; Crittenden County Extension Homemakers; Crittenden County Democratic Women; Crittenden County Retired Teachers Association; National Education Association; Kentucky Retired Teachers Association; Kentucky Library Associate; Local, District Extension Council; State Extension Council; First District Representative on Health and Insurance, Kentucky Retired Teachers; Charter Member, National History Women's Museum **Marquis Who's Who Honors:** Albert Nelson Marquis Lifetime Achievement Award; Marquis Who's Who Top Professional **Why did you become involved in your profession or industry:** Ms. Henley always wanted to become a teacher. She began on the teaching path as a child when she would tutor her nephews. Seeing her potential, Ms. Henley's mother encouraged her to become a teacher. **Avocations:** Reading; Walking; Fishing; Travel; Cooking **Political Affiliations:** Democrat

Jennifer Hennessey, DVM, CVJ

Title: Owner/Veterinarian **Industry:** Veterinary Care **Company Name:** Animal ER of Northwest Houston **Marital Status:** Married **Spouse Name:** Greg Bremseth **Children:** Two Children **Education:** GCert in Veterinary Forensics, University of Florida (2019); DVM, Texas A&M University, Cum Laude (2005); BS, University of Texas at Dallas (2000) **Certifications:** Certified Veterinary Journalist, American Society of Veterinary Journalists **Career:** Owner/President, Animal ER of Northwest Houston (2014-Present); Veterinary Tech Program Director, Pima Medical Institute (2013-Present); Member, Veterinary News Network (2011-Present); Emergency and Critical Care Veterinarian, Sugar Land Veterinary Specialist (2009-2013) **Career Related:** Co-Owner, Crowned Regent Productions, LLC; Columnist, Texas Veterinarian Magazine; Frequent Guest, Houston's Fox 26, KPRC 2 News, Houston Life, Great Day Houston **Civic:** Local Stuffed Animal Doctor (2014-Present); TVMA Public Relations Committee; Donor, Goods and Services, Animal Shelters Nationally **Awards:** Mrs. Legacy International, Double Title with Legacy US (2019); Mrs. Legacy United State (2019); Mrs. Texas Legacy (2018); Mrs. Southwest Erst (2018); NPC Universe National Championship (2018); Small Business of the Year, Woman-Owned Award (2018); Small Business of the Year (2017);Best Veterinarian (2015-2019) **Memberships:** Veterinary Emergency and Critical Care Society; The Harris County Veterinary Medical Association; The Texas Veterinary Medical Association; Veterinary News Network; The American Veterinary Medical Association; The American Association of Rehabilitation Veterinarians; The International Association of Veterinary Rehabilitation and Physical Therapy; The International Veterinarian Academy of Pain Management; The International Sled Dog Veterinary Medical Association; Veterinary Iditarod Committee **Marquis Who's Who Honors:** Marquis Who's Who Top Professional **To what do you attribute your success:** Dr. Hennessey attributes her success to her compassion. She loves finding new elements and avenues to better treat her patients. **Why did you become involved in your profession or industry:** Dr. Hennessey has always passionately cared about animals. She always does everything in her power to heal not only the suffering of her animal patients but that of their families as well. **Avocations:** International Bodybuilding Federation (IFBB); Professional athlete

Annie Belle Henry

Title: Professor Emeritus (Retired) **Industry:** Education/Educational Services **Company Name:** Bemidji State University **Date of Birth:** 06/09/1942 **Place of Birth:** Jacksonville **State/Country of Origin:** FL/USA **Parents:** Benjamin; Nellie (Bolden) Henry **Marital Status:** Single **Education:** PhD, Florida State University (1988); MA, Florida Agricultural and Mechanical University (1969); BS, Edward Waters College (1964) **Certifications:** Certified Secondary Teacher, State of Florida **Career:** Associate Professor in Education, Bemidji State University, MN (1988-2008); Teacher, Secondary Social Studies, Chair, Department, Government of Virgin Islands, St. Thomas, U.S. Virgin Islands (1968-1983); Secondary School Teacher, Department of Public Education, Bunnell, FL (1966-1968) **Career Related:** Representative-recruiter, African American Students; Presenter in Field **Creative Works:** Author, "Feeling Like a Stranger in Your Hometown? Ask the Girl from Jacksonville!" (2017); Author, "The Girl from Jacksonville Who Dared to Dream, Hope and Believe!" (2011) **Awards:** Listee, Marquis Who's Who of American Women (1999-2000); Recipient, Skipping Stones Honor Awards (1997); Award, American Red Cross Disaster Relief (1997); Listee, Who's Who in American Education (1989-1990, 1992-1993); Award, Women in Higher Education Administration, Bryn Mawr College (1991) **Memberships:** National Education Association; Minnesota Black Association; The Phi Delta Kappa Society **Marquis Who's Who Honors:** Albert Nelson Marquis Lifetime Achievement Award **To what do you attribute your success:** Dr. Henry attributes her success to her parents and the village that raised her. The village taught her that if someone is in need, you step up. **Why did you become involved in your profession or industry:** Dr. Henry became involved in her profession because she wanted to help others. **Avocations:** Volunteering; Singing; Exercising **Political Affiliations:** Independent **Religion:** Baptist **Thoughts on Life:** Dr. Henry is the author of "The Girl From Jacksonville Who Dared to Dream, Hope and Believe!" and also "Feeling Like a Stranger in Your Hometown? Ask the Girl From Jacksonville!". All proceeds from the books are put into a scholarship for the students.

Bob Herbert

Title: Journalist **Industry:** Writing and Editing **Company Name:** The New York Times **Date of Birth:** 03/07/1945 **Place of Birth:** Brooklyn **State/Country of Origin:** NY/USA **Marital Status:** Married **Spouse Name:** Suzanne Herbert **Education:** BJ, State University of New York Empire State College (1989) **Career:** Op-Ed Columnist, New York Times, New York, NY (1993-2011); National Correspondent, NBC News (1991-1993); Columnist, Editor, New York Daily News, New York, NY (1985-1993); Host, Hotlines, WNYC-TV, New York, NY (1990-1991); Panelist, Sunday Edition, WCBS-TV, New York, NY (1990-1991); City Editor, New York Daily News, New York, NY (1983-1985); City Hall Bureau Chief, New York Daily News, New York, NY (1981-1983); Reporter, New York Daily News, New York, NY (1976-1981); Reporter, Night City Editor, Star-Ledger, Newark, NJ (1970-1976) **Career Related:** Distinguished Senior Fellow, Demos (2011-Present); Chairman, Pulitzer Prize Jury for Spot News Reporting (1993); Journalism Instructor, Columbia University, Brooklyn College **Creative Works:** Writer, PolicyShop (2012-Present); Writer, The American Prospect (2012-Present); Author, "Losing Our Way: An Intimate Portrait of a Troubled America" (2014); Author, "Promises Betrayed: Waking Up from the American Dream" (2005) **Awards:** Meyer Berger Award for Coverage of New York City; Distinguished Newspaper Writing Award, American Society of Newspaper Editors **Avocations:** Reading; Tennis; Rotisserie baseball

Frank Alan Herch

Title: Law Librarian, Lawyer, Lecturer **Industry:** Law and Legal Services **Date of Birth:** 05/05/1949 **Place of Birth:** Chicago **State/Country of Origin:** IL/USA **Parents:** Robert Gilbert Herch; Shirley (Berman) Herch **Marital Status:** Married **Spouse Name:** Ruth Blackwell (12/29/1971) **Children:** Nathaniel; Rachmiel **Education:** JD, University of California Davis (1975); MLS, University of California Berkeley (1972); BA in Sociology and History, University of California Davis (1971) **Certifications:** Certified Law Librarian, American Association of Law Libraries (1978) **Career:** Legal Content/Research Advisor, Product Manager, Iron Mountain, Denver, CO (2015-Present); Research Director, Greenpoint Services, Jerusalem, Israel (2009-2015); Legal Reference Librarian/Consultant, Law Library of Congress, Washington, DC (2008-2012); Law Librarian, U.S. Department of Commerce, Trade and Business and Law Library, Washington, DC (2007); Library Manager, U.S., Federal Energy Regulatory Commission, Law Library (2005-2007); Director/Project Manager, U.S. Federal Communications Commission Library, Washington, DC (2002-2005); Project Manager/Law Librarian, U.S. Department of the Interior Law Library, Washington, DC (2000-2002); Associate Director for Public Services, San Diego County Public Law Library, San Diego, CA (1998-1999); Director, Clark County Law Library, Las Vegas, NV (1987-1997); Librarian, Cityline Information Service and City Center Bookstop, Oakland Public Library, Oakland, CA (1984-1987); Attorney, Blackwell, Herch & Herch, Oakland, CA (1981-1987); Assistant Law Librarian, Director of Public Services, Georgetown University Law Center, Washington, DC (1978-1981); Reference Librarian, Alameda County Law Library, Oakland, CA (1975-1978) **Career Related:** Lecturer, Government Information Sources, San Jose State University, M.L.S. Program, Government Information Sources (2000); Lecturer, Computer Applications Parallel Program, University of San Diego, San Diego, CA (1999) **Civic:** Member, Clark County Merit Insurance Task Force (1992); Steering Committee Second Start: Adult Literacy Program, Oakland, CA (1984-1987); Member, Executive Board, East Bay Information and Referral Network, Berkeley, CA (1984-1987) **Creative Works:** Author, "There is no workplace like Home (in the Galilee): Straddling responsibilities in two different parts of the world," American Association of Law Libraries, Spectrum (2011); Author, "Revitalizing the FCC Library," Law Librarians in the New Millennium (2006); Author, "Internet Strategies for the Paralegal in California," Eau Claire, WI: Institute for Paralegal Education (2000); Author, "Practical Legal Research and Analysis for the Paralegal in California," Eau Claire, WI: Institute for Paralegal Education (1999); Author, "Virtual Law Library II: Providing Old Wine in New Bottles, Brushfires on the Internet and Paradigm Shifts for the Legal Professions" (1995) **Awards:** Greenpoint Global Employee of the Month (2014); Federal Library of the Year, FedLink at the Library of Congress to NASA Goddard Space Flight Library (2002); Pro Bono Service Award, Nevada State Bar Association to the Staff of the Clark County Law Library (1997); Certificate of Leadership, National University, Oakland, CA (1987) **Memberships:** Member, Nominating Committee, American Association of Law Libraries (1996-1997); Chair, State Court and County Law Libraries Special Interest Section of the American Association of Law Libraries (1996-1997); Chair, State Court and County Law Libraries Special Interest Section of the American Association of Law Libraries (1996-1997); Member, Nominating Committee, American Association of Law Libraries (1996-1997); Chair, Legal Information Service to the Public Special Interest Section of the American Association of Law Libraries (1995-1997); Chair, Legal Information Service to the Public Special Interest Section of the American Association of Law Libraries (1995-1997); President, Western Pacific Chapter of the American Association of Law Libraries (1994-1995); President, Western Pacific Chapter of the American Association of Law Libraries (1994-1995); Secretary-Treasurer, State, Court and County Law Libraries Special Interest Section of the American Association of Law Libraries, (1989-1992) **Bar Admissions:** California (1981) U.S. District Court for the North District of California (1981) **Marquis Who's Who Honors:** Albert Nelson Marquis Lifetime Achievement Award **Why did you become involved in your profession or industry:** Mr. Herch became involved in his profession because his dad was an electrician and a union member; he basically developed from the influence of his dad and the rabbis from which he developed a liberal point of view in his life. That figured into so much of everything he has done, including him wanting to be a lawyer. He worked in the library for four out of five of his under graduate years. He has dual bachelor's degrees. It was his work in his undergraduate years that interested him library and he procured his master's degree in library science while his wife was in her second year of law school. When she was in her third year, he was in the first year of the same law school, so after he finished after he finished his Master of Science at Berkeley in one year; he came back to University of California Davis, which was his undergraduate school. Obviously his became the dual profession consisting of law library and practicing law. He always had a desire to protect people's civil rights. **Avocations:** Jazz performances; Acting

David M. Hercules, PhD

Title: Centennial Professor Emeritus, Consultant **Industry:** Education/Educational Services **Date of Birth:** 08/10/1932 **Place of Birth:** Somerset **State/Country of Origin:** PA/USA **Parents:** Michael George; Kathryn (Saylor) H. **Marital Status:** Married **Spouse Name:** Shirley Ann Hoover, (12/14/1970) **Children:** Sherri Sokolovich; Kevin **Education:** PhD in Analytical Chemistry, Massachusetts Institute of Technology (1957); BS in Chemistry, Juniata College (1954) **Career:** Centennial Professor Emeritus, Vanderbilt University (2007-Present); Centennial Professor, Vanderbilt University (1995–2007); Chairman, Chemistry Department, Vanderbilt University (1995-2003); Miles Professor, University of Pittsburgh (1990-1994); Chairman, Chemistry Department, Vanderbilt University (1980-1989); Professor, Vanderbilt University (1976-1994); Professor, University of Georgia (1974-1976); Associate Professor, University of Georgia (1969-1974); Associate Professor, Massachusetts Institute of Technology (1968-1969); Assistant Professor, Massachusetts Institute of Technology (1963-1968); Associate Professor, Juniata College (1960-1963); Assistant Professor, Lehigh University (1957-1960) **Career Related:** Consulting Chemical Industry and Expert Witness; Chairman, Two Gordon Research Conferences; Council on Chemical Research; NSF Visiting Scientist Program, Pittsburgh Conference Committee; VU Rep on TN STEM Development; Co-founder, International Association of Environmental Analytical Chemists (IAEAC), North American Representative, Executive Committee, IAEAC **Creative Works:** Editorial Board, Applied Spectroscopy; Editorial Board, Analytical Chemistry; Editorial Board, Journal of Electron Spectroscopy; Editorial Board, Trends in Analytical Chemistry; Editorial Board, Analytical and Bioanalytical Chemistry **Awards:** Benedetti-Pichler Award, American Microchemistry Society; Analytical Chemistry Award, Eastern Analytical Symposium; Alexander von Humboldt Foundation Prize; Distinguished Alumnus, Juniata College; President's Distinguished Research Award, University of Pittsburgh; John Simon Guggenheim Memorial Fellow; Vanderbilt Research Award; Arthur W. Adamson ACS Award in Surface Chemistry; Pittsburgh Spectroscopy Award; ACS Fisher Analytical Chemistry Award **Memberships:** American Chemical Society; Society for Applied Spectroscopy; American Society for Mass Spectrometry **Marquis Who's Who Honors:** Albert Nelson Marquis Lifetime Achievement Award; Marquis Who's Who Top Professional **Why did you become involved in your profession or industry:** Beginning with a childhood chemistry set and progressing to building fireworks in high school, Hercules was led to choosing chemistry as a college major. Having excellent professors as models in both college and graduate school instilled in him an interest in teaching and academic research. **Avocations:** Painting; Playing French horn **Religion:** Episcopalian

Enrique Hernandez Jr.

Title: Chairman, Chief Executive Officer **Industry:** Business Management/Business Services **Company Name:** Inter-Con Security Systems Inc. **Date of Birth:** 02/02/1955 **Place of Birth:** Los Angeles **State/Country of Origin:** CA/USA **Education:** JD, Harvard University (1980); AB, Harvard University, Cum Laude (1977) **Career:** Chairman, Chief Executive Officer, Inter-Con Security Systems, Inc. (1984-Present); Executive Chairman, Nordstrom Inc. (2006-2016); Co-Founder, Principal Partner, Interspan Communications; Litigation Attorney, Brobeck, Phleger & Harrison **Career Related:** Non-Executive Chairman, Nordstrom Inc. (2006-Present); Board of Directors, Wells Fargo & Co. (2003-Present); U.S. National Infrastructure Advisory Committee (2002-Present); Tribune Co. (2001-Present); Board of Directors, McDonald's Corp. (1996-Present) **Civic:** President, Board Member, Los Angeles Police Commission (1993-1995); Committee Member, Harvard University Resources Committee; Committee Member, Harvard College Visiting Committee; Board of Trustees, LA County Museum of Art; Board of Trustees, University of Notre Dame; Vice-Chairman, Board of Directors, Children's Hospital; Chairman, Board of Regents, Loyola High School, Los Angeles, CA

Robert James "Bob" Herrick

Title: Electrical Engineering Technology Educator **Industry:** Education/Educational Services **Company Name:** Purdue University **Date of Birth:** 10/30/1943 **Place of Birth:** Battle Creek **State/Country of Origin:** MI/USA **Parents:** Virgil Ellsworth Herrick; Eddie Lee (McCoy) Herrick **Marital Status:** Married **Spouse Name:** Meredyth Margaret Ponicki (07/13/1968) **Children:** Jennifer Lynn **Education:** MSEE, Purdue University (1969); BSEE, Michigan State University (1968); AAS in Electrical Engineering Technology, Kellogg Community College (1966) **Career:** Robert A. Hoffer Distinguished Professor, Electrical Engineering Technology Program, Purdue University (1998-Present); Program Leader, Electrical Engineering Technology Program, Purdue University (1989-2010); Professor, Associate Department Head, Electrical Engineering Technology Program, Purdue University (1992-2001); Associate Professor, Electrical Engineering Technology Program, Purdue University (1989-1992); Engineering Technology Department Chair, Electrical Engineering Technology Program Leader, The University of Toledo (1987-1989); With, The University of Toledo (1980-1989): Senior Member of Technical Staff, Project Leader, International Telephone and Telegraph's (ITT) Advanced International Technical Design and Development Center, CT (1979-1980); Member, Technical Staff, AT&T's Bell Telephone Laboratories, IL (1968-1979); With, Purdue University Purdue Polytechnic Institute, School of Engineering Technology, Electrical Engineering Technology Program **Career Related:** Co-founder, ET National Forum to Nationally Lead Direction of Engineering Technology (ET) Programs **Civic:** Faculty Adviser, Bicycle Team, Purdue University (1992-2000); Faculty Adviser, Epsilon Tau Sigma Veterans Fraternity (1990-1994); Minority Mentor, Purdue University (1989-1992); Residence Hall Faculty Fellow, Purdue University (1989-2016); Minority Mentor, The University of Toledo (1986-1989); Host, International Students, The University of Toledo (1980-1989); Volunteer, Special Olympics Illinois (1977-1979) **Military Service:** Navigational Aids Technician, United States Air Force (1962-1964) **Creative Works:** Author, Numerous Articles to IEEE and ASEE Professional Journals and Conferences (1990-Present); IEEE Press Publication Board (1995-2004); Former Editor-in-chief, IEEE Press Editorial Board; IEEE Series Editor; Associate Editor, National and International Proceedings; Consultant, Author, German Technical Manual **Awards:** James H. McGraw Award, ASEE (2014); IEEE Student Second Place Technical Paper Award (1967); Purdue University's Lifetime Murphy Teaching Award for Outstanding Undergraduate Teaching; Named to Purdue University's "Book of Great Teachers"; Frederick J. Berger Award, ASEE; ASEE-IEEE Ronald Schmitz Award for Outstanding Service to Frontiers in Education; Recipient, Several Other Awards **Memberships:** Campus Representative, ASEE (1986-1989, 1992-1995); Senior Member, IEEE; Fellow, ASEE; Tau Beta Pi; Charter Executive Board, Purdue University's Teaching Academy; Past President, Tau Alpha Pi **Marquis Who's Who Honors:** Albert Nelson Marquis Lifetime Achievement Award; Marquis Who's Who Top Professional **To what do you attribute your success:** Mr. Herrick attributes his success to the good Lord's faithfulness in providing the Holy Spirit leading throughout his life and providing the gifts needed to make an impact and empower others. In addition, he credits his family while growing up, including mom and dad, as well as his exceptional Uncle Harold and Aunt Lauretta, who implanted foundational values in his life. Other factors are his wife, Becky, his life's soulmate for the past 55 years, their daughter, Jenny Tucker, for being a delightful child and now an accomplished professional with her own wonderful family of husband Mike and children: Wil, Ryan and Izzy. He is also thankful for all his brothers and sisters in Christ he has met and been spiritually influenced along life's journey. **Why did you become involved in your profession or industry:** Mr. Herrick became involved in his profession because he really enjoyed math, science and solving problems. He knew he wanted to make an impact while helping others. That is why he gravitated towards engineering. For him, the purest mathematical form was found in studying electrical engineering. After becoming a professor, student feedback about their learning experience combined with his passion for teaching affirmed to him that he was on his life's true pathway. Francis Herrick, his uncle, was the only current family member to earn a college degree and become a well-recognized industrial engineer who was the top leader responsible for building factories nationally and internationally. They enjoyed solving algebra and calculus problems together via "snail" mail. His influence and these moments of solving long distance math problems together led Mr. Herrick to realize that he could make a difference in engineering and with other life experiences that he was destined to empower students as a professor. **Avocations:** Bicycling; Piano playing; Healthy living and impacting longevity **Political Affiliations:** Independent **Religion:** Evangelical Christian **Thoughts on Life:** Mr. Herrick believes life is a journey. Be bold, let the Lord lead and surround yourself with positive, can-do people. His motto is also to appreciate others and make a difference.

Gary Heuer, FIC

Title: Owner/Partner **Industry:** Financial Services **Company Name:** Pinnacle Financial Partners **Date of Birth:** 01/12/1961 **Place of Birth:** Tillamook **State/Country of Origin:** OR/USA **Year of Passing:** 32 **Parents:** Gerhard Heuer; Ilse Heuer **Marital Status:** Married **Spouse Name:** Susan Mallonee-Heuer **Children:** Sean Heuer; Timothy Heuer; Nickolas Mallonee; Angelia Moretti **Education:** AS, AA, Portland Community College **Certifications:** Licensed, 15 States, MDRT- TOT (2019) **Career:** Owner, Partner, Pinnacle Financial/Independent Finical Group (2016-Present); Financial Associate, Thrivent Financial (1988-2016) **Career Related:** Lutheran Brotherhood (1988) **Civic:** Bethesda Communities Foundation **Military Service:** U.S. Army Reserve (1986-1990); Military Police Officer, U.S. Army (1980-1983) **Creative Works:** Author, "A Determined Spirit" **Awards:** Top of the Table, Million Dollar Round Table (2019); National Quality Award; Inductee, Hall of Fame, In Faith Community Foundation (2014); Inductee, Hall of Fame, Thrivent Financial (2009) **Memberships:** The Million Dollar Round Table; National Association of Insurance and Financial Advisors (Oregon Chapter) **Marquis Who's Who Honors:** Marquis Who's Who Top Professional **To what do you attribute your success:** Mr. Heuer attributes his success to his compassion; he has an immense amount of compassion to help people through their struggles. **Why did you become involved in your profession or industry:** Growing up, Mr. Heuer and his family went through multiple hardships. When he was nine, his father died as a result of a car accident. This left his mother to raise him and his siblings on her own. Witnessing her hard work, Mr. Heuer was inspired to achieve his own success. He joined the military, got his GED, and attended community college to start a career. He now works in insurance and helps people avoid monetary issues. **Religion:** Lutheran

Joseph "Thomas" Hickman

Title: Retired **Industry:** Education/Educational Services **Date of Birth:** 03/09/1933 **Marital Status:** Married **Spouse Name:** Carolyn S. (Married 03/28/59) **Children:** Three Children **Education:** Master's in Educational Administration, George Washington University; Bachelor's in History and Science, Wittenberg University **Career:** Principal, Middle School, Montgomery County, MD (1975-2001);Teacher, George Washington University **Career Related:** Adjunct Professor, Education, George Washington University (2001-2005); Chairman of the Board, Montgomery County Teachers Federal Credit Union **Civic:** Insurance and Health Committee Chair, Montgomery County Retired Educators Association (2001-Present); Chairman of the Board, Montgomery County Teachers Federal Credit Union (1994-2014); Board Chairman, Commission on Children and Youth, Montgomery County, MD (1993-2000); Former President, Montgomery County Retired Educators Association; Board Member, Montgomery County Retired Educators Association; Former President, Board Member, Church Council; Treasurer, Ida Mae Garrett, State Senator; Treasure Delegate, Henry Heller; Board Member, Maryland Retired School Personnel Association, State of Maryland **Creative Works:** Editor, Revised Book, Purdue University Press **Awards:** Certificate of Recognition, Appreciation for the Excellence in Being the Chair, Montgomery County Department of Health and Human Services, Child Support Workgroup (1990); Excellence in Leadership, Montgomery County Council; Excellence in Leadership, Maryland Senate; Federal Government Blue Ribbon Award; Monetary Award, Montgomery County Public School **To what do you attribute your success:** Mr. Hickman attributes his success to his relationship with God. Because of this, he has received encouragement, ideas, and motivation to serve others. **Why did you become involved in your profession or industry:** In college, Mr. Hickman felt called to his profession. He knew it was always what he wanted to do with his life. Likewise, he enjoyed working with his friends, exploring his creativity, and consistently learning.

Glenda Phillips Hightower

Title: Nurse **Industry:** Medicine & Health Care **Date of Birth:** 10/12/1944 **Place of Birth:** Burlington **State/Country of Origin:** NC/USA **Parents:** Garfield; Magaline (Thompson) Phillips **Marital Status:** Divorced **Spouse Name:** Eddie James Hightower (08/21/1964, Divorced 1970) **Education:** Bachelor of Science in Nursing, University of Iowa (1979) **Certifications:** Nephrology; Venipuncture; Wound Care **Career:** Nurse, VA Medical Center, Durham, NC (1980-Present); Nurse, VA Medical Center, Iowa City, NC (1979-1980); Managing Editor, Hemisphere Publishing Company, Washington (1972-1974); Editor, American Council on Education, Washington (1971-1972); Editor, American Personnel & Guidance Association, Washington (1968-1971) **Career Related:** With, Recovery Innovations Crisis Center (2016-Present); Freedom House Crisis Center (2015-2016); Staff Nurse, Recovery Resource Center, Arizona (2007-2019); Durham Center Access Crisis Center (2007-2015) **Civic:** Local Democratic Campaign Center, Durham, NC (1990-1991); National Kidney Foundation, Durham, NC (1988-1990); Volunteer Durham chapter American Cancer Society (1988-1990) **Awards:** Doctorate of Humane Letters, Elon University (2019) **Memberships:** Executive Council, American Nephrology Nurses Association (1986-1990); Convention Planning Committee, Durham Chapter, North Carolina Nurses Association (1987-1988); Member, Cabinet on Professional and Economic Development, North Carolina Nurses Association (1989-1991); Peer Assistance Committee, North Carolina Nurses Association (1986-1991); American Association of Critical Care Nurses; Sigma Theta Tau; Chi Eta Phi **Marquis Who's Who Honors:** Albert Nelson Marquis Lifetime Achievement Award; Marquis Who's Who Top Professional **To what do you attribute your success:** Ms. Hightower credits her success to always being willing to give her best effort. **Why did you become involved in your profession or industry:** Ms. Hightower initially became involved in her field out of an abiding desire to become a doctor. She enrolled in a pre-medical program during the 1960s, and worked for the American Personnel and Guidance Association, the American Council on Education and the American Association for Higher Education, among others. These positions kept her constantly interested in information and learning. Following this period, she accepted an editor's position at a publishing company, and learned of an affirmative action initiative at her local college, which she seized upon to complete her nursing degree. **Avocations:** Sewing; Interior designing and building; Home repairs; Electrical installation; Technical writing **Political Affiliations:** Democrat **Religion:** Baptist

Norman Ty Hilbrecht

Title: Lawyer **Date of Birth:** 02/11/1933 **Place of Birth:** San Diego **State/ Country of Origin:** CA/USA **Year of Passing:** 2019 **Parents:** Norman Titus Hilbrecht; Elizabeth (Lair) Hilbrecht **Marital Status:** Married **Spouse Name:** Mercedes L. (Sharratt) Hilbrecht (10/24/1980) **Education:** JD, Yale University (1959); BA, Northwestern University (1956), Cum Laude **Career:** President, Hilbrecht & Associates (1983-2019); Managing Member, Corporate Services Group, LLC (1998-2018); Managing Member, Amcorp LLC (1999-2018); President, Nevada Incorporating Co. (1998-2018); President, Corporate Services Company (1998-2018); General Counsel, Bell United Insurance Company (1986-1994); President, Hilbrecht, Jones, Schreck & Bernhard (1969-1983); Legislative Commission (1977-1978); Nevada Senate (1974-1978); Nevada Assembly (1966-1973); Minority Leader, Nevada Assembly (1971-1972); President, Mobil Transport Corporation (1970-1972); Partner, Hilbrecht & Jones, Las Vegas, NV (1962-1969); Associate Counsel, Union Pacific R.R., Las Vegas, NV (1962) **Career Related:** Nevada Supreme Court Settlement Judge (1997); Business Law Assistant Lecturer, University of Nevada, Las Vegas (1968-1969) **Civic:** Associate for Justice National Judicial College (1993-2006); President, Nevada Arbitration Association (1984-1985); Nevada Legal Aid and Defender Association (1965-1983); Clark County Democratic Central Committee, Nevada (1959-1980); 1st Vice-Chairman (1965-1966); Delegate Western Regional Assembly as Ombudsman Chairman Clark County Democratic Convention (1966); Nevada Democratic Convention (1966); President Clark County Legal Aid Society (1964); Labor Management Committee, National Conference of Christians and Jews (1963); United Way Leadership Council **Military Service:** Captain, U.S. Army Judge Advocate General (JAG) **Creative Works:** Author, "Nevada Corporation Handbook" (1999); Author, "Nevada Motor Carrier Compendium" (1990) **Awards:** Named, Outstanding State Legislator, Eagleton Institute of Politics, Rutgers University (1969); Named, One of the Best Lawyers in America **Memberships:** President, Senior Member, Rotary, Las Vegas Rotary Foundation, (2004-2019); Chairman, Administrative Law, State Bar Nevada (1991-1996); State Legislative Committee, American Association of Retired Persons (1991-1994); Founder, German American Social Club (1971); State Vice President, Nevada Trial Lawyers (1966); American Bar Association; American Associate for Justice; American Judicature Society; American Academy Political and Social Sciences; Supreme Court Historical Society; Literary Society Las Vegas, Las Vegas Social Register; Mercedes Benz Club of America; Editor, Tri-Star Newsletter; University of Nevada-Las Vegas Foundation; Las Vegas Elks Lodge 1468; Phi Beta Kappa; Delta Phi Epsilon; Theta Chi; Phi Delta Phi; Air Force Association Thunderbird Chapter 189 **Bar Admissions:** U.S. Court of Appeals, Ninth Circuit, (1986); Supreme Court of the United States, (1963); State Bar of Nevada (1959) **Marquis Who's Who Honors:** Albert Nelson Marquis Lifetime Achievement Award; Marquis Who's Who Top Professional **Religion:** Lutheran

Don C. Hildebrand, PhD

Title: Research Plant Pathologist Emeritus **Industry:** Research **Company Name:** University of California, Berkeley **Date of Birth:** 02/27/1932 **Place of Birth:** Astoria **State/Country of Origin:** OR/USA **Parents:** Frank Frederick Theodore; Irma Amelia (Laumeister) H. **Marital Status:** Single **Spouse Name:** Mary Avarilla Nern (01/29/1973, Deceased 11/2016); Ellen Marie Primacove (09/1959, Divorced 03/1974) **Children:** Karin; Catherine; Laynie **Education:** PhD, University California, Berkeley (1962);BS, Washington State University (1953);Coursework, Northern Idaho College (1949) **Career:** Plant Pathologist, University California, Berkeley (1962-1990) **Military Service:** Air Intelligence Officer, Lieutenant, US Navy (1953-1956) **Creative Works:** Associate Editor, The Plant Disease Reporter (1980-1987); Associate Editor, Annual Review of Phytopathology (1968-1969); Contributor, Research Article, Professional Journals **Awards:** Research Career Development Award, National Institutes Of Health (1967) **Memberships:** The American Phytopathological Society; Microbiology Society; American Society of Microbiology; Subcommittee on Pseudonmonas and Related Organisms, International Committee on Systematic Bacteriology (Now International Committee on Systematics of Prokaryotes); Lake Merritt Joggers and Striders **Marquis Who's Who Honors:** Albert Nelson Marquis Lifetime Achievement Award; Marquis Who's Who Top Professional **Why did you become involved in your profession or industry:** Dr. Hildebrand became involved in his profession because of his lifelong interest in pathology and his preference of working with plants to animals. **Political Affiliations:** Republican

Gregory Hill

Title: President, Chief Operating Officer **Industry:** Oil & Energy **Company Name:** Hess Corp. (Formerly Amerada Hess) **Date of Birth:** 03/02/1961 **Place of Birth:** Springfield **State/Country of Origin:** IL/USA **Parents:** James Isaac Hill; Bonnie Lee (Ball) Hill **Marital Status:** Married **Spouse Name:** Loren Jean Hill (12/21/2012) **Children:** Justin Gregory; Brandon Andrew Kapelow **Education:** BSME, University of Wyoming (1983) **Career:** President, Chief Operating Officer, E&P, Hess Corp. (Formerly Amerada Hess) (2009-Present); Executive Vice President, Asia Division, Shell E&P International (2006-2008); Vice President, Production, Europe, Shell E&P International (2003-2006); Chief Executive Officer, Enterprise/Shell, Shell International E&P (2002-2003); Senior Operating Vice President, Aera Energy LLC (1999-2002); Senior Vice President, Innovation and Breakthrough Performance, Aera Energy LLC (1999); Vice President, Planning Executive Strategy/Affairs, Shell International (1998); Vice President, Operating, Aera Energy, LLC (1996-1997); Vice President, Operating, Calresources, LLC (1996); Area Manager, LA Basin, Calresources, LLC (1994-1995); Manager, Petroleum Engineering, Shell Western E&P (1992-1993); Strategic Planning Manager, Shell Oil Co. (1991-1992); Division Engineering Manager, Shell California Production, Inc., Bakersfield, CA (1988-1990) **Career Related:** Board Member, National Ocean Industries Association (2019-Present); Board Member, Harbour Energy (2018-Present); Board Member, Chair of Energy Committee, Greater Houston Partnership (2015-Present); Board Member, API Upstream Committee (2013-Present); Co-Chair, International Petroleum Congress (2019); Board Member, Hess Corporation (2009-2014); Chief Executive Officer, Enterprise Oil PLC (2002-2003); Chairman, Board of Directors, Terrain Tech., LLC (1999-2002); Lobbyist Shell Oil Co. (1987) **Civic:** Chairman, University of Wyoming Foundation (2018-Present); Board Member, CEOs Against Cancer (2016-Present); Executive Council Member, Blue Ribbon Panel on Sustaining Americas Diverse Fish and Wildlife (2015-Present); Co-Chair, Wyoming Governors Tier 1 Engineering Task Force (2013-Present); Chairman, Wyoming Governors ENDOW Initiative (2017-2019); Board Member, Wyoming Business Council (2016-2018); Houston SuperBowl Host Committee (2015-2017) **Memberships:** Treasurer, Tau Beta Pi (1982-1983); Pi Tau Sigma; Phi Kappa Phi **Marquis Who's Who Honors:** Albert Nelson Marquis Lifetime Achievement Award; Marquis Who's Who Top Professional; Distinguished Humanitarian **Why did you become involved in your profession or industry:** Mr. Hill became involved in his profession because of his innate curiosity as to how things worked. Hailing from Wyoming, he was always around the oil and gas industry. It was a natural progression into the field. **Avocations:** Mountain climbing; Skiing; Fishing; Hunting; Investing **Political Affiliations:** Republican **Religion:** Roman Catholic

Julie Hill

Title: Member Outreach Manager, Board President **Industry:** Financial Services **Company Name:** Navy Federal Credit Union **Children:** Two Children **Education:** Bachelor of Arts in Finance, Strayer University, Virginia **Certifications:** Certified IRA Professional; Certified Trust Professional; Pre-purchase Home Buying Educator **Career:** Branch Manager, Navy Federal Credit Union, Vienna, VA (2012-Present); Member Outreach Manager, Navy Federal Credit Union, Vienna, VA (1998-Present); Supervisor Certificate, IRA & Trust, Navy Federal Credit Union, Vienna, VA (2012-2015); Branch Manager, Navy Federal Credit Union, Vienna, VA (2009-2012) **Civic:** Board Chair, Rebuilding Together Arlington/Fairfax/Falls Church, VA (2010-Present); Team Captain, Rebuilding Together Arlington/Fairfax/Falls Church (1999-Present); Military Affairs Council, Boys and Girls Club of America; Project Neighbor; Past PTA President; Committee Chair, Pack 1831 Boy Scouts of America; Volunteer, Kaboom Project; Snowball Express **Awards:** Fairfax Volunteer of the Year **Memberships:** Association of the United States Army **To what do you attribute your success:** Ms, Hill attributes her success to her love of people, as well as small acts of kindness, which can change much in the world. **Why did you become involved in your profession or industry:** Ms. Hill was attracted by the motto of "people helping people..." at credit unions. She felt that would be a good fit for her aspirations to help others and give back to the community by using her abilities.

Ronald Charles Hill, MD, FACS

Title: Surgeon, Educator **Industry:** Medicine & Health Care **Company Name:** VA Medical Center **Date of Birth:** 09/04/1948 **Place of Birth:** Parkersburg **State/Country of Origin:** WV/USA **Parents:** Lloyd E. Hill; Margaret (Pepper) Hill **Marital Status:** Married **Spouse Name:** Lenora Jane Hill (06/12/1971) **Children:** Jeffrey Fenton Hill; Mandy Lee Cook **Education:** Diplomate, American Board of Thoracic Surgery (1987); Diplomate, American Board of Surgery (1985); Chief Resident, General and Thoracic Surgery, Duke University Medical Center (1983-1984); Senior Resident, General and Thoracic Surgery, Duke University Medical Center (1979-1983); Resident, General and Thoracic Surgery, Duke University, Durham, NC (1974-1976); Surgical Intern, Duke University Medical Center, Durham, NC (1974-1975); MD, West Virginia University (1974); BA, West Virginia University (1970) **Certifications:** Certification in Health Insurance Portability and Accountability Training, University Health Alliance (2003); Certification in Research Ethics Training, National Institutes of Health (2002); Certification in Ethics Training, National Institutes of Health (2001); Certification in Human Participant Protection, National Institutes of Health (2001); Certification in Education for Research Teams, National Institutes of Health (2001); Certification in Conscious Sedation (1998); Oxygen Provider Course, Divers Alert Network (1998); Certified in Enriched Air (1998); Nitrox Certification (1998); Certified Master Scuba Diver, Professional Association of Diving Instructors (1997); Certified, Underwater Naturalist, Professional Association of Diving Instructors (1997); Certification in Night Diving (1997); Certified Equipment Specialist (1996); Certified in Boat Diving (1996); Certification in Advanced Cardiac Life Support, American Heart Association (1996); Certification in CPR, American Red Cross (1996); Certified Rescue Diver, Professional Association of Diving Instructors (1996); Certification in First-aid, American Red Cross (1996); Certification in Underwater Photography (1995) **Career:** Consultant, North Carolina Medical Board (2016-2018); Chief, Cardiothoracic Surgery, VA Medical Center, Asheville, NC (2009-2015); Consultant, Clinical Professor of Surgery, Duke University School of Medicine (2007-2015); Clinical Professor of Surgery, School of Osteopathic Medicine, West Virginia University (1999-2007); Professor of Surgery, West Virginia University, Morgantown, WV (1996-2007); Associate Professor, West Virginia University, Morgantown, WV (1990-1996); Attending Cardiothoracic Surgeon, Monongalia General Hospital, Morgantown, WV (1987-2007); Consultant, VA Medical Center, Clarksburg, WV (1985-2007); Assistant Professor of Surgery, West Virginia University, Morgantown, WV (1985-1990); Teaching Scholar, Duke University, Durham, NC (1984-1985); Research Associate, Duke University, Durham, NC (1976-1979) **Career Related:** Director, Thoracic Surgery Program for the Protection of Human Subjects, VA Medical Center (2005-2007); Program Director, VA Medical Center (1998-2003); Chairman, Institutional Review Board, VA Medical Center (1994-2004); Surgical Education and Self-assessment Programs, VA Medical Center, Washington, DC (1988-1990); Student Coordinator, Department of Surgery, West Virginia University (1986-1997); Director, Surgical Research, Department of Surgery, West Virginia University (1986-1988) **Civic:** Board Member, Homeowners Association, North Carolina Coast (2016-Present); President, Homeowners Association (2008-Present); Chairman, Council on Evangelism, Drummond Chapel, United Methodist Church, Morgantown, WV (1999-2001); Lay Delegate, Annual Conference, Drummond Chapel, United Methodist Church, Morgantown, WV (1995-1997) **Creative Works:** Contributor, Chapters, Books; Contributor, Articles, Professional Publications; Presenter in Field; Author, "Compressive Forces of Fibrillation in Normal Hearts During Maximal Coronary Dilation by Adenosine" **Awards:** Featured Listee, "Best Doctors in America" (2013-Present); Listee, "Guide to America's Top Surgeons" (2008-Present); Listee, "The State's Best Doctors," Business North Carolina (2012-2014); Listee, "Top Surgeons" (2009-2012); Listee, "America's Top Surgeons" (2008-2013); Distinguished Service Award for Leadership Excellence, West Virginia University (2005) **Memberships:** President, American College of Surgeons (2004-2005); First Vice President, American College of Surgeons (2003-2004); Second Vice President, American College of Surgeons (2002-2003); Fellow, American College of Surgeons; Chairman, District One, Committee on Applicants, American College of Surgeons; Fellow, Association for Academic Surgery; Fellow, Sabiston Society; Fellow, Southern Thoracic Surgical Association; Fellow, Society of Thoracic Surgeons; American Heart Association; Vice President, American Heart Association **Marquis Who's Who Honors:** Albert Nelson Marquis Lifetime Achievement Award; Marquis Who's Who Top Professional **To what do you attribute your success:** Dr. Hill attributes his success to all of the wonderful mentors with whom he has worked. **Why did you become involved in your profession or industry:** After his mother passed away, Dr. Hill was invited to observe a local surgeon at his practice. After witnessing the doctor work, Dr. Hill knew he wanted to pursue medicine. **Avocations:** Fishing; Photography; Scuba; Collecting shells **Political Affiliations:** Republican **Religion:** Methodist

Monay Francis Hill-Williams

Title: Nurse Practitioner **Industry:** Medicine & Health Care **Date of Birth:** 01/28/1958 **Place of Birth:** Brooklyn **State/Country of Origin:** NY/USA **Parents:** John Lyen; Elizabeth Turner Hill **Children:** Stephen Michael Williams **Education:** MSN, CRNP, University of Pennsylvania, Graduate School of Nursing (1996); BSN, University of Pennsylvania, School of Nursing (1980) **Certifications:** ACNP-BC **Career:** Nurse Practitioner, Cigna HealthSpring-Philadelphia, PA; Nurse Practitioner, Dr Jon Fisher, Internal Medicine & Medical Weight Loss Management, Philadelphia, PA; Clinical Nursing Instructor, Widener University, Chester, PA; Clinical Nursing Instructor, Villanova University, Villanova, PA; Nurse Practitioner Heartland, HCR Manorcare, Philadelphia, PA; Nurse Practitioner, Ingrid House, Philadelphia, PA; Nurse Practitioner, Clinical Nurse Instructor, Thomas Jefferson University Hospital, Philadelphia, PA; Nurse Practitioner, Graduate Hospital, Philadelphia, PA; Case Manager, Blue Cross Blue Shield, Philadelphia, PA; Nurse Manager, Veterans Administration Hospital, Philadelphia, PA; Clinical Level 4 Nurse, CCU Hospital University of Pennsylvania, Philadelphia, PA; Nurse, Skilled Nursing Inc., Philadelphia, PA; Weekend Nursing Supervisor, Lower Bucks Hospital, Philadelphia, PA; Clinical Level IV Staff Nurse, CCU, University Hospital of Pennsylvania, Philadelphia, PA; Nurse Manager, Our Lady of Lourdes, Camden, NJ; Advanced Staff Nurse, ICU/ CCU; Assistant Nurse Manager, CCU; Evening Nursing Administrator, Presbyterian Hospital, Philadelphia, PA; Charge Nurse, Adult/Pediatric Surgical Unit, St. Mary's Hospital, Philadelphia, PA; Staff Nurse, Hospital University Pennsylvania, Philadelphia, PA **Career Related:** Sigma Theta Tau Nursing Honor Society; Secondary School Admissions Committee, University of Pennsylvania; American Diabetes Association; National Kidney Foundation; American Bariatric Society **Civic:** MILLION Woman March; Health Information Station and First Aid Station, Philadelphia, PA; Health Fairs, Philadelphia, PA; Parent Chairman, School Governance Council, Philadelphia Public Schools, Powel Elementary School, Philadelphia, PA **Creative Works:** Three Part Series for Deborah Lee WURD Radio Show, Medical Conditions Related to Obesity, Philadelphia, PA **Awards:** Cigna HealthSpring Outstanding NP Award; Alumni Award, University of Pennsylvania; Who's Who Among Nursing Professionals; Who's Who Among High School Students **Memberships:** Sigma Theta Tau; International Nursing Honor Society Chi ETA Phi; Black Nursing Sorority; Prior Vice PResidentSoutheastern Pennsylvania Area Black Nurses Association; American Cancer Society; American Diabetes Association **Marquis Who's Who Honors:** Albert Nelson Marquis Lifetime Achievement Award **Why did you become involved in your profession or industry:** Ms. Hill-Williams became involved in her profession because, when she was a young girl, her mother was diagnosed with liver cancer and died very soon thereafter. She always had an interest in medicine as a child but when her mother died of liver cancer she felt called to pursue a career in nursing because they were the patients primary contact when they were in the hospital or home. She saw nurses as angels of mercy and they were of great comfort to her mom. **Avocations:** Crochet; Charcoal and pencil sketching; Papier-mâché; Music; Cooking; Gardening **Religion:** Christian

Leonard S. Hirsch

Title: Financial Services Company Executive, Financial Analyst **Industry:** Financial Services **Date of Birth:** 01/20/1932 **Place of Birth:** New York **State/Country of Origin:** NY/USA **Parents:** Henry Sam Hirsch; Anne (Schindelheim) Hirsch **Marital Status:** Married **Spouse Name:** Elaine Jean Felberbaum (09/12/1954) **Children:** Howard Steven; Herbert Gene **Education:** BS in Accounting, Syracuse University (1955) **Career:** Vice President, Neuberger Berman, New York, NY (1991-1993); Executive Vice President, General America Investors, New York, NY (1980-1991); Vice President, Lehman Brothers, New York, NY (1977-1980); Chief Financial Officer, Payless Drug Stores, Oakland, CA (1976-1977); Vice President, Reynolds Securities, New York, NY (1973-1976); Vice President, Laird & Company, New York, NY (1970-1973); Vice President, Burnham & Co., New York, NY (1967-1970); Assistant Vice President, Kuhn Loeb & Co., New York, NY (1965-1967); Senior Analyst, Lionel D Edie & Co., New York, NY (1961-1965); Senior Analyst, Chemical Bank, New York, NY (1959-1961); Junior Analyst, Marine Midland Bank, New York, NY (1955-1959) **Civic:** Board of Directors, Franklin Township Board of Education, Somerset County, New Jersey (1964-1970); President, Somerset County Board of Education (1967-1969); Volunteer, PBS Station, San Diego, CA; Midway Museum; Library in California **Military Service:** U.S. Army (1953-1955) **Marquis Who's Who Honors:** Albert Nelson Marquis Lifetime Achievement Award; Marquis Who's Who Top Professional **Why did you become involved in your profession or industry:** Mr. Hirsch got involved in his profession when he was working in the Trust Department of the U.S. Marine Corps. He became more interested in securities and went on to study economics. **Avocations:** Gardening; Running; Reading; Travel **Religion:** Jewish

Sheila Elizabeth Fleetwood Hoen

Title: Artist, Lawyer (Retired) **Industry:** Law and Legal Services **Date of Birth:** 02/08/1935 **Place of Birth:** Victoria **State/Country of Origin:** British Columbia/Canada **Parents:** William Leslie Hardie; Winnifred Mary (Thomas) Hardie **Marital Status:** Married **Spouse Name:** Ernst Leon Wilhelm B. Hoen **Children:** Liza; Margot; Zarah **Education:** Doctor of Jurisprudence, Oklahoma City University (1981); Master of Business Administration, California State University (1975); Bachelor of Arts, University of British Columbia (1957) **Career:** Artist (2001-Present); Realtor, Priscilla Murphy Realty (1997-2000); Private Practice (1997); Partner, Co-Manager, Workman & Hoen PA, Sanibel, FL (1991-1997); Partner, Consultant, Gooderham, Hoen & Associates, Fort Myers, FL (1986-1990); Vice President, Land, General Counsel, Hoen Exploration Co., Oklahoma City, OK (1983-1986); Law Clerk, Oil and Gas Attorney, Andrews, Davis, Legg, Bixler, Milsten & Price Inc., Oklahoma City, OK (1979-1983); Financial Analyst, Manager of Gas Contracts, Grace Petroleum Corporation, Oklahoma City, OK (1975-1978); Senior Petroleum Economist, Occidental Petroleum Corporation (1974-1975); Economic Analyst, Occidental Petroleum Corporation, Bakersfield, CA (1970-1973); Scout, Assistant to Exploration Manager, Occidental Libya Inc., Tripoli, Libya (1968-1969); Teacher, British School Tripoli, Tripoli, Libya (1968-1969); Teacher, South Peace High School, Dawson Creek, British Columbia, Canada (1958-1959); Biomedical Library, Royal Victoria Hospital, Montreal, Canada (1959-1960); Biomedical Library, University of British Columbia, Vancouver (1957-1958) **Creative Works:** Impressionist, Expressionist and Abstract Painting, with Acrylics (2001-Present) **Awards:** Best New Artist of the Year, Fort Myers (2007); Recipient, Equal Rights Amendment Award (1981); Recipient, American Jurisprudence Award (1980); Recipient, Bancroft-Whitney, Lawyer's Cooperative Publishing Company (1979); Recipient, Award, The American Association of University Women **Memberships:** President, Board Member, Zonta International (1987-Present); President, Vice Board of Directors, Old Schoolhouse Theater (1994-1997); Advanced Board, Lee County Parks and Recreation (1990-1995); Chairman, Captiva Erosion Prevention District (1986-1994); President, Concerned Citizens Captiva Inc., Captiva Island, FL (1985-1988); Commissioner, Edmond Arts and Humanities Council (1985-1986); Oklahoma Zoological Society, Oklahoma City, OK (1983-1985); Member, Women's Committee Symphony, Oklahoma City, OK (1983-1984); American Bar Association; Legislative Chairman, American Association of University Women; Federation of Canadian Artists; International Association of Energy Economists; Lee County Bar; International Bar Association; Florida Bar Association; Legislative Chairman, Women's Political Caucus; Edmond Chamber of Commerce; Phi Delta Phi; Tower Gallery; Salt Spring Gallery **Bar Admissions:** United States District Court for the Middle District of Florida (1991); Certified Mediator, Florida (1991); United States District Court for the Western District of Oklahoma (1981); Oklahoma (1981) **Marquis Who's Who Honors:** Albert Nelson Marquis Lifetime Achievement Award **To what do you attribute your success:** Ms. Hoen regards her third grade teacher, Gale Bennett, as a wonderful mentor. He taught her "what to paint, how to paint and why to paint." Valerie Metz, a friend and fellow artist based in Vancouver, was also a great mentor to her and encouraged her to begin painting and continue to evolve as an artist. **Why did you become involved in your profession or industry:** Ms. Hoen chose to have several different careers because she enjoys change and growth. She has enjoyed everything that she has done thus far. She is also involved in the issue of women's rights and, although it is challenging at times to prompt change, it is an issue that she finds important for women today and in the future. **Avocations:** Ballet; Piano playing; Choral singing;

Dr. Bonnie Leah Hofer

Title: Psychologist, Researcher, Author, Health Care Administrator **Industry:** Health, Wellness and Fitness **Company Name:** Hofer Institute **Place of Birth:** Battle Creek **State/Country of Origin:** MI/USA **Parents:** James (Deceased, 2012); Miriam Brown (Deceased, 2020) **Spouse Name:** John (07/31/2004) **Children:** Erika (1995); Brandon (2000) **Education:** Ed.D. Doctor of Education: Counseling Psychology, Pastoral Community Counseling, Research (Argosy University, Phoenix, AZ, 2017); Master of Science in Administration, Health Services Administration Specialization, Central Michigan University, Mt. Pleasant, MI (1999); BA in Communication Arts, Minor in Health Sciences, Oakland University, Rochester, MI (1990) **Certifications:** Certified Stephen Leader and Stephen Minister (2013); Pastoral Ordination (2007); Certified Physical Fitness Specialist (1986) **Career:** President, Hofer Institute (2017-Present); President, Hofer International Ministries (2007-2017); Associate Pastor, Heart of the Hills Church (2011-2014); Executive Director, Alterra Wynwood Continuing Care Assisted Living (2003-2006); Regional Director, Courtyard Manor Assisted Living Memory Care (1999-2001); Regional Director of Outpatient Services and Marketing Director, Pro Therapy of America, Birmingham, MI (1994-1996); Administrator, Sterling Physical Therapy and Rehabilitation, Warren, MI (1993-1994); Administrator, Total Therapy Management, Inc., Farmington Hills, MI (1992-1993); Program Director, Crittenton Hospital, Rochester (1990-1992); Manager, Counselor, Trim 4 Life Clinic, Sterling Heights, MI (1989-1990); TV/Video Producer, KDN Videoworks, Comcast Cable, Oakland University (1989-1990); Apprentice Teacher TV production, Oakland University, Rochester (1990); Professional Model (1984-1990);Instructor, lecturer, YMCA, Warren, MI (1986-1990) **Career Related:** Ordained Minister, (2007-Present) **Civic:** Vice President, Board of Directors, Alabaster Gift (2016-2019); Volunteer, American Red Cross **Creative Works:** Setting the Captives Free: Pastoral Perceptions of Human Trafficking in the United States (2017) **Awards:** Award of Excellence, Model of the Year, USA (1990); Recipient, Excellent Leadership Award, Health Occupation Students of America (1984); Community Service Appreciation Award, ARC/Martin Pl. Hospital (1984) **Memberships:** American Psychological Association; American Association of Christian Counselors; American Association of Pastoral Counselors **Marquis Who's Who Honors:** Albert Nelson Marquis Lifetime Achievement Award **Avocations:** Education, advocacy and social justice related to advancing the cause of women and children both domestically and abroad **Religion:** Christian

Axel Hoffer, MD

Title: Psychoanalyst **Industry:** Medicine & Health Care **Date of Birth:** 07/23/1936 **Place of Birth:** Gablonz **State/Country of Origin:** Czechoslovakia **Parents:** Otto; Elsa H **Marital Status:** Married **Spouse Name:** Anita Panenka **Children:** David; Daniel **Education:** Doctor of Medicine, Harvard University, Cum Laude (1961); Bachelor of Arts, Harvard University, Magna Cum Laude (1957); Student, Konrad Adenauer Fellow, University of Munich, Germany (1955-1956) **Certifications:** Diplomate, American Board Psychiatry and Neurology; Certificate, Adult Psychoanalysis **Career:** Private Practice Of Psychoanalysis & Psychotherapy, Boston, MA (1975-Present); Associate Clinical Professor, Harvard Medical School, Boston, MA (1996-2018); Director In-Patient Services, Massachusetts Mental Health Center, Boston, MA (1977-1978); Assistant Clinical Professor, Harvard Medical School, Boston, MA (1975-1996); Associate Director, Massachusetts Mental Health Center, Boston, MA (1975-1976); Assistant Clinical Director, Massachusetts Mental Health Center, Boston, MA (1968-1975); Clinical Associate, National Institute Of Mental Health, Bethesda, MD (1966-1968); Fellow in Child Psychiatry, Massachusetts Mental Health Center, Boston, MA (1964-1966); Resident in Psychiatry, Massachusetts Mental Health Center, Boston, MA (1962-1964); Medical Intern, Massachusetts General Hospital, Boston, MA (1961-1962) **Career Related:** Faculty, Training and Supervising Analyst, Psychoanalytic Institute, New England East, Boston Psychoanalytic Society and Institute; Faculty, Supervising Analyst, Massachusetts Institute Psychoanalysis **Military Service:** Lieutenant Commander US Public Health Service, 1966-68 **Creative Works:** Editor, "Freud and The Buddha, The Couch and The Cushion" (2015); Co-translator, "A Phylogenetic Fantasy," by Sigmund Freud (1987); Editorial Board, Journal of the American Psychoanalytic Association; Author, Introduction, "The Freud-Ferenczi Correspondence, Volume Two" **Awards:** Recipient, Prize from the Journal of the American Psychoanalytic Association (1984); Honorary Member, the Prague Psychoanalytic Society and Institute **Memberships:** Boston Psychoanalytic Society; Phi Beta Kappa; Alpha Omega Alpha **Marquis Who's Who Honors:** Albert Nelson Marquis Lifetime Achievement Award; Marquis Who's Who Top Professional; Marquis Who's Who Humanitarian Award **Why did you become involved in your profession or industry:** Dr. Hoffer became involved in his profession after having drawn inspiration from Dr. John Speigel, a psychoanalyst. **Avocations:** Skiing; Hiking

James Simon Hoffman

Title: Engineering Educator (Retired) **Industry:** Education/Educational Services **Date of Birth:** 04/02/1933 **Place of Birth:** St. Paul **State/Country of Origin:** MN/USA **Parents:** Simon; Agnes (Lammers) Hoffman **Marital Status:** Married **Spouse Name:** Marilyn A. Zink (06/17/1955) **Children:** Stephen J.; Gregg A.; Ann Marie; Paul D. **Education:** BCE, North Dakota State University (1955) **Career:** Retired (1991); Senior Instructor, IBM (1974-1991); Marketing Representative, IBM, Chicago, IL (1972-1974); Systems Engineer, IBM, Austin, TX (1967-1972); Director of Data Processing, Iowa State Highway Commission (1960-1967); Programmer, Iowa State Highway Commission (1958-1960); Engineer, Iowa State Highway Commission (1955-1958) **Civic:** Volunteer, Boy Scouts of America (1964-Present) **Military Service:** Captain, U.S. Army (1955-1964) **Memberships:** Grand Knight, Knights of Columbus (1966-1967); The Tau Beta Pi Association, Inc.; The Honor Society of Phi Kappa Phi **Marquis Who's Who Honors:** Albert Nelson Marquis Lifetime Achievement Award **Why did you become involved in your profession or industry:** Mr. Hoffman became involved in his profession because of a professor at North Dakota State University. **Avocations:** Woodcarving; Taking photographs **Religion:** Roman Catholic

Carol Jane Rowland Hogue, PhD

Title: Professor Emerita of Epidemiology **Industry:** Research **Company Name:** Emory University **Date of Birth:** 12/11/1945 **Place of Birth:** Springfield **State/Country of Origin:** MO/USA **Parents:** Perry Albright Rowland; Lois Virginia (Spencer) Rowland **Marital Status:** Married **Spouse Name:** L. Lynn Hogue (05/28/1966) **Children:** Marianna Elizabeth Rowland Hogue Outerbridge **Education:** PhD in Epidemiology, University of North Carolina at Chapel Hill (1973); MPH, University of North Carolina at Chapel Hill (1971); AB in Sociology, William Jewell College, Liberty, MO, Summa Cum Laude (1966) **Career:** Retired (2019); Jules & Uldeen Terry Professor of Maternal and Child Health and Professor of Epidemiology, Rollins School of Public Health, Emory University, Atlanta, GA (1992-2019); Director, Div. of Reproductive Health, Centers for Disease Control and Prevention, Atlanta, GA (1988-1992); Chief, Pregnancy Epidemiology Branch, CDC (1983-1988); Visiting Scientist, CDC (1982-1983); Associate Professor, Division of Biometry, University of Arkansas for Medical Sciences, Little Rock, AR (1977-1982); Assistant Professor, Department of Biostatistics, University of North Carolina at Chapel Hill (1974-1977) **Career Related:** Reproductive Committee on the Quality and Safety of Abortion Services, National Academy of Medicine (2017-2018); Science and Technology Advisory Group, World Health Organization (1998-2000); Chair, Regional Advisory Panel, Human Reproduction Program, World Health Organization (1997-2000); Committee on Unintended Pregnancy, Institute of Medicine (1994-1996); Regional Advisory Panel, Human Reproduction Program, World Health Organization (1991-2000); Fellow, Environmental Health Institute, Pittsfield, MA (1990-1997); Consultant, United States Environmental Protection Agency, Washington, DC (1980-1981); Consultant, Food and Drug Administration, Washington, DC (1978-1980) **Civic:** NAACP (2013-Present); Center for Scientific Review, Infectious Diseases, Reproductive Health, Asthma, and Pulmonary Conditions Study Section, National Institutes of Health (2012-2016); Special Emphasis Panel, Car for Scientific Review, Health of the Population, NIH (2008); Special Emphasis Panel, Global Network for Women's and Children's Health, National Institute of Child Health and Human Development, NIH (2006); Ad How Review Committee on Fetal Effects on Adult Chronic Diseases, NIH (2001); Community Council, Junior League of Atlanta, (2000-2009); Subcommittee on Clinic Investigators, Peer Review Oversight Group, NIH (1997-1998); Membership Committee, American College of Epidemiology (1996-2000); Environmental Health Study Section, National Institute of Environmental Health Sciences (1993-1997); National Prenatal Health Promotion Committee, March of Dimes, White Plains, NY (1990-1993); Priority One Advisory Council, Kiwanis International (1990-1991); Epidemiology and Disease Control Study Section, NIH (1982-1986) **Creative Works:** Contributor, Articles, Professional Journals; Contributor, Chapters, Books **Awards:** Eponym, Carol J. Rowland Hogue Award for Outstanding Mid-Career Achievement (2019); Jefferson Award for Career Dedicated to Healthier Families, Emory University, Atlanta, GA (2017) **Memberships:** President-elect, President, and Past President, American College of Epidemiology (2001-2003); Board of Directors, American College of Epidemiology (1999-2004); Chair, MCH Council, Association of Schools of Public Health (1999-2001); Association of Teachers of Maternal and Child Health (1992); President-elect, President, and Past President, Society for Epidemiological Research (1987-1990); Elected Fellow, American Epidemiological Society (1983); Planned Parenthood Federation of America (1984); Population Association of America (1979); Executive Committee, Society for Epidemiological Research (1978-1981); Program Chair, Population Section, American Public Health Association (1974-1978); International Epidemiological Association (1977); Theta Chapter, Delta Omega (1975) **Marquis Who's Who Honors:** Albert Nelson Marquis Lifetime Achievement Award **To what do you attribute your success:** Dr. Hague attributes her success to standing on the shoulders of giants. **Why did you become involved in your profession or industry:** Dr. Hague became involved in her industry because of her interest in decreasing the amount of unwanted pregnancies by ensuring that couples have the pregnancies they want and when they want them, and that they are healthy in the outcome. In 1962, Dr. Hague was first introduced to the complex and important issues of population growth. She has since dedicated her career to learning about how to help couples achieve their desired family size, while maximizing health, by practicing family planning. **Avocations:** Hiking; Gardening; Reading **Religion:** Episcopalian **Thoughts on Life:** To achieve health for all, we must free ourselves of white supremacy.

Kris Holden

Title: Managing Broker/Marketing Executive **Industry:** Real Estate **Company Name:** Windermere Real Estate **Parents:** Donovan; Genevieve **Marital Status:** Divorced **Children:** Jeremy Russell; Saira (Daughter-in-law) **Career:** Managing Broker/Marketing Executive, Kris Holden/Windermere Real Estate (1992-Present); Real Estate Agent, The Heller Company, Realtors (The Heller Organization) (1989-1992); Real Estate Agent, John L. Scott Real Estate (1986-1989); Real Estate Broker, Re/MAX, LLC (1985-1986); Company Owner, LPO, Escrow and Mortgage Company, Shelter Mortgage Company, L.L.C. (1978-1985) **Career Related:** Owner, No Fear **Civic:** Fundraiser, Volunteer, Former Board Member, Pediatric Interim Care Center **Awards:** Five Star Professional Award (2006-Present); Northwest MLS Community Service Award, NWMLS **Memberships:** Northwest MLS (NWMLS); National Association of Realtors; Representative, Standards of Practice **To what do you attribute your success:** Ms. Holden attributes her success to hard work. Where there is a will, there is a way, and she has a lot of will. She is very resourceful and very social; she loves people. **Why did you become involved in your profession or industry:** Ms. Holden wanted to go to law school, but when she graduated high school she was tired of going to school; she just wanted to work. That is where she found her sense of accomplishment and joy. She decided to work for a year before going to school. She started working for a title insurance company. While there, she got promoted. One day a real estate closing attorney came in and said, "I want you to come and interview with me." He hired her and she learned that business. By the age of 19, she opened her own escrow company called No Fear. She never went to college, choosing to grow that business. She later joined forces with her biggest competitor, and later opened a branch of a mortgage company in Seattle. She really worked her tail off. She learned to be resourceful, and at 19, she didn't know everything but knew how to pick up the phone to get help. In addition, she does not like the word "no" and she was taught early on by her business banker that you never take "no" as an answer from the person who does not have the authority to say "yes." So, she learned to hang up, dial again, and get the next customer service person until she got to the person who said, "yes." **Thoughts on Life:** Ms. Holden lives by the motto, "Be kind and do what you say you're going to do and then some."

Harold Douglas Holder Sr.

Title: International Entrepreneur **Date of Birth:** 06/25/1931 **Place of Birth:** Anniston **State/Country of Origin:** Alabama/USA **Parents:** William Chester; Lucile (Kadle) H **Marital Status:** Divorced **Children:** Debra Holder Carnaroli; Harold Douglas Junior; Charlie Kadle **Education:** PhD in Economics, Richmonds University (2005); Student, Druitt School Speech (1962); Student, Jacksonville State University (1954-1957); Student, Anniston Business College (1949); Student, Advanced Executive Management, Harvard University; Masters in Merchandising and Marketing, Sears Staff School **Career:** Managing Director, The Holder Group, Incorporated (1987-Present); Chairman of the Board, Chief Executive Officer, Director, American Agronomics Corporation (1973-1986); President, Board of Directors, Rahall Communications Corporation (1971-1973); Vice President, Interstate Stores (1971); President, Board of Directors, Cunningham Drug Stores, Incorporated, Detroit, MI (1969-1970); Sales Promotion Manager, Southern Area, Sears, Roebuck & Company, Atlanta, GA (1968); Assistant General Manager, Merchandise, Sears, Roebuck & Company, Atlanta, GA (1968-1969); Operations Zone Manager, Sears, Roebuck & Company, Atlanta, GA (1967-1968); Store Manager, Sears, Roebuck & Company, Ocala, FL (1963-1965); Store Manager, Sears, Roebuck & Company, Cocoa, FL (1965-1967); Assistant Personnel Director, Sears, Roebuck & Company, Atlanta, GA (1962-1963); Director, Executive Development Program, Sears, Roebuck & Company, Atlanta, GA (1961); Director, College Recruiting, Sears, Roebuck & Company, Atlanta (1959-1961); Merchandising Manager, Sears, Roebuck & Company, Atlanta (1957-1959); Department Manager, Sears, Roebuck & Company, Anniston, AL (1954-1957); President, Harold Holder Leasing **Career Related:** CEO, Casino Management Services International (1999-2014); Stockmen's Hotel & Casino, Red Garter Hotel & Casino, Commercial Hotel & Casino, Scoreboard Sports Lounge, The Holder Group Wigwam, LLC (2005); Charlie Holder's Casino (2003-2007); CEO, Board of Directors, Cutler Manufacturing Corp., (1989-2000); Board of Directors, Treasurer, Dome Products, Inc., (1989-2000); Atlas Aircraft Corp. (1987-2000); Member, Executive Committee, Board of Directors, Coastland Corporation, FL (1979-1984); President, Board of Directors, Golden Harvest, Inc., (1976-1988); Guest Speaker, Lecturer, Ad Hoc Professor, Georgia State University, Emory University, Auburn University, University of North Carolina, University of South Florida, Harvard Business School, Young President University, among others; Speaker, National Association of Black Newspaper Publishers, National Association of Women in Radio and Television, USMC Leadership Conferences, USCG, US Army, Merchant Marine, USN; Chairman, CEO, The Holder Hospitality Group, Incorporated; CEO, Silver Club Hotel & Casino; CEO, El Capital Resort Casino; CEO, Sharkey's Nugget Casino; CEO, Sundance Casino; Model "T" Resort Casino; Fernley Truck-Inn and Casino, Joe's Tavern chairman New Dawn Resorts, Limited, Accra, Ghana chairman The Holder Group Vending Company **Civic:** Trustee, Nevada Museum of Art (2005-2011); Board Directors, United Way Hillsborough County, FL (1966); Chairman, Board Directors Miracle, Incorporated, Brevard County Chairman United Appeal, Ocala, FL (1964) Cocoa, FL; Chairman, Heart Fund Drive, Ocala, FL (1964); Chairman, Board of Trustees, Trustee Emeritus, Eckerd College; Member, Board of Directors, Southern College Placement Association; American Academy Achievement Board of directors, Marion chapter, American Red Cross, Opera Arts Association; Executive Committee Share, University of Florida; Marion (Florida) Committee of 100; Board of Trustee, University of Tampa; **Military Service:** US Marines, 1950-1953, reserves, 1953-1957 **Creative Works:** Author, "Please Leaves The Lights On" (2011); Author, "Don't Shoot, I'm Only a Trainee" (1975); Subject, "Turnaround Artist," Harvard Business School Case Study (1974) **Awards:** Nevada Entrepreneur of the Year (2009); Patriotic Employer Award, US Department Defense (2005); Named, Nevada Hotelier of the Year (2004); USMC Marine Honoree for the Year (2003); Employer of the Year Award, Nevada Disabled American Veterans Large (2003); Humanitarian Award, Florida National Association for the Advancement of Colored People (1984); Golden Plate Award (1983); Champion of Higher Education Award (1982); Distinguished Service Award, Marion County 4-H Club (1965); Harold D. Holder Chair of International Business and Finance, Eckerd College; Employer of Year Award, Nevada Disabled Veterans Large; Commandant USMC Quality Citizen Recognition Award; Secretary of the Army Freedom Team Salute Award **Memberships:** Past Chairman, Young President Organization, Florida Chapter; Chairman, Beautification Committee, Retail Business Committee, Chamber of Commerce; Chief Executives Forum; Omicron Delta Kappa **Marquis Who's Who Honors:** Albert Nelson Marquis Lifetime Achievement Award; Marquis Who's Who Top Professional **Religion:** Episcopalian

Henry Holmes, Esq.

Title: Attorney **Industry:** Law and Legal Services **Company Name:** Holmes Weinberg **Date of Birth:** 04/01/1943 **Place of Birth:** Malden **State/Country of Origin:** MA/USA **Parents:** Henry W. Holmes; Sue Cerullo Holmes **Marital Status:** Married **Spouse Name:** Lori Ann Holmes (1996) **Children:** Benjamin Holmes **Education:** JD, UC Berkeley School of Law (1969); BA, San Diego State University, San Diego, CA (1966); Coursework, University of California, Berkeley **Career:** Co-Founder, Name Partner, Holmes Weinberg, Malibu, CA (2008-Present); Sports and Entertainment Lawyer, Greenberg Traurig, LLP, Santa Monica, CA (2002-2008); Sports and Entertainment Lawyer, Weissmann, Wolff, Bergman, Coleman, Silverman & Holmes LLP, Beverly Hills, CA (1994-2002); Counsel, Cooper, Epstein & Hurewitz, Beverly Hills, CA (1984-1994); Partner, Butler, Davidson & Holmes, Beverly Hills, CA (1979-1984); Principal, Schiff, Hirsch & Schreiber, Beverly Hills, CA (1978-1979); Lawyer, Pacht, Ross, Warne, Bernhard & Sears, Los Angeles, CA (1972-1978); General Counsel, Science Fiction and Fantasy Writers of America, Inc. **Career Related:** Fellow, Ford Foundation, New Delhi, India, University of Southern California Gould School of Law (1969-1970); Speaker in the Field; Lecturer in Sports Law and Entertainment, UCLA; Adjunct Professor of Sports Law, Pepperdine University School of Law; Speaker and Lecturer on Sports and Entertainment Law; Representation, Talent and Athletes **Civic:** Board of Directors, Ranola Oil (2018-Present); Trustee, Women's Sports Foundation, New York, NY (1984-1997); Board of Directors, California Wildlife Center; Board of Advisers, Optimist Youth Programs; Member, California Police Activities League; Volunteer Member, Marine Mammals Rescue Team; The Innocence Project **Creative Works:** Author, "Motion Picture Copyright, State Bar of Wisconsin Journal"; Author, "The Indian President: Myth or Reality"; Author, "The 1969 Indian Law Journal"; Author, "The Rules of Civil Procedure for the High Court of American Samoa"; Contributor, Articles, Various Professional Journals; Editor, Autobiographies of Billie Jean King, George Foreman, and Hulk Hogan **Awards:** Named, Southern California Super Lawyers (2005); Named, One of the Top 20 Sports Lawyers, Daily Journal (1993); Recipient, Ford Foundation Berkeley Professional Studies Fellowship, Indian Law Institute, New Delhi, India (1969); Recipient, Preeminent A/V Rating, Martindale-Hubble; Named, American Registry Professional; Named, International Advisory Expert; International Who's Who of Entertainment and Sports Lawyers (2015); Super Lawyer (2013, 2005-2009); Listed, Who's Who in American Law, Who's Who in California, Who's Who in American Business **Memberships:** Screen Actors Guild (Now SAG-AFTRA); Beverly Hills Bar Association; Los Angeles Bar Association; California Bar Association; American Samoa Bar Association; Explorers Club; Malibu Film Society **Bar Admissions:** California (1970); U.S. District Court for the Central District of California (1970); U.S. Court of Appeals for the Ninth Circuit (1970); American Samoa Bar Association **Marquis Who's Who Honors:** Albert Nelson Marquis Lifetime Achievement Award; Marquis Who's Who Top Professional; Marquis Who's Who Humanitarian Award **To what do you attribute your success:** Mr. Holmes attributes his success to the power of "No" and not being afraid to say it. **Why did you become involved in your profession or industry:** Mr. Holmes became involved in his profession because he used to push carts at a supermarket, the owner of which was a dynamic and tough lawyer. This inspired him to attend law school. He was also a supporter of the civil rights movement. **Avocations:** Surfing; Acting; Appreciating art; Scuba diving **Political Affiliations:** Democrat **Religion:** Roman Catholic **Thoughts on Life:** Mr. Holmes' son plays football and works with inner city kids get through a lot of the negatives in their lives with athletics.

Stephen Paul Holowenzak, PhD, PFA, PFN, PGK

Title: Professor Emeritus **Industry:** Education/Educational Services **Company Name:** University of Maryland Global Campus (UMGC) **Date of Birth:** 11/30/1944 **Place of Birth:** Newark **State/Country of Origin:** NJ/USA **Parents:** Stephen Holowenzak; Helen Holowenzak **Marital Status:** Single **Children:** Amy Katherine Holowenzak **Education:** PhD in Educational Psychology, Statistics, Measurement, Catholic University of America (1974); MA in Counseling, Guidance, Personnel Management, The Catholic University of America (1971); BA in Philosophy and English, Mount St. Paul College, Waukesha, WI (1967) **Career:** Honorary Professor Emeritus, University of Maryland Global Campus (UMGC) (Formerly University of Maryland University College (UMUC)), Adelphi, MD (2010-Present); Collegiate Professor, University of Maryland Global Campus (UMGC), Adelphi, MD. USA, Europe, Middle East, Asia (1989-2010); Adjunct Professor of Psychology, University of Maryland Global Campus (UMGC), Adelphi, MD (2006-2010); Senior Program Manager, Faculty Services and Communication, University of Maryland Global Campus (UMGC), Adelphi, MD (2006-2010); Academic Director, Education-Student Teaching Services, University of Maryland Global Campus (UMGC), Adelphi, MD, Asia, Tokyo, Japan (1998-2006); Member, Candidate Selection Committee, Fulbright Program, Japan-U.S. Education Committee, Tokyo, Japan (2000-2001); Distance Educator, Lecturer, Computer Studies and Mathematics (1988-2006, 1984-1985), UMGC, Adelphi, MD. USA, Europe, Middle East, Asia); Senior Trainer/Evaluator, Ford Aerospace Corporation, Hanover, MD (1985-1988); Health Computer Education Coordinator, University of Maryland, Baltimore, Health Professional Schools, Cumberland Area Health Education Center, Cumberland, MD (1983-1984) **Career Related:** Humanitarian; Patriot; Industry Leader; Scholar **Civic:** Global Volunteer, God and Country (USA) When and Where Needed (1989-2006) **Military Service:** U.S. Army; U.S. Air Force; U.S. Navy; U.S. Marine Corps; Operation Desert Shield and Desert Storm; Operation Provide Comfort; Operation Northern Watch; Multi-National Force & Observers; IFOR; Operation Joint Endeavor **Creative Works:** Featured, "The Achiever," University of Maryland University College, Numerous Editions (2019, 2015, 2014, 2012, 2009, 1996, 1989); Featured, "Over There: The Adventures of Maryland's Traveling Faculty," 70th Anniversary 1947-2017, Documentary, Maryland Public Television, University System of Maryland (2018); Editor, the Patriot (2016-2017); Editor, Archangel Calling (2010-2015); Featured, "A Maryland State of Mind Special: Bullets, Books and Bosnia," Documentary by Maryland Public Television, University System of Maryland (1996); Principal Author, "9/11: We Will Never Forget"; Principal Author, "Stars and Stripes Forever"; Author, Co-Author, Contributor, Articles, Professional Journals and Books **Awards:** Knights of Columbus Star Assembly Award (2017); Sir Knight of the Year Patriotism Award, Master 4th Degree, Archdiocese of Washington District (2017); Grand Knight, Dr. Holowenzak (2014-2015); Commitment and Dedicated Service Award, 20 +Years to Military Services Globally, University of Maryland Global Campus (UMUC) (2009); Numerous Awards "for works and contributions to God and Country," US Army, US Air Force, US Navy (1992-2006); Numerous Program Awards for Excellence "for works by St. Michael the Archangel Council 15084 to Church, Council, Family, Community, Culture of Life, and Youth Services" Maryland State Council; University of Maryland Global Campus (UMUC) Operation Appreciation, Walter Reed Army Medical Center Malone House, Washington, DC **Memberships:** Franciscan Monastery of the Holy Land in America (2016-Present); Knights of Columbus Fourth Degree Assembly 386, New Haven, CT (1987-Present); Assembly 386 Member, Knights of Columbus Fourth Degree Cardinal O' Boyle (2010-2020); Member, Knights of Columbus Council 15084 (2010-2020); Faithful Admiral, Knights of Columbus Fourth Degree Cardinal O' Boyle (2017-2018); Faithful Navigator, Chief Executive Officer, Knights of Columbus (2016-2017); Grand Knight, Chief Executive Officer, Knights of Columbus (2014-2015); Apostleship of the Sea, Ministry, Archdiocese of Baltimore, MD (2012-2015); Legacy Member, Overseas Marylanders Association (OMA) **Marquis Who's Who Honors:** Albert Nelson Marquis Lifetime Achievement Award; Marquis Who's Who Humanitarian Award **To what do you attribute your success:** Dr. Holowenzak attributes his success to being an American citizen and being blessed with precious parents, Stephen and Helen, a loving sister, Phyllis, and a loving daughter, Amy. He is grateful for his own education both public and Catholic schools and institutions of higher education. He is thankful to the teachers, mentors, professionals and clergy who helped form his way in life to serve God, family, and America. **Why did you become involved in your profession or industry:** Dr. Holowenzak became involved in his profession because he wanted to serve God and country by educating active duty military members and help them to advance America's democratic society. **Religion:** Roman Catholic **Thoughts on Life:** Throughout his life, Dr. Holowenzak has aimed to serve God, America, and others in the best ways possible in the time he has and to give thanks to Him for the life He provided.

William James Hoops

Title: Clergyman **Industry:** Religious **Date of Birth:** 6/10/1957 **Place of Birth:** Welch **State/Country of Origin:** OK/USA **Parents:** Paul Raymond Hoops; Bertha Lue (Stillwell) Hoops **Marital Status:** Married **Spouse Name:** Susan Denise Towers (05/12/1983) **Children:** Robert Paul **Education:** MDiv, Golden Gate Seminary (1987); BA, Oklahoma Baptist University (1983) **Certifications:** Ordained to Ministry, Southern Baptist Church (1987) **Career:** Communications Coordinator (Amateur Radio) Disaster Relief, Southern Baptist Convention Of Pennsylvania/South Jersey (2005-Present); Chaplaincy Coordinator Disaster Relief, Southern Baptist Convention Of Pennsylvania/South Jersey (2005-Present); Institutional Minister, Federal Correctional Institution, Allenwood, PA (1999-2012); Chaplain, U.S. Air Force Reserve, Willow Grove Air Reserve Station (1999-2005); Chaplain, U.S. Air Force Reserve, March Air Force Base, California (1998-1999); Institutional Minister, Intensive Confinement Center, Lompoc, CA (1996-1999); Institutional Minister, Federal Bureau Prisons, Federal Correctional Institution, Lompoc, CA (1991-1999); Chaplain, U.S. Air Force Reserve, Travis Air Force Base, California (1993-1998); Chaplain, U.S. Air Force Reserve, Mather Air Force Base, California (1984-1993); Pastor, First Baptist Church, Marina, CA (1987-1991); Ministerial Intern, First Baptist Church, Concord, CA (1984-1987); Chaplain Assistant, U.S. Air Force Reserve, Tinker Air Force Base, Oklahoma (1979-1984); Chaplain Assistant, U.S. Air Force Reserve, Kirkland Air Force Base, New Mexico (1976-1979); Chaplain Assistant, U.S. Air Force Reserve, Lowery Air Force Base, Colorado (1975-1976) **Civic:** President, Pennsylvania/South Jersey Campers on Mission, Vice President, Pennsylvania Racing Outreach (2000-2002); Bible Teacher, First Southern Baptist Church, Lompoc, CA (1991-1999) **Military Service:** Retired Major, U.S. Air Force Reserve (2005) **Creative Works:** Producer, "Insights" (1986-1987) **Memberships:** Secretary, Milton Amateur Radio Club (2006-Present); President, Pennsylvania/South Jersey Campers on Mission (2001-Present); Vice President, California Campers on Mission (1998-1999); President, California Campers on Mission (1995-1998); Secretary, Lompoc Federal Correctional Institution Employees Club (1991-1992); Director of Evangelism, Central Coast Baptist Association (1988-1991); Revival Steering Committee, California Southern Baptist Convention (1988-1990); President, Central Coast Ministerial Alliance (1988-1989); Vice Moderator, Central Coast Baptist Association (1987-1988); Pacific Coast Baptist Association; Reserve Officers Association; Air Force Association; American Radio Relay League **Marquis Who's Who Honors:** Albert Nelson Marquis Lifetime Achievement Award; Marquis Who's Who Humanitarian Award **Why did you become involved in your profession or industry:** Mr. Hoops became involved in his profession because he believed that's what God was calling him to do. He wanted to get into the parts of ministry where he could help people. He became a chaplain and went all over the country including the federal prisons. His calling was not to run a church, but go where he could help people. He was inspired to go into the Air Force as a chaplain because it was outside the four walls of a church, where he could help people individually in disasters within the military. **Avocations:** Camping; Amateur radio **Religion:** Southern Baptist

Katherine Lacy Hoover

Title: Composer **Industry:** Media & Entertainment **Date of Birth:** 12/02/1937 **Place of Birth:** Elkins **State/Country of Origin:** VA/USA **Parents:** Samuel Randolph Hoover; Katherine (Lacy) Fletcher Hoover **Marital Status:** Married **Spouse Name:** Richard V. Goodwin (5/18/1985); J. Christopher Schwab (7/14/1964, Divorced 8/1972) **Children:** Norman Daniel Schwab **Education:** Coursework, Conductors Institute, Columbia, SC (1989-1991); MusM in Theory, Manhattan School of Music, New York (1974); Private Student, William Concave (1960-1961); MusB in Theory, Eastman School of Music, Rochester, NY (1959) **Career:** Composer (1975-2018); Theory, Composition Lessons, Teachers College, University of Columbia, New York (1984-1989); Freelance Flutist, New York, NY (1962-1985); Teacher, Theory, Manhattan School of Music, New York (1969-1984); Teacher, Flute, The Julliard School Preparatory, New York (1962-1969) **Career Related:** Distributor, Papagena Press, Theodore Presser Company (2007-2018); Partner, Papagena Press, New York (1989-2018); Originator, Director, Festivals of Women's Music, I-IV, New York (1978-1981); Guest Lecturer in Field **Creative Works:** Composer, "Requiem for the Innocent" (2016); Composer, Flute, "Four Winds" (2016); Author, Book of Poetry, "This Way About" (2015); Composer, Flute, "Spirit Flight" (2014); Composer, Flute, "To Greet the Sun" (2005); Composer, Cello, Piano, "String Quartet II" (2004); Composer, Cello, Piano, "El Andalus" (2003); Composer, Chamber, "String Quartet, Op. 58" (1999); Composer, Solo Instrumental, "Winter Spirits" (1997); Composer, Choral Music, Incantations, "Psalm 100" (1997); Composer, Solo Voice, Instruments, "The Heart Speaks" (1997); Composer, Solo Instrumental, "Stitch-Te Naku" (1996); Composer, Orchestral Composition, "Stitch-Te Naku" (1996); Composer, Solo Voice, Instruments, "Central American Songs" (1995); Composer, Composition, "Night Skies" (1994); Composer, Chamber, "Sonata, Op. 44" (1991); Composer, Solo Instrumental, "Kokopeli" (1990); Composer, Orchestral Composition, "Double Concerto, Op. 40" (1989); Composer, Orchestral Composition, "Two Sketches, Op. 42" (1989); Composer, Composition, "Quintet (Da Pacem)" (1989); Composer, Chamber, "Lyric Trio, Op. 27" (1987); Composer, Orchestral Composition, "Clarinet Concerto, Op. 38" (1987); Composer, Choral Music, "Echo" (1986); Composer, Composition, "Eleni: A Greek Tragedy" (1986); Composer, Orchestral Composition, "Summer Night, Op. 34" (1985); Composer, Composition, "Medieval Suite" (1984); Composer, Choral Music, "The Last Invocation" (1984); Composer, Solo Voice, Instruments, "Testament of Francois Villon" (1982); Composer, Solo Instrumental, "Set for Clarinet" (1978); Composer, Chamber, "Trio, Op. 14" (1978); Composer, Solo Instrumental, Various Piano Pieces (1977-1982) **Awards:** Multiple Awards, American Society of Composers (1979-2018); Lifetime Achievement Award, National Flute Association (2016); Newly Published Music, National Flute Association (2012); Newly Published Music, National Flute Association (1987-2001); Meet the Composer (1976-1994); Composition, American Academy of Arts and Letters, New York (1994); New Jersey Chamber Music Society (1991); Duologue (1991); Vinland Ensemble (1991); Composer of the Year, New York Music Teachers Association (1989); Grantee, Alice M. Ditson Fund (1984); Composers Fellowship, National Endowment for Arts, Washington (1979) **Memberships:** Board of Directors, National Flute Association (2000-2002); American Society of Composers; International Alliance of Women in Music; Bohemians; National Flute Association; Conductors Guild; American Music Center; Board Member, New York Women Composers **Marquis Who's Who Honors:** Albert Nelson Marquis Lifetime Achievement Award **Why did you become involved in your profession or industry:** Mrs. Hoover first heard Mozart when she was three years old; she was struck by the beauty of the music. She never forgot it. At five years old, she began taking piano lessons and she kept it up until high school, where her love of music blossomed further. She won an honor student with the National Honor Society; at that point in time, Mrs. Hoover was one of the 500 smartest students in the country. Though they initially held doubts, her parents eventually saw her musical talent and began to support her. However, her family couldn't afford to send her to an expensive music school, so she went to the University of Rochester and found a good music teacher with whom to work. After two years there, she transferred to a music school. Mrs. Hoover recalls walking down the hallway and hearing someone whistle Beethoven in tune; it was then that she knew she was home. **Avocations:** iUniverse (2015); Writing; Travel

Carol Sessoms Hopkins, Pastor

Title: Evangelist **Industry:** Religious **Company Name:** Soul's Saver and Worship Ministries International, Inc. **Date of Birth:** 03/15/1945 **Place of Birth:** Norfolk **State/Country of Origin:** VA/USA **Parents:** Russell Sessoms; Colona Rebecca Yeoman Sessoms **Marital Status:** Widowed **Spouse Name:** Joseph Hopkins Jr. (12/08/1941, Deceased) **Children:** Dwayne J. Wooley; David F. Wooley; Jerry Mahshan; Pierre Perrault; Terrence Johnson; Tamani T. Wooley **Education:** Bachelor's in Bible Studies, Insidious Bible College, Cleveland, MS **Certifications:** Ordained Pastor, Licensed Pastor, Temple United Church, Inc., State of Delaware (2004); Independent Pastor (2004); Licensed Local Pastor, United Methodist Church (1991) **Career:** Founder, Pastor, Victory In Grace Tabernacle, Inc. (2004-Present); Founder, President, Soul's Saver and Worship Ministries International, Inc. (1996-Present); Pastor, New Zion United Methodist Church (New Zion UMC), Laurel, DE (2001-2004); Pastor, Rock Hall-Fairlee Charge United Methodist Church (1993-2001); Pastor, Cokesbury United Methodist Church (Cokesbury UMC), Port Deposit, MD (1992-1993); Staff Assistant, Principals' Academy, University of Delaware (1992-1993); Executive Secretary to Dean, College of Marine Studies, University of Delaware (1989-1991); Executive Secretary, Center on the Study of Marine Policy, University of Delaware (1982-1989); Secretary, Institute Energy Conversion, University of Delaware (1978-1983); Secretary, Dean of Students, Office of the University of Delaware, Newark, DE (1972-1978); Secretary, Matsushita Electric Co. (Panasonic Corporation) (1968-1971); Secretary, NAACP (1964-1968); Secretary, Paul S. Gareen, Esquire, New York, NY (1963-1964) **Career Related:** Chaplain, Nanticoke Memorial Hospital, Seaford, DE (2002-Present); Director of Pastoral Care, Kent and Queen Anne Hospital, Chestertown, MD (1994-2001) **Civic:** Board Director, The Lord Servants Christian Help Ministries, Hurlock, MD (1996-Present); Member, Laurel Ministerial Association, Laurel, DE (2003); Member, Citizens Against Tobacco Smoke, Kent County Health Department, MD (1996-2001); Member, Ethics Committee, Kent County Hospice Foundation, Chestertown, MD (1996-2001); Village Crier, Speaker's Bureau Office of Prevention, State of Delaware, Dover, DE (1985); Troop Leader and Area Team Member, Chesapeake Bay Girl Scouts Council, New Castle County, DE (1978-1990); Advisory Committee, Delaware Commission for Women, Dover, DE (1975-1988); Founder, Living Stones Community Outreach **Awards:** Mayor's Citation, Mayor Margo G. Bailey (1999); Governor's Citation, Governor Parris N. Glendening (1999); Named Outstanding Young Woman in America (1986) **Memberships:** Lifetime Member, National Association for the Advancement of Colored People (NAACP) **Marquis Who's Who Honors:** Albert Nelson Marquis Lifetime Achievement Award **Why did you become involved in your profession or industry:** Pastor Hopkins received a calling to go into ministry; she said yes after she got over the shock. **Avocations:** Traveling; History; Walking; Bicycling; Sewing; Reading; Volunteering **Political Affiliations:** Democrat **Religion:** Christian **Thoughts on Life:** Pastor Hopkins taught young girls how to be sufficient and how to survive in life. She was with the Girl Scout troop for 16 years. She is the founder and pastor for Victory in Grace Tabernacle, Inc. since 2004. She helps people align with the word of God. She has grown leaps and bounds with the spiritually with heaven. The spiritual gift and words of knowledge help people identify. She will never forget the first day God gave her an anointing-the church was full people from all over; she was overcome by the spirit and 56 people received the spirit through her. Her goal is continue to try to reach a community and get people to understand the spirit.

Catherine Hopkins

Marquis Who's Who
18 | 98
Biographee

Title: Music Educator **Industry:** Education/Educational Services **Parents:** John James; Eleanor May (Hubert) Sanderson **Marital Status:** Married **Spouse Name:** Stephen Ernest Hopkins (06/26/1965) **Children:** Cheryl Lynne Hopkins Niquette; Scott Eric **Education:** Bachelor of Music in Education, New England Conservatory (1961) **Career:** Teacher, Smithfield Schools, Rhode Island (1982-Present); Teacher, Attleboro Schools, Massachusetts (1962-1968); Teacher, Nagautuck Schools, Connecticut (1961-1962) **Civic:** Advocate, North American Red Cross, Woonsocket, RI (1997-Present); Advocate, Special Olympics, Trudeau Center (1995-Present); Parent Council, Boy Scouts of America, Smithfield (1992-Present) **Awards:** State of Rhode Island, Lifetime Achievement Award (2008) **Memberships:** American Choral Directors Conference; Music Educators National Conference **Marquis Who's Who Honors:** Albert Nelson Marquis Lifetime Achievement Award **Why did you become involved in your profession or industry:** In becoming involved in her profession, Ms. Hopkins drew a great deal of influence from her high school music director, Donald Gay. She played a great deal of instruments, and was given the opportunity to direct the school band and chorus. After her director asked if she had ever considered becoming a music director herself, she began to consider it.

Edward J. Horowitz, Esq.

Title: Attorney **Industry:** Law and Legal Services **Company Name:** Edward J. Horowitz, A Professional Corporation **Date of Birth:** 02/13/1942 **Place of Birth:** Milwaukee **State/Country of Origin:** WI/USA **Parents:** Aaron Horowitz; Sue Horowitz **Marital Status:** Married **Spouse Name:** Marcia Gold Horowitz (04/29/1990) **Children:** Amy; Aaron **Education:** JD, Harvard Law School, Harvard University, Cambridge, MA (1966); BA, University of California Los Angeles, Summa Cum Laude (1963) **Certifications:** Certified Specialist in Appellate Law, Board of Legal Specialization, The State Bar of California (1996) **Career:** Lawyer, Pacific Palisades, CA (1978-Present); Partner, Horvitz, Greines & Horowitz, Encino, CA (1976-1978); Senior Attorney, 2nd District Court of Appeals, Los Angeles, CA (1972-1976); Partner, Goldhammer & Horowitz, Los Angeles, CA (1969-1972); California Deputy Attorney General, Los Angeles, CA (1966-1969); Lead Counsel, Over 540 Appellate Cases, State and Federal Appellate Courts **Civic:** Board of Directors, High School Alumni Association; Big Brothers of Greater Los Angeles **Creative Works:** Author, "Appellate Practice Handbook," Butterworth Legal Publishers (1982); Author, "Reflections on Gun Control," "Los Angeles Bar Journal" (1976); Author, "Practitioners' Guide to California Habeas Corpus," Beverly Hills Bar Association Journal (1974); Author, "Excluding the Exclusionary Rule-Can There Be an Effective Alternative?," Los Angeles Bar Bulletin (1972); Contributor, Various Legal Publications; Author, 1,000 Briefs Filed in Appellate Courts **Awards:** AV Peer Review Rating, Martindale-Hubbell, MH Sub I, LLC dba Internet Brands (1979-Present); Super Lawyers® (2004-2020); Plaque, Martindale-Hubbell, MH Sub I, LLC DBA Internet Brands (2019, 2020); Honoree, Best Lawyers in America, United States News & World Report L.P. (2017); Honoree, California Lawyer of the Year, California Journal Magazine (1999); Felix Frankfurter Scholarship Award, Student Legislative Research Bureau, Harvard University (1966); Featured Listee, Bar Register of Preeminent Lawyers, Martindale-Hubbell, MH Sub I, LLC DBA Internet Brands; Featured Listee, Best Lawyers in America©, Martindale-Hubbell, MH Sub I, LLC DBA Internet Brands **Memberships:** Fellow, American Academy of Appellate Lawyers (2000-Present); California Academy of Appellate Lawyers (1976-Present); Criminal Courts Bar Association-Los Angeles (1970-Present); Los County Bar Association (1967-Present); Emeritus, American Academy of Appellate Lawyers (2018); Chairman, Senior Lawyers Section, Los Angeles County Bar Association (2013-2014); Executive Committee, Senior Lawyers Section, Los Angeles County Bar Association (2009-2017); Appellate Advisory Committee, Judicial Council of California (2003-2006); Reporting of the Record Task Force, Judicial Council of California (2002-2005); Chairman, State Appellate Judicial Evaluation Committee, Los Angeles County Bar Association (2001-2007); Appellate Process Task Force, Judicial Council of California (1997-2001); Appellate Indigent Defense Oversight Advisory Committee, Judicial Council of California (1993-1995); Hearing Officer, Southern California Psychiatric Society (1990-1995); President, Criminal Courts Bar Association-Los Angeles (1987); President, California Academy of Appellate Lawyers (1985); Arbitrator, American Arbitration Association (1982-1995); Chair, Appellate Courts Section, Los Angeles County Bar Association (1981-1982); Appellate Courts Section, Los Angeles County Bar Association (1980-2017); Los Angeles County Bar Association (1967-2017) **Bar Admissions:** U.S. Supreme Court; California; U.S. Court of Appeals, Ninth Circuit; U.S. Court of Appeals, First Circuit **Marquis Who's Who Honors:** Marquis Who's Who Top Professional (2017); Albert Nelson Marquis Lifetime Achievement Award **To what do you attribute your success:** Mr. Horowitz attributes his success to his education from Harvard Law School and his good fortune to have learned from excellent judges and lawyer colleagues. **Why did you become involved in your profession or industry:** Mr. Horowitz became involved in his profession because he was inspired by a high school teacher, a college professor, and, most of all, his father, who was also an attorney. **Avocations:** Swimming; Skiing; Backpacking; Hiking; Writing humorous prose and poetry; Reading biographies and books on science; Playing with Golden Retriever, Jennie **Political Affiliations:** Democrat **Religion:** Jewish

William Hoskins

Title: Obstetrician, Educator, Gynecologist (Retired) **Industry:** Medicine & Health Care **Date of Birth:** 05/10/1940 **Place of Birth:** Harlan **State/Country of Origin:** KY/USA **Parents:** Lonnie S. Hoskins; Joanne (Huff) Hoskins **Marital Status:** Married **Spouse Name:** Iffath Abbasi Ahson (11/9/1985); Betty Jean Gay (9/10/1960, Divorced) **Children:** Tonya J.; William John Junior; Ahad A.; Mariya A. **Education:** Honorary DSc, Mercer University (2018); Resident, Obstetrics-Gynecology, Oakland Naval Hospital (1968-1971); Intern, Jacksonville Naval Hospital (1966-1967); MD, University of Tennessee, Memphis, TN (1965); BA, University of Tennessee, Knoxville, TN (1962) **Certifications:** Diplomate, American Board of Gynecological Oncology; American Board of Obstetrics and Gynecology **Career:** Executive Director, Surgical Activities, Department of Surgery, Memorial Sloan Kettering Cancer Center (2008-Present); Chief, Gynecology Service, Memorial Sloan Kettering Cancer Center (1990-Present); Retired (2015); Professor, Obstetrics-Gynecology, Cornell University School of Medicine (2008-2015); Professor, Obstetrics-Gynecology, Mercer Medical College, Macon, GA (2001-2007); Director, Curtis & Elizabeth Anderson Cancer Center at Memorial Health University Medical Center, Savannah, GA (2001-2007); Senior Associate Dean, School of Medicine, Mercer Medical College, Savannah, GA (2004-2005); Vice-Chairman, Gynecologic Oncology Group, Cornell University Medical College (1993-2002); Deputy Physician, Chief, Disease Management Teams, Memorial Sloan-Kettering Cancer Center (1996-2001); Professor, Obstetrics-Gynecology, Cornell University Medical College (1990-2001); Avon Chair, Gynecologic Oncology Research, Memorial Sloan-Kettering Cancer Center, New York (1995-1996); Associate Chief, Gynecology Service, Memorial Sloan-Kettering Cancer Center, New York, NY (1988-1990); Associate Professor, Obstetrics-Gynecology, Cornell University Medical Center, New York, NY (1986-1990); Associate Professor, Obsterics-Gynecology, Uniformed Services University (1976-1986); Director, Gynecological Oncology, National Naval Medical Center, Bethesda, MD (1976-1986); Fellow, Gynecological Oncology, University of Miami (1974-1976); Staff, Obstetrics-Gynecology, Pensacola Naval Hospital (1971-1974) **Career Related:** Distinguished Georgia Cancer Scholar (2001-Present); Co-Chair, NCI Cancer Steering Committee (2006-2010); Chairman, Ovarian Committee, Gynecological Oncology Group, Philadelphia, PA (1984-1989) **Military Service:** Commissioned Lieutenant, U.S. Navy (1966); Advanced Through Grades to Captain, U.S. Navy **Creative Works:** "Atlas of Procedures in Gynecologic Oncology" (2003); "Handbook of Gynecologic Oncology" (2000); "Cancer Management, A Multidisciplinary Approach" (1996); Editor, "Cervical Cancer and Perinvasive Peoplasia" (1996); Editor, "Cancer of the Ovary" (1993); Editor, "Principles and Practice of Gynecology and Oncology" (1992); Contributor, Over 224 Articles, Professional Journals; Contributor, Chapter, Books **Marquis Who's Who Honors:** Albert Nelson Marquis Lifetime Achievement Award **To what do you attribute your success:** Dr. Hoskins attributes his success to persistence and hard work. **Why did you become involved in your profession or industry:** When Dr. Hoskins was in college, he majored in English and Latin. However, he always felt drawn to pursue medicine. This is why he became a doctor. **Avocations:** Museums; Reading **Political Affiliations:** Republican **Religion:** Muslim

Melvin Howard

Title: Vice Chairman (Retired) **Industry:** Business Management/Business Services **Company Name:** Xerox Corporation **Date of Birth:** 01/05/1935 **Place of Birth:** Boston **State/Country of Origin:** MA/USA **Parents:** John M. Howard; Molly (Sagar) Howard **Marital Status:** Married **Spouse Name:** Vivien K. Weissman (10/6/2005); Beverly Ruth Kahan (06/09/1957, Deceased 2003) **Children:** Brian David; Marjorie Lyn (Deceased 2012) **Education:** MBA, Columbia University (1959); BA, University of Massachusetts (1957) **Career:** Managing Director, Taurus Advisory Group, LLC (1993-1995); President, Chief Executive Officer, Ehrlich Bober and Company (1990-1992); Vice Chairman, Board, Xerox Corporation (1986-1990); Board of Directors, Xerox Corporation (1982-1990); Executive Vice President, Chairman Financial Services, Xerox Corporation (1982-1986); Controller, Senior Vice President, Finance, Chief Financial Officer, Xerox Corporation (1970-1982); Vice President, Administration, Shoe Corporation of America, Inc., Columbus, OH (1967-1970); Financial Executive, Ford Motor Company, Dearborn, MI (1959-1967) **Career Related:** Board of Directors, Gould Pumps, Inc.; Board of Directors, Sector Management, Inc. **Civic:** Trustee, Nursing and Home Care, University of Massachusetts Amherst; Chairman, Commonwealth College **Military Service:** First Lieutenant, U.S. Army (1957) **Memberships:** Birchwood Country Club; La Gorce Country Club; Beta Gamma Sigma **Marquis Who's Who Honors:** Albert Nelson Marquis Lifetime Achievement Award; Marquis Who's Who Top Professional **Why did you become involved in your profession or industry:** Mr. Howard hoped that when he graduated from Columbia Business School that he could get a decent job. The first three years were fabulous. they put him as head of a Beta Gamma Sigma program in 1962. He was the financial head of that team and it was through that team that he met the Fords. When the program was done, the next day Mr. Ford, Sr. asked him if he could come over and talk to him. Mr. Ford, Sr. asked him to come work for him. For three months, Mr. Howard would work in the controller's office and then he was moved up to be his assistant. **Avocations:** Stock market; Traveling

John Kingman Howe

Title: Manufacturing, Sales and Marketing Executive **Industry:** Manufacturing **Company Name:** The John K. Howe Co, Inc. **Date of Birth:** 11/07/1945 **Place of Birth:** Everett **State/Country of Origin:** WA/USA **Parents:** John Cutler Howe; Nancy Carpenter (III) (Kingman) Howe **Marital Status:** Married **Spouse Name:** Loretta Kerr (08/27/1966) **Children:** Steven Cutler; Nancy Kingman Howe Jones **Education:** Coursework, The Ohio State University, Columbus, OH (1963-1965) **Career:** Chairman of the Board, The John K. Howe Company, Incorporated, Dayton, OH (2003-2019); Chairman of the Board, Chief Executive Officer, The John K. Howe Company, Incorporated, Dayton, OH (1987-2003); Director, President, Chief Executive Officer, The John K. Howe Company, Incorporated, Dayton, OH (1984-1995); Director, President, The John K. Howe Company, Incorporated, Dayton, OH (1972-1987); Director, Vice President of Sales, Springfield Binder Corporation, Ohio (1981-1984); Vice President, Vice President of Sales, Springfield Binder Corporation, Ohio (1971-1972); Vice President Sales, E.S. Klosterman Company, Incorporated, Dayton, OH (1969-1971); Sales Representative, E.S. Klosterman Company, Incorporated, Dayton, OH (1966-1971); Letter Carrier, U.S. Postal Service, Dayton, OH (1965-1966); Field Technician, Data Corporation, Dayton, OH (1965-1966); Retired, Manufacturing, Sales and Marketing Executive **Career Related:** Chairman, Chief Executive Officer, Director, The John K. Howe Company, Incorporated, Dayton, OH (1987-Present); The John K. Howe Company/Pension Plan (1976-Present); Administrator, The John K. Howe Company/Profit Sharing Plan, Cincinnati, OH (1973-Present); Owner of Cutler-Kingman, Incorporated Division of Thump Properties, Cincinnati, OH (1986-2000); Director, President, The John K. Howe Company, Incorporated, Dayton, OH (1972-1987); Design Investment Properties, Dayton, OH (1979-1986); Owner, Androscoggin Designs, Dayton, OH (1979-1986); President of Cutler-Kingman, Incorporated Division of Thump Properties, Cincinnati, OH (1979-1986); General Partner, H&B Enterprises, Dayton, OH (1977-1986); BMR Properties, Limited, Dayton, OH (1979-1982) **Civic:** President of Board of Managers, Adams Place Condominium Owners Association, Incorporated (1999-2000); Confreried de la Chaines de Rotisseurs Bailliage de Cincinnati (1993-2000); Vice President of Board of Managers, Adams Place Condominium Owners Association, Incorporated (1998-1999); Chairman of Operations Committee, Adams Place Condominium Owners Association, Incorporated (1996-1998); Chairman, South Dixie Business Association (1992-1994); President, Woods of Lincoln Park Homeowner's Association (1992-1994); Fraze Pavilion Fundraising Committee (1991-1992); President, South Dixie Business Association (1989-1991) **Marquis Who's Who Honors:** Albert Nelson Marquis Lifetime Achievement Award; Marquis Who's Who Top Professional **Why did you become involved in your profession or industry:** At first, Mr. Howe attended the Ohio State University for two years, but he left because he wanted more of a challenge. His father helped get him a job with Klosterman, but he did not want to continue with that. He and some colleagues got together and started a business. His company sold nationally, but it remained local. His children became involved in the business and now are the sole stockholders. **Avocations:** Golf; Photography; Genealogy **Political Affiliations:** Republican **Religion:** Presbyterian

James B. Howell III

Title: Agricultural Products Company Sales Consultant (Retired) **Industry:** Agriculture **Company Name:** Asgrow Seed Company **Date of Birth:** 12/11/1933 **Parents:** James Burt Howell; Catharine Stanger (Sparks) Howell **Marital Status:** Widowed **Spouse Name:** Lorraine Marie (Chanatry) Howell (02/18/1955, Deceased 2018) **Education:** MBA, University of Delaware (1980); BS, Vegetable Crops Agriculture, Rutgers, The State University of New Jersey, with High Honors (1956) **Career:** Sales Consultant, Asgrow Seed Company, Subsidiary Upjohn Company, Vineland, NJ (1960-1999); Agricultural Sales Representative, Allied Chemical Corporation, Philadelphia, PA (1957-1959) **Career Related:** Board of Directors, Advance Weight Systems, Inc., LaGrange, OH **Civic:** Trustee, First Presbyterian Church of Cedarville (2016-Present); Official Board, First Presbyterian Church of Cedarville (1960-2016); Admissions Liaison Officer, U.S. Military Academy, West Point, New York (1973-1999); Chairman, Lawrence Township Zoning Board Adjustment **Military Service:** U.S. Army (1957); Colonel, U.S. Army Reserve **Awards:** Heritage Award, New Jersey Agriculture and Business Association (2003); Horticultural Award, Rutgers, The State University of New Jersey (1955) **Memberships:** Alpha Zeta (1997); Brothers of the Century; Phi Beta Kappa; Reserve Officers Association; Vegetable Growers Association of New Jersey; Centennial Honor Roll, National Defense Industrial Association **Marquis Who's Who Honors:** Albert Nelson Marquis Lifetime Achievement Award **Why did you become involved in your profession or industry:** Mr. Howell became involved in his profession because he grew up on a vegetable crop farm; his parents always wanted to attend college, so he did. He got a bachelor's degree from Rutgers University, and later on received an MBA from there as well. His major was vegetable crops, and he has continued to explore that field with his family's asparagus farm in Cedarville, New Jersey. **Avocations:** Hunting; Fishing; Farming; Church **Political Affiliations:** Republican **Religion:** Presbyterian

Maung S. Htoo, PhD, FAIC

Title: President **Industry:** Nonprofit & Philanthropy **Company Name:** Vassar Brothers Institute **Date of Birth:** 08/17/1927 **Place of Birth:** Yenangyaung **State/Country of Origin:** Myanmar **Parents:** U Than Pe; Daw Saw Yin **Marital Status:** Widowed **Spouse Name:** Loretta Anne Htoo (01/19/1953, Deceased 2018) **Children:** Susan S. Htoo, Esq.; Nancy Rathbun; Naomi Htoo Mosher; Rhonda (Deceased) **Education:** PhD in Physical Chemistry, Rensselaer Polytechnic Institute, Troy, NY (1961); MSChemE, University of Maine, Orono, Maine (1954); BSChemE, University of Maine, Orono, Maine (1952); Fourth Year in Electrical Engineering, University of Rangoon, Rangoon, Myanmar (1949) **Career:** Adjunct Professor of Chemistry, Marist College, Poughkeepsie, NY (2006-Present); Adjunct Professor of Chemistry, State University of New York at New Paltz, New Paltz, NY (1998-2006); Adjunct Professor of Chemistry and Physical Science, Dutchess Community College, Poughkeepsie, NY (1966-2005); Adjunct Professor of Chemistry, Rensselaer Polytechnic Institute, Troy, NY (1992-1997); With, IBM, Poughkeepsie, NY (1961-1992); Senior Technical Staff Member, Manager, Chemical, Mechanical and Electrical Analysis Laboratories (1984-1991); Research Chemist, International Paper, Glens Falls, NY (1954-1961) **Career Related:** Director, Dutchess County Regional Science Fair (1989-Present); President, Technical Communications International Company (1992-1995); Organizer, Chair, International Photopolymer Conferences (1967-1991) **Civic:** Chairman, Conservation Advisory Council, LaGrange, NY (2003-Present); President, Vassar Brothers Institute, Poughkeepsie, NY (1997-Present) **Creative Works:** Editor, "Microelectronic Polymers" (1989); Guest Editor, "Polymer Engineering & Science" (1972-1993); Several Patents and Publications, Photopolymers and Semiconductors (1967-1990) **Awards:** Certificate of Special United States Congressional Recognition (2016); Lifetime Achievement Award, President Barack Obama for Lifelong Commitment to Building a Stronger Nation through Volunteer Service (2015); Honoree for Achievements in the Field of Academia and Commitment to Improve the Community through Volunteerism and Education, State of New York Legislative Resolution (2015); New York State Senate Liberty Medal for Actions on Behalf of Their Fellow New Yorkers and Their Community (2014); 300mm IBM Semiconductor Award for Contributions to IBM and Dedication to Inspire Future STEM Generations (2013); Margery Sachs Service Award for Lifelong Environmental Concern and Service (2007); Named Rotarian of the Year, Rotary Club of Arlington (1990); Named Distinguished Member, Society of Plastics Engineers (SPE-Inspiring Plastics Professionals) (1983) **Memberships:** Vice President, LaGrange Library, LaGrange, NY (2018-Present); Rotary Club of Arlington (1982-Present); Secretary Treasurer, Sigma Xi, The Scientific Research Honor Society, Vassar College Chapter (1997-Present); The New York Academy of Sciences (1972-Present); Board of Directors, New York State Association of Conservation Commissions (2004); Chairman, Town of LaGrange Conservation Advisory Council (2003); IBM Academy of Technology (1990-1992); President, Rotary Club of Arlington (1989-1990); American Men and Women of Science (1989); Fellow, American Institute of Chemists (1985); The New York Academy of Sciences (1972); Sigma Xi, The Scientific Research Society; American Chemical Society **Marquis Who's Who Honors:** Albert Nelson Marquis Lifetime Achievement Award **Why did you become involved in your profession or industry:** Dr. Htoo became involved in his profession after interning with a famous Myanmarese engineer, who encouraged Dr. Htoo to pursue engineering and learn how to make paper from bamboo. **Avocations:** Reading; Walking; Traveling

Douglas C. Huber, MD, FCAP

Title: Pathologist (Retired) **Industry:** Medicine & Health Care **Company Name:** Wellstar Health Systems **Date of Birth:** 06/11/1939 **Place of Birth:** South Charleston **State/Country of Origin:** WV/USA **Parents:** Abram Paul Huber; Mary Ashley (Grow) Huber **Marital Status:** Married **Spouse Name:** Deena Rae Freedman (8/8/1969); Angelika Madelon Pohl (6/3/1961, Divorced 1965) **Children:** Adam; Laura; HeidiMarie **Education:** DDiv, Honoris Causa, Antioch Bible Seminary (2012); MD, Emory University School of Medicine, Atlanta, GA (1964); AB in Chemistry, Emory University, Atlanta, GA (1960); Coursework, Harvard University (1958-1959) **Certifications:** Ordained Minister, Three Taverns Church, Acworth, GA (2012); Dermatopathology (1976); Anatomic and Clinical Pathology (1971); Medical Association of Georgia **Career:** Retired, Wellstar Health Systems (2006); Medical Director, Lost Mount Tissue Bank (2003-2006); Laboratory Director, Wellstar Cobb Hospital (1999-2004); Laboratory Director, Wellstar Paulding Hospital (1998-2004); Laboratory Director, Wellstar Douglas Hospital, Douglasville, GA (1980-2004); Medical Director, Roche Biomedical Laboratory, Atlanta Divison, Tucker, GA (1989-1993); General Practitioner, Leonard Morse Hospital, Natick, MA (1979-1980); Laboratory Director, Homer D. Cobb Member Hospital, Phenix City, AL (1973-1979); Associate Pathologist, Leary Laboratory, Boston, MA (1972-1973); Associate Pathologist, Baldwin County Hospital, Milledgeville, GA (1971-1972) **Career Related:** WellStar Northwest Physicians Group (1996-2006); Vice President, Alabama Association of Pathologists, Birmingham, AL (1979); Deputy State Commissioner, College of American Pathologists, Laboratory Inspection Program, Skokie, IL (1976-1979) **Civic:** President, Nam Vets of Georgia (1982-1985); Founder, Phenix City Laboratory Associates (1976-1979) **Military Service:** Commander, 346 Medical Detachment, Vietnam (1966); Captain, U.S. Army Medical Corps **Memberships:** Fellow, College of American Pathologists; American Society of Clinical Pathologists; Cobb County Medical Society; Medical Association of Georgia **Marquis Who's Who Honors:** Albert Nelson Marquis Lifetime Achievement Award; Marquis Who's Who Humanitarian Award **Why did you become involved in your profession or industry:** Dr. Huber was always good at science and chose a profession that benefited society. He chose pathology because of all the specialties in medicine, as it was the most scientific field for him. He and his team got absolute value in laboratories and absolute diagnosis on tissue specimens. **Avocations:** Missions; Visual art; Camping; Antique cars **Political Affiliations:** Republican Jewish Coalition **Religion:** Messianic Jewish

Walter F. Huebner, PhD

Title: Atomic Physicist, Astrophysicist, Space Scientist **Industry:** Sciences **Date of Birth:** 2/22/1928 **Place of Birth:** New York **State/Country of Origin:** NY/USA **Parents:** Richard Huebner; Margaret (Koch) Huebner **Marital Status:** Married **Spouse Name:** Elizabeth Putnam (4/6/1957) **Children:** Anne G.; Pieter R.; Elisabeth S.; Richard P. **Education:** PhD in Physics, Yale University, New Haven, CT (1958); MS in Physics, Yale University, New Haven, CT (1953); BS in Physics, Brooklyn Polytechnic Institute (1952) **Career:** Institute Scientist, Southwest Research Institute, San Antonio, TX (1987-2018); Deputy Group Leader, Equation of State and Opacity Group, Los Alamos National Laboratory, New Mexico (1980-1986); Group Leader, Los Alamos Scientific Laboratory (Now Los Alamos National Laboratory), New Mexico (1976-1986); Deputy Group Leader, Opacity Group, Los Alamos Scientific Laboratory (Now Los Alamos National Laboratory), New Mexico (1970-1976); Staff, Los Alamos Scientific Laboratory (Now Los Alamos National Laboratory), New Mexico (1957-1970) **Career Related:** President, Permanent Monitoring Panel for Cosmic Objects at the International Seminars on Nuclear War and Planetary Emergencies (2001-2017); Visiting Senior Scientist, Jet Propulsion Laboratory, NASA Headquarters, Washington (1994-1998); Visiting Staff, Max Planck Institute of Astrophysics, Munich, Germany (1964-1965, 1968-1970, 1982-1983); Fulbright Fellow (1968-1969); Participant, Operation Dominic, Christmas Island, Pacific (1962) **Creative Works:** Author, "Opality" (2014); Editor, "Protecting the Earth Against Collisions with Asteroids and Comet Nuclei" (2010); Editor, "Origin and Early Evolution of Comet Nuclei" (2008); Editor, "Physics and Chemistry of Comets" (1990); Editor, "Database for Rate Coefficients of Photoionization, Photodissociation, and Dissociative Ionization in Radiation Fields of the Sun, Black Bodies and the Interstellar Medium"; Editor, "Molecular Astrophysics" (1986) **Awards:** Grantee, Max Planck Society (1964, 1968-1969, 1982) **Memberships:** American Physical Society; American Astronomical Society; German Astronomical Society; International Astronomical Union; New York Academy of Science; New Mexico Academy of Science **Marquis Who's Who Honors:** Albert Nelson Marquis Lifetime Achievement Award **Why did you become involved in your profession or industry:** Dr. Huebner became involved in his profession after coming to the United States from Germany in 1946. While attending Brooklyn Polytech Institute, he developed an interest in physics. He later went to Yale University and specialized in nuclear physics. While at Yale, he worked with a well-known physicist named Prof. Breit, who arranged for him to work at Los Alamos Science Laboratory, where he later became group leader and then deputy group leader.

Kent Higgon Hughes

Title: Economist **Industry:** Financial Services **Company Name:** Woodrow Wilson International Center for Scholars **Date of Birth:** 02/23/1941 **Place of Birth:** Portland **State/Country of Origin:** OR/USA **Parents:** John Kenneth Hughes; Gwladys (Higgon) Hughes **Marital Status:** Married **Spouse Name:** Virginia Carrington Sammon **Children:** John Kenneth; Jeff; Krista **Education:** Doctor of Philosophy, Washington University (1976); Bachelor of Laws, Harvard University (1965); Bachelor of Arts, Yale University (1962) **Career:** Public Policy Fellow, Woodrow Wilson International Center for Scholars (2016-Present); Public Policy Scholar, Woodrow Wilson International Center for Scholars (2013); Program Director, American and Global Economy, Woodrow Wilson International Center for Scholars (2000); Public Policy Scholar, Woodrow Wilson International Center for Scholars, Washington, DC (1999-2001); Associate Deputy Secretary of Commerce, U.S. Department of Commerce, Washington, DC (1993-1999); President, Council on Competitiveness (1990-1993); Chief Economist, Democratic Policy Committee, U.S. Senate, Washington, DC (1987-1990); Staff Director, Trade Subcommittee, Committee on Foreign Affairs, Washington, DC (1985-1987); Policy/Legislative Director, Office of Senator Gary Hart, Washington, DC (1983-1984); Senior Economist, Joint Economic Committee, Washington, DC (1977-1982); Analyst, Congressional Research Service, Washington, DC (1973-1976); Legislative Counsel, Office of Senator Vance Hartke, Washington, DC (1971-1972); Attorney, Urban Law Institute, Washington, DC (1970-1971); Fellow, International Legal Center, Sao Paulo, Brazil (1967-1969); Latin American Teaching Fellow, Sao Paulo, Brazil (1967-1969); Adjunct Professor of Political Science, Boston University **Civic:** Executive Advisory Board, FIRST Robotics (2010-Present) **Creative Works:** Author, "Building the Next American Century" (2005); Author, "Trade, Taxes, Transnationals" (1979); Contributor, Articles, Professional Journals **Memberships:** American Bar Association; American Economic Association; The District of Columbia Bar; Cosmos Club **Bar Admissions:** District of Columbia Bar (1971) **Marquis Who's Who Honors:** Albert Nelson Marquis Lifetime Achievement Award; Marquis Who's Who Top Professional **Why did you become involved in your profession or industry:** Dr. Hughes was inspired by John F. Kennedy's proclamation to "ask not what your country can do for you, ask what you can do for your country." He was drawn to the challenge of economic development in the third world. After WWII, much of the world was destroyed, or still developing. He felt that he should help make the world a better place, and so that led him to spend time in Brazil and work on several different projects. **Avocations:** Languages; Rugby; Collecting political memorabilia

William Louis Hurlock, Esq.

Title: Managing Partner **Industry:** Law and Legal Services **Company Name:** Mueller Law LLC **State/Country of Origin:** NJ/USA **Marital Status:** Married **Education:** Doctor of Jurisprudence in Law, American University, Washington College of Law, Cum Laude (1998); Bachelor of Science in Political Science and Justice, American University, Dean's List (1988); Coursework, University of London, Dean's List **Career:** Managing Partner, Mueller Law LLC, New York and New Jersey Offices (2013-Present); First Ward Councilor, Township of Montclair, NJ (2012-Present); Partner, Seiger Gfeller Laurie LLP (2010-2013); Of Counsel, Herrick Feinstein LLP (2007-2010); Attorney, Boies, Schiller & Flexner LLP (2004-2007); Associate Independent Counsel, Office of Independent Counsel (1998-1999) **Career Related:** Adjunct Professor, Seton Hall University School of Law (2002-2013); Speaker in Field **Civic:** Board of Trustees, Family Service League/Sexual Assault and Violence Education (2018-Present); Board of Directors, American Red Cross, Northern New Jerssey (2016-Present); SobelCo. Fraud and Forensic Practice's Advisory Board (2012-Present); Montclair Board of School Estimate (2012-Present); First Ward Counselor, Township of Montclair (2002-Present); Board of Directors, National Youth Recovery Foundation (2016-2019); Board of Directors, Montclair YMCA (2013-2016); Board of Trustees, Outpost in the Burbs (2012-2015); Member, Saint Joseph's Regional Medical Center Charity Golf Outing Committee (2010-2011); Vice Chair, Board of Trustees, Newark Presbytery (2007-2012); Member, Advisory Committee, Federal Enforcement Homeland Security Foundation (2004-2010); Vice President and Barrister, Arthur T. Vanderbilt American Inn of Court (1999-2006); Former Deputy Mayor, Township of Mountclair **Creative Works:** Author, Various Articles for the SobelCo Newsletter (2013, 2014, 2015, 2016, 2017, 2018); Author, Various Articles to Legal Publications (1997, 2006, 2010, 2011) **Awards:** Lawyers of Distinction (2018); New Jersey Monthly Top Attorneys (2012); New Jersey Super Lawyer (2012); Martindale-Hubbell Peer Review Rating BV (2007); Township of Montclair, Historic Preservation Award for Saving a Historic Train Station; Lawyers in Excellence Award for Civil Litigation **Memberships:** New York State Bar Association; New Jersey Bar Association; Tax Payers Against Fraud **Bar Admissions:** New Jersey; New York; Pennsylvania; District of Columbia; Supreme Court of the United States; United States Court of Appeals for the Eleventh, Third, and Fourth Circuits; United States District Court for the District of New Jersey; United States District Court for the District of Columbia; United States District Court for the Northern, Southern, Eastern and Western Districts of New York; United States District Court for the District of Connecticut; United States District Court for the Eastern, Middle and Western Districts of Pennsylvania **Marquis Who's Who Honors:** Marquis Who's Who Top Professional **To what do you attribute your success:** Mr. Hurlock credits his success on his family, who encouraged and inspired him to pursue a career in civic society. **Why did you become involved in your profession or industry:** Mr. Hurlock was initially drawn to his career due to his upbringing and family history. His father was a police officer for 28 years and his mother has been a teachers aide, a career she remains active in at 76 years old. The family lived across the street from a town hall and local court house, and as a child he would often sneak in to watch proceedings. One day, a judge asked him what he thought of a particular case, which sparked his fascination with legal service.

Kimberly Ann Hurst

Title: Co-Owner **Industry:** Architecture & Construction **Company Name:** J&J Fencing Pros, LLC **Date of Birth:** 12/29/1974 **Marital Status:** Married **Spouse Name:** James Williams Hurst IV **Children:** Mackinzie Lynn; Abigail Bailey **Education:** CCNA, CCNP, CCSP, Southern Methodist University (2007); BS, Business Marketing, Southern Methodist University (1998); BS, Psychology & Business Management, Southern Methodist University (1998); AS, Arts in Business, Business Administration & Management, California State University, Northridge (1993) **Certifications:** Google Search Advertising Advanced (2008); Microsoft adExcellence (2008); Yahoo Ambassador (2007) **Career:** Co-Owner, J&J Fencing Pros, LLC, Denton, TX (2015-Present); Vice President, Online Marketing, Instinct Marketing, Frisco, TX (2015-2017); Vice President, Online Marketing, Traveljunction.com, Dallas/Fort Worth Area, TX (2013-2015); Director of Search Marketing, Hotels.com, Dallas/Fort Worth Area, TX (2011-2013); Vice President, Online Marketing, Hotels.com, (2007-2011); Director of Online Marketing, Nowlegal.com (2010); Senior Manager of SEM (Paid Search), Advantix Interactive (2007-2010); Optimization Account Manager/SEM Builder Lead, Idearc Media (2004-2007); Internet Consultant, Verizon Shared Services (2004-2007); Director of Accounting, Enviro~Mold IAQ Services Incorporated (2003-2004); Customer Service Lead, Fulfillment Solutions of Texas, Limited (1998-2003) **Civic:** Skills-Based Volunteer, Rise Adaptive Sports (2011-Present); Board of Directors, HOA **Awards:** Named, Best of Denton County; Named, Best of Denton; Inductee, Business Hall of Fame **To what do you attribute your success:** Ms. Hurst doesn't let anything stop her from getting to where she wants to be. She always shoots for the stars and refuses to let her gender, her age, past, or any excuse or obstacle stand in her way. She considers herself very stubborn. Any time a person tells her she cannot do something, she takes it upon herself to prove them wrong. **Why did you become involved in your profession or industry:** Ms. Hurst began her career in a completely different industry. She currently holds three college degrees. She was once vice president of online marketing. Her husband worked for a fencing company, and would come home and complain to her about the things they did wrong on the job. After about six years of complaining, she told her husband, "If you think you can do it better, then let's do it..." and began their own fencing company. She kept her position as the vice president of online marketing at the firm she was at while building the fencing business to a point she would be able to make a transition to dedicate her full time to the business. **Thoughts on Life:** Ms. Hurst's business is 100% family owned and operated. Their business motto is, "We like to under-promise and over-deliver..." Ms. Hurst had a rough childhood, which ended up with her being placed in foster care during her early teenage years. Although foster care is not an easy path, she considers herself lucky to have had someone assigned to her as a big sister while placed in Maryvale, a Catholic orphanage. She attributes much of her life path to her big sister, Lucy. She stated that if it was not for the guidance and love that Lucy provided her, she would not be where she is today. She developed the desire to constantly "pay it forward" because of the assistance she received growing up, for which she is extremely grateful. She also wants people to know two things - first, "Never let your childhood be an excuse to hold you back once you are an adult" and second, "It doesn't matter where you are in life. If you are unhappy with your position, it is possible to reinvent yourself..."

Jane Campbell Hutchison, PhD

Title: Professor Emerita of Art History **Industry:** Education/Educational Services **Company Name:** University of Wisconsin-Madison **Date of Birth:** 07/20/1932 **Place of Birth:** Washington **State/Country of Origin:** DC/USA **Year of Passing:** 2020 **Education:** PhD in Art History, University of Wisconsin-Madison (1964); Fulbright Fellow, University of Utrecht, Netherlands (1960-1961); MA in Art History, Oberlin College (1958); BFA, Western Maryland College (Now McDaniel College) (1954) **Certifications:** Certified, Print Council of America **Career:** Professor Emerita, Art History, University of Wisconsin-Madison (2012-Present); Professor, University of Wisconsin-Madison (1975-2012); Department Chairman, Art History, University of Wisconsin-Madison (1977-1980, 1992-1993); Instructor to Assistant Professor to Associate Professor, University of Wisconsin-Madison (1964-1975); Teaching Assistant, University of Wisconsin-Madison (1959-1960, 1961-1963); Research Librarian, Toledo Museum of Art (1957-1959); Technical Illustrator, U.S. Navy Department, David Taylor Model Basin, Washington, DC (1954-1956) **Career Related:** Visiting Assistant Professor, Summer Session, Temple University, Philadelphia, PA (1968); Fellow, University of Wisconsin-Madison (1959-1960, 1961-1963); Graduate Fellow, Oberlin College (1955-1957); Consultant in Field **Civic:** Secretary, Midwest Art History Society (2004-Present); President, St. Andrew's Society Madison (1995-2012); ROTC Advisory Committee, University of Wisconsin-Madison (1987-2012); Treasurer, Midwest Art History Society (2001-2004); Member, Special Committee on Arts Funding, Wisconsin State Legislative Council (2000-2001); Secretary-Treasurer, Historians of Netherlandish Art (1995-1999); Midwest Art History Society (1983-1985); President, Madison Chapter, American Association of University Professors (1979-1981) **Creative Works:** Editorial Board, Studies in Iconography (1997-2012); Editorial Board, Source (2003); Author, "Albrecht Durer: A Guide to Research," Taylor & Francis, NY (2000); Editor, "Early German Artists," Volume Eight, Part Six (1996); Author, "Albrecht Durer: A Biography," German Edition, Frankfurt am Main, Campus Verlag (1994); Editor, "Early German Artists," Volume Nine, Part Two (1991); Author, "Albrecht Durer: A Biography," Princeton University Press (1990) **Awards:** German Academy Exchange Service, Germany, Summer (1989); Alumni Award, Western Maryland College of Trustees (1987); Grant in Aid, American Council Learned Society, Amsterdam, Netherlands (1984); Research Grantee, National Endowment of the Humanities, Germany (1982); Senatorial Scholar, Western Maryland College (1950-1954); Valedictorian, Class of 1950, Maryland Park High School (1950) **Memberships:** Woman's Club of Chevy Chase (2013-Present); Board Member, Midwest Art History Society (2008-Present); Board of Directors, University Club, University of Wisconsin-Madison (1976-1980, 2005-Present); Secretary, Midwest Art History Society (2004-2008); Treasurer, Midwest Art History Society (2001-2003); Treasurer, Historians of Netherlandish Art (1995-1999); Vice President, Madison Chapter, Wisconsin Association of Scholars (1990-1995); President, Midwest Art History Society (1983-1985); President, Madison Chapter, American Association of University Professors (1979-1981); President, University Club, University of Wisconsin-Madison (1980) **Marquis Who's Who Honors:** Albert Nelson Marquis Lifetime Achievement Award; Marquis Who's Who Humanitarian Award **To what do you attribute your success:** Dr. Hutchison attributes her success to financial support from Fulbright, DAAD, ACLS and the University of Wisconsin Foundation for permitting her to conduct research for her PhD dissertation. She also credits all of her volumes for the Bartsch series of print reference works, particularly the volume on Martin Schongauer. Dr. Hutchison was successful, also, because she was able to fund her employment in Amsterdam as consultant to the Rijksmuseum in organizing the major exhibition of the anonymous 15th century Master of the Housebook, who had been the subject of her doctoral dissertation. **Why did you become involved in your profession or industry:** Dr. Hutchison had always admired the paintings, drawings, and intaglio prints of northern European old masters for their technical skill and iconographic originality, and she was fortunate to be able to study with a number of the best authorities in the field, such as Wolfgang Stechow at Oberlin, Jan Gerrit van Gelder at Utrecht, Karel G. Boon at the Rijksmuseum (Amsterdam) and James Watrous at Wisconsin. On her research travels in Europe, she was befriended by museum curators and institute directors, as well as by art collectors in Austria, Germany, Poland and Switzerland. Although in the 1950s and early 1960s, she was ineligible for admission to Harvard, Yale or Princeton, none of which accepted women as doctoral candidates in art history, Dr. Hutchison was able, through the Fulbright fellowship, to obtain the best education that Europe could offer and access to the best collections of works by Durer, Holbein, Rembrandt and Vermeer, among the other northern masters that she so admired and later would enjoy introducing to her own students. As a Wisconsin faculty member, she was also fortunate to have colleagues in the Departments of History and German, who were invaluable sources of help for her research. **Avocations:** Opera; German lieder; Theater; Watching the Washington Capitals **Political Affiliations:** Democrat **Religion:** Episcopalian

John Michael Hyde

Title: History Educator Emeritus **Industry:** Education/Educational Services **Date of Birth:** 06/16/1930 **Place of Birth:** Wichita **State/Country of Origin:** KS/USA **Parents:** George Alvan Hyde; Helen (McCarthy) Hyde **Marital Status:** Single **Education:** PhD in History, Harvard University (1963); MA in History, University of Minnesota (1957); BA in History, Williams College (1956) **Career:** Brown Professor of History Emeritus, Williams College (1995-Present); Retired, Brown Professor of History, Williams College, Williamstown, MA (1989-1995); Professor, Williams College, Williamstown, MA (1973-1995); Department Chairman, Williams College, Williamstown, MA (1982-1986); Dean of College, Williams College, Williamstown, MA (1967-1970); Dean of Freshmen, Williams College, Williamstown, MA (1963-1967); Successively Instructor, Assistant Professor, Associate Professor History, Williams College, Williamstown, MA (1959-1973) **Military Service:** U.S. Navy (1951-1955) **Memberships:** American Historical Association; Kansas Historical Society; Canadian Historical Association; Phi Beta Kappa **Marquis Who's Who Honors:** Albert Nelson Marquis Lifetime Achievement Award **Why did you become involved in your profession or industry:** Dr. Hyde dropped out of college and went into the Navy for four years, fighting in the Korean war. This meant he would have assistance in paying for college, which opened up more opportunities for him. Undecided on if he should pursue foreign services or teaching, Dr. Hyde to attend the University of Minnesota to get a master's degree. Along this journey, he found that he very much liked the life of a scholar. He then received a scholarship from Harvard to obtain a PhD. Ever since then, Dr. Hyde has loved teaching. **Avocations:** Riding trains and boats around the world **Religion:** Episcopalian

Brandy Ibos

Title: Owner **Industry:** Advertising & Marketing **Company Name:** The Sequin Siren LLC **Marital Status:** Married **Spouse Name:** Michael **Education:** BBA in Marketing, The University of Southern Mississippi (2014) **Career:** Owner, The Sequin Siren LLC (2017); Marketing Director, After The Proposal Wedding (2017-2018); NFL Cheerleader, New Orleans Saints (2013-2017); Retail Sales Associate, Maurices (2012-2013); Sales Associate, Love Ivy (2011-2012) **Civic:** Going Green Going Coastal (2016-Present) **Creative Works:** Published, Recyclable Children's Coloring Books; Hosted, 10 Beach Cleanups **Awards:** Honored, Mental Health Association of South Mississippi **Memberships:** President, Student Government Association; President, American Marketing Association; Chi Omega Sorority; Dixie Darlings Dance Team; Southern Misses Pom Squad; Krewe of Athena **Avocations:** Fishing; Boating; Paddleboarding; Going to the park with dogs; Teaching at the local dance studio

Kolapo Akanfe Ige

Title: Professor, The Provost **Industry:** Education/Educational Services **Company Name:** West Coast University International California **Date of Birth:** 01/15/1962 **State/Country of Origin:** Nigeria **Education:** PhD in Management Science, Akamai University, Hilo, HI (2018); Post-Doctorate of Science in Econometrics, West Coast University, Panama & Belize, Central America (2014); PhD in Economics, Adam Smith University, Liberia (2007); MSc in Economics, Obafemi Awolowo University, Ile-Ife, Nigeria (1998); Diploma, Computer Science, Ladoke Akintola University of Technology, Ogbomosho (1993); BSc in Economics, Education, University of Jos, Nigeria (1991) **Certifications:** National Certificate, Education (1984); Grade II Teachers' Certificate (1980) **Career:** President, Chief Executive Officer of KolagAfrimerican Institute of Scientific Research Education and Academic Development Incorporated, California; Professor, Economics and Econometrics, Faculty of Science and Technology, West Coast University Central America (2014-Present); Associate Professor, Research Fellow, Post-Doctoral Degree Studies of Economics and Econometrics, Faculty of Science and Technology, West Coast University, Central America (2009-2012); Assistant Professor, Economics and Econometrics, Faculty of Applies Sciences, Africa International Institute for Professional Training and Research, Adam Smith University of America Inc. (2007-2009) **Career Related:** Management, West Coast University, Central America (2013-Present); Communication Consultant, International Conference on Economics and Econometrics, Africa International Institute for Professional Training and Research (2013-Present); Steering Committee, International Graduate Students Seminar Presentation for Economics and Econometrics, Africa International Institute for Professional Training and Research (2011-Present); Advisory Board Member, Africa International Institute for Professional Training and Research (2012-Present); International Faculty Member, Adam Smith University of America and France (2009-Present); Editorial Board, West Africa Journal of Science, Technology and Social Sciences University of Cape Coast, Ghana, West Africa (2009-Present); Registrar, Chief Executive Officer, Organization of Economists and Business Analysts of Nigeria (2007-Present); Joseph Ayo Babalola University, Ikenji Arakeji, Osun State, Nigeria (2013-2017); Visiting Professor, Economics and Econometrics, West Coast University, Ghana Campus (2014); External Examiner, Numerous Doctoral Degree Students (2013-2014); Senior Lecturer, Ag. Head, Department of Economics, College of Social Sciences, Joseph Ayo Babalola University, Ikeji Arakeji (2012-2013) **Creative Works:** Coordinating Editor, Society for Promoting Research Education and Academic Development (SPREAD) (2012-2013); Associate Editor, JournalsBank Publishing, University of Aberdeen, United Kingdom (2012); National Editorial Adviser, International Journal of Pure and Applied Sciences, Al-Hikmah University, Ilorin- Nigeria (2009-2010); Contributor, Articles, Professional Journals **Awards:** Research Fellow, Quantitative Analysis Network-Centre for Econometric and Allied Research, University of Ibadan, Nigeria (2012); AfricanAGE International Developmental Gold Award in Public Service (2011); Listee, Who's Who in Nigeria Book of Global Professionals (2010); Fellowship Medal Award, Chartered Institute of Treasury Management, Nigeria (2009); Fellow, Research Network, International Research and Development Institute, Uyo, Akwa Ibom State, Nigeria **Memberships:** Harvard International Professionals Hall of Fame; Behavioral Economics Group, Europe; PhD Business-Economics-International Trade, Europe; American Economic Association; Austrian Economics, Austria; Institute of Data Processing Management of Nigeria (IDPM); Fellow, Director of Training, Chartered Institute of Treasury Management, Nigeria (CITMAN); Fellow, Institute of Certified Economists of Nigeria (ICEN); Fellow, Association of Business Executives of Nigeria (ABEN); Fellow, Institute of Professional Financial Managers, London (IPFML); Life Fellow, Vice World Grand President, International Affairs; World Grand Board of Directors, International Chartered World Learned Society; Most Notable and Distinguished Knight Order of Africa of the 21st Century; Chartered World Order of the Knights of Justice of Peace; Fellow, Faculty of Secretaries and Administrators, United Kingdom (FSA); Fellow, Institute of Corporate Administration of Nigeria; Research Fellow, Quantitative Analysis Network-Centre for Econometrics and Allied Research, University, Ibadan, Nigeria; Fellow, Research Network, International Research and Development Institute, Uyo, Akwa Ibom State, Nigeria; Senior Research Fellow, Organization of Economists & Business Analysts of Nigeria; Chairman, Board of Regents, Global Organization for Scientific Research, Education and Academic Development, England, Wales **To what do you attribute your success:** Dr. Ige attributes his success to the grace of God. "I can do all things through Christ that strengthens me." **Why did you become involved in your profession or industry:** While living in Nigeria, Dr. Ige was able to make connections at home with people in Nigeria. He had aspirations to use the grace of God he was provided in his life to teach professional development.

Bob Iger

Title: Chief Executive Officer **Industry:** Leisure, Travel & Tourism **Company Name:** The Walt Disney Company **Date of Birth:** 02/10/1951 **Place of Birth:** New York **State/Country of Origin:** NY/USA **Parents:** Arthur; Mimi **Marital Status:** Married **Spouse Name:** Kathleen Susan Iger (Divorced); Willow Bay **Children:** Kathleen Pamela; Amanda; Max; William **Education:** BA, Ithaca College, Magna Cum Laude (1973) **Career:** President, Chief Executive Officer, Walt Disney Company, Burbank, CA (2005-Present); President, Chief Operating Officer, Walt Disney Company, Burbank, CA (2000-2005); President, Walt Disney International (1999-2000); Chairman, ABC Group (1999-2000); President, ABC, Inc., New York, NY (1996-1999); President, Chief Operating Officer, Capital Cities/ABC Inc., New York, NY (1994-1996); Executive Vice President, Capital Cities/ABC Inc., New York, NY (1993-1994); President, ABC Entertainment (1989-1992); President, ABC TV Network Group (1992-1994); Executive Vice President, ABC TV Network Group (1988-1989); Vice President, Progressive Planning and Acquisition, ABC Sports (1987-1988); Vice President, Progressive Planning and Development, ABC Sports (1985-1987); Various Positions, ABC-TV Sports (1976-1985); Studio Supervisor, ABC-TV (1974-1976) **Career Related:** Hulu (2009-Present); The Walt Disney Company (2000-Present); Board Member, US-China Business Council (2011-Present); Member, President's Export Council, (2011-Present); Member, Board of Directors, Apple Inc. (2011-2019); Member, Board of Directors Lincoln Center Performing Arts; Board, Trustees Ithaca College, Museum TV & Radio, American Film Institute (AFI) **Civic:** Trustee, Ithaca College **Awards:** Milestone Award, Producers Guild of America (2014); Named CEO of Year, Chief Executive Magazine (2014); Award, USC Shoah Foundation Institute for Visual History and Education (2012); Named one of The Best CEOs, Institutional Investor Magazine (2008-2011); MarketWatch (2006); Named of the The 25 Most Powerful People in Business, Fortune Magazine (2006-2007); Named one of The 50 Who Matter Now, CNNMoney. com Business 2.0 (2006); Trustee Award, National Academy TV Arts & Sciences (2005); Ambassador for Humanity Award **Religion:** Jewish

Lawrence Irvine Iles

Title: Liberal Arts Educator, Historian **Industry:** Education/Educational Services **Date of Birth:** 06/08/1957 **Place of Birth:** Epsom **State/Country of Origin:** United Kingdom **Parents:** Irvine Edmund Douglas Iles; Bridget Margaret (Dobson) Iles **Marital Status:** Married **Spouse Name:** Betty Louise McLane **Education:** MA, University of Illinois (1982); MA, University of London (1978); BA, University of Newcastle Upon Tyne (1975) **Certifications:** PGCE, University of London (1977) **Career:** Private Practice Lecturer, Broadcaster Political Science and Global Perspectives, Kirksville, MO (1996-Present); Tutor, Bartholomew's College, Brighton, England (1992-1993, 1996); Lecturer, Oakland College, St. Albans, England (1993); Visiting Teacher, Roedean International College, Brighton, England (1992-1993); Adjunct Instructor, Johnson County Community College, Overland Park, KS (1991-1992); Honorary Visiting Fellow, Graduate School International Studies, Birmingham University, Edgbaston, England (1987) **Career Related:** Visiting Teacher, St. Mary's College, Brighton, England (2002); Honorary Visiting Researcher, Cambodia House Section, University of Paris Sorbonne, Paris, France (2005); Presenter In Field **Civic:** Liaison Officer, Kirksville, MO, Chapter, Truman State University (2004-Present); Deputy Chair (Hove Constituency), Brunswick And Goldsmid Branch, Labor Party (1996); State Organizer, Socialist Party USA, New York, NY (1994); U.S./Canadian Representative, British Governing Labor Party, Heritage Group Community; Active, Amnesty International **Creative Works:** Author, Three Sections, Routledge Encyclopedia of Contemporary British Culture (1999); Author, "Modern History Course Planner" (1988); Contributor, Articles, Professional Journals; Two UK TV Lead Appearances **Memberships:** Modern Language Association **Marquis Who's Who Honors:** Albert Nelson Marquis Lifetime Achievement Award **Why did you become involved in your profession or industry:** Mr. Iles had a sense of persecution and a sense of outside idealism. He comes from a skilled working class background. His parents educated both himself and his younger brother Christopher to believe that they were essentially typically lower middle class. Many people, in terms of social understanding, argue that there is not much difference of being in the humblest section of the middle class and the slightly prosperous section of the working class. His whole life he felt as illustrated that such class distinctions do matter. If a person gets their consciousness and their sense of self awareness wrong, than they can make some very big mistakes in life, whereas if they try and get it right, a person can have a better sense of bearing in life. In his decision to regard himself as somewhat persecuted, he does not want to overdue that word. However, it is important and gave him a sense of drive, which he partly he inherited from his mother, who had a strong sense of drive. He had to strive; people like him were not given to much in life. His sense of ambition came from being excluded. When he was teaching at Roedean, he remembers some of his best classes in the younger section of the school; he had discussion with his class about social mobility and he was asked by some of his female students why he was a laborer, socialist and why they should feel guilty about having a very prosperous education. His response was that he would like everyone to have the same opportunity.

Rich Imbimbo

Title: Owner **Industry:** Business Management/Business Services **Company Name:** Kingdom Cars **Place of Birth:** Summit **State/Country of Origin:** NJ/USA **Parents:** Dominic Imbimbo; Carmella Imbimbo **Marital Status:** Married **Spouse Name:** Dawn Robin **Children:** Kristen; Andrew; Emily **Education:** Governor Livingston High School, Berkeley Heights, NJ (1977) **Career:** Owner, Kingdom Cars, New Jersey (2016-Present); Rich's Automotive, New Jersey (1992-Present); 47 Years in the Auto Industry **Civic:** Volunteer Firefighter, Berkeley Heights NJ (22 Years) **To what do you attribute your success:** Mr. Imbimbo attributes his success to God and his Christian faith. **Why did you become involved in your profession or industry:** Mr. Imbimbo became involved in his profession because he began repairing cars with his father as a young boy. After awhile, he discovered his love and passion for it. Eventually he opened his own repair shop. Overtime, he developed a deeper love and compassion for people which ultimately lead to his current nonprofit auto repair for those in need. Mr. Imbimbo used his genuine care and love for people as his niche in the auto repair industry. **Thoughts on Life:** Mr. Imbimbo said, "When we're young and just beginning our professional careers, we all have big ideas on ways to excel in business, ways in which we can impact our communities. Later in years we move towards marriage, have children and again find ourselves repeating the same learning process of figuring out how to be a super husband and hero dad. For me, all this was overwhelming and brought on confusion but also a strong desire to look beyond my experiences for new answers. It became my mission to find a balance between home, God and work. Was I the same person at work that I am at home and church? After an intense study of biblical theology I began a new path in life with new meaning, new outlook with new promises. There was one passage in the scriptures that cut real deep and it's written in the book of 1st John. If anyone has material possessions and sees a brother or sister in need but has no pity on them, how can the love of God be in that person? Dear children, let us not love with words or speech but with actions and in truth. 1 John 3:17-18"

Barbara Kay Immel

Title: Management Consultant **Company Name:** Immel Resources, LLC **Date of Birth:** 07/31/1956 **Place of Birth:** Bakersfield **State/Country of Origin:** CA/USA **Marital Status:** Widowed **Spouse Name:** Joseph Herbert Immel Jr. (08/31/1979, Deceased) **Children:** Joseph Herbert Immel, III; Elizabeth "Eli" Logan **Education:** Graduate, Stanford Writer's Workshop (2009); Graduate, Stanford University Executive Public Course (2002); Graduate, Buckley School of Public Speaking (2001); Graduate, Buckley School of Public Speaking (2000); Graduate, Stanford University Executive Public Course (1982); Graduate, Stanford Professional Public Course (1981); Single Subject Teaching Credential, University of California, Santa Barbara (1979); BA in English, University of California, Santa Barbara (1978) **Career:** Consultant, President, Immel Resources, LLC, Petaluma, CA (1995-Present); Compliance Manager, Chiron Corporation, Emeryville, CA (1993-1995); Administrator, Syntex Corp., Palo Alto, CA (1986-1992); Technical Editor I-III, Syva Co., Palo Alto, CA (1982-1986); Assistant to President, Veterinary Practice Publishing Co., Santa Barbara, CA (1980-1981) **Career Related:** Consultant in Field, Guest Lecturer, Undergraduate Pharmacology Course, University of California, Berkeley (1999-Present); Co-director, Drug Development Course, University of California, Berkeley Extension, Berkeley, CA (1998-2000); Instructor, University of California, Berkeley Extension (1995-2000) **Civic:** Volunteer Librarian, Career Action Center, Palo Alto, CA (1982-1986) **Creative Works:** Editor-in-chief, Immel Report (2004-Present); Columnist, BioPharm Magazine (1996-2007); Contributor, Articles to Professional Journals, Dekker's Encyclopedia of Pharmaceutical Technology **Awards:** Scholar, President Scholar (Award and Scholarship), University of California, Santa Barbara (1974-1978); Syntex Is, Award; Teacher of the Year Award, International Co. Teaching Public Classes **Memberships:** Chair Person, Medical Device Planning Committee, FDA Inspections Summit (2006-Present); Parenteral Drug Association (PDA) (1993-1996); Training Committee, Pharmaceutical Researchers and Manufacturers of America (1988-1992) **Marquis Who's Who Honors:** Albert Nelson Marquis Lifetime Achievement Award **Why did you become involved in your profession or industry:** Ms. Immel became involved in her profession because she was very lucky to take an undergraduate course in pharmacology; at the time, UCSB was the only school offering it. She took the course with Dr. Samuel Jacobs when she was a junior; she loved the class. She loved the subject because it was a helping profession, especially the work that she was trained in by some excellent people. It fit her personality to protect patients and consumers. She was taught to always go above and beyond the minimum requirements to protect patients and consumers. **Avocations:** Reading; Travel

Joseph Herbert Immel Jr., PhD

Title: Scientist, Biologist, Physiologist, Anatomist **Industry:** Sciences **Date of Birth:** 10/28/1952 **State/Country of Origin:** Morocco **Education:** PhD, University of California Santa Barbara; MS, University of California Los Angeles; BS, University of California Santa Barbara **Creative Works:** Contributor, Scientific Papers, Journals **Marquis Who's Who Honors:** Albert Nelson Marquis Lifetime Achievement Award **Why did you become involved in your profession or industry:** Dr. Immel became involved in his profession because his dad gave him a microscope when he was very young, which prompted him to pursue a career in science. He worked hard in classes and was really inspired by his teacher, Dale Boregard. Dr. Immel later dedicated his thesis to him.

Judy Ann Immel

Title: Educator (Retired) **Industry:** Education/Educational Services **Company Name:** Los Angeles County Office of Education **Date of Birth:** 05/12/1944 **Place of Birth:** Seattle **State/Country of Origin:** WA/USA **Parents:** Morris LeRoy Rush; Rosemary Jean (Condell) Rush **Marital Status:** Divorced **Spouse Name:** John J. Immel (6/30/1961, Divorced 1986) **Children:** John Jay; Charles R.; Diana L. Immel Narey **Education:** MA in Education, California State Polytechnic University (1988); BS in Home Economics, California State Polytechnic University (1984) **Certifications:** Certified Elementary, Secondary, Adult, and Postsecondary Teacher, California; Credentials in Secondary Administration **Career:** Retired (2010); Teacher, Los Angeles County Office of Education, La Mirada, CA (1993-2010); Adjunct Professor, University of San Diego (1998-2008); Teacher, Downey Adult School (1988-2002); Teacher, Garey High School, Pomona, CA (1992-1993); Teacher, Puente Hills High School, Hacienda Heights, CA (1990-1992); Teacher, Whittier Adult and Occupational School (1988-1990); Teacher, North Orange County Community College, Fullerton, CA (1988-1990) Interior Designer, Various Companies, California (1978-1988) **Career Related:** Advisor, Home Economics, Designated Subjects Credential Board, Pomona, CA (1990-1992) **Creative Works:** Editor, Home Economic District Association (1992); Editor, Newsletter, Home Economic Alumni Association (1988-1992); Author, Curriculum in Field **Memberships:** American Home Economics Association; Golden Key National Honor Society; Phi Upsilon Omicron; Sons of Norway; District Cultural Director **Marquis Who's Who Honors:** Albert Nelson Marquis Lifetime Achievement Award; Marquis Who's Who Top Professional **Avocations:** Quilt making; Gardening; Needlework; Reading **Political Affiliations:** Independent

Marilyn Sue Immoos, PhD

Title: Senior Psychologist Specialist **Industry:** Medicine & Health Care **Company Name:** California Department of Corrections and Rehabilitation **Place of Birth:** Sacramento **State/Country of Origin:** CA/USA **Parents:** Winston Alma; Alice Laverne (Flynn) Alma **Marital Status:** Divorced **Spouse Name:** Manfred Peter Speiser; René Alfred Immoos (Divorced, 1991) **Children:** Alexandra Immoos; Maria Theresa Immoos **Education:** Post-doctoral Fellowship, Psychological Counseling Services, California State University, Sacramento; PhD in Psychology, University of Vienna, Austria (1993); MA, University of Innsbruck, Austria (1990); Mozarteum, Salzburg, Austria (1974); California State University, Sacramento, CA (1969); New England Conservatory of Music, Boston, MA (1968) **Career:** Freelance Vocal Coach, Zürich Opera (1996-Present); Teacher, Peoples' Institutes of Higher Education, Switzerland (1993-Present); Composer (1993-Present); Conductor, Community Church Choirs, Switzerland (1990-Present); Freelance Concert Singer (1990-Present); Developer, Statewide Psychology Internship Program (2015); Collaborator, Children's Choir, Zürich, Switzerland (1994-1996); Founder, Director, Center for Psychology of Voice, Zürich, Switzerland (1988); Music Therapist, Psychiatric University Clinic, Basel, Switzerland (1986); Mezzo-soprano, City Theater, Luzern, Switzerland (1981-1984); Part-time Managerial Psychologist, Fischhof Institute of Managerial Psychology (1979-1983); Part-time Assistant, Psychotherapist, Assistant Trainer, Psychiatric Rehabilitation Center, Lauzendorf, Austria (1979-1981); Concert Singer, Vienna, Austria (1974-1979); Senior Psychologist Specialist, CA Statewide Mental Health Program, Training Unit **Career Related:** Freelance Researcher, Swiss Acquired Immune Deficiency Syndrome Help, Zürich and Bern (1986); Freelance Counselor, Alcohol and Drug Addiction, Zürich, Switzerland (1986) **Creative Works:** Co-author, "Reduced Bone Strength and Muscle Force in Women 27 Years After Anorexia Nervosa," International Journal of Endocrinology; Contributor, Various Organization-internal Publications in the Areas of Differential Diagnosis of Mental Disorders; Contributor, Series of Manuals Related to Clinical Practice and Psychotherapy **Memberships:** Researcher, Organization for Parents of Children with Attention Deficit Hyperactivity Disorder, Zürich, Switzerland (1999); Voice Foundation; Swiss Federation of Psychologists; Chow-chow Club; Representative to California Board of Psychology; California Psychological Association; American Psychological Association **Marquis Who's Who Honors:** Albert Nelson Marquis Lifetime Achievement Award **To what do you attribute your success:** Dr. Immos attributes her success to a number of factors, including the excellent professional role models she has had throughout various stages of her professional development, her undying curiosity for seeking to better understand the underlying mechanisms of human behavior, her ability to research, test out and integrate some of the most unlikely components she discovers along the way, the opportunity to meet people from all walks of life who have brought a wealth of new information to the table, the ability to let go of what does not work (or apply) and to persist in attempting to find what may work (or fit) and the ability to "wait for it" while pursuing this knowledge. Dr. Immoos describes her quest as a "work in progress" and not and "end-all" solution. **Why did you become involved in your profession or industry:** Dr. Immoos became involved in her profession after starting as an opera singer in Europe. Dr. Immoos was fascinated with the human voice and began researching the effects of music on human emotion. Her almost insatiable quest for knowledge and understanding of underlying principles and mechanisms proved to be a driving force. Dr. Immoos' passion for discovering new concepts and ways to integrate these concepts into working models for helping improve the delivery of effective mental health services to people in need represented the most powerful motivations for her involvement with patient care. The same passion has kept her engaged in this endeavor, while collecting new data that has the potential to be incorporated into effective treatment methods for severe mental distress. **Avocations:** Acting; Cooking; Gardening; Dog-raising; Musical composition and conducting **Thoughts on Life:** Life is an amazing process. It's a "river" and not a "pond." Dr. Immoos marvels at the enormous variety of human behaviors and how humans have been able to step up to the plate, even under the most dire of circumstances. Humans not only have survived some of the most difficult circumstances, but, in the end, the human species has, in many areas, has survived surprisingly well. Dr. Immoos has hope and confidence that humans will find ways to continue to meet the difficult challenges they now face.

Jennifer Joan Ingmire

Title: Aerospace/Mechanical Engineer **Industry:** Engineering **Company Name:** Naval Air Systems Command (NAVAIR) **Date of Birth:** 02/07/1969 **Place of Birth:** Rochester **State/Country of Origin:** MI/USA **Parents:** Billy Raymond; Barbara Joan (Dorsch) Wheeler **Marital Status:** Married **Spouse Name:** Gordon Ingmire **Children:** Tia; Toby; Taylor; Tasha; Talea **Education:** Masters of Science in Mechanical Engineering, The University of Arizona (1995); Bachelor of Science in Aerospace Engineering, The University of Arizona (1992) **Certifications:** Engineer in Training (1993) **Career:** Mechanical Engineer, Deputy Assistant Program Manager Systems Engineering, NAWCAD, Patuxent River, MD (2003-Present); Aerospace Engineer, Human Systems, NAWCWD, China Lake, CA (2000-2003); Aerospace Engineer, Lead Engineer, Naval Aviation Depot, Jacksonville, FL (1995-2000); Research Assistant, NASA Jet Propulsion Lab (JPL), University of Arizona, Tucson, AZ (1993-1995); Teaching Assistant, Machine Shop, University of Arizona, Tucson, AZ (1991-1993) **Career Related:** Women's Initiative Network (WIN) **Civic:** Bay Community Support Services Board Member (2018-Present); Coach, Special Olympics, Skiing, Track and Field (2013-Present); Area Representative, Youth For Understanding USA (2005-Present); Volunteer, Special Olympics (2004-Present); CCD Teacher (1995-Present); Troop Leader, Girl Scouts (1994-Present) **Creative Works:** Co-Author, "Ports and Windows on Manned Spacecraft and on Lunar and Planetary Habitation Modules"; Co-Author, "Space Debris: an Engineering Solution with an Autonomous Space Robot"; Co-Author, "Teaching in Space"; Co-Author, "Optical Port Experiments"; Co-Author, "External Servicing Rack for Space Modules"; Co-Author, "Design and Development of Observation and Scientific Windows for Manned and Planetary Modules" **Awards:** ARSAG International Founders Award (2010); ARSAG International Award for ATP-56 (2007); Grantee, NASA (1994-1995) **Memberships:** American Institute of Aeronautics and Astronautics (1993-2010); Women's Initiative Network (WIN); NAVAIR Leadership Development Program (NLDP) **Marquis Who's Who Honors:** Albert Nelson Marquis Lifetime Achievement Award; Marquis Who's Who Top Professional **To what do you attribute your success:** Ms. Ingmire has never given up. She credits the wonderful support from her family to much of her success, and she feels lucky to have had several great mentors throughout her career. **Avocations:** Photography; Scrapbooking; Arts and crafts **Political Affiliations:** Moderate Republican **Religion:** Roman Catholic

Sabrina Elaine Ionescu

Title: Professional Basketball Player **Industry:** Athletics **Company Name:** New York Liberty **Date of Birth:** 12/06/1997 **Place of Birth:** Walnut Creek **State/Country of Origin:** CA/USA **Parents:** Dan Ionescu; Liliana Blaj **Education:** Diploma, University of Oregon (2020) **Career:** Professional Basketball Player, New York Liberty, WNBA (2020-Present); Basketball Player, Oregon Ducks, University of Oregon (2016-2020) **Awards:** Naismith Women's Player of the Year, NCAA (2020); AP Player of the Year (2020); Player of the Year, U.S. Basketball Writers Association (2020); Senior Class Award (2020); Honda Sports Award (2020); John R. Wooden Award (2019, 2020); Wade Trophy, NCAA (2019, 2020); Nancy Lieberman Award (2018-2020); Women's Basketball Player of the Year, Pac-12 Conferences (2018-2020); National Freshman of the Year, U.S. Basketball Writers Association (2017)

Stormy Irwin

Industry: Writing and Editing **Company Name:** Zellerbach Paper Co. **Date of Birth:** 09/04/1929 **Place of Birth:** Melrose Park **State/Country of Origin:** IL/USA **Parents:** Charles W. Irwin; Mary E. Irwin **Career:** Retired, Zellerbach Paper Co., Sacramento, CA (1952-1985) **Career Related:** Writer, Softball Summaries (2010-Present); Writer, 3-5 issues (Paper), "Softball Days of Our Lives", Sacramento CA **Civic:** Coach, Manager, Participant, Sacramento City Leagues **Creative Works:** Writer, Softball Summaries (2010-2019); Writer, Softball National News (2010-2017); Writer, Articles, Adventures from the West Coast to the East Coast (1982-2019); Writer, Articles, House-Boating Experience at Lake Shasta (1979-1984); Editor, Publisher, Owner, "Women in Softball" (1972-1978); Editor, Publisher, Owner, "Women in Sports" (1957-1971) **Awards:** Inductee, Hall of Honor, Softball Sacramento City (1980); First Place Plaque for Continuous Coverage of Softball for Non-Daily Publications with a Circulation of Under 50,000, National Softball Broadcasters and Writers Association, Amateur Softball Association of Oklahoma City (1971-1973, 1965-1968) **Marquis Who's Who Honors:** Albert Nelson Marquis Lifetime Achievement Award; Marquis Who's Who Top Professional **Why did you become involved in your profession or industry:** After attending a softball game in 1957, Ms. Irwin was awestruck; it was thrilling, and she couldn't wait to get home to write an article, take pictures, and tell her family. She felt the women's team deserved some press, which inspired her to start a publication. Though Ms. Irwin did not have a talent for softball, she was so inspired by the talented women on the team. This is what kept her writing about softball for so many years. As of 2020, she has visited numerous states and written about many different softball teams. In regard to her career at the paper company, she has excelled ever since she began working with the family-run business in 1962. It has been an exciting journey. **Avocations:** Houseboating on Lake Shasta; Writing about women's softball

Lesley Lowe Israel

Title: Political Consultant (Retired) **Industry:** Government Administration/Government Relations/Government Services **Date of Birth:** 07/21/1938 **Place of Birth:** Philadelphia **State/Country of Origin:** PA/USA **Parents:** Herman Albert Lowe; Florence (Segal) Lowe **Marital Status:** Married **Spouse Name:** Fred Israel (12/18/1960) **Children:** Herman Allen; Sanford Lawrence **Education:** BA, Smith College (1959) **Career:** President, Politics, Inc., Washington, DC (1987-1995); Chief Executive Officer, Politics, Inc. (1987-1995); Senior Vice President, The Kamber Group (1981-1987); Coordinator, National Labor, Kennedy for President (1979-1980); Special Assistant, Jackson for President (1975-1976); Director, Political Intelligence, Humphrey for President (1972); Director, Scheduling, Bayh for President (1971); Director, Media Advance, Humphrey for President (1967-1968) **Civic:** Presidential Appointment, President Barack Obama, U.S. Commission for the Preservation of America's Heritage Abroad (2016-Present); Chair, Avalon Coordination Centre (2009-Present); International Election Expert, U.S. Department of State (1997-Present); Director, IFES (1997-Present); Chair, Bender JCC of Greater Washington (1995-Present); Member, National Executive Commission, Anti-Defamation League (1994-Present); Member, National Commission, Anti-Defamation League (1991-Present); Member, Democratic Site Selection Committee (1989-Present); President, NCSEJ (2008-2009); Treasurer, IFES (2006-2017); Senior Election Officer, OSCE (1996); Chairman, Washington Regional Board, Anti-Defamation League (1991-1994); Member, Democratic Delegate Selection Commission (1983-1984); Member, Democratic Charter Commission (1982-1983); International Election Coordinator, Bender JCC of Greater Washington (1981-1983); President, Bender JCC of Greater Washington (1981-1983); Board of Managers, Adas Israel Congregation (1981-1983); Former Chairman, Washington Board, American Friends of Tel Aviv University **Awards:** Named One of the 100 Most Powerful Women, Washington Magazine (1990); Special Service Award, Jewish Community Center (1984) **Memberships:** Board Member, National Conference in Support of Eurasian Jewry (NCSEJ) **Marquis Who's Who Honors:** Albert Nelson Marquis Lifetime Achievement Award; Marquis Who's Who Top Professional **Religion:** Jewish

Anthony D. Ivankovich, MD

Title: Anesthesiologist **Industry:** Medicine & Health Care **Company Name:** Rush University Medical Center **Date of Birth:** 03/25/1939 **Place of Birth:** Debeljaca **State/Country of Origin:** Yugoslavia **Marital Status:** Married **Spouse Name:** Olga Ivankovich **Education:** Resident in Anesthesiology, The University of Chicago Hospitals (1967-1968); Rotating Intern, Edgewater Hospital, Chicago, IL (1966); Resident in Internal Medicine, County Hospital of Nunberg, Federal Republic of Germany (1963-1965); MD, University of Zagreb, Croatia (1963) **Certifications:** Licensed Physician, Illinois; Diplomate, American Board of Anesthesiology **Career:** Retired (2006); Director, Rush Pain Center, Chairman of Anesthesiology, Rush University Medical Center, Chicago, IL (1980-2006); Professor of Anesthesiology, Rush Medical College, Rush University Medical Center (1980); Faculty, School of Medicine, Cook County Postgraduate, Chicago, IL (1975-1985); Associate Professor of Anesthesiology, The University of Chicago (1972-1974); Assistant Professor in Anesthesiology, Loyola University Chicago Stritch School of Medicine, Maywood, IL (1970-1971); Instructor in Anesthesiology, The University of Chicago Pritzker School of Medicine (1969) **Career Related:** Trustee, Rush University Medical Center (2005-Present); President of Medical Staff, Director of Women and Children's Hospital, Associate Vice President, Rush University Medical Center (1994-2007); Director of Surgical Services, Associate Vice President, Rush University Medical Center (1993-2007); Chairman of the Council, Surgical Chairman, Division of Surgical Sciences and Services, Rush University Medical Center (1992-1994); Chairman of Anesthesiology, Rush University Medical Center (1980-2006); Associate Examiner, American Board of Anesthesiology (1978); Consultant in Anesthesiology, Shriners Hospital for Crippled Children (Now Shriners Hospitals for Children), Chicago, IL (1977-1982); With, Illinois Masonic Medical Center Chicago, IL (1974-1980); Associate Chief of Professional Services, 801st General Hospital, United States Army Reserve (1974-1976); Chief of Surgery, 801st General Hospital, United States Army Reserve (1973-1974); Lecturer in Anesthesiology, Loyola University Chicago Stritch School of Medicine (1971-1981); Attending Anesthesiologist, Loyola University Chicago Stritch School of Medicine (1971-1974); Director of Anesthesia Research, Loyola University Chicago Stritch School of Medicine (1971-1974); Chief of Operating Room Services, 801st General Hospital, United States Army Reserve, IL (1971-1973); Consultant in Anesthesiology, Suburban TB Sanatorium, Hinsdale, IL (1970-1971); Presenter in Field; Fellow, American College of Anesthesiologists **Creative Works:** Co-author, "Liposomes in Drug Delivery" (1992); Co-author, "Clinical Anesthesia Updates" (1992); Co-author, "Clinical Anesthesia" (1992); Co-author, "Cardiothoracic and Vascular Anesthesia Update" (1991); Co-author, "Advances in Anesthesia" (1990); Co-author, "Adjuncts to Cancer Therapy" (1989); Co-author, "Effective Hemostasis in Cardiac Surgery" (1988); Co-author, "Liposomes as Drug Carriers" (1987); Co-author, "Anesthesia and ENT Surgery" (1987); Co-author, "Current Controversies in Thoracic Surgery" (1986); Co-author, "Perspective in High Frequency Ventilation" (1983); Author, "Nitroprusside and Other Short-Acting Hypotensive Agents" (1978); Contributor, Articles and Abstracts, Professional Journals **Memberships:** American Medical Association; International Association for the Study of Pain; International Anesthesia Research Society; American Society of Anesthesiologists (ASA); American Heart Association, Inc.; American College of Chest Physicians; American Pain Society; Pan American Medical Association; Society for Intravenous Anesthesia (SIVA); Illinois State Medical Society; Illinois Society of Anesthesiologists; Society of Neurosurgical Anesthesia and Neurologic Supporting Care; Midwest Pain Society; Chicago Medical Society; Chicago Society of Anesthesiologists; Institute of Medicine of Chicago; Chicago Heart Association; Sigma Xi, the Scientific Research Honor Society **Marquis Who's Who Honors:** Albert Nelson Marquis Lifetime Achievement Award; Marquis Who's Who Top Professional **Why did you become involved in your profession or industry:** Dr. Ivankovich was a young doctor in cardiology in Germany. He came to the United States for an internship. There were a lot of cardiologists that weren't really doing too much.

Barbara Garvey Jackson, BM, MM, PhD

Title: 1) Music Educator 2) Publisher (Retired) **Industry:** Media & Entertainment **Company Name:** 1) University of Arkansas 2) ClarNan Editions **Date of Birth:** 09/27/1929 **Place of Birth:** Normal **State/Country of Origin:** IL/USA **Parents:** Neil Ford; Eva Burkhart Garvey **Marital Status:** Widow **Spouse Name:** Kern C. Jackson (03/29/1970); Malcolm Robert Seagrave (1953, Divorced 1959) **Children:** Kern; Ross; Bruce; Paul **Education:** Doctor of Philosophy in Musicology, Stanford University (1959); Master of Music, Eastman School (1952); Bachelor of Music, University of Illinois (1950) **Career:** Retired Publisher (2019); Professor Emerita, University of Arkansas (1991-Present); Publisher, ClarNan Editions (1982-2019); Professor of Music, University of Arkansas, Fayetteville, AR (1961-1991); Assistant Professor Music, Arkansas Tech University, Russellville, AR (1957-1961); Special Music Teacher, Los Angeles Public Schools, Los Angeles, CA (1956-1957); Professor of Music, University of Arkansas, Fayetteville, AR (1954-1956); Teacher (1954-1956) **Creative Works:** Co-author, "Practical Beginning Theory," Eighth Edition (2000); Editor, ClarNan Editions (1982-2019); Co-author, "The A.S.T.A. Dictionary of Bowing Terms for String Instruments" (1968); Co-author, "Practical Beginning Theory", with Dr. Bruce Benward (1963); Co-author, "The Songs of the Minnesinger, Prince Wizlaw of Rügen" **Memberships:** Phi Kappa Phi; Pi Kappa Lambda; Sigma Alpha Iota **Marquis Who's Who Honors:** Albert Nelson Marquis Lifetime Achievement Award **To what do you attribute your success:** Dr. Jackson credits his indelible success on good luck and the influence of several wonderful teachers. **Why did you become involved in your profession or industry:** Dr. Jackson has been interested in music since coming of age, having begun to play the violin at the age of 10. Upon attending college, she decided to major in music, and graduated with high honors in 1950. **Avocations:** Gardening; Photography **Political Affiliations:** Democrat **Religion:** Episcopalian

Lamar Demeatrice Jackson Jr.

Title: Professional Football Player **Industry:** Athletics **Company Name:** Baltimore Ravens **Date of Birth:** 01/07/1997 **Place of Birth:** Pompano Beach **State/Country of Origin:** FL/USA **Parents:** Lamar Jackson Sr.; Felicia Jones **Education:** Diploma in Communications, University of Louisville **Career:** Quarterback, Baltimore Ravens, National Football League (2018-Present) **Awards:** Named to the Pro Bowl (2019); Named to the First-team All-pro (2019); Named NFL Most Valuable Player (2019); Named NFL Passing Touchdowns Leader (2019); Named ACC Athlete of the Year (2018); Named Two-time ACC Offensive Player of the Year (2016, 2017); Named Two-time ACC Player of the Year (2016, 2017); Named Unanimous All-American (2016); Named Player of the Year, Sporting News (2016); Named Player of the Year, Associated Press (2016); Heisman Trophy (2016); Maxwell Award (2016); Walter Camp Award (2016); Bert Bell Award (2016)

Mona Jackson, EdD

Title: Educational Administrator, Assistant Principal **Industry:** Education/ Educational Services **Date of Birth:** 03/07/1947 **Place of Birth:** Miami **State/Country of Origin:** FL/USA **Parents:** Charles E. Bethel; Olga Isabel (Goodman) Bethel Williams **Marital Status:** Married **Spouse Name:** Herman Jackson II (12/31/1968) **Children:** Keane Sean; Herman, Jr. **Education:** EdD, Florida International University (2005); MEd, Florida Atlantic University (1973); BS, Florida A&M University (1969) **Certifications:** Certified Teacher, Florida (1969) **Career:** Assistant Principal, Dade County Public Schools (1986-Present); Mentor Principal, Miami Edison Senior High School (2008-2009); Principal, Richmond Heights Middle School (1997-2008); Middle School Liaison Principal, Miami Southridge Senior High School (1995-1999); Project Manager, Dade County Public Schools (1984-1986); Educational Specialist, Dade County Public Schools (1982-1984); Curriculum Coordinator, Perrine Crime Prevention Program, Miami, FL (1979-1982); Counselor, Dade County Public Schools (1975-1982); Science Teacher, Counselor, Dade County Public Schools (1974-1975); Science Teacher, Dade County Public Schools, Miami, FL (1970-1974) **Civic:** Presenter, "Gender Differences in Principal Motivations," National Conference, American Educational Research Association, Chicago, IL (2006); Secretary, Vestry, Christ Episcopal Church (1984-1986); President, Dade County Sickle Cell Foundation (1983-1986); Secretary, Board of Directors, Haitian Refugee Center, Miami, FL (1983-1985); President, The Episcopal Church Women for the Diocese of South Florida **Creative Works:** Co-Author, "Candlelights for Middle School Student's World" (2002); Author, "Focus on Careers" (1984) **Awards:** Certificate of Appreciation Award for Excellence, Outstanding Service, Commitment, and Dedication, Sickle Cell Community, The Sickle Cell Miami Foundation, Sickle Cell Advocacy and Outreach (2018); Inductee, George Washington Carver High School Hall of Fame (2011-2012); Award in Education, Louie Bing Scholarship Fund, Inc. (2009); "In the Company of Women" and Pillars Award for Education, Miami-Dade County Public Schools (2006); Bell Award, Principal of the Year, Dade County Council PTA/PTSA (2005); Principal Achievement Award for Outstanding Leadership, Dade Counseling Association, Florida Department of Education (2003); Middle School Administrator of the Year (2003); Principal of the Year First Runner-up, Dade County Public Schools (2003); Principal of the Year, ACCESS Center 6 (2002-2003); Middle School Administrator of the Year (1996); Plaque, Florida Association of Counseling and Development (1985); Plaque, Dade County Personnel and Guidance Association (1984); Plaque, Dade County Sickle Cell Disease Foundation (1981); One of the Teachers of the Years, Charles Drew Junior High School (1972); Unsung Hero, Booker T. Washington Alumni Association **Memberships:** President, Florida Association of Counseling and Development (1986-1987); Convention Executive, Florida Association of Counseling and Development (1986-1987); President-Elect, Florida Association of Counseling and Development (1985-1986); President, Dade County Personnel and Guidance Association (1983-1984); President, Miami Chapter, Delta Sigma Theta (1976-1980); President, Beta Alpha Chapter, Delta Sigma Theta (1967-1968); Women Involved Now, Florida Association of Science Teachers; Phi Delta Kappa **Marquis Who's Who Honors:** Albert Nelson Marquis Lifetime Achievement Award **Why did you become involved in your profession or industry:** As a student, Dr. Jackson used to help her peers. This is what inspired her to pursue teaching, as she found a passion for educating others. Likewise, she was inspired by her relatives, former teachers, and former administrators. **Avocations:** Reading; Traveling; Puzzles **Political Affiliations:** Democrat **Religion:** Episcopalian

William Richard Jackson, PhD, DSc

Title: Founder, Chairman of the Board **Industry:** Environmental Services **Company Name:** Jackson International, Inc. **Date of Birth:** 08/23/1936 **Place of Birth:** Nampa **State/Country of Origin:** ID/USA **Parents:** Richard W. Jackson; Josie P. (Mulder) Jackson **Children:** James Lee; Robbi Jo; Jolynn Kay **Education:** DSc, Northwest Nazarene University (2014); Postdoctoral Coursework, Stanford University Advanced Management College (1991); PhD in Higher Education Administration and Research, University of Denver (1991); EdM, University of Denver (1964); MEd in Secondary Education Administration, University of Northern Colorado (1961); EdB in Secondary Education, Northwest Nazarene University (1957) **Certifications:** Certification in Toxic Waste Remediation and Hyperbaric Oxygenation Medicine (1962) **Career:** Co-Founder, Environmental Care & Share, Inc. (2001-Present); President, Jackson International, Inc. (1984-Present); President, Jackson Brothers Industries (1984-Present); Founder and President, Enviro Consultant Service (1989-2003); Co-Owner, President, International Bell Museum, Inc. (1978-1986); Co-Owner, Operator, Jackson Brothers Investments (1970-1984); Director of Student Council, Brook Forest Leadership Institute, Evergreen, CO (1961-1964); Teacher in Psychology, Englewood School District (1961-1964); Teacher in Economics, Englewood Schools (1961-1964); School Teacher in Humanities, Speech and Art, Caldwell, ID (1958-1960); Football Coach, Caldwell, ID (1958-1960); Executive Insurance Director of Education Services, Idaho School of Employment, Boise, ID (1957-1958); Account Manager, Collection Contractor, Montgomery Ward, Inc., Walla Walla, WA (1953-1957); Owner, Operator, Janitorial Service (1950-1954); Chairman of the Board, Jackson International Inc. **Career Related:** Chairman of Board, Petro Silver, Inc., Denver, CO (1979-1983); Research Consultant in Agriculture; Research Consultant in Toxic Waste Remediation and Hyperbaric Oxygenation Medicine; Senior Consultant, Environmental Health Foundation 501c3; San Francisco Member of Staff, Southwest Research Institute, San Antonio, TX; Speaker on Organic Soil **Civic:** Co-Founder, Benevolent Brotherhood Foundation (1971-Present) **Creative Works:** Author, "Humic, Fulvic and Microbial Balance: Volume III - Hyperbaric Oxygen and Beyond" (2018); Author, "Humic, Fulvic and Microbial Balance: Volume II - Life: More Abundant" (2016); Author, "Blueprints for Positive Living" (2014); Author, "Hello God It's Me" (2013); Author, "Weathered Wisdom" (2004); Co-Author, "From Humic Substances in Academia To The Needs Of International Commerce", International Humic Substances 20th Anniversary Conference (2001); Author, "Environmental Care & Share" (1995); Author, "Fabulous Fulvic Electrolyte" (1995); Author, "The Arthritis, Osteoporosis and Silica Link" (1995); Author, "The Calcium Deception" (1995); Author, "Silver For Human Health", for the Environmental Health Foundation (1995); Author, "Humic, Fulvic and Microbial Balance: Volume I - Organic Soil Conditioning" (1993); Author, "Hyperbaric Oxygenation Effects on the Cognitive Function of Memory" (1991); Co-Author, "Disciplining Curriculum" (1978); Co-Author, "Brook Forest Leadership Curriculum" (1964); Author, "Barter, The History, Mystery and Mastery of Mutual Exchange" **Awards:** First Place, National Self-Publishing Award, Writer's Digest, F+W (1993); Grant, Denver Presbyterian Medical Center (Now Presbyterian/St. Luke's Medical Center), C-HCA, Inc. (1991); Grant, San Diego Center for Hyperbaric Therapy (1991); Award, Undersea & Hyperbaric Medical Society **Memberships:** Research Consultant, Undersea & Hyperbaric Medical Society (1990-Present); International Hyperbaric Medical Foundation; Alumni Association, Stanford University; Phi Delta Kappa International **Marquis Who's Who Honors:** Albert Nelson Marquis Lifetime Achievement Award; Marquis Who's Who Top Professional; Marquis Who's Who Humanitarian Award **To what do you attribute your success:** Dr. Jackson attributes his success to his love for his fellow humans and his desire to take actions every day to help everyone live a better life. **Why did you become involved in your profession or industry:** Dr. Jackson originally trained to be a minister; however, he was turned down. He broadened his love for God and humanity to encompass the Earth and help provide safe, non-toxic, and non-hazardous environments for all creatures. He helps in the production of abundant, healthy food. **Avocations:** Bartering; Writing; Reading; Travel; Artwork; Oil painting; Tesla science **Political Affiliations:** Republican **Religion:** Christian

Darleen M. Jacobs

Title: Lawyer **Industry:** Law and Legal Services **Date of Birth:** 06/18/1945 **Place of Birth:** New Orleans **State/Country of Origin:** LA/USA **Parents:** Arthur Jacobs; Ann Jacobs **Marital Status:** Widowed **Spouse Name:** Judge S. Sanford Levy (Deceased) **Education:** JD in Law, Loyola University School of Law, Chicago, IL; Master's in Admiralty Law Degree, Tulane University School of Law, Chicago, IL; BA, Louisiana State University in New Orleans (LSUNO) (Now University of New Orleans) **Certifications:** Board Certified in Civil Trial Advocacy, National Board of Trial Advocacy **Career:** Private Practice, Law Firm, Specializing in Personal Injury, General Negligence, Medical Malpractice, Maritime, the Jones Act, and Class Action Law, New Orleans, LA (1970-Present) **Career Related:** Attorney; Real Estate Broker; Auctioneer **Awards:** Recognized by the American Trial Lawyers Association in "Trial," their national publication, as "Master of the Month"; Speaker, American Trial Lawyers Association, the Melvin Belli Seminars on Two Occasions **Memberships:** Louisiana State Bar Association; National Board of Trial Advocacy; New York State Bar Association; D.C. Bar Association; New Orleans Bar Association; Louisiana State Bar Association; St. Bernard Bar Association; Louisiana Council of Women Realtors; National Realtors Association; Louisiana Auctioneers Association **Bar Admissions:** Louisiana; New York; District of Columbia **Marquis Who's Who Honors:** Albert Nelson Marquis Lifetime Achievement Award **Political Affiliations:** Democrat **Religion:** Jewish

Diane Margaret Jacobs, PhD

Title: Professor Emerita **Industry:** Education/Educational Services **Date of Birth:** 03/24/1940 **Place of Birth:** Port-of-Spain **State/Country of Origin:** Tobago **Parents:** Saul Jacobs; Eleanor (Rosenberger) Jacobs **Marital Status:** Widowed **Spouse Name:** Michael K. Shelley (06/15/1985-06/29/2012) **Children:** Three Stepchildren **Education:** Doctor of Philosophy, Harvard University (1967); Bachelor of Arts, Radcliffe College (1961) **Career:** Professor Emerita, University of Central Florida (2016-Present); Professor of Microbiology, University of Central Florida (2008-2016); Professor of Molecular Biology and Microbiology, University of Central Florida (1994-2016); Chair, Department of Health Professions, University of Central Florida (2002-2008); Vice President for Research and Graduate Studies, University of Central Florida (1994-1998); Associate Vice Chancellor of Research, East Carolina University, Greenville, North Carolina (1989-1994); Dean, Graduate School, East Carolina University, Greenville, North Carolina (1989-1994); Professor of Biology, East Carolina University, Greenville, North Carolina (1989-1994); Professor of Microbiology, University at Buffalo (1980-1989); Associate Professor of Microbiology, University at Buffalo (1976-1980); Research Associate, Salk Institute Biological Studies, La Jolla, California (1974-1976); Instructor, Hadassah Medical School, The Hebrew University of Jerusalem (1967-1971); Lecturer, Hadassah Medical School, The Hebrew University of Jerusalem (1967-1971) **Career Related:** Reviewer, National Science Foundation, Washington, DC (1989-Present); Reviewer, National Institutes of Health, Bethesda, MD (1977-Present); Board of Directors, Central Florida Innovation Corp **Civic:** Member, Condo Association **Creative Works:** Contributor, Articles, Journal of Immunology; Contributor, Articles, Journal of Experimental Medicine; Contributor, Articles, Recent Developmental Mucosal Immunity **Memberships:** Councilor, Oak Ridge Association of Universities (1993-1998); Chair, Board of Directors, Council of Graduate Schools (1996); President, Conference of Southern Graduate Schools (1995-1996); Executive Committee, Conference of Southern Graduate Schools (1993-1996); Board of Directors, Council of Graduate Schools (1993-1996); Fellow, The Association of Schools of Allied Health Professions; The American Association of Immunologists Inc.; American Society for Microbiology; The New York Academy of Sciences; Association for Women in Science **Marquis Who's Who Honors:** Albert Nelson Marquis Lifetime Achievement Award; Marquis Who's Who Top Professional **To what do you attribute your success:** Dr. Jacobs attributes her success to her mentors. She had a mathematics teacher who wanted her to become a mathematician, but while studying in college she decided to specialize in microbiology, having met the new president of Radcliffe College, an esteemed microbiologist in her own right. **Avocations:** Travel; Genealogical research

Michael S. Jacobson

Title: Doctor **Industry:** Medicine & Health Care **Company Name:** Georgia Retina **Place of Birth:** Bridgeport **State/Country of Origin:** CT/USA **Education:** MD, University of Connecticut, Farmington, CT (1982); AB in Biochemistry, Dartmouth College, Hanover, NH (1978) **Certifications:** Licensed, Georgia; Licensed, Maryland (Inactive); Licensed, Minnesota (Inactive); Licensed, Illinois (Inactive) **Career:** President, Georgia Retina, P.C., Tucker, GA (2017-Present); Co-founder, Secretary, Vice President, Georgia Retina, P.C., Tucker, GA (1995-Present); Clinical Assistant Professor, Emory University, Atlanta, GA (1993-1996); Clinical Assistant Professor, University of Minnesota, Minneapolis, MN (1989-1991); Fellow in Retina and Vitreous Surgery, Ear & Eye Infirmary at UI Health (1988-1989); Fellow in Medical Retina, Ear & Eye Infirmary at UI Health (1987-1988); Resident of Ophthalmology, University of Maryland School of Medicine, Baltimore, MD (1984-1987); Staff Physician, McGuire Veterans Administration Hospital, Richmond, VA (1983-1984); Resident in Internal Medicine, Medical College of Virginia (Now Virginia Commonwealth University School of Medicine), Richmond, VA (1982-1983) **Career Related:** Physician Board Member, EyeSouth Partners (2017-Present); Moderator, The Retina Group, LinkedIn (2010-Present) **Civic:** Interviewer, Dartmouth College, Hanover, NH (1979-Present); Class Officer, Executive Board Member, Class of 1978, Dartmouth College, Hanover, NH (2008-2010); President, Mini-Reunion Chairs Association, Dartmouth College, Hanover, NH (2010); Member, Executive Board, Dartmouth Class Officers Association (2009-2010); Vice President, Mini-Reunion Chairs Association, Dartmouth College, Hanover, NH (2009); Leadership Development Council, The Temple (2008); Volunteer, Atlanta Community Food Bank; Volunteer, Zaban Couples Shelter; Volunteer, Georgia Lighthouse **Creative Works:** Author, Book Chapter, "The Impact of Pregnancy on Ophthalmic Surgery, Non-Obstetric Surgery During Pregnancy: A Comprehensive Guide" (2018); Speaker, Annual Meetings, American Society of Retinal Specialists, British Columbia, Canada (2010, 2017); Speaker, 24th Annual Southeastern Vitreoretinal Seminar, Emory University, Atlanta, GA (2010); Speaker, Annual Summer Meeting, Georgia Society of Ophthalmology, Atlanta, GA (2010); Speaker, Annual Meeting, Vitreous Society, Anchorage, AK (1998); Speaker, Annual Meetings, Georgia Society of Ophthalmology, Atlanta, GA (1995, 1997); Speaker, Annual Meetings, Southern Educational Congress of Optometry, Atlanta, GA (1993, 1994); Co-author, Book Chapter, "Choroiditis," Clinical Ophthalmology (1991); Speaker, Annual Meeting, American Academy of Ophthalmology, New Orleans, LA (1989); Speaker, Annual Meeting, Illinois Eye and Ear Infirmary, Chicago, IL (1987); Author, Contributor, Numerous Journal Articles (1983-2017); Researcher, Numerous Abstracts (1982-1990); Speaker, Annual Meeting, Association for Research in Vision and Ophthalmology, Sarasota, FL (1982); Principal Investigator, Sub-Investigator, Numerous Research Studies; Former Contributing Editor, Ophthalmology Alert; Former Contributing Editor, Review of Ophthalmology **Awards:** Bronze Star of Excellence, Confrérie de la Chaîne des Rôtisseurs (2020); Certificate of Recognition, Sigma Xi (1982); Citation, Dartmouth College, Physics Research (1976); Harvard Book Award (1973) **Memberships:** Vice Chargé de Missions, Chaine des Rotisseurs (1994-Present); Commandeur, Chaines des Rotisseurs (1993-Present); Fellow, American Academy of Ophthalmology; Georgia Society of Ophthalmology; Medical Association of Georgia; Atlanta Ophthalmological Society; American Medical Association (resigned); Vitreous Society (now American Association of Retinal Specialists); CME Committee, Georgia Society of Ophthalmology; Former President, Minneapolis Ophthalmological Society; Former Member, Association for Research in Vision and Ophthalmology; Sigma Xi **To what do you attribute your success:** Dr. Jacobson attributes his success to dedication and sacrifice. He also attributes his success to his wife who is very supportive of his hard work and dedication to his practice, patients and referral doctors. His secret to success is to hire and surround himself with the most talented intelligent people, as this type of team stimulates creativity, inspires hard work and achieves unparalleled success. There is a special synergy that arises from this exchange of ideas among leaders. **Why did you become involved in your profession or industry:** Dr. Jacobson has always seen himself as a scientist and has always been focused on wanting to help others. Uniquely the medical profession allows one to transform scientific knowledge into helping people and that is what made the medical profession so attractive to him. His father originally had plans for him to take over his commercial equipment business but he continued to excel in math and science and did not derive the same enjoyment from working in that business. He knew that he wanted to be a doctor since childhood. He chose ophthalmology because in medical school he was having trouble working the ophthalmoscope and was determined to learn to do so. He took an ophthalmology rotation and soon gained proficiency with the device. When this breakthrough occurred, and he was able to see properly into the eye, he commented "It was like a whole new world..." and then there was no looking back. It was crystal clear that he wanted to be an ophthalmologist. **Religion:** Jewish

Annette L. James

Title: Kinleiner **Industry:** Medicine & Health Care **Date of Birth:** 04/23/1937 **Place of Birth:** West Virginia **State/Country of Origin:** WV/USA **Parents:** Two Children **Spouse Name:** Ronald **Education:** Doctor of Kinlein, Institute of Esca/ Institute of Kinlein (1998); MSN, University of Rochester; BS, Alderson-Broaddus College **Certifications:** Certified Financial Planner; Certified in the Practice of Kinlein **Career:** Private Practice, Kinleiner; Partner, James, Williams & Associates; Assistant Professor, West Virginia University, Morgantown; Assistant Professor, Alderson-Broaddus College, Philippi, WV **Career Related:** Vice President, Trustee, Alderson-Broaddus College **Civic:** Member, Partners in Education, Harrison County Public Schools, Shinnston, WV; Trustee, Alderson-Broaddus College **Creative Works:** Co-author, "The Joy of Listening," (1993) **Awards:** Distinguished Alumni Award, Alderson Broaddus College (1995); Apollo Award, Alderson-Broaddus College (1993) **Memberships:** Member WVBC Ministers Wives Association; Womans Club (Shinnston) **Marquis Who's Who Honors:** Albert Nelson Marquis Lifetime Achievement Award

R. Aileen James, DMA

Title: Concert Pianist, Educator **Industry:** Education/Educational Services **Date of Birth:** 10/24/1937 **Place of Birth:** Los Angeles **State/Country of Origin:** CA/USA **Parents:** Russell Boyd James; Mildred Maude (McPherson) James **Marital Status:** Married **Spouse Name:** Donald Martin Traeger (8/27/1982, Deceased 6/2003); Alonzo Weldon Eiseman (7/27/1958, Divorced 7/1964) **Children:** Thomas; Tamara; Teresa **Education:** DMA, Stanford University (1981); Postgraduate Coursework, University of Southern California, Los Angeles, CA (1973); MA in Piano/Music History, Pacific Union College, Angwin, CA (1969); BA, Pacific Union College, Angwin, CA (1958) **Certifications:** Certified Teacher of Music **Career:** Private Piano Teacher (1959-Present); Artistic Director, American Pianists Association, Indianapolis, IN (1986-1997); Associate Professor of Music, Santa Clara University, California (1978-1982); Teaching Assistant, Stanford University (1976-1980); Assistant Professor of Music, Pacific Union College, Angwin, CA (1969-1974) **Career Related:** Guest Lecturer, Butler University Pedagogy Clinic, Indianapolis, IN (1995-1996) **Civic:** President, Independent Presenters Network (1995-1996); Educational Chairman, Indianapolis Symphony Orchestra (1986-1989); Board of Directors, Music in the Mountains; Board of Directors, Twin Cities Concert Association **Creative Works:** Soloist, Accompanist, Chamber Music, Concerts Throughout the United States, Central America, Austria and France (1954-Present); Professional Debut in Piano, Los Angeles, CA (1953); Public Performance Debut (1945); Vice President, Twin Cities Concerto Association; Writer, Program Notes for Each Concert; Conductor, "Adult Class for Adults Who Don't Want to Perform" **Awards:** Named, Honorary Citizen, Indianapolis, IN (1997); Recipient, Key to the City, Indianapolis, IN (1995) **Memberships:** Teachers National Association; American College of Musicians; Pi Kappa Lambda; Music Teachers National Association **Marquis Who's Who Honors:** Albert Nelson Marquis Lifetime Achievement Award **To what do you attribute your success:** Dr. James attributes her success or the key to her success to having what she calls an absurd sense of humor, throughout her life. She can turn her back on this that is bad and find something good. It is not the kind of thing where everything is going badly and she has a sense of humor, but she finds the good in every situation. Her kids and grandchildren are close, and not on the same side of the country or state, but they are a very close group. And as a mother that is what she wants. **Why did you become involved in your profession or industry:** Dr. James was a child piano prodigy. She recalls growing up and living in a small town in Tennessee where her father would come and play hymns on a Chickering Spinet piano. At only 2 years old, she would sit beside him and play the melody portion of the song. By age three, Dr. James began playing with both hands. In a nearby town, there was a woman whom graduated with a degree in piano. The woman had a class for preschool students and Dr. James' mother enrolled her in the class. For the first piano recital, the other children had played pieces that they had previously practiced and rehearsed. Since Dr. James was fairly new still, she had not gotten that far to memorize a piece. In turn, at 3 years old, Dr. James improvised for her part in the recital. In response, her teacher was so impressed that she had asked her mother if she has been taught it. **Avocations:** Travel; Avid reader; Culinary arts; Spending time with family and friends **Political Affiliations:** Independent

Thomas H. Jamison

Title: 1) Principal 2) Of Counsel **Industry:** Law and Legal Services **Company Name:** 1)Thomas H Jamison, Lawyer 2)Fenton & Keller **Date of Birth:** 12/29/1947 **Place of Birth:** Fresno, CA **State/Country of Origin:** California **Parents:** Oliver Jamison; Margaret Ratcliffe Jamison **Marital Status:** Single **Spouse Name:** **Children:** Peter Holman Jamison; Sarah Jamison Messmore **Education:** JD, University of California, Hastings College of the Law (1975); BA, Williams College, Cum Laude (1970) **Career:** Attorney, Fenton & Keller **Career Related:** Golfer, NCAA Golf Championships (1970) **Civic:** Panelist, California State Bar Convention (1990) **Military Service:** Honorable Discharge, U.S. Army National Guard (1970-1976) **Creative Works:** Co-Author, "California Real Property Sales Transactions, Chapter 8, Options" (2014); Editor, Articles, Hastings Law Journal **Awards:** AV Rated, Martindale Hubbell; Benedict Prize for Achievement in French, Williams College **Memberships:** Thurston Honor Society; Order of The Coif **Bar Admissions:** California (1976); Oregon (1975) **Marquis Who's Who Honors:** Marquis Who's Who Top Professional **To what do you attribute your success:** He attributes his success to a lot of hard work over many hours. Good lawyers spend a lot of time working. He had great clients and a certain amount of luck. Monterey County, California is not a big pond but their firm is the largest in the county and he was lucky to join the firm when he started 40 years ago. As a consequence he earned a good reputation, had good clients, and achieved a lot of success for those clients. He tried to make sure he was careful as well. He was also a law clerk right after law school for a Justice on the Supreme Court of Oregon. **Why did you become involved in your profession or industry:** He comes from a long line of lawyers. His father was a lawyer, and his great-grandfather was the district attorney for Bismarck, North Dakota, and was a lawyer. His younger brother is also a lawyer. It seemed like a default profession to go to law school, so that's what he did. **Avocations:** Golf; Reading; Music festivals

Barbara Jean Janson

Title: President **Industry:** Publishing **Company Name:** Janson Associates **Date of Birth:** 03/07/1942 **Place of Birth:** Mason City **State/Country of Origin:** IA/USA **Parents:** Harley Arnold Janson; Helen Victoria (Henrickson) Janson **Marital Status:** Married **Spouse Name:** Arthur R. Hilsinger (08/31/1997); John Batty Henderson (09/08/1984, Divorced 1990); W. John Shallenberger (02/24/1963, Divorced 09/1980) **Children:** Mona; Ann **Education:** Master of Business Administration, University of Rhode Island (1982); Master of Science in Mathematics, Trinity College (1970); Bachelor of Science in Mathematics, Iowa State University (1965); Coursework, Rhode Island School of Design **Career:** International Cancer Advisory Board, Beth Israel Deaconess Medical Center (2015-Present); Overseer, Beth Israel Deaconess Medical Center (2013-Present); Board of Directors, Foundation, Iowa State University (2012-Present); Visiting Committee for American Art, Museum of Fine Arts, Boston, MA (2011-Present); Dean's Advisory Council, College of Liberal Arts and Sciences, Iowa State University (2008-Present); Mathematics Department Advisory Council, Iowa State University (2007-Present); President, Janson Associates, Dedham, MA (1996-Present); Foundation Ventures, Iowa State University (2016-2019); Executive Committee, Foundation, Iowa State University (2012-2016); Chair, Investment Committee for University Endowment, Iowa State University (2011-2016); Investment Committee for University Endowment, Iowa State University (2009-2017); Public Consultant, Everyday Learning/Tribune Education Group (1996-1998); Founder, Tribune Education Group, McGraw Hill Education (1985-1996); President, Janson Publications, Inc. (Now Tribune Education Group, McGraw Hill Education) (1985-1996); Director of Publication, American Mathematics Society, Providence, RI (1982-1985); Assistant Editorial Director, American Mathematics Society, Providence, RI (1978-1981); Mathematics Instructor, Bristol County Community College, Fall River, MA (1977-1978); Mathematics Editor, Houghton Mifflin Harcourt, Boston, MA (1974-1977); Mathematics Instructor, Ulster County Community College, Kingston, NY (1973); Mathematics Teacher, Ulster Academy, Kingston, NY (1971-1973); Mathematics Teacher, Public High Schools, Avon, Farmington, Bloomfield, CT (1966-1968) **Career Related:** Massachusetts State Advisory Board of Mathematics and Science Education (2000-2008); Expert Panel on Materials Development Reference, National Science Foundation (1996-1999); Advisory Committee, State Systemic Initiative in Mathematics and Science, Rhode Island (1993-1994); Legislative Commission for Mathematics and Science Education, Rhode Island (1991); Steering Committee, American Mathematics Project, Berkeley, CA (1986-1992); Representative, Science Publication Committee, American Heart Association Inc. (1986-1990); Oversight Committee, Resources for Mathematics Reform, Educational Development Center, Newton, MA; State Advisory Commission on Libraries, Rhode Island **Civic:** Overseer, Beth Israel Deaconess Medical Center (2013-Present); Board of Directors, Iowa State University Foundation (2012-Present); Overseer, Boston Ballet (2003-Present); Visiting Committee for American Art, Boston Museum of Fine Arts (2001-Present); Investment Committee for University Endowment, Iowa State University Foundation (2009-2017); Chair, Investment Committee for University Endowment, Iowa State University Foundation (2002-2006); Governor, Iowa State University Foundation (2000); Massachusetts Advisory Council on Mathematics Education **Creative Works:** Editor, "Scholarly Publishing: Managing Today, Planning for Tomorrow" (1986); Amateur Artist, Rhode Island School of Design **Awards:** Distinguished Alumni Award, Iowa State University (2018); Outstanding Alumni Award, Department of Mathematics, Iowa State University (2009); Rhode Island Entrepreneur of the Year Award, Ernst and Young (1987); Mortar Board Award, Iowa State University (1965) **Memberships:** Board of Directors, Society for Scholarly Publishing (1986-1990); Chair, Annual Meeting, Society for Scholarly Publishing (1985); Journals Committee, Association of American Publishers (1982-1985); American Mathematics Society; Mathematics Association of America; National Council of Teachers of Mathematics **Marquis Who's Who Honors:** Albert Nelson Marquis Lifetime Achievement Award; Marquis Who's Who Top Professional **Why did you become involved in your profession or industry:** Ms. Janson established her publishing company during a a time of concern about the performance of American students in math and science. She published materials that were either new to the curriculum or advocated new approaches to instruction. This provided an alternative to the textbooks then in use, oriented to large state adoption guidelines. The Janson materials were all research-based, and many were funded by grants from the National Science Foundation. **Avocations:** Travel sketching; Studying piano **Thoughts on Life:** In mathematics, Ms. Janson is able, through philanthropy, to extend her reach and work with people who are creating change in ways that are really important for the future. This is an extension of the mission she had at her company.

Kylie Kristen Jenner

Title: Media Personality, Founder, Owner **Industry:** Cosmetics **Company Name:** Kylie Cosmetics **Date of Birth:** 08/10/1997 **Place of Birth:** Los Angeles **State/Country of Origin:** CA/USA **Parents:** Caitlyn Jenner; Kris Jenner **Marital Status:** Single **Spouse Name:** Travis Scott (2017-2019) **Children:** Stormi **Education:** Diploma, Laurel Springs School, Ojai, CA (2015); Student, Sierra Canyon School **Career:** Founder, Kylie Skin by Kylie Jenner (2019-Present); Founder, Owner, Kylie Cosmetics by Kylie Jenner (2016-Present) **Career Related:** Launched, Makeup Line, Balmain (2020); Launched, Sunglasses Line, Quay x Kylie, Quay Australia (2017); Spokesmodel, Puma (2016); Launched, Clothing Line, Kendall + Kylie, Topshop (2015); Ambassador, Nip + Fab (2015); Launched, Hair Extension Line, Kylie Hair Kouture, Bellami Hair Europe (2014); Launched, Shoe and Handbag Line, Steve Madden's Madden Girl (2014); Launched, Jewelry Line, Metal Haven by Kendall and Kylie, Pascal Mouawad's Glamhouse (2013); Launched, Clothing Line, The Kendall and Kylie Collection, PacSun (2013); Launched, Nail Polish Line, OPI (2013) **Civic:** Participant, Kick'n It For Charity Celebrity Kickball Games, Glendale, CA (2014); Participant, Charity Game, Pinz Bowling Center, Studio City, CA (2014); Share Our Strength, No Kid Hungry; GLA VA Fisher House; Fundraiser, Children's Hospital Los Angeles **Creative Works:** Appearance, "Keeping Up with the Kardashians" (2007-Present); Cameo, "Ocean's 8" (2018); Appearance, Music Video, "Stop Trying to Be God" (2018); Appearance, "Life of Kylie" (2017); Musician, "Beautiful Day" (2016); Appearance, Music Video, "Come and See Me" (2016); Guest Appearance, "I Am Cait" (2015-2016); Appearance, Music Video, "Dope'd Up" (2015); Guest Appearance, "Kingin' with Tyga" (2015); Appearance, Music Video, "I'm Yours" (2015); Appearance, Music Video, "Stimulated" (2015); Co-Author, "Rebels: City of Indra: The Story of Lex and Livia" (2014); Guest Appearance, "Deal with It" (2014); Appearance, Music Video, "Recognize" (2014); Co-Host, Much Music Video Awards (2014); Guest Appearance, "Kourtney and Khloé Take the Hamptons" (2014); Appearance, Music Video, "Blue Ocean" (2014); Guest Appearance, "Ridiculousness" (2014); Appearance, Music Video, "Find That Girl" (2013); Guest Appearance, "Kourtney and Khloé Take Miami" (2010, 2013); Appearance, Pilot, "Million Dollar Closets" (2012); Guest Appearance, "America's Next Top Model" (2012); Co-Author, "Time of the Twins" **Awards:** The Celebrity 100, Forbes (2017); Choice TV: Female Reality/Variety Star, Keeping Up with the Kardashians, Teen Choice Awards (2013)

Mona Dickson Jensen, PhD, MBA

Title: Biochemist (Retired) **Industry:** Other **Company Name:** Jensen Craft Enterprises **Date of Birth:** 04/08/1944 **State/Country of Origin:** WA/USA **Parents:** William Oscar; Louise (Archer) Dickson **Marital Status:** Married **Spouse Name:** Thomas Carl Jensen (6/17/1967) **Children:** Carla Louise; Aaron Raymond **Education:** Master of Business Administration in Finance, Babson College (1983); Doctor of Philosophy in Biochemistry, Biostatistics and Molecular Biology, Cornell University (1973); Bachelor of Science in Biology, Massachusetts Institute of Technology (1966) **Career:** Retired (2012); Co-founder and President, Jensen Craft Enterprises Incorporated, New Hampshire (1998-Present); Manager, Veterinary Clinical Chemistry Research and Development, IDEXX Laboratory Inc., Westbrook, ME (2005-2012); R&D Manager, IDEXX Laboratory Inc. (2004-2005); Research Scientist, IDEXX Laboratory Inc. (2001-2004); R&D Manager, Startup Company, Boston, MA (1996-1998); Scientific Support, Applications Manager, Clinical Chemistry Strategic Business Unit, Instrumentation Laboratory, Lexington, MA (1995-1996); Senior Research and Development Manager, Instrumentation Laboratory, Lexington, MA (1988-1995); Manager, Reagent Systems Applications, Instrumentation Laboratory, Lexington, MA (1986-1988); Project Manager, Instrumentation Laboratory, Lexington, MA (1979-1986); Senior Scientist, Instrumentation Laboratory, Lexington, MA (1972-1979) **Career Related:** Sub-communications Advisor, National Committee on Clinical Laboratory Standards (1991-Present); Proposal Reviewer, National Science Foundation (1983-1986); Special Reviewer in vitro, National Science Foundation (1980-1981); Adjunct Faculty, W. Alton Jones Cell Science Center, Lake Placid, NY (1974-1976) **Civic:** Organist, Pianist, Island Pond Baptist Church, Hampstead, NH (1985-2017) **Creative Works:** Co-author, "Practical Tissue Culture Applications" (1979); Co-author, "Cell Culture and Its Application" (1977); Contributor, Articles to Professional Journals **Awards:** Grantee, World Health Organization (1980-1981) **Memberships:** Daughters of the American Revolution; American Chemical Society; American Association for Clinical Chemistry; American Philatelic Society; Pilgrim Edward Doty Society; Beta Gamma Sigma **Marquis Who's Who Honors:** Albert Nelson Marquis Lifetime Achievement Award **To what do you attribute your success:** Dr. Jensen attributes her success to learning how to circumvent roadblocks in research and corporate culture. **Why did you become involved in your profession or industry:** While coming of age, Dr. Jensen developed a great interest in mathematics and science. Her mother, Louise, was a math teacher who was on her way to receiving a PhD in mathematics, but had to put her ambitions on hold due to the outbreak of the Second World War. Dr. Jensen believes that her mother was an inspiration in pursuing the career path that she did. **Avocations:** Genealogy; Organ playing **Political Affiliations:** Republican **Religion:** Methodist **Thoughts on Life:** Chemically, creation is an incredibly complex series of checks and balances designed to return to equilibrium by small steps when accidents disrupt. In our lives, patience has the same effect.

William H. Jeynes

Title: Education Educator; Religious Organization Administrator; Minister **Industry:** Education/Educational Services **Company Name:** Witherspoon Institute **Date of Birth:** 03/27/1957 **Place of Birth:** New York **State/Country of Origin:** NY/USA **Parents:** Paul Hettich Jeynes; Enid Phillips Jeynes **Marital Status:** Married **Spouse Name:** Hyelee Jung Jeynes (06/17/1986) **Children:** Isaiah; Elisha; Luke **Education:** PhD, The University of Chicago, Chicago, IL (1997); MEd, Harvard University, Cambridge, MA, First in Class (1993); PhD, Freedom Seminary, Orlando, FL (1992); Doctor of Ministry, Freedom Seminary, Orlando, FL (1986); BA, University of Wisconsin-Madison, Madison, WI (1979) **Career:** Senior Fellow, Witherspoon Institute (2010-Present); Professor, California State University, Long Beach (2001-Present); Assistant Professor, Hillsdale College, MI (1999-2001); Lecturer, National Louis University, Evanston, IL (1999); Lecturer, Roosevelt University, Schaumburg, IL (1999); Lecturer, The University of Chicago (1996-1999); Lecturer, Northeastern Illinois University, Chicago, IL (1996-1999). **Career Related:** U.S. and Foreign Government Advisor/Consultant (1998-Present); Architect, South Korean Economic Stimulus Package to Arise from Asian Economic Crisis (1998); Writer, President George W. Bush Administration; Writer, President Barack Obama Administration; Advisor/Consultant for Three Presidential Administrations (George W. Bush, Barack Obama, and Donald Trump) and Former Members of the Clinton Administration; Advisor/Consultant, EU, Some G20 Governments, and United Nations; Consultant, Two U.S. Presidential Candidates, Speaker, U.S. Government: Speaker, The White House; Speaker, U.S. Department of Justice; Speaker, U.S. Department of Education; Speaker, U.S. Department of Health and Human Services; Speaker, Harvard University; Speaker, Columbia University; Speaker, University of Oxford; Speaker, University of Cambridge; Speaker, Peking University, Speaker, Moscow State University; Speaker, Imperial College, London; Speaker, National Press Club; Speaker, Harvard Family Research Project, Harvard University, Cambridge, MA; Speaker, World's Largest Church; Speaker, Various National and International Government Dignitaries; Speech and Talking Points Writer, Various Politicians Including Two U.S. Presidential Candidates, Nonresident Research Fellow, Baylor University **Civic:** President, God's Love Ministries, Huntington Beach, California (1978-Present); Trustee, International Values Education Values; North American Representative, International Values Education Values; Organizer, Bible Literature Public Schools; Columnist, Orange County Register **Creative Works:** Author, "Eliminating the Achievement Gap" (2019); Author, "Wiley Handbook of Christianity and Education" (2018); Author, "What Would Christ Do?" (2016); Author, "Ministering Spirituality to Families" (2015); Author, "School Choice: A Balanced Approach" (2014); Author, "International Handbook of Protestant Education" (2012); Author, "Getting Closer to God" (2012); Author, "Parental Involvement and Academic Success" (2011); Author, "Family Factors and Children's Educational Success" (2010); Author, "A Call for Character Education and Prayer in the Schools" (2010); Author, "American Educational History: School, Society and the Common Good" (2007); Author, "Christianity Education and Modern Society" (2007); Author, "A Hand Not Shortened" (2006); Author, "Religion, Education and Academic Success" (2003); Author, "Divorce, Family Structure and the Academic Success of Children" (2002); Columnist, LSE; Contributor, Approximately 180 Publications, Including 15 Books; Specializes in Conducting Meta-analyses **Awards:** Distinguished Achievement Award, American Educational Research Association (2015); Named California State Senate Distinguished Scholar (2012); Named California State Assembly Distinguished Scholar (2012); Named Outstanding Intellectual of Twentieth Century, Cambridge, United Kingdom (2001-2015); Named to International Network Scholars, Johns Hopkins University (2001); Rosenberger Award for Most Outstanding Cohort, The University of Chicago (1994) **Memberships:** Chair, Religion and Education Special Interest Group, American Educational Research Association (2004-2017); Executive Board, Family, School and Community Partnerships Special Interest Group, American Educational Research Association (2004-2006); American Psychological Association **Marquis Who's Who Honors:** Albert Nelson Marquis Lifetime Achievement Award **To what do you attribute your success:** Dr. Jeynes attributes his success to God's Grace. **Why did you become involved in your profession or industry:** Dr. Jeynes became involved in his profession because he believes that "children are our future." **Avocations:** Football; Baseball; Walking; Weightlifting; Chess **Thoughts on Life:** Dr. Jeynes has been interviewed or quoted by the Washington Post, the Los Angeles Times, the New York Times, the Wall Street Journal, the London Times, the Associated Press, CNN, CBS, ABC, NBC, FOX, Al Jazeera, U.S. News & World Report, USA Today, Newsweek Japan, the Atlantic, Education Week, the New York Post, Popular Science, Educational Leadership, the Japan Times, and many other media outlets. His work has been cited and quoted numerous times by the U.S. Congress, the British Parliament, the EU, and many State Supreme Courts across the United States.

Kulanand Jha

Title: Professor, Geotechnical Engineer **Industry:** Education/Educational Services **Company Name:** INDOT **Date of Birth:** 08/04/1949 **Place of Birth:** Dubrajpur **State/Country of Origin:** Jharkhand/ India **Parents:** Bimla Jha; Shukdeo Jha **Marital Status:** Married **Spouse Name:** Kiran Jha **Education:** PhD, Civil Engineering, University of Oklahoma (1977); MS, Transportation and Highway Engineering, West Virginia University (1973); BCE, National Institute of Technology, Jamshedpur, India (1970) **Certifications:** Professional Engineer (PE) **Career:** Senior Geotechnical Engineer, Department of Transportation (1999-Present); Consulting Engineer (1995-1999); University Professor (1988-1994); Research, Teaching and Consultancy (1972-1988); Fellowship, Institution of Engineers, India **Career Related:** Soil Stabilization, Clay Mineralogy, Physicochemical Properties of Soil, Soil Mechanics, Pavement and Materials **Civic:** General Community Work, Temple Committee Member **Creative Works:** Contributor, 45 Publications on Soil Stabilization, Soil Mechanics, Pavements and Rural Roads; Contributor, Books, Manual and Research Reports **Memberships:** American Society of Civil Engineers; Indian Roads Congress; Indian Geotechnical Society; Indian Society of Technical Education; Institution of Engineers, India **To what do you attribute your success:** Dr. Jha attributes his success to teaching, research and consultancy in universities, as well as professional and industrial experience, for about 25 years. **Why did you become involved in your profession or industry:** Dr. Jha was inspired to see outstanding civil engineering works in his surroundings and the world. He wanted to provide all weather rural roads in the interior and isolated communities/ villages of developing countries. **Religion:** Hindu **Thoughts on Life:** Stay persistent towards your goal in life.

Jugjit S. Johal

Title: Principal **Industry:** Law and Legal Services **Company Name:** Law Offices of Jack S. Johal **Marital Status:** Married **Children:** Two Children **Education:** Master of Laws in Taxation, New York University School of Law, New York, NY (1983); Doctor of Jurisprudence, Duquesne University School of Law, Pittsburgh, PA (1981); Bachelor of Arts in English and Economics, Occidental College, Los Angeles, CA, With Distinction (1978) **Career:** Principal, Law Offices of Jack S. Johal (2012-Present); Attorney, CVM Law Group, LLP (2009-2012); Attorney, Hanson Bridgett LLP (2003-2009); Attorney, Trainor Robertson (1988-2003); Attorney, Neumiller and Beardslee (1983-1988) **Career Related:** Teacher, Continuing Education of the Bar Courses on "Organizing and Advising Limited Liability Companies" to California Lawyers (2009); Teacher, "Advanced Course of Study: Pass Throughs: Choosing Entities and Drafting Agreements," San Francisco (2001); Teacher, Continuing Education of the Bar Courses on "Organizing and Advising Limited Liability Companies" to California Lawyers (1995, 1998-1999, 2000) **Civic:** United Way Board of San Joaquin County; President, Child Abuse Prevention Council of San Joaquin County **Creative Works:** Assistant Editor, Drafter, the Guide to Organizing and Operating a Limited Partnership in California, Report of the Partnerships and Limited Liability Committee, Business Law Section, State Bar of California (2012); Co-Speaker, Topic of "Fiduciary Duty Considerations in General Partnerships, Limited Partnerships, and Limited Liability Companies," Fourth Annual Spring Meeting, Business Law Section, State Bar of California (2003); Co-Editor, Update to the "Guide to Organizing and Operating a Limited Liability Company in California" (1999); Practice Consultant for the Limited Liability Company Chapter, "California Legal Form" by Matthew Bender (1998); Co-Author, "Practicing Under California's Version of the Revised Uniform Partnership Act" for "California Business Law News," Business Law Section, State Bar of California (1997); Presenter, Two Seminars for the Section Education Institute of the State Bar of California, "Recent Developments in Partnerships, LLC, and LLPs" and "Drafting Partnership and LLC Agreements" (1997); Assistant Editor, Drafter, "Guide to Organizing and Operating a Limited Liability Company in California," Report of the Partnerships and Unincorporated Business Organizations Committee, Business Law Section, State Bar of California (1995); Co-Author, Lead Article on Limited Liability Companies in the October and December Issues of the "California Business Law Reporter" (1994); Co-Author, Tax Chapter of the Continuing Education of the Bar's Publication, "Forming and Operating California Limited Liability Companies"; Co-Author, the Limited Liability Company Chapter for the Continuing Education of the Bar "Business Start-Up Manual"; Author, the Supplement to Several Chapters, "Buy-Sell" book for the Continuing Education of the Bar; Lecturer, Speaker in the Field **Awards:** Listee, Top 10% of Attorneys in Their Respective Field in the U.S., The Lawyers of Distinction (2018); Listee, One of Northern California's Top Rated Lawyers, ALM Media and Martindale-Hubbell (2018); Listee, Top 1% of America's Most Honored Professionals, The American Registry (2016-2019); Listee, One of the Top Business/Corporate Lawyers in Sacramento, Sacramento Magazine (2016, 2015); Five Star Wealth Manager Award (2010-2014); AV-Preeminent Rating, Martindale-Hubbell; AVVO Rating of Superb (10.0 out of 10.0) **Memberships:** State and Local Tax Committee; Chairperson, Legislative Committee, State and Local Tax Committee, Vice-Chair and Chair, State Bar Partnership Committee; Chairperson, Property Tax Subcommittee, State and Local Tax Committee; American Bar Association Committee on Trusts and Probate; Sacramento County Bar Association Probate and Real Property Sections; Monterey County Bar Association **Bar Admissions:** California (1983); Pennsylvania (1981); U.S. Court of Appeals for the Ninth Circuit; U.S. Tax Court **To what do you attribute your success:** Mr. Johal attributes his success to always being busy and taking abundant pride in his work. **Why did you become involved in your profession or industry:** Mr. Johal became involved in his profession due to his skill at public speaking, having delivered speeches at his church, high school and college.

Robert Gail Johanson, PhD

Title: Acting Quality Manager, Senior Applications Engineer **Industry:** Engineering **Date of Birth:** 08/26/1936 **Place of Birth:** San Francisco **State/Country of Origin:** CA/USA **Parents:** Robert N.; Martha A. (Peterson) J. **Marital Status:** Married **Spouse Name:** Joan B. Lee (09/25/1964) **Children:** Robert; Martha; Douglas; Wendy; Christopher **Education:** Postdoctoral Student, Case Western Reserve University (1969-1970); Doctor of Philosophy, Organic Chemistry, University of Vermont (1969); Bachelor of Arts in Chemistry, Reed College (1960) **Career:** Acting Quality Manager, Senior Applications Engineer, Indicate Technologies Incorporated, Santa Clara, CA (2008-Present); Consultant, Philips Lumileds Lighting Company, San Jose, California (2007); Consultant, Finisar Corporation, Sunnyvale, CA (2004-2007); Consultant, Genoa Corporation, Fremont, CA (2002-2004); Engineering Manager, Seagate Recording Media Operations, Milpitas, CA (1998-2000); Senior Staff Engineer, Conner Peripherals/Seagate Recording Media, Milpitas, CA (1992-1998); Director, Manufacturing Engineering, KMI Magnetics Inc., San Jose, CA (1990-1992); Manager, Process Engineering, Akashic Memories Corporation, Santa Clara, CA (1988-1990); Manager, Applications Laboratory, Circuits Processing Apparatus, Incorporated, Fremont, CA (1984-1988); Manager, Disk Operations, Datapoint Corporation, Mountain View, CA (1981-1983); Senior Member Technical Staff, Signetics Corporation, Sunnyvale, CA (1976-1981); Group Leader, Raychem Corporation, Menlo Park, CA (1972-1976); Staff Member, Raychem Corporation, Menlo Park, CA (1970-1972); Chemist, Aerojet-General Corporation, Sacramento, CA (1960-1966) **Career Related:** Disk Consultants, Sunnyvale, CA (1983-1984) **Military Service:** U.S. Army (1955-1957) **Creative Works:** Contributor, Articles to Professional Journals; Patents in field **Memberships:** American Chemical Society; American Vacuum Society; Electrochemical Society; Sigma Xi **Marquis Who's Who Honors:** Albert Nelson Marquis Lifetime Achievement Award; Marquis Who's Who Top Professional; Marquis Who's Who Humanitarian Award **To what do you attribute your success:** Dr. Johanson attributes his success to his own propensity for perseverance. **Why did you become involved in your profession or industry:** Dr. Johanson drew inspiration from his experiences while coming of age - his parents notably gifted him with a chemistry set for Christmas in 1943, which sparked his initial fascination with the field. **Avocations:** Skiing; Backpacking

Scarlett Ingrid Johansson

Title: Actress **Industry:** Media & Entertainment **Date of Birth:** 11/22/1984 **Place of Birth:** New York **State/Country of Origin:** NY/USA **Parents:** Karsten Johansson; Melanie Johansson **Marital Status:** Divorced **Spouse Name:** Romain Dauriac (10/01/2014, Divorced 09/2017); Ryan Reynolds (09/27/2008, Divorced 07/2011) **Children:** Rose Dorothy Dauriac **Education:** Diploma, Professional Children's School (2002); Coursework, Lee Strasberg Theatre Institute, New York, NY **Civic:** Participant, Women's March (2018); Collaborator, Time's Up (2018); Global Ambassador, Oxfam (2005-2014); Participant, ONE (2007); Aid Still Required; Cancer Research UK; Stand Up to Cancer; Too Many Women; USA Harvest **Creative Works:** Executive Producer, Actress, "Black Widow" (2020); Cameo, "Captain Marvel" (2019); Actress, "Avengers: Endgame" (2019); Actress, "Marriage Story" (2019); Actress, "Jojo Rabbit" (2019); Guest Host, "Saturday Night Live" (2006-2019); Voice Actress, "Isle of Dogs" (2018); Actress, "Avengers: Infinity War" (2018); Actress, "Ghost in the Shell" (2017); Actress, "Rough Night" (2017); Actress, "Captain America: Civil War" (2016); Actress, "Hail, Caesar!" (2016); Voice Actress, Video Game, "Lego Marvel's Avengers" (2016); Voice Actress, "The Jungle Book" (2016); Voice Actress, "Sing" (2016); Actress, "Avengers: Age of Ultron" (2015); Actress, "Chef" (2014); Actress, "Lucy" (2014); Guest Appearance, "HitRecord on TV" (2014); Actress, "Captain America: The Winter Soldier" (2014); Actress, "Cat on a Hot Tin Roof," Richard Rodgers Theatre (2013); Actress, "Don Jon" (2013); Actress, "Under the Skin" (2013); Voice Actress, "Her" (2013); Actress, "The Avengers" (2012); Actress, "Hitchcock" (2012); Executive Producer, Documentary, "The Whale" (2011); Actress, "We Brought a Zoo" (2011); Actress, "Iron Man 2" (2010); Actress, "A View from the Bridge," Cort Theatre (2010); Actress, "He's Just Not That Into You" (2009); Actress, "The Other Boleyn Girl" (2008); Actress, "Vicky Cristina Barcelona" (2008); Actress, "The Spirit" (2008); Appearance, Music Video, "Yes We Can" (2008); Guest Appearance, "Robot Chicken" (2005-2008); Actress, "The Nanny Diaries" (2007); Appearance, Music Video, "What Goes Around... Comes Around" (2007); Actress, "Scoop" (2006); Appearance, Music Video, "When the Deal Goes Down" (2006); Actress, "The Black Dahlia" (2006); Actress, "The Prestige" (2006); Actress, "Match Point" (2005) **Awards:** Robert Altman Award, Independent Spirit Awards (2020); Best Actress, "Marriage Story," Denver Film Critics Society (2020); Outstanding Performers of the Year Award, "Marriage Story," Santa Barbara International Film Festival (2020); Best Actress, "Marriage Story," Greater Western New York Film Critics Association (2020); Best Actress – Motion Picture Drama, "Marriage Story," Satellite Awards (2019); Best Actress, "Marriage Story," Detroit Film Critics Society (2019); Best Actress, "Marriage Story," Dallas–Fort Worth Film Critics Association (2019); Best Actress, "Marriage Story," St. Louis Film Critics Association (2019); Best Actress, "Marriage Story," Nevada Film Critic Society (2019); Choice Action Movie Actress, "Avengers: Endgame," Teen Choice Awards (2019); Best Screen Couple, "Marriage Story," Women Film Critics Circle (2019); Best Actress, "Marriage Story," Vancouver Film Critics Circle (2019); Best Actress, "Marriage Story," Utah Film Critics Association (2019); Best Actress, "Marriage Story," Florida Film Critics Circle (2019); Best Actress, "Marriage Story," Online Association of Female Film Critics (2019); Best Actress, "Marriage Story," Dublin Film Critics' Circle (2019); Female Movie Star Award, "Avengers: Infinity War," People's Choice Awards (2018); Choice Action Movie Actress, "Avengers: Infinity War," Teen Choice Awards (2018); Honorary César, César Awards (2014); Best Supporting Actress, "Her," Saturn Awards (2014); Best Depiction of Nudity, Sexuality, or Seduction, "Under the Skin," Alliance of Women Film Journalists (2014); Best Fight, "The Avengers," MTV Movie & TV Awards (2013); Best Supporting Actress, "Her," Detroit Film Critics Society (2013); Best Supporting Actress, "Her," Seattle Film Critics Society (2013); Special Honorary Award, "Her," Austin Film Critics Association (2013); Best Actress, "Her," Rome Film Festival (2013); Best Supporting Actress, "Her," Utah Film Critics Association (2013); Best Depiction of Nudity, Sexuality, or Seduction, "Her," Alliance of Women Film Journalists (2013); Best Featured Actress in a Play, "A View From the Bridge," Tony Awards (2010); Best Science Fiction Actress, "Iron Man 2," Scream Awards (2010); Theatre World Award for Outstanding Stage Debut Performance, "A View From the Bridge," Theatre World Awards (2010); Best Ensemble Cast, "Vicky Cristina Barcelona," Gotham Independent Film Awards (2008); Best Seduction, "Vicky Cristina Barcelona," Alliance of Women Film Journalists (2008); Best Actress in a Leading Role, "Lost in Translation," British Academy Film Awards (2004); Rising Star Award, "Girl with a Pearl Earring" and "Lost in Translation," Palm Springs International Film Festival (2004); Best Actress, "Lost in Translation," Boston Society of Film Critics (2003); Best Supporting Actress, "Lost in Translation," New York Film Critics Online (2003) **Political Affiliations:** Democrat

Abigail Pierrepont Johnson

Title: Chief Executive Officer, President **Industry:** Financial Services **Company Name:** Fidelity Investments **Date of Birth:** 12/19/1961 **Parents:** Edward C. Johnson III **Marital Status:** Married **Spouse Name:** Christopher John McKown (1988) **Children:** Two children **Education:** MBA, Harvard Business School (1988); BA in Art History, Hobart and William Smith Colleges (1984); Diploma, Buckingham Browne & Nichols School **Career:** Chairman, Fidelity Investments (2016-Present); Chief Executive Officer, Fidelity Investments (2014-Present); President, Fidelity Investments (2012-2014); Head of Retail, Workplace and Institutional Business, Fidelity Institutional Asset Management (2005-2012); President, Fidelity Institutional Asset Management (2001-2005); Analyst, Portfolio Manager, Fidelity Investments (1988-2001); Consultant, Booz Allen Hamilton Inc. (1985-1986) **Civic:** Donor, Jeb Bush Presidential Campaign (2016) **Awards:** Most Powerful Women in the World, Forbes (2014-2019) **Memberships:** Committee on Capital Markets Regulation; Board of Directors, Securities Industry and Financial Markets Association; Board, Financial Services Forum

Carl Johnson

Title: Marriage and Family Therapist **Industry:** Medicine & Health Care **Company Name:** Carl F. Johnson **Date of Birth:** 07/18/1947 **Place of Birth:** Minneapolis **State/Country of Origin:** MN/USA **Parents:** Gloria (Thorsen) Bennett (Deceased); Kenneth Johnson (Step-father, Deceased); Carl F. Cronemiller Jr. (Father, Deceased) **Education:** Master of Arts in Clinical Psychology, Georgia State University (1975); Bachelor of Arts in Psychology, Northwestern University (1969) **Certifications:** Licensed Marriage and Family Therapist, Georgia **Career:** Marriage and Family Therapist, Private Practice, The Family Workshop, Atlanta, GA (1980-2021); Family Therapist, The Bridge Family Center, Atlanta, GA (1972-1980) **Career Related:** Executive Director, Georgia Association for Marriage and Family Therapy, Atlanta, GA (1997-2009); Founder, President, Association of Marital and Family Therapy Regulatory Boards (1987-1991); Appointee, Georgia Composite Board of Professional Counselors, Social Workers and Marriage and Family Therapists (1985-1993); Adjunct Instructor, Dekalb Community College, Clarkston, GA (1981-1982); Graduate Teaching Assistant, Georgia State University, Atlanta, GA (1972-1973) **Creative Works:** Youtube Video, "The History of Family Therapy in Georgia - Carl F Johnson", UGA Mary Frances Early College of Education, Presented by the COE Lecture Series, UGA College of Education (2016); Contributed, Articles to Professional Journals **Awards:** Outstanding Contribution to Marriage and Family Therapy Award, American Association for Marriage and Family Therapy (2001); Lifetime Achievement and Distinguished Service Award, Georgia Association for Marriage and Family Therapy (1996); Divisional Contribution Award, American Association for Marriage and Family Therapy (1993); Outstanding Contribution Award, Georgia Association for Marriage and Family Therapy (1993, 1985, 1983) **Memberships:** Member, Georgia Association for Marriage and Family Therapy (1980-Present); Clinical Fellow, American Association for Marriage and Family Therapy (1980-Present); Chair, Legislative Affairs Committee, Georgia Association for Marriage and Family Therapy (1980-1985, 1993-1995, 2011-2018) **Marquis Who's Who Honors:** Albert Nelson Marquis Lifetime Achievement Award; Marquis Who's Who Top Professional **Why did you become involved in your profession or industry:** Mr. Johnson entered college as a pre-med student, but soon pivoted toward psychology due to the influence of a nationally-recognized social psychologist, Donald T. Campbell. Inspired by his course, and by the experience of doing undergraduate research under Professor Campbell, Mr. Johnson decided to pursue the field of psychology. Later, during his graduate studies at Georgia State University, Mr. Johnson completed a practicum placement at the Bridge Family Center working to reunite adolescent "runaways" with their families. In light of this experience, he knew he wanted to specialize in family therapy. **Avocations:** History and biography; International travel

Gregory H. Johnson, Col. (Ret.), USAF

Title: Aerospace Space/Consultant **Industry:** Aviation **Company Name:** Johnson Space Center **Date of Birth:** 05/12/1962 **Place of Birth:** South Ruislip, Middlesex **State/Country of Origin:** United Kingdom **Parents:** Harold Cumings Johnson; Marion Joyce (Frye) Johnson **Marital Status:** Married **Spouse Name:** Cari Michele Harbaugh Johnson (07/08/1989) **Children:** Matthew; Joseph; Rachel **Education:** MBA, The University of Texas at Austin (2005); MS in Flight Structures Engineering, Columbia University, NY (1985); BS in Aeronautical Engineering, United States Air Force Academy (1984) **Certifications:** Certified U.S. Air Force Pilot; Certified F-15E Fighter Pilot; Certified Test Pilot **Career:** Aerospace and Workforce Development Consultant (2018-Present); President, Executive Director, Center for the Advancement of Science in Space, ISS National Laboratory, Melbourne, FL and Houston, Texas (2013-2018); Senior Astronaut Pilot, Lead of Visiting Vehicles Technical Working Group, Johnson Space Center, Houston, Texas (2013); Associate Director of External Programs, Center Operations Directorate, NASA Glenn Research Center, Cleveland, Ohio (2011-2012); Space Shuttle Pilot, STS-134, 36th Shuttle/Station Assembly Mission, Final Flight of Endeavour, Johnson Space Center, Houston, Texas (2009-2011); Space Shuttle Pilot, Safety Branch Chief, Johnson Space Center, Houston, Texas (2008-2009); Space Shuttle Pilot, STS-123, Johnson Space Center, Houston, Texas (2006-2008); Technical Assistant to the Director, Flight Crew Operations Directorate, NASA (2000); With, Astronaut Corps, Johnson Space Center, Houston, Texas (1998-2013); Space Shuttle Astronaut/Pilot, Johnson Space Center, Houston, Texas (1998-2006); Test Pilot, F-15C/E, NF-15B, T-38A/B Aircraft, 445th Flight Test Squadron, Edwards Air Force Base, CA (1994-1997); Deployed, 27 Combat Missions in Support of Operation Southern Watch, Saudi Arabia (1992); F-15E Eagle Fighter Pilot, 335th Fighter Squadron, Seymour Johnson Air Force Base, NC (1990-1993); Deployed, 34 Combat Missions in Support of Operation Desert Storm, Al Kharj, Saudi Arabia (1990); T-38A Instructor Pilot, 54 Flying Training Squadron, Reese Air Force Base, Texas (1986-1989); Air Force Pilot, Reese Air Force Base, Texas (1986); Chief Space Officer, Space Nation **Career Related:** Crew Representative Supporting the Design and Testing of NASA's Crew Exploration Vehicle (2005); Deputy Chief, Astronaut Safety Branch (2004); Direct Support to the Crews of STS-100 and STS-108, Chief of Shuttle Abort Planning and Procedures for Contingency Scenarios, and Ascent Procedure Development, Space Shuttle Branch (2001); Assigned, Shuttle Cockpit Avionics Upgrade Council (2000); Youth Development Consultant; Guest Speaker; Lecturer; Aerospace Consultant, Boomerang Catapult, MI **Civic:** Eagle Scout, Boy Scouts of America (1978); Executive Director, Newton's Road, Nonprofit Focusing on K-STEM Development, MI; Director of Innovation and Strategic Partnerships, Boy Scouts of America **Awards:** Named Distinguished Eagle Scout (2017); Exceptional Service Medal, NASA (2012); NASA Space Medals, Superior Performance Awards, Rising Star Award, McCombs School of Business (2009); Stephen D. Thorne Top Fox Safety Award (2005); Dean's Award for Academic Excellence, McCombs School of Business (2005); Lieutenant General Bobby Bond Award, Top Test Pilot, United States Air Force (1996); Named Distinguished Graduate, U.S. Air Force Test Pilot School (1994); Decorated, Distinguished Flying Cross, Saudi Arabia (1991); Guggenheim Fellowship, Columbia University (1985); Superior Performance Award, NASA; Distinguished Flying Cross; Meritorious Service Medal; Air Medals; Aerial Achievement Medals; Commendation Medal; United States Air Force Achievement Medals; Legion of Merit **Memberships:** American Institute of Aeronautics and Astronautics; The Planetary Society; Optimist International; Advisory Board, SpaceCom; Global Entrepreneurship Network; Association of Space Explorers; The Society of Experimental Test Pilots; Rotary International; Officer, The Astronauts Memorial Foundation; Global Entrepreneurship Network; STEM Advisory Board, Boy Scouts of America **Marquis Who's Who Honors:** Albert Nelson Marquis Lifetime Achievement Award; Marquis Who's Who Top Professional **To what do you attribute your success:** Mr. Johnson attributes his success to a commitment to excellence, treating people right and doing the right thing. **Why did you become involved in your profession or industry:** Mr. Johnson was inspired to pursue his profession after Neil Armstrong's first step on the moon on July 20, 1969. **Avocations:** Bridge; Golf; Woodworking; Chess; Backgammon; Travel; Bicycling; Music **Political Affiliations:** Republican **Religion:** Methodist **Thoughts on Life:** Mr. Johnson was a key player on several "tiger teams" during the investigation into the cause of the Columbia accident in 2003. He was also the astronaut representative to the External Tank foam impact test team, which eventually proved that External Tank's foam debris on ascent could critically damage the shuttle's leading edge thermal protection system. In 2008, Mr. Johnson was the pilot on STS-123, a mission to deliver the Japanese Logistics Module and the Canadian Special Purpose Dexterous Manipulator to the International Space Station. For more information on Mr. Johnson, and his advocacy for the International Space Station, please visit the following website: https://www.youtube.com/watch?v=Dg6l1boqw00

Keith Liddell Johnson

Title: Chemical Executive, Management Consultant (Retired) **Industry:** Sciences **Company Name:** KJ Technical Directions **Date of Birth:** 07/22/1939 **Place of Birth:** Darlington **State/Country of Origin:** United Kingdom **Parents:** Arthur Henry Johnson; Beatrice (Liddell) Johnson **Marital Status:** Married **Spouse Name:** Margaret Elaine Meston (08/29/1959) **Children:** Leslie Margaret; Kevin Liddell; Gregory Norman; Kathleen Elaine; Ann Louise **Education:** BA, University of Michigan (1960) **Certifications:** Certification in International Business, California State University, Fullerton (1990) **Career:** Proprietor, KJ Technical Directions (1976-Present); Retired, Norman Fox & Company (2005); Vice Chairman, Chief Technology Officer, Norman Fox & Company (2003-2005); President, Director, Norman Fox & Company (1993-2003); Executive Vice President, Director, Norman Fox & Company (1989-1993); General Manager, Norman Fox & Company (1988-1993); Branch Manager, Norman Fox & Company (1983-1988); Technical Director, Norman Fox & Company (1982-1983); Group Manager of Plant Quality Assurance, Swift & Company (1978-1982); Quality Assurance Director, Swift & Company (1974-1978); Corporate Quality Assurance Manager, Swift Edible Oil Company (1973-1974); Quality Assurance Manager, Refinery Division, Swift Edible Oil Company (1972-1973); Administrative Assistant to Executive Vice President, Swift & Company (1971-1972); Group Leader, Research and Development Center, Swift & Company (1967-1971); Project Manager, Swift & Company (1963-1967); Research Chemist, Swift & Company (1960-1963); Chemical Technician, Ajem Laboratories, Inc. (1956-1960) **Career Related:** Member, Board of Directors, Chemical Distribution Network (2001-2004); Member, Industry Advisory Board, South Coast Air Quality Management District, CA (1982-1984); Consultant in Field **Civic:** Vestry, St. Ambrose Episcopal Church, Claremont, CA (2002-2006); Senior Warden, St. Martha's Episcopal School (2004-2005); Board of Directors, St. Martha's Episcopal School (1999-2001); Senior Warden, St. Martha's Episcopal Church (1991-1996, 1998-2001); Chairman of the Board, St. Martha's Senior Care Center (1995-1999); Vice President, Director, St. Martha's Senior Care Center (1993-1997) **Creative Works:** Contributor, Articles, Professional Journals **Memberships:** Emeritus Member, The American Oil Chemists' Society (2013); Emeritus Member, Bay Area Chapter, Society of Cosmetic Chemists (2012); Emeritus Member, American Chemical Society (2009); Member, Executive Committee, American Chemical Society (2000-2003); Chair, California Chapter, American Chemical Society (2001-2002); Chairman, Bay Area Chapter, Society of Cosmetic Chemists (1987-1988); Vice President, Chairman of the Board, Illinois Chapter, Junior Chamber International (1972); President, Illinois Chapter, Junior Chamber International (1971); Executive Vice President, Illinois Chapter, Junior Chamber International (1970); Vice President, Illinois Chamber International (1969); National Association of Chemical Distributors; IUPAC **Marquis Who's Who Honors:** Albert Nelson Marquis Lifetime Achievement Award; Marquis Who's Who Top Professional **Why did you become involved in your profession or industry:** Mr. Johnson became involved in his profession because of his experiences. He received a summer job through a friend of his father at a young age and became a chemical technician by the time he graduated high school. While serving as a technician, he had notable accomplishments that presented him with interview opportunities for companies like Proctor & Gamble, Swift and others. When he received the job at Swift, the man who interviewed him passed away between the time he was interviewed and the first day he reported for work. Mr. Johnson eventually went on to assume that man's job, making him the youngest department head in the company.

Leo Francis Johnson, PhD

Title: Physicist **Industry:** Sciences **Date of Birth:** 11/06/1928 **Place of Birth:** White Plains **State/Country of Origin:** NY/USA **Parents:** Leo Frederick; Marion (Walker) Johnson **Marital Status:** Married **Spouse Name:** Barbara Harman, (02/10/1962) **Children:** David; Kathleen; Mark; Christopher **Education:** PhD, Syracuse University (1959); MA, Syracuse University (1955); BA in Mathematics, University of Vermont, Burlington (1951) **Career:** Private Practice Consultant, Bedminster, NJ (1987-Present); Member, Technology Staff, AT&T Bell Laboratories, Murray Hill, NJ (1959-1987); Research Assistant, Syracuse University (1954-1959); Test Engineer, GE, Schenectady, NY (1951-1953) **Career Related:** Consultant, Amoco Research Center, Naperville, IL (1989-Present); Research Associate, University of Central Florida, Orlando, FL (1990-1991); Consultant, Amoco Laser Co., Naperville, IL (1987-1989) **Civic:** Member, Township Committee, Bedminster, NJ (1989-1991, 1996-1998); Mayor, Bedminster Township (1996); Member, Bedminster Planning Board (1991-1996); Member, Bedminster School Board of Education (1978-1985); Member, St. Brigid School Board Education, Peapack, NJ (1971-1972) **Creative Works:** Author, "Corruption, Fraud and Tyranny in the Science of Global Warming and Climate Change" (2019); Author, "Understanding The Global Warming Hoax-Expanded and Updated" (2009); Author, "The Layman's Guide to Understanding The Global Warming Hoax" (2008); Contributor, Articles, Professional Publications; Patentee in Field **Memberships:** Fellow, American Physical Society; Sigma Xi **Marquis Who's Who Honors:** Albert Nelson Marquis Lifetime Achievement Award; Marquis Who's Who Top Professional **Why did you become involved in your profession or industry:** Mr. Johnson became involved in his profession because back in college he liked math and physics the most. That led him into most things and he went on to get his degree. In addition, to his love for math, he chose this as a career because he wasn't sure where he would be employed as a mathematics, but it turned out that mathematics was a sideline to doing work in physics. **Avocations:** Former bowler; Golf; Fishing **Political Affiliations:** Republican

Yvonne Johnson

Title: Elementary School Educator **Industry:** Education/Educational Services **Date of Birth:** 07/01/1930 **Place of Birth:** DeKalb **State/Country of Origin:** IL/USA **Parents:** Albert O.; Virginia O. (Nelson) Johnson **Education:** Honorary Doctor of Philosophy, Sycamore Community Unit School District (2008); Master of Science in Education, Northern Illinois University (1960); Bachelor of Science in Education, Northern Illinois State Teachers College (1951) **Career:** Teacher, West Elementary School, Sycamore, IL (1953-2002); Teacher, Love Rural School, DeKalb, IL (1951-1953); Coordinator, Media Center West School **Career Related:** Organizer, Over 250 Elementary Teacher Science Workshops (1995-1998); Illinois Honors Science Teacher, Illinois State University (1985-1987) **Civic:** Volunteer, KishHealth Systems Northwestern Medicine (2011-Present); Board Member, Service Agency (2011-Present); Trustee, Midwest Museum of Natural History (2001-Present); Renaissance Scholarship; Voluntary Action Center Lifetime of Giving (2015); Board of Directors, Family Service Agency (2010-2017); President, Midwest Museum of Natural History (2006-2009); Founder, DeKalb County Excellence in Education Award (1999); President, Board of Directors, Sycamore Public Library (1984-1998); Board of Directors, Sycamore Public Library (1974-1998) **Creative Works:** Contributor, Articles to Professional Publications **Awards:** Clifford Danielson Outstanding Sycamore Citizen Award (2006); Outstanding Agricultural Teacher in the Classroom, Dekalb County Farm Bureau (1993); Scientific Literature Grantee, State of Illinois (1992-1994); Grantee, National Aeronautics and Space Administration (1988); Grantee, National Science Foundation (1985, 1986, 1987); Master Teacher, State of Illinois (1984); Named, DeKalb County Conservation Teacher (1971); Grantee, National Science Foundation (1961, 1962); Tribute Heroes Award, Boy Scouts America; Northern Illinois University, College of Education, Distinguished Alumni **Memberships:** National Education Association, National Science Teachers Association; Illinois Science Teachers Association; Illinois Education Association; Sycamore Education Association; Council for Elementary Science International **Marquis Who's Who Honors:** Albert Nelson Marquis Lifetime Achievement Award; Marquis Who's Who Top Professional; Marquis Who's Who Humanitarian Award **Why did you become involved in your profession or industry:** Following her graduation from college, Ms. Johnson briefly struggled on finding a path forward in her career. After helping her father on the family farm, she decided to apply to the nearby rural school and managed to secure a position there. **Avocations:** Gardening; Crafts **Political Affiliations:** Independent **Religion:** Lutheran ELCA

Nancy Ruth Johnson-Velazco

Title: Marketing Professional **Industry:** Consumer Goods and Services **Company Name:** Schering-Plough Corporation **Date of Birth:** 02/04/1948 **Place of Birth:** Philadelphia **State/Country of Origin:** PA/USA **Parents:** Samuel Blaine Johnson; Ruth Dorothy (Carpenter) Johnson **Marital Status:** Divorced **Spouse Name:** Julio Horacio Velazco (1982, Divorced 1984) **Children:** Christine **Education:** MBA in Marketing and Global Enterprise, The Wharton School, University of Pennsylvania, Philadelphia, PA (1978); MA in Spanish Literature, Villanova University, Villanova, PA, Summa Cum Laude (1974); BA in Spanish and French, Ursinus College, Collegeville, PA (1970) **Career:** Marketing Consultant, Enerjey Marketing Consulting, LLC, Bradenton, FL (2004-2008); Senior Marketing Director, Global Professional Services, Schering-Plough Corporation, Kenilworth, NJ (2003-2004); Senior Marking Director, Marketing Services, Global Marketing, Schering-Plough Corporation, Kenilworth, NJ (1998-2003); Director, Trainer, Market Research, Professional Services and Trademarks, Schering-Plough Corporation, Kenilworth, NJ (1998-2000); Senior Marketing Director, RAAD Business Unit, Global Marketing, Schering-Plough Corporation, Kenilworth, NJ (1991-1998); Director of Marketing, Dermatologicals/Antifungals, International Division, Schering-Plough Corporation, Kenilworth, NJ (1989-1990); Regional Marketing Director, Latin America, Schering-Plough Corporation, Miami, FL (1984-1989); Intereron Product Manager and Business Development Manager, Latin American Region, Schering-Plough Corporation, Miami, FL (1983-1984); Marketing Manager, Argentine Affiliate, Eli Lilly & Company, Indianapolis, IN (1980-1982); International Market Research Analyst, Eli Lilly & Company, Indianapolis, IN (1980); Professional Sales Representative, Eli Lilly & Company, Providence, RI (1978-1979); Business Analyst, Multinational Division, Industrial Research Unit, The Wharton School, University of Pennsylvania, Philadelphia, PA (1976-1978); Instructor, Spanish for High School Students, William Penn School District, Lansdowne, PA (1970-1976) **Civic:** Compliance Committee, Lakewood Ranch Home Owner's Association (2010-Present); Supervisor, Inter-District Authority & Community Development District 4, Lakewood Ranch, FL (2007-Present); Trustee, Board of Directors, Meadowlands Hospital, Secaucus, NJ (2001-2010); Chairman, Schering-Plough-Sponsored Charitable Events at Children's Specialized Hospital, Mountainside, NJ (1994-2004) **Creative Works:** Author, Book, "The Political, Economic, and Labor Climate in Peru" (1979); Co-Author, Book, "The Political, Economic, and Labor Climate in Mexico" (1977) **Awards:** New Jersey Humanitarian Award in Healthcare (2004); Executive Proclamation, State of New Jersey **Memberships:** Ivy League Club of Sarasota (2018-Present); Women of Manatee County Republican Club (2018-Present); Daughters of the Union Veterans of the Civil War of 1861-1865 (2017-Present); Republican Women's Club of Sarasota (2016-Present); National Society of the United States Daughters of 1812 (2014-Present); President, Genealogical Society of Sarasota (2012-Present); Compliance Committee, Lakewood Ranch Home Owners Association (2010-Present); Treasurer, National Society of the Daughters of the American Revolution, Sara de Soto Chapter (2004-2006); Treasurer, National Society of the Daughters of the American Revolution, Westfield Chapter (1995-2002) **Marquis Who's Who Honors:** Albert Nelson Marquis Lifetime Achievement Award **Why did you become involved in your profession or industry:** Ms. Johnson-Velazco became involved in her profession because, despite receiving excellent ratings during her teaching career, she wanted to pursue a different path. At first, she considered being a doctor while in high school but was discouraged because it required too many years of school. However, she completed two years in one master's degree program and another two years in a different master's degree program, both of which focused on Spanish. She was also interested in science. Ms. Johnson-Velazco attended Wharton College while the industrial research unit paid her tuition and gave her a stipend. **Avocations:** Family genealogy; International traveling; Art; Reading; Theater **Political Affiliations:** Republican **Religion:** Methodist

John Phillips "Phil" Little Johnston, JD, MBA

Title: Founder/Chief Legal Officer **Company Name:** Koolbridge Solar **Place of Birth:** Memphis **State/Country of Origin:** TN/USA **Spouse Name:** Dorothy James Johnston **Children:** Phillips; Jamie **Education:** Babcock Entrepreneurial Fellow, Wake Forest University (2010); Coursework, Directors' College, Stanford University, Stanford, CA; Coursework, Senior Managers in Government, Harvard Kennedy School, John F. Kennedy School of Government, Harvard University, Cambridge, MA; Coursework, New York University Leonard N. Stern School of Business; JD, The University of North Carolina at Chapel Hill School of Law, NC; AB in Economics, Duke University, Durham, NC **Certifications:** Certificate of Director Education, NACD Institute (2005); Top Secret Clearance, FBI (1997) **Career:** Chief Executive Officer, Pilot Biotechnologies, Winston-Salem, NC (1998-2000); Chief Executive Officer, Digital Recorders, Inc., Research Triangle Park, NC (1990-1999); President, Chief Executive Officer, Director, DataPix, Inc. (1988-1990); Administrator, North Carolina Credit Unions (1987-1989); President, Chief Executive Officer, Director, Norman Perry (1980-1985); Dewar's Profile (1980-1981); President, Chief Executive Officer, Director, Erwin-Lambeth (1979-1987); President, Chief Executive Officer, Director, Chantry Lamp Co. (1977-1987); With, Citicorp (1966); President, Chief Executive Officer, Director, Currier Piano Co. (1965-1976); Assistant Manager, Cameron-Brown Capital Corp. (1963-1966); Board of Directors, Digital Recorders, Inc., Research Triangle Park, NC; Principal, Retail Store; Real Estate Manager; Vice Chairman, Co-founder, Koolbridge Solar, Inc., High Point, NC **Career Related:** Co-founder, Rainmakers, Assisting Pro Bono Economically Disadvantaged Businesses (1998); Board of Directors, Executive Committee, Compensation Committee, Marion Manufacturing Co.; Board of Directors, Compensation Committee, Southern Film Extruders Inc.; Trustee, UNC Law Foundation, Inc.; Finance, Investment Committee, The University of North Carolina at Chapel Hill School of Law **Civic:** Advisory Board, Bryan School of Business and Economics (2013); Former Chairman, Treasurer, Marion General Hospital; Chairman, McDowell County United Way; Warden, St. John's Episcopalian Church; Trustee, North Carolina Art Museum; Trustee, Past President, North Carolina State University Friends Gallery **Creative Works:** Author, "Jokes That Span Generations" (1990); Author, "Success in Small Business is a Laughing Matter" (1980); Author, "Biscuitville: The Secret Recipe for Building a Sustainable Competitive Advantage"; Author, "True South: Leadership Lessons from Polar Extremes"; Author, Numerous Articles on Corporate Governance, National Publications **Awards:** Named Entrepreneur of the Year, Council for Entrepreneurial Development (CED) (1997); Distinguished Service Award, North Carolina Credit Union League (1988); Listed, Dewar's Profile (1982) **Memberships:** Co-founder, Chairman, Board, North Carolina Information and Technology Association (NCTA) (1993-Present); Entrepreneurial Fellow, Wake Forest University, Winston-Salem, NC (2005-Present); Co-founder, Founding Chairman, North Carolina Electronics and Information Trade Association (NCTA) (1995); Financial Expert, SEC Audit Committee; Quadrille Dance Club, High Point, NC; Kappa Alpha Fraternity, Duke University; Varsity Lacrosse, Duke University **Bar Admissions:** State of North Carolina (1963) **Marquis Who's Who Honors:** Albert Nelson Marquis Lifetime Achievement Award; Marquis Who's Who Top Professional **Why did you become involved in your profession or industry:** Mr. Johnston became involved in his profession because his father influenced him to go into law. As a lawyer, he believes you can work every day of your life. A company downsizing does not affect your work opportunity. **Avocations:** Tennis; Bridge; Pinball; Reading great classics of literature **Political Affiliations:** Republican **Religion:** Episcopalian

Virgil LLoyd Johnston

Title: Utility Consultant; Corrosion Engineer (Retired) **Industry:** Oil & Energy **Date of Birth:** 01/30/1928 **Place of Birth:** Carl **State/Country of Origin:** IA/USA **Parents:** Wilbur Bryan; Wanda Indiana (Knodle) Johnston **Marital Status:** Widowed **Spouse Name:** Laverne May Himmel (05/05/1956, Deceased) **Children:** Deborah; Karen **Education:** Diploma in Electrical Engineering, International Correspondence Schools, Scranton, PA (1963) **Career:** Utility Consultant, Arizona Corporation Commission (1986-Present); Retired (1986); Chief Corrosion Engineer, Panhandle Eastern Pipeline Company, LP, Kansas City, MO (1975-1986); Supervising Engineer, Panhandle Eastern Pipeline Company, LP, Kansas City, MO (1975); Area Superintendent, Panhandle Eastern Pipeline Company, LP, Kansas City, MO (1972-1975); Corrosion Engineer, Panhandle Eastern Pipeline Company, LP, Kansas City, MO (1963-1972); Corrosion Inspector, Panhandle Eastern Pipeline Company, LP, Kansas City, MO (1957-1963); Electrical Construction Lineman, Various Contractors (1948-1957) **Career Related:** Chairman, Arizona Corrosion Correlating Committee (1990) **Military Service:** With, United States Army (1946-1947) **Awards:** Professional of the Year Award, State of Arizona (1988); Award of Merit (1985); Service Award, Operating Section, American Gas Association (1982); Recognition for Special Service, Southern Gas Association (1980) **Memberships:** Chairman, Arizona Secretary, National Association Corrosion Engineers (NACE International) (1990); Commander, Legion of Honor, El Zaribah Shrine Temple, Shriners (1990); Commander, Legion of Honor, Ararat Shrine Temple, Shriners (1980); 33rd Degree, Masons **To what do you attribute your success:** Mr. Johnston attributes his success to family encouragement growing up, as well as some excellent teachers. **Why did you become involved in your profession or industry:** Mr. Johnston became involved in his profession because when he left the Army he knew he did not want to be a farmer as he grew up on a farm. He went to school in Chicago to be an air conditioning and refrigeration technician. However, he was starving to death and also, after World War II, farmers did not have electricity. He went to work for a contractor to become a lineman and was recently married and looking for something different. One day he was approached by another lineman who told him that another company by the name of Panhandle Eastern Pipeline Company was looking for someone like him. He ended up working for that company and moved up the ranks. **Avocations:** Fishing; Reading; Computers; Investment monitoring **Religion:** Protestant **Thoughts on Life:** Mr. Johnston's motto is "Life is what you make it to be."

Daniel E. Jolly, DDS

Title: Dental Educator and Consultant **Industry:** Medicine & Health Care **Company Name:** Daniel E. Jolly, DDS **Date of Birth:** 08/25/1952 **Place of Birth:** St. Louis **State/Country of Origin:** MO/USA **Parents:** Melvin Joseph Jolly; Betty Ehs (Koehler) Jolly **Children:** Farrell **Education:** Resident in Hospital Dentistry, VA Medical Center, Leavenworth, KS (1977-1978); DDS, University of Missouri-Kansas City (1977); BA, Biology and Chemistry, University of Missouri-Kansas City (1974) **Certifications:** Diplomate, American Board of Special Care Dentistry (2004) **Career:** Chief Forensic Dentist, Odontologist, Licking County Ohio Coroner's Office (2019-Present); Part-time Dental Director, Insurance Company (2013-Present); Chief Forensic Dentist, Odontologist, Franklin County Coroner's Office, Columbus Ohio (2000-Present); Beech Croft Family Dental (2017-2018); President, Immediadent of Ohio (2008-2013); Professor, Director, General Practice Residency Program, Ohio State University, Columbus (1993-2008); Associate Professor, Director, General Practice Residency Program, Ohio State University (1987-2008); Director of Dental Oncology, Trinity Lutheran Hospital (1982-1987); Chief of Restorative Dentistry, Truman Medical Center (1979-1987); Assistant Professor, University of Missouri (1979-1987); Private Practice, Newcastle, WY (1978-1979) **Career Related:** Director, Honduras Clinic Project (1992-Present); President, Combined Hospital Dental Staff, Columbus, OH (1991-1992); Vice President, Combined Hospital Dental Staff, Columbus, OH (1990-1991); Secretary, Combined Hospital Dental Staff, Columbus, OH (1989-1990); Consultant, Longview Nursing Center, Grandview, MO (1986-1987); Board of Directors, Rinehart Foundation, School of Dentistry, University of Missouri-Kansas City (1985-1987); Consultant, Lee's Summit Care Center, Missouri (1984-1987); Speaker, Forensic Dentistry, Medical Dentistry; Chief Forensic Odontologist, Franklin County Ohio Coroner's Office; Chief Forensic Odontologist, Licking County Ohio Coroner's Office **Civic:** Secretary, Board of Directors, Easter Seal Rehabilitation Center, Easter Seal Society, Columbus, OH (1990-1993); Professional Advisory Council, Easter Seal Society (1986-1992); Regional Council, Easter Seal Society, Kansas City (1985-1987); President, Health Professionals Serving Humanity **Military Service:** U.S. Naval Sea Cadet Corps (1998-1999) **Creative Works:** Author, "OSU Manual Hospital Dentistry" (1989-Present); Author, "Nursing Home Dentistry" (1986); Author, "Dental Oncology" (1986); Author, "Hospital Dentistry" (1985); Author, "Hospital Dental Hygiene" (1984) **Awards:** Alumni Achievement Award In Dentistry, Honduras Project, University of Missouri-Kansas City (1998, 1994-1995); Humanitarian Award, Ohio Dental Association (1998); Alumni Achievement Award in Dentistry, University of Missouri-Kansas City (1995) **Memberships:** ImmediaDent, Ohio (2008-Present); President, American Board of Special Care Dentistry (2004-Present); President, American Association of Hospital Dentists (2003-Present); Regional Vice President, American Association of Hospital Dentists (1993-Present); Secretary, President-Elect, American Association of Hospital Dentists (2002-2003); President, International Association of Dentistry for the Handicapped (1994-1996); Chairman, Federation of Special Care Dentistry Association (1992-1993); President, Academy of Dentistry for the Handicapped (1992); Fellow, Pierre Fauchard Academy; Fellow, American College of Dentistry; Fellow, Academy of Dentistry for the Handicapped; Fellow, American Society of Geriatric Dentistry; Fellow, American Dentistry International; Fellow, American Association of Hospital Dentists; Fellow, Academy of General Dentistry; American Dental Association; Ohio Dental Association; International Society of Oral Oncology; Southwest Oncology Group; Greater Kansas City Dental Society; Magna Charta Barons Club **Marquis Who's Who Honors:** Albert Nelson Marquis Lifetime Achievement Award; Marquis Who's Who Top Professional; Marquis Who's Who Humanitarian Award **To what do you attribute your success:** Dr. Jolly attributes his success to his dedication, hard work and commitment. He additionally credits his philosophy on life and service to mankind. **Why did you become involved in your profession or industry:** Dr. Jolly became involved in his profession to be of service to others. **Avocations:** Photography; Scuba diving; Swimming; Horses; Ice skating (formerly)

Charles Hill Jones

Title: President, Treasurer **Industry:** Financial Services **Company Name:** Edge Partners LPD **Date of Birth:** 07/14/1933 **Parents:** Charles Hill Jones; Susan Roy (Johnston) Jones **Marital Status:** Married **Spouse Name:** Hope Haskell (1/28/1961) **Children:** Hope H.; Charles Hill III; Henry M.T. **Education:** BA in Economics, University of Virginia, Charlottesville, VA (1956); Graduate, Groton School, Massachusetts (1952) **Career:** General Partner, President, Treasurer, Edge Partners LPD (1987-Present); Chairman, President, New Jersey Title Insurance Co. (2000-2001); Senior Vice President, Chief Investment Officer, Midlantic National Bank, Edison, NJ (1974-1987); Vice President, Director, Director of Research, Wood, Struthers & Winthrop, Inc., New York, NY (1969-1973); With, Wood, Struthers & Winthrop, Inc., New York, NY (1956-1973); General Partner, Wood, Struthers & Winthrop, Inc., New York, NY (1968-1969) **Career Related:** Chairman, Board of Directors, NJT Holdings (2000-Present) **Civic:** Trustee, Hampden-Sydney College (1995-1999, 2002-2003); President, Board of Trustees, Rumson Country Day School, New Jersey (1982-1985); Trustee, Chairman, Finance Committee, Monmouth Medical Center (1975-1981); Treasurer, New York Chapter, R.E. Lee Memorial Foundation (1964-1969) **Creative Works:** Author, "The Growth Rate Appraiser" (1968); Co-Author, "Toll Road Bonds" (1959) **Memberships:** CFA Institute **Marquis Who's Who Honors:** Albert Nelson Marquis Lifetime Achievement Award **Why did you become involved in your profession or industry:** Mr. Jones became involved in his profession because he had to get a job and found banking interesting.

Roger C. Jones, Esq.

Title: Construction Lawyer **Industry:** Law and Legal Services **Company Name:** Huddles Jones Sorteberg & Dachille **Date of Birth:** 11/27/1959 **Place of Birth:** Ithaca **State/Country of Origin:** NY/USA **Marital Status:** Married **Spouse Name:** Janet Jones **Children:** Brennan; Bradley; Blake Marie **Education:** Diplomate, School of Law, Washington University in St Louis, MO (1985); BS, Architecture and Construction Management, The Catholic University of America (1982) **Career:** Construction Attorney, Founding Partner, Huddles, Jones, Sorteberg & Dachille, PC (1995-2005); Principal, Huddles, Jones, Sorteberg & Dachille, PC (1995-2005); Managing Director, Huddles, Jones, Sorteberg & Dachille, PC (1995-2005); Principal, Braude & Margulies, P.C. (1985-1995); Managing Director, Braude & Margulies, P.C. (1985-1995) **Creative Works:** Author, "Construction Contract Changes," Lorman Education Services (2005); Author, "The Legal Implications of Construction Scheduling for Owners, Contractors & Subcontractors," Lorman Education Services (2004); Author, "Post Hoc Termination Justification: What Happened to the Logic?," Board of Contract Appeals, Judges Association Conference (1998) **Awards:** Honoree, Named Top Attorney In Maryland (2013-2015); Honoree, Named Best Lawyer in America in Construction Law (2003-2013); Honoree, U. S. News and World Report; Honoree, Maryland Super Lawyer; Honoree, America's Most Honored Professionals **Memberships:** Public Contract Law Section, American Bar Association; Construction Law Section, Maryland State Bar Association; Construction Law Section, Virginia State Bar; Boy Scouts of America **Bar Admissions:** Maryland State Bar Association; Virginia State Bar; The District Of Columbia Bar; United States District Court District of Maryland; United States District Court Eastern District of Virginia; United States District Court District of Columbia; United States Court of Appeals for the Fourth Circuit; United States Court of Appeals for the Eleventh Circuit; United States Court of Federal Claims; United States Court of Appeals for the Federal Circuit; Supreme Court of the United States **Marquis Who's Who Honors:** Albert Nelson Marquis Lifetime Achievement Award; Marquis Who's Who Top Professional **To what do you attribute your success:** Mr. Jones attributes his success to his background in architecture and construction. Due to his area of expertise, he established a law firm that specializes in construction-related disputes. **Why did you become involved in your profession or industry:** He became involved in his profession after studying architecture in college and then deciding to study law. **Avocations:** Wilderness backpacking; Hiking; Camping **Thoughts on Life:** Mr. Jones defines success as finding fulfillment in serving clients, partners, associates, and family. The advice he would give his 18 -year old self is, "A person's career is a journey that often takes that person in many different directions. It's not a destination."

Starlet "Star" Marie Jones

Title: Attorney, Advocate, Media Personality **Industry:** Consulting **Company Name:** Instant Impact Group, LLC **Date of Birth:** 03/24/1962 **Place of Birth:** Badin **State/Country of Origin:** NC/USA **Parents:** James Byard; Shirley Byard **Marital Status:** Married **Spouse Name:** Ricardo Lugo (03/25/2018); Al Reynolds (11/13/2004, Divorced 2008) **Children:** Jake (Stepson) **Education:** JD, University of Houston Law Center (1986); BA in Administration of Justice, American University, Washington, DC (1983); Diploma, Notre Dame High School, Lawrenceville, NJ **Career:** Chief Brand & Development Officer, Marquis Who's Who (2019-Present); Co-founder and Principal, Instant Impact Group LLC (2020-Present); Legal Correspondent and Commentator, NBC News (1992-2014); Host, Executive Editor, "Star Jones", Court TV Media LLC (2006-2008); Executive Editor, truTV (2007); Host, "Live from the Red Carpet!," E!, NBCUniversal Media, LLC (2004-2005); Co-host, "The View," ABC (1997-2006); Senior Correspondent, Chief Legal Analyst, "Inside Edition" (1995); Host, Syndicated TV Show, "Jones and Jury" (1994); Legal Correspondent, "Nightly News," and "Today," NBC Universal (1992-1993); Studio Commentator, Court TV Media LLC (1991); Senior Assistant District Attorney, Kings County District Attorney's Office, Brooklyn, NY (1992); Prosecutor, Kings County District Attorney's Office, Brooklyn, NY (1986-1991); National Spokesperson, Payless ShoeSource **Career Related:** Motivational Speaker; Media Appearances **Civic:** National Volunteer, Go Red for Women, American Heart Association, Inc.; National Spokesperson, International Association of Women; U.S. Representative, Women in Africa Initiative; Member, Editorial Board, Women's Forum for the Economy & Society; Founder, Co-covener, Power Rising Initiative; Board Director, Girls Inc.; Board Director, God's Love We Deliver; Board Director, Dress for Success; Board Director, The East Harlem School at Exodus House, East Harlem, NY; Launched, The Starlet Fund; Advocate, Women's Health and Workplace Issues; National Volunteer, Breast Cancer Research Foundation **Creative Works:** Executive Producer, Appearance, "Daytime Divas," VH1 (2017); Actress, TV Series, "Drop Dead Diva" (2012); Contest, Reality TV Series, "The Celebrity Apprentice," Season Four (2011); Author, "Satan's Sisters" (2011); Author, "Shine: A Physical, Emotional, and Spiritual Journey to Finding Love" (2006); Actress, Film, "Relative Strangers" (2006); Actress, TV Series, "Less Than Perfect" (2005); Actress, TV Series, "Soul Food" (2002); Actress, TV Series, "Bette" (2001); Actress, TV Series, "Strong Medicine" (2001); Actress, TV Series, "Welcome to New York" (2001); Actress, TV Series, "Spin City" (2000); Actress, TV Series, "Port Charles" (1999); Actress, TV Series, "Sports Night" (1998); Actress, TV Series, "All My Children" (1998); Author, "You Have to Stand for Something, or You'll Fall for Anything" (1998); Actress, TV Series, "Law & Order: Special Victims Unit"; Guest Host, "House Hunters," HGTV, Scripps Networks, LLC; Guest Host, "Larry King Live," Cable News Network (CNN); Host, Reunion Special, "The Bad Girls Club Season 2," Oxygen Media LLC; Guest Host, Radio Show, "The Michael Eric Dyson Show"; Legal Analyst, "The Insider," "Dr. Phil," and "The Wendy Williams Show" **Awards:** Inductee, Broadcasting and Cable Hall of Fame (2017); Woman's Day Red Dress Award (2012); American Heart Association National Volunteer Award (2012); Named Chief of Consumer Style, Payless ShoeSource (2002); Co-recipient (with co-host from "The View"), Safe Horizon Champion Award (2001); Honored for Work in Improving Educational Opportunities for Low Income Children, Exodus House, East Harlem, NY **Memberships:** Former President and National Spokesperson, International Association of Women (IAW); Former President, Professional Diversity Network; Former Second National Vice President, Alpha Kappa Alpha Sorority, Incorporated; Member, Advisory Board, Project Plié, American Ballet Theatre; Editorial Board, Women's Forum for the Economy and Society **Bar Admissions:** State of New York (1987) **To what do you attribute your success:** A strong foundation of unwavering family support, with an emphasis on excelling through education, faith, and a dedication to public and community service. **Why did you become involved in your profession or industry:** I've always had a passion for people and providing service. As a young girl, I wanted to be a public servant through the law so I could give voice to the voiceless. When I became a public prosecutor it was to speak for the victims... And in some ways I've never stopped. When I moved to work in Television, other forms of Media and then Business, I simply traded in one "jury" for another and continued to speak for the people. Every single career choice I've made always built upon the things I care most about: Women's Empowerment, Diversity & Inclusion as a business Imperative and serving my community as fierce advocate for truth, trust and integrity. **Avocations:** International cruising; Tennis; Theater **Political Affiliations:** Democrat **Religion:** Christian **Thoughts on Life:** I can do all things through God who strengthens me and when preparation meets opportunity, absolutely nothing is impossible.

Joseph Jordan

Title: Owner **Industry:** Law and Legal Services **Company Name:** The Jordan UCMJ Law Group **Marital Status:** Married **Children:** Michael; Alyssa; Nathan **Education:** Doctor of Jurisprudence, University of Arkansas at Little Rock (2006); Bachelor of Science in Justice Studies, Pittsburgh State University (2003) **Certifications:** Certification, Automated Logistical Specialist; Certification, Judge Advocate Basic Training; Certification, Brigade Judge Advocate; Certification, Collateral Damage Estimation Course **Career:** Owner, The Jordan UCMJ Law Group, Fort Hood and Killeen, TX (2011-Present); Judge Advocate, United States Army JAG Corps (2006-2011); Law Clerk, Arkansas Department of Workforce Services (2004-2006); Law Clerk, United States Army (2003-2006); Clerk, Honorable District Court Judge Donald Nolan, 11th Judicial District, Kansas (2003) **Civic:** Coach, Quarterback (2014); Football Coach (2007); Assistant Head Coach, Defensive Coordinator, Co-founder, Temple Panthers; Assistant Long Distance Track Coach, 2 Seasons; Personnel Committee Member, First Baptist Church **Military Service:** U.S. Army, served in Germany, Korea, Kuwait and continental United States **Awards:** Listee, Top 100 Trial Lawyers, National Trial Lawyers (2012-Present); Listee, Top 40 Under 40 National Trial Lawyers (2012-Present); Client's Choice, AVVO (2018); 10 Best Client Satisfaction, American Institute of Criminal Law Attorneys (2015); Listee, Lawyers of Distinction **Memberships:** American Bar Association; Arkansas Bar Association; Military Law Section for Texas Bar Association; Litigation Section for American Bar Association; Criminal Law Section for American Bar Association; National Trial Lawyers Association **To what do you attribute your success:** Mr. Jordan credits his success on the grace of God, and his ability to work hard. **Why did you become involved in your profession or industry:** Mr. Jordan initially became interested in his profession due to the thrill he derives from standing up to the government. **Religion:** Baptist

Marc Wayne Judice

Title: Lawyer **Industry:** Law and Legal Services **Company Name:** Judice & Adley, PLC **Date of Birth:** 10/22/1946 **Place of Birth:** Lafayette **State/Country of Origin:** LA/USA **Parents:** Marc Judice; Gladys B. Judice **Marital Status:** Married **Spouse Name:** Michelle Regan **Children:** Renee; Saint-Marie Judice **Education:** JD, Louisiana State University Paul M. Hebert Law Center (1977); MBA in Management and Finance, The University of Utah (1974); BS in Accounting, University of Louisiana (1969) **Certifications:** Certified in Civil Trial Law, National Board of Trial Advocacy (2015); Certified in Civil Trial Law, National Board of Trial Advocacy (2010); Certified in Civil Trial Law, National Board of Trial Advocacy (2005); Certified in Civil Trial Law, National Board of Trial Advocacy (2000); Certified in Civil Trial Law, National Board of Trial Advocacy (1995) **Career:** President, Judice & Adley, PLC (1993-Present); Partner, Juneau, Judice, Hill & Adley (1985-1993); Partner, Voorhies & Labbe (1977-1985) **Civic:** Board of Directors, Home Savings Bank, F.S.B., Lafayette, LA (1996-Present); Chairman, Board of Trustees, Medical Center of Southwest Louisiana (1999-2002); Board of Trustees, Medical Center of Southwest Louisiana (1998-2001); Board of Trustees, Women's & Children's Hospital, Lafayette, LA (1992-1994); Chairman, Board of Directors, University Medical Center (1990-1991); President, Our Lady of Fatima School Foundation, Lafayette, LA (1986-1987) **Military Service:** United States Air Force (1969-1974) **Creative Works:** Speaker, "Reflection on DPM Cases," Annual Meeting, Louisiana Podiatric Medical Association (2017); Seminar Speaker, "Expert Witness Trial Preparation & Testimony," 33rd Annual Defense Counsel Seminar, Louisiana Medical Mutual Insurance Company (2016); Co-speaker, "DPM Practice - Statute & Regulations and Louisiana State Board Medical Examiners Issues," Meeting and Seminar, Louisiana Podiatric Medical Association (2015); Speaker, "Expert Medical Testimony Viewed from the Witness Stand. Co-presentation with Dr. Weston P. Miller, III," 32nd Annual Defense Counsel Seminar, LAMMICO (2015); Speaker, "Charting Role in Defense of DPM," Meeting and Seminar, Louisiana Podiatric Medical Association (2015); Speaker, Panel Presentation, "Loss of Chance - Is There a Chance for Defense?," 29th Annual Defense Counsel Seminar, LAMMICO (2012); Speaker, "PCF and Malpractice Cap: How Medical Malpractice Has Changed in Last 30 Years," Annual Meeting, Louisiana Orthopaedic Association (2011); Speaker, "Potpourri of Medical Malpractice Legal Issues/Court Developments in Case Law," 25th Annual Defense Counsel Seminar, LAMMICO (2008); Speaker, "Direct and Re-Direct of Defendant's Expert," Masters in Trial Seminar, Louisiana Chapter, American Board of Trial Advocates (2008); Co-speaker, "Winning at the Beginning: The Importance of Jury Selection and Opening Statements," 24th Annual Defense Counsel Seminar, LAMMICO (2007); Contributing Author, "The Defendant Physician at Trial," LAMMICO, the Letter (2007); Speaker, "Medical Malpractice Update," Annual Scientific and Educational Meeting, Louisiana Orthopaedic Association (2006); Speaker, "Charting - How? Why? When?," Seminar, Louisiana Society for Healthcare Risk Management (LASHRM) (2006); Speaker, "Entanglements of the Patient/Physician Relationship," Annual Conference, Louisiana Society for Healthcare Risk Management (LASHRM) (2006); Speaker, "Risk Management and PCF for the NP," Advanced Nurse Practitioner Course, University of Louisiana at LaFayette (2005); Speaker, "Risk Management in Managed Care and Private Practice," Social Worker's Continuing Education Program, University of Houston (2004); Speaker, "Medical Malpractice Update," Annual Meeting, Louisiana Orthopaedic Association (2002) **Awards:** Honoree, Super Lawyers: Business Edition (2016); Senior Fellow, The Trial Lawyer Honorary Society, Litigation Counsel of America (2016); Honoree, Top Lawyers, Acadiana Profile (2015-2016); Honoree, Top Rated Lawyers, Louisiana's Legal Leaders (2013); Honoree, Top Lawyers, Acadiana Profile (2012); Honoree, Super Lawyers: Business Edition (2011-2017); Honoree, Super Lawyers: Corporate Counsel Edition (2009-2011); Fellow, The Trial Lawyer Honorary Society, Litigation Counsel of America (2008-2012); Honoree, Best of Acadiana, Times of Acadiana (2008-2009); Honoree, Louisiana Super Lawyers (2007-2018); Honoree, Outstanding Lawyers of America (2003); Outstanding Accounting Alumni Award, B.I. Moody III College of Business Administration, University of Louisiana at Lafayette (1996) **Memberships:** Louisiana Chapter, American Board of Trial Advocates (2016); Association of Attorney-CPAs (1995-2000); ASLME (1987-2000); State Board of Certified Public Accountants of Louisiana (1976-2012); Inactive Member, Society of Louisiana Certified Public Accountants; Inactive Member, American Institute of Certified Public Accountants; American Board of Trial Advocates **Bar Admissions:** ABA (1977-2007); Louisiana State Bar Association (1977); Lafayette Parish Bar Association **Marquis Who's Who Honors:** Albert Nelson Marquis Lifetime Achievement Award; Marquis Who's Who Top Professional **To what do you attribute your success:** Mr. Judice attributes his success to hard work. **Why did you become involved in your profession or industry:** Mr. Judice always wanted to pursue law. **Avocations:** Ragin' Cajuns Baseball Team; Basketball; Football **Political Affiliations:** Republican **Thoughts on Life:** His family came to Louisiana in the 1700s from Thaincourt, France.

John L. Juliano

Title: Trial Lawyer **Industry:** Law and Legal Services **Date of Birth:** 10/21/1944 **Parents:** John Carmine Juliano; Jeannette Helen (Ciotti) Juliano **Marital Status:** Married **Spouse Name:** Edith Helen Martuscello (08/21/2004); Maryjane T. Groccia (07/04/1966, Deceased) **Children:** Jennifer; Jonathan; John Peter Kelly; Maureen **Education:** JD, Brooklyn Law School, Brooklyn, NY (1969); BBA, St. John's University, Queens, NY (1966) **Career:** Private Practice, East Northport, NY (1972-Present); Partner, Juliano, Karlson, Weisberg (1970-1972) **Career Related:** New York State Character and Fitness Committee, Second Judicial Department for the 10th, 11th and 13th Judicial Districts (2010-Present); Chair, Judicial Screening Committee (1979-1983, 2008-2016, 2018-2019); Chair, New York State Grievance Committee, 10th Judicial District (2004-2008); Lecturer, Suffolk Academy of Law; Lecturer, Touro Law School; Lecturer, American Inns of Court; New York State Task Force; President, Director, Hillside United Van Lines, Inc.; American Association for Justice; Managing Director, Suffolk County Pro Bono Foundation Suffolk County; Director, Council of Committee Chairs; Special Master, Opioid Litigation Cases Filed in the State of New York; Suffolk County Law, Post Law School **Awards:** President's Award, Suffolk County Bar Association; Director's Award, Suffolk County Bar Association; Distinguished Service Awards, Suffolk County Bar Association **Memberships:** Board of Directors, Suffolk County Bar Association (1998-2001); President, Suffolk County Bar Association (1996-1997); Vice President, Suffolk County Bar Association (1995-1996); Treasurer, Suffolk County Bar Association (1994-1995); Secretary, Suffolk County Bar Association (1993-1994); President, Columbian Lawyers Association (1974-1975); Treasurer, Columbian Lawyers Association (1973); Secretary, Columbian Lawyers Association (1972); New York State Trial Lawyers Association; Criminal Bar Association; American Inns of Court; Suffolk County Bar Association; New York State Bar Association; New York State Trial Lawyers Association; Nassau County Bar Association; American Association for Justice (AAJ) **Bar Admissions:** New York (1970); U.S. Federal District Courts for the Eastern and Southern Districts of New York; U.S. Court of Appeals for the Second Circuit; U.S. Claims Court; U.S. Supreme Court **Marquis Who's Who Honors:** Albert Nelson Marquis Lifetime Achievement Award; Marquis Who's Who Top Professional **Why did you become involved in your profession or industry:** Mr. Juliano became involved in his profession because he believes that it is an honorable role in which one can champion the rights of the downtrodden. His goals are to level the playing field for all people presented before the court. In addition, he did not become attracted to his career because of his upbringing or because of his family; however, he went to college and decided after that to pursue law. He wanted to make a difference. **Avocations:** Musician **Religion:** Catholic

Roy Davis Jumper, PhD

Title: Writer, Educator **Industry:** Education/Educational Services **Date of Birth:** 08/30/1959 **Place of Birth:** Boston **State/Country of Origin:** MA/USA **Parents:** Roy Eulliss Jumper; Mary Ruth Linville **Education:** PhD, University of Tennessee (1996); MPA, University of Maine, Orono, ME (1985); BA, Indiana University, Bloomington, IN (1982); Coursework, American Community School, Beirut, Lebanon (1966-1972) **Career:** Adjunct Professor, Middlesex Research Center, United States Navy (1997-2004); Associate Instructor, Arizona State University, Tempe, AZ (1985-1986); Assistant Managing Director, International Business Associates, Cairo, Egypt (1983); Intern, Cummins Engine Foundation, Columbus, IN (1980-1981); Librarian's Assistant, Indiana University (1979-1980) **Career Related:** Consultant, The Linville Family LLC, South Padre Island, TX (1999-Present); Owner, CDR Press (Clint Davis Roy) **Military Service:** United States Navy Pace Program (1997-2004) **Creative Works:** Author, "When Armies Die: Kesselschlacht and Aufiragstaktic Verlorne" (2015); Author, "Ruslan of Malaysia: The Man Behind the Domino That Didn't Fall"; Author, "Death Waits in the Dark: The Senoi Praak, Malaysia's Killer Elite"; Author, "Orang Asli Now: The Orang Asli in the Malaysian Political World"; Author, "Power and Politics: The Story of Malaysia's Orang Asli"; "The US Navy Afloat Program"; Contributor, Articles, Professional Journals **Awards:** Recipient Scholar, French History and French Civil Law, University of Burgundy, France (1977-1979) **Memberships:** Association of Asian Studies; American Political Science Association; Pi Sigma Alpha; University of Maine **Marquis Who's Who Honors:** Albert Nelson Marquis Lifetime Achievement Award; Marquis Who's Who Top Professional; Distinguished Humanitarian **Why did you become involved in your profession or industry:** Mr. Jumper got involved in his profession after being offered numerous opportunities. He wanted to make a contribution to the world by writing and educating others. **Avocations:** Swimming; Table tennis **Religion:** Protestant

Barbara J. Justice, MD, ABPN, ABFP

Title: Forensic Psychiatrist **Industry:** Medicine & Health Care **Company Name:** Barbara J. Justice, MD **Date of Birth:** 08/10/1947 **Place of Birth:** Brooklyn **State/Country of Origin:** NY/USA **Parents:** Robert W. Justice, Jr.; Alma Bell Justice **Marital Status:** Single **Children:** Kamao Justice Douglas **Education:** Residency, Chief Residency General Surgery, Columbia University Harlem Medical Center; Fellowship Surgical Oncology, Howard University Cancer Center; Fellowship, Surgical Endoscopy, Columbia University, Harlem Medical Center; Residency, Chief Residency, Adult Psychiatry, Columbia University Harlem Medical Center; Fellowship Psychodynamic Psychotherapy, New York University Psychoanalytic School; Fellowship, Forensic Psychiatry, UCLA; MD, Howard University; Post-Baccalaureate Coursework, Pre-Medicine, Columbia University, BA Degree, The City University of NY, **Certifications:** Diplomate, American Board of Forensic Psychiatry (2007-Present); Diplomate, American Board of Psychiatry and Neurology Certificate (2006-Present); Qualified Medical Examiner, California (2006-Present); Board of the American Board of Medical Specialist in Forensic, Psychiatry, (2006); Certification in Psychodynamic Psychotherapy (2005); Certification in Surgical Endoscopy (1996); Certification in Surgical Oncology (1983); Board Eligible, General Surgery (1982) **Career:** Chief Executive Officer, Medical Director, Glaser Forensic Group, Woodland Hills, CA (2020–Present); Telepsychiatry Physician, Fifth Avenue Medical Associates, New York (2020–Present); Consulting Forensic Psychiatrist, Forensic MED Group, Casabas, CA (2017-Present); Psychiatrist Psychopharmacology, Center for Behavior Medicine, Whittier, CA (2007-Present); Forensic Psychiatrist, Disability, Psychopharmacology & Psychodynamic Psychotherapy, Workers' Compensation, Glaser Forensic, Woodland Hills, CA (2006-Present); Attending Forensic Psychiatrist, Metropolitan State Hospital, Norwalk, CA (2006-Present); Director, Forensic Psychiatry Training, Metropolitan State Hospital, Norwalk, CA (2007-2009); Attending Psychiatrist (Locum Tenens), Riker's Island Correctional Facility, New York, NY (2003-2009); Medical Radio Journalist, Talk Show Host, Inner City Broadcasting Corporation, New York (1984-2000); Attending, Emergency Medicine, Surgery- Methodist Hospital, New York (1984-1990); Private Practice in Surgery and General Medicine, New York (1982-2000); Co-Investigator, The Jonas Salk Institute, Therapeutic Vaccine for Human Immune Deficiency Virus (1994-1996); Principal Investigator, National Institutes of Health, Low Dose Oral Alpha Interferon Study (1993-1995); Attending, Surgery, North General Hospital, New York (1986–1990); Attending Physician, Addiction, Research and Treatment Corp, Brooklyn, NY (1985-1989); Associate Clinical Professor, Surgery, Howard University Hospital Washington, DC (1982-1984) **Career Related:** US Representative to Kenya Medical Research Institute, Nairobi, KenyaInvestigator Observed effects of low dose oral alpha interferon in treatment of AIDS, 9/91 to 9/95 **Civic:** Society for the Prevention of Cruelty to Animals; Cuban Medical School Scholarship Committee; Inter-Religious Foundation for Community Organizations **Awards:** Featured Delta Airlines Magazine (2019); Wall Street Journal Feature (2018, 2019); Elite Physicians (2014); Minority Fellowship Cultural Research in Psychiatry, American Psychiatric Association (2002); Former Mayor David Dinkins proclaimed a New York City-wide Barbara Justice Day (1996) **Memberships:** American Board of Medical Specialist in Forensic, Psychiatry (2006); American Academy of Psychiatry & the Law; American Psychiatric Association; American Board of Psychiatry & Neurology; The National Medical Association; American Board of Forensic Psychiatry; National Black Leadership Commission on AIDS, Inc. **Marquis Who's Who Honors:** Who's Who Professional Women (2020); Marquis Humanitarian Award (2020); Marquis Industry Leader (2019); Albert Nelson Marquis Lifetime Achievement Award (2018) **To what do you attribute your success:** She attributes her success to God. God has guided her steps and blessed her with skills to aide others, opportunities to make use of these gifts, a supportive family, community & a multitude of exceptional mentors. **Why did you become involved in your profession or industry:** She became involved in her profession due to her desire to use her skills in the healing arts and to make the world a little better for her having lived. She has a special commitment to her community but to all human beings and life in this universe. **Avocations:** Reading; Pets; Traveling; Exercise; Music **Political Affiliations:** Progressive **Religion:** Spiritual **Thoughts on Life:** Life is brief. We are blessed with a moment in time to chose what we will to do in this world. Dr. Justice aspires to enrich as many of her fellow human beings as possible. To heal the sick, to protect the weak, injured & unfortunate. To celebrate the best that we can be.

Richard L. Kadish

Title: Chairman, Founder **Industry:** Real Estate **Company Name:** CAPREIT **Date of Birth:** 12/01/1943 **Place of Birth:** Newark **State/Country of Origin:** NJ/ USA **Parents:** Irving Jerome Kadish (Deceased 1987); Henrietta (Appleblatt) Kadish (Deceased 1989) **Marital Status:** Married **Spouse Name:** Bethany Tortis (08/06/1972) **Children:** Jennifer Cassell; Andrew Kadish; Jill **Education:** JD, Rutgers, The State University of New Jersey (1970); MA, Rutgers, The State University of New Jersey (1968); BA, University of Pennsylvania (1965) **Career:** Chairman, CAPREIT, Rockville, MD (2014-Present); Founder, CAPREIT, Rockville, MD (1993-Present); President, CAPREIT (1998-2014); Executive Vice President, Capital Apartment Properties, Inc., Rockville, MD (1993-1998); Executive Vice President, CRI Inc., Rockville, MD (1987-1994); Senior Vice President, CRI Inc., Rockville, MD (1978-1987); Deputy Executive Director, New Jersey Housing Financial Agency (Now New Jersey Housing and Mortgage Finance Agency), Trenton, NJ (1974-1977); Deputy Attorney General, New Jersey Attorney General, Trenton, NJ (1971-1974) **Career Related:** Director, National Multifamily Housing Council (2008-2015) **Creative Works:** Contributor, Articles, Professional Journals; Lecturer in the Field **Memberships:** American Bar Association (1971); New Jersey State Bar Association (1971); National Multifamily Housing Council **Bar Admissions:** New Jersey State Bar Association (1971) **Marquis Who's Who Honors:** Albert Nelson Marquis Lifetime Achievement Award; Marquis Who's Who Top Professional **Why did you become involved in your profession or industry:** Mr. Kadish became involved in his profession because he wanted to help people. Originally, he wanted to become a dentist. However, while attending the School of Dentistry at the University of Pennsylvania, he found that his eyesight wouldn't allow him to excel as a dentist. Alternatively, he pursued a career in law. **Avocations:** Traveling; Spending time with family **Religion:** Jewish

William George Kaelin Jr., MD

Title: 1) Professor of Medicine 2) Researcher **Industry:** Education/Educational Services **Company Name:** 1) Harvard Medical School 2) Dana-Farber Cancer Institute **Date of Birth:** 11/23/1957 **Place of Birth:** Jamaica **State/Country of Origin:** NY/USA **Marital Status:** Widowed **Spouse Name:** Carolyn Kaelin, MD (1988, Deceased 2015) **Children:** Two Children **Education:** Internship and Residency, The Johns Hopkins University (1983-1986); MD, Duke University School of Medicine, Durham, NC (1982); BA in Mathematics and Chemistry, Duke University, Durham, NC (1979) **Certifications:** Certification in Medical Oncology; Diplomate, American Board of Internal Medicine **Career:** Professor, Harvard Medical School, Boston, MA (2002-Present); Associate Professor, Harvard Medical School, Boston, MA (1997-2002); Assistant Professor of Medicine, Harvard Medical School, Boston, MA (1992-1997); Clinical Fellow in Medical Oncology, Dana-Farber Cancer Institute, Boston, MA (1987-1992); Associate Director, Basic Science, Dana-Farber/Harvard Cancer Center, Boston, MA **Career Related:** Boston Investigator, Howard Hughes Medical Institute (1998-Present); Attending Physician, Adult Oncology, Dana-Farber Cancer Institute; Attending Physician, Medicine, Brigham & Women's Hospital **Creative Works:** Contributor, Articles, Professional Journals **Awards:** Nobel Prize in Physiology or Medicine (2019); Massry Prize (2018); Albert Lasker Award for Basic Medical Research (2016); Princess Takamatsu Memorial Lectureship Award, American Association for Cancer Research (2016); Science of Oncology Award, American Society of Clinical Oncology (2016); Wiley Prize in Biomedical Sciences (2014); Steven C. Beering Award (2014); Scientific Grand Prize, Fondation Lefoulon-Delalande (2012); Stanley J. Korsmeyer Award, The American Society for Clinical Investigation (2012); Canada Gairdner International Award, Gairdner Foundation (2010); Distinguished Alumni Award, School of Medicine, Duke University (2007); Richard & Hinda Rosenthal Foundation Award, American Association for Cancer Research (2006); Doris Duke Distinguished Clinical Investigator Award, School of Medicine, Duke University (2006); Paul Marks Prize for Cancer Research, Memorial Sloan-Kettering Cancer Center (2001); Richard A. Smith Prize, Dana-Farber Cancer Institute (1996-1997) **Memberships:** Fellow, American Association for Cancer Research; National Academy of Sciences; American College of Physicians; The American Society for Clinical Investigation; Institute of Medicine

Lynn R. Kahle, PhD

Title: Professor Emeritus **Industry:** Education/Educational Services **Company Name:** University of Oregon **Date of Birth:** 12/06/1950 **Place of Birth:** Hillsboro **State/Country of Origin:** OR/USA **Parents:** Walter Raymond Kahle (Deceased 2001); Dorothea Elizabeth (Schaus) Kahle (Deceased 2004) **Marital Status:** Widower **Spouse Name:** Debra Claire (08/19/1978, Deceased 2017) **Children:** Kevin; Kurtus "Kurt" **Education:** Postdoctoral Work, University of Michigan (1978-1980); PhD, University of Nebraska (1977); MA, Pacific Lutheran University (1974); BA, Concordia College, with Distinction, Fort Wayne, IN (1973); AA, Concordia University, Portland, OR (1971) **Certifications:** Blue Belt Certification, Innovation Engineering **Career:** Professor, Pace University (2018-Present); Professor Emeritus, University of Oregon (2016-Present); James Warsaw Professor, Department of Marketing, University of Oregon (1983-2017); Assistant Professor, The University of North Carolina at Chapel Hill (1980-1983); Postdoctoral Fellow, University of Michigan, Ann Arbor, MI (1978-1980); Assistant Professor, University of Nebraska-Lincoln (1977-1978) **Civic:** Board of Directors, Organization for Economic Initiatives, Inc., Eugene, OR (1988-1996); Human Rights President's Council, Eugene, OR (1988-1991); President, Commission on Rights of Aging, Eugene, OR (1987-1991) **Creative Works:** Editor, "Consumer Social Values" (2019); Author, Book, "Belief Systems, Religion, and Behavioral Economics: Marketing in Multicultural Environments" (2014); Author, "Marketplace Lifestyles in an Age of Social Media: Theory and Method" (2012); Editor, "Sport Marketing Quarterly" (1999-2000); Author, "Marketing Management" (1990); Author, Book, "Attitudes and Social Adaptation" (1983); Associate Editor, Psychology and Marketing (1983-1985); Author, "Social Values and Social Change" (1983); Editor, "Social Values and Social Change" (1983); Contributor, Articles, Professional Journals **Awards:** Stotlar Award for Education, Sport Marketing Association (2014); Thomas C. Stewart Distinguished Professor, Lundquist College of Business (2014); Lifetime Achievement Award, Consumer Behavior Special Interest Group, American Marketing Association (2013); Distinguished Career Contributions, Scientific Understanding of Sports Business, Sport Special Interest Group, American Marketing Association (2011); National Research Service Award, University of Michigan (1978-1980) **Memberships:** Policy & Planning Board, American Psychological Association, (2020-Present); Chair, Membership Board, American Psychological Association (2019); Council Representative, American Psychological Association (2013-2019); President, Society for Consumer Psychology (1997-1998); Fellow, American Psychological Association; American Marketing Association; Association for Consumer Research; Association of Psychological Science **Marquis Who's Who Honors:** Albert Nelson Marquis Lifetime Achievement Award **To what do you attribute your success:** Dr. Kahle attributes his success to his family. **Why did you become involved in your profession or industry:** Dr. Kahle became involved in his profession to create a better world. **Avocations:** Hiking; Playing tennis; Reading **Political Affiliations:** Democrat **Religion:** Lutheran **Thoughts on Life:** Dr. Kahle states, "Choose your values carefully, then strive to live by your values."

Leonard Paul "Len" Kaine

Title: Founder, President **Industry:** Nonprofit & Philanthropy **Company Name:** Golden Rule Society **Date of Birth:** 06/19/1936 **Place of Birth:** Scranton **State/Country of Origin:** PA/USA **Parents:** Adam; Theda **Marital Status:** Married **Spouse Name:** Anne **Children:** David; Glenn; Laura (Twin); Lynn (Twin) **Education:** MBA, National University, San Diego, CA, with Distinction (1977); BBA, National University, San Diego, CA, Summa Cum Laude (1976); Associate Degree, William & Mary (1965); Leadership & Psychology **Career:** Founder and President, Golden Rule Society, Inc., Coronado, CA (1972-Present); Realtor, Owner, Broker, Developer, Stand Crown, Coronado, CA (1980); Captain, US Airways (1967-1986) **Civic:** Speaker, "HOPE Collection" Radio Show; 32nd Degree Freemason, Veteran Shriner, San Diego, CA; Christ Episcopal Church, Coronado, CA **Military Service:** Fighter Pilot, United States Navy (1954-1980); Captain, United States Navy **Awards:** Five-time Nobel Peace Prize Nominee (2003, 2014, 2017, 2018, 2019); Named One of Two Live Heroes in Coronado California's Avenue of Heroes (2015); Runner Up, Nobel Peace Prize (2014); National Charity of Choice Supporting Our Troops and Veterans, American Hero Card (2012); Named Hero of the Year, CNN (2011); Named Veteran of the Year, U.S. Department of Veterans Affairs (2010); President's Lifetime Achievement Award, Medal, Citation, President George W. Bush (2006); President's Volunteer Service Award, Gold Medal, Citation, President George W. Bush (2005); Community Spirit Award, Kiwanis International (2004); National Role of Honor, Washington National Cathedral, Washington, DC (2002); Letter of Commendation, Under Secretary of Defense (2002); Hero Award, New Vision Inc. (2001); Named Alumnus of the Month, National University, San Diego, CA (1981); Noel Davis Trophy as CO of VF-301, Navy's Top Fighter Squadron, United States Navy; Aviation Safety Award, Chief of Naval Operations; J.S. McCain Trophy as Navy's Outstanding Fighter Squadron, United States Navy; All-Navy Enlisted Retention Trophy, United States Navy; Command at Sea Star, United States Navy; Recipient, Many Decorative Medals, United States Navy; Recognized, Numerous Local and National Newspaper Articles **Memberships:** Board Chairman, Nationwide Reality Pilot LLC (2013-Present) **To what do you attribute your success:** Mr. Kaine attributes his success to his goal, which is "world peace through living the Golden Rule." With five nominations for the Nobel Peace Prize as proof of this dedication, he modernized the Golden Rule from the books of the world's eight major religions. **Why did you become involved in your profession or industry:** Mr. Kaine became involved in his profession because immediately after graduating high school, he began his U.S. Navy career. Mr. Kaine scored highly on a series of tests that qualified him with a two-year college equivalency. The Navy presented him the opportunity to take the tests to enter the Naval Aviation Cadet program. He was a success and received his Navy "Wings of Gold" with an Officer's commission as a "TeenAge Ensign." **Thoughts on Life:** The motto of Mr. Kaine's nonprofit is, "with hope in your heart... treat others the way you want to be treated... truthfully, with dignity and respect..." and "to better the lives of others is your greatest reward... which makes the rest of your life the best of your life."

Walter Christian Kaiser Jr., PhD

Title: President Emeritus, Academic Administrator **Industry:** Education/Educational Services **Company Name:** Gordon-Conwell Theological Seminary **Date of Birth:** 04/11/1933 **Place of Birth:** Folcroft **State/Country of Origin:** PA/USA **Parents:** Walter Christian Kaiser; Estelle Evelyn (Jaworsky) Kaiser **Marital Status:** Married **Spouse Name:** Margaret Ruth Burk (08/24/1957) (Deceased 2013); Nancy Elizabeth Veldboom **Children:** Walter Christian III; Brian Addison; Kathleen Elise; Jonathan Kevin **Education:** PhD in Mediterranean and Near Eastern Studies, Brandeis University (1973); MA in Mediterranean Studies, Brandeis University (1962); BD in Theological Studies, Wheaton College (1958); BA in Bible Studies and Greek, Wheaton College (1955) **Career:** President Emeritus, Gordon-Conwell Theological Seminary (2005-Present); President, Gordon-Conwell Theological Seminary (1996-2005); Colman M. Mockler Distinguished Professor of Old Testament, Gordon-Conwell Theological Seminary (1993-2005); Senior Vice President of Distance Learning, Trinity International University, Deerfield, IL (1992-1993); Academic Dean, Vice President of Education, Trinity International University, Deerfield, IL (1980-1993); Senior Vice President of Education, Trinity International University, Deerfield, IL (1989-1992); Professor of Old Testament, Trinity International University, Deerfield, IL (1973-1980); Associate Professor of Old Testament, Trinity International University, Deerfield, IL (1966-1973); Assistant Professor, Wheaton College (1961-1966); Bible Instructor, Wheaton College (1958-1961) **Civic:** Trustee, Board of Directors, Wheaton College (1983-2016) **Military Service:** Reserve Officer Training Corps **Creative Works:** Author, "Walking the Ancient Paths: A Commentary on Jeremiah" (2019); Author, "Lives and Ministries of Elijah and Elisha: Demonstrating the Wonderful Power of the Word of God" (2019); Co-Author, "A History of Israel: From the Bronze Age through the Jewish Wars" (2008); Author, "The Promise-Plan of God: A Biblical Theology of the Old and New Testaments" (2008); Author, "Exodus (The Expositor's Bible Commentary)" (1990, 2008); Co-Author, Biblical Hermeneutics: The Search for Meaning" (1994, 2007); Author, "Toward Old Testament Ethics" (1993); Author, "The Communicator's Commentary: Micah-Malachi" (1992); Author, "Hard Sayings of the Old Testament" (1988); Author, "Quest for Renewal: Personal Revival in the Old Testament" (1986); Author, "The Uses of the Old Testament in the New" (1985); Author, "Malachi: God's Unchanging Love" (1984); 42 Additional Books **Awards:** Junior Teacher of the Year, Wheaton College (1966); Grant, Danforth Fellows Program (1961-1963); Faculty Fellow, Wheaton College (1957-1958) **Memberships:** Board of Directors, Near East Archaeological Society (1975-Present); Board of Directors, Bible Study Fellowship (1992-2019); National President, The Evangelical Theological Society (1977); Commission on Accrediting of the Association of Theological Schools; Institute for Biblical Research; Society of Biblical Literature **Marquis Who's Who Honors:** Albert Nelson Marquis Lifetime Achievement Award; Marquis Who's Who Top Professional **Why did you become involved in your profession or industry:** Dr. Kaiser became involved in his profession because of his lifelong love of theology and particularly, biblical manuscripts. **Avocations:** Gardening; Wood-cutting **Political Affiliations:** Independent **Religion:** Evangelical Protestant

Jon Kalina

Title: Chief Executive Officer **Industry:** Manufacturing **Company Name:** Peeled Snacks **Date of Birth:** 03/28/1969 **Parents:** Lynn Kalina; Nancy Kalina **Marital Status:** Married **Spouse Name:** Jackie Kalina **Children:** Amanda; Tyffanie; Lia; Zoe **Education:** BA in Business Management and Economics, Rockford Business College, Rockford, IL (1991) **Career:** Chief Executive Officer, Peeled Snacks, Cumberland, RI (2017-Present); Vice President of Sales, Blue Marble Brands, LLC (UNFI), Providence, RI (2006-2017); Senior Vice President of Sales, Seasons' Enterprises, Addison, IL (2005-2006); Director of National Accounts, Kettle Foods, Inc., Salem, OR (1999-2005); Sales Manager, Bin Sales and Marketing, New Port Richey, FL (1998-1999); Account Executive/Category Manager, Kuehn Prewitt Rufer, Bettendorf, IA (1990-1998) **Civic:** Volunteer, Habitat for Humanity, Local Food Pantries **Marquis Who's Who Honors:** Marquis Who's Who Top Professional **To what do you attribute your success:** Mr. Kalina attributes his success to hard work and perseverance. He prides himself on being one of the hard workers in the group and never giving up. He never takes no for an answer and encourages his staff to find the solution to make the company better. **Why did you become involved in your profession or industry:** Mr. Kalina became involved in his profession because he was in the food industry his entire life and prior to going to Peel Snacks, he spent 11 years at Blue Marble Brands. His dad spent 33 years with Coca-Cola and a lot of his family worked in the food industry. He thinks it's in his blood and when he was exposed to the natural organic side of it, he found that no matter what happened to the economy, people would want to eat and lead healthier lifestyles. He was drawn in by that and what it stood for, and enjoyed the food aspect and truly had a passion for what he did.

Ikar J. Kalogjera, MD, DFAPA, DFAACP

Title: Psychiatrist, Educator **Industry:** Social Work **Company Name:** Ikar J. Kalogjera, MD, SC **Date of Birth:** 08/30/1945 **Place of Birth:** Zagreb **State/Country of Origin:** Croatia **Parents:** Jaksa Jakov Kalogjera; Biserka Erak Kalogjera **Marital Status:** Married **Spouse Name:** Araceli Colina Cabaron (07/15/1976) **Children:** Liliana Marie **Education:** Fellow, Child and Adolescent Psychiatry, University of Cincinnati (1974-1976); Resident in Psychiatry, Medical College of Wisconsin, Wauwatosa, WI (1972-1974); Intern, University of Zagreb (1970-1971); MD, University of Zagreb, Croatia (1970) **Certifications:** Psychiatry, American Board of Psychiatry and Neurology, Inc.; Child Psychiatry, American Board of Psychiatry and Neurology, Inc.; American Board of Addiction Medicine **Career:** Psychiatrist, Private Practice, Adult, Child and Adolescent Psychiatry, Wauwatosa, WI (1981-Present); Professor, Medical College of Wisconsin (2001-2020); Director of Adolescent In-Patient Service, Medical College of Wisconsin (1980-1981); Director of Adolescent In-Patient Unit, Medical College of Wisconsin (1979-1980); Psychiatrist, Private Practice, Rockford, IL (1976-1979) **Career Related:** Honorary Staff Member, Aurora Psychiatric Hospital, Aurora Health Care, Wauwatosa, WI (1999-Present); Founder, Leader, Milwaukee Group for the Advancement of Self-Psychology (1991-Present); Clinical Professor of Psychiatry, Medical College of Wisconsin (2001-2020); Associate Clinical Professor of Psychiatry, Medical College of Wisconsin (1987-2001); Assistant Clinical Professor of Psychiatry, Medical College of Wisconsin (1981-1987); Faculty, Medical College of Wisconsin (1979-1981); Founding Fellow, Academy of Cognitive Therapy; Lifetime Fellow, American Academy of Child and Adolescent Psychiatry; Distinguished Life Fellow, American Psychiatric Association, American Child & Adolescent and Psychiatry **Civic:** Contributor, Croatian Community, Milwaukee, WI (1979-Present); Consultant, Jewish Family Services, Inc., Milwaukee, WI (1979-Present); Consultant, Lutheran Social Services of Wisconsin and Upper Michigan, Milwaukee, WI (1984-1990); Consultant, Family Service of Milwaukee, Wisconsin (1982-1989) **Creative Works:** Contributor, Book Chapter, "Disordered Couple" (1998); Author, "Hospital and Community Psychiatry" (1989); Co-author, "American Journal of Psychotherapy" (1988) **Awards:** Five-Year Honoree, Patient's Choice Award (2020); Five-Year Honoree, Compassionate Doctor Award (2020); Listed, Top Doctors in Psychiatry, Wisconsin Magazine (2020); Listed, Top Doctors in Child and Adolescent Psychiatry, Wisconsin Magazine (2019-2020); Listed, America's Most Honored Professionals – Top 1%, American Registry (2017-2020); Listed, America's Best Physicians, National Consumer Advisory Board (2016-2020); Patients' Choice Award, American Registry (2014, 2016-2020); On Time Doctor Award, American Registry (2014, 2016-2020); Most Compassionate Doctor, American Registry (2012-2014, 2016-2020); Listed, America's Most Honored Professionals – Top 5%, American Registry (2016); Honoree, Trademark's Top Doctor's Honors Edition, American Registry of Most Honored Professionals (2014-2016); Featured Listee, Top Ten Doctors in Wisconsin – Psychiatrists, American Registry (2014); Distinguished Service Award, Department of Psychiatry, Medical College of Wisconsin (2014); Listed, America's Top Psychiatrists, Consumers Research Council of America (2002-2012); Service Award, Jewish Family Service, Inc. (2010); Award for Excellence in Teaching, Child & Adolescent Psychiatry, Medical College of Wisconsin (1992, 2010); Irma Bland Award, American Psychiatric Association (2006); Community Service Honor, Jewish Family Services, Inc., Milwaukee, WI (2003); Give a Damn Award, Medical College of Wisconsin – Department of Psychiatry (1991, 2003); Featured Listee, Top Psychiatrists, Psychotherapists, Milwaukee Magazine (1994, 1996, 2001); Golden Apple Teaching Award, Department of Psychiatry, Medical College of Wisconsin (1996, 2000); Marvin Wagner Clinical Preceptor Award, Medical College of Wisconsin (1999); Award for Excellence in Teaching, Department of Psychiatry, Medical College of Wisconsin (1992); Featured Listee, Outstanding Therapists, Town and Country Magazine (1988) **Memberships:** Wisconsin Council of Child and Adolescent Psychiatry; International Association for Psychoanalytic Self Psychology; Special Member, Wisconsin Psychoanalytic Institute, Society and Foundation; Medical Society of Milwaukee County; Alumni, Family Institute at Northwestern University; American Society of Addiction Medicine; American Group Psychotherapy Association; Wisconsin Psychiatric Association; American Medical Association; Wisconsin Medical Society **Marquis Who's Who Honors:** Albert Nelson Marquis Lifetime Achievement Award; Marquis Who's Who Top Professional; Marquis Who's Who Humanitarian Award **Avocations:** Boating; Photography; Movies; Theater; Travel

Robert Kam Kamerschen

Title: Senior Business Executive, Private Investor, Consultant, Mentor **Industry:** Health, Wellness and Fitness **Company Name:** Healtheo360, LLC **Date of Birth:** 02/16/1936 **Place of Birth:** Laurium **State/Country of Origin:** MI/USA **Parents:** Robert Raymond Kamerschen; Elise D. (Barsanti) Kamerschen **Marital Status:** Married **Spouse Name:** Judith A. Campbell (07/06/1958) **Children:** Kathryn; Carol; Jean **Education:** MBA, Miami University, Oxford, OH (1958); BS, Miami University, Oxford, OH (1957) **Career:** Private Investor of Strategic Advancement, Dimac Marketing Corporation (2002-Present); Chairman, Survey Sampling International (Now Dynata) (2005-2009); Chief Executive Officer, Dimac Marketing Corporation (1999-2002); Chairman, Chief Executive Officer, ADVO, Inc., Windsor, CT (1988-1999); President, Chief Executive Officer, Wesray Capital Corporation, New York, NY (1987-1988); President, Chief Operating Officer, Marketing Corporation of America (1984-1987); Executive Vice President, Sector Executive, Office of the Chairman, Norton Simon Inc. (1981-1983); President, Chief Executive Officer, Max Factor, Hollywood, CA (1979-1983); President, Chief Operating Officer, Chanel, Christian Dior Parfums, Inc., New York, NY (1977-1979); Senior Vice President of Marketing Operations, Dunkin' Donuts, Inc., Randolph, MA (1973-1977); Vice President of Marketing, Revlon, New York, NY (1971-1973); Director of Consumer Marketing, Scott Paper Company, Philadelphia, PA (1960-1971); Management Trainee, FCB Global, Chicago, IL (1959-1960); Executive Sales Trainee, National Cash Register, Gary, IN (1958-1959); Chairman, Co-Owner, Healtheo360, LLC **Career Related:** Lecturer, College of Business Administration, University of Georgia (1979-1981); Member, 21 Public Boards; Member, 32 Private Boards; Chair, Three Boards, Vertrue Inc.; Lead Director, Chair, Two Boards, Playboy Enterprises, Inc.; Board Member, Chair of Strategic Committee, Linens 'n Things; Chair, Board Member, IMS Health Inc. (Now IQVIA); Chair, Three Boards, RadioShack; Lead Director, Chair, Three Boards, R.H. Donnelley Inc. (Now DexYP); Presiding Director, Chair, Three Boards, MDC Partners, Inc.; Guest Lecturer, Various Universities; Distinguished Practitioner, Miami University **Civic:** Regent, University of Hartford (1998-2005); Trustee, Wadsworth Atheneum Museum of Art (1990-2003); Trustee, Bushnell Hall, Columbia College (1995-2002); Trustee, Columbia College (1993-1996); Trustee, First Vice Chairman, Emerson College (1984-1989) **Memberships:** Metropolitan Club; New York Athletic Club; Sigma Alpha Epsilon; Delta Sigma Pi; Beta Gamma Sigma **Marquis Who's Who Honors:** Albert Nelson Marquis Lifetime Achievement Award; Marquis Who's Who Top Professional; Marquis Who's Who Humanitarian Award **Why did you become involved in your profession or industry:** Mr. Kamerchan became involved in his profession because of his lifelong love of business. Early in his career, his father taught him to focus on sales first because nothing happens until revenue "comes through the door." **Avocations:** Sports; Art; Collecting wine

Carolyn Kanode

Title: School Nurse Practitioner, Pediatrics Nurse **Industry:** Medicine & Health Care **Place of Birth:** Trenton **State/Country of Origin:** NJ/USA **Parents:** Lawrence Stephen Kerrigan; Louise (Welde) Kerrigan **Marital Status:** Married **Spouse Name:** Irwin Kanode (08/26/1960) **Children:** Cathy; Barbara; Teresa **Education:** MS, Pepperdine University, Malibu, CA (1984); BS, California State University, Long Beach, Cum Laude (1976) **Certifications:** New Jersey **Career:** School Nurse Practitioner; Pediatrics Nurse **Career Related:** Coordinator, Healthy Start Medical (1998-2008); Huntington Beach Union High School District **Civic:** President, American Association of University Women **Marquis Who's Who Honors:** Albert Nelson Marquis Lifetime Achievement Award; Marquis Who's Who Top Professional **Why did you become involved in your profession or industry:** Ms. Kanode became involved in nursing because initially she wanted to be an English teacher, but her parents did not have the funds. She went to Abington PA Hospital and saw that it looked like a wonderful career, so she applied to hospitals and got scholarships to two. That is how she became a nurse, but it wasn't the first thing that she was going to do. **Avocations:** Poetry; Flower arrangements; Mental illness and children's dentistry advocacy; Education; Reading autobiographies, historical novels and classics

Ravi Kant, MD

Title: Endocrinologist **Industry:** Medicine & Health Care **Company Name:** AnMed Endocrinology **Children:** Two Children **Certifications:** Certified in Endocrinology; Certified in Geriatrics, American Board of Internal Medicine **Career:** Endocrinologist, Geriatrician, AnMed Endocrinology (2014-Present); Affiliate Associate Professor, Medical University of South Carolina (2014-Present); Fellowship, Endocrinology Diabetes and Metabolism, University of Maryland (2012-2014); Fellowship, Geriatric Medicine, University of Maryland (2011-2012); Residency, Johns Hopkins University/Sinai Hospital, Baltimore MD (2008); Associate Professor, Edward Via College of Osteopathic Medicine, Virginia Polytechnic Institute and State University **Awards:** Named, Preceptor of the Year (2019); Recipient, Best Resident Award; Recipient, Best Fellow Award; Recipient, Fellowship, American Diabetes Association **Marquis Who's Who Honors:** Marquis Who's Who Top Professional **To what do you attribute your success:** Dr. Kant attributes his success to having great mentors who helped shape him into who he is today. His family has also been very supportive. Dr. Kant is grateful for all his patients during his training. He was fortunate to go through the right programs at good universities. **Why did you become involved in your profession or industry:** Dr. Kant entered his profession because of an event during his youth; when he was in middle school, his father was ill with a tumor. It was a very difficult surgery and they didn't know if he would make it through. Dr. Kant saw how he was treated and how a physician can affect the lives of a whole family. He thought this was the perfect thing, because not only is it work but it is affecting the lives of so many. Dr. Kant went on to complete medical school in India. **Avocations:** Watching sports

Tzu-Min Kao, MD

Title: Physiatrist **Industry:** Medicine & Health Care **Date of Birth:** 1939 **Place of Birth:** Taiwan **Parents:** Ya-Yuan Liu; Tieh Kao **Marital Status:** Married **Spouse Name:** Tumei Kao **Children:** Winfred; Wileen; Vivien **Education:** Degree in Clinical Neurophysiology, Harvard Medical School (1975); MS, University of Washington (1971); Fellowship in Physical Medicine and Rehabilitation, University of Washington (1970-1971); Intern, Christ Community Hospital (1967); Resident in Surgery, Kaohsiung Medical Hospital (1966-1967); Coursework, Kaohsiung Medical College (1965); Certificate, ECFMG, Association of American Medical Colleges (1965); MD, Kaohsiung Medical College (1965); Resident in Physical Medicine and Rehabilitation, New York University Medical Center **Certifications:** Fellow of the Academy, American Academy of Physical Medicine and Rehabilitation (1993); Diplomate, American Board of Physical Medicine and Rehabilitation (1973); Licensed to Practice Medicine, States of Washington, DC, New Jersey, Maryland, Virginia, Washington; Diplomate, American Board of Physical Medicine and Rehabilitation **Career:** Publisher, Taiwan Business News (2009-Present); Executive Director, Taiwan Artificial Heart Research Center (1993-2000); Clinical Professor, U.S. International University, Health Professions and Biomedical Sciences (1989-1992); Associate Professor, The George Washington University School of Medicine (1979-1981); Chief Medical Officer, The Government of DC, Department of Human Resources (1977-1987); Assistant Professor, Georgetown University School of Medicine (1976-1985); Consultant Physician, The White House Medical Unit (1974-1981); Chairman, Department of Rehabilitation Medicine, Jefferson Memorial Hospital (1974-1977); Associate Director, Physical Medicine and Rehabilitation Division, Glen Dale Hospital (1972-1974); Fellow in Physical Medicine and Rehabilitation, University of Washington (1970-1971); Resident in Physical Medicine and Rehabilitation, New York University Medical Center (1968-1970); Intern, Christ Community Hospital (1967); Private Practice; President, Asia-Pacific Medical Center, Bethesda, MD; Artificial Heart Research and Development Program, Harbin Medical University, Harbin Institute of Technology, Asia-Pacific Medical Center; Founder, P and A International Inc., Bethesda, MD; Principal Consultant, Picasso International Inc., Shanghai, China; Promoting, Trading Artwork, Asia **Career Related:** Coordinator, Artificial Heart Research and Development Program in Cooperation with Harbin Medical University, Harbin Institute of Technology, Asia-Pacific Medical Center (2014-2019); President, World Trade Center Club, Taichung (1993-1996); Legislator, Legislative Yuan, Taiwan, ROC (1990-1992) **Creative Works:** Patentee, TAH Phoenix-7k (2015-2022); Author, Books **Awards:** Special Contribution Awards, Taiwan Benevolent Association of America (2001); Physician's Recognition Award, American Medical Association (1989, 1997); Editor-in-Chief, China Times (1985-1989); The Government of DC Certificate of Appreciation for Significant and Valuable Services (1980); Outstanding Performance Award, The Government of DC (1978); Physician of the Year, Jefferson Memorial Hospital (1977) **Marquis Who's Who Honors:** Albert Nelson Marquis Lifetime Achievement Award **To what do you attribute your success:** Dr. Kao attributes his success to doing what he loves and being persistent in his work. He additionally appreciates the environment in which his parents provided to him as he grew up; it was reasonable and kind. **Why did you become involved in your profession or industry:** Dr. Kao believes in a Chinese saying that said, "Practice medicine in order to save the world." This is what inspired him to pursue medicine. **Avocations:** Art; Painting

Philip Spangler Kappes

Title: Lawyer **Industry:** Law and Legal Services **Date of Birth:** 12/24/1925 **Place of Birth:** Detroit **State/Country of Origin:** MI/USA **Parents:** Philip Alexander Kappes; Wilma Fern (Spangler) Kappes **Marital Status:** Married **Spouse Name:** Glendora Galena Miles **Children:** Susan Lea; Philip Miles; Mark William **Education:** JD, University of Michigan (1948); BA, Butler University, Cum Laude (1945); LLD, University of Michigan **Career:** Partner, Lewis Kappes PC, Indianapolis, (1993-Present); Manager, Labeco Properties, LLC, Indianapolis (1985-Present); President, Director, K&K Realty, Inc., Indianapolis (1983-Present); Active, Law Practice (1948-Present); Partner, Creston Group, Indianapolis (1989-1998); Partner, Lewis & Kappes, Indianapolis (1989-1992); Partner, Lewis Kappes Fuller & Eads, Indianapolis, (1985-1989); Of Counsel, Dutton, Kappes & Overman (1983-1985); Partner, Dutton, Kappes & Overman (1952-1985); Associate, C.B. Dutton (1950-1951); Associate, Armstrong and Gause (1948-1949) **Career Related:** James E. West Fellow, Crossroads Council, Boy Scouts of America (2014); Secretary, Board Member, Laboratory Equipment Corp., Mooresville, IN (1952-2000); Board of Trustees (1987-1990); First Chairman, Ovid Butler Society (1982-1983); Instructor, Business Law, Trustee, Butler University (1948-1949); Scholarship Review Committee, Shortridge High School **Civic:** Chairman, Membership Committee, Italian Heritage Society of Indiana (2018-Present); Ruling Elder, First Presbyterian Church, Indianapolis, IN (2015-Present); Chairman, Buildings and Grounds Committee, First Presbyterian Church, Indianapolis, IN (2015-Present); Chairman, Board of Trustees, First Meridian Heights Presbyterian Church (2014-Present); Vice Chairman, Indianapolis 32-Degree Masonic Learning Center for Children (2002-Present); Honorary Trustee (2001-Present); Director, Indianapolis 32-Degree Masonic Learning Center for Children (1998-Present); Life Director Emeritus (1994-Present); Trustee, Boy Scouts of America (1987-Present); Life Member, Board of Directors, Crossroads of America Council, Boy Scouts of America (1965-Present); First Meridian Heights Presbyterian Church (1933-Present); Chairman of the Board, Indianapolis 32-Degree Masonic Learning Center for Children (2002); Board of Distinguished Advisors (1990-2001); Chairman, Gathering of Eagles Dinner (2000); Ruling Elder, First Meridian Heights Presbyterian Church (1982-1985, 1994-1999); Planning Committee, Indianapolis 32-Degree Masonic Learning Center for Children (1997-1998); Audit and Finance Committee (1992-1994); Executive Committee (1987-1994); Board of Directors, Fairbanks Hospital, Indianapolis (1986-1994); Chairman, Trustees Endowment Fund, Boy Scouts of America (1987-1992); Chairman, Nominating Committee (1991); Chairman of the Board (1988-1991); Children's Museum, Indianapolis (1969-1988); President, Board of Trustees (1984-1985); Vice President of Finance, Executive Committee, President, Boy Scouts of America (1977-1979); Chairman, Lawyers Title Guaranty Fund Committee (1971-1973); Vice Chairman, Faculty Member, Law in American Society (1971-1973); Chairman, Board of Trustees, First Meridian Heights Presbyterian Church (1958-1961, 1969-1972); Director, Indiana Citizens for Modern Court Systems (1970); Deacon, First Meridian Heights Presbyterian Church (1950-1958) **Awards:** Professionalism Award (2014); Butler Medal, Butler University Alumni Association (2010); Legion of Merit (2010); Distinguished Barrister, Indiana Business Journal (2008); Distinguished Barrister, American Judicature Society (2008); Legendary Lawyers of Year, Indiana State Bar Association (2006); Distinguished Eagle Scout Award, National Council, Boy Scouts of America (2004); Board Managers Award for Judicial System Improvement (1995); Golden Legion (1993); Silver Beaver Award, Crossroads Council, Boy Scouts of America (1978); Nominee, One of 100 Distinguished Scouts of Past 100 Years; Paul H. Buchanan Award of Excellence, Indianapolis Bar Foundation; Distinguished Alumnus Award, Butler University Alumni Association; Mortar Award, Butler University Alumni Association **Memberships:** Indiana State Bar Association (1959-Present); Director, Chairman, Indianapolis Scottish Rite Foundation (2001-2010); American Judicature Society (2008); Chairman, Subcommittee on Merit Selection of Trial Court Judges (2005-2008); Chairman, Judicial Selection and Retention Subcommittee on Improvement in the Judicial System, Standing Committee, Indiana State Bar Association (2005); Chairman, Senior Lawyers Division, Indianapolis Bar Association (1999-2000); Chairman, Board of Trustees, Indianapolis Valley Scottish Rite (1998-1999); Trustee, Indianapolis Valley Scottish Rite (1996-1999); Past First Vice President, Director, Court Unification Implementation Committee, Chairman, Indianapolis Legal Aid Society (1995-1998); Family Law Implementation Committee, Indianapolis Bar Association (1993-1997); Committee, Board of Managers, Indianapolis Bar Association (1994-1996); Settlement Week Committee, Indianapolis Bar Association (1989-1995); Executive Counsel, Board of Managers, Indianapolis Bar Association (1994); Committee, Indianapolis Bar Association (1992-1993); Chairman, Law Day Committee, Indianapolis Bar Association (1991-1992) **Bar Admissions:** State of Indiana (1948) **Marquis Who's Who Honors:** Albert Nelson Marquis Lifetime Achievement Award; Marquis Who's Who Humanitarian Award **Political Affiliations:** Republican **Religion:** Presbyterian

Carlene M. Karavite

Title: Psychologist, Coach, Real Estate Property Manager **Industry:** Other **Date of Birth:** 01/17/1939 **Place of Birth:** Detroit **State/Country of Origin:** MI/USA **Parents:** Carl John Daniels; Leota Mae Hobbs Dunham **Marital Status:** Married **Spouse Name:** James "Jim" Karavite (1985); Charles George Schwartz Jr (1958, Divorced 1980) **Children:** Craig William; Charles Michael; Christine Marie Schwartz Mila **Education:** MS in Clinical Psychology, Eastern Michigan University (1992); BA, Wayne State University, Cum Laude (1990); Coursework, Wayne State University (1974-1980); Coursework, Oakland University (1973-1974); Coursework, Oakland Community College (1972-1973); Coursework, University of Detroit (Now University of Detroit Mercy) (1956-1957) **Certifications:** Limited Licensed Psychologist, State of Michigan **Career:** Property Manager, Leota Dunham, Royal Oak, MI (1976-2006); Limited Licensed Psychologist, Midwestern Education Resource Center, Bloomfield Hills, MI (1994-1998); Limited Licensed Psychologist, Advanced Counseling Services, Southfield, MI (1994-1997); Limited Licensed Psychologist, Evergreen Counseling Centers, Farmington Hills, Shelby and Sterling Heights, MI (1993-1994); Salesperson, AT&T, Troy, MI (1989); Real Estate Agent, Coldwell Banker Real Estate LLC, Birmingham, MI (1987-1989); Real Estate Agent, Berridge & Morrison, Royal Oak, MI (1985-1986); Secretary, Data Staff, The Dale Prentice Company, Oak Park, MI (1980-1985); Optometry Assistant, Belmont Vision Center, Detroit, MI (1979-1980); Bookkeeper, Bee Kalt Travel, Royal Oak, MI (1978-1979); Secretary, Reichhold LLC, Ferndale, MI (1957-1959) **Civic:** Supervisor, Michigan Family Court(1990-1992); Volunteer Child Advocate, Family Focus, Inc., Birmingham, MI (1976-1978) **Creative Works:** Actor, Heart of the Hills Players (2004) **Awards:** Outstanding Young Woman of the Year, Junior Women's Club of America (Now General Federation of Women's Clubs) (1966) **Memberships:** ADHD Coach, American Coaching Association (1997) **Marquis Who's Who Honors:** Albert Nelson Marquis Lifetime Achievement Award **Why did you become involved in your profession or industry:** Ms. Karavite became involved in her profession because of her appreciation for therapy and her own experiences with therapy. Grateful for how dramatically it had improved her life, she was motivated to pay it forward and provide therapy to others. Ms. Karavite also drew inspiration from a college friend who juggled full-time schoolwork and a psychology clientele. **Avocations:** Golfing; Cross-country skiing; Drawing; Painting; Roller-skating; Tap dancing; Acting; Designing costumes

Robert Frederick Karnei Jr., MD

Title: Physician **Industry:** Medicine & Health Care **Date of Birth:** 1/14/1934 **Place of Birth:** San Antonio **State/Country of Origin:** TX/USA **Parents:** Robert Frederick Karnei; Hattie (Albert) Karnei **Marital Status:** Married **Spouse Name:** Karen Zimmermann (12/19/1964) **Children:** Robert III; Kimberly; Christopher; Susan; Kathleen **Education:** MD, University of Texas, Galveston, TX (1960); BA, Rice Institute (1956) **Career:** Retired Physician, Medical Examiner (2014-Present); Board of Trustees, Wythe County Community Hospital (1995-2000); Pathologist, Medical Director Laboratory, Wythe County Community Hospital, Wytheville, VA (1992-2000); Director, Armed Forces Institute of Pathology, Washington, DC (1987-1991); Deputy Director, U.S. Navy, Armed Forces Institute of Pathology, Washington, DC (1980-1987); Head, Anatomic Pathology, National Naval Medical Center, Bethesda, MD (1972-1980); Advanced Through Grades to Captain, U.S. Navy (1975); Chief, Laboratory Service, Naval Hospital, Jacksonville, FL (1966-1970); Resident, Anatomic and Clinical Pathology, Naval Medical School, U.S. Navy, Bethesda, MD (1962-1966); Battalion Surgeon, Third MAR Division FMF, U.S. Navy (1961-1962); Commissioned Ensign, U.S. Navy (1959) **Career Related:** Professor of Pathology, Uniformed Services, University of the Health Sciences, Bethesda, MD (1976-1994); Specialty Adviser, Navy Surgeon General, Washington, DC (1980-1991); Fellow, Armed Forces Institute of Pathology, Washington, DC (1970-1972); Fellow, College of American Pathologists; Fellow, U.S. and Canadian Academy of Pathology **Civic:** Board of Governors, Armed Forces Institute of Pathology (1997-2011) **Military Service:** Retired, U.S. Navy (1991) **Creative Works:** Co-Author, "Otolaryngology Clinics of North America" (1979); Contributor, Articles, Professional Journals **Awards:** Department of the Defense Superior Service Award (1991); Meritorious Service Award (1991); Edwards Rhodes Stitt Award, Association of Military Surgeons of the U.S. (1989); Navy Commendation Medal (1980) **Memberships:** American College of Physician Executives; American Association of Blood Banks; Association of Military Surgeons of the U.S.; Washington Academy of Medicine; Washington Society of Pathologists; Blue Ridge Pathology Association **Marquis Who's Who Honors:** Albert Nelson Marquis Lifetime Achievement Award **To what do you attribute your success:** Dr. Karnei attributes his success to hard work. **Why did you become involved in your profession or industry:** Dr. Karnei wanted to become a doctor in elementary school. He later thought of being an architect. When he attended senior high school, his thoughts went back to medicine. It was unusual; he has no other relatives with a medical background. Eventually, many years later and almost about the time he was to retire from the U.S. Navy, he found out he had a distant cousin who was a doctor. That was the only connection and he did not know of him until later in his career. He is not sure of what prompted for him to be a physician, but his longing to help people brought him to medicine. **Avocations:** Woodworking; Gardening; Golf; Bridge; Gym; Walking; Reading **Political Affiliations:** Independent **Religion:** Methodist

Michael J. Kasbar

Title: President, Chief Executive Officer **Industry:** Oil & Energy **Company Name:** World Fuel Services Corporation **Career:** President, Chief Executive Officer, World Fuel Services Inc. (Subsidiary of World Fuel Services Corporation), Miami, FL (2012-Present); Board of Directors, World Fuel Services Inc. (Subsidiary of World Fuel Services Corporation), Miami, FL (1995-Present); President, Chief Operating Officer, World Fuel Services Inc. (Subsidiary of World Fuel Services Corporation), Miami, FL (2002-2012); Chief Executive Officer, Marine Fuel Service, World Fuel Services Inc. (Subsidiary of World Fuel Services Corporation), Miami, FL (1995-2002); Co-founder, Officer, Director, TransTec, NY (1985-1994)

Dr. Jane Katz

Title: Professor of Health and Physical Education **Industry:** Education/Educational Services **Company Name:** John Jay College of Criminal Justice **Date of Birth:** 04/16/1943 **Place of Birth:** Sharon **State/Country of Origin:** PA/USA **Parents:** Leon Katz; Dorothea Katz **Marital Status:** Widowed **Education:** Doctor of Education in Gerontology, Columbia University (1978); Master of Education in Therapeutic Recreation for Aging, Columbia University (1972); Master of Arts, New York University (1966); Bachelor of Science in Health and Physical Education, CCNY (1963) **Certifications:** Water Safety Instructor Trainer **Career:** Professor of Health and Physical Education **Career Related:** Faculty, City University of New York; Writer on Subjects of Swimming, Water Exercise and Fitness **Civic:** Spokesperson, CUNY Conference, NY Academy of Medicine; Fitness Ambassador to Fifty-Plus Fitness Association; Goodwill Ambassador, Hospital for Special Surgery; Keynote Speaker, Disability International Foundation; Honorary Chair, Mass. Breast Cancer Coalition; Women's Sports Foundation; Advisory Board, International Swimming Hall of Fame; Water Exercise Techniques for Veterans; Kids Aquatic ReEntry **Creative Works:** Author, DVD, "Tri-Synchro" (2018); Author, "Natacion Para Todos," Tudor, Madrid (2004); Author, "The All-American Aquatic Handbook", Allyn & Bacon, Boston (1996); Author, "Natacion Para Todos," Tudor, Madrid (1995); Author, "Swim 30 Laps in 30 Days," Putnam, NY (1991); Author, "Fitness Works," Leisure Press, IL (1988); Author, "The W.E.T. Workout," Facts on File, NY (1985); Author, "Swimming for Total Fitness, A Progressive Aerobic Program," Doubleday, NY (1981); Author of 16 books in English, Spanish and Portuguese and 4 DVDs on Fitness and Swimming **Awards:** Legends of the Maccabiah; Harold Martin Award, ISHOF; Lifetime Achievement Award, President's Council on Fitness, Sports and Nutrition; Honor Administrator, IMSHOF; Distinguished Teaching Award, John Jay College; Distinguished Educator, Alumni Association CCNY; Inductee, John Jay's Hall of Fame; Fitness Award, June Krauser Communication Award, USMS; Honoree, National Jewish Sports Hall of Fame; Certificate of Merit, IMSHOF; Distinguished Faculty Award, John Jay College; Liberty Medal, Educator of the Year Award, NY Post Newspaper; Top 25 People in Aquatics, Aquatics International Magazine; Women's Swim Coach the Year, NCAA Division III, CUNY; Distinguished Service Award, Disability International Foundation; Eponym, Dr. Jane Katz Natatorium, Children Better Health Institute, Indianapolis, IN; Honoree, National Girls and Women in Sports Day, PSAL; Certificate of Merit, Swimmer/Promoter of Aquatic Sports, FINA; Outstanding Teacher of the Year, John Jay College; Tsunami Spirit Award, Aquatic Therapy Rehab Institute; YMCA Celebrity Athlete, NYC; Paragon Award, ISHOF; Outstanding Lifetime Leadership Award, FINA; Who's Who in Aquatics, Aquatics International; Lifetime Achievement Award, Aquatic Exercise Association; Outstanding Physical Educator, President's Council on Physical Fitness and Sports; CUNY Outstanding Service Award; Annual Council Award, CUNY Council of Physical Education; New York's Finest Champion Award, Police Benevolent Association; Lifetime Achievement Award in Aquatic Fitness, United States Aquatic Fitness Association; Fitness Award, Water Fitness Association; Fin Swimming Athlete of the Year, Underwater Society of America; Townsend Harris Academic Medal, CCNY; Healthy American Fitness Leaders Award, President's Council on Physical Fitness; Athletic Hall of Fame/Swimming, CCNY; Hall of Fame Award, CCNY Athletic Varsity Association **Memberships:** National Council on Women's Health; US Committee Sports for Israel; Middle States Committee Member; Underwater Society of America; Alliance for Health; International Swimming Hall of Fame; Amateur Athletic Union; US Master Swimming; American Red Cross; Aquatic Coalition; Special Advisory Board Member, Aquatics International; Fitness Swimmer Magazine; Faculty Senate, CCNY; Leukemia Society of America; National Aquatic Council; National Fitness Leader Association; Pool and Spa Institute; AAHPERD; President's Council on Physical Fitness and Sports; Los Angeles Olympic Organizing Committee; USA Swimming; Women's Medical Association **Marquis Who's Who Honors:** Albert Nelson Marquis Lifetime Achievement Award; Marquis Who's Who Top Professional **To what do you attribute your success:** Dr. Katz attributes her success on the influence of her family, all of whom were involved in swimming. **Avocations:** Painting seashore vistas and patriotic vignettes **Religion:** Jewish

Stephen E. Kaufman, Esq.

Title: President, Attorney **Industry:** Law and Legal Services **Company Name:** Stephen E. Kaufman, P.C. **Date of Birth:** 02/16/1932 **Place of Birth:** New York **State/Country of Origin:** NY/USA **Marital Status:** Married **Spouse Name:** Marina Pinto **Children:** Andrew Herbert; Douglas Pinto **Education:** LLB, Columbia University (1957); BA, Williams College (1953) **Career:** President, Stephen E. Kaufman, P.C., New York, NY (1976-Present); Chief, Criminal Division, U.S. Department of Justice (1964-1969); Assistant U.S. Attorney, Southern District of New York, U.S. Department of Justice (1958) **Career Related:** Fellow, American College of Trial Lawyers **Civic:** Director, Police Athletic League; Vice Chairman, Museum Jewish Heritage **Memberships:** American Bar Association; New York State Bar Association; Association of the Bar of the City of New York **Bar Admissions:** U.S. Supreme Court (1963); U.S. District Court for the Southern and Eastern Districts, State of New York (1960); U.S. Court of Appeals for the Second Circuit (1958); State of New York (1958) **Marquis Who's Who Honors:** Albert Nelson Marquis Lifetime Achievement Award **Why did you become involved in your profession or industry:** Mr. Kaufman became involved in his profession because when he was in law school, he was a summer intern for the United States Attorney's Office for the Southern District of New York. He did not know what he wanted to do after law school. He was hoping to become assistant, which he did upon graduation.

Brett Michael Kavanaugh

Title: Associate Justice **Industry:** Law and Legal Services **Company Name:** Supreme Court of the United States **Date of Birth:** 02/12/1965 **Place of Birth:** Washington **State/Country of Origin:** DC/USA **Parents:** Everett Edward Kavanaugh; Martha Gamble (Murphy) Kavanaugh **Marital Status:** Married **Spouse Name:** Ashley Estes **Children:** Two Daughters **Education:** JD, Yale Law School, with Honors (1990); BA in History, Yale College, Cum Laude (1987) **Career:** Associate Justice, Supreme Court of the United States (2018-Present); Judge, United States Court of Appeals for the District of Columbia Circuit (2006-Present); Assistant to President, Staff Secretary, The White House, Washington, DC (2003-2006); Senior Associate Counsel to President, The White House, Washington, DC (2003); Associate Counsel to President, The White House, Washington, DC (2001-2003); Partner, Kirkland & Ellis LLP (1997-1998, 1999-2001); Associate Counsel, Office of Independent Counsel Kenneth W. Starr, U.S. Department of Justice (1994-1998); Law Clerk to Justice Anthony M. Kennedy, Supreme Court of the United States, Washington, DC (1993-1994); Attorney, Office of the Solicitor General, U.S. Department of Justice, Washington, DC (1992-1993); Law Clerk to Honorable Alex Kozinski, United States Court of Appeals for the Ninth Circuit (1991-1992); Law Clerk to Honorable Walter K. Stapleton, United States Court of Appeals for the Third Circuit (1990-1991) **Civic:** Lector, Shrine of the Most Blessed Sacrament, Washington, DC; Tutor, Washington Jesuit Academy **Creative Works:** Member, Notes Editor, Yale Law Journal; Contributor, Articles, Yale Daily News; Contributor, Articles, Professional Journals **Memberships:** The Federalist Society (1988-Present); Delta Kappa Epsilon **Bar Admissions:** The District of Columbia (1992); State of Maryland (1990) **Political Affiliations:** Republican **Religion:** Roman Catholic

M. Orhan Kaymakcalan, MD, FACS

Title: Doctor **Industry:** Medicine & Health Care **Date of Birth:** 06/09/1948 **Education:** MD, Hacettepe University Faculty of Medicine, Turkey (1972) **Certifications:** Re-certified in Hand Surgery, American Board of Surgery (1998, 2008); Certified in Hand Surgery, American Board of Surgery (1989); Certified, American Board of Surgery (1980) **Career:** Fellow in Hand Surgery, University of Louisville (1982-1983); Attending Surgeon, Department of Plastic and Reconstructive Surgery Burn Center, Gulhane Medical School Hospital, Ankara, Turkey (1980–1981); Company Doctor, U.S. Steel, South Works, Chicago, IL (1979–1980); Adjuvant Attending Surgeon, Mount Sinai Hospital Medical Center, Chicago, IL (1978–1980); Instructor, Department of Surgery, Rush Presbyterian Medical School, Chicago, IL (1978–1980); Resident in Surgery, Mount Sinai Medical Center, Chicago, IL (1974-1978); Resident in Surgery, Straight Surgical Internship, Jacksonville University Hospital, FL (1973-1974); Surgical Residency in Basic Science, Hacettepe University Hospital (1972-1973); Private Practice, Hand and Reconstructive Microsurgery; Chief, Division of Hand and Reconstructive Microsurgery, Mount Sinai Hospital Medical Center, Trauma One and Tertiary Hand Trauma Referral Center, IL **Career Related:** Associate Clinical Professor, Chicago Medical School (1986-Present); Principal Instructor, Plastic Surgery Residents on Hand Surgery Rotation, University of Illinois; Instructor, Plastic Surgery Residents on Hand Surgery Rotation, The University of Chicago **Civic:** Board of Trustees, Chairman, Turkish American Cultural Association (TACA), Chicago, IL (2005-Present); Doctors Without Borders **Creative Works:** Presenter, Multiple Papers, National and International Hand Society Meetings and Lectures, Canada, Greece, Finland, France, Spain, Turkey, and United States **Awards:** Named Top Doctor, Castle-Connolly (2000-Present); Compassionate Doctor Recognition (2015); Named Best Surgical Resident (1978) **Memberships:** President, Assembly of Turkish American Association (ATAA) (2000–2002); Chicago Medical Society; Illinois State Medical Society; Fellow, American College of Surgeons; Chicago Society for Surgery of the Hand; American Society for Surgery of the Hand; American Society for Reconstructive Microsurgery; Turkish Society for Reconstructive Microsurgery; Founding Fellow, Kleinert Hand Society; Founder, Midwest Turkish American Medical Association **Marquis Who's Who Honors:** Marquis Who's Who Top Professional **Why did you become involved in your profession or industry:** Dr. Kaymakcalan became involved in his profession because of his late uncle, who was a pharmacologist, and he always liked science. In his childhood, he liked the flowers that created and made something. He saw so many patients with broken fingers that he wanted to become a hand doctor. **Thoughts on Life:** Dr. Kaymakcalan worked very hard with patients having drug overdoses. In this country, the highest death rate for people from ages 14-40 is drug overdoses. The cases they do in Chicago are almost equal to the amount of gunshot wounds in Iraq and Afghanistan.

Roger Norris Keeler

Title: Physicist **Industry:** Sciences **Date of Birth:** 08/12/1930 **Place of Birth:** Houston **State/Country of Origin:** TX/USA **Parents:** Roger Maurice Keeler; Alice Marie (Tangeman) Keeler **Marital Status:** Married **Spouse Name:** Ethel Miriam Hill (12/06/1987) **Children:** Catherine Ann; John Allen; Roger David; Carolyn Elizabeth **Education:** PhD, University of California Berkeley (1962); MS, University of Colorado, Boulder (1958); BS, William M. Rice Institute for the Advancement of Literature, Science and Art (Now Rice University), Houston, TX (1952); BA, William M. Rice Institute for the Advancement of Literature, Science and Art (Now Rice University), Houston, TX (1951) **Career:** Director, Technical Marketing, Kaman Diversified Technical Corporation (1988-2005); Principal Science Advisor, Kaman Aerospace Corporation (1987-1988); Private Consultant, State of Washington (1980-1986); Director, Navy Technology (1975-1978); Staff of Director, Lawrence Livermore National Laboratory (1978-1980); Head, Physics Department, Lawrence Livermore National Laboratory (1972-1975); Deputy Head, Physics Department, Lawrence Livermore National Laboratory (1971-1972); Division Leader, University of California, Lawrence Livermore Laboratory (1969-1971); Deputy Division Leader, University of California, Lawrence Livermore Laboratory (1968-1969); Staff, University of California, Lawrence Livermore Laboratory (1963-1968) **Career Related:** Applied Physics Laboratory, Johns Hopkins University (1986-Present); Los Alamos National Laboratory (1984-Present); Expert Witness, Fires, Explosions, Chemical Effects (1970-Present); Consultant, Defense Advanced Projects Research Agency (1987-1990); National Strategic Information Center, Washington (1987-1988); Energy Conversion Devices, Troy, MI (1987); ANSER, Washington (1986-1987); Adjunct Professor, Physics and Chemistry, United States Naval Postgraduate School, Monterey, CA (1979-1981); The Valeron Corporation, Detroit, MI (1978-1983); Lecturer, Applied Science, University of California Davis (1967-1975) **Military Service:** Captain, U.S. Naval Reserve (1952-1970) **Creative Works:** Editorial Board, High Pressure (1987-Present); Editorial Board, Review of Science Instruments (1967-1971); Contributing Editor, American Institute of Physics Handbook (1968); Technical Adviser, Signal Magazine; Contributor, Articles, Book Reviews, Professional Journals **Awards:** Vavilov Gold Medal, Scientific Achievements, President of the Russian Academy of Science (2014); Inductee, Hall of Fame in Engineering, Rice University (2004); Gold Medal for Engineering (1993); Engineer of the Year, Rice University **Memberships:** Associate Director, Armed Forces Communications and Electronics Association (1992-1993); Executive Committee, Vice President, President, International High-Pressure Association (1975-1989); Fellow, American Physical Society; American Institute of Chemists; Washington Academy of Science; Lifetime Member, American Society of Naval Engineers; Capitol Hill Club **Marquis Who's Who Honors:** Albert Nelson Marquis Lifetime Achievement Award; Marquis Who's Who Top Professional **To what do you attribute your success:** Dr. Keeler attributes his success to his mother, Alice. In 1940, his father became ill with tuberculosis. His mother then became the family breadwinner, taking a teaching job at the Kinkaid School, where she eventually became the head of Kinkaid's lower school. She eventually persuaded those at Rice Institute to let Dr. Keeler take the entrance exam, which he passed. This was important as the school had no tuition at the time. **Why did you become involved in your profession or industry:** Dr. Keeler became involved in his profession because he always wanted to be a chemical engineer.

Celia Keenan-Bolger

Title: Actress, Singer **Industry:** Media & Entertainment **Date of Birth:** 01/26/1978 **Place of Birth:** Detroit **State/Country of Origin:** MI/USA **Marital Status:** Married **Spouse Name:** John Ellison Conlee (2010) **Children:** William Emmett Conlee **Education:** BFA in Musical Theater, University of Michigan; Coursework, Mosaic Detroit; Coursework, Detroit School of Arts **Creative Works:** Actress, "To Kill a Mockingbird" (2018-2019); Actress, "Diane" (2018); Actress, "Bull" (2018); Actress, "Wolverine: The Long Night" (2018); Actress, "A Parallelogram" (2017); Actress, "NCIS: New Orleans" (2017); Actress, "Blue Bloods" (2017); Actress, "Breakable You" (2017); Actress, "The Cherry Orchard" (2016); Actress, "Good Behavior" (2016); Actress, "Serial: The TV Show" (2015); Actress, "Elementary" (2015); Actress, "The Good Wife" (2015); Actress, "Louie" (2015); Actress, "The Visit" (2015); Actress, "The Oldest Boy" (2014); Actress, "Nurse Jackie" (2014); Actress, "Law & Order: Special Victims Unit" (2014); Actress, "The Glass Menagerie" (2013-2014); Actress, "Merrily We Roll Along" (2012); Actress, "Submissions Only" (2012); Actress, "Mariachi Group" (2012); Actress, "Peter and the Starcatcher" (2011-2012); Actress, "A Small Fire" (2010-2011); Actress, "Bachelorette" (2010); Actress, "The Battery's Down" (2008); Actress, "Heartland" (2007); Actress, "Law & Order" (2007); Actress, "Les Misérables" (2006-2007); Actress, "The 25ᵗʰ Annual Putnam County Spelling Bee" (2005-2006); Actress, "Sweeney Todd: The Demon Barber of Fleet Street" (2002); Actress, "The Education of Max Bickford" (2002) **Awards:** Best Performance by a Featured Actress in a Play, Tony Awards (2019); Outer Critics Circle Award for Outstanding Featured Actress in a Play (2019); Drama Desk Award for Outstanding Featured Actress in a Play (2014, 2019); Audience Choice Award for Favorite Actress in a Play, Broadway.com (2012, 2014, 2019); Award, Best Supporting Actress in a Play, New England Independent Review Board (2014); Dorothy Loudon Award for Excellence in the Theatre, Theatre World Awards, Inc. (2014); Elliot Norton Award for Outstanding Ensemble (2013); Theatre World Award (2005); Drama Desk Award for Outstanding Ensemble Performance (2005)

Dale Russell Kelley

Title: Mayor **Industry:** Government Administration/Government Relations/Government Services **Company Name:** Town of Huntingdon **Date of Birth:** 10/19/1939 **Place of Birth:** Carroll County **State/Country of Origin:** TN/USA **Parents:** Ruth (White) Williams (Deceased, 2000); William Jesse Kelley (Deceased, 1986) **Marital Status:** Married **Spouse Name:** Carlene Tullos (09/04/1965) **Children:** Cliff McKendree Kelley; Meredith Ann Kelley Surber; Amanda Beth Kelley Wallace **Education:** BS, Bethel College (Now Bethel University), McKenzie, TN (1966); Postgraduate Studies, The University of Tennessee at Martin, Martin, TN; Doctorate Degree **Certifications:** Licensed Insurance Agent and Real Estate Broker (1974-1975) **Career:** Insurance Agency Owner, Real Estate Agent, Huntingdon, TN (1974-Present); Commissioner of Transportation, State of Tennessee (1985-1987); Property Assessor, Carroll County, TN (1970-1974); Sales Representative, Mobil Oil Agricultural Chemical Division, Tennessee (1967-1970) **Career Related:** Mayor, Town of Huntingdon (1992-Present) **Civic:** State Representative; Commissioner Employment Security; District Administrator; Little League Baseball; County Official; School Board Representative **Military Service:** U.S. Air Force (1959-1963) **Awards:** Bethel College Distinguished Alumni Award (1980); Jaycees Distinguished Service Award (1972-1973); Carroll Countian of the Year; State Mayor of the Year **Memberships:** Lions; Junior Chamber of Commerce; Huntington Masonic; Scottish Rite; Shriner **Avocations:** Basketball; Sports **Political Affiliations:** Republican **Religion:** Baptist

Daniel John Kelly, MD

Title: Consolidated Pathology Consultant (Retired) **Industry:** Medicine & Health Care **Company Name:** Service Corporation **Date of Birth:** 06/23/1940 **Place of Birth:** Binghamton **State/Country of Origin:** NY/USA **Parents:** William James Kelly; Mary Elizabeth (Schmitt) Kelly **Marital Status:** Married **Spouse Name:** Lois Lanshe Kelly **Children:** Britton James; Jeffrey Daniel; Reid William; Piper Ann (Deceased) **Education:** Resident, Naval Hospital, Oakland, CA (1967-1971); Intern, Naval Hospital, Boston, MA (1966-1967); Doctor of Medicine, Jefferson Medical College (1966); Bachelor of Arts in History, Yale University (1962) **Certifications:** Diplomate, Anatomic and Clinical Pathology; Diplomate, Nuclear Medicine; Diplomate, Dermatopathology **Career:** Consolidated Pathology Consultant, Service Corporation, Lake Bluff, IL (1999-2007); Associated Laboratory Physician Services, Wauwatosa, WI (1997-1999); Director of the Laboratory, Highland Park Hospital (1996-1997); Chief of Staff, Highland Park Hospital (1994-1996); Board of Directors, Highland Park Hospital (1992-1996); Chief of Staff Elect, Highland Park Hospital (1992-1994); Director of the Laboratory, Lake Forest Hospital (1989-1991); Director of the Laboratory, Highland Park Hospital (1980-1989); Co-Director of the Laboratory, Lake Forest Hospital (1975-1997); Co-Director of the Laboratory, Highland Park Hospital (1975-1997); Dean, Hoffman & Clark Pathologists Service Corporation, Lake Forest, IL (1975-1997); Chief of Laboratory Services, Naval Hospital, Great Lakes, IL (1973-1975); Assistant Chief of the Laboratory, Naval Hospital, Great Lakes, IL (1971-1973) **Career Related:** Medical Executive Committee, Highland Park Hospital (1992-1997); Medical Executive Committee, Lake Forest Hospital (1992-1997); Medical Executive Committee, Lake Forest Hospital (1980-1989); Fellow, College of American Pathology **Civic:** Commissioner, Lake Forest Cemetery Commission (2016-Present); Clinical Laboratory and Blood Bank Advisory Board, Illinois Department of Public Health (1990-1995); Building Review Board, City Government, Lake Forest, IL (1989-1993); Board of Directors, Lake Forest Historical Preservation Foundation (1979-1988) **Military Service:** Commander, U.S. Naval Reserve (1966-1975); U.S. Navy Reserve (1962-1977) **Awards:** Navy Commendation Medal (1976) **Memberships:** American Society of Clinical Pathology; International Academy of Pathologists; American Medical Association; Illinois Society of Pathologists; American Society of Dermatopathology; International Society of Dermatopathology; Association of Military Surgeons; American Pathology Foundation **Marquis Who's Who Honors:** Albert Nelson Marquis Lifetime Achievement Award; Marquis Who's Who Top Professional **Why did you become involved in your profession or industry:** Dr. Kelly first became involved in his profession due to the influence of his uncle, Roswell Smith. He would often spend his summers with his uncle, a surgeon in Middletown, New York, who offered free medical care to hundreds of locals during the Great Depression. **Avocations:** Reading; Art; Music; Fishing **Religion:** Roman Catholic

Edward A. Kelly Jr., MD

Title: Physician **Industry:** Medicine & Health Care **Company Name:** Downingtown Family Practice **Date of Birth:** 03/16/1948 **Place of Birth:** Darby **State/Country of Origin:** PA/USA **Parents:** Edward A. Kelly; Adele R (Angelucci) Kelly **Marital Status:** Single **Children:** Kristin Colleen; Daniel Edward; Megan Grace **Education:** MD, Thomas Jefferson University, Philadelphia, PA (1973); BA in Biology, St. Joseph's University, Philadelphia, PA (1969) **Certifications:** Certification, American Board of Family Medicine (1976-2025) **Career:** Physician, Private Practice, Downingtown Family Practice, Downingtown, PA (1976-Present); Resident, Wilmington (Delaware) Medical Center (1973-1976) **Career Related:** Professional Consultant (1984-Present); Member, Professional Advisory Council, Blue Shield of Pennsylvania, Camp Hill, PA (1985-1997); Chairman, Department of Family Practice, Brandywine Hospital, Coatesville, PA (1989-1994) **Civic:** Board of Directors, Downingtown Senior Center, Downingtown, PA (1985-Present); School and Team Physician, Downingtown Area School District (1983-2001) **Memberships:** Delegate, Pennsylvania Academy of Family Physicians (1992-1993); President, Pennsylvania Academy of Family Physicians (1987-1988); Vice President, Pennsylvania Academy of Family Physicians (1985-1986); Treasurer, Pennsylvania Academy of Family Physicians (1983-1985); Fellow, American Academy of Family Physicians (1978) **Marquis Who's Who Honors:** Albert Nelson Marquis Lifetime Achievement Award; Marquis Who's Who Top Professional **To what do you attribute your success:** Dr. Kelly attributes his success to dedication, hard work, continuing education, staying healthy, and rapport with patients. **Why did you become involved in your profession or industry:** Dr. Kelly became involved in his profession because his father was a family doctor, so he was an influence on him at an early age. He likes working with people and he just wanted to make lives better. **Avocations:** Playing golf; Skiing; Music **Political Affiliations:** Democrat **Religion:** Roman Catholic **Thoughts on Life:** According to Dr. Kelly, "The best investment in life is a good education."

Roger L. Kemp, PhD

Title: Career City Manager **Industry:** Consulting **Company Name:** Kemp Consulting, LLC **Date of Birth:** 08/01/1946 **Place of Birth:** St. Paul **State/Country of Origin:** MN/USA **Parents:** Charles Woodrow; Eva Audrey Kemp **Marital Status:** Single **Children:** Jonathan David Kemp **Education:** MBA in Management, Golden Gate University (1984); PhD in Public Administration, Golden Gate University (1979); MPA in Public Administration, San Diego State University (1974); BS in Business Administration, San Diego State University (1972); AA in General Studies, Long Beach City College (1969); Diploma, Senior Executives in State and Local Government Program, Harvard University; Diploma, Advanced Government Finance Institute, Government Finance Officers Association, University of Wisconsin **Certifications:** Certificate in Urban Planning, University of California Irvine; Certificate in Real Estate, Specialization in Marketing, University of California Los Angeles; Certificate in Real Estate, Specialization in Finance, University of California Los Angeles; Certificate in Real Estate, Specialization in Appraisal, University of California Los Angeles; Certificate in Real Estate, University of California San Diego **Career:** Practitioner in Residence, Department of Public Management, University of New Haven, West Haven, CT; Distinguished Adjunct Professor, Ageno School of Business, Golden Gate University, San Francisco, CA; Former Career City Manager **Career Related:** Editorial Advisory Board, ICMA (1998); Editorial Advisory Board, ABC-CLIO, LLC (1997); Editorial Advisory Board, Macmillan (1996); Member, Connecticut State Commissions; Board of Directors, Several Non-Profit Organizations **Civic:** Citizen Ethics Advisory Commission, State of Connecticut; Regional Council of Governments, North Haven, CT; Site Visit Team, National Association of School of Public Affairs and Administration (NASPAA); Wallingford Recycling Project, Wallingford, CT; Economic Development Committee, Meriden, CT; Board of Directors, Meriden Hall of Fame, Meriden, CT **Military Service:** Yeoman, Second Class, U.S. Coast Guard (1966-1970) **Creative Works:** Author, Editor, Over 50 Books; Speaker, Various Professional Organizations, International Conferences **Awards:** Inductee, Hall of Fame, Alumni Association, Long Beach City College, Long Beach, CA (2019); Presidential Excellence Award, International Town & Gown Association, Pennsylvania (2019); Certificate of Recognition, U. S. House of Representatives (2019); Certificate of Recognition, California State Legislature (2019); Certificate of Recognition, Office of the Mayor, City of Long Beach, CA (2019); Certificate of Commendation, County of Los Angeles, CA (2019); Distinguished Alumni Award, School of Public Affairs, San Diego State University (2018); Certificate of Special Congressional Recognition, U. S. House of Representatives (2018); Certificate of Recognition, California Legislative Assembly (2018); Certificate of Special Congressional Recognition, U.S. House of Representatives, Washington, DC (2018); Outstanding Alumni of the Year Award, San Diego State University School of Public Affairs (2007) **Memberships:** Academy of Political Science; American Society for Public Administration; Government Finance Officers Association; International City/County Management Association; International Town and Gown Association; National Civic League; Pi Alpha Alpha; U.S. Association for the Club of Rome; World Future Society; Long Beach City College Alumni Association; San Diego State University Alumni Association; Golden Gate University Alumni Association; Harvard University Alumni Association **To what do you attribute your success:** After being discharged from the military, Dr. Kemp earned six college degrees. All of these educational accomplishments played a major role in his journey to fulfilling his career goals. He is proud to be a full-time city manager, working with the states of California, New Jersey, and Connecticut. He additionally enjoys his work as an adjunct professor at leading universities across the nation. **Why did you become involved in your profession or industry:** Dr. Kemp became involved in his profession because, while in the Coast Guard, he wanted to serve in the field of local government. He worked as an assistant to the city manager in the Office of the City Manager in Oakland, California, while pursuing a PhD in public administration. After graduating, he was appointed as the new city manager of Seaside, California. **Avocations:** Walking; Biking; Writing and editing books **Political Affiliations:** Unaffiliated Voter **Religion:** Believer **Thoughts on Life:** Dr. Kemp believes that America is "the land of opportunity," and if one works hard, one will be successful.

Susan O. Kennedy, PhD

Title: Physical Education Educator, Consultant, Sports Official **Industry:** Education/Educational Services **Date of Birth:** 06/01/1951 **Place of Birth:** Torrington **State/Country of Origin:** CT/USA **Parents:** Sidney Robinson Kennedy Junior, PhD, MD; Dorothy (Deering) Kennedy, RN **Education:** PhD in Physical Education/Bio Mechanics-Adapted PE, Texas Woman's University (1991); MS in Physical Education, University of Oregon (1978); BS in Physical Education, Ithaca College (1973) **Certifications:** Certified K-2 Teacher, New York **Career:** Research Assistant, Texas Woman's University (1984-1989); Instructor, Coach, Athletic Trainer, Chadron State College (1980-1984); Substitute Teacher, Girls Basketball Coach, Lake County School District #7, Lakeview, OR (1978-1980); Graduate Teaching Fellow, University of Oregon (1976-1978); Teacher, Coach, Regional District #1, Housatonic Valley Regional High School, Falls Village, CT (1973-1976) **Career Related:** Adjunct Faculty, University of North Texas (1988-1990) **Civic:** Litchfield Garden Club (2010-Present); Rating Chair, La Crosse Super Region 1 (2005-Present); Sectional Official (1992-Present); Official, U.S. Field Hockey Association (2012); National Emeritus Award Member (2012); Board of Directors, Connecticut Field Hockey Officials (1995-2012); National Official, U.S. Women's Lacrosse Association (1992-2012); Rules Interpreter, Umpire Coordinator USA Hockey Region 3 (2007-2011); Chair, Inland Wetlands Commission, Litchfield, CT (1998-2005); Volunteer, Connecticut Volunteer Services for Visually and Physically Handicapped (1992-2002); Basketball Official (1970-2000) **Creative Works:** Coordinator, Puppet Show, "Kids on the Block," Texas Woman's University (1985-1986); Author, "Prevention and Care of Athletic Injuries: Taping Techniques" (1984); Contributor, Articles, Professional Journals **Awards:** Katherine B. Pitney Award, Sasqua Garden Club (2013, 2015); Honoree, Litchfield Garden Club (2012); U.S. Lacrosse National Emeritus Award (2012); Ellen Carder Memorial Award, Federated Garden Club of CT (2012); Inductee, Hall of Fame, Connecticut Field Hockey (2007); Inductee, Northeast Women's Hall of Fame (2005); Outstanding Official, Connecticut Field Hockey Coaches Association (2001); Official of the Year, Nutmeg State Games (2000); Volunteer of the Year (2000); Scholar, All-American, U.S. Achievement Academy, (1989, 1991); Inductee, Academy of All-American (1987); WGOSC Distinguished National Service Award, Lacrosse **Memberships:** Chairman, Litchfield Wetlands Commission, Litchfield, CT (1993-2015); Alliance for Health; National Athlete Trainers Association; American College Sports Medicine; National Association of Sports Official; Connecticut Interscholastic Athletic Conference; Litchfield Garden Club; Litchfield High School Scholarship Committee; Litchfield Garden Club; Certified Election Moderator; Connecticut Orchid Society; American Orchid Society **Marquis Who's Who Honors:** Albert Nelson Marquis Lifetime Achievement Award **To what do you attribute your success:** Dr. Kennedy attributes her success to persistence. **Why did you become involved in your profession or industry:** Dr. Kennedy was an athlete when she was young. She believes if someone has a physically active body, he or she has a physically active mind. Considering a career, Dr. Kennedy knew she wanted to help young girls excel in athletics. For many years, she has been a successful teacher, coach, and athletic trainer. Her mother, Dorothy Kennedy, never doubted her, she was always supportive and gave Dr. Kennedy encouragement. **Avocations:** Sea kayaking; Weight training; Officiating; Environmental science issues; Raising orchids **Political Affiliations:** Democrat **Thoughts on Life:** Dr. Kennedy lives by the quote, "To thine own self be true," from Hamlet by William Shakespeare.

X.J. Kennedy

Title: Writer, Poet **Industry:** Writing and Editing **Date of Birth:** 08/21/1929 **Place of Birth:** Dover **State/Country of Origin:** NJ/USA **Parents:** Joseph Kennedy; Agnes Kennedy **Marital Status:** Widowed **Spouse Name:** Dorothy Kennedy (Deceased 2018) **Children:** Five Children **Education:** Honorary DLitt, Westfield State College (2002); Honorary LHD, Lawrence University (1988); MA, Columbia University (1951); BSc, Seton Hall University (1950); Honorary DFA, Adelphi University **Career:** Professor of English, Tufts University (1973-1979); Assistant Professor of English, Tufts University (1963-1973); Freelance Writer; Poet **Career Related:** Guggenheim and National Arts Council Fellowships **Military Service:** U.S. Navy (1951-1955) **Creative Works:** Author, "Fits of Concision: Collected Poems of Six or Fewer Lines" (2014); Author, "A Hoarse Half-Human Cheer" (2014); Co-Author, "Writing and Revising: A Portable Guide" (2007); Author, "In a Prominent Bar in Secaucus: New and Selected Poems, 1955-2007" (2007); Co-Author, "Handbook of Literary Terms" (2005); Author, "The Lords of Misrule: Poems, 1992-2001" (2002); Author, "Aristophanes' Lysistrata, a New English Version" (1999); Author, "Jimmy Harlow" (1994); Author, "Dark Horses: New Poems" (1992); Author, "Winter Thunder" (1990); Author, "Fresh Brats" (1990); Author, "Ghastlies, Goops, and Pincushions: Nonsense Verse" (1989); Co-Author, "The Bedford Guide for College Writers" (1987); Author, "Brats, Humorous Verse" (1986); Author, "The Forgetful Wishing Well: Poems for Young People" (1985); Author, "Cross Ties: Selected Poems" (1985); Author, "Hangover Mass" (1984); Author, "The Owlstone Crown" (1983); Author, "Translator: French Leave: Translations" (1983); Author, "Missing Link" (1983); Co-Author, "The Bedford Reader" (1982); Co-Editor, "Knock at a Star: A Child's Introduction to Poetry" (1982); Author, "Did Adam Name the Vinegarroon?" (1982); Editor, "Tygers of Wrath: Poems of Hate, Anger, and Invective" (1981); Author, "Literature: An Introduction to Fiction, Poetry, and Drama" (1976); Author, "An Introduction to Fiction" (1976); Author, "An Introduction to Poetry" (1976); Author, "The Phantom Ice Cream Man: More Nonsense Verse" (1975); Co-Author, "Three Tenors, One Vehicle" (1975); Author, "Celebrations After the Death of John Brennan" (1974); Author, "Emily Dickinson in Southern California" (1974); Editor, "Messages: A Thematic Anthology of Poetry" (1973); Co-Editor, "Pegasus Descending: A Book of the Best Bad Verse" (1971); Author, "Breaking and Entering" (1971); Author, "Blush" (1970); Author, "Growing into Love" (1969); Author, "An Introduction to Poetry" (1966); Co-Editor, "Mark Twain's Frontier: A Textbook of Primary Source Materials Research and Writing" (1963); Author, "Nude Descending a Staircase: Poems, Songs, a Ballad" (1961); Author, "One Winter Night in August and Other Nonsense Jingles" **Awards:** Poetry Society of America's Robert Frost Medal (2009); Poets' Prize (2004); Award for Excellence in Children's Poetry, National Council of Teachers of English (2000); Shelley Memorial Award (1969-1970); Michael Braude Award for Light Verse, American Academy of Arts and Letters (1961); Jackson Poetry Prize, Poets and Writers; Golden Rose, New England Poetry Club; Los Angeles Times Book Award for Poetry; Bess Hokin Prize, Poetry Magazine; Grantee, National Endowment for the Arts; Lamont Poetry Prize, Academy of American Poets **Memberships:** New England Pen Association; National Council of Teachers of English; Modern Language Association **Marquis Who's Who Honors:** Albert Nelson Marquis Lifetime Achievement Award; Marquis Who's Who Top Professional **Why did you become involved in your profession or industry:** Dr. Kennedy had a great understanding for English at the early part of his life and that is what he knew best. He taught at Tufts University as an assistant professor and professor, but quit teaching to be a writer. In addition, Dr. Kennedy starting writing poetry when he was out of college and in the Navy; he was an enlisted man in the Navy for four years and he had a lot of time to write. He started writing back when he was about 21 and he is almost 90 now, so he has been writing for about 69 years. **Avocations:** Old movies

David M. Kercher

Title: Mechanical Engineer (Retired) **Industry:** Engineering **Date of Birth:** 11/18/1931 **Place of Birth:** Goshen **State/Country of Origin:** IN/USA **Parents:** Maxwell Mease Kercher; Rosemary (Harper) Kercher **Marital Status:** Married **Spouse Name:** Betty Noreen (Raycroft) Kercher (6/7/1958) **Children:** Kimberly S. Wilson; Matthew R.; Andrew D.R.; Steven R.; Elizabeth J.; Jason R.; Amy N. **Education:** MS in Aerospace Engineering, University of Cincinnati (1967); BSME, Purdue University (1958) **Career:** Retired (2002); Principal Engineer, GE Aircraft Engines, Lynn, MA (1989-2001); Senior Engineer, GE Aircraft Engines, Lynn, MA (1985-1989); Mechanical Engineer, GE, Lynn, MA (1983-2002); Sub-section Manager, Aircraft Engine Group, GE, Lynn, MA (1983-1984); Senior Engineer, GE, Schenectady, NY (1982); Sub-section Manager, Aircraft Engine Group, GE, Schenectady, NY (1972-1982); Unit Manager, Gas Turbine Department, GE, Schenectady, NY (1972-1981); Unit Manager, GE, Cincinnati, OH (1968); Engineer, Large Jet Engine Division, GE, Cincinnati, OH (1968-1971); Senior Engineer, GE, Cincinnati, OH (1966-1971); Engineer, Large Jet Engine Division, GE, Burlington, VT (1959-1960); Engineer, Gatlin Gun Production, GE, Burlington, VT (1959-1960); Unit Manager, Gas Turbine Department, GE, Evandale, OH (1958-1971) **Civic:** Former Docent, Research Assistant, Ipswich Historical Society (now Ipswich Museum) **Military Service:** U.S. Air Force Reserve (1955-1958); Sergeant, U.S. Air Force (1951-1954) **Creative Works:** Contributor, Turbine, Heat Transfer Articles, Professional Journals; 12 Patents on Gas Turbine Cooling, Aircraft Engines **Awards:** Tau Beta Pi (1958); Pi Tau Sigma (1958) **Memberships:** Gas Turbine Heat Transfer Committee, American Society of Mechanical Engineers (1980-Present); Chairman, American Society of Mechanical Engineers (1994-1996); Vice Chairman, Committee, American Society of Mechanical Engineers (1992-1994); Fellow, American Society of Mechanical Engineers; Senior Member, American Institute of Aeronautics and Astronautics; American Society of Mechanical Engineers International Gas Turbine Institute; Life Member, American Legion; Life Member, Air Force Association; Life Member, Tau Beta Pi; Life Member, Pi Tau Sigma **Marquis Who's Who Honors:** Albert Nelson Marquis Lifetime Achievement Award; Marquis Who's Who Top Professional **To what do you attribute your success:** Mr. Kercher attributes his success to hard work, organizational skills, a good memory, and having had the opportunity to go to school because of the GI Bill. **Why did you become involved in your profession or industry:** Mr. Kercher became involved in his profession because he was in the U.S. Air Force and when he got out one of the benefits was the GI Bill. He had an interest in his field and worked towards it. **Avocations:** Reading history **Political Affiliations:** Republican **Religion:** Christian

Charles William Kern, PhD

Title: Professor of Chemistry, Emeritus **Industry:** Education/Educational Services **Company Name:** Northwestern University **Date of Birth:** 07/13/1935 **Place of Birth:** Middletown **State/Country of Origin:** OH/USA **Parents:** Charles Albert Kern; Charme (Bowman) Kern **Marital Status:** Married **Spouse Name:** Regine Bouchard **Children:** Rachelle; Scott; Jennifer **Education:** Postdoctoral Fellow in Chemical Physics, Columbia University, New York, NY (1961-1962); PhD, University of Minnesota (1961); BS, Carnegie Institute of Technology (1957) **Career:** Professor Emeritus, Northwestern University, Evanston, IL (1998-Present); Vice President, Research and Graduate Studies, Northwestern University, Evanston, IL (1993-1998); Professor in Chemistry, Northwestern University, Evanston, IL (1992-1998); Vice President of Research, Dean of the Graduate School, Northwestern University, Evanston, IL (1992-1993); Dean, Professor in Chemistry, College of Mathematics and Physical Sciences, The Ohio State University, Columbus, Ohio (1986-1992); Assistant Director, General Science, Office of Science and Technology Policy, Office of the President, Washington, DC (1986); Deputy Director, Division of Chemistry, National Science Foundation, Washington, DC (1985-1986); Acting Director, Division of Chemistry, National Science Foundation, Washington, DC (1984-1985); Program Director, Structural Chemistry and Thermodynamics, Acting Section Head of Physical Chemistry and Chemical Dynamics, Division of Chemistry, National Science Foundation, Washington, DC (1983-1984); Senior Staff Associate, Computer Science Research Network Project Director, Division of Mathematics and Computer Science, National Science Foundation, Washington, DC (1980-1983); Program Director, Theoretical Chemical Physics, Division of Chemistry, National Science Foundation, Washington, DC (1978-1980); Consultant, Director, Battelle Institute Program, Battelle Memorial Institute, Columbus, Ohio (1976-1984); Professor in Chemistry, The Ohio State University, Columbus, Ohio (1976-1980); Institute Scientist, Battelle Memorial Institute, Columbus, Ohio (1973-1976); Director, Physical Science Program, Battelle Memorial Institute, Columbus, Ohio (1973-1974); Manager, Chemical Physics Section, Battelle Memorial Institute, Columbus, Ohio (1972-1976); Academy Vice Chairman, Department of Chemistry, The Ohio State University, Columbus, Ohio (1972-1973); Adjunct Professor, Chemistry, The Ohio State University, Columbus, Ohio (1971-1976); Research Scientist, Battelle Memorial Institute, Columbus, Ohio (1966-1972); Adjunct Associate Professor, Chemistry, The Ohio State University, Columbus, Ohio (1966-1971); Assistant Professor, Chemistry, Stony Brook University, NY (1964-1966); Staff Member, IBM Watson Laboratory, Columbia University (1962-1964) **Career Related:** Executive Secretary, Director's Task Force on Advanced Science Computing Resources, National Science Foundation (1983-1984); Co-chairman, Current Biological Problems, School for Physical Scientists (1977); Summer Research Conference on Theoretical Chemistry, Boulder, CO (1975); Carnegie Mellon University Admissions Council (1970-1972); Chairman, School of Many-Body Techniques in Chemistry, Seattle, WA (1969) **Creative Works:** Associate Editor, Chemical Physics Letter (1967-1981); Contributor, Articles, Professional Journals **Memberships:** American Chemical Society **Marquis Who's Who Honors:** Albert Nelson Marquis Lifetime Achievement Award; Marquis Who's Who Top Professional **To what do you attribute your success:** Dr. Kern attributes his success to the people with whom he surrounds himself. He comes into contact with many gifted individuals, so he learns a great deal just by listening to them. Additionally, he actively tries to better himself and achieve a higher standard. **Why did you become involved in your profession or industry:** Dr. Kern grew up near a rendering plant. Unfortunately, the plant closed after the man in charge retired. However, he knew Dr. Kern's family and offered them all of the equipment from the laboratory. They accepted; Dr. Kern was able to set up all of it in his basement and make a laboratory of his own. **Avocations:** Studying the stock market

Gary Keshishyan

Title: Realtor **Industry:** Real Estate **Company Name:** Pinnacle Estate Properties Inc. **Spouse Name:** Teni Issaian **Children:** Anthony; Ella; Mila **Education:** Associate's Degree **Career:** Realtor, Pinnacle Estate Properties, Incorporated, Northridge, CA (1999-Present) **Awards:** Featured, Cover Page, Top Agents Magazine; Listee, 100 Most Influential Real Estate Agents, Real Estate Executive Magazine; Listee, Real Trends American Best Real Estate Agents; #1 Agent Company-Wide; Listee, 10 Best Agents, American Institute of Real Estate Agents; Best Agents in Los Angeles, L.A. Magazine; Featured, Top 250 Agents in America, Wall Street Journal **To what do you attribute your success:** Mr. Keshishyan has always been self-motivated; he won't let anything bring him down. He never had a mentor and had always been disciplined when it came to work. He is motivated to provide for his family and lead by a great example. **Why did you become involved in your profession or industry:** In college, Mr. Keshishyan was intending to pursue architecture because he was fascinated by homes. However, one semester before graduating, he decided to leave university and pursue a real estate career. He quickly became a top-selling agent in his company.

Emma Keulegan

Title: Retired Special Education Educator **Industry:** Education/Educational Services **Date of Birth:** 01/21/1930 **Place of Birth:** Washington **State/Country of Origin:** DC/USA **Parents:** Garbis H. Keulegan; Nellie Virginia (Moore) Keulegan **Education:** BA, Dumbarton College of Holy Cross (1954) **Certifications:** Certified Teacher, Elementary and Special Education **Career:** Substitute Teacher, Special Education, Culkin Academy (1991-2010); Teacher, Culkin Academy (1978-1991);Teacher, St. Francis Academy, Vicksburg, MS (1963-1978); Teacher, Our Lady of Victory, Washington, DC (1959-1963); Teacher, Sacred Heart Academy, Washington, DC (1956-1959); Teacher, St. Dominic's Elementary School, Washington, DC (1954-1956) **Civic:** President. Vicksburg Genealogical Society (1999); Treasurer, Parent-Teacher Association (1980) **Memberships:** Honorary State President, Daughters of the War of 1812 (1998-Present); State Vice President, State President, Colonial Dames of the 17th Century (1987-Present); Chaplain, State President, Daughters of American Colonists (1985-Present); President, Vicksburg Genealogical Society (2003); Chapter Regent, Secretary, Chapter Chaplain, Librarian, Membership Chairman, Daughters of the American Revolution (1967-2002); State Chaplain, Society of Magna Charta Dames and Barons (2001); Chapter Chaplain, President, Daughters of United Confederacy; Society of the Descendants of Knights of Most Noble Order of the Garter; Sovereign Colonial Society of America; Royal Descent; President, Warren County Chapter, International Reading Association **Marquis Who's Who Honors:** Albert Nelson Marquis Lifetime Achievement Award **Why did you become involved in your profession or industry:** In fourth grade, Ms. Keulegan encountered a mean teacher who upset one of her good friends. This lit a fire inside her to become a teacher and make all of her students happy, never sad as her fourth grade teacher had. **Avocations:** Needlecrafts; Reading; Coin collecting/numismatics; Stamp collecting/philately **Political Affiliations:** Republican **Religion:** Roman Catholic

Brad Kilgore

Title: Chef-Owner **Industry:** Food & Restaurant Services **Company Name:** Kilgore Culinary **Marital Status:** Married **Spouse Name:** Soraya **Education:** Associate of Arts in Culinary Arts, Johnson & Wales University, Colorado **Career:** Executive Chef, Owner, Kilgore Culinary (2015-Present); Executive Chef, The St. Regis Bal Harbour (2013-2015); Executive Chef, Owner, Brava; Executive Chef, Owner, Ember; Executive Chef, Owner, Kaido; Executive Chef, Owner, Alter; Co-Owner, Mad Lab Creamery **Civic:** Board, Diabetes Research **Awards:** New Best Chef in America, Best Chefs America (2017); Best New Chef in America, Food & Wine Magazine (2016); Fifth Place, James Beard Semifinalist Recognition; Second Place, Rising Star; First Place, Best Chef; South Semifinalist; Best New Restaurant; Diners Discovery, San Pellegrino's 50 Best Restaurant List **Memberships:** James Beard Foundation **To what do you attribute your success:** Mr. Kilgore attributes his success to hard work and dedication. He dreamed big and believed in himself, always remembering the famous saying from the 1989 drama, Field of Dreams, "If you build it, they will come." He believes that people can tell when a business is built with one's heart and soul, and they will then want to support it. **Why did you become involved in your profession or industry:** Mr. Kilgore got involved in the restaurant industry because he wants his customers to have the best experience possible. He wants them to leave his restaurant with a memorable experience. **Thoughts on Life:** Mr. Kilgore's motto is "Always in a hurry, never in a rush." He is usually at his second business because it just opened and needs more attention.

Unsup Kim MD, FACS

Title: University Director, Educator **Industry:** Education/Educational Services **Date of Birth:** 06/29/1934 **Place of Birth:** Seoul **State/Country of Origin:** South Korea **Parents:** Changsik Kim; Gong Kim **Marital Status:** Married **Spouse Name:** Myungsoon Kang (01/05/1963) **Children:** Kathlyn; Sandra **Education:** MD, Seoul National University (1959); Pre-Med, Seoul National University (1955) **Certifications:** Diplomate, American Board of Surgery **Career:** Attending, Mount Sinai Medical Center, New York, NY (1983-Present); Professor of Surgery, Icahn School of Medicine at Mount Sinai, New York, NY (1974-Present); Director, Surgery, Elmhurst Hospital Center, New York (1975-2011); Associate Attending, Mount Sinai Medical Center, New York, NY (1977-1983); Assistant attending, Mount Sinai Medical Center, New York, NY (1974-1977); Clinical Assistant, Surgery, Mount Sinai Medical Center, New York, NY (1972-1974);Resident, Surgery, Mount Sinai Medical Center, New York, NY (1967-1972); Staff Surgeon, First KOKA Surgical Hospital, Republic of Korea (1964-1965); Resident, Surgery, Capital Army Hospital, Seoul, South Korea (1959-1963) **Career Related:** Assistant Attending, Mount Sinai Services At Elmhurst Hospital Center (1972-1975); Chief of Surgery, Capital Army Hospital, Seoul, South Korea (1967) **Awards:** Decorated Bronze Star Medal with V (USA) (1965); Chungmu Medal, Republic of Korea (1965); Silver Star (1965) **Memberships:** Fellow, American College of Surgeons; American College of Gastroenterology; Association for Academic Surgery (AAS); Queens Medical Society (Now Medical Society of the County of Queens); Society for Surgery of the Alimentary Tract; New York Surgical Society; Collegium Internationale Chirurgiae Digestivae (CICD); International College of Surgeons **Marquis Who's Who Honors:** Albert Nelson Marquis Lifetime Achievement Award **Why did you become involved in your profession or industry:** Dr. Kim became involved in his profession because he was working as a housekeeper at a Swedish hospital during the war in 1952. He had an opportunity to watch the doctors take care of the patients, which led to an interest in medicine. **Avocations:** Playing tennis

Donald Robert Kimball

Title: Director of Regulatory Affairs (Retired) **Industry:** Agriculture **Date of Birth:** 03/04/1938 **Place of Birth:** Anderson **State/Country of Origin:** IN/USA **Parents:** Robert Martin Kimball; Mary Lucille (Gibson) Kimball **Marital Status:** Widow **Spouse Name:** Mari-Anne Talbot (4/6/1985, Deceased) **Children:** Randy; Rick; Sharon-Lee; Douglas; David **Education:** Bachelor of Science in Agriculture, Dairy Production and Biochemistry, Purdue University (1960); Coursework, Master's Degree in Health Services Administration, St. Francis College, Joliet, IL **Certifications:** Registered Professional Sanitarian (1965-Present) **Career:** Retired, Dean Foods Company, Rockford, IL (2000); Director, Farm Relations, Dean Foods Company, Rockford, IL (1990-1998); Director, Regulatory Affairs, Dean Foods Company, Rockford, IL (1987-2000); Director, Division of Dairy Products, Indiana Board of Health (1975-1987); Chief, Milk Sanitation Rating Officer, Division of Dairy Products, Indiana Board of Health (1973-1975); Milk Sanitation Rating Officer, Division of Dairy Products, Indiana Board of Health, Indianapolis, IN (1966-1975); Public Health Sanitation, Division of Dairy Products, Indiana Board of Health, LaPorte, IN (1962-1966) **Civic:** American Legion (2000); Referee, Football Games, Umpire, Baseball Games (1963-1985); Member, Youth Athletic Commission **Military Service:** Captain, U.S. Army (1960-1968) **Creative Works:** Author, "Raw Milk", Journal of Indiana State Medical Association (1982); Author, "Public Health Regulations in Milk Quality Control", Journal of the American Veterinary Medical Association; Contributor, Articles to Professional Journals **Awards:** Recipient, Distinguished Service Award, Midwest Dairy Products Association (1988) **Memberships:** With, Illinois Food Safety Task Force (1995-2000); Association of Food and Drug Officials (1989-2000); Dairy Practices Council (1985-2000); Northeast Dairy Practices Council (1985-2000); Indianapolis Dairy Technical Club (1975-1988); Indiana Public Health Association (1963-1988); Member, International Association for Food Protection; Multiple Committees, National Conference Interstate Milk Shipments **Marquis Who's Who Honors:** Albert Nelson Marquis Lifetime Achievement Award; Marquis Who's Who Top Professional **Why did you become involved in your profession or industry:** Mr. Kimball first became involved in his profession due to an interest in the dairy industry from a young age. He spent many of his summers at his grandfather's dairy farm. **Avocations:** Golf; Hiking **Religion:** Methodist

Joy Kerler King

Title: Professor Emerita **Industry:** Education/Educational Services **Company Name:** University of Colorado Boulder **Date of Birth:** 03/06/1926 **Place of Birth:** Glencoe **State/Country of Origin:** IL/USA **Parents:** William J. King; June (Bennett) King **Marital Status:** Widow **Spouse Name:** Edward L. King (12/20/1952) **Children:** Paul Gregory; Marcia (Deceased) **Education:** PhD in Classics, University of Colorado Boulder, CO (1969); MA in Latin, University of Wisconsin (1952); BA in Classical Languages, Knox College (1947) **Career:** Professor Emerita, University of Colorado Boulder (1991-Present); Associate Professor, Classics, University of Colorado Boulder (1968-1991); Chairman, Department, University of Colorado Boulder (1982-1986) **Civic:** Board Secretary, Board of Directors, Horizon West Homeowners Association (2004, 2010, 2017-Present) **Creative Works:** Contributor, "Building Newsletters" (2017); Editor, "Colorado Classics: A Newsletter" (1979-1988); Editor, "Woman's Power, Man's Game: Essays on Classical Antiquity"; Contributor, Articles on Latin Poetry **Awards:** "Ovatio" Award, Classical Association of the Middle West and South (2015); Named to Knox College Scroll of Honor (1997); University of Colorado Service Award (1991); Award, Council for Advancement and Support of Education (1991); Student-Alumni Teaching Award, University of Colorado Boulder (1974); Faculty Scholar (1946-1947) **Memberships:** President, The Classical Association of the Middle West and South (CAMWS) (1991-1992); Chair, American Philological Association (Now Society for Classical Studies) (1990); Chair, Committee on the Status of Women and Minority Groups (1988-1990); American Philological Association (1988-1990); Co-chair, Women's Classical Caucus (1983-1984); Vice President, Colorado (1982-1988); Promotion of Latin Committee, The Classical Association of the Middle West and South (CAMWS) (1982-1985); Rocky Mountain Modern Language Association; The American Classical League; The Phi Beta Kappa Society; Member, Promotion of Latin Committee (1982-1985) **Marquis Who's Who Honors:** Albert Nelson Marquis Lifetime Achievement Award; Marquis Who's Who Top Professional **Why did you become involved in your profession or industry:** It started when Dr. King was a student at Evanstown High School. At that time during the early years of World War II, there were eight Latin teachers at her school. Latin was a subject that was taught at most schools in Illinois. Her mother signed her up for a college preparation program that required four years of Latin. She started with her freshman year in high school and she loved her Latin teacher. There was a state Latin contest each year and all students taking Latin took an exam. The two best papers from each of the four years of Latin at every school in the state went on to a sectional contest. There were 19 sections in the state and those students who went to the sectionals all took the same exam for their year. The top were sent on to five district contests from which the top two students of each year went on to the state. At the state contest, the top two students in the fourth year of Latin were awarded scholarships to seven universities/colleges in the State of Illinois. Her first year, she did the exam and she had a perfect paper but there were 11 of them. They took a second exam and she did not come out in the top two. She didn't go on that year. The next year she was more determined and motivated to go on and she went to the sectionals, districts, and the states and after the state contests she was in the top two. The same thing happened her third year, and the fourth year of the contest was in the middle of World War II; there was a gas shortage due to the war effort, and so the contest was not held that year. Knox College had participated as the donor of the scholarship for fourth-year Latin people. They were persuaded to give her a scholarship for her first year in college. In college, she continued to be a good student and the scholarship was renewed each year and in her fourth year, she was chosen to be the faculty scholar. **Avocations:** Traveling **Thoughts on Life:** From March 2019 until April 9th, Dr. King was scheduled to go on a safari in Africa to visit Johannesburg, Victoria Falls, Botswana Toby National Park, Lower Zambezi National Park, and tool a city trip to Cape Town. Her best trips were Australia, New Zealand, The Fiji Museum. Another great trip was with the Denver Museum of Science to Greece and the Eastern Mediterranean.

Regina Rene King

Title: Actress **Industry:** Media & Entertainment **Date of Birth:** 01/15/1971 **Place of Birth:** Cincinnati **State/Country of Origin:** OH/USA **Parents:** Thomas King; Gloria King **Marital Status:** Divorced **Spouse Name:** Ian Alexander (4/23/1997, Divorced 2007) **Children:** Ian Alexander Jr. **Education:** Coursework, University of Southern California **Creative Works:** Director, "One Night in Miami" (2020); Actress, "Watchmen" (2019); Guest Appearance, "The Big Bang Theory" (2013-2014, 2017, 2019); Actress, "Seven Seconds" (2018); Actress, "If Beale Street Could Talk" (2018); Guest Director, "Insecure" (2018); Guest Director, "The Good Doctor" (2018); Guest Director, "Shameless" (2017); Guest Director, "This is Us" (2017); Actress, "The Leftovers" (2015-2017); Actress, "American Crime" (2015-2017); Guest Director, "Pitch" (2016); Guest Director, "Greenleaf" (2016); Guest Director, "The Catch" (2016); Guest Director, "Scandal" (2015-2016); Guest Director, "Being Mary Jane" (2015); Actress, TV Film, "The Gabby Douglas Story" (2014); Guest Appearance, "Shameless" (2014); Guest Appearance, "The Strain" (2014); Voice Actress, "Planes: Fire & Rescue" (2014); Voice Actress, "The Boondocks" (2005-2014); Director, "Let the Church Say Amen" (2013); Actress, Guest Director, "Southland" (2009-2013); Guest Judge, "RuPaul's Drag Race" (2012); Director, Music Video, "Not My Daddy" (2011); Director, Music Video, "Finding My Way Back" (2010); Actress, "Our Family Wedding" (2010); Actress, TV Film, "Living Proof" (2008); Actress, "This Christmas" (2007); Actress, "24" (2007); Actress, "Year of the Dog" (2007); Voice Actress, "The Ant Bully" (2006); Actress, Pilot, "Women in Law" (2006); Actress, "Miss Congeniality 2: Armed and Fabulous" (2005); Actress, "Ray" (2004); Actress, "A Cinderella Story" (2004); Actress, "Legally Blonde 2: Red, White & Blonde" (2003); Actress, "Daddy Day Care" (2003); Actress, "Truth Be Told" (2002); Actress, TV Film, "Damaged Care" (2002); Guest Appearance, "Leap of Faith" (2002); Actress, "Down to Earth" (2001); Actress, TV Film, "If These Walls Could Talk 2" (2000); Actress, TV Film, "Where the Truth Lies" (1999); Actress, "Love and Action in Chicago" (1999); Actress, "Mighty Joe Young" (1998); Actress, "Enemy of the State" (1998); Actress, "How Stella Got Her Groove Back" (1998); Actress, Short Film, "Rituals" (1998); Actress, "Jerry Maguire" (1996); Actress, "A Thin Line Between Love and Hate" (1996); Actress, "Friday" (1995); Guest Appearance, "Living Single" (1995); Actress, "Higher Learning" (1995); Guest Appearance, "New York Undercover" (1994); Guest Appearance, "Northern Exposure" (1994); Actress, "Poetic Justice" (1993); Actress, "Boyz n the Hood" (1991); Actress, "227" (1985-1990) **Awards:** Best Supporting Actress, "If Beale Street Could Talk," Academy Awards (2019); Best Supporting Actress in a Motion Picture, "If Beale Street Could Talk," Golden Globe Awards (2019); Best Supporting Female, "If Beale Street Could Talk," Independent Spirit Awards (2019); Best Actress in a Drama Series, "Watchmen," Critics' Choice Television Awards (2019); Best Supporting Actress, "If Beale Street Could Talk," Critics' Choice Movie Awards (2019); Best Supporting Actress, "If Beale Street Could Talk," New York Film Critics Circle (2019); Best Supporting Actress – Motion Picture, "If Beale Street Could Talk," Satellite Awards (2019); Best Supporting Actress, "If Beale Street Could Talk," San Francisco Film Critics Circle (2019); Best Supporting Actress, "If Beale Street Could Talk," National Society of Film Critics (2019); Best Supporting Actress, "If Beale Street Could Talk," Detroit Film Critics Society (2018); Best Supporting Actress, "If Beale Street Could Talk," Washington D.C. Area Film Critics Association (2018); Best Supporting Actress, "If Beale Street Could Talk," Toronto Film Critics Association (2018); Best Supporting Actress, "If Beale Street Could Talk," Los Angeles Film Critics Association and Los Angeles Online Film Critics Society Awards (2018); Outstanding Actress in a Television Movie, Mini-Series or Dramatic Special, "Seven Seconds," NAACP Image Awards (2018); Outstanding Lead Actress in a Limited Series or Television Movie, "Seven Seconds," Primetime Emmy Awards (2018); Best Supporting Actress, "If Beale Street Could Talk," National Board of Review (2018); Best Supporting Actress in a Movie/Limited Series, "American Crime," Critics' Choice Television Awards (2016); Outstanding Supporting Actress in a Drama Series, "American Crime," NAACP Image Awards (2016); Best Cast, Television Series, "American Crime," Satellite Awards (2016); Outstanding Supporting Actress in a Limited Series or Television Movie, "American Crime," Primetime Emmy Awards (2015-2016); Outstanding Actress in a Drama Series, "Southland," NAACP Image Awards (2011-2012); Best Actress in a Film, "A Cinderella Story," "Miss Congeniality 2: Armed and Fabulous" and "Ray," BET Awards (2005); Outstanding Supporting Actress in a Motion Picture, "Ray," NAACP Image Awards (2005); Best Supporting Actress in a Motion Picture, "Ray," Satellite Awards (2005)

William Richard "Bill" King, PhD

Title: Business Educator, Writer, Consultant **Industry:** Education/Educational Services **Company Name:** University of Pittsburgh **Date of Birth:** 12/24/1938 **Place of Birth:** McKeesport **State/Country of Origin:** PA/USA **Parents:** Dewey Clark King; Cambria Edith (Jones) King **Marital Status:** Married **Spouse Name:** Fay Eileen (Bickerton) King (6/20/1958) **Children:** James David; Suzan Lorain; Cambria H.L. **Education:** PhD (1964); MS, Case Institute of Technology (1962); BS, Pennsylvania State University, with Honors (1960) **Certifications:** Licensed Private Pilot; Licensed Motorcyclist; Certified SCUBA Diver; Certified Sailboat Captain; Certified Pesticide Applicator **Career:** Retired (2008); Professor, University of Pittsburgh (1969-2008); Director, Strategic Management Institute, University of Pittsburgh (1980-1985); Director, Doctoral Program, University of Pittsburgh (1971-1974); Associate Professor, Business Administration, University of Pittsburgh (1967-1968); Assistant Professor, Statistics and Operations Research, Air Force Institute of Technology (1965-1967); Assistant Professor, Operations Research (1964-1965); Instructor, Research Fellow, Research Assistant, Case Institute of Technology (1960-1964); Industrial Engineer, Pittsburgh Steel Co. (1960) **Career Related:** National Sun Yet-Sen University (2006); Chair, Co-chair, International Conference on Information Systems (1987, 2005); Visiting Professor, City University of Hong Kong (1997); Visiting Professor, National University of Singapore (1997); External Examiner, City University of Hong Kong (1996-1999); Visiting Professor, University of Auckland, New Zealand (1994); Management Consultant, Chairman, International Conference on Information Systems Professional Corp. (1987-1988); On Leave as Professional Staff Member, U.S. Senate Budget Committee (1976-1977); Vice President, Director, Co-owner, Cleland-King, Inc. (1969-1985); Visiting Research Professor, University of California Berkeley (1969) **Civic:** Active, YMCA; Vice President, Director, Pittsburgh Commerce Institute (1971-1980); Board of Directors, Western Pennsylvania Montessori School (1968-1971); President, Western Pennsylvania Montessori School (1968-1969) **Military Service:** Served to 1st Lieutenant, U.S. Air Force (1965-1967) **Creative Works:** Editor, "School Days ll" (2013); Editor, "School Days: Coming of Age in the Mid-20th Century" (2012); Editor, "Knowledge Management and Organizational Learning" (2009); Editor, "Planning for Information Systems" (2008); Co-editor, "MIS Quarterly Special Issue on Offshoring" (2007); Editor, OMEGA: International Journal of Management Science Special Issue on Knowledge Management and Oranizational Learning (2007); Co-editor, "Organizational Transformation Through Business Process Reengineering" (1998); Co-editor, "Management of Information Systems, 2nd Edition" (1994); Consultant Editor, Prentice Hall Information Management Series (1989-1999); Editor, Project Management Handbook, 2nd Edition (1989); Co-editor, "Management of Information Systems" (1989); Co-editor, "Strategic Planning and Management Handbook" (1987); Associate Editor, Strategic Management Journal (1985-1989); Associate Editor, Management Science (1971-1989); Editor-in-Chief, MIS Quarterly (1983-1985); Co-author, "Systems Analysis and Project Management, 3rd Edition" (1983); Editor, Project Management Handbook (1983); Co-author, "The Logic of Strategic Planning" (1982); Associate Editor, MIS Quarterly (1980-1982); Co-editor, "Marketing Scientific and Technical Information" (1979); Co-author, "Strategic Planning and Policy" (1978); Author, "Marketing Management Information Systems" (1977); Author, "Management: a Systems Approach" (1972); Co-editor, "Systems, Organizations, Analysis, Management" (1969); Author, "Probability for Management Decisions" (1968); Co-author, "Systems Analysis and Project Management" (1968); Author, "Quantitative Analysis for Marketing Management" (1967) **Awards:** Leo Lifetime Achievement Award, Association of Information Systems (2004); Institute Industrial Engineers Book of Year Award (1984); McKinsey Foundation Award (1969); Travelers Insurance Co. Research Fellow (1963-1964); Ford Foundation Systems Research Fellow (1960-1962) **Memberships:** Inaugural Fellow, Institute Management Science and Operations Research (2002); Founding President, Inaugural Fellow, Association of Information Systems (1999); President, Institute of Management Sciences (1989-1990); President, Institute Management Science and Operations Research (1989-1990); Vice President, Institute of Management Sciences (1986-1989); Fellow, American Association for the Advancement of Science; Fellow, Decision Science Institute; Fellow, Association of Information Systems; Planning Forum; Operations Research Society of America; Academy of Management; Strategic Management Society; Association of Computing Machinery; American Marketing Association; Society of Information Management; World Future Society; Tau Beta Pi; Beta Gamma Sigma; Alpha Pi Mu; Sigma Tau **Marquis Who's Who Honors:** Albert Nelson Marquis Lifetime Achievement Award **To what do you attribute your success:** Dr. King attributes his success initially, fear of failure and later, a desire to be the best. **Why did you become involved in your profession or industry:** He became involved in his profession because of a desire to do academic research and to lead the life of top research professors such as his mentor, Dr. Russell L. Ackoff. **Religion:** Protestant

Shawn Kinkelaar

Title: Pointing Dog Trainer **Industry:** Business Management/Business Services **Company Name:** Shawn Kinkelaar **Place of Birth:** Effingham **State/Country of Origin:** IL/USA **Career:** Pointing Dog Trainer **Creative Works:** Participant, National Radio Show (2020) **Awards:** National Handler of the Year (2019); Top Shooting Dog Award (2010); Winner, National Open Shooting Dog (2010); Handler of the Year (2009-2010); Bill Conlin Setter Shooting Dog Derby Award Winner **To what do you attribute your success:** Mr. Kinelaar attributes his success to having the ability to be so young (in his 20s at the time) and work alongside so very experienced trainers, while keeping an open mind as far as different avenues and training methods. He was very fortunate to be able to work with the best dogs and trainers in the country early in his career. Mr. Kinkelaar also recalls his first great English Pointer, Elhew Sunflower that showed him what it is to have a great dog and set the standard for him. **Why did you become involved in your profession or industry:** Mr. Kinkelaar began in junior high school with his grandfather and uncle attending hunting and walking competitions. By the time he was in high school it was all he could think about. By his sophomore year, he quit playing sports to focus on his craft and to attend competitions. He told his teachers in high school that he already had his mind made up on his career. He even attempted college three times, making the basketball and baseball team but gave it all up to continue his career in dog training.

Robert Preston Kinsman, MBA

Title: Biomedical Plastics Engineer **Industry:** Sciences **Company Name:** Kinsman & Associates **Date of Birth:** 07/25/1949 **Place of Birth:** Cambridge **State/Country of Origin:** MA/USA **Parents:** Fred Nelson Kinsman; Myra Roaxanne (Preston) Kinsman **Marital Status:** Life Partner **Spouse Name:** Mary Camilleri (Life Partner) **Education:** MBA, Pepperdine University (1982); Postgraduate Coursework in Business Administration, Air Force Institute of Technology (1972-1974); BS in Plastics Engineering, University of Massachusetts Lowell (1971) **Certifications:** Certified Veterans Service Officer, Disabled American Veterans Department of Massachusetts (2011); Licensed Real Estate Salesperson, CA (1995); Certified in Biomedical Engineering, University of California, Irvine (1984) **Career:** President, Kinsman & Associates, Billerica, MA (2001-Present); Expert/Auditor, Medical Device Certification GmbH, Memmingen, Germany (1995-Present); Director of Operations, Triage Medical, Irvine, CA (2001); Director of Biomaterials Engineering, Anchor Medical Technology, Inc., Irvine, CA (2000-2001); Director of Engineering, HemoDynamics, Inc., Irvine, CA (1999-2000); Director of Engineering, Cardio-Vascular Dynamics, Inc., Irvine, CA (1997-2000); President, Kinsman & Associates, Irvine, CA (1993-2001); Manager, Engineering and Production, Baxter Edwards Critical Care Division, Baxter Healthcare Corp., Irvine, CA (1987-1993); Project Manager, Baxter Edwards Critical Care Division, Baxter Healthcare Corp. (1984-1987); Manager, Manufacturing Engineering, Edwards Laboratories, Inc. (Subsidiary of American Hospital Supply Corp.), Anasco, Puerto Rico (1983); Senior Engineer, American Edwards Laboratories Division, American Hospital Supply Corp., Irvine, CA (1981-1982); Manufacturing Engineer, American Edwards Laboratories Division, American Hospital Supply Corp. (1978-1980); R&D Product Development Engineer, Plastics Division, General Tire Corp., Lawrence, MA (1976-1977) **Career Related:** Management, Advisory Panel, Modern Plastics Magazine, NY (1979-1980) **Civic:** Vice Commander, DAV Department of Massachusetts (2018-Present); Billerica Lions Charities, Inc.(2017-Present); Commander, DAV Chapter 47 (2014-Present); Service Officer, DAV Department of Massachusetts (2011-Present); Executive Committee, DAV Department of Massachusetts (2010-Present); DAV Department of Massachusetts, Boston, MA (2010-Present); Billerica Lions Club (2006-Present); DAV Chapter 47, Billerica, MA (2005-Present); Blood Donor (5 Gallons), The American National Red Cross, ND, MA and CA (1972-Present); President, Billerica Lions Charities, Inc. (2018-2019); President, LCIF Coordinator, Billerica Lions Club (2017-2019); Founder, First President, Billerica Lions Charities, Inc. (2017-2018); President, Billerica Lions Club (2014-2017); Treasurer, Billerica Lions Club (2009-2014); Treasurer, DAV Chapter 47 (2008-2014); President, Billerica Historical Society (2002-2005, 2008-2013); Board of Directors, Bennett Public Library Association, Billerica, MA (2007-2012); Elected Member, Town Meeting, Billerica, MA (2007-2010); Treasurer, Billerica Historical Society (2001-2002, 2005-2008); Chairman, Beginnings of Billerica 350th Anniversary Signature Event (2005); Member, Numerous Committees **Military Service:** With, United States Air Force Reserve (1975-1981); Captain, Combat Crew Commander, ICBM Launch Officer, Missile Operations Officer, United States Air Force, Minot AFB, ND (1971-1975) **Creative Works:** Newsletter Editor, Billerica Lions Club (2007-2009); Newsletter Editor, Paradise Park Owners Association (1988-1999); **Awards:** Melvin Jones Fellow, Lions Clubs International Foundation (2015); Award for Excellence, Billerica Historical Society (2008); Certificate of Recognition, US Department of Defense (2002) **Memberships:** Society for Biomaterials (1999-Present); Senior Member, American Society for Quality (1997- Present); Senior Member, SME (1996-Present); Member Emeritus, Society of Plastics Engineers (1968-Present); Member of the Month, Southern California Section, Society of Plastics Engineers (1989); Pledge Training Officer, Arnold Air Society & Silver Wings (1970-1971); Comptroller, Arnold Air Society & Silver Wings (1969-1970) **Marquis Who's Who Honors:** Albert Nelson Marquis Lifetime Achievement Award; Marquis Who's Who Top Professional **Why did you become involved in your profession or industry:** Mr. Kinsman's father, Fred Nelson Kinsman, passed away from heart disease and it was a shock to the family. Getting involved so that he could help other people was a big incentive to him and drew him to the medical device industry. His mom, Myra Roxanne Kinsman, was a college graduate and librarian, so that is where his broad interest came from; she encouraged a lot of education, research and reading. One of the reasons for Mr. Kinsman's military service was because his dad was very supportive of the military himself; he lived through World War II. **Religion:** Protestant

Wiley Price Kirk

Title: Professor of Physics, Materials Science and Electrical Engineering; Business Owner and President of Research and Development Company **Industry:** Education/Educational Services **Date of Birth:** 07/24/1942 **Place of Birth:** Joplin **State/Country of Origin:** MO/USA **Parents:** Wiley Price Kirk Senior; Inez Isabel (Watson) Kirk **Marital Status:** Widowed **Spouse Name:** Sally Ann Kirk (06/13/1964, Deceased 07/11/2019) **Children:** Camille Maura; Alexander Price (PhD) **Education:** PhD in Physics, State University of New York, Stony Brook (1970); MS in Physics, State University of New York, Stony Brook (1967); BA in Physics, Washington University, St. Louis, MO (1964) **Career:** Research Professor of Materials Science and Engineering, University of Texas at Arlington (2011-Present); Visiting Professor, Materials Science and Engineering, University of Texas (2008-2011); Professor of Electrical Engineering, University of Texas (1999-2008); NanoFAB Center Director, Texas A&M University, College Station, TX (1989-2002); Professor of Physics, Texas A&M University, College Station, TX (1984-1999); Associate Professor of Physics, Texas A&M University, College Station, TX (1978-1983); Assistant Professor of Physics, Texas A&M University, College Station, TX (1975-1977); Assistant Professor of Physics, University of Florida, Gainesville, FL (1972-1975); Postdoctoral Fellow, University of Florida, Gainesville, FL (1970-1972); Technical Collaborator, Brookhaven National Laboratory, Upton, NY (1969-1970) **Career Related:** Director, NanoFAB Center TEES (1989-2002) **Civic:** Business Owner, President, Chief Executive Officer, 3D Epitaxial Technologies, LLC (2015-Present); Board Member, Editorial Board, Superlattices and Microstructures, The Journal (1991-Present); President, American Vacuum Society, Texas Vacuum Society **Creative Works:** Editorial Board, "Superlattices and Microstructures" (1991-Present); Editor, "2D Quantum Metamaterials" (2020); Editor, "Nanostructures and Mesoscopic Systems" (1992); Editor, "Nanostructure Physics and Fabrication" (1989); Editor, "Quantum Statistics and the Many-Body Problem" (1975); Contributor, Over 120 Referred Articles, Professional Journals **Awards:** Grantee, National Science Foundation (1973-Present); Research Fellow Award, Texas Engineering Experimental Station (1992); National Bureau of Standards Precision Measurements Award, National Institute of Standards and Technology (1987); Research Corp. (1974) **Memberships:** American Association for the Advancement of Science; American Physical Society; American Vacuum Society; Materials Research Society; Senior Lifetime Member, Institute of Electrical and Electronics Engineers; Sigma Xi **Why did you become involved in your profession or industry:** Dr. Kirk got involved in physics as soon as he learned he could study the field. His introduction to the industry was at the University of Missouri, where he attended the summer program. As the United States became interested in rocket science, Dr. Kirk saw the need for professional scientists. This inspired him to work hard and pursue a career in his dream field.

Anne Saunders Kirkpatrick

Title: Systems Analyst **Industry:** Engineering **Date of Birth:** 07/04/1938 **Place of Birth:** Birmingham **State/Country of Origin:** MI/USA **Parents:** Stanley Rathbun Saunders; Esther (Casteel) Saunders **Marital Status:** Divorced **Children:** Elizabeth Macino; Martha Page Kirkpatrick; Robert Kirkpatrick; Sarah Kirkpatrick Duffy **Education:** Coursework at Oxford (1962); BA, Philosophy, University of Michigan (1961); Coursework, University of Arizona (1958-1959); Coursework, Laval University, Quebec City, Canada (1958); Coursework, Wellesley College (1956-1957) **Career:** Senior Analyst, Commonwealth Edison Company, Chicago, IL (1981-1997); Systems Engineer, IBM, Chicago, IL (1962-1964) **Civic:** President, Hinsdale Women's Republican Club, IL (1978-1981); Treasurer, Taproot Representatives, DuPage County, IL (1977-1980) **Memberships:** Board of Directors, Chicago Wellesley Club, (1972-1973) **Marquis Who's Who Honors:** Albert Nelson Marquis Lifetime Achievement Award **To what do you attribute your success:** She went to IBM right when she got out of school and she had not planned what she was going to do. To her what's significant was when she stopped working and had children. She was 40 years and started thinking about things she did and did not do and she thought what mattered was that she did not do more in business. So she thought she would get a job and her friend told her that her husband was head of data processing at Commonwealth Edison and that she should call him. She called him and went on an interview and got hired and that's how she started there. That to her was one of the most significant things she had done. **Why did you become involved in your profession or industry:** She majored in philosophy, graduated, and then decided she wanted to move to Chicago. She went to an employment agency. They gave her a test and suggested she go to IBM. She had never taken a computer course, but they gave her a test and she passed it. She loved working with the computers and customers. **Political Affiliations:** Republican

Margaret Ann Klee

Title: Software Engineer **Industry:** Information Technology and Services **Company Name:** Leidos **Date of Birth:** 02/18/1961 **Place of Birth:** Boston **State/Country of Origin:** MA/USA **Parents:** James Butt Klee; Lucille Janet (Holljes) Klee **Marital Status:** Single **Education:** MBA, Jones Graduate School of Management, Rice University (2001); MS, University of Houston - Clear Lake (1994); BA, Simons Rock College (1982) **Career:** Software Engineer, Leidos Innovations (2016-Present); Software Engineer, Lockheed Martin Corp (1991-2016); Senior Software Engineer, General Dynamics Corp. (1987-1991); Software Engineer, General Dynamics Corp., Fort Worth, TX (1985-1987); Software engineer, Goodyear Atomic Corp. (1984-1985); Programmer, Goodyear Atomic Corp., Piketon, OH (1982-1984) **Awards:** NASA Silver Snoopy (1999) **Memberships:** IEEE; IEEE-CS **Marquis Who's Who Honors:** Albert Nelson Marquis Lifetime Achievement Award; Marquis Who's Who Top Professional **Avocations:** Making jewelry; Hand analysis **Religion:** Episcopalian

Gordon Leslie Klein, MD

Title: Senior Scientist, Adjunct Professor **Industry:** Medicine & Health Care **Company Name:** University of Texas Medical Branch **Date of Birth:** 08/26/1946 **Place of Birth:** New York **State/Country of Origin:** NY/USA **Parents:** Hyman David; Ruth Harriet **Marital Status:** Married **Spouse Name:** Joann Pamela Klein **Children:** Andrew Howard; Adrienne Lindsay **Education:** Master of Public Health, University of California Los Angeles (1980); Doctor of Medicine, Albert Einstein College of Medicine (1971); Postgraduate Coursework, Cambridge University (1970-1971); Bachelor of Arts, Columbia University (1967) **Certifications:** Pediatric Gastroenterology, American Board of Pediatrics (1990, 1976) **Career:** Senior Scientist, Adjunct Professor of Orthopedic Surgery, University of Texas Medical Branch, Galveston, TX (2018-Present); Clinical Professor of Orthopedic Surgery, University of Texas Medical Branch, Galveston, TX (2010-2018); Associate to Full Professor of Pediatrics, University of Texas Medical Branch, Galveston, TX (1986-2009); Assistant Professor of Pediatrics, Tulane University Medical School, New Orleans, LA (1982-1984); Adjunct to Assistant Professor of Pediatrics, University of California Los Angeles (1980-1982); Postdoctoral Fellow, Pediatric Gastroenterology, University of California Los Angeles (1978-1980); Postdoctoral Fellow, Pediatric Nutrition, Johns Hopkins University Medical School and Nutritional Research Institute, Lima, Peru (1976-1978); Internship, Resident in Pediatrics, Stanford University Medical Center (1971-1974) **Career Related:** Editorial Board, International Journal of Molecular Sciences (2020-Present); Editorial Board, Osteoporosis and Sarcopenia (2015-Present); Editorial Board, Journal of Bone and Mineral Metabolism (2005-Present); Editorial Board, International Federation of Muscoskeletal Research Society Learning Environment (2019); Visiting Professor, Kings College Hospital and University of Sheffield (2019); Visiting Professor, Hôpital de l'Université d'État, Port-au-Prince (2010); Visiting Professor, University of Pittsburgh (2010); Visiting Professor, Cincinnati Children's Hospital (2009); Visiting Professor, Sanjay Gandhi Postgraduate Institute of Medical Sciences (2009); Invited Lecturer, Multiple Conferences and Symopsia, Including Asia Pacific Osteoporosis Conference & International Society of Clinical Denstiometry, the Scientific Advisory Committee for the International Conference on Bone and Mineral Research, the Congress of the International Society for Burn Injuries, the American Society of Bone Mineral Research and Others; Editorial Board, Journal of Bone and Mineral Research (2008-2012); Visiting Professor, Kings College Hospital and University of Sheffield (2000); Visiting Professor, Baylor College of Medicine (1999); Visiting Professor, Kyushu University (1996); Visiting Professor, Okayama University (1996); Visiting Professor, Kings College Hospital and University of Sheffield (1981); Invited Lecturer, Multiple Institutions, Including Hospital Necker in Paris, Columbia University, Harvard University, the University of Melbourne and the University of Sydney, Among Others **Military Service:** Lieutenant Commander, U.S. Navy Medical Corps (1974-1976) **Creative Works:** Guest Editor, Special Issue, "Osteoporosis and the Role of Muscle," Frontiers in Endocrinology (2019); Editor, Special Issue, Seminars in Cell and Developmental Biology (2016); Editor, Bone Drugs in Pediatrics (2014); Co-Editor, Current Opinion in Endocrine and Metabolic Research (2005); Editorial Board, Journal of Burns and Wounds (2006-2008); International Advisory Board, Journal of Bone and Mineral Metabolism; Contributor, 176 Articles in Professional Journals **Awards:** Overseas Fellow, Royal Society of Medicine (2017); Commanding General Medallion of Excellence, U.S. Army, Fourth Infantry Division, San Antonio, TX (2006); Nominee, Howard Hughes Investigatorship Translational Research (2001); Travel Award, International Conference on Calcium Regulating Hormones, Melbourne (1995); Nutrition Program Fellow, Project HOPE, Nicaragua (1992); Clinical Associate Physician, National Institutes of Health (1980-1982); National Research Service Award (1979-1980); Inaugural Fellowship, Class of 2018, American Society of Bone and Mineral Research **Memberships:** Fellow, American Academy of Pediatrics (1976-2015); Group Founder, Secretary-Treasurer, North American Pediatric Bone and Mineral Work Group (1984-1985); Fellow, American Gastroenterological Association; Society for Pediatric Research; American Society for Bone and Mineral Research; American Society for Nutrition; American Pediatric Society; Princeton Club of New York; Royal Society of Medicine **Marquis Who's Who Honors:** Albert Nelson Marquis Lifetime Achievement Award; Marquis Who's Who Top Professional

Peter Klein

Marquis Who's Who 18 98 Biographee

Title: Theatrical Producer **Industry:** Media & Entertainment **Date of Birth:** 07/22/1945 **Place of Birth:** Timisoara **State/Country of Origin:** Romania **Parents:** Andrew; Ari (Wiener) Klein **Marital Status:** Married **Spouse Name:** Phyllis Urman (06/23/1978) **Children:** Nadia; Alexis **Education:** BA, Baruch College, The City University of New York (1973) **Career:** Founder/President, Living Arts, New York, NY (1973-Present); Tour Manager, Hurok Concerts, New York, NY (1969-1974) **Career Related:** Founder, Opera Nazionale Italiana, Rome, Italy (1986); Board of Directors, Spectra Arts (Spectra NYC), New York, NY; Ballet, Manhattan, New York, NY **Creative Works:** Producer, "The Gershwins' Porgy and Bess" World Tour (1992); Organizer, Concert of Andres Segovia for President Jimmy Carter, The White House (1979); With, Productions in Europe Including "A Chorus Line," "West Side Story," and "Ain't Misbehavin'" **Why did you become involved in your profession or industry:** Mr. Klein became involved in his profession because of his love for music, dance, theater and performing arts. **Avocations:** Tennis; Basketball; Skiing

Renny D. Klein, PhD

Title: Psychotherapist, Writer, Columnist **Industry:** Medicine & Health Care **Date of Birth:** 09/29/1935 **Place of Birth:** New York **State/Country of Origin:** NY/USA **Parents:** Joseph Ferezy; Stella Benjamin **Marital Status:** Widowed **Spouse Name:** Harold Klein (Deceased 2019) **Children:** Joseph Steven; Jeffrey Michael; Deborah Lynne **Education:** PhD in Counseling Psychology, Pacific Western University (2002); Degree in Marriage, Family and Child Counseling, University of Southern California (1973); Postgraduate Coursework, University of Southern California (1970-1973); MA, San Fernando Valley State College (Now California State University, Northridge) (1970); BA, San Fernando Valley State College (Now California State University, Northridge) (1966) **Career:** Private Practice, Beverly Hills, CA (1973-1990); Private Practice, Los Angeles, CA (1973-1990); Bay Cities Mental Health Center (1970-1973); Los Angeles Psychiatric Clinic (1970-1973); Benjamin Rush Center for Mental Health & Mental Retardation (1970-1973) **Career Related:** Lecturer in Field **Civic:** Various Positions, Hadassah Southern California (1968-Present); President, Hadassah Southern California (1996-1998); Chair, Fundraisers, Technion (1985-1991); Founder, Leadership Council, Technion (1985-1991); Touring Docent, Los Angeles County Museum of Art (1980-1985) **Creative Works:** Author, "The Joy of Eating: A Simply Delicious Cookbook"; Author, "The Joy of Eating French Food"; Author, "The Love of Eating: Another Simply Delicious Cookbook"; Author, "Joy of Entertaining: A Party Planner"; Author, "Great Beginnings and Happy Endings: Hors D'Oeuvres and Desserts for Standing Ovations"; Author, "With Love from Darling's Kitchen: Treasured Recipes for Family and Friends"; Author, "Easiest and Best Coffee Cakes and Quick Breads: Great Breads and Cakes to Stir and Bake"; Author, "Entertaining Fast & Fancy"; Author, "The Moderation Diet: The "Common Sense" Way to Stay Slim and Healthy"; Author, "The New Joy of Eating: New Fast and Fancy Favorites, Leaner, Lighter and More Luscious"; Author, Happy Holidays & Great Celebrations: A Culinary Treasure"; Author, "Renny Darling's Vegetarian Fast and Fancy: The New Garden of Eating Leaner, Lighter & More Luscious"; Author, "These Are a Few of Your Favorite Things: A Treasury of Recipes to Enjoy With Love" **Memberships:** PEN International **Marquis Who's Who Honors:** Albert Nelson Marquis Lifetime Achievement Award; Marquis Who's Who Top Professional; Marquis Who's Who Humanitarian Award **Why did you become involved in your profession or industry:** Dr. Klein became involved in her profession because she wanted to be of help to others. **Avocations:** Reading; Listening to music; Art

Eric Klinger, PhD

Title: Psychologist, Educator **Industry:** Education/Educational Services **Company Name:** University of Minnesota **Date of Birth:** 05/23/1933 **Place of Birth:** Vienna **State/Country of Origin:** Austria **Parents:** Alfred Klinger; Auguste Klinger **Marital Status:** Married **Spouse Name:** Karla Ann Michelle Klinger (04/11/1960) **Children:** Heather Jill; Roderick Michael; Benjamin Karl **Education:** PhD in Psychology, The University of Chicago (1960); AB in Social Relations, Harvard University, Magna Cum Laude (1954) **Certifications:** Licensed Psychologist, Minnesota (Stopped Renewing License 2018) **Career:** Professor Emeritus of Psychology, University of Minnesota, Morris, MN (2006-Present); Professor of Psychology, University of Minnesota, Minneapolis, MN (1978-2006); Professor of Psychology, University of Minnesota, Morris, MN (1969-2006); Coordinator of Psychology Discipline, Morris, MN (1962-2006); Assistant to Associate Professor, University of Minnesota (1962-1969); Instructor in Psychology, University of Wisconsin-Madison, WI (1960-1962); Clinical Psychology Trainee, Hines and West Side VA Hospitals, Chicago, IL (1957-1960); Research Associate, Association of American Medical Colleges, Evanston, IL (1954-1960) **Career Related:** Consultant, VA Medical Center, Minneapolis, MN (1979-2002); VA Consultant (1980-1997); Visiting Professor in Psychology, University of Konstanz, Germany (1995); Consultant, Stevens Community Memorial Hospital, Morris, MN (1987-1989); Fellow, American Association for the Advancement of Science (1986); Bush Fellowship, University of Minnesota, Morris, MN (1984-1985); Visiting Professor in Psychology, Ruhr University, Bochum, Germany (1983-1984); Visiting Professor, University of Göttingen, West Germany (1981); Senior Research Fulbright, Ruhr University, Bochum, West Germany (1975-1976); Social Science Research Council Summer Undergraduate Research Training Fellowship (1953); Fellow, Divisions 1 and 8, American Psychological Association; Fellow, Association for Psychological Science; Fellow, Society for Personality and Social Psychology; Fellow, Midwestern Psychological Association **Creative Works:** Co-editor, "Handbook of Motivational Counseling: Goal-Based Approaches to Assessment and Intervention in Addiction and Other Problems," Second Edition, Wiley-Blackwell, Chichester, England, United Kingdom (2011); Co-editor, "Handbook of Motivational Counseling: Concepts, Approaches, and Assessment," Wiley, Chichester, England, United Kingdom (2004); Author, "Daydreaming," Tarcher (Putnam), Los Angeles, CA (1990); Editor, "Imagery" Plenum, New York, NY (1981); Editorial Board, Journal of Mental Imagery (1977-1982); Author, "Meaning and Void, Inner Experience and the Incentives in People's Lives," University of Minnesota Press, Minneapolis, MN (1977); Author, "Structure and Functions of Fantasy," Wiley, New York, NY (1971); Contributor, Articles and Reviews, Professional Journals; Contributor, Chapters, Books; Journal Manuscript Reviewer, 49 Journals; Book Manuscript Reviewer, Elsevier, Oxford University Press, and Psychology Press **Awards:** Named to Who's Who Among Human Services Professionals (1992-Present); Named to National Register of Health Service Providers in Psychology (1978-Present); Named to International Authors and Writers Who's Who (1977-Present); Named to The Writers Directory (1976-Present); Named to Dictionary of International Biography (1973-Present); Named to International Scholars Directory (1972-Present); Named to Contemporary Authors (1972-Present); Named to Outstanding Educators of America (1972-Present); Named to American Men and Women of Science (1961-Present); Henry A. Murray Award, Society for Personality and Social Psychology (2005); Faculty Research Award, University of Minnesota, Morris (2000); NIDRR Grantee, Rehabilitation Institute of Chicago (1991-1995); Named Outstanding Teacher in Undergraduate Psychology, Minnesota Psychological Association (1990); NIAAA Grantee, University of Health Sciences/Chicago Medical School (1989-1992); Fulbright Senior Scholar, Germany (1975-1976); Grantee, University of Minnesota Graduate School (1972-1991); Horace T. Morse Amoco Award (1972); Recipient, USOE Grant (1970-1972); National Institute of Mental Health Grantee, National Science Foundation Grantee (1964-1980) **Memberships:** External Member, Dissertation Committee, Institute for Transpersonal Psychology (Now Sofia University), Palo Alto, CA (2008-2010); External Examiner, Bangor University, Gwynedd, Wales, United Kingdom (2003-2007); Paterson Award Committee, Minnesota Psychological Association (1990-1992); International Association for the Study of Dreams (2013); Academy of Distinguished Teachers, University of Minnesota (1998-2006); Chair, Committee for the Henry A. Murray Award for Contributions to Personology, APA Division 8 (1989-1991); Scientific Advisory Council, Max Planck Institute for Psychological Research, Munich, Germany (1985-1997); President, American Association for the Study of Mental Imagery (1980-1981); Society for Personality and Social Psychology; Minnesota Psychological Association; Association for Research in Personality; Sigma Xi, the Scientific Research Honor Society **Marquis Who's Who Honors:** Albert Nelson Marquis Lifetime Achievement Award; Marquis Who's Who Top Professional; Marquis Who's Who Humanitarian Award

James Christopher Klotter

Title: State Historian, Educator **Industry:** Education/Educational Services **Date of Birth:** 01/17/1947 **Place of Birth:** Lexington **State/Country of Origin:** KY/USA **Parents:** John Charles Klotter; Marjorie Virginia Gibson Klotter **Marital Status:** Married **Spouse Name:** Freda Jean Campbell (12/28/1966) **Children:** Karen; Christopher; Katherine **Education:** LittD, Union College (1998); LittD, Eastern Kentucky University (1997); PhD, University of Kentucky (1975); MA, University of Kentucky (1969); BA, University of Kentucky (1968) **Career:** State Historian, Professor Emeritus of History, Georgetown College (1998-Present); Director, State Historian, Kentucky Historical Society (1990-1998); Assistant Director, Kentucky Historical Society (1988-1990); State Historian, Kentucky Historical Society (1980-1988); Managing Editor, Kentucky Historical Society (1978-1980); Assistant Editor, Kentucky Historical Society (1975-1978); Research Analyst, Kentucky Historical Society (1973-1975) **Career Related:** Chairman of the Board, Farmers State Bank; Member, Board of Directors, Middlefork Financial Group Inc.; Kentucky Mansions Preservation Foundation Inc. **Civic:** President, Kentucky Civil War Roundtable (1994-2007); Secretary, Kentucky Civil War Roundtable (1984-1994) **Military Service:** US Army (1970-1971) **Creative Works:** Co-Author, "A New History of Kentucky" (2018); Author, "Henry Clay: The Man Who Would Be President" (2018); Author, "William Goebel: The Politics of Wrath" (1977) **Memberships:** President, Kentucky Association of Teachers of History (1986-1987); Chairman, Kentucky Council on Archives (1980-1981); The Southern Historical Association **Marquis Who's Who Honors:** Albert Nelson Marquis Lifetime Achievement Award; Marquis Who's Who Top Professional **Why did you become involved in your profession or industry:** Dr. Klotter became involved in his profession because of his deep love of history.

Philip Hampson "Phil" Knight

Title: Retail Company Executive **Industry:** Retail/Sales **Company Name:** Nike, Inc. **Date of Birth:** 02/24/1938 **Place of Birth:** Portland **State/Country of Origin:** OR/USA **Parents:** William W. Knight; Lota (Hatfield) Knight **Marital Status:** Married **Spouse Name:** Penelope Parks (09/13/1968) **Children:** Travis; Matthew; Christina **Education:** MBA, Stanford Graduate School of Business (1962); BJ, University of Oregon, Eugene, OR (1959); BBA, University of Oregon, Eugene, OR (1959) **Certifications:** Certified Public Accountant, Oregon **Career:** Chairman, Nike, Inc., Beaverton, OR (2016-Present); Chairman, Nike, Inc., Beaverton, OR (1967-2016); President, Nike, Inc., Beaverton, OR (2000-2004); Chief Executive Officer, Nike, Inc., Beaverton, OR (1967-2004); President, Nike, Inc., Beaverton, OR (1968-1990); Assistant Professor, Business Administration, Portland State University (1964-1969); Co-Founder, Nike, Inc. (1962) **Career Related:** Owner, Laika Animation Studio **Civic:** Board of Directors, U.S.-Asian Business Council, Inc., Washington, DC; Donor, Stanford Graduate School of Business, Oregon Health & Science University, University of Oregon; Established, Knight Cancer Institute and Knight Cardiovascular Institute, Oregon Health & Science University **Military Service:** First Lieutenant, U.S. Army (1959-1960); U.S. Army Reserves **Awards:** Named, Forbes 400: Richest Americans (1999-Present); Named, World's Richest People, Forbes Magazine (1999-Present); Named, World's Richest People, Business Insider (2019); Inductee, Advertising Hall of Fame, American Advertising Federation (2013); Listee, America's Top 50 Givers, Business Week (2008); Listee, Most Influential People in the World of Sports (2007-2008); Listee, Best Managers, Business Week (1988); Oregon Businessman of the Year (1982); Inductee, World Retail Hall of Fame; Inductee, Sporting Goods Industry Hall of Fame; Inductee, Naismith Memorial Basketball Hall of Fame; Inductee, Oregon Sports Hall of Fame; Inductee, University of Oregon Hall of Fame **Memberships:** American Institute of Certified Public Accountants; Phi Gamma Delta **Avocations:** Tennis; Running; Golfing **Political Affiliations:** Republican **Religion:** Episcopalian

Arthur I. Kobrine, MD, PhD

Title: Neurosurgeon **Industry:** Medicine & Health Care **Date of Birth:** 10/09/1943 **Place of Birth:** Chicago **State/Country of Origin:** IL/USA **Parents:** Maurice William; Katherine (Lovrencic) K **Marital Status:** Married **Spouse Name:** Cynthia Elizabeth (04/19/1969) **Children:** Nicole; Steven **Education:** Doctor of Philosophy in Physiology, George Washington University (1979); Residency in Neurosurgery, Walter Reed General Hospital (1970-1973); Residency in Neurosurgery, Northwestern University (1969-1970); Intern, University of Michigan, Ann Arbor, MI (1968-1969); Doctor of Medicine, Northwestern University (1968); Bachelor of Arts in Chemistry, Northwestern University (1964) **Certifications:** Diplomate, American Board Neurological Surgery (1976) **Career:** Professor, George Washington University (1979-Present); Principal Research Investigator, Armed Forces Radiobiology Research Institute, Bethesda, MD (1973-Present); Clinical Professor of Neurosurgery, Georgetown University, Washington (1989); Attending Physician and Surgeon for, James Brady (1981); Associate Professor of Neurosurgery, George Washington University (1977-1979); Assistant Chief of Neurosurgery Service, Walter Reed General Hospital (1973-1975); Resident in Neurosurgery, Walter Reed General Hospital, Washington (1970-1973); Intern, University Hospital, Ann Arbor, MI (1968-1969); Staff Member, Georgetown University Hospital; Staff Member, Sibley Memorial Hospital; Staff Member, George Washington University Hospital; Staff Member, Washington Hospital Center **Career Related:** Member, National Advisory Neurological and Communicative Disorders and Stroke Council (1988-1991); President's Commission on Spinal Cord Injury (1980) **Civic:** Board of Directors, National Head Injury Foundation (1994-Present) **Military Service:** Assistant Chief, Neurosurgery Service, Walter Reed General Hospital, Washington DC (1973-1975); Major, United States Army Medical Corps (1970-1975) **Creative Works:** Contributor, Articles to Medical and Science Journals **Awards:** First Annual Resident Award, Congress of Neurological Surgeons (1974); Recipient, Raymond F. Metcalf Award, U.S. Army Medical Department (1971) **Memberships:** American Association of Neurological Surgeons; Society of Neurological Surgeons; Congress of Neurological Surgeons; Research Society of Neurological Surgery; American Medical Association; American Chemical Society; Society of Neuroscience; American Physiological Society; British Brain Research Association; Alpha Omega Alpha **Marquis Who's Who Honors:** Albert Nelson Marquis Lifetime Achievement Award; Marquis Who's Who Top Professional

Christina Koch

Marquis Who's Who 18 98 Biographee

Title: Astronaut, Engineer **Industry:** Sciences **Company Name:** NASA **Date of Birth:** 01/29/1979 **Place of Birth:** Grand Rapids **State/Country of Origin:** MI/USA **Parents:** Dr. Ronald Hammock; Barbara Johnsen **Marital Status:** Married **Spouse Name:** Robert Koch **Education:** MSEE, NC State University (2002); BSEE in Physics, NC State University (2001); Diploma, North Carolina School of Science and Mathematics, Durham, NC (1997); Diploma, NASA Academy Program, Goddard Space Flight Center, Greenbelt, MD **Career:** Field Engineer, Global Monitoring Division Baseline Observatory, National Oceanic and Atmospheric Administration, Barrow, AL (2012); Station Chief, American Samoa Observatory, National Oceanic and Atmospheric Administration (2012); Electrical Engineer, Applied Physics Laboratory, Space Department, John Hopkins University, Baltimore, MD (2007-2009); Research Associate, United States Antarctic Program (2004-2007); Electrical Engineer, Laboratory for High Energy Astrophysics, Goddard Space Flight Center, NASA (2002-2004); Astronaut, NASA; Station Chief, National Oceanic And Atmospheric Administration, American Samoa **Career Related:** Astronaut Group 21, NASA (2013); Ocean and Glacier Search and Rescue Teams; Adjunct Faculty Member, Physics Laboratory, Montgomery College; Crew Member, Expeditions 59, 60 and 61, Soyuz MS-12, International Space Station **Awards:** Award, Jupiter Energetic Particle Detector Instrument, Juno Mission, NASA (2012); Nominee, Invention of the Year, Applied Physics Laboratory, Johns Hopkins University (2009); Antarctic Service Medal with Winter-Over Distinction, U.S. Congress (2005); Group Achievement Award, NASA (2005); Astronaut Scholar, Astronaut Scholarship Foundation (2000-2001) **Avocations:** Backpacking; Rock climbing; Paddling; Sailing; Running; Traveling; Taking photographs; Doing yoga; Volunteering in the community

David Hamilton Koch

Title: Businessman, Philanthropist **Industry:** Business Management/Business Services **Date of Birth:** 05/03/1940 **Place of Birth:** Wichita **State/Country of Origin:** KS/USA **Parents:** Frederick Koch; Mary (Robinson) Koch **Education:** MSChemE, Massachusetts Institute of Technology (1963); BSChemE, Massachusetts Institute of Technology (1962) **Career:** With, Koch Industries, Inc., Wichita, KS (1970-Present); Executive Vice President, Koch Industries, Inc., Wichita, KS (1981-2018); Chairman, Board of Directors, Chief Executive Officer, Chemical Technology Group, LLC (Subsidiary Koch Industries, Inc.); Board of Directors, Koch Industries, Inc., Wichita, KS; Research Engineer, Process Design Engineer, Science Design Comp. (Affiliate of Halcon International, Inc.), New York, NY; Research Engineer, Process Design Engineer, Halcon International, Inc., New York, NY (1967-1970); Research Engineer, Process Design Engineer, Arthur D. Little, Inc., Cambridge, MA (1964-1967); Research Engineer, Process Design Engineer, Amicon Corp., Cambridge, MA (1963-1964) **Career Related:** Board of Directors, Hospital for Special Surgery, New York, NY **Civic:** Active, National Cancer Advisory Board, National Dinner Chairman, Republican Governor's Association (1999); Member, Libertarian Party Candidate for V.P. US (1980); Active, Library of Congress James Madison Council, Washington DC; Board of Directors, Corporate Life Member, Massachusetts Institute of Technology; Vice-chairman, Board of Directors, American Ballet Theatre; Member, Chairman's Council, Metropolitan Museum of Art, New York, NY; Board of Advisors, John Hopkins Medical Center; Board Associate, Whitehead Institute, Cambridge, MA; Board, Visiting, M.D. Anderson Cancer Advisory Board, Houston, TX; Board of Overseers, TV Station WGBH, Boston, MA; Board of Directors, CATO Institute, Washington, DC; Board of Directors, Reason Foundation, Santa Monica, CA; Board of Directors, Institute of Human Origins, Phoenix, AZ; Board of Directors, Aspen Institute, Colorado; Board of Directors, TV Station WNET, New York, NY; Board of Directors, Rockefeller University, New York, NY; Board of Directors, American Museum of Natural History, New York, NY; Board of Governors, Deerfield Academy, Massachusetts; Board of Governors, New York Presbyterian Hospital, New York, NY; Board of Trustees, Johns Hopkins University; Board of Trustees, Prostate Cancer Foundation, Los Angeles, CA; Board of Trustees, House Ear Institute, Los Angeles, CA; Member, Board of Overseers and Managers, Board of Trustees, Memorial Sloan Kettering Cancer Center, New York, NY **Awards:** Named The Forbes 400: Richest Americans (2006-Present); Named The World's Richest People (2001-Present); Named One of The 10 Most Fascinating People of 2014, Barbara Walters Special (2014); Named The 100 Most Influential People in the World, TIME Magazine (2011, 2014); Named The 50 Most Influential People in Global Finance, Bloomberg Markets (2012); Named The World's Most Powerful People, Forbes Magazine (2010-2014); Corporate Leadership Excellence Award, Society Memorial Sloan-Kettering (2005); Corporate Citizenship Award, Woodrow Wilson International Center Scholars (2004); Named 10th Annual Gala Honoree, New York Academy of Medicine (2004); Businessman of Year, Manhattan Republican Party (2002); Leadership Award, National Foundation Teaching Entrepreneurship **Memberships:** New York Explorers Club; New York Racquet & Tennis Club; New York River Club **Avocations:** Skiing; Tennis; Golf **Political Affiliations:** Republican

Randall G. Koch, MPA

Title: Hospital Administrator **Industry:** Medicine & Health Care **Date of Birth:** 10/12/1970 **Place of Birth:** Passaic **State/Country of Origin:** NJ/USA **Parents:** Gilbert William Koch; Geraldine (Abruscato) Koch **Education:** MPA, Seton Hall University (2000); Postgraduate Coursework, Seton Hall University (1993-2000); BA, William Paterson College (1993) **Career:** Financial Counciling Manager, Englewood Hospital and Medical Center, Englewood, NJ (2016-Present); Credit Manager, Englewood Hospital and Medical Center, Englewood, NJ (2002- 2016); Director, Admission Services, Jersey City Medical Center (2000-2002); Patient Account Manager, Passaic Beth Israel Hospital (1999-2000); Patient Accountant Supervisor, Englewood Hospital (1992-1999); Registration Supervisor, Kennedy Hospital, Saddlebrook, NJ (1988-1992) **Civic:** President, Garfield Library Foundation Board (2018-Present) **Memberships:** American College Healthcare Executives; American Society Public Administration; United States Golf Association; American Society of Notaries **Marquis Who's Who Honors:** Albert Nelson Marquis Lifetime Achievement Award **Why did you become involved in your profession or industry:** In 1986, Mr. Koch took a volunteer position at Kennedy hospital, as a resume booster, for college. In the process, he discovered that he loved working in the healthcare field and stuck with it.

Brooks Koepka

Title: Professional Golfer **Industry:** Athletics **Date of Birth:** 05/03/1990 **Place of Birth:** West Palm Beach **State/Country of Origin:** FL/USA **Parents:** Bob Koepka; Denise (Jakows) Koepka **Marital Status:** Single **Education:** Coursework, Florida State University, Tallahassee, FL; Diploma, Cardinal Newman High School, West Palm Beach, FL **Career:** Professional Golfer (2012-Present) **Awards:** Winner, WGC-FedEx St. Jude Invitational (2019); Winner, Masters Tournament (2019); Winner, Open Championship (2019); PGA Player of the Year (2018-2019); Winner, PGA Championship (2018-2019); PGA Tour Player of the Year (2018); Winner, CJ Cup (2018); Winner, U.S. Open (2017-2018); Winner, Presidents Cup (2017); Winner, Dunlop Phoenix Tournament (2016-2017); Winner, Ryder Cup (2016); Winner, Waste Management Phoenix Open (2015); Sir Henry Cotton Rookie of the Year (2014); Winner, Turkish Airlines Open (2014); Winner, Scottish Hydro Challenge (2013); Winner, Montecchia Golf Open (2013); Winner, Fred Olsen Challenge de España (2013); Winner, Seminole Intercollegiate, Florida Atlantic Intercollegiate (2012); Winner, Challenge de Catalunya (2012); Winner, Brickyard Collegiate (2011); Winner, Rice Planters Amateur (2009)

Hans Kok

Title: Consulting Engineer **Industry:** Engineering **Date of Birth:** 04/05/1923 **Place of Birth:** Potshausen **State/Country of Origin:** Germany **Parents:** George J. Kok; Anitina (Janssen) Kok **Marital Status:** Married **Spouse Name:** Roselle V. Venier (06/22/1960) **Children:** George H.; Karen R. **Education:** Diplom-Ingenieur, Technische Hochschule, Aachen, Germany (1950); Student, Hamburg University of Technology, Germany (1945-1946); Student, Suderburg Engineering College, Germany (1940-1942) **Certifications:** Registered Professional Engineer, States of New York, Pennsylvania, Indiana, Michigan, California, Florida, New Jersey, Arizona and Maryland **Career:** Consultant Engineer (1983); President, Treadwell Corporation Inc., Michigan (1974-1983); Director, BassetMiller Treadwell Ltd. (1973-1983); Vice President, Plant Design and Engineering Division, Treadwell Corporation, New York, NY (1973-1983); Assistant Vice President, Engineering, Treadwell Corporation, New York, NY (1969-1973); Manager, Plant Design Division, Treadwell Corporation, New York, NY (1963-1969); Chief Structural Engineer, M.H. Treadwell Corporation, New York, NY (1962-1963); Head, Structural Engineering Section, M.H. Treadwell Corporation, New York, NY (1956-1962); Structural Engineer, M.H. Treadwell Corporation, New York, NY (1953-1956); Design Engineer, Lummus Corporation, New York, NY (1951-1953) **Career Related:** Chairman, Executive Committee Council Engineering Laws (1976) **Creative Works:** Contributor, Articles, Professional Journals **Awards:** First Place Award, James F. Lincoln Arc Welding Foundation (1966) **Memberships:** Fellow, American Society of Civil Engineers; National Society of Professional Engineers; New York State Society of Professional Engineers; American Institute of Mining; Chairman, Material Shandling Committee, Metallurgical and Petroleum Engineers; American Mining Congress; American Management Association **Marquis Who's Who Honors:** Albert Nelson Marquis Lifetime Achievement Award; Marquis Who's Who Top Professional **Why did you become involved in your profession or industry:** Mr. Kok became involved in his profession after he began studying engineering.

Spiro John Kokkinos

Title: Owner **Industry:** Food & Restaurant Services **Company Name:** Greek House Cafe **Place of Birth:** Toronto **State/Country of Origin:** Canada **Parents:** Kassi Kokkinos; John Kokkinos; Niko Georgeopoulos (Step-Father) **Marital Status:** Single **Children:** Luke Liberatore (Stepson) **Education:** BS, University of Metaphysics **Career:** Owner, Greek House Café (2001-Present); Picture Framer, Art Frames and Graphics, Australia; Greek House Tavern **Awards:** Peoples Choice Award, Greek Food (2016-Present); Best Greek Food in Ventura County (2016-Present); Best Food in Los Angeles (2006-2019); All American Track Athlete, Texas A&M University (1985); Listee, Whos Who Among American High School Students (1982); Gloria Mae Walker Memorial Award (1982); All American Athlete Football Player, MVP Football Player, Ventura County (1982); All-Star MVP (1982); MVP, Track and Field, Ventura County (1982); Super Senior, Huenene High School (1982) **Memberships:** Chamber of Commerce; Better Business Bureau **To what do you attribute your success:** Mr. Kokkinos attributes his success to his ability to remain focused, responsible, and tenacious. **Why did you become involved in your profession or industry:** Mr. Kokkinos wanted to find a way to make a living while providing jobs for others. He took over the family restaurant after his family considered selling it. Not wanting to abandon the business, Mr. Kokkinos stepped into the leadership position. Growing up around Greek food and culture, he knew exactly what to do to make the restaurant thrive. It is in his blood to be hospitable to his customers.

James J. Kolb, PhD

Title: Drama Educator **Industry:** Education/Educational Services **Date of Birth:** 01/26/1944 **Place of Birth:** Rochester **State/Country of Origin:** NY/USA **Parents:** William George Kolb; Arline (Wiemer) Kolb **Marital Status:** Married **Spouse Name:** Barbara Bramlet (05/31/1969) **Education:** PhD in Theatre History and Theory, New York University, New York, NY (1974); MA in Theatre History and Theory, New York University, New York, NY (1968); BA in Philosophy, St. John Fisher College, Rochester, NY, Summa Cum Laude (1966) **Career:** Professor, Drama, Department of Drama and Dance, College of Liberal Arts and Sciences, Hofstra University, Hempstead, NY (1988-Present); Adjunct Professor, Drama, Department of Drama and Dance, College of Liberal Arts and Sciences, Hofstra University, Hempstead, NY (1987-1988); Director, Liberal Arts Studies, Hofstra University Continuing Education, Hofstra University, Hempstead, NY (1985-1988); Independent Research and Music Study, Piano Lessons and Theory, Hochstein School of Music & Dance (Now The Hochstein School), Rochester, NY (1984-1985); Professor, Theatre Arts, Nazareth College of Rochester (Now Nazareth College), Rochester, NY (1982-1984); Associate Professor, Theatre Arts, Nazareth College of Rochester (Now Nazareth College), Rochester, NY (1976-1982); Assistant Professor, Theatre Arts, Nazareth College of Rochester (Now Nazareth College), Rochester, NY (1972-1976); Instructor, Nazareth College of Rochester (Now Nazareth College), Rochester, NY (1969-1972) **Career Related:** Speaker in Humanities (1990-2005); Consultant, ArtsConnection, New York, NY (1988-1989); Theater Auditor, NYSCA, State of New York (1976-1983) **Creative Works:** Lecturer, Public Libraries (1985-Present); Director, "Madwoman of Chaillot," "Ah, Wilderness!" "Stage Door," "Merry Wives of Windsor," "A Midsummer Night's Dream," "Old Times," "Pride and Prejudice," "Awake and Sing," "Candide," "Macbeth," "Julius Caesar," "Antony and Cleopatra," "Cat on a Hot Tin Roof," "Patience," "On the Town," "Iolanthe," "Beggar's Opera," "Pajama Game," "Gypsy," "Last Five Years" (1972-2014); Director, "Bond, James Bond: The World of 007," Hofstra Cultural Center, Hofstra University (2007); Co-Editor, "Art, Glitter, and Glitz: Mainstream Playwrights and Popular Theatre in 1920s America" (2004); Co-Editor, "Experimenters, Rebels, and Disparate Voices: The Theatre of the 1920s Celebrates American Diversity" (2003); Co-Director, "The Broadway Musical: 1920-2020," Hofstra Cultural Center (2003); Author, Contributor, Professional Publications; Speaker, Presenter, Lectures and Presented Papers **Awards:** Distinguished Colleague of the Year, Nazareth College of Rochester (Now Nazareth College) (1984); Teacher of Excellence in Drama, New York State English Council (1983); New York University Tuition Scholarship (1968-1969); New York State Regents Teaching Fellowship (1966-1967, 1968-1969); New York State Regents Fellowship in the Arts and Humanities (1966); Harvard University Fellowship in the Arts and Humanities (1966); Harvard University Fellowship in Education (1966); New York State Regents Scholarship (1962-1966); Zelda Lyons Award, St. John Fisher College, Rochester, NY (1966); High School Scholarship, Aquinas Institute of Rochester (1958-1962) **Memberships:** Association for Theatre in Higher Education (ATHE); American Theatre & Drama Society; American Society for Theatre Research (ASTR); Theatre Library Association; St. Thomas Aquinas Honor Society, Aquinas Institute of Rochester; Delta Epsilon Sigma; American Theatre Association **Marquis Who's Who Honors:** Albert Nelson Marquis Lifetime Achievement Award **Why did you become involved in your profession or industry:** Mr. Kolb became involved in his profession because he was interested in teaching and academics from a young age. Once an advanced chemistry student, he later realized his academic success involved interacting with others, and shifted his areas of study to philosophy, music, art and drama. After scoring an improbable 100% on a test, Mr. Kolb was contacted by Harvard University and offered a substantial sum to come and undertake coursework in elementary education there. Mr. Kolb declined the offer upon learning the university was only inviting male students, and attended St. John Fisher College, where he was awarded Best Student in the Arts and Humanities. He found quickly that he loved teaching and loved his students. **Avocations:** Playing piano; Classical music; Videos; Collecting stamps; Exercising; Walking; Theater

George M. Kramer

Title: U.S. Senior Master Chess Player **Industry:** Professional Training & Coaching **Date of Birth:** 05/15/1929 **Place of Birth:** Brooklyn **State/Country of Origin:** NY/USA **Parents:** Daniel Kramer; Dorothy Kramer **Marital Status:** Widowed **Spouse Name:** Vivian Kaplan (2/11/1951, Deceased 11/26/2014) **Children:** Steven P. Kramer, PhD; Tina J. Garyantes **Education:** PhD, Interaction Between Helium and Nitrogen, University of Pennsylvania (1957); MS in Physical Chemistry, University of Pennsylvania (1955); BS in Chemistry, Queen's College (1951) **Career:** United States Olympic Team, Dubrovnik (1950); Participant, United States National Championships; Participant, United States Open **Career Related:** Retired, U.S. Senior Master Chess Player (1994); Senior Research Associate, Research Chemist, Exxon, Research and Engineering Company (now Mobil), Annandale, NJ (1957-1994) **Military Service:** U.S. Army (1952-1954) **Creative Works:** Author, "Mechanism of Acid-Catalyzed Reactions"; Author, "Synthesis of Volatile Uranyl Compounds"; Inventor, 22 United States Patents; Contributor, Over 50 Articles, Scholarly Journals **Awards:** Fellow, National Science Foundation **Memberships:** American Chemical Society; United States Chess Federation; Sigma Xi; B'nai B'rith **Marquis Who's Who Honors:** Albert Nelson Marquis Lifetime Achievement Award; Marquis Who's Who Top Professional **Why did you become involved in your profession or industry:** As a child, Mr. Kramer became curious about the game of chess. He would sometimes play in the yard at school. His father noticed the curiosity and decided to teach the young Mr. Kramer the game of chess. By high school, Mr. Kramer had begun playing chess more and winning local competitions. Eventually, after winning some local titles, Mr. Kramer won a competition in Detroit, Michigan, for the speed championship. As a result, he was asked to be on the Olympic team.

John Walter Kraus

Title: Aerospace Engineering Company Executive (Retired) **Industry:** Engineering **Date of Birth:** 02/05/1918 **Place of Birth:** New York **State/Country of Origin:** NY/USA **Parents:** Walter Max Kraus; Marian Florance (Nathan) Sandor Kraus **Marital Status:** Married **Spouse Name:** Jean Curtis; Janice Edna Utter (06/21/1947, Deceased 1981) **Children:** Melinda Jean Kraus-Peters; Kim Kohl-Kraus **Education:** MBA, University of Southern California, Los Angeles, CA (1972); BS, Massachusetts Institute of Technology, Cambridge, MA (1941) **Career:** Retired Aerospace Engineering Company Executive (1993); Senior Manager, McDonnell Douglas Space Systems Company, Huntington Beach, CA (1983-1993); President, Kraus and DuVall, Inc., Santa Ana, CA (1975-1983); Branch Chief, McDonnell Douglas Astronautics Company, Huntington Beach, CA (1966-1974); Special Assistant, Atomics International, Chatsworth, CA (1961-1965); Industrial Engineer to Industrial Engineer Manager, TRW, Inc., Cleveland, Ohio (1941-1961) **Career Related:** Chair, Heredity Society (2015-Present); Consultant, Technology Associates of Southern California, Santa Ana, CA (1974-1975) **Civic:** Secretary, Class of 1941, Massachusetts Institute of Technology (2008-Present); Lecturer, Northrop Institute of Technology; Secretary/Treasurer, The Residence Association, Atria Senior Plaza **Creative Works:** Author, "Handbook of Reliability Engineering and Management" (1988) **Memberships:** Chairman, Heritage Society, Friends of Oasis (2015-Present); Legacy Committee, Friends of Oasis (2013-Present); Chairman, Website Committee, Friends of Oasis (2011-Present); Secretary, Friends of Oasis, Atria Senior Plaza (2009-Present); Director, Friends of Oasis (1999-Present); Director, Oasis Sailing Club (1996-Present); Treasurer, Oasis Sailing Club (2009-2012); New Building Committee, Friends of Oasis (2007-2009); Staff Commodore, Oasis Sailing Club (2002-2009); Chairman, By-laws Committee, Friends of Oasis (2006-2008); Treasurer, Friends of Oasis (2000-2002); Commodore, Oasis Sailing Club (1996-2002); Chairman, Technical Division, American Defense Preparedness Association (Now National Defense Industries Association) (1954-1957); Life Member, American Defense Preparedness Association (Now National Defense Industries Association); Life Member, National Society of Professional Engineers; MIT Club of Southern California; Newport Beach Yacht Club **Marquis Who's Who Honors:** Albert Nelson Marquis Lifetime Achievement Award; Marquis Who's Who Top Professional; Marquis Who's Who Humanitarian Award **Why did you become involved in your profession or industry:** Mr. Kraus became involved in his profession because when he graduated from Massachusetts Institute of Technology, he was offered three jobs that involved making fuel components for military aircraft. TRW, Inc. was having problems with its liftoff and asked him to help solve the problem, which he did. He decided to move his career to another company. He received a telegram from Atomic International in California to come out for an interview, and he began working for them shortly after. They needed someone to make up a reliability program, which was approved by the Air Force. **Avocations:** Sailing; Reading **Political Affiliations:** Independent **Religion:** Lutheran

Jon Krawczyk

Title: Owner **Industry:** Business Management/Business Services **Company Name:** Superior Pools of Southwest Florida, Inc **Date of Birth:** 03/29/1982 **Place of Birth:** Lapeer **State/Country of Origin:** MI/USA **Parents:** Bill Krawczyk; Linda Krawczyk (Deceased 2011) **Marital Status:** Married **Spouse Name:** Danielle Krawczyk **Children:** JD Krawczyk; Bella Stevens **Education:** Entertainment Sports Management & Business Management, Northwood University Business School (2004); Diploma, Imlay City High School (2000) **Career:** Owner, Superior Pools of Southwest Florida, Inc. (2013-Present); Construction Manager, Superior Pools of Superior Pools (2004-2011) **Civic:** March of Dimes; Children Against Drowning **Awards:** Best Design, Harbor Lifestyle (2020); Gold Award, FSPA Design (2020); Gulf Coast Top 50 Contractors, Business Observer (2019, 2020); Best of Charlotte County Builder & Service (2019, 2020); Top 50 Builders, Pool & Spa News (2003-2007, 2016-2017, 2019, 2020); Small Business of the Year, Business Intelligence Group (2019); Florida's Top Entrepreneurs, Flvec.com (2019); Bronze Award, FSPA Design (2019); Top 50 Service Award, Nationwide Pool & Spa News (2018, 2019); Nominated for Business of the Year, North Port Chamber (2018-2020); Named #3 in Customer Service, Nationwide Pool & Spa News (2017); APSP Young Professionals of the Year (2016, 2017); Named #1 in Customer Service, Nationwide Pool & Spa News (2016); Named, 40 Under 40, Business Observer (2016); Best of Houzz Service (2015-2020); GuildMaster Award, Guild Quality (2015-2020); Guild Quality (We are the only Pool Builder that pays to have every customer surveyed) (2015-2020); Angie's List Super Service Award (2013-2020); Gulf Coast 500, Business Observer (2012-2020); Top 5 in Customer Service, Nationwide Pool & Spa News **Memberships:** FSPA; APSP BBB NPC North Port Chamber **Marquis Who's Who Honors:** Top Business Professional (2020) **Why did you become involved in your profession or industry:** Mr. Krawczyk's profession is not what he wanted to do, his dad moved from Michigan and wanted to get out of the car business. He was from the Midwest and his father was in his late 40's when he moved to Florida. So, his father wasn't looking to make millions, but to just make a living. The first year, he did what he was supposed to do by calling people back and keeping his word & built 100 pools. Then from that, the next year 300 and 500 and then 500 more for a couple of years. So, Mr. Krawczyk was doing an internship not making any money, 21 out of college, looking for a career. He started working for his dad. He didn't like it because he couldn't do anything right, but he did like to be around his family. It was not something he wanted to do. However, he saw how his father was doing it, learning about the pools, so he just did it. He saw how good his father was doing it even though he & his father are not mechanically sound, but if his dad could do it so could he. However, when he started out he thought he was going to get an office job coming from college, but his father put him out in the field building pools mastering every step of the pool process for about six to seven years and he hated it, but he did it because he had respect for his father and ended up learning the business. He would have it no other way because he learned and respected his father, plus he learned you can't be great at something without knowing how to do it. **Avocations:** Family time; Son's t-ball coach; Powerlifting; Sports **Political Affiliations:** Republican **Religion:** Christian **Thoughts on Life:** "HAVE PASSION! The strongest may survive, but it is the passionate that will thrive. Passion fuels your purpose!"

Joseph Kreines

Title: Conductor **Industry:** Media & Entertainment **Date of Birth:** 02/03/1936 **Place of Birth:** Chicago **State/Country of Origin:** IL/USA **Parents:** Leon David Kreines; Beatrice (Schoenbaum) Kreines **Marital Status:** Single **Education:** MusM, University of South Florida (1977); MusB, The University of Chicago (1956); BA in Academic, The University of Chicago (1955) **Career:** Conductor, Treasure Coast Symphony, Inc., Fort Pierce, FL (2000-2003); Conductor, Brevard Symphony Orchestra, Cocoa, FL (1965-1976); Associate Conductor, Florida Orchestra, Tampa, FL (1968-1974); Associate Conductor, Florida Symphony Orchestra, Orlando, FL (1961-1965); Conductor, University Symphony Orchestra, The University of Chicago (1957-1959) **Career Related:** Consultant in Field; Instrumental Music Clinician, Bands, Orchestras **Creative Works:** Author, "Music for Concert Band" (1989); Composer, American Song-set; Transcriber, Works for Band, Orchestra, Brass Choir; Composer, Original Music; Transcriber, Solo Works **Awards:** Named All-state Band, High School, FL (1974); Named All-state Band, Middle School, FL (1973); Recipient, Plaques for Special Clinician Conductor for Various Ensembles, FL; Named All-state 9th and 10th Grade Band, GA; Role of Distinction, Inductee, Hall of Fame, Florida Bandmasters Association **Memberships:** Music Educators National Conference (Now National Association for Music Education); Associate Member, Florida Orchestra Association; Honorary Life Member, Associate Member, Florida Bandmasters Association **Marquis Who's Who Honors:** Albert Nelson Marquis Lifetime Achievement Award; Marquis Who's Who Top Professional **Why did you become involved in your profession or industry:** Mr. Kreines started playing music at the age of 6 years old. When he was growing up there was no television, so he grew up listening to the radio. He was an avid radio listener and his ears were his most important sense. It was discovered by his piano teacher at 8 years old, that Mr. Kreines had "perfect pitch", which enabled him to hear notes perfectly and he was able to apply that to his conducting. Although Mr. Kreines did not come from a musical family, his parents, Leon David and Beatrice Kreines, did have an appreciation for his music, especially once he became an adult and started conducting. It was announced that there would be auditions for the Chicago Symphony chorus; Mr. Kreines went to audition. Margaret Hiller was the chorus founder and director for 11 years and Mr. Kreines was a member for three years. She showed Mr. Kreines about how to rehearse a group, he learned a lot from her. Mr. Kreines moved to Florida, where he encountered a number of musicians that had a great respect for Margaret Hiller. The interchange that Mr. Kreines has had moving to Florida was mostly with music teachers, band directors and orchestra directors. Mr. Kreines was invited to rehearse their groups and he had never worked with school groups before but he showed them that he knew what he was doing and that became the beginning of his career in Florida. For many years he has rehearsed middle school groups, high school groups and college groups. **Avocations:** Movies; Theater **Thoughts on Life:** Once Mr. Kreines started high school and had more homework, his practicing on the piano dwindled and he quit playing piano.

Edwin H. Krick, MPH, MD

Title: Emeritus Associate Professor of Medicine **Industry:** Education/Educational Services **Company Name:** Loma Linda University **Date of Birth:** 08/13/1935 **Place of Birth:** Takoma Park **State/Country of Origin:** MD/USA **Parents:** Russell Kenneth Krick; Flora Shaffer Parsons Krick **Marital Status:** Married **Spouse Name:** Beverly Kay Hardt; Kay Saunders Kronquest (06/02/1957, Deceased 05/1982) **Children:** Joylan Marie Grant; Edwin Harry Krick Jr. **Education:** MPH, Loma Linda University (1971); Resident in Internal Medicine, Loma Linda University Medical Center (1970-1973); Intern, White Memorial Hospital, Los Angeles, CA (1961-1962); MD, Loma Linda University (1961); BA in Chemistry, Atlantic Union College (1957) **Certifications:** Diplomate in Internal Medicine and Rheumatology, American Board of Internal Medicine; Diplomate, American Board of Allergy and Immunology: Preventive Medicine, National Board of Medicine, U.S. and Japan; Private Pilot, Over 2,000 Hours **Career:** Emeritus Associate Professor of Medicine, Linda Loma University (1980-Present); Dean of Public Health, Loma Linda University (1986-1990); Associate Professor of Medicine, Loma Linda University (1980-1986); Assistant Professor of Medicine, Loma Linda University (1976-1980); Instructor of Preventive Medicine, Loma Linda University (1971-1976); Director, Kobe Adventist Clinic, Japan Mission Seventh-Day Adventists (1966-1970); Staff Physician, Tokyo Adventist Hospital (1962-1966); Fellow in Rheumatology and Immunology, Scripps Clinic and Research Foundation (Now The Scripps Research Institute), La Jolla, CA (1974-1976) **Career Related:** Director and Founder, Rheumatology Fellowship (1993- 2014); Dean, School of Public Health (1986-1990); Chief, Section of Rheumatology, Loma Linda University School of Medicine (1977-1984); Director of Preventive Medicine, Loma Linda University School of Medicine (1973-1983) **Civic:** President, Loma Linda University School of Medicine Alumni Association (1979-1980); Treasurer, Loma Linda University School of Medicine Alumni Association (1973-1975); Assisting with Overseas Medical Work, India, Galapagos Island, Dominican Republic, Turks and Caicos Island **Awards:** Merlin A. Hendrickson Award for Outstanding Contribution Award, San Bernadino County Medical Society (2014); Named Alumnus of the Year, Loma Linda University School of Medicine Alumni Association (1988); Iner Shield- Ritchie Presidential Award **Memberships:** Fellow, American College of Physicians; Fellow, American College of Rheumatology; American Medical Association; California Medical Society; San Bernardino County Medical Society; Alpha Omega Alpha Honor Medical Society **Marquis Who's Who Honors:** Albert Nelson Marquis Lifetime Achievement Award; Marquis Who's Who Top Professional **Why did you become involved in your profession or industry:** Dr. Krick became interested in medicine because his uncle, Roy Parsons, had been a missionary in Africa for 50 years and he was Dr. Krick's inspiration. His mother was a nurse, that also helped him pursue his career goals. **Avocations:** Flying; Amateur radio; Hiking; White water rafting; Fitness/exercise **Political Affiliations:** Republican

Evelyn Sholtes Kritchevsky, PhD

Title: President **Industry:** Sciences **Company Name:** Alphatech, Inc. **Date of Birth:** 09/16/1923 **Place of Birth:** Chicago **State/Country of Origin:** IL/USA **Parents:** Stephen Sholtes; Anna Sophia (Ericsson) Sholtes **Marital Status:** Widowed **Spouse Name:** David Kritchevsky (12/21/1947, Deceased 11/20/2006) **Children:** Stephen Bennett; Barbara Ann; Janice Eileen **Education:** PhD, University of Pennsylvania (1978); MS, Northwestern University (1946); BS, Northwestern University **Career:** President, Alphatech, Inc. (1987-1990); Professor in Chemistry, Spring Garden College, Philadelphia, PA (1971-1988); Lecturer in Chemistry, Rosemont College, Lower Merion Township, PA (1965-1970); Assistant Professor in Chemistry, Upsala College, East Orange, NJ (1952-1955); Research Chemist, Tracerlab, Inc., Berkeley, CA (1950-1952); Research Chemist, Argonne National Laboratory, Chicago, IL (1946-1948) **Awards:** Outstanding Teacher, Spring Garden College (1974) **Memberships:** National Audubon Society; AAUW (American Association of University Women); American Chemical Society; Sierra Club **Marquis Who's Who Honors:** Albert Nelson Marquis Lifetime Achievement Award **To what do you attribute your success:** Dr. Kritchevsky attributes her success to her high school chemistry and math teachers. **Why did you become involved in your profession or industry:** Dr. Kritchevsky and her friend, who was also a chemist, realized how easy it was to test for radon. They bought all of the gadgets they needed and began to see how much radon was seeping into people's homes in basements. **Avocations:** Skiing; Birdwatching; Hiking; Photography; Traveling **Political Affiliations:** Democrat

David S. Kritzer

Title: Founding Partner **Industry:** Law and Legal Services **Company Name:** Kritzer Law Group **Place of Birth:** Brooklyn **State/Country of Origin:** NY/USA **Marital Status:** Married **Spouse Name:** Annmarie (2004) **Children:** Michael; Alexa; Emily; Jessica **Education:** JD, New York Law School (1992); BS in Accounting Finance, University of Buffalo (1989) **Career:** Founder, Attorney, Kritzer Law Group (1992-Present) **Awards:** Lawyers of Distinction for Excellence in Insurance Law; Named, Super Lawyers **Memberships:** National Defense Research Institute; Claims Ligation Management Alliance; Suffolk County Bar Association; American Bar Association; New York State Bar Association; American Trial Lawyers' Association; Suffolk Trial Lawyers' Association; National Retail and Restaurant Defense Association; DRI; Transportation Committee, Claims and Litigation Management Alliance; Board of Directors, Dominican Village **Marquis Who's Who Honors:** Marquis Who's Who Top Professional **To what do you attribute your success:** Mr. Kritzer attributes his success to his tenacity and the ability to have people trust and believe him. He believes that if you follow your moral compass you will do just fine. **Why did you become involved in your profession or industry:** Mr. Kritzer always knew he was supposed to be a lawyer. He is the first attorney in his family and also thought law was interesting. His father worked as a CPA and worked with a lot of attorneys. He always thought that they were interesting distinguished fellows and he really identified with them.

Herbert Kroemer, PhD

Title: Professor Emeritus **Industry:** Education/ Educational Services **Company Name:** UC Santa Barbara **Date of Birth:** 08/25/1928 **Place of Birth:** Weimar **State/Country of Origin:** Germany **Education:** Honorary Doctorate, University of Colorado (2001); Honorary Doctorate, Lund University, Sweden (1998); Honorary Doctorate, RWTH Aachen University, Germany (1985); PhD in Theoretical Physics, Georg-August-Universitat Göttingen (1952) **Career:** Professor, Department of Electrical and Computer Engineering, UC Santa Barbara (1976-2012); Faculty Research Lecturer, UC Santa Barbara (1985-1996); Teacher, Electrical Engineering, University of Colorado Boulder (1968-1976); Research Physicist, Varian Medical Systems, Inc. (1959-1966); Research Physicist, RCA Corporation (1954-1959); Semiconductor Researcher, Deutsche Post (1952-1954); Donald W. Whittier Chair, Electrical Engineering Department, UC Santa Barbara **Creative Works:** Author, "Quantum Mechanics For Engineering: Materials Science and Applied Physics" (1994); Author, "Thermal Physics" (1990); Contributor, Articles, Professional Journals **Awards:** Medal of Honor, IEEE (2002); Nobel Prize in Physics (2000); Alexander von Humboldt Medal, European Geosciences Union (1994); Jack Morton Award, IEEE (1986); Heinrich Welker Medal, International Symposium on GaAs & Related Compounds (1982); J.J. Ebers Award, Electron Devices Society, IEEE (1973); Decorated Grand Cross, Order of Merit, Federal Republic of Germany **Memberships:** IEEE; Foreign Associate, National Academy of Sciences; Foreign Member, American Physical Society; Electron Devices Society, IEEE; Foreign Associate, National Academy of Engineering

Allan E. Kroncher, PhD

Title: Economist (Retired) **Industry:** Financial Services **Date of Birth:** 06/12/1935 **Place of Birth:** Moscow **State/Country of Origin:** Russia **Parents:** Benjamin Kroncher; Ray Kroncher **Marital Status:** Widow **Spouse Name:** Rebuke A. (Greenbelt) (6/12/1975), (Deceased 12/08/2016) **Education:** PhD, Plekhanov Russian University of Economics (1962); Master's Degree, Plekhanov Russian University of Economics, Cum Laude (1957) **Career:** Retired (2017); Private Consultant, Ramat Hasharon, Israel (2014-2017); Private Consultant, Calpe, Spain (1998-2014); Private Consultant, Munich, Germany (1995-1998); Editor, Economic Program, Radio Free Europe/Radio Liberty (1987-1995); Chief, Research Unit, Radio Free Europe/Radio Liberty (1983-1987); Researcher, Radio Free Europe/Radio Liberty (1973-1983); Assistant Professor, Plekhanov Russian University of Economics (1968-1971); Lecturer, Plekhanov Russian University of Economics (1962-1968) **Career Related:** Consultant (1974-2017); Lecturer (1974-2014) **Military Service:** Reserve Officer, Russia; Private Reservist, Israel **Creative Works:** Author, "Per Aspera" (2018); Contributor, 400 Articles, Professional Journals; Contributor, "Kontinent"; Contributor, "Les Echos"; Contributor, "Soviet Analyst" **Marquis Who's Who Honors:** Albert Nelson Marquis Lifetime Achievement Award; Marquis Who's Who Top Professional **Avocations:** Studying military history; Traveling **Political Affiliations:** Conservative **Religion:** Jewish

Dolores Michael "Dee" Kulik

Title: Research Geologist, Geophysicist (Retired) **Industry:** Sciences **Company Name:** U.S. Geological Survey **Date of Birth:** 08/09/1940 **Place of Birth:** Denver **State/Country of Origin:** CO/USA **Parents:** Michael Kulik; Ella Maryver (Bryson) Kulik **Marital Status:** Divorced **Children:** Kerry Lynn; Vicky Jean; Marnie Jennifer; Three Grandchildren **Education:** Master of Arts in Elementary Education, University of Denver (1970); Bachelor of Arts in Anthropology, University of Colorado (1968) **Certifications:** Teacher, Denver Public Schools **Career:** Regional Representative, Women's Advisory Committee to Chief Geologist of U.S., US Geological Survey (1997-2000); President, Women's Advisory Committee to Chief Geologist of U.S., U.S. Geological Survey (1993-1995); With, U.S. Geological Survey (1966-2000) **Creative Works:** Basement Controls on Contractional Deformation In Foreland Thrusting (New Interpretation of Thrust Belt and Foreland Tectonics, Applicable Worldwide) **Awards:** Certificate of Sustained Achievement, US Geological Survey (1996); Special Achievement Award, U.S. Geological Survey (1975) **Memberships:** American Society for the Prevention of Cruelty to Animals; Defender Wildlife; American Humane Society; Denver Museum of Nature and Science; Smithsonian Institution; Alaskan Mensa; American Mensa; Geological Society of America; Arbor Day Society; Audubon Society **Marquis Who's Who Honors:** Albert Nelson Marquis Lifetime Achievement Award **To what do you attribute your success:** Dr. Kulik credits her success on her love for the Earth. **Why did you become involved in your profession or industry:** Dr. Kulik has long been involved in geology; when she was a small child, she often collected rocks, which provided the spark for her future interest in the subject. **Avocations:** Astrogeology; Reading; Hiking; Camping; White water; Gardening, Native American history **Political Affiliations:** Democrat **Religion:** Catholic **Thoughts on Life:** Life is strange. Strange is fun. Stay curious.

Mary La Wayne Hauser

Title: Elementary School Educator (Retired) **Industry:** Education/Educational Services **Date of Birth:** 11/06/1943 **Place of Birth:** Decatur **State/Country of Origin:** TX/USA **Parents:** Thomas Hodges; Tommie Ann Hodges **Marital Status:** Married **Spouse Name:** Karl-Heinz Hauser (11/14/1980) **Children:** Aaron Kent Cowan; Michael Dan Cowan **Education:** Postgraduate Coursework, Texas Woman's University (1985-1987); EdM, Texas Woman's University (1977); MS in Psychology, Texas Woman's University (1977); BS in Elementary Education and English, University of North Texas (1965) **Certifications:** Certified Teacher, State of Texas; National Certification for Teaching in all 50 States; Certified Professional, LLD; Certified in Gifted and Talented; Computer Proficient Certifications in Microsoft Word, Excel, PowerPoint, PC/Apple **Career:** Adjunct Professor, Northwest Campus, Tarrant County College (1999); Teacher, Birdville Independent School District, Fort Worth, TX (1974-1998); Teacher, Grapeville Independent School District, Texas (1972-1973); Teacher, Child Study Center, Fort Worth, TX (1971-1972); Teacher, Department of Defense (1967-1970); Teacher, Irving Independent School District, Texas (1966-1967); Teacher, Midland Independent School District, Texas (1965-1966) **Career Related:** Proprietor, Hauser Haus Handmade (1992-Present); Private Teacher, Private Tutor (2010-2017); Temporary Employee in Corporate World, Long Term, Special Projects, Vacations, Sick Leaves, United States Census Bureau, United States Department of Commerce (2010); Kelly Services Inc. (1999-2009); Proprietor, Hauser Haus Rental Property (1980-2003); Sponsor, Chess Club (1996-1998); Sponsor, Student Newspaper (1980-1998); Newspaper in Education Sponsor, Conferences and Programs, Fort Worth Star-Telegram (1991-1997); Chairman, Celebrity Monday Program (1993-1995); Sponsor, Student Council (1980-1989); Member, Committees, Local and State Levels, Varied School Districts of Employment **Civic:** Stakeholder Committee Member, Transportation Public Works, City of Fort Worth, Texas (2016-Present); Volunteer, Community Collaborative Rain, Hail and Snow Network, National Weather Bureau (2016-Present); Transportation/Public Works Committee, Floodplain Policy Member, City of Fort Worth, Texas (2009-Present); Editor, Newsletter, Eastern Hills Homeowners Association (2002-Present); Arts and Crafts Leader, East Fort Worth 4-H (2000-Present); Crime Watch Chair, Easter Hills Homeowners Association (1997-Present); Meadowbrook United Methodist Church; Participant, Fourth of July Parade; Volunteer Face Painter, National Night Out Event **Creative Works:** Author, Booklet, "Students Expressing Freedom of Press" (1993); Co-Author, "Teriyaki, Tea, Tokyo: A Mini Study for Third-Sixth Grades" (1986); Author, "Child Abuse: A Call for Help - A Slide Presentation" (1977) **Awards:** National Gold Award, Neighborhoods, USA, Indianapolis, IN (2012); Third Place Award, Eastern Hill Homeowners' Association, Neighborhoods USA Convention, Little Rock, AK (2010); Named, Woman of the Year, American Business Women's Association (1983); Crisco Award (1962) **Memberships:** Curator, Mary Isham Keith Executive Board, National Society Daughters of the American Revolution; General H. Tarrant Chapter, Texas Society United States Daughters of 1812; Texas Retired Teachers Association; Oak Crest Woman's Club; Scholarship and Awards Chair, Honorary Phillip Livingston Chapter, Eastside Creative Arts Club; Retired Texas Association; Eastern Hills Neighborhood Association **Marquis Who's Who Honors:** Albert Nelson Marquis Lifetime Achievement Award

Theodore P. Labuza

Title: Researcher, Educator **Industry:** Education/Educational Services **Company Name:** University of Minnesota **Date of Birth:** 11/10/1940 **Place of Birth:** Perth Amboy **State/Country of Origin:** NJ/USA **Parents:** Theodore Labuza; Catherine (Stycheck) Labuza **Marital Status:** Married **Spouse Name:** Mary K. Schmidl (11/30/1985) **Children:** Theodore J; Peter; Katherine **Education:** PhD, Massachusetts Institute of Technology, Cambridge, MA (1965); BS, Massachusetts Institute of Technology, Cambridge, MA (1962) **Career:** Researcher, Educator; Morse Alumni Distinguished Teaching Professor of Food Science and Engineering, University of Minnesota, St. Paul, MN (1983-Present); Professor, Food Science and Technology, University of Minnesota, St. Paul, MN (1973-Present); Associate Dean, Graduate School, University of Minnesota, Minneapolis, MN (1993-1996); Associate Professor, University of Minnesota, St. Paul, MN (1971-1973); Associate Professor, Massachusetts Institute of Technology, Cambridge, MA (1970-1971); Assistant Professor, Massachusetts Institute of Technology, Cambridge, MA (1965-1969) **Career Related:** Honorary Visiting Scientist, Jingnan University, Wuxi, China (2011); Co-Founder, the ISOPOW (International Symposium on the Properties of Water) Symposium; Consultant to the Food Industry; Expert Witness in the Field **Civic:** Chairman, Committee on Intercollegiate Athletics, University of Minnesota, Minneapolis, MN (1988-1992) **Creative Works:** Co-Author, Book, "Open Dating of Foods" (2001); Co-Author, Book, "Moisture Sorption: Practical Aspects of Isotherm Measurement and Use" (2000); Co-Author, Book, "Essentials of Functional Foods" (2000); Author, Book, "Food Science and Nutritional Health: An Introduction" (1984); Author, Book, "Shelf-Life Dating of Foods" (1982); Co-Author, Book, "Contemporary Nutrition Controversies" (1979); Author, Book, "Food and Your Well Being" (1977); Author, Book, "Food for Thought" (1977); Author, Co-Author, More Than 289 Scientific Refereed Research Articles, 18 Textbooks, 78 Book Chapters, Eight Patents and More Than 100 Other Semi-Technical Articles **Awards:** American Society of Nutrition/IFT Gilbert Leveille Lecturer Award (2015); IFT International Bor Luh Award (2014); IFT Minnesota Section Macy Award (2013); University of Minnesota Post-Doc Association Award for Best Research Mentoring of Post-Docs (2012); Lifetime Achievement Award, International Association of Engineering and Food (2011); IFT Reister Davis Award in Food Packaging (2006); College of Human Ecology Advisory Council Award for Innovation and Mission Advancement (2005); University of Minnesota College of Human Ecology McFarland Outstanding Teaching Award (2001); IFT Marcel Loncin Research Prize (1998); IFT Nicholas Appert Award (1998); University of Helsinki President's Award (1998); Dairy and Food Industries/American Society of Agricultural Engineers Food Engineer Award (1995); University of Minnesota H.T. Morse Alumni Distinguished Teaching Award (1988); Institute of Food Technologists Babcock Hart Nutrition Award (1988); Minnesota Student Association Gordon L. Starr Service Award (1987); IFT Cruess Award (1979); NASA Certificate of Merit (1973, 1974, 1976); IFT Samuel Cate Prescott Award (1972) **Memberships:** International Association of Food Protection (1971-Present); American Institute of Chemical Engineers (1971-Present); American Chemical Society (1962-Present); Institute of Food Technologists (1959-Present); President, Institute of Food Technologists (1988-1989); American Association of Cereal Chemists (1971-1992); Life Member, International Union of Food Science and Technology (IUFoST) **Marquis Who's Who Honors:** Albert Nelson Marquis Lifetime Achievement Award; Marquis Who's Who Top Professional **Why did you become involved in your profession or industry:** Dr. Labuza became involved in his profession because he grew up in Perth Amboy, New Jersey, and one of the things he was interested in was explosives. He built a laboratory in the basement of his family home and experimented on how to make TNT and fulminate of mercury and ammonium nitrite then he would take the explosives out to the clay pits and blow up rocks. Dr. Labuza read a lot on nuclear weapons and nuclear bombs and studied the difference between that and using it for making electricity. His father worked at the New Jersey Public Power Gas and Electric Plant in Sewaren, New Jersey. Dr. Labuza became very interested in nuclear physics and nuclear engineering, so he applied for an internship with PS and then did get one at one of the plant that his father worked at. The manager for the whole plant was an MIT graduate and he agreed to give Dr. Labuza a recommendation letter to get into MIT. Dr. Labuza's parents could not afford much, so he got a job with the nuclear engineering undergraduate program and worked in a facility that irradiated products for military and industry research. Dr. Labuza had the opportunity to meet people from the U.S Natick Laboratories, which was in Natick, Massachusetts. There were several researchers from Natick from there that were looking at using irradiation for pasteurization and sterilization of food, something that Dr. Labuza became familiar with. Dr. Labuza was introduced by them to an MIT faculty member that was on the Natick Irradation research project and in the food MIT Food engineering program. Dr. Labuza was asked by Professor Sam Goldblith to change his major to food engineering and his next three years of tuition were paid for.

Theodore H. Lackland, Esq.

Title: Lawyer **Industry:** Law and Legal Services **Company Name:** Lackland & Associates, LLC **Date of Birth:** 12/04/1943 **Place of Birth:** Chicago **State/Country of Origin:** IL/USA **Parents:** Richard Lackland; Cora Lee (Sanders) Lackland **Marital Status:** Married **Spouse Name:** Dorothy Ann Gerald (01/02/1970) **Children:** Jennifer Noel **Education:** JD, Columbia University (1975); Graduate, U.S. Army Ranger School (1968); MA in Philosophy, Howard University (1967); BS in Humanities, Loyola University Chicago (1965) **Career:** Partner, Lackland & Associates, LLC (2000-Present); Partner, Lackland & Heyward (1995-2000); Partner, Lackland & Associate (1993-1995); Partner, Arnall Golden Gregory LLP (1981-1993); Assistant U.S. Attorney, U.S District Court, District of New Jersey (1978-1981); Associate, Dewey Ballantine (1975-1978) **Career Related:** Adjunct Professor of Law, College of Law, Georgia State University (1989-1999) **Civic:** Board of Directors, APEX Museum (2002-2011); Member, Executive Committee, Leadership Atlanta (1986, 1990-1991); Advisory Director, Atlanta MBDA Business Center (1983-1991) **Military Service:** U.S. Army (1967-1971) **Creative Works:** Associate Editor, Columbia Human Rights Law Review (1974-1975); Contributor, Articles, Professional Journals **Awards:** Bronze Star, One Oak Leaf Cluster, U.S. Army; Purple Heart, U.S. Army; Air Medal, U.S. Army; Commendation Medal, U.S. Army; Combat Infantry Badge, U.S. Army **Memberships:** State Bar of Georgia; American Bar Association; American Association for Justice; Atlanta Bar Association **Bar Admissions:** United States District Court, Southern District of Georgia (2003); United States District Court, Middle District of Georgia (1985); United States Tax Court (1983); State Bar of Georgia (1982); United States District Court, Northern District of Georgia (1982); Supreme Court of the United States (1979); New Jersey State Bar Association (1975); U.S. District Court, District of New Jersey (1975) **Marquis Who's Who Honors:** Albert Nelson Marquis Lifetime Achievement Award; Marquis Who's Who Top Professional **Why did you become involved in your profession or industry:** Mr. Lackland became involved in his profession because of his interest in ethics and its role in the development of the law. This interest peaked after graduate school and his service in the U.S. Army. **Avocations:** Reading philosophy **Political Affiliations:** Democrat **Religion:** Roman Catholic

Richard J. "Dick" Lagow, PhD

Title: Chemistry Professor **Industry:** Education/Educational Services **Date of Birth:** 08/16/1945 **Place of Birth:** Albuquerque **State/Country of Origin:** NM/USA **Parents:** Faye Lagow; Ruthe Lagow **Marital Status:** Married **Spouse Name:** Roxann Parker-Lagow (06/06/1996) **Education:** National Science Foundation Postdoctoral Fellowship (1970); Doctor of Philosophy, Rice University (1969); Bachelor of Arts, Rice University (1967); Diploma, Bryan Adams High School, Dallas, TX, With Honors (1963) **Career:** L.N. Vauquelin Regents Professor of Chemistry, Department of Chemistry, University of Texas at Austin (1994-2008); Professor, Department of Chemistry, University of Texas at Austin (1980-1994); Associate Professor, Department of Chemistry, University of Texas at Austin (1976-1980); Assistant to Associate Professor, Department of Chemistry, Massachusetts Institute of Technology, Cambridge, MA (1969-1976); Instructor, Department of Chemistry, Rice University, Houston, TX (1967-1969) **Career Related:** Alfred P. Sloan Fellow (1974-1975) **Awards:** Award for Creative Work in Fluorine Chemistry, American Chemical Society (1997); Alexander von Humboldt Award (1992); I.R. 100 Award (1970) **Memberships:** Fellow, American Association for the Advancement of Science (1992) **Marquis Who's Who Honors:** Albert Nelson Marquis Lifetime Achievement Award **Why did you become involved in your profession or industry:** Dr. Lagow became involved in his profession because of his junior high school teacher, who encouraged him to do chemistry because he saw that he loved it. He always thought outside the box and when professors told him something could not be done, he would prove them wrong. He received a football and chemistry scholarship to Rice university and then went onto graduate with a bachelor's degree.

Carolyn P. Lamunière

Title: Artist **Industry:** Fine Art **Date of Birth:** 11/22/1942 **Place of Birth:** Cleveland **State/Country of Origin:** OH/USA **Parents:** Lorand Victor Johnson; Dorothy (Strom) Ussher **Marital Status:** Married **Spouse Name:** Jean Marie Lamuniere (10/23/2019); Robert Parker (09/07/1966) **Children:** Robert F. Parker Jr **Education:** BA in Art History, Skidmore College (1965) **Career:** Painter, Galleries, Main Galleries, Convergence, Santa Fe, NM, Hand Artes, Truchas, NM **Career Related:** Painter, Gallery La Forgerie, Alaigne, France **Creative Works:** Exhibitor, Group Show, Convergence Gallery, Santa Fe, NM (2000-2005, 2007); Exhibitor, Munson Gallery, Santa Fe, NM (2002); Exhibitor, Group Show, Joyce Robbins Gallery, Santa Fe, NM (1999); Exhibitor, Group Show, Elaine Beckwith Gallery, Jamaica, VT (1998); Exhibitor, Group Show, Hand Artes Gallery, Truchas, NM (1997); Exhibitor, Group Show, XX c. Art Gallery (1992, 1996-1998); Exhibitor, Group Show, The Best of Acrylic Painting (1996); Exhibitor, Group Show, Lois Hodes Gallery, Baltimore, MD (1992); Exhibitor, Group Show, Franz Bader Gallery, Washington DC (1987-1989, 1991); Exhibitor, Group Show, Peel Gallery, Danby, VT (1980, 1983, 1985, 1987-1988, 1991); Exhibitor, Group Show, Ariel Gallery, New York, NY (1990-1992); Exhibitor, Group Show, Gallaudet University, Washington DC (1988); Exhibitor, Group Show, National Society for Painters in Acrylic & Casein (1984, 1986, 1988); Exhibitor, Group Show, Albright Knox Museum, Buffalo, NY (1984, 1987); Exhibitor, Group Show, Elain Starkman Gallery, New York, NY (1980, 1984-1986); Exhibitor, Group Show, Brocton Museum (1982); Exhibitor, Group Show, Hood College, Frederick, MD (1982); Exhibitor, Group Show, Berkshire Museum, Pittsfield, MA (1977); Exhibitor, Group Show, Woman Made Gallery, Chicago, IL **Awards:** Named, One of the Best Painters, Destig (2019); Named, One of Best Acrylic Painters in United States, Artists of Southwest (2005); Many Awards from New York **Marquis Who's Who Honors:** Albert Nelson Marquis Lifetime Achievement Award **To what do you attribute your success:** Ms. Lamuniere's major decisions in life were made in three minutes. **Why did you become involved in your profession or industry:** Ms. Lamuniere always loved to paint. Growing up she would make her own toys, her own doll houses and it was never a question for her what she would do with her career. She considers it "luck" the way her career unfolded. While studying at Skidmore College, in Saratoga, New York, Ms. Lamuniere realized that Art History was the love of her life. She developed her style of painting by studying the great artists of the past, from their personal history to analyzing their styles. That love began her travels to France to study and to sell her work. Also Ms. Lamuniere's aunt and mother both painted. **Avocations:** Travel; Study of French **Political Affiliations:** Democrat **Religion:** Buddhist

Cristy Lane

Title: Country Singer **Industry:** Media & Entertainment **Date of Birth:** 01/08/1940 **Place of Birth:** Peoria **State/Country of Origin:** IL/USA **Marital Status:** Married **Spouse Name:** Leland Stoller (1959) **Creative Works:** Author, "One Day at a Time" (1985); Singer, "Lies on Your Lips" (1982); Singer, "I Have a Dream" (1981); Singer, "One Day at a Time" (1980); Singer, "Sweet Sexy Eyes" (1980); Singer, "Simple Little Word" (1979); Singer, "I'm Gonna Love You Anyway" (1978); Singer, "I Just Can't Stay Married to You" (1978); Singer, "Penny Arcade" (1978); Singer, "Tryin' to Forget About You" (1977); Singer, "Janie Took My Place"; Singer, "Let Me Down Easy"; Singer, "Shake Me I Rattle"; Album, "Cristy's Greatest Hits"; Album, "Ask Me to Dance"; Album, "Simple Little Worlds" **Marquis Who's Who Honors:** Albert Nelson Marquis Lifetime Achievement Award; Marquis Who's Who Top Professional **Why did you become involved in your profession or industry:** Ms. Lane became involved in her profession because she was shy. As a child, she had a music box. She first started singing at the Memphis church, which encouraged her when she received plenty of positive feedback. Later, when she was once again encouraged by her husband, she knew she had to pursue a career as a musician.

Edward "Beau" Lane

Title: Breeder, Trainer, Owner, Horseman **Industry:** Agriculture **Company Name:** Woodline Farm; Beau Lane Bloodstock **Date of Birth:** 03/11/1942 **Place of Birth:** Altavista **State/Country of Origin:** VA/USA **Marital Status:** Married **Spouse Name:** Gail McMichael (2008); Juliana Wright (Deceased) **Children:** Three Daughters **Career:** Breeder/Trainer/Racer/Owner/Horseman, Beau Lane Bloodstock (Over 50 Years) **Civic:** Past President, Quarter Races Order of Virginia **Awards:** National Champion, Appaloosa (1967) **To what do you attribute your success:** Mr. Lane attributes his success to hard work. When he moved to Kentucky they were basically broke. They had stayed in Virginia because he tried to get the race tracks in a position where they can succeed. He told his wife and daughter that they didn't have much money and his wife responded "The game is not over yet." **Why did you become involved in your profession or industry:** Mr. Lane was born in Altavista, Virginia, and his family owned a furniture company. They wanted him to join the company, but he was never interested in wood crafts; instead he loved horses. His parents then sent him off to military school for five years and he became a battalion commander. He received a scholarship to Virginia Tech for football but after a year, due to so many injuries, he had to stop. In search of something new to take the place of football, he moved to Wyoming and worked on a cattle ranch, where he had many great experiences. When he came back home, he married Juliana Wright, a woman who was a physical education teacher. He then joined his family's company, and shortly after bought a farm. **Avocations:** Horses **Thoughts on Life:** Mr. Lane had been married to the Juliana Wright for 45 years; he is now married to Gail McMichael. He has three daughters, one who has passed. Mr. Lane's motto is "When you are an anvil, bear - a hammer, strike."

Harris Lane

Title: President, Chief Executive Officer **Industry:** Media & Entertainment **Company Name:** Hank Lane Music and Productions **Education:** BA, Adelphi University (1992) **Career:** President, Chief Executive Officer, Hank Lane Music and Productions **Civic:** Youth America Grand Prix **To what do you attribute your success:** Mr. Lane attributes his success to his father Hank Lane, he thought him how to be successful in his profession. It is a lot of hard work, there is no nepotism. **Why did you become involved in your profession or industry:** Mr. Lane was inspired by the art of music. Not only performing but a part of people's most important days of their lives.

Joseph M. Lane, MD

Title: Professor of Orthopaedic Surgery **Industry:** Education/Educational Services **Company Name:** Hospital for Special Surgery **Date of Birth:** 10/27/1939 **Place of Birth:** New York **State/Country of Origin:** NY/USA **Parents:** Frederick Lane; Madelaine Lane **Marital Status:** Married **Spouse Name:** Barbara Greenhouse (06/23/1963) **Children:** Debra; Jennifer **Education:** MD, Harvard University, Cambridge, MA (1965); AB in Chemistry, Columbia University, New York, Magna Cum Laude (1961) **Certifications:** International Society for Clinical Densitometry (2001); Medical License, Connecticut (1990); Medical License, New York (1976); American Board of Orthopaedic Surgeons (1974); National Board of Medical Examiners **Career:** Assistant Dean, Medical Students, Weill Medical College of Cornell University and Affiliated Hospitals, New York (1997-Present); Professor of Orthopaedic Surgery, Weill Medical College of Cornell University, New York (1996-Present); Attending Orthopaedic Surgeon, Medical Director, Osteoporosis Prevention Center, Chief, Metabolic Bone Disease Service, Senior Scientist, Hospital for Special Surgery, New York (1996-Present); Director, Clinical Research Section, Hospital for Special Surgery, New York (1996-2003); Professor, Chairman, Orthopaedic Surgery, Department of Orthopaedic Surgery, University of California Los Angeles (1993-1996); Chairman, Institutional Review Board, Hospital for Special Surgery, New York (1990-1993); Associate Director, Multipurpose Arthritis Center, Hospital for Special Surgery, New York (1988-1993); Senior Scientist, Hospital for Special Surgery, New York (1984-1993); Professor of Orthopaedic Surgery, Cornell University Media College, New York (1984-1993); Chief, Bone Tumor Service, Memorial Sloan-Kettering Cancer Center, New York (1977-1991); Associate Professor of Orthopaedic Surgery, Cornell University Medical College, New York (1978-1984); Associate Clinical Professor Orthopaedic Surgery, Cornell University Medical College, New York (1976-1978); Chief Resident, Department of Orthopaedic Surgery, Hospital of the University of Pennsylvania (1972-1973); Research Associate, National Institute of Dental Research, National Institutes of Health, Bethesda, MD (1967-1969); Resident, Department of General Surgery, Hospital of the University of Pennsylvania (1966-1967); Straight Surgical Intern, Hospital of the University of Pennsylvania (1965-1966) **Career Related:** Associate Director, MultiPurpose Arthritis Center, New York, NY (1988-1993, 1996-Present); Visiting Professor, New Jersey College of Medicine & Dentistry, Newark, NJ (1978); Visiting Professor, Albert Einstein Medical College (1978); Visiting Professor, University of Pennsylvania (1976); Consultant, Genetics Institute, Andover, MA, Orquest, Mountain Side, CA, Exogen, Piscataway, NJ, VA Merit Grant Board; Visiting Professor, Numerous Colleges and Universities; Fellow, American Academy of Orthopaedic Surgeons **Military Service:** Surgeon, Research Associate, Laboratory of Biochemistry, National Institute of Dental Research, National Institutes of Health (1967-1969) **Creative Works:** Contributor, Numerous Articles to Professional Journals; Contributor, Numerous Presentations; Contributor, Book Reviews **Awards:** HSSS Life Achievement Award (2011); Excellence in Teaching Award, Weill Cornell Medical College (2005); Physician of the Year Award, CancerCare (2004); Best Scientific Presentation Award, Association of Bone and Joint Surgeons, Santa Fe, NM (1993); New York Mayoral Proclamation (1988); NIH Career Research Development Award (1977-1982); Butz Frame Development Award, University of Pennsylvania (1973-1976); Kappa Delta Award (1971); Charles Bjorkwall Prize, Columbia University (1961); Van AM Prize, Columbia University (1959) **Memberships:** President, Orthopaedic Research Society (1984-1985); President, Musculoskeletal Tumor Society (1982-1983); American Academy of Orthopaedic Surgeons; American Orthopaedic Association; American Society for Bone and Mineral Research; Medical Society of the State of New York; International Society for Fracture Repair; NIH Study Sections; FDA Orthopaedic Panel; New York State Osteoporosis and Education Program; American Rheumatism Association; Paget's Foundation; Bone Therapeutics; CollPlant, Inc.; Graftys; ON Foundation **Marquis Who's Who Honors:** Albert Nelson Marquis Lifetime Achievement Award; Marquis Who's Who Top Professional **Why did you become involved in your profession or industry:** Dr. Lane became involved in his profession because he sustained a clavicle fracture in a baseball game and the person who took care of him was ultimately taking care of the professional tennis association athletes. He amazed him with his skill and he wanted to be just like him.

Dennis H. Langer

Title: Pharmaceutical Company Executive, Board of Directors **Industry:** Pharmaceuticals **Date of Birth:** 09/08/1951 **Place of Birth:** New York **State/Country of Origin:** NY/USA **Parents:** Nathan Langer; Mira (Kenig) Langer **Marital Status:** Married **Spouse Name:** Susan F. Langer, MD (1/21/1980) **Children:** William; Thomas **Education:** JD, Harvard University, Cum Laude (1983); Intern, Resident, Chief Resident, Yale University School of Medicine, New Haven, CT (1975-1978); MD, Georgetown University (1975); BA, Columbia University (1971) **Certifications:** Diplomate, American Board of Psychiatry **Career:** Clinical Professor, Department of Psychiatry, Georgetown University School of Medicine, Washington, DC (2003-Present); Managing Partner, Phoenix IP Ventures, Philadelphia, PA (2005-2010); President, North America, Dr. Reddy's Laboratories (2004-2005); Senior Vice President, Project Management and Research and Development Strategy, Glaxo SmithKline, King of Prussia, PA (2000-2004); Senior Vice President, Product Development Strategy, Research and Development, SmithKline Beecham Pharmaceuticals (1999-2000); Senior Vice President, Research and Development, SmithKline Beecham Healthcare Services, Philadelphia, PA (1998-1999); Vice President, Health Management Services, SmithKline Beecham Pharmaceutical, Philadelphia, PA (1996-1998); Vice President, Business Strategy-U.S., SmithKline Beecham Pharmaceutical, Philadelphia, PA (1994-1996); President, Chief Executive Officer, Director, Neose Technologies Inc., Horsham, PA (1991-1994); Senior Director, Marketing, G.D. Searle and Co., Skokie, IL (1989-1991); Senior Group Product Director, G.D. Searle and Co., Skokie, IL (1988-1989); Senior Product Manager, Abbott Lab, North Chicago, IL (1987-1988); Product Manager, Abbott Lab, North Chicago, IL (1986-1987); Associate Medical Director, Abbott Laboratory, North Chicago, IL (1984-1986); Associate Clinical Investigator, Eli Lilly and Co., Indianapolis, IN (1983-1984); Instructor, Harvard Medical School, Boston, MA (1982-1983); Clinical Fellow, Harvard Medical School, Boston, MA (1980-1982); Clinical Associate, National Institute of Health, Bethesda, MD (1978-1980) **Career Related:** Clinical Clinical Professor, Georgetown University, School of Medicine (2003-Present); Associate Professor, University of Health Sciences, Chicago Medical School (1984-1991); Associate Professor, Indiana University School of Medicine, Indianapolis, IN (1983-1984); Consultant, Food and Drug Administration, Rockville (1980-1982) **Civic:** Director, Dicerna Pharmaceutical Inc. (2007-Present); Director, EnGene, Inc. (2015-Present); Director, Braeburn, Inc. (2015-Present); Deans Advisory Board, Harvard Law School (2010-Present); Emeritus, Columbia College, Columbia University (2008-Present); Board of Directors, Committee of Medical Center Affairs, Georgetown University (2007-Present); Director, Myriad Genetics, Inc. (2004-Present); Board, Visiting, Georgetwon University School of Medicine (1998-Present); Director, AdvanDx, Inc. (2012-2015); Director, Innocoll Holdings, PLC (2011-2014); Director, Myrexis Inc. (2009-2013); Director, Auxilium Pharms., Inc. (2007-2010); Director, Ception Therapeutics Inc. (2005-2010); Vice Chair, Columbia College, Columbia University (2005-2008); Director, Cytogen (2005-2008); Board of Regents, Georgetown University (2000-2010); Vice President, SmithKline Beecham Foundation (1996-2000); Vice President, Epilepsy Services, Northeast Illinois, IL (1986-1989); Board of Directors, Epilepsy Services, Northeast Illinois, IL (1985-1991); Board of Visitors, Columbia College, Columbia University **Military Service:** Surgeon, Lt. Commander, United States Public Health Service (1978-1980) **Creative Works:** Contributor, Articles, Professional Journals **Memberships:** Finance Committee, Whitehead Institute for Biomedical Research (2016) **Marquis Who's Who Honors:** Albert Nelson Marquis Lifetime Achievement Award **To what do you attribute your success:** Mr. Dennis has had many opportunities and lived in a very good time where's there's been a lot of progress and interest in healthcare. **Why did you become involved in your profession or industry:** Dr. Langer became involved in his profession because he wanted to make a difference and that's why he was attracted to health care. He thought his contribution and his calling would be in research and that's why he started his career in academics. While at NIH, he had exposure to the pharmaceutical industry as there was no biotech industry at that time so he recognized the big contribution to innovations of medicine that the companies were making. He thought that the type of things that he was interested in doing in drug development and development of products were ones that he could make a broader contribution towards than what he was doing in academia. He wanted to keep one foot in both camps, so that's what inspired him to go into industry.

Paul Anthony Lannie

Title: Executive Vice President, General Counsel **Industry:** Oil & Energy **Company Name:** Apache Corporation **Date of Birth:** 02/21/1954 **Place of Birth:** Hayti **State/Country of Origin:** MO/USA **Marital Status:** Married **Spouse Name:** Donna Dean (05/20/1977) **Children:** Heather; Anthony **Education:** JD, Vanderbilt University (1978); BA, Vanderbilt University, Magna Cum Laude (1974) **Career:** Executive Vice President, General Counsel, Apache Corporation, Houston, TX (2009-Present); Senior Vice President, General Counsel, Apache Corporation, Houston, TX (2004-2009); Vice President, General Counsel, Apache Corporation, Houston, TX (2003-2004); President, Kinder Morgan, Houston, TX (2000-2003); President, Coral Energy (1999); Senior Vice President, General Counsel, Coral Energy (1995-1999); Senior Vice President, General Counsel, Tejas Gas Corporation, Houston, TX (1994-1998); Vice President, General Counsel, Secretary, Baroid Corporation, Houston, TX (1991-1994); Executive Vice President, Greyhound Lines, Inc., Dallas, TX (1987-1991); Executive Vice President, GLI Holding Company, Dallas, TX (1987-1991); Executive Vice President, BusLease Inc., Dallas, TX (1983-1987); Associate, Johnson & Swanson, Dallas, TX (1978-1983) **Career Related:** Member, Law Committee, American Petroleum Institute **Civic:** Executive Member, Central Dallas Association (1990); Board of Directors, Dallas Industrial Development Corporation (1985-1987); Chairman, Missions Finance Subcommittee, The Woodlands UMC; Board of Directors, Foundation for Theological Education **Awards:** Best Corporate Counsel Awards, Houston Business Journal **Memberships:** The Order of the Coif; Phi Beta Kappa **Bar Admissions:** State Bar of Texas (1978) **Marquis Who's Who Honors:** Albert Nelson Marquis Lifetime Achievement Award; Marquis Who's Who Top Professional

Emma Jane Laskin

Title: Medical Doctor **Industry:** Medicine & Health Care **Company Name:** Emma Laskin, MD, PLLC **Children:** Son **Education:** Fellowship in General Psychiatry, and Child and Adolescent Psychiatry (2004); Residency in General Psychiatry, Zucker Hillside Hospital; Internship, Long Island Jewish Medical Center; MD, Cornell Medical School (1999); Post-Baccalaureate Pre-Medical Degree Program; Harvard University; Undergraduate Degree in Art History, Harvard University, Magna Cum Laude **Career:** Emma Laskin PLLC, Private Practice, (2012-Present); Psychiatric Director, Eating Disorders Center, North Shore-LIJ Health System (2008–2012) **Awards:** Patients' Choice 5th Anniversary Award, Vitals (2012); Compassionate Doctor Recognition, Vitals (2010, 2012); Patients' Choice Award, Vitals (2008-2012) **Marquis Who's Who Honors:** Albert Nelson Marquis Lifetime Achievement Award; Marquis Who's Who Top Professional **To what do you attribute your success:** Dr. Laskin attributes her success to her education, being very approachable, friendly and trustworthy and go the extra mile for her patients. **Why did you become involved in your profession or industry:** Dr. Laskin became involved in her profession because her mother is a psychoanalyst. Initially, Dr. Laskin wanted to become a pediatrician, but found that she didn't like the area. When she was completing her medical rotation, a patient who had been diagnosed with cancer intrigued her due to her need for a consultation liaison and psychologist. She enjoys talking to her patients and learning all about them and their history. **Avocations:** Oil painting-still life; Daily painting

Kaye D. Lathrop, PhD

Title: Nuclear Scientist, Educator **Industry:** Sciences **Date of Birth:** 10/08/1932 **Parents:** Arthur Quay; Helen Venita (Hoos) L **Marital Status:** Married **Spouse Name:** Judith Marie Green (6/11/1957) **Children:** Braxton Landess; Scottfield Michael **Education:** Doctor of Philosophy, California Institute of Technology (1962); Master of Science, California Institute of Technology (1959); Bachelor of Science, U.S. Military Academy (1955) **Career:** Professor Emeritus, Stanford University (1994-Present); Associate Lab Director, Professor of Applied Research, Stanford Linear Accelerator Center, Stanford University (1984-1994); Associate Director of Engineering Sciences, Los Alamos Science Laboratory (1979-1984); Division Leader, Computer Science and Services Division, Los Alamos Science Laboratory (1978-1979); Alternate Division Leader, Energy Division, Los Alamos Science Laboratory (1977-1978); Associate Division Leader, Reactor Safeguards and Reactor Safety and Technology Division, Los Alamos Science Laboratory (1975-1977); Assistant Division Leader, Theoretical Division, Los Alamos Science Laboratory (1973-1975); Group Leader, Transport Theory, Los Alamos Science Laboratory (1972-1975); Member Staff, Los Alamos Science Laboratory (1968-1972); Group Leader, Methods Development, General Atomic Co., San Diego, CA (1967-1968); Staff Member, Los Alamos Science Laboratory (1962-1967) **Career Related:** Weapons Program Review Committee, Los Alamos National Laboratory (2002-2004); Burn Code Review Panel, Department of Energy, Los Alamos National Laboratory (2000-2004); Review Committee on Applied Physics Division, Los Alamos National Laboratory (1997-2005); Membership Policy Committee, National Academy of Engineering (1997-1999); Presidential Nominating Committee, National Academy of Engineering (1996-1997); Member, University of California President's Council On National Laboratories (1995-1999); Chair, Review Committee on Technology and Safety Assessment Division, Los Alamos National Laboratory (1994-1997); Committee On Membership, National Academy of Engineering (1994-1997); Chair, Electric Power/Energy System Engineering Peer Committee, National Academy of Engineering (1994); Electric Power/Energy System Engineering Peer Committee, National Academy of Engineering (1992-1994); Advisory Committee, Nuclear Technology and Engineering Division, Los Alamos Science Laboratory (1988-1993); Steering Committee, Joint MIT-Idaho National Engineering Laboratory Research Program (1985-1989); Member, Engineering National Advisory Committee, University of Michigan (1983-1992); Management Advisory Committee, Y-12 Division Union Carbide Corp (1979-1982); Reactor Physics Visiting Committee, Argonne National Laboratory (1978-1983); Advisory Committee, Reactor Physics Energy Research and Development Administration (1973-1977); Guest Lecturer, International Atomic Energy Agency (1969); Adjunct Professor, University of New Mexico (1966-1967); Visiting Professor, University of New Mexico (1964-1965) **Military Service:** First Lieutenant, U.S. Army (1955-1958) **Creative Works:** Member, Editorial Advisory Board, Progress in Nuclear Energy (1983-1985); Author, Reports, Papers, Chapters to Books **Awards:** Distinguished Service Award, Los Alamos National Laboratory (1984); Outstanding Performance Award, American Nuclear Society (1980); E.O. Lawrence Memorial Award, Energy Research and Development Administration (1976); R.C. Baker Foundation Fellow (1961-1962); Special Fellow, Atomic Energy Commission (1958-1961) **Memberships:** Police Committee Member, National Academy of Engineering (1997-1999); Presidential Nominating Committee, National Academy of Engineering (1996-1997); National Director, American Nuclear Society (1979-1982); Treasurer, American Nuclear Society (1977-1979); National Director, American Nuclear Society (1973-1976); Chairperson, Mathematics and Computation Division, American Nuclear Society (1970-1971); American Physical Society **Marquis Who's Who Honors:** Albert Nelson Marquis Lifetime Achievement Award **Why did you become involved in your profession or industry:** Mr. Lathrop became involved in his profession because he was intrigued by it and he actually hoped that nuclear energy could provide abundant cheap energy for this country and save the country from being dependent on other sources. **Avocations:** Wrestling referee; Bicycling **Political Affiliations:** Independent **Religion:** Episcopalian

Steven Lattimore, PhD

Title: Classicist (Retired) **Industry:** Education/Educational Services **Company Name:** University of California **Date of Birth:** 5/25/1938 **Place of Birth:** Bryn Mawr **State/Country of Origin:** PA/USA **Parents:** Richmond Lattimore; Alice Bockstahler Lattimore **Marital Status:** Divorced **Spouse Name:** Deborah Lee Nourse (7/14/1976, Divorced 7/1994) **Children:** Judith; Nicholas; Isabel **Education:** PhD, Princeton University (1968); MA, Princeton University (1964); BA, Dartmouth College (1960) **Career:** Professor Emeritus, University of California Los Angeles (2005-Present); Professor, University of California Los Angeles (1998-2005); Associate Professor, University of California Los Angeles (1974-1998); Assistant Professor, University of California Los Angeles (1967-1974); Assistant Professor, Intercollegiate Center for Classical Studies, Rome, Italy (1966-1967); Instructor, Haverford College, Haverford, PA (1965-1966); Instructor, Dartmouth College, Hanover, NH (1964) **Career Related:** Fellow, John Simon Guggenheim Memorial Foundation (1975-1976) **Civic:** Program Director, Organizing Public Forums, League of Women Voters, Ventura County, California (2007-Present); Active Volunteer, Board Member, League of Women Voters, Ventura County, California **Creative Works:** Translator, "Thucydides, Peloponnesian War" (1998); Author, "Isthmia Marble Sculpture" (1996); Author, "Isthmia Marble Sculpture" (1967-1980); Author, "Marine Thiasos in Greek Sculpture" (1976) **Memberships:** Elected Member, German Archaeological Institute **Marquis Who's Who Honors:** Albert Nelson Marquis Lifetime Achievement Award; Marquis Who's Who Humanitarian Award **To what do you attribute your success:** The key to Dr. Lattimore's success was being well-rounded in many fields of study. He had many specialties. **Why did you become involved in your profession or industry:** Dr. Lattimore was inspired by his father. They were very close. When he was almost 14, his father received a fellowship and took his whole family to Greece. When he became a scholar himself, he respected his father even more and had more in common with him. Additionally, he had great teachers and fellow students. **Avocations:** Travel; Hiking **Political Affiliations:** Democrat **Religion:** Unitarian Universalist **Thoughts on Life:** Dr. Lattimore has been a board member for the League of Women Voters in Ventura County, California, for more than 10 years. He serves as the program director, where he takes the lead in organizing public forums on important topics to educate public voters.

Vincent W. Lau, JD

Title: Immigration Attorney **Industry:** Law and Legal Services **Company Name:** Clark Lau LLC **Date of Birth:** 02/27/1993 **Place of Birth:** Statesville **State/Country of Origin:** NC/USA **Education:** JD, Boston College Law School, Newton, MA (1997); MA, Higher Education Administration, Graduate School of Education, Boston College, Chestnut Hill, MA (1997); BA, Political Science, Yale University, Cum Laude (1993) **Certifications:** Diplomate, American Board of Ophthalmology **Career:** Managing Partner, Clark Lau LLC, Cambridge, MA (2012-Present); Adjunct Faculty, New England Law Boston, Boston, MA (2012-Present); Senior Associate, Flynn & Clark, Professional Corporation, Cambridge, MA (1999-2012); Associate, Fletcher, Tilton & Whipple, Professional Corporation, Worcester, MA (1998-1999); Assistant, Office of the General Counsel, Yale University, New Haven, CT (1997-1998); Law Clerk, Office of the General Counsel, Harvard University, Cambridge, MA (1997); Managing Editor, Boston College International & Comparative Law Review (1996-1997); Staff Writer, Boston College International & Comparative Law Review (1995-1996); Legal Assistant, Fallon, Bixby & Cheng, San Francisco, CA (1993-1994) **Career Related:** Vice Chair, American Immigration Lawyers Association (2017-Present); Liaison, U.S. Department of Labor, American Immigration Lawyers Association (2012-Present); Adjunct Faculty, New England Law (2012-2017) **Civic:** Board of Directors, Kendall Square Association, Cambridge, MA; Youth Counselor, Church **Creative Works:** Updating Author, "Anatomy of ETA Form 9089: An Item-by-Item Dissection," AILA's Guide to PERM Labor Certification, AILA Publications (2016-Present); Co-Author, "Chapter 5: H-1B Specialty Workers," Immigration Practice Manual, MCLE, Inc. (2004-Present); Panelist, "U.S. Department of Labor Compliance: More than Just LCAs," AILA Employer Compliance and Worksite Enforcement Conference (2018); Panelist, "PERM BALCA and FAQ Review," AILA Annual Conference on Immigration Law (2018); Panelist, "PERM Under the Trump Administration," AILA New England Immigration Conference (2018); Contributing Editor, AILA's Guide to PERM Labor Certification, AILA Publications (2016); Updating Author, "Adjustment of Status for Beginning Practitioners," Navigating the Fundamentals of Immigration Law, AILA Publications (2008-2009); Co-Editor, Advanced Immigration Practice: Agency Updates and Expert Strategy, Handbook for Sixth Annual AILA New England Law Symposium (2009); Co-Editor, Advanced Immigration Strategies, Handbook for Fifth Annual AILA New England Immigration Law Symposium (2008); Author, "From H-1B and Beyond: Exploring Nonimmigrant Options for Professionals Faced with the Limitations of H-1Bs," MCLE Immigration Law Conference (2005); Associate Editor, Advanced Immigration Options for Small Businesses and Entrepreneurs, AILA New England Chapter CLE Conference Handbook (2004); Co-Author, "Obtaining an O-1 for a Physician," Immigration Options for Physicians, 2nd Edition, AILA (2004); Co-Author, "Whose Organization is This? Institutional Liability for Student Organizations," National Association Of College And University Attorneys Annual Conference (1998); Author, "Anticipating Changes to the Form I-9 Employment Verification Process: Interim Rules and Proposed Changes," Boston Bar Association Labor & Employment Section Newsletter (1998); Author, "Post-1997 Hong Kong: Will Sufficient Educational Autonomy Remain to Safeguard Academic Freedom" (1997) **Memberships:** Board of Directors, Alumni Association, Boston College Law School (2017-Present); Board of Directors, Kendall Square Association (2016-Present); Liaison Committee, National Department of Labor, American Immigration Lawyers Association (2013-Present); PERM Conference Planning Committee, American Immigration Lawyers Association (2015, 2017); Executive Board, New England Chapter, American Immigration Lawyers Association (2009-2013); Annual Conference Planning Committee, American Immigration Lawyers Association (2011-2012); Director, Asian American Lawyers Association of Massachusetts (2006-2010); Co-chair, Community Service Committee, Asian American Lawyers Association of Massachusetts (2006-2010); Teleconference Committee, American Immigration Lawyers Association (2006-2007); Co-Chair, Ethics Committee, American Immigration Lawyers Association (2003-2004); Co-Chair, Young Lawyers' Division, American Immigration Lawyers Association (2002-2003); Board of Directors, Kendall Square Association; Director, American Immigration Lawyers Association; Rome District Chapter, American Immigration Lawyers Association **Bar Admissions:** Federal District Court of Massachusetts (1999); Massachusetts (1997) **Marquis Who's Who Honors:** Albert Nelson Marquis Lifetime Achievement Award; Marquis Who's Who Top Professional **Why did you become involved in your profession or industry:** Mr. Lau became involved in immigration law through the first job he ever had as an immigration paralegal. This position opened his eyes to a world of opportunities. **Avocations:** Running

Richard Robert Laurence

Title: History Educator **Industry:** Education/Educational Services **Company Name:** Michigan State University **Date of Birth:** 04/22/1937 **Place of Birth:** Knoxville **State/Country of Origin:** TN/USA **Parents:** Robert A. Laurence; Sally (Claxton) Laurence **Marital Status:** Married **Spouse Name:** Patricia Joan Wolthuis Laurence (05/28/2005); Gertraud Fuehrer Laurence (07/06/1961) **Children:** Daniel Robert; Sonya Christina; Alfred James **Education:** PhD, Stanford University (1968); MA, Stanford University (1962); Postgraduate Coursework, Middlebury College (1959); BA, University of Tennessee (1959) **Career:** Professor Emeritus, Department of History, Michigan State University (2007-Present); Professor, Department of History, Michigan State University (1989-2007); Associate Chairman, Department of Humanities, Michigan State University (1988-1989); Assistant Chairman, Department of Humanities, Michigan State University (1985-1988); Professor, Department of Humanities, Michigan State University (1982-1989); Associate Professor, Department of Humanities, Michigan State University (1976-1982); Assistant Professor, Department of Humanities, Michigan State University (1968-1976); Instructor, Department of Humanities, Michigan State University (1966-1968) **Career Related:** Teaching Assistant, Department of Humanities, Stanford University (1963-1964, 1965-1966) **Creative Works:** Co-Author, "Austrian History Yearbook" (1992); Co-Author, "Focus on Vienna" (1982, 1990); Co-Author, "Peace and Change" (1989); Co-Author, "Biographical Dictionary of Modern Peace Leaders" (1985); Co-Author, "Biographical Dictionary of Internationalists" (1983); Co-Author, "Michigan Academician" (1980); Co-Author, "Doves and Diplomats" (1978) **Awards:** Grantee, National Endowment of the Humanities (1979, 1990); Dissertation Fellowships (1964-1965); Woodrow Wilson Fellowship, Stanford University (1960-1963); Fulbright Scholar, University of Vienna (1959-1960); Fellow, Woodrow Wilson; Fellow, Stanford University; Austrian Government Research Fellow **Memberships:** Council, Society Study of Internationalism (1988-Present); American Historical Association; Council, Peace Research in History; Michigan Academy of Science; German Studies Association **Marquis Who's Who Honors:** Albert Nelson Marquis Lifetime Achievement Award **Why did you become involved in your profession or industry:** Dr. Laurence became involved in his profession after deciding against going into medicine. He decided to major in history and found his passion in German history. When he entered his senior year, he decided to attend graduate school for education instead of medical school, as he had initially intended. **Avocations:** Ornithology; Photography; Choral singing; Hiking; Gardening **Political Affiliations:** Independent **Religion:** Interfaith

Richard S. Lauter, JD

Title: Partner **Industry:** Law and Legal Services **Company Name:** Lewis Brisbois Bisgaard & Smith LLP **Date of Birth:** 10/04/1951 **Place of Birth:** Chicago **State/Country of Origin:** IL/USA **Parents:** Emil J. Lauter; Frances M. (Steinborn) Lauter **Education:** MSW in Clinical and Medical Social Work, Loyola University Chicago (2018); JD, Northern Illinois University College of Law (1981); BA in Political Science and Government, University of Kansas (1975) **Career:** Partner, Lewis Brisbois Bisgaard & Smith LLP (2015-Present); Equity Partner, Practice Group Leader, Freeborn & Peters LLP (2008-2015); Partner, McBride, Baker & Coles, Chicago, IL (1995-1996); Partner, Lauter & Associates, Ltd., Chicago, IL (1991-1995); Director of Economic Development, Chicago United (1990-1991); Associate Attorney, Schwartz, Cooper, Kolb & Gaynor, Chicago, IL (1987-1990); Associate Attorney, Stinson, Mag & Fizzell, Kansas City, MO (1986-1987); Associate Attorney, Mayer, Brown & Platt, Chicago, IL (1983-1986); Law Clerk, Hon. Richard L. Merrick, U.S. Bankruptcy Court, Illinois (1981-1982); Partner, Holland & Knight **Career Related:** Visiting Professor, University of Tsukuba, Tokyo, Japan **Civic:** Board of Directors, American Bankruptcy Institute (2015-Present); Sponsorship Chair, Advisory Board, Central States Regional Conference, American Bankruptcy Institute (2006-Present); Transition Chair, Advisory Board, Central States Regional Conference, American Bankruptcy Institute (2006-Present); Co-Chair, Commercial Fraud Committee, American Bankruptcy Institute (2012-2015); President and Trustee, Business and Professional Association, Chicago Symphony Orchestra (1990-1991); Volunteer, Catholic Charities of the Archdiocese of Chicago **Creative Works:** Author, "U.S. Trustee Program: Is Reduced Discretion the Better Part of Valor?", ABI Journal (2013); Co-Author, "Universal Building Products: Has the Pendulum Swung Too Far," ABI Journal (2011); Co-Author, "Commercial Fraud Manual," Fraud Task Force, American Bankruptcy Institute (2010); Author, "Privacy Concerns and Safeguards in the Governmental Dissemination of Bankruptcy Data on the Internet," ABI Journal **Awards:** Band 4, Chambers USA (2016); Illinois Leading Lawyers for Bankruptcy, Chambers USA (2015); Turnaround Atlas Award, Chapter 11 Reorganization Deal of the Year, Small Mid Markets (2014); America's Leading Lawyers for Business-Bankruptcy/Restructuring Practices, Chambers USA (2010-2011) **Memberships:** American Bankruptcy Institute; Turnaround Management Association **Bar Admissions:** State of Illinois (1981); State of Missouri (1975); U.S. District Court for the Northern District of Illinois; U.S. District Court for the Western District of Missouri; U.S. Bankruptcy Court, District of Colorado; U.S. Bankruptcy Court, Northern District, State of Illinois; U.S. Bankruptcy Court, Eastern District, State of Michigan; U.S. Bankruptcy Court, Western District, State of Missouri; U.S. Bankruptcy Court, Eastern District, State of Wisconsin; U.S. Court of Appeals for the Seventh Circuit **Marquis Who's Who Honors:** Marquis Who's Who Top Professional **Why did you become involved in your profession or industry:** Mr. Lauter became involved in his profession because of a senior lawyer at a very large Chicago-based law firm who took him under his wing. This was right after the bankruptcy code was amended in 1978, so it seemed there was a great future in restructuring and bankruptcy. His family, particularly his father and grandfather, also encouraged him to pursue the field, so he did. Over the next 40 years, he has had the opportunity to meet and work with some really great lawyers on a lot of interesting matters. Recently, however, Mr. Lauter has begun to focus on another area of interest: mental health. **Avocations:** Classical music

Betsy Lawer

Title: Banker; Small Business Owner; Vintner; Director **Date of Birth:** 07/27/1949 **Place of Birth:** Anchorage **State/Country of Origin:** AK/USA **Parents:** Daniel H. Cuddy; Betti P. Cuddy **Marital Status:** Married **Spouse Name:** David A. Lawer (06/09/1972) **Children:** One Child **Education:** BA in Economics, Duke University (1971) **Career:** President, Lawer Family Vineyard Properties, Inc. (Lawer Estates) (2005-Present); President, Lawer Family Winery Inc. (Lawer Estates) (2005-Present); Chair, Chief Executive Officer Board, First National Bank Alaska (1974) **Career Related:** Chair, Board of Directors, First National Bank Alaska (2015-Present); Member, Smithsonian National Board (2008-Present); President's Community Panel Member, Alyeska Pipeline Service Company (2001-Present); Commonwealth North (1985-Present); First National Bank Alaska (1982-Present); Director Emeritus, Providence Health Care Foundation, Providence Health & Services (2001); Board of Directors, Member, Audit Committee, Federal Reserve Bank of San Francisco, Seattle, WA (1997-2003); Board Member, Smithsonian Institution Traveling Exhibition; Board Member, Twelfth District Federal Reserve, Federal Reserve Bank of San Francisco, Seattle, WA; Advisory Board Member, Providence Hospital, Providence Health & Services **Civic:** YWCA **Creative Works:** Featured, Cover/Feature Story, Alaska Business Monthly (1999) **Awards:** Inductee, Alaska Women's Hall of Fame (2019); Named, Junior Achievement Alaska Business Hall of Fame Laureate (2007); Named, One of 25 Women to Watch, US Banker (2003); Athena Award, Anchorage ATHENA Society (2001); Named, Top 25 Most Powerful Alaskans, Alaska Journal of Commerce (1999-2003); Women Helping Women Award, Soroptimist International (1998); Commendation, Alaska State Legislature (1997); Women of Achievement Award, YWCA (1991); Named, Outstanding Young Woman of America (1982); Three-time Recipient, Alaskan State Legislative Certificates **Memberships:** Smithsonian National Board, Smithsonian Institution; Anchorage ATHENA Society **Marquis Who's Who Honors:** Albert Nelson Marquis Lifetime Achievement Award **Why did you become involved in your profession or industry:** Mrs. Lawer enjoys business because for whatever position she takes on, she has the opportunity to come to work everyday to set up the community, customers and employees for success. **Avocations:** Managing winery and vineyard businesses

Pat Lawson, ND, CNHP, CCN, CRR

Title: President **Industry:** Medicine & Health Care **Company Name:** Dr. Pat Integrative Health **Date of Birth:** 09/28/1939 **Place of Birth:** Clarksburg **State/Country of Origin:** MD/USA **Parents:** Roland Emanuel (Deceased 1955) and Eva Marie Hardy (Deceased) **Marital Status:** Widow **Spouse Name:** Kenneth Lawson **Children:** Theresa Halsey; Tamara Lawson; Kevin Lawson; Kris Lawson; Keith Lawson **Education:** Coursework, Washington School of Natural Medicine (2000-2003); Coursework, Trinity College of Natural Health; Attended, Gaithersburg High School **Certifications:** Herbology; Certified as a Clinical Nutritionist **Career:** President, Owner, Dr. Pat's Integrative Health Services (1972-Present); Instructor, International Institute of Reflexology (1972-Present); Professor, Advanced Integrative Medical Institute (1998-2003) **Creative Works:** Created YouTube Channel; Created Radio Show, "Health and Nutrition," Rhode Island; Created TV Show, Roanoke, VA; Created Fashion Show, Maryland; Wrote, Local Town Column, Newspaper "Around our Town"; Contributor, Articles to Magazines **Awards:** Featured, Cover of Health Magazine **Marquis Who's Who Honors:** Marquis Who's Who Top Professional **To what do you attribute your success:** Ms. Lawson attributes her success to a desire to help both her family and herself. **Why did you become involved in your profession or industry:** Ms. Lawson first became involved in her profession due to the loss of her parents while she came of age. Though she initially found success as a model in the fashion industry, she decided to enter the field of natural remedies out of concern for her own declining health.

Jack E. Leaman, FASLA, FAICP

Title: Landscape Architect, Community and Regional Planner **Industry:** Architecture & Construction **Date of Birth:** 01/24/1932 **Place of Birth:** Mason City **State/Country of Origin:** IA/USA **Parents:** Theodore R Leaman; Dorothy M. (Schrum) Leaman **Marital Status:** Widowed **Spouse Name:** Darlene A. McNary (06/15/1952, Deceased) **Children:** Jeffrey A.; Danna J.; Jay M.; Duree K. **Education:** Master's Degree in Community and Regional Planning, Iowa State University (1982); BS in Landscape Architecture and Urban Planning, Iowa State University (1954) **Certifications:** Registered Landscape Architect, States of California, Iowa, Minnesota, New Mexico **Career:** Private Consultant, Community and Regional Planning, Landscape Architect, Mason City, IA (1995-Present); Retired (1996); Associate Partner, Landscape Architect, Community and Regional Planner, Yaggy Colby Associates, Mason City, IA (1992-1995); Adjunct Professor, Department of Community and Regional Planning, College of Design, Iowa State University, Ames (1990- 1995); Landscape Architect, Planning Consultant, Private Practice, Mason City, IA (1990-1992); Planning Director, City of Colorado Springs, Colorado (1986-1990); Planning Director, City-County Planning, Albuquerque, NM (1982-1986); Landscape Architect, Planning Consultant, RCM Associates, Inc., Hopkins, MN (1978-1982); Landscape Architect, Planning Consultant, RCM Associates, Inc., Ames, IA (1978-1982); Landscape Architect, Planning Consultant, Sheffler, Leaman, Rova, Mason City, IA (1976-1978); Landscape Architect, Planning Consultant, Hansen, Lind, Meyer, Iowa City, IA (1974-1976); Landscape Architect, Planning Consultant, Midwest Research Institute, Kansas City, MO (1972-1974); Planning Director, City of Mason City, IA (1966-1972); Planning Director, City of Santa Barbara, CA (1963-1966); Planning Consultant, Engineering Planners, Santa Barbara, CA (1960-1963); Planning Technician, Santa Barbara County, California (1958-1960); Landscape Architect, Price Tower, Residence with Architect Frank Lloyd Wright, Bartlesville, OK (1957-1958); Landscape Architect, Phillips Petroleum Company, Bartlesville, OK (1955-1958); Landscape Architect, Sam L. Huddleston Office, Denver, CO (1954-1955) **Awards:** Design Achievement Award, College of Design, Iowa State University (1988); Residential Landscape Design Award, California Landscape Contractors Association (1962); Award of Excellence, American Society of Landscape Artists (1954); Award for Service Above Self from the Mason City Noon Rotary Club **Memberships:** President, Mason City Downtown Development (1992); Fellow American Society of Lansdscape Architects (1995); Fellow, American Institute of Certified Planners (1992); Iowa Chapter President, American Society of Landscape Architects (1990-1991); Trustee, New Mexico, American Society of Landscape Artists (1982-1986); Trustee, Iowa, American Society of Landscape Artists (1980-1982); Chapter President, Iowa Planning Association (1969-1970); Chapter President, American Society of Landscape Architects (1967-1968); Urban Land Institute; Tau Sigma Delta **Marquis Who's Who Honors:** Albert Nelson Marquis Lifetime Achievement Award **To what do you attribute your success:** Mr. Leaman was encouraged by his parents to do his best at whatever he set his mind to; this mindset has remained with him throughout his entire life. **Why did you become involved in your profession or industry:** Mr. Leaman became interested in design and planning programs in high school. He was inspired by an art teacher who took an interest in his potential. **Thoughts on Life:** Mr. Leaman emphasizing living life by doing your best at whatever you choose to do.

Paul Leblang, PhD

Title: Marketing Professional **Industry:** Advertising & Marketing **Date of Birth:** 02/05/1928 **Place of Birth:** New York **State/Country of Origin:** NY/USA **Parents:** Leon Charles Leventhal; Dorethy Leblang **Marital Status:** Married **Spouse Name:** Joan Barbara Korengold (11/19/1950) **Children:** Mark J. (Deceased); David B. (Deceased); Ellen Leblang Petrocci **Education:** PhD, New York University (1962); MBA, New York University (1957); BA, University of Minnesota (1949) **Career:** Individual Consultant (1991-1996); Senior Vice President, Director of Marketing, Saks Fifth Avenue (1975-1990); Vice President, Sales Promotion Director, G. Fox, Hartford, CT (1965-1975); Advertising Director, Abercrombie & Fitch, New York, NY (1963-1964); Advertising Manager, Gimbel Brothers, New York, NY (1950-1965) **Career Related:** Adjunct Professor, Fashion Institute of Technology (1957-1961); Vice-President, Board of Directors, Retail Adverstising Conference; Guest Speaker in Field **Military Service:** U.S. Army (1952-1954) **Awards:** Edward Mayer, Jr. Award, Direct Marketing Association (1993); Silver Medal, National Retail Merchants Association **Memberships:** Board of Directors, Retail Targeting Market Systems (1991-1995); Board of Directors, Direct Marketing Educational Foundation (1988-1990); Board of Directors, Direct Marketing Association (1981-1987); Advisory Board, Laboratory Institute of Merchandising (1978-1990); Advisory Board, Laboratory Institute of Merchandising (1978-1990) **Marquis Who's Who Honors:** Albert Nelson Marquis Lifetime Achievement Award **Why did you become involved in your profession or industry:** Mr. Leblang always wanted to be a research chemist, but starting out in that direction he figured in order to be successful in the field, he would need to pursue his PhD. To him it didn't seem like the right fit. He changed his career path and began working with an advertising agency, that was advertised in The New York Times. The agency was looking for an advertising manager with a science background, and Mr. Leblang became the perfect fit.

David J. Leciston

Title: Computer Engineer, Computer Scientist **Industry:** Engineering **Company Name:** U.S. Army **Date of Birth:** 12/25/1958 **Place of Birth:** Passaic **State/Country of Origin:** NJ/USA **Parents:** Alex Leciston; Rose (Kozmoski) Leciston **Marital Status:** Married **Spouse Name:** Deborah Ann Owens Leciston (12/30/1999); Wendie Sue Orr (02/03/1987, Divorced 10/1998); Diane Carol Hirth (06/19/1981, Divorced 04/1985) **Children:** Jennifer Ann; David Johnson; Mary Rose **Education:** BS in Computer Science, Seton Hall University (1982) **Career:** Program Executive Officer, Intelligence and Electronic Ware and Sensors, Project Manager, Distributed Common Ground System, U.S. Army (2005-Present); Computer Engineer, U.S. Army (2005-Present); Computer Engineer Software Engineering Center, U.S. Army, Fort Monmouth, NJ (2001-2005) **Military Service:** First Lieutenant, U.S. Army (1983-1987) **Awards:** Secretary of the Army Award for Outstanding Achievement in Materiel Acquisition (1997); Secretary of the Army Award for Outstanding Achievement in Materiel Acquisition (1991); Team Awards **Memberships:** Initiative on Software Engineering as a Profession (1994-Present); Life Member, AFCEA International (1987); Life and Senior Member, Association of Computing Machinery (1984); IEEE (1983-1987); Life Member, National Geographic **Avocations:** Fishing; Camping; Hiking; Computers; Tabletop war games; Tabletop role-play games **Religion:** Ukrainian Catholic

Susan J. Leclair, PhD, CLS (NCA)

Title: Chancellor Professor Emerita **Industry:** Education/Educational Services **Company Name:** University Massachusetts, Dartmouth **Date of Birth:** 02/17/1947 **Place of Birth:** New Bedford **State/Country of Origin:** MA/USA **Parents:** Joseph A. Leclair; Beatrice (Perry) Leclair **Marital Status:** Married **Spouse Name:** James T. Griffith, PhD, CLS (NCA) **Children:** Kimberly A. **Education:** PhD in Clinical Hematology, Walden University (2001); MS in Medical Laboratory Science, University of Massachusetts (1977); BS in Medical Technology, Stonehill College (1968) **Certifications:** Certified Clinical Laboratory Scientist; Certified Medical Technologist **Career:** Chancellor Professor Emerita, University of Massachusetts, Dartmouth (2015-Present); Professor, Medical Laboratory Science, University of Massachusetts, Dartmouth (1992-2015); Chancellor Professor, University of Massachusetts (2002); Associate Professor, Medical Laboratory Science, University of Massachusetts, Dartmouth (1984-1992); Assistant Professor, Medical Laboratory Science, University of Massachusetts, Dartmouth (1980-1984); Hematology Technologist, Rhode Island Hospital, Providence, RI (1979-1980); Education Coordinator, Program Director, School of Medical Technology, Miriam Hospital, Providence, RI (1972-1979); Supervisor Hematology, Morton Hospital, Taunton, MA (1970-1972); Medical Technologist, Union Hospital, New Bedford, MA (1968-1970) **Career Related:** Board of Directors, American Society of Clinical Laboratory Science (2010-Present); Consultant, Proficiency Testing, American College Of Physicians: Internal Medicine (2010-Present); President, Faculty Senate (1993-2002); Chair, Hematology/Hemostasis Committee, National Certified Agency For Medical Laboratory Personnel Exam Council (1994-1998); ASCLS Competence Assurance Council Advisory Committee (1983-1987); Chairperson, ASCLS Education & Research Fund, Inc. (1983-1985); Instructor, Hematology Courses, Brown University, Providence, RI (1978-1980) **Civic:** Reviewer, National Commission of Clinical Laboratory Sciences (1986-1989); Board of Directors, Southeastern Massachusetts Health Planning Development Inc. (1975-1988); Chairperson, Massachusetts Association of Health Planning Agencies (1986-1987); Numerous Other Offices And Committees; Planning Subcommittee, AIDS Education **Creative Works:** Creator, Director, Consumer Information Web Page (2000-Present); Editor-In-Chief, Clinical Laboratory Science (2000-2008, 2013-2017); Contributor, Articles, Professional Journals; Contributor, Articles to Journals, Chapters to Books; Author, Computer Software In Hematology **Awards:** Hero of Medicine Award, International Myeloproliferative Neoplasms Foundation, Cure Magazine (2017); Lifetime Achievement Award, American Society for Medical Laboratory Science (2015); Three-Time Recipient, Robin H. Mendleson Award, ASCLS Education & Research Fund, Inc. **Memberships:** Creator, Director, Consumer Information Web Page, American Society of Clinical Laboratory Science (1999-Present); Editor-In-Chief, CLS Journal, American Society of Clinical Laboratory Science (2001-2008); Editor, Clinical Practice Section, CLS Journal, American Society of Clinical Laboratory Science (1996-2000); President, Alpha Mu Tau (1993-1994); Chair, American Society of Medical Technology Education and Research Fund, Inc. (1983-1985); President, Massachusetts Association For Medical Technology (1977-1978); President, Southeastern Massachusetts Society of Medical Technology (1975-1976) **Marquis Who's Who Honors:** Albert Nelson Marquis Lifetime Achievement Award; Marquis Who's Who Top Professional **Avocations:** Choral singing; Cooking; Reading

Anne Lim Lee

Title: Chief, Cyber Architecture & Multi-Domain Command and Control Operations Lead **Industry:** Information Technology and Services **Parents:** Chin Yuan Lee; Chi Hing Lee **Marital Status:** Married **Spouse Name:** Dr. Alexander Lam **Education:** Master's Degree in Military Strategic Leadership and National Security Studies, Air War College, Montgomery, AL (2018); PhD in Management, Walden University, Minneapolis, MN (2017); MS in Engineering, California Institute of Technology, Pasadena, CA (2006); MSEE, California State Polytechnic University, Pomona, CA (2004); BSEE in Computer Engineering, California State Polytechnic University, Pomona, CA (2003) **Certifications:** Certified in Level III Systems Engineering and Level II Program Management, Defense Acquisition University, Fort Belvoir, VA (2016); Certified in Defense Cybersecurity and Risk Management Framework, DoD CIO, Pentagon, Arlington, VA (2014); Certified in Engineering and Technical Management, California Institute of Technology, Pasadena, CA (2006) **Career:** Chief, Cyber Architecture & MDC2 Operations Lead, U.S. Air Force Space and Missiles Systems Center, El Segundo, CA (2009-Present); Avionics Engineer, New Business Development, Northrop Grumman, El Segundo, CA (2008-Present); Senior Sensors & Communications Engineer, Boeing Company, El Segundo, CA (2007-2008); Senior Radar System Engineer Antenna Designer, Raytheon Company, El Segundo, CA (2001-2007) **Career Related:** Silicon Beach High Tech Start-up (2015-Present); Engineering Council of Publicity, California State Polytechnic University (2007-2009); Consultant, Industrial Advisory Council, California State Polytechnic University; Public Affair Officer, California State Polytechnic University **Civic:** Teaching Taoism, Lord Universal Church, Rosemead, CA (2008) **Creative Works:** Contributor, Articles, Professional Journals **Awards:** Space and Missile Systems Center Quarterly Award (2016); Best Paper Award, Global Engineering, Science, and Technology Society (2007); Aviation Week & Space Technology Achievement Award in Conformal Phase Array Radar (2006); Honor Award, IEEE (2005); First Prize, IEEE (2000); IEEE AUTOTESTCON Technical Achievement Award (2000); Space Exploration Outstanding Achievement Award, Jet Propulsion Laboratory (1999-2000); Silicon Beach Innovation Award **Memberships:** Technology Program, IEEE (2008-Present); Radar Conference Technology Program Member, IEEE (2009); Academic Success Management Related Disciplines, Sigma Iota Epsilon (2007); Co-chair, Technology Program, IEEE (2004-2006); Aerospace Conference Member, IEEE (2005); Chair, Sponsorship, Exhibitor, IEEE (2004-2005); National Management Honor Society **Marquis Who's Who Honors:** Albert Nelson Marquis Lifetime Achievement Award **Why did you become involved in your profession or industry:** Dr. Lee was inspired to get into her profession because of her first boss, a cyber expert who gave her the opportunity to get into the field. **Avocations:** Golf; Swimming; Travel; Tennis; Dance; Piano; Skiing; Running; Hiking; Reading books; Meditation **Religion:** Lord of Universe Church

Jung-Lim Lee, PhD

Title: Associate Professor **Industry:** Education/Educational Services **Company Name:** Delaware State University **Date of Birth:** 07/10/1971 **Place of Birth:** Seoul **State/Country of Origin:** Republic of Korea **Parents:** Choon-Sup Lee; Young-Lim Choi **Marital Status:** Married **Spouse Name:** Jin-Young Lee **Children:** Eric J. Lee **Education:** Post-Doctoral Fellowship, Korea Science and Engineering Foundation (2004-2005); PhD in Food Science and Biotechnology, Kyung Hee University, Republic of Korea (2003); MS in Food Science and Biotechnology, Kyung Hee University, Republic of Korea (1999); BS in Food Science and Technology, Hankyong National University, Republic of Korea (1997) **Certifications:** Certified Educator of Biotechnology Education, South Korea **Career:** Associate Professor, Delaware State University (2014-Present); Assistant Professor, Delaware State University (2009-2014) **Career Related:** Researcher; Teacher; Outreach, Food Science and Microbiology **Military Service:** Army, Republic of Korea (1991-1993) **Creative Works:** Contributor, Articles to Professional Journals **Awards:** Recipient, Faculty Excellence Award for Research, Delaware State University (2014); Recipient, Merit Award, Delaware State University (2013-2014); Recipient, Academic Enrichment Program Award, Delaware State University (2012); Recipient, Graduate Student Award for Excellence, Kyung-Hee University, Republic of Korea (1999) **Memberships:** International Association for Food Protection; Curricular Committee Member, High School **To what do you attribute your success:** For Dr. Lee, he looks to find resolutions using a novel idea. Through networking, he can collaborate in making better protection and methods for food safety. **Why did you become involved in your profession or industry:** Dr. Lee entered his profession because there are people who do not know much about food safety. His research entails the prevention of bacteria being to transferred to food sources by developing rapid molecular assays and through genomics study. **Avocations:** Watching movies; Playing Electric guitar; Collecting collectibles **Religion:** Christian

William Lamborn Lee, PhD

Title: Literature Educator **Industry:** Education/Educational Services **Company Name:** Yeshiva University **Date of Birth:** 10/17/1947 **Place of Birth:** Amarillo **State/Country of Origin:** TX/USA **Parents:** William Lamborn; Louise Monning (Elliott) Lamborn **Marital Status:** Divorced **Spouse Name:** Barbara de Cerchio (09/05/1981, Divorced 2007); Carla Jo Shatz (05/20/1973, Divorced 1978) **Children:** Morgan Monning Lee **Education:** MA, Oxford University (1986); PhD, Yale University (1980); MPhil, Yale University (1973); BA, Oxford University, England (1971); BA, Dartmouth College (1969) **Career:** Associate Professor of English Emeritus, Yeshiva University, New York, NY (2019-Present); Associate Professor, Yeshiva University, New York, NY (1998-2019); Chair, Yeshiva College Senate, Yeshiva University, New York, NY (1987-1988, 1991-1992, 1995-1996, 2001-2002); Assistant Professor, Yeshiva University, New York, NY (1983-1998); Acting Chair, English Department, Yeshiva University, New York, NY (1986-1987); Lecturer, History and Literature, Harvard University, Cambridge, MA (1980-1983); Instructor, Harvard University, Cambridge, MA (1978-1980); Instructor, Tufts University, Medford, MA (1978-1979); Instructor, Colby College, Waterville, ME (1974-1977); Instructor, Yale University, New Haven, CT (1973-1974) **Career Related:** Chair, Middle States Reaccreditation Steering Committee (2011-2012); Director, Jay and Jeanie Schottenstein Honors Program, Yeshiva College (2002-2007); Prize Teaching Fellow, Yale University (1974); Kent Fellow (1971-1974) **Civic:** Bergen County Historic Preservation Advisory Board (2006-Present); Chair, Founder, Englewood Historic Preservation Advisory Committee (1995-Present); Board, Englewood Historical Society (1992-Present); Founder and Chair, West Side Neighborhood Association, Englewood, NJ (1988-Present); Co-chair, Preservation Committee, Englewood Historical Society; Chair, Tour Planning Committee, Englewood Historical Society **Creative Works:** Literary Editor, "New Translation of the Hebrew Bible Into Contemporary American English," Koren Publications, Jerusalem, Israel (2017-2020); Co-editor, "Englewood: Historical Sketches" (2003); Contributor, Articles for Publications on Victorian Culture, Local History of Yeshiva University and of Englewood, NJ; Designer, Neo-Victorian House; Historic Preservation Consultant, Red Cross; Supervisor, Restoration of Benson House, Englewood, NJ **Awards:** Volunteer of the Year, Bergen Crossroads Chapter, American Red Cross (2003); Senior Professor Award for Distinguished Teaching, Yeshiva University (1985, 1987, 1989); Grantee, Mellon Foundation (1984); Marshall Scholar (1969-1971) **Memberships:** Program Committee, Northeast Victorian Studies Association (1986-2002, 2007-2010, 2012-2014); Executive Committee, Danforth Foundation (1971-1972); Modern Language Association; American Association of University Professors; National Council of Teachers of English; Society for Values in Higher Education; William Morris Society; Phi Beta Kappa **Marquis Who's Who Honors:** Albert Nelson Marquis Lifetime Achievement Award **To what do you attribute your success:** Dr. Lee attributes his success to his hard work, imagination, intelligence and persistence. **Why did you become involved in your profession or industry:** Dr. Lee was inspired to enter his profession by his professors at Dartmouth. **Avocations:** Reading; Arts; Films; Historic architecture; Woodworking; Tennis **Political Affiliations:** Democrat **Religion:** Multicultural Humanist

Jim Charles "Dean of Moderators" Lehrer

Title: Former News Anchor; Journalist **Industry:** Media & Entertainment **Company Name:** Public Broadcasting Service (PBS) **Date of Birth:** 05/19/1934 **Place of Birth:** Wichita **State/Country of Origin:** KS/USA **Parents:** Harry Frederick Lehrer; Lois Catherine Lehrer **Marital Status:** Married **Spouse Name:** Kate Staples **Children:** Jamie; Lucy; Amanda **Education:** Honorary PhD, McDaniel College, Westminster, MD (2004); BJ, University of Missouri (1956); AA, Victoria College, Texas (1954) **Career:** Executive Editor, Anchor, "The NewsHour with Jim Lehrer," Public Broadcasting Service (PBS) (1995-2011); Co-anchor, "The MacNeil/Lehrer NewsHour," Public Broadcasting Service (PBS) (1975-1995); Public Affairs Coordinator, Public Broadcasting Service (PBS), Washington, DC (1972-1973); Executive Producer, Correspondent, Station KERA-TV, Dallas, Texas (1970-1972); Reporter, Columnist, City Editor, Dallas Times Herald, Dallas, Texas (1961-1970); Reporter, Dallas Morning News, Dallas, Texas (1959-1961) **Career Related:** Moderator of Presidential Debates (1988, 1992, 1996, 2000, 2004, 2008, 2012); Instructor, Creative Writing, Dallas College, Dallas, Texas and Southern Methodist University, University Park, Texas (1967-1968) **Civic:** Supporter, Pacific Bus Museum, Williams, CA; Supporter, The Museum of Bus Transportation, Hershey, PA **Military Service:** Infantry Officer, United States Marine Corps **Creative Works:** Author, "Top Down: A Novel of the Kennedy Assassination" (2013); Author, "Tension City" (2011); Author, "Super" (2010); Author, "Oh Johnny" (2009); Author, "Eureka" (2007); Author, "The Phone Marine" (2006); Author, "The Franklin Affair" (2005); Author, "Flying Crows: A Novel" (2004); Author, "No Certain Rest" (2002); Author, "The Special Prisoner" (2000); Author, "Purple Dots" (1998); Author, "White Widow" (1996); Author, "The Last Debate" (1995); Author, "Fine Lines" (1994); Author, "Blue Hearts" (1993); Author, "A Bus of My Own" (1992); Author, "Short List" (1992); Author, "Lost and Found" (1991); Author, "The Sooner Spy" (1990); Author, "Crown Oklahoma" (1989); Author, "Kick the Can" (1988); Author, "We Were Dreamers" (1975); Author, "Viva Max!" (1966); Playwright, "The Will and Bart Show"; Playwright, "Church Key Charlie Blue"; Playwright, "Chili Queen"; Playwright, "Bell" **Awards:** Walter Cronkite Award for Excellence in Journalism (2008); National Humanities Medal (1999); Inductee, Television Hall of Fame (1999); Inductee, Silver Circle, The National Academy of Television Arts & Sciences (1999); Fellow, American Academy of Arts & Sciences (1991); Paul White Award, Radio Television Digital News Association (1990); Two Emmy Awards, Television Academy; Fred Friendly First Amendment Award; George Foster Peabody Award; William Allen White Foundation for Journalist Merit; Medal of Honor, University of Missouri School of Journalism; George Polk Award; Alfred I. duPont-Columbia Award, Columbia Journalism School **Memberships:** Fellow, Society of American Historians; American Academy of Arts & Sciences; Council on Foreign Relations; Texas Institute of Letters; Dramatists Guild of America, Inc.; Authors Guild; The Commission on Presidential Debates **Avocations:** Collecting bus memorabilia

Alison Ragna Lehto

Title: Middle School Educator **Industry:** Education/Educational Services **Date of Birth:** 08/26/1943 **Place of Birth:** Klamath Falls **State/Country of Origin:** OR/USA **Parents:** Lyle Frank; Alice Montana (Madison) Glenn **Marital Status:** Married **Spouse Name:** Glenn Alan Lehto (12/24/1973) **Children:** Glison Angela; Bruce Alan **Education:** Certificate of Advanced Study, University of Maine (1994); Master of Arts in English Literature, San Diego State University (1978); Bachelor of Arts in English, San Diego State University (1969) **Certifications:** Certified Teacher, Administrator, Maine; Junior College Teacher, California **Career:** Teacher, Williams Junior High School, Oakland, ME (1982-2003); Substitute Teacher, Mount Blue High School, Farmington, ME (1980-1982); Instructor, University of Maine, Farmington, ME (1980-1982); Teacher, San Diego Unified School District (1969-1980); Accounting Clerk, Chrysler Credit Corp., San Diego, CA (1967-1969); Accounting Clerk, General Motors Acceptance Corp, San Diego, CA (1963-1965) **Career Related:** Facilitator, Messalonskee Summer Institute for Teachers and Administrators, Maine School Administrative District #47, Oakland, CA (1995, 1994, 1993) **Creative Works:** Author, Poem, "Why Teach Poetry," for Anthology "Of Moonlight and Wishes" (1996); Author, Poem, "Ode to Duke"; Author of Essays and Poems **Memberships:** National Education Association; National Council of English; Maine Teachers Association; Oakland Parent Teacher Association; Michael Crawford International Fan Association **Marquis Who's Who Honors:** Albert Nelson Marquis Lifetime Achievement Award; Marquis Who's Who Top Professional **Why did you become involved in your profession or industry:** Ms. Lehto became involved in her profession because she would play teacher with her dolls, so she knew she always wanted to be a teacher. **Avocations:** Reading; Attended Michael Crawford concerts; Writing; Research; Bible study; Small group activities **Political Affiliations:** Independent **Religion:** Christian

Harry V. Leland, PhD

Title: Aquatic Ecologist (Retired) **Industry:** Sciences **Date of Birth:** 10/31/1937 **Place of Birth:** Baltimore **State/Country of Origin:** MD/USA **Parents:** Harry Valentine Leland; Edna Violet Leland **Marital Status:** Married **Spouse Name:** Gretchen Leland **Children:** Katherine Leland; Edward Harry Leland **Education:** PhD in Natural Resources, University of Michigan, Ann Arbor, MI (1968); MA in Zoology, Southern Illinois University, Carbondale, IL (1964); BA in Zoology, University of California, Riverside (1959) **Career:** Research Biologist, Water Resources Division, U.S. Geological Survey, Boulder, CO (1992-2004); Research Biologist, Water Resources Division, U.S. Geological Survey, Menlo Park, CA (1975-1992); Assistant Professor of Environmental Biology, University of Illinois, Urbana, IL (Now University of Illinois Urbana-Champaign) (1968-1975) **Career Related:** Project Director, National Water-Quality Assessment Program, U.S. Geological Survey (1989-2004); Research Adviser for Ecology, U.S. Geological Survey, (1976-1979); Research Committee, Water Pollution Control Federation (1973-1982); Founding Member, Society of Environmental Toxicology and Chemistry **Civic:** Volunteer Naturalist, Open Space and Mountain Parks, Boulder, CO (2005-2009) **Creative Works:** Contributing Senior Author, Two Book Chapters; Contributing Senior Author, 45 Articles, Professional Scientific Journals **Awards:** Outstanding Alumnus Award, University of California, Riverside (2002); Special Achievement Awards, U.S. Geological Survey (1979, 1991) **Memberships:** Society for Freshwater Science; International Society of Limnology **Marquis Who's Who Honors:** Albert Nelson Marquis Lifetime Achievement Award **Why did you become involved in your profession or industry:** Mr. Leland became involved in his profession because of his interest in the biology of rivers. **Avocations:** Traveling; Hiking; Listening to classical music **Religion:** Protestant (Methodist)

Frank Eugene LeMoine

Title: Judge, Lawyer **Industry:** Law and Legal Services **Company Name:** LeMoine Law **Date of Birth:** 10/17/1953 **Place of Birth:** Montgomery **State/Country of Origin:** LA/USA **Parents:** Frank Lucian LeMoine; Frances Pauline (Jones) LeMoine Birchfield **Marital Status:** Married **Spouse Name:** Geraldine Guidry (10/01/1971, Deceased 2012) **Children:** Frank Lucian II; Stephanie Antoinette; Monique Angele **Education:** Doctor of Jurisprudence, Southern University, Cum Laude (1986); Bachelor of Science, University of Southwestern Louisiana, Summa Cum Laude (1983) **Certifications:** U.S. Court of Appeals for the Fifth Circuit (1990); U.S. District Court for the Western District of Louisiana (1987); Louisiana (1986) **Career:** Private Practice, Abbeville, LA (1986-Present); Municipal Judge, Capalin, LA (2003-2014); Oilfield Construction Worker, Louisiana (1972-1977) **Memberships:** American Bar Association; Louisiana State Bar Association; Vermilion Parish Bar Association; American Inns of Court; Phi Eta Sigma; Phi Kappa Phi; Kappa Delta Pi; Phi Alpha Delta **Marquis Who's Who Honors:** Albert Nelson Marquis Lifetime Achievement Award; Marquis Who's Who Top Professional; Marquis Who's Who Humanitarian Award **Why did you become involved in your profession or industry:** Having endured a destitute period in his early life, Judge LeMoine decided to attend law school after working as a common laborer. **Avocations:** Woodworking; Hunting; Fishing; Knife collecting; Long range shooting **Political Affiliations:** Democrat **Religion:** Roman Catholic

Sharon J. Lemond

Title: President **Industry:** Fine Art **Company Name:** Enjolé Interiors Inc. **Marital Status:** Widowed **Children:** Jared; Morgan **Education:** Associate's Degree in Interior Design, Ivy Tech Community College (1997); Bachelor of Business Administration, University of Southern Indiana (1982) **Career:** Owner, Entwined Wine & Dine, Evansville, IN, (2020-Present); Owner, Enjolé Interiors Inc., Evansville, IN, (2016-Present); Executive Assistant, Shoe Carnival Inc. (1987-1993); Sales Assistant, Now Merrill, Bank of America Corporation (1982-1985) **Civic:** Financial Contributor, Women Build Program, Habitat for Humanity® International **Awards:** Platinum Award, Best Interior Designer, Readers Choice, courierpress.com (2018); Gold Award, Best Place to Buy Window Treatments, Readers Choice, courierpress.com (2018); Entrepreneur of the Year, Southwest Indiana Chamber (2017); Now Who's Who Among Students (1996); Top Interior Designer, Ivy Tech Community College (1996); Honor Student, Ivy Tech Community College (1996); Chamber of Commerce Award; Small Business of the Year; Best Interior Design Firm; Top 50 Retail Stores in the U.S. **Marquis Who's Who Honors:** Marquis Who's Who Top Professional **To what do you attribute your success:** Ms. Lemond attributes her success to her fantastic team, who are always empowering each other, working together and excelling in customer service. She couldn't do her job without them. **Why did you become involved in your profession or industry:** Ms. Lemond has loved interior design since childhood, but pursued a business and education degree in college for practical reasons. After her husband passed away, she immersed herself in launching her own business. Ever since, Ms. Lemond has been thrilled on a daily basis to pursue what she has always wanted. **Avocations:** Jewelry-making; Crafting

Douglas Ellis Leng, PhD

Title: Research Fellow **Industry:** Sciences **Company Name:** Dow Chemical Company **Date of Birth:** 05/28/1928 **Place of Birth:** Kitchener **State/Country of Origin:** Ontario/Canada **Parents:** Douglas Harry Leng; Blanche (Ellis) Leng **Marital Status:** Married **Spouse Name:** Dr. Marguerite Lambert (06/18/1955, Deceased 05/19/2019) **Children:** Ronald Bruce; Janet Elaine; Douglas Lambert **Education:** PhD, Purdue University, West Lafayette, IN (1956); MSc, Queen's University, Kingston, Ontario, Canada (1953); BSc, Queen's University, Kingston, Ontario, Canada (1951) **Career:** Mixing Consultant, Leng Associates, Midland, MI (1996, Retired); Fellow, Senior Research Scientist, The Dow Chemical Company, Midland, MI (1986-1996) **Career Related:** Member, Advisory Panel, National Research Council, Washington, DC (1985-1998); Advisory Board, Queen's University, Kingston, Ontario, Canada (1985-1987); Advisory Panel, National Institute of Standards and Technology (NSIT) **Civic:** President, Midland Amateur Hockey League (1965); President, Co-Founder, Midland Curling Club (1963-1964); President, Macintosh Computer Club; Commodore, Saginaw Bay Yacht Racing Association **Creative Works:** Contributor, Numerous Articles, Professional Journals; Contributor, Chapters, Books **Awards:** Procter & Gamble Mixing Forum Award (1995); Dow Gold Medal, The Dow Chemical Company (1993) **Memberships:** Fellow, American Institute of Chemical Engineers; American Chemical Society **Marquis Who's Who Honors:** Albert Nelson Marquis Lifetime Achievement Award; Marquis Who's Who Top Professional **Why did you become involved in your profession or industry:** Dr. Leng became involved in his profession because, while in high school, he began thinking he would like to be a chemical engineer. It was a notion that progressed as he attended Queen's University. **Avocations:** Sailing; Curling; Photography; Computers; Listening to classical music; Reading mysteries; Watching hockey and curling; Family visits; Playing with his two all-black cats

John Anthony Lent, PhD

Title: Researcher, Educator, Author **Industry:** Education/Educational Services **Company Name:** International Journal of Comic Art **Date of Birth:** 09/08/1936 **Place of Birth:** East Millsboro **State/Country of Origin:** PA/USA **Parents:** John Lent; Rose (Marano) Lent **Marital Status:** Married **Spouse Name:** Ying Xu (2003) **Children:** Laura Barrett; Andrea Murta; John V. Lent; Lisa K. Lent (Deceased 01/30/2013); Shahnon Lent **Education:** PhD, University of Iowa (1972); MS, Ohio University (1960); BS, Ohio University (1958) **Certifications:** Certificate, Press Institute of India, Summer School (1980); Certificate, Summer School, Sophia University, Tokyo, Japan (1965); Certificate, University of Oslo (1962); Summer School, Guadalajara, Mexico (1961) **Career:** Professor Emeritus, Temple University, Philadelphia, PA (2011-Present); Professor, Communications, Temple University (1976-2011); Associate Professor, Temple University, Philadelphia, PA (1974-1976); Founding Director, Communications Program, Universiti Sains Malaysia, Penang, Malaysia (1972-1974); Visiting Associate Professor, University of Wyoming (1969-1970); Assistant Professor of Journalism, Head Teacher's Journalism Sequence, Marshall University, Huntington, WV (1967-1970); Assistant Professor of Journalism, University of Wisconsin, Eau Claire, WI (1966-1967); Assistant Professor, West Virginia University Institute of Technology, Montgomery, WV (1965-1966); Lecturer, De La Salle College, Manila, Philippines (1964-1965); Newhouse Research Assistant, Assistant to Director of Communications Research, Syracuse University, Syracuse, NY (1962-1964); Director of Public Relations, Instructor in English, Assistant Professor, West Virginia University Institute of Technology, Montgomery, WV (1960-1962) **Career Related:** Guest Professor, University of Kebangsaan, Malaysia (2009-Present); Guest Professor, Nanjing Normal University (2009-Present); Founding Chair, APACA Center (2008-Present); Founding Chair, Asia Pacific Animation Comic Association (2008-Present); Founder, Co-Organizer, Asian Youth Animation & Comics Contest (2007-Present); Guest Professor, Animation School, Jilin College of the Arts, China (2006-Present); Honorary Chair, Asian Research Center for Animation and Comic Art, China Communications University (2005-Present); Chair, Guest Professor, Asian Research Center for Animation and Comic Art, China Communications University (2004-Present); Guest Professor, Shanghai University (2002-Present) **Creative Works:** Founding Editor, International Journal of Comic Art (1998-Present); Founding Managing Editor, WittyWorld (1987-Present); Editor, Hampton Books Popular Culture, Hampton Books Comic Art, Asian Comics (2015); Author, "Southeast Asian Cartoon Art" (2014); Author, "The First 100 years of Philippine Komiks & Cartoons" (2009); Author, "Cartooning in Africa" (2009); Author, "Comic Art of the United States Through 2000: Animation and Cartoons" (2005); Author, "Centennial Reflections on Cinematic China" (2005); Author, "Cartooning in Latin America" (2005); Author, "Comic Art in Africa, Asia, and Latin America Through 2000: An International Bibliography" (2004); Author, "Comic Art of Europe Through 2000: An International Bibliography," Two Volumes (2003); Author, "Animation in Asia and the Pacific" (2001); Author, "Illustrating Asia" (2001); Author, "Women and Mass Communications in the 1990's" (1999) **Awards:** John A. Lent Award, Comic Art Section Popular Culture Association (2011-Present); John A. Lent Award, Malaysia/Singapore/Brunei Studies Group (2007-Present); Nominee, Eisner Award (2014); President Award, Popular Culture Association (2010); John Buscema Lifetime Achievement in Comics Award (2006); Lifetime Achievement Award, Asian Media and Information Community Center (2006); John A. Lent Scholarship, ICAF (2003); Exceptional Award, Temple University (1995); Ray and Pat Browne National Book Award (1995) **Memberships:** Co-Founder, Chair, Asian Pacific Animation and Comics Association (2008-Present); Founding Chairman, Asian Popular Culture Group, Popular Culture Association (1996-Present); Asian Media and Information Community Center (2006); Chairman, Asian Cinema Studies Society (1994-2012); Visual and Comic Art Organizer, Chair, International Association of Mass Communications Research (1984-2015); Founding Chairman, Malaysia/Singapore/Brunei Studies Group (1975-1982) **Marquis Who's Who Honors:** Albert Nelson Marquis Lifetime Achievement Award **Why did you become involved in your profession or industry:** Dr. Lent got involved in journalism, and later mass communications, because his goal from grade school was to be a journalist. The degrees he obtained were in journalism. He had a lifetime interest in the field. He was interested in comic strips from a young age. His father would read them every day, and then Dr. Lent and his siblings read them. He got started in cartooning because he saw a niche he could fill, and he started to do research in the area and set up groups and publications all over the world. **Avocations:** Travel; Writing; Collecting books, artwork and cartoons

Annie Louise Leonard

Title: Executive Director **Industry:** Environmental Services **Company Name:** Greenpeace USA **Place of Birth:** Seattle **State/Country of Origin:** WA/USA **Children:** Dewi **Education:** Master's Degree in City and Regional Planning, Cornell University; Bachelor's Degree, Barnard College **Career:** Executive Director, Greenpeace USA (2014-Present); Co-creator, GAIA; With, Health Care Without Harm; With, Essential Information; With, Greenpeace International; Coordinator, Funders Workgroup for Sustainable Production and Consumption **Civic:** Board Member, Wallace Global Fund; Board Member, Ben & Jerry's Homemade Inc.; Board Member, Public Citizen; Board Member, Environmental Health Fund; Board Member, Democracy Initiative; Past Board Member, Grassroots Recycling Network; Past Board Member, GAIA; Past Board Member, Environmental Health Fund; Past Board Member, Global Greengrants India; Past Board Member, Greenpeace India; Past Board Member, International Forum on Globalization **Creative Works:** Author, "The Story of Stuff" (2010); Creator, Film, "The Story of Stuff" (2007)

Stephen Joseph Leone

Title: Deputy Secretary of Education, Commissioner for Libraries (Retired) **Industry:** Education/Educational Services **Company Name:** Westchester Community College **Date of Birth:** 09/24/1953 **Place of Birth:** Nyack **State/Country of Origin:** NY/USA **Parents:** Anthony John Leone; Anne Helen (Renella) Leone **Marital Status:** Married **Spouse Name:** Dee Ann Hammond (07/15/1989) **Children:** Stephanie Kara; Rebecca Dawn **Education:** DArts in English, St. John's University, Queens, NY (2006); MA in English, Villanova University (1982); BA in English and Education, LaSalle University, Philadelphia, PA (1975) **Certifications:** Certified Educator, State of New York, Commonwealth of Pennsylvania **Career:** Program Administrator, Westchester Community College (2001-2020); Teacher, Rockland Community College, Suffern, NY (1993-2020); Professor, Westchester Community College, Valhalla, NY (1989-2020); Teacher, Rockland Community College, Suffern, NY (1993-2003); Teacher, Manhattanville College, Purchase, NY (1990-1994); Teacher, Farmingdale High School, Farmingdale, NY (1985-1988); Teacher, The Sewanhaka Central High School District, Elmont, NY (1982-1985); Teacher, Bishop Egan High School, Catholic Schools of Philadelphia, Fairless Hills, PA (1975-1982); Co-chair, PI of the PAL-TECH National Science Foundation Grant; Acting Curriculum Chair for Networking, Westchester Community College **Career Related:** English Curriculum Coordinator, Verizon Next Step Program (2001-Present); Computer Consultant, Nyack Fire Department (1993-Present); Advisor, Drama Club, Sewanhaka High School, Central High School District, Elmont, NY (1982-1985); Advisor, Literary Magazine, Bishop Egan High School (1978-1980) **Civic:** President, Mazeppa Fire Engine Company No. 2, Nyack, NY (1991-1997); Chairman, Nyack YMCA Board of Managers (1986-1988); Chair, Mazeppa Planning Committee, Nyack, NY (1985-1995); Founding Member, Rockland County, YMCA Youth Services, Nyack, NY (1985-1988); Secretary, Mazeppa Fire Engine Company No. 2, Nyack, NY (1982-1991) **Creative Works:** Editor, D.A. Report (1996-1998) **Awards:** Next Step Recognition of Service, Next Step Program (2015); Recognition Award, Cisco Networking Academy (2008); Star Award, Verizon Next Step Program (2006); Outstanding Programs in English Award, Two Year College Association-National Council for Teachers of English (2002); Named American Legion Good Citizen, Nyack, NY **Memberships:** Modern Language Association of America; National Council of Teachers of English (NCTE); Conference on College Composition & Communication; Alliance for Computers and Writing (ACW); LaSalle Education Alumni Association; North East Cisco Networking Academy Training Alliance **Marquis Who's Who Honors:** Albert Nelson Marquis Lifetime Achievement Award; Marquis Who's Who Top Professional **To what do you attribute your success:** Dr. Leone attributes his success to being interested in science and technology. He started reading and collecting comic books as a young boy and taught himself to read. This helped Dr. Leone develop an interest in mythology and religion, as well as science fiction. **Why did you become involved in your profession or industry:** Dr. Leone became involved in his profession because of his involvement with the Boy Scouts and the YMCA. He taught classes for both when he was young and it led him in this direction.

Matt J. Lepkowski

Title: President/Business Automation Expert **Industry:** Business Management/Business Services **Company Name:** Business Automation Experts LLC **Date of Birth:** 08/21/1975 **Place of Birth:** Ann Arbor **State/Country of Origin:** MI/USA **Parents:** James Lepkowski; Alicia **Marital Status:** Married **Spouse Name:** Kathleen (07/09/2005) **Children:** Three Children **Education:** MBA, New York University Leonard N. Stern School of Business, New York, NY (2003); BSEE, Kettering University, Flint, MI (1998) **Career:** Chief Technology Architect, Lcube Advisors LLC (2014-Present); President, Founder/Owner, Business Automation Experts LLC (2005-Present); Director of Sales and Marketing, Right Decision Systems (2006-2011); Vice President, Information Systems, Total Repair Express, LLC (1999-2006) **Civic:** Volunteer, Sisters Network of Central New Jersey; Treasurer, Cub Scouts of America, Boy Scouts of America; Treasurer, Local Church; EmPoWER Somerset **Awards:** Named Healthcare Partner of the Year, Sisters Network of Central New Jersey (2019); Named One of the Top 20 Microsoft Sharepoint Partners, Seceon (2019); Men of Principal Award (2016) **Memberships:** Healthcare Information and Management Systems Society (HIMSS); Theta Zeta Pi; The Tau Beta Pi Association, Inc.; Phi Eta Sigma National Honor Society, Inc. **To what do you attribute your success:** Mr. Lepkowski attributes his success to his preparation. Although he did not enjoy the process of his father trying to instill discipline, he is grateful for it today. **Why did you become involved in your profession or industry:** Mr. Lepkowski became involved in his profession because in high school, he did not initially know what he wanted to pursue as a career. He knew that he loved math and sciences, like most engineers. He attended General Motor's Institute to receive his bachelor's degree in electrical engineering while minoring in computer science. The program that he was in required him to alternate from study for to work for three months. Part of his fifth year studies, he was required to do a capstone project which made him do work for his co-op employer. At the time, he was writing software to pay his bills. One of his clients invited him to New Jersey to become the chief information officer of a repair management company called Total Repair Express, LLC. To his surprise, working as an engineer consisted of much paper work and project design. Upon graduating, he knew that he would have to round out his skill set and decided to pursue a master of business administration as well. He learned that working for larger companies was not his desire. He found out that working for smaller companies is better for him where he can also contribute and make a bigger impact. Helping companies in his area grow became his mission, and to invest in the community to be a better neighbor. **Avocations:** Reading; Hockey (Red Wings); Sporting events; Friends **Thoughts on Life:** For more information on Mr. Lepkowski, see the following articles: https://microsoft.cioreview.com/vendor/2018/business_automation_experts; https://www.mirrorreview.com/business-automation-experts-knowledgeable-expert-technical-skills/

Wilbert Charles "Wil" Lepkowski

Title: Journalist **Industry:** Other **Date of Birth:** 09/03/1934 **Place of Birth:** Peabody **State/Country of Origin:** MA/USA **Year of Passing:** 07/16/2019 **Parents:** Charles J.; Alice (Bartnicki) A. **Marital Status:** Married **Spouse Name:** Helene Kay Hollander (2/4/1984); Jane Littlefield (10/28/1961, Divorced 05/1975) **Children:** David E.; Rebecca A.; Thomas M. C.; Katherine A.J. **Education:** MS in Biochemistry, The Ohio State University (1961); BS in Chemistry, University of Massachusetts (1956) **Career:** Columnist, Science and Policy Perspectives, The Center for Science and Society, Columbia University (2005); Contributing Editor, Chemical & Engineering News (1999-2003); Senior Correspondent, Chemical & Engineering News (1977-1999); Freelance Writer, Consultant (1975-1977); Science Correspondent, Washington Business Week (1969-1975); Head of Bureau Southeast, Chemical & Engineering News (1965-1969); Science Writer, Newhouse Newspapers, Washington (1963-1965); Science Writer, Johns Hopkins Medicine, Baltimore, MD (1961-1963); Reporter, Providence Journal, Westerly, RI (1961); Reporter, UP International, Columbus, OH (1960); Assistant Editor, CAS, A Division of the American Chemical Society, Columbus, OH (1956-1958); Assistant Chemist, Doeskin Products Inc., Easthampton, MA (1956) **Career Related:** Journalist-in-Residence, The Center for Science and Society, Columbia University (1999-2003); Adjunct Professor of Science and Technology Studies, Virginia Polytechnic Institute and State University (2002); Founder, Science and Technology Policy Conference, Gordon Research Conferences (2000); Co-Chair, New Frontiers in Science and Technology Policy, Gordon Research Conference (2000); Author, Articles, The Washington Post, Science Forum, The Progressive, Boston Globe **Creative Works:** Contributor, Articles, Professional Journals **Awards:** Sloan-Rockefeller Fellow, Advanced Science Writing Program, Graduate School of Journalism, Columbia University (1959-1960) **Memberships:** Fellow, American Association for the Advancement of Science; The National Press Club; The National Association of Science Writers, Inc.; The American Scientific Affiliation; Latin American Parents Association; Mended Hearts **Why did you become involved in your profession or industry:** Mr. Lepkowski became involved in his profession to add social, ethical and economic perspectives to science and technology and their interactions with society. **Avocations:** Reading poetry; Listening to music; Natural history; Geography **Religion:** Roman Catholic **Thoughts on Life:** Mr. Lepkowski's journalistic motto is, "Tell the truth."

Leon Maurice Lerner, PhD

Title: Professor Emeritus of Biochemistry **Industry:** Medicine & Health Care **Company Name:** State University of New York at Brooklyn **Date of Birth:** 02/02/1938 **Place of Birth:** Chicago **State/Country of Origin:** IL/USA **Parents:** Sidney Lerner; Yetta (Weiner) Lerner **Marital Status:** Married **Spouse Name:** Fern Loevsky (05/26/1996); Helen Jane Abrams (08/23/1959, Deceased 1994) **Children:** Linda; Marcia; Gary; Haley (Grandchild); Rena (Grandchild); Shayna (Grandchild) **Education:** PhD, University of Illinois (1964); MS, Illinois Institute of Technology (1961); BS, Illinois Institute of Technology (1959) **Career:** Professor Emeritus, State University of New York at Brooklyn (Downstate Medical Center) (2003-Present); Professor, State University of New York at Brooklyn (Downstate Medical Center) (1980-2003); Associate Professor, State University of New York at Brooklyn (1973-1980); Assistant Professor, State University of New York at Brooklyn (1967-1973); Instructor of Biochemistry, State University of New York at Brooklyn (1965-1967); Research Associate, University of Illinois Medical Center, Chicago, IL (1964-1965) **Creative Works:** Contributor, 75 Publications, Books, Chemistry and Biochemistry Journals **Memberships:** American Association for the Advancement of Science; American Chemical Society; Sigma Xi **Marquis Who's Who Honors:** Albert Nelson Marquis Lifetime Achievement Award **To what do you attribute your success:** Dr. Lerner attributes his success to the work ethic and kindness that his parents, Sidney and Yetta Lerner, cultivated in him. Coming to America at a time of heightened United States immigration from Russia, Dr. Lerner's father spoke seven languages and was described as a "brilliant man," but he had to work as a house painter and muralist in Chicago. Although Dr. Lerner had to care for his mother, who had multiple sclerosis, while his father worked to provide for the family, they instilled the dream of higher education in their son. This gave him a great sense of purpose and responsibility at a young age. **Why did you become involved in your profession or industry:** One of the biggest factors of Dr. Lerner choosing his career was his initial interest in biology. He also credits a book, "Microbe Hunters" by Paul de Kruif, which he read as a young teenager, for sparking his interest in the field of biological science and research, as it did for many others at the time. Dr. Lerner's uncle Eugene, was an industrial chemist that helped create the formula for spray paint, urging his nephew to consider a career in industrial chemistry. But it was the developing field of biological chemistry which turned Dr. Lerner's interest into a lifetime career. **Avocations:** Fine art drawing; Connoisseurship; Classical vocal repertoire; Cultural venues of Manhattan life **Political Affiliations:** Independent

Patrick Leung

Title: Doctor of Medicine **Industry:** Medicine & Health Care **Company Name:** Doctor Patrick Leung **Parents:** Chan Ho Mann (Mother) **Marital Status:** Married **Spouse Name:** Nancy Leung (12/09/1966) **Children:** Three Children **Education:** MD, University of Alberta-Edmonton, Canada (1968) **Career:** Private Practice, Doctor Patrick Leung (1968-2018); Professor, Texas Academy of Family Physicians **Memberships:** American Medical Association; Texas Medical Association; Texas Academy of Family Physicians; Texas Medical Association **To what do you attribute your success:** Dr. Leung attributes his success to his persistence and keeping his intentions for the good of the people rather than financial gain. He is very successful in the stock market, which allows him to be generous. "I think about helping people first before anything else..." He also attributes his success to his mother for always challenging him to do his best. **Why did you become involved in your profession or industry:** Dr. Leung wanted to help people. Seeing the immediate result, correcting the problem a patient has and finding a solution has been a fulfilling part of the profession.

Natane W. Levi-Falk

Title: Orthopedist **Industry:** Medicine & Health Care **Date of Birth:** 03/22/1957 **Place of Birth:** Pittsburgh **State/Country of Origin:** PA/USA **Marital Status:** Married **Spouse Name:** E. Cohen Levi-Falk (2010) **Children:** Liam Israel **Education:** Honorary Doctor, China (2016); Honorary DSc, UK (2013); Honorary LittD, US (2012); PhD in Orthopedic & Trauma Surgery, Hebrew Medical School & Hadassah University Hospital, Jerusalem (2012); MD in Orthopedic & Trauma Surgery, Hebrew Medical School & Hadassah University Hospital, Jerusalem (2012); Degree in Brain GHB Assessment NatCtr, France University, Summa Cum Laude (2004); Postdoctoral Studies in Research, France (2003); PhD, René Descartes University, Paris, France (2003); Diploma in Disaster Medicine (2000); Diploma in Arthroscopy, Disaster Medicine, Multiply Injured (2000); MA in Law and Anthropology, Law School, Paris, France (1999); MA in Biomechanics, René Descartes University, Magna Cum Laude, Paris, France (1991); MD in Orthopedic & Trauma Surgery, René Descartes University, Paris, France (1988); Resident, Orthopedic & Trauma Surgery, University René Descartes (1977-1980); Resident, General Surgery, UCBN Medical School, US Memorial Hospital (1975-1976); MA in Biomechanics, Harvard Medical School, Magna Cum Laude **Certifications:** Certification in Orthopedic & Trauma Surgery, France and Israel **Career:** Professor, Orthopedic & Trauma Surgery, Jerusalem (2010-President); Professor, Orthopedic & Trauma Surgery, France (2004-2010); Professor, University René Descartes (2004); Professor, Center Hospital University (2000-2010); Associate Professor and Department Head, University Hospital Centre (2000-2004); Orthopedic & Trauma Surgeon, US Memorial Hospital, South Pacific (1992-1999); Assistant, Orthopedic & Trauma Surgery, Paris Medical School (1988-1992); Orthopedic & Trauma Surgeon, University Hospital, Paris (1983-1992); Orthopedic & Trauma Surgeon, US Memorial Hospital (1980-1982) **Career Related:** Israeli Delegate, Orthopedic and Trauma Surgery, University Cooperation Programs **Civic:** Member, United Grande Loge, Israel (2012-Present); National Officer, French National Grande Lodge (2004-Present); Delegate, Mason (1993-2014); Member, Secretary, President, French Medical Boards (1993-2013); Representative, Jewish Consistory (1993); Delegate, UNO Israel; Representative, Delegate, French Ministry; Ex-President, Lions Club **Military Service:** Captain, Reserve Officer, United States Army (1985-2010); Captain, United States Army (1984); Commander, United States Army **Creative Works:** Contributor, Numerous Publications, Scientific Papers; Contributor, Writings, Books **Awards:** TESLA Award (2012); Man of the Year Award (2011-2012); Golden Medal of Honor (2011-2012); Honorary Professor, Medicine and Healthcare US; Medical Science Award; International Hippocrates Award; Lifetime Of Honor; Trauma Surgery Award; Legion D'Honneur - Ordre National Du Merite, French Government; Military Service Medal; Decorated International Merit Order, Great Minds Of 21st Century; Named One of the Top 100 World Health Professionals **Memberships:** French Society of Orthopedic & Trauma Surgery; International Society of Orthopedic & Trauma Surgery; French College of Orthopedic & Trauma Surgeons; Israel Medical Association; Israel Orthopaedic Association; Médecins Et Dentistes Israéliens Francophones; American Academy Of Orthopaedic Surgeons; French Society of Arthrocopy; International Group For Spine Surgery; European Society For Knee Surgery & Arthroscopy; Observatory of French Surgery; International Institute for Medical Research & Bioethics; Unesco Program for Research & Medical Education; Hadassah France Pour La Recherche Et La Coopération Médicale; American Medical Association; Biologic Orthopedic Society **Marquis Who's Who Honors:** Albert Nelson Marquis Lifetime Achievement Award **Avocations:** Music; Sailing; Golf; Travel; Scuba diving **Religion:** Jewish

Fredric Gerson Levin

Title: Lawyer **Industry:** Law and Legal Services **Company Name:** Levin, Papantonio, Thomas, Mitchell, Rafferty & Proctor **Date of Birth:** 03/29/1937 **Place of Birth:** Penascola **State/Country of Origin:** FL/USA **Parents:** Abraham Levin; Rose (Lefkowitz) Levin **Marital Status:** Widow **Spouse Name:** Marilyn Kapner Levin (1959, Deceased 2011) **Children:** Marci, Debra, Martin, & Kimberly **Education:** University of Florida **Career:** Lawyer, Levin Papantonio (1961-Present) **Civic:** Contributor, University of Florida; Contributor, Levin & Papantonio Family Foundation. Contributor in Wife's Name, Lubavitch-Chabad Student and Community Center, University of Florida; Contributor, YMCA of Northwest Florida; Contributor, Florida Institute for Human and Machine Cognition; Contributor, University of West Florida to Establish the Reubin O'D. Askew Institute for Multidisciplinary Studies; Contributor, Brigham & Women's Hospital to Establish the Fredric G. Levin Distinguished Chair in Thoracic Surgery and Lung Cancer Research; Contributor, University of West Florida; Contributor, 300,000 Shares of Charlotte's Web Holdings, LLC Stock, University of Florida Levin College of Law; Contributor, Dana-Farber Cancer Institute to Establish the Fredric G. Levin Endowment in Translational Cancer Research **Awards:** Trial Lawyer of the Year, National Trial Lawyers (2015); Inductee, National Trial Lawyer Hall of Fame (2009); Chief in the Republic of Ghana, United Nations (1999); National Boxing Manager of the Year, National Boxing Writers Association (1995); Perry Nichols Award (1994); Rocky Marciano National Boxing Manager of the Year Award (1994); Listee, Every Edition, Best Lawyers in America **Bar Admissions:** Florida **Marquis Who's Who Honors:** Albert Nelson Marquis Lifetime Achievement Award **To what do you attribute your success:** Mr. Levin attributes his success to always being better prepared than your opponent. **Why did you become involved in your profession or industry:** He was following the lead of his oldest brother. **Avocations:** Managing champion boxers, including Roy Jones, Jr. **Political Affiliations:** Democrat **Religion:** Jewish **Thoughts on Life:** Speaking out and being wrong does not shame me. Failing to speak out when I know I should makes my entire existence unbearable and pointless.

Gerald J. Lewis

Title: Justice **Industry:** Law and Legal Services **Date of Birth:** 09/09/1933 **Place of Birth:** Perth Amboy **State/Country of Origin:** NJ/USA **Parents:** Norman Francis Lewis; Blanche M. (Jorgensen) Lewis **Spouse Name:** Laura Susan McDonald (12/15/1973) **Children:** Michael; Marc **Education:** Doctor of Jurisprudence, Harvard Law School, Harvard University (1957); Bachelor of Arts, Tufts University, Magna Cum Laude (1954) **Career:** Private Arbitrator and Mediator (1997-2012); Of Counsel, Lathan & Watkins (1987-1997); Associate Justice, Division One, 4th District Court of Appeal, Judicial Council of California, San Diego, CA (1984-1987); Judge, Superior Court, San Diego, CA (1979-1984); Judge, Municipal Court, El Cajon, CA (1977-1979); Partner, Haskins, Lewis, Nugent & Newnham, San Diego, CA (1963-1977); Judge, Ramona Justice Court (1975-1976); Attorney, General Atomics, La Jolla, CA (1961-1963) **Career Related:** Board of Directors, Mediator, Arbitrator, Tennenbaum Opportunities Fund V, LLC (1987-2012); Executive Board, Western State College of Law, San Diego, CA (1977-1989); Adjunct Professor, Evidence, Western State College of Law, San Diego, CA (1977-1985); American Inns of Court (1984); Faculty, San Diego Inn of Court (1979); Board of Directors, Taxus Cardium; General Counsel, California Society of Anesthesiologists; General Counsel, San Diego County Medical Society **Civic:** Trustee, The San Diego Museum of Art (1986-1989); City Attorney, Coronado, CA (1972-1977); Board of Directors, Air Pollution Control District, County of San Diego (1972-1976); City Attorney, Del Mar, CA (1963-1974); Counsel, Comprehensive Planning Organization, San Diego, CA (1972-1973) **Military Service:** Lieutenant Commander, U.S. Navy (1957-1961) **Creative Works:** Consultant Editor, "California Civil Jury Instructions" (1984) **Awards:** Heritage Award, The Ireland Funds (2004); Irishman of Year, The Society of The Friendly Sons of St. Patrick (2000); Trial Judge of the Year, San Diego Trial Lawyers Association (1984) **Memberships:** President, Pauma Valley Country Club (2011); Director, La Jolla Country Club (1980-1983); American Judicature Society; Society of Inns of Court in California; Confrérie des Chevaliers du Tastevin; Knight Commander, North American Chapter, The International Order of Saint Hubert; The Society of The Friendly Sons of St. Patrick; The Irish 50 Aztec Big 50; Bohemian Club; Prophets, The K Club, Kildare, Ireland; Retired Director, Fisher Scientific International, Inc.; Retired Director, Wheelabrator Technologies Inc.; Retired Director, General Chemical Corp.; Retired Director, Henley Properties Inc; Retired Director, AIM Mutual Funds, Invesco Ltd. **Bar Admissions:** Supreme Court of the United States (1968); State of California (1962); State of New Jersey (1961); District of Columbia (1957) **Marquis Who's Who Honors:** Albert Nelson Marquis Lifetime Achievement Award **Why did you become involved in your profession or industry:** Justice Lewis grew up with the assumption that he would attend school for either law or business; he ultimately decided on Harvard Law because of its reputation. When he joined the U.S. Navy, he was assigned to be a prosecutor, and he court-martialed several significant cases. He later became a lawyer, and was the chief prosecutor for the 11th Naval District. **Political Affiliations:** Republican **Religion:** Episcopalian

John Robert Lewis

Title: Georgia Congressman **Industry:** Government Administration/Government Relations/Government Services **Date of Birth:** 02/21/1940 **Place of Birth:** Troy **State/Country of Origin:** AL/USA **Year of Passing:** 2020 **Marital Status:** Widowed **Spouse Name:** Lillian Miles (1968, Deceased 12/31/2012) **Children:** John-Miles **Education:** Honorary LLD, Yale Law School (2017); Honorary Doctor of Policy Analysis, Pardee Rand Graduate School (2016); Honorary LHD, Washington University in St. Louis (2016); Honorary LHD, Bates College (2016); Honorary LHD, New York University (2016); Honorary LHD, McCourt School of Public Policy, Georgetown University (2015); Honorary BA, Lawrence University (2014); Honorary LLD, Emory University (2014); Honorary LHD, Judson College (2013); Honorary LLD, Cleveland State University (2013); Honorary LLD, Union College (2013); Honorary LLD, Brown University (2012); Honorary LLD, University of Pennsylvania (2012); Honorary LLD, Harvard University (2012); Honorary LLD, University of Connecticut School of Law (2012); Honorary LLD, The University of Vermont (2007); Honorary LLD, University of Massachusetts Boston (1999); BA in Religion and Philosophy, Fisk University (1963); BA in Theology, American Baptist College, Nashville, TN (1961) **Career:** Member, Georgia Fifth Congressional District, United States House of Representatives, United States Congress (1987-2020); City Councilman, City of Atlanta (1983-1986); Community Affairs Director, National Cooperative Bank (1980-1982); Member, Congressional Black Caucus; Member, Ways and Means Committee, United States House of Representatives **Career Related:** Associate Director, ACTION (1977-1980); Director, Voter Education Project (1970-1977); Associate Director, Field Foundation (1966-1967); Founder, Chair, Student Nonviolent Coordinating Committee (1963-1966); Board of Directors, Robert F. Kennedy Memorial; Board of Directors, National Democratic Institute; Board of Directors, The King Center; Board of Directors, Americorps; Board of Directors, The Africa-America Institute **Civic:** Member, The King Center; Member, The Africa-America Institute; Member, Robert F. Kennedy Memorial **Creative Works:** Co-Author, "March: Book One" (2013); Co-Author, "Across That Bridge: Life Lessons and a Vision for Change" (2012); Co-Author, "Walking With the Wind: A Memoir of the Movement" (1998) **Awards:** One of the 100 Most Influential, TIME Magazine (2017); Liberty Medal, National Constitution Center (2016); Presidential Medal of Freedom, The White House (2010); Wiley A. Branton Award, Washington Lawyers' Committee (2009); Dole Leadership Award, Robert J. Dole Institute of Politics (2007); One of the Most Influential Black Americans, Ebony Magazine (2006-2008); Golden Plate Award, American Academy of Achievement (2004); Allies for Justice Award, The National LGBT Bar Association (2004); Edwin T. Dahlberg Award, American Baptist Churches USA (2003); William Mott Junior Parks Leadership Award, National Parks Conservation Association (2002); Spingarn Award, NAACP (2002); John F. Kennedy Profile in Courage Award (2001); We the People Award, National Constitution Center (2001); Helen Keller Achievement Award for Advocacy, American Foundation for the Blind (2001); Raoul Wallenberg Medal, University of Michigan (2000); Martin Luther King Junior Nonviolent Peace Prize (1999); Pinnacle Award for Lifetime Achievement, ACDelco (1999); Eleanor Roosevelt Award for Human Rights (1998) **Memberships:** President, Americans for Democratic Action (1993-1995); The Faith and Politics Institute **Political Affiliations:** Democrat **Religion:** Baptist **Thoughts on Life:** After a lifetime of service to the cause of civil rights, John Robert Lewis passed away on Friday, July 17, 2020, after a six-month battle with pancreatic cancer. He was 80 years old. Representative Lewis was mourned by presidents and political figures around the world, as well as the millions whose lives he touched through his tireless work in public service. But no tribute to Representative Lewis could be more fitting than his own words: "Do not get lost in a sea of despair. Be hopeful, be optimistic. Our struggle is not the struggle of a day, a week, a month, or a year, it is the struggle of a lifetime. Never, ever be afraid to make some noise and get in good trouble, necessary trouble."

Jonathan Joseph Lewis, MD, PhD

Title: Surgeon, Biomedical Researcher, Oncologist, Entrepreneur **Company Name:** Molecular Ninja **Date of Birth:** 05/23/1958 **Place of Birth:** Johannesburg **State/Country of Origin:** South Africa **Parents:** Myer Philip Lewis; Maisie (Bagg) Lewis **Marital Status:** Married **Education:** PhD, Yale University (1990); MB, BChir, University of the Witwatersrand, Johannesburg, South Africa (1982) **Career:** Chairman, Molecular Ninja (2015-Present); Chairman Dugri Inc, (2020 - present); Chief Executive Officer, Varian Bio (2019 - present); Chief Executive Officer, Chairman, Samus (2016-2018); Attending Surgeon, Memorial Sloan Kettering Cancer Center, New York, NY (1994-Present); Chairman, Chief Executive Officer, President, Ziopharm, New York, NY (2004-2015); Chairman, Joint Committee, Ziopharm-Intrexon (2004-2015); Fellow, Department of Surgery, Memorial Sloan Kettering Cancer Center, New York, NY (1992-1994); Chief Resident of Surgery, Yale School of Medicine, New Haven, CT (1990-1992); Postdoctoral Associate, Yale School of Medicine, New Haven, CT (1987-1990); Registrar of Surgery, School of Medicine, University of the Witwatersrand, Johannesburg, South Africa (1982-1987) **Career Related:** Lecture on Caring in Medicine, Inaugural Lecture - Sir Murray Brennan, Yale University (2018); Visiting Fellow, Churchill College, University of Cambridge (2018); Visiting Professor, St. John's College, University of Cambridge (2018); Chief Medical Officer, Antigenics Inc., New York, NY (2000-2003); Professor, Weill Cornell Medical College (Now Weill Cornell Medicine) (1999-2001); Associate Member, Memorial Sloan Kettering Cancer Center, New York, NY (1999-2001); Assistant Member, Memorial Sloan Kettering Cancer Center, New York, NY (1994-1999); Assistant Professor of Surgery, Weill Cornell Medical College (Now Weill Cornell Medicine) (1994-1999) **Civic:** Board Member, Combat Wound Initiative and Limb Salvage Program, Henry M. Jackson Foundation for the Advancement of Military Medicine; Chairman, Science Advisory Council, Hope Funds for Cancer Research; Chairman, Board of Trustees, Hope Funds for Cancer Research; Board Member, POPPA, Peer to Peer Resiliency, New York Police Department **Creative Works:** Contributor, Articles, Professional Journals; Contributor, Chapters to Books **Awards:** Carnegie Fellow, Wits University (2019); Mandela Fellow, Africa Health (2018); Brennan Award, KACR (2010); Vision of Hope Award, Sarcoma Foundation of America (2009); Outstanding Teacher Award, Memorial Sloan Kettering Cancer Center (1997); Winston Fellowship, Sloan Kettering Institute, Memorial Sloan Kettering Cancer Center (1994-1995); Traveling Fellowship Award, American Association for Cancer Research (1994); Young Investigator Award, American Society of Clinical Oncology (1994); Ohse Fellow, Yale University (1989); Trubshaw Medal, College of Surgeons, Colleges of Medicine of South Africa, Johannesburg, South Africa (1984); Abelheim Medal, South African Medical Research Council (1982); Sulliman Medal in Physiology (1979) **Memberships:** Fellow, American College of Surgeons; Fellow, Royal Society of Medicine; Fellow, Royal College of Surgeons of England; Board Member, Yale Biotechnology Society; Chairman, Rexie's LLC; American Society of Hematology; New York Academy of Sciences; Society of Surgical Oncology; Association for Academic Surgery; American Society of Clinical Oncology; American Association for Cancer Research; American Society for Cell Biology **Marquis Who's Who Honors:** Albert Nelson Marquis Lifetime Achievement Award; Marquis Who's Who Top Professional; Marquis Who's Who Humanitarian Award **Why did you become involved in your profession or industry:** Dr. Lewis was inspired by a love of humanity, a love of biology and a love of mathematics. **Religion:** Jewish

Paul Howard Lewis

Title: Professor Emeritus **Industry:** Education/Educational Services **Date of Birth:** 10/11/1934 **Place of Birth:** Appleton **State/Country of Origin:** WI/USA **Parents:** Maurice Irving Lewis; Ruth Ottilie (Birkholz) Lewis **Spouse Name:** Karen Elizabeth Everist (08/29/1964) **Children:** Anne **Education:** MS, The University of Illinois (1959); BSEE, Rose-Hulman Institute of Technology (1957) **Career:** Professor Emeritus, Michigan Technological University (1999-Present); Associate Professor, Michigan Technological University (1970-1999); Assistant Professor of Electrical Engineering, Michigan Technological University (1961-1969); Electrical Engineer, Interstate Electronics Corporation (1957-1960) **Career Related:** Various Projects, Interstate Electronics Corporation; Developer, Innovative Laboratory Equipment, Michigan Technological University **Civic:** Volunteer, Member, Building Committee, Habitat for Humanity International (2005-2015) **Creative Works:** Author, "A Proposed Z-Plane Criterion To Expedite Transient Performance Analyses," IEEE Transactions on Education (2000); Principal Author, "Basic Control Systems Engineering" (1997); Author, "A Comparison of Second, Third, and Fourth Order Phase-Locked Loops," IEEE Transactions on Aerospace and Electronic Systems (1967) **Awards:** Electrical Engineering Outstanding Professor Award, Michigan Technological University (1980, 1985, 1990); Distinguished Teaching Award, Michigan Technological University (1985); Heminway Medal, Rose-Hulman Institute of Technology (1953, 1957) **Memberships:** IEEE **Marquis Who's Who Honors:** Albert Nelson Marquis Lifetime Achievement Award; Marquis Who's Who Top Professional **To what do you attribute your success:** Mr. Lewis attributes his success to his prestigious education. **Why did you become involved in your profession or industry:** Mr. Lewis became involved in his profession because he enjoyed the challenges of the engineering industry. **Avocations:** Taking photographs outdoors; Woodworking

Ke Li, PhD

Title: Professor **Industry:** Education/Educational Services **Company Name:** Nihon University **Date of Birth:** 11/01/1969 **Place of Birth:** Nanjing **State/Country of Origin:** Jiangsu/China **Parents:** Li Songlin; Liu Yi **Education:** Postdoctoral Research Fellow in Economics, Monash University, Australian National University and Virginia Polytechnic Institute and State University; Doctor of Philosophy in Economics, Monash University; Master's Degree in Economics, Nanjing University, Johns-Hopkins University; Bachelor's Degree in Economics, Nanjing University **Certifications:** Certified Public Accountant **Career:** Professor, College of Economics and Graduate School Business of Nihon University; Assistant Professor and Associate Professor, Saint Josephs University and University of Pennsylvania; Assistant Professor, Monash University, University of Melbourne, Nanjing University and Others **Career Related:** Chairman, Director of Japan-China Management School; Chairman, Japan Economic and Technology Internationalization Association (JETIA); Lecturing Professor, Department of Economics at Saint Joseph's University; Editor, Pacific Economic Review; Visiting Adjunct Professor, City University of Hong Kong, Peking University and Others; Senior Research Associate, Advisor, Many Japanese and International Policy Institutes, Government Agencies and Business Entities, Including Daiwa Securities, Asian Development Bank, Japan Solar Energy and Economy Association **Creative Works:** Founder, Research Member on Various Market Research Models, Including for e-Commerce Pricing, New Classical Economics, Institutionalized Corruption Research, Economic Integration, Constitutional Economics, New Institutional Economics, Development Economics and Others **Awards:** National Education and Culture Award, Japan Royal Family (2016); Senior Research Fellowship, Asian Development Bank (2014-2015); Research Prize, Nihon University (2006); Senior Research Fellowship, City University of Hong Kong (2005); Senior Research Fellowship, World Bank (2004); Research Prize, Nihon University (2003); National Research Prize, Monash University and Australian National University, Ministry of Education of Australia (1995-1998) **Memberships:** Member, Standing Committee, International Entrepreneurs Association (2004); Fellow, International Entrepreneurs Association; Associate, Asian Development Bank; Associate, Monash University; Honorary President, Board of Directors, Japanese and Chinese Master of Business Administration Association; Corresponding Fellow, Australian Academy of Social Sciences; Associate, American Economic Association **Marquis Who's Who Honors:** Marquis Who's Who Top Professional (2019); Albert Nelson Marquis Lifetime Achievement Award **To what do you attribute your success:** In accounting for his success, Mr. Li credits the influence of his family, as well as his own personal mission, self-esteem and social duty. **Why did you become involved in your profession or industry:** Dr. Li initially became involved in his profession due to the influence of his family; particularly his father, who is a professor of economics. **Thoughts on Life:** Life is short, necessitating that people inspire and stimulate themselves to find valid pursuits on behalf of human society.

Marilyn Ligon, MD, FAAFP

Title: Physician **Industry:** Medicine & Health Care **Company Name:** North Alabama Family Medicine **Education:** MD, University of Alabama (2004) **Career:** Physician, North Alabama Family Medicine (2008-Present) **Civic:** Medical Missionary, Philippines **Awards:** Fellow, American Academy of Family Physicians; Best Resident, University of Alabama **Memberships:** Madison Medical Association; American Academy of Family Physicians **Why did you become involved in your profession or industry:** Dr. Ligon is originally from the Philippines. In her home country, they have government hospitals. She was studying to become a medical technologist. She remembers seeing a child fall off a transportation vehicle. After looking after the child for 24 hours, he eventually succumbed to his injuries. After that instance, she decided to apply for a medical school scholarship because she felt compelled to save as many individuals as she could. She eventually became one of five people in the Philippines to get a scholarship to an American medical school. **Avocations:** Racing cars; Ninja-style martial arts; Volleyball; Singing

William Charles Lindholm

Title: Clergyman **Industry:** Religious **Date of Birth:** 03/20/1932 **Place of Birth:** Perry **State/Country of Origin:** IA/USA **Parents:** Lester Leander Lindholm; Elizabeth (Winegar) Lindholm **Marital Status:** Widower **Spouse Name:** Patricia Ann Schneider (02/14/1953, Deceased 06/2018) **Children:** Jana Britt; William Lindholm Junior; Jonell Lindholm (Deceased, 1963) **Education:** MDiv, The Lutheran School of Theology at Chicago (1958); BA, Augustana College (1954) **Certifications:** Ordained Minister, Evangelical Lutheran Church in America (1958); Licensed FCC Engineer, Federal Communications Commission (1949) **Career:** Retired Pastor (2002); Pastor, Holy Cross, Livonia, MI (1970-2002); Pastor, Grace Lutheran Church, East Tawas, MI (1958-1970); Pastor, Hope Lutheran Church, Oscoda, MI (1958-1970) **Career Related:** Editor, "North/West Lower Michigan Synod ELCA" (1970-2002); Chairman, National Committee for Amish Religious Freedom (1967) **Civic:** Board of Directors, Carthage College, Kenosha, WI (1985-1990); Foundation Board Member, Lutheran Social Services of Michigan (Now Samaritas) **Memberships:** Trustee, Charitas Foundation **Marquis Who's Who Honors:** Albert Nelson Marquis Lifetime Achievement Award **Why did you become involved in your profession or industry:** Mr. Lindholm became involved in his profession with encouragement from his high school English teacher, who influenced him to attend a church college. **Avocations:** Piloting airplanes **Religion:** Lutheran

Ray A. Lindsay

Title: 1) Colonel (Retired) 2) Executive **Industry:** Military & Defense Services **Company Name:** 1) United States Air Force 2) Pratt & Whitney - United Technologies Corporation **Date of Birth:** 02/15/1966 **Place of Birth:** Fort Valley **State/Country of Origin:** GA/USA **Parents:** Walter T. Lindsay Sr. (Deceased); Ozie D. Lindsay **Marital Status:** Married **Spouse Name:** Delarita L. Lindsay **Children:** Heather L. Calfee; Hillary N. Lindsay; Halle D. Lindsay **Education:** Master of Science in Strategic Studies, Air War College (2009); Master of Science in Military Operational Arts, Air Command and Staff College (2002); Master of Science in Educational Leadership, Troy University (1994); Bachelor of Science in Mathematics, Angelo State University **Certifications:** Acquisition Professional Development Program Certified Acquisitions Professional Level III: Life Cycle Logistics; Acquisition Professional Development Program Certified Acquisitions Professional Level I: Program Management; Lean Six Sigma, Green Belt Certification **Career:** Senior Director, Military Engines International Operations, Pratt & Whitney, United Technologies Corporation (2018-2019); Senior Director, F135 Sustainment, Pratt & Whitney, United Technologies Corporation (2016-2018); Director of Logistics, Air Force Life Cycle Management Center, Colonel/O-6, Department of Defense, U.S. Air Force, Wright-Patterson Air Force Base, Ohio (2013-2015); Commander, 8th Maintenance Group, Colonel/O-6, Department of Defense, U.S. Air Force, Kunsan Air Base, South Korea (2012-2013); Commander, 591st Supply Chain Management Group, Colonel/O-6, Department of Defense, U.S. Air Force Global Logistics Support Center, Wright-Patterson Air Force Base, Ohio (2010-2012); Senior Adviser to Assistant Minister of Defense for Acquisitions Technology & Logistics, Colonel O-6, North Atlantic Treaty Organization Training Mission/Combined Security Training Center, Camp Eggers, Kabul, Afghanistan (2009-2010); Deputy Director, F-22 Sustainment & Logistics, Lieutenant Colonel/O-5, Department of Defense, U.S. Air Force, Aeronautics Systems Center, 478th Aeronautical Systems Wing, Wright-Patterson Air Force Base, Ohio (2006-2008); Executive to the Vice Commander, Lieutenant Colonel/O-5, Department of Defense, U.S. Air Force, Headquarters Air Force Materiel Command, Wright-Patterson Air Force Base, Ohio (2005-2006); Logistics Operations Professional (2nd Lieutenant/0-1 through Lieutenant Colonel/O-5, Department of Defense, U.S. Air Force (1988-2005) **Career Related:** Darden Executive Leadership Development; Thayer Leadership Development Group; Acquisition Leadership Challenge Program **Civic:** Project Healing Water; Rally Point **Military Service:** Colonel, U.S. Air Force (1987-2015) **Awards:** Three Legions of Merit; Bronze Star; Five Meritorious Service Medals; Two Air Force Commendation Medals; Two Air Force Achievement Medals; Air Force Material Command Thomas P. Gerrity Logistics Award; United States Air Forces in Europe Lieutenant General Leo Marquez Outstanding Aircraft Maintenance Professional Award **Memberships:** Lifetime Member, Logistics Officer Association; Military Officers Association of America; Disabled American Veterans **To what do you attribute your success:** Mr. Lindsay attributes his success to his parents and how he was raised. They impressed upon him the importance of being the best at whatever he set his mind to, and to always treat others how they would want to be treated. **Why did you become involved in your profession or industry:** Mr. Lindsay became involved in his profession due to a hallway encounter he had with his high school's Director of Air Force Junior ROTC. He was already enrolled in the University of Georgia, and followed an inquiry regarding his interest in scholarships at Angelo State University in Texas. Understanding he'd incur a service commitment as a commissioned officer, he applied and received both an academic and Air Force ROTC scholarship. **Religion:** Nondenominational Christian **Thoughts on Life:** Mr. Lindsay believes deeply in the importance of saying what one believes, and being empathetic to others.

Verna May Linzey

Title: Reverend **Industry:** Religious **Company Name:** Verna Linzey Ministries **Date of Birth:** 5/17/1919 **Place of Birth:** Coffeyville **State/Country of Origin:** KS/USA **Year of Passing:** 2016 **Parents:** Carey Franklin Hall Jr.; Alice May (Hart) (Hall) Doyle **Marital Status:** Widowed **Spouse Name:** Stanford Eugene Linzey Jr. (02/04/2010, Deceased). **Children:** Gena May English; Janice Ellen Mathis; Stanford Eugene III; Virginia Darnelle Lemons (Deceased); Sharon Faye Ackerman; George William; Vera Evelyn Nelson; Paul Edward; David Leon; James Franklin **Education:** MA, International Biographical Centre of Cambridge (2012); DD, Kingsway University (2001); DMin, Fuller Theological Seminary (1980); BA Level Coursework in Biblical Languages, Southwestern Assembly of God University (1938-1939) **Certifications:** Ordained Minister, Southern Baptist Convention (2016); Licensed Minister, Assemblies of God (1945-2016); Church Planter, Assemblies of God (1975) **Career:** Movie Actress (2010-2016); Evangelist, Singer, Songwriter, Recording Artist (1938-2016); Bible Translator, Modern English Version Bible (2014); Founder, Military Bible Association, Inc. (2010); Chief Editor, New Tyndale Version Bible (2009); Pastor, El Cajon Evangelistic Tabernacle (Assembly of God), El Cajon, CA (1946-1951) **Career Related:** Featured Guest, Prime Time Christian Broadcasting Network (2004); Featured Guest, Public Broadcasting Service (2004) **Civic:** Republican National Committee (1946-2016); Democratic National Committee (1943-1945) **Military Service:** Volunteer Military Service (1968-1970) **Creative Works:** Translator, "Modern English Version" Bible (2014); Translator, Author, "The Gifts of the Spirit" (2014); Movie Actress, "Iniquity" (2012); Editor, "Baptism in the Spirit" (2012); Host, "The Word with Dr. Verna Linzey" (2012); Chief Editor, "New Tyndale Version" Bible (2009); Radio Broadcaster, "Lectures on Pneumatology" (2007); Host, "Holy Spirit Today" (2007); Author, "Spirit Baptism" (2007); Author, "The Baptism with the Holy Spirit" (2004); Songwriter, "Oh Blessed Jesus" (1991) **Awards:** Mother of the Fleet, U.S. Navy (2016); Leader of the Year Award, Heritage Foundation (2011); National Bible Teacher of the Year (2011); Honoree, Evangelist of the Year (2010); Best Non-Fiction of the Year Award, San Diego Christian Writers' Guild (2006); Certificate of Recognition, Mayor Lori Holt Pfeiler, Escondido, CA (2001); Eponym, Congressional Proclamation, Rev. Dr. Verna May Linzey Day (2001); Gold Record Award for Best Vocals in Southern Gospel Music **Memberships:** National Wildlife Federation; National Religious Broadcasters; National Association of Evangelicals **Marquis Who's Who Honors:** Albert Nelson Marquis Lifetime Achievement Award (2017) **To what do you attribute your success:** Dr. Darrin Rodgers, who is the director of the Flower Pentecostal Heritage Center, properly attributed Rev. Linzey's success to God by saying, "Verna Hall Linzey's ministry, whose remarkable life spanned the history of the Pentecostal movement, provides a poignant example of how God has worked through Pentecostal women. Linzey was a Pentecostal evangelist before she married, she continued in pastoral and evangelistic ministry alongside her husband even while raising 10 children, and in her later years her ministry blossomed and she authored several books, spoke at conferences and crusades around the world, and even appeared in a motion picture. During her almost 80 years in ministry, Linzey prayed with countless thousands of people to receive the baptism in the Holy Spirit, and her writings and television programs faithfully shared Classical Pentecostal beliefs. Linzey's life demonstrates what God can do through a person who seeks to be fully committed to Christ and His mission." **Why did you become involved in your profession or industry:** Rev. Linzey chose her multi-faceted profession to impact the world for Christ, mainly through evangelistic crusades, making a positive impact in the movie and recording industries, and through touching an untold number of lives through her television work and Bible translation work. God had His hand on her life since she was a child and rewarded her for her faithfulness. **Avocations:** Gardening; Photography; Genealogy **Political Affiliations:** Republican **Religion:** Christian **Thoughts on Life:** "Power is not in who you think you are, for thoughts alone amount to nothing; Power is not in who you hope to be, for the future never comes; Power is who you are, for that requires work."

James Lipton

Title: Television Personality; Dean Emeritus; Actor; Author **Industry:** Media & Entertainment **Company Name:** Actors Studio Drama School at Pace University **Date of Birth:** 09/19/1926 **Place of Birth:** Detroit **State/Country of Origin:** MI/USA **Year of Passing:** 2020 **Parents:** Lawrence Lipton; Betty (Weinberg) Lipton **Marital Status:** Married **Spouse Name:** Kedakai (Turner) Lipton (1970); Nina Foch (1954, Divorced 1959) **Education:** Coursework, Wayne State University **Certifications:** Certified Pilot **Career:** Dean Emeritus, The Actors Studio Drama School, New School University, New York, NY (2004-2020); Founding Dean, The Actors Studio Drama School, New School University, New York, NY (1994-2004) **Military Service:** United States Air Force **Creative Works:** Actor, "Arrested Development" (2004, 2005, 2013, 2019); Host, Executive Producer, "Inside the Actors Studio" (1994-2018); Voice Actor, "Igor" (2008); Voice Actor, "Bolt" (2008); Author, "Inside Inside" (2007); Actor, "Cold Squad" (2005); Actor, "Bewitched" (2005); Voice Actor, "The Simpsons" (2002); Author, "Exhalation of Business and Finance" (1993); Author, "Exhalation of Home and Family" (1993); Head Writer, "Capitol" (1986-1987); Writer, Producer, "Mirrors" (1985); Writer, "Copacabana" (1985); Author, "Mirrors" (1983); Writer, Executive Producer, "Happy Birthday, Bob" (1978); Head Writer, "Guiding Light" (1973-1975); Head Writer, "Return to Peyton Place" (1972); Head Writer, "The Best of Everything" (1970); Author, "Exhalation of Larks: More Than One Thousand Terms" (1968); Lyricist, Actor, "Sherry!" (1967); Head Writer, "Another World" (1964, 1966-1968); Actor, "The Guiding Light" (1952-1962); Writer, "The Edge of Night" (1956); Actor, "Inner Sanctum" (1954); Actor, "You are There" (1953); Actor, "The Big Break" (1953); Actor, "The Autumn Garden" (1951); Producer, "The Mighty Gents"; Co-Producer, "Ain't Misbehavin'"; Producer, Two Dozen Television Specials **Awards:** Critics' Choice Award for Best Reality Show Host (2016); Primetime Emmy Award, Outstanding Nonfiction Series or Special, Television Academy (2013); Inductee, Cable Hall of Fame (2009); Lifetime Achievement Emmy, The National Academy of Television Arts & Sciences (2007); Chevalier de l'ordre des Arts et des Lettres, France **Memberships:** Aircraft Owners and Pilots Association

Jean Anne Litchfield

Title: Nurse **Industry:** Medicine & Health Care **Date of Birth:** 10/06/1942 **Place of Birth:** Gary **State/Country of Origin:** IN/USA **Parents:** Donald Kleine; Helen Louise (Sweet) Eller **Marital Status:** Widow **Spouse Name:** Norman E. Stone (12/27/1965, Divorced 1973); Frank Litchfield (01/26/1974) **Children:** Diana; David; Julie **Education:** Master of Science in Nursing, Indiana State University (1995); Bachelor of Science in Nursing, Millikin University (1993); Associate of Science in Biology, Richland Community College (1991); Licensed Practical Nurse, Indiana University Vocational Technical College (1973) **Certifications:** Registered Nurse, Indiana and Illinois **Career:** Retired (2015); Assistant Professor, Nursing Program, Richland Community College, Decatur, IL (1995-2015); Charge Nurse, Psychiatric Ward, St. Mary's Hospital, Decatur, IL (1993-1999); Nurse, St. Anthony Hospital, Terre Haute, IN (1973-1993); Nurse Assistant, St. Anthony Hospital, Terre Haute, IN (1960-1973) **Career Related:** Member, Student Welfare Committee, Millikin University, Decatur, IL (1991-1992) **Civic:** Volunteer, First Responder, CERT; Volunteer, Home for the Mentally Challenged **Creative Works:** Developed Practical Nursing Program, Richland Community College (2000) **Awards:** Excellence in Nursing Education Award, Decatur Area Task Force Nursing Education (2000); Outstanding Innovations in Teaching and Learning Award, Richland Community College (1998); Outstanding Innovations in Teaching and Learning Award, Richland Community College (1997); Clara Compton Scholar, St. Mary's Hospital (1994); Clara Compton Scholar, St. Mary's Hospital (1993); Scholar, American Legion (1992); Named, Most Caring Nurse, St. Mary's Hospital (1990); Silver Poet Award, World of Poetry (1990); Gold Poet Award, World of Poetry (1989); First Place Art Award, County Fair (1986); Second Place Art Award, County Fair (1985); First Place Art Award, County Fair (1985); First Place Art Award, County Fair (1984); Second Place Art Award, County Fair (1984) **Memberships:** Sigma Theta Tau (1995); President, Alpha Tau Delta (1992-1993); Treasurer, Alpha Tau Delta (1991-1992); Treasurer, International Platform Association, Barn Colony Artists (1986-1988); Treasurer, Beta Sigma Phi (1976-1978); Phi Theta Kappa **Marquis Who's Who Honors:** Albert Nelson Marquis Lifetime Achievement Award; Marquis Who's Who Top Professional **Why did you become involved in your profession or industry:** Ms. Litchfield became involved in her profession after being encouraged to enroll in a nursing class by two friends of hers. She attended the course for two weeks and became a certified nurse's aid, after which she eventually went to school to become a registered nurse. **Avocations:** Artist **Religion:** Catholic

John H. Litchfield, PhD

Title: Adjunct Professor **Industry:** Education/Educational Services **Company Name:** The Ohio State University **Date of Birth:** 02/13/1929 **Place of Birth:** Scituate **State/Country of Origin:** MA/USA **Parents:** Frank Albert Litchfield; Alma (Hyland) Litchfield **Marital Status:** Widowed **Spouse Name:** Dianne Chappell (04/15/1966, Deceased) **Children:** Robert Chappell **Education:** PhD in Food Technology, University of Illinois (1956); MS in Food Technology, University of Illinois (1954); BS in Food Technology, Massachusetts Institute of Technology (MIT) (1950) **Career:** Consulting Staff, Battelle Memorial Institute, Columbus, OH (1993-2013); Research Leader, Battelle Memorial Institute, Columbus, OH (1960-1993); Assistant Professor, Illinois Institute of Technology, Chicago, IL (1957-1960); Research Technologist, Swift & Co., Chicago, IL (1956-1957); Chemist, Searle Food Corp., Hollywood, FL (1950-1951) **Career Related:** Adjunct Professor, The Ohio State University, Columbus, OH (1977-Present); Fellow, Royal Society of Biology, United Kingdom (1992); Fellow, Society of Industrial Microbiology and Biotechnology (1987); Fellow, Institute of Food Technologists (1980); Fellow, American Academy of Microbiology (1970); Fellow, American Association of the Advancement of Science (1966); Food Industry Consultant, Chicago, IL (1957-1960); Fellow, American Academy of Microbiology; Fellow, American Institute of Chemists; Fellow, American Public Health Association; Fellow, Royal Society of Biology, United Kingdom; Fellow, Institute of Food Science & Technology; Fellow, Royal Society of Public Health **Civic:** Volunteer, Worthington Ohio Public Libraries **Military Service:** First Lieutenant, U.S. Army (1951-1953) **Creative Works:** Co-Author, "Food Plant Sanitation" (1962); Contributor, Articles, Scientific Journals; Patentee in the Field **Awards:** Inductee, Hall of Honor, Department of Food Science & Technology, The Ohio State University (2018); Distinguished Service Award, The Ohio State University (2016); Professor of the Year, Department of Food Science & Technology, The Ohio State University (2008); Carl R. Fellers Award, Institute of Food Technologists (1994); Distinguished Service Award, Ohio Valley Section, Institute of Food Technologists (1980); Charles Porter Award, Society of Industrial Microbiology (1977) **Memberships:** President, Institute of Food Technologists (1991-1992); President, Society of Industrial Microbiology (1970-1971); American Chemical Society; American Society for Microbiology; Life Member, Water Environmental Federation; Past President, Gardeners Club of Central Ohio; Past President, Inniswood Volunteers, Inniswood Metro Gardens **Marquis Who's Who Honors:** Albert Nelson Marquis Lifetime Achievement Award; Marquis Who's Who Top Professional **To what do you attribute your success:** Dr. Litchfield attributes his success to the talented people that he has had the fortune of working with. **Avocations:** Gardening **Thoughts on Life:** Most of Dr. Litchfield's work is in food science and technology, food industry waste treatment, food safety and industrial microbiology. He has also done research on antibiotic resistance in livestock.

R. Donald Little

Title: Real Estate Entrepreneur **Industry:** Real Estate **Date of Birth:** 03/18/1937 **Place of Birth:** Gastonia **State/Country of Origin:** NC/USA **Parents:** Coy Marshall; Stella May (Pruett) L. **Marital Status:** Married **Spouse Name:** Linda Lee Stoner (09/07/1999); Jacqueline Beatrice Mandel (06/10/1967, Deceased 03/1995) **Children:** Tina June W **Education:** MA in Architecture, Catholic University America (1983); BS in Architecture, Catholic University America (1981); BA in Philosophy & Psychology, University Maryland (1972); Coursework in Nursing, Hospital Corp. School, Chicago, IL; Coursework, Medical Technology School, U.S. Naval Hospital, Bethesda, MD **Certifications:** Ordained, Chartered Non-denominational Minister (1998) **Career:** Real Estate Entrepreneur (2002); Retired (2002); Area Administrative Officer, BARC Research Service, U.S. Department of Agriculture, Beltsville, MD (1996-2002); Supervisor Architect, Chief Facility, Engineering Branch, Agricultural Research Service, U.S. Department of Agriculture (1987-1996); Branch Head, Design Division, Naval Surface Weapons Center, Silver Spring, MD (1981-1987); Supervisor Architect, VVKR Inc., University Park, MD; Junior Architect, VVKR Inc., University Park, MD; Blood Bank and Medical Technologist, Supervisor, Central Laboratory, Doctor's Hospital, Washington DC (1959-1979); Biological Laboratory Technologist, Naval Medical Research Institute, Bethesda, MD (1966-1968); Blood Bank and Medical Technologist, Dr. Oscar B. Hunter Memorial Laboratory, Washington DC (1956-1962) **Career Related:** Project Manager, Naval Building Projects, San Diego, CA **Civic:** Hospice Volunteer, Baltimore, MD **Military Service:** U.S. Navy (1956-1962) **Creative Works:** Author, "Spirits, Angels, Demons Gods: Experiences on the Road to the Heavens and to the Hells" (2010); Author, "Mosaics of Silent Justice"; Author, "The Lesser God in Us" **Memberships:** American Association of Blood Banks; American Society of Medical Technologists; Association for Research and Enlightenment **Marquis Who's Who Honors:** Albert Nelson Marquis Lifetime Achievement Award **Why did you become involved in your profession or industry:** Mr. Little went into the Navy, he passed the test and went to three schools in nursing, medical technology, and blood bank; In addition, he went to school in the Navy as a medical technologist. He changed his profession because he wanted to go to college.

Baruch S. Littman

Title: Corporate Vice President of Development (Retired) **Industry:** Nonprofit & Philanthropy **Company Name:** Jewish Community Foundation of Los Angeles **Date of Birth:** 10/13/1946 **Marital Status:** Married **Spouse Name:** Deborah (4/5/1981) **Children:** Penina Prager; Avital Engelhardt; Shimon **Education:** MS, Baruch College; BA, Long Island University **Career:** Retired (2019-Present); Corporate Vice President if Development, Jewish Community Foundation of Los Angeles (1999-2019); American Nurses Association of Kansas City; Clairol **Memberships:** Executive Committee, Legacy Sponsor, Host, Exit Planning Institute (2017-Present); Advisors in Philanthropy (2014-Present); Senior Member, Provisors **Marquis Who's Who Honors:** Albert Nelson Marquis Lifetime Achievement Award; Marquis Who's Who Top Professional **To what do you attribute your success:** Mr. Littman attributes his success to his vigorous personality, his ability to relate to people almost immediately, being a very good listener, and delivering the message that he needs to deliver generally and as concisely as possible. He works with people until they just don't listen to him, but he works with them until they hear him. That secret was given to him by the chief executive officer at the Jewish Community Foundation of Los Angeles. Mr. Littman gets up every morning with a smile on his face. **Why did you become involved in your profession or industry:** Mr. Littman has always had the ability to understand nonprofits.

Elizabeth Liu, MD, PhD

Title: President **Industry:** Medicine & Health Care **Company Name:** Elizabeth Y. Liu, MD, PhD **Parents:** Fiang Jaixiang Ji; Zhi Xian Ma **Education:** Residency in Family Medicine, University of Medicine & Dentistry of New Jersey (UMDNJ), Capital Health System, Trenton, NJ (2002-2005); PhD in Neurosciences, University of Medicine & Dentistry of New Jersey (UMDNJ), Newark, NJ (1998); Graduate Student, City University of New York (1991-1992); MD, Guangzhou Medical College (Now Guangzhou Medical University), Guangzhou, Guangdong, China (1988) **Certifications:** Board Certification, American Board of Family Medicine (2016) **Career:** Family Medicine Practitioner, Wellness Medical Center LLC, Rochelle Park, NJ (2010-Present); Family Medicine Practitioner, Hackensack University Medical Center (2009-Present); Family Medicine Practitioner, Saint Clare's Health System, New Jersey (2007-Present); Family Medicine Practitioner, Wellness Medical Center LLC, Saddle Brook, NJ (2007-2010); Family Medicine Practitioner, Wallington Clinic LLC, Wallington, NJ (2006-2008); Family Medicine Practitioner, Beverwyck Medical Associates LLC, Parsippany, NJ (2005-2007); Family Medicine Practitioner, Saint Clare's Health System, New Jersey (2005-2007); Medical Assistant, Medical & Dental Care Center, New York (1998-2002); Assistant Professor, Guangzhou Medical College, China (1988-1990) **Awards:** Certificate of Commendation "In Honor & Recognition of Receiving the Outstanding Health Service Award," Bergen County Board of Chosen Freeholders (2019); Outstanding Medical Services Award, Certificate of Commendation, County of Bergen (2019); Certificate of Recognition, Outstanding Health Services Award, Wellness Medical Center, LLC, Bergen County, NJ (2019); Certificate of Commendation, Office of the Bergen County Sheriff (2019); Award, Patients' Choice Winner, OpenCare; Recognized, U.S. Surgeon General **Memberships:** Accountable Care Organizations (ACOs); SOMLS; Chinese Community Accountable Care Organization, Inc. (CCACO) **To what do you attribute your success:** Dr. Liu attributes her success to self-motivation and a desire to be the best at everything she does. Dr. Liu's personal motto encourages her to use positivity to make the world a better place. **Why did you become involved in your profession or industry:** In five years, Dr. Liu hopes to make a breakthrough in her field by developing a cure, treatment, or study. She would like to create and patent an idea that will benefit people all over the world.

Verdree Lockhart Sr., PhD

Title: Professional Counselor (Retired) **Industry:** Social Work **Company Name:** Atlanta Public Schools **Date of Birth:** 10/21/1923 **Place of Birth:** Louisville **State/Country of Origin:** GA/USA **Parents:** Fred Douglas Lockhart; Minnie Belle (Roberson) Lockhart **Marital Status:** Married **Spouse Name:** Louise Howard (08/05/1950) **Children:** Verdree II; Vera Louise; Fernandez; Abigail **Education:** PhD in Guidance and Counseling, Atlanta University (1975); Postgraduate Coursework in Guidance and Counseling, George Peabody College (1960); MA in Administration and Supervision, Atlanta University (1957); BS in Agricultural Education, Tuskegee University (1949) **Certifications:** Certified Counselor; Certified Principal; Certified Nursing Home Administrator; Certified Asbestos Inspector **Career:** Professional Counselor, Atlanta Public Schools (1986-2000); Regional Inspector, U.S. Environmental Protection Agency, Atlanta, GA (1985-1986); Dean of Education, Phillips College, Atlanta, GA (1984-1985); Vice President, Atlanta University (1981-1982); Trustee, Atlanta University (1975-1981); Education Consultant, Georgia Department of Education, Atlanta, GA (1963-1980); Teacher, Counselor, Jefferson County High School, Louisville, GA (1949-1963) **Civic:** Mayor's Task Force on Public Education, Atlanta, GA (1988-Present); Forest Resource Council, Tuskegee University (1972-Present); Treasurer, Board of Directors, Atlanta Branch, NAACP (1970-1995); Board of Directors, Economic Opportunity Atlanta (1985-1990); Assistant Commissioner, Atlanta Area Council, Boy Scouts of America (1972-1976) **Military Service:** Master Sergeant, U.S. Army (1943-1966) **Awards:** Named, Alumni Brother of the Year, Alpha Phi Alpha (1980); Silver Beaver Award, Boy Scouts of America (1970); Georgia Governor's Medallion Award, Executive Branch, State of Georgia (1967-1968); Named, Teacher of the Year, Georgia Chamber of Commerce (1957) **Memberships:** President, Atlanta University Consortium Chapter, Phi Delta Kappa (1988-Present); Zion Hill Baptist Church; National Education Association; Georgia Association of Educators; Atlanta Association of Educators; American Counseling Association, Inc.; Former Member, American College Personnel Association; Alpha Phi Alpha; American Legion; Boy Scouts of America; Atlanta Business League; Life Golden Heritage Member, NAACP; American Association of Retired Persons; Jefferson County Farm Bureau; American Soy Bean Association; Georgia Forestry Association; Clark Atlanta University National Alumni Association; Tuskegee University National Alumni Association; Sons of Louisville Lodge (Prince Hall Free and Accepted Masons); Georgia Community Action Association; Atlanta Tuskegee Alumni Club; Tuskegee University Agricultural, Environmental and Nutritional Sciences Alumni Association; George Washington Carver Society; Distinguished Life Member, Eminent Presidential Associates of Tuskegee University **Marquis Who's Who Honors:** Albert Nelson Marquis Lifetime Achievement Award; Marquis Who's Who Top Professional **Why did you become involved in your profession or industry:** Dr. Lockhart entered his profession because during his high school years, he was counseled by his principal. He was his role model and his hero. One day in the corridor of the high school, he said to him, "Verdree, you should be the first one to get your doctorate." That encouraged him to move forward. **Political Affiliations:** Democrat **Religion:** Baptist

Heidi Loewen

Title: Artist, Gallery Owner, Teacher **Industry:** Fine Art **Company Name:** Heidi Loewen Fine Art Gallery, School & Ceramic Restoration **Place of Birth:** Providence **State/Country of Origin:** RI/USA **Parents:** Dr. Erwin G. Loewen; Joanna Wills Loewen **Children:** Hans Christopher Loewenheath **Education:** Coursework, Anderson Ranch School of the Arts, Snowmass, CO (2006); Ceramics Program, Harvard University, Ceramics Program (1988-1991); Coursework, Haystack Mountain School of Crafts, Deere Isle, ME (1990); BS in Fine Art and Studio Arts, Art History and Languages, Skidmore College, Saratoga Springs, NY (1978); Study Abroad, Art History, Studio Art, Language, University of Paris, Sorbonne Paris, France (1976-1977) **Career:** Gallery Owner, Artist, Teacher, Corporate Team Builder, Heidi Loewen Fine Art Gallery, School & Ceramic Restoration (1998-Present); Ceramic Teacher, Santa Fe Clay (1993-1998); Assistant Art Curator, Spring Creek Art Foundation, Boston, MA (1984-1987); Business Manager, Sotheby's Art Auction House, New York, NY (1979-1984); American College of Switzerland, Admissions (1979-1980); Swiss Ski School (1979-1980); United Nations, Sudano-Sahelian Office (1980) Metropolitan Museum of Art, Intern (1977); Saratoga Performing Arts Center, Saratoga Springs, NY (1974-1978) **Career Related:** Artist; Teacher; Gallery Owner Ceramic Restorer; TV Personality; Lecturer; Curator; Photographer; Videographer **Civic:** International Folk Art Museum; Warehouse 21; New Mexico Youth Outreach; Rape Crisis Center; Santa Fe Animal Shelter; Santa Fe Show House Benefit; Carlos Slim Helu Museo Soumaya, Mexico City; Montgomery Museum of Fine Arts, Montgomery, Alabama; International Council on Foreign Relations; Cowboy Hall of Fame; Judge, SWAIA; Georgia O'Keeffe Museum **Creative Works:** Sculptor, "Un Oeuf is Enough,"; Sculptor, "It's the Shoe That Makes the Woman"; Sculptor, "Filabia Mignon" **Awards:** Santa Fe ARTsmart Artist of the Year (2019); Art Santa Fe Sculpture Award: Porcelain Sculpture with AK-47 Replica, "Un Oeuf is Enough," stand against world gun violence; Miami Basel Spectrum, Best Sculpture Honor for "It's the Shoe That Makes the Woman," 6 ft. metal sculpture, most photographed artwork in show; Honorarium and Solo Show, Western University of New Mexico; UNESCO Delegate creating porcelain with Living Treasure, Mr. Han Sug Bong, of Icheon, South Korea. **Memberships:** National Museum of Women in the Arts, Washington, DC; Santa Fe Art Gallery Association; Creative Santa Fe; Museum of New Mexico Foundation; Council on International Relations; Georgia O'Keeffe Museum **To what do you attribute your success:** Ms. Loewen attributes her success to her amazing parents, extended family, my teachers and fellow artists around the world. "My mother was a nurse during World War II, later a painter, collage artist and gourmet cook, which inspired my artistic passions. My family is filled with engineers, doctors, artists, designers, photographers, calligraphers, gilders, couturiers, and a curator at the British Museum. I learned growing up, 'Above all, be kind, smile and pursue your passions.'" **Why did you become involved in your profession or industry:** "As a child in Rochester, NY, I was blessed with a very musical, scientific and artistic family. Music has always been a source of inspiration, as well as nature. From age 2, I loved playing in mud. At age 10, my mother signed me up for pottery classes. I fell in love with squish. I had magnificent ceramic teachers at Harvard and Skidmore, but never dreamed I'd be an artist. Arts administration was my forté at Sotheby's in NYC and at William I. Koch's Spring Creek Art Foundation and Private Art Collection in Boston. Upon moving to Santa Fe, NM, I returned to my love of porcelain which blossomed into a successful career, encompassing sculpture creation, gallery ownership, teaching, corporate team building and ceramic restoration." **Avocations:** Ski instructor; Pianist; Singer; Figure skating shows; Skating and roller skating instructor; Hiker; Mountain biker; Swimmer, Dancer; Sailor; Gardener; World traveler; Gourmet cook **Thoughts on Life:** "I love traveling the world and meeting people to learn of their culture, art and languages. This energizes and invigorates my artistic life. It is important to be honorable, humorous and generous of spirit. I have a strong reputation in New Mexico for bringing together creative people from many disciplines. As an artist who has reached the height of success, giving back to others, particularly young artists, has proven to be vastly rewarding."

Samuel Johnston Losh

Title: President **Industry:** Real Estate **Company Name:** Milner Street, Inc. **Date of Birth:** 11/11/1932 **Place of Birth:** Hershey **State/Country of Origin:** PA/USA **Parents:** Charles Seibert Losh; Esther Dora (Johnston) Losh **Marital Status:** Widowed **Spouse Name:** Lorna Gail Gordon (2016, Deceased); Llewellyn Mathews Hall (1964-1994, Divorced) **Children:** Elizabeth Mathews; Stephen Johnston **Education:** Postgraduate Coursework, University of Southern California (1975-1981); Postgraduate Coursework, University of California Los Angeles (1968-1974); Postgraduate Coursework, Syracuse University (1956-1957); Bachelor of Science in Mechanical Engineering, Massachusetts Institute of Technology (1954) **Certifications:** Certified, Institute of Certified Professional Managers (1980) **Career:** President, Milner Street Inc., Pasadena, CA (1980-Present); Senior Systems Engineer, Ritec Corporation, Chatsworth, CA (1987-1989); Senior Systems Specialist, Xerox Special Information Systems, Pasadena, CA (1964-1987); Spacecraft Systems Engineer, Lockheed Aircraft Corporation, Burbank, CA (1962-1964); Systems Engineer, Hoffman Electronics, Los Angeles, CA (1959-1962); Technical Staff, TRW Inc., Los Angeles, CA (1957-1959); Instructor, Syracuse University (1956); Engineer, Technicolor SA, Camden, NJ (1954-1955); Treasurer, Milner Street Inc., Pasadena, CA **Career Related:** Secretary, Regina Properties Inc., Pasadena, CA (1981-1992) **Civic:** Chairman, Los Angeles Chapter, Massachusetts Institute of Technology Educational Council (1978-2001); Facilitator, Mathematics Standards Program, Los Angeles Unified School District (1994) **Military Service:** First Lieutenant, United States Air Force (1955-1957) **Awards:** George Morgan Award, Massachusetts Institute of Technology Educational Council (1987); Silver Knight of Management, National Management Association (1980) **Memberships:** Board of Directors, Massachusetts Institute of Technology Alumni Association (1981-1983); Institute of Electrical and Electronics Engineers; American Institute of Aeronautics and Astronautics; Pasadena Angels Inc. **Marquis Who's Who Honors:** Albert Nelson Marquis Lifetime Achievement Award **To what do you attribute your success:** Mr. Losh attributes his success to having an analytical mind. He likes to analyze situations and predict what the end result will be. **Why did you become involved in your profession or industry:** Mr. Losh became involved in his profession after a factory worker at RCA gave him a pamphlet while he was working there. It showed information on investing in real estate and how it could build wealth. He was 22 years old at the time, and didn't act on that until about four years later. He was able to buy a three-unit apartment house and built on that. **Avocations:** Traveling; Playing racquetball; Studying eclipses; Operas; Skiing **Political Affiliations:** Republican **Religion:** Unitarian Universalist **Thoughts on Life:** Mr. Losh believes that one's failures can be just as important as one's successes.

Marjorie Lott

Title: Accountant **Industry:** Financial Services **Date of Birth:** 07/23/1940 **Place of Birth:** Fort Worth **State/Country of Origin:** TX/USA **Parents:** Abraham Issac Goldberg; Florene Wilmoth (Richardson) Goldberg **Marital Status:** Widowed **Spouse Name:** Kenneth Edward Lott (1977, Deceased 2017); Ashburn Richard Piland Jr. (08/08/1959, Divorced 1975) **Children:** Ashburn Richard Piland III; Leslie Piland Sinclair **Education:** BBA in Accounting, University of Houston (1977) **Certifications:** Certified Public Accountant, Texas; Certified Management Accountant **Career:** Principal, Marjorie G. Lott, CPA, Houston, Texas (1989-2017); Director of Operations, Baca Landata, Houston, Texas (1992); Controller, Director of Finance, Houston Association of Realtors (1983-1989); Controller, Carbonite Oil Company, Houston, Texas (1981-1983); Supervisor, Tenneco Oil Company, Houston, Texas (1977-1981); Owner, Dick Piland Enterprises, GA (1969-1975) **Civic:** Audit Liaison, United Way of Greater Houston (1992-1993) **Awards:** Presidential Citation, Houston Association of Realtors (1984); Award of Merit, National Federation of Music Clubs (1975); Two-time Recipient, Five Star Wealth Manager Award **Memberships:** Legislative Regional Coordinator, Political Affairs, Houston and 13 Counties, Texas Society of CPAs (TXCPA) (1992-Present); Board of Directors, Texas Society of CPAs (TXCPA) (1987-Present); Vice President, Houston Chapter, Texas Society of CPAs (TXCPA) (1989); Founding Member, Texas Association of CPAs (TXCPA); Chairman, Houston West Chamber of Commerce **Marquis Who's Who Honors:** Albert Nelson Marquis Lifetime Achievement Award **Why did you become involved in your profession or industry:** Ms. Lott became involved in her profession because she wanted to be an engineer but they did not allow girls into engineering school. Her mother suggested she try bookkeeping in high school and she loved it. She knew she did not want to be a teacher or a nurse and people thought at that time she was crazy to go into accounting but her dad encouraged her to be anything she wanted to be; she also wanted to make more money. **Avocations:** Dancing; Traveling **Religion:** Baptist

Gary Richard Lounsberry, PhD, MPH, ACSW

Title: Professor Emeritus, Public Health Official (Retired) **Industry:** Education/Educational Services **Company Name:** Alfred State College **Date of Birth:** 05/22/1944 **Place of Birth:** Wellsville **State/Country of Origin:** NY/USA **Parents:** Alton Lewis Lounsberry; Corabelle (Buckley) Lounsberry **Spouse Name:** Chere Lea Thayer (06/09/1973) **Children:** Sarah Grace Lea; Abby Lea Edna **Education:** PhD in Social Work, University of Pittsburgh (1985); MPH, University of Pittsburgh (1981); MSW, University of Michigan (1968); AB, University of Rochester, New York (1966) **Certifications:** Licensed Specialist, Clinical Social Work, Kansas, Florida **Career:** Professor Emeritus, Alfred State College (2014-Present); Professor, Social And Behavioral Sciences, SUNY Alfred State College (2005-2014); Associate Professor, Bachelor's Program Director, School Of Social Work, Florida Gulf Coast University (1996-2005); Director of Social Services, Mental Health, Family Health Centers of Southwest Florida (1992-1996); Human Services Consultant, Indian Health Services, U.S. Public Health Service, Lawrence, KS (1981-1992); Advanced Through Grades to Captain, U.S. Public Health Service (1987); Career Development Trainee, U.S. Public Health Service, Pittsburgh, PA (1979-1981); Mental Health Consultant, Indian Health, U.S. Public Health Service, Claremore, OK (1974-1979); Service Unit Director, Indian Health, U.S. Public Health Service, Sisseton, SD (1972-1974); Social Worker Indian Health, U.S. Public Health Service, Sisseton, SD (1970-1972); Commissioned Lieutenant (Junior Grade), U.S. Public Health Service (1970); School Community Agent, Detroit Public Schools (1968-1970) **Career Related:** Field Instructor, Barry University, Miami Shores, FL (1992-Present); Field Instructor, University of Kansas, Lawrence (1983-1992); Instructor, Haskell Indian Nations University, Lawrence, KS (1982-1992); Field Instructor, University of Oklahoma, Norman, OK (1976-1979) **Civic:** Board of Directors, Salvation Army Primary Care Clinic (1993-Present); Local Episcopalian Church Board (1988-1996); Foster Home Board (1987) **Military Service:** Captain, Commissioned Corps, U. S. Public Health Service (1970-1996) **Awards:** Social Worker of the Year, American Public Health Association **Memberships:** Chair, Lawrence Area Chapter, National Association Of Social Workers (1990-1992); Secretary, Claremore Chapter, Lions (1978-1979); Program Chairman, Sisseton Chapter, Kiwanis (1972-1973); Commissioned Officers Association; U.S. Public Health Service; American Public Health Association; Academy of Certified Social Workers; Association For Applied Psychophysiology And Biofeedback **Marquis Who's Who Honors:** Albert Nelson Marquis Lifetime Achievement Award; Marquis Who's Who Top Professional **Avocations:** Gardening; Cooking; Travel; Sailing; Photography **Religion:** Episcopalian

Byron Keith Lovelace, PhD, JD

Title: Lawyer, Management Consultant **Industry:** Law and Legal Services **Company Name:** Law Offices of Keith Lovelace **Date of Birth:** 02/15/1935 **Place of Birth:** Vernon **State/Country of Origin:** TX/USA **Parents:** Joseph Edward Lovelace; Hattie Pearl (Brians) Lovelace **Marital Status:** Married **Spouse Name:** Sandra Alene (Daniel) Lovelace (06/17/1961) **Children:** Kirk Daniel; Bethany Alene; Amy Kathleen **Education:** JD, South Texas College of Law, Houston, TX (1978); PhD, The University of Texas at Austin, Austin, TX (1973); MSChemE, The University of Texas at Austin, Austin, TX (1961); BSChemE, The University of Texas at Austin, Austin, TX (1958) **Career:** Private Practice, Lawyer, Management Consultant, Law Offices of Keith Lovelace, Houston, TX (1980-Present); President, Management Resources International, Houston, TX (1980-Present); President, P-V-T Inc. (Core Laboratories, Inc.), Houston, TX (1978-1980); MOS Reliability Director, Texas Instruments, Inc., Dallas and Houston, TX (1975-1978); With, Texas Instruments, Inc., Dallas and Houston, TX (1961-1978); Reliability Manager, Metal Oxide Semicondr. (MOS) Division, Texas Instruments, Inc., Dallas and Houston, TX (1971-1975); Manager, Process Control For Advanced Tech., Texas Instruments, Inc., Dallas, TX (1969-1970); Research and Development Engineer, Core Laboratories, Dallas, TX (1960-1961) **Civic:** Chairman, Greater Southwest Houston Chamber of Commerce (1999); Board of Directors, Greater Southwest Houston Chamber of Commerce (1996-2001); Vice Chairman, Greater Southwest Houston Chamber of Commerce (1996-1997); Member, Houston Clean City Commission (1991-1994); President, Southwest Houston Chamber of Commerce (1990-1991); Board of Director, Southwest Houston Chamber of Commerce (1988-1991) **Military Service:** U.S. Army (1953) **Creative Works:** Contributor, Articles, Professional Journals; Patentee in the Field **Awards:** Fellow, Texas Instruments (1965-1968); Fellow, FMC Corp. (1958-1960); Award, American Chemical Society (1958); Eastern States Petroleum and Chemical Scholar (1957-1958); Ethyl Corp. Scholar (1956-1957); Who's Who in Finance and Industry; Who's Who in American Law; Who's Who in America **Memberships:** Board of Directors, Bellaire/Southwest Houston Rotary Club (2001-Present); Lieutenant Governor, Rotary International District 5890 (2009-2010); Assistant Governor, Rotary International District 5890 (2004-2005); President, Bellaire/Southwest Houston Rotary Club (2002-2003); Vice Chairman, Reservoir Group, Society of Petroleum Engineers (1979-1980); Chapter President, Omega Chi Epsilon (1959); American Bar Association; American Institute of Chemical Engineers; American Chemical Society; State Bar of Texas; American Association For Justice; Texas Trial Lawyers Association **Bar Admissions:** Texas (1978); Southern District of Texas; Northern District of Texas Eastern District of Texas; Western District of Texas **Marquis Who's Who Honors:** Albert Nelson Marquis Lifetime Achievement Award; Marquis Who's Who Top Professional **Why did you become involved in your profession or industry:** Dr. Lovelace became involved in his profession because his goal was to become a laboratory director; his company had a fellowship and he applied for the fellowship the first year he received it. When he got back from school after a number of years, he started getting promoted and met a few lawyers. Dr. Lovelace started law school with the company funding him. He attended school at South Texas College of Law about halfway through he knew he wanted to be a lawyer. His Business experience came from the the business jobs he had done. As a young chemical engineer, he received a job from Core Laboratories. He worked for them a couple of summers, when he finished school he went to work for them full time. He was in what was called an R&D Department and worked mostly for development. The company was much smaller than Texas Instruments. He worked for Core Laboratories for couple of years and then he got recruited to Texas Instruments and, after 17 years and after he received his law degree, he was asked to come back to Core Laboratories. He served as the president of the Houston Subsidiaries.In addition, what attracted Dr. Lovelace to his profession was that he had no interest in law until he started working for Texas Instruments and received his PhD because he wanted to be a laboratory director, which was his goal.

Daniel Lubetzky

Title: Founder, Chief Executive Officer; Philanthropist **Industry:** Food & Restaurant Services **Company Name:** KIND LLC **Place of Birth:** Mexico City **State/Country of Origin:** Mexico **Marital Status:** Married **Spouse Name:** Michelle Lynn Lieberman (2008) **Children:** Four Children **Education:** Doctor of Jurisprudence, Stanford Law School (1993); Bachelor of Arts in Economic and International Relations, Trinity University, Magna Cum Laude **Career:** Founder, Chief Executive Officer, KIND LLC (2003-Present); Founder, PeaceWorks Inc. (1994-Present); With, McKinsey & Company LLP; With, Sullivan & Cromwell; Founder, Da'Leky Times **Career Related:** Co-founder, Maiyet (2010-Present) **Civic:** Board of Directors, Anti-Defamation League (2019-Present); Founder, Feed the Truth (2017-Present); Founder, KIND Foundation (2015-Present); Co-founder, OneVoice Movement (2002-Present); President Ambassador for Global Entrepreneurship (PAGE) **Creative Works:** Author, "Do the KIND Thing" (2015); Guest Judge, "Shark Tank" **Awards:** Common Ground Award (2017); Named Entrepreneur of the Year, Ernst & Young (2013); Named, One of America's Most Promising Social Entrepreneurs, Bloomberg BusinessWeek; Named, One of the 25 Responsibility Pioneers, TIME Magazine; Named, One of the Creativity 50, Advertising Age; Named, One of the 100 Most Intriguing Entrepreneurs, Goldman Sachs; Named, Entrepreneur of the Year, Entrepreneur Magazine; Koshland Fellowship; Named, One of the 100 Global Leaders for Tomorrow, World Economic Forum; Trinity Outstanding Alumnus Award, Trinity University; Peace, Recognition and Security Award, World Association of NGOs; Blessed are the Peacemakers Award, Catholic Theological Union; King Hussein Humanitarian Leadership Prize; Young Leaders Forum Fellow, National Committee for United States-China Relations; Named, One of 43 Entrepreneurs Who are Changing the World, Fast Company; Named, Young Global Leader, World Economic Forum; Skoll Award for Social Entrepreneurship; Named One of America's Most Promising Social Entrepreneurs; Named, One of the Heroes of Conscious Capitalism; Hispanic Heritage Award; Horatio Alger Award

George Walton Lucas Jr.

Title: Film Director, Producer, Screenwriter **Industry:** Media & Entertainment **Date of Birth:** 05/14/1944 **Place of Birth:** Modest **State/Country of Origin:** CA/USA **Parents:** George Walton Lucas Sr.; Dorothy Ellinore (Bomberger) Lucas **Marital Status:** Married **Spouse Name:** Mellody Hobson (06/22/2013); Marcia Lou Griffin (1969, Divorced 1983) **Children:** Amanda (Adopted); Katie (Adopted); Jett (Adopted); Everest Hobson **Education:** BFA, University of Southern California (1966); Coursework, Modesto Junior College **Career:** Founder, Chairman, Chief Executive Officer, Lucasfilm Ltd., San Rafael, CA (1971-2012); Co-founder, American Zoetrope (1969) **Career Related:** Chairman, Film Foundation; Chairman, Joseph Campbell Foundation; Chairman, Artists Rights Foundation; Chairman, Founder, George Lucas Educational Foundation; Member, TV Board of Councilors, University of Southern California **Civic:** Member, Advisory Board, Science Fiction Museum and Hall of Fame; Founder, Lucas Museum of Narrative Art **Creative Works:** Executive Producer, Creator, "Star Wars: The Clone Wars" (2008-2014, 2020); Executive Producer, Writer, "Strange Magic" (2015); Executive Producer, "Red Tails" (2012); Executive Producer, "Double Victory: The Tuskegee Airmen at War" (2012); Executive Producer, "Manifest Destiny" (2011); Executive Producer, Writer, "Indiana Jones and the Kingdom of the Crystal Skull" (2008); Director, Executive Producer, Writer, "Star Wars: Episode III - Revenge of the Sith" (2005); Director, Executive Producer, Writer, "Star Wars: Episode II - Attack of the Clones" (2002); Director, Executive Producer, Writer, "Star Wars: Episode I - The Phantom Menace" (1999); Executive Producer, Writer, "Radioland Murders" (1994); Executive Producer, Creator, "The Young Indiana Jones Chronicles" (1992-1993); Co-executive Producer, Co-writer, "Indiana Jones and the Last Crusade" (1989); Executive Producer, Writer, "Willow" (1988); Executive Producer, "Tucker: The Man and His Dream" (1988); Executive Producer, "Labyrinth" (1986); Executive Producer, "Howard the Duck" (1986); Co-executive Producer, "Mishima: A Life in Four Chapter" (1985); Executive Producer, "Indiana Jones and the Temple of Doom" (1984); Executive Producer, Co-writer, "Star Wars: Episode VI - Return of the Jedi" (1983); Executive Producer, Writer, "Indiana Jones and the Raiders of the Lost Ark " (1981); Executive Producer, "Star Wars: Episode V - The Empire Strikes Back" (1980); Executive Producer, "More American Graffiti" (1979); Director, Writer, Executive Producer, "Star Wars: Episode IV - A New Hope" (1977); Director, Co-writer, "American Graffiti" (1973); Director, Co-writer, Editor, "THX-1138" (1971); Assistant to Francis Ford Coppola, "The Rain People" (1969); Producer, Writer, Television Shows, Films and Documentaries; Contributor, Books **Awards:** Recipient, Kennedy Center Honors, John F. Kennedy Center for the Performing Arts, Washington, DC (2015); Named Disney Legend (2015); National Medal of Arts, National Endowment for the Arts (2012); Cinema Vanguard Award, African American Film Critics Association (2011); Named One of the Forbes 400: Richest Americans (2009-2012); Named to California Hall of Fame (2009); Named to Science Fiction Hall of Fame (2009); Golden Lion for Lifetime Achievement, Venice Film Festival (2009); Named One of the 100 Most Powerful Celebrities, Forbes.com (2008); Awards for Favorite Movie and Favorite Movie Drama, People's Choice Awards (2006); Lifetime Achievement Award, American Film Institute (2005); Irving G. Thalberg Memorial Award, Academy of Motion Picture Arts & Sciences (1991); Numerous Awards **Memberships:** Honorary Member, Society of Motion Picture and Television Engineers (2014)

Robert J. Lucas

Title: Founder, Owner **Industry:** Media & Entertainment **Company Name:** Central Atlanta Props and Sets, LLC **Career:** Founder/Owner, Central Atlanta Props & Sets, LLC (2014-Present); Lead Person/Set Decoration, Motion Pictures, Santa Clarita, CA (1983-2014) **Civic:** Donates to many charitable organizations. **Memberships:** The International Alliance of Theatrical Stage Employees, Local 44 **Why did you become involved in your profession or industry:** When Mr. Lucas graduated high school, he like many other students at that age was pondering what he would do next in life. He knew that he always had a love for the film industry and intended on becoming a special effects specialist and gravitated towards the art department world of set decoration. He decided to move to Los Angeles in the early 1980's and worked on many music videos. Then he transitioned to cult classic horror movies. Over time he continued to build his career working all over the country, until 2013 he bought out an antique dealer and was able to start his prop house in Atlanta, Georgia. At the time he noticed the upswing of the film industry in Atlanta and so his business seemed to be in the perfect place, where it has now expanded greatly over the years.In addition, what attracted Mr. Lucas to his industry was that he just decided after high school that what he wanted to do with his life was to go into the motion picture industry. He moved to Los Angeles, got his foot stuck in a couple of doors, landed his first few jobs, and went from there. It was also working hard and being an assets to the companies that he worked for, along with staying at it for a long time.

Logan T. Ludwig, PhD, FMLA

Title: Former Deputy Supreme Knight, Assoc. Provost, Consultant **Industry:** Education/Educational Services **Company Name:** Knights of Columbus, Loyola University Health System **Date of Birth:** 12/23/1946 **Place of Birth:** Prairie du Rocher **State/Country of Origin:** IL/USA **Parents:** Albert Vernon Ludwig; Aurelia Marie Ludwig **Marital Status:** Married **Spouse Name:** Ina Ludwig **Children:** Ann; Doug; Amanda; Racheal **Education:** PhD in Higher Education, St. Louis University (1983); MLS, University of Missouri, Columbia (1973); BS in English, Southern Illinois University, Carbondale (1969) **Career:** Deputy Supreme Knight (2013-2016); Supreme Treasurer, Knights of Columbus (2011-2013); Associate Provost, Health Sciences, Associate Dean, Library & Telehealth Services, Loyola University Health System, Maywood, IL (1986-2011); Health Sciences Library Director, St. Louis University (1984-1985); Media Services Librarian, Assistant Professor, St. Louis University (1978-1983); Director, Learning Resources Center, Farmington Senior High School, Missouri (1973-1978) **Career Related:** Adjunct Professor, Dominican University, Riverside, IL (1986-1989); Health Sciences Library and Building Consultant, 36 National and International Facilities **Civic:** Advisory Board, Aid for Women (2011-Present); Secretary, Emeritus McGivney Center of Hope and Healing (2004-Present); Co-founder, Special Olympics Unified Football Tournament Rome, Italy (2016); Board of Directors, Supreme Council, Knights of Columbus, New Haven, CT (2007-2011); Health Sciences Communications Board of Directors (2002-2008) **Creative Works:** Contributor, Building, Technology, and Library Services Articles, Professional Journals; Contributor, Chapters, Books; Author, "In Service to One, In Service to All: A Brief History of the Illinois Knights of Columbus State Council Leadership 1898-2011" **Awards:** Named Health Sciences Librarian of the Year, Midwest Chapter, Medical Library Association (2008); William and Virginia Beatty Service Award (2008); Golden Raster, Health and Sciences Communications Association (2004); Literature Award, Journal Biomedical Communications (2001); IAIMS Planning Grant, National Library of Medicine (2000-2002) **Memberships:** President, Association of Biomedical Communications Directors (1999-2000); AAMC Council of Academic Societies; Medical Library Association; American Telemedicine Association; Health & Science Communications Association (1986-1987); Illinois Broadband Development Board; Academy of Health Information Professionals; Knights of Columbus **Marquis Who's Who Honors:** Albert Nelson Marquis Lifetime Achievement Award **Avocations:** Golf; Fishing; Stamp collecting **Political Affiliations:** Republican **Religion:** Roman Catholic

Rene Immanuel Luna, MD, FACOG

Title: Director Robotics, OB/GYN **Industry:** Medicine & Health Care **Company Name:** Intuitive Surgical **Date of Birth:** 01/17/1979 **Place of Birth:** Houston **State/Country of Origin:** TX/USA **Parents:** Rene Luna; Norma Carranza **Marital Status:** Married **Spouse Name:** Lea L Luna **Children:** Ryland Rene Luna; Ried Immanuel Luna **Education:** Resident in Obstetrics and Gynecology, Albert Einstein College of Medicine (2013); Fifth Pathway Internship, New York Medical College (2008); MD, University of Guadalajara (2007); BS in Biology, The University of Texas-Pan American (2002) **Certifications:** Diplomate, American Board of Obstetrics and Gynecology **Career:** Medical Doctor, OBGYN, Rio Grande Regional Hospital, McAllen, TX (2016-Present); Director, Women's Hospital Institute for Robotic Surgery, Doctors Hospital at Renaissance Health System (Present); Plaza OBGYN Associates, Private Practice (2013-2015) **Awards:** Named, One of the Top Doctors in Texas, Super Doctors Rising Stars, Texas Monthly Magazine (2019 & 2020); Ranked #2 in Texas, #6 in United States, Single-Site Gynecological Robotic Surgery (2017); Physician of the Quarter, Women's Hospital of Texas, Houston, TX (2015); Listee, Houston Top Docs, H Texas Magazine, Spring Editions (2014-2015); Excellence in Teaching Award, Albert Einstein College of Medicine and Montefiore Medical Center (2013) **Memberships:** American Medical Association; American College of Texas Gynecologists; Board of Obstetrics and Gynecology; Society of Laparoscopic Surgeons; Association of Gynecologic Laparoscopic Surgeons; Hidalgo-Starr County Medical Society; Texas Institute for Robotic Surgery; Texas Medical Association **Marquis Who's Who Honors:** Marquis Who's Who Top Professional **To what do you attribute your success:** Dr. Luna attributes his success to a good work ethic and always giving 110% to anything he does, whether it's the smallest thing or the biggest and always getting back on your feet and pursuing the goal. **Why did you become involved in your profession or industry:** He wanted to always help people and become a surgeon. He got into Obstetrics & Gynecology was when he was doing his rotations during residency. He would find himself immersed, losing track of time. He did not want to leave the hospital. Then he discovered robotics, The Da Vinci Surgical System, and minimally invasive gynecological surgery. It pushed his technical and surgical skills and gave him that love of surgery. He loves being innovative and using that platform to teach and spread his passion for modern innovative surgery. It continues to feed his passion to this day. **Avocations:** Motorcycles; Golf; Attending sporting events; Spending time with sons **Thoughts on Life:** Dr. Luna's motto is, "Put your heart into your patients, and treat them how you would want to be taken care of and you'll never go wrong"

Lisa Lund

Title: Owner/Broker **Industry:** Financial Services **Company Name:** Lund Mortgage Team **Marital Status:** Married **Career:** Owner, Broker, Lund Mortgage Team Incorporated, Arizona (2009-Present); Vice President, Lund Mortgage Incorporated, Arizona (2003-2009) **Civic:** Chair, Women's Affinity Group of Aime; Volunteer, ALS Charities **Awards:** Women of Vision Award (2020) **Memberships:** Arizona Association of Mortgage Professionals **To what do you attribute your success:** Ms. Lund attributes her success to never giving up and always moving forward. The knowledge that what she does helps others helps to keep her motivated. The confidence of her clients, her relationships and her team keeps her going. **Why did you become involved in your profession or industry:** Ms. Lund became involved in the banking business due to the influence of her father, who took along to a "take your daughter to work" day, which was seen as an important way to get more women involved in the professional workforce. While attending high school, Ms. Lund she worked with her father at his banking company, and eventually opened her own company in 2009.

John B. Lunseth II

Title: Shareholder **Industry:** Law and Legal Services **Company Name:** Briggs and Morgan (Now Taft Stettinius & Hollister LLP) **Date of Birth:** 04/10/1949 **Place of Birth:** Osaka **State/Country of Origin:** Japan **Parents:** John Bentley Lunseth; Cleone Beverly (Nasset) Lunseth **Marital Status:** Married **Spouse Name:** Heidi Marie Hoard (Divorced 2007) **Children:** John III; Steven James **Education:** JD, University of Minnesota, Cum Laude (1977); BA, University of Minnesota (1974) **Certifications:** United States Court of Appeals for the Eighth Circuit (1981); Minnesota State Bar Association (1977); United States District Court for the District of Minnesota (1977) **Career:** Shareholder, Briggs and Morgan (Now Taft Stettinius & Hollister LLP) (2002-Present); Partner, Rider Bennett, LLP (1983-2007); Associate, Rider Bennett, LLP (1977-1982) **Career Related:** Member, Management Committee, Rider Bennett, LLP (1989-1991); Intern, Third United Nations Conference on the Law of the Sea, Caracas, Venezuela (1974); Member, Panel of Commercial Arbitrators, American Arbitration Association; Lecturer **Civic:** The Advocates for Human Rights (1991-Present); President, Twin Cities Chapter, Ruffed Grouse Society (1990-Present); Active Member, Council Audit Committee, Medina, MN (1991); Trustee, National German Shorthaired Pointer Association, Inc.; Member, President's Council, Business Partners' Committee, Ordway Center for the Performing Arts **Memberships:** American Bar Association; Minnesota State Bar Association; Hennepin County Bar Association **Marquis Who's Who Honors:** Albert Nelson Marquis Lifetime Achievement Award **Why did you become involved in your profession or industry:** Mr. Lunseth became involved in his profession because he reached a point in his theater career where he would have to make major lifestyle changes in order to achieve more. Instead, he decided he wanted to settle down and have a family, so he attended law school and has excelled in the field ever since.

Yixiao Luo

Title: Professor, Researcher **Industry:** Research **Company Name:** Institute of Modern Physics, Chinese Academy of Sciences, Vanderbilt University, Lawrence Berkeley National Laboratory **Date of Birth:** 05/28/1944 **Place of Birth:** Sichuan, China **State/Country of Origin:** China **Parents:** Qiliang Luo; Muqing Li **Marital Status:** Married (Divorced, 2001) **Spouse Name:** Lanying Wu; Ren Guo **Children:** Xuejiao Luo **Education:** Graduate, Department of Modern Physics, University of Science and Technology of China (USTC), Beijing, China (1967) **Career:** Professor/Researcher; Senior Research Scholar, Nuclear Physics Group, Department of Physics, Vanderbilt University, Nashville, TN (2000-Present); Visiting Research Scholar, Lawrence Berkeley National Laboratory (LBNL) (2000-Present); Invited Speaker, 11 International Conferences or Symposiums (1992-Present); Deputy Director, National Laboratory of Heavy Ion Accelerator, Lanzhou, China (1991-2000); Professor of Physics, Institute of Modern Physics (IMP), Chinese Academy of Sciences, China (1988-2000); Director, Institute of Modern Physics (IMP), Chinese Academy of Sciences, China (1994-1999); Vice Director, Institute of Modern Physics (IMP), Chinese Academy of Sciences, China (1991-1994); Associate Professor of Physics, Institute of Modern Physics (IMP), Chinese Academy of Sciences, China (1982-1988); Visiting Scholar, Daresbury National Laboratory, Daresbury, England (1987); Visiting Scholar, Southern National Laboratory, Istituto Nazionale di Fisica Nucleare (INFN), Italy (1982-1984); Research Assistant, Institute of Modern Physics (IMP), Chinese Academy of Sciences, China (1977-1982) **Career Related:** Invited Member, International Advisory Committee of International Conferences (1995-Present); Invited Member, International Advisory Committee, Research Center for Nuclear Physics (RCNP), Osaka University, Suita, Japan **Creative Works:** Editor, "Proceedings of the International Workshop on NUCLEAR REACTION AND BEYOND" (2000); Associate Editor, Chinese Journal, "High Energy Physics and Nuclear Physics" (1994-2000); Contributor, More Than 100 Major Publications, Professional Journals **Awards:** First Class Award for Achievements in Science and Technology, Chinese Academy of Sciences (1999); Second Class China National Prize for Natural Sciences, Ministry of Science and Technology of China (1999); Second Class Award for Natural Sciences, Chinese Academy of Sciences (1997); Recognized, "Outstanding Scientist of the Chinese Academy of Sciences" (1995); Recognized as an "Excellent Expert of Gansu Province" (1995); First Class Award for Natural Sciences, Chinese Academy of Sciences (1994) **Memberships:** China Physics Society (1999-2001); China Nuclear Physics Society (1980-2001); President, China Nuclear Physics Society (1997-2000); Vice President, China Nuclear Physics Society (1994-1997) **Why did you become involved in your profession or industry:** In college, Mr. Luo majored in modern physics. He enjoyed fundamental nuclear physics, which is the reason get got involved in fundamental research for so many years.

Leanne Ly

Title: Managing Director **Industry:** Business Management/Business Services **Company Name:** LOL Kids Club **Marital Status:** Married **Children:** Two Children **Education:** BA in Accounting and Business Administration, University of Phoenix, AZ **Career:** Founder/Owner, Playtastic Toys, Las Vegas, NV (2018-Present); Founder/Owner, LOL Kids Club, CA (2014-Present); Business Consultant, Trucking Company; International Trader, Scrap Metal Company **Memberships:** International Amusement Association of Attraction Industry; ASTRA **Marquis Who's Who Honors:** Marquis Who's Who Top Professional **To what do you attribute your success:** Ms. Ly attributes her success to being fearless. She is never afraid to fail. She also attributes her success to her children. She always says, "Tomorrow is always going to be a better day." **Why did you become involved in your profession or industry:** Ms. Ly began her career working as an independent contractor but then became an outbound manager. That helped her gain a skill set to go back and assist her father's trucking company. At the time, she invested what she had into her father's business to take the necessary measures to keep it alive and modern. In 2009, after the trucking business became weaker, she finally decided to pull out and reach out to her global connections. She found that there was a market around the continental United States for scrap metal to be sold to overseas companies. In the years since then, she has become very successful. It was not until the recent events of mass shootings, such as the Sandy Hook Elementary School tragedy, that opened her eyes to a new idea. Concerned and wanting to establish a place of fun and safety for children and parents alike, she developed the idea for LOL Kids Club. **Avocations:** Cooking; Listening to audio books

David Lyman, Esq.

Title: Chairman, Chief Values Officer **Industry:** Law and Legal Services **Company Name:** Tilleke & Gibbins International Ltd. **Date of Birth:** 09/25/1936 **Place of Birth:** Washington **State/Country of Origin:** DC/USA **Parents:** Albert Moses Lyman; Freda (Ring) Lyman **Marital Status:** Married **Spouse Name:** Thassaneeya Pimpila (03/23/2007) **Education:** Postgraduate Coursework in Foreign and Comparative Law, Parker School of Foreign and Comparative Law, Columbia University, New York (1974); JD, University of California Hastings College Law, San Francisco, CA (1965); Certificate, U.S. Naval Officers Submarine, New London, CT (1960); BSEE, Duke University, Durham, NC (1958) **Certifications:** Certified Scuba Divemasters **Career:** Chairman, Chief Values Officer, Tilleke & Gibbins International Ltd., (2006-Present); Chief Values Officer, Advocates and Solicitors (2003-2006); Chairman, Advocates and Solicitors (2003-2006); Chairman, Senior Partner, Advocates and Solicitors, Bangkok (1984-2003); Associate Partner, Advocates and Solicitors, Bangkok (1967-1984); Associate, Lempres & Seyranian, Oakland (1966-1967); Associate, Fitzsimmons & Petris, Oakland, CA (1965-1966); Associate, Advocates and Solicitors, Bangkok; Associate, Tilleke & Gibbins International Limited **Career Related:** Board of Governors, Alumni University, California Hastings College of Law (2011-Present); Founder, Steering Committee Technology Cooperation Office, U.S. Asian Environmental Partnership Program (1994); Chairman, Foreign Chamber of Commerce, Thailand Law Change Projects for Prime Minister (1992); USAID Advisory Committee, U.S. Thai Trade and Investment (1988); Prime Minister of Thailand's Foreign Investment Advisory Council (1975); Director, Triumph International Limited, Thailand (1972-2012); Director, Goodyear Limited, Thailand (1967-2006) **Civic:** Interim Chairman, Operation Smile, Thailand, (2019-Present); Vice President, Thailand Society Prevention Cruelty to Animals (2009-Present); International Chamber of Commerce, Commission on Corruption, Paris (1996-Present); Advisory Council, International Crisis Group (2003-2013); Founder, Executive Board, National Chapter, Thailand (1999); Secretary, General, Thailand Society Prevention of Cruelty to Animals (1996-2001); Governor, Professional Services Group (1995-2005) **Military Service:** Lieutenant Commander, U.S. Navy (1967-1969); U.S. Naval Reserve (1958-1969) **Creative Works:** Author, "Lyman's Laws for Lawyers (and everybody else, too!)" (2006); Contributor, Numerous Articles, Professional Journals **Awards:** American Embassy Gold Award (2018); Phra Dulyathipat Badge, Council Judge Advocate General School Thailand (2014); Plaque of Appreciation, American Chamber of Commerce, Thailand (2006); Miniature Cartridge Pouch Pin, First Infantry Regiment, King's Own Bodyguard (2003); Boss of Year, Women Secretaries Association Thailand (1997); Honoree, Beta Gamma Sigma, Drexel University (1995); Certificate of Achievement, Thai Prime Minister (1990-1992); Distinguished Service Award, American Chamber of Commerce (1990) **Memberships:** Senior Advisor, American Chamber of Commerce, Thailand (2014-Present); Senior Advisor, Chairman, Joint Foreign Chamber of Commerce, Thailand (2013-Present); Commandeur de la Chaine, Wildlife Trust, Wildlife Fund of Thailand, Chaines Des Rotisseurs (2010-Present); Founder, Board Member, AmCham Thailand Charitable Foundation (2004-Present); Graduate Member, Thai Institute of Directors (2002-Present); Associate Member, Chartered Institute of Arbitrators (2002-Present); Dive Master, National Association Underwater Instructors (1979-Present); Phi Alpha Delta (1962-Present); Board of Governors, American Chamber of Commerce, Thailand (2010-2013); Governor, Professional Service (2003-2005) **Bar Admissions:** State of California (1966) **Marquis Who's Who Honors:** Albert Nelson Marquis Lifetime Achievement Award; Marquis Who's Who Top Professional **Why did you become involved in your profession or industry:** Mr. Lyman became involved in his profession because he grew up surrounded by lawyers. His parents were lawyers, as were his uncles and his grandfather. He actually did not want to become a lawyer because he could see how hard his family worked. Mr. Lyman's father wanted him to go into the Navy because he himself had served in World War II. During his time at Duke University, Mr. Lyman partook in the Reserve Officers' Training Corps. However, he was commissioned and went into the minesweepers; he was also accepted into submarine school. His father wanted him to stay in the navy, which Mr. Lyman could acknowledge was a good idea, but he wasn't happy. Mr. Lyman then went on to attend Hastings College of Law. After his first semester there, he knew this was what he wanted to do. Mr. Lyman has never regretted his decision to pursue law. His family history influenced him into the field as both his parents were lawyers, his father's brothers were lawyers and their father was a lawyer. **Avocations:** Swimming; Scuba diving; Photography; Travel **Religion:** Jewish.

Melody Lynd

Title: Plastic Surgeon **Industry:** Medicine & Health Care **Company Name:** Dr. Melody Lynd, Inc. **Date of Birth:** 04/22/1968 **Place of Birth:** Danville **State/Country of Origin:** IL/USA **Parents:** Hasan Yaman; Sabahat Yaman **Marital Status:** Single **Education:** MPH, George Washington University (2020); MBA, George Washington University (2016); Coursework, University of Missouri, Kansas City (1993); BA in Biology and Chemistry, University of Missouri, Kansas City (1991) **Career:** Solo Private Practice, Campbell (2002-Present); Plastic Surgeon, University of Illinois-Chicago, Cook County Hospital (1999-Present); Associate Physician, Rockefeller University (1995-2000); General Surgeon, Brookdale University Hospital and Medical Center (1993-1999); Solo Private Practice, Campbell, CA **Career Related:** Graduate Medical Education Committee, University of Illinois-Chicago (2000-2001); Board of Directors University Hospital of Brooklyn, SUNY Downstate (1998); Presenter In Field; Unit Leader, Avon Products Inc.; Physician Advisory Panel, Clinique Laboratories, LLC **Military Service:** Battalion Surgeon, United States Navy Medical Corps Reserves **Creative Works:** Contributor, Articles, Professional Journals **Awards:** Named, Outstanding Surgical Trainee, British Journal of Surgery; Outstanding Woman Resident Candidate, Association of Women Surgeons; First Place, Resident's Paper Competition Clinical Division; Service Award, Committee on Trauma, New York Organ Donor Network **Memberships:** Resident Counselor, Medical Society of the State New York (1999-2002); Associate, American College of Surgeons; National Board of Medical Examiners; Chairman, Resident's Section, Illinois State Medical Society (2000-2001); Credentials Committee, American Medical Association (1999); Resident Affiliate, American Society of Plastic Surgery; AOA; SAGES; Sapientia Est Potentia Honor Society; Mortar Board; Omicron Delta Kappa; Santa Clara County Medical Society; California Medical Society; Special Ops Medical Association **To what do you attribute your success:** Dr. Lynd attributes her success to her faith in a higher power. **Why did you become involved in your profession or industry:** Dr. Lynd never thought she would be a surgeon. However, when she began her rotations in the field as a medical student, she fell in love. She enjoyed how much the field was problem-focused; she was a good technician because she was quick to fix any problem she saw. Looking back, her decision to go to New York City was one of her best decisions. However, she left the city when she decided to pursue plastic surgery. She traveled to Chicago and then to California. It was in California that she became interested in the Army. Though she had no experience, she wanted to serve. The Marines needed a doctor, so that is where she went. She loves her experience with them and has never looked back. **Avocations:** Writing; Yoga; Fitness; Hiking; Gardening **Political Affiliations:** Independent

Stephen R. Lyne, PhD

Title: Ambassador, Professor **Industry:** Education/Educational Services **Date of Birth:** 05/20/1935 **Place of Birth:** Fall River **State/Country of Origin:** MA/USA **Parents:** Horace James Lyne; Anne (Bromley) Lyne **Marital Status:** Married **Spouse Name:** Mary (1961-2011); Shanshan Lyne **Children:** Deborah Elizabeth; Richard James **Education:** Senior Seminar in National and International Affairs, Foreign Service Institute, U.S. Department of State (1977-1978); Congressional Intern, American Political Science Association Congressional Internship Program (1973-1975); PhD in History, Stanford University (1965); MA in History, Stanford University (1961); BA in History, Amherst College (1958) **Career:** Professor of International Relations and History, Department of International Relations, Boston University (1990-Present); Professor of History and International Relations, Boston University (1980-2002); Ambassador, U.S. Embassy, Accra, Ghana (1987-1989); Diplomat-in-Residence/Adjunct Professor, Center for International Relations, Boston University, Boston, MA (1985-1986); Deputy Chief Mission, U.S. Embassy, Beirut, Lebanon (1984-1985); Deputy Chief Mission, U.S. Embassy, Canberra, ACT, Australia (1980-1984); Office Director for Vietnam, Laos and Cambodia, Bureau of East Asia, U.S. Department of State, Washington, DC (1978-1980); Senior Seminar, U.S. Department of State, Washington (1977-1978); Congressional Intern, American Political Science Association, Washington, DC (1977-1978); Deputy Chief Mission, U.S. Embassy, Algiers, Algeria (1975-1977); Deputy Chief Mission, U.S. Embassy, Libreville, Gabon (1971-1973); Section Head, South Vietnam, Laos, and Cambodia, Bureau of East Asia, U.S. Department of State, Washington, DC (1967-1971); Political Officer, American Embassies, Saigon, Vietnam (1965-1966); Political Officer, American Embassies, Phnom Penh, Cambodia (1962-1964) **Career Related:** American Special Representative for African Liaison, United Nations General Assembly (1989) **Awards:** Diplomat of the Year in Ghana (1987); Presidential Meritorious Honor Award (1986); Joint Superior Honor Award (1985); Individual Superior Honor Award (1984); Joint Superior Honor Award (1982); Individual Superior Honor Award (1971) **Marquis Who's Who Honors:** Albert Nelson Marquis Lifetime Achievement Award; Marquis Who's Who Top Professional **Why did you become involved in your profession or industry:** Dr. Lyne became involved in his profession because of his upbringing, which shaped his career. His father and mother, Horace James and Anne, introduced him to the history of the U.S. very early. He was interested in the American Revolution and the early colonization of New England. As a direct result of his historical interests, Dr. Lyne grew up hoping to serve his country in a respectful way. By the time he was 14, he knew he wanted to be a diplomat. **Avocations:** Tennis; Bridge **Political Affiliations:** Republican **Religion:** Buddhist

Kenny E. Lynn

Title: Owner **Industry:** Real Estate **Company Name:** Exit Southeast **Children:** Brittany **Education:** Coursework, College, Two Years **Certifications:** License, National Hot Rod Association **Career:** Regional Owner, EXIT Southeast (2013-Present) **Career Related:** Regional Owner, EXIT Southeast, TN, KY, GA; Regional Director, EXIT Southeast, FL; Owned Three Car Dealerships **Civic:** Founder, EXIT Realty Smart Car Race (2014) **Awards:** Finalist, Best in Business Awards for Companies with 500 or More Employees, Nashville Business Journal (2019); Ranked Number One in U.S. Region, EXIT Realty Corp. International (2017); Ranked Number One in Franchise Sales, EXIT Realty Corp. International (2016); Leaders' Leader Award for Regional Leadership and "Developing a Cohesive Team of Unstoppable Professionals," EXIT Realty Corp. International (2016); Named EXIT Realty International's Top North America Regional Owner (2015) **Marquis Who's Who Honors:** Marquis Who's Who Top Professional **Why did you become involved in your profession or industry:** Mr. Lynn initially entered his profession in 2010, having previously owned a mortgage company. He opened an independent realty office and was soon prospering enough to buy a franchise in EXIT Realty. **Avocations:** Race cars; Drag racing **Thoughts on Life:** Mr. Lynn's motto is, "If I'm not winning, I'm not happy."

Kalle J. Lyytinen

Title: Iris S. Wolstein Professor of Management Design **Industry:** Education/Educational Services **Date of Birth:** 08/09/1953 **Place of Birth:** Helsinki **State/Country of Origin:** Finland **Parents:** Veli Kaarlo Lyytinen; Raili Annikki (Lehto) Lyytinen; **Marital Status:** Married **Spouse Name:** Pirjo-Riitta Taipale (09/06/74) **Children:** Joonas; Juho (Deceased); Markus **Education:** Honorary Degree, Lappeenranta University of Technology (2017); Honorary Degree, Copenhagen Business School (2016); Honorary Degree, Umea University, Sweden (2008); Doctor of Philosophy, University Jyvaskyla, Finland (1986); Master of Arts, University Jyvaskyla Finland (1977); Bachelor of Arts, University Jyvaskyla, Finland (1976) **Career:** Distinguished Visiting Professor, Department Head, Design and Innovation Department, Aalto University (2017-2020); Distinguished University Professor, Case Western Reserve University, Cleveland, OH (2001-2019); Endowed Chair, Iris S. Wolstein Professor of Management Design (2017); Visiting Professor, London School of Economics (2013-2016); Professor, University of Jyvaskyla (1987-2016); Visiting Professor, Umea University (2008-2015); Visiting Professor, Helsinki School Of Economics (2008); Visiting Professor, University of Lausanne (2007); Dean, Information Technology, University of Jyvaskyla (1998-2000); G.E. Smith Visiting Professor, Georgia State University (1997); Professor, Hong Kong University of Science and Technology (1993-1994); Visiting Researcher, London School of Economics (1986); Principal Researcher, Academy of Finland, Jyvaskyla (1983-1985); Researcher, University of Stockholm (1981-1982) **Military Service:** Served to Third Sergeant, Infantry, Finnish Army (1972-1973) **Creative Works:** Editor, Several Professional and Academy Journals; Contributor, Numerous Articles to Professional Journals **Awards:** Leo Award (2016); Association of Information Systems Fellow (2004); IFIP Silver Core (1998) **Memberships:** Chairperson, International Conference on Information Systems Committee, International Federation of Information Processing (1998-1999); Second Chair, Technical Committee, International Federation of Information Processing (1991-1993); Academy of Management; Association of the Conquering Machinery; The Institute for Operations Research and the Management Sciences; Association of Information Systems **Marquis Who's Who Honors:** Albert Nelson Marquis Lifetime Achievement Award; Marquis Who's Who Top Professional **Avocations:** Literature; Classical music; Opera

Cathy Darlene Mabry

Title: Retired Elementary School Administrator **Industry:** Education/Educational Services **Company Name:** DeKalb County School System **Date of Birth:** 12/09/1951 **Place of Birth:** Atlanta **State/Country of Origin:** GA/USA **Parents:** G. W. Mabry; Erma Mabry **Education:** MA in Administration & Supervision Education, Georgia State University (1997); MA in Elementary Education, Oglethorpe University, Atlanta, GA (1990); BA in Sociology and Psychology, University of Georgia (1975) **Certifications:** Studies Diploma, Advance Diploma in Biblical Studies, Faith Bible Institute (2017); Bible College Diploma, Faith Bible Institute (2007); Certified in Education, Oglethorpe University, Atlanta, GA (1983); Certified in Early Childhood Education, Georgia **Career:** Retired Elementary School Administrator (2010); Teacher, DeKalb County School Systems, Decatur, GA (1984-2010); With, Rich's, Decatur, GA (1975-1976, 1979-1984); Paraprofessional, Kindergarten, DeKalb County School Systems, Decatur, GA (1979-1981); Intermediate Clerk, Superior Court of DeKalb County, Decatur, GA (1978-1981); Manager, Trainee Sales, Sears Roebuck & Co., Decatur, GA (1974-1975, 1976-1978); Charge Account Services Staff, C&S National Bank, Atlanta, GA (1974-1975) **Career Related:** Teacher Forum Representative, DeKalb County School Systems (1992-1995); Member, School-based Management Committee, Hooper Alexander School, Decatur, GA (1991-1992); Strategic Planning Committee, Hooper Alexander School, Decatur, GA (1990-1996); Member, Social Studies Curriculum Committee, DeKalb County School Systems (1990-1991) **Civic:** Member, Teach Well Wellness Program, Emory University School of Public Health (1994); Chair, Board of Directors, DeKalb Economic Opportunity Authority (Now Partnership and DeKalb), Decatur, GA (1991-1992, 1993-1994); Teen Scene, Inc., Lithonia (1993-1994); Secretary, Lithonia Civic League, Inc. (1987-1994); Active PTA **Creative Works:** Author, Poetry, American Poetry Anthology (1986) **Awards:** Teacher of the Year, DeKalb County Schools **Memberships:** National Association for the Advancement of Colored People; National Council of Negro Women, Inc.; National Geographical Society; DeKalb Association of Educators; Zeta Phi Beta **Marquis Who's Who Honors:** Albert Nelson Marquis Lifetime Achievement Award; Marquis Who's Who Top Professional **Why did you become involved in your profession or industry:** Ms. Mabry became involved in her profession because of a fifth grade teacher, Dohnnie C. Jordan, she had in elementary school whom she enjoyed so much and left an impression on her. She decided at that time that teaching was what she wanted to do. **Avocations:** Reading; Cooking; Nature walks; Poetry; Listening to gospel/jazz; Movies; Out to dinner; People watching **Political Affiliations:** Democrat **Religion:** Baptist

Priscilla Ruth MacDougall

Title: Lawyer **Industry:** Law and Legal Services **Company Name:** Columbia College Chicago **Date of Birth:** 01/20/1944 **Place of Birth:** Evanston **State/Country of Origin:** IL/USA **Parents:** Curtis Daniel MacDougall (Deceased); Genevieve Maurine (Rockwood) MacDougall (Deceased) **Marital Status:** Widowed **Spouse Name:** Lester Harrison Pierce MacDougall Brownlee (07/05/1987, Deceased) **Education:** JD, University Michigan, 1970;Master Equivalent (honorary), University Paris, 1967; BA, Barnard College, 1965 **Career:** Legal Counsel, Wisconsin Education Association Council (WEAC), Madison, WI (1975-2014); Adjunct Faculty, Columbia College Chicago, IL (1988-2013); Instructor, Law School and Undergraduate Campuses, University of Wisconsin (1973-1975); Assistant Attorney General, State of Wisconsin (1970-1974) **Career Related:** Litigator; Writer; Speaker; Educator, Women's and Children's Names and Women's Rights and Employment Issues **Civic: Creative Works:** Author, "The Right of Women to Name Their Children" (1985); Co-author, Supplement (1975); Co-author, "Booklet for Women Who Wish to Determine Their Own Names After Marriage" (1974); Author, "Married Women's Common Law Right to Their Own Surnames" (1973); Contributor, Articles to Professional Journals **Awards:** Honor Medal, Veteran Feminists of America (2008) **Memberships:** Co-founder, Chair, Section on Individual Rights and Responsibilities, State Bar of Wisconsin (1973-1975, 1978-1979); Co-founder, Legal Association for Women, WI; Women in Law Association (Now National Association of Women Lawyers) **Marquis Who's Who Honors:** Albert Nelson Marquis Lifetime Achievement Award; Marquis Who's Who Humanitarian Award **Why did you become involved in your profession or industry:** Mrs. MacDougall became involved in her profession because it was a choice between journalism and law. Mrs. MacDougall's father and mother were journalists; her father built the school for journalism at Northwestern and both were teachers. From the time she was born, her whole purpose of living was to make the world a better place. Mrs. MacDougall was in the New York Tribune when she lived in Paris. Women were not in journalism at that time; she said that she was not going to Columbia Journalism school, so she decided to go into law. She was inspired by Clarence Darrow, Thurgood Marshall and Abraham Lincoln and she knew that she could use the law for good things. She wanted to use it for civil rights because she was into the anti-war movement and civil rights. Mrs. MacDougall's first year was working with Indian Rights in the Attorney Generals Office; she did environmental law for the Native American population and she thought for awhile that she might be into their cause, however, the women's movement became her passion. **Avocations:** Pianist; Traveling; Visiting Italy every year

Cherie K. MacQueen

Title: 1) Radio & TV Broadcaster 2) Interior Designer **Industry:** Media & Entertainment **Company Name:** 1) Armed Forces Radio and Television Service **Date of Birth:** 03/20/1952 **Place of Birth:** Kansas City **State/Country of Origin:** MO/USA **Parents:** Ira Raymond Milks; Margaret Estelle (Turner) Milks; Ward L. Cruce (Stepfather) **Education:** Postgraduate Coursework, California State University, San Bernardino (1998); BS in Liberal Studies, Excelsior College (1993); AA in Liberal Arts, Los Angeles Valley College (1982) **Certifications:** Professional Certificate, Interior Design, University of California, Riverside (2002) **Career:** Owner, Ladysmythe Handcrafts (2003-2007); Owner, The Keilani Company, (2003-2007); Specialist, News and Sports, Armed Forces Radio and Television Service (AFRTS) (Now American Forces Network) (1994-1999); Manager, Internal Information, Armed Forces Radio and Television Service (AFRTS) (Now American Forces Network) (1991-1994); Support Manager, Broadcast, Armed Forces Radio and Television Service (AFRTS) (Now American Forces Network) (1990-1991); Supervisor, Specialist, Broadcast Support, Armed Forces Radio and Television Service (AFRTS) (Now American Forces Network) (1986-1990); Specialist, Radio Production, Armed Forces Radio and Television Service (AFRTS) (Now American Forces Network) (1984-1986); Specialist, Radio Traffic, Armed Forces Radio and Television Service (AFRTS) (Now American Forces Network) (1980-1984) **Military Service:** Broadcast Journalist, US Army (1977-1980); Specialist, Administrative US Army (1975-1977); Specialist, Personnel US Army (1973-1975) **Creative Works:** Author, "Sweet Pea Teddy Bear," National Library of Poetry (1995) **Awards:** Army Commendation Medal, U.S. Army (1980); National Defense Service Medal, U.S. Army (1973); Two Good Conduct Medals, U.S. Army **Memberships:** Hollywood Media Professionals, (2018-Present); Charter Member, Women's Memorial (1997-Present); Allied Member, Pasadena Chapter, American Society of Interior Designers (2004-2008); Board of Directors, Inland-Palm Springs Chapter, American Society of Interior Designers (2003-2004); Allied Member, American Society of Interior Designers (2002-2004); Pacific Pioneer Broadcasters (1999-2018); Student Member, Inland-Palm Springs Chapter, American Society of Interior Designers (1999-2002); Vice President, Los Angeles Chapter, Armed Forces Broadcasters Association (1991-1993); Association of the United States Army (1975-1980); Life Member, DAV (Disabled American Veterans) **Marquis Who's Who Honors:** Albert Nelson Marquis Lifetime Achievement Award; Marquis Who's Who Humanitarian Award **To what do you attribute your success:** Ms. MacQueen attributes her success to her education and professional experience. **Why did you become involved in your profession or industry:** Ms. MacQueen became involved in her profession because of her varied interests, including radio and television production, art, handcrafts, and drafting. **Avocations:** Crafting; Crocheting

Willis Crocker Maddrey, MD, MACP, FRCP

Title: Professor of Internal Medicine **Industry:** Education/Educational Services **Company Name:** University of Texas Southwestern Medical Center **Date of Birth:** 03/29/1939 **Place of Birth:** Roanoke Rapids **State/Country of Origin:** NC/USA **Parents:** Milner Crocker Maddrey; Sara Jean (Willis) Maddrey **Marital Status:** Married **Spouse Name:** Ann Marie Matt **Children:** Jeffrey; Gregory; Thomas **Education:** Honorary DSc, Medical College of Ohio (Now College of Medicine and Life Sciences, University of Toledo) (1994); Fellow in Liver Disease, Yale School of Medicine (1970-1971); Chief Resident, Osler Medical Residency Training Program, Johns Hopkins Hospital, Baltimore, MD (1969-1970); Senior Assistant Resident, Osler Medical Residency Training Program, Johns Hopkins Hospital, Baltimore, MD (1968-1969); Assistant Resident, Osler Medical Residency Training Program, Johns Hopkins Hospital, Baltimore, MD (1965-1966); Intern, Osler Medical Residency Training Program, Johns Hopkins Hospital, Baltimore, MD (1964-1965); MD, Johns Hopkins University School of Medicine (1964); BS, Wake Forest University, Summa Cum Laude (1960) **Certifications:** License to Practice Medicine, State of Texas (1990); License to Practice Medicine, State of Pennsylvania (1982); Diplomate, American Board Internal Medicine (1971); License to Practice Medicine, State of Maryland (1964) **Career:** Assistant to the President, University of Texas Southwestern Medical Center, Dallas, TX (2009-Present); Professor of Internal Medicine, University of Texas Southwestern Medical Center (1990-Present); Executive Vice President of Clinical Affairs, University of Texas Southwestern Medical Center, Dallas, TX (1993-2009); Vice President of Clinical Affairs, University of Texas Southwestern Medical Center, Dallas, TX (1990-1993); Magee Professor and Chairman, Department of Medicine, Jefferson Medical College (Now Sidney Kimmel Medical College), Thomas Jefferson University, Philadelphia, PA (1982-1990); Professor, Johns Hopkins University, Baltimore, MD (1980-1982); Associate Director and Associate Physician-in-Chief, Department of Medicine, Johns Hopkins University School of Medicine, Baltimore, MD (1979-1982); Associate Professor of Medicine, Johns Hopkins University School of Medicine, Baltimore, MD (1975-1979); Assistant Dean, Postdoctoral Programs and Faculty Development, Johns Hopkins University School of Medicine, Baltimore, MD (1975-1979); Assistant Professor of Medicine, Johns Hopkins University School of Medicine, Baltimore, MD (1971-1975); Chief Resident, Osler Medical Service, Johns Hopkins Hospital, Baltimore, MD (1969-1970) **Career Related:** Fellow, American College of Physicians (1971-Present); Dr. Frederick J. and Irene Stare Visiting Professor in Gastroenterology, Newton-Wellesley Hospital, Harvard Medical School, Newton, MA (2012); Address at Dedication of Michael F. Sorrell Center for Health Science Education, University of Nebraska (2008); Norton J. Greenberger, MD Distinguished Lectureship in Gastroenterology and Hepatology, University of Kansas School of Medicine, University of Kansas Medical Center (2002); Paustian Lectureship, University of Nebraska Medical Center, Omaha, NE (2000) **Civic:** Board of Directors, Chairman of the Board, UT Southwestern Moncrief Cancer Center (1999-Present); Board of Trustees, Dallas Opera (1996-Present); Board of Directors, Richardson Regional Medical Center (2005-2010); Board of Directors, Senior Citizens of Dallas (2000-2006); Chairman of the Board, Board of Directors, UT Southwestern Health Systems, Incorporated (1995-2006); Board of Directors, Dallas Zoo (1994-2000) **Military Service:** Military Service, U.S. Public Health Service, National Institutes of Health, Office of International Research, Calcutta, India (1966-1968) **Creative Works:** International Editorial Board, Hepatobiliary & Pancreatic Diseases International (2002-Present); Editorial Board, Liver Transplantation and Surgery (1995-1999); Editorial Board, Transplantation Science (1991-1998); International Advisory Board, Alimentary Pharmacology & Therapeutics (1986-1996); Associate Editor, Hepatology (1988-1995) **Awards:** Distinguished Alumnus Award, Johns Hopkins University School of Medicine (2009); Distinguished Service Award, American Association for the Study of Liver Diseases (2000); Adelyn and Edmund M. Hoffman Distinguished Chair in Medical Science, University of Texas Southwestern Medical Center, Dallas, TX (1998); Distinguished Educator Award, American Gastroenterological Association (1998) **Memberships:** Vice-Chairman at Large, American Digestive Health Association (1999-Present); Vice-Chairman, Digestive Health Initiative - Viral Hepatitis, American Digestive Health Association (1994-1999); Master, American College of Physicians (1993); President, American College of Physicians (1992); Federated Council of Internal Medicine (1991-1992); Board of Regents, American College of Physicians (1986-1992); President-Elect, American College of Physicians (1991); Chairman, Access Steering Committee, American College of Physicians (1990-1991); Co-chairman, Biliary Section, American Gastroenterological Association (1989-1990) **Why did you become involved in your profession or industry:** Dr. Maddrey's father was a surgeon, so he always knew he wanted to be a doctor because he was inspired by his father. **Political Affiliations:** Republican

John Kazuaki Maesaka, MD

Title: Nephrologist, Professor of Medicine **Industry:** Medicine & Health Care **Company Name:** NYU Winthrop Hospital **Date of Birth:** 06/23/1935 **Place of Birth:** Ewa **State/Country of Origin:** HI/USA **Marital Status:** Married **Spouse Name:** Martha Haruko Tanaka (7/21/1963) **Children:** Alan Kazumi; Robert Kazuyuki **Education:** Fellow, Postdoctoral Research, Renal Disease, Icahn School of Medicine at Mount Sinai (1967-1970); Assistant Resident, Medicine, Icahn School of Medicine at Mount Sinai (1965-1967); Assistant Resident in Medicine, Barnes Hospital, Washington University in St. Louis (1962-1963); Intern in Medicine, Barnes Hospital, Washington University in St. Louis (1961-1962); MD, School of Medicine, Boston University (1961); BA in Biology, Harvard University (1957) **Certifications:** Diplomate, Subspecialty in Nephrology, Board of Internal Medicine (1976); Diplomate, American Board of Internal Medicine (1968); Diplomate, National Board of Medicine Examiners (1961) **Career:** Emeritus Chief, Division of Nephrology & Hypertension, Department of Medicine, NYU Winthrop Hospital (2005-Present); Professor, School of Medicine, Stony Brook University (1997-Present); Director of Research, NYU Winthrop Hospital (1996-2006); Chief, Division of Nephrology, NYU Winthrop Hospital, Mineola, NY (1994-2005); Associate Professor of Medicine, Albert Einstein College of Medicine, Bronx, NY (1994); Assistant Professor of Medicine, Albert Einstein College of Medicine (1990-1994); Chief, Division of Nephrology, Long Island Jewish Medical Center, New Hyde Park, NY (1985-1994); Associate Director of Nephrology Division and Fellowship Program, University of Medicine and Dentistry (Now Rutgers, The State University of New Jersey) (1982-1985); Associate Professor of Medicine, University of Medicine and Dentistry of New Jersey, Newark, NJ (1982-1985); Assistant Professor of Medicine, University of Medicine and Dentistry (Now Rutgers, The State University of New Jersey) (1973-1982); Assistant Director of Medicine, Jersey City Medical Center (1976-1978); Medical Consultant, Control Data Corporation (1974-1978); Medical Consultant, Multiple Risk Factor Intervention Trial Program, New York, NY (1973-1978); Associate Attending Physician, Jersey City Medical Center (1973-1978); Assistant in Medicine, Washington University in St. Louis (1961-1963) **Military Service:** Captain, Medical Corps, U.S. Army (1963-1965) **Creative Works:** Editorial Board Member, BioMed Research International; Editorial Board Member, World Journal of Nephrology; Editorial Board Member, Conference Papers in Medicine; Editorial Board Member, Case Reports in Nephrology; Editorial Board Member, Journal of Translational Internal Medicine; Editorial Board Member, Journal of Nephrology and Urology; Contributor, Articles to Professional Journals; Contributor, Book Chapters; Contributor, Book Reviews; Contributor, Abstracts; Contributor, Essay, "Pearl Harbor, World War II and Experiences After" **Awards:** Eponym, Howard and Shizuko Maesaka Award, Indiana University; Pharmaceutical Grantee, American Heart Association **Memberships:** Research Committee for Clinical and Translational Science Awards, Grant Application, State University of New York at Stony Brook (2007-Present); National Advisory Board on Renal Diseases, Pfizer Inc. (2003-Present); Consultant Board of Cardiology Review (2002-Present); Grant Reviewer, Alzheimer's Association (2002-Present); Advisory Board, COX2 Inhibitors, Pfizer Inc. (1999-Present); Advisory Board, Cardiovascular Diseases, Pfizer Inc. (1999-Present); Research Committee, American Heart Council (1999-Present); Medical Advisory Board, Long Island Nassau/Suffolk Chapter, JDRF (1997-Present); Medical Advisory Board, National Kidney Foundation of New York (1992-Present); Chairman, Subcommittee on Facilitating Bedside to Bench Research Recent Research Funding (2006); Chairman, Program Committee, Nephrology Society of New Jersey (1979-1985); President, Nephrology Society of New Jersey (1977-1978); President-elect, Nephrology Society of New Jersey (1976-1977); Chairman, Program Committee, Nephrology Society of New Jersey (1975-1976); American Federation for Clinical Research; American Society of Nephrology; International Society of Nephrology; Academy of Medicine of New Jersey; American Geriatric Society **Marquis Who's Who Honors:** Albert Nelson Marquis Lifetime Achievement Award; Marquis Who's Who Top Professional **Why did you become involved in your profession or industry:** Dr. Maesaka wanted to become a doctor since he was in kindergarten. He chose nephrology because it is rational and intellectually challenging.

Robert Wyman Maguire

Title: Publisher **Industry:** Publishing **Company Name:** Maguire Newspapers **Date of Birth:** 02/26/1944 **Place of Birth:** Springfield **State/Country of Origin:** VT/USA **Parents:** Robert Wyman Maguire; Rosamond (Templeton) Maguire **Marital Status:** Widowed **Education:** Coursework, MBA Program, Boston University (1987); BS, Husson College (1967); AA, Champlain College (1964) **Career:** Retired (2008); Publisher; Maguire Ltd (1981-2008); General Manager, The Rutland Tribune & Shopper, VT (1973-1981); Law Enforcement Administrator, Governor's Crime Commission, Montpelier, VT (1971-1973) **Career Related:** Publisher, The Maguire Newspaper Group, The Rutland Tribune & Shopper, The Poultney News, VT and Bisbee Observer, AZ **Civic:** Board of Directors, Vermont Cancer Society (1996-Present); Vice President, Safer Society of America, Inc. (2017-2019); Director, Free Community Papers of New England (1997); Arizona Press Association (1994-1997); Vermont Press Association (1984-1997); New England Newspaper & Press Association (1983-1997); Clarendon Republican Committee (1985-1986); Board of Directors, Mendon United Methodist Church (1985-1986); Board of Directors, Epilepsy Foundation of Vermont (1971-1975); Member, Vermont Republican State Committee (1969-1973); Chairman, Windsor County Republican Committee, VT (1969-1971) **Memberships:** Board of Directors, Vermont Jaycees (1968-1969); Rutland Region Chamber of Commerce **Marquis Who's Who Honors:** Albert Nelson Marquis Lifetime Achievement Award; Marquis Who's Who Top Professional **To what do you attribute your success:** Mr. Maguire attributes his success to long hours and knowledge of accounting. **Why did you become involved in your profession or industry:** Mr. Maguire became involved in his profession because he was in sales and his boss, Colonel Warren Taylor, thought he had the knack to pursue the line and move up the ladder. **Avocations:** Airplane pilot; Collecting political buttons; Scuba diving; Ancient history

Dean George Makricostas

Title: Lawyer **Industry:** Law and Legal Services **Date of Birth:** 07/04/1968 **Place of Birth:** Weirton **State/Country of Origin:** WV/USA **Parents:** George James Makricostas; Eugenia George Makricostas **Marital Status:** Married **Spouse Name:** Eugenia Nikki Makricostas (12/27/1997) **Children:** George Patrick Makricostas; Kalliopi Nicole-Marie Makricostas **Education:** Doctor of Jurisprudence, Thomas M. Cooley Law School (1996); Bachelor of Arts, West Virginia University (1990) **Career:** Municipal Judge, City of Weirton (2015-Present); Partner, Dittmar Taylor Makricostas (2004-Present); Partner, Taylor & Makricostas PLLC (2003-2004); Partner, Gurrera Taylor & Makricostas, Weirton, WV (1997-2003); Clerk, Galloway & Taylor Law Office, Weirton, WV (1996-1997); Sales and Lease Consultant, Biggio Ford Lincoln Mercury & Toyota, Steubenville, OH (1991-1993); Computer Science Assistant, West Virginia University, Morgantown, WV (1988-1990); General Laborer, Weirton Steel Corporation (1987) **Career Related:** Municipal Judge, Wellsburg City, Wellsburg, WV (2003-Present); Municipal Judge, Village of Beech Bottom (2003-Present) **Civic:** Council, All Saints Greek Orthodox Church, Weirton, WV (1995-Present); American Hellenic Educational Program of America, Weirton, WV (1986-Present); County Fiduciary Commission; VP Weirton Christian Center **Awards:** Legal Network, Top Lawyers in West Virginia (2013-Present); Listee, America's Top 100 Attorney's; National League of Renounced Attorneys; Inductee, National Academy of Juris Providence Premica 100; Rue Ratings Best Attorneys of America **Memberships:** Association of Trial Lawyers of America; West Virginia Trial Lawyers Association; West Virginia Bar Association; Ohio State Bar; Ohio Trial Lawyers Association; Hancock County Bar Association; National Association of Criminal Defense Attorneys; Elks; Pennsylvania Bar Association; Jefferson County Ohio Bar Association; American Hellenic Educational Progressive Association **Bar Admissions:** States of Pennsylvania (2006); Ohio (2004); West Virginia (1997); United States District Court, Northern and Southern District of West Virginia (1997) **Marquis Who's Who Honors:** Albert Nelson Marquis Lifetime Achievement Award; Marquis Who's Who Top Professional **To what do you attribute your success:** Mr. Makricostas attributes his success to his hard work and veracity, which was instilled in him by his parents. **Why did you become involved in your profession or industry:** Mr. Makricostas has always had an interest in the law; he was driven by his desire to help people. He chose to focus on personal injury law because he wanted to ensure that people were being treated fairly. **Avocations:** Youth activities; Hockey; Public interest groups; Restoration of vehicles **Religion:** Greek Orthodox

Deepak Malhotra, MD, PhD

Title: Nephrologist **Industry:** Medicine & Health Care **Date of Birth:** 03/07/1956 **Place of Birth:** Amritsar **State/Country of Origin:** India **Parents:** Om Parkash Malhotra (Deceased 2007); Bimla (Vijh) Malhotra (Deceased 2015) **Marital Status:** Married **Spouse Name:** Judith Maria Konfal (04/20/1989) **Children:** Kristin; Nathan **Education:** MD, Case Western Reserve University (1985); PhD, Case Western Reserve University (1984); BS, Case Western Reserve University (1978) **Certifications:** Recertified (2004, 2014); Certified, Nephrology (1994); Certified, Internal Medicine (1989) **Career:** Professor, University of Toledo (2003-Present); Associate Professor, Medical College of Ohio (now University of Toledo), Toledo (1997-2003); Assistant Professor, University of New Mexico, Albuquerque, NM (1991-1997); Fellow, University of Colorado Health Sciences Center, Denver, CO (1988-1991); Resident, Cleveland Clinic Foundation (1985-1988) **Career Related:** Staff Physician, Veteran Affairs Medical Center, Albuquerque, NM (1991-1993); Chief, Division of Nephrology, University of Toledo; Medical Director, Renal Transplantation, University of Toledo; Medical Director, Southland Dialysis; Member, Institutional Review Board, University of Toledo; Member, Cancer Institutional Review Board, University of Toledo **Creative Works:** Contributor, Articles, Professional Journals **Awards:** Grantee, American Heart Association (1994) **Memberships:** International Society of Nephrology; American Heart Association; American Society of Nephrology; American Society of Transplant Physicians International; American College of Physicians; American Chemical Society; American Association for the Advancement of Science **Marquis Who's Who Honors:** Albert Nelson Marquis Lifetime Achievement Award **Why did you become involved in your profession or industry:** As an MD/PhD graduate student, Dr. Malhotra did theoretical modeling of molecules interacting with other molecules in solution. He became interested in the utilization of spectroscopy to study these interactions. After researching and reading several papers, he became interested in the molecular interactions within the kidney. However, his interest in medicine originated from his father's work as a biomedical researcher, which exposed him to medicine that he never knew existed. Additionally, Dr. Malhotra was especially intrigued by artificial materials and how it contributed to medicine. **Avocations:** Woodworking; Nature photography; Snow skiing; Home and automotive repair

Alka Manaktala

Title: Vice President **Industry:** Insurance **Company Name:** Insurance Office of America **Education:** MA, University of Delhi (1981) **Career:** Vice President, Insurance Office of America (2015-Present) **Civic:** Donor, St. Jude Children's Research Hospital **Awards:** Top Producer, Insurance Business American (2017-2019) **To what do you attribute your success:** Ms. Manaktala attributes her success to her agency and the ones with which she works.

Ronald Manderscheid, PhD

Title: Executive Director **Industry:** Health, Wellness and Fitness **Company Name:** National Association of County Behavioral Health & Developmental Disability Directors **Date of Birth:** 09/28/1943 **Place of Birth:** LcCrosse **State/Country of Origin:** WI/USA **Parents:** William Joseph; Norene Elsine Batteen **Marital Status:** Married **Spouse Name:** Frances Elizabeth Fedkiw (09/01/1973) **Children:** William Derrick; Kristen Elizabeth; Erika Marie **Education:** PhD, University of Maryland (1975); MA, Marquette University (1967); BA, Loras College, Maxima Cum Laude (1965) **Certifications:** Certified, Federal Executive Institute (1986) **Career:** Executive Director, National Association of County Behavioral Health & Developmental Disability Directors (2009-Present); Senior Principal, Director of Mental Health and Substance Use Program, Global Health Sector/SRA (2006-2011); Chief, Survey & Analysis, Center for Mental Health Services (1992-2006); Acting Director, Division of State and Community System Development, Center for Mental Health Services (1992-1993); Chief, Statistical Research Branch, National Institute of Mental Health (1981-1992); Chief, Evaluation Research Section, National Institute of Mental Health (1975-1980); Research Associate, National Institute of Mental Health (1972-1975); Research Assistant, University of Maryland (1970-1972) **Career Related:** Adjunct Professor, University of Southern California Suzanne Dworak-Peck School of Social Work (2016-Present); With, National Research Institute (2011-Present); With, The Council of Quality and Leadership, Inc. (2011-Present); With, Danya Institute (2010-Present); Adjunct Professor, Department of Mental Health, Johns Hopkins Bloomberg School of Public Health (2006-Present); Member, International Consortium of Mental Health Policy and Research (2000-Present); With, Pan American Health Organization (1995-Present); With, WHO (1993-Present); Secretary's Advisory Group of Health People 2020, U.S. Department of Health & Human Services (2008-2011); With, Columbia University (1998-2001); Consultant, George Washington University (1978-1983) **Civic:** West Montgomery Citizens Association, Potomac, MD (1983-Present); Volunteer, Chesapeake & Ohio Canal; Volunteer, Stone Ridge School of the Sacred Heart; Volunteer in Community Service, Washington, DC **Military Service:** With, United States Army (1967-1969) **Creative Works:** Co-editor, "Outcome Measurement in the Human Service" (2011); Editor, International Journal of Mental Health (1998, 2005, 2007, 2008); Author, Editor, "Mental Health in the United States" (1987, 1990, 1992, 1994, 1996, 1998, 2000, 2002, 2004); Special Editor, Journal of the Washington Academy of Sciences (2000); Producer, "Making the Numbers Works for You" (1987); Editor, "System Science and the Future of Health (1976); Contributor, Articles and Professional Journals **Awards:** Lifetime Achievement Award, New York Association of Psychiatric Rehabilitation Services, Inc. (2019); Public Policy Leadership Award, New York Association of Psychiatric Rehabilitation Services, Inc. (2014); Carl A. Taube Lifetime Achievement Award (2014); Stuart A. Rice Award, District of Columbia Sociological Society (2011); Secretary Distinguished Service Award, U.S. Department of Health & Human Services (1999, 2004-2006, 2008); Decorated Army Commendation Medal; Recipient, Numerous Awards **Memberships:** Executive Board, American College Health Administrators (2007-2015); President, American College Health Administrators (2011-2013); President, Foundation, Federal Executive Institute Alumni Association (2003-2011); Executive Board, Federal Executive Institute Alumni Association (1997-2005); President, Federal Executive Institute Alumni Association (2003); Chair, Policy Issues Committee (1995-2000); Chair of Mental Health, American Public Health Association (1997-1998); President, District of Columbia Sociological Society (1992-1993); Member, Numerous Organizations **Marquis Who's Who Honors:** Albert Nelson Marquis Lifetime Achievement Award **To what do you attribute your success:** Dr. Manderscheid attributes his success to his ability to undertake a task and to increase social justice in the world by completion of that task. **Why did you become involved in your profession or industry:** When Dr. Manderscheid was a graduate student, he had the chance to work with a very brilliant man at the National Institute of Mental Health. This man went on to win major awards in chemistry. Dr. Manderscheid became very interested in that work and stayed in the field for 40 years. His mentor taught him to think. Another colleague taught him to negotiate bureaucracy, and another person, who is the elderly father of a daughter of a schizophrenic, taught him to have heart. It's a continuation of the work he's done his whole life in the mental health field. He went from the bench to the trench; he worked in basic research when he graduated. Dr. Manderscheid also worked with a gentlemen who went on and won the noble prize in chemistry on the brain. It was very exciting work; he continued in those roles for about 10 years before going on to running and trading programs. He authored several books and ran some data systems. Eventually, he retired from the government and came to where he now works with people in the field. Dr. Manderscheid went from basic research to managing research and data programs, to working on policy and with the people in the field. **Avocations:** Coin collecting/numismatic; Reading; Visiting the Cape in Massachusetts; Relaxing with family; Furniture building

Robert D. Manfred Jr.

Title: Commissioner **Industry:** Athletics **Company Name:** Major League Baseball **Date of Birth:** 04/26/1958 **Place of Birth:** Rome **State/Country of Origin:** NY/USA **Parents:** Robert Dean Manfred; Phyllis (Aquino) Manfred **Marital Status:** Married **Spouse Name:** Colleen Feely (06/05/1982) **Children:** Megan; Francis Michael; Jane; Mary Clare **Education:** JD, Harvard Law School, Magna Cum Laude, MA (1983); BS, Cornell University, Ithaca, NY (1980); Coursework, Le Moyne College (1976-1978) **Career:** Commissioner, Major League Baseball (2015-Present); Commissioner-Elect, Major League Baseball (2014-2015); Chief Operating Officer, Major League Baseball (2013-2015); Executive Vice President, Labor Relations and Human Resources, Major League Baseball, New York, NY (1998-2013); Partner, Morgan, Lewis & Bockius LLP (1991-1998); Associate, Morgan, Lewis & Bockius LLP (1984-1991); Law Clerk, Honorable Joseph L. Tauro, United States District Court of Massachusetts (1983-1984) **Civic:** Board Member, School of the Holy Child, Rye, NY **Memberships:** Labor Section, American Bar Association; District of Columbia Bar Association; Massachusetts Bar Association **Bar Admissions:** District of Columbia (1984); Massachusetts (1983)

Carl William Mangus

Title: Technical Safety and Standards Consultant, Engineer **Industry:** Oil & Energy **Date of Birth:** 08/20/1930 **Place of Birth:** Broken Bow **State/Country of Origin:** OK/USA **Parents:** Nathaniel M. Mangus; Eva Tennessee (Johnson) Mangus **Marital Status:** Widowed **Spouse Name:** Dorotha Marie Wood Mangus (Deceased) **Children:** Steven Neal; Roy Gene (Deceased); Carla Anne **Education:** BSME, Oklahoma State University (1958) **Certifications:** Registered Professional Engineer, Louisiana (1959-1998) **Career:** Founder, TS&S Offshore Crane Services (2003-2015); Private Practice, Technical Safety and Standards, Lacombe, LA (1986-2015); Member, Senior Staff, Technical Safety Specialist, Shell Oil (1985); Regulatory Affairs, Shell Oil (1982); With Technical Safety Review Engineering Procedures, Plus Regulations and Industry Standards (1971); Offshore Production, Maintenance and Operating Standards (1970); Installation of several Gas Processing Plant Facilities such as the Calumet Gas Processing Plant (1969); Offshore Engineering Section Leader, Facilities, Calumet Gas Processing Plant (1969); Project Manager, Calumet Gas Processing Plant (1968); With, Project Development, Two Natural Gas Plants; Project Manager, N. Terrebonne Plant Expansion & Dual 36 Pipeline Loop; Project Developer, Several Natural Gas Plants; Project Manager, Chalkley Gas Processing Plant; Various Positions, Pipeline, Installations, Plant in Little Creek, Mississippi **Career Related:** Committee Member, National Academy of Sciences (1979-1984); Member, Special Advisory Ad Hoc Committee, International Association of Drilling Contractors; Consultant, State Department, International Maritime Organization, London, England; Committee Member, American Bureau Shipping, New York, NY; Representative to Exploration/Production, American Petroleum Institute; Past U.S. Industry Representative, Safety Code for Construction, Offshore Structures; Past Member, Numerous Committees; Communicator to Political Staff on Domestic and "United Nation" Issues **Military Service:** Staff Sergeant, U.S. Air Force (1951-1955) **Awards:** American Petroleum Citation for Service, American Petroleum Institute (API) (1987); **Memberships:** Past Member, Louisiana Engineering Society; Past Member, American Society of Safety Engineers; Past Member, Gulf Coast Safety and Training Group; Past Member, Society of Petroleum Engineers; American Bureau of Shipping; The International Association of Drilling Contractors (IADC); American Petroleum Institute (API) **Marquis Who's Who Honors:** Albert Nelson Marquis Lifetime Achievement Award; Marquis Who's Who Top Professional **To what do you attribute your success:** Mr. Mangus attributes his success to family and dedication. **Why did you become involved in your profession or industry:** He became involved in his profession because of his desire to construct and build things. **Avocations:** Hunting; Fishing; Woodworking; Swimming; Boating; Traveling **Political Affiliations:** Republican **Religion:** Church of Christ **Thoughts on Life:** Live a happy life for the world and especially for your family in accordance with God's will.

Winston Mendoza Manimtim, MD, FAAP

Title: Neonatologist **Industry:** Medicine & Health Care **Date of Birth:** 07/11/1961 **State/Country of Origin:** The Philippines **Parents:** Florencio Manimtim; Suprema (Mendoza) Manimtim **Marital Status:** Single **Education:** Neonatology Fellowship, University of Maryland, Baltimore (1997-2000); Pediatric Residency, Albert Einstein College Medicine, Bronx, NY (1995-1997); Pediatric Residency, Philippine Children's Medical Center (1987-1990); MD, University of St. Tomas, The Philippines (1985); BS in Zoology, University of St. Tomas, The Philippines (1981) **Certifications:** Fellow, American Board Pediatrics; Fellow, Sub-board of Neonatal-Perinatal Medicine **Career:** Associate Professor, Pediatrics, Children's Mercy-Kansas City, University of Missouri-Kansas City School of Medicine (2014-Present); Assistant Professor, Pediatrics, Children's Mercy-Kansas City, University of Missouri-Kansas City School of Medicine (2007-2014); Clinical Instructor, University of Maryland, Baltimore; Registrar Neonatology, Mercy for Hospital Women, Melbourne, Australia (1992-1994) **Career Related:** Neonatologist, Children's Mercy-Kansas City (2007-Present) Medical Director, Liberty Hospital Special Care Nursery (2007-Present); Neonatologist, Menorah Medical Center (2007-2008); Neonatologist, Medical Center of Independence (2005-2007); Chairman, Department of Pediatrics, Baptist Lutheran Medical Center (2004-2006); Neonatologist, Research Medical Center (2000-2007); Director, Children's Mercy-Kansas City Neonatal Follow-up Clinics; Medical Director, Children's Mercy-Kansas City Infant Tracheostomy and Home Ventilator Program **Awards:** United States News and World Report Top Doctors, Castle Connolly (2012-Present); Golden Apple Mercy Mentor Award, Children's Mercy-Kansas City Graduate Medical Educations (2015, 2017); Kansas City's Best Doctor's, Kansas City Business Journal (2013); Institute for International Medicine (INMED) National Healthcare Service Award (2013); Humanitarian of the Year Award, Talisay Midwest Association, Chicago, IL (2000); International Fellow, American Respiratory Care Foundation (1991); Resident Scholar, Philippine Pediatric Society (1987); Alien of Extraordinary Ability in the Field of Medicine **Memberships:** Fellow, American Academy Pediatrics; American Medical Association; Midwest Society Pediatric Research **Marquis Who's Who Honors:** Albert Nelson Marquis Lifetime Achievement Award; Marquis Who's Who Top Professional **Why did you become involved in your profession or industry:** Dr. Manimtim is the first one in his family to choose medicine as a career path. Through his pursuits he has influenced many of his nieces and nephews who are following his footsteps in the medical field as well. Dr. Manimtim was influenced by a medical school professor who happened to be a neonatologist. Manimtim had always liked babies and was exposed to the specialty early in his pursuits and decided it would be a good fit for him.

Frank Bert Mann

Title: Artist, Educator, Writer **Industry:** Fine Art **Company Name:** The Frank Mann Studio **Place of Birth:** Washington **State/Country of Origin:** DC/USA **Education:** Intern, Dorothea Rockburne, New York, NY (1986); MFA, Pratt Institute, Brooklyn, NY (1981); Whitney Graduate Seminars, The Whitney Museum of American Art, New York, NY (1980-1982); Art History, Columbia University (1980); BA, George Washington University (1978); BS, High Point University (1972) **Career:** Thorn, Los Angeles, Ca (2018-Present); Art Works 4 Charity, NY (2016-Present); Visual Aids, NY (2009-Present); Association D'Aides, Paris, France (2009-Present); Free Arts NYC, New York, NY (2018); Visiting Artist, Coalition for the Homeless Camp, Roscoe, NY (1997); Children's Friends for Life, New York, NY (1997); Project Director, St. Cyril's Church, New York, NY (1992); Director, Basic Arts Network, New York, NY (1989-1990); Executive Director, Collaborative Projects, Inc., New York, NY (1987-1988) **Career Related:** Guest Lecturer, The Frank Mann Studio (2012-Present); Guest Lecturer, The Interchurch Center, New York, NY (2011); Guest Lecturer, Educational Alliance, New York, NY (2010); Guest Lecturer, Reading College, Reading, Pa (2009); Guest Lecturer, Northampton College, Bethlehem, Pa (2009); Guest Lecturer, New Arts Program Exhibition Space, Kutztown, Pa (2009); Guest Lecturer, Iona College, New Rochelle, NY (2005); Guest Lecturer, New Jersey Institute of Technology, Newark, NJ (2002); Guest Lecturer, Parsons School of Art and Design, The New School, New York, NY (1996-1997); Guest Lecturer, Pratt Institute, Brooklyn, NY (1987-1988); Guest Lecturer, The Pennsylvania State University, Reading, Pa (1986-1987); Guest Lecturer, Corcoran College of Art, Washington, DC (1979) **Civic:** U.S. Representative, Personal Structures - Identities, Palazzo Bembo, Venice (2019); U.S. Representative, Italia Docet/Laboratorium, Palazzo Barbarigo Minotto, San Marco, Venice, Italy (2015); U.S. Representative, International Festival of Contemporary Art, Chappelle des Salelles, St. Maurice D'Ibis, France (2007); U.S. Representative, Biennale Internazionale Dell'Arte Contemporanea, Florence, Italy (1999, 2001); U.S. Representative, Recent Trends in Works of Art on Paper, Museo de Arte Moderno, Buenos Aires, Argentina (1990); U.S. Representative, Painting Today : New York to Buenos Aires, Cultural Center of Buenos Aires, Argentina (1989) **Creative Works:** Group Show, Personal Structures - Identities, the 58th Venice Biennale, Palazzo Bembo, Venice (2019); Group Show, CAP Exhibition, Infinity Gallery, Melbourne, Australia (2017); Group Show, "Art Protects," L'Space Foundation EDF, Paris, France (2016); Exhibition, Artifact Gallery, New York, NY (2015); Group Show, Italia Docet/Laboratorium, the 56th Venice Biennale, Palazzo Barbarigo Minotto, San Marco, Venice, Italy (2015); Group Show, Art Gallery of Cascais, Carcavelos, Portugal (2014); Group Show, "Leonardo Contra Canova," Galleria L'Agostiniana, Rome, Italy (2014); Author, "Then and Now, the American Society of Contemporary Artists" (2012); Group Show, Drawing Connections, Siena Art Institute, Siena, Italy (2011); Exhibition, Oculus, The Treasure Room Gallery, The Interchurch Center, New York, NY (2011); Exhibition, Oculus : A Survey Exhibition, Broome Street Gallery, New York, NY (2010) **Awards:** The Pablo Picasso Award, Accademia Italia in Arte nel Mondo Associazione Culturale, Lecce, Italy (2019); Lifetime Achievement Award, International Association of Top Professionals, New York (2019); Honorary Doctorate of Letters, The International Biographical Centre, Cambridge, England (2018); The Premier Leonardo Da Vinci International Award, International Contemporary Art Magazine, Florence, Italy (2018); Il Guerrieri di Riace, The Warriors of Riace Award, International Art Academy Award of the Accademia Italia in Arte nel Mondo Associazione Culturale, Lecce, Italy (2017); High Recognition Il Beato Angelico Award, Accademia Italia in Arte nel Mondo Associazione Culturale, Lecce, Italy (2016); International Human Rights Award, in tribute to Victor Hugo, Accademia Italia in Arte nel Mondo Associazione Culturale, Lecce, Italy (2016); The Sandro Botticelli Prize, E.A. Editore Publishers, Rome, Italy (2015); Elaine Alibrandi Award, American Society of Contemporary Artists (2013); Roy Moyer Memorial Award, American Society of Contemporary Artists (2012); Premier Certificate of Honor in Graphics, American Society of Contemporary Artists (2010); Grantee, New Arts Program, National Endowment for the Arts, Kutztown, Pa. (2009); Lorenzo Il Magnifico Medal in Painting, Biennale Internazionale Dell'Arte Contemporanea, Florence, Italy (2001); Certificate of Honors, Small Works in Venice, Art Addiction Gallery, Stockholm, Sweden (1999); Grantee, Art Matters, Inc. (1991); Grantee, Artists Space (1990); Grantee, New York City Department of Cultural Affairs (1988); Grantee, New York State Council on the Arts (1988); Grantee, New Arts Program, National Endowment for the Arts, Kutztown, Pa. (1987); Mable Sanger Webb Art Award, Ford Foundation Grant (1980) **Memberships: Marquis Who's Who Honors:** Albert Nelson Marquis Lifetime Achievement Award; Marquis Who's Who Top Professional **Avocations:** Research into structural color

Edward Manougian

Title: Physician (Retired) **Industry:** Medicine & Health Care **Date of Birth:** 04/11/1929 **Place of Birth:** Highland Park **State/Country of Origin:** MI/USA **Parents:** George Krikor Manougian; Vera Varsen (Jernukian) Manougian **Marital Status:** Married **Spouse Name:** Sylva Manougian **Children:** Yon; Tasha **Education:** Postdoctoral Fellowship, University of California Berkeley (1960-1962); Doctor of Medicine, University of Michigan (1955); Bachelor of Science, Wayne University (1951) **Career:** Medical Consultant, California State Rehabilitation (1993-2012); Medical Practice, Chronic Pain Syndrome (2003-2011); Medical Director, Hospice Contra Costa, Pleasant Hill, CA (1991-1992); Associate Medical Director, Hospice Contra Costa, Pleasant Hill, CA (1982-1990); House Physician, Peralta Hospital, Oakland, CA (1979-1981); Research Associate, Lawrence Berkeley Laboratory, California (1962-1977); Postdoctoral Fellow in Biophysics, National Institutes of Health, University of California (1960-1962); House Physician, Patton State Hospital, California (1956-1960); Intern, San Bernardino County Charity Hospital, California (1955-1956) **Career Related:** Researcher, Ocular Hazards Division, U.S. Army **Military Service:** Lieutenant Colonel, U.S. Army Reserve (1985-1994); Captain, Medical Corps, U.S. Army (1957-1959) **Creative Works:** Contributor, Articles to Professional Journals **Memberships:** American Association for the Advancement of Science; Academy Hospice Physicians; American Mathematics Society; Alameda Contra Costa County Medical Society; California Medical Society **Marquis Who's Who Honors:** Albert Nelson Marquis Lifetime Achievement Award **Why did you become involved in your profession or industry:** Dr. Manougian became involved in his profession due to an early childhood experience, wherein he broke his arm and drew inspiration from the doctor who healed him. Later on in life, while attending University of California Berkeley on a fellowship, he conducted research on glucose kinetics and breast cancer while waiting for a theoretical biology program, while spurred him to enter his area of expertise. **Avocations:** Track running **Political Affiliations:** Democrat

Lori A. Marano

Title: Partner **Industry:** Law and Legal Services **Company Name:** Gabriele Marano **Education:** JD, Hofstra University School of Law (1987); Undergraduate Coursework in Psychology, Long Island University **Career:** Partner, Gabriele Marano (2012-Present); Equity Partner, Gabriele Marano (1992) **Civic:** Former Chair, Appellate Practice Committee, Suffolk County Bar Association **Creative Works:** Co-Author, Bard & Marano, New York Medical Malpractice (1994) **Awards:** Listee, Outstanding Women in Law, Hofstra University **Memberships:** Judicial Screening Committee; National Association of Professional Women; Suffolk County Bar Association; New York State Bar Association **To what do you attribute your success:** Ms. Marano attributes her success to being involved early on with the medical malpractice treatise. Likewise, she has worked with a lot of good people and mentors. **Why did you become involved in your profession or industry:** Ms. Marano became involved in her profession because she felt it would give her an opportunity to be a leader. She chose to work in medical malpractice after writing an article on the field; from that experience, she started working for an attorney who was publishing a treatise. She then became very familiar with the body of law, which kept her interested and motivated to succeed.

Craig Brian Marcus

Title: Lawyer **Industry:** Law and Legal Services **Company Name:** Marcus, Hardee, Piñol & Davies, LLP **Date of Birth:** 05/30/1939 **Place of Birth:** Boise **State/Country of Origin:** ID/USA **Parents:** Claude Virgil Marcus; Marie Louise Marcus **Marital Status:** Married **Spouse Name:** Lynne Merryweather (09/03/1960) **Children:** Shawn; Brian; Trent **Education:** JD, University of Idaho (1963); Coursework, Mexico City College (1959-1960); Coursework, University of Pennsylvania (1958-1959); Coursework, Boise Junior College (Now Boise State University (1958) **Career:** Partner, Marcus, Hardee, Piñol & Davies, LLP and its Predecessors (MHPD Law), Boise, Idaho (1963-Present) **Civic:** Chairman, Judicial Campaign, Idaho Court of Appeals (1984, 1990); Ada County Coordinator Representative, Senatorial Campaigns, Idaho (1969); Ada County Director Representative, Congressional Campaigns, Boise, Idaho (1964-1966) **Creative Works:** Author, "Divorce in Idaho" (2018) **Awards:** 50 Year Service to Legal Profession Award, Idaho State Bar (2013); AV Preeminent Rating, Martindale-Hubbell **Memberships:** President, Lincoln Day Banquet Association (1975); Court Trial Procedural Rules Committee, Fourth District Bar Association, Idaho (1973-1974); Trial, Rules, and Peer Review Committee, Idaho Bar Association (1971-1973); Treasurer, Fourth District Bar Association, Idaho (1967-1968); BPO Elks **Bar Admissions:** Idaho (1963); United States District Court for the District of Idaho (1963) **Marquis Who's Who Honors:** Albert Nelson Marquis Lifetime Achievement Award; Marquis Who's Who Top Professional **Why did you become involved in your profession or industry:** Mr. Craig Marcus' father was an attorney and he was inspired by his father to become a lawyer. The law firm Marcus, Hardee & Davies represent three generations of lawyers in Craig Marcus' family and has been serving the community since 1963. **Avocations:** Fishing; Hunting; Golf; Skiing; Trap shooting **Political Affiliations:** Republican **Religion:** Christian **Thoughts on Life:** Mr. Marcus' father a lawyer who represented El Paso Natural Gas; his great-grandfather came through Idaho in 1867.

Rod David Margo, DCL, LLB

Title: Lawyer (Retired) **Industry:** Law and Legal Services **Company Name:** Condon & Forsyth LLP **Date of Birth:** 02/14/1950 **Place of Birth:** Johannesburg **State/Country of Origin:** South Africa **Parents:** Cecil Stanley Margo; Marguerite Giselle (Polné) Margo **Education:** DCL, McGill University, Montreal, QC, Canada (1979); LLB, University of the Witwatersrand, Cum Laude, Johannesburg, South Africa (1973); BCom, University of the Witwatersrand, Johannesburg, South Africa (1970) **Certifications:** Solicitor, New South Wales, Australia (2004) **Career:** Associate, Partner, Condon & Forsyth LLP, Los Angeles, CA (1980); Fellow, Royal Aeronautical Society **Career Related:** Lecturer of Aviation Law, UCLA (1981-1998); Adjunct Professor of Law, Institute of Air & Space Law, McGill University, Montreal, Canada **Creative Works:** Co-Author, "Shawcross & Beaumont on Air Law, Fourth Review Edition" (2009); Co-Author, "Montreal Convention, First Edition" (2007); Author, "Aviation Insurance, Third Edition" (2000) **Memberships:** Los Angeles County Bar Association **Bar Admissions:** Supreme Court of the United States (2005); New South Wales Bar Association (2004); District of Columbia Bar (1996); The State Bar of California (1981); State Bar of Georgia (1979) **Marquis Who's Who Honors:** Albert Nelson Marquis Lifetime Achievement Award; Marquis Who's Who Top Professional; Marquis Who's Who Humanitarian Award

Marion Mark, EdD

Title: Writing Educator **Industry:** Education/Educational Services **Company Name:** St. Edward's University **Date of Birth:** 09/28/1930 **Place of Birth:** Hayward **State/Country of Origin:** CA/USA **Parents:** Dr. Milton William Thorpe; Dr. Johanna Altgelt (Schwab) Thorpe **Marital Status:** Married **Spouse Name:** Hans Michael Mark (1951) **Children:** Jane; Rufus **Education:** EdD, George Washington University (1982); MEd, Boston University (1953); EdB, Boston University (1952) **Certifications:** General Teaching, Primary-12 **Career:** Instructor, Writing, Saint Edward's University, Austin, TX (1995-2008); Teacher, Advanced Placement English, Saint Michael's Catholic Academy, Austin, TX (1993-1997); Curriculum Specialist, Independent School District, Austin, TX (1984-1991); Instructor, George Washington University, Washington, DC (1981-1982); Reading Specialist, Prince Georges County, Camp Springs, MD (1971-1976); Honors English Teacher, San Mateo School District, Redwood City, CA (1971-1976); Chairman, English Department, Ravenswood High School, Redwood City, CA (1969-1971); Instructor, Reading, McKinley Continuation High School, Berkeley, CA (1968-1969); Private Tutor, Home Teacher, Berkeley, CA (1961-1968); Private Tutor, Reading, Livermore, CA (1955-1961); Teacher, Director, Remedial Reading Educational Testing and Diagnosis, Natick Public Schools, Massachusetts (1953-1955); Diagnostician, Teacher, Donald D. Durrell Reading and Writing Clinic, Boston University (1951-1953) **Career Related:** Mentor, Handicapped Students, Saint Edward's University (1997-2008); Mentor, Migrant Students, Saint Edward's University (1995-2008) **Creative Works:** Author, "The Mathematical Historian" (1986); Author, "The Scientific Grammarian" (1985); Author, "Diagnostic Test: Mathematics Skills" (1975); Author, "The Pious Tiger" (1964); Author, "Teaching Literary Appreciation" (1953) **Awards:** Leadership Award, Camp Fire (1991); Teacher of the Year, Menlo-Atherton Student Council (1975) **Memberships:** English-Speaking Union of the United States; P.E.O.; Alliance Pan American Roundtable; Austin Women's Club; American History Club; University Ladies Club; Tuesday Club; Philosophical Society of Texas **Marquis Who's Who Honors:** Albert Nelson Marquis Lifetime Achievement Award **Why did you become involved in your profession or industry:** Dr. Mark became a teacher because she was inspired by her aunt. Her aunt taught mentally challenged students. **Avocations:** Piano; Reading; Needlepoint; Antique dolls; Family history **Political Affiliations:** Democrat **Religion:** Episcopalian

Lynn McMaster Markley

Title: Rubber and Plastics Company Executive **Industry:** Manufacturing **Date of Birth:** 08/18/1938 **Place of Birth:** Carrollton **State/Country of Origin:** OH/USA **Parents:** Charles Sparks Markley; Florence Elizabeth (McMaster) Markley **Marital Status:** Married **Spouse Name:** Ina Marie Hogsed (11/01/1958) **Children:** Jerry Lynn; David Alan; Margaret Elisabeth **Education:** MBA, Akron University (1966); BS in Chemistry, Mount Union College, Alliance, OH (1960) **Career:** Manager of Quality And Technology, Bailey Transportation Products, Incorporated, Conneaut, OH (1994-2001); Director of Manufacturing Quality Assurance, Uniroyal/Goodrich Tire Company, Akron, OH (1986-1994); Director of Operations Staff, Uniroyal Incorporated, Tire Division (1986); Director of Product Engineering, Uniroyal Incorporated, Tire Division (1981-1986); Director of Materials, Uniroyal Incorporated, Tire Division (1980-1981); Director of Quality Assurance, Uniroyal Incorporated, Tire Division (1978-1980); Manager of Quality Assurance, Uniroyal Incorporated, Tire Division (1976-1978); Manager of Passenger Materials, Uniroyal Incorporated, Tire Division, Troy, MI (1974-1976); Manager of Materials, Dunlop Tire Company, Buffalo, NY (1966-1974); Laboratory Manager, General Tire Company, Akron, OH (1962-1966); Research Chemist, PPG Chemical, Barberton, OH (1960-1962); Manager of Quality and Technology, Kirkland Industries, Cleveland, OH **Memberships:** American Society of Quality Control **Marquis Who's Who Honors:** Albert Nelson Marquis Lifetime Achievement Award **Why did you become involved in your profession or industry:** Mr. Markley had always had an inquisitive mind, which is what his wife Ina believes drew him to study the sciences. She recalls their first date, describing him as "unique" and unlike anyone else she has ever met. His brilliant mind is what truly drew her to him.

Michele C. Marquardt

Title: Founding Member **Industry:** Law and Legal Services **Company Name:** DeMent and Marquardt, PLC **Date of Birth:** 05/04/1951 **Place of Birth:** Detroit **State/Country of Origin:** MI/USA **Education:** JD, Law School, Wayne State University, Cum Laude (1986); MA in Education, University of Michigan (1977); BA in French Language and Teacher Education, Albion College, Summa Cum Laude (1972) **Career:** Founding Member, DeMent and Marquardt, PLLC (1994-Present) **Civic:** Board Member, Bronson House Foundation; Member, Western Michigan Dance Board; Board Member, Local Theatre **Creative Works:** Co-Author, "Estate Administration in Michigan", 2nd Edition, Institute of Continuing Legal Education, State of Michigan (2013); Co-Author, "Incentive Trusts? Beware!", Estates, Gifts and Trusts Journal, BNA Tax Management; Co-Author, "Gifting S Corporation Stock to a Community Foundation," The Exempt Organization Tax Review; Co-Author, "Site Plan Review— Limits on Discretion," Michigan Real Property Review; Co-Author, "Share Loan Financing for the Cooperative Member," Michigan Real Property Review; Co-Author, "Revocable Living Trusts," Institute of Continuing Legal Education, State of Michigan **Awards:** Listed, Top Women Attorneys in Michigan, Hour Detroit (2017-2019); Listed, Michigan Super Lawyers, Estate Planning (2007-2017); Listed, "Who's Who of American Women" (2010-2011); Named Among the "Top 100 Attorneys in the U.S.," Worth Magazine (2006, 2007, 2008) **Memberships:** Fellow, American College of Trust and Estate Counsel; American Bar Association; Real Property & Probate Sections, State Bar of Michigan; Kalamazoo County Bar Association **Bar Admissions:** State of Michigan (1986); U.S. District Court for the Eastern District of Michigan (1986) **Marquis Who's Who Honors:** Marquis Who's Who Top Professional **To what do you attribute your success:** Ms. Marquardt attributes her success to caring about the clients. They joke in the office that their goal is to always be able to sleep at night. She has always believed "Clients first and foremost." **Why did you become involved in your profession or industry:** Ms. Marquardt became involved in her profession because it suited her and was very personal with her people. It is a positive approach to the law. They are coming to her because they are being proactive, which she really enjoyed. She gets to be creative because every family is different. There is also a lot of teaching; she taught for 10 years before she went to law school and still teaches today. That suited her, which is why she went in this direction.

C. Travis Marshall

Title: Telecommunications Executive, Government Relations Specialist **Industry:** Telecommunications **Date of Birth:** 01/31/1926 **Place of Birth:** Apalachicola **State/Country of Origin:** FL/USA **Parents:** John Marshall; Estelle (Marks) Marshall **Marital Status:** Married **Spouse Name:** Kathryn Rose Lepine Nordberg (Deceased) **Children:** Melanie Marshall-Roth; Katharine Marshall; Monica **Education:** BS, University of Notre Dame, Indiana (1948) **Career:** (Retired) Telecommunications Consultant (1992-Present); Senior Vice President, Director, Government Relations, Motorola, Washington, DC (1985-1992); Vice President, Director, Motorola, Government Relations, Washington, DC (1974-1985); Director, Government Relations, Communications Division, Motorola, Schaumburg, IL (1972-1974); Vice President, Marketing Operations, Motorola, Inc., Schaumburg, IL (1970-1972); Vice President of Marketing, E.F. Johnson, Waseca, MN (1965-1970); General Sales Manager, The Hallicrafters, Chicago, IL (1952-1965); Chief Clerk, Firestone Tire & Rubber Co., Detroit, MI (1948-1951); Telecommunications Companies **Civic:** Appointed Ambassador, Headed 35-Person U.S. Delegation by President Bush to International Telecommunications Union Conference, Geneva, Switzerland; Trustee, Maryland Youth Symphony Orchestra **Military Service:** 2nd Lieutenant, U.S. Army, Korean War; 1st Lieutenant, 28th Infantry, U.S. Army, Germany **Awards:** Distinguished Service Award, Electronics Industries Association, Washington, DC (1987) **Memberships:** Treasurer Emeritus, Electronics Industries Association (1992-Present); Treasurer, Electronics Industries Association (1982-1992); Vice President, Electronics Industries Association (1975-1988); Electronics Industries Association; Burning Tree Country Club; Columbia Country Club; Metropolitan Club; Crystal Downs Country Club **Marquis Who's Who Honors:** Albert Nelson Marquis Lifetime Achievement Award; Marquis Who's Who Top Professional **Why did you become involved in your profession or industry:** Mr. Marshall became involved in his profession because his college roommate's father worked in the electronics business, and offered him a job, thus launching a career in the field. **Avocations:** Sailing; Golf; Hand radios **Political Affiliations:** Republican **Religion:** Roman Catholic

Elizabeth Eileen Marshall

Title: Cultural Organization Administrator, Teacher **Industry:** Health, Wellness and Fitness **Date of Birth:** 12/02/1942 **Place of Birth:** Houston **State/Country of Origin:** TX/USA **Parents:** Sterling Guy Marshall; Ruth (Burke) Marshall **Marital Status:** Partner **Spouse Name:** Carol Ann Hendlmyer **Education:** PhD in Metaphysics, Esoteric Philosophy Center (1985); BS, North Texas State University (1965) **Career:** Executive Director, Harmonious Alignment Education Center, Inc., Nashville, TN (1989-2000); Admissions Representative, United Tech. Institute, Nashville, TN (1986-1987); Operations Secretary, Nelson-Westerberg of Texas, Inc., Dallas, TX (1984-1985); Sales Representative, Southern Educators Insurance, Dallas, TX (1984); Owner, Automotive Maintenance Systems, Houston, TX (1980-1984); Executive Director, Texas Nurses Association District 9, Houston, TX (1977-1980); Project Secretary, Tellepson Construction Co., Houston, TX (1974-1977); Administrative Secretary, School of Nursing, University of St. Thomas, Houston, TX (1972-1974); Teacher, Houston Independent School District (1965-1971) **Career Related:** Consultant, Harmonious Alignment Education Center, Inc., Nashville, TN (1989-Present); Private Spiritual Counselor (2000); Guest Speaker, Beyond Reason Teddy Bart Productions, Nashville, TN (1988-1991) **Creative Works:** Contributor, Articles, Professional Journals **Marquis Who's Who Honors:** Albert Nelson Marquis Lifetime Achievement Award; Marquis Who's Who Top Professional **Why did you become involved in your profession or industry:** After an unfortunate experience as a teacher, Dr. Marshall chose to change her profession. After exploring several fields, she came across meta-physics. She was intrigued by the field so much that she found comfort in pursuing a career as a healer. After earning a doctorate degree, she began working in Nashville, Tennessee, where she started the "Health Alternative" school. She feels it is her calling in life. **Avocations:** Travel; Writing books; Master jigsaw puzzle enthusiast; Reading **Political Affiliations:** Independent

Jo Taylor Marshall, MSW, LCSW, ACSW

Title: Social Worker **Industry:** Medicine & Health Care **Place of Birth:** New York **State/Country of Origin:** NY/USA **Parents:** Sydney Taylor; Ralph Taylor **Marital Status:** Married **Education:** Master of Social Work, Columbia University, New York (1959); Bachelor of Arts, Sarah Lawrence College, Bronxville, NY (1957) **Certifications:** Certified Clinical Social Worker, New York, New Jersey; Board Certified Diplomate **Career:** Retired (2002); Social Worker, Private Practice (1995-2002); Director of Social Work and Psychiatric Emergency Services, Morristown Memorial Hospital (1978-1995); Assistant Director of Fieldwork, Faculty Lecturer in Health Care, Columbia University, New York (1975-1978); Coordinator Social Work Volunteer and Student Training Programs, Saint Luke's and Roosevelt Hospital Center (1970-1975); Faculty Field Instructor of School Social Work, Columbia University, New York (1968-1970); Casework Supervisor, Louise Wise Services (1963-1968); Program Consultant, Social Work Recruiting Center (1962-1963); Caseworker, Youth Consultant Services (1960-1962) **Career Related:** Principal Speaker, Hospital Association of Tennessee (1987); Principal Speaker, Veterans Administration, East Orange, NJ (1986); Principal Speaker, Mid-Atlantic Health Congress (1985); Principal Speaker, Consultant, Hospital Association of Pennsylvania (1983); Adjunct Professor, Columbia University Advisory Board; Faculty, National Discharge Planning Institute, State University Of New York, Buffalo; Advisory Committee, Rutgers Graduate School; Social Work Member, Multidisciplinary State Review Committee for Discharge Planning Standards in New Jersey **Creative Works:** Contributor, Articles to Professional Journals; Produced and Consulted on Numerous Film and TV Productions **Awards:** Named, Director of the Year, New Jersey Hospital Social Work (1989-1990) **Memberships:** President, New Jersey Chapter, Society of Hospital Social Work Directors (1988-1989); Executive Board, Society of Hospital Social Work Directors; Chairperson, National Media Task Force, Society of Hospital Social Work Directors; National Association of Social Workers; Academy of Certified Social Workers; American Board of Examiners in Clinical Social Work; New Jersey Society for Clinical Social Work **Marquis Who's Who Honors:** Albert Nelson Marquis Lifetime Achievement Award **Why did you become involved in your profession or industry:** Ms. Marshall became involved in her profession out of a desire to pursue the performing arts. Having initially studied the subject in high school, she subsequently worked with a TV series called "Stage a Number," which was a talent show, and won an award for the choreography work on the program. She was later interviewed by a dance magazine while attending Sarah Lawrence College, and began to question whether her interests lay in dance as a medium, or working with people. Following this realization, she entered the field of social work. **Avocations:** Interest: Theater; Film; Dance; Family cat

Sheila Marshall, LLB

Title: Lawyer **Industry:** Law and Legal Services **Company Name:** Dewey & LeBoeuf **Date of Birth:** 01/17/1934 **Place of Birth:** New York **State/Country of Origin:** NY/USA **Parents:** Paul Milton Hermes; Julia Angela (Meagher) Hermes **Marital Status:** Widow **Spouse Name:** James Josiah Marshall (09/30/1967, Deceased 2015) **Children:** Five Children **Education:** LLB, New York University, New York, NY (1963); BA, St. John's University, New York, NY (1959) **Career:** Of Counsel, Dewey & LeBoeuf (Formerly LeBoeuf, Lamb, Greene & MacRae), New York, NY and Boston, MA (1994-2004); Partner, Dewey & LeBoeuf (Formerly LeBoeuf, Lamb, Greene & MacRae), New York, NY and Boston, MA (1973-1995); Associate, Dewey & LeBoeuf (Formerly LeBoeuf, Lamb, Greene & MacRae), New York, NY and Boston, MA (1963-1972) **Career Related:** Specialist in Field **Civic:** Residence Association, The Gables, Winchester, MA **Memberships:** American Bar Association (ABA); New York State Bar Association; Association of the Bar of the City of New York **Bar Admissions:** Supreme Court of the United States (1970); New York (1964); United States Court of Appeals for the Second Circuit; United States Court of Appeals for the Third Circuit; United States Court of Appeals for the Fifth Circuit; United States Court of Appeals for the District of Columbia Circuit **Marquis Who's Who Honors:** Albert Nelson Marquis Lifetime Achievement Award **To what do you attribute your success:** Ms. Marshall attributes her success to hard work, a love for the law, and being surrounded by top tier lawyers. Ms. Marshall felt she was truly partners with these lawyers, as they continuously shared their thoughts with and helped one another. **Why did you become involved in your profession or industry:** Ms. Marshall became involved in law because she has family who had already worked in the profession, and because she was inspired during her time spent working as a secretary at a law firm. After this experience, Ms. Marshall decided to pursue law school. **Avocations:** History reading **Political Affiliations:** Republican

Dennis Charles Martin, DDS

Title: Dentist **Industry:** Medicine & Health Care **Company Name:** Dennis Martin, DDS **Date of Birth:** 09/30/1960 **Place of Birth:** Osage **State/Country of Origin:** IA/USA **Parents:** Charles H. Martin; Sandra L. (Skou) Martin **Marital Status:** Divorced **Spouse Name:** Lori Jane Reisel (07/10/1982) **Children:** Andrew; Michael **Education:** DDS, University of Nebraska (1986) **Career:** Private Practice, Waverly, NE (2003-Present); Private Practice, Lincoln, NE (2000-Present); Private Practice, Clinton, IA (1986-2003); Owner, Manager, Toy Cellar, Clinton, IA (1991-2000) **Career Related:** FAGD; MAGD; Fellow, American Academy of General Dentistry **Awards:** Progress Award, River City Chamber of Commerce (1986) **Memberships:** American Dental Association; Iowa Dental Association; Chicago Dental Society; River City Chamber of Commerce; Lions; Master, American Academy of General Dentistry **Marquis Who's Who Honors:** Albert Nelson Marquis Lifetime Achievement Award **Why did you become involved in your profession or industry:** When Dr. Martin was young, he went to the local dentist and the practice was antiquated with no Novocaine, and they did not have an x-ray machine that developed his own x-rays at the office. The office was definitely backwards and a couple of years later, he went to a dentist that was modernized with better equipment and the office ran much smoother. He had decided at that point that he wanted to be a dentist, but a modernized dentist because there were too many antiquated dentists out there. **Avocations:** Computer programming; Gardening; Radio control airplane modeling; Half marathon running; Cycling; Scroll saw woodworking; Ballroom dancing; Line dancing; Tango; Volleyball; Fat tire biking; Traveling **Political Affiliations:** Republican **Religion:** Lutheran

William C. Martin Sr.

Title: Hospital Administrator (Retired) **Industry:** Medicine & Health Care **Date of Birth:** 08/16/1926 **Place of Birth:** Atlanta **State/Country of Origin:** GA/USA **Parents:** William Henry Martin; Lillian (Collier) Martin **Marital Status:** Married **Spouse Name:** Carol J. Sullivan; Alice Elizabeth Nickle (01/12/1952, Deceased) **Children:** Mary Anne; Patricia Jean; William Collier; Nancy Lee **Education:** Postgraduate Coursework, The University of Oklahoma (1969); Diploma, Charlotte Memorial Hospital (1952); Hospital Administration Intern, Charlotte Memorial Hospital, North Carolina (1950-1952); Resident, Charlotte Memorial Hospital, North Carolina (1950-1952); BS, University of Georgia (1950) **Certifications:** Lay Speaker, United Methodist Church **Career:** Director, Security Plans and Training, Fitzsimons Army Medical Center (1974-1977); Chief, Training, Exercise and Readiness, U.S. Army Medical Command, Heidelberg, Germany (1973-1974); Medical Operations Officer, VII Corps, Moehringen, Germany (1971-1973); Director, Security Plans and Operations, U.S. Army Medical Center, Camp Kue, Japan (1969-1971); Lieutenant Colonel (1969); Executive Officer, Evans Health Care Facility, Fort Buckner, Japan (1968-1969); Commanding Officer, 47th General Hospital, Fitzsimons General Hospital, Denver, CO (1967-1968); Adjunct Personnel Officer, 55th Medical Group, Qui Nhon, Vietnam (1966-1967); Adjunct Personnel Officer, 55th Medical Group, Fort Bragg, NC (1965-1966); Commanding Officer, 55th Medical Group, Fort Bragg, NC (1964-1965); Executive Officer, 5th Evacuation Hospital, Fort Bragg, NC (1964); Commanding Officer, U.S. Army Medical Service Detachment, Fort Gulick, Panama (1961-1964); Commanding Officer, Medical Corps, U.S. Army (1959-1961); Adjunct Faculty, U.S. Army, Fort Campbell, KY (1959); Commissioned 1st Lieutenant, MSC, U.S. Army (1959); Hospital Administrator, Florence-Darlington Tuberculosis Sanatorium, Florence, SC (1956-1958); Assistant Hospital Administrator, St. Agnes Hospital, Raleigh, NC (1954-1956); Hospital Administrator, Rockmart-Aragon Hospital, Rockmart, GA (1952-1954); Operating Room Technician, Athens General Hospital, Athens, GA (1949-1950) **Career Related:** Founder, Hospice of Northwest Florida (1979-1986); Executive Director, Hospice of Northwest Florida (1979-1986); President, Escambia County Public Health Trust (1978-1986); Chair, Escambia County Public Health Trust (1978-1986); Executive Director, Thomas Rehabilitation Hospital, Asheville, NC (1977-1978); Guest Lecturer, U.S. Army Medical Command in Europe (1973-1974); Healthcare Administrator, U.S. Army Medical Command in Europe (1973-1974); Fellow, American Academy of Medical Administrators **Civic:** Board of Directors, Methodist Homes for the Aging, Inc. (1990-2006); Vice President, Board of Ministries, Pensacola District United Methodist Church, Inc. (1988-1998); Director, Lay Speaking, Board of Laity, Council on Ministries, Pensacola District, United Methodist Church, Inc. (1988-1998); Director, Lay Speaking, Board of Laity, Alabama-West Florida Conference, United Methodist Church, Inc. (1988-1997); Secretary, United Methodist Board of Pastoral Care and Counseling (1988-1990); Board of Directors, Hispanic Ministries, Inc. (1986-1993); Director, Lay Speaking, Pensacola District, United Methodist Church, Inc. (1985-1988); Health and Human Services Task Force, Citizens Goals for Pensacoloa (1981-1986); Vice Chairman, Administrative Board, Pine Forest United Methodist Church, Pensacola, FL (1979-1986); Finance Committee, Pine Forest United Methodist Church, Pensacola, FL (1979-1986); President's Committee on Employment of the Handicapped (1978) **Military Service:** U.S. Navy (1944-1946) **Awards:** Decorated Legion of Merit; Bronze Star; Three Meritorious Service Medals; Vietnam Royal Cross of Gallantry with Bronze Palm **Memberships:** Board of Directors, Bob Sikes Chapter, Military Officers Association of America (1996-2000); President, ESCAROSA Chapter, Military Officers Association of America (1989-1990); Board of Directors, Escarosa Chapter, Military Officers Association of America (1985-1999); Director, Greater Gulf Coast Chapter, Association of the United States Army (1979-1986); Director, ATD (1977-1978); Director, Denver-Centennial Chapter, Association of the United States Army (1974-1977); United States Power Squadrons; Veterans of Foreign Wars; Masons; Phi Delta Theta **Marquis Who's Who Honors:** Albert Nelson Marquis Lifetime Achievement Award **Political Affiliations:** Republican

Juanita V. Martin-Davis

Title: Retired Elementary School Educator **Industry:** Education/Educational Services **Date of Birth:** 09/20/1931 **Place of Birth:** Chicago **State/Country of Origin:** IL/USA **Parents:** Alex Vivian Kinder; Lillian (Burns) Kinder **Marital Status:** Married **Spouse Name:** Sterling M. Davis (10/24/1997, Deceased 10/1998); Alfred G. Martin (06/25/1965, Deceased 06/1979) **Children:** Graham E Martin ; Marchann Simon; Lavell Brown **Education:** MA in Elementary Education, Ball State University (1979); MusB, University of St. Francis (1962); BA, University of St. Francis (1954) **Certifications:** Certified Educator, Indiana (1965); Illinois (1954) **Career:** Teacher, Elementary School Music, Kokomo Center Schools (1990-1994); Teacher, Elementary School, Kokomo Center Schools (1965-1990); Teacher, Elementary School, Joliet Public Schools (1954-1965) **Career Related:** Director, Lutheran Church Our Redeemer (1991-Present); Substitute Organist (1980-Present); Organist, Holy Cross Evangelical Lutheran Church (1970-1975); Director, Bell Choir **Civic:** Chair, Martin Luther King Junior Kokomo City-Wide Celebration (2006-2007) **Awards:** Citizen of the Year, National Association of Social Workers Region 4 (2006); Professional Service Award, College of St. Francis (1990); Community Service Award, National Association for the Advancement of Colored People (1982) **Memberships:** Alpha Kappa Alpha (1996-Present); Alpha Delta Kappa (1987-2000); Community Women's Guild; American Guild Organists; American Guild English Handbell Ringers; Kokomo Arts Commission; Democratic Women's Club; Phi Delta Kappa **Marquis Who's Who Honors:** Albert Nelson Marquis Lifetime Achievement Award **Why did you become involved in your profession or industry:** Ms. Martin-Davis decided to pursue teaching in college. Once she began student teaching, she knew that she had made the right decision. **Avocations:** Golf; Line dancing; Reading; Rug hooking; Knitting **Political Affiliations:** Democrat **Religion:** Lutheran

Jerry Martinez

Industry: Athletics **Date of Birth:** 09/30/1928 **Place of Birth:** Baytown **State/Country of Origin:** TX/USA **Parents:** Elias Martinez Sr.; Petra Barajas Martinez **Marital Status:** Married **Children:** Eleisa Maricela Martinez; James Edward Martinez **Education:** Diploma, Robert E. Lee High School (1948) **Career:** Staff, Athletic Department, Rice University, Houston, TX (1960-2001) **Career Related:** Line Manager, Steamship Agents, Houston, TX (1942); Poet **Military Service:** Staff Sergeant, US Air Force (1952) **Creative Works:** Contributor, Poetry, Special Interest Publications **Memberships:** Kingwood Poets; Poets Northwest **Marquis Who's Who Honors:** Albert Nelson Marquis Lifetime Achievement Award; Marquis Who's Who Top Professional **Political Affiliations:** Democrat **Religion:** Roman Catholic **Thoughts on Life:** Mr. Martinez is very close with his chihuahua, Chico.

JoAnn Elizabeth Maruoka

Title: Retired Information Systems Manager **Industry:** Civil Service **Date of Birth:** 01/01/1945 **Place of Birth:** Monrovia **State/Country of Origin:** CA/USA **Parents:** John Constantine Gotsinas; Pearl (Macovei) Gotsinas **Marital Status:** Divorced **Spouse Name:** Lester Hideo Maruoka (11/08/1973, Divorced 8/1992) **Children:** John Nicholas Burke; Les Scott Kaleohano Maruoka (Stepson); Lee Stewart Keola Maruoka (Stepson) **Education:** MBA in Computer Systems Management, University of Hawaii, With Honors (1971); BA in Psychology, University of California Los Angeles, With Honors (1966) **Certifications:** Various Advanced Management and Leadership Training Seminars **Career:** Retired (2001); Supervisory Information System Manager, Chief of Information Technology Plans and Programs, U.S. Army Pacific Headquarters, Honolulu, HI (1987-2001); Commanding General's Appointed Federal Women's Program Manager, U.S. Army Pacific Headquarters, Honolulu, HI (1994-1996); Computer Specialist, U.S. Army Pacific Headquarters, Honolulu, HI (1980-1987); Equal Employment Opportunity Specialist, U.S. Army Pacific Headquarters, Honolulu, HI (1979-1980); Reservations Manager, Hale Koa Hotel, Honolulu, HI (1978-1979); Computer Management Intern and System Analyst, Army Computer Systems Command, Honolulu, HI (1969-1978); Automatic Data Processing (ADP) Management Intern, U.S. Army Pacific Headquarters, Honolulu, HI (1969); Office Manager and Assistant, R. Wenkam, Photographer, Honolulu, HI (1966-1969); Deputy ITM Civilian Career Program Manager, 516th Signal Brigade, U.S. Army Pacific Headquarters, Honolulu, HI **Career Related:** Board of Directors, National High-Performance Computing and Communications Council, Tiverton, RI (1995-2018); Pacific Vice President, Federation of Government Information Processing Councils, Washington, DC (1992-1995); Past President, Hawaii Intergovernmental Information Processing Council (HIIPC); Federal Women's Council, Hawaii; Army in Hawaii Federal Women's Program Committee; Administrative Assistant, Hawaii State Land Use Commissioner Robert Wenkam; Invited Speaker, University of Hawaii **Civic:** Testifier, Various Issues at Hawaii State Legislature, League of Women Voters of Hawaii (2006-2014); National and Hawaii Women's Political Caucus, Honolulu, HI (1987-2000); Advisor, Federal Women's Council of Hawaii, Honolulu, HI (1977-2000); President, Federal Women's Council of Hawaii, Honolulu, HI (1976-1977); Past President, Army in Hawaii Federal Women's Program Committee **Awards:** Silver Order of Mercury, Army Signal Corps Regimental Association (2001); Bronze Order of Mercury, Army Signal Corps Regimental Association (1997); Named, Federal 100 Executives of the Year, Federal Computer Week (1996); Lead Dog Leadership Award, Federation of Government Information Processing Councils (1993); International Award for Information Resources Management Excellence, Hawaii Chapter, Armed Forces Communications-Electronics Association (1992); Information Resources Management Award, Federal Government Interagency Committee on Information Resources Management (1991); Pacific Federal Manager Award, Honolulu-Pacific Federal Executive Board (1990); Equal Employment Opportunity Excellence Award, Secretary of the U.S. Army (1989); Service Award, Hawaii Intergovernmental Information Processing Council (1989); Service Award, Federal Women's Council of Hawaii (1986) **Memberships:** Director, Hawaii State League of Women Voters (2005-2007); Officer, Hawaii State League of Women Voters (2004-2005); Advisor, Aloha and Rainbow Chapters, Federally Employed Women (1977-2000); President, Hawaii Intergovernmental Information Processing Council (1988-1989); American Association of University Women; National Association of Female Executives; National Women's Political Caucus; Hawaii Chapter, Armed Forces Communications-Electronics Association; Association of the U.S. Army; Army Signal Corps Regimental Association; Beta Gamma Sigma **Marquis Who's Who Honors:** Albert Nelson Marquis Lifetime Achievement Award **To what do you attribute your success:** Ms. Maruoka attributes her success to her parents, both of whom provided a shining example of important values, integrity, honor, and willingness to make good choices. **Why did you become involved in your profession or industry:** Ms. Maruoka entered federal service as one of 16 selectees for a management intern program. She is a former Honored Queen of Jobs Daughters, which helped develop her leadership abilities and point her toward her later profession and interests. In the summer before she started her freshman year at the University of California Los Angeles, she took introductory psychology and other courses there that contributed to her leadership skills. She was among the youngest in her high school class and was an award-winning editor of her high school paper. She is a cancer survivor. **Avocations:** Travel; Reading; Tai chi; Theater; Symphony; Opera **Political Affiliations:** Democrat **Religion:** Christian **Thoughts on Life:** Ms. Maruoka recognizes the many blessings in her life. She always takes a positive and loving approach to whatever she does. Likewise, she is a true and honorable friend; she is always open to others, even when they think differently. She is happy to forgive herself and others.

Louis Henry Masotti, PhD

Title: Professor Emeritus **Industry:** Education/Educational Services **Company Name:** Northwestern University **Date of Birth:** 05/16/1934 **Place of Birth:** New York **State/Country of Origin:** NY/USA **Parents:** Henry Masotti; Angela Catherine (Turi) Masotti **Marital Status:** Married **Spouse Name:** Ann Randel (Humm) Masotti (03/05/1988); Iris Patricia Leonard (08/28/1958, Divorced 1981) **Children:** Laura Lynn Masotti; Andrea Ann Masotti **Education:** PhD in Political Science, Northwestern University (1964); MA in Political Science, Northwestern University (1961); AB, Princeton University (1956) **Career:** Professor Emeritus, Northwestern University (1999-Present); Director, Guthrie Center for Real Estate Research, Kellogg School of Management, Northwestern University, Evanston, IL (1986-1988); Professor, Management and Urban Development, Kellogg School of Management, Northwestern University, Evanston, IL (1983-1994); Director, Program in Public and Not-for-Profit Management, Kellogg School of Management, Northwestern University, Evanston, IL (1979-1980); Professor, Political Science and Urban Affairs, Northwestern University, Evanston, IL (1972-1983); Director, Center of Urban Affairs, Northwestern University, Evanston, IL (1971-1980); Associate Professor, Northwestern University, Evanston, IL (1970-1972); Senior Fulbright Fellow, Johns Hopkins University, School of Advanced International Studies, Bologna, Italy (1969-1970); Director, Civil Violence Research Center, Case Western Reserve University, Cleveland, Ohio (1968-1969); Associate Professor, Case Western Reserve University, Cleveland, Ohio (1967-1969); Assistant Professor, Political Science, Case Western Reserve University, Cleveland, Ohio (1963-1967); Fellow, National Center for Education in Politics (1962) **Career Related:** Professor, Director, Real Estate Management Program, UCI Paul Merage School of Business, University of California, Irvine (1992-1998); Visiting Professor, UCLA Anderson School of Management (1989-1992); Visiting Professor, Stanford Graduate School of Business (1989-1992); Executive Director, Mayor Jane Byrne Transition Committee, Chicago, IL (1979); Visiting Associate Professor, University of Washington (1969); Board of Directors, LCPtracker, Inc.; Tucker Property Management; Imperial Credit Commissioner, Mortgage Investment Corporation; Southern California Physicians Insurance Company; International Facility Management Association; Manufactured Home Communities, Inc.; Equity Life-Style Properties, Inc. **Civic:** Development Coordinator, High Technology, Chicago, IL (1982-1983); Deputy Mayor, Chicago (1979-1980); Cleveland Heights Board of Education (1967-1969); Research Director, Carl Stokes for Mayor of Cleveland (1967); Advisor, Various Congressional, Gubernatorial and Mayoral Campaigns, States of California, New Jersey, Illinois, Ohio **Military Service:** U. S. Navy Reserve (1956-1959) **Creative Works:** Vice Chairman, Board, BOMA Office Magazine (1990-1995); Vice Chairman, Board, Illinois Issues Journal (1986-1992); Senior Editor, "Economic Development Quarterly" (1986-1992); Co-Editor, "Downtown Development, Second Edition" (1987); Co-Editor, "Downtown Development" (1985); Co-Editor, "After Daley: Chicago Politics in Transition" (1981); Author, "The New Urban Politics" (1976); Author, "The City in Comparative Perspective" (1976); Editor, "Urban Affairs Quarterly" (1973-1980); Co-Editor, "The Urbanization of the Suburbs" (1973); Author, "Suburbia in Transition" (1973); Co-Editor, "Metropolis in Crisis, Second Edition" (1971); Author, "Shootout in Cleveland" (1969); Author, "A Time to Burn?" (1969); Editor, "Education and Urban Society" (1968-1971); Co-Editor, "Riots and Rebellion" (1968); Co-Editor, "Metropolis in Crisis" (1968); Author, "Education and Politics in Suburbia" (1967) **Awards:** Senior Fulbright Fellow, School of Advanced International Studies, Johns Hopkins University, Bologna, Italy (1969-1970); Grantee, Numerous Research Grants (1963-2000); Distinguished Service Award, Cleveland Jaycees (1967); Fellow, Weimer School of Advanced Studies in Real Estate, Homer Hoyt Institute **Memberships:** International Economic Development Council; National Association for Industrial Office Properties (NAIOP); International Development Research Council (IDRC); International Association of Corporate Real Estate Executives; National Trust Historical Preservation; Habitat, Urban Land Institute; Lambda Alpha International **Marquis Who's Who Honors:** Albert Nelson Marquis Lifetime Achievement Award; Marquis Who's Who Top Professional Educators **To what do you attribute your success:** Dr. Masotti attributes his success to his commitment and hard work. **Why did you become involved in your profession or industry:** Unable to decide between a career in academics and public service, Dr. Masotti pursued both. He has spent his career teaching, writing, publishing, and consulting. **Avocations:** Sailing; Listening to jazz music; Watching baseball **Political Affiliations:** Democrat **Religion:** Christian

Joseph Anthony Materna, Esq.

Title: Attorney **Industry:** Law and Legal Services **Company Name:** Law Office of Joseph A. Materna **Date of Birth:** 6/13/1947 **Place of Birth:** Passaic **State/Country of Origin:** NJ/USA **Parents:** Anthony E.; Peggy Ann (Popowich) Materna **Marital Status:** Married **Spouse Name:** Dolores Corio (12/14/1975) **Children:** Jodi; Jennifer; Janine **Education:** JD, Columbia University (1973); BA, Columbia University (1969) **Certifications:** Accredited Estate Planner, National Association of Estate Planners (1975) **Career:** Partner, Head Trusts and Estates Department, Law Office of Joseph A. Materna (2014-Present); Partner, Head Trusts and Estates Department, Solomon Blum Heymann LLP, New York, NY (2004-2013); Partner, Head Trusts and Estates Department, Shapiro Beilly Rosenberg Aronowitz Levy & Fox LLP, New York, NY (1990-2004); Partner, Head Trusts and Estates Department, Newman Tannenbaum Helpern Syracuse & Hirschtritt, New York, NY (1985-1990); Trusts and Estates Attorney, Finley Kumble Wagner Heine Underberg Manley & Casey, New York, NY (1980-1985); Trusts and Estates Attorney, Dreyer & Traub, New York, NY (1976-1980); Trusts and Estates Attorney, Chadbourne Parke Whiteside & Wolff, New York, NY (1973-1976) **Career Related:** Expert Witness in Trusts and Estates Field Court Litigations, New York (1999-Present); Lecturer in Field **Civic:** Chairman of Planned Giving Committee, Board of Governors, New York Chapter, Arthritis Foundation, New York, NY (1980-Present); Budget and Finance Committee, New York Chapter, Arthritis Foundation, New York, NY (2001); Corporate Secretary, New York Chapter, Arthritis Foundation, New York, NY (1997); Catholic Interracial Council, New York, NY (1992); Bequests and Planned Gifts Committee, Catholic Archdiocese of New York, New York, NY (1988); Board of Trustees, Corporate Treasurer, New York Chapter, Arthritis Foundation, New York, NY (1980-1985); Memorial Sloan-Kettering National Trusts and Estates Associates **Military Service:** Active Duty, New York State National Guard, U.S. Army; Honorable Discharge, U.S. Army **Creative Works:** Contributor, Articles, Professional Journals; Contributor, Arthritis Reporter Including, "Charitable Giving Under Your Will," "New U.S. Estate and Gift Tax Rules for Non-Citizen Spouses," "The New Estate Tax Law Changes - an Update" and "The Living Will"; Extensive Lecturer, Wills & Trusts, Seminars **Awards:** Named, Top 100 Trusts & Estates Attorneys in New York State, American Society of Legal Advocates (2014-Present); A/V Rating, Martindale-Hubbell (2010-Present); Named, Top 10 Best Estate Planning Attorneys in New York for Exceptional and Outstanding Client Service, American Institute of Legal Counsel (2019); Lawyers of Distinction Award (2019); Top Trusts & Estates Attorney, Regina Coeli Legacy Society (2011); Planned Giving Award, New York Chapter, Arthritis Foundation; Discovery Alliance Award, New York Chapter, Arthritis Foundation; Named, Top Trusts & Estates Attorneys in New York City, Avenue Magazine **Memberships:** Committee on Taxation, New York County Lawyers Association (2000-Present); Committee on Trusts and Estates, Queens County Bar Association (1990-Present); Alumni Class President, Columbia College Alumni Association, Columbia University (1969-Present); Committee on Surrogates Court, New York County Lawyers Association (2007); Committee on Estates and Trusts, New York County Lawyers Association (2007); American Bar Association; Trusts and Estates Committee, Florida Bar Association; Committee on Estates and Trusts, Committee on Surrogates Court, New York State Bar Association; Committee on Surrogates Court, Committee on Estate Taxation, Bar Association of New York City; Lecturer, Author, New York City Estate Planning Council; Committee on Trusts and Estates, Committee on Professional Ethics, New York County Lawyers Association; Committee on Taxation, Committee on Professional Ethics, Committee on Surrogates Court, Queens County Bar Association; Civil Court Arbitrator, American Judges Association, New York, NY; Panel of Arbitrators, American Arbitration Association; New York State Trial Lawyers Association; Committee on Surrogates Court, Committee on Estate Taxation, Committee on Estates and Trusts, Richmond County Bar Association; New York State Bar Association; Florida Bar Association; New Jersey Bar Association; Columbia Law School Association; Staten Island Richmond Town Historical Society; Archdiocese of New York; Regina Coeli Legacy Society; Phi Delta Phi **Bar Admissions:** State of New Jersey (2019); U.S. District Court, District of New Jersey (2019); U.S. Tax Court (1978); U.S. Court of Claims (1978); Supreme Court of the United States (1977); Florida Probate Courts, All Counties, Florida (1977); State of Florida (1977); U.S. District Court, Southern District, State of New York (1977); U.S. District Court, Eastern District, State of New York (1977); State of New York (1975); U.S. Court of Appeals for the Federal Circuit (1975) **Marquis Who's Who Honors:** Albert Nelson Marquis Lifetime Achievement Award; Marquis Who's Who Top Professional **To what do you attribute your success:** Mr. Materna attributes his success to hard work, good personality and family values. **Why did you become involved in your profession or industry:** Mr. Materna always wanted to be a lawyer. **Avocations:** Music; History; Theater; Politics; Antique cars; Travel **Political Affiliations:** Republican **Religion:** Roman Catholic

Sudershan Kumar "Matt" Mathavan

Title: Principal Engineer **Industry:** Utilities **Company Name:** Next Era Energy **Date of Birth:** 08/18/1945 **Place of Birth:** Muzaffarabad **State/Country of Origin:** Kashmir/India **Parents:** Kartar Chand Mathavan; Ram Rakhi Mathavan **Marital Status:** Married **Spouse Name:** Alka Rani Mathavan **Children:** Erik; Ketan; Sarita; Manika **Education:** PhD, University of Miami (1977); MS, University of Miami (1970); BE, Regional Engineering College, National Institute of Technology, Srinagar, India (1967) **Certifications:** Registered Professional Engineer, Florida Number 16869 **Career:** Principal Engineer, Florida Power & Light Co., West Palm Beach, FL (1979-2018); Senior Engineer, Duke Power, Charlotte, NC (1977-1979); Consultant Engineer, University of Miami, Coral Gables, FL (1975-1977); Engineer, Smith, Korach A/E, Miami, FL (1973-1975); Engineer, Aircraft Equipment Company, Miami, FL (1970-1973) **Career Related:** Seismic Qualification of Equipment for Nuclear Power Plants, Electric Power Research Institute (1998-2005); Analysis Subcommittee, Westinghouse Owners Group, Pittsburgh, PA (1983-1988) **Civic:** President, Mathavan Foundation, Palm City, FL (2005-Present); Secretary, Hindu Temple, Fort Lauderdale, FL (1986-Present); Founder, Co-Chairman, Lobana Education Trust, Jammu, Jammu, and Kashmir State, India (1985-Present); Founder, Gurudwara of Treasure Coast (2005-2020); President, India Society, Miami, FL (1984-1986) **Creative Works:** Contributor, Articles, Professional Journals; Contributor, Proceedings, American Nuclear Society **Awards:** Quality Improvement Program, Florida Power and Light Company (1985) **Memberships:** American Nuclear Society; American Society of Mechanical Engineering **Marquis Who's Who Honors:** Albert Nelson Marquis Lifetime Achievement Award (2020); Distinguished Humanitarian (2020) **To what do you attribute your success:** Dr. Mathavan attributes his success to his father, who served as an inspiration to him while growing up and figuring out what he wanted to do with his life. **Why did you become involved in your profession or industry:** Growing up, Dr. Mathavan was a gifted academic. Unfortunately, his family underwent several war-related tragedies, which resulted in young Dr. Mathavan's desire to work hard. He believes he was blessed by God's grace early on in life. Likewise, physics and math came easily to him, which inspired him to pursue the field in college, going on to build a career as he got older and more experienced. **Avocations:** Bird watching; Learning and preaching Sikhism; Walking; Yoga **Political Affiliations:** Democrat **Religion:** Hindu, Sikh **Thoughts on Life:** Dr. Mathavan believes life is worthwhile if it contributes to the progress of one's tribe. In reality, the Earth and the universe as a whole is one's tribe. Thus, living a truthful life and serving God's creations is a worthwhile life. He believes in learning from mistakes, becoming better, and moving on.

Christopher C. Mathewson, PE, PG

Title: Engineer; Geologist; Educator **Industry:** Sciences **Date of Birth:** 08/12/1941 **Place of Birth:** Plainfield **State/Country of Origin:** NJ/USA **Parents:** George Anderson Mathewson; Elsa Rae (Shrimpton) Mathewson **Marital Status:** Married **Spouse Name:** Janet Marie Olmsted (11/02/1968) **Children:** Heather Alexis; Glenn George Anderson **Education:** PhD in Geological Engineering, The University of Arizona, Tucson, AZ (1971); MS in Geological Engineering, The University of Arizona, Tucson, AZ (1965); BS in Civil Engineering, Case Institute of Technology (Now Case Western Reserve University), Cleveland, Ohio (1963) **Certifications:** Registered Professional Engineer, Texas; Licensed Professional Geoscientist, Texas; Registered Professional Geological Engineer, Arizona; Registered Professional Engineering Geologist, Oregon; Licensed Geologist, Alaska; Certified Professional Geologist, American Institute of Professional Geologists; Commercial Pilot Instruments, Single Engine, Land Aircraft Certified; Industrial Drilling Fluids, Baroid; Certified, Industrial Fire Fighting, Basic, Texas A&M University; Registered Engineering Firm **Career:** Senior Training Specialist, Texas A&M Engineering Extension Service (2012); Regents Professor Emeritus, Texas A&M University (2011); Senior Professor, Geology, Texas A&M University (2011); Regents Professor, Texas A&M University (2006); Professor, Engineering Geology, Department of Geology and Geophysics, Texas A&M University (1982-2011); Director, Center for Engineering Geosciences (1982-1996); Leader, Engineering Geosciences Research Program, Texas A&M University College of Geosciences (1978 -1982); Director, Center for Applied Geosciences, Texas A&M University College of Geosciences (1977-1978); Associate Professor, Engineering Geology, Department of Geology Texas A&M University (1976-1982); Assistant Professor, Engineering Geology, Department of Geology, Texas A&M University (1971-1976) **Career Related:** Task Force on Campus Emergencies, Texas A&M University (2010-Present); Member, Council Examiners, National Association of State Boards of Geology (1994-Present); Faculty Senate, Texas A&M University (2009-2014); Sustainability and Environmental Management Committee, Texas A&M University (2007-2011); Aggie Honor Council, Texas A&M University (2004-2014); Chair, Graduate Appeals Panel, Texas A&M University (2003-2007); Academic Mentor, Texas A&M University Corps of Cadets (1988-2011); Facility Manager/Engineer and Building Proctor, Michael T. Halbouty Geoscience Building, Texas A&M University (1980-2006); Consultant, Speaker in the Field **Civic:** Trustee, Geological Society of America Foundation (2001-2003); Chairman, College Station Planning and Zoning Commission (1973-1981) **Military Service:** Commissioned Officer, Lieutenant, National Ocean Survey (1966-1970) **Creative Works:** Co-author, "The Detection of Sub-Lethal Concentrations of Cyanide in Drinking Water Using the Eclox Enhanced Chemiluminescence (ECL) Assay" (2010); Co-author, "Removal of Forest Nutrients Through Accelerated Groundwater Sapping" Gambling with Groundwater-Physical, Chemical, and Biological Aspects of Aquifer-Stream Relations (1998); Editor, "Interdisciplinary Workshop on the Physical-Chemical-Biological Processes Affecting Archaeological Sites," Department of the Army, U.S. Army Engineers (1989); Editor, "Rock Mechanics, Theory- Experiment-Practice," 24th U.S. Symposium on Rock Mechanics, Texas A&M University (1983); Editor, Contributor, Articles, Professional Journals **Awards:** Christopher C. Mathewson Scholarship in Geology (2011); Charles R. Sherman Award, National Association of State Boards of Geology (2011); Karl and Ruth Terzaghi Outstanding Mentor Award, Association of Environmental and Engineering Geologists (2008); Recipient, Numerous Awards **Memberships:** Division of Environmental Geo Sciences; American Association of Petroleum Geologists (AAPG); American Geophysical Union; American Institute of Mining, Metallurgical, and Petroleum Engineers; American Institute of Professional Geologists; American Society of Civil Engineers; American Water Resources Association; Association of Environmental and Engineering Geologists; The Geological Society of America, Inc.; IAEG; NAGT **Marquis Who's Who Honors:** Albert Nelson Marquis Lifetime Achievement Award; Marquis Who's Who Top Professional; Marquis Who's Who Humanitarian Award **Why did you become involved in your profession or industry:** Dr. Mathewson became involved in his profession because he grew up on a tree farm in NJ and the nearest kid lived miles away. He was a genuine country boy and his dad was an engineer who owned his own company. He wanted to be a civil engineer and build houses as a kid and that's what led him to go to Case Institute of Technology. He got his degree in civil engineering and was active as the student trainer on the football team and house manager of the fraternity. He graduated in four years and applied to the University of Arizona because when he was at Case he took a bunch of courses in geology from Western Reserve. That led him to theological engineering and then he completed his master's degree, which led to applying for a commission in the U.S. Coast and Geonetic Survey. When he completed his PhD, he realized what he really wanted to do was teach applied geoscience.

Molleen Matsumura

Title: Educational Organization Executive **Date of Birth:** 05/01/1948 **Place of Birth:** Riverside **State/Country of Origin:** CA/USA **Marital Status:** Married **Spouse Name:** Kenneth Naoyuki Matsumura **Children:** Miriam Ellen; Maja **Education:** BA, University of California, Berkeley (1970) **Career:** Network Project Director, National Center for Science Education, El Cerrito, CA (1993-Present); Senior Editor and Director, Alin Foundation, Berkeley (1981-Present) **Civic:** National Advisory Council, Americans United for Separation of Church and State, Washington, DC (1992-Present); Member, Feminists for Free Expression **Creative Works:** Editorial Associate, Free Inquiry Magazine, Buffalo (1989-1995); Associate Editor, Missing Link Newsletter (1995-Present); Editor, Voices for Evolution (1995); Co-author, Japan's Economy in World Perspective (1983); Co-author, Sex in China (1991); Co-author, Mother-to-be: Pregnancy and Birth for Women with Disabilities (1991); Contributor, Numerous Articles, Professional Journals **Awards:** Distinguished Service Award, Council for Secular Humanism (1993) **Memberships:** American Association of University Women; ACLU; Americans United for Separation of Church and State **Marquis Who's Who Honors:** Albert Nelson Marquis Lifetime Achievement Award; Marquis Who's Who Top Professional **Why did you become involved in your profession or industry:** Ms. Matsumura became involved in her profession because she was a gifted writer all her life. She was involved in a lot of writing and when she had her child she wanted to be able to answer questions about God. She began to read more and learn about secular humanism, which teaches that while it is not possible to know with certainty about the existence of a god, as humans we can make our world a better place by actions we take. She attended a few lectures by Paul Kurtz, who was an expert on secularism. More and more she attended many of their conferences and she became a prolific writer on secular humanism. She became one of the few female leaders. She wrote magazine articles wanting to advocate about her beliefs.

Joseph Michael Mattone

Title: Real Estate Developer, Attorney **Industry:** Real Estate **Date of Birth:** 09/15/1931 **Place of Birth:** Brooklyn **State/Country of Origin:** NY/ USA **Parents:** Vincent James Mattone; Julia (D'Amato) Mattone **Marital Status:** Married **Spouse Name:** Mary Ann Pessolano-Mattone (1991); Irene Marie Ficarra (07/14/1956, Deceased 1989) **Children:** Julia Mattone-Bello; Irene Mattone, Esq.; Carl Mattone; Joseph Mattone Jr., Esq.; Francesca Mattone-Volpe, MD; Teresa Mattone, Esq.; Michael Mattone, Esq. **Education:** Honorary Doctor of Philosophy, St. John's University, New York, NY (1993); Bachelor of Laws, St. John's University, New York, NY (1955); BA, St. John's University, New York, NY (1952); Continuing Legal Education Compliance, 24 Credits Bi-Annually **Career:** Senior Partner, The Mattone Group, Queens, NY (1976-Present); Real Estate Developer, Mannix and Mattone, Queens, NY (1963-Present); Private Practice, Law, Brooklyn, NY (1955-1976); Mattone Investors, LLC **Career Related:** Founder, St. John's University Real Estate Institute; Representative of Citibank N.A., Dime Savings Bank, Williamsburgh Savings Bank Counsel Marine Midland **Civic:** General Chairman, St. John's University 35th Annual Ball (1992); President, United Cerebral Palsy of Queens (1989); Anthropology Museum People of New York Candidate, New York Supreme Court (1968); Fundraiser, Jackson Street Settlement Association, Catholic Youth Organization; Fundraiser, Cerebral Palsy and Muscular Dystrophy Charities; Fundraiser, Saint Vincent's Home; Booth Memorial Hospital Trustee, American Cancer Society; Active in Gubernatorial Campaigns and Mayoral Campaigns **Awards:** National Education Leadership Award, Order of the Sons of Italy in America (2016); King of Queens Award, Queens Courier (2008); Faithful Steward Award, Saint Vincent Catholic Medical Center (2002); Queens Leaders' Award, New York Chapter Arthritis Foundation (2001); Business Person of the Year Award for Small Business, Queens Chamber of Commerce (1998); Italian American Man of the Year Award, Queens County Borough President (1993); Legion of Merit Award, President of the Republic of Italy (1991); Golden Lion Award, Sons of Italy (1988); President's Medal, St. John's University, New York, NY (1985); Man of the Year, Italian Charities of America (1983); Man of the Year, United Cerebral Palsy (1981) **Memberships:** President, Columbian Lawyers Association of Queens County (1989); Vice President, Columbian Lawyers Association of Queens County (1986); Secretary, Columbian Lawyers Association of Queens County (1985); New York State Bar Association; Queens Bar Association; Brooklyn Bar Association; Columbia Society Real Estate Appraisers; Queens County Builders Association; Delta Theta Pi; Knights of Columbus; Knights Equestrian Order; Holy Sepulchre Jerusalem; Board of Directors, Pride of Judea; Knights of Malta; Sons of Italy **Bar Admissions:** U.S. District Court for the Eastern and Southern Districts of New York (1957); New York (1956) **Marquis Who's Who Honors:** Albert Nelson Marquis Lifetime Achievement Award **Avocations:** Cooking; Golf; Sailing **Religion:** Roman Catholic

Rosemary McAuliffe, Esq.

Title: Lawyer **Industry:** Law and Legal Services **Date of Birth:** 05/24/1927 **Place of Birth:** New Rochelle **State/Country of Origin:** NY/USA **Parents:** William J. McAuliffe; Rose B. (Payne) McAuliffe **Education:** Honorary Doctor of Laws, New England Law School, Boston, MA (2002); Certificate, Advanced Graduate Studies, Boston State College (1981); Master of Education, Boston State College (1971); Doctor of Jurisprudence, New England Law School, Boston, MA (1954); Bachelor of Arts, Regis College (1949) **Career:** Private Practice, Boston, MA (1956-Present) **Career Related:** Teacher, Reading, City of Boston, MA (1965-1993) **Civic:** Secretary, Italian Historical Association of Massachusetts (1988-2017); Active, World Affairs Council, Boston, MA (1980-1995) **Creative Works:** Producer, Weekly TV Show, "The Legal Line," Boston Public Access Answer Channel **Memberships:** Board of Directors, Massachusetts Association of Women Lawyers (2002-Present); President, Massachusetts Association of Women Lawyers (2001); Massachusetts Bar Association; American Academy of Trial Lawyers **Bar Admissions:** Supreme Court of the United States (1961); United States District Court for the District of Massachusetts (1957); Massachusetts (1956) **Marquis Who's Who Honors:** Albert Nelson Marquis Lifetime Achievement Award **To what do you attribute your success:** Ms. McAuliffe attributes her success to her mentor, her sister, Alice. She was a lawyer for about 30 years and enjoyed practicing. **Why did you become involved in your profession or industry:** Ms. McAuliffe became an attorney because she was interested in the field, and chose to study law while attending Regis College. She taught for a couple of years and then went to law school. She also drew inspiration from her parents; her father was an immigrant, and her mother was a political progressive.

William Leon McBride, PhD

Title: Philosopher **Industry:** Education/Educational Services **Company Name:** Purdue University **Date of Birth:** 01/19/1938 **Place of Birth:** New York **State/Country of Origin:** NY/USA **Parents:** William Joseph McBride; Irene May (Choffin) McBride **Marital Status:** Married **Spouse Name:** Angela Barron (06/12/1965) **Children:** Catherine; Kara **Education:** PhD, Yale University, New Haven, CT (1964); MA, Yale University, New Haven, CT (1962); Postgraduate Studies, University of Lille (1959-1960); AB, Georgetown University, Washington, DC (1959) **Career:** Arthur G. Hansen Distinguished Professor, Purdue University, West Lafayette, IN (2001-Present); Professor, Purdue University, West Lafayette, IN (1976-2001); Associate Professor, Purdue University, West Lafayette, IN (1973-1976); Lecturer, Northwestern University, Evanston, IL (1972); Associate Professor, Yale University, New Haven (1970-1973); Assistant Professor, Yale University, New Haven, CT (1966-1970); Instructor of Philosophy, Yale University, New Haven, CT (1964-1966) **Career Related:** Senate Chairman, Purdue University (2004-2005); Fulbright Lecturer Sofia University, Bulgaria (1997); Lecturer, Korcula Summer School, Yugoslavia (1973); Lecturer, Korcula Summer School, Yugoslavia (1971) **Creative Works:** Editor, "Social and Political Philosophy" (2006); Co-editor, "Calvin O. Schrag and the Task of Philosophy after Postmodernity" (2002); The Idea of Values" (2003); Author, "From Yugoslav Praxis to Global Pathos (2001); Author, "Philosophical Reflections on the Changes in Eastern Europe" (1999); Editor, "Sartre and Existentialism, Eight Volumes" (1997); Author, "Social and Political Philosophy" (1994); Author, "Sartre's Political Theory" (1991); Co-editor, "Phenomenology in a Pluralistic Context" (1983); Co-author, "Demokrati og Autoritet" (1980); Author, "Social Theory at a Crossroads" (1980); Author, "The Philosophy of Marx" (1977); Author, "Fundamental Change in Law and Society" (1970) **Awards:** Decorated Chevalier, Ordré Des Palmes Académiques; Silver Medal, Institute of Philosophy, Russian Academy of Sciences **Memberships:** Bureau, International Council Philosophy and Human Sciences (2014-Present); Past President, Fédération Internationale des Sociétés de Philosophie (2013-Present); Steering Committee, Fédération Internationale des Sociétés de Philosophie (1998-Present); President, Fédération Internationale des Sociétés de Philosophie (2008-2013); Secretary General, Fédération Internationale des Sociétés de Philosophie (2003-2008); President, North American Society for Social Philosophy (2000-2005); Vice President, North American Society for Social Philosophy (1997-2000); President, American Society of Philosophy in the French Language (1994-1996); Board of Directors, Chairman, Committee on International Cooperation, American Philosophical Association (1992-1995); Chairman, Board of Directors, Sartre Society of North America (1991-1993); President, Indiana Conference, American Association of University Professors (1988-1989); Chairman, Board of Directors, Sartre Society of North America (1985-1988); President, Purdue Chapter, American Association of University Professors (1983-1986); Executive Co-Secretary, Society for Phenomenology and Existential Philosophy (1977-1980); American Society for Political and Legal Philosophy **Marquis Who's Who Honors:** Albert Nelson Marquis Lifetime Achievement Award; Marquis Who's Who Top Professional; Marquis Who's Who Humanitarian Award **To what do you attribute your success:** Mr. McBride attributes his success to many teachers he was lucky enough to have throughout his education, people who have simply treated him well, and his wife. **Why did you become involved in your profession or industry:** Mr. McBride became involved in his profession because he always had interest in philosophical questions and political issues. It seemed like a natural way of growing to enter the industry.

Lawrence A. "Larry" McCann

Title: Music Educator, Church Musician **Industry:** Education/Educational Services **Date of Birth:** 01/11/1951 **Place of Birth:** Sikeston **State/Country of Origin:** MO/USA **Parents:** William Alton; Billie Sue (Thomas) McCann **Marital Status:** Widowed **Spouse Name:** Vickie Dean Brown (04/14/1979, Deceased 09/25/2014) **Children:** Luke Adam; Mollie Elizabeth **Education:** Master's Degree in Educational Administration, William Woods University (2003); Bachelor's Degree in Music Education, Southeast Missouri State University (1976) **Certifications:** Certification, K-8 School Principal; Certification, Vocal Music, K-12 Teaching, Interstate School Leaders Licensure Consortium **Career:** Music Director, Temple Baptist Church, Poplar Bluff, MO (1987-Present); Elementary Music Teacher, Doniphan Elementary School, Missouri (1979-2011); Youth Music Director, Calvary Baptist Church, Dexter, MO (1982-1987); Private Guitar Teacher, Three Rivers Community College, Poplar Bluff, MO (1979-1986); News Director, Announcer, KPBM-FM, Poplar Bluff, MO (1979); Youth Music Director, Red Star Baptist Church, Cape Girardeau, MO (1977-1978); Youth Music Director, First Baptist Church, Gideon, MO (1974-1977) **Career Related:** Chairperson, Professional Development, Doniphan R-I School District (1993-2005); Owner, Luke and Mollie Music, American Society of Composers, Authors and Publishers **Civic:** Team Coach, Youth Soccer Optimist Soccer League, Poplar Bluff, MO (1988-1996); Team Coach, Youth Baseball, Parks and Recreation Department, Poplar Bluff, MO (1993); Commissioner, Planning and Zoning, City of Poplar Bluff, MO (1982); Bicentennial Choir Director, Gideon Bicentennial Committee (1976) **Creative Works:** Composer, Lyricist, Luke and Mollie Music (1993); Composer, Lyricist, Sacred Music Quarterly/Hong Kong (1993); Composer, Lyricist, Missouri State Teachers Association (1992); Composer, Lyricist, Choral Praise (1989); Composer, Lyricist, "Opus One (1988); Composer, Lyricist, Missouri Conservation Melodies (1982) **Awards:** Local Service Educator of the Year, Missouri State Teachers Association (2010); Meritorious Service Education Award, Missouri State Teachers Association (2001); Outstanding Contributor, DARE and Drug Consortium, Ripley County, MO (1993); Recipient, Community Service Award, Missouri National Guard (1991); Medium Sized School Outstanding Leadership Award for State, District and Local Service, Southeast Region, Missouri State Teachers Association **Memberships:** CTA President, Missouri State Teachers Association (2004-2005); State Executive Board, Missouri State Teachers Association (1994-2000); President, Southeast District, Missouri State Teachers Association (1992-1993); CTA President, Missouri State Teachers Association (1991-1992, 1984-1985); American Society of Composers; Music Educators National Conference; Missouri Music Educators Association; National Staff Development Council; Missouri Staff Development Council; Nashville Songwriters Association International; Gospel Music Association **Marquis Who's Who Honors:** Albert Nelson Marquis Lifetime Achievement Award; Marquis Who's Who Top Professional **Why did you become involved in your profession or industry:** Mr. McCann became involved in his profession out of an inclination toward music that extended back towards childhood. While attending high school, his choir director placed him in very selective and high achieving musical groups. **Avocations:** Photography; Sports card collecting; Record collecting; Ornament collecting **Religion:** Baptist

Paul McCartney

Title: Singer, Songwriter, Musician **Industry:** Media & Entertainment **Date of Birth:** 06/18/1942 **Place of Birth:** Liverpool **State/Country of Origin:** United Kingdom **Parents:** James McCartney; Mary Patricia (Mohin) McCartney **Marital Status:** Married **Spouse Name:** Nancy Shevell (10/09/2011); Heather Anne Mills (06/11/2002, Divorced 05/12/2008); Linda Louise Eastman (03/12/1969, Deceased 04/17/1998) **Children:** Heather (Adopted); Mary; Stella; James; Beatrice Milly **Education:** Honorary MusD, Yale University (2008); Honorary Doctorate, University of Sussex (1988) **Career:** Solo Artist (1970-Present); Singer, Guitarist, Wings (1971-1981); Singer, Guitarist, The Beatles (1960-1970); Singer, Guitarist, The Quarrymen (Later Johnny and the Moondogs, Beatals and Silver Beetles) (1957-1960) **Civic:** Performer, Benefit Concerts **Creative Works:** Appearance, "Quincy" (2018); Appearance, "Pirates of the Caribbean: Dead Men Tell No Tales" (2017); Appearance, "BoJack Horseman" (2015); Appearance, "Good Ol' Freda" (2013); Singer with Dave Grohl, Krist Novoselic and Pat Smear, "Cut Me Some Slack" (2013); Solo Singer, "New" (2013); Solo Singer, "Kisses on the Bottom" (2012); Appearance, "30 Rock" (2012); Appearance, "Al's Brain in 3-D" (2009); Solo Singer, "Memory Almost Full" (2007); Author, "High in the Clouds: An Urban Furry Tail" (2005); Performer, "Saturday Night Live" (2005); Solo Singer, "Chaos and Creation in the Backyard" (2005); Co-author, "Each One Believing: Paul McCartney On Stage, Off Stage, and Backstage" (2004); Appearance, "Tropical Island Hum" (2004); Author, "Blackbird Singing: Poems and Lyrics 1965-2001" (2002); Author, "Wingspan: Paul McCartney's Band on the Run" (2002); Solo Singer, "Driving Rain" (2001); Voice Actor, Producer, "Tuesday" (2001); Solo Singer, "Run Devil Run" (1999); Solo Singer, "Flaming Pie" (1997); Appearance, "The Simpsons" (1995); Solo Singer, "Off the Ground" (1993); Solo Singer, "Flowers in the Dirt" (1989); Appearance, "Eat the Rich" (1987); Solo Singer, "Press to Play" (1986); Solo Singer, Song, "Give My Regards to Broad Street" (1984); Actor, Writer, "Give My Regards to Broad Street" (1984); Writer, Producer, Animated Film, "Rupert and the Frog Song" (1984); Solo Singer, "Pipes of Peace" (1983); Solo Singer, "Tug of War" (1982); Solo Singer, "McCartney II" (1980); Musician with Wings, "Back to the Egg" (1979); Musician with Wings, "London Town" (1978); Musician with Wings, "Wings at the Speed of Sound" (1976); Musician with Wings, "Venus and Mars" (1975); Musician with Wings, "Red Rose Speedway" (1973); Musician with Wings, Song and Album, "Band on the Run" (1973); Musician with Wings, "Live and Let Die" (1973); Musician with Wings, "Jet" (1973); Solo Singer, "Ram" (1971); Musician with Wings, "Wild Life" (1971); Solo Singer, "McCartney" (1970); Featured, Documentary, "Let It Be" (1970); Solo Singer, "Maybe I'm Amazed" (1970); Musician with The Beatles, Song and Album, "Let It Be" (1970); Musician with The Beatles, "Abbey Road" (1969); Musician with The Beatles, "Yellow Submarine" (1969); Musician with The Beatles, "The Beatles (The White Album)" (1968); Musician with The Beatles, "Hey Jude" (1968); Featured, Animated Feature Film, "Yellow Submarine" (1968); Musician with The Beatles, "Magical Mystery Tour" (1967); Musician with The Beatles, "Sergeant Pepper's Lonely Hearts Club Band" (1967); Musician with The Beatles, "Penny Lane" (1967); Featured, Film, "Magical Mystery Tour" (1967); Musician with The Beatles, "All You Need is Love" (1967); Musician with The Beatles, "Revolver" (1966); Musician with The Beatles, "Eleanor Rigby" (1966); Musician with The Beatles, "Rubber Soul" (1965); Musician with The Beatles, "Eight Days a Week" (1965); Musician with The Beatles, "Yesterday" (1965); Musician with The Beatles, "Michelle" (1965); Musician with The Beatles, "We Can Work It Out" (1965); Featured, Film, "Help!" (1965); Musician with The Beatles, "Help!" (1965); Singer, Songwriter, Musician, Solo and Collaborations, Songs and Albums; Appearances, Television Shows, Film **Awards:** Grammy Awards for Best Rock Song, Best Music Film, The Recording Academy (2014); Lifetime Achievement Award (as Member of The Beatles), Grammy Awards, The Recording Academy (2014); Grammy Award for Best Traditional Pop Vocal Album, The Recording Academy (2013); Named to French Legion of Honour, Government of France (2012); Named Musicares Person of the Year (2012); Grammy Award for Best Historical Album, The Recording Academy (2012); Honoree, Kennedy Center Honors, John F. Kennedy Center for the Performing Arts, Washington, DC (2010); Gershwin Prize, Library of Congress (2010); BRIT Award for Outstanding Contribution to Music (2008); Named Songwriter of the Year, ASCAP (2009); Fellow, BASCA (2000); Named (as Solo Artist) to Rock and Roll Hall of Fame (1999); Decorated Knight Commander (KBE), Most Excellent Order of the British Empire (1997); Lifetime Achievement Award, PETA (1996); Award of Merit, American Music Awards (1993); Grammy Lifetime Achievement Award, The Recording Academy (1990); Ivor Novello Award, BASCA (1989); Named (as Member of The Beatles) to Rock and Roll Hall of Fame (1988); Grammy Award for Best Pop Performance by a Duo or Group with Vocal, The Recording Academy (1975); Numerous Awards **Memberships:** Fellow, American Academy of Arts & Sciences; Fellow, Royal College of Music; Honorary Member, Royal Academy of Music

Preston Moore McClanahan III

Title: Artist, Educator **Industry:** Education/Educational Services **Date of Birth:** 12/23/1933 **Place of Birth:** Charleston **State/Country of Origin:** WV/USA **Parents:** Preston Moore McClanahan Jr.; Katherine McKee (Pierson) McClanahan **Marital Status:** Married **Spouse Name:** Magdalena Maria Michels (05/16/1959) **Children:** Peter; Noel; Eve **Education:** Student, Columbia University; Student, Art Academy of Cincinnati **Career:** Program Head, Graphic Design Program, Rhode Island School of Design (1986-1988); Professor, Rhode Island School of Design (1972-1998); Professor Emeritus, Typography, Exhibition Design, Drawing, Visual Organization, Rhode Island School of Design; Graphic Designer, "The Hall of the People of the Pacific," American Museum of Natural History; Graphic Designer, Museum of Primitive Art, Columbia Records, U.S. Information Agency's Exchange Exhibition to Russia with George Nelson, Lester Beall Associate, Public Library of Cincinnati and Hamilton County, Harcourt Brace and Jovanovich, Ladislav Sutnar Associate, Proctor and Gamble, The Chase Manhattan Bank, Rhode Island Department of Health, Brown and Sharpe, Textron, Inc. **Civic:** Guest Bass Player, New Black Eagle Jazz Band **Creative Works:** Director, "Zardis: The Last of the First" and "Conversations with Paul Rand," PM Films LLC; Artist, Exhibited Kinetic Light Sculptures and Related Works, The Walker Art Center, The Whitney Museum of American Art, The Smithsonian, The Philadelphia Institute of Contemporary Arts, The Netherlands' Stedelijk van Abbe Museum, The Howard Wise Gallery, The Cincinnati Contemporary Arts Center, The Museum of Modern Art **Awards:** Keys to the Cities of Charleston, WV, and Providence, RI; Famous Person Award, Kanawha County, WV **Memberships:** AIGA **Why did you become involved in your profession or industry:** Mr. McClanahan became involved in his profession because at age eight, he found a reproduction of Ralston Crawford's "Overseas Highway," which was influential. A self portrait at age 11 was shown to Louis Bouche, an artist and educator, who recommended attending the Art Academy of Cincinnati. While enrolled there, he, in addition to the regular curriculum, was apprenticed to Noel Martin, the graphic designer for the Cincinnati Art Museum. Mr. Crawford went to Cincinnati at the same time and the two befriended each other. The first major work was for the Cincinnati Pubic Library, where he directed the Graphic Design and Exhibition Programs. His love of art and design has brought him into close association with the leading people in various fields, including Dr. Margaret Mead, Alan Lomax, Emile DeAntonio, William Russell, George Lewis, Milt Hinton, Ladislav Sutnar, Lester Beall, Dan Flavin, Howard Wise, Tom Wesselman, Robert Barry, and Robert Smithson. **Avocations:** Playing the jazz bass **Political Affiliations:** Democratic **Religion:** Catholic

Bill McCollough

Title: President, Chief Executive Officer **Industry:** Real Estate **Company Name:** McGraw Realtors **Children:** Carter **Education:** BS in Construction Management, Oklahoma State University (2000) **Career:** Chief Executive Officer, McGraw Realtors (2017-Present); President, Chief Executive Officer, McCullough Homes/Williamshare Investments (2010-2017); Owner, William Share Investments (2010); Managing Partner, Rausch Coleman Homes (2008-2010); Home Creations Executive Director of Operations (2004-2008); President, Redwood Custom Homes (2000-2003) **Civic:** Habitat for Humanity; Amethyst House; Pearl House; Tulsa Art and Humanities Association **Awards:** TulsaPeople's People's Choice Award (2013-2016) **Memberships:** National Association of Home Builders; Home Builders Association of Greater Tulsa; Oklahoma Home Builders Association **Marquis Who's Who Honors:** Marquis Who's Who Top Professional **To what do you attribute your success:** Mr. McCollough attributes his success to his ability to bounce back quickly. He learned a long time ago in his career that as long as you focus on everyone's success around it will make you more success. He also believes it's important to "Give back to the people around you." **Why did you become involved in your profession or industry:** With regard to McGraw Realtors itself, Mr. McCollough and his colleagues are all independent contractors. The Real Estate industry as whole with agents are gunslingers. He believes this matches up with his personality in general. McGraw takes care of its own business and everybody is very generous, in terms of their time. Whether it be with other agents, or helping others get into the business. **Avocations:** Playing golf; Spending time with family **Thoughts on Life:** Mr. McCollough's motto is, "Do your best until you know better and once you know better then do better."

Bill McCollum

Title: Lawyer; Former State Attorney General; Former United States Representative from Florida **Industry:** Law and Legal Services **Company Name:** Dentons US LLP **Date of Birth:** 07/12/1944 **Place of Birth:** Brooksville **State/Country of Origin:** FL/USA **Parents:** Ira William McCollum; Arline Gray (Lockhart) McCollum **Marital Status:** Married **Spouse Name:** Ingrid **Children:** Douglas; Justin; Andrew **Education:** JD, University of Florida (1968); BA, University of Florida (1965) **Career:** Partner, Dentons US LLP, Washington, DC (2011-Present); Attorney General, State of Florida (2007-2011); Partner, Baker & Hostetler LLP, Orlando, FL and Washington, DC (2001-2006); Member, United States Congress, Eighth Florida District, Washington, DC (1993-2001); Member, United States Congress, Fifth Florida District, Washington, DC (1981-1993); Partner, Pitts, Eubanks & Ross, P.A., Orlando, FL (1973-1980) **Civic:** Board Member, Step Up America Foundation, Inc. (2019-Present); Chairman, Republican State Leadership Committee (2014-Present); Board Member, American Security Council Foundation (2004-Present); Member, Board of Trustees, University of Florida Law Center Association (2011-2019); President, Chairman, Healthy Florida Foundation (2002-2018); Board Member, Enterprise Florida (2009-2011); Board Member, James Madison Institute (2002-2010); Board of Governors, State University System of Florida (2005-2006); Chairman, Seminole County Republican Party (1976-1980) **Military Service:** Commander, Judge Advocate Generals Corps, United States Naval Reserve (1969-1992); Active Duty, United States Naval Reserves (1969-1972) **Memberships:** Executive Council, Orange County Bar Association (1975-1979); President, Florida Blue Key (1968); The Florida Bar; Naval Enlisted Reserve Association; Reserve Officers Association (Now Reserve Organization of America); Kiwanis Club of Orlando; The American Legion; Omicron Delta Kappa; The International Legal Honor Society of Phi Delta Phi **Bar Admissions:** District of Columbia (2002); Florida (1968) **Political Affiliations:** Republican **Religion:** Episcopalian **Thoughts on Life:** During service in Congress from 1981-2001, Mr. McCollum was a member of the House Judiciary Committee, the Banking and Financial Services Committee and the Intelligence Committee; he chaired the Subcommittee on Crime and the Subcommittee on Human Intelligence, Analysis and Counterintelligence. He also served as Vice-Chair of the House Republican Conference for three terms and founded and chaired the House Task Force on Terrorism and Unconventional Warfare. Mr. McCollum was a member of the Committee to Investigate the Iran-Contra Affair and was House Manager of the Impeachment Trial of President William J. Clinton. At the University of Florida was President of Florida Blue Key, General Chairman of Homecoming and host of the Second 100 TV show, as well as the President of the Union Board for Student Activities.

Addison "Mitch" McConnell Jr.

Title: U.S. Senator from Kentucky; Lawyer **Industry:** Government Administration/Government Relations/Government Services **Date of Birth:** 02/20/1942 **Place of Birth:** Sheffield **State/Country of Origin:** AL/USA **Parents:** Addison Mitchell McConnell; Julia Odene (Shockley) McConnell **Marital Status:** Married **Spouse Name:** Elaine Lan Chao (2/6/1993); Sherrill Redmon (1968, Divorced 1980) **Children:** Eleanor Hayes; Claire Redmon; Marion Porter **Education:** Doctor of Jurisprudence, University of Kentucky College of Law (1967); Bachelor of Arts, University of Louisville, with Honors (1964) **Career:** Senate Majority Leader (2015-Present); U.S. Senator, State of Kentucky (1985-Present); Senate Minority Leader (2007-2015); Assistant Majority Leader (Majority Whip) (2002-2007); Judge, Jefferson County, Louisville, KY (1978-1985); Deputy Assistant Attorney General, U.S. Department of Justice, Washington, DC (1974-1975); Private Law Practice, Louisville, KY (1970-1974); Chief Legislative Assistant to Senator Marlow Cook, U.S. Senate, Washington, DC (1968-1970) **Civic:** Chairperson, Founder, Kentucky Task Force on Exploited and Missing Children (1982); Co-chairman, National Child Tragedies Coalition (1981); Chairman, Jefferson County Republican Committee (1973-1974); Member, President's Partnership on Child Safety **Awards:** Named, One of the 50 Most Powerful People in DC, GQ Magazine (2007); Sam Rainsy Pary Freedom Award (2002); Kentucky Warbler Migratory Songbird Conservation Award, U.S. Fish and Wildlife Service, Kentucky Department of Fish and Wildlife Resources (2002); Defender of Freedom Award, James Madison Center for Free Speech (2002); Distinguished Service Award, American Farm Bureau Federation (2002); Freedom Award, National Council of the Union of Burma (1999); Golden Plow Award, American Farm Bureau Federation (1996); Certificate of Appreciation, American Correctional Association (1985); Conservationist of the Year Award, League of Kentucky Sportsmen (1983); Commendation, National Trust for Historic Preservation in the United States (1982) **Memberships:** Advisory Board, National Institute of Justice (1982-1984); President, Kentucky County Judge/Executive Association (1982) **Bar Admissions:** State of Kentucky (1967) **Avocations:** Fly-fishing; Cooking **Political Affiliations:** Republican **Religion:** Baptist

Don Lewis McCord

Title: Surgeon (Retired) **Industry:** Medicine & Health Care **Date of Birth:** 08/25/1929 **Place of Birth:** Vernon **State/Country of Origin:** TX/USA **Parents:** Thomas Garfield McCord; Dola (Cavender) McCord **Marital Status:** Married **Spouse Name:** Barbara Gayle McCord (03/04/1972) **Children:** Daniel Linsey; Elizabeth Ann (Deceased); Melissa Ann Mares; Nicole Pryor **Education:** Resident in Surgery, U.S. Naval Hospital, Oakland, CA (1955-1959); Intern, University Hospital, Ann Arbor, MI (1953-1954); MD, University of Texas (1953); BS in Chemistry, Abilene Christian University (1949) **Certifications:** Diplomate, American Board of Surgery **Career:** Private Practice, Medical City, Dallas, TX (1986-2016); Section Chief, General Surgery, Medical City, Dallas, TX (1990-1992); Group Practice, Clifton, TX (1974-1986); Private Practice, Hamilton, TX (1962-1974); Assistant Chief of Surgery, U.S. Naval Hospital, Corpus Christi, TX (1959-1962) **Career Related:** Consultant in Surgery, Hamilton General Hospital (1988-1996); Consultant, De Leon Hospital **Military Service:** Lieutenant Commander, U.S. Navy (1954-1962) **Memberships:** Fellow, American College of Surgeons; American Medical Association; Texas Medical Association; Dallas County Medical Society; Dallas Society of General Surgeons; Flying Physicians Association; Alpha Omega Alpha **Marquis Who's Who Honors:** Albert Nelson Marquis Lifetime Achievement Award; Marquis Who's Who Top Professional **Why did you become involved in your profession or industry:** Growing up, Dr. McCord became interested in medicine after being around some local doctors. He followed this interest to college and then to medical school. **Avocations:** Flight instructor **Political Affiliations:** Republican

William Frederick McCormick, MD

Title: Forensic Pathologist, Neuropathologist **Industry:** Medicine & Health Care **Date of Birth:** 09/09/1933 **Place of Birth:** Riverton **State/Country of Origin:** VA/USA **Parents:** Jesse Allen; Elizabeth (Hord) McCormick **Marital Status:** Married **Spouse Name:** Deanne P. McCormick (07/02/1954, Deceased 09/09/2019) **Children:** William Frederick; Cynthia Anne **Education:** Resident in Pathology, University of Tennessee (1957-1960); MS, University of Tennessee (1957); Intern, Baptist Memorial Hospital, Memphis, TN (1956-1957); MD, University of Tennessee (1955); BS, University of Chattanooga (1953) **Certifications:** Diplomate in Forensic Pathology, American Board of Pathology (1979); Diplomate in Neuropathology, American Board of Pathology (1966); Diplomate in Anatomic Pathology, American Board of Pathology (1960) **Career:** Professor Emeritus, East Tennessee State University (2006-Present); Private Consultant, Neuropathology & Forensic Pathology (2010-2015); Retired (2010); Deputy Chief Medical Examiner, State of Tennessee (1987-2010); Professor, Head, Forensic Pathology, James H. Quillen College Medicine, East Tennessee State University (1989-1995, 2009); Professor, Pathology, Neuropathology, James H. Quillen College Medicine, East Tennessee State University (1985-1998); Clinical Professor, Pathology, University of Texas Medical Branch, Galveston, TX (1985-1989); Assistant Chief Medical Examiner, State of Tennessee (1985-1987); Professor, Pathology, Neurosurgery and Neurology, University of Texas Medical Branch, Galveston, TX (1973-1984); Professor, University of Iowa (1968-1973); Chairman, Surgery Department Review Committee, University of Iowa (1968-1969); Associate Professor, University of Iowa (1964-1968); Member, Executive Committee, Basic Medical Sciences, University of Tennessee (1963-1964); Assistant Professor, University of Tennessee (1960-1964); Deputy Chief Medical Examiner, Tennessee (1961-1963); Special Fellow, Instructor, Neuropathology, Columbia University (1961-1962); Instructor, University of Tennessee (1960); Assistant in Pathology, University of Tennessee (1957-1960) **Career Related:** Adjunct Professor, Anthropology, University of Tennessee (1997-Present); Deputy Chief Medical Examiner, Galveston County (1976-1984); Member, Committee, National Research Council (1978); Visiting Scientist, Armed Forces Institute of Pathology, Washington (1965-1966); Consultant in Field; Member, Head Injury Study Group, Department of Transportation; Visiting Professor, University of Tennessee, University of Pittsburgh, University of Virginia; 95 Presentations and Lecturers in Field; Contributor, 145 Scientific Journal Publications **Civic:** Scoutmaster, Bay Area Council, Boy Scouts of America (1975-1979) **Military Service:** Lt. Commander, U.S. Naval Reserves (Retired) **Creative Works:** Editorial Board, Association of Medical Examiners (1985-1987); Publication Advisory Board, Journal of Neuropathology & Experimental Neurology (1984-1986); Author, "Neuropathology Case Studies, 3rd Edition" (1984); Author, "Neurologic Infections in Children, 2nd Edition" (1981); Editorial Board, Focus on Neurology and Neurosurgery (1979-1981); Author, "Essentials of Neuropathology" (1979); Co-author, "Increased Intracranial Pressure in Children, 2nd Edition" (1978); Author, "Atlas of Cerebrovascular Disease" (1976); Author, "Neuropathology Case Studies" (1976); Co-author, "Syllabus of Neuropathology" (1973); Co-author, "Increased Intracranial Pressure in Children" (1972); Co-contributor, Articles, Professional Journals; Ad-hoc Reviewer, Numerous Scientific Journals; Nine Book Reviews, Various Scientific Journals; Writer, 14 Chapters, Books **Awards:** First George Perret Memorial Lecturer, University of Iowa (1990); Outstanding Contribution Award for Neuropathology Review Course, Armed Forces Institute Pathology (1990); Named, Milton Helpern Memorial Lecturer (1985); Research Grant, Wenner-Gren Foundation for Anthropological Research (1984) **Memberships:** American Association for the Advancement of Science; American Medical Association; American Society of Human Genetics; American Society of Experimental Pathology; Association of American Medical Colleges; American Association of Pathologists; American Association of Neuropathologists; National Association of Medical Examiners; New York Academy of Sciences; Texas Medical Association; American Association of Physical Anthropologists; American Academy of Neurologists; Academy of Forensic Science; Sigma Xi; National Association of Medical Examiners Paleopathology Club; College of American Pathologists; American Association of Pathologists and Bacteriologists **Marquis Who's Who Honors:** Albert Nelson Marquis Lifetime Achievement Award; Marquis Who's Who Top Professional **Why did you become involved in your profession or industry:** Dr. McCormick became involved in his profession because it was just an area of great interest to him. He also did not know anyone in the same field. In addition, he realized that he wanted to go into the area of neuropathololgy when he was an intern; It was an interest that he had.

Caia Kent McCullar

Title: Professor of Music, Program Director of Music Education **Industry:** Education/Educational Services **Company Name:** Dallas Baptist University **Parents:** JoNell Kent (Deceased 2017); Van Kent (Deceased 2004) **Marital Status:** Married **Spouse Name:** David McCullar (08/07/1976) **Education:** PhD in Fine Arts and Music Education, Vocal Performance, Texas Tech University, Lubbock, TX (1998); MA in Music Education, University of Texas at Austin, Waco, TX (1979); BA in Music Education (K-12), Baylor University, Waco, TX (1972) **Certifications:** Voice, University of Texas, Austin, TX; Certified Teacher in All-Level Music, Generic Special Education, and Elementary Education **Career:** Professor of Music, Program Director of Music Education, Music Education Division, Dallas Baptist University, Dallas, TX (2006-Present); Professor, Church Music Education, Southwestern Baptist Theological Seminary, Fort Worth, TX; Faculty Appointment, University of Mary Hardin-Baylor, Belton, TX; Faculty Appointment, Wayland Baptist University; Graded Choir Clinician and Director for Churches, Central and West Texas and the Dallas-Fort Worth Metroplex **Civic:** Vice President, College Division, Texas Music Educators Association (2008-2010); Church Volunteer, Southmont Baptist Church; Church Volunteer, St. Andrew Presbyterian Church **Creative Works:** Co-Author, "Pass the Texas Music EC-12 Study Manual" (2004) **Awards:** Outstanding Young Woman in America, Norwegian-American Historical Association **Memberships:** TMEA; Music Educators National Conference (MENC); Texas Choral Directors Association; American Choral Directors Association; National Association of Teachers of Singing; Organization of American Kodály Educators; Office of Academic and Student Affairs **Why did you become involved in your profession or industry:** Dr. McCullar became involved in her profession because she began piano lessons when she was 5 years old and ever since then, she has loved music. Her father would often sing during her childhood, and she fondly recalls his "gorgeous bass baritone voice." In fact, after her father completed his military service during World War II, he pursued proper vocal training. Dr. McCullar's parents encouraged her to explore her musical abilities and advance her education. She did so in school, where she met James Sheppard. As her music director, Sheppard inspired Dr. McCullar to further her involvement within music, education and pedagogy. **Avocations:** Reading; Traveling **Religion:** Southern Baptist **Thoughts on Life:** Dr. McCullar has twice been named in Who's Who Among America's Teachers and is recognized by the American Norwegian Historical Association as an Outstanding Young Woman in America.

Jane A. McDonald, EdD

Title: Associate Professor **Industry:** Education/Educational Services **Company Name:** 1) George Washington University 2) George Mason University **Date of Birth:** 02/22/1939 **Place of Birth:** Atlanta **State/Country of Origin:** GA/USA **Parents:** G. Byron Folmar; Helen M. Folmar **Marital Status:** Widowed **Spouse Name:** Thomas J. McDonald (11/17/1979, Deceased 2016) **Children:** J. Bradley McElroy; Michael Byron McElroy (Deceased 1988) **Education:** EdD, Virginia Tech, Blacksburg, VA (1987); MA in Education, Virginia Tech, Blacksburg, VA (1978); BA in Education, University of Florida, Gainesville, FL (1961) **Certifications:** Curriculum Auditor Certificate (1992); Strategic Planning Certificate (1988) **Career:** Associate Professor, Education Leadership, George Mason University, Fairfax, VA (1999-2008); Associate Professor, Education Leadership, George Washington University, Washington, DC (1989-1999); Assistant Superintendent of Schools, Niskayuna Public Schools, Schenectady, NY (1988-1989); Executive Fellow, National Academy of School Executives, American Association of School Administrators, Arlington, VA (1987-1988); High School Principal, Boulder Valley Public Schools, Colorado (1984-1987); High School Administrator, Curriculum Specialist, Title I Specialist, Fairfax County Public Schools, Virginia (1974-1984); Elementary Classroom Teacher, Prince George's County Public Schools, Calverton, MD (1971-1974); Elementary Classroom Teacher, Dade County Public Schools, Miami, FL (1966-1971) **Career Related:** Performance Standard Setting Committee, Virginia Reading Assessment Virginia Department Instruction, Richmond, VA (2005-Present); President, National Women's Caucus; Education Consultant to Visiting Scholars, International Research Exchange (IREX); National Review Panel, Sallie Mae Teacher Awards, Washington, DC (2000-2002); Advisory Board, Education Policy Institute, George Washington University, Washington, DC (1997-1999); Consultant, Superintendent Policy Institute, Regional III Comprehensive Center for Equity and Excellence in Education, Arlington, VA (1997-1998); Indian Policy Center Task Force (1990-1991); Executive Board, Greater Reston Arts Center (2009-2017); Co-Director, National Assistant Principals Academy (1997-1999); Director, National Superintendents Academy (1996-1999) **Civic:** Board Member, Northern Virginia Handcrafters Guild (2014-2020); Board Member, Reston Drop-In Center (2010-2016); Area Chairperson, American Heart Association, Reston, VA (2001-2002); White House Presidential Appointee to the Export/Import Bank in Washington, DC (1965) **Creative Works:** Reviewer, "International Journal of Educational Reform" (1991-1997); Author, "Social Studies Mind Stretchers: A Middle School Teacher Resource Book"; Co-Author, "Critical Thinking: Middle School Mastery Skills, Virginia Standards of Learning Graphing Calculator Activities for Algebra I"; Contributor, Articles, Professional Journals **Awards:** Outstanding Teacher Award, George Mason University (2006); Fellow, University Center for Excellence in Municipal Management (1998); Nominee, 100 Top Education Leaders in the U.S., National School Boards Association/Executive Educators (1984); Outstanding Contribution to Women's Fencing, Washington Metropolitan Fencing Association (1976); Presidential Fitness Award for Fencing, White House (1976); Presidential Appointee (1966) **Memberships:** Chapter Advisor, Phi Delta Kappa International (2000-Present); President, Virginia Professors Education Leadership (2004-2006); Former Member, Editorial Review Board, International Journal of Education Reform; Former Member, American Education Research Association; American Association of School Administrators; National Council of Professors of Educational Administration; Northern Virginia Handcrafters' Guild **Marquis Who's Who Honors:** Albert Nelson Marquis Lifetime Achievement Award; Marquis Who's Who Top Professional **To what do you attribute your success:** Dr. McDonald attributes her success to dependability, dedication, and hard work. Likewise, she credits her caring attitude, knowledge, and experience. She is thankful for the endless support from her husband, children, mentors, and friends. **Why did you become involved in your profession or industry:** All throughout her life, Dr. McDonald was told she should become a teacher. After traveling across Europe after college, she decided to finally pursue a career in the field. **Avocations:** Travel; Fencing; Dancing; Writing; Intuitive drawing **Thoughts on Life:** Dr. McDonald believes life is an experience. It is a time of rare, varied, and cherished opportunities.

Malcolm W. McDonald

Title: Real Estate Company Executive (Retired) **Industry:** Real Estate **Date of Birth:** 11/17/1936 **Place of Birth:** Minneapolis **State/Country of Origin:** MN/USA **Parents:** Malcolm Blanchard McDonald; Ruth Virginia (Stees) McDonald **Marital Status:** Widower **Spouse Name:** Patricia Kathleen C. (2005, Deceased 2018); Judy Glynn Ballard (1959, Deceased 2003) **Children:** Malcolm Scott; Margaret Alice; Philip Brian **Education:** Master of Business Administration, Harvard University (1960); Bachelor of Arts, Yale College, Magna Cum Laude with High Honors and High Orations (1958) **Career:** Retired (2004); Director, Senior Vice President, Trustee, Space Center Inc., St. Paul, MN (1977-2004); Vice President, First National Bank Building, St. Paul, MN (1960-1977) **Career Related:** With, Project Success (Present); Board Member, A Way to Grow (Present); Board of Directors, HMN Financial Inc. (2004-Present); Sherbrooke Capital (2002-Present); Vice Chair, Investment Advisory Council, Minnesota State Board of Investment, St. Paul, MN (1982-Present); Member, Advisory Board, Firstar Bank of Minnesota, St. Paul, MN (1999-2001); Scherer Brothers Lumber Company, Minneapolis, MN (1988-2012); Member, Advisory Board, Hill Monastic and Manuscript Library, Saint John's University, Collegeville, MN (1980-1997); Adjunct Professor, Graduate Programs in Management, University of St. Thomas, St. Paul, MN (1975-1994); Board Member, Yale Alumni Association of the Northwest **Civic:** Trustee Emeritus, Minnesota State Fair Foundation (2013-Present); Board of Directors, Minnesota Historical Society (2012-Present); Trustee Emeritus, Amherst H. Wilder Foundation, St. Paul, MN (2011-Present); Vice President, Grotto Foundation, St. Paul, MN (2009-Present); Trustee, Way to Grow (2006-Present); Trustee, Grotto Foundation, St. Paul, MN (1980-Present); Trustee, Founding Member, Minnesota State Fair Foundation (2002-2012); Board of Directors, Treasurer, Ready 4 K (2009-2011); Trustee, Secretary, Chairman, Audit Committee, Investment Committee, Amherst H. Wilder Foundation, St. Paul, MN (1971-2011); Second Vice President, Grotto Foundation, St. Paul, MN (2005-2009); Trustee, Episcopal Diocese in Minnesota (2004-2009); Chairman, Minnesota State Fair Foundation (2006-2008); Vice President, Episcopal Diocese in Minnesota (2005-2008); Chairman, Minnesota Landmark, Minnesota Kids First (2004-2008); Lee and Rose Warner Foundation (1990-2002); Manitou Fund (1990-2002); Adelaide and Harry G. McNeely Foundation, St. Paul, MN (1980-1998); Trustee, Bigelow & FR Bigelow Foundation, St. Paul, MN (1967-1998); Member, North Oaks Home Owners Association Board (1996); President, Board Member, Executive Committee, Minnesota Taxpayers Association (1994-1996); Member, Board of Directors, Afton Historical Society Press, Star Base Inc., Minnesota Independent School Foundation; Board Member, Dayton's Bluff Neighborhood Housing Services Inc. **Awards:** Recognition for Outstanding Service, Informal Club (2019); Bravo Awards, St. Paul Area Chamber of Commerce **Memberships:** With, Informal Club (1971-Present); Board of Governors, Board of Directors, Minneapolis Club (2002-2006); North Oaks Golf Club; North Oaks Homeowners Association; Colony Foundation; Fellow, Phi Beta Kappa Associates; Phi Beta Kappa; Phi Gamma Delta **Marquis Who's Who Honors:** Albert Nelson Marquis Lifetime Achievement Award; Marquis Who's Who Top Professional **Why did you become involved in your profession or industry:** Mr. McDonald became involved in his profession because of the influence of his parents, who were involved in real estate. **Avocations:** Exercise; Gardening; Travel **Political Affiliations:** Republican **Religion:** Episcopalian

Sharon Holliday McDonald

Title: Special Education Educator (Retired) **Industry:** Education/Educational Services **Date of Birth:** 01/15/1948 **Place of Birth:** Farmington **State/Country of Origin:** MO/USA **Parents:** Charles Douglas Holliday; Edythe Murriel Holliday **Marital Status:** Married **Spouse Name:** Gayle Dean McDonald (02/14/1969) **Children:** Leslie Douglas (Deceased 2009); Mary Elizabeth **Education:** MS in Education, Kansas State University (1973); BS in Education, University of Missouri (1969) **Certifications:** Certified K-8 Teacher (1971); Certified Professional Recognized Special Educator **Career:** Retired (2004); Teacher, Special Education, Unified School District 336, Holton, KS (1982-2004); Teacher, Special Education, Unified School District 336, Holton, KS (1971-1975, 1980-1981); Teacher, Special Education, Washington Community Schools (1969-1971); Teacher, Special Education, Ottumwa Public Schools (1969) **Career Related:** Member, Student Improvement Team, Jackson Heights Elementary School, Holton, KS (1999-Present) **Civic:** Member, Lady Belles (1993-Present); Delegate, Annual Conference, Lady Belles (1996); Chairman, Administrative Council, Lady Belles (1995); Sunday School Teacher, First United Methodist Church, Holton, KS (1991-1995); Former Church Choir, Education Committee, Lady Belles; Chair, Memorial Committee, Lady Belles; Chair, Healthy Congregations; Accompanist, Apple Red Happiness Choir **Awards:** Outstanding Scholars for the 21st Century (2000-2002); Outstanding Nutrition Educator, Midland Dairy Council (1994); Outstanding Young Women of America (1973, 1984); Dictionary of International Biography (1982); Who's Who Biographical Record, Child Development Professionals (1976); Professionally Recognized Special Educator, Council for Exceptional Children **Memberships:** President, Holton, Pilot Club (1980, 2000); Membership Committee, Holton, Delta Kappa Gamma (1998-2000); Council for Exceptional Children; Holton Education Association (1971); Kansas Education Association (1971); Lifetime Member, National Education Association (1969) **Marquis Who's Who Honors:** Albert Nelson Marquis Lifetime Achievement Award; Marquis Who's Who Top Professional **Why did you become involved in your profession or industry:** Mrs. McDonald started out as a math major in college. She was lucky enough to graduate at the top of her class in high school and received a scholarship to the University of Missouri. She went into the honors program as a math major. While enrolled in college, her roommates were education majors who had a field trip planned. In Fulton Missouri, there was a residential school for the deaf, and Mrs. McDonald accompanied her education major roommates on their trip to the school. From her profound experience on that trip, she decided to change her major and began to specialize in special education. In addition, going into her profession is what she considers a "God thing". **Avocations:** Music; Needle-crafts; Reading; General crafts; Sewing; Writing poetry; Active at church **Political Affiliations:** Republican **Religion:** United Methodist

William D. McEachern, JD, LLM

Title: Novelist **Industry:** Law and Legal Services **Date of Birth:** 01/03/1950 **Place of Birth:** New York **State/Country of Origin:** NY/USA **Parents:** George Carson; Eleanor Kinsley (Warnock) McEachern **Marital Status:** Married **Spouse Name:** Kathleen Barbara Muller (04/16/1978) **Children:** Beth; James Andrew; Mary Rose **Education:** Master of Laws, New York University (1981); Doctor of Jurisprudence, Fordham University (1977); Bachelor of Arts, Duke University (1972) **Certifications:** Board Certified, Estate Planning and Probate Law, Florida (1986) **Career:** Partner, Shutts & Bowen, West Palm Beach, FL (2001-2007); Partner, Winthrop & Stimson (1999-2001); Partner, Holland & Knight (1997-1998); Partner, Quarles & Brady, West Palm Beach, FL (1988-1997); Partner, Finley, Kumble, Wagner, Heine, Underberg, Manley, Myerson & Casey, Palm Beach, FL (1987); Associate, Gunster, Yoakley, Criser & Stewart, Palm Beach, FL (1981-1987); Trust Officer, Bankers Trust Co., New York, NY (1979-1980); Vice President and Trust Officer, United American Bank, New York, NY (1978-1979); Senior Trust Administration, Chemical Bank (1973-1974); Trust Administrator, Chemical Bank, New York, NY (1972-1974) **Career Related:** First Prize, Article Florida Bar (1981) **Civic:** President, Tax Planning Council; President, Foundation for Family Services **Creative Works:** Author, "The Life of Levi" (2019); Author, "Caledonia Lost" (2017); Author, "New Caledonia: A Song of America" (2016); Author, "Caledonia: A Song of Scotland" (2015); Author, "Casting Lots" (2014); Contributor, Estate Planning in Florida (1986); Editor, Florida Bar Journal (1984-1985); Contributor, Estate Planning in Florida (1982, 1983) **Awards:** Finalist, Best Historical Novel (2018); Finalist, Best Historical Novel (2017); Gold Medal Partner, Palm Beach County School Board **Memberships:** Florida Bar Association **Bar Admissions:** Florida (1981); New York (1978) **Marquis Who's Who Honors:** Albert Nelson Marquis Lifetime Achievement Award; Marquis Who's Who Top Professional; Marquis Who's Who Humanitarian Award **Why did you become involved in your profession or industry:** Mr. McEachern became involved in his profession because of the influence of his brother, who was also an attorney. Having worked in banking in New York City at the Chemical Bank Trust Department, he understood the legal profession intrinsically. Later on in life, Mr. McEachern leveraged his experience writing legal treatises as a professional author. **Avocations:** Astronomy; History; Literature; Civil War; Ancient Rome **Political Affiliations:** Independent **Religion:** Protestant

John P. McGee Jr., Esq.

Title: Lawyer **Industry:** Law and Legal Services **Date of Birth:** 02/21/1950 **Place of Birth:** Portsmouth **State/Country of Origin:** NH/USA **Parents:** John P. McGee; Louise (Flynn) McGee **Marital Status:** Married **Spouse Name:** Diane O'Leary (08/19/1972) **Education:** JD, William & Mary Law School, Williamsburg, VA (1975); BA in Economics, Yale University, New Haven, CT (1972) **Career:** Sole Practitioner, Flynn & McGee, P.A. (1991-Present); Partner, Flynn, McGee & Sanderson (1986-1991); Partner, Flynn & McGee (1984-1985); Associate, Flynn, McGuirk & Blanchard (1976-1983); Associate, Flynn, Powell & McGuirk (1975-1976) **Civic:** Past Eucharistic Minister; Past Parish Representative to New Hampshire Southeastern Deanery; Past Religious Education Instructor; Past Chairman, New Hampshire Labor Board of Appeals; Past Chairman, Portsmouth Republican City Committee; Past Moderator, Portsmouth Ward 1; Past Secretary, Past Vice President, Past President, Portsmouth Athenaeum; Past Member, Finance Committee, Strawbery Banke Museum; Past Board Member, Portsmouth Catholic Share; Past Member, St. Catherine's Parish Council; "New Hampshire" Commissioning Committee **Memberships:** Past Director, Wentworth-Gardner and Tobiac Lear Houses Association; New Hampshire Historical Society; U.S. Supreme Court Historical Society; Historic New England; Portsmouth Historical Society; Past Member, Warner House Association; Past Member, New Hampshire Archaeological Society; Past Member, Senior Citizens Center Advisory Board; Past Presiding Justice, Portsmouth Lodge of Elks; Past Director, Seacoast African American Cultural; Past Member, Mayor's Committee on African Burial Ground; Loyal Order of Moose Lodge, Lodge #44; Portsmouth Country Club; Portsmouth Mechanic and Fire Society **Bar Admissions:** U.S. Court of Appeals for the First Circuit (2016); Supreme Court of the United States (2003); New Hampshire (1975); U.S. District Court for the District of New Hampshire (1975) **Marquis Who's Who Honors:** Albert Nelson Marquis Lifetime Achievement Award **Why did you become involved in your profession or industry:** Mr. McGee became involved in his profession because his uncle, Tom Flynn, was a lawyer and his father was a policeman. He also used to watch the TV series, "Perry Mason," as he was growing up. Mr. McGee liked to debate and argue, especially with his mother. **Avocations:** Reading; Archaeology; History **Political Affiliations:** Republican **Religion:** Roman Catholic

Sue McGee, RN, MSN

Title: Pediatrics Nurse, Educator, Administrator (Retired) **Industry:** Education/Educational Services **Date of Birth:** 07/07/1945 **Place of Birth:** Dallas **State/Country of Origin:** TX/USA **Parents:** Dorothy Fife; James Brooks Fife **Marital Status:** Married **Spouse Name:** Lynn McGee **Children:** Troy D McGee; Misti Shelton **Education:** Postgraduate, Texas Tech University (1982); MSN, University of Texas (1979); BSN, West Texas A&M State University (1977); Diploma, Shannon Memorial Hospital, San Angelo, TX (1966) **Certifications:** Registered Nurse, Texas, Arkansas **Career:** Retired Division Chairman of Nursing, Associate Degree & Licensed Vocational Program, Amarillo College (2005); Consultant, Garland County Community College (2004-2005); Division Chairman, Nursing, Amarillo College (1994-2003); Director, Nursing Resource Center, Amarillo College (1987-1994); Staff Educator of Pediatrics, Northwest Texas Hospital, Amarillo, TX (1987-1988); Missionary, Foreign Mission Board Southern Baptist Convention, Mauritius (1982-1987); Instructor, Pediatrics, Associate Degree Nursing Program, Amarillo College (1978-1982); Staff Nurse, Pediatrics & Newborn Nursery, High Plains Baptist Hospital, Amarillo, TX (1974-1978); Pediatric Staff Nurse, Coeur d' Lane, Idaho (1970-1974); Pediatric Nurse, Diploma Nursing Instructor, Pediatrics Saint Anthony's Hospital/School of Nursing (1966-1970) **Career Related:** Hospital Accreditation Review Committee, Texas General Baptist Convention, Dallas, TX (2003-2004); Appointed by Gov. George Bush to Texas Board of Nursing Representing Texas Associate Nursing Programs (2000-2003); Consultant, Buckner Children's Home, Amarillo, TX (1992); Hot Springs Baptist Church Medical Team Member, Numerous Mission Trips to Uganda **Civic:** Secretary, Global Advance Center Conference, International Mission Board, Southern Baptist Convention, Richmond, VA (2018-Present); Instructor, Precept Bible Study, Mission Committee Chairman, Hot Springs Baptist Church (2003-Present); Board of Nurse Examiners, State of Texas (2000-2003); Board of Directors, Amarillo Pregnancy Crisis Intervention Center (1991-2003) **Awards:** Grant, Helene Fuld College of Nursing for Development of a Nursing Computer Center for Amarillo College (1992) **Memberships:** American Nurses Association; Texas Junior College Teachers Association; National Organization for the Advancement of Associate Degree Nursing; Sigma Theta Tau; Delta Delta Chapter; Harrington Supportive Care Consortium; American Association of University Women; National Council of Instructional Administrators; Texas Council of Nursing Deans and Directors; Community Health Issues Committee, Amarillo Area Foundation **Marquis Who's Who Honors:** Albert Nelson Marquis Lifetime Achievement Award; Marquis Who's Who Top Professional **Why did you become involved in your profession or industry:** Ms. McGee became involved in her profession because her paternal grandmother, Ola Joe Fife, who was an LVN and worked at a children's hospital in Fort Worth, Texas. Ms. McGee would go spend her summers going to the hospital with her and that's how her love started. She would observe her grandmother working at the children's emergency room and had the opportunity to see everything and loved every minute of it. When Ms. McGee went to high school, she joined a club called the Future Nurses of America where she was involved during her entire time at high school. She has been interested since the age of 16 and it has never changed. **Avocations:** Mission trips to Uganda; Healthcare for children and adults in Uganda **Religion:** Southern Baptist

J. Lawrence McIntyre

Title: Lawyer **Industry:** Law and Legal Services **Company Name:** The Toro Company **Date of Birth:** 04/25/1942 **Place of Birth:** St. Paul **State/Country of Origin:** MN/USA **Parents:** John F. McIntyre; Mary E. (Clancy) McIntyre **Marital Status:** Married **Spouse Name:** Mary E. Seifert (05/06/1967) **Children:** Matthew; Aimee; Brendan **Education:** Bachelor of Laws, University of Minnesota (1966); Bachelor of Arts in Philosophy, University of St. Thomas (1963) **Certifications:** Supreme Court of the United States (1984); United States Court of Appeals for the Eighth Circuit (1966) **Career:** General Counsel, The Toro Company, Minneapolis, MN (1993-Present); Vice President, The Toro Company, Minneapolis, MN (1993-Present); Secretary, The Toro Company, Minneapolis, MN (1993-Present); Doherty, Rumble and Butler, Minneapolis, MN (1967-1993); Doherty, Rumble and Butler, St. Paul, MN (1967-1963); Law Clerk to Judge, United States Court of Appeals for the Eighth Circuit (1966-1967) **Civic:** President, Board of Directors, St. Paul's Bridge Center (2015-Present) **Memberships:** Law and Accounting Committee, Business Law Section, American Bar Association; Minnesota Club, Minnesota Bar Association; Hennepin City Bar Association; Director, Counsel Association, Minnesota Corporation; Order of Coif **Bar Admissions:** Minnesota (1966) **Marquis Who's Who Honors:** Albert Nelson Marquis Lifetime Achievement Award; Marquis Who's Who Top Professional **Why did you become involved in your profession or industry:** Mr. McIntyre became involved in his profession due to a family tradition in legal service. **Avocations:** Bridge **Religion:** Roman Catholic

Ann McKee

Title: Chief Neuropathologist **Industry:** Medicine & Health Care **Company Name:** Boston University CTE Center **Place of Birth:** Appleton **State/Country of Origin:** WI/USA **Education:** Bachelor's, University of Wisconsin–MadisonCase Western Reserve University School of Medicine **Career:** Chief Neuropathologist, New England Veterans Administration Medical Centers; Director, Boston University CTE Center and Neuropathology Core for the Boston University, Alzheimer's Disease Center; Associate Director, Boston University ADC; Professor of Neurology and Pathology, Boston University, School of Medicine; Associate Professor of Neurology and Pathology, Boston University School of Medicine; Assistant Professor of Neuropathology, Harvard Medical School (1991-1994) **Awards:** Time 100 Most Influential (2018); Henry Wisniewski Lifetime Achievement Award (2018)

Andrew J. McKenna

Title: Wholesale Distribution, Printing Company Executive **Industry:** Wholesale **Date of Birth:** 09/17/1929 **Place of Birth:** Chicago **State/Country of Origin:** IL/USA **Parents:** Andrew James McKenna; Anita (Fruin) McKenna **Marital Status:** Married **Spouse Name:** Mary Joan Pickett, (6/20/1953) **Children:** Suzanne; Karen; Andrew; William; Joan; Kathleen; Margaret **Education:** JD, DePaul University (1954); BS, University of Notre Dame (1951) **Certifications:** Illinois **Career:** Chairman Emeritus, McDonald's Corp. (2016-Present); Non-executive Chairman, McDonald's Corp. (2004-2016); Chairman, Schwarz Supply Source, Morton Grove, IL (1964) **Career Related:** Board of Directors, Ryan Specialty Group (2011-Present); Board of Directors, McDonald's Corp. (1991-2016); Board Member, Chairman, Chicago Cubs (1981-1984); Board Member, Chairman, Chicago White Sox (1975-1981); Board of Directors, Chicago Bears Football Club **Civic:** Founding Chairman, Chicago Metropolis (2020); Trustee, Chairman Emeritus, University of Notre Dame; Chairman, University of Notre Dame (1992-2000); Trustee, Past Chairman, Museum Science and Industry; Director, Catholic Charities of Chicago; Director, Lurie Children's Hospital; Director, Lyric Opera **Memberships:** Member, Past Chair, Commercial Club Chicago, Member, Past Chair, Civic Committee, Commercial Club; Economic Club Chicago; Board of Directors, Lyric Opera; Executives Club of Chicago; Glenview Golf Club; Old Elm Club; Shoreacres County Club; Casino Club; Jupiter Island Club **Marquis Who's Who Honors:** Albert Nelson Marquis Lifetime Achievement Award **Why did you become involved in your profession or industry:** Mr. McKenna became involved in his profession because he desired success not only for himself but for all those around him, including his family.

John Lacy McKnight

Title: Professor Emeritus of Physics **Industry:** Education/Educational Services **Date of Birth:** 09/13/1931 **Place of Birth:** Monroe **State/Country of Origin:** MI/USA **Parents:** Joseph Daniel; Esther (Lacy) McKnight **Marital Status:** Married **Spouse Name:** Joyce Nunn (05/30/1964) **Children:** Andrew **Education:** PhD, Yale University (1957); MS, Yale University (1954); AB, University of Michigan (1953) **Career:** Professor Emeritus, Lifelong Learning Program, College of William & Mary (2000-2010); Retired (2000); Professor of Physics, Faculty, College of William & Mary (1968-1999); Member, Faculty, College of William & Mary (1957-1999) **Career Related:** Consultant on 17th and 18th Century Science Instruments, The Colonial Williamsburg Foundation **Civic:** Chairman, Board, The Nature Conservancy (1975-1977); Trustee, The Nature Conservancy, Virginia Chapter (1971-1978); Board of Directors, Conservation Council of Virginia (Now Virginia Conservation Network (VCN)) (1969-1971); President, Virginia Wilderness Committee (1969-1970); Co-founder, Virginia Wilderness Society **Creative Works:** Member, Editorial Board, Eighteenth Century Life; Author, "William Small"; Contributor, Articles to Professional Journals **Awards:** Outstanding Service Award, Research Revolution Series (2003); Certificate of Appreciation for Years of Outstanding Service and Dedication as Director of Soil and Water Conservation (1986) **Memberships:** American Association for the Advancement of Science; American Physical Society; Philosophy of Science Association; History of Science Society; Society for the History of Technology (SHOT); Scientific Instrument Society; International Scientific Instruments Commission; The Phi Beta Kappa Society; Sigma Xi, the Scientific Research Honor Society; Phi Kappa Phi **Marquis Who's Who Honors:** Albert Nelson Marquis Lifetime Achievement Award **Why did you become involved in your profession or industry:** Dr. McKnight became involved in his profession because he always loved math and science from childhood and was very much inspired by the teachers at Cadillac Elementary School, which was an experimental school. There was a garden the children tended to there. He went to the University of Michigan and took science, music and had an excellent physics teacher; he decided to major in physics. His elective was in organ building under Robert Noehren, who was one of the greatest organ builders, now deceased. Mr. Noehren used him in class because he could explain the physics of the pipe. To this day, Dr. McKnight is an organ aficionado. He was an instructor at Yale very early, even though he was a graduate student, and had a wonderful experience there. **Religion:** Episcopalian

Clara McLaughlin

Title: Owner, Publisher **Industry:** Media & Entertainment **Company Name:** The Florida Star, The Georgia Star **Date of Birth:** 10/22/1946 **Place of Birth:** Brunswick **State/Country of Origin:** GA/USA **Parents:** Dave McLaughlin; Arnetta Jackson (Lundy) McLaughlin **Marital Status:** Married **Spouse Name:** Richard A. McLaughlin (10/1968, Divorced) **Children:** Rinetta A.; Ricky A. **Education:** BA in Journalism, Howard University (1972) **Career:** Publisher, Owner, Newspapers, The Florida Star, Georgia Star (2002-Present); Founder, President, KLMG-TV and East Texas Television Network (1979-1990) **Civic:** Member, Auxiliary to American Medical Association (1974-Present); Trustee, Texas Southern University (1978-Present); Chairman of the Board, United Cerebral Palsy (1978-1980); Board of Directors, United Cerebral Palsy, Houston, TX (1976-1980) **Creative Works:** Author, "The Black Parents' Handbook: A Guide to Healthy Pregnancy, Birth, and Child Care" (1976); Contributor, Articles, Professional Journals **Awards:** Distinguished Alumni Award, Howard University; Inductee, Lincoln High School Hall of Fame, Gainesville, FL; The Kool Achievers Award; "Drum Major for Justice" Award, Southern Christian Leadership Conference (SCLC), Atlanta, GA; Female Entrepreneur of the Year Award **Memberships:** Leadership Texas **Why did you become involved in your profession or industry:** Ms. McLaughlin became involved in her profession because she started a small newsletter in high school and formed a playing group called the Golden Teardrops. She then went to Hampton University for voice studies but could not remain there because she did not have the financial means. She joined the U.S. Navy in order to complete her education. When she was in the Navy, she formed another singing group. She also worked as the secretary of a priest and would play the organ in the church every Sunday morning. She then got married, left the Navy, and continued her studies at Howard University, where she also worked within the dean's office. She ultimately graduated from the institution with honors, a degree in communications, and experience as associate editor of the university's yearbook. She and others became the first black students in the country to receive the All-American Award. She then had her daughter and found that, for the first time, she was able to "sit down and watch television" because she had a baby to take care of. However, she did not like what she saw because she noticed most shows at the time only portrayed women as waitresses and in positions of low significance, which she deemed as "ridiculous." She petitioned the SPC to remove a specific show in Houston as she wanted women to be shown in more positive ways on TV. She subsequently became the first black woman in the country to own a network, having convinced CBS to let her take over that particular station. Afterward, she had her son. Additionally, she became involved in many organizations. After her divorce, she relocated to Florida, where she was offered to run a newspaper. **Avocations:** Singing; Performing **Thoughts on Life:** For more information on Ms. McLaughlin, see:https://www.linkedin.com/in/clara-mclaughlin-a4444bb/

James McLeod

Title: Minister; Author; Teacher **Date of Birth:** 04/27/1937 **Place of Birth:** Oakdale **State/Country of Origin:** LA/USA **Parents:** The Rev. Dr. William Lasater McLeod (Deceased 1980); Sara Louise (Macaulay) McLeod (Deceased 1987) **Marital Status:** Single **Education:** Doctorate, Mississippi State University (1972); BD, Emory University (1968); MA, Emory University (1968); BA, Washington and Lee University (1959); Diploma, Princeton Theological Seminary, Princeton, NJ **Certifications:** Ordained to Ministry, Presbyterian Church (1963) **Career:** President, Brunswick Gallery (1993-2003); President, Brunswick Financial, GA (1991-2003); Minister, Synod, The Associate Reformed Presbyterian Church (1985-Present); Minister, The Associate Reformed Presbyterian Church, Augusta, GA (1988-1999); Educator, Georgia State Schools (1972-1991); Minister, U.S.-Southern Presbyterian Church (1963-1985) **Civic:** Mayor Pro Tempore, City of Brunswick (1996-1998); Councilman, City of Brunswick (1994-1996); Member, Society of the Cincinnati, Washington, DC (1970) **Creative Works:** Author, "Flannery O'Connor and Me" (2017); Author, "Great Dr. Waddel" (1985); Author, "Presbyterian Tradition in the South" (1978); Author, "A Season of Grace" (1974); Author, "1918: Needed: National Referendums on Important Issues in the U.S.A. Today" **Awards:** Scholar, National Endowment of the Humanities (1986) **Memberships:** Fellow, Society of Antiquaries of Scotland; National Education Association; Georgia Association of Educators; Fulbright Alumni Association; The Pinnacle Club, Augusta, GA; Phi Delta Kappa (PDK International) **Marquis Who's Who Honors:** Albert Nelson Marquis Lifetime Achievement Award **Avocations:** Reading; Opera **Political Affiliations:** Republican **Religion:** Presbyterian **Thoughts on Life:** Albert Marquis Lifetime Achievement Award

Walton James McLeod III

Title: Lawyer, Former State Legislator, Businessman **Industry:** Law and Legal Services **Company Name:** McLeod Law Office **Date of Birth:** 6/30/1937 **Place of Birth:** Walterboro **State/Country of Origin:** SC/USA **Parents:** Walton James McLeod Jr.; Rhoda Lane (Brown) McLeod **Marital Status:** Married **Spouse Name:** Julie Edwina Hamiter (2/15/1969) **Children:** Walton James IV **Education:** Postgraduate Coursework, University of Minnesota Public Health School (1972); LLB, University of South Carolina (1964); BA, Yale University (1959) **Career:** Special Counsel, South Carolina Department of Health and Environmental Control, Columbia, SC (1994-1996); General Counsel, South Carolina of Department Health and Environmental Control, Columbia, SC (1968-1994); Deputy South Carolina Attorney General, Columbia, SC (1987-1988); Assistant U.S. Attorney, Columbia, SC (1967-1968); Associate, Pope and Schumpert, Newberry, SC (1965-1967); Law Clerk, Chief Judge Clement Haynsworth, U.S. Court of Appeals for the Fourth Circuit, Richmond, VA (1964-1965) **Career Related:** State Representative, District 40, South Carolina House of Representatives (1996-2016); Mayor, Town of Little Mountain (1983-1989, 1993-1996); Municipal Judge (1981-1983); Magistrate Judge, Newberry County (1973-1981); Fellow, South Carolina Bar Foundation **Civic:** Board Member, South Carolina Alzheimer's Association (2007-Present); Board Member, Newberry College Foundation (2005-Present); Board Member, Newberry County Council on Aging (2001-Present); Assistant House Democratic Leader (2013-2016); South Carolina State House Committee (2010-2016); South Carolina Legislative Audit Council (2008-2016); Board Member, South Carolina Humanities Council (2008-2014); Board Member, Southeastern Institute for Women in Politics (2007-2012); First Vice Chair, House Judiciary Committee (2006-2008); Chair, Central Midlands Council of Governments, Columbia, SC (1981-1982, 2001-2003); Board Member, South Carolina Housing Finance and Development Authority, Columbia, SC (1977-1996); Trustee, South Carolina State Museum, Columbia, SC (1981-1985); President, Newberry Jaycees, South Carolina (1967) **Military Service:** U.S. Navy Reserve (1961-1992); Lieutenant Junior Grade to Captain, U.S. Navy (1961-1992); Active Duty, U.S. Navy (1959-1961,1963, 1990) **Creative Works:** Co¬author, "Hospital Franchising Law and Regulation" (1979); Co¬author, "Environmental Quality Law" (1975); Author, "Legal Perspectives of Environmental Health" (1973) **Awards:** Legislator of the Year Award, South Carolina Human Service Providers Association (2008); Legislative Appreciation Award, South Carolina Association of Conservation Districts (2006); Outstanding Service Award, South Carolina American Legion (2006); Outstanding Legislator Award, Gift of Life Trust Fund (1999); Named, Reserve Officer of the Year (1998); Named, Outstanding Freshman Representative of the Year, South Carolina Historical Foundation Society, Inc. (1997); Howell Excellence Award, Naval Reserve Law Program, Washington, DC (1991); Distinguished Judicial Service Award (1975); Outstanding Jaycee Award, Newberry Jaycees (1967) **Memberships:** President, South Carolina Society, University of South Carolina (1990-1993); National President, Judge Advocates Committee (1991-1992); State President, Reserve Officers Association, South Carolina (1981-1982); President, South Carolina Magistrates Association (1976-1977); President, Clariosophic Society, University of South Carolina **Bar Admissions:** Supreme Court of the United States (1974); State of South Carolina (1964) **Avocations:** Reading; Physical fitness **Political Affiliations:** Democrat **Religion:** Protestant (Lutheran)

Joseph Hamilton "Joe" McMakin

Title: Chemical Industry Executive **Industry:** Sciences **Date of Birth:** 01/28/1946 **Place of Birth:** Wilmington **State/Country of Origin:** DE/USA **Parents:** Joseph Purple McMakin; Bernadine Joan (Hamilton) McMakin **Marital Status:** Married **Spouse Name:** Diane Rose Sidoti (04/28/1984); Gail Lynn Pierce, (01/24/1970, Divorced 08/1982) **Children:** Sean Joseph, Dana Lynn; Lauren Taylor McMakin; Ryan Signarovitz (Step-child) **Education:** BS ChemE, University of Delaware (1968) **Career:** Consultant (2003-2007); Chief Information Officer, Air Products and Chemicals, Inc., Allentown, PA (1996-2003); Vice President, General Manager, Polyurethane and Performance Chemicals, Air Products and Chemicals, Inc., Allentown, PA (1993-1996); General Manager, Performance Chemicals, Air Products and Chemicals, Inc., Allentown, PA (1990-1993); General Manager, Business Development, Air Products and Chemicals, Inc., Allentown, PA (1987-1990); Business Manager, Amines, Air Products and Chemicals, Inc., Allentown, PA (1985-1987); Director, Marketing Industrial Chemicals, Air Products and Chemicals, Inc., Allentown, PA (1981-1985); Technology Director, Plastics, Air Products and Chemicals, Inc., Allentown, PA (1979-1981) **Civic:** Advisory Committee, 3COM (1997-2001); Trustee, Good Shepherd Hospital (1998); Trustee, Hillside School, Allentown, PA (1997); Member, Governor of PA I.T. Advisory Committee (1997); Vice President, YMCA, Allentown, PA (1991) **Creative Works:** Co-Author, Encyclopedia of Chemical Technology (1977) **Awards:** Gartner CIO Choice Award **Memberships:** American Institute of Chemical Engineers; Brookside Country Club; Sons of the American Revolution; Lehigh Country Club; Windstar on Naples Bay Country Club; Commercial Development Association; Chemical Information Technology Association; Research Board **Marquis Who's Who Honors:** Albert Nelson Marquis Lifetime Achievement Award **Why did you become involved in your profession or industry:** Mr. McMakin became involved in his profession indirectly. He grew up in Delaware and the University of Delaware was an economically driven choice. Since Delaware was a top five rated chemical engineering school in the United States, Mr. McMakin pursued that degree which led him into the Chemical Industry upon graduation. **Avocations:** Golf; Woodworking **Religion:** Roman Catholic

Rodney McMullen

Title: Chairman, Chief Executive Officer **Industry:** Retail/Sales **Company Name:** Kroger **Place of Birth:** Willamstown **State/Country of Origin:** KY/USA **Education:** MS in Accounting, University of Kentucky (1982); BBA in Finance, University of Kentucky (1981); BS in Accounting, University of Kentucky (1981) **Certifications:** Certified Public Accountant **Career:** Chairman, Chief Executive Officer, Kroger (2014-Present); President, Chief Operating Officer, Kroger (2009-2013); Vice Chairman, Kroger (2003-2009); Executive Vice President of Strategy, Planning and Finance, Kroger (2000-2003); Senior Vice President, Chief Financial Officer, Kroger (1997-2000); Group Vice President, Chief Financial Officer, Kroger (1995-1997); Vice President of Financial Services and Control, Kroger (1993-1995); Vice President of Planning and Capital Management, Kroger (1990-1993); Assistant Treasurer, Kroger (1988-1990); Financial Analyst, Kroger (1985-1988) **Career Related:** Board of Directors, Kroger (2003-Present); Board of Directors, The Cincinnati Insurance Companies (2001-Present) **Civic:** Trustee, Xavier University; Trustee, Business Partnership Foundation, Gatton College of Business and Economics, University of Kentucky

Thomas Joseph McPartland, PhD

Title: Director (Retired) **Industry:** Education/Educational Services **Company Name:** Whitney Yong School of Honors and Liberal Studies at Kentucky State University **Date of Birth:** 07/30/1945 **Place of Birth:** Oakland **State/Country of Origin:** CA/USA **Parents:** Richard Joseph McPartland; Anne Josephine (Calmes) McPartland **Education:** PhD in Electrical History, University of Washington (1976); MA, University of Washington (1969); BA, University of Santa Clara (1967) **Career:** Retired (2016); Director, Whitney Yong School of Honors and Liberal Studies (2006-2016); Professor, Kentucky State University (1996-2016); Associate Professor, Kentucky State University, Frankfort, KY (1992-1996); Acting Dean, Whitney Young College, Kentucky State University, Frankfort, KY (1993-1994); Assistant Professor, Kentucky State University (1988-1992); Assistant Professor, Seattle University (1987-1989); Instructor, Bellevue Community College (1981-1987); Lecturer, University of Washington, Seattle, WA (1985); Acting Assistant Professor, University of Washington, Seattle, WA (1976-1979); Lecturer, Pacific Lutheran University, Tacoma, WA (1977) **Career Related:** President, Kentucky Honors Roundtable (2006-2016); President, Academy Senate, Kentucky State University (2003-2004); Northern Kentucky University (1993); Murray State University (1992); Kentucky State University (1991); Governor's Scholar Program, Western Kentucky University (1990); Consultant to Psychotherapists, Seattle, WA (1977-1988); Instructor, Issaquah, WA (1986-1987); Instructor, Telos, Clyde Hill, WA (1985-1986); Editorial Board, "Method: A Journal of Lonergan Studies" **Creative Works:** Author, Book, "Lonergan and the Philosophy of Historical Existence"; Author, Book, "Lonergan and Historiography: The Epistemological Philosophy of History"; Contributor, Book, "Philosophy of Bernard Lonergan"; Contributor, Book, "Philosophy of History"; Contributor, Book "History of Revolutions"; Speaker, International Conferences at Rome, Mainz, Germany, Toronto, and Hong Kong; Speaker, Over 40 Presentations, American Political Science Association, Lonergan Workshop, Boston College, West Coast Methods Institute **Awards:** Kentucky State University Distinguished Professor (2002-2003) **Memberships:** Southern Regional Honors Council (1992-2016); National Collegiate Honors Council (1992-2016); American Political Science Association; West Coast Methods Institute; Honorary Order of Kentucky Colonels **Marquis Who's Who Honors:** Albert Nelson Marquis Lifetime Achievement Award; Marquis Who's Who Top Professional **Why did you become involved in your profession or industry:** Dr. McPartland became involved in his profession because he had a wealth of experience in philosophy due to the readings and thinking he participated in during his undergraduate years. **Avocations:** Watching sports; Exercise; Running

Lawrence "Larry" McPhail

Title: Executive Director **Industry:** Nonprofit & Philanthropy **Company Name:** The New Non-Profit Institute (NNPI INC) **Date of Birth:** 03/25/1963 **Place of Birth:** Saskatchewan **State/Country of Origin:** Canada **Parents:** Lawrence D. McPhail (Deceased 2019); Pamela M. (Wakeling) McPhail (Deceased 2018) **Education:** Pursuing MBA, University of the People, Pasadena, CA; BS in Management Science, Southern Methodist University, Dallas, Texas (1988); Diploma, Lenape Valley Regional High School, Stanhope, NJ (1981) **Certifications:** Documentation and Analysis (2020); Quantitative Methods in Systems Engineering (2020); Certified, Model-Based Systems Engineering, Architecture of Complex Systems, MIT xPRO (2019); Models in Engineering, MIT xPRO (2019); edX101: Creating an edX Course (2017); Managing Projects with Microsoft Project (2017); Microsoft Azure Virtual Networks (2017); ICT100x: ICT Accessibility GTx (2016); xSeries: HTML5 from W3C Record (2016); edX Verified Certificates **Career:** Executive Director, The New Non-Profit Institute (NNPI INC) (2019-Present); Travel Advisor, Cruise Planners, First Response Travel LLC, www.98cruise. com (2019-Present); Technology Consultant, Priority IT LLC, Newton, NJ (2019-Present); Past President, Sussex Technical School PTA, Sparta, NJ (2014-2019); Senior Systems Engineer, Atlantic Technology Systems, Newton, NJ (2010-2019); System Administration Analyst, Dell (2008-2010); Network Engineer, Tellurian Networks (2003-2008); Technical Support Manager, Tellurian Networks (2005-2007); Cisco Regional Academy Coordinator, Sussex County Community College (2002-2003); CCE Coordinator of Technology, Sussex County Community College (2001-2003); Citi-Group Global Help Desk, Butler International, Inc. (2001); Vice President, Sales and Marketing, Software Engineer, Westech Corporation (1987-2000); Chief Executive Officer, Captain, Sparta Ambulance Service, Inc., Sparta, NJ (1983-2009) **Career Related:** With, Travel Agency (Present) **Civic:** Member, President, Chairman, Board of Trustees, Emergency Medical Technician (EMT), Glenwood Pochuck Volunteer Ambulance Corps (2017-Present); President, Chairman, Board of Trustees, NJ Fair Play (Vernon Vipers) (2015-Present); Member, Board of Directors, Safety Officer, Information Officer, Vernon Little League Baseball (2013-Present); Life Member, Sparta Ambulance Service, Inc. (1983-2009); Member, Community Dispute Resolution Committee, Superior Court of New Jersey (1996-2008) **Memberships:** National Association of Emergency Medical Technicians; Professional Member, National Association of EMS Physicians; American Society of Association Executives (ASAE); Individual Member, Cruise Line Industry Association (CLIA); Institute of Electrical and Electronics Engineers (IEEE); IEEE Technology and Engineering Management Society (IEEE-TEMS); IEEE Systems Council; National Systems Contractors Association (NSCA) **To what do you attribute your success:** Mr. McPhail's motto is "I never lose. I either win or I learn," by Nelson Mandela. **Why did you become involved in your profession or industry:** Mr. McPhail became involved in non-profit community service when he became an emergency medical technician after the death of a childhood friend, Jeff Ford, and joined the Sparta Ambulance Service as a volunteer EMT, which resulted in a 30 year career as a volunteer EMT, educator, officer, and board member in two EMS organizations, Sparta Ambulance Service (27 years) and Glenwood Pochuck Volunteer Ambulance Corps (three years). He is also involved in community service as a board member and founder of other non-profit organizations, including the New Non-Profit Institute and the New Jersey EMS Project. The Institute recently awarded Vernon Little League a grant from the L.D. and Pamela McPhail Public Access Defibrillation Program for two defibrillators, CPR and AED training by Glenwood Pochuck VAC. Mr. McPhail's technology career began when he took a computer programming course in high school – FORTRAN and punch cards! – from one of his favorite teachers, David Naysmith. Mr. McPhail's father, L.D. McPhail, purchased a used TRS-80 Model I computer from a friend, Vic Haines, and the rest is history. Mr. McPhail went to work as a programmer for a small company, Westech Corporation, and for 13 years helped build that company into an international supplier of point-of-sale systems before moving on to CitiGroup, Sussex County Community College, Tellurian Networks, Perot Systems, Dell, and Atlantic Technology Systems, ultimately starting Priority IT LLC and working as a technology consultant. **Avocations:** Avid hockey fan (New Jersey Devils)

Alice R. McPherson

Title: Ophthalmology Department **Industry:** Medicine & Health Care **Date of Birth:** 06/30/1926 **Place of Birth:** Regina **State/Country of Origin:** Saskatchewan/Canada **Parents:** Gordon; Viola **Education:** Honorary Doctor of Science, University of Wisconsin (1997); Doctor of Medicine, University of Wisconsin (1951); Bachelor of Science, University of Wisconsin (1948) **Certifications:** Diplomate, American Board of Ophthalmology **Career:** President, Retina Research Foundation, Houston, TX (1969-Present); Private Ophthalmologist Practice, Houston, TX (1960-Present); Ophthalmologist, Scott and White Clinic, Temple, TX (1958-1960); Fellow in Retina Service, Massachusetts Eye and Ear Infirmary (1957-1958); Clinical Instructor, University of Wisconsin (1956-1957); Ophthalmologist, Davis and Duehr Eye Clinic, Madison, WI (1956-1957); Resident of Ophthalmology, University of Wisconsin Hospitals (1953-1955); Resident of Ophthalmology, Chicago Eye, Ear, Nose and Throat Hospital (1953); Resident of Anesthesiology, Hartford Hospital, Connecticut (1952); Intern, Santa Barbara Cottage Hospital, California (1951-1952) **Career Related:** Professor, Baylor College of Medicine (1998-Present); Consultant in Retinal Diseases, Veterans Administration Hospital, Houston, TX (1960-Present); Consultant, Ben Taub Hospital, Houston, TX (1960-Present); Clinical Professor, Baylor College of Medicine (1975-1998); Member, Grievance Panel, Methodist Hospital (1997); Member, Equipment Committee, Methodist Hospital (1993-1995); Volunteer, Clinical Faculty Appointments and Promotions Committee, Methodist Hospital (1993); Member, Advisory Committee for Active Staff Appointment, Ophthalmology Section, Methodist Hospital (1986-1991); Clinical Associate Professor, Baylor College of Medicine (1969-1975); Assistant Professor of Ophthalmology, Baylor College of Medicine (1961-1969); Clinical Assistant Professor, Baylor College of Medicine (1959-1961); Staff Methodist, Saint Lukes Texas Children's Hospital, Harris County Hospital District, Houston, TX; Board Director, Highlights of Ophthalmology; Vice President, North America Highlights of Ophthalmology International **Civic:** External Advisory Board Member, University of Wisconsin Eye Research Institute (2010); Madison Board Member, International Council of the Ophthalmology Foundation (2008); Board Director, University of Wisconsin Foundation; Ambassador, Houston Ballet; Member, Houston Ballet Foundation **Creative Works:** Editor, "Retinopathy of Prematurity: Current Concepts and Controversies" (1986); Editor, "New and Controversial Aspects of Vitreoretinal Surgery" (1977); Editor, "New and Controversial Aspects of Retinal Detachment" (1968) **Awards:** Retina Hall of Fame Award, American Academy of Ophthalmology (2019); Honoree, ARVO Foundation (2018); Distinguished Alumni Award and Presidents Circle Award, Wisconsin Alumni Association (2015); Master Clinician Award, Baylor College of Medicine (2014); Gonin Medal (2014); Honored Guest, Pan-American Congress of Ophthalmology (2013); Establishment of McPherson Eye Research Institute Lectureship, Dr. Jean Bennett, Inaugural Lecturer (2013); Dedication of the McPherson Eye Research Institute, University of Wisconsin (2012); Distinguished Alumni Professional Achievement Award, Harvard Medical School (2012); Circle of Vision, Member at Gold Level, American Academy of Ophthalmology (2011); Women of Vision, Houston Delta Gamma Foundation (2002); Philip Corboy Memorial Award, Distinguished Service in Ophthalmology (2002); Benjamin Boyd Humanitarian Award, Pan-American Association Ophthalmology (2001); Crystal Award, Recognizing Generous Support-Partners, Eye for Vision Foundation, American Academy Ophthalmology (2000); Woodlands Medal for Outstanding Contributions to the Economic Development of Community (1988); Alice R. McPherson Laboratory for Retina Research Dedicated Baylor Center for Biotechnology (1988); Alice R. McPherson Day Proclaimed in Her Honor, Mayor of the City of Houston, TX (03/12/1988); Award of Appreciation, Knights Templar Eye Foundation (1978) **Memberships:** Board of Directors, International Council of the Ophthalmology Foundation (2006-Present); President, Schepens International Society (1995-1997); President, Pan American Association of Opthalmology (1995-1997); Fellow, Member of Several Committees, American College of Surgeons; Fellow, Member and Leader of Several Committees, American Academy of Ophthalmology; American Medical Association; Highlights of Ophthalmology International; University of Wisconsin Ophthalmology Alumni Association; Association of Research Surgeons; Pan-American Association of Ophthalmology Foundation; Texas Ophthalmological Association; Southern Medical Society; Research to Prevent Blindness; Macula Society; International Society of Eye Research; Houston Ophthalmological Society; Harris County Medical Society; American Board of Laser Surgery; American Society of Contemporary Ophthalmology; International College of Ocular Surgeons; Retina Society; American Medical Women's Association; International College of Surgeons; Texas Medical Association; Vitreous Society; Jules Gonin Club **Marquis Who's Who Honors:** Albert Nelson Marquis Lifetime Achievement Award

Sharon Louise McWhorter

Title: President **Industry:** Consulting **Company Name:** McWhorter Development Company, Inc. **Date of Birth:** 02/22/1951 **Place of Birth:** Detroit **State/Country of Origin:** MI/USA **Parents:** Leroy Byron Harris Jr.; Josiebell (Richards) Harris Azeez **Marital Status:** Divorced **Spouse Name:** Abner McWhorter II, (03/15/1969, Divorced 08/1974) **Children:** Abner III (Deceased 2011); Zuri McWhorter **Education:** BA, Wayne State University (1988) **Certifications:** Certified in Sound Engineering, Detroit Recording Institute, Warren, MI (1982); Certified, Small Business Administration, Detroit, MI (1978) **Career:** Consultant, Galactic Concepts & Designs, Detroit, MI (1983-Present); Member, Library Standing Committee and Open House Committee, Wayne County Community College District, Detroit, MI (1983-1984); President, Galactic Concepts & Designs, Detroit, MI (1977-1988); Circulation Clerk, Wayne County Community College District, Detroit, MI (1977-1985); Quality Control Clerk, Chevrolet Gear & Axle, Detroit, MI (1971-1974); Directory Assistant, Michigan Bell Telephone Company, Detroit, MI (1969) **Career Related:** Lecturer, Consultant, President, McWhorter Development Company, Inc. (1994-Present); Lecturer, Consultant, President, American Resource Training System, Inc. (1990-Present); Elected Alternate Michigan Delegate, White House Conference on Small Business (WHCSB), Washington, DC (1985-1986); General Partner, Manager, S.M.J. Corridor Development, Detroit, MI (1982-Present); Historical Researcher (1982); Ad Hoc Member, National Minority Technology Council (1981-1982); Delegate, Small Business Conference (1981); Partner, 18943 John R, LLC; Partner, KFM, LLC **Civic:** Board of Directors, Corporate Chair, Detroit Empowerment Zone Development Corp. (1997-Present); Detroit Empowerment Zone Development Corp., Detroit, MI (1996-Present); Appointed Member, Citizen Review Committee (1988-Present); President, MADD, Wayne County Chapter, MI (1987-1988); Cass Corridor Citizens Patrol, Detroit, MI (1983-1984); Active, Concerned Citizens of Cass Corridor, Detroit, MI (1982-1987); Volunteer, Counselor, Barat House/March of Dimes, Detroit, MI (1977); Member, Advisory Board, Neighborhood and Family Initiative; President, Southeastern Community Foundation; Board Member, Volunteers of America Michigan (VOAMI), Women's Informal Network, Global Ties U.S., and Women Veteran Resource Center **Creative Works:** Contributor, "Poetry, Volume One," Alkebulanian (1989); Author, Editor, Creative Dilemma Newsletter (1985); Author, Editor, Several Course Books Including "How to Start Your Own Business," "Patent Trademark and Copyright," "Consumer Awareness and Your Right," and "Advanced Business"; Co-patentee, Cup Holding Apparatus; Writer, Publisher, Songs for Artists **Awards:** Certified Appreciation, Tri-County Substance Abuse Awareness Committee (1984); Historical Landmark Award, U.S. Department of the Interior (1983) **Memberships:** President, South Cass Business Association (1988-1989); Vice President, South Cass Business Association (1987-1988); Board of Directors, Inventors Council Mid-Michigan (1985-1988); Secretary, Black Women in Business (1984-1985); Former Member, Inventors Council Mid-Michigan; Former Member, Black Women in Business; Member, Greater Detroit Chamber of Commerce (Now Detroit Regional Chamber); Former Member, South Cass Business Association; Detroit Athletic Club; Wyandotte Yacht Club **Why did you become involved in your profession or industry:** Ms. McWhorter became involved in her profession because of her mother. Her mother always treated them as though they were her most valuable asset and as such she encouraged them to follow their dreams. Part of Ms. McWhorter's dream was to one day be an inventor and so each one of the little things that she wanted to do, whether it was to be a writer, and at one point modelling, she was able to achieve each one of them. She wanted to be a writer so she wrote and her poems were published. They were the little things but she realized that it was the small accomplishments that led to bigger ones and the goals she set could be achieved even though they were small goals. **Avocations:** Photography; Filmmaking; Cycling; Writing **Political Affiliations:** Democrat **Religion:** Methodist

Annie Mecias-Murphy

Title: Co-Owner, President **Industry:** Architecture & Construction **Company Name:** JA&M Developing Corporation **Education:** PhD, Barry University (2007) **Certifications:** Certified General Contractor; Certified Therapist **Career:** Co-Owner, President, JA&M Developing Corporation (2005-Present) **Civic:** Metro Life Church; Hollywood Police Department **Awards:** Woman of the Year (2016); Numerous Excellence in Construction Awards **Memberships:** Board of Directors, Executive Committee, Associated Builders and Contractors, Inc.; Board of Directors, Boys & Girls Clubs of Broward County; Executive Board Member, Epic Foundation **To what do you attribute your success:** Dr. Mecias-Murphy attributes her success to the drive and work ethic her parents instilled in her, as well as her faith and respecting others regardless of who they are. **Why did you become involved in your profession or industry:** Dr. Mecias-Murphy became involved in her profession because it is a family tradition. They came to the United States and pursued the American Dream. **Religion:** Christian

Jean Edith Melton

Title: Retired Elementary Education Educator **Industry:** Education/Educational Services **Date of Birth:** 11/17/1926 **Place of Birth:** Monticello **State/Country of Origin:** IA/USA **Parents:** James Calvin Bender; Edith C (Schneider) Bender **Marital Status:** Married **Spouse Name:** Thomas Greenleaf Melton (09/09/1947) **Children:** Nancy Jean; Thomas Mark; David Myron **Education:** MEd, University of Missouri, Kansas City, MO (1978); BA, Central Missouri State University (1971); AA, Dubuque University, Iowa **Certifications:** Certified Elementary Teacher **Career:** Elementary Teacher, Mill Street Elementary School, Independence, IA **Memberships:** Local Board, Missouri State Teachers Association; Board of Directors, International Reading Association; Delta Kappa Gamma; Honorary Christian Education Member, Presbyterian Women's Organization); P.E.O. **Marquis Who's Who Honors:** Albert Nelson Marquis Lifetime Achievement Award **Why did you become involved in your profession or industry:** Ms. Melton grew up in a small town and had one class that went through kindergarten all the way through high school. She has always wanted to teach and she gained her inspiration from the teachers who taught her. **Avocations:** Church travel tours **Religion:** Presbyterian **Thoughts on Life:** Ms. Melton has had and interesting life; as the wife of a minister, they have moved to several different places. They landed in Independence, Missouri, and lived across the street from President Truman. She flew on Air Force One with the president of Malawi to Washington, DC, to visit the president of the United States.

Howard Shigeharu Mende

Title: Mechanical Engineer **Industry:** Engineering **Company Name:** Defense Contracts Management West **Date of Birth:** 11/19/1947 **Place of Birth:** Hilo **State/Country of Origin:** HI/USA **Parents:** Tsutomu Mende; Harue (Kubomitsu) Mende **Education:** MME, University of Southern California (1975); BS in Mechanical Engineering, University of Hawaii (1969) **Certifications:** Registered Professional Engineer, State of California **Career:** Electronics Engineer, Defense Contracts Management West, Santa Ana, CA (1994-Present); Mechanical Engineer, Defense Contracts Management West, Santa Ana, CA (1987-1994); Technical Staff IV, Rockwell International, Los Angeles, CA (1984-1986); Development Engineer, AiRsch. Manufacturing Company, Torrance, CA (1977-1983); Technical Staff II, Rockwell International, Los Angeles, CA (1973-1977); Technical Staff I, Rockwell International, Los Angeles, CA (1971-1973); Technical Staff I, Rockwell International, Anaheim, CA (1970-1971) **Career Related:** Lecturer, Pacific States University, Los Angeles, CA (1974-1975) **Memberships:** American Society of Mechanical Engineers **Marquis Who's Who Honors:** Albert Nelson Marquis Lifetime Achievement Award; Marquis Who's Who Top Professional; Marquis Who's Who Humanitarian Award **Why did you become involved in your profession or industry:** Mr. Mende became involved in his profession because his father was a mechanic, but always told him to become an engineer so he could enter a profession that makes great money. What inspired him was to try to understand and learn about things. In addition, Mr. Mende's big break that lead him to being a mechanical engineer is when he was fortunate enough to work during the time President Nixon had a federal job freeze on. He wasn't able to apply for a job at Pearl Harbor and luckily, Rockwell International came by the University of Hawaii and he was fortunate enough to get a job. He had the opportunity to work with people who were doing work on defense projects, more specifically the minute man missile. He got to be very close to Dr. George R. Talbert; they use to go out and eat dinner. Dr. Talbert also acknowledged him for all the insightful discussions that they had in his book called "Philosophy of Unified Science" in the 1970s. **Avocations:** Gardening; Home improvements **Political Affiliations:** Democrat **Religion:** Buddhist

Michael Drew Mendelson

Title: Writer, Novelist **Industry:** Writing and Editing **Date of Birth:** 12/13/1945 **Place of Birth:** Kansas City **State/Country of Origin:** MO/USA **Parents:** Harry Mendelson (Deceased, 2000); Marilyn Drew Mendelson (Deceased, 2016) **Marital Status:** Married **Spouse Name:** Susan Lee Aguilar (05/02/1992) **Children:** Alexandra (1983); Eric (1987); Max (1993); Jacob (1997) **Education:** MA in English Literature (Concentration in Creative Writing), San Francisco State University (1980); BA in Journalism and English, Sonoma State University, with Honors (1977); Coursework, Artillery Officer Candidate School, Fort Sill, Oklahoma **Career:** Retired (2019); Founder, Owner, Mendelson Communications (2009-2019); Senior Policy Advisor, California State Treasurers Phil Angelides, Bill Lockyer and John Chiang (2005-2017); Chief Writer, California Senate Democratic Caucus (2004-2005); Deputy Communications Director, California Governor Gray Davis (1999-2003); Director of Communications, the California Democratic Party (1994); Senior Communications Specialist, California State Employees Association (1986-1999); Editor-in-Chief, The St. Paul Union Advocate, St. Paul, MN (1983-1986); Reporter, Photographer, The Kansas City Labor Beacon, Kansas City, MO (1981-1983); Managing Editor, The Lancaster Excelsior, Lancaster, MO (1980-1981); Associate Editor, The Cotati Call, Cotati, CA (1975-1977) **Career Related:** Writer, Novelist, Editor **Civic:** Political Activist; Volunteer for Democratic Candidates **Military Service:** Battalion Artillery Liaison Officer, Fire Support Coordinator, United States Army, Vietnam War (1970); Artillery Forward Observer, United States Army, Vietnam War (1969-1970); First Lieutenant, United States Army (1969); Assistant Battery Executive Officer, United States Army, Fort Lewis, Washington (1968-1969); Second oLieutenant, United States Army (1968); United States Army (1967-1970) **Creative Works:** Co-Author, Barry Broad, "Dark Sea Rising," Edge Science Fiction (2018); Author, "Song Ba To," Mira Digital Publishing, Amazon Books (2010); Author, "Marin 2120 A.D.," Pacific Sun Publishing (1980); Author, "Pilgrimage," DAW Books (1980); Contributor, New Dimensions; Author, "A Shepherd to Fools"; Author, "Chief to Smoke"; Author, "The Folly of a Dream" **Awards:** Recipient, Various Awards for Editorial Excellence, News and Feature Writing, Photography, International Labor Communications Association, Western Labor Press Association (1983-Present); Finalist, Ted Sorensen Speech Writing Award (2009) **To what do you attribute your success:** Mr. Mendelson attributes his success to the depth of his education in writing. He feels that certain writers get by with strength only in language; however, there is more to it than that, such as grammar and style. **Why did you become involved in your profession or industry:** Mr. Mendelson entered his profession after moving to California with the goal of becoming an astronomer. He loved astronomy, but he didn't possess the mathematical strength that the field required. As a result, he began writing fiction. At 16, he started working on a novel. Ever since then, he has built on his skills during his many years as a journalist, speech-writer, and press relations professional. **Avocations:** Photography; Traveling; Biking; Hiking; Camping **Political Affiliations:** Democratic Party **Religion:** Jewish **Thoughts on Life:** Life is both real and earnest; a joy and a labor to live well. Live for today but dream for tomorrow. Be active, be productive and take great joy in all. As an old friend once said, live a worthy life, you can sleep when you are dead.

Peter C. Merani, Esq.

Title: Principal Partner **Industry:** Law and Legal Services **Company Name:** Peter C. Merani PC **State/Country of Origin:** NY/USA **Parents:** Peter; Arlene **Marital Status:** Married **Spouse Name:** Maria **Education:** JD, Saint Johns University School of Law (1990); BS in Accounting, St. Johns University (1989) **Career:** Founding Member, Owner, Managing Principal Attorney, Office of Peter C. Merani, P.C. (1993-Present); Staff Attorney, Large Insurance Company **Career Related:** Lecturer on No-Fault Insurance Law, Continued Legal Education Programs; Lecturer, Seminars on No-Fault Insurance Law, Insurance Companies; Program Teacher, Coordinator, Street Law Trial Program **Creative Works:** Featured, New York Magazine **Awards:** Lawyer of Distinction, New York Magazine **Memberships:** New York State Bar Association; American Bar Association; Lawyers of Distinction; The District of Columbia Bar **Bar Admissions:** New York; Washington, DC; New Jersey; United States District Court for the Southern District of New York; United States District Court for the Eastern District of New York; United States District Court for the District of New Jersey **Marquis Who's Who Honors:** Marquis Who's Who Top Professional **To what do you attribute your success:** Mr. Merani attributes his success to many long hours of dedication, as well as to his knowledge in his field. **Why did you become involved in your profession or industry:** Mr. Merani became a lawyer to help other people. **Religion:** Catholic

Carolyn Merchant, PhD

Title: Professor Emerita **Industry:** Education/Educational Services **Company Name:** University of California Berkeley **Date of Birth:** 07/12/1936 **Place of Birth:** Rochester **State/Country of Origin:** NY/USA **Parents:** George Eugene Merchant; Elizabeth Merchant **Marital Status:** Married **Spouse Name:** Charles Grier Sellers (9/5/1993); Hugh Iltis (8/5/1961, Divorced) **Children:** David Iltis; John Iltis **Education:** Honorary Doctorate, Umea University, Sweden (1995); PhD, University of Wisconsin, Madison (1967); MA, University of Wisconsin, Madison (1962); AB, Vassar College (1958) **Career:** Assistant Professor to Professor, University of California Berkeley (1979-2018); Assistant to Associate Professor, University of San Francisco (1969-1978) **Career Related:** Fellow, Center for Advanced Study in the Behavioral Sciences, Stanford University (2017); Institute for Advanced Study, Princeton University (2012); Visiting Fellow, School of Social Sciences, Murdoch University, Perth, Australia (1991); Visiting Professor, Ecole Normale Superieure, Paris, France (1986); Fulbright Fellow, Umea University, Sweden (1983); Fellow, Center for Advanced Study in the Behavioral Sciences, Stanford University (1978); Chancellor's Professor, Environmental History, Philosophy and Ethics, University of California Berkeley; Chair, Department of Conservation and Resource Studies, University of California Berkeley; Lecturer, Consultant in Field **Creative Works:** Contributor, "Afterword," "After the Death of Nature, Carolyn Merchant and the Future of Human-Nature Relations" (2019); Contributor, "Science and Nature, Past, Present, and Future" (2018); Contributor, "Autonomous Nature, Problems of Prediction and Control from Ancient Times to the Scientific Revolution" (2016); Contributor, "Spare the Birds! George Bird Grinnell and the First Audubon Society" (2016); Editor, Contributing Author, "Major Problems in American Environmental History, Documents and Essays, 3rd Edition" (2013); Author, "Reinventing Eden, The Fate of Nature in Western Culture, 2nd Edition" (2013); Author, "Ecological Revolutions, Nature, Gender and Science in New England, 2nd Edition" (2010); Editor, Contributing Author, "Key Concepts in Critical Theory, Ecology, 2nd Edition" (2008); Co-Editor, "American Environmental History: An Introduction" (2007); Author, "Radical Ecology, The Search for a Livable World, 2nd Edition" (2005); Editor, Contributing Author, "Major Problems in American Environmental History, Documents and Essays, 2nd Edition" (2004); Author, "Reinventing Eden, The Fate of Nature in Western Culture" (2003); Co-Editor, 3 Volumes, Encyclopedia of World Environmental History (2003); Author, "Columbia Guide to American Environmental History" (2002); Editor, Contributing Author, "Green Versus Gold, Sources in California's Environmental History" (1998); Author, "Earthcare, Women and the Environment" (1996); Editor, Contributing Author, "Key Concepts in Critical Theory, Ecology" (1994); Editor, Contributing Author, "Major Problems in American Environmental History, Documents and Essays" (1993); Author, "Radical Ecology, The Search for a Livable World" (1992); Author, "The Death of Nature: Women, Ecology and the Scientific Revolution, 2nd Edition" (1990); Author, "Ecological Revolutions, Nature, Gender and Science in New England" (1989); Author, "The Death of Nature: Women, Ecology and the Scientific Revolution" (1980); Contributor, Articles, Professional Journals **Awards:** Grantee, American Association for the Advancement of Science (2011); Fellow, National Humanities Center (2001); Grantee, California Council for the Humanities (1997-1998); John Simon Guggenheim Fellow (1995); Grantee, Nathan Cummings Foundation (1992) **Memberships:** Advisory Board, Ethics and the Environment (1997-Present); Advisory Board, Organization and Environment (1997-Present); Advisory Board, Interdisciplinary Studies in Literature and Environment (1993-Present); Society of Woman Geographers (1985-Present); President, American Society for Environmental History (2001-2003) **Marquis Who's Who Honors:** Albert Nelson Marquis Lifetime Achievement Award **To what do you attribute your success:** Professor Merchant attributes her success to the support of her husband, historian Charles Grier Sellers, who she met in 1972. He inspired the advancement of her work on her first and second books, "The Death of Nature: Women, Ecology and the Scientific Revolution" and "Ecological Revolutions, Nature, Gender and Science in New England." **Why did you become involved in your profession or industry:** Professor Merchant became involved in her profession because she took a class in physics at Vassar College and the professor, Margaret Waggoner, taught it from the perspective of history. Professor Merchant found the work to be fascinating. She still didn't know what she wanted to do after she graduated, however. She then consulted Professor Waggoner and another professor, Phillip Macklin. They recommended she pursue the history of science, and she followed their advice.

Keith E. Meredith, PhD

Title: Academic Administrator, Educator (Retired) **Industry:** Education/Educational Services **Date of Birth:** 10/13/1943 **Place of Birth:** Clay Center **State/Country of Origin:** KS/USA **Parents:** Joseph Edward Meredith; Eulah Mae Meredith **Marital Status:** Widowed **Spouse Name:** Margaret Rose Meek Meredith (05/29/1964, Deceased) **Children:** Kurt Edward Meredith; Mark David; Scott Thomas **Education:** PhD, The University of Arizona, Tucson, AZ (1973); MS, Kansas State University, Manhattan, KS (1968); BS, Kansas State University, Manhattan, KS (1965) **Career:** Director, Gerontological Studies, Interdisciplinary Studies Program, The University of Arizona, Tucson, AZ (1993-1999); Associate Director, Arizona Center of Aging, The University of Arizona, Tucson, AZ (1991-1998); Adjunct Associate Professor, College of Education, The University of Arizona, Tucson, AZ (1986-1999); Associate Director, Division of Restorative Medicine, The University of Arizona, Tucson, AZ (1985-1991); Associate Director, Southwest Arthritis Center, The University of Arizona, Tucson, AZ (1981-1985); Assistant Professor, College of Education, The University of Arizona, Tucson, AZ (1974-1981); Research Associate, The University of Arizona, Tucson, AZ (1972-1973); Assistant Director of Bands, Kansas State University, Manhattan, KS (1966-1968); Member, Faculty, Manhattan Public Schools, Manhattan, KS (1965-1966) **Career Related:** Chairman, Board of Trustees, Arizona State Retired Systems (2004-2008); Arizona Board of Trustees, Arizona State Retired Systems (2003-2008); President, University of Arizona Retirees Association (1999-2005); Chairman, OASIS, Tucson, AZ (2001-2002) **Civic:** Chairman, Planning Division, United Way of Greater Tucson (Now United Way of Tucson and Southern Arizona), Tucson, AZ (1988-Present); Chairman, Board of Directors, United Way Capital Support Corp., Tucson, AZ (1999-2005); Chairman, United Way of Greater Tucson (Now United Way of Tucson and Southern Arizona), AZ (1994-1995); Member, Advisory Council for Aging, Arizona Governor's Office, Phoenix, AZ (1991-1994); Board of Directors, United Way of Greater Tucson (Now United Way of Tucson and Southern Arizona), Tucson, AZ (1985-1999); Chairman, Board of Trustees, Sonora Desert Hospital, Tucson, AZ **Creative Works:** Author, Co-Author, More Than 80 Articles, Professional Journals; Principal Investigator, Co-Investigator, More Than 40 Grants **Awards:** Volunteer of the Year Award, United Way of Greater Tucson (Now United Way of Tucson and Southern Arizona) (1989); Research Award, Association for Specialists in Group Work (1988); Meritorious Performance in Teaching Award, The University of Arizona Foundation (1972) **Memberships:** American Educational Research Association **Marquis Who's Who Honors:** Albert Nelson Marquis Lifetime Achievement Award **Why did you become involved in your profession or industry:** Dr. Meredith became involved in his profession because he started out as a math major in college but realized after his first semester that it wasn't for him. He switched over to music and music education, and ultimately earned bachelor's and master's degrees at Kansas State University. His goals shifted as his life shifted. He really didn't have a goal to become a teacher but that's what he wound up doing. That was the path that just kept coming and he kept enjoying the opportunities. Even while studying music education, he was teaching private lessons on his instrument and then got into working with school bands and programs with school bands. After he finished his bachelor's degree, he went and taught for one year in the public schools in Manhattan, Kansas, and served as the assistant director of bands there. He went back to get his master's and was subsequently hired as an assistant director of bands at Kansas State University. **Avocations:** Reading; Playing golf; Music; Architectural design **Political Affiliations:** Democrat

Tony C. Merry

Title: Owner **Industry:** Law and Legal Services **Company Name:** Law Offices of Tony C. Merry LLC **Date of Birth:** 10/16/1951 **Place of Birth:** Dell Rapids **State/Country of Origin:** SD/USA **Parents:** Howard Jerome Merry; Reda May (Schuldt) Merry **Marital Status:** Married **Spouse Name:** Margaret Ann Gizzi (5/27/1997) **Children:** Megan Elizabeth; Tony Antonopolous **Education:** JD, Harvard University, Cum Laude (1989); BA, Sioux Falls College (1973) **Career:** Law Offices of Tony C. Merry LLC (2006-Present); Partner, McCarthy, Palmer, Volkema, Boyd and Thomas (1995-2006); Private Practice, Blacklick, OH (1994-1995); Partner, The Benefits Department Law Firm, Pittsburgh, PA (1993-1994); Associate, Vorys, Sater, Seymour And Pease, Columbus, OH (1989-1993); Chief of Staff to Governor of South Dakota, State of South Dakota, Pierre, SD (1983-1987); Commissioner, State Planning Agency, State South Dakota, Pierre, SD (1981-1983); Deputy State Auditor, State South Dakota, Pierre, SD (1979-1981); Assistant Executive Director, South Dakota Municipal League, Pierre, SD (1975-1979); Elementary Music Teacher, Beresford Public Schools (1973-1975) **Career Related:** Lecturer, Duquesne University Benefits Institute, Pittsburgh, PA (1994) **Civic:** City Commissioner, City of Pierre, South Dakota (1980-1982); Volunteer, Mediator, Federal Court of Columbus, Ohio; Church Organist **Memberships:** American Bar Association; Association of Trial Lawyers of America; Columbus Bar Association; Ohio State Bar Association; Federal Bar Association **Bar Admissions:** U.S. Court of Appeals for the Sixth Circuit (1991); State of Ohio (1989); U.S. District Court, Southern District, State of Ohio (1989) **Marquis Who's Who Honors:** Albert Nelson Marquis Lifetime Achievement Award; Marquis Who's Who Top Professional; Marquis Who's Who Humanitarian Award **Why did you become involved in your profession or industry:** When Mr. Merry graduated from college, he taught school for awhile and then got involved working in the South Dakota state government. He had worked directly for the South Dakota State governor from 1978 to 1986, eventually working his way up to the chief of staff. Most of the people around the governor were lawyers, but he was not. The governor strongly encouraged him to go to law school, so he enrolled. **Avocations:** Music; Golf; Reading; Organ **Political Affiliations:** Republican **Religion:** Methodist

Maggie Cole Messina

Title: 1) Owner, Master Instructor 2) Founder **Industry:** Athletics **Company Name:** Taecole Tae Kwon Do and Fitness Inc. **Place of Birth:** Nyack **State/Country of Origin:** NY **Marital Status:** Married **Spouse Name:** Raymond Messina **Children:** Brandon **Certifications:** Certified, International Taekwon-Do Federation (2011); CDA National Credentials (2011); CPR Certified; Certified, Life Guard; Certified, Epipen; American Black Belt Certified; KATU-ITF U-ITF-ABBF Certified; Certified International (#A-17-Class A) Master Instructor; Certified International **Career:** Owner, Master Instructor, TaeCole Tae Kwon Do & Fitness Inc, New York (1997-Present); Project Coordinator, PACs Team, Memorial Sloan Kettering Cancer Center (1987-2001); Founder, President, Swerv.change Inc. **Career Related:** Taekwondo Director, Hampton Elementary, Mineola, NY (2017); Taekwondo Director, Jackson Elementary, New Hyde Park, NY (2017); Ranked First Twice, World Karate Commission, USA Team, Traditional Forms (2015); Director, Temple Sinai Nursery School Martial Arts Program (2014); Master Instructor, Buckley Day School After School Martial Arts Program (2013); Host, Long Island Martial Arts Winter Open (2012); Personal Fitness Merit Badge Counselor, Boy Scouts of America (2011); Regional Director, New York and New Jersey, International Taekwon-Do Federation (2007); Master Instructor, Beth Shalom Early Childhood Programs, East Hills, NY; Master Instructor, JCC of East Hill Martial Arts Programs; Director, TaeCole Tae Kwon Do; Fitness House Call Network; Master Instructor, JCC/Searingtown After School Tae Kwon Do Program; Master Instructor, Shelter Rock Early Childhood Programs; Master Instructor, Herricks Schools Community Center Martial Arts Program; Solo Fitness Instructor, Lennox Hill Fitness NYC **Civic:** Founder, Female Fighters Matter 2 (2018); Founder, SWERV.CHANGE (2018); Mineola Chamber of Commerce; Roslyn Chamber of Commerce; Volunteer, Girls, Inc.; Volunteer, Isaacs Park and Recreation **Creative Works:** Author, Memoir, Making Maggie "Little Miss Tri-County" (2011) **Awards:** Named, One of the Most Powerful Business Women (2019); Best Martial Arts School, Long Island, NY (2017-2019); Gold Medalist, 2018 United States Martial Arts Team, World Karate Kickboxing Commission, Dublin, Ireland (2018); Women of High Honors Distinction Award (2017); Best Martial Arts Business, Long Island, NY (2016, 2017); Gold Medalist, Team USA, Traditional Forms (2015); World Champion, Women's Lightweight BB Fighting, North American Sport Karate Association (2015); World Champion, BB Tradition, Creative Forms, North American Sport Karate Association (2015); Inductee, Twin Towers Hall of Fame (2014); ISKA Forms Champion (2014); World Champion Women's Forms, North American Sport Karate Association (2014); Inductee, Martial Arts Hall of Fame (2012); Hall of Fame Golden Warrior Lifetime Achievement Award (2010); New York State Champion, Woman's Black Belt Fighting (2008); Woman's Grand World Champion in Fighting (2008); World Champion, Forms & Sparring, Woman's Grand World Champion in Fighting (2006); New York State Champion, Open and Traditional Forms, Fighting (2004-2006); Instructor of the Year, Buzz Martial Arts, LLC (2004); Best Adult Black Belt of the Year, Woman's Grand World Champion in Fighting (2003, 2001); National Champion (1991); Special Congressional Recognition Award, United States of America; New York States Assembly Certificate of Merit; Awarded for Giving Tirelessly and Endlessly to the State of New York, Senator Joseph P. Addabbo, Jr. **To what do you attribute your success:** Ms. Messina attributes her success to her tenacity and her fighting spirit. She also credits her perseverance in not letting anyone keep her down, which was a driving force in her success. **Why did you become involved in your profession or industry:** Growing up, Ms. Messina was in the foster care system and, at times, unfortunately, was homeless. She believes that her fighting spirit originated during the darker times of her life. When she graduated high school, Ms. Messina began searching for a purpose in life. Her sister-in-law was heavily involved in martial arts; Ms. Messina had always admired her. She decided to begin practicing martial arts and she never stopped. As soon as she started, she knew she had found the purpose she was looking for and more. Ms. Messina quickly discovered that she was born to teach martial arts. Once, when she had just started, one of her instructors promised Ms. Messina that she would be able to teach until she didn't want to anymore. As of today, she has been teaching for over 30 years. **Thoughts on Life:** Ms. Messina believes in finding what fuels oneself and continuing to practice it. She additionally recommends surrounding oneself with positive influences. Anything is possible with hard work and perseverance.

Frances Anthony Meyer, PhD, CHES

Title: Executive Director **Industry:** Education/Educational Services **Company Name:** 1) National Dance Society 2) Society of State Leaders of Health & Physical Education **Date of Birth:** 11/15/1947 **Place of Birth:** Stella **State/Country of Origin:** VA/USA **Parents:** Arthur Abner Anthony, Jr.; Emmie Adeline (Murray) Anthony **Marital Status:** Married **Spouse Name:** Stephen Leroy Meyer (08/02/1975) **Education:** PhD in Educational Leadership and Public Management, Virginia Commonwealth University, Richmond, VA (1996); MS VSU in Physical Education-Elementary and Adaptive Concentration, Virginia Commonwealth University, Richmond, VA (1982); BS in Health, Physical Education, and Driver Education, Longwood College (Now Longwood University), Farmville, VA (1970) **Certifications:** Comprehensive Health Education Specialist (CHES) (1992-Present); Graduate Professional License (1982-2005); Professional License (1970-1982); Cert. teacher Virginia (1970) **Career:** Educational Consultant, Fredericksburg, VA (2003-2015); Specialist, Comprehensive School Health Program, Virginia Department of Education, Richmond, VA (1994-2003); Specialist, Health Education, Virginia Department of Education, Richmond, VA (1990-1994); Coordinator, AIDS Education, Virginia Department of Education, Richmond, VA (1989-1990); Teacher, Health, Physical Education, and Dance, Fredericksburg City Public Schools, Virginia (1970-1989) **Career Related:** The National Public Health Leadership Institute (2001); Review Board, National Commission for Health Education and Credentialing, Inc., Conference and Professional Development Review (1996-2000); Executive Director, National Dance Society; Executive Director, Society of State Leaders of Health & Physical Education **Civic:** Virginia Heart Disease & Stroke Alliance (2008-Present); American Heart Association (2004-Present); Health Committee, Virginia Healthy Pathways Coalition (2004-2008); Mentor, Public Health Leadership Institute (2001); Board of Directors, Virginia HIV/AIDS Network, American Red Cross (1997-2001); Virginia Alliance Adolescents and School Health (1990-2004); Director, Virginia Children's Dance Festival (1981-1996); Volunteer, American Red Cross, Fredericksburg, VA (1976-1984); Comprehensive School Health Education Team; Public Health Education Council; Virginia Affiliate, American Cancer Society; Central Steering Committee **Creative Works:** Author, Editor, "Implementing the National Dance Education Standards" (2010); Author, Editor, "Dance Education: What is it? Why is it Important?" (2002); Co-Author, "Elementary Physical Education: Growing Through Movement — A Curriculum Guide" (1982); Contributor, Articles, Professional Journals; Editor, Manuscripts **Awards:** Professionals Who Make a Difference Award, College of Education & Human Services, Longwood University, Farmville, VA (2006); Virginia Coordinated School Health Leadership Fellow (2006); Distinguished Leadership in Physical Education Award, National Association for Sport and Physical Education (2004); Youth Education award for Leadership in the Healthy Development of Children, American Cancer Society (2002); Alumni Community Service Award, Virginia Commonwealth University, Richmond, VA (1998); Governor's Award for Substance Abuse Prevention, Office of the Governor, State of Virginia (1996-1997); Service Award, VAHPERD (1982, 1984, 1987); Virginia's Outstanding Elementary Physical Education Teacher of the Year Award, VAHPERD (1983) **Memberships:** International Association of Dance Medicine Science (IADMS) (2015-Present); Dance and Child International (2000-Present); International Council for Health, Physical Education, Recreation, Sport & Dance (1994-Present); Association for Middle Level Education (1988-Present); Delta Kappa Gamma Society International (1979-Present); Strategic Planning Committee, AAPHERD (2002-2004); Board of Directors, Longwood College Alumni Council (1987-1990); Life Member, American School Health Association; National Education Association; Society of Health and Physical Educators; Society of State Leaders for Health & Physical Education; National Dance Association; ASCD; SHAPE America; Virginia Association for Health, Physical Education, Recreation, and Dance (VAHPERD); International Alliance for Health, Physical Education, Dance & Sport **Marquis Who's Who Honors:** Albert Nelson Marquis Lifetime Achievement Award **Why did you become involved in your profession or industry:** Dr. Meyers knew since the fifth grade that she wanted to be a teacher. While she faced some initial discouragement, she knew she had made the right decision when she pursued health education. **Avocations:** Travel; Dance; Swimming; Reading; Theatrical performances; Working out at the gym **Political Affiliations:** Independent

Robert Eugene Meyer

Title: Owner **Industry:** Business Management/Business Services **Company Name:** R.E. Meyer & Associates **Date of Birth:** 09/28/1929 **Place of Birth:** Fairmont **State/Country of Origin:** MN/USA **Parents:** William Carl Henry Meyer; Meta Anna (Kramer) Meyer **Marital Status:** Married **Spouse Name:** Angeline Esther Schwarz, (05/31/1953) **Children:** Robert Jon; Russell William **Education:** BS, BME, University of Minnesota (1954) **Certifications:** Registered Professional Engineer, Minnesota **Career:** Owner, R.E. Meyer & Associates, Edina, MN (1995-Present); Vice President, Quality Assurance and Regulatory Affairs, Cascade Medical, Inc., Eden Prairie, MN (1989-1995); Director, Quality Assurance and Regulatory Affairs, Garid, Inc., Eden Prairie, MN (1986-1989); Director, Quality Assurance, Dahlberg, Inc., Golden Valley, MN (1982-1986); Manager, Quality Assurance, Maico, Inc., Edina, MN (1977-1982); Principal, R.E. Meyer & Associates, Edina, MN (1972-1977); Program Manager, Control Data Corp., Bloomington, MN (1971-1972); Manager, Quality Assurance System, Government System Division, Control Data Corp., Bloomington, MN (1968-1970); Configuration Manager, Univac, St. Paul, MN (1966-1968); Program Manager, Defense System Division, Univac, St. Paul, MN (1964-1966) **Career Related:** Consultant, Bayer & MacElrath, Detroit, MI (1975); President, Institute for Basic Church Management, Minneapolis, MN (1973-1976); Presenter in Field **Civic:** Member, Quality Advisory Board, St. Cloud State University (1993-Present); Senior Examiner, Minnesota Council for Quality, Bloomington (1993-Present) **Military Service:** U.S. Army (1947-1949) **Creative Works:** Author, "One Mortal Chance: Don't Blow It"; Contributor, Articles, Professional Publications **Awards:** Top Achievement Award, Section Management Program, American Society for Quality Control (1992) **Memberships:** Board of Directors, American Society for Quality Control (1992-1997); Head Council, Past Chairman, American Society for Quality Control (1992-1994); Chairman, American Society for Quality Control (1991-1992); Senior Vice Chairman, American Society for Quality Control (1990-1991); Vice Chairman, Minnesota Section, American Society for Quality Control (1988-1990); Vice Chairman, Engineers in Industry, Minnesota Chapter, National Society of Professional Engineers (1962) **Marquis Who's Who Honors:** Albert Nelson Marquis Lifetime Achievement Award; Marquis Who's Who Top Professional **Why did you become involved in your profession or industry:** Mr. Meyer became involved in his profession because he was a very logical thinker so he had a good gift of bringing facts together into a continuous improvement mode. He found that engineering best represented that area of interest and he got involved with that in both defense and military manufacture as well as in the health area in his later years. **Avocations:** Jogging; Woodcarving; Painting; Golf; Travel **Religion:** Lutheran

Kevin Richard Michaels

Title: Attorney **Industry:** Law and Legal Services **Company Name:** Law Offices of Kevin Richard Michaels PC **Date of Birth:** 02/09/1960 **Place of Birth:** Buffalo **State/Country of Origin:** NY/USA **Parents:** Richard Ronald Michaels; Marlene Constance (Mnich) Michaels **Marital Status:** Married **Spouse Name:** Beatrice Mary Szeliga (01/15/1983) **Children:** Jaena René **Education:** Doctor of Jurisprudence, South Texas College of Law Houston (1992); Bachelor of Science in Government, University of Houston (1987) **Career:** Attorney, Law Offices of Kevin R. Michaels PC (2000-Present); Senior Associate Attorney, Davis & Shank PC (1997-1999); Associate Attorney, O'Quinn & Laminack PC (1992-1997); Paralegal, O'Quinn, Kerensky, McAninch & Laminack (1988-1992); Court Coordinator, Office of Harris County District Clerk (1985-1988) **Career Related:** Invited Speaker, Presentations, Houston Chapter, American Institute of Graphic Arts; Invited Speaker, Presentations, Services Cooperative Association; Invited Speaker, Presentations, China Symposium, International Trade Center of Houston **Civic:** Attorney, Veteran's Clinics, Katy Bar Association (2012); Chapter Director, Sigma Pi Fraternity, Texas A&M University (2006-2010); Vice President, Fine Arts Council, Houston Christian High School (2005-2006); 12th Grade Representative, Campus Advisory Team, Houston Christian High School (2005-2006); Director, Harris County Municipal Utility District 238 (1989-2003); President, Harris County Municipal Utility District 238 (1989-2003); Third Degree, Memorial Council No. 6527 Knights of Columbus **Military Service:** U.S. Army (1983-1985) **Awards:** Honoree, Top Lawyer in Texas, The Legal Network (2016); Honoree, Top Rated Litigator, American Legal Media and Martindale-Hubbell (2016); Honoree, Top Lawyers, Commercial Litigation, H Texas Magazine (2015); Honoree, Top Professional, H Texas Magazine (2014); Honoree, Top Lawyer in Texas, The Legal Network (2013); Commendation Medal, Oak Leaf Cluster, U.S. Army (1985); Good Conduct Medal, U.S. Army (1985); Commendation Medal, U.S. Army (1984); Honoree, Dean's List, South Texas College of Law Houston; American Jurisprudence Award in Professional Responsibility, South Texas College of Law Houston; Honoree, AV Preeminent Rating, Martindale-Hubbell **Memberships:** Chair, Law Practice Management Committee, Houston Bar Association (2017); Secretary, Law Practice Management Committee, Houston Bar Association (2015); Administration of Justice Committee, Houston Bar Association (2012-2016); Professionalism Committee, Houston Bar Association (2012-2013); Member, The Pro Bono College, State Bar of Texas (2011-2014); Fee Dispute Committee, Houston Bar Association (2003-2007); Texas Governor, New Lawyers Division, American Association for Justice (1994-1997); Texas Mediator Credentialing Association; National Arbitration and Mediation; Texas Bar Foundation **Bar Admissions:** Supreme Court of the United States (2016); United States District Court for the Western District of Texas (2016); United States District Court for the Northern District of Texas (2003); United States District Court for the Eastern District of Texas (2003); United States Court of Appeals for the Fifth Circuit (2002); United States District Court for the Southern District of Texas (1996); State of Texas (1992) **Marquis Who's Who Honors:** Albert Nelson Marquis Lifetime Achievement Award; Marquis Who's Who Top Professional **Why did you become involved in your profession or industry:** While coming of age, Mr. Michaels dreamed of becoming a lawyer. After he completed college and started practicing, he found that he enjoys the area of commercial litigation the most. **Avocations:** Golfing; Camping

Gildo A. Micheletti

Title: Dermatologist **Industry:** Medicine & Health Care **Parents:** Guildo Micheletti; Madeline Micheletti **Marital Status:** Widower **Spouse Name:** Mary Micheletti (Deceased 2016) **Children:** Robert; David **Education:** Resident, Dermatology, Emory University School of Medicine (1974-1977); MD, University of Texas (1973); Intern, Scott and White Memorial Hospital; BA, Rice University **Certifications:** Diplomate, American Board of Dermatology (1977) **Career:** Private Practice, Sterlock Towers; Physician, Head of Dermatology Park Plaza Hospital **Career Related:** Instructor **Civic:** Medical Executive Committee, Park Plaza Hospital **Creative Works:** Contributor, Articles, Journals; Author, Article, International Conference on Aids; Author, Chapter, "Manage Venous Insufficient of the Leg and the Skinned that Accompanied it" **Memberships:** President, Houston Dermatological Society (2009); American Academy of Dermatology **Marquis Who's Who Honors:** Albert Nelson Marquis Lifetime Achievement Award **Why did you become involved in your profession or industry:** Dr. Gildo Micheletti wanted to be a doctor at the age of 7. A family friend, Dr. Dunkin would come into his father's store and would hear his father talk about his grades and Dr. Dunkin requested the Dr. Micheletti go and work with him in the anatomy department. He worked with Dr. Dunkin from the age of 8 until he was 19. His father took him to Rice University to see a football game and he fell in love with the campus and told his father that is were he wanted to go to college, it was the only school he applied to. Dr. Micheletti attended Rice University and was taking child psychiatry, he received very little exposure about dermatology. The only exposure he did receive was when Dr. Orville Stone gave 10 lectures in dermatology in his junior year and he fell in love with dermatology. When he graduated, he did a pre-dermatology internship that he designed himself at Scott Weis Hospital in Temple, Texas, which gave him a view of other specialties that were connected with dermatology. Shortly after, he applied for residency and was accepted at Emory University School of Medicine. **Avocations:** Bridge 55 sectional championships; 13 regional championships

Eric Michrowski

Title: President, Chief Executive Officer **Industry:** Business Management/Business Services **Company Name:** Propulo **Marital Status:** Married **Education:** Licentiate of Laws, University of Ottawa (1996) **Certifications:** Project Management Professional (PMP); Lean Six Sigma Master Black Belt; Deployment Leader **Career:** President, Chief Executive Officer, Propulo Consulting (2013-Present); Chief Executive Officer, Sentis-Americas & Europe (2016-2018); Chief Operating Officer, Head, Sentis-Americas & Europe (2013-2016); Head, Quality & Process Improvement, TELUS (2008-2013); Vice President, Director, Fixed Income Operations, TD Securities (2006-2008); Vice President, Director, Process Improvement, TD Securities (2005-2006); General Manager, Business Process Improvement, CP Ships (now Hapag-Lloyd) (2003-2005); Leadership Portfolios, Safety, Process, Transformational & Organizational Change, Air Canada (1995-2003) **Career Related:** Speaker in Field, National and International Conferences **Memberships:** American Society of Equality **To what do you attribute your success:** Mr. Michrowski attributes his success to hard work, perseverance, and always having the courage to venture into unknown fields. **Why did you become involved in your profession or industry:** Mr. Michrowski's vast experience in different roles at varying organizations provided him with an abundance of useful information to take with him into his leadership roles. His insight into team members and their strengths and weaknesses resulted in his confidence as a chief executive officer.

Ronald Eldon Mickel, PhD

Title: Historian, Educator **Industry:** Education/Educational Services **Date of Birth:** 12/09/1935 **Place of Birth:** Alum Bank **State/Country of Origin:** PA/USA **Parents:** Ralph Andrew Mickel; Lillian A. (Burkett) Mickel **Marital Status:** Married **Spouse Name:** Jane Marie Pederson (08/12/1983); Mary Jean Kukuska (09/05/1965, Divorced 1977) **Children:** Marisa K. Mickel **Education:** Fellowship, National Endowment for the Humanities (NEH) (1976-1977); Postdoctoral Studies, University of California, Berkeley (1966-1967); PhD, Wayne State University (1961); MA, Wayne State University (1958); BA, Eastern Nazarene College, Valedictorian, Summa Cum Laude (1957) **Career:** Professor Emeritus (2003-Present); Coordinator, Network for Excellence in Teaching (1993-2003); Director, University Honors Program, UW-Eau Claire (1983-2003); Professor, UW-Eau Claire (1970-2003); Interim Dean, School of Graduate Studies, UW-Eau Claire (1982-1983); Chair, Department, UW-Eau Claire (1972-1982); Associate Professor, UW-Eau Claire (1965-1970); Assistant Professor of History, UW-Eau Claire (1961-1965) **Career Related:** President, Upper Midwest Honors Council (1991-1992, 1999-2001); Editor, Wisconsin Dialogue (1984-1994); Co-Founder, Wisconsin Association for the Promotion of History; Founder, Wisconsin Collegiate Honors Council (President for Three Years) **Civic:** Member, Board of Directors, Chippewa Valley Museum (2006-2015); Member, Board of Directors, Eau Claire Historic Preservation Foundation (2004-2013) **Awards:** Outstanding University Student in History, Wayne State University (1961) **Memberships:** Member, Board of Governors, Upper Midwest Honors Council (1986-1990, 1992-Present); Board of Directors, Wisconsin Association for Promotion of History (1984-Present); President, Upper Midwest Honors Council (1991-1992); Vice President, Upper Midwest Honors Council (1990-1991); President, Board of Directors, Wisconsin Association for Promotion of History (1986-1987); American Historical Association; Organization American History; American Studies Association; National Collegiate Honors Council Mid-America; American Studies Association; Agricultural History Society; Immigration History Society; Phi Alpha Theta **Marquis Who's Who Honors:** Albert Nelson Marquis Lifetime Achievement Award **Why did you become involved in your profession or industry:** Mr. Mickel became involved in his profession because it was an inspiration from his history professor, Timothy L. Smith, whom he admired very much. It led him to get his master's degree in history before continuing to pursue a law degree and in the end he continued for his PhD and go on to a career in teaching and research. **Avocations:** Gardening; Traveling; Biking; Gourmet cooking; Reading **Political Affiliations:** Democrat

Janet Mae Micklos

Title: County Agency Administrator (Retired); Human Services Director **Industry:** Law and Legal Services **Company Name:** Rockingham County Department of Corrections **Date of Birth:** 07/24/1947 **Place of Birth:** Jacksonville **State/Country of Origin:** FL/USA **Parents:** Thomas Anthony Micklos; Yolanda Mae (Murphy) Micklos **Marital Status:** Widowed **Spouse Name:** Terry Mercer Maisey (05/28/1988, Deceased) **Children:** Ryan W. Satterthwaite; Shawn E. Satterthwaite Hanscom **Education:** Graduate, New Hampshire Part-time Police Officer Academy, New Hampshire Police Standards and Training Council (1995); MA, Webster University, Distinguished Graduate (1985); BA, University of Northern Colorado (1969) **Certifications:** Certified New Hampshire Police Officer (PT) (1995); U.S. Government Security Clearance: SECRET, U.S. Department of State (1983); Teaching Certificate, Grades K-12, State of Colorado (1969) **Career:** Director, Human Services, Rockingham County Department of Corrections, Brentwood, NH (1989-2009); Psychiatric Counselor, Portsmouth Pavilion, NH (1988-1989); Admissions Coordinator, Horizon Hospital, San Antonio, Texas (1988); Director, Alamo Area Rape Crisis Center, San Antonio, Texas (1986-1988); Secretarial Support, United States Logistics Group, Ankara, Turkey (1982-1983); Secretarial Support, Joint United States Military Mission for Aid to Turkey (JUSMMAT), Ankara, Turkey (1981-1982); Director, Physical Department, Victor Valley YMCA, Victorville, CA (1978-1979); Fitness Instructor/Gymnastics Coach, Victor Valley Community College, Apple Valley, CA (1977-1979); Physical Education Teacher, Terrell Wells Middle School, San Antonio, Texas (1969-1970); Public Education **Civic:** Team Leader, Destination Imagination Competitions (2015-Present); Served on Church Mission Trips to Mozambique, Africa (2012-Present); Served on Prison Ministry Team to Regional Youth Detention Centers (2009-Present); Member, New Hampshire Sex Offender Management Advisory Committee (2004-2009); Special Deputy, Rockingham County Sheriff's Department (1995-2000); Police Officer, Newfields Police Department, NH (1995-2000); Trustee, Newfields Community Church (1994-2000); Member, Task Force on Victim Restitution, Rockingham County, NH (1992-2000); Member, Advisory Task Force, New Hampshire Council of Churches (1992); Member, Government's Council on Volunteerism, Seacoast, NH (1990-1993); Chairman, Outreach Commission, First United Methodist Church, Portsmouth, NH (1990-1993) **Memberships:** American Correctional Association (1988-2009); AJA (1988-2009); Life Member, Sigma Kappa Sorority **Marquis Who's Who Honors:** Albert Nelson Marquis Lifetime Achievement Award **To what do you attribute your success:** Mrs. Micklos has always tried to honor her Lord and Savior. Her parents were amazing people with great values. **Why did you become involved in your profession or industry:** With extensive experience as a victim advocate and public educator in the field of sexual assault, the transition to working with offenders meant Mrs. Micklos could bring a grounded understanding to that population. **Avocations:** Gardening; Reading

Lucille Catherine Miera

Title: Artist, Educator, Engineering Draftsman **Industry:** Fine Art **Date of Birth:** 11/25/1931 **Place of Birth:** Socorro **State/Country of Origin:** New Mexico **Parents:** Stephen Maurice Miera; Carmen Rosela (Baca) Miera **Marital Status:** Widowed **Spouse Name:** Vito Modesto Miera Jr. (8/22/1953, Deceased 2004) **Children:** Stephanie Lucille Miera Mansfield; Jennifer Ann Miera Eberhart **Education:** Educational Specialist School Administration, University of New Mexico (1984); MA, University of New Mexico (1976); BA, University of New Mexico (1973); Student, La Romita School of Art, Turin, Italy **Certifications:** Certified Teacher; Administrator, New Mexico; Certified Professional Engineering Draftsman, U.S. Civil Service Commission **Career:** Art Teacher, Art Department Chair, APS (1973-1993); Engineering Draftsman, U.S. Department of Interior, Albuquerque, NM (1957-1959); Typist, Engineering Draftsman, U.S. Army Corps Engineers, Albuquerque, NM (1950-1957); Typist, Albuquerque Abstract & Title (1950); Apprentice Land Surveying And Draftsmen, Stephen M. Miera, Regional Land Surveyor, Albuquerque, NM (1944-1949) **Career Related:** Art Teacher, Board of Directors, Technical Vocational Institute (1997-Present); President, Art Teacher, New Mexico Art League, Albuquerque, NM (1996-1997, 1999); Founder, Art Program, Emeritus Academy, Technical Vocational Institute (1997); Middle School Articulation Representative, Taylor Middle School, Albuquerque, NM 1974-1983); Art Representative, North Central Evaluation Middle School, Albuquerque, NM (1978); Professor Assistant, University of New Mexico, Albuquerque, NM (1974) **Civic:** President, National Area Director, Reserve Officers Association of Ladies, Washington, DC (1989-1991); President, Glenwood Neighborhood Association, Albuquerque, NM (1984-1987); Leader, Campfire USA, Albuquerque, NM (1966, 1980); Treasurer, Manzano Band, Albuquerque, NM (1977); Poll Clerk, Bernalillo County, Albuquerque, NM (1960); Flyer Distributor, Republican Party, Albuquerque, NM (1954); Active, Docent Vietnam Memorial, Albuquerque, NM **Military Service:** Emeritus Area 8 Director, Reserve Officers Association of Ladies, (ROAL) New Mexico, Colorado, Utah, Texas and Arizona, Headquarters in Washington, DC; Past President, ROAL, New Mexico **Creative Works:** Exhibited, University of New Mexico (1969-1976, 1999-2000); Exhibited, Albuquerque Chamber of Commerce (1999); Exhibited, APS Administration Building (1973-1993); Exhibited, Kirtland Air Force Base Officers Club, Albuquerque, NM (1967-1968); Exhibited, Museum of Art, Toledo, OH (1964); Exhibited, New Mexico State Fair Fine Arts Gallery, Hispanic Art Gallery, Scottsdale Village, Old Town Albuquerque Galleries; Juror, "Contemporary Hispanic Art," Santa Fe, NM; Host, International Artists, Monastery, Northern Rome, Italy; Painter, Sketches, Umbrian Hill Towns, Portugal, Spain, Italy, England, Belgium, Budapest, Hungary, Vienna, Austria, Slovakia, Passau, Germany, Aruba, Mexico, Panama, Costa Rica and Canada **Awards:** Ribbon, Mayor Chavez, Fine Arts Booth, Albuquerque, NM (2002); Acknowledgement, Siegfried Hahn; Dedication, Honors Assembly, Taylor Middle School, Albuquerque, NM **Memberships:** President, New Mexico Archdiocesan Council on Catholic Women (1974); Charter Member, National Museum of Women's Art; National Historical Society; Retired Member, New Mexico Association of Educators; New Mexico Watercolor Society; President, New Mexico Reserve Officer Ladies; Epsilon Sigma Alpha; Spouse Member, MOAA and U.S. Army **Marquis Who's Who Honors:** Albert Nelson Marquis Lifetime Achievement Award **To what do you attribute your success:** Whenever Ms. Miera starts to do something, she evaluates the situation, sets a goal, follows a plan of action and tries to complete the project to the best of her ability. **Why did you become involved in your profession or industry:** When Ms. Miera was in grade school, she opened a book to a beautiful picture. She was inspired by it and knew that she had to try to duplicate it. New Mexico's "The Land of Enchantment," known for its beautiful skies, has been an inspiration to her. In 1944, she was 13, but her father became ill and he was a registered land surveyor, so when she arrived home from school, she would go with him and she learned how to do land surveying, note taking and drafting. **Avocations:** Travel; Instructing and displaying art to promote art in the community **Political Affiliations:** Republican **Religion:** Roman Catholic

Joanna Miles

Title: Actress **Industry:** Media & Entertainment **Date of Birth:** 03/06/1940 **Place of Birth:** Nice **State/Country of Origin:** France **Parents:** Johannes Schiefer; Jeanne Miles **Marital Status:** Married **Spouse Name:** Michael Brandman (04/29/1978); William Burns (05/23/1970, Divorced 1977) **Children:** Miles Brandman; Mercedes Brandman **Education:** Diploma, High School, Putney, VT (1958) **Career:** Founder, "The Playwright's Group", Los Angeles, CA (1990-1999); Co-founder, LA Classic Theater (1986) **Civic:** Founder, President, "Children Giving to Children" **Creative Works:** Actor, Play, "Portrait of the Widow Kinski," (2017); Actor, Play, "Anna by Savannah" (2016); Actor, Play, "Front Door Open" (2015); Actor, Play, "Women on Time," (2014); Actor, TV Film, "Hunt for the Labyrinth Killer" (2013); Actor, Play, "Women in Shorts," (2010); Actor, Play, "Chairwoman," (2008); Actor, TV Film, "Thin Ice" (2008); Actor, TV Film, "Grave Misconduct" (2007); Actor, Film, "Sex & Breakfast" (2006); Actor, TV, Film "Judging Amy" (2003); Actor, TV, Film, "Monte Walsh" (2002); Actor, TV, Film, "Crossfire Trail" (1999); Actor, TV, Film, "Thin Air" (1999); Actor, TV, Film "Chicago Hope" (1998); Actor, TV, Film "Nothing Sacred" (1998); Actor, TV Film, "Small Vices" (1998); Actor, Film, "Alone" (1996); Actor, TV Film, "Everything to Gain" (1995); Actor, Play, "Cut Flowers," LA, CA (1994); Actor, Film, "Judge Dredd" (1994); Actor, TV, Film, "The American Clock" (1993); Actor, TV Film, "Cooperstown" (1992); Actor, TV, Film, "Willing to Kill" (1992); Actor, TV Film, "The Habitation of Dragons" (1991); Actor, TV Film, "The Heart of Justice" (1991); Actor, TV Film, "The Water Engine" (1991); Actor, Film, "Rosencrantz and Guildenstern Are Dead" (1991); Actor, TV Episodes, "Star Trek: The Next Generation" (1990-1991); Actor, Play, "Growing Gracefully," LA, CA (1990); Actor, TV Film, "All My Sons" (1987); Actor, TV Film, "The Right to Die" (1987); Actor, Film, "As Is" (1986); Actor, Play, "The Debutante Ball," LA, CA (1985); Actor, TV Film, "The Sound of Murder" (1983); Actor, Film, "Cross Creek" (1983); Actor, TV Film, "Promise of Love" (1982); Actor, TV, Film "Barney Miller" (1980); Actor, TV Film, "Sophisticated Gents" (1979); Actor, TV, "The Incredible Hulk"(1979); Actor, TV Film, "Fire in the Sky" (1978); Actor, TV Film "Kaz" (1978): Actor, TV, Film, "Harvest Home" (1977); Actor, Play, "Kramer" (1977); Actor, Play, "Dancing for the Kaiser," NY (1976); Actor, Film, "Bug" (1975); Actor, Film, "The Ultimate Warrior" (1975); Actor, TV Film, "The Trial of Chaplain Jensen" (1975); Actor, TV Film and Film, "The Glass Menagerie" (1973); Actor, TV Film, "Born Innocent" (1974); Actor, TV Film, "Aloha Means Goodbye" (1974); Actor, Play, "Dylan," New York (1973); Actor, Play, "One Night Stands of a Noisy Passenger," NY (1972); Actor, Film, "The Way We Live Now" (1969); Actor, Play, "Drums in the Night," NY (1968); Actor, Play, "Dracula," NY (1968); Actor, TV Film, "In What America" (1965); Actor, Play, "Home Free," NY (1964); Actor, Play, "Cave Dwellers" (1964); Actor, TV Film, "My Mother's House" (1963); Actor, Play, "Once in a Lifetime" NY (1963); Actor, Play, "One Flew Over the Cuckoo's Nest"; Actor, TV Episodes, "Dallas"; Playwright, Brandman Productions; "Euthanasia"; "A Woman in Reconstruction", "Hostages", "Feathers", "On the Shelf", "Lunch"; Memoir "Mischievous Memories"; Screenwriter, "An Offering of Oranges"; "Breaking the Rules" **Awards:** Edon Award (2015); Vision Award (2003); Dramaloge Award (1996); The Actors Studio Achievement Award (1980); Emmy Award for Outstanding Performance by a Supporting Actress in a Drama (1974); Emmy Award for Supporting Actress of the Year (1974); Women in Radio and TV Award (1974); Nominee, Golden Globe Award (1974) **Memberships:** The Actors Studio NY, NY (1966); Lifetime Member; The Actors Studio LA, CA (1999) Playwrights and Directors Workshop, Academy of Motion Picture Arts and Sciences. **Marquis Who's Who Honors:** Albert Nelson Marquis Lifetime Achievement Award **To what do you attribute your success:** Ms. Miles credits her success on the influence of her education, having attended Putney High School, a progressive boarding school. Likewise, she has drawn a great deal of inspiration from reading books.

Aaron L. Miller

Title: Owner & Manager **Industry:** Business Management/Business Services **Company Name:** ALK Miller Brothers **Marital Status:** Married **Children:** Three sons **Career:** Owner & Manager, ALK Brothers LLC (1979-Present) **Civic:** Volunteer, Omega Nu Sorority **To what do you attribute your success:** Mr. Miller attributes his success to his blood, sweat, and tears. Having a goal and being dedicated to one's goal is something he feels that all people should strive for. **Why did you become involved in your profession or industry:** Mr. Miller grew up on an almond ranch so he was always around it. His goal was to go through high school, and to Fresno State to get a degree in agriculture, but he met the girl of his life while he was in junior college. He never finished junior college because he got married. That meant he had to go to work, so he started farming and it was all around almonds. He was involved with his father at first then he and his wife decided he needed to go out on his own. In 1979 he started his company. The company name are his sons initials. He has done a lot of other types of farming as well, but now they are 100% almonds.

Andrew Pickens Miller

Title: Attorney (Retired) **Industry:** Law and Legal Services **Date of Birth:** 12/21/1932 **Place of Birth:** Fairfax **State/Country of Origin:** VA/USA **Parents:** Francis Pickens Miller; Helen (Hill) Miller **Marital Status:** Married **Spouse Name:** Penelope Farthing (11/18/1990) **Children:** Winfield Scott; Lucia Holcombe; Julia Lane; Andrew Pickens (Deceased 2013); Elise Givhan **Education:** LLB, University of Virginia, Charlottesville, VA (1960); Postgraduate Coursework, New College, University of Oxford, England (1954-1955); AB, Princeton University, New Jersey, Magna Cum Laude (1954) **Career:** Counsel, Hunton Williams LLP (2009-2011); Partner, Powell Goldstein LLP, Washington, DC (2002-2008); Partner, Dickstein, Shapiro, Morin & Oshinsky, LLP, Washington, DC (1979-2002); Partner, Mays, Valentine, Davenport & Moore, Richmond, VA (1977-1978); Attorney General, Commonwealth of Virginia (1970-1977); Partner, Penn, Stuart & Miller, Abingdon, VA (1963-1969); Associate, Penn, Stuart & Stuart (1960-1962) **Career Related:** Executive Committee, Virginia Bar Association (1985-1988); Action Commission to Reduce Court Costs and Delay (1979-1984); Executive Committee, American Judicature Society (1974-1976); Board of Directors, American Judicature Society (1973-1976); Chairman of Antitrust Committee, National Association of Attorneys General (1971-1976); House of Delegates, American Bar Association (1971-1976); Executive Committee, National Association of Attorneys General (1973-1974); Vice Chairman, Southern Conference of Attorneys General (1972-1973); Chairman, Young Lawyers Section, Virginia Bar Association (1967-1968); Fellow, American Bar Foundation; Fellow, Virginia Bar Foundation; Phi Beta Kappa; Omicron Delta Kappa **Civic:** Vice Chairman, Virginia Board of Corrections (1983-1986); Center for Oceans Law and Policy, University of Virginia (1975-1979); Democratic Nominee for the United States Senate from Virginia (1978); Advisory Board, Americans for Effective Law Enforcement (AELE) (1973-1977); Trustee, King College (1966-1974); Chairman, Washington County Democratic Committee (1967-1969); Board of Directors, Barter Foundation (1962-1969); President, Young Democratic Clubs of Virginia (1966-1967) **Military Service:** First Lieutenant, U.S. Army, Republic of Korea (1955-1957) **Awards:** Kelley-Wyman Award, National Association of Attorneys General (NAAG) (1976) **Memberships:** President, Coalition to Preserve an Independent Supreme Court (2019-Present); Vice President, National Maritime Heritage Foundation (2008-2011); Board of Directors, National Maritime Heritage Foundation (2005-2011); Secretary General, Society of the Cincinnati (1995-1998); Virginia Standing Committee, Society of the Cincinnati (1993-1996); Assistant Secretary General, Society of the Cincinnati (1992-1995); Commission on Public Understanding About the Law (1992-1995); Founder and President, John Marshall Foundation (1987-1989); Virginia Standing Committee, Society of the Cincinnati (1986-1989) **Bar Admissions:** District of Columbia (1979); Supreme Court of the United States (1967); Virginia (1960) **Marquis Who's Who Honors:** Albert Nelson Marquis Lifetime Achievement Award; Marquis Who's Who Top Professional **To what do you attribute your success:** Mr. Miller attributes his success to great colleagues, good fortune and hard work. **Why did you become involved in your profession or industry:** Mr. Miller became involved in his profession because of the potential the law has for settling controversies in a civil manner; he believes that, in light of the severe and chronic tensions in American society currently, the need for dedication to the rule of law is even greater than it was when he launched his career. **Avocations:** Baseball; Watching Jeopardy **Political Affiliations:** Independent **Religion:** Presbyterian **Thoughts on Life:** Mr. Miller's mother, Helen (Hill) Miller, was an author and journalist, who was disappointed in his decision to enter law school (but eventually forgave him). At his office, his major services have involved advising corporations and trade associations on the obstacles and opportunities of working with state governments. For example, he is still representing a company that has developed Medicaid-monitoring technology. Millions of dollars are wasted by federal and state governments because Medicaid payments are being made for services not rendered due to provider error or fraud. This technology will detect if the patient's records support the invoice so as to allow regulatory agencies to respond appropriately. That is why he enjoys his practice so much because something new comes up frequently, and he is then faced with a variety of challenges. When these issues arise, he devises appropriate strategies to advance the client's interests. What makes his work interesting, he believes, is the complexity of the governmental matters with which he is presented.

Beverly Miller, RN, MSN, GNP-C, APRN, BC

Title: Geriatric Nurse Practitioner (Retired) **Industry:** Medicine & Health Care **Date of Birth:** 08/01/1942 **Place of Birth:** Memphis **State/Country of Origin:** TN/USA **Parents:** William C. McDonald; Inez (Travis) McDonald **Marital Status:** Married **Spouse Name:** William L. Miller (12/16/1962) **Children:** Travis Andrew; Susan M. Wright; Sean Mark **Education:** Graduate Coursework, Vanderbilt University (1996); MS in Nursing, University of Tennessee (1981); BSN, University of Tennessee (1980); Diploma, Baptist Memorial Hospital (1963) **Certifications:** Certified Geriatric Nurse Practitioner; Clinical Specialist; Health Education Specialist **Career:** Geriatric Nurse Practitioner (Retired), Veterans Affairs Hospital, Memphis, TN (1995-2008); Patient Health Education Coordinator, Veterans Affairs Hospital, Memphis, TN (1988-1995); Clinical Specialist, Staff Development, Veterans Affairs Hospital, Memphis, TN (1988-1989); Clinical Specialist, Veterans Affairs Hospital, Memphis, TN (1986-1988); Staff Nurse, Veterans Affairs Hospital, Memphis, TN (1981-1985) **Career Related:** Presenter, International Nursing Conference **Civic:** Volunteer, Orpheum, Orphan Theater (1995-Present) **Creative Works:** Contributor, Research Articles, Professional Peer-Reviewed Journals **Awards:** Named, Excellent 11 Top Nurses, Shelby and Fayette County; Administrator's Award for Excellence in Nursing; West Tennessee Employee Award for Outstanding Scientific Professional Employee **Memberships:** Board of Directors, Tennessee Nurses Association; Past President, Sigma Theta Tau International Honor Society of Nursing **Marquis Who's Who Honors:** Albert Nelson Marquis Lifetime Achievement Award; Marquis Who's Who Top Professional **Why did you become involved in your profession or industry:** Ms. Miller became involved in her profession because ever since she was a child, she wanted to be a nurse. **Avocations:** Geriatrics; Literacy

Carolyn A. Miller

Title: Nurse Midwife, Educator **Industry:** Medicine & Health Care **Date of Birth:** 05/03/1937 **Place of Birth:** Burlington **State/Country of Origin:** IA/USA **Parents:** Glenn B.; Vivian (Milton) Miller **Marital Status:** Single **Education:** Certified Nurse Midwife, Booth Maternity Hospital, Philadelphia, PA (1977); Master of Arts, Nursing of Children, University of Iowa (1971); State Certified Midwife, Elsie Inglis Maternity Hospital, Edinburgh, Scotland (1966); Bachelor of Science in Nursing, University of Iowa (1962); Diploma, Lutheran Hospital School for Nurses, Moline, IL (1959) **Certifications:** Registered Nurse, Iowa **Career:** Clinical Staff, Certified Nurse Midwife, Maternal Health Center, Bettendorf, IA (1990-Present); Founder, Faculty of Nurse Midwifery Educational Program, Phebe Hospital and School of Nursing, Suakoko (1984-1990); Coordinator of Midwifery Education, Instructor, Frontier Nursing Service, Hyden, KY (1977-1979); Chairman, Division of Nursing, Cuttington University College, Suakoko, Liberia (1971-1976); Supervisor, Midwifery Clinic and Inpatient Department of Obstetrics, Phebe Hospital, Suakoko, Liberia (1966-1969); Founder, Instructor, Supervisor, Midwifery Education Department, Phebe Hospital, Suakoko, Liberia (1966-1969); Instructor, Supervisor of Bachelor of Science in Nursing Students, Cuttington University College, Suakoko, Liberia (1966-1969); Instructor, Supervisor of Practical Nursing, University of Iowa, Iowa City, IA (1962-1964); Staff Nurse, University of Iowa Hospital and Clinics, Iowa City, IA (1959-1962) **Career Related:** Instructor of Continuing Nursing Education, University of Iowa, College of Nursing, Iowa City, IA (1982-1984); Volunteer, Faculty Member, University of Kentucky, College of Nursing, Lexington, KY (1978-1979) **Civic:** Volunteer, Southeast Iowa Synod, Global Health Ministries, Minneapolis, MN (1993-Present); Member, Synod Global Mission Committee Southeast Iowa, Iowa City, IA (1990-1997); Missionary-in-Residence, Evangelical Lutheran Church in America, Chicago, IL (1990); Active Phebe Connection Project, Liberia; Active in Liberian Civil Activism **Awards:** Gratitude for Outstanding Service, Cuttington College Board of Directors, Baltimore (1994); Named, Distinguished Alumnus, Lutheran Hospital School for Nurses, Moline, IA (1990); Recipient, Knight Commander of Liberian Humane Order of African Redemption, President of Liberia William Tolbert Junior (1976) **Memberships:** Member, American College Nurse Midwifery; Sigma Theta Tau **Marquis Who's Who Honors:** Albert Nelson Marquis Lifetime Achievement Award; Marquis Who's Who Top Professional **Avocations:** Reading; Writing **Religion:** Lutheran

Charles E. Miller, MD

Title: Gynecologist **Industry:** Medicine & Health Care **Date of Birth:** 08/18/1953 **Place of Birth:** Iron Mountain **State/Country of Origin:** MI/USA **Parents:** Alfred Miller; Muriel Miller **Marital Status:** Married **Spouse Name:** Laura Miller **Children:** Benjamin; Abagayle; Alec **Education:** MD, Feinberg School of Medicine, Northwestern University (1977); BS in Medicine, Northwestern University (1975) **Certifications:** Diplomate, American Board of Obstetrics and Gynecology, Inc. (1984); Licensed, State of Texas; Licensed, State of Illinois; Licensed, State of New York **Career:** Director, Fellowship in Minimally Invasive Gynecologic Surgery, Advocate Lutheran General Hospital, Park Ridge, IL (2010-Present); Attending Physician, Northwestern Medicine Central DuPage Hospital, Winfield, IL (2010-Present); Director of Minimally Invasive Gynecological Surgery, Lutheran General Hospital, Winfield, IL (2005-Present); President, Medical Director, The Advanced IVF Institute Dr. Charles Miller (2001-Present); Attending Physician, Edward-Elmhurst Health (2000-Present); Physician, St. Alexius Medical Center Hoffman Estates, AMITA Health (1994-Present); Physician, Northwestern Medicine Lake Forest Hospital (1992-Present); Attending Physician, Advocate Lutheran General Hospital (1983-Present); Attending Physician, Northwest Community Healthcare (1995-2005); Medical Director, Center for Minimally Invasive Gynecologic Surgery, Evanston Hospital, Glenbrook Hospital (1997-2001) **Career Related:** Consulting Reproductive Endocrinologist, Hematopoietic Progenitor Cell Transplantation Program, Advocate Lutheran General Hospital (2017-Present); Clinical Associate Professor, Department of Obstetrics and Gynecology, University of Illinois Chicago (1997-Present) **Creative Works:** Advisory Board Member, The Journal of Minimally Invasive Gynecology; Member, Editorial Board, OB/GYN News; Contributor, Numerous Research Projects; Contributor, Book Chapters; Contributor, Articles, Professional Journals **Awards:** Top Doctor, Castle Connolly (2001-Present); John F. Steege Mentorship Award, AAGL (2018); National Faculty Award for Promoting High Standards of Residency Education in the Field of Obstetrics and Gynecology, American College of Obstetricians and Gynecologists (2012); Lifetime Achievement Award, RESOLVE: The National Infertility Association (2005) **Memberships:** Board Member, Fellowship Committee, Society of Reproductive Surgeons (2015-Present); Treasurer, The International Society for Gynecologic Endoscopy (2013-Present); Member, National Advisory Board, Society of Laparoscopic & Robotic Surgeons (2011-Present); Member, National Clinical Advisory Board, RESOLVE: The National Infertility Association (2003-Present); Vice Chair, Reproductive Surgery/Endometriosis Special Interest Group, AAGL (2019-2020); Video Committee Member, American Society for Reproductive Medicine (2017-2020); Board Member, Fellowship in Minimally Invasive Gynecology, AAGL (2013-2015); Board Member, The Global Surgical Consortium (2012-2014); President, International Society for Gynecologic Endoscopy (2011-2013); Chairman, Reproductive Surgery/Endometriosis Special Interest Group, AAGL (2011-2012); Vice Chair, Reproductive Surgery/Endometriosis Special Interest Group, AAGL (2010-2011); Chairman, Advisory Board, International Institute of Minimally Invasive Surgery (2010); Vice President, International Society for Gynecologic Endoscopy (2009-2011); Board Member, Sociedad Argentina Medica de Histeroscopia (2008-2009); Chair, Scientific Program, Global Congress of Minimally Invasive Gynecology, 36th Annual Meeting, AAGL, Washington, DC (2007) **Marquis Who's Who Honors:** Albert Nelson Marquis Lifetime Achievement Award **Why did you become involved in your profession or industry:** Dr. Miller became involved in his profession because of his desire to help others on their journey to create a family.

Linda Karen Miller, EdD

Title: Educator (Retired) **Industry:** Education/Educational Services **Date of Birth:** 01/22/1948 **Place of Birth:** Kansas City **State/Country of Origin:** KS/USA **Parents:** Bennie Chris Miller; Thelma Jane (Richey) Miller **Marital Status:** Single **Education:** Doctor of Education, University of Virginia (1991); Master of Education in Secondary Education, University of Virginia (1978); Bachelor of Science in Secondary Education, University of Kansas (1970) **Certifications:** Education, Environment and Interpretation, University of Nevada, Las Vegas (2009) **Career:** Instructor, Department of Education, College of Southern Nevada (2003-2010); Social Studies Teacher, Fairfax High School (1978-2002); Social Studies Teacher, Herndon Middle School (1975-1978); Social Studies Teacher, Mark Twain Middle School (1974-1975); Reading Aide, Lake Braddock Secondary School, Fairfax County Public Schools (1973-1974); Substitute Teacher, Fairfax County Public Schools (1972-1973); Social Studies Teacher, Pierson Junior High School (1970-1972); Teacher, Turner Unified Schools, Kansas City, KS **Career Related:** Delegate to Turkey, People to People International (2010); Delegate to Egypt, People to People International (2007); Delegate to China, People to People International (2005); Delegated Consultant in Field **Civic:** Board of Directors, East-West Center, University of Hawaii at Manoa (2016-Present); Historical Interpreter, Helen J. Stewart, First Lady of Las Vegas (2004-Present); President, Southern Nevada Peace Corps Association (2009-2010); President, Nevada Women's History Project (2008-2009); Nevada Coordinator, National Council for History Education (2005-2010); Various Offices, 15 Genealogical Societies **Creative Works:** Author, "USS Nevada BB36" (2017); Author, Book, "Early Las Vegas," Arcadia Publishing (2013); Author, Book, "Put a Little Acting Into Your Teaching," National Social Science Association (2006) **Awards:** History Award, National Society US Daughters of 1812 (2017); Historic Preservation Medal, National Society Daughters of the American Revolution (2016); Diversity Award, College of Southern Nevada (2009); Woman of Excellence Award, College of Southern Nevada (2009); Outstanding Leadership, People to People International (2009); Asia-Pacific Islander Award, College of Southern Nevada (2008); Fellow, The Korea Society (2004); National Peace Educator, National Peace Corps Association (2002); World History Teaching Prize, The World History Association (2002); American Revolution Fellow, New-York Historical Society (2001); Fellow, The Korea Society (2000); Teacher of the Year, Global Teachnet (1999); Teacher of the Year, Virginia Geographical Society (1999); Excellence in Teaching Award, School of Education, The University of Kansas (1999); Celebrating Teaching Excellence Award, The American Council of Teachers of Russian (1998); Honoree, Outstanding Secondary Teacher, Virginia Historical Society (1998); George Washington Medal, Freedoms Foundation at Valley Forge (1998); Secondary Teacher of the Year, University of Virginia (1997); Secondary Teacher of the Year, National Council for the Social Studies (1996); Pre-Collegiate Teacher of the Year, The Organization of American Historians (1996); Teacher Historian, U.S. Capitol Historical Association (1986) **Memberships:** University of Virginia Alumni Association; University of Kansas Alumni Association; National Society Daughters of the American Revolution (NSDAR); National Society US Daughters of 1812; National Society Colonial Dames XVII Century; Daughters of Union Veterans of the Civil War; Ladies of the Grand Army of the Republic; National Society Magna Charta Dames and Barons; Continental Society Daughters of Indian Wars, Inc.; National Society Daughters of Colonial Wars; The National Society of the Dames of the Court of Honor; National Society Daughters of the American Colonists; League of Women Voters of Las Vegas Valley; East West Center, University of Hawai'i CTAPS Alumni **Marquis Who's Who Honors:** Albert Nelson Marquis Lifetime Achievement Award; Marquis Who's Who Top Professional **To what do you attribute your success:** Dr. Miller attributes her success to her parents, who took her to historical places since she was 7 years old. She also drew inspiration from her high school history teacher, Mrs. Zimmerman, who ignited her love for history. **Why did you become involved in your profession or industry:** Dr. Miller became involved in her profession because her teachers, Mr. Toothaker and Mrs. Zimmerman, instilled within her a love for history. **Avocations:** Doll collecting **Political Affiliations:** Republican **Religion:** Episcopalian

Ronald H. Miller, PhD

Title: President **Industry:** Business Management/Business Services **Company Name:** Ronald H. Miller, PhD, LLC **Date of Birth:** 03/13/1948 **Place of Birth:** Saint Louis **State/Country of Origin:** MO/USA **Parents:** Ilion Louis Miller (Deceased); Joyce Gloria Rimerman (Deceased) **Marital Status:** Single **Children:** Nathan Joel Samuel Miller **Education:** MA, Teaching, Lindenwood University, Saint Charles, MO (2007); PhD, Public Administration, New York University (1990); MPP, Public Policy Studies, University of Michigan (1978); MCP, City & Regional Planning, The Ohio State University (1972); BA, Journalism, Indiana University (1970) **Certifications:** Certified Teacher, K-12 Vocal Music Education, State of Missouri; Certified, 9th-12th Grade Social Sciences, State of Missouri **Career:** President, Ronald H. Miller, PhD, LLC **Civic:** Treasurer, Lilian Circle Neighborhood Development Association **Creative Works:** Author or Editor, 40 Publications; Presenter, More than 35 Events **Awards:** Newcomer Award, MAACCE (1997) **Memberships:** Phi Eta Sigma (1967) **Marquis Who's Who Honors:** Albert Nelson Marquis Lifetime Achievement Award; Marquis Who's Who Top Professional; Marquis Who's Who Humanitarian Award **To what do you attribute your success:** Dr. Miller attributes his success to his knowledge in the sectors of the education and the tax preparation fields **Why did you become involved in your profession or industry:** Dr. Miller became involved in his profession because of his interest and background in education and tax preparation **Avocations:** Singing in church choirs, Jewish temples, and community choirs; Watching Major League Baseball; Watching college basketball

Stephen Ralph Miller, JD

Title: Lawyer **Industry:** Law and Legal Services **Company Name:** McDermott Will & Emery **Date of Birth:** 11/28/1950 **Place of Birth:** Chicago **State/Country of Origin:** IL/USA **Parents:** Ralph Miller; Karin Ann (Olson) Miller **Marital Status:** Divorced **Spouse Name:** Sheila L. Krysiak (02/02/1998) **Children:** David Williams; Lindsay Christine **Education:** JD, Cornell University (1975); BA, Yale University, Cum Laude (1972) **Career:** Counsel, McDermott Will & Emery (2006-2011); Equity Partner, McDermott Will & Emery (1986-2006); Management Committee Member, McDermott Will & Emery (1992-1995); Income Partner, McDermott Will & Emery (1981-1985); Associate, McDermott Will & Emery (1975-1980) **Career Related:** Member, Special Task Force on Post-Employment Benefits, Financial Accounting Standards Board, Norwalk, CT (1987-1991) **Civic:** Member, The Chicago Council on Global Affairs (1978-Present); Member, President's Circle Steering Committee, The Chicago Council on Foreign Relations (2005-2009); Member, Seabury Council (2004-2007); Chancellor, Bexley Seabury Seminary, Evanston, IL (2004-2005); Member, External Relations Committee, The Chicago on Council Foreign Relations (2002-2003); Chair, Trusteeship Committee, Bexley Seabury Seminary, Evanston, IL (2000-2002); Chair, Development Committee, The Chicago Council on Foreign Relations (1999-2002); Development Committee Member, The Chicago Council on Foreign Relations (1997-2002); Trustee, Bexley Seabury Seminary, Evanston, IL (1994-2002); Police and Firefighters' Pension Board of Trustees, Wilmette, IL (1992-1998); Chancellor, Bexley Seabury Seminary, Evanston, IL (1996-1997) **Creative Works:** Contributor, Articles, Professional Journals **Awards:** Honoree, Illinois Super Lawyers (2010-Present) **Memberships:** Board of Directors, Center for Companies That Care (2011-Present); Nordic Law Club of Chicago; Worldwide Employee Benefits Network; 100 Club of Chicago; Cornell Club of Chicago; Lawyers Club of Chicago; Yale Club of Chicago; Illinois State Bar Association; American Bar Association; Associate, Chicago Bar Association **Bar Admissions:** Illinois State Bar Association **Marquis Who's Who Honors:** Albert Nelson Marquis Lifetime Achievement Award; Marquis Who's Who Top Professional **Why did you become involved in your profession or industry:** Mr. Miller became involved in his profession because of his innate desire to pursue a career in public service. Additionally, he was inspired by his father, who was also an attorney. **Avocations:** Sailing; Water skiing; Cross-country skiing; Walking

Charles Blanchard Millham, PhD

Title: Mathematician, Environmental Scientist, Educator, Consultant **Industry:** Education/Educational Services **Date of Birth:** 11/01/1936 **Place of Birth:** Liberal **State/Country of Origin:** KS/USA **Parents:** Charles B. Millham; Abbie Estella (Lowrance) Millham; **Marital Status:** Married **Spouse Name:** Bonnie May Miller; **Children:** Michael B. Millham; Stacy S. Dayley (Stepchild); Orion Cassetto (Stepchild); Angela Sperandio (Stepchild, Deceased) **Education:** PhD in Economics, Iowa State University (1962); MS in Mathematics, Iowa State University (1961);BA in Foreign Trade and Service, Iowa State University (1958); Student, Carleton College (1954-1956) **Career:** Professional Consultant, Professor (1974-2001); Associate Professor, Washington State University, Pullman, WA (1969-1974); Assistant Professor, Washington State University, Pullman, WA (1966-1969); Assistant Professor, Iowa State University (1964-1966); Instructor of Mathematics, Iowa State University (1962-1964); Former Chairman, Environmental Science and Regional Planning **Career Related:** Acting Chair, Computer Science, Washington State University; Chair, Environmental Science and Regional Planning, Washington State University; Numerous Campus-Wide and Departmental Committees **Creative Works:** Co-Author, "Mathematics and Statistics for Economists" (1969, 1970); Contributor, Articles, Professional Journals; Contributor, Chapters, Book **Awards:** Charles "Chuck" Millham Endowed Scholarship in Mathematics, Department of Mathematics, Washington State University, Endowed by Mr. Mrs. Chris Carlson (2012); Fulbright Grant, University of Jordan, Amman (1976-1977); Citation Award, Royal Scientific Society of Jordan **Memberships:** Founding Member, Past President, Association of Research Professors, Washington State University; Association for Computing Machinery; Past Member, American Economic Association; Institute for Operations Research and Management Science; Past Member, Mathematics Programming Society; Society for Industrial and Applied Mathematics (SIAM) **Marquis Who's Who Honors:** Albert Nelson Marquis Lifetime Achievement Award; Marquis Who's Who Top Professional; Marquis Who's Who Humanitarian Award **To what do you attribute your success:** Dr. Millham attributes his success to hard work, dedication, and long hours. **Why did you become involved in your profession or industry:** Dr. Millham became involved in his profession because the high school he attended, a the time, had a very poor curriculum in mathematics and sciences and he went to college at a very selective small school. He did very poorly in math the first time he took it and his professor said he would pass him if he promised he would never take anymore mathematics. He took the deal and he spent some number years trying to prove to himself that he really could do mathematics and that led to one thing to another, He had a undergraduate minor in mathematics then early in his graduate education he decided he would get a master's in mathematics and he succeeded. For a long time he tried to prove to himself that he could do something for which he had no high school background, competing with students who did. **Avocations:** Military and intelligence history; Black-powder firearms; Camping; Repairing antique outboard motors; Writing a new book titled "A River Boyhood" **Political Affiliations:** Independent **Religion:** Roman Catholic **Thoughts on Life:** Dr. Millham said, "Pass up no chance to contribute. Maintain your integrity and honesty. Get as much education as you can, then work as hard as you can. Nothing worth doing is ever easy. Value the accomplishments of others, and congratulate them. Seek advice from those much older and more experienced. When giving a talk, practice giving it numerous times until it is all but memorized. Be gracious to everyone. If a student disagrees with you in class, consider it carefully: the student may be right."

John David Minor

Title: Physician **Industry:** Medicine & Health Care **Date of Birth:** 02/19/1943 **State/Country of Origin:** WA/USA **Parents:** Harold Lee; Lusia (Teetz) Minor **Marital Status:** Married **Spouse Name:** Susan W. Withers Minor (06/10/1972) **Children:** David (Deceased); Kevin **Education:** Chief Resident in Pediatrics, University of Florida (1970); Resident, Pediatrics, College of Medicine, University of Florida, Gainesville, FL (1968-1970); Intern, College of Medicine, University of Florida, Gainesville, FL (1967); Doctor of Medicine, University of Tennessee Health Science Center (1963-1966); Pre-medical Coursework, University of Florida (1960-1963) **Certifications:** Diplomate, American Board of Allergy and Immunology; Diplomate, American Board of Pediatrics **Career:** Retired (2009); Clinical Assistant Professor Medicine Division Immunology, Allergy and Rheumatology, Oregon Health & Science University Hospital, Portland, OR (1979-2009); Private Practice, Medicine Specializing in Allergy, Eugene, OR (1974-2009); Medical Director, Camp Asthmatic Children, Oregon Lung Association (1975-1990); Research Fellow, Allergy & Immunology, University of California-San Francisco (1972-1974); Staff Member, McKenzie-Willamette Hospital, Springfield, OR; Member, Staff, Sacred Heart Hospital **Career Related:** Trustee, Oregon Medical Association (1991-1996); President, Lane County Medical Society (1990-1991); Delegate, Oregon Medical Association (1989-1990); President, Lane Individual Practice Association (1989-1990); Trustee, Oregon Medical Association (1987-1989); President, Oregon Society of Allergy, Asthma and Immunology (1984-1986); Member, Citizens Advisory Committee, Lane Regional Air Protection Agency (1980-1988); Medical Adviser, Lane Community College, Eugene, OR (1974) **Military Service:** Major, U.S. Air Force (1970-1972); Chief of Pediatrics Homestead Air Force TAC Base (Homestead ARB), Miami–Dade County, FL **Creative Works:** Author, UCLA Paper, "Antagonism of experimentally induced bronco-constriction by chronically impressed electric current," American Physiology Society, UCLA 17th Meeting (1965) **Awards:** Humanitarian Award, Oregon Lung Association (1990); Service to Camp Christmas Seal (1973-1990); Wildlife Photography, PrintDivision Everglades National Park, Homestead **Memberships:** President, Oregon Society of Allergy, Asthma and Immunology (1984-1986); Fellow, American Academy of Pediatrics; American Academy of Allergy & Immunology; Alpha Omega Alpha; Alpha Epsilon Delta **Marquis Who's Who Honors:** Albert Nelson Marquis Lifetime Achievement Award **To what do you attribute your success:** Dr. Minor credits his success on the love and support of his parents, as well as his wife. **Why did you become involved in your profession or industry:** Dr. Minor became involved in his profession because of his lifelong interest in science. By the time he graduated from high school, he had resolved to enter the field of medicine, specializing in pediatrics. **Avocations:** Heli-skiing; Former motorcycle rider; History; Backpacking; River rafting; Traveling; Former guitar player **Political Affiliations:** Republican

Alan Huntress Minter, JD

Title: Lawyer **Industry:** Law and Legal Services **Date of Birth:** 02/21/1939 **Place of Birth:** San Antonio **State/Country of Origin:** TX/USA **Parents:** Dr. Merton Melrose Minter; Katherine Logan Huntress **Marital Status:** Married **Spouse Name:** Patricia West Minter (05/31/1964) **Children:** Katherine Ruth Minter Cary; Patricia West Minter Bland **Education:** JD, University of Texas (1965); BA, University of Texas (1962); Coursework, Brown University (1957-1959); Preparatory School, Phillips Exeter Academy (1953-1957) **Career:** Private practice, Austin, TX (1971-Present); Assistant Attorney, Attorney General's Office, State of Texas, Austin, TX (1965-1971) **Civic:** Member, Exeter Alumni Counsel (1989-Present); Class President, 50th Year Reunion, Phillips Exeter Academy (2007); Treasurer, Winedale Historical Center, University of Texas (1984-1985); Board of Directors, Texas Historic Foundation (1983-1985); Member, Steering Committee, Texas Heritage Council Board (1983-1985); Chairman, City Austin Texas Library Commission (1981-1984); Vice-chairman, City Austin Texas Library Commission (1980-1981); Trustee, Elisabet Ney Museum Association (1980-1981); Member, Advisory Council, Winedale Historical Center, University of Texas (1978-1987); Board of Directors, Les Patrons Paramount Theatre Performing Arts (1978-1982); Vice President, Education, Texas Historical Foundation (1978-1980); 2nd Vice President, Austin Heritage Society (1978-1979); Member, Steering Committee, Texas Historical Foundation (1977-1983); Trustee, Austin Natural Science Assoc Board (1977-1980); Co-chairman, Properties Committee, Austin Heritage Society (1976-1977); Chairman, Properties Committee, Austin Heritage Society (1975-1976); Board of Directors, Austin Heritage Society (1974-1981); Board of Directors, St. Andrew's Episcopal School, Austin, TX (1973-1976); Member, Ad Hoc Historical Zoning Committee, City of Austin (1973); Member, Citizen Advisory Committee, Texas Constitutional Revision Committee (1973); Board of Directors, Young Man's Business League, Austin, TX (1972); Member, National Advisory Committee, Deganawidah Quetzalcoatl University, Davis, CA; Member, History Aviation Collection, University of Texas **Creative Works:** Author, "The Tigua Indians of the Pueblo de Ysleta del Sur," Volume XLV, West Texas Historical Association Year Book (1969); Author, "Preserving Your Historical Legislation," Texas Historical Commission Reference Series **Awards:** Self Storage Hall of Fame (2006); Award of Excellence, American Indian Law Section of the State Bar of Texas (2005); Appointed by United States President, U.S. Associate Government Appeal Agent Certificate of Appreciation (1971) **Memberships:** Chair, Travis County Senior Law Section (2004-2007); Board of Directors, Bankruptcy Law Section, Travis County Bar Association (2001-2004); Board of Directors, Estate Planning and Probate Law Section, Travis County Bar Association (1995-1996); Board of Directors, Chairman, Estate Planning and Probate Law Section, Travis County Bar Association (1994-2001); Vice Chairman, American Bar Association (1981-1985); Fellow, Texas Bar Foundation; State Bar of Texas; Texas Old Forts and Missions Restoration Association; Old Trail Drivers Association Texas; State Association Texas Pioneers; Sons Republic Texas; Order Alamo; Order Sons Hermann State Texas; German Club; Phi Alpha Delta; Historical Preservation and Easement Committee Real Property, Probate and Trust Law Section, American Bar Association; Associate, Sheriff's Association Texas **Bar Admissions:** Texas; Supreme Court of the United States; U.S. Tax Court; U.S. Court of Claims; U.S. Court of Military Appeals; U.S. Court of Customs and Patent Appeals; United States Court of Appeals for the Fifth Circuit; United States District Court for the Western District of Texas; United States District Court for the Northern District of Texas; United States District Court for the Eastern District of Texas; United States District Court for the Southern District of Texas **Marquis Who's Who Honors:** Albert Nelson Marquis Lifetime Achievement Award; Marquis Who's Who Top Professional; Marquis Who's Who Humanitarian Award **Why did you become involved in your profession or industry:** Mr. Minter was suppose to be a doctor and headed to medical school. He attended an event with his father and the Dean of the law school was there, explained to the dean that he had no business background and that he had only taken science courses, he asked could he attend summer law school for something other than science, the dean said yes all your need to know, is land, contract, and consumer protection. He attended law school for the summer. Mr. Minter attended MD Anderson in Houston, because his dad was a doctor, Dr. Merton Mintor, he helped found MD Anderson when he was chairman of the board of Regents, So Mr. Minter got to attend MD Anderson with VIP treatment, got in to a special program and started his career. He worked for the Attorney General Office and he spent his time learning and after he left he opened his own practice. **Avocations:** Hunting; Fishing; Travel; Reading; Writing **Religion:** Episcopalian

William C. Mirams

Title: Construction Executive **Industry:** Architecture & Construction **Company Name:** Marinita Development Company **Date of Birth:** 04/24/1934 **Place of Birth:** Alhambra **State/Country of Origin:** CA/USA **Parents:** William Roy Mirams; Mary Louise Clarke **Marital Status:** Married **Spouse Name:** Lisa Ann Richmond (12/05/1969); Judith Ann Hamilton (02/20/1956-1961) **Children:** Deborah; Sheryl; Bruce; Lisa **Education:** Bachelor of Science in Engineering, Stanford University (1956) **Career:** Executive, Marinita Development Company (1974-Present); Owner and President, Various Companies, California and Idaho (1961-Present); With, Capri Builders, Inc. (1961-1985); With, Mirams & Smith, Inc. (1961-1975) **Military Service:** Fighter Pilot, Captain, U.S. Marine Corps (1956-1960) **Marquis Who's Who Honors:** Albert Nelson Marquis Lifetime Achievement Award **To what do you attribute your success:** Mr. Mirams attributes his success to diligence and luck. **Why did you become involved in your profession or industry:** Mr. Mirams has been interested in real estate development, building and land-planning since childhood. **Avocations:** Skiing; Sailing

Leona Lousin Mirza, EdD

Title: Mathematics Statistics Professor **Industry:** Education/Educational Services **Date of Birth:** 07/01/1944 **Place of Birth:** Chicago **State/Country of Origin:** IL/USA **Parents:** Max B. Lousin; Opal Lousin **Marital Status:** Married **Spouse Name:** David B. Mirza **Children:** Sara Anush; Elizabeth Ann **Education:** Coursework, Statistics, North Park College (1990); EdD, Western Michigan University, Kalamazoo (1972); MEd, Western Michigan University, Kalamazoo (1967); BA in Mathematics, North Park College, Chicago, IL (1965) **Certifications:** Certified in Computer Studies, North Park College (1983); Specialist in Elementary Curriculum and Administration **Career:** Professor, Mathematics Education, North Park University, Chicago, IL (1969-Present); Chair, Department of Mathematics and Statistics, North Park University, Chicago, IL (2004-2013); Director, Institute for International and Cultural Studies (2001-2006); Assistant Academy Dean, North Park University, Chicago, IL (1999-2001); Teacher, Kalamazoo Public Schools (1965-1969) **Civic:** President, Chicago Armenian Generals Union (2008-2013); Chairman, Advisory Committee on Education in Illinois (1975-1977) **Creative Works:** Editor, The Illinois Mathematics Teacher (1992-1995); Contributor, Articles, Professional Journals **Awards:** Fred Flener Award, Illinois Council of Teachers of Mathematics (2015); Woman of the Year, Armenian International Women's Association (2015); Max Beberman Award (1997) **Memberships:** National Council of Teachers of Mathematics; Illinois Council of Teachers of Mathematics; Illinois Association of Colleges of Teacher Education **Marquis Who's Who Honors:** Albert Nelson Marquis Lifetime Achievement Award; Marquis Who's Who Top Professional **To what do you attribute your success:** Dr. Mirza attributes her success to doing the best that she can. **Why did you become involved in your profession or industry:** When Dr. Mirza graduated in the 1960s, there were really only two options available to women - education and nursing. She chose education and has now been in the field for 53 years. Dr. Mirza's mother had a teaching degree, but she never worked as a teacher. Her father was a survivor of the Armenian Genocide and valued education very highly. He really encouraged her to become a teacher. Dr. Mirza was always interested in mathematics and problem solving since she was little girl. Her parents played cards that were board games and strategy oriented, which peaked her interest in math. Further in school, the more interesting the math became, such as coding, bar codes and how systems are set up, etc., she developed an interest in math. **Avocations:** Traveling; Gardening; Writing math questions for high school contests; Interacting with other cultures **Thoughts on Life:** Dr. Mirza's advice to her 18-year-old self is that she would encourage whatever position, whatever job the person wanted to be something that would make this world a better place. Whether it would be teaching or making the IT area a better place, but that would be it. Whatever you become passionate about, follow your dream.

David Vokes Mitchell

Industry: Media & Entertainment **Date of Birth:** 11/23/1943 **Place of Birth:** San Francisco **State/Country of Origin:** CA/USA **Parents:** Herbert Houston Mitchell; Edith (Vokes) Mitchell **Marital Status:** Married **Spouse Name:** Lynn Axelrod Mitchell (2018); Linda Foor; Catherine "Cathy" Casto; Cynthia Clark; Ana Carolina Monterroso **Education:** Master of Arts in Communication, Stanford University (1967); Bachelor of Arts in English, Stanford University (1965) **Career:** Editor, Publisher, Owner, Point Reyes Light, Point Reyes Station, CA (1984-2005); Reporter, San Francisco Examiner (1981-1983); Editor, Publisher, Owner, Point Reyes Light, Point Reyes Station, CA (1975-1981); Editor, Sebastopol Times (1973-1975); Reporter, Union Democrat (1971-1973); Reporter, Council Bluffs Nonpareil (1970); Instructor, English, Upper Iowa College (1968-1970); Instructor, English, Leesburg High (1968); Instructor, Marvel Academy (1967) **Civic:** Advisory Board Member, California Marine Mammal Center (1984-1985) **Creative Works:** Author, "The Light on the Coast: 65 Years of News Big and Small As Reported in The Point Reyes Light" (2013); Author, "The Light on Synanon: How a Country Weekly Exposed a Corporate Cult and Won the Pulitzer Prize" (1982) **Awards:** Eugene Cervi Award, International Society of Weekly Newspaper Editors (2014); James Madison Freedom of Information Award, Northern California Chapter, Society of Professional Journalists (2006); More Than 100 State, Regional and National Journalism Awards (1973-2005); Pulitzer Prize for Meritorious Public Service, Point Reyes Light (1979) **Memberships:** California Newspaper Publishers Association; International Society of Weekly Newspaper Editors **Why did you become involved in your profession or industry:** Mr. Mitchell became involved in his profession after struggling for a long time to find himself, enduring multiple hardships before he attended Stanford University, where majored in journalism. **Avocations:** Photography; Writing for his blog; Maintaining his home property **Political Affiliations:** Democrat

Jere Holloway Mitchell, MD

Title: Cardiovascular and Exercise Physiologist **Industry:** Health, Wellness and Fitness **Company Name:** UT Southwestern Medical Center **Date of Birth:** 10/17/1928 **Place of Birth:** Longview **State/Country of Origin:** TX/USA **Parents:** William Holloway Mitchell; Dorothea (Turner) Mitchell **Marital Status:** Married **Spouse Name:** Pamela Battey (10/1/1960, Deceased 2010) **Children:** Wendy Mitchell O'Sullivan; Laurie Mitchell Woods; Amy Mitchell Poeppel **Education:** Honorary PhD, University of Copenhagen (2000); Cardiology Fellow, UT Southwestern Medical Center (1956-1958); Resident, Internal Medicine (1955-1956); Intern, Parkland Health and Hospital System, Dallas, TX (1954-1955); MD, UT Southwestern Medical Center (1954); BS, Virginia Military Institute, with Honors (1950) **Career:** Courtesy Staff, Zale Lipshy University Hospital (1990-Present); Holder, Carolyn P. and S. Roger Horchow Chair in Cardiac Research (1989-Present); Attending Physician, VA Medical Center, Dallas, TX (1969-Present); Professor (1969-Present); Attending Physician, St. Paul Family Medical Center (1966-Present); Attending Physician, Parkland Health & Hospital System (1963-Present); Holder, Frank M. Ryburn Junior Chair in Heart Research (1982-2000); Director, Harry S. Moss Heart Center (1976-2000); Director, Weinberger Laboratory for Cardiopulmonary Research (1966-1999); Associate Professor (1966-1969); Assistant Professor of Medicine and Physiology, UT Southwestern Medical Center, Dallas, TX (1962-1966); Public Health Service, Laboratory of Cardiac Energetics, National Heart, Lung, and Blood Institute, Bethesda, MD (1958-1962); Fellow, American College of Cardiology Foundation **Career Related:** Research Review Committee A, National Heart, Lung and Blood Institute (1992-1997); Percy Russo Lecturer, Professor, School of Health Sciences, The University of Sydney (1991); Pfizer Visiting Professor, The Pennsylvania State University (1990); Science Advisory Board, U.S. Air Force (1988-1990); Respiratory & Applied Physiology Study Section, National Institutes of Health (1981-1982); Applied Physiological Orthopedic Study Section, National Institutes of Health (1979-1981); Established Investigator, American Heart Association, Inc. (1962-1967) **Creative Works:** Editorial Board, "Clinical Physiology and Functional Imaging" (1981-Present); Editorial Board, "Circulation" (1993-2004); Associate Editor, "Experimental Physiology" (1993-2000); Associate Editor, Journal of Applied Physiology (1984-1993); Editorial Board, Journal of Cardiopulmonary Rehabilitation and Prevention (1981-1991); Editorial Board, "Cardiovascular Research" (1979-1987); Editorial Board, American Journal of Cardiology (1982-1984); Associate Editor, Journal of Applied Physiology (1978-1982); Editorial Board, "Circulation" (1978-1981); Editorial Board, American Journal of Physiology (1972-1976); Editorial Board, American Journal of Cardiology (1965-1974) **Awards:** Paton Prize, The Physiological Society (2012); Honor Award, The American Physiological Society (2007); Edward Adolph Distinguished Lecturer, Environmental and Exercise Physiology Section, The American Physiological Society (2003); Distinguished Scientist Award, American College of Cardiology Foundation (1999); Carl J. Wiggers Award, Cardiovascular Section, The American Physiological Society (1992); Honor Award, ACSM (1988); Award of Merit, American Heart Association, Inc. (1984); Citation Award, ACSM (1983); Donald W. Seldin Research Award, The University of Texas Southwestern Medical Center (1978); Career Development Award, U.S. Public Health Service (1968-1973); Young Investigators Award, American College of Cardiology Foundation (1961) **Memberships:** Medical Science Committee, American Association for the Advancement of Science (1988-Present); Council, Cardiac Rehabilitation, International Society for Heart Research (1981-Present); Commission on Cardiovascular Physiology, International Union of Physiological Sciences (1977-Present); National Vice President, American Heart Association, Inc. (1990-1991); Joseph B. Wolffe Lecturer, ACSM (1989); President, Texas Affiliate, American Heart Association, Inc. (1983-1984); President, Dallas Division, American Heart Association, Inc. (1977-1978); Emeritus Member, American Federation for Clinical Research; Emeritus Member, The American Society for Clinical Investigation; Association of American Physicians; The American Physiological Society; Association of University Cardiologists; The Physiological Society; Alpha Omega Alpha **Marquis Who's Who Honors:** Albert Nelson Marquis Lifetime Achievement Award; Marquis Who's Who Top Professional; Marquis Who's Who Humanitarian Award

Imogene Mathison Mixson, PhD

Title: Academic Dean (Retired) **Company Name:** Wallace State Community College **Date of Birth:** 12/11/1936 **Place of Birth:** Skipperville **State/Country of Origin:** AL/USA **Parents:** John Thomas Mathison (Deceased 1981); Sarah Myrtis (Watson) Mathison (Deceased 2002) **Marital Status:** Widowed **Spouse Name:** David Whigham Mixson (Deceased 2007) **Education:** Postdoctoral Coursework, The University of Southern Mississippi (1981, 1982); Postdoctoral Coursework, Troy University (1980, 1982); PhD, Florida State University (1972); MS, Auburn University (1963); BS, Troy University (1959) **Career:** Retired (1996); Academic Dean, Wallace State Community College, Dothan, AL (1983-1996); English Instructor, English Department Chairperson, Assistant Academic Dean, Wallace State Community College, Dothan, AL (1982-1983); English Instructor, Enterprise State Community College (1966-1982); English Department Chairperson, Enterprise State Community College (1968-1982); Professional Leave, Doctoral Study, Florida State University (1969-1970); English Teacher, Dothan High School (1959-1966) **Career Related:** Interim President, Alabama Aviation College (1996-1997); Interim President, Wallace State Community College (1991); Advisory Board, Caroline Marshall Draughon Center for the Arts & Humanities, Auburn University (1986-2006); Coordinator, Professional Development Task Force, Alabama Community College System (1984-1986) **Civic:** Board of Directors, Ozark Dale County Library, Inc., Ozark, AL (1981-1989; 1999-Present); Board of Directors, Alabama Humanities Foundation (1993-1997); Advisory Board, Dothan Kellogg Center, Alabama Institute for Deaf and Blind (1986-1988); Conference Board of Trustees, United Methodist Church (2008-2017) **Awards:** Named Outstanding Alumnus, Auburn University College of Education (2016); Distinguished Educator, Florida State University College of Education (2016); Alumnus of the Year Award, Troy University (2016); Outstanding Auburn University Woman Graduate Award, Centennial of Women's Admission to Auburn University Celebration, Auburn University (1992); Distinguished Leadership Award, Alabama Community College System (1991); Administrator of the Year Award, Alabama Community College System (1990); Teacher of Year Award, Enterprise State Community College (1973, 1977, 1980) **Memberships:** Legacy Giving Council, Troy University (2014-Present); Ozark Literary Club (2001-Present); Dale County Education Retirees Association (1998-Present); Development Leadership Team, Auburn University College of Education (2013-2017); National Advisory Council, Auburn University College of Education (2008-2013) **Marquis Who's Who Honors:** Marquis Millennium Magazine (2019); Marquis Distinguished Worldwide Humanitarian Award (2020); Marquis Industry Leaders (2020); Marquis Who's Who in America (2019-2020); Marquis Top Professionals (2019); Marquis Top Educators (2019); Albert Nelson Marquis Lifetime Achievement Award (2018) **To what do you attribute your success:** Dr. Mixson's attributes her success to strong support from parents and husband, a strong desire to make positive differences, the ability to work well with others and extraordinary opportunities. She also credits a strong value system and sense of purpose, outstanding educators and inspiring students. **Why did you become involved in your profession or industry:** Dr. Mixson became involved in her profession because she always knew that she wanted to become a teacher. She was always very excited by, interested in, and excelled at school. She was the valedictorian of her class in sixth grade, ninth grade, and twelfth grade. Her decision to become a teacher was supported by her loving parents. **Avocations:** Reading; Church activities; Music; Community service; Support for student scholarships and faculty/staff professional development (high schools, community colleges, and universities) **Religion:** United Methodist **Thoughts on Life:** Dr. Mixson's motto is to discover a meaningful purpose and work diligently, enthusiastically, and consistently to make positive contributions for the common good! She believes in developing significant relationships and always find places to serve. She also believes in maintaining the personal integrity that ensures self respect and respect from others.

Steven Terner Mnuchin

Title: United States Secretary of the Treasury **Industry:** Government Administration/Government Relations/Government Services **Date of Birth:** 12/21/1962 **Place of Birth:** New York **State/Country of Origin:** NY/USA **Parents:** Robert E. Mnuchin; Elaine Terner Cooper **Marital Status:** Married **Spouse Name:** Louise Linton (06/24/2017); Heather Mnuchin (1999, Divorced 2014); Kathryn Leigh McCarver (1992, Divorced 1999) **Children:** Three Children **Education:** BA, Yale University (1985) **Career:** United States Secretary of the Treasury, United States Department of the Treasury, Washington, DC (2017-Present); Chairman, Chief Executive Officer, Dune Capital Management, LP (2004-Present); Chairman, Chief Executive Officer, OneWest Bank Group, LLC (2009-2017); Chief Executive Officer, SFM Capital Management LP (2003-2004); Vice Chairman, English as Second Language Investments Inc. (2003); Executive Vice President, Chief Information Officer, Goldman Sachs Group, Inc. (Formerly Goldman, Sachs & Co.) (2001-2002); Various Management Positions, Goldman Sachs Group, Inc. (Formerly Goldman, Sachs & Co.) (1985-2001) **Civic:** Board of Trustees, New York-Presbyterian Medical Center (2004-Present); Board of Directors, Kmart Holding Corporation (Merged Sears Holding Corporation) (2003-Present); Yale Development Board; Trustee, Whitney Museum of American Art; Trustee, Hirshhorn Museum and Sculpture Garden; Trustee, Riverdale Country School; Senior Member, Junior Achievement USA **Creative Works:** Publisher, Yale Daily News **Memberships:** Skull and Bones, Yale University (1985) **Political Affiliations:** Republican

Karen Mochan

Title: Secondary School Educator **Industry:** Education/Educational Services **Date of Birth:** 05/02/1973 **Place of Birth:** Scranton **State/Country of Origin:** PA/USA **Parents:** Gary William Haas (1944); Vincentina Rose (Salerno) Haas (1946) **Marital Status:** Married **Spouse Name:** John Mochan III (07/28/2007) **Education:** Master's Degree in 21st Century Teaching and Learning, Wilkes University (2014); Master's Degree in Educational Development and Strategy, Wilkes University (2006); Bachelor of Science, Marywood University, with Honors (1995) **Certifications:** Certified Secondary Teacher, Commonwealth of Pennsylvania (1997); Certified Level II Mathematics Teacher, Commonwealth of Pennsylvania (1997); Certified Level II Elementary Education Teacher, Commonwealth of Pennsylvania (1995) **Career:** Chairperson, Mathematics Department, East Stroudsburg Area High School North, Dingmans Ferry, PA (2000-Present); Teacher of Mathematics, East Stroudsburg Area High School North, Dingmans Ferry, PA (1998-Present); Ballet Instructor, Illusions Performing Arts Studio, Old Forge, PA (1999-2004) **Career Related:** School Growth and Action Plan Team, East Stroudsburg Area High School North, Dingmans Ferry, PA (2000-Present); Mentor, East Stroudsburg Area High School North, Dingmans Ferry, PA (2000-Present); Mathematics Tutor, Club Z Tutoring, Olyphant, PA (2003-2005); Scholastic Scrimmage Coach, East Stroudsburg Area High School South, East Stroudsburg, PA (1998-2000); Private Tutor, Old Forge, Moosic, Taylor and Scranton, PA (1995-1997) **Creative Works:** Author, "Protected" (2007); Author, "Wakiza" (1997) **Awards:** Editor's Choice Award For Poetry, World Of Poetry (1993-1997, 1990) **Memberships:** Treasurer, Kappa Delta Pi (1994-1995); Formerly, Keystone State Reading Association; Formerly, Northeastern Pennsylvania Reading Association; Formerly, International Reading Association; Pennsylvania Council Teachers Mathematics; Mathematics Association America; National Council Teachers Mathematics; Life Member, International Society of Poets **Marquis Who's Who Honors:** Albert Nelson Marquis Lifetime Achievement Award **Why did you become involved in your profession or industry:** Ms. Mochan was inspired to become a teacher by her third grade instructor, who made learning fun. She was also influenced by her high school mathematics teacher. **Avocations:** Ballet; Poetry

Jacqueline C. Mohen

Title: Research Fellow **Industry:** Sciences **Company Name:** Rowan University **Education:** MS in Pharmaceutical Sciences, Rowan University, Glassboro, NJ (2019); Prerequisite Courses for PhD in Pharmaceuticals, University of the Sciences in Philadelphia, PA (2015-2016); BS in Textile Design, Minor in Mathematics, Philadelphia University, With Honors (2013) **Certifications:** Associate Member of the Royal Society of Chemistry (2019) **Career:** Research Fellow, Rowan University, Glassboro, NJ (2016-Present); Pharmacy Technician, CVS Pharmacy (2019-Present); Crest Pier Playmates Summer Camp Counselor, "Professor J," Wildwood Crest Pier Recreation Center, Wildwood Crest, NJ (2019); Event Co-Chair, Fragrance Today NYSCC-ASP Joint Meeting, New York Society of Cosmetic Chemists (NYSCC) and American Society of Perfumers (ASP) (2017-2018); Technical Department Staff, Volunteer, Première Vision (2015); Showroom Organizer and Sales Assistant Intern, Bradlee International Ltd., New York, NY (2011) **Career Related:** District Boardworker, Burlington County Board of Elections, Mount Holly, NJ (2019-Present); Nesbit Information Center of Wildwood Crest Staff, Borough of Wildwood Crest, Wildwood Crest, NJ (2019); Exam Scorer and Test Proctor, MATHCOUNTS NJ State Competition, New Jersey Society of Professional Engineers (NJSPE), Somerset, NJ (2012) **Civic:** Software Beta-Testing (2016-Present); Bottle Collection Project, Kingsessing Library, Southwest Philadelphia, PA (2015-Present); College Advisement in New York-New Jersey-Pennsylvania Tri-State Area (2015-Present); Hazardous Pesticide Chemical Substance Awareness, Moorestown, NJ (2014-2016); Delegate, American Legion Auxiliary Jersey Girls State, Georgian Court University, Lakewood, NJ (2009) **Creative Works:** Author, Master of Science Thesis, "Investigating Color Additive Molecules for Pharmaceutical and Cosmetic Applications: A Comparison of Theoretical and Experimental UV-Visible Absorbance Spectra in Tunable Solvents" (2019); Contributor, Numerous Presentations (2017-2018); Published Revision, JacqCAD Instructional Material, Philadelphia University, Philadelphia, PA (2012) **Awards:** Dean's List, Rowan University (2018); Nominee, Best Poster Award, 256th ACS National Meeting Physical Chemistry Poster Session (2018); Presidential Scholar's Award, Rowan University (2017-2018); Fifth Place Winner, Student Fashion Textile Design Competition, Alpaca Owners and Breeders Association (2013); American Association of Textile Chemists & Colorists (AATCC) Award, Philadelphia University School of Design and Engineering (2013); Second Place Winner, Drawing I Award, Philadelphia University Foundations Push Pin Exhibition (2011); Outstanding Mentor Award, Big Sister, Camden County Mentoring Initiative (2010); Dean's List, Philadelphia University (2010) **Memberships:** Associate Member, Royal Society of Chemistry (2019-Present); Upsilon Chapter, Alpha Epsilon Lambda, Rowan University (2018-Present); Member, Society of Cosmetic Chemists (2016-Present); American Institute of Chemical Engineers (2015-Present); American Chemical Society (2014-Present); American Association of Textile Chemists & Colorists (2010-Present); Alpha Lambda Delta, Philadelphia University (2011) **To what do you attribute your success:** Ms. Mohen was fueled by cold, hard ambition to achieve her dreams. This, coupled with the determination to achieve a sustainable outcome, is what made her so successful. Each of her works is truly unique, as they have all taken their own form upon completion. **Why did you become involved in your profession or industry:** Ms. Mohen embraced her artistic talents early in life. As time moved forward, she learned that in order to make her creations come to life, she had to merge the concepts of applied design, sciences, and mathematics. Acknowledging these boundaries was essential to the beginning of her creative journey, as was the wisdom to decide when such boundaries can be lifted, broken, or reformed to make further progress. **Thoughts on Life:** Ms. Mohen always looks for new ways to push boundaries in how she represents herself, whether it be through light, color, texture, scent, taste, or sound. She feels everyone should do so.

Paula Mokulis

Title: Director, Visual Information Directorate **Industry:** Military & Defense Services **Place of Birth:** Hartford **State/Country of Origin:** CT/USA **Education:** Graduate Coursework, Army Management Staff College (1991); AAS, North Virginia Community College, Summa Cum Laude, Alexandria, VA (1984); BA, University of Connecticut (1969) **Career:** Director, Visual Information Directorate, Secretary, U.S. Army (2002); Chief of Plans and Programs, Visual Information Center, U.S. Army (1990-2002); System Administrator, Computer Network, Visual Information Center, U.S. Army (1986-1990); Graphic Arts Analyst, Visual Information Center, U.S. Army (1980-1986); Management Assistant, U.S. Secretary of Defense, Washington, DC (1979-1980); Secretary, Joint Chiefs of Staff, Washington, DC (1979); Executive Secretary, Defense Resource Management Study, Washington, DC (1978-1979); Secretary, Secretary of Defense, Washington, DC (1974-1978); Writer, Editor, Medicine Magazine, U.S. Navy, Washington, DC (1973-1974); Clerk Typist, Bureau of Medicine and Surgery, U.S. Navy, Washington, DC (1973); Assistant Editor, TV Guide Magazine, Atlanta, GA (1972); Management Analyst, Travelers Insurance Co., Hartford, CT (1971-1972); Writer, Editor, Hartford Insurance Group (1969-1971) **Career Related:** Designer, Creator, Cover for Army Reserve Magazine (1981); Copywriter, Station WETA, Public Radio **Creative Works:** Designer, Exhibit Panels, General Floyd Parks Memorial Corridor, The Pentagon (1988); Contributing Designer, Bicentennial Medallion, Department of Defense (1988); Contributing Poet, Poetry, Published Anthology **Awards:** President's Volunteer Gold Service Award (2018); Fairfax County Outstanding Senior Adult Award (2013); SAAA Meritorious Civilian Service Award (2002); Army Review Boards Agency (2002); ADFCR for Career Program 34 (1998-2002); DISC4 Coin for Civilian Service (1996); Commander's Award for Civilian Service (1988); 1st Prize in Illustration, NOVA (1984) **Memberships:** Appointed, Army Board for Correction of Military Records (ABCMR) (2002); President's Quality Award Board of Examiners (2001); OAASA Strategic Planning Board (2000-2001) **Marquis Who's Who Honors:** Albert Nelson Marquis Lifetime Achievement Award **Why did you become involved in your profession or industry:** Unsure of what she wanted to do, Ms. Mokulis began working in insurance while she pursued teaching and creative writing. She joined the military after being invited by her brother, which is how she began working for the U.S. Navy magazine. The rest is history, she says. **Avocations:** Writing poetry; Piano; Portrait artist; Violin; Dance teacher; Hollin Hall band member; Tai Chi instructor **Political Affiliations:** Democrat

J. Paul Montgomery

Title: Foundation Administrator **Company Name:** Hero's **Date of Birth:** 07/19/1941 **Parents:** James Montgomery; Julia Montgomery **Marital Status:** Widower **Spouse Name:** Robbie A. Washington (Deceased, 2020) **Children:** Joe; Sydnee; James; Jon **Education:** Master's Degree, University South Carolina (1986); AA, Columbia College (1980); Master's Degree, US Government Employment **Certifications:** Baptist Minister **Career:** Founder, Hero's, Austin, TX (1995-Present); Founder, COTA, Inc. (1984-1987); Retired (1980); Recruiter, U.S. Army, Killeen, TX (1973-1984); Army intelligence, U.S. Army (1966-1973) **Military Service:** U.S. Army (1959-1980) **Creative Works:** Author: "Mama's Black Child" (2011) **Awards:** Meritorious Service Medal, U.S. Army (1978); Driver Badge, U.S. Army; Vietnam Service Medal, U.S. Army; Defense Service Medal, U.S. Army; Good Conduct Medal and Clasp, U.S. Army; Bronze 5 Loops, U.S. Army; Army Commendation Medal, U.S. Army; The President Unit Citation Award, U.S. Army **Memberships:** Veterans of Foreign Wars; Disabled American Veterans **Marquis Who's Who Honors:** Marquis Lifetime Achievement Award **Why did you become involved in your profession or industry:** Mr. Montgomery became involved with the Army because he was raised in the south, where there weren't many opportunities for African American men at the time. His company, Hero's, came about when, as a recruiter, he acquired a strong record, though he often found himself enlisting men who had poor test scores. This was when Mr. Montgomery began a mentoring program for families with less than $50,000 in income annually. He wanted to help children who did not have the capabilities to attend college, which is how his business started various scholarship funds. **Avocations:** Writing **Political Affiliations:** Democrat **Religion:** Baptist Minister

John Richard Montgomery, MD

Title: Pediatrician **Industry:** Medicine & Health Care **Date of Birth:** 10/24/1934 **Place of Birth:** Burnsville **State/Country of Origin:** MS/USA **Parents: Spouse Name:** Dottye Ann Newell (06/26/1965) **Children:** John Newell; Michelle Elizabeth **Education:** MD, University of Alabama (1958); BS, University of Alabama (1955) **Career:** Professor Emeritus, University of Alabama at Birmingham School of Medicine, Huntsville, AL (1997-Present); Professor, University of Alabama at Birmingham School of Medicine, Huntsville, AL (1975-1997); Associate Professor, Baylor University (1970-1975); Assistant Professor of Pediatrics, Baylor University (1966-1970) **Military Service:** Colonel U.S. Army Reserve (1999); With, U.S. Army, Korea (1961-1962) **Awards:** 9A Proficiency Designator, U.S. Army **Memberships:** President, Alabama Chapter, American Academy of Pediatrics (1991-1993); Sigma Xi; Phi Beta Kappa **Thoughts on Life:** "Dr. Montgomery taught pediatrics at Baylor University between 1966 and 1975. During this time, he became known for the co-implementation of the environmental bubble used to protect David Vetter from infection by external germs. In 1975, he became a full professor of pediatrics at University of Alabama School of Medicine, Huntsville campus, and in 1997 he became professor emeritus at the University of Alabama School of Medicine. John Richard Montgomery was born on October 24, 1934 in Burnsville, Mississippi. He received a BS Degree in 1955 from the University of Alabama. He also became a member of Phi Beta Kappa. Dr. Montgomery received an MD in 1958 from the Medical College of Alabama. He joined the U.S. military and served as the Chief of Pediatrics at Seoul Military Hospital until 1963. In 1966, he became an assistant professor of pediatrics at Baylor and was promoted to associate professor in 1970. He remained at the college until 1975 when he became the chief of pediatric programs and full professor at the University of Alabama School of Medicine, Huntsville campus. In 1997, he became a professor emeritus at the University of Alabama School of Medicine, where he has continued teaching medical students and serving on advisory boards. Dr. Montgomery is best known for his assistance in the implementation of the first germ-free environmental bubble in the United States for newborn patients with no natural immune system. The first newborn patient to be placed in the bubble was David Vetter, who was placed in the environment soon after his birth under the care of the Texas Children's Hospital Team, which also included Mary Ann South and Joseph. The patient died in 1984, and, afterward, his life was the subject of a PBS American Experience documentary featuring Dr. Montgomery. The documentary featured the major points of Vetter's life and complications, including Dr. Montgomery first breaking the news of the boy's diagnosis soon after he was born. He served as his physician until 1975 when he moved from Baylor to the University of Alabama. Dr. Montgomery has also researched congenital rubella syndrome and transplant rejection in heart transplant patients. He has been a member of the American Association of Immunologists, the Infectious Diseases Society of America, the International Experimental Hematology Society, the Society of Paediatric Research, and the New York Academy of Sciences. He has also published more than 80 academic articles. Dr. Montgomery married his wife Dottye Ann Newell in June 1965."

Will Montgomery

Title: Chief Executive Officer **Industry:** Insurance **Company Name:** Montgomery & Associates Insurance & Financial Services **Children:** One Daughter **Education:** High School Diploma **Certifications:** Life, Accident & Health Insurance License, Property & Casualty License, Department of Commerce & Insurance, State of Tennessee **Career:** Founder, Chief Executive Officer, Montgomery & Associates Insurance & Financial Services (2010-Present); Agent, Owner, Family Insurance and Financial Group, LLC (2005-2010) **Civic:** Volunteer, American Liver Foundation; Volunteer, JDRF; Volunteer, HFH of Greater Nashville, Habitat for Humanity International; Volunteer, Hands on Nashville; Volunteer, Second Harvest Food Bank of Middle Tennessee; The Fatherhood Project; Big Brother Big Sisters of America; GiGi's Playhouse **Awards:** Sizzle Award, Best Financial Services, Williamson County, TN (2018); Sizzle Award, Best Insurance Agency, Williamson County, TN (2018); Named One of the Best Practices Agencies, Independent Insurance Agents & Brokers of America, Inc. (2016-2020); Ruthies Award, Favorite Insurance Agent, Rutherford County, TN (2016-2018); Young Guns Award, Insurance Business America, Key Media (2016); Small Business Award Winner in Category (1-10 Employee Range), Nashville Business Journal, American Business Journals (2015); Named to MetLife Leaders Conference (2012-2019) **Memberships:** Round Table Experience; National Advisory Panel, Nationwide Private Client, Nationwide Mutual Insurance Company; Advisory Panel, Selective Insurance Group, Inc.; Advisory Panel, MetLife Insurance, MetLife Services and Solutions, LLC; EO Nashville, Entrepreneurs' Organization **To what do you attribute your success:** Mr. Montgomery attributes much of his success to his late father, who was a successful real estate investor, worked as a veterinarian in his private practice in Knoxville, and assisted the Knoxville Zoo with the Zoo Director Jack Hannah. Mr. Montgomery's professional success is also attributed to creating an abundant life for his 3-year-old daughter. **Why did you become involved in your profession or industry:** Mr. Montgomery became involved in his profession as a young man; while he worked at a bicycle shop, he was contacted by a man who presented a marketing opportunity to him. Open to a change of pace, Mr. Montgomery realized he didn't want to resign himself to being someone else's employee for the rest of his life. At the age of 21, he officially became self-employed, and reaped success quickly. He remembers learning the power of a passive income, and made the decision to invest in insurance. As an insurance advisor and young entrepreneur, Mr. Montgomery learned to value earning the trust of his business-to-business and business-to-customer clients. In the time since, Mr. Montgomery has built a knowledgeable reputation, mastered his services and started three successful companies. **Avocations:** Coaching and mentoring others; Reading; Road and mountain bike racing; Lifting weights; Hiking; Traveling; Mountain unicycling; Skate boarding; Surfing; Snowboarding; Rock climbing **Thoughts on Life:** As a team-building exercise, Mr. Montgomery conducts quarterly masterminded book studies, encouraging discussion and reflection among his employees. In the office, he occasionally dresses up as Gumby, a character known for being malleable and making the best of any situation. Mr. Montgomery's guiding principles call for disposing negativity, keeping your mind right and separating good from bad in the name of perseverance.

Carissa Kainani Moore

Title: Professional Surfer **Industry:** Athletics **Date of Birth:** 08/27/1992 **Place of Birth:** Honolulu **State/Country of Origin:** HI/USA **Parents:** Chris Moore; Carol Lum **Marital Status:** Married **Spouse Name:** Luke Untermann **Career Related:** Team Member, U.S. Team, Olympic Games, Tokyo, Japan; Spokesmodel, Nike, Red Bull, Target, Hurley, Subaru Hawaii **Awards:** Winner, Corona Open J-Bay (2019); Winner, Roxy Pro France (2016-2017, 2019); World Champion, ASP Women's World Tour (2011, 2013, 2015, 2019); Winner, Beachwater Maui Pro (2018); Winner, Surf Ranch Pro (2018); Winner, Swatch Women's Pro (2015); Winner, Rip Curl Women's Pro Bells Beach (2015); Winner, Target Maui Pro (2014-2015); Winner, Roxy Pro Gold Coast (2011, 2015); Winner, Drug Aware Margaret River Women's Pro (2013-2014); Winner, Rip Curl Pro (2013-2014); Winner, Cascais Women's Pro (2013); Winner, U.S. Open of Surfing (2010, 2013); Winner, Billabong Pro Rio (2011); Winner, Commonwealth Bank Beachley Classic (2011); Winner, Rip Curl Pro Portugal (2010); Named ASP Rookie of the Year (2010); Winner, U.S. Open of Surfing (2010); Winner, TSB Bank Women's Surf Festival (2010); Winner, Gidget Pro (2009); Winner, Reef Hawaiian Pro (2008); Triple Crown of Surfing, Reef Hawaiian Pro (2008); Named Adventurer of the Year, National Geographic Society; Named Woman of the Year, Glamour Magazine; Named Top Female Surfer, SURFER Magazine; Inductee, Surfers' Hall of Fame

Rose Moorman

Title: County Administrator, Systems Analyst **Industry:** Information Technology and Services **Date of Birth:** 05/13/1945 **Place of Birth:** Miami **State/Country of Origin:** FL/USA **Parents:** Willie Moorman; Claudia (Fluker) Moorman **Children:** William Christopher Mitchell **Education:** MS in Engineering in Computer and Information Sciences, University of Pennsylvania Moore School of Electrical Engineering (Now University of Pennsylvania School of Engineering and Applied Science) (1976); BA in Mathematics, Fisk University (1967); Diploma, Booker T. Washington High School (1963) **Career:** Senior Systems Analyst, Miami-Dade County, FL (1997-2008); Executive Administrator to County Commissioner, Metro-Dade County (Miami-Dade County), FL (1996-1997); Coordinator of Diversity, City of Miami, FL (1994-1995); Technical Support Manager, Internal Audits & Review Department, City of Miami, FL (1988-1994); Owner, Chief Executive Officer, Computer and Information Management, Incorporated, Miami, FL (1983-1988); Director of Technology Services, Gill Associates, Incorporated, WA (1978-1983); Systems Analyst, Honeywell International, Inc., Fort Washington, PA (1977-1978); Senior Programmer and Analyst, Institute for Environmental Medicine, University of Pennsylvania, Philadelphia, PA (1972-1977); Programmer/Analyst, PwC, Philadelphia, PA (1970-1972); Computer Programmer, General Electric Missile and Space Division, Valley Forge, PA (1967-1970) **Career Related:** Facilitator, Computer Education Advisory Panel, Miami-Dade County Public Schools (1984-1988); Facilitator, "Women in Information Processing," Washington, DC (1979-1983); President, South Florida Chapter, Black Data Processing Associates **Civic:** Treasurer, Chair, Finance Committee, The Family Christian Association of America, Inc. (1992-Present); Ebenezer United Methodist Church, Miami, FL (1954-Present); Board Director, Epworth Village (2007-2008) Miami-Dade County Historical Preservation Board (1996-1998); Dade Heritage Trust, Miami, FL (1994); New Miami Group, Incorporated (1994); Treasurer, Board of Directors, Overtown Community Health Clinic, Miami, FL (1992-1995); President, Loran Park School PTA, Miami, FL (1991-1993); Troop Leader, Girl Scouts of the United States of America (1990-1992); The Family Christian Association of America, Inc. (1989-1994); Vice President to President, United Methodist Women Administrative Board; Staff Chair, Pastor-Parish Relations Committee **Creative Works:** Editor (2009-Present); Co-editor, Newsletter, "Ebenezer Speaks" (1992-1994); Editor, Newsletter, "Bits and Bytes" (1979-1982) **Awards:** Living Legends Awards for Community Service, BTW Alumni Association, Miami, FL (2012); Meritorious Service Award, Fisk University (1992); Service Excellence Award, Delta Sigma Theta Sorority, Inc. (1986); Listee, Who's Who Among Students in American Colleges and Universities (1967); Bronze Medallion for Community Service, National Conference of Christians and Jews, Presented by Elliot Roosevelt (1963); Leadership Award, The American National Red Cross (1957) **Memberships:** President, Black Data Processing Associates of South Florida (BDPA) (2001-2002); Board of Directors, Black Data Processing Associates of South Florida (BDPA) (2001-2002); Board of Directors, National Forum for Black Public Administrators (1993-1995); 2nd Vice President, National Forum for Black Public Administrators (1993-1995); Miami Alumnae Chapter, Delta Sigma Theta Sorority, Inc.; Miami Fisk Club; Dade Heritage Trust; Fairchild Tropical Botanic Gardens; NAACP; The Family Christian Association of America, Inc.; National Council of Negro Women, Inc.; National Wildlife Federation; Board of Directors, Overtown Community Health Clinic; Miami Chapter, Jack and Jill of America, Inc.; Smithsonian Institution **Marquis Who's Who Honors:** Albert Nelson Marquis Lifetime Achievement Award **Why did you become involved in your profession or industry:** Ms. Moorman originally wanted to be a doctor but she did not have the means to go to medical school. She was a good math student and General Electric recruited her out of college. Ms. Moorman was hired into STEP (the Space Technological Engineering Program). She was hired at a time when women were not going into math and science fields. **Avocations:** Bridge; Competition of Games such as chess, checkers, monopoly, scrabble, sudoku; Crossword puzzles; Gardening; Tutoring; Music; Collecting cookbooks; Collecting coins; Collecting kaleidoscopes **Political Affiliations:** Democrat **Religion:** United Methodist

James Calvin Mordy, JD, BA

Title: Lawyer **Industry:** Law and Legal Services **Date of Birth:** 01/03/1927 **Place of Birth:** Ashland **State/Country of Origin:** KS/USA **Parents:** Thomas Robson (Pastor) Mordy; Ruth (Floyd) Mordy **Marital Status:** Widowed **Spouse Name:** Marjory Ellen Nelson (11/17/1951, Deceased 2018) **Children:** Jean Claire Mordy Jongeling; Rebecca Jane Mordy King; James Nelson **Education:** Postgraduate Coursework, George Washington University (1952-1953); JD, University of Michigan (1950); BA in Chemistry, University of Kansas (1947) **Certifications:** Certified, Business Bankruptcy Law, American Bankruptcy Board (1994) **Career:** Counsel, Morrison & Hecker LLP, Kansas City, MO (1997-2000); Senior Counsel, Morrison & Hecker LLP, Kansas City, MO (1996-1997); Partner, Chairman, Executive Communications, Morrison & Hecker LLP, Kansas City, MO (1959-1996); Associate, Morrison, Hecker, Buck, Cozad & Rogers, Kansas City, MO (1950-1959) **Civic:** Council Member, St. Paul School of Theology, Kansas City, MO (1986-Present); Secretary, Kingswood Senior Living Community (2011-2014); Vice Chairman, Kingswood Senior Living Community (2005-2010); Board of Directors, Kingswood Senior Living Community, Kansas City, MO (2004-2014); Board of Directors, Treasurer, Friends of Sacred Structures, Kansas City, MO (2000-2007); Delegate, 17th World Methodist Conference, Rio de Janeiro, Brazil (1996); Board of Directors, Counsel, Broadway Child Enrichment Center (1980-2006); Board of Directors, Executive Committee, Della Lamb Neighborhood House, Kansas City, MO (1973-1980); Chairman, Board of Directors, Broadway United Methodist Church, Kansas City, MO (1964-1970); Ranger, Rocky Mountain National Park (1948-1949) **Military Service:** Commander, Navel Intelligence, Washington, DC (1952-1953); Active Duty (1951-1953, 1945-1946); U.S. Naval Reserve (1945-1973) **Creative Works:** Contributing Author, "Missouri Bar Bankruptcy Handbook" (1991); Contributing Author, "Missouri Bar Insurance Handbook" (1968); Member, Michigan Law Review (1948-1949); Contributor, Article, Professional Journals **Awards:** President's Award, St. Paul School of Theology, John Wesley Society (2011); Shepherd of the Lamb Award, Della Lamb Neighborhood House (1980); Summerfield Scholar (1943-1947) **Memberships:** Fellow, American College of Bankruptcy (1996); Life Member, American Bar Foundation (1996); American Bar Association; American Judicature Society; American Bankruptcy Institute; Missouri Bar Association; Kansas City Metropolitan Bar Association; Lawyers Association Kansas City; Workout Professors Association Kansas City; University Club; Barristers Society; Phi Beta Kappa; Delta Tau Delta; Alpha Chi Sigma; Phi Alpha Delta **Bar Admissions:** Missouri State Bar (1950); Kansas State Bar (1950) **Marquis Who's Who Honors:** Albert Nelson Marquis Lifetime Achievement Award; Marquis Who's Who Top Professional **To what do you attribute your success:** Mr. Mordy attributes his success to his curiosity and perseverance. **Why did you become involved in your profession or industry:** Mr. Mordy was inspired to become an attorney after interviewing with the Texas Oil company for an entry-level position. Mr. Mordy was told that that he'd need to get a PhD, so he decided to go to law school instead. Mr. Mordy enjoyed analysis and research, so he felt law would be a good fit. **Avocations:** Travel; Geography; History; Music; Theology **Religion:** United Methodist

Mayer Morganroth

Title: Attorney **Industry:** Law and Legal Services **Company Name:** Morganroth & Morganroth, PLLC **Date of Birth:** 03/20/1931 **Place of Birth:** Detroit **State/Country of Origin:** MI/USA **Parents:** Maurice Jack Morganroth; Sophie (Reisman) Blum **Marital Status:** Married **Spouse Name:** Sheila Rubinstein (08/16/1958) **Children:** Lauri; Jeffrey; Cherie **Education:** JD, Detroit College of (Now Law Michigan State University College of Law) (1954); Undergraduate Degree in Psychology and History, Michigan State University, East Lansing, MI **Career:** Sole Practice, Morganroth & Morganroth, PLLC, Birmingham, AL (1955-Present); Founding Partner, Morganroth & Morganroth, PLLC, Birmingham, MI (1989) **Career Related:** Entertainment Industry Consultant, Numerous Films; Speaker, Lecturer in the Field, Various Universities and Law Schools Throughout the Country **Civic:** Trustee, Board of Trustees, Michigan State University Law School (2014-Present); Appointed Trustee, Michigan State University College of Law **Military Service:** U.S. Navy (1948-1950) **Awards:** Preeminent Lawyer, Martindale-Hubbell; North America's Top Attorneys; New York Top Trial Lawyers, National Trial Lawyers; Top 100, American Academy of Trial Attorneys; Distinguished Lawyer, Lifetime Achievement, Michigan State University College of Law **Memberships:** American Association for Justice; Federal Bar Association; American Bar Association; American Judicature Society; National Criminal Defense Lawyers Association; State Bar of Michigan; Oakland County Bar Association; New York State Bar Association; Supreme Court Historical Society **Bar Admissions:** U.S. District Court for the District of Columbia (2002); U.S. District Court, Michigan (1996); U.S. Court of Appeals for the Eighth Circuit (1994); U.S. Court of Federal Claims (1993); U.S. Tax Court (1993); U.S. Court of Appeals for the Second Circuit (1986); U.S. Court of Appeals for the Fourth Circuit (1985); U.S. District Court for the Eastern District of New York (1985); U.S. Supreme Court (1971); U.S. Court of Appeals for the Sixth Circuit (1968); U.S. District Court for the Northern District of Ohio (1958); U.S. District Court for the Eastern District of Michigan (1955) **Marquis Who's Who Honors:** Albert Nelson Marquis Lifetime Achievement Award **To what do you attribute your success:** Mr. Morganroth attributes his success to being in the right place at the right time. Success means to him happiness and satisfaction and comfort **Why did you become involved in your profession or industry:** Mr. Morganroth became involved in his profession after leaving the U.S. Army when he was 19. Mr. Morganroth began studying pre-med, but eventually found that he was more interested in studying law. **Avocations:** Golf; Travel **Political Affiliations:** Democrat **Religion:** Jewish

John Selwyn Morris, PhD, DLitt, LLD, MA

Title: Philosopher, Educator, Academic Administrator (Retired) **Industry:** Education/Educational Services **Company Name:** Union College **Date of Birth:** 06/02/1925 **Place of Birth:** Tonypandy **State/Country of Origin:** Wales/UK **Parents:** Jenkin Morris; Hannah M. (Williams) Morris **Children:** Paul John **Education:** DLitt, Skidmore College (1991); Honorary LHD, Elmira College (1990); Honorary LLD, Hartwick College (1979); PhD, Columbia University (1961); MA, Colgate University (1961); Coursework, Union Theological Seminary (1957-1960); MA, University of Cambridge (1953); BA, The University College of South Wales and Monmouthshire (now Cardiff University) (1951) **Career:** President Emeritus, Research Professor of Philosophy, Union College, Schenectady, NY (1990-Present); Chancellor, Union University (1979-1990); President, Union College, Schenectady, NY (1979-1990); Professor of Philosophy, Union College, Schenectady, NY (1979-1990); Provost, Dean of Faculty, Colgate University (1973-1979); Professor of Philosophy and Religion, Colgate University (1970-1979); Acting President, Colgate University (1977); Director, Division of University Studies, Colgate University (1972-1973); Director, Division of Humanities, Colgate University (1970-1972); Associate Professor, Colgate University (1966-1970); Assistant Professor, Colgate University (1963-1966); Instructor, Colgate University (1960-1963); Minister, Vernon Center Presbyterian Churches (1954-1957); Ordained to Ministry, Presbyterian Church (1954) **Career Related:** Chairman, Indiana Commission for Higher Education (1984-1986); Leverhulme Visiting Fellow, University of Exeter, England (1968-1969); Trustee, Cazenovia College **Civic:** Trustee, Skidmore College **Military Service:** Royal Air Force (1943-1947) **Awards:** Founders Medal, Union College (1990); Schenectady Patroon Award (1989); Colgate University Alumni Corporation (1978); Distinguished Service Award; Fellow, Cardiff University **Memberships:** American Association of University Professors; The American Philosophical Association; American Academy of Religion; Royal Institute of Philosophy; Society for the Study of Theology; Former Member, Board of Directors, National Welsh American Foundation **Marquis Who's Who Honors:** Albert Nelson Marquis Lifetime Achievement Award; Marquis Who's Who Top Professional **Why did you become involved in your profession or industry:** Dr. Morris became involved in his profession because of his work as a minister in Wales. **Avocations:** Reading **Religion:** Presbyterian

Jaydene Morrison

Title: Education Counseling Firm Executive **Industry:** Education/Educational Services **Date of Birth:** 08/22/1933 **Place of Birth:** Cherokee **State/Country of Origin:** OK/USA **Parents:** Jay Frank Walker; Kathryn D. (Johnson) Walker **Marital Status:** Married **Spouse Name:** Ross Peterson (Deceased 2017); Michael H. Morrison, (07/11/1955, Deceased 1991) **Children:** Jay; Mac **Education:** Postgraduate Coursework, Central State University, Oklahoma (1967-1970, 1984); Postgraduate Coursework, University of Denver (1981-1982); Postgraduate Coursework, University of Colorado (1965); MS, Oklahoma State University (1957); BS, Oklahoma State University (1955) **Certifications:** Certified Counselor; Certified School Psychologist; Licensed Marriage and Family Therapist; Licensed Council, Oklahoma **Career:** President, Director, Ventures in Learning, Inc., Helena, OK (1984-Present); School Psychologist, Oklahoma State Department Education, Enid, OK (1977-1985); Psychometrist, Oklahoma State Title III Program, Alva, OK; Counselor, Teacher, Special Education, Helena-Goltry Public Schools, Oklahoma (1965-1973); Educator, Indianapolis Public Schools (1958-1959); Educator, Cushing Public Schools, Oklahoma (1955-1957) **Career Related:** With, Department Education Behavior Management Central District, Hawaii (1995-2000); Coordinator, Statewide Farm Stress Program (1994-1995); Therapist, Public School Liaison, Chisholm Trail Counseling Service (1993-1995); Consultant, Oklahoma Family Institute (1990-1993); School Psychologist, Oklahoma City Public Schools (1988-1993); Secretary, Treasurer, Oklahoma Pure Therapist Greenleaf Drug/Alcohol Rehabilitation (1988-1989); Vice President, Secretary/Treasurer, Oklahoma Made, Inc., Oklahoma City, OK (1988-1989); Part-time Counselor, Clayton Clinic (1987-1989); Rural Specialist, Oklahoma Conference Churches AG LINK (1986-1988); Career Counselor, Oklahoma City, OK (1985-1986) **Civic:** Counselor, United Methodist Counseling Center (1987-1988); Secretary-treasurer, 6th District of Oklahoma, Democratic State Executive Board (1983-1987); Assistant State Coordinator, Oklahoma American Agriculture Movement, Oklahoma City, OK (1982-1983); Chairman, Alfalfa County Excise and Equalization Board, Cherokee (1979-1983); Co-chairman, Alfalfa County Democratic Party, Cherokee (1976-1983); Member, Elder, Christian Church; Deacon, Presbyterian Church, Nederland, CO **Creative Works:** Author, "I'm Not Sick, Society Is-A 5 Step Drug-Free Parent/Teacher Guide" (2006); Author, "Coping with ADD/ADHD" (1995); Co-author, "Coping With a Learning Disability" (1992); Author, "I Hate You Miss Bliss" **Awards:** Named Outstanding Citizen of Year, Oklahoma Chapter, National Association Social Workers (1988); Special Award, Oklahoma Women for Agriculture (1979); Teacher of Year Award, Helena Masonic Lodge (1967) **Memberships:** Oklahoma Association Learning Disabilities; Garfield County Interagency Task Force; Oklahoma School Psychologists Association; National Association School Psychologists; Oklahoma Society Advancement Biofeedback; Biofeedback Society America; National School Psychologist; National Board for School Counselors; Chi Omega Alumni; Delta Kappa Gamma **Marquis Who's Who Honors:** Albert Nelson Marquis Lifetime Achievement Award; Marquis Who's Who Top Professional; Marquis Who's Who Humanitarian Award **Why did you become involved in your profession or industry:** Ms. Morrison became involved in her profession because of a commitment to children and their well being. She got into psychology and counseling because she was looking for answers. **Avocations:** Reading; Enjoying people and being involved with people; Travel **Political Affiliations:** Democrat **Religion:** Presbyterian

Wendell R. Mortimer

Title: Judge **Industry:** Law and Legal Services **Company Name:** ADR Services **Date of Birth:** 04/07/1937 **Place of Birth:** Alhambra **State/Country of Origin:** CA/USA **Parents:** Wendell Reed Mortimer; Blanche (Wilson) Mortimer **Marital Status:** Married **Spouse Name:** Cecilia Vick Mortimer (08/11/1962) **Children:** Michelle Dawn; Kimberly Grace **Education:** Doctorate of Letters (2016); JD, University Southern California (1965); AB, Occidental College (1958) **Certifications:** Judge, California Superior Court (1995-2007); Attorney, State of California (1966) **Career:** Arbitrator, Mediator, ADR Services Inc. (2008-Present); Complex Civil Litigation Panel, L.A. Superior Court (2000-2008); Judge, L.A. Superior Court (1995-2008); Private Practice, San Marino, CA (1994-1995); Partner, Thelen, Marrin, Johnson & Bridges (1976-1993); Associate, Thelen, Marrin, Johnson & Bridges (1973-1976); Trial Attorney, Legal Division, State of California (1965-1973) **Military Service:** U.S. Army (1960-1962) **Awards:** Judicial Civility Award, American Board of Trial Advocates (2000) **Memberships:** President, LA Railroad Heritage Foundation (2012-Present); American Board Trial Advocacy (1988-Present); American Judicature Society (2006); Past President, San Marino City Club (2006); International Academy of Trial Judges (2000); California Judges Association (2000); American Judges Association (2000); American Bar Association (1966); Los Angeles County Bar Association (1966); Legion Lexington, Irish-American Bar Association; Pasadena Bar Association; Balboa Yacht Club; San Gabriel Country Club; The Twilight Club **Bar Admissions:** California **Marquis Who's Who Honors:** Albert Nelson Marquis Lifetime Achievement Award; Marquis Who's Who Top Professional **Why did you become involved in your profession or industry:** After leaving the Army, Mr. Mortimer wanted to go back to school. He decided to go to law school, though he was not set on pursuing a career in law. However, he found a passion for the field and has since excelled as a lawyer and judge. **Avocations:** Photography; Railroads **Religion:** Presbyterian

Karl H. Muench

Title: Professor of Medicine **Industry:** Medicine & Health Care **Date of Birth:** 05/03/1934 **Place of Birth:** St. Louis **State/Country of Origin:** MO/USA **Parents:** Albert F. Muench; Virginia C. Kueter **Marital Status:** Married **Spouse Name:** Anyltha Torres Muench (1976) **Children:** Julia; Laura; Anita; Michael; Natalie **Education:** Doctor of Medicine, Washington University, Magna Cum Laude, St. Louis, MO (1960); Bachelor of Arts in Chemistry, Princeton University, Magna Cum Laude (1956) **Certifications:** Diplomate, American Board of Medical Genetics **Career:** Fellow in Biological Chemistry, Stanford University School of Medicine (1961-1965); Intern, Barnes Hospital, St. Louis, MO (1960-1961); Instructor to Full Professor of Medicine, University of Miami School of Medicine; Staff Member, Jackson Memorial Hospital, Miami, FL **Career Related:** Lecturer in Field **Civic:** Fundraiser, Princeton University **Creative Works:** Contributor, Articles to Professional Journals **Memberships:** American Medical Association; American College of Physicians; American College of Medical Genetics and Genomics **Marquis Who's Who Honors:** Albert Nelson Marquis Lifetime Achievement Award **Why did you become involved in your profession or industry:** Dr. Muench became involved in his profession while attending medical school at Washington University, during which time he extensively studied the structure and replication methods of DNA. He drew a wealth of inspiration from his professor, renowned microbiologist Arthur Kornberg. **Avocations:** Genealogy **Political Affiliations:** Democrat **Religion:** Christian

Walter Edward Mullendore, PhD

Title: Economist (Retired) **Industry:** Financial Services **Company Name:** University of Texas at Arlington **Date of Birth:** 04/22/1940 **Place of Birth:** Harrah **State/Country of Origin:** OK/USA **Parents:** Newton; Ida Minnie (Lohmann) M **Marital Status:** Married **Spouse Name:** Edra Janell Havenstrite (7/4/1963) **Children:** Matthew Edward; Karen Kay; Mark Andrew **Education:** Doctor of Philosophy in Economics, Iowa State University (1968); Master of Science, Oklahoma State University (1963); Bachelor of Science, Oklahoma State University (1961) **Career:** Retired (2002); Professor, University of Texas, Arlington (1975-2002); Faculty Member, Department of Economics, University of Texas, Arlington (1968-2002); Dean, College of Business, University of Texas, Arlington (1980-1993); Instructor, Iowa State University (1965-1967); Graduate Assistant, Oklahoma State University (1961-1963) **Military Service:** U.S. Army (1963-1965) **Creative Works:** Contributor, Articles to Professional Journals **Memberships:** President, Great Southwest Rotary (1989-1990); President, Missouri Valley Economic Association (1982-1983); Vice President, Missouri Valley Economic Association (1980-1981); Omicron Delta Epsilon **Marquis Who's Who Honors:** Albert Nelson Marquis Lifetime Achievement Award **To what do you attribute your success:** Mr. Mullendore attributes his success to hard work and the amazing tenacity of his graduate students. **Why did you become involved in your profession or industry:** Mr. Mullendore became involved in his profession because he was interested in economics and he was also an agriculture major. **Avocations:** Photography **Religion:** Methodist

Oscar Munoz

Title: Chief Executive Officer and President **Industry:** Business Management/Business Services **Company Name:** United Continental Holdings Inc. **State/Country of Origin:** CA/USA **Education:** MBA, Pepperdine University (1986); BS, University of Southern California (1982) **Career:** President, Chief Executive Officer, United Continental Holdings, Inc., (2016-Present); President, Chief Executive Officer, United Continental Holdings, Inc., Chicago, IL (2015-Present); Medical Leave, United Continental Holdings, Inc. (2015-2016); Executive Vice President, Chief Financial Officer, CSX Corp., Jacksonville, FL (2003-2015); Chief Financial Officer, Vice President, AT&T Consumer Services, AT&T Corp., Basking Ridge, NJ (2001-2003); Senior Vice President, Finance and Administration, Qwest Comms. International Inc., Denver, CO (2000); Chief Financial Officer, Vice President, U.S. West Retail Markets, Denver, CO (1999-2000); Vice President, Finance, Controller, USWEST Comms. Inc., Denver, CO (1997-1999); Executive Director, Coca-Cola Co., Atlanta, GA (1996-1997); Chief Financial Officer, Region Vice President, Coca-Cola Enterprises, Inc., Hollywood, CA (1991-1996); Division Controller, Director, Financial Operations, Assistant Corporate Controller, Coca-Cola Enterprises, Inc., Los Angeles and Atlanta (1986-1991); Financial Analyst, Accounting Manager, Manager, Financial Control, Pepsico Inc., Los Angeles and Purchase, New York (1983-1986) **Memberships:** Financial Executives Institute

Harry Munsinger, JD, PhD

Title: Owner **Industry:** Law and Legal Services **Company Name:** Law Office of Harry L. Munsinger **Spouse Name:** Kim M. Munsinger (02/09/1970, Divorced 04/15/2016) **Children:** Inga; Brita **Education:** Doctor of Jurisprudence, Duke University (1985); Doctor of Philosophy, Experimental and Clinical Psychology, University of Oregon (1958); Bachelor of Arts, University of California Berkeley, CA **Career:** Owner, Law Office of Harry L. Munsinger (2012-Present); Of Counsel, Bretton and Hall, San Antonio, TX (2008-2012) **Creative Works:** Author, "The History of Marriage and Divorce" (2019); Author, "The Texas Divorce Guide" (2018) **Awards:** Best Series of Three Articles (2019); Writing Award, The Best Featured Article in Texas (2013) **Bar Admissions:** Federal Court (2000); Texas State Bar (1995) **Avocations:** Bridge; Sail; Running; Reading; Swimming; Cooking; Visiting museums

Lilit Muradyan

Title: Chief Executive Officer **Industry:** Health, Wellness and Fitness **Company Name:** Licasa, Inc./DBA Resilient Recovery Center/New Road **Date of Birth:** 11/06/1986 **State/Country of Origin:** Armenia **Parents:** Zaven Manukyan Muradyan; Svetlana Muradyan **Marital Status:** Widow **Spouse Name:** Hobit Krboyan (Deceased, 09/13/2016) **Children:** Anna Diamond (Recording Artist) **Education:** BS, PharmD, Armenia **Certifications:** Interior Design, New York School of Interior Design **Career:** Chief Executive Officer, Licasa, Inc./DBA Resilient Recovery Center (2016-Present) **To what do you attribute your success:** Ms. Muradyan attributes her success to loving to make another mother smile. Working tirelessly to help others in need has helped her through her traumatic experiences. She understands the struggles that the people she helps are going through. **Why did you become involved in your profession or industry:** Ms. Muradyan became involved in her profession after witnessing the murder of her husband in 2016. To this day, she doesn't know who did it and why. To heal her pain, she decided to get involved in helping others in unfortunate situations. Initially, she had plans to open an orphanage to save children that needed structure in their lives. After some time trying to figure out how to do so, someone finally suggested that she begin work in the field of abuse and addiction, due to her ability to effectively communicate with others. She is now a mentor at a law school and owns her own company, which treats those with substance abuse and mental health issues.

James Michael Murray, Esq.

Title: Retired Law Librarian, Lawyer **Industry:** Law and Legal Services **Company Name:** United States Courts for the Ninth Circuit **Date of Birth:** 11/08/1944 **Place of Birth:** Seattle **State/Country of Origin:** WA/USA **Parents:** Clarence Nicholas; Della May (Snyder) M. **Marital Status:** Married **Spouse Name:** Linda Monthy Murray **Education:** MLaw Librarianship, University Washington (1978); JD, Gonzaga University (1971) **Career:** Lawyer; Retired Law Librarian, United States Courts for the Ninth Circuit, Spokane, WA (1997-2014); Librarian, East Bonner County Library District (1991-1997); Law librarian, assistant professor, Gonzaga University School Law, Spokane (1984-1991); Associate Law Librarian, Washington University of Law Library, St. Louis (1981-1984); Reference/Resource Librarian, University of Texas Law Library, Austin, TX (1978-1981) **Career Related:** National Reporter on Legal Ethics and Professional Responsibility (1982-1991); Member, State Advisory Board; Consultant in Field **Civic:** Board of Directors, Spokane Chapter, ACLU (1987-1991); Washington Volunteer Lawyers for the Arts (1976-1978) **Creative Works:** Author (with Gasaway and Johnson), "Law Library Administration During Fiscal Austerity" (1992); Author (with Reams and McDermott), "American Legal Literature: Bibliography of Selected Legal Resources" (1985); Editor, Book Appraisals Column, "Texas Bar Journal" (1979-1982); Contributor, Numerous Articles and Reviews to Professional Journals, Acknowledgements and Bibliographies in Field **Memberships:** Law School Liaison Committee, Washington State Bar Association (1986-1988); American Bar Association, Idaho Library Association **Bar Admissions:** U.S. District Court, Eastern District of Washington (1985); U.S. District Court, Western District of Washington (1975); Washington (1974) **Marquis Who's Who Honors:** Albert Nelson Marquis Lifetime Achievement Award **Why did you become involved in your profession or industry:** Mr. Murray simply wanted to be of service to people. **Avocations:** Travel; Exercise **Religion:** Roman Catholic

John E. Murray

Title: Vice President of Commercial Lending **Industry:** Financial Services **Company Name:** Foundation One Bank **Marital Status:** Married **Spouse Name:** Lynn **Children:** John; Bobby **Education:** BS in Criminal Justice (1990); Diploma, Omaha South High Magnet School (1983) **Certifications:** Real Estate License **Career:** Vice President of Commercial Lending, Foundation One Bank (2014-Present); Vice President, Mid City Bank, Inc. (1993-2011) **Civic:** Volunteer, Homeless Shelter **Memberships:** Rotary Club of Omaha Millard **To what do you attribute your success:** Mr. Murray attributes his success to listening to his father-in-law. **Why did you become involved in your profession or industry:** Mr. Murray became involved in his profession because of his father-in-law, who worked in the finance industry for more than 40 years and taught him everything he knows. **Avocations:** Watching football; Car enthusiast

Matt Murray

Title: Deputy Editor-in-chief **Industry:** Writing and Editing **Company Name:** The Wall Street Journal **Education:** MJ, Northwestern University; BJ, Northwestern University **Career:** Deputy Editor-in-chief, The Wall Street Journal, Dow Jones & Co. (2013-Present); Deputy Managing Editor, The Wall Street Journal, Dow Jones & Co. (2008-2013); Deputy National Editor to National News Editor, Management Group, General Electric (2004-2008); Senior Special Writer, Management Group Beat, General Electric (1999-2001); Banking Reporter, Money & Investing Section, The Wall Street Journal, Dow Jones & Co. (1997-1999); Reporter, Pittsburgh Bureau, Dow Jones & Co. (1994-1997) **Creative Works:** Author, "The Father and the Son"; Co-author, "Strong of Heart"

Denise Murrell, PhD

Title: Curator **Industry:** Museums & Institutions **Company Name:** Metropolitan Museum of Art **Education:** MBA, Harvard Business School (1980); PhD and Master's Degree in Art History, Columbia University; Coursework in Art History, Hunter College **Career:** Associate Curator, Metropolitan Museum of Art **Career Related:** Research Fellow, Ford Foundation (2014) **Creative Works:** Curator, "Posing Modernity: The Black Model from Manet and Matisse to Today," Wallach Art Gallery, Columbia University (2018); Curator, "Black Models: From Géricault to Matisse," Musée d'Orsay, Paris, France

Vanukuri Krishna Murthy, PhD, PE, MASCE

Title: Civil Engineer **Industry:** Engineering **Date of Birth:** 06/20/1928 **State/Country of Origin:** Hyderabad/India **Parents:** Rama Vannkuri; Sita (Dittakavi) Rao **Marital Status:** Married **Spouse Name:** Lakshmi Gruha Gadiraju (09/12/1952) **Children:** Siva; Prabha; Jyothy; Lata **Education:** Doctor of Philosophy, University of Pennsylvania (1967); Master of Science in Engineering, University of Florida (1964); Bachelor of Civil Engineering, Osmania University (1949) **Certifications:** Registered Professional Engineer, Texas **Career:** Consultant, Water Resources (1991-Present); Chief Engineer, Texas Water Commission (1990-1991); Head, Basin Modeling, Texas Water Commission, Austin, TX (1978-1990); Head, Hydraulics Design Section, Texas Water Rights Commission, Austin, TX (1972-1977); Hydrologist, Texas Water Rights Commission, Austin, TX (1968-1971); Instructor, University of Pennsylvania, Philadelphia, PA (1967-1968); Graduate Research Assistant, University of Pennsylvania, Philadelphia, PA (1966-1967); Graduate Research Assistant, University of Delaware, Newark, DE (1964-1966); Graduate Research Assistant, University of Florida, Gainesville, FL (1963-1964); Engineer, Government of Andhra Pradesh, Hyderabad, India (1949-1962) **Career Related:** Engineer Advisor to Commissioner, Pecos River Compact Commission, Austin, TX (1987-1991); Chairman, Engineering Advisory Committee (1987-1991); Principal Expert Witness in Interstate Law Suit, Texas v. New Mexico (1977-1990) **Creative Works:** Author, "Allocation of Pecos River Basin Water" (1991); Editor, Journal of Pipeline Division, American Society of Civil Engineers (1969-1974); Contributor, Articles, Professional Journals **Awards:** Travel Grant, National Science Foundation (1975) **Memberships:** Life Member, American Society of Civil Engineers; Sigma Xi **Marquis Who's Who Honors:** Albert Nelson Marquis Lifetime Achievement Award; Marquis Who's Who Top Professional

Janet Myhre

Title: Doctor, Professor Emerita **Industry:** Education/Educational Services **Company Name:** Claremont McKenna College **Date of Birth:** 09/24/1932 **Place of Birth:** Tacoma **State/Country of Origin:** WA/USA **Parents:** Leif Christian Klippen (Deceased); Thelma Gladys Klippen (Deceased) **Marital Status:** Married **Spouse Name:** Leon Hollerman (05/29/1988, Deceased 2006); Philip Cushman Myhre (06/12/1954, Divorced 1984) **Children:** Karin Elizabeth; Jeremy Hollerman **Education:** PhD in Mathematical Statistics, Stockholm University (1968); MA, University of Washington (1956); BA, Pacific Lutheran University, Summa Cum Laude (1954) **Career:** Doctor, Professor Emerita, Claremont McKenna College, Claremont, CA (2008-Present); Professor of Mathematics, Claremont McKenna College, Claremont, CA (1962-2008) **Career Related:** Founder, President, Mathematical Analysis Research Corporation, Claremont, CA (1973-Present); Consultant, Data Analyst, Strategic Systems Programs, US Navy, Washington, DC (1968-Present); Professor of Mathematics, Claremont Graduate University (1968-Present); Director, Reed Institute for Decision Science, Claremont McKenna College, Claremont, CA (1975-2008); Visiting Professor, Washington State University, Pullman, WA (1978); Consultant, Environmental Protection Agency (1976-1977); Associate Editor, Technometrics, American Statistical Association (ASA) (1969-1975); Instructor, Eidgenössische Technische Hochschule Zürich (1971-1972); Instructor, Stockholm University (1971-1972) **Civic:** Member, Reliability, Nuclear Safety and Risk Assessment, US Navy (1972-Present); Officer, Padua Hills Homeowners Association, Claremont, CA (1988-1994); Member, Board of Trustees, The Webb Schools, Claremont, CA (1984-1988); Member, Numerous Blue Ribbon Committees, US Navy **Creative Works:** Contributor, Chapters, Book; Contributor, Articles, Professional Journals **Awards:** Honorary Alumna, Claremont McKenna College (1996); Austin Bonis Award, American Society for Quality Control (Now American Society for Quality) (1984); Research Grant, Office of Naval Research (1973-1983); Lifetime Achievement Award, US Navy **Memberships:** Board of Trustees, Claremont Museum of Art (2007-Present); President, Claremont McKenna College, Chapter, Phi Beta Kappa (2004-2007); President, Southern California Chapter, American Statistical Association (ASA) (2003-2005); Council Representative, American Statistical Association (ASA) (2001-2003); Fellow, American Statistical Association (ASA); Padua Hills Museum Committee **Marquis Who's Who Honors:** Albert Nelson Marquis Lifetime Achievement Award **Avocations:** Gardening; Cooking; Used to go hiking; Used to spend time weaving **Religion:** Lutheran

Michael J. "Mike" Nadeau

Title: Staff Assistant (Retired), Purchasing Agent (Retired) **Industry:** Education/Educational Services **Company Name:** Passaic County Community College **Date of Birth:** 12/19/1949 **Place of Birth:** Glens Falls **State/Country of Origin:** NY/USA **Parents:** John Long; Mary Catherine (Cimo) N. **Marital Status:** Married **Spouse Name:** Charles J. Shanley Jr. **Education:** AA in English, Borough of Manhattan Community College, with Honors (1992) **Career:** Staff Assistant, Wanaque Academic Center, Passaic County Community College, Paterson, NJ (1999-2005); College Service Assistant, Passaic County Community College, Paterson, NJ (1993-1999); Purchasing Agent, Maersk Inc., Madison, NJ (1975-1993); Record Storage Clerk, Continental Insurance Co., Glens Falls, NY (1972-1975); Orderly, Glens Falls Hospital, Glens Falls, NY (1969-1971) **Military Service:** U.S. Navy (1969-1970) **Creative Works:** Author, "The Adventures of Prudence Longface" (1993) **Memberships:** The American Legion **Why did you become involved in your profession or industry:** Mr. Nadeau grew up in a small town called Fort Edward, and was interested in poetry and English from a young age. In 1975, he moved to Manhattan in search of meaningful work. Two years later, he met the knowledge of Eli Siegel, whose philosophy changed Mr. Nadeau's approach to life. He pins his success on the principles of Siegel's Aesthetic Realism, including the oneness of opposites and an understanding of liking the world on an honest basis. **Avocations:** Bowling; Swimming; Boating; Woodworking; Singing **Political Affiliations:** Democrat **Religion:** Roman Catholic **Thoughts on Life:** Mr. Nadeau is the proud owner of three dogs, a parrot and a parakeet. Between 1979 and 1981, he worked alongside blind performers during his time as an actor and singer with the Elbee Audio Players of New York.

Catherine Raseh Nagi

Title: Retired Community School Superintendent; Financial Planner **Industry:** Education/Educational Services **Company Name:** District 28 (Queens) **Date of Birth:** 10/13/1940 **Place of Birth:** Brooklyn **State/Country of Origin:** NY/USA **Parents:** Massed Nagi; Catherine (Irateo) Nagi **Education:** Postgraduate Coursework, St. John's University, Queens, NY (1976-1978); Postgraduate Coursework, Hofstra University (1967-1976); Postgraduate Coursework, Brooklyn College (1965-1967); MS, Brooklyn College (1964); BS, Brooklyn College (1962) **Certifications:** Financial Planning License **Career:** Retired (1997); Community School Superintendent, District 28 Board of Education, Queens, NY (1990-1997); Acting Principal, Public School 217-District 22, Brooklyn, NY (1980); Deputy Superintendent, District 22 Board of Education, Brooklyn, NY (1984-1990); Supervisor Comprehensive Planning, District 22 Board of Education, Brooklyn, NY (1979-1984); Supervisor Reimbursable Programs, District 22 Board of Education, Brooklyn, NY (1975-1979); Supervisor Health/Drug Education/Services, District 19 Board of Education, Brooklyn, NY (1973-1975); Narcotics Education Teacher Trainer, District 19 Board of Education, Brooklyn, NY (1971-1973); Acting Assistant Principal, Intermediate School 302-Dist. 19, Brooklyn, NY (1970-1971); Teacher, Acting Chair, Junior High School 78-District 22, Brooklyn, NY (1963-1970); Teacher, Health/Physical Education, Bay Ridge High School, Brooklyn, NY (1962-1963); Teacher Health/Physical Education, Junior High School 211-Dist. 18, Brooklyn, NY (1962) **Career Related:** Universities Grant Writer, New York City Board of Education (1973-Present); Teacher Adult Education/Community Centers, New York, NY (1959-1965); Presenter, New York City and New York State Educational Conferences **Creative Works:** Co-Author, Consultant, "Get Ahead In Math" (1985); Creator, Editor, "Gateways To Learning" (1977-1990); Creator, Developer Educational Data System (1976); Developer, First NYC/NY State Early Identification Learning Disabilities Program (1975) **Awards:** Recognition Award, Forestdale Foster and Adoptive Parents Association, Queens, NY (1992); Legislature Resolution, New York State Assembly/Senate (1991-1997); Congressional Record Recognition, U.S. Congress (1991-1997); City Council Proclamation, New York City Council (1991-1997); Educator of the Year, Association of Teachers of New York (1980); Queensboro President Proclamation; Superintendents Network Recognition, Fordham University New York City; Recognition, 112 Precinct Community Council **Memberships:** Association for Supervision and Curriculum Development; American Association of School Administrators; New York City Association of Superintendents; New York City Administrative Women in Education; Brooklyn/New York State Reading Counsel Association; Thomas Jefferson Democratic Club; Kings County Democratic Committee **Marquis Who's Who Honors:** Albert Nelson Marquis Lifetime Achievement Award; Marquis Who's Who Top Professional **Why did you become involved in your profession or industry:** Growing up, Ms. Nagi and her family experienced financial hardships. She was motivated to pursue a formal education, start a career, and free her family of their debt. She knew she wanted to be a teacher, but after discovering the lack of women in physical education, she knew she wanted to work in that field. **Avocations:** Travel; Languages; Sports; Singing; Gourmet cooking; Collecting stamps, coins, and pens **Political Affiliations:** Democrat

Theresa Napolitano

Marquis Who's Who
18 | 98
Biographee

Title: Attorney **Industry:** Law and Legal Services **Company Name:** TN Global Law **Children:** Madelena **Education:** Doctor of Jurisprudence, Seton Hall Law School (1997); Fulbright Scholar, University of Lund, Sweden (1996) **Certifications:** Comparative Religious Studies, Harvard; Human Rights Studies, Rutgers University **Career:** Owner, Lawyer, TN Global Law, New York, NY (2000-Present) **Civic:** Volunteer, Numerous Animal Shelters **Memberships:** National Rifle Association; New Jersey Bar Association; American Bar Association; American Immigration Lawyers Association; Association of New Jersey Rifle and Pistol Clubs **To what do you attribute your success:** Ms. Napolitano attributes her success to her Christian faith. **Why did you become involved in your profession or industry:** Mrs. Napolitano had always been sympathetic towards those who have suffered persecution. Once she started witnessing asylum interviews, she became more intrigued, witnessing firsthand what was going on in Egypt at the time, and felt compelled to help.

S. David Nathanson, MD, FRCS, FACS

Title: Oncologist, Surgeon, Educator **Industry:** Medicine & Health Care **Company Name:** Henry Ford Hospital **Date of Birth:** 12/12/1943 **Place of Birth:** Johannesburg **State/Country of Origin:** South Africa **Parents:** Hymie Barnett; Freda Charlotte (Weinberg) N. **Marital Status:** Married **Spouse Name:** Jerrilyn Marie B. (02/18/1979); Maxine Elaine Zacks, (11/29/1966, Divorced 09/1978) **Children:** Laurence Cecil; Joshua Russel; Abigail, Alison **Education:** MD, University of the Witwatersrand, Johannesburg, South Africa (1966) **Certifications:** Diplomate, American Board of Surgery (1983) **Career:** Professor of Surgery, Wayne State University School of Medicine (2008-Present); Director, Breast Cancer Center, Henry Ford Health Systems, Detroit, MI (1995-Present); Surgical Oncologist, Henry Ford Health Systems, Detroit, MI (1982-Present); Professor of Surgery, Case Western Reserve University, Cleveland, OH (1993-2005); Chief Resident in Surgery, University of California Davis, Sacramento, CA (1980-1982); Fellow in Surgical Oncology, University of California Los Angeles (1977-1980); Fellow in Immunology, University of California Los Angeles (1975-1977); Resident in Surgery, University of the Witwatersrand (1967-1974); Director, Breast Center Henry Ford Hospital, West Bloomfield, MI **Career Related:** Adjunct Associate Professor, Medical Physics, Oakland University, Rochester, MI (1993-Present); Cancer Liaison Physician (1988-2011); Endowed Chair, Breast Cancer Research, American College Of Surgeons Oncology Group (2001); Associate Clinical Professor, Surgery, University of Michigan, Ann Arbor, MI (1985-2000); Commission On Cancer Principal Investigator, HFHS; Fellow, American College of Surgeons; Fellow, Society of Surgical Oncology; Fellow, Royal College of Surgeons **Creative Works:** Author, "Surviving Arrogance" (2020); Author, "Ordinary Miracles" (2007); Author, "The Concealed Revealed"; Contributor, Over 200 Articles and Abstracts to Scientific Journals, Chapters to Books **Awards:** Surgical Oncologist of the Year, Henry Ford Health Systems (2017); Jae Ho Kim Award, Outstanding Surgical Oncologist, HFHS (2017); White House Distinguished Career Award (2007); Humanitarian Cancer Award (2006); Resident Teacher of the Year, Henry Ford Health Systems Department of Surgery (2006); Outstanding Teacher Awards, University of Michigan (1982-2000); National Institutes of Health Grantee, National Cancer Institute (1989) **Memberships:** Alternate Delegate, Wayne County Medical Society (1994-1996); American Society of Clinical Oncology; Western Surgical Association; American Association of Cancer Research **Marquis Who's Who Honors:** Albert Nelson Marquis Lifetime Achievement Award **Why did you become involved in your profession or industry:** Dr. Nathanson's mother taught him all sorts of things when he was a kid. When he was about 16, he had some exposure to illness. His grandmother got a condition, which seemed to be incurable. During his time at the University of California Los Angeles, he was doing immunology and he saw people who were surgical oncologists, and they looked like they really loved what they were doing. He spoke with them and a position became available, and he applied and got it. **Avocations:** Photography; Landscapes and portraits; Writing creative non-fiction; Writing memoirs **Thoughts on Life:** We should wake up every day and practice gratefulness, a way to feel happy without waiting for the world or events or people to make us feel happy. Take every opportunity we have to feel grateful and happiness will follow. Remember also that every living being is precious and valuable.

Ronald Clinton Naugle, PhD

Title: Historian, Professor Emeritus **Industry:** Education/Educational Services **Company Name:** Nebraska Wesleyan University **Date of Birth:** 09/18/1942 **Place of Birth:** Mitchell **State/Country of Origin:** IN/USA **Parents:** Durward Clinton Naugle; Martha May Naugle **Marital Status:** Married **Spouse Name:** Gretchen Rohn (06/02/1963) **Children:** Meredith **Education:** Doctor of Philosophy in American Studies, University of Kansas (1976); Master of Arts in American History, Purdue University (1966); Bachelor of Arts in American Government and Politics, Purdue University (1964) **Career:** Professor Emeritus of History, Nebraska Wesleyan University (2004-Present); Director, Historical Studies Graduate Program, Nebraska Wesleyan University (2004-2006); Chairman, Graduate Program, Nebraska Wesleyan University (2002-2005); Huge-Kinne Professor of History, Nebraska Wesleyan University (1985-2004); Chairman, Department of History, Nebraska Wesleyan University (1985-2004); Director, Wesleyan Honors Academy, Nebraska Wesleyan University (2001-2003); Associate Professor, Nebraska Wesleyan University (1980-1985); Huge-Kinne Endowed Chairman of History, Nebraska Wesleyan University (1980-1984); Assistant Professor, Nebraska Wesleyan University, Lincoln (1971-1980); Instructor of History, Nebraska Wesleyan University (1966-1971) **Career Related:** Chair, The Willa Cather Statutory Hall Project (2019); Representative, Mountain-Plains States Coordinators, Executive Committee of State Coordinators (1997-2005); Director, Nebraska Summer Institute for High School History and Social Studies Teachers (1991-2006); Co-Coordinator, "We the People" Program for High School History and Social Studies Students, Nebraska (1990-2003); State Coordinator, National History Day, Nebraska (1985-2005); Associate Fellow, Center for Great Plains Studies **Civic:** Chairman, Nebraska Hall of Fame Commission (2015-Present); Director, Honors Academy Dual Credit, Nebraska Wesleyan University (2006-Present); Emeritus Member, Honors Academy Dual Credit, Nebraska Wesleyan University (2006-Present); Nebraska Hall of Fame Commission (2003-Present); National Alliance of Concurrent Enrollment Partnerships (2001-Present); Representative, Four-Year Private College and Universities, National Board (2003-2006); Founder, Nebraska Foundation for the Preservation of Oral History (2001-2006); Treasurer, Nebraska Foundation for the Preservation of Oral History (2001-2006); Creator, Two-Week Educational Program for Social Studies Teachers, Fort Robinson, NE (1992-2003); Affiliate, Seven Denominational-Sponsored Ministries for Inner-City Omaha National Americans (1996-2001); Chairman, Native-American Strategy and Action Team of Interchurch Ministries of Nebraska (1985-2000); Multi-Cultural Education Training Team (1990-1993); Planning Committee, Healing the Hoop (1992); Head, One-Week Immersion Experiences for College Juniors, Omaha and Winnebago Indian Reservations (1991); Congregational Council, First Lutheran Church, Lincoln, NE (1981-1984); Chairman, Property Committee, University of Nebraska-Lincoln, Lutheran Student Center, Lincoln, NE (1974-1976); President, University Lutheran Church, The University of Kansas, Lawrence, KS (1971-1972); Multicultural Ministries Commission, Nebraska Synod, Evangelical Lutheran Church in America **Creative Works:** Editor, "Short History of Nebraska" (2018); Editor, "History of Nebraska" (2015); Co-Author, "Nebraska Quilts and Quiltmakers" (2003); Editor, "Life, Liberty and the Pursuit of Happiness, Volume II", McGraw Hill, (2003); Editor, "Ham, Eggs and Corncakes, A Nebraska Territorial Diary" (2001); Co-Author, "History of Nebraska (1997); Co-Author, "In the White Man's Image" (1992); Co-Author, "Nebraska Quilts and Quiltmakers" (1991); Co-Author, "White Man's Way" (1986) **Awards:** Award, "History of Nebraska, Fourth Edition," Nebraska Center for the Book (2015); Paul Beck Social Studies Teacher of the Year, Nebraska State Council of Social Studies (2003); Nebraska Sower Award, Nebraska Humanities Council (2003); Addison E. Sheldon Award, Nebraska Historical Society (1998); Frost Award for the Book, "Nebraska Quilts and Quiltmakers," Smithsonian Institution (1993); Clarion Award for the Film, "White Man's Way," Women In Communications (1987) **Memberships:** Chairman, Nebraska Hall of Fame Commission (2015-Present); President, Nebraska State Council History Education (2005-2008); Associate, International Quilt Study Center; Nebraska Historical Society; Lifetime Member, Phi Kappa Phi; Phi Alpha Theta, International History Honor Society **Marquis Who's Who Honors:** Albert Nelson Marquis Lifetime Achievement Award; Marquis Who's Who Top Professional; Marquis Who's Who Humanitarian Award **Why did you become involved in your profession or industry:** Dr. Naugle became involved in his profession after initially studying engineering in college. However, he soon pivoted towards history, and hasn't looked back since. **Avocations:** Carpentry; Cooking **Political Affiliations:** Democrat **Religion:** Episcopalian

Kourosh "Cyrus" Naziri

Title: General Manager **Industry:** Engineering **Company Name:** Cyrus 21st Century Entrepeneurship LLC **Date of Birth:** 10/31/1958 **Place of Birth:** Tehran **State/Country of Origin:** Iran **Marital Status:** Single **Education:** MS in Telecommunications/Engineering, The George Washington University (1988); BA, The George Washington University (1982) **Career:** General Manager, Cyrus 21st Century Entrepeneurship, LLC (2020); General Manager, Naziri Dental Corp (2003-2020); Lecturer, Washington DC Metropolitan Area; Data Network Specialist, World Bank **Career Related:** Science and Technology Research **Civic:** Salvation Army **Creative Works:** New Science Fiction Style; Original Style of Comedy **To what do you attribute your success:** Mr. Naziri attributes his success to hard work and innovation. **Why did you become involved in your profession or industry:** Mr. Naziri became involved in his profession because he always had a fascination with medical science and came from a family of doctors, dentist and health professionals. They had over 100 doctors in the extended family and that was part of the reason he wrote a book. He also enjoyed science fiction and always wanted to get into management. He was happy to be doing that currently. **Thoughts on Life:** Make the first move and God will bless you along the way.

Gail Neal, PT

Title: President/Owner (Retired) **Industry:** Health, Wellness and Fitness **Company Name:** Capital Physical Therapy Associates **Date of Birth:** 05/06/1938 **Place of Birth:** New Haven **State/Country of Origin:** CT/USA **Parents:** Edward Francis Fallon; Ruth Alexina (Hutchinson) Fallon **Marital Status:** Widowed **Spouse Name:** Marcus Pinson Neal Jr., MD (Deceased 12/23/2009) **Children:** Sandra Neal Dawson; Marcus Pinson III; Ruth-Catherine "Boo" Neal Perkins **Education:** BS in Physical Therapy, Medical College of Virginia (Now Virginia Commonwealth University School of Medicine) (1959); Coursework, Mary Washington College (Now University of Mary Washington) (1955-1957) **Certifications:** Licensed Physical Therapist (1959) **Career:** President, Owner, Capital Physical Therapy Associates, Richmond, VA (1989-2013); Physical Therapist On-call, St. Mary's Hospital, Richmond, VA (1968-1974); Interim Director, Stuart Circle Hospital, Richmond, VA (1968-1969); Private Practice, Richmond, VA (1965-1968); Chief, Physical Therapy, Stoughton Community Hospital, WI (1961-1963); Staff Physical Therapist, University Hospitals, University of Wisconsin-Madison, WI (1959-1961) **Career Related:** Chairman, Virginia Board of Physical Therapy (1995-1996); John Tyler Community College, Richmond, VA (1992-1994); Vice Chairman, Virginia Board of Physical Therapy (1992-1993); Lecturer, Medical College of Virginia (Now Virginia Commonwealth University School of Medicine), Richmond, VA (1992-1993); Advisory Board, Physical Therapy Virginia State Board of Medicine (Now Virginia Board of Physical Therapy) (1990-1996); Physical Therapist, St. Mary's Hospital, Richmond, VA (1975-1988); Governor Committee, Community Work; Consultant in Field **Civic:** President, Richmond Symphony Orchestra League (1986-1988); Rector of the Board of Visitors, University of Mary Washington (1982-1984); Board of Visitors, Mary Washington College (Now University of Mary Washington), Fredericksburg, VA (1980-1982); Advisory Board, Virginia Opera (1979-2010); Volunteer, Physical Therapy, Cerebral Palsy Center, Richmond, VA (1963-1964) **Awards:** Named Clubwoman of the Year, Richmond Newsleader (1972) **Memberships:** President, Medical Society of Virginia Alliance (1980-1981); President, Medical College of Virginia Hospitals Auxiliary (1973-1975); President, Richmond Academy of Medicine Auxiliary (1967-1968); American Physical Therapy Association; Richmond Academy of Medicine Auxiliary; Medical Society of Virginia Alliance; Medical College Virginia Hospitals Auxiliary; Virginia Cultural Laureate Society; Female Voice Club; Advisory Board, American Cancer Society, Inc.; Science Museum of Virginia; Virginia Museum of Fine Arts (VMFA) **Marquis Who's Who Honors:** Albert Nelson Marquis Lifetime Achievement Award **Why did you become involved in your profession or industry:** Mrs. Neal wanted to be a physical therapist from the fourth grade. She had a cousin who had brain surgery, and he never got better. He had to stay in an institution but on the weekends he would come home. It made her realize that people needed help. There were two people who came from London, Bo Bass; one was a psychiatrist and the other was a physical therapist and they did a lot to help people who had strokes, and children. She took their course and it was wonderful. Recently, when she fell, she was at an orthopedic hospital and they asked her if she ever did Bo Bass, and she told them yes she trained with them. **Avocations:** Reading; Music; Indian folklore; Horsemanship

Aleksandra Nejman

Title: President/CEO/CFO **Industry:** Financial Services **Company Name:** Aleksandra Nejman Holding Company I **Date of Birth:** 07/18/1985 **State/Country of Origin:** Poland **Education:** BA in Pre-Law and Business, Dominican University, River Forest, IL **Career:** Founder, President, CEO, CFO, Aleksandra Nejman Holding Company I (2017-Present); Executive Management, Wedgewood Investment Group, LLC (2014-2016); Physicist, Fermilab (2001) **Career Related:** Consultant, Robert Half Legal (2016-Present) **Civic:** Arbitrator, Mediator, Animal Custody Warriors (2015-Present) **Memberships:** ASPCA; Soi Dog **To what do you attribute your success:** Ms. Nejman attributes her success to training. **Why did you become involved in your profession or industry:** While working for a private equity firm, Ms. Nejman's chief executive officer would fund large projects for commercial development, which is what inspired her to pursue her current path. Throughout middle school, Ms. Nejman's keen interest was physics. As a freshman in high school, she regularly participated in particle physics seminars at Fermilab Particle Accelerator Laboratory. She was a particle physics researcher and collaborated with a German physicist on a paper regarding the particle nature of matter, a topic she still approaches in her studies today. Inspired by Albert Einstein's treatise on quantum mechanics, she pursued a topic many researchers simply did not approach, a theory known as simply too theoretical - is it possible to induce inception in particle mechanics? She is pursuing laboratories now for access to the particle accelerator for the purpose of induction research. **Thoughts on Life:** Ms. Nejman has obtained eight vertical loans for up to $1 billion a piece, so $8 billion for skyscrapers. Currently, she is negotiating the governing law behind each one and trying to narrow down a location for each one. The first vertical should be in the United States. She also obtained $1 billion in funding for an airline.

Richard C. "Rich" Nemanick Sr., JD, LLM

Title: Business Executive (Retired) **Industry:** Pharmaceuticals **Company Name:** The Lorvic Corp. **Date of Birth:** 12/08/1942 **Place of Birth:** St. Louis **State/Country of Origin:** MS/USA **Parents:** Charles Nemanick; Kathryn (Shank) Nemanick **Marital Status:** Married **Spouse Name:** Linda Nemanick (10/08/1999 -Present); Colleen Elizabeth Hennessy (08/26/1967-1/30/1996) **Children:** Richard C. Junior; Jeffrey R; Eric J; Nicholas Holzworth (Stepchild); Jill Garver (Stepchild); Elizabeth Noeth (Stepchild); James Thompson (Stepchild) **Education:** LLM, Washington University, St. Louis, MO (1978); JD, St. Louis University, Cum Laude (1967); BS, University of Missouri (1964) **Career:** President, The Lorvic Corp., St. Louis, MO (1986-1995);Vice President, Young Dental Inc. (1995-1999); Vice President, The Lorvic Corp., St. Louis, MO (1969-1986); Vice President, North America Security Corp., St. Louis, MO (1967-1970) **Career Related:** President, CKN Inc. (1984-Present) **Civic:** Alderman City of Town and Country (1986-1994); Chairman, Police and Fire Commission, Town and Country (1986-1994); Board of Directors, Century County Dispatching, Ballwin, MS (1986-1994); Board Member, Boys Hope Girls Hope of St. Louis; Founders Circle, Lydia House of St. Louis; Salvation Army; William Booth Society; Phi Delta Phi; Delta Sigma Pi **Military Service:** Staff Sargent, U. S. Army Reserves, Honorable Discharge (1973) **Creative Works:** Three Articles, Published, St. Louis University Law Journal **Awards:** Scholastic Award, Gamma Pi Epsilon, Jesuit Honor Society (1967); Scholastic Achievement, St. Louis University Law School (1967); Listee, Who's Who in MRHA (1964) **Memberships:** American Contract Bridge League; Phi Delta Phi; Order of the Woolsack; Delta Sigma Pi, Alpha Beta Chapter; Board Member, Chairman, The Lorvic Corp; Young Dental Inc.; North American Securities; Lindell Bank; CKN **Bar Admissions:** Missouri; St. Louis Bar; Missouri Bar **Marquis Who's Who Honors:** Albert Nelson Marquis Lifetime Achievement Award **To what do you attribute your success:** Mr. Nemanick attributes his success to his perseverance and confidence. He took advantage of every opportunity that came his way because he was never afraid to fail. **Why did you become involved in your profession or industry:** Mr. Nemanick chose to go into his family business, which put him in a great position to pursue civic work. **Avocations:** Golf; Swimming; Fishing; Reading; Walking; Playing bridge **Thoughts on Life:** Mr. Nemanick always looks for the big picture. He believes the most important responsibility in life is always to take care of his family.

Eric J. Nestler, MD, PhD

Title: Neuroscientist, Medical Educator **Industry:** Medicine & Health Care **Company Name:** The Friedman Brain Institute **Date of Birth:** 07/07/1954 **Place of Birth:** New York **State/Country of Origin:** NY/USA **Parents:** Herbert A. Nestler; Mildred D. Nestler **Marital Status:** Married **Spouse Name:** Susan DeRenzo (12/06/1980) **Children:** David I.; Matthew E.; Jane D. **Education:** Honorary PhD, Uppsala University (2011); MD, PhD, Yale University (1983); BA, Yale University (1976); Residency in Psychiatry, McLean Hospital **Certifications:** Diplomate, American Board of Psychiatry and Neurology, Inc. **Career:** Nash Family Professor of Neuroscience, Department of Neuroscience, Icahn School of Medicine at Mount Sinai (2008-Present); Director, Friedman Brain Institute, Icahn School of Medicine at Mount Sinai (2008-Present); Distinguished Professor, Chairman, Department of Psychiatry, The University of Texas Southwestern Medical Center, Dallas, TX (2000-2008); Professor, Director, Division of Molecular Psychiatry, Yale School of Medicine (1987-2000); Former Chairman, Department of Neuroscience, Icahn School of Medicine at Mount Sinai **Career Related:** Sloan Research Fellowship (1987) **Civic:** Former President, Society for Neuroscience (2017); Former President, American College of Neuropsychopharmacology (2011) **Creative Works:** Co-Author, "Neurobiology of Mental Illness"; Co-Author, "Molecular Neuropharmacology: A Foundation for Clinical Neuroscience"; Contributor, Articles, Medical Journals **Awards:** Wilbur Cross Medal for Alumni Achievement, Yale University (2017); The Rhoda and Bernard Sarnat International Prize in Mental Health, National Academy of Medicine (2010); Falcone Prize (2009); Goldman-Rakic Prize for Outstanding Achievement in Cognitive Neuroscience, The Brain & Behavior Research Foundation (2008); Neuroscience Research Grant, Freedom to Discover Program, Bristol-Myers Squibb Company (2004); Jordi Folch-Pi Award, American Society of Neurochemistry (1990); Scholar Award, McKnight Foundation (1989); Scholar Award, Pfizer Inc. (1987) **Memberships:** Fellow, American Association for the Advancement of Science; National Academy of Medicine; American Academy of Arts & Sciences **Marquis Who's Who Honors:** Albert Nelson Marquis Lifetime Achievement Award **Why did you become involved in your profession or industry:** Dr. Nestler became involved in his profession because of his lifelong interest in medicine. He was inspired by his father, a high school biology teacher.

Charles H. Neumann

Title: Professor Emeritus **Industry:** Education/Educational Services **Date of Birth:** 01/30/1943 **Place of Birth:** Washington **State/Country of Origin:** DC/USA **Parents:** Bernhardt Walter; Emma (Habitz) Neumann **Marital Status:** Married **Spouse Name:** Cheryl Elaine Girard (06/18/1965) **Children:** Matthew Roy; Kristen Elizabeth **Education:** MAT in Mathematics, Michigan State University (1965); BS in Mathematics, Michigan State University (1964); AS, Alpena Community College, Michigan (1962) **Career:** Professor Emeritus, Oakland Community College (2009-Present); Professor, Mathematics and Statistics, Oakland Community College, Bloomfield Hills, MI (1984-2009); Mathematics Science Department Chair, Alpena Community College (1969-1984); Instructor, Mathematics, Alpena Community College (1966-1984); Science Teacher, Alpena Public Schools (1965-1966) **Career Related:** Member, Consumers Advisory Committee, Delta Dental of Michigan, Ohio and Indiana (2006-Present) **Civic:** Vice President, Michigan Education Special Services (2005-Present); Trustee, Michigan Education Special Services (2002-Present); Chairman, Board, Lutheran Social Services of Michigan (2004-2005); Board of Directors, Lutheran Social Services of Michigan (1996-2005); Vice Chair, Board, Lutheran Social Services of Michigan (1999-2003); Member, Executive Committee, Oakland County Democratic Committee, Michigan (1995-1996); Board of Directors, Blue Cross Blue Shield of Michigan (1986-1994); Trustee, Michigan Education Special Services (1975-1993); President, Michigan Education Special Services (1976-1993); Board of Directors, Ohio Vision Service Association (1988-1989); Board of Directors, Michigan Vision Service Association (1985-1989); Scoutmaster, Troop 92, Boy Scouts of America, Alpena, MI (1981-1984) **Memberships:** Vice President, Two-year Colleges, Michigan Association Higher Education (1970-1996, 2002-2004); Vice President, Oakland Community College Faculty Association (1998-2001); President, Oakland Community College Faculty Association (1995-1998); Advisory Committee Membership, National Education Association (1993-1996); Vice President, Oakland Community College Faculty Association (1994-1995); President, MESSA (1976); Board of Directors, Michigan Education Association (1974-1980); Delegate, National Education Association (1974-1980); American Mathematics Association Two-Year Colleges; Michigan Mathematics Association Two-Year Colleges; Mathematics Association America; Phi Kappa Phi **Marquis Who's Who Honors:** Albert Nelson Marquis Lifetime Achievement Award; Marquis Who's Who Top Professional; Marquis Who's Who Humanitarian Award **Why did you become involved in your profession or industry:** Mr. Neumann started out as an electrical engineer, and was so taken with mathematics he decided to emphasize his studies in mathematics. **Avocations:** Collecting antique books; Racquetball; Cross country skiing **Religion:** Lutheran

Samuel Ralph Newcom, MD

Title: Professor of Medicine (Emeritus) **Industry:** Medicine & Health Care **Company Name:** Emory University **Date of Birth:** 06/14/1943 **Place of Birth:** Bastrop **State/Country of Origin:** TX/USA **Parents:** Samuel George Newcom; Grethel Joy (Conklin) Newcom **Marital Status:** Married **Spouse Name:** Janis Sue (Williams) **Children:** Samuel Joshua; Cassandra Lynn (Carr); Seth Emerson **Education:** Fellow, University of California San Francisco (1972-1974); Resident, University of Southern California (1970-1972); MD, University of Southern California (1969); BA in Psychology, Berkeley and Santa Barbara Campuses, University of California **Certifications:** Diplomate, American Board of Internal Medicine - Internal Medicine, Hematology, Medical Oncology **Career:** Professor of Medicine, Emory University, Atlanta, GA (1984-Present); Associate Professor and Head of Medical Oncology, Oregon Health & Science University Portland, OR (1979-1984); Assistant Professor and Chief, Medical Oncology Clinic, University of California San Francisco (1975-1979); Instructor, Medicine, University of Oregon, Portland, OR, Medical Oncologist, Hematologist, Portland Clinic (1974-1975); Intern, U.S. Public Health Service, Staten Island, NY (1969-1970); Professor of Medicine (Emeritus), Emory University, Atlanta, GA **Career Related:** Chief, Lymphoma Leukemia Service, Grady Memorial Hospital; Chief, Hematology/Oncology Service, Atlanta Veterans Affairs Medical Center; Presenter, Local, National, and International Scientific Organizations **Military Service:** Senior Assistant Surgeon, U.S. Public Health Service **Creative Works:** Assistant Editor, American Journal of The Medical Sciences (1995); Editor, "Hematologic Malignancies in the Adult" (1979); Editor, "Supplemental 5 Blood" (1977); Contributor, Articles, Professional Journals **Awards:** Grantee, National Institutes of Health (1981, 1984, 1990); Fellow, American Cancer Society (1980-1983); Grantee, M.J. Murdock Trust (1981); Grantee, American Cancer Society (1980) **Memberships:** Fellow, American College of Physicians; American Society of Clinical Oncology; American Association for Cancer Research; American Society of Hematology; American Federation for Clinical Research (AFCR); Southern Society; Southern Society for Clinical Investigation; American Association for the Advancement of Science; American Medical Association **Marquis Who's Who Honors:** Albert Nelson Marquis Lifetime Achievement Award; Marquis Who's Who Top Professional **To what do you attribute your success:** Dr. Newcom attributes his success to excellent mentors including Dwight Conklin, MD, Georgia Friou, MD (Immunology/Rheumatology), Samuel Rapaport, MD James Linman, MD, and Steve Shohet, MD (Hematology), Joe Bateman, MD, Martin J. Cline, MD, and Ted Jacobs, MD (Medical Oncology), Marshall Kadin, MD, and Charles Huguley, MD from Emory University. **Why did you become involved in your profession or industry:** Dr. Newcom became involved in his profession because his parents grew up on Iowa Farms and physicians were prominent in the small towns of Griswold and Denison, where they went to high school. By the time he was two or three years old, his mother told him that he should become a doctor; her younger brother went to the University of Iowa School of Medicine and practiced medicine. Dr. Newcom spent summers with him observing and assisting in Lake City and Oakland in Iowa. In addition, medicine was being celebrated via television and movies, further glamorizing the profession. **Political Affiliations:** Democrat **Religion:** Methodist **Thoughts on Life:** Dr. Newcom said, "There is no more rewarding or exciting life than that provided by the practice of medicine - particularly when interwoven with active investigation and research."

Roger Austin Newell, PhD

Title: Geologist, Mining Executive, Consultant **Industry:** Mining & Metals **Date of Birth:** 03/01/1943 **Place of Birth:** Portland **State/Country of Origin:** OR/USA **Parents:** Lester Judson; Myrtle Elizabeth (Reisner) Newell **Marital Status:** Married **Spouse Name:** Mary Anne Norman (06/18/1965) **Children:** Andrea; Heidi **Education:** PhD, Applied Earth Sciences in Specialty in Minerals Exploration, Stanford University (1975);MSc in Geology and Economic Geology, Colorado School of Mines (1971); BSc in Geology, University of Oregon (1965) **Certifications:** Qualified Person Geologist (Retired), Maine Mathematics and Science Alliance **Career:** Consulting Geologist (2016-Present); Director, Midway Gold Inc. (2012-2016); President, Chief Executive Officer, Lake Victoria Mining Company, Inc. (2009-2015); Vice President of Development, Capital Gold, Inc. (2000-2009);Vice President of Development, Western Exploration Inc. (1995-2000); Regional Manager, Gold Fields Mining Company, Denver, CO (1992-1995); Exploration Manager, Gold Fields Mining Company, Reno, NV (1989-1992); Exploration Manager, Newmont Exploration Ltd., Danbury, CT (1984-1989); Exploration Geologist, Newmont Exploration Ltd., Tucson, AZ (1977-1983); Geologist, Researcher, Kennecott Exploration Ltd., Salt Lake City, UT (1974-1977) **Civic:** Director, National Mining Hall of Fame (2009-Present); Alumni Board President, Colorado School of Mines (2007-2008); U.S Peace Corps, Malaysia (1965-1968); Stanford University PhD, Research Topic Geology & Geochemistry at Tombstone, Arizona **Awards:** Henry DeWitt Smith Scholar, Stanford University (1972) **Memberships:** Foundation President, Society of Economic Geologists (1999-2000); Fellow, Society Economic Geologists; 50+ Year Member, American Institute of Mining and Exploration; Society of Mining Engineers (AIME/ SME); Fellow, Geological Society America; Nevada Geological Society; Past Member, Sigma Xi **Marquis Who's Who Honors:** Albert Nelson Marquis Lifetime Achievement Award; Marquis Who's Who Top Professional **Why did you become involved in your profession or industry:** Dr. Newell became involved in his profession because in high school a neighbor was taking a university geology course and loaned him the textbook, saying he might be interested in being a geologist; this sparked a lifelong career. He wanted to be a geologist since he was a junior in high school. He was lucky as he was in the right place at the right time. **Avocations:** Skiing; Traveling; Playing tennis **Religion:** Episcopalian

Patricia H. Newsome, MEd

Title: Elementary School Educator (Retired) **Industry:** Education/Educational Services **Company Name:** Muscogee County School District **Date of Birth:** 07/12/1939 **Place of Birth:** Athens **State/Country of Origin:** GA/USA **Parents:** Charles N. Harris; Frances (Cummings) Harris **Marital Status:** Widow **Spouse Name:** Paul W. Newsome (Deceased) **Children:** Marti Hinds-Kurtz; Brad Newsome; Robin N. Vircsik; Burt Newsome; Regina Newsome (step-daughter) **Education:** Master of Education, Georgia State University (1974); Bachelor of Science in Education, Auburn University (1961) **Career:** Elementary School Educator, Muscogee County School District, Columbus, GA (1968-1999) **Civic:** President, Free Spirits-Senior Adults, Saint Luke United Methodist Church; Tutor, Our House, Board of Directors, Second Harvest Food Bank; Board of Directors, Older Adult Council, St. Luke Methodist Church; Delegate, South Georgia United Methodist Conference **Awards:** Reading Teacher of Year, Muscogee County (1987-1988) **Memberships:** President, Alpha Chi Chapter, Alpha Delta Kappa (2004-2006); Chairman, Necrology, Muscogee Retired Educators Association; Chair, Muscogee County Council IRA; Executive, Mr. & Mrs. Club; Fellow, Jesus Is Lord Sunday School Class, Saint Luke United Methodist Church; President, Circle 3, United Methodist Women; President, Prayer Room, Chain and Meals on Wheels Program; Georgia Council IRA; Georgia Science Teachers Association; District VI Science Teachers Association; Georgia Retired Educators Association, Circle 3, United Methodist Women; Alpha Delta Gamma Sorority **Marquis Who's Who Honors:** Albert Nelson Marquis Lifetime Achievement Award; Marquis Who's Who Top Professional **Why did you become involved in your profession or industry:** Mrs. Newsome became involved in education when she returned home after her sophomore year of college and was asked to work in bible school. She had previously been frustrated with her experiences working in music, and found that she liked working with children much better, so she changed her major and focused on education.In her church, she was a music major. She was not a sight reader and she couldn't play by ear so she had to practice three times as much as her fellow players. **Avocations:** Reading; Traveling; Dining; Church service **Political Affiliations:** Republican **Religion:** Methodist

George Durfee Newton Jr., LLB

Title: Lawyer (Retired) **Industry:** Law and Legal Services **Date of Birth:** 04/19/1931 **Place of Birth:** Rochester **State/Country of Origin:** NY/USA **Parents:** George Durfee Newton; Nora (Dexter) Newton **Marital Status:** Married **Spouse Name:** Marja H. Newton (07/16/1955) **Children:** Patricia; George Durfee, III; Melinda; Deborah **Education:** Coursework, "Complex Litigation," Wake Forest Law School (1991-2003); LLB, Yale College (1958); Director, Moot Court (1956-1957); BA in Government, Harvard College, Cum Laude (1953) **Career:** Retired, RJR Nabisco, Inc., Winston-Salem, NC (1991); Vice President, Deputy General Counsel, RJR Nabisco, Inc., Winston-Salem, NC (1985-1991); Partner, Kirkland & Ellis (1964-1985); Associate, Kirkland & Ellis, Chicago, IL (1958-1964) **Civic:** Director, Task Force on Firearms National Commission Causes and Prevention of Violence, Washington, DC (1968-1969); Member, Episcopal Church, Congregational Church **Military Service:** Counter Intelligence Corps, U.S. Army, Korea (1953-1955) **Creative Works:** Author, "My Life Inside Big-Case Litigation," Blue Moon Books (2017); Author, "Firearms and Violence in American Life" (1969) **Memberships:** Indian Hill Landings, Old Town, Piedmont **Bar Admissions:** North Carolina (1989); Illinois (1958) **Marquis Who's Who Honors:** Albert Nelson Marquis Lifetime Achievement Award; Marquis Who's Who Top Professional **Why did you become involved in your profession or industry:** Mr. Newton was influenced by his grandfather and father who were both lawyers. **Avocations:** Scuba diving (1973-2001); Stamps; Coins; Tennis; Baseball fan; Spending Time with Family **Political Affiliations:** Republican **Religion:** Episcopalian, Congregationalist

Samuel John Nicholas Jr.

Title: Arbitrator and Mediator **Industry:** Law and Legal Services **Date of Birth:** 07/04/1937 **Place of Birth:** Yazoo City **State/Country of Origin:** MS/USA **Parents:** Samuel J. Nicholas; Mildred Lucille (Jefferies) Nicholas **Marital Status:** Divorced **Spouse Name:** Olivia Thomas Nicholas **Children:** Samuel John III; Christopher Walter; John Thomas **Education:** Student, University of Notre Dame, Notre Dame, IN; BBA, MBA, University of Mississippi, Oxford, MS; JD, LLM, Mississippi College School of Law, Jackson, MS **Career:** Arbitrator (1968-Present); Chairman of the Board, Southland Management Corporation (1968-Present) **Career Related:** Consultant, Office of Governor of Mississippi; Adjunct Professor of Law, University of Mississippi, Oxford, MS, and Mississippi College, Jackson, MS; Assistant Professor of Economics, Millsaps College, Jackson, MS; Lecturer, Amos Tuck School of Business, Dartmouth College, Hanover, NH **Civic:** Several Local and State Boards and Commissions; Active Participant, Local and State Civic, Educational and Religious Projects **Military Service:** U.S. Marine Corps **Creative Works:** Featured, Video, "A Conversation with Sam Nicholas, Jr. '66" (2015) **Awards:** 50-Year Member, AAA; 50-Year Member, NAA **Memberships:** Federal Mediation and Conciliation Service (FMCS); American Arbitration Association (AAA); National Academy of Arbitrators (NAA); Supreme Court Historical Society; American Bar Association; American Business Law Association; Bar Association Ethics Committee; Christian Conciliation Service of Central MS, Inc.; Federal Bar Association; Industrial Relations Research Association; International Labor Law Society; Mississippi Arbitration Advisory Council; National Association of Railway Referees **Bar Admissions:** Mississippi Bar; Federal Bar Association **Marquis Who's Who Honors:** Albert Nelson Marquis Lifetime Achievement Award; Marquis Who's Who Top Professional **To what do you attribute your success:** Mr. Nicholas' success can be attributed to having many quality mentors in his life. **Why did you become involved in your profession or industry:** Mr. Nicholas became involved in this profession because he was invited by labor, management and courts. **Avocations:** Reading; Playing sports; Working out; Keeping up with Notre Dame and Dartmouth; Hiking; Camping; Hunting; Traveling **Religion:** Roman Catholic **Thoughts on Life:** Develop an "attitude of gratitude." Say thank you to everyone you meet for everything you do for you. Managing his charities keeps Mr. Nicholas grateful for how blessed he is. He makes sure that he keeps a stack of ones in his glove box so that he may give a dollar to someone in need, and often takes time to stop and talk. He prays for them, but he tells them he wants something in return for his $1 - he asks them to pray for him.

Richard Allen Nicholls, MA

Title: Educator (Retired) **Industry:** Education/Educational Services **Company Name:** Palos Community Consolidated School District 118 **Date of Birth:** 09/01/1944 **Place of Birth:** Chicago **State/Country of Origin:** IL/USA **Parents:** Harry Allen Nicholls (Deceased 2012); Rita Mae (O'Connell) Nicholls (Deceased 2007) **Marital Status:** Single **Spouse Name:** Karen Ann Miller; Linda Lee Soderberg (03/27/1969, Divorced 1980) **Education:** MA, National Louis University (1991); Postgraduate Coursework, Loyola University Chicago (1967); BA, MacMurray College (1966); AA, Lincoln College (1964) **Certifications:** National, Certified Volleyball Coach (1981-1996) **Career:** Retired (2001); Seventh and Eighth Grade Teacher, Palos Community Consolidated School District 118, Palos Park, IL (1967-2001); Sixth Grade Teacher, Chicago Public Schools (1966-1967) **Career Related:** Retired Coach (1996); Co-Writer, Curriculum for Development of Thematic Units for Transition of Palos South Junior High School to Palos Middle School (1995); Illinois Goals Assessment Program Committee for School Standards (1992-1993); Volleyball Coach, Carl Sandburg High School (1985-1991); Volleyball Coach, Palos South Junior High School (Now Palos South Middle School) (1977-1990); Volleyball Coach, Victor J. Andrew High School (1981-1984); Sponsor, Student Government, Palos Community Consolidated School District 118 (1971-1973); Sponsor, Pompom Squad (1971-1973); Curriculum Development Committee (1970-1972) **Creative Works:** Guest Speaker, United States History, Various Schools and Organizations (2001-2009) **Awards:** Finalist, Amateur Athletic Union of the United States, Inc. (1996); National Champion, Amateur Athletic Union of the United States, Inc. (1981-1982, 1995); Fifth Place, Junior Olympics National Tournament (1985, 1994); Citizenship Award, American Legion (1964); Runner-Up, Chicago City Champion in Baseball (1962); Chicago City Champion in Baseball (1960-1961); Co-Rookie of the Year, Palos Athletics; Marquis Who's Who of American Educators; Who's Who of America's Best Teachers **Memberships:** Volleyball Coach, Amateur Athletic Union of the United States, Inc. (1981-1982, 1984-1985, 1987, 1995-1996); Volleyball Coach, Junior Olympics National Tournament (1985, 1994); National Education Association; Illinois Education Association; United States Volleyball Association; Phi Theta Kappa Honor Society **Marquis Who's Who Honors:** Albert Nelson Marquis Lifetime Achievement Award **Why did you become involved in your profession or industry:** Mr. Nicholls became involved in his professional because of his faith. He looked to Jesus Christ for inspiration, as Jesus was a teacher and walked with the people. **Avocations:** Coaching volleyball; Sponsoring school trips to Washington, DC and Springfield, IL for 22 years; Personal training for physical fitness **Political Affiliations:** Moderate Conservative Republican **Religion:** Methodist

Carol J. Nichols, EdS

Title: Retired Nurse Educator **Industry:** Education/Educational Services **Parents:** Cecil Guy; Augusta Nichols **Marital Status:** Widowed **Spouse Name:** Roy E. Mitchell **Education:** EdS, Georgia State University (1987); MEd, Georgia State University (1980); BS in Vocational Education, Georgia State University, Cum Laude (1978); Diploma in Nursing, Greenville Hospital, South Carolina (1963) **Career:** Retired (2001); Instructor, Pediatrics, Atlanta Technical College (1974-2001); Coordinator, Infection Control, Atlanta Technical College (1993-2000); Assistant Supervisor, Operating Room, Joan Glancey Hospital, Duluth, GA (1974); Staff Nurse, Operating Room, Northeast Georgia Medical Center, Gainesville, GA (1974); Supervisor, Psychiatric Area, Touro Infirmary, New Orleans, LA (1973); Staff Nurse to Head Nurse, Doctors Memorial Hospital, Atlanta, GA (1971-1973); Assistant Head Nurse, Radiation Therapy Department, Nurse Educator, Shands Teaching Hospital, Gainesville, FL (1969-1971); Nurse Educator, Instructor, Staff Nurse, Shands Medical Center Teaching Hospital, Gainesville, FL (1968-1969); Staff Nurse, Psychiatric Unit, Greenville General Hospital (1963-1968) **Civic:** Project Manager, Fundraiser, American Family Foundation Inc.; Contributor, Sewing, Charity **Awards:** Deans List **Memberships:** Treasurer 4th District, Georgia Nurses Association; American Heart Association; Past Vice President, First Vice President, Region I, Georgia Vocational Association; American Vocational Association; Mortar Board; Golden Key; Blue Key; Kappa Delta Pi **Marquis Who's Who Honors:** Albert Nelson Marquis Lifetime Achievement Award **Why did you become involved in your profession or industry:** Ms. Nichols always wanted to be a nurse. At a very young age she knew she wanted to be a nurse. If she didn't become a nurse she would have been a dress designer. **Avocations:** Sewing; Machine embroidery **Political Affiliations:** Republican **Religion:** Methodist

Jan Hildreth Nichols

Title: Elementary School Educator, Childbirth and Parenting Educator (Retired) **Industry:** Education/Educational Services **Company Name:** Rocky Mountain School for the Gifted and Creative **Date of Birth:** 07/01/1948 **Place of Birth:** Glenwood Springs **State/Country of Origin:** CO/USA **Parents:** Pershing Loveland Nichols; Myrna Jean Nichols **Children:** Carrie Christine Schultz; Taylor James Pruss **Education:** MA, University of Northern Colorado (1973); BA, University of Northern Colorado (1971) **Certifications:** Certified Prenatal Parenting Instructor, Prenatal Parenting (2003); Licensed Childbirth Educator, Lamaze International (1982); Certified Doula **Career:** Retired (2008); Teacher, Rocky Mountain School for the Gifted and Creative (2006-2008); Kindergarten and Elementary Teacher, Douglass Elementary School (1992-2005); Pre-academic Teacher, Boulder Valley Schools (1987-1992); Teacher, Physically Handicapped, St. Vrain Public Schools, Longmont, CO (1985-1987); Lead Teacher, Mountain View Pre-school, Boulder, CO (1983-1984); Child Evaluator, St. Vrain Public Schools, Longmont, CO (1979-1980); Special Education Teacher, Jefferson County Schools, Lakewood, CO (1973-1974); Special Education Teacher, Ouray Public Schools, CO (1971-1972) **Career Related:** Childbirth and Parenting Instructor, Boulder Community Hospital (1990-Present) **Civic:** Contributor, Head Start, Boulder, CO (1988-1989); Volunteer, Visiting Angels; Volunteer, Egypt, Kenya, Ghana, South Africa and Thailand **Awards:** Recipient, Mapmaking Grant, Foundation for Boulder Valley Schools (Now Impact on Education) (2003); Recipient, Reading Comprehension Grant (2002); Recipient, Math Education Grant (1995) **Memberships:** Lamaze International **Marquis Who's Who Honors:** Marquis Who's Who Humanitarian Award **Why did you become involved in your profession or industry:** Ms. Nichols' sister is a nurse, and watching her teach child birth classes inspired her. Having her own children was also something that spurred her on. **Avocations:** Spending time with her family and friends; Gardening; Making art; Reading; Outdoor activities **Thoughts on Life:** Ms. Nichols was once hired as a tutor for a family who was travelling around the world. She traveled with them for three months, and taught the four young girls in the family. They spent time volunteering, especially in Africa. Ms. Nichols has five grandchildren; Alex and Austin from her daughter, Carrie Christine Schultz, and Brie, Brooklyn and Blake from her son, Taylor James Pruss.

William J. Nicholson

Title: Energy and Environmental Consultant (Retired) **Industry:** Oil & Energy **Company Name:** Potlatch Corporation **Date of Birth:** 08/24/1938 **Place of Birth:** Tacoma **State/Country of Origin:** WA/USA **Parents:** Ferris Frank Nicholson; Athyleen Myrtle (Fesenmaier) Nicholson **Marital Status:** Married **Spouse Name:** Carland Elaine Crook (10/10/1964) **Children:** Courtney; Brian; Kay; Benjamin **Education:** Master of Business Administration, Pacific Lutheran University, Tacoma, WA (1969); Doctor of Philosophy in Chemical Engineering, Cornell University, Ithaca, NY (1965); Master of Science in Chemical Engineering Practice, Massachusetts Institute of Technology, Cambridge, MA (1961); Bachelor of Science in Chemical Engineering, Massachusetts Institute of Technology, Cambridge, MA (1960); Graduate, Stadium High School (1956) **Certifications:** Registered Professional Chemical Engineer, Washington **Career:** Retired (2015); Independent Energy and Environmental Consultant, Potlatch Corporation, American Forest and Paper Association, Washington (2002-2015); Chair Energy Council, American Forest and Paper Association, Washington (1998-2002); Director, Corporation Energy and Environmental Services, Potlatch Corporation, San Francisco (1994-2002); Manager, Corporation Energy Service, Potlatch Corporation, San Francisco, CA (1976-1994); Planning Associate, Potlatch Corporation, San Francisco, CA (1970-1975); Senior Development Engineer, Battelle Northwest, Richland, WA (1969-1970); Senior Development Engineer, Hooker Chemical Company, Tacoma, WA (1964-1969) **Career Related:** Member, Massachusetts Institute of Technology Educational Council (1971-Present); Expert Energy Management, US Technical Advisory Group International Standards Organization (2008-2014); Project Peer Reviewer, U.S. Department of Energy (2004-2008); Advisory Committee, Federal Biomass (2000-2005); Chairman, Advisory Board (2003); United States Expert, Environmental Labeling International Standards Organization (1994-2000); Advisory Board College Natural Resources, University of California, Berkeley, (1993-1995); Chairman, Advisory Board (1993-1995); Advisory Board, Forest Products Laboratory (1992-2003); Expert Witness, Public Utility Regulatory Policy Act; Expert Witness, Rate Hearings, Public Utility Commissions of Idaho, Minnesota, Arkansas, Washington **Civic:** First Presbyterian Church, San Anselmo, CA (1970); Chair, Electricity Committee (21 Years); Supporter, Boy Scouts of America **Awards:** George B. Morgan Award, MIT Educational Council (2000) **Memberships:** American Association for the Advancement of Science; Associate, American Institute of Chemical Engineers; American Chemical Society; Environmental Council; Sigma Xi; Sons in Retirement **Marquis Who's Who Honors:** Albert Nelson Marquis Lifetime Achievement Award; Marquis Who's Who Top Professional **Why did you become involved in your profession or industry:** Dr. Nicholson was inspired to enter his profession by a family friend, who was a chemical engineer. **Avocations:** History; Genealogy; Playing bridge **Political Affiliations:** Republican **Religion:** Presbyterian

Robert M. Niecestro

Title: Managing Director **Industry:** Financial Services **Company Name:** AccelaPHARM Investment, LLC **Place of Birth:** Chicago **State/Country of Origin:** IL/USA **Parents:** James; Josephine **Marital Status:** Married **Spouse Name:** Caryn **Children:** Arielle; Aaron **Education:** Postgraduate Coursework, University of Illinois (1985-1987); PhD in Biochemistry, University of Illinois at Chicago (1985); BS in Biological Science, University of Illinois at Chicago (1979) **Career:** Head of Investments, AccelaPHARM Investment, LLC (2012-Present); Managing Director, General Partner, AccelaPHARM (2004-Present); Founder, Head of Regulatory Affairs and Vice President, Axsome Therapeutics (2012-2018); Founder, Executive Vice President, Clinical & Regulatory, TG Therapeutics, Incorporated (2012-2018); Executive Vice President, Clinical and Regulatory Affairs, Keryx Biopharmaceuticals, Incorporated (2004-2016); Executive Vice President, Clinical Development (2002-2004); Senior Director, Research and Development, Eisai Incorporated, Teaneck, NJ (1997-2000); Organon Incorporated, Azko Nobel Pharma Division, West Orange, NJ (1991-1997) **Career Related:** Regulatory Consultant, Stemline Therapeutics (2006-2012); Strategic Regulatory-Development Consultant, Over 10 Biotechnology and Pharmaceutical Companies; Adjunct Professor, Muhlenberg College, Allentown, PA; Adjunct Professor, City College of New York **Civic:** Board of Directors, Collaborative Study Group, Vanderbilt University (2014-Present); Managing Director, AccelaPHARM Investment, LLC; Scientific Advisory Board, Oncolix **Creative Works:** Contributor, Over 60 Peer-Reviewed Publications; Three Patents Pending **To what do you attribute your success:** Mr. Niecestro attributes his success to his quest for knowledge and to gain answers to the unknown. **Why did you become involved in your profession or industry:** Mr. Niecestro loved research and answering questions. In science, there are always questions to be answered.

Dale Frederick Nitzschke, PhD

Title: Chancellor (Retired) **Industry:** Education/Educational Services **Company Name:** Southeast Missouri State University **Date of Birth:** 09/16/1937 **Place of Birth:** Remsen **State/Country of Origin:** IA/USA **Marital Status:** Married **Spouse Name:** Linda Hutchinson (06/24/1971) **Children:** Mary Beth; Stephen; Lori; Eric; David **Education:** PhD in Guidance and Counseling, Ohio University, Athens, OH (1964); MEd in Guidance and Counseling, Ohio University, Athens, OH (1960); EdB, Loras College, Dubuque, IA, Cum Laude (1959) **Career:** Chancellor, Southeast Missouri State University, Cape Girardeau, MO (1999-2001); President, Southeast Missouri State University, Cape Girardeau, MO (1996-1999); President, University of New Hampshire, Durham, NH (1990-1994); President, Marshall University, Huntington, WV (1984-1990); Vice President of Academy Affairs, University of Nevada, Las Vegas, NV (1980-1984); Professor of Education, University of Nevada, Las Vegas, NV (1980-1984); Dean, College of Education, University of Northern Iowa (1976-1980); Professor of Education, University of Northern Iowa (1976-1980); Associate Dean of Professional and General Studies, School of Arts and Sciences, State University of New York, Plattsburgh, NY (1972-1976); Dean of Education, School of Arts and Sciences, State University of New York, Plattsburgh, NY (1972-1976); Associate Dean, College of Education, Ohio University, Athens, OH (1967-1972); Associate Professor of Education, Ohio University, Athens, OH (1967-1972); Chairman, Department of Education, Loras College, Dubuque, IA (1965-1967); Instructor of Education, Loras College, Dubuque, IA (1961-1963) **Career Related:** Workshop Director, Evaluation of Elementary Schools; Director, Martha Holden Jennings Foundation's Lectureship Series; Consultant, Athens Non-graded High School; Consultant on Personnel Management, University of Nevada, Reno School of Medicine **Civic:** Greater St. Louis Council, Boy Scouts of America (1997-Present); Board of Directors, The New England Council (1991-1995); Ex-officio Member, New Hampshire Post-secondary Education Commission (1991-1995); New England Board of Higher Education (1991-1995); New Hampshire Economic Development Commission (1991-1995); Panel of Judges, New Hampshire High Tech Entrepreneur Awards (1991); Chairperson, Board of Regents State Advisory Committee for the Iowa Braille and Sight Saving School (1978); Chairperson, Board of Regents State Advisory Committee for the Iowa School for the Deaf (1978); New York State Policy Board in Special Education (1975-1976) **Creative Works:** Peer Reviewer, Committee on Athletics Certification, National Collegiate Athletic Association (NCAA) (1996-1998); Author, "Endorsement of State Government Can Enhance Opportunities for Research and Development Funding at Land-grant Universities," Boston Globe (1993); Author, "Putting Education and Research to Work," New Hampshire Premier (1993); Author, "A New Day for the University," New Hampshire Premier (1993); Author, "Economic Development Talk is Cheap...But Costly," Higher Education Reform in Europe and America Conference, Innsbruck, Austria (1992); Author, "Our Quality of Life: A Gathering of People is an Essential Beginning," New Hampshire Premier (1992); Author, "Beyond Mandates: Public Service to Public Schools," New Hampshire Premier (1992); Co-author, "Graduate Education: Some Issues, Concerns, and Challenge," AACTE, ERIC, SP013795 (1979) **Awards:** John T. Crowe Award, Regional Commerce and Growth Association (1998); George E. Hill Distinguished Alumni Award, Ohio University (1988); Administrator of the Year, West Virginia Association for Counseling and Development (1987); West Virginian of the Year Award, West Virginia Chapter, Public Relations Society of America (PRSA-WV) (1987); Kappan of the Year, Phi Delta Kappa Chapter, Marshall University (1987); Distinguished Speaker Award, Huntington Jaycees (1987); West Virginian of the Year Award, Marshall University, State of West Virginia (1986); Excellence in Communication Community Award, River Cities Chapter, International Association of Business Communicators (1986); George Van Zandt Community Service Award, Huntington Jaycees (1986) **Memberships:** Rotary Club of Cape Girardeau (1997-Present); Missouri Slope Areawide United Way (1999); Commission on Women, American Council on Education (1999); President, Ohio Valley Conference (1997-1998); Planning & Development Committee, Ohio Valley Conference (1997-1998); Academic Excellence Committee, Rotary International (1997-1998); Hall of Fame Committee, Ohio Valley Conference (1997-1998); Chairperson, Hall of Fame Committee, Ohio Valley Conference (1996-1997); Vice President, Ohio Valley Conference (1996-1997); Public Affairs Committee, Ohio Valley Conference (1996-1997); New England Defense Conversion Task Force (1994-1995); New England Council of Presidents (1994); Golden Key National Honor Society (1993-1995); Board of Directors, Public Service of New Hampshire (1992-1995); Board of Trustees, Nature Conservancy, New Hampshire Chapter (1992-1995); Ex-officio Member, Board of Trustees, University System of New Hampshire (1990-1995); Chief Executive Officer, New Hampshire Public Television (New Hampshire Public Broadcasting) (1990-1995) **Marquis Who's Who Honors:** Albert Nelson Marquis Lifetime Achievement Award; Marquis Who's Who Top Professional

George Harry Nolan, MD

Title: Obstetrician/Gynecologist **Industry:** Medicine & Health Care **Date of Birth:** 12/20/1935 **Place of Birth:** Kansas City **State/Country of Origin:** MO/USA **Parents:** Edward P.; P. Lee (Boykin) N **Marital Status:** Married **Spouse Name:** Leila R. Hajjar-Nolan **Children:** Philip; Nicole; Monique; Justin; Yasmeen; Jason **Education:** MPH, University of Michigan (1970); MD, Howard University (1962); BA in Biological Sciences, Drake University (1957) **Certifications:** Diplomate National Board Medical Examiners; American Board of Obstetrics-Gynecology; American Board of Maternal-Fetal Medicine **Career:** Acting Chairman, OBGYN. Henry Ford Health System (1995-1996); Chief of Obstetrics Division and Head of Maternal-Fetal Medicine, Henry Ford Medical Center, Detroit (1988-1997); Professor, Chairman of Obstetrics-Gynecology, Howard University College of Medicine, Washington (1980-1988); Fellow, Maternal-child Health Nutrition, National Foundation March of Dimes, Montreal, Canada (1978); Associate Professor Maternal Child Health, Population Planning (1976-1980); Associate Professor of Obstetrics-Gynecology, University of Michigan, Ann Arbor, (1976-1980); Assistant Professor, Maternal Child Health, Population Planning (1970-1980); Assistant Professor of Obstetrics-Gynecology, University of Michigan, Ann Arbor, (1973-1976); Faculty Fellow, J. Macy Foundation, Ann Arbor, MI (1973-1976); Acting Director, obstetrics-gynecology, University of Missouri Medical School, Kansas City, MO (1966-1967); Intern, Then Resident, Obstetrics-Gynecology, University of Missouri, Kansas City, (1962-1966) **Career Related:** Board Examiner, American Board of Obstetrics and Gynecology (1980-1990) **Civic:** Board Regents National Library. Medicine; Commander. United States Public Health Service (1967-1969) **Military Service:** U.S Public Health Service Commissioned Corp. (1967-1970); Deputy Chief Obstetrics and Gynecology: Staten, Island N.Y.; Final Rank Commander **Awards:** Firestone Fellowship in Tropical Medicine; Harbel, Liberia, West Africa USPHS Fellowship, Maternal Child Health; Population Planning Josiah Macy Jr, Faculty Fellow **Memberships:** Fellow, American College of Obstetrics-Gynecology; Member, Society Perinatal Obstetrics-Gynecology **Marquis Who's Who Honors:** Albert Nelson Marquis Lifetime Achievement Award **To what do you attribute your success:** Dr. Harry attributes his success to his parents, teachers and those who gave him a chance. **Religion:** Episcopalian

Janiece Simmons Nolan, PhD

Title: Retired Health System Chief Executive Officer, Scientist and Board Director **Industry:** Health, Wellness and Fitness **Place of Birth:** Fort Worth **State/Country of Origin:** TX/USA **Parents:** James Coleman Simmons (Deceased 1976); Berenice Johnson Simmons (Deceased 1999) **Marital Status:** Married **Spouse Name:** Robert L. Nolan, MD, JD, MPH **Children:** Douglas; Patricia; Nancy; Margo; Sheffield; Gemini **Education:** Master of Public Health in Hospital Administration, School of Public Health and Business School, University of California Berkeley (1975); Postdoctoral Fellow, Physiology/Anatomy Department, University of California Berkeley (1970-1973); PhD in Biology, Tulane University (1968); MA in Botany, University of Texas, Austin (1963); BA in Plan II (Accelerated Liberal Arts), University of Texas, Austin, with High Honors (1961) **Certifications:** Diplomate, American College of Healthcare Executives **Career:** Retired 2008, Chief Executive Officer and Board Member, John Muir Physician Network, a California medical foundation owning physician practices and negotiating health plan contracts (1997-2008); Chief Operating Officer and other titles, John Muir Medical Center, a 512-bed acute care private hospital and regional trauma center, Walnut Creek, CA (1977-1997); Assistant Director, Hospitals and Clinics, University of California, San Francisco Medical Center, the research and teaching hospital of the University of California, San Francisco (1975-1977); Post Doctoral Fellow, Physiology/Anatomy Department, University of California Berkeley (1970-1973); Research Physiologist, Acting Associate Chief of Staff for Research and Education, Chief, Tissue Culture Laboratory, Veterans Administration Hospital, a 400-bed acute care hospital, Martinez, CA (1970-1973); Head of Cell Biology, Gulf South Research Institute, New Orleans, LA (1968-1970); Chief Biologist, Aerospace Medicine, Texas Nuclear Corporation (Nuclear Chicago), a nuclear research facility producing neutron generators, Austin, TX (1963-1965) **Career Related:** Published 23 peer reviewed articles in scientific journals (1962-1978); Calstar (medical helicopters) Board (1984-1985); Mosquito Cell Culture, Water Pollution by Polio Virus and Aging of Human Cells in Culture (1968-1970); Aerospace Medicine Research on the Effects of Radiation on Human Cells in Space Travel (1963-1965) **Civic:** Member, Industry Advisory Board, Center Health Management Research (2004-2008); Member, Corporate Advisory Board for Graduate Program in Health Management Research, University of California Berkeley (2003-2008); Commissioner, State Commission on Emergency Services, Sacramento, CA (1997-2000) **Military Service:** Navy Veteran, Captain (O-6) U.S. Naval Reserve, Medical Service Corps (Retired); Commanding Officer of Reserve Hospital Units, including a Marine Support Detachment; Three-Time Recipient, Navy Commendation Medal; Recipient, Humanitarian Service Medal; Recipient, Armed Forces Reserve Medal **Creative Works:** Historical Fiction/Family Biography on Amazon: "Son of a Civil War Surgeon" (2017) and "Up From Hester Street" (2012) **Awards:** Distinguished Leadership Award, Graduate Program for Health Management, Alumni Association, University of California, Berkeley (2009); Inductee, Women's Hall of Fame for Leadership, Contra Costa County Commission for Women (2008); Woman of the Year, Women Health Care Executives, San Francisco (1989); Mortar Board, University of Texas, Austin (1960); Phi Beta Kappa (1960); Woodrow Wilson Fellow (1960) **Memberships:** Life Member, Naval Reserve Association; University of California, Berkeley Section Club (2008-Present); Daughters of the American Revolution (DAR) (2017-present); Member, Colonial Dames of the 17th Century, 2019-present; Board of Directors, Phi Beta Kappa Northern California Association (2005-2011); Alumna, Delta Gamma Sorority (President, Beta Eta Collegiate Chapter) (1959-1960) **Marquis Who's Who Honors:** Albert Nelson Marquis Lifetime Achievement Award **To what do you attribute your success:** Dr. Nolan attributes her success to serendipity and a very supportive husband and family. **Why did you become involved in your profession or industry:** Beginning in 1963, Dr. Nolan had a successful 10-year career as a research scientist in cell biology in laboratories in Austin, New Orleans and Berkeley. In 1973, she shifted career focus, becoming one of 12 students accepted for the two-year Master of Public Health program in Hospital Administration at the University of California Berkeley. Her employer, the Veterans Administration appointed her to their national Graduate Education Program. Her relationship with the Veterans Administration did not continue. Her first hospital management position was in the private sector. **Avocations:** Modeling - print ads/commercials (Agent: Models, Inc., Pleasanton, CA); Writing; International travel; Genealogical research **Political Affiliations:** Democrat **Thoughts on Life:** Dr. Nolan believes she has successfully combined demanding careers with being a devoted wife, mother and grandmother.

Tyler Norman

Title: Chief Executive Officer **Industry:** Aviation **Company Name:** Aero Engine Solutions **Children:** Three Children **Education:** MBA in Aviation, Embry-Riddle Aeronautical University (2016); BS in Aeronautics, Aviation, Aerospace and Technology, Embry-Riddle Aeronautical University (2012) **Career:** President and Chief Executive Officer, Aero Engine Solutions (2015-Present); Whole Asset Manager, Intertrade (2015); Principal Product Line Manager, Intertrade (2014-2015); Senior Product Line Manager (Engines), Intertrade (2013-2014); Product Line Representative, AeroTurbine, Inc. (2011-2013); Owner, Air and Land Partners, LLC **Civic:** Sponsor, FLORIDAAVIATIONNETWORK.COM; Sponsor, Wounded Warrior Project; Sponsor, 22KILL **Military Service:** Sergeant, U.S. Marine Corps (2004-2009) **Awards:** Good Conduct Medal; Humanitarian Service Medal; Certificate of Appreciation; Global War on Terrorism Expeditionary Medal; Sea Service Deployment Ribbon; National Defense Service Medal; Certificate of Commendation; Marine Corps Pistol Qualification Badge; Letter of Appreciation; Global War on Terrorism Service Medal **To what do you attribute your success:** Mr. Norman attributes his success to hard work and family stability. He also credits his knack for hiring people who are smarter than him. His military background has provided him with excellent training and leadership skills, as well as a network of military professionals with whom he's made great relationships over time. **Why did you become involved in your profession or industry:** Mr. Norman became involved in his career when he began working at a large aircraft company. There, he learned a great deal about the industry and engines in particular. When he chose to leave the company, Mr. Norman was hired by Rockwell Collins and tasked with heading their engine division. He was successful in this position but made the difficult decision to leave in favor of being closer to his son. With encouragement from his father, Jeff, Mr. Norman decided to start his own business. **Avocations:** Golf; Boating; Fishing; Coaching baseball

Frank Nosek

Title: Senior Attorney **Industry:** Law and Legal Services **Company Name:** Nosek Law Group, LLC **Date of Birth:** 04/13/1934 **Place of Birth:** Evanston **State/Country of Origin:** IL/US **Parents:** Francis J. Nosek; Loretto (Brannan) Nosek **Marital Status:** Married **Spouse Name:** Janet Child (12/30/1964) **Children:** Francis J. III; Peter C. **Education:** JD, University of Idaho (1960); BA in Political Science, University of Idaho, Moscow (1956) **Certifications:** Supreme Court of the United States (2004); The District of Columbia (1978); Alaska (1962); United States District Court for the District of Alaska (1962); United States Court of Appeals for the Ninth Circuit (1961); United States District Court for the Northern District of California (1961); California (1961) **Career:** Hon. Counsel General for the State of Alaska on behalf of the Czech Republic (1990-Present); Senior partner, Nosek, Bradberry, Wolf and Schlossberg, Anchorage (1967-1975); Associate, Bell, Sanders & Tallman, Anchorage (1961-1962); Private practice, Anchorage (1960-1967, 1975) **Career Related:** Adjunct Professor, University of Alaska, Anchorage Graduate Business School (2007-2010); Editor, State of Alaska Real Estate Commission, Anchorage (1983); Lecturer, Anchorage Community College (1979-1983); Adjunct Professor, University of Alaska, Mat-Su Community College, Anchorage (1976-1982); Small Business Administration (1975-1997) **Civic:** Honorary Consul General (2009-Present); Honorary Consul for Czech Republic (1999); IIHF World Junior Championships, Anchorage (1988); Chairman Anchorage Parks and Recreation (1968-1983) **Creative Works:** Author, "Alaska Mortgage Law, How to Buy and Sell a Business"; Contributor Articles, Law Journals **Awards:** Super Lawyers (2007-2017); Honorary Consul General for Alaska, Ministry of Foreign Affairs - Czech Republic (1999) **Memberships:** American College of Real Estate Lawyers, Alaska Bar Association; California Bar Association, Real Estate Law Committees; The District of Columbia Bar Association, International Law Committee; Anchorage Bar Association **Marquis Who's Who Honors:** Albert Nelson Marquis Lifetime Achievement Award; Marquis Who's Who Top Professional **Why did you become involved in your profession or industry:** He had lots of lawyers in his family including his father and grandfather. He knew from an early age he was going to be a lawyer and is delighted he did. He also knew in high school that from reading lots of Jack London books on Alaska, that he was coming to Alaska. His connection to the Czech Republic came from a Czech man who called his office, probably based on his Czech last name-Nosek, and that man wanted to go over and help the developing country of Czechoslovakia. Mr. Nosek got interested in wanting to help. He starting going to the Czech Republic, did lots of business transactions, helped the U.S. governemnt set up its aide program for what became the Czech Republic, finding office space for US aide to monitor the large federal grant, and lots and lots of legal transactions. Then in 1998, the Czech Repulic began to require licensing of lawyers doing legal work for Czechs and he stopped doing the work there. **Avocations:** Mountain climbing; Ice hockey; Antique cars

Sally Johnson Novetzke

Title: Former Ambassador **Industry:** Government Administration/Government Relations/Government Services **Date of Birth:** 01/12/1932 **Place of Birth:** Stillwater **State/Country of Origin:** MN/USA **Marital Status:** Widow **Spouse Name:** Richard (Deceased 2013) **Children:** Sara Elliot; Beth Johnsen; Chip Novetzke; Drew Novetzke **Education:** Honorary PhD, Mount Mercy College (1991); Coursework, Carleton College (1950-1952) **Career:** Chairman of the Board, Family Company, U.S. Name Plate Inc. (1970-Present); Ambassador to Malta, American Embassy, Valletta, Malta (1989-1993) **Career Related:** Founder, Sunday School, Oklahoma City Catholic Church **Civic:** Trustee, American University in Rome (2001-Present); Vice Chairman, Life Trustee, Member, Executive Committee, Hoover Presidential Library (1982-Present); Member, Advisory Board, National Representative of Women (1987-1989); State Chairman, Iowa Representative Central Committee (1984-1986); Chairman, Linn County Republican Committee (1980-1983); Co-chaiman, Vice President Bush Inauguration (1980); Advisory Council, Shattuck-St. Mary's School, Faribault, MN; Chairman, National Council Youth Leadership, Trustee, 4-Oaks Juvenile Facility; Member, Council, American Ambassador, Vice President Hoover; Past Trustee, Vice President, Board Director, Mount Mercy College, Cedar Rapids, IA; Past Trustee, Vice President, Board Director, Shattuck-St. Mary's School, Faribault, MN; Past Board Director, James Baker III Public Policy Institute, Rice University; Board Director, Life Trustee, Cedar Rapids Community Theater, Cedar Rapids, IA; Past Member, Advisory Council for Career Education; Past Member, Planning Council, Kirkwood Community College; Past Member, Legislature Representative, National Council on Vocational Education; Iowa Co-chairman, George Bush for President; Co-chair, Representative, Central Committee; Board Director, Ambassador Forum, Garden Club of America **Awards:** Distinguished Alumni Award for Outstanding Achievement, Carleton College (1994); Distinguished Alumnus Award, Stillwater High School (1991); Decorated Dame, Order of Knights of Malta **Marquis Who's Who Honors:** Albert Nelson Marquis Lifetime Achievement Award **To what do you attribute your success:** Success for Ms. Novetzke is being happy, and happy at what she's doing: that's success. She enjoyed doing what she does, she didn't get paid she volunteered but that was part of the enjoyment doing things for people. **Why did you become involved in your profession or industry:** Mrs. Novetzke has always been interested in politics, and so was her father. She attended college during the Korean War and unfortunately she could not finish. Mrs. Novetzke decided she could always attend college where ever she went. She moved to Hawaii and three months later she began her family and that was not the right time for her to start school however what Mrs. Novetzke gained was life experience. She lived in Oklahoma City for six years and became involved with the republican party. She worked for Barry Goldwater and held various positions and that open the door to many civic opportunities. She started the Sunday School in an Oklahoma City Catholic Church and also started a Brownie troop in her town. She worked for George Bush and became very good friends with him. She was co-chairman of his inauguration. When George Bush was elected president, he called Mrs. Novetzke and asked if she would be the 11th Ambassador of Malta. **Avocations:** Gardening; Used to ski and sail; Sports **Political Affiliations:** Republican **Religion:** Catholic

Deanna Kuiper Noyes, PhD

Title: Professor **Industry:** Education/Educational Services **Company Name:** Dallas Baptist University **Date of Birth:** 09/25/1961 **Place of Birth:** Muskegan **State/Country of Origin:** MI/USA **Parents:** Ronald Jay Kupier; Eilene Joyce Kuiper **Spouse Name:** Stephen Casper Noyes (04/11/1985) **Children:** Johnathan Caleb; Joshua David **Education:** PhD, University of Southern Mississippi, Hattiesburg (1997); MS in Medical Genetics, University of Mississippi, Jackson, MS (1987); BS in Biology, Belhaven College, Jackson, MS (1983) **Career:** Full Professor, Biology, Dallas Baptist University (2003-Present); Full Professor, Dallas Baptist University (1999-Present); Adjunct Professor, Biology, Dallas Baptist University (1997-2003); Adjunct Professor, Physics, University of North Texas, Denton, TX (1997-1999); Adjunct Professor, Geology, Texas Women's University, Denton, TX (1997); Adjunct Professor, Physical Science, William Carey College, Hattiesburg, MS (1995-1997); Adjunct Professor, Science Education, University of Southern Mississippi, Hattiesburg, MS (1994-1997); Teacher, Chemistry, Physics, Jackson Preparatory School, Mississippi (1987-1994) **Career Related:** School Board, Sachse Christian Academy, Texas (2005-Present); Content Editor, Cook Museum of Natural Sciences, Huntsville, AL (2017-2019); Ecological Society of America National Conference, Austin, TX (2011); Native Plant Conference, Stephen F. Austin (2008-2011); Speaker in Field **Civic:** Representative Club, Sachse, TX (2004); Band Member, First Baptist Church, Sachse, TX (2003-2015); Leader, Awana, Richardson, TX (1998-2003); Science Content Advisor, Cook Natural Science Museum, Huntsville, AL; Christian Ecologist Speaker's Bureau, Earth Stewardship Outreach, Faith Communities; Preservation Society, Spring Creek Forest, Richardson, TX **Awards:** Inductee, Beta Beta Beta Biological Honor Society (2012); Featured Listee, Who's Who in American Professionals (2008); Featured Listee, Who's Who Among Women (2006); Inductee, Phi Delta Kappa (1995); Featured Listee, Who's Who Among America's Teachers (1994-2004); Distinguished Teacher, White House Commission on Presidential Scholars (1994); Inductee, Sigma Zeta, National Honor Society for Math and Science Majors (1983); Inductee, University Honor Committee (1982-1983) **Memberships:** Texas Association of Science Teachers; National Association for Research in Science Teaching; National Association of Science Teachers; Ecological Society of America; American Association for the Advancement of Science **Marquis Who's Who Honors:** Albert Nelson Marquis Lifetime Achievement Award **Why did you become involved in your profession or industry:** In high school, Dr. Noyes was inspired by her science teacher, who enlightened her to the world of genetics and physics. In college, Dr. Noyes further pursued a career in science and consequently fell in love with the field. Though she initially intended to pursue a career in medicine, she quickly found that her heart could not handle witnessing death; this inspired her to transition to medical education. **Avocations:** Flute; Singing; Swimming; Travel; Owning treasures of nature jewelry **Political Affiliations:** Republican **Religion:** Baptist

Geoffrey D. Nusbaum, PhD

Title: Psychotherapist **Industry:** Health, Wellness and Fitness **Company Name:** Medpsych Associates **Date of Birth:** 04/01/1946 **Place of Birth:** Berkeley **State/Country of Origin:** CA/USA **Parents:** Wayne Dale Nusbaum; Jeanne (Hankins) Nusbaum **Marital Status:** Married **Spouse Name:** Barbara Ann Pierfy (06/01/1986) **Children:** Michael Wayne Nusbaum **Education:** Fellow, American University (1981); PhD, Hartford Seminary (1978); MA, Hartford Seminary (1971); BA, Washington University in St. Louis (1967) **Certifications:** Diplomate, American Board of Medical Psychotherapy; Certified Therapist, American Association for Marriage and Family Therapy; Licensed Therapist, State of New Jersey **Career:** Psychotherapist, Medpsych Associates (1972-Present); Private Practice, Marlton, NJ, Philadelphia, PA and Greater New York Area (1972-Present); Consultant, Bancroft School, Haddonfield, NJ (1983-1987); Consultant, New York Fertility Research Foundation, New York, NY (1978-1983) **Career Related:** International Council, Sex Education and Parenthood, American University **Civic:** Board Member, Calcutta House AIDS Hospice (Founded by Mother Theresa's Missionary Brothers of Charity) **Creative Works:** Author, Chapter, "The Country Place: An Intentional Therapeutic Community," Community, Self, and Identity Textbook (1978); Peer Manuscript Reviewer, Various Scientific Journals **Memberships:** Fellow, American Board of Medical Psychotherapy; American Society for Reproductive Medicine; Co-founder, Psychological Issues Section, American Society for Reproductive Medicine; North American Society for Psychosocial Obstetrics & Gynecology (NASPOG); The New York Academy of Science; American Academy of Psychotherapists; World Federation for Mental Health; Fallopius International Society; International Psychosomatic Institute; Mensa International Limited **Marquis Who's Who Honors:** Albert Nelson Marquis Lifetime Achievement Award; Marquis Who's Who Top Professional **Why did you become involved in your profession or industry:** Dr. Nusbaum is a product of his generation. Dr. Martin Luther King was his hero and he wanted to be like him and uplift people from hurt and pain. **Avocations:** Bicycle riding; Reading; British TV; Animals; Music and opera

Jesse A. Nusbaum

Title: Bronze Sculptor **Industry:** Fine Art **Date of Birth:** 09/21/1989 **State/ Country of Origin:** CT/USA **Education:** BA in Art, Muhlenburg College, PA (2013) **Career:** Bronze Sculptor, Jesse Nusbaum (2015-Present) **Career Related:** Guilford Craft EXPO, Guilford, CT (2019); Art Basel, Miami, FL (2015, 2017, 2018); Artist, Gallery Features and Exhibitions; Mamaroneck Artist Guild, Mamaroneck, NY; Stamford Art Association, Stamford, CT; Martin Art Gallery, Allentown, PA; Limner Gallery, Hudson, NY; Ridgefield Artist Guild, Ridgefield, CT; Juried Member, AreaArtist.com; Zenith Art & Fashion Gallery, Miami, FL; University of Connecticut Trophy Rooms; Carriage Barn Arts Center, New Canaan, CT; Greenwich Art Society, Greenwich, CT; Connecticut Academy of Fine Arts, Mystic, CT **Creative Works:** Published, 100 Artists of the Future, Contemporary Art Curator Magazine (2019); Published, A New Conceptual Art and Fashion, Original Living Magazine (2018); Published, The Art Album Live, Dawud Knuckles, (2015); Husky Busts, University of Connecticut (2014) **Awards:** Listee, 100 Artists of the Future, Contemporary Art Curator Magazine (2019); Listee, International Contemporary Masters, World Wide Art Books (2019); Listee, Important World Artists, World Wide Art Books (2018); "Best New Exhibitor Award" and "Spotlight Award," at Red Dot Venue, Art Basel Miami (2018); Inducted, The Silvermine Guild of Artists (2017); Inducted, Connecticut Academy of Fine Arts (2018); Nominated, Top 40 Under 40: Class of 2019, Connecticut Magazine **Memberships:** Juried Member, Silvermine Artist Guild; Juried Member, Connecticut Academy of Fine Arts; Juried Member, The Greenwich Art Society; Juried Member, Chartered Financial Analysts; Juried Member, Zenith Art and Fashion, Miami, FL; Juried Member, AreaArtist.com **To what do you attribute your success:** Mr. Nusbaum attributes his success to the subject of his sculptures. He says, "I strive to replicate the actual subject; utilizing micro-detail encourages an intimate, close-up view." His love for animals is what inspires him. As opposed to sculpting human figures, he aims to sculpt animals that strike a sense of familiarity and relatability to all. Furthermore, Mr. Nusbaum believes the key to success is to "Follow your passion; your most successful work will come from doing what you truly love and enjoy." **Why did you become involved in your profession or industry:** Mr. Nusbaum always had a knack for art growing up. He additionally was a great athlete, honored as a First-Team All-State baseball player in high school, and then continued his athletic career as a collegiate player. Most people, friends included, were not aware of his artistic abilities. "It came as a surprise to many," he says. He continued to pursue art throughout his schooling and won many awards. When he began college, he majored in political science with intentions of going to law school. While he was not practicing and creating art, he could not ignore how much he missed it. This motivated him to enroll in a sculpture class. It was in this class that he fell back in love. He immediately switched his major to focus on art again.

Ronald A. Nussbaum, PhD

Title: Professor Emeritus of Ecology and Evolutionary Biology, Curator Emeritus of Herpetology **Industry:** Education/Educational Services **Company Name:** University of Michigan **Date of Birth:** 02/09/1942 **Place of Birth:** Rupert **State/Country of Origin:** ID/USA **Parents:** Walter Werner Nussbaum; Dollres Rice Nussbaum **Marital Status:** Married **Spouse Name:** Jeanne d'Arc Nussbaum **Children:** Kim Michelle; Ronna Melinda; Ronald Archie II; Rebecka Lee; Nicole; Nevada; Alene; Meade; Colter; Ulani; Malone; Tara; Myriam **Education:** PhD in Biology, Oregon State University, Corvallis, OR (1968-1972); MS in Biology, Central Washington University (1968); BS in Biology, University of Idaho (1960-1967) **Career:** Professor Emeritus of Ecology and Evolutionary Biology, Curator Emeritus of Herpetology, University of Michigan, Ann Arbor (2016-Present); Professor of Ecology and Evolutionary Biology, Curator of Herpetology, University of Michigan, Ann Arbor (1974-2016); Research Associate, Oregon State University, Corvallis, OR (1972-1974) **Career Related:** Director, Edwin S. George Reserve, Pinckney, MI (1983-2006) **Creative Works:** Contributor, 190 Articles, Research Publications; Author, "Amphibians and Reptiles of the Pacific Northwest" **Awards:** Inductee, Honor Societies **Marquis Who's Who Honors:** Albert Nelson Marquis Lifetime Achievement Award; Marquis Who's Who Top Professional **Why did you become involved in your profession or industry:** Growing up on a ranch, Dr. Nussbaum had four sisters and no brothers so he spent a lot of time on his own in the woods and rivers. This is how he became interested in field research. **Avocations:** Old time movies, actors and actresses, the directors and the dynamics of the people involved in the film; History of the Western US **Religion:** Roman Catholic

Molly Oberbillig

Title: Founding Sponsor **Industry:** Civil Service **Company Name:** Martin Luther King Junior National Memorial **Date of Birth:** 02/11/1934 **Place of Birth:** Gibraltar **Parents:** William Ferguson Cavenaugh; Mary (Davis) Cavenaugh **Marital Status:** Married **Spouse Name:** Gary Joel Oberbillig (11/08/1961) **Children:** Andrew Ferguson; Julie Anne **Education:** Coursework, San Jose State University (1963-1964); Coursework, University of Washington, Seattle, WA (1954-1955); Coursework, Antioch College, Yellow Springs, OH (1953-1954); Coursework, Reed College, Portland, OR (1951-1953) **Career:** Conservation Manager, Mason County Public Utility District No. 1 (1975-1990) **Civic:** Charter Member, Wellstone Action Leadership Council (2012-Present); Board Treasurer, All Souls Unitarian Universalist Church (2010-Present); Founding Sponsor, Martin Luther King Jr. National Memorial, Washington, DC (2005-Present); Charter Member, National Women's History Museum (2003-Present); Sustainer, Rural Advancement Fund International (1995-Present); Founder and Chairman, Thurston Council on Cultural Diversity and Human Rights (1995-Present); Leadership Council, Southern Poverty Law Center (1992-Present); Founding Trustee, Anne Williston Scholarship, Seattle, WA (1988-2007); Vice Chairman, Democratic Central Committee, Shelton, WA (1991-1992); Secretary, Mason Council Fire District, Lilliwaup, WA (1979-1981); Founding Member, Progressive Patriots Club; Nordiska Folkdance Exhibition Team (1953-1961); Charter Member, National Museum of African-American History and Culture; Charter Member, Food and Water Watch Leader's Circle **Creative Works:** Contributor, Articles, Professional Journals **Awards:** Woman of the Year, National Association of Professional Women (2012-2013); Youth Diversity Award, Thurston Council Cultural Diversity and Human Rights **Memberships:** American Association of University Women; National Association of Professional Women; Thurston Diversity Council **Marquis Who's Who Honors:** Albert Nelson Marquis Lifetime Achievement Award; Marquis Who's Who Top Professional; Marquis Who's Who Humanitarian Award **Why did you become involved in your profession or industry:** Ms. Oberbillig became involved in her profession because she was always interested in conservation. Her great uncle, who was born the same day as she was, invented the Rural Electrification Administration under former President Roosevelt, which was a big inspiration. In addition, she always valued fairness as a child, as she had an experience with neighborhood bullies who invaded her property when she was 9. The bullies tried to hold her captive and force her into saying something, but she didn't comply; she punched one of the boys. Ever since then, Ms. Oberbillig has been fighting for equality. **Avocations:** Gardening

Mary O'Brien

Title: Commissioner, Acting President **Industry:** Financial Services **Company Name:** The Essex County Tax Board in New Jersey **Date of Birth:** 02/13/1944 **Place of Birth:** Buenos Aires **State/Country of Origin:** Argentina **Parents:** George Earle Owen; Margaret Frances (Richards) Owen **Marital Status:** Married **Spouse Name:** Gordon Covert O'Brien (02/16/1962, Divorced 08/1982); Christopher G. **Children:** Christopher Covert; Devon Elizabeth **Education:** MBA, Rutgers, The State University of New Jersey (1976); BA, Rutgers, The State University of New Jersey (1975) **Certifications:** Certification in Project Management (1989) **Career:** Commissioner, Essex County Tax Board (2008-Present); President, Anamex, Inc. (1995-Present); Consultant, Strategic Planning, Avionics Division ITT, Nutley, NJ (1983-1995); Senior Manager, Projects, Avionics Division ITT, Nutley, NJ (1981-1993); Manager, Project, Avionics Division ITT, Nutley, NJ (1980-1981); Voice Processing Project, Defense Communications Division ITT, Nutley, NJ (1979-1980); Controller, Manpower, Defense Communications Division ITT, Nutley, NJ (1977-1980); Manager, Cost, Schedule Control, Defense Communications Division ITT, Nutley, NJ (1978-1979); Administrator, Program, Defense Communications Division ITT, Nutley, NJ (1977-1978) **Career Related:** Chairman, Board of Trustees, South Mountain Counseling Center (1994-Present); Board of Trustees, South Mountain Counseling Center (1987-1998); Keynote Speaker, New Zealand (1995); Speaker, Session Leader, Vancouver, Canada (1994); Session Moderator, Panel Member, MES Conference, Cairo, Egypt (1993); Board Director, New Jersey Eye Institute Session Leader Internet Conference, Florence, Italy (1992); Lecturer in Field **Civic:** President, Essex County Tax Board (2018-Present); President, Maplewood Civic Association (2000-Present); Chairman, Maplewood Republican County Committee (1996-Present); Appointed Fellow, Leadership New Jersey (1993-Present); Chairman, Leadership Division, Chairman, Speakers Bureau, United Way of Essex and West Hudson (1991-Present); Chairman, Council Chapter, President Interaction Committee (1991-Present); Chairman, Community Service Council of Oranges and Maplewood Homelessness, Affordable Housing, Shelter Committee (1988-Present); Board of Trustees, United Way Essex and West Hudson Community Service Council (1988-Present); Trustee, Community Service Council and Education Program, United Way of Essex and West Hudson (1988-Present); Advisory Board, New Jersey PMI Educational (1987-Present); Long Range Planning and Steering Committee, International Project Management Institute Journal and Membership Survey (1987-Present); Officer, Member, Executive Board, New Jersey Project Management Institute (1985-Present); Board of Directors, Officer, Maplewood Civic Association (1984-Present) **Creative Works:** Author, "Voices" (1982); Author, "Pace: System Manual" (1979); Contributor, Articles, Professional Journals; Contributor, Maplewood Community Calendar; Author, Poetry; Contributor, Articles, Maplewood Civic Association **Awards:** Maplewood New Jersey Chamber of Commerce Distinguished Service Award (2005); Fellow, International Project Management Institute (1995); New Jersey Leadership Fellow (1993); Citation, New Hampshire General Assembly Senate Resolution Community Leadership and Service (1992); U.S. House Representatives Citation (1992); Phoebe and Benjamin Shackelford Award, United Way (1992); Maple Leaf Award for Outstanding Community Service (1992) **Memberships:** 3rd Vice Chairman, Lions Clubs International (2005-Present); State Advisor, Lions Clubs International (2004-Present); District MD16 Treasurer, Lions Clubs International (1999-Present); International District 16-E Governor, Lions Clubs International (1999-Present); Secretary, Lions Clubs International (1997-Present); Liaison Officer, President, IPMA (1991-Present); Trustee, Eye Bank of Delaware Valley, Secretary-Treasurer, Lions Clubs International (2003-2005); Youth Opportunities Chairman, N.J District MD-16, Council Chairman, Lions Clubs International (2003-2004); NAFE; The International Platform Association; Grand Jury Association; Telecommunications Group and Aerospace Industries Association; Women's Career Network; National Security Industrial Association; AIIM; PMA; Labor and Employment Relations Association **Marquis Who's Who Honors:** Albert Nelson Marquis Lifetime Achievement Award; Marquis Who's Who Top Professional; Distinguished Humanitarian **To what do you attribute your success:** Ms. O'Brien attributes her success to her parents. Watching them strive for education motivated her to do the same. They believed in keeping an open mind, serving their community, and making the world a better place. **Why did you become involved in your profession or industry:** Ms. O'Brien's career path has taken many unexpected turns over the years. After marrying and having children, she worked in information technology before venturing into communications and project management. In 2008, she became a commissioner on the Essex County Tax Board, for which she has also served as president.

Michael Occhiato

Title: Municipal Official **Place of Birth:** Pueblo **State/Country of Origin:** CO/ USA **Parents:** Joseph Michael Occhiato (Deceased 1982); Joan Occhiato **Marital Status:** Single **Children:** Michael; James; Jennifer; Nick **Education:** Coursework, U.S. Brewers Academy; Postgraduate Coursework, University of Southern Colorado; MBA, University of Colorado (1984); BBA, University of Denver (1961) **Career:** Broker Associate, Jones Healy Better Homes & Gardens (1998-Present); Independent Consultant, Pueblo, CO (1983-Present); Broker Associate, Sound Venture Realty, With, Coldwell Banker Partners (2006-2012); Elect Member, City Council (2002-2010); President, Council, Bergamo, Italy (2007); President, City Council (2001-2006); Broker Associate, Sound Venture Realty, Pueblo, CO (1996-1998); Member, Electro Pueblo City Council (1978-1993); President, Council (1991-1992); With Registered Sellers, Occhiato Land & Cattle LLC (1985-1990); President, Council (1985-1986); With, Die Marketing Development Lambs Information Systems (1983-1985); Owner, Occhiato Land and Cattle LLC (1984); Area Vice President, Pepsi-Cola Bottling Group Division, PepsiCompany, Pueblo, CO (1982-1983); President, Pepsi-Cola Bottling Group Division, Pepsi Company, Pueblo, CO (1982); President, Pepsi-Cola Bottling Company, Pueblo, CO (1978-1982); Vice President, Pepsi-Cola Batt Company (1976-1978); Owner, Peps Advertising Company (1976-1978); Operations Manager, Canners Incorporated, Pepsi-Cola Bottling Company, Pueblo, CO (1970-1976); Administrative Manager, King Resources Co., Denver Air Motive, Broomfield, CO (1969-1970); Plant Manager, Tivoli Brewing company, Denver, CO (1968-1969); Acting Brewmaster, Production Control Manager, Tivoli Brewing Company, Denver, CO (1967-1968); Sales Manager, Tivoli Brewing Company, Denver, CO (1965-1967) **Career Related:** President, Ethnic Foods International dba Taco Rancho, Pueblo, Exodus 20 (1996-Present); Land Developer, Real Estate Broker Associate (1996-Present); Chairman, Weifang Sister City, Delaware (1991-Present); Board of Directors, Pueblo Diversified Industries, Pueblo Crime Stoppers, Pueblo Regional Building Rancher (1976-Present); Regional Director, Pepsi Cola Management Institute Division, Pepsi Company (1979-1982); President, Colorado Soft Drink Association (1979); Vice President, Colorado Soft Drink Association (1978); Foundation Board Member, Colorado State University **Civic:** President, Pueblo City Council (2006-Present, 2002-2003, 1991-1992, 1986-1987); Active, Pueblo Regional Building Board (2003-Present); Member, Pueblo City Council (2001-Present, 1978-1993); Board of Directors, Pueblo Crime Stoppers (2001-Present); Board Directors, Pueblo Urban Renewal Authority (1993-Present); Chairman, Fundraising, Pueblo Chapter, American Heart Association (1983-Present); Representative in Signing Sister City Agreement with Bergamo, Italy, City of Pueblo, CO (2004); Active, Earth Wise Pueblo (1991); Member, Pueblo Economic Development Corporation (1983-1991); Delegate, 1st World Conference Local Elected Officials to 1st UN International Council for Local Environmental Initiative (1990); Member, Pueblo Planning and Zoning Commission (1985); Chairman, Pueblo Area Council Governments (1984-1985); Chairman, Pueblo Area Council Governments (1980-1982); President, Colorado Soft Drink Association (1980-1981); Member, Pueblo Regional Planning Commission (1980-1981); Vice President, Colorado Soft Drink Association (1979-1980); Member, Pueblo Board of Health (1978-1980); Member, Pueblo Action Incorporated (1978-1980); Board of Directors, El Pueblo Boys Ranch **Military Service:** U.S. Navy **Awards:** Named Italian Citizen of Year, Pueblo, CO (2008) **Memberships:** President, Southern Colorado Emergency Medical Technicians Association (1975); Vice President, Pi Kappa Alpha (1960); Former, Southern Colorado Emergency Medical Technicians Association Former, American Saler Association, Colorado; American Quarter Horse Association; Colorado Cattle Association; Pueblo Chamber of Commerce; Rotary **Marquis Who's Who Honors:** Albert Nelson Marquis Lifetime Achievement Award; Marquis Who's Who Top Professional **Why did you become involved in your profession or industry:** In the eighth grade, Mr. Occhiato was involved in the Eisenhower-Stevenson campaign. Influenced by his father who was heavily involved in politics, Mr. Occhiato followed his footsteps and was always encouraged to take leadership positions. **Avocations:** Fixing up his ranch (second home) **Political Affiliations:** Republican **Religion:** Catholic

Wendy Odell

Title: President, Chief Executive Officer **Industry:** Business Management/Business Services **Company Name:** Silverado Roofing Group LLC **Marital Status:** Married **Spouse Name:** Michael Odell **Children:** One Child **Education:** Coursework, University of North Carolina at Chapel Hill (1981-1982) **Certifications:** Minority Woman's Business Enterprise (MWBE) **Career:** Owner, Silverado Roofing Group LLC, McKinney, TX (2014-Present); Independent Owner, Genesis PURE Corporation, Frisco, TX (2012-2014); Owner, Speed Camp (2004-2009); Administrative Management, Top 10 Earner, AdvoCare, Plano, TX (1999-2006) **Awards:** Master 10 Awards **To what do you attribute your success:** Ms. Odell attributes her success to her willingness to give back and "pay it forward". **Why did you become involved in your profession or industry:** Ms. Odell had never originally been in the roofing business. She had always been business savvy and was looking for a new idea for a successful business venture. She was able to pick up on the ins and outs of the roofing industry fairly quickly. **Thoughts on Life:** "Never quit, and take care of others..."

William D. Odell, MD, PhD, MACP

Title: Physician, Educator, Research Scientist **Industry:** Education/Educational Services **Company Name:** University of Utah School of Medicine **Date of Birth:** 06/11/1929 **Place of Birth:** Oakland **State/Country of Origin:** CA/USA **Parents:** Ernest A. Odell; Emma L. (Mayer) Odell **Marital Status:** Married **Spouse Name:** Margaret F. Reilly (08/19/1950) **Children:** Michael; Timothy; John D.; Debbie; Charles **Education:** PhD in Biochemistry and Physiology, The George Washington University, Washington, DC (1965); MD and MS in Physiology, The University of Chicago, Chicago, IL (1956); AB, University of California Berkeley, Berkeley, CA (1952) **Career:** Professor Emeritus, Medicine and Physiology, University of Utah School of Medicine, Salt Lake City, UT (1999-Present); Professor, Medicine and Physiology, University of Utah School of Medicine, Salt Lake City, UT (1980-1999); Chairman, Department of Internal Medicine, University of Utah School of Medicine, Salt Lake City, UT (1980-1996); Visiting Professor, Medicine, School of Medicine, The University of Auckland, New Zealand (1979-1980); Chairman, Department of Medicine, Harbor-UCLA Medical Center, Torrance, CA (1972-1979); Chief, Endocrinology, Harbor-UCLA Medical Center, Torrance, CA (1966-1972); Chief, Endocrine Service, Eunice Kennedy Shriver National Institute of Child Health and Human Development (NICHD) (1965-1966); Senior Investigator, Endocrine Branch, National Cancer Institute, Bethesda, MD (1960-1965); Postdoctoral Fellow in Endocrinology and Metabolism, University of Washington, Seattle, WA (1957-1958) **Career Related:** President, Medical Staff, University of Utah School of Medicine, Salt Lake City, UT (1995-1996); Intern, Resident, Chief Resident in Medicine, University of Washington, Seattle, WA (1956-1960) **Civic:** U.S. Public Health Service (1960-1966) **Creative Works:** Editorial Boards, Medical Journals; Author, Editor, Eight Books in Field; Contributor, Over 330 Articles, Medical Journals **Awards:** Robert Williams Award, Endocrine Society (1991); Governor Award, Science and Technology, State of Utah (1988); Mastership Award, American College of Physicians (1987); Pharmacia Award for Outstanding Contribution to Clinical Chemistry (1977); Distinguished Service Award, The University of Chicago (1973); Research Awards; Laureate Award, Utah; Mayo Soley Award, Western Society for Clinical Research **Memberships:** Society for Experimental Biology and Medicine; Councillor, Society for Experimental Biology and Medicine; Western Society for Clinical Research; President, Western Association of Physicians; Western Association of Physicians; Pacific Coast Fertility Society (Now Pacific Coast Reproductive Society); Society for the Study of Reproduction; Board of Directors, Society for the Study of Reproduction; Endocrine Society; Vice President, Endocrine Society; American Society of Andrology; President, American Society of Andrology; Association of American Physicians (AAP); The American Physiological Society; The American Society for Clinical Investigation; Alpha Omega Alpha Honor Medical Society **Marquis Who's Who Honors:** Albert Nelson Marquis Lifetime Achievement Award; Marquis Who's Who Top Professional **Why did you become involved in your profession or industry:** Dr. Odell became involved in his profession because he wanted to be a scientist since he was 12 years old. He did a lot of home research and then pursued formal education in the field. **Avocations:** Golf; Carpentry; Formerly Backpacking **Political Affiliations:** Democrat

Joyce Lanier Ogburn

Title: Professor of Practice **Industry:** Education/Educational Services **Company Name:** University of North Carolina at Chapel Hill **Place of Birth:** Richmond **State/Country of Origin:** VA/USA **Parents:** Thomas Ogburn; Dorothy Ogburn **Marital Status:** Married **Spouse Name:** Steven Eichner **Education:** MA in Anthropology, Indiana University; MS in Library Sciences, University of North Carolina at Chapel Hill; Bachelor in Anthropology, University of North Carolina, Greensboro **Career:** Principal and Founder, FarView Insights, (2019-Present); Professor of Practice, University of Norths Carolina at Chapel Hill (2020); Intellectual Property Consultant, Appalachian State University (2018-2019); Professor and Digital Strategies and Partnerships Librarian, Appalachian State University (2016-2019); Dean and Distinguished Professor, Appalachian State University (2013-2016); Special Assistant to Senior Vice President of Academic Affairs, University of Utah, Salt Lake City, UT (2011-2013); Dean, University Librarian, J. Willard Marriott Library, University of Utah, Salt Lake City, UT (2005-2011); Associate Director of Libraries, Resources and Collection Management Services, University of Washington (1999-2005); Assistant University Librarian, Information Resources and Systems, Old Dominion University; Chief Acquisitions Librarian, Anthropology Bibliographer, Yale University; Librarian, Pennsylvania State University **Career Related:** Board of Visitors, School of Information and Library Science, University of North Carolina at Chapel Hill (2014-Present); Vice President, Association of College & Research Librarians, 2010-2011; President, Association of College & Research Libraries (ACRL) (2011-2012); **Civic:** Watauga Humane Society Board of Directors **Creative Works:** Author, "Extending the Principles and Promise of Scholarly Communication Reform: A Chronicle and Future Glimpse in Creating the 21st Century Academic Library: Open Access Volume One – Policy and Infrastructure," Rowman & Littlefield, Lanham, MD (2016); Author, Foreword, "Closing the Gap between Information Literacy and Scholarly Communication," in "Common Ground at the Nexus of Information Literacy and Scholarly Communication," Association of College and Research Libraries, Chicago, IL (2013); Co-author, "Library Publishing Services: Strategies for Success: Final Research Report," SPARC, WA (2012); Author, "The Imperative for Data Curation," in "Portal: Libraries and the Academy" (2010); Author, "Defining and Achieving Success in the Movement to Change Scholarly Communication," "Library Resources and Technical Services" (2008); Co-author, "Developing a Consortial Approach to Cataloging and Intellectual Access," in "Library Acquisitions, Collections and Technical Services" (2000) **Awards:** Distinguished Alumna, School of Information and Library Science, University of North Carolina at Chapel Hill (2013); Named One of 30 Women to Watch, Utah (2012); Selected University of California Los Angeles Senior Fellow Program (2001); Phi Beta Kappa (1978) **Memberships:** American Library Association; Association of College & Research Libraries (ACRL); American Anthropological Association **Marquis Who's Who Honors:** Albert Nelson Marquis Lifetime Achievement Award **Why did you become involved in your profession or industry:** As a teenager, Mrs. Ogburn worked in a seminary library in Virginia. Working there and the support of other librarians made her become interested in going into this field. They inspired her and encouraged her to go to library school, insisting that she go to Chapel Hill because they had the best program. **Avocations:** Music

Heather Ogburn-Stokes

Industry: Health, Wellness and Fitness **Company Name:** Serenity Light Recovery **Marital Status:** Married **Children:** Stepson **Education:** BA, Psychology, University of Houston, Clear Lake (2013) **Career:** Founder, CEO, Rehabilitation Director, Serenity Light Recovery, LLC, (2014-Present); Agent, US Jesco International Ltd, Inc. (2013); Show Condition Home Staging, Style & Design Coordinator (2010-2013); Teacher, Kids R Kids (2007-2008) **Civic:** Raising Awareness, Talking to Representatives **Awards:** Best of Hartford Magazine **Memberships:** International Women Society **Marquis Who's Who Honors:** Marquis Who's Who Top Professional **Why did you become involved in your profession or industry:** Mrs. Stokes became involved in this profession because she is long term recovery herself. She experienced the darkness and the depths of addiction and saw how it derailed her goals in life. She was once premed, and on the dean's list doing really well, until addiction through a curve ball at her and that caused her life to go spiraling for the worst. She does not wish the disease of addiction on any one. Mrs. Stokes was given another chance at life, so she strives to give back to others. She is dedicated to her new life and seeing what recovery can bring and how it will change the lives of others. She is the women he is today because of her past. 95% of her team is in recovery themselves, and the other 5% have family members or friends battling addiction or in recovery. Already having the knowledge of addiction, they can relate to clients on a more personal level and help them be everything they can be. A quote she lives by is "I am not what I have done, I am what I have overcome." **Avocations:** Yoga; Spending time with family

Maureen B. Ogden

Title: State Legislator for Environmental Issues (Retired) **Industry:** Government Administration/Government Relations/Government Services **Date of Birth:** 11/01/1928 **State/Country of Origin:** Vancouver/British Columbia **Parents:** William Moore Black; Margaret Hunter (Leitch) Black **Marital Status:** Widowed **Spouse Name:** Robert Moore Ogden III (06/23/1956, Deceased 2010) **Children:** Thomas (Deceased); Henry; Peter **Education:** Master in City and Regional Planning, Rutgers, The State University of New Jersey (1977); MA, Columbia University (1963); BA, Smith College (1950) **Career:** Retired State Legislator for Environmental Issues (1996); Member, New Jersey General Assembly, Trenton, NJ (1982-1996); Mayor, Township of Millburn, NJ (1979-1981); Member, Millburn Township Committee, NJ (1976-1981); Staff Associate, Foreign Policy Association, New York, NY (1956-1958); Researcher, Staff Assistant, Ford Foundation, New York, NY (1951-1956) **Career Related:** Member, Advisory Board, School of Policy and Planning, Rutgers, The State University of New Jersey (1992-1996); Chairman, Energy and Public Utilities Committee, Council of State Governments (1991-1992); Chairman, Assembly Environment Committee, New Jersey General Assembly; Vice Chair, National Affairs and Legislative Committee on Energy Sources **Civic:** Trustee, Policy Committee, New Jersey Conservation Foundation (2006-Present); Co-chair, Policy Committee, New Jersey Conservation Foundation (2000-Present); Chair, Garden State Preservation Trust (1999-Present); Board of Governors, New Jersey Historical Society, Newark, NJ (1992-2000); Chair, Governor's Council on New Jersey Outdoors (1996-1999); Member, Palisades Interstate Park Commission (1996-1999); Trustee, New Jersey Chapter, The Nature Conservancy (1994-1999); Honorary Trustee, Paper Mill Playhouse, Millburn, NJ (1990); Former Trustee, St. Barnabas Medical Center, Livingston, NJ; Former President, New Jersey Drug Abuse Advisory Council; Member, Steering Committee, Highlands Coalition of NJ-NY-Conn; Member, Advisory Committee, Greenwood Gardens **Creative Works:** Author, "Natural Resources Inventory, Township of Millburn" (1974) **Awards:** President's Award, The Nature Conservancy (1995); Public Policy Award, National Trust for Historical Preservation (1995); Award, New Jersey School for Conservation (1990); Award, New Jersey Historical Sites Council (1989); Citation, The Humane Society of the United States (1989); Annual Environmental Quality Award, EPA Region II (1988); Citation, National Association for State Outdoors Recreation Liaison Officers (1987); Certificate of Appreciation, John F. Kennedy Center for the Performing Arts, The Alliance for Art Education (1987); Distinguished Service Award, Art Educators of New Jersey (1987) **Memberships:** Vice Chair, Energy Sources, National Affairs and Legislation Committee, The Garden Club of America (2005-Present) **Marquis Who's Who Honors:** Albert Nelson Marquis Lifetime Achievement Award; Marquis Who's Who Humanitarian Award **To what do you attribute your success:** Ms. Ogden attributes her success to being passionate about what she does. She saw what happened when we just let things go and didn't preserve our water supply. She wanted to help people from being flooded. **Why did you become involved in your profession or industry:** Ms. Ogden became involved in her profession because the appointments were being dominated by business people, who had a financial interest, and she was really interested in what makes a community distinctive and valuable. It is really natural things like trees and rivers. **Avocations:** Gardening; Birdwatching; Bridge **Political Affiliations:** Republican **Religion:** Episcopalian

Lloyd John Ogilvie, DD

Title: Clergyman **Industry:** Religious **Company Name:** First Presbyterian Church **Date of Birth:** 09/02/1930 **Place of Birth:** Kenosha **State/Country of Origin:** WI/USA **Parents:** Varde Spencer Ogilvie; Katheryn (Jacobson) Ogilvie **Marital Status:** Married **Spouse Name:** Doris Kaiser (Somner) (04/09/2005); Mary Jane Jenkins (03/25/1951, Deceased 04/2003) **Children:** Heather Anne Shuemaker; Scott Varde Ogilvie; Andrew Ghlee Ogilvie **Education:** LittD, King's College (2008); DD, Asbury College, Baltimore, MD (2008); DD, Carthage College, Kenosha, WI (2004); DD, University of Edinburgh, Edinburgh, Scotland (2003); LLD, Belhaven College, Jackson, MS (2001); DD, Azusa Pacific College, Azusa, CA (2001); DST, Roberts Wesleyan College, Rochester, NY (2000); DD, Lehigh University, Bethlehem, PA (1999); HHD, Dickinson College, Carlisle, PA (1998); LLD, Pepperdine University, Malibu, CA (1998); LLD, George Fox University, Newburg, OR (1997); DD, Westmont College, Montecito, CA (1997); DD, Lake Forest College, Lake Forest, IL (1997); LHD, Seattle Pacific University, Seattle, WA (1995); LLD, Eastern University, St. Davids, PA (1988); HHD, Moravian College, Bethlehem, PA (1975); LHD, University of Redlands, Redlands, CA (1974); DD, Whitworth College, Spokane, WA (1973); MA, Garrett Theological Seminary, Evanston, IL (1957); Postgraduate Coursework, New College, University of Edinburgh, Edinburgh, Scotland (1955-1956); BA, Lake Forest College, Lake Forest, IL (1952) **Certifications:** Ordained to Ministry, Presbyterian Church (1956) **Career:** Pastor, First Presbyterian Church, Hollywood, CA (1972-1995); Pastor, Presbyterian Church, Bethlehem, PA (1962-1972); First Pastor, Winnetka Presbyterian Church, Winnetka, IL (1956-1962); Student Pastor, Gurnee, IL (1952-1956) **Career Related:** Chaplain, U.S. Senate (1995-2003); Preacher, Chicago Sunday Evening Club (1963-1989) **Civic:** President, Leadership Unlimited, Lloyd John Ogilvie Institute of Preaching, Fuller Theological Seminary, Pasadena, CA **Creative Works:** Editor, "A Passionate Calling" (2014); Editor, "Experiencing the Power of the Holy Spirit" (2013); Author, "Praying Through the Tough Times" (2007-2008); Author, "The Essence of His Presence" (2007); Author, "The Red Ember in the White Ash" (2006); Author, "Quiet Moments with God" (1998); Author, "Perfect Peace" (1997); Author, "The Greatest Counselor in the World" (1994); Author, "Conversation with God" (1992); Author, "The Lord of the Loose Ends" (1991); Author, "Enjoying God" (1990); Author, "Silent Strength" (1990); Author, "A Future and a Hope" (1988); Author, "12 Steps to Living Without Fear" (1987); Author, "Understanding the Hard Sayings of Jesus" (1986); Author, "If God Cares, Why Do I Still Have Problems?" (1985); Author, "Why Not Accept Christ's Healing and Wholeness" (1984); Author, "The Lord of the Impossible" (1984); Author, "Freedom in the Spirit" (1984); Author, "Making Stress Work For You" (1984); Author, "Falling into Greatness" (1983); Author, "Praying with Power" (1983); Author, "Commentary on Book of Acts" (1983); Author, "Ask Him Anything" (1982); Author, "God's Will in Your Life" (1982); Author, "God's Best for My Life" (1981); Author, "The Beauty of Caring, The Beauty of Sharing" (1981); Author, "The Beauty of Love, The Beauty of Friendship" (1981); Author, "Life as it Was Meant to Be" (1981); Author, "Congratulations, God Believes in You" (1981); Author, "The Radiance of the Inner Splendor" (1980); Author, "The Bush is Still Burning" (1980); Author, "The Autobiography of God" (1979); Editor, "Communicator's Commentary Series of the Bible," 32 Volumes (1978-1995); Author, "When God First Thought of You" (1978) **Awards:** Lifetime Achievement Award, Christian Publications Association (2004); William Booth Award, Salvation Army (1992); Angel Award, Religion in Media (1986); Gold Medallion Book Award (1985); Preacher of the Year, Religion in Media (1982); Named One of the 12 Most Effective Preachers in the English-Speaking World, Baylor University; Silver Angel Award, G200 Association; Distinguished Service Citation, Lake Forest College **Memberships:** 100 Club of Los Angeles; Los Angeles Country Club; St. Andrew's Society **Marquis Who's Who Honors:** Albert Nelson Marquis Lifetime Achievement Award **To what do you attribute your success:** Rev. Ogilvie attributes his success to Dr. James Stewart, one of the best preachers of the 20th century, and Dr. Thomas F. Torrance of the famous Torrance family, who was the only theologist admitted to the Albert Einstein Society. **Avocations:** Playing golf; Fishing **Political Affiliations:** Non-Partisan Republican **Religion:** Presbyterian **Thoughts on Life:** Rev. Ogilvie was given the privilege of having very dynamic friends who together formed the Covenant Group that consisted of outstanding pastors across the nation. Those people inspired and encouraged him, and he worked with leaders in each one of his churches. He had great scholars, business leaders, and community leaders, and was inspired by them as he tried to inspire them to live out their faith and work.

Tommy O'Grady

Title: President **Industry:** Food & Restaurant Services **Company Name:** Tuscany Gourmet Market **Children:** Two Sons; One Daughter **Career:** President, Chief Executive Officer, Tuscany Gourmet Market **Awards:** Man of the Year, Local Fire Departments; Business of the Year, ALS **To what do you attribute your success:** His hard work, self esteem, and his love for people and what he does. **Why did you become involved in your profession or industry:** Mr. O'Grady grew up in the industry. His father had a small meat market but they didn't get along and his father didn't like the stuff that he did. He learned how to cook by watching and seeing others and going to seminars. **Thoughts on Life:** He always lives by the golden rule, treat others how you would like to be treated.

Richard P. O'Hamill

Title: Chief Executive Officer **Industry:** Other **Company Name:** Stealth Belt Inc. **Education:** AS in Marketing, East Tennessee State University (2004); AS in Advertising, Northeast State (2003); AS in Business Administration and Management, College of Charleston (2002); Coursework in Public Relations, Trident Technical College (1999) **Certifications:** Certified Assistant Instructor, International WingTsun Association **Career:** Martial Arts Instructor, Tri-Cities Lifestyle Center (2014-Present); Chief Executive Officer, Smart Arts Director, Instructor, Smart Arts Academy (2013-Present); Founder, Medical Research Coordinator, Emerging Medical Technology Global Network (2012-Present); Chief Executive Officer, Stealth Belt Inc. (2009-Present); Assistant Instructor, Tri-Cities WingTsun Kung Fu (2014-2015) **Memberships:** International WingTsun Association **Why did you become involved in your profession or industry:** Mr. O'Hamill became involved in his profession after being diagnosed with Crohn's disease back in 2001. Once his colon was removed in 2008, he had an ostomy bag and began to struggle mentally and emotionally. Alongside his mother, he developed a belt that would conceal the ostomy bag, which he hoped would help him feel normal again. Inventing the belt was life changing for him, so he decided to try and sell one online to see if someone else could benefit from it. After a young gentleman purchased it and had some complaints, he spent time talking to the man to troubleshoot the issues he had and ended up developing a custom belt for him, for which he received rave reviews. In 2009, he decided to establish Stealth Belt Inc. in order to help others like him.

Antony Oldknow

Title: English Educator; Writer; Publisher; Visual Artist **Industry:** Education/Educational Services **Date of Birth:** 08/15/1939 **Place of Birth:** Peterborough **State/Country of Origin:** England/United Kingdom **Parents:** William Fleming; Gertrude Ada (Webster) G. **Marital Status:** Married **Spouse Name:** Cheryll Kay Powell Hendershot (05/2016); Meriel Dorothy Batchelor Steines (08/18/1962, Divorced 04/1969) **Education:** PhD in English, University of North Dakota (1983); Graduate Coursework in Linguistics and Computer Programming, The University of Chicago (1968-1969); MS in Phonetics, The University of Edinburgh, Scotland, United Kingdom (1964); MEd, University of Leeds, England, United Kingdom (1963); BA in English, Minors in History and Italian, University Leeds, England, United Kingdom, with Honors (1961) **Certifications:** Certified Teacher in English and History, Grades K-12, United Kingdom Ministry of Education (1961) **Career:** Professor Emeritus, Eastern New Mexico University, Portales, NM (2012-Present); Professor of English, Eastern New Mexico University, Portales, NM (1996-2012); Associate Professor of English, Eastern New Mexico University, Portales, NM (1990-1994); Assistant Professor, Eastern New Mexico University, Portales, NM (1987-1990); Instructor of English, The University of Kansas, Lawrence, KS (1984-1987); Academic Coordinator, University of Wisconsin-Stevens Point, WI (1980-1984); Instructor of English, University of Wisconsin-Stevens Point, WI (1976-1979); Instructor of English, University of North Dakota (1976); Graduate Teaching Assistant, Department of English, University of North Dakota, Grand Forks, ND (1972-1976); Assistant Professor of English, North Dakota State University, Fargo, ND (1966-1972); Assistant Professor of Linguistics, Université Laval, Quebec, Canada (1964-1966); Lecturer of English, Cowdenbeath Technical College, Scotland, United Kingdom (1962-1964) **Career Related:** Chair, Council of Chairs, Eastern New Mexico University (1993-1999); Chair, Department of Language and Literature, Eastern New Mexico State University (1991-1999); Poetry Reader, Cottonwood Magazine, Lawrence, KS (1985-1987); Visiting Assistant Professor of English, Mankato State University (Now Minnesota State University, Mankata), MN (1982-1983) **Civic:** Former Chair, Budgeting and Planning Committee **Creative Works:** Editor, Blackwater Magazine (1995-Present); General Editor, Publisher, The Scopcraeft Press, Portales, NM (1966-Present); Author, Short Story Collection, "Dr. Upex and the Great God Ing-Fifteen Weird Unexpected Stories" (2016); Author, Paperback, "Five Haunted House Stories, By Antony Oldknow" (2013); Author, "The Passion Play and Other Ghost Stories" (2006); Editor, Eastern New Mexico University Gallery Paintings (2006); Co-author with Caryl Johnson and Kodzxo Gavua, "Educated: An Intercultural Perspective on Ghana" (2006); Author, "Wanderers" (1995); Co-author with Cynthia Hendershot and Jesse Swan, "A Short Book of Literary Terms" (1995); Translator, "Clara d'ell Beuse," Jammes (1992); Author, "Miniature Clouds" (1981); Traveling Writer, Plains Book Bus, Fargo, ND (1980-1981); Author, "Consolation for Beggars" (1978); Author, Poems, "Anthem for Rusty Saw and Blue Sky" (1975); Editor, Art Exhibition of the University of North Dakota Poetry Prize (1974); Editor, The Mainstreeter Magazine (1971-1979); Author, "The Rod of the Lord" (1971); Editor, The Fifth Horseman Magazine (1967-1968); Editor, Scopcraeft Magazine (1966-1972) **Awards:** Named Distinguished Professor Emeritus of English, Eastern New Mexico University (2017); President's Award for Service, Eastern New Mexico University (1991); Citation as a North Dakota Distinguished Writer, Governor of North Dakota (1972) **Memberships:** Academy of American Poets **Marquis Who's Who Honors:** Albert Nelson Marquis Lifetime Achievement Award; Marquis Who's Who Top Professional **Why did you become involved in your profession or industry:** Dr. Oldknow was inspired to write by a school teacher named John D. Mowat. His teacher introduced him to the poet Gerard Manley Hopkins. Dr. Oldknow immediately was intrigued by Hopkins' writing style and began to mimic his style. Eventually, Dr. Oldknow's writing manifested into its' own and he followed his dream of becoming a writer. **Avocations:** Painting; Railroads; Film; Photography; Piano; Sports; Music **Political Affiliations:** Democrat **Thoughts on Life:** Dr. Oldknow was mainly raised by his step-grandmother, Theodosia Millins. She taught Dr. Oldknow how to read and write using the King James Bible.

Nancy Helen Olney

Title: Secondary School Educator (Retired) **Industry:** Education/Educational Services **Date of Birth:** 01/01/1954 **Place of Birth:** Montgomery **State/Country of Origin:** AL/USA **Parents:** Lieutenant Colonel George W. Olney; Virginia E. Olney **Education:** Bachelor of Science in Education, Auburn University, Auburn, AL **Certifications:** Certified Teacher, State of Georgia; Certified in Insurance, State of Georgia **Career:** Retired (2015); Executive Assistant, Lafayette Society for Performing Arts (2009-2015); Director of Education, LaGrange Art Museum (2007-2009); Teacher, Chair of Fine Arts, LaGrange High School; Teacher, Troup County School Systems, LaGrange, GA **Career Related:** Artist-in-Residence, Georgia National Fair, Perry, GA (1997); Teacher, Chattahoochee Valley Art Museum, LaGrange, GA **Civic:** Board of Directors, Art Director, Miss Troup County, LaGrange, GA (1993-1996); Board of Directors, Lafayette Society for Performing Arts, LaGrange, GA; Vice President, LaGrange International Friendship Exchange; LaGrange Woman's Club **Creative Works:** Exhibited, Group Show, Governor's Show (2000-2003); Artist in Residence Invitational, Electronic Gallery, Miami, FL (2002); Artist in Residence Invitational, Electronic Gallery, New York (2001); Exhibited, Group Show, Jasper Fine Arts Festival (1994-2001); Exhibited, Group Show, Moultrie Traveling Exhibit (1999-2000); Exhibited, Group Show, Chattahoochee Valley Art Museum Exhibit of Art Educators (1997-1999); Exhibited, Group Show, Wesleyan University (1998); Exhibited, Group Show, Chattahoochee Valley Exhibit (1998); Exhibited, Group Show, Breneau University (1998); Exhibited, Group Show, Governor's Show (1996-1998); Exhibited, Group Show, Governor's Show, Kennesaw State University (1997); Exhibited, Group Show, Wesleyan University (1996); Exhibited, Group Show, Breneau University (1995); Exhibited, Group Show, LaGrange City School Teachers' Exhibit (1993) **Memberships:** Georgia Art Educators Association; National Art Educators Association; Retired Teachers Association of LaGrange; Daughters of the American Revolution **Marquis Who's Who Honors:** Albert Nelson Marquis Lifetime Achievement Award; Marquis Who's Who Top Professional **Why did you become involved in your profession or industry:** In becoming involved in her profession, Ms. Olney drew inspiration from a wonderful high school art teacher, who encouraged her to enter the field of education. Likewise, she was influenced by her upbringing and family history.

Keith Waldemar Olson

Title: Historian **Industry:** Education/Educational Services **Date of Birth:** 08/04/1931 **Place of Birth:** Poughkeepsie **State/Country of Origin:** NY/USA **Parents:** Ernest Waldemar (Deceased); Elin Ingeborg (Rehnstrom) Olson **Marital Status:** Widower **Spouse Name:** Marilyn Joyce Wittschen (09/10/1955, Deceased 10/2017) **Children:** Paula; Judy **Education:** Honorary Doctor of Philosophy, University of Tampere, Finland (2000); Doctor of Philosophy, University of Wisconsin (1964); Master of Arts, State University of New York at Albany (1959); Bachelor of Arts, State University of New York at Albany (1957) **Career:** Professor Emeritus of History, University of Maryland (2008); Instructor of History, University of Maryland (1966-2008); Instructor of History, Syracuse University (1963-1966) **Career Related:** Fulbright Professor, University of Tampere (2004, 2005); Fulbright Professor, University of Jyväskylä, Finland (1994); Fulbright Professor, University of Oulu, Finland (1993); Fulbright Professor, University of Tampere (1986-1987) **Civic:** President American Scandinavian Foundation, Washington, DC (1977-1979) **Military Service:** Served with US Army (1952-1954) **Creative Works:** Author, "Watergate: The Presidential Scandal That Shook America" (2003); Author, "Biography of a Progressive: Franklin K. Lane" (1979); Author, "The G.I. Bill, the Veterans and the Colleges" (1974) **Awards:** Grantee, University of Maryland (1971, 1976, 1978); Grantee, U.S. Office of Education (1965-1966) **Memberships:** President, American Scandinavian Association (1998-1999); American Historical Association; Organization of American Historians; Wisconsin Historical Society; Swedish American Historical Society; Honorary Member, Finnish Historical Society; Society of Historians of American Foreign Relations; Center for the Study of the Presidency and Congress **Marquis Who's Who Honors:** Albert Nelson Marquis Lifetime Achievement Award; Marquis Who's Who Top Professional **To what do you attribute your success:** Mr. Olson attributes his success to being happy with his career - job satisfaction is key to one's success. **Why did you become involved in your profession or industry:** Mr. Olson initially became involved in his profession out of a love for history, having always wanted to become an educator. He also bore a great appreciation for his Swedish heritage. **Avocations:** Travel; Family; Keeping up the yard **Religion:** Unitarian Universalist

Lois Ruth Olson, MEd

Title: Mathematics Teacher; Learning Disability & Emotionally Disturbed Professional **Industry:** Education/Educational Services **Date of Birth:** 07/07/1945 **Place of Birth:** Shanghai **State/Country of Origin:** China **Parents:** Dr. Joseph Tsoti Ling; Rose Shui-Yueh (Shu) Ling **Marital Status:** Divorced **Children:** Susan Lynn; Sandra Rose **Education:** MEd, University of Minnesota (1983); BS in Mathematics and Sciences K-12, University of Minnesota (1967) **Certifications:** Certified Teacher, Mathematics, Grades 7-12; Special Education, Learning Disabilities/Emotional Behavioral Disability K-12; Middle School Mathematics License; Emotional and Behavioral Degree **Career:** Teacher, Mathematics and Special Education, John Glenn Middle School, Maplewood, MN (1986); Teacher, Mathematics, John Glenn Junior High School, Maplewood, MN (1976-1985); Teacher, Mathematics, North St. Paul High School, North St. Paul, MN (1970-1976); Teacher, Mathematics, Highland Park Junior High School, St. Paul, MN (1967-1969); After School Program, Tartan High School, Oakdale, MN **Career Related:** Teacher, Presenter, Local, State, and National Conferences (1992); Mentorship, St. Paul, MN (1987); Teacher, Business Mentor, 3M Co. **Creative Works:** Video Mathematics Teacher, Video Lessons on Statistics for local Middle Schools (1994); Co-Creator, Lessons, Woodrow Wilson Uncertainty (1992) **Awards:** Woodrow Wilson Fellow, Mathematics Institute (1992) **Memberships:** National Council of Teachers of Mathematics; Minnesota Council of Teachers of Mathematics **Marquis Who's Who Honors:** Albert Nelson Marquis Lifetime Achievement Award **Why did you become involved in your profession or industry:** Mrs. Olson always liked numbers. Her family was science and math minded, as both of her parents were engineers in chemical and civil engineering. She is the oldest in the family and she attended the University of Minnesota, where she enjoyed the classes that she took. There, she decided that would focus on mathematics education. Mrs. Olson has always liked kids because they inspire her to grow in many ways and she has always enjoyed talking to them. **Avocations:** Travel; Golf; Exercise; Skiing; Dance; Talking to people **Religion:** Lutheran

Lisa Onishi

Title: Chemical Engineer, Senior Process Enigineer **Industry:** Engineering **Company Name:** Intel **Date of Birth:** 08/14/1978 **Place of Birth:** Richland **State/Country of Origin:** WA/USA **Parents:** Yasuo Onishi; Esther Onishi **Education:** PhD in Chemical Engineering, University of California, Berkeley (2009); BS in Chemical Engineering, University of Washington, Seattle, WA (2000) **Career:** Chemical Engineer & Researcher, Senior Process Engineer, Intel, Santa Clara, CA (2010-Present); Engineer, UTC Fuel Cells, South Windsor **Civic:** Committee Member, United Way UTC Fuel Cells (2001-2002) **Creative Works:** Contributor, Journal of Physical Chemistry (2007); Contributor, Articles, Professional Journals **Awards:** Achievement Award, UTC Fuel Cells (2003); Outstanding Performance Award (2002); Most Popular Poster Presentation Award, Gorden Research Conference (2002); Award, Golden Key International Honor Society **Marquis Who's Who Honors:** Albert Nelson Marquis Lifetime Achievement Award; Marquis Who's Who Top Professional **Why did you become involved in your profession or industry:** Ms. Onishi became involved in her profession because she believed that being an engineer would permit her to use an applicable, practical form of science. Additionally, she liked chemistry and the idea that she could make an impact with her work. An application that could be rolled out and then people could use and apply. In addition, what attracted her to her profession is that she likes science and math. She thought that it would be easier to apply it. **Avocations:** Taking classes; Throwing dinner parties; Dancing; Exercising; Being out in nature; Meeting people

Kim Opperman

Title: President, Founder **Industry:** Nonprofit & Philanthropy **Company Name:** Socks for Soldiers Inc. **Date of Birth:** 09/25/2020 **Place of Birth:** Norwalk **State/Country of Origin:** OH/USA **Parents:** Donald Nutter; P. Alice Nutter **Marital Status:** Single **Children:** Tom Edwards; Jason Edwards; Luke Edwards; James Opperman; Joe Opperman; Rachel Opperman **Education:** Coursework, The Ohio State University; Coursework, Mansfield Campus, North Central State College, Dean's List **Certifications:** EMT Certification; Behavior Management Certificate **Career:** President, Founder, Socks for Soldiers Inc. (2006-Present); Para-Professional Tutor for Multi-Disability Students, Shelby City Schools (2001-2017); Founder and Owner, Gourmet Bakery; Pastry Chef, Westbrook Country Club; Co-Founder, The Entrepreneur Group, Richland County **Career Related:** Motivational Speaker; Author; Published Articles in Newspapers, Magazines and Several Books in Progress **Civic:** Visiting Classrooms and Other Public Audiences to Inspire Active Patriotism **Creative Works:** Featured, Country Woman Magazine (2017); Creator, Bagel Recipe with 37 Flavors in a Gourmet Bakery Called "The Bagel Lady" and the Prototype Bagel for McDonald's; Creator, "All Season Superwash Wool" Yarn; Designer, Official Military Regulation Sock Pattern and Caps for Socks, Soldiers Inc. Organization **Awards:** Featured, Numerous Televisions Appearances, Specials (2009); Nominated, "Women of Worth" Award, L'Oreal Paris (2008); Awarded by the Governor, State of Ohio (2008); Finalist, Above and Beyond Award, Microsoft (2007); Endorsed, Vogue Knitting, Knitting Simple; Featured, Numerous Newspaper, Magazine Articles; Awarded the Medal of Excellence by the Ohio National Guard, Ohio Generals and the Governor; Countless Military Missions Honoring Her, and the Organization, Complete with Mission Certificates, and Flags Sent to Organization; Other Unit Gifts and Military Medals of Honor; Featured, Socks for Soldiers, in Addicted to Sock Knitting Magazine. Featured story in Country Woman magazine, titled "Sergeant at Yarns." **Marquis Who's Who Honors:** Distinguished Humanitarian Award **To what do you attribute your success:** Ms. Opperman attributes her success to her strong faith, persistence and hard work. **Why did you become involved in your profession or industry:** Ms. Opperman became involved in in her profession because she wanted to honor her son, Senior Master Sergeant Tom Edwards, Jr. of the U.S. Air Force, who retired after 25 years of service. Additionally, viewing Vietnam through the eyes of a child, impacted her life, having seen the negative treatment of deployed troops and returning service members. She felt it immoral to blame the warriors for the political climate and decisions of its leaders. She was determined to create an environment where troops would be supported in a world outside of politics. **Avocations:** Family; Christian ministry; Knitting; Gardening; Gourmet baking and cooking **Political Affiliations:** Independent, Republican **Religion:** Non-denominational, Baptist **Thoughts on Life:** A personal opinion from Ms. Opperman: "As I reflect back on my life and my diverse accomplishments, both public and personal, I have noticed that for every step forward, and ultimate success of that goal, came with it many steps backwards, and obstacles that seemed bent on hindering my progress. For many years I put a name, a face on that shadowy force, and called it failure. I was a failure. I did not recognize that in fact it was a test, many tests, necessary to stay the course and complete my journey. I adopted a personal philosophy for life from the U.S. Marine Corp, of things I must do: Keep going, keep others going, set the example and complete the mission. I applied those to my personal faith in God. Also using two specific strategies for success were "How to Eat an Elephant," and making a checklist of seven priority tasks, inspired from the real life story of the "$25,000 Question." But my biggest motivator to success was an inborn Irish stubbornness, when facing my critics, and defeat that said, "Oh Yea, Watch Me." Thank you to all those supported me, and for those that hindered me. I give equal gratitude and credit for helping make my life and this organization a success! It helped me to try harder, do it better, and to figure out a way to conquer many obstacles, and personal demons. It caused me to draw upon something you could not give me, nor take from me. It was my inner strength, courage, and fighting faith to go on and get the job done. My life was then marked by a God, a life of faith, not failure. I would not be defined by the opinions of others. God was to be my lighthouse. I am blessed and honored by the high calling upon my life, and the 14+ years of being "Sarge" of Socks for Soldiers. The non profit mission continues, with bigger goals to attain, until they all come home. In the meantime I have eight grandchildren to love on, books and memoirs to finish, knitting my endless stash of yarn into more socks, and gardens to tend. Most importantly, I will be sharing the love of God until He says my mission on earth is complete."

Pamela D. Orsak, JD

Title: Attorney **Industry:** Law and Legal Services **Company Name:** The Law Office of Pamela D. Orsak **Children:** Two Children **Education:** JD, Duke University School of Law (1999); BBA in Accounting, University of Houston, Summa Cum Laude (1996) **Certifications:** Board Certified in Estate Planning and Probate, Texas Board of Legal Specialization; Certified Guardian Ad Litem **Career:** Attorney, The Law Office Of Pamela D. Orsak (2011-Present); Attorney, Anderson, Smith, Null & Stofer, L.L.P. (2006-2011); Attorney, Ware, Jackson, Lee & Chambers (Now Ware, Jackson, Lee, O'Neill, Smith & Barrow, LLP) (2004-2006); Attorney, Ware, Snow, Fogel & Jackson (Now Ware, Jackson, Lee, O'Neill, Smith & Barrow, LLP) (2002-2004); Staff Attorney, Harris County Probate Court Number Three (2000-2002); Briefing Attorney, Fourteenth Court of Appeals (1999-2000); Law Clerk, Griggs and Harrison (1994-1997) **Career Related:** Speaker, "Administering the Estate," State Bar of Texas Building Blocks of Wills, Estates and Probate Course (2019); Speaker, "Estate Planning: Who, What, Why & How," Victoria College Foundation, Victoria, Texas (2015); Speaker, "Unintended Consequences of TOD, POD and Other Beneficiary Designations," Victoria Area Estate Planning Council, Victoria, Texas (2014); Speaker, "Estate Planning Post 2010," First Victoria National Bank, Victoria, Texas (2011); Speaker, "Trusts: Who Needs Them," Victoria Professional Express Network, Victoria, Texas (2010); Speaker, "Why Do I Need a Will," Victoria Professional Express Network, Victoria, Texas (2008) **Civic:** Secretary, Presbyterian Day School (2011-2012) **Creative Works:** Author/Speaker, "Techniques for Avoiding Probate for Real Estate: Old Foundations, New Foundations, or Wrecking Balls," Corpus Christi Estate Planning Council (2018); Author/Speaker, "Transfer Techniques for Real Estate That Can Avoid Probate: Old Foundations, New Foundations, or Wrecking Balls," Notre Dame Estate Planning Institute (2017); Author/Speaker, "Save Me from Probate: Transfer on Death Deeds and Lady Bird Deeds," Stanley M. Johanson Estate Planning Workshop (2016); Author/Speaker, "Save Me from Probate: Transfer on Death Deeds and Lady Bird Deeds," State Bar of Texas 40th Annual Advanced Estate Planning & Probate Course (2016); Author/Speaker, "Use and Abuse of Show Cause Motions in Probate Proceedings," State Bar of Texas 39th Annual Advanced Estate Planning & Probate Course (2015); Author, Numerous Papers; Speaker, Various State and Local Professional Organizations; Yearly Speaker, State Bar of Texas Continuing Education (TexasBarCLE) **Memberships:** Victoria Area Estate Planning Council (2008-Present); Victoria County Bar Association (2007-Present); The Junior League of Victoria, Texas Inc. (2006-Present); College of the State Bar (Texas Bar College) (2002-Present); Public Relations Chair, The Junior League of Victoria, Texas Inc. (2013-2014); Membership Development Chair, The Junior League of Victoria, Texas Inc. (2012-2013); Treasurer, The Junior League of Victoria, Texas Inc. (2010-2011); President, Victoria Area Estate Planning Council (2009-2010); Victoria Professional Express Network, American Business Women's Association (ABWA Management LLC) (2008-2012); President, Victoria County Bar Association (2008-2009); Lifetime Member, Houston Livestock Show and Rodeo; The Junior League of Houston, Inc. (2002-2006); Breeders Greeters Committee, Houston Livestock Show and Rodeo (2001-2006); State Bar of Texas **Bar Admissions:** United States District Court for the Southern District of Texas (2000); State of Texas (1999) **Marquis Who's Who Honors:** Marquis Who's Who Top Professional **To what do you attribute your success:** Being very honest and fair with people, Ms. Orsak has been very blessed to some extent in being at the right place at the right time. She has a reputation for being fair and honest in the community with business people. She would say 90% of her business comes from referrals from either accountants, bankers, financial planners or prior clients or attorneys. She doesn't market; at this point, she has been blessed with enough business and she feels that is because she tries to give everyone a fair shake. She isn't the cheapest in town, but they get the most for their money when they go to her. **Why did you become involved in your profession or industry:** Ms. Orsak has an undergraduate degree in accounting and estate planning, and probate allows her to utilize that degree in a way that other areas of law don't. The main reason she loves what she does is because she gets the opportunity to help people who are struggling through very difficult times. A lot of people don't really understand the necessity or why they would even need to plan their estates. If someone has passed away and hasn't planned and you need a guardianship, just helping the family through a difficult time and making it as easy as possible is satisfying. She has done other areas of law; she has done commercial litigation and that certainly has it benefits, but she finds it more satisfying dealing with people on a more personal level. **Avocations:** Biking; Hunting; Guitar; Scuba diving; Skiing; Reading

Charles D. Orth, PhD

Title: Physicist **Industry:** Sciences **Company Name:** Lawrence Livermore National Security, LLC **Date of Birth:** 06/01/1942 **Place of Birth:** Seattle **State/Country of Origin:** WA/USA **Parents:** William Harold Orth; Lois Janet (Sims) Orth **Marital Status:** Married **Spouse Name:** Teresa Ann Stout (08/30/1992); Shirley Lee Crouse (06/14/1964, Divorced 05/20/1992) **Children:** Kenneth James; Michael Douglas **Education:** PhD, California Institute of Technology, Pasadena, CA (1970); BS, University of Washington, Seattle, WA (1964) **Career:** Physicist, Lawrence Livermore National Laboratory, Lawrence Livermore National Security, LLC, Livermore, CA (1978-Present); Physicist, University of California Berkeley (1972-1978); Research Associate, Manned Spacecraft Center (Now Johnson Space Center), National Aeronautics and Space Administration, Houston, TX (1970-1972) **Career Related:** Physicist **Creative Works:** Author, "Spallation as a Dominant Source of Pusher-Fuel and Hot-Spot Mix in Inertial Confinement Fusion Capsules," AIP Physics of Plasmas (2016); Author, "VISTA – A Vehicle for Interplanetary Space Transport Application Powered by Inertial Confinement Fusion," LLNL Report UCRL-TR-110500 (2003); Co-author, "A Diode Pumped Solid State Laser Driver For Inertial Fusion Energy," Nuclear Fusion (1996) **Awards:** Award, National Ignition Facility Advanced Radiographic Capability, Lawrence Livermore National Laboratory (2016) **Memberships:** Sigma Xi; Phi Beta Kappa Society; American Physical Society **Marquis Who's Who Honors:** Albert Nelson Marquis Lifetime Achievement Award (2017); Marquis Who's Who Top Professional **To what do you attribute your success:** Dr. Orth attributes his success to his close relationship with God. **Why did you become involved in your profession or industry:** Dr. Orth became involved in his profession because he wanted to understand lightning after seeing it hit the top of a flagpole a few hundred yards away from where he was sleeping as a young child. **Avocations:** Piano **Religion:** Christian

Roger Harold Ostdahl

Title: Neurological Surgeon **Industry:** Medicine & Health Care **Date of Birth:** 05/01/1946 **Place of Birth:** Richland **State/Country of Origin:** WA/USA **Parents:** Harold Everett; Lorraine (DeWall) Ostdahl **Marital Status:** Widowed **Spouse Name:** Maureen Callahan (05/08/1976, Deceased 2013) **Children:** Maggie Ostdahl; Shannon Killian **Education:** Doctor of Medicine, Duke University (1973); Bachelor of Arts in Chemistry, Duke University, Magna Cum Laude (1969); Exchange Student to Switzerland, Lehrerseminar Wettingen, American Field Service (1964-1965); Diploma, Alexis I. DuPont High School, Wilmington, DE (1964); Assistant Resident in General Surgery and Neurological Surgery, Duke University Medical Center; Chief Resident in Neurosurgery, Duke University Medical Center **Certifications:** Board Certified, American Board of Neurological Surgery (1981); Board Certified, National Board of Medical Examiners (1974) **Career:** Retired (2011); Neurological Surgeon, Pinnacle Health Systems, Harrisburg, PA (2008-2011); Neurological Surgeon, Consulting Staff, Department of Surgery, Carlisle Hospital, Carlisle, PA (1979-2009); Neurological Surgeon, Harrisburg Hospital, Harrisburg, PA (1979-2008); Neurological Surgeon, Holy Spirit Hospital, Camp Hill, PA (1979-2007); Chairperson, Surgical Quality Assessment Committee, Polyclinic Medical Center, Harrisburg, PA (1994-1998); Neurological Surgeon, Polyclinic Hospital, Harrisburg, PA (1979-1996); Chief of Neurosurgery, Holy Spirit Hospital, Camp Hill, PA (1984-1989); Clinical Assistant Professor of Surgery, The Milton S. Hershey Medical Center, College of Medicine, Pennsylvania State University, Hershey, PA (1988) **Career Related:** Presenter, Numerous Symposia and Conferences (1971-2010) **Civic:** Volunteer, World Surgical Foundation (2012, 2013); Neurological Coordinator, Think First Program, Harrisburg, PA (1988-1994); World Wildlife Fund **Creative Works:** Contributing Author, "The Drez Operation" (1996); Contributing Author, Book Chapter, "Neurosurgery" (1985); Contributor, Articles to Professional Journals; Contributor, Chapters to Books **Awards:** Duke Endowment Scholarship in Community Health Sciences (1971); Order of Hippocrates; Merck Index Award (1969); Phi Eta Sigma, Duke University; Phi Lambda Upsilon; Phi Beta Kappa; Alpha Omega Alpha; Physicians Recognition Award, American Medical Association **Memberships:** Board of Directors, Pennsylvania Division, American Trauma Society (1989-2005); Fellow, American College of Surgeons; American Medical Association; American Association of Neurological Surgeons; Congress of Neurological Surgeons; Pennsylvania Medical Society; Pennsylvania Neurological Society; Alpha Omega Alpha; Dauphin County Medical Society; Durham-Orange County Medical Society; North Carolina Medical Society **Marquis Who's Who Honors:** Albert Nelson Marquis Lifetime Achievement Award (2019) **To what do you attribute your success:** Dr. Ostdahl credits his success on his propensity for hard work and constant awareness of the example set by his parents and several respected mentors. **Why did you become involved in your profession or industry:** Dr. Ostdahl was inspired to become involved in his profession due to the influence of his uncle, Dr. Richard DeWall, who invented the DeWall bubble oxygenator, which allowed open heart surgeries to happen at the University of Minnesota. After finishing high school, he spent a year in Switzerland as an American Field Service exchange student, after which he attended Duke University. He later worked with a community neurosurgeon in Wilmington, Delaware, which inspired him to specialize in the field. **Avocations:** Tennis; Skiing; Reading; Travel; Scuba diving **Political Affiliations:** Independent **Thoughts on Life:** If you have integrity, nothing else matters; if you don't have integrity, nothing else matters.

Marie Otto

Title: Educational Administrator, Educational Consulting Company Executive **Industry:** Education/Educational Services **Date of Birth:** 07/11/1930 **Place of Birth:** Houston **State/Country of Origin:** TX/USA **Parents:** Robert Lillard Davis; Bertha Irene Allen Davis **Marital Status:** Widowed **Spouse Name:** Robert Lee Otto **Children:** Lois Buschmann; Barbara Hunt; Robert Lee Otto jr **Education:** Coursework, Hardin-Simmons University, Texas Christian University, North Texas State University, Sul-Ross State University, University of Wyoming, University of California Santa Barbara, California State University Long Beach, Golden West College, California State University, Northridge, Cal State University, Fullerton **Certifications:** Licensed Teacher, Texas; Secondary Teacher, Wyoming, California; Licensed Psychologist; Licensed Marriage and Family Counselor **Career:** Superintendent Emeritus, Huntington Beach Union High School District, California (1988-Present); Superintendent, Huntington Beach Union High School District, California (1984-1988); Assistant Superintendent, Huntington Beach Union High School District, California (1980-1984); Project Manager, Director of Pupil Personnel, Huntington Beach Union High School District, California (1974-1980); Psychologist, Huntington Beach Union High School District, California (1969-1974); Counselor, Neff High School, La Mirada, CA (1966-1969); Teacher, Counselor, Excelsior High School, Norwalk, CA (1964-1966); Teacher, High Schools, Texas, Wyoming and California (1956-1964) **Career Related:** Secretary-Treasurer, Center for Teaching Thinking, Huntington Beach, CA (1991-Present); Supervisor, Student Teachers, Chapman University, Orange, CA (1988-Present); President, Marie Otto Associates, Fountain Valley, CA (1979-Present); Private Practice, Marriage and Family Counselor, Fountain Valley, CA (1970-Present); Vice President, Poole-Young-Koehler Associates Inc., Long Beach, CA (1964-1979) **Civic:** Secretary, Treasurer, Center For Teaching of Thinking, Huntington Beach, CA (1992-Present); No On Drugs, Santa Ana, CA (1988-Present); President, Special Education Local Plan Organization (1983-1984); Member, Fountain Valley Human Services Committee, Huntington Beach Human Resources Commission, State Planning Committee Girl Scouts of America, Worland, WY (1959-1961); Board of Directors, Humana Hospital of Huntington Beach, CA; Board of Directors, Golden West College Foundation, Huntington Beach, CA; Board of Directors, Huntington Beach Community Clinic, Orange County Chapter, American Red Cross **Awards:** Distinguished Alumnus, Graduate School of Education California State University, Long Beach, CA (1988); Recipient, Plaque, Fountain Valley Human Services Committee (1988); Recipient, Plaque, Huntington Beach, CA (1988); Recipient, Plaque, Fountain Valley Chamber of Commerce (1988); Recipient, Plaque, City of Westminster (1988); Recipient, Plaque, Orange Coast College (1988); Recipient, Plaque, Golden West College (1988); Recipient, Plaque, Ocean View School District (1988); Recipient, Plaque, Special Education Local Plan Organization (1984); Named, Woman of the Year, Soroptimist Club, Westminster (1984) **Marquis Who's Who Honors:** Albert Nelson Marquis Lifetime Achievement Award; Marquis Who's Who Top Professional **Why did you become involved in your profession or industry:** Ms. Otto became involved in her profession because she had an interest in special education when she was in college. She did a lot of speech correcting and had a career as a speech pathologist. **Avocations:** Bridge **Political Affiliations:** Democrat **Religion:** Methodist

John Arthur Owens, Esq.

Title: Senior Partner **Industry:** Law and Legal Services **Company Name:** Owens & Millsaps, LLP **Date of Birth:** 07/07/1939 **Place of Birth:** Birmingham **State/Country of Origin:** AL/USA **Parents:** James King Owens; Beatrice (Geer) Owens **Marital Status:** Married **Spouse Name:** Dorothy Terry (07/07/1962) **Children:** Apsilah (Appie) Geer Owens-Millsaps; Terry Owens-Alvarez **Education:** LLB, University of Alabama (1967); BS in Commerce and Business Administration, University of Alabama (1961) **Career:** Senior Partner, Owens & Millsaps, LLP, Tuscaloosa, AL (2003-Present); Partner, Owens and Almond, Tuscaloosa, AL (1997-2002); Founder, Owens and Carver, Tuscaloosa, AL (1994-1996); Partner, Phelps, Jenkins, Gibson & Fowler, Tuscaloosa, AL (1969-1994); Associate, Sam M. Phelps, Tuscaloosa, AL (1968-1969); Associate, Spiro & Phelps, Tuscaloosa, AL (1967-1968) **Career Related:** Fellow, American Bar Foundation; Fellow, Alabama Bar Foundation; Fellow, Tuscaloosa County Bar Association **Civic:** Board of Directors, Tuscaloosa Symphony Orchestra (1989-2017); Chairman, Board of Trustees, First United Methodist Church Tuscaloosa (1967-2012); Board of Directors, Professional Division, United Way of West Alabama (1997-2003); The Arts and Humanities Council of Tuscaloosa County, Inc. (1980-2002); President, Tuscaloosa Symphony Orchestra (1997-1999); Chair, Professional Division, United Way of West Alabama (1997); President, The Arts and Humanities Council of Tuscaloosa County, Inc. (1993-1994); Board of Directors, Children's Hands-On Museum of Tuscaloosa, Tuscaloosa, AL (1985-1989); President, The Arts and Humanities Council of Tuscaloosa County, Inc. (1981-1982); Advisory Committee Member, The Junior League of Tuscaloosa, Inc.; Former Member, Officer, Tuscaloosa County Solid Waste Authority; Chairman, Jemison–Van de Graaff Mansion Foundation; Genesis House Board; The Arts and Humanities Council of Tuscaloosa County, Inc. **Military Service:** Lieutenant, U.S. Naval Reserve (1964-1975); U.S. Navy (1961-1964) **Awards:** Distinguished Alumnus Award, The University of Alabama (2012); Honoree, Alumni of the Year, The University of Alabama (2012); Pillar of the Bar Award, Tuscaloosa Co. Bar Association (2010); Distinguished Service Award, The Arts and Humanities Council of Tuscaloosa County, Inc. (1995); Patron of the Arts Award, The Arts and Humanities Council of Tuscaloosa County, Inc. (1985); Honoree, AV Preeminent Rating, Martindale-Hubbell; Honoree, 50 Year Recognition, Alabama State Bar Association **Memberships:** Tuscaloosa Rotary Club (1969-Present); President, Alabama Law Foundation (2005-2007); Vice President, Alabama Law Foundation (2003-2005); Board of Directors, Alabama Law Foundation (1994-1997); President, Alabama State Bar Association (1995-1996); President-elect, Alabama State Bar Association (1994-1995); President, Farrah Order, Order of the Coif (1994-1995); Vice President, Alabama State Bar Association (1990-1991); Commissioner, Alabama State Bar Association (1987-1994); Director, Alabama Defense Lawyers Association (1984-1987); President, Tuscaloosa Rotary Club (1983-1984); Alabama State Bar Association; Alabama Defense Lawyers Association; International Association of Defense Counsel; Omicron Delta Kappa **Bar Admissions:** Supreme Court of the United States (1990); United States District Court Northern District of Alabama (1975); Alabama (1967); United States Court of Appeals for the Fifth Circuit; United States Court of Appeals for the Eleventh Circuit **Marquis Who's Who Honors:** Albert Nelson Marquis Lifetime Achievement Award; Marquis Who's Who Top Professional **Why did you become involved in your profession or industry:** Mr. Owens became involved in his profession after taking business law courses in commerce school. After becoming familiar with the field, he found that he had a true passion for the work. **Religion:** Methodist

Carolyn Sheets Owen-Towle

Title: Minister (Retired) **Industry:** Religious **Date of Birth:** 07/27/1935 **Place of Birth:** Upland **State/Country of Origin:** CA/USA **Parents:** Millard Owen Sheets; Mary (Baskerville) Sheets **Marital Status:** Married **Spouse Name:** Thomas A. Owen-Towle (11/16/1973) **Children:** Christopher Charles; Jennifer Anne; Russell Owen; Erin Michelle **Education:** Doctor of Divinity, Meadville Lombard Theological School, Chicago (1994); Postgraduate Coursework in Religion, University of Iowa (1977); Bachelor of Science in Art and Art History, Scripps College (1957) **Certifications:** Ordained, Unitarian-Universalist Church (1978) **Career:** Minister, First Unitarian Universalist Church, San Diego, CA (1978-2002) **Career Related:** President, Unitarian Universalist Service Committee, Unitarian Universalist Church (1983-1985); Unitarian Universalist Service Committee (1979-1985); President, Ministerial Sisterhood, Unitarian Universalist Church (1980-1982) **Civic:** Chaplain, Interfaith AIDS Task Force, San Diego, CA (1988-Present); U.S. Republican Jim Bates Hunger Advisory Committee, San Diego, CA (1983-1987); Board of Directors, Planned Parenthood, San Diego, CA (1980-1986); Clergy Advisory Committee, Hospice, San Diego, CA (1980-1983); Board Member, Mingei International Craft and Design Museum; Former President, Mingei International Craft and Design Museum; Board Member, James Hubbell, Ilan Lael Foundation; Board Member, Sam and Freda Maloof Foundation; Volunteer, Planned Giving Committee, 1st Unitarian Universalist Church **Creative Works:** Author, "Damngorgeous: A Daughter's Memoir of Millard Owen Sheets" (2008) **Awards:** Creative Sageing Award, Unitarian Universalist Retired Ministers Association (2019); Distinguished Alumna, Scripps College (2017) **Memberships:** African American Minister's Action Committee, Unitarian Universalist Ministers Association (1995-1998); President, Unitarian Universalist Ministers Association (1989-1991); Executive Committee, Unitarian Universalist Ministers Association (1988) **Marquis Who's Who Honors:** Albert Nelson Marquis Lifetime Achievement Award **Why did you become involved in your profession or industry:** With a well-known artist for a father, Ms. Owen-Towle came of age in the art world. She was surrounded by beauty and those who created it much earlier than most children. In college, Ms. Owen-Towle invested much in her artistic studies, and received a Bachelor of Arts in both art and art history. After getting married and becoming a mother, Ms. Owen-Towle found a new home inside the church, where she volunteered for several years, and eventually decided to become a minister. As she was already married to a minister, the four-year program came easily to her. Once she was officially ordained, she and her husband were called to their church in San Diego, where they served for 24 years. **Avocations:** Reading; Walking; Promoting human rights

David T. Owsley

Title: Art Consultant, Appraiser, Lecturer, Author **Industry:** Fine Art **Date of Birth:** 08/20/1929 **Place of Birth:** Dallas **State/Country of Origin:** TX/USA **Parents:** Alvin Mansfield Owsley; Lucy (Ball) Owsley **Education:** Doctor of Humanities, Ball State University (2005); Fellow, Metropolitan Museum, American Wing (1964); MFA, New York University (1964); AB, Harvard University, (1951); Graduate, Phillips Andover Academy (1947) **Career:** Curator, Antiquities, Oriental and Decorative Arts, Museum of Art, Carnegie Institute, Pittsburgh, PA (1968-1978); Visitor, Victoria and Albert Museum, London, England (1966-1968); Assistant Curator, Department of Decorative Arts and Sculpture, Boston Museum of Fine Arts (1965-1966); Patron, David Owsley Museum of Art, Ball State University **Career Related:** Collections Committee, Dallas Museum of Art (1994) **Civic:** Donor, David Owsley Museum of Art, Ball State University **Military Service:** First Lieutenant, U.S. Air Force (1952-1954) **Creative Works:** Contributor, Articles, Professional Journals **Awards:** Gold Medal, Westmoreland Society (1991); Presidents Medal of Distinction, Ball State University (1989); Eponym, Dallas Museum of Art, The David T. Owsley Galleries of Indian, Southeast Asian and Himalayan Art **Memberships:** D.U., Harvard College; Leland Country, Michigan; Knickerbocker, New York, NY **Marquis Who's Who Honors:** Albert Nelson Marquis Lifetime Achievement Award **Why did you become involved in your profession or industry:** Mr. Owsley's grandparents were collectors, they curated the founding collection at the Ball State University Art Museum. Mr. Owsley always wanted to follow his grandparent's footsteps and have a career in the arts. When the opportunity arose, Mr. Owsley quit his job in public relations to become a museum curator.

R. Wayne Pace, PhD

Title: Professor Emeritus **Industry:** Education/Educational Services **Company Name:** Brigham Young University **Date of Birth:** 5/15/1931 **Place of Birth:** Wanship **State/Country of Origin:** UT/USA **Parents:** Ralph W. Pace; Elda (Fernelius) Pace **Marital Status:** Married **Spouse Name:** Gae Tueller (03/19/1953) **Children:** Michael; Rebecca; Lucinda; Gregory; Angela; Lavinia **Education:** PhD, Organizational Communications, Purdue University (1960); MS, Rhetoric and Public Address, Brigham Young University (1957); BS in Language Arts, University of Utah (1953) **Certifications:** High School Teaching Certificate; Certified Organizational Communication Auditor **Career:** Professor, Emeritus, Brigham Young University (1996-Present); Professor, Organizational Behavior, Management, Brigham Young University (1986-1996); Professor, Human Resource Development, Brigham Young University, Laie, HI (1987-1988); Professor, Communications, Director of Research Center, Coordinator of Human Resource Department, Brigham Young University (1978-1985); Professor, Chairman of Communication, University of New Mexico (1972-1978); Lecturer, School for Administrative Leadership (1968-1972); Professor, Chairman, Communication, University of Montana (1966-1972); Fellow, AAAS (1971); Assistant Professor, California State University, Fresno (1962-1966); Associate Professor, Communication, Parsons College, Fairfield, IA (1960-1962); Visiting Professor, Bowdoin College, Brunswick, ME (1961) **Career Related:** Fulbright Senior Specialist, University Of Twente, Enschede, Netherlands (2007); Visiting Professor, Australian Graduate School of Entrepreneurship, Swinburne University Of Technology, Hawthorn, VIC, Australia (2002); Adjunct Professor, Training and Development, Southern Cross University (1999-2002); Senior Partner, Organizational Associates (1970-2000); Visiting Professor, Human Resource Development Program, University Of Georgia, Athens, GA (1997); Visiting Professor, Department Of Management, University Of Canterbury, Christchurch, New Zealand (1996); Research Fellow, Southern Cross University, Lismore, NWS, Australia (1995-1996); Distinguished Visiting Professor, Boise State University (1992); Editor, Series, Human Resource Department, Prentice Hall Publishing Co. (1989-1992) **Military Service:** Honorable Discharge, U.S. Army (1961); Inactive, U.S. Army Reserve (1955-1961); U.S. Army, Fort Ord, CA (1953-1955) **Creative Works:** Author, "Communication and Work Systems" (2018); Author, "How to Avoid Making a Fool of Yourself" (2017); Co-Author, "Easy Leadership" (2015); Co-Author, "The Gentle Juggernaut: the Amazing Power of Leaning in Influencing Others" (2008); Co-Author, "The 7 Secrets of Successful and Happy People" (2007); Author, "The Pees/Pace Family from Germany, Vol I, II, III" (2006); Co-Author, "When You Receive the Aaronic Priesthood" (2006); Co-Author, "The Common Sense of Research" (2004); Co-Author, "Powerful Leadership" (2002); Author, "Organizational Dynamism" (2002); Co-Author, "Training Across Multiple Locations" (2001); Co-Author, "Me Mum Sez" (1994); Co-Author, "Organizational Communication" (1983, 1989, 1994); Co-Author, "Human Resource Development" (1991); Co-Author, "The Perfect Leader" (1990); Co-Author, "Bibliography of Management Development Literature" (1987, 1990); Co-Author, "Analysis in Human Resource Training and Development" (1989); Co-Author, "Communication Probes" (1982); Co-Author, "Techniques for Effective Communication" (1979); Author, "Communication Experiments" (1975); Co-Author, "Communication Behavior: A Scientific Approach" (1975); Co-Author, "Communicating Interpersonally: A Reader" (1973); Co-Author, "The Human Transaction: Facets, Functions and Forms of Interpersonal Communication" (1973) **Awards:** Modern Pioneer Award, National Society of the SUP (2008); R. Wayne Pace Human Resource Department Book of the Year, AHRD (2006); Spec Recognition, Alumni Association, Brigham Young University (2006); Management Development Award, ASTD (1992); Distinguished Service, SUP (1987); Research Award, Brigham Young University (1985); Outstanding Member, Division 4, ICA (1985); Master M-Man, Latter-Day Saints Church (1960) **Memberships:** President, Academy of Human Resource Development (1993); National Vice President, Sons of Utah Pioneers (1986-1987); President, Brigham Young Chapter, Sons of Utah Pioneers (1986); President, Western States Communication Association (1978); President, International Committee Association (1971); International Society of General Semantics; American Business Communication Association; National Communication Association; Academy of Management; American Association for the Advancement of Science; American Society for Training and Development **Marquis Who's Who Honors:** Albert Nelson Marquis Lifetime Achievement Award **Why did you become involved in your profession or industry:** Dr. Pace was the first doctoral candidate of the person who started the field of organizational communication, W. Charles Redding, at Purdue University; they were starting a new field of activity. He taught high school for a year and that did not appeal to him, so he went to graduate school at Purdue. He became involved with the National Society for the Study of Communication, which eventually became the International Communication Association. He was kind of swept into it through a lot of activities, such as being executive secretary of NSSC. **Avocations:** Founder and President, St. George Club; Coordinator, Sandstone Quarry Project; Coordinator, WWI Veterans Project **Political Affiliations:** Republican **Religion:** Latter-Day Saints

Mary Ann Pacella-Sams

Title: 1) Educational Administrator (Retired) 2) Corporate Executive **Industry:** Education/ Educational Services **Company Name:** 1) Oakland Unified School District 2) Behavioral Research Laboratories **Date of Birth:** 09/14/1933 **Place of Birth:** Chicago **State/Country of Origin:** IL/USA **Parents:** Carmen Harold; Helen Frances (Strauk) Pacella **Marital Status:** Married **Spouse Name:** Wendell M. Sams (08/12/1973) **Children:** Derek John **Education:** Postgraduate, All but Dissertation, University San Francisco, CA (1977); Master of Education, University of Puget Sound (1970); Bachelor of Arts, Mundelein College, Cum Laude (1958) **Career:** San Francisco and Bay Area Tour Guide (2005-Present); Mentor Director of Early Childhood, California (2003-2013); Retired (2003); Site Administrator, Harriet Tubman and Henry Longfellow Child Development Centers (1995-2003); Principal, Piedmont Avenue School (1989-1995); Principal, Piedmont Avenue School and Child Development Center (1986-1989); Administrator, Child Development, Piedmont Children's Center (1981-1986); Director, Children's Centers Department, Oakland Unified School District, California (1979-1980); Program Manager, Children's Centers Department (1978-1979); Supervisor Personnel, San Francisco Unified School District (1975-1978); Program Director, Western Region Mini-Skools Limited, Irving, CA (1974-1975); Coordinator, Reading and English as a Second Language, Department of Defense Military Dependents Schools, Japan (1973-1974); Executive Director, Curriculum and Personnel, Sullivan Preschool and Sullivan Elementary School, Irving, CA (1971-1973); Director, Sullivan Preschool and Sullivan School, Redwood City, CA (1971); Project Manager, Project Learn, Behavioral Research Laboratories, Menlo Park, CA (1970-1971); Early Childhood Specialist, Franklin Pierce Public School District, Tacoma, WA (1969-1970); Instructor, University Puget Sound, Tacoma, WA (1968-1970); Teacher, Annie Wright Seminary, Tacoma, WA (1968-1969); Master Teacher & Teacher Trainer, Spring Valley Montessori School, Federal Way, Washington (1967-1968); Master Teacher & Teacher Trainer, Park Ridge Montessori School, Illinois (1966-1967); Social and Personnel Adjustment Teacher, Vocational Rehabilitation Division, Topeka, WA (1962-1964); Teacher, Kindergarten & Primary Grades, Chicago Public Schools (1964-1966); Special Services Teacher, Chicago Public Schools (1958-1961) **Career Related:** Lecturer in Field; Consultant In Field; Graduate Instructor; Early Childhood Education, University of San Francisco **Civic:** Board of Trustees, San Francisco Tour Guide Guild (2014) **Creative Works:** Contributor, Articles to Professional Journals **Awards:** Member of the Year, California Child Development Administrator Association (1982); Keeper of the Dream Award, California Child Developmental Administrators Association (1981); Excellence Award, California Child Developmental Administrators Association (1980); Award, Oakland Unified School District Board Education (1980); Appreciation Award, Oakland Department of Children's Centers (1980); San Francisco Unified School District, Board of Education (1978) **Memberships:** State Executive Board, California Child Developmental Administrators Association (1979-1981); Association of California School Administrators; Association of Montessori International; National Black Child Developmental Institute; American Montessori Society; Bay Area School Personnel Association; American Society of Personnel Administrators; American Association of School Personnel Administrators; Council for Exceptional Children; National Association of Education Young Children; United Administrators of Oakland Schools; Phi Delta Kappa; San Francisco Tour Guide Guild **Marquis Who's Who Honors:** Albert Nelson Marquis Lifetime Achievement Award; Marquis Who's Who Top Professional **To what do you attribute your success:** Ms. Pacella-Sams credits her success on the influence of her mother, who served as a neighborhood nurse during the Second World War. **Why did you become involved in your profession or industry:** Having come of age in a poor immigrant neighborhood, Ms. Pacella-Sams was notably the first member of her family to receive a college education, as well as the first woman in her community. Drawing a wealth of inspiration from her teachers, she was encouraged to enter the field of education for herself. **Avocations:** Reading; Swimming; Historical research **Political Affiliations:** Democrat **Religion:** Roman Catholic

Martin Everett Packard, PhD

Title: Electronics Company Executive (Retired) **Industry:** Sciences **Company Name:** Varian Associates **Date of Birth:** 03/10/1921 **Place of Birth:** Eugene **State/Country of Origin:** OR/USA **Year of Passing:** 2020 **Parents:** Earl Leroy Packard; LeFay V. (Davy) Packard **Marital Status:** Widowed **Spouse Name:** Barbara (Grafton) Packard (1943, Deceased) **Children:** George G. Packard; Jane M. Packard **Education:** PhD, Stanford University, Stanford, CA (1949); BA, Oregon State University, Corvallis, OR (1942) **Career:** Assistant to Executive Vice President, Instrument Division, Varian Associates, Palo Alto, CA (1984-1990); Assistant to Chairman, Instrument Division (1975-1984); Corporate Vice President, Instrument Division (1969-1975); Vice President, Analytical Instrument Division (1963-1969); Director of Research, Instrument Division (1953-1963); Research Physicist, Varian Associates, Palo Alto, CA (1951-1953) **Career Related:** Chairman, Addiction Research Foundation, Palo Alto, CA; Chairman, Vega Biotechnologies, Inc., Tucson, AZ; Research Team, Nuclear Magnetic Resonance Magnetic Field Stabilizing Method and Apparatus, Stanford, CA **Civic:** Committee Member, Boys Scouts of America-Stanford Area Council, Palo Alto, CA (1972-1980); President, Ravenswood School Board, Palo Alto, CA (1960) **Creative Works:** Author, "Nuclear Induction at Stanford and the Transition to Varian," Encyclopedia of Magnetic Resonance (2007); Co-Author, "Evaluation of the Genetic Basis of Tricuspid valve Dysplasia in Labrador Retrievers," American Journal of Veterinary Research (2002); Co-Author, "Elbow Incongruity and Developmental Elbow Diseases In the Dog," Journal of the American Animal Hospital Association (1986); Author, "Eastern-Bloc Technology," Harvard Business Review (1982); Co-Author, "Effect of Canine Para-Influenza Vaccine on The Spread of Tracheobronchial Coughs in a Boarding Kennel," Journal of the American Animal Hospital Association (1979); Author, "New Techniques in Nuclear Magnetic Resonance," Acta Cientifica Venezolana (1964); Co-Author, "Magnets and Magnetic Field Measurements," Science (1955); Co-Author, "Nuclear Relaxation Time of Hydrogen Gas," Physical Review (1952); Co-Author, "Chemical Effects on Nuclear Induction Signals from Organic Compounds," Journal of Chemical Physics (1951); Co-Author, "Variations In Absolute Chemical Shift Of Nuclear Induction Signals Of Hydroxyl Groups Of Methyl And Ethyl Alcohol," Journal Of Chemical Physics (1951); Co-Author, "A Fine Structure In Nuclear Induction Signals From Ethyl Alcohol," Journal Of Chemical Physics (1951); Co-Author, "Nuclear Induction Apparatus For Observing Signals In Gases," Physical Review (1950); Author, "A Proton-Controlled Magnetic Field Regulator," Physical Review (1948); Author, "Relative Nuclear Moments Of H-1 And H-2," Review Of Scientific Instruments (1947); Co-Author, "Relative Moments of H1 and H3," Physical Review (1947); Co-Author "Spin and Magnetic Moment of Tritium," Physical Review (1947); Co-Author "Nuclear Induction," Physical Review (1946); Co-Author "Nuclear Induction," Comment in Physical Review (1946); Co-Author, "The Nuclear Induction Experiment," (1946) **Awards:** Service Award, International Elbow Working Group (2000); Award Commemorating 50 Years of NMR Spectroscopy, ENC Experimental NMR Conference (1995); Service Award, Bernese Mountain Dog Club of America (1990); Morris E. Leeds Award, IEEE (1971) **Memberships:** International Society of Magnetic Resonance; Bioelectromagnetics Society; New York Academy of Sciences; American Physical Society; American Chemical Society; Association for the Advancement of Science; Sigma Xi; International Elbow Working Group; Bernese Mountain Dog Club of America; The Packard Club (PAC) **Marquis Who's Who Honors:** Albert Nelson Marquis Lifetime Achievement Award **To what do you attribute your success:** Dr. Packard attributes his success to innovation, resilience, and sustainability. **Why did you become involved in your profession or industry:** Dr. Packard always liked to tinker with electronics. After Pearl Harbor, he wanted to help with the war efforts and was recruited by Westinghouse Research Labs; he was fresh out of college with a BA in physics from Oregon State University. He and his team worked on developing the IB24 tube still used in navigation systems. He was fortunate enough to be involved with projects that engaged other curious and inventive individuals. **Avocations:** Electronics; Photography; Packard cars **Political Affiliations:** Independent **Religion:** Agnostic **Thoughts on Life:** https://www.24-7pressrelease.com/press-release/466183/martin-everett-packard-phd-presented-with-the-albert-nelson-marquis-lifetime-achievement-award-by-marquis-whos-who

Douglas L. Packer, MD

Title: Cardiologist **Industry:** Medicine & Health Care **Company Name:** Mayo Clinic Hospital - Saint Mary's Campus **Date of Birth:** 12/21/1953 **Place of Birth:** Brigham City **State/Country of Origin:** UT/USA **Parents:** Leon C. Packer; Lou Jean Scoffield-Packer **Marital Status:** Married **Spouse Name:** Janet M. Moyes **Children:** Ryan D.; Gregory R.; Bradley D.; Aaron S. **Education:** Resident in Internal Medicine, Duke University (1981-1983); Intern in Internal Medicine, Duke University (1980-1981); MD, The University of Utah, Salt Lake City, Utah (1980); BA in Chemistry, Brigham Young University, Provo, Utah, Summa Cum Laude, with Highest Honors (1976) **Certifications:** Minnesota State Medical License (1989-Present); Diplomat in Cardiology, American Board of Internal Medicine (1985-Present); Diplomat, American Board of Internal Medicine (1983-Present); North Carolina Medical License (1982-Present) **Career:** John M. Nasseff, Sr., Professor in Cardiovascular Diseases, Mayo Clinic Alix School of Medicine (2009-Present); Professor in Medicine, Mayo Clinic Alix School of Medicine (1998-Present); Associate Professor in Medicine, Mayo Clinic Alix School of Medicine (1993-1998); Assistant Professor in Medicine, Mayo Clinic Alix School of Medicine (1989-1993); Assistant Professor in Medicine, Duke University (1987-1989); Associate in Medicine, Duke University (1985-1987); Fellow in Cardiology/Electrophysiology, Duke University (1983-1985); Assistant Chief Resident in Internal Medicine, Duke University (1982) **Creative Works:** Member, Editorial Board, Journal of the American College of Cardiology; Member, Editorial Board, American Heart Journal; Reviewer, Circulation; Reviewer, American Journal of Cardiology; Contributor, Numerous Articles to Professional Journals; Reviewer, Numerous Manuscripts **Awards:** ACC 2019 Distinguished Scientist Award, Translational Domain, American College of Cardiology (2019) **Memberships:** European Heart Rhythm Association/European Society of Cardiology (2016-Present); Asia Pacific Heart Rhythm Society (APHRS) (2009-Present); American College of Cardiology (1988-Present); Cardiac Electrophysiology Society (1985-Present); American Heart Association, Inc. (1985-Present); Founding Member, European Cardiac Arrhythmia Society (ECAS) (2017); Founder, Heart Rhythm Foundation (2004); Biophysical Society (1990-2004); American Society of Echocardiography; Fellow, American Heart Association, Inc.; Heart Rhythm Society **Marquis Who's Who Honors:** Albert Nelson Marquis Lifetime Achievement Award **Why did you become involved in your profession or industry:** Dr. Packer became involved in medicine in the seventh grade. He thinks the reason was that he had the opportunity to interact with several doctors in his hometown for a variety of reasons and it just seemed to click with what his nature was. Then, as time went on, the question was whether he was going to be a cardiologist or a cardiac surgeon. In 1978, he decided or predicted that both of those things that surgeons do they would be able to do. So, the next decision was pursuing electronics and physics. Cardiac electrophysiology meshed the subjects best. His undergraduate degree was in chemistry with an emphasis on physical chemistry or quantum mechanics or physics. Things just kind of played out.

Nancy Huddleston Packer

Title: Educator, Writer, Professor Emerita **Industry:** Education/Educational Services **Company Name:** English Department, Stanford University **Date of Birth:** 05/02/1925 **Place of Birth:** Washington **State/Country of Origin:** DC/USA **Parents:** George Huddleston; Bertha Baxley Huddleston **Marital Status:** Widowed **Spouse Name:** Herbert L. Packer (03/15/1958, Deceased 12/1972) **Children:** Ann; George **Education:** ThM, University of Chicago (1947); BA, Birmingham-Southern College, Alabama (1945) **Career:** Professor Emerita, Stanford University, California (1993-Present); Professor, Stanford University, California (1980-1993); Associate Professor, Stanford University, California (1974-1980); Assistant Professor, Stanford University, California (1968-1974); Lecturer, Stanford University, California (1960-1968); Lecturer, Birmingham-Southern College (1947-1948) **Career Related:** Teacher, Writer **Creative Works:** Author, "Funny Little Pictures" (2010); Author, "Jealous-Hearted Me" (1997); Author, "The Women Who Walk" (1989); Author, "In My Father's House" (1988); Author, "Small Moments" (1976) **Awards:** American Library Association Award (1998); O'Henry Prize, Doubleday & Company (1981); Outstanding Alumna Award, Birmingham-Southern College (1980); Award for Fiction, National Endowment for the Arts (1980); O'Henry Prize, Doubleday & Company (1968); Commonwealth Award **Marquis Who's Who Honors:** Albert Nelson Marquis Lifetime Achievement Award; Marquis Who's Who Top Professional **Why did you become involved in your profession or industry:** Ms. Packer became involved in her profession because she was always a reader and she did not have anything else to do. She worked in a bookstore when she got out of college. She received a master's degree in theology. She taught at Birmingham Southern College and Stanford University. **Avocations:** Travel; Spectator sports; Reading; Going out to eat with friends **Political Affiliations:** Democrat **Thoughts on Life:** Ms. Packer has two children, Ann and George, both whom are writers.

James Joseph Palmer

Title: Arbitrator and Mediator, Labor/Employee Relations Consultant **Industry:** Law and Legal Services **Company Name:** ADR NEUTRALS, LLC **Date of Birth:** 09/28/1943 **Place of Birth:** Detroit **State/Country of Origin:** MI/USA **Parents:** James J. Palmer; Mary M. (Stockoski) Palmer **Marital Status:** Divorced **Children:** Jennifer L.; Julianne M. **Education:** MBA, University of Detroit Mercy, Detroit, MI (1975) **Certifications:** Master Conflict Resolution Specialist, Macomb Community College Center for Continuing Education (2009) **Career:** Principal (Arbitrator and Mediator), ADR Neutrals, LLC (2010-Present); Principal Consultant, Center For Creative Employee Relations, LLC (2001-Present); Director, Union Relations, Daimler Chrysler Corporation (1998-2001); Manager, Union Relations, Chrysler Corporation, Highland Park and Auburn Hills, MI (1992-1998); Manager, Group Human Resources, Procurement and Supplier Operations, Chrysler Corporation, Highland Park, MI (1991-1992); Manager, Employee and Community Relations, Allis-Chalmers Corporation, Independence, MO (1983-1985); Manager, Employee and Community Relations, Allis-Chalmers Corporation, La Porte, IN (1981-1983); Numerous Personnel and Human Resources and Manufacturing Positions, Chrysler Corporation and Its Subsidiary ACUSTAR, Detroit, Highland Park and Troy, MI (1968-1981) **Career Related:** Arbitrator and Mediator, ADR Neutrals, LLC, MI and FL (2010-Present); Employee and Labor Relations Consultant, MI and FL (2001-Present); Consultant, Palmer/Roe & Associate, Orchard Lake, MI (1988-Present); Educator, Michigan (1975-2012); Consultant, Palmer/Roe & Associate, Troy, MI (1985-1988); Consultant, Palmer/Palmer and Associate, Blue Springs, MO (1984-1985) **Civic:** Hearings Officer, Hillsborough County Discipline Appeal Process Panel (2020-Present); Assistant Secretary of State, U.S. Department of State, Lansing, MI (1965-1968) **Awards:** Outstanding Career Achievement and Exemplary Professional Leadership, Top 100 Registry (2020); Man of the Year in Recognition of Outstanding Effort and Achievements in the Field of Human Resources, Top 10 Registry (2020); Certificate of Achievement, Roundtable Magazine (2020); Best International Labour Management Relations Firm, Acquisition International Magazine (2016) **Memberships:** Labor and Employment Relations Association (LERA); Alpha Sigma Nu; Beta Gamma Sigma **Bar Admissions:** Labor and Employment Law Section, State Bar of Michigan; Alternate Dispute Resolution Section, State Bar of Michigan **Marquis Who's Who Honors:** Albert Nelson Marquis Lifetime Achievement Award (2019); Marquis Industry Leaders (2019) **To what do you attribute your success:** Mr. Palmer believes in the need for continuous improvement, and urges others to adopt and practice the related principles. **Why did you become involved in your profession or industry:** Mr. Palmer became involved in his profession after a short career in government as a legislative staff assistant to two committees of the Michigan House of Representatives and as an Assistant Secretary of State, where his role was to manage the legislative programs of the Michigan Department of State. When he felt that the nature of his work with the Department of State no longer served what he desired for his career, he made his departure from government for industry and his long career at Chrysler Corporation and its successors. **Political Affiliations:** Democrat **Religion:** Roman Catholic **Thoughts on Life:** Continuous improvement is vital in a competitive environment. Things rarely get better unless and until there is a change in the process or processes. Don't ever give up. Reward success.

Ramesh C. Pandey, PhD

Title: Chemist, Educator, Entrepreneur, Motivator, Pharmaceutical Executive **Industry:** Sciences **Date of Birth:** 11/05/1938 **Place of Birth:** Naugaon, Taragtal, Uttarakhand **State/Country of Origin:** India **Parents:** Raj Vaidaya; (Dr.) Gauri Dutt Pandey; Jivanti Pandey **Marital Status:** Single **Education:** PhD, University of Pune (Now Savitribai Phule Pune University), India (1965); MSc, Gorakhpur University, India (1960); BSc, University Allahabad, India (1958) **Career:** Chairman, Director, RaMed Pharm Inc. (2009-Present); Chairman, President, G.D. Pandey Ayurvedic University (2001-Present); Chairman, Chief Executive Officer, Xechem International Inc. (2004-2007); Chairman, Chief Executive Officer, President, Xetapharm Inc. (1996-2007); Chairman, Chief Executive Officer, President, Xechem International Inc. (1994-2004); President, Chief Executive Officer, Director, Technology Development, Xechem, Inc., New Brunswick, NJ (1990-2003); President, Xechem, Inc., Melrose Park, IL (1984-1990); Senior Scientist, Abbott Laboratories, North Chicago, IL (1983-1984); Head, Chemistry Section, National Cancer Institute, Frederick Cancer Research Facility, Maryland (1982-1983); Senior Scientist, Fermentation Program, National Cancer Institute, Frederick Cancer Research Facility, Maryland (1977-1982); Visiting Scientist, University of Illinois Urbana-Champaign (1972-1977); Scientist, Organic Division, CSIR National Chemical Laboratory, Pune, India (1970-1972); Research Associate, Department of Chemistry, University of Illinois Urbana-Champaign (1967-1970); Research Officer, CSIR National Chemical Laboratory, Pune, India (1965-1967); Junior Research Fellow, CSIR National Chemical Laboratory, Pune, India (1960-1964) **Career Related:** Member, Life Science Advisory Board, New Jersey Tech Council (1999-Present); Consultant, Rutgers State University New Jersey in Biotechnology (2002-2010); Founder, G.D. Pandey Ayurvedic University (GDPAU), New Brunswick, NJ (2001); Consultant, LyphoMed, Inc., Melrose Park, IL (1984-1990); Visiting Professor, Waksman Institute of Microbiology, Rutgers University, Piscataway, NJ (1984-1986); Consultant, Washington University School of Medicine in St. Louis (1976-1985); Member, Statewide Advisory Committee Board of Managers, New Jersey Agricultural Experimental Station **Civic:** Member, Middlesex County Work Force Investment Board (1999-2005); Member, Advisory Committee for Science Transfer and Science Technology Program, Middlesex County College, Edison, NJ (1999-2001) **Creative Works:** Member, Editorial Board, International Journal of Antibiotics (1986-Present); Patentee, Graft Thin Layer Chromatography; Numerous U.S. and International Patents for the Isolation and Purification of Antibiotics and Anticancer Agents **Awards:** Lifetime Achievement Award, President HE Route Sir A. Jugnauth, Mautitius (2009); P. Ray Memorial Award, Indian Chemical Society (2006); Named Readers Choice CEO of the Year, CBS Marketwatch.com (2006) **Memberships:** Paul Harris Fellow, Rotary Club (1996-Present); President, New Brunswick Club, Rotary Club (1999-2000); Fellow, Royal Society Tropical Medicine & Hygiene; Emeritus Member, American Society for Microbiology; Emeritus Member, American Chemical Society; Emeritus Fellow, American Institute of Chemists; American Society of Hospital Pharmacists; American Society of Pharmacognosy; American Association for the Advancement of Science; New York Academy of Science; American Council for Medicinally Active Plants; Indian Science Congress Association; Founder, Executive Trustee, American Academy of Ayurvedic Medicine **Marquis Who's Who Honors:** Albert Nelson Marquis Lifetime Achievement Award **Why did you become involved in your profession or industry:** Dr. Pandey became involved in his profession because his father, Dr. Gauri Dutt Pandey, was the physician for the royal family in his home country. His mother was a homemaker but she encouraged him in his career. He moved from India 55 years ago; in the 1960s, he came to the University of Illinois. Since his father was the doctor for the royal family, Dr. Pandey had an interest in natural medicine since he was young. Medicine chemistry was an interest to him and when he came to the University of Illinois, he noticed that people were suffering and that when people were going to the doctor, the doctor sometimes has a difficult time determining a diagnosis. They give the patients a broad spectrum of antibiotics. He knew that although antibiotics make you feel better, it eventually kills the immune system because everything in the body is based on immunity. This sparked a drive to further his research. Shortly after Dr. Pandey received his PhD in chemistry, his research began in natural medicines, creating many breakthroughs in science and in the world of medicine, inspiring others to follow in his footsteps. **Political Affiliations:** Life Member, National Republican Senatorial Inner Circle **Religion:** Hindu

Bernard J. Paris, PhD

Title: Emeritus Professor of English **Industry:** Education/Educational Services **Company Name:** Bernard J. Paris **Date of Birth:** 08/19/1931 **Place of Birth:** Baltimore **State/Country of Origin:** MD/USA **Parents:** Albert Paris; Anna (Richmond) Paris **Spouse Name:** Shirley Helen Freedman (04/01/1949) **Children:** Mark Eliot; Shoshana **Education:** PhD, Johns Hopkins University, Baltimore, MD (1959); AB, Johns Hopkins University, Baltimore, MD (1952) **Career:** Professor Emeritus, University of Florida, Gainesville, FL (1996-Present); Director, International Karen Horney Society (1991-1996); English Professor, University of Florida, Gainesville, FL (1981-1996); Director, Institute for Psychological Study of Arts, Gainesville, FL (1985-1992); From Assistant Professor to English Professor, Michigan State University, East Lansing, MI (1960-1981); English Instructor, Lehigh University, Bethlehem, PA (1956-1960) **Career Related:** Visiting Professor, Victorian Studies Centre, University of Leicester, England (1972); Editorial Board, American Journal of Psychoanalysis **Creative Works:** Author, "A General Drama in Pain: Character and Faith in Hardy's Major Novel" (2009); Co-Editor, "Karen Horney: A Psychoanalyst's Search for Self-Understanding" (1994); Co-Editor, "Character as a Subversive Force in Shakespeare: The History and the Roman Plays" (1991); Co-Editor, "Bargains with Fate: Psychological Crises and Conflicts in Shakespeare and his Plays" (1991); Co-Editor, "Shakespeare's Personality" (1990); Editor, Book, "Third Force Psychology and the Study of Literature" (1986); Author, Book, "Character and Conflict in Jane Austen's Novels" (1978); Author, Book, "A Psychological Approach to Fiction" (1974); Author, Book, "Experiments in Life: George Eliot's Quest for Values" (1965); Contributor, More Than 40 Articles, Professional Tour **Awards:** Guggenheim Fellow (1974-1975); National Endowment for the Humanities Fellow (1969-1970) **Memberships:** Founder, Founding Director, International Karen Horney Society; National Association for the Advancement of Psychoanalysis; American Academy of Psychoanalysis and Dynamic Psychiatry; Modern Language Association; Phi Beta Kappa **Why did you become involved in your profession or industry:** Dr. Paris was drawn to English and writing because of his talents for the field. By his early 20s, he knew he would pursue a career as an educator and writer. **Avocations:** Travel; Photography

Barry R. Parker

Title: Physics Educator (Ret.) **Industry:** Education/Educational Services **Date of Birth:** 04/13/1935 **Place of Birth:** Penticton **State/Country of Origin:** British Columbia/Canada **Parents:** Gladstone Parker; Olive (Young) Parker **Marital Status:** Married **Spouse Name:** Gloria Parker (1960) **Children:** David **Education:** PhD, Utah State University (1967); MSc, University of British Columbia (1961); BA in Physics, With Honors, University of British Columbia (1959) **Career:** Professor, Idaho State University (1975-1998); Assistant Professor, Physics, Idaho State University, Pocatello, ID (1967-1975); Assistant Professor, Physics, Weber State College, Ogden, UT (1963-1966) **Career Related:** Director, 19 Master's Degree Students **Civic:** Piano Performer, Numerous Nursing Homes and Community Centers **Creative Works:** Author, "Physics of War" (2014); Author, "Young Einstein" (2010); Author, "Good Vibrations (Physics of Music)" (2009); Author, "Einstein's Vision" (2004); Author, "Mystery of Gravity" (2003); Author, "Isaac Newton School of Driving" (2003); Author, "Quantum Legacy" (2002); Author, "Einstein's Brainchild" (2000); Author, "Alien Life: The Search for Extraterrestrials and Beyond" (1998); Author, "Chaos in the Cosmos" (1996); Author, "Stairway to the Stars" (1994); Author, "Vindication for the Big Bang" (1993); Author, "Cosmic Time Travel" (1991); Author, "Colliding Galaxies" (1990); Author, "Invisible Matter" (1989); Author, "Creation" (1988); Author, "Search for a Supertheory" (1987); Author, "Einstein's Dream" (1986); Author, 29 Books; Author, Articles for Encyclopedia Brittanica, Time-Life Books, The New York Times; Author, Scientific Papers, Scientific Journals **Awards:** "Outstanding Educator of America" (1971); Writing Award, University of Texas-McDonald Observatory **Marquis Who's Who Honors:** Albert Nelson Marquis Lifetime Achievement Award; Marquis Who's Who Top Professional **To what do you attribute your success:** Dr. Parker attributes his success to hard work and intense interest in his field. **Why did you become involved in your profession or industry:** When Dr. Parker was a teenager, he read popular science books, which got him interested in the field. **Avocations:** Playing piano; Photography; Skiing; Fly fishing

Mark G. Parker

Title: Chairman, President, Chief Executive Officer **Industry:** Business Management/Business Services **Company Name:** Nike, Inc. **Date of Birth:** 10/21/1955 **Place of Birth:** Poughkeepsie **State/Country of Origin:** NY/USA **Parents:** Bruce Parker; Meg Parker **Marital Status:** Married **Spouse Name:** Kathy Parker **Children:** Three Children **Education:** BS in Political Science, Pennsylvania State University (1977) **Career:** Chairman, Nike, Inc. (2016-Present); President, Chief Executive Officer, Nike, Inc. (2006-Present); President, Nike Brand, Nike, Inc. (2001-2006); Vice President, General Manager, Global Footwear, Nike, Inc. (1998-2001); Vice President, Consumer Product Marketing, Nike, Inc. (1993-1998); Corporate Vice President, Research Design and Development, Nike, Inc. (1988-1993); Division Vice President, Footwear Research, Design and Development, Nike, Inc. (1987-1988); Head, Special Design Project Teams, Nike, Inc. (1985-1987); Manager, Footwear Marketing, Nike, Inc. (1983-1985); Director, Footwear Design, Nike, Inc. (1982-1983); Director, Design Concepts & Engineering, Nike, Inc., Beaverton, OR (1981-1982); Manager, Advanced Product Design, Nike, Inc. (1980-1981); Designer, Development Manager, Nike, Inc., Exeter, NH (1979-1980); Joined, Nike, Inc. (1979) **Awards:** Named, Top 50 Best CEOs of Large Companies, Comparably (2018); Power Player, Advertising Age (2009); Named, 50 Most Influential People in Sports Business, Street & Smith's SportsBusiness Journal (2009); Named, Most Influential People in the World of Sports, Business Week (2007-2008) **Avocations:** Running; Rock climbing; Bicycling; Sailing; Kayaking; Art

William Watts Parmley, MD

Title: Doctor (Retired), Professor Emeritus **Industry:** Medicine & Health Care **Company Name:** University of California, San Francisco **Date of Birth:** 01/22/1936 **Place of Birth:** Salt Lake City **State/Country of Origin:** UT/USA **Parents:** Thomas Jennison Parmley; Martha Lavern (Watts) Parmley **Marital Status:** Married **Spouse Name:** Shanna Lee Nielsen (08/17/1961) **Children:** Michael William; John Nielsen; Todd Jennison; Ann **Education:** MD, Johns Hopkins University (1963); AB, Harvard University, Summa Cum Laude (1957) **Certifications:** Subspecialty Board of Cardiovascular Disease (1972); Diplomate, American Board of Internal Medicine (1970); California Medical License (1970); Maryland Board of Medical Examiners (1963) **Career:** Doctor (Retired), Professor Emeritus of Medicine, University of California, San Francisco (UCSF) (2003-Present); Araxe Vilensky Endowed Chair in Cardiology, University of California, San Francisco (UCSF) (1997-2003); Professor of Medicine, University of California, San Francisco (UCSF) (1976-2004); Chief of Cardiology, Moffitt Hospital, San Francisco, CA (1974-1997); Associate Professor of Medicine, University of California, San Francisco (UCSF) (1974-1976); Associate Professor of Medicine, UCLA (1973); Associate Director, Department of Cardiology, Cedars-Sinai Medical Center, Los Angeles, CA (1970); Associate Director of Cardiology, Cedars-Sinai Medical Center, Los Angeles, CA (1969-1973); Associate in Medicine, Peter Bent Brigham Hospital, Boston, MA (1969); Instructor in Medicine, Harvard Medical School, Boston, MA (1969); Fellow in Cardiology, Peter Bent Brigham Hospital, Boston, MA (1967-1969); Clinical Associate, Cardiology Branch, National Heart Institute, National Institutes of Health, Bethesda, MD (1965-1967); Resident in Medicine, Osler Medical Service, Johns Hopkins Hospital (1964-1965); Intern, Osler Medical Service, Johns Hopkins Hospital, Baltimore, MD (1963-1964) **Career Related:** Visiting Professorships and Named Lectures, Numerous Institutions (1982-2002); Served, Numerous Committees, American College of Cardiology (1973-2002); Numerous Committees, American Board of Internal Medicine (1981-1993); Served, Served, Numerous Committees, American Heart Association (1973-1992); Chairman, Cardiovascular Boards (1985-1987); Fellow, American College of Cardiology; President, American College of Cardiology (1985-1986); Established Investigator, American Heart Association (1971-1974) **Civic:** Missionary, Humanitarian, Africa, Salt Lake City, UT, Sacramento, CA (2009-2019); General Authority Seventy, Sacramento LDS Temple (Sacramento California Temple) (2003-2010); Stake President, Sacramento LDS Temple (Sacramento California Temple) (1986-1993); Bishop, Mormon Church (1977-1982); President, Sacramento LDS Temple (Sacramento California Temple) **Military Service:** Surgeon, Commissioned Corps of the U.S. Public Health Service (1965-1967) **Creative Works:** Editor, Journal of the American College of Cardiology (1992-2002); Associate Editor, Circulation (1976-1983); Associate Editor, Circulation Research (1976-1979); Associate Editor, American Journal of Physiology (1976-1978); Section Editor, Journal of Applied Physiology (1974-1976); Section Editor, Circulation, American Journal of Physiology (1974-1976); Contributor, 300 Articles, Professional Journals; Contributor, 300 Abstracts Published in the Field; Contributor, More Than 130 Chapters, Books; Contributor, More Than 120 Editorials Published in the Field **Awards:** Special Award, Laennec Society, Council on Clinical Cardiology, American Heart Association (2001); Heart Saver Award, Save A Heart Foundation (1996); Distinguished Service Award, Collegium Aesculapium, Brigham Young University, Academy of Medicine, Salt Lake City, UT (1986); May Order of Merit, Argentina (1985); Theodore and Susan Cummings Humanitarian Award, American College of Cardiology (1971, 1974); Johns Hopkins Medical Society Annual Student Research Award (1963) **Memberships:** American Heart Association (2001); Heart Failure Society of America (1997); Musser-Burch Society (1994); Association of Professors of Cardiology (1990); Honorary Fellow, American College of Chest Physicians (1988); President, American College of Cardiology (1985-1986); American Medical Association (1985); Honorary Member, Colombian Society of Cardiology and Cardiovascular Surgery (1979); Fellow, American Heart Association (1978); Association of University Cardiologists (1976); Western Association of Physicians (1975); Association of American Physicians (1975); San Francisco Heart Association (1974); Honorary Member, Chilean Society of Cardiology and Cardiovascular Surgery (1973); American Society for Clinical Investigation (1973); Cardiac Muscle Society (1973); Council on Clinical Cardiology (CLCD), American Heart Association (1972); Council on Circulation, American Heart Association (1972) **Marquis Who's Who Honors:** Albert Nelson Marquis Lifetime Achievement Award; Marquis Who's Who Top Professional **To what do you attribute your success:** Dr. Parmley attributes his success to good luck, hard work, and the influence of superb colleagues and mentors. **Why did you become involved in your profession or industry:** Dr. Parmley became involved in his profession because he was inspired by Dr. Frank J. Winget, the family practitioner he had in Salt Lake City, Utah, who came out to homes in the area and took care of everyone. **Political Affiliations:** Republican **Religion:** Mormon

Anthony Daniel Parone, Esq.

Title: Attorney at Law **Industry:** Law and Legal Services **Date of Birth:** 12/01/1934 **Place of Birth:** Niagara Falls **State/Country of Origin:** NY/USA **Parents:** Daniel Parone; Jessie Elaine (West) Parone **Marital Status:** Married **Spouse Name:** Josephine A. Zoda (02/13/1965) **Children:** Deborah Lyn **Education:** JD, University at Buffalo, NY (1968); LLM in Taxation, New York University (1961); LLB, University at Buffalo, NY (1960); BA, University at Buffalo, NY (1957) **Career:** Lawyer, Private Practice, Niagara Falls, NY (1968-Present); Associate, Saperston, Wiltse, Duke, Day & Wilson, Buffalo, NY (1966-1968); Assistant General Counsel, National General Corporation, Los Angeles, CA (1965-1966); Lawyer, Gellman & Gellman (1961-1965); General Counsel, Conbow Corporation, Niagara Falls, NY (1961-1965) **Career Related:** Trustee, Stella Niagara Education Park, NY (1978-1990) **Memberships:** President, Bar Association of Niagara Falls (1983); Bar Association of Niagara County New York **Bar Admissions:** United States District Court for the Western District of New York (1980); United States District Court for the Southern District of California (1966); California (1966); New York (1960) **Marquis Who's Who Honors:** Albert Nelson Marquis Lifetime Achievement Award; Marquis Who's Who Top Professional **To what do you attribute your success:** Mr. Parone attributes his success to Jack E. Gellman, his employer when he first started. **Why did you become involved in your profession or industry:** Mr. Parone had no idea why he wanted to be a lawyer, but he knew he wanted to go to law school. His uncle influenced him greatly; although he wasn't a lawyer himself, he pushed his nephew to be a lawyer. **Avocations:** Golf; Travel to Florida **Political Affiliations:** Democrat

Carmelita Beal Parrish, MA, MED, BSED, AA

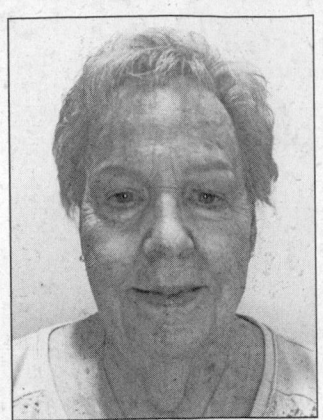

Title: Secondary School Educator, Language Educator (Retired) **Industry:** Education/Educational Services **Date of Birth:** 03/19/1934 **Place of Birth:** Varina **State/Country of Origin:** NC/USA **Parents:** Nita Mae (Webb) Beal (Deceased, 1992); James Robert (Deceased, 1967) **Marital Status:** Widow **Spouse Name:** John J. Parrish (07/24/1953, Deceased, 1987) **Children:** Deborah Joy Parrish White; Toni Lynne Parrish Altenburg **Education:** MA, University of Georgia (1993); MEd, Valdosta State University (1988); BS in Education, Georgia Southern University (1981); AA, Middle Georgia College (1979) **Certifications:** Certified, Secondary English & Spanish, State of Georgia (1981) **Career:** Teacher, Macon State College (1999-2006); Retired (1998); Teacher, Spanish, English, Pickens County High School, Jasper, GA (1992-1998); Teacher, Spanish, English, Telfair County Board Education, McRae, GA (1991-1992); Secondary Teacher, English, Graphic Arts, Spanish, Ware County Board of Education, Waycross, GA (1981-1991) **Career Related:** Adjunct Instructor, Spanish, Macon State College, GA (1999-2006) **Civic:** Band Chaperone, Tour Leader, Student Travel in Europe (1973-Present); Cadet Troop Leader, Trainer (1966-1969); Former Leader, Girl Scouts of the United States; Spanish Teacher, Area Sunday School; Former Member, Baptist Church Choir; Leader, Women's Bible Study; Adult Choir, Baptist Church; Neighborhood Chairman, The Troops on Foreign Soil, Spain **Creative Works:** Author, Poem, "Shawn" (2005); Author, Poem, "Dreams" (2000); Author, Poem, "Tequiro" (1999) **Awards:** Star Teacher Award, Waycross-Ware County Chamber of Commerce (1987) **Memberships:** National Education Association; National Council of Teachers of English; Local Associate President, Legislator Contact Team, Georgia Association of Educators; Evaluation Committee, Southern Association Colleges and Schools; Phi Kappa Phi **Marquis Who's Who Honors:** Albert Nelson Marquis Lifetime Achievement Award; Listee, Who's Who Among America's Teachers; Listee, Who's Who in the South; Listee, Who's Who Among Women **Why did you become involved in your profession or industry:** Ms. Parrish became interested in teaching from her Latin teacher and her junior homeroom teacher. Both teachers were strong individuals that Ms. Parrish learned to respect. They exhibited neatness, professionalism, and kindness. Their aptitude for teaching was so admirable that Ms. Parrish was inspired to be a teacher herself. **Avocations:** Cross stitch; Reading **Political Affiliations:** Republican **Religion:** Baptist

Delores L. Parron-Ragland, PhD

Title: Federal Agency Administrator (Retired) **Industry:** Social Work **Date of Birth:** 01/14/1944 **Place of Birth:** Red Bank **State/Country of Origin:** NJ/USA **Parents:** James W. Parron; Ruth Pitts Parron **Marital Status:** Married **Spouse Name:** Col. Sherman L. Ragland **Education:** PhD in Philosophy, Catholic University (1977); MSW, Catholic University (1968); BA, Georgian Court College (1966) **Career:** Scientific Advisor for Capacity Development, National Institutes of Health, Bethesda, MD (2001-2007); Deputy Assistant Secretary for Planning and Evaluation, United States Department of Health & Human Services, Washington, DC (1999-2001); Associate Director, National Institute of Mental Health, National Institutes of Mental Health, Rockville, MD (1983-1999); Senior Program Officer, Institute of Medicine, National Academy of Sciences, Washington, DC (1978-1983); Social Science Analyst, Presidential Commission on Mental Health, Washington, DC (1977-1978); Assistant Professor, Department of Psychiatry, Howard University College of Medicine, Washington, DC (1971-1978); Psychiatric Social Worker, Hillcrest Children's Center, Washington, DC (1969-1971) **Civic:** Trustee, Georgian Court College, Lakewood, NJ (1996-2001); Trustee, Center for the Advancement of Health, Washington, DC (1995-2001) **Awards:** Pioneer in Recognition of Exceptional Contributions to the Profession and its Ability to Meet the Needs of All People, National Association of Social Work (2013); Alumnae Service Award, Georgian Court University (2011); Distinguished Leader for Women in Psychology, American Psychological Association (2003); Distinguished Alumnae Award, The Catholic University of America (1993) **Memberships:** Fellow, National Academy of Public Administration; National Association of Social Workers; American Psychological Association **Marquis Who's Who Honors:** Distinguished Humanitarian (2004); Albert Nelson Marquis Lifetime Achievement Award; Marquis Who's Who Top Professional **To what do you attribute your success:** The overarching goal of Dr. Parron-Ragland's work has been to address the concerns of racial and ethnic populations, especially for women. She has approached this complex task with good judgment, which has yielded superb results. **Why did you become involved in your profession or industry:** During her time in college, Dr. Parron-Ragland found an interest in sociology and American history. Her thinking and belief system was shaped by the core values of justice, compassion, service, respect, and integrity. All of these principles have guided her to find success throughout her career. **Religion:** Roman Catholic **Thoughts on Life:** Dr. Parron-Ragland feels fortunate to be blessed with a great life. She worked hard to achieve her dreams, and she encouraged all others to do the same.

James Alphonso Paschal

Title: College Professor; Family Counseling Center Director (Retired) **Industry:** Education/Educational Services **Date of Birth:** 08/11/1931 **Place of Birth:** Americus **State/Country of Origin:** GA/USA **Parents:** Bouie L.; Mary L. (Jackson) Paschal **Marital Status:** Married **Spouse Name:** Zelma L. Paschal **Children:** Maret Elvara **Education:** EdD, University of South Carolina (1977); MS, Fort Valley State College (Now Fort Valley University) (1963); BA, Xavier University of Louisiana, New Orleans, LA (1957) **Certifications:** Certified Administrator, Teacher, Counselor, Social Worker **Career:** Retired (2015); Owner, Director, Pro Bono Work, Family Counseling Center, Atlanta, GA (2005-2015); Head of Counseling Program, Albany State University, Albany, GA (2000-2005); Counselor, Monroe High School, Albany, GA (1991-1999); Counselor, Swainsboro High School, Swainsboro, GA (1990-1991); Coordinator of Facilities and Planning, South Carolina Commission on Higher Education, Columbia, SC (1982-1990); Director of Counseling Center and Student Affairs, Benedict College, Columbia, SC (1978-1982); Assistant Coordinator of Student Services, Augusta Technical School, Augusta, GA (1971-1978); Coordinator of Student Services, Augusta Technical School, Augusta, GA (1967-1978); Teacher, Librarian, Counselor, Social Worker, Americus City Schools (Sumter County Schools), Americus, GA (1957-1967); School Social Worker, Americus City System (1965-1967); Library, Counselor, Staley Junior High School (Now Staley Middle School), Americus, GA (1959-1965); Teacher, Grade 5, East View Elementary School, Americus, GA (1957-1959) **Civic:** Member, Board of Governors, National Alumni Association of Xavier University of Louisiana, New Orleans, LA (2019-Present); President, National Alumni Association of Xavier University of Louisiana, New Orleans, LA (2015-2019); President, Xavier University of Louisiana, Atlanta Alumni Chapter, Atlanta, GA (2005-2015); Lieutenant Governor, Division 16, Georgia District of Kiwanis International (2012-2013); Volunteer, Caritas, New Orleans, LA (1953-1957); Volunteer, Friendship House, New Orleans, LA (1955-1956); Member, St. Paul of the Cross Holy Catholic Church **Military Service:** Served, United States Army, Korean Conflict Era (1951-1953) **Creative Works: Awards:** Whitney M. Young Jr. Service Award, Atlanta Area Council, Boy Scouts of America, Atlanta, GA (2014); Named Alumnus of the Year, Xavier University of Louisiana, New Orleans, LA (2014); Named Outstanding Alumni, Xavier University of Louisiana, New Orleans, LA (2013); Graduate Assistantship, Fort Valley State College (Now Fort Valley State University), Fort Valley, GA (1962-1963); Bronze Service Medal, United States Army (1953); Recipient, Scholarship, Fort Valley State College (Now Fort Valley State University), Fort Valley, GA (1948) **Memberships:** National Education Association; American Counseling Association; Georgia Counseling Association; Life Member, Alpha Phi Alpha Fraternity, Inc.; Life Member, Kiwanis International; 100 Black Men of South Metro Atlanta, Inc.; Life Member, Optimist International **Marquis Who's Who Honors:** Albert Nelson Marquis Lifetime Achievement Award; Marquis Who's Who Top Professional; Marquis Who's Who Humanitarian Award **To what do you attribute your success:** Dr. Paschal attributes his success to God, and his mother and father, who instilled in him a desire for knowledge and taught him to give back and help those who were not in a position to help themselves. **Why did you become involved in your profession or industry:** After serving in the US Army, Dr. Paschal reentered college and with a developing love for people, he entered a Franciscan Seminary for priesthood. Due to an illness, he left the seminary and returned to college. After graduation, he decided that he wanted to spend his life helping other people with problems that they could eliminate together. **Avocations:** Reading; Walking; Helping Others **Political Affiliations:** Democrat **Religion:** Roman Catholic **Thoughts on Life:** Dr. Paschal is the owner and operator of Family Counseling Center for 10 years doing pro bono work for individuals unable to pay for services. Dr. Paschal's daughter followed in his footsteps and is an elementary school counselor; his wife is a high school math teacher.

Saundra Paschal

Title: Mathematics Teacher **Industry:** Education/Educational Services **Company Name:** San Angelo Independent School District **Education:** BS in Mathematics, Minor in Biology, Angelo State University (1980) **Career:** Teacher of Honors Algebra II and Precalculus, Lake View High School, San Angelo Independent School District **Career Related:** Coach, Mathematics Team, Lake View High School; Coordinator, University Interscholastic League, Lake View High School **Civic:** Local Church; Local Charitable Organizations **Creative Works:** Advisor, Books for Publication **Awards:** Educator Hall of Fame, IAOTP (International Association of Top Professionals) (2019); IAOTP Teacher of the Year (2019); Top Educator of the Year of 2017; Teacher of the Year Award (2014); VIP of the Year Award (2011-2012); Teacher of the Year Award (2000); Top 12 Educators of the Year Calendar; 35-Year Pin **Memberships:** Curriculum Writing Team, San Angelo Independent School District; Texas Math and Science Coaches Association; Association for Supervision and Curriculum Development **Marquis Who's Who Honors:** Albert Nelson Marquis Lifetime Achievement Award; Marquis Who's Who Top Professional; Marquis Who's Who Humanitarian Award **To what do you attribute your success:** Ms. Paschal attributes her success to her ability to teach students and the support she has received from her high school teachers. **Why did you become involved in your profession or industry:** Ms. Paschal became involved in her profession after starting her career as a teacher's aide. **Avocations:** Playing the organ at church; Photographing high school sports teams and natural landscapes; Reading

James Brendan Patterson

Title: Author; Former Advertising Executive **Industry:** Writing and Editing **Date of Birth:** 02/22/1947 **Place of Birth:** Newburgh **State/Country of Origin:** NY/USA **Parents:** Charles Patterson; Isabelle (Morris) Patterson **Marital Status:** Married **Spouse Name:** Susan Patterson **Children:** Jack **Education:** Master of Arts, Vanderbilt University, Nashville, TN (1970); Bachelor of Arts in English, Manhattan College, Summa Cum Laude (1969) **Career:** Author (1996-Present); Chairman, J. Walter Thompson U.S. (Now Wunderman Thompson) (1990-1996); Advertising Executive, J. Walter Thompson Co. (Now Wunderman Thompson), New York, NY (1971-1996) **Civic:** Founder, James Patterson Teacher Education Scholarship, Appalachian State University, Michigan State University, Florida Atlantic University and University of Florida; Founder, College Book Bucks Scholarship Program **Creative Works:** Co-author, with Cynthia Fagen, "The House of Kennedy" (2020); Co-author, with Andrew Bourelle, "Texas Outlaw" (2020); Co-author, with James O. Born, "Lost" (2020); Co-author, with Max DiLallo, "The Chef" (2019); Co-author, with David Ellis, "Unsolved" (2019); Co-author, with Howard Roughan, "Killer Instinct" (2019); Author, "Out of Sight" (2019); Co-author, with Brendan DuBois, "The Cornwalls are Gone" (2019); Co-author, with Robison Wells, "The Warning" (2019); Co-author, with Candice Fox, "The Inn" (2019); Co-author, with Tim Arnold, "We. Are. Not. Alone" (2019); Co-author, with Max DiLallo, "The Killer's Wife" (2019); Co-author, with Susan DiLallo, "The House Next Door" (2019); Co-author, with Connor Hyde, "The Doctor's Plot" (2018); Co-author, with Andrew Holmes, "Revenge" (2018); Co-author, with Gabrielle Charbonnet, "Fall of Crazy House" (2018); Co-author, with Andrew Bourelle, "Texas Ranger" (2018); Co-author, with Duane Swierczynski, "Unbelievably Boring Bart" (2018); Co-author, with Bill Clinton, "The President is Missing" (2018); Co-author, with Brendan DuBois, "The First Lady" (2018); Co-author, with Shan Serafin, "The 13-Minute Murder" (2018); Co-author, with Nancy Allen, "Juror No. 3" (2018); Co-author, with Richard DiLallo, "The Store" (2017); Co-author, with Gabrielle Charbonnet, "Crazy House" (2017); Co-author, with Howard Roughan, "Murder Games" (2017); Co-author, with David Ellis, "The Black Book" (2017); Co-author, with Emily Raymond, "Expelled" (2017); Author, "Black Dress Affair" (2017); Co-author, with Derek Nikitas, "You've Been Warned" (2017); Co-author, with Loren D. Estleman, "The Moores are Missing" (2017); Co-author with Duane Swierczynski, "The Shut-In" (2017); Co-author, with Scott Slaven, "Steeplechase" (2017); Author, "Stingrays" (2017); Co-author, with Emily Raymond, "Tell Me Your Best Story" (2017), Co-author, with Kecia Bal, "The Dolls" (2017); Co-author, with Alison Joseph, "The Exile" (2017); Co-author, with Robert Rotstein, "The Family Lawyer" (2017); Co-author, with Rachel Howzell Hall, "The Good Sister" (2017); Co-author, with Frank Constantini and Brian Sitts, "The Lifesaver" (2017; Co-author, with Doug Allyn, "The Lawyer Lifeguard" (2017); Co-author, with Duane Swierczynski, "The House Husband" (2017); Co-author, with Sam Hawken, "The Housewife" (2017); Co-author, with Max DiLallo, "Stealing Gulfstreams" (2017); Co-author, with Rob Hart, "Scott Free" (2017); Co-author, with Ed Chatterton, "Absolute Zero" (2017); Author, "Achilles" (2017); Co-author, with David Inglish, "Avalanche" (2017); Co-author, with Lauren Hawkeye, "Christmas Sanctuary" (2017); Co-author, with Christopher Farnsworth, "Dead Man Running" (2017); Co-author, with Derek Nikitas, "Diary of a Succubus" (2017); Co-author, with Scott Slaven, "Kill and Tell" (2017); Co-author, with Laurie Horowitz, "Love Me Tender" (2017); Co-author, with Christopher Charles, "Night Sniper" (2017); Author, "Nooners" (2017); Co-author, with Maxine Paetro, "Woman of God" (2016); Co-author, with Andrew Holmes, "Hunted" (2016); Co-author, with Jeffrey J. Keyes, "Killer Chef" (2016); Co-author, with Shan Serafin, "Come and Get Us" (2016); Co-author, with Michael White, "Airport: Code Red" (2016); Co-author, with Rees Jones, "Heist" (2016); Co-author, with Lee Stone, "Dead Heat" (2016); Co-author, with James O. Born, "Let's Play Make-Believe" (2016); Co-author, with Emily Raymond, "Little Black Dress" (2016); Co-author, with Scott Slaven, "Taking the Titanic" (2016); Co-author, with Laurie Horowitz, "The Mating Season" (2016); Co-author, with Andrew Bourelle, "The Pretender" (2016); Co-author, with Shan Serafin, "The Women's War" (2016); Co-author, with Max DiLallo, "113 Minutes" (2016); Co-author, with Hilary Liftin, "$10,000,000 Marriage Proposal" (2016); Co-author, with Howard Roughan, "Truth or Die" (2015); Co-author, with David Ellis, "The Murder House" (2015); Co-author, with David Ellis, "Invisible" (2014); Co-author, with Howard Roughan, "Second Honeymoon" (2013); Co-author, with David Ellis, "Mistress" (2013); Co-author, with David Ellis, "Guilty Wives" (2012); Co-author, with Michael Ledwidge, "Zoo" (2012); Co-author, with Neil McMahon, "Toys" (2011) **Awards:** Literarian Award, National Book Foundation (2015); Named One of the Highest-paid Authors, Forbes (2014-2016); Named One of the 100 Most Powerful Celebrities, Forbes.com (2008); Effie Award (1983); Six Clio Awards (1983)

William Brown Patterson

Title: Professor Emeritus of History, Dean (Retired) **Industry:** Education/ Educational Services **Company Name:** The University of the South at Sewanee **Date of Birth:** 04/08/1930 **Place of Birth:** Charlotte **State/Country of Origin:** NC/USA **Parents:** William Brown Patterson; Eleanor Selden (Miller) Patterson **Marital Status:** Widower **Spouse Name:** Evelyn Byrd Hawkins (11/27/1959, Deceased 01/21/2012) **Children:** William Brown Patterson; Evelyn Byrd Donatelli; Lucy Patterson Murray; Emily Patterson Higgs **Education:** DLitt, Sewanee, The University of The South (2012); PhD, Harvard University (1966); MA, Oxford University, England (1959); MDiv, Episcopal Theological School, Cambridge, MA (1958); BA, Oxford University, England (1955); MA, Harvard University (1954); BA, Sewanee, The University of The South (1952) **Certifications:** Certificate, Educational Management, Harvard University (1982);Ordained to Ministry, Priest (1959); Deacon, The Episcopal Church (1958) **Career:** Francis S. Houghteling Professor, History (2001-2005); Dean, College of Arts and Sciences, Sewanee: The University of The South, Sewanee, TN (1980-1991); Professor, History, Sewanee: The University of The South (1980-2005); Professor, History, Davidson College, NC (1976-1980); Associate Professor, History, Davidson College (1966-1976); Assistant Professor, History, Davidson College (1963-1966); Professor Emeritus of History, Retired Dean **Civic:** President, Southern College and University Union, Organizer, Associated Colleges of the South (1988-1989); Member, International Advisory Committee, University of Buckingham, England (1977-1993); Trustee, Sewanee, The University of The South (1968-1971) **Creative Works:** Author, "Thomas Fuller: Discovering England's Religious Past" (2018); Author, "William Perkins and the Making of a Protestant England" (2014); Author, "The Liberal Arts at Sewanee: A History of Teaching and Learning at the University of the South" (2009); Co-Author, "Lutheran and Anglican: Essays in Honour of Egil Grislis" (2009); Co-Author, "A Companion to Richard Hooker" (2008); Co-Author, "Richard Hooker and The Construction of Christian Community" (1997); Author, "King James VI and I and the Reunion of Christendom" (1997); Co-Author, "This Sacred History: Anglican Reflections for John Booty" (1990); Member of the Board of Editors, "St Luke's Journal of Theology" (1982-1990); Co-Author, "Discord. Dialogue, and Concord" (1977); Contributor, Numerous Articles, Professional Journals **Awards:** National Endowment for the Humanities (1967); American Council of Learned Societies First-Year Graduate Fellowship (1952-1953) **Memberships:** American Historical Association; American Society of Church History; North American Conference on British Studies; Ecclesiastical History Society England; Royal Historical Society England; Southern Historical Association; Society for Values in Higher Education; Episcopal Divinity School Alumni/ae Association; Phi Beta Kappa; Omicron Delta Kappa, Beta Theta Pi **Marquis Who's Who Honors:** Albert Nelson Marquis Lifetime Achievement Award **Why did you become involved in your profession or industry:** During his years as an undergraduate and graduate student, Dr. Patterson aspired to be a scholar as well as a leader in academic and religious endeavors. While at Oxford on a Rhodes Scholarship, he studied under C.S. Lewis, the eminent literary historian and theologian. Lewis became a model for him. After two years at Oxford, Dr. Patterson entered the Episcopal Theological School in Cambridge, Massachusetts, and, following graduation, he was ordained. He subsequently served parish churches on a part-time basis. He enrolled in an interdisciplinary doctoral program in history and religion at Harvard. This led to his being appointed to the history department and to the faculty team serving the humanities program at Davidson College. After seventeen years, he was called to be dean of the College of Arts and Sciences at Sewanee. He continued teaching, conducting research, writing, and publishing during his tenure as dean and after he returned to full-time service as a faculty member. **Avocations:** Gardening; Tennis **Religion:** The Episcopal Church

Basil Mantas Paulus, MD

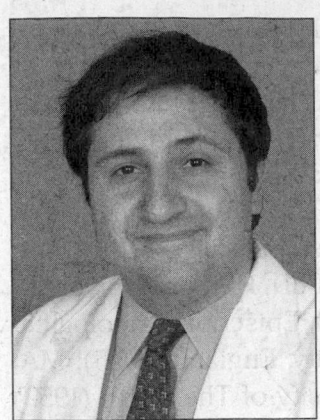

Title: Physician, Medical Director **Industry:** Medicine & Health Care **Company Name:** The Stern Cardiovascular Foundation **Marital Status:** Married **Children:** One Child **Education:** Interventional Cardiology Fellowship, Borgess Heart Institute, Michigan State University, Kalamazoo, MI (2009-2010); Cardiology Fellowship, University of Tennessee Health Science Center, Memphis, TN (2006-2009); Internal Medicine Residency, University of Tennessee Health Science Center, Memphis, TN (2003-2006); MD, Albany Medical College, Albany, NY (1999-2003); BS in Biology, Rensselaer Polytechnic Institute, Cum Laude, Troy, NY (1997-2001) **Certifications:** Interventional Cardiology, American Board of Internal Medicine (2011-Present); Cardiovascular Disease, American Board of Internal Medicine (2009-2019); Internal Medicine, American Board of Internal Medicine (2007-2017) **Career:** Physician, Medical Director, Heart Valve Program, Baptist Memorial Hospital, Memphis, TN; Physician, The Stern Cardiovascular Foundation **Civic:** Volunteer, Local Church **Creative Works:** Contributor, Articles, Professional Journals **Awards:** Top 10 Doctors, Vitals (2014); Patient Choice Award, Vitals (2014); America's Top Cardiologists, Consumers' Research Council of America (2013); Patents' Choice Award, Vitals (2013); Patients' Choice Award (2010-2012); Top 40 Under 40, Memphis Business Journal (2012); Most Compassionate Doctor Award (2012); Most Compassionate Doctor Award (2011); Most Compassionate Doctor Award (2010); Physician of the Month, St. Francis Hospital, Memphis, TN (2010); America's Top Cardiologists, Consumers' Research Council of America (2009); Excellence in Teaching Fellow Award, University of Tennessee Health Science Center, Department of Internal Medicine, Memphis, TN (2008); Outstanding Case Report, Social Scientists Citation Index (2008); Innovative Research Project, Social Science Citation Index (2007); National Merit Based Scholarship (1997-1999); Dean's Award, Merit Based Scholarship, Rensselaer Polytechnic Institute, Troy, New York (1997-1999); Best Teacher, Internal Medicine Residents and Interns; Cardiovascular Case Reports Scholar, Southern Society for Clinical Investigation, New Orleans, LA; Trainee Award, Southern Society for Clinical Investigation, New Orleans, LA; American Hellenic Educational Progressive Association Scholarship, Rensselaer Polytechnic Institute, Troy, NY; **Memberships:** American Heart Association; American Medical Association; American College of Cardiology; Society for Cardiovascular Angiography and Interventions **Marquis Who's Who Honors:** Albert Nelson Marquis Lifetime Achievement Award; Marquis Who's Who Top Professional **Why did you become involved in your profession or industry:** Dr. Paulus became involved in his profession because he was inspired by his father, brother and sister, who are all physicians. Dr. Paulus was drawn to cardiology because of his mentors. **Avocations:** Basketball; Swimming; Reading; Alto saxophone; Piano; Guitar

Mary Libby Payne, JD, LLD (Hon.)

Title: Emerita Dean, Professor, Judge (Retired) **Industry:** Law and Legal Services **Date of Birth:** 03/27/1932 **Place of Birth:** Gulfport **State/Country of Origin:** MS/USA **Parents:** Reece O. Bickerstaff; Emily Augusta (Cook) Bickerstaff **Marital Status:** Widowed **Spouse Name:** Bobby R. Payne (1955, Deceased 02/15/2018) **Children:** Reece Allen; Glenn Russell **Education:** Honorary LLD, Mississippi College (2013); JD, University of Mississippi (1955); BA in Political Science, University of Mississippi, With Distinction (1954); Coursework, Mississippi University for Women (1950-1952) **Career:** Scholar in Residence, Professor Emerita, Professor, and Founding Dean, Mississippi College School of Law, Clinton, MS (1975-1994, 2003-2011); Retired, Judge, Mississippi Court of Appeals, Jackson, MS (1995-2001); Assistant Attorney General, State Attorney General Office, Jackson, MS (1972-1975); Chief, Legislative Services, Mississippi House of Representatives, Jackson, MS (1970-1972); Executive Director, Mississippi Judiciary Commission, Jackson, MS (1968-1970); Solo Practitioner, Brandon, MS (1963-1968); Freelance Researcher, Pearl, MS (1961-1963); Associate, Henley, Jones, & Henley, Jackson, MS (1958-1961); Partner, Bickerstaff & Bickerstaff, Gulfport, MS (1955-1958) **Career Related:** Board of Distinguished Alumnae, Mississippi University for Women (1988-2000); Fellow, American Bar Foundation **Civic:** Advisor, Covenant Ministerial Fellowship (1995-2002); Board of Directors, Exchange Club's Child Abuse Prevention Center, Jackson, MS (1999-2001); National Board of Directors, Christian Legal Society (1992-2001); Founder, Board of Directors, Christian Conciliation Service, Jackson, MS (1983-1993); Counsel, Christian Action Committee, Rankin Baptist Association, Pearl, MS (1968-1992) **Creative Works:** Author, "A Goodly Heritage: A Memoir of Mississippi College, School of Law" (2011); Contributor, Articles, Professional Journals **Awards:** Law Alumni Hall of Fame, School of Law, University of Mississippi (2015); Mississippi Medal of Service, Governor of Mississippi (2011); Lifetime Achievement Award, Mississippi Women Lawyers Association (2010); Lifetime Achievement Award, Mississippi Bar (2005); Distinguished Jurist Award, Pre-Law Group, Mississippi State University (2004); Lifetime Achievement Award, National Christian Legal Society (2002); Susie Blue Buchanan Award, Women in Profession Committee, Mississippi Bar (2000); Mississippi College Lawyer of the Year, Mississippi College School of Law Alumni Association (1998); Excellence Medallion, Mississippi University for Women (1990); Woman of the Year Award, Mississippi Association of Women in Higher Education (1989); Book of Golden Deeds Award, Pearl Exchange Club (1989) **Memberships:** Mississippi Bar Foundation **Bar Admissions:** State of Mississippi (1955) **Marquis Who's Who Honors:** Albert Nelson Marquis Lifetime Achievement Award; Marquis Who's Who Top Professional and Humanitarian Awards **To what do you attribute your success:** Judge Payne attributes her success to her father's example and God's blessings. **Why did you become involved in your profession or industry:** Judge Payne's father was a lawyer and a legislator. He included his family in everything and when political dignitaries would come, he would be the legislator to take them to dinner, where she loved the conversations. She was in public school at this time. When she was in second grade, she went to her cousin's graduation at Mississippi State College for Women, where she decided to go to study ballet. Around junior high school, Judge Payne realized that if she were going to make a living out of ballet, she would have to move to New York, which is a long way from Mississippi. She couldn't handle the thought of being away from her father. She put a lot of faith in God at this time and considered going into law. Between Judge Payne's freshman and sophomore years of college, she was on the staff at Ridgecrest Baptist Assembly. She had some free time when she would miss a meal and go to the prayer garden to pray. She thought God might be calling her to become a social worker. Dr. Chester Swor, a Christian mentor, helped her realize the five specific reasons why he thought she needed to become a lawyer. Judge Payne wanted to do God's will in her life, and she looked at her dad's library and thought the books would be interesting to read. She did an aptitude test, which showed she should be a lawyer, and after much counseling with spiritual mentors, she came to realize that God's will for her was in the "ministry of jurisprudence." She then was able to plan her college schedule toward that end. **Avocations:** Public speaking; Travel; Needlepoint; Sewing; Reading; Writing; History **Religion:** Baptist **Thoughts on Life:** Judge Payne's husband, Bobby, recently passed away. She says it takes a special kind of husband to be married to a woman lawyer, at least in the 20th century, and he was a man who was so secure in his own person-hood that he freed her up to become all that God intended for her to be. Although Judge Payne worked hard and wrote many opinions, she believes that her greatest contribution to the court of appeals was her efficiency (she never missed a deadline) and her congeniality.

R. Samuel Paz

Title: Chief Executive Officer, Civil Rights Lawyer **Industry:** Law and Legal Services **Company Name:** Law Offices of R. Samuel Paz **Place of Birth:** Los Angeles **State/Country of Origin:** CA/USA **Marital Status:** Married **Spouse Name:** Sonia Maria Mercado **Children:** Tomas, Andres, Paloma, and Sonia Isabel; Nicolas (Grandchild); Deven (Grandchild); Tomasito (Odin) (Grandchild) **Education:** JD, University of Southern California Gould School of Law (1974); BA in Psychology, University of California Los Angeles, Cum Laude (1971) **Career:** President, Chief Executive Officer, Law Offices of R. Samuel Paz, Culver City, CA (1985-Present); Senior Partner, Law Offices of Romero, Paz, Rodriguez and Sanora, Alhambra, CA (1975-1986); Staff Attorney, Legal Services of San Gabriel Valley, El Monte, CA (1974-1975) **Career Related:** Faculty Member, Southern California Regional Program, National Institute for Trial Advocacy (1995-2004); Adjunct Professor, Loyola Law School (1990-1998); Instructor, Torts and Evidence, Peoples College of Law **Civic:** American Civil Liberties Union; American Civil Liberties Union of Southern California; National Police Accountability Project; Los Angeles Legal Aid Foundation; The UCLA Foundation **Military Service:** U.S. Navy **Creative Works:** Author, Co-Author, Numerous Articles, Professional Journals; Guest Lecturer, Guest Presenter, Guest Panelist, Numerous Presentations and Conferences **Awards:** ACLU National Board 30 Year of Service Award (2019); Decades of Service Award, National Lawyers' Guild (2018); Johnnie L. Cochran Jr. Public Service Award (2018); Los Angeles County Board of Supervisors' Commendation (2016); Service to the Affairs of the Community, County Supervisor Mark Ridley-Thomas (2013); City of Los Angeles Certificate of Recognition for Outstanding Achievements (2013); Honorable Robert W. Kenny Award for Being a Pioneer involving the Constitutional Rights of Persons in Jails, the National Lawyer's Guide (2007); Certificate of Recognition for Dedication to the Community, State of California Senate Majority Leader (2007); Eason Monroe Courageous Advocate Award for a Lifetime of Advocacy for Civil and Human Rights, ACLU-SC (2002); Inspirational Alumnus Award for Distinguished Advocacy of Human Rights, U.S.C. Law School (2002); Assembly Resolution of Commendation for Dedication to Civil Rights, Assembly Member Antonio Villaraigosa (1995); Frank E. Munoz Award Protecting Legal and Human Rights, Mexican American Bar Association (1994); and Cruz Reynoso Award for Outstanding Community Service and Contribution to the Legal Community, California La Raza Lawyers Association & National Hispanic Bar Association (1993) **Memberships:** Consumer Attorneys Association of Los Angeles (1982-Present); California State Bar Association (1974-Present); Mexican American Bar Association (1974-Present); American Trial Lawyers Association (1984-1994); Hispanic National Bar Association **Bar Admissions:** United States District Court for the Eastern District of California (2005); United States District Court for the Southern District of California (1990); Supreme Court of the United States (1983); United States Court of Appeals for the Ninth Circuit (1975); United States District Court for the Central District of California (1975); California State Bar (1974) **Marquis Who's Who Honors:** Marquis Who's Who Top Professional **To what do you attribute your success:** Mr. Paz attributes his success to the lessons he learned to "take yourself extremely seriously and hold yourself to a higher level of competence, honesty, and integrity than any other lawyer because asserting civil rights requires challenging your government to hold them accountable to the constitution. His colleagues demand of themselves to be highly professional, squeaky clean and to be better than good. **Why did you become involved in your profession or industry:** Growing up in a Mexican community in Los Angeles he and his friends were constantly stopped and searched by the heavy police presence and their racially biased treatment. The Navy experience sharpened his awareness of the not so subtle attitudes of discrimination against brown and black Americans. In the 1960s in college, he planned to be a psychologist, but Anti-War protests and the Chicano Movement made civil rights and human rights primary to his life's ambition. There was just one lawyer in Southern California who had the courage to sue when police abused and killed. In the early 1980s, the local papers would not publish the verdicts for fear of exposing police officers to negative publicity. It took several months to get an article published and years until enough people were unjustly killed that the country became outraged.

Robert Lawrence Pearson

Title: Executive Recruiter **Industry:** Staffing and Recruiting **Company Name:** Pearson Partners International Inc. **Date of Birth:** 04/19/1939 **Place of Birth:** Chicago **State/Country of Origin:** IL/USA **Parents:** Jonas Peter Pearson; Caroline Margaret (Reilly) Pearson **Marital Status:** Married **Spouse Name:** Norma Eloise Dale (04/27/1963) **Children:** Jill Caroline; Keith Donald **Education:** Master of Science, Massachusetts Institute of Technology, Magna Cum Laude (1963); Bachelor of Science in Electrical Engineering, Michigan State University (1961) **Career:** Chairman, Pearson Partners International Inc. (2001-Present); Member, Board of Directors, Baird Capital Partners Inc. (2000-Present); Member, Board of Directors, Pentagon Technologies Inc. (2000-2019); Member, Board of Directors, Tatum CFO Inc. (1999-2003); Chairman, Chief Executive Officer, Lamalie Amrop International (1994-1999); President, Lamalie Amrop International (1994-1998); Chairman, Lamalie Associate Inc. (1989-1994); Managing Director, Lamalie Associate Inc. (1984-1989); Executive Director, Russell Reynolds Associate Inc. (1981-1983); President, Pearson Inc. (1971-1981); President, Pearson Wade and Co. Inc. (1970-1971); Vice President, Raymond James and Associate (1968-1970); Consultant, McKinsey and Co. Inc. (1964-1968) **Civic:** Member, Board of Directors, Dallas Museum of Natural History (1985-Present); Member, Dallas Mayor's Inaugural Campaign (2011); Member, Board of Directors, YMCA Dallas (1988-1990); Member, Fundraising Committee, Dallas Museum of Art (1983-1985); Speechwriter, Governor's Campaign, Chicago (1968); Patron, Ronald McDonald House of Dallas **Creative Works:** Contributor, Numerous Articles to Newspapers and Professional Journals **Awards:** Lifetime Achievement Award, Association of Executive Search and Leadership Consultants (2013) **Memberships:** Dallas President, Massachusetts Institute of Technology Alumni Club (1993-1996); President, Chapter, Phi Delta Theta Michigan Beta (1959-1961); Founding Sponsor, Gilda's Club North Texas; Massachusetts Institute of Technology Enterprise Forum; Dallas National Golf Club; Broadmoor Golf Club; Dallas Chamber of Commerce; Charter Member, Tower Club Dallas; Phi Beta Kappa **Marquis Who's Who Honors:** Albert Nelson Marquis Lifetime Achievement Award **To what do you attribute your success:** Mr. Pearson attributes his success to working hard, playing hard, and always remembering that "whatever happens, the sun will be up tomorrow." **Why did you become involved in your profession or industry:** Mr. Pearson became involved in his profession because he joined executive search legend Russell Reynolds Jr. in Dallas, Texas, in 1982. They became fast friends and have been close ever since. **Avocations:** Squash; Jogging; Deep sea fishing; Hunting; Marathon running **Religion:** Catholic

Paul F. Pedigo, BA, BEChE, JD

Title: Managing Attorney **Industry:** Law and Legal Services **Company Name:** Pedigo Law Firm PLLC **Date of Birth:** 10/22/1954 **Place of Birth:** Chattanooga **State/Country of Origin:** TN/USA **Marital Status:** Married **Spouse Name:** Leigh **Children:** Richardson; Harrison; Coleman **Education:** JD, Loyola University of Chicago School of Law (1985); BEChE in Chemical Engineering, Vanderbilt University (1980); BA in English, Minor in Philosophy, Coursework in Anthropology, Botany, and Zoolology, Vanderbilt University (1976) **Certifications:** Registered, U.S. Patent and Trademark Office (1984) **Career:** Managing Attorney, Pedigo Law, Intellectual Property Law and Management (2009-Present); Partner, Summa, Additon & Ashe, P.A. (2005-2009); Group Leader, Chemical and Pharmaceutical Patent Solicitation, Alston & Bird LLP (1997-2005); Partner, Bell, Seltzer, Park & Gibson, P.A. (1988-1997); Associate, Leydig, Voit & Mayer, Ltd. (1985-1987) **Career Related:** Chemical Engineer, UOP, Inc., Chicago, IL (1980-1984) **Civic:** Committee on Ministry, Presbytery of Charlotte (2017-2020); Patron Sponsor, Charlotte Biotechnology Conference (2011); Patron Sponsor, Five Ventures Conference (2011); Board of Directors, Mecklenburg County Bar (2002-2005); Access to Justice Campaign (2000-2001); Chair, Bar's Publications Committee (1997-2002); Bar's Family Liaison, Habitat for Humanity Houses (1988-1989) **Awards:** Listee, Business North Carolina's Legal Elite (2006, 2012-2014); AV Preeminent Peer Review, Martindale-Hubbell; Listee, Bar Register of Preeminent Lawyers **Bar Admissions:** North Carolina (1988); Illinois (1986) **Marquis Who's Who Honors:** Marquis Who's Who Top Professional **Why did you become involved in your profession or industry:** Mr. Pedigo began his journey to a career in law by enrolling in engineering school. After graduating, he got his first job, which gave him the opportunity to enroll in law school. Taking advantage of what was being offered, Mr. Pedigo attended law school and decided to become a patent attorney. He feels the transition from engineering to law was natural. It came easily to him because he was able to combine both of his degrees into a profession by making use of his excellent writing skills. **Avocations:** Cross-country mountain biking; Iconography; Study and teaching in the area of stained glass symbolism and iconography; Postmodern influences in current iconography **Religion:** Presbyterian Church

Stuart P. Pegg, MD, AM

Title: Emeritus Professor **Industry:** Education/Educational Services **Company Name:** University of Queensland **Date of Birth:** 03/13/1932 **Place of Birth:** Gladstone **State/Country of Origin:** Queensland/Australia **Parents:** Harry Thomas Pegg (Deceased 1971); Eileen (Standish) Pegg (Deceased 1978) **Marital Status:** Married **Spouse Name:** Gwenda Mary Smart (12/12/1958) **Children:** David Andrew (1962); Susan Mary (1960); Michael Stuart (1959) **Education:** MD, University of Queensland, Brisbane, Australia (2006); MBBS, University of Queensland, Brisbane, Australia, With Honors (1956) **Certifications:** Pediatric Surgery, Medical Board of Australia (1970s); Registered in General Surgery, Medical Board of Australia (1964) **Career:** Emeritus Professor, University of Queensland, Brisbane, Australia (2006); Professor, University of Queensland, Brisbane, Australia (1996-2006); Associate Professor, Burn Surgery, University of Queensland, Brisbane, Australia (1994-1996); Director, Surgery, Royal Brisbane Hospital (1977-1994); Surgical Supervisor, Royal Brisbane Hospital (1967-1977); Surgical Registrar, Royal Berkshire Hospital, England (1965-1966); Surgical Registrar, Princess Alexandra Hospital, Brisbane, Australia (1962-1964); Medical Superintendent, Julia Creek, Queensland, Australia (1958-1961); Intern, Royal Brisbane Hospital (1957) **Military Service:** Major, Australian Army Reserve (1981-1987); Captain, U.S. Army Reserve (1957) **Creative Works:** Contributor, Chapters, Books; Contributor, Articles, Professional Journals **Awards:** Vice Chancellor Alumni Award of Excellence, University of Queensland (2018); G. Whitaker International Burn Prize, Sicily (2003); Decorated Order of Australia; Australian Fellowship RICS in 1964; **Memberships:** Honorary Life Member, International Society for Burn Injuries (2004); President, Churchill Fellows' Association of Queensland (1995-1998); Vice President, International Society for Burn Injuries (1990-1998); President, Australian and New Zealand Burn Association (1980-1982); Fellow, Royal Australian College Surgery; Honorary, American Association for Surgery of Trauma; Royal College of Surgeons (England); Royal Australasian College of Medical Administrators; Australian Medical Association; American Burn Association; South African Burn Society **Marquis Who's Who Honors:** Albert Nelson Marquis Lifetime Achievement Award **Why did you become involved in your profession or industry:** Dr. Pegg became involved in his profession because he wanted to pursue medicine since he was 13. **Avocations:** Orchids; Gardening **Religion:** Anglican

Karen Sue Pence

Title: Second Lady of the United States; Teacher **Industry:** Government Administration/Government Relations/Government Services **Date of Birth:** 01/01/1957 **Place of Birth:** McConnell Air Force Base **State/Country of Origin:** KS/USA **Parents:** John M. Batten; Lillian (Hacker) Batten **Marital Status:** Married **Spouse Name:** Mike Pence (06/08/1985); John Steven Whitaker (08/04/1978, Divorced) **Children:** Michael; Charlotte; Audrey **Education:** MS in Elementary Education, Butler University; BS in Elementary Education, Butler University **Career:** Teacher, Arts, Immanuel Christian School (2019-Present); Second Lady of the United States (2017-Present); First Lady of Indiana (2013-2017); Teacher, John Strange Elementary, Indianapolis, IN; Teacher, Acton Elementary, Indianapolis, IN; Teacher, Fall Creek Elementary, Indianapolis, IN; Teacher, Orchard School, Indianapolis, IN; Painter **Civic:** Founder, Indiana First Lady's Charitable Foundation

Ewell Dean "Bub" Pendergrass

Title: Communications Executive (Retired) **Industry:** Technology **Company Name:** LED Communications **Date of Birth:** 12/24/1945 **Place of Birth:** Houston **State/Country of Origin:** TX/USA **Parents:** Ewell Burl Pendergrass (1912-1990); Mary LaVerne (Sharp) Pendergrass (1913-1973) **Marital Status:** Married **Spouse Name:** Linda Jo Williams (12/20/1973) **Children:** William Dean Pendergrass; Douglas Aaron Pendergrass; Nagaya Jo Pendergrass **Education:** AAS in Electronics, Westark Community College (1979) **Career:** Electronics Supervisor, Fort Smith, AR (1975-2016); Co-Owner, LED Communications (1975-2016); Electronics Technician, Fort Smith, AR (1973-2010); Communications Technician, Murdock Communications, Fort Smith, AR (1966-1973); Adjunct Faculty, Southern Arkansas University Tech, Camden, AR **Career Related:** Broadcast Engineer, Station KFSA (1975-1976); Broadcast Engineer, Station KWHN (1972-1973); Arkansas Department of Pollution and Ecology Wastewater; Licensing Board Member, Arkansas Licensing Commission **Civic:** Contributor, Little League Baseball; Leader, Boy Scouts of America **Awards:** Appreciation for Dedication and Outstanding Service, Wastewater Licensing Committee (1994-2003); Appreciation for Dedication and Outstanding Service, District of Arkansas Water Works & Water Environment Association (AWW&WEA) (1993); Water Operator of the Year (1992); Appreciation for Dedication and Outstanding Service, Arkansas Waterworks and Water Environment Association Western District (25 Years); Appreciation for Dedication and Outstanding Service, City of Fort Smith, AR (26 Years) **Memberships:** President, Border Amateur Radio Club (1974-1975); Chairman, Western District Director, Arkansas Water Works and Pollution Control Association; American Water Works Association **Marquis Who's Who Honors:** Albert Nelson Marquis Lifetime Achievement Award **Avocations:** Call signs, WA5AER, W5BUB (1960-2016); Amateur radio; Fishing; Little league baseball; Being a Boy Scouts leader **Political Affiliations:** Democrat **Religion:** Methodist

Roger S. Penske Jr.

Title: Chairman, Chief Executive Officer **Industry:** Automotive **Company Name:** Penske Corporation **Date of Birth:** 02/20/1937 **Place of Birth:** Shaker Heights **State/Country of Origin:** OH/USA **Marital Status:** Married **Spouse Name:** Kathy; Lissa **Children:** Roger Jr.; Gregory; Blair; Mark; Jay **Education:** Gradate, Lehigh University (1959) **Career:** Chairman, Chief Executive Officer, Penske Automotive Group, Inc. (1999-Present); Chairman, President, Pennsylvania International Raceway, Inc. (1986-Present); Chairman, Penske Truck Leasing Company (1982-Present); Chairman, Chief Executive Officer, Penske Corporation (1969-Present); Founder, Owner, Team Leader, Penske Racing (Now Team Penske), IndyCar Series, NASCAR (1966-Present); Chairman, United Auto Group Inc. (1999); Chairman, Penske Motorsports (Acquired by Penske Automotive Group, Inc.) (1996-1999); Member, Board of Directors, Penske Motorsports (Acquired by Penske Automotive Group, Inc.) (1995); Chairman, California Speedway Corporation (1994); Chairman, Detroit Diesel Corporation (1987); Chairman, Michigan International Speedway, Inc. (1973); Race Car Driver, NASCAR (1960-1965); Managing Director, Transportation Resource Partners, LP; Chairman, Detroit Investment Fund; Former Member, Board of Directors, Delphi Corporation; Founder, Penske Racing South Inc.; Founder, Penske Racing Inc.; Founder, Penske Logistics; Senior Adviser to the Board of Directors, Delphi Corporation **Career Related:** Detroit Renaissance Vice Chairman, CarsDirect.com, Inc. (2000-Present); Board of Directors, International Speedway Corporation (1999-Present); Board of Directors, General Electric Company (1994-Present); Chairman, Super Bowl XI, Detroit, MI (2006); Board of Directors, Home Depot, Inc. (2000); Board of Directors, Gulfstream Aerospace Corporation (1993); Former Member, Board of Directors, Delphi Automotive Systems Corporation; Former Member, Board of Directors, Internet Brands, Inc. **Civic:** Board of Directors, Business Leaders for Michigan, Universal Tech. Institute (2002-Present); Chairman, Downtown Detroit Partnership; Donor, $500,000, Restore Our Future **Awards:** Presidential Medal of Freedom, President Donald Trump (2019); Inductee, NASCAR Hall of Fame (2019); Five-Time IndyCar Series Champion (2006, 2014, 2016, 2017, 2019); Two-Time NASCAR Cup Series Champion (2012, 2018); Inductee, Automotive Hall of Fame (2015); Inductee, Indianapolis Motor Speedway Hall of Fame (2002); Inductee, International Motorsports Hall of Fame (1998); Inductee, Motorsports Hall of Fame America (1995); Sports Car Club of America Driver of the Year, Sports Illustrated (1961); Spirit of Competition Award, Simeone Foundation **Memberships:** The Business Council; Phi Gamma Delta **Avocations:** Collecting cars

Frank A. Pepe

Title: Cell and Developmental Biology Educator **Industry:** Education/ Educational Services **Company Name:** University of Pennsylvania **Date of Birth:** 05/22/1931 **Place of Birth:** Schenectady **State/Country of Origin:** NY/USA **Parents:** Rocco Pepe; Margherita (Ruggiero) Pepe **Marital Status:** Single **Education:** PhD in Physical Chemistry, Yale University (1957); BS in Chemistry, Union College (1953) **Career:** Professor Emeritus, University of Pennsylvania, Philadelphia, PA (1996-Present); Professor, Cellular and Development Biology, University of Pennsylvania, Philadelphia, PA (1992-1996); Chairman, Department of Anatomy, University of Pennsylvania (1977-1990); Professor, University of Pennsylvania, Philadelphia, PA (1970-1992); Associate Professor, University of Pennsylvania, Philadelphia, PA (1965-1970); Professor, University of Pennsylvania, Philadelphia, PA (1970-1977); Assistant Professor, University of Pennsylvania, Philadelphia, PA (1963-1965); Associate in Anatomy, University of Pennsylvania, Philadelphia, PA (1960-1963); Instructor, Anatomy, University of Pennsylvania, Philadelphia, PA (1957-1960) **Creative Works:** Speaker, "Pepe Lecture," University of Pennsylvania, Philadelphia, PA (1999-2009); Editor, "Motility in Cell Function" (1979) **Awards:** Raymond C. Truex Distinguished Lecture Award, Hahneman University (1988); Research Career Development Award, U.S. Public Health Service (1968-1973) **Memberships:** Fellow, American Association for the Advancement of Science; American Association of Anatomists; American Chemical Society; Biophysics Society; Microscopy Society of America; Sigma Xi, The Scientific Research Honor Society **Marquis Who's Who Honors:** Albert Nelson Marquis Lifetime Achievement Award **To what do you attribute your success:** Dr. Pepe attributes his success to having had some very good people who have been very kind to him. Dr. Louis B. Fleckner was Chairman of the department at Penn; he and his wife Pepita, who is also a doctor, were very good to him, Dr. Pepe was very close to them. **Why did you become involved in your profession or industry:** Dr. Pepe became involved in his profession because he started out as a PhD in Chemistry from Yale University. His thesis subject was "Thermodynamics of the Antigen Antibody Reaction." From his deep studies of the subject he became heavily interested and began to pursue the subject further. Eventually, he asked the university for the use of their electron microscope to study his subject in even more visual detail. Constantly being around the subjects related to anatomy and biology, his scientific background transformed him to achieve the career he has had today. **Avocations:** Painting; Gardening; Ballroom dancing **Political Affiliations:** Democrat **Religion:** Roman Catholic

Fred M. Perilstein

Title: Electrical Engineering Consultant **Industry:** Engineering **Date of Birth:** 10/25/1945 **Place of Birth:** Philadelphia **State/Country of Origin:** PA/USA **Parents:** Paul Pincus Perilstein; Adeline Sylvia (Schneyer) Perilstein **Marital Status:** Widower **Spouse Name:** Abigail Siff (Married 6/13/1971, Deceased 03/25/2011) **Education:** MSEE, Power, New Jersey Institute of Technology (1977); BSEE, Newark College of Engineering (1972); BS in Economics, City College of New York (1968) **Certifications:** Registered Professional Engineer, States of California, New Jersey, New York, Pennsylvania, Texas **Career:** Consultant, Envar Services Incorporated (1997-Present); President, Tramlec Corporation, Consulting Engineers, Springfield, NJ (1982-1997); Consultant in Field (1978-1982); Engineer, Switchgear Applications, Federal Pacific Electric Corporation, Newark, NJ (1972-1978) **Career Related:** ASME/IEEE Joint R.R. Conferences (1994, 1997, 2000); IEEE Consultants, Network, NJ (1992-1996); Lecturer, Institute of Electrical and Electronics Engineers Montech 86, Montreal, Canada (1986); Seminar Instructor, Multi-Amp Conference, Springfield, NJ (1980) **Military Service:** United States Army Reserve (1968-1974) **Creative Works:** Contributor, Articles, Institute of Electrical and Electronics Engineers Transactions; Consultant in Field **Awards:** 3rd Prize Trophy, World Wide Inventor Expo (1982); Regents Scholar, New York Board of Regents (1963) **Memberships:** Institute of Electrical and Electronics Engineers **Marquis Who's Who Honors:** Albert Nelson Marquis Lifetime Achievement Award; Marquis Who's Who Top Professional **To what do you attribute your success:** Mr. Perilstein attributes his success to his continued interest in developments in power electrical engineering. **Why did you become involved in your profession or industry:** As a toddler, Mr. Perilstein recalls visiting the Pennsylvania Rail Road's 30th Street Station. He was fascinated by its then-vast collection of overhead catenary wires. This sparked his interest in engineering, as did having a model train set, which piqued his equally strong interest in electricity.

Thomas J. Perrone, JD

Title: Systems Analyst, Consultant **Industry:** Consulting **Company Name:** Thomas J. Perrone Consulting **Date of Birth:** 11/02/1941 **Place of Birth:** Haverhill **State/Country of Origin:** MA/USA **Parents:** Winfred Mose Perrone; Josephine Jennie (Azzatto) Perrone **Marital Status:** Married **Spouse Name:** Jeanne Frances Munroe (02/13/1982) **Education:** MS in Systems Management, University of Denver (1990-1991); JD, Lincoln University, San Jose, CA (1974-1978); BS in Meteorology, Pennsylvania State University (1966-1967); BS in Economics, Politics, Engineering, Massachusetts Institute of Technology (1959-1965) **Career:** Private Practice Consultant, Clarksburg, MD (2015-Present); Senior Systems Engineer, ITT, Washington (2009-2010); Senior Systems Analyst, BAE Systems, Washington (1994-2009); Senior Computer Scientist, Logicon, Inc., Washington (1984-1993); Research Meteorologist, Techniques Development Laboratory, National Weather Service, Silver Spring, MD (1980-1984); Marine Meteorologist, Marine Weather Branch, National Weather Service Headquarters, Silver Spring, MD (1979-1980); Research Meteorologist, Naval Environmental Prediction Research Facility, Monterey, CA (1974-1979); Marine Meteorologist, Ocean Routes, Inc., Palo Alto, CA (1973-1974); Marine Meteorologist, IMCOS Marine Limited, London (1971-1973); Statistician, New York Department of Motor Vehicles (1965-1966) **Military Service:** Air National Guard, California, New Jersey, Virginia (1975-1993); 1st Lt., Captain, U.S. Air Force, Vietnam (1969-1970); Aviation Meteorologist, U.S. Air Force, New York, Maine, Vietnam (1966-1970) **Creative Works:** Contributor, Articles, Professional Journals, Meteorology **Memberships:** Retired Member, American Meteorological Society; American Legion; Former Member, American Statistical Association; Retired Member, California Bar Association; Former Member, National Weather Association **Bar Admissions:** California (1978) **Marquis Who's Who Honors:** Albert Nelson Marquis Lifetime Achievement Award; Marquis Who's Who Top Professional **Why did you become involved in your profession or industry:** Mr. Perrone became involved in his profession because he was facing the draft in the Vietnam era, so he began to look at options in which he could use his intelligence to make a contribution. While looking into the officer programs, he saw opportunities for pilots, navigators, and meteorologists. Because Mr. Perrone had some interest in statistics and computer science as well as physics, he chose meteorology, and later worked in applying statistical techniques and computer programming to his research efforts. After entering the military, he quickly became very involved in weather forecasting and figured out that even after he was done serving the military, he would continue to pursue meteorology. **Avocations:** Music **Political Affiliations:** Republican **Religion:** Roman Catholic

Natalie L.M. Petesch, PhD

Title: Author **Industry:** Writing and Editing **Date of Birth:** 07/06/1924 **Place of Birth:** Detroit **State/Country of Origin:** MI/USA **Parents:** Samuel Levin; Anna Goldman Levin **Marital Status:** Married **Spouse Name:** Donald Anthony Petesch (1959) **Children:** Rachel Pearl Maines; Nicholas Petesch **Education:** PhD, University of Texas (1962); MA, Brandeis University (1956); BS, Boston University, Magna Cum Laude (1955) **Career:** Assistant Professor, Department of English, San Francisco State University (1961-1962); Special Instructor, University of Texas, Austin, TX (1959-1960); Teaching Fellow, University of Texas, Austin, TX (1956-1959); Author, Short Stories, Novels, and Novellas; Assistant Professor, Department of English, Southwest Texas State University **Career Related:** Distinguished Visiting Professor, Creative Writing, University of Idaho (1982); Pennsylvania Council on the Arts Literary Fellowship (1980); Presenter in Field **Creative Works:** Author, "Stories of the Civil Rights Movement: Selma 1965" (2006); Author, "The Confessions of Señora Francesca Navarro" (2005); Author, "The Immigrant Train and Other Stories" (1996); Author, "North of the Rio Grande, The Mexican-American Experience in Short Fiction, Ramon El Conejo, 1965" (1992); Artist Statement, Pittsburgh Cultural Trust (1991); Author, "Justina of Andalusia and Other Stories" (1990); Author, "Contemporary Authors Autobiography Series," Vol. 12 (1990); Author, "Flowering Mimosa" (1987); Author, "Wild With All Regret" (1986); Author, "Duncan's Colony" (1982); Author, "Soul Clap Its Hands And Sing" (1981); Author, "The Leprosarium" (1979); Author, "The Long Hot Summers of Yasha K." (1979); Author, "After the First Death, There is No Other" (1974); Author, "The Odyssey Of Katinou Kalokovich" (1974); Author, Autobiography, "The Laughter of Hastings Street: An Autobiographical Memoir" **Awards:** Pittsburgh Cultural Trust Award for Outstanding Established Artist (1991); Harvey Curtis Webster Award for Best Story (1989); Swallow's Tale Award (1985); Best American Short Stories (1979); Louisville Review Fiction Prize (1978); New Letters Summer Prize Book Award (1978); Kanwaw Quarterly Fiction Award (1974); Iowa School of Letters Award for Short Fiction, University of Iowa (1974) **Memberships:** Supporter, Numerous Liberal and Progressive Organizations **Marquis Who's Who Honors:** Albert Nelson Marquis Lifetime Achievement Award; Marquis Who's Who Top Professional **Why did you become involved in your profession or industry:** At 9 years old, Dr. Petesch knew she wanted to be a writer. It has been a life long passion of hers. **Avocations:** Travel; Walking; Reading; Music

Renee Danette Petrola

Title: Retired Teacher, Author **Industry:** Education/Educational Services **Company Name:** Mt. Sinai School District **Date of Birth:** 03/01/1948 **Place of Birth:** Mineola **State/Country of Origin:** NY/USA **Parents:** Phyllis Petrola **Education:** Master's Degree in Liberal Studies, Stony Brook University (1974); BA in Elementary Education and Teaching, Bethany College (1970) **Career:** Retired Teacher (2013); Sixth Grade Teacher, Writing, Mount Sinai School District, Mount Sinai, NY (1970-2013); Author, Self-Employed **Career Related:** Conflict Mediator; Counselor; Instructor, Swimming Lessons **Civic:** Participant, Rocky Point Relay for Life (2012); Volunteer, Beach Cleanups; Volunteer, Relay for Life; Participant, Mount Sinai Relay for Life; American Cancer Society, Inc.; Volunteer, Ride For Life Inc; Volunteer, ASPCA; Volunteer, Greenpeace **Creative Works:** Author, "Fragment from the Shadows", BookStand, (2016); Author, "The Healing Tree, Volume Three," BookStand Publishing (2015); Author, "Woman on the Edge of Time", Self Published (2013); Author, "Primitive Dancer," BookStand Publishing (2014) **Awards:** Walt Whitman, Excellence in Education, Blue Ribbon (2013); Professional of the Year in Education (2010); Certificate of Recognition, Elite American Educators **Memberships:** Mt. Sinai Teachers Association; American Federation of Teachers; National Education Association **Marquis Who's Who Honors:** Albert Nelson Marquis Lifetime Achievement Award; Marquis Who's Who Top Professional; Marquis Who's Who Humanitarian Award **To what do you attribute your success:** Ms. Petrola attributes her success to her passion, as well as her listening and observational skills. **Why did you become involved in your profession or industry:** Ms. Petrola became involved in her profession because of the inspiration she received from her mother, Phyllis Petrola, who was also an elementary teacher, and her experience as a babysitter. **Avocations:** Designing jewellery; Writing; Swimming; Kayaking; Spending time at the beach; Riding her bike; Running; Rescuing and adopting Irish Setters; Yoga; Meditation; Taichi class

Christy Pettit

Title: Owner **Industry:** Education/Educational Services **Company Name:** First Impressions **Marital Status:** Widow **Spouse Name:** JP **Children:** Two Sons; One Daughter **Education:** Master of Arts in Special Education, Phoenix University (2006); Bachelor of Arts in Special Education and the Psychology of the Exceptional Child, State University of New York College at Cortland (2003) **Career:** With, JP's Jump Masters (2018-Present); Owner, First Impressions (2009-Present); Teacher, Cumberland County, NC (2006-2008); Special Education Teacher, Hawaii; Itinerant Teacher, Long Island, New York **Civic:** With, FIA Gives Back **Why did you become involved in your profession or industry:** Having struggled academically, Ms. Pettit encountered many structural difficulties in education, and eventually decided to open her own school in order to make a difference on her own terms.

Wayne Howe Phelps, PhD

Title: Director of Planning and Educational Research (Retired) **Industry:** Education/ Educational Services **Company Name:** West Virginia Board of Regents **Parents:** Elmer R. Phelps; Floy E. (Howe) Phelps **Education:** PhD in English, Princeton University, NJ (1965); MA in English, Princeton University, NJ (1961); BA in English, St. Lawrence University, Magna Cum Laude, Canton, NY (1959) **Career:** Retired (1986); Director, Planning and Educational Research, West Virginia Board of Regents, Charleston, WV (1982-1986); Coordinator, Institutional Approval, State Council of Higher Education for Virginia, Richmond, VA (1980-1982); Research Associate, Institutional Approval, State Council for Higher Education for Virginia, Richmond, VA (1980); Research Associate, Academy Programs, State Council for Higher Education for Virginia, Richmond, VA (1978-1980); Assistant Professor, Virginia Polytechnic Institute and State University, Blacksburg, VA (1972-1977); Instructor to Assistant Professor of English, University of Pennsylvania, Philadelphia, PA (1962-1972) **Career Related:** Editorial Consultant, University of Self-Study, Virginia Polytechnic Institute and State University (1975-1976); Student Personnel Officer, University of Pennsylvania, Philadelphia, PA (1963-1966)

Civic: Board of Directors, Friends of the Owen D. Young and Launders Libraries, St. Lawrence University (1989-2009) **Creative Works:** Author, "Plymouth Brethren Hymnody," Notes and Queries (1998); Author, "Charles Bagot Cayley, Poems and Translations 1880," Notes and Queries (1998); Author, "Thomas Holmes, Esquire: The Dedicatee of Middleton's The Witch," Notes and Queries (1980); Author, "The Date of Ben Jonson's Death," Notes and Queries (1980); Author, "Sir Henry Helmes, Prince of Purpoole," Notes and Queries (1980); Author, "John Gerard, the Herbalist," The Library (1980); Author, "The Early Life of Robert Daborne," Philological Quarterly (1980); Author, "The Second Night of Davenant's Salmacida Spolia," Notes and Queries (1979); Author, "Thomas Jordan and His Family," Notes and Queries (1979); Author, "Two Notes on Thomas May," Notes and Queries (1979); Author, "Ruskin's Contribution to the Metropolitan Tabernacle: An Acknowledgement from C. H. Spurgeon," English Language Notes (1979); Author, "The Merry Loungers: An Eighteenth-Century Satirical Play from Clare Hall," Theatre Survey (1979); Author, "Dickens to Bradbury and Evans: An Unnoted Letter, and Cruikshank to Chapman and Hall: A Letter Concerning Sketches by 'Boz,'" The Dickensian (1979); Author, "John Edwards and the Date of the Lost Saturnalia," Notes and Queries (1979); Author, "Nathaniel Johnson, a Seventeenth-Century Playwright," Notes and Queries (1979); Author, "Cosmo Manuche, Royalist Playwright of the Commonwealth," English Language Notes (1979); Author, "The Leakes of St. Dunstan's in the West: A Family of Seventeenth-Century Stationers," Papers of the Bibliographical Society of America (1979); Author, "Thomas Gainsford (1566-1624), the 'Grandfather of English Editors,'" Papers of the Bibliographical Society of America (1979); Author, "Some Sixteeth-Century Stationers' Wills," Studies in Bibliography (1979); Author, "The Will of Randall Taylor, a Restoration Bookseller," Papers of the Bibliographical Society of America (1978); Author, "Simon Baylie (1644-1679) and the Date of the Wizard," Papers of the Bibliographical Society of America (1978); Author, "The Date of Lewis Wager's Death," Notes and Queries (1978); Author, "Philip Gerrard, Translator of Erasmus," Erasmus in English (1978); Author, "Edmund Shakespeare at St. Leonard's, Shoreditch," Shakespeare Quarterly (1978); Author, "John Ford's Perkin Warbeck and the Pretender Plays: 1634-1746," Dissertation, Princeton University (1965); Contributor, Articles to Various Professional Publications (1962-1998); Author, "Deor Daedscua: A Note on the Old English Christ," Notes and Queries (1962); Author, "Dickens to Bradbury and Evans: An Unnoted Letter, and Cruikshank to Chapman and Hall: A Letter Concerning Sketches by 'Boz,'" The Letters of Charles Dickens **Awards:** Summer Fellow, Princeton University (1961, 1962); Charles Scribner Junior Fellow, Princeton University (1961-1962); Junior Fellow, Princeton University (1960-1961); Woodrow Wilson National Fellow, Princeton University (1959-1960) **Memberships:** The Phi Beta Kappa Society; Pi Mu Epsilon; Former Secretary, Club, Modern Square Dancing **Marquis Who's Who Honors:** Albert Nelson Marquis Lifetime Achievement Award

John G. Pierce, JD

Title: Attorney (Retired) **Industry:** Law and Legal Services **Company Name:** Pierce & Associates PL **Date of Birth:** 01/12/1937 **Place of Birth:** Winter Haven **State/Country of Origin:** FL/USA **Parents:** Francis E. Pierce; Margaret (Butler) Pierce **Marital Status:** Married **Spouse Name:** Kathleen E. (12/1/1989) **Children:** Kathleen M. Cooke; Nancy A., John Gerald Jr.; Michael J.; Kevin J. Klein **Education:** JD, University of Florida, Gainesville, FL, With Honors (1965); BSChemE, University of Florida, Gainesville, FL (1959) **Career:** Principal Owner, Pierce & Associates PL, Orlando, FL (2003-Present); Owner, Private Practice, Orlando, FL (1974-2002); Partner, Pierce, Lewis & Dolan, Orlando, FL (1970-1974); Associate, Arnold, Matheny & Eagen, Orlando, FL (1968-1970); Associate, Anderson, Rush, Dean & Lowndes, Orlando, FL (1966-1968) **Military Service:** First Lieutenant, U.S. Army (1959-1965) **Awards:** Pinnacle Profession Member Award, Continental Who's Who (2014); Businessman of the Year, National Republican Congressional Committee (2004) **Memberships:** American Bar Association; Florida Bar Association; Orange County Bar Association **Bar Admissions:** U.S. Court of Appeals for the 11th Circuit (1983); U.S. District Court, Middle District, State of Florida (1966); State of Florida (1966) **Marquis Who's Who Honors:** Albert Nelson Marquis Lifetime Achievement Award; Marquis Who's Who Top Professional **Why did you become involved in your profession or industry:** Mr. Pierce's brother, who is seven years old than he is, was a lawyer. When he retired out of the military pilot, he worked at Cape Canaveral; he decided after three years he wanted to find something a little more inspiring in terms of dealing with people. He saw what his brother was able to do for people, as well as a few uncles, and decided to change his direction and went back to law school. **Avocations:** Golf; Boating; Skiing **Political Affiliations:** Republican **Religion:** Roman Catholic

Stacia Pierce

Title: Owner **Industry:** Consulting **Company Name:** Lifecoach2women.com **Date of Birth:** 06/08/1967 **Place of Birth:** Grand Rapids **State/Country of Origin:** MI/USA **Parents:** Alfred Scott; Phyllis Scott **Marital Status:** Married **Spouse Name:** Dr. James Pierce **Children:** Ariana, Ryan **Education:** PhD in Divinity, Friends University (2001); MA in Theology, Friends University; Counseling Degree **Career:** Founder, Women and Wealth Club; Founder, Success Mastery Business Academy; Founder, Chief Executive Officer, Life Coaching, LifeCoach2Women.com **Creative Works:** Author, 23 Books; Course Creator, 37 Journaling Secrets to Success Attraction Course; Course Creator, The Go Big Coaching Program; Course Creator, Success Mastery Coaching Program; Course Creator, Over 200 Female-Empowerment Courses; Creator, Inspire Perfume; Creator, Superstar Nail Lacquer; Creator, StyleShoppe. com; Founder, 089pWomen's Success Conference **Awards:** Congressional Tribute for Service as Exemplary Life Coach, Rep. Congressman Mike Rogers; Honored, Women's Success Conference Weekend, Lansing, MI; Woman of Distinction, Girl Scouts of America; 3rd Place Winner, Oprah Winfrey's OWN Contest; Eponym, Stacia Pierce Day; Most Valued Member in the Community, Key to the City, Lansing MI; Listee, Top Influential Women Over 50, Better Homes and Garden **To what do you attribute your success:** Ms. Pierce's late father, Alfred Scott, was a serial entrepreneur. When she was 13, he gave her an ice cream shop and arcade to manage, consequently giving her the gift of entrepreneurship. Likewise, Ms. Pierce's father taught her to read and how to sell products. She is endlessly grateful. **Why did you become involved in your profession or industry:** For as long as she can remember, Ms. Pierce has wanted to help women find their passion and profit from it. She began by hosting events to help other women, and when she started receiving follow-up phone calls from her participants, she knew she wanted to become a success coach. Ms. Pierce found that by serving as a success coach, she could do what she loves and simultaneously help others do what they love. This was when she started LifeCoach2Women. com. **Avocations:** Reading; Researching **Religion:** Christian **Thoughts on Life:** Ms. Pierce believes everyone was created for a significant purpose. One finds personal success when one begins to unleash this potential and pursue one's purpose.

William Peter Pinna

Title: Lawyer **Industry:** Law and Legal Services **Company Name:** Pinna, Johnston & Burwell, P.A. **Date of Birth:** 08/11/1943 **Place of Birth:** Chicago **State/Country of Origin:** IL/USA **Parents:** Peter Bernard Pinna; Adelle (Hruska) Pinna **Marital Status:** Married **Spouse Name:** Barbara Sue Nelson (08/27/1966) **Children:** James Michael; Jennifer Anne **Education:** Doctor of Jurisprudence, Duke University (1968); Bachelor of Science in Commerce, DePaul University (1966) **Career:** Partner, President, Pinna, Johnston & Burwell PA, Raleigh, NC (1974-Present); Associate and Partner, Spears, Spears, Barnes & Baker, Durham, NC (1969-1974); Tax Specialist, A.M. Pullen & Co., Raleigh, NC (1968-1969); Accountant, Arthur Andersen & Co., Chicago, IL (1963-1967); Accountant, Borg-Warner Corp., Chicago, IL (1962-1963) **Career Related:** Hospital Board Member, Wake County (2003-2010); Hospital Board Member, Wake County (1996-2001); Board of Adjustment, Wake County (1994-1996); Chairman, Property Tax Commission, North Carolina Department of Revenue, Raleigh, NC (1987-1991); Adjunct Professor of Law, Duke University School of Law, Durham, NC (1978-1987); Assistant Professor, North Carolina State University, Raleigh, NC (1968-1981); ABA Speakers Bureau in Law Practice Management in areas of Retirement Planning, Estate Planning, Methods of Income Distribution in Small & Medium Law Firms; Lecturer, Wake Forest University Seminars, North Carolina Bar Seminar, North Carolina CPA Symposiums; Reported Cases, United States Tax Court, United States Court of Appeals for the Fourth Circuit; Managing Partner, Director, More than 35 Real Estate and Financial Partnerships and Limited Liability Companies; Founder, Lawyers Mutual **Civic:** Member, St. Andrew Parish Finance Committee, Apex, NC **Creative Works:** Contributor, Articles on Use of Credit Cards and Fee Collections, Legal Economic (1979-1980) **Awards:** Named, Outstanding Professor, North Carolina State University (1975-1976, 1969-1970) **Memberships:** Sub-Chairman of Law Practice Management Subcommittee, American Bar Association (1980-1990); North Carolina Bar Association; Wake County Bar Association; Chairman of Subcommittees in Legal Economics and Agricultural Tax Laws, Secretary of Taxation, American Bar Association **Bar Admissions:** North Carolina (1970); Illinois (1968); United States District Court for the Eastern District of North Carolina; United States Tax Court; United States Court of Appeals for the Fourth Circuit; United States Court of Claims for the Eastern Federal District Court **To what do you attribute your success:** Mr. Pinna credits his success on the influence of his family, who have consistently inspired him to go above and beyond. **Why did you become involved in your profession or industry:** Mr. Pinna became involved in his profession due to his family's history with the legal profession, as well as the circumstances of his childhood. **Avocations:** Skiing; Hiking; Fishing **Political Affiliations:** Independent/Republican **Religion:** Roman Catholic

Diane Elaine Pirlot

Title: Special Education Educator **Industry:** Education/Educational Services **Company Name:** Ivey Ranch Elementary (Oceanside Unified School District) **Date of Birth:** 07/15/1944 **Place of Birth:** Detroit **State/Country of Origin:** MI/USA **Parents:** Clarence B. Welker; Betty M. Welker **Marital Status:** Married **Spouse Name:** Wayne Charles Pirlot (6/16/1962) **Children:** Rene A. Galarza; Keith A. Stern-Pirlot **Education:** MS, National University, La Jolla, CA; BS, National University, La Jolla, CA; AB, National University, La Jolla, CA **Certifications:** Teaching Certification, State of California **Career:** Owner, Fairy Dust Farms (2019-Present); Owner, Farms of Ta-Dae, Winchester, CA (2000-Present); Special Education Teacher, Elementary Teacher, Ivey Ranch Elementary (Oceanside Unified School District), Oceanside, CA (1994-Present); Resort Owner, Welker's Lodge, Inc., Grand Marais, MI (1970-2000) **Career Related:** President, Chamber of Commerce, Grand Marais, MN (1973-1977) **Civic:** Leader, 4-H, Vista, CA (1994-2000); President, National Federation of Women's Clubs, Grand Marais, MI (1977-1979); United States Representative, Bicentennial Committee, Washington, DC (1976) **Memberships:** Special Education Caucus, National Education Association; Women's Caucus, National Education Association; CARS **Marquis Who's Who Honors:** Albert Nelson Marquis Lifetime Achievement Award **Why did you become involved in your profession or industry:** When Ms. Pirlot's grandchild was diagnosed with dyscalculia, a learning disorder, she was inspired to help. Though she had never considered pursuing a career in teaching, she found a passion for the field quickly. She has since impacted many other children positively as a result. Outside of her educational endeavors, she owns a ranch with approximately 100 horses. It all started when her daughter expressed interest in getting a horse. Once the family bought one, they decided to expand their property and buy more horses. The ranch is now thriving, and they since have begun performing shows for local visitors. **Avocations:** Travel **Religion:** Lutheran

Anthony Michael Pisani

Title: Architect **Industry:** Architecture & Construction **Company Name:** Anthony M. Pisani & Associates, Architects **Date of Birth:** 05/18/1943 **Place of Birth:** Cambridge **State/Country of Origin:** MA/USA **Parents:** Anthony Joseph Pisani; Josephine Ann (Tortorella) Pisani **Marital Status:** Married **Spouse Name:** Emilia D'Agostino (08/27/1967) **Children:** Emiliabianca; Giancarlo **Education:** MArch, Harvard University (1971); BFA, Tufts University (1966); Diploma, Museum School (1966) **Certifications:** Registered Architect, State of Massachusetts; Registered Architect, State of California; Registered Architect, State of Maine; Registered Architect, State of Michigan; Registered Architect, State of New York; Registered Architect, State of New Hampshire; Registered Architect, State of Texas; Registered Architect, State of Vermont **Career:** President, Anthony M. Pisani & Associates, Architects, Boston, MA (1978-Present); Project Architect, Desmond & Lord, Architects, Boston, MA (1974-1977); Project Architect, Charles G. Hilgenhurst & Associates, Boston, MA (1973-1974); Project Architect, Kallmann & McKinell, Architects, Boston, MA (1971-1973) **Career Related:** Vice Chairman, Boston Landmarks Commission (1987-1995); Instructor of Design, Boston Architectural Center (1971-1974) **Civic:** Boston Zoning Board of Appeals (1998-Present) **Creative Works:** Architect, Major Works in the Eastern United States, Ireland, Canada, Mexico, Puerto Rico, Japan, Italy (Italian Consulate); Contributor, Articles to Professional Journals **Memberships:** American Institute of Architects; Boston Society of Architects; Construction Specifications Institute; Urban Land Institute; National Council of Architectural Registration Boards; Society of Architectural Historians **Marquis Who's Who Honors:** Albert Nelson Marquis Lifetime Achievement Award; Marquis Who's Who Top Professional; Marquis Who's Who Humanitarian Award

Brad Pitt

Title: Actor, Film Producer **Industry:** Media & Entertainment **Date of Birth:** 12/18/1963 **Place of Birth:** Shawnee **State/Country of Origin:** OK/USA **Parents:** Bill Pitt; Jane Pitt **Marital Status:** Divorced **Spouse Name:** Angelina Jolie (08/23/2014, Divorced 2019); Jennifer Aniston (07/29/2000, Divorced 2005) **Children:** Shiloh Nouvel; Knox Leon; Vivie **Education:** Coursework in Journalism, University of Missouri **Career:** Founder, Make It Right Foundation (2007-Present); Co-founder, Maddox Jolie-Pitt Foundation (MJP Foundation) (2006-Present); Co-founder, Plan B Entertainment (2001-Present) **Creative Works:** Producer, "Americanah" (2020); Producer, "Blonde" (2020); Producer, "Irresistible" (2020); Executive Producer, "The Underground Railraod" (2020); Executive Producer, "Lego Masters" (2020); Actor, Producer, "Ad Astra" (2019); Actor, "Once Upon a Time... in Hollywood" (2019); Actor, "The Jim Jefferies Show" (2018, 2017); Actor, "Deadpool 2" (2018); Actor, "War Machine" (2017); Actor, "Allied" (2016); Narrator, "Voyage of Time: The IMAX Experience" (2016); Actor, "The Big Short" (2015); Actor, "By the Sea" (2015); Actor, "The Audition" (2015); Actor, "Fury" (2014); Actor, "The Counselor" (2013); Actor, Producer, "12 Years a Slave" (2013); Actor, Producer, "World War Z" (2013); Producer, "Kick-Ass 2" (2013); Actor, "Killing Them Softly" (2012); Actor, "8" (2012); Actor, "Touch of Evil" (2011); Voice Actor, "Happy Feet Two" (2011); Actor, "Moneyball" (2011); Actor, "The Tree of Life" (2011); Executive Producer, "Eat Pray Love" (2010); Voice Actor, "Megamind" (2010); Producer, "Kick-Ass" (2010); Voice Actor, "Beyond All Boundaries" (2009); Actor, "Inglourious Basterds" (2009); Executive Producer, "The Time Traveler's Wife" (2009); Actor, "The Curious Case of Benjamin Button" (2008); Actor, "Burn After Reading" (2008); Actor, Producer, "The Assassination of Jesse James by the Coward Robert Ford" (2007); Actor, "Ocean's Thirteen" (2007); Actor, "Babel" (2006); Actor, "Mr. & Mrs. Smith" (2005); Actor, "Ocean's Twelve" (2004); Actor, "Troy" (2004); Actor, "Freedom: A History of US" (2003); Voice Actor, "King of the Hill" (2003); Voice Actor, "Sinbad: Legend of the Seven Seas" (2003); Actor, "Confessions of a Dangerous Mind" (2002); Actor, "Ocean's Eleven" (2001); Actor, "Friends" (2001); Actor, "Spy Game" (2001); Actor, "The Mexican" (2001); Actor, "Snatch" (2000); Actor, "Fight Club" (1999); Guest Appearance, "Being John Malkovich" (1999); Actor, "Meet Joe Black" (1998); Actor, "Seven Years in Tibet" (1997); Actor, "The Devil's Own" (1997); Actor, "Sleepers" (1996); Actor, "12 Monkeys" (1995); Actor, "Se7en" (1995); Actor, "Legends of the Fall" (1994); Actor, "Interview with the Vampire: The Vampire Chronicles" (1994); Actor, "The Favor" (1994); Actor, "True Romance" (1993); Actor, "Kalifornia" (1993); Actor, "Contact" (1993); Actor, "A River Runs Through It" (1992); Actor, "Tales from the Crypt" (1992); Actor, "Cool World" (1992); Actor, "Two-Fisted Tales" (1992); Actor, "Johnny Suede" (1991); Actor, "Thelma & Louise" (1991); Actor, "Glory Days" (1990); Actress, "Across the Tracks" (1990); Actress, "Too Young to Die?" (1990); Actor, "The Image" (1990); Actor, "Growing Pains" (1989, 1987); Producer, Executive Producer, Actor, Numerous Films **Awards:** Academy Award for Best Performance by an Actor in a Supporting Role, Academy of Motion Picture Arts and Sciences (2020); Golden Globe for Best Performance by an Actor in a Supporting Role in a Motion Picture, Hollywood Foreign Press Association (2020); BAFTA Film Award for Best Supporting Actor (2020); AACTA International Award for Best Supporting Actor (2020); EDA Award for Best Supporting Actor, Alliance of Women Film Journalists (2020); AFCA Award for Best Supporting Actor, Austin Film Critics Association (2020); Named Best Movie Supporting Actor, Critics' Choice Movie Awards (2020); AFCC Award for Best Supporting Actor, Atlanta Film Critics Circle (2019); Named Best Supporting Actor, Chicago Film Critics Association (2019); Named Best Supporting Actor, Dallas-Fort Worth Film Critics Association (2019); Named Best Supporting Actor, Houston Film Critics Society (2019); Named Best Supporting Actor, National Society of Film Critics (2019); Named Best Supporting Actor, Online Film Critics Society (2019); Named Best Supporting Actor, San Diego Film Critics Society (2019); Named Best Supporting Actor, Toronto Film Critics Association (2019); Named Best Supporting Actor, Washington DC Area Film Critics Association (2019); Visionary Award, Stanley Kramer Award, Producers Guild of America Awards (2015); Co-recipient, Academy Award for Best Picture, Academy of Motion Picture Arts and Sciences (2014); Co-recipient, BAFTA Film Award for Best Film (2014); Named Guy of the Year, Guys Choice (2012); Desert Palm Achievement Award, Palm Springs International Film Festival (2011); Named Best Actor, Boston Society of Film Critics (2011); Named Best Actor, Georgia Film Critics Association (2011); Named Best Supporting Actor, Georgia Film Critics Association (2011); Named Best Actor, New York Film Critics Circle (2011); Named Best Actor, New York Film Critics Circle (2011); Named One of the "100 Most Influential People in the World," Time Magazine (2009, 2008, 2007); Recipient, Numerous Awards and Accolades

Nicholas Platt

Title: Consultant, Ambassador (Retired); President Emeritus **Industry:** Government Administration/Government Relations/Government Services **Date of Birth:** 03/10/1936 **Place of Birth:** New York **State/Country of Origin:** NY/USA **Parents:** Geoffrey Platt; Helen (Choate) Platt **Marital Status:** Widowed **Spouse Name:** Sheila Maynard (06/28/1957, Deceased 05/15/2018) **Children:** Adam; Oliver; Nicholas **Education:** Master of Arts, Johns Hopkins University School of Advanced International Studies (1959); Bachelor of Arts, Harvard University, Cum Laude (1957) **Career:** President Emeritus, Asia Society (2004-Present); President, Asia Society, New York (1992-2004); U.S. Ambassador to Pakistan, U.S. Department of State, Islamabad (1991-1992); U.S. Ambassador to The Philippines, U.S. Department of State, Manila (1987-1991); Executive Secretary, Special Assistant to Secretary, U.S. Department of State, Washington (1985-1987); United States Ambassador to Zambia, U.S. Department of State, Lusaka (1982-1984); Deputy Assistant, Secretary, International Organization Affairs, U.S. Department of State (1981-1982); Deputy Assistant, Secretary for International Security Affairs, U.S. Department of Defense (1980-1981); Staff, National Security Council, White House (1978-1979); Director Office of Japanese Affairs, U.S. Department of State (1977-1978); First Secretary, United States Embassy, Tokyo (1974-1977); Chief, Political Section, United States Embassy, Peking, China (1973-1974); Director, Staff, Bureau of Intelligence and Research, U.S. Department of State, Washington (1972-1973); Deputy Director, Executive Secretariat Staff, Bureau of Intelligence and Research, U.S. Department of State, Washington (1971-1973); Chief, North Asia Division, Bureau of Intelligence & Research, U.S. Department of State, Washington (1970); Chief, Asian Communist Areas Division, Bureau of Intelligence & Research, U.S. Department of State, Washington (1969); Political Officer, Consulate General, United States Consulate, Hong Kong (1964-1968); Chinese Language Trainee, Foreign Service Institute (1962-1963); United States Consulate, Windsor, Canada (1959-1961); Commissioned Foreign Service Officer, U.S. Department of State (1959) **Career Related:** Senior Advisor, Philadelphia Orchestra China Programs (2011-Present); Consultant in Field (2005-Present); Adjunct Professor, Chinese Domestic Politics, Johns Hopkins University (1975); Board of Directors, Scenic Hudson, Fiduciary Trust International **Civic:** Board Chairman, United States China Education Trust **Creative Works:** Author, "China Boys" (2010) **Awards:** Lifetime Award, Chinese Cultural Foundation (2018); Wilbur Carr Award (1992); Distinguished Honor Award, United States Department State (1991, 1987); Presidential Merit Award (1987, 1985); Distinguished Civilian Service Medal, United States Department of Defense (1981); Meritorious Award, William A. Jump Foundation (1973) **Memberships:** New York Council on Foreign Relations; Metropolitan Club, Washington; Century Club; Union Club; Board Member, United States China Education Trust **Marquis Who's Who Honors:** Albert Nelson Marquis Lifetime Achievement Award; Marquis Who's Who Top Professional **Why did you become involved in your profession or industry:** Mr. Platt was always interested in history and pursued a profession whereby he could witness history in the making. He was drawn to diplomatic service from the beginning. While serving overseas in London around 1955, he worked as a volunteer in the East End, repairing the area post-World War II. **Avocations:** Reading; Walking; Watching television

Dennis D. Porter, BA, MA, PhD

Title: Professor of French and Comparative Literary Studies (Retired) **Industry:** Education/Educational Services **Company Name:** University of Massachusetts Amherst **Date of Birth:** 12/03/1933 **Place of Birth:** Rayleigh **State/Country of Origin:** Essex/United Kingdom **Parents:** William Arthur Porter; Annie (Prangley) Porter **Marital Status:** Married **Spouse Name:** Annick F. Leitner **Children:** Gregory Y.; Thomas A.; Benjamin W. **Education:** PhD, University of California, Berkeley (1966); BA, Cambridge University, England (1957); MA, Cambridge University, England (1957) **Career:** Director, Center for Studies in Contemporary Culture, University of Massachusetts Amherst (1988-1991); Professor, Modern European Literature and Theory, Department of French and Italian, University of Massachusetts Amherst (1971-1974); Assistant Professor, University of California, Berkeley (1966-1971); Professor, French and Comparative Literary Studies **Career Related:** Playwright, Numerous Plays; Visiting Professor, University of Freiburg **Military Service:** Pilot Officer, Royal Air Force (1952-1954) **Creative Works:** Translator, Play, "WOYSECK" (2019); Playwright, "Adele's Way," Broadway Bound Theatre Festival (2018); Author, "Rousseau's Legacy," Oxford University Press (1995); Translator, "The Seminar of Jacques Lacan: The Ethics of Psychoanalysis," W. W. Norton & Company (1992); Author, "Haunted Journeys," Princeton University Press (1991); Author, "Pursuit of Crime," Yale University Press (1981); Playwright, "Between Men," Julien Dubuque International Film Festival, Midtown International Theatre Festival, Off-Broadway; Playwright, "Surprised by Love Again," Remy Bumppo Theatre, Chicago, IL; Contributor, Articles, Professional Journals **Awards:** Recipient, John Gassner Memorial Playwriting Award; Recipient, Julie Harris Playwright Award **Memberships:** Humanities Research Center, Australian National University (1994); American Council of Learned Societies (1985-1986); Research Fellow, National Endowment of the Humanities (1977-1978); Modern Language Association; Dramatists Guild of America **Marquis Who's Who Honors:** Albert Nelson Marquis Lifetime Achievement Award; Marquis Who's Who Top Professional **Why did you become involved in your profession or industry:** Dr. Porter became involved in his profession because he was interested in foreign language and culture. He studied French and German at Cambridge University, and because he was so interested in the culture of each country, he lived in Germany for a year, and then France for a year. He met his wife in Bordeaux, France, and they came to America so he could pursue a PhD. Dr. Porter became a playwright through teaching French novels and theater and decided to write critiques on European literature.

Jeanne S. Porter

Title: Civic Worker **Industry:** Civil Service **Date of Birth:** 02/27/1930 **Place of Birth:** Hammond **State/Country of Origin:** IN/USA **Parents:** Cyril Augustus; Mary (Mabley) Smith **Marital Status:** Widowed **Spouse Name:** William Harry Porter (04/01/1953, Deceased) **Children:** Wendy Alice; David William; Mary Elizabeth; Audrey Jeanne **Education:** Bachelor of Arts in Literature, Indiana University, with Honors (1953); Student, Hanover College (1948-1950) **Civic:** Supporter, Imago Dei Middle School, Tucson, AZ (2000-Present); Supporter, The Drawing Studio, Tucson, AZ (2000-Present); Supporter, St. Philips Episcopal Church, Tucson, AZ (1994-Present); Organizer, Planner, Columbarium Garden, Episcopal Church, Helena, MT (1988-Present); Board of Directors, Library Chairman, Montana Alliance For the Mentally Ill, Helena, MT (1979-Present); Developer Social Club for the Mentally Ill (1968-Present); Organizer, T-House Project, Mental Health Services (1983-1988); Advisory Board, Montana House Day Treatment Center, Helena, MT (1980-1993); Developer, Area Leader, Recovery Incorporated, Montana (1971-1982); Library Committee, Tucson Episcopal Church **Creative Works:** One-woman Shows Include Art Works Gallery, Holter Museum, Helena, MT (2003) **Awards:** Dignity Award, Golden Triangle Mental Health Center (2001); Long Term Service Award, Montana Alliance for the Mentally Ill (1989); Volunteer of the Year Award, Mental Health Association of Montana (1989); Electrum Award, Helena Arts Council (1988); Community Service Award, Carroll College (1986); Distinguished Service Award, Jaycees Helena (1974) **Memberships:** Philanthropic Committee, P.E.O. International (1994-Present); Southwest Arizona Watercolor Guild **Marquis Who's Who Honors:** Albert Nelson Marquis Lifetime Achievement Award **Avocations:** Painting; Drawing; Gardening; Travel; Reading; Giving painting tips to older women interested in learning how to paint

Robin Portman

Title: President, Chief Executive Officer **Industry:** Research **Company Name:** Atlas Research **Education:** MA, University of Maryland (1989) **Career:** President, Chief Executive Officer, Atlas Research (2017-Present); Adjunct Professor, Business Innovations, Georgetown University School of Nursing and Health Studies (2015-Present); Director, Strategic Innovations, Georgetown University School of Nursing and Health Studies (2016-2017); Executive Vice President, Booz Allen Hamilton (1994-2016) **Civic:** Board Member, Easter Seals DC/MD/VA; Service Source; PsychArmor Institute, University of Maryland; CPark Foundation; E. Dole Foundation

Zac Posen

Title: Apparel Designer **Industry:** Business Management/Business Services **Date of Birth:** 10/24/1980 **Place of Birth:** New York **State/Country of Origin:** NY/USA **Parents:** Stephen Posen; Susan (Orzack) Posen **Marital Status:** Partnered **Spouse Name:** Christopher Niquet **Education:** Coursework, Womenswear Degree Program, Central Saint Martins College of Art and Design, University of the Arts London (1999-2001); Coursework, The Costume Institute of the Metropolitan Museum of Art (Three Years); Coursework, Pre-College Program, Parsons The New School for Design **Career:** Launched Bridal Gowns, Truly Zac Posen (2014-Present); Creative Director, Women's Collection and Accessories, Brooks Brothers (2014-Present); Founder, Designer, Outspoke LLC, New York, NY (2001-Present); Launched, Zac Posen for Target (2008); Launched, Handbags, Accessories, Hosiery, Eyewear, Fure, and Fine Jewelry; Launched, Red Carpet Make-up Collection; Intern, Tocca; Intern, Nicole Miller; Intern, New York Costume Institute of the Metropolitan Museum of Art **Career Related:** Designer, Uniforms, Delta Air Lines (2018) **Creative Works:** Creator, Documentary, "House of Z" (2017); Judge, "Project Runway" (2013-2018) **Awards:** Named Among the "40 Under 40," Crain's New York Business (2004); Swarovski Perry Ellis Award for Womenswear, Council Fashion Designers of America (2004); Swarovski's Perry Ellis Award for Womenswear (2004); Scholastic Art and Writing Award

Jerome Hayden "Jay" Powell

Title: Chair **Industry:** Financial Services **Company Name:** Federal Reserve System **Date of Birth:** 02/04/1953 **Place of Birth:** Washington **State/Country of Origin:** DC/USA **Parents:** Jerome Powell; Patricia (Hayden) Powell **Marital Status:** Married **Spouse Name:** Elissa Leonard (9/14/1985) **Children:** Samuel; Hayden; Lucy Leonard **Education:** JD, Georgetown University Law Center (1979); AB, Princeton University (1975) **Career:** Chair, Board of Governors, Federal Reserve System, Washington, DC (2018-Present); Board of Governors, Federal Reserve System, Washington, DC (2012-Present); Partner, The Carlyle Group (1997-2005); Under, Secretary of the Treasury, Domestic Finance, U.S. Department of the Treasury (1992-1993); Assistant Secretary for Domestic Finance, U.S. Department of the Treasury (1990-1992); Consultant, U.S. Department of the Treasury, Washington, DC (1990); Senior Vice President, Dillon Read & Co., Inc. (1984-1990); Associate, Werbel, McMillin & Carnelutti (1982-1984); Associate, Davis Polk & Wardwell LLP, New York, NY (1981-1982); Law Clerk, Hon. E.A. Van Graafeiland, U.S. Court of Appeals for the Second Circuit (1979-1980); Legislative Assistant, Sen. Richard S. Schweiker, U.S. Senate, Washington, DC (1976) **Career Related:** Visiting Scholar, Bipartisan Policy Center, Washington, DC (2010-2012); Senior Advisor, Global Environment Fund (2008-2012) **Civic:** Founding Chair, Center City Consortium, Washington, DC; Board of Directors, The Nature Conservancy of Maryland/DC; Board of Directors, Bendheim Center for Finance, Princeton University; Board of Directors, DC Prep, Washington, DC **Political Affiliations:** Republican

Elbert Charlton Prather Sr., MD

Title: State Health Officer **Industry:** Government Administration/Government Relations/Government Services **Date of Birth:** 03/13/1930 **Place of Birth:** Jasper **State/Country of Origin:** FL/USA **Parents:** Walter J.; Myrtle (Wetherington) P. **Marital Status:** Married **Spouse Name:** Annie Louise Leigh, (02/14/1954) **Children:** E. Charlton Jr.; Walter Franklin **Education:** Master of Public Health in Epidemiology, University of North Carolina (1963); Doctor of Medicine, Bowman Gray School of Medicine (1959); Master of Science, University of Florida (1954); Bachelor of Science in Bacteriology, University of Florida (1952) **Career:** State Health Officer, Department of Health and Rehabilitation Services, Florida (1986-1987); Health Program Supervisor, Department of Health and Rehabilitation Services, Florida (1979-1985); State Health Officer, Department of Health and Rehabilitation Services, Florida (1978-1979); Staff Director, Health Program Office, Department of Health and Rehabilitation Services, Tallahassee, FL (1974-1978); Chief, Bureau of Preventable Disease, Florida Department of Health (1970-1974); State Epidemiologist, Florida Department of Health, Jacksonville, FL (1964-1970); Public Health Resident, Hillsborough County Health Department, Tampa, FL (1963-64); Intern, Jackson Memorial Hospital, Miami, FL (1961-1962); Research Epidemiologist, Florida State Board of Health (1959-1961) **Military Service:** U.S. Army (1954-1959) **Awards:** Certificate of Merit, Florida Medical Association (2009); Volunteer of the Year, City of Tallahassee, FL (1993, 1997) **Memberships:** American Public Health Association; Florida Public Health Association; Association of State and Territorial Health Officials; Florida Medical Association; Delta Omega; Phi Sigma; Advisory Committee on Indian Health, United States Department of the Interior **Marquis Who's Who Honors:** Albert Nelson Marquis Lifetime Achievement Award **Why did you become involved in your profession or industry:** While attending school during the ninth grade Dr. Prather was assigned to do a book report on "Microbe Hunters" by Paul de Kruif. The material fascinated him greatly, and he decided that he would aspire to become a biologist. **Avocations:** Blacksmithing; Fly fishing **Political Affiliations:** Democrat **Religion:** Presbyterian

Laurence Pressly

Title: Executive Vice President **Industry:** Media & Entertainment **Company Name:** American Royal Association **Date of Birth:** 06/02/1931 **Place of Birth:** Lee's Summit **State/Country of Origin:** MO/USA **Parents:** John L. Pressly; Katherine L. (Lienweber) Pressly **Marital Status:** Widowed **Spouse Name:** Janet Wilson Pressly **Children:** Laura M. Schwab **Education:** Bachelor of Science in Agriculture, University of Missouri (1953) **Career:** Executive Vice President, General Manager, American Royal Association (1975-1985); Agribusiness Manager, Greater Kansas City Chamber of Commerce, Missouri (1973-1974); County Agent, Farm Management & Area Dairy Specialist, University of Missouri Extension Service (1956-1972); County Agent, Family Farm Partnership (1953-1961); Advisory Director, Charter Bank, Lee's Summit, MO **Career Related:** Associate Broker, Sales Agent, Reece Nichols, Lee's Summit, Greater Kansas City, MO (1985-Present); Member, Lee's Summit Industrial Development Authority (1978-2017); Member, Lee's Summit Board Zoning & Adjustment (1976-2015); Member, Lee's Summit City Council (1969-1972); Member, Lee's Summit Planning & Zoning Board (1964); Member, Westminster Gerontology Foundation (1960-1974); Vice President, Hospital Association; Chairman, Show-Me Vienna Committee **Civic:** Served, Jackson County Grand Jury **Awards:** Civic Leadership Award, Missouri Municipal League (2017); Named, Citizen of the Year, Lee's Summit (2017); Proclamation in Recognition & Appreciation for 58 Years of Civic Service, City Lee's Summit (2016); Inductee, High School Hall of Fame (2016); Named, Alpha Gamma Rho Fraternity "Brothers of the Century" (2004); Distinguished Service Award, Missouri Holstein Association (1980); Honorary Award, American Farmer Degree, Future Farmers of America (1974); Distinguished Award, Lee's Summit Jaycees (1956) **Memberships:** President, Charter Member, Optimist (1968); NALS & RMA; The International Association of Fairs and Expositions; Hillcrest Country Club; Kansas City Club; Rotary International; Saddle & Sirloin Club; International Agribusiness Club **Marquis Who's Who Honors:** Albert Nelson Marquis Lifetime Achievement Award; Marquis Who's Who Top Professional **Why did you become involved in your profession or industry:** Mr. Pressly was active in a farm program and in dairy herd protection. The University of Missouri extension program approached him about joining and, finding this prospect interesting, he remained affiliated with the university for more than 15 years. **Avocations:** Civic events; Conventions; Visiting cities **Political Affiliations:** Republican **Religion:** Episcopal

Shirley Pritchett-Hilton

Title: 21st Century Foundational Hematologist, Oncologist, Neurologist, and Biologist **Industry:** Medicine & Health Care **Company Name:** 1) Glory International University (GIU) 2) Glory Music Academy **Date of Birth:** 04/11/1939 **Place of Birth:** Atlanta **State/Country of Origin:** GA/USA **Parents:** William Hiram Pritchett; Bertha (Giles) Pritchett **Children:** Michele Rene Hilton; Michael John Hilton Sr. **Education:** PhD in 21st Foundational Hematology, Oncology, Neurology, and Biology, Glory International University (GIU) & Music Academy, Commonwealth of Heaven, Cum Laude (2011); MAR in 21st Century Congregational Dynamics, Lutheran Theological Seminary at Philadelphia (2004); ThD in Divine Hematology, Victorious Living: Family Prayer Ministries, Inc., Commonwealth of Pennsylvania (2001); DMin, Certificate, Eastern Baptist Theological Seminary; MDiv, Urban Theological Institute, Lutheran Theological Seminary at Philadelphia; DDiv, Biblical Definitions of Spirituality, Jameston Christian College, Caguas, Puerto Rico; MA in Communication, Norfolk State College, Magna Cum Laude; BS in Early Childhood Education, Temple University, Magna Cum Laude; Student, Voice Major, Boyer College of Music and Dance, Temple University **Certifications:** "Chosen Global Pastor" **Career:** Administrative Judiciary Secretary, Honorable Juanita Kidd Stout, Pennsylvania (1974-1989); The Lord's Chosen Global Pastor, Teacher, and Christian Counselor, Medical Counseling; Professor of Foundational Hematology, Oncology, Neurology, and Biology; The Lord's Chosen Typist and Editor; Retired Public School Teacher, Philadelphia Board of Education; President, Senior Pastor, Glory International University (GIU) & Ministries; International Chief Executive Officer, International Warriors for Equality and Justice (IWEJ); Member, Enon Tabernacle Baptist Church; Associate Minister, Pinn Memorial Baptist Church; Associate Minister, Canaan Baptist Church; Affiliate, New Gethsemane Baptist Church, East Bethel Baptist Church **Career Related:** Typist, Editor, Zega-Eminent Professor Dr. Yeshua/Jesus **Civic:** Block Captain Emeritus 900 Block East Stafford Street, Philadelphia, PA 19138 (Philosophy, Sharing Flowers with the Living); Awbury Neighbors; W. Russell Johnson Music Guild, Inc. of the National Association of Negro Musicians, Inc.; NOW 2019 and 2020; Retiree, Chapter, American Federation of State, County and Municipal Employees (AFSCME) **Creative Works:** Editor, "Unveiling the Mystery of Dahm" (Hebrew for Blood) (2020); Editor, "Moments of Sharing about The Great Lady on the Bench: Justice Juanita Kid Stout" (2019); Author, "Liquid Gold (H3OAu)®™ = Zero [0]" (2010); Editor, "I Confess, There Was Never a Dull Moment on the Bench"; Author, "Banned from the Pulpit"; Author, "I, Too, Have a Journey to Justice"; Editor, Documentary Film, "Day Zero Positive of World History"; Editor, "Liquid Gold (H/Trinity/O)"; Editor, "Songs of Zion"; Editor, Songwriter, Two Gospel Musicals; Contributor, Numerous Chapters, Books **Awards:** Recipient, Numerous Academic, Civic, Literary, and Talent Awards **Marquis Who's Who Honors:** Albert Nelson Marquis Lifetime Achievement Award **To what do you attribute your success:** Ms. Pritchett-Hilton attributes her success to her healer, the Lord, Redeemer Yeshua/Jesus, the late Justice Juanita Kidd Stout, the late Mary Reason Henderson, the late Reverend Howard O. Jameson, ThD, PhD, Elsie Jameson, ThD, PhD, and the late Reverend Green and Mrs. Eugenie Sanders. **Why did you become involved in your profession or industry:** Ms. Pritchett-Hilton became involved in her profession because she was chosen by the creator of Heaven and Earth, the ancient native "Golden Ebony Hebrew Israelite Atomic Human" and "Divine Family of Heaven" with the "Royal Insignia of the Star of David," who are the "Royal Incorruptible Blueboods" and "Living Water (H/Trinity/O)." **Political Affiliations:** Democrat **Religion:** Baptist

Dora Puig

Title: Owner, Founder **Industry:** Real Estate **Company Name:** Luxe Living Realty **Education:** MBA in International Business, The George Washington University, School of Business, Washington, DC (1998); BBA in International Finance & Marketing, University of Miami, School of Business, FL (1986) **Career:** Director of Sales & Marketing, Palazzo Del Sol, Fisher Island, FL (2014-Present); Real Estate Broker, Luxe Living Realty, FL (2013-Present); Director of Sales & Marketing, Riva Bay Harbor, FL (2013-2016); Principal Real Estate Broker, Owner, PuigWerner Real Estate Services, FL (2006-2015); Professional Sales & Marketing Consultant, AstorHome Condon-Hotel, FL (2006-2007); Director of Sales & Marketing, The Residences at the Bath Club, FL (2001-2005); Top Sales Producer, Fortune International Realty, FL (1998-2001); Professional Real Estate Marketing Consultant, LaSalle International Group (1999-2000); Director of Sales Marketing, Santa Maria, FL (1994-1997); Director of Sales & Marketing, Bristol Tower, FL (1994-1997); Estates Division Sales Specialist, Jon Douglas Properties, CA (1993-1994); Real Estate Associate, Director's Office, Fred Sands Estatesm CA (1989-1993) **Civic:** Founder, Women of Tomorrow; National Association of Professional; Master Broker's Forum **Awards:** #1 Broker in Dade County, The Wall Street Journal (2016-2018); Most influential Businesswomen in Florida, South Florida Business Journal **To what do you attribute your success:** Ms. Puig attributes her success to he consistency, she is detail-oriented, and very thorough. She loves what she does. "Find something you love doing because then it isn't work... it is just doing what you love, most of the time..." **Why did you become involved in your profession or industry:** Ms. Puig always knew that she wanted to do something in international sales. She speaks three languages, is well traveled and is highly educated. After graduating school, she was hired by Columbia Pictures and moved to Los Angeles. She was one of nine MBAs recruited to do international sales packaging for films. The year she went out there, Columbia was bought by SONY. Her job was put on hold for nearly a year. In that year, she did many odd-jobs, one of which was for one of the top brokers in Beverly Hills. Right there is when she found her calling. She loved architecture, understood big business, the numbers were big and she really felt a pull away from nepotism and a male-dominated industry. She received her California sales license, and never went back to the sales distribution job.

Ganapathi Pulipaka, PhD

Title: Chief Data Scientist **Industry:** Sciences **Company Name:** Accenture **Marital Status:** Married **Education:** Postdoctoral Coursework, DeepSingularity LLC (2016-2018); PhD in Computer Science, Engineering and Computer Science, Machine Learning, Big Data Analytics, Colorado Technical University, Colorado Springs, CO (2017); PhD in Business Administration, Information Systems, Data Analytics & ERM, University of California Irvine, Irvine, CA (2015) **Career:** Chief Data Scientist, SAP Technical Lead, Accenture (2018-Present); Chief Executive Officer, Chief Data Scientist, SAP Technical Lead, DeepSingularity LLC (2016-2018); SAP Senior Manager, Prosum (2012-2016); SAP CRM 7.0/IPM 2008 Product Development Consultant (2008); SAP Delivery Project Manager, Telecom Media Entertainment North America, Burbank, Capgemini US LLC (2006-2012) **Career Related:** Keynote Speaker, Intercon World Conference, Las Vegas, NV (2019); Speaker, VIP-Only AI Executive Conference, Venture Beat Magazine, San Francisco, CA (2019); Speaker, SAPPHIRE Conference, Orlando, FL (2019); Global Premier Speaker, Robotics and Artificial Intelligence International Conference, Los Angeles, CA (2018); Speaker and Presenter in the Field **Creative Works:** Interviewee, "A Data Science Guide and Predictions for the Future with Onalytica and Joe Fields" (2018); Author, eBook, "The Digital Evolution of Supply Chain Management with @SAPLeonardo," SAP Leonardo IoT (2017); Author, eBook, "Machine Learning and Artificial Intelligence for Enterprise HealthCare and Health Technology Solutions," Change HealthCare, McKesson HealthCare Corp. (2017); Author, Book, "The Future of Data Science and Parallel Computing: A Road to Technological Singularity"; Author, Book, "Big Data Appliances for In-Memory Computing: A Real-World Research Guide for Corporations to Tame and Wrangle Their Data"; Author, Contributor, More Than 400 AI Research Papers; Featured, Top 22 Artificial Intelligence Experts, Microsoft's Partner Acuvate; Featured, "8 AI Influencers You Must Follow On Twitter To Stay On Top Of Your Game"; Featured, "Top Data Superheroes Among US: The Whole Next Level Of Human Brain"; Featured, "The Future Of Humanity: Artificial Intelligence," BuzzFeed Magazine; Featured, Top 10 AI Technologies and Courses to Learn for a Great Data Science Career in Today's Era, Launchora Magazine **Awards:** Top 50 Technology Leaders in AI Award, Machine Learning, Data Science, Mathematics, and Statistics, Intercon, Las Vegas Intercon Conference (2019); Ranked, Top 5 Supply Chain Management and SAP Machine Learning Experts, SAP (2019); Ranked, Machine Learning and AI Influencers, DigitalBbanking World (2019); Ranked, Most Influential Artificial Intelligence Executives in the World, Analytics Insight Magazine (2019); Listed, Top Twitter Influencers in Artificial Intelligence (2019); Ranked, Data Science Influencer, Business Intelligence Influencer, Onalytica and Joe Fields (2018); Listed, Top 10 Most Inspiring Tweets On AI That Blew Our Mind (2018); Named, SAP and AI Solution Providers, Mirror Review Magazine, Insights Success Magazine (2018); Ranked, Machine Learning Influencer, Deep Learning Influencer, KCore Analytics and Hernan Makse (2018); Ranked, Data Science Influencer, Machine Learning Influencer, KCore Analytics and Hernan Makse (2017); Named, CXO Leaders and SAP Innovative Solution Providers, SAP Special Annual Edition, CIOReview (2017); Levi Strauss and Co., Jeff Gordon Award for On-Time and On-Budget Software Delivery of Projects as SAP Technical Lead (2011); HP Award of Excellence as ABAP Developer (2002-2003); SAP Pinnacle Award for North America's First SAP CRM 7.0 Project; Two Best-Selling Author Awards; Top 50 Tech Leaders Award; Ranked, #1 IoT Influencer in the World, 10 Fold Communications, San Francisco, CA; Ranked, 14 Best Books of All Time, Book Authority; Trending Daily AI Influencer, TweetsonTech Influential Platform; Named, Two Indian American Artificial Intelligence Executives, "10 Most Influential" List, Analytics Insight Magazine **To what do you attribute your success:** Dr. Pulipaka attributes his success to his specializations in artificial intelligence, high-performance consulting, machine learning, data science, mathematics, SAP, the internet of things, and statistics. **Why did you become involved in your profession or industry:** Dr. Pulipaka became involved in his profession because when he was 16 years old, he started writing programs in C, C++, VC++ and Java. At this stage, as a freelancer, he implemented a vast number of commercial projects while attending school for clients. Significant customers included the United States Air Force and the State Electricity Board, in C and C++. Programming competitions take an entirely different approach from building enterprise grade software systems. Mathematics and programming correlate; the former aims at solving the abstract problem and the latter requires a particular skill set and programming framework to develop design patterns in object-oriented programming and addressing the particular commercial complex conundrums. **Political Affiliations:** Republican **Thoughts on Life:** For more information on Dr. Pulipaka's written work, see: https://www.amazon.com/s?i=stripbooks&rh=p_27%3ADr.+Ganapathi+Pulipaka&s=relevancerank&text=Dr.+Ganapathi+Pulipaka&ref=dp_byline_sr_book_1

John Michael Quinn

Title: Physicist, Geophysicist **Industry:** Sciences **Date of Birth:** 05/08/1946 **Place of Birth:** Denver **State/Country of Origin:** CO/USA **Parents:** Leonard Simon Quinn; Winifred Ruth (Doolan) Quinn **Marital Status:** Married **Spouse Name:** Pamela Dagmar-Shield (05/28/1983) **Education:** MS in Physics, University of Colorado (1982); BS in Physics, University of Virginia (1968) **Career:** Owner, Consultant, Solar Terrestrial Environmental Research Institute, LLC. (2010-Present); Retired (2002); Research Geophysicist, U.S. Geological Survey, Denver, CO (1995-2002); Geophysicist, Mathematician, U.S. Naval Oceanography Office, Stennis Space Center (1985-1995); Geophysicist, U.S. Naval Oceanography Office, Stennis Space Center (1982-1985); Geophysicist, U.S. Naval Oceanography Office, Stennis Space Center (1974-1979); Research Physicist, U.S. Naval Research Laboratory, Washington, DC (1979-1980); Principal Engineer, Singer Simulation Products, Silver Spring, MD (1973-1974); Physicist, U.S. Naval Research Laboratory, Washington, DC (1967-1973) **Career Related:** Visiting Scientist, National Oceanographic and Atmospheric Administration (2003-Present); U.S. Delegate, United Nations International Standards Organization (2000-2002); International Geomagnetic Ref. Field Committee (1989-2002); Principal Investigator, National Polar-Orbiting Environmental Satellite Systems (1989-2002); Chairman, Committee on Earth and Planetary Geomagnetic Survey, Satellites International Association of Geomagnetism and Aeronomy (1991-1999); Investigator, Polar-Orbiting Geomagnetic Survey Experiment (1990-1994); Project Coordinator, U.S. Navy Project MAGNET; Consultant In Field **Military Service:** U.S. Army (1968-1971) **Creative Works:** Author, "Epoch World Geomagnetic Model" (1985, 1990, 1995, 2000) **Memberships:** American Geophysical Union; American Mathematics Society; European Geophysical Society; Mathematics Association American **Marquis Who's Who Honors:** Albert Nelson Marquis Lifetime Achievement Award **Why did you become involved in your profession or industry:** By the 7th grade, Mr. Quinn became very fascinated with mathematics, algebra, and trigonometry. In the 9th grade, he read a book written by a French physicist by the name of Lichnerwicz called "Relativity." Intrigued by what he read, he decided that he wanted to become a physicist. He has been working on furthering Einstein's research on magnetic fields for much of his career.

Nathalie Racine

Title: Portfolio Manager **Industry:** Financial Services **Company Name:** The Racine-Marcotte Advisory Group **Education:** Fellow, Canadian Securities Institute (1999); Coursework, University of Montreal **Certifications:** Coach Certification, Life Coach, The John Maxwell Team (2017); Wealth Advisory, RBC Dominion Securities (2016); Hedge Fund Certified Advisor, Man Group (2010); Strategic Coach (2013); Canadian Investment Management CIM I & II, Canadian Securities Institute (1997); Options and Futures, Canadian Securities Institute (1995); PIM, FCSI, CIM, Options & Futures, Canadian Securities Institute **Career:** Vice President, The Racine-Marcotte Advisory Group (2005-Present); Portfolio Manager, The Racine-Marcotte Advisory Group (1994-Present); President, Cemos International, Noord Holland, Netherlands (1991-1993) **Civic:** Organizing Committee Member, Muscular Dystrophy, Canada (2000-Present) **Awards:** Nominee for the Mackenzie Female Trailblazer of the Year, Wealth Professional (2018); Canada's Top 50 Advisory, Wealth Professional, Canada (2016, 2018); Canada's Top 10 Investment Advisory Team, Wealth Professional, Canada (2017); Honorable Mention, Canadian Securities Course, Canadian Securities Institute (1994) **To what do you attribute your success:** She is a workaholic. Consistency and being reliable and dependable. One trait that lacks in society today is people taking on responsibility and being accounted for. That is the first character trait of her personality. People shy away from taking on responsibility she is the opposite she likes to take care of people. Her success is because she really takes helping people to heart, to add value to their life. **Why did you become involved in your profession or industry:** Ms. Racine has always loved the market, and money. She always loved to add value to people and help them get to their goals. Most entrepreneurs have a vision and have a dream with their company but they put so much into the company but they never think about the plan B to try to build something for themselves. They only think in terms of the company, so it is her job to help prioritize and say yes the company is great but we also need to think about you and make sure you are ok financially.

Sharon Lee Radashaw

Title: Music Educator(Retired), Entertainer **Industry:** Education/Educational Services **Company Name:** Lawrence Middle School, Los Angeles Unified School District **Date of Birth:** 03/07/1937 **Place of Birth:** Grosse Pointe **State/Country of Origin:** MI/USA **Parents:** Henry Paul Fleischmann; Daisy (Hein) Fleischmann **Marital Status:** Widowed **Spouse Name:** Denny Dmitri Radashaw (07/25/1959, Deceased 2009) **Children:** Todd Warren; Joy Noelle; Shana Lee **Education:** Postgraduate Coursework, University of San Diego (1992-1996); Postgraduate Coursework, UC Santa Barbara (1965-1990); MusM, Michigan State University, East Lansing, MI (1962); MusB in Music Education, Eastern Michigan University, East Lansing, MI (1959) **Certifications:** Secondary Music Credential, State of California; General Secondary Credential, Michigan State Special Music Credential **Career:** Music Specialist, California Arts Project, Northridge, CA (1991-2000); Teacher, Music, Drama, Math, Los Angeles Unified School District, Chatsworth, CA (1980-2007); Creative Arts Teacher, California Lutheran University, Thousand Oaks, CA (1980); Music Consultant, Conejo Unified School District, Thousand Oaks, CA (1978-1980); Creative Arts Teacher, California Lutheran University, Thousand Oaks, CA (1969-1970); Music Consultant, Valley Oak District & Ventura County, Thousand Oaks, CA (1965-1967); Music Teacher, Garden Grove Unified School District (1962-1963); Music Teacher, Waverly Schools, Lansing, MI (1960-1962); Music Teacher, Mason Public Schools (1959-1960); Music Educator (Retired), Entertainer;Master Teacher, California State University, Northridge (Three Years Part-Time) **Career Related:** Chair, Electives Department, Lawrence Middle School, Chatsworth, CA (1988-Present); Music and Drama Counselor, Boy Scouts of America (1981-Present); Extra, Singer, Television, Stage, and Movies, Hollywood, CA (1965-Present); Cyber Chorus Singer, Carnegie Hall, New York, NY (1998); Singer, Dancer, Macy's Thanksgiving Parade (1998); Singer, Ventura County Master Chorale (1965-1970) **Civic:** Art Show Judge, Thousand Oaks City Council (1985-Present); California Towards Arts Assessment Project, Sacramento, CA (1993); Arts Commissioner and Hostess, Thousand Oaks Art Commission (1985-1994); Executive Producer, Conejo Players Theatre (1980-1992) **Creative Works:** Actress, "The Stingiest Man in Town"; Actress, "A Little Night Music"; Actress, "Desert Song"; Actress, "Dido and Aeneas"; Actress, "Fiddler on the Roof"; Actress, "The Music Man"; Director, "The King and I"; Director, "Beauty and the Beast"; Director, "Aladdin"; Director, "Guys and Dolls"; Director, "Finian's Rainbow"; Director, "Oliver"; Director, "Annie"; Director, "Grease"; Director, "Peter Pan"; Director, "Kiss Me Kate"; Director, "Sound of Music, Bye-Bye Birdie"; Director, "Wizard of Oz"; Director, "Willy Wonka and the Chocolate Factory"; Director, "Blithe Spirit"; Director, "The Pink Panther Strikes Again"; Director, "Scrooge"; Singer **Awards:** Fulbright-Hays Scholar, Japan (2007); Fulbright-Hays Scholar, Japan (2003); Fulbright-Hays Scholar, Turkey (2002); Commendation for Multi-Cultural Contribution to Youth, Los Angeles Mayor and City Council (2001); Fulbright-Hays Scholar, Romania-Bulgaria (1997); Bravo Award, Los Angeles Music Center (1992) **Memberships:** Conejo Players Theatre (1970-Present); National Educators Association (NEA); National Association for Music Education; California Teachers Association; CMEA; California Math Educators Association; Drama Teachers Association of Southern California; UTLA **Marquis Who's Who Honors:** Albert Nelson Marquis Lifetime Achievement Award; Marquis Who's Who Top Professional **To what do you attribute your success:** Ms. Radashaw attributes her success to her good upbringing, her faith, and her tenacity. **Why did you become involved in your profession or industry:** Ms. Radashaw became involved in her profession because her parents were very supportive, and told her that she could do anything she wanted to. She started tap dancing at the age of four. **Avocations:** World traveling (60 countries); Skiing; Gourmet cooking; Costume construction; Hosting exchange students; Reading; Genealogy; Singing and acting professionally and locally **Religion:** Baptist **Thoughts on Life:** Ms. Radashaw has been to 60 countries and is still traveling.

Nathaniel Joseph Raggette

Title: Chairman, Chief Executive Officer **Industry:** Oil & Energy **Company Name:** Scorpion Oil & Gas **Date of Birth:** 04/27/1974 **Place of Birth:** New Iberia **State/Country of Origin:** LA/USA **Parents:** Alfred Raggette; Gail Raggette **Marital Status:** Married **Spouse Name:** Charlotte Castillo Raggette **Children:** Nathaniel Joseph Raggette II **Education:** MBA in Finance, Harvard Business School (2001); BSM in Accounting, Tulane University, AB Freeman School of Business, Magna Cum Laude (1997) **Certifications:** Certified Public Accountant **Career:** Founder, Chief Executive Officer, Scorpion Oil and Gas (2018-Present); Managing Director, RBC Capital Markets (2015-2018); Chief Financial Officer, Bright Horizon Resources LLC (2014-2015); Director, RBC Capital Markets (2010-2014); Director, RBC Capital Markets (2010-2014); Board of Directors, Volunteer, Houston Area Urban League (2008-2011); Vice President, GE Energy Financial Services (2007-2010); Associate, Morgan Stanley (2004-2007); Associate, Goldman Sachs (2001-2003); Accountant, KPMG (1995-1999) **Civic:** Coach, Soccer and Baseball **Awards:** Academic All American, Baseball, Tulane University; IMA's Outstanding Junior, Tulane University; Dean's Honor Scholar, Tulane University **Memberships:** Board of Sienna Plantation; University of the Ozarks, Clarksville AR; Beta Gamma Sigma **To what do you attribute your success:** Mr. Raggette feels if you are willing to work hard and learn, and understand what is in front of you, then you can be successful in anything you are passionate about. **Why did you become involved in your profession or industry:** Mr. Raggette felt that was a void in the market place. The public EMP Companies have been limited in their buying capacity because public investors have no energy good returns. So when public investors don't have access to equity capital to support acquisitions, they don't have to the liberty to by assets. The life blood of the oil and gas industry is to recycle assets. Mr Raggeette's company. **Thoughts on Life:** Mr. Ragette's motto is, "Hard work over the long term will always pay off."

Terry Eugene "Gene" Ragland, MD

Title: Emergency Physician **Industry:** Medicine & Health Care **Company Name:** Gene Ragland MD,PC **Date of Birth:** 06/14/1944 **Place of Birth:** Greensboro **State/Country of Origin:** NC/USA **Parents:** Terry Porter Ragland; Virginia Lucile (Stowe) Ragland **Marital Status:** Married **Spouse Name:** Marguerite Elizabeth Ragland **Children:** John McConnell; Ryan Ragland **Education:** Internal Medicine Resident, St. Joseph Mercy Hospital, Ann Arbor, MI (1974-1977); Intern, St. Joseph Mercy Hospital, Ann Arbor, MI (1970-1971); MD, University of Michigan Medical School, Ann Arbor, MI (1970); BS, Central Michigan University, Mount Pleasant, MI (1966) **Certifications:** Diplomate, American Board Internal Medicine; American Board Emergency Medicine **Career:** Founder, President, Chief Executive Officer, Secure Care, Inc. (1992-2003); Clinical Assistant Professor of Emergency Medicine, University of Michigan Medical School (1994-2001); Emergency Physician, St. Joseph Mercy Hospital, Ann Arbor, MI (1977-2001); Principal, Emergency Physicians Medical Group (1979-2001); President, Huron Valley Physician Association (1997-2000); Associate Director, Department of Emergency Medicine, SJMH (1985-2000); Chief of Staff, St. Joseph Mercy Hospital, Ann Arbor, MI (1996-1997); Medical Director, Emergency Center, St. Joseph Mercy Hospital, Ann Arbor, MI (1985-1997); Clinical Instructor, Department of Surgery, University of Michigan Medical School (1981-1994); President, Washtenaw County Medical Society (1994); Chief Resident, Internal Medicine, St. Joseph Mercy Hospital, Ann Arbor, MI (1975-1976) **Career Related:** Founder, Chairman, Advisory Board, College of Health Professions, Central Michigan University, Mount Pleasant, MI (2001-2004); Member, Science Advisory Committee, Ecology Center/Michigan Environmental Council (2001-2003); Member, Mercy Health Plans Board (1999-2000); Consultant, Guam Memorial Hospital, Mercy International Health Services (1990); Examiner, American Board of Emergency Medicine (1983-2001); Founding Member, Medical Director, Life Support Services, Ann Arbor, MI (1983-1992); Member, University of Michigan Classified Research Committee (1969-1970); Externship, Ralph Nader, Center for Study of Responsive Law, Washington, DC (1970); Member, Victor Vaughan Society for the History and Philosophy of Medicine (1966-1970) **Civic:** Member, Medical Marijuana Licensing Board, Ann Arbor City Council (2001); Trustee, Ann Arbor Township Board (2002-2006); Board Member, Domestic Violence Project, SAFE House (1992-2001) **Military Service:** U.S. Naval Academy, Annapolis, MD (1973-1974); General Medical Officer, Lieutenant, U.S. Navy (1972-1974); Naval Hospital, Guantanamo Bay, Cuba (1972-1973) **Creative Works:** Keynote Speaker, Medical Emergencies 93, Kingdom of Saudi Arabia (1993); Author, Bitterman RA, Ragland G: Updates in Acute Medicine, Vol 5, American Health Consultants (1993); Author, Ragland G, Spivey Wm., STAT!CARDS!, The rapid guide to medical emergencies, STAT Medical Publishing Company (1992); Contributor, "Emergency Medicine: A Comprehensive Study Guide" (1985-2000); Medical Lecturer, Five Cities in China, China/U.S. Exchange Project (1985); Author, "Endocrine Emergencies" Section, Eight Chapters, "A Study Guide in Emergency" (1981) **Awards:** Distinguished Alumni Award, Central Michigan University (2020); The 1997 WCA Spirit Award, Washtenaw Council of Alcoholism (1997); Spirit Award, Mercy International Health Services (1995); David H. Morgan Leadership Award (1965); Senator of the Year, Student Senate, Central Michigan University (1964) **Memberships:** President, Huron Valley Physicians Association (1997-2000); President, Washtenaw County Medical Society (1993); Delegate, Michigan State Medical Society (1991-1994); Alternate Delegate, Michigan State Medical Society (1989-1990, 1982-1984); National Association of Emergency Medical Technicians (NAEMT); Michigan Association of Emergency Medical Technicians **Marquis Who's Who Honors:** Albert Nelson Marquis Lifetime Achievement Award; Marquis Who's Who Top Professional **To what do you attribute your success:** Dr. Ragland's parents grew up during the Great Depression. Both pursued education while raising a family. His father attained and ABD, all but dissertation, for a PhD in Philosophy and his mother had a Masters in Library Science. His two older sisters have PhDs. He followed their steps and made the most of opportunities. He was a pioneer in Emergency Medicine working his first solo shift in 1973, six years before Emergency Medicine became a specialty. **Why did you become involved in your profession or industry:** Dr. Ragland became involved in his profession because of his religious upbringing. His father was a minister for 55 years and he was raised to believe in service to others. **Avocations:** Gardening; Skiing; Bicycling; Hiking **Political Affiliations:** Democrat **Religion:** Universalist **Thoughts on Life:** "All humans have lack and should accept fallibility in themselves and in others. We must remain true to our values and beliefs regardless of the consequences. Look to the future but live in the moment!"

Manjula Raguthu, MD

Title: Physician, Director **Industry:** Health, Wellness and Fitness **Company Name:** Proage Institute **Date of Birth:** 07/07/1964 **Place of Birth:** Guntur **State/Country of Origin:** India **Parents:** Dr. Ramnath Singh, Murali Bai **Marital Status:** Married **Spouse Name:** Surya Raguthu MD **Children:** Sharvani Raguthu; Chetan Raguthu; Neil Raguthu **Education:** Postgraduate Diploma in Obstetrics and Gynecology (1993); MBBS, Guntur Medical College (1990) **Certifications:** Re-Certified in Family Practice (2008); Board Certified in Family Practice (2001); Board Certified in Anti-Aging and Integrative Medicine; Certification in Advanced Trauma Life Support; Certified Medical Coder; Certification in Medical Office Management Certification; Certified Compliance Officer **Career:** Physican, Director, Proage Institute (2001-Present) **Civic:** Various Nonprofit Organizations; Provides Healthcare for Immigrant Children **Awards:** Best Family Physicians in America, Consumer's Research Council of America (2009); Best Family Physician, Consumer's Research Council of America (2008); Best Family Physicians in America, Consumer's Research Council of America (2006); Best Family Physician, Consumer's Research Council of America (2006); Best Family Physicians in America, Consumer's Research Council of America (2004); Exemplary Leadership Award (2001); 32nd Rank in Family Practice Boards in America; Distinction in Microbiology; Distinction in Ophthalmology; Overall Percentile of 97.3 in Medical School; Topper in Physiology, Surgery, and Obstetrics and Gynecology **Memberships:** American Academy of Family Physicians; American Medical Association; American Association of Physicians of Indian Origin; Texas Academy of Family Physicians; American Anti-Aging Academy **Marquis Who's Who Honors:** Albert Nelson Marquis Lifetime Achievement Award; Marquis Who's Who Top Professional; Marquis Who's Who Humanitarian Award **To what do you attribute your success:** She attributes her success to her hard work and dedication. **Why did you become involved in your profession or industry:** She became involved in her profession because of her desire to care for people. **Avocations:** Badminton; Photography; Handicrafts **Thoughts on Life:** The focus of the practice is to deliver quality, comprehensive, compassionate health care for the entire family. They care for patients from infancy to the elderly throughout the life cycle. She believes strongly that "HEALTH IS WEALTH."

Keshava Rajagopal, MD, PhD

Title: Associate Professor, Cardiothoracic/Vascular Surgery **Industry:** Education/Educational Services **Company Name:** University of Texas-Houston **Marital Status:** Married **Spouse Name:** Shilpa **Children:** Hari; Leela; Shriram **Education:** Residency, Cardiothoracic Surgery, Duke University Medical Center (2009-2012); Residency, Surgery, Duke University Medical Center (2002-2009); Postdoctoral Fellowship, Molecular Cardiololgy/Physiology, Duke University Medical Center (2004-2006); MD, PhD, Medicine, Immunology, University of Chicago-The Prizker School of Medicine, With Honors (2002); BS in Chemistry, University of Pittsburgh, Magna Cum Laude (1994) **Certifications:** American Board of Thoracic Surgery; American Board of Surgery **Career:** Assistant Professor, Cardiothoracic/Vascular Surgery, The University of Texas Health Science Center at Houston (UTHealth) (2015-Present); Assistant Professor, Cardiac Surgery, University of Maryland Medical Center (2012-2015) **Awards:** The Norman Shumway Career Development Award, International Society of Heart and Lung Transplantation (2014); Resident Research Award, Duke (2009); National Research Service Award, National Institute of Health (2004) **Memberships:** Phi Beta Kappa **To what do you attribute your success:** Dr. Rajagopal attributes his success to hard work, determination, focus, and discipline. **Why did you become involved in your profession or industry:** Dr. Rajagopal became involved in his profession because his father is an engineering professor who exposed him to biomedical engineering. His brother, who is a cardiologist at Duke, was born with a minor heart defect, so that exposed him to cardiac work at a young age.

José Ramírez-Rivera, MD, FCCP, MACP

Title: Professor Emeritus, Professor of Medicine, Physician (Retired) **Industry:** Education/Educational Services **Company Name:** UPR, UCC **Date of Birth:** 06/26/1929 **Place of Birth:** Mayaquez **State/Country of Origin:** Puerto Rico **Parents:** Jesus Ramirez; Nieves Rivera **Marital Status:** Married **Spouse Name:** Sally P. Wheeler (06/20/1952) **Children:** Frederico; Steven; Sally; Juliette; Natasha; Leila **Education:** Resident, University of Maryland Medical Center (UMMC) (1959); Fellow in Hematology, University of Maryland Medical Center (UMMC) (1958-1959); Resident in Medicine, University of Maryland Medical Center (UMMC) (1954-1955); Intern, University of Maryland Medical Center (UMMC) (1953-1954); MD, Yale University (1953); BA, Johns Hopkins University (1949); Fellow, Royal College of Physicians, London, United Kingdom; Fellow, College of Chest Physicians, Royal Society of Medicine, London, United Kingdom **Certifications:** Re-certified, Diplomate, American Board of Internal Medicine (1974) **Career:** Professor Emeritus, University of Puerto Rico (2017-Present); Associate Chief, Staff for Education, VA Hospital, Puerto Rico (1980-1982); Professor of Medicine, University of Puerto Rico (1972-2017); Chief of Medicine, Mayaguez Medical Center (1971-1982); Director, Medical Education and Clinical Investigation, Puerto Rico (1970-1980); Chief of Professional Services, Mayaguez Medical Center (1970-1978); Assistant Chief of Medicine, VA Hospital, Durham, NC (1968-1970); Chief, Pulmonary Disease Section, VA Hospital, Durham, NC (1968-1970); Associate Professor, Duke University (1968-1970); Instructor in Medicine, Johns Hopkins University (1967-1968); Associate Chief of Staff, VA Hospital, Baltimore, MD (1962-1968); Assistant Professor of Medicine, University of Maryland (1961-1968); Assistant in Medicine, Johns Hopkins University (1960-1967); Staff Physician, VA Hospital, Baltimore, MD (1960-1967) **Career Related:** Professor of Medicine, Universidad Central del Caribe (1998-Present); Director, Clinical Investigation, La Concepcion Hospital, Puerto Rico (1996-Present); Professor of Medicine, University Medical Services, Medical Sciences Campus, University of Puerto Rico (1974-Present); Associate Chief of Staff Education, VA Medical Center, Puerto Rico (1990-1992) **Civic:** President, Puerto Rican Bioethics Society (2000-2010); Board of Directors, Southwest Society of Educators **Military Service:** U.S. Public Health Service (1955-1957) **Creative Works:** Featured Biography, "A Todo Bulmon," by Juan Ramon Saravia (2011); Translator; Author, Books of Puerto Rican Legends; Contributor, Articles to Medical Journals **Awards:** Abelardo Diaz Alfaro Prize, Imperial Orden Hispanica de Carlos V (2010); Laureate Award, American College of Physicians (2005); Named Man of the Year, Puerto Rico Medical Society Western Section (1975, 1981); Decorated Comendador, Imperial Orden Hispanica de Carlos V **Memberships:** Board of Directors, Alianza Francesa de Puerto Rico (2006-2009); President, Puerto Rican Federation of Bioethics (2002-2010); Board of Directors, Puerto Rican Federation of Bioethics (1999-2012); Casa Espanã (1998-2009) **Marquis Who's Who Honors:** Albert Nelson Marquis Lifetime Achievement Award; Marquis Who's Who Top Professional; Marquis Who's Who Humanitarian Award **To what do you attribute your success:** Dr. Ramirez-Rivera attributes his success to his desire to find a treatment for a disease that people were dying from. His main contribution is the treatment he invented, lung lavage. **Why did you become involved in your profession or industry:** Dr. Ramírez-Rivera's mother wanted him to be a doctor. He had two uncles that were doctors. At age 15, he moved to the U.S. to improve his English and attend Johns Hopkins University like his mother wanted him to. He was living in Baltimore, MD, at the time, but he applied to Yale instead. **Avocations:** Classical music; Literature **Religion:** Roman Catholic **Thoughts on Life:** When Dr. Ramírez-Rivera was 19 years old, he went to Paris and studied literature and philosophy at the Sorbonne for a summer. He wrote to his mother and she wrote back every week. She collected all the letters he wrote to her. Yesterday, he was reading all of them; they were typed, very well protected, and very readable, too, despite the fact that they are more than 50 years old. He studied two years of French at Johns Hopkins, traveling to France the summer of 1948; he studied at the Sorbonne after his third year of college. They gave him the equivalent of a year's credit for his time at the Sorbonne because they were impressed when he came back speaking fluent French. The Sorbonne began earlier in May and they gave him the final exams two weeks before so he could get to there on time for the course. The Sorbonne is the University of Paris, and in the morning, they studied grammar composition and literature, while the afternoons were dedicated to French philosophers. There were people all over the world in that course, including Japan, Africa, Argentina, England, and Europe. It was very interesting.

Tammy Ramsay

Title: Realtor **Industry:** Real Estate **Company Name:** Ramsay Realtors **Marital Status:** Married **Spouse Name:** Rick Ramsay **Children:** Three Children **Education:** BBA in Management, Dowling College (1994) **Career:** Realtor, Real Estate Sales, Eric G. Ramsay, JR, Associates, LLC (Ramsey Realtors) (1995-Present); Kindergarten Teacher, East Islip School District **Civic:** Sponsor, Charlie's Champions **Awards:** Named, Top 10 Best Agents (2019); Named, Best of Zillow (2019); Named, America's Top 100 Real Estate Agents (2018) **To what do you attribute your success:** Ms. Ramsay attributes her success to having a sales background from her experiences working with her father in his car dealerships. **Why did you become involved in your profession or industry:** Ms. Ramsay grew up working with her father, who owned car dealerships, since she was about 12 years old. Eventually, she went to school and became a teacher. She only worked as a teacher for about two years before getting married and having children. Initially, she planned to go back, but things changed. Her husband Rick's family owned a real estate company. Her father-in-law told her to get her real estate license and she did so. Being around a family that ate, breathed and slept real estate, she developed a genuine love and passion for the business.In addition, what attracted Ms. Ramsay to real estate was that she married into it. She got married, then got a real estate license at the same time.

William Louis Ramstein, MBA, CPA

Title: Retired Manufacturing Executive **Industry:** Manufacturing **Place of Birth:** Los Angeles California **State/Country of Origin:** CA/USA **Parents:** Robert James Ramstein; Norma Elaine (Knapp) Ramstein **Marital Status:** Divorced **Education:** MBA, University of Southern California (1984); BSBA, California State University, Northridge, Magna Cum Laude (1975) **Certifications:** CPA, California; Certified, Internal Auditor **Career:** Independent Financial And Systems Consultant (2011-2013); Senior Business Manager, Velocium Products, Northop Grumman (2003-2010); Manager, Special Projects and Systems, Space and Electronics Group, TRW Inc., Redondo Beach, CA (1998-2003); Manager, Financial Reporting, Space and Electronics Group, TRW Inc., Redondo Beach, CA (1989-1998); Head, Accounting Section, Hughes Aircraft Co., Missile Systems Group, Canoga Park, CA (1980-1989); Management Consultant, Alexander Grant & Co., Van Nuys, CA (1978-1980); Senior Internal Auditor, County of Los Angeles, LA (1975-1978) **Career Related:** Financial Consultant **Memberships:** American Institute of Certified Public Accountants; Beta Gamma Sigma **Marquis Who's Who Honors:** Albert Nelson Marquis Lifetime Achievement Award **To what do you attribute your success:** Mr. Ramstein attributes his success to his mathematical and analytical abilities, combined with the substantial time and effort he put forth in order to succeed. **Why did you become involved in your profession or industry:** Mr. Ramstein was always interested in how businesses operate, which drew him to finance, economics, and accounting coursework. The experience helped him understand the world of business and the challenges that are present. **Avocations:** Acting; Piano; Songwriting; Fitness; Ocean sports **Thoughts on Life:** Mr. Ramstein believes continued learning and growth are necessary. Without personal growth, life doesn't exist.

George Ranalli

Title: Architect, Educator **Industry:** Education/Educational Services **Date of Birth:** 11/27/1946 **Place of Birth:** Bronx **State/Country of Origin:** NY/ USA **Parents:** George S. Ranalli; Kathryn (Heilbron) Ranalli **Marital Status:** Married **Spouse Name:** Anne J. Valentino **Education:** Honorary MA, Yale University (1996); MArch, Harvard University (1974); BArch, Pratt Institute, Brooklyn, NY (1972); Coursework, New York Institute of Technology (1967-1968) **Certifications:** Registered Architect, State of New York; Registered Architect, State of Connecticut; Certification, National Council of Architectural Registration Boards **Career:** William Henry Bishop Chair, Visiting Professor, Architectural Design, School of Architecture, Yale University, New Haven, CT (1988-1989); Professor, Architectural Design, School of Architecture, Yale University, New Haven, CT (1976-1999); Architect, Max O. Urbahn and Associates, New York, NY (1973-1976) **Career Related:** Visiting Professor, School of Architecture, The Cooper Union for the Advancement of Science and Art; Member, Advisory Board, The New York Landmarks Conservancy **Creative Works:** Solo Exhibitor, Yale University (1999); Exhibitor, Group Shows, Canadian Society for Architect, Montreal, Canada (1999); Author, "CASAS: George Ranalli" (1998); Solo Exhibitor, Artists Space Gallery, New York, NY (1997-1998); Exhibitor, Group Shows, Whitney Museum of Art, New York, NY (1997); Exhibitor, Group Shows, Denver Art Museum (1992, 1996); Exhibitor, Group Shows, Canadian Centre for Architecture, Montreal, Canada (1996); Exhibitor, Group Shows, Museum of Modern Art, New York, NY (1994); Exhibitor, Group Shows, Metropolitan Museum of Art, New York, NY (1991); Author, "George Ranalli: Bauten und Projekte; Constructions et Projets" (1990); Exhibitor, Group Shows, Deutsches Architekturmuseum, Frankfurt am Main, Germany (1989); Exhibitor, Group Shows, American Institute of Architects (1988-1989); Author, "George Ranalli: Buildings and Projects" (1988); Exhibitor, Group Shows, Yale University (1987, 1978); Exhibitor, Group Shows, Centre Pompidou (1986); Exhibitor, Group Shows, Il Progetto Domestico XVII Milan Triennale (1986); Exhibitor, Group Shows, Udine, Italy (1985); Exhibitor, Group Shows, Young-Hoffman Gallery, Chicago, IL (1980); Solo Exhibitor, Architectural Projects (1980); Exhibitor, Group Shows, Museum of Contemporary Art, Chicago, IL (1980); Exhibitor, Group Shows, Museum of Finnish Architecture, Helsinki, Finland (1980); Exhibitor, Group Shows, American Architectural Alternatives, Europe (1979-1980); Solo Exhibitor, UNC Charlotte (1979); Exhibitor, Group Shows, Hudson River Museum (1979); Exhibitor, Group Shows, Cooper-Hewitt Museum, New York, NY (1979); Exhibitor, Group Shows, New Americans, Rome, Italy (1979); Exhibitor, Group Shows, Sperone, Westwater and Fisher Gallery, New York, NY (1979); Exhibitor, Group Shows, Drawing Center and Cooper-Hewitt Museum, New York, NY (1977); Exhibitor, Group Shows, Otis Art Institute, Los Angeles, CA (1977); Contributor, Articles, Professional Journals; Contributor, Chapters, Books; Author, "In Situ, George Ranalli" **Awards:** Projects Award, AIA (1997); Projects Citations, AIA (1995-1996); Architecture Award, AIA (1994); Artist Fellowship in Architecture, New York Foundation for the Arts (1988) Design Award, Citation, Progressive Architecture (1980); James Stewardson Traveling Fellowship, AIA (1976); Matthew del Gaudio Memorial Award, New York Society Architects (1972) **Memberships:** AIA; New York Society Architects **Marquis Who's Who Honors:** Albert Nelson Marquis Lifetime Achievement Award

James Byrne Ranck Jr., MD

Title: Neuroscience Researcher, Educator **Industry:** Education/Educational Services **Company Name:** SUNY Downstate Medical Center **Date of Birth:** 08/17/1930 **Place of Birth:** Frederick **State/Country of Origin:** MD/USA **Parents:** James Byrne Ranck; Dorothy Irene (Schwieger) Ranck **Marital Status:** Married **Spouse Name:** Helen Haukeness (06/09/1961) **Children:** Mary Ranck-Bolieu **Education:** Honorary Doctorate, SUNY Downstate Medical Center (2017); Postdoctoral Fellow, Laboratory of Walter Woodbury, University of Washington, Seattle, WA (1959-1961); Intern, The University of Chicago Medicine (1955-1956); MD, Columbia University (1955); BA, Haverford College (1952) **Career:** Retired 2015; Emeritus (2015); Distinguished Teaching Professor in Physiology, SUNY Downstate Medical Center (2005-2015); Professor, Department of Physiology, SUNY Downstate Medical Center, Brooklyn, NY (1975-2005); Professor, Department of Physiology, University of Michigan, Ann Arbor, MI (1962-1975); Assistant Professor, Department of Physiology, University of Michigan, Ann Arbor, MI (1962-1975); Instructor of Biophysics, Department of Physiology, University of Washington, Seattle, WA (1960-1961); Scientist, Laboratory of Neuroanatomy, National Institutes of Health, Bethesda, MD (1956-1958); Intern, University of Chicago Clinics (1955-1956) **Military Service:** Public Health Service, counted as uniformed service time; **Creative Works:** Co-author, "Head-Direction Cells Recorded from the Postsubiculum in Freely Moving Rats. I. Description and Quantitative Analysis" (1990); Co-author, "Spatial Firing Patterns of Hippocampal Complex-Spike Cells in a Fixed Environment" (1987); Author, "Head Direction Cells in the Deep Layer of Dorsal Presubiculum in Freely Moving Rats" (1984); Co-author, "Sensory-Behavioral Correlates of Individual Hippocampal Neurons in Three Situations: Space and Context," Neurobiology of the Hippocampus (1983); Author, "Which Elements are Excited in Electrical Stimulation of Mammalian Central Nervous System: A Review" (1975); Author, "Studies on Single Neurons in Dorsal Hippocampal Formation and Septum in Unrestrained Rats. I. Behavioral Correlates and Firing Repertoires" (1973); Co-author, "Studies on Single Neurons in Dorsal Hippocampal Formation and Septum in Unrestrained Rats. II. Hippocampal Slow Waves and Theta Cell Firing During Bar Pressing and Other Behaviors" (1973); Author, "Electrical Impedance in the Subicular Area of Rats During Paradoxical Sleep" (1966); Contributor, Book Chapters; Contributor, Articles, Professional Journals **Marquis Who's Who Honors:** Albert Nelson Marquis Lifetime Achievement Award **To what do you attribute your success:** Dr. Ranck attributes his success to being accepted into the public health service in 1956. **Why did you become involved in your profession or industry:** Dr. Ranck was inspired to enter his profession during the doctors' draft of 1955. He was recruited by the National Institutes of Health to perform research. He enjoyed research, and decided to stay with it. **Avocations:** Reading; Tennis

Arun A. Rangaswami

Title: Associate Professor of Pediatrics **Industry:** Medicine & Health Care **Company Name:** Stanford University **Education:** Fellow, Stanford University (1996); Resident, St. Louis Children's Hospital (1993); Intern, St. Louis Children's Hospital (1993); MD, Washington University (1990); BS, Johns Hopkins University (1986) **Career:** Clinical Associate Professor of Pediatrics, Stanford University (2006-Present); Assistant Professor, University of California, Davis (1996-2001) **Civic:** Mentorship Program, Stanford University **Awards:** C. John Tupper Teaching Award for Excellence in Medical Education, University of California Davis (1999) **Memberships:** FIOP FIOPEL; The Children's Oncology Group; ACLOU **To what do you attribute your success:** Dr. Rangaswami has always been critical of himself, to which he attributes much of his success. He believes that, as a surgeon, one must be overly critical of oneself in order to succeed. Criticism is the key to improvement. **Why did you become involved in your profession or industry:** Dr. Rangaswami has always liked science. Both of his parents were scientists, which motivated him to pursue a career in medicine. Though he was initially interested in surgery, he found a passion for pediatric oncology.

Megan Anna Rapinoe

Title: Professional Soccer Player **Industry:** Athletics **Company Name:** OL Reign **Date of Birth:** 07/05/1985 **Place of Birth:** Redding **State/Country of Origin:** CA/USA **Parents:** Jim Rapinoe; Denise Rapinoe **Education:** Coursework, University of Portland; Diploma, Foothill High School **Career:** Professional Soccer Player, OL Reign (2013-Present); Professional Soccer Player, Olympique Lyonnais (2013-2014); Professional Soccer Player, Seattle Sounders Women (2012); Professional Soccer Player, Sydney FC (2011); Professional Soccer Player, MagicJack (2011); Professional Soccer Player, Philadelphia Independence (2011); Professional Soccer Player, Chicago Red Stars (2009-2010); Soccer Player, University of Portland (2005-2008); Soccer Player, Elk Grove Pride (2002-2005) **Career Related:** Professional Soccer Player, U.S National Team (2006-Present); Professional Soccer Player, U.S. U-20 (2003-2005); Endorser, Multiple Branding, Including Nike, Samsung, Wildfang, DJO Global, Vitamin Water, Procter & Gamble, BodyArmor, Hulu, LUNA Bar and VISA **Civic:** Participant, Common Goal (2017); Ambassador, Athlete Ally (2013); Gay, Lesbian & Straight Education Network; U.S. Olympic & Paralympic Committee **Awards:** CONCACAF Women's Olympic Qualifying Tournament Champion (2020); SheBelieves Cup Champion (2018, 2020); Ballon d'Or Féminin (2019); FIFA Women's World Cup Final Player of the Match (2019); FIFPro World XI Champion (2019); FIFA Women's World Cup Golden Boot and Ball (2019); Best FIFA Women's Player (2019); IFFHS World's Best Woman Playmaker (2019); FIFA Women's World Cup Champion (2015, 2019); NWSL Second XI Champion (2013, 2015, 2017, 2019); Tournament of Nations Champion (2018); NWSL Best XI Champion (2018); CONCACAF Women's Championship Winner (2014, 2018); NWSL Player of the Week (2013, 2015, 2017-2018); Inductee, National Gay and Lesbian Sports Hall of Fame (2015); NWSL Shield Champion (2014-2015); Algarve Cup Champion (2011, 2013, 2015); Inductee, Shasta County Sports Hall of Fame (2014); Coupe de France Féminine Champion (2012-2013); Division 1 Féminine Champion (2012-2013); Algarve Cup MVP (2013); Olympic Gold Medal (2012); Board of Directors Award, Los Angeles Gay and Lesbian Center (2012); Finalist, Sports Illustrated's Most Inspiring Performers (2012); Harry Glickman Professional Female Athlete of the Year Award, Oregon Sports Awards (2012) **Political Affiliations:** Democrat

Laurian Rauen

Title: Chief Executive Officer **Industry:** Environmental Services **Company Name:** Wings to New Horizons, Inc. **Career:** Founder and Chief Executive Officer, Wings to New Horizons, Inc. (2000-Present); Handler, Orlando Dog Training Club, Inc.; Secretary, Sunshine State Cage Bird Society, Inc.; Wintermiles Trotting Center (Now Burke Training Center); ERC Horizon Farms **Civic:** Board of Directors, Oviedo-Winter Springs Regional Chamber of Commerce **Awards:** Ambassador of the Year, Oviedo-Winter Springs Regional Chamber of Commerce; Non-Profit of the Year, Oviedo-Winter Springs Regional Chamber of Commerce **Memberships:** Oviedo-Winter Springs Regional Chamber of Commerce **To what do you attribute your success:** Mrs. Rauen attributes her success to her faith in God, to whom she credits for opening doors she never could have on her own. She has experienced her share of setbacks but finds comfort in her tribulations. Mrs. Rauen values extreme honesty and emphasizes that while lies are exposed over time, the truth will always be the truth. **Why did you become involved in your profession or industry:** Overall, a natural interest in birds and profound love for animals has always informed Mrs. Rauen's career path. From an early age, she wanted to be a veterinarian. She recalls rescuing and hand-feeding birds as a child; in high school, she would hang out at a local veterinary office just for exposure to the profession. Mrs. Rauen applied and was accepted to veterinary school twice, but following that path would have risked her relationship with her mother. She ultimately did not pursue her veterinary dream but remained involved with animals throughout her working life. She adopted her first parrot several decades ago and has continued to rescue parrots since. Mrs. Rauen's career was disrupted when a sanctuary of hers was, devastatingly, burglarized; precious macaws and cockatoos were stolen, and this proved to be a turning point in her mission. The event opened her eyes to "the plight of the parrot", and by 1995, she found that the global parrot trade had largely disappeared. Mrs. Rauen grew concerned about the impacts on her industry, realizing the United States may no longer have access to exotic birds native to other continents.

Judith Rawie-Rook

Title: Co-Founder, President, Producer/Writer **Industry:** Writing and Editing **Company Name:** R2 Group **Parents:** Wilmer Ernest Rawie; Margaret Jane (Towle) Rawie **Marital Status:** Widowed **Spouse Name:** Tim Rook (1993, Deceased 2016); Dr. John Holland (1964, Divorced 1978) **Children:** Daryn Simons; Dawn Reinard **Education:** Postgraduate Coursework in Visual Arts & Communications, University of California, San Diego (1978); Postgraduate Coursework, University of California, Irvine (1976); BBA, Loyola-Marymount University (1964) **Career:** Founder, President, R2 Group (1990-Present); Producer, Writer, Partner, BrantHol Productions (1990-1993); Co-Sponsorship, The Last Emperor (1987-1989); Co-Sponsorship, Beetle Juice (1987-1989); Partner, Real Magic (1987-1989); Director of Development, Embassy/Nelson Home Entertainment (1985-1987); Director of Programming, Westinghouse Cable (1983-1985); Director of Video, IABC, San Francisco, CA (1982); Syndicated Columnist, Environmental Forum (1971-1974); International Market Researcher, Smith, Kline & French (1964-1966) **Civic:** Board, Getty Museum (2005-2007); Editor, Board League of Women Voters, Santa Monica, CA (2004-2005); Board Secretary, Counseling 4 Kids (2001-2005); Member, Board of Directors, Counseling 4 Kids (1998-2005); Advisory Board Member, Screenwriting/Film Production, University of California Irvine (1996-2000); Advisory Board, University of Art Museum (1996-1997); Co-President, Contemporary Council, University of Art Museum (1996-1997); Executive Board Member, Long Beach Museum of Art (1995-1996) **Creative Works:** Producer, "Ed Mieczkowski: Visual Paradox" (2010-Present); Co-Producer, "Boots Across The Divide: The Love Story" (2005-Present); Associate Producer, "Highway 101" (2005-Present); Producer, "Somewhere in Between" (2005); Playwright, "Anniversary for Three," Theatre 40 Writer's Workshop (2003); Associate Producer, Fox Latin American Billboard Music Awards (1998-2000); Producer, "Close Up: The 60s" (1995-1997); Producer, "One Creative Moment" (1992); Producer, Writer, CNN Pilot, "Clever Encounters" (1991); Producer, Writer, NBC Pilot, "Christmas Comes to Silverton" (1990-1993); Producer, Writer, "Achieving" (1982); Associate Director, "The Man Who Came to Dinner" (1981); Producer, Writer, PBS Series, "Focus" (1980); Associate Director, "Arms and the Man" (1967); Executive Producer, "Neighborhood Without Bars"; Associate Producer, TV Pilot, "Fempresario" **Awards:** Emmy Award (1986); Nominee, Award; ACE Award; Nominee, Award, PBS **Memberships:** American Film Institute; Director, Seminars on Women in Film, Women in Film; International Documentary Association; Independent Feature Project; National Women's History Museum; California Jazz Foundation; Library Foundation of Los Angeles **Marquis Who's Who Honors:** Albert Nelson Marquis Lifetime Achievement Award; Marquis Who's Who Top Professional **Why did you become involved in your profession or industry:** Ms. Rook entered her profession because after her first divorce she gave herself permission to do what she always loved and that was film and production. **Political Affiliations:** Democrat **Religion:** Episcopalian

Robert R. Read, PhD

Title: Mathematical Statistics Educator (Retired) **Industry:** Education/ Educational Services **Date of Birth:** 10/05/1929 **Place of Birth:** Columbus **State/Country of Origin:** OH/USA **Parents:** Ira Jay Read; Pearl V. (Scott) Read **Marital Status:** Married **Spouse Name:** Dagmar Ann Ruud (12/19/1963, Divorced 1974) **Children:** Darren James; Steven Michael; Christopher Scott **Education:** PhD, University of California Berkeley (1958); BSc, Ohio State University (1951) **Career:** Retired (2004); Professor Emeritus, Navy Postgraduate School, Monterey, CA (1961-2004); Assistant Professor, University of Chicago (1961-2004); Lecturer, Research Statistician, University of California Berkeley (1957-1960) **Career Related:** United Technical Center, Sunnyvale, CA (1962-1965); Consultant, Maritime Cargo Transportation Conference, San Francisco, CA (1959) **Civic:** Monterey Cypress Aires, Chapter Chorus (2002-2010); Coach, Baseball Teams, Local Pony-Colt Youth League (1986); Monterey Cypress Aires, Chapter Chorus (1961-1964); Berkeley Californians, Chapter Chorus (1957-1960); Participant, International Barbershop Chorus Championship (1957); Participant, Bridge Golf, Formal Duplicate Bridge Competition (1948); Barbershop Harmony Society **Creative Works:** Contributor, Research Articles, Professional Journals **Awards:** Winner, International Barbershop Chorus Championship (1957) **Memberships:** Institute of Mathematical Statistics; American Statistical Association; Sigma Xi, the Scientific Research Honor Society **Marquis Who's Who Honors:** Albert Nelson Marquis Lifetime Achievement Award **Why did you become involved in your profession or industry:** Dr. Read received a Bachelor of Science in mathematics, which exposed him to statistics. He started out in engineering, but he soon found an opportunity in math and teaching. The Math Department at his university requested for stronger students to become full-time faculty. He was drawn to this field and, consequently, away from engineering. **Avocations:** Bridge; Golf; Skiing

Harry M. Reasoner

Title: Lawyer **Industry:** Law and Legal Services **Date of Birth:** 07/15/1939 **Place of Birth:** San Marcos **State/Country of Origin:** TX/USA **Parents:** Harry Edward Reasoner; Joyce Marjorie (Barrett) Reasoner **Marital Status:** Married **Spouse Name:** Elizabeth Macey Hodges (04/15/1963) **Children:** Barrett Reasoner; Macey Reasoner Stokes **Education:** Postgraduate Studies, LSE (1963); JD, University of Texas, with Honors (1962); BA in Philosophy, Rice University, Summa Cum Laude (1960) **Career:** Partner, Vinson & Elkins (1970-Present); Managing Partner, Vinson & Elkins (1992-2001); Associate, Vinson & Elkins, Houston, TX (1964-1969); Law Clerk, U.S. Court of Appeals for the Second Circuit (1963-1964) **Career Related:** Chair, Texas Access to Justice Commission, Supreme Court of Texas (2009-2019); At-Large Representative (2006); Adjunct Professor, University of Texas School of Law, University of Texas at Austin (2002); Chair, Advisory Group, U.S. District Court for the Southern District of Texas (1990); Advisory Committee, Supreme Court of Texas (1984-1990); Visiting Professor, University of Houston Law Center (1977); Visiting Professor, Rice University (1976); Visiting Professor, University of Texas School of Law, University of Texas at Austin (1971) **Civic:** Advisory Board, Baker Institute for Public Policy, Rice University (2011-Present); Trustee Emeritus, Center for American and International Law (CAIL) (2008-Present); Member, Board of Trustees, Supreme Court Historical Society (2000-Present); Life Trustee, University of Texas Law School Foundation (1980-Present); President, University of Texas Law School Foundation (1998-2001); Member, Board of Directors, Houston A+ Challenge (1997-2009); Trustee, Baylor College of Medicine (1992-2018); Chair, Texas Higher Education Coordinating Board (THECB) (1991) **Creative Works:** Co-Author, Book, "Procedure, The Handmaid of Justice" (1965) **Awards:** Lifetime Achievement Award, Anti-Defamation League (2016); Outstanding 50 Year Lawyer Award, Texas Bar Foundation (2012); Lola Wright Foundation Award (2011); Named One of "The 25 Greatest Lawyers of Past Quarter-Century," Texas Lawyer (2010); Lifetime Achievement Award, The American Lawyer Magazine (2009); Named Distinguished Alumnus, Rice University (2003); Named Distinguished Alumnus, University Texas School Law (1998); Named Distinguished Alumnus, University of Texas (1997); Professionalism Award, U.S. Court of Appeals For The Fifth Circuit, American Inns Court Foundation **Memberships:** Board of Directors, International Academy of Trial Lawyers (2005-2013); Chairman, Antitrust Section, American Bar Association (1989-1990); Fellow, Texas Bar Foundation; American Bar Association Foundation; International Society of Barristers; American College of Trial Lawyers; American Law Institute; District of Columbia Bar; American Board of Trial Advisors; Philosophical Society of Texas; Houston Philosophical Society; Association of the Bar of the City of New York; Houston Bar Association; Century Association; Cosmos Club; Phi Delta Phi; Phi Beta Kappa **Bar Admissions:** New York (2000); District of Columbia (1974); Texas (1962) **Marquis Who's Who Honors:** Albert Nelson Marquis Lifetime Achievement Award; Marquis Who's Who Top Professional **Why did you become involved in your profession or industry:** Mr. Reasoner became involved in his profession because he received one of the first national merit scholarships in 1956 and was thinking he should go into science. He won the state debate championship and later went to Rice university. He was grateful for the education and, at one point, thought about going to law school, which he did and loved. He studied comparative law, international law, and economics at London School of Economics and then became a law clerk for a judge at Yale. **Avocations:** Reading; Traveling; Pilates

Robert Ray Redfield Jr., MD

Title: Director; Virologist **Industry:** Sciences **Company Name:** Center for Disease Control and Prevention **Date of Birth:** 07/10/1951 **Place of Birth:** Chicago **State/Country of Origin:** IL/USA **Marital Status:** Married **Spouse Name:** Joyce Hoke **Children:** Six Children **Education:** Honorary Degree, New York Medical College; Fellow in Tropical Medicine, Walter Reed National Military Army Medical Center (1982); Fellow in Infectious Diseases, Walter Reed National Military Army Medical Center (1980-1982); Resident in Medicine, Walter Reed National Military Army Medical Center (1980-1982); Intern, Walter Reed National Military Army Medical Center (1977-1978); MD, Georgetown University School of Medicine (1977); BS, Georgetown University (1973) **Career:** Director, Centers of Disease Control and Prevention (2018-Present); Administrator, Agency for Toxic Substances and Disease Registry (2018-Present); Director, Adult HIV Program, University of Maryland Medical Center; Professor of Medicine, Immunology, Microbiology, Department of Infectious Disease, University of Maryland School of Medicine; Director, Clinical Care & Research Division, Institute of Human Virology, University of Maryland School of Medicine, Baltimore, MD; Co-founder, Associate Director, Institute of Human Virology, University of Maryland School of Medicine, Baltimore, MD; Project Director, HIV Vaccine Development for Treatment and Prevention, Military Medical Consortium for Applied Retroviral Research, U.S. Department of Defense; Chief, Department of Retroviral Research, Walter Reed Army Institute of Research (WRAIR); Project Director, HIV Immunotherapy, Walter Reed Army Institute of Research (WRAIR) **Career Related:** Member, AIDS Research Advisory Council, National Institutes of Health; Member, Advisory Board, Fogarty International Center **Civic:** Board of Directors, The Pendulum Project **Military Service:** Advanced through Grades to Colonel, United States Army (1977-1996) **Awards:** Multiple Medals in Virology, United States Army; Physician Recognition Award, Surgeon General; Highest Achievement in Clinical Virology Award, Ortho Diagnostic Systems Inc.; Lifetime Science Award, Institute of Advanced Studies in Immunology and Aging

Shari Ellin Redstone

Title: Chairwoman **Industry:** Media & Entertainment **Company Name:** ViacomCBS Inc. **Date of Birth:** 04/14/1954 **Place of Birth:** Washington, DC **State/Country of Origin:** DC/USA **Parents:** Sumner Redstone; Phyllis Redstone **Marital Status:** Divorced **Spouse Name:** Ira A. Korff **Children:** Three Children **Education:** LLM, Boston University School of Law (1980); JD in Tax Law, Boston University School of Law (1978); BS, Tufts University (1975) **Career:** Chairwoman, ViacomCBS, Inc.; Co-founder and Managing Partner, Advancit Capital; Vice Chair, Board of Directors, Viacom Inc. (Now ViacomCBS, Inc.); Vice Chair, Board of CBS Corporation (Now ViacomCBS, Inc.); President, National Amusements, Inc.; Co-chairman, MovieTickets.com (Now Fandango) **Career Related:** Owner, Rising Star Media (2002-2011) **Civic:** Member, Board of Directors, The National Center on Addiction and Substance Abuse (CASA), Columbia University (2003-2012); Member, Board of Directors, OurTime.com; Member, Local Advisory Board and Executive Committee, Build.com, Inc.; Member, Board of Trustees, Dana-Farber Cancer Institute **Memberships:** Board of Directors and Executive Committee, National Theatre Owners Association (Now National Association of Theatre Owners); Member, Board of Directors, Combined Jewish Philanthropies of Greater Boston; Member, Board of Directors, John F. Kennedy Library Foundation

George Elliott Reed, DVM, MD

Title: Scholar, Surgeon and Healer **Industry:** Medicine & Health Care **Date of Birth:** 08/04/1923 **Place of Birth:** New York **State/Country of Origin:** NY/USA **Marital Status:** Married **Spouse Name:** Anne Miller Moore (1995); Thelma Bilik Reed **Children:** Elizabeth E.; George E. Jr; Patrick M. Moore; Alissa Moore Sims; Greta Moore Scott **Education:** Fellow in Surgery, New York University College of Medicine (1956); MD, New York University College of Medicine (1951); DVM, Cornell University College of Veterinary Medicine (1944) **Certifications:** Diplomate, American Board of Thoracic Surgery; Diplomate, American Board of Surgery **Career:** Professor of Surgery, Chief of Cardiac Surgery, Vice Dean, New York Medical College, Westchester, NY (1977-2004); Director of Residency Program, New York University Bellevue Medical Center (1965-1977); Professor of Surgery, New York University Bellevue Medical Center; Chief of Cardiovascular Surgery, New York University/ Bellevue Medical Center **Career Related:** Board of Directors, Mid-Hudson Family Health Institute (2000-2004); Board of Directors, Westchester Health Care Corporation (1998-2004); President, Medical Faculty Health Alliance (1994-2004); Medical Director, Westchester County Medical Center (1994-2004); President of Medical Staff, Chair, Executive Committee, Westchester County Medical Center (1989-1993); Founder, President, East-View Foundation (1992); Vice Dean, New York Medical College; Fellow, American College of Surgeons **Civic:** Endowment of Thelma Bilik Reed Carrel, Uris Library, Cornell University; Endowment of George E. Reed Chair of Writing and Rhetoric, Cornell University; Endowment of Elizabeth Reed Fund for Rare Books and Manuscripts, Cornell University; Endowment of Chair of Pediatric Cardiac Surgery, School of Medicine, New York University; Endowment of John H. Mulholland Fellowship in Surgery, Langone/NYU College of Medicine; Cardiac Surgeon for the Bellevue Thursday Night Cardiac Clinic and Irvington House, Both Icons of Cardiac Care at the Time, and Available to Anyone Who Could Not Afford Private Medical Care of the Loss of Wages **Military Service:** Honorably Separated as Captain, AUS, 5th Army, Veterinary Corp. (1947); Enlisted as a Private, AUS, U.S. Army (1944) **Creative Works:** Reviewer, Editorial Board, Asian Cardiovascular Annals; Editorial Consultant, Cardiovascular Reviews and Reports; Section Editor, Heart Disease; Editor, Section of Surgery, Heart and Health Reports; Advisory Board, American Heart Journal; Reviewer, American Journal of Cardiology; Reviewer, Annals of Thoracic Surgery; Reviewer, Artificial Organs **Memberships:** Founding Member, North American Society of Pacing and Electrophysiology; Founding Member, American Trauma Society; Founding Member, Heart Rhythm Society; Founding Member, International Association for Cardiac Biological Implants; Founding Member, American Trauma Society; American College of Cardiology; International Society for Artificial Internal Organs; International Association of Cardiac Biological Implants; Society of Thoracic Surgeons; American Association for Thoracic Surgery; Harvey Society; American Trudeau Society; Alpha Omega Alpha; American College of Cardiology; American College of Surgeons; American Association for Thoracic Surgery; American Heart Association; American Society for Artificial Internal Organs; International Study Group for Research in Cardiac Metabolism; New York Society for Cardiovascular Surgery; New York Society for Thoracic Surgery **Marquis Who's Who Honors:** Albert Nelson Marquis Lifetime Achievement Award; Marquis Who's Who Top Professional; Marquis Who's Who Humanitarian Award **Why did you become involved in your profession or industry:** Dr. Reed became involved in his profession because he was raised by the belief that he needed to pay it forward and make contributions to the community. He ultimately decided that this track was the most rewarding way in which he could do that. **Avocations:** Woodworking (Furniture); Landscape design **Thoughts on Life:** As an undergraduate at Cornell, Dr. Reed tutored in math, captained the Varsity Fencing Team, and won the Intracollegiate 3-Weapon Championship for three consecutive years, thereby retiring the Iron Man Trophy. He was the instructor and coach for the women's fencing program for two years after Coach Cointe left to join the Free French Army in World War II. He involved himself in World War II by rejecting his draft deferment in 1944 to join the U.S. Army as a Private. He was separated in 1947 as a Captain, AUS, after having developed a very successful school for training veterinary technicians in the 5th Army.

William Piper Reed Jr., MD, FACS

Title: Emeritus Professor **Industry:** Medicine & Health Care **Date of Birth:** 05/24/1942 **Place of Birth:** Melrose **State/Country of Origin:** MA/USA **Parents:** William Piper Reed; Gertrude Harriett (Irons) Reed **Marital Status:** Married **Spouse Name:** Martine Francoise Valentine Billet (10/16/1963) **Children:** Antoinette Elsa Rose; Christopher LLewellyn **Education:** Diploma in Head and Neck Cancer Surgery, University of Paris-Sud, Paris, France (1977); Fellow in Surgical Oncology, Institut Gustave-Roussy, Villejuif (Paris) France (1976-1977); Residency in General Surgery, Stanford University Medical Center, Stanford, CA (1968-1970, 1972-1976); MD, Harvard Medical School, Boston, MA (1968); AB, Harvard College, Cambridge, MA (1964) **Certifications:** Licensure, State of New York (1999), Commonwealth of Massachusetts (1986), State of Maryland (1978), State of California (1969); Diplomate, American Board of Surgery; Diplomate, National Board Of Medical Examiners **Career:** Professor, Department of Surgery, State University of New York at Stony Brook (2001-Present); Chairman, Department of Surgery, Winthrop University Hospital, Mineola, NY (2000-2013); Professor, Department of Surgery, Tufts University School of Medicine, Boston, MA (1992-2000); Director, Surgical Oncology, Baystate Medical Center, Springfield, MA (1986-2000); Associate Professor, Department of Surgery, Tufts University School of Medicine, Boston, MA (1986-1992); Associate Professor, Department of Surgery, Surgical Oncology Program, University of Maryland, Baltimore, MD (1983-1986); Assistant Professor, General Surgery, University of Maryland, Baltimore, MD (1978-1981) **Career Related:** Program Surveyor, Commission on Cancer, American College of Surgeons (2000-Present); Leadership Group, Commission on Cancer, American College of Surgeons (2004, 2009, 2012); Accreditation Chair, Commission on Cancer, American College of Surgeons (1999-2009); Program Review Subcommittee of the Committee on Approvals, Commission on Cancer, American College of Surgeons (2001-2004); State Chair for Massachusetts, Cancer Liaison Program, Commission on Cancer, American College of Surgeons (1997-2000); Chairman, Promotion Committee, Tufts University School of Medicine (1997-1998); Medical Vice President, Springfield Unit, American Cancer Society (1987-1993); Co-Principal Investigator, National Surgical Adjuvant Breast & Bowel Project, Baystate Medical Center (1986-2000); NIH Fellowship (1968) **Civic:** Board of Directors, American Cancer Society, Massachusetts (1989-Present); Conservation Commissioner, Longmeadow, MA (1989-1995); President of Local Chapter, State Board, American Cancer Society, Maryland and Massachusetts **Military Service:** Captain, Commanding Officer, Company D, U.S. Army, Vietnam (1970-1972, Honorably Discharged); Bronze Star with Oak Lead Cluster (1971) **Creative Works:** Reviewer, Annals of Surgical Oncology (2011); Reviewer, European Journal of Gastroenterology & Hepatology (2007); Reviewer, World Journal of Surgery (2006); Reviewer, Surgical Endoscopy (1992); Reviewer, Artificial Organs (1989-1995); Contributor, Articles to Professional Journals, Chapters to Books and Textbooks; Contributor, Numerous Bibliography Papers **Awards:** Healing Hero, Nassau County Legislative Citation, Breast Cancer Summit (2011); Surgery Attending of the Year, SUNY Stony Brook (2003); The Best Doctors in America, New York Region (2002); The Best Doctors in America, Northeast Region (1996); Life Saver Award, Massachusetts Division, American Cancer Society (1994); Margery Sadowski Memorial Cancer Foundation Award (1988); Golden Apple Award (1988); American Cancer Society Grant, Maryland Division (1983-1985); National Institutes of Health Training Grant (1973-1975); National Institutes of Health Fellowship (1969-1970); Preceptorship in Anesthesiology Awarded by the American Society of Anesthesiology, Lahey Clinic Foundation, Boston, MA (1966) **Memberships:** American Society of Breast Surgeons (2007-Present); Fellow, American College of Surgeons (2000-Present); New York Surgical Society (2001-Present); New England Surgical Society (1989-Present); Society of University Surgeons (1987-Present); Society of Surgical Oncology (1982-Present); American College of Surgeons (1981-Present); American Hernia Society (2007-2013) **Marquis Who's Who Honors:** Albert Nelson Marquis Lifetime Achievement Award; Marquis Who's Who Top Professional **Avocations:** Opera; Hiking; Solar eclipses; Reading American history books **Thoughts on Life:** Dr. Reed's current professional activities carry him around the country to survey cancer centers and breast programs on behalf of the American College of Surgeons. This has given him a chance to follow a good portion of the route taken by Lewis and Clark on the Corps of Discovery Expedition and to visit many of the battlefields of the American Revolution. Growing up in the Boston area, he was already familiar with Lexington, Concord and Bunker Hill, but the crucial battles in the Carolinas got short shrift. He has also been attending opera at the Met for some 30 years and enjoy symphony as well. On a more exotic level, he and his wife Martine have been chasing solar eclipses since 1999. This has taken them to Germany, Turkey, China, Australia, Wyoming and most recently to Chile. The most adventurous trip was to Western Mongolia in 2008, which involved a three-hour plane ride from Ulan Bator (where he paid a house call on one of his patients) followed by an eight-hour jeep trip over dirt roads.

Terry Dalton "Tiger" Rees, DDS, MSD

Title: Professor Emeritus **Industry:** Education/Educational Services **Company Name:** Texas A&M University College of Dentistry **Date of Birth:** 08/27/1934 **Place of Birth:** Hattiesburg **State/Country of Origin:** MS/USA **Parents:** John Lacy Rees; Myrna Gay Rees **Marital Status:** Married **Spouse Name:** Greta **Children:** Mark; David; William (Deceased); Matthew; Mary; Benjamin **Education:** MSD, Brooke Army Medical Center, College of Dentistry, Baylor University (1966-1969); DDS, College of Dentistry, The University of Tennessee Health Science Center (1957) **Certifications:** Licensed Dentist, State of Oregon (1980-Present); Diplomate, The American Board of Oral Medicine (1985); Diplomate, The American Board of Periodontology (1975); Certificate in Periodontology (1969); Certification of Completion, Army Medical Career Course, Medical Field Service School, Brooke Army Medical Center, Fort Sam Houston, Texas (1963-1964); Certificate of Completion in Advanced Dentistry, United States Army Institute of Dental Research, Walter Reed Army Medical Center (1961-1962) **Career:** Professor Emeritus, College of Dentistry, Texas A&M University (2017-Present); Professor of Periodontics, College of Dentistry, Texas A&M University (1984-2017); Chairman, Professor, Director, Stomatology Center, College of Dentistry, Texas A&M University **Career Related:** Consultant, Committee on Scientific Affairs, American Dental Association (2004-2017); Member, Board of Directors, American Academy of Periodontology Foundation (2010-2016); Consultant, American Board of Dental Examiners (2006-2014); Chair, American Board of Periodontology (2002-2003); Chair, Southwest Society of Periodontists (1991-1992) **Military Service:** Dentist, U.S. Army (1957-1984) **Creative Works:** Author, Contributor, More Than 300 Scientific Publications; Author, Contributor, More Than 450 Invited Lecture Presentations; Reviewer, 19 Peer-Reviewed Journals; Consultant, Two Professional Journals, Eight Organizations; Participant, Contributor, Numerous State, National and International Workshops **Awards:** Outstanding Periodontal Educator Award, American Academy of Periodontology (2013); Fellowship, International College of Dentists (2007); Fellowship, American Academy of Periodontology (2001); Gies Award for Contributions to Periodontology, American Dental Association (2001); Fellowship, American College of Dentists (1987); Named, Extraordinary Professor of Graduate Periodontics, Universidad Autónoma de Nuevo León (1987); Geriatric Dental Health Award, American Dental Association (1985); Fairbanks Medal (1964) **Memberships:** Member, Co-Founder, International Oral Lichen Planus Support Group (1996-Present); Member, 13 Dental Organizations **Marquis Who's Who Honors:** Marquis Who's Who Top Professional (2021) **To what do you attribute your success:** Dr. Rees attributes his success to the people that influenced him during the early years in his life. His mentor, Dr. William Hurt, was very interested in oral medicine and taught him a great deal about it. **Why did you become involved in your profession or industry:** Dr. Rees became involved in his profession because when he was in high school, a physician and a dentist came to speak to one of his classes. The dentist impressed him the most because he wasn't going to spend his entire life with patients. He was able to have a personal life as well as a career. As far as periodontics is concerned, he was influenced by a number of factors. He liked all aspects of periodontal therapy and he wanted all patients to understand the gingival disease processes and the individuals' role in its management. **Avocations:** Spending time with family; Traveling; Liaising with graduate students **Religion:** Presbyterian

Joy Harriman Reilly, PhD

Title: Associate Professor Emeritus **Industry:** Education/Educational Services **Company Name:** Ohio State University **Date of Birth:** 05/17/1942 **Place of Birth:** Dublin, Ireland **State/Country of Origin:** Ireland **Parents:** Rene William; Sybil Mary (MacGowan) Harriman **Marital Status:** Married **Spouse Name:** Richard Reilly (06/23/1978) **Children:** Patrick Harriman **Education:** Doctor of Philosophy, Ohio State University (1984); Master of Arts, Ohio State University (1979); Bachelor of Fine Arts, Ohio State University (1977) **Career:** Associate Professor Emeritus, Ohio State University, Columbus, OH (1985-Present); Part-time, The Newark Advocate, Newark, OH (1973-1980); Copy Editor, Journalist, The Newark Advocate, Newark, OH (1970-1983); Assistant, Radio-TV Production, J. Walter Thompson Advertising, London and Frankfurt (1962-1967); Intern, The Times, London, England (1961-1962) **Career Related:** Theater Critic, Station Wosu Radio, Columbus, OH (1979-Present); Presenter, Disney Institute, Orlando, FL (1999); Presenter, First National Festival Senior Theater (1993, 1995); Presenter. Papers, Dublin Eire (1992); Presenter, First International Festival Senior Adult Theater, Cologne, Germany (1991); Presenter. Papers, Association For Theater In Higher Education, Multiple Cities including New York, Chicago, Seattle, Atlanta, Philadelphia, San Francisco and San Antonio (1989-1998); Presenter. Papers, International Foundation For Theater Research, Stockholm, Sweden (1989); Founding Artistic Director, Grandparents Living Theater, Columbus, OH (1984) **Civic:** Commissioner, Upper Arlington Arts Council, OH (1987) **Creative Works:** Author, Play, "I've Almost Got the Hang of It" (1998); Author, Play, "Woman" (1995); Author, Play, "A Picket Fence, Two Kids and a Dog Named Spot" (1993); Author, Play, "I Was Young, Now I'm Wonderful!"(1991); Author, Play, "Golden Age is All the Rage" (1989); Author, Book Chapter, "Olga Nethersole's Sapho" (1989); Author, Play, "A Grandparent's Scrapbook" (1986) **Awards:** Golden Achievement Award, Doctors Hospital (1997); Battelle Endowment for Technology and Human Affairs Grantee (1994); Distinguished Teaching Award, Ohio State University (1994); Living Faith Award, Columbus Metropolitan Area Church Council (1992); Outstanding Achievement in Theater Award Ohio Theater Alliance (1991); Woman of Achievement Award, YWCA (1991); Ohioana Citation, Ohioana Library Association (1989); Columbus Mayor's Award For Volunteer Services In Arts (1986) **Memberships:** American Theater Association; American Society for Theater Research; International Federation for Theater Research; Association for Theater in Higher Education; Ohio Theater Alliance **Marquis Who's Who Honors:** Albert Nelson Marquis Lifetime Achievement Award; Marquis Who's Who Top Professional **Why did you become involved in your profession or industry:** Dr. Reilly initially aspired to become involved in a career path where she could exercise his creative impulses. After graduating, she was asked to teach at the school, and decided to implement her interests, like comedy improvisation, into her teaching. Not only did Dr. Reilly enjoy the work, her students did as well. After receiving awards for her unique teaching style, Dr. Reilly continued the path.Additionally, Dr. Reilly started working at the Times newspaper in London as an intern. A year later, she was employed by an advertising agency creating commercials, which dispatched her to Germany to learn more about creating TV commercials that ran between 60 and 30 seconds. **Avocations:** Playwriting; Gardening; Reading; Theater **Religion:** Roman Catholic

Katalin Reimann, MA

Title: President **Industry:** Health, Wellness and Fitness **Company Name:** Method Aesthetics & Wellness Spa **State/Country of Origin:** Hungary **Marital Status:** Married **Education:** Degree in Dermatology and Nutrition, Medizinische Berufsfachschule Dresden (1984); Jozsef Attila Gimnazium-Szekesfehervar (1976) **Certifications:** Transition Lifestyle and Wellness Coach **Career:** Owner, Method Aesthetics & Wellness (2012-Present); Owner, Aesthetics and Wellness (2012-2014); Coach, Peak Potentials (2007-2009); Coach Peak Potentials (2007-2009); Owner, Golden Spoon Spa (1999-2009); Participant, Landmark Education (1997-2004); Owner, Spa New Life, Spa Results (1989-1995) **Career Related:** Teaching, Aesthetics and Nutrition **Civic:** Volunteer, Constant Contact **Memberships:** American Academy of Anti-Aging Medicine; NASTO

William John Reinke

Title: Lawyer (Retired) **Industry:** Law and Legal Services **Date of Birth:** 08/07/1930 **Place of Birth:** South Bend **State/Country of Origin:** IN/USA **Parents:** William August Reinke; Eva Marie (Hein) Reinke **Marital Status:** Married **Spouse Name:** Elizabeth Beck Lockwood (1991); Sue Carol Colvin (1951, Divorced 1988) **Children:** Sally Sue Taelman; William A. Reinke II; Andrew J. Reinke **Education:** JD, The University of Chicago (1955); AB, Wabash College, Cum Laude (1952) **Career:** Of Counsel, Barnes & Thornburg and Predecessors (1996); Partner, Barnes & Thornburg and Predecessors (1961-1996); Associate, Barnes & Thornburg and Predecessors, South Bend, IN (1957-1996); Former Chairman, Compensation Committee, Management Committee, Barnes & Thornburg and Predecessors **Career Related:** Member, Management Committee, Barnes & Thornburg and Predecessors **Civic:** Life Member, Advisory Board, The Salvation Army USA (1973-Present); Trustee, First Methodist Church (1976-1970, 2005-2007); Board of Directors, South Bend Civic Theatre (1997-2003); President, National Association for Bilingual Education (NABE), Michigan Chapter (1993-1994); Board of Directors, National Association for Bilingual Education (NABE), Michigan Chapter (1990-1994); President, The Salvation Army USA (1990-1992); Board of Directors, United Way (1979-1981); Board of Directors, Isaac Walton League (1970-1981); President, Stanley Clark School (1977-1980); Trustee, The Stanley Clark School (1969-1980); President, South Bend Round Table (1963-1965) **Military Service:** Sergeant, United States Fifth Army Headquarters, Chicago, IL (1955-1957) **Creative Works:** Author, "A Hoosier Trial Lawyer's Notebook" (2019) **Awards:** Wabash College Richard O. Ristine Award (2018); Life Patron Fellow, St. Joseph County Bar Foundation (2018); Boss of the Year Award (1979); Named South Bend Outstanding Young Man of the Year (1961); Outstanding Local President Award, Indiana Jaycees (1960-1961) **Memberships:** Board of Directors, Rotary International (1970-1973, 1994-1997); Member, Management Planning Unit, United States Fifth Army Headquarters, Chicago, IL (1955-1957); Lifetime Member, Board Director, The Salvation Army USA; ABA; Indiana State Bar Association; St. Joseph County Bar Association; Patron Fellow, Indiana State Bar Foundation; American Judicature Society; Founders Committee, Summit Club **Bar Admissions:** Indiana (1955) **Marquis Who's Who Honors:** Albert Nelson Marquis Lifetime Achievement Award; Marquis Who's Who Top Professional **To what do you attribute your success:** Mr. Reinke attributes his success to following the admonition of Winston Churchill to never give up, as well as thinking and writing on a constant basis. **Why did you become involved in your profession or industry:** When Mr. Reinke was in college, the dean of his school, Bryon Trippett, taught a course called English Institutional History. One of the things he learned was the institution of law, and he saw that lawyers were the center of everything. So he said to himself "If I'm going to go through this life once, then I want to be in the center of the action" and he went into law. **Avocations:** Photography; Golf **Political Affiliations:** Republican **Religion:** Methodist

John F. Reintjes, PhD

Title: Senior Research Physicist **Industry:** Sciences **Company Name:** KeyW Corp **Parents:** J. Francis; Elizabeth **Marital Status:** Married **Spouse Name:** Maura **Children:** Christopher **Education:** Doctor of Philosophy, Harvard University (1972); Bachelor of Science, Massachusetts Institute of Technology (1966) **Career:** Full Time Research Physicist, KeyW Corp (2007-Present); Research Physicist, US Naval Research Laboratory, Washington (1973-2007); Lecturer, Catholic University (1984-1992); Postdoctoral Fellow, IBM Watson Research Center, Yorktown Heights, NY (1971-1973) **Creative Works:** Author, Nonlinear Optical Parametric (1984); Holder, 24 Patents; Contributor, Papers to Scientific Journals **Awards:** Presidential Rank Award, Meritorious Senior Professional (2003); Recipient, Meritorious Civilian Service Award (1985) **Memberships:** Chapter President, Sigma Xi (1985-1986); Chapter Secretary, Sigma Xi (1982-1984); Fellow, Optical Society America; Washington Academy of Sciences; American Physical Society **Marquis Who's Who Honors:** Albert Nelson Marquis Lifetime Achievement Award; Marquis Who's Who Top Professional **To what do you attribute your success:** Dr. Reintjes attributes his success to a mixture of talent and serendipity, as well as having the benefit of several mentors. **Why did you become involved in your profession or industry:** Mr. Reintjes became involved in his profession because he was fascinated with the subject of research. He also enjoyed the issues problem solving, as well as developing an understanding of various issues. **Avocations:** House maintenance; Travel; Photography

Noel Reitmeister, PhD

Title: Certified Financial Planner **Industry:** Financial Services **Company Name:** Wachovia Securities, LLC (Now Wells Fargo Advisors, LLC) **Date of Birth:** 08/12/1938 **Place of Birth:** Brooklyn **State/Country of Origin:** NY/USA **Parents:** Morris G. Reitmeister; Anna (Miller) Reitmeister **Marital Status:** Married **Spouse Name:** Elaine Schendelman (09/16/1961) **Children:** Gregg Allen; Stephen Michael **Education:** PhD, American Western University (1982); Degree in Financial Planning, College of Financial Planning, Denver, CO (1974); Diploma, New York Institute of Finance (1969); MBA in Industrial Psychology and Management, Erikson School, Baruch College (1969); BA in Economics and Political Science, Queens College, CUNY (1960); Honorary Diploma in Math and Science, Stuyvesant High School **Certifications:** Registered Investment Advisory Representative (IAR); Licensed in Investments, Commodities and Futures, Options **Career:** Certified Financial Planner, A.G. Edwards & Sons, Inc. (1992-Present); Financial Adviser, Senior Vice President, Investment Officer, Wachovia Securities, LLC (Now Wells Fargo Advisors, LLC) (2007-2009); Senior Vice President of Investments, A.G. Edwards & Sons, Inc. (1999-2007); Senior Vice President, Investment Officer, Wells Fargo Advisors, LLC (1999); Wells Fargo Advisors, LLC (1992-2016); Vice President of Investments, A.G. Edwards & Sons, Inc. (1979-1999); Senior Financial Consultant, A.G. Edwards & Sons, Inc. (1974-1979); Accountant Executive, Branch Coordinator, Special Partner, DuPont Walston (1969-1974); Insurance and Investment Consultant, John Hancock (1968-1969); Project Director of Advertising Research, Toni Division, Gillette Company (1967-1968); Regional Manager, Cosmair Division, L'Oréal, Paris, France (1963-1967); Associate Merchandise Manager, Bloomingdale's, New York, NY (1962-1963) **Career Related:** Commerce Point, LLC (2004-2010); Hearings Officer (2000-2002); Committee to Design Exam Questions, Board Professional Review (2000); Examination Criteria Committee (1999); American Medical News Journal, The Times (1996-2008); Adjunct Faculty in Finance, Purdue University (1992-1997); C.B. Geigy Pharmaceutical (1991-1993); Anglo American Productions (1987-1998); Ford Motor Co. (1987-1991); Conducted Roundtable at Advanced Conference on Retirement Planning, Washington, DC (1986); Columnist, Daily Southtown Star (1984-1986); Inland Steel (1983-1994); Rollingbrook Properties, LLC (1983-1992); Adjunct Professor, Finance Executive, LTV (1982-1992); Nora Associates (1981-2000) **Civic:** Sinai Veterans of Foreign Wars (2010-Present); Chicago Sinai Congregation (2008-Present); Jewish War Veterans (1971-Present); Chair, Vice President, Pet Committee (2008-2009); Kol Ami, Chicago, IL (2006-2008); Chair of Pet Committee, Pinnacle Condominium Association (2006-2008); House Committee, Pinnacle Condominium Association (2006-2007); Chairman of Marketing Committee, Executive Committee, Planning Committee, Pinnacle Condominium Association (2004-2009); Board Member, Illinois Philharmonic Orchestra (2002-2015); Director, Visiting Nurse Association of Northwest Indiana (2000-2002); Financial Committee, Executive Committee, Visiting Nurse Association of Northwest Indiana (1992-2005); Temple's Endowment Committee, Visiting Nurse Association of Northwest Indiana (1992-2001); Director, Visiting Nurse Association of Northwest Indiana (1992-1998); Development Committee, Chairman, By-Laws Committee, Executive Committee, Co-Chairman, Northwest Indiana Public Broadcasting WYIN (1992-1998) **Military Service:** 197th U.S. Army Security Agency Company, Fort Dix, Fort Devens, Fort Hamilton, and Fort Drum (2005-2008); Northwest Staff Sergeant, U.S. Army (1960-1965) **Creative Works:** Producer, "Market Crisis of October," Public Broadcasting Service (1987); Producer, Host, "Money Doctor" (1985-1994); Author, "Portfolios, Inc. Key Objectives in Investments"; Co-Author, "Retirement Planning for College Finance Planning"; Contributor, Articles, Professional Journals **Awards:** Man of the Year Award, Jewish Federation of Chicago (2005); Appointed, Colonel on Staff, Governor of Kentucky (1988); Honoree, Man of the Year, B'nai B'rith International (1986); Excellence Award, National Association of Accountants (1985); Decorated, Order of William Tell, Switzerland **Memberships:** Ambassador, Illiana Society, Institute for Certified Financial Planners (1997-Present); Chairman, Illiana Society, Institute for Certified Financial Planners (1993-1997); Founder, Illiana Society, Institute for Certified Financial Planners (1985-1993); Charterer, Registry for Financial Planning Practitioners (1983-1995); Chicago Association of Financial Planners (1973-1978); President, Chicago Association of Financial Planners (1975); President of Pledge Class, Zeta Beta Tau (1956-1957); Social Chairman, Zeta Beta Tau (1956-1957); National President of Beta Chapter, Delta Omega Kappa (1955-1960) **Marquis Who's Who Honors:** Albert Nelson Marquis Lifetime Achievement Award; Marquis Who's Who Humanitarian Award **Why did you become involved in your profession or industry:** Dr. Reitmeister became involved in his profession because he always had an interest in economics and finance. **Avocations:** Taking classes at the university; Spending time with his family and friends

William Childs Rense, PhD

Title: Geography Educator (Retired) **Industry:** Education/Educational Services **Company Name:** Shippensburg University **Date of Birth:** 09/02/1944 **Place of Birth:** Baton Rouge **State/Country of Origin:** LA/USA **Parents:** William Alphonsus Rense; Wanda Evelyn (Childs) Rense **Marital Status:** Single **Education:** PhD in Physical Geography, Oregon State University (1974); MA, University of Southwestern Louisiana (1969); BA, University of Southwestern Louisiana (1967) **Career:** Retired (2004); Professor, Geography and Earth Science, Shippensburg University, Pennsylvania (1980-2004); Assistant Professor, University of Southwestern Louisiana, Lafayette, LA (1973-1980); Instructor, University of Southwestern Louisiana, Lafayette, LA (1968-1970) **Creative Works:** Author, Numerous Papers in Field; Contributor, Article, World Book Encyclopedia **Memberships:** American Association of Geographers; American Water Resources Association; Pennsylvania Geographical Society; Rocky Mountain Hydrologic Research Center **Marquis Who's Who Honors:** Albert Nelson Marquis Lifetime Achievement Award; Marquis Who's Who Top Professional **Why did you become involved in your profession or industry:** Dr. Rense's father was a professor, he grew up in highly educational environment. He started weather as a hobby, his earliest childhood memories started out with weather factors. Climatology is one of the things that he specialized in when he was working on his college degree. He also had an interest in physical geography and hydrology as a child. He thinks that he subconsciously knew that he would go into education. When he started moving toward education he realized that his talents dealt with young adults rather than younger kids, college level. He would not be effective in high school or grade school and that he needed to deal with college level people this was an assessment of his own abilities. **Avocations:** Traveling (Alaska, Hawaii, Munich, Paris, etc.); Opera; Opera festival

John A. Repicci, DDS, MD

Title: Doctor (Retired) **Industry:** Medicine & Health Care **Date of Birth:** 12/29/1936 **Marital Status:** Married **Spouse Name:** Lorey Huber Repicci (1962) **Children:** Thomas; Cindy; Julie **Education:** MD, State University of New York at Buffalo, NY (1963); DDS, State University of New York at Buffalo (1960) **Certifications:** Board Certified, American Board of Orthopedics (1971) **Career:** Retired (2019); Residency in Orthopedics, Buffalo Veterans Administration (1968-1969); Residency in Orthopedics, Buffalo Children's Hospital (1967-1968); Residency in Orthopedics, Buffalo General Hospital (1965-1967); Residency in General Surgery, Buffalo Veterans Administration (1964-1965); Rotating Intern, Buffalo General Hospital (1963-1964); Clinical Instructor in Surgery, State University of New York at Buffalo; Active Staff, Kenmore Mercy Hospital; Active Staff, Sisters of Charity Hospital; Active Staff, Buffalo General Hospital; Active Staff, Erie County Medical Center **Career Related:** More than 120 Presentations on Surgical Procedures both Domestically and Internationally (1987-2009); Presenter, Lectures on The Repicci II Unicondylar Knee System, University of New Jersey, University of New London, State University of New York at Buffalo, University of Texas, University of Rochester, University of Gottenberg, University of Texas, University of Gottingen, University of California Irvine, University of Louisville Kentucky, Unicondylar Knee International Symposium, Charnley ERA Meeting, University of Arkansas for Medical Sciences (1992-1998); Consultant, Biomet Company, MAKO Surgical Corp. **Creative Works:** Co-Author, "Minimally Invasive in Orthopedics; Unicondylar Arthroplasty: Bone Sparing Technique" (2009); Co-Author, "Minimally Invasive Unicondylar Knee Arthroplasty for the Treatment of Unicompartmental Osteoarthritis: an Out-patient Arthritic Bypass Procedure (2004); Co-Author, "Unicondylar Knee Surgery, Development of the Minimally Invasive Surgical Approach" (2004); Author, "Minimally Invasive Knee Unicompartmental Arthroplasty: Bone-Sparing Technique," Surgical Technology International XI (2003); Co-Author, "Unicondylar Arthroplasty: My Technique and Early Discharge" (2003); Co-Author, "Unicondylar Knee Replacement: The American Experience" (2003); Co-Author, "Technical Aspects of Medial Versus Lateral Minimally Invasive Unicondylar Arthroplasty" (2003); Co-Author, "Total Knee or Uni? Benefits and limitations of the unicondylar Knee Prosthesis" (2003); Co-Author, "Mini-Invasive Knee Unicompartmental Arthroplasty: Bone Sparing Technique" (2003); Co-Author, "Minimally Invasive Unicondylar Knee Arthroplasty: Eight-Year Follow-Up" (2002); Co-Author, "Tracing The Evolution Unicondylar Arthroplasty" (2000); Co-Author, "A Minimally Invasive Surgical Technique for Unicondylar Knee Arthroplasty" (1999); Producer, Video, "The Repicci II Unicondylar Knee Program" (1999); Author, "Repicci II Unicondylar Program" (1998); Contributor, The Journal of Bone and Joint Surgery (1997); Author, "Repicci II Unicondylar Program - A Unique Approach to the Treatment of Unicondylar Osteoarthritis" (1995); Author, "Anatomic Articular Reconstructive Surgery System" (1992); Co-Author, "Unicondylar Minimally Invasive Approach to Knee Arthritis"; Co-Author, Chapter, "Unicondylar Knee Replacement: The American Experience," "Management of Osteoarthritis of the Knee: An International Consensus," American Academy of Orthopaedic Surgeons **Awards:** Inventor of the Year Award, City of Buffalo, NY (2003) **Marquis Who's Who Honors:** Marquis Who's Who Top Professional **To what do you attribute your success:** Mr. Repicci attributes his success to the fact that he always enjoyed mechanical arts. His professions required a great deal of mechanical art, which made him enthusiastic and led him to find genuine enjoyment in his work. **Why did you become involved in your profession or industry:** Mr. Repicci originally enrolled in medical school. It was common for dentists to transition into plastic surgery, so when he finished his medical degree, that is what he planned to do. However, after some experience in dental school, he realized that some techniques overlapped with orthopedics, so he transitioned into that field instead. **Avocations:** Farming; Spending time with family

Juliana T. Rhoten

Title: Principal (Retired) **Industry:** Education/Educational Services **Company Name:** Parkview School, Milwaukee Public Schools **Place of Birth:** Manhattan **State/Country of Origin:** NY/USA **Parents:** Julius Joseph Bastian; Gladys Maude (Grant) Bastian (Deceased) **Marital Status:** Widowed **Spouse Name:** Marion Rhoten (08/07/1956, Deceased 1990) **Children:** Don Carlos Rhoten **Education:** EdS, University of Wisconsin-Milwaukee (1977); MS, Hunter College (1956); BA, Hunter College (1954) **Career:** Principal, Parkview School, Milwaukee Public Schools, Milwaukee, WI (1983-1990); Principal, Ninth St. School, Milwaukee, WI (1980-1983); Assistant Principal, 21st Street School and Clarke Street School (1977-1980); Administrator of Program, Radio Program, "The Sound House" (1974-1977); Visitor, Technical Assistance Program, Administrator, Milwaukee, WI (1971-1974); Reading Specialist, Milwaukee, WI (1965-1971); Teacher, Elementary Schools, Milwaukee, WI (1956-1965) **Civic:** Board of Directors, Eisenhower Group, Milwaukee, WI (1990-Present); Board of Directors, Eisenhower Center (1994) **Creative Works:** Contributor, Radio Program, "The Sound House" (1974-1977); Producer, Documentary Film, "You Wouldn't Believe it, But Here it Is" (1972) **Awards:** Golden Soror, Alpha Kappa Alpha Sorority, Incorporated **Memberships:** Alpha Kappa Alpha Sorority, Incorporated (1954-Present); Association for Supervision and Curriculum Development (ASCD); Administrators & Supervisors Council; National Council of Teachers of English (NCTE); National Association of Elementary School Principals; International Reading Association; Phi Delta Kappa (PDK International); Retired Administrators Association **Marquis Who's Who Honors:** Albert Nelson Marquis Lifetime Achievement Award; Marquis Who's Who Humanitarian Award **Why did you become involved in your profession or industry:** Mrs. Rhoten attended Catholic school from first grade and she always enjoyed reading and going to school. Her mother passed away when she was in high school, but she still enjoyed going to school every day. She never missed a single day of high school and was never late or absent through all the years. In college, Mrs. Rhoten joined the sorority Alpha Kappa Alpha. Education has been a very strong value for her since childhood. Mrs. Rhoten became a reading specialist while in New York and moved to Milwaukee, Wisconsin, when she got married. **Avocations:** Reading; Classical music; Traveling **Thoughts on Life:** Mrs. Rhoten was in the administrator position for the visitor technical assistance program in Milwaukee, Wisconsin, which included her doing a film. She made a documentary about the reading program because it was excellent at that time. Mrs. Rhoten also brought in visitors from the surrounding states to look at the film and then decide on a program. When they came, she would take them around to the various programs that they wanted to look at and allow them time to spend time looking at the programs. They would return to their home districts from which they came, which was around the surrounding states, such as Minnesota, Iowa, and places like that, with the information. The whole idea was for them to look at the programs to see if they wanted to use them in their districts. Mrs. Rhoten did that from 1971 to 1974. From 1977 to 1980, Mrs. Rhoten worked with teachers who went into the homes of parents of kindergarten-age children, and they helped the children get ready for school. Notably, she had a student that she taught in third grade and she still communicates with her every Christmas. When on a trip to Rome, she once shook hands with Pope John Paul II.

Denis Timlin Rice, JD

Title: Senior Counsel **Industry:** Law and Legal Services **Company Name:** Arnold & Porter LLP **Date of Birth:** 07/11/1932 **Place of Birth:** Milwaukee **State/Country of Origin:** WI/USA **Parents:** Cyrus Francis Rice; Kathleen (Timlin) Rice **Marital Status:** Married **Spouse Name:** Pamela Stefania Rice (05/08/2007) **Children:** James Connelly; Tracy Ellen **Education:** Doctor of Jurisprudence, University of Michigan (1959); Bachelor of Arts in Public and International Affairs, Princeton University (1954) **Career:** Senior Counsel, Arnold & Porter LLP (2012-Present); Principal, Howard, Rice, Nemerovski, Canady, Falk & Rabkin (1964-2012); Associate, Howard & Prim (1961-1963); Associate, Pillsbury, Madison & Sutro (1959-1961) **Career Related:** Board of Directors, Ironstone Group Inc. (2016); Managing Committee, San Francisco Institute of Financial Services (1983-1992) **Civic:** Board of Directors, Planning and Conservation League (1981-2006); President, Digital Village Foundation (1997-2001); Board of Directors, Digital Village Foundation (1995-2001); Board of Directors, Marin Conservation League (1995-2000); Board of Directors, Marin Theatre Co. (1987-1997); Board of Directors, Marin Symphony (1984-1992); Member, Metropolitan Transportation Commission (1980-1988); Member, San Francisco Bay Conservation and Development Commission (1977-1983); Chairman, Marin County Transit District (1979-1981); Director, Marin County Transit District (1977-1981); Commissioner, Marin Housing Authority (1977-1981); Director, Marin County Transit District (1970-1972); Mayor, City of Tiburon, California (1970-1972); Councilman, City of Tiburon, California (1968-1972); Member, Board of Visitors, University of Michigan Law School **Military Service:** First Lieutenant, Artillery Branch, United States Army (1955-1957) **Creative Works:** Contributor, Articles, Law Reviews; Presenter in Field **Awards:** Lifetime Achievement Award in Business Law, The State Bar of California (2012); Recipient Freedom Foundation Medal, U.S. Army (1956) **Memberships:** Board of Directors, ITechLaw (2002-2008); Vice Chairman, Securities Committee, Inter-Pacific Bar Association (2002-2006); Chair, Committee on Cyberspace Law, The State Bar of California (1997-2001); Chair, Committee on Administration Justice, The State Bar of California (1997-1998); Editor, The State Bar of California (1978-1980); Vice Chair, Section on Business Law, The State Bar of California (1978-1980); Fellow, American Bar Foundation; Federal Regulation of Securities Committee, American Bar Association; Chair, Asia-Pacific Business Law Committee, American Bar Association; Chairman, Subcommittee on International Venture Law, American Bar Association; San Francisco Bar Association; American Judicature Society; American Intellectual Property Law Association; South End Rowing Club; Tiburon Peninsula Club; Pacific-Union Club; The Olympic Club; Order of the Coif; The Phi Beta Kappa Society; The International Legal Honor Society of Phi Delta Phi **Bar Admissions:** Supreme Court of the United States (1963); State of California (1960) **Marquis Who's Who Honors:** Albert Nelson Marquis Lifetime Achievement Award; Marquis Who's Who Top Professional **To what do you attribute your success:** Mr. Rice attributes his success to his former partner, Henry Howard. When they established the Howard Rice Firm, Henry Howard had a wonderful personality and the ability to not stress about problems. Mr. Rice was inspired by the idea of stability and continuity in the law. **Why did you become involved in your profession or industry:** Mr. Rice first became involved in his profession due to his fascination with the law, particularly in how it was fashioned and interpreted. He has become committed to enshrining the legal system as an important fixture in a strong and progressive society. **Avocations:** Competitive swimming; Long distance swimming

Camala Richardson

Title: Attorney **Industry:** Law and Legal Services **Company Name:** Richardson Law **Education:** Doctor of Jurisprudence, University of Massachusetts School of Law (2012); Bachelor of Science in Marketing, Rochester Institute of Technology (1991); Diploma, Newark Senior High School (1987) **Certifications:** Trained, Mediation Works Incorporated (2007) **Career:** Owner, Attorney at Law, Private Practice (2012-Present); Account Specialist, AT&T (2005-2009); Emerging Markets, Cisco (1997-2005) **Civic:** Attorney Representing Children, Barnstable Probate and Family Court; Board of Directors, Women's Bar Association of Massachusetts; Pro Bono Attorney, We Can; Volunteer, Cape Cod Center for Women; Lawyer of the Day, Barnstable Probate and Family Court **Awards:** Nery Arrano Pro Bono Award, for Dedication for Representing Low Income Individuals Who are Survivors of Domestic Violence (2018); First Justices' Award for Pro Bono Publico Excellence; Dean Fellowship Award, Southern New England School of Law; Delta Theta Phi Award **Memberships:** Board of Directors, Women's Bar Association; Member, Barnstable Bar Association; Board of Directors, Falmouth Art Center; Member, Massachusetts Bar Association; Leadership Academy; Member, American Bar Association **To what do you attribute your success:** Ms. Richardson credits her success on her difficult upbringing, which taught her the value in hard work, as well as other lessons that she would leverage well into the future. **Why did you become involved in your profession or industry:** Ms. Richardson worked in software for almost 20 years and was doing well, but she eventually reached a point in her life where she realized that she was making companies like Cisco and AT&T millions of dollars, and that she wanted to do something that would help make the world a better place to live in. **Thoughts on Life:** Ms. Richardson is motivated by the saying; "If you want it, then you can achieve it." She greatly believes in the value of paying it forward.

Elisha Roscoe Richardson

Title: Dentist, Educator **Industry:** Medicine & Health Care **Date of Birth:** 08/15/1931 **Place of Birth:** Monroe **State/Country of Origin:** LA/USA **Parents:** Warren Carter Richardson; Hannah Mariah (Goins) Richardson **Marital Status:** Widower **Spouse Name:** Pattye Sue Whyte (05/28/1967) **Children:** Scott Carter; Jonathan Edward; Mark David **Education:** PhD in Human Growth & Development, University of Michigan (1988); MS, University of Illinois (1963); DDS, Meharry Medical College, Nashville, TN (1955); BS, Southern University, Baton Rouge, LA (1951) **Certifications:** American Board of Orthodontics **Career:** Dean, School of Dentistry, Meharry Medical College, Nashville, TN (1988); Professor, Chairman, Orthodontics, University of Colorado Health Science Center, Denver, CO (1985-1988); Associate Dean, School of Dentistry, Meharry Medical College (1977-1985); Professor, School of Dentistry, Meharry Medical College (1976-1985); Associate Professor, School of Dentistry, Meharry Medical College (1967-1976); Assistant Professor, Orthodontics, School of Dentistry, Meharry Medical College (1962-1967); United States Air Force Hospital, Wiesbaden, Germany; Chief of Clinic, Wiesbaden Air Force Base, Germany; United States Air Force Hospital, Wright-Patterson AFB **Career Related:** National Advancement Dental Research Council (Now National Institutes of Health) (1980-1984); President, Medical and Dental Staff, Hubbard Hospital, Meharry Medical College School of Dentistry (1971-1972); Consultant, VA Hospital, Nashville, TN (1968) **Military Service:** Served to Captain, Dental Corps, U.S. Air Force (1955-1960) **Creative Works:** Contributor, Articles, Profession Journals; Researcher, Three-Dimensional Longitude Study on Facial Growth **Awards:** Most Outstanding Sophomore Dental Student, Meharry Medical College **Memberships:** Chairman, Council of Education, American Association of Orthodontists (1987-Present); Secretary, Orthodontic Section, American Association of Dental Schools (1987-Present); President, National Dental Association (1981-Present); President, Craniofacial Biology Group, American Association of Dental Research (1978-1979); Chairman, American Association of Dental Schools (1972-1973); President, Nashville Section, International Association of Dental Research (1968-1972); President, Pan-Tenn. Dental Association (1968-1970); President, Capital City Dental Society (1964-1966); American Association for the Advancement of Science; American Dental Association; Craniofacial Biology Group; University of Illinois Orthodontics Alumni Association; American Omicron Kappa Upsilon; Kappa Sigma Pi; Beta Kappa Chi; Physiology Society of the Upper One-Tenth; NIH Research Fellow; Early Periodic Screening Diagnosis and Treatment Advisory Committee for Medicare and Medicaid-Dental Rep. for the State of Tennessee; College Advisory Council to the President; Budget and Finance Committee, Supreme Chapter, Omicron Kappa Upsilon National Honorary Dental Society; National Advisory Council for Dental Research; Councilor, Craniofacial Biology Group for IADR and AADP; Master's Theses Committee, University of Tennessee Health Sciences Center, Memphis, TN; Fellow, American College of Dentists; Diplomates of the American Board of Orthodontics **Marquis Who's Who Honors:** Albert Nelson Marquis Lifetime Achievement Award; Marquis Who's Who Top Professional **Why did you become involved in your profession or industry:** Dr. Richardson became involved in his profession because he did not have access to dental care while growing up. His decision to pursue orthodontics was also motivated by his drive to research the faces and teeth of African-American descent. **Religion:** Baptist

David W. Richerson

Title: Ceramic Engineer, Educator **Industry:** Engineering **Date of Birth:** 02/13/1944 **Place of Birth:** Llano **State/Country of Origin:** TX/USA **Parents:** James Walter Richerson; Viola Ruth (Nicholson) Richerson **Marital Status:** Married **Spouse Name:** Michael Anne Todd (09/06/1967) **Children:** Jennifer; Heather **Education:** Master of Science in Ceramic Science and Engineering, Pennsylvania State University, University Park, PA (1969); Bachelor of Science in Ceramic Science and Engineering, University of Utah, Salt Lake City, UT (1967) **Career:** Manager of Minerals, Natural History Museum of Utah (2010-Present); President, Richerson and Associates, Salt Lake City, UT (1991-Present); Co-Founder, Vice President, Advanced Energy Devices (1995-1999); Adjunct Associate Professor, University of Utah, Salt Lake City, UT (1991-2013); Vice President, Applied Technology, Ceramatec Inc. (1988); Director, Research and Development, Ceramatec Inc., Salt Lake City, UT (1985-1991); Adjunct Faculty, Arizona State University, Tempe, AZ (1979-1985); Senior Research Engineer, Supervisor, Advanced Materials, Garrett Turbine Engine Company, Phoenix, AZ (1973-1985); Research Engineer, Senior Research Engineer, Norton Company, Worcester, MA (1969-1973) **Career Related:** Member, Committee for Tribology of Ceramics, National Materials Advisory Board (1986-1987); Participant, Ceramic Technology Assessment, U.S. Congress (1985); Member, Committee on the Reliability of Ceramics for Heat Engine Applications, National Materials Advisory Board (1979); Instructor, Short Courses for the American Ceramic Society, American Institute of Chemical Engineers, Continuing Education Institute-Europe and ASM International; Lecturer in the Field **Civic:** Principal Investigator, Program Manager, Multiple STEM Education Outreach Projects for the 4th to 6th Grade Levels and at the University Level; Leader in Local Community Sustainability Task Force **Creative Works:** Co-Author, "Modern Ceramic Engineering" (1982, 1992, 2006, 2018); Author, "The Magic of Ceramics" (2000, 2011); Co-Designer, Co-Editor, Treatise, "Ceramic Gas Turbine Component Development and Characterization" (2003); Co-Designer, Co-Editor, Treatise, "Ceramic Gas Turbine Design and Test Experience" (2002); Co-Author, "Oxide Ceramics" (1985); Author, "Modern Engineering"; Author, "The Magic of Ceramics"; Patentee in the Field; Contributor, Numerous Articles to Professional Journals; Contributor, Numerous Chapters to Books **Awards:** Outstanding Service Award, University of Utah College of Engineering (2009); Admiral Earle Award for "Work in the Field of Ceramics," Worcester Engineering Society (1972) **Memberships:** American Ceramic Society Board of Directors (2000-2003); Chairman, Organizer, Arizona Section, Instructor of Short Courses, Chair, Education Committee, American Ceramic Society (1990-2002); National Institute of Ceramic Engineers; National Council on Education for the Ceramic Arts **Marquis Who's Who Honors:** Albert Nelson Marquis Lifetime Achievement Award; Marquis Who's Who Top Professional **Why did you become involved in your profession or industry:** Mr. Richerson became involved in his profession because, since he was a child, he was interested in rocks, minerals and fossils. His initial major in college was in mineralogy, but after his first year, he decided there were better opportunities in the field of ceramic science and engineering. **Avocations:** Writing; Tennis; Skiing; Mineralogy; Art; Volunteering

Jack Wayne Richeson

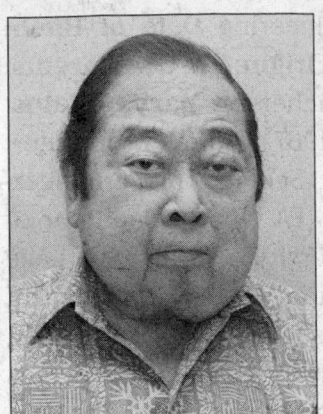

Title: Realtor **Industry:** Real Estate **State/Country of Origin:** Korea **Marital Status:** Married **Spouse Name:** Diane M. Richeson **Children:** One Son **Education:** BA in Accounting, University of Hawaii (1973) **Career:** Independent Realtor, Century 21, Prudential Locations, Electronic Realty Associates, Hawaii (Retired) **Awards:** Certified, Residential Broker; Certified, Residential Specialist; Broker in Charge **Memberships:** Emeritus Honolulu Board **To what do you attribute your success:** Mr. Richeson attributes his success to patience and sharing. He donated half of his commission to his trainees to help them get off their feet. Money has never been Mr. Richeson's top priority. He was always more concerned with his security, confidence, family, and other individuals who are close to him. **Why did you become involved in your profession or industry:** Mr. Richeson's adopted parents came from Indiana to Korea during the "Christian Movement." When they came to Korea, a lieutenant was trying to adopt him. As a child, Mr. Richeson was found naked in-between two snow banks by an army troop marching to get more ammunition. They recall a little girl standing perhaps 50-60 yards away who may have been his sister. They believe that she stripped him naked in the snow to make him cry so that he would be found by the soldiers. The sergeant tucked him in his jacket and took him to the army camp. Mr. Richeson lived at the camp until he was about 7 years old. The lieutenant that wanted to adopt him was not allowed because they did not allow adoption to single parents. It just so happened that his adopted parents were looking for a son because they could not conceive another child. His parents were just in time because the government was about to stop letting children out of the country. The first president of the country, Syngman Rhee, had to sign off on his release to the United States. His father was a journalist and had a job lined up in Bloomington, Illinois. Mr. Richeson was the forest Korean orphan during that time to be brought to the states. His father took him to Peoria to become naturalized.

Nancy T. Richmond

Title: State Agency Administrator (Retired) **Industry:** Government Administration/Government Relations/Government Services **Company Name:** Massachusetts Rehabilitation Commission **Date of Birth:** 03/14/1933 **Place of Birth:** Buxton **State/Country of Origin:** ME/USA **Parents:** Ansel Robert Mason; Kate Douglas (Libby) Mason **Marital Status:** Married **Spouse Name:** Stephen L. Richmond (11/10/2006) **Education:** Postgraduate Coursework, The Auditor's Institute (1988); Postgraduate Coursework, Institute for Governmental Services, Boston, MA (1985); BA, University of Massachusetts, Boston, MA (1977); Diploma, Bryant College (Now Bryant University), Providence, RI (1952) **Career:** Director of Contracts, Massachusetts Rehabilitation Commission, Boston, MA (1986-1998); Assistant Director, Massachusetts Office of Deafness (Now Commission for the Deaf and Hard of Hearing), Boston, MA (1978-1986); Management Consultant, East Boston Community Development Association (EBCDC), Boston, MA (1973-1978); Community Liaison, Action for Boston Community Development, Boston, MA (1968-1973); Assistant to Chief Justice, Massachusetts Superior Court, Boston, MA (1964-1968) **Career Related:** Consultant, NetWorks, Inc. (2003-2005); Consultant, Radio Station WFCC, Cape Cod Broadcasting, Chatham, MA (1987-1991); Consultant, Jos. A Ryan & Associates, Boston and Orleans, MA (1981-1986) **Civic:** Member, Vestry Trinity Episcopal Church, Saco, Maine (2005-2007); Treasurer, Highland Cemetery Association (2002); Board of Directors, Sunset Bay Condo Association (1998-2001); Treasurer, Sunset Bay Condo Association (1998-1999); Tax Equity Alliance of Massachusetts (1994); Board of Directors, Deaf-Blind Contact Center, Boston, MA (1988-1991); Volunteer, American Cancer Society, Inc., Winchester, MA (1986-1993) **Creative Works:** Co-author, "How to Start Your Own Small Business" (1981); Author, "Reorganization of East Boston Community Development Corporation" (1976); Author, "Mayor's Safe Streets Act: Bromley-Heath Security Patrols" (1974) **Awards:** Governor's Citation for Outstanding Performance (1993); Community Service Award, Northeastern University (1986); Named to Outstanding Young Women of America (1965); Good Citizen Award, Daughters of the American Revolution (1950); Named Valedictorian, Samuel D. Hanson High School, Buxton, Maine (1950) **Memberships:** Co-chair, "Take Your Daughters to Work Day" (1998-1999); Procurement Management Team, Massachusetts Rehabilitation Commission (1997-1998); Chair, Statewide Central Office of Directors, Massachusetts Rehabilitation Commission (1995-1998); National Organization of Women; Massachusetts State Association of the Deaf (MSAD); The Red Hat Society, Inc. **Marquis Who's Who Honors:** Albert Nelson Marquis Lifetime Achievement Award **To what do you attribute your success:** Mrs. Richmond could not have advanced in her career without obtaining a bachelor's degree. Her subsequent positions required a degree. **Why did you become involved in your profession or industry:** Mrs. Richmond's career started when she was 19 and she became a member of the Episcopal church. The priest there was very civic minded and believed in volunteering so she got involved in the community. Her parents did not have a lot, however, they mortgaged their house for Mrs. Richmond to attend school. **Avocations:** Reading; Music; Swimming; Sign language; Traveling and making stops around the world **Political Affiliations:** Democrat **Religion:** Episcopalian **Thoughts on Life:** Mrs. Richmond's mother was an avid reader and she encouraged Nancy to become interested in books. With the help of Mrs. Richmond's sister and a friend, she learned to read at age 4. This early beginning was the key to doing well throughout her life.

William Frederick Richmond

Title: Lawyer **Industry:** Law and Legal Services **Company Name:** Richmond Law Office **Date of Birth:** 06/07/1943 **Place of Birth:** Albany **State/Country of Origin:** OR/USA **Parents:** William Frederick Richmond; Mary Jane (McQuilkin) Richmond **Marital Status:** Married **Spouse Name:** Carolyn Jean Whealtey (03/03/1973) **Children:** Frederick Scott; Christina Jean **Education:** JD, The University of Tennessee (1972); BBA, Marshall University (1967) **Career:** Assistant Prosecuting Attorney, Raleigh County, WV (1996-Present); Private Practice, Beckley, WV (1972-Present); Partner, Abrams, Byron, Henderson & Richmond, Beckley, WV (1984-1996); Partner, Bowers, Hodson, Henderson & Richmond, Beckley, WV (1976-1984); Associate, Bowers, Hodson, Henderson, Beckley, WV (1974-1976); **Career Related:** Associate Professor, Real Property Law and Administrative Law, Paralegal Program, College of West Virginia, Beckley, WV (1990-1993) **Civic:** President, Beckley-Raleigh Citizens Development Council (1985-Present); Republican Ballot Commissioner, Raleigh County, WV (1972-Present); Vice Chairman, Historical Landmark Commission (1991-2012); Member, Design Standards Committee, City of Beckley, WV (1987-1990); Founding Counsel, Beckley-Raleigh Citizens Development Council (1985-1994); Founding Counsel, Secretary, Beckley-Raleigh County Policeman-Fireman Relief Fund (1982-1994); Chairman, Beckley Human Rights Commission (1979-1980); Founding Counsel, Beckley Contact Teleministries, Inc. (1976-1978); Mental Hygiene Commissioner, Raleigh County, WV (1973-1977); Counsel, Beckley Human Rights Commission (1972-1980) **Awards:** Presidential Award, Home Builders Association of West Virginia (2014); Meritorious Service, Home Builders Association of West Virginia (1999) **Memberships:** General Counsel, West Virginia Home Builders Association (1992-Present); Counsel, Board of Directors, Southern West Virginia Home Builders Association (1986-Present); President, Woodrow Wilson High School Alumni Association, Inc. (1982-Present); President, Raleigh County Bar Association (1992-1993); Board Directors, West Virginia Home Builders Association (1988); President, Black Knight Country Club (1985); Board of Directors, Black Knight Country Club (1983-1986); American Bar Association (ABA); American Judicature Society; West Virginia State Bar Association; West Virginia Defense Lawyers Association; Defense Research Institute (DRI); Southern West Virginia Home Builders Association; Moose International; BPO Elks **Bar Admissions:** West Virginia (1972) **Marquis Who's Who Honors:** Albert Nelson Marquis Lifetime Achievement Award; Marquis Who's Who Top Professional **Why did you become involved in your profession or industry:** Mr. William Richmond had never thought about law as he was going to school. He graduated from Marshall University in 1967 and it was during the draft for Vietnam that he considered it; he was drafted after he got out of college. He was a management trainee, and he left the job. A friend's mother got him a position as a probation officer and social worker. He was the only male social worker in the county at the time. He turned 26 and everybody over the age of 26 was excluded; the judge he worked for asked him if he ever thought about going to law school and he had never thought about it. The judge told him if he was interested he could get him in. He took the LSAT and he attended college. He started his own firm, and went to work for another firm but it did not work out, so he re-established his own firm. **Avocations:** Swimming; Tennis; Photography; Hiking; Whitewater rafting **Political Affiliations:** Republican **Religion:** Presbyterian

Karl Rickels, MD

Title: Psychiatrist **Industry:** Medicine & Health Care **Company Name:** University of Pennsylvania **Date of Birth:** 08/17/1924 **Place of Birth:** Wihelmshaven **State/Country of Origin:** Germany **Parents:** Karl E. Rickels; Stephanie (Roehrhoff) Rickels **Marital Status:** Widowed **Spouse Name:** Rosalind Wilson (06/27/1964, Deceased 2008) **Children:** Laurence; Stephen; Michael; Andrew (Grandchild); Peter (Grandchild); Caroline (Grandchild); Claudia (Grandchild); Aiden (Grandchild); Ashley (Grandchild) **Education:** MD, University of Muenster, Germany (1951) **Career:** Professor Emeritus (2019); Stuart and Emily B.H. Mudd Professor of Human Behavior, University of Pennsylvania (1977-2019); Professor of Psychiatry, University of Pennsylvania (1969-2019); Chief, Mood and Anxiety Disorders Program, University of Pennsylvania (1964-2010); Chairman, Committee on Studies Involving Human Beings, University of Pennsylvania (1985-1998); Professor of Pharmacology, University of Pennsylvania (1976-1998); Instructor to Associate Professor, University of Pennsylvania (1957-1969); Resident in Psychiatry, Hospital University of Pennsylvania (1955-1957); Resident in Psychiatry, Mental Health Institute, Cherokee, IA (1954-1955); Postgraduate Training, Universities of Erlangen and Frankfurt, City Hospital Kassel (1952-1954); Intern, Dortmund City Hospital, Germany (1951-1952) **Career Related:** Chief, Psychiatry, Philadelphia General Hospital (1975-1977) **Civic:** Board Member, Waverly Heights Life Care Facility **Creative Works:** Editor, Author, 10 Books; Contributor, Over 620 Articles, Professional Publications **Awards:** Distinguished Graduate Award, University of Pennsylvania (2018); Pioneer in Psychopharmacology Award, CINP (2012); William Osler Patient-Oriented Research Award, University of Pennsylvania (2008); Lifetime Achievement Award, Pennsylvania Psychiatric Society (2003) **Memberships:** Fellow, Life Charter, American College of Neuropsychopharmacology; Life Member, American Psychiatric Association; College of Physicians of Philadelphia; Collegium International Neuro-Psychopharmacologicum; Corresponding Member, European College of Neuropsychopharmacology **Marquis Who's Who Honors:** Albert Nelson Marquis Lifetime Achievement Award **Why did you become involved in your profession or industry:** When Dr. Rickels came to America, he signed up to work at the Cherokee Mental Hospital to receive his immigration papers. There, he discovered a passion for psychology.

John Addison Ricks III

Title: Professor Emeritus **Industry:** Education/Educational Services **Company Name:** Middle Georgia State College **Date of Birth:** 08/18/1939 **Place of Birth:** Charlotte **State/Country of Origin:** NC/USA **Parents:** John Addison Ricks Jr.; Mamye Snow (Turner) Ricks **Marital Status:** Married **Spouse Name:** Nancy Elaine Ricks (1966) **Children:** Elizabeth Anne Lampton; John Addison Ricks IV. **Education:** PhD, University of North Carolina (1974); MA, Tulane University (1963); BA, Davidson College (1961) **Career:** Professor Emeritus, Middle Georgia State College, Cochran, GA (2003-Present); Professor, Chairman, History, Social Sciences, Education, Business Administration Division, Middle Georgia State College, Cochran, GA (1988-2003); Instructor, Professor, Valdosta State University, Georgia (1968-1988); Instructor, History, Montreat-Anderson College (Now Montreat College), North Carolina (1966-1968) **Civic:** Clerk of Session, Elder First Presbyterian Church, Eastman, GA (1990-1993, 1998-2001, 2011-2014); President, Friends of Librarians, Cochran, GA (1989-1990); Scoutmaster, Boy Scouts America, Valdosta, GA (1982-1984); Member, Valdosta Board of Education (1976-1980); Chair, Democratic Party of Bleckley County **Military Service:** 1st Lt., 2nd Lt. U.S. Army (1963-1965) **Creative Works:** Contributor, Articles, Professional Journals, Newspapers **Awards:** Rotarian of the Year (1997); Fulbright Foundation Grantee (1992, 1997); Kiwanian of the Year (1979) **Memberships:** President, Rotary District 6920, Rotary International (2019); President-Elect, Rotary District 6920, Rotary International (2018); Will Watt Fellow, Rotary International (2013); Commander, American Legion Post 107 (2008-2016); President, Local Chapter, AARP (2007-2009); Assistant Governor, Rotary District 6920, Rotary International (2005-2008); Program Manager, Cochran-Bleckley Better Hometown Inc. (2003-2010); Paul Harris Fellow, Rotary International (2001); President, Georgia Association of Historians (1994-1995); President, Rotary District 6920, Rotary International (1993-1994); Visiting Team, Southern Association of Secondary Schools and Colleges (1979)(1990); Treasurer, Azalea City Kiwanis Club (1980-1982); Cochran Chamber of Commerce **Marquis Who's Who Honors:** Albert Nelson Marquis Lifetime Achievement Award **Why did you become involved in your profession or industry:** Professor Ricks became involved in his profession because of his mother, a high school teacher with a master's degree who inspired him to teach. He always enjoyed history and historical figures. He likes to read biographies and tries to measure himself against the biography he is reading and what the subject has accomplished. He feels that for young people to know their history, they need to be more versed in it. **Avocations:** Playing piano; Weightlifting; Nordic Track Exercise; Reading; Playing chess **Political Affiliations:** Democratic **Religion:** Presbyterian

George F. Riess, Esq.

Title: Lawyer, Educator **Industry:** Law and Legal Services **Company Name:** Law Offices of George F. Riess **Parents:** Frank Riess; Jane (Kelleher) Riess **Marital Status:** Married **Spouse Name:** Maida Magee (08/23/1980, Deceased 1996); Cheryl Lambert Riess (06/22/1968, Divorced 1976) **Children:** Katherine Cody; Frank Henry; Carson Magee; Maida Jean **Education:** JD, Louisiana State University, Baton Rouge, LA (1969); BA, Tulane University, New Orleans, LA (1965) **Career:** Managing Partner, Law Offices of George R. Riess (2000-Present); Partner, Polack, Rosenberg, Endom & Riess, LLP, New Orleans, LA (1996-2000); Partner, Monroe & Lemann Law Firm, New Orleans, LA (1976-1996); Managing Partner, Johnson & Riess Law Firm, New Orleans, LA (1970-1976) **Career Related:** Adjunct Professor, Law, Tulane University Law School, New Orleans, LA (1987-2008); Board of Directors, Plaquemines Oil & Development Company, New Orleans, LA **Civic:** Parishioner, Vestry, St. Martin's Episcopal Church (1998-2004); Secretary of Vestry, St. Martin Episcopal Church, Metairie, LA (1992-1995) **Creative Works:** Published Poet **Awards:** Grantee, Ford Foundation (1969); Chair, Flory Trial Board; Member and Associate, New Orleans Friends of Music **Memberships:** Fellow, Louisiana State Bar Foundation; American Bar Association; American Judicature Society; Federal Bar Association; Louisiana Association of Defense Counsel; Louisiana State Bar Association; Former Member, Southern Yacht Club; New Orleans Lawn Tennis Club **Bar Admissions:** Michigan (1972); U.S. District of the Eastern, Western, and Middle Districts of Louisiana (1970); Louisiana (1969) **Marquis Who's Who Honors:** Albert Nelson Marquis Lifetime Achievement Award **To what do you attribute your success:** Mr. Riess attributes his success to him liking what he does. If he did not, he would not be successful as he as been. He likes the various discipline that trial lawyers know about, as well as taking deposition and trying cases in appellate court. **Why did you become involved in your profession or industry:** Mr. Riess became involved in his profession because he initially majored in English and music, having played the piano and harpsichord as an undergraduate at Tulane University. However he has always enjoyed politics because of a desire to be able to help people. So he decided to pursue his Judicial Doctorate from Louisiana State University and become a lawyer. In 1970, he became the managing partner of Johnson & Riess law firm. Shortly after, he began to partner up with a prestigious law firm, Monroe & Lemann, and stayed there for 20 years. He wanted to also pursue the education aspect of law and became an adjunct professor at partners with Polack, Rosenberg, Endom and Riess, LLP. He decided to open his own practice in 2000 while teaching and although he is somewhat retired. Mr. Riess is still very active in law and helping people. He is also very proud of his trial work and ability to help clients. **Avocations:** Running and walking long distances; Music; Classical piano **Political Affiliations:** Democrat **Religion:** Episcopalian

Robert Dale Riggs, PhD

Title: Plant Pathology and Nematology Educator, Researcher **Industry:** Sciences **Date of Birth:** 06/15/1932 **Place of Birth:** Pocahontas **State/Country of Origin:** AR/USA **Parents:** Rosa MacDowell Riggs; Grace (Million) Riggs **Marital Status:** Widowed **Spouse Name:** Jennie Lee Willis (06/06/1954, Deceased 2013) **Children:** Rebecca Dawn; Deborah Lee; Robert Dale Jr.; James Michael **Education:** PhD in Plant Pathology, NC State University (1958); MS in Plant Pathology, University of Arkansas, Fayetteville, AR (1956); BS in Agriculture, University of Arkansas, Fayetteville, AR (1954) **Career:** Plant Pathology and Nematology Educator, Researcher;Professor, University of Arkansas, Fayetteville, AR (1967-2019); Graduate Assistant, NC State University, Raleigh, NC (1955-1958); Associate Professor, University of Arkansas, Fayetteville, AR (1962-1967); Assistant Professor, University of Arkansas, Fayetteville, AR (1958-1962); Graduate Assistant, University of Arkansas, Fayetteville, AR (1954-1955) **Career Related:** Chair of the Faculty, College of Agricultural, Food and Life Sciences (1999) **Creative Works:** Co-Editor, "Biology and Management of the Soybean Cyst Nematode" (1992); Editor-in-Chief, Journal of Nematology (1987-1990); Editor, Nematology in the Southern United States (1982); Contributor, Articles, Professional Nematology and Plant Pathology Journals; Inventor, Fungal Control of Nematodes **Awards:** Meritorious Service Award, United Soybean Board (2002); Spitze Land Grant University Faculty Award (2001); Outstanding Researcher Award, Association of Arkansas Extension Specialists (AACES) (2000); Honor Award For Research In Environmental Protection, U.S. Department Of Agriculture (1994); District Faculty Achievement Award, University of Arkansas Alumni Association (1993); John W. White Award, College of Agriculture And Home Economics (1989); Distinguished Service Award, Southern Soybean Disease Workers (1987); Outstanding Plant Pathologist Award, Southern Division, American Phytopathological Society (APS) **Memberships:** President, Society of Nematologists (1993-1994); Vice President, Society of Nematologists (1991-1992); American Phytopathological Society; Southern Soybean Disease Workers; Arkansas Alumni Association, University of Arkansas; Organization of Nematologists of Tropical America FL, Inc.; Sigma Xi; Gamma Sigma Delta **Marquis Who's Who Honors:** Albert Nelson Marquis Lifetime Achievement Award; Marquis Who's Who Top Professional **Why did you become involved in your profession or industry:** Dr. Riggs became involved in his profession because he grew up on a farm and recognized the need for solutions for the diseases that he noticed were on the plants. When he graduated from high school, he had a $200 grant, so he went to the University of Arkansas and after that, he received additional grants. He also received money to go to NC State University to earn his PhD. **Avocations:** Collecting coins; Photography; Puzzles; Enjoying retirement and family time **Political Affiliations:** Democrat **Religion:** Baptist

Michael "Mike" Rikon, CRE

Title: Partner **Industry:** Law and Legal Services **Company Name:** Goldstein, Rikon, Rikon & Houghton, P.C **Date of Birth:** 02/02/1945 **Place of Birth:** Brooklyn **State/Country of Origin:** NY/USA **Parents:** Charles Rikon (deceased 1971); Ruth (Shapiro) Rikon (deceased 1976) **Marital Status:** Married **Spouse Name:** Leslie Sharon Rein (2/11/1968) **Children:** Carrie Rachel; Joshua Howard **Education:** LLM, New York University (1974); JD, Brooklyn Law School (1969); BS, New York Institute of Technology (1966) **Certifications:** CRE (Counselor of Real Estate) (2016) **Career:** Partner, Goldstein, Rikon, Rikon & Houghton, P.C, Professional Corporation, New York (1994-Present); Private Practice, New York (1988-1994); Partner, Rudick and Rikon, Professional Corporation, New York (1980-1988); Law Clerk, New York State Court of Claims (1973-1980); Law Clerk to Honorable Albert A. Blinder, New York State Court of Claims (1969-1973); Assistant Corporate Counsel, City of New York (1969-1973) **Career Related:** Former Assistant Corporation Counsel, Condemnation Division, City of New York **Civic:** President, Village Greens Residents Association (1978-1980); Member, President, Community Board, Staten Island Borough (1977); Chairman of the Board, Arden Heights Jewish Center, Staten Island, New York (1976-1977); New York Designee, Owners Counsel of America **Military Service:** SSGT 99th Signal Batallion, U.S. Army Reserve (1969-1975) **Creative Works:** Contributor, Articles, Professional Journals; Blog Contributor, Bulldozers at Your Doorstep; Contributor, New York Law Journal **Awards:** A.V. Preeminent, Martindale-Hubbell (2010-Present); Named Top Lawyer of New York (2019); Named a Super Lawyer, Eminent Domain Law (2011); Best Lawyers in Eminent Domain and Condemnation Law, New York (2006-2009); Business Leadership Award, NYIT Alumni Federal (2006) **Memberships:** Fellow, American Bar Foundation; Chair, Committee of Condemnation, American Bar Association; Special Committee of Condemnation Law, New York State Bar Association; Suffolk County Bar Association; Nassau County Bar Association; Chair Condemnation Committee, New York County Lawyers Association; Condemnation Committee, Association of the Bar City of New York; Director, Owners Counsel America **Bar Admissions:** United States Court of Appeals for the Fifth Circuit (1981); United States Court of Appeals for the Eleventh Circuit (1981); Supreme Court of the United States (1973); United States Court of Appeals for the Second Circuit (1972); United States District Court for the Eastern District of New York (1971); United States District Court for the Southern District of New York (1971); New York (1970) **Marquis Who's Who Honors:** Albert Nelson Marquis Lifetime Achievement Award; Marquis Who's Who Top Professional **Why did you become involved in your profession or industry:** Mr. Rikon was in law school and it was his last year which was 1969. His draft status had changed from 2S to 1A, it was the height of the Vietnam War. He joined the reserves so he wasn't drafted and he was given an extension until after the bar exam. When he went for interviews they asked if he has served his active duty, they all said to come back and see them after he did his service. The city announced an exam for an attorney trainee, it was a civil service position, he was number three out of 155 that took the test. They only had one position to be on the corporation counsel, that is where you wanted to work because that was the ligation office of the city. He got that position and it happened to be in the condemnation division. **Avocations:** Photography; Stamp collecting/philately **Religion:** Jewish

Thurlow Richard Robe

Title: Dean Emeritus, Cruse W. Moss Professor Emeritus **Industry:** Education/Educational Services **Company Name:** Russ College of Engineering and Technology, Ohio University **Place of Birth:** Petersburg **State/Country of Origin:** OH/USA **Parents:** Thurlow Scott Robe; Mary Alice (McKibben) Robe **Marital Status:** Married **Spouse Name:** Eleanora C. Komyati (08/27/1955) **Children:** Julia; Kevin; Stephen; Edward **Education:** PhD in Applied Mechanics, Stanford University (1966); MS in Mechanical Engineering, Ohio University (1962); BS in Civil Engineering, Ohio University (1955) **Career:** Dean Emeritus, Cruse W. Moss Professor Emeritus, Russ College of Engineering and Technology, Ohio University, Athens, Ohio (1996-Present); Founding Director, T. Richard and Eleanora K. Robe Leadership Institute, Ohio University (1996-2005); Cruse W. Moss Professor of Engineering Education, Ohio University, Athens, Ohio (1992-1996); Chair, Ohio Engineering Deans Council (1985-1987); Dean, Russ College of Engineering and Technology, Ohio University, Athens, Ohio (1980-1996); President, Chairman, Board, Q.E.D. Associates, Incorporated, Lexington, KY (1975-1983); Research Fellow, Postgraduate School of Applied Dynamics, University of Edinburgh, Scotland, United Kingdom (1973); Assistant Professor to Professor, Associate Dean, Special Assistant to President, University of Kentucky, Lexington, KY (1965-1980); Acting Instructor to Instructor, Ohio University, Athens, Ohio (1960-1963); Engineer, General Electric, Niles and Evendale, Ohio, Cleveland and Erie, PA (1954-1960) **Career Related:** Member, Advisory Board, Robe Leadership Institute (1996-Present); Liaison, Engineering Accreditation Commission, Accreditation Board of Engineering and Technology (1989-1991); Trustee, Engineers Foundation of Ohio (1988-1994); Board of Governors, Edison Materials Technical Center (1987-1996); Director, Innovation Center of Authority, Ohio University (1983-1986) **Civic:** Trustee Emeritus, Ohio University Foundation (2007-Present); Advisory Board Member, Salvation Army of Oconee County (2010-2014); Member-at-large, Oconee District, Boy Scouts of America (2007-2009); Member, Russ Prize Selection Committee, National Academy of Engineering (2000-2016); Trustee, Ohio University Foundation (1998-2007); Board of Trustees, Association of Ohio Commodores (1995-1997); Board of Directors, Athens County Community Redevelopment Corporation (1980-1986); Treasurer, South Lexington Little League (1976-1980); Vice Chairman, Thoroughbred District, Boy Scouts of America (1975-1977); Board of Directors, University Kentucky Athletics Association (1975-1980); President, Tates Creek High School PTA, Lexington, KY (1975-1976) **Military Service:** Liaison Officer, United States Air Force Academy (1975-1980); Officer, Jet Fighter Pilot, United States Air Force (1956-1959); Major, United States Air Force Reserve (1955-1985) **Creative Works:** Contributor, Articles to Professional Journals; Patentee, Trailer Hitch **Awards:** Recipient, Match Play Champion Keowee Key, SC (2010); Inductee, Academy of Distinguished Graduates, Russ College Engineering and Technology (2001); Named Ohio University Alumnus of the Year (1996); Alumni Medal of Merit, Ohio University (1993); Fellow, American Council on Education Administration (1970-1971); Outstanding Contribution in Research Award, American Society of Engineering Education (ASEE) (1966); Eagle Scout Award (1951) **Memberships:** Professional Engineering in Education Executive Board, Central Region Vice Chairman, National Society of Professional Engineers (1987-1989); The American Society of Mechanical Engineers; American Society Engineering Education; Athens Reading Club; Athens Symposiarchs; Rotary International; Sigma Xi, The Scientific Research Honor Society; The Tau Beta Pi Association, Inc.; Omicron Delta Kappa; Alpha Lambda Delta; The American Legion **Marquis Who's Who Honors:** Albert Nelson Marquis Lifetime Achievement Award; Marquis Who's Who Top Professional; Marquis Who's Who Humanitarian Award **Why did you become involved in your profession or industry:** Dr. Robe went into engineering because he admired engineers he encountered in Athens, Ohio where he grew up. He liked knowing that engineers can be a part of making things that have an affect on people's lives. In addition, he liked the general challenge of doing things. He enjoyed helping students. He liked the diversity and dealing with different people. **Avocations:** Reading; Tennis; Golf **Thoughts on Life:** The T. Richard and Eleanora K. Robe Leadership Institute was established in 1996 by the Ohio University Board of Trustees. It selects students to participate in special seminars and programs that will teach and demonstrate how they can guide the future of engineering and technology - and of society as a whole. It was named in behalf of Dr. Robe's wife, as well for all her support that she gave Thurlow all throughout his career.

Robert S. Roberson

Title: Investment Company Executive **Industry:** Financial Services **Company Name:** Weaver Bros, Inc. **Place of Birth:** Mount Kisco **State/Country of Origin:** NY/USA **Marital Status:** Married **Spouse Name:** Barbara C. Drane (1967) **Children:** Elizabeth de V.; Merritt B.; Barbara D. **Education:** Master of Business Administration, College of William and Mary (1973); Postgraduate Coursework, Washington and Lee University School of Law (1966); Postgraduate Coursework, New York University Leonard N. Stern School of Business (1964); Bachelor of Science, New York University (1964) **Career:** President, Director, Weaver Bros Incorporated, Newport News, VA (1967-Present); Board of Directors, First Peninsula Bank and Trust Company, Hampton, VA (1977-1978); Member, New York Produce Exchange (1965-1966); Various Positions in Financial and Building Industries (1964-1967) **Civic:** Former Member, Board of Directors, Peninsula Unit, American Cancer Society, Inc., Newport News, VA; Former Member, Board of Directors, Heritage Council, Girl Scouts of the United States of America, Hampton, VA; Former Member, Board of Trustees, Newport News Public Library; Former Member, Board of Trustees, Virginia Living Museum, Newport News, VA; Former Member, Board of Trustees, Chairman, Committee on Development, Hampton Roads Academy, Newport News, VA; Former Member, Board of Visitors, George Washingtons Mount Vernon National Shrine, Mount Vernon, VA; Former Member, Board of Trustees, President, Chief Curator, Golf Museum, Newport News, VA; Member, Board of Trustees, Randolph College/Randolph-Macon Womans College, Lynchburg, VA; Former Commissioner, Chairman, Newport News Arts Commission, Virginia; Former Commissioner, Vice Chairman, Williamsburg Area Arts Commission, VA; Former Member, Board of Directors, Muscarelle Museum of Art, Williamsburg, VA; Founding Member, Board of Trustees, Executive Committee, Chairman, Vice Chairman, Muscarelle Museum of Art Foundation, Williamsburg, VA; Member, Board of Trustees, Maier Museum of Art, Lynchburg, VA; Former Member, Board of Trustees, President, Virginia War Museum Foundation, Newport News, VA; Former Member, Governing Board of Visitors, Executive Committee, Chairman, Committee on Development and Alumni Affairs, College of William and Mary, Williamsburg, VA; Member, Board of Trustees, Executive Committee, Treasurer, Roberson Museum and Science Center/ Planetarium, Binghamton, NY; Member, Board of Trustees, Chairman, The Roberson Foundation, Binghamton, NY; Member, Board of Trustees, Former Vice Chairman, Former Chairman, Ad Hoc Institutional Transition Committee, Member, Executive Committee, Chairman, Audit Committee, New York Genealogical & Biographical Society, New York, NY; Former Member, Governing Board of Visitors, Member, Executive Committee, Richard Bland College, Petersburg, VA; Member, Board of Trustees, Woodrow Wilson Presidential Library and Museum, Staunton, VA; Former Member, Museum Committee, Virginia State Golf Association Foundation, Midlothian VA; Former Member, Board of Visitors, Virginia Institute of Marine Science, Gloucester Point, VA; Former Member, Veteran Corps of Artillery, State of New York (VCASNY) **Awards:** Patrick Henry Award, Commonwealth of Virginia (2001); Inductee, New York University Honorary Society (1964); Decorated Knight, Officer, Order of Saint John, England; Knight, Order of Saints Maurice and Lazarus, Royal House Savoy, Italy; Honorary Deputy Chief, New York City Fire Department **Memberships:** Newcomen Society of the United States; Former National Committeeman, United States Golf Association, Far Hills, NJ; General Society of Colonial Wars; The Saint Nicholas Society of the City of New York; Colonial Order of the Acorn; Knight Commander, Sovereign Military Order of the Temple of Jerusalem; Squadron A Association; Pilgrims of the United States/Pilgrims of Great Britain; Union Club of the City of New York; Down Town Association, NY; Library and Arts Committee, The Brook Club, NY; The Church Club of New York, NY; Royal Enclosure at Royal Ascot Racecourse (England); The Metropolitan Club of the City of Washington, Washington, DC; Southampton Club, Long Island, NY; Farmington Country Club, Charlottesville, VA; Executive Committee, Vice President, Cypher Society of William and Mary; James River Country Club; Former President, Hampton Roads German Club; Hampton Roads Assembly; The Hundred Club, Newport News, VA; Williamsburg German Club; America's Cup Archives and Library Committee, New York Yacht Club; Fishers Island Yacht Club, Long Island, New York; Former Member, Fishers Island Club, Long Island, NY; Social Register Association, New York, NY; The Blue Book of the Hamptons, Long Island, NY; Paul Harris Fellow, Rotary International; Blue Key Honor Society; Delta Sigma Pi; Doubles Club, New York, NY **Marquis Who's Who Honors:** Albert Nelson Marquis Lifetime Achievement Award **Political Affiliations:** Republican **Religion:** Episcopalian

Bill Roberts

Title: Fire Chief (Retired) **Industry:** Other **Date of Birth:** 06/02/1938 **Place of Birth:** Deport **State/Country of Origin:** TX/USA **Parents:** Samuel Westbrook Roberts; Ann Lee (Rhodes) Roberts **Marital Status:** Widowed **Spouse Name:** Johana R. Caines (10/14/2000, Deceased 2018); Ramona Ryall (06/01/1963, Deceased 1988) **Children:** Renee Ann **Education:** Graduate, Executive Fire Officer Program, National Fire Academy (1989); AAS, El Centro Junior College, Dallas, TX (1980); Graduate, Executive Program for Fire Service, Texas Agricultural and Mechanical University (Now Texas A&M University) (1978); Graduate, Paramedic Course, UT Southwestern Medical School (1974); Student, North Texas State University (Now University of North Texas) (1974); Student, Southern Methodist University (1968) **Career:** Fire Chief, Austin Fire Department (1983-1994); With, Dallas Fire Department (1958-1983); Assistant Fire Chief, Dallas Fire Department (1979-1983); Division Fire Chief, Dallas Fire Department (1971-1979); Captain, Dallas Fire Department (1967-1971); Lieutenant, Dallas Fire Department (1964-1967) **Career Related:** Member, Adjunct Faculty, National Fire Academy (1981-1986); Technical Board of Directors, Foundation Fire Safety, Washington (1982-1985); Texas Department, Health Resources (1973-1978); Georgia Institute of Technology (1974); Consultant, University of Tennessee (1974); Field Engineer, IBM Corporation, Dallas, TX (1968); Salesman, Intercommunications Equipment, Chandler Sound, Dallas, TX (1966-1967); Real Estate Salesman, Dale Copus Realtor, Dallas, TX (1963-1966); Owner, Personnel Testing Laboratory, Dallas, TX (1963); State Life of Indianapolis, Dallas, TX (1962); Rand Corporation, Washington, Mission Research, Santa Barbara, CA, Macro **Civic:** Board of Directors, Rehabilitation Hospital Austin (1992-1994); Capitol Area Council, Boy Scouts of America (1989-1992); Board of Directors, Brackenridge Hospital (1989); Board of Directors, Austin Police Pensions Board (1989); Task Force, American Heart Association, Austin, TX (1973-1983); Committee Chairman Dallas Jaycees (1962-1965) **Creative Works:** Co-Author, "EMS Measures to Improve Care" (1980); Author, "EMS Dallas" (1978); Co-Author, "Anesthesia for Surgery Trauma" (1976); Contributor, Articles, Periodicals **Awards:** John Stemmons Service Award, Dallas Fire Department (1979); Scholar, International Association of Fire Chiefs Foundation (1967) **Memberships:** Technical Board of Directors, Foundation Fire Safety (1982-1985); Regional Emergency Service Advisory Council, North Texas Council of Governments (1973-1979); International Association Fire Chiefs; American Heart Association; Texas Association of REALTORS; Rotary Club of Austin; Rotary Club of Asheville **Marquis Who's Who Honors:** Albert Nelson Marquis Lifetime Achievement Award **Why did you become involved in your profession or industry:** Mr. Roberts became involved in his profession by accident. A friend of his decided to go to Dallas to apply for a position in the fire department. He and another friend went out with the friend the night before he was leaving for Dallas and they decided to go with him and also apply. They arrived in Dallas later than they were supposed to, but were allowed to take the test anyway. The guy who wanted to join did not pass, but Mr. Roberts and his other friend did. **Religion:** Methodist

Joan Roberts

Title: English Language Professor **Industry:** Education/Educational Services **Date of Birth:** 03/04/1930 **Place of Birth:** Buffalo **State/Country of Origin:** NY/USA **Parents:** Cyril Gyrard Warthling; Edith Irene (Patterson) Warthling **Marital Status:** Married **Spouse Name:** Edward McCreery, PhD (05/08/1954) **Children:** Christopher; Elizabeth; Cecily; Julia; Margaret; Anne **Education:** PhD, University of Cincinnati, Cincinnati, OH (1975); MA, University of Cincinnati, Cincinnati, OH (1969); AB, Nazareth College, Rochester, NY (1951) **Certifications:** Permanent Certification in Secondary English, New York State **Career:** Professor, English, State University College at Buffalo, Buffalo, NY (1978-2000); Adjunct Assistant Professor, Manhattanville College, Harrison, NY (1976-1977); Director, Academy Remediation, Mercy College, Dobbs Ferry, NY (1974-1976); Instructor, English, University of Cincinnati, Cincinnati, OH (1969-1973) **Creative Works:** Co-Author, "Oxford Companion to Mystery/Detective Fiction" (1996); Co-Author, "Feminism in Women's Detective Fiction" (1995); Co-Author, "Great Women Mystery Writers" (1994); Contributor, "Great Women Mystery Writers: A Biocritical Dictionary" (1994); Presenter, Exhibition at Burchfield Center, "The Work of Charles Rohlfs and Anna Katharine Green Exhibit Catalog" (1994); Author, Article, "A Haverstraw Mystery Writer," South of the Mountains: A Quarterly Publication of the Historical Society of Rockland County (1992); Editor, Book, "Sicily and Naples, Or, A Fatall Union: A Tragedy" (1986); Author, Article, "Before 'Sherlock Holmes' There was Anna Katharine Green," MS Magazine (1985); Author, "Excuse me, Sir. I am an Intelligent Woman: Critical Response to The Leavenworth Case in 1878," Submitted to American Literature; Author, Book in Progress, "Why Did She Do It? A Literary/Critical Biography of Anna Katharine Green, The 'Mother of the Detective Novel'" **Awards:** Fellowship, Danforth Foundation (1967-1975) **Memberships:** Modern Language Association; College English Association **Marquis Who's Who Honors:** Albert Nelson Marquis Lifetime Achievement Award **Why did you become involved in your profession or industry:** Ms. Roberts became involved in her profession because her mother was a registered nurse and she thought that maybe she would follow in her footsteps and do medicine. However, at the time, women were not welcome into medical school. So she thought that, because she loved reading and the language, she should proceed in that direction and become an English professor.

Edwin David Robertson

Title: Lawyer **Industry:** Law and Legal Services **Date of Birth:** 07/05/1946 **Place of Birth:** Roanoke **State/Country of Origin:** VA/USA **Parents:** Edwin Traylor Robertson; Norma Burns (Bowles) Robertson **Marital Status:** Married **Spouse Name:** Anne Littelle Ferratt, (9/7/1968); Catherine Roberta Britt **Children:** Thomas Therit **Education:** LLB, University of Virginia (1971); BA, University of Virginia, with Honors (1968) **Career:** Retired (2017); Senior Counsel, Cadwalader, Wickersham & Taft (2012-2017); Partner, Cadwalader, Wickersham & Taft, New York, NY (1980-2012); Associate, Cadwalader, Wickersham & Taft, New York, NY (1971-1980) **Civic:** President, Disciplinary Board Episcopal Diocese of New York (2010-2017); New York State Independent Judicial Screen Commission, 1st Judicial District (2007-2015); Secretary, Oratorio Society of New York City (1991-2004); Board of Directors, Oratorio Society of New York City (1988-2004); Judge, Court of Review, Episcopal Church (2001-2003); Chairman, Early Music Foundation, New York, NY (1993-1999); Board of Directors, Early Music Foundation, New York, NY (1983-1999); Confidential Consulting **Military Service:** First Lieutenant, U.S. Air Force (1971-1972) **Creative Works:** Contributing Author, "Kassoff on Elder Law and Guardianship" (2011-2012); Contributing Editor, "The New York Rules of Professional Conduct" (2010); Author, "Brethren and Sisters of the Bar" (2008) **Awards:** Echols Scholar, Servant of Justice Award (2014) **Memberships:** House of Delegates, New York State Bar Association (2001-Present); Board of Directors, New York County Lawyers Association (1985-1988, 1995-1999, 2000-Present); Secretary, Sons of the Revolution in the State of New York (2014-2017); Council of Administration, Military Society War 1812 (2014-2017); Board of Managers, Sons of the Revolution in the State of New York (2009-2017); President, New York County Lawyers Association (2006-2007); House of Delegates, American Bar Association (2004-2007); Nominating Committee, New York State Bar Association (2002-2007); Vice President, New York County Lawyers Association (2002-2004); Treasurer, New York County Lawyers Association (2001-2002); Chairman, Finance Committee, New York County Lawyers Association (1999); Executive Committee, New York County Lawyers Association (1996-2008); Investment Committee, New York County Lawyers Association (1992-2007); Chairman, Bankruptcy Committee, New York County Lawyers Association (1983-1987); National Conference Bar Presidents; Federal Bar Council; Association of the Bar of the City New York; Society of Colonial Wars; Jefferson Society; Sons of Confederate Veterans; Order of the Coif; Phi Beta Kappa; Phi Kappa Psi; Jamestowne Society; Shenandoah Club **Bar Admissions:** United States District Court for the Eastern District of Michigan (1986); Supreme Court of the United States (1975); United States District Court for the Southern District of New York (1973); United States District Court for the Eastern District of New York (1973); New York (1972); United States Court of Appeals for the Second Circuit (1972) **Marquis Who's Who Honors:** Albert Nelson Marquis Lifetime Achievement Award; Marquis Who's Who Top Professional; Marquis Who's Who Humanitarian Award **Why did you become involved in your profession or industry:** Mr. Robertson became involved in his profession because it looked like it was going to be fun. His focus was on trial law. **Political Affiliations:** Republican **Religion:** Episcopalian

Barbara S. Robinson

Title: Cultural Organization Consultant **Industry:** Consulting **Date of Birth:** 01/07/1930 **Place of Birth:** Cleveland **State/Country of Origin:** OH/USA **Parents:** Alfred Cass Schultz; Rose (Markey) Shultz **Marital Status:** Widowed **Spouse Name:** Larry Robinson (05/23/1953) **Children:** Lisa; John; James **Education:** MBA, Radcliffe Institute for Advanced Study at Harvard (1952); BA, Wellesley College, Wellesley, MA (1951) **Career:** Chair Emeritus, Ohio Arts Council (2001-Present); Chair, Arts Midwest (1996-2002); Chair, National Assembly State Arts Agencies, Washington, DC (1991-1995); Chair, Ohio Arts Council (1987-2000); Advanced Arts Manager, Internship Program, Cleveland Area Arts Council (1969-1973); Marketing Research, Harvard Business School (1956-1958); Assistant Director, Public and Public Relations, Wellesley College, Massachusetts (1953-1956); Administrative Assistant to the Manager, Bonwit Teller, Cleveland, OH (1952-1953); Chairman, Vice Chairman, Policy and Planning Committee, Ohio Arts Council; Seminar Leader, Project Planner, Leadership Development Program, Cleveland Area Arts Council; Coordinator, Arts in Education Project, Cleveland Area Arts Council; Artist in the Classroom, Cleveland Area Arts Council **Career Related:** Trustee, New Organization Director, Founding Member, National Cultural Alliance, Washington, DC (1991-Present); Board of Trustees, Executive Committee, Cleveland Cultural Coalition (1987-Present); Chair, Arts and Access Celebration and Awards (1993); Member, Ohio Arts and Sports Facilities Commission (1992); Chairman, Cleveland Chamber Music Seminar (1979-1985); President, Cleveland Ballet (1978-1983); Member, Preparatory Faculty, Cleveland Institute of Music (1968-1972); Vice President, National Board Young Audiences, New York; Panel Chair of the States and Regional Program, National Endowment for the Arts, Chairman and Founder, Young Audiences, Cleveland, OH; Member, Cleveland Foundation Commission of Performing Arts; Opera Council, Cleveland Opera; Advisory Committee, Ohio Light Opera; Program Advisory Committee, Visual and Performing Arts Center Jewish Committee Center; Cultural Initiative Task Force; Advisory Committee, Harvard Institute Arts Management; Ohio Chamber Orchestra; Advisory Panel, States and Regions Program, National Education Association **Civic:** Trustee, Leadership Cleveland (1990-Present); Honorary Chairman, YWCA Corp. Campaign (1987); Chairman, Capital Projects Committee, Wooster College (1983-1990); Member, Executive Committee, University Hospitals; Chairman, Member, University Council, Case Western Reserve University; Member, Citizens Advisory Committee, Cuyahoga Community College; Trustee, Western Reserve AIDS Foundation; Board Member, Cleveland Convention and Visitors Bureau, Shaker Heights PTA Council, Ohio **Creative Works:** Soloist, Boston Pops Orchestra (1951); Columnist, Spotlight Magazine **Awards:** Barbara Robinson Prize for Arts Advocacy, Cleveland Arts Prize (2018); Cleveland Arts Prize Special Award (2014); Irma Lazarus Award for Lifetime Achievement, Governor's Award for the Arts, State of Ohio (2012); Named, "Treasures of Cleveland," Leadership in Cleveland's Art Community, Visiting Nurse Association, Cleveland, OH (2011); Named, Difference Maker, Crain's Cleveland Business 30th Anniversary - 30 Difference Makers, Cleveland, OH (2010); Named, Outstanding Woman in the Arts, Ohio Opera League (2009); Samuel Mather Visionary Award, University Hospitals Case Medical Center, Cleveland, OH (2008); Awardee, National Philanthropy Day, Honor Roll of Philanthropy, Cleveland, OH (2008); Named, Outstanding Northeast Ohio Arts Advocate, Friends of Solon Center for the Arts, Solon, OH (2007); Bravo! Award for Support of the Arts in Ohio, Ohio Ballet (2005); Named, Outstanding Friend of Community Shares, Cleveland, OH (2002); Cleveland Arts Prize, Special Citation for Distinguished Service to the Arts (2001); Distinguished Public Service Award, National Assembly of State Arts Agencies (2001); Honoree, Golden Achievement Award for Community Service, The Golden Age Centers of Greater Cleveland (1999); Named, 29 Most Influential Women in Business, Inside Business (1997); Named, Most Interesting People of 1994, Cleveland Magazine (1994); Leadership Cleveland Volunteer of the Year Award, Governor's Award, Ohio Newspaper Association (1991) **Memberships:** Trustee, Executive Committee Member, Musical Arts Association; Cleveland Orchestra; The Print Club of Cleveland; Cleveland Society of Contemporary Arts; Musical Arts Association, Cleveland Orchestra; Wellesley Club; Radcliffe Club; Alzheimer's Association, Cleveland Area Chapter **Marquis Who's Who Honors:** Albert Nelson Marquis Lifetime Achievement Award **Why did you become involved in your profession or industry:** Ms. Robinson became involved in her profession because she was brought up in a very civic society as an only child, and participated in lots of activities for nonprofits, particularly in arts and culture. She started out in a program started by the Harvard Business School, which did not accept women, but put them in a special category. **Avocations:** Reading; Travel; Art performances; Exhibits; Tennis **Religion:** Jewish

Nicole Robinson

Title: Senior Vice President – Global Government **Industry:** Government Administration/Government Relations/Government Services **Company Name:** SES **Marital Status:** Married **Spouse Name:** Michael **Children:** Mackenzie; Skylar; Michael **Education:** Senior Executives in National and International Security, Harvard Kennedy School (2012); MBA, Liberty University (2007); BS, Communications, Radford University (2002); MCA in Computer Applications, Liberty University **Career:** Senior Vice President, Global Government, SES (2017-Present); Corporate Vice President, Global Government, SES (2007-2017); Strategic Communications Lead for U.S. Standing Joint Force Headquarters (SJFHQ), General Dynamics (2004-2007); Communications Manager, SUPRA Corporation, National Museum of the U.S. Army (2000-2004) **Civic:** Chairman of the Board, REDU Space Services (2018-Present); Director of the Board, Luxdovesat; Board Member, Society of Satellite Professionals International (SSPI) **Awards:** Future Leaders Award, SSTI (2012) **To what do you attribute your success:** Ms. Robinson attributes her success to putting her hand up and not being afraid to be counted, and taking on a new area of responsibility even if it was outside of her comfort zone. She has advised others, "Take on a new role, don't wait to be offered your next opportunity. Just prove yourself even when it makes you uncomfortable operating in a new area." She feels that is where true growth comes from. **Why did you become involved in your profession or industry:** Ms. Robinson became involved in her profession because after college, she found an early opportunity with the U.S. Army Center of Military History. It was not a path she was setting out for or something she envisioned for herself. The opportunity was presented to her and she took it, and it really became a glide path to what she wanted to build a career around. She considers herself very fortunate to have had that initial opportunity, from which she was able to learn and build a career. **Avocations:** Hiking; Kayaking; Skiing

Ruth Freddie Carleson Robinson

Title: Secondary School Educator (Retired) **Industry:** Education/Educational Services **Date of Birth:** 08/27/1937 **Place of Birth:** Salem **State/Country of Origin:** OR/USA **Parents:** Richard Victor Carleson; Opal Charlotte (Mespelt) Carleson **Marital Status:** Widowed **Spouse Name:** Kenneth Oliver Robinson (Deceased) **Children:** Grant Kenneth; Victoria Ruth **Education:** Bachelor of Science, Oregon State University (1959); Coursework, Oregon State University; Coursework, Portland State University **Career:** High School Teacher, Gresham-Barlow School District, Oregon (1976-2002); High School Teacher, Hillsboro School District, Oregon (1959-1960) **Career Related:** Served, Gresham-Barlow Education Association (2002); Chair, Site Council, Sam Barlow High School, Gresham, OR (1994-2002); Secretary, Multnomah County UniServ Office (1992); President, Multnomah County UniServ Office (1995) **Civic:** Contributor, Portland Opera Association (1982-2014) **Creative Works:** President, American Association of Individual Investors, Oregon (2008-2015); Vice President, American Association of Individual Investors, Oregon (2004-2008) **Awards:** Valedictorian, Dallas High School Graduation (1955); Valedictorian, 8th Grade Graduation (1951) **Memberships:** President, American Association of Individual Investors, Portland, OR (2008-2015); Vice President, American Association of Individual Investors, Portland, OR (2004-2008); Gresham-Barlow Education Association (1994-1995); President, Multnomah County UniServ (1993-1995); Secretary, Multnomah County UniServ (1989-1992); Portland Japanese Garden; Asia Art Council, Portland, OR; Asian Art Museum, San Francisco, CA; Portland Art Museum; Metropolitan Museum of Art, New York, NY; Portland Classical Chinese Garden; BMW Car Club America; International Ivory Association; Sleuth Sisters Book Club; Modern Fiction Book Club; Barlow Book Club; Vice President, Oregon Education Association **Marquis Who's Who Honors:** Albert Nelson Marquis Lifetime Achievement Award; Marquis Who's Who Humanitarian Award **To what do you attribute your success:** Ms. Robinson attributes her success to her parents, as well as her first and second grade teachers, who encouraged her to be the best she could be. **Why did you become involved in your profession or industry:** Having always been curious about teaching, Ms. Robinson was encouraged to enter the field of economics education by her grandfather. **Avocations:** Opera; Travel; Collecting; Ballroom dancing **Political Affiliations:** Democrat **Religion:** Unitarian

Sir James L. "Jackrabbit" Robinson, OSJ

Title: Architect Planner/Developer **Industry:** Architecture & Construction **Company Name:** Robinson Architects PC **Date of Birth:** 07/12/1940 **Place of Birth:** Longview **State/Country of Origin:** TX/USA **Parents:** Ruby Nell Robinson; W.L. Robinson **Marital Status:** Widowed **Spouse Name:** Lady Martha Robinson (Deceased) **Children:** Kenneth; Gudonna; Maria Theresa; Cherrie; Jasmin Marisol; Ruby Nell; James II **Education:** MCP, Pratt Institute (1972); BArch, Southern University (1964) **Certifications:** Licensed Architect, New York, New Jersey, Connecticut, Pennsylvania, Wyoming, Virginia, Ohio, Florida **Career:** President, Architect Planner/Developer, Robinson Architects PC, Professional Corporation, New York, NY (1969-Present); Architect-Associate, Beyer Blinder Belle, New York, NY (1969); Architect, Kennerly, Slomanson & Smith, New York, NY (1967-1969); Architect, Carson, Lundin & Shaw, New York, NY (1966); With, Herbst & Rusciano, American Institute of Architects (1965); Architect, Store Planner, W.T. Grant (1964); Architect, Pt. of New York Authority (1964) **Career Related:** Vice President, R & S Construction; Visiting Professor, City University of New York; Adjunct Professor, Pratt Institute **Civic:** Board of Directors, Boys Club of America **Military Service:** Private-E1, United States Army (1966) **Creative Works:** Architect, Principal Works, Stuyvesant Heights Christian Church, David Chavis House, Fulton Court Houses, Sinclair Houses, Hamilton Heights Terrace, Eliot Graham Houses, Sojourner Truth Houses, Nehemiah Plan, Casas Theresa, New York City Postal Data Center, Mount Carmel Baptist Church, Consolidated Edison Collection Center, Jasmin Houses, CityHomes CD&E, The Promenade, Gore Residence & Tse Residence, Paramount Best Western, Sealy Funeral Home, Nanking Restaurant, Parkview Family Life Center, Jerome Charter School **Awards:** Decorated Knight, Order of St. John (1985); American Institute of Architects Design Award (1976); Fellow, Pratt Institute (1972); Bard Award (1972); Decorate Knight, Knight of Malta; Martin Luther King **Memberships:** Arbitrator, American Arbitrators Association **Marquis Who's Who Honors:** Albert Nelson Marquis Lifetime Achievement Award; Marquis Who's Who Top Professional **To what do you attribute your success:** Mr. Robinson attributes his success to perseverance. **Why did you become involved in your profession or industry:** Mr. Robinson started out as a chemistry major, but after taking a couple of courses he decided that he didn't want to live his life in a laboratory. This was around the time of the Russian launch of Sputnik. So due to an extreme scramble for advancement of American technology, most students switched careers to fields like engineering or some sort of science. Engineering seemed like the best choice for Mr. Robinson, with a focus on architecture.In addition, being an architect is something that he did not always want to do because he is from a small town of 40,000 people. He never remembered hearing the word architect, but he went to the university on a baseball and football scholarship. So right after sputnik, anybody that could read wanted to be an engineer. So, he wanted to be a chemical engineer. He took three or four courses in chemistry and advanced chemistry. He realized that is not how he wanted to spend the rest of his life. He also realized that in engineering, the courses always had something to do with math such as differential equations or logic. He thought that was too much. But, architecture only had one calculus course. He tried that and ended up enjoying the drawing and it came easy to him because he realized he could draw. He also had an imagination, which you can not teach. **Political Affiliations:** Democrat **Religion:** Baptist

Heidrun S. Robitshek

Title: Artistic Director **Industry:** Fine Art **Company Name:** Virginia Regional Ballet **Place of Birth:** Karlovy Vary **State/Country of Origin:** Czech Republic **Parents:** Alois Sichert (Deceased 1954); Johanna Sichert (Deceased 2003) **Marital Status:** Widow **Spouse Name:** Irving H. Robitshek, (4/22/1966, Deceased 1992) **Education:** Junior College Graduate, Heidelberg, Germany; Coursework in Martha Graham Technique, Advanced Modern Dance, Dance Workshops, College of William & Mary; Coursework, Palucca School, Dresden, Germany **Career:** Artistic Director, Instructor, Virginia Regional Ballet (2006-Present); Instructor, Chamber Ballet (1976-2006); Founder, The Ballet Studio, Williamsburg, VA (1968); Assistant Dance Director, Choreographer, "The Common Glory" **Creative Works:** Producer, Choreographer, "The Nutcracker", Chamber Ballet (1984); Producer, Choreographer, "A Midsummer Night's Dream", Chamber Ballet; Producer, Choreographer, "La Fille Mal Gardee", Chamber Ballet; Producer, Choreographer, "Les Patineurs", Chamber Ballet; Producer, Choreographer, "The Blue Danube", Chamber Ballet; Producer, Choreographer, "Alice in Wonderland", Chamber Ballet; Producer, Choreographer, "Beauty and the Beast", Chamber Ballet; Producer, Choreographer, "Fairy Tale to Fairy Tale", Chamber Ballet; Producer, Choreographer, "The Secret Garden", Chamber Ballet; Producer, Choreographer, "The Magic Flute", Chamber Ballet; Producer, Choreographer, "The Tales of Beatrix Potter", Chamber Ballet **To what do you attribute your success:** She attributes her success to her husband who financed a majority of the spring shows. **Why did you become involved in your profession or industry:** It was always Ms. Robitshek's dream to dance. Her parents did not have the money, so she went to a local school once a week. But that was not enough for her, she ended up going multiple times a week. Another school came to town so she ended up going to both, one school in the morning. She was an extra in the local theater. She was very grateful that someone believed in her and gave her lessons even though her family could not afford it. **Religion:** Catholic **Thoughts on Life:** Doing the best you can.

S. Kay Rockwell, PhD

Title: Educator **Industry:** Education/Educational Services **Date of Birth:** 02/28/1940 **Place of Birth:** Columbus **State/Country of Origin:** NE/USA **Parents:** Carrol Albert Becher; Lauretta Susanna (Grossnicklaus) Becher **Marital Status:** Married **Spouse Name:** Lee V. Rockwell (06/16/1962) **Children:** Kent Alan; Susan Kay Rockwell Downing; Keri Lynn **Education:** PhD in Community and Human Resources, University of Nebraska-Lincoln (1984); MA in Adult and Continuing Education, University of Nebraska-Lincoln (1975); BSN, University of Nebraska-Lincoln (1962); Graduate Coursework in Nursing, Lincoln General Hospital (Now Bryan Medical Center West) (1960) **Certifications:** Registered Nurse, State of Nebraska **Career:** Professor, Department of Agricultural Leadership, Education and Communication, University of Nebraska-Lincoln, Lincoln, NE (1990-2003); Specialist, Evaluation, University of Nebraska-Lincoln, Lincoln, NE (1984-2003); Professor, Cooperative Extension Division, Institute of Agriculture and Natural Resources, University of Nebraska-Lincoln, Lincoln, NE (1984-1990); Advisory Board, Department of Adult Education and Social Foundation, University of Nebraska-Lincoln, Lincoln, NE (1984-1986); Evaluation Technologist, University of Nebraska-Lincoln, Lincoln, NE (1979-1984); Instructor, Lincoln General Hospital (Now Bryan Medical Center West) (1962-1967); Acting Assistant Director, Nursing Education, Lincoln General Hospital (Now Bryan Medical Center West) (1965-1966) **Career Related:** Consultant, Trainer, Extension and Program Evaluation, Nebraska Extension, University of Nebraska-Lincoln **Civic:** Volunteer, USAID (2002-Present); Chairman, Social Ministry Committee, Nebraska Synod ELCA; Board Member, Advocacy Office, Evangelical Lutheran Church in America **Creative Works:** Research-in-Brief Editor, Extension Journal, Inc. (1987-1990); Contributor, Articles, Professional Journals; Presenter, Workshops and Symposia **Awards:** Wisherd Award for Outstanding International Community Service, UNL Emeriti Association (2020); Humanitarian Award, Friendship Force International (2018); Exceptional Support to the Open World Program, Open World Leadership Center, Library of Congress (2008) **Memberships:** American Evaluation Association (1990-Present); Representative, North Central Region, NACD; Extension Education Evaluation Topical Interest Group, American Evaluation Association; Nebraska Cooperative Extension Association, Inc.; Adult and Continuing Education Association of Nebraska; Epsilon Sigma Phi; Gamma Sigma Delta **Marquis Who's Who Honors:** Albert Nelson Marquis Lifetime Achievement Award; Marquis Who's Who Top Professional; Marquis Who's Who Humanitarian Award **To what do you attribute your success:** Dr. Rockwell attributes her success to her major influences, early aspirations and role models, all of which were crucial to her upbringing. She ultimately chose her profession because of her ambition to help others. **Why did you become involved in your profession or industry:** Dr. Rockwell became involved in her career with encouragement from her mother and one influential teacher, both of whom helped her in the process of applying to nursing school. She pursued nursing because it excited her and seemed a financially wise decision; she was also given the flexibility to raise her children while continuing to work. She has always followed the path of least resistance, taking advantage of what is available to her along the way. **Avocations:** Book club; Reading; Bridge; Traveling **Political Affiliations:** Democrat **Religion:** Protestant (Lutheran) **Thoughts on Life:** Dr. Rockwell particularly enjoyed the challenge of participating in monitoring and evaluation guidelines during her career. She is the proud grandmother of Sidney, Alex, Kyle, Shelby, Grace, Allison, Luna, Athena and Serena, and great-grandmother of Silas.

Hugh Roff Jr.

Title: Energy Executive **Industry:** Law and Legal Services **Company Name:** Roff Resources LLC **Date of Birth:** 10/27/1931 **Place of Birth:** Wewoka **State/Country of Origin:** OK/USA **Parents:** Hugh Roff; Louise Roff **Marital Status:** Married **Spouse Name:** Ann Roff **Children:** John; Charles; Andrew; Elizabeth; Jennifer **Education:** LLB, College of Law, University of Oklahoma (1955); AB, University of Oklahoma (1954) **Career:** Chairman, Roff Resources LLC, Houston, TX (1998-Present); Chairman of the Board, PetroUnited Terminals Incorporated, Houston, TX (1986-1998); Chairman of the Board, Alabama Methane Production Company, Inc. (1986-1989); Chairman, President, Chief Executive Officer, United Energy Resources, Houston, TX (1974-1985); General Attorney, Long Lines, New York, NY (1973-1974); Vice President, General Attorney, Long Lines, New York, NY (1969-1973); Attorney, AT&T, New York, NY (1964-1968); Attorney, Southwestern Bell Telephone Company, St. Louis, MO (1959-1963); Law Clerk to Presiding Justice A.P. Murrah, United States Court Appeals for the Tenth Circuit (1958) **Career Related:** Board of Trustees, Baylor College of Medicine (1983-Present); Director, Tidewater, Inc. (1986-2004); Advisory Director, Chase Bank of Texas (1998-2002); Director, Texas Commerce Bancshares (1981-1997); Board of Directors, Central Houston, Inc. (1983-1994); Executive Committee, Central Houston, Inc. (1983-1988); Director, Gas Research Institute (1984-1987); Advisory Director, Interstate Natural Gas Association of America (1982-1986); Chairman, Central Houston, Inc. (1983-1984); Director, Institute of Gas Technology (1974-1983); Director, Interstate Natural Gas Association of America (1974-1982); Chairman, Institute of Gas Technology (1980-1982); Chairman, Interstate Natural Gas Association of America (1978-1979); Advisory Director, Center for Strategic & International Studies, Washington, DC; Former Chairman, Houston Roundtable, Houston, TX **Civic:** Past Chairman, Central Houston Incorporated; Advisory Board, Center for Strategic and International Studies, Washington, DC; Trustee, Baylor College of Medicine; Past Chairman of Advisory Board, The Salvation Army, Houston, TX; Director, Inasmuch Foundation; Ethics and Excellence in Journalism Foundation; Life Trustee, Houston Symphony **Military Service:** First Lieutenant, Judge Advocate General's Corps, United States Army (1955-1958) **Awards:** Freshman Award, Pe-et Society, University of Oklahoma **Memberships:** Order of Coif; Phi Beta Kappa; Beta Theta Pi; Pe-et Society; Beta Theta Pi; Phi Delta Phi; American Bar Association; New York City Bar Association; Missouri Bar Association; Oklahoma Bar Association **Bar Admissions:** Oklahoma; Missouri; New York **Marquis Who's Who Honors:** Albert Nelson Marquis Lifetime Achievement Award; Marquis Who's Who Top Professional; Distinguished Humanitarian **Why did you become involved in your profession or industry:** Mr. Roff chose law as a career path because he felt that there was a larger scope of activities in the profession to make a difference. Growing up, both of his parents were attorneys in Oklahoma, which introduced him to the field. His mother and father were very influential in his life and his career progression.

Who's Who in America   Distinguished Listees • 1073

John Francis Rogan

Title: Private Practice Consultant **Industry:** Financial Services **Date of Birth:** 07/10/1926 **Place of Birth:** New York **State/Country of Origin:** NY/USA **Parents:** John Rogan; Susan (O'Doherty) Rogan **Marital Status:** Married **Spouse Name:** Anna Mae Cogan (07/19/1950, Deceased 01/28/2015) **Children:** Suzanne; John Junior; Kathleen; Patricia; Colleen; Michael; Kevin; David; Maureen **Education:** MBA, Indiana University, with Distinction (1960); BS, Indiana University, with Distinction (1959) **Career:** Private Practice Consultant, Middleton, WI (1983-Present); State Finance Director, Wisconsin Department of Administration, Madison, WI (1970-1983); Director, Settlement Operations, United States Army Financial Center, IN (1968-1970); Finance and Accounting Officer, Chief, Finance and Accounting Policy Division, Office of the Comptroller, United States Eighth Army, Korea (1967-1968); Finance and Accounting Officer, U.S. Military Academy, West Point, NY (1963-1967); With, Commando and General Staff College, Fort Leavenworth, KS (1962-1963); Deputy Director, Finance Department, United States Civil Administration, Okinawa, Japan (1960-1962); Member, Faculty, United States Army Financial School, Fort Benjamin, Harrison, ID (1955-1958); Finance Officer, Advanced Course, United States Army (1954-1955); Finance Disbursing Officer, United States Army, Japan (1948-1952); Member, Faculty, United States Army Finance School, St. Louis, MO (1946-1948) **Career Related:** Central Corporate Board, Diocese of Madison, WI (1994-Present); Co-chairman, State/Federal Cash Management Task Force, Washington, DC (1982-1983); National Council on Governmental Accounting, Chicago, IL (1980-1983); Cemetery Board Member, National Government Accounting Research Project, Lexington, KY (1977-1982); Financial Advisor, Diocese of Madison, WI (1970-2008) **Civic:** Chairperson, Advisory Board, Holy Name Seminary, Madison, WI (1973-Present); Member, Diocesan Appeals Committee, Madison, WI (1973-Present); Board of Directors, St. Raphael Society, Madison, WI (1975-Present); Board of Directors, Advisor, State and University Employees Charity Campaign, Madison, WI (1977-1983); Chairperson, State and University Employees Charity Campaign, Madison, WI (1975-1976) **Military Service:** Retired, United States Army (1970); Advanced through Grades to Colonel, United States Army (1968); Enlisted, United States Army (1945) **Creative Works:** Author, Paperback, "Our Wartime Love Story" (2018); Featured, "Know Your Madisonian," Wisconsin State Journal (1983) **Awards:** Leadership Award, Catholic Charities of the Diocese of Madison, Faith in Action (2017); Inductee, Officer Candidate School Hall of Fame (2016); Veteran Lifetime Achievement Award, Wisconsin Board of Veterans Affairs (2009); Named Serran of the Year, Madison Serra Club (2004); Family of the Year Award, Wisconsin Knights of Columbus (2003); Special Recognition Award, National Association of State Auditors, Comptrollers, and Treasurers (1984); Outstanding Leadership and Service Award, Wisconsin Governor and State Legislature (1983); Inductee, Army Finance Corps Hall of Fame **Memberships:** President, Madison Serra Club (2001-2002); President, National Association of State Auditors, Comptrollers and Treasurers (1982-1983); Executive Committee, National Association of State Auditors, Comptrollers and Treasurers (1979-1983); Association of Government Accountants; Retired Officers' Association (Now Military Officers Association of America); Association of the United States Army; National Association for Uniformed Services (NAUS); Army Finance Corps Association; Society of Retired Army Finance Officers; Beta Gamma Sigma; Beta Alpha Psi; National Council on Governmental Accounting; Executive Committee, The Council of State Governments and National State Comptroller's Association; Governmental Accounting Standards Board (GASB); U.S. Catholic Bishops' National Advisory Council; Order of St. Gregory the Great; Equestrian Order of the Holy Sepulcher of Jerusalem; Fourth Degree Member, Knights of Columbus; President, National Association of the Holy Name Society **Marquis Who's Who Honors:** Albert Nelson Marquis Lifetime Achievement Award; Marquis Who's Who Top Professional **Avocations:** Biking; Walking; Bowling; Softball; Movies; Church **Religion:** Roman Catholic

Alan Ernest Exel Rogers

Title: Research Scientist **Industry:** Research **Date of Birth:** 10/03/1941 **Place of Birth:** Harare **State/Country of Origin:** Zimbabwe **Parents:** John Exel Rogers; Leonara Violet (De Smidt) Rogers **Marital Status:** Married **Spouse Name:** Louise Marilyn Holland (02/24/1968) **Children:** Heather; David **Education:** Doctor of Philosophy in Electrical Engineering, Massachusetts Institute of Technology, Cambridge, MA (1967); Master of Science in Electrical Engineering, Massachusetts Institute of Technology, Cambridge, MA (1964); Bachelor of Science in Mathematics and Physics, University of Zimbabwe (1962) **Career:** Research Affiliate, MIT Haystack Observatory (2006-Present); Associate Director, MIT Haystack Observatory (1993-2006); Senior Research Scientist, MIT Haystack Observatory (1968-2006); Lecturer, University of Zimbabwe (1968); Research Assistant, Massachusetts Institute of Technology (1962-1967) **Creative Works:** Author, Co-Author, Contributor, Numerous Publications **Awards:** Grote Reber Medal (2010); John Howard Dellinger Medal (2008) **Memberships:** Institute of Electrical and Electronics Engineers; American Astronomical Society; American Geophysical Union; American Association for the Advancement of Science **Marquis Who's Who Honors:** Albert Nelson Marquis Lifetime Achievement Award; Marquis Who's Who Top Professional; Marquis Who's Who Humanitarian Award **Why did you become involved in your profession or industry:** Dr. Rogers initially became involved in his industry due to the influence of his father, who was a radio operator and pilot during the Second World War. Likewise, his father built a satellite tracking station, and was able to record data from early satellites that were not capable of recording on-board data. **Religion:** Episcopalian

Jon M. Rogers, PhD, ChFC, MRFC, CKA

Title: Chairman, Chief Executive Officer **Industry:** Financial Services **Company Name:** Rogers Financial Group, LLC, Rogers Financial Advisory Group, LLC **Date of Birth:** 06/04/1942 **Place of Birth:** Piedmont **State/Country of Origin:** SC/USA **Parents:** James Robert (1993); Eunice (Ashley) Rogers (1998) **Marital Status:** Married **Spouse Name:** Jeanette O. Rogers (6/16/62) **Children:** Elaine R. Walsh; Joni R. Foy; Melissa R. King **Education:** PhD in Financial Management, LaSalle University (1994); MS, Clemson University (1966); BS, Clemson University (1964) **Certifications:** Senior Leaders Greenville, SC (2018); MRFC (2017); Accredited Asset Specialists (AAMS), College for Financial Planning, CKA (2016); Chartered Finanical Consultant (1984); Chartered Life Underwriter (1973); Certified Kingdom Advisor **Career:** Chief Executive Officers, Rogers Fin. Group LLC, Greenville, SC (2000-Present); Partner, J&J Enterprises, Piemont, SC (1975-Present); Chairman, Board of Directors, Chief Executive Officer, Rogers Fin. Group LLC, Greenville, SC (1989-2000); Regional Sales Manager, Liberty Corp., Greenville, SC (1982-1988); Regional Sales Manager, Metropolitan Life, Milwaukee, WI (1975-1981); District Sales Manager, Metropolitan Life, Atlanta, GA (1972-1974); Sales Representative, Metropolitan Life, Greenville, SC (1969-1971) **Career Related:** Registered Securities Representative, Royal Alliance Associates, Inc., New York, NY (1986-Present); Adjunct Professor, Webster University; Member, Masters Club with Royal Alliance Associate **Civic:** Life Member, Rotary Intl. (1989-Present); Deacon, Chairman, Washington Church, Pelzer, SC (1993-1994); Board of Directors, Child Evangelism Fellowship (1988-1989); President, Republican Precinct, Piedmont, SC (1988); Deacon, Chairman, Washington Church, Pelzer, SC (1985-1987); Top of Table, Life Member, Washington Church, Pelzer, SC; Paul Harris Fellow **Military Service:** Captain, U.S. Army, Vietnam (1967-1969); U.S. Army Reserve (1964-1975) **Creative Works:** Co-author, "21st Century Wealth, Essential Financial Planning Principles," Quantum Press LLC (2000) **Awards:** Top 5% of Financial Consultant Ambassador Award (2018); IARFC Lorea Donton Award (2015); Decorated Bronze Star; Army Air Medal; Army Commendation Medal Oak Leaf Cluster **Memberships:** Board of Directors, President, Rotary (1996-1997); South Carolina President, Gideons International Club (1985-1987); Vice President, National Association of Life Underwriters (1972-1973); Million Dollar Round Table; National Association of Securities Dealers; International Association of Financial Planners **Marquis Who's Who Honors:** Albert Nelson Marquis Lifetime Achievement Award **To what do you attribute your success:** He attributes his success to Jeremiah 29: 11, Phil 4: 13 and excellent mentors in his life that believed in him. **Why did you become involved in your profession or industry:** After his service in Vietnam, jobs were not readily available. He started marketing life Insurance and mutual funds to clients with a need and really enjoyed helping with their financial goals. Offered a management training program with a large insurance co. advanced very rapidly. **Avocations:** Photography; Golf; Walking; Community theatre; Reading; Studying and teaching Bible; Traveling to other countries with his wife; Vacations with family; Attending Clemson football games **Political Affiliations:** Republicans **Religion:** Baptist

Lee Frank Rogers, MD

Title: Professor Emeritus of Radiology **Industry:** Education/Educational Services **Company Name:** Wake Forest University; Northwestern University **Date of Birth:** 09/24/1934 **Place of Birth:** Colchester **State/Country of Origin:** VT/USA **Parents:** Watson Frank Rogers (Deceased 1981); Marguerite Mortimer (Cole) Rogers (Deceased 1988) **Marital Status:** Married **Spouse Name:** Donna Mae Brinker (06/20/1956) **Children:** Michelle; Cynthia; Christopher; Matthew **Education:** Resident in Radiology, Fitzsimons General Hospital (1960-1963); Rotating Intern, Walter Reed General Hospital (1959-1960); MD, Northwestern University (1959); BS, Northwestern University (1956) **Career:** Retired (2014); Professor of Radiology, The University of Arizona Health Sciences Center (2003-2014); Isadore Meschan Distinguished Professor of Radiology, Wake Forest University School of Medicine, Winston-Salem, NC (1995-2004); The Bradd and Kennedy Professor of Radiology, Northwestern University Medical School, Chicago, IL (1986-1995); Professor, Chairman, Department of Radiology, Northwestern University Medical School, Chicago, IL (1974-1995); Director, Residency Training, Radiologist, University of Texas Medical School (Now The University of Texas Health Science Center at Houston (UTHealth)), Houston, Texas (1972-1974); Radiologist, University of Texas Medical School (Now The University of Texas Health Science Center at Houston (UTHealth)), San Antonio, Texas (1968-1971); Radiologist, Baptist Memorial Hospital, San Antonio, Texas (1967-1968) **Career Related:** Visiting Professor, 115 Occasions; Given 30 Named Lectures **Military Service:** Advanced to Major, United States Army (1967); Commissioned First Lieutenant, United States Army (1959) **Creative Works:** Author, "Imaging of Skeletal Trauma" (2015); Editor-in-chief, American Journal of Roentgenology, Winston-Salem, NC (1995-2003); Author, "Radiology of Skeletal Trauma", First Edition (1982); Author, Over 150 Scientific Articles, 100 Editorials; Author, Three Books; Presenter, Over 100 Scientific Exhibits; Exhibitor, "A Multisystem Radiographic Analysis of Complications in the Burn Patient" **Awards:** Named Educator of the Year, American Roentgen Ray Society (2011); Magna Cum Laude Award for "A Multisystem Radiographic Analysis of Complications in the Burn Patient," 57th Annual Meeting, Radiological Society of North America (1971); Gold Medal Award, American College of Radiology; Gold Medal Award, Association of University Radiologists; Gold Medal Award, Chicago Radiological Society; Gold Medal Award, American Society of Emergency Radiology; Gold Medal Award, Radiology Society of North America; Distinguished Service Medal, Chicago Radiological Society; Grubb Medal, Illinois Radiological Society; Founder's Medal, International Skeletal Society **Memberships:** President, American Board of Radiology; Chairman, Board of Chancellors, American College of Radiology; American Roentgen Ray Society (ARRS); Association of University Radiologists; Chicago Radiological Society; Society of Chairs of Academic Radiology Departments; First Vice President, Radiological Society of North America; American Society of Neuroradiology; American Association of Women in Radiology (AAWR); Society for Pediatric Radiology; Royal Australasian College of Radiologists (Now The Royal Australian and New Zealand College of Radiologists) **Marquis Who's Who Honors:** Albert Nelson Marquis Lifetime Achievement Award **Why did you become involved in your profession or industry:** There were a lot of physicians in Professor Rogers' family and he was the oldest one, so he chose to continue the family legacy. He chose radiology because the rest of the physicians in his family were internists.

Raymond Stephen Roginski, MD, PhD

Title: Medical Educator, Staff Anesthesiologist **Industry:** Medicine & Health Care **Date of Birth:** 11/27/1955 **Place of Birth:** Jersey City **State/Country of Origin:** NJ/USA **Parents:** Edward Stanley Roginski; Carmella Phyllis (Maiuro) Roginski **Spouse Name:** Sharon Claire Krieger (1988) **Children:** Melissa Rae; Vanessa Kristine; Grant Edward **Education:** Resident in Anesthesiology, Albert Einstein College of Medicine, Bronx, NY (1985-1989); MD, PhD, Albert Einstein College Medicine (1985); MS, Albert Einstein College Medicine (1981); BS, MS, Yale University (1977) **Certifications:** Diplomate, American Board of Anesthesiology (1992) **Career:** Clinical Assistant Professor, University of Pennsylvania (2009-Present); Staff Anesthesiologist, Philadelphia VA Medical Center (2009-Present); Assistant Professor, Anesthesiology and Critical Care, University of Pennsylvania (2002-2009); Clinical Assistant Professor, Anesthesiology, UMDNJ University Hospital, New Brunswick, NJ (1991-2002); Instructor, Department of Neuroscience, Albert Einstein College of Medicine, Bronx, NY (1989-1991); Clinical Assistant Professor, Anesthesiology, University of Medicine and Dentistry of New Jersey, Newark, NJ (1989-1991) **Civic:** Parishioner, St Bartholomews Episcopal Church **Creative Works:** Contributor, Numerous Scientific Papers, Articles, Scientific and Biomedical Journals **Awards:** UMDNJ Anesthesiology Research Award (1998); Anesthesiology Young Investigator Award, Burroughs Wellcome Company/Foundation for Anesthesia Education and Research (1993) **Memberships:** Alpha Chapter, Yale University; American Society of Anesthesiologists; Society of Neuroscience; International Anesthesia Research Society; Society of Neuroscience, Anesthesiology, and Critical Care; Phi Beta Kappa **Marquis Who's Who Honors:** Albert Nelson Marquis Lifetime Achievement Award **Avocations:** Golf; Running; Chess **Religion:** Episcopalian

Jim R. Ropchan, PhD

Title: Research Scientist **Industry:** Research **Company Name:** Yale University **Place of Birth:** Leamington **State/Country of Origin:** ON/Canada **Parents:** William George Ropchan; Katie (Rudyka) Ropchan **Marital Status:** Single **Education:** Postdoctoral Studies, University of California Los Angeles (1981-1985); PhD, Synthetic Organic Chemistry, University of Detroit (1981); BS, Detroit Institute of Technology, With Honors (1972); Degree in Chemical Engineering Technology, St. Clair College of Applied Arts and Technology, Ontario, Canada (1971) **Certifications:** PETtrace Cyclotron Advanced Training and Certification, GE Center, Sweden (2009); PETtrace Cyclotron Training and Certification, Yale University by GE (2006); RDS 111 Cyclotron Training and Certification, CTI, San Diego, CA (2000) **Career:** Lead Production Chemist of Radiopharmaceutical and Cyclotron Operations at Yale (2006-Present); Director of Radiopharmaceutical and Cyclotron Operations, Molecular Imaging/UCSD (2003-2006); Vice President of Radiopharmaceuticals and Cyclotron Operations, Vital Imaging/UCSD, San Diego, CA (2000-2003); President of JR Consulting Services, San Diego, CA (1995-2000); Instructor in Radiopharmacy and PET Courses, Veterans Affairs Medical Center, Los Angeles, CA (1987-1995); Secretary of Radioactive Drug Research Committee, Veterans Affairs Medical Center, Los Angeles, CA (1987-1995); Director, Chief Chemist of Chemistry Section, Positron Emission Tomography Facility, Veterans Affairs Medical Center, Los Angeles, CA (1986-1995); Associate Investigator, Division of Nuclear Medicine and Biophysics, University of California Los Angeles (1983-1985); Postdoctoral Scholar, University of California Los Angeles (1981-1985); Quality Control Chemist, Ford Motor Co., Windsor, ON, Canada (1973-1976) **Career Related:** Director, Cyclotron Facility (1992-1995); Director, Cyclotron Targetry Development (1989-1995); Supervisor of Radiopharmaceutical/PET Facility, Veterans Affairs Medical Center, Los Angeles, CA (1987-1995); Director of Radiopharmacy Chemistry Research/ Positron Emission Tomography Facility (1987-1995); Radiation Safety Committee (1986-1995); Lecturer on Radiopharmaceutical Chemistry/ Cyclotron Research, Switzerland (1991); Lecturer on Radiopharmaceutical Chemistry/Cyclotron Research, Canada (1989); Lecturer on Radiopharmaceutical Chemistry/Cyclotron Research, Italy (1984); Part-Time Teacher, High School Mathematics and Science, Windsor, Ontario, Canada (1977); Part-Time Instructor of Organic Chemistry, Detroit Institute of Technology (1977); Fellow, IBC; Fellow, American Institute of Chemists; Research Fellow, ABI **Creative Works:** Designer, Fabricator, New Cyclotron Targetry/Chemistry Systems (1991-Present); Contributor, Over 175 Articles, Abstracts to Professional Journals; Inventor, Laboratory Accessories **Awards:** American Way Scientist Award (2020); Honorable Mention, Wall Street Journal (2019); ABI Shield of Valor Award; Presidential Seal of Honor Award, ABI (1996); Dictionary of International Biography, IBC (1995); Named, Man of the Year, IBC (1992); Supervisor Performance Award, Veterans Affairs Medical Center, Los Angeles (1991-1992); Named, Man of the Year, ABI (1991); Associate Investigator Award, University of California Los Angeles, International Register of Profiles, Ed X, IBC (1990); Supervisor Performance Award, Veterans Affairs Medical Center, Los Angeles (1989); Grantee, University of California Los Angeles (1983); Outstanding Scholar Award, Detroit Institute of Technology (1972); 20th Century Award for Achievement **Memberships:** American Association for the Advancement of Science (1990); American Management Association (1990); American Chemical Society (1979); New York Academy of Sciences; Cousteau Society; Planetary Society; Keepers Club; American Heart Association; Diamond Club **Marquis Who's Who Honors:** Albert Nelson Marquis Lifetime Achievement Award (2020); Marquis Who's Who Top Professional (2019-2020) **To what do you attribute your success:** Dr. Ropchan attributes his success to dedication, natural and acquired skills, the desire to learn from his failures, and a lot of determination and hard work. If you do not apply your acquired skills and work hard toward your objective in life, you cannot be disappointed if you do not succeed. **Why did you become involved in your profession or industry:** As a young boy, Dr. Ropchan always loved to create things and to explore how things worked, and then apply them to help others. In PET, it is one of the few professions where you can synthesize a radiopharmaceutical for a specific use and send it to imaging, where you can obtain a 3-D image of the specific area in the human body that provides valuable information for you, all in the same day. **Religion:** Protestant **Thoughts on Life:** "We all go through this life only once and we should try to do the very best at what vocation we have chosen. What we do should be something we have a passion for, and then apply all your skills and compassion for the area you have chosen and pursue it with our entire being."

Daniel Rose

Title: Chairman **Industry:** Financial Services **Company Name:** Rose Associates, Inc. **Date of Birth:** 10/31/1929 **Place of Birth:** New York **State/Country of Origin:** NY/USA **Parents:** Samuel B. Rose; Belle (Bernstein) Rose **Marital Status:** Married **Spouse Name:** Joanna Semel (09/16/1956) **Children:** David Semel; Joseph Benedict; Emily; Gideon Gregory **Education:** Certificate of Proficiency in Russian Language, U.S. Air Force (1952); BA, Syracuse University (1952); Coursework, Yale University (1947-1950); Honorary Doctor of Science, Technion Israel; Honorary Doctor of Humane Letters, Long Island University; Honorary Doctor of Engineering, New York University; Postgraduate Studies, University of Paris (Now Sorbonne University) **Career:** Chairman, Rose Associates, Inc. (formerly Dwelling Managers, Inc.), New York, NY (1955-Present); Director, U.S. Trust Company of New York, New York, NY (1982-1999); Director, Dreyfus Tax-Exempt Bond Fund (Now Dreyfus New York Tax Exempt Bond Fund, Inc.) (1976-1982); Director, Dreyfus Money Market Fund, Inc. (1980-1980) **Career Related:** Governor, Urban Land Foundation (Now ULI Foundation) (1993-Present); Board Member, 22 Dreyfus Funds, MBSC Securities Corporation (1992-Present); Executive Committee, Urban Land Foundation (Now ULI Foundation) (1989-Present); Vice-Chairman, Lionel Trilling Seminars, Columbia University (1977-Present); Associate Fellow, Pierson College, Yale University (1974-Present); Fellow, American Academy Arts and Sciences (2012); Trustee, Mixed Use Development Council, Urban Land Institute (1986-1993); Vice-Chairman, Mixed Use Development Council, Urban Land Institute (1986-1993); Trustee, Executive and Compensation and Benefits Committees, U.S. Trust Company of New York (1982-1992); Executive and Compensation and Benefits Committees, U.S. Trust Company of New York (1982-1992); Board of Governors, Technion - Israel Institute of Technology; Board of Directors, Grants Committee, Realty Foundation of New York; Designated Certified Property Manager, Institute for Real Estate Management; Chairman, Forum for Urban Design (Now Urban Design Forum, Inc.); Vice Chairman, Baltic American Enterprise Fund **Civic:** Board of Trustees, MBA of New York Scholarship Foundation, Inc. (1996-Present); National Convention Board of Advisors, Democratic Leadership Council (1992-Present); Honorary Trustee, Horace Mann-Barnard School (Now Horace Mann School) (1989-Present); Director, New York Council of Humanities (1980-Present); Chairman Emeritus, Jewish Community Centers Association (Now JCC Association of North America) (1978-Present); Board of Directors, Citizens Housing and Planning Council of New York (CHPC New York) (1972-Present); Board of Directors, Jewish Community Centers Association (Now JCC Association of North America) (1970-Present); Overseers Committee, Visitor Center of International Affairs (Now Weatherhead Center for International Affairs), Harvard University (1992-1998); Get Ahead Foundation (CGAP) (1989-1998); Fifth Avenue Association (Now Fifth Avenue Association BID) (1989-1998); Progressive Policy Institute Trustee, Democratic National Committee (DNC) (1988); Board Member, Museum of the City of New York (1984-1990); Consultant, U.S. Housing and Urban Development Panel on Urban Development (1984-1986); Chairman, Democratic Platform Advisory Committee (1984); New York Convention Center Development Corporation (1980-1990); Vice President, Board of Directors, New York Landmarks Conservancy (1977-1990) **Military Service:** United States Air Force Russian Program (1951-1954) **Creative Works:** Author "The Examined Life" (2020) **Awards:** Entrepreneur of the Year, Ernst & Young (EY) (2003); Harlem Renaissance Award, Abyssinian Development Corporation; Joseph Papp Racial Harmony Award, Foundation for Ethnic Understanding (FFEU); Mayor's Award of Honor for Arts and Culture, City of New York; Man of the Year Award, Realty Foundation of New York; Award, Urban Land Institute; Community Service Award, Building Owners & Managers Association (BOMA) International; Eight Cicero Speechwriting Awards; James E. Landauer Award, American Society of Real Estate Counselors (Now The Counselors of Real Estate) **Memberships:** Chairman, Executive Committee, East-West Institute (2000-Present); Board of Governors, Real Estate Board of New York (REBNY) (1990-Present); Director, American Committee, International Institute for Strategic Studies (IISS) (1987-Present); Chairman, Housing Committee, Real Estate Board of New York (REBNY) (1975-Present); Board of Directors, Council on Foreign Relations, Foreign Policy Association (1971-Present); Co-chairman, Financial Committee, EastWest Institute (1990-2010); Class of 1951 Delegate, Association of Yale Alumni (1986-1989); REBNY Foundation; The Century Association, New York, NY; The Union League Club; Cosmos Club, Washington, DC; Quaker Ridge Country Club (Now Quaker Ridge Golf Club); Noyac Country Club (Now Noyac Golf Club); The Economic Club New York; Honorary Life Member, Technion, Israel Institute of Technology **Marquis Who's Who Honors:** Albert Nelson Marquis Lifetime Achievement Award; Marquis Who's Who Top Professional

Susan Porter Rose, LHD (Hon.)

Title: Former Chief of Staff to Barbara Bush **Industry:** Government Administration/Government Relations/Government Services **Company Name:** The White House **Date of Birth:** 09/20/1941 **Place of Birth:** Cincinnati **State/Country of Origin:** OH/USA **Parents:** Elmer Johnson Porter; Dorothy (Wurst) Porter **Marital Status:** Married **Spouse Name:** Jonathan Chapman Rose (01/26/1980) **Children:** Benjamin Chapman Rose **Education:** Honorary LHD, Rose-Hulman Institute of Technology (2002); MA, Indiana State University (1970); BA, Earlham College (1963) **Career:** Retired, Commissioner, U.S. Commission of Fine Arts (1993-1998); Deputy Assistant to the President, George H.W. Bush (1989-1993); Chief of Staff to the First Lady, Barbara Bush (1989-1993); Assistant to the Vice President, George H.W. Bush (1981-1989); Chief of Staff, Barbara Bush (1981-1989); Special Assistant to Assistant Attorney General, Justice Management Division, U.S. Department of Justice (1978-1981); Special Assistant to Assistant Attorney General, Office for Improvements in The Administration of Justice, U.S. Department of Justice (1977-1979); Head of Scheduling and Projects, First Lady Betty Ford (1974-1977); Head of Scheduling and Projects, First Lady Pat Nixon (1972-1974); Assistant Director of Correspondence, First Lady Pat Nixon (1971-1972); Assistant Director of Admissions, Mount Holyoke College (1966-1971); Assistant Dean, George School (1964-1966); Staff Assistant, Congressman Richard L. Roudebush (1963-1964) **Civic:** Trustee, George H.W. Bush Presidential Library and Museum (1994-Present); Spouse Participant, Yale Global Alumni Leadership Exchange Program "Participants in Yale-GALE" (2008-2017); Participant, Renaissance Weekend (1986-2012); Board of Directors, Barbara Bush Foundation for Family Literacy (1993-2002); Commissioner, United States Commission of Fine Arts (1993-1998); Effecter (1992); President, Alumni Association, Earlham College (1978-1981); Alumni Council, Earlham College (1975-1978) **Memberships:** Indiana Academy (1991) **Marquis Who's Who Honors:** Albert Nelson Marquis Lifetime Achievement Award; Marquis Who's Who Top Professional; Marquis Who's Who Humanitarian Award **To what do you attribute your success:** Mrs. Rose attributes her success to her wonderful, creative, hard-working parents with many interests. She was fortunate to have an excellent liberal arts education and people in her life that included her in very interesting and significant endeavors. **Why did you become involved in your profession or industry:** Mrs. Rose became involved in her profession because she was always interested in government and education. Mrs. Rose gave careful, creative thought to where she actually wanted to be situated in life. **Avocations:** Worldwide politics; Travel; Books; Family; Pets; Golf **Political Affiliations:** Republican **Religion:** Quaker, Congregational, Episcopalian **Thoughts on Life:** Mrs. Rose served as Chief of Staff to Barbara Bush for 12 years. Susan Porter Rose and her husband, Jonathan C. Rose, have participated in a Yale University Alumni program, Yale/Global Alumni Leadership Exchange (Yale GALE). She also worked with Foreign Universities on their alumni programs.

William A. Rosoff

Title: Counsel **Industry:** Law and Legal Services **Company Name:** Dechert LLP **Date of Birth:** 06/21/1943 **Place of Birth:** Philadelphia **State/Country of Origin:** PA/USA **Parents:** Herbert Rosoff; Estelle (Finkel) Rosoff **Marital Status:** Married **Spouse Name:** Beverly Rae Rifkin (02/07/1970) **Children:** Catherine D.; Andrew M. **Education:** LLB, University of Pennsylvania, Magna Cum Laude (1967); BS, Accounting, Temple University, With High Honors (1964) **Career:** Counsel, Dechert LLP (2011-Present); President, Advanta Corp. (1999-2011); Vice Chairman, Board of Directors, Advanta Corp. (1996-2011); Chairman, Tax Department, Wolf Block, Schorr & Solis Cohen (1995-1996), Partner, Wolf, Block, Schorr & Solis-Cohen (1975-1996); Chairman, Executive Committee, Wolf, Block, Schorr & Solis-Cohen (1987-1988); Associate, Wolf, Block, Schorr & Solis-Cohen (1969-1975); Instructor, University of Pennsylvania Law School (1968-1969); Law Clerk to Hon. Abraham L. Freedman, U.S. Court of Appeals for the Third Circuit (1967-1968) **Career Related:** Trustee, Atlantic Realty Trust (1996-2006); Chairman, Board of Directors, RMH Teleservices, Inc. (1997-1999); Tax Advisory Board Member, Little, Brown and Company, Hachette Book Group, Inc. (1994-1996); Trustee, RPS Realty Trust (1990-1996); Legal Activities Policy Board of Tax Analysts (1978-1995); Tax Advisory Board, CCH Incorporated (1983-1994); Presenter in Field Including to the National Office of the Internal Revenue Service and Harvard Law School's Tax Policy Institute; Fellow, American College of Tax Counsel **Civic:** Board of Directors, Rothman Institute (2011-Present); Dean's Counsel, Fox School of Business, Temple University (2012-2019); Board of Visitors, Fox School of Business, Temple University (2005-2012); Past Member, Committee on Law and Social Action, Philadelphia Council, American Jewish Committee **Creative Works:** Associate Reporter, American Law Institute's Proposals on the Taxation of Partners (1984); Editor, University of Pennsylvania Law Review (1965-1967); Contributor, Articles, Professional Journals; Presenter in Field **Awards:** Co-Recipient, Martin D. Ginsburg Award, Cedille Chicago, NFP (2017) **Memberships:** Advisory Group, Federal Income Tax Project, American Law Institute (1982-Present); Consultant for Taxation of Pass-through Entities, American Law Institute (1995-2000); Associate Reporter for Taxation of Partnerships, American Law Institute (1978-1982); Consultant for Taxation of Partnerships, American Law Institute (1976-1978); Order of the Coif; Beta Gamma Sigma, Inc.; Beta Alpha Psi **Bar Admissions:** State of New York (2017); U.S. District Court for the Eastern District of Pennsylvania (1968); State of Pennsylvania (1968) **Marquis Who's Who Honors:** Albert Nelson Marquis Lifetime Achievement Award; Marquis Who's Who Top Professional **Why did you become involved in your profession or industry:** Mr. Rosoff was an accounting major in college and assumed he should focus on tax. He also had an exceptional tax law professor, who guided him into tax. Therefore, after clerking and teaching at Pennsylvania State University for a year, he joined Wolf, Block, Schorr & Solis-Cohen's Tax Department. After extensive tax experience, clients asked him to handle other matters and eventually to oversee their overall legal affairs. In late 1995, a client, Advanta Corp., one of the largest credit card issuers in the country, asked him to join as vice chairman of the board of directors and later as president as well.

Hugh Courtney Ross

Title: Electrical Engineer **Industry:** Engineering **Company Name:** Ross Engineering Corporation **Date of Birth:** 12/31/1923 **Parents:** Clare W. Ross; Jeanne F. Ross **Marital Status:** Married **Spouse Name:** Patricia A. Malloy; Sarah A. Gordon (Deceased) **Children:** John C.; James G.; Robert W. **Education:** Postgraduate Coursework, Stanford University (1954); BEE, Stanford University (1950); Coursework, San Jose State University (1946-1947); Coursework, California Institute of Technology (1942) **Certifications:** Registered Professional Electrical Engineer, California **Career:** President, Electrical Engineer, Ross Engineering Corporation, Campbell, CA (1964-Present); Chief Engineer, ITT Jennings, San Jose, CA (1962-1964); Chief Engineer, Vacuum Power Switches, Jennings Radio Manufacturing Corporation, San Jose, CA (1951-1962); Instructor, San Benito High School and Junior College (1950-1951) **Career Related:** Fellow, IEEE (Institute of Electrical and Electronics Engineers) **Military Service:** U.S. Air Force (1943-1946) **Creative Works:** Contributor, Articles, Professional Journals; Developer **Awards:** OSS/CIA Congressional Medal of Honor for Secret Service Assisting the European Resistance in 1945, Secret Air Force "Carpet Baggers" (2018) **Memberships:** Chairman, Santa Clara Valley Subsection, IEEE (Institute of Electrical and Electronics Engineers) (1960-1961); American Vacuum Society; American Society of Metals **Marquis Who's Who Honors:** Albert Nelson Marquis Lifetime Achievement Award **Why did you become involved in your profession or industry:** Mr. Ross was attracted to his profession because of his father, who was an electrical contractor. He was inspired by watching his father excel in the field. **Religion:** Protestant

Thomas David Roti

Title: Judge **Industry:** Law and Legal Services **Company Name:** Circuit Court of Cook County **Parents:** Sam N. Roti; Theresa S. (Salerno) Roti **Marital Status:** Married **Spouse Name:** Donna Sumichrast (1972) **Children:** Thomas S.; Kyle D.; Rebecca D.; Gregory J. **Education:** JD, Loyola University Chicago, Cum Laude (1970); BS, Loyola University Chicago (1967) **Career:** Mentor, Circuit Court Cook County (2005-Present); The Honorable Judge, Circuit Court Cook County (2000-Present); Vice President, General Counsel, Dominick's Finer Foods, Inc., Northlake, IL (1977-1997); Assistant General Counsel, Dominick's Finer Foods, Inc., Northlake, IL (1975-1977); Associate, Boodell, Sears et al, Chicago, IL (1973-1975); Associate, Arnstein, Gluck & Lehr, Chicago, IL (1972-1973); Senior Law Clerk to Judge Frank McGarr, United States District Court for the Northern District of Illinois (1971-1972) **Career Related:** Trustee, National Conference on Community and Justice (1995-2000); Legislation Committee, Illinois Retail Merchants Association, Chicago, IL (1987-1997); National Conference Lawyers and Economics Committee, Food Marketing Institute, Washington, DC (1987-1997) **Civic:** Director, Chicago Clean Streak (1990-1997); Trustee, Joint Civic Committee on Italian Americans, Chicago, IL (1986-1995); Chicago Council, EDU-CARE Scholarship Program (1988) **Military Service:** Major, Quartermaster Corps, United States Army Reserve (1967-1983) **Creative Works:** Contributor, Articles, Professional Journals **Awards:** Mock Trial Special Service Award, Northwest Suburban Bar Association (2015); American Jurisprudence Award (1970); Alumni Association Award, Loyola University (1970) **Memberships:** Co-chair, Civil Practice Committee, Public Services Award (2011); Board of Directors, Illinois Judges Association (2005-2011); Nomination Committee, Board of Trustees, Illinois Judges Association Foundation (2007-2008); Board of Governors, Northwest Suburban Bar Association (2006-2008); Board Governors, Director, The Catholic Lawyers Guild of Chicago (2004-2007); Phi Alpha Delta; Alpha Sigma Nu; Justinian Society of Lawyers; Chicago Bar Association; Illinois Bar Association **Bar Admissions:** United States District Court for the Northern District of Illinois (1971); United States Court of Appeals for the Seventh Circuit (1971); Illinois State Bar (1970) **Marquis Who's Who Honors:** Albert Nelson Marquis Lifetime Achievement Award; Marquis Who's Who Top Professional **To what do you attribute your success:** Judge Roti attributes his success to his parents, two brothers and wife, all whom were his mentors. He was also inspired by Judge Frank McGarr because he believes he was the perfect example of how to be a judge. **Why did you become involved in your profession or industry:** Judge Roti became involved in his profession because he always wanted to be a lawyer; he always loved the law. **Religion:** Roman Catholic

Jack Rounick

Title: Lawyer **Industry:** Law and Legal Services **Company Name:** Law Offices of Jack A. Rounick, LLC **Date of Birth:** 06/05/1935 **Place of Birth:** Philadelphia **State/Country of Origin:** PA/USA **Parents:** Philip Rounick; Nettie (Brownstein) Rounick **Marital Status:** Married **Spouse Name:** Noreen A. Garrigan (09/04/1970) **Children:** Ellen; Eric; Amy; Michelle **Education:** JD, University of Pennsylvania, Philadelphia, PA (1959); BBA, University of Michigan, Ann Arbor, MI (1956) **Certifications:** Diplomate, The American College of Family Trial Lawyers **Career:** Of Counsel, Law Offices Jack A. Rounick LLC (2012-Present); Of Counsel, Flamm Walton PC, (2010-2012); Of Counsel, Flamm, Boroff & Bacine, Professional Corporation, Blue Bell, PA (2006-2010); Director, Deb Shops, Inc. (1974-2007); Assistant Secretary, Deb Shops, Inc. (1974-2007); Counsel to Firm, Wolf Block, Schorr & Solis-Cohen LLP (1997-2006); Director, Martin Lawrence Limited Editions, Inc. (1984-1995); Vice President, General Counsel, Martin Lawrence Limited Editions, Inc. (1987-1993); Partner, Pechner, Dorfman, Wolffe, Rounick and Cabot, Norristown, PA (1973-1987); Partner, Moss & Rounick, Norristown, PA (1972-1973); Partner, Moss, Rounick & Hurowitz, Norristown, PA (1969-1972); Special Assistant Attorney General (1963-1971); Partner, Moss & Rounick (1968-1969); Partner, Israelit & Rounick (1960-1967) **Civic:** Chairman, American Friends of the Hebrew University (1970); Chairman, Pennsylvania Young Republicans (1968-1970); Treasurer, Pennsylvania Young Republicans (1966-1968); Finance Chairman, Pennsylvania Young Republicans (1964-1966) **Creative Works:** Author, "Pennsylvania Matrimonial Practice, 6 Volumes" (1982); Editor, "Pennsylvania Family Lawyer" (1980-1987); Board of Editors, Family Advocate **Awards:** Honored, Attorney of the Year, IAOTT (2019); Eric Turner Award, Family Law Section, Pennsylvania Bar Association (2009); Named One of Top 100 Attorneys, Worth Magazine (2005); Certificate of Appreciation, Pennsylvania Bar Institute (1980); Special Achievement Award, Pennsylvania Bar Association (1979-1980); Boss of Year Award, Montgomery County Legal Secretaries Association (1970) **Memberships:** Chairman, Scope and Correlation Committee (2005-2006); Council, ABA (2000-2003); Chairman, Board Review, American Academy of Matrimonial Lawyers (1997-1998); Vice President, American Friends of the Hebrew University (1990-1991); President, Philadelphia Chapter, American Friends of the Hebrew University (1988-1991); Board of Trustees, American Friends of the Hebrew University (1987-2006); National Council of Trustees, American Friends of the Hebrew University (1987-1993); Board of Directors, American Friends of the Hebrew University (1987-1993); Vice President, American Academy of Matrimonial Lawyers (1985-1987); Governor, American Academy of Matrimonial Lawyers (1983-1985); Council, Family Law Section, ABA (1982-1987); President, Pennsylvania Chapter, American Academy of Matrimonial Lawyers (1982-1984); Past Chairman, Family Law Section, Pennsylvania Bar Association (1978-1980); Fellow, American Academy of Matrimonial Lawyers; Fellow, IAFL; FLS; Montgomery Bar Association **Bar Admissions:** United States District Court Eastern District of Pennsylvania (1960); Pennsylvania (1960) **Marquis Who's Who Honors:** Albert Nelson Marquis Lifetime Achievement Award; Marquis Who's Who Top Professional; Marquis Who's Who Humanitarian Award **Avocations:** Football; Hockey **Political Affiliations:** Republican **Religion:** Jewish

Robert Richard Rounsley, PhD

Title: Chemical Engineer, Educator (Retired) **Industry:** Engineering **Date of Birth:** 01/11/1931 **Place of Birth:** Detroit **State/Country of Origin:** MI/USA **Parents:** John Roland Rounsley; Verna E. (Clark) Rounsley **Marital Status:** Widowed **Spouse Name:** Beatrice Anne Fulton (03/07/1953, Deceased) **Children:** Richard; Suzanne; Pamela; Deborah; David **Education:** PhD in Chemical Engineering, Iowa State University (1957); MSChemE, Michigan Technological University, Houghton, MI (1954); BSChemE, Michigan Technological University, Houghton, MI (1952) **Certifications:** Registered Professional Engineer, Ohio **Career:** Retired (1996-Present); Research Fellow, Mead Corporation, Chillicothe, Ohio (1957-1996); Instructor, Iowa State University, Ames, Iowa (1954-1957); Associate, Argonne National Laboratory, Lemont, IL (1953-1954) **Career Related:** Instructor, Ohio University, Chillicothe, Ohio (1963-1968) **Creative Works:** Editorial Board, Technical Association of Pulp and Paper Industry (TAPPI) (1988-1989); Patent in Field; Contributor, 10 Articles to Professional Journals; Author, 12 Papers on Heat Transfer **Memberships:** Chairman, Lions Clubs International (1975-1976, 1992-1993); Chairman, Simulation Committee, Technical Association of Pulp and Paper Industry (TAPPI) (1991-1993); Project Advisory Committee, Institute of Paper Science and Technology (1986-1989); President, Central Ohio Section, American Institute of Chemical Engineers (1977-1978); Senior Member, American Institute of Chemical Engineers; American Chemical Society; Senior Member, Society for Computer Simulation (Now Society for Modeling & Simulation International); Technical Association of Pulp and Paper Industry (TAPPI); Institute of Paper Science and Technology; Lions Clubs International **Marquis Who's Who Honors:** Albert Nelson Marquis Lifetime Achievement Award; Marquis Who's Who Top Professional **Why did you become involved in your profession or industry:** When Dr. Robert Rounsley attended college, he started in chemical engineering because it seemed to offer more opportunities. He decided to stay with that career choice and as a result he has been chairman of local societies for chemical engineers. His parents also urged him to try the field. **Avocations:** Music; Photography **Religion:** Methodist

Thomas Jerome "Jerry" Royer, RFC

Title: Chief Executive Officer **Industry:** Financial Services **Company Name:** Group 10 Financial **Date of Birth:** 06/17/1943 **Place of Birth:** Coshocton **State/Country of Origin:** OH/USA **Parents:** Walter H. Royer Sr.; Francis (Guerke) Royer **Marital Status:** Married **Spouse Name:** Felipa T. Pagal (12/24/1965) **Children:** Matthew Vincent; Brian Eugene; Nicholas Alexander **Education:** Diploma, Life Underwriter Training Council (1967) **Certifications:** Registered Financial Consultant (2002) **Career:** Founder, Chief Executive Officer, Group 10 Financial, Maitland, FL (1988- Present); General Agent, Summit National Life Insurance Company, Akron, Ohio (1970-Present); Founder, Chief Executive Officer, United Group Marketing, Altamonte Springs, FL (1996); Founder, Chief Executive Officer, United Group Marketing, Cincinnati, Ohio (1993); Principal, Royer & Co., Fairfield, Ohio (1985-1988); General Agent, American Life & Casualty Co. (Now Metropolitan Life Insurance Company) (1997); General Agent, Life USA (1990); General Agent, Community National, Worthington, Ohio (1989); Manager, Metropolitan Life Insurance Co., New York, NY (1968-1970); Agent, Metropolitan Life Insurance Company, New York, NY (1966-1968) **Civic:** Honorable Order of Kentucky Colonels **Military Service:** United States Navy (1961-1966) **Creative Works:** Author, "Defuse, 7 Steps to Saving your 401K from the IRS" (2018); Author, "Its Your Money" (2001) **Awards:** American Flag Flown Over U.S. Capitol in Recognition of His Work Nationally and Internationally in Assisting Americans Accomplish Their Money Goals and Related Objectives (2008); Named to Dean's List, Brookstone Capital Management, Wheaton, IL **Memberships:** International Association of Registered Financial Consultants (IARFC) **Marquis Who's Who Honors:** Marquis Who's Who Top Professional **To what do you attribute your success:** Mr. Royer attributes his success to lessons learned from his own poor dad. **Why did you become involved in your profession or industry:** Mr. Royer became involved in his profession after growing up in a home where his father didn't save for his future. He had lost his desire to save, after losing all his savings accumulated over 12 years when the markets crashed in 1929. **Avocations:** Consumer advocate; Lifelong crusader to mentor, coach and inspire people to take control of their financial decisions **Political Affiliations:** Republican **Religion:** Roman Catholic **Thoughts on Life:** Mr. Royer's new book, "Defuse, 7 Steps to Saving your 401K from the IRS," is available on amazon.com.

Donald C. "Don" Royston

Title: Former President **Industry:** Automotive **Company Name:** Vintage Motor Car Club of America **Date of Birth:** 06/06/1933 **Place of Birth:** Reisterstown **State/Country of Origin:** MD/USA **Year of Passing:** 11/19/2018 **Parents:** George Royston; Hilda Royston **Marital Status:** Married **Spouse Name:** Leona "Lee" Royston **Children:** One Daughter; Two Step-daughters **Education:** Coursework, United States Army/OFC Training; Coursework, Auctioneer's School, Clear Lake, Iowa **Certifications: Career:** Founder, Former President, Vintage Motor Car Club of America, Southwest Florida Region (Formerly Veteran Motor Car Club of America, South West Florida Chapter) (1999-2018); Founder, Veteran Motor Car Club of America, South West Florida Chapter (1997); Retired, Eastern Savings Bank, MD (1989, 1990); With, Eastern Savings Bank, MD (28 Years) **Career Related:** Land Developer and Active Member in the Stock Market (1961-2018); Founder, 500-Member Antique Car Club of Greater Baltimore (Now Antique Motor Club of Greater Baltimore (AMCGB) (1960); Member, Rolls Royce/Clenet Registry **Civic:** Volunteer, The Salvation Army USA (20 Years); Punta Gorda Chamber of Commerce (17 Years); Charlotte County Chamber of Commerce (17 Years) **Military Service:** With, United States Army, Washington, DC; Officer Training, United States Army **Creative Works:** Columnist, Weekly Column, "You Auto Know," Sun Newspaper (2008-2018); Guest Appearance, "The Tonight Show with Jay Leno" (1996) **Awards:** Award for Recruiting the Most New Members (1999-2018); Hog-Calling Trophy (1996); Governor's Citation, Community Service (1990); Several National Veteran Awards for Doing the Most for the Club, Vintage Motor Car Club of America (VMCCA) **Memberships:** Antique Automobile Club of America, Hershey, PA (1958-2018); Charlotte County Chamber of Commerce; Punta Gorda Chamber of Commerce; Baltimore City Chamber of Commerce, Inc.; Vintage Car Club (Now Vintage Motor Car Club of America (VMCCA) **Marquis Who's Who Honors:** Albert Nelson Marquis Lifetime Achievement Award; Marquis Who's Who Top Professional **To what do you attribute your success:** Mr. Royston attributed his success to being very bold. He never met a stranger. He would shop at the supermarket and talk to someone at the grocery check-out and by the time he had paid, he knew everything about that person. **Why did you become involved in your profession or industry:** Mr. Royston became involved in his profession at age 14 when, after earning enough money exercising race horses, he bought a 1941 Lincoln Continental — this began his lifelong passion for car-owning. He eventually owned more than 79 different convertibles, his theory being that if the "top goes down, the price goes up," which served him well throughout his colorful life. **Avocations:** Magistrate of the Baltimore County Court **Religion:** Methodist **Thoughts on Life:** Mr. Royston's mother's side of the family (Chilcoat) founded Dover Methodist Church in 1808. He had been married to his wife, Leona "Lee" Royston, for 12 years. His wife is now the president of the car club. Mr. Royston always said, "We've seen the good times."

Alan Miles Ruben, JD

Title: 1) Advisory Professor 2) Emeritus Professor of Law **Industry:** Education/Educational Services **Company Name:** 1) Fudan University 2) Cleveland-Marshall College of Law **Date of Birth:** 05/31/1931 **Place of Birth:** Philadelphia **State/Country of Origin:** PA/USA **Parents:** Maurice Robert Ruben; Ruth (Blatt) Ruben **Marital Status:** Married **Spouse Name:** Betty Jane Willis (5/23/1965) **Education:** JD, University of Pennsylvania (1956); MA, University of Pennsylvania (1956); AB, University of Pennsylvania (1953) **Career:** Professor of Law Emeritus, Cleveland-Marshall College of Law, Cleveland State University (2003-Present); Advisory Law Professor, Fudan University, Shanghai, People's Republic of China (1993-Present); Commentator, Higher Education Issues, Station WCLV-FM, Cleveland, OH (1975-1987); Professor, Cleveland-Marshall College of Law, Cleveland State University (1970-2003); Corporate Counsel, Lubrizol Corporate, Cleveland, OH (1969-1970); Associate Counsel, Aetna Life & Casualty Co., Hartford, CT (1965-1969); Special Counsel, U.S. Senate Subcommittee on National Stockpile (1962); Deputy Attorney General, State of Pennsylvania (1961-1965); Private Practice, PA (1958-1965); Deputy to City Solicitor, Philadelphia, PA (1958-1961); Law Clerk, Supreme Court of Pennsylvania (1956-1958) **Career Related:** Consultant, Shanghai Law Office for Foreign Economy and Trade, People's Republic of China (1991-1994); Visiting Professor, Law School, Fudan University, Shanghai, People's Republic of China (1988-1989); Lecturer, School of Law, University of Connecticut (1968); National Panel, Labor Arbitrators, National Academy Arbitrators; Federal Mediation and Conciliation Service, American Arbitration Association; Ohio State Employment Relations Board **Civic:** Trustee, Verb Ballet (2009-2012); Trustee, Cleveland-San Jose Ballet (1999-2001); Board of Directors, Legal Aid Society of Cleveland (1973-1977); U.S. Olympic Fencing Team (1972); Captain, U.S. Pan-American Fencing Team (1971); Chairman, U.S. Olympic Fencing Sport Committee (1969-1973); Board of Directors, U.S. Olympic Committee (1968-1973); President, U.S. Fencing Association (1968-1973) **Creative Works:** Editor-in-Chief, "How Arbitration Works," Supplement (2008); Editor-in-Chief, "How Arbitration Works," 6th Edition (2003); Co-Editor, "How Arbitration Works" (1997); Contributor, Practice Guides, Ohio Limited Liability Company (1995-2006); Ohio Limited Partnership Law (1992-2002); Contributor, "An American Lawyer's Observations on the Inauguration of the Shanghai Stock Exchange" (1989); Contributor, "Modern Corporation Law," Supplement Edition (1978); Contributor, Model Public Employees Labor Relations Act (1972); Author, "Sentencing the Corporate Criminal" (1972); Author, "Arbitration in Public Employee Labor Disputes, Myth, Shibboleth and Reality" (1971); Author, "Illicit Sex of Campus, Federal Remedies for Employment Discrimination" (1971); Author, "The Constitutionality of Basic Protection for the Automobile Accident Victim" (1968); Author, "Unauthorized Insurance, The Regulation of the Unregulated" (1968); Contributor, "With an Eye to Tomorrow, The Future Outlook of the Life Insurance Industry" (1968); The Computer in Court, Computer Simulation and the Robinson Patman Act (1964); Contributor, The Administrative Agency Law, Reform of Adjudicative Procedure and the Revised Model Act (1963); Contributor, The Urban Transportation Crisis, The Philadelphia Plan (1961); Contributor, Philadelphia's Union Shop Contract (1961); Contributor, "The Top Ten Judicial Decisions Affecting Labor Relations in Public Education During the Decade of the 1990s" **Awards:** Elect, Cleveland-Marshall College of Law Hall of Fame (2018); Fulbright Scholar, Fudan University, Shanghai (1993-1994); Prize Winner, Harrison Tweed Bowl, National Moot Court Competition (1955); Prize Winner, American Law Institute, National Moot Court Competition (1955); Winner, International Debate Championship, International Institute of Education (1953); Guggenheim Scholar (1949-1953) **Memberships:** Securities Law Institute, Cleveland Metro Bar Association (1995-2002); Chairman, Law and Education Section, Association of American Law Schools (1976-1978); President, Ohio Conference, American Association of University Professors (1974-1975); Fellow, College of Labor and Employment Lawyers Inc; American Bar Association; Professional Responsibility Committee, Ohio Bar Association; International Industrial Relations Research Association; International Society for Labor Law and Social Security; International Bar Association; Union Internationale Des Avocats; International Law Association; Rowfant Club; Phi Beta Kappa; Pi Gamma Mu **Bar Admissions:** Ohio (1972); Pennsylvania (1957) **Marquis Who's Who Honors:** Albert Nelson Marquis Lifetime Achievement Award; Marquis Who's Who Top Professional **Why did you become involved in your profession or industry:** Professor Ruben became involved in his profession because he felt that law was the most optimal fit for him, making it his first choice by default.

Evan A. Rubinson

Title: Chief Executive Officer, President **Industry:** Media & Entertainment **Company Name:** Armadillo Enterprises **Date of Birth:** 09/23/1991 **Parents:** Elliott & Pamela Rubinson **Marital Status:** Single **Education:** Bachelor of Arts in Economics and Public Policy, Specialization in International Trade, Duke University (2014) **Certifications:** 2-15 Health & Life Agent Licenses, State of Florida, Office the Chief Financial Officer; Core Comprehensive Analyst and Associate Training Program, Training The Street **Career:** Chief Executive Officer, President, Armadillo Enterprises (2016-Present); Chief Executive Officer, Chief Information Officer, Koroit Capital (2015-2016); Self-Employed Portfolio Manager, Financial Services (2014-2015); International Sales Strategist, Financial Analyst, Armadillo Enterprises (2013); Private Equity Analyst, Prometheus Partners (2012) **Civic:** Volunteer, RCS Food Bank (2011-Present) **Memberships:** National Association Music Merchants **To what do you attribute your success:** Mr. Rubinson attributes his success to his education at Duke University, where he benefited greatly from the influence of his professors and coaches. Likewise, he drew great inspiration from his parents. **Why did you become involved in your profession or industry:** Mr. Rubinson became involved in his profession due to his father, who owned a massive retail music store during the younger man's early childhood. Being surrounded by music inspired him to enter the field himself.

Kal Solomon Rudman, EdM

Title: Humanitarian, Philanthropist, Media Executive, Educator **Industry:** Nonprofit & Philanthropy **Company Name:** Kal and Lucille Rudman Foundation **Date of Birth:** 03/06/1930 **Place of Birth:** Philadelphia **State/Country of Origin:** PA/USA **Parents:** Benjamin Rudman; Lena (Holtzman) Rudman **Marital Status:** Married **Spouse Name:** Lucille Steinhauer (6/29/1958) **Children:** Mitchell **Education:** Honorary PhD, University of the Arts, Philadelphia, PA (2006); Honorary LHD, University of the Arts, Philadelphia, PA (2005); Honorary LHD, University of the Arts, Philadelphia, PA (2003); Honorary LHD, Holy Family University, Philadelphia, PA (2002); Honorary HHD, Drexel University, Philadelphia, PA (1970); EdM, Temple University, Philadelphia, PA (1957); EdB, University of Pennsylvania, Philadelphia, PA (1951) **Career:** Co-Founder, Kal and Lucille Rudman Foundation (1993-Present); Publisher, Premier Record, Radio Trade, "Friday Morning Quarterback," Cherry Hill, NJ (1968-Present); Chairman, Department of Special Education, Franklin D. Roosevelt School, Bristol Township, Pennsylvania (1960-1968); Color Announcer, World Wrestling Federation; R&B Editor/Columnist, Billboard Magazine; Special Education Teacher **Career Related:** Co-Host, "The Merv Griffin Show" (1981-1982); Music Expert, "The Today Show" (1981-1982); Music Expert, "Tomorrow Show" (1981-1982); Board of Directors, Variety Club; Board of Directors, The Recording Academy; Board of Directors, Crime Commission, State of Pennsylvania; Board of Directors, Crime Commission, State of New Jersey; Board of Directors, Crime Commission, State of Delaware; Music Expert, "Tom Sny- der TV Show"; Host, Mobile Science Programs, The Franklin Institute of Science Museum and Fels Planetarium; Host, Entertainment Shows, Philadelphia Senior Citizens; Host, Entertainment Shows, New Jersey Senior Citizens' Homes; Host, Entertainment Shows, Children's Hospitals; Host, Entertainment Shows, Veterans Affairs Hospitals; Co-Host, Tal- ent Booker, Easter Seals Telethon; Creator, High School Jazz Piano Competition, University of the Arts, Philadelphia, PA; Eponym, Kal and Lucille Rudman Institute, Drexel University; Financial Supporter, National Academy of Television Arts and Sciences; Founder, Media Center and Financial Digital TV Station, Temple University **Civic:** Founder, Kal and Lucille Rudman Institute for Entertainment Studies, Westphal College of Media Arts & Designs, Drexel University, Philadelphia, PA (1974); Board of Directors, Philadelphia Broadcast Pioneers; Elected Vice President, Philadelphia Broadcast Pioneers; Sponsor, Carillon Bells, Avenue of the Arts Inc., Philadelphia, PA; Sponsor, TV Cameras, Temple University School of Communications; Sponsor, Alert Systems, Police Dog Cars, Philadelphia, PA; Sponsor, The Franklin Institute Travelling Science Show, Philadelphia Elementary Schools; Sponsor, First Annual Classical Piano High School Competition, Citizens' Crime Commission, Chestnut Hill College **Creative Works:** Publisher, "Modern QB"; Producer, CDs, Advance Hits; Founder, "Pro QB" Music Trade Magazine; Founder, Q-Beatl; Creator, 50 Billboards, Mothers in Charge **Awards:** Philanthropist of the Year (2007); Person of the Year, Philadelphia Art Community College (1970); Lifetime Achievement Award, Philadelphia Music Conference; Lifetime Music Achievement Award, Delaware Valley Music Poll; Presidential Citation, Citizens Crime Commission; Plaque on Walk of Fame, Avenue of the Arts Inc.; Enforcement Award, United States Marine Corps; Radio Milestone Award to Philadelphia Radio Legends, March of Dimes Foundation; T. Seddon Duke Award; Bennell Award; Top Civilian Award, Philadelphia Fire Department; Marshall Award, Citizens Crime Commission; Award, National Academy of Television Arts & Sciences; Top Civilian Award, Citizens Crime Commission of Delaware Valley; Top Award, Citizens Crime Commission, Philadelphia, PA; Named, Penndelphia Humanitarian of the Year; Named, Humanitarian of the Year, National Sunshine Federation; Named, Honorary Deputy Commissioner, Philadelphia Police Department; Named, Honorary Fire Commissioner; Named, Person of the Year, The Broadcast Pioneers of Philadelphia; Named, Community Philanthropic of the Year; Named, Broadcast Pioneers Hall of Fame, Philadelphia, PA; Honoree, Hall of Fame, Klein College of Media and Com- munication, Temple University; Golden Gavel Award, Community College of Philadelphia; Scholarship, Hahnemann Medical School, Drexel University, Philadelphia, PA; Mini-Medical Scholarships, Hahnemann Medical School, Drexel University; 15th-Year Scholarship, Olney High School; 15th-Year Scholarship Program, St. Christopher's Hospital for Children; College Communication Grant, Temple University **Memberships:** Board of Directors, Philadelphia Music Alliance; Board of Directors, National Arthritis Foundation; Board of Directors, Recording Academy; Grand Master, Freemasons **Marquis Who's Who Honors:** Albert Nelson Marquis Lifetime Achievement Award; Marquis Who's Who Top Professional; Marquis Who's Who Humanitarian Award

John "Jan" Rudolf, MS, PE

Title: Chief Structural Engineer **Industry:** Engineering **Company Name:** Gall Zeidler Consultants (GZ Consultants) **Marital Status:** Married **Spouse Name:** Bozena (Jenny) Rudolf **Children:** Two Children **Education:** BS and MS in Civil Engineering, Wroclaw Polytechnic (Now Wroclaw University of Science and Technology), Poland **Certifications:** Registration, Virginia (1974-2022); Registration, Maryland (1974-2020); Registered Professional Engineer, New York (1972-2013); Registered Professional Engineer Trough Exam, New York State University (1972); Registration, District of Columbia **Career:** Chief Structural Engineer, Gall Zeidler Consultants, (GZ Consultants), Ashburn, VA, (2013-Present); Engineering Chief, Silver Line Metro; Chief/Project Engineer, Supervisor, The Design Builder Project, Construction Site of Metro at Tysons Corner, Dulles, Virginia; Engineer, HNTB Corporation, New York, NY **Career Related:** Presenter, Domestic and International Conferences, Metro Tunnels, Aerial Structures Design, and Construction Experience; Lecturer in Field **Creative Works:** Author, Numerous Technical Papers **Awards:** General Manager Meritorious Achievement Award, Honor Roll, Washington Metropolitan Area Transit Authority (WMATA) (1998); Letter of Appreciation, Washington Metropolitan Area Transit Authority (WMATA) (1982) **Memberships:** Society for Mining, Metallurgy & Exploration (SME); Former Member, American Concrete Institute (ACI); Former Member, American Physical Therapy Association (APTA); Former Member, American Segmental Bridge Institute (ASBI); Former Member, International Tunneling Association (ITA); Former Member, Real Estate Training Center; Former Member, PCA; Former Member, NAT; Former Member, FIB/PCI **To what do you attribute your success:** Mr. Rudolf attributes his success to wanting to contribute to a better society. He accomplished this through hard work and determination to learn the language to get a job in his profession; he was not afraid of tough and demanding work. **Why did you become involved in your profession or industry:** Mr. Rudolf became involved in his profession because he was good at mathematics and physics. His math teacher suggested applying for an admission exam at the Polytechnic Institute instead of the Medical Academy, which was always his original interest. **Thoughts on Life:** Mr. Rudolf's motto is, "Who said one cannot become valuable in a free society of a beautiful country with opportunity for all, and love for family that gives the motivation to contribute for their good when there is a determination to accept challenges? If there is a will, there is a way, even starting without knowing the language of a new country."

Brunilda "Brunie" Ruiz

Title: Dancer, Dance Instructor, Choreographer **Industry:** Media & Entertainment **Date of Birth:** 06/01/1936 **Place of Birth:** Rincon **State/Country of Origin:** Puerto Rico **Year of Passing:** 08/13/2019 **Parents:** Eusebio Ruiz; Maria (Perez) Ruiz **Marital Status:** Married **Spouse Name:** Paul Sutherland (1968); John Wilson (Divorced 1968) **Children:** Alicia; Mhari **Education:** BA, State University of New York at Empire State College, New York, NY (1995); Diploma, High School of Performing Arts (Now Fiorello H. LaGuardia School of Music and Art and Performing Arts), New York, NY, With Honors (1954) **Career:** Instructor of Ballet, New Jersey Ballet School, West Orange, NJ (1987-Present); Instructor of Ballet, Fiorello H. LaGuardia High School of Music & Art and Performing Arts, New York, NY (1988-2001); Ballet Mistress, Milwaukee Ballet Company (1983-1986); Associate Director, Baron Ballet Company, Waldwick, NJ (1976-1983); Founding Member, Puerto Rico Dance Theatre, New York, NY (1971-1973); Charter Member, Principal Dancer, Harkness Ballet, New York, NY (1964-1970); Charter Member, Principal Dancer, Joffrey Ballet, New York, NY (1955-1964); Soloist, New York City Opera (1959-1961); Ballet Mistress, The Julliard School, New York, NY **Career Related:** Instructor of Ballet, The New Ballet School, Feld Ballet, New York, NY (1976-1984); Instructor of Ballet, Helena Baron School of Ballet, Waldwick, NJ (1971-1973); Guest Artist, Ballets de San Juan, Puerto Rico (1964-1965); Guest Artist, Philadelphia Opera (1960); Guest Teacher, Northeast Regional Ballet; Guest Teacher, New Jersey Ballet; Guest Teacher, Cecchetti Council Summer Workshop; Guest Teacher, Joffrey Ballet Summer Workshop; Guest Teacher, Bartholin Seminar, Copenhagen, Denmark; Guest Teacher, Tomoko Cultural Center, Hong Kong, China **Creative Works:** Choreographer, "Holberg Suite" (1991); Choreographer, "Ballet Espanol" (1990); Choreographer, "Ritmo Indio" (1987); Choreographer, "Variations on a Theme by Chopin" (1986); Choreographer, "Ebony Concerto" (1983); Choreographer, "Pelleas and Melisande" (1982); Choreographer, "Concerto for Cello" (1977); Choreographer, "Birthday Variations", "I've Got Rhythm", "Can Can", "Handel Suite", "Variations Serieuse", "Tango" **Awards:** Grantee, New Jersey State Council of the Arts (1983-1984, 1989); National Choreographic Award, National Association for Regional Ballet (1982-1983); Named, Dancer of the Month, Dance Magazine (1965) **Marquis Who's Who Honors:** Albert Nelson Marquis Lifetime Achievement Award; Marquis Who's Who Top Professional **Why did you become involved in your profession or industry:** Ms. Ruiz became a dancer because she saw a girl dancing around; she asked the little girl where she learned how to dance and the little girl told her to go to the YMCA on 59th Street. She told her brother that she wanted to be a ballerina and to take her there. The class was full there; she started to cry and someone told her to go to the class on 92nd Street. She went there and became a student of Martha Melinkoff. **Avocations:** Crocheting **Political Affiliations:** Democrat **Religion:** Roman Catholic

Rusen Rusev

Title: Managing Broker **Industry:** Real Estate **Company Name:** Runway Realty, Inc. **Date of Birth:** 04/14/1967 **Place of Birth:** Kazanlak **State/Country of Origin:** Bulgaria **Marital Status:** Married **Spouse Name:** Nina Ruseva **Children:** Aleksandrina; Nicholas **Education:** MA in Engineering, Military Pilot Training, Military Academia, Bulgaria **Career:** Managing Broker, Runway Realty, Inc. (2004); Military Pilot **Military Service:** Bulgarian Air Force **Awards:** Top 1% Realtor (2009-Present); Five Stars Reals Estate Agent Award (2014, 2015) **Memberships:** Chicago Association of Realtors; Illinois Association of Realtors; National Association of Realtors **To what do you attribute your success:** Mr. Rusev attributes his success to self-discipline. **Why did you become involved in your profession or industry:** Mr. Rusev became involved in real estate after having an experience with a realtor who was not helpful to him. This individual was not focused on what Mr. Rusev was looking for in a home, which inspired him to become a real estate agent. He always gives his clients the exact home for which they are looking. **Avocations:** Skiing; Biking; Reading; Gardening **Thoughts on Life:** Mr. Rusev believes in helping others achieve their dreams.

Gerard Rushton, PhD

Title: Professor Emeritus, Researcher **Industry:** Education/Educational Services **Company Name:** University of Iowa **Date of Birth:** 03/03/1938 **Place of Birth:** Burnley **State/Country of Origin:** England **Parents:** James; Alice Rushton **Marital Status:** Married **Spouse Name:** Carolyn Arnell Lucken (09/21/1963) **Children:** Edward James; John Palmer **Education:** PhD, University of Iowa (1964); MA, University of Wales, Aberystwyth, Wales (1961); BA, University of Wales, Aberystwyth, Wales (1959) **Career:** Retired Geography Professor, Researcher (2013-Present); Professor Emeritus, University of Iowa (2013-Present); Full Professor, University of Iowa, Iowa City, IA (1972-2013); Associate Professor, University of Iowa, Iowa City, IA (1969-1972); Assistant Professor, Michigan State University, Lansing, MI (1967-1969); Assistant Professor, McMaster University, Hamilton, ON, Canada (1964-1967) **Career Related:** Professor, San Diego University (2005-2007); Reviewer, National Institutes of Health **Civic:** Consultant, Iowa City Community School Board (1990-Present); Consultant, National Science Foundation (1978-1983); Consultant, Ford Foundation, India (1971-1974) **Creative Works:** Editorial Board Member, Association of American Geographers (2000-2003); Contributor, Articles, Professional Journals **Awards:** Award, Association for American Geographers **Marquis Who's Who Honors:** Albert Nelson Marquis Lifetime Achievement Award; Marquis Who's Who Top Professional **To what do you attribute your success:** Dr. Rushton attributes his success to the variety of experiences at an early age. **Why did you become involved in your profession or industry:** Dr. Rushton saw that bringing the developments in computerization of geography to him was something he could see coming in the future. If you look at the history of computers in geography, around 1962 in the United States is when it began. His roommate was studying hydraulics, who introduced him to a professor who was teaching the use of computers. He started attending his classes in the computerization in hydraulics. He found himself in a field where very few people went, so he was one of a kind. Within a number of years, more people studying geography followed his path. In 1969, he got called by the Ford Foundation and asked if he would review a piece of work they were doing in India. **Avocations:** Squash

Richard A. Russel, DCS, AeE

Title: Space Systems Engineer (Retired) **Industry:** Aviation **Company Name:** Northrup Grumman Corporation **Date of Birth:** 01/24/1958 **Place of Birth:** Shreveport **State/Country of Origin:** LA/USA **Parents:** Robert Lee Russel; Gloria Jeanette (Gile) Russel **Marital Status:** Married **Spouse Name:** Kathryn Joy Koehler (12/30/1983) **Children:** Richard; Kammie; Jonathan; Stephen; Katie **Education:** DCS, Colorado Technical University (2003); MSc in Astronomical Engineering, Naval Postgraduate School, Monterrey, CA (1994); AeE in Aerospace and Astronautics, Naval Postgraduate School, Monterrey, CA (1994); BSEE, University of New Mexico, Albuquerque, NM (1980) **Certifications:** Navy Space Systems Engineer; Navy Nuclear Engineer **Career:** Adjunct Full Professor, Webster University (2006-Present); Board of Directors, Deep Space Exploration Society (DSES Science) (2017-2020); Business Development, Price to Win and Competitive Analyst, Northrop Grumman (2008-2015); Board of Directors, Object Management Group Inc (omg.org) (2009–2014); Chief Architect, Air Force Satellite Control Network, Northrop Grumman (2002-2008); Director, System Engineering, Maxim Systems Inc., Colorado Springs, CO (2002-2002); Director, Space and Communications, Predicate Logic Inc., Colorado Springs, CO (1997-2000); Project Manager for Spacecraft Communications., Booz-Allen and Hamilton, Inc., San Diego, CA (1996-1997); UHF/EHF Satellite Navy Rep. PEO-SCS, El Segundo, CA (1994-1996); Navigator, Operations Officer, USS Indianapolis, Pearl Harbor, HI (1989-1992); Combat Systems Officer, USS TAUTUG, Pearl Harbor, HI (1987-1989); Antisubmarine Analyst, Nuclear Engineer, Commander, Third Fleet, Pearl Harbor, HI (1985-1987); MPA, USS Puffer, Pearl Harbor, HI (1981-1985) **Career Related:** Special Service Citation for Developing Internet Capability, American Institute of Aeronautics and Astronautics (1996); Chief Engineer, Center Y2K Strategic Stability; Systems Engineer, Space Battle Management Laboratory; Fellow, Institute for the Advancement of Engineering; Associate Fellow, American Institute of Aeronautics and Astronautics **Civic:** Emergency Coordinator, Colorado, El Paso and Teller County Amateur Radio Emergency Service (ARES) (2013-2016); President, Redeemer Lutheran Church, Colorado Springs, CO (2006-2010); Telecommunication Policy Advisory Committee, Colorado Springs City Council (2000-2002); Chairman, Board of Directors, Christ the Cornerstone Lutheran Church (1998-1999); President, Christ the Cornerstone Lutheran Church (1985-1987); School Board, Our Savior Lutheran School, Aiea, HI (1985-1987); Board of Directors, Children's Angelcare Aid International (1985-1987) **Military Service:** Retired, U.S. Navy (1996); UHF/EHF PEO-SCS (1994-1996); Naval Postgraduate School (1992-1996) **Awards:** Astronomical League Gold Level Observing Award for Radio Astronomy (2017); University of Colorado at Colorado Springs Leadership in Education Award (2006); Northrop Grumman Mission Systems Technologist of the Year Award (2004) **Memberships:** Society of Amateur Radio Astronomers (2016-Present); Deep Space Exploration Society (2015-Present); Astronomical League Board of Directors (2016-2018); Adventurers Club of Los Angeles; Eta Kappa Nu **Marquis Who's Who Honors:** Albert Nelson Marquis Lifetime Achievement Award; Marquis Who's Who Top Professional **Why did you become involved in your profession or industry:** Mr. Russel's father was a lawyer and his mother was a teacher, and he got involved in a seventh grade science fair. One of the nuns in his catholic grade school wanted him to do this science fair. Science fairs are where he got his jump start. He did science fairs all through high school, which helped get him a Navy scholarship and then to Navy ROTC program. While completing a bachelor's degree, he made the switch to electrical engineering. **Avocations:** Radio astronomy; Amateur radio (AC0UB) **Political Affiliations:** Republican **Religion:** Lutheran

Danny Russo

Title: Creative Director of Design **Industry:** Architecture & Construction **Company Name:** Daniel Russo Home **Date of Birth:** 03/23/1980 **Place of Birth:** Youngstown **State/Country of Origin:** OH/USA **Parents:** Connie Russo-Dudley; John M. Porinchak Sr. **Marital Status:** Married **Education:** Youngstown State University, Youngstown, Ohio; Boardman High School, Boardman, Ohio **Certifications:** American Society of Interior Designers (ASID) **Career:** Chief Executive Officer, SRG Interiors Incorporated (2008-Present); Creative Director, Daniel Russo Home, OH (2017-Present) **Civic:** Stonewall Columbus; Design-Build Committee, New Facility **Creative Works:** Author, "The Book of Russo According to Danny" Crazy by Design (2021); Published Designer, "Best of Show" with Donna Moss (2021); Design Star, "Danny Does Design" (2021); Featured Designer, Home Design Television (2020); Designer, Columbus Museum of Art "Designer Showcase" Dining Room (2019); Featured Designer, Central Ohio Science and Industry Museum (2017-2018); Designer, Columbus Museum of Art "Designer Showcase" Living Room (2017); Guest Designer, "Best of Show"; Host, "The Design Exchange Podcast" **Memberships:** American Society of Interior Designers (ASID); Builders Industry Association (BIA) **Marquis Who's Who Honors:** Marquis Who's Who Top Professional **To what do you attribute your success:** Mr. Russo attributes his success to the team he works with and the great clients he has had over the course of his career. His motto, when approaching design and engaging his clients, is "Anyone can design a space, but only a designer can make a space magical."Mr. Russo is inspired by Alexander McQueen, Tom Ford, Kelly Hoppen, and Martin Lawrence Bullard. **Why did you become involved in your profession or industry:** Mr. Russo became involved in his profession after he began working at Dillard's department store in the home department. He then moved from Youngstown to Columbus, Ohio, taking on work in the construction industry by helping people select their finishes and plans for their new homes. After building a bit of a reputation, he began receiving inquiries from people to design their homes. He had one client with a townhome, which he designed. It went well and, eventually, Mr. Russo's designs progressed to salons, retail stores, dental offices, medical offices, and hospitality projects. His career continued to rapidly progress. He then began attending and participating in industry shows throughout the country, which brought him to where he is today. His passion has always been furniture and how things are made. Mr. Russo excels in color selection, lighting, home accessories, and space planning. **Religion:** Roman Catholic **Thoughts on Life:** Mr. Russo says, "Design is all about storytelling these days. It is about communicating that story, bringing out my client's desires in their homes which are their calling-cards. I never stop learning and, when I was younger, I thought I knew everything; I learned quickly that I do not know everything and I am always excited to learn new things and meet new people. Animals bring so much spice and enjoyment to life! I am currently obsessed with my muse, Orso Russo."

Robert W. Rust

Title: Lawyer (Retired), Colonel (Retired), U.S. Marine Corps Forces Reserve **Industry:** Law and Legal Services **Date of Birth:** 08/16/1928 **Place of Birth:** Jamaica **State/Country of Origin:** NY/USA **Parents:** Adolf H. Rust (Deceased); Helen Margaret Rust (Deceased) **Marital Status:** Married **Spouse Name:** Theresa N. Rust (1982); Mary Ruth Duncan (1953, Deceased 1981) **Children:** Benjamin; Lani; Debra; Bonnie; Randall; Wendy; Brandon Walsh (Stepson) **Education:** Postgraduate Studies, Naval War College (1975); JD, University of Miami, Coral Gables, FL (1954); Student, St. Lawrence University (1946-1948); Student, St. Lawrence University (1946-1948) **Certifications:** U.S. Supreme Court (1960); U.S. Customs Court (1960); U.S. District Court of Appeals for the Fifth Circuit (1959) **Career:** Partner, Rust & Rust, Miami (1977-1989); U.S. Attorney Department of Justice, Southern District Florida, Miami (1969-1977); Chief Counsel, House Crime Committee, Tallahassee, FL (1968-1969); Florida House of Representative for Palm Beach, Martin County, FL (1966-1968); Chief Assistant County Prosecutor, Palm Beach County, West Palm Beach, FL (1963-1966); Associate Attorney, Shutts & Bowen, Miami, FL (1961-1963); Assistant U.S. Attorney, Department of Justice, Southern District of Florida, Miami, FL (1958-1961); Associate Attorney, Smathers, Thompson & Dyer, Miami, FL (1956-1957); Assistant Auditor, First National Bank, Miami, FL (1954-1956); Police Officer, City of Miami (Florida) Police Department (1953-1954) **Military Service:** Private, Colonel, U.S. Marine Corps Forces Reserve (1947-1988) **Awards:** Outstanding Service Award, National Executive Board of Federal Criminal Investigators (1977); Southern Florida Law Enforcement Community Award for Honesty, Integrity and Leadership as U.S. Attorney, (1977); Outstanding Legislator Award, St. Petersburg Times (1967); Outstanding Legislator Award, Florida State Fraternal Order of Police (1967); Award of Merit "for assisting in preventing the assassination of the President of U.S.," Secretary of Treasury and Chief, U.S. Secret Service (1964); Heritage Foundation Award **Memberships:** President, West Palm Beach Chapter, Marine Corps Reserve Officers Association (1964-1965); Florida Bar; Miami Dade County Association of Chiefs of Police; Member National Rifle Association; Navy League; American Legion; Military Order World Wars; Reserve Officers Association; Key Biscayne Yacht Club; Capitol Hill Club; Audubon Society; Rotary Club; The Union League; Miami University Alumni Association; Cat Cay Club; Knights of Columbus **Bar Admissions:** Florida Bar (1954) **Marquis Who's Who Honors:** Albert Nelson Marquis Lifetime Achievement Award **Why did you become involved in your profession or industry:** Mr. Rust became involved in his profession because his father was a private in the Marine Corps during World War I and he wanted to follow in his footsteps as that was part of his culture growing up. In September 1946, he started at St. Lawrence University; he had not served in World War II because he was not old enough but was among those men who did, which was very inspiring. He then became a volunteer as a police officer for one year and went to law school at night. Being a police officer allowed him to go to law school so that he could support his family as the GI bill could not do so. When he graduated from law school, he left the police department and became an assistant auditor a First National Bank in Miami. **Avocations:** Shooting; Skiing; Dog sledding; Boating and fishing **Political Affiliations:** Republican **Religion:** Catholic

Diane Phyllis "Di" Ryan, PhD, AGPCNP-BC, FNP-BC

Title: Nurse **Industry:** Medicine & Health Care **Company Name:** VA Western New York Healthcare Center/Batavia Site **Date of Birth:** 06/19/1954 **Place of Birth:** Buffalo **State/Country of Origin:** NY/USA **Parents:** Edward John Vnuk; Helen (Pasko) Vnuk **Marital Status:** Married **Spouse Name:** Terrance Patrick Ryan (05/14/1977) **Children:** Kevin Daniel; Jaclyn Nicole; Amanda Leigh; Scott Michael **Education:** PhD in Nursing, University at Buffalo (2010) MS in Nursing, State University of New York (1980); BSN, D'Youville College (1976) **Certifications:** Certified, Family Nurse Practitioner (2003); Certified, Adult-Gerontology; Primary Care Nurse Practitioner; Certified, Public Health Nurse Specialist; Certified Nurse Educator **Career:** Nurse Practitioner, Buffalo VA Medical Center (2018-Present); Associate Professor, Daemen College (2004-2018); Associate Professor, St. John Fisher College (2001-2004); Nurse Practitioner, Buffalo VA Medical Center (1992-2001); Community Referral Nurse Coordinator, Buffalo VA Medical Center (1983-1992); Nurse Practitioner, Buffalo VA Medical Center (1980-1983); Staff Nurse, Buffalo VA Medical Center (1976-1979) **Career Related:** Nurse Practitioner, Trinity Cardiology; Nurse Practitioner, Dr. Nora Meaney-Elman; Nurse Practitioner, Dr. Piwko; Contributor, Articles, Professional Journals; Speaker, Poster Presentation, Various Topics **Civic:** Evaluation and Review Panel Member, Accreditation Commission for Education in Nursing **Awards:** Carol Sinicki Manuscript Award, American Diabetes Educators (1984); Continuing Education Award, Homemaker's Upjohn, Buffalo, NY (1976); Proficiency Medal in Nursing (1975); 1st Place Award, 11th Annual Discharge Planning Symposium, Society Hospital Social Work Directors, American Hospital **Memberships:** Western New York Nurse Practitioners; Nurse Practitioners Association of New York State; Sigma Theta Tau **Marquis Who's Who Honors:** Albert Nelson Marquis Lifetime Achievement Award (2019) **To what do you attribute your success:** Dr. Ryan attributes her success to how much she loves nursing. She has always been persistent when it comes to her goals. **Why did you become involved in your profession or industry:** Dr. Ryan pursued nursing because of her interest in healthcare. **Avocations:** Dancing; Gardening **Thoughts on Life:** Ms. Ryan believes life is all about following your passion, helping others, and doing what you love.

Dewey Doo-Young Ryu, PhD

Title: Professor Emeritus **Industry:** Education/Educational Services **Company Name:** Dewey Consultants Inc. **Parents:** Han Sang Ryu; Sonam Kim **Marital Status:** Married **Spouse Name:** Sunny Choi **Children:** Mina Ryu; Regina Ryu **Education:** PhD in Biochemical Engineering, Massachusetts Institute of Technology (1967); BS in Chemical Engineering, Massachusetts Institute of Technology (1961) **Career:** Maynard Amerine Endowed Chair Professor and Director of Biochemical Engineering Program, University of California, Davis, CA (1982-Present); President, Dewey Consultants, Inc. (2013-Present); Invited Fulbright Distinguished Professor Lectureship, College of Biosystems and Biotechnology and College of Pharmaceutical Science, Yonsei University, Seoul, Korea, (US Department of State Grant) (2012-2013); Invited Distinguished Professorship, Advisor to the President, Industry-Government-Academia Programs, Nara Advanced Institute of Science and Technology, Kyoto, Japan (2011-2012); Director of Biotechnology and Biochemical Engineering Programs, National Science Foundation, Washington, DC (2000-2002); President, Korean-American Community Association of Greater Sacramento (1996-1998); President, Vice-President, Korean-American Scientists and Engineers Association, Washington, DC (1993-1996); Professor, Director of Biochemical Engineering Program, State University of New York at Buffalo (1992-1993); Visiting Professor, Department of Chemical and Biochemical Engineering, Seoul National University (1989); Distinguished Visiting Professor, International Center for Biotechnology, Osaka University (1985-2007); Senior Visiting Research Associate, U.S. National Academy of Science, National Research Council Research Associateship, U. S. Army Natick Research Laboratory (1978-1979); Professor, Director of Biochemical Engineering Program, The Texas A & M University, College Station, TX (1976); Professor and Chairman, Departments of Chemical Engineering and of Biological Science and Engineering, Korea Advanced Institute of Science and Technology (1973-1982); Associate Professor, Departments of Chemical Engineering and Applied Biological Science, Massachusetts Institute of Technology, Cambridge, MA (1972-1973); Adjunct Professor, Department of Chemical and Biochemical Engineering, Rutgers University, New Brunswick, NJ (1969-1972); Senior Research Engineer, Squibb Institute for Medical Research (now Bristol-Myer Squibb), Princeton, NJ (1967-1972) **Career Related:** Editorial Board, Journal of Biotechnology and Biochemical Engineering (1996-Present); Editorial Board, Journal of Bioscience and Bioengineering (1986-Present); Director, Biochemical Engineering Program, University of California, Davis (1986-Present); Editorial Board, Applied Biochemistry and Biotechnology (1981-Present); Division of Biochemical Engineering and Biotechnology, Korean Institute of Chemical Engineers (1978-Present); Advisory Committee, Brain Korea 21st Century Program (2004); Advisory Committee, International Biochemical Engineering Conferences (2002-2003) **Civic:** National Institutes of Health Research Program Workshop, University of California Berkeley (2004); Recent Advances, Flow Cytometry, Davis, CA (2003); National Institutes of Health, Regional Seminar on Research Programs and Funding, Stanford University, CA (2003); Cell Reactor Engineering, Minneapolis, MN (2003); American Institute of Medical and Biological Engineering, Washington, DC (2003); Cell Culture Engineering Conference, Snowmass, CO (2002); Stem Cell Technology, Research Opportunities, Johns Hopkins University, Baltimore, MD (2002); American Society of Cell Biology, San Francisco, CA (2002); Bioengineering Consortium, National Institutes of Health, Bethesda, MD (2002) **Creative Works:** Author, 224 Scientific Research Publications; Inventor, 16 Patents; Speaker, 311 Invited Lectures, Presentations **Awards:** Founding Fellow, American Institute of Medical and Biological Engineering (1992-Present); Distinguished Chair Professor Fulbright Scholar Award, U.S. State Department (2012); Japan Science Promotion Society Senior Fellow Award (2011); International Enzyme Engineering Conferences Award (2005); International Biochemical Engineering Award Asia-Pacific (2005); Special Award for Valuable Contributions, Asia-Pacific Biochemical Engineering Congregate (2005); Ho-Am Award for Outstanding Accomplishment in Biomolecular Engineering, Samsung (2004); International Enzyme Engineering Conference Special Award for Outstanding Contributions (2004); Ho-Am Foundation Special Prize in Biomolecular Engineering, Korea (2004) **Memberships:** Founding Fellow, Engineering Society (1992-Present); American Chemical Society; American Institute of Chemical Engineers; American Society for Microbiology; American Association for the Advancement of Science; Japanese Society of Bioscience and Biotechnology; Korean Society of Biochemical Engineering and Biotechnology; American Institute of Medical and Biological Engineering; American Society of Biological Engineering; American Institute of Chemical Engineers; American Association for the Advancement of Science; American Society of Microbiology; American Chemical Society; National Academy of Science Engineering; Korean-American Institute of Medical Biology **Marquis Who's Who Honors:** Albert Nelson Marquis Lifetime Achievement Award **Avocations:** Skiing; Mountain hiking; Global healthcare and environment movements

Muthukrishna Sabanayagam, MD

Title: Neuropsychiatrist **Industry:** Medicine & Health Care **Date of Birth:** 01/15/1940 **Place of Birth:** Chidambaram **State/Country of Origin:** Tamilnadu/India **Parents:** Muthukrishna Sabanayagam ; Marimuthu (Krishnan) Sabanayagam **Marital Status:** Married **Spouse Name:** Madelyn Garcia (08/1987); Cheryl Braun (Divorced, 1975) **Children:** Mari Suzanne **Education:** Resident in Neurology, New York Medical College, New York, NY (1972-1974); Postgraduate Coursework, New York School of Psychiatry, New York, NY (1969-1972); Resident in Psychiatry, Central Islip Psychiatric Center (1968-1972); Medical Intern, St. Francis Hospital, Poughkeepsie, NY (1967-1968); MD, University of Madras (1965) **Certifications:** Diplomate, American Board of Psychiatry and Neurology (1974) **Career:** Associate Medical Director, Kings Park Psychiatric Center (1983-Present); Private Practice, Bay Shore, NY (1974-Present); President, Medical Staff, Kings Park Psychiatric Center (1981-1995) **Career Related:** Psychiatrist III (1981-1983); Psychiatrist II, University Service, State University of New York at Stony Brook (1978-1982); Psychiatric Consultant, Hoch Psychiatric Center, Brentwood, NY (1975-1978); Consultant, Neurology, New York Medical Development Institute, New York, NY (1974-1977) **Memberships:** American Academy of Neurology; American Psychiatric Association; American Geriatric Society; American Neurophysiology Society; New York Medical Society; Suffolk County Medical Society **Marquis Who's Who Honors:** Albert Nelson Marquis Lifetime Achievement Award **Why did you become involved in your profession or industry:** Mr. Sabanayagam became involved in his profession because after graduating from medical school and coming to the United States. After completing a psychiatric residency, he knew he wanted to help individuals struggling with mental disorders. **Avocations:** Photography

Ronald William Sabo, Esq.

Title: Lawyer, Financial Consultant **Industry:** Law and Legal Services **Company Name:** Ronald Sabo, Attorney **Date of Birth:** 10/13/1944 **Place of Birth:** Pottstown **State/Country of Origin:** PA/USA **Parents:** William Sabo; Margaret (Dutchman) Sabo **Marital Status:** Widowed **Spouse Name:** Mary Jane **Children:** Richard; Five Step-Children **Education:** JD, University of Miami, Cum Laude (1969); BBA, University of Miami, Cum Laude (1966) **Career:** Private Practice, Lompoc, Cambria, CA (1985-Present); Special Assistant District Attorney, Ventura County, California (1979-1984); Director of Research, National Legal Data Center, Thousand Oaks, CA (1974-1978); Assistant Counsel, Ventura County, California (1972-1973); Assistant Attorney General, State of Florida, Tallahassee, FL (1970-1971); Research Attorney, Florida Court of Appeals for the Third District, Miami, FL (1969) **Career Related:** Consultant, RAND Corporation, Santa Monica, CA (1976-1978); Consultant, Battelle Memorial Institute, Seattle, WA (1975); Lecturer, FBI National Academy, Quantico, VA (1974); Consultant, Rules Committee, California Senate **Awards:** Named, Honorary Citizen of New Orleans (1978) **Memberships:** ABA; Disciplinary Examiner, California Bar Association **Bar Admissions:** United States Tax Court (1985); California (1972); Florida (1969) **Marquis Who's Who Honors:** Albert Nelson Marquis Lifetime Achievement Award; Marquis Who's Who Top Professional **To what do you attribute your success:** Mr. Sabo attributes his success to perseverance. **Why did you become involved in your profession or industry:** Mr. Sabo became involved in his profession because it just happened organically. **Avocations:** Sailing; Cooking **Political Affiliations:** Republican **Religion:** Methodist Episcopalian

Sneha Sabu

Title: Coordinator, Corporate Planning and Reporting **Industry:** Government Administration/Government Relations/Government Services **Company Name:** Waverley Council **Parents:** Sudha Sabu (Mother); Sabu Thomas (Father); Cyriack (Brother) **Marital Status:** Married **Spouse Name:** Vinu Thomas **Education:** MBA Essentials, London School of Economics and Political Science (2021); Coursework in Executive Education in Strategy Frameworks, Harvard Kennedy School, (2012); Diploma in Government Management, Australian Institute of Management, North Sydney, New South Wales, Australia (2011); Executive Education in Strategic Management, International Institute of Management (2008); MA in Communication, Madras Christian College, University of Madras, India, (2004); Bachelor's Degree in Communicative English (III Main), Christian Missionary Services College, Mahatma Gandhi University, India, (2002) **Certifications:** Certificate in Economics for Managers, Harvard Business School (2020); Course in Workforce Planning, Local Government NSW (2015); Master Certificate in Project Leadership & System Design, Cornell University (2013); Certificate in Financial Management, Cornell University (2013); Program in Successfully Executing Strategic Change, Conner Partners – Habitat for Humanity (2012); Certificate Course on Gender and Development Training, Global Human Rights Leadership Training Institute (2012); Developing and writing operational policy and procedures, Institute of Public Administration Australia NSW (2011); Course work in Business Process Design and Implementation, The University of Sydney (2011); Coursework in Making the Business Case, The University of Sydney (2011); IAP2 Certification in Public Participation, International Association for Public Participation (2011) **Career:** Coordinator, Corporate Planning and Reporting, Waverley Council (2015-Present); Senior Project Officer, Strategy and Performance, Liverpool City Council (2014-2015); Full-time Consultant, Strategy and Business Planning, Asia Pacific, Habitat for Humanity International (2013-2014); Associate Director, Strategy Management, Asia Pacific, Habitat for Humanity International (2011-2013); Governance Officer (Corporate Planning & Governance), Lane Cove Council (2010-2011); Casual Projects Officer (Strategy & Projects), City of Ryde Council (2010); Project Coordinator, Integrated Planning Volunteer (Corporate Planning & Governance), North Sydney Council (2010); Consultant of Strategy Management and Communications, Channel One Entertainment Pvt Ltd. (2009); Corporate Planner, World Vision India (2006-2008); Chief Operating Officer, NMTv Pvt Ltd. (2005-2006); Head of Client Servicing, IcPAR, Planman Consulting (2004) **Civic:** Prepared and rolled out a Pandemic Prioritization Matrix to more than 60 councils in NSW, Australia to support decision making on services and projects impacting the community in a pandemic context (2020); Represented Habitat for Humanity International Asia Pacific Office at the United Nations Asia Pacific Post Millennium Development Goals (MDGs) 2015 discussions and advocated to include issues related to housing as part of the next MDGs (2012-2013), Asia Pacific **Creative Works:** Author, Contributor, 30 Short Stories for Children; Former Host, Television and Stage Shows, Artist **Awards:** Waverley Council Staff Award (2018); Runner-up, Champion of TREC Values "for demonstrating outstanding contributions as an employee that works Together, Responsible, Engaging and Creative," Waverley Council (2018) **Marquis Who's Who Honors:** Marquis Who's Who in the World **To what do you attribute your success:** Ms. Sabu attributes her success to being a believer and having strong spiritual values. She is driven by strong morals in terms of having a discipline of spiritual connection. The people around her have been very supportive, starting with her mother. She would attribute her success firstly to God and then her family, which includes her mother, brother and husband. **Why did you become involved in your profession or industry:** Ms. Sabu became involved in her profession because when she started her career in corporate planning, she had no clue what it entailed. It was very intriguing, and she really wanted to find out what it was. Several years back when the whole idea of corporate planning sprouted, she went back home and had a chat to understand this concept better. Her grandmother spoke of the lawyers and judges in the family who were organized and meticulous – key planning skills. Her forefathers were planners as well. For her, it was a big triggering point. She saw it was closely related to that, and for her, that was a triggering factor in terms of giving her more confidence; it was in her blood and that is what triggered her to pursue it because there were members in the family who already did it. Thanks to her organization, World Vision India, they had several international mentors who used to work with organizations. Since 2006, it started off like that and is how she continued to be in this field. **Avocations:** Traveling; Painting; Writing **Religion:** Christian **Thoughts on Life:** "Six feet of land is all that you have to take along. So let us cut the chase, love yourself, the creator and creation. Co-exist and live life to the fullest for you may not have a second chance!"

Jeremy Saenz

Title: Founder, Owner **Industry:** Business Management/Business Services **Company Name:** The American Dream **Parents:** Rick Saenz; Linda Saenz **Marital Status:** Single **Spouse Name:** Samantha (Girlfriend) **Education:** High School Diploma **Career:** Owner, Partner, The American Dream **Career Related:** Co-Creater, Lucky Habanero Salsa **Civic:** Fundraiser, Donor, Local Schools and Local People **To what do you attribute your success:** Mr. Saenz believes that there are a lot of factors that play into being success. Location is very important, he has a beach front property. The quality of your product is important as well. **Why did you become involved in your profession or industry:** Mr. Saenz and his mom made all natural, no-preservatives salsa. It was the first time you could get a homemade flavor in a store bought situation. He thought to himself that most restaurants salsas that contain preservatives, and thought it would be great for his places to start using natural ingredients/ high quality ingredients to make better food. He wanted to bring that to the public.

Robert Howard Sagerman, MD, FACR

Title: Professor Emeritus **Industry:** Education/Educational Services **Company Name:** State University of New York Health Science Center **Date of Birth:** 01/23/1930 **Place of Birth:** Kings County **State/Country of Origin:** NY/USA **Parents:** Irving R. Sagerman; Ethel Sagerman **Marital Status:** Married **Spouse Name:** Malyne Barnett Sagerman (12/23/1954) **Children:** Jason E.; Eric S.; Evan C.; Roger F. **Education:** Resident in Radiology, Montefiore Hospital (Now Montefiore Medical Center), Bronx, NY (1959-1961); Resident in Radiology, Charity Hospital, New Orleans, LA (1956-1957); Intern, Meadowbrook Hospital (Now Nassau University Medical Center), NuHealth, Hempstead, NY (1955-1956); MD, New York University College of Medicine (1955); BA, New York University, Magna Cum Laude (1951) **Certifications:** Diplomate, American Board of Radiology **Career:** Professor Emeritus, Department of Radiation Oncology, State University of New York Health Science Center, Syracuse, NY (2003-Present); Professor, Department of Radiation Oncology, State University of New York Health Science Center, Syracuse, NY (1995-2003); Professor, Department of Radiology, Division of Radiation Oncology, State University of New York Health Science Center, Syracuse, NY (1968-1995); Director, Division of Radiation Oncology, State University of New York Health Science Center, Syracuse, NY (1968-1992); Assistant Professor, Division of Radiation Oncology, Department of Radiology, NewYork-Presbyterian/Columbia University Irving Medical Center, New York, NY (1964-1968); Instructor, Division of Radiation Oncology, Department of Radiology, Stanford University School of Medicine, Palo Alto, CA (1961-1964); Clinical Instructor, Department of Radiology, Tulane University School of Medicine, New Orleans, LA (1956-1957) **Career Related:** Fellow, American College of Radiation Oncology (2003-Present); Fellow, American College of Radiology (1981-Present); Fellow, American Society of Therapeutic Radiology and Oncology (ASTRO) (2008); Consultant, Department of Radiology, United Health Services Hospitals, Johnson City, NY (1998-2003); Consultant, Department of Radiology, Oswego Hospital, Oswego, NY (1994-2003); Consultant, Department of Radiology, Community General Hospital, Syracuse, NY (1968-2003); Attending Physician, Department of Radiology, St. Joseph's Hospital Health Center, Syracuse, NY (1968-2003); Attending Physician, Department of Radiology, Crouse Irving Memorial Hospital (Now Crouse Health), Syracuse, NY (1968-2003); Attending Physician, Department of Radiology, Syracuse VA Medical Center, Syracuse, NY (1968-2003); Attending Physician, Radiation Oncology, University Hospital, State University of New York Health Science Center, Syracuse, NY (1968-2003); Invited Lecturer, Society of Radiation Oncology Administrators (1998); Invited Lecturer, Betty Schmidt Memorial Lecture, State University of New York Health Science Center, Syracuse, NY (1998) **Military Service:** Captain, U.S. Air Force (1957-1959); Roentgenologist and Chairman of the Department, 5060th USAF Hospital, U.S. Air Force, Fairbanks, AK (1957-1959) **Creative Works:** Editorial Board, Radiographics (1998-Present); Author, Co-editor, "Radiotherapy of Intraocular and Orbital Tumors," Second Edition, Springer-Verlag (2002); Author, Co-editor, "Age Related Molecular Degeneration," Springer (2001) **Awards:** Named, Best Doctors in America (1993-2002); Certification of Appreciation, Residency Review Committee for Radiation Oncology, ACGME (1993-1998); Distinguished Commission Service Award, American College of Radiology (1997); Named, Most Prolific Reviewer, Radiology (1985-1996); Editor's Recognition Award, Radiology (1994); Editors Recognition Award, Radiographics (1993); President's Award for Research, State University of New York (1991) **Memberships:** Chairman, Radiation Oncology Scientific Exhibit Committee, Radiological Society of North America (1998-Present); Public Information Advisory Board, Radiological Society of North America (1995-Present); Commission on Human Resources, American College of Radiology (1991-Present); Upstate New York Society for Therapeutic Radiology and Oncology (1990-Present); Therapeutic Radiology Accreditation Appeals Panel, ACGME (1986-Present); Associated Science Committee, Radiological Society of North America (1986-Present); Bureau of Radiological Health, MRAC, Department of Health, Education & Welfare (1980-Present); Radiological Society of North America (1961-Present); Radiation Oncology Test Writing Committee (1980-2002); Guest Examiner, American Board of Radiology (1965-2002); Career Advisor Committee, Radiation Oncology Representative, New York State Radiological Society (1998-2000) **Marquis Who's Who Honors:** Albert Nelson Marquis Lifetime Achievement Award; Marquis Who's Who Top Professional **Why did you become involved in your profession or industry:** As a boy, Dr. Sagerman always admired the work of his father, a physician. He went on to complete medical school and became a radiologist. **Avocations:** Travel

Ivan S. Salgo, MD

Title: Cardiothoracic Anesthesiologist **Industry:** Medicine & Health Care **Company Name:** Philips **Date of Birth:** 11/06/1962 **Place of Birth:** New York **State/Country of Origin:** NY/USA **Parents:** Ivan L. Salgo; Madeleine M. Salgo **Education:** MBA, Massachusetts Institute of Technology (2012); Fellow, Hospital of the University of Pennsylvania, Philadelphia, PA (1994-1996); Resident in Anesthesiology, Hospital of the University of Pennsylvania, Philadelphia, PA (1991-1994); Intern, North Shore University Hospital, Manhasset, NY (1990-1991); MD, Mount Sinai School of Medicine (1990); MS, Columbia University (1987); BS, Columbia University (1985) **Certifications:** Diplomate, American Board of Anesthesiology (1996) **Career:** Associate Chief Medical Officer, Philips Monitoring and Analytics (2015-Present); Cardiology Segment Leader, Senior Director, Philips Ultrasounds (2010-2015); Chief of Cardiovascular Medical Investigations, Philips Healthcare (2008-2011); Strategic Initiative Team Leader, Ultrasound & Monitoring Group, Philips Healthcare (2004-2008); Senior Scientist of Research & Development, Ultrasound & Monitoring Group, Philips Healthcare (2000-2004); Assistant Professor, University of Pennsylvania, Philadelphia, PA (1996-2000) **Career Related:** Chair, Philips Global Innovation Drive & Event, Philips Corporate (2016); Referee; Presenter in Field **Creative Works:** Contributor, Chapters, Caplan's Cardiac Anesthesia (2011, 2016); Author, "Pare-operative trans-esophageal eco-cardiography" (2014) **Memberships:** American Society of Echocardiography; American Society of Anesthesiologists **Marquis Who's Who Honors:** Albert Nelson Marquis Lifetime Achievement Award; Marquis Who's Who Top Professional **Why did you become involved in your profession or industry:** Dr. Salgo was interested in heart surgery and engineering from a young age. During the early part of his career, he was inspired by someone who one of the first to use echocardiography in heart surgery. He likes to push the envelope of medicine to help patients. He wants to ultimately be known for bringing technology forth to advance medicine. **Avocations:** Cycling; Hiking; Traveling

Richard Arlen Saliterman

Title: President **Industry:** Law and Legal Services **Company Name:** Saliterman & Siefferman PC **Date of Birth:** 08/03/1946 **Parents:** Leonard Slitz Saliterman; Dorothy (Sloan) Saliterman **Children:** Robert Saliterman **Education:** Graduate, FBI Citizens Academy, Minneapolis, MN, Washington, DC (2006); Master of Laws, New York University (1974); Coursework, United States Naval Justice School (1972); Doctor of Jurisprudence, Columbia Law School (1971); Bachelor of Arts, University of Minnesota, Summa Cum Laude (1968); Coursework, History of U.S. Diplomacy and Development of Constitutional Concepts, Harvard University (1965) **Career:** President, Saliterman & Siefferman PC, Minneapolis, MN (1975-Present); Military Attorney, Presidential Clemency Board, White House, Washington, DC (1975); Acting Director and Deputy Director, Compliance and Enforcement Division, Federal Energy Office, New York, NY (1974); Legal Staff Subcommittee on Antitrust and Monopoly, United States Senate, Washington, DC (1971-1972) **Career Related:** Adjunct Professor of Corporation Law, Business Organization Law and Fundamental Income Taxation, Hamline University School of Law (1976-1981); Teaching Fellow in Anti-Trust Law, Columbia Law School; Professor, University of Minnesota Law School; Guest Lecturer on Franchise Law, University of Minnesota School of Business **Civic:** National Board of Directors, Navy League of the United States, Washington, DC (1997-Present); Board of Directors, Secretary, The Pavek Museum (1992-Present); National Judge Advisor (2001-2002); Trustee, W. Harry Davis Foundation (1990-1996); Board of Directors, Minneapolis Urban League (1983-1987); Trustee, Secretary, Hopkins Education Foundation; President, Twin Cities Council; Attendee, Citizens Academy, Federal Bureau of Investigation; Citizens Advisory Panel, Hennepin County Sheriffs Office **Military Service:** United States Navy Reserve (1975-Present); Lieutenant, JAG Corps, United States Navy (1972-1975) **Creative Works:** Co-author, "Advising Minnesota Corporations and Other Business Organizations, Second Edition," Four Volumes, Juris Publishing (2011); Chairman, Hennepin County Bar Journal (1985-1987); Co-author, "Advising Minnesota Corporations and Other Business Organizations," Four Volumes, Juris Publishing (1975); Student Editor, Columbia Human Rights Law Review (1969-1971) **Awards:** Super Lawyer; AV-Rating, Martindale-Hubbell; Five-Star Professional, Minneapolis/St. Paul Magazine; Bar Registration of Preeminent Lawyers **Memberships:** Founding Board Member, Hopkins Education Foundation; Board of Directors, Secretary, Pavek Museum; Trustee and Officer, W. Harry Davis Foundation for Black Leadership; Honorary Commissioning Committee, USS Minnesota; Board of Directors, Minnesota Urban League; Officer and Board Member, Pavek Museum of Broadcasting; Alumni Group, Citizens Academy, Federal Bureau of Investigation **Bar Admissions:** Washington, DC (1974); Minnesota (1972) **Marquis Who's Who Honors:** Albert Nelson Marquis Lifetime Achievement Award; Marquis Who's Who Top Professional **Why did you become involved in your profession or industry:** Mr. Saliterman became involved in his profession to help others find justice.

Marc Sallus

Title: Partner **Industry:** Law and Legal Services **Company Name:** Oldman, Cooley, Sallus, Birnberg, Coleman & Gold, LLP **Date of Birth:** 09/14/1954 **Place of Birth:** Washington **State/Country of Origin:** DC/USA **Marital Status:** Married **Education:** JD, Hastings College of the Law, University of California (1979); BA, Claremont McKenna College, Cum Laude (1976) **Career:** Partner, Oldman, Cooley, Sallus, Birnberg, Coleman & Gold, LLP **Civic:** Las Angeles Law Philharmonic **Creative Works:** Research Editor, Hastings International and Comparative Law Review, Special Edition, Japan; Lecturer in Field **Awards:** LA County Bar Outstanding Law Award (2004, 2017); Beverly Hills Bar Presidents Award (2004); Southern California Super Lawyer; Listee, Southern California Best Lawyers **Memberships:** Executive Committee, Trust and Estate Section, State Bar of California; Chair, Board of Directors, Conference of Delegates of California Bar Association; Executive Committee, Board of Trustees, President, Barristers Big Band; Litigation Section Executive Committee, Trusts and Estates Section, Executive Committee, Chair, Los Angeles County Bar Delegation to the Conference of Delegates of the State Bar, Los Angeles County Bar Association; President, President-Elect, Beverly Hills Bar Association; First Vice President, Board of Governors; Probate and Trust Section, Chair and Executive Committee, Beverly Hills Bar Foundation Board; House of Delegates, American Bar Association; Chair, ABA Center on Children and the Law Advisory Board; Council, American Bar Association's Family Law Section; Chair, Task Force on Children Needs and Juvenile Justice Committee; Board of Trustees, Historian, Treasurer, Mexican American Bar Association; San Fernando Valley Bar Association; Board Member, Public Counsel; CEB Probate/Estate Planning Advisory Subcommittee; American College of Trust and Estate Counsel; Los Angeles Lawyers Philharmonic Orchestra; Order of the Coif **Bar Admissions:** Central District of California, United States District Court; Eastern District of California, United States District Court; Northern District of California, United States District Court; Southern District of California, United States District Court; United States Tax Court; United States Ninth Circuit **Marquis Who's Who Honors:** Albert Nelson Marquis Lifetime Achievement Award; Marquis Who's Who Top Professional **Why did you become involved in your profession or industry:** Mr. Sallus' family instilled the duty to serve his community in him from a young age, which resulted in his motivation to pursue his career.

Alfred L. Salt, Rev.

Title: Priest **Industry:** Religious **Date of Birth:** 04/30/1927 **Place of Birth:** Hackensack **State/Country of Origin:** NJ/USA **Parents:** Alfred John; Lily (Tittle) Salt **Marital Status:** Married **Spouse Name:** Elizabeth May Loveland, (06/18/1949) **Children:** Richard John; Michael Rob; Christopher William; Katharine Anne **Education:** Doctor of Ministry, Graduate Theological Foundation (1988); Graduate, Advanced Management Program, Harvard University (1970); Bachelor of Divinity, Bishop's University, Lennoxville, Canada (1960); MA in History, Bishop's University, Lennoxville, Canada (1951); BA in History, Bishop's University, with Honors, Lennoxville, Canada (1949) **Certifications:** Ordained Priest, Cathedral of Holy Trinity (1952); Ordained Deacon, Cathedral of Holy Trinity (1951) **Career:** Retired; Honorary Assistant, St. Mary's, Bonita Springs, FL (2007-Present); Assisting Priest, St. Mary's, Bonita Springs, FL; Honorary Assistant, St. John's Church, Naples, FL (2004-2006); Honorary Assistant, St. Monica's Church, Naples, FL (2002-2003); Honorary Assistant, Trinity Church, Lexington, MI (1998-2001); Honorary Assistant, Grace Church, Port Huron, MI (1993-1998); Rector, All Saints Church, Millington, NJ (1972-1993); Rector, St. Michael's Church, Sillery (1962-1972); Rector, Christ Church, Stanstead (1954-1962); Parish Priest, St. George's Church (1952-1954) **Career Related:** Retreat Conductor, Morris Convocation, Morris County, NJ (1979-Present); Director, VMTC Canada (1995-2002); Vice President, Victorious Ministry Through Christ, Orlando, FL (1989-1992); Director, Victorious Ministry Through Christ, Orlando, FL (1986-1992); With, Victorious Ministry Through Christ, Orlando, FL (1981-1992); President, Morris Convocation, Morris County, NJ (1974-1978); Honorary Canon, Diocese of Quebec (1970); Quebec Bishop's Chaplain Diocese of Quebec (1962); Honorary Canon, Cathedral of Holy Trinity **Civic:** Member, Passaic Township Welfare Board, Millington (1977-1978, 1982); Trustee, Heath Village, Hackettstown, NJ (1974-1976); Commissioner, Quebec Protestant School Board (1970-1972); Member, Superior Council Education, Quebec, Canada (1964-1970); Active, St. Barnabas, North Hatley, Quebec **Military Service:** U.S. Navy (1945-1946); With, USAAC Reserve (1944-1945) **Creative Works:** Author, "Compass Book on Healing" (1996); Contributor, Articles, Religious Journal **Memberships:** Naples Deanery Clericus; Chaplain, Order of St. Luke; Harvard Club of Naples; Worker Sisters of Holy Spirit/Worker Brothers of Holy Spirit **Marquis Who's Who Honors:** Albert Nelson Marquis Lifetime Achievement Award; Marquis Who's Who Humanitarian Award **Why did you become involved in your profession or industry:** Rev. Salt became involved in his profession because he started off as an engineer and had two friends in the service that were killed. So that made him take a long hard look at what he wanted to do. He also had a calling to the ministry.

Dorothy Myers Sampas, PhD

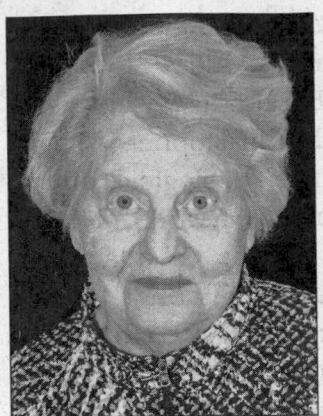

Title: Government Official (Retired) **Industry:** Government Administration/Government Relations/Government Services **Date of Birth:** 08/24/1933 **Place of Birth:** Washington **State/Country of Origin:** DC/USA **Parents:** Lawrence Myers; Anna Cornelia (Henkel) Myers **Marital Status:** Married **Spouse Name:** James George Sampas (12/08/1962) **Children:** George; Lawrence James **Education:** PhD, Georgetown University (1970); Additional Coursework, University of Paris, École libre des sciences politiques (1955-1956); AB, University of Michigan (1955) **Certifications:** Certificate, Defense Resource Management Institute, Naval Postgraduate School (1993); Certificate, National War College, Washington DC (1987) **Career:** Foreign Service Officer (1998); American Ambassador, Islamic Republic of Mauritania (1994-1997); Minister-Counselor, United States Mission to the United Nations, New York, NY (1991-1994); Embassy Minister-Counselor, Embassy of the United States, Beijing, China (1987-1990); Director, Office of Management, United States State Department, Washington, DC (1984-1986); Division Chief, Office of Management, United States State Department, Washington, DC (1983-1984); Division Chief, Deputy Chief, Office of Position and Pay Management, United Stats State Department, Washington, DC (1979-1983); General Services Officer, United States Embassy in Belgium (1975-1979); Analyst, Bureau of Administration, United States State Department, Washington, DC (1973-1975); Consultant, Transcentury Corporation, Washington, DC (1972); Vice-Consul, United States Consulate General Hamburg, Federal Republic of Germany (1960-1962); Member, Bureau of Public Affairs, United States State Department, Washington, DC (1958-1960); Registered Lobbyist, The Michigan Legislature (1954-1955); City Editor, The Michigan Daily (1954-1955) **Civic:** Volunteer, Sibley Memorial Hospital, Johns Hopkins Health System (1999-2013) **Memberships:** Cosmos Club **Marquis Who's Who Honors:** Albert Nelson Marquis Lifetime Achievement Award; Marquis Who's Who Top Professional; Marquis Who's Who Humanitarian Award **To what do you attribute your success:** Dr. Sampas attributes her success to hard work and listening to others. **Why did you become involved in your profession or industry:** She became involved in her profession because her father Lawrence Myers did similar work. He was an agricultural economist and for several years director of the Sugar Program for The Department of Agriculture. Dr. Sampas believes that she has always had an interest with politics and foreign policy from youth on up. **Avocations:** Reading; Theatre **Religion:** Presbyterian

Sheryl Kara Sandberg

Title: Executive, Chief Operating Officer **Industry:** Internet **Company Name:** Facebook **Date of Birth:** 08/28/1969 **Place of Birth:** Washington, DC **State/Country of Origin:** DC/USA **Parents:** Joel Sandberg; Adele (Einhorn) Sandberg **Marital Status:** Widowed **Spouse Name:** David Bruce Goldberg (04/17/2004, Deceased 05/2015); Brian Kraff (1993, Divorced 1994) **Children:** Two Children **Education:** MBA, Harvard Business School, with Highest Distinction (1995); BA in Economics, Harvard University, Summa Cum Laude (1991) **Career:** Chief Operating Officer, Facebook, Menlo Park, CA (2008-Present); Vice President, Global Online Sales & Operations, Google, Inc., Mountain View, CA (2001-2008); Chief of Staff to Secretary Larry Summers, U.S. Department of the Treasury, Washington, DC (1999-2001); Chief of Staff to Deputy Secretary Larry Summers, U.S. Department of the Treasury, Washington, DC (1996-1999); Management Consultant, McKinsey & Company, New York, NY (1996); Research Assistant, The World Bank Group, New York, NY (1991-1993) **Career Related:** Board of Directors, SurveyMonkey.com, LLC (2015-Present); Board of Directors, Facebook (2012-Present); Board of Directors, Walt Disney Company (2009-Present); Board of Directors, Starbucks Coffee Company (2009-2012); Board of Directors, eHealth, Inc. (2006-2008) **Civic:** Founder, LeanIn.org; Board Member, V-Day; Board Member, Center for Global Development; Board Member, Women for Women International **Creative Works:** Co-author, "Option B: Facing Adversity, Building Resilience and Finding Joy" (2017); Co-author, "Lean In: Women, Work and the Will to Lead" (2013) **Awards:** Named One of the 50 Most Powerful Women in Business, Fortune Magazine (2007-2015); Named One of the 100 Most Powerful Women, Forbes Magazine (2010-2014); Named One of the 50 Most Influential People in Global Finance, Bloomberg Markets (2013); Named One of the 100 Most Influential People in the World, Time Magazine (2012-2013); Named One of the Most Influential Players in Marketing, Advertising Age (2011); Named One of the 10 Most Powerful Women in Silicon Valley, San Jose Mercury News (2011); Named One of the Most Influential Women in Technology, Fast Company Magazine (2009); Named Woman to Watch, Advertising Age (2009); Named One of the 25 Most Influential People on the Web, Businessweek (Now Bloomberg Businessweek) (2008); Named One of the 50 Women to Watch, The Wall Street Journal (2007-2008); John H. Williams Prize, Harvard University (1991) **Memberships:** The Phi Beta Kappa Society **Political Affiliations:** Democrat **Religion:** Jewish

Bernard "Bernie" Sanders

Title: U.S. Senator from Vermont **Industry:** Government Administration/Government Relations/Government Services **Date of Birth:** 12/08/1941 **Place of Birth:** Brooklyn **State/Country of Origin:** NY/USA **Parents:** Eli Ben Yehuda Sanders; Dorothy (Glassberg) Sanders **Marital Status:** Married **Spouse Name:** Jane O'Meara (1988); Deborah Shiling Messing (1964, Divorced 1966) **Children:** Levi; Heather; Carina; David **Education:** Honorary LHD, Brooklyn College (2017); BA, The University of Chicago (1964); Coursework, Brooklyn College **Career:** Ranking Member, Senate Budget Committee (2015-Present); U.S. Senator, State of Vermont (2007-Present); Chairman, U.S. Senate Committee on Veterans' Affairs (2013-2015); U.S. House of Representatives, Vermont's At-large Congressional District, United States Congress, Washington, DC (1991-2007); Faculty, Hamilton College, Clinton, NY (1991); Faculty Member, Harvard University, Cambridge, MA (1989); Mayor, City of Burlington, VT (1981-1989); Director, American People's Historical Society, Burlington, VT (1976-1981); Freelance Writer, Carpenter, Youth Counselor (1964-1976) **Career Related:** Candidate, Democratic Party Presidential Nomination (2016, 2020) **Civic:** Candidate, Vermont Governor (1972, 1976, 1986); Chairman, Vermont Liberty Union Party (1975-1976); Candidate, United States Senate (1971, 1974) **Creative Works:** Appearance, Television Show, "Saturday Night Live" (2016); Author, "The Speech: A Historic Filibuster on Corporate Greed and the Decline of Our Middle Class" (2011); Appearance, "My X-Girlfriend's Wedding Reception" (1999); Author, "Outsider in the House" (1997); Appearance, Film, "Sweet Hearts Dance" (1988); Artist, Folk Album, "We Shall Overcome" (1987) **Awards:** Named, One of the 10 Most Fascinating People of 2015, Barbara Walters Special (2015) **Political Affiliations:** Independent **Religion:** Jewish

Daljit Singh Sandhu

Title: Retired **Industry:** Food & Restaurant Services **Company Name:** India House Indian Restaurant **Date of Birth:** 02/01/1949 **Place of Birth:** Amritsar **State/Country of Origin:** Punjab, India **Parents:** S. Kashmir Singh Sandhu; Sdrn. Gurbachan Kaur Sandhu **Marital Status:** Married **Spouse Name:** Lakhwinder Kaur Sandhu **Children:** Two daughters; Two sons **Education:** MA in Economics, Khalsa College, Guru Nanak Dev University (1971); BA, Punjab University (1968) **Career:** Owner, India House, Indian Restaurant (2007-2015); Bank Manager, Punjab and Sind Bank (1971-2001) **Career Related:** President, Bank Officer Association, India North Zone, Amritsar **Civic:** Donor, Restoration of Khalsa College Amritsar, India (1996); Arranged Kirtan Smagam, Prayers; Member, Governing Council, Khalsa College, Amritsar, India; Commissioner, Board Member, Elk Grove Historic Preservation; Member, Committee, Rotary Club; Vice President, Indus Valley American Chamber of Commerce Sacramento; Convener, Coordinator, Khalsa College of Education Society Amritsar for California **Awards:** Certificate of Recognition, Mayor of Elk Grove City Mr. Steve Ly (2019); Heritage Award, Governing Council Khalsa College and Punjab Cultural Promotion Chandigarh (2017); State Assembly Recognition Award, Jim Cooper (2016); Certificate of Recognition, Assembly Member Beth Gains (2008-2015); Small Business Man of the Year, California State (2014); Honoree, 59th All India Sikh Education Conference, Chief Khalsa Dewan (1996); Honoree, World Sikh Conference, Mini Sikh Parliament (SGPC) (1996); Honoree, California State Flag, Six State Assembly Members **To what do you attribute your success:** He attributes his success to his parents and family. There is no substitute for hard work, honesty and sincerity. **Why did you become involved in your profession or industry:** Mr. Sandhu worked as a bank manager for over thirty years in India. When he came to America he did not want to work for someone else he wanted to have his own business. Mr. Sandhu and his sons sold ice cream out of small vans when they first came to America. They made a little money and used that money to buy the restaurant. They successfully ran it for nine years. **Avocations:** Gardening; Community services **Religion:** Sikh **Thoughts on Life:** Satisfactory Customer and community services is the key to success.

M. Akram Sandhu

Title: Co-Owner, Chemist, Business Executive **Date of Birth:** 03/26/1936 **Parents:** Ch. Fateh Ali Sandhu; Sadiqa (Bhaigam) Sandhu **Marital Status:** Married **Spouse Name:** Bushra N. Sandhu (10/06/1962) **Children:** Aqeel A; Faheem A; Fazeelah A; Chappell **Education:** Postdoctoral Fellowship, Walter Reed Army Research Command, University of Minnesota (1967-1970); Doctor of Philosophy, University of Strathclyde, Glasgow, Scotland (1967); Master of Science in Technology, University of Punjab, Lahore, Pakistan (1961) **Career:** Co-Owner, Chemist, Business Executive, Chairman, ADI LLC, Rochester, NY (2000-2018); Co-Founder, President, AKSA-SDS, Rochester, NY (2000-2018); Chief Executive Officer, President, AKSA Corporation, Rochester, NY (1999-2018); Board of Directors, AKSA-SDS, Rochester, NY (1999-2018); Vice President, Nanosystems LLC, Rochester, NY (1994-1998); Director, Business Development, Kodak, Rochester, NY (1985-1994); Senior Research Associate, Kodak, Rochester, NY (1982-1985); Laboratory Head, Eastman Kodak Company, Kingsport, TN (1978-1982); Senior Research Chemist, Eastman Kodak Company, Rochester, NY (1970-1978); National Institutes of Health Fellow, University of Minnesota, Minneapolis (1967-1970) **Civic:** Chairman, Islamic Center Rochester (1994-2000) **Creative Works:** Contributor, Many Articles to Professional Journals; Creator, Over 40 U.S. Patents **Awards:** Hamilton Barrett Research Prize (1965); Grantee, University of Strathclyde (1964-1967) **Memberships:** President, Pakistani American Society (1992-1998); Chairman, Pakistani American Society (1989-1990); Fellow, Royal Society of Chemistry, England; Royal Institute of Chemistry, England; Founder, Pakistani American Society; Sigma Xi **Marquis Who's Who Honors:** Albert Nelson Marquis Lifetime Achievement Award; Marquis Who's Who Top Professional **Why did you become involved in your profession or industry:** Hailing from a renowned family in Pakistan, Dr. Sandhu drew a great deal of influence from his grandfather, whose decision making process contributed greatly to the younger man's business training. His mother, likewise, consistently encouraged him to become more educated. Since coming of age, he was fascinated by how the universe fits together, and this led him toward the field of chemistry.

Chitto Priyo Sarkar, DO, PhD

Title: Family Medicine Physician, Research Scientist **Industry:** Medicine & Health Care **Company Name:** St. Lucie Family Doctor **Date of Birth:** 06/01/1951 **Place of Birth:** West Bengal **State/Country of Origin:** India **Parents:** Bimala Kanto Sarkar; Labonyamoyee (Mitra) Sarkar **Marital Status:** Divorced **Spouse Name:** Maria Lourdes Uceta (02/11/1998, Divorced April 2006); Patricia A. Matthews (05/27/1987, Divorced July 1996) **Children:** Danny Lee; Christopher J.; Emily I. **Education:** DO, Kirksville College of Osteopathic Medicine (Now A.T. Still University of Health Sciences (ATSU)), Kirksville, MO (1987); PhD in Biochemistry, University of Calcutta, Kolkata, India (1977); MSc in Biochemistry, University of Calcutta, Kolkata, India (1971); BSc in Chemistry, University of Calcutta, Kolkata, India (1969) **Certifications:** Board-Certified in Family Practice, American Board of Osteopathic Family Physician **Career:** Owner, Physician, Private Practice, St. Lucie Family Doctor, Port St. Lucie, FL (1992-Present); Physician, Infectious Disease Center, Fort Pierce, FL (1991-1992); Physician, Okeechobee Community Health Center, Florida (1989-1991); Resident, General Family Practice, Oakland General Hospital, Madison Heights, MI (1988-1989); Intern, Botsford General Hospital, Farmington Hills, MI (1987-1988); Member, Research Science Staff, Dalton Research Center, University of Missouri, Columbia, MO (1982-1983); Research Associate, Kirksville College of Osteopathic Medicine (Now A.T. Still University of Health Sciences (ATSU)), Kirksville, MO (1980-1982); Research Associate, Tulane University Medical Center, Department of Biochemistry, New Orleans, LA (1979-1980) **Career Related:** Instructor, Southeast College Osteopathic Medicine, North Miami Beach, Florida (1989-1995); Staff Physician, Lawnwood Regional Medical Center, Ft Pierce FL (1992-2007); St. Lucie Medical Center, Port St. Lucie, FL (1994-Present); Cleveland Clinic, Stuart, FL (2014-Present); Instructor, Associates, Florida State University College of Medicine, Ft. Pierce Regional Campus, FL (2017-2018) **Civic:** Sponsored Several Years, Little Leagues of Port St Lucie as well as Jensen Beach High School Band Program **Creative Works:** Contributor, Numerous Articles to Professional Journals, Including Journal Of Neurochemistry, Epilepsy, and Various Other International Journals and Publications; Contributor, Author, Numerous Abstracts, Including "Effect of Delta 9-Tetrahydrocannabinol on Gangliosides," "Gangliosides in normal and cataractous lenses of several species," "Reactivity of key metabolic sterols in standard colorimetric assays for cholesterol," and "Studies on the Mechanism of the Epileptiform Activity Induced by U18666A. I. Gross Alteration of the Lipids of Synaptosomes and Myelin" **Awards:** America's Top Family Doctors (2007) **Memberships:** American Medical Association; American Osteopathic Medical Association; American Academy of Family Physicians; Florida Osteopathic Medical Association (FOMA) **Marquis Who's Who Honors:** Albert Nelson Marquis Lifetime Achievement Award (1993-1994) **To what do you attribute your success:** He attributes his success to perseverance, which he feels is a pillar of any successful career. "It is very important to set up your goal, long-term or short-term, and stay determined to achieve that goal no matter what kind of obstacles come on the path." He also credits his faith and trust in God. "With hard work, good faith and perseverance one can achieve what he or she wants. I always tried to keep feet on the ground and looked for the stars." **Why did you become involved in your profession or industry:** Dr. Sarkar did not plan to be a physician from the beginning. However, he feels it was his destiny, which was determined by God. He became involved in family/general practice after going through training and experience in research in biochemistry; he found he was most interested in treating and taking care of patients and helping patients at a primary care level after giving up an idea to be a neurologist since he had the background in neurobiochemical pharmacology including extensive research background in cannabis or THC (TetrahydroCannabinol) **Avocations:** Photography; Reading; Music; Traveling the world **Political Affiliations:** Independent **Religion:** Spiritual (Non-Religious) **Thoughts on Life:** In his life, if Dr. Sarkar could do one thing, which is practice medicine for patients regardless of age, race or sex or financial status without any restrictions from the Insurance company or inability to pay for the healthcare, he would have been really happy in life! He feels that the medical system is so pathetic in this country that it is hard to believe that this country claims to be the best in the world. Life couldn't be any worse when a physician cannot treat a patient or prevent preventable disease for lack of financial ability or restrictions by health insurance and pharmaceutical companies. He feels that it is a shame that pets get better medical care than humans, but there is always a hope that this will change someday. Dr. Sarkar would also like to mention his grandchildren: Danny, who is 2 years old, and Matthew, who is 9 months old.

David Satinsky, MD

Title: Medical Doctor (Retired) **Industry:** Medicine & Health Care **Company Name:** The Neurology Center **Marital Status:** Married **Spouse Name:** Carla (1960) **Children:** Andrew; Stephen; Deborah; Adam **Education:** MD, University of Pennsylvania School of Medicine, Philadelphia, PA (1964); BA, Chemistry, University of Pennsylvania, Philadelphia, PA (1960) **Certifications:** American Board of Qualification in Electroencephalography (1977); American Board of Psychiatry & Neurology (1972); State of Maryland Medical License (1970); Licensed, DEA **Career:** Private Practice, The Neurology Center, Rockville, MD (1971-2019); Director, Headache Clinic, The Neurology Center, Chevy Chase, MD (1979-1985); Attending Neurologist, National Children's Rehabilitation Center, Leesburg, VA (1970-1972); Private Practice, Neurology, Riverdale, MD (1971); Neurology Residency, Hospital of the University of Pennsylvania, Philadelphia, PA (1967-1970); Research Associate, National Institutes of Mental Health, Washington, DC (1965-1967); Internship, Bronx Municipal Hospital Center, Bronx, NY (1964-1965) **Career Related:** Assistant Clinical Professor of Neurology, George Washington University School of Medicine, Washington, DC (1971-2019) **Civic:** Board Member, Center for Unique Learners (1985-1986) **Creative Works:** Contributor, Numerous Articles, Professional Journals **Memberships:** President, Alpha Omega Alpha (1963-1964); President, Epsilon Chapter, Alpha Epsilon Delta (1959-1960); American Epilepsy Society; American Association for the Study of Headache (Now The American Headache Society); American Board of Clinical Biofeedback; American Academy of Neurology; American Medical Association; Montgomery County Medical Society; American Electroencephalographic Society; Phi Beta Kappa; Pi Mu Epsilon; Alpha Chi Sigma **To what do you attribute your success:** Dr. Satinsky attributes his success to loving his work. He has more than the usual powers of observation, so when he interviews patients about their disease, the diagnosis is primarily in the history, not in the exams or testing. He remembers one of his teachers saying to him listen to the patient he is giving you the diagnosis. That was a critical piece of information that stuck. He spent as much time as he needed listening and looking, verbal and visual information from the patient until he knows what is wrong with the patient. Once you know what is wrong treatment is easy. He has a keen interest in observing. **Why did you become involved in your profession or industry:** Dr. Satinsky became involved in his profession because he had two uncles who were physicians, one was a surgeon and one was a general physician. They were highly respected in the city of Philadelphia where he lived. He loved them both and they certainly had an effect on him. Dr. Satinsky started playing the violin when he was 8 years old, and he was pretty good. He was the concert master in high school and the concert master in the Pennsylvania State Orchestra. He went up to his violin teacher when he was a senior in high school, and he asked him if he thought he could become a musician and his teachers response was you will make a great physician. So he didn't pursue music professionally but continued to play chamber music. **Avocations:** Plays violin; Photography; Volunteer position at the national zoo in Washington DC

Warren S. Satterlee II

Title: Retail Management Professional, Writer **Industry:** Retail/Sales **Date of Birth:** 12/08/1946 **Place of Birth:** Harlingen **State/Country of Origin:** TX/USA **Parents:** Ralph Pickard Satterlee; Diane (Royall-Mann) Satterlee **Marital Status:** Married **Spouse Name:** Virginia Lou Schumacher (07/17/1971, Deceased 05/24/2011) **Children:** Heather Irene **Education:** BA, St. Cloud State University (1974); AA, Cayuga Community College, Auburn, NY (1972) **Certifications:** Graduate Certificate in Theological Studies, Brite Divinity School, Texas Christian University (1991) **Career:** Retired (2006); Retail Management Staff, Ross Dress For Less, Fort Worth (2000-2006); Retail Management, Eckerd Drug #3156, Arlington (1995-2000); Member, Supervisory Training Program, Eckerd Drug (1999); Member, Management Training Program Retail Management Practices, Eckerd Drug (1999); Member, Customer Service Staff, Office Depot, Arlington (1998); Supervisor, Bakery Support Staff, Schlotzskys Deli Sandwich Shop, Arlington (1993-1996); Supervisor, Bakery Support Staff, Schlotzskys, Arlington, TX (1989-1993); Retail Management Staff, AARP Southwest Chapter **Civic:** Member, St. Timothy Anglican Catholic Church Choir (2017-Present); Member, Rite I Choir (2012-2017); Monthly Refreshment Committee, AARP Chapter 4116, Fort Worth, TX (2009-2011); Member, Rite I, Church of Saint Peter and Paul Anglican Church Choir, Arlington, TX (1999-2006); Member, Church Choir (1999-2001); Volunteer, Cowtown Marathon, Fort Worth, TX (1991-2011) Past Member, Fort Worth Genealogical Society, Crowley Art Guild; Contributor, Hereditary Register of the USA **Military Service:** U.S. Air Force (1966-1970), Honorable Discharge **Creative Works:** Author, "Meditation" (1997); Author, "Meditation III" (1997); Author, Numerous Poems; Contributor, Articles, Professional Journals **Memberships:** International Order of St. Luke the Physician **Marquis Who's Who Honors:** Albert Nelson Marquis Lifetime Achievement Award; Marquis Who's Who Top Professional; Marquis Who's Who Humanitarian Award **Avocations:** Creative writing; Making church worship banners and visuals; Music; Crafts **Religion:** Anglican

Benjamin Saunders

Title: Attorney **Industry:** Law and Legal Services **Company Name:** Davis, Saunders & Miller, PLC **Place of Birth:** New Orleans **State/Country of Origin:** LA/USA **Marital Status:** Married **Children:** Rachel; Rebeca **Education:** JD, Loyola University College of Law, New Orleans, LA (1969); BS in Pre-Medicine, Louisiana State University, Baton Rouge, LA (1966); Coursework in Negotiation Projects for Lawyers, Harvard Law School, Harvard University, Cambridge, MA **Career:** Attorney, Davis, Saunders, Miller & Oden Law Firm **Career Related:** Lecturer, Continuing Legal Education Programs, Railroad Law Section, Association of Trial Lawyers of America (1993-Present); Chairman, Designated Legal Counsel, BLE **Civic:** Board Member, Loyola Law Alumni (2005-Present); Chairman of the Designated Legal Counsel, Brotherhood of Locomotive Engineers (1999-2002); President, American Rail Labor Attorneys (1999-2000); Chairman, Railroad Law Section, Association of Trial Lawyers of America (1994) **Creative Works:** Contributor, "Preparing the Plaintiff for Direct Examination in a FELA Case," Trial Magazine (1994); Managing Editor, Loyola Law Review (1967-1969); Speaker, Television Program, "It's the Law," New Orleans Bar Association; Contributor, "Truth Wins Lawsuits," NOBA Legal Seminar; Contributor, Articles, Loyola Law Review; Contributor, "Rules of Conduct," NOBA Designated Legal Counsel Program **Awards:** Named, One of the Best Lawyers in New Orleans in the Field of Railroad Law, New Orleans Magazine (2000-Present); Named, Best Lawyers of America (1999-Present); Lifetime Achievement Award, Railroad Section, American Trial Lawyers (2000) **Memberships:** Board of Governors, Louisiana Trial Lawyers (1992-1997); Louisiana Trial Lawyers; Chairman, Railroad Law Section, American Association for Justice; New Orleans Bar Association; Jefferson Parish Bar Association; Louisiana State Bar Association; Federal Bar Association; Section on Litigation, ABA; Academy of New Orleans Trial Lawyers; Harvard Law School Negotiation Project for Lawyers; Delta Theta Phi; Past President's Advisory Committee, American Rail Labor Attorneys; Chair, Legislative and Government Affairs Committee, Compliance Committee, American Rail Labor Attorneys **Bar Admissions:** All Federal Courts (1970); State of Louisiana (1969); U.S. District Court, Eastern District, State of Louisiana (1969); U.S. District Court, Western District, State of Louisiana (1969); U.S. District Court, Middle District, State of Louisiana; U.S. Court of Appeals for the Fourth Circuit; U.S. Court of Appeals for the Fifth Circuit; U.S. Court of Appeals for the 11th Circuit **Marquis Who's Who Honors:** Marquis Who's Who Top Professional **To what do you attribute your success:** Mr. Saunders attributes his success to hard work. **Why did you become involved in your profession or industry:** Mr. Saunders started out as a pre-medicine major, focusing on molecular biology, and was accepted to medical school, but the dean put him on hold for a year because he could get some students from Harvard University. Mr. Saunders' plan was to go attend law school for a year and then go to medical school. However, when he attended law school, he fell in love with it.

Diane Sawyer

Title: Broadcast Journalist **Industry:** Media & Entertainment **Company Name:** ABC News **Date of Birth:** 12/22/1945 **Place of Birth:** Glasgow **State/Country of Origin:** KY/USA **Parents:** Erbon Powers Sawyer; Jean W. (Dunagan) Sawyer **Marital Status:** Widowed **Spouse Name:** Mike Nichols (04/29/1988, Deceased 11/19/2014) **Children:** Daisy (Stepchild); Max (Stepchild); Jenny (Stepchild) **Education:** Honorary LHD, Brown University (2012); BA in English, Wellesley College, MA (1967) **Career:** Special Interview Correspondent, ABC News (2014-Present); Correspondent, "20/20," ABC News (2000-Present); Anchor, "ABC World News Tonight," ABC News, New York, NY (2009-2014); Co-anchor, "Primetime Live" (Now "PrimeTime"), ABC News (2000-2009); Co-anchor, "Good Morning America," ABC News, New York, NY (1999-2009); Co-anchor, "20/20," ABC News (1998-2000); Co-anchor, "Primetime Live," ABC News (1989-1998); Correspondent, Co-editor, "60 Minutes," CBS News (1984-1989); Co-anchor Early Morning News, CBS News (1981-1984); General Assignment Reporter, Then Department State Correspondent, CBS News (1978-1981); Literary Assistant to Former President Richard Nixon (1974-1978); Press Office Administrator, The White House, Washington, DC (1970-1974); Reporter, Station WLKY-TV, Louisville, KY (1967-1970) **Awards:** Disney Legend Award (2019); Named One of the 100 Most Powerful Women, Forbes Magazine (2005, 2007-2008, 2010-2013); RFK Journalism Award, Robert F. Kennedy Center for Justice & Human Rights (Now Robert F. Kennedy Human Rights) (2007, 2010); Walter Cronkite Award for Excellence in Journalism (2010); George Foster Peabody Award for Excellence in TV Broadcasting (2009); Named One of the 50 Most Powerful Women in New York City, New York Post (2007); George Polk Award for TV Reporting (2004); Named One of the 30 Most Powerful Women in America, Ladies' Home Journal (2001); Named to the Broadcast Magazine Hall of Fame (1997); Named to the Television Academy Hall of Fame (1997); George Foster Peabody Award for Public Service (1988); Numerous Emmy Awards, Television Academy; Numerous Alfred I. duPont-Columbia University Awards; Distinguished Achievement in Journalism Award, University of Southern California; Lifetime Achievement Award, Investigative Reporters & Editors (IRE)

Nancy Lee Saylor, BS

Title: Teacher (Retired) **Industry:** Education/Educational Services **Company Name:** Dallas Independent School District **Date of Birth:** 05/11/1941 **Place of Birth:** Tucson **State/Country of Origin:** AZ/USA **Parents:** Ellmont Meredith Saylor; Margaret Ann (Simmons) Saylor **Marital Status:** Married **Spouse Name:** James A. Wingrove (07/29/2009, Deceased 2019) **Education:** BS in Health, Physical Education, Recreation, and Dance, Texas Woman's University (1962) **Certifications:** Secondary Education, State of Texas; Physical Education and Recreation, State of Texas; Driver's Education, State of Texas; Elementary Education, State of Texas; Computer Literacy, State of Texas **Career:** Teacher, Computer Literacy, Dallas Independent School District (1989-1997); Teacher, Physical Education, Dallas Independent School District (1986-1990); Teacher, Driver's Education, Dallas Independent School District (1983-1995); Teacher, Physical Education, Dallas Independent School District (1976-1986); Girl's Gymnastics Coach, Dallas Independent School District (1976-1986); Teacher, Elementary and Physical Education, Dallas Independent School District (1963-1976) **Career Related:** Bus Driving Instructor, Trainer, Dallas County Schools, Region 10 Education Service Center (1997-2017); Assistant Director, Recreation, Denton State School, Texas (1962-1963) **Civic:** Educators Political Action Committee, Austin, TX (1983-1996); Texas Parent-Teacher Association (1969); Project 1000, Texas; Teacher, Sunday School **Awards:** Favorite Teacher Award, Positive Parents of Dallas (1983) **Memberships:** Regional Representative, TAHPERD (1984-1987); President, Physical Education and Recreation (1981-1983); Alliance for Health **Marquis Who's Who Honors:** Albert Nelson Marquis Lifetime Achievement Award **Why did you become involved in your profession or industry:** Ms. Saylor became involved in her field as a result of her decision to major in health, physical education, recreation, and dance in college. Once she began working as an elementary teacher, she put all of her core college classes to use in her lesson plans. **Avocations:** Reading **Political Affiliations:** Democrat **Religion:** Church of Jesus Christ of Latter Day Saints

Dorothy Ray Scarbrough, RNC, BSN, MSN

Title: Nursing Educator; Consultant **Industry:** Medicine & Health Care **Date of Birth:** 09/17/1932 **Place of Birth:** Cottonwood **State/Country of Origin:** AL/USA **Parents:** Theo; Bonnylin Elizabeth (Adams) Ray **Marital Status:** Widow **Spouse Name:** John William Scarbrough (06/01/1952, Deceased 08/2019) **Children:** Mary Jane; Lisa Ann; Tina Marie **Education:** MS in Nursing, The University of Alabama (1960); BS in Nursing, The University of Alabama (1954) **Certifications:** Registered Nurse; Certified Gerontological Nurse **Career:** Associate Chief, Nursing Service Nursing Home Care and Extended Care, Tuscaloosa VA Medical Center (1987-1994); Nursing Supervisor, Tuscaloosa VA Medical Center (1981-1987); Consultant, Lecturer, International Center Disabled (ICD), New York, NY (1982-1983); Workshop Planner, Participant, Southeastern Regional Medical Center, Birmingham, AL (1976-1983); Lecturer, New Brunswick Department of Health, Fredericton, Canada (1982); Director, Reality Orientation Training Program, Tuscaloosa VA Medical Center (1969-1981); Workshop Coordinator, Consultant, VA Medical Centers (1973-1980); Advisory Committee, Region 4 Education Service Center, Raleigh, NC (1975-1977); Advisory Board, Reality Orientation Project, American Hospital Association, Chicago, IL (1973-1974); Assistant Professor, Nursing, The University of Alabama, Tuscaloosa, AL (1962-1969); Staff Nurse, Druid City Hospital (DCH Health System), Tuscaloosa, AL (1960-1962); Instructor, The University of Alabama, Tuscaloosa, AL (1954-1959); Workshop Coordinator, Consultant, Hillhaven Foundation, Tacoma, WA; Associate Chief of Nursing, Long Term Care, Veterans Administration Hospital, Tuscaloosa, AL; Technical Adviser, Films Reality Orientation, International Center Disabled (ICD), New York, NY **Career Related:** Co-organizer, Tuscaloosa Alzheimer's Support Group (1983); Southeastern Assembly, The American Assembly, Columbia University, Sea Island, GA (1972); Alabama Delegate, White House Conference on Aging (WHCOA), Washington, DC (1971) **Civic:** Member, Advisory Council, Retired Senior Volunteer Program (RSVP), Tuscaloosa, AL (1981-1991); Member, Professional Advisory Board, Mental Health Association in Tuscaloosa County, AL (1980-1990) **Creative Works:** Author, Book, "I am Still with You: Our Fight Against the Losses from Alzheimer's and Dementia Diseases" (2017); Author, Textbook Chapter, "Nursing of the Confused Patient," Nursing and the Aged Gerontological Nursing (1981); Co-producer, Workbook, Cassette, International Center for the Disabled (ICD), New York, NY; Co-author, Self-instruction Materials; Contributor, Chapters, Books; Contributor, Articles, Professional Journals **Awards:** Outstanding Nurse Administrator Award, Alabama State Nurses Association (ASNA) (1993); Meritorious Service Award, LeadingAge Texas (Formerly the Texas Association of Homes and Services for the Aging - TAHSA) (1974) **Memberships:** Secretary-treasurer, Alabama Organization of Nurse Executives (AlaONL), West Alabama Chapter (1988-1992); State Treasurer, Director, Alabama League for Nursing, National League for Nursing (1956-1958); Alabama Organization of Nurse Executives (AlaONL); Local Nomination Committee, American Nurses Association; The Gerontological Society of America; The University of Alabama Capstone College of Nursing Honor Society; Sigma Theta Tau International Honor Society of Nursing **Why did you become involved in your profession or industry:** Mrs. Scarbrough became involved in her profession because of the influence of her two aunts, who were nurses. When she was 9 years old, her father passed away in an accident. Ever since then, she has wanted to work in the medical field and help other people. Additionally, her mother was adamant about the importance of a college education, which was another reason she pursued nursing. **Avocations:** Traveling; Jewelry making; Writing; Journals; Painting; Children playing on the beach in Panama City **Political Affiliations:** Democrat **Religion:** Methodist

Joyce Schafer

Title: Investment Broker **Industry:** Financial Services **Date of Birth:** 08/28/1934 **Place of Birth:** Bainbridge **State/Country of Origin:** GA/USA **Parents:** Alton Reuben Reddick; Nita Ethelyn (Knighton) Reddick **Marital Status:** Married **Spouse Name:** Lawrence Schafer (01/29/1961) **Children:** Arthur Reuben **Education:** PhD, Georgia State University (1978); MS, Smith College, Northampton, MA (1958); BBS, Wesleyan College, Macon, GA (1955) **Career:** Vice President, Smith, Brown & Groover, Inc., Macon, GA (1985-Present); Registered Representative, Smith, Brown & Groover, Inc., Macon, GA (1980-1985); Vice President, Student Affairs, Wesleyan College (1978-1980); Dean of Students, Wesleyan College (1972-1978); Department Chairman, Wesleyan College (1962-1972); Associate Professor, Wesleyan College (1958-1962) **Career Related:** Secretary-Treasurer, Big Daddy's Package Store, Macon, GA (1990); Advisory Council, John Nuveen & Co., Chicago, IL (1985); Board of Governors, Golden Seale, Putnam Cos., Boston, MA (1984); Stockbroker, Macon, GA **Civic:** Chairman, Board of Commissioners, Macon Housing Authority (1985-1996); Chairman, Board of Governors, River North Country Club, Macon, GA (1995); President, Career Women's Network, Macon, GA (1995); Chairman, Budget Review Board of Education, Macon, GA (1994-1995); Committee Vice President, Macon Chamber of Commerce, Macon, GA (1994); Treasurer, Women's Political Organization, Macon, GA (1992); President, Dunes of Panama Management Association, Panama City, FL (1988); First Women of the Boys Scout Board of Macon **Creative Works:** Syndicated, Finest Columnist, Various Newspapers (1989-Present) **Awards:** Woman of Achievement Award, Career Women's Network, Macon, GA (1994); Humanity Award, American Red Cross, Macon, GA (1967); Honorable Aide-deCamp, Governor of Georgia, Atlanta, GA (1975); Alumnae Distinguished Achievement, Wesleyan College; Inductee, Career Women's Network of Achievement; Jean Harris Award, Rotary International; Silver Bell Award, Bibb Court Board of Education; The Scouting Heritage Boy Scouts Award **Memberships:** Navicent Macon Hospital Authority Board (2018-Present); McCon Housing Authority Board (2000-2019); Medical Center Board Authority (2000-2001); International President, Quota International, Inc.(1978-1979); Secretary, Board Member, Daughters of the American Revolution (1975); Phi Kappa Phi; Career Women's Network; Deacon, Adult Sunday School, St. Andrews Presbyterian Church; Healy Point Ladies Golf Association **Marquis Who's Who Honors:** Albert Nelson Marquis Lifetime Achievement Award **Why did you become involved in your profession or industry:** Ms. Shaefer was encouraged by her father to pursue higher education, which inevitably led to her professional success. She was additionally inspired by her brother, who fought in World War II. **Avocations:** Golf; Reading **Political Affiliations:** Democrat **Religion:** Presbyterian

Mark A. Schaffer

Title: President, Owner **Industry:** Agriculture **Company Name:** Mark Schaffer Excavating and Trucking Inc., Mark Schaffer Farms **Date of Birth:** 10/28/1955 **Place of Birth:** Norwalk **State/Country of Origin:** OH/USA **Parents:** John A.; Doris A. (White) Schaffer **Marital Status:** Married **Spouse Name:** Diane M. Cutnaw (11/27/1976) **Children:** Jason A.; Amy M.; Julie B **Career:** Proprietor, Mark Schaffer Farms (1994-Present); President, Mark Schaffer Excavating and Trucking Inc., Norwalk, OH (1983-Present) **Awards:** Inductee, Saint Paul High School Hall of Fame **Marquis Who's Who Honors:** Albert Nelson Marquis Lifetime Achievement Award; Marquis Who's Who Top Professional **Why did you become involved in your profession or industry:** Mr. Schaffer became involved in his profession because he was inspired by his father, John A. who set the ground work for his work ethic and allowed him to dream. He believed his early childhood work ethic played an instrumental role in setting the tone for the remainder of his career. **Avocations:** Family **Political Affiliations:** Republican **Religion:** Catholic

Willi Georg Schalk

Title: Founder **Industry:** Advertising & Marketing **Company Name:** Team Consulting GmbH **Date of Birth:** 03/07/1940 **Place of Birth:** Aschaffenburg **State/Country of Origin:** Germany **Marital Status:** Widowed **Spouse Name:** Gerdi Goehler **Children:** Silke; Sven **Career:** Chief Executive Officer, McCann Erickson Worldwide (Now McCann, A McCann Worldgroup Agency), Germany (1997-2000); Chairman, McCann Erickson Worldwide (Now McCann, A McCann Worldgroup Agency), Germany (1997-2000); President, Chief Operating Officer, BBDO Worldwide (1986-1990); President, BBDO International Group (Now BBDO Worldwide), New York, NY (1980-1986); Executive Vice President, General Manager, International Operations, BBDO International, Inc. (Now BBDO Worldwide), New York, NY (1978-1980); Chairman, BBDO Group Germany, Düsseldorf, Federal Republic of Germany (1969-1990); Chief Executive Officer, BBDO Group Germany, Düsseldorf, Federal Republic of Germany (1969-1990); Director, BBDO International Group (Now BBDO Worldwide) (1969-1990); Managing Partner, Special Team Advertising Agency, Duesseldorf, Federal Republic of Germany (1967-1970); Marketing Manager, Enka Glanzstoff AG, Wuppertal, Federal Republic of Germany (1963-1966); Product Manager, Enka Glanzstoff AG, Wuppertal, Federal Republic of Germany (1959-1963) **Career Related:** Founder, Team Consulting GmbH (2000-Present); Chairman, BBDO Group (Now BBDO Worldwide), Düsseldorf, Federal Republic of Germany (1981); Chief Executive Officer, BBDO Group (Now BBDO Worldwide), Düsseldorf, Federal Republic of Germany (1981); Board of Directors, Omnicom Group Inc., New York, NY; Chief Executive Officer, M.DuMont Schauberg, Cologne, Germany **Civic:** Pro Bono Work, UNICEF; Pro Bono Work, UNESCO; Wir für Deutschland, AMD-Networks **Creative Works:** Author, "Future of the Advertising Industry" (2020) **Awards:** Inductee, Hall of Fame for Advertising, Germany (1997) **Memberships:** Board of Directors, International Advertising Association (Now IAA Global) (1986-Present); Industrie Düsseldorf; Ocean Reef Club, Key Largo, FL; Marketing Club Düsseldorf; Wissenschaftliche Gesellschaft, Germany **Marquis Who's Who Honors:** Albert Nelson Marquis Lifetime Achievement Award; Marquis Who's Who Top Professional **Why did you become involved in your profession or industry:** Mr. Schalk broke into the advertisement industry by initially working in the client sector. He later transitioned to the advertising side of the business, as well as the media sector. However, he eventually found himself back in advertising, where he has stayed since. **Avocations:** Scuba diving

Susan O. Schall, DEng

Title: Founder & Lead Consultant **Industry:** Consulting **Company Name:** SOS Consulting, LLC **Date of Birth:** 05/26/1959 **Place of Birth:** Buffalo **State/Country of Origin:** NY/USA **Parents:** William Edward; Carol Ruth **Marital Status:** Married **Spouse Name:** Gary Lyle Morrison (05/08/1999) **Education:** DEng in Industrial Engineering, Pennsylvania State University (1988); MS in Industrial Engineering, Pennsylvania State University (1986); BS in Industrial Engineering, Pennsylvania State University (1982); BS in Mathematics, State University of New York at Fredonia (1981) **Certifications:** ASQ Manager of Quality/Organizational Excellence (2016); Certified Lay Servant, Front Royal United Methodist Church, Virginia (2008-2014); ASQ Certified Quality Engineer (1989); Six Sigma Master Black Belt **Career:** Authorized Partner, Everything Disc, John Wiley & Sons, Inc. (2017-Present); Authorized Partner, Five Behaviors of a Cohesive Team, John Wiley & Sons, Inc. (2017-Present); Founder, Operations Leader, SOS Consulting, LLC. (2004-Present); Methodology Director, RR Donnelley & Sons Company Inc., Downer's Grove, IL (2002-2004); President, Susan O. Schall Process Improvement Consulting, Front Royal, VA (1999-2002); Technical Superintendent, Control System Engineering, DuPont Engineering Polymers, Parkersburg, WV (1997-1998); Consulting Engineer, DuPont Quality Management & Technology Center, Wilmington, DE (1990-1997); Quality Engineer, Eastman Kodak, Rochester, NY (1982-1984, 1988-1989) **Career Related:** Consultant, ABET Foundation, Inc. (2014-Present); Industrial and Professional Advisory Council, Harold and Inge Marcus Department of Industrial and Systems Engineering, Pennsylvania State University (1993-2014); Adjunct Training Director, ABET Foundation, Inc. (2008-2011); Board of Directors, ABET Foundation, Inc. (2005-2008); Engineering Accreditation Commission Commissioner, ABET (1997-2003); President, Engineering Alumni Society, Pennsylvania State University (1996-1998); Fellow, ABET Foundation, Inc. **Civic:** Project Lead the Way, Warren County Public Schools, Front Royal, VA (2010-2020); Lay Leader, Front Royal United Methodist Church (2010-2012); Board of Examiners, Malcolm Baldrige National Quality Award (2006, 2008) **Creative Works:** Contributor, "Is Your Organization Healthy Enough for Six Sigma?" ASQ Six Sigma Forum Magazine (2015); Contributor, "Variability Reduction: A Statistical Engineering Approach to Engage Operations Teams in Process Improvement," Quality Engineering (2012); Contributor, Articles, Professional Journals and Conferences **Awards:** Fellow Award, Institute of Industrial and Systems Engineers (2020); Medallion Award, Institute of Industrial and Systems Engineers (2018); Outstanding Engineering Alumna Award, College of Engineering, Pennsylvania State University (2009); Distinguished Service Award, Engineering Alumni Society, Pennsylvania State University (1999); Engineering Excellence Silver Award, DuPont Engineering (1992); Engineering Excellence Bronze Award, DuPont Engineering (1990) **Memberships:** Chair, Freund-Marquardt Medal Committee, American Society for Quality (2014-Present); Treasurer and Internet Liaison, Northern Shenandoah Valley Section, American Society for Quality (2014-Present); Awards Board Member, American Society for Quality (2008-2013); Chair, Northern Shenandoah Valley Section, American Society for Quality (2001-2003); American Society of Engineering Education; Senior Member, American Society of Quality; Senior Member, Institute of Industrial and Systems Engineers **Marquis Who's Who Honors:** Albert Nelson Marquis Lifetime Achievement Award; Marquis Who's Who Top Professional; Marquis Who's Who Humanitarian Award **To what do you attribute your success:** Dr. Schall attributes her success to persistence. **Why did you become involved in your profession or industry:** Dr. Schall became involved in her profession because she always enjoyed studying mathematics and science. With encouragement from her father, a vocal advocate for women in STEM, she chose to study engineering. Her grandfather, a carpenter, helped her to develop a love of putting things together. As a high school student, she wanted to be a patent lawyer, but after visiting a string of universities and learning about their pre-law programs, she decided not to pursue the field. Once she began her engineering program, she never considered law again. Now, she pays it forward by mentoring young women. **Avocations:** Travel; Baking; Reading **Political Affiliations:** Democrat **Religion:** United Methodist **Thoughts on Life:** Dr. Schall is an integrator. She takes different tools and concepts and unites them to help with the issue at hand. She works with the clients, and has compassion and empathy to set her clients up for success. She enjoys mentoring to help others have the tools and mindset to always make a difference.

David T. Schiff

Title: Investment Banker **Industry:** Financial Services **Company Name:** Kuhn, Loeb & Co. **Date of Birth:** 09/03/1936 **Place of Birth:** New York **State/Country of Origin:** NY/USA **Parents:** John Mortimer Schiff; Edith Brevoort (Baker) Schiff **Marital Status:** Married **Spouse Name:** Martha Elisabeth Lawler (05/11/1963) **Children:** Andrew Newman; David Baker; Ashley Reynolds **Education:** BS in Engineering, Yale University (1958); Graduate, Brooks School (1954) **Career:** Managing Partner, Kuhn, Loeb & Co. (1993-Present); Managing Partner, KLS Enterprises (1984-1993); Managing Director, Lehman Brothers Kuhn Loeb Inc. (1977-1983); Vice Chairman, Kuhn Loeb & Co. Inc. (1977); General Partner, Kuhn, Loeb & Co. (1967-1977); Associate, Kuhn, Loeb & Co. (1963-1966); Analyst, Madison Fund Inc. (1962); Trainee, Chemical Bank New York Trust Company (Now JP Morgan Chase & Co.) (1959-1962) **Career Related:** Advisory Board, Yale Center Environmental Law & Policy (2006-Present); Advisory Board, Venture Capital Fund of America (1999-Present); Board of Advisors, VCFA Group (1996-Present); Partner, Rabbit Hollow Partners (1981-Present); Lifetime Fellow, The Morgan Library & Museum (1973-Present); Leadership Council, Yale School of Forestry & Environmental Studies (2000-2008); Director, Vice Chairman, Crown Life, Canada (1981-1995); Board of Directors, Crown Life, Canada (1971-1992); Director, Distribix Inc., St. Louis, MO (1985-1990); Lower Manhattan Advisory Board, Chemical Bank New York Trust Company (Now JP Morgan Chase & Co.) (1977-1985); Director, Distribix Inc., St. Louis, MO (1977-1983); Board of Directors, Kuhn, Loeb & Co. **Civic:** Chairman Emeritus, Wildlife Conservation Society (2013-Present); Trustee Emeritus, Citizens Budget Commission (2009-Present); Trustee Emeritus, Metropolitan Museum of Art (2008-Present); Board of Governors, Federal Hall Memorial Association (1970-Present); Provident Loan Society of New York (1968-Present); Director and Vice Chairman, Schiff Foundation (1964-Present); Lifetime Trustee, Wildlife Conservation Society (1965-2013); Trustee, Citizens Budget Commission (1973-2009); Trustee, Metropolitan Museum of Art (1971-2008); Chairman, Wildlife Conservation Society (1996-2007); Board of Directors, American Hospital of Paris Foundation (1987-2006); Advisory Board of Directors, Outward Bound (1983-1999); Board of Governors, Yale University Art Gallery (1973-1997); Trustee, Greater New York Council, Boy Scouts of America (1965-1991); Treasurer, Brooks School (1987-1990); Trustee, Brooks School (1972-1990); Trustee, Beekman Downtown Hospital (Now Lower Manhattan Hospital), New York-Presbyterian Hospital (1966-1982); Chairman, Beekman Downtown Hospital (Now Lower Manhattan Hospital), New York-Presbyterian Hospital (1975-1979) **Military Service:** U.S. Army (1959) **Memberships:** Lifetime Member, Executive Committee, Pilgrims of the United States (1992-Present); Governor, Federal Hall Memorial Associates (1970-Present); Century Association; Yale Club, New York, NY; Mill Reef Club, Antigua; Maroon Creek Club, Aspen, CO; Brook Club **Marquis Who's Who Honors:** Albert Nelson Marquis Lifetime Achievement Award; Marquis Who's Who Top Professional; Marquis Who's Who Humanitarian Award **To what do you attribute your success:** Mr. Schiff attributes his success to his non-confronting and quiet approach. **Why did you become involved in your profession or industry:** Mr. Schiff entered his profession because his family was always in investment banking. The firm included his father, grandfather and great-grandfather. **Avocations:** Tennis; Biking **Political Affiliations:** Republican **Religion:** Episcopalian

Marlene Sandler Schiff

Title: Entrepreneur **Industry:** Financial Services **Company Name:** MSS Associates, Inc. **Place of Birth:** Great Barrington **State/Country of Origin:** MA/USA **Parents:** Jacob Sandler; Lena Yetta (Klein) Sandler **Marital Status:** Widowed **Spouse Name:** Dr. Haskel Schiff (1967, Deceased) **Children:** Melissa Robin **Education:** Diploma, OPM, Harvard University, Cambridge, MA (1985); BA, University of Massachusetts Amherst, MA (1960) **Career:** Founder, Chief Executive Officer, President, MSS Associates, Inc., New York, NY (1995-Present); Founder, Chairman, and Chief Executive Officer, Transceiver East Inc. (1971-1988); With, American Facsimile Systems (AFS) (1971-1988) **Career Related:** Elected Chairperson, Sol C. Snider Entrepreneurial Center Advisory Board, The Wharton School, The University of Pennsylvania (1991-1994); Invited to Join, Sol C. Snider Entrepreneurial Center Advisory Board, The Wharton School, The University of Pennsylvania (1988); Mentor, Advisor and Consultant to Various Individuals and Corporations **Civic:** Vice President, Board of Directors, Fight For Sight (2003-2006); Member, Advisory Committee as Woman Entrepreneur, White House Conference on Small Business (1995); Member, Advisory Board, White House Research Project on Small Business and Entrepreneurship in the 21st Century; Member, Advisory Board, Regulation and Taxation Group, White House Research Project on Small Business and Entrepreneurship in the 21st Century, Center for Entrepreneurial Leadership, Inc., Ewing M. Kauffman Foundation; Eye Advisory Committee, NewYork-Presbyterian Weill Cornell Medical Center; Advisory Board, Nutrition and Fitness Project, Harvard T.H. Chan School of Public Health, Cambridge, MA; Theater Gala Event Chair, The American Federation of Arts **Creative Works:** Provisional Patent for Smartphone Application to Provide Learning Feedback System from Acoustical Signature of a Ball Being Struck by a Golf Club, Tennis Racquet, Baseball Bat, or Cricket Bat (2015); Publisher, "Best of American Lifestyle Catalog," Published in Japanese for Japanese Markets, and in English for Singapore Markets, Providing Editorial and Cutting-Edge Fashion Advice (1995-1997); Music Publisher, Molly-O Music Corp. (1976); Producer, MOM Records (1976) **Memberships:** Board Member and Foundation Board Member, Committee of 200 (Now C200); Harvard Club of New York City **Marquis Who's Who Honors:** Albert Nelson Marquis Lifetime Achievement Award (2019) **To what do you attribute your success:** Mrs. Schiff attributes some of her success to her grammar school education, which took place in a one-room schoolhouse. **Avocations:** Bridge; Sailing; Skiing; Travel; Opera and jazz; Theater **Thoughts on Life:** As the founder, chief executive officer and president of MSS Associates, Mrs. Schiff is a deal-maker, an identifier, a finder, an adviser, a creator and a connector. She has raised venture capital, arranged mezzanine financing and participated in an advisory capacity to many companies and individuals. She had also developed a strategy to roll-up government health insurance companies, which resulted in an acquisition by a private equity fund. She has the innate ability to recognize opportunities, advise and bring fresh perspective to mentor those with whom she brainstorms and consults. Mrs. Schiff is also the founder, chairman, and chief executive officer of Transceiver East Inc., a facsimile communication network providing services between governmental agencies in the U.S. and Canada to the transportation industry. She was with the American Facsimile Systems (AFS), a money transfer business servicing the trucking industry, competing successfully against Western Union. AFS eventually became the company under which the Transceiver network and other businesses were sold to a public company in 1988.

Katherine R. Schlaerth

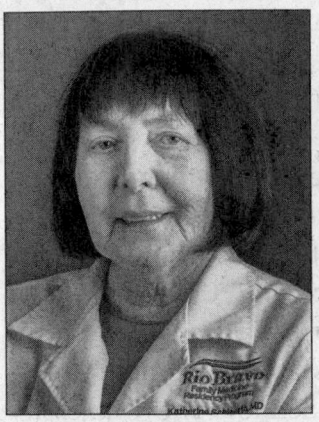

Title: Physician **Industry:** Medicine & Health Care **Company Name:** Family Health Center Pomona California **Date of Birth:** 12/30/1942 **Place of Birth:** Norristown **State/Country of Origin:** PA/USA **Parents:** Alan Frances Dowling, DDS; Mary Dowling **Marital Status:** Married **Spouse Name:** John Schlaerth, MD **Children:** John Jr.; Alan; William; Elizabeth; Michael; Mary; James **Education:** MD, State University of New York at Buffalo School of Medicine (Now Jacobs School of Medicine and Biomedical Sciences), Buffalo, NY (1968); BA in Natural Science, Manhattanville College, Purchase. NY (1964) **Certifications:** Certification, American Board of Family Medicine (1979, 1985, 1991, 1997, 2003, 2012, 2021); Certificate of Added Qualification in Geriatrics (1992, 2001, 2010); Board-Certified in Pediatric Infectious Diseases (2001, 2008-2021); Certification, Advanced Cardiovascular Life Support (ACLS) (1994-2021); Certification, American Board of Pediatrics (1975, 1986); Licensure, California **Career:** Coordinator, Pediatrics Curriculum, Family Medicine Residency Program (FMRP), Pomona Valley Hospital Medical Center, Pomona, CA (2013-Present); Preceptor, PVHC Pomona (Family Health Center), Pomona Valley Hospital Medical Center, Pomona, CA (2011-Present); Preceptor, Family Health Center, Lecturer, School of Allied Health Professionals, Loma Linda University, Loma Linda, CA (2011-Present); Physician, Rio Bravo Medicine Residency Program (2011-Present); Physician, Teacher, PVHMC, Family Medicine Residency Program (FMRP) at Pomona Valley Hospital Medical Center, Pomona, CA (2010-Present); Attending Physician, Pediatrics and Family Medicine, California Hospital Medical Center (1999-2001); Preceptor, Family Practice Residency Program, USC Family Medicine Center at California Hospital, Los Angeles, CA (1986-1995, 1999-2001); Preceptor, USC Multi-Site Family Practice Residency Program, Acute Care Center, USC University Hospital, Avalon Hospital, St. Luke's Medical Center (1997-2000); In-Patient Attending Physician, Family Medicine, USC University Hospital (Now Keck Medicine of USC), Los Angeles, CA (1997-1999); Preceptor, Family Medicine Residency Program, Natividad, Salinas, CA (1996-1997); Faculty Adviser, African-Americans in Medicine, University of Southern California (USC), Los Angeles, CA (1993-1995); Coordinator, Pediatrics Curriculum, CHMC Family Medicine Residency Program, Los Angeles, CA (1984-1995); Preceptor, Family Medicine Residency Program, Whittier - PIH Health (1978-1980); Academic Adviser, Department of Family Medicine, University of Southern California (USC), Los Angeles, CA (1977-2010); ward Attending Physician, Pediatrics Residency Program, LAC+USC Medical Center, Los Angeles, CA (1976-1995); Fellowship, Infectious Disease, Los Angeles County-USC Medical Center, Los Angeles, CA (1970-1973); Residency, Pediatrics, Children's Hospital of Los Angeles, Los Angeles, CA (1969-1970); Internship, Pediatrics, Children's Hospital of Los Angeles, Los Angeles, CA (1968-1969); CURE Faculty, Rio Bravo Family Medicine Residency Program, Bakersfield, CA **Career Related:** Adjunct Associate Professor, Davis School of Gerontology, University of Southern California (USC), Los Angeles, CA (2015); Associate Professor, Family Medicine, School of Medicine, Loma Linda University, Loma Linda, CA (2002-2011); Adjunct Professor, Undergraduate Course on Medical Aspects of Geriatrics, Andrus Gerontology Center (2011); Associate Clinical Professor Emeritus, Pediatrics and Family Medicine, University of Southern California School of Medicine (Keck School of Medicine of USC), Los Angeles, CA; Instructor, School of Allied Health Professionals, Loma Linda University, Loma Linda, CA; Researcher in Field **Creative Works:** Author, Book, "Raising a Large Family" (1991); Speaker, Presenter, Numerous Scientific Meetings and Presentations (1982-2014); Guest, "The Oprah Winfrey Show"; Contributor, Articles, Numerous Magazines; Author, Editorials, Newspapers; Author, Book, "The Physiology of Aging" **Awards:** Teacher of the Year, Family Medicine Residency Program (FMRP), Pomona Valley Hospital Medical Cente (2012, 2013); Teacher of the Year Loma Linda Family Practice Residency Program (2004, 2005); Teacher of the Year, USC/CHMC Family Practice Residency Program (2001) **Memberships:** Executive Committee for Physician Education, American Geriatrics Society (1999-2001); American Academy of Pediatrics; American Academy of Family Medicine; American Geriatrics Society; Pediatrics Infectious Disease Society **To what do you attribute your success:** Dr. Schlaerth doesn't need much sleep; she works very hard. She attributes her work ethic to her parents. **Why did you become involved in your profession or industry:** Dr. Schlaerth became involved in her profession because she had a brother with cerebral palsy, who she spent a lot of time caring for. She decided early on that she wanted to pursue pediatrics as a career. She grandfathered into family medicine, which was possible at the time with enough of an educational background; she had completed a fellowship in infectious diseases, which allowed her to get board certifications in pediatric infectious disease. Later, she was offered a position in geriatrics at a clinic in the San Francisco Bay Area. Dr. Schlaerth learned geriatrics, took her board exams, and eventually found success in the field. **Avocations:** Seeing grandchildren; Jogging

Carol Schneider, PhD

Title: 1) Attendant and Clinical Professor Emerita 2) Psychologist **Industry:** Social Work **Company Name:** 1) University of Colorado 2) Colorado Center for Biobehavioral Health **Date of Birth:** 05/05/1938 **Place of Birth:** Appleton **State/Country of Origin:** WI/USA **Parents:** Richard Coppel Joyce; Lorraine (Hendrickson) Joyce **Marital Status:** Divorced **Spouse Name:** Robert Schneider (1963, Divorced 1970) **Children:** Kayt Whitebird Orange; Jay **Education:** Doctor of Philosophy, University of Colorado (1965); Bachelor of Science, University of Wisconsin (1960) **Certifications:** Psychology License, State of Colorado **Career:** Attendant and Clinical Professor Emerita, Department of Psychology & University of Colorado Medical School, Department of Psychiatry, Division of Clinical Psychiatry, University of Colorado (1990-Present); Director, Colorado Center for Bio-behavioral Health, Boulder, CO (1976-Present); Psychologist, Private Practice (1974-Present); Attendant Professor, University of Colorado School of Medicine (1972-1990); Adjunct Professor, Department of Psychology, University of Colorado (1972-1990); Director of Biofeedback, Relaxation and Stress Management Clinic, Student Health Program, University Colorado (1970-1987) **Career Related:** Special Project Psychology and Treatment Committee, Medicare, Colorado State Health Department, Denver, CO (1975-1978); Prediction of Abuse Project, Michigan State University College of Human Development, East Lansing, CO (1969-1982); Consultant Psychologist, Battered Child Treatment Project, Adams County, CO (1968-1970) **Civic:** Board of Directors, Former Vice President, Brain Injury Hope Foundation (1986-Present); Chairman, Donated Computers Project (1986-Present); Board of Directors, Boulder International Chamber Players (1984-Present); Committee Chairman, Legislative Public Policy Committee, Several Projects, Denver, CO (1986-1990) **Creative Works:** Co-author, "The Challenge of Chronic Muscle Pain" (1989); Co-author, "Foundations of Biofeedback Practice" (1985); Co-author, "Bolder Bodies: A Physical and Emotional Wellness Guidebook" (1977); Contributor, Articles to Professional Journals **Awards:** Grantee, Creative Research Council, University of Colorado School of Medicine (1967); James T. Lewis Prize, University of Wisconsin (1957) **Memberships:** President, International Society for the Study of Subtle Energy and Energy Medicine (1994); Board of Directors, International Society for the Study of Subtle Energy and Energy Medicine (1990); President, Association for Applied Psychophysiology and Biofeedback (1986); The Phi Beta Kappa; Former Member, American Psychological Association **Marquis Who's Who Honors:** Albert Nelson Marquis Lifetime Achievement Award; Marquis Who's Who Top Professional **Why did you become involved in your profession or industry:** Dr. Schneider initially became involved in her profession at a young age after winning a scientific talent search contest by Westinghouse. She subsequently worked at an atomic energy plant in Pittsburgh, which was the first nuclear reactor in the world. She helped program the plant reactor, and worked in that position for two summers. Dr. Schneider later transitioned toward psychology after attending the University of Wisconsin and studying under Dr. Harry Harlow, who worked extensively with monkeys. She became interested in the bonding of primates, which led to her extensive research and career in the field. **Avocations:** Classical piano; Hiking **Political Affiliations:** Democrat

Frederick R. Schneider

Title: Professor of Law Emeritus **Industry:** Education/Educational Services **Company Name:** Northern Kentucky University **Date of Birth:** 07/11/1939 **Place of Birth:** Milwaukee **State/Country of Origin:** WI/USA **Parents:** Clifford R. Schneider; Eunice R. (Druse) Schneider **Marital Status:** Widowed **Spouse Name:** Karen M. Anderson (12/21/1963, Deceased 2017) **Children:** Kari; Richard; Carl **Education:** JD, The University of Chicago (1964); BA, Luther College (1961) **Career:** Professor Emeritus of Law, North Kentucky University Salmon P. Chase College of Law, Highland Heights, KY (2009-2013); Assistant Dean, North Kentucky University Salmon P. Chase College of Law, Highland Heights, KY (1974-1976); Professor, North Kentucky University Salmon P. Chase College of Law, Highland Heights, KY (1973-2008); Associate Professor, North Kentucky University Salmon P. Chase College of Law, Highland Heights, KY (1972-1973); Assistant Professor of Law, North Kentucky University Salmon P. Chase College of Law, Highland Heights, KY (1969-1972); Associate, Steele, Smyth, Klos & Flynn, La Crosse, WI (1964-1969) **Career Related:** Vice Chair, Task Force of Faculties, North Kentucky University Salmon P. Chase College of Law, Highland Heights, KY (1998-2000); Vice President, Faculty Senate, North Kentucky University Salmon P. Chase College of Law, Highland Heights, KY (1998-2000); Fas Hearing Committee, North Kentucky University Salmon P. Chase College of Law, Highland Heights, KY (1988-2000); Dean, Search School Committee, North Kentucky University Salmon P. Chase College of Law, Highland Heights, KY (1998-1999); Chair, Professional Concerns Committee, North Kentucky University Salmon P. Chase College of Law, Highland Heights, KY (1993-1994, 1996-1998); President's Special Task Force, Faculty of Reassigned Time, North Kentucky University Salmon P. Chase College of Law, Highland Heights, KY (1997); Chair, Faculty Handbook Religion Committee, North Kentucky University Salmon P. Chase College of Law, Highland Heights, KY (1986-1989); Parliamentarian, Faculty, North Kentucky University Salmon P. Chase College of Law, Highland Heights, KY (1983-1989); Ad Hock Committee, North Kentucky University Salmon P. Chase College of Law, Highland Heights, KY (1984-1985) **Civic:** Consultant, Ohio District, American Lutheran Church, Columbus, Ohio (1997-1987); Inspection Team, Various Universities, Southern Association of Colleges and Universities **Creative Works:** Contributor, Articles, Professional Journals **Awards:** Faculty Leadership Award, Northern Kentucky University (2000); Foundation Merit Professorship Award, North Kentucky University Salmon P. Chase College of Law (1996); Five-time Recipient, Lukowski Award for Teaching **Memberships:** State Bar of Wisconsin (1964-Present); Reporter, Arbitration Rules Committee, United State District Court for the Southern District of Ohio (1984-1987); President, Trinity Lutheran Church, Ohio (1983-1985); Troop Committee, Boy Scout Troop 858, Boy Scouts of America, Cincinnati, Ohio (1978-1981); Chairman, Boy Scout Troop 858, Boy Scouts of America, Cincinnati, Ohio (1981-1989); Consultant, Organization of Vietnamese Refugees, Hamilton County, Ohio (1976-1977); Professional Ethics Committee, Cincinnati Bar Association (1975-2008); President, Trinity Lutheran Church, Ohio (1974-1976); Leader, Stephen Ministry; Church Council, Trinity Lutheran Church **Bar Admissions:** United States Tax Court (1967); United States District Court for the Western District of Wisconsin (1964); Wisconsin (1964) **Marquis Who's Who Honors:** Albert Nelson Marquis Lifetime Achievement Award; Marquis Who's Who Top Professional; Distinguished Humanitarian **Why did you become involved in your profession or industry:** Mr. Schneider became involved in education because it interested him. It was an opportunity to serve the universities and students he came across, which was hard to resist. Mr. Schneider's father was a doctor, and his mother taught and worked for a church group, so the desire to serve others was a value instilled in him from childhood. **Avocations:** Amateur radio; Photography **Religion:** Lutheran

Valerie Lois Schneider, PhD

Title: Professor of Speech Communication (Retired) **Industry:** Education/Educational Services **Company Name:** East Tennessee State University **Date of Birth:** 02/12/1941 **Place of Birth:** Chicago **State/Country of Origin:** IL/USA **Parents:** Ralph Joseph Schneider; Gertrude Blanche (Gaffron) Schneider **Marital Status:** Single **Education:** PhD in Speech Communication, Minor in Sociology, University of Florida (1969); MA in Speech Communication, University of Wisconsin (1966); BA in English and History, Minor in Secondary Education, Carroll College (1963) **Certifications:** Certificate of Advanced Study, Developmental Education, Appalachian State University (1981) **Career:** Professor of Speech, East Tennessee State University, Johnson City, TN (1976-1997); Associate Professor of Speech, East Tennessee State University, Johnson City, TN (1971-1976); Assistant Professor of Speech, Edinboro State College (1970-1971); Assistant Professor of Speech, University of Florida, Gainesville, FL (1969-1970); Instructor, Speech, University of Florida, Gainesville, FL (1966-1968); Teacher, English and History, Director, Forensics and Drama, Montello High School (1963-1964) **Career Related:** Member, Investor Panel, USA Today (1991-1992); Instructor, Newspaper Course, Elizabethton Star, Erwin Record, Mountain City Tomahawk, Jonesboro Herald and Tribune (1980); Instructor, Newspaper Course, Johnson City Press Chronicle (1979); Developer, One Week Intensive Weekend Course on Business and Professional Speech; Teacher, Kingsport Extension Center **Civic:** Adult Bible Teacher, Zion Covenant Church, Sheboygan, WI (2009-Present); Self Funded Mission Trip a Year (1997-Present); Adult Bible Teacher, First Presbyterian Church, Johnson City, TN (1988-2008); Chairman, American Association of University Women Mass Media Study Group Committee, Johnson City, TN (1973-1974) **Creative Works:** Editor, East Tennessee State University Evening and Off-Campus Newsletter (1984-1991); Book Reviewer, Pulpit Digest (1986-1990); Columnist, Video Visions, Kingsport Times-News (1984-1986); Associate Editor, Homiletic (1974-1976); Contributor, Articles, Professional Journals **Awards:** Honorable Mention, Essay on Abraham Lincoln, C-SPAN, "American President's Life Portraits" National Contest (2000); Finalist, Writer's Digest Contest (2000); Honorary Life Member, Tennessee Presbyterian Women (2000); Finalist, Money Magazine Contest (1994); Award, Kingsport Times News (1984-1985); Award, Tri-Cities Metropolitan Advertising Federation (1983-1984); Recognition, Best Debate Judge, University of Richmond Tournament (1982); Named, Danforth Associate (1977); Best Article Award, Religious Speech Communication Association (1976); Creative Writing Award, Virginia Highlands Arts Festival (1973) **Memberships:** World Missions Alliance (1999-Present); President, Johnson City Book Club (2001-2003); President, Tennessee Basic Skills Council (1981-1982); Vice President, Tennessee Basic Skills Council (1980-1981); Executive Board, Tennessee Basic Skills Council (1979-1980); First Woman President, Tennessee Speech Communication Association (1977-1978); Vice President, Business and Professional Women's Club (1976-1977); President, American Association of University Women (1975-1976); Former Member, Tennessee Basic Skills Council (1975-1976); Publications Board, Tennessee Speech Communication Association (1974-1978); Executive Board, Tennessee Speech Communication Association (1974-1977); Tennessee Representative to States Advisory Council, Speech Communication Association (1974-1975); Vice President, Chapter, American Association of University Women (1974-1975); Chapter Executive Board, Business and Professional Women's Club (1972-1973); Former Member, American Association of University Women; Former Member, Religious Speech Communication Association; Former Member, Tennessee Speech Communication Association; Former Member, Southern Speech Communication Association; Former Member, Speech Communication Association; Former Member, Mensa; Former Member, Johnson City Book Club; Pi Gamma Mu; Phi Delta Kappa; Tau Kappa Alpha; Delta Sigma Rho **Marquis Who's Who Honors:** Albert Nelson Marquis Lifetime Achievement Award; Marquis Who's Who Top Professional **To what do you attribute your success:** Ms. Schneider attributes her success to hard work, good planning, and an analytical mind. **Why did you become involved in your profession or industry:** Ms. Schneider became involved in her profession because much of her activity was always related primarily to teaching or learning. She chose communications as her teaching field because it conveys concepts and skills crucial to success in most professions and relational situations. **Avocations:** Traveling; Writing; Reading **Political Affiliations:** Republican **Religion:** Protestant **Thoughts on Life:** Ms. Schneider's skills in money management and investing enabled her to retire from academia at age 56. Then she continued her educational services work with adult bible teaching, programming, and writing projects in the local church. She also did at least one self-funded international mission trip a year; doing adult bible teaching and leadership training. She's also funded 53,000 Chinese bibles and other teaching media in her mission trips to different countries.

Jacob "Jack" Schneps, PhD

Title: Emeritus Professor of Physics, Department Chairman **Industry:** Sciences **Date of Birth:** 08/18/1929 **Place of Birth:** New York **State/Country of Origin:** NY/USA **Year of Passing:** 2019 **Parents:** Elias Schneps; Rose (Rephen) Schneps **Marital Status:** Married **Spouse Name:** Lucia De Marchi **Children:** Loredana; Melissa; Leila **Education:** Postdoctoral Fellow, National Science Foundation, University of Padua, Italy (1958-1959); PhD, University of Wisconsin-Madison, Madison, WI (1956); MS, University of Wisconsin-Madison, Madison, WI (1953); BA, New York University, New York, NY (1951) **Career:** Vannevar Bush Professor Emeritus, Tufts University, Massachusetts (2011-Present); Vannevar Bush Chair, Tufts University, Massachusetts (1995-2011); Chairman, Department Physics, Tufts University, Massachusetts (1980-1989); Professor, Tufts University, Massachusetts (1963-2011); Associate Professor, Tufts University, Massachusetts (1960-1963); Assistant Professor Physics, Tufts University, Massachusetts (1956-1960) **Career Related:** Visiting Scholar, Associate, Harvard University, Cambridge, MA (2005-2017); Chairman, International Neutrino Committee (2002-2014); Visiting Professor, Paris Diderot University, Paris, France (2011); Visiting Scientist, Paris Diderot University, Paris, France (2010); Visiting Professor, College de France, Paris, France (1997); Visiting Professor, The Technion, Haifa, Israel (1989-1990); Visiting Professor, École Polytechnique, Palaiseau, France (1982-1983); Visiting Research Fellow, University College London, London, England (1973-1974); Lecturer, International School of Elementary Particle Physics, Yugoslavia (1968); Visiting Scientist, European Organization for Nuclear Research, Geneva, Switzerland (1965-1966); Visiting Physicist, University of Padua, Padua, Italy (1958-1959) **Creative Works:** Editor, "Proceedings of Neutrino 88" (1989); Contributing Author, "Methods in Subnuclear Physics, Volume IV" (1970); Contributor, Numerous Articles, Professional Journals **Memberships:** Fellow, American Physical Society; American Association of University Professors; Phi Beta Kappa; Sigma Xi **Marquis Who's Who Honors:** Albert Nelson Marquis Lifetime Achievement Award **Why did you become involved in your profession or industry:** Dr. Schneps became involved in his profession because he was in the 10th grade when World War II had finally ended. He found himself highly fascinated by the science behind the atomic bomb. He then began to read about nuclear physics. At the end of his senior year of high school, his teacher allowed all students to write about topics of their choice for their term papers. Dr. Schneps chose to write his paper about nuclear physics and atomic energy. His teacher was highly impressed by his work and so he decided to pursue a career in physics. **Avocations:** Baseball (New York Yankees); Music; Violin; Mandolin; Writing **Thoughts on Life:** Dr. Schneps passed away on July 12, 2019.

Michael P. A. Schoch

Title: Chief Executive Officer **Industry:** Business Management/Business Services **Company Name:** MPA Enterprises **Place of Birth:** Quincy **State/Country of Origin:** IL/USA **Education:** MS in Industrial and Systems Engineering, The Ohio State University (1974); BS in Mechanical Engineering, General Motors Institute (1965) **Certifications:** B-727 Captain, Federal Aviation Administration (2010); Captain B-727, UPS, B-727 Airline Captain (1990-2007) **Career:** Chief Executive Officer, MPA Enterprises (1980-Present); Design Development Engineer, Program Test Engineer, Special Problems Engineer, General Motors Corporation, Engineering Department, Pontiac Motors Division (1961-1969) **Civic:** Church Choir **Military Service:** Pilot, Aircraft Commander, Program Manager, Maintenance Director, United States Air Force (1969-1990) **Awards:** Decorated, Distinguished Flying Cross **Memberships:** The Royal Order of Ponce De Leon; Veterans of Foreign Wars; Aircraft Owners and Pilots Association; Veterans Motor Car Club of America **To what do you attribute your success:** Mr. Schoch attributes his success to his hard work and determination. **Why did you become involved in your profession or industry:** Mr. Schoch became involved in his profession after originally starting in real estate and property management in Ohio. He then sold everything and started this business in Florida. **Avocations:** Golfing; Airplanes

Jonathan Schochor, JD

Title: Lawyer; Law Educator **Industry:** Law and Legal Services **Company Name:** Schochor, Federico & Staton, P.A. **Date of Birth:** 09/09/1946 **Place of Birth:** Suffern **State/Country of Origin:** NY/USA **Parents:** Abraham Schochor; Betty (Hechtor) Schochor **Marital Status:** Married **Spouse Name:** Joan Elaine Brown (05/31/1970) **Children:** Lauren Aimee; Daniel Ross **Education:** JD, American University School of Law (1971); BA, The Pennsylvania State University (1968) **Career:** Senior Managing Partner, Schochor, Federico & Staton, P.A., Baltimore, MD (1984-Present); Associate, Ellin & Baker, Baltimore, MD (1974-1984); Associate, McKenna, Wilkinson & Kittner, Washington, DC (1970-1974) **Career Related:** Guest Expert, Numerous Radio and TV Programs; Expert Witness to State Legislature; Lecturer in Law, Johns Hopkins Hospital, Johns Hopkins School of Medicine; American Association of Medical Dosimetrists **Civic:** Two Scholarship Endowments, The University of Pennsylvania **Creative Works:** Editor-in-chief, American University Law Review (1970-1971) **Awards:** Named to Best Lawyers in America (2016); Named Lawyer of the Year, Medical Malpractice Law - Plaintiffs in Baltimore, Best Lawyers (2016); Named Trial Lawyer of the Year, Maryland Association for Justice (2015); Cornerstone Award, SmartCEO Magazine (2015); Named to Influential Marylanders, Daily Record (2015); Ranked Top One Percent, National Association of Distinguished Counsel (2015); Named One of the Top 100 Litigation Lawyers in the State of Maryland, American Society of Legal Advocates (2013); Named to Maryland Super Lawyers; Named Lawyer of the Year, Baltimore, MD; Named One of the Top 100 Lawyers, American Trial Lawyers Association; Named to Baltimore and Washington, DC's Best Lawyers; Bar Register of Pre-Eminent Lawyers; AV Rating, Martindale-Hubbell; Named to Million Dollar Advocates Forum; Named to Multi-Million Dollar Advocates Forum; Outstanding Liberal Arts Alumni Award, The Pennsylvania State University **Memberships:** Membership Committee, American Board of Trial Advocates (1994-Present); Circuit Court for Baltimore City Task Force, Civil Document Management System, Baltimore City Bar Association (1994-1995); State Governor, Association of Trial Lawyers of America (1992-1995); State Delegate, Association of Trial Lawyers of America (1991); American Association for Justice; Leaders Forum, American Association for Justice; American Bar Association (ABA); American Judicature Society; American Board of Trial Advocates; Association of Trial Lawyers of America; President, Maryland Trial Lawyers Association (1990-1991); Medicolegal Committee, Baltimore City Bar Association (1989-1990); President-elect, Maryland Trial Lawyers Association (1989); Executive Committee, Maryland Trial Lawyers Association (1987-1992); Vice President, Maryland Trial Lawyers Association (1987-1988); Secretary, Maryland Trial Lawyers Association (1987-1988); Board of Governors, Maryland Trial Lawyers Association (1986-1987); Chairman, Legislative Committee, Maryland Trial Lawyers Association (1986-1987); Legislative Committee, Baltimore City Bar Association (1986-1987); Special Committee on Tort Reform, Baltimore City Bar Association (1986); Legislative Committee, Maryland Trial Lawyers Association (1985-1988); Special Committee on Health Claims Arbitration, Maryland State Bar Association (1983); Maryland State Bar Association; Maryland Association for Justice; Baltimore City Bar Association; DC Bar Association; Melvin M. Belli Society; The College of Master, Advocates and Barristers; Phi Alpha Delta Law Fraternity; Development Council for the College of Liberal Art and Professional Studies, The University of Pennsylvania **Bar Admissions:** Supreme Court of the United States (1986); United States District Court for the District of Maryland (1974); Maryland State Bar (1974); District of Columbia Bar (1971); United States District Court for the District of Columbia (1971); United States Court of Appeals for the District of Columbia Circuit (1971); Baltimore City Bar Association; American Bar Association **Marquis Who's Who Honors:** Albert Nelson Marquis Lifetime Achievement Award; Marquis Who's Who Top Professional; Marquis Who's Who Humanitarian Award **Avocations:** Travel; Reading; Golf; Fishing

John J. Schornack

Title: Vice Chairman, Retired **Industry:** Business Management/Business Services **Company Name:** Ernst & Young **Date of Birth:** 11/22/1930 **Place of Birth:** Chicago **State/Country of Origin:** IL/USA **Parents:** John Joseph Schornack; Helen Patricia (Patrickus) Schornack **Marital Status:** Married **Spouse Name:** Barbara Anne Lelli (06/05/1965) **Children:** Mark Boyd; Anne Marguerite Schornack Trueman; Erin Keeley Schornack Dickes; Tracy Bevan Schorn **Education:** Graduate Coursework, Advanced Management Program, Harvard Business School (1969); MBA, Northwestern University (1956); BS, Loyola University (1951) **Career:** Managing Partner, Midwest Region, Vice Chairman (Retired), Ernst & Young LLP (1985-1991); Partner, Ernst & Young (1964-1991); With, Ernst & Young LLP (1955-1991); Managing Partner, Chicago Office, Ernst & Young LLP (1976-1985); Managing Partner, Ernst & Young LLP (1972-1974); Assistant Managing Partner, New York City Office, Ernst & Young LLP (1971-1972); Firm Director Personnel, Ernst & Young LLP (1966-1971) **Career Related:** Wintrust Financial Corp. (1996-2008); Chairman, Board of Directors, North Shore Bancorp, Inc. (1992-2008); Management Committee, Arthur Young & Co.; Vice-Chairman, Managing Partner, Midwest Region, Ernst & Young LLP (1989-1991); Board of Directors, Chairman, Ernst & Young Foundation (1981-1991) **Civic:** Catholic Charities of Chicago (2004-Present); Trustee, Kohl Children's Museum (1994-2005); Life Trustee, Vice Chairman, Chairman, Trustee Night Ministry (1985-2004); Graham Foundation (1992-1998); Trustee, Barat College (1983-1998); Catholic Theological Union (1992-1997); Board of Directors, Metropolitan Planning Council (1992-1995); President, Chicago Youth Centers (1979-1995); Loyola University Citizens Board (1977-1994); Trustee, Lyric Opera (1984-1992); Life Trustee, Volunteer United Way (1975-1992); Advisory Committee, Northwestern University Graduate School of Management (1967-1991); Council, University of Chicago Graduate School of Business (1982-1991); Board of Governors, Chicago Symphony (1979-1985); Visiting Advisory Committee, School of Accountancy, Depaul University (1980-1983) **Military Service:** U.S. Navy (1952-1956) **Awards:** Order of the Sacred Treasurer, Emperor of Japan (1999) **Memberships:** Chairman, Midwest-Japan Association (1983-1999); American Institute of Certified Public Accountants; American Accounting Association; Illinois Society of CPAs; Japan American Society; Chicago Club; Glen View Club; The Little Club **Marquis Who's Who Honors:** Albert Nelson Marquis Lifetime Achievement Award; Marquis Who's Who Top Professional **Why did you become involved in your profession or industry:** After studying philosophy in college, Mr. Schornack enlisted in the United States Navy. There, his responsibilities consisted of making sure his peers had everything they needed and keeping count of the supplies. This was how he became interested in accounting. In the years that followed his exit from the military, he pursued a career in accounting.

Mitch J. Schroder

Title: Owner **Industry:** Health, Wellness and Fitness **Company Name:** Better Bodies, Inc **Education:** MS in Physical Therapy, University of Iowa (1992); BPE, Computer Science, Iowa State University (1990); AS in Bio-technology, Ellsworth Community College (1987) **Certifications:** Certified, Health & Fitness Instructor, American College of Sports Medicine (1995); Certified, Physical Therapy, Indiana State, Iowa State (1992); CPR, American Red Cross; Certified, Strength & Conditioning Coach, NSCA; Elite & Master Level Personal Fitness Trainer, IDEA Health & Fitness Association **Career:** President, Owner, Personal Trainer, Physical Therapist, Better Bodies Incorporated (1994-Present); Medical Advisory Panel, Physical Therapist Representative, Biersdorff Incorporated, Cincinnati, OH (2003-2005); Lead Acute Rehabilitation Physical Therapist, Industrial Rehabilitation Associates, Waterloo, IA (1998-2000); Clinic Director, Industrial Rehab Associate, Indianapolis, IN (1998-1999); Lead Acute Rehabilitation Physical Therapist, Staff Physical Therapist, Clinical Instructor, Geriatric Physical Therapy Aide, Pediatric Physical Therapy Aide Inpatient, Outpatient Hydrotherapy Aide, Covenant Medical Center, Systems Unlimited, Iowa Methodist Medical Center, Waterloo, IA (1989-1994) **Civic:** Founding President, Saint Maria Goretti Parish, Westfield, IN (2000); Board Member, Rotary Club, Carmel, IN; Precinct Committeeman, Westfield, IN; Fitness Badge Director, Boy Scouts of America, Carmel, Westfield, IN **Memberships:** Rotary International **To what do you attribute your success:** Mr. Schroder attributes his success to his ability and willingness to care for every patient that walks through his door. He also credits his strong work ethic. **Why did you become involved in your profession or industry:** Mr. Schroder originally wanted to become a physician because he received a perfect score on the science portion of his ACT test. However, he changed his mind after his grandfather had a stroke. When he saw how hard the physical therapists worked with his grandfather to help him regain his independence, he became very interested in physical therapy. Once he became certified in the field, he wondered why he was only treating people that had already been hurt instead of taking preventative measures to avoid injury. He compared his professional role to that of an individual tasked with putting a shattered vase back together instead of simply caring for the vase so it would never break in the first place. He wanted to help others be the best version of themselves. He has achieved this goal by working with his patients to set goals and practice extensive assessments to get them to where they want to be. **Thoughts on Life:** Mr. Schroder has three patents and is planning to have more in the future.

Charles Ellis "Chuck" Schumer

Title: U.S. Senator from New York **Industry:** Government Administration/ Government Relations/Government Services **Date of Birth:** 11/23/1950 **Place of Birth:** Brooklyn **State/Country of Origin:** NY/USA **Parents:** Abraham Schumer; Selma (Rosen) Schumer **Marital Status:** Married **Spouse Name:** Iris Weinshall (09/21/1980) **Children:** Jessica Emily; Alison **Education:** Honorary LLD, Brooklyn Law School (2015); Honorary JD, Touro Law Center (2007); Honorary LDH, Pace University (2004); Honorary LLD, New York Law School (2002); Honorary LDH, Adelphi University (2000); Honorary LDH, Hunter College (1999); Honorary Doctorate, Hofstra University (1999); JD, Harvard University, with Honors (1974); BA, Harvard University, Magna Cum Laude (1971) **Career:** Senate Minority Leader (2017-Present); U.S. Senator, State of New York (1998-Present); Chairman, U.S. Senate Democratic Policy Committee (2011-2017); Chairman, U.S. Senate Rules and Administration Committee (2009-2015); Vice Chairman, U.S. Senate Democratic Conference (2007-2017); Chairman, Joint Economic Committee (2007-2009); Chairman, Democratic Senatorial Campaign Committee (2005-2009); Member, U.S. House of Representatives from New York's Ninth Congressional District, United States Congress, Washington, DC (1993-1999); Member, U.S. House of Representatives from New York's 10th Congressional District, United States Congress, Washington, DC (1983-1993); Member, U.S. House of Representatives from New York's 16th Congressional District, United States Congress, Washington, DC (1981-1983); Chairman, Committee on Oversight and Investigation, New York State Assembly (1979); Chairman, Subcommittee on City Management and Governance, New York State Assembly (1977); Member, New York State Assembly (1975-1980); Associate, Paul, Weiss, Rifkind, Wharton & Garrison LLP (1974); Staff Member to Senator Claiborne Pell, U.S. Senate (1973) **Civic:** Board of Directors, New York Philharmonic **Creative Works:** Co-author with Daniel Squadron, "Positively American: Winning Back the Middle-Class Majority One Family at a Time" (2007) **Awards:** Sound Guardian Award, Audubon New York and Construction Industry Council of Westchester & Hudson Valley, Inc. (2002); Public Policy Achievement Award, American Cancer Society, Inc. (2000); Criminal Justice Legislative Award, New York State Bar Association (1999); Leadership in Government Award, Columbia Business School, Columbia University (1999); Travers J. Bell Memorial Award of Distinction, New York District Economic Education Foundation, Securities Industry Foundation (1999); Herbert Tenzer Award for Public Service, Five Towns Jewish Council (1995) **Memberships:** Jewish War Veterans of the United States of America; B'nai Brith International; The Phi Beta Kappa Society **Bar Admissions:** State of New York (1975) **Political Affiliations:** Democrat **Religion:** Jewish

Scott C. Schurz

Title: Chairman of the Board **Industry:** Technology **Company Name:** Schurz Communications Inc. **Date of Birth:** 02/23/1936 **Place of Birth:** South Bend **State/Country of Origin:** IN/USA **Parents:** Franklin Dunn Schurz; Martha (Montgomery) Schurz **Marital Status:** Married **Spouse Name:** Kathryn Joan Foley (08/05/1967) **Children:** Scott Clark; Alexandra Carol; John Danforth **Education:** LHD (Honorary), Indiana University (2000); BA, Denison University (1957) **Career:** Chairman of the Board, Schurz Communications Inc. (1970-Present); Circulation Consultant, Imperial Valley Press, El Centro, CA (1966); Administrative Assistant, South Bend Tribune (1960-1966); Assistant Instructor, University Maryland (1957-1958); Director, Vice Chairman, Schurz Communications Inc.; Chairman, Hoosier Times, Inc. **Civic:** Board of Directors, United Way of Monroe County Inc. (1979-1981); Junior Achievement of Monroe County (1971-1973); President, Bloomington Boys' Club (1970-1971); Community Foundation, Area Arts Council **Military Service:** Served, U.S. Army (1958-1960) **Memberships:** Board of Directors, Inter-American Press Association (1995-Present); Board of Directors, Indiana University Foundation (1986-Present); Treasurer, International Newspaper Marketing Association (1997-2004); President, Hoosier State Press Association (1989, 1997); Board of Directors, Newspaper Association of America (1992-1995); Newspaper Advertising Bureau (1987-1992); President, Inland Daily Press Association (1989); International Newspaper Marketing Association (1986); Honorary President, Life, Inter-American Press Association; Board Member, International Press Institute; Advisory Board, World Press Freedom Committee; Board of Directors, Executive Committee, Vice President, World Association of Newspapers and News Publishers **Marquis Who's Who Honors:** Albert Nelson Marquis Lifetime Achievement Award; Marquis Who's Who Top Professional **To what do you attribute your success:** Mr. Schurz attributes his success to having a good education, the ability to listen, and not minding making mistakes as long as he realized it and stopped doing it. **Why did you become involved in your profession or industry:** Mr. Schurz became involved in his profession because of family ties. He was the last of four children but once he got in, he was very much involved. He graduated from Denison University and was recognized with an honorary degree. **Political Affiliations:** Republican **Religion:** Presbyterian

Walter Richard Schwartz, MD, FACOG

Title: Obstetrician/Gynecologist (Retired) **Industry:** Medicine & Health Care **Date of Birth:** 01/02/1931 **Place of Birth:** Lancaster **State/Country of Origin:** WI/USA **Marital Status:** Married **Spouse Name:** June (Ladelske) (08/11/1956, Deceased 12/13/2018) **Children:** Linda Hutchins; Richard Schwartz; John Schwartz (Deceased 07/08/2018) **Education:** Doctor of Medicine, University of Wisconsin Medical School (1955); Bachelor of Arts, University of Wisconsin (1952) **Certifications:** Diplomate, American Board of Obstetrics and Gynecology **Career:** Staff, Milwaukee Children's Hospital (1964-Present); Associate Attending Staff, Milwaukee County General Staff (1961-Present); Retired (1994); Senior Staff, Department of Obstetrics and Gynecology, Lutheran Hospital of Milwaukee (1992-1994); Associate Clinical Professor of Obstetrics and Gynecology, Medical College of Wisconsin (1976-1994);Courtesy Staff, Department of Obstetrics and Gynecology, Lutheran Hospital of Milwaukee (1990-1992); Staff, Elmbrook Memorial Hospital (1971-1994); Staff, Sinai Samaritan Hospital (1961-1994); Staff, West Allis Hospital, Wisconsin (1961-1994); Attending Staff, Department of Obstetrics and Gynecology, Lutheran Hospital of Milwaukee (1967-1990); Assistant Clinical Professor, Department of Gynecology and Obstetrics, Medical College of Wisconsin (1968-1976); Clinical Instructor in Obstetrics and Gynecology, Marquette County General Hospital (1961-1968); Associate Staff, Department of Obstetrics and Gynecology, Lutheran Hospital of Milwaukee (1964-1967); Courtesy Staff, Department of Obstetrics and Gynecology, Lutheran Hospital of Milwaukee (1961-1964); Resident in Obstetrics and Gynecology, Milwaukee County Hospital (1958-1961); Intern, St. Josephs Hospital, Marshfield, WI (1955-1956); Member, Chairman, Various Committees, Lutheran Hospital of Milwaukee; Member, Various Committees, Department of Obstetrics and Gynecology, West Allis Memorial Hospital **Career Related:** Medical Examining Board, Wisconsin (1991-1999); Professional Review Committee, West Allis Physicians Association (1985-1994); Maternal and Child Health Coalition (1983-1994); Visiting Staff, Froedtert Memorial Lutheran Hospital (1981-1994); James E. Fitzgerald Obstetrics and Gynecology Society (1987-1993); Consulting Staff, Saint Joseph's Community Hospital, West Bend, WI (1961-1990); Professional Review Committee, Samaritan Health Plan (1984); Professional Review Committee, Samaritan Health Plan (1982, 1983) **Civic:** Volunteer, Local Church **Military Service:** Captain, U.S. Army Aviation Medical Officer (1956-1958) **Creative Works:** Contributor, Articles to Professional Journals **Memberships:** Central Association of Obstetricians and Gynecologists (1967-Present); Fred J. Hofmeister Travel Club (1961-Present); American Association of Gynecological Laparoscopists (1979-1989); Continental Gynecologic Society (1967-2001); Wisconsin Society of Obstetrics and Gynecology (1963-1995); Milwaukee Gynecological Society (1962-1995); Medical Society of Milwaukee County (1961-1994); State Medical Society of Wisconsin (1961-1994); Wisconsin Medical Alumni Association (1956); Fellow, American College of Obstetricians and Gynecologists; Fellow, American College of Surgeons; American Medical Association; American College of Obstetrics and Gynecology **Marquis Who's Who Honors:** Albert Nelson Marquis Lifetime Achievement Award; Marquis Who's Who Top Professional **Why did you become involved in your profession or industry:** Dr. Schwartz became involved in his profession after attending medical school, where he drew inspiration from working with several obstetricians.

Martin Scorsese

Title: Film Director, Film Producer **Industry:** Media & Entertainment **Company Name:** World Cinema Foundation **Date of Birth:** 11/17/1942 **Place of Birth:** Flushing **State/Country of Origin:** NY/USA **Parents:** Charles Scorsese; Catherine (Cappa) Scorsese **Marital Status:** Married **Spouse Name:** Helen Morris (1999); Barbara De Fina (1985, Divorced 1991); Isabella Rossellini (1979, Divorced 1982); Julia Cameron (12/30/1975, Divorced 1977); Laraine Marie Brennan (05/15/1965, Divorced 1971) **Children:** Catherine Terese Glinora Sophia; Domenica Elizabeth; Francesca **Education:** Honorary Doctorate, Royal College Art; Honorary Doctorate, Yale University; Honorary Doctorate, Williams College; Honorary Doctorate, Bard College; Honorary Doctorate, Wesleyan University; Honorary Doctorate, Princeton University; Honorary Doctorate, New York University; MA in Film, New York University's School of the Arts (Now Tisch School of the Arts) (1966); BA in English, New York University (1964) **Career:** Founder, World Cinema Foundation (Now World Cinema Project) (2007-Present); Faculty Assistant, Instructor of Film, New York University, New York, NY (1963-1970) **Creative Works:** Director, Producer, "The Irishman" (2019); Director, Documentary, "Rolling Thunder Revue: A Bob Dylan Story by Martin Scorsese" (2019); Executive Producer, "Uncut Gems" (2019); Director, Co-screenwriter, "Silence" (2016); Director, "Vinyl" (2016); Director, "The Audition" (2015); Executive Producer, "The Third Side of the River" (2014); Director, Producer, Documentary, "The 50 Year Argument" (2014); Executive Producer, "The Wannabe" (2014); Executive Producer, "Glickman" (2013); Executive Producer, "The Family" (2013); Director, Producer, "The Wolf of Wall Street" (2013); Executive Producer, "Surviving Progress" (2011); Director, Executive Producer, Documentary, "George Harrison: Living in the Material World" (2011); Director, Executive Producer, "Boardwalk Empire" (2010-2014); Director, Producer, "Hugo" (2011); Director, Documentary, "A Letter to Elia" (2010); Director, Documentary, "Public Speaking" (2010); Director, Producer, "Shutter Island" (2010); Appearance, "30 Rock" (2009); Producer, "The Young Victoria" (2009); Appearance, "Entourage" (2008); Executive Producer, "Lymelife" (2008); Director, Documentary, "Shine a Light" (2008); Director, "The Departed" (2006); Director, Producer, Documentary, "No Direction Home: Bob Dylan" (2005); Director, Executive Producer, "The Aviator" (2004); Director, "The Gangs of New York" (2002); Appearance, "Curb Your Enthusiasm" (2002); Director, "Bringing Out the Dead" (1999); Director, Documentary, "My Voyage to Italy" (1999); Producer, "The Hi-Lo Country" (1998); Executive Producer, "Kicked in the Head" (1997); Director, "Kundun" (1997); Executive Producer, "Grace of My Heart" (1996); Producer, "Clockers" (1995); Director, Co-screenwriter, "Casino" (1995); Director, Documentary, "A Personal Journey with Martin Scorsese Through American Movies" (1995); Executive Producer, "Quiz Show" (1994); Executive Producer, "Naked in New York" (1994); Producer, "Mad Dog and Glory" (1993); Director, Co-screenwriter, "The Age of Innocence" (1993); Executive Producer, "Guilty by Suspicion" (1991); Director, "Cape Fear" (1991); Executive Producer, "Akira Kurosawa's Dreams" (1990); Producer, "The Grifters" (1990); Director, Co-Screenwriter, "Goodfellas" (1990); Director, "New York Stories" (1989); Director, "The Last Temptation of Christ" (1988); Executive Producer, "Round Midnight" (1986); Director, "The Color of Money" (1986); Director, "After Hours" (1985); Director, Screenwriter, Producer, Numerous Films **Awards:** Spotlight Award for Career Collaboration with Leonardo DiCaprio, National Board of Review (2013); Golden Globe Award for Best Director, "Hugo" (2012); Fellow, BAFTA (2012); Primetime Emmy Award for Outstanding Documentary or Nonfiction Special (2012); National Board of Review Award for Best Director, Best Film (2011); Boston Society Film Critics Award for Best Director (2011); Primetime Emmy Award for Outstanding Directing for a Drama Series (2011); Directors Guild of America Award for Outstanding Directing - Drama Series (2010); Cecil B. DeMille Award, Hollywood Foreign Press Association (2010); Columbia-DuPont Journalism Award (2007); Golden Globe Award for Best Director, Hollywood Foreign Press Association (2007); Named, One of the World's Most Influential People, TIME Magazine (2007); Academy Award for Best Director, "The Departed" (2007); Directors Guild of America Award for Outstanding Directing - Feature Film (2007); Honoree, Kennedy Center Honors, John F. Kennedy Center for the Performing Arts (2007); New York Film Critics Circle Award for Best Director (2006); National Board of Review Award for Best Director (2006); Grammy Award for Best Music Film, The Recording Academy (2006); Ellis Island Family Heritage Award (2004); Evelyn F. Burkey Award, Writers Guild of America East (2003); Lifetime Achievement Award, Directors Guild of America (2003); Golden Globe Award for Best Director, Hollywood Foreign Press Association (2002); Peabody Award; Decorated Commandeur, De La Legion D'Honneur France; Honoree, Star, Hollywood Walk of Fame **Memberships:** Fellow, American Academy of Arts & Sciences; Jefferson Humanities Lecturer, National Endowment for the Humanities; Honorary Member, American Academy of Arts and Letters **Marquis Who's Who Honors:** Albert Nelson Marquis Lifetime Achievement Award

Freida Scott

Title: Parent Educator Coordinator **Industry:** Education/Educational Services **Company Name:** RISE (Raising Innovations In Special Education) **Date of Birth:** 01/06/1939 **Children:** Three Children **Education:** ThD in Theology, United Bible College and Seminary (1984); MA in Teaching and Curriculum, Columbia University (1980); BA in Early Childhood Education, Jersey City University (1977) **Career:** Parent Educator Coordinator, RISE (Raising Innovations In Special Education) **Career Related:** Associate Pastor, Local Church **Awards:** Award, East Florence Board of Education; A+ Teachers Award, New Jersey Jets; Excellence in Teaching Award, Evangelical Bible Institute **Memberships:** Association for Supervision and Curriculum Development **Marquis Who's Who Honors:** Marquis Who's Who Top Professional **To what do you attribute your success:** Ms. Scott attributes her success to knowing what her purpose in life is and pursuing it wholeheartedly. **Why did you become involved in your profession or industry:** Dr. Scott lives by her philosophy in life. She will always do what is best for thy neighbor and for herself. She became involved in her profession because of her child's classification. She started working to assist other parents. Her objective was to get others to see that children are so much more than their labels. She wanted to reinforce the idea that a label has no power to control what one's child is capable of achieving. Inside of every child is a desire to be accepted like everyone else, and Dr. Scott has made it her mission to make that possible. In addition, the reason why Dr. Scott became involved in her profession as an educator is because she was always sharing stories no matter how good they were, but how they impacted and did for her. However she wanted to be a nurse because her mother was a nurse. So, when she decided not to do nursing she decided to be a teacher. **Thoughts on Life:** Dr. Scott's motto is, "No one can make you inferior without your consent."

Robert A. Sedler

Title: Distinguished Professor of Law **Industry:** Law and Legal Services **Company Name:** Wayne State University **Date of Birth:** 09/11/1935 **Place of Birth:** Pittsburgh **State/Country of Origin:** PA/USA **Parents:** Jerome Sedler; Esther (Rosenberg) Sedler **Marital Status:** Married **Spouse Name:** Rozanne Friedlander (01/24/1960) **Children:** Eric; Beth **Education:** JD, University of Pittsburgh (1959); BA, University of Pittsburgh (1956) **Career:** Distinguished Professor, Law, Wayne State University (2000-Present); Professor, Law, Wayne State University, Detroit, MI (1977-Present); President, Wayne State Academy Scholars (2007-2008); Gibbs Chair, Civil Rights and Civil Liberty, Wayne State University (2000-2005); Associate Professor to Professor, Law, University of Kentucky, Lexington, KY (1966-1977); Associate Professor, Law, Assistant Dean, Addis Ababa University, Ethiopia (1963-1966); Assistant Professor, Associate Professor, Law, St. Louis University (1961-1965) **Civic:** General Counsel, ACLU Kentucky (1971-1976) **Creative Works:** Author, "Constitutional Law in The United States, 4th Edition" (2019); Author, "Constitutional Law in the United States" (2017); Author, "Constitutional Law in The United States, 1st Edition" (1994); Author, "Across State Lines: Applying the Conflict of Law to Your Practice" (1989); Co-author, "The Sum and Substance of Conflict of Laws" (1987); Author, "Ethiopian Civil Procedure" (1968); Contributor, Articles, Professional Journals **Awards:** Champion of Justice Award, Michigan Association for Justice (2019); Champion of Justice Award, State Bar of Michigan (2014); John W. Reed Michigan Lawyer Legacy Award (2012); Named Gershenson Distinguished Faculty Fellow, Wayne State University (1985-1987); Phi Beta Kappa; Order of the Coif; Champion of Justice- Michigan Association for Justice; Honorary Professor, Ural State Law University, Yekateringburg, Russia; Bernard Gottfried Bill of Rights Day Award, Metropolitan Detroit Branch of the American Civil Liberties Union **Memberships:** American Bar Association; American Association of University Professors; Phi Beta Kappa; Order of the Coif **Bar Admissions:** Michigan (1979); Supreme Court of the United States (1969); Kentucky (1968); The District of Columbia (1959) **Marquis Who's Who Honors:** Albert Nelson Marquis Lifetime Achievement Award **Why did you become involved in your profession or industry:** Mr. Sedler became involved in his profession because when he was 14 years old he knew he wanted to be a lawyer. **Political Affiliations:** Democrat **Religion:** Jewish

Rena Segal

Title: Artist **Industry:** Fine Art **Date of Birth:** 05/27/1953 **Place of Birth:** New Brunswick **State/Country of Origin:** NJ/USA **Parents:** George Segal; Helen (Steinberg) Segal **Education:** MFA, Rutgers, the State University of New Jersey (1977); BFA, Montclair State College, Montclair, NJ (1975) **Career Related:** Fellow, New Jersey State Council on the Arts (1985) **Civic:** President, George and Helen Segal Foundation **Creative Works:** Guest Curator, "It Runs in the Family Barnet/Segal," Montclair State University, Montclair, NJ (2012); Subject, Numerous Reviews and Articles in Professional Publications, including News Tribune Review, Sunday Home News, Star Ledger, Village Voice, The New Yorker, The New York Times, Trenton Times, South Brunswick Post, and the Sentinel, Among Others (1980-2012); Artist, One-Person Exhibition, The Heldrich Hotel, New Brunswick, NJ (2009); Artist, One-Person Exhibition, Rabbet Art Gallery, New Brunswick, NJ (2008); Artist, One-Person Exhibition, CAS Gallery, Kean University, Union, NJ (2005); Artist, One-Person Exhibition, Rutgers University Art Library, New Brunswick, NJ (2004); Curator, Forging Memorial Art for Public Memory, Rutgers Art Library, New Brunswick, NJ (2003); Artist, One-Person Exhibition, Gratz Gallery, New Hope, PA (2001); Artist, Group Exhibition, Marsh Insurance Company, Morristown, NJ (2000); Artist, Group Exhibition, Visual Arts Center of New Jersey, Summit (1999); Curator, Woman in the Weisman Collection, the Frederick R. Weisman Art Museum, University of Minnesota, Twin Cities, Minneapolis, MN (1998); Curator, Father and Daughter George and Rena Segal, The Gallery at Bristol-Meyer Squibb, Princeton, NJ (1998); Artist, Group Exhibition, Sound Shore Gallery, Stamford, CT (1994-1996); Artist, Curator, Altered Images, Gallery at Bristol-Myers Squibb, Princeton, NJ (1995); Curator, American Art, Frederick R. Weisman Art Foundation, University of Minnesota, Twin Cities, Minneapolis, MN (1992); Curator, Feast Your Eyes, Hunterdon Art Museum, Clinton, NJ (1990); Artist, One-Person Exhibition, Mystic Knight Gallery, New Brunswick, NJ (1990); Artist, One-Person Exhibition, Rena Segal Paintings, New Jersey State Museum, Trenton, NJ (1989); Fellowship Exhibition, Morris Museum, Morristown, NJ (1987); Artist, Group Exhibition, Laforet Museum, Harajuku, Tokyo, Japan (1986); Artist, Exhibition, Cork Gallery Avery Fisher Hall, Lincoln Center, New York, NY (1985); Artist, One-Person Show, Johnson and Johnson, New Brunswick, NJ (1985); Artist, Group Exhibition, Sidney Janis Gallery, New York, NY (1984); Artist, One-Person Exhibition, Piscataway Municipal Building, New Jersey (1983); Artist, Group Exhibition, Dumont Landis Gallery, New Brunswick, NJ (1981); Artist, One-Person Exhibition, Ocean County College, Toms River, NJ (1978); Artist, Permanent Collection, Public Service Electric & Gas Company (PSE&G), Newark, NJ; Artist, Permanent Collection, Pepsico, Purchase, NY; Artist, Permanent Collection, Bristol-Meyers Squibb, Lawrenceville, NJ; Artist, Permanent Collection, Johnson & Johnson, New Brunswick, NJ; Artist, Permanent Collection, Chase Manhattan Bank, New York, NY; Artist, Permanent Collection, Marsh Insurance Company, Morristown, NJ; Artist, Permanent Collection, Frederick R. Weisman Foundation, Los Angeles, CA **Marquis Who's Who Honors:** Albert Nelson Marquis Lifetime Achievement Award; Marquis Who's Who Top Professional **Why did you become involved in your profession or industry:** Ms. Segal became involved in her profession because she wanted to be a painter since high school. By the time graduate school came around, she decided to test her talents by making a full-time career out of it. She can remember being 4 years old and picking up her first crayon.

Romualdo Segurola Jr., MD

Title: Chief of Cardiac Surgery **Industry:** Medicine & Health Care **Company Name:** Jackson Memorial Hospital/Jackson Health Systems **Parents:** Elena Segurola **Education:** Diploma, CVTS Surgery, Cardiac Surgery, University of Minnesota Medical School, Minneapolis, MN **Certifications:** American Board of Surgery, Critical Care; Diplomate, American Board of Surgery; American Board of Thoracic Surgery **Career:** Chief of Cardiac Surgery, Jackson Memorial Hospital, Jackson Health Systems (2019-Present); Division Chief of Cardiothoracic Surgery, Department of Surgery, Nova Southeastern University (2017-Present); Clinical Associate Professor, Nova Southern University (2014-Present); Chief, Chairman, Department of Cardiac Surgery, Palmetto General Hospital, TH Medical (2006-2019); Cardiovascular and Thoracic Surgeon, South Florida Heart and Lung Institute (2004-2019) **Awards:** Cor Vitae Award, American Heart Association, Inc. (2014); Excellence in Cardiac Surgery, Healthgrades (2012-2014); Salute, City of Miami, FL (2009); Mayor's Award, City of Hialeah, FL (2009); Recognition Award, City of Doral, FL (2009) **Memberships:** The Society of Thoracic Surgeons; Heart Rhythm Society (HRS) **Marquis Who's Who Honors:** Marquis Who's Who Top Professional **To what do you attribute your success:** Dr. Segurola attributes his success to his mother and her philosophy. She advised him to "just care." He believes that the best doctor is not the one that is the smartest or the brightest, it's the one that cares the most. **Why did you become involved in your profession or industry:** Dr. Segurola became involved in his profession because he is a Cuban American and he was on one of the last freedom flights from Cuba back during the revolution. He came to America in 1967 and in 1985, his father disappeared, however, he regards his mother as a saint. She cleaned houses and took care of elderly people. She did not speak English but prayed a lot. He is an American success story; his mother did whatever she could to make sure her three children had an education. **Avocations:** Advent boater **Thoughts on Life:** Dr. Segurola's motto is "as long as you're a Miami-Dade resident, then the doors are open. It doesn't matter where you are economically or if you are an immigrant or not."

Petra Seidler

Title: Team Leader **Industry:** Business Managemen Business Services **Company Name:** COWI **Date of Birth:** 05/14/1963 **Parents:** Dr. Siegfried; Christa Siegfried **Marital Status:** Divorced **Education:** PhD in International Economic Relations, Saint Petersburg State University of Economics and Finance (1989); Diploma in Economics, Saint Petersburg State University of Economics and Finance (1986); PhD in Finance Credit Procurement, European University at St. Petersburg **Certifications:** Chartered Translator in Russian; Chartered Translator in German; Certified Expert of Consolidation; Chartered Interpreter in Russian; Chartered Interpreter in German **Career:** Team Leader, Consultancy Services to Prime Minister's Strategy Unit, Ukraine Municipal Infrastructure Program, European Investment Bank, COWI, Kiev Region, Ukraine (2018-Present); Head of Programme, Team Leader, Regional Infrastructure Development Fund, Afghanistan (2011-2018); Administrator, Finance Director, Head of Press Office, Darya Management, Afghanistan (2009-2012); Adviser to the Board of Directors and Senior Management, Da Afghanistan Breshna Sherkat (DABS), Asian Development Bank (ADB) (2010); Team Leader and Change Management Expert, Da Afghanistan Breshna Sherkat (DABS), Asian Development Bank (ADB) Financed, MVV decon GmbH, Kabul, Afghanistan (2009-2010); Project Director, Change Management Expert for Corporatization and Commercialization of Da Afghanistan Breshna Moassassa (DABM), Kabul, Afghanistan (2006-2009) **Civic:** Sponsor, Various Students; Sponsor, Families in Need; Ongoing Contributor, Various Charitable Organizations **Awards:** Consultant of the Decade, International Association of Top Professionals (IAOTP) (2020); Empowered Woman of the Year (2019); Top Consultant of the Year, International Association of Top Professionals (IAOTP) (2018) **Marquis Who's Who Honors:** Albert Nelson Marquis Lifetime Achievement Award; Marquis Who's Who Top Professional; Marquis Who's Who Humanitarian Award **To what do you attribute your success:** Dr. Seidler attributes her success to being a results-oriented individual and having the ability to bring change. She also credits her recognition and respect for cultural diversity. **Why did you become involved in your profession or industry:** Dr. Seidler became involved in her current profession because of her focus on change management. She is always looking for great challenges and works hard to achieve the best results under difficult circumstances. She got the opportunity to go to Saint Petersburg, Russia, and study at the Institute for Economics and Finance. There were only two universities in Russia like this and they are still internationally recognized. There were more than 10,000 students, out of which 3,000 were international students. After Dr. Seidler's third year, she was elected president of the international students. It was sometimes very difficult because there were students from countries around the world, including China, Cuba and Libya, but it was a great experience overall. During her first year at the university, Dr. Seidler started scientific research in addition to her regular studies. She was one of the only students that spoke English, German and Russian perfectly, which enabled her to enter a restricted area of the public library. Dr. Seidler was able to read and learn a lot about economics and how capitalism worked. When she was there, she recognized that there were also problems with the environment. Her professor was one of the first scientists in recycling and ecology. Dr. Seidler received a red diploma after five years, which means she finished her coursework with distinction. After receiving this certification, individuals have the opportunity to either join a PhD program or go into research. In socialist countries, it was regulated where recipients have to go after. Dr. Seidler was lucky and obtained a PhD after three years. She studied international economics and enterprise, as well as national economy. During those three years, she was working very hard, but enjoyed it a lot. She got married in her second year of study to a Russian native and he subsequently joined her in Germany. Her parents supported her by helping set up her new living place. It was really great what they made. Her father and uncle always said, "You have to think what will be done with your knowledge." This is one of the reasons she studied economics because she felt it is relative to all people. **Avocations:** Writing; Swimming; Diving; Painting; Music

Karl E. Seifert, PhD

Title: Geology Educator **Industry:** Education/Educational Services **Date of Birth:** 03/16/1934 **Place of Birth:** Orangeville **State/Country of Origin:** OH/USA **Parents:** Allan L. Seifert; Elma I. (Cassidy) Seifert **Spouse Name:** Carole Ann Aselman (06/19/1981); Norma L. Scroggy (12/18/1954, Divorced 1981) **Children:** Keith Alan; Lynnette Kay; Kendall Curtis **Education:** PhD, University Wisconsin, Madison, WI (1963); MS, University of Wisconsin, Madison, WI (1959); BS, Bowling Green State University, Bowling Green, OH (1956) **Career:** Professor, Geology, Iowa State University, Ames, IA (1972-2002); Department Chair, Geology, Iowa State University, Ames, IA (1988-1991); Associate Professor, Iowa State University, Ames, IA (1968-1972); Assistant Professor, Geology, Iowa State University, Ames, IA (1965-1968) **Career Related:** Ocean Drilling Project, Atlantic Ocean (1993); Visiting Scientist Fellow, Geological Museum, Oslo, Norway (1979); Shipboard Scientist, Deep Sea Drilling Project, Pacific Ocean (1978); Speaker in Field **Military Service:** Captain, U.S. Air Force (1961-1965) **Creative Works:** Contributor, Professional Publications **Awards:** Distinguished Visitor, Washington University, St. Louis, MO (1980-1981) **Memberships:** Fellow, Geological Society of America; Geochemical Society; American Geophysical Union **Marquis Who's Who Honors:** Albert Nelson Marquis Lifetime Achievement Award **Why did you become involved in your profession or industry:** Dr. Seifert became involved in his profession because he has always been interested, and skilled, in math and science, and he believed that geology was the most interesting science that he came across. His pursuits in math and science go beyond the family tree, as nobody in the family was a scientist. In addition, Dr. Seifert chose his profession because it combined the mental stimulation of mathematics, computers, and science. It also involved outdoor activity during the summer; he could get out and work in the woods and mountains, where he could collect rocks. So, it was both physically and mentally invigorating for him. **Avocations:** Computer; Reading; Studying science; Playing Racquetball; Playing tennis; Backpacking **Political Affiliations:** Democrat

Jerome M. Selby

Title: Municipal and Business Consultant **Industry:** Consulting **Company Name:** Kodiak Tax Service **Date of Birth:** 9/4/1948 **Place of Birth:** Wheatland **State/Country of Origin:** WY/USA **Parents:** John Franklin Selby; Claudia Meredith (Hudson) Selby **Marital Status:** Married **Spouse Name:** Gloria Jean Nelson (6/14/1969) **Children:** Tyan; Cameronn; Kalen **Education:** MPA, Boise State University (1978); MA, Educational Administration, College of Idaho (1974); BS in Mathematics, College of Idaho (1969) **Certifications:** Enrolled Agent, Enrolled to Practiced Before IRS (1987-Present) **Career:** Municipal and Business Consultant (1998-Present); Mayor, Kodiak Island Borough (2004-2013); Interim Executive Director, Kodiak Island Convention & Visitors (2007); Interim Executive Director, Kodiak Chamber of Commerce (2004); Regional Director, Planning and Development, Providence Health System (1998-2003); Mayor, Kodiak Island Borough (1983-1998); Manager, Kodiak Island Borough (1984-1985); Director of Health, Kodiak Area Native Association, Alaska (1978-1983); Health Policy Analysis and Accountability, Mountain States Health Corp., Boise, ID (1976-1978); Director, Evaluation, Mountain States Health Corp., Boise, ID (1974-1976); Director, Research, Mountain States Health Corp., Boise, ID (1974-1976); Director, Evaluation, WICHE, Mountain States Regional Medical Program, Boise, ID (1971-1974); Associate Engineer, Boeing Co., Seattle, WA (1969-1971) **Career Related:** Proprietor, Kodiak Tax Service (1978-Present); Paul Harris Fellow (1987-1988, 1991-1992, 1996, 2005); Registered Guide, Kodiak, Alaska (1987-2004); Consultant, National Cancer Institute, Washington, DC (1973-1978) **Civic:** Vice President, Providence Kodiak Island Medical Center Advisory Board (2018-Present); Vice Chairman, Alaska Mental Health Trust Authority (2018-Present); Chair, Finance Committee, Alaska Mental Health Trust Authority (2017-Present); Governor, Appointed to Alaska Mental Health Trust Authority (2016-Present); Advisory Board, Providence Kodiak Island Medical Center (2014-Present); Wells Fargo Community Advisory Board (2005-Present); Development Committee, Koniag Education Foundation (2002-2015); President, Western Interstate Region National Association Counties (2012-2013); Treasurer, Kodiak Health Care Foundation (2010-2013); Western Interstate Region National Association Counties Board (2007-2013); Board of Directors, Alaska Municipal League (2004-2013); Board of Directors, Alaska Municipal League (2004-2013); Board of Directors, Alaska Municipal League Joint Insurance Association Board (1995-2013); Board of Directors, Kodiak Health Care Foundation (1992-2013); First Vice President, Western Interstate Region National Association Counties (2011-2012); Second Vice President, Western Interstate Region National Association Counties (2010-2011); President, Oiled Regions of Alaska (2002-2010); Oiled Regions of Alaska Board (2001-2010); Vice President, Kodiak Health Care Foundation (1992-2010); Board of Directors, American Red Cross Alaska Statewide Chapter (2002-2009); Council on Economic Policy for Rural Alaska (2006-2007); Board of Directors, Alaska State Chamber of Commerce (2000-2007); Executive Committee, Alaska State Chamber of Commerce (2002-2006) **Creative Works:** Contributor, Articles, Professional Journals **Awards:** Vic Fischer Local Government Leadership Award (2013); Member of the Year, Kodiak Chamber of Commerce (2005); Award of Appreciation, U.S. Secretary of Interior (2000); Lifetime Achievement Award, Alaska Municipal League (1998); Distinguished Alumni Award, College of Idaho (1997); Outstanding Contribution Award, Alaska Municipal League (1994) **Memberships:** Board of Directors, Kodiak Rotary International (2004-2011); President, Kodiak Rotary International (2009-2010); President-elect, Kodiak Rotary International (2008-2009); Vice President, Rotary International (2007-2008); Director, Kodiak Chamber of Commerce (1983-1999); Board of Directors, Kodiak Rotary International (1989-1997); President, Kodiak Rotary International (1995-1996); President-elect, Kodiak Rotary International (1994-1995); Vice President, Kodiak Rotary International (1993-1994); Treasurer, Kodiak Rotary International (1989-1993); Alaska Conference of Mayors; National Society of Tax Professionals; Academy of Political Science; Alaska Municipal Managers Association **Marquis Who's Who Honors:** Albert Nelson Marquis Lifetime Achievement Award (2019); Marquis Humanitarian Award (2018) **To what do you attribute your success:** Mr. Selby attributes his success to the good fortune of being born to honest, hardworking parents with old-school American values, who taught him that hard work was the key to achieving success. Growing up in the American West, helping your neighbor was a way of life and this was a major influence on him as well. **Why did you become involved in your profession or industry:** Mr. Selby became involved in his profession because it was something he was interested in. He took an H&R Block study course, picked up some knowledge about taxes and leveraged that experience to go into the industry. During his Master of Public Administration studies, he developed an interest in public service, which led to service as mayor, and participation on numerous boards and committees. These opportunities fit well with a mindset that we are here to help and serve our fellow man. **Avocations:** Fishing; Hunting **Religion:** Protestant

Wayne Steven Sellman, PhD

Title: Vice President for Strategic Planning (Retired) **Industry:** Government Administration/Government Relations/Government Services **Company Name:** The Human Resources Research Organization **Date of Birth:** 08/30/1940 **Place of Birth:** Texarkana **State/Country of Origin:** TX/USA **Parents:** Albert Clay Sellman; Irene Lois (Baird) Sellman **Marital Status:** Married **Spouse Name:** Elaine Elizabeth Sellman **Children:** Christine Lynn Grisler; Margaret Elaine Hennessy **Education:** Diploma in National and International Security, Harvard University (1986); PhD in Industrial and Organizational Psychology, Purdue University (1968); MEd in Counseling Psychology, Texas A&M University (1963); BA in Psychology and History, Texas A&M University (1962) **Career:** Retired (2015); Vice President for Strategic Planning, The Human Resources Research Organization, Alexandria, VA (2002-2015); Civilian, U.S. Senior Executive Service, Director, Accession Policy, U.S. Department of Defense, Washington, DC (1984-2002); Lecturer, Texas Lutheran College, Seguin, Texas (1976-1977); Staff Officer, Enlistment Testing and Entrance Standards, United States Air Force, Washington, DC (1974-1978); Lecturer, University of Colorado at Denver, CO (1970-1971); Lecturer, Our Lady of the Lake College, San Antonio, Texas (1968-1969); Lecturer, St. Mary's University, San Antonio, Texas (1968-1969) **Career Related:** Advisory Committee, National General Educational Development (GED) Program, Washington, DC (1981-1986) **Military Service:** Retired (1980); Chief, Air Force Personnel Testing, Enlistment Testing and Entrance Standards, Headquarters, United States Air Force, Washington, DC (1974-1978); Exchange Officer, Royal Australian Air Force, Melbourne, VIC, Australia (1972-1974); Research Psychologist, Lowry Air Force Base, Denver, CO (1969-1972); Chief, Test Review Section, Air Force Human Resources Laboratory, Lackland Air Force Base, San Antonio, Texas (1968-1969); Operational Psychologist, 3320th Retraining Group, Amarillo Air Force Base, Amarillo, Texas (1963-1965); Advanced through Grades to Major, United States Air Force (1974); Commissioned Second Lieutenant, United States Air Force (1962) **Creative Works:** Contributor, Over 150 Articles, Professional Publications, Book Chapters, and Technical Reports; Co-author, Book on Cognitive Differences in Youth Over Time by Demographic Variables; Contributor, Over 60 Reports, U.S. Congress. **Awards:** Civilian Distinguished Service Medal, U.S. Department of Defense (2002); U.S. Selective Service System Meritorious Achievement Medal (2002); Presidential Meritorious Executive Award (1999); Certificate of Merit Award, U.S. Department of Defense (1995); Society for Military Psychology Lifetime Achievement Award (1995); Air Force Systems Command Technical Achievement Award (1971); Air Force Human Resources Laboratory Scientific Achievement Award (1971) **Memberships:** President, Society for Military Psychology, American Psychological Association (1989-1990); Fellow, American Psychological Association; Fellow, Society for Industrial and Organizational Psychology, Inc.; Fellow, Society for Military Psychology; Fellow, Armed Forces & Society; National Council on Measurement in Education; American Educational Research Association; Armed Forces and Society; Masons; Phi Delta Kappa (PDK International); Phi Eta Sigma National Honor Society, Inc.; Psi Chi, The International Honor Society in Psychology; The Honor Society of Phi Kappa Phi **Marquis Who's Who Honors:** Albert Nelson Marquis Lifetime Achievement Award; Marquis Who's Who Top Professional; Marquis Who's Who Humanitarian Award **To what do you attribute your success:** Dr. Sellman attributes his success to his mentors, and working at jobs he felt were valuable to his organizations and his country. **Why did you become involved in your profession or industry:** Dr. Sellman became involved in his profession after wanting to be both in the Air Force, and being interested in psychology. He always liked to do things for people. In high school, he delivered boxes of food around the holiday time to people who were homeless or indigent. He also enjoyed helping kids when he was progressing through the Boy Scouts of America; Dr. Sellman was an Eagle Scout. **Avocations:** Reading; Golf **Religion:** Methodist **Thoughts on Life:** Dr. Sellman separated from the Air Force in 1980 to become a U.S. Department of Defense civilian. He worked as a senior executive in the Office of the Secretary of Defense till 2002; he then went into the corporate arena and retired in 2015.

Gregg Leonard Semenza, MD, PhD

Title: Professor of Genetic Medicine; Director of Vascular Program **Industry:** Medicine & Health Care **Company Name:** Johns Hopkins University School of Medicine; Institute for Cell Engineering **Date of Birth:** 07/12/1956 **Place of Birth:** Flushing **State/Country of Origin:** NY/USA **Marital Status:** Married **Spouse Name:** Laura Kasch-Semenza **Education:** Postdoctorate Fellow, Medical Genetics, Johns Hopkins University School of Medicine, Baltimore, MD (1986-1990); Intern, Resident in Pediatrics, Duke University Medical Center, Durham, NC (1984-1986); MD, University of Pennsylvania, Philadelphia, PA (1984); PhD in Genetics, University of Pennsylvania, Philadelphia, PA (1984); AB in Biology, Harvard College, Magna Cum Laude, Cambridge, MA (1974) **Certifications:** Diplomate, American Board of Medical Genetics; Diplomate, American Board of Pediatrics; Diplomate, National Board of Medical Examiners **Career:** Founding Director, Vascular Program, Institute for Cell Engineering, Johns Hopkins University School of Medicine, Baltimore, MD (2003-Present); Professor, Johns Hopkins University School of Medicine, Baltimore, MD (1999-Present); Associate Professor, Johns Hopkins University School of Medicine, Baltimore, MD (1994-1999); Assistant Professor, Department of Pediatrics, Johns Hopkins University School of Medicine, Baltimore, MD (1990-1994); Professor, Department of Medicine, Oncology and Radiation Oncology, McKusick-Nathans Institute of Genetic Medicine, Johns Hopkins University School of Medicine, Baltimore, MD **Career Related:** Fisher Distinguished Lecturer, Tulane University School of Medicine, New Orleans, LA (2003); Woznicki Lecturer, Cardiovascular Pathology and Genetics, Baylor College of Medicine, Houston, Texas (2001); Abelson Memorial Visiting Professor, Washington University School of Medicine, St. Louis, MI (2001); Iyengar Memorial Lecturer, University of Pennsylvania School of Veterinary Medicine (2001); Visiting Professor, Department of Physiology, Medical College of Wisconsin, Milwaukee, WI (1998) **Creative Works:** Contributor, Molecular & Cellular Biology (2008-Present); Editor-in-Chief, Journal of Molecular Medicine (2007-Present); Contributor, Antioxidants & Redox Signaling (2003-Present); Contributor, Cancer Research (2003-Present); Member, Editorial Board, Journal of Clinical Investigation (2000-Present); Author, "Transcription Factors and Human Disease" (1998); Contributor, Articles, Professional Journals **Awards:** Co-Recipient, Nobel Prize in Physiology or Medicine (2019); Co-Recipient, Albert Lasker Award for Basic Medical Research (2016); Wiley Prize (2014); Stanley J. Korsmeyer Award, The American Society for Clinical Investigation (2012); Scientific Grand Prize, Lefoulon-Delalande Foundation (2012); Gairdner Foundation International Award, Canada (2010); Chancellor's Award in Neuroscience, Louisiana State University Health Sciences Center (2002); E. Mead Johnson Award for Research in Pediatrics, Society for Pediatric Research (2000); Jean & Nicholas Leone Award, Children's Brain Tumor Foundation (1999); Established Investigator Award, American Heart Association, Inc. (1994); Lucille P. Markey Scholar Award in Biomedical Science, Markey Trust (1989) **Memberships:** Founding Fellow, American College of Medical Genetics and Genomics (1992); National Academy of Sciences; The American Society of Clinical Investigation; Society of Pediatric Research; Association of American Physicians; Alpha Omega Alpha Honor Medical Society; Institute of Medicine

Barry Sendel

Title: Founder & Chief Executive Officer **Industry:** Food & Restaurant Services **Company Name:** Chef Minute Meals Inc. **Marital Status:** Married **Children:** Three Children **Education:** Doctor of Philosophy in Mathematics, Sir George Williams University, Montreal, Quebec (1964) **Career:** Founder, Hand of Hope (2012-Present); Co-Founder, Chief Executive Officer, Chef Minute Meals Inc. (2011-Present); Founder, Innovatek, Inc. (1985); Founder, Norsofco Group Ltd., Toronto, Canada (1968); Founder, Montreal Open Woodhaven, Home Renovation Depot & Building Supply House, Montreal, Canada (1964-1967); Founder, Kyoto Fibers **Career Related:** Packaged Food Industry (1997-Present); Co-Founder, Chief Executive Officer, President, Director, D&B Specialty Foods Inc. (2001) **Creative Works:** Producer, Film, "Playgirl Killer" (1967); With, Monticana Records and Carnival Records (1962-1964) **Awards:** Citizen of the Year Award, U.S. Deputy Sheriff's Association (2019); Honored Member, Trademark Business Leaders of America (2018); Grand Prix Award for Originality & Innovation, New Products Category (2000-2001) **Memberships:** U.S. Chamber of Commerce; Johnson City Chamber of Commerce; National Republican Senate Committee; Lions; Canadian Film Development Corporation; Toastmasters International **Marquis Who's Who Honors:** Albert Nelson Marquis Lifetime Achievement Award; Marquis Who's Who Top Professional **To what do you attribute your success:** Dr. Sendel attributes his success to perseverance and believing in what he does. **Why did you become involved in your profession or industry:** Dr. Sendel fell into his career due to his ability to maximize his profit-making abilities, having joined a canned tuna company in Mexico and selling the product in Canada.

Edward Joseph Seppi

Title: Physicist (Retired) **Industry:** Research **Company Name:** SLAC and Varian Associates Inc. **Date of Birth:** 12/16/1930 **Place of Birth:** Price **State/Country of Origin:** UT/USA **Parents:** Joseph Seppi; Fortunata Seppi **Marital Status:** Married **Spouse Name:** Betty Rae Stowell Seppi (08/25/1953) **Children:** Duane Joseph; Kevin Darrell; Cynthia Rae **Education:** Doctor of Philosophy, California Institute of Technology (1962); Research Fellow, California Institute of Technology, Pasadena, CA (1962); Master of Science, University of Idaho (1956); Bachelor of Science, Brigham Young University (1952) **Career:** Retired (2012); Principal Scientist, Varian Ginzton Research Center, Palo Alto, CA (1993-2012); Senior Scientist, Varian Associates, Palo Alto, CA (1987-1992); Technical Director, Varian Associates, Palo Alto, CA (1985-1986); Engineering Manager of Radiation Division, Varian Associates, Palo Alto, CA (1983-1985); Manager of Computer Tomography Division, Varian Associates, Palo Alto, CA (1977-1978); Manager of Medical Diagnostic Instrumentation, Varian Associates, Palo Alto, CA (1974-1982); Head of Experimental Facility Department, Stanford Linear Accelerator Center (SLAC), Stanford, CA (1968-1974); Research Area Department Head, Stanford Linear Accelerator Center, Stanford, CA (1966-1968); Staff Physicist, Institute for Defense Analyses, Washington, DC (1962-1964); Staff Physicist, General Electric at Hanford Atomic Works (1952-1958); Active Member, Physics of Medical Imaging **Career Related:** Scientist, Superconducting Super Collider, Dallas, TX (1990-1991); Consultant, Institute of Defense Analysis, Washington, DC (1964-1972) **Civic:** Board of Directors, Ladera Community Association (1988-1990); Assistant Scoutmaster, Boy Scouts of America, Menlo Park, CA (1969-1975) **Creative Works:** Co-Author, with others, "The Stanford Two-Mile Accelerator" (1968); Contributor, Articles to More than 50 Scientific Publications; Co-Author, Numerous Technical Papers on CT and Digital X-Ray Photography **Memberships:** American Physical Society **Marquis Who's Who Honors:** Albert Nelson Marquis Lifetime Achievement Award; Marquis Who's Who Top Professional **Why did you become involved in your profession or industry:** Dr. Seppi became involved in his profession because he was interested in doing research in high school. He loved his science classes, which got him into teaching. But as time went on, Dr. Seppi realized that he could go to a university and do research. **Avocations:** Football; Tennis

David Joseph Sessa

Title: Chemist, Biochemist **Industry:** Sciences **Date of Birth:** 03/03/1938 **Place of Birth:** Hackensack **State/Country of Origin:** NJ/USA **Parents:** Joseph Stephen Sessa; Anne (Ullersberger) Sessa **Marital Status:** Married **Spouse Name:** Irene Barnes (06/03/1960, Divorced 1976); Virginia Lee Morse **Children:** Brian David; Valerie Irene; Kenneth Gregory; Jennifer Danielle **Education:** Postgraduate Coursework, Bradley University (1965-1969); Postgraduate Coursework, Oklahoma State University (1962-1963); BS in Chemistry, Tufts University (1959) **Career:** Research Chemist, North Regional Research Center, Agricultural Research Service, U.S. Department of Agriculture, Peoria, IL (1968-Present); Associate Chemist, North Regional Research Center, Agricultural Research Service, U.S. Department of Agriculture, Peoria, IL (1963-1968) **Career Related:** Organizing Committee Officer, World Congress on Vegetable Protein (1988) **Civic:** Illinois Corn Marketing Board **Military Service:** U.S. Army (1959-1962) **Creative Works:** Contributor Author, Lecithins (1985); Contributor, Articles, Professional Journals **Awards:** Outstanding Presentations, American Oil Chemistry Society; Certificate of Appreciation Award for Commercial Support of Civil Rights Activities and Efforts in Community Outreach Program, United States Department of Agriculture (USDA); American Men and Women in Spence **Memberships:** American Oil Chemists Society (1983-Present); Vice President, Kiwanis (1975-1976); Institute of Food Technologists **Marquis Who's Who Honors:** Albert Nelson Marquis Lifetime Achievement Award; Marquis Who's Who Top Professional **Why did you become involved in your profession or industry:** Mr. Sessa attributes his success to his upbringing. He had a positive environment around him constantly, which enabled him to take a liking to chemistry. He has always had a scientific mind. **Avocations:** Investments; Culinary arts; Gardening; Bicycling

Richard Burt Seymour

Title: President, Chief Executive Officer; Author; Health Educator (Retired) **Industry:** Writing and Editing **Company Name:** Westwind Associates **Date of Birth:** 08/01/1937 **Place of Birth:** San Francisco **State/Country of Origin:** CA/USA **Parents:** Arnold Burt-Oakley Seymour; Florence Marguerite (Burt) Seymour **Marital Status:** Married **Spouse Name:** Sharon Harkless (01/05/1973); Michelle Driscoll (09/15/1963, Divorced 1972) **Children:** Brian Geoffrey; Kyra Daleth **Education:** Master of Arts in English and Comparative Literature, Emphasis on Creative Writing, Sonoma State University (1970); Bachelor of Arts in English, Sonoma State University (1969) **Career:** President, Chief Executive Officer, Westwind Associates, Sausalito, CA (1988-Present); Freelance Writer, Sausalito, CA (1960-Present); Instructor, John F. Kennedy University, Orinda, CA (1986-2007); Assistant Professor, Sonoma State University, Rohnert Park, CA (1985-2007); Executive Administrator, Director of Training and Education Projects, Height Ashbury Free Clinics, San Francisco, CA (1977-1987); Business Manager, Haight Ashbury Free Clinics, San Francisco, CA (1973-1977); Coordinator, Administrator, College of Mendocino, Boonville, CA (1971-1973) **Career Related:** Coordinator, California Collaborative Center for Substance Abuse Policy Research (1997-Present); Treasurer, Board of Directors, Chairman, World Drug Abuse Treatment Network, San Francisco, CA (1988-Present); Consultant, Haight Ashbury Free Clinics, San Francisco, CA (1987-2007); Board of Directors, Slide Ranch **Civic:** Alcohol and Drug Counselors Education Project (1985-Present); San Francisco Delinquency Prevention Commission (1981-Present); California Primary Prevention Network (1980-Present); Chairman, Marin Drug Abuse Advisory Board, San Rafael, CA (1979-1981); California Health Profiles for New Health Policy, Washington, DC (1976-1980); CalDrug Abuse Services Association, Sacramento, CA (1975-1979) **Creative Works:** Executive Editor, Alcohol MD.com (1999-Present); Author, "Murder on the Dock of the Bay" (2018-2019); Author, "Ariadne's Thread" (2015); Author, "Death Comes to the Reunion" (2014); Author, "If It's Tuesday It Must Be Murder" (2013); Author, "The Red Tide Murders" (2014); Author, "Clinicians' Guide to Substance Abuse" (2001); Author, "Compost College" (1997); Editor-in-chief, Journal of Psychoactive Drugs (1996); Editor-in-chief, International Addictions Infoline (1995); Author, "The Psychedelic Resurgence" (1993); Author, "The New Drugs" (1989); Author, "Physician's Guide to Psychoactive Drugs" (1987); Author, "Drug Free" (1987); Contributor, Articles, Professional Journals **Awards:** Grantee, National Institute of Mental Health (1974-2007); Grantee, National Institute on Drug Abuse (1974-2007) **Memberships:** Board of Directors, Treasurer, International Society of Addiction Journal Editors (2000-2007); International Platform Association; Commonwealth Club of California; Board of Directors, Sausalito Village **Marquis Who's Who Honors:** Albert Nelson Marquis Lifetime Achievement Award; Marquis Who's Who Top Professional; Marquis Who's Who Humanitarian Award **To what do you attribute your success:** Mr. Seymour attributes his success to being good at what he does. **Why did you become involved in your profession or industry:** Mr. Seymour entered his profession due to his early involvement in the communal movement in the United States, having seen that families become broken by the experience of having to travel and take jobs in different areas. He co-founded an experimental college, the College of Mendocino, also known as Compost College, which he wrote a book on. Mr. Seymour has worked in a variety of professions, including the Air Force, newspaper reporting, and writing. He began as a janitor and secretary at the Haight Ashbury Clinic, and, within eight months, became the chief executive. **Avocations:** Travel; Writing; Landscape painting; Camping **Political Affiliations:** Democrat **Religion:** Episcoplian

David R. Shaheen, Esq.

Title: Trial Attorney **Industry:** Law and Legal Services **Company Name:** Ged Lawyers, LLP **Parents:** Bob Shaheen; Patricia Shaheen **Education:** JD, Shepard Broad College of Law, Nova Southeastern University, Davie, FL, Summa Cum Laude (2015); BS in Business, Villanova University (2011) **Certifications:** The Florida Bar; United States District Court, Southern District of Florida **Career:** Attorney, Ged Lawyers, LLP (2018-Present); Attorney, Kanner & Pintaluga (2015-2018); Attorney, Simon & Sigalos, Boca Raton, FL (2015); Legal Clerk, McIntosh Schwartz, Fort Lauderdale, FL (2015); 17th Judicial Circuit, Office of the State Attorney, Fort Lauderdale, FL (2014); Summer Associate, Law Offices of Kubicki Draper, Fort Lauderdale, FL (2014) **Civic:** Boca Helping Hands; 4KIDS of South Florida, Inc.; High School Ministry, Boca Raton Community Church **Awards:** Legal Elite Up & Comers (2020); Top Lawyer, Palm Beach Illustrated (2019-2020); Red Pen Award; Merit Scholar, Shepard Broad College of Law, Nova Southeastern University; Simonhoff Scholar, Shepard Broad College of Law, Nova Southeastern University; Top 10 Finish at Nationals, Moot Court Society, Shepard Broad College of Law, Nova Southeastern University **Memberships:** Florida Justice Association; Broward County Trial Lawyers Association; Trial Lawyers Section, The Florida Bar; Rotary Club of Downtown Boca Raton **To what do you attribute your success:** Mr. Shaheen attributes his success to God. He also thanks his father for teaching him the core principles of being a man. **Why did you become involved in your profession or industry:** Mr. Shaheen became involved in his profession because studying law was in his blood; his father was involved in a lawsuit where he was wronged, but was misrepresented by the attorney handling his case. Watching this experience play out as a teenager, Mr. Shaheen believed that he could go to law school and overturn the case his father had lost because he knew that what had happened was wrong. "When you're involved in ligation," he said, "you have to explain things to a jury and sometimes they don't necessarily understand the complexity of the terms. If you can't explain what's happening to your community and why there is an injustice occurring in our midst, then you're not representing your client properly." His father's attorney was more concerned about being an advocate than he was about his client's case. Mr. Shaheen became a lawyer because he never wanted anyone in his community to commit blatant injustices and get away with them because of poor representation. He now strives to change the culture of the profession, and leave behind him a trail of fire. **Religion:** Christian

Robert Leslie Shapiro

Title: Attorney **Industry:** Law and Legal Services **Company Name:** Glaser Weil Fink Howard Avchen & Shapiro LLP **Date of Birth:** 09/02/1942 **Place of Birth:** Plainfield **State/Country of Origin:** NJ/USA **Spouse Name:** Linell (Thomas) Shapiro (03/08/1971) **Children:** Brent (Deceased); Grant **Education:** JD, Loyola Law School, Loyola Marymount University, Los Angeles, CA (1968); BS in Finance, UCLA (1965) **Career:** Senior Attorney, Glaser Weil Fink Howard Avchen & Shapiro LLP, Los Angeles, CA (1995-Present); Of Counsel, Christensen, Miller, Fink, Jacobs, Glaser, Weil & Shapiro (Now Glaser Weil Fink Howard Avchen & Shapiro LLP), Los Angeles, CA (1988-1995); Of Counsel, Bushkin, Gaims, Gaines and Jonas, Los Angeles, CA (1987-1988); Private Practice, Los Angeles, CA (1972-1987); Deputy District Attorney, Los Angeles County District Attorney's Office, Los Angeles, CA (1969-1972) **Career Related:** Co-Founder, LegalZoom.com, Inc.; Co-Founder, RightCounsel; Co-Founder, Shoedazzle.com, TechStyle Fashion Group; Co-Founder, BizCounsel, Inc.; Lecturer in Field **Civic:** Board Member, EarthWater (2016-Present); Founder, Chairman of the Board, Brent Shapiro Foundation for Drug Prevention **Creative Works:** Co-Author (with Walt W. Becker), "Misconception" (2001); Contributor, "On Second Thought," "California Lawyer" (1997); Author, "The Search for Justice: A Defense Attorney's Brief on the O.J. Simpson Case" (1996); Contributor, "For the Defense," "Loyola Law Review" (1996); Contributor, "Using the Media to Your Advantage," NACDL (1993); Contributor, "When the Press Calls: A Lawyer's View," "California Litigation," CLA (1991); Contributor, Op-Ed Pieces and Legal Articles; Frequent Guest, Network and Cable Television Programs **Awards:** The 100 Most Influential Lawyers in America, The National Law Journal, ALM Media Properties, LLC (2013); Pro-Bono Lawyer of the Year, State of Nevada (2008); Best Criminal Defense Attorney, Century City Bar Association (1993); American Jurisprudence Award (1968, 1969); Nation's Top 100 Attorneys, National Association of Distinguished Counsel; Top 100 Litigation Lawyers in the State of California, American Society of Legal Advocates; Premier 100 Trial Attorneys, National Academy of Jurisprudence; Top 100 Trial Lawyers, The National Trial Lawyers; 100 Super Lawyers, LA Daily Journal, Daily Journal Corporation; Top California Litigator, Benchmark Litigation; Lifetime Charter Member, Best Attorneys of America, LLC; 50 Inspirational Alumni, Loyola Law School, Loyola Marymount University; Southern California Super Lawyers **Memberships:** Founding Member, Trial Lawyers for Public Justice (1982); Founding Member, National Association of Distinguished Counsel; NACDL; California Attorneys for Criminal Justice; Century City Bar Association **Bar Admissions:** The United States District Court for the Southern District of California (1982); The United States District Court for the Central District of California (1982); The United States District Court for the Northern District of California (1982); United States Court of Appeals for the Ninth Circuit (1972); State of California (1969) **Marquis Who's Who Honors:** Albert Nelson Marquis Lifetime Achievement Award **Avocations:** Watching basketball and boxing events

Alan Roger Shaw

Title: Market Analyst, Stock Brokerage Company Executive (Retired) **Industry:** Financial Services **Date of Birth:** 07/07/1938 **Place of Birth:** Brooklyn **State/Country of Origin:** NY/USA **Parents:** Sewall Shaw; Vera (Dimmick) Shaw **Spouse Name:** Barbara Ann Phillips-Cole (09/28/2013) **Children:** Stephen S.; Todd J.; Bradley C. **Education:** LLD, Susquehanna University, with Honors (1999); Coursework, Adelphi University (1963-1966); Coursework, Susquehanna University (1957) **Career:** Senior Vice President, Managing Director, Smith Barney, New York (1980-2004); 1st Vice President, Smith, Barney, Harris, Upham & Company, New York (1975-1980); Vice President, Harris Upham & Company, New York, NY (1973-1975); Assistant Vice President, Harris Upham & Company, New York, NY (1971-1973); Teacher, New York Institute of Finance (1966-2004); Analyst, Harris Upham & Company, New York (1958-1971) **Memberships:** Commodore, Unqua Corinthian Yacht Club (1988-1990); Trustee, Securities Industry Association Institute (1986-1992); President, Market Technicians Association (1974); New York Athletic Club **Marquis Who's Who Honors:** Albert Nelson Marquis Lifetime Achievement Award; Marquis Who's Who Top Professional **Avocations:** Crossword puzzles; Jigsaw puzzles; Reading; Model trains

E. Dorinda Shelley, MD

Title: Dermatologist, Author **Industry:** Museums & Institutions **Date of Birth:** 10/28/1940 **Place of Birth:** St. Louis **State/Country of Origin:** MO/USA **Parents:** Robert G. Loeffel; Ellen (Shattuck) Loeffel, MD **Marital Status:** Widowed **Spouse Name:** Walter B. Shelley, MD, PhD **Children:** Thomas R. Shelley; Katharine D. Shelley; William L. Shelley **Education:** Postdoctoral Fellow, Stanford University, Palo Alto, CA (1970-1971); Resident in Dermatology, University of Missouri, Columbia, MO (1967-1970); Intern, Saint Luke's Hospital, St. Louis, MO (1966-1967); MD, University of Missouri (1966); BA, Mount Holyoke College (1962) **Certifications:** Certification, American Board of Dermatology (1971) **Career:** Clinical Professor of Dermatology, The University of Toledo, Toledo, OH (1997-Present); Professor, Chief of Dermatology, Medical College of Ohio, Toledo, OH (1983-1997); Professor, Chairman, Peoria School of Medicine (University of Illinois) (1978-1983); Associate Professor, University of Illinois at Chicago (1975-1978); Assistant Professor of Dermatology, University of Illinois at Chicago (1974-1975); Assistant Professor of Dermatology, Stanford University, Palo Alto, CA (1971-1974); Author **Career Related:** Consultant, Food and Drug Administration, Rockville, MD (1974-1982) **Civic:** Grand Rapids Arts Council (2011-2020) **Creative Works:** Editor, "Earl W. North, American Landscape Painter" (2014, 2018); Editor, "Bernadine Stetzel's Our Town" (2014, 2018); Co-Author, "Toronto and Ted", (2016); Author, "Dasher and the Sleigh-Train" (2015); Author, "Helium Heels" (2014); Co-Editor, "A Community of Scholars: Recollections of the Early Years of the Medical College of Ohio" (2011); Author, "The Helium Table" (2010); Author, "The Helium Egg" (2010); Co-Author, "Consultations in Dermatology" (2006); Co-Author, "Shelley's 77 Skins" (2002); Co-Author, "Advanced Dermatologic Therapy II" (2001); Co- Author, "Advanced Dermatologic Diagnosis" (1992); Co-Author, "A Century of International Dermatological Congresses" (1992); Co-Author, "Advanced Dermatologic Therapy" (1986); Co-Editor, "Adolescent Dermatology" (1978); Contributor, Over 200 Articles, Professional Journals **Awards:** Recipient, Walter B. Shelley MD Leadership Award, Women's Dermatologic Society (2012); Named, Honorary Member, American Academy of Dermatology (2009); Recipient, Rose Hirschler Award, Women's Dermatologic Society (2007); Recipient, Faculty-Alumni Award, University of Missouri (1996) **Memberships:** Board of Trustees, Noah Worcester Dermatological Society (2002-2005); Historian, Women's Dermatologic Society (1996-2005); Chairman of Evaluation Committee on Annual Program, American Academy of Dermatology (1994-1999); Board of Directors, Women's Dermatologic Society (1980); President, Women's Dermatologic Society (1980); American Dermatological Association; Ohio Dermatological Association; Cosmos Club, Washington, DC **Marquis Who's Who Honors:** Albert Nelson Marquis Lifetime Achievement Award; Marquis Who's Who Top Professional; Distinguished Humanitarian **Why did you become involved in your profession or industry:** Dr. Shelley was inspired to be a dermatologist by her dermatology professor in medical school, Dr. Philip C. Anderson, who became her mentor. **Avocations:** Gardening; Library sales; Antique auctions; Art collecting; Owning and directing book shops, art galleries, and antique stores in Grand Rapids, Ohio **Political Affiliations:** Democrat **Religion:** Protestant

Estherina Shems, MD

Title: Child Psychiatrist (Retired) **Date of Birth:** 04/15/1932 **Place of Birth:** Tel Aviv **State/Country of Origin:** Israel **Parents:** Aaron Shems; Rachel Yehuda Shems **Marital Status:** Widowed **Spouse Name:** Donald L. Schotland,MD (01/11/1976, Deceased 2015) **Education:** Honorary DSc, Lynchburg College (Now University of Lynchburg) (2009); Fellowship in Adult Psychiatry, School of Medicine, University of Pennsylvania, Philadelphia, PA (1960-1963); Internship, Lankenau Hospital (Now Lankenau Medical Center, Main Line Health), Wynnewood, PA (1958-1959); MD, Woman's Medical College of Pennsylvania (Now Drexel University College of Medicine) (1958); BS, Lynchburg College (Now University of Lynchburg), Cum Laude (1954) **Career:** Retired, Child Psychiatrist (2002); Consultant, Early Intervention Programs, Community Council Health Services, Philadelphia, PA (1981-2002); Clinical Associate, Department of Psychiatry, School of Medicine, University of Pennsylvania, Philadelphia, PA (1979-1981); Staff, Administration, Irving Schwartz Institute for Children and Youth, Philadelphia Psychiatric Center, Philadelphia, PA (1964-1981); Assistant Instructor, Irving Schwartz Institute for Children and Youth, Philadelphia Psychiatric Center (1964-1966); Assistant Instructor, Department of Psychiatry, School of Medicine, University of Pennsylvania, Philadelphia, PA (1962-1963); Affiliate, Child Psychiatry, Child Study Center, Philadelphia, PA (1961-1963) **Career Related:** Invited Lecturer, Institute of Pediatrics, Chinese Academy of Medical Sciences & Peking Union Medical College, Beijing, China **Civic:** Executive Board, Trust Fund of the Alumnae/Alumni Association of the Medical College of Pennsylvania, Drexel University College of Medicine (2001-2015); Vice-Chairman, Medical College of Pennsylvania (Now Drexel University College of Medicine) (2003-2012) **Creative Works:** Author, Article; **Awards:** Distinguished Life Member, American Psychiatric Association (2013); Bertha Van Hoosen Award, American Medical Women's Association (2002); Lifetime Achievement Award, Virginia Foundation for Independent Colleges (2002); Richard H. Thornton Award for Excellence, Lynchburg College (Now University of Lynchburg) (1995); Distinguished Alumni Award, Lynchburg College (Now University of Lynchburg) (1990); T. Gibson Hobbs Memorial Award, Lynchburg College (Now University of Lynchburg) (1969); Outstanding Young Women of America (1967); Outstanding Young Women of Pennsylvania (1967) **Memberships:** Committees, Task Forces, American Medical Women's Association (1970-Present); Executive Board, Vice President, North America, Medical Woman's International Association (1998-2001); Executive Committee, Board of Directors, American Medical Women's Association (1986-1988, 1992-1998); National Coordinator, United States, Medical Woman's International Association (1992-1998); Science Research Committee, Medical Woman's International Association (1990-1998); Delegate, Session Co-Chairman, United States, XXII Congress, Medical Woman's International Association (1995); Councilor, American Medical Women's Association (1986-1988); Delegate, Session Co-Chairman, United States, XX International Congress, Medical Woman's International Association (1987); Delegate, Session Co-Chairman, United States, XIX International Congress, Medical Woman's International Association (1984); Life Member, American Medical Women's Association; Fellow, American Orthopsychiatric Association; Fellow, The College of Physicians of Philadelphia; Medical Woman's International Association; American Psychiatric Association; Psychiatric Physicians of Pennsylvania; Philadelphia Chapter, Pennsylvania Psychiatric Society; The Honor Society of Phi Kappa Phi; Various Offices, Chi Beta Phi National Scientific Honorary **Marquis Who's Who Honors:** Albert Nelson Marquis Lifetime Achievement Award **Why did you become involved in your profession or industry:** Dr. Shems was always committed to attending medical school, and knew from an early age that she would become a doctor. Having grown up in the Middle East, where women aren't afforded the same opportunities as men, Dr. Shems's pursuit of medicine was also one of equity. She ultimately chose the field of psychiatry because of how it is applied to the patient as a whole, as opposed to a specialized area.

Mark R. Shenkman

Title: Founder and President **Industry:** Financial Services **Company Name:** Shenkman Capital Management, Inc. **Date of Birth:** 8/17/1943 **Place of Birth:** Providence **State/Country of Origin:** NY/USA **Parents:** George Shenkman; Florence Shenkman **Marital Status:** Married **Spouse Name:** Rosalind E. Shenkman **Children:** Andrew Harris; Gregory Alexander; Justin Warren Slatky; 10 Grandchildren **Education:** LHD Honoris Causa, University of Connecticut, Storrs, CT (2007); MBA, George Washington University, Washington, DC (1967); BA in Political Science, University of Connecticut, Storrs, CT (1965) **Career:** Founder and President, Shenkman Capital Management Inc., New York, NY, Stamford, CT, London, England (1985-Present); President, First Investors Asset Management Company, New York, NY (1983-1985); Vice President, Lehman Brothers Kuhn Loeb, New York, NY (1979-1983); Research Analyst, Portfolio Manager, Fidelity Management & Research Company, Boston, MA (1973-1979); Financial Analyst, Stone & Webster Securities Corporation, Boston, MA (1971-1973); Security Analyst, New England Merchants National Bank, Boston, MA (1969-1971) **Civic:** Board of Governors and Treasurer, Union League Club, New York; Vice Chairman, Board of Trustees, Wilbraham & Monson Academy, Wilbraham, MA; Board of Trustees, Museum of American Finance; Board of Directors, Museum of the American Revolution; Emeritus Trustee, George Washington University; Former Chairman, University of Connecticut Foundation; Emeritus Board of Governors, University of Connecticut Foundation; Former Board of Directors, Mason School of Business, College of William and Mary **Military Service:** First Lieutenant, U.S. Army Computer Systems Command, Fort Lee, VA (1967-1969) **Creative Works:** Co-Author, Professional Textbooks, "High-Yield Bonds," "Leveraged Financial Markets" **Awards:** Inductee, Fixed Income Analysts Society Hall of Fame; Inductee, University of Connecticut School of Business Hall of Fame; George Washington University Distinguished Alumni Award; Hillel's Renaissance Award **Memberships:** American Bankruptcy Institute; New York Society of Security Analysts; Boston Security Analysts Society; American Statistical Association; Business Executives for National Security **Marquis Who's Who Honors:** Albert Nelson Marquis Lifetime Achievement Award **To what do you attribute your success:** Mr. Shenkman attributes his success to integrity, goal-oriented, planning, preparation and persistence. **Why did you become involved in your profession or industry:** Mr. Shenkman's father was a businessman and entrepreneur, who instilled in him a great passion for business and investing. **Avocations:** Yachting; Travel; Collecting American political flags and banners **Thoughts on Life:** Find your niche and then become the best in the world.

Kikuko T. Shepherd

Title: Artist **Industry:** Fine Art **Date of Birth:** 01/28/1934 **Place of Birth:** Nagano **State/Country of Origin:** Japan **Parents:** Kataro Takemura; Hana Takemura **Marital Status:** Widowed **Spouse Name:** James B. Shepherd Jr. (Deceased 1959) **Children:** Kenneth S.; Scott L.; Craig S. **Education:** Master's Equivalent, Ikenobo, Japan (1968) **Career:** Artist, Lewisburg, WV (1987-Present); Interpreter, Private Practice, Okinawa, Japan (1966-1971); Lecturer, Private Practice, Dayton, Ohio (1960-1965); Translator, United States Air Force, Yokota, Japan (1957-1959); Translator, Japan Public Trading Company, Tokyo, Japan (1952-1955) **Civic:** Volunteer, Homeless Veterans and Abused Women and Children in the Community **Memberships:** The Sumi-e Society of America, Inc.; Watercolor USA Honor Society **Marquis Who's Who Honors:** Albert Nelson Marquis Lifetime Achievement Award; Marquis Who's Who Top Professional **Why did you become involved in your profession or industry:** Mrs. Shepherd always liked painting and her passion for it motivated her to study it more in depth and pursue a career in art. After her children enrolled in college, she began her career with the encouragement and support of her husband. **Thoughts on Life:** Mrs. Shepherd currently volunteers helping homeless veterans, as well as abused women and children in her community.

Mikaela Pauline Shiffrin

Title: Alpine Skier **Industry:** Athletics **Date of Birth:** 03/13/1995 **Place of Birth:** Vail **State/Country of Origin:** CO/USA **Parents:** Jeff Shiffrin; Eileen (Condron) Shiffrin **Career:** Competitive Alpine Skier, World Cup (2011-2020); Competitive Alpine Skier, World Championships (2013-2019); Competitive Alpine Skier, Winter Olympics (2014, 2018) **Military Service:** Featured, "How to Raise an Olympian" (2014); Appearances, Television Shows **Awards:** Two Gold Medals, Bronze Medal, World Championships (2019); Gold Medal, Silver Medal, Winter Olympics (2018); Gold Medal, Two Silver Medals, World Championships (2017); Gold Medal, World Championship (2015); Gold Medal, Winter Olympics (2014); Gold Medal, World Championship (2013); Bronze Medal, Junior World Championship (2011)

Hong Shih

Title: Fellow **Industry:** Research **Company Name:** Lam Research Corporation **Date of Birth:** 12/02/1945 **Place of Birth:** Qingdao **State/Country of Origin:** People's Republic of China **Parents:** Lin Shih; Yan Wang **Marital Status:** Married **Spouse Name:** Shaoping Chen (10/01/1976) **Children:** Alice (Yunyu) Shih **Education:** Postdoctoral Fellow, University of Southern California, Los Angeles, CA (1986-1988); PhD in Metallurgy, Department of Materials Sciences and Engineering, Pennsylvania State University (1986); MS in Electrochemistry, Academia Sinica, Electric Power Institute, People's Republic of China (1981); BS in Chemistry, Peking University, People's Republic of China (1970) **Career:** Fellow, Etch Products Group (2014-Present); Director, Senior Director, and Managing Director, Lam Research Corporation, Fremont, CA (2002-2014); Director, Metal Etch, Applied Materials (1999-2002); Member of Technical Staff, Applied Materials, San Jose, CA (1994-1998); President, Chief Research Scientist, Cortech Corporation Company, Los Angeles, CA (1992-1994); Member of Technical Staff, FMC Corporation Technical Center, San Jose, CA (1991-1992); Senior Scientist, Physical Chemistry Department, GM Research Lab, Warren, MI (1990-1991); Research Assistant Professor, University of Southern California, Los Angeles, CA (1988-1990); Post Doctor, University of Southern California, Los Angeles, CA (1986-1989); Research Assistant, Pennsylvania State University, University Park, PA (1981-1986); Research Engineer, Academia Sinica, Xian, People's Republic of China (1978-1981); Analytical Chemistry Engineer, Electric Power and Machinery Factory, Xian, People's Republic of China (1973-1978); Heat Treat Engineer, Electric Power and Machinery Factory, Xian, People's Republic of China (1970-1973) **Career Related:** Consultant, Applied Materials, San Jose, CA (1992-1994); Consultant, BASF Corporation, Wyandotte, MI (1992-1994); Consultant, GM Research Laboratory, Warren, MI (1991-1994); Consultant, Leviton Manufacturing Company, Inc., Los Angeles, CA (1989-1994); Technical Consultant, 20 United States Leading Companies, Universities and Research Laboratories (1989-1994); Consultant, Schlumberger Technologies, Inc. (1988-1994); Presenter, National and International Conferences (1986-2019); Member of Planning Committee, Sixth Pennsylvania State University Readers Conference on Electroplating (1985) **Creative Works:** Author, "Corrosion Resistance" (2012); Author, 20 Technical Papers, Pennsylvania State University; Author, Co-Author, 120 Publications, Referred Journals, Books and Proceedings; Author, More than 100 Confidential Technical Reports; Inventor, Patent, Chromate-free Conversion Coatings, Aluminum Based Materials; Inventor, Patent, Chromate, Phosphate Coatings Online Monitoring; Inventor, Patent, Anodic Inhibition, Carbon Steel in High Temperature Sulfuric Acid; Inventor, Patent, Electrochemical Techniques and Software Development; Contributor, 100 Articles, Professional Journals; More Than 80 US Patents and 250 International Patents Awarded in Semiconductor IC industry **Awards:** Recognition of Outstanding Technical Achievement, ET Conference, Lam Research Corporation (2017); Lam Fellowship (2014); McFarland Award, Pennsylvania State University (2004); Wesley W. Founder Award (1993); Named, First Place Winner, Graduate Student Poster Contest, National Association of Corrosion Engineers (1984); Numerous Awards, Applied Materials, Lam Research Corporation **Memberships:** ASTM International; NACE International; The Electrochemical Society (ECS) **Marquis Who's Who Honors:** Albert Nelson Marquis Lifetime Achievement Award; Marquis Who's Who Top Professional **Why did you become involved in your profession or industry:** Dr. Hong Shih became involved in his profession because he has loved science since he was in high school. This prompted him to attend Peking University with the goal of becoming a scientist; he received a bachelor's degree in chemistry. During his time growing up in China, Dr. Shih was surrounded by civil revolutions. He was faced with the ultimatum of joining the revolution or enrolling in university. By choosing the latter, Dr. Shih propelled himself into an educational journey that took longer than he expected. When he was working in the factory, technology was not fully recognized so he had to pause his work. However, Dr. Shih didn't want to give up. As a result, he received the chance to come to the United States as a graduate student. **Avocations:** Ballroom dancing (20 years) **Thoughts on Life:** For more information about Dr. Shih, please visit the following website: https://www.intechopen.com/profiles/89658/shih.

L. Zane Shuck, PhD, PE

Title: Distinguished Research Scientist; Founder, President **Industry:** Research **Company Name:** Technology Development Inc. **Date of Birth:** 10/23/1936 **Place of Birth:** Bluefield **State/Country of Origin:** WV/USA **Parents:** Carl O. Notre Dame (Wright) Shuck **Marital Status:** Single **Children:** Kirsten Berman **Education:** PhD in Theoretical and Applied Mechanics, Biomechanics, West Virginia University (1970); Postdoctoral Coursework, Wayne State University (1965); Coursework, Iowa State University (1962); MSME, West Virginia University (1965); Special Postdoctoral Program Coursework, Massachusetts Institute of Technology (1961-1965); BS in Mechanical Energy, West Virginia Institute of Technology (1958) **Certifications:** Registered Professional Engineer, Licensed Surveyor, States of West Virginia and Ohio; Certified, National Council of Engineering Examiners; Certified, U.S. Security Q. Clearance **Career:** Founder, President, Technology Development Inc. (1980-Present); Adjunct Professor, West Virginia University (1980-1985); Professor of Mechanical Engineering, Associate Director of Energy Experiment Station, Member of Graduate Faculty, Doctoral Dissertation Advisor, West Virginia University, Morgantown, WV (1976-1980); Supervisory Mechanical Engineer, U. S. Department of Energy (1970-1976); National Science Foundation Science Faculty Fellow, Research Engineer, West Virginia University, Morgantown, WV (1968-1970); Instructor, Associate Professor, Chairman of the Mechanical Engineering Department, West Virginia Institute of Technology (1960-1965); Sales and Design Engineer, West Virginia Armature Co., Bluefield, WV (1958-1959) **Career Related:** Developed, Completed, Over 65 Oil and Gas Wells, West Virginia, Ohio (1980-Present); Science Advisor, West Virginia Governor Jay Rockefeller; Energy Consultant, FMC Corp.; Energy Consultant, South Charleston, WV; Energy Consultant, United Fuel Gas Company, South Public Service Co.; Air Pollution Control Comm., Gravely Tractor Division; Energy Consultant, Studebaker Corp.; Energy Consultant, METC-U.S. Department of Energy,; Energy Consultant, Mound Labs, Numerous O & Gas Companies; Advisory Committee, West Virginia Coal and Energy; West Virginia Inventors Council **Civic:** Founder, President, The WMAC Foundation (1997-Present); Member, Advisory Capacity, West Virginia University Tech, West Virginia University Colleges of Engineering Advisory Committee (2002-2018); Science Advisor, W.V. Governor John D. Rockefeller IV (1978-1981); Appointed Science and Technology Coordinator, W.V. Legislature (1979-1980) **Creative Works:** Author, Five U.S. Patents, Human Healthcare Gastrointestinal Research & Patient Treatment System (2013-2018); Producer, Three Technical Films, U. S. Dept. of Energy; Editorial Board, IN SITU Journal; Associate Editor, ASME Journal of Energy Resources Technology; Author, 62 Publications; Author, 23 U.S. Patents; Speaker, 18 Invited Lectures; Organizer, Numerous Professional Society Conferences; Editor, Transactions Journals and Symposia Proceedings **Awards:** Eponym, L. Zane Shuck Nanobiotechnology Lab., West Virginia University (2016); Ralph James National Award, American Society of Mechanical Engineers (1980); Award, "Most U.S. Patents Awarded in One Year Ever to A Federal Government Employee" U. S. Department of Energy (1975); Materials Testing Award, American Society for Testing Materials (1970); Four-Time Recipient, Fellowship, Ford Foundation; Three-Time Recipient, Graduate Scholarship, National Science Foundation; Special Summer Program, Iowa State University; Special Summer Program, Wayne State University; Four-Time Recipient, Summer Program, Massachusetts Institute of Technology **Memberships:** W.V. Region Planning and Development Council (2000-Present); West Virginia University Institute of Technology, Colleges of Energy Advisory Committee (2002-2019); Dunkard Creek Watershed Association (1997-2005); Vision 2000 Infrastructure Committee, Morgantown Chamber of Commerce (1992-2001); Chairperson, Monongalia Co. West Run Expressway Committee (2000); Founder, Chair, Appalachian Rivers Conference & Exhibit (1998-2000); W.V. Governor Rockefeller Appointed Coal and Energy Advisory Committee (1978-1981); Tau Beta Pi Engineering Honorary Society **Marquis Who's Who Honors:** Albert Nelson Marquis Lifetime Achievement Award; Marquis Who's Who Top Professional **Avocations:** Buying and renovating many real estate rental properties; Pursuing research in gastroenterology, oil and gas extraction technology, unconventional well stimulation without fracking, and use of water

Abraham Shulman, MD, FACS

Title: Otolaryngology Educator; Hospital Administrator **Industry:** Medicine & Health Care **Date of Birth:** 02/24/1929 **Place of Birth:** New York **State/Country of Origin:** NY/USA **Parents:** Ben Shulman; Libby (Sarnoff) Shulman **Marital Status:** Married **Spouse Name:** Arlene P. (09/08/1957) **Children:** Rachel; Melanie **Education:** Pursuing PhD, Martha Entenmann Tinnitus Research Center (2010-Present); Residency in Otolaryngology, Kings County Hospital, Brooklyn, NY (1957-1960); Rotating Internship, Queens County General Hospital (1955-1956); MD, University of Bern, Switzerland (1955); BS, City College of New York (1950) **Certifications:** Diplomate, American Board of Otolaryngology (1962); Diploma, Lempert Ear Institute (1956) **Career:** Professor Emeritus, Clinical Otolaryngology, State University of New York Health Science Center at Brooklyn (Now SUNY Downstate Health Sciences University) (1992); Assistant Clinical Professor, Otolaryngological Surgery, Albert Einstein College of Medicine (1968-1975); Clinical Instructor, Albert Einstein College of Medicine (1966-1968); Professor, Clinical Otolaryngology, State University of New York Health Science Center at Brooklyn (Now SUNY Downstate Health Sciences University) (1989-1992); Acting Director, Division of Otolaryngology, State University of New York (1990-1991); Director, Division of Otolaryngology, Center for Communicative Sciences Health Science Center, SUNY Downstate Health Sciences University (1980-1985); Acting Director, Division of Otolaryngology, State University of New York (1975-1980); Associate Professor, SUNY Downstate Health Sciences University (1975-1989); Clinical Instructor, SUNY Downstate Health Sciences University (1962-1964) **Career Related:** Chief, Otolaryngology, Staff Attending Otolaryngologist (1985-Present); Attending Otolayngologist (1975-Present); Director, Otology Neurotology, Martha Entenmann Tinnitus Research Center (1995-2017); Chairman, International Tinnitus Forum (1982-2017); Chief, Otolaryngology, Brooklyn VA Medical Center (1977-2013); Chief and Attending Otolaryngologist, Catholic Medical Center, Brooklyn and Queens, NY (1969-1994); Director, Otolaryngology (1975-1992); Attending Otolaryngologist, Brookdale Medical Center (Now Brookdale University Hospital Medical Center) (1982-1986); Lecturer, Otolaryngology, The Mount Sinai Hospital (1974); Chief, Otolaryngology, Lincoln Hospital (1967-1970); Assistant Surgeon, Brooklyn Eye and Ear Hospital (1966-1969); Assistant Attending Otolaryngologist, Kings County Hospital (1962-1964) **Civic:** Member, Medical Scientific Advisory Board, American Translators Association (ATA) (1980-2001); Consultant, Children's Development Centers, Inc. (1975); Medical Consultant, Office of Vocational Rehabilitation (1974); Director, Medical Service, Lexington School for the Deaf (1972-1974) **Military Service:** Lieutenant Commander, United States Naval Reserve (1960-1962) **Creative Works:** Editor, "Tinnitus Diagnosis and Treatment" (1991-Present); Author, "Gabadur Trial - Cortical Impact-induced Neurodegeneration" (2018); Co-author, "Neurodegeneration" (2014-2015); Emeritus Editor, International Tinnitus Journal (2011); Co-chief Editor, International Tinnitus Journal (1994-2017); Chairman, First International Tinnitus Seminar, New York, NY (1979); Author, Contributor, Numerous Articles **Awards:** Certificate of Appreciation, American Speech and Hearing Association (Now American Speech-Language-Hearing Association) (1989-Present); Named One of the Leading Figures in the Field of Tinnitus Spotlight on Dr. Abraham Shulman (2018); Named Top Doctor (2015-2019); Recognition of Exemplary Expertise and Knowledge in the Field of Tinnitus Research and Treatment, Expertscape (2013); Department of Veteran Affairs Service Award (2012); Neurotology Research Award, NES (2010); Named to Faculty of 1000 UK, F1000 Research Ltd (2010); 2010 Myrtle Reed Award, SUNY Downstate Health Sciences University (2010); Certificate of Merit, American Medical Association (2005); Named to Best Doctors, Castle Connolly (1998-2019); Honor Award, American Academy of Otolaryngology - Head and Neck Surgery (1994); Hocks Award, American Translators Association (ATA) (1990) **Memberships:** Centurion Club, American Academy of Otolaryngology - Head and Neck Surgery (2017); Fellow, The Harvey Society (1999); Emeritus Member, American Academy of Facial Plastic and Reconstructive Surgery (AAFPRS) (1997); Sigma Xi, the Scientific Research Honor Society (1982); Fellow, American College of Surgeons (1974); The American Neurotology Society (1974); Association for Research in Otolaryngology (1964); The New York Academy of Science (1962); American Medical Association (1960); Queens County Medical Society (1960); American Academy of Ophthalmology and Otolaryngology (Now American Academy of Ophthalmology); The American Auditory Society; International College of Surgeons; Politzer Society **Marquis Who's Who Honors:** Albert Nelson Marquis Lifetime Achievement Award

M. Ross Shulmister

Title: Attorney **Company Name:** M. Ross Shulmister, Attorney, PLLC **Date of Birth:** 01/06/1940 **Place of Birth:** Atlanta **State/Country of Origin:** GA/ USA **Education:** JD, University of Florida (1973); BEE, University of Florida (1962) **Certifications:** Board Certified Civil Trial Lawyer, Board of Legal Specialization & Education, The Florida Bar (1984-1999) **Career:** Attorney, Private Practice, M. Ross Shulmister, Attorney, PLLC (1980-Present); Attorney, Josias, Shulmister & Goren (1975-1979); Attorney, Zeiher & Brinkley (1974); Attorney, Alachua County State Attorney's Office (1973-1974) **Career Related:** Pompano Beach Special Master for Code Enforcement (1991-1992); City Prosecutor, Pembroke Pines, FL (1979-1980); Assistant State Attorney, Eighth Judicial Circuit of Florida (1973-1974) **Civic:** Airpark Advisory Committee (2019-Present); Chair, Charter Amendment Advisory Board, Pompano Beach, FL (2008-Present); Zoning Board of Appeals, Pompano Beach, FL (2008-Present); Vice Chair, Bench-Bar Liaison Committee (1999-Present); Treasurer, Pompano Civic Action Committee (1998-Present); Professional Responsibility Committee (1997-Present); Chair, Pompano Beach Mayor-at-Large Initiative Committee (1997-Present); Construction Law Committee (1994-Present); Construction Law Subcommittee (1978-Present); Chair, Broward County Consumer Protection Board (1999-2000); Clerk-Bar Liaison Committee (1998-1999); Bench-Bar Liaison Committee (1996-1998); President, Director, South Pompano Civic Association (1992-1998); Chair, Charter Amendment Advisory Board, Pompano Beach, FL (1994-1997); Fee Arbitration Committee (1988-1989); Landlord-Tenant Subcommittee (1983-1987); Courts Committee (1982-1983); Judicial Selection and Tenure Committee (1979-1983); Broward County Mobile Home Advisory Board (1979-1982) **Military Service:** With, United States Air Force Reserves (1970-1993); With, United States Air Force (1964-1970) **Creative Works:** Editor, The Examiner (1998-2000); Editor, The Sentry (1982-2000) **Awards:** Distinguished Flying Award; 10 Air Medals **Memberships:** Arbitrator, American Arbitration Association; Broward County Bar Association; Florida Bar Association **Bar Admissions:** United States Court of Appeals for the Fifth Circuit (1981); United States Court of Appeals for Eleventh Circuits (1981); United States District Court for the Southern District of Florida (1974); Florida Public Service Commission (1974); State of Florida (1974); Florida Supreme Court (1973)

Jean-Philippe Siblet

Title: Museum Director **Industry:** Museums & Institutions **Company Name:** National Museum of Natural History **Date of Birth:** 03/29/1957 **Place of Birth:** Paris **State/Country of Origin:** France **Parents:** Guy Siblet; Suzanne Siblet **Marital Status:** Married **Spouse Name:** Corinne Siblet (06/16/1984) **Education:** Degree in Bird Censusing Methods, University of Burgundy (2000); Degree in Public Law, University Paris II Panthéon-Assas (1980) **Career:** Director, Natural Heritage Service, National Museum of Natural History, Paris, France (2007-Present); Director of Expetise, National Museum of Natural History, Paris, France (2017); Head, Nature Protection Service, Regional Direction of Environment, Paris, France (1988-2007) **Civic:** General Secretary, French Society of Ornithological Studies, Paris, France (2009-2014); President, Association Naturaliste d'Ouessant, Lampaul, France (2009-2014); President, Forest Naturalists' Association, Fontainebleau, France (2008-2014) **Awards:** Honoree, National Merit Order Officer Medal, French Republic President (2016); Honoree, National Merit Order Chevalier Medal, French Republic President (1997); Vermeil Medal, French Agriculture Academy **Memberships:** WPCA; International Union for Conservation of Nature, Gland, Switzerland; National Council of Nature Protection, Paris, France **Avocations:** Birdwatching

Richard Leon "Dick" Sidman, MD

Title: Neuroscientist, Educator **Industry:** Medicine & Health Care **Company Name:** Harvard Medical School **Date of Birth:** 09/19/1928 **Place of Birth:** Boston **State/Country of Origin:** MA/USA **Parents:** Manuel Sidman; Annabelle (Seltzer) Sidman **Marital Status:** Married **Spouse Name:** Ljiljana Lekic-Sidman (1974) **Children:** David Sidman **Education:** Assistant Resident in Neurology, Massachusetts General Hospital, Boston, MA (1955-1956); Intern in Medicine, Boston City Hospital (1953-1954); MD, Harvard University (1953); AB, Harvard University (1949) **Career:** Professor of Neuropathology, Emeritus, Department of Neurosurgery, Brigham and Women's Hospital, Boston (1999-Present); Professor Emeritus, Harvard University Medical School, Boston, MA (1999-Present); Senior Research Associate, Department of Neurology, Beth Israel Deaconess Medical Center, Boston, MA (2001-2016); Chief, Division of Neurogenetics, New England Regional Primate Research Center, Harvard Medical School, Southborough, MA (1991-1999); Bullard Professor, Harvard University Medical School, Boston, MA (1969-1999); Instructor to Professor Neuropathology, Harvard University Medical School, Boston, MA (1959-1969); Staff Scientist, National Institutes of Health, Bethesda, MD (1956-1958) **Career Related:** Bailey Memorial Lecturer, University of Saskatchewan, Canada (1978); Chief, Department of Neuroscience, Children's Hospital, Boston, MA (1972-1988); First Richard Stearns Memorial Lecturer, Albert Einstein College Medicine (1958); Lecturer, University of Texas MD Anderson Cancer Center; Lecturer, Albert Einstein Medical School; Waisman Memorial Lecturer, University of Wisconsin **Civic:** U.S. Public Health Service (1956-1958); Board of Science Overseers, Jackson Laboratory, Bar Harbor, ME; Scientific Advisory Committee, Retinitis Pigmentosa Foundation **Military Service:** Senior Assistant Surgeon (R), USPHS., Laboratory of Neuroanatomical Sciences, NINDB, NIH (1956-1959) **Creative Works:** Co-author, "Atlas of the Mouse Brain and Spinal Cord" (1971); Co-author, "Introduction to Neuropathology" (1968); Co-author, "Neuroanatomy - A Programmed Text, vol. 1" (1965); Co-author, "Catalog of the Neurological Mutants of the Mouse" (1965); Contributor, Numerous Articles, Book Chapters, Reviews on Neuroembryology Pathology and Genetics, Professional Publications **Awards:** Fellow, Neuroscience Research Program (1971-1979); Mosley Traveling Fellow, Harvard University (1954-1955); Boylston Society Essay Prize, Harvard University Medical School (1953); Jeffries Wyman Scholar, Harvard University (1953); Soma Weiss Student Research Prizes (1951-1953) **Memberships:** Fellow, National Academy of Sciences; Fellow, American Academy of Arts and Sciences; American Association for the Advancement of Science; Tissue Culture Association; Society of Neuroscience; Society for Development of Neuroscience; International Society for Development of Neurobiology; Society for Development of Biology; International Brain Research Organization; Histochemical Society; American Society for Cell Biology; American Association of Neuropathologists; American Association of Anatomists; American Academy of Neurology **Marquis Who's Who Honors:** Albert Nelson Marquis Lifetime Achievement Award; Marquis Who's Who Top Professional; Marquis Who's Who Humanitarian Award **To what do you attribute your success:** Concentration on Biomedical Research; Willingness to seek and develop tests for undiscovered biomedical ideas. **Why did you become involved in your profession or industry:** Richard Sidman was a student at Harvard University and he applied to Harvard Medical School as well as a number of other medical schools. He was rejected, so he reached out to his professor, who directed him to a former student who was an assistant professor at a medical school. Mr. Sidman did a year of research, reapplied, and was accepted. He continued his research during his four years in medical school and had a publication record by the time he graduated. Mr. Sidman completed a medical internship, and afterwards he was granted a Harvard traveling research fellowship to England. He ended his clinical research as a physician's assistant resident in neurology. He was assigned to The National Institutes of Health from 1956 to 1959 and built his reputation around his important work.

Arthur Charles Silverman, Esq.

Title: Building Construction Lawyer **Industry:** Law and Legal Services **Company Name:** Rosenberg & Estis, P.C. **Date of Birth:** 06/13/1938 **Place of Birth:** Lewiston **State/Country of Origin:** ME/USA **Parents:** Louis A. Silverman; Frances (Brownstone) Silverman **Marital Status:** Married **Spouse Name:** Donna Zolov (06/18/1961) **Children:** Leonard; Daniel **Education:** JD, Columbia Law School (1964); BS in Industrial Management, Massachusetts Institute of Technology (1961); BEE, Massachusetts Institute of Technology (1960) **Career:** Head, Building Construction Group, Rosenberg & Estis, P.C. (2018-Present); Partner, Duane Morris LLP (2008-2018); Partner, Thelen LLP (Formerly Thelen Reid & Priest) (1989-2008); Partner, Golenbock and Barell (1972-1989); Associate, Golenbock and Barell, NY (1968-1972); Associate, Baer & Marks, NY (1965-1968); Law Clerk for Chief Judge Lumbard, United States Court of Appeals for the Second Circuit (1964-1965); Engineering Assistant, Missile and Space Vehicles and Ordnance Divisions, General Electric, Pittsfield, MA and Philadelphia, PA (1958-1962) **Career Related:** Lawyer, Owner Advisors, Owner Representatives and Construction Managers, Lehrer McGovern, Inc. (Now Lehrer LLC), Lehrer McGovern Bovis, Inc. (Now Lendlease Corporation), Boris Lend Lease LMB, Inc., Schal Bovis Inc., McDevitt Street Bovis Inc., and Bovis Lend Lease Americas (1979-2001); Lawyer, Owners and Developers; Lawyer, National September 11 Memorial & Museum; Lawyer, JetBlue Terminal, John F. Kennedy International Airport, The Port Authority of New York and New Jersey; Lawyer, iTech Uplink Facilities, Home Box Office, Inc.; Lawyer, New Harlem Campus, Lois V. and Samuel J. Silberman School of Social Work at Hunter College; Lawyer, Barbara Walters Campus Center, Sarah Lawrence College; Lawyer, New Learning Center, Barnard College; Lawyer, Eataly Restaurants and Food Markets, Eataly Net USA LLC, Flat Iron District and World Trade Center, New York, NY and Prudential Center, Boston, MA **Civic:** Commission Appointed by New York City Mayor Michael Bloomberg to Find Ways to Reduce Construction Costs of New York City Public Schools (2001); Executive Committee, National Jewish Center for Learning & Leadership (Now CLAL) (1984-1990); Board of Governors, Massachusetts Institute of Technology Hillel International (1979-1984); Past Chair, Board of Trustees, The Ramaz School, New York, NY **Creative Works:** Author, "Getting the Most for Owners in Construction Contracting," The Voice, Construction Users Roundtable (2009) **Awards:** Listee, Top Rated Lawyers in Construction and Super Lawyers Business Edition (2014-2015); Listee, Corporate Counsel's Best Lawyers (2011-2013); Listee, Avenue Magazine's Legal Elite (2010-2014); Listee, America's Leading Lawyers, Chambers & Partners (2008-2017); Listee, The Best Lawyers in America, Construction Law Section, U.S. News & World Report L.P./Best Lawyers (2007-2018); Listee, New York Super Lawyers (2006-2018); Listee, Super Lawyers Corporate Counsel Edition (2006-2013); Named, Leading Construction Lawyer in New York, Chambers & Partners; AV Preeminent Rating, State of Maryland, Martindale-Hubbell; Named, Best Presentation in Moot Court, Columbia Law School **Memberships:** Committee on Construction Law, Association of the Bar of the City of New York (2011-Present); Forum on the Construction Industry, ABA; Section of Litigation, Committee on Construction, ABA; Committee on Design Construction, Section of Real Property, ABA; Business Law Section, ABA; Section on Real Estate, New York State Bar Association; Dispute Resolution Section, New York State Bar Association; Section on Torts, New York State Bar Association; Section on Insurance and Commerce, New York State Bar Association; New York State Society of Professional Engineers; Professional Member, Construction Specifications Institute; Federal Bar Council; Associate Member, National Society of Professional Engineers; Planning, Growth and Sustainability Committee, Higher Education Committee, Healthcare Committee, New York Building Congress **Bar Admissions:** Supreme Court of the United States (1971); New York (1965); United States District Court for the Eastern District of New York; United States District Court for the Southern District of New York **Marquis Who's Who Honors:** Albert Nelson Marquis Lifetime Achievement Award; Marquis Who's Who Top Professional; Marquis Who's Who Humanitarian Award **To what do you attribute your success:** Mr. Silverman attributes his success to the love of what he does. He had an understanding of the construction and design process since his early years in high school. Mr. Silverman also credits his diligence and dedication. **Why did you become involved in your profession or industry:** Mr. Silverman became involved in his profession because he had a passion and interest in construction and design from a young age. **Religion:** Jewish **Thoughts on Life:** Mr. and Mrs. Silverman are the proud grandparents of Jonathan, Rebecca, Gabriel, Benjamin, Jennifer, David, Sarah, Rachel and Ariana. Mr. Silverman has represented owners and developers including the National September 11 Memorial & Museum, the JetBlue Terminal at JFK Airport, high-tech uplink facilities for HBO, the new Harlem campus for the Hunter College School of Social Work of the City University of New York, Eataly, the largest artisan Italian food and wine marketplace in the world and located in a landmark building, and City Point, a complex urban redevelopment, condominium, multi-use project in New York.

Robert Maurer Simmonds

Title: Educator, Web Developer, Operations Research Analyst (Retired) **Industry:** Consulting **Company Name:** Neighborhood Webmaster **Date of Birth:** 04/16/1947 **Place of Birth:** Beaver Falls **State/Country of Origin:** PA/USA **Marital Status:** Married **Spouse Name:** Deborah Lynne Carawan (06/25/1977) **Children:** Stephen Maurer; Kenneth Hayes **Education:** MA, Naval War College (2008); Army Senior Fellowship Program (2006-2009), John F. Kennedy School of Government, Harvard University (2004); EdD, William & Mary (1985); MS, Youngstown State University (1975); BS, Youngstown State University (1972) **Certifications:** Advanced Certification in Education, College of William & Mary (1983) **Career:** Educator, Web Developer, Operations Research Analyst, Neighborhood Webmaster, (2014-Present); Deputy Director, Office and Enlisted Personnel Management, Military Personnel Policy OSD (2008-2012); Senior Army Fellow (2006-2009); Deputy Undersecretary (2006-2009); Senior Operations Researcher, Analyst, U.S. Army Human Resources Command, Washington, DC (2006); Department Chairman, System Engineering Department, U.S. Army Logistics Management College, Fort Lee, NJ (2001-2006); Associate Professor, Florida Institute of Technology (2000-2006); Full Professor, U.S. Army Logistics Management College, Fort Lee, NJ (1988-2001) **Civic:** Elks Lodge 1693, Southern Pines, NC **Military Service:** U.S. Navy, Vietnam War (1965-1968) **Creative Works:** Contributor, "Analysis of Complex Threats (ACT)," Resource Analysis Division (2000); Author, "Adhesive Selection Export System: A Summary Report" (1995); Author, "Neural Networks at ALMC is a SNNAP (Statistical Neural Network Analysis Package)" (1995); Author, "Drug Abuse: A PROBLEM OF SOCIALIZATION," Journal of Drug Education (1987); Contributor, "State Court Caseload Summary Annual Report 1976 -1978" (1979) **Awards:** Featured Listee, Who's Who in America; Featured Listee, Who's Who in Education; Defense Medal for Exceptional Civilian Service, U.S. Navy; Superior Civilian Service Award **Memberships:** Treasurer, Combat Veterans Motorcycle Association (2016-Present); Webmaster, Combat Veterans Motorcycle Association (2015-Present); Board Member, Line Nine Conservation Inc. **Marquis Who's Who Honors:** Albert Nelson Marquis Lifetime Achievement Award; Marquis Who's Who Top Professional **To what do you attribute your success:** Dr. Simmonds attributes his success to his wife, Deborah. He additionally credits education, passion for continuous learning, and his children. **Why did you become involved in your profession or industry:** Dr. Simmonds became involved in his profession because he wanted to serve the Department of Defense and the federal government. **Avocations:** Golfing; Walking dogs; Riding bike with the Combat Veterans Motorcycle Association **Thoughts on Life:** Dr. Simmonds' treats others the way he would like to be treated. He additionally believes that respect is the most important part of any profession. As a veteran, his motto is, "Vets help vets."

Adele Simmons, PhD

Title: Foundation Administrator **Industry:** Nonprofit & Philanthropy **Company Name:** Chicago Metropolis 2020 **Date of Birth:** 06/21/1941 **Place of Birth:** Lake Forest **State/Country of Origin:** IL/USA **Parents:** Hermon Dunlap Smith; Ellen T. (Thorne) Smith **Marital Status:** Married **Spouse Name:** John L. Simmons **Children:** Ian; Erica; Kevin **Education:** Honorary LHD, Tufts University (1994); Honorary LHD, American University (1992); Honorary LHD, Mount Holyoke College (1989); Honorary LHD, Smith College (1988); Honorary LHD, Marlboro College (1987); Honorary LHD, Alverno College (1982); Honorary LHD, University of Massachusetts (1978); Honorary LHD, Franklin Pierce College (1978); Honorary LHD, Amherst College (1977); Honorary LHD, Lake Forest College (1976); PhD, Oxford University, England (1969); BA in Social Studies, Harvard University, with Honors (1963) **Career:** The Chicago Community Trust, Chicago, IL, (Present); Vice Chair, Senior Executive, Chicago Metropolis 2020 (1999-2009); Senior Associate, Center for International Studies, University of Chicago (1999-2005); President, John D. and Catherine T. MacArthur Foundation (1989-1999); President, Hampshire College, Amherst, Massachusetts (1977-1989); Assistant Professor of History, Dean of Student Affairs, Princeton University (1972-1977); Dean, Jackson College (1970-1972); Assistant Professor, Tufts University (1969-1972) **Career Related:** High Level Advisory Board UN (1993-Present); Board of Overseers, Harvard University (1972-1978); Board of Directors Marsh & McLennan Companies; Shorebank Corporation, Chicago; Union of Concerned Scientists; Synergos Institute; Environmental Defense; Board Member, American Prospect; Board of Directors, Field Museum, Chicago; Mexican Fine Arts Center Museum; Chicago Council on Foreign Relations; Winning Workplaces; Emeritus Member, Board of Directors, Rocky Mountain Institute; Advisory Committee, World Bank Institute; Chairman, Fair Labor Association; Senior Advisor, World Economic Forum **Civic:** Chair, Mayor Richard Daley's Youth Development Task Force (1993-1995); President's Commission on Environmental Quality (1991-1992); Global Governance Trustee, Carnegie Foundation for Advancement Teaching (1978-1986); Commissioner, President's Commission on World Hunger (1978-1980) **Creative Works:** Author, "Modern Mauritius" (1982); Co-author, "Exploitation from 9 to 5: Twentieth Century Fund Task Force Report on Working Women" (1975); Contributor, Articles on Education and Public Policy **Awards:** One of Chicago's 100 Most Influential Women, Crain's Chicago Busines (2004) **Memberships:** Fellow, American Academy of Arts and Sciences; Phi Beta Kappa **Marquis Who's Who Honors:** Albert Nelson Marquis Lifetime Achievement Award **Why did you become involved in your profession or industry:** What initially inspired Dr. Simmons to get involved in her profession is her father Hermon Dunlap Smith. He was very engaged in civil society issues and a leading corporate business man. Her great-grandmother founded the first juvenile court in the United States. She has a long family history of being engaged in important civic issues. Her god-father was Adlai Stevenson whom ran for President. She had many chances to talk with amazing people who inspired her to get involved in things at a time when women were not. **Avocations:** Hiking; Sailing; Water skiing

Lee Guyton Simmons Jr., DVM

Title: Chairman of the Board **Industry:** Veterinary Care **Company Name:** Omaha Zoo Foundation **Date of Birth:** 02/20/1938 **Place of Birth:** Tucson **State/Country of Origin:** AZ/USA **Parents:** Lee Guyton Simmons Sr.; Dorothy Esther (Taylor) Simmons **Marital Status:** Married **Spouse Name:** Marie Annette Geim Simmons (09/06/1959) **Children:** Lee Guyton III; Heather Ann; Heidi Marie **Education:** Honorary Doctor of Science, Midland Lutheran College (2009); Honorary Doctor of Science, University of Nebraska at Omaha (2002); Honorary Doctorate in Zoological Science, Creighton University (1993); Doctor of Veterinary Medicine, Oklahoma State University, Stillwater, OK (1963); Pre-Veterinary Studies, Central State College, Edmond, OK (1957-1959) **Certifications:** Veterinary Medical License, Nebraska (1967); Veterinary Medical License, Ohio (1964); Veterinary Medical License, Oklahoma (1963) **Career:** Chairman of the Board, Omaha Zoo Foundation (2009-Present); Board of Directors, Treasurer, Omaha Zoo Foundation (1982-2009); Executive Director, Omaha's Henry Doorly Zoo and Aquarium (1970-2009); Associate Director, Omaha's Henry Doorly Zoo and Aquarium (1967-1970); Resident Veterinarian, Omaha's Henry Doorly Zoo and Aquarium (1966-1970); Mammals Curator, Columbus Municipal Zoo, Powell, OH (1963-1964); Assistant Superintendent & Resident Veterinarian, Columbus Municipal Zoo, Ohio; (1964-1966) **Career Related:** Associate Clinical Professor, Oral Biology, Creighton University School of Dentistry (1989); North American Species Coordinator, Gaur (1981-2009); Chairman, Animal Research Committee, VA Hospital, Omaha, NE (1980-1990); Research Consultant, VA Hospital, Omaha, NE (1967-1990); Guest Lecturer, College of Veterinary Medicine, Ohio State University (1963-1966) **Civic:** Advisory Board, Salvation Army (2009-Present); Save the Tiger Fund, Exxon Corporation, National Fish & Wildlife Foundation (1995-1999); Board of Directors, Nebraska State Museum, Lincoln, NE; National Advisory Board, Platte River Whooping Crane Maintenance Trust Inc. **Military Service:** Medical Assistant, 179th Battle Group Surgeon, Oklahoma National Guard (1963); Military Police, U.S. Army Reserves (1959-1963, 1955-1959); Board of Directors, 55th Wing; Co-Commander, Civil Engineering, Offutt Air Force Base Advisory Council **Creative Works:** United States Patent 3,880,162, Simmons Pole Syringe (1975); Author, Memoir, "Doc – Zoo Memories and Animal Stories"; Author, "The Lied Jungle"; Author, Contributor, 95 Medical and Scientific Articles, Professional Journals; Inventor, Manufacturer, Five Models, The Zoolu Arms **Awards:** Nebraskalander Legend, Nebraska Press Association (2019); Conservationist of the Year, Royal Game Dinner, Nebraska Game and Parks Commission (2019); Distinguished Citizen Award, West Point Society of Nebraska and Western Iowa (2015); Citizen of the Year, Mid-America Council, Boy Scouts of America (2014); Ulysses S. Seal Innovation in Conservation Award, CBSG (2013); Inductee, Business Hall of Fame, Nebraska Chamber of Commerce (2013); D.J.'s Hero Award, Salvation Army (2010); Named, King of Quivira 113th, Knights of Aksarben (2009); Man of the Year Award, Suburban Rotary (2009); Center for Veterinary Health Sciences Distinguished Alumnus, Oklahoma State University (2007); Co-Recipient, Jason Award, Childrens Square USA (2007); Inductee, Court of Honor, Knights of Aksarben (2005); Inductee, Business Hall of Fame, Greater Omaha Chamber of Commerce (2004); Henry Fonda Nebraskan Award, Gov. Mike Johanns of the Nebraska Division of Travel and Tourism (2003); Pathfinder Award, Fremont Area Art Association (1998); Prestigious Vision Award, State of Nebraska (1995); Humanitarian of the Year, Sons of Italy Nebraska State Lodge (1995) **Memberships:** Founding Board Member, Global Conservation Network (1991-Present); Board of Scientific Advisors, International Wildlife Institute (2003); Acting Chairman, Steering Committee, Conservation Breeding Specialist Group (2002-2003); Quarantine Specialist Committee, American Zoo and Aquarium Association (2000); University of Nebraska at Omaha Chapter, Omicron Delta Kappa (1993); President, American Association of Zoo Veterinarians (1987); Board of Directors, American Association of Zoos, Parks and Aquariums (1985-1988); Secretary, Treasurer, Vice President, Board of Directors, American Association of Zoo Veterinarians (1984-1986); President, Nebraska Academy of Veterinary Medicine (1980); Executive Board, Omaha Zoological Society (1970-2009); Fellow, Life Member, American Veterinary Medical Association; World Zoo Association; International Union for Conservation of Nature; Board of Directors, Nebraska Veterinary Medical Association **To what do you attribute your success:** Dr. Simmons attributes his success to being lucky enough to find a profession that not only was challenging and stimulating, but also fun to do. He loves the surprises and challenges of what he will face every day at work. **Why did you become involved in your profession or industry:** Dr. Simmons' original passion was herpetology. He initially sought to become a herpetologist specializing in reptile curation but, while volunteering at the Omaha City Zoo, decided that he wanted to have a say in zoo policy and knowledge. With encouragement from a veterinarian colleague, he entered the field of veterinary medicine. **Avocations:** Fishing; Working shop; Wildlife photography **Religion:** Christian

John G. Simon

Title: Augustus Lines Professor Emeritus of Law **Industry:** Education/Educational Services **Date of Birth:** 09/19/1928 **Place of Birth:** New York **State/Country of Origin:** NY/USA **Parents:** Robert Alfred; Madeleine (Marshall) Simon **Marital Status:** Married **Spouse Name:** Claire Aloise Bising, (6/14/1958) **Children:** John Kirby (deceased) **Education:** LLD (honorary), Indiana University (1989); LLB, Yale University (1953); AB, Harvard University (1950); Graduate, Ethical Culture Fieldston School (1946) **Certifications:** New York (1953) **Career:** Augustus Lines Professor Emeritus Law, Yale Law School (2003-Present); Acting Dean, Yale Law School (1991); Deputy Dean, Yale Law School (1985-1990); Acting Dean, Yale University (1977-1988); Augustus Lines Professor of Law, Yale Law School (1976-2003); Professor law, Yale Law School, (1967-1976); Member faculty, Yale Law School (1962-2003); With firm, Paul, Weiss, Rifkind, Wharton & Garrison, New York, (1958-1962); Assistant to General Counsel, United States Secretary of the Army (1956-1958) **Civic:** President, Taconic Foundation (1967-Present); Trustee, Secretary Potomac Institute (1961-1993); Member, Graduate Board, Harvard Crimson (1950-Present); Chairman, Board of Directors, Cooperative Assistance Fund (1970-1976) Vice Chairman (1977-Present); Member, Governing Council, Rockefeller Archives Center (1982-1986); Trustee, The Foundation Center (1983-1992); Open Society Foundations, NY (1996-2007) **Military Service:** 1st lieutenant, U.S. Army, (1953-1956) **Creative Works:** Co-Author, with Powers and Gunnemann, "The Ethical Investor" (1972) **Awards:** Recipient, Certificate of Achievement, The United States Department of the Army (1956) **Memberships:** Member, Phi Beta Kappa **Marquis Who's Who Honors:** Albert Nelson Marquis Lifetime Achievement Award **Why did you become involved in your profession or industry:** Mr. Simon became involved in his profession because he saw various controversies in the newspaper that were resolved successfully and honorably by attorneys and he thought that was a good profession to be in.

Harold Yazzie Simpson

Title: Founder, Owner **Industry:** Leisure, Travel & Tourism **Company Name:** Simpson's Trailhandler Tours **Place of Birth:** Oljato-Monument Valley **State/Country of Origin:** UT/USA **Career:** Founder, Owner, Operator, Simpson's Trailhandler Tours, Monument Valley, UT (1996-Present) **Civic:** Volunteer, Reaching the Summit **Marquis Who's Who Honors:** Marquis Who's Who Top Professional **To what do you attribute your success:** Mr. Simpson attributes his success to networking. **Why did you become involved in your profession or industry:** Mr. Simpson became involved in his profession because he was inspired by the beautiful area where he grew up called Monument Valley. Born and raised in a Native American environment, he felt a natural pull to establish his company.

Michael Simpson

Title: Retired Metals Service Center Executive **Industry:** Utilities **Company Name:** A.M. Castle & Co. **Date of Birth:** 12/10/1938 **Place of Birth:** Albany **State/Country of Origin:** NY/USA **Parents:** John McLaren Simpson; Constance (Hasler) Ames **Marital Status:** Married **Spouse Name:** Barbara Ann Bodtke (01/05/1963) **Children:** Leslie Ann; Elizabeth S. Wessel **Education:** MBA, Marketing, University of Michigan (1966); BA, Economics, University of Michigan (1965) **Career:** Chairman Emeritus, A.M. Castle & Co. (2004-2012); Board of Directors, A.M. Castle & Co. (1973-2012); With, A.M. Castle & Co., Franklin Park, IL (1968-2012); Chairman of the Board, A.M. Castle & Co. (1979-2004); Vice President, Midwestern Region, A.M. Castle & Co. (1977-1979); President, Hy-Alloy Steels Co. Division, A.M. Castle & Co. (1974-1979); Product Manager, Armour & Co., Chicago, IL (1966-1968) **Career Related:** Chairman, Executive Committee, Steel Service Center Institute, (Now Metal Service Center Institute (MSCI)) (1982-1984) **Civic:** Life Trustee, Rush University Medical Center, Chicago, IL (2009-Present); Chairman of the Board of Overseers, Rush University, Chicago, IL (1996-2009); Vice Chairman, Rush University Medical Center, Chicago, IL (1991-2009); Executive Committee, Rush University Medical Center, Chicago, IL (1982-2009); Trustee, Rush University Medical Center, Chicago, IL (1978-2009); Board of Directors, Lake Forest Hospital Foundation and Lake Forest Hospital, IL (1998-2008); Trustee, Oldfields School, Glencoe, MD (1982-1987, 1995-2003); Chairman of the Board, Oldfields School, Glencoe, MD (1998-2000) **Military Service:** U.S. Marine Corps Reserve (1957-1963) **Marquis Who's Who Honors:** Albert Nelson Marquis Lifetime Achievement Award

Allen L. Sinai, PhD

Title: Chief Global Economist/Strategist & President **Company Name:** Decision Economics, Inc **Date of Birth:** 04/04/1939 **Place of Birth:** Detroit **State/Country of Origin:** MI/USA **Parents:** Joseph Sinai; Betty Paula (Feinberg) Sinai **Marital Status:** Married **Spouse Name:** Lee Davis Etsten (06/23/1963) **Children:** Lauren Beth; Todd Michael **Education:** PhD in Economics, Northwestern University (1969); MA in Economics, Northwestern University (1966); AB in Economics (Honors), University of Michigan, with Honors (1961) **Career:** Chief Global Economist/Strategist & President, Decision Economics, Inc., New York, Boston, London (1996-Present); President, Laural Consulting, Evanston, IL, Lexington, MA (1969-Present); Global Chief Economist, Executive Vice President, Global Insight, Inc., Lexington, MA (2001-2003); Chief Global Economist, Vice-Chairman, WEFA Group (1997-2000); Managing Director, Chief Global Economist, Lehman Brothers Inc., New York, NY (1993-1996); President, Chief Executive Officer, Boston Co. Economic Advisors Inc., Boston, New York (1988-1993); Chief Economist, Executive Vice President, The Boston Co. Inc. (1988-1993); Chief Economist, Managing Director, Lehman Brothers Global Economics, New York, NY (1983-1988); Senior Vice President, Co-Chairman, Financial Information Group, Chief Financial Economist, Data Resources, Lexington, MA (1971-1983). **Career Related:** Economic Leadership Council, University of Michigan (2007-Present); Advisory Board Gerald R. Ford School of Public Policy, University of Michigan (2004-Present); Board of Directors, Boston Private Financial Holdings, Inc. (1995-2014); Boston Private Bank (1992-1995); Board of Economists, Time Magazine (1991-2003); Visiting Faculty, MIT (1976-1979), Sloan School, Massachusetts Institute of Technology, Cambridge (1989-1991); Adjunct Professor of Economics and Finance, Lemberg School, Brandeis University (1988-1995); Adjunct Professor of Economics, New York University, New York, NY (1984-1988); Boston University (1981-1983); Boston University(1975-1977) (1977-1978) Visiting Associate Professor of Economics and Finance; From Assistant Professor to Professor of Economics, University of Illinois, Chicago, IL (1966-1975) **Civic:** Economic Policy Adviser, Republican and Democratic Administrations, U.S. Congress, Congressional Testimonies, Washington, DC (1975-Present); Consultant, Board of Governors, Federal Reserve (1995); Board of Directors, International Banking Economics and Finance Association; Economists for Peace & Security (1994-Present); Committee on Developing American Capitalism (1990-1995) and member (1984-1996); Reducing Federal Budget Deficit Task Force, Roosevelt Center, Washington, DC (1984) **Creative Works:** Contributor, over 100 articles to Professional and Academic Journals; Contributor, Chapters to Books, Lectures, Conferences and Speeches **Awards:** John Sweetland Award, University of Michigan Department of Economics (2016); Named Top Forecaster, Market Watch (2004); USA Today (2003) (2005); Wall St. Journal (2006); Business Week (1997); named One of Ten Smartest Men in Boston, Boston Magazine (1993); Otto Eckstein Prize (1988); Alumnus Merit Award, Northwestern University (1985) **Memberships:** President, North America Economics and Financial Association (2004-2005); Vice President, North America Economics and Finance Association (2003-2004); Board of Directors; Western Economic Association (1995-1997); President, Eastern Economics Association (1990-1991); Vice President, Eastern Economics Association (1988-1989); Econometric Society, American Economics Association. **Marquis Who's Who Honors:** Albert Nelson Marquis Lifetime Achievement Award; Marquis Who's Who Top Professional **Why did you become involved in your profession or industry:** Mr. Sinai became involved in his profession to discover what makes the world tick using the window of economics and markets. He feels he has a window on the world as an economist, analyst, observer, researcher, forecaster, investor and business person. For him, economics and its applications open the world to someone who is extremely curious, always learning, and wants to know why things happen the way they do. He came from a poor background in Detroit. His father Joseph was an immigrant from Russia/Poland who had no education, but what he did have was honesty and a hard working ethic that made it possible for his son Allen to go to the University of Michigan. That changed his world. His mother was a bookkeeper. **Avocations:** Tennis; Skiing; Golf; Bicycling; Wellness **Religion:** Jewish

Frederick Raphael Singer, MD

Title: Medical Researcher **Industry:** Medicine & Health Care **Company Name:** John Wayne Cancer Institute **Date of Birth:** 06/27/1939 **Place of Birth:** St. Louis **State/Country of Origin:** MO/USA **Parents:** Meyer Singer; Lee (Minkle) Singer **Marital Status:** Married **Spouse Name:** Sandra Joy Singer (08/16/1964) **Children:** Stephanie; Jeffrey **Education:** Resident, Veterans Affairs Hospital, Los Angeles, CA (1968-1969); Resident, Veterans Affairs Hospital, Los Angeles, CA (1964-1965); Intern, University of California, Los Angeles Affiliated Hospital (1963-1964); MD, University of California San Francisco (1963); BS, University of California Berkeley (1960); Coursework, University of California Los Angeles (1956-1959) **Certifications:** Diplomate, American Board of Internal Medicine; Diplomate, American Board of Endocrinology and Metabolism **Career:** Clinical Professor of Medicine, David Geffen School of Medicine, University of California Los Angeles (1992-Present); Director of Bone Center, Cedars-Sinai Medical Center, Los Angeles, CA (1989-1992); Professor of Orthopedic Surgery, University of Southern California, Los Angeles, CA (1980-1989); Professor, University of Southern California, Los Angeles, CA (1978-1989); Associate Professor, University of Southern California, Los Angeles, CA (1974-1978); Assistant Professor of Medicine, University of Southern California, Los Angeles, CA (1973-1974); Assistant Professor of Medicine, University of California, Los Angeles (1972-1973); Instructor in Medicine, Harvard University, Boston, MA (1971-1972); Medical Researcher **Career Related:** Director, Osteoporosis/Metabolic Bone Disease Program, St. John's Hospital and Health Center, Santa Monica, CA (1992-Present); Director, Skeletal Biology Lab, John Wayne Cancer Institute, Santa Monica, CA (1992-Present); Endocrine and Metabolic Drug Advisory Committee, Food and Drug Administration, Bethesda, MD (1983-1987) **Civic:** Vice Chairman, Community Advisory Committee, University High School, Los Angeles, CA (1984); Clinical Investigator, Veterans Affairs Hospital (1971-1973) **Military Service:** Captain, U.S. Air Force (1965-1967) **Creative Works:** Author, "Paget's Disease of Bone" (1977); Contributor, Articles and Reviews, Professional Journals; Contributor, Chapters, Books **Awards:** William H. Oldendorf Lifetime Achievement Award, West Los Angeles Veterans Affairs Medical Center (2014); Constellation Award, Fibrous Dysplasia Foundation (2008); John Johnson Award, The Paget Foundation (1990); California State Scholarship (1956-1960) **Memberships:** Board of Trustees, National Osteoporosis Foundation (2017-Present); Board of Directors, Fibrosis Dysplasia Foundation (2006-Present); Chairman, Board of Directors, Paget's Disease Foundation (1990-2006); President, American Society of Bone and Mineral Research (1990); President-Elect, American Society of Bone and Mineral Research (1989); Council, American Society of Bone and Mineral Research (1987); Chairman of Public Affairs, American Society of Bone and Mineral Research (1981-1986); Endocrine Society; American Society of Clinical Investigation **Marquis Who's Who Honors:** Albert Nelson Marquis Lifetime Achievement Award; Marquis Who's Who Top Professional; Distinguished Humanitarian **Why did you become involved in your profession or industry:** In high school, Dr. Singer was talking with a teacher and he told him he didn't know what he wanted to do. The teacher replied, "Be a doctor!" Consequently, that's how Dr. Singer was inspired to enter his career. **Avocations:** Music; Theater; Tennis **Political Affiliations:** Independent

1186 • Distinguished Listees

Jag Jeet Singh, PhD

Title: Research Physicist **Industry:** Sciences **Date of Birth:** 05/20/1926 **Place of Birth:** Rohtak **State/Country of Origin:** Haryana/India **Parents:** Shubh Ram Singh; Dhan Kaur (Nandal) Singh **Marital Status:** Single **Children:** Surinder Kumar **Education:** Postdoctoral Research Associate, University of Kansas, Lawrence (1958-1960); PhD, University of Liverpool, England (1956); MSc, Panjab University, Chandigarh, India (1950) **Certifications:** Chartered Physicist, United Kingdom **Career:** Chief Scientist, Instrument Research Division, NASA Langley Research Center, Hampton, VA (1980-2015); Research Scientist, NASA Langley Research Center, Hampton, VA (1964-1980); Associate Professor, Physics, College William and Mary, Williamsburg, VA (1962-1964); Associate Professor, Physics, West Virginia State College, Institute (1960-1962); Lecturer, Physics, Panjab Educational Service, Ludhiana, India (1950-1953) **Career Related:** Promoted to Senior Executive Service (SES) (1991); Appointed Associate Chief, Division of the Experimental Testing and Technology Division (ETTD) (1991); Joined NASA Langley-Research Center, Hampton, VA (1964); Member, Advisory Board to Governor, State of Virginia (1962-1964) **Civic:** Consultant, Nuclear-radiology Department, York County CD, Yorktown, VA (1985); Board of Directors, Council for Environmental Quality, Hampton, VA (1972-1974) **Creative Works:** Editor, "Environmental and Climatic Impacts" (1980); Contributor, Over 200 Articles, Professional Journals **Awards:** Designated "Distinguished Research Scientist (1991); Medal for Exceptional Science Achievements, NASA (1990); Special Science Achievement Award (1990); Technology Utilization Awards, NASA Langley Research Center (1977, 1983, 1986-1988, 1990); Outstanding Performance Award (1981, 1986, 1989); Scholar, Panjab University (1943, 1945, 1947); Awarded Honorary DSc, Honorary LittD, International Biographical Center, Cambridge, England **Memberships:** Fellow, American Association for the Advancement of Science; Fellow, American Institute of Aeronautics and Astronautics; Fellow, American Physical Society; Fellow, British Institute Physics; Fellow, Explorers Society; Elected Fellow, British Physical Society (IOP); Elected Fellow, American Physical Society (APS); Elected Fellow, American Association for Advancement of Science (AAAS); Elected Fellow, American Institute of Aeronautics and Astronauts (AIAA) **Marquis Who's Who Honors:** Albert Nelson Marquis Lifetime Achievement Award **Why did you become involved in your profession or industry:** Dr. Jag Singh has always liked science and mathematics as a young boy and combining physics and mathematics led him to being a physicist and a scientist. His father was a general in the British Indian Army and he wanted Dr. Singh to do his best, he told Dr. Singh, he should decide what his best was going to be. His mother told him to treat everybody like a lady or a gentleman until they prove themselves otherwise, Dr. Singh was greatly encouraged by his parents.

John Francis Sipos Jr.

Title: Historian for Village of Cassadaga, and Town of Stockton, NY **Industry:** Education/Educational Services **Company Name:** Chautauqua County New York Historians **Date of Birth:** 07/06/1944 **Place of Birth:** Homer City **State/Country of Origin:** PA/USA **Parents:** John Francis Sipos; Katherine Bracken Sipos **Marital Status:** Married **Spouse Name:** Susan Washington Sipos (08/22/1970) **Education:** MS in Mathematics, The State University of New York Fredonia (1983); BS in Mathematics, The State University of New York Geneseo (1966) **Certifications:** Secondary Mathematics in Education **Career:** Retired from Education (1999); Historian, Village of Cassadaga, NY (15 Years); Historian, Town of Stockton, NY (Three Years); Education Field (33 Years) **Career Related:** Mathematics Department Chairman, Frontier Central High School, Hamburg, NY (17 Years); Coordinator, Gifted and Talented Program, Junior High School **Civic:** Vice President, Meals on Wheels, Cassadaga Valley, NY (1999-Present); Historian, Secretary, The Thule Lodge #127 Swedish Organization (1999-Present); Chautauqua County Genealogical Society(1999-Present); Member, of the Hamburg Presbyterian Church, NY (1956-Present); Moderator, Sunday School Teacher, Vacation Bible School Director, and Sunday School Superintendent, Cassadaga Community Baptist Church, NY (24 Years); Former Board member, Cassadaga Cemetery Association (Seven Years); Advisor, Cassadaga Cemetery Association; Treasurer, Cassadaga Valley Historical Society (Now The Valley Historical Society); Served, Bicentennial Celebration Committee, Village of Cassadaga, NY **Awards:** National Community Service Award, Jamestown Chapter, National Society Daughters of the American Revolution, Jamestown Chapter, NY (2015); Named Kiwanian of the Year, Cassadaga Valley Kiwanis (2005); Named Outstanding Teacher of the Year, PTA (1995); Named to First Edition of Who's Who in America's Teachers (1990); Named Sixth-time Parade Marshall, Annual Cassadaga Memorial Day Parade **Memberships:** Chautauqua County Historical Society; Association of Public Historians of New York State (APHNYS); Western New York Association of Historical Agencies (WNYAHA); Government Appointed Historians of Western New York (GAHWNY); The Valley Historical Society; New York State Retired Teachers' Association (NYSRTA); Hilltop Spinning Wheel Association; Thule Lodge Swedish Organization #127; Ingald Lodge Vikings #65; Library Association, Cassadaga, NY **Marquis Who's Who Honors:** Marquis Who's Who Top Professional **To what do you attribute your success:** Mr. Sipos attributes his success to his interest in the field of education, his interest in the community, and his willingness to share his historical knowledge. **Thoughts on Life:** Mr. Sipos was a four-year member of the varsity swimming team at the State University of New York Geneseo.

Morton Sipress

Title: Political Scientist, Professor Emeritus **Industry:** Education/Educational Services **Company Name:** University of Wisconsin-Eau Claire **Date of Birth:** 03/23/1938 **Place of Birth:** Brooklyn **State/Country of Origin:** NY/USA **Parents:** Philip Sipress; Delia (Shapiro) Sipress **Marital Status:** Widower **Spouse Name:** Sylvia Ruth Margulies, (08/20/1967, Deceased 2016) **Children:** Neal; Matthew; Judith **Education:** Postgraduate Coursework, University of Minnesota (1966); MA in Political Science, University of Minnesota (1964); BA in Political Science, City College of New York (1961) **Career:** Emeritus, University of Wisconsin-Eau Claire (2000-Present); Chair, University Senate, University of Wisconsin-Eau Claire (1993-1995); Associate Professor, University of Wisconsin-Eau Claire (1985-2000); Assistant Professor, University of Wisconsin-Eau Claire (1971-1985); Instructor, Wisconsin State University, Eau Claire (1966-1971); Teaching Assistant, University of Minnesota, Minneapolis, MI (1962-1966); Residence Counselor, University of Minnesota, Minneapolis, MI (1961-1965) **Career Related:** Political Campaign Consultant (1989-Present); Radio and TV Election Analyst, Eau Claire, WI (1978-Present) **Civic:** Chair, A-Team, Western Wisconsin-Advocacy for the Disabled (2014-2017); President, Temple Sholom, Eau Claire, WI (1972-1990); 3rd Congressional District (1985-1988); Future Directions Commission (1984-1986); Caucus Implementation Commission (1983-1984); Board of Directors, Child and Family Service Society, Eau Claire, WI (1979-1985); Chairman, Platform Committee Democratic Party of Wisconsin (1978-1982) **Creative Works:** Editor, "Wisconsin Political Scientist" (1992-Present); Co-Author, "Wisconsin Government and Politics" (1987); Author, "Instructor's Manual to Government in America" 2nd Edition (1983) **Awards:** Teaching Assistantship, University of Minnesota (1962-1965) **Memberships:** President, Wisconsin Political Science Association (1985-1986); President, B'nai B'rith, Eau Claire Chapter (1972-1990); American Political Science Association; Midwest Political Science Association **Marquis Who's Who Honors:** Albert Nelson Marquis Lifetime Achievement Award; Marquis Who's Who Top Professional **Why did you become involved in your profession or industry:** Interested in politics for quite some time, Professor Sipress majored in the field in college. When he graduated, he attended the University of Minnesota Graduate School, which motivated him to pursue a career in education. **Avocations:** Photography of landscapes and flowers; Advocate for people with disabilities **Religion:** Jewish

Vicki Skeen

Title: Director of Delivery and Customer Enablement **Industry:** Business Management/Business Services **Company Name:** Openet, Inc. **Education:** BBA, Eastern Michigan University (1986) **Career:** Director of Delivery and Customer Enablement, Openet, (2019-Present)Director, High Touch Customer Care, Openet (2017-2019) Director, PMO, Openet (2009-2017)Executive Director, Customer Support and Operations, Ardacom (2008-2009) Language Production Manager, SpinVox (2007-2008)Director, Service Account Management, SpinVox (2007)Global Manager, Program Operations, Project Operations & Training, IP Unity Glenayre (1996-2007) **Memberships:** Project Management Association; SpinBox Alumni Association; Glenayre Alumni Association; Eastern Michigan Alumni Association **Marquis Who's Who Honors:** Marquis Who's Who Top Professional **To what do you attribute your success:** She attributes her success to her love of being challenged. She wants to be excited every morning when her feet hit the floor **Why did you become involved in your profession or industry:** She fell into the profession, when she was in college she wanted to be a nurse, she made the grades, by the time she was a junior she didn't get in because there were so many applicants. So she had do decide what to do and she switched directions to a business degree. An old boss of hers said her husband worked for a company and he was looking for someone to do business proposals and she went to work for him and she moved up and it blossomed from there.

Andrew E. Sloan, MD, FACS

Title: Professor, Vice Chair of Neurosurgery **Industry:** Medicine & Health Care **Company Name:** University Hospitals, Case Western Reserve University **State/Country of Origin:** MI/USA **Marital Status:** Married **Spouse Name:** Jill **Children:** Chase **Education:** Fellow in Neurosurgery, University of Texas MD Anderson Cancer Center (1997-1998); Chief Resident in Neurosurgery, University of California Los Angeles (1996-1997); Resident in Neurosurgery, University of California Los Angeles (1991-1996); MD, Harvard Medical School, Harvard University (1990); BS in Biology, Yale University (1985) **Certifications:** Neurological Surgery, American Board of Neurological Surgery **Career:** Case Medical Center, University Hospitals (2015-Present); Professor, Case Western Reserve University (2014-Present); Vice-Chair, Department of Neurological Surgery, Case Western Reserve University (2014-Present); Director of Stereotactic Radiosurgery, Case Medical Center, University Hospital Seidman Cancer Center (2007-Present); Peter D. Cristal Chair of Neurosurgery, Center for Translational Neuroscience, University Hospitals (2007-Present); Director, Brain Tumor and Neuro-oncology Center, Seidman Cancer Center, University Hospitals (2007-Present); Director of Stereotactic Radiosurgery, Moffitt Cancer Center (2004-2007); Associate Professor, Wayne State University (1999-2004); Director, Brain Tumor Program, Karmanos Cancer Institute (1998-2004); Director, Brain Tumor and Neuro-oncology Center, Wayne State University (1997-2004) **Creative Works:** Author, 200 Publications, Peer-Reviewed Journals; Author, Numerous Editorials, Reviews, 35 Book Chapters; Speaker, Over 525 Invited Presentations; Patentee, Four Patents, Investigational New Drug (IND) Applications **Awards:** Top Surgeons in America (2007-Present); Best Doctors in America (2003-Present); Grantee, Chemoprotection and Immune Remodeling After Hematopoietic Progenitor Cell Gene Therapy for Glioblastoma, National Cancer Institute (2019); Neuro-oncology Award, Congress of Neurological Surgery (2016); Dean's Research Award (2016); Distinguished Doctor Award, Expert Network/Castle Connolly (2016); Neuro-Oncology Award, Congress of Neurological Surgeons (2016); Exemplary Teaching Award, Case Western University School of Medicine (2015); Mahaley Award for Clinical Research, American Association of Neurological Surgeons and National Brain Tumor Foundation (2013); Clinical Research Career Development Award, American Society of Clinical Oncology (2000); Clinician Investigator Award, American Brain Tumor Association (1999) **Memberships:** Congress of Neurological Surgeons (1995-Present); President, Ohio State Neurosurgical Society (2014-2015); American Association of Neurological Surgeons (1990-2013); Fellow, American College of Surgeons Oncology Group; American Society of Clinical Oncology; American Association of Neurological Surgeons; Tumors Executive Committee, Joint Section, Congress of Neurological Surgeons **Marquis Who's Who Honors:** Albert Nelson Marquis Lifetime Achievement Award; Marquis Who's Who Top Professional **To what do you attribute your success:** Dr. Sloan attributes his success to hard work and preparation. **Why did you become involved in your profession or industry:** Dr. Sloan has always been fascinated by the brain and science. Fortunately, he had the opportunity to find a field that would blend the two, incorporating the inner workings of the brain and his fascination regarding science. **Thoughts on Life:** Dr. Sloan lives by the motto, "Aim high."

Kathleen Overin Slobin, PhD

Title: Professor Emerita, Consultant **Industry:** Education/Educational Services **Date of Birth:** 07/18/1942 **Place of Birth:** Santa Ana **State/Country of Origin:** CA/USA **Parents:** Courtenay Stuyvesant Overin; Janet Kathleen (Raitt) Church **Marital Status:** Widow. **Spouse Name:** Margaret K. Scott (10/21/2008, Deceased 2018); Dan Isaac Slobin (05/21/1969, Divorced 1983); Barry A. Gordon (1962-1968, Divorced) **Children:** Heida Q. Slobin Shoemaker; Shem Alexander Slobin **Education:** PhD in Medical Sociology, University of California, San Francisco (1991); MPA, California State University, Hayward (now California State University, East Bay) (1984); MFA in Fine Arts-Painting, California College of the Arts (1980); BA in Psychology, Pomona College, Claremont, CA (1964) **Career:** Professor Emerita, North Dakota State University, Fargo, ND (2007-Present); Professor, North Dakota State University, Fargo, ND (2004-2007); Chair, Department of Sociology-Anthropology, North Dakota State University, Fargo, ND (2003-2006); Director, Women's Studies and Founder of WISMET (Women in Science, Math, Engineering, & Technology) North Dakota State University, Fargo, ND (1997-2002); Associate Professor, North Dakota State University, Fargo, ND (1997-2004); Assistant Professor, Sociology, North Dakota State University, Fargo, ND (1991-1996); Staff Research Associate, University of California (1990); Research Assistant, University of California (1986-1990); Associate Director, Continuing Education Department of Psychiatry, University of California (1983-1986); Coordinator, Education, National Energy Foundation, San Francisco, CA (1982); Instructor, Fine Arts, Indian Valley Community College, Novato, CA (1981-1982) **Career Related:** Instructor, Cappadocia University Community College, Mustafa Pasa, Turkey (2010-2011); Research Associate, Center for Study of Women in Society, Graduate Center, City University of New York (2002-2003); Research Analyst, Refugees in the Community, Fargo, ND (2002, 1993-1995); Researcher, Consultant, West River Regional Medical Center, Hettinger, ND (1994-1998) **Civic:** Society of Asian Arts, Board Member, San Francisco, CA (2019-Present); Storyteller, Asian Art Museum, San Francisco, CA (2010-Present); Docent, California Academy Sciences (2008-Present) **Creative Works:** Group Coordinator, California Pacific Medical Center (2018-Present); "Repairing Broken Rules: Care Seeking Narratives for Menstrual Problems in Mali," Medical Anthropology Quarterly (1998); Editor, SWS Network News, Society for Women Sociologists (1997-2000); Co-Author, Journal, Book Chapter, "Refugees in the Fargo Community: A Research Agenda" (1996); Author, "Healing Through the Use of Symbolic Technology Among the Dogon of Mali," High Plains Applied Anthropology (1996); Author, Journal, Book Chapter, "Field Work and Subjectivity: On the Ritualization of Seeing a Burned Child," Symbolic Interaction (1995); Author, Journal, "Family Mediation of Health Care in an African Community" (1991); Contributor, Articles, Professional Journals, Book Chapters **Awards:** Inducted into Tapestry of Diverse Talents (2006); Presidents Development Award, American Sociological Association (2006); Presidents Professional Development Award, Womens World, Kampala, Uganda (2002); Bison Ambassadors Teaching Award, North Dakota State University (1999); Bison Ambassadors Teaching Award, North Dakota State University (1997); Anthony Fellow, University of California, San Francisco (1988); First Place Award, Graduate Student Research Day, Social Science Division, University of California, San Francisco (1987) **Memberships:** American Sociological Association; African Studies Association; Society for Symbolic Interaction; San Francisco Asian Art Museum; Society of Asian Arts; California Academy of Sciences **Marquis Who's Who Honors:** Albert Nelson Marquis Lifetime Achievement Award **To what do you attribute your success:** During her childhood, Dr. Slobin learned to work hard. She prioritized doing well in school and taking extracurricular activities. **Why did you become involved in your profession or industry:** Dr. Slobin became involved in her profession because, as a young artist, she was pulled into more practical affairs. She pursued additional graduate education in public administration and medical sociology with the goal of a career in research and teaching. **Avocations:** Painting; Music; Wildlife Photography; Theater; Symphony; Art galleries; Lessons in classical guitar; Staying healthy; Exercise; Nature; Writing; Journaling **Political Affiliations:** Democrat **Religion:** Unitarian Universalist; American Friends (Quaker) **Thoughts on Life:** Dr. Slobin believes life should be cherished.

Marilynn Jean Smiley, PhD

Title: Professor Emerita **Company Name:** State University of New York at Oswego **Date of Birth:** 06/05/1932 **Place of Birth:** Columbia City **State/Country of Origin:** IN/USA **Parents:** Orla Raymond Smiley; Mary Jane (Bailey) Smiley **Marital Status:** Single **Education:** PhD, University of Illinois (1970); MusM, Northwestern University (1958); BS, Ball State University (1954) **Certifications:** Certification, Ecoles d'Art Americaines, Fontainebleau, France (1959) **Career:** Professor Emeritus, State University of New York at Oswego (2014-Present); Distinguished Teaching Professor, State University of New York at Oswego (1974-2014); Faculty Member, Music Department, State University of New York at Oswego (1961-2014); Chairman, Music Department, State University of New York at Oswego (1976-1981); Public School Music Teacher, Logansport, IN (1954-1961) **Career Related:** Presenter, Conference Papers, Oswego Opera Theater (2009-Present); President, Board of Directors, Oswego Opera Theater (2009-Present); Early American Interest Group (2012-2014); Honorary Fellow, State University of New York Research Foundation (1974); Honorary Fellow, State University of New York Research Foundation (1972); Honorary Fellow, State University of New York Research Foundation (1971) **Civic:** Member, Board of Directors, Oswego Opera Theater (1978-Present); Member, Board of Directors, Oswego County Historical Society; Member, Board of Directors, H. Lee Maritime Museum; Member, Board of Directors, Safe Haven; Member, Board of Directors, Friends of Fort Ontario **Creative Works:** Co-Editor, "Remarkable Women in New York State History," History Press (2013); Contributor, Articles on Renaissance and American Music, Professional Journals **Awards:** National Endowment of the Humanities Grantee (1990-1991); Grantee, AAUW (1984); State University of New York Research Foundation Fellow, Summers (1974, 1972, 1971); Chancellor's Award for Excellence in Teaching (1973); Delta Kappa Gamma International Scholarship (1964-1965) **Memberships:** Co-President, Oswego Branch, AAUW (2007-Present); Diversity Chairperson, Oswego Branch, AAUW (1995-Present); Historian, New York State Division, AAUW (2004-2013); Membership Committee, Society for American Music (2003-2004); Unofficial Historian, New York State Division, AAUW (2000-2004); Membership Chairperson, Society for American Music (1998-2003); Status of Women Committee, American Musical Society (1997-2000); Diversity Director, New York State Division, AAUW (1993-1996); Chapter Representative, Council, American Musical Society (1993-1996); Board of Directors, New York State-St. Lawrence Chapter, American Musical Society (1993-1996); New York Division Area Interest Representative, Cultural Interests, AAUW (1990-1992); Branch Council Coordinator, New York State Division, AAUW (1988-1990); Branch Council Representative, District III, New York State Division, AAUW (1986-1988); President, Oswego Branch, AAUW (1984-1986); Chairman, New York Chapter, American Musical Society (1975-1977); Music Chairperson, New York Chapter, Delta Kappa Gamma (1968); Music Chairperson, Indiana Chapter, Delta Kappa Gamma (1961); National Organization for Women; Oswego County Historical Society Safe Haven; Early Music America; American Recorder Society; The Renaissance Society of America; The College Music Society; Music Library Association; The Medieval Academy of America; Oswego Recorder Consort; Affiliate, Ontario Singers; Heritage Foundation of Oswego; Phi Kappa Phi; Kappa Delta Pi; Sigma Tau Delta; Sigma Alpha Iota; Pi Kappa Lambda; Delta Phi Alpha; Phi Delta Kappa **Marquis Who's Who Honors:** Albert Nelson Marquis Lifetime Achievement Award; Marquis Who's Who Top Professional **To what do you attribute your success:** Dr. Smiley attributes her success to having inspirational teachers. **Why did you become involved in your profession or industry:** Dr. Smiley became involved in her profession because of her tremendous love of music. She learned to play the piano at 7 years old and the flute at 12 years old, which she continued all throughout high school. **Avocations:** Traveling; Collecting flutes; Photography; Traveling across 50 states, 10 Canadian provinces, and six continents **Political Affiliations:** Democrat **Religion:** Methodist

Allie Maitland Smith, PhD

Title: Engineering Educator (Retired) **Industry:** Education/Educational Services **Company Name:** University of Mississippi **Date of Birth:** 06/09/1934 **Place of Birth:** Lumberton **State/Country of Origin:** NC/USA **Parents:** Allie McCoy Smith; Emma Hattie (Wright) Smith **Marital Status:** Married **Spouse Name:** Sarah Louise Whitlock (06/16/1957) **Children:** Sara Leianne; Hollis Duval; Meredith Lorren **Education:** PhD in Aerospace Engineering, North Carolina State University, Raleigh, NC (1966); MS in Aerospace Engineering, North Carolina State University, Raleigh, NC (1961); BS in Mechanical Engineering, North Carolina State University, with Honors (1956) **Career:** Emeritus Professor, University of Mississippi (2008-Present); Emeritus Dean, University of Mississippi (2000-Present); Professor of Mechanical Engineering, University of Mississippi (1979-2008); Dean, School of Engineering, University of Mississippi (1979-2000); Adjunct Professor, University of Tennessee Space Institute, Tullahoma, TN (1967-1979); Research Supervisor, Sverdrup/ARO, Inc., Arnold Air Force Base, Tennessee (1966-1979); Research Project Engineer, RTI International, Durham, NC (1962-1966); Technical Staff, Bell Telephone Laboratories, Burlington, NC (1960-1962); Instructor then Assistant Professor Extension, North Carolina State University (1958-1962); Development Engineer, Western Electric Company (1957-1960); Associate Engineer, Glenn L. Martin Company, Baltimore, MD (1956-1957) **Career Related:** Keynote Lecturer, Third International Conference on Hydroscience and Engineering, Berlin, Germany (1998); Chair of Plenary Session, Third International Conference on Hydroscience and Engineering, Berlin, Germany (1998); Chair of Plenary Session, Conference on Management of Landscapes Disturbed by Channel Incision (1997); Presiding Officer of Plenary Session, International Conference on Hydroscience and Engineering (1995); Session Chair, Conferences on Theoretical and Applied Mechanics, SECTAM (1994); Presiding Officer of Plenary Session, International Conference on Hydroscience and Engineering (1993); Operations Committee, Conferences on Theoretical and Applied Mechanics, SECTAM (1990-1999); Policy Committee, Conferences on Theoretical and Applied Mechanics, SECTAM (1990-1999); Board of Directors, Scholarship Board, Mississippi Mineral Resources Institute, University of Mississippi; Executive Chairman, 14th Southeastern Conference on Theoretical and Applied Mechanics, SECTAM; Executive Committee, 13th to 16th Conferences on Theoretical and Applied Mechanics, SECTAM; Organizing Committee, International Scientific Advisory Board; Conference on Management of Landscapes Disturbed by Channel Incision **Civic:** Member, Rotary International (1980-2000) **Creative Works:** Editor, "Radiative Heat Transfer" (1997); Editor, "Solution Methods for Radiative Heat Transfer in Participating Media" (1996); Editor, "Radiative Heat Transfer: Theory and Applications" (1993); Editor, "Fundamentals of Radiation Heat Transfer" (1991); Editor, "Radiation Heat Transfer: Fundamentals and Applications" (1990); Editor, "Developments in Theoretical and Applied Mechanics, Volume XIV" (1988); Editor, "Fundamentals and Applications of Radiation Heat Transfer" (1987); Associate Editor, Journal of Thermophysics and Heat Transfer (1986-2007); Editor, "Thermophysics of Spacecraft and Outer Planet Entry Probes" (1977); Editor, "Radiative Transfer and Thermal Control" (1976); Associate Editor, Journal, American Institute of Aeronautics and Astronautics (AIAA) (1975-1977); Author, "Fundamentals of Silicon Integrated Device Technology, Volume I: Oxidation, Diffusion and Epitaxy" (1967); Contributor, Articles and Reviews to Professional Journals **Awards:** Inductee, Hall of Fame for Mechanical and Aerospace Department, North Carolina State University, Raleigh, NC (2018); Hermann Oberth Award, American Institute of Aeronautics and Astronautics (AIAA) (1984-1985); Space Shuttle Flag Challenger Plaque, American Institute of Aeronautics and Astronautics (AIAA) (1984); Thermophysics Award, American Institute of Aeronautics and Astronautics (AIAA) (1978); Scholarship, Sigma Pi Fraternity International **Memberships:** Aerospace Heat Transfer Committee, American Society of Mechanical Engineers (1975-2007); Chairman, Radiation Heat Transfer II Session, American Society of Mechanical Engineers, St. Louis, MO (2002); Chairman, Radiative Heat Transfer I and II Sessions, American Society of Mechanical Engineers, Pittsburgh, PA (2000); Supernumerary Director, Alabama-Mississippi Section, American Institute of Aeronautics and Astronautics (AIAA) (1994-2000); Host, General Chairman, Engineering Deans Institute, American Society for Engineering Education (1991); Fellow, American Institute of Aeronautics and Astronautics (AIAA); American Association of University Professors; New York Academy of Sciences; Sigma Xi, The Scientific Research Honor Society; The Tau Beta Pi Association, Inc.; Pi Tau Sigma; Upsilon Pi Epsilon; Sigma Pi Fraternity International; Notable Member, Order of the Engineer; Fellow, American Society of Mechanical Engineers **Marquis Who's Who Honors:** Albert Nelson Marquis Lifetime Achievement Award; Marquis Who's Who Top Professional; Marquis Who's Who Humanitarian Award

Daniel Owen Smith

Title: Consultant, Thermal Engineer **Industry:** Engineering **Date of Birth:** 11/04/1951 **Place of Birth:** Fort Worth **State/Country of Origin:** TX/USA **Children:** Four Children **Career:** Consultant, Extreme Temperature Thermal Application, Southern Thermal Fabricators; General Superintendent, Refractory Installation; Owner, AAP (Absolute Accurate Products); Employee, International Association of Heat and Frost Insulators and Allied Workers **Career Related:** Instructor, Train-the-trainer Programs **Creative Works:** Author, "Industrial Insulation: A General Guide to Fabrication and Instillation in Shop and Field" (2010); Author, "Cloth Removable and Reusable Insulation for General Industry" **Why did you become involved in your profession or industry:** Mr. Smith became involved in his profession because the family business began with his stepfather, uncles and kinsmen, who served in the U.S. Navy during World War II. They maintained the boilers and steam systems, which served to power the navy's warships, and after the war, the family business came ashore in the form of coal, gas and oil powerhouses. He originally went to college to become a mechanical engineer, but during summer break, his uncle asked him to help him out. He never returned to college and stayed in the family business, working on project sites and rising through the ranks, becoming a foreman, job supervisor and project superintendent. Mr. Smith later moved into office work, becoming an estimator, project manager and international project manager on large projects overseas. Following the retirement of Mr. Smith's older relatives, he worked for several large firms and finally, he opened his own business, where he supplied pre-fabricated high-temperature removable insulation systems for use in domestic and international power plants. Though they are both closed now, his companies were Southern Thermal Fabricators and Absolute Accurate Products, and he continues to apply his expertise as a consultant in the field to this day. He was also employed by the International Association of Heat and Frost Insulators and Allied Workers. Mr. Smith has found success through his written works, authoring "Industrial Insulation: A General Guide to Fabrication and Installation in Shop and Field" in 2010 and "Cloth Removable and Reusable Insulation for General Industry." In addition, he is an instructor and in his free time, he enjoys fishing, hunting and visiting industrial museums. **Avocations:** Fishing; Hunting; Visiting industrial museums **Thoughts on Life:** Mr. Smith's motto is, "Get it done."

Dawn E. Smith

Title: Owner, Chief Executive Officer **Industry:** Financial Services **Company Name:** Oasis Financial Services **Date of Birth:** 08/20/1970 **Marital Status:** Married **Children:** Four Children **Education:** BA, Psychology, Dartmouth College, Hanover, NH (1992) **Certifications:** Accredited Portfolio Management Advisor, College for Financial Planning; Certified Divorce Financial Analyst, Institute for Divorce Financial Analysts; Certified Financial Planner, Practitioner, CFP Board; Certified in Long Term Care, CLTC Board of Standards, Incorporated; Chartered Retirement Planning Counselor, College for Financial Planning; Chartered Financial Consultant, American College **Career:** Oasis Financial Services, Hopkinton, MA (2009-Present); Private Wealth Advisor & Chief Executive Officer, Ameriprise Financial Services, Incorporated (1993-Present) **Civic:** Board Member, Various Civic Boards; Pro Bono, Financial Planning & Advisement **Awards:** Forbes Best-in-State Wealth Advisors (2018-2019); Five Star Wealth Manager (2013, 2015-2019); Ameriprise Circle of Success (2007-2019); Named, Forbes Top Women Wealth Advisors (2017-2018); Working Mother, Top Wealth Advisor Moms (2017-2018) **Memberships:** Button Hole Short Course and Teaching Center; Dana Farber Cancer Research Institute; Junior Achievement Academy; National Association of Professional Women; Financial Planning Association; NAPW; FPA **To what do you attribute your success:** Ms. Smith's life motto is, "Fall down seven times, but get up eight..." She has the ability to push through short term defeats. She is persistent, competitive and a very hard worker."I love helping people find financial freedom... I don't find money in itself, to be very interesting... I find people to be interesting... and I find money traps people to a large extent... Having the ability to see through that, come out on the far side of that is empowering and freeing... and it can change people's lives and that is something worth getting up daily and going to work to do...." **Why did you become involved in your profession or industry:** Ms. Smith began her career as a financial advisor at a young age. Because she was so young, she initially did not think she would make a career out of it. Her first two or three years were very difficult. It took her nearly five years for her to begin to feel like it would be something she could do well as a career. What occurred to her is that people put their faith and trust in her. It was the people who made her feel like she was making a true difference in the lives of others and, as she says, "held my feet to the ground, when I questioned my ability to do what needed to be done..." She also attributes her competitive nature. When she saw other advisors she felt were not smarter than her becoming more successful than her, that drove her to be even better. **Thoughts on Life:** To be a successful financial advisor, you must, "Have the mind of a capitalist, and the heart of a social worker..." Ms. Smith also wants there to be changes in the finance industry, and see more women as financial advisors and in executive positions.

G. Louis Smith

Title: Senior Research Scientist **Industry:** Research **Company Name:** Science Systems and Applications, Inc. **Date of Birth:** 01/07/1938 **Place of Birth:** Perquimans County **State/Country of Origin:** NC/USA **Parents:** Louis Norman Smith; Viola Ruth (Rogerson) Smith **Marital Status:** Married **Spouse Name:** Olivia Chaney (06/25/1960) **Children:** Joni Lynn; Diann Patsy; Laurie Ruth **Education:** PhD in Aerospace Engineering, Virginia Polytechnic Institute and State University (1968); MS in Aerospace Engineering, Virginia Polytechnic Institute and State University (1963); BS, Virginia Polytechnic Institute and State University, With Honors (1960); Coursework, George Washington University **Career:** Senior Scientist, Science Systems Applications, Inc. (2000-Present); International Science Working Group for Scanner for Radiation Budget (SCARAB), Centre Nationale Etudes Spatiale, Paris, France (1995-2000); Research Scientist, Clouds and Earth Radiant Energy System (CERES), Langley Research Center, National Aeronautics and Space Administration (NASA) (1991-Present); Research Scientist, Earth Radiation Budget Experiment (ERBE), NASA (1975-1990); Research Scientist, Satellite Project Support and Planetary Reentry Analysis, NASA, (1960-1974); Trainee, NASA (1956-1959) **Civic:** The Yorktown Rotary Club **Creative Works:** Contributor, Numerous Research Articles, Professional Journals **Awards:** H.J.E. Reid Award for Best Publication, Langley Research Center, NASA (1981); Langley's Technical Excellence Award, NASA; Group Achievement Award, NASA; Group Achievement Award to CERES Team for Outstanding Group Achievement, NASA **Memberships:** American Meteorological Society; American Geophysical Union **Marquis Who's Who Honors:** Albert Nelson Marquis Lifetime Achievement Award; Marquis Who's Who Top Professionals **To what do you attribute your success:** Mr. Smith learned the importance of work and education from his parents. He also had the steadfast support of his wife, Libby. He also credits his success to working with highly motivated and skilled people. **Why did you become involved in your profession or industry:** As a young boy, Mr. Smith was fascinated by air crafts and it was natural to attend college in engineering. He further realized that it fit his interest in technical subjects. **Avocations:** Exercise; Gardening; Karate **Religion:** Baptist **Thoughts on Life:** Mr. Smith believes is not a gregarious person, but needs interaction with other people.

James E. Smith II, MSW, PhD, LSCSW

Title: Professor/Licensed Specialist Clinical Social Worker **Industry:** Education/Educational Services **Company Name:** Washburn University, Dept of Social Work, **State/Country of Origin:** KS/USA **Marital Status:** Married **Education:** PhD in Family Life Education and Consultation, Kansas State University, Manhattan, KS (2000); MPA, University of La Verne, La Verne, CA (1988); MSW, Virginia Commonwealth University, Richmond, VA (1977); BA in Sociology, Hampton University, Hampton, VA (1975) **Certifications:** Licensed Specialist Clinical Social Worker, State of Kansas (2019); Licensed Clinical Social Worker, State of Wyoming (2018); Clinical Associate, American Board of Medical Psychotherapists and Psychodiagnosticians (1988-2000); Licensed Clinical Social Worker, State of North Carolina (Retired) **Career:** Professor, Department of Social Work, School of Applied Studies, Washburn University, Topeka, KS (2011-Present); Associate Professor, Department of Social Work, School of Applied Studies, Washburn University, Topeka, KS (2008-2011); Marital and Family Therapist, Licensed Clinical Social Worker, The Alliance for Growth: Counseling & Consulting, LLC, Laramie, WY (2008); Marital and Family Therapist, Licensed Clinical Social Worker, The Psychology Clinic, LLC, Laramie, WY (2001-2008); Associate Professor, Division of Social Work, College of Health Sciences, University of Wyoming, Laramie, WY (1999-2008); Clinical Social Worker, Outpatient Therapist, Pawnee Mental Health Services, Junction City, KS (1993-1999); Social Work Officer, Major, U.S. Army Medical Service Corps, U.S. Army Reserve, Topeka, KS (1993-1999); Division Social Worker Officer, Major, 1st Infantry Division, Fort Riley, KS (1990-1992); Chief, Social Work Division, Major, U.S. Army Correctional Brigade, Fort Riley, KS (1988-1990); Chief, Social Work Services, Major, Bassett Army Community Hospital, Fort Wainwright, AK (1987-1988); Chief, Family Support Division, Major, U.S. Army Garrison, Fort Wainwright, AK (1986-1987); Chief, Human Resources Division, Captain, U.S. Army Garrison, Fort Wainwright, AK (1985-1986); Chief, Army Community Services, Captain, U.S. Army Garrison, Fort Wainwright, AK (1983-1985); Chief, Community Mental Health Activity, Captain, U.S. Army Health Clinic, Fort Greely, AK (1982-1983); Unit Social Work Officer, First Lieutenant, U.S. Army Retraining Brigade, Fort Riley, KS (1978-1982); Caseworker, Service to Military Families and Veterans, American National Red Cross, Richmond Virginia Chapter, Richmond, VA (1977-1978) **Civic:** Social Worker, Home Care and Hospice, Topeka, KS (2018-Present); Board of Directors, Valeo Behavioral Health (2013-Present); Narrator, Children & Family Services Training Video Course Series, Kansas Department of Social & Rehabilitation Services, Topeka, KS (2010); Board of Directors, Kansas Medical Education Foundation (2009-2015) **Military Service:** Active Duty, U.S. Army (1978-1993, Honorably Discharged)Joined Reserves in 1993 and Retired in 2003 **Creative Works:** Contributor, Numerous National and International Presentations (1992-2018); Contributor, Numerous Local and Regional Presentations (1990-2018); Author, Contributor, Numerous Publications (Refereed Journals) (2002-2015); Author, Review of the Book "The Mindful Path to Self-Compassion: Freeing Yourself from Destructive Thoughts and Emotions," Bulletin of the Menninger Clinic (2011); Author, Review of the Book, "Imprisoned Intellectuals: American's Political Prisoners Write on Life, Liberation, and Rebellion," Criminal Justice Review (2005) **Awards:** Distinguished Alumni, St. Luke's School, Founder's Day, New Canaan, CT (2011); Army Reserve Component Achievement Medal with Oak Leaf Cluster (1996, 1999); Armed Forces Reserve Ribbon (1997); Meritorious Service Medal with Oak Leaf Cluster (1982, 1993); Army Commendation Medal with Oak Leaf Cluster (1982, 1983, 1992); Combat Medical Badge (1992); Army Service Ribbon (1992); Liberation of Kuwait Medal, Kingdom of Saudi Arabia (1992); Unit Commendation Ribbon with Oak Leaf Cluster (1992); Army Achievement Medal with Oak Leaf Cluster (1985, 1991); Southwest Asia Service Medal (1991); National Defense Service Medal (1991); Overseas Ribbon (1983); Expert Field Medical Badge (1981); Distinguished military Graduate, Reserve Officers' Training Corps (ROTC) (1975); Distinguished Military Student, Reserve Officers' Training Corps (ROTC) (1973-1975); Reserve Officers' Training Corps (ROTC) Scholarship Award (1973-1975) **Memberships:** Council on Social Work Education (2000-Present); Society for Spirituality and Social Work (1994-Present); Academy of Certified Social Workers (1983-Present); National Association of Social Workers (1977-Present); National council on Family Relations (1996-2000); Charter Member, National Council of African-American Men (1992); Phi Beta Delta; Phi Alpha Honor Society; Kappa Omricon Nu Honor Society **Marquis Who's Who Honors:** Albert Nelson Marquis Lifetime Achievement Award **To what do you attribute your success:** He attributes his success to determination, having a Vision, willingness to over come obstacles, accept challenges and reject the nay-sayers. **Avocations:** Astronomy; Photography; Chess, Landscaping, Traveling, Building and Collecting Model Airplanes, Art Collector, Collecting Star Trek Memorabilia **Thoughts on Life:** From Carl Sandburg - Nothing Happens, unless first a Dream. From the Bible - Where there is no vision, the people perish

Glen Miller Smyth

Title: Management Consultant, Human Resources Executive **Industry:** Human Resources **Date of Birth:** 07/26/1929 **Place of Birth:** Abingdon **State/Country of Origin:** VA/USA **Parents:** Glen Miller Smyth; Kathleen (Dunn) Smyth **Marital Status:** Married **Spouse Name:** Lilian Castel Edgar (10/31/1968); Olson (08/25/1954, Divorced 1967) **Children:** Catherine Ellen; Glen Miller III; Cynthia Allison; Stephanie Eisenstein; Kimberly Boyce; Lindsay McConeghy; Cameron (deceased); Valerie (deceased) **Education:** MS in Psychology, Rutgers University, the State University of New Jersey (1958); BA, Yale University (1951) **Career:** Vice President, Spherion (1998-2005); President, Chief Executive Officer, Smyth, Fuchs & Co., Inc. (1995-2002); President, Fuchs & Co. (1993-1994); President, Fuchs, Cuthrell & Co., Inc. (1987-1993); Vice President, Career Transition Group (1985-1987); Senior Vice President, California Federal Savings (1983-1985); Senior Vice President of Human Resources, Northwest Bancorp., Minneapolis, MN (1973-1982); Manager, Organization and Manpower International, Can. Group, General Electric Co., New York, NY (1971-1973); Personnel Director, Celanese International, New York, NY (1958-1971); Marketing Representative, Wheeling Stamping Co., New York, NY (1953-1956) **Career Related:** Leader, Seminars, National Foreign Trade Council **Military Service:** U.S. Army (1951-1953) **Creative Works:** Co-Author, "International Career Pathing" (1971); Contributor, Articles, Professional Journals **Awards:** Emirate of International Honors **Memberships:** Founder, Past Chairman, Organization Committee, National Foreign Trade Council (1966-Present); American Psychological Association; Human Resources Planning Society; Employment Management Association; Jonathan Club; North Ranch Country Club; Phi Gamma Delta **Marquis Who's Who Honors:** Albert Nelson Marquis Lifetime Achievement Award **Why did you become involved in your profession or industry:** After Mr. Smyth left the Army, he pursued work in sales. In the years that followed, he found success; however, he knew he did not want to work as a salesman for the rest of his life. He decided to go back to school and work towards a career in human resources. After attaining the necessary credentials, he began working at Celanese International. **Avocations:** Tennis; Golf

Jean Snyder

Title: Lawyer **Industry:** Law and Legal Services **Company Name:** University Chicago **Date of Birth:** 01/26/1942 **Place of Birth:** Chicago **State/ Country of Origin:** IL/USA **Parents:** Norman Fitzroy Maclean; Jessie (Burns) Maclean **Marital Status:** Married **Spouse Name:** Joel Martin Snyder (9/4/1964) **Children:** Jacob Samuel; Noah Scot **Education:** JD, University of Chicago (1979); BA, University of Chicago (1963) **Career:** Teaching Team Member, Intensive Trial Practice Workshop, University of Chicago (2009-Present); Principal, Law Office of Jean Maclean Snyder (2004-Present); Independent Advisor, Midwest Coalition Human Rights (2000-Present); Of Counsel, University of Chicago Law School (2004-2005); Trial Counsel, The MacArthur Justice Center, University of Chicago Law School (1997-2004); Principal, Law Office of Jean Maclean Snyder, Chicago, IL (1993-1997); Partner, D'Ancona & Pflaum, Chicago, IL (1979-1992) **Civic:** Board of Directors, Citizens Alert (2005-2007) **Creative Works:** Contributor, Articles to Professional Journals **Awards:** Excellence Award, United States District Court of the Northern District of Illinois (2012) **Memberships:** Co-Chair, Section Litigation Task Force on Gender, Racial and Ethnic Bias (1998-2001); Standing Committee on Strategic Communications (1996-2001); American Civil Liberties Union of Illinois (1996-1999); Board of Directors, Lawyers for the Creative Arts (1995-1997); Co-Chair, First Amendment and Media Litigation Committee (1995-1996); Member Council, Litigation Section, American Bar Association (1989-1992); Editor-in-Chief, Litigation Magazine (1987-1988) **Bar Admissions:** United States Court of Appeals for the Seventh Circuit (1981); Illinois (1979); United States District Court for the Northern District of Illinois (1979)

Ned Snyder IV, MD

Title: President/Plastic Surgeon **Industry:** Medicine & Health Care **Company Name:** Snyder Dermatology and Plastic Surgery **Parents:** Ned Snyder III; Dot Snyder **Marital Status:** Married **Spouse Name:** Dr. Renee Snyder **Children:** Cinco; Remi; Gigi **Education:** Residency, Plastic Surgery, University of Texas Medical Branch, Galveston, TX (2000-2005); Doctor of Medicine, University of Texas Medical Branch, Galveston, TX (2000); Bachelor of Arts, Plan II Honors, University of Texas, Austin (1996); Fellowship, Perforator Flaps and DIEP Flaps for Breast Reconstruction, Universiteit Gen **Certifications:** Board Certified in Plastic and Reconstructive Surgery (2007); American Board of Plastic Surgery **Career:** Founder/President, Snyder Dermatology and Plastic Surgery at The Breast and Body Center of Austin (2005-Present) **Civic:** Vice President, Board Member, Austin Smiles; Medical Advisory Board, Breast Cancer Resource Center of Austin; President, Austin Society of Plastic Surgeons **Creative Works:** Published in Multiple Peer Reviewed Medical Journals, Numerous Presentations on Plastic Surgery and Reconstruction **Awards:** Named to Austin Monthly's Top Doctors List (2019); Named, Best Doctors in America (2014); Recipient, First Humanitarian Award, Saint David's Medical Center in Austin, Texas (2014); Named, Texas Rising Star Super Doctor (2012-2014); Blocker-Lewis Invited Lecturer, University of Texas Medical Branch for the Graduating Surgical Residents Ceremony (2011) **Memberships:** Alpha Omega Alpha; American Society of Plastic Surgeons; American Society of Reconstructive Microsurgeons **To what do you attribute your success:** Dr. Snyder attributes his success to hard work. **Why did you become involved in your profession or industry:** Dr. Snyder was inspired to enter the field of plastic surgery due to his mother, who was afflicted with breast cancer. **Avocations:** Hunting; Fishing; Skiing; Cars **Religion:** Catholic

John Sodolski

Title: President (Retired) **Industry:** Telecommunications **Company Name:** Global Integrated Communications **Date of Birth:** 04/11/1931 **Place of Birth:** Menasha **State/Country of Origin:** WI/USA **Parents:** L.V. Sodolski; L.W. (Pinkowski) Sodolski **Marital Status:** Married **Spouse Name:** Carol Jan Eppard Sodolski **Education:** Bachelor of Science, University of Wisconsin (1953) **Career:** Retired (1993); President, USTelecom, Washington, DC (1983-1993); Vice President, Electronic Industries Association, Washington, DC (1961-1983) **Military Service:** Served to First Lieutenant, United States Marine Corps (1955) **Awards:** Certificate of Appreciation Award, Telecommunication Industry Association; Framed Plaque for Three Decades of Outstanding Service and Decisive Leadership, Board of Directors, Telecommunication Industry Association **Memberships:** Member, U.S. Naval Institute **Marquis Who's Who Honors:** Albert Nelson Marquis Lifetime Achievement Award **Why did you become involved in your profession or industry:** Mr. Sodolski became involved in his profession after moving to Washington, DC, after graduating from the University of Wisconsin, after which he joined the Electronic Industries Association. **Avocations:** Reading books, newspaper and magazines; Spending time with cats and dog

Arturo Soler

Title: Real Estate Investor, Entreprenuer **Industry:** Real Estate **Company Name:** Arturo Soler **Place of Birth:** Mexico City **State/Country of Origin:** Mexico **Parents:** Arturo Soler; Virginia Soler **Marital Status:** Married **Spouse Name:** Maria A Lopez Moreno **Children:** Alejandro; Amelie; Enrique **Education:** MLS in Business Law, University UABC (1995); Bachelor Degree, University UABC (1994); High School Centro Universitario Franco Mexicano de Monterrey (1990); Middle School Instituto Mexico (1985-1988) **Certifications:** University of San Diego Real Estate Investment and Income Analysis (2019); University of San Diego Legal Aspects of Real Estate (2015); University of San Diego Development Feasibility (2015); DRE Real Estate License (2006-2016); Certification in Canaco Human Resources ABC (1998-1999); Certification in Coparmex Business Rules (1997) **Career:** Entrepreneur, ARSO Real Estate Investments, San Diego County (2008-Present); Business Owner, Juice, Salads and Sandwich Bar, Candy Shop, Ice Cream Shop (1997-Present); Lawyer, Mexico **Awards:** The 100 Top Real Estate Agents in California (2016); Top 2% Nationwide Sales Volume (2015); Best Real Estate Agent in San Diego (2014-2016) **Memberships:** PSAR South Bay San Diego Association of Realtors; SDAR San Diego County Association of Realtors; REBBA La Jolla Ca Associaton of Realtors; SDAR Coronado Ca division of Association of Realtors **Bar Admissions:** California; Mexico **To what do you attribute your success:** Mr. Soler attributes his success to his consistency. **Thoughts on Life:** "Live Happy, Love, Support and Respect."

David Michael Solomon

Title: Chief Executive Officer, Chairman **Industry:** Financial Services **Company Name:** Goldman Sachs Group, Inc. **Place of Birth:** Hartsdale **State/Country of Origin:** NY/USA **Parents:** Alan Solomon; Sandra Solomon **Marital Status:** Divorced **Spouse Name:** Mary Elizabeth (Coffey) Solomon (1989, Divorced 2018) **Education:** BA in Political Science and Government, Hamilton College, Clinton, NY **Career:** Chairman, Goldman Sachs Group, Inc. (2019-Present); Chief Executive Officer, Goldman Sachs Group, Inc. (2018-Present); President, Chief Operating Officer, Goldman Sachs Group, Inc. (2017-2018); Co-Head, International Banking Division, Goldman Sachs Group, Inc. (2006-2016); Partner, Goldman Sachs Group, Inc. (1999) **Civic:** Board of Trustees, Hamilton College (2005-Present); Board of Directors, Robin Hood Foundation **Memberships:** Alpha Delta Phi **Avocations:** Disc jockey (DJ D-Sol)

Ryan P. Somers

Title: Owner **Industry:** Architecture & Construction **Company Name:** Somers Painting LLC **Education:** Bachelor of Fine Arts in Ceramics, Glass Blowing and Painting, Jacksonville University (1996) **Certifications:** Benjamin Moore Staining Certification **Career:** Owner, Somers Painting LLC (2003-Present); Construction Worker and Painter, Thomas Construction (2001-2003); Manager, Surf Shop (1996-2001); Lifeguard **Career Related:** Benjamin Moore Planning and Advisory Board **Civic:** Donates to Charities; Volunteers for Beach Clean Ups **Awards:** Gold Design Award, Residential Interior Design, Rhode Island Monthly Magazine (2014); Silver Design Award, Residential Interior Design, Rhode Island Monthly Magazine (2013) **To what do you attribute your success:** Mr. Somers attributes his success to his hard work and dedication. He has a very strong work ethic and he is not afraid of a challenge. Further, he has drawn a wealth of influence from his mentor, Ben Mondor, the late owner of the Pawtucket Red Sox. **Why did you become involved in your profession or industry:** Mr. Somers started working in construction with Thomas Construction in 2001, after returning to Rhode Island from Duxbury, Massachusetts. Due to the amazing response his painting skills garnered, he decided to launch his own independent venture, Somers Painting LLC, in 2003. **Avocations:** Classic cars; Cooking

Ojars Juris Sovers, PhD

Title: Research Physicist **Industry:** Sciences **Company Name:** NASA Jet Propulsion Laboratory **Date of Birth:** 07/11/1937 **Place of Birth:** Riga **State/Country of Origin:** Latvia **Parents:** Karlis Sovers; Olga (Kaneps) Sovers **Marital Status:** Married **Spouse Name:** Zinta Armande Aisters (1959) **Education:** Postdoctoral Coursework, Columbia University (1962-1964); National Science Foundation Postdoctoral Fellowship for One Years Studies with Dr. J.W. Linnett, Inorganic Chemistry Laboratory, University of Oxford, England, United Kingdom (1962); PhD in Physics and Physical Chemistry, Princeton University (1962); National Science Foundation Fellowship for Graduate Study in Chemistry, Princeton University (1958); BS in Psychics and Chemistry, Brooklyn College, Magna Cum Laude (1958) **Career:** Retired (2015); Contractor, NASA Jet Propulsion Laboratory, Pasadena, CA (1998-2008); With, Technical Staff, NASA Jet Propulsion Laboratory, Pasadena, CA (1979-2015); With, Technical Staff, Development Division, Sony Corporation, Tokyo, Japan (1972-1978); With, Technical Staff, GTE Laboratories, Bayside, NY (1964-1972); With, Argonne National Laboratory, IL (1958) **Career Related:** Worked in Three Aspects of Physics and Chemistry, Theoretical Chemistry of Molecular Structures, Lanthanide Ion Spectroscopy in Solids, and Radio Interferometric (VLBI) Measurements to Establish a Coordinate Reference Frame for Interplanetary Spacecraft Navigation; Lecturer in Field **Creative Works:** Co-author, Book Detailing Work Leading to New Celestial Reference Frame (2000); Contributor, "Astrometry of Fundamental Catalogues," Spring, Germany (2000); Co-author, VLBI Summary Article, Reviews of Modern Physics (1996); Author, Thesis, "d-Hybridization in Pi Bonds" (1961); Author, "d-Hybridization in Pi Bonds," Journal of Chemical Physics; Author, Two Papers, Discussions of the Faraday Society; Contributor, Articles on Physics and Chemistry to Professional Journals **Memberships:** Former Member, American Association for the Advancement of Science; American Physical Society; Former Member, American Geophysical Union; Sigma Xi, The Scientific Research Honor Society; International VLBI Service **Marquis Who's Who Honors:** Albert Nelson Marquis Lifetime Achievement Award; Marquis Who's Who Top Professional **Why did you become involved in your profession or industry:** Dr. Sovers became involved in his profession because it was random and not chosen. In 1970, there was a big problem for physicists to get jobs and that was how he ended up in Japan for six years. **Avocations:** Backpacking; Hiking **Thoughts on Life:** The Sovers left Riga, Latvia in 1944 for Germany in order to avoid Soviet occupation. In late 1944 until the end of the war in 1945, they lived on a farm near Kempten, Bavaria. In 1945-1946, Dr. Sovers and his family were held in a displaced persons camp in Kempten, and in 1946-1950, they were in a Latvian displaced persons camp in Augsburg. He was able to complete the 7th grade in the elementary Latvian school in the camp. In December of 1950, they emigrated to the U.S. to a farm near Harrisburg, PA, where he once again completed 7th grade to improve his English language skills. In 1951, the Sovers moved to Brooklyn, NY. He attended Brooklyn public high schools, Jefferson and Lincoln, and graduated in 1954 with a Lincoln service award and a biology medal. He enrolled in Brooklyn College in 1954, intending to study chemical engineering. Some of Dr. Sovers' memorable mentors include Prof. Bernhard Kurrelmeyer in physics and Prof. Albert Levine in chemistry. Both were helpful in establishing future direction, decisions of physics vs. chemistry and the choice of graduate schools. Fellow physics students formed a group helping each other in studying material related to course work. One memorable person, Julius Frankel, has remained a friend for 50+ years. Dr. Sovers met his future wife, Zinta Aisters, who studied French and Russian literature.

Amy B. Sowers

Title: Speech-Language Pathologist **Industry:** Medicine & Health Care **Date of Birth:** 03/13/1952 **Place of Birth:** Houston **State/Country of Origin:** TX/USA **Parents:** Albert Glenn Sowers; Helen June (Meador) Barnet Sowers **Marital Status:** Married **Spouse Name:** George Vernon Sowers Jr. (08/23/1975) **Children:** George Vernon III; Adam Glenn **Education:** MA, University of Houston (1993); BA, University of Houston (1975) **Certifications:** Certified Speech-language Pathologist, State of Texas **Career:** Supervisory Position, Home Health Care (2016-2018); Private Practice (1996-2016); Consultant Service, Montgomery Independent School District (1996-2000); Lead Therapist, Montgomery Independent School District (1996-2000); Speech-language Pathologist, Conroe Independent School District, Texas (1984-1996); Speech-language Pathologist, Tomball Independent School District, Texas (1978-1983); Speech-language Pathologist, Aldine Independent School District, Houston, TX (1976-1978) **Civic:** Member, Crighton Players; Founder, Crighton Kidz; Fundraiser, Chairperson, Crighton Theatre (-Present); Executive Director, Bravo Company (2009-Present); Executive Director, Crighton Players, Performing Arts School for Youth (1998-2008); President, Crighton Theatre Foundation (1999-2001); Clinical Supervisor, Graduate School, Texas Women's University (1997-1998); City of Conroe Commission on Arts & Culture **Awards:** Pursuit of Excellence Award, Crighton Theatre Foundation **Memberships:** President, Stage Right (2010); President, Conroe Service League (2005-2006); Vice President, Conroe Service League (2004-2005); National Education Association; American Speech, Language and Hearing Association; Texas Speech and Hearing Association; Texas Educators Association; Houston Association of Communications Disorders; Committee, Montgomery County Performing Arts Society; University of Houston Alumni Association **Marquis Who's Who Honors:** Albert Nelson Marquis Lifetime Achievement Award; Marquis Who's Who Top Professional; Marquis Who's Who Humanitarian Award **Why did you become involved in your profession or industry:** Mrs. Sowers was inspired to become a speech-language pathologist because of her grandmother. Mrs. Sowers' grandmother encouraged her to work hard. **Avocations:** Reading; Crafts; Dance; Theater; Traveling **Religion:** Methodist

Catherine Spalding, Esq.

Title: Family Court Attorney, Guardian Ad Litem **Industry:** Law and Legal Services **Company Name:** Catherine Spalding Attorney at Law **Place of Birth:** Lebanon **State/Country of Origin:** KY/USA **Parents:** Hugh C. Spalding (deceased); Bernadette (Hill) Spalding (deceased) **Marital Status:** Married **Spouse Name:** Martin **Children:** Hugh **Education:** JD, University of Louisville (1983); BS in Biology, Spalding University, Louisville, KY (1970) **Career:** Family Court Attorney, Guardian Ad Litem, Jefferson County, Kentucky (2000-Present); Private Practice in Law, Louisville, KY (1983-Present); Assistant County Attorney, Jefferson County, Kentucky (1993-2000) **Civic:** Past Board of Directors, League of Women Voters, Portland Museum, Louisville, KY **Creative Works:** Editor, "Kentucky Family Law" (1990); Speaker in Field **Memberships:** Chair, Social Security Section, Louisville Bar Association (1992-1993); Chair, Family Law Section, Kentucky Bar Association (1990-1991); American Bar Association; Past Newsletter Editor, Speaker, Moderator of Seminars, Kentucky Bar Association; Past Board of Directors, American Association of University Women; Past Board of Directors, Daughters of the American Revolution; Past Board of Directors, Optimist Club; Past Board of Directors, League of Women Voters; Colonial Dames **Bar Admissions:** State of Kentucky; Sixth Circuit, U.S. Court of Appeals; Court of Veterans Appeals; Federal District Court **Marquis Who's Who Honors:** Albert Nelson Marquis Lifetime Achievement Award; Marquis Who's Who Top Professional **To what do you attribute your success:** Mrs. Spaldine attributes her success to determination, working hard, and the desire to want to help others. Her dad (Hugh C. Spalding) worked hard, he was the school superintendent for 37 years, and she never heard of anyone working in that position for so long. He would come home, eat dinner, go to bed, and go back to work. She would feel sorry for him at night because he would work until about midnight. So she would go over there to be with him sometimes so he wasn't there by himself, all the time. **Why did you become involved in your profession or industry:** She had a great grandfather who was a lawyer. He enjoyed his job. He passed away before she was born, but she always heard about him. Her great-grandmother was a writer and wrote for a national magazine that Edgar Allan Poe had written in as well. She had copies of her old letters. So, there was that in the family. **Avocations:** Skiing; Watching son's soccer games

Barbara L. Sparks, MBA

Title: Pharmaceutical Manager (Retired) **Industry:** Pharmaceuticals **Company Name:** 1) Cephalon 2) Sanofi-Aventis 3) GlaxoSmithKline **Date of Birth:** 11/08/1947 **Place of Birth:** Oreland **State/Country of Origin:** PA/USA **Parents:** Joseph D. Sparks; Lena A. (McDowell) Sparks **Education:** MBA in Finance, Wharton School of the University of Pennsylvania, with Distinction, Philadelphia, PA (1975); BA in Economics, University of Massachusetts Amherst, Cum Laude (1970); Diploma, Washington Township High School, Sewell, NJ (1966) **Certifications:** Certified Secondary Social Studies (Economics) Teacher, States of New Jersey, Pennsylvania, Massachusetts; New Jersey Business Administrator Provisional Certificate **Career:** Director of Commercial Operations, Cephalon, Inc. (Now a Subsidiary of Teva Pharmaceutical Industries, Ltd.), Malvern/Frazer, PA (1999-2008); Consultant, Owner, Sparks Consulting, Business Financial Planning and Control, Mullica Hill, NJ (1995-1998); Director of Global Planning and Forecasting, Sterling Winthrop Pharmaceutical Research Division, Malvern, PA (1992-1995); Consultant, Owner, Sparks Consulting, Business Financial Planning & Control, Mullica Hill, NJ (1990-1992); Manager of International Financial Planning and Analysis, SmithKline Consumer Products/Menley & James, Smith Kline Beckman, Philadelphia, PA (1977-1990); Senior Financial Analyst of Bankruptcy Re-Organization, Penn Central Railroad, Philadelphia, PA (1977); Financial Analyst, CertainTeed Corp., Valley Forge, PA (1975-1977); Relocation Planner, United States Department of Housing and Urban Development, Philadelphia, PA (1970-1974); Director, Agnes Flood Temporary Housing Office for Montgomery and Philadelphia Counties, Pottstown, PA (1972) **Career Related:** From Co-Chairperson of Alumni Advisory Board to Emeritus, Department of Economics, University of Massachusetts Amherst (1990-Present); Member, Business Technology Committee on Healthcare Distribution Management Association, Reston, VA (2000-2003); Member, Entrepreneurial Executive Review Board, Graduate School of Business, LaSalle University, Philadelphia, PA (1995-2000); Pharmaceutical Consulting Consortium, Inc. (1995-2000); Alumni College Recruiter, University of Massachusetts (1980-2000); Co-Chairperson, Class of 1970, 25th Reunion Committee, University of Massachusetts (1994-1995) **Civic:** Volunteer Marketing Adviser, Fox Chase Cancer Center, Philadelphia, PA (1996-2000) **Awards:** Named Valedictorian, Washington Township High School, Sewell, NJ (1966); Inductee, National Honor Society, Washington Township High School, Sewell, NJ (1964); Full Tuition, Two-Year Director's Scholarship, Wharton School of the University of Pennsylvania; Dean's List, Wharton School of the University of Pennsylvania **Memberships:** Sierra Club (2008-Present); Sigma Kappa Sorority, University of Massachusetts Amherst (1968-Present); Camden County Branch, American Association of University Women (2009-2017); Co-Membership Chair, Camden County Branch, American Association of University Women (2010-2016); Board of Directors, Camden County Branch, American Association of University Women (2010-2015); Annual Book Sale Committee, Camden County Branch, American Association of University Women (2010-2015); Network of Women in Computers and Technology, Philadelphia, PA (1995-2000); Wharton Alumni Club, Philadelphia, PA (1990-1999); Phi Kappa Phi National Honor Society (1970) **Marquis Who's Who Honors:** Albert Nelson Marquis Lifetime Achievement Award **To what do you attribute your success:** Ms. Sparks attributes her success to her persistence and positive attitude. **Avocations:** Jogging; Traveling; Snowshoeing; Playing golf; Reading; Downhill skiing; Sailing **Thoughts on Life:** Ms. Sparks' expertise lies in managing finance and business planning activities with the vice president and chief financial officer, budgeting, evaluating business projections, forecasting accuracy and strategic planning.As a temporary disaster housing manager during Hurricane Agnes, she directed an on-site disaster housing office to locate temporary housing for 300 displaced families and individuals.

Dale Arthur Speelman

Title: Proprietor **Industry:** Media & Entertainment **Company Name:** Dickens Carolers of Branson **Date of Birth:** 05/08/1953 **Place of Birth:** Vance Air Force Base, Enid **State/Country of Origin:** OK/USA **Parents:** Lettie Speelman (Deceased 2016); William Speelman (Deceased 1992) **Marital Status:** Divorced **Children:** Anne; Andrew **Education:** BA in Music, Conservatory of Music, University of Missouri, Kansas City, MO; Diploma in Russian Language, Defense Language Institute, Presidio of Monterey, Monterey, CA; Diploma, Center for Russian Studies, Garmisch, Germany; Diploma, Cryptologic Studies, National Cryptologic School; Cryptologic Instructor Rating, National Cryptologic School, Fort Meade, MD; United States Army NCO Professional Education Program **Certifications:** Certificate, German as a Foreign Language, Goethe Institute; Cryptologic Instructor Rating, National Cryptologic School, Ft Meade, MD **Career:** Proprietor, Dickens Carolers of Branson, Dickens Singers of Branson (2013-Present); Performer, Encore Theatre, Independence, MO, Singer with "The Bavarians," Kansas City, MO; Proprietor, Speelman Photography; Singer, Soloist, Community of Christ Church, Kansas City, MO; Singer, Soloist, Roanoke Presbyterian Church, Kansas City, MO **Career Related:** Fort McHenry Guard; Historical Interpreter, Fort McHenry National Monument and Historic Shrine, Baltimore, MD; Vocalist, Kansas City Chorale, Kansas City, MO; Singer and Performer Hallmarks Maxines Christmas Carol, Branson, MO; Performer in "Sound of Music," City Theatre of Independence, MO, Performer in "Life of Rosie O'Neill," Branson, MO; Capt Brackett, "South Pacific," University of Maryland, Munich, Germany **Civic:** Singer, Branson Chorale Community Choir, First Presbyterian Church; Volunteer, Board Member, Taney Hills Community Library; German Liederkranz Society Community Choir, Idar-Oberstein, Germany; Choir Member, Perlacher Forst Community Chapel, Munich, Germany; Counselor, Leader, Boy Scouts of America; Board Member, Savannah Place Home Owners Association **Military Service:** U.S. Army Senior Non-Commissioned Officer, Russian and German Linguist (Retired) (1977-1995); Visual Information Chief, Tracked Vehicle Mechanic, Wheeled Vehicle Mechanic, Barracks Security Guard, Floor Polishing Specialist, Training Aids Developer, Mobile Training Team Instructor, TAREX Representative, Field First Sergeant, Platoon Sergeant, Squad Leader, Team Leader **Creative Works:** Photograph, "The Launch"; Photograph, "Change of Seasons"; Photograph, "Holiday Rush" **Awards:** First Place Ribbons for Photography; Volunteer, Service Awards, National Park Service, Baltimore, MD; Armistead Award, Fort McHenry, Baltimore, MD; "Thank You" Award, 126th Anniversary of Liederkranz, Idar-Oberstein, Germany; Award for Merit, Hohl Soccer Club, Idar-Oberstein, Germany; Meritorious Service Medal; Army Commendation Medal; Army Achievement Medal; Five Good Conduct Medal Awards; Army Superior Unit Award; National Defense Ribbon; Army of Occupation Ribbon; Overseas Service Ribbon; Three Awards, NCO Development Ribbon; Army Service Ribbon; Order of Fred, TAREX Detachment-Europe; Apfelkorn Anonymous Medal, CPAR, Ft Meade, MD **Memberships:** Boy Scouts of America; Mic-O-Say, Heart of America Council; Friends of Taneyhills Library; Branson Regional Arts Council; Branson Chorale; Life Member, Veterans of Foreign Wars; Phi Mu Alpha Sinfonia **Marquis Who's Who Honors:** Albert Nelson Marquis Lifetime Achievement Award **To what do you attribute your success:** Mr. Speelman attributes his success to a lot of luck. He said, "How could a mook like me achieve this great singing group?" **Why did you become involved in your profession or industry:** Mr. Speelman became involved in carol singing groups while in high school and college in Kansas City. He continued forming caroling groups while in the Army to visit Army hospitals on post where he was stationed. After he retired, he became involved in several professional caroling groups in his hometown of Kansas City, MO. When he moved to Branson, he noticed there were no professional caroling groups available during the long Christmas season, and wondered if a professional caroling group could fit in. When he became involved with the Branson Chorale, he felt he could make the Dickens Carolers a reality. He formed the Dickens Carolers of Branson in 2014. They sing Christmas carols and do things that other caroling groups do not do. For instance, the carolers sing a Japanese version of "Rudolph the Red Nosed Reindeer." Mr. Speelmans' group encourages kids to come up and play the jingle bells on a number of secular, holiday songs. **Avocations:** Photography; Music; History; Star gazing; Petting cats; Trivia contests; Traveling; Drinking German beer; Linguistics; Performing onstage; Good comedy; Movies; Gazing upon the standing support systems of certain feminine creatures **Political Affiliations:** Whoever will do the best for the country despite political affiliation **Religion:** Spiritual/Nondenominational **Thoughts on Life:** Mr. Speelman said, "The Dickens Carolers of Branson have taught me tolerance, especially when trying to sing in this many languages: German, Japanese, French, Latin and Spanish. The Army is a hard habit to break."

Richard Speer

Title: Senior Security Analyst **Industry:** Military & Defense Services **Company Name:** ARES Security Corporation **Date of Birth:** 08/21/1958 **Place of Birth:** Oxnard **State/Country of Origin:** CA/USA **Parents:** Richard McCord Speer; Betty Jean (Wilson) Speer **Education:** Diploma, Las Vegas High School, Nevada **Career:** Senior Security Analyst, Ares Security Corporation (2019-Present); Duke Energy Corporate Office, Nuclear Protective Services (2017-2018); Duke Energy Corporation Loanee to Nuclear Energy Institute, Washington DC (2014-2016); Supervisor for Fitness of Duty, Duke Energy Corporation (2013-2014); U.S. Congressional Candidate, North Carolina Congressional District 2 (2012); Lead Security Specialist, Corporate Operations, Nuclear Department, Progress Energy Services Company, LLC (2008-2012); Operations Support Manager, Nuclear Security Consultant, Securitas Security Services, NJ (1998-2008); Project Manager of Special Projects, U.S. Army, Fort Bragg, NC (1995-1998); Heavy Weapons Specialist, Special Forces, U.S. Army, Fort Bragg, NC (1988-1994); Infantry Squad Leader, 4th Infantry Division, U.S. Army, Fort Carson, CO (1987-1988); Infantry Squad Leader, U.S. Army, Fort Bragg, NC (1981-1987); Infantryman 82nd Airborne Division, U.S. Army, Fort Bragg, NC (1976-1981); Sergeant First Class, U.S. Army (1990); Enlisted, U.S. Army (1976) **Civic:** National Representative, Congressional Committee (2003-Present); National Representative, Senatorial Committee (2003-Present); Life Member, Representative, National Committee, Washington (1994-Present); Representative, Presidential Task Force (2005) **Military Service:** U.S. Army (1976-1998) **Awards:** Meritorious Services Medals, U.S. Army (1991, 1996, 1998); Decorated Army Commendation Medal, 3rd Award, U.S. Army (1984) **Memberships:** Heritage Foundation; Former Member, Cumberland County Representative Men's Club; Former Member, Hope Mills Area Chamber of Commerce, North Carolina Representative Party; North America Hunting Club; American Legion, Chapter 1-18, Special Forces Association; Legacy Member, President's Club; Heritage Foundation President's Club; Legacy Member, President's Club; Young American's Foundation **Marquis Who's Who Honors:** Albert Nelson Marquis Lifetime Achievement Award **Why did you become involved in your profession or industry:** Mr. Speer became involved in his profession because his dad was in the military and the Air Force. His father's influence, coupled with the fact that he didn't fare well as a student, made his decision to join the Army easy. **Avocations:** Amateur philatelist; Hunting; Fishing; Bird watching; Collecting firearms **Political Affiliations:** Conservative

Ralph Eugene Spelbring

Title: Chemist (Retired) **Industry:** Sciences **Company Name:** Whitehall Laboratories **Date of Birth:** 05/09/1945 **Place of Birth:** Brazil **State/Country of Origin:** IN/USA **Parents:** Harold Eugene Spelbring; Virginia Kathryn (Craft) Spelbring **Education:** BA in Chemistry, DePauw University (1967) **Certifications:** Teachers License, Indiana State University (1971) **Career:** Chemist, Apex Pharmaceutical, Elkhart, IN (1993-1995); Chemist, Whitehall Laboratories, Elkhart, IN (1972-1991); Teacher, Chemistry, LaSalle High School, South Bend, IN (1971); Teacher, Science, Corydon High School (1968-1969) **Career Related:** Commercial Delivery Driver (2011-Present); Substitute Teacher, Michigan Schools (1997-2007); Substitute Teacher, Indiana High Schools (1997-2007) **Civic:** Vice President, Elkhart Jaycees (1981); Treasurer, Elkhart Jaycees (1979-1980) **Creative Works:** Author, Letters to the Editor, Several Indiana Newspapers, Chicago Tribune, BARRON'S **Awards:** Sigma Xi; Lifetime Member, Elkhart Jaycees **Memberships:** League of Women Voters of Elkhart County (1988-Present); American Chemical Society (1969-Present); Economic Club of Michiana (1986-2016); Elkhart Chamber (1979-1999) **To what do you attribute your success:** Mr. Spelbring attributes his success is being analytical and good with numbers. **Why did you become involved in your profession or industry:** Mr. Spelbring became involved in his profession because there was an emphasis on science after the Russians launched sputnik. **Avocations:** Reading; Sports; Bowling **Political Affiliations:** Democrat

Steven Allan Spielberg

Title: Film Director, Producer **Industry:** Media & Entertainment **Date of Birth:** 12/18/1946 **Place of Birth:** Cincinnati **State/Country of Origin:** OH/USA **Parents:** Arnold Spielberg; Leah (Posner) Adler Spielberg **Marital Status:** Married **Spouse Name:** Kate Capshaw (10/12/1991); Amy Irving (11/27/1985, Divorced 1989) **Children:** Max Samuel; Sasha Rebecca; Sawyer Avery; Destry Allyn; Jessica Capshaw (Stepdaughter); Theo (Adopted); Mikaela George (Adopted) **Education:** DA (Honorary), Harvard University (2016); LHD (Honorary), Boston University (2009); BA in Film and Electronic Arts, California State University Long Beach (2002); DHL (Honorary), Yale University (2002); Honorary Degree, Brown University (1999); Honorary Doctorate, University of Southern California (1994); Coursework, Brookdale Community College; Coursework, California State University Long Beach **Career:** Co-Founder, DreamWorks Pictures (1994-Present); Co-Founder, Amblin Entertainment (1981-Present) **Career Related:** Frequent Collaborator, Partner, EA Games (2005-Present) **Civic:** Advisory Board, Science Fiction Museum and Hall of Fame **Creative Works:** Producer, "Bernstein" (2021); Executive Producer, "Halo" (2021); Executive Producer, "Jurassic World: Dominion" (2021); Director, Producer, "West Side Story" (2020); Executive Producer, "Animaniacs" (2020); Executive Producer, Episode, "Amazing Stories" (2020); Executive Producer, "Cats" (2019); Executive Producer, "Why We Hate" (2019); Executive Producer, "Men in Black: International" (2019); Director, Producer, "Ready Player One" (2018); Executive Producer, "Bumblebee" (2018); Executive Producer, "First Man" (2018); Executive Producer, "Jurassic World: Fallen Kingdom" (2018); Director, Producer, "The Post" (2017); Executive Producer, "Transformers: The Last Knight" (2017); Executive Producer, "Five Came Back" (2017); Executive Producer, "Bull" (2016-2019); Director, Producer, "The BFG" (2016); Executive Producer, "Finding Oscar" (2016); Executive Producer, TV Movie, "All the Way" (2016); Director, Producer, "Bridge of Spies" (2015); Executive Producer, "Public Morals" (2015); Executive Producer, Four Episodes, "Minority Report" (2015); Executive Producer, Producer, "The Whispers" (2015); Executive Producer, "Jurassic World" (2015); Producer, "Auschwitz" (2015); Executive Producer, "Extant" (2014-2015); Executive Producer, "Transformers: Age of Extinction" (2014); Executive Producer, "Under the Dome" (2013-2015); Executive Producer, "Don't Say No Until I Finish Talking: The Story of Richard D. Zanuck" (2013); Executive Producer, "Smash" (2012-2013); Director, "Lincoln" (2012); Executive Producer, "Falling Skies" (2011-2015); Director, Producer, "War Horse" (2011); Director, Producer, "The Adventures of Tintin" (2011); Executive Producer, "Terra Nova" (2011); Voice Actor, "Paul" (2011); Executive Producer, "Real Steel" (2011); Executive Producer, "Cowboys & Aliens" (2011); Executive Producer, "Transformers: Dark of the Moon" (2011); Producer, "Super 8" (2011); Executive Producer, "True Grit" (2010); Executive Producer, "The Pacific" (2010); Executive Producer, "United States of Tara" (2009-2011); Executive Producer, "Transformers: Revenge of the Fallen" (2009); Director, "Indiana Jones and the Kingdom of the Crystal Skull" (2008); Executive Producer, "Transformers" (2007); Executive Producer, "Monster House" (2006); Director, Producer, "Munich" (2005); Director, "War of the Worlds" (2005); Executive Producer, Six Episodes, "Into the West" (2005); Director, Producer, "The Terminal" (2004); Himself, "Austin Powers in Goldmember" (2002); Director, Producer, Catch Me If You Can" (2002); Director, "Minority Report" (2002); Executive Producer, 10 Episodes, "Taken" (2002); Executive Producer, "Men in Black II" (2002); Director, Producer, "A.I. Artificial Intelligence" (2001); Executive Producer, 10 Episodes, "Band of Brothers" (2001); Executive Producer, "Jurassic Park III" (2001); Actor, "Vanilla Sky" (2001); Director, Producer, "Saving Private Ryan" (1998); Executive Producer, "Small Soldiers" (1998); Director, Producer, "Amistad" (1997); Director, "The Lost World: Jurassic Park" (1997); Executive Producer,"Men in Black" (1997); Executive Producer, "Pinky and the Brain" (1995-1998); Executive Producer, "Freakazoid!" (1995-1997); Executive Producer, "Casper" (1995); Executive Producer, "The Flinstones" (1994); Executive Producer, "Animaniacs" (1993-1998); Executive Producer, "Seaquest 2032" (1993-1995); Director, "Schindler's List" (1993); Executive Producer, Producer, Numerous Films and TV Shows **Awards:** Presidential Medal of Freedom, President Barack Obama (2015); Honoree, Records of Achievement Award, National Archives and Records Administration (2013); David O. Selznick Achievement Award in Theatrical Motion Pictures, Producers Guild of America (2012); Liberty Medal, National Constitution Center (2009); Cecil B. DeMille Award, Hollywood Foreign Press Association (2009); Lifetime Achievement Award, Visual Effects Society Awards (2009); Honoree, French Legion of Honor (2008); Honoree, Kennedy Center Honor, John F. Kennedy Center for Performing Arts (2006); Inductee, Science Fiction Hall of Fame (2005); Honoree, Knight Commander of the Order of the British Empire (2001); Lifetime Achievement Award, Directors Guild of America (2000); Numerous Awards and Accolades **Memberships:** Fellow, British Academy of Film and Television Arts; Theta Chi Fraternity

John K. Spitznagel, MD, FACP

Title: Microbiologist, Immunologist, Physician (Retired) **Industry:** Medicine & Health Care **Date of Birth:** 04/11/1923 **Place of Birth:** Peoria **State/Country of Origin:** IL/USA **Parents:** Elmer Florian Spitznagel (Deceased); Anna S. (Kolb) Spitznagel (Deceased) **Marital Status:** Married **Spouse Name:** Anne Moulton Sirch (02/02/1947) **Children:** John; Jean; Margaret; Elizabeth; Paul **Education:** Doctor of Medicine, Columbia University (1946); Bachelor of Arts, Columbia University (1943) **Certifications:** Diplomate, National Board of Medical Examiners, American Board of Internal Medicine (1953) **Career:** Professor Emeritus of Microbiology and Immunology, Emory University, Atlanta, GA (1993-Present); Chairman, Executive Board, Chief Executive Officer, Good Samaritan Health and Wellness Center (2004-2006); Co-founder, Attending Physician, Good Samaritan Health and Wellness Center, Jasper, GA (2002-2012); Associate Dean of Research, Emory University, Atlanta, GA (1997-1998); Professor of Microbiology and Immunology, Department Chairman, Emory University, Atlanta, GA (1979-1993); Consultant, North Carolina Memorial Hospital, Chapel Hill, NC (1974-1979); Ad-hoc Adviser, National Institutes of Health (1971-2000); Visiting Investigator, National Institute of Medical Research, London, England (1967-1968); Professor of Microbiology and Infectious Diseases, Professor of Medicine, University of North Carolina (1957-1979); Faculty, University of North Carolina, Chapel Hill, NC (1957-1979); Visiting Investigator, Rockefeller Institute, New York, NY (1952-1953); Resident in Internal Medicine, Barnes Hospital, St. Louis, MO (1949-1951); Intern, Johns Hopkins Hospital, Baltimore, MD (1946-1947) **Career Related:** Chairperson, Health and Safety Committee, Cedars Chapel Hill (2014); Member, Bacteriology and Mycology Study Section, National Institutes of Health (1985-1989); Chairperson, Bacteriology and Mycology Study Section, National Institutes of Health (1977-1979); Member, Bacteriology and Mycology Study Section, National Institutes of Health (1975-1979) **Military Service:** Medical Corps, U.S. Army (1947-1957) **Creative Works:** Editor, Journal of Immunology (1973-1980); Editor, Journal of the Reticuloendothelial Society (1973-1980); Editor, Infection and Immunity (1970-1980) **Awards:** Lectureship Named in His Honor, Spitznagel Lectureship on Host Antimicrobial Defense, Emory University (1998); Distinguished Service Award, University of North Carolina School of Medicine, Chapel Hill, NC (1987); Postdoctoral Fellow, U.S. Public Health Service (1968); Research Career Development Award, U.S. Public Health Service (1957-1967); Grantee, U.S. Public Health Service and Atomic Energy Commission **Memberships:** President, American Medical School of Microbiology and Immunology (1990-1991); President, Reticuloendothelial Society (1982); Division Group Councilor, American Society of Microbiology (1977-1979); Fellow, American College of Physicians (1953); Infectious Disease Society; American Association for the Advancement of Science; American Association of Immunologists; Infectious Disease Society; Southern Society of Clinical Research Association; Sigma Xi; Kiwanis Knights of Pythias **Marquis Who's Who Honors:** Albert Nelson Marquis Lifetime Achievement Award **Why did you become involved in your profession or industry:** Dr. Spitznagel became interested in medicine at an early age, having suffered from appendicitis with a rupture and peritonitis, a combination of afflictions that necessitated a surgery. During this time, he learned much about microbiology, which evolved into a broader interest in medicine. **Avocations:** Water color painting; Sketching **Religion:** Episcopalian

Barbara Stanislawski

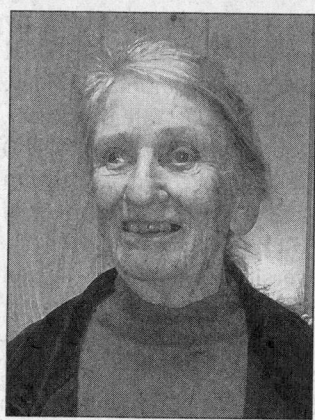

Title: Curator, Secondary School Educator **Industry:** Education/Educational Services **Date of Birth:** 05/17/1936 **Place of Birth:** Oakland **State/Country of Origin:** CA/USA **Parents:** Lewis Hart Bishop; Edna Frances (Shestek) Bishop **Marital Status:** Married **Spouse Name:** Michael Barr Stanislawski (1958) **Education:** BS in Psychology, Stanford University (1958) **Career:** Curator, Museum, National Park Service, Santa Fe, NM (1984-2006); Manager of Collections, School of American Research, Santa Fe, NM (1975-1983); Director, Head Start, Manhattan Public Schools, Manhattan, KS (1964-1968); Elementary Teacher, Davis School, Tucson, AZ (1959-1963) **Civic:** Board, League of Women Voters, Manhattan, KS (1964-1966) **Creative Works:** Contributor, Articles, Professional Journals **Awards:** Outstanding Young Woman in America, Outstanding Americans Foundation, Chicago, IL (1967) **Memberships:** Board of Directors, National New Deal Preservation Association (1998-Present); New Mexico Museum Association (1980-Present) **Marquis Who's Who Honors:** Albert Nelson Marquis Lifetime Achievement Award; Marquis Who's Who Top Professional **Why did you become involved in your profession or industry:** Mrs. Stanislawski found her passion for teaching after working for the Head Start program in Kansas. Mrs. Stanislawski found that she enjoyed teaching, and wanted to teach children as if they were her own. Mrs. Stanislawski later became interested in ancient Native American societies, and went on to become a curator for the National Park Service. **Avocations:** Reading; Hiking; Writing

Steven Mitchell Stanley, PhD

Title: 1) Paleontologist 2) Professor **Industry:** Education/Educational Services **Company Name:** 1) Florida State University 2) The Smithsonian Institution **Date of Birth:** 11/02/1941 **Place of Birth:** Detroit **State/Country of Origin:** MI/USA **Parents:** William Thomas Stanley; Mildred Elizabeth (Baker) Stanley **Children:** One Daughter **Education:** PhD, Yale University, New Haven, CT (1968); AB, Princeton University, Princeton, NJ, Summa Cum Laude (1963) **Career:** Research Professor, Florida State University, Tallahassee, FL (2019-Present); Research Professor, University of Hawaii at Manoa, Honolulu, HI (2005-2019); Chair, Department of Earth and Planetary Science, Johns Hopkins University (1987-1988); Professor, Johns Hopkins University (1974-2005); Associate Professor, Johns Hopkins University (1971-1974); Assistant Professor, Johns Hopkins University (1969-1971); Assistant Professor, University of Rochester (1967-1969) **Career Related:** Member, Editorial Board, American Journal of Science (1975-Present); President, Executive Committee, American Geosciences Institute (2002); Member, Executive Committee, American Geosciences Institute (1997-2001); Member, Commission on Geoscience, Environment, and Resources (1990-1996); Member, Advisory Committee, Earth Science, National Science Foundation (NSF) (1990-1993); Member, Editorial Board, Paleobiology (1988-1990, 1975-1982); Member, Board on Earth Science and Resources (1988-1990); Member, Board on Earth Science, National Research Council (1985-1988) **Creative Works:** Author, "Earth System History" (1999); Author, "Children of the Ice Age: How a Global Catastrophe Allowed Humans to Evolve" (1996); Author, "Exploring Earth and Life Through Time" (1992); Author, "Extinction" (1987); Author, "Earth and Life Through Time" (1986); Author, "The New Evolutionary Timetable: Fossils, Genes, and the Origin of Species" (1981); Author, "Macroevolution: Pattern and Process" (1979); Co-Author, "Principles and Paleontology" (1971); Author, "Relation of Shell Form to Life Habits in the Bivalvia" (1970) **Awards:** Penrose Medal, Geological Society of America (2013); Twenhofel Medal, Society for Sedimentary Geology (2008); Paleontological Society (2007); Mary Clark Thompson Medal, National Academy of Sciences (2006); Shea Award, National Association of Geoscience Teachers (2004); Bownocker Medal, Medial, Ohio State University (1997); Outstanding Technical Paper Award, Washington Geological Society (1986); Guggenheim Fellowship (1981); Allan C. Davis Medal, Maryland Academy of Sciences (1973); Outstanding Paper Award, Journal of Paleontology (1968) **Memberships:** Fellow, National Academy of Science (1994-Present); Public Affairs Committee, American Geophysics Union (2002-2004); Penrose Medal Committee, Geological Society of America (1996-1998, 1986-1988); President, Paleontological Society (1993-1994); Senior Councilor, Paleontological Society (1991-1993); Fellow, American Academy of Arts and Science (1988); Councilor, Society for the Study of Evolution (1982-1984); Penrose Grant Committee, Geological Society of America (1976-1978); Councilor Under Age 40, Paleontological Society (1976-1977); Society for Sedimentary Geology **Marquis Who's Who Honors:** Albert Nelson Marquis Lifetime Achievement Award; Marquis Who's Who Top Professional; Distinguished Humanitarian **To what do you attribute your success:** Professor Stanley attributes his success to being good at deductive reasoning and fundamentally creative with the courage to tolerate controversy. **Why did you become involved in your profession or industry:** A famous medical researcher invited him at the age of 15 for a month of mineral collecting in Colorado. For a thesis topic at his boys' school, Prof. Stanley chose the geological and economic history of Ohio's Chagrin River Valley where he lived. At Princeton U. he took a biology course for which the main theme was evolution, which intrigued Prof. Stanley. In a paleontology course Prof. Al Fisher brought fossils to life for Prof. Stanley and became his life-long friend. Paleontology was for him. Professor Stanley graduated summa cum laude from Princeton in 1963 and from Yale U. with a doctorate in 1968. His doctoral dissertation, "Relation of Shell Form to Life Habits in the Bivalvia (Mollusca)," is the largest body of work produced by any one person on the functional skeletal morphology of a single class of animals. At the age of 32 he became the youngest full professor at Johns Hopkins University, where he later founded and chaired a part-time evening master's program in environmental sciences and policy. Since 1972, Prof. Stanley has been a Research Associate at the Smithsonian Institution, where he has a laboratory. His textbook "Principles of Paleontology," coauthored with David Raup in 1971, changed the way paleontology was taught, and his historical geology text, now in its seventh edition and titled "Earth System History," has been used by about half a million students. **Avocations:** Landscape architecture; Gardening **Thoughts on Life:** Professor Stanley believes it is important that prominent people reach out to support young people to help them receive the appreciation they deserve.

M. Duncan Stanton, PhD

Title: Professor Emeritus **Industry:** Education/Educational Services **Company Name:** Spalding University **State/Country of Origin:** NY/USA **Marital Status:** Married **Education:** PhD in Clinical and Community Psychology (Minors in Experimental and Social Psychology), University of Maryland (1968); MA in Clinical Psychology, George Washington University, Washington, DC (1964); BA in Psychology, Alfred University, Alfred, NY (1962) **Certifications:** Certification or Diplomate Status, Seven National Specialty Boards; Licensed Psychologist, Three States **Career:** Professor Emeritus of Psychology, Spalding University, Louisville, KY (1999-Present); Vice President for Academic Research (1999); Dean/Professor, School of Professional Psychology and Social Work, Spalding University (1997-1999); Professor of Psychiatry (Psychology), Director, Division of Family Programs, University of Rochester School of Medicine and Dentistry (1983-1997); Visiting Faculty, Harvard Medical School (1989); Assistant to Associate Professor of Psychiatry (Psychology), with Appointments at Philadelphia General Hospital and the Philadelphia Child Guidance Clinic, University of Pennsylvania School of Medicine, Philadelphia, PA (1972-1983) **Career Related:** Consultant, Advisory Board Member, More than 75 Governmental and Private Agencies and Organizations (1970-Present); Consultantship, The White House Office of Drug Abuse Policy, Washington, DC (1977-1981); Chair, Multiple Task Forces, Review Committees and Site Visit Teams, National Institute on Drug Abuse (NIDA), National Institute of Mental Health (NIMH), National Institute on Alcohol Abuse and Alcoholism (NIAAA) (1975-1998); Ad Hoc Committee, Special Action Office on Drug Abuse Policy, The White House, Washington, DC (1974); U.S. Department of Defense, Task Group on Alcoholism, The Pentagon, Washington, DC (1971-1972) **Civic:** Committee and Program Appointments, Various Cities and States (1972-1999); Consultant, Sponsor, and Supervisor, Fulbright Commission (1987-1992) **Military Service:** Second Lieutenant to Captain, United States Army (1962-1972); Assistant Chief of Psychology and Director of Psychology Training, Walter Reed General Hospital, Washington, DC (1971-1972); Chief Psychologist, Fort Meade, MD (1970-1971); 98th Medical Detachment, Vietnam (1969-1970); Fort Dix, NJ (1968-1969) **Creative Works:** Author, More Than 150 Professional Publications (1968-Present); 16 Editorial Boards (1980-2008); Director, Anonymous Survey, U.S. Army (1971); Speaker, Presenter, Over 500 Invited Presentations and Workshops in 27 Different Countries Across Five Continents **Awards:** Inductee, Hall of Fame, Schenectady City School District (2008); Cumulative Contribution to Family Therapy Research Award, American Association for Marriage and Family Therapy (AAMFT) (2003); Presidential Citation, American Psychological Association (APA) (2001); Legacy Circle Award, National Council on Family Relations (NCFR) (1999); Award for Distinguished Contribution to Family Systems Research, American Family Therapy Academy (AFTA) (1997); Decorated, Bronze Star Medal, United States Army (1971); Grantee (Principal Investigator), Eight Research Grants; Recipient, Various Prestigious Honors and Awards **Memberships:** Kentucky Psychological Association (1998-Present); International Family Therapy Association (1987-Present); AAMFT (1978-Present); AFTA (1979-Present); NCFR (1974-Present); APA (1969-Present) **Marquis Who's Who Honors:** Albert Nelson Marquis Lifetime Achievement Award (2018); Marquis Who's Who Top Educator (2018) **Why did you become involved in your profession or industry:** Dr. Stanton became involved in psychology largely because of his parents and their effect on his upbringing. His father was a physics and math teacher with an interest in science, and his mother was an outgoing "people person." This combination of influences shaped his career path.

Roger D. Stanton

Title: Attorney **Industry:** Law and Legal Services **Company Name:** Roger D. Stanton Attorney At Law **Date of Birth:** 10/04/1938 **Place of Birth:** Waterville **State/Country of Origin:** KS/USA **Parents:** George W. Stanton; Helen V. (Peterson) Stanton **Marital Status:** Married **Spouse Name:** Judith L. Duncan (01/27/1962) **Children:** Jeffrey B.; Brady D. (Deceased); Todd A. **Education:** JD, University of Kansas (1963); AB, University of Kansas (1960) **Career:** Private Practice, Roger D. Stanton Attorney At Law, Overland Park, KS (2005-2012); Partner, Litigation Practice, Berkowitz Stanton Brandt Williams & Shaw LLP, Prairie Village, KS (1997-2005); Partner, Stinson, Mag & Fizzell, Kansas City, MO (1983-1996); Chairman, Products Practice Group, Board of Directors, Stinson, Mag & Fizzell, Kansas City, MO (1993-1995); Board of Directors, Chairman, Executive Committee, Weeks, Thomas & Lysaught, Kansas City, MO (1981-1982); Partner, Weeks, Thomas & Lysaught, Kansas City, MO (1969-1981); Associate, Stanley, Schroeder, Weeks, Thomas & Lysaught, Kansas City, MO (1963-1968) **Career Related:** Fellow, American Bar Foundation **Civic:** Board of Directors, Kansas Appleseed Foundation (2000); Co-Chairman, Civil Justice Reform Act Committee, District of Kansas (1991-1995); President, YMCA Youth Football Club (1980-1982); Active, Boy Scouts America (1973-1979); Former Chairman, Johnson County 302 Baseball; Former Chairman, Johnson County 302 Baseball Foundation **Creative Works:** Chairman, Board of Editors, Journal of Kansas Bar Association (1975-1983); Contributor, Articles, Professional Journals **Memberships:** Founding Member, Earl O'Conner Inn of Court (1991-Present); American College of Trial Lawyers (1981-Present); Johnson County Bar Association (2010-2011); Johnson County Bar Foundation (1997-2010); Board of Directors, History Society of the 10th Circuit (2005-2007); Defense Research Institute (1979-1990); President, Kansas Association Defense Counsel (1977-1978); University of Kansas School of Law Alumni Association (1975-1976); Kansas Bar Association; International Association of Defense Counsel; Board of Directors, University of Kansas Kansas City Alumni; Club Kansas City; Phi Delta Phi; 40 Years Club; Civil War Round Table **Bar Admissions:** Supreme Court of the United States (1973); U.S. Court of Appeals for the 10th Circuit (1972); State of Kansas (1963); U.S. District Court of Kansas (1963) **Marquis Who's Who Honors:** Albert Nelson Marquis Lifetime Achievement Award; Marquis Who's Who Top Professional **Why did you become involved in your profession or industry:** When Mr. Stanton got out of undergraduate school, he was thinking about pursuing law school. He did well early on, as he made law review and was editor of the Kansas Law Review several times. This felt like his path; he knew he should continue. Through his work, he got to meet a lot of people and learned a lot from them. He truly enjoyed what he was doing. **Avocations:** Reading Civil War history; Reading biographies; Watching historical television shows

Sylvia Doucet Stanton

Title: Artist, Gallery Owner, Author **Industry:** Fine Art **Date of Birth:** 09/21/1935 **Place of Birth:** New Orleans **State/Country of Origin:** LA/USA **Parents:** Clifton Leo Doucet Sr.; Maria Delbert (Alfonso Swiber) Doucet **Marital Status:** Married **Spouse Name:** Robert Elmer Stanton (01/03/1953) **Children:** Robert; Sylvia; Barbara; Richard; Laura; Cheri **Education:** Graduate, High School, New Orleans, LA (1952) **Certifications:** Certified Jewelry Appraiser **Career:** Owner, Gallery at Milbrook, Picayune, MS (2001-2005); Owner, Doucet-Stanton Ltd., Slidell, LA (1988-1997); Owner, Magnolia Plantation, Slidell, LA (1988-1997); Real Estate Agent, Century 21, Slidell, LA (1982-1988); Owner, Plantation Antiques, Slidell, LA (1974-1988); Partner, Doucet's Jewelry, Slidell, LA (1969-1982) **Career Related:** Appraiser Jewelry, Antiques, Real Estate (1969-Present); Artist, Painter (1950-Present) **Civic:** Founding Chairman, President, Council of Le Cotillion (1987); Co-Founder, Le Cotillion, Slidell, LA (1975) **Creative Works:** Exhibited, Montserrat Gallery, New York, NY, Agora Gallery, New York, NY, Stanton Gallery in Bay, St. Louis, MO, Maggie May's in Bay, St. Louis, MO, Art Center, Foley, AL; Permanent Collections, New Orleans, LA; Author, "A Grandmother's Happy Tales" **Awards:** Named, Countess De Miron Delbert, Greece (1988) **Memberships:** Secretary, Bayou Liberty Garden Club (1988-Present); District Chairman, 6840, Inner Wheel (1990-1991); Founding President, Inner Wheel, Slidell, LA (1989); Albuquerque Art League; Allied Artists of America; New Orleans Art Association; Former Member, Albuquerque Art League; Bayou Liberty Garden Club; Picayune Garden Club; Ozone Camellia Club **Marquis Who's Who Honors:** Albert Nelson Marquis Lifetime Achievement Award; Marquis Who's Who Top Professional **Why did you become involved in your profession or industry:** Ms. Stanton became involved in her profession because her mother, Maria Delbert (Alfonso Swiber) Doucet, ran a jewelry store in 1944 and back then, it was not common to see a woman doing that. Her mother raised her to believe she could do anything she set her mind to and only recently her sister closed the store. When Ms. Stanton was in kindergarten, her teacher gave everyone finger paints and she got brown finger paints, and she was trying to figure out what she could do with brown finger paint. She made tall grass, soldiers and jeeps going through the grass, and her teacher loved it so much she made her knock on all the doors of the school so that she could show off her artwork. **Avocations:** Art; Antiques; Gardening; Interior decorating **Political Affiliations:** Republican **Religion:** Roman Catholic

Irving C. Statler, PhD

Title: Associate Emeritus **Industry:** Research **Company Name:** NASA Ames Research Center **Date of Birth:** 11/23/1923 **Place of Birth:** Buffalo **State/Country of Origin:** NY/USA **Year of Passing:** 2020 **Parents:** Samuel William Statler; Sarah (Strauss) Statler **Marital Status:** Married **Spouse Name:** Renée Roll Statler (08/23/1953) **Children:** William Scott; Thomas Stuart **Education:** PhD in Aeronautics and Mathematics, California Institute of Technology, Pasadena, CA (1956); BS in Engineering Mathematics and Aeronautical Engineering, University of Michigan, Ann Arbor, MI (1945) **Career:** Associate Emeritus, NASA Ames Research Center (2008-2014); Level 3 Lead, Data Analysis Tool Development and Intramural Monitoring, Aviation Safety and Security Program, NASA (1999-2008); Project Manager, Aviation Performance Measuring System, NASA (1994-2008); Lead, AOS MASSS (1998-1999); Chief, Aerospace Human Factors Research Division, NASA (1992-1994); Principal Engineer, NASA Ames Research Center (1988-1992); Director, Advisory Group for Aerospace R&D (AGARD), NATO (1985-1988); Director, Aeromechanics Laboratory, U.S. Army Aviation Systems Command's Research and Technology Laboratories (1972-1985); Research Scientist, U.S. Army Air Mobility Research and Development Laboratory, Moffett Field, CA (1970-1972); Senior Staff Scientist, Aerosciences Division, Cornell Aeronautical Laboratory (Now Calspan) (1969-1970); Head, Applied Mechanics Department, Cornell Aeronautical Laboratory (1963-1970); Assistant Head, Aeromechanics Department, Cornell Aeronautical Laboratory (1957-1963); Principal Engineer, Flight Research Department, Cornell Aeronautical Laboratory (1955-1957); Research Engineer, Flight Research Department, Cornell Aeronautical Laboratory (1946-1953) **Career Related:** Human Factors Research Scientist, NASA Ames Research Center (1988-2014); Project Officer, Letter of Agreement, NASA Ames Research Center and Office National d'Etudeset de Recherches Aérospatiales (ONERA) (1992-1999); Project Officer, Letter of Agreement, NASA Ames Research Center and the National Aerospace Laboratory NLR (1989-1994); Initiator, U.S.-Israel MOU for Cooperative Research in Helicopter Flight Controls and Display Technologies (1984-1985); Project Officer, U.S.-Italy MOU for Cooperative Research in Helicopter Dynamics and Simulation (1981-1985); Project Officer, U.S.-German MOU for Cooperative Research in Rotary Wing Flight Control and Handling Qualities (1978-1985); Project Officer, U.S.-France MOU for Cooperative Research in Helicopter Aerodynamics (1972-1985); Project Officer, U.S.-Japan Data Exchange Agreement on Rotary Wing Technology (1972-1985); Director, Army Aeromechanics Laboratory (1971-1985); Chairman, Flight Mechanics Panel Advisory Group, Aerospace Research and Development, NATO (1974-1976); Lecturer, University of Buffalo, Millard Fillmore College, Buffalo, NY (1957-1958); Research Scientist, Research Analysis Group, Jet Propulsion Laboratory, Pasadena, CA (1953-1955); Fellow, American Institute of Aeronautics and Astronautics; Fellow, American Association for the Advancement of Science; Fellow, Royal Aeronautical Society; Fellow, German Aerospace Society **Military Service:** U.S. Army Air Forces (1945-1946) **Creative Works:** Author, "Human Consciousnesses: the Evolution of Our Sensor of Society" (2020); Author, "Distributed National FOQA Program" (2002); Author, "Aviation Performance Measuring System (APMS)" (1980) **Awards:** Wesley L. McDonald Distinguished Statesman of Aviation Award (2012); Embry-Riddle Aeronautical University President's Special Recognition for Exemplary Dedication to Safety (2007); NASA Outstanding Leadership Medal (2006); R&D 100 Award (2005); NASA TIGE Administrators Award for Performance Data Analysis and Reporting System (2003); NASA Group Achievement Award to the Aviation Performance Measuring Systems Project Team (1999); NASA Group Achievement Award to the PI-in-a-Box Project Team (1993); AIAA Medal for International Cooperation (1992); U.S. Air Force Exceptional Civilian Service Medal (1988); NATO Military Committee, Chairman's Medal (1988); Ministry of Defense of France, La Medaille de l'Aeronautique (1986); U.S. Army Exceptional Civilian Service Medal (1985); Presidential Meritorious Executive Rank (1981); U.S. Army Meritorious Civilian Service Medal (1979); Charter Member, Senior Executive Service (1978); U.S. Army Certificate of Achievement (1975) **Memberships:** U.S. Air Force Scientific Advisory Board (1985-1988); NATO/AGARD Flight Mechanics Panel (1972-1983); German Aerospace Society; American Helicopter Society; Sigma Xi; Human Factors Society **Marquis Who's Who Honors:** Albert Nelson Marquis Lifetime Achievement Award; Marquis Who's Who Top Professional **To what do you attribute your success:** Dr. Statler attributes his success to having leadership over an extraordinarily competent group of dedicated research scientists and engineers. **Why did you become involved in your profession or industry:** Dr. Statler followed airplanes since the day he could ride his bicycle and he always wanted to be an aerospace engineer. As he looks back, he spent his entire life in human factors. **Avocations:** Drawing

John Vance Stechman

Title: Rangeland Management Educator, Owner **Industry:** Agriculture **Company Name:** La Cuesta Consulting **Date of Birth:** 08/01/1934 **Place of Birth:** Peoria **State/Country of Origin:** IL/USA **Parents:** John Henry Stechman; Helen Jean (Vance) Stechman **Marital Status:** Married **Spouse Name:** Dorothy Jean McKowan (08/18/1956, Deceased) **Children:** John Carl; Jennifer Jean; Laurie Joan **Education:** Federal, State, and County Agency, and University and Society Sponsored Workshops (1986-2009); MS, University of California Davis (1960); BS, University of California Davis (1956); Coursework, Occidental College, University of California Davis, University of California Berkeley (1952-1956) **Certifications:** Certified Nationally Range Management Consultant **Career:** Consultant, Rangeland Resources Management (1964-Present); Rancher, San Luis Obispo, CA (1971-1991); Professor of Range Management, California Polytechnic State University San Luis Obispo (1960-1992); Research Assistant, University of California Davis Department of Agronomy, (1959-1960); Research Assistant, U.S. Department of Agriculture Agricultural Research Service, Davis, Susanville, CA (1955-1956); Fire Guard, U.S. Department of Agriculture Forest Service, El Dorado National Forest, CA (1954) **Career Related:** Board of Directors, San Miguelito Mutual Water Company (1997-2002); Technical Advisory Committee, Morro Bay Watershed (1995-1997); Rangeland Manager, California Board of Forestry (1995); Range Science Education Council (1965-1990); Advisory Committee, Montana de Oro State Park (1965-1974); Rancher, Managed 83 Beef Cattle Cow Herd **Civic:** Team Tennis Champion, San Luis Obispo Country Club (1989); Water Board, San Miguelito Water Company; Honorary Chapter Farmer, Vocational FFA **Military Service:** U.S. Army, Quartermaster Corps Food & Container Institute (1957-1960) **Creative Works:** Author, "Agricultural cartographer - Ranches of California Poly State University, 2nd Edition" (1991); Author, "Agricultural cartographer - Ranches of California Poly State University" (1988); Author, "Common Western Range Plants, 3rd Edition" (1986); Author, "An Illustrated History of University Land, Agriculture" (1985); Contributor, Articles, Professional Journals **Awards:** Golden State Award, Who's Who Historical Society (1994); Lili Research Laboratories Grantee (1981); U.S. Army Suggestion Awards (1958); California Range Manager of the Year; Two Awards for Cross Country Horsemanship **Memberships:** Historian, Society for Range Management California (1990); Range Science Education Council; National Cattlemans Association; California Cattlemans Association; California Range Improvement Association; Alpha Zeta; Future Farmers of America; Soil and Water Conservation Society **Marquis Who's Who Honors:** Albert Nelson Marquis Lifetime Achievement Award **To what do you attribute your success:** Mr. Stechman attributes his success to lots of interests in a lot of our world, and most of all being married for 65 years to a great, kind, intelligent woman, Dottie Jean. Also his two fine parents, who encouraged him to go to college. **Why did you become involved in your profession or industry:** Mr. Stechman read an entire textbook on Range Management, the original copy by Dr. Samson which was written in 1948 as a new agricultural science that had been recognized as range land management. When he was working in the forest has a fire guard he read the entire book and knew that is what he wanted to do. He got off to a good start reading that textbook, and decided to major in that field after he graduated from junior college. He was one of the first nine students in the state of California to graduate with a range management degree. **Avocations:** Watercolor art; Piano composition; Tennis; Reading **Political Affiliations:** Independent **Religion:** Lutheran and Presbyterian

Jack Steele, PhD

Title: Professor Emeritus of Chemistry **Industry:** Education/Educational Services **Company Name:** Albany State University **Date of Birth:** 1942 **Place of Birth:** Indianapolis **State/Country of Origin:** IN/USA **Marital Status:** Widowed **Spouse Name:** Carolyn J. Botts (05/18/1968, Deceased 2017) **Children:** Two Sons (One Deceased); One Daughter **Education:** Postdoctoral Research, Teaching Intern, Washington State University, Pullman, WA (1968-1970); PhD in Inorganic Chemistry, University of Kentucky, Lexington, KY (1968); BA in Chemistry, DePauw University, Greencastle, IN (1964) **Certifications:** Handling Controlled Substances, Georgia Board of Pharmacy, United States Drug Enforcement Administration **Career:** Professor Emeritus of Chemistry, Albany State University, Albany, GA (2006-Present); Full Professor, Albany State University, Albany, GA (1980-2005); Coordinator, Chemistry and Physics, Albany State University, Albany, GA (1985-2003); Chairman, Chemistry and Physics, Albany State University, Albany, GA (1981-1985); Associate Professor, Albany State University, Albany, GA (1975-1980); Assistant Professor of Chemistry, Albany State University, Albany, GA (1970-1975) **Career Related:** Reviewer, Journal of Chemical Education (1985-2003); Contributor, Writer, MCAT (1993-1998); Extramural Reviewer, National Science Foundation (1975-1980); Extramural Reviewer, U.S. Environmental Protection Agency (1977-1980); Recitation Instructor, University of Kentucky (1967-1968); Graduate Research Assistant, National Science Foundation (1967); Graduate Teaching Assistant in General and Analytical Chemistry (1964-1966); Undergraduate Laboratory Assistant, General and Analytical Chemistry, DePauw University, Greencastle, IN (1963-1964); Instructor, Drug Identification Course, U.S. Marine Corps Logistics, Albany, GA; Presenter in Field, National, Regional and State Meetings **Civic:** Assistant Starter for Local and State BMX Bicycle Races; Assistant Den Leader, Cub Scouts of America; Co-Founder, Southwest Georgia Section, American Chemical Society; Founder, Air Force ROTC Drill Team, Clinical Chemistry Programs, Forensic Science Programs; Finance Committee, St. Teresa's School, Albany, GA **Creative Works:** Interviewee, Hurricane Andrew, WALB News 10, WFXL Fox 31, Albany, GA (1994); Cast and Crew, Late Night Show, WFXL Fox 31, Albany, GA; Contributor, Numerous Papers in Field, Scientific Journals; Verbal Contributor, Papers, Regional and National American Chemical Society Meetings **Awards:** Grantee, National Institutes of Health (1988-2005); Grantee, Charles Stewart Mott Foundation (1988-1994); Grantee, Minority Schools of Biomedical Support (1972-1977); Grantee, National Science Foundation (1972-1973); Doctoral Year Fellowship, University of Kentucky Foundation (1967-1968); Variety Athletic Letter, Letter Jacket Award, DePauw University (1960-1964); Commander Award, ROTC Drill Team, DePauw University (1962); Four Gun Drill, Honor Group, Culver Military Academy (1959-1960); Silver A Award, Culver Military Academy (1958); Blue Key Honor Society Awards; One of Five NSF Science Summer Scholars of Electrochemical Research; Clinical Chemistry Recognition Award; Outstanding Service Award; Started Best and Most Popular Teacher as Selected by the Students, Albany State University **Memberships:** Co-Founder, Chairman, Southwest Georgia Section, Referee Journal, American Chemical Society (1986-Present); Sigma Xi, the Scientific Research Honor Society; American Association for Clinical Chemistry; Organizer, Founder, Air Force ROTC Drill Team; Vice President to President, Student Study Affiliates, American Chemical Society; Georgia Academy of Science **Marquis Who's Who Honors:** Albert Nelson Marquis Lifetime Achievement Award; Marquis Who's Who Top Professional **To what do you attribute your success:** Dr. Steele attributes his success to mentors in his life. First and foremost, he credits his late wife, Carolyn B. Steele. Dr. Laurence T. Crimmins, MD, and Dr. Tom Johnson, MD, of Albany Internal Medicine invited him to join the weekly seminars at both hospitals and earned continuing medical credits in internal medicine from the Medical College of Georgia. Dr. Don Williams directed his research at the University of Kentucky. Dr. Don Sands and Dr. Joe Wilson were, without a doubt, the best teachers Dr. Steele ever had. Dr. James A. Hotz, MD, the original and real "Doc Hollywood," Dr. Thomas F. Neal, MD, and Dr. John Schilling, MD, saved his life in 2014 from thrombocytopenia. They did not have to remove any toes, feet, lower legs, or upper legs, and gave super encouragement in healing. It's been six years since the procedure. Dr. J. Ivan Legg of Washington State University directed his postdoctoral research and taught him a number of other procedures on molecular structure. Colonel John R. Mars-Culver was his military counselor for Battery B, and later head of Culver Military Academy. He also gave moral guidance and fatherly advice. Dr. John Ricketts, Dr. Eugene Schwartz, Dr. Howard Burkett, and Dr. Jack Cook from DePauw University encouraged Dr. Steele and gave him a love for chemistry. Dr. Russell Compton, head of the department of philosophy and religion, gave enough advice and teachings of Dr. Steele to form his own thoughts on ethics. **Avocations:** Reading; Cooking; Overseas traveling; Genealogy **Religion:** Catholic

Robin Faith Steinberg

Title: Ophthalmologist **Industry:** Medicine & Health Care **Company Name:** Burlington Eye Associates **Date of Birth:** 02/23/1954 **Place of Birth:** Kansas City **State/Country of Origin:** MO/USA **Parents:** Dr. Milton Stanley Steinberg; Norma (Cohen) Steinberg **Marital Status:** Married **Spouse Name:** Dr. Phillip M. Gendelman **Children:** Alana; Joshua; Ashira; Mirit **Education:** Resident, Tufts/New England Medical Center, Boston, MA (1982-1984); Resident, Barnes Hospital/Washington University Medical Center, St. Louis, MO (1981-1982); Intern, Lenox Hill Hospital, New York, NY (1980-1981); MD, Columbia University (1980); BA, Smith College (1976) **Certifications:** Diplomate, American Board of Ophthalmology **Career:** Attending Ophthalmologist, Burlington Eye Associates (1984-Present) **Career Related:** Reviewer, Massachusetts Peer Review Organization, Waltham, MA (1994-Present); Instructor, Clinical Diagnosis, Boston University Medical School **Awards:** Listee, Top Docs; Electee, Best of Boston, Boston Magazine **Memberships:** American Academy of Ophthalmology; Massachusets Medical Society; Massachusets Society of Eye Physicians & Surgeons **Marquis Who's Who Honors:** Albert Nelson Marquis Lifetime Achievement Award **To what do you attribute your success:** Dr. Steinberg attributes her success to a great education, wonderful role models, and mentors. She also credits a healthy dose of stamina, fortitude, and persistence. **Why did you become involved in your profession or industry:** Dr. Steinberg became involved in her profession because she was interested in medicine from an early age. Her father, Milton Stanley, was a cardiologist. He served as an inspiration to her because of his industry success. After taking college courses covering Hubel and Wiesel's fascinating studies, she decided to specialize in ophthalmology. **Avocations:** Reading; Theater; Languages; World travel **Religion:** Jewish **Thoughts on Life:** Dr. Steinberg believes the most important part of life is following one's dreams.

Donald M. Steinwachs, PhD

Title: Public Health Educator, Academic Administrator **Industry:** Education/Educational Services **Date of Birth:** 09/09/1946 **Place of Birth:** Boise **State/Country of Origin:** Idaho/USA **Parents:** Don Peter Steinwachs; Emma Bertha (Weisshaupt) Steinwachs; **Marital Status:** Married **Spouse Name:** Sharon Steinwachs **Education:** PhD, Johns Hopkins University (1973); MS, University of Arizona (1970) **Career:** Professor Emeritus (2016); Professor, Health policy and management, Johns Hopkins University (1986-2016); Professor, Health Policy and Management (2005-2016); Director Health Services Research & Development Center, Johns Hopkins University, (1982-2010); Interim Provost, Johns Hopkins University (2007); Chair, Department of Health Policy and Management, Johns Hopkins University, (1994-2005); Associate professor, Health policy and management, Johns Hopkins University (1979-1986); Assistant professor, Health services administration, Johns Hopkins University (1973-1979) **Career Related:** Secretary, Advisory committee Department of Veteran Affairs, Washington, DC (1991-1992); Board of directors, Mathematica Policy Research, Inc., **Civic:** Board directors, President, Foundation for Health Service Research, Active, Governors, Commission on Health Policy Research and Finances (1988-1990) **Military Service:** Reserve Officer, Captain, United States Army (1969-1975) **Creative Works:** Contributor, Articles, Professional Journals **Awards:** Grantee, Robert Wood Johnson Foundation, Agency for Health Care Policy and Research, National Institute of Mental Health **Memberships:** Board of Directors, President, Member, Institute Medicine National Academy of Sciences (1993); Association Health Service Research **Marquis Who's Who Honors:** Albert Nelson Marquis Lifetime Achievement Award; Marquis Who's Who Top Professionals **Why did you become involved in your profession or industry:** Mr. Steinwachs received his bachelor's degree in engineering and a master's degree also, which was in engineering. He soon realized that he wanted to purse a career in system engineering. **Avocations:** Traveling; Sailing **Political Affiliations:** Democrat **Religion:** Baha'i Faith

Walter W. Stern III

Title: Consultant, Senior Emeritus Attorney **Industry:** Law and Legal Services **Company Name:** Walter W. Stern Attorney at Law **Date of Birth:** 03/25/1946 **Place of Birth:** Cincinnati **State/Country of Origin:** OH/USA **Parents:** Walter W. Stern Jr.; Harriet Louise Stern **Children:** Rachael Louise **Education:** JD, Marquette University (1974); BA, Carthage College (1969) **Career:** Retired Lawyer, Private Practice Walter W. Stern Attorney at Law, (2007-2019); Lawyer, Private Practice (1991-2007); Senior Partner, Caviali & Stern (1985-1991); Senior Partner, Joling Rizzo Willems Stern & Burroughs (1982-1985); Lawyer, Private Practice (1974-1983); Consultant, Senior Emeritus Attorney **Career Related:** Lecturer in Criminal Law, Carthage College (1976-2005) **Civic:** State Board, Board Member, Advocacy, NAMI (National Alliance of Mentally Ill) (2004-Present); Candidate for Circuit Judge (2005); Hearing Examiner, General Relief (1990-1995); Educator, Domestic Violence Project (1983-1994) **Memberships:** Fellow, American Academy of Forensic Sciences; Advisory Branch, NAMI **Bar Admissions:** State of Illinois (1999); Supreme Court of the United States (1983); U.S. Court of Appeals for the Seventh Circuit (1981); State of Wisconsin (1974); U.S. District Court, Eastern District, State of Wisconsin (1974); U.S. District Court, Western District, State of Wisconsin (1974) **Marquis Who's Who Honors:** Albert Nelson Marquis Lifetime Achievement Award; Marquis Who's Who Top Professional; Marquis Who's Who Humanitarian Award **To what do you attribute your success:** Mr. Stern attributes his success to his tenacity. **Why did you become involved in your profession or industry:** Mr. Stern was a school teacher. He taught in high school and he didn't see it going anywhere, although he liked the kids. He wanted to make a difference and do something positive. His generation, the baby boomers, wanted civil rights. They didn't like that there was a rigid class system where people couldn't advance whether race or poverty. People who actually tried to make it couldn't make it. There were too many institutional barriers to their success. He went into the law because he wanted to defend these underdogs. In the past 15-20 years, the underdog was basically the middle class. No political party is for the middle class. The Republicans say they're for the middle class, but their actions show they are for big businesses. The Democrats say they're for the middle class and end up coddling people, and doing well doesn't get rewarded. In a way, they enslave the people trying to help. He sees that. When he was a kid, people with a high school education who worked hard could make it and do well, but that isn't true anymore. If you work hard, put the effort in and have a reasonably good mind, you should be able to make it in this country successfully. He has never been for coddling people; he is not a liberal, but he just thinks there should be more opportunities. **Avocations:** Golf; Fishing; Hunting; Jogging; Reading; Creative writing; Fencing; Yoga

Sandra G. Stevens, CLU, CFC

Title: Financial Services Representative **Industry:** Insurance **Company Name:** Ohio National Financial Services Inc. **Date of Birth:** 02/01/1953 **Place of Birth:** Clarksville **State/Country of Origin:** IN/USA **Parents:** Samuel T. Gose (Deceased 1999); Eva (Hahn) Gose (Deceased 1998) **Marital Status:** Widow **Spouse Name:** Christopher W. Allen (10/21/1989) (deceased 2007); Mark T. Stevens (09/28/1974, Divorced 1985) (Deceased) **Children:** Garrett Allen **Education:** Bachelor of Arts in Psychology and Sociology, Indiana University (1974) **Certifications:** Chartered Financial Consultant (1989); Chartered Life Underwriter (1981) **Career:** Financial Services Inc. Representative, Ohio National Financial (2018-Present); Financial Services Representative, Rabjohns Financial Group, Chicago, IL (1988-2015); Sales Manager, New England Mutual Life, Chicago, IL (1984-1988); Sales Manager, LaVan Insurance Agency, Chicago, IL (1981-1984); Sales Representative, Aetna Life & Casualty, Oak Brook, IL (1974-1981) **Career Related:** Life Underwriters, Training Council, Bethesda, MD (1994); Instructor, American College, Bryn Mawr, PA (1992) **Civic:** Task Force, Committee of Illinois Insurance Code, Springfield, IL (1981); Advisory Board Department, Insurance, State of Illinois, Springfield, IL (1979-1981) **Memberships:** Board of Directors, First Christian Church of Downers Grove (2019); President, Darien Woman's Club (2013); District Board of Directors, DuPage Business and Professional Women (1994-1995); President, Hinsdale Business and Professional Women's Club (1989-1992); Board of Directors, DuPage Life Underwriters (1979-1983); Young Career Woman Award (1979); National Association of Insurance and Financial Advisors; Arbutus Society, Indiana University; Indiana University Alumni Association; Southern Shore Yacht Club **Marquis Who's Who Honors:** Albert Nelson Marquis Lifetime Achievement Award **Why did you become involved in your profession or industry:** Ms. Stevens became involved in her profession after studying psychology and sociology at Indiana University. Aetna was one of the few companies recruiting at the university's psychology department. Ms. Stevens worked at Aetna and eventually became one of their top producing employees. **Avocations:** Boating; Skiing; Golfing **Religion:** Christian

Joyce Louise Stevos, PhD

Title: Adjunct Professor **Industry:** Education/Educational Services **Date of Birth:** 05/22/1943 **Place of Birth:** Providence **State/Country of Origin:** RI/USA **Parents:** Josephus Caldwell; Patricia Anita (Strong) Caldwell Smith **Marital Status:** Divorced **Spouse Name:** Manuel Joseph Stevos (10/22/1966, Divorced 1981) **Children:** Manuel Joaquim **Education:** PhD, University of Rhode Island College, Rhode Island College (2005); MEd, Rhode Island College (1997) **Certifications:** Certified Teacher and Principal, Superintendent of Schools, Rhode Island **Career:** Adjunct Faculty, Rhode Island College (2005-Present, 1997-1999); Adjunct Faculty, Salve Regina University (2003-2005); Director, Salve Regina University (1992-2001); Supervisor, Social Studies, Salve Regina University (1976-1990); Teacher, Providence School Department (1965-1976) **Career Related:** Planning Committee, First Steps and Next Steps: Teaching African-American History in RI Classrooms (2016, 2018); Consultant in Developing Trinity Academy for the Performing Arts Charter School (2007-2009); Disciplinary Literacy Development Team, Evaluator, Connections: The Deborah McCrea Memorial Lecture Series: Congdon St. Church, Providence, RI (2002-2003); Evaluator, Langston Hughes Centennial Birthday Celebration, Museum of Art, RISD (2002); Facilitator; Teacher Quality Institutes, and Evaluator, Model Professional Development/Awards, U.S. Dept of Ed (2000); Mt. Hope High School, RI Visiting Committee for NEASC (1996); NCSS, Carter G. Woodson Book Award Committee (1993-1996); Cumberland High School, RI Visiting Committee for NEASC (1993); U.S. History NAEP Planning Committee (1991-1992, 1994); NCSS- Children's Book Council Review Committee (1990-1993) **Civic:** RI College Foundation Trustee (2018-Present); Board of Directors, RI Heritage Hall of Fame (2017-Present); Board of Directors, Heritage Harbor Foundation (2017-Present); RI Board of Education (2015-2017); 1696 Historical Commission Member, Appointed by Governor (2015-2017); Board President, Trinity Academy for the Performing Arts Charter School (2009-2016); Board of Directors, Fund for UCAP (2007-2012); Board of Trustees, Providence Public Library (1992-1999); Board of Directors, Providence Preservation Society (1991-1996); Board of Directors, RI College Alumni Association (1990-1997); President, Urban League of RI, (1983-1987) **Creative Works:** Senior Consultant, "Creating America: A History of the United States" (1999, 2002); Author, "Review of Till Victory is Won," Social Education (1996); Author, "The Constitution" (1987, 1977) **Awards:** Charles B. Willard Award, RI College Alumni Association (2019); Living the Dream Award, Martin Luther King Jr. State Commission (2019); All Kids Award, UCAP (2018); Distinguished Alumni Award, Classical High School (2014); Big Brothers Big Sisters of the Ocean State Legacy Award (2012); Northern YWCA Woman of Achievement Award (2011); George T. Downing Award for Education, RI Black Heritage Society (2007); RI College Alumni Honor Roll (1999); National Educator Award, Milken Family Foundation (1992); Education Award, Providence NAACP (1991); Community Service Award, John Hope Settlement House (1987); Never Again Award, Jewish Federation of RI (1983) **Memberships:** Alpha Omega State of RI (2015-Present); President, RI Black Heritage Society (1989-1995, 2011-2015); Treasurer, Delta Sigma Theta (1989-1991); Secretary, National Council for Social Studies (1979-1980); Secretary, Social Studies Supervisors Association (1979-1980); Trustee, Program Committee, National Conference of Christians and Jews; Daughters of the American Revolution; Delta Kappa Gamma Society International **Bar Admissions: Marquis Who's Who Honors:** Albert Nelson Marquis Lifetime Achievement Award; Marquis Who's Who Top Professional; Marquis Who's Who Humanitarian Award **To what do you attribute your success:** Setting goals and focussing on achieving them. Never taking "no" for an answer. **Why did you become involved in your profession or industry:** Dr. Stevos became involved in her profession because she knew she was destined to receive a college education. She liked reading and studying history. When she went to Rhode Island College, she majored in education and history. Not until her supervisor in student teaching had evaluated her, did she realize how much she enjoyed teaching. She then was able to relax and she began to enjoy herself as she was teaching and that is when she knew that teaching was what she wanted to do. From then on she knew teaching was her avocation and through it she could make a difference in the education of many young people. **Avocations:** Cooking; Family history; Reading

David James Stewart

Title: Cardiologist **Industry:** Medicine & Health Care **Date of Birth:** 12/27/1934 **Place of Birth:** Midland **State/Country of Origin:** MI/USA **Parents:** Leroy Hepburn Stewart; Zoa Irene (Hatchet) Stewart **Marital Status:** Widowed **Spouse Name:** Abbie Gale Pickett (09/07/1957, Deceased) **Children:** Kirk; Julia; Laura; Kenneth **Education:** Resident in Cardiology, Cleveland Metropolitan General Hospital, The MetroHealth System (1965-1967); Resident, Cincinnati General Hospital (1962-1963); Rotating Intern, Cincinnati General Hospital (1961-1962); MD, University of Colorado Denver, CO (1961); BS in Chemical Engineering, University of Colorado Boulder (1957) **Certifications:** Diplomate, American Board of Internal Medicine and Cardiovascular Disease **Career:** Director, Heart Center, Providence Regional Medical Center, Everett, WA (1995-2011); Cardiologist, The Everett Clinic, WA (1968-1995); Chief Resident, Medicine, Cleveland Metropolitan General Hospital, The MetroHealth System, Cleveland, Ohio (1967-1968) **Career Related:** Medical Coordinator, Cardiac Emergency Network (1988-2011); Medical Director, Saunders Regional Heart Center (1987-2011); Director, Heart Center, General Hospital Medical Center, Everett, WA (1984-1987); Medical Director, Medic One Program **Civic:** President, Snohomish Division (1995-1996); Board of Directors, General Hospital Medical Center, Everett, WA (1975-1995); Board of Directors, American Heart Association, Inc., Seattle, WA (1970-1990); Member, Advisory Board, Prosecuting Attorney, Snohomish County, WA (1985-1986); President, The Everett Clinic (1979); Board of Directors, The Everett Clinic (1975-1979); Volunteer Teacher, Nursing School **Military Service:** Captain, Deputy Hospital Commander, United States Air Force, (1963-1965) **Creative Works:** Editor, Newspaper, Cardiac Emergency Network (1988-1991) **Awards:** Budd Gould Award for Outstanding Community Service **Memberships:** Fellow, American College of Cardiology; American College of Internal Medicine; North Pacific Society of Internal Medicine **Marquis Who's Who Honors:** Albert Nelson Marquis Lifetime Achievement Award; Marquis Who's Who Top Professional **Why did you become involved in your profession or industry:** Dr. Stewart's oldest brother was a physician and continued to encourage him. After he got his degree in chemical engineering, he had a summer job and realized it was not very fulfilling trying to make other companies wealthier. His brother always encouraged him to get his pre-med out of the way, so he could change his mind if he wanted to. He decided to go to medical school, during his senior year. Dr. Stewart was the first one from the Chemical Engineering Department at the University of Colorado to go to medical school, and now 1/3 of the students go to medical school. The two are a natural fit. You learn fluid flow, chemistry, chemical reactions, and overall the human body. Dr. Stewart always liked cardiology, but it wasn't really a specialty when he was in school. When he got to Cleveland, it became apparent there was a lot he could do, and that is when he got interested in it. **Avocations:** Tennis; Computers; Bible; Spending time with grandchildren

David Wayne Stewart, PhD

Title: President's Professor of Marketing and Business Law **Industry:** Education/Educational Services **Company Name:** Loyola Marymount University **Date of Birth:** 10/23/1951 **Place of Birth:** Baton Rouge **State/Country of Origin:** LA/USA **Parents:** Wesley A. Stewart, Jr.; Edith L. (Richhart) Moore **Marital Status:** Married **Spouse Name:** Lenora Francois (06/06/1975) **Children:** Sarah Elizabeth; Rachel Dawn **Education:** PhD, Baylor University (1974); MA, Baylor University (1973); BA, Northeast Louisiana University (Now The University of Louisiana Monroe) (1972); Graduate, Leadership Riverside, Greater Riverside Chambers of Commerce; Graduate, Leadership Los Angeles, Los Angeles Area Chamber of Commerce **Career:** President's Professor of Marketing and Law, Loyola Marymount University (2012-Present); Professor Emeritus, University of California, Riverside (2012-Present); Professor, Marketing & Law, University of California, Riverside (2012-Present); Professor, Management & Marketing, University of California, Riverside (2007-2012); Dean, The A. Gary Anderson Graduate School of Management, University of California, Riverside (2007-2011); Chairman, Department of Marketing, University of Southern California, Los Angeles, CA (2006-2007); Robert E. Brooker Professor of Marketing, University of Southern California, Los Angeles, CA (1991-2007); Deputy Dean, Marshall School of Business, University of Southern California, Los Angeles, CA (1999-2001); Chairman, Department of Marketing, University of Southern California, Los Angeles, CA (1994-1999); Ernest W. Hahn Professor of Marketing, University of Southern California, Los Angeles, CA (1990-1991); Professor, University of Southern California, Los Angeles, CA (1986-1990); Senior Associate Dean, Vanderbilt University, Nashville, TN (1984-1986); Associate Professor, Vanderbilt University, Nashville, TN (1980-1986); Associate Professor, Jacksonville State University, AL (1978-1980); Research Manager, Needham, Harper & Steers Advertising (Now DDB Worldwide), Chicago, IL (1976-1978); Research Psychologist, Department of Health and Human Services, LA (1974-1976) **Career Related:** Management Consultant (1978-Present) **Civic:** Member and Chair, United States Census Bureau Advisory Committee; Chair, City of Riverside Economic Development Planning Task Force ("Seizing Our Destiny") **Creative Works:** Editor, Journal of Public Policy & Marketing (2012-2017); Editor-in-Chief, Oxford Online Bibliography in Marketing (2012-2015); Editor, Journal of the Academy of Marketing Science (2006-2009); Editor, Journal of Marketing (1999-2002); Author, "Secondary Research: Information Sources and Methods"; Co-author, "Effective Television Advertising: A Study of 1000 Commercials"; Co-author, "Consumer Behavior and the Practice of Marketing"; Co-author, "Focus Groups: Theory and Practice"; Co-author, "Attention, Attitude, and Affect in Response to Advertising"; Co-author, "Nonverbal Communication in Advertising"; Co-author, "Marketing Champions"; Author, "Handbook of Persuasion and Social Marketing"; Co-author, "Accountable Marketing: Linking Marketing Action to Financial Performance"; Author, "A Primer on Consumer Behavior"; Author, "Financial Dimensions of Marketing"; Co-author: "How to Get Published in the Best Marketing Journals"; Contributor, Articles to Professional Journals; Editorial Boards, Journal of Public Policy & Marketing, Journal of Marketing, Journal of Marketing Research, Journal of Advertising, The Journal of Advertising Research, Journal of International Advertising, Journal of Interactive Marketing, Journal of Interactive Advertising, Journal of Promotion Management, Current Issues & Research in Advertising, Journal of International Consumer Marketing, Journal of Managerial Issues and Other Journals **Awards:** American Marketing Association Award for Lifetime Contributions to Marketing and Public Policy (2015); Chairman's Award, Greater Riverside Chambers of Commerce (2010); Elsevier Distinguished Marketing Scholar Award, Society for Marketing Advances (2007); Cutco/Vector Distinguished Marketing Educator, Academy of Marketing Science (2006); Outstanding Contribution to Advertising Research Award, American Academy of Advertising (1998); Man of Merit Award, Omicron Delta Kappa **Memberships:** Founding Chair, Marketing Accountability Standards Board (2004-Present); Vice President for Publications, American Marketing Association (2017-Present); Board of Governors, Academy of Marketing Science (2004-2010); Vice President of Finances, American Marketing Association (1998-1999); President, Academic Council, American Marketing Association (1997-1998); Chair, Section on Statistics in Marketing, American Statistical Association (1997); Past President, Policy Board, Journal of Consumer Research; Fellow, American Psychological Association; Council Representative, American Psychological Association; Charter Fellow, American Psychological Society (Now Association for Psychological Science); Past President, Society for Consumer Psychology; INFORMS **Marquis Who's Who Honors:** Albert Nelson Marquis Lifetime Achievement Award **To what do you attribute your success:** He attributes his success to hard work and persistence. **Why did you become involved in your profession or industry:** He became involved in his profession because of his interest in people and their behavior, in addition to his desire to contribute to community. **Avocations:** Traveling; Live theatre **Political Affiliations:** Republican **Religion:** Baptist

James H. Stewart

Title: President/Managing Director **Industry:** Pharmaceuticals **Company Name:** The Stewart Group **Date of Birth:** 07/15/1941 **Place of Birth:** Boston **State/Country of Origin:** MA/USA **Parents:** James Henry; Mary E. (Cummins) Stewart **Marital Status:** Married **Spouse Name:** Linda (10/24/1964) **Children:** Laurie; Cathi; Brian; Daniel "Dan" **Education:** Master of Business Administration, Pepperdine University (1988); Bachelor of Science in Pharmacy, Massachusetts College Pharmacy (1964) **Certifications:** Registered Pharmacist (1964) **Career:** President, Managing Director, The Stewart Group (1988-Present); Manager, Industry Affairs, Syntex Laboratories Inc., Palo Alto, CA (1984-1988); Executive Director, Massachusetts State Pharmaceutical Association, Boston, MA (1978-1984); Director, Professional Relations, Pilgrim Health Applications, Bedford, MA (1974-1978); Registered Pharmacist, Various Pharmacies, Boston, MA (1964-1974) **Career Related:** Volunteer Positions at Associations and other Organizations **Civic:** Finance Committee, Town of Kingston, MA (1974-1977); Capital Budget Committee, Town of Marshfield, MA (1980-1983); Member, University of Southern California; Advisory Board, School of Business, School of Pharmacy, University of Southern California **Creative Works:** Editorial Board, U.S. Pharmacist Magazine **Awards:** Several **Memberships:** Fellow, American College Apothecaries; American Pharmaceutical Association; California Pharmaceutical Association; Society of Consumer Affairs Professionals; California Association of Personnel Consultants; Grand Knight and District Deputy, Knights of Columbus **To what do you attribute your success:** Mr. Stewart attributes his success to the support of his family, as well as his own personal dedication. **Why did you become involved in your profession or industry:** Mr. Stewart became involved in his profession out of a desire to be a health care practitioner. **Avocations:** Golf; Tennis **Political Affiliations:** Republican **Religion:** Roman Catholic

Michael Glenn Stewart, MD, MPH

Title: Vice Dean, Professor, Chairman **Industry:** Health, Wellness and Fitness **Company Name:** NewYork-Presbyterian Weill Cornell Medical Center **Date of Birth:** 09/17/1962 **Place of Birth:** Bowling Green **State/Country of Origin:** KY/USA **Parents:** Michael Joseph Stewart; Barbara (Weisser) Stewart **Education:** MPH, The University of Texas (1996); MD, Johns Hopkins University (1988); Bachelor's Degree in Engineering, Vanderbilt University, Summa Cum Laude (1984) **Certifications:** Diplomate, American Board of Otolaryngology **Career:** Vice Dean, Weill Cornell Medical College (2012-Present); Professor, Chairman, Department of Otolaryngology, Weill Cornell Medical College, New York, NY (2005-Present); Otolaryngologist-in-chief, NewYork-Presbyterian Hospital (2005-Present); Senior Associate Dean, Clinical Affairs, Weill Cornell Medical College (2010-2017); Associate Dean of Clinical Affairs, Baylor College of Medicine, Houston, Texas (2000-2005); Associate Professor, Baylor College of Medicine, Houston, Texas (1999-2005); General Director, Affiliated Medical Service, Baylor College of Medicine, Houston, Texas (1999-2005); Residency Director, Education Department of Otolaryngology, Baylor College of Medicine, Houston, Texas (1996-2005); Assistant Dean, Clinical Affairs, Baylor College of Medicine, Houston, Texas (1998-2000); Assistant Professor, Baylor College of Medicine, Houston, Texas (1994-1999) **Career Related:** Director, American Board of Otolaryngology (2008-Present); Senior Examiner, American Board of Otolaryngology (2007-2008); Chief Otolaryngology, Ben Taub Hospital, Harris Health (1994-2005); Chairman, Medical Board, Harris County Hospital District, Houston, Texas (1999-2000) **Creative Works:** Editor-in-chief, The Laryngoscope (2011-Present); Reviewer, Cancer (2001-Present); Reviewer, Journal of Trauma (1998-Present); Reviewer, Otolaryngology-Head and Neck Surgery (1998-Present); Reviewer, Archive Otolaryngology-Head and Neck Surgery (1997-Present); Editor, Reviewer, Head & Neck (1994-Present); Associate Editor, Editorial Board Member, Allergy & Rhinology (2010-2011); Editorial Board Member, Archives of Otolaryngology-Head and Neck Surgery (2005-2011); Associate Editor, Editorial Board Member, American Journal of Rhinology (2003-2010); Editorial Board Member, ENT Today; Contributor, Two Textbooks, More than 30 Textbook Chapters, More than 110 Peer-Reviewed Publications **Awards:** Presidential Citation Award, American Academy of Otolaryngology-Head and Neck Surgery (2017); Resident Teaching Award, NewYork-Presbyterian-Columbia and Cornell (2013); Distinguished Service Awards, Cornell Otolarynology-Head and Neck Surgery (2012); Distinguished Service Award, American Academy of Otolaryngology-Head and Neck Surgery (2012); Distinguished Service Award, American Academy of Otolaryngology-Head & Neck Surgery (2012); Presidential Citation Award, American Academy of Otolaryngology-Head and Neck Surgery (2010); Resident Teaching Award, NewYork-Presbyterian-Columbia and Cornell (2006); Houston Distinguished Surgeon Award, Association of Perioperative Nurses (2005); Distinguished Service Award, American Academy of Otolaryngology-Head and Neck Surgery (2004); Distinguished Service Award, American Academy of Otolaryngology-Head & Neck Surgery (2004); Outstanding Clinical Research Award, Kelsey-Seybold Foundation (1992-1993) **Memberships:** Board of Directors, American Rhinologic Society (2011-Present); American Rhinologic Society (2011-Present); Board of Directors, American Academy of Otolaryngology–Head and Neck Surgery (2011-Present); Board of Directors, Association of Academic Departments of Otolaryngology (2007-2014); President, Association of Academic Departments of Otolaryngology (2011-2013); Vice President, Eastern Section, Triological Society (2012); Chair, Research Advisory Board, American Academy of Otolaryngology–Head and Neck Surgery (2008-2010); Board of Directors, Society of University Otolaryngologists (2005-2009); Board of Directors, Society of University Otolaryngologists (2007-2008); American Laryngological, Rhinological and Otological Society; Fellow, American College of Surgeons **Marquis Who's Who Honors:** Albert Nelson Marquis Lifetime Achievement Award **Why did you become involved in your profession or industry:** Dr. Stewart became involved in his profession when he went to medical school and got an interest there. **Avocations:** Music; Performing arts

Venetia Stifler

Title: Artistic and Executive Director **Industry:** Fine Art **Company Name:** Ruth Page Center for the Arts **Parents:** Theodore Chakos; Ruth (Pastirsky) Chakos **Marital Status:** Married **Spouse Name:** Michael Hugos (1994); John G. Stifler (01/28/1972, Deceased 1977) **Education:** PhD, Union Institute (Now Union Institute & University), Cincinnati, OH (1992); MFA in Equivalency, Union Institute (Union Institute & University), Cincinnati, OH (1987); BA, University of Illinois at Chicago (1983) **Career:** Professor Emerita, Northeastern Illinois University (2014-Present); Assistant Professor, Chair, Dance Program, Northeastern Illinois University, Chicago, IL (1987-Present); Teacher, Modern, Jazz, Ballet, Venetia Stifler & Concert Dance, Inc., Chicago, IL (1978-Present); Teacher, Artist in Residence, Mundelein College, Chicago, IL (1982-1990); Teacher, Choreography Workshop, Bell Elementary School, Chicago, IL (1987); Guest Teacher, Artistic Director Composition/Improvisation, University of Wisconsin, Madison (1980-1987); Teacher, Wilson College, Chambersburg, Pennsylvania (1984); Teacher, Chicago Dance Center, Chicago, IL (1971-1978); Teacher Workshops, Urban Gateways, Chicago, IL (1977); Teacher, Modern Technique, Southern Illinois University, Carbondale (1975); Teacher, Smith College, Northampton, MA (1975) **Career Related:** Executive Director, Ruth Page Foundation (2000-Present); Artistic and Executive Director, Artistic Director, Ruth Page Nonprofit Dance Series (1992-Present); Centennial Director, Ruth Page Foundation Centennial (1999); Guest Speaker, Chicago Office of Fine Arts (1987); Program Director, Choreographer, Special Programs Chicago Symphony Orchestra (1985, 1987); Lecturer, Mundelein College, Chicago, IL (1983-1986); Chicago Office of Fine Arts (1983-1986); Choreographer, Sears Fashion Files, Bombay Productions (1983-1986); President, Board of Directors, Chicago Dance Arts Coalition (1983-1985); Advisory Dance Panel, Illinois Arts Council (1983-1985); Mayor's Office Of Special Events, Chicago, IL (1980); Production Assistant, Audio Visual Productions (1970-1971); Choreographer in Residence, Ruth Page Foundation **Civic:** Ruth Page Foundation **Creative Works:** Choreographer, "Three German Songs" (1999); Choreographer, "Over Weight Over Wrought Over You" (1997); Choreographer, "Veils" (1996); Choreographer, "Chicago Sketches" (1995); Choreographer, "Between Us" (1991); Choreographer, "Corporate Cases" (1988); Choreographer, "Private Places" (1987); Choreographer, "Bell School Scrimmage" (1987); Choreographer, "Blessings" (1986); Choreographer, "Don't Dance with Your Back to the Moon" (1986); Choreographer, "Magic Spaces" (1985-1986); Choreographer, "Imagery & Concept in the Dances of Venetia Stifler" (1985); Choreographer, "Rhymes" (1984); Choreographer, "Arriving at Onion" (1984); Choreographer, "Pulse" (1983); Choreographer, "Haiku" (1982); Choreographer, "Fugues" (1981-1982); Choreographer, "Mundelein Madness" (1981); Choreographer, "Solo Crane" (1981); Choreographer, "Tales of a Winter's Night" (1980); Choreographer, "Jackson Park-Howard" (1979); Choreographer, Opera, "La Gaite Parisienne" (1976) **Awards:** Named For Outstanding Artistic Achievement, Chicago Dance Coalition (1985); Creative Grant, Poetry Foundation; Emmy Nominated Choreographer, Director; Ruth Page Award **Memberships:** Water Tower Cultural District; See Chicago Dance; The Magnificent Mile **Why did you become involved in your profession or industry:** Ms. Stifler became involved in her profession because she has always known dance and the arts. It was the only career she wanted to pursue. Once she found work in the university setting, she knew she would want to do the best for her students for as long as she could. **Avocations:** Films; Art; Family time; Traveling **Thoughts on Life:** "Do on to others as they would do on to you."

Sheila S. Stiles Jewell, PhD

Title: Research Geneticist, Marine Biologist **Industry:** Sciences **Company Name:** U.S. Department of Commerce, (USDOC) (National Oceanic and Atmospheric Administration) NOAA, National Marine Fisheries Service (NMFS), Northeast Fisheries Science Center (NEFSC) **Date of Birth:** 09/28/1942 **Place of Birth:** Memphis **State/Country of Origin:** TN/USA **Parents:** Westley Robert Stiles; Ellen Louise (Dunford) Stiles **Marital Status:** Widowed **Education:** PhD, University of Massachusetts (1994); MS in Zoology and Ecology, University of Connecticut (1973); BS in Biology, Xavier University (1964); Diploma, Father Bertrand's/St. Augustine High School, Memphis, TN, Valedictorian (1960) **Career:** Geneticist, Northeast Fisheries Science Center (1985-Present); Team/Unit/Project Leader, Geneticist (1980-1985); Research Geneticist, Conducting Aquaculture Genetics, Breeding and Genomics Research, Former Biologist (1971-1980); Fishery Biologist, U.S. Department of the Interior, Milford, CT (1966-1971) **Career Related:** Co-Convener, Genetics Theme Session, ICES 100th Anniversary Conference, Denmark (2003); Mentor, New England Board of Higher Education, Massachusetts Institute of Technology (MIT), Boston, MA (1992); Local Coordinator, Training Program, Howard University/Rockefeller Foundation (1987-1988); Temporary Special Assistant to the Director of Science and Research (1987); Consultant, Science Textbook, Addison Wesley (1987); Former President, Sound (Aquaculture) School, Yale Peabody Museum Associates Council; Volunteer, Yale Peabody Museum; Chairperson, Milford Lab Open House; Representative, Scientific Meetings in Canada, China, Germany and Iceland; Collaborator, Yale University Scholars Program for Youth **Civic:** Former President, Interfaith Volunteer Caregivers, New Haven, CT (1991); Treasurer, Board of Directors, Stetson Library, New Haven, CT (1989-1991); Chairperson, Board of Directors, HiTech Learning Center, New Haven, CT (1990); Past President, New Haven Section, National Council of Negro Women; Past President, New Haven, National Council of Catholic Women; Head, Ladies Auxiliary of the Knights of Peter Claver, Fourth Degree Ladies, Knights of Peter Claver; Charter Member, Ladies Guild, St. Martin DePorres; Charter Member, Secretary, Greater New Haven African American Historical Society; Co-Founder, African American Women's Summit; Mayor-Appointed Board Member, New Haven Public Library; Co-Founder, Stetson Library Book Club, New Haven, CT; Delta Sigma Theta Sorority; Soul Passages Book Club **Creative Works:** Contributor, 40 Articles, Professional Journals **Awards:** Inductee, Memphis Catholic Hall of Fame (2020); Service Award for "54 Years of Exceptional Government Service and Advancing the Science of Genetics," NEFSC, NOAA, USDOC (2018); NTA Achievement Award (1996-1997, 2012); Sustained Superior and Outstanding Performance and QSI Awards (1974, 1985, 1987, 1995); Best Poster Paper Award, World Mariculture Society (1982); NOAA Unit Citation, Environmental Studies (1974); Legendary Women's Award, Perfect Blend Organization; Humanitarian Award, Interfaith Ministries; Minority Women in Science Award, National Technical Association; National Technical Association AT Weathers Technical Award; New Haven Leadership Award **Memberships:** Secretary-Treasurer, Atlantic Fisheries Biologists (1973); American Association for the Advancement of Science (AAAS); American Fisheries Society; Genetics Society of America; Former Member, Genetics Society of Canada; American Men and Women of Science; Northeastern Regional Director, National Technical Association; Former Member, National Shellfisheries Association; East Coast Shellfish Growers Association; Former Member, Genetics Working Group Committee, ICES (International Council for the Exploration of the Sea); African Scientific Institute; Sigma Xi **Why did you become involved in your profession or industry:** Dr. Stiles became involved in her profession because her mother, an educator, was an excellent role model who encouraged her children to be whatever they wanted to be in life. Her father, siblings and extended family also supported her. In addition, she had a brother who liked birds; he built a birdhouse for migrating birds, which still exists today. After she graduated with a Bachelor of Science, she was offered an internship at the Milford Laboratory. She also had a mentor, Dr. Arlene Longwell, who was one of her first supervisors, and helped her in terms of providing information and inspiring her to go into the field of genetics. That internship helped guide her in her career path. **Avocations:** Photography; Music

Robert Wayne Stinson

Title: Meat Company Executive **Industry:** Food & Restaurant Services **Date of Birth:** 01/11/1936 **Place of Birth:** Pierson **State/Country of Origin:** MI/USA **Parents:** Thomas Levi Stinson; Esther Amy (Smith) Stinson **Marital Status:** Married **Spouse Name:** Altha Jane Irwin (03/04/1961) **Children:** Robert Wayne; Debra Anne **Education:** AS, Davenport College (1970) **Career:** Retired, Kroger Co., Cincinnati, OH (1998); Vice President, National Sales, Grove Meat Co. (1986-1998); Corporate Office of Meat Procurement, Kroger Co., Cincinnati, OH (1977-1986); Meat Plant Procurement, Kroger Co., Indianapolis, IN (1975-1977); Meat Merchandising, Kroger Co., Grand Rapids, MI (1973-1975); Meat Merchandising, Kroger Co., Fort Wayne, IN (1971-1973); Assistant Meat Buyer, Kroger Co., Detroit, MI (1970-1971); Meat Manager, Kroger Co., Grand Rapids, MI (1963-1970) **Career Related:** Grove Lamb Co., Chicago, IL (1986-1998) **Military Service:** Military (1958-1960) **Memberships:** American Meat Institute **Marquis Who's Who Honors:** Albert Nelson Marquis Lifetime Achievement Award **Why did you become involved in your profession or industry:** After growing up on a farm, Mr. Stinson was inspired to pursue a career in the meat business. **Avocations:** Travel; Beach walking

Neal Richard Stoll

Title: Retired Partner **Industry:** Law and Legal Services **Company Name:** Skadden Arps LLP **Date of Birth:** 11/07/1948 **Place of Birth:** Philadelphia **State/Country of Origin:** PA/USA **Parents:** Mervin Stoll; Goldie Louise (Serody) Stoll Wilf **Marital Status:** Married **Spouse Name:** Linda G. Seligman (05/25/1972) **Children:** Meredith Anne; Alexis Blythe **Education:** JD, Fordham University (1973); BA in History, Pennsylvania State University, With Distinction (1970) **Career:** Retired Partner, Skadden Arps LLP (2017-Present); Partner, Skadden, Arps, Slate, Meagher & Flom, LLP, New York, NY (1981-2017); Associate, Skadden, Arps, Slate, Meagher & Flom, LLP, New York, NY (1973-1981) **Career Related:** Lecturer, Practicing Law-Institute, New York, NY (1998) **Creative Works:** Co-Author, Antitrust and Trade Regulation Column, New York Law Journal (1981-2013); Co-author, "Acquisitions Under the Hart Scott Rodino Antitrust Improvements Act" (1980, 1988, 2008); Contributor, Articles, Professional Publications **Awards:** Penn State Liberal Arts Graduate Achievement Annual Award (2001); Nominee, Wood Wilson Scholarship, Department of History in the Liberal Arts College (1969); Top New York Lawyer Award **Memberships:** Trade Regulation Committee, Association of the Bar of the City of New York (1974); ABA (1974); New York State Bar Association (1974) **Bar Admissions:** Supreme Court of the United States (1986); New York (1974); U.S. District Court Eastern District of New York (1974); U.S. Court of Appeals for the Second Circuit (1974); U.S. District Court Southern District of New York (1974) **Marquis Who's Who Honors:** Albert Nelson Marquis Lifetime Achievement Award; Marquis Who's Who Top Professional **Why did you become involved in your profession or industry:** Mr. Stoll initially wanted to earn a PhD in European history and then teach at the college level. His college advisor essentially became probably the most important influence in his life. His father had passed when he was 12 years old, and he just sat him down and told him it was difficult to get the position he was striving for. He made a suggestion that he should consider getting a law degree because once you get a law degree, your options are very wide. If you want to teach, you can teach; if you want to do history, you can always come back, get advanced degrees and do that. It opens up the world of finance and industry. **Avocations:** Collecting fountain pens and vintage wrist watches **Political Affiliations:** Democrat

James Bernard Stoltman

Title: Professor Emeritus, Anthropology **Industry:** Education/Educational Services **Company Name:** University of Wisconsin-Madison **Date of Birth:** 02/06/1935 **Place of Birth:** Minneapolis **State/Country of Origin:** MN/USA **Year of Passing:** 2019 **Parents:** Bernard Edward Stoltman; Sophia Ann (Kalitowski) Stoltman **Marital Status:** Married **Spouse Name:** Sarah Ruth Voelker (07/16/1960) **Children:** Wendy; Jeffrey; Andrew **Education:** PhD, Harvard University (1967); MA, University of Minnesota (1962); BA, University of Minnesota, Cum Laude (1957) **Career:** Professor Emeritus, Anthropology, University of Wisconsin-Madison (2000-Present); From Assistant Professor to Professor of Anthropology, University of Wisconsin-Madison (1966-2000); Instructor, Department of Anthropology, Tulane University, New Orleans, LA (1965-1966) **Career Related:** Wisconsin Burial Sites Preservation Board, Madison, WI (1989-Present); Governor's Appointee, Historic Preservation Review Board, Madison, WI (1972-1980); Fellow, American Association for the Advancement of Sciences **Military Service:** Junior Grade Lieutenant, U.S. Navy (1957-1960) **Creative Works:** Contributing Editor, Review of Archaeology (1986-Present); Editorial Board, Midcontinental Journal of Archaeology (1976-Present); Author, "Ceramic Petrography and Hopewell Interaction," University of Alabama Press (2005); Author, "New Perspectives on Cahokia: Views from the Periphery" (1991); Author, "Prehistoric Mound Builders in the Mississippi Valley" (1986); Editor, The Wisconsin Archaeologist (1973-1976); Author, "Groton Plantation" (1974); Author, "The Laurel Culture in Minnesota" (1973) **Awards:** Distinguished Career Award, Midwest Archaeological Conference (2015); Lapham Research Medal, Wisconsin Archaeological Society (1979) **Memberships:** President, Wisconsin Archaeological Society (1971-1973); Society of American Archaeology **Marquis Who's Who Honors:** Albert Nelson Marquis Lifetime Achievement Award **Why did you become involved in your profession or industry:** Mr. Stoltman wanted to work outside and not sit behind a desk. In the 1950s, everyone was going to be an engineer and he was in line to enroll in engineering school. He got off the line and enrolled in Letters and Sciences. He received a degree in geology and while he was doing this, he took courses in archaeology and anthropology. He had an ROTC scholarship and had to serve three years of active duty after college. While he was in the U.S. Navy, he did a lot of reading and settled on archaeology. **Avocations:** Tennis; Fishing

Howard L. Stone, CPA, CFE, JD

Title: Partner **Industry:** Law and Legal Services **Company Name:** Stone McGuire & Siegel PC **Date of Birth:** 09/16/1941 **Place of Birth:** Chicago **State/ Country of Origin:** IL/USA **Parents:** Ceale (Perlik) Stone Tandet **Marital Status:** Married **Spouse Name:** Susan L. Saltzman (06/02/1963) **Children:** Lauren; David **Education:** JD, DePaul University (1972); BSBA, Roosevelt University (1963); Coursework, University of Illinois (1960-1961) **Certifications:** Certified Public Accountant, Illinois **Career:** Senior Partner, Stone, McGuire & Siegel, P.C. Chicago, IL (1976-Present); With, Altshuler, Melvoin & Glasser; Special Assistant, U.S. Attorney, Chief Financial Auditor, Investigator, North District Illinois, Department of Justice, Chicago, IL (1972-1976); Agent, IRS, Chicago, IL (1964-1972); Lecturer in Taxation **Career Related:** Chairman, University of Illinois Foundation Fund for Gerontology Research (1984-2015) **Creative Works:** Co-author, "Federal Civil Tax Law" (1982, 1988); Co-author, "Handling Criminal Tax Cases: A Lawyers Guide" (1982, 1987); Co-author, "Negotiating to Win" (1985); Author, "Client Tax Fraud- A Practical Guide to Protecting Your Rights" (1984); Author, "Defending the Federal Tax Case: What To Do When the IRS Steps In" (1978) **Memberships:** Resident Lecturer, Tax Fraud, C.P.A. Society (1976-1984, 1990-1991); Chairman, Investment Advisers Act Task Force, C.P.A. Society (1983-1984); American Association Attorney-C.P.A.s; Illinois C.P.A. Foundation; American Institute C.P.A.s; Decalogue Society Lawyers; American Bar Association; Federal Bar Association; Illinois State Bar Association; Chicago Bar Association; Association of certified fraud examiners; American Health Wire Association **Bar Admissions:** Supreme Court of the United States (1982); U.S. Tax Court (1972); United States District Court for the Northern District of Illinois (1972); Illinois (1972) **Marquis Who's Who Honors:** Albert Nelson Marquis Lifetime Achievement Award **Why did you become involved in your profession or industry:** Mr. Howard Stone started as a CPA and then he transitioned to being lawyer, it started with the Internal Revenue Service (IRS), his goal was to serve the country through public service. He has been in private practice for over 40 years. As a successful Federal Prosecutor and defense criminal lawyer for white collar crimes, his focus was to defend individuals who may not have committed the crime, also representing executives and owners of businesses who may be falsely accused of criminal allegations. **Religion:** Jewish

Paul "Paulie" Straface

Title: Service Manager/Technician **Industry:** Other **Company Name:** Res-Com Heating & Air-Conditioning Inc. **Date of Birth:** 09/18/1988 **Place of Birth:** Harrison **State/Country of Origin:** NY/USA **Parents:** Steve Straface Sr.; Donna (Defonce) Straface **Certifications:** R-410A Puron Certificate (2009); Environmental Protection Agency Certified (2006) **Career:** Service Manager/Technician, Res-Com Heating & Air Conditioning Inc. (2006-Present) **Awards:** Named One of the Top 40 Under 40 in HVAC in the United States **Memberships:** Refrigeration Specialty Association **To what do you attribute your success:** Mr. Straface attributes his success to wanting to be the best. He always wanted to be the "go-to guy" whenever someone needed help. "I am always ready and always there when people need me... day or night..." **Why did you become involved in your profession or industry:** Mr. Straface is a part of a family business, that his father started about 22 years ago. He had the desire to follow his father Steve's footsteps. He fell in love with the way his father loves his craft, takes care of his customers and is always available when people need him. **Thoughts on Life:** Mr. Straface would like people to know that he is trustworthy.

John Henry Strathman

Title: Electrical Engineer (Retired) **Industry:** Engineering **Company Name:** HP Development Company, L.P. **Date of Birth:** 03/24/1933 **Place of Birth:** Peoria **State/Country of Origin:** IL/USA **Parents:** John Herman Strathman; Esther Sophie (Reinhardt) Strathman **Marital Status:** Widowed **Spouse Name:** Sarah Louise Mefford (07/20/1957) (Deceased 2005) **Children:** Stanley David; Sarah Jane Rockwell **Education:** MSEE, Stanford University (1959); BSEE, University of Illinois (1955) **Career:** Retired (1997); Quality Manager, HP Development Company, L.P. (1992-1997); General Manager, Technical Center, Integrated Circuit Division, HP Development Company, L.P. (1972-1992); Research and Development Section Manager, HP Development Company, L.P. (1966-1972); Research and Development Project Manager, HP Development Company, L.P. (1959-1966); Research and Development Engineer, HP Development Company, L.P. (1957-1959) **Civic:** Member, Board of Directors, Griffith Centers, Inc. (1998-2004); Member, Board of Trustees, Citizens' Goals (1989-1994); President, Board of Directors, HPC Credit Union (1976-1992); Member, Engineering Dean's Advisory Board, University of Colorado (1981-1983); Member, Chairman, Planning and Community Development Committee, El Paso County, Colorado Springs (1969-1974); Springs Rescue Mission **Military Service:** Lieutenant, U.S. Navy (1955-1957) **Creative Works:** Contributor, Articles, Professional Journals; Lecturer in Field **Memberships:** Pi Mu Epsilon; Sigma Tau; The Tau Beta Pi Association, Inc.; IEEE Eta Kappa Nu; American Society for Quality **Marquis Who's Who Honors:** Albert Nelson Marquis Lifetime Achievement Award **Why did you become involved in your profession or industry:** Mr. Strathman became involved in his profession because of his interest in radio and electronics. His father was a radio operator on a ship in the Navy during WWI. **Avocations:** Golfing; Sailing **Religion:** Presbyterian

Howard Stringer, PhD

Title: Electronics Executive **Industry:** Media & Entertainment **Company Name:** American Film Institute **Date of Birth:** 02/19/1942 **Place of Birth:** Cardiff **State/Country of Origin:** Wales/United Kingdom **Parents:** Harry Stringer; Marjorie Mary (Pook) Stringer **Marital Status:** Married **Spouse Name:** Jennifer Kinmond Patterson (07/29/1978) **Children:** David Ridley; Harriet Kinmond **Education:** Honorary PhD, American Film Institute (2007); Honorary PhD, University of Glamorgan (2005); Honorary PhD, University of Arts London (2003); BA, MA in Modern History, Oxford University, England, UK (1964) **Career:** Chairman, Sony Corporation (2012-2013); President, Sony Corporation (2009-2012); Chairman, Chief Executive Officer, Sony Corporation (2005-2012); Representative, The Americas, Officer-in-Charge, Entertainment Business Group, Sony Corporation (2003-2012); Vice-Chairman, Sony Corporation (2003); President, Sony Entertainment, Inc. (2000-2012); Chairman, Chief Executive Officer, Sony Corporation of America (1998-2012); Group Executive Officer, Sony Corporation (1998); Chairman, Sony Pictures Entertainment, Inc. (1998); Chairman, Sony Electronics, Inc. (1998); Chairman, Chief Executive Officer, Sony of Canada, Ltd. (1997-2012); President, Sony Corporation of America (1997-1998); Chairman, Chief Executive Officer, Tele-TV (1995-1997); President, CBS Broadcast Group (1988-1995); President, CBS News (1986-1988); Executive Vice President, CBS News (1984-1986); Executive Producer, "CBS Evening News," CBS News (1981-1984); Executive Producer, "CBS Reports," CBS News (1976-1981); Producer, Director, CBS News, New York, NY (1973-1976) **Career Related:** Member, Board of Directors, Talk Talk Telecom Group PLC (2012-Present); Member, Board of Directors, Intercontinental Hotels Group PLC (2003-2006); Member, Board of Directors, Sony Corporation (1999-2013); Chairman, Saïd Business School, University of Oxford **Civic:** Member, Non-Executive Board, Time Inc. (2014-Present); Member, Non-Executive Board, BBC (2013-Present); Non-Executive Director, BBC; Board Member, Center for Communications; Board Member, Carnegie Hall; Board Member, Teach for America; Board Member, Corporate Leadership Committee, Lincoln Center for the Performing Arts; Board Member, American Friends of the British Museum; Board Member, New York Presbyterian Hospital; Board Member, American Theatre Wing; Member, Board of Trustees, Paley Center for Media (Formerly Museum of Television & Radio (MT&R)); Chairman, Board of Trustees, American Film Institute; Member, Chancellor's Court of Benefactors, Oxford University; President, Merton Society; North American Chairman, British Army Benevolent Fund; Chairman, New York Presbyterian Hospital Ophthalmology Center **Military Service:** Sergeant, U.S. Army, Vietnam (1965-1967) **Awards:** Lifetime Achievement Award in Technology & Engineering, National Academy of Television Arts & Sciences (NATAS) (2011); Henry A. Grunwald Award for Public Service, Lighthouse International (2009); Honorary Award, Partnership for a Drug-Free America (Now Partnership for Drug-Free Kids) (2008); Honoree for Dedication To The Arts And Extraordinary Personal Achievements In Media And Communications, Metropolitan Opera, New York, NY (2008); Visionary Award for Innovative Leadership in Media and Entertainment, Paley Center for Media (Formerly Museum of Television & Radio (MT&R)) (2007); Honoree, Alliance Lupus Research (2007); Distinguished Service Award, Lincoln Center For The Performing Arts (2006); Living Landmarks Honoree, New York Landmarks Conservancy (2005); Honoree, Sidewalks Of New York Awards, Big Brothers Big Sisters of New York City (2005); Named, One Of The 100 Most Influential People In The World, TIME Magazine (2005); Medal Of Honor, St. George's Society of New York (2004); Award, New York Hall Of Science (2003); Distinguished Leadership Award, International Emmy Founders (2002-2003); Dinner Champions Honoree, National Multiple Sclerosis Society (2002); Public Service Award, Phoenix House (2002); Award, Literary Partners (2002); Teach for America Annual Award For Commitment To Expanding Educational Opportunity For Children (2001); Honorary Fellow, Welsh College of Music & Drama (2001); Honorary Fellow, Merton College, Oxford, England (2000); Highest Award, Center For Communications (2000); Steven J. Ross Humanitarian Award, UJA-Federation of New York (1999); Named, Knight Commander Of The British Empire (KBE), Her Majesty Queen Elizabeth II (1999); Named To Royal TV Society Welsh Hall Of Fame, Wales, UK (1999); Broadcasting And Cable Hall Of Fame (1996); First Amendment Leadership Award, Radio & TV News Directors Foundation (1996); Honored Uncommon Vision Media Industry, Museum Moving Image (1994); IRTS Foundation Award (1994); Overseas Press Club Awards (1982, 1979, 1974); DuPont Journalism Award, Columbia Journalism School, Columbia University (1981, 1979); Decorated U.S. Army Commendation Medal For Meritorious Achievement for Service in Vietnam **Memberships:** Council on Foreign Relations (CFR) **Why did you become involved in your profession or industry:** Dr. Stringer became involved in his profession because he believes reading history at university enables you to learn to draw a straight line to the news of the day while learning to understand the value of objectivity. **Avocations:** Remaining active

Carolyn Ray Strong

Title: Information Designer (Retired) **Industry:** Information Technology and Services **Date of Birth:** 01/09/1951 **Place of Birth:** Pasadena **State/Country of Origin:** CA/USA **Parents:** Albert Charles Strong; Juliana (Ray) Strong **Education:** Master of Science in Applied Information Management, University of Oregon (1992); Postgraduate Coursework, DeVry Institute of Technology (1975-1977); Bachelor of Arts in Mathematics and Journalism, Whitworth University (1973) **Career:** Retired (2015-Present); Autism Integration and Program Assistant, Beaverton School District (2005-2015); Owner, Consultant, Strong Strategic Consulting (1999-2010); Tektronix Internet Strategist (1998-1999); Director, Worldwide Customer Communications, Tektronix Inc. (1995-1998); Director, Adjunct Professor, Applied Information Management Master's Program, University of Oregon (1992-2008); Manager of Test and Measurement Customer Documentation (1991-1995); Manager of Oscilloscope Group Documentation (1990-1991); Manager of Laboratory Instruments Marketing Support (1989-1990); Manager of Laboratory Instruments Documentation (1986-1989); Manager of Technical Publications and Computer Training (1985-1986); Manager of Technical Communications (1979-1985); Group Manager, Technical Publications (1976-1979); Documentation Manager & Technical Writer, Tektronix Inc., Beaverton, OR (1973-1976); Mathematics and Aerospace Demonstrator, Pacific Science Center, Seattle, WA (1970-1971) **Civic:** Emeritus Board Member, First Tech Federal Credit Union (2015-2017); Volunteer, Bereavement Team, Serenity Hospice & Palliative Care (2014-2020); Chairman of the Board, Secretary of the Board, First Tech Federal Credit Union (1984-2015) **Awards:** Named, Print on Demand Innovator and Keynote Speaker (1996) **Memberships:** President, Willamette Valley Chapter, Society for Technical Communications (1979-1982); Treasurer, Willamette Valley Chapter, Society for Technical Communications (1979); Secretary, Willamette Valley Chapter, Society for Technical Communications (1978); Senior Member, Society for Technical Communications; Association for Computer Machinery; Special Interest Group on the Design of Communication **Marquis Who's Who Honors:** Albert Nelson Marquis Lifetime Achievement Award; Marquis Who's Who Top Professional **To what do you attribute your success:** Ms. Strong attributes her success to her independence and adaptability, as well as the experiences of her family. **Why did you become involved in your profession or industry:** Ms. Strong initially became involved in her profession after deciding to pursue a degree in math, journalism and psychology. Those areas, when combined, provided a natural stepping stone into technical writing. After leaving the technical industry, Ms. Strong became involved in education, having garnered a great deal of personal experience with her disabled niece. She applied the knowledge she gleaned in the tech industry to her position at her local school district, and was able to advocate for getting iPads in the classroom. **Avocations:** Collecting Coca-Cola memorabilia; Rose gardening; Learning Japanese and Spanish, Building Legos; Technology trends; Reading **Political Affiliations:** Independent

Donald C. Stubbs

Title: Secondary School Educator (Retired) **Industry:** Education/Educational Services **Date of Birth:** 03/06/1935 **Place of Birth:** Providence **State/Country of Origin:** RI/USA **Parents:** Edward J. Stubbs; Margaret Eleanor (Clark) Stubbs **Marital Status:** Married **Spouse Name:** Sarah E. Andrews (04/23/1999); Lorraine Alice Thivierge (04/03/1969, Deceased 01/1986) **Children:** Derek C.; Greg Mete (Stepchild); Jay A. Mete (Stepchild, Deceased 08/2006); Lisa M. Doherty (Stepchild); Linda A. Lovett (Stepchild); David J. Andrews (Stepchild); Daniel J. Andrews (Stepchild, Deceased 01/2014) **Education:** Master of Science in Microbiology, The Catholic University of America, Washington, DC (1966); Postgraduate Coursework, St. John's University, New York, NY (1960); Bachelor of Arts, The Catholic University of America, Washington, DC (1959) **Career:** Retired (2000); Teacher of Chemistry, Science Department Chair, Ponaganset Regional High School, Glocester, RI (1969-2000); Teacher, Science Department Chair, LaSalle Military Academy, Oakdale, NY (1966-1969); Teacher, Bishop Bradley High School, Manchester, NH (1961-1966); Teacher, Bishop Loughlin Memorial High School, Brooklyn, NY (1959-1961) **Civic:** Knights of Columbus; Alliance for Better Long Term Care; Project 2061 **Memberships:** American Association for the Advancement of Science; Association for Supervision and Curriculum Development **Marquis Who's Who Honors:** Albert Nelson Marquis Lifetime Achievement Award; Marquis Who's Who Top Professional; Marquis Who's Who Humanitarian Award **Why did you become involved in your profession or industry:** Mr. Stubbs entered his profession because he was impressed by many of his high school teachers and their teaching, so he decided to follow that route and become a teacher. Science was his first love. He was leaning toward chemistry, but when he got into a program with microbiology, he decided to stay there. As a teacher, Mr. Stubbs taught mostly chemistry.

Robert Thomas "Bob" Stumpff

Title: Director of Public Works (Retired) **Industry:** Government Administration/Government Relations/Government Services **Company Name:** City of College Park **Date of Birth:** 6/25/1945 **Place of Birth:** Lewistown **State/Country of Origin:** PA/USA **Parents:** Harry Clarence Stumpff; Marjorie Louise (Bossinger) Stumpff **Marital Status:** Married **Spouse Name:** Sylvia Simmons (1972) **Children:** Robert Dale; Cherie Lynn Stumpff-Zimmer **Education:** BS, University of Maryland, College Park (1968) **Certifications:** APPA Institute for Facilities Management (1989); Certificate, College Business Management Institute, University of Kentucky (1978); Municipal Solid Waste Manager, Solid Waste Association of North America **Career:** Director, Public Works, City of College Park (2005-2018); Assistant Director, General Services, Facilities Management, University of Maryland (1988-2005); Assistant Athletic Director, University of Maryland (1980-1988); Associate/Assistant Director, Maryland Student Union, University of Maryland (1970-1980); Assistant Director Athletics, University of Maryland, College Park (1968-1969) **Career Related:** Tournament Director, NCAA Wrestling Championships, University of Maryland (1987); Tournament Director, ACC Wrestling Championships, University of Maryland (1983); Assistant Tournament Director, NCAA Wrestling Championships, University of Maryland (1978); Tournament Director, ACC Wrestling Championships, University of Maryland (1977); Assistant Tournament Director, NCAA Wrestling Championships, University of Maryland (1972); Assistant Tournament Director, NCAA East Regional Basketball Tournament, University of Maryland(1969); Tournament Manager, ACC Wrestling Championships, University of Maryland (1968-1969); Staff Member, NCAA East Regional Basketball Tournament, University of Maryland (1968); Staff Member, First Round NCAA Basketball Tournament, University of Maryland (1968); Tournament Manager, NCAA Soccer Championships, University of Maryland (1968); Staff Member, NCAA East Regional Basketball Tournament, University of Maryland (1967); Staff Member, NCAA Basketball Finals, University of Maryland (1966); Tournament Manager, ACC Wrestling Championships, University of Maryland (1964-1966); Presentations on Operating Athletic Tournaments and Events, Performing Arts, On Campus Operation of a Movie Theater, Solid Waste Removal/Recycling Services/ Programs and Snow Removal Services from Mid-Sized City **Civic:** Assisting Minister, St. Paul's Lutheran Church, Fulton, MD (1996-Present); Lutheran Campus Ministry Board, University of Maryland (1995-2006); Church Council **Military Service:** Honorable Discharge, Cadet Lieutenant Colonel, U.S. Air Force (1968); U.S. Air Force ROTC (1963-1968) **Creative Works:** Assistant Editor, Maryland Football Guide (1965-1969); Assistant Editor, Maryland Basketball (1964-1969); Author, Editor, Maryland Wrestling (1964-1969); Editor, Contributor, Articles, Professional Journals **Awards:** Proclamations from Maryland Gov. Lawrence Hogan and Mayor Patrick Wojahn, City of College Park (2018); Outstanding Service Award from the Maryland Municipal Public Works Officials Association (2016); Certificate from Maryland Municipal League (2015); Proclamations from C.D. Mote Jr., University of Maryland and Gov. Robert E. Ehrlich, State of Maryland (2005); President's Distinguished Service Award, University of Maryland (2001); M Club Award in Recognition of Outstanding Wrestling Publication (1967-1969); Charles Leroy Mackert Award, Senior Who Has Contributed Most to Wrestling (1967) **Memberships:** Chair, Maryland Recycling Network (2003-Present); Board of Directors, Maryland Recycling Network (1997-Present); Board of Directors, M Club, University of Maryland (1970-Present); Maryland Municipal Public Works Officials Association (2005-2018); President, Maryland Municipal Public Works Officials (2013-2015); Maryland Municipal League, Legislative Committee (2009-2013); Vice President, Maryland Municipal Public Works Officials Association (2009-2013); Board of Directors, Mid-Atlantic Chapter, Solid Waste Association of North America (1992-1994); Faculty Secretary-Treasurer, Sigma Chapter, Omicron Delta Kappa (1972-1976); National Recycling Coalition; Maryland-Delaware Solid Waste Association; National Waste & Recycling Association; American Public Works Association; Lifetime Member and Past President, M Club, University of Maryland; Lifetime Member, University of Maryland Alumni Association; Terrapin Club, University of Maryland **Marquis Who's Who Honors:** Albert Nelson Marquis Lifetime Achievement Award; Marquis Who's Who Top Professional **To what do you attribute your success:** Mr. Stumpff attributes his success to the desire to learn something new and being able to accomplish things that are beneficial to the organization. **Why did you become involved in your profession or industry:** Mr. Stumpff became involved in his profession by accident. He was offered a job by the athletic director at Pennsylvania State University. When he spoke about the offer to his mentor at the University of Maryland, they wanted him to stay at the university, so they offered him a position. **Avocations:** Reading; Sightseeing **Religion:** Lutheran **Thoughts on Life:** Mr. Stumpff will continue to learn new information.

Charles L. Stuppard, PhD

Title: Chief Executive Officer, Founder, Owner **Company Name:** CLS Consulting & Leadership Services, LLC **Place of Birth:** St. Marc **State/Country of Origin:** Haiti **Parents:** Rev. Maurice P. Stuppard; Gracieuse M. Stuppard **Education:** PhD in Humanities, Salve Regina University, Newport, RI; MA in National Security & Strategic Studies, Naval War College, Newport, RI; BS in Mechanical & Aerospace Engineering, Cornell University, Ithaca, NY; Joint Professional Military Education Phase II, Joint Forces Staff College, Norfolk, VA; Executive Business Course, Naval Postgraduate School, Monterrey, CA **Certifications:** Black Belt Instructor in Tae Kwon Do; 360 Psychometric Assessment Tool; Shiphandling (Officer of the Deck, Underway); Tactical Action Officer (TAO) **Career:** Owner, Chief Executive Officer, CLS Consulting & Leadership Services, Virginia Beach, VA (2020-Present); General Manager, Canopy Defense, Lowell, MA (2018-2020); Chief Operating Officer, The BLUESTONE Group & Constellation Blue Group, Washington, DC (2017-2018); Vice President & Director, Defense Operations, Maintenance & Training, Middle East, AECOM Management Services, Saudi Arabia (2016-2017); Professor, Strategic Leadership, Naval War College, Newport, RI (2014-2015); Chief, U.S. Naval Forces Division, Kingdom of Saudi Arabia, Security Cooperation, Riyadh, Saudi Arabia (2013-2014); Commander, Joint Expeditionary Base Little Creek - Fort Story, Virginia (2010-2013); Chief of Staff (EA), Navy Installations Command (CNIC), Washington DC (2008-2009); Leadership Instructor, Command Leadership School (Navy Leadership & Ethics Center), Newport, RI (2006-2008); Commanding Officer, USS ARLEIGH BURKE (DDG-51), Norfolk, VA (2004-2006); Politico-Military Affairs Officer, The Joint Staff (CJCS), The Pentagon (2000-2003); Executive Officer, USS NICHOLAS (FFG 47), Norfolk, VA (1999-2000); US Naval War College Student, Newport RI (1997-1998); Pre-Commissioning Combat System Officer, USS GONZALEZ (DDG 66), Norfolk, VA (1994-1997); Combat System Officer, USS SIDES (FFG 14), San Diego, CA (1993-1994); Missiles Officer, USS REEVES (CG 24), Pearl Harbor, HI (1990-1992); Boilers Officer, USS BIDDLE (CG 34), Norfolk, VA (1987-1990); Student Naval Aviator, Mather AFB, Sacramento, CA (1986-1987) & Pensacola, FL (1985-1986); Aviation Officer Candidate School, AOCS 27-85, Pensacola, FL; Mechanical Design Engineer; Aircraft Designer in the A-10A and T-46 Flight Programs, Fairchild Republic Corporation, Long Island, NY (1982-1985) **Civic:** Executive Advisory Board Member (Vice-Chair), Cornell University Council, Ithaca, New York; Co-President, Cornell University Class of 1982; Philanthropy & Charity for Haiti; Member of Board of Directors, Community Work Services, Boston, MA; Board Member, Military Economic Development Advisory Committee, Virginia Beach, VA; Board Treasurer, Castleton Homeowners Association. **Military Service:** Retired US Navy Captain (1985-2015) **Awards:** Two-time Recipient, Defense Superior Service Medal; Three-time Recipient, Legion of Merit; Defense Meritorious Service Medal; Three-time Recipient, Meritorious Service Medal; Four-time Recipient, Navy/Marine Corps Commendation Medal; Joint Service Achievement Medal; Navy Unit Commendation Medal; Meritorious Unit Commendation Medal; Navy Expeditionary Medal; Two-time Recipient, National Defense Service Medal; Global War on Terrorism Expeditionary Medal; Global War on Terrorism Service Medal; Sea Service Deployment Ribbons; NATO Medal; Expert Rifleman Medal; Expert Pistol Shot Medal; US Coast Guard Special Operations; Surface Warfare Officer Insignia **Memberships:** Surface Navy Association; National Naval Officers Association; Cornell University Council; Cornell Association of Class Officers; Life Member, Washington DC Scottish Rite; Naval Lodge #4, Washington DC; Founding Member, L'Haitienne Lodge #925, Washington DC. **Thoughts on Life:** "That people are good! That we also need an anchor in life; for me it is my God, My family and my friends."

Siva Subramanian, MD, FAAP

Title: Professor, Neonatologist **Industry:** Medicine & Health Care **Company Name:** Medstar Georgetown University Hospital **Date of Birth:** 05/09/1945 **Place of Birth:** Coimbatore **State/Country of Origin:** India **Year of Passing:** 1969 **Parents:** Kolinjavadi Ramaswamy; Sukanthi (Subramanian) Nagarajan **Marital Status:** Married **Spouse Name:** Kalyani Hariharier (02/05/1975) **Children:** Ramya; Rajeev; Ranjan **Education:** Bachelor of Medicine and Bachelor of Surgery, Madras University (1969); Bachelor of Science, Madras University (1964); Bachelor of Arts in Pediatrics; Bachelor of Arts in Neonatal Perinatal Medicine **Certifications:** Diplomate, American Board of Pediatrics; Diplomate, American Board of Neonatal-Perinatal Medicine **Career:** Director of Nurseries, Chief of Neonatology, Medstar Georgetown University Hospital, Washington, DC (1981-Present); Attending Neonatologist, Medstar Georgetown University Hospital, Washington, DC (1976-Present); Professor of Pediatrics and Obstetrics/Gynecology, Medstar Georgetown University Hospital, Washington, DC (1974-Present); Vice Chair of Pediatrics, Medstar Georgetown University Hospital, Washington, DC (1988-1998); Fellow in Neonatology, Medstar Georgetown University Hospital, Washington, DC (1974-1976); Resident in Pediatrics, University Maryland Hospital, Baltimore, MD (1972-1974); Intern in Pediatrics, Jewish Hospital and Medical Center, New York (1971-1972) **Career Related:** Co-chair, Children's Health and Development Department, Medstar Georgetown University Medical Center (2005-Present); Co-chair, Research Committee, Medstar Georgetown University Medical Center (2005-2010) **Civic:** Past District of Columbia Board Director, National Youth Leadership Forum; Coordinator, AIM for Seva (2010-Present); Helping Refugees in the United States (2008-Present); Organizer, Service, Innovation and Entrepreneurship Conference at White House and Georgetown University (2012); Organizer, Hindu American Community Services Conference at White House and Georgetown University (2011); Organizer, Medical Mission to Haiti (2010); Co-founder, Hindu American Community Services Inc. (2009); President, USA's One America Meeting with Religious Leaders (2000); President, The National Conference for Community and Justice, White House, Washington, DC (2000); Member, Fetus and New Born Committee, Washington, DC (1988); Chairman, Siva Vishnu Temple, Lanham, MD (1981-1991); Chairman, Siva Vishnu Temple, Lanham, MD (1981-1991); Founder, Board of Directors, Council of Hindu Temples; Founder, United Hindu Temples of Metropolitan Washington; First Vice President, Interfaith Council of Metropolitan Washington, DC; Board Director, EVERMORE **Creative Works:** Editor, Current Concepts in Neonatology, India (1990-Present); International Editor, Indian Journal of Pediatrics, India (1988-Present); Editor, Trace Elements/Mineral Metabolism During Development (1993); Editor, Publisher, SIDS Series (1985) **Awards:** Lifetime Achievement Award by American Diversity Group (2019); Interfaith Leadership Award (2019); Clinical Teacher of Year Award, Kaiser Permanente (2007); MAGIS Master Teacher Award (2007); Featured, Georgetown University Medical Center Web Magazine (2007); Interfaith Bridge Builder Award (2006); Featured, Washingtonian Journal (2005); Featured, Georgetown University Medical Center Web Magazine (2003); Featured, Washingtonian Journal (1996); Recipient, "Preemies" Cover Article, Newsweek (1988) **Memberships:** Committee Member on Medicine and Ethics, American Pediatric Society (2019); Fellow, American College of Nutrition; Fellow of American Academy of Pediatrics; Past Member, American Association for the Advancement of Science; New York Academy Sciences; International Society for Trace Element Research in Humans; Society for Bioethics Consultation; American Society of Law **Marquis Who's Who Honors:** Albert Nelson Marquis Lifetime Achievement Award (2019) **To what do you attribute your success:** Dr. Siva attributes his success to his wonderful family, as well as his propensity for optimism. **Why did you become involved in your profession or industry:** Though Dr. Siva was initially interested in agriculture, he transitioned toward pediatric medicine. While working as an intern, he visited the neonatal care unit while doing his rounds and became fascinated. **Avocations:** Community service; Spiritual engagements; Youth development **Religion:** Hindu

Paul Augustine Suhr, Esq.

Title: Managing Member **Industry:** Law and Legal Services **Company Name:** Mitchell & Suhr PLLC **Date of Birth:** 01/20/1940 **Place of Birth:** Sonwunri, Chonbuk **State/Country of Origin:** Republic of Korea **Parents:** Chong-ju So; Oksuk (Bang) So **Marital Status:** Married **Spouse Name:** Angeline M. Kang Suhr **Children:** Christopher **Education:** JD, North Carolina Central University, Durham, NC (1988); MS, University of North Carolina at Chapel Hill, NC (1975); MA, The University of North Carolina at Greensboro, NC (1970); BA, Campbell College, Buies Creek, NC (1968) **Career:** Partner, Mitchell & Suhr PLLC (1989-Present); Private Practice, Paul A. Suhr: Attorney at Law, Raleigh and Fayetteville, NC (1989-Present); Librarian, Tob. Literary Service, North Carolina State University, Raleigh, NC (1980-1985); Director, Pender County Public Library, Burgaw, NC (1978-1980); Bibliographer, North Carolina Division of State Library, Raleigh, NC (1975-1978) **Civic:** Chairman, Human Resources and Human Relations Advisory Commission, Raleigh, NC (1994-1995); Member, Human Resources and Human Relations Advisory Commission, Raleigh, NC (1990-1995) **Creative Works:** Author, Short Stories and Novelettes, Various Literary Magazines, Journals and Reviews **Awards:** Presidential Award, President of Korea (1992); Grantee, North Carolina Humanities Committee (1979-1980) **Memberships:** Board of Directors, Wake County Bar Association (1996-1997, 2003-2004, 2012-2013); ABA; American Association for Justice; American Immigration Lawyers Association: AILA; North Carolina Bar Association; North Carolina Advocates for Justice **Bar Admissions:** Supreme Court of the United States (2011); United States Court of Appeals for the Eleventh Circuit (2008); United States Court of Appeals for the Fourth Circuit (1992); United States Court of Appeals for the District of Columbia (1990); North Carolina (1989); United States District Court for the Eastern of North Carolina (1989); United States District Court for the Middle District of North Carolina (1989) **Marquis Who's Who Honors:** Albert Nelson Marquis Lifetime Achievement Award; Marquis Who's Who Top Professional; Marquis Who's Who Humanitarian Award **To what do you attribute your success:** Mr. Suhr attributes his success to being born in empathy. **Why did you become involved in your profession or industry:** Mr. Suhr became involved in his profession because he found himself useful when it came to helping others and seeing the results. **Avocations:** Gardening; Fishing; Writing; Walking; **Political Affiliations:** Democrat **Religion:** Roman Catholic

Jean Luena Mestres Sulc

Title: Lobbyist, Consultant (Retired) **Industry:** Oil & Energy **Date of Birth:** 03/17/1939 **Place of Birth:** Worcester **State/Country of Origin:** MA/USA **Parents:** Emilio Luena; Julia Bulan **Marital Status:** Widowed **Spouse Name:** Lawrence Bradley Sulc (11/04/1983, Deceased (02/01/2017); Lee Gwynne Mestres (10/09/1965, Divorced 1973) **Children:** Bradley D. Sulc (Stepson); Wayne S. Sulc (Stepson); Katherine Sulc Dwyer (Stepdaughter); Brian L. Sulc (Stepson) **Education:** Master's Degree in Urban and Regional Planning, University of Colorado Denver, Denver, CO (1976); BS in Psychology, Tufts University, Medford, MA (1961) **Certifications:** Licensed, Real Estate, Virginia; Licensed Private Pilot, Airplane, Single Engine, Land Certificate; Certified Business Retention & Expansion Consultant (Clemson Extension) **Career:** President, EdgeSystem.XXI, Washington, DC (1996-Present); Manager, Federal Relations, OXY USA Inc., Washington, DC (1990-1995); Government Affairs Representative, Cities Service, OXY USA Inc., Washington, DC (1982-1989); Assistant, Director international, Cities Service Oil & Gas Corporation, Washington, DC (1980-1981); Program Director, Council International Urban Liaison, Washington, DC (1976-1979); Consultant, Office of Policy Analysis, City and County of Denver, CO (1976); Intern, Adams County Planning Department, Brighton, CO (1974-1975); Staff, Clandestine Service, Central Intelligence Agency (1962-1967) **Career Related:** Chair, Savannah River Site (SRS) Citizens Advisory Board, Aiken, SC; Chair, Beaufort County Board of Elections and Voter Registration **Civic:** Secretary, Beaufort Aviation Association (2019-2020); Mission Trip to Zambia (2019); Ambassador for Christ International, Mission to Philippines (2018); Member, National Panel Consumer Arbitration, Better Business Bureau, Virginia (1991-1992); Chairman, Government Affairs Committee, L.P. Gas Clean Fuel Coalition, Inc., Irvine, CA (1990-1992); Volunteer, Reagan/Bush and Bush/Quayle Presidential Campaigns and Inaugural Committees, Washington, DC (1984-1989); President, Hale Foundation, Nathan Hale Institute, Washington, DC (1984-1985); Churchwork, Community Bible Church **Creative Works:** The Angel Lady Self Defense Series, for Beaufort Community (2006); Editor, Newsletter for Beaufort Republican Women's Club, "The Elephant's Ear" (2000-2004); Author, Editor, Newsletter, Dayton Climate Project (1979-1980) **Awards:** Beaufort Gazette's "Bouquet" For Addressing Top 2006 Issue (Violent Crime) Through "Angel Lady" Personal Security Series (2006); Presidential Citation, National Propane Gas Association (1992); Minority Intern Grantee, Denver Regional Council Governments (1974-1976); Two-Time Nominee, "S.C. Woman of the Year" **Memberships:** Emeritus, American League of Lobbyists (Now Association of Government Relations Professionals) (1999-Present); Eastern Regional Adviser, Association of Image Consultants International (1998-1999); Second Vice President, American League of Lobbyists (Now Association of Government Relations Professionals) (1996-1997); Board of Directors, American League of Lobbyists (Now Association of Government Relations Professionals) (1994-1997); American Society for Training and Development; Associate, Arbitration Section, American Bar Association; Greater Beaufort Chamber of Commerce; Vice President, Delta Chapter, Alpha Omicron Pi Sorority; President, Northern Virginia Alumnae Chapter, Alpha Omicron Pi Sorority; Psi Chi, International Honor Society in Psychology **Marquis Who's Who Honors:** Albert Nelson Marquis Lifetime Achievement Award; Marquis Who's Who Humanitarian Award **To what do you attribute your success:** Ms. Sulc attributes her success to a quote from Coach Dabo Swinney when his Clemson team won the National Championship in 2019, which was, "To God be the Glory." **Why did you become involved in your profession or industry:** Ms. Sulc became involved in her profession because the source of energy in local government is "community-driven needs"; in the country's survival, it is "good national security and intelligence"; in powering the economy, it is "the oil/gas sectors contributions"; and in the continued existence of the Republic, it is a return to "In God We Trust." **Avocations:** Playing the cello; Skiing; Sports shooting **Political Affiliations:** President, Beaufort Republican Women's Club (2016); Editor, "The Elephants Ear," Newsletter for BRWC (2000-2004) **Religion:** Evangelical Christian

Cornelius Wayne Sullivan

Title: Marine Biology Educator, University Research Foundation and Government Agency Administrator **Industry:** Sciences **Date of Birth:** 06/11/1943 **Place of Birth:** Pittsburgh **State/Country of Origin:** PA/USA **Parents:** John Wayne Sullivan; Hilda Sullivan **Marital Status:** Married **Spouse Name:** Jill Hajjar (10/28/1966) **Children:** Shane; Preston; Chelsea **Education:** Postdoctoral Work, Scripps Institution of Oceanography (1971-1974); PhD in Marine Biology, UC San Diego (1971); MS in Microbiology, The Pennsylvania State University (1967); BS in Biochemistry, The Pennsylvania State University (1965) **Career:** Professor, University of Southern California (1985-Present); Director, Office of Polar Programs, National Science Foundation (1993-1997); Director, Hancock Institute for Marine Studies (1991-1993); Director, Marine Biology Section, Department of Biological Sciences, University of Southern California (1982-1991); Associate Professor, University of Southern California (1980-1985); Assistant Professor of Marine Biology, University of Southern California (1974-1980) **Career Related:** Member, Board of Directors, Alfred E. MannInstitute of Biomedical Engineering (1999-2005);Vice Provost for Research, University of Southern California (1994-1997); Member, Director's Policy Group, National Science Foundation (1993-1997); Director, United States Antarctic Program (1993-1997); Visiting Scientist, Goddard Space Flight Center, NASA (1991); Visiting Senior Scholar, Cold Regions Research & Engineering Laboratory, US Army (1990-1991); Scientific Committee on Oceanic Research on the Ecology of Sea Ice (1987-1993); Scientific Committee of Antarctic Research, Specialist Group on Southern Ocean Ecology(1986-1993); Chair, Committee to Evaluate Polar Research Platforms, Polar Research Board, National Research Council (1985-1989); Member, Steering Committee, Antarctic Marine Research at the Ice Edge Zone (1982-1989); Member, BIOMASS Working Party on Pack-Ice Zone Studies (1983-1986); Ecological Research Project Review Board, Department of the Navy (1982-1985); Visiting Professor, University of Colorado Boulder (1981-1982); Visiting Professor, Massachusetts Institute of Technology (1981-1982); Field Team Leader on Sea Ice Microbial Communities Studies, McMurdo Sound (1980-1986) **Civic:** Delegation Head, Council of Managers of National Antarctic Programs (1993-1997); US Representative, Antarctic Treaty Consultative Meeting (1993-1997) **Creative Works:** Member, Editorial Board, Polar Biology (1987-1998); Member, Editorial Board, Journal of Microbiological Methods (1982-1985); Contributor, 150 Articles, Professional Scientific Journals; Patent, Heat Sensitive Bacterial Alkaline Phosphatase **Awards:** Antarctica Service Medal, National Science Foundation (1981); Fellowship, U.S. Public Health Service (1969-1971) **Memberships:** California Council on Science and Technology; Fellow, American Association for the Advancement of Science **Marquis Who's Who Honors:** Albert Nelson Marquis Lifetime Achievement Award **Why did you become involved in your profession or industry:** Dr. Sullivan became involved in his profession because of his lifelong love of fishing and marine science. **Avocations:** Fishing **Political Affiliations:** Democrat

James Gerald Sullivan

Title: Small Business Owner **Industry:** Business Management/Business Services **Company Name:** Jerry's Barber Shop **Date of Birth:** 09/13/1935 **Place of Birth:** Bad Axe **State/Country of Origin:** MI/USA **Parents:** John Thomas Sullivan; Frances Eugena (O'Henley) Sullivan **Marital Status:** Married **Spouse Name:** Florence Marie Tack (09/12/1959) **Children:** Kevin Michael (Deceased); Kathleen Marie **Education:** Coursework, Highland Park College (1959-1960); Coursework, University of Detroit Mercy (1957-1958); Coursework, Central Michigan University **Career:** Owner, Jerry's Barber Shop, Kinde, Bad Axe, MI (1963-Present); Senior Member, MoneySports.com Investor Relations (2014); Senior Member, GNLD International (2013-2015); Member, Independent Ionways Associates (2013); Distributor, AlkaViva Distributor (2013); Water Specialist, AlkaViva Distributor (2013); Water Distributor, Ionized Antioxdant (2010); Director, ASEA (2010); Distributor, ASEA (2010); Regional Manager, Primerica Financial Services, Michigan (2010); Elected Member, Executive Committee, Veterans Club, National Rural Letter Carriers' Association (2009); Distributor, Water Specialist, Enagic USA Inc. (2009); Regional Manager, Primerica Financial Services, Bad Axe, MI (1985-1998); Rural Letter Carrier, United States Postal Service, Bad Axe, MI (1982-1998); Sales Representative, WLEW Radio Station, Bad Axe, MI (1981-1982); Sales Representative, Thumb Blanket, Bad Axe, MI (1980-1981); Treasurer, Colfax Township, Bad Axe, MI (1979-1990); Purchasing Agent, Walbro Corporation, Cass City, MI (1979-1980); Purchasing Agent, Thumb Electric Cooperative, Ubly, MI (1966-1980) **Career Related:** Member, Michigan Chapter, National Rural Letter Carriers' Association (2015); Professional Tee.com Golf Partnership (2014); Elected President, Armed Forces Veterans Club (2011); Assistant National Secretary, Armed Forces Veterans Club (2011); Treasurer, Armed Forces Veterans Club (2011); Distributor, Ionized Antioxidant Water (2010); Distributor, Water Specialist, Enagic USA Inc., Kangen Water (2009); Elected Member, Executive Committee, Veterans Club, National Rural Letter Carriers' Association (2009); Notary Public, State of Michigan (1968); Loss Clerk, Toplis & Harding Wagner & Gliddon, Detroit, MI (1959-1961); Inventory Control Clerk, Carrick Products Co., Royal Oak, MI (1957-1959); Independent Distributor, Alkaline Antioxidant Ionized Multi-Clustered Water **Civic:** President, Huron County Township Association, Michigan (1988-1990); Leader, Boy Scouts of America, Bad Axe, MI (1975-1977); Eucharistic Minister, Lector, Ushers Club, Sacred Heart Church **Military Service:** U.S. Army (1954-1956) **Creative Works:** Honoree, National Profile Plus (2017) **Awards:** Featured, National Profile Plus Magazine (2017); Voted, Most Famous Classmate **Memberships:** Past President, Tip of the Thumb Dance Club (2005); Member, Tip of the Thumb Dance Club (2009-Present); State Secretary, Michigan Division, National Rural Letter Carriers' Association (1999-Present); Re-Elected National Secretary-Treasurer, Armed Forces Veterans Club of the National Rural Letter Carriers Association (2018, 2012); President, Bad Axe Lions Club, Lions Club International (2009-2010); President, Bad Axe Lions Club, Lions Club International (2006-2007); President, Huron County Rural Letter Carriers Association (1988-2003); President and member, Bad Axe Lions Club, Lions Club International (1979-1980), (2000), (2006-2007), (2009-2010); President, Community Club (1976-1977); President, 4-H Club (1948-1950); Associate, The American Legion; Lion Tamer, Chaplain, Lions Club International; Council 1546, Knights of Columbus; President, Michigan Armed Forces Veterans Club **Marquis Who's Who Honors:** Albert Nelson Marquis Lifetime Achievement Award; Marquis Who's Who Top Professional; Marquis Who's Who Humanitarian Award **To what do you attribute your success:** Mr. Sullivan attributes his success to being honest and hardworking. **Why did you become involved in your profession or industry:** Mr. Sullivan became involved in his profession because he was trying to make a difference. **Avocations:** Gardening; Playing golf; Swimming; Fishing **Political Affiliations:** Republican **Religion:** Roman Catholic

David Sumo Meltzer

Title: Owner **Industry:** Food & Restaurant Services **Company Name:** Sumo San Antonio, LLC **Marital Status:** Married **Spouse Name:** Rosemarie **Children:** Mekayla **Career:** Owner, Sumo San Antonio, LLC (2016-Present); Employee, Sumo San Antonio (2011-2016); Benihana, San Antonio, TX **Awards:** Readers Choice Award, San Antonio News (2018); Gold Award; Awarded Private, Texas Ranger Foundation **Marquis Who's Who Honors:** Marquis Who's Who Top Professional **To what do you attribute your success:** He attributes his success to his father Bradley Meltzer for giving him the start. **Why did you become involved in your profession or industry:** Mr. Meltzer started because he wanted to prove to his father, but it also had to do with an older gentleman from Japan who is the first master of sushi to come to Texas. He taught him everything about sushi restaurants and Japanese restaurants.

Don Sundquist

Title: Former Governor **Industry:** Government Administration/Government Relations/Government Services **Company Name:** State of Tennessee **Date of Birth:** 03/15/1936 **Place of Birth:** Moline **State/Country of Origin:** IL/USA **Parents:** Kenneth M. Sundquist; Louise (Rohren) Sundquist **Marital Status:** Married **Spouse Name:** Martha Swanson (10/03/1959) **Children:** Tania Sundquist; Andrea; Donald Kenneth (Deke) Sundquist **Education:** BA, Augustana College, Rock Island, IL (1957) **Career:** Co-Founder, Principal, Sundquist Anthony LLC, Washington, DC (2003-2013); Governor, State of Tennessee, Nashville, TN (1995-2003); U.S. Congress From Seventh Tennessee District, Washington, DC (1983-1995); President, Graphic Sales of America, Memphis, TN (1973-1982); Executive Vice President, Graphic Sales of America, Memphis, TN (1972); Division Manager, Josten's, Inc. (1961-1972); Former Governor, State of Tennessee **Career Related:** Six Term Member, United States Congress; Two Term, State of Tennessee **Civic:** Chairman, Congressional Steering Committee, George Bush for President (1992); Chairman, Congressional Steering Committee, George Bush for President (1988); Director, Committee of Operations, Alternate Delegate, Republican National Convention (1980); National Campaign Manager, Howard Baker for President (1979); U.S. Delegate, Study Tour, People's Republic of China (1978); Alternate Delegate, Republican National Convention (1976); Chairman, Shelby County Republican Party (1975-1977); U.S. Delegate, Study Tour, USSR (1975); U.S. Youth Council (1972-1975); Director, Mid-South Coliseum, American Council on Young Political Leaders (1972-1974); Executive Committee, Republican National Committee (1971-1973); National Chairman, Young Republican National Federation (1971-1973); Chairman, Tennessee Young Republican Federation (1969-1970); Secretary, Bedford County Election Commission (1968-1970); Board of Governors, Charles Edison Memorial Youth Fund; National Advisory Board, Distributive Education Clubs of America **Military Service:** Active Duty, U.S. Navy (1957-1959) **Awards:** Gold and Silver Star, Order of the Rising Sun, Emperor of Japan (2018) **Memberships:** Kiwanis Club **Marquis Who's Who Honors:** Albert Nelson Marquis Lifetime Achievement Award **Avocations:** Golf; Politics **Political Affiliations:** Republican **Religion:** Methodist

Robert W. Surplus

Title: Music Educator (Retired) **Industry:** Education/Educational Services **Company Name:** Surge Promotions **Date of Birth:** 09/01/1923 **Place of Birth:** Scranton **State/Country of Origin:** PA/USA **Parents:** Willard K. Surplus; Olive T. (Wrightson) Surplus **Marital Status:** Married **Spouse Name:** Jean Craig (06/25/1976, Deceased 2015) **Children:** Amy; Melanie **Education:** EdD, Columbia University, New York, NY (1968); MA, Columbia University, New York, NY (1947); BS, Susquehanna University, Selinsgrove, PA (1945) **Career:** Retired (1994); Professor, Music, Eastern Kentucky University, Richmond, KY (1965-1994); Assistant Professor, University Minnesota, Minneapolis, MN (1961-1965);Assistant to Norval Church in Conducting, Columbia University, New York, NY (1961); Assistant to Dr. Gladys Tipton in Music Education, Columbia University, New York, NY (1959-1961); Instructor, Columbia University, New York, NY (1959-1961); Music Teacher, Fox Lane School, Bedford, NY (1958-1959); Associate Professor, Shippensburg State University, Shippensburg, PA (1956-1958); Music Supervisor, Red Lion, PA (1947-1956); Music Teacher, Butler, NJ (1946-1947); Music Teacher, Mineola, NY (1945-1946) **Career Related:** Research Council Member (1974-1980); Consultant, National Association of Junior Colleges (1973-1975); Research Chairman, Southern Division, Music Educators National Conference **Military Service:** Served Briefly in the 17th Airborne Division, U.S. Army **Creative Works:** Author, "Beyond the Classroom: Informing Others" (1987); Editor, "A Guidebook for State Music Education Associations" (1985); Author, "The Story of Musical Organizations" (1963); Author, "The Alphabet of Music" (1963); Author, "Follow the Leader" (1962); Author, Brochures, "Working together for quality music education for all students"; Contributor, Articles, Professional Journals; Edited Works by Jean Craig, Danny Tetzlaff, Lee Gilmore, Robert Krishef, Sharon Lerner, and Lional & Edith Davis **Awards:** Citation for Service, Kentucky Music Educators Association (2004); Distinguished Service Award, Kentucky Music Educators Association (1983) **Memberships:** President, Southern Division, Music Educators National Conference (1982-1984); President, Kentucky Alliance for Arts Education (1974-1982); President, Board of Directors, Kentucky Music Educators Association (1971-1973) **Marquis Who's Who Honors:** Albert Nelson Marquis Lifetime Achievement Award; Marquis Who's Who Top Professional **To what do you attribute your success:** Mr. Surplus attributes his success to hard work and keeping at things until they are completed. **Why did you become involved in your profession or industry:** Mr. Surplus became involved in his profession because when he was young, he was crazy about Hawaii and played the Hawaiian guitar along with his younger brother. His other brother played the regular guitar. His brother played the guitar and banjo. At the age of 10, he played his guitar on the radio in WGBI in Scranton, Pennsylvania, and he also played the trumpet in the high school band for four years as first trumpet. When he was in high school, he did not know what he wanted to do in college, he was interested in history and music. He looked at various things and the local band director of the high school sent him to the guidance counselor and together they decided that he should go into music, so he did. **Avocations:** Reading **Religion:** Methodist

Gary Mark Sussman

Title: Assistant Treasurer **Industry:** Insurance **Date of Birth:** 03/01/1954 **Place of Birth:** Dayton **State/Country of Origin:** OH/USA **Parents:** Meyer Sussman; Sylvia Florence (Oltusky) Lehman **Marital Status:** Married **Spouse Name:** Susan Sussman **Children:** Eric Sussman; Steven Sussman **Education:** MBA, The University of Chicago (1978); BSBA, The Ohio State University, Cum Laude (1976) **Certifications:** Certified Public Accountant (CPA), State of Texas **Career:** Supervisor, Armco, Inc. (1988-Present); Supervising Auditor, Northwestern National Insurance Company (1987-1988); Auditor, Armco, Inc., Houston, TX (1980-1983); Associate Auditor, Armco, Inc., Middletown, OH (1978-1979); Assistant Treasurer, Treasurer, Statutory Accounting Manager, Northwestern National Insurance Company, Middletown, OH **Awards:** Outstanding Young Men of America (1986) **Memberships:** Charter Member, Treasurer, South Dayton Chapter, B'nai Brith (1991-Present); Treasurer, Alpha Kappa Psi Fraternity (1974-1975); TXCPA; The Institute of Internal Auditors; The Ohio Society of Certified Public Accountants; IASA **Marquis Who's Who Honors:** Albert Nelson Marquis Lifetime Achievement Award **Why did you become involved in your profession or industry:** Mr. Sussman became involved in his profession because of his interest in accounting and business. **Avocations:** Oil painting; Woodworking **Religion:** Jewish

Martha B. "Marti" Swanson

Title: Secondary Educator (Retired), Consultant **Industry:** Consulting **Date of Birth:** 06/08/1935 **Place of Birth:** Berwyn **State/Country of Origin:** IL/USA **Parents:** Francis M. Baldwin; Irville (Miller) Baldwin **Marital Status:** Widowed **Spouse Name:** Kenneth A. Swanson (03/27/1954, Deceased 2013) **Children:** Richard R. Swanson (Deceased 2006); Gary E. Swanson (Deceased 2010); Laura Ruth Swanson Bender **Education:** MS in English and Education, Northern Illinois University (1973); EdB, Northern Illinois University, With Honors (1967) **Certifications:** Licensed Teacher, State of Illinois (1967) **Career:** Classroom Teacher, Grant Community High School, Fox Lake, IL (1986-1992); Teacher, President, Grant Council Union, Grant Community High School, Fox Lake, IL (1983-1992); English, Grant Community High School, Fox Lake, IL (1967-1992); Chair, English Department, Grant Community High School, Fox Lake, IL (1975-1986); Secretary, Local 504, Lake County Federation of Teachers Local 504, AFL-CIO (1975-1983) **Career Related:** Local Site Coordinator, American Federation Teacher, Educational Research and Dissemination Project, Lake County Federation of Teachers Local 504, AFL-CIO, Waukegan, IL (1987-1994); Selection Panel, All-State Academic Team, Chicago Tribune (1992); Judge, Annual Achievement Awards in Writing, NCTE (1978-1992); Secretary, Illinois Association of Teachers of English, Department of English, Illinois State University (1977-1989); In-Field Consultant, Inventory Educational Progress, Illinois State Board of Education, Springfield, IL (1985); Workshop Presenter **Civic:** Precinct Committeeperson, McHenry 01, Democratic Party of McHenry County (1992-Present); Treasurer, Wildflower Preservation & Propagation Committee (1993-2004); Board of Trustees, Village of Ringwood (1995-1999); Environmental Defenders of McHenry County **Creative Works:** Editor, "Baldwin Family Bulletin" (2001-Present); Editor, "Citizens for Ringwood Organization" (1993-1998); Editor, "Five-Oh for Retirees" (1992-1998); Editor, "Grant Slant" (1986-1988); Author, Essays **Awards:** Unit Honoree, Lake County Retired Teachers Association, Teachers' Retirement System of the State of Illinois (2011); Retired Teacher of the Year, McHenry County Retired Teachers Association (1998); Retired Teacher of the Year, Lake County Retired Teachers Association (1998); Superintendent's G Award, Grant Community High School (1989) **Memberships:** Chair, Legislative Committee, Lake County Retired Teachers Association (2010-Present); Representative, Area II, IRTA (2008-2015); Secretary, Jacob Hochstetler Family Association (2003-2013); Treasurer, McHenry County Illinois Genealogical Society (2000-2011); President, McHenry County Illinois Genealogical Society (2005-2008); Legislative Committee, Lake County Retired Teachers Association (2006-2007); President, McHenry County Retired Teachers Association (2002-2005); Vice President, McHenry County Retired Teachers Association (2000-2001); Chair, State Legislative Committee, IRTA (1995-1999); Secretary, Retirees Council, Lake County Federation of Teachers Local 504 (1992-1998); Chair, Region 2 Legislative Committee, IRTA (1994-1995); Chairman, Legislative Committee, McHenry County Retired Teachers Association (1992-1995); Secretary, Lake County Federation of Teachers Local 504 (1984-1995); Co-Chairman, Educational Excellence Committee, Illinois Federation of Teachers (1989-1993); President, Grant Council, Lake County Federation of Teachers Local 504, AFL-CIO (1983-1992); Secretary, Illinois Association of Teachers of English, Department of English, Illinois State University (1977-1989); Executive Board, Illinois Association of Teachers of English, Department of English, Illinois State University (1971-1989); Secretary, Grant Council, Lake County Federation of Teachers Local 504, AFL-CIO (1975-1983); Honorary Lifetime Member, Illinois Association of Teachers of English, Department of English, Illinois State University; McHenry County Chapter, Citizens' Climate Lobby, Spring Grove, IL; Numerous Genealogical Societies **Marquis Who's Who Honors:** Albert Nelson Marquis Lifetime Achievement Award **Why did you become involved in your profession or industry:** Ms. Swanson became involved in her profession with mutual inspiration from her husband, who, halfway through college, decided he would like to be a teacher. She took time off to have children, but worked hard to earn a bachelor's degree at night school and a master's degree through summer school. **Avocations:** Camping; Photography; Family history; Genealogy **Political Affiliations:** Democrat **Religion:** United Church of Christ

Mary Eva Swigar, MD

Title: 1) Neuro-Psychiatry Educator 2) Chair **Industry:** Medicine & Health Care **Company Name:** 1) Rutgers University, Institutional Review Board/ Robert Wood Johnson Medical School 2) Institutional Review Board **Date of Birth:** 10/17/1940 **Place of Birth:** Nesquehoning **State/Country of Origin:** PA/ USA **Education:** Doctor of Medicine, Temple University (1966); Bachelor of Science, Muhlenberg College (1962) **Certifications:** Registered Psychiatrist, New Jersey **Career:** Professor Emerita (2013); Institutional Review Board, Piscataway, New Brunswick, NJ (1988-2013); Chief, Psychiatry Department, Robert Wood Johnson Hospital, New Brunswick, NJ (1988-2000); Associate Professor of Psychiatry, Yale University (1977-1988); Associate Professor, Psychiatry & Neuro-Psychiatry Educator, Rutgers University; Institutional Review Board, Robert Wood Johnson Medical School **Career Related:** Chair, Executive Committee Institutional Review Board, Robert Wood Johnson University Hospital (2004-2010); Ex-Officio, Conductor, Research Committee, Robert Wood Johnson University Hospital (1993-2010); Chair Institutional Review Board, Robert Wood Johnson University Hospital (1993-2010); Member, Institutional Review Board, Robert Wood Johnson University Hospital (1990-2010); Member, Geriatrics Providers Group, Robert Wood Johnson University Hospital (1990-1991); Member, Credentials Committee, Robert Wood Johnson University Hospital (1988-2000); Member, Medical Board, Robert Wood Johnson University Hospital (1988-2000) **Creative Works:** Contributor, Articles and Book Chapters to Professional Journals and Publications **Awards:** Lifetime Achievement Award, Muhlenberg College **Memberships:** Fellow, International College of Psychosomatic Medicine; Royal Society of Medicine; New York Academy of Science; Retired Faculty Association-Rutgers Robert Wood Johnson Medical School; Medical Historical Society of New Jersey **Marquis Who's Who Honors:** Albert Nelson Marquis Lifetime Achievement Award; Marquis Who's Who Top Professional **To what do you attribute your success:** Dr. Swigar attributes her success to the support of her family, as well as hard work, persistence and wonderful mentors. **Why did you become involved in your profession or industry:** Dr. Swigar initially became involved in her profession after dabbling with the field of neurosurgery. She decided to study psychiatry, as that field was entering a time of transition, and it seemed more interesting. **Avocations:** Hiking; Music; Theater; Classical music; Mushroom hunting; Reading **Religion:** Orthodox Christian

Carol Swinford

Title: Manager **Industry:** Agriculture **Company Name:** Shades of Blue Ranch **Marital Status:** Married **Spouse Name:** Gary Swinford **Education:** Certified Nurse's Aid; Coursework, McHenry County College (One Year) **Career:** Owner, Founder, Shades of Blue Ranch (1990-Present); Pioneer, Center for Training, Center for Mentally Challenged Adults, Carostoel Nursing Home (1982); With, Valley Hi Nursing Home (1981); With, Easter Seals Therapy Center for Physically and Mentally Challenged Children, Wood Stock, IL (1978) **Civic:** Volunteer, Journey Care Hospice; Vice President, Falabella international Preservation Association, FL; Treasurer, Heart of America Miniature Equine Club; Falabella Breeders and Owners Society **Awards:** HAME Award for Excellent Leadership and Ever Present Dedication, Heart of America Miniature Equine Club (2018) **Marquis Who's Who Honors:** Albert Nelson Marquis Lifetime Achievement Award; Marquis Who's Who Top Professional; Marquis Who's Who Humanitarian Award **Why did you become involved in your profession or industry:** Every time Mrs. Swinford's husband built a new barn, it ended up being a new shade of blue; that is why it is called Shades of Blue Ranch. After the barns were built, they bought horses and the equipment for riding. She did not grow up on a farm, but in Chicago. Her dad moved them out when she was four years old, and it was only a couple of acres in the country. She kept asking her dad when she was in fifth or sixth grade for a pony. Her dad did surprise her with a pony, and she grew up with it; later on, when she got older, her dad got her a horse. But the big break that allowed her to have this incredible life came when she was working as a nurse's aide in the nursing home where they had just bought a couple of miniature horses. She broke the ice by asking the executor of the nursing home if she could bring her horse there for the patients because she saw the need, to give them something to look forward to, something different, something for them to talk about. That was back in 1998. But, in the meantime and up until that time she had horses that she enjoyed. She has been doing it ever since, and it is rewarding. **Thoughts on Life:** Shades of Blue Ranch houses 21 Miniature horses; four visit the nursing homes and the rest are breeding mares. Mrs. Swinford performs memorial services, as well as dressing the horses in costumes, tennis shoes and combat boots for occasions.She takes the horses into people's home for their last request, so they can pet a horse, smell a horse, or whatever their association was with horses. She works with schools when they have special occasions. For more information on Mrs. Swinford's work, please visit: http://www.shadesofblueranch.com

Lee Merriam Talbot, PhD

Title: Professor **Industry:** Education/Educational Services **Company Name:** George Mason University **Date of Birth:** 08/02/1930 **Place of Birth:** New Bedford **State/Country of Origin:** MA/USA **Parents:** Murrell Williams Talbot; Zenaida (Merriam) Talbot **Marital Status:** Married **Spouse Name:** Martha Walcott Hayne (05/16/1959) **Children:** Lawrence Hayne; Russell Merriam **Education:** PhD, University of California Berkeley (1963); MA, University of California Berkeley (1963); BA, University of California Berkeley (1953) **Career:** Affiliate of Geography, Full Professor of Environmental Science and Policy, Ecologist, Geographer, George Mason University (2007-Present); Senior Professor of Environmental Sciences, International Affairs and Public Policy, George Mason University, Virginia (1994-Present); President, Lee Talbot Associates International (1991-Present); Senior Environmental Adviser, The World Bank Group (1984-Present); Visiting Fellow, World Resources Institute, Washington, DC (1984-1989); Research Fellow, East-West Center (1983-1987); Director General, International Union for Conservation of Nature, Gland, Switzerland (1980-1983); Senior Science Adviser, International Science Council, Paris, France (1978-1983); Director of Conservation, Special Science Adviser, WWF - World Wide Fund For Nature (1978-1980); Senior Scientist, Director of International Activities, Council on Environmental Quality, Washington, DC (1970-1978); Resident Ecologist, Field Representative for International Affairs, Smithsonian, Washington, DC (1966-1970); Director, Southeast Asia Project, International Union for Conservation of Nature (1964-1965); Wildlife Advisor, United Nations Special Fund, Africa (1963-1964); Ecologist, Director, East African Ecological Research Project, National Academy of Sciences, Governments of Kenya and Tanzania (1959-1963); Staff Ecologist, International Union for Conservation, Brussels, Belgium (1954-1956); Biologist, Arctic Research Laboratory, Point Barrow, AK (1951) **Career Related:** President's Council, Population Reference Bureau (2007-Present); Founding Trustee, Cary Institute of Ecosystem Studies, New York (2006); Coordinator, International Biological Program (1965-1970); Consultant, US Government, United Nations Special Fund, World Health Organization, The World Bank Group, The Nature Conservancy, UNEP; Member, Board of Directors, Defenders of Wildlife; Science Advisor, National Parks Conservation Association **Civic:** Active Member, Boy Scouts of America, Washington, DC (1987-1995); Active Member, Boy Scouts of America, Geneva, Switzerland (1980-1982) **Military Service:** US Marine Corps (1953-1954) **Creative Works:** Author, 17 Books and Monographs; Contributor, More Than 300 Articles, Professional Journals **Awards:** The Benton H. Box Award, Clemson University (2013); Secretary Interior Award for the Development and Implementation of the World Heritage Convention, US Secretary of State (2012); Flag Award, The Explorers Club (2003-2005, 2007, 2011); Driver of the Year, SVRA (2010); Roll of Honor Award, Species Survival Commission, International Union for Conservation of Nature (2010); Medal, The Explorers Club (2009); Excellence in Achievement Award, University of California (2008); East Asia Award, World Commission on Protected Areas, International Union for Conservation of Nature (2005); Eponym, Centenary Symposium, BNHS (2003); Officer, Candidate School, US Marine Corps (2003); Career Accomplishment Award, George Mason University (2003); Pierre Chaleur Prize, French Academy of Sciences (1993); Regents Lectureship Award, UC Santa Barbara (1986); Distinguished Scientist Award, American Institute of Biological Sciences (1979); Outstanding Publication Award, The Wildlife Society (1963); Distinguished Alumnus (1953); Decorated Officer, National Order of the Lion, Senegal **Memberships:** Fellow, Royal Geographical Society; Fellow, The RSA; Fellow, American Association for the Advancement of Science; Fellow, New York Zoological Society; American Institute of Biological Sciences; The Club of Rome U.S. Association; The American Society of Mammalogists; The Wildlife Society; Ecological Society of America; Society for Conservation Biology; The International Society for Ecological Economics; The Explorers Club; Boone and Crockett Club; Cosmos Club Washington DC; Sigma Xi, The Scientific Research Honor Society; Phi Kappa Sigma International Fraternity **Marquis Who's Who Honors:** Albert Nelson Marquis Lifetime Achievement Award **Why did you become involved in your profession or industry:** Dr. Talbot became involved in his profession because his parents were both ecologists and his father was head of research for Forest in the West. His father worked with Aldo Leopold to start a wilderness area in New Mexico. His grandfather was the founder of the Fish and Wildlife Service.

Ilkka Talvi

Title: Concert Violinist **Industry:** Education/Educational Services **Company Name:** Seattle Pacific University **Date of Birth:** 10/22/1948 **Place of Birth:** Kuusankoski **State/Country of Origin:** Finland **Parents:** Veikko Tuomo Talvi; Irja Margareta (Saajos) Talvi **Marital Status:** Married **Spouse Name:** Marjorie Kransberg-Talvi **Children:** Silja Joanna; Sonja Louisa Rosen; Anna Mirjan Blick; Sarah Lillian Duncan **Education:** Coursework, Curtis Institute of Music, Philadelphia, PA (1968-1969); Coursework, Heifetz Master Class, University of Southern California (1967-1968); Private Studies, Gabrielle Bouillon, Ricardo Odnoposoff, Paris, France (1965-1967); Private Studies, Gabrielle Bouillon, Ricardo Odnoposoff, Vienna, Austria (1965-1967); Diploma in Violin, Sibelius Academy, Helsinki, Finland (1966) **Career:** Concertmaster, Rainier Symphony (2006-Present); Professor, Concert Violinist, Seattle Pacific University, (2005-Present); Concertmaster, Mostly Mozart Festival, New York, NY (1999-2001); Concertmaster, Waterloo Festival, NJ (1988-1992); Concertmaster, Seattle Opera (1985-2004); Concertmaster, Seattle Symphony (1985-2004); Principal, Los Angeles Chamber Orchestra, Pasadena, CA (1979-1985); Concertmaster, Malmö Symphony Orchestra, Sweden (1976-1977); Lecturer, Porin Musiikkiopisto, Pori, Finland (1970-1976); Lecturer, Sibelius Academy, Helsinki, Finland (1969-1975) **Career Related:** Guest Concertmaster, Seattle Symphony (1983-1985); Freelance Violinist, Los Angeles, CA (1977-1980); Freelance Violinist, Film and Television, Los Angeles, CA (1977-1980); Recording Industries, Los Angeles, CA (1977-1980) **Creative Works:** Violinist, Finland and United States (1972-Present); Soloist, Recitals, Europe and United States (1965-Present); Performer, "Klami Violin Concerto," "In Concordian," "Diamond 2. Violin Concerto," and "Ein Heldenleben"; Performer, Numerous Recordings; Numerous CDs **Awards:** Kuusankoski Award, Finland (1967); Numerous Grants, Finland (1965-1975) **Memberships:** Association of Soloists, Finland (1965-Present) **Marquis Who's Who Honors:** Albert Nelson Marquis Lifetime Achievement Award; Marquis Who's Who Top Professional **Why did you become involved in your profession or industry:** Mr. Talvi found his love for music at 3 years old. When Mr. Talvi was young, he composed a piece for his father, a violinist in a community orchestra. Mr. Talvi taught himself to play violin until he was 10 years old, when he joined his father's orchestra and performed in the United States and Canada. Mr. Talvi also started playing piano at 3. He picked up his father's violin as they were taking a walk. When they came home, he began to show him a piece he composed right then and there. His father brought home a violin teacher because it is very hard for a parent to teach their own child. **Avocations:** Computers; Science; Geography; Medicine

Raquel Tamez

Title: Chief Executive Officer **Industry:** Law and Legal Services **Company Name:** Society of Hispanic Professional Engineers **Parents:** Cecilia Gloria Uresti Tamez Juventino Tamez **Education:** Doctor of Jurisprudence, St. Mary's University School of Law, San Antonio, TX (1998); Bachelor of Arts in Government, Business, and Spanish, University of Texas at Austin, Texas (1994) **Certifications:** ELI Certified Trainer in "Strengthening Employee Relations" (2010); Certified Mediator (2002) **Career:** Chief Executive Officer, Society of Hispanic Professional Engineers, Los Angeles, CA (2017-Present); Chief Legal Officer, SourceAmerica, Washington, DC (2014-2017); Deputy General Counsel, Computer Sciences Corporation, Falls Church, VA (2010-2014); Counsel, Sumner, Schick, Pace, Dallas, TX (2009-2010); Vice President, Corporate Counsel, Affiliated Computer Services Inc., Dallas, TX (2007-2009); Partner, Nace & Motley LLP, Dallas, TX (2006-2007); Assistant General Counsel, Benefit Partners Inc., Dallas, TX (2004-2006); Corporate Counsel, Mary Kay Inc., Dallas, TX (2002-2004); Prosecutor, Solicitor's Office, U.S. Department of Labor, Region VI, Dallas, TX (1998-2002) **Career Related:** Advisory Board Member, Base 11 Space Challenge (2018-Present); Advisory Board Member, Rutgers University Customer Experience (2018-Present); Advisory Council Member, digitalNow Advisory Group (2018-Present); Advisory Board Member, Internet of Things in Manufacturing (2018-Present); STEM Ed Coalition (2017-Present); Board Member, AIDS Arms Inc. (2004-2007) **Civic:** Board Member, Council of Engineering and Scientific Society Executives; Board Member, Hispanic Association on Corporate Responsibility **Creative Works:** Featured as a Leader, Numerous Media Outlets **Awards:** Young Hispanic Corporate Achievers National Award, Hispanic Association on Corporate Responsibility (2008) **Memberships:** Fellow, Leadership Council on Legal Diversity Talent Development Program (2011); Hispanic Bar Association of the District of Columbia (2010-2017); Dallas Association of Young Lawyers Leadership Class (2009); Dallas Bar Association (1998-2010) **Bar Admissions:** State Bar of Texas **To what do you attribute your success:** Ms. Tamez feels that this job is her calling and vocation. She is very passionate about what she does, and is grateful and humbled to serve in that capacity. She attributes her success to the values her parents instilled within her, such as hard work, persistence and integrity. She has a great relationship with her father, and he has always made her feel like she can do anything. **Why did you become involved in your profession or industry:** Ms. Tamez became involved in her profession because she grew up in a deprived neighborhood, to immigrant parents. When an executive search firm approached her and asked her if she would be interested in the CEO role of the Society of Hispanic Professional Engineers, she was not aware of what the organization was but did her due diligence and found out. After researching the company and the role, she realized how great of an opportunity it was and decided to transition from her law career into her new role.

Jay Harvey Tanenbaum

Title: Lawyer **Industry:** Law and Legal Services **Company Name:** The Law Offices of Jay H. Tanenbaum **Date of Birth:** 11/17/1933 **Place of Birth:** New York **State/Country of Origin:** NY/USA **Parents:** Leo Aaron Tanenbaum; Regina (Stein) Tanenbaum **Marital Status:** Single **Spouse Name:** Linda Goldman (05/28/1961, Deceased 2010) **Children:** Susan Hillary; Steven Eric **Education:** JD, Union College (1961); LLB, Albany Law School (1957); BA, Hobart and William Smith Colleges (1954) **Certifications:** Supreme Court of the United States (1967); United States District Court for the Southern District of New York (1961); New York (1957) **Career:** Lawyer, Private Practice, The Law Offices of Jay H. Tanenbaum, New York, NY (1964-Present); International Trader, Associated Metals and Minerals Corporation, New York, NY (1960-1964) **Career Related:** Corporate Counsel, International Gate Corporation; Corporate Counsel, General Gate Corporation **Awards:** Named to Knighthood, His Royal Highness The Prince of Cittanova and His Royal Highness The Prince of Trabzon (2001) **Memberships:** New York State Bar Association; New York Trial Lawyers Association; Bronx County Bar Association; St. James Hotel and Club; Le Club, New York **Marquis Who's Who Honors:** Albert Nelson Marquis Lifetime Achievement Award; Marquis Who's Who Top Professional **Why did you become involved in your profession or industry:** Mr. Tanenbaum became involved in his profession because of his strong tenacity from a young age. When he was 9, he was shining shoes at the Saratoga Race Course and by age 12, he was getting up at four in the morning with his father and driving to the market, where he watched his father buy fruits and vegetables and learned how to do it. At 16, he borrowed $300 and bought himself a black Pontiac 1940 convertible with red leather seats and a tan top. By that age, he was also finished with high school and drove himself to college in his car. By 19 1/2, he graduated college and when he was 22, he became a lawyer.

Eric S. Tautfest

Title: Lawyer **Industry:** Law and Legal Services **Parents:** David La Roy Tautfest; Linda Kay Mathis **Marital Status:** Married **Spouse Name:** Rebecca Suzanne Moss (08/13/1991) **Children:** Jessica Marie; Alexa Suzanne; Matthew Sean **Education:** JD, Southern Methodist University (2000); BA, Brigham Young University (1996) **Career:** Participating Associate, Godwin Gruber LLP, Dallas, TX (2003-Present); Associate, McKool Smith, Professional Corporation, Dallas, TX (2000-2003); Partner, Gray Reed & McGraw LLP; Tautfest Bond PLLC **Civic:** Member, Eagle Scout, Missionary, The Latter Day Saints Church, Seoul, South Korea (1988-1990); Pro Bono Lawyer; Service Work, Church; Missionary, Seoul, South Korea **Awards:** Scholar, SMU Law Review Association, SMU Dedman School of Law (1998-2000); Duty to God Award, The Latter Day Saints Church **Memberships:** Board Member, J. Reuben Clark Law Society (2004-Present); Voting Member, Patent Litigation Committee, American Intellectual Property Association (2003); Officer, Executive Board, Phi Delta Phi (1998-2000); Federal Bar Association; American Bar Association; Texas Young Lawyer's Association; Dallas Association Young Lawyers; Dallas Bar Association; Life Member, Phi Delta Phi **Bar Admissions:** U.S. District Court for the Western District of Texas (2005); U.S. District Court for the Southern District of Texas (2003); U.S. District Court for the Eastern District of Texas (2003); U.S. Court of Appeals For The Fifth Circuit (2002); U.S. District Court for the Northern District of Texas (2000); Texas (2000) **Marquis Who's Who Honors:** Albert Nelson Marquis Lifetime Achievement Award **Why did you become involved in your profession or industry:** Mr. Tautfest became involved in his profession because he always wanted to be a surgeon until a family friend, who is a heart surgeon, let him stand in watch him perform heart surgery. The family friend thought it may change his mind, but Mr. Tautfest thought it was "the coolest thing." The family friend then tried a different approach: he told him about all the years of school and training, and the debt he was in from student loans. Eventually, he decided he didn't want to be a doctor, but he didn't know what he wanted to do until college. He took a political science class on legal theory and loved it; he knew right then that that was what he had to do. He graduated with a degree in political science, with a minor in Japanese literature, and then went to law school. In addition, he grew up in humble circumstances and always thought there was a way to help those who couldn't help themselves. He believes that this profession really lends itself for that, being able to step up for people when they need it and for companies when they need help. He has always strived to use his knowledge of the law, his skills, and advocacy to do what he can for them. **Avocations:** Sports; Boating; Playing drums in a rock band; Spending time with family and grandson **Political Affiliations:** Republican **Religion:** Member The Church of Jesus Christ of Latter-day Saints

David L. Taylor

Title: President **Industry:** Law and Legal Services **Company Name:** Adams & Blinn Counsellors at Law, P.C. **Date of Birth:** 02/01/1945 **Place of Birth:** Boston **State/Country of Origin:** MA/USA **Parents:** A. Leavitt Taylor; Jean B. Taylor **Marital Status:** Married **Spouse Name:** Linda **Children:** Two Children **Education:** JD, Boston University School of Law, Boston, MA (1970); BA in Economics, Brown University, Providence, RI (1967) **Certifications:** Registered Investment Adviser (RIA) **Career:** Owner, Attorney, Adams & Blinn Counsellors at Law, P.C. (1970-Present) **Civic:** Member, Various Non-Profits **Military Service:** U.S. Army Reserve (1969-1975) **Memberships:** Christian Legal Society; Cambridge Trustee Advisors, Inc.; Chairman, Board, 2=1 Inc. **Bar Admissions:** Supreme Court of the United States; United States Court of Appeals for the First Circuit; United States Tax Court; Massachusetts **Marquis Who's Who Honors:** Marquis Who's Who Top Professional **To what do you attribute your success:** Mr. Taylor attributes his success to hard work and attention to detail. **Why did you become involved in your profession or industry:** Mr. Taylor, a third-generation attorney, became involved in his profession with inspiration from his father and grandfather, who also worked at Adams & Blinn. His younger brother has also pursued the legal profession. **Avocations:** Sailing **Religion:** Christian

Jean Tenore

Title: Real Estate Professional **Industry:** Real Estate **Company Name:** Coldwell Banker Residential Brokerage **Marital Status:** Married **Spouse Name:** Rick Pfaff **Children:** Alice **Career:** Luxury Specialist, Coldwell Banker Residential Brokerage, Los Gatos, CA (2018-Present); Real Estate Professional, Jean Tenore Team, Los Gatos, CA (1996-Present) **Awards:** First Place, Snowboarding, Utah Winter Games (1999) **Memberships:** Silicon Valley Women's Council of Realtors; Women's Council of Realtors **To what do you attribute your success:** Ms. Tenore would like to attribute some of her success to her daughter Alice. In her life journey, her daughter taught her so many things, mainly how to remain humble, to name one. Also her parents have been extremely supportive. Her father gave her the business knowledge and her mother Alice, gave her the greatest support in all areas in her life. **Why did you become involved in your profession or industry:** Ms. Tenore, somewhat grew up in the real estate industry. Her father had a business for 45 years in the area she grew up in. As early as 13 years old, she would take phone calls for her father at his business. She tried to find a path of her own, and found a somewhat successful career in snowboarding, but when she had her first child, mainly out of the convenience of being able to spend more time raising her child, she came back home and took up the real estate business that she had known for much of her early life. In that time, she fell in love with the industry and the feeling of gratitude she gets from assisting others. **Thoughts on Life:** Carpe Diem

Ward Edgar Terry Jr.

Title: Lawyer **Industry:** Law and Legal Services **Date of Birth:** 08/01/1943 **Place of Birth:** Denver **State/Country of Origin:** CO/USA **Parents:** Ward E. Terry; Helen (known as Peggy) Louise (Smith) Terry **Marital Status:** Married **Spouse Name:** Juliann "Julie" DiRe Terry (04/08/1967) **Children:** Seth S.; Nicole E. **Education:** LLM in Taxation, University of Denver (1976); JD, University of Colorado (1968); BA, University of Colorado (1965) **Career:** Retired (2019); Solo Practitioner (2007-2019); Shareholder, Krys Boyle (2002-2007); Shareholder, Director, Clanahan, Tanner, Downing & Knolton (1997-2002); Shareholder, Officer, Director, Terry, Syke and Graham (1996-1997); Practitioner of Tax, Securities and Corporate Finance Law, Vice President, Member of Board of Directors, Shareholder, Hopper and Kanouff Professional Corporation, Denver, CO (1976-1996); Secretary, Director, Ward Terry and Company, Denver, CO (1972-1976); Associate, Gorsuch, Kirgis, Campbell, Walker & Grover, Denver, CO (1971-1972); Associate, Modesitt & Shaw, Denver, CO (1970-1971); Associate, McMartin & Burk, Englewood, CO (1968-1970) **Career Related:** General Partner, PSW Investments Limited, Denver, CO (1984-1996) **Civic:** Campaign Chair, Roseanne Ball Election Committee, Denver, CO (1974); Trustee, Denver Country Day School, Englewood, CO (1969-1970) **Memberships:** President, Denver Gyro Club (1994-1995); Vice President, Denver Gyro Club (1993-1994); Membership Chairman, Denver Gyro Club (1991-1992); Business Law Section, Real Estate and Probate Section, Taxation Section, Antitrust Section, ABA; Business Law and Taxation Section, Colorado Bar Association; Denver Bar Association; Phi Alpha Delta **Bar Admissions:** United States Tax Court (1980); Colorado (1968); United States District Court for the District of Colorado (1968) **Marquis Who's Who Honors:** Albert Nelson Marquis Lifetime Achievement Award; Marquis Who's Who Top Professional **Why did you become involved in your profession or industry:** Mr. Terry became involved in his profession because his grandfather on his father's side was a lawyer in New York. He was involved as a district attorney for the City of New York and helped found the Boy Scouts of America and that became his inspiration. Mr. Terry took a career test and it indicated that law is what he should do and it was also what he wanted to do. **Avocations:** Currently a weight trainer; Golfing; Reading; Bible study **Political Affiliations:** Republican **Religion:** Presbyterian

Jekan Thangavelautham

Title: Assistant Professor **Industry:** Education/Educational Services **Company Name:** University of Arizona **Education:** Postdoctoral Training, Robotics and Energy Systems (2013); Doctor of Philosophy in Space Robotics (2008); Bachelor of Science in Engineering Science and Aerospace, University of Toronto (2002) **Career:** Assistant Professor, Head of SpaceTREx, University of Arizona (2017-Present); Assistant Professor, Arizona State University (2013-2017); Research Associate, University of Toronto Institute for Aerospace Studies (2008-2009); Instructor, University of Toronto, DaVinci Engineering Enrichment Program (2004-2006); Software/Systems Engineering, MDA Space Missions (2000-2001); Postdoctoral Fellow, Associate, Massachusetts Institute of Technology **Career Related:** Reviewer, IEEE Transaction on Robotics (2018-Present); Reviewer, Neural Networks (2017-Present); Reviewer, Robotics and Automation Letters (2017-Present); Reviewer, Advances in Space Research (2017-Present); Reviewer, Acta Astronautica (2016-Present); Editorial Board, Nature Microgravity (2015-Present); Reviewer, Journal of Hydrogen Energy (2015-Present); Reviewer, Journal of Genetic Programming and Evolvable Machines (2012-Present); Conference Co-Chair, AstroRecon (2015); Reviewer, ASME International Conference on Advanced Intelligent Mechatronics (2013); Reviewer, ASME Mechanics and Robotics Conference (2012); Reviewer, IEEE/RSJ International Conference on Intelligent Robots and Systems (2012); Judge, MIT De Florez Award Competition (2012); Judge, University of Toronto, Space Systems Design Contest (2008-2009); Reviewer, Journal of Robotics; Reviewer, Journal of Energies; Reviewer, Journal of Sensors; Reviewer, Journal of Mechatronics; Reviewer, Journal of Technologies; Committee Member, In-Situ Resource Utilization Technical Committee; Committee Member, IEEE Space Robotics Technical Committee **Creative Works:** Author, "Cooperative Multi-Spacecraft Observation of Incoming Space Threats" (2019); Creator, Patents, Laser Beam for External Position Control and Traffic Management of On-Orbit Satellites (2018); Low-Cost, Long-Distance, High-Bandwidth Laser Communication System for Small Mobile Devices and Spacecraft (2018); Novel Shape Identification, Classification in Autonomous Exploration (2017); Hydrogen Generator and Fuel Cell and System (2014) **Awards:** Winner, Space Settlement Challenge, Dubai Future Foundation (2018); Winner, HeroX CubeSat Challenge (2017); Best Student Paper, Presentation Award, Himangshu Kalita, AAS Guidance, Navigation and Control Conference (2017); Top 5 Winner, Tech Briefs Design the Future (2017); Top Achievements of the Year, Arizona State University (2016); Best Presentation Award, National Aeronautics and Space Administration (2019); Popular Mechanics Breakthrough Award (2016); Popular Mechanics, Hearst Corporation (2016); Peer Nomination, ENI Energy Award (2013-2014); Recipient, Travel Fellowship (2005-2006); Principal Achievement Award (1997); Recipient, Scarborough Lion's Club University Entrance Scholarship; Best Team Design, 4th Year Space Systems **Memberships:** American Institute of Aeronautics and Astronautics; American Society of Mechanical Engineers; Institute of Electrical and Electronics Engineers **Marquis Who's Who Honors:** Marquis Who's Who Top Professional **To what do you attribute your success:** Mr. Thangavelautham attributes his success to his mentors during university and postdoctoral years, including Professor Gabriel D'eleuterio and Dr. Steven Dubowsky at the Massachusetts Institute of Technology. **Why did you become involved in your profession or industry:** When Mr. Thangavelautham first got recruited into his profession, he worked on three projects that were quite distinct, but operated at the same time, particularly in the realm of space robotics. **Avocations:** Traveling

Larry Alan Tharp

Title: Chemical Engineer **Industry:** Manufacturing **Company Name:** Advance Research Chemicals, Inc. **Date of Birth:** 09/25/1938 **Place of Birth:** Chicago **State/Country of Origin:** IL/USA **Parents:** Garland Edgar Tharp; Zola Louise (Grigor) Tharp **Marital Status:** Married **Spouse Name:** Paula Jane Keesee (09/08/1962) **Children:** Julie Ann Tharp Cotherman; Janet Dawn Tharp **Education:** MBA, Oklahoma City University (1991); BSChemE, The University of Tulsa (1963) **Career:** Director of Engineering, Advance Research Chemicals, Inc. (2015-Present); Chemical Engineering Consultant, President, The Latest, Inc. (1993-2020); Senior Chemical Engineer, Muskogee Pulp & Paper Mill, Georgia-Pacific (1998-2015); Chemical Engineer, Babcock Wilcox (now BWXT Naval Nuclear Fuels Division) (1996-1998); Senior Staff Engineer, Sequoyah Fuels Corporation (1993-1995); Manager, Engineering Department, Sequoyah Fuels Corporation (1991-1993); Production Manager, Sequoyah Fuels Corporation (1989-1991); Process Engineering Manager, Sequoyah Fuels Corporation (1988-1989); Production Manager, Sequoyah Fuels Corporation (1986-1988); Senior Process Engineer, Kerr-McGee Corporation (Now Sequoyah Fuels Corporation) (1980-1986); Product and Project Engineer, Kerr-McGee Corporation (Now Sequoyah Fuels Corporation) (1969-1980); Engineering Technology Assistant to Paper Mill Manager, Pine Bluff Pulp & Paper Mill, International Paper (1963-1969); Summer Student Research Chemist, Bartlesville Petroleum Experiment Station, Bureau of Mines, U.S. Department of the Interior (1960-1962) **Career Related:** President, Tenkiller Valley Ranch, Gore, OK (1974-Present); Chairman, Board I-40, Industrial Park and Port, Gore, OK (1995) **Civic:** Board of Directors, Lake Tenkiller Association, Cookson, OK (1975-1996) **Awards:** Eagle Scout Award, Boys Scouts of America **Memberships:** American Institute of Chemical Engineers; American Chemical Society; Gore-Webbers Falls Lions Club; Squadron Three, Air Scouts; Boy Scouts of America; President, Independent Students Association, The University of Tulsa **Marquis Who's Who Honors:** Albert Nelson Marquis Lifetime Achievement Award **To what do you attribute your success:** Mr. Tharp attributes his success to support parents, amazing teachers, his experiences in the Boy Scouts and his science and engineering professors at The University of Tulsa. **Why did you become involved in your profession or industry:** Mr. Tharp became involved in his profession because of his childhood experiences. After playing with chemistry puzzles at a friend's house, he discovered his love of the field. **Avocations:** Flying private aircraft; Appreciating photography; Collecting arrowheads; Scuba diving **Political Affiliations:** Constitutional Conservative **Religion:** Methodist

Gordon Henry Theilen, DVM, DACVIM

Title: Veterinary Surgery Scientist Educator **Industry:** Education/Educational Services **Date of Birth:** 05/29/1928 **Place of Birth:** Montevideo **State/Country of Origin:** MN/USA **Parents:** Lou Ernst Theilen; Ema Kathryn (Schaller) Theilen **Marital Status:** Married **Spouse Name:** Carolyn June Simon (03/06/1953) **Children:** Kyle; John; Ann **Education:** BS, DVM, DACVIM, University of California Davis (1953, 1955) **Career:** Professor Emeritus, University of California Davis (1993-Present); Director, Center for Comparative Cancer Medicine (1980-1993); Professor, University of California Davis (1991); Chief Clinical Oncology, University of California Davis (1970-1990); Associate Professor, University of California Davis (1962-1970); Assistant Professor, University of California Davis (1957-1962); Instructor, University of California Davis (1956-1957); Private Practice, Tillamook, OR (1955-1956) **Career Related:** Leukemia and Lymphoma Society USA (1970-1975); Board of Directors, WHO Committee Staging Tumors in Animals (1970-1975); Board Member, American Association for Cancer Research (1970); International Association for Comparative Research on Leukemia and Related Diseases (1962); First President, Veterinary Cancer Society; Scientific Review Committee **Military Service:** U.S. Army (1946-1968) **Creative Works:** Lead Speaker, "One Medicine," 20th Anniversary Establishment of the Comparative Center of Medicine on UC Davis Campus (2018); Author, "Boy with the Wounded Thumb" (2017); Author, "One Medicine War on Cancer: How Discoveries in Veterinary Oncology Led to Advancement in Comparative Medicine" (2017); Faculty Guest Speaker, "History of Veterinary Cancer Medicine," UCD School of Veterinary Medicine (2017); Keynote Speaker, "One Medicine War on Cancer," Third World Veterinary Cancer Congress, Foz de Iguassu, Brazil (2016); Co-Author, "Veterinary Cancer Medicine" (1987); Co-Discoverer, "Feline and Simian Sarcoma Viruses" (1969, 1971); Co-Discoverer, Reticuloendotheliosis (1966); Contributor, Articles to Numerous Professional Journals; Author, Chapter, "Immune Therapy Against Cancer and Prevention"; Keynote Speaker, Upcoming Fourth Veterinarian Cancer Congress, Tokyo, Japan **Awards:** Theilen Tribute Award, Given to Outstanding Veterinary Oncologist of the Year (2008-Present); Nominating Committee Japanese Prize (2017); Lifetime Member, Northern California Brittany Club (2010); American Field Hall of Fame for Brittanys (2007); American Field Nominating Committee Dog(s) and Person(s) for the Year Award (2007); American Brittany Club Hall of Fame (2006); Alumni Achievement Award, University of California Davis (1987); Fleishmann Foundation Award (1980-1985); Ralston Purina Award in Small Animal Medicine (1982); Alexander Von Humboldt Senior Scientist Award, Department of Virology, Justus Liebig University (1979-1980); New York Cancer Immunology Fellow (1972-1973); Alexander Von Humboldt Senior Fellowships, National Cancer Institute (1964-1965) **Memberships:** Board of Directors, American Brittany Club (1992-Present); World Committee, International Association for Comparative Research on Leukemia and Related Diseases (1990-1998); Scientific Board, Leukemia Society of America (1985-1990); American Veterinary Medical Association; Veterinary Internal Medicine; American Association of Veterinary Clinicians; American Association for Cancer Research; Veterinary Cancer Society; Phi Zeta; Sigma Xi **Marquis Who's Who Honors:** Albert Nelson Marquis Lifetime Achievement Award; Marquis Who's Who Top Professional **Why did you become involved in your profession or industry:** Dr. Theilen became involved in his profession from an early age. When he was 5 years old, he almost lost his right thumb due to a hatchet accident and a veterinarian by the name of Dr. Rasmussen, who was doing work on his parent's farm at the time, put a tourniquet on it, cleaned it and put a bandage on it. He became his hero and the reason why he wanted to become a veterinarian. In addition, Dr. Theilen found his focus in oncology in veterinary school, having a desire to know more about cancer by doing research. He was the first in the world, with assistance, to show infectious nature of leukemia in cattle than any place in the world, and he got so involved and intrigued that he started cancer research. At that point and time, he never left to go into practice. He has been with the university for over 37 years. **Avocations:** Reading; Writing; Training bird dogs (Brittanys) for field; Geography; History connected with biological sciences **Political Affiliations:** Independent **Religion:** Lutheran

Brian David Thiessen

Title: Lawyer **Industry:** Law and Legal Services **Company Name:** Law Offices of Brian D. Thiessen **Date of Birth:** 07/27/1939 **Place of Birth:** Grass Valley **State/Country of Origin:** California/USA **Parents:** John J. Thiessen; Ellen Emily Agnes (Larsen) Thiessen **Marital Status:** Married **Spouse Name:** Carolyn Owen Thiessen **Children:** Robert Thiessen; Bill Thiessen; Erica Thiessen House **Education:** JD, Hastings College of Law (1967); Postgraduate Coursework, State University of New York, Plattsburg (1962); AB, Duke University (1960) **Certifications:** Certified, Family Law Specialist **Career:** Founder, Mount Diablo Courthouse Alternatives Program (1990-Present); Arbitrator, Mediator, Contra Costa Superior Court, Martinez, CA (1980-Present); Judge Pro Tempore, Various Municipal and Superior Courts, Contra Costa County, California (1975-Present); Professor, John F. Kennedy University, Orinda, CA (1977-1979); With, Kaiser Industries (1964-1967); Secretary, Director, First Western Savings and Loan Association **Career Related:** Past President, Contra Costa County Bar Association **Civic:** Scoutmaster, National Chair Community Relations Committee (2004-Present); Scoutmaster, Mount Diablo Council, Boy Scouts of America, Alamo (1986-1989); President, Mount Diablo Council, Boy Scouts of America, Walnut Creek, CA (1986-1987); Chairman, Alamo Park and Recreation Commission (1986-1987); Member, Alamo Park and Recreation Commission (1984-1988); Member, Governing Board, East Bay Community Foundation (1973-1979); Chairman, San Ramon Valley Planning Committee (1973); Member, Diablo Valley Foundation for Aging; Past President, Las Aguilas de Diablo; Past Board Member, East Bay Community Foundation **Military Service:** U.S. Air Force Reserves (1963-1965); Captain, U.S. Air Force (1960-1963) **Awards:** Alumnus of the Year, Hastings College Law Alumni Association (2000); Silver Beaver Award, Boy Scouts of America (1989); Alamo Citizen of the Year (1987); Named San Ramon Valley Citizen of the Year, Valley Pioneer Newspaper (1973); Silver Wheel, IFSR; Cliff Dochterman Award, IFSR **Memberships:** Hearing Referee, State Bar Association (1980-Present); Governor, Rotary International District, Alamo Rotary (2005-2006); President, Alamo Rotary (1991); Past President, Vice President, 1066 Foundation, Hastings College Law Alumni Association; California Trial Lawyers; Trial Lawyers America; International Bar Association; American Bar Association; Past President, Contra Costa County Bar Association; American Arbitration Association; Past President, Markham Regional Arboretum; Past President, Danville Area Jaycees; Past President, San Ramon Valley Lions **Bar Admissions:** Supreme Court of the United States (1982); United States Court of Appeals for the Ninth Circuit (1968); California (1967);United States District Court for the Northern District of California (1967); United States District Court for the Southern District of California (1967); United States District Court for the Eastern District of California (1967); United States District Court for the Western District of California (1967) **Marquis Who's Who Honors:** Albert Nelson Marquis Lifetime Achievement Award; Marquis Who's Who Top Professional **Avocations:** Backpacking; Hiking; Horticulture; Scouting nationally and internationally **Political Affiliations:** Republican **Religion:** Congregationalist

James Tate Thigpen, MD

Title: Oncologist **Industry:** Health, Wellness and Fitness **Company Name:** NRG Oncology **Date of Birth:** 06/08/1944 **Place of Birth:** Columbia **State/Country of Origin:** MI/USA **Parents:** Monroe Tate Thigpen; Janet (Crestnan) Thigpen **Marital Status:** Married **Spouse Name:** Louisa Berdie Kessler (06/14/1969) **Children:** Monroe Tate; James Howard; Samuel Calvin; Richard Allen; David Albert **Education:** Fellowship, Division of Hematology and Oncology, Department of Medicine, The University of Mississippi (1971-1973); Resident, The University of Mississippi (1970-1971); Intern, Strong Memorial Hospital, University of Rochester (1969-1970); MD, The University of Mississippi (1969); BS, The University of Mississippi (1964) **Certifications:** Certified in Oncology, American Board of Internal Medicine (1975); Certified in Hematology, American Board of Internal Medicine (1974); Certification, American Board of Internal Medicine (1972) **Career:** LS Professor Emeritus, The University of Mississippi Medical Center (2016-Present); Retired (2016); Director, Division of Medical Oncology, Department of Internal Medicine, The University of Mississippi (1973-2016); Professor, The University of Mississippi (1985-2016); Associate Professor, The University of Mississippi (1980-1985); Assistant Professor, The University of Mississippi (1973-1980) **Career Related:** Division Director, NRG Oncology (2014-Present); Vice Chairman, Oncology Research Strategy Committee (2018-Present); Deputy Chair, NRG Oncology (2013-2018); Chairman, Cancer Clinical Investigations Review Committee, National Cancer Institute, National Institutes of Health (1993-1995); Cancer Clinical Investigations Review Committee, National Cancer Institute, National Institutes of Health (1990-1995); National Medical Development from Mississippi, American Cancer Society, Inc. (1983-1985); National Public Issues Committee, American Cancer Society, Inc. (1983-1985) **Civic:** National Board of Governors, The American National Red Cross (1981-1987) **Creative Works:** Contributor, 270 Articles, Professional Publications **Awards:** Distinguished Leadership Award, Society of Gynecologic Oncology (2017) **Memberships:** Vice Chairman, Sciences Group, The GOG Foundation, Inc. (1988-Present); International President, Optimist International (1990-1991); President, Society Association of Oncology (1988-1990); International Vice President, Optimist International (1983-1984); American Medical Association; Mississippi State Medical Association; Central Medical Society; Jackson Academy of Medicine; MAS; SWOG; American Federation for Medical Research; American Association for Cancer Education; American Society of Clinical Oncology; American Association for Cancer Research; American Society of Hematology; Society of Gynecologic Oncology; American Radium Society; Fellow, American College of Physicians; Fellow, Mississippi Medical Association; Fellow, Central Medical Society; Fellow, American Federation for Clinical Research **Marquis Who's Who Honors:** Albert Nelson Marquis Lifetime Achievement Award; Marquis Who's Who Top Professional **Why did you become involved in your profession or industry:** There is no one specific thing that made Dr. Thigpen go into medicine. Out of all the professions in the world, he only had two choices: either medicine or law, so he picked medicine. As far as the GYN cancer area, which is where he worked most of his life, there was a GYN oncologist in Jackson, Mississippi, named Dr. Richard Borno, who was responsible for that. He dragged Dr. Thigpen, kicking and screaming, to his first gynecological meeting back in 1974. He was one of his first mentors. **Avocations:** Photography; Golf; Backyard table tennis **Political Affiliations:** Republican **Religion:** Baptist

D. Russell D. Thomas

Title: Owner/President **Industry:** Law and Legal Services **Company Name:** The Thomas Law Firm **Date of Birth:** 08/03/1952 **Place of Birth:** Murfreesboro **State/Country of Origin:** TN/USA **Parents:** Ellis; Mable (Bowen) Thomas **Marital Status:** Married **Spouse Name:** Jeanmarie **Children:** Six Children **Education:** Coursework, College, Atlanta, GA (2019); Graduate, ATLA's Advanced Civil Litigation Course (1985); JD, Memphis State University (1977); BS, Middle Tennessee State University (1974) **Career:** Owner, President, The Thomas Law Firm **Career Related:** Guest Lecturer, Tennessee Trial Lawyers Association (1992-Present) **Civic:** Board of Governors, Representative for the Tennessee Trial Lawyers Association, 6th District of Tennessee (1991-2005) **Creative Works:** Author, "Automobile Liability in Tennessee," Trial Magazine **Awards:** AV Preeminent Rating, Martindale-Hubbell (2019) **Memberships:** President, Andrew Jackson American Inns of Court (2005-2006); Legislative Committee, The Tennessee Association for Justice (2000-2004); Rutherford County Bar Association; Tennessee Bar Association; American Bar Association; The American Association for Justice; Trial Master; Kappa Sigma; Phi Alpha Delta **Bar Admissions:** United States District Court for the Middle District of Tennessee (1978); Tennessee (1978); United States District Court for the Eastern District of Tennessee **Marquis Who's Who Honors:** Albert Nelson Marquis Lifetime Achievement Award; Marquis Who's Who Top Professional **To what do you attribute your success:** Mr. Thomas attributes his success to the focus to get up every day and help people. **Why did you become involved in your profession or industry:** Mr. Thomas became involved in his profession because he desired to help people and personal injury was always an uneven playing field. At one time he did a lot of workers compensation. In addition, Mr. Thomas decided early on when he was in high school that he wanted to get involved in his field and the deciding factor was having an interest in the law. **Avocations:** Scuba diver; Taekwondo; Water skier; Music

Billy Thompson

Title: President/CEO **Industry:** Advertising & Marketing **Company Name:** Lumegent **Marital Status:** Married **Spouse Name:** Jillian (Married 09/27/2003) **Children:** Keiren Thompson **Education:** BA, Business Administration, Purdue University (2020); AA, Business Management, University of Phoenix (2010) **Career:** President/CEO, Lumegent (2016-2020); Managing Partner, Janess Print & Marketing (2011-2016); Regional Director, Sales, Holiday Retirement (2010-2011); Senior Director, Marketing, Bonaventure Senior Living (2009-2010); Director, Marketing and Sales, Highland Village (2007-2009); Store Manager, Janess Business Services (2004-2007); Store Manager, Foot Locker (2002-2004) **Civic:** Contributor, Various Charitable Organizations; Program Sponsorship **Awards:** CEO of the Year, International Association of Top Professionals (2020);Top 100 Marketing and Advertising Leaders, MadCon (2020); Nominated, Person of the Year (2019); Effective Marketing Award, Chamber of Commerce (2018); Business Leader of the Year, Chamber of Commerce (2017); Marketing of the Year, Chamber of Commerce (2017); Sales Person of the Year (2012, 2013, 2014, 2015, 2016); Key to Success Award (2014); Excellence Award (2013); Top Sales Achievement Award (2012) **Memberships:** Purdue Alumni Association; Golden Rule International Honor Society; International Association of Top Professionals; Society for Collegiate Leadership and Achievement **To what do you attribute your success:** Mr. Thompson attributes his success to his wife, Jillian. He met his wife in high school, only about a month before his dad died. She has been there for him from that moment forward through anything and everything. They have been together happily for 18 years. She's the reason why he has been able to get through his tragedies and why he has been able to become successful. Along with their daughter, Keiren, they continue to be the driving force for success in Mr. Thompson's career and life. **Why did you become involved in your profession or industry:** Mr. Thompson become involved in the industry when he joined ownership of an organization by becoming a joint-partner in a struggling company where he was brought on to redeveloped and mature it toward profitability. The development he created boomed as it skyrocketed into 100% year over year growth six years in a row, sometimes peaking higher. The result morphed the organization into a new realm as a profitable multi-million-dollar organization resulting in a buy-out. However, the acquisition also resulted in disbanding the company with releases to the team that he had created. With the determination to keep employment for the team he built, and an idea of a unique business structure, he found myself in another opportunistic situation and decided to create a new organization and his current venture that he named Lumegent. Mr. Thompson's long-standing dream to work for an organization that differed from the typical approach to business, team and client relationships was yet to be found so he decided to create it. At 34, he now oversees the direction of a multi-million-dollar organization. With connections throughout the US, Canada and Europe, the organization continues to grow toward becoming the leader in client/vendor relationships worldwide in printing, marketing, consulting and advertising. Mr. Thompson has had the opportunity to consult for Fortune 500 companies, restructure departments for large organizations, and travel the world to support international clients. **Avocations:** Anime; American history; Japanese culture; Dallas Cowboy football; Traveling the world; Disney **Thoughts on Life:** Motto: Results are generated through effort.

Ival Crandall "Val" Thornton

Title: Interior Architect **Industry:** Architecture & Construction **Company Name:** Val Thornton Design Concepts **Date of Birth:** 04/28/1932 **Place of Birth:** American Falls **State/Country of Origin:** ID/USA **Parents:** Crandall Dunn Thornton; Enid Rosalie (Walker) Thornton **Spouse Name:** Cheryl Lynn Bader (07/13/1974); Bonnie Jean Larson (06/10/1951, Divorced 05/1961) **Children:** Blake; Brek (Deceased); Anne Bader **Education:** Student, Art Center School of Design, Los Angeles, CA (1963-1964); Student, Colorado Institute of Art (1959-1960); Student, Weber State College (1956-1958) **Career:** Senior Associate, Arthur Gensler Associates, San Francisco, CA; Illustrator, Carlos Diniz Associates, Los Angeles, CA; Illustrator, Luckman and Associates, Los Angeles, CA; Illustrator, Victor Gruen & Associates, Los Angeles, CA; Artist, Richard Daly Art Studio, Salt Lake City, UT; Conceptual Architectural and Interior Designer, Paul Steelman Associates, Las Vegas, NV; Architectural and Interior Design, Bergman, Walls and Associates, Las Vegas, NV; Architectural Design Consultant, Howard Perlman and Associates, Las Vegas, NV; Architectural Designer, Rodgers, Nagle and Langhart, Denver, CO and Los Angeles, CA; Architectural and Interior Designer, Cannell and Chaffin, Inc., Denver, CO, Seattle, WA and Los Angeles, CA; Conceptual Architectural and Interior Designer, Bergman, Walls and Youngblood, Ltd, Las Vegas, NV; Conceptual Architectural Designer, Klai, Juba and Associates, Las Vegas, NV; Conceptual Architectural Designer, Howard Perlman Architects, Las Vegas, NV **Military Service:** U.S. Marine Corps **Creative Works:** Principal Works Include Investment Mortgage International, San Francisco, CA, Mountain Bell Training Center, Denver, CO, Denver Sporting House Interior, Interior Design Public Service Company, Denver, CO, Caesar's Palace Forum Shops, Las Vegas, NV, Gateway International Cruise Ships and Corp.; Interior Designer, Two Jets for Frank Sinatra, Ford Motor Company, Superior Oil Company, Mellon Family, Meshulem Ricklis, Pia Zadora, Cary Grant, Danny Kaye, His Highness Sheikh Mohamed Bin Zayed Of Dubai, William Oldenburg, Hughes Tool Company, Hilton Hotels, Triad Holdings Of Lebanon; Original Concept Artist, Shah Of Iran's 747 Jet Interiors And Paint Scheme, SS U.S. Cruise Vessel-Complete Interior Restoration, Elitch's Amusement Park (Now Six Flags), Denver, CO, Princess Cruises Grand Princess 97; Interior Designer, King Fahd's Summer Palace Taif, Saudi Arabia, Two Schools, Commissioned Officers Club and Non-Commissioned Officers Club for the Saudi Air Force, Jeddah, Saudi Arabia; Painter, 44,000 Square Feet Of Murals, Church Of Jesus Christ Of the Latter Day Saints, Salt Lake Temple (1962); Painter, Bass Pro Shops, Las Vegas, NV, Shark Reef Aquarium at Mandalay Bay Resort, Las Vegas, NV; Interior And Exterior Designer, Paris Las Vegas Resort And Casino, Forum Shops at Caesar's Palace, Las Vegas, NV, Well Fargo Banks, Denver, CO And Seattle, WA, Lodges For Princess Cruises-Denali Park, Alaska, Justice Center And Library, Longmont, CO, Broadway Plaza, Los Angeles, CA, Yacht Club, Seattle, WA; Architectural And Interior Designer, B And C Concourses, Denver International Airport, Sahara Resort And Casino, Las Vegas, NV, Sheraton Hotel And Resort, Tokyo, Japan; Storyboard Artist, Cannon Films, Barona Ranch Resort And Casino, San Diego, CA; Architectural Designer, Albertson's Headquarters, Boise, ID; Interior Designer, Joe Albertson's Executive Office, Boise, ID, Katherine Albertson Park, Boise, ID, Hudson Gardens Arboretum, Denver, CO, Hard Rock Hotel And Casinos, Hollywood, CA And Tampa, FL; Conceptual Designer, Paradise Beach Hotel, Pusan, Korea; Complete Interior Restoration, New Mexico State Capitol, Santa Fe, NM, Chateau Marriott, Las Vegas, NV, MGM Grand Hotel And Casino Bronze Lion And Art-Deco Facade, Studio 54; Las Vegas, NV, Four Seasons Hotel, Las Vegas, NV, Trump Tower, Las Vegas, NV, Alexis Park Hotel, Las Vegas, NV, Copa Casinos, Gulfport, MS, Bermuda Star Cruise Ship, Sundancer Cruise Ship, Star Dancer Cruise Ship, Nordic Empress Cruise Ship, Trump Riverboat, Gaudin Jaguar, Las Vegas, NV, Memphis Barbecue, Las Vegas, NV, Turnberry Towers, Las Vegas, NV, High Roller, Las Vegas, NV, Mardi Gras World, New Orleans, LA **Awards:** Inductee, Mountain Bell Training Center Hall of Fame, Colorado Institute of Art (1995); Denver Drawings by American Architects (1974); Design Awards; IMI, San Francisco Denver Sporting House **Marquis Who's Who Honors:** Albert Nelson Marquis Lifetime Achievement Award **Avocations:** Skiing; Sailing; Painting; Golf; Music **Political Affiliations:** Republican **Religion:** Church of Jesus Christ of the Latter Day Saints

Greta Tintin Eleonora Thunberg

Title: Climate Activist **Industry:** Environmental Services **Date of Birth:** 01/03/2003 **Place of Birth:** Stockholm **State/Country of Origin:** Sweden **Parents:** Svante Thunberg; Malena Ernman **Marital Status:** Single **Education:** Doctor Honoris Causa, University of Mons (2019) **Creative Works:** Speaker, Austrian World Summit R20 (2019); Speaker, European Parliament, Strasbourg, France (2019); Speaker, Brandenburg Gate, Berlin, Germany (2019); Speaker, Davos, World Economic Forum (2019); Speaker, European Economic and Social Committee (2019); Featured, Cover, "Next Generation Leader," Time Magazine (2019); Author, "No One is Too Small to Make a Difference," Penguin Books (2019); Author, "Scenes from the Heart" (2019); Featured, Documentary, "Make the World Greta Again" (2019); Speaker, TedxStockholm (2018); Speaker, COP24 Summit (2018) **Awards:** Nominee, Nobel Peace Prize (2019-2020); Named, Maphiyata Echiyatan Hin Win ("Woman Who Came from the Heavens"), Standing Rock Indian Reservation (2019); Named One of the 100 Most Powerful Women, Forbes Magazine (2019); Named One of Nature's 10, Springer Nature Limited (2019); Named Person of the Year, Time Magazine (2019); Named Glamour Woman of the Year Award, Glamour Magazine (2019); Co-recipient, Fritt Ord Award (2019); The Right Livelihood Award, Right Livelihood Foundation (2019); Co-recipient, International Children's Peace Prize, KidsRights Foundation (2019); Geddes Environmental Medal, Royal Scottish Geographical Society (2019); Keys to the City of Montréal (2019); Named One of the 100 Most Influential People of 2019, Time Magazine (2019); Ambassador of Conscience Award, Amnesty International (2019); Nordic Council Environment Prize (2019); Named Swedish Woman of the Year, SWEA International (Swedish Women's Educational Association International, Inc.) (2019); Rachel Carson Prize (2019); Laudato Si' Prize, University of St. Andrews (2019); Goldene Kamera, German Special Climate Protection Award (2019); Prix Liberte, Normandy, France (2019); Named Most Important Woman of the Year in Sweden (2019); Fryshuset Scholarship of the Young Role Model of the Year (2018); Nominee, Children's Climate Prize, Telge Energi (2018); Winner, Debate Article Writing Competition, Svenska Dagbladet (2018); Winner, Climate Change Essay Competition, Svenska Dagbladet (2018); Named One of the 25 Most Influential Teens, Time Magazine (2018) **Memberships:** Honorary Fellowship, Royal Scottish Geographical Society (2019)

Virginia Beth "Ginny" Tigue

Title: Community Volunteer **Date of Birth:** 09/10/1945 **Place of Birth:** Owosso **State/Country of Origin:** Michigan/USA **Parents:** Joseph Frederick; Florence Marion Sahlmark **Spouse Name:** Joseph James Tigue Junior, (08/12/1967) **Children:** James Christopher; Molly Elizabeth **Education:** BS in Physical Therapy, University of Michigan (1967) **Certifications:** Registered Physical Therapist, Michigan, California **Career:** Physical Therapist, Hospitals, Rehabilitation Centers, Private Practices **Career Related:** Co-owner, Tigue Property Company; Former Co-owner, Texas Toyota of Grapevine and Westway Ford, Irving, TX **Civic:** Chairman, Arts Council of Fort Worth Tarrant County (2011-Present); Board Chairman, Tarrant County College Foundation (2011-Present); Board Chairman, Toast Town (2011-Present); Chairman, Board, Arts Council of Fort Worth Tarrant County (2011-Present); Board of Directors, Arts Council of Fort Worth Tarrant County (2008-Present); Board of Directors, Safehaven (2007-Present); Art Council Fort Worth and Tarrant County Board, Fort Worth, TX (1997-2005, 2007-Present); Executive Board Director, United Way of Metropolitan Tarrant County (2002-Present); Founding Board of Directors, Tarrant County College Foundation (2001-Present); Board of Directors, N.E Leadership Forum (1999-Present); Member, Women's Policy Forum (1999-Present); Board of Directors, Colleyville Chamber of Commerce (1991-Present); Sustaining Member, Dallas Junior League (1991-Present); Board Chair, Tarrant County College Foundation (2010-2012); Chairman, Tarrant County College Foundation (2010-2011); Gala Chairman, Arts Council of Fort Worth Tarrant County (2010); Co-chair, Toast Town (2010); Member, Women Leader's Summit, Washington DC (1995, 1996, 1998, 1999, 2005, 2008); Chairman, Legacy Woman Luncheon (2008); Chairman, Texas Health Harris Methodist Heb Hospital (2007); Board of Trustees, Texas Health Harris Methodist Heb Hospital (1998-2007); Vice Chairman, Texas Health Harris Methodist Heb Hospital (2005); Councilman, Place 5, City of Colleyville (1998-2004); Founding Board of Directors, Grapevine-Colleyville Independent School District Education Foundation (1998-2004); Chairman, N.E Leadership Forum (2004); Board of Directors, Origins Museum (1998-2004); Board of Directors, Volunteer Center of Tarrant County (1998-2002); Board, Methodist Health Harris Foundation (2001-2009); Women's Foundation of Tarrant County (2000-2008); Board of Directors, United Way of Metropolitan Tarrant County (2000-2007); Board of Trustees, Texas Health Harris Methodist Heb Hospital (1999-2007); Mayor Pro Tempore, City of Colleyville (2000-2004); Vice President, Origins Museum (2000-2001); Chairman, Volunteer Center of Tarrant County (2000); Board of Directors, Dallas Museum Art League (1999-2000); Chairman, Community Center Advisory Committee, City of Colleyville (1998); Master Plan Revision Committee, City of Colleyville (1997-1998); Member, Advisory Board, Women's Shelter (1996-1998); Co-chairman, Gala, Northeast Tarrant County Division, American Heart Association (1997); Fashion Show Chairman, Colleyville Women's Club (1996); Home Tour Committee, Colleyville Women's Club (1990, 1993, 1996); Chairman, Arts Council Northeast Tarrant (1995-1996) **Awards:** Distinguished Leadership Award, Colleyville Area Chamber of Commerce (2007-Present); Easter Seal Hats Off to Mothers Award (2011); Fort Worth Texas Magazine-Art of Giving Award (2010); Leadership Award, North East Leadership Forum (2008); Colleyville Rotary Citizen of the Year (2002); Citizen of Year, Colleyville Area Chamber of Commerce (2001); Named, Most Influential Business Woman, The Business Press (1997); Volunteer of the Year, City Of Colleyville (1997); Legacy of Women Award, The Women's Shelter (1995); Proclamation as Outstanding Citizen of Colleyville (1995); Herman J. Smith Leadership Award, Colleyville Chamber of Commerce (1994) **Memberships:** Executive Board, Colleyville Area Chamber of Commerce (2003-Present); Vice-chairman, Community Development, Colleyville Area Chamber of Commerce (1998, 2003, 2005); Vice-chairman, Business Development, Colleyville Area Chamber of Commerce (2004); Vice-chairman, Membership Development, Colleyville Area Chamber of Commerce (1997); President, Colleyville Area Chamber of Commerce (1994); President-elect, Colleyville Area Chamber of Commerce (1993); Board of Directors, Colleyville Area Chamber of Commerce (1990-1998); Advisory Board Member, Texas Westland University, Fort Worth, TX; Board Member, Texas for the Arts; Honorary Life Member, Texas Congress Parents and Teachers **Marquis Who's Who Honors:** Albert Nelson Marquis Lifetime Achievement Award; Marquis Who's Who Humanitarian Award **Why did you become involved in your profession or industry:** Mrs. Tigue went into the physical therapy field because physical therapy had more regarding patient care than nurses do. Physical therapists are more flexible and work in more areas. She switched to volunteer work because of her children; they did not want her to return to work, and since her husband owned a car dealership, she did not have to work. **Avocations:** Golf; Travel; Reading; The arts **Political Affiliations:** Republican **Religion:** Methodist

Joseph William Tobin

Title: Archbishop **Industry:** Religious **Date of Birth:** 05/03/1952 **Place of Birth:** Detroit **State/ Country of Origin:** MI/USA **Parents:** Joseph Tobin; Marie Terese (Kerwin) Tobin **Education:** MDiv in Pastoral Theology, Mount St. Alphonsus Seminary (1979); MA in Religious Education, Mount St. Alphonsus Seminary (1977); BA in Philosophy, Holy Redeemer College (1975) **Career:** Archbishop, Newark (2017-Present); Cardinal-Priest, Santa Maria delle Grazie a Via Trionfale (2016-Present); Archbishop, Indianapolis (2012-2017); Secretary, Congregation for Institutes of Consecrated Life and Societies of Apostolic Life (CICLSAL) (2010-2012); Titular Archbishop, Obba (2010-2012); Superior General, Congregation of the Most Holy Redeemer (1997-2009); General Consultor, Redemptorist Fathers (1991-1997); Pastor, St. Alphonsus Parish (1990-1991); Pastor, Holy Redeemer Parish (1984-1990); Episcopal Vicar, Archdiocese of Detroit (1980-1986); Ordained Priest, Congregation of the Most Holy Redeemer (1978); Congregation of the Most Holy Redeemer (1972) **Career Related:** Overseer, Sodalitium Christianae Vitae (2016); Participant, Synod of Bishops, Rome, Italy (2005) **Memberships:** Pontifical Council for Culture (2019-Present); Canon Law Society of America (1985-Present) **Religion:** Roman Catholic

Joseph B. Tompkins Jr.

Title: Lawyer **Industry:** Law and Legal Services **Company Name:** Sidley Austin LLP **Date of Birth:** 04/04/1950 **Place of Birth:** Roanoke **State/Country of Origin:** VA/USA **Parents:** Joseph Buford; Rebecca Louise (Johnston) T. **Children:** Edward Graves; Claiborne Forbes **Education:** Doctor of Jurisprudence, Harvard Law School, Harvard University (1975); Master of Public Policy, Harvard Kennedy School, Harvard University (1975); Bachelor of Arts in Politics, Washington and Lee University, Summa Cum Laude (1971) **Career:** Partner, Sidley & Austin LLP, Washington, DC (1982-Present); Deputy Chief, Fraud Section, Criminal Division, US Department of Justice, Washington, DC (1980-1982); Associate Director, Office of Policy and Management Analysis Criminal Division, US Department of Justice, Washington, DC (1979-1980); Associate, Sidley & Austin LLP, Washington, DC (1975-1979) **Civic:** Chairman, Virginia State Board of Health (1986-1988, 1990-1991); With, Virginia State Board of Health Professions, Richmond, VA (1984-1992); Vice Chairman, Virginia State Board of Health (1984-1986) **Creative Works:** Contributor, Various Articles to Professional Journals **Memberships:** White Collar Crime Committee, Criminal Justice Section, American Bar Association (1980-Present); Chairman, Task Force on Computer Crime, American Bar Association (1982-1992); Virginia Bar Association; District of Columbia Bar; Phi Beta Kappa **Bar Admissions:** United States Court of International Trade (1996); United States Court of Appeals for the Fourth Circuit (1993); United States Court of Appeals for the Seventh Circuit (1991); United States Court of Appeals for the Sixth Circuit (1985); United States Court of Appeals for the Third Circuit (1983); United States Court of Appeals for the 11th Circuit (1982); United States District Court for the District of Columbia (1982); Supreme Court of the United States (1977); United States Court of Appeals for the Fifth Circuit (1977); Virginia State Bar (1975); United States Court of Appeals for the District of Columbia Circuit

Marco E. Tonietti, PhD

Title: Professor Emeritus **Industry:** Education/Educational Services **Date of Birth:** 11/17/1935 **Place of Birth:** Baghdad **State/Country of Origin:** Iraq **Parents:** Emile Tonietti; Najiba (Basmaji) Tonietti **Marital Status:** Married **Spouse Name:** Suzanne Tonietti (06/15/1968) **Children:** One Child (Deceased 1995) **Education:** Doctor of Philosophy in Business Administration, Saint Louis University (1971); Master of Business Administration, University of California, Los Angeles (1964); Master of Science in Accounting, University of Illinois (1961) **Career:** Professor, California State University, Fullerton (1970-2000); Auditor, Civic Financial Corp., Beverly Hills, CA (1964-1965); Accountant, Eitel McCullough Inc., San Carlos, CA (1961-1962) **Creative Works:** Contributor, Articles to Professional Journals (1976-1984) **Marquis Who's Who Honors:** Albert Nelson Marquis Lifetime Achievement Award; Marquis Who's Who Top Professional **Why did you become involved in your profession or industry:** Dr. Tonietti first became involved in his profession due to the influence of his father and brother, who were accountants. After earning his degree, he decided to transition toward finance, and subsequently chose to enter the field of education. **Avocations:** Travel **Religion:** Roman Catholic

Hampton Scott Tonk

Title: President **Company Name:** MPCSC, LLC **Parents:** Hampton E. Tonk; Jean W. Tonk Peacock **Children:** Noah; Seth **Education:** Keller Graduate School of Management, Chicago (1980-1981); MDiv in Pastoral Care, Bible, and Theology, Episcopal Theological School, Cambridge, MA (1972); BA in History, DePauw University, Greencastle, IN (1965); High School Diploma, New Trier High School, Illinois (1961) **Certifications:** Certification, Quality Improvement Associate, American Society for Quality (2002-Present) **Career:** Management Profitability Consultant and Success Coach (MPCSC), LLC, North Fort Myers, FL (1998-Present); Criminal Investigations Consultant and Data Forensics Expert (2006-Present); Investor, Hampton S. Tonk, North Fort Myers, FL (2016-Present); Founder, Principal, Share the Word Ministries, North Fort Myers, FL (2007-Present); Past Enterprises: Owner, HST TeleSales Services, Chicago; Managing Partner, Cash Flow Associates, Chicago; Owner, Tri-R Solutions, Chicago; Owner, Corporate Acquisition Finder and Referral Service (2004-Present); Affiliated Educational Consultants Limited, Florida (2006-2009); Sales Rep to Chief Executive Officer, Affiliated Educational Consultants Limited, Chicago (1997-2004); Sales Representative, Smedberg Machine Corporation, Chicago (1995-1997); Hydraulic Brake and Clutch, Chicago (1993-1994); Sales, Universal Automotive Industries, Chicago (1991-1995); Pastor, Parish Minister, Episcopal Church in Chicago, Western Michigan, Western Massachusetts (1972-1979); Owner, H. Scott Tonk, Copywriter, Business Writer; Owner, The Turnaround Management Group, Chicago; Owner, Professional Quality Sales International, Chicago; Owner, The Solutions Guy, North Fort Meyers, FL; Owner, Capital Funding of Southwest Florida, North Fort Meyers, FL; Chief Executive Officer, Proprietor, Owner, Corporate Opportunity Engineering; Christian Writer; Public Speaker; Independent Contractor, Kids Party Pals **Career Related:** Priest, Episcopal Church (1972-1984) **Civic:** Monthly Contributor to 40 Charities including Jewish National Fund; International Fund of Christians and Jews; Volunteer, Secretary, Men's Club, Church of the Resurrection of Our Lord, Fort Myers, FL **Military Service:** Company Clerk, U.S. Army, Germany (1965-1968) **Creative Works:** Author, "The Reunion of the Churches of East and West: Reversing the Great Schism of 1054 A.D. – A Theological and Ecclesiological Reconciliation (Multi-volume Magnum Opus Forthcoming in 2023 or 2024); Author, "How I Became Successful in Business and in Life – and Why My Failures, Mistakes, and Experiences of Being Fired Were the Best Things That Ever Happened to Me" (2021); Author, "YES, LORD – A Conversion Story" (2020); Author, "How I Became Successful in Business and in Life – and How My Failures, Mistakes, and Experiences of Being Fired Were the Best Things That Ever Happened to Me" (2020); Author, "God's Opportunity: How God Is Pouring Out His Holy Spirit, Reuniting His People, Evangelizing the World, and Showing Forth the Glory of His People Israel" (Second Revised and Expanded Edition, 2020); Author, "Yes Lord! A Conversion Story" (2020); Author, "God's Opportunity: How God is Reuniting His Church and Evangelizing the World" (2016) **Memberships:** American Society for Quality (1998-2017); Turnaround Management Association; American Society for Training and Development; American Society of Safety Engineers; Midwest Business Brokers and Intermediaries Association; Society of Manufacturing Engineers; SAE International; The Above Board Chamber of Commerce, Fort Meyers, FL; Florida Catholic Chamber of Commerce; Faith Fellowship Writer's Club **To what do you attribute your success:** Mr. Tonk attributes his success to coming from a very entrepreneurial family. The family founded the Tonk Manufacturing Company in the early 19th century. **Why did you become involved in your profession or industry:** Mr. Tonk became involved in the ministry because in high school, he had a call to the ordained ministry. He stayed active in the ministry for seven years. For the last five years as an Episcopal Priest he supported himself with a secular job. He then discovered that he had more aptitude towards business than the ministry. **Avocations:** Singing **Thoughts on Life:** Mr. Tonk's motto is, "Now that I'm retired, I love my work!" Mr. Tonk has a rich genealogy with a German, English, Irish, Scottish, French, Dutch, Cherokee and Jewish ancestry. Though he is not fully Jewish, Mr. Tonk identifies himself with Jewish people because of his interest in the history of Nazi Germany. He has a strong opposition to anti-semitism; in fact, in the 1980s, Mr. Tonk chased off a neo-Nazi by reciting a list of the Nazi concentration and extermination camps of the Holocaust. He never saw the neo-Nazi again. He has always been passionate about helping persecuted, helpless and innocent people; he wants to see the underdogs succeed

Craig Aaron Tovey, PhD

Title: Engineering Educator **Industry:** Education/Educational Services **Company Name:** Georgia Institute of Technology **Date of Birth:** 10/01/1955 **Place of Birth:** Washington **State/Country of Origin:** DC/USA **Parents:** Henry Tovey; Bella Tovey **Marital Status:** Married **Spouse Name:** Gail Ann Foorman (06/11/2000); Duif Calvin (Divorced) **Children:** William Noah; Kendl SoonMee; David MinHyeok; Leo Oscar **Education:** PhD in Operations Research, Stanford University (1981); MS in Computer Science, Stanford University (1981); AB in Applied Mathematics, Harvard College, Magna Cum Laude (1977) **Career:** Vice-Chair, Faculty Executive Board, Georgia Institute of Technology (2019-Present); Professor, H. Milton Stewart School of Industrial and Systems Engineering (ISyE), Georgia Institute of Technology (1993-Present); Associate Professor, H. Milton Stewart School of Industrial and Systems Engineering (ISyE), Georgia Institute of Technology (1986-1992); Assistant Professor, H. Milton Stewart School of Industrial and Systems Engineering (ISyE), Georgia Institute of Technology (1981-1985) **Career Related:** Co-Director, Center for Biologically Inspired Design (CBID), Georgia Tech (2006-2009); Senior Research Associate, National Research Council, Monterey, CA (1990-1991); Consultant, AT&T Bell Laboratories, Weyerhaeuser Paper Co. (1984-1992) **Creative Works:** Co-Author, "How Hard Is It to Control an Election?" (2016); Editor, "Modeling in Industrial Engineering" **Awards:** Biologically Inspired Design Education Grant (2009-Present); Golden Goose Award (2016); Sig-Econ Test of Time Award (2016); Auction-Based Coordination Grant, United States Army Research (2008-2009); Fundamentals and Applications Grant, National Science Foundation (2006-2009); Online Planning Methods Grant (2001-2005); Research Fellow, Georgia Institute of Technology (1995-1999); Jacob Wolfowitz Prize, American Journal of Medicine and Medical Sciences (1989); Presidential Young Investigator Award, National Science Foundation (1985); Research Initiation Grant (1983-1985); Test of Time Award, ACM Special Interest Group on Electric Commerce **Memberships:** INFORMS (Institute for Operations Research and the Management Sciences); Society for Neuroscience **Marquis Who's Who Honors:** Albert Nelson Marquis Lifetime Achievement Award; Marquis Who's Who Top Professional; Distinguished Humanitarian **Why did you become involved in your profession or industry:** Dr. Tovey became involved in his profession because he always wanted to explain the unexplained through teaching and research. **Avocations:** Reading; Singing; Music **Religion:** Jewish **Thoughts on Life:** Dr. Tovey is writing a paper with Paul Erdos.

Cynthia Merle "Cindy" Towsner

Title: Academic Administrator, Educator **Industry:** Education/Educational Services **Company Name:** U.S. Department of Education **Place of Birth:** Washington, DC **Parents:** A. Philip Towsner; Edith Towsner **Marital Status:** Divorced **Children:** Scott David Garrison (Deceased 2004); Lorienne Schwenk **Education:** Postgraduate Coursework, American University (1987); Postgraduate, University of Maryland (1964-1965); Bachelor of Science, University of Maryland (1961) **Certifications:** Certified Contracting Officer's Representative, United States Department of Education **Career:** Retired (2010); Coordinator, Literacy Volunteers, Health Literacy, U.S. Department of Education, Washington, DC (2005-2010); Coordinator, Literacy Volunteers, U.S. Department of Education (1996-2010); National Coordinator, Health Literacy and Literacy Volunteers for Adults, U.S. Department of Education, Washington, DC (1996-2002); Education Program Specialist, Bilingual Vocational Training, U.S. Department of Education, Washington, DC (1993-1996); Educational Program Specialist, Office of Bilingual Education & Minority Languages Affairs, U.S. Department of Education, Washington, DC (1987-1993); Acting Director, Intergovernmental Affairs Office, U.S. Department of Education, Washington, DC (1987); Special Assistant to the Director, Office of Intergovernmental & Interagency Affairs, U.S. Department of Education, Washington, DC (1985-1987); Special Assistant to Commissioner, Rehabilitation Services Administration, U.S. Department of Education, Washington, DC (1981-1985); Teacher, Montgomery County Public Schools, Rockville, MD (1961-1966, 1972-1980) **Career Related:** Vice President, Dalmahoy Group International, Chevy Chase, MD (1997-2005); Consultant, R.J. Comer Communications, Inc., Jacksonville, FL (1995-1997); Program Administrator, Office of Vocational Adult Education, U.S. Department of Education, Washington, DC (1992-2010); Special Assistant, Office of Vocational and Adult Education, U.S. Department of Education, Washington, DC (1988-1992); Educare Programs Inc., Chevy Chase, MD (1988-2004); Special Assistant, Rehabilitation Services Administration, U.S. Department of Education, Washington, DC (1981-1988) **Civic:** Annual Ball Committee, Hospital Relief Fund for the Caribbean, Chevy Chase, MD (1989-1994); Volunteer Tutor, Laubach Literacy Action, Literacy Volunteers in America, Chevy Chase, MD (1989-1993); Chair, Corporation and Business Contributions, Hospital Relief Fund for the Caribbean, Chevy Chase, MD (1989-1991); Member, Renaissance Women, Washington, DC (1983-1987); Board of Directors, Membership Chair, Citizens for Education, Montgomery County, MD (1977-1982); PTA, Larchmont Elementary School, Montgomery County, MD (1976-1978); Assistant to the President, Education Issues; Chair, International Festival, Washington, DC (1973-1975); Volunteer, Holy Cross Hospital, Silver Spring, MD (1969-1974); Vice-president, Chair, Youth Rally, Chair, Radiothon Publicity, St. Jude's Children's Research Hospital, Memphis, TN (1969-1981); Chair, Nominating Committee, Chair Community Directory, Rock Creek Hills Civic Association, Kensington, MD (1968-1985) **Creative Works:** Photographer, "Crowing About Life: Voyage Through Time," International Library of Photography (2000); Photographer, Project Education Reform, Time for Results, Volume One (1987) **Awards:** Achievement in Amateur Photography Award, International Library of Photographs (2004); First Place Award, Maryland State Fair (2000); First Place, Second Place Ribbons, Photography, Maryland State Fair, Timonium, MD (1999); First, Second, Third Place Ribbons, Photography, Montgomery County Agricultural Fair, Gaithersburg, MD (1999, 1998); Hammer Award, Vice President of the United States, Washington, DC (1996); President's Award, Combined Federal Campaign, Washington, DC (1987); Honors Award, Rock Creek Hills Civic Association, Kensington, MD (1979); Meritorious Service Medal, American Automobile Association, Washington, DC **Memberships:** Master Photographer, International Freelance Photographers Organization (2002); Association for Career and Technical Education; Society of Government Meeting Planners, Washington, DC; National Trust for Scotland; Founding Member, National Museum of Women in the Arts; Charter Member, National Women's History Museum; American Association of University Women **Marquis Who's Who Honors:** Albert Nelson Marquis Lifetime Achievement Award; Marquis Who's Who Top Professional **Why did you become involved in your profession or industry:** Ms. Towsner became involved in her profession after graduating from the University of Maryland in journalism and public relations. She began working for a Maryland newspaper, but discovered that she wasn't interested in journalism as a career. On a date, someone dared Ms. Towsner to get into teaching. She was interested in the idea, and went on to become an educator. **Avocations:** Photography; Reading; Travel

Matthew J. Trachtenberg, Esq.

Title: Chairman, President, Chief Executive Officer **Industry:** Nonprofit & Philanthropy **Company Name:** The National Orchestral Association **Date of Birth:** 06/20/1953 **Place of Birth:** New York **State/Country of Origin:** NY/USA **Parents:** Mark Trachtenberg; Joanne Horne **Education:** MBA in Finance, Fordham University (1982); JD, Brooklyn Law School (1977); BA, New York University, Magna Cum Laude (1974) **Career:** Chairman, President, Chief Executive Officer, The National Orchestral Association (2006-Present); Senior Vice President, U.S. Trust Co. (2004-2006); Managing Director, First Republic Bank (2002-2004); Vice President, Senior Private Banker, Fleet Bank (2000-2002); Vice President, Senior Private Banker, The PNC Financial Services Group, Inc. (1999-2000); Vice President, Deputy Corporate Secretary, Regional Advisory Board, Chase Manhattan Bank (1996-1998); Vice President, Deputy Corporate Secretary, Regional Advisory Board, Chemical Bank (1992-1996); Agent, Officer-in-Charge, Vice President, Corporate Secretary, Manufacturers Hanover Foundation (1987-1992); Vice President, Manufacturers Hanover Trust Co. (1982-1986); Assistant Vice President, Manufacturers Hanover Trust Co. (1982); Assistant Secretary, Manufacturers Hanover Trust Co. (1980-1982); Corporate Banking Representative, Manufacturers Hanover Trust Co. (1979-1980); Credit Analyst, Manufacturers Hanover Trust Co. (1978-1979); Management Training Program, Manufacturers Hanover Trust Company (1977-1978) **Civic:** Board of Directors, Chairman, Audit Committee, The Macula Foundation, Inc. (2014-Present); Board of Directors, Treasurer, Secretary, The Pat Palmer Foundation (2010-Present); Board of Directors, Chairman, President, Chief Executive Officer, The National Orchestral Association (2006-Present); Former Member, Board of Directors, Joffrey Ballet School; Former Member, Board of Directors, Continuum Health Partners; Former Member, Board of Directors, Treasurer and Chairman of Finance Committee, New York Eye and Ear Infirmary of Mount Sinai; Former Member, Board of Directors, Past President, USO Metropolitan New York; Former Member, Education Advisory Committee, Lighthouse Guild; Former Chairman, Creative Arts Committee, Lighthouse Guild; Former Member, Direct Services Council, Lighthouse Guild; Former Member/Director, The Friends of Thirteen, Inc., WNET **Creative Works:** Producer, Director, "Leon Barzin and the National Orchestral Association" **Awards:** Recognition for Years of Service, Board of Directors, Lighthouse International (2000); Distinguished Hospital Trustee Award, United Hospital Fund (1998); Certificate of Meritorious Service Recognizing Tenure as Managing Editor, The Justinian, Brooklyn Law School (1975-1976); Founders' Day Award, New York University (1974) **Memberships:** New York State Bar Association; Phi Beta Kappa; Pi Sigma Alpha **Bar Admissions:** New York State Bar Association (1979) **Marquis Who's Who Honors:** Albert Nelson Marquis Lifetime Achievement Award; Marquis Who's Who Top Professional **To what do you attribute your success:** Mr. Trachtenberg attributes his success to the mentors and self-made individuals who have inspired him, including John McGillicuddy and Edward D. Miller. Both men taught him that banking was not just about business, but helping others. Another man, J. Bruce Llewellyn taught him about the kind of courage an African-American man must have in order to rise from humble beginnings into positions of power. Finally, Cyrus R. Vance taught him the value of friendship, the value of listening to the opinions of others and how to lead a life dedicated to service. **Why did you become involved in your profession or industry:** Mr. Trachtenberg became involved in his profession because of the intellectual challenges it provided, as well as the opportunities to liaise with a wide variety of business leaders and institutions. **Avocations:** Listening to music; Watching classic cinema; Painting; Writing **Political Affiliations:** Independent **Religion:** Christian and Jewish **Thoughts on Life:** Mr. Trachtenberg believes in always respecting the opinions of others, not only because our own thoughts are fluid and capable of change, but because listening to the opinions of others promotes intellectual growth. Respect for others' opinions is the cornerstone of civil discourse.

Raymond Mattern Trageser

Title: Insurance Executive **Industry:** Insurance **Date of Birth:** 09/30/1934 **Place of Birth:** Pittsburgh **State/Country of Origin:** PA/USA **Parents:** Raymond Michael; Marcella Cecilia (Mattern) Trageser **Marital Status:** Widower **Spouse Name:** Anne Marie Kois (6/4/1960, Deceased) **Children:** Debra Anne **Education:** Coursework, University of Pittsburgh (1959-1961); Coursework, Duquesne University (1952-1954) **Certifications:** Fully Licensed **Career:** Insurance Company Executive, Regional Manager, Transamerica Insurance, Philadelphia, PA (1985-1990); Branch Manager, Transamerica Insurance, Pittsburgh, PA (1984-1985); Manager, Marketing, Transamerica Insurance, Pittsburgh, PA (1969-1984); Manager, Underwriting, Transamerica Insurance, Pittsburgh, PA (1965-1969); Superintendent, Casualty, Continental Insurance, Pittsburgh, PA (1963-1965); Assistant Superintendent, Casualty, Continental Insurance, Pittsburgh, PA (1959-1963); Senior Underwriter, Continental Insurance, Pittsburgh, PA (1958-1959); Underwriter, Continental Insurance, Pittsburgh, PA (1957-1958) **Career Related:** Self Employed, Commercial Editing, State of Pennsylvania and Others (1992-2004); Speaker, Representative, Insurance Information Institute, New York **Military Service:** U.S. Army, Germany (1955-1957) **Memberships:** President, Casualty Association Pittsburgh (1965-1967); Insurance Clubs Pittsburgh; Casualty and Property Managers Association Philadelphia; Insurance Federation Pennsylvania; Vesper; Urban; Rotary **Marquis Who's Who Honors:** Albert Nelson Marquis Lifetime Achievement Award; Marquis Who's Who Top Professional **Why did you become involved in your profession or industry:** Mr. Trageser became involved in his profession because he came from a middle class family and was always interested in investing when he was in high school. He also collected coins and so he pursued finance and when he got discharged from the U.S. Army, he wanted a job in insurance or banking. He got a job one week after being discharged at Continental Insurance. **Avocations:** Numismatist; Fishing; Travel **Political Affiliations:** Democrat **Religion:** Roman Catholic

Stephen I. Traub

Title: Senior Partner (Retired) **Industry:** Law and Legal Services **Company Name:** Lynch, Traub, Keefe & Errante **Date of Birth:** 04/01/1930 **Place of Birth:** McKeesport **State/Country of Origin:** PA/USA **Parents:** David Traub; Lilian Traub **Marital Status:** Widow **Spouse Name:** Rosemary Nolan (Deceased, 2007) **Children:** David; Leslie; Michael; Christopher; Five Stepchildren **Education:** JD, University of Virginia School of Law, Charlottesville, VA (1960); LLB, University of Virginia School of Law, Charlottesville, VA (1960); BS in Economics, University of Connecticut, Storrs, CT (1957) **Certifications:** Licensed Pilot **Career:** Assistant City Attorney, Trial Counsel, City of Milford (1966-1973); Senior Partner, Lynch, Traub, Keefe, Errante (1960-1999) **Career Related:** Fellowship, American College of Trial Lawyers **Civic:** Vice-Chairman, Board of Finance, City of Milford (1996-Present); State Committee Member, American College of Trial Lawyers (1995-2000); Vice President, New Haven County Bar Association (1974-1975); Chairman, Lawyer Referral Service, New Haven County (1970-1978); Board of Finance, City of Milford (1964-1966); Chairman, Grievance Committee, Connecticut Bar Association; Executive Board Member, Quinnipiac School of Law **Military Service:** Captain, United States Army Reserve (1951-1955); Korean War Veteran (1951-1953) **Creative Works:** Author, "Medical Malpractice in Connecticut," (1986); Author, "Medical Malpractice in Connecticut," (1985); Lecturer, "Structured Insurance Settlements," Connecticut Bar Association (1980); Lecturer, "Third Party Claims," Connecticut Trial Lawyers Association (1980); Instructor, "Trial Practice and Procedure," Quinnipiac College (1978-1979); Lecturer, "Continuing Legal Education Seminar, Medical Malpractice in Connecticut," Connecticut Bar Association (1978); Lecturer, "Continuing Legal Education Seminar, Using the Economist," Connecticut Bar Association (1978); Lecturer, "Seminar on Connecticut Civil Trial Advocacy," Connecticut Bar Association, (1977-1990); Co-Author, "Preparation, Pleadings and Trial of a Medical Malpractice Case in Connecticut," Connecticut Law (1976); Co-Author, "Economic Loss in Death and Disability Cases in Connecticut," Connecticut Bar Association Continuing Legal Education Book (1976); Co-Author, "Pre-Trial Investigation and Discovery, a Must," Connecticut Law Tribune (1972); Lecturer, "Structured Settlements," The Association of Trial Lawyers of America **Awards:** Fellow, American College of Trial Lawyers; Super Lawyers; AV Preeminent Rated; Personal Injury Hall of Fame; Top Attorneys in Connecticut; Listee, Top 40 Under 40, the National Trial Lawyers; Best Lawyers; Four Bronze Stars for Valor; Combat Infantry Badge **Memberships:** American Bar Foundation; Connecticut Bar Foundation; Former President, Connecticut State Bar Association; Phi Alpha Delta; American Board of Trial Advocates; American Association for Justice **Bar Admissions:** United States Court of Appeals Second Circuit (1969); United States Supreme Court (1967); United States District Court District of Connecticut (1961); State of Connecticut (1960) **To what do you attribute your success:** Mr. Traub attributes his success to hard work, diligence, integrity, and honesty, all of which he learned from his mother. **Why did you become involved in your profession or industry:** Mr. Traub was inspired by his education. He wanted to go to college or university, but due to financial reasons, he couldn't. He studied well and benefited from his studies by being admitted to three law schools that he had selected. **Thoughts on Life:** Mr. Traub's motto is, "Honesty, integrity, and hard work."

Natalia Alexandrova Trayanova, PhD

Title: Biomedical Engineering Educator **Industry:** Education/Educational Services **Company Name:** Johns Hopkins University **Date of Birth:** 04/22/1956 **Place of Birth:** Sofia **State/Country of Origin:** Bulgaria **Parents:** Alexander Atanasov Gydikov; Vera Dimitrova Ivanova **Children:** Boyanna Atanasova **Education:** PhD in Biophysics, Section on Bioengineering, Bulgarian Academy of Sciences, Sofia, Bulgaria (1982); MS in Physics, Department of Physics, Sofia University (1980); Postdoctoral Coursework in Biomedical Engineering, Duke University **Career:** Professor, Department of Medicine, Johns Hopkins School of Medicine, Baltimore, MD (2012-Present); Professor, Murray B. Sachs Endowed Chair, Department of Biomedical Engineering, Johns Hopkins University, Baltimore, MD (2012-Present); Professor, Department of Biomedical Engineering and Institute for Computational Science, Johns Hopkins University, Baltimore, MD (2006-Present); Professor, Department of Biomedical Engineering, Tulane University, New Orleans, LA (2002-2006); Distinguished Fulbright Visiting Professor, Laboratory of Physiology, University of Oxford (2002); Associate Professor, Department of Biomedical Engineering, Tulane University (1995-2002); Assistant Research Professor, Department of Biomedical Engineering, Duke University, Durham, NC (1990-1994); Assistant Professor, Bulgarian Academy of Sciences, Sofia, Bulgaria (1988-1989); Visiting Research Fellow, Department of Biomedical Engineering, Duke University, Durham, NC (1986-1988); Assistant Professor, Bulgarian Academy of Sciences, Sofia, Bulgaria (1986) **Career Related:** Session Chairman, 17th Conference, IEEE/EMBS, Amsterdam, Netherlands (1996); World Congress on Medical Physical and Biomedical Engineering, Rio de Janeiro, Brazil (1994); Lecturer, International Meetings of BMES, Tempe, AZ (1994); Session Chairman, 14th Conference, Paris, France (1992); Lecturer, Cray Conference on High Performance Computing Biomedical Research, Research Triangle Park, NC (1992); Lecturer, 13th Conference, IEEE/EMBS, Orlando, FL (1991); Lecturer, International Meetings of BMES, Charlottesville, VA (1991) **Civic:** Chair, Gordon Research Conference on Cardiac Arrhythmia Mechanisms (2009); Vice Chair, Gordon Research Conference on Cardiac Arrhythmia Mechanisms (2007); Numerous External Advisory Boards **Creative Works:** Presenter, TEDxTalk (2017); Astor Visiting Lecturer, University of Oxford (2004); Associate Editor, IEEE Transactions on Biomedical Engineering; Reviewer/Editor, Annals of Biomedical Engineering, Journal of Mathematical Biology, Journal of Cardiac Electrophysiology, Circulation, Biophysics Journal, Others; Contributor, Articles, Professional Journals; Editorial Boards, Heart Rhythm, Circulation: Arrhythmias and Electrophysiology, Journal of Interventional Cardiology, Frontiers in Computational Physiology and Medicine; Presenter in Field **Awards:** Inductee, Women in Tech International Hall of Fame (2019); Capitol Hill Briefing, United for Medical Research (2017); Discovery Innovation Award, Johns Hopkins School of Medicine (2015); Director's Pioneer Award, National Institutes of Health (2013); William R. Brody Faculty Scholar, Johns Hopkins University (2009); Established Investigator Award, American Heart Association, Inc. (2002-2006); Excellence in Research and Scholarship Award, Tulane University (2005); Outstanding Researcher Award, Tulane University (2002); Fulbright Distinguished Scholars Research Award (2001-2002); Lee H. Johnson Award for Teaching Excellence, Tulane University (2000); AETMB Teaching Award, Department of Biomedical Engineering, Tulane University (1999-2000); Whitaker Foundation Award (1992); Discovery Innovation Award, Johns Hopkins University **Memberships:** Fellow, International Academy of Medical and Biological Engineering (2017); Fellow, Biomedical Engineering Society (2010); Fellow, American Heart Association, Inc. (2010); Fellow, Heart Rhythm Society (2008); Fellow, American Institute for Medical and Biological Engineering (AIMBE) (2003); Fellow, U.S. National Academy of Sciences (Now National Academy of Sciences) (1986-1987); Senior Member, IEEE; FDA CIPA Steering Committee; Research Funding Subcommittee, American Heart Association, Inc.; International Society for Heart Research; International Society for Computerized Electrocardiology; Society for Industrial and Applied Mathematics; American Association for the Advancement of Science; Cardiac Muscle Society; Cardiac Electrophysiology Society; Biophysical Society; The New York Academy of Sciences; American Society for Engineering Education (ASEE); Sigma Xi, The Scientific Research Honor Society **Avocations:** Travel; Skiing

Alex Trebek

Title: Television Personality, Game Show Host **Industry:** Media & Entertainment **Date of Birth:** 07/22/1940 **Place of Birth:** Sudbury, Ontario **State/Country of Origin:** Canada **Year of Passing:** 2020 **Parents:** George Edward Trebek; Lucille (Lagacé) Trebek **Marital Status:** Married **Spouse Name:** Jean Currivan-Trebek (04/30/1990); Elaine (Callei) Trebek Kares (1974, Divorced 1981) **Children:** Matthew; Emily **Education:** Honorary Doctorate, University of Ottawa, Ontario, Canada (1997); PhB, University of Ottawa, Ontario, Canada (1961) **Career Related:** Owner, Creston Vineyards; Host, "Great Canadian Geography Challenge," Canada; Host, National Geographic Bee **Civic:** Donor, Hope of the Valley Rescue Mission (2020); Donor, Alex Trebek Forum for Dialogue, University of Ottawa (2016); Donor, Santa Monica Mountains Conservancy (1998); USO, Inc. (1995); World Vision Canada **Creative Works:** Game Show Host, "Jeopardy!," CA (1984-Present); Host, "Jeopardy! The Greatest of All Time" (2020); Host, Executive Producer, "Game Changers" (2017); Executive Producer, "Prey" (2013); Guest Appearance, "How I Met Your Mother" (2010, 2013); Guest Appearance, "FCU: Fact Checker Unit" (2010); Guest Appearance, "Arthur" (2000); Guest Appearance, "The Male Swagger" (1999); Host, "Live from the Hollywood Bowl" (1999); Host, "Pillsbury Bake-Off" (1996-1998); Guest Host, "Wheel of Fortune" (1997); Guest Appearance, "Spy Hard" (1996); Guest Appearance, "The X-Files" (1996); Guest Appearance, "The Magic School Bus" (1996); Guest Appearance, "Seinfeld" (1996); Guest Appearance, "Dave's World" (1995); Guest Appearance, "The Larry Sanders Show" (1993-1994); Host, "The Red Badge of Courage/Heart of Courage" (1993); Guest Appearance, "Rugrats" (1993); Guest Appearance, "Dying Young" (1991); Game Show Host, "To Tell The Truth" (1991); Host, "Super Jeopardy!" (1990); Game Show Host, "Classic Concentration," CA (1987-1991); Co-host, "VTV-Value Television" (1987); Host, "Lucky Numbers" (1985); Producer, "Jeopardy!," CA (1984-1987); Host, "Starcade" (1983); Host, "Malcolm" (1983); Game Show Host, "Battlestars," NBC, CA (1981-1983); Host, "Pitfall" (1981-1982); Host, "Wall $treet" (1980-1981); Guest Appearance, "Vega$" (1978); Game Show Host, "The $128,000 Question," Global TV, Canada (1977-1978); Game Show Host, "Stars on Ice," Canada (1976-1980); Game Show Host, "Double Dare," CBS, CA (1976-1977); Game Show Host, "High Rollers," NBC, CA (1974-1980); Game Show Host, "The Wizard of Odds," NBC, CA (1973); Announcer, "TGIF" (1973); Host, "Reach for the Top" (1966-1973); Host, "Outside/Inside" (1972); Host, "Pick and Choose" (1971); Announcer, "CBC Championship Curling" (1966-1970); Host, "Strategy" (1969); Co-host, Announcer, "Barris & Company" (1969); Co-host, "Vacation Time" (1964); Host, "Music Hop" (1963-1964); Staff Announcer, Canadian Broadcasting Co. (Now CBC/Radio-Canada), Toronto, Ontario, Canada (1961-1973); Numerous Guest Appearances **Awards:** Americanism Award, Daughters of the American Revolution (2019); Daytime Emmy Award for Outstanding Game Show Host, The National Academy of Television Arts & Sciences (1989, 1990, 2003, 2006, 2008, 2019); Alex Trebek Leadership Award, University of Ottawa (2017); Named Officer, Order of Canada, Governor General David Johnston (2017); Daytime Entertainment Emmy Lifetime Achievement Award, The National Academy of Television Arts & Sciences (2011); Gold Medal, The Royal Canadian Geographical Society (2010); Access Award, American Foundation for the Blind (2001); Recipient, Star, Canada's Walk of Fame (2006); Recipient, Star, Hollywood Walk of Fame (1999) **Memberships:** Honorary President, The Royal Canadian Geographical Society (2016); American Federation of TV and Radio Artists (Now SAG-AFTRA); Screen Actors Guild (Now SAG-AFTRA); ACTRA **Political Affiliations:** Independent **Religion:** Roman Catholic

James Alfred Trent

Title: Founder/President **Industry:** Museums & Institutions **Company Name:** Queens County Farm Museum **Date of Birth:** 05/25/1946 **Place of Birth:** Brooklyn **State/Country of Origin:** NY/USA **Parents:** Alfred Trent; Helen (Vanasco) Trent **Marital Status:** Single **Education:** BArch in Landscape Architecture, University of Georgia, Athens, GA (1969); AAS, State University of New York, Farmingdale, NY (1966); Academic Diploma, Martin Van Buren High School, Queens Village, NY (1964) **Career:** Chief Professional, Contracts Section, New York City Department Of Design And Construction (1996-2001); Chief, Professional Contracts Section, New York City Department Of General Services (1993-1996); Project Manager, Architectural Specialties Unit, New York City Department Of General Services (1992-1993); Deputy Chief, Professional Contracts Management Section, New York City Department Of Design And Construction, New York, NY (1987-1992); Assistant To The Director, Bureau Of Building Design, New York City Department Of Design And Construction (1984-1987); Chief, Professional Contracts Section, New York City Department Of Design And Construction (1979-1984); Assistant Landscape Architect, New York City Department Of Design And Construction (1970-1979); Junior Landscape Architect, New York City Department Of Public Works (1969-1970) **Career Related:** Vice President, Joint Bellerose Business District Development Corporation, Incorporated (1997-Present); Charter Member, Joint Bellerose Business District Development Corporation, Incorporated (1995-1997); Assistant Editor, The Georgia Agriculturalist, University of Georgia School of Agriculture (1968); Assistant Editor and Acting Editor-in-Chief, Student Newspaper, The Rambler, State University of New York, Farmingdale, NY (1966) **Civic:** Second Vice President, Bowne House Historical Society (2017-Present); Preservation Committee, Bowne House Historical Society (2013-Present); President, Board Director, Four Borough Neighborhood Preservation Alliance Foundation (2006-Present); Historian, Community Board 13 Queens (2005-Present); President, Board Director, Four Borough Neighborhood Preservation Alliance Foundation (2005-Present); Treasurer, Queens Civic Congress Trust Foundation (2003-Present); Treasurer, Queens Civic Congress (1997-Present); Chairman, Board of Directors, Queens Village Republican Club (1993-Present); Treasurer, Creedmoor Civic Association Incorporated, Bellerose, NY (1989-Present); Founder, President, Queens County Farm Museum (1975-Present); Queens County Committee of the Republican Party (1968-Present); Board of Directors, Preservation Committee, Bowne House Historical Society (2014-2017) **Creative Works:** Editor, Author, The Creedmoor Civic News (1994-Present); Author, Article, "The Queens County Farm Museum", Juniper Berry (2007); Author, Article, "The Development of the Queens County Farm Museum", Municipal Engineers Journal (1998); Author, Preface, "The Construction and Restoration of the Manhattan Municipal Building", Journal of the Municipal Engineers of the City of New York (1995); Author, Foreword, "Illustrated History of the Manhattan Municipal Building" (1989); Contributor, Article About the RESTORE Program for Historical Buildings, Journal of the Municipal Engineers of the City of New York (1982); Editor, Author, The Creedmoor Civic News (1967-1980) **Awards:** Certificate of Recognition, State Sen. Leroy Comrie (2016); Queens Impact Award, Times-Ledger Newspapers (2016); Lifetime Achievement Award, Queens Village Republican Club (2014); Certificate, Nassau County Legislature (2013); Plaque, Oyster Bay Historical Society, Class of 2013 Education in Preservation Awards (2013); 85th Anniversary Plaque, Creedmoor Civic Association (2012); 25th Anniversary Plaque, Queens County Farm Museum (2007); Farm Museum Plaque from the Queens Coalition for Parks and Green Spaces (2006); Proclamation from the City Council for Work with Bellerose Business District (2004); Plaque, Joint Bellerose Business District Development Corporation (2004); Plaque, Queens Civic Congress (2004); Queens County Farm Museum Service Citation, New York State Assembly (2002); Liberty Award Medal, New York State Senate (2002); Plaque, Poppenhusen Institute (2001) **Memberships:** President, Metropolitan Historic Structures Association (2005-2011); Vice President, Metropolitan Historic Structures Association (2003-2005); President, Poppenhusen Institute (1995-2003); Board Member, Metropolitan Historic Structures Association (1977-2003); Board of Directors, Municipal Engineers of the City of New York (1995-2002); Co-Editor, Journal of the Municipal Engineers City of New York (1995-1997); Board of Directors, Poppenhusen Institute (1991-1995); Board Member, Queens Historical Society, Inc. (1970-1973); Gamma Sigma Delta (1969); Knights of Columbus **Marquis Who's Who Honors:** Marquis Who's Who Industry Leader Award (2018); Albert Nelson Marquis Lifetime Achievement Award **Why did you become involved in your profession or industry:** Mr. Trent became involved in his profession because he was interested in horticulture. He eventually transitioned into more civic related endeavors. He was taken by his mother to his first civic meeting when he was 12 years old. He was the youngest president of a civic organization in New York, being elected at 23. **Avocations:** Gardening; Traveling **Political Affiliations:** Republican **Religion:** Roman Catholic

Thomas P. Trevisani

Title: Chief Surgeon **Industry:** Medicine & Health Care **Company Name:** Plastic Surgery Practice **Children:** Two Children **Education:** Doctor of Medicine, University of Nebraska Medical Center, Omaha, NE (1975); Master of Science in Physiology and Biophysics, University of Nebraska Medical Center, Omaha, NE (1972); Bachelor of Science in Biology, Midland Lutheran College, Fremont, NE (1970) **Certifications:** Certification, American Board of Plastic Surgery (1983); Certified, National Board of Medical Examiners (1976) **Career:** Chief Surgeon, Private Practice in General Plastic and Reconstructive Surgery, Winter Park, FL (1981-Present); Resident, Plastic Surgery, Medical College of Wisconsin, Milwaukee, WI (1979-1981); Resident, General Surgery, Jackson Memorial Hospital, University of Miami School of Medicine, Miami, FL (1977-1979); Part-Time Staff Physician, Kaiser Foundation Hospital Emergency Room, Oakland, CA (1976); Private Practice, Utica, NY (1976); Emergency Room Staff Physician, Utica, NY (1976); Surgical Internship, Kaiser Foundation Hospital, Oakland, CA (1975-1976) **Career Related:** Member, Hospital Staff, Orlando Regional Health Systems **Civic:** Board Member, Families and Children of Florida **Creative Works:** Presenter, "The Medial Arm Neurovascular Free Flap," Annual Meering, American Society of Plastic and Reconstructive Surgeons (1981); Co-author, "Reversal of Myocardial Depression with Angiotensin II in the Dog," Radiology (1975); Author, "Neurofibroma of the Ear: Function and Aesthetics," Journal of Plastic and Reconstructive Surgery; Author, "The Medial Arm Neurovascular Free Flap," Journal of Plastic and Reconstructive Surgery; Presenter, "Breast Reconstruction Following Mastectomy," Surgical Grand Rounds, Medical College of Wisconsin, Milwaukee, WI; Presenter, "Replantation and Free Tissue Transfer," Surgical Grand Rounds, Medical College of Wisconsin, Milwaukee, WI; Presenter, "Current Concepts in Tendon Repair," Surgical Grand Rounds, Medical College of Wisconsin, Milwaukee, WI; Presenter, "Free Flap Coverage of the Lower Extremity," Milwaukee Academy of Orthopedic Surgeons, Milwaukee, WI; Presenter, "The Scope of Plastic Surgery," Midwest Society of Operating Room Technologists and Nurses, Brookfield, WI; Presenter, "Aesthetic Cosmetic Surgery," Midwest Society of Operating Room Technologists and Nurses, Brookfield, WI; Presenter, "Pressure Sores: Prevention and Treatment," Veteran's Administration Spinal Cord Rehabilitation Conference, Milwaukee, WI; Presenter, "New Wrinkles in Facelift," Continuing Education Conference, Milwaukee Plastic Surgeons, Milwaukee, WI; Presenter, "Mandibular Reconstruction," Continuing Education Conference, Milwaukee Plastic Surgeons, Milwaukee, WI; Presenter, "Medical Arm Neurovascular Free Flap," Annual Meeting, American Society of Plastic and Reconstructive Surgeons, New York, NY **Awards:** "Best Cosmetic Surgeon," Orlando Sentinel Reader's Choice Awards (2017, 2016, 2015); Realself 100 Top Doctors (2012-2017); Realself Top Doctor **Memberships:** Research Fellow, Nebraska Heart Association (1975); American Society of Plastic and Reconstructive Surgeons Inc.; Orange County Medical Society; Florida Medical Association; American Medical Association; American Board of Plastic and Reconstructive Surgery; Board of Directors, American Cancer Society; Qualify for Aesthetic Society **To what do you attribute your success:** Dr. Trevisani credits his success on the influence of his Christian faith, as well as his traditional Italian American background. **Why did you become involved in your profession or industry:** Dr. Trevisani became involved in his profession because he had always been attracted to the study of anatomy. After graduating from medical school, he worked in an emergency room and became inspired by the example of local plastic surgeons.

Robert Bogue Trimble, PhD

Title: Research Scientist (Retired) **Industry:** Sciences **Date of Birth:** 07/02/1943 **Place of Birth:** Baltimore **State/Country of Origin:** MD/USA **Parents:** George Simpson Trimble; Janet Anna (Bogue) Trimble **Marital Status:** Married **Spouse Name:** Elizabeth Ann Gould Belden (12/03/1994); Marie Davis (05/17/1969, Deceased 08/1988) **Children:** Alison Bogue **Education:** PhD in Biology, Rensselaer Polytechnic Institute (1969); MS in Biology, Rensselaer Polytechnic Institute (1967); BS in Biology, Rensselaer Polytechnic Institute (1965) **Career:** Professor Emeritus, State University of New York (2007-Present); Director, Wadsworth Center Office of Research (2003-2007); Professor, Department of Biomedical Science, School of Public Health at University, Albany, State University of New York (1989-2007); Retired, Research Scientist VIII, New York State Department of Health, Wadsworth Center, Albany, NY (2004); From Research Scientist I to Research Scientist VI, New York State Department of Health, Wadsworth Center, Albany, NY (1970-2004); Deputy Director, Wadsworth Center Office of Research (2002-2003); Associate Chairman, Department of Biomedical Science, School of Public Health at University, Albany, State University of New York (1999-2003); Executive Committee on Graduate Studies, Albany Medical College (1998-2003) **Career Related:** Personnel Review Group, American Cancer Society Personnel, Atlanta, GA (1991-1996); Reserve Panel, United States Public Health Service Review, Bethesda, MD (1989-1993); U.S. Public Health Service on Cell Biology and Physiological I Study Section, Bethesda, MD (1985-1989) **Civic:** International Skeet/Trap Director, New York Empire State Games (1993-2001, 2003-2008); Volunteer, New York State Office of Parks, Recreation and Historic Preservation **Creative Works:** Editorial Board, Analytical Biochemistry (1997-2006); Editorial Board, Glycobiology (1996-2005); Editorial Board, Journal on Biological Chemistry (1992-1997); Contributor, More than 80 Articles, Professional Journals and Technical Manual Chapters **Awards:** Grantee, National Center for Research Resources (2002-2007); Grantee, National Institute on General Medical Science (1977-2007); Recognition Award, Wadsworth Center (2005); Recognition Award, New York State Commissioner of Health (2003, 2005); Named, International Skeet Champion, New York State (1994); Grantee, National Institute on Aging (1977-1981) **Memberships:** Executive Board, Society for Glycobiology (1995-1998); American Society for Biochemistry and Molecular Biology; American Society for Microbiology; American Association for the Advancement of Science; Sigma Xi **Marquis Who's Who Honors:** Albert Nelson Marquis Lifetime Achievement Award **Why did you become involved in your profession or industry:** Dr. Trimble became involved in his profession because he had an inquiring mind. There were a lot of competition in the engineering fields at Rensselaer Polytechnic Institute, and he started in architecture and found that the program did not involve building beautiful houses like the ones Frank Lloyd Wright was known for, nor did it call for doing landscape gardening. Instead, the program focused on building large, edifice-type buildings. After a year, he switched his major to biology, thinking that he would do general biology. However, the program also drew heavily from chemistry and geology. **Avocations:** Travel; Model railroads; Shotgun sports; Yachting **Political Affiliations:** Independent **Religion:** Episcopalian

Russell W. Tripp

Title: Real Estate Company Officer **Industry:** Real Estate **Date of Birth:** 02/09/1927 **Place of Birth:** Albany **State/Country of Origin:** OR/USA **Parents:** Rufus Winfield Tripp; Elsie (Powell) Tripp **Marital Status:** Married **Spouse Name:** Barbara "Duffy" Tripp **Children:** Heather Young; Wendy Tripp; Alison Pontynen **Education:** MA, Stanford University (1953); BA, Willamette University (1950); Graduate Coursework, Victoria University of Wellington and University of New Zealand **Career:** Partner, Tripp & Tripp, Albany, OR (1952-Present); Chairman, Board, State Sav., Albany, NY (1963-1982); Russ Tripp Investment Real Estate; Founder, President, Linn-Benton Community College **Career Related:** Developed Subdivision, Hawthorne Park, Hillway Addition; Developed Subdivision, Orchard Park; Developed Subdivision, Fir Oaks-all, Albany, OR **Civic:** Mayor, City of Albany, OR (1964-1970); Board Chairman, Linn-Benton Community College; President, Oregon Community College Association; President, Albany Kiwanis; President, World Championship, Timber Carnival; Secretary, League of Oregon Cities; Albany Public Library Board; President, Linn County Chamber of Commerce **Military Service:** Sergeant, United States Army (1945-1946) **Awards:** Legacy Distinguished Service Award, Albany Area Chamber of Commerce (2018); Alumni Citation, Willamette University (1976); Named First Citizen, Albany, OR (1971); Named Realtor of the Year (1968); Named Albany Junior First Citizen (1962); Rotary Scholar **Memberships:** Oregon Community College Association (1977); Albany Tennis Club (1973); President, Albany Board of Realtors (1957) **Marquis Who's Who Honors:** Albert Nelson Marquis Lifetime Achievement Award **Avocations:** Golfing; Walking **Political Affiliations:** Republican **Religion:** Methodist

Alvin W. Trivelpiece, PhD

Title: Scientist (Retired) **Industry:** Sciences **Company Name:** Sandia National Laboratories **Date of Birth:** 03/15/1931 **Place of Birth:** Stockton **State/Country of Origin:** CA/USA **Marital Status:** Single **Spouse Name:** Shirley Ann Ross (03/23/1953, Deceased 04/26/2009) **Children:** Craig Evan; Steve Edward; Keith Eric **Education:** PhD in Electrical Engineering and Physics, California Institute of Technology, Pasadena, CA (1958); MEE, California Institute of Technology, Pasadena, CA (1955); BEE, California Polytechnic State University, San Luis Obispo, CA (1953) **Career:** Board of Trustees, Atomic Testing Museum (2017-2018); Consultant, Lawrence Livermore National Laboratory (2009-2014); Consultant, Sandia National Laboratories, Albuquerque, NM (2000-2017); President, Lockheed Martin Corporation (1996-2000); Director, Oak Ridge National Laboratory, Oak Ridge, TN (1989-2000); Vice President, Lockheed Martin Corporation (1995); Vice President, Martin Marietta (1989-1995); Executive Officer, American Association for the Advancement of Science, Washington, DC (1987-1988); Director, Office of Energy Research, United States Department of Energy, Washington, DC (1981-1987); Corporate Vice President, Science Applications International Corporation, La Jolla, CA (1978-1981); Vice President, Maxwell Technologies, San Diego, CA (1976-1978); Assistant Director, Atomic Energy Commission, Washington, DC (1973-1975); Professor of Physics, University of Maryland (1966-1976); Associate Professor, University of California Berkeley (1959-1966); Assistant Professor, University of California Berkeley (1959-1966); Fulbright Scholar, Delft University of Technology, Delft, Netherlands (1958-1959) **Career Related:** Founding Board Member, American Council on Global Nuclear Competitiveness (2006-2012); Secretary, American Council on Global Nuclear Competitiveness (2006-2012); Treasurer, American Council on Global Nuclear Competitiveness (2006-2012); Chairman, Committee on Science and Technology in Kazakhstan, National Research Council, National Academy of Sciences (2006-2007); Workshop Chairman, National Academy of Sciences (2004); Workshop Chairman, Russian Academy of Sciences, Yekaterinburg, Russia (2004); Member, Committee on Technical Issues Related to Comprehensive Test Bane Treaty, National Academy of Sciences (2000-2002); Chairman, Committees, Small Innovative Firms, Nuclear Cities, Russia (2001); Chairman, Tennessee Technology Development Corporation (1998-2000); President, Tennessee Technology Development Corporation (1998-2000); Chairman, Tennessee Advisory Commission on Intergovernmental Relations (1996-1999); Member, Commission on Physical Sciences, Mathematics, and Applications, National Academy of Sciences (1993-1996); Member, Tennessee Advisory Commission on Intergovernmental Relations (1993-1996); Chairman, Advisory Committee, Federal Networking Council (1992-1996); Chairman, Coordinating Council for Education (1991-1993); Chairman, Mathematical Sciences Education Board, National Academy of Sciences (1990-1993); Head Delegate, Conference on Energy and Global Ecological Problems, National Academy of Sciences (1989); Head Delegate, Conference on Energy and Global Ecological Problems, Soviet Academy of Sciences (1989) **Creative Works:** Author, "Principles of Plasma Physics" (1973); Author, "Slow-Wave Propagation in Plasma Wave Guides" (1967); Contributor, Articles, Professional Journals **Awards:** Prize, Global Energy International (2009-2014); Tennessee Outstanding Service Commendation, Senate Joint Resolution #530 (2000); Distinguished Associate Award (2000); Outstanding Engineer Award, Region Three, IEEE (1995); Named, Distinguished Alumnus, California Institute of Technology, Pasadena, CA (1987); Gold Medal for Distinguished Service, United States Secretary of Energy (1986); Named, Distinguished Alumnus, California Polytechnic State University, San Luis Obispo, CA (1978) **Memberships:** Fellow, John Simon Guggenheim Foundation (1966); Fellow, IEEE (Institute of Electrical and Electronics Engineers); Fellow, American Association for the Advancement of Science; Fellow, American Physical Society; National Academy of Engineering; American Association of University Professors; International Award Committee, Global Energy International; American Association of Physics Teachers; American Nuclear Society; National Press Club; Capital Hill Club; Tau Beta Pi; Sigma Xi **Marquis Who's Who Honors:** Albert Nelson Marquis Lifetime Achievement Award; Marquis Who's Who Top Professional **Avocations:** Running; Golf

Monroe Eugene Trout, MD, JD

Title: Health Facility Administrator **Industry:** Health, Wellness and Fitness **Date of Birth:** 04/05/1931 **Place of Birth:** Harrisburg **State/Country of Origin:** PA/USA **Parents:** Florence Margaret (Kashner) Trout; David Michael Trout **Marital Status:** Married **Spouse Name:** Sandra Lemke Trout (06/11/1960) **Children:** Monroe Eugene, Jr.; Timothy William (Deceased) **Education:** Honorary LLD, Cumberland College (2003); AB, University of Pennsylvania (19 College (2003); Honorary LLD, Penn State Dickinson Law, The Pennsylvania State University (1996); Honorary LLD, Penn State Dickinson Law, The Pennsylvania State University (1996); Honorary LLD, Bloomfield College (1994); Honorary LLD, Bloomfield College (1994); JD, Penn State Dickinson Law, The Pennsylvania State University (1969); JD, Penn State Dickinson Law, The Pennsylvania State University (1969); LLB, Penn State Dickinson Law, The Pennsylvania State University (1964); LLB, Penn State Dickinson Law, The Pennsylvania State University (1964); MD, University of Pennsylvania (1957); MD, University of Pennsylvania (1957); AB, University of Pennsylvania (1953) **Certifications:** Certified in Medicine, State of New York (1961); Certified in Medicine, Commonwealth of Pennsylvania (1958) **Career:** Chairman Emeritus, American Healthcare Systems, Inc. (1995-Present); Interim CEO, Cytran Inc. (1996); Chairman, American Healthcare Systems, Inc. (1987-1995); President, American Healthcare Systems, Inc. (1986-1995); Chief Executive Officer, American Healthcare Systems, Inc. (1986-1995); Senior Vice President, Sterling Drug, Inc. (1978-1986); Director of Medical Affairs, Sterling Drug, Inc. (1978-1986); Board of Directors, Sterling Drug, Inc. (1978-1986); Executive Committee Member, Sterling Drug, Inc. (1978-1986); Vice President, Sterling Drug, Inc. (1974-1978); Director of Medical Affairs, Sterling Drug, Inc. (1974-1978); Medical Director, Sterling Drug, Inc. (1970-1974); Vice President, Winthrop Laboratories (1968-1970); Medical Director, Sterling Drug, Inc. (1968-1970); Director of Drug Regulatory Affairs, Pfizer Inc. (1964-1968); Chief of Medical Department, Harrisburg State Hospital (1961-1964); Resident in Internal Medicine, Naval Medical Center Portsmouth (1959-1961); Intern, Great Lakes Naval Hospital, (1957-1958); Consultant, State Department; Consultant to the Secretary of Health and Education; Spy, Central Intelligence Agency (CIA) (25 Years) **Career Related:** Chairman, Board of Directors, Cytyc, Inc. (Now Hologic, Inc.) (1998-2002); Chairman, Board of Directors, AEIX (1990-1995); Co-Chairman, Health and Human Services Agency, County of San Diego (1992-1994); Trustee, College of Health Solutions, Arizona State University (1988-1991); Research Board Member, Sterling Drug, Inc. (1977-1986); Member, The Joint Commission on Drug Use (1976-1980); Secretary, Commission on Medical Malpractice, Department of Health (1971-1973); Special Lecturer in Legal Medicine, Penn State Dickinson Law, The Pennsylvania State University (1970-1993); Trustee, Penn State Dickinson Law, The Pennsylvania State University (1970-1993) **Civic:** Member, Board of Directors, The International Churchill Society (2016-Present); Board of Directors, East Tennessee Historical Society (2003-2004); Member, Board of Directors, Knoxville Opera (2001-2004); Board of Directors, Knoxville Symphony Orchestra (2001-2004); Trustee, Baptist Health Foundation (1999-2007); Trustee, The San Diego Museum of Art (1996-1998); President, Board of Trustees, University of California San Diego Foundation (1994-1997); Trustee, Thornton Pavilion, UC San Diego (1990-1997) **Military Service:** Regimental Surgeon, 3rd Marine Division; U.S. Navy (1953-1961) **Creative Works:** Editorial Board Member, Medical Malpractice Prevention (1985-Present); Editorial Board Member, Forensic Science (1971-Present); Author, Winter Galley (2008); Editorial Board Member, Regulatory Toxicity and Pharmacology, Elsevier (1981-1987); Editorial Board Member, Journal of Legal Medicine, Taylor & Francis Group, Informa UK Limited (1973-1979); Editorial Board Member, Hospital Formulary Management (1969-1979); Editorial Reviewer, Annals of Internal Medicine; Contributor, 190 Articles, Professional Journals **Awards:** Lifetime Leadership Award, University Of Cumberlands (2014); Eponym, Monroe E. Trout Day, Knoxville Tennessee (2007); Caring Servant Award, Cumberland College (2005); Knoxville Philanthropist of the Year (2004); Visionary Award, Baptist Health Foundation (2002); 100 Most Influential Deltas of Twentieth Century, Delta Tau Delta (2000); Gold Medal Award, American College of Legal Medicine (1999); Civis Universitatus Award, UC San Diego (1997); Salvation Army Tradition of Caring Award (1996); Alumni Achievement Award, Delta Tau Delta (1996) **Memberships:** President, Medical Executives (1975-1976); Bridge Bronze Life Master; President, American College of Legal Medicine; Vice President, American College of Legal Medicine, Fellow, American College of Legal Medicine; American Medical Association; Delta Tau Delta; Founding Sponsor, Rossini Festival, City of Knoxville **Marquis Who's Who Honors:** Albert Nelson Marquis Lifetime Achievement Award **Why did you become involved in your profession or industry:** At 7 years old, Dr. Trout worked for a doctor by cleaning out the furnaces and cleaning his office to help his family. This doctor encouraged him to pursue medicine. As a result, Dr. Trout received several scholarships to the University of Pennsylvania and was able to attend. **Avocations:** Tennis; Bridge; Oil painting **Political Affiliations:** Republican **Religion:** Lutheran

Donald John Trump

Title: 45th President of the United States; Real Estate Developer **Industry:** Government Administration/Government Relations/Government Services **Date of Birth:** 06/14/1946 **Place of Birth:** Queens **State/Country of Origin:** NY/USA **Parents:** Fred C. Trump; Mary Trump **Marital Status:** Married **Spouse Name:** Melania Knauss (01/22/2005); Marla Maples (12/30/1993, Divorced 06/08/1999); Ivana Zelnicek (04/09/1977, Divorced 1991) **Children:** Donald Jr.; Ivanka; Eric; Tiffany Ariana; Barron William **Education:** BS in Economics, The Wharton School, The University of Pennsylvania (1968) **Career:** 45th President of the United States (2017-Present); Chairman, Chief Executive Officer, The Trump Organization, LLC, New York, NY (1980-Present); Chairman, Trump Entertainment Resorts, Inc., Atlantic City, NJ (2005-2009); Owner, Trump Casino Riverboat, Buffington Harbor, IN; Partner, Owner, Trump International Hotel and Tower, Chicago, IL; Owner, Trump International Hotel and Tower, New York, NY; Owner, Trump Tower, Trump Parc, Trump Palace, Trump Building (40 Wall Street), New York, NY; Owner, Trump Grande Ocean Resort and Residences, Miami Beach, FL; Owner, Trump Park Avenue (Formerly Delmonico Hotel); Owner, 610 Park Ave (Formerly Mayfair Hotel), NY; Owner, Trump World Tower, New York, NY; Owner, The Mar-a-Lago Club, Palm Beach, FL; Owner, Mansion at Seven Springs, Bedford, NY; Owner, West Side Rail Yards (Trump Place), New York, NY; Owner, Trump 29 Casino, Palm Springs, CA **Career Related:** Republican Nominee, Presidential Election of the United States (2016); Owner, Trump Golf Links, Ferry Point, NY (2015); Owner, International Trump Golf Links, Doonbeg, Ireland (2014); Owner, Trump International Golf Club, Dubai, United Arab Emirates (2013); Owner, Trump National Golf Club, Charlotte, NC and Jupiter, FL (2012); Owner, Trump Vineyard Estates, Charlottesville, VA (2011); Trump University, Online Courses, CD-ROMS, Blogs, Consulting Services and Learning Annex-type Seminars (2005-2010); Owner, Fashion Line of Men's Suits (2004); Launched Signature Fragrance, Donald Trump the Fragrance (2004); Owner, Beauty Pageants, Including Miss Universe, Miss USA and Miss Teen USA, Trump Pageants, Inc. (1996-2015); Owner, Trump Model Management/Talent Agency; Owner, Trump National Golf, Bedminster, NJ; Owner, Trump International Golf Club, Palm Beach, CA; Owner, Trump National Golf Club, Briarcliff Manor, NY; Owner, Ocean Trails Golf Course, Trump National Golf Course, Palos Verdes, CA **Civic:** Grand Marshall, Nation's Parade (1995); Chairman, New York Citizens Committee, 78th Annual NAACP Convention (1987); Committee Member, Celebration of Nations Commemorating 50th Anniversary of United Nations and UNICEF; Co-Chairman, New York Vietnam Veterans Memorial Fund; Founding Member, Construction Committee, Cathedral Church of Saint John the Divine; New York Citizens Tax Council; Fifth Avenue Association; Realty Foundation of New York; Real Estate Council, Metropolitan Museum of Art; Advisory Board, Lenox Hill Hospital, Northwell Health; United Cerebral Palsy Association; Special Advisor to President's Council on Physical Fitness and Sports; New York Sportsplex Commission; Board of Directors, Police Athletic League of New York City; Board of Overseers, The Wharton School, The University of Pennsylvania; Founding Member, Advisory Board, Wharton Real Estate Center (Now Samuel Zell and Robert Lurie Real Estate Center); Board of Directors, Fred C. Trump Foundation; Chairman, Donald J. Trump Foundation **Creative Works:** Author, "Crippled America: How to Make America Great Again" (2015); Author, "Time to Get Tough: Making America #1 Again" (2011); Co-Author, "Midas Touch: Why Some Entrepreneurs Get Rich - And Why Most Don't" (2011); Co-Author, "Think Like a Champion - An Informal Education in Business and Life" (2009); Co-Author, "Think Big and Kick Butt - in Business and Life" (2007); Co-Author, "Why We Want You to Be Rich: Two Men - One Message (2006); Author, "Trump: The Best Golf Advice I Ever Received" (2005); Host, Executive Producer, Television Series, "The Apprentice" (2004-2015); Author, "Trump: The Way to the Top: The Best Real Estate Advice I Ever Received: 100 Top Experts Share Their Strategies" (2004); Co-Author, "Think Like a Billionaire: Everything You Need to Know About Success, Real Estate and Life" (2004); Launched, Trump World Magazine (2004); Host, Syndicated Radio Program, "Trumped!," Premiere Radio Networks (2004); Co-Author, "The America We Deserve" (2000); Co-Author, "Trump: The Art of the Comeback" (1997); Co-Author, "Surviving at the Top/Trump: The Art of Survival" (1990); Co-Author, "Trump: The Art of the Deal" (1987) **Awards:** Named, One of the Forbes 400: Richest Americans (2006-Present); Named, One of the 100 Most Influential People in the World, Time Magazine (2016); Person of the Year, Time Magazine (2016); Named, One of the 10 Most Fascinating People of 2015, Barbara Walters Special (2015); Named, One of the 10 Most Fascinating People of 2011, Barbara Walters Special (2011); Named, One of the 100 Most Powerful Celebrities, Forbes.com (2008); Inductee, Wharton Hall of Fame (2003); Named, Benefactor, Board of Directors, Historical Society of Palm Beach County (2003); Hotel and Real Estate Visionary of the Century, UTA Federation (2000) **Political Affiliations:** Republican

Edwin Fred Tulloch, PhD

Title: Minister, Chaplain, Psychotherapist **Industry:** Religious **Date of Birth:** 08/19/1937 **Place of Birth:** Belton **State/Country of Origin:** TX/USA **Parents:** Robert Euclid Tulloch; Clara Laura (Muehlhause) Tulloch **Marital Status:** Widowed **Spouse Name:** Marianne Brevard (09/19/1959, Deceased 09/19/14) **Children:** Melanie Ruth; Valerie Anne **Education:** MS, East Texas State University (Now Texas A&M University-Commerce) (1987); PhD, East Texas State University (Now Texas A&M University-Commerce) (1985); DMin, Southern Methodist University (1978); ThM, Austin Presbyterian Theological Seminary (1969); MDiv, Austin Presbyterian Theological Seminary (1962); BA, Baylor University (1959); AA Degree, Temple College, Temple, TX, With Honors (1957) **Certifications:** Licensed Marriage and Family Therapist (1987); Licensed Professional Counselor, State of Texas; Certified Pastoral Counselor **Career:** Private Practice, Counseling (1992-Present); Psychotherapist of Pastoral Counseling and Education Center, Dallas, TX (1988-Present); Chaplain, Texas Health Presbyterian Hospital Dallas (1988-Present); Associate Pastor, First Presbyterian Church, Dallas, TX (1969-1987); Pastor, First Presbyterian Church, Dickinson, TX (1966-1969); Pastor, Highland Presbyterian Church, Hot Springs, AK (1962-1966) **Career Related:** Guest Lecturer, East Texas State University (Now Texas A&M University-Commerce) (1987); Guest Lecturer, Southern Methodist University; Guest Lecturer, Austin Presbyterian Theological Seminary; Chaplin, Proletarian Hospital, Dallas, TX **Civic:** Founder, The Stew Pot, Dallas, TX (2008) **Creative Works:** Advisory Board Editor, "Kerygma: Bible Study in Depth" (1984) **Awards:** Named, Outstanding Alumni in Commerce, East Texas State University (Now Texas A&M University-Commerce) (1987); Eastern Star Religious Award, Belton, TX (1960-1961); Named, MVP of Basketball Team (1957); Selected, All-district and Invitational Tournament from Various Teams, Temple High School, Texas; Honorable Mention, All-state in Basketball **Memberships:** Clinical Member, American Association for Marriage and Family Therapy; Certified Member, American Association of Pastoral Counselors **Marquis Who's Who Honors:** Albert Nelson Marquis Lifetime Achievement Award; Marquis Who's Who Top Professional **Why did you become involved in your profession or industry:** Dr. Tulloch went into ministry because of the example set by his parents. When he told his mother that he wanted to go into ministry, his mother replied that she had always prayed that he would go into the ministry. He felt like when he was in ministry, he was doing a lot of pastoral counseling unofficially. More and more, he became people-oriented. He became more interested in people, as well as the teaching part of ministry. **Avocations:** Tennis; Hiking; Running; Sports

Lewis Putnam "Turk" Turco

Title: Professor Emeritus **Industry:** Education/Educational Services **Company Name:** State University of New York at Oswego **Date of Birth:** 05/02/1934 **Place of Birth:** Buffalo **State/Country of Origin:** NY/USA **Parents:** Luigi Turco; May Laura (Putnam) Turco **Marital Status:** Married **Spouse Name:** Jean Cate Houdlette (5/29/1934) **Children:** Melora Ann; Christopher Cameron **Education:** Honorary DAH, Unity College (2012); Honorary LHD, University of Maine at Fort Kent (2009); Honorary LHD, Ashland University, Ashland, OH (2000); MA, University of Iowa, Iowa City, IA (1962); BA, University of Connecticut, Storrs, CT (1959); Diploma, High School, Meriden, CT (1952) **Career:** Professor Emeritus, State University of New York at Oswego (1996); Poet-in-Residence, State University of New York at Oswego (1995-1996); Assistant Professor to Full Professor, State University of New York at Oswego (1965-1996); Assistant Professor, Hillsdale College, Hillsdale, MI (1964-1965); Instructor, Cleveland State University (1960-1964) **Career Related:** Graduate Assistant, English, University of Connecticut (1959); Editorial Assistant, Writer's Workshop, University of Iowa (1959-1960); Visiting Professor, State University of New York at Potsdam (1968-1969); Bingham Poet-in-Residence, University of Louisville (1982); Writer-in-Residence, Ashland University (1991); Founding Director, Cleveland State University Poetry Center (1962); Program in Creative Writing, State University of New York at Oswego (1968) **Civic:** Secretary, City of Oswego Charter Revision Commission (1990-1991); Active, Oswego Opera Theater Chorus, Oswego Festival Chorus, (1986-1996) **Military Service:** U.S Navy, U.S.S. Hornet (CVA12) (1952-1956) **Creative Works:** Author, "The Book of Forms: A Handbook of Poetics" (2020); Author, "The Book of Dialogue" (2020); Author, "The Book of Literary Terms" (2020); "The Sonnetarium" (2018); "The Hero Enkidu: An Epic" (2015); Author, "Satan's Scourge: A Narrative of the Age of Witchcraft in England and New England 1580-1697" (2007); Author, "Fantaseers, A Book of Memories" (2005); Author, "A Sheaf of Leaves: Literary Memoirs" (2004), Author, "The Book of Literary Terms" (1999); Editor, "The Life and Poetry of Manoah Bodman" (1999); Author, "A Book of Fears" (1998); Author, "Emily Dickinson, Woman of Letters" (1993); Author, "The Shifting Web: New and Selected Poems" (1989); Author, "Visions and Revisions of American Poetry" (1986); Author, "The Book of Forms: A Handbook of Poetics" (1968); Author, "First Poems" (1960); Author, "Awaken"; Author, "Bells Falling: Poems" (1959-1968); Author, "Fearful Pleasures: The Complete Poems" (1953-2007); Author, "The Collected Lyrics of Lewis Turco/Wesli Court" (1953-2004); Author, Numerous Nonfiction Works; Contributor, Articles, Professional Journals; Blog, "Poetics and Ruminations" **Awards:** Award for "Satan's Scourge," New England Book Festival (2010); Award, New England Book Festival (2009); Robert Fitzgerald Award, West Chester University Poetry Conference (2008); Choice Outstanding Academic Title, "The Book of Literary Terms" (2000); John Ciardi Award for Lifetime Achievement in Poetry, Italian-American Foundation (1999); Bordighera Bilingual Poetry Prize, Sonia Raiziss-Giop Charitable Foundation (1997); Inductee, Meriden Hall of Fame (1993); Distinguished Alumnus Award (1992); Exhibit Certificate of Award, for "The Compleat Melancholick" National Endowment for the Arts, New American Writing Exhibits, International Book Fairs of Frankfurt and Liber (1986); Melville Cane Award, Poetry Society America (1986); Resident Fellowship, Yaddo Foundation (1977); Grant-in-Aid (1969); Faculty Fellowships, Research Foundation of State University of New York (1966-1978); Resident Fellowship, Yaddo Foundation (1959); Distinguished Alumnus Award, Alumni Association of the University of Connecticut; Poetry Fellow, Bread Loaf Writers Conference **Memberships:** Poetry Society of America; P.E.N **Marquis Who's Who Honors:** Albert Nelson Marquis Lifetime Achievement Award; Marquis Who's Who Top Professional **To what do you attribute your success:** Mr. Turco attributes his success to talent, luck, and hard work. **Why did you become involved in your profession or industry:** From a young age, Mr. Turco loved to read. He longed to do for others what his favorite authors had done for him, which inspired him to pursue writing. **Avocations:** Gardening **Political Affiliations:** Democrat **Thoughts on Life:** Mr. Turco makes the most of his life.

Gerard Michael Turino

Title: John H. Keating Sr. Professor of Medicine Emeritus **Industry:** Medicine & Health Care **Company Name:** Columbia University **Date of Birth:** 05/16/1924 **Place of Birth:** New York **State/Country of Origin:** NY/USA **Parents:** Michael Turino; Lucy (Arciero) Turino **Marital Status:** Married **Spouse Name:** Dorothy Estes **Children:** Peter; Phillip; James **Education:** Resident in Medicine, New Haven Hospital (1950-1951); Assistant Resident in Medicine, Columbia University, Bellevue Hospital (1949-1950); Intern, Columbia University, Bellevue Hospital (1948-1949); MD, Columbia University (1948); AB, Princeton University (1945) **Certifications:** Diplomate, American Board of Internal Medicine **Career:** Director, St. Luke's-Roosevelt Hospital James P. Mara Center (1997-Present); Professor Emeritus, Columbia University (2016); John H. Keating Professor of Medicine, Columbia University (1983-2016); Director, Medical Services, St. Luke's-Roosevelt Hospital, New York, NY (1983-1992); Professor of Medicine, Columbia University (1973-1983); Associate of Professor, Columbia University (1967-1972); Career Investigator, Health Research Council City of New York (1961-1971); Attending Physician, Presbyterian Hospital (1960-1983); Staff, Presbyterian Hospital, New York, NY (1960-1983); Assistant Professor of Medicine, Columbia University (1960-1967); Senior Fellow, New York Heart Association (1956-1960); Chief Resident in Medicine, Columbia University Division, Bellevue Hospital (1953-1954) **Career Related:** President, East Hampton Health Foundation (2005-Present); Chairman, American Bureau Medical Advancement in China (2001-Present); Consultant, Science Affairs, American Thoracic Society (1992-Present); Chairman, Board of Directors, Chronic Obstructive Pulmonary Disease Foundation (2004); President, American Bureau Medical Advancement in China (1994-2001); Consultant, VA Hospital, East Orange, NJ (1962-1967); Science Advisory Committee, National Heart, Lung, and Blood Institute; Member, Science Advisory Committee, American Lung Association; Science Advisory Committee, American Heart Association; Science Advisory Committee, New York Lung Association; Science Advisory Committee, New York Heart Association; Consultant in Medicine, Englewood Hospital; American Bureau Medical Advancement in China **Civic:** Chairman, Chronic Obstructive Pulmonary Disease Foundation (2004); Board of Education, Alpine, NJ (1960-1967) **Military Service:** Served to Captain, U.S. Air Force (1951-1953) **Creative Works:** Contributor, Articles, Medical Journals **Awards:** First Visionary Award, COPD Foundation (2017); St. Luke's Roosevelt Hospital Alumni Award (2014); Breathing for Life Award, American Thoracic Society (2013); Lifetime Achievement Award, Birmingham UK 7 Conference (2010); Research Achievement Award, Copd Foundation (2010); Edward Livingston Trudeau Medal, American Lung Association (2003); Edward Livingston Trudeau Prize, American Thoracic Society (2003); Gold Medal, Alumni Association of College Physicians and Surgeons, Columbia University (1986); Alumni Medal, Columbia University (1983); Silver Medal, Alumni Association of College Physicians and Surgeons, Columbia University (1979); Joseph Mather Smith Prize, Columbia University (1965) **Memberships:** Board of Directors, COPD Association (2004-Present); President, New York Medical-Surgical Society (1995); Distinguished Achievement Award, American Heart Association (1989); President, American Thoracic Society (1987-1988); President, New York Heart Association (1981-1983); Award of Merit, American Heart Association (1980); Fellow, American Association for the Advancement of Science; Association of American Physicians; American Society Clinical Investigation; Harvey Society; American Thoracic Society; American Federation Clinical Research; American Physiological Society; American Heart Association; Board of Directors, American Heart Association; New York Heart Association; Director, New York Lung Association; New York Medical-Surgical Society; New York Clinical Society; Princeton Club; Maidstone Club; Devon Yacht Club; Century Association Club **Marquis Who's Who Honors:** Albert Nelson Marquis Lifetime Achievement Award; Marquis Who's Who Top Professional; Distinguished Humanitarian

Natalie Ann Turner

Title: Consultant (Retired) **Industry:** Consulting **Place of Birth:** Vancouver, British Columbia, Canada **State/Country of Origin:** Canada **Parents:** Walter P. (Deceased); Jenny (Ferley) Koohtow (Deceased) **Marital Status:** Widow **Spouse Name:** George M. Turner, Junior (08/1991, Deceased) **Education:** BSc, McGill University (1949) **Career:** Retired (1989); Chemical Program Manager in R&D, Technical Service Manager to International Operations, Clearance Officer for Latin-America and Asia-Pacific Companies, Gillette Company, Boston, MA (1954-1988); Research Assistant, Harvard Medical School, Boston, MA (1951-1954); Research Assistant in Neurophysiology, Allen Memorial Institute, Montreal, Canada (1949-1951) **Career Related:** Technician, Red Cross Blood Transfusion Service, Montreal, Canada (1949); Technical Consultant, Damon Biotech, Boston, MA (1988-1989); Research assistant, Harvard School of Public Health **Civic:** Board of directors, Children's Museum, Easton, MA (1989-2005) **Creative Works:** Co-author, Research publications in field **Memberships:** National Association of Female Executives; International Congress Physiology; American Chemical Society; Society Cosmetic Chemists; New England Women Business Owners; Kappa Alpha Theta **Marquis Who's Who Honors:** Albert Nelson Marquis Lifetime Achievement Award **To what do you attribute your success:** Ms. Turner attributes her success to the mindset that her parents Jenny and Walter had instilled in her from a very young age. **Why did you become involved in your profession or industry:** Ms. Turner's mother, Jenny, always pushed the philosophy to her children to pursue an education and job in an area that they can attain a good income, just in case her children have to fend for themselves due to unexpected circumstances. Ms.Turner chose to pursue the sciences by high school, because her motto was "body, mind & soul". She decided that she was entitled to develop all of those aspects. **Avocations:** Sewing; Golfing; Creating portraits in fabric and oils

Juan A. Umanzor Jr.

Title: Realtor **Industry:** Real Estate **Company Name:** Long and Foster Real Estate, Inc. **Date of Birth:** 12/04/1975 **Place of Birth:** San Salvador **State/Country of Origin:** El Salvador **Parents:** Juan A. Unmanzor; Romana Martinez **Marital Status:** Married **Spouse Name:** Andrea (2010) **Children:** Nicole; Samuel; David **Education:** BA in Business Administration and Management (2001) **Certifications:** Short Sales & Foreclosure Resource (SFR) Certification **Career:** Umanzor & Associates, Long & Foster Companies (2005-Present); Real Estate Agent, Long & Foster Companies (2003-2005) **Civic:** Board Member, Latino Association of Realtors **Awards:** Best of Homelight Award; Best of Zillow Award; The Masters' Club Award **Memberships:** Salvadoran Chamber of Commerce; GCAAR; NAR; NAREHP **Marquis Who's Who Honors:** Marquis Who's Who Top Professional **To what do you attribute your success:** Mr. Umanzor attributes his success to his passion for helping others; when he started his own business, he was never, and still isn't, driven by the money. His success comes from helping others and the desire to better himself. **Why did you become involved in your profession or industry:** Mr. Umanzor became involved in his profession because he moved to the United States when he was 20 years old and had to start from scratch; he didn't have anyone here when he arrived. He wanted to change his life and the lives of those behind him. He is also a believer of God. **Avocations:** Traveling; Experiencing different cultures with the family; Networking **Religion:** Christian

Carrie Marie Underwood

Title: Singer **Industry:** Media & Entertainment **Date of Birth:** 3/10/1983 **Place of Birth:** Muskogee **State/Country of Origin:** OK/USA **Parents:** Stephen Underwood; Carol Underwood **Marital Status:** Married **Spouse Name:** Mike Fisher (07/10/2010) **Children:** Isaiah Michael Fisher; Jacob Bryan Fisher **Education:** Bachelor's Degree in Mass Communication, Northeastern State University, Magna Cum Laude (2006) **Career:** Founder, Fitness Clothing Line, "CALIA by Carrie" (2015-Present); Recording Artist (2005-Present) **Civic:** Donor, $1 Million, Red Cross (2013); Donor, Canadian and American Red Cross (2012); Donor, $140,125," Save the Children (2011); Founder, Academy of Country Music Lifting Lives Temporary Home Fund (2010); Founder, Checotah Animal, Town, and School Foundation (2009); Supporter, Humane Society of the United States; Supporter, United Services Organization; Supporter, Clothes Off Our Back; Supporter, Habitat For Humanity; Supporter, Arts Education; Supporter, Animal Welfare **Creative Works:** Author, "Find Your Path" (2020); Singer, Songwriter, Producer, Album, "Cry Pretty" (2018); Featured Artist, "The Fighter" by Keith Urban (2017); Featured Artist, "We Can't Stand Each Other" by Bobby Bones (2016); Singer, Songwriter, Album, "Storyteller" (2015); Herself, "Nashville" (2014, 2013); Singer, Songwriter, Producer, Compilation Album, "Greatest Hits: Decade #1" (2014); Featured Artist, "Somethin' Bad" by Miranda Lambert (2014); Performer, Video Album, "The Blown Away Tour: Live" (2013); Featured Artist, "Can't Stop Lovin' You" by Aerosmith (2013); Actress, "The Sound of Music Live!" (2013); Singer, Songwriter, Album, "Blown Away" (2012); Herself, "Zendaya: Behind the Scenes" (2012); Featured Artist, "Remind Me" by Brad Paisley (2011); Actress, "Soul Surfer" (2011); Herself, "Blue Bloods" (2011); Actress, "How I Met Your Mother" (2010); Herself, "The Buried Life" (2010); Voice Actress, "Sesame Street" (2009); Singer, Songwriter, Album, "Play On" (2009); Performer, "Saturday Night Live" (2008, 2007); Singer, Songwriter, Album, "Carnival Ride" (2007); Singer, Songwriter, Album, "Some Hearts" (2005); Contestant, Winner, "American Idol" (2004-2005) **Awards:** Honoree, CMT Artist of the Year Awards (2019, 2018, 2016, 2012, 2010); Video of the Year, "Cry Pretty," CMT Music Awards (2019); Female Video of the Year, "Love Wins," CMT Music Awards (2019); Songwriting Award, "Cry Pretty," BMI Country Awards (2019); Top Female Country Artist, Billboard Music Awards (2019); Favorite Country Album, "Cry Pretty," American Music Awards (2019); Favorite Female Country Artist, American Music Awards (2019); Vocal Event of the Year, With Keith Urban, "The Fighter," Academy of Country Music Awards (2018); Favorite Female Country Artist, American Music Awards (2018); Female Vocalist of the Year, Country Music Association Awards (2018); Female Video of the Year, "The Champion," CMY Music Awards (2018); Favorite Female Country Artist, American Music Awards (2017); Video of the Year, "Forever Country," Academy of Country Music Awards (2017); ACM Lifting Lives Gary Haber Award, Academy of Country Music Awards (2017); Female Video of the Year, "Church Bells," CMY Music Awards (2017); Songwriting Award, "Heartbreak," "Smoke Break," "Little Toy Guns," BMI Country Awards (2016); Female Vocalist of the Year, American Country Countdown Awards (2016); Favorite Country Album, "Storyteller," American Music Awards (2016); Best Country Solo Performance, "Something in the Water," Grammy Awards (2015); Songwriting Award, "Something in the Water," BMI Country Awards (2015); Favorite Female Country Artist, American Music Awards (2015); Top Christian Music, "Something in the Water," Billboard Music Awards (2015); Songwriting Award, "See You Again," BMI Country Awards (2014); Gene Weed Special Achievement Award, Academy of Country Music Awards (2014); Favorite Female Country Artist, American Music Awards (2014); Milestone Award, Billboard Music Awards (2014); Named One of "The 100 Most Influential People in the World," Time (2014); Best Country Solo Performance, "Blown Away," Grammy Awards (2013); Female Music Video of the Year, "Blown Away," American Country Awards (2013); Songwriting Award, "Two Black Cadillacs," "Good Girl," BMI Country Awards (2013); International Album of the Year, "Blown Away," British Country Music Awards (2013); Vocal Collaboration of the Year, With Brad Paisley, "Remind Me," American Country Awards (2012); Female Artist of the Year, American Country Awards (2012); Favorite Country Album, "Blown Away," American Music Awards (2012); Songwriting Award, "Mama's Song," "Undo It," "Temporary Home," BMI Country Awards (2011); Favorite Country Album, "Play On," American Music Awards (2010); Female Music Video of the Year, "Mama's Song," American Country Awards (2011); Female Single of the Year, "Mama's Song," American Country Awards (2011); Best Country Collaboration with Vocals, "I Told You So," Grammy Awards (2010); Triple Crown Award, Academy of Country Music Awards (2010); Songwriting Award, "Cowboy Casanova," BMI Country Awards (2010); Entertainer of the Year, Academy of Country Music Awards (2010); Album of the Year, "Play On," American Country Awards (2010); Female Music Video of the Year, "Cowboy Casanova," American Country Awards (2010); Female Single of the Year, "Cowboy Casanova," American Country Awards (2010) **Religion:** Baptist

Manuel Urbina II, PhD, JD

Title: Founder, Curator **Industry:** Museums & Institutions **Company Name:** Museo Urbina de Historia de Mexico **Date of Birth:** 9/23/1939 **Place of Birth:** Rodriguez **State/Country of Origin:** Nuevo Leon/Mexico **Parents:** Rev. Manuel Urbina; Irene (Salce) de Urbina **Education:** JD, University of Houston (1983); Postgraduate, Cambridge University, England (1982); PhD, University of Texas (1976); MA, University of Texas (1967); Postgraduate Coursework, National Autonomous University of Mexico, Mexico City, Mexico (1963-1964); BA, Howard Payne University (1962) **Certifications:** Diploma, Sistema Legal Mexicano **Career:** Professor of Latin American History, College of the Mainland, Texas City, TX (1967-1974) **Career Related:** Founder, Curator, Urbina Museum of History of Mexico, Houston, TX (1990-Present); Chairman, Legal Counsel, Urbina Foundation, Houston, TX (1985-Present); Chairman, Chief Executive Officer, Urbina Publishing Co. Inc., Houston, TX, Mexico City, Mexico (1985-Present) **Civic:** Founder, Faculty Sponsor, Mexico American Student Association, College of the Mainland (1974-2014); Founder, Organizer, Cinco de Mayo Festival (1974-2014); Organizer, National Reunion of Veterans of the Mexican Revolution (1988); Founder, Cinco de Mayo Association, Galveston County, Texas (1976); Founder, COM AMIGOS (1974); Interpreter, 33 Missionary Trips, Mexico **Creative Works:** Author, "The Impact of the Texas Revolution on the Government, Politics and Society of Mexico, 1836-1846," National Autonomous University of Mexico (2009); Featured, "General Pancho Villa in International Law" (1999); Featured, "Bilingual Dollars of the Bank of Texas (1835) in the Context of the Separation of Texas from Mexico" (1998); Featured, "The Mexican War in the United States Constitutional Law" (1996); Featured, "Efectos de la Independencia de Texas Sobre el Gobierno, la Politica, y la Sociedad de Mexico" (1996); Featured, "The Mexican War in International Law" (1995); Featured, "General Emiliano Zapata in North American Historiography" (1989); Featured, "Relations Between the United States and Mexico" (1987); Featured, "The Battle of the Alamo: A Mexican Viewpoint (1986); Featured, "The Mexican Side of the Texas Revolution" (1985); Featured, "The Mexican Side of the Mexican War" (1985); Featured, "The Battle of San Jacinto: A Mexican Viewpoint" (1985); Editor, Interviewer, History Videos, Oral History Interviews with Participants in the Mexican Revolution; Contributor, Articles to Newspapers and Magazines including Houston Chronicle, Mexico City Novedades, San Antonio Light, Boletin Del Archivo General Del Estado de Nuevo Leon, Boletin de la Sociedad Numismatica de Mexico **Awards:** Outstanding Leadership Diploma, U.S. Congress (2010); Named, Hispanic of the Year, Galveston County League of United Latin American Citizens (1982); Named, Scholar Diplomat, U.S. Department of the State (1979); Grantee, National Endowment of the Humanities (1971-1972) **Memberships:** League of United Latin American Citizens; Texas State Historical Association; Howard Payne University Alumni Association; University of Houston Law Alumni Association; University of Texas Alumni Association; Inter-American Chamber of Commerce; Mexican Numismatic Society; LULAC Council 255; Familias Unidas; Club Latino; Organizaciones Mexicanas de Texas City; Hispanic League of Galveston County; HOLA; Cinco de Mayo Association, Inc **Marquis Who's Who Honors:** Albert Nelson Marquis Lifetime Achievement Award; Marquis Who's Who Top Professional **Why did you become involved in your profession or industry:** Dr. Urbina was inspired by his parents. They were an immigrant family from Mexico. His father was a Baptist pastor in a theological seminary in Mexico and his mother was a trained school teacher. They stressed education. The reason they immigrated from Mexico was because his parents thought that they would have a better chance for educational achievement in the United States. **Avocations:** Reading; Research; Travel; Trumpet; Volunteer work; Missionary trips **Political Affiliations:** Democrat **Religion:** Baptist

Benny "The Jet" Urquidez

Marquis Who's Who
18 98
Biographee

Title: Kickboxer, Martial Arts Choreographer, Actor **Industry:** Athletics **Date of Birth:** 06/20/1952 **Place of Birth:** Tarzana **State/Country of Origin:** CA/USA **Career:** Retired (1989-1993); Co-Founder, Los Angeles Film Fighting Institute (2000); Founder, Ukidokan Karate **Career Related:** Teacher, The Jets Gym, North Hollywood, CA, Team Karate Center, Woodland Hills, CA **Creative Works:** Author, "King of The Ring," Pro Action Publishing (1995); Author, "Karate Dynamics: The Ukidokan System," Pro Action Publishing (1991); Featured, "Martial Arts: Traditions, History, People" (1983); Appearance, "World of Martial Arts" (1982); Contributor, "Living on the Martial Arts," Sports Life Publications, Inc., Japan (1982); Author, "Practical Kick-Boxing: Strategy in Training & Technique," Pro Action Publishing (1982); Featured, "The Baddest Dude In The World, Hustler Magazine (1979); Author, "Training and Fighting Skills" **Awards:** Inductee, International Sports Hall of Fame (2019); Inductee, Hall of Fame, World Kickboxing League W.K.L (2013); Super-Welterweight World Champion, World Kickboxing Association (1993); Undisputed Welterweight Champion, STAR System World Kickboxing Ratings (1985); Welterweight World Champion, World Kickboxing Association (1985); Super-Lightweight World Champion, World Kickboxing Association (1977-1985); Welterweight World Champion, Muay Thai Bond Nederland (1984); Competitor of the Year, Black Belt Magazine (1978); Super-Lightweight (-63.6 kg) World Champion, KATOGI (1978); Lightweight World Champion, Professional Karate Association (1976-1977); Lightweight World Champion, World Series of Martial Arts Championships (1975-1976); Openweight World Champion, World Series of Martial Arts Championships (1974-1976); Lightweight World Champion, World Professional Karate Organization (1975); Lightweight World Champion, National Karate League (1974-1975); Undisputed Super-Welterweight World Champion, STAR System World Kickboxing Ratings (1974) **Memberships:** NKL; WPKO; Professional Karate Association (PKA); World Kickboxing Association (WKA); AJKBA; Shin-Kakutojutsu Federation; NJPW; MTN

Kathleen W. Uy, MD

Title: Medical Director, Fresenius Medical Care Lakeshore Unit, Medical Director, Acute Dialysis Services, Advocate Aurora Healthcare **Industry:** Medicine & Health Care **Company Name:** Midwest Nephrology Associates, LLC **Date of Birth:** 12/27/1969 **Place of Birth:** Quezon City **State/Country of Origin:** Philippines **Parents:** Cesar Lim Uy; Elena Leano Wan **Education:** Nephrology Fellowship, University of Chicago, Chicago, IL (2000); Residency, Louis A. Weiss Memorial Hospital, Chicago, IL (1998); MD, University of the East Ramon Magsaysay Memorial Medical Center, Quezon City, Philippines (1993) **Certifications:** Certified in Internal Medicine, American Board of Internal Medicine; Certified in Nephrology, American Board of Internal Medicine **Career:** Medical Director, Fresenius Medical Care, Midwest Nephrology Associates (2001-Present); Medical Director, Acute Dialysis Services, Advocate Aurora Healthcare, Milwaukee, WI **Awards:** Top Doctor Milwaukee Magazine (2015-2016, 2018, 2020); Recognition of Service, Philippine Medical Association; Outstanding Leadership Award; Patient Care Advocate Award **Memberships:** Past President, Philippine Medical Association (2016); National Kidney Foundation **Marquis Who's Who Honors:** Marquis Who's Who Top Professional **To what do you attribute your success:** Dr. Uy attributes her success to her desire to always want to learn. She tries to make sure that she learns something daily and that each patient gets the attention they need. She is always willing to do the necessary work to do the right thing and lead her patients down the right path of treatment. **Why did you become involved in your profession or industry:** Dr. Uy became involved in her profession because of her father, Dr. Cesar L. Uy, is a surgeon. He was her inspiration for going into medicine. He still practices in the Philippines and she would assist him with his surgical cases in the operating room when she was young. In the Philippines, poverty was and still is a very common issue. She recalls an instance where a patient thanked her father for saving his life, despite knowing that he could not pay for his services. Her family is involved in health care. Her brother, Edmund, is a physician. Some of her cousins are physicians as well. Her family has always been very loving and supportive, and she dedicates her success to them. Her mother, Elena, had instilled in her the discipline in her studies. Her brother, Cezar, helped focus on her decision to go into medicine. Her sister, Christine, has always been the cheerleader by her side. She saw in her youngest brother, Christian, the same drive that runs in her family to strive for the best. **Avocations:** Ballroom dancing; Scuba diving **Thoughts on Life:** Dr. Uy aims for knowledge and wisdom to use her knowledge. She believes in working with others to achieve the greater good. She believes in perseverance and work to achieve goals. Loving what she does makes everything easier. Sharing with loved ones warms her heart.

Antonio "Tony" Valdovinos De La Mora

Title: Chief Executive Officer, Founder **Industry:** Machinery **Company Name:** La Machine Strategic Electoral Operations LLC **Date of Birth:** 06/19/1990 **Place of Birth:** Colima **State/Country of Origin:** Mexico **Parents:** Felicitas De La Mora; Martin Valdovinos De La Mora **Education:** Associate Degree in Political Science and Government, Phoenix College (2016); Associate Degree in Art, Gateway Community College (2011); Diploma, Camelback High School (2008) **Career:** Founder, La Machine Strategic Electoral Operations, LLC. (2015); Founding Members, Team Awesome (2011) **Awards:** Labor Activist Award (2016); Profile in the Hispanic Chamber of Commerce **Marquis Who's Who Honors:** Albert Nelson Marquis Lifetime Achievement Award **To what do you attribute your success:** Mr. Valdovinos is perhaps best known for being a fierce community agent for Dreamers and his grit and relentless determination to improve the lives of other undocumented youth. He discovered his undocumented status on his 18th birthday when he was unable to enlist into the Marines because of his legal status. Since then he has served patriotically by registering people to vote and helping the state of Arizona turn blue through his civic-engagement work. He attributes his success to the example of leadership and social awareness that his mother Felicitas De La Mora modeled for him. **Why did you become involved in your profession or industry:** Mr. Valdovinos became inspired to pursue his career path by simply being told "No". His biggest career aspiration as a young man was to become a United States Marine after watching the terrorist attacks of 9/11. When he went to enlist, he was denied because he was not a United States citizen. He then attended college but due to tuition hikes, he was unable to continue. He felt it was unfair to be priced out of an education. He then chose to find another way to serve his community and country. **Political Affiliations:** Democrat

Ivan P. Vamos, AICP

Title: State Agency Administrator (Retired) **Industry:** Government Administration/Government Relations/Government Services **Date of Birth:** 03/14/1938 **Place of Birth:** Budapest **State/Country of Origin:** Hungary **Parents:** Zoltan Vamos; Ilona (Leon) Vamos **Marital Status:** Married **Spouse Name:** Maria G.A. Vanderweerd, (06/30/1965) **Children:** David; Igor; Tara **Education:** Postgraduate Coursework in Public Affairs, State University of New York, Albany (1968-1974); MS in Urban Planning, Columbia University (1965); AB, Columbia University (1960) **Certifications:** Certified, American Institute Professional Planners **Career:** Retired, State Agency Administrator; Associate, Hudson Group LLC, Planning and Engineering Consultants (1994-2016); Deputy Commissioner, Planning and Development, New York State Parks, Albany, NY (1980-1994); Assistant Commissioner, Environment, New York State Parks, Albany, NY (1974-1980); Director, Planning, New York State Parks, Albany, NY (1968-1974); Associate Transportation Planner, New York State Department of Public Works (DOT), Albany, NY (1965-1968); Engineering Geologist, Snowy Mountain, Australia (1963); Engineering Geologist, Geotechnics and Resources, Inc., White Plains, NY (1962) **Career Related:** Holocaust Survivor Speaker, Local Schools and Organizations within 100 Miles of Albany, NY; Promoter, Safe Bicycle Trails and Pedestrian Trails **Civic:** Section Chief, Berkshires (1989-1990); Senior Patroller, National Ski Patrol (1967-1990) **Military Service:** Leiutenant, Junior Grade (1962); Naval Control of Shipping Officer, Reykjavik, Iceland (1961); Ensign U.S. Navy Shipboard Engineering Officer, TAP 115 (1960); Officer in Charge, Site H2, Iceland; Leiutenant, U.S. Naval Reserve **Memberships:** American Institute Professional Planners **Marquis Who's Who Honors:** Albert Nelson Marquis Lifetime Achievement Award; Marquis Who's Who Top Professional **Why did you become involved in your profession or industry:** Mr. Vamos became involved in his profession because he was interested in land and land form and the puzzles some of the environmental issues presented them, both as an engineer and land management stewardship. **Avocations:** Traveling

Dirk Van de Put

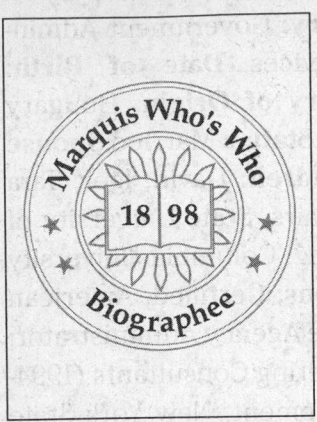

Title: Chairman, Chief Executive Officer **Industry:** Food & Restaurant Services **Company Name:** Mondelez International **Place of Birth:** Mechelen **State/Country of Origin:** Belgium **Education:** Veterinary Medicine Degree, Ghent University; Master's Degree in Business, University of Antwerp **Career:** Chairman, Chief Executive Officer, Mondelez International (2018-Present); Chief Executive Officer, Mondelez International (2017-Present); Chief Executive Officer, McCain Foods (2010-2017); President, Coca Cola Caribbean; President, Global OTC Division, Novartis, Inc.; President, Americas Division, Freshy Dairy Division, Groupe Danone; Non-Executive Director, Mattell Inc. **Career Related:** Member, Board of Directors, Consumers Goods Forum

Carolena Adrianna van den Berk

Industry: Architecture & Construction **Date of Birth:** 02/03/1941 **Place of Birth:** Eindhoven **State/Country of Origin:** Netherlands **Parents:** Lambert Jacobus Marinus van den Berk; C. A. van den Eeden **Marital Status:** Married **Spouse Name:** Prof. John Clark **Children:** Marcel; Andre; Carissa; Jessica; Sabrina; Eugene **Career:** Artist/Interior Designer/Builder, Van Den Berk-Clark Properties, Inc. **Marquis Who's Who Honors:** Albert Nelson Marquis Lifetime Achievement Award **To what do you attribute your success:** Ms. van den Berk attributes her success to hard work. She has enormous drive. A lot of people obstructed her because she is female. Ms. van den Berk's father was a writer for politics and economics, and she gets her business sense from him. **Why did you become involved in your profession or industry:** Ms. van den Berk became involved in her profession because when she was little, she saw broken down villas in Berlin after the war, which is when she got interested. She was always drawing houses over and over since she was little, so it was something there subconsciously and she didn't know. She tried to image what the building would look like in real life after restoration. There were many broken down villas that really set her off, so when her last child was born, she couldn't wait to go after her dream, which was something that was promised. When Ms. van den Berk came to St. Louis, she saw all of the big beautiful buildings standing vacant. It was similar to Berlin during the war with buildings that were there that were neglected and run down. She didn't come from a poor family. She had a very different background. She didn't believe that was possible and that is how she started working on the rehabbing of buildings. When she was young, she had money to buy her own house and didn't have a job; she never had a job and she always worked for herself. Basically, she tried to run a family and a business at the same time. It wasn't because of the money that she did it. **Religion:** Catholic

Jan van Eys, MD, PhD

Title: Retired Pediatrician, Educator, Administrator **Industry:** Medicine & Health Care **Date of Birth:** 01/25/1929 **Place of Birth:** Hilversum **State/Country of Origin:** The Netherlands **Parents:** Jan van Eys; Geertruida (Floor) van Eys **Marital Status:** Widowed **Spouse Name:** Catherine Travis **Children:** Jan Peter; D. Catherine **Education:** MD, University of Washington (1966); PhD in Biochemistry, Vanderbilt University (1955) **Certifications:** Diplomate, National Board of Medical Examiners; American Board of Pediatric Hematology/Oncology **Career:** Clinical Professor of Pediatrics Emeritus, School of Medicine, Vanderbilt University (2006-Present); Clinical Professor, Pediatrics, School of Medicine, Vanderbilt University (1994-2006); David R. Park Professor of Pediatrics, University of Texas Medical School, Houston, TX (1990-1994); Chairman, Department of Pediatrics, University of Texas Medical School (1987-1994); Head, Division, M.D. Anderson Hospital, University of Texas (1983-1990); Mosbacher Chair, M.D. Anderson Hospital, University of Texas (1979-1987); Mosbacher Professor of Pediatrics, M.D. Anderson Hospital, University of Texas (1979-1987); Chairman, Department of Experimental Pediatrics, M.D. Anderson Hospital, University of Texas (1973-1990); Professor, Pediatrics, M.D. Anderson Hospital, University Texas (1973-1994); Pediatrician, M.D. Anderson Hospital, University of Texas (1973-1994); Head, Division of Pediatrics, M.D. Anderson Hospital, University of Texas (1973-1988); Professor, Vanderbilt University, Nashville, TN (1971-1973); Intern, Resident in Pediatrics, Vanderbilt University Hospitals, Nashville, TN (1966-1969); Associate Professor, Vanderbilt University, Nashville, TN (1962-1971); Assistant Professor, Biochemistry, Vanderbilt University, Nashville, TN (1957-1962); Postdoctoral Fellow, Mccollum Pratt Institute, Johns Hopkins University, Baltimore, MD (1955-1957) **Career Related:** Consultant, Cancer Information Services for Code Ethics and Pediatric Cancers (1986-1989) **Civic:** Vanderbilt University Wesley Foundation (2003-Present); Tennessee Hemophilia and Bleeding Disorder Foundation (2003-Present); Alive Hospice, Nashville, TN (1998-2004); National Hemophilia Foundation (1997-2003); Board of Directors, Mckendree Senior Care Corp., Nashville, TN (1996-2005); Chairman, Health and Welfare Tennessee Annual Conference, United Methodist Church (1996-2004); President, Board of Trustees Institute of Religion, Houston, TX (1989-1994); Administrative Board, Westbury United Methodist Church, Houston, TX (1989-1994); Miriam's Promise, Adoption and Counseling Agency **Creative Works:** Associate Editor, The Pharos (1994-Present); Associate Editor, Cancer Prevention International (1993-2000); Editor, "Cancer in the Very Young" (1989); Editor, "The Child With Cancer in the Community" (1988); Associate Editor, Houston Medical Journal (1986-1993); Editor, "Human Values in Pediatric Hematology/Oncology" (1986); Co-Author, "Nicotinic Acid, Drug, Nutrient and Cofactor" (1983); Associate Editor, Journal of Pediatric Hematology/Oncology (1982-1992); Co-Author, "Humanity and Personhood: Personal Reactions to a World in Which Children Can Die" (1981); Co-Author, "The Howell Kindred" (1979); Associate Editor, "Nutrition and Cancer" (1978-1995); Chief Editor, Pediatric Section, Year Book of Cancer (1978-1987); Contributor, Numerous Articles, Abstracts, Papers, Book Chapters, Reviews, Professional Publications; Proctor, Workshops, Clinical and Mental Health Conferences, Annual Symposiums **Awards:** Lifetime Board Member, Tennessee Hemophilia; Lifetime Board Member, Bleeding Disorder Foundation; Lifetime Board Member, Miriam's Promise Adoption Agency **Memberships:** President, Houston Pediatric Society (1981-1982); Fellow, American Academy of Pediatrics; American College of Nutrition; American Pediatric Society; American Society of Hematology; American Society of Clinical Oncology; American Medical Writers Association; American Society for Parenteral and Enteral Nutrition; Southern Medical Association; World Federation for Hemophilia; Texas Pediatric Society; Houston Academy of Medicine; Harris County Medical Association; University of Texas M.D. Anderson Cancer Center Associates; Nashville Academy of Medicine; Davidson County Pediatrics Society; Sigma Xi; Alpha Omega Alpha **Marquis Who's Who Honors:** Albert Nelson Marquis Lifetime Achievement Award; Marquis Who's Who Top Professional **Why did you become involved in your profession or industry:** Dr. van Eys became involved in his profession because he had many role models. These included Professor van Creveld, his children, and one of his father's friends. **Religion:** Methodist

Dolores M. Van Rensalier

Title: Chief Executive Officer, President, Founder **Industry:** Nonprofit & Philanthropy **Company Name:** Huntoon-Van Rensalier Underground Railroad Foundation **Date of Birth:** 10/08/1940 **Place of Birth:** Queens **State/Country of Origin:** NY/USA **Parents:** Elwood Joseph Addison-Madeo; Ruth Veronica Van Rensalier **Marital Status:** Married **Spouse Name:** Dr. John E. Warren (2009) **Children:** Michael; Latanya West **Education:** BA in English, California State University, Long Beach (1976) **Certifications:** Certified Advanced Management Analyst, University of Southern California **Career:** Research Genealogist (1964-Present); Rehabilitation Counsel, New Jersey Council of the Blind (1985-1988); Management Analyst, WLCAC (1981-1984); Recreation Leader to Project Manager, City of Los Angeles Department of Recreation and Parks (1970-1998) **Career Related:** Consultant, Speaker (1998-Present) **Civic:** Leader, Historic Monument Committee, Paterson, NJ (1996); Founder, Watts Senior Citizen Center and Rose Garden, Los Angeles, CA (1994); Co-Founder, Monitoring Unit, City of Los Angeles Department of Aging (1977); Director, Curator, Los Angeles Festival, Watts Arts Festival (1972); President, Chief Executive Officer, Founder, Huntoon-Van Rensalier Underground Railroad Foundation; Founder, Seniors of Watts Oral History Project, Los Angeles City Hall Rotunda **Creative Works:** Author, "Bridge Street to Freedom: Landmarking a Station on the Underground Railroad" (2017); Author, "Documentation Underground Railroad Essay," Paterson, NJ (1994); Author, "Hidden Roots: When Racism is Stronger Than Love" **Awards:** Four Book Awards (2015-2016); Historic Monument Site Award, Passaic County Board of Chosen Freeholders (2014); $271,000 Historic Parks Preservation Grant, Passaic County, NJ (2013); $106,000 Historic Monument Grant, Paterson Parking Authority (2012); Outstanding Leadership Role in Public Culture of Los Angeles Award, California State Assembly (1999); 30 Community, City, County and State Awards, State of California (1972-1998); Historic Site Preservation Award, Historic Preservation Commission, State of New Jersey (1997); Bill Pascrell Jr. Award, Paterson, NJ (1996); Mayor's Award, Paterson, NJ (1996); Historic Site Preservation Award, Paterson Historic Preservation Commission (1996) **Memberships:** National Council of Negro Women, San Diego, CA (2017-Present); Rotary Club (1992-1998); President, Crenshaw Watts Rotary Club, Los Angeles, CA (1996-1997); Soroptimist (1975-1976) **Marquis Who's Who Honors:** Albert Nelson Marquis Lifetime Achievement Award; Marquis Who's Who Top Professional; Marquis Who's Who Humanitarian Award **To what do you attribute your success:** Ms. Van Rensalier attributes her success to her four-page documentation essay, Bridge Street to Freedom, which informed people of her documentation of the historic site. It helped successfully unify the city to save the historic site from being sold. **Why did you become involved in your profession or industry:** Ms. Van Rensalier became involved in her profession because of her African-American ancestry. After discovering the knowledge at the age of 17, she became inspired to fight for the civil rights of others and honor her African-American roots. **Avocations:** Researching Black history; Reading biographies; Playing bridge and cards **Political Affiliations:** Democrat **Religion:** Christian; Nonsectarian

Jaap van Zweden

Title: Music Director **Industry:** Media & Entertainment **Company Name:** New York Philharmonic **Date of Birth:** 12/12/1960 **Place of Birth:** Amsterdam **State/Country of Origin:** Netherlands **Marital Status:** Married **Spouse Name:** Aaltje van Zweden-van Buuren **Children:** Anna-Sophia; Daniel; Benjamin; Alexander **Education:** Coursework, The Juilliard School, New York, NY **Career:** Music Director, New York Philharmonic (2016-Present); Conductor Laureate, Dallas Symphony Orchestra (2018-2021); Music Director, Hong Kong Philharmonic Orchestra (2012-2022); Music Director, Dallas Symphony (2008-2019); Chief Conductor, Antwerp Symphony Orchestra (2008-2011); Chief Conductor, Artistic Leader, Radio Filharmonisch Orkest (2005-2012); Chief Conductor, Residentie Orchestra, The Hague, Netherlands (2000-2005); Chief Conductor, Orkest van het Oosten, Netherlands (1996-2000); Co-concertmaster, Concertgebouw Orchestra (1979-1995) **Career Related:** Conductor, Guest Conductor, Chicago Symphony Orchestra Association, The Cleveland Orchestra and Musical Arts Association, Netherlands Radio Philharmonic, Shanghai Symphony Orchestra, Royal Concertbegouw Orchestra, Orchestre de Paris, Liepzig Gewandhaus Orchester, Los Angeles Philharmonic (Los Angeles Philharmonic Association), Vienna Philharmonic Orchestra (Wiener Philharmoniker), London Symphony Orchestra, Rotterdam Philharmonic (Rotterdams Philharminisch Orkest), Vienna Philharmonic, Berlin Philharmonica (Berliner Philharmoniker), Saint Petersburg Philharmonia, Oslo Philharmonic, St. Louis Symphony Orchestra **Civic:** Co-founder, Papageno Foundation **Creative Works:** Conductor, Album, "Wolfe: Fire in My Mouth," New York Philharmonic (2019); Conductor, Album, "Stravinsky: Le Sacre du Preintemps," New York Philharmonic (2019); Conductor, Album, "Beethoven: Symphonies Nos. 5 & 7," New York Philharmonic (2018); Conductor, "Live from Lincoln Center" (2018); Music Director Designate, "New York Philharmonic: Chinese New Year - Year of the Dog" (2018); Appearance, "60 Minutes" (2018) **Awards:** Concertgebouw Prize (2020); Named Conductor of the Year, Musical America (2012)

Robert Leon Vander Aarde

Title: Minister, Clergyman **Industry:** Religious **Company Name:** Christ's Church on the Hill **Date of Birth:** 08/20/1936 **Place of Birth:** Orange City **State/Country of Origin:** IA/USA **Parents:** Bernard John Vander Aarde; Christina (Luchtenburg) Vander Aarde **Marital Status:** Married **Spouse Name:** Marjorie Ielleen Hartog (06/18/1960) **Children:** Tamela Joy Vander Aarde-Scholten, MD; Liesl Renee Vander Aarde, MBA **Education:** Trained in Prepare/Enrich Advanced Training (1994); Postgraduate Coursework in Clinical Pastoral Education, Lutheran Deaconess Hospital, Minneapolis, MN (1969); Postgraduate Coursework in Pastoral Counseling, Luther Theological Seminary, St. Paul, MN (1968-1970); Postgraduate Coursework in Clinical Pastoral Education, University Hospital, Ann Arbor, MI (1962); MDiv, Western Theological Seminary, Holland, MI (1961); BA, Hope College, Holland, MI (1958); AA, Northwestern College, Orange City, Iowa (1956) **Certifications:** Ordained to Ministry, Reformed Church in America (1961) **Career:** Pastor, Minister, Clergyman, Christ's Church on the Hill, Great Falls, MT (1970-2001); Missionary, Board of World Ministries, Reformed Church in America (1961-1968); Hospital Chaplain, American Mission Hospital, Kuwait; Chief Executive Officer, American Mission Hospital, Kuwait; Assistant Pastor, The National Evangelical Church, Kuwait **Career Related:** Board of Trustees, Northwestern College, Orange City, Iowa (1979-1983); Member, Executive Committee, Arabian Mission, Kuwait (1964-1967) **Civic:** Cascade County Sheriff's Chaplaincy Program (1999-Present); Chair, Language Bank of Big Sky Chapter (1977-Present); Board of Directors, Gateway Recovery Center (1996-2015); Big Sky Chapter, The American National Red Cross, Great Falls, MT (1977-2004); Continuum of Care for the Homeless, Great Falls, MT (1998-2004); Lewis and Clark Region Blood Services Committee (1993-2004); Secretary, Lewis and Clark Region Blood Services Committee (2000-2004); Chair, Service to Delivery Committee (1994-2004); President, Board, Mental Health Association of Montana (1999-2001); Board of Directors, Mental Health Association of Great Falls (1993-1996, 1998-2001); Member, Public Affairs Committee, Mental Health Association of Great Falls (1993-2001); Building a Healthy Coalition (1998-2001); Board of Directors, Mental Health Association of Montana (1996-2001); President, Board, Gateway Recovery Center (1999, 2000); Organizational Chair of Arrangements, Crop Walk for World Hunger (1987-2000); Human Resources Committee, Mountain West Region (1997, 1998, 1999); Founding Member, Executive Committee, Alliance for Youth, Inc. (1990-1996); President, Board, Mental Health Association of Great Falls (1994-1995); Youth Volunteer Services, United Way Advisory Committee (1991-1993); Treasurer, Montana Affiliate, American Heart Association, Inc. (1989-1993); Board of Directors, American Heart Association, Inc. (1979-1986, 1987-1993); Montana Region Blood Services Committee (1986-1993); Planning Committee Chair, Youth Detention Center for Cascade County (1990-1992); Chair, Past President's Council, Big Sky Chapter (1988-1990); Member, Service to Military Families and Veterans Committee (1977-1985, 1988-1990); Great Falls Mercy Home for Battered Women and Children (1977-1990); President, Board of Directors, Big Sky Chapter, The American National Red Cross (1985-1988); Member, Northwest/Rocky Mountain Regional Heart Committee, American Heart Association, Inc. (1984-1986); Second Vice President, Big Sky Chapter, The American National Red Cross (1983-1985); Chair, Service to Military Families and Veterans Committee (1981-1985); Great Falls Crisis and Information Center (1971-1985); President, Board of Directors, Great Falls Mercy Home for Battered Women and Children (1982); Founding Member, Board of Directors, Great Falls Crisis and Information Center; Founding Member, Board of Directors, Great Falls Mercy Home for Battered Women and Children; Montana Affiliate, American Heart Association, Inc.; Alliance for Youth Action, Inc., Great Falls, MT; Gateway Recovery Center, Great Falls, MT **Awards:** Distinguished Alumni Award, Service to Humankind, Northwestern College, Orange City, Iowa (2001); Montana Volunteer of the Year Award, The American National Red Cross (1999); Counselor of the Year Award, Great Falls Counseling Association (1986); Volunteer Merit Award, Big Sky Chapter, The American National Red Cross (1985); Listed, Who's Who in Religion, First Edition **Memberships:** Amnesty International (1991-Present); Treasurer, Great Falls Area Church Association (1986-Present); National Association of Evangelicals (1980-Present); Bread for the World (1977-Present); International Association for Mission Studies (1977-Present); Great Falls Ministerial Association (1970-Present); American Society of Missiology (1962-Present); Chair, Counselor of the Year Award Committee, Great Falls Counseling Association (1988-2001); Great Falls Area Church Association; Classis of Cascades' Committees, Various Times **Marquis Who's Who Honors:** Albert Nelson Marquis Lifetime Achievement Award **Why did you become involved in your profession or industry:** Mr. Vander Aarde became involved in his profession because he got the call. He was in junior college at the time and they had a religious emphasis week. The speaker talked about Christian service, and Mr. Vander Aarde felt as though he was speaking to him. He decided to change his direction of mathematics, physics and biology into the work of the ministry.

Diane Mary Vanderwalker, PhD

Title: Materials Research Engineer (Retired) **Industry:** Research **Company Name:** Army Research Laboratory **Date of Birth:** 11/01/1955 **Place of Birth:** Springfield **State/Country of Origin:** MA/USA **Parents:** Wallace Vanderwalker (Deceased 1987); Mary (Wrzesien) Vanderwalker **Marital Status:** Single **Education:** Doctor of Philosophy, Massachusetts Institute of Technology (1981); Bachelor of Science, Boston College (1977) **Career:** Retired (1994); Materials Research Engineer, Army Research Laboratory, Watertown, MA (1986-1994); Assistant Professor, State University of New York at Stony Brook (1983-1985); NATO Fellow, University of Oxford, England (1981-1982) **Career Related:** Consultant, IBM, Yorktown Heights, NY **Creative Works:** Contributor, Articles, Professional Publications **Memberships:** New York Academy of Sciences **Marquis Who's Who Honors:** Marquis Who's Who Top Professional **Why did you become involved in your profession or industry:** Dr. Vanderwalker was always interested in science. As she went through school, she eventually specialized in material science and chose to work on dislocations of precipitation and materials. **Avocations:** Oil painting **Religion:** Roman Catholic

Erwin Vanhaecke, PhD

Title: Pharmaceutical Executive **Industry:** Pharmaceuticals **Date of Birth:** 10/10/1960 **Place of Birth:** Brugge **State/Country of Origin:** Belgium **Parents:** Robert; Liliane (Boghmans) V. **Marital Status:** Married **Spouse Name:** Kathleen Van Den Haesevelde (09/10/1988) **Children:** Laurens; Liselotte **Education:** Postgraduate Coursework in Business Management, Vlaamse Ekonomische Hoge School, Brussels, Belgium (1989); Doctor of Philosophy in Pharmacy, State University, Ghent, Belgium (1989); Pharmacist, State University, Ghent, Belgium (1983) **Certifications:** Industrial Pharmacist, Belgium (1985) **Career:** Strategic Advisor Quality, Novartis (2018-2019); Executive Senior Vice-President, Head Group Quality, Novartis (2012-2018); Senior Vice President, Corporate Quality Assurance (2001-2012); Group Director, Quality Assurance, Pharmaceuticals Alcon, Fort Worth, TX (2000-2001); Quality Assurance and Regulatory Affairs Manager, Alcon-Couvreur, Puurs, Belgium (1999-2000); Quality Assurance Manager, Alcon-Couvreur, Puurs, Belgium (1990-1998); Lecturer, Ghent University, Belgium (1987-1989); Research Assistant, State University, Ghent, Belgium (1983-1989) **Career Related:** Global Head Quality Alcon; Global Head Quality Novartis **Civic:** Chairman, Opthalmic Special Interest Group (1996-1998) **Military Service:** Lieutenant, Belgian Medical Corps (1985-1986) **Creative Works:** Co-author, "Aseptic Pharmaceutical Manufacturing," Interpharm Press (1987); Contributor, Numerous Articles to Professional Journals, such as the Journal of Clinical Microbiology, Journal of Applied and Environmental Microbiology, the Regulatory Affairs Journal, the International Journal of Artificial Organs and the Journal Veterinary Pharmacological Therapy **Awards:** Novartis Excellence Award (2015); Cross of Knight in the Order of the Crown (1999) **Memberships:** Parenteral Drug Association; Team Elevate Racing. **Marquis Who's Who Honors:** Albert Nelson Marquis Lifetime Achievement Award; Marquis Who's Who Top Professional **To what do you attribute your success:** Dr. Vanhaecke attributes his success to his belief in people, and his discipline in the execution of long term planning. **Why did you become involved in your profession or industry:** Dr. Vanhaecke was inspired to make a difference in the manufacturing of high quality medicines and devices. **Avocations:** Cycling; Scuba diving, Genealogy **Thoughts on Life:** Authenticity is key to earn the trust of people.

Joseph William Vattilana

Title: Chief State Safety Inspector (Retired) **Industry:** Business Management/Business Services **Company Name:** Joe V. Safety, LLC **Date of Birth:** 03/22/1928 **Place of Birth:** Wilmington **State/Country of Origin:** DE/USA **Parents:** Andrew Vattilana; Elizabeth (Castiglione) Vattilana **Marital Status:** Married **Spouse Name:** Gladys Mary Spence (11/28/1978); Annmarie **Children:** Joseph W.; Joy Ann **Education:** Coursework, Pennsylvania State University, University Park, PA (1976-1980); Coursework, Delaware Technical Community College, Dover, DE (1966-1970) **Certifications:** Field Instructor; Instructor for Radiation Control; Work Zone Safety Supervisor; Director, Fleet Maintenance; Flagger Instructor **Career:** Owner, Joe V. Safety, LLC (1994-Present); Chief Safety Inspector, Department of Highways and Transportation, Bear, DE (1984-Present); Highway Safety Engineer, Department of Highways and Transportation, Bear, DE (1979-1984); Equipment Supervisor, Department of Highways and Transportation, Bear, DE (1970-1979); Heavy Equipment Mechanic, Department of Highways and Transportation, Bear, DE (1963-1970) **Career Related:** Safety Consultant for Private Engineering Company (1994-Present); Instructor, Flagger, National Safety Council (1997); Speaker and Instructor in the Field **Civic:** Honored Life Member, Wilmington Manor Volunteer Fire Company (1985-Present); Instructor, Delaware Chapter, American Red Cross, Wilmington, DE (1956-Present); Secretary, Talleyville Volunteer Fire Company, Delaware (1946-1998); Board of Directors, Captain of Rescue; Department Chief Assistant, Chief-Chief Driver **Military Service:** Sergeant First Class, 4th Infantry Division, U.S. Army (1950); Drafted, U.S. Army (1946) **Creative Works:** Author, "Do Something-Traffic Controls for Emergency Services Personnel" (1999); Contributor, "Delaware Traffic Control Manual" (1990); Author, "Equipment Certification Manual" (1987); Author, Safety Manual, "Pass the Word" (1986) **Awards:** Outstanding Volunteer of the Year Award, Delaware Safety Counsel (1996); Man of the Year, American Society of Highway Engineers (1994); Special Recognition Safety Award, Federal Highway Administration (1994); Honorable Staff Officer, Delaware State Police (1994); National Safety Award, American Traffic Safety Services (1992); Lamont DuPont Jr. Memorial Award, Delaware Chapter, American Red Cross, Wilmington, DE (1989); Distinguished Service Award, State of Delaware (1986) **Memberships:** Executive Director, First State Chapter, American Society of Highway Engineers (1997); President, Delaware State Fire Chief's Association (1993-1994); President, First State Chapter, American Society of Highway Engineers (1988-1990); Vice President, Delaware Highway Engineers (1987-1989); President, New Castle County Volunteer Firefighter's Association (1986-1987); President, New Castle County Volunteer Fire Chief's Association (1985-1986); Honorable Life Member, Delaware State Fire Police Association; Life Member, American Legion; Life Member, Veterans of Foreign Wars **Marquis Who's Who Honors:** Albert Nelson Marquis Lifetime Achievement Award **Why did you become involved in your profession or industry:** Mr. Vattilana became involved in his field after exploring several other options first. He spent several years working with his family business, which was followed by time at the Department of Transportation in Delaware. In the years following this position, Mr. Vattilana chose to return to school and further his education at Penn State University. There, he studied rotor programs, which provided him with a foundation off which to grow his career in transportation; it eventually led to a career in safety for the state of Delaware. **Avocations:** Woodworking; Gardening; Fishing **Religion:** Roman Catholic

Heea Vazirani-Fales, JD

Title: Legislative Staff Member(Retired), Lawyer (Retired) **Industry:** Government Administration/Government Relations/Government Services **Company Name:** U.S. House of Representatives **Place of Birth:** Calcutta **State/Country of Origin:** India **Parents:** Dr. Ras Mohun Halder; Sulekha Halder **Marital Status:** Widow **Spouse Name:** John Fales, Jr (1978, Deceased 11/2018) **Children:** Deepika; Reetika; Ashish; Monika; Jyotika; Denise **Education:** JD, Howard University (1979); AB in Psychology, History, Political Science, Guilford College (1959) **Career:** Legislative Staff Member(Retired), Lawyer (Retired);Counsel Subcommittee on Civil Service, U.S. House of Representatives (2003); Deputy Staff Director, Counsel Subordinate Command, D.C. Government Reform, U.S. House of Representatives, Washington (2000-2002); Counsel Subcommittee on Postal Service, Committee on Government Reform, U.S. House of Representatives, Washington (1995-2000); Legislature Counsel, Congresswoman Constance A. Morella, U.S. House of Representatives, Washington (1987-1994); Staff, Legislature Director, Montgomery County Delegation General Assembly of Maryland (1981-1987) **Civic:** Board of Directors, Manipal Education and Medical Foundation (1970-1992); Board of Directors (1979-1981); Staff, Volunteers for Visually Handicapped (1973-1979) **Memberships:** Phi Delta Phi **Marquis Who's Who Honors:** Albert Nelson Marquis Lifetime Achievement Award; Marquis Who's Who Top Professional **Why did you become involved in your profession or industry:** Ms. Vazirani-Fales was heavily influenced by her parents, Dr. Ras Halder and Sulekha Halder. Her father had a PhD and specialized in education for the blind; he additionally participated in the embassy of India. **Avocations:** Seeing family and friends

Leo A. Vecellio Jr.

Title: Construction, Mining and Petroleum Company Executive **Industry:** Oil & Energy **Date of Birth:** 10/26/1946 **Place of Birth:** Beckley **State/Country of Origin:** WV/USA **Parents:** Leo Arthur Vecellio; Evelyn (Pais) Vecellio **Marital Status:** Married **Spouse Name:** Kathryn Cottrill Vecellio (11/29/1975) **Children:** Christopher Scott; Michael Andrew **Education:** LLD, Northwood University (1992); MCE, Georgia Institute of Technology (1969); BCE, Virginia Polytechnic Institute and State University (1968) **Career:** Hal Jones Contractor, Jacksonville, FL (2018-Present); Vecellio & Grogan, Divisions, Sharpe Brothers, Greensboro (2006-Present); Chief Executive Officer, South Florida Materials Corp., South Florida Petroleum Services (2002-Present); Chairman, President, Chief Executive Officer, The Vecellio Group-Holding Co., West Palm Beach, FL (2002-Present); President, Chief Executive Officer, Chairman, Board of Directors, Vecellio & Grogan, Inc., Beckley, WV (1996-Present); Managing Partner, WRQ Property Association Ltd. (1997-2004); Managing Partner, Orlando Property Association Ltd. (1997-2004); President, Vecellio Realty Inc., Palm Beach, FL (1997-2004); Managing Partner, Vecellio Realty Co., Palm Beach, FL (1990-2004); Senior Vice President, Vecellio & Grogan, Inc., West Palm Beach, FL (1973-1996) **Career Related:** President, Vecellio Contracting Corp. and Subsidiary Ranger Construction Industries, West Palm Beach, dba Ranger Construction, South, Deerfield Beach, White Rock Quarries, Miami, FL (1990-Present); President, Vecellio Contracting Corp. and Subsidiary Ranger Construction Industries, Florida (1982-Present); Member, Advisory Board, Sun Trust (2002-2018); Bank Director, Raleigh County National Bank (now United National Bank), West Virginia (1975-1987); Founder, Past Director, Gulf National Bank, Sophia, WV, National Bankers Trust, Beckley; Banks Board of Directors, Natural Resource Partners (NYSE) **Civic:** President, Trustee, Vecellio Family Foundation, Beckley (1996-Present); Executive Committee Corporator, Schepens Eye Research Institute, Harvard University (1993-Present); Vice-chairman, Mini-Grace Commission, Florida Council 100 (1991-Present); Active, Mini-Grace Commission, Florida Council 100 (1989-Present); Chairman, Board Director, Economic Council Palm Beach County, Florida (1985-Present); Governor, Northwood University, West Palm Beach, FL (1985-Present); Executive Committee, Virginia Tech. Foundation (2004-2005); Trustee, Chair, Investment Committee, Virginia Tech. Foundation (2001); Member, President's Advisory Board, Georgia Institute of Technology (2000-2006); Organizer, Trustee, Beckley Area Foundation (1985); Vice President, Trustee, Vecellio Family Foundation, Beckley (1972-1996); Chairman, Economic Council Palm Beach County, Florida (1989); Chairman-elect, Economic Council Palm Beach County, Florida (1987); Commission Director, Vice President, Criminal Justice Commission; Chairman, Budget Review Task Force, Budget Oversight Task Force; Board Director, Palm Beach County Cultural Council and Art School Task Force, Florida Council 100, Floridians for Better Transportation; Member, Engineering Council 100, Virginia Polytechnic Institute and State University **Military Service:** Captain, U.S. Air Force (1969-1973) **Awards:** Georgia Tech Engineering Hall of Fame (2018); National Academy of Construction Hall of Fame (2016); American Road & Transportation Builders Association Hall of Fame (2015); Distinguished Civil Engineering Award, Virginia Polytechnic Institute and State University (2006); Distinguished Engineering Alumni Award, Georgia Institute of Technology (2002); Free Enterprise Medal, Palm Beach Atlantic University (1988) **Memberships:** Founder, Board Director, Flexible Pavements Association (1979-Present); Board Director, Contractors Association W. (1975-Present); Chairman, American Road and Transportation Builders Association (2008); First Vice President, American Road and Transportation Builders Association (2007); Regional Vice Chairman, American Road and Transportation Builders Association (2002-2005); Director, American Road and Transportation Builders Association (2000); Jupiter Hills Club (Florida); Everglades Club; Club Colette; Greenbrier Sporting Club; Glade Springs Club **Marquis Who's Who Honors:** Albert Nelson Marquis Lifetime Achievement Award **Why did you become involved in your profession or industry:** Mr. Vecellio became involved in his profession because he was the third generation in a family business and his two sons in the business were the fourth. His grandparents came from Northern Italy around the turn of the century in the 1900s and his grandfather got into the construction business fairly early on. His father followed in his footsteps and when he came back from the military in 1973, he spearheaded the expansion to Florida and the expansion into the limestone mining. **Avocations:** Golf; Boating; Skiing **Political Affiliations:** Republican **Religion:** Roman Catholic

Janet Frances "Jan" Velicer-Geiger

Title: Elementary School Educator (Retired) **Industry:** Education/Educational Services **Company Name:** Okemos Public Schools **Date of Birth:** 08/27/1941 **Place of Birth:** Cedar Rapids **State/Country of Origin:** IA/USA **Parents:** Allan J. Schafbuch; Geraldine Frances (Stuart) Schafbuch **Marital Status:** Married **Spouse Name:** James Joseph Geiger (08/22/1937); Leland Frank Velicer (10/16/1939-12/27/2000) **Children:** Mark Allan Velicer; Gregory Jon Velicer; Daniel James Velicer **Education:** Master of Science in Food Science and Human Nutrition, Iowa State University of Science and Technology (1966); Bachelor of Science in Home Economics Education, Iowa State University of Science and Technology (1963); Attended Clarke College (1959-1961) **Certifications:** Certificate in K-8 Elementary Education, Michigan State University (1976) **Career:** Fourth Grade Teacher, Wardcliff Elementary School, Okemos, MI (1995-2001); Fourth/Fifth Grade Teacher, Gifted and Talented Alternative Program, Hiawatha Elementary School, Okemos, MI (1994-1995); Elementary School Teacher, Wardcliff Elementary School, Okemos, MI (1978-1994); Elementary School Teacher, Winans Elementary School, Waverly, MI (1976-1978); Substitute Teacher, Pennsylvania and Michigan (1967-1976); Home Economics Teacher, Cardinal O'Hara High School, Springfield, PA (1965-1966); Chemistry Teacher, Monsignor Bonner and Archbishop Prendergast High School, Drexel Hill, PA (1964-1965) **Career Related:** Michigan Education Exchange Opportunity Program, Germany (1999); Chairman, Wellness Committee, Okemos Public Schools (1993-1995); Member, District Committees on Mathematics, Computers, Substance Abuse and Cable Television, Evaluation, Okemos Public Schools; Executive Council, Okemos Education Association; Instructional Council, Okemos Education Association; Computer Coordinator, Great Books Coordinator, Budget Committee, Wardcliff Elementary School **Civic:** Member, Greater Kansas City Association of Family and Consumer Sciences (2019-Present); Chaperone, Spanish Club Exchange, Benton Community High School, Spain (2003); Chaperone, Spanish Club Exchange, Benton Community High School, Spain (2001); Chaperone, Spanish Club Exchange, Benton Community High School, Costa Rica (1999); Leadership Council, National Institute for the Clinical Application of Behavioral Medicine (1998-2011); Chaperone, Spanish Club Exchange, Benton Community High School, Mexico (1995); Faculty Representative, Bonding Election Steering Committee, Okemos Public Schools (1991); Faculty Representative, Taking Our Schools into Tomorrow Committee (1990-1991); Chaperone, German Club Exchange, Okemos Public Schools (1990); Faculty Representative, Strategic Planning Steering Committee (1989-1990); Chaperone, German Club Exchange, Okemos Public Schools (1987); Co-President, Okemos Music Patrons (1984-1986); Faculty Representative, Community Use of Schools Advisory Committee (1984-1985); Faculty Representative, Building Utilization Advisory Committee (1983-1984); Faculty Representative, Citizens Advisory Committee (1982-1983); Member, Board of Directors, Okemos Music Patrons (1981-1986); Swimming Instructor, American Red Cross (1959-1961); Lifeguard, American Red Cross (1957-1959) **Creative Works:** Author and Film Editor, "The Integrated Arts Program of the Okemos Elementary Schools," Okemos Public Schools (1983); Author and Film Editor, "Wardcliff School Documentary," Okemos Public Schools (1982); Producer, Annual Classroom Plays **Awards:** Recipient, Classrooms of Tomorrow Teacher Award, Department of Education, State of Michigan (1990); Recipient, General Foods Fund Fellowship (1963-1964); Fellow, Michigan Council of Teachers of Mathematics **Memberships:** Lansing Woman's Club (2003-2006); National Education Association; Michigan Education Association; National Association for Female Executives; National Retired Teachers Association, AARP; Michigan Association of Retired School Personnel; Michigan State University Alumni Club of Kansas City; Iowa State University Alumni Club of Kansas City; Kappa Delta; Phi Kappa Phi; Omicron Nu; Iota Sigma Pi **Marquis Who's Who Honors:** Albert Nelson Marquis Lifetime Achievement Award **To what do you attribute your success:** Mrs. Velicer-Geiger attributes her success to hard work, persistence and the contagious optimism and enthusiasm of her pupils. **Why did you become involved in your profession or industry:** Mrs. Velicer-Geiger's parents encouraged her to attend college and become a teacher. Likewise, she drew inspiration from her local 4-H Club, which provided many broadening experiences at the local, county and state levels. **Avocations:** Family; Travel; Classical and folk music; Cultural events; Photography; Reading; Walking; Swimming **Political Affiliations:** Democrat **Religion:** Unitarian Universalist **Thoughts on Life:** Mrs. Velicer-Geiger is grateful for the many opportunities which teaching offered. She made connections with numerous people all over the world, as well as within her own community and state. She was able to work with and learn from many diverse people.

Grant Delbert Venerable II, PhD

Title: Artist, Teacher, Chemical Scientist **Industry:** Education/Educational Services **Company Name:** ArtMolecular Concepts, LLC **Date of Birth:** 08/31/1942 **Place of Birth:** Los Angeles **State/Country of Origin:** CA/USA **Parents:** Grant Delbert Venerable; Thelma L. (Scott) Venerable **Marital Status:** Single **Spouse Name:** N/A **Education:** United States Atomic Energy Commission Postdoctoral Fellow, Laboratory of Nuclear Medicine, University of California, Los Angeles (1970-1971); PhD, Physical Chemistry, The University of Chicago (1970); MS, Chemistry, The University of Chicago (1967); BS, Chemistry, University of California, Los Angeles (1965) **Career:** Chemistry Adjunct Instructor, Georgia Military College (2017-2019); Chemistry Visiting Lecturer, California Polytechnic State University, San Luis Obispo, CA (2016-2017); Provost and Senior Vice President for Academic and Student Affairs (2010-2011), Vice President for Academic Affairs, (2002-2010) Lincoln University; Chair, Council of Chief Academic Officers, Atlanta University Center (2001-2002); Dean of Faculty, Provost and Vice President for Academy Affairs, Morris Brown College (1999-2002); Associate Provost, Associate Vice President, Professor, Chemistry and African-American Studies, Chicago State University (1996-1999); President, Chief Executive Officer, Ventek Software, Inc. (1992-1999); Lecturer, College of Ethnic Studies, San Francisco State University (1989-1996); Executive Vice President, Omnitrom Associates (1982-1989); Sloan Lecturer in Chemistry, University of California, Santa Cruz (1978-1980); Associate Professor of Chemistry, California Polytechnic State University, San Luis Obispo, CA (1972-1978); Chemistry and Biology Instructor, Duarte Unified School District (1971-1972) **Career Related:** Adjunct Instructor, Laney College (1995); Adjunct Instructor, California Institute of Integral Studies (1995); Keynote Speaker, National Conference on Arts Education, John F. Kennedy Center for the Performing Arts (1985, 1987); Secretary, State Board, California Alliance for Arts Education (1985-1991); Keynote Speaker, National Conference on Arts Education, Chemistry Lecturer, California State University Los Angeles (1971); Pianist; Concert Organist; Oil Painter **Civic:** Board of Directors, City Quest, Chicago, IL (1998-2000); Secretary, State Board, California Alliance for Arts Education (1985-1991) **Creative Works:** Books: Author,"Footsteps in the Chaotic Unknown: Art Science Oracles Kinfolk" (2020); Author, "Managing in a Five Dimension Economy: Ven Matrix Architectures for New Organizations" (1999); Author, "The Paradox of the Silicon Savior: Charting the Reformation of the High-Tech Super State" (1988); Author, "The Natural Flow: an Alchemy of Mind (1976); Author, "The Discovery of a Calculus of Transformations in Chemistry" (1974) **Awards:** National Educational Leadership Award, JGT Foundation of San Francisco (1996); "Step To" College Distinguished Teaching Award, San Francisco State University (1991); Outstanding Achievement Award, California Alliance for Arts Education (1990); Molecular Art Appreciation Award, Alpha Chi Sigma Chemical Fraternity(1984); National Endowment for the Humanities Faculty Fellow, Michigan State University (1978); Outstanding Teaching Award for Chemistry, California Polytechnic State University (1977); Danforth Associate, The Danforth Foundation (1974); United States Atomic Energy Commission Postdoctoral Research Fellow, University of California, Los Angeles (1970-1971); Argonne Universities Association Predoctoral Fellowship, The University of Chicago and Argonne National Laboratory (1967-1970) **Memberships:** American Association for the Advancement of Science; American Chemical Society; Alpha Chi Sigma **Marquis Who's Who Honors:** Albert Nelson Marquis Lifetime Achievement Award; Marquis Who's Who Top Professional (2019-2020) **To what do you attribute your success:** Dr. Venerable attributes his success to his creative imagination, long-range vision, determination, and persistence. He received a PhD in chemistry at The University of Chicago which provide him the intellectual foundation for his development of the Ven Matrix of an Optimum System and its application to teaching, research and organization management. **Why did you become involved in your profession or industry:** Dr. Venerable's involvement in a multi-faceted career began during his creative experiences and and intellectual foundation he received in his undergraduate studies at the University of California Los Angeles (UCLA).

Krish Venkataraman

Title: Chief Financial Officer **Industry:** Financial Services **Company Name:** KnowBe4 **Marital Status:** Married **Children:** One Daughter **Education:** MBA, S.C. Johnson Graduate School of Management, Cornell University (2004); BA in Finance, Tepper School of Business, Carnegie Mellon University (1999) **Certifications:** Series 7, Financial Industry Regulatory Authority; Series 55, Equity Trader, Financial Industry Regulatory Authority; Series 63, Financial Industry Regulatory Authority **Career:** Chief Financial Officer, Board Observer, KnowBe4 (2018-Present); Chief Financial Officer, Dealogic (2016-2018); Chief Financial Officer, Chief Operating Officer, Syncsort (2014-2016); Chief Financial Officer, Chief Administrative Officer, NYSE Global Technology, NYSE Euronext (2008-2014); Chief Administrative Officer, Equities Liquid Markets, Electronic, Programs & Syndicate, Lehman Brothers (2004-2008); Senior Manager, Strategy (2002-2004); Senior Consultant, FSi Strategy, Deloitte Consulting (1999-2002) **Career Related:** Consultant in Field **Civic:** Board of Directors, SR Labs (2014-2016) **Awards:** CFO of the Year, Tampa Journal (2019) **To what do you attribute your success:** Mr. Venkataraman attributes his success to his background in the strategic side of the business industry. As an experienced manager, he was able to bring strong skills to each organization with whom he worked. This resulted in his strength as a chief financial officer in the modern world. He enjoys combining old and new practices to create a unique work environment. **Why did you become involved in your profession or industry:** Mr. Venkataraman became involved in finance because he feels that a strong finance organization is the backbone of every company. He is always excited by the transactions on which he works, and he is never bored with his responsibilities. He feels lucky to work with one of America's oldest banks.

Richard Carl Vie

Title: Chairman Emeritus **Industry:** Insurance **Company Name:** Kemper Corporation **Date of Birth:** 09/26/1937 **Place of Birth:** St. Louis **State/Country of Origin:** MO/USA **Marital Status:** Married **Spouse Name:** Joan Wilschetz Vie (1950) **Children:** Laura; Mark; Amy; Paul; Sarah; Todd **Education:** Coursework, University of Missouri; Coursework, Saint Louis University **Career:** Chairman, Unitrin, Inc. (Now Kemper Corporation) (2006-2009); Chairman Emeritus, Chief Executive Officer, Unitrin, Inc. (Now Kemper Corporation) (2005); President, Chief Executive Officer, Chairman, Unitrin, Inc. (Now Kemper Corporation) (1999-2006); President, Chief Executive Officer, Unitrin, Inc. (Now Kemper Corporation) (1992-1999); Senior Vice President, Board of Directors, Unitrin, Inc. (Now Kemper Corporation), Subsidiary of Teledyne, Inc. (1990-1992); Chief Executive Officer, Chairman, Board of Directors, United Insurance Company (1983-1990); President, Commonwealth Annuity and Life Insurance Company (1979-1982); Affiliate, Reliable Life Insurance Company (1962-1979) **Career Related:** Chairman, Life Insurance Conference (1994); Trustee, Life Underwriters Training Council, National Association of Insurance and Financial Advisors **Civic:** Co-founder, Chairman, Military Outreach USA (2010-Present); Director, National Museum of the American Sailor Foundation (2017); Affiliate, U.S. Navy Memorial, Washington, DC (2009-2015); Co-chairman, Chicago Navy Memorial at Navy Pier, Chicago Navy Memorial Foundation Inc. (2012); Board of Directors, Valparaiso University (1995); Board of Directors, Concordia University Foundation, Concordia University, WI (1985-1994); Board of Directors, Concordia University, WI; Board of Directors, Concordia University, Irvine, CA; Serves on Several Military Support Boards, United Service Organizations (USO) **Military Service:** Lieutenant, United States Navy (1958-1962); Navy Pilot **Creative Works:** Co-author, Autobiography **Memberships:** Chairman, U.S. Navy Memorial, Washington, DC (2010-2017); Chairman, The Executives' Club of Chicago (2010); Chicago Navy Memorial Foundation Inc., Chicago, IL (2010); Racquet Club Ladue **Marquis Who's Who Honors:** Albert Nelson Marquis Lifetime Achievement Award; Marquis Who's Who Humanitarian Award **Thoughts on Life:** Mr. Vie was a survivor of a crash on Midway Island, where nine of 21 men perished and he was the co-pilot. Mr. Vie was born during the Great Depression, grew up during World War II, and went to high school in the early 1950s. He began serving in the military in 1958 during the Cold War, and received his Wings in Commission in June of 1960. He was then deployed to Barbara Point, Hawaii, and was stationed in Midway Island. The forward of Mr. Vie's biography was written by the Chairman and Joint Chief of Staff in the Reagan administration, General John Vessey, and Jim Lovell, who was a participant on Apollo 13, a good friend, and a part of the steering committee of the Chicago Navy Memorial at Navy Pier Foundation.

Linda Marie Vieira

Title: Chief Financial Officer, Secretary **Industry:** Financial Services **Date of Birth:** 07/08/1961 **Place of Birth:** San Jose **State/Country of Origin:** CA/USA **Parents:** Albert Viera; Catherine Viera **Spouse Name:** Patrick Boring (2012) **Education:** AS in Nursing, De Anza College, Cupertino, CA (2000); BA, St. Mary's College California, Moraga (1988); AA, De Anza College (1986) **Certifications:** Registered Nurse, California **Career:** Chief Financial Officer, Secretary, Vieira Enterprises, Santa Clara, CA (2012-Present); Administrative/Technical Coordinator, South Bay Endoscopy Center, San Jose, CA (1997-2014); Lead Nurse, Surgical Care Affiliates (2011-2013); Treasurer, Vieira Enterprise, Santa Clara, CA (1999-2012); Lead Nurse, Surgery Center Partners (2008-2011); Endoscopy Nurse, Good Samaritan Health Systems, Los Gatos, CA (1994-2002); Nurse, GI Laboratory/Santa Clara Valley Medical Center, San Jose, CA (2001); Endoscopy Nurse, Regional Medical Center San Jose (Formerly Alexian Brothers Hospital), San Jose, CA (1995-2001); Endoscopy Technician, O'Connor Hospital, San Jose, CA (1979-1994) **Career Related:** Aerobic Instructor, Club One@Silicon Valley Athletic Club (1995-2000); Aerobic Instructor, Golds Gym, Mountain View, CA (1994-2002); Aerobic Instructor, Decathlon Club, Santa Clara, CA (1991); Aerobic Instructor, Mountain View Athletic Club (1984-1995) **Civic:** Chairman of the Board, Luso-American Financial, Fraternal Benefit Society (2014-Present); Director, Luso-American Financial, Fraternal Benefit Society (2007-Present); Class Representative, DeAnza College Inter Club Council (1999); Active Campaign, Santa Clara City Council (1980-1981); Volunteer, O'Connor Hospital (1975-1979) **Creative Works:** Contributor, Articles, Professional Journals **Memberships:** Chairman of the Board, Luso American Fraternal Federation State (2007-2008); President, Luso American Fraternal Federation State (2006-2007); Chair, Youth Directors, Luso American Fraternal Federation State (1998-1999); State Director, Luso American Fraternal Federation State (1994-2000); American Council Exercise Certified Aerobics Instructor (1991-2002); State Director, Youth Programs, Luso American Fraternal Federation State (1988-1994); State 20-30 President, Luso American Fraternal Federation State (1984-1985); President Local Region, Mountain View-Santa Clara Chapter, Luso American Fraternal Federation State (1980-1984); Founder, Organizer, Mountain View-Santa Clara Chapter, Luso American Fraternal Federation State (1980); Youth Leader, Local Council, Santa Clara Mountain View Chapter, Luso American Fraternal Federation State (1979-1987); State Youth President, Luso American Fraternal Federation State (1979-1980); Treasurer, Local Council, Santa Clara/Mountain View, Scholar (1979); Queen, Irmandade Da Festa Do Espirto Santo (1975-1976); Secretary, Irmandade Da Festa Do Espirto Santo (1974-1985); Society Epspirito Santo of Santa Clara; North Society Gastrointestinal Assistants; Society of Gastrointestinal Assistants; Fellow, Luso American Fraternal Federation State **Marquis Who's Who Honors:** Albert Nelson Marquis Lifetime Achievement Award **Why did you become involved in your profession or industry:** Ms. Viera, has always had a passion for nursing and the science behind it and the challenges that medical professionals face in treating patients with gastrointestinal ailments. Ms. Viera was introduced to endoscopy when she was a volunteer at the hospital. She was able to observe some procedures and the technology fascinated her until she focused into that area as a technician. When the opportunity presented itself for her to work in that area she went back to school and received her registered nursing degree. She had so much work experience and expertise in that area that she decided to continue to stay and pursue her career. Ms. Viera became interested in Viera Enterprises after the loss of her father, Albert Viera, in 2012. **Avocations:** Promotion of Portuguese language and culture through involvement in Fraternal Beneifit Society; Aerobic dance; Weightlifting; Gardening; Wine tasting **Political Affiliations:** Republican

Miguel Villanueva

Title: Administrator **Industry:** Medicine & Health Care **Company Name:** Abundant Living Home Health **Marital Status:** Married **Children:** Christian **Education:** Coursework, University of Phoenix (2006) **Career:** Administrator, Abundant Living Home Health (2013-Present) **Civic:** Volunteer, Abundant Living Faith Center; Volunteer, Viviendo Enn Abundancia **To what do you attribute your success:** Mr. Villanueva credits his standout success on every employee who worked under him - their contributions were invaluable. **Why did you become involved in your profession or industry:** Mr. Villanueva became involved in his profession due to the fact that the business has long existed under his family's care. He also aspired to help the elderly.

Maryann Villone, RN

Title: Nursing Consultant **Industry:** Medicine & Health Care **Date of Birth:** 01/11/1951 **Place of Birth:** Clifton **State/Country of Origin:** NJ/USA **Parents:** Edward J.; Joan C. (Strominski) Kraiger **Marital Status:** Married **Spouse Name:** Dennis Alan Villone (05/03/1975) **Children:** Dennis Edward; Richard Alan **Education:** Associate of Applied Science, County College of Morris (1971) **Certifications:** Registered Nurse (1971) **Career:** Nursing Consultant; Automated External Defibrillator Program Manager, State of New Jersey; Atlantic HeartSmart Automated External Defibrillator Program, State of New Jersey; Home IV Therapist, Director of Customer Service, At Home Medical; Director, Dialysis Program; Manager of Dialysis Unit, Dialysis Program, Morristown Medical Center **Civic:** Active, Chester Parent Teacher Association (1985-1990) **Memberships:** John Taylor Babbitt Foundation (2006-2010); Hypertrophic Cardiomyopathy Foundation (2000-2010); Atlantic Training Center Faculty (2000-2010) **Marquis Who's Who Honors:** Albert Nelson Marquis Lifetime Achievement Award; Marquis Who's Who Top Professional **To what do you attribute your success:** Ms. Villone credits her standout success on her propensity for hard work, proactivity, empathy and dedication to the profession. **Why did you become involved in your profession or industry:** Ms. Villone became involved in her profession due to her experiences with her father while coming of age. He was critically ill, but managed to survive, and she was inspired to become a nurse. **Avocations:** Gardening; Spending time with her four grandchildren

Frank Vite

Title: Realtor **Industry:** Real Estate **Date of Birth:** 02/09/1930 **Place of Birth:** Aurora **State/Country of Origin:** IL/USA **Parents:** Frank A.; Rose (Cosentino) Vite **Marital Status:** Married **Spouse Name:** Barbara Ann Decio (10/23/1954) **Children:** Bradley Scott; Mark Steven; Michael Lee; Leslie Ann; Lisa Ann **Education:** DBA, Hillsdale College, with Honors (1972); Coursework, School of Management, University of Notre Dame (1958); Graduate, Marmion Military Academy (1948) **Career:** Business Broker for Mergers and Acquisitions (1996-Present); Sales Manager, Skyline Homes, Inc. (1954); Purchasing Agent, Lyon Metal Products (1953-1954); Plant Engineer, Lyon Metal Products (1951-1952); Owner, Golden Falcon Homes, Inc.; Owner, Northern Industrial Appraisal Company; Owner, B&F Realty, Inc.; Director, First National Bank; Director Owner, Executive Vice President, Skyline Homes, Inc. **Civic:** Board of Directors, Indiana Commission for Higher Education; Trustee, Holy Cross College; Trustee, Hillsdale College; Board of Directors, Elkhart County Sheriff; Ohana House Military Service: U.S. Army, Republic of Korea (1952-1953) **Awards:** Commandment to Service Award, Sheriff Department, Elkhart County (2018); Liberty Bell Award (1971); Bronze Medal, Junior Achievement (1967-1970); Lifetime Award, Elkhart County Board of Realtors; Outstanding Dedication and Leadership Award, Elkhart County Board of Realtors; Bronze Star; Combat Infantry Badge **Memberships:** Knight of Malta; Holy Name Society; Former Member, National Institute of Real Estate Brokers; Indiana Real Estate Association; National Sales Executives Association; Former Member, Elkhart County Board of Realtors **Marquis Who's Who Honors:** Albert Nelson Marquis Lifetime Achievement Award **Why did you become involved in your profession or industry?:** Mr. Vite became involved in his profession because his brother-in-law and himself went to the military academy and when they came back from Korea he didn't know what he wanted to do. Though he had a baseball career waiting for him and entertained becoming a priest, he decided to go into a similar line of work as his brother-in-law and marry his now wife of 65 years. **What do you consider to be the highlight of your career?:** The highlight of Mr. Vite's career was having a story done on him regarding his stance on success in business. He stated that what made him successful was his family; he could have all the money in the world, but without a happy wife and family that money would mean nothing. **Political Affiliations:** Republican

Roman Vnoukov

Title: Principal Designer **Industry:** Architecture & Construction **Company Name:** Design Studio Romani Inc. **Career:** Principal Designer, Design Studio Romani Inc. (1991-Present) **Creative Works:** Exhibition, "Roman Vnoukov, The Retrospective: Architecture, Design, Photography" National Arts Club, Gregg Gallery **To what do you attribute your success:** He attributes his success to hard work, and never starting a project if he doesn't like the idea.

Cedric Wakelee Vogel, Esq.

Title: Lawyer **Industry:** Law and Legal Services **Date of Birth:** 06/04/1946 **Place of Birth:** Cincinnati **State/Country of Origin:** OH/USA **Parents:** Cedric Vogel; Patricia (Woodruff) Vogel **Education:** JD, Harvard Law School, Harvard University, Cambridge, MA (1971); BA, Yale College, New Haven, CT (1968) **Certifications:** Real Estate License **Career:** Solo Practice (1997-Present); Partner, Vogel, Heis & Wenstrup (Formerly Vogel, Heis, Wenstrup & Cameron), Cincinnati, OH (1972-1996);   Board of Directors, Pro Seniors, 1998-2001 **Career Related:** Cincinnati Delegate, YAA Assemblies (2016-2019) **Civic:** Member, Cincinnati Opera Guild (1997-1999); Chairman, Keep Cincinnati Beautiful, Inc. (1994-1996); Board of Directors, Mercantile Library (1991-1999); Board of Directors, Cincinnati Preservation Association (1990-1993); Vice Chairman, Children's Heart Association of Reds Rally (1989); Bravo! Cincinnati Ballet (1989); Treasurer, The Heimlich Institute (1987-1990); Chairman, Act II Nutcracker Ball (1987-1988); Chairman, Men's Committee, Cincinnati Art Museum (1987-1988); Chairman, Auction, Cincinnati Historical Society (1985); Alumni Committee Chairman, Cincinnati Regatta, National Intercollegiate Rowing Championship (1984-1987); Board of Directors, Cincinnati Country Day School (1983); President, Alumni Council and Ann Fund for Cincinnati Country Day School (1983); National Board of Directors, English-Speaking Union (1981); President, Cincinnati Branch, English-Speaking Union (1979-1981) **Military Service:** U.S. Army Reserve Officer Training Corps (ROTC) (1969-1970) **Awards:** Outstanding Small Cities Award, Yale Alumni Association (2015) **Memberships:** The Cincinnati Bar Association; The Florida Bar; Cincinnatus Association; The Harvard Club of Cincinnati; The Harvard Law School Association of Cincinnati; The Cincinnati Yale Club; Cincinnati Country Club; University Club of Cincinnati; Queen City Club; English-Speaking Union, Cincinnati Branch; Friends of Music Hall; Travel Club of Cincinnati; The Lawyers Club of Cincinnati; The Cincinnati Art Museum; The Cincinnati Museum Center; The Taft Museum of Art; Manorial Society of Great Britain; The Somerset Chapter, Magna Charta Barons; Americans of Royal Descent; Plantagenet Society; Descendant of a Knight of the Most Noble Order of the Garter; Colonial Order of the Crown; The Social Register; the Society of Colonial Wars in the State of Ohio; Fellow, Samuel Victor Constant Society of the General Society of Colonial Wars **Bar Admissions:** Supreme Court of the United States (1975); Florida (1973); United States Tax Court (1972); Ohio (1972) **Marquis Who's Who Honors:** Albert Nelson Marquis Lifetime Achievement Award; Marquis Who's Who Top Professional **Political Affiliations:** Republican

Edward Fuller von Briesen

Title: Builder, Real Estate Developer **Industry:** Architecture & Construction **Date of Birth:** 09/21/1948 **Place of Birth:** Glen Cove **State/Country of Origin:** NY/USA **Parents:** Elizabeth Schermerhorn (Suydam) von Briesen **Marital Status:** Married **Spouse Name:** Alice Ruth Marvin **Education:** BSEE, Tufts University (1970) **Certifications:** Lead Inspections; Asbestos, Mold, Home Inspections **Career:** President, Sole Proprietor, Long Island Lead Assessment and Control (1996-Present); President, Breza Enterprises Inc., Oyster Bay, NY (1982-1996); President, Briesmar Inc., Oyster Bay, NY (1973-1982); Engineer, Long Island Lighting Co., Hicksville, NY (1970-1972) **Civic:** Public Works Commissioner, Road Commissioner Inc., Village of Matinicock (2005-Present); Board Member, Grenville Baker Boys and Girls Club, Locust Valley, NY (1991-Present); Public Works Commission, Village of Oyster Bay Cove (1979-Present); Former Member, Board of Directors, Nassau County Chapter, American Red Cross (1998) **Memberships:** Former Member, Piping Rock, Locust Valley, NY **Marquis Who's Who Honors:** Albert Nelson Marquis Lifetime Achievement Award **Why did you become involved in your profession or industry:** Mr. von Briesen became involved in his profession after the real estate crash of the 1990s. His work took a hit, which motivated him to become certified and work in lead painting. During that time, he also became involved in home inspections, which encouraged him to further this career path by becoming certified in asbestos and mold inspections. **Avocations:** Flying; Restoring antique automobiles **Political Affiliations:** Republican **Religion:** Episcopalian

Leonid Ya Vulakh, PhD

Title: Mathematics Educator (Retired) **Industry:** Education/Educational Services **Date of Birth:** 08/28/1940 **Place of Birth:** Ukraine **State/Country of Origin:** Russia **Parents:** Yakov Vulakh; Betya (Nikelshparg) Blam **Marital Status:** Widowed **Spouse Name:** Gita Fainbron (04/26/1969) **Children:** Yakov Vulakh; Yelena Vulakh **Education:** PhD in Mathematics, Lomonosov Moscow State University, Moscow, Russia (1971); MA in Mathematics, Lomonosov Moscow State University, Moscow, Russia (1965); MS in Control Science, Moscow Aviation Institute, Russia (1963) **Career:** Retired (2020); Professor, Cooper Union, New York, NY (1994-2020); Associate Professor, Cooper Union, New York, NY (1988-1994); Associate Professor, St. John's University, Staten Island, NY (1987-1988); Visiting Professor, Cooper Union, New York, NY (1986-1987); Substitute Professor, Baruch College, City University of New York, New York, NY (1986); Adjunct Professor, Brooklyn College, City University of New York, Brooklyn, NY (1985-1986); Associate Professor, Institute of Radio Engineering, Electronics and Automatics, Moscow, Russia (1972-1984); Assistant Professor, Institute of Radio Engineering, Electronics and Automatics, Moscow, Russia (1969-1972) **Career Related:** Senior Researcher, Manager, All-Union Research Radio Engineering Institute, Moscow, Russia (1969-1979) **Creative Works:** Author, "Discreet Mathematics, Third Edition" (2010); Author, "Discreet Mathematics" (1985); Co-author with A.G. Aslanyan, "Matrix Theory" (1974) **Memberships:** American Mathematical Society; Mathematical Association of America; The New York Academy of Sciences **Marquis Who's Who Honors:** Albert Nelson Marquis Lifetime Achievement Award **Why did you become involved in your profession or industry:** Dr. Vulakh became involved in his profession because he had a love for mathematics. He started off going for his engineering degree but he chose to be a mathematician. **Religion:** Jewish

Romesh Wadhwani

Title: Application Developer **Industry:** Technology **State/Country of Origin:** India **Marital Status:** Married **Spouse Name:** Kathleen "Kathy" Wadhwani **Children:** Melina **Education:** Honorary Doctorate, Indian Institute of Technology Bombay (2018); PhD in Electrical Engineering, Carnegie Mellon University (1972); MS in Electrical Engineering, Carnegie Mellon University; BS in Electrical Engineering, Indian Institute of Technology Bombay **Career:** Founding Chairman, Symphony AI (2018); Co-Chairman, Lawson Software, Inc. (2006-Present); Founder, Chairman, Chief Executive Officer, Symphony Technology Group (2002-Present); Founder, Chairman, Chief Executive Officer, Aspect Development, Inc. (1991-1999); Co-Chairman, Intentia **Career Related:** Inaugurator, Research Centre, National Centre for Biological Sciences (2012); Member, Board, John F. Kennedy Center for the Performing Arts; Member, Board, Center for Strategic and International Studies **Civic:** Founder, Wadhwani Foundation (2000-Present) **Creative Works:** Member, Giving Pledge **Awards:** Named Among the "Wealthiest Billionaires in USA," Forbes (2019); Ranked #222, Forbes 400 Richest Americans (2016); India Abroad Award for Lifetime Achievement (2013); Ranked #277, Forbes 400 Richest Americans (2009) **Memberships:** Board of Trustees, John F. Kennedy Center for the Performing Arts

Charolette Jo Wagner

Title: State Legislator (Retired) **Industry:** Government Administration/Government Relations/Government Services **Date of Birth:** 08/12/1946 **Place of Birth:** Monette **State/Country of Origin:** AR/USA **Parents:** Gordon Green; Flossie Green **Marital Status:** Married **Spouse Name:** Wayne Wagner **Children:** Tommy; Wes **Education:** MA, University of Kentucky, Lexington, KY (1975); BS in English, Arkansas State University, Jonesboro, AR (1967) **Certifications:** Certified, Arkansas School Administrator (2001); Certified, Gifted and Talented Education (1987); Real Estate Broker License (1975-1985) **Career:** District 77, Arkansas House of Representatives (2007-2012); Sales Representative, Harcourt Rigby Steck-Vaughn Book Publishing Co. (2004-2008); Superintendent, Manila Public Schools (2001-2003); Coordinator, Federal Programs and Gifted and Talented Programs, Technology Coordinator, and Grant Writer, Manila Public Schools, Manila, AR (1987-2001); Superintendent, Etowah School District, Gadsden, AL (1986-1987) **Career Related:** Real Estate Broker (1975-1985); Assistant to the Dean of the College of Arts and Sciences, University of Arkansas, Fayetteville, AR **Civic:** Chairperson, Division of Communication and Arts, Mississippi County Community College, Blytheville, AR **Awards:** Outstanding Young Woman of America (1979) **Memberships:** Honorary Member, Arkansas Northeastern College Foundation Board; Mississippi County Retired Teachers Association; Manila Business & Professional Women; Former Member, Osceola South Mississippi County Chamber of Commerce; Blytheville Gosnell Chamber of Commerce; Former Member, Executive Committee, Economics Arkansas **Marquis Who's Who Honors:** Albert Nelson Marquis Lifetime Achievement Award **To what do you attribute your success:** Ms. Wagner attributes her success to her love of learning and her determination to work in those particular fields, along strong family support. **Why did you become involved in your profession or industry:** Ms. Wagner became involved in her profession because of the role models she had when she was in school. **Avocations:** Reading; Traveling **Political Affiliations:** Republican **Religion:** Methodist

Jack Andrew Wagner, Jr.

Title: Electrical Engineer (Retired) **Industry:** Engineering **Date of Birth:** 07/18/1949 **Place of Birth:** Borger **State/Country of Origin:** TX/USA **Parents:** Jack Andrew (1920-2010); Marjory (Willson) (1921-1996) **Marital Status:** Married **Spouse Name:** Linda Mae Beavers (09/04/1971) **Children:** Julie Elaine Knight (1979); Lance Andrew Wagner (1977); Melinda Mae Hamby (1974) **Education:** Bachelor of Science in Electrical Engineering, University of Tennessee, Knoxville, TN (1972) **Certifications:** Registered Professional Engineer, State of Tennessee; Certified Data Professional **Career:** Retired (2015); Sargent and Lundy (2004-2015); Tennessee Valley Authority (2003-2004); Manager, Distribution Engineering, Chattanooga Electric Power Board (1972-2003) **Civic:** Co-Chair, Chattanooga Regional Engineering and Science Fair **Memberships:** President, Chattanooga Engineers Club (1998); Eta Kappa Nu **Marquis Who's Who Honors:** Albert Nelson Marquis Lifetime Achievement Award **Why did you become involved in your profession or industry:** Mr. Wagner's father was a chemical engineer, which is where his interest in the field originated. One day, Mr. Wagner found an old, broken radio. He brought it home and, with the help of his father, repaired the radio. Ever since then, he knew chemical engineering was the field for him. **Avocations:** Magic; Flower gardening **Religion:** Christian

C.L. Wales

Title: Assistant Project Manager **Industry:** Consulting **Company Name:** C.L. Wales Consulting **Date of Birth:** 07/20/1956 **Marital Status:** Single **Children:** Son **Education:** BA in Environmental Design, Architectural Design and Construction, Texas A&M University (1978) **Career:** Assistant Project Manager, TX Morrow Construction, Inc., Dallas, TX (2016-Present); Assistant Project Manager, Cardinal Construction (2020); Assistant Project Manager, Alta General Contractors Inc. (2015-2016); Assistant Project Manager, Stanford Construction Inc., Dallas TX (2014-2015) **Civic:** Volunteering **Memberships:** Associate Member, Treasurer, American Institute of Architects; Member, National Association of Professional Women **Marquis Who's Who Honors:** Albert Nelson Marquis Lifetime Achievement Award **To what do you attribute your success:** C.L. Wales attributes her success to her attention to detail, tenacity, and her persistence. She always meets her deadlines. **Why did you become involved in your profession or industry:** C.L. Wales started off in architecture, worked for community development department. She was the total sum project manager on each project. **Avocations:** Antiquing; Reading; Practicing architecture

Darren Walker

Title: Foundation Administrator **Industry:** Nonprofit & Philanthropy **Date of Birth:** 08/28/1959 **Place of Birth:** Lafayette **State/Country of Origin:** LA/USA **Marital Status:** Single **Spouse Name:** David Beitzel (Partner of 26 Years, Deceased 2019) **Education:** DHL (Honorary), Amherst College (2019); JD, University of Texas School of Law (1986); BS in Speech Communication, University of Texas at Austin (1982); BA in Government, University of Texas at Austin (1982) **Career:** President, Ford Foundation (2013-Present); Mayor Bill de Blasio's November 2013 Transition Advisory Team (2013); Vice President for Education, Creativity, and Free Expression, Ford Foundation (2010-2013); Vice President, Rockefeller Foundation (2006-2010); Working Communities Program Director, Rockefeller Foundation (2002-2006); Chief Operating Officer, Abyssinian Development Corporation (1994-2001); Volunteer, Associate, Union Bank of Switzerland (UBS) (1988-1995); Cleary Gottlieb Steen & Hamilton (1986-1988) **Career Related:** Instructor, Housing, Law, Urban Development, New York University School of Law; Instructor, Housing, Law, Urban Development, Robert F. Wagner Graduate School of Public Service; Member, Board of Directors, Committee to Protect Journalists; Vice Chairman, Board of Directors, New York City Ballet; Board Member, Arcus Foundation; Board Member, Friends of the High Line; Board Member, Rockefeller Philanthropy Advisors; Board Member, Foundation for Art and Preservation in Embassies **Creative Works:** Author, "From Generosity to Justice: A New Gospel of Wealth" (2019) **Awards:** Alan Reich Award, National Organization on Disability (NOD) (2019); Director's Award, 2018 National Design Awards (2018); Listee, "100 Most Influential People in the World," Time (2016); Preston Robert Tisch 2015 Award in Civic Leadership, Aspen Institute (2015); Civic Inspiration Award, Ballet Hispanico (2014); Distinguished Alumnus Award, University of Texas at Austin; Recipient, 10 Honorary Degrees and University Awards **Memberships:** Fellow, Institute for Urban Design; Council on Foreign Relations; American Academy of Arts and Sciences

William Walker

Title: Investment Banker **Industry:** Financial Services **Date of Birth:** 09/05/1931 **Place of Birth:** Detroit **State/Country of Origin:** MI/USA **Parents:** William Tidd; Irene (Rhode) W. **Marital Status:** Married **Spouse Name:** Patricia Louise Frazier (09/10/1953) **Children:** Donna Louise; Carol Ann; Sally Lynn; Alyssa Jane **Education:** Coursework, Stanford University (1950) **Career:** Executive Vice President, Bateman Eichler, Hill Richards Inc., Los Angeles, CA (1969-1985); Partner, Executive Committee, Lester, Ryons & Co., Los Angeles, CA (1968); Senior Vice President, Glore Forgan, William R. Staats Inc., New York, NY (1965-1968); Syndicate Partner, William R. Staats & Co., (1958-1965); Sales Manager, William R. Staats & Co., (1957-1958); Stockbroker, William R. Staats & Co., Los Angeles, CA (1952-1957) **Career Related:** Member, American Stock Exchange (1981); President, Chief Executive Officer, WTW Inc.; Chairperson, Chief Executive Officer, Walker Associates **Military Service:** U.S. Air Force (1949-1952) **Memberships:** President, Bond Club of Los Angeles (1973); Board of Governors, Pacific Coast Stock Exchange (1971-1972); National Public Relations Committee, Investment Bankers Association (1966); Director, National Syndicate Committee, Securities Industry Association; Chairperson, California District 10, Securities Industry Association **Marquis Who's Who Honors:** Albert Nelson Marquis Lifetime Achievement Award; Marquis Who's Who Top Professional **Why did you become involved in your profession or industry:** Mr. Walker became involved in his profession because he had a father-in-law, Edward Frazier, who was a New York Stock Exchange member. He invited the younger man to register himself and become a stock broker, which led to him working on Wall Street for a decade.

Gerald T. Walsh

Title: Roman Catholic Priest, Bishop **Industry:** Religious **Company Name:** St. Joseph's Seminary **Date of Birth:** 04/25/1942 **Place of Birth:** New York **State/Country of Origin:** NY/USA **Parents:** Thomas Walsh; Anne Haggerty Walsh **Marital Status:** Single **Education:** MSW, Fordham University, New York, NY (1983); MDiv, St. Joseph's Seminary, New York, NY (1967) **Certifications:** Ordained Bishop (2004) **Career:** Roman Catholic Priest, Bishop, Vicar for Clergy, Archdiocese of New York (2012-Present); Auxiliary Bishop, Archdiocese of New York (2004-Present); Vicar for Development, Archdiocese of New York (2003-Present); Rector, President, St. Joseph's Seminary, Yonkers, NY (2007-2012); Vicar, North Manhattan Vicariate, New York, NY (1998-2007); Pastor, St. Elizabeth Parish, New York, NY (1998-2007); Priest Secretary to John Cardinal O'Connor (1996-1998); Pastor, Incarnation Parish, New York, NY (1989-1996); Named Monsignor (1990); Director, Department of Family & Children's Services, Catholic Charities, New York, NY (1980-1989); Parochial Vicar, Holy Trinity Parish, New York, NY (1967-1980); Ordained Priest, Archdiocese of New York, New York (1967) **Civic:** Associate Chaplain, Knights of Columbus, New York, NY (1980-Present); Associate Chaplain, Cardinal Mccloskey Services, Arc for Washington Senior Center; Associate Chaplain, Isabella Geriatric Center; Associate Chaplain, St. Elizabeth Pediatric Center, Yonkers, NY; Archcare Board **Marquis Who's Who Honors:** Albert Nelson Marquis Lifetime Achievement Award; Marquis Who's Who Top Professional; Marquis Who's Who Humanitarian Award **Why did you become involved in your profession or industry:** Bishop Walsh became involved in his profession because when he was growing up he lived in a big parish and the parish priest was omnipresent in the school and neighborhood. He was very interested in young people, the elderly and people who were having difficulty making ends meet and because of that he felt it was something he would like to pursue. **Religion:** Roman Catholic

R. Lynette "Lyn" Walsh, OTR

Title: Occupational Therapist (Retired) **Date of Birth:** 02/23/1944 **Place of Birth:** Wellington **State/Country of Origin:** Somerset/UK **Parents:** Thomas Fox; Marguerite Alexandra Fox **Marital Status:** Widowed **Spouse Name:** Jack Walsh (06/04/1977, Deceased 03/15/2011) **Education:** MEd, Salisbury State College (1977); Diploma, St. Loyes School of Occupational Therapy, Exeter, Devon, UK (1965) **Certifications:** Registered Occupational Therapist; State Registered Occupational Therapist **Career:** Occupational Therapist, Beverly Rehabilitation, Monrovia & Country Villa, Arcadia, CA (1994-2004); Occupational Therapist, Casa Colina Hospital for Rehabilitation Medicine, Pomona, CA (1986-1994); Occupational Therapist II, City of Hope National Medical Center, Duarte, CA (1977-1986); Chief Occupational Therapist, Deers Head Center, Salisbury, MD (1975-1977); Consultant Occupational Therapist, Wicomico County Health Department, Salisbury, MD (1973-1975); Staff Occupational Therapist, University of Texas Medical Branch, Galveston, TX (1971-1973); Staff Occupational Therapist, Cherry Hospital, Goldsboro, NC (1970-1971); Senior Occupational Therapist, Cowley Road. Hospital, Oxford, England (1967-1970); Occupational Therapist, Exe Vale Hospitals, Exeter, England (1965-1967) **Career Related:** Preceptor, Guest Lecturer, Loma Linda University (1989-2004); Preceptor, Occupational Therapy, University Of Southern California, Los Angeles, CA (1977-1998); Preceptor, Occupational Therapy, University Of Boston (1971-1977); Preceptor, Occupational Therapy, University Of Texas, Galveston, TX (1971-1977); Preceptor, Occupational Therapy, University of Puget Sound, Seattle, WA (1971-1977) **Civic:** Vestry Member, St. Luke's Episcopal Church, Monrovia, CA (2015-2017, 2020-Present); Volunteer, Unity Center, San Gabriel Valley, Monrovia, CA (2014-Present); Junior Warden, St. Luke's Episcopal Church, Monrovia, CA (1984, 1992); Choir Member, St. Luke's Episcopal Church, Monrovia, CA (1978) **Creative Works:** Contributor, Chapters to Books, Articles to Professional Journals; Author, Travel Journals and Travel Scrapbooks **Awards:** Distinction in Psychological Occupational Therapy Practical Exam, Britain Association of Occupational Therapy, London, England (1965) **Memberships:** Occupational Therapy Association of California (1977); Registered Occupational Therapist, American Occupational Therapy Association (1971); British Association of Occupational Therapy (1965) **Marquis Who's Who Honors:** Albert Nelson Marquis Lifetime Achievement Award; Marquis Who's Who Top Professional; Who's Who of American Women **To what do you attribute your success:** Ms. Walsh attributes her success to being good to the people around her and having a good work ethic, keeping her promises and confidentiality, and being fair as a supervisor at work. **Why did you become involved in your profession or industry:** Ms. Walsh attended boarding school and was encouraged to think about what she wanted to do as a career. Her family thought it was a bit morbid, but she was really interested in accidents, as she was more interested on the things that went on after the accident. That directed her towards health care, but she decided nursing was not an option because she disliked the hours. Her mother was an artist and she was extremely creative, so she taught her how to sew, knit and crochet when she was quite young. Her mother would make toys and taught others the art of toy making. She grew up in a small village of Somerset and they had Women's Institute groups. Right after World War II, everybody was making do and creating things they needed with what they had at hand. Her father had a full workshop in their house, so she learned at an early age about how to use and respect tools. If he didn't have a tool that he needed, he would make the tool so he could do the job that he was working on. This background drew her towards occupational therapy. **Avocations:** Travel; Photography; Reading; Music; Hiking; Church choir; Theatre; Concerts; Art; Financial management; Writing; Swimming; Interior design **Religion:** Christian **Thoughts on Life:** Timing is the axle grease of life. One of Ms. Walsh's favorite prayers is, "God, give us grace to accept with serenity the things that cannot be changed, courage to change the things that should be changed, and the wisdom to distinguish the one from the other."

Martha Bosse Walsh-McGehee

Title: Ornithologist **Industry:** Sciences **Date of Birth:** 09/21/1947 **Place of Birth:** Kansas City **State/Country of Origin:** MO/USA **Parents:** Leon Bosse (Deceased); Lenore (Carter) Bosse (Deceased) **Marital Status:** Married **Spouse Name:** Donald B. McGehee (08/06/1992, Deceased 2016); Leo S. Walsh (09/30/1972, Divorced 1982, Deceased) **Children:** Stepchildren **Education:** Student, Marymount Manhattan College (1980-1982); Student, Baker University (1966-1967); Student, University of Missouri (1966) **Career:** Conservationist, President, Island Conservation Effort (1988-2004); Flight Attendant, Trans World Airlines (TWA) New York, NY (1967-1978) **Career Related:** Chairman, Board of Directors, The Tortoise Preserve Trustee, Rare Center for Tropical Bird Conservation, Philadelphia, PA (1987-1991); Research Associate, North Carolina Museum of Natural Sciences **Civic:** Associate, World Resources Institute, Washington DC (1987-Present); Member, St. Croix Environmental Association (1987); Partner, World Wildlife Fund, Washington DC (1986-1992); Member, Saba Conservation Foundation **Memberships:** Caribbean Conservation Association; St. Lucia Naturalists Society; Cedam International; Executive Council, Board of Directors, Society of Caribbean Ornithology; Friends of Abaco Parrot; Association Parrot Conservation; Tropical Audubon; Center for Marine Conservation **Marquis Who's Who Honors:** Albert Nelson Marquis Lifetime Achievement Award **Why did you become involved in your profession or industry:** Ms. Walsh-McGehee became involved in her profession because she read and saw the treatment of animals such as birds. **Avocations:** Reading; Bird watching; Horseback riding; Former scuba diving **Political Affiliations:** Republican

James Carr "Jim" Walton

Title: 1) Retail Company Executive 2) Bank Executive **Industry:** Other **Company Name:** 1) Walmart 2) Arvest Bank **Date of Birth:** 06/07/1948 **Place of Birth:** Newport **State/Country of Origin:** AR/USA **Parents:** Samuel Moore Walton; Helen Walton **Marital Status:** Married **Spouse Name:** Lynne McNabb Walton **Children:** Alice A. Proietti; Steuart Walton; Thomas L. Walton; James M. Walton **Education:** BBA in Marketing, University of Arkansas (1971) **Career:** Board of Directors, Strategic Planning and Finance Committee, Walmart (2005-Present); President, Walton Enterprises, Inc. (1975); President, Chairman, Chief Executive Officer, Arvest Bank, Bentonville, AR **Career Related:** Member, Dean's Executive Advisory Board, The Sam M. Walton College of Business, University of Arkansas; Member-at-Large, Executive Committee, Arkansas State Council on Economic Education **Civic:** Member, National Board of Advisers, Children's Scholarship Fund; Member, Walton Family Foundation **Awards:** The Forbes 400: The Richest Americans (2006-Present); One of the World's Richest People, Forbes Magazine (2001-Present); One of the World's Richest People, Business Insider, Insider Inc. (2019)

Harold Joseph Wanebo, MD, FACS

Title: Cancer Surgeon, Investigator **Industry:** Medicine & Health Care **Company Name:** Chemo Enhanced **Date of Birth:** 08/12/1935 **Place of Birth:** Denver, CO **State/Country of Origin:** CO/USA **Parents:** Clifford P. Wanebo; JoAnn (Curtin) Wanebo **Marital Status:** Married **Spouse Name:** Claire Anne Wanebo (10/27/1964) **Children:** John Eric; Michael David; Jacqueline Elise **Education:** Surgical Fellow, Memorial Sloan Kettering Cancer Center, NY (1973-1975); Surgical Resident, University of California San Francisco (1967-1969); Fellow, Tumor Immunology, Memorial Sloan Kettering Cancer Center, New York, NY (1965-1967); Surgical Resident, University of California San Francisco (1963-1965); Resident, Cornell Medical Division, Bellevue Hospital (1961-1963); MD, University of Colorado (1961); BS, Regis College (1957) **Certifications:** Fellow, American College of Surgeons **Career:** Professor of Surgery, Boston University Medical School (1998-Present); Director, Surgical Oncology, Landmark Med Center, Woonsocket, RI (2007-2015); Professor of Surgery, Director of Surgical Oncology, Brown University, Providence, RI (1987-2007); Consultant, Clinical Immunology, Memorial Sloan Kettering Cancer Center, New York (1977-1990); Professor, Surgery, Chief, Division of Surgical Oncology, University of Virginia, Charlottesville, VA (1977-1987); Associate Scientist, Memorial Sloan Kettering Cancer Center, New York (1977-1983); Professor, Assistant of Surgery, Weill Cornell Medicine, Cornell University (1975-1977); Assistant Attending Surgeon, Memorial Sloan Kettering Cancer Center, New York (1974-1977); Associate, Memorial Sloan Kettering Cancer Center, New York (1973-1977); Instructor, Surgery, Weill Cornell Medicine, Cornell University (1973-1975); Clinical Assistant, Attending Surgeon, Memorial Sloan-Kettering Cancer Center, New York (1973-1974); Founder, Chemo Enhanced, Providence, RI **Career Related:** Advanced Training Council, American Head and Neck Society (1997-2002); Consultant, Ad Hoc Study Section, Allergy and Infectious Diseases, National Institutes of Health; Endowed Chair, Harold Wanebo Professorship of Surgical Oncology, Rodger Williams Medical Center, Providence, RI; Associate Editor, Gastric Cancer, Japan; International Adviser, Journal of Surgical Association, Taiwan, China **Military Service:** Major, U.S. Army, Vietnam (1969-1971) **Creative Works:** Editor, "Regional Therapy of Malignancy," Surgical Clinics of North America (2008); Editor, "Surgical Management for Pelvic Malignancy" (2005); Editor, "Surgery for Gastrointestinal Cancer" (1996); Editor, "Colorectal Cancer" (1993); Editor, "Common Problems in Cancer Surgery" (1990); Contributor, Journal of Cancer Education (1988-1992); Editor, "Hepatic and Biliary Cancer" (1987); Editor, Surgical Clinics of North America; Editorial Board Member, Head and Neck, Annals of Surgical Oncology; Contributor, Presentation Papers; Contributor, Books; Contributor, Articles, Professional Journals **Awards:** Special Award, University of Colorado Medical School (2007); Special Award, University of Colorado Medical School (2007); Junior Faculty Clinical Fellowship Award, American Cancer Society (1974-1977); Bronze Star Medal; Commendation Medal, Valor Device, U.S. Army Service, Vietnam (1971) **Memberships:** American College of Surgeons; American Association for Cancer Education; American Association for Cancer Research; American Association of Immunologists; American Cancer Society; American Surgical Association; American Society of Clinical Oncology; Association of American Physicians and Surgeons; Medical Society of the State of New York; Medical Society of Rhode Island; Medical Society of Virginia; Naffziger Surgical Society; New England Surgical Society; New York Academy of Sciences; New York Surgical Society; Society for Surgery of the Alimentary Tract; Society of Surgical Oncology; Society of University Surgeons; Southeastern Surgical Congress; Southern Surgical Association; American Head & Neck Society **Marquis Who's Who Honors:** Albert Nelson Marquis Lifetime Achievement Award; Marquis Who's Who Top Professional **To what do you attribute your success:** Dr. Wanebo credits his success to his parents, as he was raised with a passion for a rigorous education. He feels fortunate to have participated in numerous aspects of surgery in various high-quality academic centers, all of which are directed by highly respected academic surgeons. **Why did you become involved in your profession or industry:** After being exposed to numerous high-level and internationally respected surgeons, Dr. Wanebo knew he wanted to become a doctor. His colleagues, all of whom have various educational backgrounds and skillsets, also served as inspiration. **Avocations:** Skiing; Classical piano; Exercise **Political Affiliations:** Republican **Religion:** Catholic

James Chung Fang Wang

Title: Mechanical Engineer (Retired) **Industry:** Engineering **Date of Birth:** 07/12/1944 **State/Country of Origin:** China **Marital Status:** Married **Spouse Name:** Vivian H.W. Tan (06/07/1969) **Children:** Edward C.L.; Lorraine C.L. **Education:** PhD in Aeronautics and Astronautics, Massachusetts Institute of Technology (MIT) (1972); MS in Aeronautics and Astronautics, Massachusetts Institute of Technology (1968); BS in Mechanical Engineering, National Taiwan University (1965) **Career:** Director, DOE Metal Hydride Center of Excellence (MHCoE) (2005-2007); Manager, Analytical Materials Science Department, Sandia National Laboratories (1992-2007); Distinguished Member, Technical Staff, Sandia National Laboratories (1989-1992); Senior Member, Technical Staff, Sandia National Laboratories (1978-1989); Mechanical Engineer, General Electric Corporate Research Center (1972-1978); Research Associate (Postdoc), University of Michigan (1971-1972); Research Assistant, Massachusetts Institute of Technology (MIT) (1966-1971) **Career Related:** Director in Research, Department of Energy **Creative Works:** Co-Author, "Real-time laser spark spectroscopy of particulates in combustion environments," Applied Spectroscopy (1989); Co-Author, "Real-Time Particulate Mass and Size Fraction Measurements in a PFB Combustion Exhaust," Aerosol Science and Technology (1985); Co-Author, "Particle Collection by Cyclone at High Temperature and Pressure," Proceedings of 1982 Symposium on Instrumentation and Control for Fossil Energy Processes (1982); Co-Author, "Measurements of Spatial Distribution of Species in Helium-Argon Gas Mixtures Expanding in Supersonic Jets," Rarefied Gas Dynamics, Sixth International Symposium (1969); Author, Contributor, Numerous Journal Articles **Awards:** Five-Star Award for "Development of Tapered Element Oscillation Micro-Balance," Pollution Engineering Magazine (1981) **Memberships:** Associate Fellow, Sensor Systems Technical Committee, American Institute of Aeronautics and Astronautics (1999); Electrochemical Society; Associates Fellow, Aeronautical Society; Sigma Xi **Marquis Who's Who Honors:** Albert Nelson Marquis Lifetime Achievement Award **Why did you become involved in your profession or industry:** Dr. Wang became involved in his profession because his father worked in the Air Force in Taiwan. Growing up, he developed a strong interest in aeronautics, which gave him the ambition to study mechanical engineering. Mr. Wang then came to the United States because, at the time, there was an advance education offered and he was on top of the technological logic side. **Avocations:** Golf; Chinese calligraphy; Spending quality time with family

Xingwu Wang, PhD

Title: Professor of Electrical Engineering **Industry:** Education/Educational Services **Company Name:** Alfred University **Date of Birth:** 02/19/1953 **Place of Birth:** Hangzhou **State/Country of Origin:** China **Parents:** Jinguang Wang; Xiuying Lin **Education:** PhD in Physics, State University of New York at Buffalo (1987); MS in Physics, Hangzhou University, China (1981); BS in Electric Engineering, Harbin N. England Institute, China (1978) **Career:** Professor, Electrical Engineering, Alfred University, Alfred, NY (1997-Present); Associate Professor, Alfred University, Alfred, NY (1993-1997); Assistant Professor, Electrical Engineering, Alfred University, Alfred, NY (1988-1993); Research Associate, State University of New York at Buffalo (1987-1988); Research Assistant, State University of New York at Buffalo (1984-1987); Teacher, Physics, Hangzhou University, China (1981-1984); Teacher, Technician, Hangzhou N. School, China (1978-1981); Speaker for U.S. Congress Forum on the Future of the Electrical Power Grid with Renewable Energy **Creative Works:** Author, Contributor, 100 Papers Published in the Physical Review Journal **Memberships:** American Physical Society **Marquis Who's Who Honors:** Albert Nelson Marquis Lifetime Achievement Award; Marquis Who's Who Top Professional **Why did you become involved in your profession or industry:** Dr. Wang became involved in his profession because his father, Jinguang Wang, taught physics at Hangzhou University in China from 1952 until he passed away in 2008. He was Dr. Wang's biggest influence for becoming successful. In addition, Prof. Wang chose electrical engineering because his first degree was electrical engineering and his family was asking him to look more at the less hands on career which was considered better choice based on traditional Chinese culture. It is how he was brought up. Having a pure scientist approach to more of the applied field. The electrician job before college really made him more in favor of electrical engineering. **Avocations:** Home maintenance; Movies; Spending time with his wife

Nicholas Donnell Ward

Title: Lawyer **Industry:** Law and Legal Services **Date of Birth:** 07/30/1941 **Place of Birth:** New York **State/Country of Origin:** NY/USA **Parents:** Francis Xavier Ward; Sarah Delamater (Donnell) Ward **Marital Status:** Married **Spouse Name:** Robin Lepard (2012); Virginia Ann McArthur (06/07/1985, Divorced 1993); Elizabeth Reed Lowman (09/06/1968, Deceased 12/22/1984) **Education:** LLB, Georgetown University, Washington, DC (1966); Coursework, Trinity School, New York, NY (1959); BA, Columbia College, New York, NY (1963) **Career:** Principal, Law Office of Nicholas D. Ward (2006-); Partner, Hamilton & Hamilton, P.C. (1973-1986); Associate, Hamilton & Hamilton, P.C. (1967-1972) **Career Related:** Fellow, The American College of Trust and Estate Counsel (1978-Present); Fellow, National Association of College and University Attorneys (1991); Consultant, Register of Wills (1987-1988); Adjunct Professor, The Catholic University of America Columbus School of Law, Washington, DC (1986-1988); Member, Faculty, Museum Management Institute, Berkeley, CA (1979-1986); Faculty and Planning Committee, ALI-ABA's Legal Problems of Museum Administration (1976-1987); Member, Advisory Committee on Superior Court Rules of Probate and Fiduciary Procedure, Superior Court of the District of Columbia (1975-2018); Chairman, Estates and Trusts Section, The District of Columbia Bar (1984-86); Faculty, Seminar for Historical Administration, Williamsburg, VA (1987-1997); President, The Barristers (1993) **Civic:** Officer, Most Venerable Order of Hospital of St. John of Jerusalem (1992); Member, Steering Committee, Friends of Music at the Smithsonian (1986-2005); Former Board Member, Foundation for the Preservation of Historic Georgetown; Former Chairman of Trustees, Client Security Trust Fund, The District of Columbia Bar; Member, Downtown Jaycees, Washington, DC **Military Service:** Staff Sergeant, Counter Intelligence, United States Army Reserve (1966-1972) **Creative Works:** Author, "Dancing Across The Years: The History of the Georgetown Assembly" (2016); Author, "Magna Carta and American Law," The St. Croix Review, Vol. XLVIII (2015); Co-author, "Wills, Trusts and Estates for the D.C. Area Practitioner, Fourth Edition," Matthew Bender & Co. (2004); Co-author, "Wills, Trusts and Estates for the D.C. Area Practitioner," Matthew Bender & Co., (1974, 1982, 1993); Performer, Author, Phonograph Record, "The Roast Beef of Old England" (1983); Author "The Georgia Grind: Can the Common Law Accommodate the Problems of Title in the Art World," Observations on a Recent Case (1982); Author "Adverse Possession of Loaned or Stolen Objects - Is Possession Still 9/10^{ths} of the Law," Legal Problems of Museum Administration (1980) **Awards:** Samuel Green Award (1991); Special Recognition Award for "Will and Testamentary Trust Forms," ABA (1982); Marvin E. Preis Award, Bar Association of the District of Columbia (1980); Jaycee of the Year (1973); Named to Barrister Inn, The International Legal Honor Society of Phi Delta Phi **Memberships:** President, The Society of the Cincinnati in the State of New Hampshire (2013-2016); President, National Gavel Society (2013-2016); President General, Order of the Crown of Charlemagne in the USA (2012-2015); President General, National Society of Americans of Royal Descent (2004-2011); President General, General Society of the War of 1812 (1984-1987); Secretary, Cosmos Club (1986-1987); Governor General, Hereditary Order of Descendants of Colonial Governors (1983-1985); General Secretary, Songs of the Revolution (1976-1985); Governor, Society of Colonial Wars, Washington, DC (1982-1984); Governor, Society of Mayflower Descendants in the District of Columbia (1978-1980); President, Aztec Club of 1847 (1979); Former Chairman, Art Committee, Chevy Chase Club; Former Member, Library Committee, The Metropolitan Club of the City of Washington; Former President, City Tavern Club; Former Secretary/Treasurer, The Georgetown Assembly; Military Order of the Stars and Bars; Sons of Confederate Veterans; Order of Colonial Lords of Manors in America; Ancient and Honorable Artillery Company, MA; Order of the Crown in America; BOMC; Order of Indian Wars in the United States of America; Colonial Order of the Acorn; One Hundred Living Descendants of Blood Royal; Order of Albion; The Huguenot Society of America; Order of Americans of Armorial Ancestry; The Order of the Founders and Patriots of America; The Lawyers Club; The Counsellors; The International Legal Honor Society of Phi Delta Phi; Alpha Delta Phi Fraternity **Bar Admissions:** Supreme Court of the United States (1977); District of Columbia (1967) **Marquis Who's Who Honors:** Albert Nelson Marquis Lifetime Achievement Award **To what do you attribute your success:** Mr. Ward attributes his success to aspirations, good luck and willingness to work. **Why did you become involved in your profession or industry:** Mr. Ward became involved in his profession due to being a linguistic flop and unable to see anything with a microscope, save his eyelash, and hardly being athletic. Upon learning that a wrong answer on the bar exam, but with a good argument permits passing, the law was a natural outlet for him to pursue. **Avocations:** Golf; Flutist; Genealogy; Reading **Political Affiliations:** Republican **Religion:** Episcopalian

Kathy J. Warden

Title: President, Chief Executive Officer **Industry:** Military & Defense Services **Company Name:** Northrop Grumman Corporation **Education:** Master of Business Administration, George Washington University (1999); Bachelor of Business Administration, James Madison University (1992) **Career:** President, Chief Executive Officer, Northrop Grumman Corporation, Linthicum, MD (2019-Present); President, Chief Operating Officer, Northrop Grumman Corporation, Linthicum, MD (2017-Present); Vice President, President of Mission Systems, Northrop Grumman Corporation, Linthicum, MD (2016-2018); Vice President, President of Information Systems, Northrop Grumman Corporation (2013-2016); Vice President, General Manager of Cyber Intelligence, Northrop Grumman Corporation (2011-2012); Vice President of Strategic Initiatives, Northrop Grumman Corporation (2008-2019); Executive Position, Veridian Corporation; Executive Position, General Dynamics; Principal, Venture Internet Firm **Career Related:** Chairman, Board of Directors, Northrop Grumman Corporation (2019-Present); Member, Board of Directors, Northrop Grumman Corporation (2018-Present); Member, Board of Visitors, James Madison University (2018-Present); Chair, Board of Directors, Federal Reserve Bank of Richmond (2018-Present); Vice Chair, Aerospace Industries Association; Member, Internet Advisory Council, Clinton Administration **Civic:** Member, Board, College of Business, James Madison University (2016-Present); Member, Board, Wolf Trap National Park for the Performing Arts; Computer, Security Strategy Group, Aspen Institute; Member, Board of Directors, Catalyst **Awards:** Named, Washington's Top Tech Leaders, Washingtonian Magazine (2018); Business Achievement Award, Beta Gamma Sigma, James Madison University (2018); Named, Most Powerful Women in Washington, Washingtonian (2017); Named among the "Federal 100" List, Federal Computer Week (2015); Ranked #22, List of "Most Powerful Women," Fortune Magazine; Ranked #80, List of "Most Powerful Women," CEOWORLD Magazine

Neari F. Warner, PhD

Title: Visiting Clinical Professor; Former Acting University President **Industry:** Education/ Educational Services **Company Name:** Jackson State University **Date of Birth:** 07/20/1945 **Place of Birth:** New Orleans **State/Country of Origin:** LA/USA **Parents:** Cornelius Francois; Enell (Brimmer) Francois **Marital Status:** Divorced **Spouse Name:** Jimmie Duel Warner Sr. (Divorced 1983) **Children:** Jimmie Duel Jr. **Education:** PhD in Curriculum and Instruction, Louisiana State University, Baton Rouge, LA (1992); MA in English Education, Atlanta University, Atlanta, GA (1968); BS, Grambling State University, Grambling, LA, Magna Cum Laude (1967) **Career:** Visiting Clinical Professor, Executive PhD Program, Jackson State University, Jackson, MS (2005-2019); Acting President, Grambling State University, Grambling, LA (2001-2004); Provost, Vice President for Academic Affairs, Grambling State University, Grambling, LA (1999-2004); Nissan/ETS Fellow, Institute for Chief Academic Officers at Historically Black Colleges and Universities, New Orleans, LA (2000); Acting Vice President for Academic Affairs, Grambling State University, Grambling, LA (1998-1999); Special Assistant to the President, Grambling State University, Grambling, LA (1998); Acting Vice President for Academic Affairs, Grambling State University, Grambling, LA (1997-1998) **Career Related:** Secretary, The Conference of Louisiana Colleges & Universities (1999-Present); Member, Board of Directors, Louisiana Endowment for the Humanities (1998-Present); Member, Funding Task Force, State of Louisiana (1998-1999); President, Louisiana Association of Student Assistant Programs (1986-1988) **Civic:** Task Force Six, Louisiana Board of Regents (1999-Present); Board of Directors, Louisiana Endowment for the Humanities (1998-Present); Member, Education Committee, Bring Back New Orleans Task Force (2006); Curriculum Task Force, Monroe City Schools (1995); Mayor's Task Force for Education, New Orleans, LA (1994) **Creative Works:** Author, "Honoring the Call: Odyssey of an Acting University President" Xlibris LLC (2016); Co-Author, "INQUIRY: Investigative Nuances, Questions, Understandings in Educational Research Yield," Academica Press (2015); Author, "Be Secure in Who You Are: Justice Bernette Joshua Johnson," Voices of Historical and Contemporary Black American Pioneers (2012); Author, "Fight for the Things You Believe: Clarence Ray Nagin," Voices of Historical and Contemporary Black American Pioneers (2012); Author, "The 'Katrina' General: Lieutenant General Russel L. Honore," Voices of Historical and Contemporary Black American Pioneers (2012); Author, "A Gift to Yourself: The Doctorate Degree," "The Black Student's Guide to Graduate and Professional School Success," Greenwood Press (2003); Author, "Racism in the Classroom: Case Respondent," Association of Childhood Education International (2002); Author, "Understanding the Issues: A Study of African American First Generation College Students," "Meeting the Challenge of Cultural Diversity in Higher Education," Wyndham Hall Press (2002); Co-Author, "Employing Collaborative Learning Across Disciplines to Enhance Teaching and Learning," "Teaching Culturally Diverse College Students in a Pluralistic Society," Wyndham Hall Press (2002); Co-Author, "Enhancing Academic Achievement Through a Continuum of Literacy Activities," "Developing Literacy Skills Across the Curriculum," The Edwin Mellen Press (2001); Co-Author, "Developing a Perspective for an Assessment Model for Evaluating Developmental Education Programs," "Selected Models of Developmental Education Programs in Higher Education," University Press of America (2001); Author, "Preface, An Interdisciplinary Approach to Issues and Practices in Teacher Education" Mellen Press (1998); Preface Writer, "Interdisciplinary Approach" (1998); Author, "From Their Perspective: Issues of Schooling and Family Culture of Four African American, First Generation College Students," Louisiana State University (1992); Author, "Pre-College Compensatory Programs: Science in Upward Bound," National Council of Educational Opportunity Associations, Washington, DC (1989); Author, Three Editions, "Handbook for Upward Bound Participants," Southern University, New Orleans, LA (1980-1987); Contributor, Articles, Professional Journals; Contributor, Book Chapters **Awards:** Superior Service Award, Omicron Lambda Omega Chapter, Alpha Kappa Alpha Sorority, Inc. (2017); Beacon Award for Education, Grambling University Foundation (2016); Outstanding Teacher Award, College of Education and Human Development, Jackson State University (2014-2015); Jake Ayers Research Center Award, Jackson State University (2013); Inductee, Hall of Fame, Grambling State University (2008); Eponym, Dr. Neari F. Warner Endowed Student Scholarship, Grambling State University (2008); Glass Ceiling Award, Louisiana Association of Women in Higher Education (2003); Outstanding Public Service Award, 71st South Central Regional Conference, Alpha Kappa Alpha Sorority, Inc. (2003); Star Performance Award, Student Government Association, Grambling State University (2003); Mary B. Singleton Award, The Sigma Delta Chapter, Alpha Phi Alpha Fraternity, Inc. (2003); Citizen of the Year, Gamma Chapter, Omega Psi Phi Fraternity, Inc. (2002); Powerful Black Woman Award, Groove Phi Groove Social Fellowship Inc. (2001) **Religion:** Baptist

Tarik Wasfie, MD, FACS, FICS

Title: Surgeon, Educator **Industry:** Medicine & Health Care **Date of Birth:** 07/01/1946 **Place of Birth:** Baghdad **State/Country of Origin:** Iraq **Marital Status:** Married **Spouse Name:** Barina Y. Zado **Children:** Giselle; Nissan **Education:** Resident, College of Physicians & Surgeons, Columbia University, New York, NY (1985-1991); MD, College Of Medicine, University Of Baghdad, Baghdad, Iraq (1970); BS, University of Technology, Iraq, Baghdad, Iraq (1964) **Certifications:** Developing Faculty Competencies in Assessment, Michigan State University (2018); Teaching for Quality, Michigan State University Osteopathic School of Medicine (2016-2018); Diplomate, American Board of Surgery (1996, 2004, 2014); Diplomate, American Board of Forensic Examiners (1996). **Career:** Attending Surgeon, General and Laparoscopic Surgery, Trauma and Acute Care Surgery, Genesys Regional Medical Center, Grand Blanc, MI (1991-Present); Postdoctoral Research Scientist, Department of Surgery, Division of Transplant Surgery, Columbia University, New York, NY (1987-1989); Resident, General Surgery, Oncology, Transplant Surgery, College of Physicians & Surgeons, Columbia University, New York, NY (1985-1991); Research Associate, Cardiovascular Research, Surgical Research Laboratory, Sinai-Grace Hospital - Detroit Medical Center, DMC (1981-1985); Registrar, Sr. House Officer, Intern, General Surgery and Cardio-Thoracic Surgery, Baghdad Medical City, Diwaniya Hospital, Medway Hospital, Freeman Hospital (1970-1981) **Career Related:** Member, Genesys Hospital Institutional Review Board (2017-Present); Member, Post-Operative Complications Committee (2016-Present); Member, Trauma Quality Improvement committee (2015-Present); Member, Board of Managers Committee (2015-Present); Member, Post-Operative Glycemic Control Committee (2014-Present); Member, Implementation WHO Checklist Committee (2013-Present); Member, Post-Operative Patient Preparation Committee (2012-Present); Member, Patient Satisfaction Committee (2012-Present); Member, Genesys Ambulatory Surgery Operating Committee (2008-Present); Member, Professional Review Organization, State of Michigan (2000-Present); Member, Community Health Coalition Genesee County Medical Society (1996-Present); Member, International Medical Graduate Committee for Genesee County Medical Society (1996-Present); Member, Surgical Service Supply Committee (2013-2015); Member, Research and Education Committee (2012-2014) **Civic:** Community Health Coalition, Genesse County Medical Society (1996-Present) **Creative Works:** Co-Author, Textbook, "Elderly Care - Options, Challenges and Trends" (2018); Journal Articles, "Effect of Single Dose of Decamethasone for Control of Postoperative Nausea on the Management of Blood Glucose level in Diabetic Patients," American Journal of Surgery (2018); "Does a fracture liaison service program minimize recurrent fragility fractures in the elderly with osteoporotic vertebral compression fracture?" American Journal of Surgery (2018); Numerous Abstracts and Presentations (1984-2018); "Comparative Analysis of Paravertebral Continuous Local Anesthetics Pump Catheter with Epidural Catheter in Elderly Trauma Patients," American Surgeons (2017); "Mediastinal Hematoma Secondary to Syndesmophyte Fracture in Ankylosing Spondylitis," Journal of Trauma (2017); Co-Author, Journal Article, "Value of Extended Warming in Patients Undergoing Elective Surgery" (2015); Co-Author, Journal Article, "Acute Traumatic Subdural Hematoma Among the Elderly - Reducing Readmission Rate" (2014); Author, Contributor, 41 Articles, Professional Journals (1981-2014); Co-Author, Journal Article, "Abdominal Wall Endometrioma After Cesarean Section: A Preventable Complication" (2002); Author "A Laparoscopic Approach to the Diagnosis of a Morganic Hernia," Surgical Rounds (1993); Co-Author, Journal Articles, "The Effect of Anti-idiotypic Antibodies in the Rat: Correlation of In-Vitro Blocking Activity and Immunopathology with Cardiac Allograft Survival," Transplantation Proceedings (1991); Co-Author, Journal Article, "The Role of Passenger Leukocytes in the Immunogenicity of Intestinal and Cardiac Allografts in the Rat," Transplantation Proceedings (1991); "The Role of Passenger Leukocytes in Small Bowel Allograft Transplant in the Rat," Surgical Forum (1990) **Awards:** Men of Achievement (1995-Present); Fellow, International College of Surgeons (1997); Fellow, American College of Surgeons (1996); Grantee, National Institutes of Health (1984) **Memberships:** Genesee County Medical Society (1991, 2000-Present); Midwestern Surgical Association (2018); Fellow, American College of Forensic Examiners (1997); Society of American Gastro-Endoscopic Surgeons (1993); American Medical Association (1991) New York Academy of Science (1988); International Society for Artificial Organs (1982); American Society for Artificial Internal Organs (1982) **Marquis Who's Who Honors:** Albert Nelson Marquis Lifetime Achievement Award **Why did you become involved in your profession or industry:** Dr. Wasfie wanted a career where he could use his mind and energy to challenge existing facts and improve on them. He became involved in education because the the most noble profession was teaching. **Thoughts on Life:** Dr. Wasfie believes that true happiness is when your thoughts, wards and actions are in harmony .

John Rosser "Jack" Washburn

Title: Entrepreneur **Industry:** Pharmaceuticals **Company Name:** Washburn & Associates **Date of Birth:** 07/24/1943 **Place of Birth:** Hopewell **State/Country of Origin:** VA/USA **Parents:** Winthrop Doane Washburn; Mary Virginia (Overstreet) Washburn **Marital Status:** Married **Spouse Name:** Rebecca Wells (09/1991) **Children:** Amanda Ashley Washburn; Eric Joseph Harrison; Leo M. Cicone; Suzann Weldon **Education:** Coursework, Stanford University (1986-1987); Coursework, Williams College (1985); Coursework, University of Richmond Extension (1967-1969); Coursework, Louisburg College (1963-1964) **Career:** Owner, Principal Agent, Washburn Insurance and Financial Services Group, Richmond, VA (1996-2005); Investment Consultant, Jago Enterprises Corp., Richmond, VA (1982-1998); Corporate Credit Management, Owens & Minor, Inc., Richmond, VA (1974-1988); Regional Credit and Sales Supervisor, Moore's Lumber and Building Supplies, Inc., Roanoke, VA (1969-1974); Loan Interviewer, Central Fidelity Bank, Richmond, VA (1967-1969); Assistant Manager, Liberty Loan Corporation, Richmond, VA (1965-1967) **Career Related:** Board of Directors, Mathews Yacht Club (2012-Present); Board Member, Pharmacy Advisory Board, Greenwoods State Bank (2007-Present); Retail Pharmacy Specialist, President, Chief Executive Officer, Washburn & Associates (2003-Present); Executive Senior Vice President, ECom Consultant, Inc., Richmond, VA (1998-Present); Retail Pharmacy Consultant, Washburn Enterprises (1970-Present); Board of Directors, Pharmacy Advisory Board (2007-2013); Senior Vice President, American Wellness Alliance, Immune Health Management Group LLC (2005-2006); Director, Vice President, Forbes Clinical Research Group, Richmond, VA (1995-2005); Charter Member, Partner, Nations Business Consultant Group, Tysons Corner, VA (1998-2003); Agent, New York Life Insurance Company, Richmond, VA (1994-1998); Secretary-Treasurer, Multi-Enterprises, Inc., Richmond, VA (1988-1998); Board of Directors, DaneVest Capital LLC (1972) **Civic:** American Museum of National History (1982-Present); U.S. Defense Committee (1981-Present); NRCC (1980-Present); YMCA (1979-2006); Member, The Credit Research Foundation **Military Service:** Vessel Examiner Officer, U.S. Coast Guard Auxiliary (2007-Present); Flotilla Commander, U.S. Coast Guard Auxiliary (2009-2011) **Awards:** National Quality Award, National Association of Insurance and Financial Advisors (1996-1997); Appreciation Certificate for Outstanding Service, National Association of Credit Management (1980-1981) **Memberships:** Director, National Association of Credit Management (1983-Present); National Association of Insurance and Financial Advisors (1985-2005); President, Central Virginia Section, National Association of Credit Management (1979-1980); Chairman, Legislative Committee, National Association of Credit Management (1977-1979); The International Platform Association; American Management Association; National Wildlife Federation; Virginia Association of Health Underwriters; American Pharmacists Association; Congressional Club; Hopewell Yacht Club; Mathews Yacht Club; Classic Yacht Club of America **Marquis Who's Who Honors:** Albert Nelson Marquis Lifetime Achievement Award; Marquis Who's Who Top Professional **Avocations:** Boating; Sports **Religion:** Episcopalian **Thoughts on Life:** Mr. Washburn's advice to his 18-year-old self: "I worked hard, did well, and had a father who gave me great advice so I wouldn't change a thing. A lot of what I learned was from the school of hard knocks and I worked hard to pay for a Stanford education."

Leonard M. Wasserman, Esq.

Title: 1) Consultant 2) Adjunct Professor **Company Name:** 1) NYCEDC 2) Brooklyn Law School **Date of Birth:** 03/06/1946 **Place of Birth:** Wilmington **State/Country of Origin:** DE/USA **Children:** One Son **Education:** JD, Brooklyn Law School (1972); BA, Columbia University (1968) **Career:** Adjunct Professor, Brooklyn Law School (2006-Present); Consultant, NYCEDC (2011); Chief, Economic Development Division, New York City Law Department, City of New York **Civic:** Volunteer, Local Homeless Shelter; Volunteer, Masbia; Volunteer, Our Place in NY Inc.; Volunteer, Urban Land Institute; Volunteer, New Israel Fund **Awards:** AV Peer Review Rating, Martindale-Hubbell, MH Sub I, LLC dba Internet Brands **Memberships:** Jewish Studies Advisory Board, The Jewish Theological Seminary; New York State Bar Association; American Bar Association **Marquis Who's Who Honors:** Albert Nelson Marquis Lifetime Achievement Award; Marquis Who's Who Humanitarian Award **To what do you attribute your success:** Mr. Wasserman attributes his success to his devotion to achieve public benefits through a socially sensitive, equitable approach to urban development projects. **Why did you become involved in your profession or industry:** Mr. Wasserman became involved in his profession with an administration internship. There, he engaged with young college graduates interested in the municipal sector. He had considered a degree in urban planning, but was encouraged by his supervisor to pursue law. **Avocations:** Teaching Jewish text study **Religion:** Jewish

Denton L. Watson

Title: Professor **Industry:** Education/Educational Services **Company Name:** State University of New York at Old Westbury **Date of Birth:** 08/19/1935 **Place of Birth:** Jamaica **State/Country of Origin:** NY/USA **Parents:** Audley Granville Watson; Ivy Louise Watson **Marital Status:** Widowed **Spouse Name:** Rosa Louise (Balfour) Watson (09/01/1962) **Children:** Victor C; Dawn M. Edwards **Education:** MSc, Columbia University Graduate School in Journalism, New York, NY (1965); BA in English, University of Hartford (1964) **Career:** Professor, State University of New York at Old Westbury (1992-Present); Project Director and Editor, The Papers of Clarence Mitchell Jr. (Present); Director, Public Relations, National Association for the Advancement of Colored People, New York, NY (1983-1985); Public Relations, National Association for the Advancement of Colored People, New York, NY (1971-1983) **Career Related:** Editorial Writer, Baltimore Sun (1979-1981) **Civic:** Member, Board of Trustees, Freeport Memorial Library (26 Years) **Military Service:** US Navy (1957-1959) **Creative Works:** Author, "Lion in the Lobby: Clarence Mitchell, Jr.'s Struggle for the Passage of Civil Rights Laws" (2014); Author, Publications of Volumes 1 - 6 of "Papers of Clarence Mitchell, Jr." **Awards:** Inter American Press Association Scholarship, Chile (1967-1968) **Memberships:** NAACP; American Historical Association **Marquis Who's Who Honors:** Albert Nelson Marquis Lifetime Achievement Award; Marquis Who's Who Top Professional **To what do you attribute your success:** Professor Watson attributes his success to the strength of his family and belief in God. **Why did you become involved in your profession or industry:** Professor Watson became involved in his profession because he has always had an interesting life around him and was always able to see a storyline in every event that has happened in his life. He attended Columbia University Graduate School of Journalism because it was one of the top schools for Journalism and writing, which was his career path. Professor Watson worked with the Leaders of the NAACP who directed the flagship organization through the modern civil rights movement, notably, Roy Wilkins, executive director; Henry Lee Moon, director of public relations and editor of the Crisis magazine; Gloster B. Current, director of branches and field administration; and Clarence Mitchell Jr, director of NAACP Washington Bureau, who led the struggle for passage of the civil rights laws. As Clarence Mitchell's biographer, Professor Watson is editing his papers, which are the archival NAACP Washington Bureau Collection at the Library of Congress. **Avocations:** Photography **Political Affiliations:** Democrat **Religion:** Methodist **Thoughts on Life:** For additional information on Professor Watson and his work, see: https://www.ohioswallow.com/author/Denton+L+Watsonhttps://www.amazon.com/Lion-Lobby-Clarence-Mitchell-Struggle/dp/0761864504https://rowman.com/ISBN/9780761864509/Lion-in-the-Lobby-Clarence-Mitchell-Jr-%27s-Struggle-for-the-Passage-of-Civil-Rights-Laws-Revised-Editionhttps://www.clarencemitchellpapers.com/content/lion-lobby

George Elder Watson III

Title: Ornithologist **Industry:** Sciences **Date of Birth:** 08/13/1931 **Place of Birth:** New York **State/Country of Origin:** NY/USA **Parents:** George Elder Watson Junior; Forsyth (Patterson) Watson **Marital Status:** Married **Spouse Name:** Louisa Carter Johnson (12/10/1966) **Children:** Elisabeth Carter; George Elder IV **Education:** PhD, Yale University (1964); MS, Yale University (1961); Postgraduate Coursework, American School of Classical Studies (1953-1954, 1958-1960); BA, Yale University (1953) **Career:** Ornithological Consultant (1985-Present); Curator of Birds, National Museum of National History, Smithsonian Institution, Washington, DC (1966-1985); Chairman, Department of Vertebrate Zoology, National Museum of National History, Smithsonian Institution, Washington, DC (1967-1972); Associate Curator, National Museum of National History, Smithsonian Institution, Washington, DC (1964-1965); Assistant Curator, National Museum of National History, Smithsonian Institution, Washington, DC (1962-1964) **Creative Works:** Co-Author, "Birds of the World, Vol. 11" (1986); Author, "Birds of the Antarctic and Sub-Antarctic" (1975); Co-Author, "Antarctic Map Folio 14, Birds of the Antarctic and Sub-Antarctic" (1971); Author, "Birds of the Tropical Atlantic Ocean" (1966); Co-Author, "Preliminary Field Guide to the Birds of the Indian Ocean" (1963); Contributor, Bird Articles, Encyclopedia Americana, Encyclopedia Britannica; Contributor, Articles, Professional Journals **Awards:** Recipient, Research Grants, Contracts, National Science Foundation; Awarded, Office of Naval Research; Awarded, Army Research Office **Memberships:** Trustee, Cosmos Club Foundation (2018-Present); American Ornithological Society (2017-Present); Committee on Research and Exploration, Emeritus Member, National Geographic Society (2001-Present); Vice President, Literary Society (1993-Present); Fellow, Secretary, Council, Vice President, American Ornithologist's Union (1973-1985); President, Washington Biologists Field Club (1981-1984); Governing Board, Cosmos Club (1981-1984); Fellow, American Association for the Advancement of Science; Wilson Ornithology Society; British Ornithology; Union, Correspondence Member, Deutsche Ornithologen Gesellschaft **Marquis Who's Who Honors:** Albert Nelson Marquis Lifetime Achievement Award; Marquis Who's Who Top Professional **Why did you become involved in your profession or industry:** As a child, Dr. Watson was always interested in taxidermy. It started in fourth grade when he was assigned to collect flowers for a school competition, which led to his decision to study biology in college. He was encouraged to pursue a career in museum work by every one of his future teachers. **Avocations:** Gardening **Political Affiliations:** Republican **Religion:** Episcopalian

Raymond Coke Watson, PhD, PE

Title: Lead Consultant **Industry:** Consulting **Company Name:** R.C. Watson & Associates **Date of Birth:** 08/31/1926 **Place of Birth:** Anniston **State/Country of Origin:** AL/USA **Children:** Lee; Coke; Anne; Joseph **Education:** Wartime Certificate in Electrical Engineering, Auburn University (1942); MBA, California Coast University; PhD in Engineering Science, California Coast University; MS, University of Florida; MS in Engineering, University of Alabama; BS, Jacksonville State University **Career:** Lead Consultant, R.C. Watson & Associates (1980-Present); President, Vision Technologies Systems, Inc. (2000-2003); Chief Executive Officer, Vision Technologies Systems, Inc. (2000-2003); Chief Engineer, Teledyne Brown Engineering (1990-2001); Chief Scientist, Teledyne Brown Engineering (1990-2001); President, Professor of Engineering and Professor of Mathematics, Southeastern Institute of Technology (1976-2004); Director of Continuing Education, University of Alabama in Huntsville (1970-1976); Director of Engineering, University of Alabama in Huntsville (1970-1976); Director of Mathematics, University of Alabama in Huntsville (1970-1976); Vice President of Engineering and Research, Teledyne Brown Engineering (1960-1970); Head of Physics and Engineering Department, Jacksonville State University (1954-1960); Chief Engineer, Dixie Service Company (1948-1954) **Career Related:** Adjunct Associate Professor, University of Alabama in Huntsville (1961-1970); Science Faculty Fellowship, National Science Foundation **Civic:** Chairman, Electrical Engineering Advisory Board, Alabama A&M University **Creative Works:** Contributor, Articles, Professional Journals; Contributor, Reports, Professional Journals **Awards:** Public Service Award, National Aeronautics and Space Administration **Memberships:** IEEE; American Institute of Aeronautics and Astronautics; Optical Society; Operations Research Society of America; Institute of Management Sciences (Now INFORMS); SPIE; Institute of Industrial and Systems Engineers **Marquis Who's Who Honors:** Albert Nelson Marquis Lifetime Achievement Award; Marquis Who's Who Top Professional

Leroy Edward Weathers

Title: Retired **Industry:** Consumer Goods and Services **Date of Birth:** 12/02/1933 **Place of Birth:** Barton County **State/Country of Origin:** KS/USA **Parents:** George Edward Weathers; Edith Marie (Erbe) Weathers **Marital Status:** Widower **Spouse Name:** Juanita Eve Richter, (09/22/1957, Deceased 01/31/18) **Children:** Ronald Leroy; Terry Lee **Education:** Coursework, Kansas State University (1951-1952) **Career:** Divisional Customer Service Supervisor, Centel Electric (1977-1995); Assistant to Divisional Superintendent, Centel Electric (1966-1977); Serviceman, Centel Electric (1960-1966) **Civic:** Pawnee Valley Scout Museum (1987-Present); Vice Chairman, Boy Scouts America, Great Bend, KS (1988); Board of Directors, Great Bend Economic Development Commission (1984-1986); Representative, 4-H Clubs of America, Great Bend, KS (1968-1971) **Military Service:** Active Duty and Reserves, U.S. Military (1952-1987) **Awards:** Vons Plaque for Commissioner, Boy Scouts of America (1992); Silver Beaver Award, Boy Scouts America (1984); Big Plaque, Chamber of Commerce (1984); District Award of Merits (1981); Alumni Award Kansas 4-H, Great Bend, KS (1971) **Memberships:** Former Member, President, Great Bend Chamber of Commerce (1984); Former Show Chairman, Three-Eye Show (1984); Ambassadors Club; President, Kiwanis; The First Congregation United Church of Christ **Marquis Who's Who Honors:** Albert Nelson Marquis Lifetime Achievement Award **Why did you become involved in your profession or industry:** Mr. Weathers went into his profession because he was laid off from a mobile home company. As he was exploring his options, a friend of his told him about a service job at Centel Electric; Mr. Weathers took the job. Over the years, he continually moved up the ranks. **Avocations:** Woodworking **Political Affiliations:** Republican **Religion:** Christian

Robert Weber, EdD

Title: Adapted Physical Education Educator, Academic Administrator **Industry:** Education/ Educational Services **Date of Birth:** 10/11/1948 **Place of Birth:** West Union **State/Country of Origin:** IA/USA **Parents:** Victor Duane Weber; Elaine I. (Johnson) Weber **Marital Status:** Divorced **Spouse Name:** Debra Elaine Nay (08/12/1972, Divorced 1980) **Children:** Heidi Harris; Mindy Weber; Ryan Weber **Education:** EdD in Special Physical Education and Administration, University of Utah (1985); MS in Physical Education, Eastern Illinois University (1973); BS in Physical Education and Health, Bemidji State University, MN (1971) **Certifications:** Teaching Certificate, States of Minnesota, Illinois, Utah, Texas, North Carolina, Wisconsin (1971); Water Safety Instructor; Red Cross First Aid Instructor **Career:** Graduate Coordinator, Adapted Physical Education, Part-Time Graduate Teacher, Department of Kinesiology and Health, University of Wisconsin Oshkosh (2011-2014); Professor, Department of Kinesiology and Health, University of Wisconsin Oshkosh (2009-2011); Chair, Division of Health, Physical Education, and Recreation, Associate Professor, Division of Health, Physical Education, and Recreation, The University of South Dakota (2007-2009); Coordinator, Adapted Physical Education, Associate Professor, Division of Health, Physical Education, and Recreation, The University of South Dakota (2007-2009); Coordinator, Adapted Physical Education, University of Wisconsin Oshkosh (2002-2008); Associate Professor, Physical Education, Minnesota State University, Mankato, MN (2000-2002); Physical Education Teacher, Dakota Memorial School (1999-2000); Assistant Professor, Physical Education, Minot State University, Minot, MN (1998-1999); Assistant Professor, Physical Education, Bemidji State University (1996-1997); Assistant Professor, Coordinator, Adapted Physical Education Program, Texas Tech University, Lubbock, TX (1996); Assistant Professor, Eastern Illinois University, Charleston, IL (1987-1989); Supervisor, Special Physical Education, Lubbock State School (1981-1983); Assistant Professor, Health and Physical Education, Coach, Dakota State College (now Dakota State University), Madison, SD (1978-1980); Teacher, Driver's Education, Football and Track Coach, Virden High School (1975-1978); Instructor, Coach, Director, Intramural Sports, Iowa Wesleyan College, Mount Pleasant, IA (1973-1975); Graduate Assistant, Eastern Illinois University, Charleston, IL (1972-1973); Teacher, Elementary Physical Education, Assistant Basketball Coach, Charleston Public Schools (1972-1973); Director, Recreation and Adult Education, Coach, Cass Lake Public Schools (1971-1972) **Career Related:** Adjunct Professor of Education (1996-Present); Kicking Coach, Football Team, Bemidji State University (2014); Assistant Editor (2004-2011); Southern Illinois University, Carbondale, IL (1986-1987); Adjunct Professor of Education (1985-1986); Lecturer, University of North Carolina, Wilmington, NC (1983-1984); Instructor, University of Utah, Salt Lake City, UT (1981); Counselor, Therapeutic Recreation, Camp Kostopulos, Salt Lake City, UT (1981); Salt Lake City EBD and TMR Group (1981); Counselor, Northwest Juvenile Training Center, Bemidji State University (1980); Consultant, Lecturer in Field **Civic:** Treasurer, Bemidji Lions Club (2015-Present); United States Coordinator, Lions Clubs District 5M 10, Special Olympics (2013-Present); Board of Directors, Bemidji Lions Club (2012-Present); Board of Directors, Paul Bunyan Chapter, Fishing Has No Boundaries (2012-Present); Advisory Board, Region 17 (1989-Present); Advisor South Plains Wheelchair Spokers (1989-Present); Volunteer, Special Olympics (1987-Present) **Creative Works:** Developer, Audio-Visual Aids, 4 Books; Author, 160 Abstracts, Professional Journals; Author, "Dealing with Teaching Motor Skills to Genetic Degenerate Youngster"; Speaker, 120 Presentations, National and International Professional Conferences **Awards:** International President's Certificate of Appreciation Award for Recognition of Distinguished Achievement, Lions Club International (2016-2017); Adapted Physical Council's Service Award, American Alliance for Health, Physical Education, Recreation and AAALF (2011); Evening of Stars, Civic Engagement Award, Oshkosh Chamber of Commerce, University of Wisconsin Oshkosh, Outstanding Service to the Community and Use of Service Learning (2007); Tommy Wilson Award for Significant Contribution to Recreation for Individuals with Disabilities, American Alliance for Health, Physical Education, Recreation, Dance National Convention (2005); In-Fisherman Fox Valley Award, Significant Contribution to Fishing, Wisconsin (2004) **Memberships:** Physical Education, Recreation, and Dance Representative, Region 17 (1989-Present); Presenter, Various Conferences, Alliance for Health; National Association of Sports and Physical Education; Adapted Physical Education Academy; National Consortium on Physical Education and Recreation for Handicapped; International Federation for Adapted Physical Activities; Leisure Special Populations **Marquis Who's Who Honors:** Albert Nelson Marquis Lifetime Achievement Award **Why did you become involved in your profession or industry:** Dr. Weber chose to pursue a career in education and coaching during his time in college. **Avocations:** Golf; Hunting; Fishing; Reading; Travel **Political Affiliations:** Independent **Religion:** Presbyterian

Robert E. Weems Jr.

Title: Willard W. Garvey Distinguished Professor of Business History **Industry:** Education/Educational Services **Company Name:** Wichita State University **Date of Birth:** 10/17/1951 **Place of Birth:** Chicago **State/Country of Origin:** IL/USA **Parents:** Robert Everett Weems Senior; Dolores Jean Weems **Marital Status:** Married **Spouse Name:** Clenora Hudson **Children:** Nima **Education:** PhD in History, University of Wisconsin Madison (1987); MA in History, University of Wisconsin Milwaukee (1982); MA in Afro-American Studies, Boston University (1975); BA in History, Western Illinois University (1973) **Career:** Professor, History, University of Missouri, Columbia (1999-Present); Interim Associate Vice Chancellor for Equity, University of Missouri, Columbia; Assistant Professor, Associate Professor, History, University of Missouri, Columbia (1990-1999); Assistant Professor, History and African American Studies, University of Iowa (1988-1990); Teacher, History, Milwaukee Public Schools, Milwaukee, WI (1977-1983); Instructor, History, Middlesex Community College, Boston, MA (1974-1975); Willard W. Garvey Distinguished Professor of Business & History, Wichita State University **Civic:** Minority Men's Network, Columbia; Board of directors, Kansas African Museum, (2013-Present); Former Chair, Kansas African Museum; Board of Directors, Heartland Wichita Black Chamber of Commerce **Creative Works:** "The Merchant Prince of Black Chicago: Anthony Overton and the Building of a Financial Empire" (2020); Historical Adviser, Appeared in Documentary, "Boss: The African American Experience in Business," PBS (2019); "Building the Black Metropolis: African American Entrepreneurship in Chicago" (2017); "Business in Black and White: American Presidents and Black Entrepreneurs in the Twentieth Century" (2009); "Desegregating the Dollar: African American Consumerism in the Twentieth Century" (1998); "Black Business in the Black Metropolis: The Chicago Metropolitan Assurance Company, 1925-1985" (1996) **Memberships:** Organization of American Historians; American Historical Association; Association for Study of African American Life and History, Inc.; Phi Alpha Theta **Marquis Who's Who Honors:** Albert Nelson Marquis Lifetime Achievement Award; Marquis Who's Who Top Professional **Why did you become involved in your profession or industry:** Mr. Weems completed his PhD dissertation on an African American insurance company in Chicago that he later revised in his first book. He did not know a lot about the insurance industry before he began doing that research, but within a short period of time, as he learned more about the insurance business, it became clear to him why that business was so important in a lot of African-American communities. At any given time, there were more people alive paying premiums than there were dying and causing the company to pay death benefits. These companies had to figure out how to invest their surpluses, which caused a lot of African-American insurance companies to reinvest their surpluses back into their communities in the form of mortgage loans and other types of money. To Mr. Weems, that was so fascinating and important, especially in terms of community economic development. **Avocations:** Jazz enthusiast; Music; Documentaries; Exercise; Staying fit

Donald Charles "Don" Wegmiller, MHA, FACHE

Title: Chairman, Chief Executive Officer **Industry:** Health, Wellness and Fitness **Company Name:** Scottsdale Institute, C-Suite Resources **Date of Birth:** 09/25/1938 **Place of Birth:** Cloquet **State/Country of Origin:** MN/USA **Marital Status:** Married **Spouse Name:** Janet A. Listerud (04/27/1957) **Children:** Katherine; Mark; Dean **Education:** MHA, University of Minnesota (1962); BA, University of Minnesota (1960) **Certifications:** FACHE **Career:** Chairman, Chief Executive Officer, Scottsdale Institute (2012-Present); Chairman, Founder, C-Suite Resources (2010-Present); Chairman Emeritus, Gallagher Integrated Healthcare (Formerly Clark/Bardes Consulting-Healthcare Group) (2008-Present); Chairman, Clark/Bardes Consulting-Healthcare Group, Minneapolis, MN (2002-2008); Vice Chairman, Scottsdale Institute (1993-2012); President, Chief Executive Officer, Clark/Bardes Consulting-Healthcare Group, Minneapolis, MN (1993-2002); President, HealthSpan, Minneapolis, MN (1992-1993); President, Chief Executive Officer, Health One Corp., Minneapolis, MN (1987-1992); President, Health Central Corp., Minneapolis, MN (1980-1987); President, Health Central, Inc., Minneapolis, MN (1978-1980); Senior Vice President, Health Central System, Minneapolis, MN (1976-1978); Administrator, Fairview-Southdale Hospital, Minneapolis, MN (1966-1976); Assistant Administrator, Fairview-Southdale Hospital, Minneapolis, MN (1965-1966); Assistant Administrator, Fairview Hospital, Minneapolis, MN (1962-1965) **Career Related:** Clinical Faculty, Lecturer, Duke University (1981-Present); Lecturer, Adjunct Faculty, University of Minnesota (1980-Present); Preceptor, Clinical Faculty, University of Minnesota (1975-Present); Member, Leadership Advisory Committee, American College of Healthcare Executives (1994); Keynote Speaker, Australian Private Hospitals Association 10th National Congress (1990); National Coordinator, U.S. International Hospital Federation (1987); Board of Directors, Allete, ADESA, Omnicell, CareMedic, MedAssets, Third Millenium Healthcare, Vivius, JLJ Medical Devices, LecTec, SelectCare, Possis Medical, McKesson HBOC, INPhyNet Medical Management, LifeRate Systems, International Clinical Laboratories, Richfield Bank & Trust; Chairman, American Hospital Association (1986-1988); National Coordinator, Health Providers Insurance Co., Hospital Research and Educational Trust, Medical Graphics Corp., HBO & Co., G.D. Searle & Co., Minnesota Power, Profile Group, LifeRate U.S. Del. Kings's Fund International (1985); Board of Directors, Health Providers Insurance Co., Hospital Research and Educational Trust, Medical Graphics Corp., HBO & Co., G.D. Searle & Co., Minnesota Power, Profile Group, LifeRate U.S. Del. Kings's Fund International (1979-1985); Consultant, Division of Medical Services, U.S. Department of State, Washington DC (1975) **Civic:** Trustee, National Advisory Council on Social Security (1989-Present); Advisory Committee, Sen. Durenberger's Health Care, Minneapolis, MN (1979-Present); Staff Assistant to Presidents Nixon, Ford and Reagan (1972-1988); Chairman, Board Education, Richfield, MN (1971-1974) **Creative Works:** Member, Advisory Board, Health Management Quarterly Magazine; Editorial Board, Frontiers, American College of Healthcare Executives Publication; Contributor, Over 200 Articles, Professional Journals **Awards:** Healthcare Hall of Fame (2013); Merit Award, Duke University Program in Healthcare Administration Alumni Association (1990); Distinguished Service Award, Minnesota Hospital Association (1988); National Healthcare Award, B'nai B'rith (1987); Young Man of the Year Award (1971); Outstanding President of the Year Award, Minneapolis Jaycees (1969); Robert S. Hudgen's Award, American College of Health Care Executives (1969); Outstanding Director, Minneapolis Business Magazine **Memberships:** Chairman, Board of Trustees, American Hospital Association (1987); Fellow, American College of Health Care Executives; Minnesota Hospital Association; Lodges; Rotary **Marquis Who's Who Honors:** Albert Nelson Marquis Lifetime Achievement Award **To what do you attribute your success:** Mr. Wegmiller attributes his success to great teams of co-workers in every business organization he was a part of. **Why did you become involved in your profession or industry:** Mr. Wegmiller became involved in his profession because when he was in high school he started thinking ahead of what he wanted to do with his life. He was always interested in things related to medicine and he was very impressed with physicians and nurses and what they did with humanity. So he was trying to decide whether medicine should be his career or business should be his career. He felt something in medicine would be better for him to study. He was lucky to run into someone who was in his residency year of a degree in healthcare administration and he asked him what he was thinking of doing. He told him he was thinking of going into medicine or business and the resident told him that he might consider thinking of doing what he was doing which was hospital administration which was a side of business and a side of medicine. He thought about it and felt it might be a good way to blend both of his interest and so that was why he chose to do his graduate education in healthcare administration and it went on from there. **Avocations:** Golf; Skiing; Travel **Political Affiliations:** Republican **Religion:** Methodist

Douglas John Weichman

Title: Fleet Manager of County Government **Industry:** Automotive **Date of Birth:** 05/23/1956 **Place of Birth:** Lakeview **State/Country of Origin:** MI/USA **Parents:** George Ludwig Weichman; Phyllis Bertha (Baker) Weichman **Marital Status:** Married **Spouse Name:** Teresa Marie Bevier (05/03/1980) **Children:** Kyle Douglas; Rebecca Marie **Education:** Postgraduate Coursework, Instructions Course on Alternate Fuel, U.S. Department of Transportation, Tampa, FL (1995); BSc, Ferris State University (1978) **Certifications:** Certified Automotive Fleet Manager **Career:** Director, City Fleet Management, City of Gainesville/Gainesville Regional Utility, FL (2017-Present); Director, Fleet Management, Palm Beach County, West Palm Beach, FL (1990-2017); Fleet Service Manager, Metropolitan Dade County, Miami, FL (1982-1990); Shop Supervisor, McLouth Steel, Trenton, MI (1979-1981); Supervisor, Equipment Maintenance, Purolator Security (Purolator, Inc.), Detroit, MI (1978-1979) **Career Related:** Member, Accident Review Board, West Palm Beach, FL (1995-2017); Instructor, Various Fleet Management Programs and Conferences **Civic:** Chairman, City of Gainesville Charitable Giving Campaign (2018); Chairman, School Advisor Committee, Palm Beach County, FL (1998, 2000); Cub Scout Leader, Boy Scouts of America, Jupiter, FL (1995-2000); Government Appointee Chairman, United Way of Palm Beach County, West Palm Beach, FL (1996); Board of Directors, Clean Cities Coalition, Hollywood, FL (1996) **Creative Works:** Presenter, Television Program, Government Service TV Network; Contributor, Articles to Professional Journals **Awards:** Recipient, Alternative Fuels Grant, State of Florida, Department of Community Affairs (1994, 1995) **Memberships:** Past President, NAFA Fleet Management Association; Florida Association of Governmental Fleet Administrators (FLAGFA) **Marquis Who's Who Honors:** Albert Nelson Marquis Lifetime Achievement Award **Why did you become involved in your profession or industry:** When Mr. Weichman was about 5 years old, he took his parents' lawn mower apart; he has always been mechanically inclined and he has always wanted to be in the mechanical industry. Through high school, Mr. Weichman followed that routine, and at the time, he was attending college. He had a choice of two colleges that offered automotive and heavy equipment technology; he attended Ferris State University for his four year degree. **Avocations:** Boating; Golf; Racquetball; Corvette activities and associations; Fishing **Thoughts on Life:** Mr. Weichman is involved on the NAFA Foundation board, which was established to interact with universities regarding certification. They provide a $2,500 scholarship to a student each year.

Wanda Opal Weickert

Title: Child Welfare and Attendance Counselor, Psychotherapist, Educator (Retired) **Industry:** Social Work **Date of Birth:** 04/10/1941 **Place of Birth:** LaCygne **State/Country of Origin:** KS/USA **Parents:** Frank W. Weickert; Opal M. Weickert **Marital Status:** Widowed **Spouse Name:** Janice Parnell (Deceased 2018); Carol Cichowski (Deceased 2007) **Education:** MA in Marriage and Family Therapy, Phillips Graduate Institute (1983-1985); MPE, Kansas State College (1963-1966); BPE, Kansas State College (1959-1963) **Certifications:** Marriage, Family, Child Therapist, Board of Behavioral Sciences, State of California (1991); Pupil Personnel Services Credential, California Lutheran College (1987-1989); Teaching Credential, State of California (1969); Teaching Credential, State of Kansas (1963) **Career:** Marriage, Family, Child Therapist, Self Employed, Los Angeles, CA (1991-2010); Child Welfare & Attendance Counselor, Los Angeles Unified School District (1989-2001); Career Education, Coach, Teacher, Kennedy Senior High School, Los Angeles, CA (1981-1989); Coach & Physical Education Teacher, Reseda Senior High School, Los Angeles, CA (1973-1981); Physical Education Teacher, Nightingale Middle School, Los Angeles, CA (1969-1973); Health and Physical Education Teacher, Circle High School, Towanda, KS (1963-1969) **Career Related:** Crisis Team Leader, Los Angeles Unified Schools (1996-2001); Advisory Board, School Attendance Review Board, Los Angeles Unified School District, Los Angeles, CA (1991-2001); Counselor, Valley Community Clinic, North Hollywood, CA (1989-1992); Drug Prevention Program Director, Kennedy High School, Los Angeles, CA (1987-1989); Counselor, San Fernando Valley Mental Health Clinic, Van Nuys, CA (1985-1988); Coach, Third Place Gymnast All-around Events, City Championships (1980); Coach, Third Place Volleyball Team, City Championships (1979); Coach, First Place Gymnast Floor Exercise, City Championships (1976); Coordinator, Cheerleaders, Kayettes and Pep Club, Circle High School, Towanda, KS (1963-1969); Director, Camp Waterfront, Young Women's Christian Association, Wichita, KS **Civic:** Volunteer, RVing Women (2013-Present); Volunteer, Girl Scouts of the United States, Los Angeles, CA (1994-1995); Presidents Club Contributor, Pittsburg State University, Kansas; Contributor, Civitan, Burbank, CA **Creative Works:** Choreographer, Hollywood Christmas Parades (1984-1986); Choreographer, Drill Team Performance, Los Angeles Coliseum (1977) **Awards:** Commendation for 32 Years of Public School Service, Mayor Jim Hahn, Los Angeles, CA (2001); First Place, Band and Drill Team Championships, Los Angeles Unified Schools (1978) **Memberships:** California Association of Marriage and Family Therapists; California Teachers Association; Life Member, Delta Psi Kappa; Life Member, Alpha Sigma Alpha **Marquis Who's Who Honors:** Albert Nelson Marquis Lifetime Achievement Award **To what do you attribute your success:** Ms. Weickert's parents gave her a strong work ethic. **Why did you become involved in your profession or industry:** Ms. Weickert did not know that she wanted to go into teaching until after high school. She went to work for a bank and realized she did not want to sit behind a machine for the rest of her life. She went to college, and discovered the Physical Education Department and loved it. She realized that she wanted to teach physical education to children. She then discovered she was interested in child welfare and attendance, and she was interested in the welfare of children. From that point, she found her way to marriage and family counseling. It seemed to be a natural progression, all three areas tied together. **Avocations:** Quilting; Gardening; RVing; Swimming; Walking

Florence May Weinberg, PhD

Title: Modern Language and Literature Educator (Retired) **Industry:** Education/Educational Services **Date of Birth:** 12/03/1933 **Place of Birth:** Alamogordo **State/Country of Origin:** NM/USA **Parents:** Steven Horace Byham; Olive Gladys (Edgington) Byham **Marital Status:** Widowed **Spouse Name:** Kurt Weinberg (05/08/1955, Deceased 1996) **Education:** Resident, Hambidge Center for the Creative Arts & Sciences (1999-2001, 2003-2007, 2009-2010); PhD, University of Rochester (1968); MA, Spanish, University of British Columbia (1962); AB, Foreign Languages (Spanish and French), Park College (1954); Graduate Studies, University of Iowa **Career:** Author, Novels (1999-Present); Professor of French, Trinity University, San Antonio, TX (1989-1999); Professor of Spanish, Trinity University, San Antonio, TX (1989-1999); Chairman, Department of Modern Languages and Literature, Trinity University, San Antonio, TX (1989-1995); Professor of Modern Languages, St. John Fisher College, Rochester, NY (1975-1989); Director of International Studies, St. John Fisher College, Rochester, NY (1983-1986); Chairman, Department of Modern Languages, St. John Fisher College, Rochester, NY (1972-1979); Associate Professor of Modern Languages, St. John Fisher College, Rochester, NY (1971-1975); Assistant Professor of Modern Languages, St. John Fisher College, Rochester, NY (1967-1971); Instructor of Modern Languages, St. John Fisher College, Rochester, NY (1967) **Career Related:** Senior Fellowship, National Endowment for the Humanities (1979-1980) **Civic:** Board Member, Zapatos **Creative Works:** Author, "Dolet" (2015); Author, "Anselm: a Metamorphosis" (2013); Author, "Unruhe im Paradies" (2012); Author, "Unrest in Eden" (2011); Author, "El Jesuita y el brujo" (2011); Author, "El Jesuita y la Tormenta" (2011); Author, "El Jesuita y la Caridad" (2011); Author, "Sonora Wind" (2009); Author, "Seven Cities of Mud" (2008); Author, "Sonora Moonlight" (2008); Author, "The Storks of La Caridad" (2005); Author, "Apache Lance, Franciscan Cross" (2005); Author, "Sonora Wind, Ill Wind" (2002); Author, "Longs désirs" (2002); Author, "I'll Come to Thee By Moonlight" (2002); Author, "Les Leçons du rire" (2000); Author, "Gargantua in a Convex Mirror" (1986); Author, "The Cave" (1986); Author, "The Wine and the Will" (1972) **Awards:** Pinnacle Book Achievement Award (2012, 2014-2015); Finalist, Indie Next Generation Book Award (2012); Arts & Letters Award, Friends of the San Antonio Public Library (2012); Finalist, Indie Book Award (2012); New Mexico Book Award (2011); Finalist, Indie Next Generation Book Award (2010); Finalist, Eric Hoffer Award (2009); Alumna of the Year Award, Park University (2008); Finalist, New Mexico Book Award (2007-2008); Finalist, WILLA Literary Award (2006); Research Grant, Ludwig Vogelstein Foundation (1986); Grantee, National Endowment for the Humanities (1983); Grantee-in-Aid, American Council of Learned Societies (1974-1975) **Memberships:** Modern Language Association; PEN; Renaissance Society of America; Sixteenth Century Society & Conference; Women Writing the West; Toastmasters International **Marquis Who's Who Honors:** Albert Nelson Marquis Lifetime Achievement Award; Marquis Who's Who Top Professional **Why did you become involved in your profession or industry:** Both of Dr. Weinberg 's parents were teachers; her mother taught elementary school age children. She taught them to love reading. She feels that is one of the most important phases of anybody's development, to learn how to read and to love books, not just do it because someone forced you to. Her father was teaching at the high school level and became a high school principle for some years; later. he got a doctorate and became the dean of a junior college in Highland, Kansas. He was the CEO, so his title should have been president, but it was "dean" instead. He passed away from injuries from World War II two years after he accepted this position. **Avocations:** Swimming; Hiking; Weightlifting; Exercise **Political Affiliations:** Democrat **Thoughts on Life:** In Shakespeare's "Hamlet," Polonius tells his son Laertes, "This above all, to thine own self be true, and it must follow, as the night the day, thou canst not then be false to any man." Polonius was an old fool. Nevertheless, these words have come down to us as pure wisdom. Dr. Weinberg quoted them in her valedictory speech on graduating from high school; she quotes them now. Human nature can be warped, but she believes it is basically good. If you follow your conscience, you will do the right thing. Heed your inner voice. The philosopher Immanuel Kant believed it and so does she.

Gerson Weiss, MD

Title: Reproductive Endocrinologist, Educator (Retired) **Industry:** Medicine & Health Care **Date of Birth:** 08/01/1939 **Place of Birth:** New York **State/Country of Origin:** NY/USA **Parents:** Samuel Weiss; Lillian (Wolpe) Weiss **Marital Status:** Married **Spouse Name:** Laura Goldsmith, PhD; Linda M. Gordon (12/24/1959, Deceased 2/10/2011) **Children:** Jonathan; David; Andrew; Michele **Education:** Resident, Obstetrics and Gynecology, New York University Medical Center, New York, NY (1965-1969); Fellow, Medicine, Johns Hopkins School of Medicine, Baltimore, MD (1964-1965); Intern, Straight Medicine, Baltimore City Hospital, Baltimore, MD (1964-1965); MD, New York University (1964); BA in Biology, New York University, Magna Cum Laude (1960) **Certifications:** Certified, Reproductive Endocrinology, American Board of Obstetrics and Gynecology (1993); Certified, American Board of Obstetrics and Gynecology (1981) **Career:** Emeritus Professor, Obstetrics and Gynecology, Rutgers, the State University of New Jersey, Medical School (2014-Present); Retired Professor, Obstetrics and Gynecology, Rutgers University, State University of New Jersey, Medical School (1986-2014); Director, Reproductive Endocrinology, Hackensack University Medical Center (1996-2002); Consultant, Booth Memorial Hospital, Queens, NY (1978-1995); Director, Reproductive Endocrinology, New York University Medical Center (1975-1985); Professor, Obstetrics and Gynecology, New York University Medical Center (1980-1985); Associate Professor, Obstetrics and Gynecology, New York University Medical Center (1976-1980); Assistant Professor, Obstetrics and Gynecology, New York University Medical Center (1971-1976) **Career Related:** Board of Directors, American Board of Medical Specialties (2004-Present); Task Force on Recruitment, Retention and Integrity in Clinical Studies, Office of Research on Women's Health (2003); Scientific Advisory Panel, Second International Congress of Hormone Relaxing (1994); Advisory Committee, Society for Implantation and Early Pregnancy in Humans (1993); Reproductive Scientist Training Program (RSTP) Selection Committee (1988-1993); Ad Hoc Task Force on New Reproductive Practices, New Jersey Bio-ethics Commission, State of New Jersey (1988-1992); Research Fellow, John Polachek Foundation (1975-1976); President, Pittsburgh Free Clinic (1972-1973) **Military Service:** Major, Medical Corps, U.S. Army (1969-1971) **Creative Works:** Editorial Board, Women's Health (2004-Present); Editorial Board, Endocrinology and Metabolism (2001-2004); Editorial Board, Fertility and Sterility Journal (1986-1993); Editorial Board, Obstetrics and Gynecology (1988-1991); Editorial Board, Gynecological-Obstetrics Investigation; Contributor, 300 Scientific Papers, Professional Journals **Awards:** Research Grants, National Institutes of Health (1975-2010); Research Grantee, Mellon Foundation (1982-1985); Research Grant, United Cerebral Palsy Foundation (1977-1983); Army Commendation Award (1971) **Memberships:** Advisory Committee, Women's Health Research, National Institutes of Health (2011-Present); New York Obstetrics Society (1977-Present); Society of Gynecological Investigation (1976-Present); Chair, Liaison Committee, American College of Obstetrics and Gynecology (2009-2011); Chairman, American Board of Obstetrics and Gynecology (2002-2006); President, American Board of Obstetrics and Gynecology (1998-2002); Obstetrics and Gynecology Residency Review Committee, American Board of Obstetrics and Gynecology (1995-2000); Board of Directors, Treasurer, American Board of Obstetrics and Gynecology (1997-1998); President, Society Study of Reproduction; New York Gynecological Society (1989-1990); Division of Reproductive Endocrinology, American Board of Obstetrics and Gynecology (1985-1990); Alpha Omega Alpha; Endocrine Society; Sigma Xi; Phi Beta Kappa; American Board of Medical Specialties **Marquis Who's Who Honors:** Albert Nelson Marquis Lifetime Achievement Award; Marquis Who's Who Top Professional **To what do you attribute your success:** Dr. Weiss says one has to have a sense of humor to some extent; what one needs for practice is somewhat different than what one needs for research. If one is practicing, one has to listen. That is critical. One has to be able to determine a diagnosis from a patient's information, no matter how vague. If he sees referred patients from other doctors, he always thanks them. He additionally attributes his success to compassion and kindness. **Why did you become involved in your profession or industry:** Dr. Weiss was always curious on how things worked, but especially how they worked with people. He decided what he really wanted to do was be a clinical investigator. He then determined that being a clinical investigator without practicing medicine would be unsatisfactory. He wanted to be able to take care of the patients that he was dealing with and that worked out very well because he had patients who had interesting problems. He was able to help them and he was able to continue doing research; he additionally had fellows and graduate students who worked with him.

Aaron Max Weitzenhoffer

Title: Theatrical Producer **Industry:** Media & Entertainment **Company Name:** Nimax Theatres Ltd **Date of Birth:** 10/30/1939 **Place of Birth:** Oklahoma City **State/Country of Origin:** OK/USA **Parents:** Aaron Max Weitzenhoffer; Clara Irene (Rosenthal) Weitzenhoffer **Marital Status:** Married **Spouse Name:** Ayako **Children:** Nikki; Owen **Education:** Honorary Doctorate, The University of Oklahoma (2000); BFA, The University of Oklahoma (1961) **Career:** Chairman, Theatrical Producer, Nimax Theatres Ltd (1965-Present); President, Weitzenhoffer Productions, Ltd. (1965-Present); Director, Findlay Galleries (1965-1969); Co-Manager, La Jolla Playhouse (1963-1964) **Career Related:** Chief of Public Relations, Oklahoma State Department of Health (1964-1965); Adjunct Drama Professor, The University of Oklahoma; President, Chief Executive Officer, Chairman, Seminole Manufacturing Company **Civic:** Vice President, New Dramatists; Trustee, American Academy of Dramatic Arts; Treasurer, Stage Directors and Choreographers Foundation; Theater Investment Fund **Creative Works:** Featured, "To The Max: Max Weitzenhoffer's Magical Trip from Oklahoma to New York and London-and Back," By Tom Lindley **Awards:** Olivier Award, Society of London Theatre (2000); Inductee, Oklahoma Hall of Fame (1994); Tony Award (1978, 1991); Distinguished Service Citation, The University of Oklahoma (1988) **Memberships:** The League of American Theatres and Producers; Society of London Theatre; The Players; The Century Association; Delta Kappa Epsilon; Friars Club **Marquis Who's Who Honors:** Albert Nelson Marquis Lifetime Achievement Award **To what do you attribute your success:** Mr. Weitzenhoffer attributes his success to never being bored and being mentored by his peers. **Why did you become involved in your profession or industry:** Mr. Weitzenhoffer became involved in his profession because of his childhood. His parents immersed him in theater, so he felt a natural pull to enter the field. **Avocations:** Traveling; Antiquing **Political Affiliations:** Republican

John Francis "Jack" Welch Jr., PhD

Title: Former Chairman, Chief Executive Officer **Industry:** Other **Company Name:** General Electric **Date of Birth:** 11/19/1935 **Place of Birth:** Peabody **State/Country of Origin:** MA/USA **Year of Passing:** 2020 **Parents:** John Francis Welch Sr.; Grace (Andrews) Welch **Marital Status:** Married **Spouse Name:** Suzy Wetlaufer (2004); Jane Beasley (1989, Divorced 2003); Carolyn B. Osburn (1959, Divorced 1987) **Children:** Four Children **Education:** PhD in Chemical Engineering, University of Illinois at Urbana-Champaign (1960); Master's Degree in Chemical Engineering, University of Illinois at Urbana-Champaign (1960); BS in Chemical Engineering, University of Massachusetts Amherst (1957) **Career:** Chairman, Chief Executive Officer, General Electric (1981-2001); Vice Chairman, General Electric (1979-1981); Senior Vice President, Consumer Products and Services Division, General Electric (1977-1979); Head of Strategic Planning, General Electric (1973-1979); Vice President, Metallurgical and Chemical Division, General Electric (1971-1973); Vice President, Plastics Division, General Electric (1968); Junior Chemical Engineer, General Electric, Pittsfield, MA (1960) **Career Related:** Founder, Jack Welch Management Institute, Strayer University (2011-Present) **Civic:** Chairman, The Business Council (1991-1992) **Political Affiliations:** Republican

Vernon E. Wendt, MD

Title: Internist, Cardiologist **Industry:** Medicine & Health Care **Date of Birth:** 03/26/1931 **Place of Birth:** Cleveland **State/Country of Origin:** OH/USA **Parents:** Raymond C. Wendt; Esther L. (Naujoks) Wendt **Marital Status:** Widowed **Spouse Name:** Hildegarde Caroline Moeller (08/14/1953) **Children:** David; Frederick; Kathryn; Elizabeth; Doralyn; James; Vernon Earl Jr. **Education:** Postdoctoral Fellowship in Cardiology, U.S. Public Health Service, School of Medicine, Wayne State University (1962-1965); Residency, Detroit Receiving Hospital (1959-1962); Internship, Detroit Receiving Hospital (1956-1957); MD, Columbia University (1956); BS in Zoology and Chemistry, Baldwin Wallace University, Cum Laude (1952) **Certifications:** Diplomate, American Board of Internal Medicine **Career:** Private Practice, Grand Rapids, MI (1967-2000);Research Director, Blodgett Hospital, Grand Rapids, MI (1965-1967); Instructor, Assistant Professor of Medicine, School of Medicine, Wayne State University, Detroit, MI (1961-1965) **Civic:** Head Elder, Grace Lutheran Church, Wyoming, MI (2008-2012) **Military Service:** Captain, Medical Service Corps Officers, Air Force Reserve (1957-1959) **Memberships:** Trustee, Michigan Health Council (1998-Present); Trustee, Michigan Chapter, American Heart Association (1973-1993); President, Michigan Chapter, American Heart Association (1987-1988); Michigan Chapter, American Lung Association (1978-1980); Fellow, American College of Physicians; American Society of Angiology; American College of Cardiology; American Medical Association; Michigan State Medical Society; KCMS; A4M (American Academy of Anti-Aging Medicine) **Marquis Who's Who Honors:** Albert Nelson Marquis Lifetime Achievement Award **Why did you become involved in your profession or industry:** Dr. Wendt became involved in his profession because he was inspired by his childhood family doctor. **Avocations:** Golfing; Gardening; Walking **Religion:** Lutheran

Mark H. Werner, MD

Title: Neurologist, Researcher **Industry:** Medicine & Health Care **Date of Birth:** 06/10/1954 **Place of Birth:** Louisville **State/Country of Origin:** KY/USA **Parents:** Stanley Gerald Werner; Sara (Berolzheimer) Werner **Spouse Name:** Yana Serita Banks, MD **Children:** Adam; Isaac **Education:** MD, Bowman Gray Center for Medical Education, Wake Forest School of Medicine (1981); BA, University of North Carolina (1975) **Certifications:** Board Certified, American Academy of Neurology **Career:** Private Practice, Gainesville, FL (1994-2013); Research Associate, Duke Medical Center (1987-1991); Neuro-Oncology Fellow, Duke Medical Center (1985-1987); Neurology Resident, Vanderbilt University Medical Center (1982-1985); Resident, New Hanover Regional Medical Center (1981-1982) **Civic:** Democratic Party Volunteer, Durham, NC (1990); Democratic Party Volunteer, Precinct Chairman, Gainesville, FL **Creative Works:** Contributor, Articles, Professional Journals **Awards:** Fellowship, American Heart Association (1989-1991); Fellowship, American Brain Tumor Association (1986-1988, 1989-1991); Fellowship, National Cancer Center (1986-1987) **Memberships:** American Academy of Neurology; The Phi Beta Kappa Society **Marquis Who's Who Honors:** Albert Nelson Marquis Lifetime Achievement Award; Marquis Who's Who Top Professional; Marquis Who's Who Humanitarian Award **Why did you become involved in your profession or industry:** Dr. Werner became involved in his profession because of his interest in humanities and science. Studying medicine and becoming a physician was the best way to combine the two. **Avocations:** Playing guitar **Political Affiliations:** Democrat **Religion:** Jewish

Jacqueline Irene Wert, MSW, LCSW

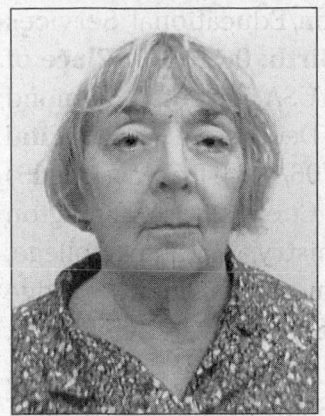

Title: Private Practice/ Licensed Clinical Social Worker **Industry:** Social Work **Company Name:** Jacqueline I. Wert, MSW, LCSW **Date of Birth:** 01/24/1942 **Place of Birth:** Newton **State/Country of Origin:** IA/USA **Parents:** John Alvin Wert; Sarah Irene (Jacobs) Wert **Marital Status:** Single **Education:** Certificate in Medical Billing and Coding, Harry S. Truman College Continuing Education Department (2009); Substance Abuse Training (1984); Certificate, Family Institute of Chicago/Center for Family Studies, Institute of Psychiatry, Northwestern Memorial Hospital, Northwestern University Medical School (1982); MSW, Jane Addams School of Social Work, University of Illinois (1974); BS in Psychology, University of Iowa (1964) **Certifications:** Certified, Council on Affordable Quality Healthcare (CAQH) (2007-Present); LCSW, Illinois (1993-Present); Iowa Board of Professional Licensure/Social Work, Social Worker Independent Level (2019-2020); Certified, Elite CME (2017); Certified in Cinema Therapy, Zur Institute, Inc. (2011); Certified in Ethics for Social Work, Affect Plus (2011); Certified in Practical Psychopharmacology, Professional Education Systems, Inc. (PESI) (2009); Certified, Gottman Institute (2009); Certified Billing and Coding Specialist, National Healthcareer Association (2009); Healthcare Training Institute (2005); Trainer, Substance Affected Families Policy and Practice (1999); Certified, Conflict Resolution and Divorce Mediation Institute (1996); Illinois Child Welfare Employee License (1990-1994); CSW, Illinois (1969-1993); Certified, Quality Care for HIV Infected Children and Their Families (1990); Certified, Academy of Certified Social Workers, National Association of Social Work (1981); Certified, Medicare Learning Network **Career:** Licensed Clinical Social Worker, Jacqueline I. Wert, MSW, LCSW (1993-Present); Private Practice, Jacqueline I. Wert, MSW, LCSW, (1982-Present); Social Work Field Experience Placement (1973-1974); Child Welfare Worker, Illinois Department of Children & Family Services, Chicago, IL (1968-2001); Case Worker in Public Assistance, Cook County Department of Public Assistance, Chicago, IL (1965-1968); Nursing Aide, Psychopathic Hospital, Iowa City, IA (1964-1965) **Career Related:** Part-Time Worker, The Youth Campus (2009); Part-Time Worker, Elk Grove Schaumburg Family Service (1982-1984); Presenter in the Field **Awards:** Certificate of Recognition for Team Performance (2000); Certificate of Recognition for Team Performance (1998); Director's Award, Director of Illinois Children and Family Services (1989) **Memberships:** Academy of Certified Social Workers; National Association of Social Work **Marquis Who's Who Honors:** Albert Nelson Marquis Lifetime Achievement Award; Marquis Who's Who Top Professional; Marquis Who's Who Industry Leader; Who's Who of Professional Women **Why did you become involved in your profession or industry:** Ms. Wert became involved in her profession because she had an interest in social services, which emerged while in college. She had plans for graduate school after receiving a position at the psychopathic hospital, but was not sure if she truly would want to endure more schooling. She began job hunting further. She developed a serious interest in psychosocial issues and helping others. She received an opportunity with the Cook County Department of Public Aid in Chicago. She was also accepted to the University of Illinois. **Avocations:** Photography; Crafts; Dance; Hiking **Religion:** Presbyterian

Douglas Xavier West, PhD

Title: Professor of Chemistry **Industry:** Education/Educational Services **Company Name:** Illinois State University **Date of Birth:** 06/11/1937 **Place of Birth:** Tacoma, WA **State/Country of Origin:** WA/USA **Parents:** Raymond Idaho West (Deceased 1997); Myrtle Agnes West (Deceased 1986) **Marital Status:** Widowed **Spouse Name:** Gayl Lee West (06/06/1964, Deceased 2016) **Children:** Gregory; Gabriel **Education:** PhD in Chemistry, Washington State University, Pullman, WA (1964); AB in Chemistry, Whitman College, Walla Walla, WA (1959) **Certifications:** Director, American Contract Bridge League (1967) **Career:** Professor Emeritus, Illinois State University, Normal, IL (2000-Present); Affiliate Professor, University of Washington, Seattle, WA (2000-2002); Distinguished Professor, Illinois State University, Normal, IL (1993-2000); Professor, Illinois State University, Normal, IL (1986-1993); Chairman and Professor, Inorganic Chemistry, Illinois State University, Normal, IL (1975-1986); Professor, Central Michigan University, Mount Pleasant, MI (1972-1975); Director, University Honors Programs, Central Michigan University, Mount Pleasant, MI (1973-1974); Associate Professor, Central Michigan University, Mount Pleasant, MI (1968-1972); Assistant Professor, Central Michigan University, Mount Pleasant, MI (1965-1968); Instructor, Upsala College, East Orange, NJ (1964-1965) **Civic:** President, Seaside Unit Board (2012, 2015); President, Peninsula Duplicate Bridge Club Board (2005); President, Eastern Michigan Bridge Unit Board (1974) **Creative Works:** Contributor, Articles, Professional Journals **Awards:** Grantee, Senior Scholar, The Camille & Henry Dreyfus Foundation (2000-2002); Recipient, Purdue Research Foundation Grants, American Chemical Society (1988-1990, 1990-1992, 1993-1995, 1997-1999); Dreyfus Scholar (1994-1996); Distinguished Professor, Illinois State University (1993); Award, Council for the International Exchange of Scholars (1990); Recipient, Travel Grant, NATO (1985-1997); Instrumentation Award, National Science Foundation (1979, 1984); Indo-American Fellowship **Memberships:** Board of Directors, Seaside Unit (2007, 2009, 2014); President, Seaside Unit (2010); Board of Directors, American Contract Bridge League, Eastern Michigan Bridge Unit (1973); Silver Life Master **Marquis Who's Who Honors:** Albert Nelson Marquis Lifetime Achievement Award **Why did you become involved in your profession or industry:** Dr. West got involved in his profession after picking chemistry over economics at Whitman College. **Avocations:** Golf; Surf-fishing; Razor clamming; Hiking; Beach walking; Stamp collecting/Philately; Gardening

Shannon Wettstein

Title: Experimental Classical Pianist **Industry:** Media & Entertainment **Company Name:** Saint Cloud State University **Date of Birth:** 06/16/1968 **Place of Birth:** Fort Scott **State/Country of Origin:** KS/USA **Parents:** Walter Lee Wettstein; Dorothe Ann Wettstein **Marital Status:** Married **Spouse Name:** William Sadler **Education:** Doctor in Musical Arts, University of California San Diego (2000); MusM, New England Conservatory of Music (1992); MusB, University of Kansas (1990) **Career:** Assistant Professor of Music, St. Cloud State University (2015-Present); Summer Session Artist Faculty, New England Conservatory, Boston, MA (1998-Present); Studio Artist in Music, Augsburg University (2005-2015); Pianist, Zeitgeist New Music (2005-2015); Assistant Professor of Music, Bemidji State University (2000-2005); Artist-in-Residence, Walden School **Civic:** Board Member, 113- Composers Collective; Judge, American Classical Pianist International Piano Competition, China **Creative Works:** Musician, Concert, Sounds Modern, Fort Worth Modern Art Museum, Fort Worth, Texas (2019); Musician, Shannon Wettstein Performs Music of Chopin, Berg, Ferneyhough and Debussy (2003); Musician, Catfish and Disciplines, Including Performances of Music By Applebaum; Musician, Concert, University of North Texas, Intermedia Festival **Awards:** Grantee, United States Artists International (2019); Saigo Excellence Award, St. Clouds University (2018); Minnesota State Arts Award, Artist Initiative Grants (2010); American Composers Forum Commissioning (2008); Grantee, American Composers Forum (2001, 2004); Individual Artist Grantee, Minnesota Region 2 Arts Council (2001); Merle Montgomery Fellow, Mu Phi Epsilon (1999); Grantee, Aaron Copland Foundation; Grantee, National Endowment for the Arts with Zeitgeist **Memberships:** American Composers Forum; College Music Society; Music Teachers National Association; Minnesota Music Teachers Association **Marquis Who's Who Honors:** Albert Nelson Marquis Lifetime Achievement Award; Marquis Who's Who Top Professional **Why did you become involved in your profession or industry:** Growing up, Ms. Wettstein could not imagine doing anything other than music. **Avocations:** Yoga; Pilates; Cooking; Reading

Lois Deimel Whealey

Title: Citizen Activist **Industry:** Civil Service **Company Name:** City of Athens, Ohio **Date of Birth:** 06/20/1932 **Place of Birth:** New York **State/Country of Origin:** NY/USA **Parents:** Edgar Bertram Deimel (1902, Deceased 1937); Lois Elizabeth (Hatch) Washburn (1902, Deceased 1959) **Marital Status:** Married **Spouse Name:** Robert Howard Whealey (07/02/1954) **Children:** Richard William; David John; Alice Ann **Education:** Master's Degree, Social Science, The Ohio University (2007); MA, Political Science, The Ohio University (1975); MEd, University of Michigan (1955); BA, History, Stanford University (1951) **Career:** Administrative Assistant, Humanities Conference, Ohio University, Athens, OH (1983); Administrative Assistant, Humanities Conference, Ohio University, Athens, OH (1974-1976); Teacher, English and Social Studies, Slauson Junior High School (Now Slauson Middle School), Ann Arbor, MI (1958-1959); Sixth-Grade Teacher, Amerman School (Now Amerman Elementary School), Northville, MI (1957-1958); Teacher, Adult Basic Education, United States Air Force, Oxford, England (1956-1957); Seventh-Grade Teacher, Fort Knox Dependent Schools, Kentucky (1955-1956); Fifth-Grade Teacher, Swayne School (Now Owyhee Combined School), Owyhee, NV (1952-1953); Citizen Activist, City of Athens, OH **Career Related:** Rural Action AmeriCorps VISTA (1996-1998); Part-Time Instructor, Ohio University (1975); Part-Time Instructor, Athens, OH (1966-1968) **Civic:** Athens Community Television, Cable Channel 1017 (Now Athens Community Television, Inc.) (2006-Present); Secretary, Ohio Women Inc. (1997-Present); Board of Directors, Ohio Women Inc. (1995-Present); Co-Chair, Unitarian Universalist Service Committee, National Volunteer Network (Now National Volunteer Caregiving Network) (2003-2005); Board President, Organize! Ohio (2001-2007); Board of Directors, Unitarian Universalist Service Committee (2001-2003); Board of Directors, Organize! Ohio (1999-2007); Ohio Outreach Liaison, National Town Meeting for a Sustainable America (1999); Vice President, Ohio Alliance for the Environment (1998); Board of Directors, Ohio Alliance for the Environment (1994-1998); Vice President, Tri-County Vocational School Board (Now Tri-County Career Center), Nelsonville, OH (1988-1989); Member, Advertising Committee, Ohio River Valley Water Sanitation Commission (Now ORSANCO) (1986-1995); Secretary, Ohio Environmental Council (1986-1990); President, Athens City School District Board of Education (1985); Board of Directors, Ohio Environmental Council (1984-1990); Tri-County Vocational School Board (Now Tri-County Career Center), Nelsonville, OH (1984-1990); Athens City School District Board of Education (1984-1990); Vice President, Athens City School District Board of Education (1984); Chair, New Day for Equal Rights Amendment, Athens, OH (1982); Vice President, Black Diamond Girl Scout Council (Now Girl Scouts of Black Diamond) (1980-1986); Member of Ohio Coordinator Committee, International Women's Year (1977); Treasurer, Athens County Regional Planning Commission (1976-1978); Board of Directors, Ohio-Meadville District Unitarian-Universalist Association (1975-1981); Member, Athens County Regional Planning Commission (1974-1978); Executive Committee, Democracy Over Corporations; Host, Women Today and Yesterday **Creative Works:** Contributor, Articles, Professional Journals **Awards:** Social Justice Award for Contributions Over a Lifetime, United Campus Ministry (Now UCM), Ohio University (2016); Nora Price Award, SEOH Planned Parenthood (2009); Social Justice Award, United Campus Ministry (Now UCM), Ohio University (2008); Spirit Award, League of Women Voters of Athens County (2002); Award for Individual Contribution Over a Lifetime, Ohio Alliance Environment (2002); Outstanding Feminist, Athens Herstory Celebration (2002); Peacemaker, Appalachian Peace & Justice Network (1998); Community Service Award, Athens County Community Services Council (1998); Donna Chen Women's Equity Award, Ohio University (1994); How-To Award, Educational Press Association of America (1990); Woman of Achievement, Black Diamond Girl Scout Council (Now Girl Scouts of Black Diamond) (1987); Thanks Badge, Black Diamond Girl Scout Council (Now Girl Scouts of Black Diamond) (1986); Unsung Unitarian Universalist Award, Ohio-Meadville District Unitarian Universalist Association (1984) **Memberships:** Ohio Board Member, American Association of University Women (1995-2004); President, Athens Branch, American Association of University Women (1993-2001); President, Athens Branch, American Association of University Women (1989-1990); President, League of Women Voters of Athens County (1975-1977); President, Athens Branch, American Association of University Women (1969-1970); Phi Kappa Phi (Now The Honor Society of Phi Kappa Phi); Pi Lambda Theta; League of Women Voters; Executive Committee, Democracy Over Corporations **Marquis Who's Who Honors:** Albert Nelson Marquis Lifetime Achievement Award; Marquis Who's Who Humanitarian Award **Avocations:** Genealogy; Arts; Music **Political Affiliations:** Democrat

Robert Howard Whealey, PhD

Title: Historian **Industry:** Education/Educational Services **Company Name:** Ohio University **Date of Birth:** 05/16/1930 **Place of Birth:** Freeport **State/Country of Origin:** NY/USA **Parents:** Howard Edgar Whealey; Ethel Ann (Rooney) Whealey **Marital Status:** Married **Spouse Name:** Lois Deimel (07/02/1954) **Children:** Richard; David; Alice **Education:** PhD, University of Michigan (1963); Graduate Coursework, University of Oxford (1956-1957); MA, University of Michigan (1954); BA, University of Delaware (1952); Coursework, Bates College **Career:** Professor Emeritus, Ohio University (2001-Present); Associate Professor, Ohio University, Athens, OH (1967-2001); Assistant Professor, Ohio University, Athens, OH (1964-1967); Instructor, University of Maine, Orono, ME (1961-1964) **Civic:** Candidate, Democratic U.S. Congress, Athens, OH (1972) **Military Service:** U.S. Army (1955-1956); Seventh Army, Hauptgefreiter, Stuttgart, Germany (1955-1956); 12th Historical Battalion **Creative Works:** Featured, "Athens Speak Out," Athens Community TV (2006-Present); Author, "Hitler and Spain" (1989) **Awards:** Fulbright Foundation Award, Spain (1977-1978) **Memberships:** Board of Directors, Athens Chapter, American Civil Liberties Union (1994-Present); American Historical Association **Marquis Who's Who Honors:** Albert Nelson Marquis Lifetime Achievement Award **Why did you become involved in your profession or industry:** Dr. Whealey was inspired by his father, a World War I veteran. He got involved in his profession after attending Bates College in Maine. He thought he wanted to be a chemist, but found that he wasn't passionate about it. Next, he considered biology, then dentistry, but found that they weren't the right fit for him. He wanted to solve the world's problems, so eventually he settled on history. **Avocations:** Stamp collecting; Swimming; Politics **Political Affiliations:** Democrat **Religion:** Unitarian Universalist

James W. Wheless, BScPharm, MD, FAAP, FACP, FAAN, FAES

Title: Neurologist **Industry:** Medicine & Health Care **Company Name:** The University of Tennessee Health Science Center **Date of Birth:** 04/18/1956 **Place of Birth:** Glens Falls **State/Country of Origin:** NY/USA **Parents:** True Wheless; Adelphine Ada (Bump) Wheless **Marital Status:** Married **Spouse Name:** Annette Carolyn Hyland (04/07/1984) **Children:** Catherine; Margaret **Education:** Fellow in Clinical Neurophysiology/Epilepsy, Augusta University Medical College of Georgia (1988-1989); Fellow in Child Neurology, Ann & Robert H. Lurie Children's Hospital of Chicago, Northwestern University (1985-1988); Intern and Pediatric Resident, The University of Oklahoma-Tulsa School of Community Medicine (1982-1985); MD, The University of Oklahoma, Oklahoma City, OK (1982); BS in Pharmacy, The University of Oklahoma, Norman, OK (1978) **Certifications:** Board Certified in Psychiatry and Neurology, American Board of Psychiatry and Neurology (2013); Board Certified in Clinical Neurophysiology, American Board of Psychiatry and Neurology (1996); Board Certified in Child Neurology, American Board of Psychiatry and Neurology (1989); Board Certified, American Board of Pediatrics (1987); Medical License, State of Oklahoma (1983); Oklahoma Pharmacy License (1979) **Career:** Professor and Chief of Pediatric Neurology, Le Bonheur Chair in Pediatric Neurology, Director, Le Bonheur Comprehensive Epilepsy Program and Neuroscience Institute, Le Bonheur Children's Hospital, The University of Tennessee Health Science Center (2005-Present); Associate Professor of Neurology and Pediatrics, Medical Director of Epilepsy Monitoring Unit and Texas Comprehensive Epilepsy Program, The University of Texas at Houston (2000-2005); Director of Pediatrics Epilepsy Section, Head of Clinical EEG, Director and Founder, Texas Comprehensive Epilepsy Program (1998-2005); Assistant Professor of Neurology and Pediatrics, The University of Texas Health Science Center at Houston (UTHealth) (1989-2005); Associate Professor of Neurology and Pediatrics, The University of Texas Health Science Center at Houston (UTHealth) (1995-2000) **Career Related:** Clinical Director, Chief of Pediatric Neurology, St. Jude Children's Research Hospital, Memphis, TN (2005-2012); Director, Neuroscience Institute and Le Bonheur Comprehensive Epilepsy Program, Le Bonheur Children's Hospital **Civic:** Founding Member, Rare Epilepsy Network Advisory Board, Epilepsy Foundation of America (2016-Present); Chair, Targeted Research Initiative for Severe Symptomatic Epilepsies, Epilepsy Foundation of America (2011-Present); MED, Regional Medical Center at Memphis (2005-Present); Epilepsy Foundation of America (1989-Present); Professional Advisory Board, Advocacy Committee, Epilepsy Foundation of America (2009-2018); Professional Advisory Board, LGS Foundation (2010-2016); Scientific Advisory Board, Charlie Foundation to Help Cure Pediatric Epilepsy (2008-2016); Professional Advisory Board Member, Epilepsy.com (2001-2014); Scientific Advisory Board, CURE (1998-2010); Camp Physician, Kamp Kaleidoscope, Epilepsy Foundation Texas (1995-2005); Executive CME Committee, University of Texas Health Science Center (1995-2005); Several Committees **Creative Works:** Editorial Board, Neurotherapeutics (2010-Present); Associate Editor, Special Issues Editor (2000-Present); Editorial Board, Journal of Child Neurology (1998-Present); Editorial Board, Epilepsy.com (2003-2013); Editorial Board, Formulary, Neurologychannel.com (2000-2010); Editorial Board, WebMD (2004-2006); Guest Editor, Neurology (2002); Editorial Board, Journal of Pediatric Neurology (2003-2008); Contributor, Articles to Professional Journals, Chapters to Books; Ad Hoc Referee, Over 300 Publications **Awards:** Named, Best Doctors in America (2003, 1998-2000, 2011-2016); Named Top Doctor in Child Neurology, Memphis Magazine (2010-2011); John Bodensteiner Presidential Lecture, Southern Pediatric Neurology Society, New Orleans, LA (2010); Named, Best Doctors in America (2005-2010); Named, America's Top Pediatricians (2009); Named, Guide to America's Top Pediatricians (2008); Hans Berger Lecturer Award, VCU Medical Center, Virginia Commonwealth University School of Medicine (2007); Named, America's Top Doctors (2007); Named, Houston's Best Doctors (2002); Named International Scientist of the Year (2002); J. Kiffin Penry Eagle Award, American Epilepsy Society Meeting, Cyberonics (1998); Grantee in Field; Recipient, Multiple Awards **Memberships:** European Paediatric Neurology Society (2017-Present); Advisory Board, Rare Disease Report (2015-Present); Professors of Child Neurology, Child Neurology Society (2012-Present); Tuberous Sclerosis Alliance (2011-Present); Professional Advisory Board, Co-director of Regional TSA Clinic at LeBonheur Children's Hospital, Tuberous Sclerosis Alliance (2010-Present); The American Clinical Magnetoencephalography Society (2010-Present); ASENT (2010-Present); Fellow, American College of Pediatricians (2006-Present); International Society for the Advancement of Clinical Magnetoencephalography (2005-Present); International Child Neurology Society (1995-Present); Fellow, American Academy of Pediatrics (1983-Present); Fellow, Child Neurology Society; Fellow, Several Committees, American Academy of Neurology; Fellow, Several Committees, American Epilepsy Society; Member, Numerous Organizations **Marquis Who's Who Honors:** Albert Nelson Marquis Lifetime Achievement Award **Avocations:** Running; Camping; Hiking; Travel; Reading

Stephen Halley White

Title: Biophysicist, Educator **Industry:** Education/Educational Services **Company Name:** University of California Irvine **Date of Birth:** 05/14/1940 **Place of Birth:** Wewoka **State/Country of Origin:** OK/USA **Parents:** James Halley White; Gertrude June (Wyatt) White **Marital Status:** Married **Spouse Name:** Jackie Marie Dooley (04/14/1984); Buff Ertl (08/20/1961, Divorced 1982) **Children:** Saill; Shell; Storn; Sharr; Skye; Sunde **Education:** Honorary PhD, Stockholm University (2008); United States Public Health Service Post-doctoral Fellow, Biochemistry, University of Virginia, Charlottesville (1971-1972); PhD, Physiology and Biophysics, University of Washington (1969); MS in Physics, University of Washington (1965); BS in Physics, University of Colorado (1963) **Career:** Professor Emeritus, Physiology and Biophysics, University of California, Irvine (2012-Present); Professor, Physiology and Biophysics, University of California, Irvine (1978-Present); Chairman, Physiology and Biophysics, University of California, Irvine (1977-1989); Vice Chairman, Physiology and Biophysics, University of California, Irvine (1974-1975); Associate Professor, Physiology and Biophysics, University of California, Irvine (1975-1978); Assistant Professor, Physiology and Biophysics, University of California, Irvine (1972-1975) **Career Related:** National Institutes of Health, BBM Study Section (2005-2010); Guest Biophysicist, Brookhaven National Laboratory, Upton, New York (1977-1999); Biophysics Lab, Membrane Protein Folding, University of California Irvine **Military Service:** Captain, United States Army Reserves (1969-1971) **Creative Works:** Contributor, Numerous Articles, Professional Journals **Awards:** Grantee, National Institutes of Health (1971-Present); Fellow, American Association for the Advancement of Science (2018); Fellow, Neutron Scattering Society of America (2016); Protein Society Carl Brändén Award (2014); O'Malley Lectures in Chemical Biology, Boston College (2011); Frederic M. Richards Lecture, Yale University (2010); Avanti Award in Lipids, Biophysical Society (2009); Fellow, Biophysical Society (2002); Kaiser-Permanente Teaching Award (1975, 1992); Research Career Development Award, U.S. Public Health Service (1975-1980); Grantee, National Science Foundation (1971-1985) **Memberships:** Electronic Public Coordinator, The Protein Society (1993-2007); Chairman, United States National Committee, International Union Pure and Applied Biophysics (1997-2004); Board of Directors, Federation America Society For Experimental Biology (1998-2002); Chairman, Membrane Biophysics Subgroup, Acting Secretary, Treasurer, Executive Board, Biophysics Society (1977-1999); Advisory Panel for Molecular Biology, National Steering Committee Advanced Neutron Source, National Science Foundation (1982-1995); Editorial Board, Membership Committee, Publication Committee, American Physiological Society (1981-1991); Treasurer, Society of General Physiologists (1985-1988); Association Chairman, Departments of Physiology (1981-1987) **Marquis Who's Who Honors:** Albert Nelson Marquis Lifetime Achievement Award **To what do you attribute your success:** Dr. White attributes his success to persistence. **Why did you become involved in your profession or industry:** He became involved in his profession because of his love of science. **Avocations:** Skiing; Cooking; Travel **Thoughts on Life:** Do what you love, work hard, never give up, be fair, and remember that all lives matter.

Michael Anthony Whitehead, DSc, PhD

Title: Professor Emeritus **Industry:** Education/Educational Services **Company Name:** McGill University **Date of Birth:** 06/30/1935 **Place of Birth:** London **State/Country of Origin:** England **Parents:** Francis Henry Whitehead; Edith Downes (Rotherham) Whitehead **Children:** Christopher Mark **Education:** DSc, Queen Mary College, University of London (1974); PhD, Queen Mary College, University of London (1960); BSc in Chemistry, Queen Mary College, University of London, With Honors (1956) **Career:** Professor Emeritus, McGill University (1999-Present); Professor, McGill University (1974-1999); Associate Professor, McGill University (1966-1974); Assistant Professor, Theoretical Chemistry, McGill University, Montreal, QC, Canada (1962-1966); Assistant Professor, University of Cincinnati (1961); Postdoctoral Fellow, University of Cincinnati (1960); Assistant Lecturer, Queen Mary College, University of London (1958-1960) **Career Related:** Center for Molecular Modelling, Concordia University, Montreal, QC, Canada (2005-Present); Advisor, Fundamental Applied Pulp and Paper Modelling Symposium (2011); Honorary Chair, Fundamental Applied Pulp and Paper Modelling Symposium (2008); Joint Chairman, First Applied Pulp and Paper Molecular Modelling Symposium (2005); Visiting Erskine Fellow, University of Canterbury, Christchurch, New Zealand (2000); Visiting Professorial Fellow, University of Oxford (1990-1991); Invited Professor, University of Geneva (1983-1984); Co-chairman, Seventh International Symposium on Nuclear Quadrupole Resonance, Ontario, Canada (1983); Visiting Professor, University of Oxford, England (1972-1974); Visiting Professor, University of Cambridge, England (1971-1972); Fulbright Fellowship, University of Cincinnati (1960-1962); Life Guest Professor, National University of Defense Technology, Changsha, People's Republic of China; International Committee on Nuclear Quadrupole Resonance; Fellow, Royal Chemical Society; Fellow, Chemical Institute of Canada; Fellow, Royal Society of the Arts **Civic:** Chairman, Montreal School of Theology (2006-2009); Stewardship Environmental Committee, Planned Giving Committee, Montreal Anglican Diocese (2004-2009); Executive Council, Canadian Science and Christian Affiliation; Parish Council, St. John the Evangelist **Creative Works:** Editor, The Evangelical (2013-Present); Contributor, Articles, Professional Journals **Awards:** Evan Ferguson Award, Sigma Xi (2013) **Memberships:** President, McGill Chapter, Sigma Xi (2008-Present); President, Sigma Xi (2007-Present); Evan Ferguson Award, Sigma Xi (2013); Chair, Awards Committee, Sigma Xi (2001-2006); President, James McGill Society (1993-1995); American Chemical Society; American Physical Society; James McGill Society; Sigma Xi; Founder, McGill Savoy Society; Phi Lambda Upsilon **Marquis Who's Who Honors:** Albert Nelson Marquis Lifetime Achievement Award; Marquis Who's Who Top Professional **Avocations:** Walking **Religion:** Anglican

C. Barton Whitehouse, EdD

Title: Avionics & Aviation History instructor **Industry:** Aviation **Company Name:** Inter-Tech Aviation Services **Date of Birth:** 09/07/1933 **Place of Birth:** Boston **State/Country of Origin:** MA/USA **Parents:** John Clifford Whitehouse; Pauline Barbara (Larkin) Whitehouse **Marital Status:** Married **Spouse Name:** Diane Bernier Whitehouse (06/09/1962) **Children:** Clifford Bernard (1968) **Education:** EdD, University of North Colorado (1977); MS, University of North Colorado (1974); BS, Central Connecticut State College (Now Central Connecticut State University) (1957); Coursework, Industry Technical Schools, Bendix, Collins, Frasca, E.F. Johnson, King Avionics, Motorola, Raytheon, Radio Corporation of America, Sunair, Universal Avionics **Certifications:** Certified Professional Teacher, State of Colorado (1959); Certified Flight Instructor, FAA; Accident Prevention Counselor, FAA; General Radiotelephone/Radar Operator License, FCC; Commercial Pilot Single & Multi-Engine Land, Single-Engine Sea, FAA; Instrument Rated, FAA **Career:** Founder, Owner, Seminar Leader, Manufacturer, InterTech Aviation Services, Inc., Littleton, CO (1980-Present); Professor, Aviation History, Aerospace, Metropolitan State College of Denver (Now MSU Denver) (1990-2012); Avionics for Aviators, Aviation History and Aviation Development, Metropolitan State College of Denver (Now MSU Denver) (1990-2010); Instructor, Avionics, Communications, Emily Griffith Opportunity School (Now Emily Griffith Technical College), Denver, CO (1968-1992); Instructor, Avionics, Electronic Technology, Emily Griffith Opportunity School (Now Emily Griffith Technical College) (1958-1991); Electrical Instructor, Emily Griffith Opportunity School (Now Emily Griffith Technical College), Denver, CO (1960-1968); Technician, Electric Curriculum, Emily Griffith Opportunity School (Now Emily Griffith Technical College), Denver, CO (1958-1960); Electrician, Guerard Electrical Co., New Britain, CT (1956-1957); Electrician, Killywatt Electrical Co., Newington, CT (1951-1956) **Career Related:** Curator, Avionics Exhibit, "Wings Over the Rockies," Air & Space Museum (1998-Present); Radio Engineer, Pacific Nomad, TIGHAR (1989) **Creative Works:** Author, "Aviation History and Aerospace Development: A Profile of History" (1998); Author, "Avionics for Aviators: Lab Manual & Study Guide" (1994); Author, "FCC Exam Guide" (1991); Contributor, Manuals, Study Guides; Contributor, Articles, Various Aviation & Radio Communication Journals **Awards:** FAA Wright Brothers Master Pilot Award (2011); Radio Club of America Ralph Batcher Memorial Award for Preservation of Radio History (2009); FAA Flight Standards "Golden Eagle" Award (2006); Laureate, Colorado Aviation Hall of Fame (2003); Metropolitan State College Certificate of Distinction (1993) **Memberships:** American Association for Advancement of Science; Aircraft Owners & Pilots Association; American Radio Relay League; Colorado Aviation Historical Society; Colorado Radio Collectors; Experimental Aircraft Association; International Group for Aircraft Recovery; Radio Club of America; Silver Wings Aviation Fraternity; Wings Over the Rockies Air & Space Museum **Marquis Who's Who Honors:** Albert Nelson Marquis Lifetime Achievement Award **Why did you become involved in your profession or industry:** Dr. C. Barton Whitehouse has been interested in electricity and aviation since the age of 6. He began working as an electrician at Killywatt Electrical in order to pay his way through school instead of relying on his parents, who had lived through the Depression era. He was an only child and was raised in a conservative Protestant family. **Avocations:** Amateur radio; Bicycling; Volunteer curation; Airport radio communications monitoring; Reading **Political Affiliations:** Independent **Thoughts on Life:** In 1972, Dr. Whitehouse visited the native Xingu peoples of Posto Leonardo Villas Boas, deep in the interior of Brazil, alongside other professors. As a graduate student, he was invited to Brazil's Instituto Tecnológico Aeronáutica in Sao Jose dos Campos, Brazil, in 1972 by physicist Dr. Lawrence Holland. This integrated circuit study/project resulted in a variable frequency audio signal generator, which was later manufactured by Equilab Co. for use in schools and laboratories. He flew a Cessna 205 to Brazil for the project. Over the course of his career, he has directed and prepared over 350 students in the subjects of aviation, radio communication and navigation. An accomplished pilot, he has flown a Cessna 172 plane into the jungles of Guatemala and a Cessna 205 plane to a remote site in Alaska; these missions were for field research in both tropical and arctic high frequency radio propagation. His wife was a therapeutic dietitian. The couple has traveled frequently throughout their 57-year marriage. His son builds one-of-a-kind wooden furniture at Bernwood Custom Design.

Dolores T. Whitelaw

Title: Artist **Industry:** Fine Art **Date of Birth:** 06/12/1941 **Place of Birth:** Brooklyn **State/Country of Origin:** NY/USA **Parents:** John Michael Fahey; Irene Marie (Bulger) Fahey **Marital Status:** Married **Spouse Name:** Bruce David Whitelaw (06/23/1962) **Children:** Erin Carolyn; Casey Bruce **Education:** Coursework, Art Student League (1962-1963);Coursework, Newark School of Fine and Industrial Art (1959-1960) **Creative Works:** Group Show, Sueanne Shirzay Gallery, Island Park, NY (2007-2008); One-Woman Show, E3 Gallery, New York, NY (2004); One-Woman Show, Les Malamut Art Gallery, Union, NJ (1998); Group Show, La MaMa La Galleria (1998); Group Show, Westbeth Gallery (1998); Group Show, Carole Franklin Gallery, Emerson, NJ (1997); JCB International, New York, NY (1997); One-Woman Show, E3 Gallery, New York, NY (1996) **Memberships:** Organization of Industrial Artists; City Without Walls **Marquis Who's Who Honors:** Albert Nelson Marquis Lifetime Achievement Award; Marquis Who's Who Top Professional **Why did you become involved in your profession or industry:** Mrs. Whitelaw knew from a young age that she had a talent for art. She quickly mastered acrylic, oil, and watercolor paintings.

Betsy Ann Whitenight Strunk, MEd

Title: Retired Education Educator **Industry:** Education/Educational Services **Date of Birth:** 05/28/1942 **Place of Birth:** Bloomsburg **State/Country of Origin:** PA/USA **Parents:** Mathias Clarence Whitenight; Marianna (Naunas) Whitenight **Marital Status:** Divorced **Spouse Name:** Robert J. Strunk (Divorced 1991) **Children:** Robert J. Strunk, Jr; Geoffrey M. Strunk, Esq. **Education:** Postgraduate Coursework, Western Maryland College (Now McDaniel College), Westminster, MD (1987); Postgraduate Coursework, Drexel University, Philadelphia, PA (1986); Postgraduate Coursework, Saint Joseph's University, Philadelphia, PA (1986); Postgraduate Coursework, Wilkes University, Wilkes-Barre, PA (1985); Certificate, Mentally/Physically Handicapped, PennState Brandywine, The Pennsylvania State University, Delaware County, PA (1981); MEd, West Chester University, PA (1969); BS in Education, Bloomsburg University, PA (1964) **Certifications:** Certified, Single Engine Private Pilot, Brandywine Airport, West Chester, PA (1984); Certified, Special Education Teacher, Commonwealth of Pennsylvania (1981); Certified, Elementary Education (1964) **Career:** Retired (2005); Teacher, Rose Tree Media School District (1977-2005); Instructor, Drexel University, Philadelphia, PA (1989-2001); Representative, Federal Aviation Administration, Philadelphia, PA (1986-1988); Instructor, Ground School Education, Brandywine Airport, West Chester, PA (1986-1988); Director, Ground School Education, Brandywine Airport, West Chester, PA (1986-1988); Adjunct Professor, Drexel University (1986-1990); Instructor, Delaware County Community College, Media, PA (1986); Instructor, Performance Learning Systems, Inc., Emerson, NJ and Nevada City, CA (1981-2001); Adjunct Professor, Wilkes University, Wilkes-Barre, PA (1981-1986); Teacher, Lima Elementary School, Rose Tree Media School District (1966-1969); Teacher, Eddystone Elementary School (1964-1966); Teacher, Faust School, Bensalem Township, PA (1964) **Career Related:** Owner, Stitches of Love (Stitches of Love Knitting, LLC), Savannah, GA (2006-2016); Designer, Stitches of Love (Stitches of Love Knitting, LLC), Savannah, GA (2006-2016); Teacher, Academically Gifted Program, Indian Lane and Glenwood Elementary Schools (1998-2005); Member, Educator's Advisory Committee, The Franklin Institute, PA (1995-2005) **Civic:** Volunteer, The American National Red Cross (2007-Present); Volunteer, Brandywine River Museum of Art (2005-Present); Deployed and Welcomed Home Army Soldiers, The American National Red Cross, Fort Stewart-Hunter Army Airfield, Savannah, GA (2005-Present); Captain, American Heart Association (2014-2017); Reunion Chairperson, Ben Franklin Laboratory School, Bloomsburg University (2004) **Creative Works:** Editor, "Deerfield Knoll Quarterly Newsletter" (1999-2003); Chairperson, "Deerfield Knoll Quarterly Newsletter" (1999-2003); Program Director, Video Documentaries, Including "Learning Through Live Events" and "Teaching Skills for the 21st Century" (1995); Contributor, Articles, Professional Journals **Awards:** First Place, Color Division in Photography, Bloomsburg Fair (1994); Grantee, Fine Arts in Special Education, Pennsylvania Department of Education, Commonwealth of Pennsylvania (1993-1994); Performance Learning Systems Championship Teacher Award (1993); First Place, Color Division in Photography, Colonial Pennsylvania Plantation **Memberships:** Signature Gold Member, First City Club (2008); Chairman, Public Relations, Alpha Delta Kappa (2004-2005); Program Committee, Alpha Delta Kappa (2003-2004); Program Committee, Alpha Delta Kappa (2003-2004); House of Delegates, PSEA (1999-2005) **Marquis Who's Who Honors:** Albert Nelson Marquis Lifetime Achievement Award **Why did you become involved in your profession or industry:** She was inspired by her love of children and by Mr. Warren I. Johnson, her sixth grade teacher. When she went to Bloomsburg University, he was her psychology professor, became her student teacher and advisor, and they became friends. He was the greatest teacher and made you feel like you were contributing to the class. **Avocations:** Reading; Writing; Interior Decorating; Gardening; Walking; Knitting **Political Affiliations:** Democrat **Religion:** United Methodist Church, West Chester, PA

Gretchen Esther Whitmer

Title: Governor of Michigan **Industry:** Government Administration/Government Relations/Government Services **Date of Birth:** 08/23/1971 **Place of Birth:** Lansing **State/Country of Origin:** MI/USA **Parents:** Richard Whitmer; Sharon "Sherry" H. Reisig **Marital Status:** Married **Spouse Name:** Marc Mallory (2011); Gary Shrewsbury (Divorced) **Children:** Sherry; Sydney; Alex (Stepson); Mason (Stepson); Winston (Stepson) **Education:** JD, Michigan State University College of Law (1998); BA in Communications, Michigan State University (1993) **Career:** Governor, State of Michigan (2019-Present); Prosecutor, Ingham County, MI (2016); Minority Leader, Michigan Senate (2011-2015); Member, District 23, Michigan State Senate (2006-2015); Member, District 69, Michigan House of Representatives (2003-2006); Member, District 70, Michigan House of Representatives (2001-2002); Former Member, Appropriations Committee **Political Affiliations:** Democrat

Ralph Roy Whitney Jr.

Title: 1) Partner 2) Director 3) Owner **Industry:** Business Management/ Business Services **Company Name:** 1) Monument Partners 2) First Internet Bank 3) Red Mountain Ranch **Date of Birth:** 12/10/1934 **Place of Birth:** Philadelphia **State/Country of Origin:** PA/USA **Parents:** Ralph Royal Whitney; Florence Elizabeth (Whitney) Whitney **Marital Status:** Married **Spouse Name:** Fay Wadsworth Whitney (04/04/1959) **Children:** Lynn Marie; Paula Sue; Brian Ralph **Education:** MBA, University of Rochester (1972); BA in English and History, University of Rochester (1957) **Certifications:** Certified Twin Engine Pilot; Certified Sea Captain **Career:** Partner, Monument Partners (2018-Present); Chairman, Hammond Kennedy & Whitney, New York, NY (1972-2007); President, Warren Components Corp. (1968-1972); President, Wadsworth Manufacturing Associates Inc., Syracuse, NY (1968-1971); Vice President, Wadsworth Manufacturing Associates Inc., Syracuse, NY (1965-1968); Controller, Wadsworth Manufacturing Associates Inc., Syracuse, NY (1964-1965); General Agent, National Life Vermont, Syracuse, NY (1963-1964); Division Manager, Prudential Insurance Co., Rochester, NY (1959-1963); Special Agent, Prudential Insurance Co., Rochester, NY (1958-1959); Owner, Red Mountain Ranch **Career Related:** Board Member, Seneca Printing, Inc., Dura Automobile Systems Inc., Cheyenne Capital (1990-2005); Chairman, Chief Executive Officer, Grobet File Co.; Board of Directors, Baldwin Tech. Corp.; Board of Directors, MedTek Inc.; Board of Directors, First Internet Bank **Civic:** Trustee, University of Rochester; Past Chairman, Director, University of Wyoming Foundation **Military Service:** U.S. Army (1958-1963) **Memberships:** First Technology-London, Keene Corp. (2000-2010); New York Yacht Club; Lotus Club; Century Club; Naples Yacht & Sailing Club; Princeton Club **Marquis Who's Who Honors:** Albert Nelson Marquis Lifetime Achievement Award; Marquis Who's Who Top Professional **To what do you attribute your success:** Mr. Whitney attributes his success to persistence, good communication skills, and strong leadership ability. **Why did you become involved in your profession or industry:** Mr. Whitney became involved in his profession because of the opportunities in the profession that were presented to him, both financially and professionally. After graduating, he knew that he wanted to pursue a career in business. **Avocations:** Boating in Florida; Tennis; Flying plane **Religion:** Episcopalian

Anthony D. Whittemore, MD

Title: Chief Medical Officer (Emeritus) **Industry:** Medicine & Health Care **Company Name:** Harvard Medical School Brigham and Women's Hospital **Date of Birth:** 11/05/1944 **Place of Birth:** Boston **State/Country of Origin:** MA/USA **Parents:** Anthony Rogers Whittemore; Kathrine Gansevoort Binnian Howe **Marital Status:** Married **Spouse Name:** Rhoda S. Whittemore (06/18/1966) **Children:** Anthony; Joshua; Sarah **Education:** Vascular Fellow, Peter Bent Brigham Hospital, Boston, MA (1976-1977); Resident Surgery, Columbia Presbyterian Medical Center (1970-1976); Doctor of Medicine, Columbia University (1970); Bachelor of Science in Biology, Trinity College (1966) **Career:** Professor of Surgery, Harvard Medical School, Harvard University (1993-Present); Associate Professor of Surgery, Harvard University (1987-1993); Assistant Professor of Surgery, Harvard University (1981-1987); Instructor of Surgery, Harvard Medical School/Peter Bent Brigham Hospital, Boston, MA (1979-1980); Chief of Vascular Surgery, Naval Regional Medical Center, Portsmouth, VA (1977-1979); Trainee, National Institutes of Health (1975-1976); Research Associate, Columbia University, New York, NY (1972-1973) **Career Related:** Chief Medical Officer Emeritus, Harvard Medical School, Brigham and Women's Hospital (1999-Present); Consultant, Meadox Medical School, Oakland, NJ (1983-Present); Bard Cardiopulmonary & Cardiosurgery, Billerica, MA (1982-Present); Consultant, Instrumentation Laboratories, North Andover, MA (1980-Present); Member of Medical Staff, Brigham and Women's Hospital (1979-Present); Appointed Director of Vascular Center, Brigham and Women's Hospital (1991); Chief, Division on Vascular Surgery, Brigham and Women's Hospital (1990-1999); Grant Investigator, National Institutes of Health (1979, 1983); Director, Surgical Training Program, Harvard Medical School/ Brigham and Women's Hospital (1979) **Military Service:** Lieutenant Commander, U.S. Navy (1977-1979) **Creative Works:** Contributor, More than 300 Articles to Professional Journals; Artist, Model Ships, Galleries **Awards:** Decorated, Commendation Award, U.S. Navy **Memberships:** Program Committee, American Society for Artificial Internal Organs (1982-Present); President, American Surgical Society (1991); Fellow, American College of Surgeons; Society International de Chirurgie; President, New England Society for Vascular Surgery; New England Surgical Society; Society for Vascular Surgery; President, International Cardiovascular Society; President, Boston Surgical Society; Society of University Surgeons; President, American Surgical Association; Association for Academy Surgery; Country Club **Marquis Who's Who Honors:** Albert Nelson Marquis Lifetime Achievement Award; Marquis Who's Who Top Professional **Why did you become involved in your profession or industry:** After enduring two early tragedies while coming of age, Mr. Whittemore dedicated himself to the medical profession to try and prevent such horrors from afflicting others. **Avocations:** Skiing; Sailing; Model ship building

Ronald Clarence "Ron" Whittemore

Title: Senior Olympian; Computer Program Analyst **Industry:** Information Technology and Services **Company Name:** Datamann, Inc. **Date of Birth:** 04/03/1938 **Place of Birth:** Saco **State/Country of Origin:** ME/USA **Parents:** Kenneth Edward Whittemore; Bertha Dorkas (Grace) Whittemore **Marital Status:** Married **Spouse Name:** Lois J. (03/25/2017); Lillian Marie Therriault (11/24/1962, Deceased 2016) **Children:** Deborah Lorraine (Adopted at six weeks old) **Education:** BSBA, Hawthorne College (1984) **Certifications:** Masters All-American Certificate **Career:** Programming Manager, Datamann, Wilder, VT (1979-Present); Senior Programmer, Computac, LLC, West Lebanon, NH (1973-1979); Senior Programmer, Joy Manufacturing, Claremont, NH (1968-1973); Computer Programmer, Cross Company, Hartford, VT (1966-1968); Senior Olympian; Computer Program Analyst **Civic:** President, Claremont Bridge Club (2006-2019); President, Claremont Men's Softball League (1980); Chess Coach, Stevens High School (1972) **Military Service:** United States Air Force (1961-1965); United States Navy (1956-1960) **Creative Works:** Featured, Sports, The Eagle Times (2008, 2011, 2018); Featured, Valley News (2010, 2011); Featured, Valley News (2010) **Awards:** First Place Gold Medal, Long Jump, Senior Olympic Qualifying Track, National Senior Games, Burlington, VT (2018); First Place Gold Medal, Triple Jump, Senior Olympic Qualifying Track, National Senior Games, Burlington, VT (2018); Fourth Overall, Senior Olympics (2018); First Place Gold Medal, 100 Meter Dash, Senior Olympic Qualifying Track and Field, National Senior Games, Burlington, VT (2018); Second Place, Triple Jump, National Senior Games (2017); Fourth Place, Triple Jump, National Senior Olympics (2013); Bronze Medal, Triple Jump, National Senior Games, Humble, Texas (2011); Fourth Place, Long Jump, National Senior Games, Humble, Texas (2011); Placed 18th, 200 Meter Dash, National Senior Games, Humble, Texas (2011); Placed 21st, 100 Meter Dash, National Senior Games (2011); First Place, Long Jump, Dartmouth Relays, Hanover, NH (2010); Second Place, 60 Meters, Dartmouth Relays, Hanover, NH (2010); Eighth Place Ribbon, Triple Jump, National Senior Games, San Francisco, CA (2009); Four Gold Medals, Vermont Senior Games (2008); Named Marquis Who's Who Industry Leader **Memberships:** Board of Directors, Circle 8 Square Dance (1984-1985); President, White Mountain Chess (1971-1980); Fellow, Data Processing Management Association (Now Association of Information Technology Professionals (AITP)); Veterans of Foreign Wars; Circle 8 Square Dance; Knights of Columbus **Marquis Who's Who Honors:** Albert Nelson Marquis Lifetime Achievement Award; Marquis Who's Who Top Professional; Marquis Who's Who Humanitarian Award **Why did you become involved in your profession or industry:** Mr. Whittemore was planning on making a career in the Air Force, but he got married and his next tour was going to be in Vietnam. He decided to get out of the Air force. He went to programming school, where he graduated magna cum laude. **Avocations:** Running; Chess; Softball; Reading; Bicycling; Long jump; Triple jump; Playing bridge; Playing cribbage **Political Affiliations:** Republican **Religion:** Roman Catholic **Thoughts on Life:** Mr. Whittemore started running to stay in shape, and then it became a habit. A few years ago, he started running everyday. He still holds the record in Claremont for the most consecutive days without missing a day, ranking second in New Hampshire.

Mary Kathryne Wiedebusch

Title: Dancer **Industry:** Other **Place of Birth:** Clarksburg **State/Country of Origin:** WV/USA **Parents:** Danton Leon; Mary Margaret (Dixon) Caussin **Marital Status:** Married **Spouse Name:** Charles Edward Wiedebusch (07/12/1952, Deceased) **Children:** Carole Jean; Charles Edward II **Education:** Postgraduate, Duke University (1980); Postgraduate, American University (1979); Postgraduate, Radford University (1975); MA, West Virginia University (1974); BS, West Virginia University (1951) **Career:** Director, Orchesis Dance Ensemble, West Virginia University, Morgantown (1993-2006); Professor of Dance, Coordinator, Dance Program, West Virginia University, Morgantown, WV (1993-2006); Associate Professor, Director, Choreographer, West Virginia University, Morgantown, WV (1990-1993); Assistant Professor, Choreographer, Orchesis Modern Dance Ensemble, West Virginia University, Morgantown, WV (1955-1990); Teacher, Choreographer, Morgantown High School (1951) **Career Related:** Director, Fundraiser Project, Residency Program, West Virginia University (1978-2006); Founder, Director, Artist-in-Residence Program, West Virginia University (1978-2006); West Virginia University Honor Dance Gala, Metropolitan Theatre Commission (2005); Member, Commission Board, Metropolitan Theatre Foundation (2003); Faculty Member, Governor's Schools of West Virginia (1997); Faculty Member, Fine Arts Music Camp, West Virginia University (1976); Professor, Coordinator, Artistic Director, Choreographer, Order of Vandalia, West Virginia University **Civic:** Chair, Golf Classic (1993-1995) **Creative Works:** London Contemporary Dance School (1991-Present); Choreographer, Director, Loulie, Valerie and William Canady Creative Arts Center, West Virginia University (1976-2006); Gala Performance Choreographer, West Virginia Dance Festival (1975-1995) **Awards:** Award, Metropolitan Theatre (2016); Woman of Distinction Award, Alpha Xi Delta (2009); Paul Martin Alumni Service Award, Physical Education Gala, West Virginia University (2006); Inductee, Hall of Fame, School of Physical Education, West Virginia University (1994); Outstanding Leadership Award **Memberships:** National Awards, American College Dance Association (1990-1991); Founding Member, Board of Directors, American College Dance Association (1973-1987) **Marquis Who's Who Honors:** Albert Nelson Marquis Lifetime Achievement Award **Avocations:** Golf; Boating

Dale Lee Wilcox

Title: Executive Director, General Counsel **Industry:** Law and Legal Services **Company Name:** Immigration Reform Law Institute **Date of Birth:** 07/24/1968 **Place of Birth:** Caribou **State/Country of Origin:** ME/USA **Parents:** Alden A. Wilcox; Gail V. Wilcox **Marital Status:** Married **Spouse Name:** Elma Oliveira Wilcox **Children:** Isabella Grace Oliveira Wilcox **Education:** JD, Regent University School of Law, Virginia Beach, VA, Cum Laude (1996); BA in Political Science, University of Louisville, Louisville, KY (1992) **Career:** Chief Executive Officer, General Counsel, Immigration Reform Law Institute (2014-Present); State and Local Affairs Director, Federation for American Immigration Reform (2012-2014); Of Counsel (2005-2011), Executive Director of Mid-Atlantic Regional Headquarters, Norfolk, Virginia (2002-2005), Counsel (2001-2002), Judicial Watch, Inc.; Associate Attorney, Bopp, Coleson, & Bostrom (1996-2000) **Career Related:** Clerk for the Honorable Steven M. Fleece, Clark Superior Court III, Jeffersonville, Indiana; Expert Witness, Various Issues, State Legislative Committees **Civic:** Active Member, Community and Church; Volunteer, Vice President of Church Board of Directors; Volunteer, Nursing Home Ministry; Volunteer, Youth Ministry; Volunteer, Bible School Teacher; Volunteer, Greeter; Volunteer, Usher; Volunteer, Alter Care Ministry, Volunteer, Stepping Stone Mission; Co-Organizer, Numerous Missions Trips to Brazil, Provide Food and Medical Care to the Poor and Minister in Churches, City-Wide Crusades, Conferences, and Prisons **Creative Works:** Contributor, More than 100 Published Articles; Appearance, National Television and Radio; Speaker, Major Groups Across America; Participant, Academic Forum Panels **Bar Admissions:** Supreme Court of the United States; United States Court of Appeals for the Fourth Circuit; United States Court of Appeals for the Fifth Circuit; United States Court of Appeals for the Seventh Circuit; United States Court of Appeals for the Ninth Circuit; United States Court of Appeals for the Tenth Circuit; United States Court of Appeals for the Eleventh Circuit; United States Court of Appeals for the District of Columbia Circuit; United States District Court for the District of Columbia; United States District Court for the Northern District of Indiana; United States District Court for the Southern District of Indiana; Supreme Court of Indiana; District of Columbia Court of Appeals **Marquis Who's Who Honors:** Marquis Who's Who Top Professional; Marquis Who's Who Humanitarian Award **To what do you attribute your success:** Mr. Wilcox attributes his success to hard work, and, above all, his faith. His character, integrity, confidence, and desire to help others have been instrumental to his accomplishments, not to mention the numerous opportunities and open doors that have sprung from God. The advice that Mr. Wilcox can offer the next generation or others aspiring to work in his profession would be to not pursue fortune and fame, but do what you enjoy. Let your natural gifts, talents, and abilities dictate what you do. It will bring long-lasting success and personal satisfaction. Have integrity. Do not compromise your values for anyone. Be kind. Always being a good and decent person opens doors. Be faithful. Work diligently and give your best to every project and in the end you will be rewarded. Push through fear. Do it scared if you must because fear of failure will rob you of many great opportunities. **Why did you become involved in your profession or industry:** Mr. Wilcox became involved in his profession because he wanted to defend and protect the vulnerable, good values, and the rule of law. **Avocations:** Reading; Mountain biking **Religion:** Christian **Thoughts on Life:** Mr. Wilcox's motto is: "Do justice, love mercy, walk humbly."

David Eric Wilcox, MS, PE

Title: Electrical Engineer, Educator, Consultant, Federal Agency Executive, President & Chief Executive Officer **Industry:** Engineering **Company Name:** Global Skills Exchange Corporation **Date of Birth:** 09/04/1939 **Place of Birth:** Cortland **State/Country of Origin:** NY/USA **Parents:** James A. Wilcox; Lucille C. (Fiske) Wilcox **Marital Status:** Married **Spouse Name:** Phillipa Ann Wilcox (01/23/1977) **Children:** Terri L.; Cindy A.; Jana L. **Education:** Postgraduate Coursework, The State University of New Jersey Rutgers (1980-1983); MS in Electrical Engineering, University of Bridgeport (1977); MS in Counseling and Human Resources, University of Bridgeport (1977); Business, Postgraduate Coursework, Marist College (1976); Postgraduate Coursework, Electronic Engineering, Syracuse University (1965); BSEE, University at Buffalo (1961) **Certifications:** Registered Professional Engineer, State of New York (1968) **Career:** President, Global Skills Exchange Corporation, Alexandria, VA (2003-Present); Chief Executive Officer, Global Skills Exchange Corporation, Alexandria, VA (2003-Present); Executive Deputy Director, National Skills Standards Board, Washington DC (1998-2003); President, Wilcox Industries, Corp. (1973-1998); Director of Sales, Mercom Corporation, Winooski, VT (1970-1973); Research Engineering Manager, Input/Output Devices Section, Air Force Research Laboratory, Rome, NY (1961-1970) **Career Related:** Board Member, Mercom Corporation (1970-1973); Board of Directors Principal, Executive Effectiveness Inc., New York, NY; Instructor, Dale Carnegie & Associates, Inc. **Civic:** Examiner, New York State Excelsior Program (1995); Member, Orange County Private Industry Council (1995); Treasurer, Board of Directors, Family Counseling Service, Inc. (1980-1984); Board Chairman, New York State Jaycees (1973-1974); President, New York State Jaycees (1972-1973); Vice President, Board of Directors, Special Olympics New York (1972-1973); Director, JCI, Inc. (1970-1971); Member, Various National Committees; Member, Various Advisory Committees **Military Service:** Lieutenant, U.S. Air Force (1961-1965) **Creative Works:** Author, "Information System Sciences"; Contributor, Articles, Professional Journals **Memberships:** IEEE; Society for Information Display (SID); NYSSPE; International Transactional Analysis Association (ITAA); American Society for Quality (ASQ); Platform-The International Platform Association; SHRM; ICE **Marquis Who's Who Honors:** Albert Nelson Marquis Lifetime Achievement Award **Religion:** Methodist

Roger Wilcox

Title: Psychologist, Researcher **Industry:** Research **Date of Birth:** 04/01/1934 **Place of Birth:** Zanesville **State/Country of Origin:** OH/USA **Parents:** Clark Lewis Wilcox; Mildred Adelaide (O'Hara) Wilcox **Marital Status:** Married **Spouse Name:** Joy Ann Barr (11/02/1956) **Children:** Beth Hartigan, Wells Lewis, Judd O'Hara **Education:** PhD, University of Tennessee (1968); MA, Ohio State University (1960); BA, Ohio State University (1959) **Certifications:** Licensed Psychologist, Ohio **Career:** Principal, Roger Wilcox, PhD, Inc., Zanesville, OH (1976) **Career Related:** Administrative Consultant, Community Mental Health, St. Clairsville, OH (1967-1999); Industrial Consultant, Visual Information Institute, Xenia, OH (1967-1990); Director of Administration, Comprehensive Mental Health, Zanesville, OH (1974-1976); Professor, Ohio University, Zanesville, OH (1970-1974); Department Chairman, California Polytechnic State University (1968-1970); Wilberforce University (1966-1968); Board Member, Zanesville Ohio Design Review Architectural Board; Board of Directors, Goodwill Industries; Board of Directors, City of Zanesville Architectural Design and Review Board **Civic:** Co-Founder, Ohio Association Mental Health Directors, Columbus, OH (1976); Budget Chairman, United Way of America (United Way Worldwide), Zanesville, Muskingum County, OH (1970-1973) **Military Service:** U.S. Army (1953-1956) **Creative Works:** Author, "Psychological Consequences of Being a Black American" (1971); Contributor, More Than 15 Articles on Verbal Learning and Verbal Behavior, Professional Journals; Presenter, Speeches and Research Papers, 25 Symposiums in Professional Field **Awards:** Fellow, U.S. Office of Education (1968); Fellow, U.S. Public Health Service (1960) **Memberships:** American Psychological Association (1961-Present); Ohio Psychological Association (1979); American Arbitration Association **Marquis Who's Who Honors:** Albert Nelson Marquis Lifetime Achievement Award **Why did you become involved in your profession or industry:** Dr. Wilcox became involved in his profession because he lived in Tennessee and enlisted in the Korean War; they sent him to Europe to work as a photo engraver and assignment photographer for Stars and Stripes and, additionally for international news, at the time called New York Times offshore sight. He managed a couple of laboratories in France and would get telegrams that would tell him about the photographs to honor the deceased and to send pictures to the paper for consideration. He later got sent to Germany. There, he worked in the European photo center and went on assignments. He photographed the homecoming queen and others and went to the American headquarters in Europe but couldn't work in their lab unless he had clearance. So they sent him to another lab where he did a little bit of work there. However, he decided to pursue a career in psychology when he was studying physics. He was in an astronomy class and was so bored, so he transferred his major to psychology. **Avocations:** Playing golf; Photography; Computer technology; Statistical analysis; Writing **Political Affiliations:** Democrat

Marjory Wildcraft

Title: Chief Executive Officer, President, Owner **Industry:** Business Management/Business Services **Company Name:** Grow Network **Marital Status:** Married **Spouse Name:** Dave **Education:** BA, Business Finishing School (2017); MA in Trans-Personal Psychology, Sofia University (1997); BS in Electrical and Electronics Engineering, Cum Laude (1986) **Career:** Chief Executive Officer, President, Owner, Grow Network (2009-Present); Chief Executive Officer, Backyard Food Production Inc. (2005-2009); Investment Manager, ENP Network (1996-2003); Senior Engineering Consultant, Synergy Engineering Ltd. (1993-1998); Senior Manager of Engineering Operations, Motorola Solutions, Inc. (1991-1993); Senior Engineer, Motorola Solutions, Inc. (1989-1991); U.S. Department of Defense (1986-1988) **Civic:** Host, Home Grown Food Summit; Volunteer, Trail Clean Up Crest Butte, U.S. Forest Service; Volunteer, Animals Shelters **Creative Works:** Author, "7 Shortcuts to Finding the Perfect Survival Retreat"; Author, "How To Grow Half Of Your Own Food"; Author "Snakebite!"; Producer, DVD Series, "Grow Your Own Groceries" **Awards:** Featured, Winning Article, "Food Sustainability Media," Reuters (2017); Student of the Year, Business Finishing School (2017) **Memberships:** Mainstream Preppers; Association for the Study of Peak Oil & Gas - USA; Organic Consumers Association; Ecology Action, Biointensive Mini-Farming; Transition Town, Transition Network; Survival Podcast; Permaculture Activist; American Botanical Council; Seed Savers Exchange; National Gardening Association **Why did you become involved in your profession or industry:** Ms. Wildcraft became involved in her profession because of her experiences as a volunteer to get local grown food into elementary schools in Texas. However, due to the lack of farmers in the area, the initiative was difficult to implement. In order to build resiliency in the food system in the United States, she established Grow Network. **Avocations:** Running; Doing gymnastics; Skateboarding

Donny Wilder

Title: Editor, Publisher, Owner, Retired State Legislature **Industry:** Writing and Editing **Company Name:** Chronicle Publishing Company **Date of Birth:** 03/09/1932 **Place of Birth:** Woodruff **State/Country of Origin:** SC/USA **Parents:** Robert Perry Wilder; Shadie (Skinner) Wilder **Marital Status:** Widowed **Spouse Name:** Gene Marshall (08/28/1954) **Children:** Robert Perry II **Education:** BA, Furman University (1954) **Career:** South Carolina House Of Representatives (1992-Present); President, Laurens County Communications Inc. (1985-1993); President, Chronicle Publishing Company (1967-1987); Editor-Publisher, The Chronicle, Clinton, SC (1967-1987); Managing Editor, The Daily Star, Shelby, NC (1963-1967); Assistant Managing Editor, Herald-Tribune, Sarasota, FL (1961-1963); Associate Editor, Evening Herald, Rock Hill, SC (1955-1960); Sports Writer, Spartanburg (1954-1955); Sports Editor, Cautavet News-Times (1954); Editor, Publisher, Owner, Chronicle Publishing Company **Career Related:** Board Visitors, Presbyterian College, Clinton, SC (1986-1987); Economic Task Force, State of South Carolina (1979-1983); President, South Carolina Press Association (1974) **Awards:** Award for Public Service; Honorary Degree, Presbyterian College; Order of the Palmetto, South Carolina's Highest Civilian Honor; Henry Laurens Award for Service to Laurens County **Memberships:** Rotary Club; SAE International **Marquis Who's Who Honors:** Albert Nelson Marquis Lifetime Achievement Award **To what do you attribute your success:** Mr. Wilder attributes his success to enjoying his job, as he always felt it was worthwhile. **Why did you become involved in your profession or industry:** In high school, Mr. Wilder played sports, though he had to stop when he was injured. However, he never let go of his love for all things athletic, which proved useful when he began writing about sports for the school paper. As he gained more experience as a writer, he began to cover legislature and local government. This prompted him to run for a seat in the State House in a special election. Fortunately, Mr. Wilder won and spent the next 10 years as a member of the House of Representatives. **Political Affiliations:** Democrat **Religion:** Presbyterian **Thoughts on Life:** Mr. Wilder prioritizes treating others the way he wants to be treated.

Raymond Leigh Wilder

Title: Statistician; Consultant **Industry:** Financial Services **Date of Birth:** 08/19/1927 **Place of Birth:** Tacoma **State/Country of Origin:** WA/USA **Year of Passing:** 2019 **Parents:** Raymond Dabney; Edna Mabel (Leigh) Wilder **Marital Status:** Married **Spouse Name:** Janice Epps (08/23/2000); Marion Shirley Champagne (01/22/1972); Alois DenBeste (1957) **Children:** Michael Jon; Leslie Ann **Education:** MS in Quantitative Business Analysis, University of Southern California, Los Angeles, CA (1965); Postgraduate Coursework, University of Delaware, Newark, DE (1958-1959); Postgraduate Coursework, University of Oregon, Eugene, OR (1956-1957); Postgraduate Coursework, University of Washington, Seattle, WA (1955); Postgraduate Coursework, University of California Los Angeles, Los Angeles, CA; BS in Mathematics, Oregon State University, Corvallis, OR (1952) **Career:** Treasurer, Board Directors, Seal Rock Rural Fire Protection District (1979-1987); Senior Associate, Wilder Associates, Inc., Sunset Beach, CA and Seal Rock, OR (1974-1982); Consultant, Teacher in the Field, Member, Advisory Committee, Waldport Schools, Lincoln County Schools, Waldport, OR (1978-1979); Group Engineer, Huntington Beach, CA (1972-1974); Assistant to the Director, Santa Monica, CA (1963-1972); Group Engineer, McDonnell Douglas, Culver City, CA (1960-1963); Consultant Statistician, Niagara Falls, NY (1959-1960); Consultant Statistician, E.I. du Pont de Nemours & Co., Wilmington, DE (1957-1959); Computing Engineer, Northwest Natural Gas Corporation (NW Natural), Portland, OR (1956-1957); Computing Analyst, Douglas Aircraft Corporation, Long Beach, CA (1953-1955); Applied Statistician, Washington Public Opinion Laboratory, Seattle, WA (1953) **Career Related:** Member, Endowment Committee, YMCA, Newport, OR (1983-2019); Member, Beaver Creek Citizens Advisory Committee, Oregon Department of Land Conservation and Development Commission (1980-1981) **Civic:** Member, Track & Basketball, Kellogg High School; Manager, Track, Oregon State **Military Service:** Fire Controlman, United States Navy (1945-1948) **Creative Works:** Rating for Reliability Allocation **Awards:** Lettered, Track & Basketball, Kellogg High School **Memberships:** President, Chi Phi; Pi Mu Epsilon; The Honor Society of Phi Kappa Phi; American Statistical Association; Student Athletic Managers Association; Endowment Committee, Oregon Coast Commission for the Arts; Seal Rock Water District Board **Marquis Who's Who Honors:** Albert Nelson Marquis Lifetime Achievement Award **Why did you become involved in your profession or industry:** Mr. Wilder became involved in his profession because he had loved numbers and looking for solutions since he was young; he quickly found his interest in math. **Avocations:** Followed the stock market; Collected yellow business pads **Political Affiliations:** Democrat **Religion:** Episcopalian **Thoughts on Life:** Mr. Wilder always had a passion for statistics, had to settle for math when deciding for a field, since at the time there was no major field in statistics. His younger years were in Kellogg, Idaho, which was a mining town at the time, he then moved to Portland for his high school days. Mr. Wilder passed away on August 21, 2019.

Thomas Wilhelmy

Title: Attorney, Vice President **Industry:** Law and Legal Services **Company Name:** Fredrikson & Byron, P.A. **Children:** Five Children **Education:** JD, University of Chicago Law School (1978); BBA, University of Notre Dame, Summa Cum Laude (1975); St. Thomas Academy, Summa Cum Laude (1971) **Certifications:** MSBA Board-Certified Specialist in Real Property Law, Real Property Section, Minnesota Bar Association **Career:** Attorney, Shareholder, Fredrikson & Byron, P.A. (1988-Present); Shareholder, Gray Plant Mooty (1978-1985) **Civic:** Committee Co-Chair, ABA/IPT Advanced Property Tax Seminar (2010-Present) **Awards:** ICFM 500 Leading Lawyer, by Inter Continental Finance & Law (2016-Present); Best Corporate Tax Law Firm, USA by Lawyers World Law Awards (2016-Present); The Best Lawyers in America, Litigation and Controversy, Tax (2015-Present); Tax Law Firm of the Year, Finance Monthly (2014-Present); Best Corporate Tax Law Firm, USA, LegalComprehensive.com; Lawyer Monthly Legal Awards, Corporate Tax Lawyer of the Year (2013-Present); Corporate Tax Lawyer of the Year, USA, by Lawyer Monthly Legal Awards (2013-Present); Corporate Tax Lawyer of the Year, USA, Global Venture Annual Awards (2019); Corporate Tax Lawyer of the Year, USA, Corporate America Today (2019); Most Influential Property Tax Lawyer of the Year, Minnesota, AI Global Media Corporate Excellence Awards (2019); M&A Today Global Corporate Tax Lawyer of the Year, USA (2016, 2019); Lawyer International, Legal 100 Award Corporate Tax Lawyer of the Year, USA (2016, 2019); Best Corporate Tax Law Firm – USA (with Fredrikson & Byron), Lawyer's World (2016, 2019); America's Most Honored Professional by American Registry (2016); 2015 Legal Award, Excellence in Tax Litigation, Minnesota, International Association of Lawyers and Swissportl Golden Globe 100 Award – Corporate Tax Lawyer of the Year, USA by KMH Media Group (2015); Minnesota Super Lawyers, Super Lawyer (2008, 2010-2017); Top Rated Lawyer in Taxation Law, by American Lawyer Media; Top Rated Lawyer in Taxation Law, Martindale Hubbell; Leading Lawyer Global 250 for 2014, Lawyer Monthly; Martindale-Hubbell, AV Preeminent Peer Review Rated **Memberships:** Real Property, Urban, State and Local Law and Tax Sections, State and Local Taxation Committee, American Bar Association; Board of Directors and Member, National Association of Property Tax Attorneys; Real Property and Tax Sections, Minnesota State Bar Association; Minnesota Corporate Counsel Association; Institute for Professionals in Taxation; Retail Committee, Institute for Professionals in Taxation; Minneapolis and St. Paul Building Owners and Managers Association; National Association of Industrial and Office Properties; Minnesota Shopping Center Association; Hennepin County Bar Association **Bar Admissions:** Wisconsin (2018); Federal Courts (1988); Minnesota (1978) **To what do you attribute your success:** Mr. Wilhelmy attributes his success to being blessed with some very intelligent and supportive clients. He was raised to have a strong sense of justice and fairness and to fight against the abuse of power. **Why did you become involved in your profession or industry:** Mr. Wilhelmy became involved in his profession because he is the oldest of nine children and when he was 5 years old, he would stand and argue with his mother when she asked him to do something. From a young age, everyone told him he should be a lawyer some day.

Alfred B. Williams, PhD

Title: Management Educator (Retired) **Industry:** Education/Educational Services **Date of Birth:** 09/17/1940 **Place of Birth:** Oakland City **State/Country of Origin:** IN/USA **Parents:** Ross Merl Williams; Jesse Adell (Helsley) Williams **Marital Status:** Married **Spouse Name:** Francis Allen Duhe (09/26/2015) **Education:** PhD in Educational Administration and Business Communications, Georgia State University (1974); MS in Business Education, Indiana University (1964); BS, Oakland City University, Cum Laude (1963) **Career:** Professor Emeritus (2002); Professor of Management and Business Communications, University of Louisiana at Lafayette (1975-2002); Chairman, Department of Business Administration, University of Louisiana at Lafayette (1986-1996); Consultant, South-Western Publishing Company, Cincinnati, OH (1981-1993); Adjunct Professor, Georgia State University, Atlanta, GA (1972-1974); Editor, South-Western Publishing Company, Cincinnati, OH (1969-1972); Teacher, Oakland City University (1965-1969); Teacher, Arlington High School, Indianapolis, IN (1964-1965) **Career Related:** Adjunct Professor, University of Louisiana at Lafayette (2004-2005); Irwin Publishing (1989); Consultant, John Wiley & Sons, Inc. (1988-1989) **Civic:** Reading Mentor, North Lewis Elementary, New Iberia, LA (2003-2007) **Military Service:** US Air Force (1958-1960) **Creative Works:** Editor, Professional Journal (1983, 1993); Author, Study Guides **Awards:** Award of Merit in Memory of Francis W. Weeks, Association for Business Communications (1984); Outstanding Teacher, College of Business Administration **Memberships:** Association for Business Communications (1986-1990); American Association of University Professors; Louisiana Association of Independent Colleges & Universities; Sierra Club; PDK International; The Honor Society of Phi Kappa Phi; Delta Pi Epsilon; Beta Gamma Sigma **Marquis Who's Who Honors:** Albert Nelson Marquis Lifetime Achievement Award **Why did you become involved in your profession or industry:** Mr. Williams became involved in his profession because of his father, a deep vein coal miner, and one of his mentors in college, Olive Smith, who helped him obtain admission to Indiana University. **Avocations:** Exercising; Gardening; Reading; Socializing **Religion:** Protestant

Cory Williams

Title: Chief Executive Officer, Entrepreneur **Industry:** Medicine & Health Care **Company Name:** EPIC Health Partners **Date of Birth:** 08/31/1984 **Place of Birth:** Chatham **State/Country of Origin:** VA/USA **Parents:** Roger Williams; Deborah Williams **Education:** MBA, Ashford University (2010); MS in Computer Science, Averett University (2006) **Career:** Chairman of the Board, Epic Health Partners and Epic Management Group (2015-Present); Founder, Chief Executive Officer, Epic Health Partners (2012-Present); Director of Operations, Troxler Electronic Laboratories, Inc. (2012-2016); Manager, MRT Operations, The Goodyear Tire & Rubber Company (2008-2012); Supply Chain Analyst, The Goodyear Tire & Rubber Company (2006-2008) **Civic:** Board Member, PDC Capital Group, LLC **Awards:** Employee of the Year, Goodyear; Employee of the Year, Troxler Electronics Laboratories **Memberships:** Business Leadership Council; Chamber of Commerce **To what do you attribute your success:** Mr. Williams attributes his success to his upbringing. He grew up in a two-family household and his family wasn't wealthy. He watched his parents work hard everyday to make sure they provided for him and his two sisters. He wanted to be in a position where he would enable his kids to have a better start than he was able to. He also wanted to make a difference in the community and make a name for himself across the globe. A part of his competitive spirit comes from playing sports, he hated to lose but he understood the value of losing. He has learned to never make the same mistake twice. His grandmother was very inspirational in pushing him to be the best he could be and telling him and instilling in him that he could be whatever he wanted to be if he put his mind to it. **Why did you become involved in your profession or industry:** Mr. Williams became involved in his profession because he had a family member that had a mental illness, which inspired him to do more research in the area. When he was 19, he started a medical transportation business which wasn't very successful. He interned at Goodyear while in college but always had an entrepreneur spirit, so that spiked his journey.

DeWayne A. Williams

Title: Artist **Industry:** Writing and Editing **Company Name:** Artistwork Publishers **Date of Birth:** 08/20/1943 **Place of Birth:** San Diego **State/Country of Origin:** CA/USA **Parents:** DeWayne Arthur Williams Senior; Mary Elizabeth (Cardell) Williams **Marital Status:** Married **Spouse Name:** Suelynn Davison (01/18/1964) **Children:** Regan Lane; Rani Chellane Garcia; DeWayne Arthur III **Education:** Postgraduate Coursework, University of Idaho (1997-1999); Bachelor of Arts in Biological Sciences, Florida State University (1966); Master of Arts in Interdisciplinary Studies, Oregon State University (1974) **Career:** Full-time Artist (2002-Present); Exhibit Specialist, National Park Service, Mammoth, WY (2001-2002); Fish and Wildlife Biologist, United States Fish and Wildlife Service, Sacramento, CA (2000-2001); Environmental Protection Assistant, United States Army Corps of Engineers, Boise, ID (1996-2000); Exhibit Specialist, National Park Service, Homestead, FL (1994-1996); Biological Technician (Fish), National Marine Fisheries Service, Honolulu, HI (1994); Artist, Author, Editor, Photographer, Missoula, MT (1988-1993); Artist, Museum Curator, University of Montana, Missoula, MT (1980-1988); Arts and Crafts Director and Instructor, United States Army in the Canal Zone (1975-1979); Biological Technician, Environmental Protection Agency, Corvallis, OR (1974-1975); Aquatic Biologist, Oregon Game Commission, Corvallis, OR (1966-1972) **Career Related:** Curator, Artist, Dooby Avenue Art Installation, Gerlach, NV (1973-1995); Fine Arts Director, Student Union, Oregon State University, Corvallis, OR (1973) **Civic:** Boy Scout Leader (1967-1993) **Creative Works:** Contributing Photographer, "Photographic Possibilities" (1991); Author, Editor, Photographer, and Publisher, "Montana Tribute" (1990); Contributing Photographer, "American Photographers" (1989); Contributing Photographer, "Living Artists in America" (1989); Contributing Photographer, "Erotic Art by Living Artists" (1988); Creator, Correlative Composite Photograph, Idaho State University, Oregon State University (1976); Photo in Collection, Center for Creative Photography, Tucson, AZ **Awards:** Employee of the Quarter, University of Montana (1988); Outstanding Performance Rating for Proficiency in Teaching Art in the Canal Zone (1976) **Memberships:** Phi Kappa Phi (1974) **Marquis Who's Who Honors:** Albert Nelson Marquis Lifetime Achievement Award; Marquis Who's Who Top Professional **Avocations:** Hunting; Fishing; Camping **Political Affiliations:** Democrat **Religion:** Episcopalian

Ebb Harry Williams III

Title: Lawyer **Industry:** Law and Legal Services **Date of Birth:** 12/13/1939 **Place of Birth:** Danville **State/Country of Origin:** VA/USA **Parents:** Ebb Harry Williams Jr.; Lillian (Shuping) Williams **Marital Status:** Married **Spouse Name:** Gayle G. Williams (12/31/1960) **Children:** Kevin T. Williams; Christa W. Stultz **Education:** JD, University of Richmond, Richmond, VA, With Honors (1964); BA, University of Richmond, Richmond, VA, With Honors (1961) **Career:** Private Practice, Martinsville, VA (1973-Present); Partner, Broaddus, Epperly, Broaddus and Williams, Martinsville, VA (1964-1973) **Career Related:** Substitute Judge, Domestic Relations Court, General District Court, Counties of Henry, Patrick, City of Martinsville (1969-1981); Associate Professor, Law, Patrick Henry Community College, Martinsville, VA (1974-1973) **Civic:** Board of Trustees, Averett University, Danville, VA (1970-1982, 1982-1990, 1994-2002, 2003-2011); Board of Trustees, University of Richmond (1994-2000); Instructor, Political Action Course, Martinsville Henry County Chamber of Commerce; District Chair, Boy Scouts of America; Chairman, Board of Directors, Martinsville Chapter, The American National Red Cross; Advisory Board, The Salvation Army USA; Board of Directors, Piedmont Community Services; Guest Speaker, Numerous Civic and Service Club Meetings **Awards:** Listee, Top 100 Registry Book (2019); Top 100 Registry Book, (2017-2018); Tradition of Excellence Award, Virginia State Bar (2000) **Memberships:** President, Martinsville-Henry County Bar Association (1973-1974); Secretary, Virginia State Bar (1968-1969); Lifetime Member, Virginia State Bar **Bar Admissions:** United States Court of Appeals for the Fourth Circuit (1988); United States District Court for the Western District of Virginia (1984); Virginia (1964); Supreme Court of the United States **Marquis Who's Who Honors:** Albert Nelson Marquis Lifetime Achievement Award **To what do you attribute your success:** Mr. Williams attributes his success to a strong work ethic, which he learned from his parents. He is also grateful for his wife's superb love and support. Above all, Mr. Williams loves helping people and is confident that he has saved many lives. **Why did you become involved in your profession or industry:** From a young age, Mr. Williams has been an advocate for the rights of other people, his family, and himself; this strong conviction led him to his profession. In his years of practice, he has become an expert in acknowledging, using, and applying the law, but he has most especially enjoyed helping people. **Avocations:** Watching football and basketball; Electric trains; Sculpture

Tonda Williams

Title: Entrepreneur, Consultant **Industry:** Consulting **Company Name:** Omni-Data Technology **Date of Birth:** 11/21/1949 **Place of Birth:** New York **State/Country of Origin:** NY/USA **Parents:** William Williams; Juanita (Rainey) Williams **Marital Status:** Married **Spouse Name:** Richard K. Frasca **Children:** Tywana Williams **Education:** Graduate, Long Island Business Institute, New York (1996); MBA in Business Management, American National University, Phoenix, AZ (1987); BA in Business Management, American National University, Phoenix, AZ (1983); Student, C.W. Post College (Now LIU Post), Brookville, NY (1981-1983); Student, Collegiate Institute, New York, NY (1975-1978) **Certifications:** Notary Public, New York **Career:** President, Omni Data Technology, Bay Shore, NY (1995-Present); Controller, LaMar Lighting Co., Freeport, NY (1987-Present); Owner, President, Omni-Star, Brooklyn, NY (1981-Present); Specialist Computer, RGM Liquid Waste Removal, Deer Park, NY (1985-1987); Manager, Office, Chapman-Apex Construction Co., Bay Shore, NY (1982-1984); Assistant Controller, Academy Educational Development, New York, NY (1971-1981) **Career Related:** Controller, E2LI, LLC., Bay Shore, NY (2017-Present); Controller, Phil Loft Productions, Bay Shore, NY (2017-Present); Vice President, Spero Lighting East Inc., Rockville Centre, NY (1999-Present); Business Development Consultant (1998-2018) **Civic:** Most Influential Business Women & Organizations, Long Island Business News (2003) **Creative Works:** Author, "The Magic of Life" (1991); Co-Author, "Computer Management of Liquid Waste Industry" (1986); Author, "Tonda's Songs in Poetry" (1978) **Awards:** Golden Poet Award, World of Poetry (1992) **Memberships:** American Museum of Natural History; American Society of Notary Publics **Marquis Who's Who Honors:** Albert Nelson Marquis Lifetime Achievement Award **Avocations:** Bowling; Chess; Singing

Bobby L. Wilson, PhD

Title: L. Lloyd Woods Distinguished Professor of Chemistry and Shell Oil Endowed Chaired Professor of Environmental Toxicology **Industry:** Education/Educational Services **Company Name:** Texas Southern University **Date of Birth:** 09/30/1942 **Place of Birth:** Columbus **State/Country of Origin:** MS/USA **Parents:** Johnny B.; Lillie M. Wilson **Marital Status:** Married **Spouse Name:** Mary Ann Wilson **Children:** Anthony; Melanie; Malissa; Malinda **Education:** Doctor of Philosophy, Michigan State University, East Lansing, MI (1976); Master of Science in Chemistry, Southern University, Baton Rouge, LA (1972); Bachelor of Science in Chemistry, Alabama State University, Montgomery, AL (1966) **Career:** L. Lloyd Woods Distinguished Professor of Chemistry and Shell Oil Endowed Chaired Professor of Environmental Toxicology, Texas Southern University, Houston, TX (2001-Present); Interim Provost and Vice President for Academic Affairs, Texas Southern University, Houston, TX (2016-2018); L. Lloyd Woods Southern University, Houston, TX (2008-2016); Acting President and/or Provost, L. Lloyd Woods Distinguished Professor of Chemistry and Shell Oil Endowed Chaired Professor of Environmental Toxicology, Texas Southern University, Houston, TX (2006-2008); Provost, L. Lloyd Woods Distinguished Professor of Chemistry and Shell Oil Endowed Chaired Professor of Environmental Toxicology, Texas Southern University, Houston, TX (2004-2006); Provost, Texas Southern University, Houston, TX (2001-2004); Provost and Professor of Chemistry, Texas Southern University, Houston, TX (1999-2001); Professor and Chair of Chemistry, Texas Southern University, Houston, TX (1997-1999) **Career Related:** Program Director for the Centers of Research Excellence in Science and Technology at the National Science Foundation in Washington, DC (1995-1997); Visiting Research Professor, Exxon Research and Engineering Company, Baytown, TX (1982-1983) **Creative Works:** Author, "General Chemistry Laboratory 2 Manual" (1989); Author, "General Chemistry Laboratory 1 Manual" (1988); Contributor, Numerous Articles to Professional Journals and Publications; Contributor, Numerous Presentations; Contributor, Book Chapters **Awards:** The Albert Nelson Marquis Lifetime Achievement Award, Marquis Who's Who Publications Board (2019); Percy L. Julian Award, National Organization for the Professional Advancement of Black Chemists and Chemical Engineers (2018); Faculty Senate Outstanding Alumni Award, Michigan State University's College of Natural Science (2012); Leadership Award, College of Science and Technology, Texas Southern University (2011); Minority Access Mentor Award (2009); Alabama State University Alumni of Distinction Award (1997) **Memberships:** American Chemical Society; National Organization for the Professional Advancement of Black Chemists and Chemical Engineers; African Scientific Institute; Texas Academy of Science; Texas Association of College Teachers; The American Institute of Chemists; American Association for the Advancement of Science; American Institute of Chemists; Sigma XI, The Scientific Research Society. **Marquis Who's Who Honors:** Albert Nelson Marquis Lifetime Achievement Award; Marquis Who's Who Top Professional **To what do you attribute your success:** Dr. Wilson credits his success on the grace of God and his own propensity for hard work. **Why did you become involved in your profession or industry:** Coming of age on an 80-acre farm that was purchased by his family after the conclusion of the Civil War, Dr. Wilson was the oldest of 10 children, and strived to serve as an example to his younger sibling. Attending college, he picked a STEM field and pursued chemistry. **Political Affiliations:** Democrat **Religion:** Baptist

Janice Crabtree Wilson, PhD

Title: Vice President **Industry:** Education/Educational Services **Date of Birth:** 01/18/1938 **Place of Birth:** War **State/Country of Origin:** WV/USA **Parents:** Walter Hash Crabtree; Faye (Presley) Crabtree **Marital Status:** Divorced **Spouse Name:** Arthur Lee Wilson (05/28/1961, Divorced 1981) **Children:** Leslie Megan Wilson; Melissa Jill Wilson Jones **Education:** Coursework, Appalachian Writers Workshop, Hindman, KY (2010-2015); Coursework, Antioch Writers Workshop, Yellow Springs, OH (2000-2009); PhD in American Literature, University of Cincinnati (1990); MA, Miami University, Oxford, OH (1964); BA, Berea College (1959) **Career:** Retired (2002); Curriculum Coordinator, Beaver Creek City Schools (1997-2002); Curriculum Coordinator, Van Wert County Schools (1995-1997); Corporate Education Director, Vernay Laboratories, Yellow Springs, OH (1993-1995); Vice President, Pacer Group, Dayton, OH (1989-1992); Various Positions, NCR Corp., Dayton, OH (1980-1989); Assistant Director, University Honors Program, Wright State University, Dayton, OH (1973-1976); Instructor, Wright State University, Dayton, OH (1964-1975); Teacher, Beavercreek School, Xenia, OH (1962-1966); Teacher, Xenia City School (1959-1962) **Career Related:** Independent Consultant, Quality Management (1992-1993); Adjunct Instructor, College of Medicine, Wright State University (1976-1979) **Civic:** Board of Directors, Investment Committee, Program Committee, Greene County Historical Society (2012-2018); Board of Directors, Xenia Area Community Theater (2004-2016); Board of Directors, Antioch Writers Workshop (2002-2009); Board of Directors, Multiple Sclerosis Society of Dayton (1988-1995); Board of Directors, Greene County Easter Seal Society for Crippled Children, Xenia, OH (1970-1975); Camp Director (1969) **Creative Works:** Author, Short Story, "What They Do When Somebody Kills a Baby" (1993); Associate Editor, "A Comprehensive Bibliography for the Study of American Minorities" (1986); Author, Short Story, "Washed in the Blood of the Lamb" (1982); Contributed, Articles, Professional Journals **Awards:** Taft Fellowship, University of Cincinnati (1977-1979); Full Tuition Scholarship, University of Cincinnati **Memberships:** Phi Kappa Phi; American Society for Training and Development; American Society for Quality Control; Founding Member, Quality Dayton; The Woman's Club of Xenia; Xenia Friends of the Library **Marquis Who's Who Honors:** Albert Nelson Marquis Lifetime Achievement Award **To what do you attribute your success:** Dr. Wilson attributes her success to her confidence in recognizing and saying "yes" when an amazing opportunity presented itself. She has always been eager to develop expertise and excel in professional areas. **Why did you become involved in your profession or industry:** In high school, Dr. WIlson joined three high school clubs, Future Teachers of America, Future Nurses of America, and Future Business Leaders of America. However, in college, she discovered biology and English, the latter of which she loved. She decided to major in English, going on to take courses in pursuit of a teaching certificate. **Avocations:** Reading; Devoted movie fan; Theater; Gardening; Cooking **Thoughts on Life:** Dr. Wilson is open to any opportunity that comes her way. Over the years, she has developed the courage to take these opportunities. She sees fear as a challenge; it will never stop her.

John David Wilson

Title: Founder, Chairman **Industry:** Engineering **Company Name:** ABEC Inc. **Date of Birth:** 07/23/1925 **Place of Birth:** Corning **State/Country of Origin:** NY/USA **Parents:** Paul Fleming Wilson; Lois Dorothy Shomper **Marital Status:** Widowed **Spouse Name:** Jean Ann (DeVoe) Wilson (12/26/1953, Deceased 01/18/2018) **Children:** Terri Ann; Steve DeVoe; Julie Lynn; Paula Jean; Susan Lee **Education:** Bachelor's Degree in Mechanical Engineering, Yale University (1948); Bachelor's Degree in Naval Engineering, Yale University (1946); Coursework, V-12 Program, Stevens Technical Institute, Hoboken, NJ (1943-1944); Diploma, Northside High School, Corning, NY Salutatorian (1943) **Career:** Founder, Chairman of the Board, Associated Bio-Engineers and Consultants (ABEC) Inc., Bethlehem, PA (1974-Present); President, Fermentation Design (Acquired by New Brunswick Scientific) (1967-1974); Sales Manager, Cryotherm, Bethlehem, PA (1960-1967); Sales Manager, Isocyanate Products, New Castle, DE (1955-1958); "La Creaole," Standard Oil, Venezuela (1949-1950); Junior Engineer, Manufacturing Department, Corning Glass Works (1946-1947); Construction Department, Glass Blowing, Corning Glass Works (1942-1943); Bellhop, Baron Steuben Hotel, Corning, NY (1937-1938); Salesman, Saturday Evening Post (1935-1937); Salesman, Collier Magazine; Joe's Esso Station **Career Related:** President, Fermentation Design; Pitcher, La Ba Nius, Venezuela **Civic:** UNICEF (1960-Present); Jack & Jean D. Wilson Fund Lehigh Valley Community Foundation (2018); Wounded Warrior (2018); Meals on Wheels (2018); Salvation Army **Military Service:** Engineering Officer, Assistant Engineer, U.S. Navy, Guam (1945-1946); U.S. Navy Reserve (1943-1946); Commissioned Ensign, Central Pacific, U.S. Navy (1945); Naval Reserve Officers' Training Corps, Yale University (1944-1945) **Creative Works:** Biographee, "We'll Think of Something: the Life of Jack Wilson," Real Life Stories, LLC, Montreat, NC (2017); Three Patents in Field; Author, Numerous Papers and Textbook Chapters **Awards:** Inductee, Lehigh Valley Business Hall of Fame (2014); Pennsylvania Employer of the Year (2013); Major "Y" in Baseball, Yale University Athletic Association (1945) **Memberships:** Sports Car Club of America; Senior Class Vice President; Homer Society; North Star Yearbook; Service Squad; French Club; Camera Club; Student Council; Football; Basketball; Baseball **Marquis Who's Who Honors:** Albert Nelson Marquis Lifetime Achievement Award **To what do you attribute your success:** Mr. Wilson attributes his success to hard work, integrity, focus on quality, honesty, and sincerity. He also credits his wife, Jean D. Wilson, his children, and his grandchildren. **Why did you become involved in your profession or industry:** Mr. Wilson wanted to contribute to the world in any way he could, which is why he became involved in his work. **Avocations:** Building and shooting guns; Swimming; Amateur photography; Baseball **Religion:** Episcopalian

Lorraine McCarty Wilson, PhD, RN

Title: Professor Emerita **Industry:** Education/Educational Services **Company Name:** Eastern Michigan University **Date of Birth:** 11/18/1931 **State/Country of Origin:** MI/USA **Parents:** Bert McCarty; Frances Fern (White) McCarty **Marital Status:** Widow **Spouse Name:** Harold A. Wilson (Deceased, 2004) **Children:** David S. Wilson; Ann E. Wilson Barnes **Education:** PhD, Wayne State University, (1985); MS, University of Michigan (1972); BS in Chemistry, Siena Heights College (1969); Diploma in Nursing, Bronson School of Nursing, Kalamazoo, MI (1953) **Certifications:** RN, Michigan **Career:** Professor Emerita, Eastern Michigan University, (2014-Present); Professor in Nursing, Eastern Michigan University (1989-2014); Associate Professor, Nursing, School of Nursing, Oakland University of Rochester (1986-1989); Assistant Professor, Nursing, Wayne State University, Detroit, MI (1978-1979); Assistant Professor, Nursing, University of Michigan, Ann Arbor (1972-1978); Staff Nurse, Herrick Memorial Hospital, Tecumseh, MI (1954-1969); Staff Nurse, University of Michigan Medical Center, Ann Arbor (1953-1954) **Career Related:** Consultant, Faculty Liaison, Nurse Extern Program on Critical Care, Eastern Michigan University Catherine Mcauley Health Center (1989-Present); Board of Advisors, Professional Fitness Systems, Warren, MI (1986-Present); Consultant, Wellness and Exercise Program, GM CPC Headquarters (1986); Researcher In Field **Civic:** Volunteer, Community Health Screening Drs. (1960-1970); Parent-Teacher Association; Leader, Girl Scouts of the United States (1960); Sunday School Teacher, Gloria Dei Lutheran Church (1960) **Creative Works:** Co-Author, "Pathophysiology, 6th Edition" (2004); Co-Author, "Pathophysiology: Clinical Concepts of Disease-Processes, 6th Edition" (2003); Contributor, Articles, Professional Journals **Awards:** Grantee, R. C. Mahon Foundation (1988); Michigan Heart Association (1984, 1988); Books of the Year Award, American Journal of Nursing (1979) **Memberships:** National Organization of Women; American Nurses Association; National League Nursing; Michigan Nurses Association; Midwest Nursing Research Society; Sigma Theta Tau **Marquis Who's Who Honors:** Albert Nelson Marquis Lifetime Achievement Award; Marquis Who's Who Top Professional **To what do you attribute your success:** Dr. Wilson attributes her success to her background in science, as she is always teaching people to think clinically. **Why did you become involved in your profession or industry:** Dr. Wilson was raised by her grandmother, who unfortunately died of cancer when she was 8. Helping to care for her grandmother inspired Dr. Wilson to pursue a career in medicine. **Avocations:** Travel; Theater; Jogging **Religion:** Lutheran

Paula J. Wilson, DNM

Title: President, Owner, Doctor **Industry:** Health, Wellness and Fitness **Company Name:** Energy Medicine, LLC **Education:** Doctor of Natural Medicine, The Examining Board of Natural Medicine Practitioners, North America; Master's Degree in Medical Radiesthesia; Master's Degree in Telecommunications, Concentration in Educational Documentary, Kutztown University of Pennsylvania; Bachelor of Music in Professional Music, Berklee College of Music **Certifications:** Quantum Healing License; Quantum Instructor License; License in Traditional Naturopathy; Licensed Thoroughbred Trainer; Certification in Equine Studies, Cornell University; Board-Certified Natural Therapy Practitioner, Vibrational Energy Research and Technology Center **Career:** Physical Therapy and Naturopath (2000-Present); Licensed Thoroughbred Trainer (1989-2000) **Awards:** ABI Fellow (2010); National Professional Women Award in Health Care and Medicine; Great Minds of the 21st Century Award; International Peace Prize, United Cultural Convention **Marquis Who's Who Honors:** Marquis Who's Who Top Professional **To what do you attribute your success:** Dr. Wilson attributes her success to her upbringing, open-mindedness and focus on progression. **Why did you become involved in your profession or industry:** Dr. Wilson became involved in her profession after beginning her career in physical therapy and integrating complementary medicines when working with animals and people. **Avocations:** Spending time outdoors; Breeding and training horses **Thoughts on Life:** Dr. Wilson serves on the board of ABEC, Inc., a biopharmaceutical manufacturing company in Bethlehem, Pennsylvania. It was recently awarded a certificate for export achievement from Senator Bob Casey of Pennsylvania and the Mayor of Bethlehem, Mr. John Callaghan. She is setting up an endowment fund for Cedar Crest College.

R. Marshall Wilson, PhD

Title: Research Professor **Industry:** Education/Educational Services **Company Name:** Bowling Green State University **Date of Birth:** 10/18/1939 **Place of Birth:** Reading **State/Country of Origin:** PA/USA **Parents:** Robert Fitzpatrick Wilson; Eugenia (Kyle) Wilson **Marital Status:** Married **Spouse Name:** Antonia Gigliello (06/17/1967) **Children:** Daniel Lee; Laura Jean **Education:** Summer Faculty Fellow, University of Cincinnati (1972); Postdoctoral Fellow, Harvard University (1965-1967); PhD in Organic Chemistry, Massachusetts Institute of Technology (1965); BS in Chemical Engineering, The Pennsylvania State University (1961) **Career:** Andrew Schmitt Wealth Advisers; Distinguished Research Professor, Department of Chemistry, Center for Photochemical Sciences (Now Center for Pure and Applied Photosciences), Bowling Green State University (2005-Present); Fellow, Graduate School, University of Cincinnati (1988-Present); Interim Director, Center for Photochemical Sciences, Bowling Green State University (2013-2015); Professor Emeritus, Department of Chemistry, University of Cincinnati (2005); Head, Department of Chemistry, University of Cincinnati (1998-2004); Acting Head, Department of Chemistry, University of Cincinnati (1997-1998); Distinguished Research Professor, University of Cincinnati (1995-2005); Visiting Professor of Chemistry, The Ohio State University, Columbus, OH (1990-1991); Adjunct Professor, Center for Photochemical Sciences, Bowling Green State University (1987-2005); Senior Scientist Fellowship, North Atlantic Treaty Organization (1982); Visiting Professor of Chemistry, Julius-Maximilians-Universität Würzburg, Germany (1982); Professor of Chemistry, University of Cincinnati (1976-1995); Visiting Professor of Chemistry, University of Wisconsin-Madison (1974); Associate Professor of Chemistry, University of Cincinnati (1972-1976); Assistant Professor of Chemistry, University of Cincinnati (1967-1972); Fellow, National Institutes of Health, Massachusetts Institute of Technology (1962-1965); Graduate Assistant, Massachusetts Institute of Technology (1961-1962); Engineer, American Cyanamide; Engineer, Texas Instruments; Engineer, Johnson Services **Career Related:** Advisory Board, Biomedical Research Center, Department of Chemistry, University of Cincinnati (1986-Present); Lecturer, "Pyridinium Salts as Photoinduced Electron Traps," 4th International Conference on Physical and Theoretical Chemistry, Dublin, Ireland (2017); Lecturer, "Pyridinium Salts of Dihydrodioxins as Photoinduced Electron Traps in DNA Cleaving; Quantum Chemical and Experimental Study," 16th International Photodynamic Association Meeting, Coimbra, Portugal (2017); Lecturer, "Pyridinium Salts as Photoinduced Electron Traps in Dihydrodioxin DNA Cleaving Agents," 3rd World Conference of Smart Molecules, Bangkok, Thailand (2017); Lecturer, "Pyridinium Salts Acting as Photoinduced Electron Traps Studied by Ultrafast Transient Absorption Spectroscopy," Sarasota, FL (2017); Lecturer, "Pyridinium and Dipyridinium Salts as Electron Traps: An Ultrafast Transient Absorption Spectroscopy Study," 25th I-APS Meeting, Santiago, Chile (2016) **Creative Works:** Co-Author, "Oxidation of Adenosine and Inosine: The Chemistry of 8-Oxo-7,8-dihydropurines, Purine Iminoquinones and Purine Quinones as Observed by Ultrafast Spectroscopy," American Chemical Society (2013); Co-Author, "Nitrenium Ions and Related Species in Photoaffinity Labeling," Nitrenes and Nitrenium Ions, Wiley Interscience (2013); Co-Author, "Photoaffinity Labeling via Nitrenium Ion Chemistry: Protonation of the Nitrene Derived from 4-Amino-3-nitrophenyl Azide to Afford Reactive Nitrenium Ion Pairs," American Chemical Society (2009); Co-Author, "Photoaffinity Labeling with 8-Azidoadenosine and Its Derivatives: The Chemistry of Closed and Open Adenosine Diazaquinodimethanes," Biochemistry (2005) **Awards:** Private Funding, Bowling Green Effort Foundation (2007-Present); The Inter-American Photochemical Society Fellow Award For Outstanding Lifetime Contribution to the Advancement of the Photochemical and Photophysical Sciences and Services to the Inter-American Photochemical Society as a Whole (2019); Grant, Hoke S. and Stella Greene Chair in Biocatalysis (2006); Hans H. Jaffe Award for Distinguished Scholarship, Department of Chemistry, University of Cincinnati (2005) **Memberships:** Co-Organizer, Luminating Molecules Symposium, Central Region, American Chemical Society (2007); Organizer, Meetings, Ohio Photochemistry Society (2005); Organizer, Oesper Symposium (2004); Organizer, Meetings, Ohio Photochemistry Society (2002); Session Leader, Gordon Conference on Organic Photochemistry, Connecticut College (2001); Organizer, Symposium on "Photochemical Manipulation of Biological Molecules," Central Region, American Chemical Society (2000) **Marquis Who's Who Honors:** Albert Nelson Marquis Lifetime Achievement Award **Why did you become involved in your profession or industry:** Dr. Wilson became involved in his profession while he was a chemical engineer at Pennsylvania State University, and worked for three companies during the summers. He decided, as a result of his industry experience, that he wanted to go into academics. **Avocations:** Biology

1390 • Distinguished Listees

Who's Who in America

Thomas Matthew Wilson III

Title: Of Counsel (Retired) **Industry:** Law and Legal Services **Company Name:** Tydings & Rosenberg **Date of Birth:** 02/22/1936 **Place of Birth:** Ware **State/Country of Origin:** MA/USA **Parents:** Thomas Matthew Wilson, Jr.; Ann Veronica (Shea) Wilson **Marital Status:** Married **Spouse Name:** Deborah Ord Lockhart (02/10/1962) **Children:** Deborah Veronica; Leslie Lockhart; Thomas Matthew, IV **Education:** JD, University of Maryland (1971); BA, Brown University (1958) **Career:** Retired (2017); Of Counsel, Tydings & Rosenberg, LLP, Baltimore, MD (2012-2017); Partner, Tydings & Rosenberg, LLP, Baltimore, MD (1979-2012); Assistant Attorney General, Chief of Antitrust Division, State of Maryland, Baltimore, MD (1974-1979); Sales Manager, Mideastern Box Manufacturing Company, Baltimore, MD (1966-1974) **Creative Works:** Member, Editorial Advisory Board, "Bureau of National Affairs Antitrust and Trade Regulation Report" (1979-2016); Co-Author, "Intentional Grounding of an Implied Antitrust Exemption" (2011); Author, "An Unintended Consequence of Leegin" (2007); Author, "The Spectre of Double Recovery in Antitrust Federalism" (1989); Author, "Defending an Antitrust Action Brought by a State Attorney General" (1987); Co-Author, "Reciprocity and the Private Plaintiff" (1972) **Awards:** Honoree, Best Lawyers in Baltimore Anti-Trust Law & Government Relations, Best Lawyers (2017); Honoree, AV Preeminent Rated Attorney, Martindale-Hubbell; Featured Listee, 23rd Edition, The Best Lawyers in America **Memberships:** Antitrust Law and Monopolies Committee, Section on Business Law, International Bar Association (1983-Present); Section on Antitrust Law, ABA (1974-Present); Coordinator, Committee on Legal Education, American Bar Foundation (1993-1994); Antitrust Section Council, ABA (1990-1993); Chairman, State Antitrust Enforcement Committee, ABA (1986-1989); Antitrust Subcommittee, Maryland State Bar Association (1975-1978); Fellow, American Bar Foundation; Section on Business Law, International Bar Association; Churchwarden's Chess Club; Annapolis Yacht Club; Metropolitan Club of the City of Washington **Bar Admissions:** Supreme Court of the United States (1977); United States Court of Appeals for the Fourth Circuit (1976); Maryland (1972) **Marquis Who's Who Honors:** Albert Nelson Marquis Lifetime Achievement Award; Marquis Who's Who Top Professional **To what do you attribute your success:** Mr. Wilson attributes his success to his desire for helping others. **Why did you become involved in your profession or industry:** Mr. Wilson entered his profession because he thought that he was having antitrust problems and started looking into law. **Avocations:** Chess **Political Affiliations:** Republican

Jeffrey L. Wilt, MD

Title: Pulmonary and Critical Care Physician, Educator **Industry:** Medicine & Health Care **Date of Birth:** 11/15/1963 **Place of Birth:** Fairmont **State/Country of Origin:** WV/USA **Parents:** Paul Lynn Wilt; Linda (Amos) Wilt **Children:** Alexander; Derek **Education:** MD, University Michigan, 1988;BA, University Michigan, 198 **Certifications:** Diplomate American Board Internal Medicine; American Board Pulmonary Diseases; American Board Critical Care Medicine; American Board Medical Examiners; American Board Nutrition Support; certified ACLS instructor **Career:** Director of Medical Critical Care, Ascension Borgess Hospital (2009-Present); Chief, Department of Critical Care, Ascension Borgess Hospital (2009-Present); Private Practice, Grand Rapids, MI (1995-2007); Director of Pulmonary and Critical Care, Associate Clinical Professor of Medicine, Homer Stryker M.D. School of Medicine, Western Michigan University **Career Related:** Associate Program Director, Internal Medicine Residency, Michigan State University (1999-Present); Associate Professor, Michigan State University (2003-Present); Assistant Professor of Medicine, Michigan State University (1999-2003); Program Director, Michigan State University (1998-1999); Chief Operating Officer, Internal Medicine Residency, Michigan State University (1998); Assistant Director, Intensive Care Unit, Blodgett Memorial Medical Center (1997-1998); Assistant Director, Internal Medicine Residency, Mercy Health Saint Mary's, Grand Rapids, MI (1991-1992) **Civic:** Volunteer, Baseball Coach **Creative Works:** Author, Books, Book Chapters, Publications **Awards:** Outstanding Teaching Award, Department of Internal Medicine, Homer Stryker M.D. School of Medicine, Western Michigan University (2018); Young Investigator's Award, American College of Chest Physicians (1993); Winner, Clinical Vignette, American College of Physicians (1991); Several Teaching Awards **Memberships:** Fellow, American College of Physicians; American College of Chest Physicians; American Medical Association; Society of Critical Care Medicine; American Thoracic Society **Marquis Who's Who Honors:** Albert Nelson Marquis Lifetime Achievement Award **Why did you become involved in your profession or industry:** Dr. Wilt became involved in his profession because, as a child, he was always the first one to help if he saw someone in pain. **Avocations:** Reading; Writing poetry; Martial arts **Political Affiliations:** Republican

Jeff Wine

Title: Chief Executive Officer **Industry:** Automotive **Company Name:** Wine Automotive **Place of Birth:** 11/30/1964 **Marital Status:** Married **Spouse Name:** Mary (Lewis) **Children:** Jakob; Joshua; Kiki **Education:** Coursework in Business, College of William & Mary **Certifications:** Notary Public, State of Virginia **Career:** CEO, Wine Automotive (2013-Present) **Awards:** Top Dealership in the Country for Customer Service **Memberships:** Chamber of Commerce **Marquis Who's Who Honors:** Marquis Who's Who Top Professional **To what do you attribute your success:** Mr. Wine attributes his success to hard work and his faith in the Good Lord. **Why did you become involved in your profession or industry:** Mr. Wine became involved in his industry as a means to give back to his community. Once a month, his dealership gives away a free car. Though he started out as a car wash owner, he has since expanded his business and hopes to do more in the future. **Avocations:** Exercise; Reading; Hiking; Outdoor activities; Fishing

Raymond Norman Winkel

Title: Aerospace Industry Consultant **Industry:** Sciences **Date of Birth:** 12/08/2028 **Place of Birth:** Flint **State/Country of Origin:** MI/USA **Parents:** Norman Martin Winkel; Evelyn Matilda (Hylen) Winkel **Marital Status:** Widowed **Spouse Name:** Ellen Stefula (12/29/1955, Deceased 2005) **Children:** Raymond Norman; Ann; Maryellen **Education:** Graduate, Advanced Management Program, Harvard University (1973); MS in Mathematics, Villanova University, PA (1967); BS, Naval Postgraduate School, Monterrey, CA (1964) **Career:** Aerospace Industry Consultant, Heathsville, VA (1994-1995); Vice President of Programs and Contracts, Astronautics Corporation of America, Milwaukee, WI (1982-1994); Vice President, Washington Operations Telephonic Corporation, Huntington, NY (1981-1982) **Military Service:** Retired, United States Navy (1981); Rear Admiral, United States Navy (1979); General Manager, LAMPS Mark III Project, United States Navy (1978-1981); Project Manager, Navy/Marine Corps Heavy Lift Helicopter (1976-1978); Director of Avionics, United States Navy (1973-1976); Commanding Officer, Naval Electronics Systems Test and Evaluation Facility, St. Inigoes, MD (1969-1971); With, United States Navy (1951) **Awards:** Decorated Legion of Merit; Air Medal; Navy Achievement Medal **Memberships:** National Rifle Association of America; U.S. Naval Institute; Association of Naval Aviation; Military Officers Association of America; Kiwanis International; Indian Creek Yacht & Country Club; Experimental Aircraft Association; Amateur Radio KM4AAI; The American Legion **Marquis Who's Who Honors:** Albert Nelson Marquis Lifetime Achievement Award **Why did you become involved in your profession or industry:** Mr. Winkel became involved in his profession because he was interested in electronics ever since he built a radio when he was 17 years old. He has always wanted to learn more about electronics. He had an opportunity in 1946, after passing a test for the United States Navy to measure the correlation of success on the test and success in any given professional field. After scoring well on the test, he enlisted in the Navy. He attended boot camp and then aviation electronics school, where he graduated at the top of his class. This was a significant achievement for him because, as he jokingly notes, his high school major was "girls," and he graduated at the bottom of his class as a result. The Navy taught him that he had a brain. A year later, the Navy opened up an opportunity for young enlistees who had very high test scores. He was selected to be promoted to the rank of Naval Aviation Cadet and to go to Flight Training School. In 1951, his mother pinned his gold Navy wings on his uniform as his father put the shoulder boards on his uniform; he was commissioned without any college. **Avocations:** Traveling; Cruises; YMCA to workout three days a week

Dolores Eugenia Winkler

Title: Health Facility Administrator **Industry:** Financial Services **Company Name:** West Allis Memorial Hospital **Date of Birth:** 08/10/1929 **Place of Birth:** Milwaukee **State/Country of Origin:** WI/USA **Parents:** Charles Peter Kowalski; Eugenia Anne (Zamka) Kowalski **Marital Status:** Married **Spouse Name:** Donald James Winkler (08/18/1951) **Children:** David John Winkler **Education:** Milwaukee Business Institute (1949) **Career:** Director, Budgets and Reimbursement, West Allis Memorial Hospital (1985-1995); Reimbursement Analyst, West Allis Memorial Hospital (1978-1985); Chief Accountant, West Allis Memorial Hospital (1970-1978); Staff Accountant, West Allis Memorial Hospital (1968-1970); Accountant, Curative Rehabilitation Center, Milwaukee, WI (1949-1960) **Career Related:** Advisory Council, Financial Committee, Tau Home Health Care Agency, Milwaukee, WI (1981-1983) **Civic:** St. Mary's Seniors **Awards:** Medal of Honor, Healthcare Financial Management Association (1993); Award of Excellence, Institute of Management Accountants (1989); Muncie Gold Award, Healthcare Financial Management Association (1989); Reeves Silver Award, Healthcare Financial Management Association (1986); Follmer Bronze Award, Healthcare Financial Management Association (1980) **Memberships:** President, Healthcare Financial Management Association (1989-1990); President, Mid-American Regional Council, Institute of Management Accountants (1988-1989); National Director, Institute of Management Accountants (1986-1988); President, Institute of Management Accountants (1983-1984); Governor, Beta Chi Rho (1948); National Association of Accountants **Marquis Who's Who Honors:** Albert Nelson Marquis Lifetime Achievement Award **To what do you attribute your success:** Mrs. Winkler wanted to make her parents proud, as they worked hard throughout the Great Depression. She had a strong desire to succeed. **Why did you become involved in your profession or industry:** Mrs. Winkler became involved in finances and accounting because of her affinity for mathematics. **Avocations:** Travel; Photography; Golf **Religion:** Catholic

Derek Winstanley

Title: Chief Emeritus, Illinois State Water Survey **Industry:** Civil Service **Date of Birth:** 05/19/1945 **Place of Birth:** Wigan **State/Country of Origin:** England **Parents:** Thomas; Bessie Winstanley **Marital Status:** Married **Spouse Name:** Linda Winstanley **Children:** Deborah Lon; Stuart Neil; Kay Dee **Education:** Doctor of Philosophy, Oxford University, England (1970); Master of Arts, Oxford University, England (1970); Bachelor of Arts, Oxford University, England (1966); Diploma, Wigan Grammar School, England (1956-1963) **Career:** Chief, Illinois State Water Survey, Champaign, IL (1997-2008); Deputy Chief Scientist, National Oceanic and Atmospheric Administration, Washington, DC (1994-1997); Director, National Acid Precipitation Assessment Program, Executive Office of The President, Washington DC (1992-1994); Senior Atmospheric Scientist, National Acid Precipitation Assessment Program, Executive Office of The President, Washington, DC; Program Analyst, U.S. Department of Energy, Germantown, MD; Climatologist, National Center for Atmospheric Research, Boulder, CO; Hydroclimatologist, Banjul, The Gambia; Consultant, Food and Agriculture Organization of the United Nations; Climatologist, Environment Canada; Meteorologist, Anti-Locust Research Center, London, England; Radcliffe Meteorological Observer, Oxford University, UK. **Civic:** Science Advisory Committee, Illinois River Coordination Council, Springfield, IL; Chair, Illinois Global Climate Change Work Group, Springfield, IL; Mahomet Aquifer Consortium, Champaign, IL; Krannert Art Museum Council, Urbana, IL **Creative Works:** Contributed, Numerous Articles to Professional Journals **Awards:** Proxime Accessit, Henry Oliver Becket Memorial Prize, School of Geography, Oxford University, Oxford, England; Alstead Geography Prizes, Wigan Grammar School, Wigan, England **Marquis Who's Who Honors:** Albert Nelson Marquis Lifetime Achievement Award; Marquis Who's Who Top Professional. **To what do you attribute your success:** Dr. Winstanley attributes his success to his propensity for determination and taking risks. **Why did you become involved in your profession or industry:** Dr. Winstanley became involved in his profession when one of his neighbors in Northern England had his own weather station and got him interested in the subject. So he installed instruments in his own yard and took daily records. He later became a meteorological observer at Oxford University and, for his doctorate, conducted research on the climate of the eastern Mediterranean area. **Avocations:** Wood and stone sculpture; Furniture making; Photography; Local history

Joseph Stephen Wise

Title: Secondary Education Educator, Artist **Industry:** Education/Educational Services **Date of Birth:** 11/26/1939 **Place of Birth:** Seattle **State/Country of Origin:** WA/USA **Parents:** Prentice Lafayette Wise; Norma Fay (Freeman) Wise **Marital Status:** Married **Spouse Name:** Jeanne Marie Avila (8/27/1977); Virginia Mae Linstrom (11/15/1960, Divorced 10/1961) **Children:** Three Children **Education:** MA in Art, San Jose State University (1966); BS in Education, Indiana University (1963) **Certifications:** Certified Kindergarten through Junior College Teacher, California **Career:** Teacher, English, Art, Gunderson High School, San Jose, CA (1995-2001); Teacher, Art, Physical Education, English, Social Studies, Steinbeck Middle School, San Jose, CA (1968-1995); Art Teacher, Santa Venetia Middle School, San Rafael, CA (1967-1968); Art Teacher, Meany Middle School, Seattle, WA (1963-1964); Art Teacher, Studebaker Middle School, South Bend, IN (1963) **Creative Works:** Exhibitor, Group Show, Los Gatos Art Museum (1990-2006); Exhibitor, Group Show, Filoli Estate (2006); Solo Exhibitor, The Granary, Morgan Hill, California (2005); Solo Exhibitor, Hidden Villa, California (2005); Solo Exhibitor, Toll House House Hotel, Los Gatos, CA (1998); Exhibitor, Group Show, Tait Museum, Los Gatos, CA (1990-1998); Solo Exhibitor, Bingham Gallery, San Jose, CA (1987); Exhibitor, Group Show, Ages Gallery, San Jose, CA (1986); Exhibitor, Group Show, Discovery Gallery, San Jose, CA (1980); Exhibitor, Group Show, Greenleaf Gallery, Saratoga, CA (1979-1983); Solo Exhibitor, Cabrillo Junior College Gallery, Santa Cruz, CA (1973); Exhibitor, Group Show, Pavilion Gallery, Los Gatos, CA (1972); Solo Exhibitor, Mankato State College Union, Minnesota (1972); Exhibitor, Group Show, Owens Corning Fiberglas Corp., Santa Clara, CA (1972); Solo Exhibitor, San Jose State University Union Art Gallery (1971); Solo Exhibitor, Los Robles Gallery, Palo Alto, CA (1970); Solo Exhibitor, Stanford University International Center, Palo Alto, CA (1969); Solo Exhibitor, Washington State College Union Gallery (1968); Solo Exhibitor, Idaho State College Union Gallery, Moscow (1968); Solo Exhibitor, Triton Museum, San Jose, CA (1967); Exhibitor, Group Show, Museum Art, San Francisco, CA (1967); Solo Exhibitor, Casa Gallery, San Juan Baptista, CA; Exhibitor, Permanent Collections, IBM Corp., San Jose, Amdahl Corp., Sunnyvale, CA, Owens Corning Fiberglas Corp., Calvary Community Church, San Jose, CA, Mankato State College, San Jose Public Library, De Saisset Museum, Santa Clara, CA, San Jose Museum Art, Dunn Instruments, San Francisco, CA, St. Johns Episcopal Church, Capitola, CA; Exhibitor, Numerous Private Collections **Awards:** Plein Air Contest Winner, Hidden Villa, Los Altos, CA (2005) **Marquis Who's Who Honors:** Albert Nelson Marquis Lifetime Achievement Award **Avocations:** Golf; Tennis; Hiking; Bicycling **Political Affiliations:** Republican

Anne E. Wojcicki

Title: Co-Founder, Genomics and Biotechnology Company Executive **Industry:** Biotechnology **Company Name:** 23andMe, Inc. **Date of Birth:** 07/28/1973 **Place of Birth:** San Mateo County **State/Country of Origin:** CA/USA **Parents:** Stanley George Wojcicki; Esther Denise (Hochman) Wojcicki **Marital Status:** Divorced **Spouse Name:** Sergey Brin (05/2007, Divorced 2015) **Children:** Benji Wojin; Chloe Wojin **Education:** BS in Biology, Yale University, New Haven, CT (1996); Diploma, Gunn High School, Palo Alto, CA **Career:** Chief Executive Officer, 23andMe, Inc. (2006-Present); Co-Founder, 23andMe, Inc. (2006); General Partner, Covalence Life Sciences Partners; Senior Research, Analyst for Health Care, Amerindo Investment Advisors Inc.; Research Associate, Biochemistry Department, Yale University; Research Associate, Biochemistry, Weizman Institute; Research Associate, Oncology and Hematology, National Institutes of Health; Senior Health Care Analyst, Investor AB; Health Care Analyst, Ardsley Partners; Health Care Analyst, Andor Capital Management **Civic:** Co-Founder, Board Member, Breakthrough Prize **Creative Works:** Editor, The Oracle, Gunn High School **Awards:** Named, Top 50 Health Care Technology CEOs, Healthcare Technology Report (2019); Most Daring CEO, Fast Company (2013); Invention of the Year, TIME Magazine (2008) **Memberships:** Xconomists **Avocations:** Ice skating; Hockey **Religion:** Atheist

Julia Wolfe

Title: Composer **Industry:** Medicine & Health Care **Date of Birth:** 12/18/1958 **Place of Birth:** Philadelphia **State/Country of Origin:** PA/USA **Marital Status:** Married **Spouse Name:** Michael Gordon (1984) **Children:** Two Children **Education:** Honorary Degree, Drew University (2018); PhD, Princeton University (2012); MusM, Yale University (1986); BA in Music and Theater, University of Michigan (1982) **Career:** Professor of Music Composition, Steinhardt School of Culture, Education and Human Development, New York University (2009-Present); Co-Founder, Cantaloupe Music (2001); Co-Founder, Red Poppy Music (1993); Co-Founder, Bang on a Can (1987) **Career Related:** MacArthur Fellowship (2016); Former Adjunct Professor, Manhattan School of Music **Creative Works:** Composer, "Spinning" (2018); Composer, "Fire in My Mouth" (2018); Co-Composer, "Road Trip" (2017); Composer, "Retrieve" (2016); Composer, "Splendid Hopes" (2016); Composer, "Spinning Jenny" (2016); Featured, "Julia Wolfe's Pulitzer-winning 'Anthracite Fields' makes its West Coast debut at Disney Hall," Los Angeles Times (2016); Featured, "A Dark But Redeeming Tour Of Coal Country, With Composer Julia Wolfe," "Julia Wolfe Wins Music Pulitzer For Anthracite Fields," NPR's Deceptive Cadence (2015); Featured, "Pulitzer-winning music a tribute to Pennsylvania coal miners," Pittsburgh Tribune-Review (2015); Composer, "Emunah" (2015); Composer, "Blue Dress for String Quartet" (2015); Composer, "Cha" (2015); Co-Composer, "Cloud-River-Mountain" (2015); Composer, "Anthracite Fields" (2014); Featured, "The Sound of (New) Music," NEPR (2014); Featured, "Questions of Practice: Composer Julia Wolfe on the Transformation of Research into Art," Pew Center for Arts and Heritage (2014); Composer, "Lass" (2014); Composer, "You Breathe" (2013); Composer, "Reeling" (2012); Composer, "riSE and fLY" (2012); Composer, "Combat de Boxe" (2011); Composer, "Iron Maiden" (2011); Featured, "Post-Minimalism and Folk Ballads Fuel a Composer," The New York Times (2011); Composer, "With a Blue Dress On" (2010); Composer, "Steel Hammer" (2009); Featured, "Her radical, rumbling vision," Philadelphia Inquirer (2009); Composer, "Guard My Tongue" (2009); Composer, "Traveling Music" (2009); Composer, "Thirst" (2008); Co-Composer, "Water" (2008); Composer, "Stronghold" (2008); Composer, "Singing in the Dead of Night" (2008); Composer, "Fuel" (2007); Composer, "Lad" (2007); Composer, "Impatience" (2005); Co-Composer, "Shelter" (2005); Composer, "Accordion Concerto (True Love)" (2005); Composer, "Cruel Sister" (2004); Contributor, "Artists on Artists: Suzanne Bocanegra," Bomb Magazine (2004); Featured, "Classing Rock, or Rocking Classical?," WNYC Soundcheck (2003); Composer, "My Beautiful Scream" (2003); Composer, "Big Beautiful Dark and Scary" (2002); Contributor, "Steve Reich & Beryl Korot," Bomb Magazine (2002); Composer, "Dark Full Ride" (2002); Composer, "Compassion" (2001); Co-Composer, "Lost Objects" (2001); Composer, "Earring" (2001); Composer, "Close Together" (2000); Co-Composer, "The Carbon Copy Building" (1999); Arranger, "Music for Airports" (1998); Composer, "Believing" (1997); Composer, "Mink Stole" (1997); Composer, "New York Composers: Searching for a New Music" (1997); Composer, "East Broadway" (1996); Composer, "Dig Deep" (1995); Composer, "Steam" (1995); Composer, "Lick" (1994); Composer, "Tell Me Everything" (1994); Composer, "My Lips from Speaking" (1993); Composer, "Arsenal of Democracy" (1993); Composer, "Early That Summer" (1993); Composer, "Four Marys" (1991); Composer, "Window of Vulnerability" (1991); Composer, "The Vermeer Room" (1989); Composer, "Girlfriend" (1988); Composer, "Amber Waves of Grain" (1988); Composer, "On Seven-Star-Shoes" (1985) **Awards:** Pulitzer Prize for Music, "Anthracite Fields" (2015); Fulbright Scholarship (1992) **Memberships:** Phi Beta Kappa

Manfred P. "Fred" Wolff, PhD

Title: Geologist, Educator, Environmental Scientist, Consultant **Industry:** Education/Educational Services **Date of Birth:** 04/26/1938 **Place of Birth:** New York **State/Country of Origin:** NY/USA **Parents:** Kurt F. Wolff (1904-1989); Marie M. Mueller (1912-1999) **Marital Status:** Married **Spouse Name:** Suzanne Charlene Mosier (07/02/1988) **Children:** Brian P.; Mark P. **Education:** PhD in Geology, Cornell University (1967); MS, University of Rochester (1963); BS, Hofstra University (1961) **Career:** Chairman, Geology Department, Hofstra University (2000-2004); Professor of Geology, Hofstra University (1981-2004); Associate Professor of Geology, Hofstra University (1974-1981); Assistant Professor of Geology, Hofstra University (1967-1974) **Civic:** Member, Citizens Advisory Committee, Long Island Regional Planning Council (2008-Present); Member, Science Advisory Committee, New York State Disaster Preparedness Commission (1989-1999); Wastewater Management Program, Hauppauge, NY (1981-1992); Executive Secretary, NYSGA, New York, NY (1978-1990) **Military Service:** U.S. Army Reserve (1956-1960) **Creative Works:** Lead Author, Textbook, Introductory Geology Course **Awards:** Scholarship, Cornell University (1963-1967); Penrose Bequest Grantee, Geological Society of America (1966); Wilson P. Foss Senior Fellow, New York State Geological Survey (1963-1964); Scholarship, University of Rochester (1961-1962); Grantee, Hofstra University **Memberships:** Co-Chairman, Nassau Science Exploration Day Committee (2002-2003); The Explorers Club; Geological Society of America, Inc.; Society of Economic Geologists; NYSCPG **Marquis Who's Who Honors:** Albert Nelson Marquis Lifetime Achievement Award **Why did you become involved in your profession or industry:** Dr. Wolff became involved in his profession because he was interested in nature and the outdoors from the time he was a teenager. **Avocations:** Traveling; Hiking; Biking; Taking photographs; Computer scanning and printing **Political Affiliations:** Independent Democrat **Religion:** Roman Catholic

Vivian C. Wolf-Wilets, PhD, RN

Title: Clinical Nursing Educator **Industry:** Education/Educational Services **Date of Birth:** 11/10/1937 **Place of Birth:** Norcross **State/Country of Origin:** MN/USA **Parents:** Hiram Thomas Ricks; Florence Myrdal (Brewster) Ricks **Marital Status:** Widowed **Spouse Name:** Lawrence Wilets **Children:** Ross Thomas; Ilana Wilets (Stepchild); Edward Wilets (Step child); James Wilets (Stepchild) **Education:** PhD, University of Chicago (1969); Fellowship, Postmaster Study, University of Marquette (1965); MA in Education, University of Chicago (1964); BSN, North Central College (1960) **Career:** Retired (1999); Assistant Professor, University of Washington, School of Nursing (1969-1999); Professor, University of Washington, Seattle, WA (1988-1999); Distinguished Visiting Professor, University of California San Francisco (1987-1988); Professor, Chair, University of Washington, Seattle, WA (1982-1987); Associate Professor, University of Washington, Seattle, WA (1974-1982); Assistant Professor, University of Washington, Seattle, WA (1969-1974) **Career Related:** Consultant, Speaker, Numerous Schools of Nursing, Nursing Organizations, China, Norway, Israel, Brazil, Australia, and Taiwan (1970-1994) **Civic:** Former Board Review Member, National League of Nursing; Former Member, Visiting Committees, Baccalaureate Nursing Programs, United States **Creative Works:** Contributor, Chapters, Books; Contributor, Articles, Professional Journals **Awards:** Grantee, Department of Health (1971); Outstanding Young Women of Washington, Outstanding Young Women of America (1971) **Memberships:** President-Elect, President, Washington League for Nursing (1993-1997); Fellow, American Academy of Nursing **Marquis Who's Who Honors:** Albert Nelson Marquis Lifetime Achievement Award; Marquis Who's Who Top Professional **To what do you attribute your success:** Dr. Wolf-Wilets attributes her success to her tenacious nature and her resilient attitude. When times are tough, she has always pushed forward. **Why did you become involved in your profession or industry:** Dr. Wolf-Wilets was inspired by her mother, who encouraged her to pursue nursing. **Avocations:** Watercolor art; Reading; Creative writing; Singing; Music; Exercising **Political Affiliations:** Democrat **Religion:** United Methodist

Chorng-Huey Wong, PhD

Title: Former Deputy Director of IMF Institute, International Monetary Fund **Industry:** Financial Services **Date of Birth:** 11/03/1940 **Place of Birth:** Yichu **State/Country of Origin:** Chiayi County,Taiwan **Parents:** Tai-Ge Wong; Lien (Liu) Wong **Marital Status:** Married **Spouse Name:** Wan-Jong (Chen) Wong (08/30/1968) **Children:** Christine; Patricia **Education:** PhD in Economics, University of Minnesota, Minneapolis, MN (1970); Graduate Studies in Economics, National Taiwan University, Taipei, Taiwan (1964); BA in Economics, National Taiwan University, Taipei, Taiwan (1962) **Career:** Deputy Director, IMF Institute, International Monetary Fund, Washington, DC (2002-2005); Senior Adviser, IMF Institute, International Monetary Fund (1997-2002); Assistant Director, IMF Institute, International Monetary Fund (1992-1997); Division Chief, Central Asia Department, International Monetary Fund (1991-1992); Division Chief, Asian Department, International Monetary Fund (1991); Adviser, Asian Department, International Monetary Fund (1989-1991); Adviser, IMF Institute, International Monetary Fund (1987-1989); Division Chief, IMF Institute, International Monetary Fund (1982-1987); Adviser, IMF Institute, International Monetary Fund (1981-1982); Deputy Division Chief, IMF Institute, International Monetary Fund (1979-1981); Senior Economist, International Monetary Fund (1975-1979); Economist, International Monetary Fund (1970-1975) **Career Related:** Consultant/Visiting Scholar, IMF Institute (2005-2017); Senior Personnel Manager, IMF Institute (1995-2005); Senior Budget Manager, IMF Institute (1992-1995); Acting Director, IMF Institute (On Occasion) **Creative Works:** Contributor of articles in professional journals, including Journal of Monetary Economics, Journal of Finance, Weltwirtchaftliches Archiv, and IMF Staff Papers (Now Known as IMF Economic Review); Co-editor of four books, "Macroeconomic Management: Programs and Policies," "Trade Policy Issues," "Coordinating Stabilization and Structural Reform," and "Approaches to Exchange Rate Policy." Most of his research and publications have focused on monetary and exchange rate policies, financial programming, and the prevention and management of financial crisis. **Awards:** Albert Nelson Marquis Lifetime Achievement Award (2019); Tainan First High School's Outstanding Alumni Award (2011) **Memberships:** American Economic Association; Taiwanese American Senior Society; Taiwanese Association of America, Greater Washington Chapter; Taiwanese Presbyterian Church of Washington **Marquis Who's Who Honors:** Albert Nelson Marquis Lifetime Achievement Award **To what do you attribute your success:** Aside from the great influences of his loving parents, siblings, wife and daughters, as well as dedicated teachers and professors, he attributes his success to hard work and God's grace. **Why did you become involved in your profession or industry:** Dr. Wong became involved in his profession because he has been interested in economics since high school when his father, Tai-Ge Wong, instilled in him the importance of economics. During his high-school years, he observed many economic problems in Taiwan, which was an emerging market economy at that time, and he wanted to find solutions. When he took the college entrance examination, Dr. Wong selected economics as his main focus. After graduating from National Taiwan University with a BA in Economics, he was offered a full scholarship at the University of Minnesota, where he got a PhD in Economics. He was the first Taiwanese to be recruited by the IMF immediately following the completion of a doctorate. **Avocations:** Plein-air oil painting **Religion:** Christian

Sun Yet Wong

Title: Engineer, Consultant (Retired) **Industry:** Engineering **Date of Birth:** 12/06/1932 **Place of Birth:** Honolulu **State/Country of Origin:** HI/USA **Parents:** Chip Tong Wong; Shiu Inn (Chang) Wong **Marital Status:** Married **Spouse Name:** Janet Siu Hung (Lau) Wong (08/08/1954) **Children:** Cathleen Wai Hin Wong; Bryan Sun Keong Wong; Jonathan Sun Tuck Wong **Education:** Master of Science in Civil Engineering, Yale University (1955); Bachelor of Science in Civil Engineering, University of Hawaii, with Honors (1954) **Career:** Independent Consultant, Rolling Hills Estates, California (1981-2014); Chairman of Board, President, Treasurer, Applied Research Incorporated, El Segundo, CA (1979-1981); Treasurer, System Development Corporation, Santa Monica, CA (1977-1978); Executive Vice President, Treasurer, Technical Director, Mechanics Research Incorporated, El Segundo, CA (1964-1977); Member of Technical Staff, Ramo Woolridge Space Technical Laboratories, Redondo Beach, CA (1958-1964); Engineer, North America Aviation, Downey, CA (1955-1958) **Career Related:** Consultant, TriSept, Washington, DC (2003-2014); Consultant, Boeing Space Systems, El Segundo, CA (2000-2012); Consultant, Boeing Space and Intelligence, Seal Beach, CA (2003-2006); Consultant, Tompkins and Associates, Torrance, CA (1984-2003); Consultant, Lion Engineering, Rancho Palos Verdes, California (1994-2002); Consultant, Raytheon, El Segundo, CA (2000-2002); Consultant, Hughes Space and Communications, El Segundo, CA (1996-2000); Consultant, NASA Goddard, Greenbelt, MD (1997); Consultant, Measurement Analysis Corporation, Torrance, CA (1984-1996); Consultant, Swales & Associates, Beltsville, MD (1992-1993); Consultant, E Systems, Garland, TX (1986-1993); Consultant, Ampex, Redwood City, CA (1991); Consultant, Odectics, Anaheim, CA (1990); Consultant, Kodak Datatape, Pasadena, CA (1989); Consultant, Statistical Sciences, Incorporated, Beverly Hills, CA (1986); Consultant, Applied Technology, Mountain View, CA (1983-1985); Consultant, Astron, Mountain View, CA (1983-1985); Consultant, TRW, Redondo Beach, CA (1984); Consultant, MRJ, Fairfax, VA (1984); Consultant, Electromechanics Systems Incorporated, Anaheim, CA (1984); Consultant, Acurex, Mountain View, CA (1983); Consultant, Intercon, Cerritos, CA (1982-1984); Consultant, J.H. Wiggins Company, Redondo Beach, CA (1982-1984) **Awards:** Recipient, 71st Award, United States Government National Reconnaissance Office (2007); Recipient, National Reconnaissance Office Director's Medal, United States Government (2007); Recipient, Technical Excellence Award, Boeing Company (2002); Recipient, National Reconnaissance Office Director's Medal, United States Government (2001); Recipient, 137th Seal Medallion Award, United States Government Central Intelligence Agency (2001) **Marquis Who's Who Honors:** Albert Nelson Marquis Lifetime Achievement Award; Marquis Who's Who Top Professional **To what do you attribute your success:** Mr. Wong attributes his success to authoring and implementing improvements "outside the box." **Why did you become involved in your profession or industry:** Mr. Wong was requested by United States government representatives to consult on an individual business. **Avocations:** Metal machining; Machine shop work in his garage **Religion:** Christian

Frederick S. Wonham

Title: Trust Bank Executive, Investment Banking Executive **Industry:** Financial Services **Date of Birth:** 04/08/1931 **Place of Birth:** New York **State/Country of Origin:** NY/USA **Parents:** W. Stapley Wonham; Mary Knight (Lincoln) Wonham **Marital Status:** Married **Spouse Name:** Suzanne Butler Wonham (05/09/2017); Ann Hayden Brunie (06/18/1953, Deceased) **Children:** Stapley Emberling; Henry Brunie Wonham; Frederick Lincoln Wonham **Education:** Postgraduate Coursework, New York University (1956-1958); BA, Princeton University (1953) **Career:** Retired (1994); Vice Chairman, United States Trust Company of New York (Now Bank of America Corporation), New York, NY (1980-1994); President, White Weld & Company Incorporated (1975-1978); President, G.H.Walker & Company, Incorporated (1970-1974); Executive Vice President, Director, United States Trust Company of New York (Now Bank of America Corporation), New York, NY (1982-1989); Senior Vice President, United States Trust Company of New York, (Bank of America Corporation), New York, NY (1979-1981); President, Chief Operating Officer, White, Weld and Company, Inc., New York, NY (1976-1978); Senior Vice President, White, Weld and Company, Incorporated, New York, NY (1974-1975); President, Chief Executive Officer, G.H. Walker and Company, New York, NY (1971-1974); General Partner, G.H. Walker and Company, New York, NY (1961-1970); Associate, G.H. Walker and Company, New York, NY (1955-1960) **Civic:** Trustee, Provident Loan Society of New York (1973-Present); Chairman, Provident Loan Society of New York (1977-1978); ETO **Military Service:** First Lieutenant, United States Army, Trieste, Italy and Linz, Austria (1953-1955) **Memberships:** Governor, The Municipal Bond Club of New York (1976-1980); President, Investment Association of New York (1968); President, Round Hill Club, Greenwich, CT (1986-1989); Ausable Club, Keene Valley, NY; Racquet and Tennis Club, New York, NY; Riomar Country Club, Vero Beach, FL **Marquis Who's Who Honors:** Albert Nelson Marquis Lifetime Achievement Award **Why did you become involved in your profession or industry:** Mr. Wonham worked many summers in New York City while growing up. After he graduated college, he decided he would try his luck in New York City again. He received a job at the same company he worked for in the summers and began his professional career in finance. **Avocations:** Golf; Fishing **Political Affiliations:** Republican **Religion:** Episcopalian

Peng-Yung "吴本荣" Woo

Title: Electrical Engineering Educator and Researcher **Industry:** Engineering **Company Name:** Northern Illinois University **Date of Birth:** 08/30/1949 **Place of Birth:** Shanghai **State/Country of Origin:** China **Parents:** Donald D.S. Woo; Jane Q. (Liu) Woo **Marital Status:** Married **Spouse Name:** Eva Yi-hui Yu **Children:** Grace; Joyce **Education:** PhD, University of Pennsylvania (1988); MS, Drexel University (1983); BS, Fudan University, China (1982) **Career:** Emeritus Professor, Northern Illinois University, DeKalb (2015-Present); Professor, Northern Illinois University (2000-2014); Associate Professor, Northern Illinois University (1994-2000); Assistant Professor, Northern Illinois University (1988-1994); Teaching Assistant, University of Pennsylvania, Philadelphia, PA (1983-1988); Research Assistant, Drexel University, Philadelphia, PA (1982-1983); Electrical Tech, Shanghai 4th Instruments Co. (1976-1977); English French Translator, Shanghai 4th Instruments Co. (1976-1977); Mechanical, Electrical Technician, Shanghai Analytical Instruments Co. (1968-1976) **Career Related:** Invited Editor, Special Issue of International Journal of Distributed Sensor Network (2014); Invited Lecturer, Fudan University, Tongjii University (2000); Invited Lecturer, Fudan University, Tsinghua University, Jiaoton University, Tongjii University (1996); Member, Various Committees, Northern Illinois University; Thesis Advisor, Northern Illinois University; Editor, Software Engineering; Editor, International Journal of Computer Science and Information Technology Applications; Advisory Professor, Tongjii University, Shanghai, China; Invited Presentation, Seminar, Fudan University, China **Creative Works:** Contributor, Over 50 Articles, International Journals; Contributor, Over 60 Papers, International Conferences; Contributor, 8 Sections, Books **Awards:** Named, IBC Formost Educators of World, Cambridge (2008); Listee, Dictionary of International Biography (1997-1998); The 20th Century Award (1996); International Man of Year (1995); Listee, Men of Achievements (1994, 1996); **Memberships:** Senior Member, Institute of Electrical and Electronics Engineers (IEEE); Standing Technical Committee Member, International Association of Science and Technology for Development (IASTED) **Marquis Who's Who Honors:** Albert Nelson Marquis Lifetime Achievement Award **Why did you become involved in your profession or industry:** When Dr. Woo was 28, he came upon the opportunity to come to the United States and further his education. He attended Drexel University, earning a Master's and then a PhD. He then embarked on his path to success, beginning his career at Northwestern University as an assistant professor. **Avocations:** Reading; Stamp collecting; Music; Peking opera

Kay Ellen Woolridge

Title: Music Educator **Industry:** Education/ Educational Services **Company Name:** Colonial Heights Public Schools **Date of Birth:** 12/16/1953 **Place of Birth:** Petersburg **State/Country of Origin:** VA/USA **Parents:** Roland Page; Vivian Mae Williams Jones **Marital Status:** Widowed **Spouse Name:** Thomas C. Woolridge, Jr. (Deceased 02/01/2019) **Children:** Robert (Bobby) Thomas Woolridge; Michael; Mark; Lisa; Meredith **Education:** Bachelor's Degree in Music Education, Longwood University (1977) **Career:** Music Teacher, Colonial Heights Public Schools (1977-2007) **Civic:** Volunteer, Mission Work; St. Jude Children's Research Hospital **Awards:** Teacher of the Year, Tussing Elementary School (2000-2001) **Memberships:** The Heights Baptist Church **Marquis Who's Who Honors:** Albert Nelson Marquis Lifetime Achievement Award **To what do you attribute your success:** Ms. Woolridge attributed her success to hard work, enthusiasm, optimism, persistence and a positive outlook on life. **Why did you become involved in your profession or industry:** Ms. Woolridge became involved in her profession because of her love of working with children and her passion for music. **Avocations:** Reading; Listening to music; Going to the beach; Spending time with family **Political Affiliations:** Republican **Religion:** Southern Baptist

Robert James Wren

Title: Aerospace Engineering Manager **Industry:** Aviation **Date of Birth:** 05/12/1935 **Place of Birth:** Moline **State/Country of Origin:** IL/USA **Parents:** James O. Wren; Gladys W. Wren **Marital Status:** Married **Spouse Name:** Jordis Wren; Shirley (Divorced); Jean (Divorced) **Children:** James; Patrick; Kiley **Education:** Master of Science in Chemical Engineering, Southern Methodist University (1962); Bachelor of Science in Chemical Engineering, University of Texas (1956); Doctoral Candidate, University of Houston **Certifications:** Registered Professional Engineer, Texas **Career:** Member, Space Shuttle Payload Safety Review Panel, NASA, Johnson Space Center, Houston, TX (1984-2000); Alternate Chairman, Space Shuttle Payload Safety Review Panel, NASA, Johnson Space Center, Houston, TX (1990-2000); Manager, Engineering Director, Vehicle and Payload Flight System Safety, NASA, Johnson Space Center, Houston, TX (1995-2000); Manager, Engineering Directorate for Space Shuttle Payload Safety, NASA, Johnson Space Center, Houston, TX (1984-1995); Manager, Structural Division Space Shuttle Payload Systems, NASA, Johnson Space Center, Houston, TX (1972-1984); Manager Structural Design and Development, Space Shuttle Carrier Aircraft-747, NASA, Johnson Space Center, Houston, TX (1975-1977); Manager, Structural Design Space Station, Space Base, Lunar Base, Mars Mission, NASA, Manned Spacecraft Center, Houston, TX (1969-1975); Head Experimental Dynamics Section, NASA, Manned Spacecraft Center, Houston TX (1966-1970); Manager, Apollo Lunar Module-2 Drop Test Program (1968-1969); Manager, Apollo Spacecraft 2TV-1 CSM Test Program (1967-1968); Senior Structural Dynamics Engineer, Manager, Vibration and Acoustic Test Facility, NASA, Manned Spacecraft Center, Houston, TX (1962-1963, 1963-1966); Structural Test Engineer, General Dynamics, Fort Worth, TX (1957-1962); Associate Engineer, Hydraulic Engineer, U.S. Bureau of Reclamation, Austin, TX (1955-1957); Station Clerk, City of Austin Power Plant, Texas (1954-1955); Engineering Aide, Central Power and Light Co., Corpus Christi, TX (1954) **Career Related:** Aerospace Consultant (2003-Present); Director, Safety and Mission Assurance, International Space Station Program Office, United Space Alliance Headquarters, Houston, TX (2000-2003); Member, System Safety Panel, NASA International Space Station Flight (1994-2000) **Civic:** Board of Directors, Bay Area YMCA, Houston, TX (1980-2007); Chairperson, Bay Area YMCA, Houston, TX (1983-1984); President, Friendswood Little League Baseball (1980-1983) **Creative Works:** Contributor, "Eight Years to the Moon," by Nancy Atkinson **Awards:** Recipient, Sustained Superior Performance Award, National Aeronautics and Space Administration; Personal Letter of Commendation, George Low NASA Apollo Program; Outstanding Service Award, NASA; Group Achievement Awards, NASA; Paul Harris Fellow, Rotary, Floyd Boze Fellow, Rotary **Memberships:** Co-founder, Board of Directors, Space Center Rotary Memorial Foundation (1987-Present); Co-founder, Board of Directors, Rotary World Health Foundation Plastic Surgery for Children (1985-Present); Co-founder, Board of Directors, Rotary National Award for Space Achievement Foundation (1984-Present); Chairperson, District Assembly, Rotary Club of Space Center (1993-1994); Finance Committee, Rotary Club of Space Center (1989-1991); Chairperson, District Assembly, Rotary Club of Space Center (1989-1990); Governor's Aide, Rotary Club of Space Center (1989-1990); Zone Leader, Rotary Club of Space Center (1988-1989); Area Coordinator, Rotary Club of Space Center (1987-1989); Government Representative, Rotary Club of Space Center (1986-1987); President, Rotary Club of Space Center (1985-1986); Director, Treasurer, Secretary, Vice President, Rotary Club of Space Center (1979-1985) **Marquis Who's Who Honors:** Albert Nelson Marquis Lifetime Achievement Award; Marquis Who's Who Top Professional **Why did you become involved in your profession or industry:** Mr. Wren became involved in his profession due to the influence of his father, who excelled in the industry of heavy construction. **Avocations:** Snow and water skiing; Running; Scuba diving; Tennis; Sailing **Religion:** Methodist

Erich-Oskar Wruck, PhD

Title: Foreign Language Educator, Administrator (Retired) **Industry:** Education/Educational Services **Date of Birth:** 10/29/1928 **Place of Birth:** Gross-Kroessin **State/Country of Origin:** Pomerania/Germany **Parents:** Erich Albert Wruck; Erna (Kroening) Wruck **Marital Status:** Married **Spouse Name:** Esther Emmy Schmidt (10/03/1953) **Children:** Dr. Eric Gordon (Deceased); Karin Esther (Deceased); Krista Elisabeth **Education:** PhD, Rutgers, the State University of New Jersey (1969); MA, Rutgers, the State University of New Jersey (1961); BA, Rutgers, the State University of New Jersey, Magna Cum Laude (1959) **Career:** Retired (1994-Present); Junior Year Abroad Program, Wuerzburg, Germany (1989-1992); University of Wuerzburg, Germany (1986-1992); Junior Year Abroad Program, Wuerzburg, Germany (1986-1987); Professor, Chairman of German Department, Davidson College, North Carolina (1983-1987); Established Exchange Program, Marburg University, University of Wuerzburg, Germany (1985); Associate Professor, Davidson College, North Carolina (1969-1983); Director, Davidson Abroad Program, Marburg University (1971-1972); Assistant Professor, Davidson College, North Carolina (1962-1969); Director, Davidson Abroad Program, Marburg University (1966-1967); Established Exchange Program, Marburg University, Germany (1963); Assistant instructor, Rutgers, the State University of New Jersey, New Brunswick, NJ (1959-1962) **Career Related:** West Point Liaison Officer for Ninth (Parts of Eighth and 10th) North Carolina Congressional Districts (1982-1986); Consultant, Faculty, U.S. Army Command and General Staff College (1974-1985); Operations and Plans Staff Officer, Headquarters, Department of the Army, Office of the Deputy Joint Chiefs of Staff For Military Operations (1973-1985) **Military Service:** Colonel, U.S. Army Reserve (1986); First Lieutenant, U.S. Army (1953-1957) **Awards:** Named, Artillery OCS Hall Of Fame (1996); Julius Maximilians Medal, University of Wuerzburg (1987); Achievement Medal In Gold, West German Armed Forces (1979); West German Athletic Medal In Gold (1979); Henry Rutgers Scholar (1959); Three Meritorious Service Medals **Memberships:** Charter, Goethe Society of North America; Society of German American Studies **Marquis Who's Who Honors:** Albert Nelson Marquis Lifetime Achievement Award **Why did you become involved in your profession or industry:** Dr. Wruck was inspired to go into his profession because of a ski trip he went on. He met an American girl, got engaged and came to America in 1952. He went to school, got married and was drafted into the Army in 1953. **Avocations:** Painting; Photography; Soaring; Skiing; Running; Woodworking **Religion:** Lutheran

Lynn Ruth Wurth

Title: Advertising Executive **Industry:** Advertising & Marketing **Company Name:** The Catholic Sun **Date of Birth:** 06/19/1933 **Place of Birth:** Paducah **State/Country of Origin:** KY/USA **Parents:** Anthony I. Wurth; Mildred L. (Ross) White (Deceased 2007) **Education:** Coursework, Phoenix Junior College (Now Phoenix College), Phoenix, AZ (1978-1980); Diploma in Business, Bowling Green University, Bowling Green, Ohio (1956) **Career:** Advertising and Business Manager, The Catholic Sun, Phoenix, AZ (1985-2004); Account and Sales Representative, Computer Graphics, Phoenix, AZ (1981-1985); Account Representative, Data Corporation, Phoenix, AZ (1978-1981); Branch Manager, National Auto Glass, Phoenix, AZ (1976-1978); President, Newman Auto Glass, Phoenix, AZ (1958-1976) **Memberships:** Governor, Soroptimist International of the Americas (1984-1986); President, National Association of Insurance Women (1982-1983); Catholic Press Association; The Associated Church Press; Arizona Newspapers Association **Marquis Who's Who Honors:** Albert Nelson Marquis Lifetime Achievement Award; Marquis Who's Who Top Professional **Why did you become involved in your profession or industry:** Ms. Wurth became involved in her profession through her faith. She prayed for guidance and was led in the right direction. **Avocations:** Golf; Theater; Music **Religion:** Methodist

Gerald Joseph Yakatan, PhD

Title: Chairman, Chief Executive Officer **Industry:** Pharmaceuticals **Company Name:** IRISYS, LLC **Date of Birth:** 05/20/1942 **Place of Birth:** Philadelphia **State/Country of Origin:** PA/USA **Parents:** Nathan Yakatan; Bella (Resnick) Yakatan **Marital Status:** Married **Spouse Name:** Una Gittleman (12/20/1964) **Children:** Nicole Blayne; Brook Noel **Education:** PhD, Pharmaceutical Sciences, University of Florida (1971); MS, Pharmaceutical Chemistry, Temple University (1965); BS, Pharmacy, Temple University (1963) **Career:** Founder & Chairman, IriSys, LLC (1996-Present); Founder, Chief Executive Officer, Avanir Pharmaceuticals, San Diego, CA (1998-2005); Founder, President, Chief Executive Officer, Tanabe Research Laboratories USA Inc., San Diego, CA (1990-1995); Executive Vice President, Research and Development, Immunetech Pharmaceutical, San Diego, CA (1987-1990); Vice President, Product Development, Warner Lambert Co., Morris Plains, NJ (1983-1987); Director, Pharmacokinetics and Drug Metabolism, Warner Lambert Co., Ann Arbor, MI (1980-1983); Chairman, Department of Pharmaceutics; Assistant Director Drug Dynamics Institute, College of Pharmacy, University of Texas, Austin, Texas (1971-1980); Associate (1976-1988) and Assistant Professor, The University of Texas (1971-1976) **Awards:** President, ATS(American Technion Society) San Diego (2004-2009);Director of the Year, Corporate Directors Forum, San Diego, CA (2003); Distinguished Alumnus, Temple University (2003); AMGEN Honorary Lecturer, 9th Annual CSU Biotechnology Symposium (1997); ACCP Distinguished Service Award (1996); Distinguished Service Award, American College of Clinical Pharmacy (1996); Distinguished Alumnus, University of Florida College of Pharmacy (1993); Fellowship, National Institutes of Health (1965-1969) **Memberships:** National Science Foundation (1964); Fellow, Honorary Regent, American College of Clinical Pharmacology; Fellow, American Association of Pharmaceutical Scientists; Academy of Pharmaceutical Sciences; United States Professional Tennis Registry; Florida Blue Key; Rho Chi Society; Temple University Sword Society; National Board of Directors, American Technion Society **Marquis Who's Who Honors:** Albert Nelson Marquis Lifetime Achievement Award; Marquis Who's Who Top Professional; Marquis' Industry Leader; **To what do you attribute your success:** Dr. Yakatan attributes his success to the PASSION in pursuing pharmaceutical creativity, the VISION in integrating economic development and social responsibility and the DECISION making skill in achieving accelerated program results. **Why did you become involved in your profession or industry:** Dr. Yakatan became interested in pharmacology when he was an adolescent. As a teen, Dr. Yakatan worked the soda fountain at a pharmacy. The pharmacy later promoted Dr. Yakatan and allowed him to work with prescriptions. Because of this job and his interest in chemistry, Dr. Yakatan chose to pursue a career in pharmacology and earned his master's degree and later his PhD. **Avocations:** Tennis; Reading; Traveling **Political Affiliations:** Democrat **Religion:** Jewish **Thoughts on Life:** Touch the data and talk with data; the data will tell you where to go. Agree to disagree. One should have enough courage and passion to pursue what he wants to accomplish, at peril of being judged not to have lived.

Richard Charles Yancey

Title: Investment Banker (Retired) **Industry:** Financial Services **Date of Birth:** 05/28/1926 **Place of Birth:** Spokane **State/Country of Origin:** WA/USA **Parents:** George R. Yancey; M. Ruth (Yenney) Yancey **Marital Status:** Married **Spouse Name:** Mary Anne Shaffer (2/5/1956) **Children:** Leslie; Jennifer; Richard C. Yancey, Jr. **Education:** MBA, Harvard University, with Distinction (1952); BA in Economics, Whitman College, Walla Walla, WA (1949) **Career:** (Retired) Senior Advisor, Dillon, Read & Co., New York, NY (1992); Director, Dillon, Read & Co., New York, NY (1990); Managing Director, Dillon, Read & Co., New York, NY (1975-1989); Vice President, Dillon, Read & Co., New York, NY (1963-1975); Associate, Dillon, Read & Co., New York, NY (1952-1963) **Career Related:** Senior Advisor, Ad Media Partners, Inc., New York, NY; Chairman, Director, Czech and Slovak American Enterprise Fund, Massapequa, NY; Past Partnership, Board Whittle Communications L.P., Knoxville, TN; Former Board of Directors, Principal Funds, Des Moines, IA **Civic:** Trustee, Brooklyn Youth Chorus Academy; Former Chairman, Board of Directors, WM Group of Funds, Seattle, WA; Former Member, Board of Overseers, Whitman College; Former Trustee, Plymouth Church, Brooklyn, NY; Former President, Plymouth Church, Brooklyn, NY; Former Trustee, New York Infirmary-Beekman Downtown Hospital (Now NewYork-Presbyterian Lower Manhattan Hospital); Board of Directors, Brooklyn Chamber Music Society **Military Service:** U.S. Navy Reserve (1944-1946) **Awards:** President's USA Freedom Corps Call to Service Award, USAID (2006) **Memberships:** Harvard Club of New York City; The Pilgrims of the United States; Former Member, NYSSA **Marquis Who's Who Honors:** Albert Nelson Marquis Lifetime Achievement Award; Marquis Who's Who Top Professional; Marquis Who's Who Humanitarian Award **Why did you become involved in your profession or industry:** Mr. Yancey became involved in his profession because it was a good field to go into after the war; he wanted to provide financing to companies in the United States and abroad. **Political Affiliations:** Democrat

Andrew Yang

Title: Entrepreneur, Philantrhopist; Lawyer **Industry:** Nonprofit & Philanthropy **Date of Birth:** 01/13/1975 **Place of Birth:** Schenectady **State/Country of Origin:** NY/USA **Marital Status:** Married **Spouse Name:** Evelyn Lu (2011) **Children:** Two Sons **Education:** Doctor of Jurisprudence, Columbia Law School (1999); Bachelor of Arts in Economics and Political Science, Brown University (1996) **Career:** Founder, Venture for America (2011-Present); Candidate, Democratic Nominee, U.S. Presidential Election (2017-2020); Chief Executive Officer, Venture for America (2011-2017); President, Manhattan Prep (2009-2012); Chief Executive Officer, President, Manhattan Prep (2006-2009); Vice President, MMF Systems Inc. (2001-2005); Launched, Stargiving. com (2000-2001); Corporate Attorney, Davis Polk & Wardwell, NY (1999-2000) **Creative Works:** Author, "The War on Normal People: The Truth About America's Disappearing Jobs and Why Universal Basic Income is Our Future" (2018); Author, "Smart People Should Build Things: How to Restore Our Culture of Achievement, Build a Path for Entrepreneurs, and Create New Jobs in America" (2014) **Awards:** Presidential Ambassador for Global Entrepreneurship (2015); Champion of Change, White House (2012) **Political Affiliations:** Democrat

Ismael Duran Yanga

Title: Surgeon, Primary Care Physician **Industry:** Medicine & Health Care **Date of Birth:** 02/05/1932 **Place of Birth:** Bocaue **State/Country of Origin:** Philippines **Parents:** Ismael Eusebio Yanga Sr.; Sofia Rodriguez Duran **Marital Status:** Married **Spouse Name:** Ruth Morter (12/17/1971) **Children:** Michele Marie; Dr. I. David III **Education:** Fellow in Surgery, Hurley Medical Center, Flint, M (1969-1970); Surgical Resident, Hurley Medical Center, Flint, MI (1965-1969); Surgical Resident, Albany Memorial Hospital, Albany, NY (1964); Rotating Intern, Mercy Hospital, Buffalo, NY (1963); MD, University of Santo Thomas, Manila, Philippines (1956); AA, University of Santo Thomas, Manila, Philippines (1951) **Certifications:** Diplomate, American Board of Surgery, American Board of Disability Analysts (ABDA) **Career:** Practice of Medicine, Specializing in Surgery, Howell, MI (1973) **Career Related:** President, Dr. Yanga's Hospital, Inc., Bocaue Bulacan, Philippines (2000); Chief, Medical Staff, McPherson Hospital, Howell, MI (1994-1995); Board of Directors, Dr. Yanga's Hospital, Inc., Bocaue Bulacan, Philippines **Civic:** President, Mission Board, Christ for the Philippines **Memberships:** Chairman, Board of Directors, Livingston Physicians Group (1994-Present); President, Livingston Physicians Group (1991-1994); President, Medical Society of Livingston, Inc. (1979); Fellow, American College of Surgeons; Diplomate, American Society for Laser Medicine and Surgery, Inc. (ASLMS); Fellow, International College of Surgeons; American Medical Association; Michigan State Medical Society (MSMS); American Board of Disability Analysts (ABDA); Livingston Physicians Organization; Diplomate, American College of Managed Care Medicine; American College of Medical Quality; Howell Area Chamber of Commerce **Marquis Who's Who Honors:** Albert Nelson Marquis Lifetime Achievement Award; Marquis Who's Who Top Professional **Why did you become involved in your profession or industry:** Dr. Yanga became involved in his profession because his father was a doctor who inspired him to follow in his footsteps. **Religion:** Baptist

Brent Yonts

Title: State Legislator **Industry:** Government Administration/Government Relations/Government Services **Date of Birth:** 03/21/1949 **Place of Birth:** Greenville **State/Country of Origin:** KY/USA **Parents:** Larry Ray Yonts; Dorothy Nell (Sweeney) Yonts **Marital Status:** Married **Spouse Name:** Janice Faye Covington (11/20/1976) **Children:** Emily Sparks; Ellen Suetholz; Harrison **Education:** JD, University of Kentucky, Lexington, KY (1975); BS, Murray State University, Murray, KY (1971) **Career:** Owner, Partner, Yonts, Sherman & Driskill, PSC, Yonts Attorney at Law, Yonts & Packford (1978-Present); Associate, Streets & Cisney, Greenville, KY (1976-1978) **Civic:** Deacon, First Baptist Church (1995-Present); Treasurer, First Baptist Church, APX (1993-2013); Board of Directors, Owensboro Museum of Fine Art **Military Service:** 1st Lieutenant, U.S. Army (1971-1973); 2nd Lieutenant, U.S. Army **Creative Works:** Author, Weekly Column, Legislators, Regional and Local Newspapers; Participant, Essay Contests; Participant, High School Public Speaking **Memberships:** Muhlenberg Community Theatre (2018-Present); Member District 15, Kentucky House of Representatives (1997-2016); Member, Greenville Board Education (1978-1983); Former President, Kiwanis International; Kentucky Bar Association **Bar Admissions:** Kentucky (1976); License, Supreme Court of Kentucky (1976); U.S. District Court for the Western District of Kentucky; U.S. Court of Appeals for the Sixth Circuit, Cincinnati **Marquis Who's Who Honors:** Albert Nelson Marquis Lifetime Achievement Award **Why did you become involved in your profession or industry:** Mr. Yonts became involved in his profession because he started out wanting to be a teacher, specifically of agriculture as he grew up on a farm in Kentucky. But after his first semester in college, he changed his major. He graduated with honors after four years as a political science major, with minors in agriculture, English, education, and military science. He was commissioned when he graduated and went into the military for two years. Mr. Yonts went to law school because his ultimate long-range goal was to go into public service and he thought the best way to do that was to go into the law. He graduated from law school in two-and-a-half years. **Political Affiliations:** Democrat **Religion:** Baptist **Thoughts on Life:** Mr. Yonts' early education — from first to sixth grade — took place in one of the last one-room schools in Kentucky under the guidance of the same teacher. In the classroom, there was a potbelly coal-fired stove, and outside, there were toilets and a well to draw water from. He remembers students oiling down the wooden floor to keep dust down during the year and competitive math matches on the blackboard between grades. "A good education there," he later said.

Jonathon C. York

Title: Professor of Government **Industry:** Education/Educational Services **Company Name:** Mountain View College **Date of Birth:** 08/17/1972 **Place of Birth:** Manhattan **State/Country of Origin:** KS/USA **Parents:** Thomas F. York; Florence D. York-Carpenter **Education:** Master of Arts, Politics, Braniff Graduate School of Liberal Arts, University of Dallas, Irving, TX (1999); Bachelor of Arts, Politics, Constantin College of Liberal Arts, University of Dallas, Irving, TX (1994) **Career:** Professor of Government, Mountain View College, Dallas, TX (2005-Present); Visiting Scholar in Government, North Lake College, Irving, TX (2003-2005); Adjunct Instructor in Government and Developmental Writing, North Lake College, Irving, TX (2001-2003); Adjunct Instructor, Government, Tarrant County College, Northwest Campus (2001-2003) **Career Related:** Resident, Armature Astronomer, Mountain View College; Coordinator of Star Parties, Mountain View College; Tutoring, Mountain View College; Department Coordinator, Mountain View College; Chair, Astronomy Club; Chair, Library Committee; Chair, Search Committee for Faculty and Government; Chair, Former Discipline Committee in Government; Guitarist, Faculty Garage Band **Creative Works:** Contributor, book chapter, "Honoring the Circle", published by Waterside (2019); Former Musician, Music Educator, Primrose School Musical Workshop; Musician, Mountain View College Astronomy Day; Contributor, The Leo Test **Memberships:** Political Information Officer, Mountain View College Faculty Association (2009-2010); Indigenous Studies Network; American Political Science Association; McDonald Observatory; Planetary Society **Marquis Who's Who Honors:** Albert Nelson Marquis Lifetime Achievement Award; Marquis Who's Who Top Professional; Marquis Who's Who Humanitarian Award **To what do you attribute your success:** Mr. York attributes his success to his mentors, including Wayne Ambler and Sally Fisher Hicks, who were his former professors. When he started teaching, he adopted a style similar to that of Thomas West. He also attributes Sister Susan Kongs, his social science teacher in middle school. **Why did you become involved in your profession or industry:** Mr. York became involved in his profession out of a desire to learn more about politics, which was a gap in his educational experience. **Avocations:** Music; Astronomy

Richard Yost

Title: Founder, Chief Executive Officer **Industry:** Business Management/Business Services **Company Name:** Airo Brands Inc. **Education:** BS in Business Management, Northwood University, Midland, MI (2017) **Certifications:** Medical Marijuana License, State of New York (2015) **Career:** Founder, Chief Executive Officer, Airo Brands Inc. (2017-Present); Angel Investor, Various Companies Specializing in Health and Wellness, Urban Agriculture, Soil Science, Cannabis Science and Delivery, Consumer Products, Alternate Energy and Energy Efficiency **Civic:** Vertical Agriculture Project, Staten Island, NY; Financial Donor, Juvenile Diabetes; First, Free-standing Hospice Residence on the Grounds of Eger Health Care & Rehabilitation Center, Egbertville, Staten Island, NY **Awards:** Named One of the 100 Most Influential People in Cannabis (2019); Innovation Award, Product Technology (2017); Product Innovation Award, Cannabis Concentrate (2017) **To what do you attribute your success:** Mr. Yost attributes his success to his dedication to making a difference and building systems and processes that serves as a model for others. He is driven to make an impact on the quality of life of the people his products serve. He has a hunger to build teams and organizations that are leaders in their industries. Mr. Yost starts by identifying what the consumer really needs, and asks, "Is there a better way?" **Why did you become involved in your profession or industry:** Mr. Yost became involved in his profession after an experience providing fully organic, contaminant-free soil to a United States veteran, who was a home cannabis gardener; this changed his perspective about the value of using natural compounds, like cannabis, as medicine and the critical importance of going back to natural cultivation methods for all crops. The youngest entrepreneur to be awarded a medical marijuana license in New York, Mr. Yost focused on building a best-in-class business with responsible environmental design that allowed the cultivation and delivery of the purest plant-based medicine in a comforting and caring environment. His long-term commitment has evolved from developing a portfolio of businesses that leverage the latest technology in plant and soil science to creating an approach to farming and plant-based medicine that is cleaner, safer, and healthier for farmers and consumers. With Airo Brands, a non-cannabis touching company, Mr. Yost has built a model that supplies revolutionary technology with formulation processes, cutting-edge science, and go-to market strategy for partners on a state-by-state basis that allows delivery of the most consistent product nationally, while remaining compliant with federal and state regulations around cannabis.

Sara Young

Title: OB/GYN Clinical Nurse Specialist/IBCLC **Industry:** Medicine & Health Care **Date of Birth:** 06/05/1948 **Place of Birth:** Parkersburg **State/Country of Origin:** WV/USA **Parents:** Jack H. Young; Jean L. (Ankrom) Young (Deceased) **Marital Status:** Single **Education:** MS in Nursing, Catholic University America (1977); BSN, West Virginia University (1970) **Certifications:** International Board Certified Lactation Consultant (IBCLC) (1994-2014); Certified Bereavement Counselor (1989) **Career:** Retired, RN, West Virginia (2018); Obstetrics-Gynecology Clinical Nurse Specialist, Hartford Hospital (1978-2011); Staff Nurse, George Washington University Hospital, Washington, DC (1974-1978); Head Nurse, Labor and Delivery, Camden Clark Memorial Hospital, Parkersburg, WV (1972-1974); Staff Nurse, Camden Clark Memorial Hospital, Parkersburg, WV (1970-1972) **Career Related:** Clinical Associate II, University of Connecticut School of Nursing **Awards:** Professional Award, La Leche League of Connecticut (2001); Co-recipient, Wyeth Laboratory Plaque, AWHONN (1989) **Memberships:** American Nurses Association; AWHONN **Marquis Who's Who Honors:** Albert Nelson Marquis Lifetime Achievement Award (2018); Marquis Who's Who Top Professional (2020) **To what do you attribute your success:** She has always loved learning, doing the best possible by working hard, following up as she is a detailed person in doing a task and is very organized with her work and she cares about those who are suffering and want to help relieve that suffering as well as prepare others for what to expect and how to help themselves with an issue in a timely way with available resources. **Why did you become involved in your profession or industry:** Inspired by her mother who was also a nurse. Ms. Young loved the different components and challenges of the clinical nurse specialist role- hands on clinical at bedside, leadership, education, consultant, and research. **Avocations:** Oil painting **Political Affiliations:** Republican **Religion:** Methodist

Virgil M. Young, EdD

Title: Education Educator **Industry:** Education/Educational Services **Date of Birth:** 09/24/1936 **Place of Birth:** Santa Rosa **State/Country of Origin:** CA/USA **Parents:** Virgil M.; Vesta May (Huyett) Williams **Marital Status:** Married **Spouse Name:** Katherine Ann Young (12/20/1964) **Children:** Susan Annette; Louis H. Young (Stepson) **Education:** EdD, University of Idaho (1967); BS, University of Idaho (1958) **Certifications:** Certified Advanced Secondary Education Educator, School Superintendent, State of Idaho **Career:** Professor Emeritus, Boise State University, Idaho (1996-Present); Head, Department of Education, Boise State University, Idaho (1989-1996); Professor of Education, Boise State University, Idaho (1967-1996); Administrative Assistant to the Superintendent, Coeur d'Alene School District, Idaho (1965-1967); Teacher, Moscow School District, Idaho (1959-1963) **Military Service:** Captain, United States Army Reserve **Creative Works:** Designer, Author, Educational and Commercial Internet Websites (1999-Present); Co-author, "Legends of the West" (2014); Co-author, "Quilters Garden of Verse" (2013); Co-author, "The Story of the Idaho Guide and Resource Book" (1993); Author, "The Year 2000 Grolier Multimedia Encyclopedia" (2000); Author, Elementary Textbook, "The Story of Idaho, Four Editions" **Memberships:** Past President, Northwest Association of Teacher Educators; Past President, Idaho Association of Colleges for Teacher Education; Past President, Phi Delta Kappa (PDK International) **Marquis Who's Who Honors:** Albert Nelson Marquis Lifetime Achievement Award; Marquis Who's Who Top Professional **Why did you become involved in your profession or industry:** Dr. Young became involved in his profession because he admired teachers he had in school. **Avocations:** Reading

Wael Zatar

Title: Dean, J. H. Distinguished Engineering Chair, Interim Chair **Industry:** Education/Educational Services **Company Name:** Marshal University **Parents:** Abdelhalim Mohamed Zatar; Yussr Elsheihy **Marital Status:** Married **Spouse Name:** Gehan Elsayed **Children:** Jana Wael Abdelhalim Mohamed Zatar; Ahmed Wael Abdelhalim Mohamed Zatar **Education:** Doctor of Engineering in Civil Engineering, Saitama University (1999); Master of Science in Civil Engineering, Cairo University (1994); Bachelor of Science in Civil Engineering, Cairo University (1990) **Career:** Dean, J. H. Distinguished Engineering Chair, College of Engineering and Computer Sciences, Marshall University, West Virginia (2011-Present); Professor, Marshall University, West Virginia (2006-2011); Professor of Civil Engineering, West Virginia University Institute of Technology (2004-2006); Visiting Professor, University of Kentucky (2001-2003); Faculty Fellow, Saitama University (1999-2001); Research Assistant, Department of Civil Engineering, Saitama University, Japan (1996-1999); Senior Design Eengineer, Ferrometalco International Company, Cairo, Egypt (1991-1996); Design Engineer, Dars Consultant and Engineers, Cairo, Egypt (1990-1991) **Career Related:** Associate Editor, American Society for Civil Engineers Journal of Performance of Constructed Facilities **Creative Works:** Contributor, Chapters to Books; Contributor, Research Articles to Technical Publications **Awards:** Grantee, WV-ASCE Outstanding Educator Award (2019); Fellow, Prestressed Concrete Institute (2017); Distinguished Educator Award, Prestressed Concrete Institute (2016); Grantee, WV-ASCE Outstanding Educator Award (2015); Distinguished Educator Award, Prestressed Concrete Institute (2009); Grantee, Prestressed Concrete Institute (2006); Faculty Advisor Certificate of Commendation, American Society of Civil Engineers (2005); Fellow, Japan Society for the Promotion of Sciences (2001); Grantee, Ministry of Education, Culture and Science (1996-1999) **Memberships:** Transportation Research Board; American Concrete Institute; Fellow, Prestressed Concrete Institute; American Society of CivilEngineers; American Society of Engineering Education; American Society for Non-destructive Testing; Global Engineering Dean's Council; European Academy of Science; Japan Concrete Institute; Japan Society for Civil Engineers; Egyptian Syndicate of Engineers **Marquis Who's Who Honors:** Albert Nelson Marquis Lifetime Achievement Award; Marquis Who's Who Top Professional **Why did you become involved in your profession or industry:** Dr. Zatar became involved in his profession due to the influence of his father, who was a civil engineer. After working in the field for six years, he felt satisfied with all he had achieved, and decided to share his knowledge with others. **Avocations:** Sightseeing; Travel; Soccer; Tennis; Time with the family; Outdoors

Renée Zellweger

Title: Actress, Producer **Industry:** Media & Entertainment **Date of Birth:** 04/25/1969 **Place of Birth:** Katy **State/Country of Origin:** TX/USA **Parents:** Emil Erich Zellweger; Kjellfrid Irene Andreassen **Marital Status:** Single **Spouse Name:** Kenny Chesney (05/09/2005, Annulled 12/20/2005) **Education:** BA in English, University of Texas at Austin (1991) **Career:** Actress, Film, Television (1992-Present) **Civic:** Participant, 2005 HIV Prevention Campaign of the Swiss Federal Health Department (2005); Patron, The GREAT Initiative **Creative Works:** Actress, Film, "Judy" (2019); Actress, Television Series, "What/If" (2019); Actress, Film, "Here and Now" (2018); Actress, Film, "Same Kind of Different as Me" (2017); Actress, Film, "Bridget Jones's Baby" (2016); Actress, Film, "The Whole Truth" (2016); Executive Producer, Writer, Television Film, "Cinnamon Girl" (2013); Actress, Film, "My Own Love Song" (2010); Actress, Film, "Case 39" (2009); Actress, Film, "My One and Only" (2009); Voice Actress, Film, "Monsters vs. Aliens" (2009); Actress, Film, "New in Town" (2009); Actress, Film, "Appaloosa" (2008); Actress, Film, "Leatherheads" (2008); Executive Producer, Television Film, "Living Proof" (2008); Voice Actress, Film, "Bee Movie" (2007); Actress, Executive Producer, Film, "Miss Potter" (2006); Actress, Film, "Cinderella Man" (2005); Actress, Film, "Bridget Jones: The Edge of Reason" (2004); Voice Actress, Film, "Shark Tale" (2004); Actress, Film, "Cold Mountain" (2003); Actress, Film, "Down with Love" (2003); Actress, Film, "Chicago" (2002); Actress, Film, "Bridget Jones's Diary" (2001); Voice Actress, Film, "King of the Hill" (2001); Actress, Film, "Nurse Betty" (2000); Actress, Film, "Me, Myself & Irene" (2000); Actress, Film, "The Bachelor" (1999); Actress, Film, "One True Thing" (1998); Actress, Film, "A Price Above Rubies" (1998); Actress, Film, "Deceiver" (1997); Actress, Film, "Jerry Maguire" (1996); Actress, Film, "The Whole Wide World" (1996); Actress, Film, "The Low Life" (1995); Actress, Film, "Empire Records" (1995); Actress, Film, "Texas Chainsaw Massacre: The Next Generation" (1994); Actress, Film, "Love and a .45" (1994); Actress, Film, "8 Seconds" (1994); Actress, Film, "Shake, Rattle and Rock!" (1994); Actress, Film, "Reality Bites" (1994); Actress, Film, "My Boyfriend's Back" (1993); Actress, Film, "Dazed and Confused" (1993); Actress, Miniseries, "Murder in the Heartland" (1993); Actress, Television Film, "A Taste for Killing" (1992) **Awards:** Best Actress, "Judy," Academy Awards (2020); Best Film Actress in a Leading Role, "Judy," BAFTA Awards (2020); Best Actress in a Motion Picture - Drama, "Judy," Golden Globe Awards (2020); Outstanding Performance by a Female Actor in a Leading Role in a Motion Picture, "Judy," Screen Actors Guild Awards (2020); Best Actress, "Judy," Critics' Choice Movie Awards (2020); Best Actress, "Judy," Hollywood Critics Association (2020); American Riviera Award, "Judy," Santa Barbara International Film Festival (2020); Desert Palm Achievement Award, "Judy," Palm Springs International Film Festival (2020); Best Actress in a Motion Picture, "Judy," Satellite Awards (2020); Best Actress, "Judy," Houston Film Critics Society (2019); Best Lead Actress, "Judy," Atlanta Film Critics Circle (2019); Best Actress in a British Independent Film, "Judy," British Independent Film Awards (2019); Best Female Lead, "Judy," Independent Spirit Awards (2019); Best Actress, "Judy," Kansas City Film Critics Circle (2019); Nominee, Best International Lead Actress - Cinema, "Judy," AACTA International Awards (2019); Best Actress, "Judy," AARP's Movies for Grownups Awards (2019); Silver Medallion, Telluride Film Festival (2019); Nominee, Most Daring Performance, Alliance of Women Film Journalists (2019); Actress of the Year, "Judy," London Film Critics' Circle (2019); Nominee, Best Actress, "Judy," Alliance of Women Film Journalists (2019); Nominee, Best Actress, "Judy," Austin Film Critics Association (2019); Best Actress, "Judy," Awards Circuit Community Awards (2019); Nominee, Best Actress, "Judy," Chicago Film Critics Association (2019); Nominee, Best Actress, "Judy," Detroit Film Critics Society (2019); Film Performance of the Year - Actress, "Judy," Dorian Awards (2019); Nominee, Best Actress, "Judy," San Diego Film Critics Society (2019); Nominee, Best Actress, "Judy," Florida Film Critics Circle (2019); Nominee, Best Actress, "Judy," Georgia Film Critics Association (2019); Best Actress, "Judy," National Board of Review (2019); Nominee, Best Actress, "Judy," North Carolina Film Critics Association (2019); Nominee, Best Actress, "Judy," Seattle Film Critics Society (2019); Best Actress, "Judy," Online Association of Female Film Critics (2019); Best Actress, "Judy," Phoenix Film Critics Society (2019); Nominee, Best Actress, "Judy," Toronto Film Critics Association (2019); Nominee, Best Actress, "Judy," Washington D.C. Area Film Critics Association (2019); Best Actress, "Judy," Online Film Critics Society (2019); Inductee, Texas Film Hall of Fame, Texas Film Awards (2011); Best International Actress, Goldene Kamera (2010); Woman of the Year, Hasty Pudding Theatricals (2009); Numerous Television Appearances; Appearance, Cover Story and Photo, Numerous Magazines

Walter Zemialkowski Jr.

Title: Airport Consultant **Industry:** Aviation **Company Name:** AMS - Airport Management Services **Marital Status:** Married **Children:** One Son; One Daughter **Education:** MBA, SIUE (1994) **Career:** Airport Consultant, Airport Management Services, Punta Cana (2019-Present); Director of Operations, Airport Management Services, Punta Cana (2000-2019); Airside Operations Supervisor, Fort Lauderdale-Hollywood International Airport **Military Service:** US Air Force (Retired) **Awards:** Graduate Division Award, Gateway Chapter, Industrial Relations Research Association (1989) **Memberships:** Beta Gamma Sigma; Former Member, Rotary International **Marquis Who's Who Honors:** Marquis Who's Who Top Professional **To what do you attribute your success:** Mr. Zemialkowski attributes his success to hard work, dedication and considerable patience. **Why did you become involved in your profession or industry:** Mr. Zemialkowski became involved in his profession because of his military experiences. After serving as a crew member on a B-52 while stationed in Homestead, Puerto Rico, the military wanted to transfer him to North Dakota. However, with a heavily-pregnant wife and a sick mother-in-law this wasn't possible, so he requested to change to airport management. **Avocations:** Golfing **Thoughts on Life:** Mr. Zemialkowski's motto is "Integrity above all. Selfless before self. Excellence in all you do."

Tikey A. Zes

Title: Music Minister **Industry:** Media & Entertainment **Date of Birth:** 10/10/1927 **Place of Birth:** Long Beach **State/Country of Origin:** CA/USA **Parents:** Athanasios Zes; Anna Zes **Marital Status:** Married **Spouse Name:** Theodore P. Chlentzos-Zes (09/08/1963) **Children:** Athan; Evan; Anna-Matina; Evans Zesl; Christine Zes (Daughter-in-law) **Education:** Doctor in Musical Arts, University of Southern California (1969); MusM, Double Major in Volin and Composition, University of Southern California (1951, 1953) **Career:** Music Minister, San Francisco Greek Orthodox Metropolitan (1993-Present); Professor Emeritus, San Jose State University (1991-Present); Professor of Music, San Jose State University (1964-1991) **Career Related:** Choir Director, Greek Orthodox, Long Beach, San Francisco, Oakland, San Jose, CA (1950-Present) **Military Service:** Corporal, U.S. Army (1951-1953) **Creative Works:** Composer, "The Divine Liturgy in Greek and English" (2004); Composer, "Memorial Service for the Orthodox Church" (1996); Composer, "A Liturgy with English Text" (1992); Composer, "The Choral Music for Mixed Voices for the Divine Liturgy" (1991); Composer, "The Choral Music for the Liturgy of St. John Chrysostom" (1977); Composer, "A Unison Liturgy for Greek Orthodox Choirs" (1976); Composer, "Unison Doxology, Cherubic Hymn, propers for major feast days"; Composer, "Concert Liturgy for Chorus and Orchestra"; Processional for Chorus, Organ and Brass Quintet; Five Greek Songs, High Voice, Piano; Composer, "Nonet for Strings"; Composer, "Trio for Violin, Clarinet and Cello"; Composer, "French Overture for Orchestra"; Composer, Greek Folk and Urban Songs, Chorus, Piano, Chorus, Chamber Orchestra **Awards:** Axion Award, Hellenic American Professional Society of California (1989); Archon, Patriarch Demetrios of the Greek Orthodox Church, San Jose, CA (1977) **Memberships:** National Forum, Greek Orthodox Church Musicians; American Choral Directors Association **Marquis Who's Who Honors:** Albert Nelson Marquis Lifetime Achievement Award **Why did you become involved in your profession or industry:** Mr. Zes always had a love for music that stemmed from his family. Mr. Zes' mother insisted that he take music lessons, and consequently volunteered him as an organ player for their church. Mr. Zes also played the violin and eventually got involved in an orchestra in Hollywood, California. **Avocations:** History; Politics; Chamber music **Political Affiliations:** Democrat **Religion:** Greek Orthodox

Henry Steinway Ziegler, Esq.

Title: Partner **Industry:** Law and Legal Services **Company Name:** Withers Beigman LLP **Date of Birth:** 06/21/1933 **Place of Birth:** Utica **State/Country of Origin:** NY/USA **Parents:** Frederick J. Ziegler; Alice (Cantwell) Ziegler **Marital Status:** Married **Spouse Name:** Jourdan Arpelle-Ziegler (4/06/1991); Patricia Blackmore (Divorced) **Children:** Frederick S.; Alicia P.; Timothy O. **Education:** LLB, Columbia University (1958); AB, Harvard University (1955) **Career:** Of Counsel, Withers Beigman LLP (2006-2007); President, Consultant, Governance and Transfer of Family Wealth, HSZ Consultant LLC (2003-2006); Senior Vice President, Fiduciary Trust Company International, New York, NY (1999-2003); Trust Estate Planning Director, Deutsche Bank Trust Company (1998-1999); Chairman, Chief Executive Officer, Deutsche Bank Trust Company (1995-1997); Partner, Shearman and Sterling, New York, NY (1967-1992); Associate, Shearman and Sterling, New York, NY (1958-1967) **Civic:** Board of Directors, The Chamber Music Society of Lincoln Center (2004-Present); Board of Regents, The American College of Trust Estate Counsel (1988-1994); Trustee, Lincoln Center for the Performing Arts, New York, NY (1985-1989); President, The Chamber Music Society of Lincoln Center (1983-1989); Honorary Trustee, St. Luke's-Roosevelt Hospital Center; Trustee, Outward Bound **Military Service:** With, United States Army (1958-1962) **Creative Works:** Contributor, Articles, Bar Associations **Awards:** Decorated, Army Commendation Award **Memberships:** Former Vice Chairman, International Committee on Property Probate and Trust Law, ABA; Vice President, Member of Executive Council, Academy of International Trust and Estate Law; New York State Bar Association; Association of the Bar of the City of New York; The Century Association; Order of St. John of Jerusalem; Racquet and Tennis Club; Knickerbocker Club; Somerset Club **Bar Admissions:** United States Tax Court (1972); United States Court of Appeals for the Second Circuit (1963); United States District Court for the Eastern District of New York (1962); United States District Court for Southern District of New York (1962); New York (1961) **Marquis Who's Who Honors:** Albert Nelson Marquis Lifetime Achievement Award **Why did you become involved in your profession or industry:** Mr. Ziegler knew as a child that he wanted to be an attorney. After being a chairman and chief executive officer, he needed a change of career. **Avocations:** Classical piano; Music composition; Writing **Political Affiliations:** Independent

Thomas Callander Price Zimmermann, PhD

Title: Historian, Educator (Retired) **Industry:** Education/Educational Services **Company Name:** Davidson College **Date of Birth:** 08/22/1934 **Place of Birth:** Bryn Mawr **State/Country of Origin:** PA/USA **Parents:** R.Z. Zimmermann; Susan (Goodman) Zimmermann **Marital Status:** Married **Spouse Name:** Margaret Upham Ferris **Education:** Fellowship, American Council of Learned Societies, New York, NY (1975-1976); Villa "I Tatti" Fellowship, Harvard University (1970-1971); PhD, Harvard University (1964); MA, University of Oxford (1964); Fulbright Fellowship, Italy (1962-1964); Danforth Fellowship (1956-1962); AM, Harvard University (1960); BA, University of Oxford (1958); BA, Williams College (1956) **Career:** Charles A. Dana Professor Emeritus, History, Davidson College, Davidson, NC (1999-2000); Charles A. Dana Professor, History, Davidson College, Davidson, NC (1986-1999); Vice President, Academic Affairs, Davidson College, Davidson, NC (1977-1986); Professor, History, Reed College, Portland, OR (1973-1977); Chairman, Department of History, Reed College, Portland, OR (1973-1975); Associate Professor, Reed College, Portland, OR (1967-1973); Assistant Professor, Reed College, Portland, OR (1964-1967) **Career Related:** Member, Oregon Committee, National Endowment for the Humanities (1971-1977); Member, Region 14 Selection Committee, Woodrow Wilson National Fellowship Foundation, Princeton, NJ (1967-1970) **Civic:** Advisory Council, Botanical Gardens, University of North Carolina, Charlotte, NC (2007-2008); Rome Prize Jury, Post-classical Humanistic Studies, American Academy, Rome, Italy (1993); Board of Advisors, Lowell Observatory (1988-1993); Board of Directors, Opera Carolina, Charlotte, NC (1980-1982); President, The American Alpine Club, New York, NY (1979-1982); Board of Directors, North Carolina Outward Bound School, Morganton, NC (1978-1981); Board of Directors, The American Alpine Club, New York, NY (1975-1983); Member, Region 14 Selection Committee, Woodrow Wilson National Fellowship Foundation, Princeton, NJ (1967-1970) **Creative Works:** Author, "Paolo Giovio: The Historian and the Crisis of Sixteenth-Century Italy," Italian Translation (2012); Author, "Paolo Giovio: Uno storico e la crisi italiana del XVI secolo" (1995); Co-editor, "Collected Works of Paolo Giovio" (1985); Author, "April in Alaska," Mazama Annual (1972); Contributor, Articles, Professional Journals **Awards:** Helen & Stewart F. Blake Philanthropy Award, Opera Carolina (2015); Presidential Book Award, American Association for Italian Studies (1997); Helen and Howard R. Marraro Prize, American Historical Association (1996); Fellowship, American Council of Learned Societies (1975-1976); Villa "I Tatti" Fellowship, Harvard Center for Italian Renaissance Studies (1970-1971) **Memberships:** Board of Advisers, Opera Carolina Endowment Campaign (2008-2012); Renaissance Society of America; Society for Italian Historical Studies; American Association for Italian Studies; The Phi Beta Kappa Society **Marquis Who's Who Honors:** Albert Nelson Marquis Lifetime Achievement Award; Marquis Who's Who Top Professional; Marquis Who's Who Humanitarian Award **Why did you become involved in your profession or industry:** Dr. Zimmermann always wanted to be a professor. He was originally interested in teaching chemistry, but shifted his focus to history after being inspired by his history professor. Dr. Zimmermann was attracted to the field because of his love for medieval and Renaissance history. He thought it would make a good career because he could learn more through research and share his love of history with students. **Avocations:** Mountaineering; Listening to Music; Gardening; Visiting old friends

Everett Igor Zlatoff-Mirsky

Title: Violinist **Industry:** Media & Entertainment **Company Name:** Chicago Performing Arts Academy **Date of Birth:** 12/29/1937 **Place of Birth:** Evanston **State/Country of Origin:** IL/USA **Year of Passing:** 2020 **Parents:** Alexander Igor Zlatoff-Mirsky; Evelyn Ola (Hill) Zlatoff-Mirsky **Marital Status:** Widowed **Spouse Name:** Janet (Dalbey) Zlatoff-Mirsky (1976) **Children:** Tania; Laura **Education:** MusM, Roosevelt University (1961); MusB, Roosevelt University (1960) **Career:** Faculty, Music Department, Roosevelt University, Chicago, IL (1961-1966); Freelance Musician, Chicago, IL; Soloist; Founder, Chicago Performing Arts Incorporated (Chicago Performing Arts Academy) **Career Related:** Violinist, Lyrics Opera Orchestra, Lyric Opera of Chicago (1974-2003); Concert Master, Personnel Manager (1974-2003); Founding Member, Violinist, Violist Music of the Baroque (1971-2003); Solo Violinist, Bach Society (1966-1983); Violist, Violinist, Lexington String Quartet (1966-1981); With, Recording Studios; Contractor for Musicians, Shows and Commercials **Civic:** Board of Directors, The Santa Fe Symphony Orchestra & Chorus, Santa Fe, NM; Board of Directors, Recording Academy, Chicago Federation of Musicians, Local 10-208, Chicago, IL **Creative Works:** Violinist, Violist, Founding Member, Contemporary Chamber Players, The University of Chicago (1964-1982); Recording Artist, Numerous Records, Radio, Television and Films; Solo Violinist, United States **Awards:** Inductee, Franklin Honor Society (1961); Olive Ditson Award; Inductee, 2000 Outstanding Musicians of the 20th Century, International Biographical Centre, Cambridge, England, United Kingdom; Dal Segno Honoree Award **Memberships:** Recording Academy, Chicago Federation of Musicians, Local 10-208; The Arts Club of Chicago **Marquis Who's Who Honors:** Albert Nelson Marquis Lifetime Achievement Award; Marquis Who's Who Top Professional **Why did you become involved in your profession or industry:** Mr. Zlatoff-Mirsky's father, Alexander, was an opera singer, as well as a portrait painter and sculptor. It was his father that said maybe he could become an opera singer, since he showed that he had musical ability at an early age. At about age three, Mr. Zlatoff-Mirsky enjoyed singing and would repeat commercial tunes that he heard on the radio after only hearing them one time; he had a beautiful boy soprano voice. Mr. Zlatoff-Mirsky's father encouraged him to sing and play music, and at age 7 he began singing in the St. Peter's Episcopalian choir as their boy soprano soloist. In order that he would be a well-rounded musician, he also studied the piano and violin. When Mr. Zlatoff-Mirsky's voice changed, it was obvious after a few months that he would never be a professional singer. So his father gave him a choice, either become a violinist or a pianist; a professional singer was not in the cards. Since the violin was closer to singing than playing the piano (at least in Mr. Zlatoff-Mirsky's adolescent mind), he chose to become a violinist. It was Mr. Zlatoff-Mirsky's father that in essence guided his decision to become a violinist. **Avocations:** Photography; Traveling **Political Affiliations:** Republican **Religion:** Roman Catholic

Irena Zubcevic, OISC/DESA

Title: Chief of Branch DESA **Industry:** Government Administration/Government Relations/Government Services **Company Name:** United Nations **Place of Birth:** Zagreb **State/Country of Origin:** Croatia **Education:** MS in Humanities and Social Sciences, University of Zagreb; BS in Humanities and Linguistics, University of Zagreb **Certifications:** Certificate in Project Management, United Nations (2010); Certificate in Public Administration, Harvard University (2000); Certificate in Diplomacy, Diplomatic Academy of Vienna, Austria (2000); Certificate in Public Diplomacy, Centre for Diplomatic Studies, Cambridge, United Kingdom (1998); Certificate in Diplomacy and Counselor Examination, Croatian Foreign Ministry Diplomatic Academy (1997) **Career:** Chief of Intergovernmental Policy and Review Branch, Office of Intergovernmental Support and Coordination for Sustainable Development, United Nations Department of Economic and Social Affairs (2018-Present); Chief, Small island Developing States, Oceans and Climate Branch, Division for Sustainable Development, United Nations Department of Economic and Social Affairs (2016-2018); Senior Sustainable Development Officer, United Nations (2008-2016); Minister, Plenipotentiary, Ministry of Foreign Affairs of the Republic of Croatia (1992-2008); Head, English News Service, Croatian News Agency-HINA (1991-1992); Adviser, Ministry of Information of the Republic of Croatia (1990-1991) **Creative Works:** Author, "Gateway Portals to the City: Reshaping Cities and the Urban Rural Continuum Through Gateway Portals," Consortium for Sustainable Urbanization (2017); Author, Global Mobility for All Report 2017, World Bank (2017); Author, "The Potential of Blue Economy", World Bank (2017); Author, "Inclusive Institutions for Sustainable Development", Global Sustainable Development Report, United Nations (2016); Author, "Countries in Special Situations", Global Sustainable Development Report, United Nations, (2015); Author, "Economic Diplomacy" Yearbook of the Croatian Diplomatic Academy (2002); Contributor, Professional Journals **Awards:** Top Chief of the Year in Sustainable Development by International Association of Top Professionals (2019); Certificate of Appreciation for Dedicated Service to the United Nations Conference on Sustainable Development (2012) **Memberships:** International Professional Women's Society; International Society of Sustainability Professionals; International Association of Top Professionals; International Leadership Association; Soroptimist International of New York City **Marquis Who's Who Honors:** Albert Nelson Marquis Lifetime Achievement Award **To what do you attribute your success:** Ms. Zubcevic attributes her success to her love for what she does, and her ability to make a difference and empower people around her so they can also make a difference and empower other people to do the same. **Why did you become involved in your profession or industry:** Ms. Zubcevic became involved in her profession because she believes in sustainable development and the goals of sustainable development, which, if achieved, will change the world in terms of the planet's health, prosperity and the well being of mankind. **Thoughts on Life:** Ms. Zubcevic thinks that the United Nations is an amazing place to work. First of all, there are people from all different parts of the world with all different backgrounds and it is just such an enriching experience to work with these people. That has helped her a lot. The United Nations is an organization that tries to make this world a better place. She has always been interested in other parts of the world and where the world is going, but her working for the United Nations has really deepened that and has helped her grow and understand different issues. She is looking forward to continuing making a difference in this and other settings.

Mark Elliot Zuckerberg

Title: Co-Founder, Chairman, Chief Executive Officer, Controlling Shareholder **Industry:** Other **Company Name:** Facebook **Date of Birth:** 05/14/1984 **Place of Birth:** White Plains **State/Country of Origin:** NY/USA **Parents:** Edward Zuckerberg; Karen (Kempner) Zuckerberg **Marital Status:** Married **Spouse Name:** Priscilla Chan (05/19/2012) **Children:** Maxima Chan Zuckerberg; August Zuckerberg **Education:** Honorary Degree, Harvard University (2017); Coursework in Psychology and Computer Science, Harvard University (2002-2004) **Career:** Chairman, Chief Executive Officer, Co-Founder, Controlling Shareholder, Facebook, Menlo Park, CA (2012-Present); Chief Executive Officer, Facebook, Palo Alto, CA (2004-2012); Co-Founder, Facebook, Palo Alto, CA (2004) **Career Related:** Member, Board of Directors, Facebook (2004-Present); Founder, Internet.org by Facebook (2013); Co-Founder, Board Member, Breakthrough Starshot, Breakthrough Initiatives **Civic:** Host, A Year of Books (2015); Co-Owner, Donor, The Chan Zuckerberg Initiative (2015); Donor, 18 Million Facebook Shares, Silicon Valley Community Foundation (2013); Initiative Co-Signer, Advocate, The Giving Pledge (2010); Donor, $100 Million, Newark Public Schools, Newark, NJ; Founder, Education Start-up; Donor, Diaspora **Creative Works:** Appearance, Documentary, "Terms and Conditions May Apply" (2013); Guest Appearance, "Saturday Night Live" (2011); Voice Actor, "The Simpsons" (2010) **Awards:** The Forbes 400: The Richest People in American, Forbes (2009-Present); TIME 100: The Most Influential People in the World, TIME Magazine (2008, 2011, 2016); Tenth Place, "The World's Most Powerful People," Forbes (2016); Top 10 Business Visionaries Creating Value for the World, Business Insider (2016); Axel Springer Award (2016); The World's Most Powerful People, Forbes (2010-2014); 40 Under 40, Fortune (2009-2014); Chief Executive Officer of the Year, Sixth Annual Crunchies Awards (2013); Named, The Philanthropy 50, The Chronicle of Philanthropy (2013); 50 Most Influential Jews, The Jerusalem Post (2011-2013); 50 Most Influential, Bloomberg (2012); Ten Smartest People in Tech, Forbes (2010); "Barbara Walters Presents: The 10 Most Fascinating People of 2010" (2010); Person of the Year, TIME Magazine (2010); Media Person of the Year Award, 57th International Advertising Festival, Palais des Festivals et des Congrès (2010); 100 Agents of Change, Rolling Stone, LLC (2009); Best Start-Up Chief Executive Officer, Crunchbase, Inc. (2007); Most Influential Person in Tech Industry, Agenda Setters (2007); Media Achiever of the Year, Campaign Media Awards (2007); The Web Celeb 25, Forbes (2007); The 50 Who Matter Now, Business 2.0 (2006) **Memberships:** Advisory Board, Tsinghua University School of Economics and Management (2014-Present)

Gordon Nathaniel Zuckerman

Title: President **Industry:** Insurance **Company Name:** Murray & Zuckerman, Inc. **Date of Birth:** 03/18/1942 **Place of Birth:** Schenectady **State/Country of Origin:** NY/USA **Marital Status:** Married **Spouse Name:** Linda Zuckerman **Children:** Miriam Zuckerman-Smith; CJ Wiley **Education:** BS, Union College, Schenectady, NY (1970); AAS in Chemistry, Hudson Valley Community College, Troy, NY (1962) **Career:** President, Murray & Zuckerman, Inc., Schenectady, NY (1991) **Career Related:** Board of Directors, New York State Association of Health Underwriters **Civic:** Member, Shared Decision-Making Committee, Niskayuna High School, Schenectady, NY (1997-Present); Fire Commissioner, Secretary, Niskayuna Fire District #2 (1984-Present); Brown School, Schenectady, NY (1991-1997); Mentor, Chairperson, Shared Decision-Making Committee, Pleasant Valley School District, Pennsylvania (1989, 1992-1993); Board of Directors, Holocaust Survivors & Friends in Pursuit of Justice, Inc. (1978-1985, 1994-1997) **Military Service:** U.S. Army, Vietnam (1968-1969) **Creative Works:** Contributor, Articles, Trade Journals **Awards:** Mary G. Breslin Volunteer Service Award, De La Salle Christian Brothers, LaSalle School, Albany, NY (2016); Outstanding Philanthropist Award, Hudson Valley Community College Foundation (2015); Spencer L. McCarty Award, New York Chapter, NAIFA (2009); Ben Brewster Government Relations Award, New York Chapter, NAIFA (2007); Hudson Valley Community College Humanitarian Award (2006); Sidney Albert Community Service Award, Jewish Federation of Northeastern New York (1999); Berger Award for Community Services, Maimonides Hebrew Day School, Lake Grove, NY (1997); Community Volunteer Award, Maimonides Hebrew Day School, Lake Grove, NY (1997); Volunteer of the Year, Jewish Family Services (1997); B'nai B'rith Youth Service Award (1996); First Recipient, Dr. Robert S. Hoffman Distinguished Service Award, Arthritis Foundation (1990) **Memberships:** President, Autism Society of the Greater Capital Region (2013-2016); Board Member, National Association of Independent Life Brokerage Agencies (2010-2013); Schenectady Local Development Corporation Board (2001-2011); Chairman, Northeastern New York Chapter, Arthritis Foundation (1987-1989, 1993-1994, 2007-2009); President, New York State Association of Health Underwriters (2004-2005); Board Member, Jewish Federation of Northeastern New York (1987-2003); Chair, Shared Decision Making Committee, Pleasant Valley School (1994-1998); Board Member, Congregation Gates of Heaven (1978-1985, 1994-1997); Chairman, Board of Governors, Endowment Fund, Jewish Federation of Northeastern New York (1989-1995); Hemochromatosis Foundation Board (1988-1995); Nominating Committee, Albany League of Arts (1987); New York State Association of Health Underwriters (1977-1987); Leadership Positions, Schenectady Jewish Community Center (1981-1986); President, Albany Association of Life Underwriters (1977-1978, 1981-1982) **Marquis Who's Who Honors:** Albert Nelson Marquis Lifetime Achievement Award **Why did you become involved in your profession or industry:** Mr. Zuckerman became involved in his profession because when he returned from Vietnam in 1969, he was a research chemist working for Albany International. They wanted him and his wife to move to and work in Buffalo, New York, but they didn't want to, so he talked to a lot of agents about his GI insurance and converting it. Someone offered him an opportunity to work for New York Life Insurance Company, and he thought it would be a good career change with a good living. About 10 years later, he and his partner formed their brokerage firm of Murray & Zuckerman, Inc. as wholesalers, which means they do not sell to the public; they deal only with agents and brokers because he didn't want to sell anybody anything.

Alfred Zweidler

Title: Doctor of Natural Philosophy, Biomedical Scientist, Educator (Retired) **Industry:** Medicine & Health Care **Company Name:** Fox Chase Cancer Center **Date of Birth:** 02/01/1937 **Place of Birth:** Dübendorf **State/Country of Origin:** Switzerland **Parents:** Hermann Zweidler; Mina (Nyffeler) Zweidler **Marital Status:** Married **Spouse Name:** Irène Erika Baertschi (04/06/1963) **Children:** Regula Sullivan-Zweidler; Patrick Zweidler-McKay; Stephan Zweidler-White **Education:** Postdoctoral Fellow, Cell Research Institute, The University of Texas at Austin (1966-1969); Welch Foundation Fellowship, University of Texas (1966-1969); Doctor of Philosophy, University of Zürich (1966); Research Fellow, Institute for Cancer Research, Department of Pathology, University of Zürich (1964-1966) **Certifications:** Mathematics Diplomate Type B, Institute Juventus, Zürich, Switzerland (1960); Business Diplomate, Kaufmännischer Verband Zürich, Switzerland (1955) **Career:** Biomedical Scientist, Educator, Fox Chase Cancer Center, Philadelphia, PA (1980-1997); Associate Member, Fox Chase Cancer Center, Philadelphia, PA (1976-1980); Assistant Member, Institute for Cancer Research, Philadelphia, PA (1972-1976); Senior Research Associate, Department of Botany, The University of Texas at Austin (1970-1971); Visiting Scientist, Institute for Cancer Research, Philadelphia, PA (1969-1970); Research Associate, Experimental Cancer Research, University Hospital of Zürich (1964-1966); Teaching Assistant, Department of Botany, University of Zurich (1962-1964); Teacher for Biology and Chemistry, Kantonsschule Schaffhausen (1962-1964); Notary Assistant, Notariat Schwamendingen-Zürich (1956-1959); Apprentice, Notariat Zürich-Altstadt, Business School (1952-1955) **Career Related:** Adjunct Associate Professor, University of Pennsylvania Medical School, Philadelphia, PA (1984-1997) **Civic:** Director, M. Rohrbach Cultural Fund, Philadelphia, PA (1984-1996); President, New Helvetic Society, Philadelphia, PA (1978-1984) **Creative Works:** Co-Author, "Histone Genes and Histone Gene Expression" (1984); Editor, "Histones and Cancer" (1979); Contributor, More than 40 Articles, Professional Journals, Scientific Conventions **Awards:** Grantee, National Cancer Institute (1972-1991); Outstanding Student Research Award, University of Zürich (1964) **Memberships:** Fox Chase Cancer Center; American Association for the Advancement Science; American Society for Development and Cell Biology; The Protein Society; Swiss Genetic Society; Sigma Xi **Marquis Who's Who Honors:** Albert Nelson Marquis Lifetime Achievement Award; Marquis Who's Who Top Professional **To what do you attribute your success:** Dr. Zweifler attributes his success to his father, who raised three children during World War II in Switzerland. The man taught his children to confront and overcome adversity. Dr. Zweifler also credits his wife, Irène, who was a good sport during the meager years of his life as a postdoctoral fellow in a foreign country while raising three children. **Why did you become involved in your profession or industry:** Dr. Zweifler became involved in his profession because he worked in a government office dealing with the law. After finishing his apprenticeship, he received a diploma in business administration. Dr. Zweifler was then instructed to attend law school, but he did not have a proper education. While in night school, his teachers advised him that the best fit for him would be a career in natural sciences. He finally decided on studying biology. **Avocations:** Gardening; Collecting tropical fruit plants and flowers; Swimming; Monitoring the health of Clear Lake for Florida Lakewatch at the University of Florida; Traveling the world to study the origin of Western Civilization

ACCLAIMED LISTEES

73rd Edition

Amanda Ackerman

Title: Chief Financial Officer **Industry:** Consumer Goods and Services **Company Name:** RPM Storage Management Services **Date of Birth:** 11/10/1978 **Place of Birth:** Houston **State/Country of Origin:** TX/USA **Marital Status:** Married **Children:** Brittany; Wyatt; Lacey **Education:** AS, St. Philips College, San Antonio, Texas (1999) **Certifications:** Licensed Vocational Nurse **Career:** Co-owner/Chief Financial Officer, RPM Storage Management Services (2014-Present); License Vocational Nurse (6 Years); With, Criminal and Collections, Comal County District Court Office; With, Child Support Division, Hays County District Court Office; Project Management Assistant, Construction Company **Memberships:** The Republican Women Association (National Federation of Republican Women (NFRW)); Comal County Republican Party **Marquis Who's Who Honors:** Marquis Who's Who Top Professional **To what do you attribute your success:** Mrs. Ackerman attributes her success to her strong sense of family. She has a wonderful husband who supports her. **Why did you become involved in your profession or industry:** Mrs. Ackerman's father opened up the RPM Storage Management Services. She was a stay at home mom. They started with only five properties, now they have 23 that they manage. She does all of the HR and payroll for all of her employees. She has two bookkeepers that she manages. **Thoughts on Life:** Mrs. Ackerman's motto is, "God, family, community; do unto others as others would do unto you. Be a good human being."

Frederick Adams

Title: Shareholder **Industry:** Law and Legal Services **Company Name:** KoonsFuller Family Law **Date of Birth:** 10/06/1955 **Place of Birth:** Dallas **State/Country of Origin:** TX/USA **Marital Status:** Married **Children:** Two Daughters **Education:** JD, Baylor Law School, Waco, TX (1981); BBA, University of Texas, Austin, Austin, TX (1978) **Certifications:** Certified Mediator; Family Law Arbitrator; Board Certified, Family Law, Texas Board of Legal Specialization **Career:** Shareholder, KoonsFuller Family Law (2014-Present); Shareholder, Quilling, Selander, Lownds, Winslett & Moser, Dallas, TX (2011-2014); Owner, Law Offices of Frederick S. Adams, Jr. (1989-2011); Attorney, Adams & Sherwood (1987-1988); Associate Attorney, Graham, Bright & Smith (1981-1986) **Creative Works:** Author, "Three Key Considerations for Texas Gun Owners in Divorce." TexasDivorceBlog.com (2019); Author, Contributor, Numerous Articles/Presentations (1997-2018); Speaker, "Federal Firearms Law Related to Family Law," Dallas Bar Association Family Law Section Meeting, Dallas, TX (2011); Speaker, "Family Law Essentials," State Bar of Texas Family Law Section Pro Bono Committee Meetings, Waco, TX (2011); Speaker, "Family Law Essentials," State Bar of Texas Family Law Section Pro Bono Committee Meetings, Plainview, TX (2010); Speaker, "Civil and Criminal Ramifications of a Family Violence Protective Order," State Bar of Texas Advanced Family Seminar, San Antonio, TX (2010) **Awards:** Listee, The Best Lawyers in America© in Family Law, Best Lawyers, LLC (2016-2020); Listee, Top 100 DFW (2019); Honoree, Texas Super Lawyers (2003-2019); Recognized, Elite Lawyer by Elite Lawyer (2018) **Memberships:** College of the State Bar of Texas (1996-Present); Family Law Section, American Bar Association (1981-Present) **Bar Admissions:** Federal District Court for the Western District of Texas (1987); The Federal District Court of the Northern District of Texas (1982); Federal District Court of the Northern District of Texas (1982); The U.S. Court of Appeals for the 5th Circuit (1982); U.S. Court of Appeals for the 11th Circuit (1982); Texas State Bar (1981) **To what do you attribute your success:** Mr. Adams attributes his success to preparation. At Baylor University, a trial court teacher stressed that the single biggest determining factor deciding who comes up on top in a trial is preparation. He never forgot this statement. **Why did you become involved in your profession or industry:** Mr. Adams became involved in his profession because he had worked in every field except criminal law. Corporations suing each other was not very inspiring work to him; he wanted to help save children and resolve family situations.

Jerome Michael Adams, MD, MPH

Title: U.S. Surgeon General; Vice Admiral **Industry:** Medicine & Health Care **Company Name:** U.S. Department of Health & Human Services **Date of Birth:** 9/22/1974 **Place of Birth:** Orange **State/Country of Origin:** NJ/USA **Parents:** Richard Adams; Edrena Adams **Marital Status:** Married **Spouse Name:** Lacey Adams **Children:** Caden; Eli; Millie **Education:** Residency in Anesthesiology, Indiana University (2003-2006); Intern in Internal Medicine, St. Vincent Indianapolis Hospital (2002-2003); MD, Indiana University School of Medicine; MPH, University of California Berkeley (2000); BS in Biochemistry, University of Maryland; BA in Psychology, University of Maryland **Certifications:** Board Certified in Anesthesiology **Career:** U.S. Surgeon General , U.S. Department of Health & Human Services (2017-Present); Indiana State Health Commissioner (2014-2017); Vice Admiral, U.S. Public Health Service Commissioned Corps; Secretary, Executive Board, Indiana State Department of Health; Assistant Professor of Anesthesiology, Indiana University; Private Practice, Ball Memorial Hospital, Indiana University Health **Civic:** Member, COVID-19 Pandemic Task Force, The White House (2020-Present) **Creative Works:** Contributor, "Anesthesia Student Survival Guide: A Case-based Approach"; Contributor, "Are Pain Management Questions in Patient Satisfaction Surveys Driving the Opiod Epidemic?," American Journal of Public Health; Author, Several Academic Papers and Book Chapters **Awards:** Public Health Service Outstanding Service Medal; Public Health Service Unit Citation; Public Health Service Unit Commendation; Public Health Service Crisis Response Service Award; Humanitarian Service Medal; Public Health Service Regular Corps Ribbon; Commissioned Corps Training Ribbon; Eli Lilly and Company Scholarship; Meyerhoff Scholarship

James Alston

Title: Chief Executive Officer **Industry:** Business Management/Business Services **Company Name:** McCall's Bronxwood Funeral Home **Place of Birth:** Harlem **State/Country of Origin:** NY/USA **Children:** Four Sons **Education:** JD, Howard University School of Law (1965); BS in Economics, New York University, New York, NY (1962) **Certifications:** Building Operator Certification **Career:** Owner, Chief Executive Officer, McCall's Bronxwood Funeral Home, Bronx, NY (2005-Present); Practicing Attorney (1965-2005); McCall's Bronxwood Funeral Home, Bronx, NY (1966-2005) **Career Related:** Former Assistant District Attorney, Bronx, NY; Former Law Secretary, New York Civil Court; Former Trustee, Audrey Cohen College; Former President, Dewitt Clinton High School Alumni Association **Civic:** Chair, Barbara M. Simpson Memorial Fund; Donor, 25 $1,000 Scholarships a Year **Awards:** Businessman of the Year Award, Macedonia Baptist Church; International Excellence Award in Scholarship Support, NANBPWC; The International Lawyers Award, Manila College of Law; "Take It To The Hill" Award, The Harriet Tubman Humanitarian Achievement Awards Jubilee, Inc.; Distinguished Service Award, Bronx-Manhattan North Association of Realtors, Inc.; Joseph L. Galiber Award, New York State Association of Black and Puerto Rican Legislators; A Fe WE Cultural Award for Leadership; "Community Service Award," 47th Precinct Community Council; Community Honoree, New York Chapter, Mico Old Students Association, Inc.; Honoree, Lehman College's Urban Male Leadership Program **Memberships:** Gold Life Member, NAACP; Northeast Bronx Child Care Centers; Williamsbridge NAACP Child Care Center; Thru Way Home Owners Association; New York State Bar; Federal Bars; Fellow, American Bar Association Foundation **Marquis Who's Who Honors:** Marquis Who's Who Top Professional **To what do you attribute your success:** Mr. Alston attributes his success to his work ethic — continuous, unrelenting daily hard work. He also went through many challenges before coming into his present role. Being exposed to both the public and private sector has also been very instructive in his ability to perform. **Why did you become involved in your profession or industry:** Mr. Alston became involved in his profession when he took over his family business.

Robert "Bob" Alvine

Title: Industrialist, Entrepreneur, Board Leader, Strategist, Financier **Company Name:** i-TEN Management Corp. **Date of Birth:** 08/25/1938 **Place of Birth:** Newark **State/Country of Origin:** NJ/USA **Parents:** James C. Alvine; Marie Alvine **Marital Status:** Married **Spouse Name:** Joann Thompson (1995) **Children:** Robert; Laurie; Heather **Education:** DHL, University of New Haven, Summa Cum Laude (2000); Executive Master's, Harvard Business School (1972); Diploma, School Sales Management & Marketing Executives International, Syracuse University Graduate School, with Honors (1968); Diploma, Field Sales Management Institute Sales and Marketing Executives International, Syracuse University Graduate School, with Honors (1966); Diploma in Cryptography and Codes, United States Military Signal School, Fort Gordon, Georgia, with High Honors (1962); BS in Chemistry, Chemical Engineering, Minor Physics and Biology, Rutgers University, State University of New Jersey (1960) **Certifications:** Code Breaker, Cryptography, United States Signal Corporation (1962) **Career:** Founder, Chairman, Chief Executive Officer, Aim Capital Group (1987-Present); Founder, Principal Owner, Chairman, Chief Executive Officer, President, i-TEN Management Corp, i-TEN Capital (1987-Present); Principal Owner, Chairman, Premier KIA LLC (2011-2019); Principal Owner, Chairman, Premier Automotive Group LLC (2011-2019); Principal Owner, Chairman, Premier International Motors Cars LLC (2008-2019); Principal Owner, Chairman, Premier Realty LLC (2000-2019); Principal Owner, Chairman, Premier Subaru, Branford, CT (1999-2019); Principal Owner, Chairman, Global Automotive Reins, LLC (2005-2017); Senior Operating Partner, Investment Committee, Desai Capital Private Equity Investors (1998-2009); Principal, Director, Chairman, International Automobile Products Holdings Corporation (1990-1997); President, Chief Executive Officer, Uniroyal Inc. (1980-1987) **Career Related:** Chair Emeritus The Jackson Laboratory (2012-Present); Connecticut Life Science Group (2011-Present); Board Chair, Numerous Profit, Non-Profit Civic, Industrial Organization Governor, Harvard Global Health Institute (2010-Present); Founder, Jackson Laboratory National Council (2007-Present) **Military Service:** U.S. Army Reserves (1964-1968) **Awards:** Recipient, Over 50 Awards in Field **Memberships:** Member, Various Professional Organizations **Marquis Who's Who Honors:** Albert Nelson Marquis Lifetime Achievement Award

K. Owusu Amaning

Title: President; Civil Engineer **Industry:** Engineering **Company Name:** GCI Inc. **Date of Birth:** 02/12/1956 **Place of Birth:** Accra **State/Country of Origin:** Ghana **Parents:** Samuel Lawrence Amaning; Gladys Oforiwa Addo Amaning **Marital Status:** Married **Spouse Name:** Adwoa Adu Ampaw (08/24/1985) **Children:** Akua Asantewa Amaning; Nana Yaa O. Amaning **Education:** Diploma of Advanced Studies, University Pierre et Marie Curie/Ecole Centrale, Paris, France (1981); Diploma in French Language, Institut Catholique de Paris, France (1980); Bachelor of Science in Civil Engineering, Kwame Nkrumah University of Science and Technology, with Honors, Ghana (1978) **Career:** President, GCI Inc., Longwood, FL (1993-Present); Project Engineer, Jammal & Associates, Winter Park, FL (1988-1993); Civil Engineer, Manager of Material Inspection, Robert W. Hunt Company, Chicago, IL (1986-1988); Lecturer, L'Ecole National d'Ingenieurs, Oran, Algeria (1983-1986); Soils Engineer, Laboratory des Travaux Publics de l'Quest, Oran, Algeria (1981-1986); Research Assistant, Laboratoire Central des Ponts et Chaussees, Paris, France (1981); Civil Engineer, Structural, Asafo Boakye & Partners, Accra-North, Ghana (1979); Civil Engineer, Milton & Richards, Architects, Engineers Associates, Monrovia, Liberia (1979); Trainee, Building & Road Research Institute, Kumasi, Ghana (1977-1978); Trainee Supervisor, Babtie, Shaw & Morton, Glasgow, Scotland (1977) **Civic:** Governing Elder, Chairman, Northland Church (2002-2008, 2010-2016); Chairman, Human Relations Board, City of Orlando, FL (1998-2002) **Awards:** Engineering Excellence Award, American Council of Engineering Companies (2017); Engineering Excellence Grand Award, Florida Institute of Consulting Engineers (2000, 2017) **Memberships:** Associate Member, Ghana Institute of Engineers; Société des Ingénieurs et Scientifiques de France (ISF); American Society of Civil Engineers **Marquis Who's Who Honors:** Albert Nelson Marquis Lifetime Achievement Award **Why did you become involved in your profession or industry:** Mr. Amaning became involved in his profession because he enjoyed mathematics and science studies in school. **Religion:** Christian

Robert A. Andersen

Title: Federal Official (Retired) **Date of Birth:** 08/27/1936 **Place of Birth:** Denver **State/Country of Origin:** CO/USA **Parents:** Emmett Christian Andersen; Margaret Irene (Maupin) Andersen **Marital Status:** Widowed **Spouse Name:** Jane Eng (05/13/1967, Deceased 1994) **Children:** Nimi R.B. Manpin-Andersen; Saquan Bull Andersen **Education:** PhD in International Relations, American University School of International Service (1973); MA in Political Science, University of South Carolina (1961); Postgraduate Coursework in Law, University of Colorado (1958-1959); AB in Political Science, University of South Carolina (1958) **Certifications:** Certified, United States Federal Government (1962-1996) **Career:** Retired (1997); Director, Quality Assurance Review, Office of Inspector General, U.S. Department of Justice, Washington, DC (1990-1997); Director, Management, Planning and Review, Office of Inspector General, U.S. Department of Justice (1988-1990); Director, Office of Program Inspection, Immigration and Naturalization Service, Washington, DC (1986-1988); Director, Evaluation, Immigration and Naturalization Service (1974-1986); Senior Planning Officer, USPS (1972-1974); Staff Assistant to Deputy Postmaster General, USPS (1967-1972); Implementation Programming, Planning and Budgeting System, Office of Program Planning and Evaluation, Office of Education (1966-1967); Acting Director, Urban Projects Division, Program Officer, Chief Project Administration, Volunteers in Service to America, Office of Economic Opportunity, Washington, DC (1964-1966); Area Coordinator, Economic Development, Area Redevelopment Administration, U.S. Department of Commerce (1962-1964) **Career Related:** Night School Teacher, Reading and Writing Comprehension, Grammar, The Lab School of Washington (1997-2017); Private Tutor, High School and College Students (1997-2017) **Civic:** Chairman, Diocese and Personnel Committee (27 Years); Past President, Board of Directors, The Arc; Past Secretary, The Arc; Senior Warden, Youth Leader, Episcopal Church **Awards:** Blue Key Award; Outstanding Senior Award; Omicron Delta Kappa Award **Memberships:** The Arc (46 Years) **Marquis Who's Who Honors:** Albert Nelson Marquis Lifetime Achievement Award; Marquis Who's Who Top Professional

Gregg G. Antonsen

Title: Senior Vice President, Manager **Industry:** Real Estate **Company Name:** Sotheby's International Realty **Education:** JD, William Mitchell College of Law, St. Paul, MN (1979); BS in History and Political Science, Gustavus Adolphus College, St. Peter, MN (1975) **Career:** Senior Vice President, Manager, Qualifying Broker, Sotheby's International Realty, Santa Fe (2011-Present); Senior Vice President, Business Development, Christie's Great Estates (2003-2011); Founder, Antonsen Garrett & Associates, Ltd.; Owner, Real Estate Company (1979-1993); Attorney, Private Practice (1979-1993) **Career Related:** Lecturer, Adjunct Professor, University of Hawaii, Manoa Campus **Civic:** Board of Directors, Performance Santa Fe; Advisory Board, Enterprise Bank and Trust of Santa Fe **Bar Admissions:** Hawaii **To what do you attribute your success:** Goal setting, he was raised to set goals and to achieve goals. Through law, he found that he really enjoyed working in real estate. It was a perfect segway for him. While he was in Honolulu, he taught business law in addition to having a law practice and a real estate company. **Why did you become involved in your profession or industry:** Mr. Antonsen moved to Santa Fe in 2003, and what brought him there at the time was the position with Christie's Great Estates. He was brought here to be their senior vice president of business development.

William Eugene Artz

Title: Associate Professor Emeritus **Industry:** Education/Educational Services **Company Name:** University of Illinois at Urbana-Champaign **Date of Birth:** 06/30/1950 **State/Country of Origin:** IA/USA **Parents:** Buddie Eugene Artz; Margaret Mary Artz **Marital Status:** Married **Spouse Name:** Elisangela Gomes Artz (2006) **Children:** Mary; Michael; AnaCelina **Education:** PhD in Food Science, Washington State University (1984); MS in Food Science, Washington State University (1978); BS in Agriculture and Natural Sciences, University of Wisconsin-Madison (1972, 1973) **Career:** Associate Professor Emeritus, University of Illinois at Urbana-Champaign (2012-Present); Assistant Professor, Associate Professor, University of Illinois at Urbana-Champaign (1984-1992, 1992-2012) **Career Related:** Consultant in Field (1984-Present) **Creative Works:** Contributor, Numerous Articles, Scientific Publications; Contributor, Book Chapters; Speakers, Numerous Invited Lectures **Awards:** President, Vice-President, University of Illinois Chapter, Gamma Sigma Delta (GSD) **Memberships:** Institute of Food Technologists; American Chemical Society; American Oil Chemists Society; GSD **Marquis Who's Who Honors:** Albert Nelson Marquis Lifetime Achievement Award; Marquis Who's Who Top Professional **To what do you attribute your success:** Dr. Artz attributes his success to a wealth of excellent professors with whom he worked during his college studies. In particular, he credits Professor Barry G. Swanson, an emeritus regents professor at Washington State University, who directed both Dr. Artz's Master's and PhD research programs. **Why did you become involved in your profession or industry:** In searching for a college major, Dr. Artz found the perfect fit for his interests in science and math when he discovered food chemistry. **Avocations:** Golfing; Bicycling; Reading; Basketball; Investing; Fermenting and distilling beverages; Exploring computers **Political Affiliations:** Democrat

Stephen H. Atkins, PhD

Title: Owner, Director **Industry:** Medicine & Health Care **Company Name:** Atkins Integrative Wellness Solutions **Marital Status:** Married **Spouse Name:** Christina **Children:** Lily **Education:** PhD in Integrative Medicine, Capitol Technology University, Laurel, MD (2001) **Certifications:** Board Certified in Holistic Health **Career:** Owner, Director of Clinical Services, Atkins Integrative Wellness Solutions (1984-Present); Director of Clinical Services, BioEnergetic Clinic (1991-1995) **Awards:** Best of Health & Medicine in Huntington, NY (2015-2019) **Memberships:** International Oxidative Medicine Association; American College for Advancement in Medicine; AAEM; American Academy of Anti-Aging Medicine; American Association of Nutritional Consultants; Nutritional Therapy Association; American Association of Drugless Practitioners; ACIMD; The Institute for Functional Medicine; National Paramedical for Technicians & Assistants Association **Marquis Who's Who Honors:** Marquis Who's Who Top Professional **To what do you attribute your success:** Dr. Atkins attributes his success to practice, patience, love, and tolerance with all of his patients. He treats them as a family member rather than a statistic. He is truly dedicated to finding the cause of a patients health problem and assisting them in overcoming the issue. **Why did you become involved in your profession or industry:** Dr. Atkins became involved in his profession because of his experiences as a paramedic in Harlem during the early-1980s. At the time, most of the people he tended to were victims of violent crimes. During one particular job, he responded to a gunshot victim and ended up in the line of fire. Upon his safe return, he quit that job and pursued a career in medicine so that he could continue to help people.

Vincent Auricchio, Esq.

Title: Managing Partner **Industry:** Law and Legal Services **Company Name:** Auricchio Law Offices **Place of Birth:** New York **State/Country of Origin:** NY/USA **Marital Status:** Married **Spouse Name:** Tori **Children:** Three children **Education:** JD, College of Law, DePaul University (1997); BS in Human and Organizational Development, Vanderbilt University (1993); Graduate, Hunter College High School **Career:** Managing Partner, Auricchio Law Offices (2006-Present); Senior Associate Attorney, McBreen & Kopko (2000-2006); Langhenry, Gillen, Lundquist & Johnson LLC (1997-2000) **Career Related:** Featured Speaker, National Business Institute; Annual Speaker, American Association of Neurological Surgeons **Civic:** Mentor, Dream on Education (2017-Present); President, Via Como Due Townhomes Homeowners' Association (2009-2014); Master, Cub Scouts, Boy Scouts of America (2009-2013); Big Brother, Mentor, Partners in Education (1999-2006); Former President, Parent Teacher Organization, LaSalle II Magnet School **Creative Works:** Author, "Taking Medicare's Interest Into Consideration: Mandatory Insurer Reporting," National Business Institute (2010) **Awards:** Legal Elite Award for Real Estate Counsel of the Year, U.S. Business News (2019); Top One Percent, National Association of Distinguished Counsel (2015, 2017); Top 40 Under 40 Personal Injury Litigator, National Trial Lawyers (2012); Top Attorney in Illinois in Real Estate Law and Business Litigation (2008-2011); Outstanding Young Attorney **Memberships:** Team Leader, CBMC, Inc. (2000-2016); Christian Legal Society; Alliance Defending Freedom; National Association of Distinguished Counsel; Former Member, American Bar Association; Former Member, Illinois State Bar Association; Former Member, Chicago Bar Association **Bar Admissions:** Illinois State Bar Association; United States District Court Northern District of Illinois **Marquis Who's Who Honors:** Marquis Who's Who Top Professional **To what do you attribute your success:** Mr. Auricchio attributes his success to following the Golden Rule and putting others first. **Why did you become involved in your profession or industry:** Mr. Auricchio became involved in his profession because of a law for human resources class he took during his junior year of college. He was exposed to how the law could help people and it piqued his interest.

Bi Awosika, MD, FACP, FHM

Title: Associate Professor of Medicine **Company Name:** University of Cincinnati Medical Center, UC Health **Place of Birth:** Chicago **State/Country of Origin:** IL/USA **Marital Status:** Married **Children:** Three children **Education:** MD, College of Medicine, The University of Illinois, Chicago, IL (2008); BA in Human Biology, Stanford University (2002) **Certifications:** Board Certified, American Board of Internal Medicine; Licensed Physician, State of Ohio **Career:** Associate Professor of Clinical Medicine; Associate Program Director, Internal Medicine Residency Program, Department of Medicine, University of Cincinnati Medical Center (2018-Present); Academic Hospitalist, Attending Physician, Assistant Professor of Clinical Medicine, Division of General Internal Medicine, Hospital Medicine, College of Medicine, University of Cincinnati Medical Center, Cincinnati, OH (2016-Present) **Career Related:** Faculty Judge, Annual Resident and Student Clinical and Research Poster Presentations, Department of Internal Residency Program, University of Cincinnati (2017-Present); Interviewer, Candidates for Resident Positions, Internal Medicine Residency Program (2017-Present) **Civic:** Member, Outreach Ministry, Montgomery Community Church (2018-Present); Teacher, Children's Ministry, Montgomery Community Church (2017-Present); Attendance Chair, Committee Member, Alumni Class Reunion Committee, Stanford University (2007-Present) **Creative Works:** Commencement Speaker, DePaul Cristo Rey High School (2020); **Awards:** Richard W. Vilter Award, University of Cincinnati (2019); Nominee, Excellence in Mentoring Award, College of Medicine, University of Cincinnati (2019); Young Alumna Award, Trinity High School (2019) **Memberships:** Academy of Medicine of Cincinnati (2019-Present); Association of Program Directors in Internal Medicine (2019-Present); Society of Hospital Medicine (2013-Present); American College of Physicians (2010-Present) **To what do you attribute your success:** Dr. Awosika attributes her success to her faith as well as family, friends, and mentors who have paved the way before her. **Why did you become involved in your profession or industry:** Dr. Awosika became involved in her profession because of her parents, who relocated to America, specifically to the northwest of Chicago, from West Africa in pursuit of a higher education, both seeking their PhDs. Even at a young age, she saw how they wanted to provide service and make an impact, and she was inspired to do the same. **Avocations:** Singing; Running; Volunteering at church

E. Maurlea Babb, LMFT, LPHA, QE

Title: Marriage and Family Therapist **Company Name:** Chrysalis Center for Individual & Family Development **Date of Birth:** 06/22/1927 **Place of Birth:** Newtown **State/Country of Origin:** IN/USA **Parents:** B. Dewey C.; Arlotta Bessie (Fine) Scannel **Marital Status:** Married **Spouse Name:** John L. Marteja (12/04/2015); Russell W. Babb 02/09/1947 (Deceased 2013) **Children:** A. Sue; Joyce A.; Janet I.; Julia Martega (Stepdaughter); Edward Marteja (Stepson) **Education:** EdD, Northern Illinois University (1984); MS in Engineering, Northern Illinois University (1964); Bachelor of Music Education, American Conservatory (1949); Coursework, DePauw University (1945-1947) **Career:** Owner, Director, Marriage and Family Therapist (LMFT, LPHA, QE), Chrysalis Center for Individual & Family Development, Wheaton, IL (1977-Present); Consultant, Agencies for the Handicapped, Chrysalis Center for Individual & Family Development (1977-Present); Executive Director, IAMFT (1993-2016); Consultant, Lecturer, Family Dynamics to Hospitals, Schools and Churches, IAMFT; Counselor, Glenbard West High School (1964-1977); Counselor, Geneva High School (1961-1963); Teacher, Glen Ellyn School District 41 (1958-1961); Supervisor, Teacher, Midlothian School District 143 (1950-1958) **Career Related:** Drug Abuse Community Action Team (1978); Chairman, Milton Township Youth Committee (1970-1978); Coordinator, American Group Psychotherapy Association Conference; Member, Vice President, Nurture & Outreach, United Methodist Church; Local Unit Member, Children's Ministries Committees; Bishops' Initiative on Children and Poverty; Member, Aurora District Council Ministries; Staff-parish Relations Committee, United Methodist Church; Member, Task Force, Northern Illinois Conference, The Ad Council and Finance Community **Civic:** Board Member, IAMFT (Present); Board of Directors, Emeritus Board Member, Chicago Methodist Senior Services; Member, United Methodist Church and United Methodist Women **Creative Works:** Contributor, Numerous Articles, Professional Journals and Family Matters and Church Conferences **Memberships:** Member, Several Organizations **Marquis Who's Who Honors:** Albert Nelson Marquis Lifetime Achievement Award **Why did you become involved in your profession or industry:** Dr. Babb spent a lot of her childhood in foster homes and learned a lot about families. She started as a teacher, and then a high school counselor until she became a therapist. **Avocations:** Singing; Reading **Religion:** United Methodist

Thomas Robert Bailey

Title: President **Industry:** Pharmaceuticals **Company Name:** TR Bailey Consulting LLC **Date of Birth:** 07/08/1956 **Place of Birth:** Lansing **State/Country of Origin:** Michigan **Parents:** Gilbert Lee; Alexandria (Thomas) Bailey **Marital Status:** Married **Spouse Name:** Catherine Ann Yambor (8/2/1980) **Children:** Nicole Cherisse; Melanie Renee; Jacob Thomas **Education:** PhD in Chemistry, Pennsylvania State University (1983);BS, The Ohio State University (1978) **Career:** President, TR Bailey Consulting LLC, Phoenixville, Pennsylvania (2012-present); Senior Scientist II, Cephalon Inc., West Chester, PA (2004-2011); Senior Scientist, ViroPharma Inc., Exton, PA (1995-2004); Principal Research Investigator, Sterling-Winthrop, Inc., Collegeville, PA (1993-1995); Principal Research Investigator, Sterling-Winthrop, Inc., Rensselaer, NY (1992-1993); Senior Research Investigator, Sterling-Winthrop, Inc., Rensselaer, NY (1989-1992); Senior Research Chemist, Sterling-Winthrop, Inc., Rensselaer, NY (1985-1988); Postdoctoral Fellow, Colorado State University, Fort Collins, TX (1983-1985) **Career Related:** Reviewer, Journal of Medicinal Chemistry **Civic:** Past Member, Church of the Epiphany, Royersford, PA **Creative Works:** Contributor, Professional Journals; Inventor, 50 United States; Associated, Seven Clinical Candidates; Inventor, Tecovirimat **Memberships:** Am. Chemical Society; New York Academy Science **Marquis Who's Who Honors:** Albert Nelson Marquis Lifetime Achievement Award; Marquis Who's Who Top Professional **To what do you attribute your success:** Dr. Bailey attributes his success to an open, prepared mind, and welcoming to new opportunities. **Why did you become involved in your profession or industry:** Dr. Bailey became involved in his profession while he was at Ohio state in pre-medicine and he was not a chemistry major. He was thinking about majoring in classics such as Latin and Greek. Extensive chemistry was required for medical school. He discovered organic chemistry at the Ohio State University where he worked for Professor L.A. Paquette, and later went on to graduate school. **Avocations:** Reading; Problem Solving **Religion:** Episcopalian **Thoughts on Life:** Seek success outside your comfort zone.

Royce Eugene Ballinger, PhD

Title: Professor Emeritus, Academic Administrator, Educator **Industry:** Education/Educational Services **Company Name:** University of Nebraska-Lincoln **Date of Birth:** 02/21/1942 **Place of Birth:** Burkburnett **State/Country of Origin:** TX/USA **Parents:** Royce Ballinger; Luceil Evelyn (Tucker) Ballinger **Marital Status:** Widowed **Spouse Name:** Ruth Ann Hamshar (05/15/1976) (Deceased 2003) **Children:** One Son; One Daughter; Three Stepchildren **Education:** PhD, Texas A&M University (1971); MS, Texas Tech University (1967); BA, University of Texas (1964) **Career:** Professor Emeritus, University of Nebraska-Lincoln (2004-Present); Assistant Executive Vice President, Provost, University of Nebraska (2000-2005); Director, Established Program to Stimulate Competitive Research, University of Nebraska (1993-2005); Professor, University of Nebraska-Lincoln (1982-2005); Associate Vice Chancellor of Research, University of Nebraska-Lincoln (1993-2000); Director of Biological Sciences, University of Nebraska-Lincoln (1982-1990); Associate Professor, University of Nebraska-Lincoln (1976-1982); Assistant and Associate Professor, Angelo State University (1971-1976) **Career Related:** Board of Governors, Center for Great Plains Studies, University of Nebraska-Lincoln; International Advisory Panel, Chinese University Development Project, World Bank; National Advisory Council, Biocom; President, Academic Senate, University of Nebraska-Lincoln **Civic:** Board Member, Established Program to Stimulate Competitive Research; Friends of Ironwood Forest **Creative Works:** Author, "Natural History of the Ironwood Forest National Monument: A Sonoran Desert Primer" (2014); Author, "Amphibians and Reptiles of Nebraska" (2010); Author, "How to Know Amphibians and Reptile" (1983); Contributor, 140 Articles, Professional Journals **Awards:** Research Grantee, National Science Foundation; Sigma Xi, The Scientific Research Honor Society **Memberships:** American Society of Ichthyologists and Herpetologists; Southwestern Association of Naturalists; Herpetologists' League; American Association for the Advancement of Science; Ecological Society of America **Marquis Who's Who Honors:** Albert Nelson Marquis Lifetime Achievement Award **Why did you become involved in your profession or industry:** Dr. Ballinger became involved in his profession at the insistence of Professor W.F. Blair. **Avocations:** Golfing; Birding

Richard W. Bank, MD

Title: Portfolio Manager **Industry:** Financial Services **Company Name:** BioVest Advisors LLC **Children:** Two children **Education:** BS in Pre-Med, Washington & Lee (1965-1969); MD in Oncology, Immuno-oncolgy and Blood Tumors, Pritzker School of Medicine, The University of Chicago **Career:** Chief Medical Officer, Liquid Biosciences (2017-Present); President, Portfolio Manager, BioVest Advisors, LLC (1996-Present); Senior Director of Strategic Operations, Bradmer Pharmaceuticals (Now Takeda Pharmaceutical Company Limited) (2006-2008); Director, Arbios Systems (2003-2006); Portfolio Manager, Managing Partner, First-Tier Partners (1995-2004) **Awards:** Emeritus Professor of the Year, Keck School of Medicine, University of Southern California (2012); Emeritus Professor of the Year, Norris Comprehensive Cancer Center, University of Southern California (1984); Fellowship, National Institutes of Health **Memberships:** American Medical Association; Fellow, The Royal Academy of Medicine; Fellow, American College of Obstetricians and Gynecologists **Why did you become involved in your profession or industry:** Mr. Bank became involved in his profession because a friend, who was an analyst on Wall Street, would frequently send him research reports. At that time, he fell in love with the biotechnology industry because it was on the cutting-edge of the future of medicine. **Avocations:** Reading prosaic literature; Listening to classical music; Watching sports

Pauline C. Barbin, CRNA, MEd

Title: Academic Director **Industry:** Education/Educational Services **Date of Birth:** 09/25/1933 **Place of Birth:** Berlin **State/Country of Origin:** NH/USA **Parents:** Wilfrid J. Barbin; Juliette B. (Gagnon) Barbin **Marital Status:** Single **Education:** MEd, University of Maine (1983); BS, Thomas College, Waterville, Maine, Magna Cum Laude (1980); Certificate, Carney Hospital School of Anesthesia, Steward Health Care, Boston, MA (1956); Diploma, St. Louis Hospital (1954); Diploma, School of Nursing, Berlin, New Hampshire (1954) **Career:** Director, School Anesthetist, Eastern Maine Medical Center (Now Northern Light Eastern Maine Medical Center), Northern Light Health, Bangor, Maine; Director, Surgery Complex, Eastern Maine Medical Center (Now Northern Light Eastern Maine Medical Center), Northern Light Health; Chief Nurse Anesthetist, Eastern Maine Medical Center (Now Northern Light Eastern Maine Medical Center), Northern Light Health **Creative Works:** Author, "Nurse Anesthesia Programs: Who Benefits?," American Association of Nurse Anesthetists, Volume 32, No. 1 (1984); Professional Speaker, 14 Workshops, Conferences, and Symposia (1977-1987); Presenter, Paper, ""Cold Alert" Team Approach for the Treatment of Malignant Hyperpryexia," MeANA Meeting (1973) **Awards:** Helen Lamb Outstanding Educator Award, AANA **Memberships:** Council on Accreditation, American Association of Nurse Anesthetists (AANA); Past President, Maine Association of Nurse Anesthetists; New England Assembly of School Faculty; New England Assembly of Nurse Anesthetists (NEANA) **Marquis Who's Who Honors:** Albert Nelson Marquis Lifetime Achievement Award **Why did you become involved in your profession or industry:** In high school, Ms. Barbin's class had to dissect a rabbit. She volunteered to be the one to give the rabbit anesthesia. Since then she wanted to pursue a career as an anesthetist. Eastern Maine Medical Center started the first school of anesthesia in the state of Maine and Ms. Barbin was the chief nurse anesthetist and worked her way to eventually becoming the director. Dr. Clement Dwyer, Chief Anesthesiologist, was a huge influence as well as Sylvia Durepos, who was in the class with Ms. Barbin. She not only encouraged her to succeed, but also became her best friend. After they started the school, Ms. Barbin was instrumental in starting a nursing anesthetist society in Maine and that is when she became the president of the Maine Association of Nurse Anesthetists. **Avocations:** Gardening; Crafts

Margaret Louise Barron

Title: Elementary and Music Educator **Company Name:** Toledo Public Schools **Date of Birth:** 08/03/1933 **Place of Birth:** Yazoo City **State/Country of Origin:** MS/USA **Parents:** Beauford Howard Barron; Annie (Harmon) Barron **Education:** MusM, Boston Conservatory (1960); BS, Arkansas State University (1954); Postgraduate Coursework, Mozarteum, Salzburg, Austria and Zagreb, Yugoslovia **Career:** Teacher, Toledo Public Schools (1975-Present); Teacher, American School, Zagreb, Croatia (1972-1975); Teacher, Boston Public Schools (1960-1971); Teacher, Yazoo City Training School (1954-1958) **Career Related:** Singer, Toledo Opera Chorus (1986-Present); Singer, Boston Opera Chorus (1960-1966); Singer, Concerts, "Standing Ovation," Miles College; Singer, "Virtue, Violence and Vengeance Inspired by the Virtue of Lucretia by Cades"; Singer, "A Journey Through the Live of African Americans"; Museum Work, Themes at the Museum the Emancipation and March on Washington; Museum Work, African Americans in Times of War; Museum Work, Movement of African Americans to New Destinations; Museum Work, Civil War and Emancipation; Museum Work, Hip Hop Culture; Represented Toledo in Hungary; Singer, Concert, Cambridge College, MA and England **Civic:** Volunteer, Campaign of Mike Sturdivant for Governor, Jackson, MS (1984) **Memberships:** Ohio Music Education Association; National Association for Female Executives; Delta Kappa Gamma Society International; Delta Sigma Theta Society, Inc. **Marquis Who's Who Honors:** Albert Nelson Marquis Lifetime Achievement Award; Marquis Who's Who Top Professional **Avocations:** Music **Political Affiliations:** Democrat **Religion:** Methodist

Nancy Marshall Bauer

Title: TV and Radio Network Executive, Retired **Industry:** Education/Educational Services **Company Name:** Wisconsin Public Television **Date of Birth:** 03/17/1929 **Place of Birth:** Madison **State/Country of Origin:** WI/USA **Parents:** Richard Hughes Marshall; Lucy (Whitaker) Marshall **Marital Status:** Widow **Spouse Name:** Helmut R. Bauer (3/4/1974, Deceased); Joseph B. McNamara (12/29/1952, Divorced 1962) **Children:** Margaret; Patrick **Education:** MS, University of Wisconsin (1963); BA, University of Wisconsin (1950) **Career:** Executive Committee, Central Educational Network (1989-1998); Retired, Wisconsin Educational TV and Radio Networks (1989); Director, Educative Services, Wisconsin Educational TV and Radio Networks, Madison, WI (1972-1989); Director, Central Educational Network (1973-1980); Assistant Professor, University of Wisconsin-Extension (1968-1973); Specialist, Educational Communications, University of Wisconsin-Madison (1966-1971); Elementary Teacher, Madison, WI (1963-1968) **Career Related:** ITV Study Committee (1983-1985); Board Member, PBS (1980-1983); Instructional Radio Advisory Committee, National Public Radio (NPR) (1979-1982); ITV Advisory Committee (1978-1979); Executive Committee, ITV Cooperative (1976-1977) **Creative Works:** Producer, Writer, "Inquiry: The Justice Thing" (1973); Producer, Writer, "Patterns in Arithmetic" (1967); Producer, Writer, Numerous Nationally Distributed ITV Radio Series; Writer, Publisher, Family History; Contributor, Articles, Historical and Genelogical Magazines **Awards:** Golden Mike Award, American Legion (1976); Gavel Award, American Bar Association (1975); Ohio State Award (1975); Ford Foundation Scholar (1961-1963) **Memberships:** National Association of Educational Broadcasters **Marquis Who's Who Honors:** Albert Nelson Marquis Lifetime Achievement Award **Why did you become involved in your profession or industry:** Ms. Bauer began her career as a teacher. When assigned to teach experimental television mathematics to her class, she became interested and decided to visit the television station on her day off. The woman in charge of the program had just announced her retirement, and luckily for Ms. Bauer, she was in the right place at the right time. **Avocations:** Traveling; Gardening

Nancy Ann Beasom

Title: Occupational Therapist, Consultant **Industry:** Consulting **Date of Birth:** 11/02/1936 **Place of Birth:** Kansas City **State/Country of Origin:** KS/USA **Year of Passing:** May 2020 **Parents:** Albert Lawrence Hibbs; Ruth Augusta (Badgley) Hibbs **Marital Status:** Married **Spouse Name:** Ronald Lightner Beasom (6/14/1958) **Children:** Kim Schwab; Jeffrey Beasom; Bryn Fay **Education:** BS, University of Pennsylvania (1958) **Certifications:** Registered and Licensed Occupational Therapist, PA, FL **Career:** Occupational Therapy Consultant, Elwyn, Inc., PA (1989-1999); Occupational Therapist, DPW/Embreeville Center, Coatesville, PA (1975-1982, 1985-1996); Occupational Therapy Consultant, Chester County MH/MR Unit, West Chester, PA (1988-1991); Mental Retardation, Unit Manager, Occupational Therapy Supervisor, DPW/Embreeville Center, Coatesville, PA (1982-1985); Occupational Therapy Consultant, Private Practice, West Chester, PA (1978-1981); Artist, Craftsman, West Chester, PA (1965-1975) **Career Related:** Occupational Therapy Consultant, Home Health Care Agency, West Reading, PA (1981-1982); Occupational Therapy Consultant, Brian's House, West Chester, PA (1978-1980); Pottery Instructor, Princess Cruise Line **Civic:** Vice President, First Presbyterian Church of Punta Gorda; Elder, First Presbyterian Church; **Creative Works:** Author, Poetry Book, "Growing and Knowing" (2012) **Memberships:** American Occupational Therapy Association; Vice president, Church Corporation **Marquis Who's Who Honors:** Albert Nelson Marquis Lifetime Achievement Award **Why did you become involved in your profession or industry:** Ms. Beasom became involved in her profession while attending the University of Pennsylvania and majoring in their occupational therapy program. During that time, many clinical courses were offered, as well as art courses, and occupational therapy had a lot to do with the art part of it. She also became very interested in silversmithing. She graduated from college married with one child. Rather than go back to work right away, she made silver jewelry. **Avocations:** Basketry; Gardening; Poetry; Art **Political Affiliations:** Republican **Religion:** Presbyterian

Margaret Beggs Towle

Title: Senior Vice President, Financial Advisor **Industry:** Financial Services **Company Name:** Wealth Enhancement Group **Marital Status:** Married **Spouse Name:** Timothy **Education:** Bachelor of Science in Accounting, Metropolitan State University (1996); Coursework, University of Minnesota **Certifications:** Certified Public Accountant; Minnesota Insurance License **Career:** Senior Vice President, Financial Advisor, Wealth Enhancement Group (2004-Present); Certified Public Accountant, Senior Tax Accountant, Redpath and Company Limited (2000-2004); Fiduciary Tax Accountant, United States Bank (1998-2000); Assistant to the Controller, Honeywell (1997-1998) **Civic:** Volunteer, Best Prep; Former Member, Governmental Issues Committee, Minnesota Society of Certified Public Accountants **Awards:** Top Women in Business & Finance, Minnesota (2014); 5-Star Financial Advisor Award, Minneapolis, St. Paul Magazine, Minneapolis Business Journal **Memberships:** Minnesota Society of Certified Public Accountants **To what do you attribute your success:** Ms. Beggs Towle attributes her success to having great parents that instilled within her the importance of a good education. She also credits her own passion for educating people and helping them through difficult situations. **Why did you become involved in your profession or industry:** Ms. Beggs Towle became involved in her profession due to her lifelong interest in education, public service and finance.

Cody James Bellinger

Title: Professional Baseball Player **Industry:** Athletics **Company Name:** Los Angeles Dodgers **Date of Birth:** 07/13/1995 **Place of Birth:** Scottsdale **State/Country of Origin:** AZ/USA **Parents:** Clay Bellinger **Career:** First Baseman, Outfielder, Los Angeles Dodgers, Major League Baseball (2017-Present) **Awards:** Named Two-time National League All-star (2017, 2019); Rawlings Gold Glove Award (2019); Fielding Bible Award for Right Field (2019); Fielding Bible Award for Multi-positional (2019); National League Most Valuable Player Award (2019); Named National League Championship Series MVP (2018); National League Rookie of the Year Award (2017); Named Players Choice National League Outstanding Rookie (2017); Named Sportsman of the Year, Los Angeles Sports Council (2017); Named Sporting News National League Rookie of the Year (2017); Named to Topps All-star Rookie Team (2017); Named to Arizona Fall League Fall Stars Game (2016); Named California League Mid-season All-star (2015); Named California League Post-season All-star (2015);

Scott L. Bennett, Esq.

Title: Lawyer **Industry:** Law and Legal Services **Date of Birth:** 07/08/1949 **Place of Birth:** New York **State/Country of Origin:** NY/USA **Parents:** Allen J. Bennett; Rhoda Bennett **Marital Status:** Single **Education:** JD, Cornell University (1974); BA, University of Michigan, with High Distinction (1971) **Career:** Retired (2016); Former Senior Vice President, Associate General Counsel, Secretary, McGraw Hill Financial, Inc. (Now S&P Global), New York, NY (1979-2016); Associate, Donovan, Leisure, Newton & Irvine, New York, NY (1974-1979) **Civic:** Director, SAGE USA; Chairman, Board of Directors, New York Chapter, Our Fund Foundation; Volunteer, Outshine LGBTQ+ Film Festival, Equality Florida, Ft. Lauderdale, FL **Memberships:** American Bar Association (ABA); Association of the Bar of the City of New York; New York State Bar Association; The Phi Beta Kappa Society **Bar Admissions:** Supreme Court of the United States (1976); United States District Court for the Southern District of New York (1975); United States District Court for the Eastern District of New York (1975); United States Court of Appeals for the Second Circuit (1975); New York (1975) **Marquis Who's Who Honors:** Albert Nelson Marquis Lifetime Achievement Award; Marquis Who's Who Top Professional

Christine D. Berg, MD

Title: Radiation Oncologist; Special Volunteer **Company Name:** National Cancer Institute **Date of Birth:** 11/18/1954 **Place of Birth:** Chicago **State/Country of Origin:** IL/USA **Parents:** Roy Albert Berg; Dorothy (Dahlberg) Berg **Marital Status:** Married **Spouse Name:** Cyril W. Draffin Jr. (1990) **Children:** Cyril William Draffin III; Benjamin Philip Draffin **Education:** MD, Northwestern University Feinberg School of Medicine (1977); BS, Northwestern University (1975) **Certifications:** Certified, Therapeutic Radiology, American Board of Radiology (1986); Certified, Medical Oncology, American Board of Internal Medicine (1983); Certified, Internal Medicine, American Board of Internal Medicine (1980); Licensed, District of Columbia and State of Maryland **Career:** Special Adviser, Director, Division of Cancer Epidemiology and Genetics, National Cancer Institute, National Institutes of Health (2015-Present); Adjunct Professor, Department of Radiation Oncology and Molecular Radiation Sciences, Sidney Kimmel Comprehensive Care Center, Johns Hopkins Medicine (2013-Present); Chief, Early Detection Research Group, Division of Cancer Prevention, National Cancer Institute, National Institutes of Health (2004-2012); Cancer Center Director, Suburban Hospital Cancer Program, Bethesda, MD (2000-2003); Chief, Lung and Upper Aerodigestive Cancer Research Group, Division of Cancer Prevention, National Cancer Institute (1999-2000); Associate Professor, Department of Radiation Medicine, Division of Medical Oncology, Department of Medicine, Georgetown University School of Medicine (1994-1998); Director, Breast Radiation Therapy, Vincent T. Lombardi Comprehensive Cancer Center, Georgetown University Medical Center (1992-1998); Director, Residency Training Program, Department of Radiation Medicine, Georgetown University Medical Center (1993-1997); Assistant Professor, Department of Radiation Medicine, Department of Medicine, Medical Oncology, Georgetown University Medical School (1986-1993); Clinical Director, Georgetown Radiation Medicine Associates at Shady Grove, Rockville, MD (1986-1992) **Career Related:** Consultant, GRAIL, Inc. (2017-Present) **Civic:** Climate Victory Council, League of Conservation Voters; Advisory Board, Chesapeake PSR **Creative Works:** Author, Over 130 Peer-reviewed Original Scientific Publications, 10 Publications, New England Journal of Medicine, Scientific Journals **Awards:** Recipient, Numerous Awards **Memberships:** Member, Numerous Organizations **Marquis Who's Who Honors:** Albert Nelson Marquis Lifetime Achievement Award; Marquis Who's Who Top Professional

Nikhil K. Bhayani, MD, FIDSA

Title: Physician **Industry:** Medicine & Health Care **Company Name:** DFW ID, PLLC **Date of Birth:** 06/10/1976 **Place of Birth:** Roanoke **State/Country of Origin:** VA/USA **Parents:** Kiran; Chandra **Spouse Name:** Chanda **Children:** Krish; Prem **Education:** Infectious Diseases Fellow, University of Illinois, Chicago, IL (2006-2008); Resident Physician, Mercy Hospital and Medical Center, Chicago, IL (2003-2006); MD in Medicine, Ross University School of Medicine, Miramir, FL, Bridgetown, Barbados (2003); BS in Biology, University of Utah, Salt Lake City, UT (1998) **Certifications:** Diplomate in Infectious Disease, American Board of Internal Medicine (2008, 2018); Licensed, State of Illinois (2008); Licensed, State of Texas (2008); Diplomate in Internal Medicine, American Board of Internal Medicine (2006); Licensed, State of Illinois (2005) **Career:** Assistant Professor, TCU and UNTHSC School of Medicine, Fort Worth, TX (2019-Present); Physician Adviser, Department of Quality, Patient Safety, and Infection Prevention, Texas Health Resources, Arlington, TX (2018-Present); Owner, Infectious Disease Consultant, Nikhil K Bhayani, MD, PA (DFW Infectious Diseases, PLLC) (2016-Present); Adjunct Clinical Instructor, University of Texas at Arlington College of Nursing (2019-2020); Consulting Physician, Infectious Disease Doctors, P.A., Dallas, TX (2008-2016) **Career Related:** Secretary of Medical Staff, Member of Medical Executive Committee, Texas Health Resources Arlington Memorial (2018-Present); Chair, Department of Adult Medicine, Texas Health Resources, Texas Health Arlington Memorial Hospital (2014-2018) **Civic:** Member, Executive Board, Pratham DFW (2013-Present); Member, Numerous Hospital Committee Memberships (2008-Present) **Creative Works:** Speaker, Presenter, Numerous Local and Intramural Presentations **Awards:** Top Doctor Award of Tarrant County, 360 West Magazine (2018-2019); Physician of the Year, Texas Health Arlington Memorial Hospital (2016); Recognition Award, Illinois Mathematics and Science Academy (IMSA) (2008) **Memberships:** Texas Indo-American Physicians Society (2018-Present); Crimson Laureate Society, University of Utah (2017); Elected Member, Texas Health Resources Infectious Disease Congress (2008-2010) **Marquis Who's Who Honors:** Marquis Who's Who Top Professional

Martin George Bialer, MD, PhD

Title: Geneticist **Industry:** Medicine & Health Care **Company Name:** NYU Grossman School of Medicine **Date of Birth:** 06/10/1952 **Place of Birth:** New York **State/Country of Origin:** NY/USA **Parents:** Henry Bialer; Ethel (Raffel) Albert Bialer **Marital Status:** Married **Spouse Name:** Rachel Sydney Baron (05/05/1991) **Children:** Daniel; Aaron **Education:** Fellow in Genetics, University of Virginia, Charlottesville, VA (1986-1989); Intern and Resident in Pediatrics, North Shore University Hospital (Now Northwell Health), Manhasset, NY (1983-1986); MD, Medical University of South Carolina, Charleston, SC (1983); PhD, Medical University of South Carolina, Charleston, SC (1980); BA, Cornell University, Ithaca, NY (1973) **Certifications:** Diplomate, American Board of Medical Genetics and Genomics (1990); Diplomate, American Board Pediatrics (1987) **Career:** Section Head of Clinical Metabolism, New York University School of Medicine (Now NYU Grossman School of Medicine) (2010-Present); Chief Division, Medical Genetics, New York University School of Medicine (Now NYU Grossman School of Medicine), New York, NY (1999-2010); Associate Professor of Pediatrics, Hofstra, North Shore LIJ School of Medicine (Now Donald and Barbara Zucker School of Medicine at Hofstra/Northwell) (1999-2010); Associate in Genetics, North Shore University Hospital (Now Northwell Health), Manhasset, NY (1989-1999); Assistant Professor of Pediatrics, New York University School of Medicine (Now NYU Grossman School of Medicine), New York, NY (1997-1999); Assistant Professor of Pediatrics, Cornell University, New York, NY (1989-1997) **Creative Works:** Contributor, Articles to Professional Journals Including Clinical Cardiology, Clinical Chemistry, American Journal of Medical Genetics and European Journal of Pediatrics **Awards:** Fellow, Muscular Dystrophy Association (1988-1989) **Memberships:** Fellow, American Academy Pediatrics; Former Member, American Medical Association; American Society Human Genetics; American College Medical Genetics; Previous member Nassau Pediatrics Society; Alpha Omega Alpha **Marquis Who's Who Honors:** Albert Nelson Marquis Lifetime Achievement Award **Why did you become involved in your profession or industry:** Dr. Bialer became involved in his profession because he knew since high school that it was what he wanted to do. He remembered reading "Microbe Hunters" for the first time about Louie Pasteur and Robert Koch and being fascinated by it. **Avocations:** Photography **Political Affiliations:** Democrat **Religion:** Jewish

Blake Biernacki

Title: Managing Director **Industry:** Engineering **Company Name:** ProLytx **Place of Birth:** , **Marital Status:** Married **Spouse Name:** Andrea Biernacki **Children:** Amelia; Emmett **Education:** Bachelor of Science, Coventry University (2010-2013); Associate of Science, Lee College (2001-2004) **Career:** Owner, Managing Director, ProLytx (2015-Present); Subject Matter Expert, Intergraph (2014-2015); Smartplant Administartor, Wood Group Mustang (2008-2014); Control System, The Automation Group (2006-2008) **Civic:** Vice Chairman, Technical User Forum Instrumentation, Houston, Texas; Volunteer, Church **Awards:** Top 10 Engineering Technology Start-ups **Memberships:** Instrument Society of America **To what do you attribute your success:** Mr. Biernacki credits his success on his employees, as well as his customers. Without either, his business would never have become successful. **Why did you become involved in your profession or industry:** Mr. Biernacki became involved in his profession due to the influence of his uncle, who was a chemical engineer. After maintaining involvement in the field for several years, he received an opportunity to start his own business, which could fulfill the need for information that business executives required to succeed.

Terri Ellen Bigler, MD

Title: Internal Medicine and Pediatrics Doctor **Industry:** Medicine & Health Care **Company Name:** Dignity Health **Marital Status:** Married **Education:** MD, School of Medicine, University of Nevada, Reno (1992) **Certifications:** Licensed, State of California (1994) **Career:** Doctor, Dignity Health Medical Foundation (2000-Present); Specialist in Internal Medicine, Mercy General Hospital, Dignity Health; Specialist in Internal Medicine, Mercy Hospital of Folsom, Dignity Health; Specialist in Internal Medicine, Mercy San Juan Medical Center, Dignity Health; Coordinator, Medical Groups, Dignity Health Medical Foundation **Civic:** Advisory Committee, Physician Assistance Program, University of the Pacific **Awards:** Distinguished Doctor Recognition (2016); Best Doctor, Roseville Tribune, Gold Country Media (2016); One of the Top Ten Internal Medicine Doctors in Roseville, CA, Vitals.com (2014); Most Compassionate Doctor (2009, 2011, 2012); Featured Listee, American Registry, American Top Doctors (2005-2012) **Memberships:** American Board of Internal Medicine; American College of Physicians; Sierra Sacramento Valley Medical Society **Marquis Who's Who Honors:** Marquis Who's Who Top Professional **To what do you attribute your success:** Dr. Bigler attributes her success to her religion and faith. **Why did you become involved in your profession or industry:** Dr. Bigler became involved in her profession because she has always been driven to help others; becoming a doctor was a calling. **Avocations:** Reading; Playing piano; Traveling

Simone Arianne Biles

Title: Professional Gymnast **Industry:** Athletics **Date of Birth:** 3/14/1997 **Place of Birth:** Columbus **State/Country of Origin:** OH/USA **Parents:** Shanon Biles (Mother); Ron Biles (Adoptive Father); Nellie Cayetano Biles (Adoptive Mother) **Education:** Coursework, University of the People **Creative Works:** Contestant, "Dancing with the Stars" (2017); Co-author, "Courage to Soar: A Body in Motion, A Life in Balance" (2016) **Awards:** Award for Sportswoman of the Year, Laureus World Sports Awards Ltd. (2017, 2019, 2020); Award for Game Changer of the Year, People's Choice Awards, E! Entertainment Television, LLC (2019); International Listee, L'Équipe Champion of Champions, L'Équipe Magazine (2016, 2018, 2019); Most Dominant Athlete of the Year, ESPN The Magazine, ESPN (2018); Arthur Ashe Courage Award, ESPN (2018); TIME 100, TIME USA, LLC (2017); ESPY Award for Best Female Athlete, ESPN (2017); Teen Choice Award for Choice Female Athlete, Fox Media LLC (2017); Overseas Sports Personality of the Year, BBC (2016); Honoree, Women of the Year Awards, Glamour, Condé Nast (2016); Listee, 100 Women, BBC (2016); Listee, Impact 25, espnW, ESPN (2016); Sports-Woman of the Year, United States Olympic & Paralympic Committee (2014, 2015); WSF Individual Sportswoman of the Year, Women's Sports Foundation (2014) **Religion:** Catholic

Carol I. Black

Title: Elementary School Educator, Principal (Retired) **Industry:** Education/Educational Services **Date of Birth:** 05/26/1937 **Place of Birth:** Bremerton **State/Country of Origin:** WA/USA **Parents:** Jack Lester; Lillian Gertrude (Hall) Zander **Marital Status:** Widow **Spouse Name:** Richard Black (08/1/1981, Deceased); Bruce Craig Matheny, (06/4/1955, Divorced 04/1972) **Children:** Craig Matheny; David; Matheny; Victoria Black-Miller; Jon Black **Education:** Master of Arts, U.S. International University (1987); Bachelor of Science, Southern Oregon State College (1972) **Certifications:** Certified, Elementary Teacher, Administrative Services **Career:** Retired (1996); Elementary Principal, Fairfield-Suisun Unified School District, California (1991-1996); Assistant Principal, Fairfield-Suisun Unified School District, California (1991); Summer School Principal, Fairfield-Suisun Unified School District, California (1990); Expulsion Hearing Panel, Fairfield-Suisun Unified School District, California (1990); Teacher, Program Manager, Fairfield-Suisun Unified School District, California (1985-1990); Teacher, Program Manager, Visalia Unified School District, California (1973-1985); Teacher, Rogue River, OR (1972-1973); Principal, Teacher, Applegate Kindergarten, Oregon (1965-1967) **Career Related:** Reviewer, Compensatory Education National Awards, California (1988-1990); Presenter, Compensatory Education Conference, California Department of Education (1989) **Creative Works:** Featured Artist, Bakersfield Art Association (2017); Author, "Never Ask Permission" (2006); Featured, Art Exhibition (1972) **Awards:** Golden Bell Award, California School Boards Foundation (1995) **Memberships:** National Education Association; Association for Supervision and Curriculum Development; Association of California School Administrators; Fairfield-Suisun Unified Administration Association; Phi Delta Kappa **Why did you become involved in your profession or industry:** Ms. Black became involved in her profession because she loved working with children. having two of her own at the time. Her husband was a school principal and superintendent. Already deeply involved in education, she realized she aspired to do the same thing. **Avocations:** Golf; Reading; Travel; Home remodeling; Gardening; Music **Religion:** Presbyterian

Eilene Bloom

Title: Director **Industry:** Staffing and Recruiting **Company Name:** Eilene Bloom Group LLC **Education:** BS, Queens College, Cum Laude (1975) **Career:** Founding Partner, Eilene Bloom Group, LLC (2016-Present); Partner, Foster, Bloom Legal Search LLC (2014-2015); Managing Director, Major, Lindsey & Africa (2013-2014); Director, Mestel & Company (2004-2012); Vice President, Reliance Group Holdings, Inc. (1980-2000) **Civic:** Volunteer, Numerous Charities at Local Temple **Awards:** Named One of the "100 Leading Legal Consultants," Law Dragon (2019) **To what do you attribute your success:** Ms. Bloom attributes her success to her perseverance. She does not take no for an answer. She believes that you cannot just be technically smart, but also emotionally smart. Emotional intelligence adds so much credibility because it allows you to understand people and their situations. **Thoughts on Life:** Ms. Bloom's motto is, "Honesty is the best policy." She leads a legal search and recruiting company that connects lawyers, practice groups, and firms in combinations that allow them to thrive. Her early career experience hiring talent for a public company and building its corporate legal department grounded her in what it takes for a recruiter to add value. Now the people she works with — the lawyers who are moving and the firms that are expanding – recognize the value when her knowledge and emotional intelligence and their interests and strategies drive the recruiting process. Thinking hard and realistically about the complementarity of practices, economics, personalities, and philosophies, she gives honest and insightful guidance about fit. With the determination to demonstrably add value, she has orchestrated the placement of partners across legal practices – litigation, corporate, IP, real estate, bankruptcy, regulatory, and tax; partners focusing on industries from finance to pharmaceuticals, technology to manufacturing; and for firms from boutiques to global leaders. Consequently, she is a sought-after adviser both to law firm leaders and to partners considering their career options. In recognition of her accomplishments, in 2019 she was named by Law Dragon as one of the 100 Leading Legal Consultants. A New York City native and veteran of 20 years in legal recruiting, she launched her own firm in 2016 and previously worked at other leading recruiting firms.

Douglas Ray Bohi, PhD

Title: Economist **Industry:** Financial Services **Date of Birth:** 09/09/1939 **Place of Birth:** Pocatello **State/Country of Origin:** ID/USA **Parents:** Clarence R. Bohi; Florence E. (Karstad) Bohi **Marital Status:** Married **Spouse Name:** Marjorie Brenner Bohi **Children:** Heidi; James **Education:** PhD in Economics, Washington State University (1967); BS in Economics, Idaho State University (1962) **Career:** Vice President, CRA International, Inc. (1994-2004); Division Director, Resources for the Future (1988-1994); Chief Economist, FERC (1987-1988); Senior Fellow, Resources for the Future (1978-1987); Professor of Economics, Southern Illinois University (1970-1978); Economist, Caterpillar (1969-1970) **Career Related:** Visiting Professor, Monash University (1982) **Military Service:** U.S. Army (1976-1978) **Creative Works:** Author, "Analyzing Nonrenewable Resource Supply" (1984, 2015); Author, "The Economics of Energy Security (1996); Co-Author, "The Energy Upheavals of the 1970s: Policy Watershed or Aberration?" (1994); Author, "Utility Investment Behavior and the Emission Trading Market" (1991); Author, "Understanding Nonrenewable Resource Supply Behavior" (1983); Author, "Oil Prices, Energy Security, and Import Policy" (1982); Author, "Analyzing Demand Behavior: A Study of Energy Elasticities" (1981); Co-Author, "Limiting Oil Imports: An Economic History and Analysis" (1978); Author, "U.S. Energy Policy: Alternatives for Security" (1975) **Awards:** Fulbright Scholar, Erasmus University Rotterdam (1977) **Marquis Who's Who Honors:** Albert Nelson Marquis Lifetime Achievement Award **Why did you become involved in your profession or industry:** Dr. Bohi became involved in his profession because he was inspired by several university professors.

Donna Bonin

Title: Owner **Industry:** Fine Art **Company Name:** Back in Time Gallery **Date of Birth:** 01/03/1946 **Place of Birth:** Hamilton **State/Country of Origin:** Ontario/Canada **Parents:** Robert M. (1902, Deceased 1996); Ruth C. (1906, Deceased 1967) **Marital Status:** Widowed **Spouse Name:** Oscar Bonin (10/10/1981, Deceased 1990) **Children:** Lisa; Nicole **Education:** BA in History and English, Queen's University, Kingston, Ontario, Canada (1969) **Certifications:** Certified, Physical Education Specialist **Career:** Owner, Back in Time Gallery (2000-Present); Artist, Watercolor Instructor, Loyalist College, Belleville, Ontario, Canada (2000-Present); Retired Teacher (2000); Teacher, Secondary School (1969-2000) **Career Related:** Creator, Art Workshop, Portugal; Teacher, Art Classes, France and Barcelona, Spain; Leader, Instructor, Travel Art Workshops, Europe and North America; Instructor, Workshops, British Columbia, Bavarian Alps, Amalfi Coast, Greek Islands and Malta; Invited Biannual Instructor, Le Monastere, Limoux, France **Creative Works:** Artist, Exhibit, Back in Time Gallery; Artist, Various International Galleries and Venues; Artist, Showings, New York, NY, Miami, FL, Florence, Italy, Cannes, France, Brussels, Belgium, Vienna, Austria, Paris, France, and Montreal and Toronto, Canada; Artist, Watercolor, Oil and Pastel Paintings, Horse and Pet Portraits **Awards:** Recipient, Multiple Awards, Juried Shows **Memberships:** ArtTour International; Artist Inspo; Farscec International; Vivid Arts Network; Create 4 Peace; Artist's Info; Arts Quinte West; Belleville Art Association; Quinte Arts Council **To what do you attribute your success:** Mrs. Bonin attributes her success to perseverance and her motivation to experiment and expand her artistic horizons. She also credits her decision to allow her paintings to "speak" to her and tell her what they need for greatest effect. Often, they suggest things she never thought of. **Avocations:** Painting; Travel **Thoughts on Life:** Mrs. Bonin's motto is, "Stay Inspired."

Denis Bouboulis

Title: MD **Industry:** Medicine & Health Care **Company Name:** Advanced Allergy, Immunology & Asthma, P.C. **Education:** Fellowship, Albert Einstein College of Medicine of the Yeshiva University (1993); MD, New York Medical College (1986); BA, New York University; Internship, SUNY Medical Center; Residency, Stamford Hospital **Career:** Physician, Immunologist, Advanced Allergy, Immunology & Asthma, PC (1993-Present) **Career Related:** Clinical staff, Columbia University; Professor, Stamford Hospital **Civic:** Board member, Parish Council **Creative Works:** Writer, Christmas Album for Charity (St. Basil's Academy); Contributed articles, Journal of Neurology Research (2015, 2016) **Memberships:** Fellow, American College of Allergy; American Academy of Allergy & Immunology; Fellow, American Board of Certified Allergists; Connecticut Medical Society; Fairfield County Medical Society **To what do you attribute your success:** Dr. Bouboulis has a passion for what he does and goes to the highest degree to do what needs to be done to treat his patients. He is also very persistent in treating his patients. I live by the morals and principals that I think are the basic foundation in medicine. I don't view myself as unique... I think that the way that I practice should be inherent in other physicians, regardless of the discipline... you must have a passion and persevere... **Why did you become involved in your profession or industry:** Dr. Bouboulis remembers receiving a call from a colleague name Dr. Jim Lectus, that asked him to treat a patient for him. The patient was a 13 year old Chinese boy who had been suffering from a movement disorder since the age of 3. The family was in America from Japan on business, so they were able to receive treatment at Yale. After the successful treatment of the child, Dr. Bouboulis began to see more patients in the related discipline an study it much further. Dr. Bouboulis was always interested in physiology, and how things work. He was never attracted to surgical specialties because they were more technical and not cerebral enough. He felt the the immune system is the most complex and intriguing part of the human body.

Mike Bowie

Title: Owner and President **Industry:** Leisure, Travel & Tourism **Company Name:** Dunbar Yachts **Marital Status:** Married **Career:** Owner and President, Dunbar Yachts (2015-Present) **Memberships:** Georgia Marine Business Association, Savannah, GA; American Boat & Yacht Council; Yacht Brokers Association of America **To what do you attribute your success:** Mr. Bowie attributes his success to his life experience in corporate grounding. **Why did you become involved in your profession or industry:** Mr. Bowie became involved in his profession because of his father, who had a passion for boating and the outdoors. Because of illness, his father was not able to enjoy these activities, but he was able to influence his son to value these hobbies and pursue them on his career path.

Thomas Joseph Bowles, PhD

Title: Fellow **Industry:** Sciences **Company Name:** Los Alamos National Laboratory **Date of Birth:** 06/27/1950 **Place of Birth:** Denver **State/Country of Origin:** CO/USA **Parents:** Joseph Shipman Bowles; Mary Virginia (Belle) Bowles **Marital Status:** Married **Spouse Name:** Jeanne Marie Smith (05/30/1987) **Children:** Kathleen; Liana **Education:** PhD in Physics, Princeton University (1978); BS in Physics, Mathematics, minor in German, University of Colorado (1973) **Career:** Chief Executive Officer, Board Chair, New Mexico Computing Applications Center (2007-Present); Affiliate Professor, Physics Department, University of Washington, Seattle, WA (1995-Present); Staff Member, Los Alamos National Laboratory (1979-Present); Science Advisor, New Mexico Governor Bill Richardson (2006-2010); Chief Scientist, Los Alamos National Laboratory (2006); Chief Science Officer, Los Alamos National Laboratory (2004-2006); Nuclear Physics Program Manager, Los Alamos National Laboratory (2002-2004); Postdoctoral Fellow, Argonne National Laboratory (1976-1979); Laboratory Instructor, Physics Department, Princeton University (1974-1975); WICHE Fellow, Environmental Protection Agency, Denver Federal Center, Danver, CO (1973); Undergraduate Research Assistant, Nuclear Physics Laboratory, University of Colorado (1972-1973); NSF Undergraduate Research Fellow, Denver Center, University of Colorado (1972-1973) **Career Related:** Chairman, Postdoctoral Committee, Los Alamos National Laboratory (1989-1991) **Civic:** Organizer, Re-Energizing America Conference (2009); Representative, Science and Technology Table, Border Governor's Conference, New Mexico (2006-2010) **Creative Works:** Contributor, Over 20 Articles, Professional Journals **Awards:** New Mexico Nonprofit Titan of Information Technology (2012); New Mexico Climate Change Leadership Institute Innovation Award (2012); New Mexico Rainmaker Award (2010); Who's Who in Technology Facilitator Award, New Mexico (2009); New Mexico Energy Executive of 2009, New Mexico Association of Energy Engineers (2009) **Memberships:** Vice Chair, United States, Mexico Foundation for Science (2015-Present); Council Member, Entrepreneurship and Innovation Council, Mexico, United States (2013-Present) **Marquis Who's Who Honors:** Marquis Who's Who Top Professional; Marquis Who's Who Humanitarian Award; Albert Nelson Marquis Lifetime Achievement Award **Affiliations:** Democrat **Religion:** Roman Catholic

Frank Boyer Salisbury, PhD

Title: Professor Emeritus; Botanist; Author **Industry:** Education/Educational Services **Date of Birth:** 08/03/1926 **Place of Birth:** Provo **State/Country of Origin:** UT/USA **Year of Passing:** 2015 **Parents:** Frank Maine Salisbury; Catherine (Boyer) Salisbury **Marital Status:** Married **Spouse Name:** Helene Hancock Coats (08/03/2012); Mary Thorpe (1991, Deceased 2011); Lois Marilyn Olson (09/01/1949, Divorced) **Children:** Clark; Steven Scott; Michael James; Cynthia Kay; Phillip Boyer (Deceased); Rebecca Lynn; Blake **Education:** PhD in Plant Physiology, California Institute of Technology, Pasadena, CA (1955); MA, University of Utah, Salt Lake City, UT(1952); BS, University of Utah, Salt Lake City, UT (1951); Diploma, South High School, Salt Lake City, UT **Career:** Professor Emeritus, Utah State University, Logan, UT (1997-Present); Distinguished Professor of Agriculture, Utah State University, Logan, UT (1987-1997); Technical Representative of Plant Physiology, Atomic Energy Commission, Germantown, MD (1973-1974); Professor of Plant Physiology, Utah State University, Logan, UT (1966-1997); Head, Department of Plant Science, Utah State University, Logan, UT (1966-1970); Plant Physiologist, Experiment Station (1961-1966); Professor of Plant Physiology, Colorado State University, Fort Collins, CO (1961-1966); Assistant Professor, Colorado State University, Fort Collins, CO (1955-1961) **Career Related:** Leader, Project to Grow Wheat Through a Life Cycle in Russian Space Station, Mir (1990-1997); Chairman, NASA Controlled Ecological Life Support System Discipline Working Group (1989-1994); Aerospace Medicine Advisory Committee, NASA (1988-1993) **Civic:** Financial Secretary, Mission, Latter-day Saints Church, Columbus, OH (1997-1999) **Military Service:** U.S. Army, World War II **Creative Works:** Editor, Contributor, "Units, Symbols, and Terminology for Plant Physiology" (1996); Co-author, "Plant Physiology," Fourth Edition (1992) **Awards:** Founder's Award, American Society for Gravitational and Space Biology (1994); Merit Award, Botanical Society of America (1982) **Memberships:** American Society for Gravitational and Space Biology; Botanical Society of America; Sigma Xi; Phi Kappa Phi **Marquis Who's Who Honors:** Albert Nelson Marquis Lifetime Achievement Award **Avocations:** Photography **Religion:** Mormon

Dana G. Bradford II

Title: Partner; Lawyer **Industry:** Law and Legal Services **Company Name:** Smith, Gambrell & Russell, LLP **Date of Birth:** 09/29/1948 **Place of Birth:** Coral Gables **State/Country of Origin:** FL/USA **Parents:** Dana Gibson Bradford; Jeanette (Ellis) Bradford **Marital Status:** Married **Spouse Name:** Donna P. Bradford (04/14/1984); Mary E. Bradford (06/20/1970, Divorced 01/1982) **Children:** Jeffrey Dana; Shannon Claire **Education:** JD, Duke University School of Law (1973); BA, University of Florida (1970) **Certifications:** Board Certified Civil Trial Lawyer, Board of Legal Specialization and Education, The Florida Bar **Career:** Partner, Smith, Gambrell & Russell, LLP, Jacksonville, FL (2000-Present); Partner, Baumer, Bradford & Walters, Jacksonville, FL (1982-2000); Partner, Mahoney, Hadlow & Adams, Jacksonville, FL (1973-1982) **Career Related:** Member, Florida Supreme Court Commission on Professionalism (1996-1998); Chairman, Florida Board of Bar Examiners (1992-1993) **Civic:** Member, Leadership Jacksonville Inc. (1982); Special Counsel, Sports Authority, Jacksonville, FL **Military Service:** Honorable Discharge, United States Army Reserve (1980); Captain, United States Army Reserve (1972-1980); Commissioned Second Lieutenant, United States Army ROTC **Creative Works:** Contributor, Chapters to Books; Contributor, Articles, Professional Journals; Contributor, Treatises and Continuing Legal Education Materials **Awards:** Named, AV Rated Attorney, Martindale-Hubbell (1982-Present); Named, Best Lawyer, Best Lawyers in America (2019); Named, Lawyer of the Year, Best Lawyers in America (2019); Listed, Florida Super Lawyers (2006-2018); Lifetime Achievement Award, America's Top 100 Attorneys, FL **Memberships:** Board of Governors, Boys & Girls Clubs of Northeast Florida (2002-Present); Chairman of Trial Sections, Jacksonville Bar Association (1989-1990) **Bar Admissions:** United States Court of Appeals for the Eleventh Circuit (1982); United States District Court for the Southern District of Florida (1979); United States District Court for the Northern District of Florida (1979); Supreme Court of the United States (1979); United States District Court for the Middle District of Florida (1974); United States Court of Appeals for the Fifth Circuit (1974) **Marquis Who's Who Honors:** Albert Nelson Marquis Lifetime Achievement Award; Marquis Who's Who Top Professional **Avocations:** Golfing; Sports; Traveling **Political Affiliations:** Republican **Religion:** Methodist

M. Christine Braithwaite

Title: Elementary School Educator (Retired) **Industry:** Education/Educational Services **Date of Birth:** 09/09/1945 **Place of Birth:** Toledo **State/Country of Origin:** OH/USA **Parents:** John William Braithwaite; Eleanor Margaret (Gedert) Braithwaite **Marital Status:** Married **Spouse Name:** David R. Johnston (08/20/1996) **Education:** Bachelor of Science in Education, University of Toledo (1968) **Certifications:** Certified Private Glider Pilot, Advanced Ground Instructor (1986) **Career:** Teacher, 1st-8th Grades, Toledo Public Schools (1958-1999) **Career Related:** Resource Facilitator, Project S.T.A.R., Toledo Public Schools **Civic:** Volunteer Work for State Senator (2009-2014) **Memberships:** Vice President, Women's Educational Club; Past President, Adrian Soaring Club; Toledo Federation of Retired Teachers; Lucas County Retired Teachers Association; Ohio Retired Teachers Association; Women Soaring Pilots Association; Chair, Program of Works Committee, Delta Kappa Gamma **Marquis Who's Who Honors:** Albert Nelson Marquis Lifetime Achievement Award **Why did you become involved in your profession or industry:** Mrs. Braithwaite became involved in her profession after initially aspiring to become a chemical engineer. However, she found it difficult to secure employment in the field, and decided to become a kindergarten teacher instead. **Avocations:** Soaring; Photography; Travel; Computers; Gardening; Sewing; Gem mining

Michelle L. Brandriss

Title: Founder, President **Company Name:** NameBubbles, LLC **Date of Birth:** 08/13/1969 **Place of Birth:** Sacramento **State/Country of Origin:** CA/USA **Marital Status:** Married **Spouse Name:** David **Children:** Cooper **Education:** BA in International/Global Studies, University of the Pacific (1991) **Career:** Founder, President, NameBubbles, LLC (2009-Present) **Civic:** Donor, NameBubbles Giving Program, Blessings in a Backpack (2009-Present); Co-founding Member, Troy Rensselaer Women's Organization **Awards:** Excellence in Small Business Award, U.S. Small Business Administration (2017); Gold Medal Winner, Mom's Choice Awards (2014); Seal of Approval, Parent Tested Parent Approved (PTPA Media Inc.) (2012, 2014); Named Outstanding Product, iParenting Media Awards (2009); SheKnows Parenting Award for Best School Supply, SheKnows Media, LLC; Listee, "Back to School List," The New York Times **Memberships:** Women Presidents' Organization (WPO) (2020) **Marquis Who's Who Honors:** Marquis Who's Who Top Professional **To what do you attribute your success:** Mrs. Brandriss attributes her success to setting up her short-term and long-term goals and checking them off. **Why did you become involved in your profession or industry:** Mrs. Brandriss was working in advertising and her son was 18 months old; when you have a young child, you are suddenly exposed to all these new products in this new area. When she was dropping him off at daycare, she would use masking tape and Sharpies. The product just made sense. **Thoughts on Life:** Mrs. Brandriss is an entrepreneur at heart who works to create a brand and team that produces the best quality personalized waterproof labels to help keep families happy and organized. After working for multiple companies during the dotcom boom and bust, followed by years in the advertising industry, she has seen firsthand how important both internal morale and a good business model and budgets are for long-term growth of a startup. It is her goal to be a fair and mindful employer while always delivering the best customer experience. Mrs. Brandriss is proud to be a woman-owned manufacturer with highly valued and hardworking employees producing superior products. NameBubbles utilizes top of the line materials and supports an open and collaborative environment for employees to experiment and create high quality label products that customers have come to expect. Inspired by her son's need for labels at daycare, NameBubbles has grown from an idea in a basement over 10 years ago, to a thriving business that continually grows a loyal customer following around the world. Established to help busy families stay organized, the creation of NameBubbles' dishwasher and laundry safe labels combines style and function to create a series of products for any stage in life.

Earlene Brasher

Title: Music Educator **Industry:** Education/Educational Services **Date of Birth:** 05/02/1932 **Place of Birth:** Albertville **State/Country of Origin:** AL/USA **Parents:** David Frank; Luna (Pearson) Decker **Spouse Name:** Francis Eugene Brasher (1956-1976) **Children:** Julia Brasher Thorn; Celia Kay Brasher (Deceased) **Education:** PhD, The University of Southern Mississippi (1988); MusM, Georgia State University (1981); MusM in Sacred Music, New Orleans Baptist Theological Seminary (1959); MusB, The University of Alabama (1952) **Career:** Coordinator of Choral Music, DeKalb County Board of Education (1989-2002); Organist, Briarcliff Baptist Church (1979-2002); Elementary Music Specialist, DeKalb County Board of Education (1979-1989); Music Resource Teacher, NOLA Public Schools (1970-1979); Music Supervisor, Thomasville City Schools (1969-1970); Music Teacher, Whitesburg Elementary School (1965-1969); Organist, First Baptist Church, Columbia, SC (1954-1956); Choral Director, Tuscaloosa County High School (1953-1954) **Career Related:** The Atlanta Boy Choir (1995-Present); Advisory Board, Atlanta Young Singers of Callanwolde (1989-2002); Education Advisory Board, Spivey Hall, Clayton State University (1990) **Civic:** Chorus Member, Atlanta Symphony Orchestra (1979-1996) **Awards:** Mary Clark Award, Decatur Civic Chorus (2003); Lifetime Achievement Award, Georgia Music Educators Association (2001); Miss Alabama (1952); President, Student Government Association (1951-1952) **Memberships:** Advisory Committee for Young Audiences, Atlanta Symphony Associates (1989-Present); Music Educators National Conference, National Association for Music Education; American Choral Directors Association; Alpha Delta Kappa **Marquis Who's Who Honors:** Albert Nelson Marquis Lifetime Achievement Award; Marquis Who's Who Top Professional **Why did you become involved in your profession or industry:** Ms. Brasher became involved in her profession because she was inspired by her piano teacher from junior high school. Ms. Brasher and her teacher attended a college recruitment event together, and during the event she decided to attend the college. **Religion:** Presbyterian

Sylvia A. Brodsky

Title: Psychologist, Consultant **Industry:** Social Work **Parents:** Edward Cassell; Goldie (Yarnoff) Cassell **Marital Status:** Widow **Spouse Name:** Benjamin Z. Brodsky **Children:** Allen; Sandra; Marla **Education:** Certified in Family Therapy, Family Institute of Philadelphia (1974); Master of Education, Temple University (1949); Bachelor of Arts, Temple University (1945) **Certifications:** Licensed Psychologist, Pennsylvania (1949) **Career:** Private Practice, Philadelphia, PA (1982-2005); Family Therapist, Therapeutic Center, Fox Chase, PA (1978-1982); Consultant, Bensalem School District, Pennsylvania (1976-1978); Family Therapist, Paley Day Care Center, Philadelphia, PA (1972-1975); Director, Early Childhood Education, Germantown Jewish Center, Philadelphia, PA (1947-1949); Director, Social Services, Jewish Federation, Camden County, New Jersey (1945-1947) **Career Related:** Montgomery County Mental Health Committee, Norristown, PA (1983-Present); Board of Directors, Carbon, Monroe, Pike Drug and Alcohol Commission, Stroudsburg, PA; Board of Directors, Aldersgate Youth Service Bureau, Willow Grove, PA **Civic:** First Vice President, York Road Council, Abington, PA (1962-1972); Chairperson, Anti-Defamation League of B'nai B'rith Women, Philadelphia, PA (1969-1971) **Creative Works:** Established, Sylvia A. Brodsky Psychological Walk-In Service at Ben Gurion University (2006); Established, Outpatient Clinic at Residential Treatment Center for Children in Jerusalem **Awards:** Outstanding Mental Health Volunteer Award, Red Cross for Disaster Relief Efforts (2007); Outstanding Service Award, Jewish Women International (1998); Certificate of Merit for Girl Scouting Beyond Bars, Girl Scouts of America (1997); Distinguished Service Award, Southeast Mental Health Association, Philadelphia (1989); Certificate of Appreciation, Eastern State School and Hospital, Trevose, PA (1989); Achievement Award, March of Dimes, Cheltenham Township, PA (1970) **Memberships:** American Psychological Association; Pennsylvania Psychological Association; Philadelphia Society of Clinical Psychologists; Society of Personality Assessment **Why did you become involved in your profession or industry:** Ms. Brodsky initially became involved in her profession after having studied to become a doctor. She eventually decided to take a course in psychology and found that field very illuminating.

Paul Broussard

Title: Pastor **Industry:** Religious **Company Name:** Saint Leo IV Roman Catholic Church **Place of Birth:** Abbeville **State/Country of Origin:** LA/USA **Education:** MA, Pontifical University of Saint Thomas Aquinas, Rome, Italy (1998); STB in Sacred Theology, Pontifical University of Saint Thomas Aquinas, Rome, Italy (1997); BA in Philosophy, Saint Joseph Seminary College (1994) **Career:** Pastor, Saint Leo IV Roman Catholic Church (2001-Present); Roman Catholic Priest (1998-Present) **Memberships:** Equestrian Order of the Holy Sepulchre of Jerusalem; The Military and Hospitaller Order of Saint Lazarus of Jerusalem; Knights of Columbus **To what do you attribute your success:** Father Broussard attributes his success to his faithful parents and the fellow priests who worked in his home parish. **Why did you become involved in your profession or industry:** Father Broussard became involved in his profession because he was inspired by the priests in his parish. **Religion:** Roman Catholic **Thoughts on Life:** Father Broussard states, "faith through truth."

Laura Brown

Title: Editor-in-chief **Industry:** Writing and Editing **Company Name:** InStyle Magazine **Date of Birth:** 5/27/1974 **State/Country of Origin:** Australia **Parents:** Lola Brown **Education:** Coursework, Charles Sturt University, Bathurst, Australia **Career:** Editor-in-chief, InStyle Magazine (2016-Present); With, Harper's Bazaar, NY (2005-2016); Articles Editor, Details Magazine; Senior Editor, W Magazine; With, Talk Magazine; Features Editor, Harper's Bazaar Australia; Freelancer; Production Editor, Mode **Creative Works:** Appearance, "Good Morning America," "Today," and "American Morning" **Awards:** Best Fashion and Beauty Cover, American Society of Magazine Editors (2016)

Justin Bryan

Title: Partner **Industry:** Law and Legal Services **Company Name:** McCathern PLLC **Date of Birth:** 12/27/1984 **Marital Status:** Married **Spouse Name:** Jessica Bryan **Children:** Anderson; Benjamin **Education:** JD, Texas Tech University School of Law (2010); BS, Political Science, Philosophy, Texas A&M University (2007) **Career:** Partner, McCathern, PLLC (2016-Present);Attorney, Fee, Smith, Sharp & Vitullo, LLP (2014-2016); JAG, Judge Advocate General Corps, United States Armed Forces (2010-2014) **Military Service:** Judge Advocate General, United States Armed Forces **Awards:** Super Lawyers Rising Star (2019, 2020) **Memberships:** American Bar Association; Texas Aggie Bar Association; Dallas Bar Association; Dallas Association of Young Lawyers; Phi Delta Phi; Corps of Cadets **Bar Admissions:** Texas; U.S. District Courts for Texas; Court of Appeals for the Armed Forces; Air Force Court of Criminal Appeals **Marquis Who's Who Honors:** Marquis Who's Who Top Professional **To what do you attribute your success:** Mr. Bryan attributes his success to his role models, professors, senior military officers, colleagues and his employers. They deserve all the credit for any success of his. Whether professional or personal success with my loving family, he is the product of the investment of others who understood the importance of helping others. He hopes to provide the same support and opportunities for as many others as possible. **Why did you become involved in your profession or industry:** Mr. Bryan has desired becoming a lawyer for a long time because the values instilled in him resonate strongly with fairness, equality, and justice.

Richard Snowden Bucy

Title: Aerospace Engineering and Mathematics Educator, Consultant **Date of Birth:** 07/20/1935 **Place of Birth:** Washington **State/Country of Origin:** DC/USA **Year of Passing:** 2019 **Parents:** Edmond Howard; Marie (Glinke) Bucy **Marital Status:** Married **Spouse Name:** Ofelia **Children:** Phillip; Erwin **Education:** PhD in Math., Statistics, University California-Berkeley (1963); BS in Mathematics, Massachusetts Institute of Technology (1957) **Career:** Professor Associe, French Government, NICE (1983-1984, 1990-1991); Professor Associe, French Government, Toulouse (1973-1974); Professor of Aerospace Engineering and Mathematics, University of Southern California, Los Angeles (1966); Associate Professor of Aerospace Engineering, University of Colorado, Boulder (1965-1966); Assistant Professor of Mathematics, University of Maryland, College Park (1964-1965); Research Assistant, University of California, Berkeley (1961-1963); Researcher in Mathematics, Research Institute Advanced Studies, Towson, MD (1960-1961, 1963-1964) **Career Related:** Visiting Professor, Technische Universitt Berlin (1975-1976); Co-director, NATO Advanced Study Institute on Non-linear Scholastic Problems, Algarve, Portugal; Consultant **Creative Works:** Author, "Filtering for Stochastic Processes" (1968, Second edition, 1987); Nonlinear Stochastic Problems (1984); Lectures on Discrete Filtering Theory (1994); Editor, Journal Information Sciences, Journal Mathematics Modeling and Science Computing; Founding, Editor Stochastics (1971-1977); Contributor, Articles to Professional Publications **Awards:** Recipient, Humboldt Prize (1975-1976); NATO Research Grantee (1979) **Memberships:** Fellow, IEEE; American Mathematical Society **Political Affiliations:** Republican

Michael Buffer

Title: Boxing Announcer; Actor **Industry:** Media & Entertainment **Date of Birth:** 11/2/1944 **Place of Birth:** Lancaster **State/Country of Origin:** PA/USA **Marital Status:** Married **Children:** Two Sons **Career:** Boxing Announcer, Boxing Matches Broadcasts, DAZN (2018); Guest Announcer, United States Grand Prix (2017); Guest Announcer, Indianapolos 500 (1999); Boxing Ring Announcer (1982); Announcer, Wrestling Matches, World Championship Wrestling (WCW); Announcer, UFC Fights; Announcer, Various Sporting Events Including the World Series, Stanley Cup Final, NBA Finals, Volunteer 500 at Bristol Motor Speedway, and NFL Playoff Games **Creative Works:** Actor, "Dumbo" (2019); Appearance, "Holmes & Watson" (2018); Appearance, Announcer, "Creed II" (2018); Appearance, Announcer, "Creed" (2015); Appearance, Announcer, "Grudge Match" (2013); Appearance, "Maravilla, la Pelicula" (2013); Appearance, "Vanilla Ice Archive" (2012); Appearance, Announcer, "The Green Card Tour: Live from the O2 Arena" (2011); Announcer, "The Fighter" (2010); Appearance, Announcer, "Love and Other Drugs" (2010); Appearance, Announcer, "2012" (2009); Actor, "You Don't Mess with the Zohan" (2008); Appearance, "Cornered: A Life Caught in the Ring" (2008); Voice Actor, "BoxinBuddies: Knockout Juvenile Diabetes" (2006); Appearance, Announcer, "Rocky Balboa" (2006); Appearance, "The L.A. Riot Spectacular" (2005); Appearance, Announcer, "Against the Ropes" (2004); Appearance, "Fade to Black" (2004); Appearance, "Dickie Roberts: Former Child Star" (2003); Appearance, Announcer, "Game Over" (2003); Appearance, "More than Famous" (2003); Announcer, "Promi-Boxen" (2002-2013); Appearance, Announcer, "Ready to Rumble" (2000); Appearance, Announcer, "The Extreme Adventures of Super Dave" (2000); Appearance, Announcer, "Play It to the Bone" (1999); Appearance, "Ready 2 Rumble Boxing" (1999); Announcer, "ClayFighter 63 1/3" (1997); Announcer, "Pitball" (1996); Appearance, Announcer, "Virtuosity" (1995); Appearance, Announcer, "Prize Fighter" (1993); Announcer, Master of Ceremonies, "Sky Sports World Championship Boxing" (1991-2017); Appearance, Announcer, "Rocky V" (1990); Appearance, Announcer, "Harlem Nights" (1989); Announcer, "HBO Boxing" (1988-2017); Appearance, Announcer, "Homeboy" (1988); Appearances, Announcer, Actor, Numerous Television Series **Awards:** Inductee, International Sports Hall of Fame (2019)

Jennifer A. Burget

Title: Owner, Hearing Instrument Specialist **Industry:** Health, Wellness and Fitness **Company Name:** Artisan Hearing Technologies LLC **Children:** Five Children **Career:** Owner, Artisan Hearing Technologies LLC (2015-Present); Hearing Instrument Specialist, Microtone Hearing Instruments (2011-2014); Certified Nursing Assistant, Ellen Memorial Nursing Home (1998-2014); Audiology Technician, Wayne Memorial Hospital (2004-2011) **Awards:** Named Healthcare Hero (2020); Distinguished Woman's Award, Distinguished Women's Magazine (2018) **To what do you attribute your success:** Mrs. Burget came from a very difficult upbringing. She lived on her own since she was 15 years old, working between two and four jobs at a time. Learning from the mistakes that her parents made is what drew her to her success. She was determined to "break the cycle" and not let her children live that way. Today, all of her children so far are in college and her daughter, Veronika Yerke, is following in her footsteps to create a family business for years to come. Her love for hearing will live on longer than she will through the heart of her family to continue to help. **Why did you become involved in your profession or industry:** Mrs. Burget worked in a nursing home for six years. While working there, she noticed that most of the people that lived there could not hear her. Looking at statistics, she noticed that two out of three people over the age of 70 experience hearing loss. It makes life difficult if they cannot communicate with their healthcare providers or their families. She created a program to create better lives for people. Her program, "Smart Hearing for Life," will help those in need now and those in need with terminal illness at no charge. Through her time in her career, her husband became deaf without the use of hearing aids due to kidney failure. This has made her even more driven to help every person she can. **Thoughts on Life:** Mrs. Burget is a part of her local builders association. Her main goal is to also prevent hearing loss in the future as well. "Protect your hearing now or come see me later," she said.

Charlene Burr

Title: Administrative Assistant to the Managing Director **Industry:** Financial Services **Company Name:** Santora CPA Group **Parents:** Joan Carpenter **Marital Status:** Married **Spouse Name:** Tony Burr (1/23/1982) **Children:** Joshua; Jennifer **Education:** AA in Business Administration, Goldey-Beacom College (2012) **Career:** Administrative Assistant to the Managing Director, Santora CPA Group (2015-Present); Instructional Coordinator, Reading ASSIST Institute (2011-2015); Administrative Assistant, New Hire and Division Support, Avon Products, Inc. (2005-2009); Division Sales Administrative Assistant, Avon Products, Inc. (1999-2005); Fundraiser, Large Order Clerk, Olsten Staffing Services (1998-1999); Customer Service Agent, Telephone Support Specialist, Olsten Staffing Services (1996-1998); Head Teacher, Hockessin Friends Pre-School (1991-1998); Mail Room, Secretary, Administrative Assistant, DuPont, DE (1977-1982) **Civic:** Former PTA Coordinator; Various School Committees; Former Volunteer, NAMI; Former Board Member, Family Education Center **Memberships:** Administrative Professionals Today; Business Management Daily **To what do you attribute your success:** She wants to do a great job, she wants to excel at what she does, and she loves working. **Why did you become involved in your profession or industry:** Ms. Burr has always had a love of business, in high school she took college prep and business. Upon graduation her parents told her if she wanted to go to college she would have to find her own way. Out of high school she started working for a big company DuPont, and as long as she received a B they reimbursed her for her education. So she was able to work and go to school and they paid. **Avocations:** Gardening; Reading; Family time

Michael Daniel Buzash

Title: Professor Emeritus **Industry:** Education/Educational Services **Company Name:** Indiana State University **Parents:** Mike Buzash; Flora (Urden) Buzash **Marital Status:** Single **Education:** Postgraduate Coursework, University of Wisconsin (1963-1969); MA in Romance Languages, University of Western Reserve (Now Case Western Reserve University) (1960); BA in French and Spanish, Indiana State University (1953); Coursework, University of Mexico, Mexico City, Mexico (1952) **Certifications:** Certified de Stage, University of Illinois (1995); Certified de Stage, Michigan State University (1994); Certified de Stage, University of Wisconsin (1993); Certified Superior Rating, American Council on the Teaching of Foreign Languages (1986); Certified de Stage, Purdue University (1984-1986) **Career:** Professor Emeritus, Indiana State University (1998-Present); Associate Professor, Romance Languages, Indiana State University (1959-1998); Director, Pilot Program in French and Spanish Honors, Summer, Indiana State University (1981-1997); Director, French Honors Program, Indiana State University (1980-1997); Teacher, French, Spanish, English, Lawrence High School (1954-1959) **Creative Works:** Author, "ERIC Database" (1990-1998); Contributor, Honors Program Research Projects (1986, 1992, 1998); Contributor, European Studies Conference (1971-1997); Author, Honors Edition, "Revision Pratique de Francais" (1994-1996); Author, "Repetition et Acquisition Pratique" (1983-1995); Contributor, "Proceedings of Black Studies Conferences" (1989-1991); Author, Honors Edition, "Revision Pratique de Francais" (1989-1990); Author, Manual and Tape, "Exercices Pratiques de Francais Oral" (1983-1990); Contributor, Book Chapter, "From Third World to One World" (1988); Author, "Revision Pratique de Francais" (1980-1986); Author, Honors Edition, "Revision Pratique de Francais" (1981) **Awards:** Meritorious Service Award, Scottish Rite Council of Deliberation (2018); 50-Year Award, Masons (2006); Service and Honorary Teaching Awards, Theta Alpha Phi (1967, 1969, 1975, 1989, 1994, 1996, 1997, 1998, 2005) **Marquis Who's Who Honors:** Albert Nelson Marquis Lifetime Achievement Award

Elizabeth Byam

Title: Chief Operating Officer **Industry:** Technology **Date of Birth:** 10/31/1949 **Place of Birth:** Cooperstown **State/Country of Origin:** NY/USA **Parents:** Harmon Leigh Byam; Elizabeth Virginia (Baldo) Byam **Children:** Leslie Anne Epps Richards **Education:** MBA, University of New Mexico (1997); Postgraduate Coursework, Columbia Southern University School of Law (1976-1978); BA, Georgia State University (1972) **Certifications:** Project Management Professional (PMP); Systems Professional **Career:** Chief Operating Officer, Advisory Platform Solution (2009-Present); Managing Partner, Benetechs (2018-Present); Program Director, Advisory Platform Solutions (2005-2009); Senior Program Manager, Government Telecom Inc. (2002-2004); Director, Business Solutions, Explore Reasoning Systems (1998-2001); Enterprise Applications Program Manager, Intel Corporation, Rio Rancho, NM (1992-1997); Owner, Principal Consultant, MEB Associates, Winnetka, CA (1984-1992); Senior Consultant, Field Manager, Computer Dynamics, Woodland Hills, CA (1983-1984); Consultant, Computer Programming (1978-1982); Programmer, Analyst, Southern Airways (1975-1976); Programmer, Coastal States Life Insurance Company (1973-1975) **Career Related:** Speaker, Career Planning and Information Processing, Local Schools, Professional Conferences, Meetings, Radio Shows **Civic:** Board of Directors, Opera Guild of Southern California (1984-1988) **Memberships:** Publications Director, Treasurer, Data Processing Management Association (1988-1991); President, Association of Women in Computing (1985-1987); Project Management Institute **Marquis Who's Who Honors:** Albert Nelson Marquis Lifetime Achievement Award; Marquis Who's Who Top Professional **Why did you become involved in your profession or industry:** Growing up, Ms. Byam enjoyed math and science, as well as being social. Searching for a career, she enrolled in a training program for computer programming. From there, her career progressed organically. **Avocations:** Reading; Crafting; Traveling; Mentoring; Playing music; Spending time with family

S. Sammy Cacciatore

Title: Partner; Attorney **Company Name:** Nance Cacciatore **Date of Birth:** 08/2/1942 **Place of Birth:** Tampa **State/Country of Origin:** FL/USA **Parents:** Sam Cacciatore; Margarita Cacciatore **Marital Status:** Married **Spouse Name:** Carolyn Michels (08/10/1963) **Children:** Elaine Michel; Sammy Michel **Education:** JD, Stetson University School of Law, Gulf Port, FL (1966); BA, Stetson University, DeLand, FL (1966); AA, Orlando Junior College (1962) **Certifications:** Board Certified in Medical Malpractice, American Board of Professional Liability Attorneys; Board Certified in Civil Trial Law, The Florida Bar; Board Certified in Civil Trial Advocacy, National Board of Trial Advocacy **Career:** Partner, Nance, Cacciatore, Hamilton, Barger, Nance & Cacciatore (Now Nance Cacciatore), Melbourne, FL (2003-Present); Private Practice, Melbourne, FL (1967-Present); Partner, Nance, Cacciatore & Hamilton (1999-2003); Partner, Nance, Cacciatore, Sisserson, Duryea & Hamilton (1991-1999); Partner, Nance, Cacciatore, Sisserson & Duryea (1983-1991); Partner, Nance, Cacciatore & Sisserson (1977-1983); Partner, Nance & Cacciatore (1970-1977); With, Law Offices of James H. Nance (1967-1970); With, Associate Firm, Billings, Frederick and Rumberger, Orlando, FL (1966-1967); Assistant Public Defender, Ninth Judicial Circuit Court, State of Florida (1966) **Civic:** Trustee, Stetson University (2000-Present); Board of Overseers, Stetson University College of Law (1995-Present); Chairperson, Stetson University College of Law (2006-2008); Trustee, A. Max Brewer Memorial Law Library, Brevard County, FL (1972-1976); Chairman, A. Max Brewer Memorial Law Library, Brevard County, FL (1972-1975); Overseer, Stetson University College of Law **Creative Works:** Contributor, Articles, Professional Journals; Contributor, Chapters, Books **Awards:** Named, America's Top 100 Attorneys (2016); B. Masterson Professional Award, Florida Justice Association (2011); President's Award, Florida Justice Association (1983); President's Award, Brevard County Bar Association (1975) **Memberships:** Chairman, Constitutional Revision Committee, The Florida Bar (1997-Present); Fellow, Board Director, Florida Justice Association (1970-Present); Jury Instruction Committee, Florida Supreme Court, The Florida Bar (2001-2010); Chairman, The Florida Bar (1996, 1998-1999); Legislative Committee, The Florida Bar (1995-1999); Executive Committee, The Florida Bar (1995-1999) **Bar Admissions:** District of Columbia Court of Appeals (1982); U.S. Court of Appeals for the Eleventh Circuit (1981); Supreme Court of the United States (1971); U.S. Court of Appeals for the Fifth Circuit (1967); U.S. District Court, Middle District, State of Florida (1966); State of Florida (1966)

Rose Marie Taylor Calhoun, RN, MEd, CPHQ, MBBLSS

Title: Healthcare Quality Consultant **Industry:** Medicine & Health Care **Date of Birth:** 08/24/1950 **Place of Birth:** Kaufman **State/Country of Origin:** TX/USA **Parents:** Harvey Stokely Taylor; Theresa Marie (Dendy) Taylor **Marital Status:** Married **Spouse Name:** William Benjamin Calhoun III **Education:** Master of Education, University of Houston (1980); Bachelor of Science in Nursing, Texas Woman's University (1976) **Certifications:** Lean Six Sigma Master Black Belt (2014); Certified Professional in Healthcare Quality (2007) **Career:** Healthcare Quality Consultant (2018-Present); Adjunct Professor, Nursing for Target Populations, The University of Texas at Houston (2016-2017); Director Quality and Outcomes Management, Texas Children's Health Plan (2007-2017); Associate Vice President of Quality, Amerigroup Texas (2006); Manager, Clinical Quality Improvement, Blue Cross of California (1999-2006); Chief Executive Officer, The Victorian, Ventura, CA (1994-1998); Administrator, Chief Executive Officer, Victoria Care Center, Ventura, CA (1993-1998); Vice President, Channel Islands Associates, Camarillo, CA (1990-1992) **Career Related:** Health Services Value Based Purchasing and Quality Improvement Committee, State of Texas (2016-Present); Chair, Health Sciences Advisory Board, Oxnard Adult School, CA (1990-1999) **Civic:** Special Attractions Committee, Houston Livestock Show and Rodeo (2006-Present); Endowed William and Rose Calhoun Scholarships at University of Houston and Southwestern University **Creative Works:** Contributor, Journal of Managed Care Nursing (2014, 2015, 2018); Contributor, Chest (2015); Contributor, Ethnicity & Disease (2007); Contributor, Journal of School Health (1982); Contributor, The American Journal of Maternal Child Nursing (1977) **Awards:** 150 Top Nurses in Houston, Houston Chronicle (2017); Seven Best of Blue Awards from Blue Cross Blue Shield Association for Quality Improvement Projects (2001-2005) **Memberships:** Daughters of the Republic of Texas (2014-Present); Sigma Theta Tau (1976-Present) **Religion:** Methodist

Blake Callahan, CRFP, CPA, CVA, CCIFP

Title: Chief Financial Officer **Industry:** Financial Services **Company Name:** MC Builder LLC; Blake Callahan, CPA **Marital Status:** Married **Spouse Name:** Megan **Children:** Sydni; Cooper; Noah **Education:** BS in Accounting/Management, University of Tennessee at Chattanooga (1998) **Career:** Chief Financial Officer, MC Builders, LLC (2013-Present); Owner, Blake Callahan, Certified Public Accountant, CVA (2013-Present) **Memberships:** American Institute of Certified Public Accountants (AICPA); Tennessee Institute of Certified Public Accountants (Now Tennessee Society of Certified Public Accountants (TSCPA)) **Marquis Who's Who Honors:** Marquis Who's Who Top Professional **To what do you attribute your success:** Mr. Callahan attributes his success to hard work, dedication and sleepless nights. **Why did you become involved in your profession or industry:** Mr. Callahan grew up on a farm and did plenty of construction. He was always good at math; it was his favorite subject, so he went in that direction in college. **Avocations:** Traveling

Magda Campbell, MD

Title: Professor Emeritus; Child Psychiatrist; Researcher **Industry:** Education/Educational Services **Company Name:** New York University **Date of Birth:** 01/22/1928 **Place of Birth:** Subotica **State/Country of Origin:** Former Yugoslavia **Parents:** Bela Pijukovic; Marija Lipozencic **Marital Status:** Widowed **Spouse Name:** Francis P. Campbell (1962, Deceased 2008) **Children:** Maria D.; John F. **Education:** MD, University of Belgrade, Former Yugoslavia (1953) **Certifications:** Diplomate in Psychiatry, Child Psychiatry, American Board of Psychiatry and Neurology **Career:** Professor Emeritus, New York University, New York, NY (1995-Present); Director, Training Education, New York University (1990-1991); Director, Division of Child Adolescent Psychiatry, New York University (1987-1991); Teaching Assistant to Professor of Psychiatry, New York University, New York, NY (1963-1995) **Creative Works:** Co-author, "Clinical Evaluation of Psychotropic Drugs for Psychiatric Disorders" (1993); Co-author, "Child and Adolescent Psychopharmacology" (1985); Contributor, 225 Articles, Professional Journals; Contributor, Chapters, Books **Awards:** Virginia Q. Anthony Outstanding Woman Leader Award (2013); Grantee, National Institute of Mental Health (1973-1995) **Memberships:** Fellow, Emeritus, American College of Neuropsychopharmacology; American Academy of Child Adolescent Psychiatry; American Psychiatric Association **Marquis Who's Who Honors:** Albert Nelson Marquis Lifetime Achievement Award **Avocations:** Reading; Gardening

Kimberly Cargile

Title: Owner **Industry:** Business Management/Business Services **Company Name:** A Therapeutic Alternative **Education:** BS in Liberal Studies and Psychology, Focus on Social Justice, Humboldt State University, CA (2006); AA in University Studies, College of the Redwoods, CA (2003) **Career:** Owner, A Therapeutic Alternative; Owner, Khemia Manufacturing; Owner, Napa Cannabis Collective; Owner, Yolo Family Farms Inc.; Owner, Davis Cannabis Collective; Owner, Dixon Wellness; Director, Owner, Woodland Roots Inc. **Civic:** Medical Cannabis Patients' Rights Advocate, National Organization for Reform of Marijuana Laws, California Growers Association, California Cannabis Industry Association, Women Grow, The National Cannabis Industry Association (2007-Present) **Awards:** Best Cannabis Advocate, Sacramento News & Review; Luminary Nominee, NAWBO; 5 Women to Watch, Sacramento News & Review; 40 Under 40, Marijuana Venture Magazine; Women Who Mean Business Award, Sacramento Business Journal; 40 Under 40, Sacramento Business Journal **To what do you attribute your success:** Ms. Cargile has experienced considerable hardships in her career. She's never relented, and believes that her mindset and mission are what sustain her success. She lives by the motto, "if you don't give up, you will eventually win." **Why did you become involved in your profession or industry:** Ms. Cargile became involved in her industry while she attended Humboldt State University. It is there that she began studying medicinal cannabis, which, despite its centuries-long practical use, was banned in the U.S. in 1937. She spent two more years in college, fully immersing herself in social justice studies, which prepared her to advocate for the systemically oppressed. In the time since, Ms. Cargile has sat on advocacy boards and helped to pass local and state pro-cannabis legislation. She has also conducted over 100 cannabis education tours for state and local governments, during which she discusses the industry and science behind cannabis. Today, Ms. Cargile owns eight state-licensed companies, including five dispensaries, two farms and one manufacturing company.

Ira Harris Carmen, PhD

Title: Professor Emeritus **Industry:** Education/Educational Services **Company Name:** University of Illinois **Date of Birth:** 12/03/1934 **Place of Birth:** Boston **State/Country of Origin:** MA/USA **Parents:** Jacob Carmen; Lida (Rosenman) Carmen **Marital Status:** Married **Spouse Name:** Lawrence Lowell Putnam (03/16/2000); Sandra Vineberg (09/06/1958, Divorced 06/1999) **Children:** Gail Deborah; Amy Rebecca **Education:** PhD, University of Michigan (1964); MA, University of Michigan (1959); BA, University of New Hampshire (1957) **Career:** Professor Emeritus of Political Science, University of Illinois (2009-Present); Professor of Political Science, University of Illinois (1968-2009); Associate Professor, Coe College (1966-1968); Assistant Professor, Ball State University (1963-1966) **Career Related:** Member, Institute of Genomic Biology, University of Illinois (2004-2009); Visiting Lecturer, Tamkang University, Taiwan (1991); Member, Recombinant DNA Advisory Committee, National Institutes of Health (1990-1994); Organizer, Numerous International Meetings **Civic:** Guest Delegate, Republican National Convention (1992); Member, President George Bush's Inaugural Educators Advisory Committee (1989); Senior Advisor, Bush-Quayle National Jewish Campaign Committee (1988); Leadership Council, Republican Jewish Coalition **Creative Works:** Author, "Politics in the Laboratory: The Constitution of Human Genomics" (2004); Author, "Cloning and the Constitution" (1986); Author, "Power and Balance" (1978); Author, "Movies, Censorship, and the Law" (1966); Contributor, Articles to Professional Journals **Awards:** Grantee, National Science Foundation (2007-2008); Visiting Scholar, Yale Law School (1981) **Memberships:** Chairman Council, Association for Politics and the Life Sciences (2000-2003); Human Genome Organization; The Phi Beta Kappa Society; American Association for the Advancement of Science **Avocations:** Competitive running **Religion:** Jewish

John Carreyrou

Title: Reporter **Industry:** Writing and Editing **Company Name:** The Wall Street Journal **Place of Birth:** Paris **State/Country of Origin:** France **Parents:** Gérard Carreyrou **Marital Status:** Married **Spouse Name:** Molly Schuetz **Children:** Three Children **Education:** BA in Political Science and Government, Duke University (1994) **Career:** Investigative Reporter, The Wall Street Journal (1999-2019); Dow Jones Newswires **Creative Works:** Author, "Bad Blood: Secrets and Lies in a Silicon Valley Startup" (2018); Contributor, "Damage Control: How Messier Kept Cash Crisis at Vivendi Hidden for Months" (2002); Appearance, Documentary, "The Inventor: Out for Blood in Silicon Valley" **Awards:** Financial Times and McKinsey Business Book of the Year Award (2018); George Polk Awards in Journalism for Financial Reporting (2016); Co-Recipient, Pulitzer Prize for Investigative Reporting (2015); Co-Recipient, Gerald Loeb Award (2015); Co-Recipient, German Marshall Fund's Peter R. Weitz Sr. Prize (2004); Pulitzer Prize for Explanatory Reporting (2003); German Marshall Fund's Peter R. Weitz Jr. Prize (2003)

Betty Jane Edna Carrington, EdD, FACNM

Title: Certified Nurse-midwife, Educator **Date of Birth:** 03/14/1936 **State/Country of Origin:** WV/USA **Parents:** James Henry; Odessa E. Watts **Marital Status:** Widowed **Spouse Name:** Homer Smith Isiah Carrington (08/17/1958, Deceased) **Children:** Michael S.; Lynn Ellen **Education:** EdD, Columbia University (1986); MS, Columbia University (1971); BSN, University of Michigan (1958); Diploma, Walnut Hills High School, Cincinnati, Ohio (1954) **Certifications:** Certified Nurse-midwife **Career:** Retired (1998); Nurse-midwife Research Associate, Department of Obstetrics-gynecology, Harlem Hospital Center (Now NYC Health + Hospitals/Harlem) (1989-1997); Director, Graduate Program in Nurse-midwifery, Columbia University School of Nursing (1986-1991); Associate Professor of Nurse-midwifery, SUNY Downstate Health Sciences University (1979-1986); Director, Nurse-midwifery Service, Maternity-Infant Care Project/Brookdale University Hospital Medical Center Affiliation, Brooklyn, NY (1972-1979) **Career Related:** Consultant, Minority Recruitment and Retention (1981-Present) **Civic:** Second Vice President, Executive Secretary, Recording Secretary, Charter Member, Active Member, National Association of University Women, Northeast Section (2013-2018); Board Member, Alpha Phi Alpha Senior Citizens Center, Jamaica, Queens, NY (2006-2011); Queens Sickle Cell Advocacy Network Inc. **Creative Works:** Contributor, Articles to Professional Journals **Awards:** Award, National Association of University Women (2017); Award for Community Services, Kiwanis of Cambria Heights, NY (2008); Hattie Hemschemeyer Award, American College of Nurse Midwives (2001); Bishop's Cross Award, St. David's Episcopal Church (1997); Fellow, WHO, Tanzania (1983); Distinguished Alumni Award, Michigan State University (1973); Distinguished Service Award, United States Navy; NOGI Award, AUAS **Memberships:** Chairperson, National Program Standards Committee (1994-Present); Chair Division of Accreditation, American College of Nurse Midwives (1999-2004); President, Long Island Branch, National Association of University Women (1986-1990); National Vice President, American College of Nurse Midwives (1973-1974); Sigma Theta Tau International Honor Society of Nursing; Golden Member, Alpha Kappa Alpha Sorority, Incorporated, Epsilon Pi Omega Chapter; Life Member, Fellow, American College of Nurse Midwives **Marquis Who's Who Honors:** Albert Nelson Marquis Lifetime Achievement Award; Marquis Who's Who Top Professional **Avocations:** Knitting; Painting; Advocate for quality healthcare for mothers and babies and persons living with sickle cell disease; Arts and crafts; Handwork; Acrylic and oil painting; Reading; Singing at her church choir

DeVallo Francis Cassidy

Title: Film Manager, Writer, Consultant **Industry:** Media & Entertainment **Date of Birth:** 07/07/1937 **State/Country of Origin:** IL/USA **Parents:** DeVallo Francis Cassidy; Catherine Mary (Crowe) Cassidy **Marital Status:** Single **Education:** Graduate, St. Mary's College, Winona, MN (1959) **Career:** Ex Producer, Stiles-Bishop Productions Inc., Hollywood, CA (1982-Retired); Production Manager, Rapport Films Inc., Hollywood, CA (1988-1990); Production Manager, Colman Group Inc., Hollywood, CA (1982-1988); Production Coordinator, Osmond Productions, Hollywood, CA (1980-1982); Production Coordinator, 7-West, Hollywood, CA (1979); Head Division Writer, McMaster Carr Supply Co., Chicago, IL (1966-1979); Advertising Writer, Planner, Cada Inc., Chicago, IL (1964-1965) **Career Related:** Consultant, Various Waiver Theaters, Los Angeles, CA (1982-1988); Consultant, Various Independent Production Companies, Los Angeles, CA (1982); Director, Various Community and Regional Theatres, Chicago, IL (1964-1979); Consultant, Plays; Consultant, Film; Consultant, TV **Military Service:** Combat Intelligence, U.S. Air Force (1960-1964) **Creative Works:** Author, Poetry Review (1972, 1974); Author, Editor, Skunk Hollow Ski Magazine (1972-1973); Author, Articles, Popular Science (1972); Author, Combat Survival Soft Books (1962-1963); Author, Articles, Popular Mechanics **Awards:** Best in AF (1963) **Memberships:** American Film Institute; National Geographic Society; National Associates, Smithsonian Institute **Marquis Who's Who Honors:** Albert Nelson Marquis Lifetime Achievement Award; Marquis Who's Who Top Professional **Why did you become involved in your profession or industry:** After Mr. Cassidy attended college, he joined the Air Force and they decided to place him in combat intelligence. He started to write up escapes and teach them to the tactical crew members. When Mr. Cassidy was not on a mission he primarily created inquiries and did write-ups on what routes to take and how they could escape. When he got out of the service he wanted to go back into intelligence, however the pay was not what he expected so he went to Chicago to be a writer, he wrote about technical items. Shortly after, he moved to Hollywood, California, he met up with contacts that he met in the service and ended up working for a commercial production company and he also worked for the Osmonds for a while. **Avocations:** Riding; Hiking; Amateur archaeology **Religion:** Roman Catholic

Manuel Castaneda

Title: President **Industry:** Engineering **Company Name:** PLI Systems Inc. **Place of Birth:** , **Marital Status:** Married **Spouse Name:** Rosa **Children:** Brandon; Savannah **Career:** President, PLI Systems Inc. (1987-Present) **Civic:** Volunteer, Oversight Committee for Metro; Co-Founder, Washington County Business Counsel; Board of Trustees, Pacific University; Board Member, Executive Committee, Chairman of the Lawn Committee, Vina Community Bank; Appointed by Governor to the Commission on Hispanic Affairs, State of Oregon; Volunteer Radio Host, KPOO-FM **Awards:** Minority Business of the Year in the State of Oregon, Small Business Administration; Chairman's Award, Hillsborough Chamber of Commerce, Oregon **Memberships:** American Society of Civil Engineers **To what do you attribute your success:** Mr. Castaneda attributes his success to the value of hard work, as well as the influence of his father. **Why did you become involved in your profession or industry:** Mr. Castaneda entered his profession due to the impoverishment he experienced early in life.

Gary L. Catchen, PhD

Title: Professor Emeritus; Nuclear Engineer; Photographer **Date of Birth:** 08/09/1950 **Place of Birth:** Johnstown **State/Country of Origin:** PA/USA **Parents:** Michael Catchen; Sylvia Fay (Levine) Catchen **Marital Status:** Divorced **Spouse Name:** Gwen Davey (04/21/1974, Divorced 2003) **Children:** Aaron Russell; Julian Michael **Education:** Doctor of Philosophy in Chemistry, Columbia University (1979); Bachelor of Arts in German, The Pennsylvania State University (2000); Bachelor of Science in Chemistry, The Pennsylvania State University (1971) **Career:** Professor Emeritus, The Pennsylvania State University, University Park, PA (2014-Present); Professor, The Pennsylvania State University, University Park, PA (1996-2013); Associate Professor, The Pennsylvania State University, University Park, PA (1990-1996); Assistant Professor, Department of Nuclear Engineering, The Pennsylvania State University, University Park, PA (1982-1990); Research Chemist, Conoco Inc., Ponca City, OK (1979-1982) **Military Service:** With, United States Army (1971-1974) **Memberships:** American Chemical Society; American Physical Society; American Association of University Professors **Marquis Who's Who Honors:** Albert Nelson Marquis Lifetime Achievement Award **Why did you become involved in your profession or industry:** Dr. Catchen became involved in his profession because he was always interested in science from an early age. He went to graduate school, then ended up working in an army hospital for three years. Following his service, he benefited from the G.I. Bill and started work as a chemist. **Avocations:** Photography; Reading; History **Thoughts on Life:** Dr. Catchen's father, Michael Catchen, passed away in 2003.

Eric Caturia

Title: Owner **Industry:** Architecture & Construction **Company Name:** Hustad Companies, Inc. **Marital Status:** Married **Spouse Name:** Hilary **Children:** Izel; Marshal; Levent; Isla; Evelyn; Unity **Career:** Executive Vice President, Hustad Companies, Inc. (2008-Present) **Civic:** Volunteer, The Salvation Army of USA; Volunteer, Ronald McDonald House (RMHC) **Awards:** Award for Perfect Installation, GAF **Memberships:** National Roofing Contractors Association; GAF **To what do you attribute your success:** Mr. Caturia attributes his success to being passionate; he loves developing and maintaining relationships and being a point of contact that people can reach out to. He also likes being apart of large projects. **Why did you become involved in your profession or industry:** Mr. Caturia started in construction during his college years as a part-time job; he didn't know that he would fall in love with the industry. He was inspired by the fact that Lee Hustad, the founder of the company, has developed and maintained relationships with large real estate developers and property management companies. He felt there was a big need in the field when he was starting out.

Harold L. Chapel, MD, FACC

Title: Physician **Company Name:** Banner Health **Date of Birth:** 06/26/1956 **Place of Birth:** Sterling **State/Country of Origin:** CO/USA **Parents:** Gerald (1925-1963); Hilda (1924-) **Marital Status:** Married **Spouse Name:** Vicki Paula Moore (06/06/1983) **Children:** Kaitlin (1987); Kelsea (1992) **Education:** Fellowship in Cardiology, The University of Tennessee Health Science Center (1993-1996); MD, University of Colorado, Denver (1982); Residency in Internal Medicine, Creighton Affiliated Hospitals **Certifications:** Board Certified in Nuclear Cardiology (2017); Certified in Advance Heart Failure and Transplant, American Board of Internal Medicine (2014); Certified in Cardiovascular Disease, American Board of Internal Medicine (1997); Board Certified in Geriatric Medicine (1991); Lifetime Certification in Internal Medicine, American Board of Internal Medicine (1985); Licensed Physician, States of Colorado, Wyoming, Nebraska, Tennessee and Texas **Career:** Physician, Cardiologist, Banner Health (2002-2019) **Career Related:** Presenter in Field **Creative Works:** Published, Top Cat Trial, New England Journal of Medicine (2014); Author, Article, Journal of American Chemical Society (1979) **Memberships:** The Phi Beta Kappa Society (1978); Fellow, American College of Cardiology; American Society of Nuclear Cardiology; American College of Physicians **To what do you attribute your success:** Dr. Chapel attributes his success to his mentors, including Dr. Clyde Yancey. **Why did you become involved in your profession or industry:** Dr. Chapel became involved in his profession because of an unfortunate accident. His father developed a brain tumor and died at 38, when Dr. Chapel was just 7 years old. **Avocations:** Spending time with family; Skiing; Gardening **Political Affiliations:** Republican **Religion:** Lutheran

Vernon Lee "Vern" Chartier

Title: Electrical Engineer (Retired) **Industry:** Utilities **Date of Birth:** 02/14/1939 **Place of Birth:** Fort Morgan **State/Country of Origin:** CO/USA **Parents:** Raymond Earl; Margaret Clara (Winegar) Chartier **Marital Status:** Married **Spouse Name:** Lois Marie Schwartz **Children:** Neal Raymond Chartier **Education:** Bachelor of Science in Electrical Engineering, Bachelor of Science in Business, University of Colorado (1963) **Career:** Power System EMC Consultant, Portland, OR (1995-2015); Principal Engineer, High Voltage Phenomena, Bonneville Power Administration, Vancouver, WA (1975-1995); Research Engineer, Consultant, Westinghouse Electric Co., East Pittsburgh, PA (1963-1975) **Civic:** Treasurer, First Baptist Church, Portland, OR **Creative Works:** Co-author, Five Chapters in EPRI Reference Books; Contributor, Over 50 articles to Professional Journals **Awards:** National Academy of Engineers (2004); Institute of Electrical and Electronics Engineers Third Millennium Medal (2000); Herman Halperin Transmission and Distribution Award (1995); Fellow, Institute of Electrical and Electronics Engineers (1980) **Memberships:** Institute of Electrical and Electronics Engineers; International Council on Large Electric Systems **Marquis Who's Who Honors:** Albert Nelson Marquis Lifetime Achievement Award; Marquis Who's Who Top Professional **To what do you attribute your success:** Mr. Chartier attributes his success to the experience he accrued while working on the Apple Grove 750-kV Project at Westinghouse, which set the stage for the rest of his career. **Why did you become involved in your profession or industry:** Mr. Chartier became involved in his profession due to his childhood interest in chemistry. He was encouraged to become an engineer by his teacher, and he also took inspiration from his father, who ran a radio and TV repair business. **Avocations:** Genealogy **Political Affiliations:** Independent **Religion:** Baptist

Aparna Chattoraj

Title: Gynecologist, Educator **Date of Birth:** 12/01/1935 **Place of Birth:** Calcutta **State/Country of Origin:** India **Parents:** Tarak N.; Kashi Bhattacharya **Marital Status:** Married **Spouse Name:** Sati C. Chattoraj (07/31/1961) **Children:** Partha P. **Education:** Doctor of Philosophy, Boston University (1965); Doctor of Medicine, University of Calcutta (1958) **Certifications:** Diplomate, American Board of Obstetrics and Gynecology **Career:** Private Practice, Needham, MA (1983-Present); Assistant Professor, Boston University Medical School (1965) **Career Related:** With, University of Massachusetts Student Health, Boston Harbor Campus (1983-Present); Practicing and Attending Physician, Deaconess Glover Hospital, Needham, MA (1978-Present); Gynecologist, Boston University Student Health Services (1975-1993); Consultant Gynecologist, Curry College, Milton, MA (1980-1990); Clinical Instructor, Harvard Medical School, Boston, MA (1978-1990); With, Wheaton College, Norton, MA (1975-1983); With, Babson College, Wellesley, MA (1978-1982) **Civic:** Active, Prabasi Inc., Boston, MA (1963-Present) **Creative Works:** Contributor, Over 20 Scientific Articles to Professional Journals **Awards:** Award, Leukemia Foundation (1966-1968) **Memberships:** Federation of American Societies for Experimental Biology; American Association of Immunologists **Marquis Who's Who Honors:** Albert Nelson Marquis Lifetime Achievement Award **Why did you become involved in your profession or industry:** Born under British rule in India, Ms. Chattoraj was the youngest of several children, and lost her mother due to the country's antiquated health system. Following this tragic experience, she felt compelled to become a physician in her own right and heal as many people as she could. **Avocations:** Speed walking; Bridge

Richard C. Chou

Title: Mechanical Engineer (Retired) **Industry:** Engineering **Date of Birth:** 02/07/1934 **Place of Birth:** Peking **State/Country of Origin:** China **Parents:** Kuan-Shih; Chi-Chung (Chang) Chou **Marital Status:** Married **Spouse Name:** Roseanna Chou **Children:** Henry; Jerry; Karol **Education:** Postgraduate Coursework in Mechanical Engineering, University of Pennsylvania (1963); Bachelor of Science in Applied Mathematics, Milton College (1961); Bachelor of Mechanical Engineering, Purdue University (1959) **Career:** Retired (2000); President, Nusat International, Ltd (1994-2000); Senior Member, Technical Ataff, ITT-Gilfillan, Van Nuys, CA (1985-1993); Principal Engineer, Franklin Institute, Philadelphia, PA (1961-1985) **Awards:** Space Act Award, NASA (1988); Silver Medal, German Industry Innovation Award (1986) **Memberships:** Case School Nursing Alumni Board (2007-Present); National Defense Industrial Association; Sigma Xi **Marquis Who's Who Honors:** Albert Nelson Marquis Lifetime Achievement Award **Why did you become involved in your profession or industry:** Mr. Chou became involved with his profession because whilst growing up in China, he would play around and tinker with machines (including army Jeeps) quite often.

Jimmy Coco

Title: Founder; Celebrity Tanning Expert; Visionary Inventor **Industry:** Consumer Goods and Services **Company Name:** Jimmy Jimmy Coco **Date of Birth:** 04/20/1972 **Place of Birth:** WA **State/Country of Origin:** CA/USA **Marital Status:** Single **Education:** Coursework, Two-year Junior College **Career:** Founder, Jimmy Jimmy Coco (2004-Present); Launched, Mobile Tanning Business (2004) **Career Related:** Founder, Jimmy Coco International Pro Training & Education; Global Spokesman, Sunless Tan, Hollywood Beauty Industry; Keynote Speaker; "Official Tan Man," Victoria's Secret Fashion Show (10 Years) **Civic:** Supporter, Best Friends Animal Society, St. Jude Children's Research Hospital, Help Ban Yulin Campaign, Ric O'Barry's Dolphin Project **Creative Works:** Tanning Artist, Heart-shape Butt-lift Contour Famously Applied to Kim Kardashian; Producer, Short film Documentary, "Sunergize"; Inventor, Buff 'N' Glow 3 in 1 Exfoliate & Apply Beauty Mitt; Tan Expert, Golden Globe Awards, Academy Awards, American Music Awards, Grammy Awards, European Music Awards, Video Music Awards, Emmy Awards and SAG Awards **Awards:** Recipient, Multiple Best of Beauty Awards Including Vogue, Allure, and InStyle; Named to Alt Time 100, Time Magazine; Honoree, Named "The Luxury Tan," Harper's Bazaar; Named to "Best of LA," Los Angeles Magazine **Marquis Who's Who Honors:** Albert Nelson Marquis Lifetime Achievement (2019) **To what do you attribute your success:** Birthing his industry in Hollywood lured a celebrity clientele. Mr. Coco's trusting nature and professionalism provided his clients a safe environment. **Why did you become involved in your profession or industry:** Working as a sportswear model and actor (Jimmy told Arnold to "talk to the hand" in "Terminator 3,") required him to maintain a tan physique. Using body makeup and fake tan to mask a birthmark on his chest inspired him to start his business. **Avocations:** Body art/painting; Human anatomy studies **Thoughts on Life:** As a child, Mr. Coco was a victim of bullying. Surviving abuse, his father's sudden death at a young age, and an unstable home environment, instilled strength and courage in him. Today, it is Mr. Coco's will to help people feel good about themselves, and that anything in life can be achieved with proper focus, work ethic, and discipline. He is a self-taught airbrush artist. In 2004, he launched his first mobile tanning business, an innovative concept, and instantly changed the way Hollywood celebrities prepare for and attend red carpet events. He has remained Hollywood's tan authority for almost two decades.

Alan Cohen

Title: Professor of Interventional Radiology **Industry:** Education/Educational Services **Company Name:** University of Texas Houston **Marital Status:** Widowed **Children:** Two sons **Education:** Doctor of Medicine, Case Western Reserve University School of Medicine (1972); Bachelor of Science in Molecular Biology, Massachusetts Institute of Technology (1968) **Certifications:** Certificate of Added Qualification, Vascular and Interventional Radiology (2007); Certified, American Board of Radiology (1997); Board Certified, Diagnostic Radiology (1976) **Career:** Medical Director, Memorial Hermann Hospital (2005-Present); Staff Radiologist, Chief, Vascular and Interventional Radiology, Lyndon B. Johnson General Hospital (1994-Present); Staff Radiologist, Chief, Vascular and Interventional Radiology, Hermann Hospital (1994-Present); Staff Radiologist, Department of Diagnostic and Therapeutic Care Line and Radiology, Michael E. DeBakey Veterans Affairs Medical Center (2008-2009) **Career Related:** Professor of Interventional Radiology, University of Texas Houston Medical School (1994-Present); Associate Professor of Surgery, Case Western Reserve University School of Medicine (1989-1994); Associate Professor, Department of Radiology, Case Western Reserve University School of Medicine (1985-1994); Assistant Professor, Department of Radiology, Case Western Reserve University School of Medicine (1976-1985) **Creative Works:** Contributor, Articles to Professional Journals **Awards:** Listee, Texas Top Docs (2018); Listee, Houstonia Top Doctors (2013, 2014, 2015, 2016); Listee, America's Best Physicians (2015); Distinguished Reviewer, Journal of Vascular and Interventional Radiology (2006); Outstanding Achievement in Clinical Service, University of Texas Health Science Center, Department of Radiology (1997); Distinguished Reviewer, Journal of Vascular and Interventional Radiology (1994); Recognition, Leading Cardiovascular Radiologist, MetroHealth Medical Center (1993) **Memberships:** Academy of Transcatheter Cardiovascular Therapeutics (2005-Present); Houston Radiological Society (1994-Present); American Roentgen Ray Society (1987-Present); American College of Radiology (1978-Present); Radiologic Society of North America (1978-Present); Fellow, Society of Interventional Radiology; Fellow, American Heart Association **To what do you attribute your success:** Dr. Cohen credits his success on his upbringing, curiosity, hard work and the support of his family. **Why did you become involved in your profession or industry:** Dr. Cohen became involved in his profession due to the revolutionary nature of radiology at the time. He also benefited from the tutelage of Bill Phelson, the chief of radiology during his internship.

Freddie Duane Coleman

Title: Host, Commentator **Industry:** Media & Entertainment **Company Name:** ESPN Radio **Date of Birth:** 12/19/1965 **Place of Birth:** Brooklyn **State/Country of Origin:** NY/USA **Parents:** Mattie Coleman; Freddie Coleman **Marital Status:** Married **Spouse Name:** Denise **Children:** Briana **Education:** BA in Mass Communication, Minor in Journalism, Mansfield University of Pennsylvania (1987) **Career:** Football and Basketball Color Analyst, Sacred Heart University (2017-Present); Host, Commentator, Freddie and Fitzsimmons, ESPN Radio (2016-Present); GameNight (2004-2016); The Freddie Coleman Show (2004-2016); Host, Weekday PM Drive-Time, Fox Sports 980 & 95.9 FM, Albany's Sports Radio (2002-2004); Co-Host, SportsScene (1999-2002); Color Analyst for Basketball, Marist College Athletics (1999-2002); Program Director, Oldies 97 WCZX-FM (1999-2000); On-Air Host, 101.5 WPDH-FM (1996-1999); Host, 1600-AM WWRL NYC (1997-1998); Music Director, Thunder-107 FM (1989-1990) **Civic:** Speaker, Mansfield University of Pennsylvania, Sacred Heart University, Manchester Community College, Hofstra University, Eastern University **Awards:** Inductee, Athletic Hall of Fame, Mansfield University of Pennsylvania (2017) **Memberships:** National Association of Black Journalists; Football Writers Association of America; U.S. Basketball Writers Association **To what do you attribute your success:** Mr. Coleman attributes his success to his belief and trust in himself and his abilities. **Why did you become involved in your profession or industry:** Mr. Coleman became involved in his profession because he loved radio growing up in Brooklyn, New York. As soon as he joined his college radio station, he knew he wanted to pursue a career in the field. **Thoughts on Life:** Mr. Coleman states "Fear the known, leave the unknown alone."

Mary Alice Collins, PhD

Title: Psychotherapist; Social Worker; Educator (Retired) **Industry:** Health, Wellness and Fitness **Date of Birth:** 04/20/1937 **Place of Birth:** Everett **State/Country of Origin:** WA/USA **Parents:** Harry Edward Caton; Mary (Yates) Caton **Marital Status:** Married **Spouse Name:** Gerald C. Brocker (03/24/1980) **Education:** PhD, Michigan State University (1974); MSW, University of Michigan (1966); BA in Sociology, Seattle Pacific College (1959) **Certifications:** Diplomate, American Board Clinical Social Workers **Career:** Retired (2005); Part-time Adjunct Assistant Professor, Michigan State University (1993-2005); Private Practice, East Lansing, MI (1984-2005); Vice President, Brief Psychotherapy Coalition (1994); Lecturer, Michigan State University (1987-1993); Clinical Social Worker, Psychological Evaluation and Treatment Center, East Lansing, MI (1982-1984); Visiting Professor, Hurley Medical Center (1979-1984); Clinical Social Worker, Genesee Psychiatric Center, Genesee Health System, Flint, MI (1974-1982); Lecturer, Michigan State University (1974); Social Worker, Ingham Medical Mental Health Center, Lansing, MI (1971-1973); Consultant, Ingham County Department Social Services (1971-1973); Social Worker, Catholic Social Services, Flint, MI (1969-1971); Director, Teenage, Adult and Counseling Departments, YWCA, Flint, MI (1959-1964, 1966-1968); Instructor of Social Work, Lansing Community College **Career Related:** President, Round Lake Improvement Association (1984-1987); Advisor, Human Relations Youth League, Flint Council CHS (1964-1965); Secretary, Genesee County Young Democrats (1960-1961) **Civic:** Volunteer **Creative Works:** Contributor, Articles, Professional Journals **Memberships:** National Association of Social Workers; Academy of Certified Social Workers (ACSW); Alpha Kappa Sigma; The Honor Society of Phi Kappa Phi **Why did you become involved in your profession or industry:** Dr. Collins became involved in her profession because in the 9th grade they were going over what they could be and she knew she wanted to do something that was helpful to people. When she was in college at Seattle Pacific, she worked one summer as a camp counselor for kids that were troubled. She was always torn between sociology and psychology because she found them both interesting. She believed in working with individuals and groups as well. **Avocations:** Exercise; Reading like an addict; Swimming in the summer; Lunch with friends; Talk and laughter for mental development; Slow jogging **Political Affiliations:** Democrat

Suzanne Collins

Title: Author **Industry:** Writing and Editing **Date of Birth:** 08/10/1962 **Place of Birth:** Hartford **State/Country of Origin:** CT/USA **Parents:** Lt. Col. Michael John Collins; Jane Brady Collins **Marital Status:** Married **Spouse Name:** Charles Pryor **Children:** Charlie; Isabella **Education:** MFA in Dramatic Writing, Tisch School of the Arts, New York University (1989); BA in Theater and Telecommunications, Indiana University Bloomington (1985); Diploma in Theater Arts, Alabama School of Fine Arts, Birmingham, AL (1980) **Career:** Children's Television Writer, Scholastic Entertainment (1991-Present); Children's Television Writer, Kids WB (1991-Present); Children's Television Writer, Nickelodeon (1991) **Creative Works:** Author, "The Ballad of Songbirds and Snakes" (2020); Author, "Year of the Jungle" (2013); Author, "Mockingjay" (2010); Author, "Catching Fire" (2009); Author, "The Hunger Games" (2008); Author, "Gregor and the Code of Claw" (2007); Author, "Gregor and the Marks of Secret" (2006); Author, "When Charlie McButton Lost Power" (2005); Author, "Gregor and the Curse of the Warmbloods" (2005); Author, "Gregor and the Prophecy of Bane" (2004); Author, "Gregor the Overlander" (2003); Author, "Fire Proof: Shelby Woo #111" (1999) **Awards:** Authors Guild Award for Distinguished Service to the Literary Community (2016); California Young Reader Medal (2011); Book List Editor's Choice (2008); Cybils Award for Fantasy & Science Fiction (2008); Listee, School Library Journal Best Books (2008); Best Young Adult Book, Kirkus Reviews (2008); ALSC Notable Children's Recording (2006); NAIBA Children's Novel Award (2004); Listee, New York Public Library's 100 Titles for Reading and Sharing; Horn Book Fanfare; Notable Children's Book, American Library Association; Listee, American Library Association's Top 10 Best Books For Young Adult Selection; Listee, Best Books of the Year: Children's Fiction, Publisher Weekly

Judi Combs

Title: Chief Executive Officer, Partner **Industry:** Fine Art **Company Name:** Arizona Fine Art Expo **Date of Birth:** 07/22/1944 **Place of Birth:** Southgate **State/Country of Origin:** CA **Parents:** Lewis Lee, Marie Ellen (Peat) Long **Marital Status:** Married **Spouse Name:** Roger Combs (1967) **Children:** Mike Combs; Brett Combs; Kim Bulot; Denise Colter **Career:** Chief Executive Officer, Partner, Arizona Fine Art EXPO, Scottsdale, AZ (2005-Present); Founder, Chief Executive Officer, American Healing Arts Foundation, Arizona (1981-Present) **Creative Works:** Exhibition, Care Free Art Show; Mentioned in "The Best Laid Plans," by Sidney Sheldon **Awards:** Over 50 Awards and Accolades **To what do you attribute your success:** Ms. Combs attributes her success to being surrounded by so much love. Her family is constantly present to support her events, which is a major contributing factor in keeping her motivated and focused. Cognizant that artists are often abused by their promoters, she considers herself a "producer" of art shows, rather than someone who is solely driven by financial gain. **Why did you become involved in your profession or industry:** Ms. Combs became involved in her profession after her father passed away, whereupon she began to spend a great deal of time with her mother. They began to attend art classes together, and she became interested in the field herself. Ms. Combs feels that art can be very therapeutic, and it offers an opportunity to escape from the daily travails of life.

Janis L. Comstock-Jones

Title: Business Owner, Consultant **Company Name:** Gallifrey Enterprises **Date of Birth:** 11/17/1956 **Place of Birth:** Royal Oak **State/Country of Origin:** MI/USA **Parents:** Robert Ulysses; Mary Sue Comstock **Marital Status:** Widowed **Spouse Name:** David Todd Jones (07/29/1981, Deceased 2019) **Education:** Postgraduate Coursework, Columbus Technical College (1986-1987); Postgraduate Coursework, Ohio University (1978-1979); BS, Rio Grande College (1978); MS, Tiffin University **Certifications:** Certified Specialist, IBM **Career:** President, Gallifrey Enterprises (1995-Present); Director of Information Technology, The American National Red Cross (1993-1995); Assistant Director, The American National Red Cross (1992-1993); Data Processing Coordinator, The American National Red Cross (1987-1992); Instructor, Columbus Technical College (1986-1987); Fiscal Officer, County Government, Columbus, OH (1979-1985) **Career Related:** National Instructor, The American National Red Cross (1990-1995) **Civic:** President, Central Ohio Driving Association (1992-Present); Director, National Standardbred Pleasure Horse Organization (1989-2003); Fundraising Chair, Columbus Area United Way (1990-1991) **Creative Works:** Author, "MIS Manual" (1992) **Awards:** Employee of the Year, The American National Red Cross **Memberships:** IAEM; Ohio Thoroughbred Breeders & Owners; Ohio Harness Horsemen's Association; The United States Trotting Association **Why did you become involved in your profession or industry:** Ms. Comstock-Jones became involved in her profession because she wanted to know everything about everything. **Avocations:** Traveling; Antiquing

Catherine Connely

Title: Associate Broker **Industry:** Real Estate **Company Name:** Tom Shaw Realty **Marital Status:** Married **Children:** Sheena; Billy **Career:** Agent, Broker, Tom Shaw Realtors, St. Louis, MO (1978-Present) **Awards:** St. Louis Magazine Five Star Real Estate Agent Award (2006-2020) **To what do you attribute your success:** Ms. Connely attributes her success to caring about her customers, being there for them, doing the right by them, and working hard for them. **Why did you become involved in your profession or industry:** Ms. Connely became involved in her profession because her grandfather, Charles A. Shaw, who also developed the city of Clayton, Missouri, and became its first mayor, opened the business in 1922. The business remained in the family, where Ms. Connely got her start more than 40 years ago. She was only 18 when she first received her real estate license. She began practicing real estate as her full-time career in 1982 at the height of the 1980s recession. Through hard work and perseverance, she became knowledgeable in marketing and well-informed in regards to financing in the real estate industry. Forty-two years later, she is a successful and highly respected agent and broker. She prides herself on superior service, follow up and being available to her clients. She has worked extensively over the years in all areas of the real estate market, including St. Louis, Chesterfield, Wildwood, St. Charles, Franklin and Jefferson counties. **Thoughts on Life:** Ms. Connely plans to continue moving forward and growing the firm. She plans to work as long as she can like her father did and not retire.

Thomas Ernest Constance, Esq.

Title: Partner; Lawyer **Industry:** Law and Legal Services **Company Name:** Kramer Levin Naftalis & Frankel LLP **Date of Birth:** 05/16/1936 **Place of Birth:** Union City **State/Country of Origin:** NJ/USA **Parents:** James Constance; Effie (Economides) Constance **Marital Status:** Married **Spouse Name:** Janet Barbara Raynor (11/21/1970) **Children:** Nicole Susan; Jo Anne Barbara; Patricia Anne **Education:** JD, St. John's University (1964); BS, New York University (1958) **Career:** Partner, Co-chairman, Kramer Levin Naftalis & Frankel LLP, New York, NY (1994-Present); Partner, Chairman, Executive Committee, Shea & Gould (1971-1994) **Career Related:** Advisory Board, Barington Capital Group, LP; Board of Directors, Premier American Bank, Siga Technologies **Civic:** Board of Directors, The Sass Foundation; Board of Directors, St. Vincent Services, Inc. **Military Service:** Lieutenant, United States Army (1958-1960) **Memberships:** Corporate Governance Committee, ABA; Association of the Bar of the City of New York; Florida Community Bank Board; SIGA Technologies; MD-SAS Cancer Research; Advisory Board, U.S. Trust, Bank of America **Bar Admissions:** New York (1965) **Marquis Who's Who Honors:** Albert Nelson Marquis Lifetime Achievement Award; Marquis Who's Who Top Professional **Why did you become involved in your profession or industry:** Mr. Constance was always interested in law.

Beverly E. Conway

Title: Associate Professor of Science and Nutrition **Industry:** Education/Educational Services **Company Name:** Williston State College **Marital Status:** Married **Spouse Name:** Bruce Conway **Children:** Three Sons **Education:** Master of Science in Nutrition, Washington State University (1977); Bachelor of Science in Biology, University of North Dakota (1974); Associate of Science, University of North Dakota (1972) **Career:** Associate Professor, Sciences and Nutrition, Williston State College, ND (1998-Present); Research Assistant, South West Foundation Biomedical Research, San Antonio, Texas (1985-1988); Biology LHR Assistant, Bentley College, Waltham, MA (1982-1983); Graduate Research Teaching Assistant, Washington State University (1974-1977) **Career Related:** Guest Speaker on Nutrition, Cancer Support Group and Other Health Organizations **Civic:** Judge, Little Miss & Pre-Teen Miss North Dakota Pageant, Williston, ND **Awards:** Outstanding Alumni Award, Williston State College Foundation and Alumni Association **Memberships:** Foundation Director, Sons of Norway (2004-2005); Sons of Norway; Northern Plains Sustainable Agriculture Society **Marquis Who's Who Honors:** Albert Nelson Marquis Lifetime Achievement Award; Marquis Who's Who Top Professional; Who's Who in American Junior Colleges **To what do you attribute your success:** Ms. Conway attributes her success to her loving of teaching. **Why did you become involved in your profession or industry:** Mrs. Conway became involved in her profession unexpectedly. She never intended on entering the field of education, but had goals of doing research. She did get to pursue research on premature baboons as human infant models, but after supporting her husband in his military career, they moved to Williston, North Dakota. She accepted a position at Williston State College, at which point she discovered her passion for teaching. **Avocations:** Gardening; Refinishing furniture

Anderson Hays Cooper

Title: Broadcast Journalist, News Correspondent **Industry:** Media & Entertainment **Date of Birth:** 06/03/1967 **Place of Birth:** New York **State/Country of Origin:** NY/USA **Parents:** Wyatt Emory Cooper; Gloria Vanderbilt **Education:** BA in Political Science, Yale University, New Haven, CT (1989); Coursework, Vietnam National University, Hanoi **Career:** Correspondent, "60 Minutes," CBS News (2007-Present); Anchor, Host, "Anderson Cooper 360," Cable News Network (CNN) (2003-Present); Host, "Anderson Live" (2011-2013); Co-Anchor, "NewsNight," CNN (2005); Weekend Primetime Anchor, CNN (2002-2003); Co-Anchor, "American Morning," CNN (2002); Host, "The Mole," ABC (2001-2002); Co-Anchor, "World News Now," ABC News (1999-2000); Correspondent, "ABC News" (1995-1999); Producer, Chief International Correspondent, "Channel One News" **Career Related:** Host, "New Year's Eve Special from Times Square," CNN (2002-Present); Contributing Editor, "Details Magazine" **Creative Works:** Host, "CNN Heroes: An All-Star Tribute" (2007-Present); Co-Author, "The Rainbow Comes and Goes: A Mother and Son on Life, Love, and Loss" (2016); Narrator, "How to Succeed in Business Without Really Trying" (2011); Co-Host, "Planet in Peril: Battle Lines" (2008); Co-Host, "Planet in Peril" (2007); Author, "Dispatches From the Edge: A Memoir of War, Disasters and Survival" (2006) **Awards:** Vito Russo Award, Gay & Lesbian Alliance Against Defamation (2013); Emmy Award for Outstanding Live Coverage of a Current News Story - Long Form (2011); Emmy Award for Outstanding Coverage of a Breaking News Story in a Regularly Scheduled Newscast (2011); National Order for Honour & Merit, Government of Haiti (2010); Listee, 100 Agents of Change, Rolling Stone Magazine (2009); Action Against Hunger Humanitarian Award (2008); Emmy Award for Outstanding Feature Story in a Regularly Scheduled Newscast (2006); Emmy Award for Outstanding Live Coverage of Breaking News Story - Long Form (2006); National Headliners Award, Press Club Atlantic City (2005); Peabody Award, Henry W. Grady College of Journalism & Mass Communications, University of Georgia (2005); GLAAD Media Award, Gay & Lesbian Alliance Against Defamation (2001); Emmy Award (1997); Bronze Award, National Education Film & Video Festival; Silver Plaque, Chicago International Film Festival

Bradley Cooper

Title: Actor **Date of Birth:** 01/05/1975 **Place of Birth:** Philadelphia **State/Country of Origin:** PA/ USA **Parents:** Charles J. Cooper; Gloria (Campano) Cooper **Spouse Name:** Jennifer Esposito (12/21/2006, Divorced 11/2007) **Education:** MFA, Actors Studio Drama School, New York, NY; BA in English, Georgetown University (1997) **Creative Works:** Actor, "Atlantic Wall" (2021); Actor, "Bernstein" (2021); Actor, "Guardians of the Galaxy Vol. 3" (2021); Actor, "Nightmare Alley" (2021); Actor, "Avengers: Endgame" (2019); Actor, "The Mule" (2018); Actor, "A Star is Born" (2018); Actor, "Avengers: Infinity War" (2018); Actor, "Guardians of the Galaxy Vol. 2" (2017); Producer, "War Dogs" (2016); Actor, "10 Cloverfield Lane" (2016); Actor, "Aloha" (2015); Actor, "Wet Hot American Summer: First Day of Camp" (2015); Actor, "Adam Jones" (2015); Actor, "Burnt" (2015); Actor, "Joy" (2015); Actor, Producer, "American Sniper" (2014); Actor, "The Elephant Man" (2014); Voice Actor, "Guardians of the Galaxy" (2014); Actor, "Serena" (2014); Actor, "The Hangover Part III" (2013); Actor, "American Hustle" (2013); Actor, "Silver Linings Playbook" (2012); Actor, "Hit and Run" (2012); Actor, "The Place Beyond the Pines" (2012); Actor, "The Words" (2012); Actor, Executive Producer, "Limitless" (2011); Actor, "The Hangover Part II" (2011); Actor, "The A-Team" (2010); Actor, "Valentine's Day" (2010); Actor, "He's Just Not That Into You" (2009); Actor, "The Hangover" (2009); Actor, "All About Steve" (2009); Actor, "Case 39" (2009); Actor, "Nip/Tuck" (2007-2008); Actor, "The Understudy" (2008); Actor, "Older Than America" (2008); Actor, "The Rocker" (2008); Actor, "The Midnight Meat Train" (2008); Actor, "New York, I Love You" (2008); Actor, "Yes Man" (2008); Actor, "The Comebacks" (2007); Actor, "Three Days of Rain" (2006); Actor, "Failure to Launch" (2006); Actor, "Kitchen Confidential" (2005-2006); Actor, "Jack & Bobby" (2004-2005); Actor, "Alias" (2001-2006); Actor, "Wedding Crashers" (2005); Actor, "I Want to Marry Ryan Banks" (2004); Actor, "Touching Evil" (2004); Actor, "The Last Cowboy" (2003); Actor, "My Little Eye" (2002) **Awards:** Grammy for Best Pop Duo/Group Performance, "Shallow," (2018); 10 Most Fascinating People of 2015 (2016); Critics' Choice Award for Best Actor in an Action Movie (2015); MTV Movie Award for Best Male Performance (2015); Critics' Choice Award for Best Actor in a Comedy Movie (2013); National Board Review Award for Best Actor (2012); International Man of Year Award, GQ (2011); Sexiest Man Alive, People Magazine (2011)

Mary Sandra "Sandy" Copley, MD

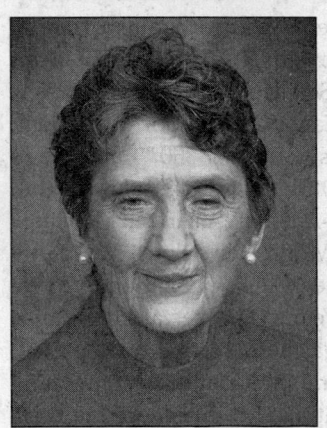

Title: Physician **Industry:** Medicine & Health Care **Company Name:** Ebenezer Medical Clinic **Date of Birth:** 07/13/1947 **Place of Birth:** Milton **State/Country of Origin:** WV/USA **Parents:** Edward Wendel Copley; Mary Rena Copley **Children:** Tracie; Sandra **Education:** MD, Marshall University Medical School (1990); MS; BS, Religion & Bible Studies **Career:** Ebenezer Medical Clinic, Huntington, WV **Civic:** Piano Player, Local Church **Awards:** Graduated Second in Class, Marshall University (1990) **Memberships:** American Academy of Family Physicians **Marquis Who's Who Honors:** Who's Who in 2020 **To what do you attribute your success:** Ms. Copley attributes her success to the changes she had to make due to her hearing limitations. She knew that she wanted to go to medical school, and found ways to do the things she knew that she could do, the best that she could, to make up for the areas she lacked in. Her motto is to "Do what God tells me to do, and treat people with grace and dignity at all times..." **Why did you become involved in your profession or industry:** Ms. Copley always knew that she wanted to be in the medical profession. From the time that she knew what medicine was, she knew what she wanted to do. She was always great in math and science although her bachelor's degree was in biblical studies. She used that degree for her to find jobs in order to fund her plans for medical school. Although she had great grades, she always feared that her hearing impairment may stop her from achieving her goal. With great support from the community around her, they helped encourage her that they did not think it would be able to stop her and she would be a great doctor. While in pursuit of her master's degree, Ms. Copley worked as a social worker in the time she was funding her education. **Avocations:** Playing piano **Religion:** Christian

Addie Cormier

Title: Process Safety Consultant **Company Name:** Siemens Energy **Children:** Two Children **Career:** Process Engineer Consultant, Siemens Energy (2012-Present); Design Engineer, Shaw Stone & Webster, Inc. (2005-2012) **Civic:** Church Volunteer, Youth Applying to College **Creative Works:** Author, Article, "Integrating Cybersecurity in Hazard and Risk Analyses" (2020) **Memberships:** American Institute of Chemical Engineers **Bar Admissions:** MS in Advanced Safety Engineering, The University of Alabama at Birmingham, AL (2018); BSChE in Chemical Engineering, Prairie View A&M University (1990); BS in Chemistry, Prairie View A&M University (1980) **To what do you attribute your success:** Ms. Cormier attributes her success to working with different people and learning from them. **Why did you become involved in your profession or industry:** Ms. Comier works with high-risk, low-income kids with low GPAs. Ms. Cormier always had a decent GPA, but she had friends that were falling behind. She tried her best to help them. She promised herself that once she had the time, she would help them find a way to go to college. **Thoughts on Life:** Ms. Cormier's motto is, "Live and let live." She respects people and respects knowledge.

Charles N. Cornell, MD

Title: Professor of Clinical Orthopedic Surgery **Industry:** Medicine & Health Care **Company Name:** Hospital for Special Surgery **Date of Birth:** 05/21/1954 **Place of Birth:** New York **State/Country of Origin:** NY/USA **Parents:** Geroge Nelson; Jeanne Lawless Cornell **Marital Status:** Married **Spouse Name:** Priscilla Brawley (06/16/1977) **Children:** Kate Lizabeth; Peter Trip; William Brawley **Education:** MD, Cornell University Medical College, New York, NY (1980); BS in Chemistry and Physics, Williams College, Williamstown, MA **Career:** Member, Board of Directors, Hospital Special Surgery (2006-Present); Attending Orthopedic Surgeon, Director, Hospital Special Surgery, New York, NY (2004-Present); Professor, Clinical Orthopedic Surgery, Weill Cornell Medicine, New York, NY (2004-Present) **Creative Works:** Editor-in-Chief, Journal for the Hospital of Special Surgery **Awards:** Career Service Award, American Academy of Orthopedic Surgeons; Phillip D. Wilson Teaching Award, Hospital for Special Surgery **Memberships:** American Academy of Orthopedic Surgery; American College of Surgeons; Association of Bone and Joint Surgeons **Marquis Who's Who Honors:** Marquis Who's Who Top Professional **To what do you attribute your success:** Mr. Cornell attributes his success to good education and training as well as his hard work and love for the field. **Why did you become involved in your profession or industry:** Mr. Cornell became involved in his profession because he came from a family of doctors and wanted to be able to apply science in a very practical field. His grandfather, Nelson Warren Cornell, and father, George Nelson Cornell, were both general surgeons. In his family it was also expected that he would pursue a career in medicine.

Michael A. Costa

Industry: Real Estate **Company Name:** Highridge Costa Housing Partners LLC **Marital Status:** Married **Spouse Name:** Cheryl **Children:** Three Children **Education:** Bachelor of Science in Engineering and Information Technology, California Polytechnic State University, San Luis Obispo, CA (1979) **Career:** President, Chief Executive Officer, Highridge Costa (1994-Present); President, Chief Executive Officer, MacFarlane Costa LLC (1994-2007); President, KB Home Multifamily Division (1994-2000); President, Multifamily Division, Calmark (1979-1992) **Civic:** Board Member, California Housing Consortium; California Council of Affordable Housing; Chairman, RISE **Awards:** Top Design for Senior Housing, Texas; California Hall of Fame, Affordable Housing Finance; National Hall of Fame, Affordable Housing Finance **Why did you become involved in your profession or industry:** Mr. Costa became involved in his profession due to the influence of his father, who was deeply involved in their local community.

James Hicklin Craig

Title: Fine Arts Consultant **Industry:** Fine Art **Company Name:** James Craig Fine & Decorative Arts **Date of Birth:** 07/23/1937 **Place of Birth:** Chester **State/Country of Origin:** SC/USA **Parents:** John Edward Craig; Una Bee (Martin) Craig **Marital Status:** Life Partner **Spouse Name:** Randy S. Johnson **Education:** Coursework, Paris, France (1960); Coursework, The Juilliard School (1960); Coursework, College-Conservatory of Music, University of Cincinnati (1956-1959); Coursework, University of South Carolina (1955-1956) **Career:** Fine Arts Consultant, Independence, VA (1985-Present); Owner, James Craig Fine & Decorative Arts (1985-Present); President, Craig & Tarlton Inc., Raleigh, NC (1969-1985); Principal, James Craig Fine & Decorative Arts (1965-1969); Curator, Decorative Arts, North Carolina Office of Archives & History, Raleigh, NC (1962-1964) **Career Related:** Consultant, North Carolina Executive Mansion **Civic:** Trustee, The Mint Museum, Charlotte, NC (2000-2006); Board Member, Chamber Opera Theater of New York (1982-1985); Board of Directors, Chamber Music Raleigh; Board of Directors, Chamber Opera Theater of New York; Board of Directors, The Mint Museum, Charlotte, NC; Board Member, Acquisitions Committee, North Carolina Executive Mansion; Patron, The Metropolitan Opera, New York, NY; Board of Directors, Sparta Museum Project, NC **Creative Works:** Author, "The Arts and Crafts in North Carolina 1699-1840" (1965); Writer, Book, North Carolina Decorative Arts, The Museum of Early Southern Decorative Arts (1964-1965) **Awards:** Grantee, North Carolina Decorative Arts, The Museum of Early Southern Decorative Arts (1964-1965); Named One of the 100 Best in Field, Montgomery **Marquis Who's Who Honors:** Albert Nelson Marquis Lifetime Achievement Award; Marquis Who's Who Top Professional **Avocations:** Art; Antiques; Gardening

Patrick Crone

Title: Owner, President **Industry:** Engineering **Company Name:** Imperial Pools & Design **Marital Status:** Married **Spouse Name:** Alyssa (12/16/2011) **Children:** Four Children **Education:** Bachelor of Science in Mechanical Engineering, Embry–Riddle Aeronautical University (2009) **Certifications:** License, Mechanical Engineering (2007) **Career:** Owner, Imperial Pools & Design (2017-Present); Owner, Dynamics (2014-2017); Nights Shift Engineer, Bombardier **Awards:** Listed, #39, Top 50 Pool Service in the Country; Best Pool Builder; Best Pool Design; Best Pool Service in Tuscon **Why did you become involved in your profession or industry:** Mr. Crone became involved in his profession after meeting a man who had patented and invented a method for cleaning pool tiles with salt. He subsequently accepted a job in Tucson and soon established his own business performing pool renovations. **Avocations:** Basketball; Yard care; Spending time with family

Rosalina Sedillo Cruz

Title: Marriage and Family Therapist **Industry:** Medicine & Health Care **Date of Birth:** 04/01/1933 **Place of Birth:** Dumaguete **State/Country of Origin:** The Philippines **Parents:** Dionisio Sedillo; Simplicia Raagas **Marital Status:** Married **Spouse Name:** Anatolio Benedicto Cruz Jr. (04/28/1955) **Children:** Raquel Regina; Anatolio Benedicto III; Anthony Bradley; Roselle Regina **Education:** Specialist Degree in Marriage and Family Therapy, St. Mary's University, San Antonio, TX (1980); MEd in Guidance Counseling, Trinity University (1972); BS in Education, University of the Philippines (1955) **Certifications:** Certified Marriage and Family Therapist, State of Texas; Diplomate, American Psychotherapy Association **Career:** Part-Time Counselor, Church of the Holy Spirit (1990-Present); Private Practice in Marriage and Family Therapy (1980-Present); Counselor, Church of the Holy Spirit (1972-1975); Teacher, Holy Spirit Catholic School (1968-1970); Teacher, Roosevelt High School (Now Far Eastern University Roosevelt) (1955-1957) **Civic:** Advisory Board, Child Abuse Prevention Services, San Antonio, TX (1994-Present); Chairman, Family Advisory Board, St. Mary's University, San Antonio, TX (1985-1986) **Creative Works:** Author, Child Abuse Programs **Awards:** Volunteer of the Year, Child Abuse Prevention Services (1991); Community Service Award **Memberships:** President, San Antonio Marriage and Family Therapy (1985-1986); Member, Lobbying Licensure Committee, Texas Counseling Association (1980); Clinical Member, American Association for Marriage and Family Therapy; Texas Association for Marriage and Family Therapy **Marquis Who's Who Honors:** Albert Nelson Marquis Lifetime Achievement Award; Marquis Who's Who Top Professional **Avocations:** Playing tennis; Cooking; Jogging; Reading; Swimming

George Woody Cunningham, PhD

Title: Federal Official, Nuclear Scientist (Retired) **Date of Birth:** 12/03/1930 **Place of Birth:** Union City **State/Country of Origin:** TN/USA **Parents:** Mose Marshall Cunningham; Zula Ethel (Easterwood) Cunningham **Marital Status:** Married **Spouse Name:** Jesse M. Harris (10/02/2010); Patricia G. Pate (12/31/1954, Deceased 04/15/2007) **Children:** John; Ann **Education:** PhD in Metallurgical Engineering, The Ohio State University (1960); MS in Metallurgy, University of Tennessee (1955); BSChemE, University of Tennessee (1954) **Career:** Retired (2004); Consultant (2000-2004); Career Technical Director, Defense Nuclear Facilities Safety Board, Washington, DC (1990-2000); Director, Mitre Institute, The Mitre Corporation, McLean, VA (1984-1990); Director, Nuclear Studies, The Mitre Corporation, McLean, VA (1981-1984); Assistant Secretary for Nuclear Energy, Department of Energy (1980-1981); Counselor, Atomic Energy U.S. Mission to International Atomic Energy Association, Vienna, Department of Energy, Washington, DC (1978-1979); Director, Division of Waste Management, Program Director for Nuclear Energy, Department of Energy, Washington, DC (1977-1978); Deputy Director, Reactor Development Division, Energy Research and Development Administration, Washington, DC (1975-1976); Assistant Director, Engineering and Technician, Atomic Energy Commission, Washington, DC (1973-1975); Chief, Liquid Metal Products Branch, Atomic Energy Commission, Washington, DC (1970-1973); Member, Fuel and Materials Branch Division, Reactor Developer and Technician, Atomic Energy Commission, Washington, DC (1966-1970); Chief, Materials Thermodynamics Division, Battelle Memorial Institute, Columbus, Ohio (1965-1966); Principal Metallurgical Engineer, Battelle Memorial Institute, Columbus, Ohio (1955-1962) **Career Related:** American Delegate, International Working Group on Fast Reactors (1976); U.S.-USSR Coordinating Committee on Fast Reactors (1976); U.S. Fast Breeder Reactor Team, Japan (1971); Chairman, U.S.-U.K. Libby-Cockcroft Exchange of Ceramic Fuels (1967) **Creative Works:** Contributor, Articles, Professional Journals **Awards:** Ranked Distinguished Executive, Senior Executive Service, Presented by President Bill Clinton **Memberships:** American Society of Metals; Sigma Xi; Tau Beta Pi Association, Inc.; Lamda Chi Upsilon; Alpha Chi Sigma **Marquis Who's Who Honors:** Albert Nelson Marquis Lifetime Achievement Award; Marquis Who's Who Top Professional **Avocations:** Writing **Religion:** Presbyterian

David N. Danforth

Title: Associate Research Physician, Surgical Oncologist **Industry:** Medicine & Health Care **Date of Birth:** 06/25/1942 **Place of Birth:** New York **State/Country of Origin:** NY/USA **Parents:** David Newton Danforth; Gladys Margaret (Blaine) Danforth **Spouse Name:** Anne Walker Nickson (4/13/1985) **Children:** Laura **Education:** MD, Northwestern University (1971); MS, University of New Mexico (1967); BA, Northwestern University (1965) **Certifications:** Diplomate, American Board of Surgery **Career:** Associate Research Physician, National Cancer Institute, National Institutes of Health, Bethesda, MD (2012-Present); Senior Investigator, National Cancer Institute, National Institutes of Health, Bethesda, MD (1985-2012); Senior Staff Fellow, National Institutes of Health, Bethesda, MD (1980-1982); Surgical Fellow, M.D. Anderson Hospital, Houston, TX (1979-1980); Internship, Residency, New York-Presbyterian Hospital, Cornell University, New York, NY (1971-1974, 1977-1979); Clinical Associate, National Institutes of Health, Bethesda, MD (1974-1977) **Civic:** Lieutenant Commander, U.S. Public Health Service (1974-1976) **Creative Works:** Editor, "Diagnosis and Management of Breast Cancer" (1988); Editor, Over 100 Publications, Scientific Peer Review Journals; Contributor, Chapters, Books; Contributor, Articles, Professional Journals **Awards:** Fellowship, American Cancer Society (1979-1980) **Memberships:** Fellow, American College of Surgeons; Society of Surgical Oncology; American Society of Clinical Oncology; American Association of Cancer Research; American Society of Breast Surgeons **Why did you become involved in your profession or industry:** Encouraged to pursue medicine from a young age by his parents, Dr. Danforth decided to attend medical school right after completing high school. He had been inspired by his father, a well-respected gynecologist, which played a major role in his decision to specialize in surgical oncology. This decision was affirmed even more when Dr. Danforth completed rotations in medical school. Through this process, he specifically became interested in breast cancer. From there, he began working with the National Institutes of Health. **Avocations:** Traveling; Watching sports; Reading **Political Affiliations:** Republican **Religion:** Episcopalian

Judith Margaret Deegan Hill

Title: Attorney **Date of Birth:** 12/13/1939 **Place of Birth:** Chicago **State/Country of Origin:** IL/USA **Parents:** William J. Deegan; Ida May Deegan **Marital Status:** Single **Children:** Colette; Cristina **Education:** Postgraduate Coursework, Harvard University, Cambridge, MA (1984); JD, Marquette University Law School (1971); BA, Western Michigan University, Kalamazoo, MI (1960) **Certifications:** Paris-Sorbonne University, Paris, France (1962) **Career:** Attorney Private Practice (1989-1999); Deputy City Attorney, Criminal Division, City of Las Vegas (1984-1989); Attorney, Civil and Criminal Law, Coleman Law Associates, Las Vegas (1983-1984); Criminal Prosecutor, Deputy District Attorney, District Attorney, Clark City, Las Vegas (1977-1983); Attorney, Morse, Foley, Las Vegas (1976-1977); Senior Trust, Continental Illinois National Bank & Trust Co., Chicago, IL (1972-1976); Corporate Attorney, First Howard Paper Co, Green Bay, WI (1971-1972); Teacher, Shorewood School District (1964-1968); Teacher, Maple Heights City School, Maple Heights, OH (1963-1964); Teacher, Kalamazoo Public School (1960-1962); Plymouth Drama Fest, MA (1957) **Civic:** Red Hats, Las Vegas, NV (2005-Present); Mentor, Clark County School District (1999-2003); St. Jude Children's Research Hospital (1999-2001); Judical Candidate, Las Vegas Municipal Court System (1987); St. Charles Nevada Legal Services (1984-1987); Board of Directors, Clark County Legal Services, Las Vegas, NV (1980-1987); Nevada Legal Services, Carson City, NV (1979-1987); Planned Parenthood of Southern Nevada (1977-1978); Secretary, Student Council (1955-1957); Member, National Honor Society (1955-1957) **Creative Works:** Radio Performer, 94.9 WSJM, St Joe, MI (1957-1958) **Awards:** Listee, 1st 100 Woman Attorneys in Nevada; Internship, Juvenile Law, Marquette University Law School (1970); St. Thomas More Scholarship, Marquette University Law School (1968-1969); Auto Spec Scholarship, St. Joe, MI (1957-1960) **Bar Admissions:** District of Columbia (1979); Nevada (1976); Illinois (1973); Wisconsin (1971) **Marquis Who's Who Honors:** Albert N Marquis Lifetime Achievement Award; Marquis Who's Who Top Prof **To what do you attribute your success:** Ms. Hill attributes her success to hard work, discipline & faith in God. **Why did you become involved in your profession or industry:** At 26, Ms. Hill read "Those Who Love," a novel focused on John Adams career as an itinerant lawyer. Within a year, she was accepted to law school. At 28, Ms. Hill read about the Miranda warning in Time magazine & was further inspired.

Christopher Delgado

Title: Chef, Owner **Industry:** Food & Restaurant Services **Company Name:** The Wood Shack **Place of Birth:** , **Marital Status:** Married **Spouse Name:** Hope Delgado **Career:** Owner, Chef, The Wood Shack, St. Louis, MO (2017-Present); Executive Chef, 119 North, St. Louis, MO **To what do you attribute your success:** Mr. Delgado attributes his success to thoroughly enjoying his profession, having always felt a great sense of energy and enthusiasm while working in the industry. Likewise, he benefited from the tutelage of several wonderful chefs, including Pierre Chambrin, who had worked at the White House. **Why did you become involved in your profession or industry:** Mr. Delgado became involved in his profession after attending school, whereupon he began cooking professionally, which he greatly enjoyed.

Paula der Boghosian

Title: Retired Computer Business Consultant **Industry:** Business Management/Business Services **Date of Birth:** 11/19/1933 **Place of Birth:** Watervliet **State/Country of Origin:** NY/USA **Parents:** Harry der Boghosian; Osgi (Piligian) der Boghosian **Education:** Postgraduate Coursework, State University of New York at Albany (1974); Postgraduate Coursework, State University of New York at Oswego (1972); MS, Syracuse University (1967); BS, Syracuse University, Magna Cum Laude (1964) **Certifications:** Certified Professional Secretary **Career:** Consultant in Computer Business, Principal, Syracuse, NY (1984-Present); Director, Business Careers, Board of Cooperative, Syracuse, NY (1976-1992); Instructor, Board of Cooperative, Syracuse, NY (1973-1976); Assistant Professor, Cazenovia College (1964-1973) **Awards:** Jessie Smith Noyes Grantee, Syracuse University (1965); Zonta Scholar (1964); Inductee, International Professional and Business Women Hall of Fame **Memberships:** Vice President, International Training Communications (1985-1986); Committee Chairman, Association of Information Systems Professionals; Business Teachers Association of New York State; Administrative Management Society; Eastern Business Teachers Association; Association for Supervision and Curriculum Development; Association of American Junior Colleges; Association of American University Professors; National Association for Armenian Studies and Research, Harvard University; Delta Pi Epsilon; Beta Gamma Sigma; Phi Kappa Phi; Pi Lambda Theta; Sigma Lambda Delta **Marquis Who's Who Honors:** Albert Nelson Marquis Lifetime Achievement Award **Why did you become involved in your profession or industry:** Ms. der Boghosian wanted to pursue a career in teaching from a young age. **Avocations:** Listening to music; Golfing; Traveling; Painting **Political Affiliations:** Republican **Religion:** Armenian Apostolic

Thomas Sieger Derr Jr., PhD

Title: Professor Emeritus of Religion and Biblical Literature **Industry:** Education/Educational Services **Company Name:** Smith College **Date of Birth:** 06/18/1931 **Place of Birth:** Boston **State/Country of Origin:** MA/USA **Parents:** Thomas Sieger; Mary Ferguson (Sebring) Derr **Marital Status:** Married **Spouse Name:** Linda Vincent (02/14/1986) **Children:** Peter Bulkeley; Laura Seely; Mary Williams; Erin Vincent; Philip Henry **Education:** PhD, Columbia University (1972); MDiv, Union Theological Seminary (1956); AB, Harvard University (1953) **Certifications:** Ordained to Ministry, United Church of Christ (1956) **Career:** Professor Emeritus of Religion and Biblical Literature, Smith College, Northampton, MA (2005-Present); Professor, Smith College, Northampton, MA (1977-2005); Associate Professor, Smith College, Northampton, MA (1972-1977); Assistant Professor, Religion, Smith College, Northampton, MA (1965-1971); Assistant Chaplain, Smith College, Northampton, MA (1963-1965); Assistant Chaplain, Stanford University, CA (1956-1959); Researcher, World Council of Churches, Geneva, Switzerland (1961-1962) **Career Related:** Consultant, World Council of Churches (1965-Present); Ethics Consultant, Baystate Medical Center, Springfield, MA (1995-2012); Member, Compartmental Faculty, Rush Medical College, Chicago, IL (1979-1984); Consultant, Institute on Religion in Public Life, New York, NY **Creative Works:** Author, "Environmental Ethics and Christian Humanism" (1996); Author, "Creation at Risk? Religion, Science, and Environmentalism" (1995); Author, "Believable Futures of American Protestantism" (1988); Author, "Barriers to Ecumenism: The Holy See and the World Council of Churches on Social Questions" (1983); Author, "Church, State and Politics" (1981); Author, "Ecology and Human Need" (1975); Author, "The Political Thought of the Ecumenical Movement" (1972); Contributor, Articles to Professional Journals **Awards:** Fellow, The University of Chicago Institute for Advanced Study of Religion (Now Martin Marty Center for the Advanced Study of Religion) (1981); Grantee, Danforth Foundation (1959-1960, 1965-1966) **Memberships:** Society for Christian Ethics **Marquis Who's Who Honors:** Albert Nelson Marquis Lifetime Achievement Award **Religion:** Christian

Alan Morton Dershowitz

Title: Scholar of Constitutional Law, Lawyer **Industry:** Law and Legal Services **Date of Birth:** 09/1/1938 **Place of Birth:** New York **State/Country of Origin:** NY/USA **Parents:** Harry Dershowitz; Claire (Ringel) Dershowitz **Marital Status:** Married **Spouse Name:** Carolyn Cohen, PhD; Sue Barlach (1959, Divorced 1976, Deceased 1983) **Children:** Elon; Jamin; Ella **Education:** LLB, Yale Law School (1962); BA in Political Science, Brooklyn College (1959); Diploma, Yeshiva University High School **Career:** Felix Frankfurter Professor of Law Emeritus, Harvard Law School; Law Clerk, Judge David Bazelon and Justice Arthur Goldberg **Career Related:** Guggenheim Fellowship; Fellow, Center for the Advanced Study of Behavioral Sciences; Lecturer in Field **Creative Works:** Author, "Taking the Stand: My Life in the Law" (2013); Contributor, 1000 Articles in Magazines, Newspapers, Journals and Blogs Including The New York Times Magazine, The Washington Post, The Wall Street Journal, Harvard Law Review, Yale Law Journal, Huffington Post, Newsmax, Jerusalem Post, Ha'aretz; Author, 30 Fiction and Nonfiction Works; Author, "Rights from Wrong: The Case for Israel"; Author, "The Case for Peace"; Author, "Blasphemy"; Author, "Preemption"; Author, "Finding Jefferson"; Author, "Shouting Fire" **Awards:** William O. Douglas First Amendment Award, Anti-Defamation League of the B'nai B'rith (1983); Valedictorian, Yale Law School (1962); Numerous Dean's Awards

Michael Edward Diskin

Title: President, Chief Executive Officer & Owner Diskin Enterprises LLC **Industry:** Manufacturing **Company Name:** Diskin Enterprises LLC **Date of Birth:** 08/08/1946 **Place of Birth:** Dallas **State/Country of Origin:** Texas **Parents:** William Michael Diskin; Edna Patricia (Loughran) Diskin **Marital Status:** Married **Spouse Name:** Mary Jean Fraser (10/08/1972) **Children:** Robyn Kristine; Karyn Marie; Michael Alexander; Stephen James; Alisyn Krystal **Education:** Bachelor of Science in Business Administration and Economics, Northern Michigan University (1971) **Career:** President, Chief Executive Officer & Owner, Diskin Enterprises LLC, Garrettsville, OH (1998-Present); Executive Vice President, Specrete-Ip Inc., Cleveland, OH (1992-1998); Director of Marketing, Master Builders Technologies, Cleveland, OH (1987-1992); From Product Manager Assistant to Senior Marketing Manager, Durkee Foods, Westlake, OH (1978-1987); Sales Manager, Durkee Foods, Cleveland, OH (1975-1978); Sales Representative, Durkee Foods, Dayton, OH (1973-1975); Sales Representative, Lincoln National Life, Fort Wayne, IN (1971-1973) **Civic:** Member, Board of Directors, Put-in-Bay Township Port Authority (2004-2013); Vice President, Put-in-Bay Property Owners Association, Ohio **Military Service:** United States Marine Corps (1966-1972) **Memberships:** Lake Erie Islands Historical Society; Crews Nest Club; Put-in-Bay Yacht Club **Marquis Who's Who Honors:** Albert Nelson Marquis Lifetime Achievement Award **Why did you become involved in your profession or industry:** Mr. Diskin initially became involved in plastic manufacturing due to a strong desire to own his own business. **Avocations:** Boating; Fishing; Reading; International travel **Political Affiliations:** Republican **Religion:** Roman Catholic

Callitia M. Domzalski

Title: Insurance Agent **Industry:** Insurance **Company Name:** Axxcess Insurance Agencies Ltd **Date of Birth:** 07/11/1978 **Place of Birth:** , **Marital Status:** Married **Children:** Two Daughters **Education:** Master of Science in Education, Buffalo State College (2007); Bachelor of Fine Arts in Illustration Design, State University of New York at Buffalo (2001); Bachelor of Arts in English Language and Literature, State University of New York at Buffalo (2001); Associate of Science in Commercial and Advertising Art, Syracuse University (1999) **Certifications:** Licensed Insurance Broker, New York (2012); Teacher Certification, Buffalo State College (2004) **Career Related:** Instructor, High School Art in Buffalo (2004-2007) **Civic:** Jesse's Children; Buffalo Area Charities; Diabetes Run **To what do you attribute your success:** Ms. Domzalski attributes her success to hard work and perseverance. **Why did you become involved in your profession or industry:** Ms. Domzalski took over the company her father who passed away. She relied heavy on her brothers, and is now the sole owner. **Avocations:** Painting; Sculpting; Reading

William Alan Donovan

Title: Public Service Librarian (Ret.) **Industry:** Library Management/Library Services **Date of Birth:** 01/29/1937 **Place of Birth:** Rochester **State/Country of Origin:** NY/USA **Parents:** Joseph Leo Donovan; Wilhelmina (Fawcett) Donovan **Education:** MA, University of Chicago (1981); BA, St. John Fisher College (1958); Coursework, Hollywood School of Comedy Writing; Coursework, Famous Writers Course **Certifications:** Catechist, St. Charles Borromeo Church, Diocese of Venice, Florida **Career:** Librarian, Chicago Public Library (1961-1993) **Civic:** Teacher, Sunday School, St. Charles Borromeo Church; Sponsor, Childfun, Unbound Organizations **Military Service:** U.S. Army (1958-1961) **Creative Works:** Writer, Various Cartoon Gags; Contributor, Articles, Book Reviews, Professional Journals **Awards:** Volunteer of the Month, St. Charles Borromeo Church **Memberships:** Phi Kappa Phi; Beta Phi Mu; Knights of Columbus; Couples for Christ **Marquis Who's Who Honors:** Albert Nelson Marquis Lifetime Achievement Award **Why did you become involved in your profession or industry:** After serving in the military, Mr. Donovan decided to become a librarian. He was always an avid reader, so it felt natural. **Avocations:** Collecting baseball cards; Philately **Religion:** Roman Catholic

Clifford J. Drew, PhD

Title: Vice President for Academic Affairs (Retired) **Company Name:** The University of Utah **Date of Birth:** 03/09/1943 **Place of Birth:** Eugene **State/Country of Origin:** OR/USA **Parents:** Albert C.; Violet M. (Caskey) Drew **Education:** Honorary PhD, University of Oregon (1968); EdM, University of Illinois (1966); BS, Eastern Oregon University, Magna Cum Laude (1965) **Career:** Retired (2013); Professor of Special Education and Educational Psychology, The University of Utah (1979-2013); Professor, The University of Utah (1977-2013); Associate Dean, College of Education, The University of Utah (2004-2009); Associate Academy Vice President, The University of Utah (1997-2004); Coordinator of Instructional Technology, Academy Vice President Office, The University of Utah (1995-1997); Associate Dean, The University of Utah (1977-1979, 1989-1995); Assistant Dean, The Graduate School, The University of Utah (1974-1977); Associate Professor of Special Education, The University of Utah (1971-1976); Assistant Professor, Director of Research and Special Education, The University of Texas at Austin (1969-1971); Assistant Professor of Education, Kent State University (1968-1969) **Career Related:** Board of Directors, Far West Laboratory Educational Research and Development, (Now WestEd) (1974-1980); Consultant, Department of Health (1969-1980); Member, Executive Board, Salt Lake County Association for Retarded Children (1971-1972); Member, Advisory Committee, Texas Department of Mental Health and Mental Retardation (1969-1970) **Creative Works:** Co-Author, "Human Exceptionality: School, Community, and Family" (2008); Co-Author, "Designing and Conducting Research in Education" (2008); Co-Author, "Human Exceptionality: School, Community, and Family" (2006); Co-Author, "Intellectual Disabilities Across the Lifespan" (2006); Co-Author, "Understanding Child Behavior Disorders: An Introduction to Child Psychopathology" (2003); Co-Author, "Designing and Conducting Research: Inquiry in Education and Social Science" (1996); Co-Author, "Theory and Application of Statistics" (1990); Author, "Introduction to Designing and Conducting Research" (1976) **Awards:** Fellow, U.S. Department of Education (1966-1968); Fellow, National Defense Education Act (1965-1966) **Memberships:** Fellow, American Association on Intellectual and Development Disabilities; American Psychological Association; American Educational Research Association **Marquis Who's Who Honors:** Albert Nelson Marquis Lifetime Achievement Award

Lawrence K. Duffy, PhD

Title: Professor, Biochemist **Company Name:** University of Alaska Fairbanks **Date of Birth:** 02/1/1948 **Place of Birth:** Brooklyn **State/Country of Origin:** NY/USA **Parents:** Michael Duffy; Anne (Browne) Duffy **Marital Status:** Married **Spouse Name:** Geraldine Antoinette Sheridan (11/10/1972) **Children:** Anne Marie; Kevin Michael; Ryan Sheridan **Education:** Postdoctoral Fellow, Roche Institute of Molecular Biology (1978-1980); Postdoctoral Fellow, Boston University (1977-1978); PhD, University of Alaska Fairbanks (1977); MS, University of Alaska Fairbanks (1972); BS, Fordham University (1969) **Certifications:** Chemist, American Institute of Chemistry (1985) **Career:** Director, Resilience & Adaptation Program, University of Alaska Fairbanks (2013-Present); Professor of Chemistry and Biochemistry, University of Alaska Fairbanks (1992-Present); Co-leader, Graduate Studies Area, University of the Arctic (2007-2012); Interim Dean, University of Alaska Fairbanks Graduate School (2007-2012); Associate Dean for Graduate Studies and Outreach, University of Alaska Fairbanks College of Natural Science and Mathematics (2000-2006); Head, Department of Chemistry and Biochemistry, University of Alaska Fairbanks (1994-1999) **Career Related:** Fellow, American Association for the Advancement of Science (2017); Curriculum Advisory Board, Ilisaguik College (2014); Advisory Board, Pollution Control Commission (2004-2014); Director, Alaska Basic Neuroscience Program (2000-2012); Curriculum Advisory Board, Fairbanks North Star Borough School District (2002-2004); President, Faculty Senate, University of Alaska Fairbanks (2000-2001) **Civic:** President, Board of Directors, Alzheimer's Disease Association of Alaska (1994-1995); Science Advisory Board, American Federation for Aging Research (1994-1995); Institutional Review Board, Fairbanks Memorial Hospital (1990) **Military Service:** Lieutenant, U.S. Navy Reserve (1971-1973) **Creative Works:** Editorial Board, Science of Total Environment (2000-2002) **Awards:** Irish Educator Award, Irish Voice (2013); Excellence Interdisciplinary Science Award, Western Alabama Interdisciplinary Science Conference (2012); Chancellors Diversity Award, University of Alaska Fairbanks (2011); Leadership Fellow, SENCER (2008); Sven Ebbesson Neuroscience Service Award (2007); Carol Fiest Outstanding Adviser Award (1994, 1997, 2005); Usibelli Professional Activity Award (2002) **Memberships:** Board of Directors, American Society of Circumpolar Health (2003-2018); President, American Society of Circumpolar Health (2008); President, American Institute of Chemists (2006); Associate Regional Director, Sigma Xi (2000-2002); President, Sigma Xi (1991) **Marquis Who's Who Honors:** Albert Nelson Marquis Lifetime Achievement Award

Arthur McKee Dula, Esq.

Title: Lawyer; Aerospace Transportation Executive **Industry:** Law and Legal Services **Company Name:** The Law Office of Art Dula **Date of Birth:** 02/06/1947 **Place of Birth:** Arlington **State/Country of Origin:** VA/USA **Parents:** Arthur M. Dula; Lorraine S. Dula **Marital Status:** Married **Spouse Name:** Tamea Ann Dula (12/27/1971) **Children:** Russell E. Dula; Austin Dula **Education:** JD, Tulane University (1975); BS, Eastern New Mexico University (1970) **Career:** Lawyer, The Law Office of Art Dula, Houston, Texas (1979-Present); Associate, Butler & Binion, Houston, Texas (1975-1979) **Career Related:** Visiting Distinguished Professor of Law, University of Akron (1992-1993); Faculty of Law, South Texas College of Law (1985-1997); Faculty of Law, University of Houston (1977-2018); Co-Founder, Eagle Aerospace, Space Services Inc.; Co-Founder, Space Commerce Corp.; Co-Founder, Spacehab Inc.; Co-Founder, Tethers Unlimited Inc.; Co-Founder, Excalibur Almaz Limited **Civic:** Executor, Literary Estate of Robert A. Heinlein (2003-Present); Trustee, Robert A. & Virginia Heinlein Prize Trust (1991-Present); Board of Governors, International Space University; Board of Governors, Board of Directors, U.S. National Space Society; Academician, International Academy of Astronautics; Legal Advisor, Chinese Space Program **Military Service:** With, United States Army (1967-1968) **Creative Works:** Editorial Board, University of Houston Law Review (1978-1984); Editorial Board, Tulane Law Review (1973-1974); Contributor, Articles, Professional Journals **Awards:** Award, ABA (1982); Gagarin Medal, Russian Federation of Cosmonautics; Space Pioneer Award, U.S. National Space Society; Eponym, Minor Planet, 44455Artdula, International Astronomical Union; National Defense Service Medal, Expert; Medal Pistol & Rifle, United States Army **Memberships:** Chairman, Science and Technology Section, ABA (1982-1983); Fellow, American Institute of Aeronautics and Astronautics; International Institute of Space Law, Paris, France; Fellow, Britain Interplanetary Society **Bar Admissions:** Supreme Court of the United States (1978); State of Texas (1975); United States Patent and Trademark Office (1975) **Marquis Who's Who Honors:** Albert Nelson Marquis Lifetime Achievement Award **Avocations:** Reading; Science fiction

Mary Ellen Duncan, PhD

Title: President Emeritus **Company Name:** Howard Community College **Date of Birth:** 08/29/1941 **Place of Birth:** New York **State/Country of Origin:** NY/USA **Parents:** Harry Fielder; Mary (Laveglia) Fielder **Marital Status:** Married **Spouse Name:** John M. Kingsmore (Deceased) **Children:** Kathryn Marie Dickens **Education:** Doctor of Philosophy, University of Connecticut (1982); Master of Arts, University of Connecticut (1973); Bachelor of Science, St. John's University (1963) **Career:** President Emeritus, Howard Community College, Columbia, MD (2008-Present); President, Howard Community College, Columbia, MD (1998-2008); President of Technical College, SUNY Delhi (1991-1998); Director, Eastern Region, Tri-County Technical College, Pendleton, SC (1980-1992); Dean, Planning and Development, Catonsville Community College, Baltimore, MD (1988-1991); Interim President, Catonsville Community College, Baltimore, MD (1989-1990); Dean, Tri-County Technical College, Pendleton, SC (1987-1988); Director of Institutional Development, Tri-County Technical College, Pendleton, SC (1982-1983); Instructional Associate, ACCTion Center, Tri-County Technical College, Pendleton, SC (1976-1982); Instructor, Tri-County Technical College, Pendleton, SC (1975-1976); Graduate Research Assistant, University of Connecticut, Storrs, CT (1971-1975); Instructor of English and Latin, West Islip Public Schools, NY (1963-1971) **Creative Works:** Author, "Indicators of Institutional Effectiveness" (1989) **Awards:** Named, One of Maryland's Top 100 Women, The Daily Record (2002); Merit Award, South Carolina Women in Higher Education (1985); Merit Award, American Association of Community and Junior Colleges (1982); John Fry Award, American Association of Community and Junior Colleges (1981) **Memberships:** Legislative Liaison, National Council for Resource Development (1990-Present); Federal Relations Task Force, American Association of Community and Junior Colleges (1990-1991); American Association of Women in Community Colleges **Marquis Who's Who Honors:** Albert Nelson Marquis Lifetime Achievement Award; Marquis Who's Who Top Professional; Marquis Who's Who Humanitarian Award **Why did you become involved in your profession or industry:** Dr. Duncan did not aspire to become a president of a community college. She entered her profession because she always felt that things needed to be done wherever she was. When Dr. Duncan first arrived at Howard Community College, she felt that things needed to be done and she got them done. **Avocations:** Golf **Religion:** Roman Catholic

Tyrone "Ty" Dunham

Title: Owner, Engineer and Entrepreneur **Industry:** Engineering **Company Name:** Oa Products **Date of Birth:** 06/18/1955 **Place of Birth:** Truckee **State/Country of Origin:** CA/USA **Parents:** Alice Slettedahl; Farnum Dunham **Marital Status:** Divorced **Spouse Name:** Jeanne Marie Brilliante **Children:** Shanna Rae Dunham; Cherie Alana Dunham **Education:** Coursework for Bachelor of Business Administration, College of the Desert, Palm Desert, CA (1973-1977) **Certifications:** Institute of Inspection Cleaning & Restoration Certification, Las Vegas, NV (2001); Master Textile Cleaner and Mold Remediation Specialist **Career:** Owner, Engineer, Entrepreneur, Oa Products, Desert Hot Springs, CA (2016-Present); Master Technician, Prestige Flooring Center, Cathedral City, CA (2002-Present); Carpet Cleaning Technician, Powers Carpet One, Rancho Mirage, CA (1998-2002); Production Operations, Tacmir Corporation and ALMA Inc., Palm Springs, CA (1982-1997) **Career Related:** Production Engineer for Tacmir Corporation and ALMA Inc. **Creative Works:** Patent for Contamination Control Mats, ALMA Inc. **Awards:** Multiple Awards in Gymnastics and Martial Arts **Memberships:** Institute of Inspection Cleaning & Restoration Certification **To what do you attribute your success:** Mr. Dunham attributes his success to being willing to take risks and go above and beyond where other people are willing to go. He does not place limitations on his abilities in procedures, when it comes to discovering new and effective ways to accomplish tasks. He has an intuitive nature that causes him to constantly explore things of interest. **Why did you become involved in your profession or industry:** Mr. Dunham became involved in his profession after cleaning carpets for his best friends for several years. He soon realized he had a knack for this line of work, and eventually established his own business. **Political Affiliations:** Democratic **Religion:** Spiritual

Janice Dutcher

Title: Associate Director **Company Name:** Cancer Research Foundation **Date of Birth:** 11/10/1950 **Place of Birth:** Bend **State/Country of Origin:** OR/USA **Parents:** Charles Glen Phillips; MayBelle (Fluit) Phillips **Marital Status:** Divorced **Spouse Name:** John Dutcher (09/08/1972, Divorced 1981) **Education:** Resident, Rush-Presbyterian-St. Luke's Medical Center, Chicago, IL (1976-1978); Intern, Rush-Presbyterian-St. Luke's Medical Center, Chicago, IL (1975-1976); MD, University of California Davis School of Medicine (1975); BA, The University of Utah, with Honors (1971) **Certifications:** Diplomate, American Board of Internal Medicine; Diplomate, American Board of Medical Oncology; Licenses, Maryland and New York **Career:** Co-founder, Associate Director, Cancer Research Foundation (1998-Present); Professor Medicine, New York Medical College (1998-Present); Director of Immunotherapy Program, Division of Hematology/Oncology, St. Luke's - Roosevelt Hospital Center, Continuum Cancer Centers, NY (2010-2012); Site Director, Oncology, Montefiore North Division, Montefiore Medical Center (2009-2010); Associate Director for Clinical Affairs, Comprehensive Cancer Center, Director of Oncology Apheresis, Our Lady of Mercy Medical Center, Bronx, NY (1998-2008); Professor, Albert Einstein College of Medicine, New York, NY (1992-1998); Associate Professor, Albert Einstein College of Medicine (1986-1992); Course Co-director, Advances in Cancer Treatment Research, Albert Einstein College Medicine (1984-1986); Assistant Professor, Albert Einstein College of Medicine (1983-1986); Assistant Professor, University of Maryland (1982); Senior Investigator, Baltimore Cancer Research, National Cancer Institute (1981-1982); Clinical Associate, Baltimore Cancer Research, National Cancer Institute (1978-1981) **Career Related:** Co-chair, Medical Oncology, National Institutes of Health Renal Cancer Task Force (2015-Present); Advisory Board Member, ECOG-ACRIN Cancer Research Foundation (2010-Present); National Institutes of Health Renal Cancer Task Force (2009-Present); Member, Publishing Committee, ECOG-ACRIN Cancer Research Group (2000-Present); Member, National Institutes of Health Genitourinary Cancer Steering Committee (2009-2011); Member, Data Safety Committee, National Heart, Lung, and Blood Institute (1990-1995); Member, Numerous Committees, Organizations **Military Service:** Inactive Reserve, U.S. Public Health (1982-Present); Commissioned Officer, U.S. Public Health Service (1978-1982) **Creative Works:** Contributor, Editor, Editorial Board; Numerous Professional Journals **Awards:** Recipient, Numerous Grants and Awards **Memberships:** Member, Numerous Organizations **Marquis Who's Who Honors:** Albert Nelson Marquis Lifetime Achievement Award

Alexandra Dylong, RN, BSN, CNOR

Title: Registered Nurse (Retired) **Industry:** Medicine & Health Care **Date of Birth:** 08/03/1950 **State/Country of Origin:** Jersey City **Marital Status:** NJ/USA **Spouse Name:** Walter (Deceased) **Children:** Michael; Meeghan; Mathew **Education:** BA in Health Science and Education **Career:** Registered Nurse, Monmouth Medical Center, Long Branch, NJ (1979-2003); Registered Nurse, Christ Hospital, Jersey City, NJ (1968-1979) **Awards:** Excellence in Education Award **Marquis Who's Who Honors:** Marquis Who's Who Top Professional; Marquis Who's Who Humanitarian Award **Why did you become involved in your profession or industry:** Ms. Dylong became involved in her profession because of her desire to help others, which is reflected in her first name, Alexandra, which translates to "helper of mankind."

Carolyn Eaglehouse

Title: Manager, President **Industry:** Business Management/Business Services **Company Name:** Milky Way Farm/Chester Springs Creamery **Education:** Master of Education **Certifications:** Elementary Education **Career:** Manager, President, Milky Way Farm/Chester Springs Creamery **Civic:** Pumpkin Operation **Creative Works:** Author, "The Magic of Milky Way Farm" (2005) **Awards:** Best Ice Cream in the Area; Best Ice Cream in Pennsylvania **Marquis Who's Who Honors:** Albert Nelson Marquis Lifetime Achievement Award **To what do you attribute your success:** Ms. Eaglehouse had tremendous community support on her journey to success. To this day, the community invests in the farm and, in turn, the farm invests in the community. **Why did you become involved in your profession or industry:** Milky Way Farm has been home to the Matthews family for four generations. Ms. Eaglehouse always knew she would pursue a career in the family business. **Avocations:** Spending time with kids; Supporting others in agriculture; Working with summer camp

Thomas S. Edwards Jr.

Title: Senior Partner **Industry:** Law and Legal Services **Company Name:** Edwards & Ragatz, PA **Place of Birth:** Jacksonville **State/Country of Origin:** FL/USA **Parents:** Thomas Seth Edwards, MD; Hazel Crawford Hetzel **Marital Status:** Married **Spouse Name:** Julie Edwards **Children:** Thomas S. Edwards IV; Jerry C. Edwards; Jennie R. Edwards **Education:** Washington and Lee University **Career:** Senior Partner, Edwards & Ragatz, PA (2008); Predecessor, Edwards & Ragatz, PA **Creative Works:** Author, Articles, Chapters in Legal Books, Books **Awards:** Listed, Best Lawyers in America (2012-Present); "AV" Rated in Martindale-Hubbell (1995-Present); Lawyer of the Year, Medical Malpractice Law, Plaintiffs, Jacksonville, FL (2012, 2015, 2019); Top 100 Trial Lawyers, The National Trial Lawyers (2013-2019); Martindale-Hubbell 35-Year Anniversary Award (2019); Lawyer of the Year, Personal Injury Litigation, Plaintiffs, Jacksonville, FL (2017); B.J. Masterson Award for Professionalism, Florida Justice Association (2014); FJA President's Horsemen Award for "legislative work for consumers and victims" (2014); Justice Raymond Ehrlich Trial Advocacy Award, Jacksonville Bar Association (2013); Trial Lawyer of the Year, Jacksonville Chapter, American Board of Trial Advocates (2009); Spartans at Thermopylae Award "for great personal sacrifice in protecting the justice system," North Florida Trial Lawyers (2009); AFTL FLAG Award (2003, 2004, 2005, 2006, 2007); AFTL Gold Eagle (2003, 2004, 2005, 2007); AFTL Silver Eagle (2006); FJS President's Rough Rider Award for "legislative work for consumers and victims" (2005); AFTL Staff Appreciation Award (2003); AFTL Legislative Leadership Award (2002, 2003); AFTL Bronze Eagle (2002); Barbra Sanders Legal Writing Award, The Florida Bar (1993); Florida Trend Magazine, "Legal Elite"; Florida "Super Lawyer; Listed, Best Law Firms – Tier 1 **Memberships:** Past President, Florida Justice Association (State Trial Lawyers); Past President, Jacksonville Bar Association; Past President, Jacksonville Chapter, ABOTA; Florida Supreme Court Judicial Management Council; Florida Commission on Access to Justice; National Board of Directors, American Board of Trial Advocates; National Board of Directors, The International Academy of Trial Lawyers; The Florida Bar Trial Lawyers Section Executive Counsel; Florida Supreme Court Civil Jury Instructions Committee; Florida Supreme Court Business Jury Instruction Committee; 4th Judicial Circuit Grievance Committee, Florida **To what do you attribute your success:** Mr. Edwards attributes his success to hard work. **Avocations:** Hunting; Fishing

Billie Eilish

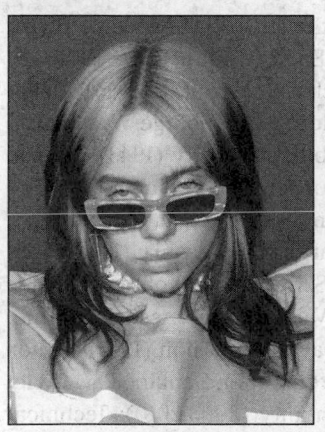

Title: Singer **Industry:** Media & Entertainment **Date of Birth:** 12/18/2001 **Place of Birth:** Los Angeles **State/Country of Origin:** CA/USA **Parents:** Patrick O'Connell; Maggie Baird **Marital Status:** Single **Creative Works:** Singer, "When We All Fall Asleep, Where Do We Go?" (2019); Singer, "Everything I Wanted" (2019); Singer, "All the Good Girls Go to Hell" (2019); Singer, "Bad Guy" (2019); Singer, "Wish You Were Gay" (2019); Singer, "Bury a Friend" (2019); Singer, "When I Was Older" (2019); Singer, "Come Out and Play" (2019); Singer, "You Should See Me in a Crown" (2018); Singer, "Party Favor" (2018); Singer, "Lovely" (2018); Singer, "Bitches Broken Hearts" (2018); Singer, "My Boy" (2018); Singer, "Idontwannabeyouanymore" (2018); Singer, "Copycat" (2017); Singer, "Watch" (2017); Singer, "Bored" (2017); Singer, "Bellyache" (2017); Singer, "Six Feet Under" (2016); Singer, "Ocean Eyes" (2015) **Awards:** Album of the Year, Grammy Awards (2020); Song of the Year, Grammy Awards (2020); Best New Artist, Grammy Awards (2020); Record of the Year, Grammy Awards (2020); Best Pop Vocal Album, Grammy Awards (2020); Best Pop Solo Performance, Grammy Awards (2020); Most Simultaneous U.S. Hot 100 Entries by a Female, Guinness World Records (2020) Best Solo Female Act, Telehit Awards (2019); Best Anglo Song, Telehit Awards (2019); Best Anglo Song, Telehit (2019); Choice Breakout Artist, Teen Choice Awards (2019); Choice Female Artist, Teen Choice Awards (2019); Beginner, Rolling Stone's International Music Awards (2019); Female Artist of 2019, People's Choice Awards (2019); International Breakthrough of the Year, NRJ Music Awards (2019); Favorite Breakout Artist, Nickelodeon Kids' Choice Awards (2019); Favorite International Star, Nickelodeon Kids' Choice Awards Abu Dhabi (2019); Winning Video, MTV Video Play Awards (2019); Best New International Artist Video, MTV Video Music Awards Japan (2019); Best Editing, MTV Video Music Awards (2019); Push Artist of the Year, MTV Video Music Awards (2019); Best New Artist, MTV Video Music Awards (2019); Global Hit, MTV Millennial Awards (2019); Best New Act, MTV Europe Music Awards (2019); Best Song, MTV Europe Music Awards (2019); Best Pop Song, Melon Music Awards (2019); Best International Album, LOS40 Music Awards (2019); Best Foreign New Act, GAFFA Awards (Sweden) (2019); Foreign Album of the Year, Danish Music Awards (2019); 61 Seconds to Five Minutes - Clio Grand, Clio Awards (2019); Woman of the Year, Billboard Women in Music Awards (2019); Vanguard Award, ASCAP Pop Music Awards (2019)

Nicholas Elefterakis

Title: Founding Partner **Industry:** Law and Legal Services **Company Name:** Elefterakis, Elefterakis & Panek **Date of Birth:** 11/07/1985 **Place of Birth:** Brooklyn **State/Country of Origin:** NY/USA **Parents:** John Elefterakis; Dory Elefterakis **Marital Status:** Married **Spouse Name:** Monique **Children:** Neeko; Taso; Penelope **Education:** JD, Hofstra University Maurice A. Deane School of Law (2010); BS in Business Management, Fordham University, NY (2007) **Career:** Partner, Elefterakis, Elefterakis & Panek (2010-Present) **Civic:** Founder, Youth Sports Program, EEP Sports (2017-Present) **Memberships:** New York State Bar Association; New York State Trial Lawyers (NYSTLA) **Why did you become involved in your profession or industry:** Mr. Elefterakis had been a competitive athlete his entire life. What intrigued him about the law was the competitive nature of the business. He was also inspired by family members who he had that were also lawyers. His brother is a lawyer as well, and the two decided to go into business together right after graduating law school. **Thoughts on Life:** Mr. Elefterakis says "It is important that people are treated with respect and dignity... We genuinely care about our clients. It is more than a business... it is real life and has real life impacts on people."

Roy T. Englert, JD

Title: Lawyer **Industry:** Law and Legal Services **Date of Birth:** 09/11/1922 **Place of Birth:** Nashville **State/Country of Origin:** TN/USA **Parents:** Roy T. Englert; Ruth Rowe (Tindall) Englert **Marital Status:** Married **Spouse Name:** Maureen Backof Englert (3/4/2015); Helen Frances Wiggs (9/25/1948) **Children:** Lee Ann; Roy Jr. **Education:** LLM, George Washington University (1953); JD, Columbia University (1951); BA, Vanderbilt University (1943) **Career:** Sole Practice, Washington, DC (1973-1996); Deputy General Counsel, U.S. Department of the Treasury (1966-1973); Assistant General Counsel, U.S. Department of the Treasury (1962-1966); Chief Counsel, Office Comptroller of Currency, U.S. Department of the Treasury (1958-1962); Assistant Counsel, Office of the Comptroller of the Currency, U.S. Department of the Treasury (1951-1958) **Career Related:** Secretary, Board of Directors, Walker/Potter Associates, Inc. (Now, Potter Associates), Washington, DC (1973-1996); U.S. Assay Commission (1975); Senior Seminar, Foreign Policy, Department of State (1963-1964); Lecturer, Writer, Banking Law **Civic:** Board Director, Westminster at Lake Ridge Retirement Community (2003-2010); Technical Official, Judo, Atlanta Olympics **Military Service:** Lieutenant, U.S. Navy Reserve (1943-1946) **Creative Works:** Contributor, Articles, Professional Journals **Awards:** General Counsel's Award (1973); Exceptional Service Award, U.S. Treasury (1972) **Memberships:** ABA; Tennessee Bar Association **Bar Admissions:** U.S. Court of International Trade (1975); Supreme Court of the United States (1955); State of Tennessee (1951); U.S. District Court for the District of Columbia (1951) **Marquis Who's Who Honors:** Albert Nelson Marquis Lifetime Achievement Award **Why did you become involved in your profession or industry:** Mr. Englert became involved in his profession because he loved reading. **Religion:** Presbyterian

Sandra "Sandee" Evans

Title: Director of Academic Services (Ret.) **Industry:** Education/Educational Services **Company Name:** Cumberland County College **Date of Birth:** 03/01/1934 **Place of Birth:** Amherst **State/Country of Origin:** MA/USA **Parents:** Alfred George Wheeler; Isabelle (Hoelzle) Wheeler **Marital Status:** Widower **Children:** Charles Douglas; Darcie L.; Dana L. **Education:** Postgraduate Coursework, Virginia Polytechnic Institute and State University; Kellogg Fellow, The Kellogg Institute at Appalachian State University (1981, 1984)Degree in reading, Glassboro State College, 1980; MA, Reading Specialization, Glassboro State College, (now Rowan University), 1980;BS, Business Education, Grove City College, (1956) **Certifications:** Certified Developmental Education Specialist **Career:** Retired Director of Academic Services (2004); Director, Success Center, Cumberland County College, Vineland, NJ (1984-2004); Mathematics Instructor, Cumberland County College, Vineland, NJ (1979-1984); Coordinator, Learning Laboratory, Cumberland County College, Vineland, NJ (1974-1978); Teacher, East Washington High School (1956-1957) **Career Related:** Project Director, National Workplace Literacy Project, Millville, NJ (1991-2000); Project Director, Retention Initiative Project, Vineland, NJ (1991); Chairman, Board of Directors, Literacy Volunteers of America, Cumberland County, Vineland, NJ (1989-2000); Trainer, Tutor (1989-1991) **Civic:** Creator, Board of Directors for Literacy Volunteers of America **Awards:** Literacy Citation, State Assembly of New Jersey (1990); Literacy Award, International Reading Association (1988) **Memberships:** Research Club, Bridgeton (2005-Present); American Association of University Women (1980-2002); New Jersey Association of Development Educators (1980); International Reading Association (1980); National Education Association (1976) **Marquis Who's Who Honors:** Albert Nelson Marquis Lifetime Achievement Award; Marquis Who's Who Top Professional **Why did you become involved in your profession or industry:** Ms. Evans became involved in her profession because she always wanted to be a teacher. She had a large black board since was 5 or 6 years old and would play school with her sister who was the student and she was the teacher. **Avocations:** Reading; Gardening; Crewel embroidery; Bridge; Tutoring **Political Affiliations:** Independent **Religion:** Presbyterian

Gloria "Laiinie" Everhart

Title: Music Educator **Industry:** Education/Educational Services **Date of Birth:** 02/28/1945 **Place of Birth:** Olney **State/Country of Origin:** MD/USA **Parents:** Thomas Oland; Catherine Rosalie Oland **Marital Status:** Widow **Spouse Name:** Frederick F. Everhart DVM (Deceased) **Children:** April Elayne Woodall; Joy Elizabeth Kang (Stepdaughter); Gregory Duke Everhart (Stepson); Carolyn Whitworth Everhart (Stepdaughter); 11 Grandchildren; Five Great-grandchildren **Education:** Postgraduate Coursework, Towson State University; Postgraduate Coursework, University of Illinois; MusB, Peabody Conservatory of Music (1967) **Career:** Music Director, Rolling Hills Baptist (2002-Present); Teacher, Piano, Voice, Music Theory, Everhart Piano Studio, Columbia, MD (1960-Present); Long Term Substitute Music Teacher, Glenelg Country School (2002); Music Director, Bethel Baptist (1997-2002); Teacher, High School Vocal Music, Howard County Public Schools (1984-1986); Teacher, Vocal Music, Howard County Public Schools (1967-1974) **Career Related:** Choir Director, Christian Choir Howard County (2013-Present); Accompanist, Maryland (2007-2013); Music Director, The Alleluias, Inc., Columbia, MD (1987-2004) **Civic:** Minister, Music and Worship, Rolling Hills Baptist Church, Clarksville, MD (2002-Present); Music Director, The Alleluias, Inc., Columbia, MD (1987-2005); Music Minister, Bethel Baptist Church, Ellicott City, MD (1997-2002); Secretary, Treasurer, Board of Directors, Everhart Animal Hospital, Inc. (1975-1991); Music Director, Bethany Lane Baptist Church, Ellicott City, MD (1968-1975) **Creative Works:** Director, Choral Performances, The Alleluias in Concert **Memberships:** Associate Member, American Choral Directors Association **Marquis Who's Who Honors:** Marquis Who's Who Top Professional **To what do you attribute your success:** Ms. Everhart's success belongs to her parents, teachers and husband. Each one encouraged and supported her in many ways with their love and wisdom. **Why did you become involved in your profession or industry:** She became involved with her profession because she enjoyed her music training that officially began at 8 years of age. **Avocations:** Reading; Internet studies; Ethnomusicology; Jumble word puzzles; Scrabble; Dogs; Playing the piano **Religion:** Christian **Thoughts on Life:** Put God first and the rest will come.

David Albert Ezzo, PhD

Marquis Who's Who
18 98
Biographee

Title: Nonprofit Executive; Anthropologist; Educator **Industry:** Education/Educational Services **Date of Birth:** 06/09/1963 **Place of Birth:** Buffalo **State/Country of Origin:** NY/USA **Parents:** Albert Ezzo; Ann Ezzo **Marital Status:** Married **Spouse Name:** Michelle Martin (08/13/2005) **Education:** PhD in Anthropology, Richardson University (2005); MPA, Hamilton University (2005); Coursework, New York University, New York, NY (1996); MA in Anthropology, University of Oklahoma, Norman, OK (1987); BA in Anthropology, State University of New York at Fredonia (1985) **Certifications:** Certified, Fundraising Executive (1997); Certified, Nonprofit Management, University of South Florida, Tampa (1997); Certified, Personnel Management, State University of New York at Buffalo (1991) **Career:** Adjunct Professor, Sociology and Anthropology, Erie Community College (2010-Present); Director, Endowment, Boy Scouts of America (2005-Present); Adjunct Professor of Anthropology, Villa Maria College, Buffalo, NY (2011); Director, Community Development, YMCA, Burbank, CA (2002); Director, Development and Public Relations, YMCA, St. Petersburg, FL (1996-1998); From Staff Member to Director of Endowment, Boy Scouts of America, Buffalo, NY (1987-2005); Adjunct Teacher, Sociology, Niagara University; Lecturer, Anthropology, Villa Maria College; Adjunct Assistant Professor of Sociology and Anthropology, Genesee Community College **Career Related:** Lecturer in Field **Civic:** Member, Board of Directors, Delaware Family YMCA, Buffalo, NY (2014-Present); Member, Board of Directors, Friend of Camp Turner (2013-Present) **Creative Works:** Author, "Cannibalism & Cross-Cultural Perspective," Dog Ear Press (2008); Co-author, "Papers on Historical Algonquin & Iroquois Topics," Dog Ear Press (2007); Contributor, Scientific Papers **Awards:** Vigil Honor Award, Boy Scouts of America (1981); Eagle Scout Award, Boy Scouts of America (1977) **Marquis Who's Who Honors:** Albert Nelson Marquis Lifetime Achievement Award; Marquis Who's Who Top Professional **Why did you become involved in your profession or industry:** Professor Ezzo became involved in his field because of an interest in Native American culture over a course of four summers. When he went to college, he became a double major in music and anthropology, and graduate school for anthropology. **Avocations:** Fitness; Tennis; Music; Travel

Paul Joseph Fellers, PhD

Title: Research Scientist III **Industry:** Research **Date of Birth:** 03/10/1933 **Place of Birth:** Northampton **State/Country of Origin:** MA/USA **Parents:** Dr. Carl Raymond; Josephine F. **Marital Status:** Married **Spouse Name:** Donna Mavis Fellers (06/30/1962) **Children:** Rebecca; Annette **Education:** PhD in Food Sciences, Michigan State University (1964); MS in Food Processing, Virginia Polytechnic Institute and State University (1957); BS in Food Technology, University of Massachusetts (1955) **Career:** Retired (1995); Research Scientist III, Florida Department of Citrus (1964-1995) **Civic:** President, Interim Vice President, Lake Region Audubon Society **Military Service:** Meteorological Observer, Fort Huachuca, U.S. Army (1957-1959) **Creative Works:** Contributor, Articles, Professional Journals **Awards:** Blazing Star Award, Green Horizon Land Trust (2018) **Memberships:** Phi Tau Sigma The Honor Society of Food Science and Technology; Sigma Xi, The Scientific Research Honor Society **Marquis Who's Who Honors:** Albert Nelson Marquis Lifetime Achievement Award; Marquis Who's Who Top Professional **Why did you become involved in your profession or industry:** Dr. Fellers became involved in his profession because his father was one of the founder of the field of food technology during the early-1930s. Inspired by his father, he followed his father's footsteps and pursued a similar path. **Avocations:** Leading nature field trips; Teaching ornithology; Taking photographs; Dancing

Patrick H. Fernandez

Title: Crime Lab Technician Supervisor (Retired) **Industry:** Sciences **Marital Status:** Married **Spouse Name:** Glenda Harris **Education:** Postgraduate Coursework, Survey of Forensic Science, The George Washington University (1973); BS in Biology, Morgan State University (1971) **Certifications:** Certified Crime Scene Investigation Expert; Diplomate, Various Courses in Crime Scene Investigation Field **Career:** Retired (2011); Crime Lab Technician Supervisor, Mobile Unit, Baltimore Police Department (1980-2011); Crime Laboratory Technician, Mobile Unit, Baltimore Police Department (1971-1979); Substitute Teacher, Baltimore City Public Schools (1971) **Civic:** Rainbow Unit; The American National Red Cross; Colleges and High Schools; Numerous Charitable Organizations **Awards:** Certificate for Service, Baltimore Police Department (2011); Special Service Commendation with Ribbon (1999, 2008); Two Letters of Commendation, Mobile Unit, Baltimore Police Department; Unit Citation with Ribbon **Memberships:** Vanguard Justice Society, Inc. **Marquis Who's Who Honors:** Albert Nelson Marquis Lifetime Achievement Award; Marquis Who's Who Top Professional **Why did you become involved in your profession or industry:** Mr. Fernandez become involved in his profession because he needed a job. He spent the summer after he graduated looking for work, and he wound up substitute teaching for about a month. Most of his family are school teachers. There was no desire prior to teaching to get into law enforcement. **Avocations:** Ravens fan; Music; Wine collector; Gourmet cooking; Gardening

Andrew Taylor Fisher

Title: Website Designer **Industry:** Internet **Date of Birth:** 11/22/1950 **Place of Birth:** Oakland **State/Country of Origin:** CA/USA **Parents:** Walter Dummer Fisher; Marjorie Catherine Lynis Smith **Education:** Diploma in Web Development, DePaul University, Chicago, IL (2001); Bachelor of Arts in Computer Studies, Northwestern University, Evanston, IL (1988) **Career:** Webmaster, Website Design and Management (2000-Present); Database, Office Manager, SCORE Association, Chicago, IL (2003-2006); Programmer, Financial Statistical Analyst, Business Decisions Economics, Inc., Northbrook, IL (2001-2002); Database Programmer, Technology Writer, The Good Group, Inc., Evanston, IL (1997-2000); Programming Contractor, Northrop Grumman Corporation, Rolling Meadows, IL (1996); Data Management Software Developmental Consultant, Amoco, Chicago, IL (1995) **Career Related:** Editor, Newsletter, Unitarian Universalists for Social Justice, Northeast Illinois, Wisconsin, Northwest Indiana, Michigan (2008-Present); Webmaster, Hyde Park and Kenwood Interfaith Council (2009-2013); Nutrition for Optimal Health Association (1997-2008) **Civic:** Commission Director, Unitarian Universalists for Social Justice, Northeast Illinois, Wisconsin, Northwest Indiana, Michigan (2008-Present); Chair, Environmental Task Force, Unitarian Universalists for Social Justice, Northeast Illinois, Wisconsin, Northwest Indiana, Michigan (2004-Present); Baritone Singer, North Shore Choral Society (1999-Present); Choir Baritone Singer, Unitarian Church of Evanston, Evanston, IL (1976-Present) **Creative Works:** Author, "The Lifelong Search for Truth - Photo Autobiography" (2017); Cast Member, "The Mikado" (2000) **Awards:** Fleet Championship Award, Sheridan Shores Yacht Club (2007); First Place Trophy, Art McGee Sailing Race (2004); Second Place Trophy, Art McGee Sailing Race (2003); Co-recipient, Arthur B. Hanson Rescue Medal, United States Sailing Association (2000) **Memberships:** Webmaster, Snowsneeker Club (2004-2006); Recording Secretary, Snowsneeker Club (1995-1996); Founder, First President, Students for Ecological and Environmental Development, Northwestern University (1986-1988) **Marquis Who's Who Honors:** Albert Nelson Marquis Lifetime Achievement Award **Why did you become involved in your profession or industry:** Mr. Fisher went into web design because he knew computers were an expanding field. He went to DePaul University to further his education in computers. **Avocations:** Choral singing; Biking; Skiing; Sailing; Website designing; Jogging; Sculling **Political Affiliations:** Democrat **Religion:** Unitarian Universalist

Terri L. Fitzpatrick

Title: Chief Operating Officer, Vice President of Development **Industry:** Business Management/Business Services **Company Name:** Boji Group, LLC **Parents:** Terry; Sharron **Children:** Paul; Andy; Sam **Education:** Graduate Coursework, Michigan Political Leadership Program, Michigan State University, East Lansing, MI; Coursework, Lake Superior State University, Sault Ste. Marie, MI **Career:** Chief Operating Officer, Vice President of Development, Boji Group, LLC, Lansing, MI (2014-Present); Vice President, Tribal Business Development/Federal Procurement, Michigan Economic Development Corporation (2010-2014); Real Estate Director, Strategic Development Director, State of Michigan, DTMB (2004-2010); Real Estate Director, Sault Tribe/Vice President of Development, Kewadin and Greektown Casinos, Sault Ste. Marie Tribe of Chippewa Indians (1994-2004) **Career Related:** Chairperson, Board of Directors, Waseyabek Development Company (2014-2016) **Civic:** First Chairperson, Nottawaseppi Huron Band of the Potawatomi's Business Development Board, Waseyabek Development Company (2014-2016) **Awards:** Notable Women in Real Estate, Detroit Crain's (2019); Innovations Award for Public Private Partnership for Delivery of Real Estate Services, National Association of State Facility Administrators; Award for Work for Securing a Forensic Lab, Michigan State Police **Memberships:** Sault Ste. Marie Tribe of Chippewa Indians **To what do you attribute your success:** Ms. Fitzpatrick attributes her success to her mom and dad. They are very humble working class people who always worked really hard. They were community oriented. Her dad was extremely creative, they were both very resourceful, and her mom was never daunted by any task. She also feels she had great teachers when she was in grade school who were very encouraging. **Why did you become involved in your profession or industry:** Ms. Fitzpatrick became involved in her profession because she grew up in a very rural area and spent a lot of time with uncles and family members who property walk and could tell where lines were, she always found that so interesting. She found the history of land ownership really interesting and helped form basis for successful development. **Avocations:** Reading (historical readings); Time with friends; Family time

Rose Ann Fleming, PhD, JD, SNDdeN

Title: Special Assistant to the President **Industry:** Education/Educational Services **Company Name:** Xavier University **Date of Birth:** 08/23/1932 **Place of Birth:** Cincinatti **State/Country of Origin:** OH/USA **Parents:** Thomas John Fleming; Mary Gertrude (Sullivan) Fleming **Education:** JD, Salmon P. Chase School of Law, Northern Kentucky University (1988); MBA, Xavier University, Cincinnati, OH (1984); PhD in Educational Administration, Miami University, Oxford, OH (1973); MEd, Xavier University, Cincinnati, OH (1969); MA in English, University of Detroit Mercy (1964); BA, Mount St. Joseph University (1954) **Certifications:** Sisters of Notre Dame de Namur, Roman Catholic Church (1954) **Career:** Special Assistant to the President, Xavier University (2010-Present); Lawyer, Private Practice, Cincinnati, OH (1989-Present); Academy Administrator, Xavier University, Cincinnati, OH (1982-Present); President, Trinity College (1975-1982); Supervisor, Summit Country Day School, Cincinnati, OH (1967-1975); Faculty, Summit Country Day School, Cincinnati, OH (1960-1975); Teacher, Latin, Social Studies, English, Mount Notre Dame High School, Reading, OH (1954-1960) **Civic:** Board Member, Friars Club; Board Member, Legal Aid Society; Volunteer, Lawyers Project; Xavier Players, Charleston, SC **Creative Works:** Co-Author, "Out of Habit" **Awards:** One of Four Great Cincinnatians, Chamber of Commerce (2019); Friars Award, Friars Club (2019) **Bar Admissions:** Ohio (1989) **Marquis Who's Who Honors:** Marquis Who's Who Top Professional; Distinguished Humanitarian **To what do you attribute your success:** Dr. Fleming is fortunate to have been blessed by God in many ways. She has had wonderful advantages in terms of education and travel, all of which have provided her with the knowledge to succeed. Likewise, she has always been able to relate to others, which has benefitted her career in both education and law. **Why did you become involved in your profession or industry:** Dr. Fleming became involved in education and law because she wanted to serve others. Throughout her career, she has also done a lot of volunteer work, especially with the Sisters of Notre Dame de Namur.

Martin Floch, MD

Title: Professor of Gastroenterology and Nutrition **Industry:** Education/Educational Services **Company Name:** Yale University **Date of Birth:** 07/24/1928 **Place of Birth:** New York **State/Country of Origin:** NY/USA **Parents:** Samuel Floch; Jean (Scheinman) Floch **Marital Status:** Married **Spouse Name:** Gladys Wisser (11/24/1954) **Children:** Dr. Jeffrey Aaron; Dr. Craig Lawrence; Lisa Suzanne; Dr. Neil Robert **Education:** Fellow in Gastroenterology, Seton Hall College of Medicine (Now Hackensack Meridian School of Medicine at Seton Hall University) (1959-1960); Resident in Medicine, Beth Israel Hospital (Now Mount Sinai Beth Israel Hospital) (1957-1959); Intern, Beth Israel Hospital (Now Mount Sinai Beth Israel Hospital) (1956-1957); MD, New York Medical College (1956); MS, University of New Hampshire (1950); BA, New York University (1949) **Certifications:** Diplomate, American Board of Internal Medicine, American Board of Gastroenterology, and American Clinical Board of Nutrition (ACBN) **Career:** Clinical Professor, Conference Coordinator, Yale University (2011-Present); Clinical Professor, Medicine, Yale University (1976-Present); Member, Staff, Norwalk Hospital, Western Connecticut Health Network (1964-Present); Director, Ambulatory Gastroenterology Services, Yale University (2005-2011); Chief, Gastroenterology and Nutrition, Norwalk Hospital, Western Connecticut Health Network (1970-1998); Chairman, Department of Medicine, Norwalk Hospital, Western Connecticut Health Network (1970-1994); Assistant Attending Physician, Montefiore Medical Center (1962-1964); Instructor, Medicine, University of Puerto Rico (1960-1962) **Career Related:** Board of Directors, Norwalk Bank (1987) **Civic:** Trustee, Aspetuck Valley Health District (Now Naugatuck Valley Health District) (1974-1976); Trustee, Norwalk Hospital, Western Connecticut Health Network (1972-1978) **Military Service:** Served, Medical Corps, United States Army (1960-1962) **Creative Works:** Editor, Textbooks, Journals; Contributor, Articles, Professional Journals **Awards:** Samuel S. Weiss Award, American College of Gastroenterology (2010); Grantee, EFA (1989-1992, 2001-2003); Named Master, American College of Gastroenterology (1985); George Thornton Teaching Award, Connecticut Medical Society (1984); Grantee, The Carson Leslie Foundation (1980); Grantee, National Institutes of Health (1975-1978); Grantee, United States Army Medical Research (1964-1967) **Memberships:** Member, Numerous Organizations

H. Eugene Forrester, BS, BE

Title: Agriculture Educator **Date of Birth:** 05/16/1928 **Place of Birth:** Grass Valley **State/Country of Origin:** OR/USA **Parents:** Charles Scott Forrester; Edna Minna (Hoffmeister) Forrester **Marital Status:** Married **Spouse Name:** Vivian Eloise Roberts (07/19/1953) **Children:** Melissa D. Mattick; Beverley Garcia; Marilyn D. Finley; Pamela Forrester **Education:** BS,BE, Washington State University **Certifications:** Certified Teacher and Vocational Director, State of Washington **Career:** Owner, Consultant, Forrester Consulting Service (1991-Present); Administrator of Vocational Education, Superintendent of Public Instruction (1989-1991); Director of Agricultural Education, Superintendent of Public Instruction (1982-1989); Supervisor of Agricultural Education, Superintendent of Public Instruction (1972-1982); Teacher of Agricultural Education, Ellensburg School District (1951-1954, 1956-1972) **Career Related:** Owner, Commercial Hay and Cattle Ranch, Ellensburg (1960-1976); Liaison Officer, United States Air Force Academy (1960-1970) **Civic:** Director, Washington FFA Association (1982-Present); President, Washington State School Retirees' Association (2008); Chair, WSFA (1955-1958, 1991-1993); Member, WSFA (1988-1993); Board Member, Thurston County Fair (1976-1988) **Military Service:** Air Force Reserve (1951-1974); Lieutenant Colonel, U.S. Air Force (1954-1956) **Creative Works:** Contributor, Articles, Professional Journals **Awards:** Distinguished Alumnus Award, Alumni Association, Washington State University (2010); Governor's Citation, State of Washington (1991); Outstanding Service Award, NAAE (1984, 1987); Meritorious Service Award, Washington Commission for Vocational Education (1985); State Teacher of the Year, Washington Association of Agricultural Educators (1969) **Memberships:** President, Thurston County School Retirees' Association (1994-1995); President, Washington Association of Agricultural Educators (1971-1972); Member, National Policy Council; Former President, Lieutenant Governor, Kiwanis International **Marquis Who's Who Honors:** Albert Nelson Marquis Lifetime Achievement Award; Marquis Who's Who Top Professional **Why did you become involved in your profession or industry:** Mr. Forrester became involved in his profession because of his high school teachers, Mr. Gronewald and Mr. McKay. **Avocations:** Gardening; Hunting elk; Playing softball; Spending time with three grandsons and two granddaughters **Political Affiliations:** Republican

Nancy Fortunato

Title: Artist, Educator **Industry:** Education/Educational Services **Parents:** Charles Fortunato; Virginia Niemuth Fortunato **Marital Status:** Widowed **Spouse Name:** Donald William Anstedt (Deceased, 2015) **Education:** Coursework, China Academy of Art (1984) **Career:** Art Instructor **Career Related:** Board of Directors, National Arts Foundation **Civic:** President Emeritus, International Society of Marine Painters, Inc. (2004-Present); President, International Society of Marine Painters, Inc. (2002-2004) **Creative Works:** Author, "Splash 14 Book" (2013); Author, "Splash 12 Book" (2011); Author, "Splash 11 Book" (2010); Author, "How to Capture Movement Book" (2001); Author, "Artists of the Renown Book" (2001); Author, "Watercolor Tips" (1982, 2001); Author, "Artistic Touch Book, First Edition" (1999); Author, "So You Want to be An Artist" (1980); Author, Five Volumes, "Coffee Book for Thinkers" **Awards:** Award, Arizona Watercolor Association Inc. (2008, 2019); Medal, Pennsylvania Watercolor Society (2013); Grand Paint America, Western Federation of Watercolor Societies (2009); Academic Artist Award, Transparent Watercolor Society of America (2002-2003); Purchase Award, Merit Award, Academic Artists Association (2002); Excellence Awards, Texas Watercolor Society (1989) **Memberships:** Master, Transparent Watercolor Society of America; Fellow, The American Artists Professional League, Inc.; Signature Member, Watercolor West; The American Society of Marine Artists; Watercolor Honor Society USA; Western Federation of Watercolor Societies; Academic Artists Association; Arizona Watercolor Association Inc.; Texas Watercolor Society; Purple Sage Honor Society; Artists for Conservation Foundation, Inc. **Marquis Who's Who Honors:** Albert Nelson Marquis Lifetime Achievement Award; Marquis Who's Who Top Professional **Why did you become involved in your profession or industry:** Ms. Fortunato became involved in her profession because she grew up an only child and was able to spend time alone in nature, which made her want to preserve it through the arts. **Avocations:** Taking photographs; Watching birds; Traveling

James Mark Fragomeni, PhD

Title: Technical Consultant, Educator, Metallurgical and Mechanical Engineer **Industry:** Consulting **Company Name:** Metallurgy & Science Consulting Services **Date of Birth:** 09/24/1962 **Place of Birth:** Columbus **State/Country of Origin:** OH/USA **Marital Status:** Single **Education:** PhD, Purdue University, West Lafayette, IN (1994); MS in Engineering, Purdue University, West Lafayette, IN (1988); BS in Metallurgical Engineering, University of Pittsburgh, Pittsburgh, PA (1985) **Certifications:** Construction Quality Management, U.S. Army Corps Engineers (2009); Quality Technician, American Society for Quality (ASQ) (2005) **Career:** Assistant Professor, University of Detroit Mercy, Detroit, MI (2000-2004); Summer Faculty Fellow, AFB Materials and Manufacturing Directorate, AFOSR, Wright Patterson Air Force Base, Dayton, OH (1998); Assistant Professor, Ohio University, Athens, OH (1997-2000); Assistant Professor, University of Alabama, Tuscaloosa, AL (1995-1997); Assistant Researcher, Department of Defense Analysis Center, Purdue University, West Lafayette, IN (1995); Management Associate Engineer, United States Steel Corporation, Gary, IN (1985-1986); Research Intern, Allegheny Ludlum Steel Corporation, Research Center, Brackenridge, PA (1984) **Career Related:** Quality Systems Manager, Distel Tool and Machine Company, St. Clair Shores, MI (2008-2010); Metallurgical Engineering Consultant, Westmoreland Mechanical Testing and Research, Inc., Youngstown, PA (2007-2008); Instructor with University of Detroit at Ford (2001-2004); Engineering Instructor, Lawrence Tech at Focus Hope, Detroit, MI (2002-2003); Summer Faculty Fellow, NASA Marshall Space Flight Center, Huntsville, AL (1996-1997); Graduate Research Assistant, Engineering Research Center, Purdue University, West Lafayette, IN (1986-1994) **Civic:** Volunteer, Comcast Television Studio, Southfield, MI (2005-2008) **Creative Works:** Contributor, Numerous Articles to Professional Science and Engineering Journals and Conferences **Awards:** Inductee, Pi Tau Sigma (1998); Merit Scholarship, University of Pittsburgh (1981-1985); Inductee, Omicron Delta Kappa (1984); Order of Engineer (1983); Inductee, Tau Beta Pi (1982); Inductee, Phi Eta Sigma (1981) **Marquis Who's Who Honors:** Albert Nelson Marquis Lifetime Achievement Award (2018)

Stephen Field Franks

Title: Judge (Retired) **Company Name:** District Court of North Carolina **Date of Birth:** 06/12/1930 **Place of Birth:** Biltmore **State/Country of Origin:** NC/USA **Parents:** Thomas Hendricks; Margaret (Field) Franks **Marital Status:** Married **Spouse Name:** Betty J. Causey (11/21/2004); Mary Elizabeth Volbeda (4/28/1962, Divorced 2004) **Children:** Stephen Bruce; Andrea Carol; Craig Thomas **Education:** JD, University of North Carolina (1955); LLB, University of North Carolina (1955); BA, Duke University (1952) **Career:** Judge, District Court of North Carolina, Hendersonville, NC (1988-2002); Private Practice, Hendersonville, NC (1981-1988); Legislative Advisor, County of San Bernardino, Sacramento, CA (1970-1981); Counsel to Mayor, Mayor's Office, San Bernardino, CA (1966-1969); Deputy City Attorney, City Attorney Office, San Bernardino, CA (1964-1966) **Career Related:** Federal Aid Coordinator, City of San Bernardino, CA (1966-1969) **Civic:** Member, Child Fatality Prevention Team, Hendersonville, NC (2002); Chairman, San Juan Unified School District, Sacramento, CA (1979); Member, San Juan Unified School District, Sacramento, CA (1978-1981); President, Sacramento County Mental Health Association, Sacramento, CA (1978-1979); President, County Board of Education (1977-1978); Director, Sacramento County Mental Health Association, Sacramento, CA (1973-1980) **Military Service:** Commander, United States Navy Judge Advocate General's Corps (1955-1960) **Memberships:** Fellow, Association of Trial Lawyers of America (Now American Association for Justice); North Carolina Bar Association; University Club; Elks; Board of Directors, Rotary International; Active Member, Senior Warden; Vestry Governing Board; Historic Saint John's Church; Flat Rocks **Bar Admissions:** Supreme Court of the United States (1966); California (1964); North Carolina (1955) **Marquis Who's Who Honors:** Albert Nelson Marquis Lifetime Achievement Award; Marquis Who's Who Top Professional **Why did you become involved in your profession or industry:** Mr. Franks became involved in his profession as a judge because he was working for an insurance company while he was studying for the bar, and then after he passed the bar he took a job with the city of San Bernardino as a deputy attorney. He did that for about four years and then took a position as a staff attorney for the mayor of San Bernardino. He was practicing law in a private practice in Henersonville for about six years before he was elected judge. **Avocations:** Hiking **Religion:** Episcopalian

William G.D. Frederick, PhD

Title: Research Scientist **Industry:** Research **Date of Birth:** 06/23/1936 **Place of Birth:** Toledo **State/Country of Origin:** OH/USA **Parents:** Rolland Leslie Frederick; Ruth Matilda Frederick **Marital Status:** Married **Spouse Name:** Geralyn Goldman Middleton (08/14/1981); Nancy Lee Spalding (06/14/1958, Divorced 07/14/1981) **Children:** William George DeMott Frederick; Rebecca Ann Rudich; Frank Gibson Goldman **Education:** Diploma in Systems Planning, Research, Development, and Engineering, Level III, Defense Acquisition University, Fort Belvoir, VA (1997); MS in Management, Massachusetts Institute of Technology (1980); PhD in Materials Science, University of Cincinnati (1973); MS in Physics, University of Dayton (1968); BS in Engineering Physics, The University of Toledo (1958) **Career:** Executive Director, Photon Research Associates Inc., (Now Raytheon Company) (2004-2010); Corporate Vice President, Photon Research Associates Inc., (Now Raytheon Company) (2001-2004); Deputy for Special Projects, Ballistic Missile Defense Organization (Now Missile Defense Agency), U.S. Department of Defense (2000-2001); Chief Scientist, Ballistic Missile Defense Organization, (Now Missile Defense Agency), U.S. Department of Defense (1999-2000); Assistant Deputy for Technology, Ballistic Missile Defense Organization, (Now Missile Defense Agency), U.S. Department of Defense (1992-1999); Director of Sensor Technology, Strategic Defense Initiative Organization, U.S. Department of Defense (1984-1992); Staff Specialist for Early Warning, Air Defense and Attack Assessment, Office of the Secretary of Defense (1983-1984); Physicist, Air Force Materials Laboratory, U.S. Air Force, Dayton, Ohio (1958-1983) **Creative Works:** Editor, "Strategic Defense Initiative Launch Phenomenology" (1994-1997) **Awards:** Decorated Pioneer Award, Ballistic Missile Defense Organization, (Now Missile Defense Agency), U.S. Department of Defense (2007); John A. Jamieson Memorial Award in Sensors, Environments and Algorithms, Military Sensing Symposium (2001); Fellowship, Military Sensing Symposium (2001) **Memberships:** American Institute of Aeronautics and Astronautics; Infrared Information Symposium; Military Sensing Symposium; National Space Society **Marquis Who's Who Honors:** Albert Nelson Marquis Lifetime Achievement Award; Marquis Who's Who Top Professional **Why did you become involved in your profession or industry:** Dr. Frederick became involved in his profession after listening to the late, former President Ronald Reagan. **Avocations:** Traveling; Spending time with family

Darryl E. Freling

Title: Managing Principal **Industry:** Real Estate **Company Name:** Med-Properties Realty Advisors **Place of Birth:** 03/24/1957 **Marital Status:** Married **Spouse Name:** Emily **Children:** Alexandra Michelle **Education:** Doctor of Jurisprudence, The University of Texas at Austin (1984); Master of Business Administration in Finance, The University of Texas at Austin **Career:** Managing Principal, Co-Founder, MedProperties Realty Advisors LLC (2007-Present); Senior Director of Acquisitions, Mack-Cali Realty Corp. (1997-2001); With, Patriot American Hospitality Inc., Patriot American Office Group (1996-1997) **Career Related:** Member, MedProperties Investment Committee; Member, MedProperties Management Committee **Creative Works:** Speaker in Field **Marquis Who's Who Honors:** Marquis Who's Who Top Professional **To what do you attribute your success:** Mr. Freling credits his success on a propensity for hard work, as well as wonderful employees. Likewise, he benefited from his early successes and initial investments. **Why did you become involved in your profession or industry:** After graduating from law school, Mr. Freling became involved in the real estate development business in Dallas, Texas. In 2006, he and three other individuals seized upon the opportunity to establish their own business endeavor.

Lawrence Samuel Friedman, MD

Title: Anton R. Fried, MD, Chair; Gastroenterologist; Educator **Company Name:** Newton-Wellesley Hospital **Date of Birth:** 05/11/1953 **Place of Birth:** Newark **State/Country of Origin:** NJ/USA **Parents:** Maurice Friedman; Esther (Slansky) Friedman **Marital Status:** Married **Spouse Name:** Mary Jo Cappuccilli (04/12/1981) **Children:** Matthew Jacob **Education:** Fellow, Massachusetts General Hospital/Harvard Medical School, Boston, MA (1981-1984); Resident, Department of Medicine, Johns Hopkins Hospital, Baltimore, MD (1979-1981); Intern, Department of Medicine, Johns Hopkins Hospital, Baltimore, MD (1978-1979); MD, Johns Hopkins University, Baltimore, MD (1978); BA, Johns Hopkins University, Baltimore, MD (1975); Coursework, Princeton University, Princeton, NJ (1971-1973) **Certifications:** Diplomate, Pennsylvania Board of Medical Education and Licensure (1984); Diplomate, American Board of Internal Medicine, Subspecialty of Gastroenterology (1983); Diplomate, Massachusetts Board of Registration in Medicine (1981); Diplomate, Maryland Board of Medical Examiners (1979); Diplomate, National Board of Medical Examiners (1979) **Career:** Anton R. Fried, MD, Chair, Department of Medicine, Newton-Wellesley Hospital (2013-Present); Clinical Professor, Massachusetts College of Pharmacy and Health Science (2011-Present); Clinical Affiliate, Massachusetts General Hospital (2009-Present); Professor, Medicine, Tufts University School of Medicine, Boston, MA (2006-Present); Assistant Chief, Medicine, Massachusetts General Hospital (2003-Present); Professor, Medicine, Harvard Medical School, Boston, MA (2001-Present); Trustee, Newton-Wellesley Hospital (2013-2017); Chairman, Department of Medicine, Newton-Wellesley Hospital, Newton, MA (2003-2013); Physician, Massachusetts General Hospital, Boston, MA (1993-2008); Chief, Bauer Firm (1997-2003); Associate Professor, Harvard Medical School, Boston, MA (1993-2001) **Career Related:** Consultant, Antimicrobial Drugs Advisory Committee (2015-Present); U.S. Food and Drug Administration Antiviral Drugs Advisory Committee (2013-2015); Chairman, Multisociety Task Force (2008-2011); Treasurer, Digestive Disease Week Council (2005-2008) **Creative Works:** Editor, "Sleisenger & Fordtran's Gastrointestinal and Liver Disease" (2002, 2006, 2010, 2016, Present); Editor, "Essentials of Gastroenterology" (2012, 2018) **Awards:** Crystal Award for Service as Editor of ASGE News and ASGE Connection, American Society for Gastrointestinal Endoscopy (2018); Newton-Wellesley Hospital Faculty Teaching Award, Massachusetts General Hospital Medical House Staff (2014) **Marquis Who's Who Honors:** Albert Nelson Marquis Lifetime Achievement Award **Avocations:** Woodwind instruments; Travel; Basketball; Reading; Computers **Religion:** Jewish

Leslie Frimerman

Title: Senior Vice-President of Global Technologies **Date of Birth:** 11/25/1943 **Place of Birth:** Brooklyn **State/Country of Origin:** NY/USA **Parents:** Abe Frimerman; Shirley Frimerman **Marital Status:** Married **Spouse Name:** Roberta Frimerman **Education:** MBA, Adelphi University, Garden City, NY, With Distinction (1978); BBA in Finance, Baruch College, New York, NY (1974) **Career:** Assistant Professor, Mathematics, Nassau Community College, Garden City, NY (2000-Present); New Accounts Analyst, Systems Analyst, Vice-President of Finance, Senior Vice-President of Global Technologies, American Express Company, New York, NY (1965-1999) **Career Related:** Finance Officer, National Computer Conference (1980-1981) **Civic:** Treasurer, Weather Vane Cooperative; President, Pebble Cove Homeowners Association; Commissioner, Board of Zoning Appeals, Atlantic Beach, NY **Creative Works:** Author, "Selected Functions of the TI-83/84 Calculators For Studying Statistics" (2005) **Awards:** Chancellor Award, State University of New York (2009) **Memberships:** New York State Mathematics Association of Two-Year Colleges; Sigma Alpha; Delta Mu Delta **Marquis Who's Who Honors:** Albert Nelson Marquis Lifetime Achievement Award **To what do you attribute your success:** Mr. Frimerman attributes his success to honesty, setting tough goals, perseverance, and caring for others. **Why did you become involved in your profession or industry:** Mr. Frimerman became involved in his profession because, during his career at American Express, he began conceptualizing product quality and productivity opportunities by using technologies. He taught himself how to design software applications and computer programming, which eventually led to his successful career in technologies. **Avocations:** Skiing; Scuba diving; Exploring electronics; Practicing photography; Traveling; Model railroading; Hiking **Thoughts on Life:** In 1996, Mr. Frimerman and nine other Information Technology experts were invited to the U.S. Congress House Committee on Ways and Means to present the requirements of re-designing every government computer application that uses date information from before the year 2000. Mr. Frimerman presented the need to expand the year data field from YY (two data positions) to YYYY (four data positions). The recommendations were accepted. This change was not trivial. Billions of dollars were spent across the globe by every commercial entity and government to make the required changes. As 2000 became a reality, there were no interruptions in processing date-sensitive data around the globe. Success was achieved.

Katherine Frost

Title: Chief Executive Officer **Industry:** Events Services **Company Name:** A Frosted Affair **Date of Birth:** 07/01/1988 **State/Country of Origin:** TX/USA **Education:** BA in Art, Southern Methodist University, Dallas, Texas (2011) **Certifications:** Certified Event Planner, Event Integrity **Career:** Chief Executive Officer, Owner, A Frosted Affair, Denver, CO (2015-Present); Sales and Account Coordinator, Destination Services Corporation, Denver, CO (2013-2015) **Career Related:** Community Relations Chair, Colorado Thought Leaders Forum; Luxury Wedding Expert, The Huffington Post (Now HuffPost), Verizon Media **Civic:** Volunteer, Two Hearts Foundation **Awards:** Named Colorado's Up-and-Coming Special Events Professional, Colorado Meetings + Events (2019); Red Carpet Treatment Award, Colorado Meetings + Events **Memberships:** Board Member, Two Hearts Foundation; President, Denver Metro Chamber, Leads Group 7 **To what do you attribute your success:** Ms. Frost attributes her success to her ability to make lasting relationship with their clients. They are a referral-based business and it's key to have clients who recommend them every year. **Why did you become involved in your profession or industry:** Ms. Frost became involved in her profession because she loves helping people and making their day special. It's a very important day for people; she loves being a part of the family and making their event fun and beautiful for everyone. **Thoughts on Life:** Ms. Frost's motto is to "make memorable events."

Arnold Fuchs

Title: President **Industry:** Manufacturing **Company Name:** Harris Thermal Transfer Products **Place of Birth:** Nezperce **State/Country of Origin:** ID/USA **Parents:** Anthony Joseph Fuchs; Rosa (Lauby) Fuchs **Marital Status:** Married **Spouse Name:** Shirley Seubert (08/29/1964) **Children:** Paula; Gregory; Donald; Patrick **Education:** MBA, Washington State University (1964); BA, Saint Martin's University, Olympia, WA (1962) **Career:** Chairman, Board, Executive Vice President, Anctil Sheet Metal Company, Portland, OR (1986-Present); President, Systems Piping, Incorporated (1984-1986); Board of Directors, Northwest Medical Equipment Distributors; Board of Directors, Northwest Copper Works, Inc.; President, Northwest Copper Works, Inc. (1984-1986); Executive Vice President, Northwest Copperworks, Inc. (1978-1984); Financial Vice President, Northwest Copper Works, Inc. (1975-1978); With, Northwest Copper Works, Inc., Portland, OR (1968-1986); Senior Audit Staff, Peat, Marwick, Mitchell & Company, C.P.A. (Now KPMG International) (1964-1968); Board of Directors, Systems Piping, Incorporated **Memberships:** American Management Association; American Society of CPAs (Now AICPA); Oregon Society of CPAs; American Institute of CPAs (AICPA); Fraternal Order of Eagles; Multnomah Athletic Club **Why did you become involved in your profession or industry:** What attracted Mr. Fuchs to his career was just the opportunities that were available. He liked manufacturing, taking on materials and making something useful out of them; that is his joy. **Political Affiliations:** Republican **Religion:** Roman Catholic

Gloria Jean Fulton, MLS, MA

Title: Librarian, Educator **Industry:** Library Management/Library Services **Date of Birth:** 11/20/1940 **Place of Birth:** Sterling **State/Country of Origin:** IL/USA **Parents:** Reese H.; Aldine (Hansen) Hinton **Marital Status:** Widowed **Children:** Alexander; Rolf Fulton **Education:** MA, Humboldt State University (1976); MLS, University of California Los Angeles (1968);BA, University of California Los Angeles (1963) **Career:** Retired Librarian, Educator (2000); Librarian, Humboldt State University (1970-2000); Professor, Russian Language, Humboldt State University (1979-1989); Librarian, Santa Monica Public Library (1969-1970); Consultant, RAND Corporation (1965-1966) **Career Related:** Consultant, Oscar Larson & Associates (1990-1991); Library, College of the Redwoods (1970-1972) **Awards:** Fellow, ALA/USIA, Yugoslavia (1991-1992); Council Library Resources Fellow (1976-1977); Higher Education Act Fellow (1967-1968); Fellow, Institute of International Education, Inc., University of Zagreb (1964-1965); Fellow, Woodrow Wilson Foundation (1963-1964); National Defense Education Act Fellow (1963); The American Legion School Award **Memberships:** American Library Association; Association for Slavic, East European, and Eurasian Studies; The Phi Beta Kappa Society **Marquis Who's Who Honors:** Albert Nelson Marquis Lifetime Achievement Award **Why did you become involved in your profession or industry:** Mrs. Fulton grew up fairly poor but her parents worked very hard for a living. In search of opportunity for their daughter, her parents moved to California where she attended UCLA due to the cheap cost of education. At the time, Mrs. Fulton worked in a bar to help support herself and also receive honors for her good grades. She felt that libraries are great places for people who don't have many educational resources in life, and so she began to pursue a career working in a library. Libraries helped broaden her horizons growing up. In addition, Mrs. Fulton became involved as a librarian after working at RAND Corporation and doing work for a machine translation. Her boss suggested that she become a librarian because the grant was going to run out. So, she applied, got into UCLA, and worked for the scan department for six months before becoming a librarian. She was always good at math and language. She was kind of lucky in the process ability for numerous inputs. **Avocations:** Folk dancing; Cooking; Travel; Gardening **Political Affiliations:** Democrat

Gal Gadot

Title: Actress **Industry:** Media & Entertainment **Date of Birth:** 04/30/1985 **Place of Birth:** Petah Tikva **State/Country of Origin:** Israel **Parents:** Michael Gadot; Irit (Weiss) Gadot **Marital Status:** Married **Spouse Name:** Yaron Varsano (2008) **Children:** Two Children **Education:** Coursework in Law and International Relations, IDC Herzliya **Career Related:** Winner, Miss Israel (2004); Participant, Miss Universe (2004) **Military Service:** Combat Instructor, Israel Defense Forces **Creative Works:** Producer, Actress, "Wonder Woman 1984" (2020); Appearance, "Imagine (Stand for Corona)" (2020); Actress, "Death on the Nile" (2020); Guest, Eurovision Song Contest (2019); Cameo, "Between Two Ferns: The Movie" (2019); Voice Actress, "Ralph Breaks the Internet" (2018); Appearance, "Girls Like You" (2018); Voice Actress, "The Simpsons" (2018); Actress, "Wonder Woman" (2017); Host, "Saturday Night Live" (2017); Actress, "Justice League" (2017); Actress, "Batman v Superman: Dawn of Justice" (2016); Actress, "Criminal" (2016); Actress, "Keeping Up with the Joneses" (2016); Actress, "Triple 9" (2016); Actress, "Furious 7" (2015); Actress, "Kicking Out Shoshana" (2014); Actress, "Fast and Furious 6" (2013); Guest Appearance, "Eretz Nehederet" (2012); Guest Appearance, "Asfur" (2011); Actress, "Fast Five" (2011); Actress, "Date Night" (2010); Actress, "Knight and Day" (2010); Guest Appearance, "The Beautiful Life" (2009); Guest Appearance, "Entourage" (2009); Actress, "Fast and Furious" (2009); Guest Appearance, "Bubot" (2007); Actress, "Red Notice"; Producer, Actress, "Irena Sendler"; Co-Executive Producer, Untitled Showtime Limited Series; Appearances, Several Commercials **Awards:** #SeeHer Award, Critics' Choice Awards (2018); Listee, Time 100 Most Influential (2018); Best International Actress, "Wonder Woman," Jupiter Awards (2018); Best Fight, "Wonder Woman," MTV Movie & TV Awards (2018); Rising Star Award - Actress, "Wonder Woman," Palm Springs International Film Festival (2018); Virtuosos Award, "Wonder Woman," Santa Barbara Film Festival (2018); Best Actress, "Wonder Woman," Saturn Awards (2018); Spotlight Award, "Wonder Woman," National Board of Review Awards (2017); Choice Movie: Action Actress, "Wonder Woman," Teen Choice Awards (2017); Most Popular U.S. Actress in China, "Batman v Superman: Dawn of Justice," Chinese American Film Festival (2016)

Connie R. Gard

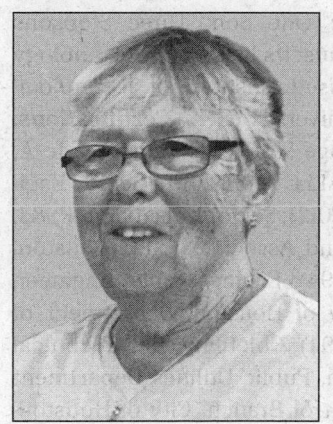

Industry: Real Estate **Company Name:** Rancho Cabeza Mobile Estates **Date of Birth:** 01/16/1936 **Place of Birth:** Glasgow **State/Country of Origin:** MT/USA **Parents:** Arthur Alexander Osland; Margaret (Crest) Osland **Education:** Degree, System Science Institute (1980); Degree, Greenes Business College (1966); Coursework, Santa Rosa Junior College (1958-1960) **Certifications:** Certified Property Manager **Career:** Property Manager, Rancho Cabeza Mobile Estates (2001-Present); Consultant, Chips & Bits Micros, Santa Rosa, CA (1984-2001); Assistant Operations Manager, Sonoma County Data Processing, Santa Rosa, CA (1969-1995); Office Manager, Anchorage Drug Supply, Alaska (1963-1967) **Career Related:** Manager, Senior Mobile Home Park (2000-Present); President, Wine Country Chapter, Western Manufactured Housing Communities Association (2004-2018) **Military Service:** With, U.S. Navy (1954-1957) **Memberships:** Treasurer, Data Processing Management Association (1981-1983); National Association of Female Executives; American Management Association **Marquis Who's Who Honors:** Albert Nelson Marquis Lifetime Achievement Award; Marquis Who's Who Top Professional **To what do you attribute your success:** Ms. Gard attributes her success to her ability to listen to other people. **Why did you become involved in your profession or industry:** After joining the U.S. Navy, Ms. Gard began specializing in computer science, and owned her own business in this field for five years. Shortly thereafter, she became a property manager for a mobile home park. **Political Affiliations:** Democrat **Religion:** Lutheran

Eric J. Garofano

Title: Attorney **Industry:** Law and Legal Services **Company Name:** Conway, Londregan, Sheehan & Monaco, P.C. **Education:** JD, Albany Law School, Albany, NY, Summa Cum Laude (2011); BA in History and Political Science, Minor in Philosophy, Union College, Schenectady, NY, Cum Laude (2008) **Career:** Associate, Conway, Londregan, Sheehan & Monaco, PC, New London, CT (2013-Present); Assistant Clerk, Connecticut Superior Court (2013-2013); Law Clerk, Connecticut Superior Court (2011-2012); Intern, U.S. Attorney's Office, Northern District of New York, Albany, NY (2010-2011); Research Assistant, Professor Patrick Connors, Professor Timothy Lytton, Albany Law School (2010-2011); Judicial Intern, Honorary Lawrence E. Kahn, U.S. District Court, Northern District of New York, Albany, NY (2010) **Career Related:** Honors Teaching Fellowship, Albany Law School (2009) **Civic:** Board President, Board Member, Stonington Community Center; Board Member, Southeastern Connecticut Cultural Coalition; Mystic Lions Club; Board President, Board Member, Mystic Flag Committee; Board President, Board Member, Mystic Lions Club; Board Member, New London County Bar Association **Creative Works:** Author, "Losing Power: Siting Power Plants in New York State," Albany Government Law Review (2011) **Awards:** Rising Star, SuperLawyers (2016-Present); Dean's List, Albany Law School (2009-2011); Dean's List, Union College (2006-2008); Certificate of Recognition for State and Local Government, American Bar Association **Bar Admissions:** Mohegan Tribal & Gaming Disputes Courts (2016); U.S. District Court, Rhode Island (2016); Rhode Island (2014); U.S. District Court, Connecticut (2013); Connecticut (2012); New York (2012) **To what do you attribute your success:** Mr. Garofano attributes his success to hard work, as well as his passion and love for what he is doing. **Why did you become involved in your profession or industry:** Mr. Garofano wanted to make a positive improvement in the world. He felt that pursuing a career in the legal profession would be a good way to do so. **Avocations:** Running

---

Melrose Garrett

Title: Engineer (Retired) **Industry:** Engineering **Children:** One Son; Three Stepsons **Education:** Doctor of Science in Sanitary Engineering, Massachusetts Institute of Technology (1952); Master of Science in Sanitary Engineering, Massachusetts Institute of Technology (1949); Bachelor of Science in Civil Engineering, Texas A&M University (1948) **Certifications:** Professional Engineer, Texas No. 10959 (1953); Certified Sewage Works Operator, Grade A, Texas, No. 56 **Career:** President, M.T. Garrett and Associates LLC (2012-2019); Senior Engineering Consultant, Atkins North America, Houston, TX (2011-2012); Senior Consultant, PS&J, Houston, TX (1998-2011); Senior Consultant, Espey, Huston and Associates, Inc., Houston, TX (1994-1998); Environmental Engineer, City of Houston (1994); Engineer Chief Engineer, Technical Director for Wastewater Operations Division, City of Houston, Department of Public Works and Engineering, Public Utilities Group (1993-1994); Chief Engineer, Technical Director for Wastewater Operations Division, City of Houston, Public Utilities Department (1991-1993); Engineer VI, Manager of Wastewater Quality Control Branch, City of Houston, Department of Public Works, Utility Operations Division (1985-1990) **Career Related:** Adjunct Professor, Department of Civil and Environmental Engineering, University of Houston, TX **Civic:** Past President, Director, Water Environment Federation; Past President, Director, Water Environment Association of Texas; Past President, Texas Water Utilities Association **Military Service:** Active, U.S. Air Force Reserves (1945-1952); 2nd Lieutenant, Air Corps, Army of the United States (1943-1945) **Creative Works:** Presenter, Numerous Seminars to Various Conferences and Symposia; Co-author, Several Articles on Environmental Engineering **Awards:** Pillars of the Profession Award, Water Environment Association of Texas (2009); Lifetime Achievement Award, Water Environment Association of Texas (2003); Hatfield Award, Water Environment Federation (1978); Man of the Year Award, Sam Houston Water Utilities Association (1972) **Memberships:** International Water Association; American Society of Civil Engineers; American Chemical Society; International Society on Automation; Texas Natural Resources Conservation Commission; Texas Department of Health; Texas Water Commission; Texas Natural Resources Conservation Commission; National Council on Public Works Improvement; Water and Wastewater Instrumentation Testing Association of North America Inc., Texas Water Utilities Association

---

Norwood Gay III

Title: Senior Vice President, Chief Legal Officer (Retired) **Industry:** Law and Legal Services **Company Name:** Attorneys' Title Fund Services, LLC. **Marital Status:** Widowed **Children:** Two children **Education:** JD, University of Florida (1965) **Career:** Retired (2012); Senior Vice President, Chief Legal Officer, Corporate Secretary, Special Counsel, Attorneys' Title Fund Services, LLC. (2009-2012); Senior Vice President, General Counsel, Corporate Secretary, Attorneys' Title Fund Services, LLC. (1991-2009) **Marquis Who's Who Honors:** Marquis Who's Who Top Professional **To what do you attribute your success:** Mr. Gay attributes his success to simple hard work. **Why did you become involved in your profession or industry:** Mr. Gay became involved in his profession because of his experiences in the Navy. After returning, he went to law school and became interested in maritime law.

Margaret Joan Geller

Title: Astrophysicist **Industry:** Sciences **Date of Birth:** 12/08/1947 **Place of Birth:** Ithaca **State/Country of Origin:** NY/USA **Education:** Honorary Doctorate, University of Turin (2017); Honorary Doctorate of Health Science, Dartmouth College (2014); Honorary Doctorate of Health Science, Colby College (2009); PhD, Princeton University (1975); BA, University of California, Berkeley (1970); Four Additional Honorary Degrees **Career:** Assistant Professor of Astronomy, Harvard University (1980-1983); Research Fellowship, Center for Astrophysics, Harvard & Smithsonian; Research Fellowship, Institute of Astronomy, University of Cambridge **Career Related:** Fellow, American Academy of Arts & Sciences (1990); Fellowship, John D. and Catherine T. MacArthur Foundation (1990); Scientific Staff, Smithsonian Astrophysical Observatory; Fellow, American Association for the Advancement of Science; Fellow, American Physical Society **Civic:** Council, National Academy of Sciences (2000-2003) **Creative Works:** Author, "Mapping the Universe" (2014); Appearance, "Where the Galaxies Are" (1989); Appearance, "So Many Galaxies...So Little Time"; Lecturer in Field **Awards:** Karl Schwarzschild Medal, German Astronomical Society (2014); Julius Edgar Lilienfeld Prize, American Physical Society (2013); James Craig Watson Medal, National Academy of Sciences (2010); Henry Norris Russell Lectureship, American Astronomical Society (2010); Magellanic Premium, American Philosophical Society (2008); La Medaille de l'ADION, Nice Observatory (2003); New York Public Library Lion (1997); Klopsteg Memorial Award, American Association of Physics Teachers (1996); Helen Sawyer Hogg Lecturer, Canadian Astronomical Society (1993); Co-Recipient, Newcomb Cleveland Prize, American Association for the Advancement of Science (1989); Best Commencement Speeches Ever, NPR **Memberships:** National Academy of Sciences (1992); American Academy of Arts & Sciences (1990)

Wayne Gentry

Title: Owner **Industry:** Medicine & Health Care **Company Name:** Home Helpers Home Care of Somerset and London **Marital Status:** Married **Children:** Will; Nathan; Hopper; Danielle; Caitlyn; Elizabeth; Anderson **Education:** Bachelor of Science in Business Management and Asset Protection Management, Eastern Kentucky University (1993) **Certifications:** Certified, Alzheimer's Education, National Certification Board for Alzheimer Care (2016) **Career:** Owner, Home Helpers & Direct Link of London, KY (2016-Present); Zone Manager, The Schwan Food Company (1996-2016) **Civic:** Board of Directors, London Laurel Optimist Club (2013-Present); Board of Directors, Cornerstone Christian School; Ambassador, London Laurel Chamber of Commerce **Awards:** Brand Champion Award, Home Helpers Home Care National Conference (2019); Veteran Advocate of the Year, Home Helpers Home Care National Conference (2019); Top Growth in the History of the Franchise, Home Helpers Home Care (2018) **To what do you attribute your success:** Mr. Gentry attributes his success to the experience and mentors he enjoyed with the Schwan Food Company, where he was able to connect himself to several amazing leaders and learned much about marketing and self-training. **Why did you become involved in your profession or industry:** Mr. Gentry became involved in home healthcare because of his grandparents, who endured far too much hardship in the twilight of their lives. On a more professional level, Mr. Gentry began speaking to Home Helpers after retiring from his previous position. Due to his experiences with his grandparents, he became interested and joined the company.

Vincent Paul Gibbons, MD

Title: Pediatric Neurologist; Educator **Industry:** Medicine & Health Care **Date of Birth:** 04/21/1949 **Place of Birth:** Cambridge **State/Country of Origin:** MA/USA **Parents:** Edward F. Gibbons; Elizabeth A. (Ring) Gibbons **Marital Status:** Married **Spouse Name:** Marcellina Murphy **Children:** Joshua; Liam; Gabriel Gibbons **Education:** Fellowship in Neurophysiology, Boston Children's Hospital (1978-1982); Resident in Child Neurology, George Washington University Medical Center (1977-1978); Resident in Pediatrics, Children's National Hospital, Washington, DC (1976-1977); Intern in Pediatrics, Children's National Hospital, Washington, DC (1975-1976); MD, Georgetown University, Washington, DC (1975); BA in Biochemical Sciences, Harvard College, Magna Cum Laude (1971) **Certifications:** Diplomate, Pediatric Neurology, Epilepsy, Clinical Neurophysiology, American Board of Psychiatry and Neurology, Inc.; Diplomate, American Board of Pediatrics **Career:** Head, Division of Pediatrics Neurology, Albany Medical Center, NY (2007-2009); Associate Clinical Professor, Pediatrics and Neurology, University of California San Francisco School Medicine (2001-2007); Associate Professor, Neurology, Southern Illinois University, Springfield, IL (1999-2000); Assistant Professor, Neurology, University of Illinois, Peoria, IL (1997-1999); Assistant Professor, Neurology, St. Louis University School of Medicine (1987-1997); Attending Physician, University of San Francisco (2000); Attending Physician, St. John's Hospital, HSHS Hospital Sisters Health Systems, Springfield, IL (1999-2000); Attending Physician, Methodist Medical Center (UnityPoint Health), IL (1997-1999); Attending Physician, SSM Cardinal Glennon Children's Hospital, SSM Health, St. Louis, MO (1987-1997) **Creative Works:** Contributor, Articles to Professional Journals **Memberships:** American Epilepsy Society; American Academy of Clinical Neurophysiology; American Clinical Neurophysiology Society (ACNS); American Academy of Neurology **Marquis Who's Who Honors:** Albert Nelson Marquis Lifetime Achievement Award **Why did you become involved in your profession or industry:** Dr. Gibbons became involved in his profession because he felt that it was fun to be an undergraduate. He was at Harvard and did very well. **Avocations:** Sailboat racing; Kayak expeditions **Political Affiliations:** Democrat **Religion:** Catholic

Paul M. Glenn

Title: United States Bankruptcy Judge **Industry:** Law and Legal Services **Company Name:** U.S. Bankruptcy Court **Education:** JD, Duke University (1970); BA, Florida State University, Cum Laude (1967) **Career:** Bankruptcy Judge, U.S. Bankruptcy Court, Middle District, Tampa, FL (1993-Present); Shareholder, Dale & Bald, Jacksonville, FL (1989-1993); Executive Vice President, Chief Administrative Officer, The Dependable Insurance Group, Inc. of America and Subsidiaries, Jacksonville, FL (1987-1988); Shareholder, Bledsoe, Schmidt & Glenn, P.A., Jacksonville, FL (1985-1987); President, Chief Executive Officer, Mobile America Corporation and Subsidiaries, Jacksonville, FL (1981-1985); Associate, Shareholder, Mahoney, Hadlow & Adams, P.A., Jacksonville, Miami, FL (1970-1981) **Career Related:** Fellow, American College of Bankruptcy (2005); Guest Lecturer, University of Florida; Guest Lecturer, Stetson University College of Law **Creative Works:** Contributing Editor, Norton Handbook for Bankruptcy Trustees; Contributing Editor, Debtors in Possession; Contributing Editor, Various Committees **Awards:** Distinguished Service Award, Bankruptcy Inn Alliance, America Inns of Court, National Conference of Bankruptcy Judges (2014); Robert W. Patton Outstanding Jurist Award, Hillsborough County Bar Association (2007) **Memberships:** Budget Committee, Judicial Conference of the United States (2013-2017); National Board of Trustees, American Inns of Court Foundation (2010) **Marquis Who's Who Honors:** Albert Nelson Marquis Lifetime Achievement Award; Marquis Who's Who Top Professional; Marquis Who's Who Humanitarian Award **To what do you attribute your success:** The Honorable Judge Glenn attributed his success to the many people whom he admired and relied on throughout his life. **Why did you become involved in your profession or industry:** Judge Glenn knew, as he went through his formative years and his high school years, that the people in the city where he grew up were both doctors and lawyers, and he talked with them during this time to determine the kind of preparation that he should have as he moved into adult life. He met some very good people, and he focused on those two professions. In talking with lawyers, he considered after graduating from college to go to law school rather then medical school.

Ronald John Glossop, PhD

Title: Professor Emeritus **Company Name:** Southern Illinois University-Edwardsville **Date of Birth:** 02/17/1933 **Place of Birth:** Aurora **State/Country of Origin:** IL/USA **Parents:** Donald LeRoy Glossop Sr.; Helen M. (Johnson) Glossop **Marital Status:** Married **Spouse Name:** Audrey Yvonne (Lutz) Glossop **Children:** Kent David Glossop **Education:** Doctor of Philosophy, Washington University in St. Louis, MO (1960); Postgraduate study, Chicago Lutheran Theological Seminary (1955-1956); Bachelor of Arts, Carthage College, Summa Cum Laude, Carthage, IL (1955) **Career:** Professor Emeritus, Southern Illinois University-Edwardsville (1998-Present); Assistant Professor to Professor, Southern Illinois University Edwardsville (1965-1998); Instructor to Assistant Professor, Portland State University (1961-1965); Instructor, Boise Junior College (1960-1961) **Career Related:** Coordinator, Peace Studies Program, Southern Illinois University Edwardsville (1974-1998); Executive of Communications, The Hume Society (1976-1978). **Military Service:** U.S. Army Reserve (1957-1963) **Creative Works:** Author, "Confronting War," (1983, 1987, 1994, 2001); Author, "World Federation?" (1993); Author, "Philosophy: An Introduction to its Problems and Vocabulary" (1974); Author, Articles in Journals **Awards:** Lifetime Achievement Award, Citizens for Global Solutions (2017) **Memberships:** Chair, St. Louis Chapter, World Federalist Association and Citizens for Global Solutions (1970-2021); National Board, World Federalist Association and Citizens for Global Solutions (1986-2020); Member, International League of Instructors of Esperanto (2018); President, American Association of Teachers of Esperanto (2009-2018); Vice President, American Association of Teachers of Esperanto (1988-2018); Member, Esperanto-USA (2012); Vice President, World Federalist Association (1990-2003); Vice President, Internacia Ligo de Esperantistaj Instruistoj (1991-1993); Board of Directors, Esperanto League for North America (1985-1987); American Philosophical Association; Consortium on Peace, Research & Development; Concerned Philosophers for Peace; Phi Beta Kappa **Marquis Who's Who Honors:** Albert Nelson Marquis Lifetime Achievement Award; Marquis Who's Who Humanitarian Award **To what do you attribute your success:** Dr. Glossop credits his success on good luck and hard work. **Avocations:** Promoting world federation and esperanto **Political Affiliations:** Democrat **Religion:** Unitarian Universalist

Ruthee Goldkorn

Title: Owner **Company Name:** No Barriers Disabled Access and Advocacy Consulting 2) Californians for Disability Rights, Inc. **Marital Status:** Married **Children:** One Daughter **Education:** Coursework, Community College, San Fernando Valley, CA (1974-1981); MA, Bryman School, Santa Monica, California (1973); Postgraduate Coursework (1973) **Certifications:** Trained Consultant, Access Compliance, California Department of Rehabilitation (1994); Certified, Child Birth Educator, Labor Adviser (1980) **Career:** Ambassador, The Abilities Expo (2011-Present); Founder, No Barriers Disabled Access Consulting and Advocacy Services (1995-Present); Management, Business Development, Beverly Hills, CA (1975-1989); Owner, The Baby Biz (1980-1984); Specialist, Obstetrics, Genecology (1974-1982); Anchor, Cable News Program, California **Career Related:** Training, California Department of Justice, Federal Department of Justice, National Association of Americans with Disability Act Coordinators, California Department of Rehabilitation, National Americans with Disability Act Centers, Riverside Community College, Riverside, CA (1998) **Civic:** Voters Accessibility Advisory Committee, Riverside County Registrar of Voters (2015-Present); President Emeritus, Ms. Wheelchair California Pageant (2013-Present); California Democratic Party Standing Committee, Affirmative Action, Diversity, Inclusion (2017-2018); Access Advisory Committee, San Bernardino, CA (2009-2015); Ambassador, Abilities Expo, Los Angeles, California (2011-2014); President, Ms. Wheelchair California Pageant (2012-2013); United States Golf Association, Executive Director, Ms. Wheelchair California Pageant (2001-2012); Mentor, North High School Education and Human Services Academy (2009-2010); Volunteer, Ability Awareness, Habitat for Humanity, Downey, CA (2009) **Awards:** Hero Award, Americans with Disabilities Act, Californians for Disability Rights Inc., Los Angeles, CA (2019); Hero Award, No Barriers Disables Access Consulting and Advocacy Services (2019); Volunteer of the Year, California Democratic Party for Disability Rights Advocacy (2017); Inductee, International Women's Leadership Association (2012-2014); Inductee, Latino American Who's Who (2012); President's Call to Service Award, President Barack Obama (2009); Volunteer of the Year, Riverside County Democratic Party (2007); Title, Ms. Wheelchair California (2001); Scholarship Winner, Academic, Community Achievements (1992-1997); Man of the Year Meritorious Award, Federation of Jewish Men's Clubs (1992) **Marquis Who's Who Honors:** Marquis Who's Who Top Professional

Laurence Goldman

Title: Senior Attorney **Education:** JD, University of San Fernando Valley College of Law, California (1976); BS in Business Administration & Accounting, California State University, Northridge, CA (1973) **Certifications:** Certified Rescue Diver (1994); Certified Specialist in Family Law, California Board of Legal Specialization, State Bar of California (1990); Certified Law Clerk, Los Angeles City Attorney's Office (1976); Certified Scuba Diver **Career:** Senior Attorney, The Reape-Rickett Law Firm, Calabasas, CA (2018-Present); Senior Counsel, Einstein Pham & Glass (2017-2018); Partner, Freid & Goldsman, APLC, Los Angeles, CA (2004-2017); Sole Practitioner, Law Offices of Laurence R. Goldman, Calabasas, CA (2003-2004); Hersh, Mannis & Bogen, LLP, Beverly Hills, CA (2001-2003); Sole Practitioner, Law Offices of Laurence R. Goldman, Woodland Hills, CA (1996-2001); Trope and Trope, Los Angeles, CA (1994-1996); Partner, Freid & Goldman, Los Angeles, CA (1985-1993); Law Office of Marvin Mitchelson, Los Angeles, CA (1985); Sole Practitioner, Law Offices of Laurence R. Goldman, Los Angeles and Woodland Hills, CA (1978-1985) **Civic:** Chair, Board of Trustees, West Hills Hospital and Medical Center (2008-2009); Board of Directors, Valley Economic Alliance (2003-2016); Member, West Hills Neighborhood Council (2003-2005) **Awards:** President's Award for Dedicated Service, Beverly Hills Bar Association (2000) **Memberships:** Board of Directors, Public Counsel (2009-Present); Family Law Section, Beverly Hills Bar Association (1982-Present); Family Law Section, Los Angeles County Bar Association (1978-Present); Board of Directors, Conference of California Bar Associations (2007-2012); President, Beverly Hills Bar Association (2006-2007) **Bar Admissions:** Supreme Court of the United States (2004); U.S. Tax Court (1981); U.S. Court of Appeals for the Ninth Circuit (1981); State Bar of California (1978); U.S. District Court for the Central District of California (1978) **Marquis Who's Who Honors:** Marquis Who's Who Top Professional **To what do you attribute your success:** Mr. Goldman never thought he would do Family Law, but he found out that he had the temperament every case is different and every case requires a different strategy and that's part of what he enjoys. **Why did you become involved in your profession or industry:** Mr. Goldman became involved in his profession because even though he was an accounting and tax major in college, he always enjoyed his business law courses and knew that he wanted to work with the legal community in some capacity. **Avocations:** High performance sports cars (Two Dodge Pipers); Driving and going to the track; Ocean and beach; Hiking; Traveling; Being with family and friends

Stephen Gottesman, PhD

Title: Professor Emeritus **Company Name:** University of Florida **Date of Birth:** 02/23/1939 **Place of Birth:** New York **State/Country of Origin:** NY/USA **Parents:** Jacob Gottesman; Edna Beatrice Gottesman **Marital Status:** Married **Spouse Name:** Mariou Barr (10/20/1990) **Children:** Lorna Rachel; Ian Kenneth Jacob; Emily Caitlin; Erika Barr (Step); Alexander Barr (Step) **Education:** PhD, University of Manchester, (1967); BA, Colgate University, Magna Cum Laude (1960) **Career:** Professor Emeritus, University of Florida (2007); Chairman, Astronomy, University of Florida (1988-1993); Professor, University of Florida (1981-2007); Research Fellow, California Institute of Technology (1971); Research Associate, National Radio Astronomy Observatory (1969-1971); Lecturer, Keele University, (1968-1969) **Career Related:** Visiting Professor, Instituto Astrofisica de Canarias (1995-1996); Visiting Professor, Onsala Space Observatory, (1983); Visiting Professor, Royal Observatory, Edinburgh, (1983) **Civic:** Docent, Harn Museum of Art, (2012-2018); Treasurer, American Civil Liberties Union, Gainesville, FL (1988-1992) **Creative Works:** Co-Ed, "Nonlinear Dynamics in Astronomy and Physics..." (2005); Co-Ed, "Nonlinear Dynamics and Chaos in Astrophysics..." (1998); Contributor, More than 100 Articles, Professional Astrophysical and Astronomical Journals **Awards:** Eponym, Asteroid "Dr. G. 17602" (2007); Leverhulme Fellow, University of Manchester (1961-1964); Fulbright Scholar (1961) **Memberships:** President, Beta Chapter Florida, Phi Beta Kappa Society (2005-2007); American Astronomical Society; International Astronomical Union; International Union of Radio Science; Astronomical Society of the Pacific; Harn Museum of Art **Marquis Who's Who Honors:** Albert Nelson Marquis Lifetime Achievement Award; Who's Who in the World (2011) **To what do you attribute your success:** Encouraged by parents and teachers in school and college. **Why did you become involved in your profession or industry:** As a child I was inspired by many visits to the Hayden Planetarium. In college I wrote my Honors Thesis on Cosmology. A Fulbright enabled me to study radio astronomy at the University of Manchester. **What do you consider to be the highlight of your career?:** I mentored 18 graduate students to their PhD. My legacy resides in their achievements. **Avocations:** Flute; Classical music; Jazz; Blues; Collecting coins and stamps; Long walks **Political Affiliations:** Democrat **Religion:** Atheist

Marta Grace

Title: Owner, Managing Broker **Industry:** Real Estate **Company Name:** United Real Estate Kansas City **Children:** Three Children **Education:** BS in Nursing, Graceland University, Lamoni, IA (2000); Coursework, Scaling Program, Latino Business Action Network (LBAN), Stanford Graduate School of Business, Stanford, CA **Career:** Real Estate Broker, United Real Estate Kansas City, Kansas City, MO (2001-Present) **Civic:** Northeast Community Housing and Development; Habitat for Humanity **Awards:** United Real Estate Velocity Award (2017-2018); United Real Estate Leadership Excellence Award (2017); Listee, Superstar Entrepreneurs Inc. 5000 (2000) **Memberships:** Hispanic Chamber of Commerce; Kansas City Association of Realtors; National Association of Realtors **To what do you attribute your success:** Ms. Grace attributes her success to her hard work and dedication to the long hours she puts in. She loves and is passionate about her work. **Why did you become involved in your profession or industry:** Ms. Grace became involved in her profession because a career change from nursing to real estate made for more freedom in her schedule. Although she loved nursing and working in the labor delivery unit, the freedom she got from real estate allowed her to be the mother she wanted to be and have the relationship that she wanted to have with her children. **Thoughts on Life:** Ms. Grace is a Latina Broker, wife, and mother of three. She is driven by her passion to change the real estate industry in Kansas City and owns and manages two real estate brokerages in Kansas and Missouri with over 230 agents closing 178 million in sales volume in 2017 and over 200 million in 2018. She is also the broker and owner for a property management company in which she manages over $67 million in assets. She personally owns 15 million dollars in assets as residential and commercial buildings throughout Missouri and Kansas. As a broker for these companies, her goal is to train her agents to bring back customer service and integrity into these industries. She has been recognized with awards for Excellence in Leadership by the international United Real Estate Headquarters in 2017 and received a Velocity Award in 2018 for rapid growth. United was featured in Inc. 5000 as one of KC's fastest growing companies in 2016 and 2017. Outside of real estate, her passion is to give back to the communities that she services by serving as a board member for two charities called Reverse Retts and Northeast Community Housing and Development. She is also a proud and active member of the Hispanic Chamber of Commerce.

Coty Graff

Title: Owner **Industry:** Automotive **Company Name:** Coty's Auto Body Inc **Education:** Doctor of Philosophy, Pipe Organ Performance, Yale University (2000); Master of Business Administration, University of Connecticut (1998); Bachelor of Music, University of Connecticut **Career:** Owner, Coty's Auto Body, Inc. (2015-Present) **Career Related:** Church Organist/Choir Director, Trinity Episcopal Church (2010-Present) **Civic:** Sponsor, Martinsburg Bulldogs; Sponsor, Scholarship Program; Sponsor, Various Community Organizations **Military Service:** Tech Sergent, Engineer, U.S. Air Force (2001-2007) **To what do you attribute your success:** Mr. Graff attributes his success to the community, which is the reason he has been successful. **Why did you become involved in your profession or industry:** Mr. Graff entered the auto body profession because he wanted to put people back into safe cars. If someone is in a car wreck they have to be put back into a safe vehicle; he cares deeply about every customer's life. **Avocations:** Barbecue

Ariana Grande

Title: Singer; Actress **Industry:** Media & Entertainment **Date of Birth:** 06/26/1993 **Place of Birth:** Boca Raton **State/Country of Origin:** FL/USA **Parents:** Edward Butera; Joan Grande **Career:** Performer, South Florida Symphony Orchestra; Florida Children's Theatre **Career Related:** Launched, Fragrance, Thank U Next Eau de Parfum, Luxe Brands (2019); Launched, Fragrance, Cloud, Luxe Brands (2018); Launched, Fragrance, Moonlight, Luxe Brands (2017); Launched, Limited Edition Fragrance, Sweet Like Candy, Luxe Brands (2017); Brand Ambassador, Reebok (2017); Launched, Limited Edition Fragrance, Frankie, Luxe Brands (2016); Launched, Fragrance, Sweet Like Candy, Luxe Brands (2016); Launched, Ariana Grande's MAC Viva Glam, MAC Cosmetics (2016); Launched, Fragrance, Ari by Ariana Grande, Luxe Brands (2015); Equity Holder, Partner, WAT-AAH! (2014); Appearances, Commercials, T-Mobile, Macy's, American Express **Civic:** Co-Founder, Kids Who Care; Member, Broadway in South Africa; Performer, Various Benefit Concerts **Creative Works:** Performer, "The Disney Family Sing-a-long" (2020); Appearance, "Kidding" (2020); Singer, "Thank U, Next" (2019); Performer, "Carpool Karaoke: The Series" (2017); Performer, "Hairspray Live!" (2016); Appearance, "Zoolander 2" (2016); Singer, "Sweetener" (2018); Singer, "Dangerous Woman" (2016); Singer, "My Everything" (2014); Singer, "Yours Truly" (2013); Actress, "Sam & Cat" (2013-2014); Actress, "Swindle" (2013); Actress, "Cuba Libre" (2012); Actress, "A Snow White Christmas" (2012); Voice Actress, "Snowflake, the White Gorilla" (2011); Actress, "Victorious" (2010-2013); Actress, "7 Secrets with Victoria Justice" (2010); Actress, Broadway, "13" (2008); Singer, Solo and Collaborations, Songs and Albums; Appearances, Television Shows **Awards:** The World's Highest Paid Women in Music, Forbes (2019, 2020); 100 Most Influential People in the World, TIME Magazine (2016, 2019); Grammy Award for Best Pop Vocal Album, Recording Academy (2019); Woman of the Year, Billboard (2018); Award for Favorite Female Pop/Rock Artist, American Music Awards (2015); Favorite Breakout Artist, People's Choice Awards (2014); New Artist of the Year, American Music Awards (2013); Numerous Awards

Douglas Grauer

Title: Civil Engineer **Industry:** Engineering **Date of Birth:** 06/27/1956 **Place of Birth:** Marysville **State/Country of Origin:** KS/USA **Parents:** Norman Wayne; Ruth Ann (Schwindaman) G. **Marital Status:** Married **Spouse Name:** Bette Lynn Bohnenblust (08/16/1980) **Children:** Diana Kathryn; Laura Jaclyn **Education:** Bachelor of Science in Chemical Engineering, Kansas State University (1979); Coursework, Baker University (1976) **Certifications:** Management Certificate, Wichita State University W. Frank Barton School of Business (2000); Certificate, University of Texas at Austin School of Pipeline Technology (1979); Licensed Professional Engineer in Iowa, Kansas, Nebraska and Oklahoma **Career:** Superintendent, Products Pipeline and Terminal, National Cooperative Refinery Association, McPherson, KS (1996-2015); Superintendent, Products Pipeline and Terminal, National Cooperative Refinery Association, Blue Rapids, KS (1990-1996); Assistant Products Pipeline and Terminal Superintendent, National Cooperative Refinery Association, Blue Rapids, KS (1985-1990); Staff Engineer, Cities Service Oil and Gas Corp., Tulsa, OK (1983-1985); Project Engineer, Cities Service Co., Tulsa, OK (1981-1983); Products Terminal Engineer, Cities Service Co., Braintree, MA (1980-1981); Pipeline Engineer, Cities Service Pipeline Co., Shreveport, LA (1979-1980) **Civic:** Board of Directors, McPherson Optimist Club; President, McPherson County Catbackers; Children's Ministry Team, Countryside Covenant Church; Industry Representative, Kansas Commission on Emergency Planning and Response **Awards:** Engineer of the Year, Smoky Valley Chapter, Kansas Society of Professional Engineers (2012-2013) **Memberships:** American Society of Civil Engineers; National Society of Professional Engineers; Kansas Society of Professional Engineers; National Association of Corrosion Engineers; Chi Epsilon; Vice President, Iowa Pipeline Association; President, Kansas Pipeline Association; President, Nebraska Pipeline Association **To what do you attribute your success:** Mr. Grauer credits his success on integrity, good morals, honesty and hard work. **Why did you become involved in your profession or industry:** Mr. Grauer became involved in his profession due to his longtime interest in carpentry, which led him to become a civil engineer. **Avocations:** Golf; Fishing; Woodworking **Political Affiliations:** Republican **Religion:** Christian

Paul Wesley Gray, EdD

Title: Dean Emeritus **Company Name:** Azusa Pacific University **Date of Birth:** 01/30/1947 **Place of Birth:** Berwyn **State/Country of Origin:** IL/USA **Parents:** Harry Ben Gray; Audrey (Tong) Gray **Marital Status:** Married **Spouse Name:** Rachel E. (Boehr) Gray **Children:** John M. Gray; Janel E. Alagoz; Robert B. Gray **Education:** EdD in Commerce, Texas A&M University (1980); MA in Library Science, Texas Woman's University (1989); MSLS, East Texas State University (1977); ThM, Dallas Theological Seminary (1975); BA, Faith Baptist Bible College (1970) **Certifications:** Certified, Reality Therapy Counselor (1978); Pilot's License, Single Engine Land (1968) **Career:** Dean Emeritus, University Libraries, Azusa Pacific University (2018-Present); Dean, University Libraries, Azusa Pacific University (2012-2018); Dean, University Libraries, Azusa Pacific University (1989-2018); Vice Provost, Graduate Programs & Research, Azusa Pacific University (2008-2011); Vice Provost, Academic Affairs, Azusa Pacific University (2006-2007); Interim Dean, School of Education and Behavioral Studies, Azusa Pacific University (2005-2006); Interim Dean, School of Theology, Azusa Pacific University (2004-2005); Dean, Academic Computer Services, University Librarian, Azusa Pacific University (1997-2000); Dean, Computer Services, University Librarian, Azusa Pacific University (1994-1996); Director, Library, Letourneau University (1984-1989); Vice President, Golden Triangle Christian Academy (1979-1983) **Career Related:** Past President, CalPALs (California Private Academic Libraries); Team Visits, WASC, North Central Regional Accreditation Association, Southern Association of Colleges and Schools Commission on Colleges, and Middle States Association of Colleges and Schools; Past Search Committee, Chairs for Provost, Dean, School of Education and Behavioral Studies, Dean, School of Nursing, and Dean, School of Theology, Azusa Pacific University; Past Chair, Several Organizations **Civic:** President Emeritus, General Society Sons of the Revolution; President Emeritus, Rotary Club of Azusa; Sunday School Teacher, First Baptist Church; Grace Baptist Church; Church of the Open Door; Member, Several Organizations **Military Service:** With, ROTC Band, Central High School (1963-1964) **Creative Works:** Author, "Blackland Memories: Photographic History of the City of Greenville, Texas," Greenville Historical Society (1979); Author, Theses and Dissertation **Awards:** Recipient, Several Awards **Memberships:** Member, Numerous Organizations **Marquis Who's Who Honors:** Albert Nelson Marquis Lifetime Achievement Award **Avocations:** Fishing; Crossword puzzles; Family; Travel; Reading in theology and philosophy; Riding a Harley Road King **Political Affiliations:** Republican **Religion:** Baptist

Judson A. Grenier

Title: History Educator **Date of Birth:** 03/06/1930 **Place of Birth:** Indianapolis **State/Country of Origin:** IN/USA **Parents:** Judson A Grenier Sr; Beatrice Olivia (Bjeldanes) Grenier **Marital Status:** Married **Spouse Name:** Nancy Hicks Grenier (08/09/1954) **Children:** Karen; Eric; Jonathan; Katherine (Caddie) **Education:** Doctor of Philosophy in History, University of California Los Angeles (1965); Master of Arts in Journalism, University of California Berkeley (1952); Bachelor of Arts in Journalism, University of Minnesota (1951) **Certifications:** General Secondary Credential, University of California Berkeley (1956); Certificate, Proficiency in Russian, Army Language School, Monterey, CA (1954) **Career:** Professor Emeritus, California State University, Dominguez Hills, CA (1995-Present); Professor, California State University, Dominguez Hills, CA (1966-1995); Instructor, El Camino College, Torrance, CA (1956-1965); Reporter, L.A. Mirror-News (1958, 1959) **Career Related:** Director, Oral History Project (1986-1989, 1994-Present); Secretary, Archivist, California State University, Emeritus Faculty Association (2000-2014); Consultant, City of Redondo Beach, California (1985-1987); Consultant, City of Gardena, California (1980-1987); Consultant, El Pueblo State Historic Park, Los Angeles, CA (1980-1983);Member, Academic Senate, California State University (1974-1983); Consultant, City of Torrance, California (1980-1982) **Military Service:** Intelligence Analyst, Army Security Agency (1952-1955) **Creative Works:** Author, "George Carlson, Los Angeles Pioneer" (2014); Author, "Golden Odyssey: John Stroud Houston: California's First Controller and the Origins of State Government" (1999); Author, "California Legacy: Watson-Dominguez Family" (1987) **Awards:** Wheat Award (1993); Newberry Fellow (1991); Pflueger Award, Historical Society of Southern California (1991); Community Distinguished Service Award, California State University (1987); Huntington-Haynes Fellow (1985); National Endowment of the Humanities Fellow (1984) **Memberships:** Vice President, Historical Society of Southern California (1981-1983); Los Angeles Bicentennial Committee, California Historical Society (1973-1976) **Why did you become involved in your profession or industry:** Professor Grenier became involved in his profession due to the influence of his mother, who introduced him to literature and submitted a poem of his to Story Parade, a publication of the Junior Literary Guild. This experience gave him an appetite to become a prominent author.

Joseph Griffin

Title: Chief Executive Officer **Industry:** Financial Services **Company Name:** TrueNorth Wealth **Parents:** Deloy Griffin **Children:** Three Children **Education:** BS, Charter Oaks State College (2016) **Career:** Chief Executive Officer, TrueNorth Wealth (2019-Present); President, TrueNorth Wealth (2016-2018) **To what do you attribute your success:** Mr. Griffin attributes his success to the great leaders with whom he worked. His father had a tremendous impact on his work ethic, as did the founder of his firm, Martin Watkins. He was a great influence and mentor. Mr. Watkins saw great potential in Mr. Griffin, putting him in leadership positions even though Mr. Griffin had little experience. Even when others questioned Mr. Watkins' decision, he always backed Mr. Griffin. Throughout his entire career, Mr. Griffin felt a responsibility to live up to, and perhaps exceed, Mr. Watkins' expectations to validate that he made the right choice. **Why did you become involved in your profession or industry:** From an early age, Mr. Griffin was taught all about business. He helped his father at their family-owned grocery store for many years, starting at the early age of 9. From this experience, he grew an appreciation for analytics and knew that he wanted to be involved in leadership. It was this foundation that caused Mr. Griffin to keep moving forward in his career. He never became complacent in any one job until he found a position that was both rewarding and aptly challenging.

Jeff Grippando

Title: Senior Vice President, General Manager **Industry:** Advertising & Marketing **Company Name:** Petty Marketing Group Inc. **Place of Birth:** , **Parents:** Gerald Grippando **Marital Status:** Married **Spouse Name:** Tracey Grippando **Children:** Casey Grippando; Sam Grippando **Education:** Bachelor of Science, California State University, Chico (1990) **Career:** Executive Vice President, General Manager, Petty Marketing Group (2017–Present); Vice President, General Manager, Promotional Marketing Operations, City Paper Company (2014–2017); Vice President, General Manager, Branded Merchandise Division, WorkflowOne (2005–2014); Regional Sales Manager, Wallace, Moore Wallace, RRD (1994–2005); Sales Representative and Marketing Manager, Wallace, Moore Wallace and RRD (1990–1994) **Awards:** Rookie of the Year **Memberships:** Wallace Computer Services; Chico State Alumni Business Networking Group; Workflow One Customer Solutions "Promotional"; ANA Business Marketing-Atlanta; ASI Show; Idealliance; TMSA; Promotional Products & Advertising Specialty Forum; Gwinnett County Connections, Georgia; PPAI Industry Professionals Networking **To what do you attribute your success:** Mr. Grippando attributes his success to the great mentors he has had, including his father, his first manager, his marketing manager, and the chief executive officer of WorkflowOne. **Why did you become involved in your profession or industry:** Mr. Grippando became involved in his profession due to the inspiration of his father, who had been an accountant. However, he soon discovered his interest in sales and marketing while studying in college, and decided to pursue that career instead. **Thoughts on Life:** The world is about real-time responses, so one must constantly pay attention and keep moving.

Agnes Gund

Title: President Emerita; Arts Patron **Company Name:** The Museum of Modern Art **Date of Birth:** 08/13/1938 **Place of Birth:** Cleveland **State/Country of Origin:** OH/USA **Parents:** George Gund II; Jessica Laidlaw Gund **Marital Status:** Married **Spouse Name:** Daniel Shapiro (06/13/1987); Albrecht "Brec" Saalfield (1963, Divorced 1981) **Children:** David; Catherine; Jessica; Anna **Education:** Honorary Doctorate, Bowdoin College (2012); Honorary Doctorate, The Graduate Center, CUNY (2007); Honorary Doctorate, University of Illinois (2002); Honorary Doctorte, Kenyon College (1996); Honorary LHD, Brown University (1996); Honorary LHD, Case Western Reserve University (1995); Honorary Doctorate, Hamilton College (1994); MA in Art History, Fogg Museum, Harvard University (1980); BA in Art History, Connecticut College (1960) **Career:** President Emerita, The Museum of Modern Art, New York, NY (2002-Present); President, The Museum of Modern Art, New York, NY (1991-2002); Vice President, The Museum of Modern Art, New York, NY (1988-1991) **Civic:** Chair, Mayor's Cultural Affairs Advisory Commission, New York, NY (2003-Present); Board of Trustees, Wexner Center Foundation (1997-Present); Trustee, The Museum of Modern Art, New York, NY (1976-Present); Board of Trustees, National Council on the Arts (2011); Museum Council, Cleveland Museum of Art; Trustee, J. Paul Getty Trust, CA; Trustee, Institute for Advanced Study, Princeton University, NJ; Trustee, Aaran Diamond AIDS Research Center; Trustee, Brown University; Board Member, Foundation for Contemporary Arts, Foundation for Art and Preservation in Embassies, Morgan Library and Museum, and National YoungArts Foundation; Honorary Trustee, Independent Curators International and Museum of Contemporary Art, Cleveland, Ohio **Awards:** Inaugural Justice Ruth Bader Ginsburg Woman of Leadership Award (2020); Carnegie Medal of Philanthropy (2005); Named, Top 200 Collectors, ArtNews Magazine (2004-2008); Centennial Medal, Harvard University Graduate School of Arts And Sciences (2003); Evan Burger Donaldson Achievement Award, Miss Porter's School (2003); Arts Education Award, Americans for the Arts (1999); National Medal of Arts (1997); Montblanc De La Culture Award (1997); Art Table Award For Distinguished Service to the Arts (1994); Governor's Art Award, Studio in a School Association, NY (1988); Dorothy Freeman Award, Studio in a School Association, NY (1988); Women in the Arts Award, College Art Association **Memberships:** Fellow, American Academy of Arts & Sciences; Honorary Fellow, Royal Academy of Arts **Avocations:** Collecting contemporary African and Chinese Art

Arnold Albert Hafford

Title: Attorney **Industry:** Law and Legal Services **Company Name:** Pearlman, Brown & Wax, LLP **Date of Birth:** 05/31/1957 **Place of Birth:** Reno **State/Country of Origin:** NV/USA **Parents:** Ralph Stanley Hafford; Alvida Josephine (Arena) Hafford **Marital Status:** Married **Spouse Name:** Linda Melody Davis (08/20/1982) **Children:** Joshua Adam; Celeste Melody; Daniel Charles; Alisa Ra'Chelle; Aaron Michael; Holly Noelle **Education:** JD, McGeorge School of Law, University of the Pacific, Sacramento, CA (1982); BA in Criminal Justice, University of Nevada, Reno, with Distinction (1979) **Career:** Attorney, Pearlman, Brown & Wax, LLP (2019-Present); Attorney, Coleman Chavez & Associates LLP (2018-2019); Attorney, Cipolla, Calaba & Wollman (2017-2018); Attorney, Chernow & Lieb, Zenith Insurance Company (2003-2017); Attorney, Mullen & Filippi (2002-2003); Owner, Law Offices of Arnold A. Hafford, Reno, NV (1996-2002); Attorney, Edward M. Bernstein & Associates (1993-1996); Attorney, Hill, Cassas, DeLipkau, & Erwin (1983-1993); Law Clerk, Bailiff to the Honorable District Judge John W. Barrett (1982-1983); Legal Intern, Supreme Court of Nevada (1981) **Civic:** Little League Coach; Softball Coach; Various Roles, Youth Organizations **Memberships:** American Bar Association; American Association for Justice; Washoe County Bar Association; Litigation Section, The State Bar of California; The Church of Jesus Christ of Latter-Day Saints **Bar Admissions:** The State Bar of California (1983-Present); State Bar of Nevada (1982-Present); U.S. District Court, District of Nevada (1982-Present) **Marquis Who's Who Honors:** Albert Nelson Marquis Lifetime Achievement Award; Marquis Who's Who Top Professional **Why did you become involved in your profession or industry:** Mr. Hafford became involved in his profession because he wanted to help others and was inspired by his father's hard work and dedication. **Avocations:** Playing softball and basketball **Religion:** Mormonism; Nontrinitarian

Arthur Ainsworth Hagen, PhD

Title: Professor, Pharmacologist (Retired) **Industry:** Education/Educational Services **Company Name:** Sanford School of Medicine, University of South Dakota **Date of Birth:** 10/09/1933 **Place of Birth:** Hot Springs **State/Country of Origin:** SD/USA **Parents:** Arthur Hagen; Gussie (Aldyne) Ainsworth Hagen **Marital Status:** Widowed **Spouse Name:** Laurin Kirley (06/01/1957, Deceased) **Children:** Kristen K.; Karol L.; Sandra L.; Sharon A. **Education:** Fellowship, Swedish Medical Research Council, Karolinska Hospital, Karolinska Institutet, Stockholm, Sweden (1963-1965); National Institutes of Health Trainee in Steroid Biochemistry, The University of Utah (1961-1963); PhD, The University of Tennessee (1961); MA, University of South Dakota (1957) **Career:** Retired (1998); Professor, Chairman, Department of Physiology and Pharmacology, University of South Dakota, Vermillion, SD (1983-1998); Professor, College of Medicine, The University of Tennessee Health Science Center, Memphis, TN (1980-1983); Associate Professor, College of Medicine, The University of Tennessee Health Science Center, Memphis, TN (1969-1980); Assistant Professor, College of Medicine, The University of Tennessee Health Science Center, Memphis, TN (1965-1969) **Career Related:** Visiting Professor, College of Pharmacy, South Dakota State University; Visiting Professor, School of Medicine & Health Sciences, University of North Dakota; Visiting Professor, Nurse Anesthetist Program, University of South Dakota; Visiting Professor, Nurse Anesthetist Program, Mount Marty University; Visiting Professor, School of Medicine, Ross University; Visiting Professor, Nurse Anesthetist Program, St. Joseph Mercy Hospital Georgetown **Awards:** Class Sponsor, Numerous Classes, University of Tennessee Health Science Center **Memberships:** Endocrine Society; American Society for Pharmacology and Experimental Therapeutics; Society for the Study of Reproduction; Western Pharmacology Society; Indian Academy of Neuroscience; Alpha Omega Alpha Honor Medical Society **Marquis Who's Who Honors:** Albert Nelson Marquis Lifetime Achievement Award **Why did you become involved in your profession or industry:** Dr. Hagen became involved in his profession because he wanted to be involved in the medical field since he was a young child. **Avocations:** Woodworking; Polishing rocks; Making jewelry **Religion:** Methodist

Edward Payson Hall Jr., PhD

Title: Professor Emeritus **Industry:** Education/Educational Services **Company Name:** Western New Mexico University **Date of Birth:** 11/13/1938 **Place of Birth:** St. Louis **State/Country of Origin:** MO/USA **Parents:** Edward Payson Hall Sr.; Marjorie (LeMasters) Hall **Marital Status:** Married **Spouse Name:** Jean Quintero Hall **Children:** Edward Payson Hall, III; Ken Payson Hall; Akiko Eileen Hall; Michael Joe Hall; Junko Michelle Hall **Education:** PhD University of Washington, International Communication (1980); MA University of Hawaii, Intercultural Communication (1974); BA , University of Washington, East Asian Studies (1972) **Career:** Western New Mexico University: Professor Emeritus, Western New Mexico University (2010-Present); Professor of Communications, Western New Mexico University, Silver City, NM (1995-2010); Chair of Humanities, Western New Mexico University (2003); Coordinator of Institutional Assessment, Western New Mexico University, Silver City, NM (1997-2000); Founding Director, Academy Support Department, Western New Mexico University, Silver City, NM (1997-1998); Coordinator of Accreditation/Self-Study, Western New Mexico University, Silver City, NM (1995-1997); Director of Communication Minor, Associate Professor, Western New Mexico University, Silver City, NM (1993-1995); Coordinator of Planning, Radford University New College of Global Studies (Now Center for Global Education and Engagement), VA (1989-1993); Associate Professor of Communications, Radford University, VA (1988-1993); Founding Director of Communications Graduate Program, Radford University, VA (1988-1990); Assistant Professor of Communications, Radford University, VA (1986-1988); Assistant Professor of Communications, University of Hawai'i, Honolulu, Hawaii (1984-1986); Assistant Professor of Communications, University of Delaware, Newark, DE (1980-1984) **Military Service:** U.S. Marine Corps (1957-1967) **Awards:** Planning Grantee, Commonwealth of Virginia, Commission on the University of the 21st Century, Radford University (1991) **Marquis Who's Who Honors:** Albert Nelson Marquis Lifetime Achievement Award

Jean Quintero Hall, MPA

Title: Communication Faculty Member (Retired) **Industry:** Education/Educational Services **Company Name:** Western New Mexico University **Date of Birth:** 07/28/1946 **Place of Birth:** Manila **State/Country of Origin:** Philippines **Parents:** Evan Drake Moody; Victoria Quintero **Marital Status:** Married **Spouse Name:** Edward Payson Hall **Education:** MPA, University of Delaware (1984); BA in Communications, University of Washington (1978) **Career:** Faculty Member, Western New Mexico University (1994-2010); Faculty Member, Radford University (1989-1992); Faculty Member, New River Community College (1986-1990); Administrator, Radford University (1987-1989); Administrator, Contracts Department & Job Training Partnership Act (JTPA), City/County of Honolulu (1985-1986); Community Development, Catholic Social Services (1985); Faculty Member, Kapi'lani Community College (1984-1985); Coordinator, Title XII (USAID) Office, University of Delaware (1980-1982) **Career Related:** Advisory Board, International Federation of Knights of Rizal, Canada (2008-2011); President, Asian Resource Group (2006-2007); Columnist, Fil-Am Journal, Phoenix, AZ (1999-2003); Board Member, Women in Development of the UN (1980-1982); Hospitality Communications, Seattle, WA (1974-1978); Speaker in Field **Creative Works:** Author, "Rizal - Our Beloved Beacon," (1996); Author, "Desiderate Melodies" (1990); Author, Newspaper Column on the Life of the Hero, Dr. Jose Rizal **Awards:** Lifetime Achievement, International Federation of Knights of Rizal, Canada (2008); 2000 Notable American Women, American Institute of Biological Sciences (2000); 2000 Outstanding Scholars of the Century, Cambridge, England (1999); Honoree, Accomplished Fil-Am Poster Exhibit, Filipino American National Historical Society (1999); Grantee, 21st Century Education Commission, Virginia (1991); Graduate, Fellowship, Delaware (1982-1984); Outstanding Filipino University Graduate, University of Washington Fil-Am Alumni Association, Seattle, WA (1978) **Marquis Who's Who Honors:** Albert Nelson Marquis Lifetime Achievement Award; Marquis Who's Who Top Professional **To what do you attribute your success:** Ms. Hall attributes her success to the teachings of her family, the nuns, and the Jesuit priests in her youth. **Why did you become involved in your profession or industry:** Ms. Hall became involved in her profession because of those who recognized her desire to guide young people in their quest for life's meaning.

Sherry Reneé Hall, PA-C

Title: Physician Assistant **Industry:** Medicine & Health Care **Company Name:** Desert Orthopaedic Center **Parents:** Paul Hall; Kay Hall **Marital Status:** Married **Spouse Name:** Michael Reulbach **Education:** Master's Degree in Physician Assistant Studies, University of Nebraska Medical Center (2007); BS in Specialized Studies, Ohio University, Cum Laude; AS in Applied Science, Cuyahoga Community College, Magna Cum Laude **Certifications:** Basic Cardiac Life Support (2018); Authorized Registrant, Drug Enforcement Administration (2017); Licensed Physician Assistant, Nevada Medical Board (2016); National Commission on Certification of Physician Assistants (2002) **Career:** Physician Assistant, Desert Orthopedic Center, Las Vegas, NV (2016-Present); Physician Assistant, St. Francis Orthopedic Institute, Columbus, GA (2014-2016); Physician Assistant, Blue Ridge Bone & Joint (2013); Physician Assistant, Pinehurst Hip and Knee Center, North Carolina (2011-2013); Physician Assistant, Center for Orthopedics, Elyria, OH (2005-2011); Physician Assistant in Surgery, EMH Regional Healthcare System, Elyria, OH (2002-2004) **Memberships:** Fellow, American Association for Orthopedics (Now American Academy of Orthopaedic Surgeons); American Academy of PAs **To what do you attribute your success:** Ms. Hall attributes her success to the support of her family. She spent many hours away from them due to the demanding hours of her career. Despite her distance, Ms. Hall's family has been supportive throughout the process, which has led to her continued success. **Why did you become involved in your profession or industry:** Ms. Hall became involved in her profession because of her desire to help others. It was also very important to her to walk a patient through the process of surgery from the educational aspects to the physical and emotional care. She has always wanted her patients to feel as safe and secure in their surgical intervention as they possibly could be.

Peter L. Halvorson, PhD

Title: Professor Emeritus **Company Name:** University of Connecticut **Date of Birth:** 09/07/1940 **Place of Birth:** Berlin **State/Country of Origin:** OH/USA **Parents:** Otto P. Halverson; Adele B. (Chase) Halverson **Marital Status:** Married **Spouse Name:** Judith A. Devaud (02/04/1964) **Children:** Peter C. **Education:** Doctor of Philosophy, University of Cincinnati (1970); Master of Arts, University of Cincinnati (1965); Bachelor of Arts, Dartmouth College (1962) **Career:** Professor Emeritus, Department of Geography, University of Connecticut, Storrs, CT (2003-Present); Professor, University of Connecticut, Storrs, CT (1983-2003); Special Assistant to President, University of Connecticut, Storrs, CT (1986-1988); Department Head, University of Connecticut, Storrs, CT (1981-1986); From Assistant Professor to Associate Professor, University of Connecticut, Storrs, CT (1970-1983); Assistant Professor, University of Northern Colorado, Greeley, CO (1968-1970); Geographer, United States Army Corps of Engineers, Cincinnati, Ohio (1967-1968); Instructor, University of Cincinnati (1965-1967) **Career Related:** Chair, University Senate, University of Connecticut (1984-1986, 1990-1993, 1994-2000, 2001-2002); Chairperson, Commencement Committee, University of Connecticut (1985-2002); Executive Committee, University Senate, University of Connecticut (1983-1986, 1987-1993, 1994-2000) **Civic:** Connecticut Central Housing Committee, Statewide Body (1978-1988, 1993-Present); Member, Town Council, Coventry, CT (1988-1993); Chairman, Connecticut Central Housing Committee (1980-1982) **Creative Works:** Co-author, Monographs, "Atlas of Religious Change in America" (1987, 1994, 2000); Co-author, Monograph, "Patterns in Pluralism: A Portrait of American Religion"; Co-author, Textbook, "The City in the Western Tradition" **Awards:** Excellence in Service Award, University of Connecticut (2002, 2016); Outstanding Faculty Advisor, University of Connecticut (2002); Award, American Association of University Professors **Memberships:** Executive Committee, American Association of University Professors (1978-1985, 1990-1993); President, American Association of University Professors (1980-1981); Vice President, American Association of University Professors (1979-1980) **Marquis Who's Who Honors:** Albert Nelson Marquis Lifetime Achievement Award **Why did you become involved in your profession or industry:** Dr. Halvorson went into education in part because his mother was a teacher. He wanted to be a city planner when he graduated from school, but he was asked if he wanted to be a teaching assistant. He took the position and enjoyed it.

Susan Owens Hamilton

Title: Attorney; Transportation Executive (Retired) **Company Name:** Springboard Consulting LLC **Date of Birth:** 08/07/1951 **Place of Birth:** Birmingham **State/Country of Origin:** AL/USA **Parents:** William Lewis Owens; Vonnette (Wilson) Owens **Marital Status:** Divorced **Spouse Name:** M. Raymond Hamilton (06/08/1974) **Education:** Doctor of Jurisprudence, Samford University (1977); Bachelor of Arts, Auburn University (1973) **Career:** Part-time Legal Counsel, Springboard Consulting LLC (2012-Present); Legal Counsel, Springboard Consulting LLC, FL (2019); Emeritus Advisory Council, Auburn University College of Business (2007-2017); Advisory Council, Cumberland School of Law (2003-2005); Chief Diversity Officer, Chief Compliance Officer; CSX Transportation (2002-2012); Assistant Vice President, Casualty Prevention, Chessie System R.R.'s, Baltimore, MD (1985-1986); General Manager, Freight Claim Services, Seaboard System R.R., Jacksonville, FL (1984-1985) **Civic:** Trustee, Gator Bowl (2004-Present); Past Chairman, Co-founder, Seamark Ranch (2001-Present); Board Chairman, Pine Castle, Inc. (2006-2008); Chairman, Gator Bowl (2003); Chairman, Board of Directors, United Way of Northeast Florida (1996-1997) **Awards:** Inaugural Wolf Award, Women's Leadership Forum (2015); Corporate Leader Award, Hands on Jacksonville (2014); Club Honor Key, Named Member of the Year, Uptown Civitan (2010); Named, Corporate Leader of the Year, Women in Business, Jacksonville Business Journal (2007); Named, Women's History Month Poster, Jacksonville Mayor (2006) **Memberships:** Downtown Rotary Club (2000-2012); President, Jacksonville Chapter, Business and Professional Women's Foundation (1984-1985); American Bar Association; Jacksonville Bar Association; President, First Coast Chapter, Ladies Professional Golf Association Amateurs **Bar Admissions:** Alabama; Florida **Marquis Who's Who Honors:** Albert Nelson Marquis Lifetime Achievement Award **To what do you attribute your success:** Ms. Hamilton attributes her success to her Christian faith. **Why did you become involved in your profession or industry:** Ms. Hamilton's parents were very active in their community, which inspired her to follow their example. She planned on pursuing math, but after taking some college courses, realized the subject wasn't for her. Ms. Hamilton decided to study pre-law instead, and she never looked back. **Avocations:** Singing; Golf; Football **Religion:** Methodist

Winborne Leigh "Winnie" Hamlin

Title: English, Religion and Art Teacher **Company Name:** Lancaster Middle and High School; Eastern High School **Date of Birth:** 08/12/1937 **Place of Birth:** Norfolk **State/Country of Origin:** VA/USA **Parents:** Dr. Southgate; Maud Winborne Leigh **Marital Status:** Married **Spouse Name:** Jefferson Davis Hamlin (06/27/1959) **Children:** Jeff; John; Frank **Education:** Master of Arts in Teaching, Johns Hopkins University (1959); Bachelor of Arts, Sweet Briar College, Magna Cum Laude (1958); Coursework, The Graham School, Norfolk, VA **Career:** English Teacher, Lancaster Middle and High Schools, SC (1959-1963); English Teacher, Eastern High School, Baltimore, MD (1958-1959); With, Sweet Briar College (1955-1958): Student Waitress, Alumnae/President's Office (1954-1958); With, Seaboard Citizen's National Bank, Norfolk, VA (1953-1957) **Career Related:** Docent, Dallas Museum of Art (1992-2005); Board of Directors, St. Michael School (1989-1993); Vestry, St. Michael and All Angels Church (1990-1992); President, Friends of the Library for Park Cities (1988-1991); Executive Council, Diocese of Dallas (1988-1990); National Selection Committee, Jefferson Scholars Program, University of Virginia (1989); Delegate, Triennial Conventions of Episcopal Church (1988); Board, Episcopal Province VII (1984-1987); Board of Directors, Highland Park High School (1985-1986) **Civic:** Volunteer, St. Michael and All Angels Church; Volunteer, YMCA **Awards:** Acorn Award for the Establishment of the University Park Library (2013); Most Popular and Best All-around, The Graham School, Norfolk, VA (1954); Highest SAT Senior Award; Benedict Scholar, Sweet Briar College **Memberships:** Executive Board, Judicial Board, Vice President, Joint Council, Tau Phi, Q.V., Sweet Briar College Alumnae Association (1977-1983, 1985-1989); Student Representative, Board of Overseers, Sweet Briar College (1957-1958); President, Fellowship of Young Churchmen, Diocese of Southern Virginia (1954-1955); Psi Mu Nu Citywide High School Sorority (1952-1954) **Marquis Who's Who Honors:** Albert Nelson Marquis Lifetime Achievement Award; Marquis Who's Who Top Professional; Marquis Who's Who Humanitarian Award **Why did you become involved in your profession or industry:** Ms. Hamlin initially became involved in her profession after receiving a master's degree in teaching, whereupon she began to teach in public schools. **Avocations:** Art; Reading; Taking children to museums **Political Affiliations:** Independent **Religion:** Episcopalian

Mia Margaret Hamm

Title: Professional Soccer Player **Industry:** Athletics **Date of Birth:** 03/17/1972 **Place of Birth:** Selma **State/Country of Origin:** AL/USA **Parents:** Bill Hamm; Stephanie Hamm **Marital Status:** Married **Spouse Name:** Nomar Garciaparra (11/22/2003); Christiaan Corry (1994, Divorced 2001) **Children:** Grace Isabella; Ava Caroline; Garrett Anthony **Education:** BS in Political Science, University of North Carolina (1994) **Career:** Forward, U.S. Women's National Soccer Team (1987-2004); Professional Soccer Player, Washington Freedom (2001-2003); Soccer Player, North Carolina Tar Heels (1989-1993); Soccer Player, Lake Braddock Bruins (1989); Soccer Player, Notre Dame Knights (1986-1988) **Career Related:** U.S. Women's Soccer Team, Olympic Games, Athens, Greece (2004) **Civic:** Founder, Mia Hamm Foundation (1999); Fundraiser, UNC Health and Children's Hospital Los Angeles **Creative Works:** Author, "Go for the Goal: A Champions Guide to Winning in Soccer and Life" (1999) **Awards:** Golden Foot Legends Award (2014); Listee, ESPNW's Impact 25 (2014); U.S. Soccer's USWNT All-Time Best XI (2013); Inductee, World Football Hall of Fame (2013); Greatest Female Athlete, ESPN (2012); Inductee, Texas Sports Hall of Fame (2008); Inductee, National Soccer Hall of Fame (2007); Inductee, Alabama Sports Hall of Fame (2006); Gold Medal, Olympics Games, Athens, Greece (2004); Listee, FIFA 100 (2004); Bronze Medal, FIFA Women's World Cup (2003); Silver Medal, Olympic Games, Sydney, NSW, Australia (2000); FIFA Female Player of the Century Award (2000); Winner, FIFA Women's World Cup (1999); Sportswoman of the Year, Women's Sports Foundation (1997, 1999); U.S. Soccer Female Athlete of the Year (1994-1998); Gold Medal, Olympic Games, Atlanta, GA (1996); Bronze Medal, FIFA Women's World Cup (1995); Honda-Broderick Cup (1994); Honda Sports Award (1993-1994); Winner, FIFA Women's World Cup, China (1991); Three-Time Recipient, ESPY Awards

Brett Gene Hardcastle

Title: Master Sergeant (Retired) **Industry:** Military & Defense Services **Company Name:** U.S. Army **Date of Birth:** 05/06/1953 **Place of Birth:** Twin Falls **State/Country of Origin:** ID/USA **Parents:** Sgt. Hal Gene Hardcastle; Marian Fellows **Marital Status:** Married **Spouse Name:** Kim (Shewell) (12/31/2011) **Children:** 13 Children **Education:** AS in Liberal Arts, Columbia College, Salt Lake City, UT; AA, Columbia College **Career:** Teacher, U.S. Army Junior ROTC, Salt Lake City, UT (2009-2013) **Civic:** Former Volunteer, Big Brothers Big Sisters of America (1984-1991) **Military Service:** Combat Engineer, U.S. Army (1987); Reserve, U.S. Army, Salt Lake City, UT (1971-1977); Platoon Sergeant, U.S. Army, Iraq War; Recruiter, U.S. Army, Salt Lake City, UT **Awards:** Eagle Scout Award (2004, 2007); Academic Leadership & Excellence, SALUTE Veterans National Honor Society (1996); Meritorious Service Medal; Glen R. Morrell Award, U.S. Army **Memberships:** BPO Elks; Utah Sports Hall of Fame Foundation; SALUTE Veterans National Honor Society **To what do you attribute your success:** Mr. Hardcastle attributes his success to the incredible influencers, leaders, and young people he has associated with; he also praises the Army for setting him up for success. When he re-enlisted in the early 1980s, he served with some outstanding Americans. He loved representing and wearing the uniform of the U.S. Army. **Why did you become involved in your profession or industry:** Mr. Hardcastle became involved in his profession because his parents taught him the value of service from an early age. His father, who was a high school coach, counselor and educator, served in the U.S. Army Reserve; Mr. Hardcastle calls him his biggest influence. He fondly remembers fun family vacations taking place around his father's two weeks of annual training, and it is at this time that he became familiar with the importance of serving. His sense of duty has always been strong, so much so that he didn't want to wait to be drafted. Inspired by his father, who joined the Korean War, Mr. Hardcastle grew to believe that every able-bodied male should serve. **Thoughts on Life:** In career accomplishments, Mr. Hardcastle completed a successful one-year mission in Kirkuk, Iraq as a platoon sergeant in support of Operation Iraqi Freedom. When he was in high school, he was a student body officer and a two-time regional wrestling champion. As a young man, he won third place in the Rocky Mountain Athletic Conference Wrestling Championships, where he represented the College of Eastern Utah (now Utah State University). Today, Mr. Hardcastle is a proud husband and grandfather to 15 grandchildren.

Duncan Hartley, PhD

Title: Owner, Duncan Hartley Fine Art Photography **Industry:** Fine Art **Company Name:** Duncan Hartley Fine Art Photography **Date of Birth:** 09/27/1941 **Place of Birth:** Detroit **State/Country of Origin:** MI/USA **Parents:** Harold Shephard Hartley; Catherine Carmichael Hartley **Marital Status:** Widowed **Spouse Name:** Adrienne Ashley Hartley (Deceased 2014) **Education:** PhD in English Literature, Wayne State University, Detroit, MI (1971); MA in English Literature, Wayne State University, Detroit, MI (1966); BA in English Literature, University of Michigan (1964) **Career:** Owner, Duncan Hartley Fine Art Photography (2008-Present); Associate Dean, Case Western Reserve University School of Medicine, Cleveland, OH (1996-2003); Executive Director of the President's Council, Memorial Sloan Kettering Cancer Center, New York, NY (1984-1996); Administrator, Educational Resources, Chapter Liaison, Young Presidents Organization (YPO), New York, NY (1973-1978) **Civic:** Member, Princeton United Methodist Church. **Creative Works:** Photograph, Harvard Museums of Art (2020); Portfolios on New York City, Little Italy; Birth of the Revolution: Concord and Ipswich; More than 150 Prints, Permanent Collections of Museums **Memberships:** KelbyOne (2006-Present); Tim Grey (2006-Present); The New-York Historical Society; Princeton University Art Museum; The Princeton Club of New York; The Audiophile Society **Why did you become involved in your profession or industry:** Dr. Hartley grew up in a family dedicated to the arts. His mother attended art school, and later opened an art gallery. His father was a poet, a Thoreau scholar and wood sculptor. He began a career in professional photography while in the eighth grade when he was offered a job working in a darkroom. He held that job until he graduated college and stuck to it with the profession. **Avocations:** Audio equipment reviewing; Arts and culture; Environment; Health; Improving cooking skills; Museums; Jazz and classical music **Religion:** Methodist

Deirdre Anne Shanahan Harvey

Title: Construction Manager **Industry:** Engineering **Company Name:** MTA New York City Transit **Date of Birth:** 01/17/1968 **Parents:** John Shanahan; Anne Shanahan **Marital Status:** Married **Spouse Name:** Robert **Education:** Mechanical Engineer Intern, MTA New York City Transit (1991-1992); BS in Mechanical Engineer, New York Institute of Technology, Old Westbury, NY (1991) **Certifications:** Certified Building Commissioning Professional (2016-Present): Certified Construction Manager (2006-Present) **Career:** Construction Administrator, MTA New York City Transit, New York, NY (2016-Present); Project Administrator, MTA New York City Transit (2014-2016); City Planner IV, MTA New York City Transit (2011-2014); Associate Project Manager III, MTA New York City Transit (2010-2011); Associate Project Manager II, MTA New York City Transit (2001-2009); Associate Transit Management Analyst, MTA New York City Transit (1994-2001); Assistant Mechanical Engineer, MTA New York City Transit (1992-1993) **Career Related:** Teacher, Construction Project Management, Pace University, New York, NY **Civic:** Chair, Construction Management Association of America (CMAA) Public Owners Caucus; Chair, Constructors Managers Professional Forum **Awards:** Recipient, Area and Division Awards, Toastmasters International (2006-2019); Diamond Award for Emergency Stabilization of Rockaway Line, American Council of Engineering Companies of New York (2014); Recognition for Dedication of Service, Construction Management Association of America (CMAA) (2011); Project of the Year, Construction Management Association of America (CMAA) (2010); Award of Merit for Best of Construction (2004) **Memberships:** Construction Management Association of America (CMAA); New York InterAgency Engineering Council (NYIEC); The Association of Energy Engineers (AEE) **To what do you attribute your success:** Mrs. Harvey attributes her success and tenacity to how her family raised her. **Why did you become involved in your profession or industry:** Mrs. Harvey turned toward her profession in high school. She took Mr. D'Antoni's physics class and thought that was interesting. She also took Brother Louie's course, introduction to aeronautics, and got sold on the engineering aspect of it. **Avocations:** Exercise; Occasional 5k; Painting; Drawing; Writing; Former soccer coach; Public speaking; Teaching **Political Affiliations:** Right to Life Republican, Fiscal Conservative **Religion:** Catholic

Michael L. Haskett

Title: Founder, Chief Executive Officer **Industry:** Insurance **Company Name:** Cornerstone Wealth Advisory Group **Marital Status:** Married **Spouse Name:** Jennifer Haskett **Children:** Michael Lee Haskett III (Max) **Education:** BBA in Business, Management, Marketing and Related Support Services, Clemson University, SC (1994) **Certifications:** Certified, Long-term Care; Fellow, Life Underwriter Training Council; Chartered Life Underwriter **Career:** Founder, Chief Executive Officer, Cornerstone Wealth Advisory Group, North Charleston, SC (2007-Present); Executive Counsel, American Senior Benefits (2013-2018); Owner, Regional Manager, Universal American (Now WellCare Health Plans, Inc.) (2008-2011); Branch Manager, Bankers Life and Casualty (2004-2007); Branch Manager, ING (1999-2004) **Civic:** Supporter, Dorchester Two Educational Foundation (2018-Present); Supporter, Miracle League of Northern Charleston, NC (2018-Present); Supporter, Young Life (2018); Supporter, COPS Athletic Program (2018); Supporter, Knightsville Elementary School (2015); Supporter, Chase After a Cure (CAAC) (2013-2017); Team Leader, Alzheimer's Association (2004-2007); Supporter, North Charleston POPS! **Creative Works:** Featured Author, "Baby Boomers Are Demanding More from Their Financial Advisors," Kiplinger; Featured Author, Bloomberg Businessweek, Fortune and Money **Awards:** Large Business Torch Award for Ethics, Better Business Bureau (2017) **Marquis Who's Who Honors:** Marquis Who's Who Top Professional; Marquis Who's Who Humanitarian Award **To what do you attribute your success:** Mr. Haskett attributes his success to hard work and surrounding himself with a great team. He also attributes much of the success and efficiency of his business to having great team chemistry. He also believes that you have to empower people and they will perform if you give them the room to do it, so he urges how important it is to "give them the ability to shine and they will." **Why did you become involved in your profession or industry:** Mr. Haskett became involved in his profession because he was working a job in the corporate sector and worked his way up to a supervisor position. He then began to feel as though he was not using his abilities to their full potential. His wife suggested he look into a career in financial services due to his skill with numbers and his overwhelming desire to help others. Mr. Haskett followed his wife's advice and walked away from his corporate position to take on a career as a wealth adviser. **Avocations:** Traveling with his wife and kids in the family RV

Ronald R. Hatch

Title: Engineer **Industry:** Engineering **Date of Birth:** 12/28/1938 **Place of Birth:** Freedom **State/Country of Origin:** OK/USA **Parents:** Richard Verni; Elma Lottie (Carberry) H. **Marital Status:** Married **Spouse Name:** Nancy Elene Bates (30/12/1960) **Children:** Richard; Rebecca; Sondra; Wendy; Randall; Ronald; Jeffrey; Nathan; Abigail; Peter; Robert; Marcy; Melanie **Education:** Bachelor of Science in Physics and Mathematics, Seattle Pacific College (1962) **Career:** Retired (2014); With, John Deere (1995-2014); With, NavCom Tech. Inc. (1995-1999); Consultant, Wilmington, CA (1993-1995); Engineer, Magnavox, Torrance, CA (1970-1993); Engineer, Boeing Co., Seattle, OR (1965-1970); Physicist, Johns Hopkins Applied Physics Laboratory, Silver Spring, MD (1963-1965) **Career Related:** With, U.S. Space-Based Positioning, Navigation and Timing Advisory Board (PNT Advisory Board) **Creative Works:** Author, "Escape from Einstein" (1992); Contributor, Numerous Articles to Professional Journals **Awards:** Fellow, Institute of Navigation (2000); Colonel Thomas Thurlow Award, Institute of Navigation (2000); Johannes Kepler Award, Institute of Navigation (1994) **Memberships:** President, Institute of Navigation (2001-2002); Chairperson, Satellite Division, Institute of Navigation (1998-2000); Western Region Vice President, Institute of Navigation (1992-1993); Marine Representative, Institute of Navigation (1991-1993) **Marquis Who's Who Honors:** Albert Nelson Marquis Lifetime Achievement Award **Why did you become involved in your profession or industry:** Mr. Hatch became involved in his profession because he enjoyed mathematics and finding any particular way to do something. **Avocations:** Studying and writing on relatively theory; Written numerous articles about need to revise relativity theory **Political Affiliations:** Republican **Religion:** Baptist

Carla Diane Hayden

Title: 14th Librarian **Company Name:** Library of Congress **Date of Birth:** 08/10/1952 **Place of Birth:** Tallahassee **State/Country of Origin:** FL/USA **Parents:** Bruce Kennard Hayden Jr.; Colleen (Dowling) Hayden **Education:** Honorary LHD, New York University (2019); Honorary Degree, College of William and Mary (2017); PhD in Library Science, Graduate Library School, The University of Chicago (1987); MLS, Graduate Library School, The University of Chicago (1977); Bachelor's Degree in Political Science and African History, Roosevelt University; Honorary LHD, Wake Forest University; Honorary LHD, McDaniel College; Honorary LHD, Morgan State University; Honorary LHD, University of Baltimore **Career:** 14th Librarian of Congress, Library of Congress (2016-Present); Executive Director, Enoch Pratt Free Library (1993-2016); Deputy Commissioner, Chief Librarian, Chicago Public Library (1991-1993); Associate Professor, School of Computing and Information, University of Pittsburgh (1987-1991); Library Services Coordinator, Museum of Science and Industry, Chicago (1982-1987); Young Adult Services Coordinator, Chicago Public Library (1979-1982); Associate, Children's Librarian, Chicago Public Library (1973-1979) **Civic:** National Foundation on the Arts and the Humanities (2010-Present); Board Member, Institute of Museum and Library Services (2010-Present); Board Member, Baltimore Gas and Electric (2007-Present); Trustee, Baltimore Community Foundation (2015-2016); Board Member, Urban Libraries Council; Board Member, YWCA USA; Board Member, Maryland African American Museum Corporation; Board Member, Kennedy Krieger Institute; Board Member, The American Institute for Urban Psychological Studies, Inc. **Creative Works:** Contributor, "From Outreach to Equity: Innovative Models of Library Policy and Practice" (2004); Contributor, "The Black Librarian in America Revisited" (1994); Contributor, "Your Right to Know: Librarians Make It Happen: Conference Within a Conference Background Papers" (1992) **Awards:** World's 50 Greatest Leaders, Fortune (2016); Jean E. Coleman Library Outreach Lecturer, American Library Association (2006, 2015); Joseph W. Lippincott Award, American Library Association (2013); Woman of the Year, Ms. Magazine (2003); Maryland's Top 100 Women, The Daily Record (2003); President's Medal, Johns Hopkins University (1998); Legacy of Literacy Award, The DuBois Circle, Baltimore, MD (1996); Andrew White Medal, Loyola University Maryland (1995); Librarian of the Year Award, Library Journal (1995) **Memberships:** Honorary Member, American Library Association (2018); President, American Library Association (2003-2004)

William S. Haynes Jr., MD

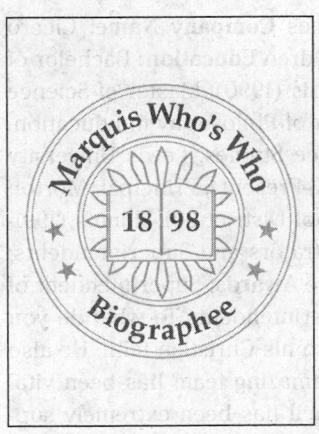

Title: Internist, Cardiologist, Educator (Retired) **Industry:** Medicine & Health Care **Date of Birth:** 06/06/1926 **Place of Birth:** Newark **State/Country of Origin:** NJ/USA **Parents:** William Forby Haynes; Grace (Brien) Haynes **Marital Status:** Married **Spouse Name:** Aline Linehan (08/25/1984); Constance Simpson (07/02/1960) **Children:** William; Suzanne; David **Education:** MA in Theology, La Salle University (2001); Fellow, Cardiology, St. Luke's Medical Center (Now Mount Sinai Morningside) (1959-1960); Medical Resident, St. Luke's Medical Center, (Now Mount Sinai Morningside) (1957-1959); Intern, St. Luke's Medical Center (Now Mount Sinai Morningside) (1954-1955, 1957-1959); MD, Columbia University (1954); AB, Princeton University (1950); BS, United States Merchant Marine Academy (1946) **Certifications:** Diplomate, Sub-certified in Cardiovascular Diseases, American Board of Internal Medicine; National Board of Medical Examiners (NBME) **Career:** Retired (1997); Private Practice Specializing in Internal Medicine/Cardiology, Princeton, NJ (1960-1997); New York Cardiology Resident, New York Heart Association (NYHA) (1959-1960); Ship's Medical Officer, United States Navy (1955-1957) **Career Related:** Retired, Honorary Staff, Princeton Medical Staff (1997-Present); Lecturer on Spirituality and Medical Practice, Princeton Medical Center (1982-Present); Assistant Clinical Professor, Medicine, Robert Wood Johnson Medical School, Rutgers, The State University of New Jersey (1972-Present); President, Class of 1950, Princeton University (2010-2015); Member, Advisor Council, Center for Study of Religion, Princeton University (2000-2009); Senior Attending Intern Medical (1960-1997); Senior Attending, Internal Medicine, Princeton Medical Center (1960-1989); Guest Lecturer, Princeton Theological Seminary (1959-1960); Adjunct Professor, Theology, La Salle University **Civic:** Cadet, Pacific Theater (1944-1945); Vestry, Trinity Episcopal Church, Princeton, NJ; Member, Third Order of St. Francis, NJ **Military Service:** Lieutenant, Medical Officer, Navy Medical Corps, United States Navy (1955-1957) **Creative Works:** Author Four Books; Contributor, Articles, Professional Journals **Awards:** Member, Several Awards **Memberships:** Member, Numerous Organizations **Marquis Who's Who Honors:** Albert Nelson Marquis Lifetime Achievement Award **Avocations:** Swimming; Reading **Religion:** Episcopalian

Beth Hedva, PhD, DABPS

Title: Psychologist **Industry:** Medicine & Health Care **Date of Birth:** 08/27/1955 **Place of Birth:** Detroit **State/Country of Origin:** MI/USA **Parents:** Harold Chaim Milinsky; Tova Sylvia Snyder **Marital Status:** Spouse **Spouse Name:** Harold Finkleman **Education:** PhD, Psychology, School of Health and Human Services, Columbia Pacific University, San Rafael, CA, with Distinction (1989); MA, Clinical Psychology, Graduate School of Professional Psychology, John F. Kennedy University, Orinda, CA (1981); MA, Transpersonal Counseling Psychology, Graduate School of Consciousness Studies, John F. Kennedy University, Orinda, CA (1981); BS, Psychology, College of Social Sciences, Michigan State University, East Lansing, MI (1977) **Certifications:** Psychologist, AB, Canada; (2007-Present); Canadian Registry of Marriage & Family Therapists (1998-Present); Certified Provider of Continuing Education, CAMFT, California (1983-Present); Psychologist, NWT Canada (2000-2011); Diplomate in Clinical Psychology (1999); MFT, Board of Behavioral Sciences, CA (1983) **Career:** Director, Training and Counseling Services, Psychologist, Finkleman Communications (1995-Present); Co-Founder, Canadian Institute of Transpersonal and Integrative Sciences (2007) **Career Related:** United Nations Panelist, "Human Rights Violations & Recovery: Body, Mind and Spirit Symposium," New York, NY (2007); Panelist, "A Year After the Tsunami in Banda Aceh," Peace International Relations and Human Rights Symposium, Greece (2006); Panelist, "Addressing Racism Between Aboriginal and Non-Aboriginal Canadians," Peace International Relations & Human Rights Symposium (2003); Lecturer, Department of Psychology, Tarumanagara University, West Jakarta, Indonesia (2008, 2006, 2005, 2001); Faculty, Department of Clinical Psychology, Antioch University, San Francisco, CA (1986-1989) **Creative Works:** Author, Book, Award-Winner "Betrayal, Trust and Forgiveness (2013); Author, "Traumatisme Collectif en Haiiti et Endurance Morale du Peuple Haitien" (2011); Author; "Unlearning Racism" Opinion Canada, Vol. 5, No. 29 (2003); Conferences & Presentations (1982-2019); Author, Contributor, Articles, Numerous Publications **Avocations:** Ceramics; Mysticism **Religion:** Anamism

Rudy Hernandez

Title: Superintendent **Industry:** Education/Educational Services **Company Name:** Cicero School District 99 **Marital Status:** Married **Children:** Seven Children **Education:** Bachelor of Science in Education and Spanish, North Park University, Illinois (1990); Master of Science in Bilingual Education, Chicago State University, Illinois; Doctor of Philosophy in Education, Aurora University, Illinois **Certifications:** Certificate of Advance Studies, Lewis University **Career:** Superintendent, Cicero School District 99, Illinois (2013-Present); Principal, Morton District 201, Illinois (2000-2013); Teacher, Mornings High School District 201, Illinois (1991-2000) **Civic:** President, Illinois Association of School Administrators and Superintendents; Strategic Committee, Diverse Learner Ready Teacher Committee **Awards:** Superintendent of the Year, Illinois Association of School Administrators and Superintendents **To what do you attribute your success:** Mr. Hernandez attributes his success to his Christian faith. He also believes that having a supportive family, community and an amazing team has been vital in him achieving his goals. Likewise, his superintendent council has been extremely supportive, as well as the entire District 99 community. **Why did you become involved in your profession or industry:** Mr. Hernandez began working with the Chicago public schools as a teachers assistant. As a student and assistant, he saw a greater need for resource services and began to develop his own idea of what the educational system should be like. Working with children and trying to address their needs was enough for Mr. Hernandez to set out on the path to make an impact on education and ensure that children were receiving the best possible service. Despite the lack of funding they receive, they have achieved so much progress for their community at no additional cost to the community. **Avocations:** Listening to music; Playing golf

Carol Ann Hilleary, MEd

Title: Realtor; Elementary School Principal (Retired) **Industry:** Real Estate **Company Name:** Sellstate Priority Realty LLC **Date of Birth:** 11/15/1945 **Place of Birth:** Baltimore **State/Country of Origin:** MD/USA **Parents:** Joseph Martin Schepers; Evelyn Dorothy (Shivoder) Schepers **Marital Status:** Married **Spouse Name:** Gary Wayne Hilleary (07/23/1981) **Children:** Robert Hilleary (Stepson); Dawn Hilleary (Stepdaughter) **Education:** MS in Elementary Education, Towson University (1975); BS in Elementary Education and Psychology, Towson University (1971) **Certifications:** Realtor (2006-2021); Certified Elementary Teacher, Grades 1-8; Certified, Elementary Middle School Principal, Supervisor; Advanced Professional State Certificate **Career:** Realtor, Sellstate Priority Realty LLC (2013-2021); Realtor, BMI International (2006-2013); Executive Director of Marketing and Call Centers, Sylvan Learning Centers, Southwest FL (2002-2010); Principal, Orems Elementary School Then Riderwood Elementary School (1989-2001); Assistant Principal, Baltimore County Public Schools (1984-1988); Chapter I/Resource Teacher, Baltimore County Public Schools (1979-1983); Elementary Classroom Teacher, Baltimore County Public Schools (1966-76, 1978-1979); Math Science Resource Teacher, Victory Villa Elementary School (1977-1978); Demonstration/Supervising Teacher, Baltimore County Public Schools/Towson University (1968-1977) **Career Related:** Realtor (2006-Present); Board of Directors, Sellstate Priority Realty LLC (2011-2018); Member, Baltimore County Public Schools Based Management Team (1994-1995); Consultant/Speaker, Towson University (1994); Presenter in Field **Civic:** Baltimore County Public Schools Central Area Liaison Johns Hopkins Childrens' Center, Baltimore, MD (1994-1995); Host-organizer/Planner, Maryland Hunger Summit, Riderwood Elementary School (1994); Member, Architectural Planning Committee, Wellington Valley Improvement Association (Now Wellington Valley Homeowners Association), Lutherville, MD (1988-1990); Lector, St. Isaac Jogues Church, Baltimore, MD (1976-1979); CCD Teacher (1973-1976); Member, Summit Church, University Campus, Estero, FL **Creative Works:** Contributor, Editor, Books **Awards:** Gold and Platinum Awards for Real Estate Sales (2013-2019); Recipient, Several Awards/Grants **Memberships:** Member, Numerous Organizations **Avocations:** Bible study; Exercise; Boating; Dog handling and breeding; Music; Reading **Political Affiliations:** Republican **Religion:** Baptist **Thoughts on Life:** Mrs. Hilleary's motto is, "Attitude is everything in life. Start and end each day with a thankful heart."

John Hoard

Title: Partner **Company Name:** Rubin & Levin P.C. **Marital Status:** Married **Spouse Name:** Nancy F. Hoard **Children:** John (33); Jennifer (31); Jason (27) **Education:** J.D., The Indiana University Robert H. McKinney School of Law (IU McKinney) (1980); BS, Northwestern University (1977) **Career:** Partner, Rubin & Levin P.C. (2000-Present); Attorney, Rubin & Levin P.C. (1992-2000); Attorney, Baker & Daniels (1989-1992); Certified Public Accountant, Ernst & Young **Career Related:** Owner, International Traders Ltd **Civic:** Treasurer, President, Board, Neighborhood Christian Legal Clinic **Awards:** Indianapolis Business Journal's Distinguished Barrister Award (2019); Named a Super Lawyer, which recognizes the top 5% of attorneys in the State of Indiana (2007, 2009, 2010-2019); Named Top 50 Lawyers in the State of Indiana (2012); AV Rated, Martindale Hubbel **Memberships:** St. Richard's School Foundation Board (2012-Present); Strategic Planning Finance Committee, St. Paul's Episcopal Church (2012-Present); Treasurer, Ex Officio Member, Executive Committee, Neighborhood Christian Legal Clinic (2011-Present); Board Member, Neighborhood Christian Legal Clinic (2004-Present); Distinguished Fellow, American Bar Association (2013); Fellows of the American Bar Foundation (2013); Treasurer, Board Member, National Episcopal Health Ministry (1999-2012); Brebeuf Finance Committee, Brebeuf Dad's Club (2010-2011); President, Brebeuf Dad's Club (2009–2011); Treasurer, Chair, Bankruptcy and Creditors' Rights Section, Indiana State Bar Association (2005-2007); Treasurer, St. Paul's Episcopal Church (2002-2006); Judges and Lawyers Assistance Committee, Indianapolis Bar Association (1998-2006); Development Committee, Indianapolis Bar Foundation (2003-2005); Senior Warden, St. Paul's Episcopal Church (2000-2002); Vestry Member, St. Paul's Episcopal Church (1999-2002) **Bar Admissions:** Certified Public Accountant in the State of Indiana (1988); Indiana State Bar; U.S. Court of Appeals for the Seventh Circuit; U.S. District Court for the Northern and Southern Districts of Indiana; U.S. Tax Court **Marquis Who's Who Honors:** Marquis Who's Who Top Professional **To what do you attribute your success:** Mr. Hoard's parents were very open minded to people of all colors and religions. They tried to spread the good word thorough out Indiana. He was instilled with social justice at a very early age from his parents. His mother graduated phi beta kappa. His grandma also graduated from college. His father is a podiatrist. **Why did you become involved in your profession or industry:** Mr. Hoard was always very impressed by the public persona of lawyers in America. They were agents for good and justice and protected the rights of individuals.

Kimberly Hoehing

Title: Associate **Industry:** Law and Legal Services **Company Name:** Kotlar, Hernandez & Cohen, LLC **Marital Status:** Married **Spouse Name:** Patrick **Education:** JD, Widener University School of Law (2004); BBA, Business, Management, Marketing, and Related Support Services, Temple University, Fox School of Business and Management (2001) **Certifications:** Certified, Civil Trial Attorney, Supreme Court of New Jersey **Career:** Associate, Kotlar, Hernandez & Cohen, LLC (2018-Present); Defense Attorney, Geico (2009-2018) **Career Related:** Speaker, Educator, National Business Institute (NBI) **Memberships:** Camden County Bar Association; Burlington County Bar Association; New Jersey Association for Justice **Marquis Who's Who Honors:** Marquis Who's Who Top Professional **To what do you attribute your success:** Ms. Hoehing attributes her success to the support of her family and friends. **Why did you become involved in your profession or industry:** Ms. Hoehing became involved in profession from watching Matlock with her mother when she was a little girl. She always wanted to be a lawyer. **Avocations:** Traveling with family

Linda Hoffman

Title: President, Chief Executive Officer **Company Name:** New York Foundation for Senior Citizens **Date of Birth:** 07/23/1940 **Place of Birth:** New Haven **State/Country of Origin:** CT/USA **Parents:** Bernard Harry Rosenfield; Sylvia (Paul) Rosenfield **Marital Status:** Married **Spouse Name:** Peter A. Hoffman (09/25/1965) **Children:** Tracie Hoffman Cohen **Education:** MSW, Columbia School of Social Work, New York, NY (1968); BA, Russell Sage College, Troy, NY (1962) **Certifications:** Licensed Master Social Worker, State of New York; Certified, National Association of Social Workers **Career:** President, Chief Executive Officer, New York Foundation for Senior Citizens, New York, NY (1979-Present); Special Assistant to Commissioner, New York City Special Service for Children, New York, NY (1972-1979) **Career Related:** Consultant, Government Programs; Adjunct Professor, Columbia University School of Social Work **Creative Works:** Author, "Introduction, The Columbia Guide to Social Work Writing," Columbia University Press (2012); Author, "In China, Many Signs Point to Growing Awareness of the Challenge Accompanying an Aging Population," The National Council of Aging Perspective on Aging, July-October Edition (1992) **Awards:** Recognition Award for Many Contributions, Order of St. John of Jerusalem, Knights Hospitaller (2012); Inductee, Columbia School of Social Work Hall of Fame (2000) **Memberships:** National Association of Social Workers; Women Creating Change **Marquis Who's Who Honors:** Albert Nelson Marquis Lifetime Achievement Award **Avocations:** Boating; Fishing; Opera **Thoughts on Life:** New York Foundation for Senior Citizens must continue its mission of providing services that meet the needs of the growing older adult population while seeking more solutions that work.

Nichole Holland, MSN, CRMP

Title: MSN, RN **Industry:** Medicine & Health Care **Company Name:** 1) ForeverCare 2) Mallard Bay, Signature HealthCARE **Children:** Two Children **Education:** MSN (2019); BS, Drexel University (2015) **Certifications:** NP (Nurse Practitioner), State of Maryland **Career:** RN, Rehabilitation, Long-Term Care, ForeverCare (2014-Present); RN, Rehabilitation, Long-Term Care, Mallard Bay, Signature HealthCARE (2014-Present); Nursing Assistant, Step Down Unit, ICU (1999) **Memberships:** American Nurses Association; American Nurses Credentialing Center; Maryland Nurses Association **To what do you attribute your success:** Ms. Holland attributes her success to her father, who influenced her to never give up. He always gave support when she wasn't doing well, and encouraged her to strive to be the best. **Why did you become involved in your profession or industry:** Ms. Holland became involved in her profession at age 19 after her mother passed away. She had spent a great deal of time in the hospital by her mother's side and felt motivated to be in a position to help others. **Thoughts on Life:** Ms. Holland strives to make every day count. She is inspired by Muhammad Ali's saying, "the man who views the world at 50 the same as he did at 20 has wasted 30 years of his life."

Carol Hoskins, PhD

Title: Professor Emeritus, Director, PhD Program in Nursing & Nursing Research **Industry:** Education/Educational Services **Company Name:** New York University **Date of Birth:** 12/25/1932 **Place of Birth:** New York **State/Country of Origin:** NY/USA **Parents:** Victor Herbert Noll; Rachel (Perkins) Noll **Marital Status:** Married **Spouse Name:** Donald William Hoskins (12/19/1955) **Children:** Lauren Hoskins-Lingley; David William; Bruce Noll **Education:** Honorary PhD, National and Kapodistrian University of Athens, Greece (1998); PhD in Nursing, New York University (1978); MA in Community Health, New York University (1973); BSN in Nursing, Cornell University, New York Hospital (1955) **Certifications:** Registered Nurse **Career:** Professor Emeritus, Director, PhD Program in Nursing and Nursing Research, New York University (2003-2008); Senior Research Scientist, New York University (2003-2008); Professor of Nursing, New York University (1987-2003); Director, PhD Program in Nursing & Nursing Research, New York University (1985-1990); Associate Professor of Nursing, New York University (1982-1987); Assistant Professor of Nursing, New York University (1977-1982); Public Health Nurse, Visiting Nurse Service of New York (1955-1958) **Career Related:** Visiting Professor, University of Catalonia (2000); Elected Fellow, American Academy of Nursing (1992); Postdoctoral Nurse Fellowship, National Research Service Award, PHS (1980-1982) **Civic:** Case Manager, American Red Cross Family Emergency Relief Services **Creative Works:** Co-author, "The Breast Cancer Treatment Response Inventory: Development, Psychometric Testing, and Refinement for Use in Practice," Oncology Nursing Forum (2008); Co-author, "Breast Cancer-Education, Counseling, and Adjustment Among Patients and Partners: A Randomized Clinical Trial," Nursing Research (2008) **Awards:** Grantee, National Cancer Institute, National Institutes of Health (1999-Present); Worldwide Lifetime Achievement (2018); Joseph and Violet Pless Faculty Award, New York University College of Nursing (2006) **Memberships:** American Nurses Association; Fulbright Association; Sigma Theta Tau **Marquis Who's Who Honors:** Albert Nelson Marquis Lifetime Achievement Award **Avocations:** Swimming; Skiing; Gardening; Quilting

Carl E. Hostler

Title: Attorney, Associate **Industry:** Law and Legal Services **Company Name:** Prim Law Firm, PLLC **Date of Birth:** 10/28/1960 **Place of Birth:** Morgantown **State/Country of Origin:** WV/USA **Parents:** Stanley Hostler; Jessie (Buckel) Hostler **Marital Status:** Married **Spouse Name:** Janet Clarke Hostler **Education:** JD, West Virginia University College of Law, Morgantown, WV (1989); BA in History, University of Maryland, College Park, MD (1984); Diploma, South Charleston High School, South Charleston, WV (1978) **Career:** Attorney, Associate, Prim Law Firm, PLLC (2007-Present); Self-employed with Focus on Criminal and Juvenile Cases in State Courts, Wilmington, NC (2005-2007); Managing Partner, Hostler and Donnelly, PLLC, Charleston, WV (1992-1998); Attorney, Hostler and Segal, LC (1989-1991); Full-time and Part-time Paralegal, Hostler and Segal, LC (1985-1989); Various Contractors (1978-1985) **Civic:** Guardian Ad Litem Assistant, Brunswick County, NC (2001-2002); Volunteer, Habitat for Humanity, Alaska, Charleston, WV, Wilmington, NC, and Myrtle Beach, SC (1995-2005); Member, Volunteer Guardian Ad Litem Program, Brunswick County, NC (1999-2005); Pro Bono Work, Legal Aid of West Virginia; Volunteer, Big Brothers Big Sisters of America, Charleston, WV **Awards:** Award, Leadership West Virginia; Certificate of Appreciation, Big Brothers Big Sisters of America **Memberships:** National Association of Criminal Defense Lawyers; West Virginia Association for Justice (WVAJ); Habitat for Humanity International; Big Brothers Big Sisters of America **Bar Admissions:** North Carolina State Bar (1991, 1999); United States District Court for the Southern District of West Virginia (1989); The West Virginia State Bar (1989) **To what do you attribute your success:** Mr. Hostler attributes his success to common sense and patience. He likes to think things through and does not "fly off the handle." **Why did you become involved in your profession or industry:** Mr. Hostler became involved in his profession because he believes that everyone deserves a fair day in court. There was not much more to his pursuit of his career path. **Avocations:** Woodworking; Fishing; Reading; Spending time with his family

Patrick Kuo-Heng Hsu

Title: Language Educator (Retired); Former Librarian **Industry:** Education/Educational Services **Company Name:** Texas Lutheran University **Date of Birth:** 07/3/1936 **Place of Birth:** Hefei **State/Country of Origin:** Anhui/China **Parents:** Hsiang-Chang Hsu; Yi-Yun (Tan) Hsu **Marital Status:** Married **Spouse Name:** You-Wei Gina Wang (02/1/1962) **Children:** David Shing; James C. **Education:** MLS, Western Michigan University (1968); BA, National Cheng-Chi University, Mucha, Taipei, Taiwan (1960) **Career:** Professor, University Librarian, Director of Information Service, Texas Lutheran University, Seguin, TX (1991-2002); Associate Professor, Library Director, Texas Lutheran University, Seguin, TX (1985-1991); Librarian, Ripon College (1985); Associate Librarian, Ripon College, Wisconsin (1977-1985); Assistant Librarian, Ripon College, Wisconsin (1968-1977) **Career Related:** Director, University Students in America from Taiwan Consortium, Seguin, TX (1990-1996) **Civic:** World Affairs Council of San Antonio (1993-Present); Advisor, Overseas Chinese Affairs Commission, Republic of China (1994-1996); Chairman, Board, San Antonio Chinese Cultural Institute (1994-1995); Director, Chinese Society of San Antonio (1989-1995) **Creative Works:** Translator, "Theory of Literature" (1976); Translator, Editor, "A Selection of Modern One-Act-Plays" (1971) **Memberships:** American Library Association; Modern Language Association; Association for Asian Studies; Chinese Language Teachers Association; Texas Library Association; Seguin Lions **Marquis Who's Who Honors:** Albert Nelson Marquis Lifetime Achievement Award **Why did you become involved in your profession or industry:** Prof. Hsu was inspired to go into his profession because he was interested in literature. He was a writer in college, so when he came to America, he wanted to continue studying literature. Library science was an extension of his studying literature; technology helped him to continue his growth. **Avocations:** Travel; Photography; Chinese art collecting **Thoughts on Life:** After his retirement in 2002, Prof. Hsu wrote articles for papers in Taiwan and Taipei, the INC monthly publication on various topics.

Charlotte Thomson Iserbyt

Title: Researcher, Writer, Educational Consultant **Industry:** Education/Educational Services **Company Name:** 3D Research Co. **Date of Birth:** 10/26/1930 **Place of Birth:** Brooklyn **State/Country of Origin:** NY/USA **Parents:** Clifton Samuel; Charlotte Deyer Thomson **Marital Status:** Widow **Spouse Name:** Johan Louis Iserbyt (09/26/1964, Deceased 05/2009) **Children:** Robert Louis; Samuel Thomson **Education:** Diploma in Secretarial, Executive, and Academic Studies, Katharine Gibbs School, with Honors (1949) **Career:** President, 3D Research Co., Bath, ME (1999-Present); Senior Policy Advisor, Office of Educational Research and Improvement, U.S. Department of Education, Washington DC (1980-1982); Co-founder, Guardians of Education for Maine, Camden, ME (1978-2000); Secretary to Ambassador, U.S. Department of State, Brussels (1961-1963); Secretary to Ambassador, U.S. Department of State, Pretoria, South Africa (1959-1960); Social Worker, American Red Cross, Anderson AFB (1953-1955) **Career Related:** Host, Guest, Radio Talk Shows (1999-2005); Freelance Writer (1973-2005) **Civic:** Elected School Board Member, Camden-Rockport School District (1976-1979) **Creative Works:** Author, Book, "The Deliberate Dumbing Down of America...A Chronological Paper Trail, 3rd Edition" (2003); Author, Book, "The Deliberate Dumbing Down of America...A Chronological Paper Trail" (1999); Author, Book, "Back to Basics Reform or...OBE*Skinnerian International Curriculum, 2nd Edition" (1993); Author, Book, "Back to Basics Reform or...OBE*Skinnerian International Curriculum" (1985) **Memberships:** Co-founder, Maine Conservative Union; Affiliate, National American Conservative Union; Daughters of the American Revolution **Marquis Who's Who Honors:** Albert Nelson Marquis Lifetime Achievement Award **Why did you become involved in your profession or industry:** Ms. Iserbyt became involved in her profession because of her experience overseas. She started her career as a social worker on an Air Force base in Guam, after two years, she decided she wanted to change things around. Many of the men she met didn't have a great education, and she wanted to do something to help. This inspired her to pursue education. **Avocations:** Languages; Collecting old books; History **Political Affiliations:** Independent **Religion:** Roman Catholic

Henry Woodrow "Woody" Jackson, PhD

Title: Physicist, Researcher **Industry:** Sciences **Date of Birth:** 10/30/1931 **Place of Birth:** Nassau **State/Country of Origin:** The Bahamas **Parents:** Robert Jackson; Mary Louise (Watler) Jackson **Marital Status:** Married **Spouse Name:** Jean Ellen Jackson (04/25/1987) **Children:** Brent Nelson (Stepchild); Larry Nelson (Stepchild); Carl Nelson (Stepchild); Warren Nelson (Stepchild); Eight Step-Grandchildren **Education:** PhD in Physics, Washington University (1962); BA in Mathematics, University of Texas (1958); BS in Physics, University of Texas (1958) **Career:** Research Scientist, Jet Propulsion Laboratory, Pasadena, CA (1987-1999); Private Consultant, Pasadena, CA (1982-1987); National Research Council Senior Resident Research Associate, Jet Propulsion Laboratory, Pasadena, CA (1981-1982); Visiting Faculty, Washington University (1980); Visiting Faculty, St. Louis University (1976-1977); Visiting Faculty, Washington University (1965-1966, 1974-1976); Staff Scientist, Scientific Research Laboratory, Ford Motor Co., Dearborn, MI (1966-1974); Assistant Professor, Physics, North Texas State University (1964-1965); Postdoctoral Research Associate, Washington University (1962-1964) **Career Related:** Researcher, Consultant, LaVerne, CA (1999-Present) **Military Service:** U.S. Army (1952-1954) **Creative Works:** Contributor, 53 Articles, Professional Journals; Patentee, 15 Patents **Awards:** Predoctoral Fellow, National Science Foundation, Washington University (1961, 1962) **Memberships:** American Physical Society; American Ceramic Society; Materials Research Society; Phi Beta Kappa; Sigma Xi **Marquis Who's Who Honors:** Albert Nelson Marquis Lifetime Achievement Award; Marquis Who's Who Top Professional; Distinguished Humanitarian **Why did you become involved in your profession or industry:** Dr. Jackson wanted to be a scientist all his life; as he progressed in school and attended Washington University, he met a research director, Eugene Feenberg, who was an inspiration to him. He started his research under Dr. Feenberg. Since then, many of his papers have been based on further developing the microscopic based theory on superfluid helium.

Tze-Chi Jao, PhD

Title: Research and Development Scientist (Retired) **Industry:** Research **Company Name:** Afton Chemical **Date of Birth:** 04/03/1940 **State/Country of Origin:** Taiwan **Parents:** Wei-de Jao; Chao-Mei Hsi **Marital Status:** Married **Spouse Name:** Carmen Jao **Children:** Shui-Yang, Meilin; Eugene **Education:** PhD in Physical Chemistry, University of Florida (1973) **Career:** Consultant (2010-2019); Distinguished Adviser, Research and Development Fellow, Afton Chemical (1996-2010); Research and Development Chemist, Research Fellow, Texaco Research Center (1981-1995); Visiting Associate Professor, Texas A&M University (1980); Assistant and Associate Professor, University of Puerto Rico (1974-1980); Postdoctoral Fellow, Royal Holloway, University of London **Civic:** Donor, Various Charitable Organizations **Creative Works:** Author, Co-Author, 100 Technical Papers; Contributor, Three Book Chapters **Awards:** Captain Alfred E. Hunt Award, Society of Tribologists and Lubrication Engineers (2011); Forest R. McFarland Award, SAE International (2010); Outstanding Industrial Innovator Award, Virginia Section, American Chemical Society (2010); Research Award on Automotive Lubricants, SAE International (2009); Annual Recognition Award for Creativity, Texaco Research Center (1989); Research Award, Mid-Hudson Section, American Chemical Society (1988) **Memberships:** Chair, Mid-Hudson Section (1991); SAE International; The American Oil Chemists' Society; American Chemical Society; Society of Tribologists and Lubrication Engineers **To what do you attribute your success:** Dr. Jao attributes his success to his father, Wei-de Jao, and Professor Jose Martinez Pico of the University of Puerto Rico at Mayaguez. **Why did you become involved in your profession or industry:** Dr. Jao became involved in his profession because of his lifelong interest in mathematics and science.

Beryl Jacqueline Jazvic

Title: Professional Artist, Art Teacher **Industry:** Education/Educational Services **Company Name:** Prince William County Public Schools **Date of Birth:** 12/15/1963 **Place of Birth:** Nassau **State/Country of Origin:** Bahamas **Marital Status:** Married **Spouse Name:** Josef **Children:** Ashlynn; Josef; Aston **Education:** MS in Teaching, Saint Mary University (2012); BFA, Savannah College of Arts and Design **Certifications:** Certified Teacher, K-12 Art **Career:** Teacher, Mary Williams Elementary School (2006-Present); Professional Artist (1995-Present); Art Educator (1992-Present); Art Teacher, Prince William County Public Schools **Creative Works:** Artist, "America Is...", Touchstone Gallery (2019); Artist, Messenger, CATO Freedom Art (2019); FCCA Artist Choice (2019); Virginia MOCA New Waves (2019); The Healing Power of ART, Manhatten Arts (2019); Featured Artist, Creative Quarterly Issue 51 (2018); Art impact International Golden Art Exhibition (2018); Art Impact International Light of the Caribbean (2018); Featured Artist, Creative Quarterly Issue 49-50 (2017); Contemporary Art Gallery Online (2017); Featured, Fredericksburg Fine Arts Exhibit (2017) **Awards:** Honorable Mention, CATO Freedom Art as the Messenger (2019); Second Place, FCCA Artist Choice (2019); Runner Up, Creative Quarterly Issue 51 (2018); Seascape Winner, Contemporary Art Gallery Online (2017); Fredericksburg Dorothy Hart Award, Fredericksburg Fine Arts Exhibit (2016); Third Place, Fredericksburg Fine Arts Exhibit (2016) **Memberships:** Poetry Society of America; Contemporary Online Gallery; American Impressionist Society, Inc. **To what do you attribute your success:** Mrs. Jazvic attributes her success to her parents and her consistency. She could have given up painting many times due to interrupting life factors; however, she never did. Her love and passion for painting outweighed any possible interruptions. **Why did you become involved in your profession or industry:** Mrs. Jazvic began painting when she was in high school. Her philosophy is to create and share, as she has a lot to share with the world. She uses artwork to express her emotions.

Melissa Viviane "Lizzo" Jefferson

Title: Singer, Rapper, Songwriter **Industry:** Media & Entertainment **Date of Birth:** 04/27/1988 **Place of Birth:** Detroit **State/Country of Origin:** MI/USA **Marital Status:** Single **Education:** Diploma, University of Houston; Diploma, Alief Elsik High School **Career:** Singer, Lizzo, The Larva Ink **Career Related:** Performer, Coachella (2019); Headline Performer, Glastonbury Festival (2019); Headline Performer, Indianapolis Pride Festival (2019); Headline Performer, Sacramento Pride Festival (2019); Performer, Har Mar Superstar; Tour, St. Paul and the Broken Bones; Performer, HAIM; Performer, Florence and the Machine; King Soupers **Creative Works:** Actress, "Hustlers" (2019); Voice Actress, "Ugly Dolls" (2019); Solo Artist, "Cuz I Love You" (2019); Model, Say It Louder Campaign, ModCloth (2018); Model, Future of Fashion Runway Show, Grace Insogna, Pride Island LGBTQ, Fashion Institute of Technology (2019); Voice Actress, "Yeti! Yeti!" (2018); Actress, "Wonderland" (2016); Voice Actress, "Brad Neely's Harg Nallin' Sclopio Peepio" (2016); Solo Artist, "Coconut Oil" (2016); Solo Artist, "Big Grrrl World" (2015); Solo Artist, "Lizzobangers" (2013); Singer, "We Art the Chalice" (2012); Featured Singer, "BoyTrouble," "Plectrumelectrum" **Awards:** Entertainer of the Year, NAACP Image Awards (2020); Best Pop Solo Performance, Grammy Awards (2020); Best Traditional R&B Performance, Grammy Awards (2020); Best Urban Contemporary Album (2020); Named, Pride50, Queerty (2019) Nominee, Push Artist Award, MTV Video Music Awards (2019); Nominee, Best New Artist, MTV Video Music Awards (2019); Nominee, Best Power Anthem (2019); Nominee, Song of the Summer, MTV Video Awards (2019); Nominee, Album of the Year, BET Hip Hop Awards (2019); Nominee, Impact Track (2019); Nominee, Choice Breakout Artist, Teen Choice Awards (2019); Nominee, Choice Summer Female Artist, Teen Choice Awards (2019); Nominee, Choice Summer Song, Teen Choice Awards (2019); Named, Billboard Hot 100 (2019); Featured, Music Issue, Teen Vogue (2018); Named, One to watch, Time Magazine (2014) **Avocations:** Flute

Arthur Kirk Jenne

Title: Secondary School Educator **Industry:** Education/Educational Services **Company Name:** Baltimore County Public Schools **Date of Birth:** 01/15/1942 **Place of Birth:** Pikeville, **State/Country of Origin:** KY/USA **Parents:** William Kendrick Jenne; Robina Laurie (Kirk) Jenne **Marital Status:** Married **Spouse Name:** Linda Louise Morris **Children:** Karen Jenne Stevens; Arthur Kirk II **Education:** MEd, Western Maryland College (Now McDaniel College) (1973); BS, Towson University (1970) **Career:** Retired (1999); Instructor, Baltimore County Public Schools, Towson, MD (1970-1999) **Career Related:** Designer, Computer Learning Center, Baltimore County Public Schools (1986) **Civic:** CCUCC Lay, Kirkridge Associate Reformed Presbyterian Church Fellowship (1994-1996); President, St. Matthew's United Church of Christ Council, Pleasant Valley, MD (1994) **Military Service:** With, United States Marine Corps (1961-1965); Radio Relay Repairman, United States Marine Corps (1963); Motor Vehicle Operator Course, United States Marine Corps (1962); Radio Electronics School, United States Marine Corps (1962) **Creative Works:** Author, "Computer Utilization of T.G." (1987); Author, "Read, Study, Think...Reading Comprehension" (1973) **Awards:** Good Conduct, Corporal Rank, United States Marine Corps (1963) **Memberships:** President, Valley Lions (1991-1992); Maryland Instructional Computer Coordinator, State of Maryland International Reading Association (Now SoMLA, State of Maryland Literacy Association); Marine Corps League; The American Legion **Marquis Who's Who Honors:** Albert Nelson Marquis Lifetime Achievement Award; Marquis Who's Who Top Professional; Marquis Who's Who Humanitarian Award **Why did you become involved in your profession or industry:** Mr. Jenne became involved in his profession because when he was in elementary school, he had a sixth grade teacher who taught him a lot. Later on in high school, his teacher, John Lowe, who was his wrestling coach, set a good example for him and the students. Mr. Lowe was the primary reason for him getting a good education along with the support of his dad and mom, William Kendrick Jenne and Robina Laurie (Kirk) Jenne. **Avocations:** Photography; Wood working; Genealogy; Family history **Religion:** Reformed Presbyterian **Thoughts on Life:** Mr. Jenne has two children; Karen Jenne Stevens who is married to Bradley, and Arthur Kirk II, married to Caryn. He has five grandchildren, Abigail Stevens, Maghan Stevens, Benjamin Stevens, Allison Elizabeth Jenne and Arthur Kirk Jenne III.

Raymond Franklin "Soames" Job, PhD

Title: Global Lead for Road Safety **Industry:** Infrastructure **Company Name:** The World Bank Group **Date of Birth:** 07/13/1954 **Place of Birth:** Dubbo **State/Country of Origin:** Australia **Parents:** Raymond Wallace Job; Nancy Colleen (Cook) Job **Marital Status:** Married **Spouse Name:** Chika Sakashita (2003) **Children:** Shannon; Lara; Lawson **Education:** PhD in Psychology, The University of Sydney (1985); BA in Psychology, The University of Sydney (1977) **Certifications:** Graduate, Australian Institute of Company Directors (2009) **Career:** Head of Global Road Safety Facility, Global Lead for Road Safety, The World Bank Group (2015-Present); Principal, Managing Director, Global Road Safety Solutions (2011-Present); Executive Director, Member, National Road Safety Council, Australia (2009-2012); Director, Centre for Road Safety, Transport for NSW (2003-2011); Chairperson, International Commission on Biological Effects of Noise; Founder, Managing Director, Global Road Safety Solutions; Director, Health and Safety Psychology Research Unit, The University of Sydney;; Head, Socio-Acoustics Section, Department of Health, Commonwealth of Australia; Senior Behavioral Scientist, Traffic Accident Research Unit, NSW Government **Creative Works:** Author, Co-Author, 400 Scientific Journal Papers, Conference Papers, Manuals, Book Chapters and Books; "Australia's Adolescents: A Health Psychology Perspective"; "Pedestrian Safety: A Road Safety Manual for Decision-Makers and Practitioners"; Editor, Journal of Road Safety; Associate Editor, Editorial Board Member, Numerous Journals **Awards:** Fellow, Australasian College of Road Safety; Two-Time Winner, Prince Michael International Road Safety Award; Two-Time Winner, Caples International Award; NSW Premier's Public Sector Gold Award; AdNews National Award for Campaign of the Year; Grand EFFIE for Most Effective Campaign, Advertising Foundation of Australia; Swedish Institute Award **Avocations:** Scuba diving; Surfing; Skiing **Religion:** Christian

David S. Johnson

Title: Civil Engineer **Industry:** Engineering **Date of Birth:** 04/10/1935 **Place of Birth:** Minneapolis **State/Country of Origin:** MN/USA **Parents:** Milton Edward Johnson; Helen M. (Sellie) Johnson **Education:** BS, Montana College of Mineral Science and Technology (1958) **Certifications:** Registered Professional Engineer, State of Montana **Career:** Director of Marketing, Jacobs (1994-2008); Preconstruction Chief, Department of Highways, Montana Department of Transportation (1989-1993); Engineering Specialties Supervisor, Department of Highways, Montana Department of Transportation (1972-1989); Regional Engineer, Department of Highways, Montana Department of Transportation (1968-1972); Assistant Preconstruction Engineer, Department of Highways, Montana Department of Transportation (1966-1968); Designer, Department of Highways, Montana Department of Transportation (1959-1966); Trainee, Department of Highways, Montana Department of Transportation (1958-1959); Traffic Accident Reconstructionist, Department of Highways, Montana Department of Transportation; Forensic Engineer, Department of Highways, Montana Department of Transportation **Career Related:** Consulting Engineer (1985-Present) **Civic:** Advisory Board Member, Helena Vocational-Technical Center (1972-1973) **Military Service:** U.S. Army Reserve (1959-1966) **Creative Works:** Contributor, Articles, Professional Journals **Memberships:** Fellow, Expert Witness Council, Institute of Transportation Engineers; National Society of Professional Engineers; Fellow, National Academy of Forensic Engineers; Montana Society of Engineers; Tort Liability Committee, Geometric Design Committee, Transportation Research Board; Washington Association of Technical Accident Investigators; Corvette Club; Shriners International **Marquis Who's Who Honors:** Albert Nelson Marquis Lifetime Achievement Award **Why did you become involved in your profession or industry:** Mr. Johnson became involved in his profession because of the challenges of being an engineer. **Avocations:** Taking photographs; Racing sports cars

Brenda Gail Jones

Title: School District Administrator (Retired) **Industry:** Education/Educational Services **Date of Birth:** 11/05/1949 **Place of Birth:** Winnipeg **State/Country of Origin:** MB/Canada **Parents:** Glen Allen McGregor; Joyce Catherine (Peckham) McGregor **Marital Status:** Divorced **Education:** Master of Arts, University of San Francisco (1983); Bachelor of Arts, San Francisco State University (1972) **Certifications:** Certified Teacher, School Administrator, State of California **Career:** Retired (2014); Principal and Program Manager of Special Education, Santa Clara County Office of Education (2003-2014); Director, Pupil Personnel Services, Redwood City School District, CA (2000-2003); Director, Educational Services and Special Projects, Lakeport Unified School District, CA (1988-2000); Assistant Principal, Lakeport Unified School District, CA (1982-1988); Teacher, Lakeport Unified School District, CA (1973-1982) **Career Related:** Management Team, Co-chairman, Santa Clara County Office of Education (2005-2007); Instructor of English, Mendocino College, Ukiah, CA (1977-1982) **Civic:** Volunteer Leader, Church Groups **Memberships:** Deputy Grand Matron, Order of the Eastern Star (1999); Past Matron, Clear Lake Chapter, Order of the Eastern Star (1995); Past President, Association of California School Administrators (1987); Lake County Charter Member, Association of California School Administrators **Marquis Who's Who Honors:** Albert Nelson Marquis Lifetime Achievement Award; Marquis Who's Who Top Professional; Marquis Who's Who Humanitarian Award **Avocations:** Health; Exercise; Walking; Reading; Gardening; Animals; Church; Extensive travel **Political Affiliations:** Republican **Religion:** Episcopalian

Edwin Channing Jones Jr., BSEE, PhD

Title: University Professor Emeritus **Industry:** Education/Educational Services **Company Name:** Iowa State University of Science and Technology **Date of Birth:** 06/27/1934 **Place of Birth:** Parkersburg **State/Country of Origin:** WV/USA **Parents:** Edwin Channing; Helen M.J. **Marital Status:** Married **Spouse Name:** Ruth Carol Miller (08/14/1960) **Children:** Charles; Cathleen; Helene **Education:** PhD University of Illinois (1962); Diploma, University of London (1956); BSEE, West Virginia University (1955) **Certifications:** Registered Professional Engineer, State of West Virginia **Career:** Professor Emeritus, Iowa State University (2001-Present); Associate Department Chair, Iowa State University (1997-2001); Professor, Iowa State University (1972-2001); Associate Professor, Iowa State University (1967-1972); Assistant Professor, Iowa State University (1966-1967); Assistant Professor of Electrical Engineering, University of Illinois at Urbana-Champaign (1962-1966); Engineer, GE (1955, 1962); Engineer, Westinghouse Electric Corporation (1959) **Career Related:** Director, ABET (1984-1987) **Military Service:** Lieutenant, U.S. Army (1956-1958) **Creative Works:** Author, Chapters, Handbook on Electronic Engineering **Awards:** Linton F. Grinter Distinguished Service Award, ABET (2001) **Memberships:** Fellowship for Advanced International Study, Rotary International (1955-1956); Fellow, American Association for the Advancement of Science; Fellow, IEEE; Fellow, ASEE; Sigma Xi, The Scientific Research Honor Society; The Tau Beta Pi Association, Inc.; Eta Kappa Nu, IEEE; Phi Beta Delta Honor Society **Marquis Who's Who Honors:** Albert Nelson Marquis Lifetime Achievement Award; Marquis Who's Who Top Professional **Why did you become involved in your profession or industry:** Dr. Jones became involved in his profession because he was inspired by his father, an electrical engineer. **Avocations:** Taking photographs; Collecting slide rules

Sharon Kaiser-Botsai

Title: Primary School Educator (Retired) **Place of Birth:** Waterloo **State/Country of Origin:** IA/USA **Parents:** Peter A. Ley; Lorraine Burton Ley **Marital Status:** Widowed **Spouse Name:** Dr. Elmer E. Botsai (12/5/1981, Deceased 8/28/2013); Hugh W. Kaiser (12/28/1968, Divorced 1981) **Children:** Kiana; Donald; Kurt **Education:** Postgraduate Coursework, University of Hawai'i (1972-1988); MEd, University of Hawai'i, Honolulu, HI (1970); BSBA, University of Arizona (1963) **Certifications:** Certified Elementary Education Teacher, Hawaii (1971-2004) **Career:** Substitute Teacher, Honolulu, HI (2003-Present); Teacher of Kindergarten, Waialae Chartered School (1997-2003); Teacher of Kindergarten, Palolo School, Honolulu, HI (1991-1997); Teacher of Students of Limited English Proficiency, Kaahumanu School, Honolulu, HI (1990-1991); Teacher of Staff Instruction, Honolulu District Department of Education (1989-1990); Curriculum Coordinator, Teacher, Waiokeola Preschool, Honolulu, HI (1977-1988); Part-time Lecturer, Honolulu Community College (Creative Approach to Language Skills for Young Children) (1986); Head Teacher, Central Union Preschool, Honolulu, HI (1967-1977); Teacher, Waiokeola Preschool, Honolulu, HI (1974-1976); Teacher, St. Mark's Kindergarten, Honolulu, HI (1966-1973); Secretary, Donald M. Drake, San Francisco, CA (1964-1966) **Career Related:** Validator, Accreditation Program, National Academy for the Education of Young Children (1986-Present); Workshop Leader on Multiple Intelligence (1998); Drama Workshop (1994); Representative, Palolo School, Hawaii State Teachers Association (1993); Assistant to Co-chair, Conference, Hawaii Association for the Education Young Children (1987-1988); Workshop Leader, HAEYC Conference (1984-1986); Workshop Leader, MECAP Conference (1985); Speaker, Creative Communications (1984); Workshop Leader, HAEYC Conference (1982); Workshop Leader, Drama National Conference (1982) **Civic:** Volunteer, Angel Network Charities (2006-Present); Trustee, Stewardship Chairman, Waiokeola Church (1986-1988); Board of Directors, Zoo Hui (1984-1986); Troop Co-leader, Girl Scouts of the United States of America (1981-1984) **Creative Works:** Author, "Creative Dramatics" (1990); Co-author, "Preschool Activities" (1990) **Awards:** First Recipient, Phyllis Loveless Excellence in Teaching Award (1979) **Memberships:** Hawaii Association for the Education Young Children; Delta Delta Delta; Calvary by the Sea Church **Marquis Who's Who Honors:** Albert Nelson Marquis Lifetime Achievement Award **Avocations:** Travel; Line dancing; Watercolor art **Religion:** Lutheran

Sean P. Kavanagh

Title: Partner **Industry:** Law and Legal Services **Company Name:** Harbison & Kavanagh **Marital Status:** Married **Spouse Name:** Jennifer Kavanagh **Children:** Kaitlyn; Conall **Education:** JD, University of Baltimore, MD (1991); Diploma, College of William & Mary, VA (1988) **Career:** Partner, Harbison & Kavanagh (2012-Present); Partner, Jenkins Block & Associates (1992-2012) **Memberships:** National Organization of Social Security Claimants Representatives (NOSSCR) **To what do you attribute your success:** Mr. Kavanagh attributes his success to thousands of satisfied clients he has had over the years. His motto is, "Do your best for your clients and give them your best efforts every time..." **Why did you become involved in your profession or industry:** Mr. Kavanagh chose a career as a lawyer because it is a rewarding and honorable profession which would allow him to really make a difference in peoples' lives and help them through difficult times. He was exposed to Social Security disability claims and workers' compensation claims while clerking for a private firm during law school and has dedicated his practice to those areas ever since.

David Blair Kay, PhD

Title: Principal Optical Scientist (Retired) **Industry:** Research **Company Name:** Quality Vision International, Inc. **Date of Birth:** 10/21/1942 **Place of Birth:** Decatur **State/Country of Origin:** IL/USA **Parents:** Alvin Reuel Kay; Harriet Marjorie (Blair) Kay **Marital Status:** Married **Spouse Name:** Bonnie Lea Elliott Kay (10/19/1974); Barbara Weeks Kay (06/01/1967, Deceased 10/9/1970) **Children:** Christina Leigh Kay Kirivong; Laura Elliott Kay Passic **Education:** Doctor of Philosophy in Optics, University of Rochester, NY (1976); Master of Science in Optics, University of Rochester, NY (1973); Master of Science in Physics, University of Arkansas (1967); Bachelor of Science in Physics, University of Arkansas (1965) **Career:** Principal Optical Scientist, QVI Inc. (2006-2019); Research Associate, Senior Staff, Group Leader, Research Labs, Eastman Kodak Company, Rochester, NY (1980-2005); Associate Scientist, Xerox Corp., Webster, NY (1978-1980); Assistant Professor of Pathology and Optics, University of Rochester Medical Center (1976-1978); Research Associate in Pathology, University of Rochester Medical Center (1974-1976); Technical Staff, Texas Instruments, Dallas, TX (1966-1970) **Career Related:** Kodak Fellow, University of Rochester (1973-1974); NSF Traineeship, University of Rochester (1971-1972) **Civic:** Treasurer, Pultneyville Yacht Club (2018-2019); Trustee, Asbury First UMC, Rochester, NY (2006-2008); Elder, 12 Corners Presbyterian Church (1988-1990); Elder, 12 Corners Presbyterian Church (1981-1984); Elder, South Presbyterian Church (1973-1976) **Creative Works:** Co-author, "Multichannel Laser Thermal Printhead Technology," Handbook of Optical Laser Scanning (2004); Co-author, "Optical Heads and Lasers," Handbook of Magneto-Optical Data Recording (1997); Co-editor, Co-chair, "Optical Data Storage," Proc. of SPIE (1992); Contributor to 17 Publications in Physical Review, Journal of Nuclear Medicine, Optical Engineering, Proceedings of SPIE; Contributor, 23 Presentations at Conference and Meetings; Author or Co-author, 35+ Patents **Awards:** Kingslake Medal SPIE (1978); Itek Award, SPIE (1976) **Memberships:** Honorary Member, Rochester Section OSA (2006-Present); President, Rochester Section OSA (1989-1990); President Elect, Rochester Section OSA (1988-1989); Secretary, Rochester Section OSA (1987-1988); Treasurer, Rochester Section OSA (1984-1985); Program Chair, Rochester Section OSA (1982-1983) **Marquis Who's Who Honors:** Albert Nelson Marquis Lifetime Achievement Award **Avocations:** Sailing; Swimming **Political Affiliations:** Democrat **Religion:** Methodist

Peter Kehoe, PhD

Title: President **Industry:** Engineering **Company Name:** The Blasket Group, Ltd **State/Country of Origin:** England **Marital Status:** Married **Spouse Name:** Brigid Ann Kehoe **Children:** Breffni; Cormac; Ciera; Lochlann **Education:** PhD in Chemical Engineering, Yale University (1970); MS, Cistercian College, Roscrea, County Tipperary, Ireland (1970); Master's Degree in Engineering Science, University College Dublin, First-class Honors (1966); BE, University College Dublin, First-class Honors (1966) **Career:** President, The Blasket Group, Ltd., Wilmington, DE (2004-2016); President, The Blasket Group, Ltd., Chadds Ford, PA (2004-2016); Technical and Product Manager, Director, DuPont (1973-2004) **Career Related:** ICI Research Fellow, Cambridge University, Cambridge, England (1971-1973); Research Fellow, Irish Institute for Industrial Research, Dublin, Ireland (1970-1971) **Marquis Who's Who Honors:** Albert Nelson Marquis Lifetime Achievement Award; Marquis Who's Who Top Professional **To what do you attribute your success:** Dr. Kehoe attributes his success to his parents; both were very intelligent. He also credits his interest in learning new things. **Why did you become involved in your profession or industry:** Dr. Kehoe was very good at mathematics; he graduated first in his class and came in first in Ireland's National University Exam. Dr. Kehoe decided to become an chemical engineer because his father was a civil engineer. **Avocations:** Exercise; Reading; Attending plays

David Stewart Kennedy

Title: Chief United States Bankruptcy Judge **Industry:** Government Administration/Government Relations/Government Services **Date of Birth:** 04/09/1944 **Place of Birth:** Reagan **State/Country of Origin:** TN/USA **Parents:** Charles Elco Kennedy; Ethelyn (Stewart) Kennedy **Marital Status:** Married **Spouse Name:** Patricia Kelly (06/18/1977) **Education:** JD, (1970); BA, The University of Memphis **Certifications:** Tennessee Bar Association (1971) **Career:** Judge, United State Bankruptcy Court (1980-Present); Adjunct Professor, Cecil C. Humphreys School of Law, The University of Memphis (1982); Member, Private Panel of Bankruptcy Trustees, Private Practice (1971-1973, 1976-1980); Administrative Assistant, Chief Clerk, United States Bankruptcy Court, Western District of Tennessee (1974-1976); Law Clerk, United States Bankruptcy Court, Western District of Tennessee (1970-1971); Bankruptcy Representative, Governance & the Judicial Conference, United States Courts; Member, Former Chair, Bankruptcy Judicial Advisory Group, Administrative Office of the U.S. Courts **Creative Works:** Contributor, Articles, Professional Journals **Awards:** Pillars of Excellence Award, Alumni Association, The University of Memphis **Memberships:** Member, President, Alumni National Council, Cecil C. Humphreys School of Law; Memphis Bar Association; Tennessee Bar Association; American Bar Association; American College of Bankruptcy **Marquis Who's Who Honors:** Albert Nelson Marquis Lifetime Achievement Award; Marquis Who's Who Top Professional **Why did you become involved in your profession or industry:** Judge Kennedy became involved in his profession because his dad was a lawyer and he was also a big fan of Atticus Finch, the lawyer in the novel "To Kill a Mockingbird."

James A. Kenney III

Title: Senior Judge **Industry:** Law and Legal Services **Company Name:** Court of Special Appeals, Maryland **Date of Birth:** 03/26/1937 **Place of Birth:** Salisbury **State/Country of Origin:** MD/USA **Marital Status:** Married **Spouse Name:** Karen H. Abrams **Education:** JD, George Washington University, (1963); Postgraduate Coursework, Yale Divinity School (1959-1960); BA, Dickinson College (1959) **Career:** Senior Status (2007-Present); Judge, Court of Special Appeals of Maryland (1997-2007) Partner, Briscoe Kenney, and Successors, Lexington Park, MD (1966-2007); Assistant State's Attorney, St. Mary's County, MD (1964-1967); Associate, Barco Cook Patton, Washington, DC (1963-1964) **Career Related:** Chair, Senior Judge Committee, Maryland Judicial Council; Board Member, Maryland Judicial Ethics Committee; Adjunct Professor, St. Mary's College; Maryland General Assembly Land Use and Alcohol Beverage Code Revision Committees; Business and Technology Case Management Committee **Civic:** Housing Code Revision Committee; Governor's Advisory Commission, Maryland Higher Education Plan; St. Mary's College Foundation; Board of Governors, Southern Maryland Higher Education Center; Chair, Governmental Regulation of Land Use Committee; Advisor, American Bar Association; National Conference on Uniform State Laws on Planned Communities **Creative Works:** Contributor, "Land Use Regulation"; Author, "The Problem of People: Critical Areas and Floating Zones in the Chesapeake," Virginia Journal of Natural Resources Law; Co-Author, "Codifying the Law of Homeowners Associations: The Uniform Planned Community Act," Real Property, Probate and Trust Journal; Contributor, Community Association Law Reporter, American Bar Association Journal **Awards:** Leadership in Law Award, Daily Record **Memberships:** St. Mary's County Bar Association; Board of Governors, Maryland State Bar Association; Committee on Laws, Maryland State Bar Association; Advisor, National Conference of Commissioners on Uniform State Laws for Planned and Common Interest Communities; American College of Real Estate Lawyers **Bar Admissions:** U.S. Supreme Court (1977); U.S. Court Appeals (1974); U.S. District Court for the District of Maryland (1965); U.S. District Court for the District of Columbia (1964); Court of Appeals of Maryland (1963) **Marquis Who's Who Honors:** Albert Nelson Marquis Lifetime Achievement Award; Distinguished Humanitarian

Christian Randolph Kerns

Title: Chemist (Retired) **Industry:** Sciences **Company Name:** SPECTRO Analytical Instruments **Date of Birth:** 04/08/1953 **Place of Birth:** Fredericksburg **State/Country of Origin:** VA/USA **Parents:** Terrill D. Kerns; Mary Barbe Kerns **Marital Status:** Single **Education:** BS in Chemistry, West Virginia University (1978) **Career:** Retired (2008); Chemist, Adecco, Leominster, MA (2002-2008); Engineer, Spectro Analytical Instruments GmbH, Fitchburg, MA (2000-2001); Chemist, Aerotek Sciences (Now Aerotek, an Allegis Group Company), Fort Lauderdale, FL (1999-2000); Chemist, Harbor Branch Oceanographic Institution, Florida Atlantic University, Fort Pierce, FL (1997); Chemist, Florida Department of Agriculture and Consumer Services, Tallahassee, FL (1986-1996) **Civic:** President, United Methodist Men, Wesley United Methodist Church, Worcester, MA (2010-2012); Member, Membership and Evangelism Committee, Wesley United Methodist Church, Worcester, MA (2002-2008); Chairman, Mission Committee, Saint Paul's United Methodist Church, Tallahassee, FL (1994-1996); Captain, Colorado State Championship Basketball Team (1971); Charter Board Member, Interfaith Hospitality Network; Providing Food and Shelter to Homeless Families, Worcester Area, MA **Awards:** Science Excellence Award, American Biographical Institute (2011); Honoree, Named Man of the Year, American Biographical Institute (2011); Honoree, First Team, All State Colorado Men's Basketball Team (1971) **Memberships:** American Chemical Society; Past President, Lions Club; Honorary Member, Phi Theta Kappa Honor Society **Marquis Who's Who Honors:** Albert Nelson Marquis Lifetime Achievement Award **To what do you attribute your success:** Mr. Kerns attributes his success to his education. **Avocations:** Stained glass artist **Religion:** Methodist **Thoughts on Life:** Mr. Kerns follows the motto: "Life isn't about waiting for storms to pass. It's about learning to dance in the rain."

Mary Kieler

Title: Nurse **Industry:** Medicine & Health Care **Company Name:** Canonsburg General Hospital, Allegheny Health Network **Marital Status:** Married **Spouse Name:** Mark **Education:** MS in Fraud and Forensics, Carlow University (2016); BSN, Carlow University (1995); Diploma, Jameson School of Nursing (1990) **Certifications:** Certified Fraud Examiner, Association of Certified Fraud Examiners (2017); Paralegal Certificate, Duquesne University (1998) **Career:** Clinical Documentation Improvement Specialist, Canonsburg General Hospital, Allegheny Health Network (2015-Present); Medical Records Review Nurse, UPMC Health Plan (2005-2015); Legal Nurse Consultant, Downtown Pittsburgh Law Firms (1999-2004); RN, Staff Nurse, Mercy Hospital (1992-1999) **Memberships:** Former Member, Toast Masters International **To what do you attribute your success:** Ms. Kieler attributes her success to hard work and persistence. In everything she does, she performs to the best of her ability. **Why did you become involved in your profession or industry:** Ms. Kieler's mother was a nurse; she served as her primary inspiration to pursue a career in nursing.

Ellen Jane Killebrew, MD

Title: Cardiologist, Educator **Industry:** Health, Wellness and Fitness **Date of Birth:** 10/08/1937 **Place of Birth:** Tiffin **State/Country of Origin:** OH/USA **Parents:** Joseph Arthur Killebrew; Stephanie (Beriont) Killebrew **Marital Status:** Married **Spouse Name:** Edward S. Graves (09/12/1970, Deceased, 2016) **Education:** MD, University of Medicine and Dentistry of New Jersey (1965) **Certifications:** Certified in Cardiovascular Diseases (1982); Certified in Internal Medicine (1978) **Career:** Clinical Professor of Medicine, University of California, San Francisco (1992-Present) **Career Related:** Board of Medical Examiners of California (1999-2002) **Civic:** Mentor, University of California Berkeley (1985-2016); Contributor, Resolution Firm California State Assembly (2005) **Creative Works:** Co-Author, Chapter, "Difficult Diagnosis II" (1991) **Awards:** Special Recognition, Outstanding Contribution on Clinical Faculty, University of California San Francisco School of Medicine (2014); Certificate of Congressional Recognition, Permante Medical Group (2010); Commendation, State Assembly of California for Contributor to Women and Heart Disease (2005) **Memberships:** President, East Bay Chapter, American Heart Association (1995-Present); President, Oakland Piedmont Branch (1995-1996); Research Chairman, American Heart Association, Contra Costa Chapter (1975-1985); Chairman, CPR Committee, Alameda Chapter (1984); President, Contra Costa Chapter, American Heart Association (1980-1982); Fellow, American College of Physicians; American College of Cardiology; Board of Directors, Western Affiliate; Former Member, Federation of Clinical Research **To what do you attribute your success:** Dr. Killebrew attributes his success to the support of his family and friends. **Why did you become involved in your profession or industry:** When Dr. Killebrew was 13, she developed severe gastroenteritis. The family doctor came and gave Dr. Killebrew a shot from his bag. In the morning, she was well. Since then, she wanted to have her own "magic" bag full of magic remedies. **Avocations:** Equitation; Skiing; Sailing; Boating; Hiking; Reading; Scuba diving; Water skiing; Swimming; Horses **Political Affiliations:** Independent

Chris Kim

Title: Coordinator **Industry:** Law and Legal Services **Company Name:** CrimeStoppers Honolulu **Education:** BS in Liberal Arts, University of Hawaii (1998) **Career:** Coordinator, CrimeStoppers Honolulu (2017-Present); Detective, Homicide Unit, Honolulu Police Department, Honolulu, HI **Civic:** Volunteer Speaker, 59 Schools in Hawaii; Volunteer Speaker, Rotatory Club **Awards:** Coordinator of the Year, Crime Stoppers USA National Conference **To what do you attribute your success:** Mr. Kim attributes his success to the work ethic his parents instilled in him. He works hard in everything he does. His philosophy is to make everyone matter. **Why did you become involved in your profession or industry:** Mr. Kim is currently a police officer for the Hawaii Police Department. In 2017, the previous CrimeStoppers coordinator retired and a replacement was needed. Mr. Kim was asked if he would take over the program, and he did.

Toby Kimball

Title: Founder, President **Industry:** Food & Restaurant Services **Company Name:** Cajun Works: The Real Cajun Deal **Place of Birth:** Atchafalaya Basin **State/Country of Origin:** LA/USA **Marital Status:** Married **Education:** Coursework, Melville High School, Melville, LA **Career:** President, Founder, Cajun Works Incorporated, Krotz Springs, LA (2011-Present); President, Founder, Self-employed, Krotz Springs, Breaux Bridge, LA (2011-2016); Co-owner, Cajun Works Incorporated, Krotz Springs, LA (2005-2011); Owner, Kimball's Auto, Krotz Springs, LA (1998-2005); Auto Technician, Gerry Lane Chevrolet, Baton Rouge, LA (1993-1998); Mechanic, Santa Marta Golf Course, Baton Rouge, LA (1986-1988) **Military Service:** Aviation Machinist Mate, Second Class, United States Navy (1988-1992) **Why did you become involved in your profession or industry:** Mr. Kimball has been cooking for as long as he can remember. Having been raised in Atchafalaya Basin, a swamp in Louisiana, he grew up enjoying simple activities like hunting, fishing, camping, friendship, food and family. He started his career as a mechanic, although he still enjoyed to cook. When he joined the military, Cajun culture was a popular topic of curiosity. Mr. Kimball began to feel that he could take this culture and present it to people outside Louisiana so they can learn about the culture, history, beliefs and food.

Tommie Kirkendoll

Title: Education **Industry:** Other **Company Name:** National Alumni Association Officers **Parents:** JB Jones; Estella Crawley Jones **Marital Status:** Married **Spouse Name:** Leland Kapel Kirkendoll (06/07/1969) **Children:** Leland Kapel Kirkendoll, Jr. (11/24/1969); Chester Arthur Kirkendoll, IV (07/17/1973) **Education:** Degree, The University of Memphis (1976); BS in Health and Physical Education, Lane College **Career:** Teacher of Health and Physical Education (1974-2016); National Alumni Association Officers **Civic:** Volunteer, Lincoln Elementary School **Awards:** Teacher of the Year, I.B. Tigrett Middle School (2015); Teacher of the Year, Lane College **Memberships:** Sigma Gamma Rho Sorority, Inc.; Jackson Tennessee Chapter, The Links, Incorporated; PDK International **To what do you attribute your success:** Ms. Kirkendoll attributes her success to her desire to serve others, as well as her parents. **Why did you become involved in your profession or industry:** Ms. Kirkendoll became involved in her profession because she wanted to stay active and help others stay active, which pushed her into teaching human anatomy. **Avocations:** Gardening; Traveling; Listening to music

John "Jack" Knowlton, CPBD, GMB, CAPS

Title: President **Industry:** Architecture & Construction **Company Name:** Envision Design Build **Date of Birth:** 02/13/1955 **State/Country of Origin:** TX/USA **Parents:** John A Knowlton; Mary Louise Knowlton **Marital Status:** Married **Spouse Name:** Diana **Children:** Andrea **Education:** High School Diploma **Certifications:** CPBD (Certified Professional Building Designer); GMB (Graduate Master Builder); CAPS (Certified Aging-in-Place Specialist) **Career:** Owner, Founder, Envision Design Build **Civic:** Board Member, Lakeside Forest Homeowner Association **Awards:** Recipient, GHBA PRISM Awards **Memberships:** American Institute of Building Design; Greater Houston Builders Association; Board Member, Remodelers Council, Greater Houston Builders Association; National Association of Home Builders **To what do you attribute your success:** Mr. Knowlton attributes his success to his clients. He has never advertised, as his business is fully based on referrals. Mr. Knowlton is a talented, trustworthy designer and builder. **Why did you become involved in your profession or industry:** Mr. Knowlton became involved in his profession when he began designing homes in the late 1970s. Before going into business for himself, he worked for a building design firm and eventually became its vice president. Later, he and a partner opened a successful architectural firm, which was successful for seven years. Mr. Knowlton built his own home, which he still lives in today.

Jill L. Koch

Title: Owner **Industry:** Real Estate **Company Name:** JK Property Management **Date of Birth:** 02/22/1980 **Marital Status:** Married **Spouse Name:** Brian Koch **Children:** Three Children **Education:** BA in Business Administration and Early Childhood Education, University of Central Florida (2002) **Certifications:** Real Estate Certification; Property Management Certification **Career:** President, JK Property Management (2014-Present); CV Property Management (2007-2013); Gable Property Management (2005-2007); Florida Executive Realty (2002-2005) **Civic:** Executive Vice President, Best Torah; Fundraiser, The Leukemia & Lymphoma Society **Awards:** Best Management, South Florida Business Journal (2020); Best Full Service Property Management Firm (2019); Largest Homeowners Association (2019); Listee, Women of Distinction (2018); Listee, Best of 2018, Hollywood, FL (2018); Best South Florida Homeowners Association (2018); Largest Homeowners Association Management (2017); Listee, Top 25 Property Management, South Florida Business Journal **Marquis Who's Who Honors:** Marquis Who's Who Top Professional **To what do you attribute your success:** Ms. Koch attributes her success to her husband and her children, as well as a great support staff of friends and colleagues. **Why did you become involved in your profession or industry:** Ms. Koch became involved in her profession because real estate runs in her blood. Her parents owner commercial real estate and she married a real estate agent as well. **Avocations:** Shopping; Spending time with her family **Religion:** Jewish

David G. Korn, PhD

Title: Computer Scientist, Researcher **Industry:** Sciences **Date of Birth:** 08/28/1943 **Place of Birth:** New York **State/Country of Origin:** NY/USA **Parents:** Nathaniel Korn; Florence (Weider) Korn **Marital Status:** Married **Spouse Name:** Susan Lyn Weiner (08/16/1967) **Children:** Phillip; Jeffrey; Adam **Education:** PhD in Mathematics, Courant Institute of Mathematical Sciences, New York University, NY (1969); BS in Mathematics, Rensselaer Polytechnic Institute (1965) **Career:** Research Associate, Google (2014-2018); Research Associate, AT&T Laboratories (1993-2014); Distinguished Member, Technical Staff, AT&T Bell Laboratories, Murray Hills, NJ (1984-1993); Technical Staff, AT&T Bell Laboratories, Murray Hills, NJ (1981-84); Adjunct Professor, Computer Science, New York University (1980-1981); Supervisor, Bell Telephone Laboratories, Holmdel, NJ (1978-1980); Technical Staff, Bell Telephone Laboratories, Holmdel, NJ (1976-1978); Senior Research Scientist, New York University (1971-1976); Research Associate, New York University (1969-1971) **Civic:** Snug Harbor Owners, Inc., New York (1987-1993); Treasurer Pompeii Nursery Center (1976) **Creative Works:** Creator, Korn Shell Language (1988); Co-author, "Supercritical Wing Sections" (1973); Contributor, Articles, Professional Journals **Awards:** National Science Foundation Fellow (1968); AT&T Bell Laboratories Fellow (1986) **Memberships:** Senior, American Institute of Aeronautics and Astronautics; Association for Computing Machinery (ACM, Inc.); IEEE Computer Society; USENIX Association **Marquis Who's Who Honors:** Albert Nelson Marquis Lifetime Achievement Award; Marquis Who's Who Top Professional **Why did you become involved in your profession or industry:** Dr. Korn chose math because it came easily to him. As for computer science, he started reading the Knuth books on software and became very interested in their material. He consequently switched his profession to computer science. As he was already doing a lot of computing for his earlier position, it was a natural and comfortable transition. **Political Affiliations:** Democrat

Russell B. Korner Jr.

Title: Lawyer **Industry:** Law and Legal Services **Date of Birth:** 03/19/1957 **Place of Birth:** Manchester **State/Country of Origin:** CT/USA **Parents:** Edward George; Esther Jeanne (Lawrence) Washco **Education:** Doctor of Jurisprudence, Ohio Northern University, Pettit School of Law (1984); Bachelor of Arts in History, Political Science and Sociology, Waynesburg University (1979) **Career:** Assistant Public Defender, County Of Washington, PA (1998-Present); Sole Practice, Uniontown, PA (1984-Present); First Administrative Assistant District Attorney, Fayette County, Uniontown, PA (1990-1991); First Trial Assistant District Attorney, County Of Fayette Uniontown, PA (1990); Assistant District Attorney, Fayette County, Uniontown, PA (1987-1990); Assistant Trust Officer, Fayette Bank & Trust Company, Uniontown, PA (1985-1986) **Career Related:** Adjunct Instructor, California University of Pennsylvania (1991-Present); Adjunct Instructor, Waynesburg College (1988-Present); Adjunct Instructor, Moorelands County Community College (1988-Present); Constable Training Program Instructor, Pennsylvania Commission on Crime & Decency; Deputy Sheriff Training Program Instructor, Pennsylvania Commission on Crime & Decency; Municipal Police Officer Training Program Instructor; Adjunct Instructor, Pennsylvania State University, Fayette Campus, Uniontown, PA **Memberships:** Pennsylvania Bar Association; Order of Barristers; Phi Alpha Theta; Pi Gamma Mu; Xi Psi Epsilon **Bar Admissions:** United States Court of Appeals for the Fourth Circuit (1989); Supreme Court of the United States (1988); United States Court of Appeals for the Third Circuit (1988); United States District Court for the Southern District of West Virginia (1985); West Virginia (1985); United States District Court for the Western District of Pennsylvania (1984); Pennsylvania (1984) **Marquis Who's Who Honors:** Albert Nelson Marquis Lifetime Achievement Award **Why did you become involved in your profession or industry:** Having always had an interest in history and the law while attending school, Mr. Korner decided to focus on his talent in writing, oratory and law.

Jagannadham Kottha

Title: Chief Executive Officer **Industry:** Technology **Company Name:** CQI J Kottha **State/Country of Origin:** India **Children:** Anjali Kottha **Education:** Master of Business Administration, Baldwin Wallace College, Cleveland, OH (1978); Master of Science in Biomedical Engineering, Case Western Reserve University, Cleveland, OH (1976); Bachelor of Electronics Engineering, Osmania University, Hyderabad, India (1967) **Certifications:** RAB QSA Certified AS 9100 Auditor; Certification, Lead Auditor for ISO-17025 for Testing and Calibration Labs; Certification, CMMI Introduction Course and Registered with SEI; Certification, ATM Registered with SEI; Certification, NIAHO Lead Auditor: Accreditation for Hospitals **Career:** President, Crestbest Quality Institute (2003-Present); Chief Executive Officer, Lead Auditor, GMS Registrar (2003-Present); Owner, Crestbest Quality Institute (1995-Present); President, General Systems Inc., Cleveland, OH (1978-1988); Vice President, Engineering, Environmental Control of Life Systems, Cleveland, OH (1976-1977); R&D Engineer, Electronics Corporation of India Limited (ECIL), Hyderabad, India (1968-1970); Owner, BPX Technologies **Career Related:** Adjunct Professor, Instructor, Quality-Related Courses, Kent State University, Cuyahoga Valley Career Center, University of Findlay, Cuyahoga Community College; Teacher, Various Business and Quality Systems Related Courses Along with Supporting the Continuing Education and Work-Site Training Programs; Member, Technical Committee and the Education Committee; Project Coordinator, ASQC Cleveland Chapter, ISO Focus Group; Course Director, Numerous Educational Workshops, Association for the Advancement of Medical Instrumentation (AAMI) Regional; Program Director, ISO-9000/QS-9000 Consortium, Kent State University, University of Findlay, and Cuyahoga Valley Career Center **Civic:** Chairman, American Society of Engineers of Indian Origin **Awards:** Lifetime Achievement Award, American Society of Engineers of Indian Origin **Memberships:** American Society for Quality; Project Management Institute; CMMI Institute **To what do you attribute your success:** Mr. Kottha attributes his success to good karma, persistence and his habit for not giving up.

John W. "Jack" Lacey III, MD

Title: Chief Medical Officer Emeritus **Company Name:** University of Tennessee Medical Center **Date of Birth:** 10/10/1947 **Place of Birth:** Knoxville **State/Country of Origin:** TN **Parents:** John W. Lacey Jr.; Louise S. Lacey **Marital Status:** Married **Spouse Name:** Slyvia **Children:** John; Jennifer; James T. (BO) **Education:** Residency in Internal Medicine, The University of Tennessee Graduate School of Medicine (1973-1977); MD, University of Tennessee at Memphis (The University of Tennessee Health Science Center), Memphis, TN (1973); BS in Nuclear Engineering, The University of Tennessee Knoxville, TN (1970) **Career:** Board of Directors, Provectus Biopharmaceuticals, Inc. (2018-Present); Chair, Ionogen Science and Medical Board (2020-Present); Medical Director, Knoxville Area Project Access (2005-Present); Board, Home Federal Bank of Tennessee (2003-Present); Board of Directors, Knox County Board of Health (1995-2020); Chief Medical Officer and Senior Vice President, The University of Tennessee Medical Center (1998-2016); Practicing General Internist, The University of Tennessee Medical Center, Knoxville, TN (1977-2016); Inaugural Chair, Governor's Health and Wellness Task Force, TN (2011-2013); Chairman of the Board, Tennessee Health Partnership (1999-2000); Medical Director, Board Member, Tennessee Health Partnership (1995-2000); Medical Director, University of Tennessee Health Plan, Inc. **Career Related:** Assistant Professor, Department of Internal Medicine, College of Medicine (Now The University of Tennessee Graduate School of Medicine), Knoxville, TN (1992-2017); Physician Leader, Co-founder, Knoxville Area Project Access, Knoxville Academy of Medicine, Knoxville, TN **Civic:** Board, Seniors Project Director, Leadership Knoxville (2016-Present); Elder, Grace Presbyterian Church of Knoxville (2015-Present); Board Member, United Way of Greater Knoxville (2015-2019), Campaign Co-Chair (2015-2016); Member, Several Organizations **Creative Works:** Co-author, "Reading, Writing, Arithmetic...and Tennesseans Health," Tennessee Medical Journal Quarter 2 (2018); Speaker, Presenter, Numerous Presentations **Awards:** Award of Excellence and Meritorious Service Award, Tennessee Hospital Association (2015); Tennessee Certificate of Appreciation for Outstanding Service, Governor's Health and Wellness Task Force, TN (2013); Commissioner of Health Award for Outstanding Service to Population Health in Tennessee (2013); TMA Outstanding Physician Award (2011); Recognized by three Tennessee Governors for outstanding contributions and Tennessee House and Senate Resolutions (2010 and 2016); Eagle Scout, Boy Scouts of America; Recipient, Numerous Awards **Memberships:** Board of Directors, National Kidney Foundation Inc., TN (2007-2010); Scarrabbean Senior Society, The University of Tennessee; Tennessee Medical Association; American Medical Association; Sigma Nu; Member, Several Organizations **Marquis Who's Who Honors:** Marquis Who's Who Humanitarian (2019) **Religion:** Christian

Louise Lamphere, PhD

Title: Anthropologist **Date of Birth:** 10/04/1940 **Place of Birth:** St. Louis **State/Country of Origin:** MO/USA **Parents:** Harold Lamphere; Miriam (Bretschneider) Lamphere **Marital Status:** Life Partner **Spouse Name:** Peter B. Evans **Children:** Peter Bret (1980) **Education:** LHD, Brown University (2015); PhD, Harvard University (1968); MA, Harvard University (1966); BA, Stanford University (1962) **Career:** Distinguished Professor Emeritus of Anthropology, The University of New Mexico (2009-Present); Distinguished Professor, The University of New Mexico (2001-2008); Regent's Professor, The University of New Mexico (1999-2002); Visiting Scholar, Russell Sage Foundation (2001-2002); Full Professor, The University of New Mexico (1986-1999); Professor, Brown University (1985-1986); Associate Professor, Brown University (1979-1985); Associate Professor, The University of New Mexico (1976-1979); Assistant Professor, Brown (1968-1975); Fellow, Radcliffe Institute for Advanced Study, Harvard University (1971-1972); Academic Visitor, LSE (1971-1972); Visiting Assistant Professor, Department of Anthropology, University of Rochester (1967-1968); Visiting Professor, University of California, Berkeley **Creative Works:** Co-Author, "Weaving Women's Lives: Three Generations in a Navajo Family" (2007); Co-Editor, "Situated Lives: Gender and Culture in Everyday Life" (1997); Co-Editor, "Newcomers in the Workplace: Immigrants and the Restructuring of the U.S. Economy (Labor and Social Change)" (1994); Co-Author, "Sunbelt Working Mothers: Reconciling Family and Factory (The Anthropology of Contemporary Issues)" (1993); Editor, Edition One, "Structuring Diversity: Ethnographic Perspectives on the New Immigration" (1992); Author, "From Working Daughters to Working Mothers: Immigrant Women in a New England Industrial Community" (1987); Author, "To Run After Them: Cultural and Social Bases of Cooperation in a Navajo Community" (1977); Co-Editor, "Woman, Culture, and Society" (1974) **Awards:** Bronislaw Malinowski Award for Exemplary Professional Achievement, Society for Applied Anthropology (2017); Franz Boas Award for Exemplary Service to Anthropology, American Anthropological Association (2013); The Squeaky Wheel Award, Committee on the Status of Women in Anthropology, American Anthropological Association (1998); SANA Prize for Critical Study of North America (1995); Conrad Arensberg Award, Society for the Anthropology of Work (1994) **Memberships:** President, American Anthropological Association (1999-2001); Chair, Association for Feminist Anthropology (1995-1997); President, American Ethnological Association (1987-1989)

Barbara Lang

Title: Chief Executive Officer **Industry:** Religious **Company Name:** West Street Baptist Church **Education:** BA in Sociology and Psychology, Jarvis Christian College (1972) **Career:** Chief Executive Officer, West Street Baptist Church (1978-Present); Senior Residential Administrative, Clausen House **Civic:** Volunteer, Special Olympics **Awards:** Lifetime Achievement Award, Alameda Contra Costa **To what do you attribute your success:** She attributes her success to her love for people. **Avocations:** Spending time with her family; Going to church **Thoughts on Life:** Ms. Lang has assisted individuals with mental disabilities. She was the residential administrator at Clausen House for 44 years. She supervised staff and clients in a residential community setting, and helped with developmentally disabled adults.

Joseph Laquatra Jr., PhD

Title: Professor Emeritus **Industry:** Education/Educational Services **Company Name:** Cornell University **Date of Birth:** 04/28/1952 **Place of Birth:** Pittsburgh **State/Country of Origin:** PA/USA **Parents:** Joseph Laquatra Sr.; Carmela Zito **Marital Status:** Married **Spouse Name:** Gregory Lee Potter (08/03/2011) **Education:** PhD in Consumer Economics and Housing, Cornell University (1984); MS in Consumer Economics and Housing, Cornell University (1982); BS in Hotel Administration, Cornell University (1974) **Career:** Professor Emeritus, Department of Design and Environmental Analysis, Cornell University (2017-Present); Professor, Home Builders Institute (2009-2017); Professor, Department of Design and Environmental Analysis, Cornell University (2008-2017); Hazel E. Reed Human Ecology Professor of Family Policy, Cornell University (2004-2008); Professor, Extension Housing Specialist, Department of Design and Environmental Analysis, Cornell University (2003-2004); Associate Professor, Cornell University (1992-2003); Director for Advanced Education, Home Builders Institute, Washington, DC (1996-1997); Scholar-in-Residence, American-Polish Home Builders Institute, Gdansk, Poland (1994); Associate Professor, Extension Housing Specialist, Department of Design and Environmental Analysis, Cornell University (1992); Assistant Professor, Extension Housing Specialist, Department of Design and Environmental Analysis, Cornell University (1986-1992); Extension Associate, Cornell University (1984-1986); Visiting Staff Member, Los Alamos National Laboratory, NM (1981); Housing Director, Project Reach, Wayland, NY (1977-1979); General Contractor, Self-Employed, Wayland, NY (1976-1977) **Civic:** Chair, Several Government Advisory Groups and Academic Organizations **Creative Works:** Contributor, Articles, Refereed Journals; Contributor, Book Chapters, Books; Speaker, National and International Conferences **Awards:** Several Awards, Professional Organizations and Government Agencies **Why did you become involved in your profession or industry:** Dr. Laquatra became involved in his profession to focus on sustainable aspects of housing. **Avocations:** Swimming; Cooking; Hiking; Woodworking; Building things **Political Affiliations:** Democrat

Robert James Lavigne, PhD

Title: Entomologist, Educator, Researcher **Date of Birth:** 05/30/1930 **Place of Birth:** Herkimer **State/Country of Origin:** NY/USA **Parents:** Robert James Lavigne; Dorothea Eckerson Lavigne **Marital Status:** Married **Spouse Name:** Judith Jane (Deceased) **Children:** Jay Wayne; Michelle Renee; Todd Jeffrey; Cathleen Jeanette; Flavia Beatriz Ascani **Education:** Doctor of Philosophy in Entomology, University of Massachusetts (1961); Master of Science in Entomology, University of Massachusetts (1958); Bachelor of Arts in Biology, American International College, Springfield, MA (1952); Coursework, Animal Behavior Institute **Career:** Professor Emeritus, University of Wyoming, Laramie, WY (1994-Present); Professor, University of Wyoming (1971-1994); Associate Professor, University of Wyoming (1965-1971); Assistant Professor, University of Wyoming, Laramie, WY (1959-1965); Instructor, University of Massachusetts at Amherst (1956-1959) **Career Related:** Honorary Research Associate, South Australian Museum (2004-Present); Chief of Party, Wyoming Team, Baidoa, Somalia (1985-1988); Environmental Advisory Committee, Basin Electric Power Corp. (1973-1976); Consultant, Thorne Ecological Institute (1973-1975) **Civic:** Founding Member, Rotary, Blakiston, South Australia **Military Service:** U.S. Army (1953-1955) **Creative Works:** Co-Author, "Ants of Yellowstone National Park" (2004); Co-Author, "Rangeland Entomology" (1989); Editor, "Crop Care in Wyoming" (1962-1969); Contributor, 120 Plus Papers in Professional Journals; Webmaster of Internet Site, 'Australian Asilidae' **Awards:** Award for initiating "Road Watch" in South Australia (2005); Grantee, National Science Foundation; Grantee, United States Department of Agriculture; Grantee, Wyoming Weed & Pest District; Grantee, U.S. Bureau of Reclamation; Grantee, Pacific Power & Light Co.; Distinguished Service Award, University of Wyoming **Memberships:** Co-Editor, Journal of Economic Entomology (1982-1985); Editorial Board, Pan-Pacific Entomological Society of America; Editorial Board, Pan American Acridological Society; Editorial Board, Kansas Entomological Society; Editorial Board, Animal Behavioral Society; Range Management Society; Australian Entomological Society; Alpha Chi; Phi Kappa Phi **To what do you attribute your success:** Dr. Lavigne attributes his success to hard work. **Why did you become involved in your profession or industry:** Dr. Lavigne became involved in his profession due to the influence of Dr. C.P. Alexander, a famous crane fly specialist. **Avocations:** Philately; Gardening **Political Affiliations:** Independent

Sean Lazarus, DPM

Title: Podiatrist **Company Name:** West Haven Foot and Ankle Center **Marital Status:** Married **Children:** One Child **Education:** Fellowship in Pediatric Orthopedics and Biomechanics, New York College of Podiatric Medicine Orthopedic Fellowship (1994-1995); Doctor of Podiatric Medicine, New York College of Podiatric Medicine, New York, NY, Cum Laude (1993); National Diploma in Podiatry, University of Witwatersrand, Johannesburg, South Africa (1988) **Certifications:** Diplomate, American Board of Podiatric Surgery (Now American Board of Foot and Ankle Surgery (ABFAS)) (2000) **Career:** Podiatrist, West Haven Foot and Ankle Center, CT (2015-Present); Attending, Podiatric Surgery, Hospital of St. Raphael (1996-Present); Doctor of Podiatric Medicine, Surgery, Advanced Foot Care, P.C. (1995-2015) **Awards:** Listee, Leading Physicians in the World (2018); Named to National Dean's List (1991-1993); Inductee, Pi Delta **Memberships:** Connecticut Podiatric Medical Association (CPMA); American Podiatric Medical Association; American College of Foot and Ankle Surgeons; Alumni Association; New York State Podiatric Medical Association (NYSPMA) **To what do you attribute your success:** Dr. Lazarus attributes his success to working with the right people and being open-minded in the medical profession. He says, "When you look at the field of medicine, you must look at it from all angles, and align yourself with different types of doctors who practice alternative medicines." **Why did you become involved in your profession or industry:** Dr. Lazarus discovered more about neuropathy when he began speaking to fellow doctors; he found out about the new technologies available, and he began speaking to doctors from an integrated practice, who guided him into realizing what he should be doing. This was all in research for his podiatry practice. These doctors did not believe in putting their patients on different medications with countless side effects. They felt proposed diet changes and vitamin boosts would help more substantially. He began to realize the things that they were saying were true and he applied it to his practice. That is when he began to see the biggest results in his practice. **Thoughts on Life:** Dr. Lazarus says, "I just try to improve the quality of life for people through pain reduction/elimination... to me that is priceless...You have to work hard in life, as I have... There are always good and bad things in life, but you have to find the good in the bad and apply it, and improve the quality of your life..."

Eduardo Leite

Title: Chairman Emeritus, Senior Partner **Industry:** Law and Legal Services **Company Name:** Baker McKenzie **Date of Birth:** 08/07/1950 **Place of Birth:** Montevideo **State/Country of Origin:** Urugay **Parents:** Eduardo C. Leite; Amanda E. (Mendez) Leite **Marital Status:** Married **Spouse Name:** Yolanda Amaral C. (02/26/1977) **Children:** Juliana; Natalia **Education:** LLM, New York University (1980); JD, University of Sao Paulo (1978); BA, Institute Osimani y Llerena, Salto, Uruguay (1970) **Career:** Chairman Emeritus, Baker & Mckenzie (2017- Present);Executive Committee, Baker & Mckenzie (1999-2003); Partner, Baker & Mckenzie (1988-Present); Chairman, Executive Committee, Baker & Mckenzie (2010-2016); Managing Partner, Baker & Mckenzie, Brazil (2003-2010); Partner, Stroeter, Trench E Veirano, Sao Paulo, Brazil (1986-1988); Associate, Stroeter, Trench E Veirano, Sao Paulo, Brazil (1981-1986); Associate, Baker & Mckenzie (1980-1981); Associate, Stroeter, Trench E Veirano, Sao Paulo, Brazil (1975-1979); Law Clerk, Dr. Benedito A.P. D'Olival, Sao Paulo, Brazil (1974-1975); Law Clerk, Dr. Maria C. Cebrian, Sao Paulo, Brazil (1973-1974) **Career Related:** Chairman, Latin American Regional Council (1999-2003); Executive Vice President, China-Brazil Business Council **Civic:** Secretary, President, Fellowship Community Church, Sao Paulo, Brazil (1982-1988); Rocky Mountain Mineral Law Foundation; Grupo de Lideres Empresariais **Awards:** Medal Carlos Gomes Lodge, Carlos Gomes 1598 (1988); Medal Jose Bonifacio Society Bras. de Heraldica **Memberships:** International Business Committee, Coral Gables Chamber of Commerce (1988-1989); French Chamber of Commerce (1987-1988); Legal Committee, American Chamber of Commerce (1982-1988); Brazilian Bar Association **To what do you attribute your success:** Mr. Leite attributes his success to discipline, understanding his next step, and objective patience. **Why did you become involved in your profession or industry:** Mr. Leite was introduced to legal work by working for a retired judge while he was in high school. From that experience, he found that he liked the law. He had always been interested in history, politics, and philosophy, all of which are prominent in legal work. Likewise, he loves to help others, which only further inspired him to pursue a career in the field. **Avocations:** Studying languages; Listening to music; Learning **Religion:** Presbyterian

Martha Lepow, MD

Title: Professor Emeritus of Pediatrics, Director of Division of Pediatric Infectious Disease **Industry:** Medicine & Health Care **Company Name:** Albany Medical College **Date of Birth:** 03/28/1927 **Parents:** Harry A. Lipson; Anna (Miller) Lipson **Marital Status:** Widowed **Spouse Name:** Irwin H. Lepow (02/07/1958, Deceased 1984) **Children:** Lauren; David; Daniel **Education:** Honorary DSc, Oberlin College and Conservatory, Ohio (2009); Fellow, Case Western Reserve University, Cleveland, Ohio (1958-1967); Intern, Resident in Pediatrics, Case Western Reserve University (1952-1956); MD, Case Western Reserve University (1952); BA, Oberlin College and Conservatory, Ohio (1948) **Career:** Attending Physician, Albany Medical Center Hospital, Albany, NY (1979-Present); Professor of Pediatrics, Albany Medical College, Albany, NY (1978-Present); Director, Pediatric HIV Program, Albany Medical Center Hospital, Albany, NY (2006-2012); Head, Division of Pediatric Infectious Diseases, Albany Medical Center Hospital, Albany, NY (1979-2012); Chairman, Pediatrics, Albany Medical College, Albany, NY (1994-1997); Vice Chairman, Pediatrics, Albany Medical College, Albany, NY (1981-1994); Director, Clinical Studies Center, Albany Medical College, Albany, NY (1979-1987) **Career Related:** Board of Directors, Albany College of Pharmacy and Health Sciences (1987-1989); Consultant, Pediatrics Infectious Disease, St. Peter's Hospital (1978-1982); Member, Study Section, Epidemiology and Disease Control, National Institutes of Health (1972-1976); Special Fellow, U.S. Public Health Service, Oxford, England, United Kingdom (1961-1962) **Civic:** Board of Directors, WYHCR Foundation (2005-2006); Board of Directors, Whitney M. Young Health Center, Albany, NY (1985-2004); Member, Advisory Committee, National Institute of Allergy and Infectious Diseases, National Institutes of Health (1978-1982) **Creative Works:** Member, Editorial Board, Pediatrics (1976-1981); Associate Editor, Reports, American Academy of Pediatrics **Awards:** Best Doctor Award (2014); Named One of the Best Doctors in New York (2013); Lifelong Award, American Academy of Pediatrics (2012) **Marquis Who's Who Honors:** Marquis Who's Who Top Professional

Leonard Levine

Title: Attorney at Law **Industry:** Law and Legal Services **Company Name:** Leonard S. Levine, Attorney at Law **Marital Status:** Married **Spouse Name:** Pamela Levine **Education:** AB, LLD, Harvard Law School, Cum Laude (1959); BA, Economics, Harvard College, Magna Cum Laude (1956); Intern, Office of the U.S. Attorney General; Law Clerk, U.S. Court of Appeals **Career:** Real Estate Attorney, Leonard S. Levine, Attorney at Law (1959-Present); Law Associate, Rosenman Colin Kaye Petschek & Freund (1961-1964); Law Clerk, U.S. Court of Appeals, Judge Calvert McGuder and Judge William Orr **Creative Works:** Director, Northern Westchester Center for the Arts **Awards:** Martindale-Hubbell Client Silver Service Champion Award (2019, 2020) **Bar Admissions:** New York (1960) **To what do you attribute your success:** Mr. Levine attributes his success to his expertise, service and a lot of experience. **Why did you become involved in your profession or industry:** Mr. Levine was with a large law firm who assigned him to real estate department. He enjoyed it and did very well with it, and was highly regarded at the firm for it. **Avocations:** Watching sports

Thomas R. LeViness

Title: President **Industry:** Law and Legal Services **Company Name:** Pell & LeViness P.C. **Date of Birth:** 07/30/1940 **Place of Birth:** Floral Park **State/Country of Origin:** NY/USA **Parents:** John F. LeViness; Juliette Q. LeViness; **Marital Status:** Married **Spouse Name:** Grace LeVineess (1991) **Children:** Thomas, Jr.; Christine Miller; Suzanne Meador; Kathryn Murray; Alissa Hinkson; Mary Kate LeViness **Education:** LLB, St. Johns University (1964) **Career:** President, Pell & LeViness, PC (1967-Present); Attorney, Estate Department, J.P. Morgan (1965-1966) **Career Related:** Counsel, Trustee, Earl C. Sams Foundation; Volunteer Attorney, Families of 911 Victims **Civic:** Deans Council, Stony Brook Medical School (1990-2000); Trustee, Champlain College (1970-1990) **Awards:** Martindale-Hubbell AV Rated (1970-Present); Named, Super Lawyers (2009) **Memberships:** Faculty, New York State Bankers Association Estate Planning School and Estate and Trust Administration Schools (1980-Present); American Bar Association; New York State Bar Association; New York City Bar Association; Board Member, Stony Brook Medical School; Board of Directors, Champagne College; Lecturer, Marino Bar Review Course, New York State Bar Association; Faculty Member, Tax and Retirement Lecturer, CBS, Chemical Bank, ASCAP, Airline Pilots Association, Long Island Estate Planning Council, Connecticut Banking Association **Bar Admissions:** New York State **To what do you attribute your success:** Mr. LeViness attributes his success to his hard work, concentration and honesty. **Why did you become involved in your profession or industry:** Raised in a family of attorneys, he recognized law as a profession that provided the opportunity to help and assist people in need and those treated unfairly. **Religion:** Roman Catholic, Jesuit trained

David Carleton Lewis, MD

Title: Professor Emeritus, Donald G. Millar Distinguished Professor of Alcohol and Addiction Studies **Industry:** Medicine & Health Care **Company Name:** Brown University **Date of Birth:** 05/19/1935 **Place of Birth:** Hartford **State/Country of Origin:** CT/USA **Parents:** Theodore Lewis; Lillian (Levin) Lewis **Marital Status:** Widowed **Spouse Name:** Eleanor Grace Levinson (08/23/1959, Deceased) **Children:** Deborah; Steven **Education:** Chief Medical Resident, Beth Israel Hospital (Now Beth Israel Deaconess Medical Center) (1966-1967); Junior Resident, Beth Israel Deaconess Medical Center (1962-1963); Intern, Beth Israel Deaconess Medical Center (1961-1962); MD, Harvard University (1961); AB, Brown University, Magna Cum Laude (1957) **Career:** Professor Emeritus, Brown University (2012-Present); Donald G. Millar Professor of Alcohol and Addiction Studies, Brown University (1987-2012); Professor, Brown University (1982-2012); Director, Center for Alcohol and Addiction Studies, Brown University (1982-2000); Chairman, Department of Community Health, Brown University (1981-1986); Director, Program in Alcoholism and Drug Abuse, Brown University (1976-1982); Director, Division of Alcohol and Substance Abuse, Roger Williams General Hospital (1976-1982); Medical Director, Washingtonian Center for Addictions (1972-1977); Sloan Foundation Fellow, Harvard Medical School (1971-1972); Fellow, The University of Texas Southwestern Medical Center (1964-1966); Senior Resident, Parkland Memorial Hospital, Dallas, Texas (1964-1966); Senior Resident, University Hospitals Cleveland (1963-1964); Director, Emergency Unit and Medical Outpatient Department, Beth Israel Deaconess Medical Center (1969-1971) **Career Related:** Board of Directors, Drug Policy Alliance (2000-Present); Board of Directors, NCADD (1995-Present); Chair, NCADD (2004-2008); Chair, Physicians and Lawyers for National Drug Policy (1997-2004); National Advisory Committee, Robert Wood Johnson Foundation Fighting Back Program (1996-2002); Director, WHO Collaborating Center at Brown University (1995-2000); Member, Numerous Committees, Organizations **Civic:** Board of Directors, Physicians and Lawyers for National Drug Policy (2004-Present); Project Director, Physician Leadership on National Drug Policy (1997-2004); Chairman, Mayor's Council on Drug Abuse, Boston, MA (1972-1980); Medical Director, Beacon Hill Free Clinic (1968-1971) **Creative Works:** Editor, Contributor, Numerous Articles to Professional Journals **Awards:** Recipient, Several Grants, Awards **Memberships:** Board of Directors, AMERSA (1985-Present); Secretary, American Society of Addiction Medicine (2003-2005); Member, Numerous Organizations **Marquis Who's Who Honors:** Albert Nelson Marquis Lifetime Achievement Award; Marquis Who's Who Top Professional **Avocations:** Photography

David Arthur Lienhart

Title: Forensic Engineering Geologist **Industry:** Engineering **Company Name:** DAL Engineering Geologic & Petrographic Services **Date of Birth:** 09/28/1939 **Place of Birth:** Cincinnati **State/Country of Origin:** OH/USA **Parents:** Arthur C.; Grace H. (Burger) Lienhart **Marital Status:** Married **Spouse Name:** Donna (Klosterman) Lienhart **Children:** Devin S. Lienhart; Dana Ann (Lienhart) Boehmer **Education:** Coursework in Advanced Rock Mechanics Engineering, Massachusetts Institute of Technology (1978); Coursework in Nuclear Radiology, U.S. Army Chemical School, Fort McClellan, AL (1969); Master of Science, University of Cincinnati (1964); Bachelor of Arts, University of Cincinnati (1961) **Certifications:** Certified Professional Geologist, Indiana; Research Geologist, Delaware; Licensed Professional Geologist, North Carolina **Career:** Hydrologist, U.S. Army Corps Engineers (1990-1995); Geologist, Laboratory Director, Ohio River Division Laboratories (1976-1990); Geologist, Ohio River Division Laboratories, Cincinnati, OH (1970-1976); Petrographer, Ohio River Division Laboratories, Cincinnati, OH (1964-1970) **Career Related:** Consultant, Dal Engineering Geologic & Petrographic Services (2000-2015); Consultant, Construction Rock Properties and Evaluation of Rock for Erosion Control (1995); Partner, Rock Products Consultants; Guest Speaker, University of Warwick; International Reviewer, British CIRIA Publication, "Handbook on Rock for Construction" **Civic:** Advisor, Department of Geology, University of Cincinnati, Ohio **Creative Works:** Contributor, Numerous Articles to Professional Journals; Author, Editor, Technical Publications; Designer, Rock Mechanics Direct Shear Device for Rock Sold to an Engineering Firm, Lexington, KY **Awards:** Publication of the Year Award (2013); Special Publication Award, ASTM International (1995); Recipient, Outstanding Public Service Award, City of Cincinnati (1994); Department of the Army Fellow, University of Cincinnati (1986-1987) **Memberships:** Fellow, Geological Society of America; Fellow, Geological Society of London; American Society of Civil Engineers; ASTM International; Association of Environmental & Engineering Geologists; International Society of Engineering Geologists **To what do you attribute your success:** Mr. Lienhart credits his success on his grandfather, Wilbur E. Burger, who was a lifetime student of the arts and sciences. Likewise, he was inspired by Paul E. Potter, who had a doctorate in sedimentary geology. **Why did you become involved in your profession or industry:** Mr. Lienhart initially became involved in his profession due to his childhood interest in rocks, fossils and minerals.

Kathyrn Loper

Title: Director of Special Events & International Tours **Industry:** Leisure, Travel & Tourism **Company Name:** Kathy Loper Events **Date of Birth:** 06/02/1942 **Place of Birth:** Clinton **State/Country of Origin:** IA/USA **Parents:** Richard Dennes; Vivian Dennes **Marital Status:** Widowed **Children:** Kathy; Nancy (Deceased) **Education:** MEd, Eastern Washington State College (1968); BS in Physical Education, Adrian College (1964) **Career:** Owner, Director, Special Events & International Tours, Kathy Loper Events (1980-Present) **Civic:** Water for Children Africa; Fundraiser, Volunteer, Rady Children's Hospital; Volunteer, Stand Down; Fundraiser, End of Summer Run, Local High Schools **Awards:** Presidential Award, Fundraising, USA Track & Field **Memberships:** San Diego Business Bureau (Serving Pacific Southwest) **Marquis Who's Who Honors:** Marquis Who's Who Top Professional **To what do you attribute your success:** Ms. Loper attributes her success to her ability to be flexible; she is always willing to give and learn. **Why did you become involved in your profession or industry:** Ms. Loper became involved in her profession because she grew up in a small town in Illinois with parents who were both involved in giving back to the community. Her father told her once, "you will get more out of giving than you ever will out of receiving." This lesson stuck with her throughout her life, and she takes it with her anywhere she goes. She actively tries to give back whatever kindness has been bestowed on her. **Religion:** Protestant **Thoughts on Life:** Ms. Loper said, "My father also stressed to me that one received so much more in giving than in receiving."

Mi Lu, PhD

Title: Professor; Computer Engineer **Industry:** Education/Educational Services **Company Name:** Texas A&M University **Date of Birth:** 07/22/1949 **Place of Birth:** Chongqing **State/Country of Origin:** China **Parents:** Chong Pu Lu; Shu Sheng Fan **Marital Status:** Married **Children:** Luke Yin **Education:** PhD, Rice University (1987); MS, Rice University (1984) **Certifications:** Registered Professional Engineer **Career:** Professor, Texas A&M University (1998-Present); Associate Professor, Texas A&M University (1993-1998); Assistant Professor, Texas A&M University (1987-1993) **Career Related:** General Chair, International Conference on Control Engineering and Mechanical Design (2017); Co-chair, Third Annual International Conference on Computer Science and Mechanical Automation (2017); Keynote Speaker, Third Annual International Conference on Management, Economic and Social Development (2017); Conference Chair, Fifth, Sixth and Seventh International Conference of Computer Science and Informatics (2000, 2002, 2003) **Creative Works:** Honorable Editor, Robotics & Automation Journal (2017); Guest Editor, Journal of Computer Science and Engineering, Scientific & Academic Publishing (2015); Associate Editor, Information Science (1996-1997, 2002-2003); Associate Editor, Journal of Computing and Information (1995-1997); Book Author, "Arithmetic and Logic in Computer Systems"; Contributor, Articles, Professional Journals **Memberships:** Senior Member, IEEE Computer Society **To what do you attribute your success:** Dr. Lu attributes her success to hard work and perseverance. **Why did you become involved in your profession or industry:** Dr. Lu became involved in her profession as she came from an engineering family. Her father devoted his whole life to hydroelectric power projects benefiting mankind by converting nature and its resources. Her mother designed all kinds of buildings still standing there today to serve the generations in the community. Dr. Lu chose her career since she wanted to contribute and to be a useful person to society. **Avocations:** Playing piano; Traveling; Poetry

Oscar Lua

Title: Partner; Former Professional Football Player **Industry:** Architecture & Construction **Company Name:** Statewide Services **Children:** Three Daughters **Education:** Bachelor of Arts and Sciences (BASc) in Urban Planning and Development, University of Southern California (2006) **Career:** Co-founder/Business Partner, Statewide Service (2015-Present); Property Manager, Weststar Management (2008-2016); President, Shadow Rock Properties, LLC (2008-2016) **Career Related:** Professional Football Player, Linebacker, New England Patriots (2007-2008) **Civic:** Vice President, Trojan Club of the Desert, University of Southern California Athletics (2008-2010) **Awards:** Named One of the Top 40 Under 40 Business Men in California **To what do you attribute your success:** Mr. Lua attributes his success to his mentors and his upbringing. His father was a business owner. **Thoughts on Life:** Mr. Lua's motto is, "Do what you say you're going to do and always be honest."

John Stanley Mackiewicz, PhD

Title: Distinguished Teaching Professor Emeritus **Industry:** Education/Educational Services **Company Name:** State University of New York at Albany **Parents:** William Witold Vincent; Antonina Mackiewicz **Marital Status:** Widowed **Spouse Name:** Shirley Williams Miller, PhD (08/27/1957, Deceased 11/28/2008) **Children:** Janina Ann Harfmann **Education:** Postdoctoral Fellow, National Institutes of Health, Institute of Zoology, Neuchâtel, Switzerland (1960-1961); Doctor of Philosophy in Biology, Cornell University, Ithaca, NY (1960); Master of Science, Cornell University (1954); Bachelor of Science, Cornell University (1953) **Career:** Distinguished Teaching Professor Emeritus, State University of New York, Albany (2017-Present); Part-time Distinguished Teaching Professor, State University of New York, Albany (2002-2017); Full-time Distinguished Teaching Professor, State University of New York, Albany (1961-2002); Instructor, Cornell University (1957-1959) **Creative Works:** Contributor, 90 Articles, Scientific Publications; Author, Only Review on Non-segmented Tapeworms **Memberships:** American Association for the Advancement of Science; American Society of Parasitologists; Life Member, Helminthological Society of Washington **Marquis Who's Who Honors:** Albert Nelson Marquis Lifetime Achievement Award; Marquis Who's Who Top Professional **Avocations:** Fly fishing **Religion:** Christian

John Macleod

Title: Lawyer (Retired) **Industry:** Law and Legal Services **Date of Birth:** 06/05/1942 **Place of Birth:** Manila **State/Country of Origin:** Philippines **Parents:** Anthony Macaulay Macleod; Dorothy Lillian (Amend) Macleod **Marital Status:** Married **Spouse Name:** Ann Klee **Children:** Kerry; Jack **Education:** JD, University of Notre Dame (1969); BBA, University of Notre Dame (1963) **Career:** Retired (2015); Partner, Crowell & Moring LLP, Washington, DC (1979-2015) Partner, Jones, Day, Reavis & Pogue, Washington, DC (1974-1979); Associate, Jones, Day, Reavis & Pogue, Washington, DC (1969-1973) **Career Related:** Chairman Emeritus (2006-Present); Chairman (1984-1985, 1993-1994, 2000-2006); Member, Management Committee (1979-1982, 1983-1986, 1991-1994, 1999-2000, 2000-2006) **Military Service:** First Lieutenant, U.S. Army (1963-1965) **Creative Works:** Author, "Justice Hill" (2020); Author, "Snippets" (2018); Author, "A Lawyer or a Priest" (2016); Editor-in-chief, Notre Dame Law Review (1968-1969); Contributor, Articles, Professional Journals **Awards:** Crowell & Moring Leadership Award (2010); Distinguished Mining Lawyer Award, National Mining Association (1995); Forest Industry Victory of the Year Award, American Forest and Paper Association (1994) **Memberships:** American Bar Association; The District of Columbia BarAspetuck Valley Country Club; Member, Various Directorships and Trusteeships **Bar Admissions:** Supreme Court of the United States (1980); The District of Columbia Bar (1969) **Marquis Who's Who Honors:** Albert Nelson Marquis Lifetime Achievement Award **To what do you attribute your success:** Mr. Macleod attributes his success to hard work, luck, optimism, integrity, and surrounding himself with influential individuals in his field. **Why did you become involved in your profession or industry:** Mr. Macleod became involved in law because he enjoyed reading, writing, and communicating, which are prominent skills for a lawyer. He believes in idealism and fairness. **Avocations:** Viewing contemporary art; Drinking wine; Reading; Writing; Playing with dogs **Thoughts on Life:** Mr. Macleod believes integrity, balance, and optimism are indispensable ingredients of a happy life.

Rachel Anne Maddow

Title: Television and Radio Personality; Political Commentator **Company Name:** MSNBC **Date of Birth:** 04/1/1973 **Place of Birth:** Castro Valley **State/Country of Origin:** CA/USA **Parents:** Robert B. Maddow; Elaine (Gosse) Maddow **Marital Status:** Life Partner **Spouse Name:** Susan Mikula **Education:** Honorary LLD, Smith College, Northampton, MA (2010); DPhil in Political Science, Lincoln College, University of Oxford, England, United Kingdom (2001); BA in Public Policy, Stanford University, CA (1994) **Career:** Host, "The Rachel Maddow Show," MSNBC, NBC Universal (2008-Present); Political Analyst, MSNBC (2008-Present); Host, "The Rachel Maddow Show," Air America Radio, New York, NY (2005-2010); Co-host with Chuck D. and Liz Winstead, "Unfiltered," Air America Radio, New York, NY; Host, "Big Breakfast," WRSI, Saga Communications, Inc., Northhampton, MA (2002-2004); Co-host, "Dave in the Morning Show," Station WRNX-100.9 FM (1999-2002) **Career Related:** Panelist, "Race for the White House with David Gregory" (2008-2009); Panelist, "Tucker," MSNBC (2005-2008); Regular Contributor, Former Guest Host, "Countdown with Keith Olbermann" **Creative Works:** Author, "Blowout: Corrupted Democracy, Rogue State Russia, and the Richest, Most Destructive Industry on Earth" (2019); Host, Podcast, "Bag Man" (2018); Writer, Monthly Opinion Column, Washington Post (2013); Voice Actor, "The Simpsons" (2013); Author, "Drift: The Unmooring of American Military Power" (2012); Voice Actor, "Batwoman"; Appearance, Television Shows **Awards:** Emmy Awards for Outstanding News Discussion and Analysis, Academy of Television Arts & Sciences (2011, 2017); Emmy Award for Outstanding Live Interview, Academy of Television Arts & Sciences (2017); Named Outstanding Host, Gracie Allen Award (2012); John Steinbeck Award, Martha Heasley Cox Center for Steinbeck Studies, San Jose State University (2012); Walter Cronkite Faith & Freedom Award, Interfaith Alliance (2010); Maggie Award, Planned Parenthood Federation America Inc. (2010); GLAAD Media Award, GLAAD (2010); Named One of the 100 Most Powerful Women, Forbes Magazine (2010); Named One of the 50 Highest-Earning Political Figures, Newsweek (2010); Named One of the 100 Agents of Change, Rolling Stone Magazine (2009); Proclamation of Honor, California State Senate (2009); Gracie Award, Alliance for Women in Media and Foundation (2009); Named One of the 40 Under 40, The Advocate (2009); Named One of the 40 Under 40, Crain's New York Business (2009); Named Lesbian/Bi Woman of the Year, AfterEllen.com's Visibility Awards (2008); Named One of the Top 100 Gay Men & Women Who Moved Culture, Out Magazine (2008); Grantee, Rhodes Scholar (1995)

Mary Hoyle Mahan, EdD

Title: Physical Educator, Athletics Administrator (Retired) **Industry:** Education/Educational Services **Company Name:** Miami Dade College **Date of Birth:** 07/19/1939 **Place of Birth:** Boston **State/Country of Origin:** MA/USA **Parents:** Frederick John; Mary Dwyer Hoyle **Marital Status:** Widow **Spouse Name:** J. Roger Mahan (Deceased) **Education:** Doctor of Education, Nova Southeastern University; Master of Science, University of North Carolina; Bachelor of Science, Bridgewater State University **Certifications:** ARC First Aid & CPR Instructor; Paramedic 1; ARC Water Safety Instructor & Trainer **Career:** Professor Emeritus, Associate Athletics Director, Chair, Department of Physical Education, Miami Dade College; Professor of Physical Education, Coach, Central Connecticut State University; Teacher, Coach, Locust Valley High School, New York; Teacher, Coach, Stoughton Junior High School, Massachusetts **Career Related:** President, Chief Executive Officer, The Teaching Well **Civic:** President, Woodlands Women's Golf Association; Education Foundation, Villanova University; Bridgewater State University Foundation **Awards:** Inductee, Florida College System Activities Association Hall of Fame; Inductee, National Association of Collegiate Directors of Athletics Hall of Fame; Inductee, Bridgewater State University Athletics Hall of Fame; Inductee, Miami Sports Society Hall of Fame; Dr. Catherine Comeau Outstanding Bridgewater State University Alumni Award; American Alliance for Health, Physical Education, Recreation and Dance, Honor Award; Delta Psi Kappa Alumna of Year Award; DSK Lifetime of Giving Award; Cheshire Academy Bowden Award; Miami Dade College Endowed Teaching Chair; Case Professor of the Year Award, University of Texas; Three Miami Dade College Outstanding Faculty Awards **Memberships:** National Alliance of Two Year College Athletic Administrators; Delta Psi Kappa; Women's Sports Society; Women Leaders in College Sports **Marquis Who's Who Honors:** Albert Nelson Marquis Lifetime Achievement Award **To what do you attribute your success:** Ms. Mahan attributes her success to the love and support of her family and mentors. **Why did you become involved in your profession or industry:** Ms. Mahan became involved in her profession due to the influence of her junior high school teacher, who encouraged her to enter the field of physical education. **Avocations:** Golf; Interior design; Travel **Political Affiliations:** Independent **Religion:** Roman Catholic

Justin Marchetta

Title: Partner **Industry:** Law and Legal Services **Company Name:** Inglesino, Webster, Wyciskala & Taylor LLC **Place of Birth:** , **Marital Status:** Married **Children:** Three Children **Education:** Doctor of Jurisprudence, Seton Hall University School of Law, Cum Laude (2009); Bachelor of Arts in U.S. History, Rutgers College (2004) **Certifications:** Licensed Amateur Radio Operator **Career:** Partner, Aviation Attorney, Inglesino, Webster, Wyciskala & Taylor LLC (2017-Present); Associate, Aviation Attorney, Inglesino, Webster, Wyciskala & Taylor LLC (2010-2016); Associate, Stern & Kilcullen (2009-2010); Law Clerk, Stern & Kilcullen (2006-2009); Judicial Intern, Honorable Madeline Cox Arleo, United States District Court, District of New Jersey (2008); Dispatcher, Franklin Township Police Department (2002-2006) **Civic:** Founding Member, Aviation Law Section, New Jersey State Bar Association (2016-Present); Board Member, Mid-Atlantic Aviation Coalition (2016-Present); Member, Lawyer, Pilots Bar Association (2012-Present); Panel Attorney, Aircraft Owners and Pilots Association Legal Services Plan; Volunteer Counsel, American Radio Relay League **Creative Works:** Author, "Safety Sales and the Owner Managed Crew," LinkedIn (2017); Author, "Aviation Finance, The Crew Dilemma and More," LinkedIn (2016); Author, "The Aviation Fiance Twilight Zone," LinkedIn (2016); Guest on Attorney Talk, Casual Conversations About the Law, Episode 16 "Aviation Law," with Justin Marchetta (2016); Co-author, "Municipal Computers Under Attack," New Jersey Municipalities (2013) **Awards:** New Jersey Rising Stars List for Aviation Law, Thomson Reuters' Super Lawyers (2014–2019) **Memberships:** New Jersey Bar Association; American Bar Association; Aircraft Owners and Pilots Association; National Business Aviation Association; International Aviation and Transportation Safety Bar Association; Lawyer Pilots Bar Association; American Radio Relay League **Bar Admissions:** Supreme Court of the United States (2014); District of Columbia (2011); U.S. Court of Appeals for the Third Circuit (2010); U.S. District Court for the Eastern District of New York (2010); U.S. District Court for the Southern District of New York (2010); New York (2010); U.S. District Court for the District of New Jersey (2009); New Jersey (2009) **To what do you attribute your success:** Mr. Marchetta attributes his success to hard work. **Why did you become involved in your profession or industry:** Mr. Marchetta became involved in his profession after serving as a dispatcher for public safety services. He applied to law school, and, having already gained experience as an amateur pilot, decided to specialize in aviation law.

Howard Leslie Marren

Title: Composer **Industry:** Other **Date of Birth:** 05/02/1946 **Place of Birth:** Brooklyn **State/Country of Origin:** NY/USA **Parents:** Dr. Murray Marren; Sylvia (Levin) Marren **Marital Status:** Married **Spouse Name:** Robert Myers **Education:** MA, Tufts University (1969); BA, Tufts University (1967) **Career:** Composer **Creative Works:** Composer, "Valentino" (2019); Composer, "Night Without a Moon" (2018); Composer, "Snapshots" (1996); Composer, "Paramour" (1996); Composer, "Open House" (1995); Composer, "Beyond the Sea" (1993); Composer, "Sesame Street" (1993); Composer, "Making Memories" (1991); Composer, "Fauntleroy" (1990); Composer, "Georgia Avenue" (1985); Composer, "Captain Kangaroo" (1975-1985); Composer, "Love" (1983); Composer, "Portrait of Jennie (1982); Composer, "Games" (1974) **Awards:** Nominee, Emmy Award, "Sesame Street" (1996-1997); New Music Theatre Award (1988); Best Musical of the Year Award (1987); Outer Critics Circle Award for Best Off-Broadway Score, "Love" (1983-1984); Richard Rodgers Production Award, "Portrait of Jennie" (1982) **Memberships:** Dramatists Guild **Marquis Who's Who Honors:** Albert Nelson Marquis Lifetime Achievement Award; Marquis Who's Who Top Professional **To what do you attribute your success:** Mr. Marren attributes his success to having shows Off-Broadway and all over the world, as well as wonderful collaborators and mentors, and a lot of luck. **Why did you become involved in your profession or industry:** Mr. Marren became involved in his career because of his early experiences as a singer and actor. He was asked to write a couple of songs for the musical, "Games," for which he eventually wrote the entire score. Shortly after, he was accepted into BMI Lehman Engel Musical Theatre Workshop. He hasn't looked back since. **Avocations:** Collecting enamel boxes; Cooking; Traveling; Reading; Attending theatre and movies

Dan Merrill Martin, PhD

Title: Foundation Executive (Retired) **Industry:** Other **Date of Birth:** 12/27/1939 **Place of Birth:** Waterloo **State/Country of Origin:** IA/USA **Parents:** Cecil Parr Martin; Violet (Strother) Martin **Marital Status:** Divorced **Spouse Name:** Susan Paxton Parker (1970, Divorced 1992) **Education:** PhD in Political Theory, Princeton University, NJ (1968); MA in Political Theory, Princeton University, NJ (1963); BA in Political Science, Knox College, Galesburg, IL (1961) **Career:** Consultant, Climate Reality Project, Washington, DC (2014-2015); Senior Associate, Arabella Philanthropic Advisers, Washington, DC (2009-2011); Senior Managing Director, Critical Ecosystem Partnership Fund, Washington, DC (2004-2007); Chief Research Officer, Gordon & Betty Moore Foundation, San Francisco, CA (2001-2004); Program Director, John D. & Catherine T. MacArthur Foundation, Chicago, IL (1986-2001); President, Jessie Smith Noyes Foundation, New York, NY (1984-1986); President, Cranbrook Educational Community, Bloomfield Hills, MI (1980-1984); Assistant Professor, Social Science, Rush Medical School, Chicago, IL (1973-1980); President, Associate Colleges of the Midwest, Chicago, IL (1972-1980); Assistant to Chancellor, Assistant Professor of Political Science, Vanderbilt University, Nashville, TN (1969-1972); Executive Assistant, John and Mary R. Markle Foundation, New York, NY (1966-1969) **Career Related:** President, Consultative Group on Biological Diversity **Civic:** Trustee, Knox College (1987-Present); Full-time Volunteer, Barack Obama Presidential Campaign (2007-2008, 2012); Vice Chairman, Illinois Board of Regents (1975-1980); National Commission, Financing of Postsecondary Education, Washington DC (1972-1973) **Military Service:** Captain, U.S. Army (1964-1966) **Memberships:** Cosmos Club, Washington, DC; University Club of Chicago **Marquis Who's Who Honors:** Albert Nelson Marquis Lifetime Achievement Award **Avocations:** Traveling; Collecting maps **Political Affiliations:** Republican **Religion:** Episcopalian

Bonita Martinez

Title: Attorney-at-Law **Industry:** Law and Legal Services **Company Name:** Law Offices of Bonita P. Martinez **Marital Status:** Married **Spouse Name:** Gody Martinez **Children:** Two Children **Education:** JD, Western State University College of Law; BS in Business Administration, University of the Redlands; Coursework, Sacred Heart Hospital School of Cytology; Coursework, University of the East, The Philippines **Career:** Attorney at Law, Law Offices of Bonita P. Martinez (1991-Present); Cytotechnologist, Scripps Clinic (1981-1991) **To what do you attribute your success:** It is apparent to Ms. Martinez that knowledge and truth are helpful to humans. She feels the need to contribute to humanity. Ms. Martinez has a good rapport in her field, even with her adversaries in court. She attributes all of her success to God.

Why did you become involved in your profession or industry: Ms. Martinez thought that becoming a scientist would be a fulfilling job and put her in a position to affect change on a large scale. The focus of her goals as a cytologist was to alleviate disease and prolong life. While doing the work, she saw many other things that she could contribute to as well. However, she quickly felt that she had maximized her skills in the cytology field. She saw a lot of errors in the fields of medicine, therapy, and pharmacology, which bothered her enough to make a change. She now specializes in medical malpractice. Likewise, Ms. Martinez was drawn to litigation because she likes the "drama of life," as she calls it; she also likes working with people, which is prevalent in her work as a lawyer.

Anthony William "Tony" Marx

Title: President and Chief Executive Officer; Former Academic Administrator **Industry:** Library Management/Library Services **Company Name:** The New York Public Library **Date of Birth:** 02/28/1959 **Place of Birth:** New York **State/Country of Origin:** NY/USA **Parents:** Peter Marx; Marion (Mankin) Marx **Children:** Josh; Anna-Claire **Education:** Honorary Degree, Amherst College (2012); PhD, Princeton University (1990); MA, Princeton University (1987); MPA, Princeton University (1986); BA, Yale University, Magna Cum Laude, New Haven, CT (1981); Coursework, Wesleyan University, Middletown, CT **Career:** President, Chief Executive Officer, The New York Public Library, New York, NY (2011-Present); President, Amherst College (2003-2011); Professor of Political Science, Columbia University, New York, NY (1990-2003); Visiting Scholar, Community Agency for Social Enquiry, Johannesburg, South Africa (1988, 1990); Consultant, South African Committee of Higher Education Trust, Johannesburg, South Africa (1984, 1986); Research Assistant, Center for Educational Research & Development, Santiago, Chile (1985); Administrative Aide to President, University of Pennsylvania, Philadelphia, PA (1981-1984) **Career Related:** Visiting Scholar, Center of Afro-Asian Studies, Rio de Janeiro, Brazil (1993); Consultant, United Nations Development Programme (UNDP), New York, NY (1991) **Civic:** Director, Early College HS Initiative, Woodrow Wilson National Fellowship Foundation, Princeton, NJ (2002-2003); Trustee, Treasurer, Fund for Education in South Africa, New York, NY (1991-1994) **Creative Works:** Author, "Faith in Nation: Exclusionary Origins of Nationalism" (2003); Author, "Making Race and Nation: A Comparison of the United States, South Africa and Brazil" (1998); Author, "Lessons of Struggle: South African Internal Opposition" (1960-1990, 1992); Contributor, Articles, Professional Journals **Awards:** Barrington Moore Prize, American Sociological Association (2000); Ralph J. Bunche Award, American Political Science Association (1999); Fellow, National Humanities Center (1997-1998); Fellow, John Simon Guggenheim Memorial Foundation (1997); Fellow, Harry Frank Guggenheim Foundation (1994); Fellow, United States Institute of Peace (1992-1993); Fellow, John D. & Catherine T. MacArthur Foundation (1989-1990)

Richard A. Maxwell

Title: Retail Executive **Industry:** Retail/Sales **Company Name:** Associated Dry Goods Inc. **Date of Birth:** 04/01/1933 **Place of Birth:** New York **State/Country of Origin:** NY/USA **Parents:** Arthur William Maxwell; Mary Ellen (Winestock) Maxwell **Marital Status:** Widowed **Spouse Name:** Jacqueline Ann Creamer (10/27/1962, Deceased 11/2018) **Education:** Coursework, Academy of Advanced Traffic (Now William Loveland College) (1959); Coursework, New York University (1958-1959) **Career:** Chief Operating Officer, Fire Block International (2010-2011); Chief Logistics Officer, Zeroignition Technologies (2009-2014); President, Home Farms Technologies Inc. (2002-2009); Chief Financial Officer, IGW Trust (1995-2001); Executive Vice President, Matol World Corporation (1989-1994); Independent Consultant (1986-1989); Executive Vice President of Marketing, Associated Dry Goods Corporation (1981-1986) **Career Related:** Member, Industry Sector Advisory Committee, United States Department of Commerce; Member, Shippers Advisory Committee, National Maritime Council; Consultant **Military Service:** Armament Specialist, United States Air Force (1952-1956) **Awards:** Honoree, Commander in Order of Merit in Recognition of Improvement of Trade Between Italy and United States, Republic of Italy (1985); Silver Medal for Contributions to Trade Expansion, People's Republic of China (1980) **Memberships:** President, Italy-America Chamber of Commerce (1981-1983); President, American Association of Exporters and Importers (1979-1981); President, Shippers Conference of Greater New York (1965-1966) **Marquis Who's Who Honors:** Albert Nelson Marquis Lifetime Achievement Award **Why did you become involved in your profession or industry:** Mr. Maxwell didn't choose his career path but he fell into it as a mail messenger boy at a company that consulted for department stores. He worked for them for a few years and then went into the service for four and a half years. When he came out, he went back with them and they put him into the import department. One of the competitors, a $5 billion dollar company that owns Lord & Taylor of New York, heard about Mr. Maxwell through the exporter and importers association and he began to work for them. **Avocations:** Former Shooting; Hunting

Michel Gustave Edouard Mayor, PhD

Title: Professor Emeritus; Astrophysicist **Company Name:** University of Geneva **Date of Birth:** 01/12/1942 **Place of Birth:** Lausanne **State/Country of Origin:** Switzerland **Education:** Honorary Degree, Joseph Fourier University (Now Grenoble Alpes University), Grenoble, France (2014); Honorary Degree, University of Provence (Now Aix-Marseille University), Marseille, France (2011); Honorary Degree, Free University of Brussels, Belgium (2009); Honorary Degree, Paris Observatory, France (2008); Honorary Degree, Uppsala University, Sweden (2007); Honorary Degree, Federal University of Rio Grande do Norte, Brazil (2006); Honorary Degree, Swiss Federal Institute of Technology of Lausanne, Switzerland (2002); Honorary Degree, Catholic University of Leuven, Belgium (2001); PhD, University of Geneva, Switzerland (1971); MS in Physics, University of Lausanne, Switzerland (1966) **Career:** Professor Emeritus, University of Geneva (2007-Present); Director, Observatory of Geneva (1998-2004); Professor of Astronomy, University of Geneva (1988-2007); Associate Professor, University of Geneva (1984-1988); Research Associate, University of Geneva (1971-1984) **Career Related:** Swiss Delegate, ESO Council (2003-2007); With, University of Hawai'i (1994-1995); Member, Science and Technical Committee, European Southern Observatory (ESO) (1990-1993); Swiss Delegate, Astronomical Working Group, European Space Agency (1985-1987); With, Cambridge Observatory (1971); Astronomer, Science Contributor, Chile; With, Haute-Provence Observatory, Centre National de la Recherche Scientifique (CNRS), France **Creative Works:** Editorial Board, Europhysics News (1985-1990); Co-author, "Les Nouveaux Mondes du Cosmos"; Publisher, Organizer, Nine Saas-Fee Advanced Courses, Swiss Society of Astrophysics and Astronomy **Awards:** Co-recipient, Nobel Prize in Physics (2019); Wolf Prize in Physics, Wolf Foundation (2017); Gold Medal, Royal Astronomical Society (2015); Frontiers of Knowledge Award of Basic Sciences, BBVA Foundation (2011); Viktor Ambartsumian International Science Prize (2010); Co-recipient, Shaw Prize in Astronomy, The Shaw Prize Foundation, Hong Kong (2005); Recipient, Numerous Awards **Memberships:** Fellow, Royal Astronomical Society (2015); Foreign Associate, American Association for the Advancement of Science (2010); European Academy of Sciences (2004); Committee Member, Swiss Society for Astrophysics and Astronomy, Zürich, Switzerland (1990-1993); National Academy of Sciences; French Academy of Sciences; Various Commissions, International Astronomical Union; Honorary Member, American Astronomical Society

Joanne McBride, ABR, GRI

Title: Realtor **Industry:** Real Estate **Company Name:** Berkshire Hathaway HomeServices Fox & Roach, Realtors **Marital Status:** Widowed **Spouse Name:** Don McBride (Deceased 2018) **Children:** Five children **Education:** BA, Chestnut Hill College (1963) **Career:** Realtor, Berkshire Hathaway HomeServices Fox & Roach, Realtors (2010-Present) **Civic:** Board of Directors, Chestnut Hill College; Volunteer, Speak Up; Volunteer, Fox & Roach Charities **Awards:** Chairman Circle Award, Berkshire Hathaway HomeServices Fox & Roach, Realtors (2019); Top Real Estate Producer, Philadelphia Magazine (2019); Top Agent, Main Line Today (2017); 100 Award, Pension Real Estate Association **To what do you attribute your success:** Ms. McBride attributes her success to hard work. **Why did you become involved in your profession or industry:** Ms. McBride became involved in her profession because a friend, Tony Hayden, suggested she pursue a career in real estate. Upon completion of her training, she received a job with Weigert Realtors and confided in her friend. However, he did not seem pleased. Just days later, a representative of his from Fox & Roach, called her back and offered her a job with their company.

Robert McCarthy

Title: Physics Professor, Researcher **Industry:** Education/Educational Services **Date of Birth:** 01/14/1943 **State/Country of Origin:** IL/USA **Children:** Michael; Daniel **Education:** Doctor of Philosophy, University of California Berkeley (1971); Bachelor of Arts in Physics, Harvard University, Summa Cum Laude (1965); Russell Shaw Traveling Fellowship **Career:** Director, Undergraduate Studies in Physics, Stony Brook University (2014-Present); Professor of Physics, Stony Brook University (1986-Present); Director, Undergraduate Studies in Physics, Stony Brook University (1989-1996); Associate Professor, Stony Brook University (1978-1986); Assistant Professor of Physics, Stony Brook University (1972-1978); Enrico Fermi Fellow, University of Chicago (1971-1972) **Career Related:** Chairman, Users Executive Committee, Fermi National Accelerator Laboratory, Batavia, IL (1984-1985); Contributor, Fermi National Accelerator Laboratory, Batavia, IL (1971-1989) **Creative Works:** Author, Numerous Articles, Scientific and Academic Journals **Awards:** Numerous Grants, National Science Foundation (1972-2015) **Memberships:** American Association for the Advancement of Science; American Association of Physics Teachers; Fellow, American Physical Society **Marquis Who's Who Honors:** Who's Who in American Education; Who's Who in Science and Engineering

William James McCoy, PE

Title: Electrical Engineer; Consultant **Industry:** Consulting **Date of Birth:** 09/29/1951 **State/Country of Origin:** WV/USA **Education:** MBA, LeTourneau University (1998); MSEE, West Virginia University (1977); BSEE, West Virginia University Institute of Technology, Cum Laude (1974); ASEE in Computer Option, West Virginia University Institute of Technology (1971); Diploma, Iaeger High School, with Honors (1969) **Certifications:** Licensed Professional Engineer by Examination, States of West Virginia and Texas; Chief Electrician, Commonwealth of Virginia **Career:** Independent Consultant (2007-Present); With, Verizon Wireless (2000-2007); With, Verizon Communications (1999-2000); With, GTE Financial (1977-1999); Research Assistant, West Virginia University, Morgantown, WV (1976-1977); Electrical Engineer, Pittston Coal Company, Lebanon, VA (1974-1976) **Career Related:** Invited Speaker, Two Verizon Wireless Leadership Conferences; Presenter, Several Engineering Conferences; Guest Lecturer, Several Universities and Trade Schools **Creative Works:** Author, Master's Thesis, "Cable Splices and Some of Their Effects on the Safety Ground System"; Co-contributor, Articles to Professional Journals; Author, Co-author, Published Papers **Awards:** Listee, Lexington Who's Who of Executives and Professionals, Millennium Edition (1999-2000); Listee, Marquis Who's Who in the World, 16th Edition (1999); Listee, Marquis Who's Who in America for Science and Engineering, Fourth Edition (1998-1999); Listee, Who's Who Among Students in American Universities and Colleges (1973-1974); Two GTE President's Team Gold Awards **Memberships:** IEEE-Eta Kappa Nu (1974); The Tau Beta Pi Association, Inc. (1972); Alpha Chi Honor Society (1972); National Society of Professional Engineers; Life Senior Member, IEEE; National Fire Protection Association (NFPA); Senior Professional Member, International Association of Electrical Inspectors (IAEI); Underwriters Laboratories Standards Technical Panel 497; Texas Society of Professional Engineers; Pi Kappa Phi Fraternity **Marquis Who's Who Honors:** Albert Nelson Marquis Lifetime Achievement Award **Religion:** Christian

Linda Marie McGuffie

Title: Chief Operating Officer **Industry:** Manufacturing **Company Name:** King Paper Limited **Place of Birth:** Hartford **State/Country of Origin:** CT/USA **Education:** MS, Science and Management, Purdue University, Krannert School of Management, 2000; BA,Business Administration, Georgia College, 1988; AA, Business Administration, Community College of the Air Force, 1985 **Career:** Chief Operating Officer, King Paper Limited (2004-Present); Vice President, Paccess (1991-2003); Manager, Perry H. Koplik And Sons (1991-1994) **Civic:** Donor, Care Kits for Battered Women and Children; Shoes That Fit **Military Service:** Non-Commissioned Officer-in-Charge, U.S. Air Force (1980-1988) **Memberships:** TAPPI **To what do you attribute your success:** Ms. McGuffie attributes her success to her willingness to listen to her customers. **Why did you become involved in your profession or industry:** Ms. McGuffie became involved in her profession because she sought out a job after leaving the U.S. Air Force. She fell in love with the profession and never looked back. **Religion:** Catholic

John McGuire

Title: Partner **Industry:** Law and Legal Services **Company Name:** Thorsnes Bartolotta McGuire LLP **Date of Birth:** 08/29/1945 **Place of Birth:** New York **State/Country of Origin:** NY/USA **Parents:** John F. McGuire Sr.; Gertrude (Quast) McGuire **Marital Status:** Married **Spouse Name:** Lynne Marie Randazzo (06/09/1968) **Children:** Kerry L.; John F. III; Patrice M.; Brian W. **Education:** JD, Marquette University, Cum Laude (1975); MS, Southern Illinois University (1973); BS, U.S. Naval Academy (1968) **Career:** Partner, Thorsnes, Bartolotta, McGuire & Padilla, San Diego, CA (1978-Present); Associate, McInnis, Fitzgerald, Rees, Sharkey & McIntyre, San Diego, CA (1976-1978) **Career Related:** Board of Directors, Bank, Rancho Bernardo, San Diego, CA **Military Service:** Captain, U.S. Navy, Vietnam **Awards:** 2019 America's Top 100 Personal Injury Attorneys (2019); 2018 The Best Lawyers in America (2018); 2015 Best Lawyers in America (2015); 2013 Best Lawyers in America (2013); Daily Transcript's San Diego Top Attorney Award (2005-2012); 2010 Daily Transcript's San Diego Top Attorney Award (2010); 2010 Daniel T. Broderick Award for Civility, Integrity and Professionalism (2010); Trial Lawyer of the Year, San Diego Trial Lawyers Association (1983, 1988, 1991); 1989 Outstanding Trial Lawyer (1989); Outstanding Trial Lawyer, San Diego Trial Lawyers Association (1982); Thomas Moore Scholar, Marquette Board of Governors (1975); Decorated Purple Heart; 22nd Recipient of the Daniel T. Broderick Award for Civility, Integrity and Professionalism; Super Lawyer **Memberships:** California Bar Association; San Diego County Bar Association; Association of Trial Lawyers of America; California Trial Lawyers Association; San Diego Trial Lawyers Association; Order of Barristers; President, San Diego Chapter, American Board of Trial Advocates **Bar Admissions:** California (1976); Wisconsin (1976) **Avocations:** All water sports; Biking; Hiking; Amateur and professional theater; Playing golf; Being a grandad; Surfing **Political Affiliations:** Democrat **Religion:** Roman Catholic

Megan McGuire, Esq.

Title: 1) Attorney 2) Associate Attorney **Industry:** Law and Legal Services **Company Name:** 1) McGuire Law Firm 2) Juvenile Defense Panel **Parents:** Aaron McGuire; Meri McGuire **Marital Status:** Married **Spouse Name:** Bryan Noyes **Children:** Jack; Kaity; Ally; Connor **Education:** JD, Dale E. Fowler School of Law, Chapman University (2002); BS in Political Science and Psychology, California State University, Fullerton **Career:** Attorney, McGuire Law Firm (2008-Present); Associate Attorney, Juvenile Defense Panel (2007-Present) **Civic:** Youth Accountability Team **Awards:** Dean's Award, Chapman University **To what do you attribute your success:** Ms. McGuire attributes her success to her wonderful, strong, supportive family. **Why did you become involved in your profession or industry:** Ms. McGuire became involved in her profession because of her lifelong interest in law. She went to law school with the intention of becoming a prosecutor, but eventually began working with the Juvenile Defense Panel, which sparked her desire to work with children and make a difference. **Thoughts on Life:** Ms. McGuire would like for people to know that she loves what she does and loves working with and helping people. Everyone, no matter the crime, deserves someone to help and support them. She believes that even in our darkest hours, people deserve help and support.

Alfred Don McInturff

Title: Physicist **Industry:** Sciences **Date of Birth:** 02/24/1937 **Place of Birth:** Clinton **State/Country of Origin:** OK/USA **Parents:** Eunice Marie Barton; Herman Alfred McInturff **Marital Status:** Widowed **Spouse Name:** Sandra Lynne Jernigan McInturff **Children:** Jennifer Lynne; Micheal Eric; Timothy Aaron **Education:** Postdoctoral Research Fellow, Vanderbilt University, Nashville, TN (1964-1966); PhD in High Energy Physics, Vanderbilt University (1964);MS, Vanderbilt University (1960); BS, Oklahoma State University (1959) **Career:** Professor, Physics, Graduate School, Texas A&M University (2004-2017); Physicist, Superconducting Magnet Development Group, Lawrence Berkeley Lab (1994-2014); Task Leader, CERN LHC String Team (1996-1997); Senior Scientist, Superconducting Super Collider Laboratories, Waxahachie, TX (1992-1994);Physicist III, Fermi National Accelerator Laboratory, Batavia, IL (1980-1992);Physicist, Brookhaven National Laboratory, Upton, NY (1966-1980); Senior Research Engineer, North America Aviation, Canoga Park, CA (1966-1967); Graduate Research Associate, Postdoctoral Research Associate, Synchrotron Laboratory, California Institute of Technology (1960-1966) **Career Related:** Visiting Professor, Physics Department, Texas A&M University (2001-2005); Science Attaché, CERN, the European Organization for Nuclear Research, Geneva, Switzerland (1988-1989); Visiting Scientist, Rutherford Laboratory, Chilton Didcot, Oxfordshire, England (1973-1974) **Creative Works:** Contributor, More Than 100 Articles, Professional Journals; Author, Chapters, 225 Books; Co-Author, Book Chapter, "100 Years Anniversary Book of the Discovery of Super Conductivity" **Awards:** IEEE Council on Superconductivity (2004); Special Fellowship, Atomic Energy Commission (1961-1964); ORINS Scholar (1959-1960); Award for Continuing and Significant Contributions in the Field of Applied Superconductivity **Memberships:** Senior Member, IEEE **Marquis Who's Who Honors:** Albert Nelson Marquis Lifetime Achievement Award **Why did you become involved in your profession or industry:** Mr. McInturff became involved in his profession because he started out as a coach and was a football player and wrestler in college but got injured. He wanted to become a high school football and wrestling coach and he wanted to go to a big high school, which required a big reputation. He could do it with academics, which he was good at, and came from a very good high school. He took physics and math in college because he figured a major high school would hire him as a math and science teacher and he would become an assistant coach and he would get it all in one shot. However, his knee injury prevented him from doing any coaching. Therefore, he pursued math and science.

Michael McManus

Title: Vice Chairman **Industry:** Financial Services **Company Name:** United States Olympic Trust **Parents:** Michael McManus; Mary F. (Glynn) McManus **Education:** JD, Georgetown University Law Center (1967); BA in Economics, University of Notre Dame, (1964) **Career:** Retired (2000); President, Chief Executive Officer, Misonix, Farmingdale, NY (1998-2000); President, Chief Executive Officer, Home Federal Savings Bank (Subsidiary of New York Community Bancorp, Inc.) (1995-1998); President, Chief Executive Officer and Member, Board of Directors, New York Community Bancorp, Inc. (1991-1998); Vice President, Strategic Planning, Vice President, Business Planning and Development, Consumer-Pfizer, Inc. (1986-1991); Executive Vice President, Pantry Pride, Inc., Fort Lauderdale, FL (1985-1986); Assistant to President Regan, White House, Washington, DC (1982-1985); Corporate Counsel, Pfizer, Inc., New York, NY (1977-1982); Special Assistant to Secretary, U.S. Department of Commerce, Washington, DC (1975-1977); Associate, Cadwalader, Wickersham & Taft LLP, New York, NY (1970-1975); President, Chief Executive Officer, Jamcor Pharmaceuticals Inc.; Various Positions, Revlon, Inc. **Career Related:** Board Member, The Eastern Company (2015-Present); Board Member, Novavax Inc. (2005-Present); Vice Chairman, Board, United States Olympic Trust (2003-Present); Advisory Board Member, Barington Capital Group, L.P. (2000-2017); Board Member, Communications Satellite Corporation (COMSAT); Board of Directors, A. Schulman, Inc. (Now LyondellBasell Industries Holdings B.V.) **Military Service:** Sergeant, Infantry, United States Army (1968-1970) **Awards:** Named Super CEO, Long Island (2016); Named One of the Leading CEOs of a Micro Cap Company (2015); Ellis Island Medal of Honor, 1998 **Why did you become involved in your profession or industry:** Mr. McManus started out as a lawyer and went into government; he started managing public companies. Now he's on boards and charitable organizations.

Mae Frances McMillan, MD

Title: Child Psychiatrist **Date of Birth:** 05/12/1936 **Place of Birth:** Austin **State/Country of Origin:** TX/USA **Parents:** Ben Sanders McMillan Sr. (1904-1999); Annie Mae (Walker) McMillan (1905-2000) **Education:** MD, Meharry Medical College, Nashville, TN, with Honors (1959); BS, Wiley College, Marshall, Texas, with Honors (1955) **Certifications:** Medical Diplomate (1959) **Career:** Private Practice, Child Psychiatry, Houston, Texas (1985-1994); Unit Director, Latency Service, DePelchin Children's Center, Houston, Texas (1985-1990); Director, Child Therapy and Clinic for Early Childhood Disorders, Texas Research Institute of Medical Sciences (1980-1985); Associate Professor, Baylor College of Medicine, Houston, Texas (1975-2018); Assistant Director, Division of Child Psychiatry, Texas Research Institute of Medical Sciences, Houston, Texas (1968-1975); Resident Child Psychoanalysis, Hampstead Clinic, London, England (1967); Assistant Professor, Department of Psychiatry, Baylor College of Medicine, Houston, Texas (1965-1975); Resident, General and Child Psychiatry, Baylor College Medicine, Houston, Texas (1963-1965); Associate Professor, Menninger Clinic, Department of Psychiatry, Baylor College of Medicine, Houston, Texas **Career Related:** With, Harris County Mental Health, Mental Retardation Association (Now The Harris Center for Mental Health and IDD), Houston, Texas (2000-Present); Consultant, Teen-Parent Services, Institute of Child and Family Psychiatry, Houston, Texas (1990-Present); Board Member, Consultant, Harris County Mental Health, Mental Retardation Association (Now The Harris Center for Mental Health and IDD), Houston, Texas (1988-Present) **Civic:** Vice Chair, Board of Higher Education, Restorative Justice Ministry (2008-Present); Board Member, Treasurer, Texas Community Corporation, Houston, Texas (1995-Present); Certified Lay Speaker, Texas Conference United Methodist Church, Houston, Texas (1990-Present) **Creative Works:** Author, Editor, "Child Psychiatry: Treatment and Research" (1970); Contributor, Articles to Professional Journals **Awards:** Best Supervisor Award (2007); Excellence Award, Texas Society of Psychiatric Physicians (2004); Named Outstanding Woman, YWCA (Young Women's Christian Association), Houston, Texas (1978) **Memberships:** Distinguished Fellow, Mentor, Life Member, American Psychiatric Association (2009-Present); Chair, Children's Committee, Houston Psychiatric Society (1990-1994); Chair, Life Member, Thelma Patten Law Lectureship, National Council of Negro Women (1977) **Marquis Who's Who Honors:** Albert Nelson Marquis Lifetime Achievement Award **Avocations:** Travel; Fine Arts; Physical Fitness; Volunteerism **Political Affiliations:** Democrat **Religion:** United Methodist Church

Irvine G. "Irv" McQuarrie, MD, PhD

Title: Associate Professor; Neurosurgeon; Financier **Company Name:** Case Western Reserve University **Date of Birth:** 06/27/1939 **Place of Birth:** Ogden **State/Country of Origin:** UT/USA **Parents:** Irwin Bruce McQuarrie; Ruby Loretta (Epperson) McQuarrie **Marital Status:** Divorced **Spouse Name:** Maryann Kaminski (08/14/1980, Divorced); Katharine Gamble Rogers (03/11/1967, Divorced) **Children:** Michael Gray; Mollie; Morgan Elizabeth; Gray Luke **Education:** MBA, Case Western Reserve University (2007); PhD, Cornell University (1977); Research Fellow, Department of Physiology, Cornell University Medical College, New York, NY (1974-1976); Intern, Assistant Surgeon, Surgeon, New York Hospital, New York, NY (1972-1973); Research Fellow, Department of Physiology, Cornell University Medical College, New York, NY (1971-1972); Assistant Surgeon, Surgeon, New York Hospital, New York, NY (1974-1981); Intern, Assistant Surgeon, New York Hospital, New York, NY (1965-1973); MD, Cornell University (1965); BS in Biology, The University of Utah (1961) **Certifications:** Diplomate, American Board of Neurological Surgery **Career:** Associate Professor of Neuroscience, Case Western Reserve University, Cleveland, OH (1988-Present); Associate Professor of Neuroscience, Case Western Reserve University, Cleveland, OH (1985-2002); Associate Professor of Neurosurgery, Case Western Reserve University, Cleveland, OH (1985-2002); Assistant Professor of Neurosurgery, Case Western Reserve University, Cleveland, OH (1981-1987); Assistant Professor of Developmental Genetics and Anatomy, Case Western Reserve University, Cleveland, OH (1981-1985); Visiting Assistant Professor of Anatomy, Department of Anatomy, Case Western Reserve University, Cleveland, OH (1979-1981); Assistant Professor of Physiology, Cornell University Medical College, New York, NY (1976-1981); Chief of Neurosurgery, Boston Naval Hospital (1973-1974) **Career Related:** Staff Neurologist, Veterans Affairs Medical Center, Cleveland, Ohio (2002-2011); Chief of Neurosurgery, Veterans Affairs Medical Center, Cleveland, Ohio (1999-2002); Elizabeth Crosby Lecturer, University of Michigan (1989); Chairman, Veterans Affairs Office Regeneration Research Programs (1988-1989) **Military Service:** Retired, U.S. Navy Reserve (2005); Commander, Medical Corps, U. S. Navy Reserve **Creative Works:** Contributor, Medical Research Articles to Professional Journals. **Awards:** Decorated, Legion of Merit, United States Marine Corps (2005); Grantee, Spinal Cord Society (1986-1988); Grantee, National Institutes of Health (1982-1989); Grantee, Veterans Affairs Individual Research (1981-2002) **Marquis Who's Who Honors:** Albert Nelson Marquis Lifetime Achievement Award; Marquis Who's Who Top Professional

Jessica Ulrika Meir

Title: Astronaut **Industry:** Sciences **Company Name:** NASA **Date of Birth:** 07/01/1977 **Place of Birth:** Caribou **State/Country of Origin:** ME/USA **Education:** PhD in Marine Biology, Scripps Institution of Oceanography (2009); Postdoctoral Research, The University of British Columbia **Career:** Experiment Support Scientist, Human Research Facility, Johnson Space Center, NASA, Houston, TX (2000-2003) **Career Related:** Astronaut Candidate, Astronaut Group 21, NASA (2009-2015); Assistant Professor of Anesthesia, Massachusetts General Hospital, Harvard Medical School (2012); Fellow, Achievement Rewards for College Scientists Foundation, Inc. (2006); Aquanaut, NASA Extreme Environment Mission Operations (2002) **Awards:** Scholar Award, P.E.O. Sisterhood (2008); Special Recognition Award, Lockheed Martin Space, Lockheed Martin Corporation (2002); Special Professional Achievement Award, Space and Life Sciences Directorate, Johnson Space Center, NASA (2002); Lightning Award, Lockheed Martin Corporation (2002) **Avocations:** Reading classical literature; Playing flute, piccolo and saxophone; Cycling; Hiking; Running; Skiing; Playing soccer; Scuba diving; Flying

Regina G. Mellinger

Title: President, Chief Executive Officer **Industry:** Staffing and Recruiting **Company Name:** Primary Services, LP **Children:** Heather; Collin; John **Education:** BFA, Kutztown University of Pennsylvania, Kutztown, PA (1978) **Certifications:** GLOBALG.A.P. Certification; Leadership Courses, Garcia Ladera Consulting Ltd; Maslin Scale **Career:** President, Chief Executive Officer, Primary Services LP, Houston, TX (1988-Present); Art Direction, NY (1986-1988) **Civic:** Board Member, Women's Business Enterprise Alliance; Change Happens! **Awards:** Top 25, 2017 Women Who Mean Business, Houston Business Journal, American City Business Journals; Top 30 Influential Women of Houston, Top 30 Women; Top 10 in Houston, Women on the Move, Texas Executive Women; National Star Award, Women's Business Enterprise National Council **To what do you attribute your success:** Ms. Mellinger attributes her success to her family and values. For all that she has been given, she would love to give the same back to others. **Why did you become involved in your profession or industry:** Ms. Mellinger became involved in her profession because she studied fine arts, and for the first two years, she worked in the art direction industry. She decided she wanted to be in business for herself as she wanted to be responsible for both making decisions and making an impact. She drew inspiration from her father, an expert in sales, marketing, and leadership. His happiness, which stemmed from a career he loved, motivated her. Galvanized, she moved to Houston and applied for sales jobs. However, her fine arts degree proved to be an obstacle and she was often advised to pursue recruiting instead. She soon accepted a recruiting position that included a sales training program. She stayed in the position and enjoyed the work for eight years, but recruiting was still a developing field; the company she worked for began to suffer, and she chose to finally pursue my entrepreneurial dream in 1998. Primary has thrived since its inception and has been in business for 32 years. **Thoughts on Life:** Ms. Mellinger lives by the saying, "it's a wonderful life."

Frank Harrison Merrill

Title: Contract Developer; Software Developer **Industry:** Technology **Company Name:** TEKsystems Inc. **Date of Birth:** 06/20/1953 **Place of Birth:** Pittsburgh **State/Country of Origin:** PA/USA **Parents:** Edgar Frank Merrill; Harriet Margaret Merrill **Marital Status:** Married **Spouse Name:** Rita Alice May Merrill **Children:** Laura Margaret **Education:** Master of Computer Information Systems, University of Denver (1988); BS in Metallurgical Engineering, Colorado School of Kingdom Ministry (1976) **Certifications:** ICCP Certified Systems Professional (Inactive); ICCP Certified Computer Professional (Inactive); Certified PICK Professional; A+, Microsoft Certified Systems Engineer (Inactive) **Career:** Contract Developer, TEKsystems Inc. (2019-Present); Developer II, HealthLink (2012-2019); Senior Development Programmer, Trust Company of America (2006-2011); Director of Software Development, Drycreek Associates Corporation (2004-2010); Owner, System Consultant, Dynamic Solutions, Denver, CO (1986-2004); Data Processing Manager, PBI/BAXA, Inc., Denver, CO (1983-1986); Programmer, Analyst, Titsch & Associates, Denver, CO (1983); Programmer, Analyst, M.L. Foss, Inc., Denver, CO (1981-1983); Metallurgical Engineer, Cominco American, Inc., Bixby, MO (1980-1981); Metallurgical Engineer, Inspiration Copper Co., Miami, AZ (1979-1980) **Career Related:** Co-owner, Drycreek Associates Corporation (2004-2010); Consultant in Field, Denver, CO (1985-2009); Instructor, Continuing Education User's Group, Denver, CO (1985-2001); Instructor, Computer Information System, University of Denver (1990-1997); Board of Directors, Institute for Certification of Computing Professionals (1993-1996); Member, Graduate Computer Information System Faculty, Colorado Campus, University of Phoenix (1991-1994) **Military Service:** National Staff, IT Fellow, U.S. Coast Guard Auxiliary (2016-Present); With, U.S. Coast Guard Auxiliary (2013-Present); Commander, U.S. Coast Guard Auxiliary, Flotilla 085-01-04 Denver, CO (2017); National Staff, Division Chief for National Systems Support, U.S. Coast Guard Auxiliary (2014-2016); First Lieutenant, U.S. Army (1977-1983) **Creative Works:** Author, "Security on the Picket System," International Spectrum Magazine (1995); Author, "Automating the Information and Referral Function at a Regional Senior Citizens Center," Journal of Systems Management (1992); Author, Articles, Professional Journals **Awards:** Coast Guard Auxiliary Commandant's Letter of Commendation (2017); Coast Guard Auxiliary Achievement Medal (2016); Army Commendation Medal (1979) **Marquis Who's Who Honors:** Albert Nelson Marquis Lifetime Achievement Award **Avocations:** Model railroading; Model rocketry; Hiking; Camping; Mountain climbing **Religion:** Christian

Lori Miller

Title: Humanities Educator **Industry:** Education/Educational Services **Date of Birth:** 10/01/1945 **Place of Birth:** Denver **State/Country of Origin:** CO/USA **Parents:** Raymond Albert; Audrey Marilyn Berwick Brown **Marital Status:** Divorced **Children:** Robert Capron Funk **Education:** Doctor of Philosophy in English Literature and Writing Theory, International College, Los Angeles, CA (1983); All But Dissertation, University of Southern California, California (1981); Bachelor of Arts, University of California, Riverside (1967); Master of Arts, California State University, Northridge **Certifications:** Lifetime Credential, California College **Career:** Faculty Staff Member, Department of English, Moreno Valley College, Moreno Valley, CA (2007-2020); Freelance Writer, Editor, Millers Editing Service (1994-2020); Freshman Core Course Writing Director, Department of Humanities, University of California Irvine (2006-2009); Scholarship Advisor, University of California Irvine (2006-2008); Faculty Staff Member, Communications and Advertising, California State University, Fullerton (1997-2005); Freelance Writing Workshops (1980-1998); Director, Freshman Composition, Upper Division Writing, University of California Irvine (1985-1997); Faculty Staff Member, Department of English, University of California Irvine (1985-1997); Theater Critic, LA Reader (1980-1985) **Civic:** Business Coach, San Diego Employers Association (2004-Present); Board of Directors, Hospice of the Valley (2003); Meditation Facilitator, Vipassana Support Institute; MVC Mentor **Creative Works:** Author, "Cat Signs" (2004); Author, "No Self, No Problem" (2003); Author, UCI Freshman Upper Division Composition Guides (1989-1996); Author, "To the Far Side of Darkness" (1986) **Awards:** Outstanding Faculty Award, Department of Communications, California State University Fullerton (2001); Travel Fellowship, Dean of Humanities, University of California Irvine (1978); Fellow, Cambridge University, England (1974); Fellow, Universita per Stranieri, Perugia, Italy **Marquis Who's Who Honors:** Albert Nelson Marquis Lifetime Achievement Award **To what do you attribute your success:** Ms. Miller attributes her success to her sense of perseverance, inspiration and the great fortune she has had to live a sober life. **Why did you become involved in your profession or industry:** Ms. Miller became involved in her profession due to her lifetime interest in excelling as a teacher. **Avocations:** Oil painting; Musician; Mindfulness meditation

Tara L. Milligan

Title: Assistant Clinical Professor **Industry:** Education/Educational Services **Company Name:** Mississippi State University - Meridian **Date of Birth:** 02/12/1980 **Place of Birth:** Natchez **State/Country of Origin:** MS/USA **Education:** Master's Degree, UNT Health Science Center (2013); BS in Medical Technology, Louisiana Tech University; BS in Biology, Louisiana Tech University **Career:** Assistant Clinical Professor, Mississippi State University - Meridian (2019-Present); Physician Assistant, Wellness in Sleep **Civic:** Volunteer, Free Clinic of Meridian **Awards:** Leadership Lauderdale Class of 2020 (Honor), East Mississippi Business Development Corporation (2019) **Memberships:** Physician Assistant Education Association (PAEA); Copyright American Academy of PAs; Louisiana Academy of Physician Assistants; Young Professionals of Meridian **To what do you attribute your success:** Ms. Milligan attributes her success to the dedication to her profession, as well as her faith in God for giving her the inspiration and ability to want to help people. **Why did you become involved in your profession or industry:** Ms. Milligan became involved in her profession because she simply wanted to help others. She was aware of the need for adequate and competent providers who know how to communicate well with people. She had always been interested in science. In undergrad, she studied medical technology but wet back because she felt that she needed more training. She wanted to see patients, diagnose and interact with them. **Avocations:** Leadership Waterdale Group

Elizabeth "Betsy" Mills

Title: Art Educator **Date of Birth:** 02/19/1947 **Place of Birth:** Baton Rouge **State/Country of Origin:** LA/USA **Parents:** Robert Bernard Jennings; Virginia Adelia (Lobdell) Jennings **Marital Status:** Married **Spouse Name:** Wilmer Riddle Mills (12/28/1967) **Children:** Wilmer Hastings (Deceased 2011); Evelyn Kate Irby; Virginia Young Musacchia; John Jennings **Education:** Postgraduate Coursework, Studio Art, Louisiana State University (1991-1993); BA in Studio Art and English, Louisiana State University (1969); Diploma, Louise S. McGehee School, New Orleans, LA (1965) **Career:** Cattle Farm Rancher (1983-2016); Private Teacher, Art, Zachary, LA (1986-1995); Orthodontic Assistant, Jeffrey K. Machen, DDS, Zachary, LA (1987-1991); Teacher, Art, St. Patrick's Episcopalian Day School (1982-1984); Agricultural Missionary to Brazil, Presbyterian Church, LA (1972-1980) **Career Related:** Weaving Demonstrator, Church and Civic Groups, St. Francisville, LA (1983-Present); Bookmaking Instructor, Belhaven University (1998); Guest Lecturer, James Madison University, Harrisonburg, VA (1995) **Civic:** Member, Officer, Study Clubs/Book Clubs, Baton Rouge and Zachary, LA (1982-Present); Member, Officer, Teacher, Plains Presbyterian Church, Zachary, LA (1980-Present); Lecturer, Art Nouveau Artists (2017); Chairman, "Louisiana Roads," "Remembering the Poet Wilmer Hastings Mills," Zachary Branch Library (2014); Member, Zachary Fall Festival Art Show (2009); President, Harness Club (2000, 2001, 2007); Member, Art Committee, Zachary Community School District (2004); Member, Award Grants Panel, East Baton Rouge Parish (2003); Volunteer, Baton Rouge Symphony Orchestra (1987-1990); Tour Guide, Plantation Homes, St. Francisville Pilgrimage, West Feliciana, LA (1985-1990); Teacher, Women's Bible Study, Local Church (20 Years); Presbyterian Church in America **Creative Works:** Contributor, Louisiana Sportsman Magazine (2017); Contributor, "International Grand Isle Tarpon Rodeo Guide Book" (2014); Article, "The Natural Gardener," The Advocate (2013); Article, "Art Show to Accompany Home Tours", Zachary Post (2009); Artist, Exhibitions; Contributor, Articles, Professional Journals **Memberships:** The Reading Group (1996-Present); Edna Heft '32 Society (2019); The Study Club (1995); Board of Directors, Artist Guild of West Feliciana (1992-1995); Secretary, Associate Women in the Arts (1991-1993); The Weaving Group; Lagniappe Dulcimer Society; Delta Delta Delta Fraternity **Marquis Who's Who Honors:** Albert Nelson Marquis Lifetime Achievement Award; Marquis Who's Who Top Professional **Political Affiliations:** Republican **Religion:** Presbyterian

James "Jim" Minard, PhD

Title: Psychologist, Associate Professor, Research Chief **Date of Birth:** 03/23/1933 **Place of Birth:** Spokane **State/Country of Origin:** WA/USA **Parents:** Glen Minard (Deceased); Irene Elaine Minard (Deceased 1973) **Marital Status:** Married **Spouse Name:** Nancy Ann Croyle (06/27/59) **Children:** Annette Gil; Katherline "Kate" Thomas **Education:** PhD in Psychology, University of Colorado (1963); MS in Psychology, University of Washington (1959); BS in Biology, Whitworth University (1955) **Certifications:** Certified, School Psychologist, WA (2002) **Career:** Retired (2005); Associate Professor (Tenured), Consultant, Private Practice (2002-2005); Intern Psychology, East Valley School District (2001-2002); Director, Sleep and Vigilance Laboratory, Rutgers School of Biomedical and Health Sciences (1987-1998); Associate Professor, Rutgers School of Biomedical and Health Sciences (1973-1998); Associate Professor, Rutgers School of Biomedical and Health Sciences (1973-1987); Research Chief, Maryland Psychiatric Research Center (1971-1973); Instructor, Assistant Professor, University Pittsburgh School of Medicine (1963-1971); Instructor, SUNY Downstate Health Sciences University (1962-1963); Teaching, Research Assistant, University of Colorado (1960-1961); Teaching, Research Assistant, University of Washington (1957-1960) **Career Related:** Medical Advisory Committee, Narcolepsy Network (1987-Present); Essex County College (1997-1998); Adjunct Faculty, Department of Psychology, University of Maryland (1972-1973); Board of Directors, Spokane Falls Community College **Civic:** Health Research Team, Spokane Alliance (2003-Present); Teacher, Safer Driving Program, AARP (2004-2007); Moderator, Education, United Church Christ (2003-2007); Lecturer, Maryland State Police Training Program (1972) **Creative Works:** Producer, Film; Contributor, Articles on Science, Professional Scientific Journals **Awards:** Recipient, Awards, Washington State Psychological Association, Eastern Psychological Association, and Associated Professional Sleep Societies, LLC **Memberships:** Washington State Psychological Association; Eastern Psychological Association; Associated Professional Sleep Societies, LLC **Marquis Who's Who Honors:** Albert Nelson Marquis Lifetime Achievement Award **Why did you become involved in your profession or industry:** Dr. Minard has always had an interest in science. However, as a young child, he was very sick. In fact, two pediatricians told his father that he was at risk of death. His father got them both fired. He found another doctor, who he felt was better grounded in science, and they pulled Dr. Minard through. Ever since then, he has held a high level of respect for science. **Avocations:** Writing; Drawing; Magic **Political Affiliations:** Independent **Religion:** Unitarian Universalist

Helen Lydia Mirren

Title: Actress **Date of Birth:** 07/26/1945 **Place of Birth:** London **State/Country of Origin:** United Kingdom **Parents:** Vasily "Basil" Petrovich Mironoff; Kathleen Alexandrina Eva Matilda (Rogers) Mironoff **Marital Status:** Married **Spouse Name:** Taylor Hackford (12/31/1997) **Education:** Coursework, National Youth Theatre; Coursework, The Royal Central School of Speech and Drama **Career:** International Centre for Theatre Research, Africa (1972-1973); Joined, Royal Shakespeare Company (1967) **Abridged Creative Works:** Actress, "Woman in Gold" (2015); Actress, "Eye in the Sky" (2015); Actress, "Trumbo" (2015); Actress, "The Hundred-Foot Journey" (2014); Actress, "Red 2" (2013); Actress, "The Audience" (2013); Actress, "The Door" (2012); Actress, "Hitchcock" (2012); Actress, "Arthur" (2011); Actress, "Love Ranch" (2010); Actress, "Red" (2010); Actress, "The Tempest" (2010); Actress, "Brighton Rock" (2010); Actress, "The Debt" (2010); Actress, "The Last Station" (2009); Actress, "State of Play" (2009); Actress, "Inkheart," (2008); Actress, "National Treasure: Book of Secrets" (2007); Actress, "The Queen" (2006); Actress, "Shadowboxer" (2005); Actress, "Elizabeth I" (2005); Actress, "The Clearing" (2004); Actress, "Raising Helen" (2004); Actress, "Calendar Girls" (2003); Actress, "The Roman Spring of Mrs. Stone" (2003); Actress, "Prime Suspect 6: The Last Witness" (2003); Actress, "Door to Door" (2002); Actress, "Georgetown" (2002) **Abridged Awards:** Drama Desk Award for Outstanding Actress in a Play (2015); Tony Award for Best Performance by an Actress in a Leading Role in a Play (2015); Fellowship Award, BAFTA (2014); Sherry Lansing Leadership Award, The Hollywood Reporter (2010); Distinction in Theatre Award, Geffen Playhouse (2007); Golden Globe Award for Best Performance by an Actress in a Miniseries or Motion Picture Made for TV, Hollywood Foreign Press Association (2007); National Society Film Critics Award for Best Actress (2007); Critics' Choice Award for Best Actress (2007); Golden Globe Award for Best Performance by an Actress in a Motion Picture - Drama, Hollywood Foreign Press Association (2007); Academy Award for Best Actress in a Leading Role, Academy of Motion Picture Arts and Sciences (2007); BAFTA Award for Best Actress in a Leading Role (2007); Screen Actors Guild Award for Outstanding Performance by a Female Actor in a Leading Role, SAG-AFTRA (2007); New York Film Critics Circle Award for Best Actress (2006); National Board of Review Award for Best Actress (2006); Emmy Award for Outstanding Lead Actress in a Miniseries or Movie, Academy of Television Arts and Sciences (2006); Named Dame Commander of the Most Excellent Order of the British Empire, Her Majesty Queen Elizabeth II (2003); National Society Film Critics Award for Best Supporting Actress (2002)

Dawn T. Mistretta, JD

Title: Partner **Industry:** Law and Legal Services **Company Name:** Strauch Green & Mistretta P C **Marital Status:** Married **Spouse Name:** Sam Green **Education:** JD, Norman Adrian Wiggins School of Law, Campbell University (2003); BA in History, Louisiana State University (1996) **Career:** Partner, Strauch Green & Mistretta, PC (2013-Present); Partner, Strauch Fitzgerald & Green, PC (2010-2013); Attorney, Womble Carlyle Sandridge & Rice, PLLC (2003-2010) **Civic:** Community Involvement Committee, YMCA (Youth Men's Christian Association) **Awards:** Best Lawyers, Family Law (2019, 2020); Texas Super Lawyers, Thomson Reuters (2009-2019); Texas Board of Legal Specialization, Family Law (1993); AV Preeminent Rating, Martindale Hubbell **Memberships:** North Carolina Bar Association; American Bar Association; Wake County Bar Association **To what do you attribute your success:** Ms. Mistretta attributes her success to hard work and her refusal to give up. Her profession is not easy and not for the faint-hearted. **Why did you become involved in your profession or industry:** Ms. Mistretta became a paralegal when she first graduated as an undergraduate. She had a degree in history but there were not many options in the field. She had great typing skills and began working for lawyers as a legal secretary. After a few years, she realized that she was interested in becoming a lawyer. She had pragmatic exposure to the field before going to law school, which gave her an advantage over her classmates. In the years since then, she has thoroughly excelled as a lawyer.

Mario Jose Molina, PhD

Title: Founder; Physical Chemist; Professor **Company Name:** Molina Center for Energy and the Environment **Date of Birth:** 03/19/1943 **Place of Birth:** Mexico City **State/Country of Origin:** Mexico **Parents:** Roberto Molina-Pasquel; Leonor Henriquez Molina **Marital Status:** Married **Spouse Name:** Guadalupe Alvarez (02/11/2006) **Children:** Felipe **Education:** Doctor of Philosophy, University of California, Berkeley (1972); Master of Science, University of Freiburg, Germany (1967); Bachelor of Science in Chemical Engieering, National Autonomous University of Mexico (1965) **Career:** Founder, President, Molina Center for Energy and the Environment, Mexico City, Mexico (2005-Present); Professor, Department of Chemistry and Biochemistry, Scripps Institution of Oceanography, University of California, San Diego (2004-Present); Institute Professor, Massachusetts Institute of Technology, Cambridge, MA (1997-2004); Martin Professor of Atmospheric Chemistry, Massachusetts Institute of Technology (1989-1996); Senior Research Scientist, Jet Propulsion Laboratory, California Institute of Technology (1983-1989); Associate Professor, University of California, Irvine (1979-1982) **Career Related:** United States President's Council of Advisors on Science and Technology (1994-2000, 2008-2015) **Awards:** Presidential Medal of Freedom, The White House (2013); Named One of the 50 Most Important Hispanics in Government & Education, Hispanic Engineer & Information Technology Magazine (2005); Trailblazer in Science, Science Spectrum Magazine (2005); Volvo Environment Prize (2004); Heinz Award in Environment, Heinz Family Foundation (2003); Sasakawa Prize, UN Environment Programme (1999); Willard Gibbs Medal, Chicago Section, American Chemical Society (1998); Prize for Creative Advances in Environmental Technology & Science, American Chemical Society (1998); Nobel Prize in Chemistry, Royal Swedish Academy of Sciences (1995); NASA Exceptional Science Achievement Medal (1989) **Memberships:** National Academy of Sciences; Pontifical Academy of Science; Institute of Medicine; American Geophysical Union; American Physical Society; American Chemical Society **Marquis Who's Who Honors:** Albert Nelson Marquis Lifetime Achievement Award; Marquis Who's Who Top Professional **Why did you become involved in your profession or industry:** Professor Molina became interested in science at 11 years old. He realized that he could make a career out of his love of science, and decided to teach. **Avocations:** Classical music; Tennis

Minerva Houston Montooth

Title: Coordinator of Social Events **Industry:** Architecture & Construction **Company Name:** Frank Lloyd Wright Foundation **Date of Birth:** 02/21/1924 **Place of Birth:** Rushville **State/Country of Origin:** IL/USA **Parents:** Walter Scripps Houston; Margaret Allen Houston **Marital Status:** Widowed **Spouse Name:** Charles Montooth (1952, Deceased 12/31/2014) **Children:** Susan Priscilla Montooth; Margaret Allen Montooth; James Andrew Montooth **Education:** BSc in English Language and Literature, Northwestern University (1945); Coursework, MacMurray College (1941-1943) **Certifications:** Certificate from Frank Lloyd Wright School of Architecture (Now The School of Architecture at Taliesin) **Career:** Coordinator of Social Events, Frank Lloyd Wright Foundation, Taliesin, WI (1985-Present); Personal Assistant to Olgivanna Lloyd Wright (Mrs. Frank Lloyd Wright) (1962-1985) **Career Related:** Member, Board of Trustee, Frank Lloyd Wright Foundation (2000-2008); Member, Taliesin Preservation Board (2000-2008); Library Research, Encyclopedia Britannica and Ellington Advertising Agency (1945-1948) **Civic:** Phoenix Symphony Auxiliary (1953-1980); Phoenix Light Opera Auxiliary (1953-1980) **Creative Works:** Contributor, Frank Lloyd Wright Foundation Publications (1980-1999) **Awards:** Honoree, Shining Brow Award, Taliesin Preservation (2018) **Memberships:** Taliesin Tables (2008-Present) **Marquis Who's Who Honors:** Albert Nelson Marquis Lifetime Achievement Award **To what do you attribute your success:** Mrs. Montooth attributes her success to her years of study and work learning with Mrs. Frank Lloyd Wright, the Frank Lloyd Wright Foundation and the Taliesin Fellowship. **Why did you become involved in your profession or industry:** Mrs. Montooth became involved in her profession because Frank Lloyd Wright's Taliesin is unique and superior in education in the world. **Avocations:** Photography; Travel **Political Affiliations:** Democrat **Religion:** Christian **Thoughts on Life:** Mrs. Montooth's hopes and prayers are for world peace.

Alfred V. Morgan

Title: Management Consulting Company Executive **Industry:** Financial Services **Date of Birth:** 04/13/1936 **Place of Birth:** Liberal **State/Country of Origin:** KS/USA **Parents:** Forest Francis Morgan; Gertrude Irene (Henning) Morgan **Marital Status:** Married **Spouse Name:** Peggy Ann Riley (06/29/1960) **Children:** Trudie Marie; Vance Riley; Allen Forest; Bradley Augustus; Kelly James (Deceased 07/25/1999) **Education:** Postgraduate Diploma, American Institute of Banking (AIB) (1965); MBA, University of Southern California, Los Angeles, CA (1966); BBA, The University of Kansas, Lawrence, KS (1958) **Career:** President, Morgan Business Associates, Inc., Santa Barbara, CA and Boston, MA (1971-2019); Instructor, Management, Santa Barbara City College, Santa Barbara, CA (1973); Instructor, Business, Los Angeles City College, Los Angeles, CA (1971-1972); Consultant, Harbridge House, Inc., Boston, MA (1966-1971); Marketing Executive, Doyle, Dane, Bernbach Advertising (Now DDB Worldwide) (1965-1966); Assistant Marketing Director, Security Pacific National Bank (1961-1965); Assistant Manager, Fruehauf Trailer Company, Vernon, CA (1960-1961) **Career Related:** President, The Experimental in International Living, World Learning (1980-1981) **Civic:** Junior Warden, Financial Committee, All Saints-by-the-Sea Episcopal Church (2006-2019); Vice President, El Escorial Condo Association (2003-2008); Member, Vestry, All Saints-by-the-Sea Episcopal Church (2003-2006); Member, Lobero Theatre Board (1984-1988) **Military Service:** With, United States Army Reserve (1960-1964); With, United States Army (1958-1960) **Creative Works:** Contributor, Articles to Professional Publications **Memberships:** American Society for Training and Development (Now ATD); American Marketing Association Los Angeles; American Society of Professional Consultants; University Southern California Marshall Alumni Association; Los Rancheros Pobres; Los Fiesteros Dance Club **Marquis Who's Who Honors:** Albert Nelson Marquis Lifetime Achievement Award **Why did you become involved in your profession or industry:** Mr. Morgan became involved in his profession because he started his career with a group called Harbridge House, Incorporated. He found that he enjoyed helping people develop their skills and talents in order to be better at their jobs. **Avocations:** Dancing; Horseback riding **Religion:** Episcopal **Thoughts on Life:** Mr. Morgan's motto was, "Don't give up if you don't get it right the first time..." It is important to know that in the beginning of his career, he wasn't always successful. He lost jobs in the past before finally finding the right career path for himself.

Jeffrey Morgan

Title: Chief Financing Officer, Treasurer **Industry:** Financial Services **Company Name:** Finger Lakes Regional Health System, Inc. **Date of Birth:** 08/09/1966 **Place of Birth:** Westerly **State/Country of Origin:** RI/USA **Marital Status:** Married **Spouse Name:** Kelly Morgan **Education:** MBA, University of Miami, Coral Gables, FL; BBA, Florida Atlantic University, Boca Raton, FL; BS in Secondary Education, University of Rhode Island, Kingston, RI **Certifications:** Certified Public Accountant (CPA), State of Delaware; Delaware State Board of Accountancy **Career:** Chief Financial Officer and Treasurer, Finger Lakes Health System, Inc., Geneva, NY (2019-Present); Vice President of Finance and Chief Financial Officer, Brooks-TLC Hospital System, Inc., Dunkirk, NY (2013-2018); Interim Vice President for Finance, Administrative Director of Finance, Miami Children's Hospital, Miami, FL (2012-2013); Vice President for Financial Performance and Improvement, Canton-Potsdam Hospital, Potsdam, NY (2010-2012); Area Finance Officer, San Jose Market Area, Kaiser Foundation Hospitals/Health Plan, Inc., Oakland, CA (2008-2010); Owner, Jeff Morgan Consulting, Chapel Hill, NC (2005-2008); Interim Senior Vice President for Finance at Southside Hospital, Bay Shore, NY (2004-2005); Chief Financial Officer, Charles Cole Memorial Hospital, Coudersport, PA (2002-2004); Chief Financial Officer, Carlisle Regional Medical Center, Carlisle, PA (2001-2002) **Memberships:** Fellow, American College of Healthcare Executives (1996); Fellow, Healthcare Financial Management Association (1996) **Marquis Who's Who Honors:** Marquis Who's Who Top Professional **To what do you attribute your success:** Mr. Morgan attributes his success to his strong education and work experience. **Why did you become involved in your profession or industry:** Mr. Morgan became involved in his profession because he comes from a family of health care professionals. However, he never liked the sight of blood, so he chose to pursue the financial side of health care. **Avocations:** Restoring old cars

Mendell D. Morgan Jr.

Title: Director **Industry:** Library Management/Library Services **Company Name:** El Progreso Memorial Library **Date of Birth:** 11/29/1940 **Place of Birth:** Alice **State/Country of Origin:** TX/USA **Parents:** Mendell D. Morgan Sr.; Laura Elizabeth (Fowler) Morgan **Marital Status:** Widowed **Spouse Name:** Jean Marie Winn (12/07/1963, Deceased 10/10/2008) **Children:** Mendell David Morgan **Education:** MSLS, Louisiana State University (1964); BA, The University of Texas at Austin (1963) **Certifications:** American Library Association **Career:** Library Director, El Progreso Memorial Library, Uvalde, Texas (2014-Present); Dean, Library Information Services, Former Director, Library Services, J.E. and L.E. Mabee Library, Incarnate Word College (Now University of the Incarnate Word), San Antonio, TX(1975-2008); Library Director, Mountain View College, Dallas, TX (1970-1975); Field Consultant, Assistant Director, Field Services, Texas State Library, Austin, TX (1965-1970); With, Public Services, Baltimore County Public Library, Catonsville Branch, MD (1964-1965) **Civic:** Live Oak City Councilman (2014-Present); Vestry, St. Matthew's Episcopal Church, Universal City, TX (1985-1988, 1995-1998); Campus Chairman, United Way, San Antonio, TX (1980-1990); Past Club President, Lieutenant Governor Division 5, TX-OK Kiwanis **Creative Works:** Author, Articles, Professional Journals **Memberships:** American Library Association; Texas Library Association **Marquis Who's Who Honors:** Albert Nelson Marquis Lifetime Achievement Award **Why did you become involved in your profession or industry:** Mr. Morgan loves to help other people. He became involved in the library profession due to being hired as a student assistant in his university career at the University of Texas at Austin. He really enjoyed the work and it blossomed from there. **Avocations:** Traveling; Reading; Art appreciation **Political Affiliations:** Republican **Religion:** Episcopalian

Art Morrical

Title: Quality Manager (Retired) **Industry:** Telecommunications **Company Name:** AT&T Bell Laboratories/Lucent/Alcatel-Lucent/Nokia **Date of Birth:** 03/22/1960 **Place of Birth:** Kankakee **State/Country of Origin:** IL/USA **Parents:** Victor Morrical; Helen Morrical **Marital Status:** Divorced **Children:** Jeffery; Linda **Education:** Master of Science in Computer Science, North Central College, Naperville, IL (1989); Bachelor of Science in Electrical Engineering Technology, Bradley University, Peoria, IL (1982) **Certifications:** Certified, Project Management Professional, Project Management Institute (2007); Lead Assessor, British Standards Institution, London (1995); Quality Engineer, American Society of Quality (1989) **Career:** Quality Manager, AT&T Bell Laboratories, Lucent Technologies/Alcatel-Lucent, Naperville, IL (1985-2016); Senior Engineer, GTE Communications Systems, Northlake, IL (1982-1985) **Civic:** Vice President, Sugar Grove Public Library (2011-Present); Vice Chair, Telecom Business Excellence Quest Forum (2010-Present); Global Business Excellence, QUEST Forum Leadership (2011-2012); President, Board of Trustees, Sugar Grove Public Library (1999-2011); Vice Chair, American Region QUEST Forum (2008-2009); Founder, Chair, Great Lakes TL 9000 Special Interest Group, Naperville, IL (2003-2009); Secretary, North American Region, Quest Forum (2007-2008); Founding Contributor, Quest Forum (1997-2007); Vice President, Sugar Grove Public Library (1997-1999); Trustee, Sugar Grove Public Library (1996-1997) **Creative Works:** Co-author, "TL9000 Requirements and Measurements," Quest Forum (1998) **Awards:** Lifetime Fellowship, Quest Forum (2015); Quest Forum COO Award (2012); COO Award, Quest Forum (2012); Outstanding Leadership and Contribution Award (2007-2012); Leadership Award (2001) **Memberships:** Illinois Library Association; American Library Association; Project Management Institute; American Society of Quality **Marquis Who's Who Honors:** Albert Nelson Marquis Lifetime Achievement Award **To what do you attribute your success:** Mr. Morrical is an avid reader, which propelled him to be able to excel at research for Bell Laboratories Libraries online. His ability to prepare and execute corporate strategy provided leadership to his team members that led to the worldwide adoption of QuEST Forum and TL 9000 standards. **Why did you become involved in your profession or industry:** Mr. Morrical learned much about wavelengths in science, which led to his career in communications technology. **Avocations:** Juggling; Genealogy

Audrey Farrar Morton

Title: Public Administrator **Industry:** Government Administration/Government Relations/Government Services **Date of Birth:** 06/24/1937 **Place of Birth:** Washington, DC **State/Country of Origin:** USA **Parents:** John Ollie; Massie Hollard Farrar **Marital Status:** Divorced **Children:** Michelle Bernadette; Michael Nathaniel (Deceased); Brian Anthony; Brenda Anne **Education:** Doctoral Studies in Public Administration, University of Colorado, Denver, CO; Master of Public Affairs, University of Colorado, Boulder, CO; Bachelor of Arts, Regis University, Denver, CO **Career:** Legislative Assistant, United States House of Representatives; Deputy Assistant Secretary, Equal Employment Opportunity and Civil Rights, U.S. Department of State; Director, Office for Civil Rights, U.S. Department of Health and Human Services; Special Assistant to Director, Office of Minority Health, U.S. Department of Health and Human Services; Deputy Regional VIII Director & Director of Intergovernmental and Congressional Affairs, U.S. Department of Health and Human Services, Denver, CO; Doctoral Program Coordinator, University of Colorado, Denver, CO; Assistant to the City Manager, Aurora, CO **Civic:** Human Services Council, Fairfax County, VA (2016-2019); Civil Service Commission, Fairfax County, VA (1994-2016); Republican Candidate, Colorado House of Representatives District 7, Denver, CO (1981-1982) **Creative Works:** Sculpture, "Circle of Life," George Mason University **Awards:** Masters of Public Administration Fellowship, United States Department of Housing and Urban Development (1972-1973) **Memberships:** President, Colorado City Management Assistants Association (1976-1977); Life Member, Alpha Kappa Alpha Sorority Inc. **Marquis Who's Who Honors:** Albert Nelson Marquis Lifetime Achievement Award; Marquis Who's Who Top Professional **To what do you attribute your success:** Ms. Morton attributes her success to the foundation provided by her parents, which allowed her to follow her interests throughout life. **Why did you become involved in your profession or industry:** Ms. Morton became involved in her profession out of a desire to influence decisions that improve conditions in society. **Avocations:** Music; Travel; Sports; Reading **Political Affiliations:** Republican **Religion:** Roman Catholic

Maxine Mulligan

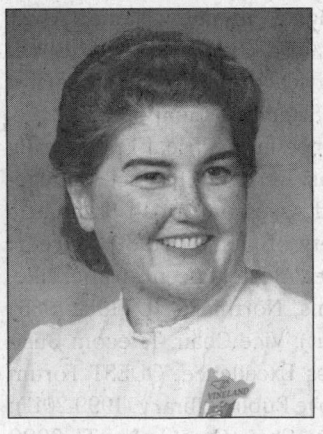

Title: Secondary School Educator (Retired) **Date of Birth:** 10/26/1937 **Place of Birth:** Vineland **State/Country of Origin:** NJ/USA **Parents:** Firman John Rogers; Vera Virginia (Saul) Rogers **Marital Status:** Married **Spouse Name:** Rodney W. Mulligan (10/01/1960) **Children:** Kelly J. **Education:** MA, Glassboro State College (1987); BA, Glassboro State College (1980) **Certifications:** Secondary English Education, State of New Jersey **Career:** Retired (1998); High School Teacher, Educational Secretary, Vineland Board of Education **Civic:** Vineland High School All Sports Booster Club; Vineland Secretarial Association; Delaware Bay Lighthouse Keepers and Friends Association; Vineland High School Historical Committee **Creative Works:** Contributor, Contract Structure for Secretarial Group; Author, Numerous Works **Awards:** Inductee, Vineland High School Wall of Warriors (2014); Named, Vineland Hometown Heroes (2009); Teacher of Year, Governors Teachers Recognition Program (1986) **Memberships:** National Education Association; New Jersey Education Association; Cumberland County Education Association; Representative, Vineland Education Association; National Council of Teachers of English **Marquis Who's Who Honors:** Albert Nelson Marquis Lifetime Achievement Award; Marquis Who's Who Top Professional **To what do you attribute your success:** Mrs. Mulligan attributes her success to setting goals, working to reach them, never giving up, and staying active. **Why did you become involved in your profession or industry:** For 26 years, Mrs. Mulligan excelled as a secretary at Memorial Junior High School. It was in this role that she discovered she would like to become a teacher. From there, she did everything she could to further pursue her career in education. **Avocations:** Traveling; Listening to music

Paul Mulzoff

Title: Project Manager **Industry:** Technology **Company Name:** Verizon Communications Inc. **Education:** MBA in Marketing, Hagan School of Business, Iona College (2007); BA in Business Administration, Empire State College **Certifications:** Master's Certificate, Management Information Systems and Services, Iona College **Career:** PMO/Tech Integration, Verizon Global Corporation Citizenship (The Verizon Foundation) (2015-Present); Lean Six Sigma Black Belt, Verizon (2013-2015); Senior Systems Engineer, Verizon (1993-2013) **Civic:** Abberley Park Homeowner's Association **To what do you attribute your success:** Mr. Mulzoff attributes his success to networking, willingness to adapt to new environments and keep learning, as well as his ability to notice new opportunities and take advantage of them. **Why did you become involved in your profession or industry:** While working in IT-Network infrastructure, as social media began in the early 2000s, Mr. Mulzoff was involved in a lot of planning and problem-solving discussions, mainly involving the marketing team as they tried to figure out how to reach out to customers in the new channel. He saw an opportunity as an IT person to become a liaison between the coding people and the business side of the industry.

Pearl Marie Murphy, RNC

Title: Medical and Surgical Nurse **Date of Birth:** 02/09/1954 **Place of Birth:** Portsmouth **State/Country of Origin:** OH/USA **Parents:** Chester Eugene Murphy; Eunice Jean (Windsor) Murphy **Marital Status:** Single **Education:** BSN, Ohio University (1989); Associate Degree in Nursing, Hocking College (1980) **Certifications:** Licensed Practical Nurse, Scioto County Career Technical Center (1973); Certified Medical-Surgical Nurse, American Nursing Credentialing Center, American Nurses Association **Career:** Staff Nurse, Medical-Surgical Vascular Care Unit, Southern Ohio Medical Center (1989-Present); Staff Nurse, Diabetic Unit, Scioto Memorial Hospital (1988-1989); Staff Nurse, Psychiatric Unit, Mercy Hospital (1987-1988); Staff Nurse, Psychiatric Unit, Southern Hills Hospital (1980-1987); Staff Nurse, Psychiatric-Alcohol Unit, Southern Hills Hospital (1975-1979); Staff Nurse, Medical-Surgical Unit, Southern Hills Hospital (1973-1975) **Career Related:** Nursing Assistant Program Coordinator, Instructor, Scioto County Career Technical Center (1991-1992) **Memberships:** Ohio Nurses Association; The Order of the Eastern Star **Marquis Who's Who Honors:** Albert Nelson Marquis Lifetime Achievement Award **To what do you attribute your success:** Ms. Murphy attributes her success to hard work. **Why did you become involved in your profession or industry:** Ms. Murphy became involved in her profession because her mother, Eunice Jean Murphy, worked as a nursing assistant. Additionally, her friend, Jessie, inspired her by how she acted and presented herself to others. **Avocations:** Camping; Hiking; Fishing; Working in church **Religion:** Baptist

Walter Mitsuo Nakatsukasa, PhD

Title: Microbiologist **Industry:** Biotechnology **Date of Birth:** 10/16/1934 **Place of Birth:** Haiku **State/Country of Origin:** HI/USA **Parents:** Yutaka; Fusayo (Okunaga) Nakatsukasa **Marital Status:** Married **Spouse Name:** Shirley Toshiko Takeuchi (6/22/1957) **Children:** Wendy Chieko **Education:** Postdoctoral, University of Washington (1969-1971); PhD, University of Kansas (1969); MA, Indiana University, (1961); BA, University of Hawaii (1956) **Career:** Retired (1992); Research Scientist, Eli Lilly & Co., Indianapolis, IN (1980-1992); Senior Microbiologist, Eli Lilly & Co., Indianapolis, IN (1971-1979); Postdoctoral Fellow, University Washington, Seattle, WA (1969-1971); Associate Microbiologist, Eli Lilly & Co., Indianapolis, IN (1961-1965); Laboratory Technician, U.S. Army (1957-1959) **Creative Works:** Contributor, 25 Articles to Professional Journals **Awards:** Recipient, Postdoctoral Fellowship, National Institutes of Health (1969-1971) **Memberships:** Member, Japanese American Citizens League (President 1986-1987); American Society for Microbiology **Why did you become involved in your profession or industry:** Dr. Nakatsukasa became involved in his profession because he was always interested in science in particular micro-organisms ever since he was a child growing up. So that in a nutshell was the reason why he went into his field.

Marie Napoli, Esq.

Title: Partner **Company Name:** Napoli Shkolnik PLLC **Date of Birth:** 04/12/1967 **Place of Birth:** New York **State/Country of Origin:** NY/USA **Parents:** John Kaiser; Dolores Kaiser **Marital Status:** Married **Spouse Name:** Paul Napoli **Children:** Three Children **Education:** LLM, New York University School of Law; JD, St. John's University School of Law, Queens, NY (1994); BS in Psychology, St. John's University, Queens, NY (1989) **Career:** Partner, Napoli Shkolnik PLLC (2015-Present); Partner, Napoli Law (1997-Present) **Civic:** Marie and Paul Kaiser Napoli Foundation (2005-Present); Board Member, Bone Marrow & Cancer Foundation; Former Board Member, Glen Cove Boys & Girls Club **Creative Works:** Author, "Child Victims Act is a Step Toward Healing"; Featured Speaker, "America on Opioids: The Issues, the Claims, and the Coverage," Perrin Conference Webinars **Awards:** Named to Women in Law, Business Edition, Best Lawyers (2019); Named to New York Division, Super Lawyers (2018-2019); Litigator Awards, Trial Lawyers Board of Regents (2015-2016); Top Lawyer for Women's Rights, The National Trial Lawyers; Named One of the Best Law Firms in New York, U.S. News & World Report L.P.; Named One of the Top 100 Attorneys in Personal Injury Law, American Academy of Attorneys; Recipient, Numerous Awards **Memberships:** American Association for Justice; Brooklyn Women's Bar Association; Nassau County Bar Association; New York State Academy of Trial Lawyers; New York State Bar Association; Board of Directors, New York State Trial Lawyers Association (NYSTLA); New York Women's Bar Association; Suffolk County Bar Association **Bar Admissions:** New York; United States District Court for the Eastern District of New York; United States District Court for the Southern District of New York; New York Supreme Court; Supreme Court of the United States; United States District Court for the Eastern District of Michigan **To what do you attribute your success:** Mrs. Napoli attributes her success to perseverance and self-assurance. Her personal drive empowers her to ignore naysayers. Mrs. Napoli emphasizes that if you believe in something, always keep going, regardless of the motives of others. **Why did you become involved in your profession or industry:** From a young age, Mrs. Napoli spent time working in her father's law firm learning the importance of psychology in jury selection. Her path in law is meaningful to her; she believes that helping others when they are most in need has always been her calling. She chose to help and represent 9/11 victims, and took on difficult, extensive cases. While most lawyers turned these victims away, Mrs. Napoli stepped up to the challenge, crediting her empathy and belief in herself. **Avocations:** Skiing; Running; Charitable foundations; Family time

Samer Narouze, MD, PhD, DABPM, FIPP

Title: Founder, President; Clinical Professor; Physician **Company Name:** American Interventional Headache Society; The Ohio State University **Date of Birth:** 09/14/1966 **Place of Birth:** Cairo **State/Country of Origin:** Egypt **Marital Status:** Married **Education:** PhD in Cervicogenic Headaches, Maastricht University (2012); Chief Fellow in Pain Medicine, Cleveland Clinic (2002); Resident in Anesthesiology, Cleveland Clinic (1999-2002); Intern in Internal Medicine, Cleveland Clinic (1998-1999); Externship, Internal Medicine Program, Cleveland Clinic (1997-1998); MSc in Anesthesia, Pain and Intensive Care, Ain Shams University (1993); MD, Ain Shams University (1989) **Certifications:** Certified in Interventional Pain Management, World Institute of Pain (2008); Certified in Acupuncture, Stamford University (2006); Certified in Headache Medicine, United Council for Neurologic Subspecialties (2006); Certified in Pain Medicine Subspeciality, The American Board of Anesthesiology (2003); Diplomate, American Board of Pain Medicine (2003); Diplomate, The American Board of Anesthesiology (2001); Medical Licenses, Ohio and FL **Career:** President, Founder, American Interventional Headache Society (2015-Present); Clinical Professor, Consultant, The Ohio State University (2011-Present); Associate Professor, Surgery, Northeast Ohio Medical University (2011-Present); Chairman, Western Reserve Hospital (2010-Present); Clinical Professor, Ohio University Heritage College of Osteopathic Medicine (2010-Present); Associate Professor, Cleveland Clinic Lerner College of Medicine (2010); Staff, Center for Neurological Restoration, Cleveland Clinic (2008-2010); Program Director, Pain Medicine Fellowship, Cleveland Clinic (2007-2010); Assistant Professor, Anesthesiology, Cleveland Clinic Lerner College of Medicine (2007-2010); Associate Program Director, Pain Medicine Fellowship, Cleveland Clinic Foundation (2006-2007); Staff, Anesthesiology Institute, Cleveland Clinic (2005-2010); Anesthesia and Pain Management Staff, The Aultman Foundation (2003-2004); Assistant Professor, Ain Shams University (1994-1997) **Career Related:** President, Ohio Pain and Headache Institute (2010-Present); Member, Anesthesiology Institute Advisory Board, Cleveland Clinic (2009-2010); Member, Several Committees, Organizations **Creative Works:** Contributor, Over 200 Peer-reviewed Articles; Author/Co-author, Chapters, Books; Invited Speaker/Presenter in the Field; Editor-in-chief, Editor, Editorial Boards, Medical Reviewer, Professional Journals and Books; Contributor, Numerous Abstracts and Case Reports **Awards:** Recipient, Numerous Awards

Nicole Naylor-Wells, DDS

Title: Dentist **Industry:** Health, Wellness and Fitness **Company Name:** West Lake Dentistry **Parents:** Arley L.; Kimberly R. **Marital Status:** Married **Spouse Name:** John D. (06/07/2014) **Children:** Ava; Lucas **Education:** DDS, West Virginia University (2010); BA in Biology, West Virginia University (2006) **Certifications:** Permit, Minimal Sedation, State of North Carolina (2013) **Career:** Owner, Dentist, West Lake Dentistry (2011-Present) **Civic:** Missions of Mercy, The North Carolina Dental Society Foundation **Awards:** 40 Under 40 Dental Professionals in the U.S., Incisal Edge – A Lifestyle Magazine for Dental Professionals (2019); Normy Award, Best Pediatric Dentist, Best Dentist, Lake Norman Media Group (2018, 2019) **Memberships:** North Carolina Dental Society; American Dental Association; American Academy of Cosmetic Dentistry **To what do you attribute your success:** Dr. Naylor-Wells attributes her success to her commitments to be genuine and to always do her best. She believes that if you truly love what you're doing, you will do well without rushing. Dr. Naylor-Wells is always willing to learn and improve as a person and a dentist. **Why did you become involved in your profession or industry:** Dr. Naylor-Wells became involved in her profession with encouragement from a friend, whose husband was a dentist. Initially interested in medical school, dentistry was something she had always kept in mind, and she could see that it was a great profession for women. Dr. Naylor-Wells was especially attracted to the idea of being able to help countless people while maintaining her own work-life balance. **Avocations:** Cooking; Exercising; Spending time with family **Thoughts on Life:** Dr. Naylor-Wells stands by the principle of treating others the way she would like to be treated. She regards her team and her patients as if they are family, and is devoted to making procedures as easy and comfortable as possible. Dr. Naylor-Wells's husband is also a dentist.

Louis I. Newman

Title: Attorney, Managing Partner **Industry:** Law and Legal Services **Company Name:** Newman Law Group P.C. **Marital Status:** Married **Education:** JD, New York Law School, New York, NY (1967); BS in Accounting, Queens College, Queens, NY (1965) **Career:** Attorney, Managing Partner, Newman Law Group P.C. (2010-Present) **Creative Works:** Contributor, Numerous Professional Presentations; Contributor, Articles, Professional Publications; Media Appearances for Matrimonial Topics, Television Shows; Speaker, Various Radio Talk Shows **Awards:** AV Rating, Martindale Hubbell; Listee, Super Lawyers **Memberships:** Family Law Committee, New York State Bar Association; Matrimonial Law Committee, New York County Lawyers Association; Family Law Section, American Bar Association **Bar Admissions:** New York State Bar (1968); U.S. District Court for the Southern District of New York; U.S. District Court for the Eastern District of New York; U.S. District Court for the Western District of New York; U.S. Court of Appeals for the Second Circuit; U.S. Supreme Court **Marquis Who's Who Honors:** Marquis Who's Who Top Professional **To what do you attribute your success:** Mr. Newman attributes his success to seeing clients at their worst moments and being able to make them feel special while helping them. **Why did you become involved in your profession or industry:** Mr. Newman became involved in his profession because his graduate work was in accounting and he wanted to be able to help others beyond simply crunching numbers. He then chose to attend law school. After graduating, Mr. Newman's adversaries didn't want to practice matrimonial law, so they would refer their cases to him. Gradually, he became a well-respected individual in the field. It is rewarding in many of the practice areas because of the vast opportunities to help people. **Thoughts on Life:** Mr. Newman's motto is, "If you can help somebody, all the better."

Robert Lee Nicholls, PhD

Title: Civil Engineer, Educator **Industry:** Engineering **Date of Birth:** 06/11/1929 **Place of Birth:** Lincoln **State/Country of Origin:** NE/USA **Parents:** Carrol Nicholls; Claire Nicholls **Marital Status:** Married **Spouse Name:** Ruth Ann Allen (8/30/1958) **Children:** David; Jonathan; Carol **Education:** Postgraduate Coursework in Engineering Systems Optimization, University of Colorado (1967); Postgraduate Coursework in Engineering Materials Science, Stevens Institute (1963); Postgraduate Coursework in Matrices and Probability, Lehigh University (1962); PhD in Civil Engineering, Iowa State University (1957); MSCE in Civil Engineering, Iowa State University (1952); BSCE in Civil Engineering, University of Colorado, with Honors (1951) **Certifications:** Registered Civil Engineer, States of Delaware, Pennsylvania, Iowa, Maryland; Aircraft Pilots License **Career:** Professor, Civil Engineering, University of Delaware (1959-1993); Chief Materials Engineer, Highway Design Engineer, Gannett & Fleming, Harrisburg, PA (1957-1959); Design Engineer, Construction Supervisor, U.S. Army Corps Engineers (1953-1955); Concrete Materials and Metal Structures Inspector, Canyon Ferry Dam, U.S. Bureau of Reclamation (1951); Laboratory Research Assistant, Bituminous and Concrete Materials Research Laboratories, U.S. Bureau of Reclamation (1950); Survey Instrument Man, U.S. Bureau of Reclamation (1949); Surveyor, U.S. Geological Survey (1948) **Career Related:** Geotechnical Engineering and Construction Materials Consultant (1960-2006); Economic Analyst, Applied American Technology Corp., Houston, TX (1992-1996); Evaluator, Reemay Inc., Old Hickory, TN (1992-1995); Construction Surveyor, Albanian Transportation Ministry, U.S. Mission Aviation Fellowship, Redlands, CA (1993); Consultant, Diversitech Inc., Conyers, GA (1992-1993) **Civic:** Consultant, Concrete Products Plants International Executive Service Corp. (1993-Present); Consultant, Airfield and Hanger Designs, Engineering Ministries International (1993-Present) **Creative Works:** Author, Editor, "American Society of Civil Engineers Structural Plastics Selection Manual" (1984); Author, "Composite Construction Materials" (1976); Co-Author, "Civil Engineering Systems" (1972); Author, Articles, Professional Journals; Patentee, Seven Patents in Field **Awards:** University Outstanding Teaching Award (1962) **Memberships:** Life Member, Fellow, President, American Society of Civil Engineers (1974-1975); Operations Research Society of America; International Society of Soil Mechanics; Transportation Research Board; American Concrete Institute; Pi Mu Epsilon; Tau Beta Pi; Chi Epsilon; Sigma Xi **Marquis Who's Who Honors:** Albert Nelson Marquis Lifetime Achievement Award; Marquis Who's Who Top Professional

Cathrene Nichols

Title: Administrator **Industry:** Government Administration/Government Relations/Government Services **Company Name:** Washington State Department of Veterans Affairs **Marital Status:** Married **Children:** Five Children **Education:** Bachelor of Arts in English, Spanish and Education, Eastern Washington University, Cheney, WA (2008); Undergraduate Student, English Language and Literature, Gonzaga University, Spokane, WA (1996); Undergraduate Work, Sophomore, Central Texas College (1994-1995) **Career:** Board of Directors, National Coalition for Homeless Veterans (2018-Present); Director, Spokane County Regional Veterans Service Center (2017-Present); Strategic Operations Manager, Washington State Department of Veterans Affairs (2015-Present); Chairman, Veterans Employee Resource Group (2014-2015); Program Manager, Washington State Department of Veterans Affairs (2013-2015); Disabled Veterans Outreach Specialist, Washington State Employment Security Department (2009-2012) **Civic:** Chair, Washington State Veterans Employment Resource Group (2014-2016); Vice President, Veterans of Foreign Wars Post 6963 Auxiliary (2012); Stevens County Veterans Advisory Board Member (2010-2012); Government & Public Sector Lead, Washington State Military Transition Council **Military Service:** Ammunition Specialist U.S. Army (1991-1996) **Awards:** Director's Award, Washington State Department of Veterans Affairs (2016); Disabled Veterans' Outreach Program Specialist of the Year Award, American Legion (2010) **Memberships:** National Coalition of Homeless Veterans; Lifetime Member, Disabled American Veterans **Marquis Who's Who Honors:** Marquis Who's Who Top Professional **To what do you attribute your success:** Ms. Nichols credits her success on her Christian faith, as well as the influence of many amazing leaders and mentors she has worked under. **Why did you become involved in your profession or industry:** Ms. Nichols became involved in her profession because she is a veteran, alongside her husband and father. When she graduated from Eastern Washington University, her goal was to become a teacher, but she ended up working for the state in a veteran-oriented role and fell in love with taking care of those who had served. **Religion:** Christian

Stevie Lynn Nicks

Title: Singer, Songwriter **Industry:** Media & Entertainment **Date of Birth:** 05/26/1948 **Place of Birth:** Phoenix **State/Country of Origin:** AZ/USA **Parents:** Jesse Nicks; Barbara Nicks **Marital Status:** Divorced **Spouse Name:** Kim Anderson (01/29/1983, Divorced 1983) **Education:** Coursework, San Jose State University (1966-1968) **Career:** Solo Artist, Singer, Songwriter (1981-Present); Singer, Songwriter, Fleetwood Mac (1974-Present); Singer, Songwriter, Fritz (1968-1972) **Civic:** Founder, Stevie Nicks' Band of Soldiers; Supporter, Army and Navy Medical Centers, Washington, DC **Creative Works:** Appearance, "American Horror Story: Coven" (2013); Appearance, "Up All Night" (2012); Solo Artist, "24 Karat Gold: Songs from the Vault" (2014); Solo Artist, "In Your Dreams" (2011); Solo Artist, "The Soundstage Sessions" (2009); Featured, "Soundstage" (2008); Solo Artist, "Crystal Visions - The Very Best of Stevie Nicks" (2007); Featured, "Live in Boston" (2004); Featured, "Destiny Rules" (2004); Singer, Fleetwood Mac, "Live in Boston" (2004); Singer, Fleetwood Mac, "Say You Will" (2003); Singer, Fleetwood Mac, "The Very Best of Fleetwood Mac" (2002); Solo Artist, "Trouble in Shangri-La" (2001); Solo Artist, "Enchanted: The Works of Stevie Nicks" (1998); Singer, Fleetwood Mac, "The Dance" (1997); Featured, "Fleetwood Mac: The Dance" (1997); Solo Artist, "Street Angel" (1994); Singer, Fleetwood Mac, "25 Years - The Chain" (1992); Solo Artist, "Time Space: The Best of Stevie Nicks" (1991); Singer, Fleetwood Mac, "Behind the Mask" (1990); Solo Artist, "The Other Side of the Mirror" (1989); Singer, Fleetwood Mac, "Greatest Hits" (1989); Singer, Fleetwood Mac, "Tango in the Night" (1987); Featured, "Stevie Nicks: Live at Red Rocks" (1987); Solo Artist, "Rock a Little" (1985); Featured, "Fleetwood Mac in Concert: Mirage Tour" (1983); Solo Artist, "The Wild Heart" (1983); Featured, "Stevie Nicks in Concert" (1982); Singer, Fleetwood Mac, "Mirage" (1982); Solo Artist, "Bella Donna" (1981); Singer, Fleetwood Mac, "Fleetwood Mac Live" (1980); Singer, Fleetwood Mac, "Tusk" (1979); Singer, Fleetwood Mac, "Rumours" (1977); Singer, Fleetwood Mac, "Fleetwood Mac" (1975); Singer, "Buckingham Nicks" (1973) **Awards:** Inductee, Rock and Roll Hall of Fame (2019); Grammy Hall of Fame Award (With Fleetwood Mac), The Recording Academy (2003); Inductee (With Fleetwood Mac), Rock and Roll Hall of Fame (1998); Grammy Award for Album of the Year, The Recording Academy (1977); Listee, 100 Greatest Songwriters of All Time, Rolling Stone

Wayland Evan Noland, PhD

Title: Professor Emeritus **Industry:** Education/Educational Services **Company Name:** University of Minnesota **Date of Birth:** 12/08/1926 **State/Country of Origin:** WI/USA **Education:** Doctor of Philosophy in Chemistry, Harvard University, Cambridge, MA (1952); Master of Science, Harvard University, Cambridge, MA (1950); Bachelor of Science, University of Wisconsin-Madison, Madison, WI (1948) **Career:** Professor Emeritus, University of Minnesota, Minneapolis, MN (2016-Present); Interim Chair, Department of Chemistry, University of Minnesota, Minneapolis, MN (1967-1969); Professor, Department of Chemistry, University of Minnesota, Minneapolis, MN (1952-2016) **Career Related:** Director, National Science Foundation Research Experiences for Undergraduates (1959-1970, 1987-1993); Consultant, Petroleum Technology and Heterocyclic Chemistry, Sun Oil Co., Marcus Hook, PA (1958-1970) **Civic:** Judge, Local Elections, Prospect Park, Seward, NY (1990-2004); East River Gorge Citizens Advisory Committee (1990-1994); Organic Synthesis Inc. **Creative Works:** Editor-in-chief, "Organic Syntheses" (1988); Contributor, Chapter to Book, Articles to Professional Journals **Awards:** Charles E. Brown Faculty Teaching Award (2006); Best Instructor in Chemistry, Institute of Technology Student Board (1999); Minnesota Award, Minnesota Section, American Chemical Society (1997); Honoree, Wayland E. Nolan Symposium, University of Minnesota (1996); Distinguished Service Medal, Chapter of Sigma Xi, University of Minnesota (1994); Fellow, American Association for the Advancement of Science (1987); Institute of Technology Distinguished Teaching Award (1964) **Memberships:** Minnesota Section, American Chemical Society **Marquis Who's Who Honors:** Albert Nelson Marquis Lifetime Achievement Award; Marquis Who's Who Top Professional **Why did you become involved in your profession or industry:** Dr. Noland became involved in his profession because he grew up with a strong interest in science. His parents, who were zoologists, met in graduate school at Wisconsin, and he hoped to follow in the footsteps of his father, who was a noted professor at the University of Wisconsin. **Avocations:** Investments; Fishing

Judith Norback, PhD

Title: Academic Faculty & Director of Workplace & Academic Communication **Industry:** Education/Educational Services **Company Name:** H. Milton Stewart School of Industrial & Systems Engineering **Date of Birth:** 07/05/1953 **Place of Birth:** Rochester **State/Country of Origin:** NY/USA **Parents:** John Daley Shaul; Barbara (Bark) Shaul **Marital Status:** DIvorced **Children:** One Son **Education:** Doctor of Philosophy and Master of Arts, Princeton University (1979); Bachelor of Arts in Psychology and Philosophy, Cornell University, Magna Cum Laude (1975) **Career:** President, Director, Center for Skills Enhancement Inc., Princeton, NJ (1993-2001); Research Associate to Research Scientist, Educational Testing Service (1987-1993) **Civic:** Member, Church Choir, Encouragement Program, Peachtree Church, Atlanta, GA **Creative Works:** Author, "Oral Communication Excellence for Engineers and Scientists (2013); Author, "The Complete Guide to Computer Careers: (1987); Co-author or Author of Five Handbooks; Contributor or Co-contributor, 40 Research Articles in Professional Journals **Awards:** Best Paper Award, Industrial Engineering Division, American Society for Engineering Education (2003); Senior of the Year, Cornell University, Mortarboard Honorary Society **Memberships:** American Society for Engineering Education; Institute for Operations Research and Management Sciences; Institute of Electrical and Electronics Engineers Professional Communication Society; American Psychological Association; American Association for the Advancement of Science; MENSA; Association of Princeton Graduate Alumni; Cornell Alumni Association **Marquis Who's Who Honors:** Marquis Lifetime Achievement Award **To what do you attribute your success:** Dr. Norback attributes her success toward her persistence, consistency and compassion for people. **Why did you become involved in your profession or industry:** Dr. Norback initially became involved in her profession as an assistant teacher in high school, and greatly enjoyed delivering presentations on a variety of subjects. She decided to continue in this vein as she attended Georgia Tech.

Kayla Northcutt

Title: Teacher **Industry:** Education/Educational Services **Company Name:** Frenship Independent School District **Date of Birth:** 04/30/1994 **Place of Birth:** Carlsbad **State/Country of Origin:** NM/USA **Parents:** Cody Northcutt; Jacqueline Northcutt **Education:** MEd, Texas Tech University (2020); China Fellowship (2019); BS in Early Childhood Education and Teaching, Texas Tech University (2017); Australia Internship Teacher, Kindergarten/First Grade (2016) **Certifications:** Early Childhood Teacher, EC- 6th Grade, State of Texas; Educator- Type 4, Special Education; English as a Second Language **Career:** Frenship Independent School District (2017-Present); Second Grade Teacher (2020-2021); Pre-Kindergarten Teacher (2017-2020) **Creative Works:** Presenter, KDP National Conference, Kappa Delta Pi, International Honor Society in Education; Presenter, Texas Association of Literacy Education Conference; Collaboration Through Co-teaching **Awards:** Named to Kappa Delta Pi, International Honor Society in Education; Named to The Honor Society of Phi Kappa Phi; Named to Aspiring Administrators Leadership Academy; Named to Australia Internship Program; International Scholar, Laureate Program, Texas Education Policy Fellowship Program **Memberships:** Kappa Delta Pi, International Honor Society in Education; Golden Key International Honor Society; The Honor Society of Phi Kappa Phi; National Academy of Sciences **Marquis Who's Who Honors:** Who's Who's in America 73rd Edition;Top Featured Educator for Millennium Magazine **To what do you attribute your success:** Ms. Northcutt attributes her success to her mentors in the past and the present. They have helped shape her and her career. **Why did you become involved in your profession or industry:** Ms. Northcutt has a love for children and wants to be able to be an influence for them and an impact on their overall educational career. **Avocations:** Going to the beach for scuba diving **Thoughts on Life:** Ms. Northcutt's motto is, "Be kind and do your best every day. Education is such an important aspect of everyone's life that they will embark on, which makes a teachers job truly rewarding to be able to touch so many lives."

Justin Noseff

Title: President **Industry:** Business Management/Business Services **Company Name:** Divine Energy Services **Date of Birth:** 09/29/1983 **Place of Birth:** Hobbs **State/Country of Origin:** NM/USA **Children:** Finley; Blakely; Cage **Education:** Coursework, New Mexico Junior College **Career:** President, Divine Energy Services (2006-Present) **Marquis Who's Who Honors:** Marquis Who's Who Top Professional; Distinguished Humanitarian **To what do you attribute your success:** Mr. Noseff attributes his success to hard work. **Why did you become involved in your profession or industry:** Mr. Noseff's family consisted of many successful business moguls. Seeing the opportunity from a young age, he sought his own success immediately after graduating from high school.

Michelle LaVaughn Obama

Title: Former First Lady of the United States; Lawyer; University Administrator **Industry:** Government Administration/Government Relations/Government Services **Date of Birth:** 2/17/1964 **Place of Birth:** Chicago **State/Country of Origin:** IL/USA **Parents:** Fraser C. Robinson; Marian Lois (Shields) Robinson **Marital Status:** Married **Spouse Name:** Barack Hussein Obama Jr. (10/18/1992) **Children:** Malia Ann; Natasha ("Sasha") **Education:** JD, Harvard Law School (1988); BA in Sociology, Princeton University, Cum Laude (1985) **Career:** First Lady of the United States (2009-2017); Vice President, Community and External Affairs, University of Chicago Medical Center (2005-2008); Manager, Business Diversity Program, University of Chicago Medical Center (2005-2008); Executive Director, Community and External Affairs, University of Chicago Medical Center (2002-2005); Associate Dean of Students, Director of Community Service, The University of Chicago (1997-2005); Founding Executive Director, Public Allies - Chicago (1993-1996); Assistant to Mayor Richard M. Daley, Assistant Commissioner of Planning and Development, City of Chicago, IL (1991-1993); Associate Marketing and Intellectual Property, Sidley Austin LLP, Chicago, IL (1988-1991) **Career Related:** Honorary Chairwoman, President Barack Obama's Committee on Arts and Humanities (2009-Present); Board of Directors, Chicago Council on Global Affairs, TreeHouse Foods, Inc. (2005-2007) **Civic:** Honorary Board Chair, Girls Inc. (2010-Present); Board Member, Muntu Dance Theatre; Board Member, Facing History and Ourselves; Board Member, Otho S.A. Sprague Memorial Institute **Creative Works:** Author, "Becoming" (2018); Author, "American Grown: How the White House Kitchen Garden Inspires Families, Schools and Communities" (2012); Appearance, Documentary, "By the People: The Election of Barack Obama" (2009); **Awards:** Named One of the 100 Most Influential People in the World, TIME Magazine (2009, 2011, 2013); Named One of the 100 Most Powerful Women, Forbes Magazine (2009-2014); Named a Woman to Watch, Crain's Chicago Business (2008, 2009); Named One of the 100 Most Powerful Women in DC, Washingtonian Magazine (2009); Woman of the Year Award, Glamour Magazine (2009); Named One of the World's 25 Most Inspiring Women, Essence Magazine (2006) **Memberships:** Honorary Member, Alpha Kappa Alpha Sorority, Incorporated **Political Affiliations:** Democrat **Religion:** Protestant

Alexandria Ocasio-Cortez

Title: U.S. Representative from New York **Industry:** Government Administration/Government Relations/Government Services **Date of Birth:** 10/13/1989 **Place of Birth:** New York **State/Country of Origin:** NY/USA **Parents:** Sergio Ocasio; Blanca Ocasio-Cortez **Education:** BA in International Relations and Economics, Boston University College of Arts and Sciences, Cum Laude (2011); Intern, Foreign Affairs and Immigration Issues, U.S. Senator Ted Kennedy **Career:** Member, U.S. House of Representatives from New York's 14th Congressional District (2019-Present); Organizer, Bernie Sanders' Presidential Campaign (2016); Founder, Brook Avenue Press **Civic:** With, National Hispanic Institute **Awards:** Named Person of the Year, National Hispanic Institute (2017); John F. Lopez Fellowship **Political Affiliations:** Democrat **Religion:** Catholic

Mark O'Connell

Title: Auxiliary Bishop **Industry:** Religious **Company Name:** Archdiocese of Boston **Date of Birth:** 06/25/1964 **Place of Birth:** Toronto **State/Country of Origin:** Ontario/Canada **Parents:** Thomas F. O'Connell; Margaret M. (Delaney) O'Connell **Education:** Doctor of Canon Law, University della Santa Croce, Rome (2002); Divinity Degree, Priesthood, Saint John's Seminary, Boston, MA (1990); BA in English, Boston College (1986) **Career:** Auxiliary Bishop, Diocese of Boston (2016-Present); Priest, Archdiocese of Boston (1990-Present) **Civic:** Senior Consultant, Canon Law Society of America (2009-2012) **Bar Admissions:** Judicial Vicor **To what do you attribute your success:** Bishop O'Connell attributes his success to "We have found the Messiah..." **Why did you become involved in your profession or industry:** Bishop O'Connell comes from a religious family. His uncle was a priest, his aunt was a nun, along with other family members who were n the clergy. He made the decision before age 18 that he would join the priesthood and never looked back.

M. Kent Olsen, Esq.

Title: Lawyer, Educator **Industry:** Law and Legal Services **Company Name:** Law Office of M. Kent Olsen **Date of Birth:** 03/10/1948 **Place of Birth:** Denver **State/Country of Origin:** CO/USA **Parents:** Marvin Olsen; F. Winona (Wilker) Olsen **Marital Status:** Married **Spouse Name:** Dr. Shauna L. Casement (07/08/2000) **Children:** Kristofer Anders Olsen; Alexander Lee Olsen; Nikolaus Alrik Olsen; Amanda Elizabeth Hill **Education:** JD, University of Denver(1975); BS, Colorado State University, Fort Collins, CO (1970) **Career:** Lawyer, Law Offices of M. Kent Olsen (2017-Present); Partner, Olsen Traeger & Ursery, LLP (2001-2016); Private Practice, Denver, CO (1995-2001); Partner, Haines & Olsen, Professional Corporation, Denver, CO (1989-1995); Referee, Denver Probate Court, Denver, CO (1983-1989); Associate, William E. Myrick, Professional Corporation, Denver, CO (1982-1983); Associate, Buchanan, Thomas and Johnson, Lakewood, CO (1981-1982); Associate Partner, Johnson & McLachlan, Lamar, CO (1975-1980); Law Clerk, Denver Probate Court (1973-1975) **Career Related:** Advisory Board, Elder Law Institute (1994-2010); Denver Career College (1993-2004) **Civic:** President, Colorado Fund for People with Disabilities (2010-Present); Board of Directors, The Arc of Colorado (2004-Present); Member, Colorado Fund for People with Disabilities (1994-Present) **Creative Works:** Author, Manual, "Instruction at the Denver College, for Trusts & Estates" (1993-2004) **Awards:** Colorado Super Lawyers (2006-2019); Elder Law Pioneers Award, Colorado Gerontological Society (2015); Advanced Denver Schenkein Award (2012); Five Star Wealth Manager, ColoradoBiz Magazine (2011-2012); President's Award, The Arc of Colorado (1998, 2002) **Memberships:** Denver Estate Planning Council (1993); Past Chair, Probate Section, American Bar Association (1988); First Judicial District Bar Association (1980); Colorado Bar Association (1975); Denver Bar Association (1975); American Bar Association (1975); Colorado Association of Homes and Services for the Aging **Bar Admissions:** The United States District Court District of Colorado (1982); United States Tax Court (1982); Colorado Bar Association (1975) **Marquis Who's Who Honors:** Albert Nelson Marquis Lifetime Achievement Award **Why did you become involved in your profession or industry:** Mr. Olsen became involved in his profession because he wanted to make a difference in society. **Avocations:** Running; Skiing; Racquetball; Art; Hiking; Traveling

Thomas Opre

Title: President, Chief Executive Officer (Retired) **Industry:** Writing and Editing **Company Name:** TOP Safaris, Inc. **Date of Birth:** 11/06/1943 **Place of Birth:** Evansville **State/Country of Origin:** IN/USA **Parents:** William Jennings Opre; Ruth (Strouss) Opre **Children:** Thomas Andrew; William Hartley **Education:** AB in Journalism, Indiana University (1965) **Career:** President, Tom Opre Productions (1967-2004); Editor-at-Large, Sports Vehicles Editor, Outdoor Life Magazine (1981-1993); Outdoor Editor, Detroit Free Press (1966-1991); Field Editor, Midwest Division, Field and Stream Magazine (1971-1981); Editorial Director, Great Lakes Sportsman Magazine (1972-1975); Writer, Sports and Outdoors, Herald & Review (1965-1966); Retired Editor, Film Company Executive **Career Related:** President, Chief Executive Officer, TOP Safaris, Inc. (1988-2003) **Civic:** Chairman, Livingston County Planning Commission **Creative Works:** Author, Numerous Articles, Outdoor and Travel Magazines **Awards:** Conservation Communicator of the Year (1985); World Wildlife Foundation Award (1981); Environmental Award, Environmental Protection Association (1977); National Writer's Award, Safari Club International (1977); Deep Woods Writing Award Outdoor Writers Association of America (1977); Conservation Service Award, Ducks Unlimited (1977); Teddy Award, International Outdoor Travel Film Festival (1973); James Henshall Award, American Fish Tackle Manufacturers Association (1969); Inductee, International Fishing Hall of Fame (1968) **Memberships:** Past Director, President, Vice President, Chairman of the Board, Outdoor Writers Association of America; Past Director, Chairman of the Board, President, Vice President, Association of Great Lakes Outdoor Writers; Vice President, President, Chairman of the Board of Directors, Michigan Outdoor Writers Association; Alpha Tau Omega **Marquis Who's Who Honors:** Albert Nelson Marquis Lifetime Achievement Award; Marquis Who's Who Top Professional **Why did you become involved in your profession or industry:** Though Mr. Opre never intended to become a writer, he found the field after exploring several others. In college, he initially wanted to become a lawyer but felt it would take too long to acquire the necessary degrees. He then spent some time in Florida as a fishing guide before deciding to enroll in journalism classes, which led to his career in writing. **Avocations:** Hunting; Fishing

Fredy Oyuela

Title: Installation Manager **Industry:** Information Technology and Services **Company Name:** Northland Controls Systems **Date of Birth:** 08/22/1967 **Place of Birth:** Tegucigalpa **State/Country of Origin:** Honduras **Parents:** Gregario Antonio Oyuela Aguilar; Gloria Jerrardina Oveido Pas **Marital Status:** Married **Spouse Name:** Sonia Aramubro Oyuela (04/19/1965) **Children:** Tracey Viviana Oyuela; Carlos Oyuela Moda **Education:** Construction Management and Inspection, San Jose State University; Computer Electronics Technology, Mission Community College **Certifications:** Electronic Security Networking Certification, BICSI Education; C-CURE 9000 Systems Installer, American Dynamics; ONSSI Certified, On-Net Surveillance Systems; Lenel Onguard, Lenel Fire and Security Company; Win-Pak Pro Certification, Northern Computers; Fire Alarm Systems 1, National Institute for Certification in Engineering Technologies **Career:** Installation Manager, Northland Control Systems (2015-2019); Field Superintend, RFI Communications and Security Systems (1992-2015) **Civic:** Volunteer, Local Church; President, Mano a Mano **Military Service:** Honduras Air Force (1984-1988); Defense Language Institute **Memberships:** Nesdu Union National; Communication Workers of America (CWA); Electrical Brotherhood of Electrical Workers, IBW Local 332 **Marquis Who's Who Honors:** Marquis Who's Who Top Professional **To what do you attribute your success:** Coming from a third-world country, Mr. Oyuela always wanted to do something meaningful with his life. The United States has provided that opportunity for him. He has a house, other properties, a retirement plan and a beautiful family. Both of his children are college graduates as well. He attributes his success to his desire to be the best at what he does and to live the American dream. **Why did you become involved in your profession or industry:** Mr. Oyuela is a native of Honduras. His father, Gregorio Antonio Oyuela, passed when he was only 12 years old. He was his inspiration for choosing his career path. While living in Honduras, Mr. Oyuela joined the Air Force, which worked with the United States Military, and received his training in San Antonio, Texas. Mr. Oyuela considers his mission in his work, in his own words, to be "to prevent bad things from happening to good people." He has always been interested in increasing security and preventing theft or other issues. **Avocations:** Watching sports; Soccer connoisseur; Hiking; Eating good food **Religion:** Catholic **Thoughts on Life:** "You must keep working hard... Try to do your best and good things will happen to you..."

J.D. Packwood Jr., JD, MA

Title: Owner, Solo Practitioner **Industry:** Law and Legal Services **Company Name:** J. D. Packwood, Jr., Attorney-At-Law **Marital Status:** Married **Spouse Name:** Annette **Education:** MA in Biblical Studies, Conservative Theological University (2018); JD, School of Law, Howard University (1969); BA in Government, Louisiana State University (1966) **Certifications:** Ordained Minister **Career:** Owner, J. D. Packwood, Jr., Attorney-At-Law (2004-Present); Attorney, Director, Supervisor, U.S. Equal Employment Opportunity Commission (1970-2002) **Civic:** Volunteer; Community Speaker; Mentor **Creative Works:** Author, Poetry Book (1997); Author, Poem, "Born to Write" (1996) **Awards:** Top 100 for State of Florida, National Black Lawyers (2018-Present) **Bar Admissions:** Nebraska State Bar Association (1972); The Florida Bar; The Virginia Bar Association; The District of Columbia Bar **Marquis Who's Who Honors:** Marquis Who's Who Top Professional **To what do you attribute your success:** Mr. Packwood attributes his success to a strong faith in God, which was instilled in him by his mother, a single parent. **Why did you become involved in your profession or industry:** Mr. Packwood became involved in his profession because of the racial disparities in the law. When he was 11, he read bout Emmett Till, a 14-year-old Black kid from Chicago who was beaten, shot and killed for allegedly flirting with a white woman at a grocery store. He recalls crying and being angry about the injustice, which encouraged him to pursue a career in law. **Avocations:** Writing; Teaching Sunday school

David R. Panza, CEBS, RHU

Title: AVP, Underwriting Consultant **Industry:** Insurance **Company Name:** Alliant Insurance Services **Education:** Bachelor of Arts in Mathematics, Pace University (1980) **Certifications:** Registered Health Underwriter **Career:** Assistant Vice President, Underwriting Consultant, Alliant Insurance Services (2014-Present); Account Manager, Alliant Insurance Services (1985-2014) **Civic:** President, Staten Island Athletic Club **Creative Works:** Speaker, Conferences and Meetings **Awards:** Lou Marli Lifetime Service Award, Staten Island Athletic Club (2010); Fellow, International Society of Certified Employee Benefit Specialists **Marquis Who's Who Honors:** Marquis Who's Who Top Professional **To what do you attribute your success:** Mr. Panza attributes his success on his propensity for hard work and dedication. He takes his work and clients seriously. **Why did you become involved in your profession or industry:** Mr. Panza became involved in his profession due to his strength in mathematics. Though he originally wished to become an actuary, he transitioned toward insurance. **Thoughts on Life:** Work hard and always be honest with what you do.

Arva Moore Parks

Title: President; Historian; Author **Company Name:** Arva Parks & Company **Date of Birth:** 01/19/1939 **Place of Birth:** Miami **State/Country of Origin:** FL/USA **Parents:** Jack Moore; Anne (Parker) Moore **Marital Status:** Widowed **Spouse Name:** Robert Howard McCabe (06/1992, Deceased 01/2015); Robert Lyle Parks (08/1959, Divorced 1986) **Children:** Jacqueline Carey; Robert Downing; Gregory Moore **Education:** Honorary LLD, Barry University (1996); MA in History, University of Miami (1971); BA, University of Florida (1960); Coursework, Florida State University (1956-1958) **Career:** President, Arva Parks & Company, Miami, FL (1986-2020); Freelance Research Historian, Miami, FL (1970-2020); Acting Director, Chief Curator, Coral Gables Museum (2011-2012); Adjunct Professor, University of Miami (1986-1987); Consultant (1966-1970); Teacher, Everglades School for Girls (Now Ransom Everglades School), Miami, FL (1965-1966); Graduate Assistant, University of Miami (1964-1965); Teacher, Miami Edison Senior High School (1963-1964); Teacher, Rollingcrest Junior High School, West Hyattsville, MD (1960-1963) **Career Related:** President, Centennial Press (1991-2020) **Civic:** Board Member, Dade Heritage Trust (2016-Present); Board Member, Historic St. Augustine, University of Florida (2013-2020); Trustee, University of Miami (1994-2020); Board of Directors, Orange Bowl Committee (1989-2020); Member, National Trust for Historic Preservation, Preservation Pennsylvania (2013); Board Member, Coral Gables Museum Corp. (2005-2017); Board Member, Bok Sanctuary (Now Bok Tower Gardens) (2005-2010); Member, Numerous Committees, Organizations **Creative Works:** Co-author, "George Merrick: Son of the South Wind; Visionary Creator of Coral Gables" (2015); Co-author, "Miami - A Sense of Place" (2014); Co-author, "Legendary Locals" (2013); Author, "Harry Truman and the Little White House in Key West" (2012); Co-author, "Coconut Grove" (2010); Author, "Miami the Magic City," Revised Edition (2008); Film Writer; Author, Books; Editor, Journals **Awards:** Named to Alumni Hall of Fame, Miami-Dade County Public Schools (2017); Florida Book Award, Nonfiction (2015); Distinguished Florida Author Award, Florida House (2014); Finer Womanhood Community Fellowship Award, Zeta Phi Beta Sorority, Inc. (2011) **Memberships:** Board of Directors, Florida Chapter, International Women's Forum (2005-2009); President, Florida Chapter, International Women's Forum (2003-2005); Foundation Board Member, International Women's Forum (2001-2005); The Association Junior Leagues International; Zeta Phi Beta Sorority, Inc. **Marquis Who's Who Honors:** Albert Nelson Marquis Lifetime Achievement Award; Marquis Who's Who Humanitarian Award **Avocations:** Photography **Political Affiliations:** Democrat **Religion:** Methodist

William A. Perry III

Title: Health Care Sales Executive **Industry:** Health, Wellness and Fitness **Company Name:** PDI Healthcare **Education:** MBA, Texas Woman's University, Denton, TX, Magna Cum Laude (2007); BBA, Northeastern State University, Tulsa, OK, Cum Laude (2003) **Career:** Director of Sales, Government Liaison, Interim Vice President, Sales, PDI Healthcare (2015-Present); District Sales Manager, Danaher (2011-2015); Regional Sales Manager, Biomedical Systems (2009-2011); Access Division Territory Manager, AngioDynamics (2008-2009); Sales Representative IV (2004-2008) **Civic:** Volunteer, Church Organizations **Military Service:** U.S. Marine Corps (1996-2001) **Awards:** Seven-Time Award, Recipient at Director Level; Multiple Military Leadership Awards **Memberships:** Texas Society of Infection Control Practitioners (2011); Association for Professionals in Infection Prevention & Epidemiology (Now Association for Professionals in Infection Control and Epidemiology (APIC)) (2011); National Society of High School Scholars (2007); National Rifle Association (2004); Marine Corps Association & Foundation (2001) **Marquis Who's Who Honors:** Marquis Who's Who Top Professional **To what do you attribute your success:** Mr. Perry attributes his success to having people who fertilized the idea of being an entrepreneur. For example, his uncle knew he was getting in trouble in school for selling things, so he would give him ideas to sell things outside of school. **Why did you become involved in your profession or industry:** Mr. Perry became involved in his profession because he always knew he had the ability to sell. In fact, he often got in trouble in school for selling things. He had the entrepreneurial spirit as a kid and he applied that to his future endeavors. **Thoughts on Life:** Mr. Perry's motto is, "Control your controllable."

Delaney Philbrick

Title: Real Estate Agent **Industry:** Real Estate **Company Name:** Philbrick's of Rye **Parents:** Dan Philbrick **Education:** High School Diploma, Forth Smith High School (2017) **Certifications:** Certified Real Estate Agent **Career:** Real Estate Agent, Philbrick's of Rye (2017-Present); Property Manager, Philbrick's by the Sea (2015-Present) **Awards:** Named Real Estate Newsmaker of the Year, Trendsetter Category (2019) **Memberships:** Realtor Society (National Association of Realtors); East Coast Board of Realtors **To what do you attribute your success:** Ms. Philbrick attributes her success to the support she received. Her father always knew the answer to her questions. **Why did you become involved in your profession or industry:** Ms. Philbrick's father always had rental properties. When he bought Philbrick's by the Sea, it used to be called Crown Colony Cottages. She started working for him and rebuilt them. They redid all of the units and changed the name. She started by cleaning the cottages and going to the stores for supplies. She then started working there full-time, taking reservations, checking guests in, and doing floor plans. Until she started to run the office, she ran the books and wrote out checks for employees. Ms. Philbrick knew that she always wanted to do real estate since third grade. Her father did real estate and her favorite game was Monopoly. Her nanny at the time, named Missy, taught her and her brother how to play. Also, when she was younger, she would skip school and go to real estate showings/closing with her father. She graduated high school six months early and received her real estate license at age 18. From that point, she went into real estate with her father. Her dad was her broker. **Thoughts on Life:** Philbrick's by the Sea is ocean front property in Rye, New Hampshire. There are 17 units where tourists rent out cottages weekly. Ms. Philbrick's motto is, "If you find a job that you love, you never work a day in your life."

Laramie Phillips

Title: IT Manager **Industry:** Government Administration/Government Relations/Government Services **Company Name:** FEMA **Date of Birth:** 09/26/1991 **Place of Birth:** Orange **State/Country of Origin:** TX/USA **Parents:** Larry; Vicki **Education:** MS in Management Information Systems, Strayer University (2020); BS in Computer Science Information Assurance, Sam Houston State University (2016) **Career:** IT Manager Candidate, FEMA (2019-Present); IT Specialist, FEMA (2017-Present); Application Specialist, FEMA (2017); Teacher Parent, Bayes Achievement Center (2016-2017); Distributor, AdvoCare (2015-2017); Supervisor, Sam's Club (2014); Night Auditor, Assistant Manager, Comfort Suites Hotel (2012-2014) **Civic:** Member, New Perspective Development (2017-Present); Treasure/Active Member, The Exceptional Men of The Talented Tenth (2011-2015); Community Service Chair, Men of Honor (2012-2013); Member, InfraGard **Awards:** Golden Key International Honour Society **Memberships:** Black Alumni Association of Sam Houston State University **To what do you attribute your success:** Mr. Phillips attributes his success to his family. His family has been the biggest drive, having come from a small town. **Why did you become involved in your profession or industry:** Mr. Phillips became involved in his profession because he had interest in building a network/computer in high school. **Avocations:** Music; Cooking; Exercising; Concerts; Sports (football/Atlanta Falcons)

Joaquin Raphael Phoenix

Title: Actor **Date of Birth:** 10/28/1974 **Place of Birth:** San Juan **State/Country of Origin:** Puerto Rico **Parents:** John Bottom; Arlyn Dunetz **Marital Status:** Engaged **Spouse Name:** Rooney Mara (2019) **Civic:** Social Activist, Numerous Charities and Humanitarian Organizations; Animal Rights Advocate; Member, Board of Directors, The Lunchbox Fund; Member, In Defense of Animals; Member, PETA **Creative Works:** Actor, "C'mon C'mon" (2020); Executive Producer, Documentary, "Gunda" (2020); Actor, Short Film, "Guardians of Life" (2020); Actor, "Joker" (2019); Executive Producer, Documentary, "The Animal People" (2019); Actor, Short Film, "Lou" (2018); Actor, "The Sisters Brothers" (2018); Actor, "Mary Magdalene" (2018); Actor, "Don't Worry, He Won't Get Far on Foot" (2018); Actor, "You Were Never Really Here" (2017); Executive Producer, Documentary, "What the Health" (2017); Executive Producer, Documentary, "What the Health" (2017); Executive Producer, Short Film, "Across My Land" (2017); Associate Producer, Documentary, "CAMP: The Documentary" (2016); Actor, "Irrational Man" (2015); Narrator, Documentary, "Unity" (2015); Executive Producer, Documentary, "I Am Dying" (2015); Actor, "Inherent Vice" (2014) **Awards:** Oscar for Best Performance by an Actor in a Leading Role, "Joker," Academy Awards (2020); Best Performance by an Actor in a Motion Picture - Drama, "Joker," Golden Globes (2020); BAFTA Film Award for Best Leading Actor, "Joker," BAFTA Awards (2020); Critics Choice Award for Best Actor, "Joker," Broadcast Film Critics Association Awards (2020); Best Actor - International Competition, "Joker," CinEuphoria Awards (2020); Best Actor, "Joker," Denver Film Critics Society (2020); Best Foreign Actor, "Joker," Días de Cine Awards (2020); Gold Derby Award for Lead Actor, "Joker" (2020); Best Actor, "Joker," Hawaii Film Critics Society (2020); Best Actor, "Joker," Hollywood Critics Association (2020); Best Actor, "Joker," Iowa Film Critics Awards (2020); Best Performance by an Actor in a Leading Role, "Joker," Latino Entertainment Journalists Association Film Awards (2020); Actor of the Year, "Joker," London Critics Circle Film Awards (2020); Best Actor, "Joker," North Dakota Film Society (2020); Chairman's Award, "Joker," Palm Springs International Film Festival (2020); Outstanding Performance by a Male Actor in a Leading Role, "Joker," Screen Actors Guild Awards (2020); Best Lead Performer in a Movie, "Joker," IGN Summer Movie Awards (2019); Capri Actor Award, "Joker," Capri, Hollywood (2019); Best Actor of the Year, "Joker," Golden Schmoes Awards (2019); Best Actor, "Joker," New York Film Critics, Online (2019)

Bruce Piasecki

Title: President, Founder **Industry:** Consulting **Company Name:** AHC Group Inc. **Date of Birth:** 02/01/1955 **Spouse Name:** Andrea Masters **Education:** Doctor of Philosophy in American Studies and Cultural History, Cornell University (1981); Bachelor of Arts in American Studies and American Literature, Cornell University (1976) **Career:** President, Founder, American Hazard Control Group Inc. (1981-Present) **Career Related:** Chairperson, Working Group on Reinventing EPA, National Environmental Policy Institute, Washington, DC (1994-Present); Member, National Advisory Council, Environmental Protection Agency, Washington, DC (1992-Present); Director, Master of Science Program in Environmental Management and Policy, Rensselaer Polytechnic Institute; Professor of School Management, Rensselaer Polytechnic Institute; Instructor, Cornell University, Clarkson University and Rensselaer Polytechnic Institute **Civic:** Vice Chairperson, Solid Waste Authority; Board Member, Osiris Labs; Board Member, Company in Waste Management **Creative Works:** Editor-in-Chief, Corporate Environmental Strategy (1993-Present); Author, "Doing More with Teams" (2013); Author, "Doing More with Less" (2012); Author, "The Surprising Solution: Creating Possibility in a Swift and Severe World" (2009); Author, "World Inc." (2007); Author, "Environmental Management and Business Strategy: Leadership Skills for the 21st Century" (1998); Author, "Corporate Environmental Strategy: The Avalanche of Change Since Bhopal" (1995); Author, "In Search of Environmental Excellence: Moving Beyond Blame" (1990); Author, "Americas Future in Toxic Waste Management" (1988); Author, "Beyond Dumping" (1984); Editor-in-Chief, New World Companies: The Future of Capitalism, and Missing Persons **Awards:** Grantee, Numerous Organizations, Including German Marshall Fund and Joyce Foundation **Memberships:** Member, National Press Club **Marquis Who's Who Honors:** Marquis Who's Who Top Professional **To what do you attribute your success:** Mr. Piasecki credits his success on his determination, intelligence and the influence of his mother. **Why did you become involved in your profession or industry:** Mr. Piasecki became involved in his profession due to the influence of several of his mentors, including A. R. Ammons and M.H. Abrams at Cornell University. **Avocations:** Volunteer, Saratoga YMCA **Political Affiliations:** Democrat **Religion:** Catholic

Thomas H. Pollihan

Title: Corporate Lawyer **Industry:** Law and Legal Services **Date of Birth:** 11/15/1949 **Place of Birth:** St. Louis **State/Country of Origin:** MO/USA **Parents:** C.H. Pollihan Jr.; Patricia Ann (O'Brien) Pollihan **Marital Status:** Married **Spouse Name:** Donna M. Bickhaus (08/25/1973) **Children:** Emily Christine Pollihan Givens **Education:** Executive Masters in International Business, Saint Louis University (1992); JD, University of Notre Dame (1975); BA in Sociology, Quincy University (1972) **Career:** Executive Vice President, General Counsel and Secretary, Kellwood Company (Now Kellwood Apparel), St. Louis, MO (2005-2008); Senior Vice President, Kellwood Company (Now Kellwood Apparel) (2002-2005); Vice President, Kellwood Company (Now Kellwood Apparel) (1993-2002); Assistant General Counsel, Kellwood Company (Now Kellwood Apparel) (1982-1989); From Associate to Partner, Greenfield, Davidson, Mandelstamm & Voorhees, St. Louis, MO (1976-1982); Judicial Law Clerk to Judge Joseph Stewart, Missouri Court of Appeals, St. Louis, MO (1975-1976) **Career Related:** Adjunct Professor, Saint Louis University Cook School of Business (Now Richard A. Chaifetz School of Business) (2001-2004) **Civic:** With, Quincy University Foundation (1993-1994, 1997-Present); Trustee, Quincy University, IL (1987-1993, 1997-2004, 2009-2016); Board President, Lake St. Louis Community Association (2011-2014); Director, Secretary, New Piasa Chautauqua, IL (1996-1997); President, Alumni Board, Quincy University (1986-1987); Past Board Member, Boys Hope Girls Hope, St. Louis; Past Board Member, World Affairs Council of St. Louis; Current Member, Ambassadors of Lake St. Louis **Awards:** Inductee, St. Louis Soccer Hall of Fame (2014); Named Quincy University Alumnus of the Year (1997); Outstanding Alumni Award IIB, Saint Louis University (1997); Inductee, Quincy University Sports Hall of Fame (1988) **Memberships:** The Bar Association of Metropolitan St. Louis (BAMSL) **Bar Admissions:** Illinois (1976); Missouri (1975) **Marquis Who's Who Honors:** Albert Nelson Marquis Lifetime Achievement Award **Why did you become involved in your profession or industry:** Mr. Pollihan did very well on the law school entrance exam and received several law school scholarships, including one to Notre Dame, where he studied in London his second year. **Avocations:** Soccer; Bicycling **Political Affiliations:** Republican **Religion:** Roman Catholic

Melissa Powell

Title: President, Chief Operating Officer **Industry:** Medicine & Health Care **Company Name:** The Allure Group **Parents:** Sylvester; Lois **Marital Status:** Married **Spouse Name:** Matt **Children:** Rebecca; Lexi **Education:** BS in Reaction and Leisure, York College of Pennsylvania (1998) **Certifications:** Certified, Nursing Home Administrator **Career:** President, Chief Operating Officer, The Allure Group (2012-Present); Vice President of Operations, AristaCare Health Services (2006-2011) **Civic:** Volunteer, St. Rayfield Baptist Church **Memberships:** American Health Care Association; LTC 100, Lincoln Healthcare Leadership; New York State Housing Finance Agency **To what do you attribute your success:** Mrs. Powell attributes her success to living by the golden rule; treat others as you wish to be treated. It is through this philosophy that Mrs. Powell continues to bring out the very best in her employees, which has enabled her company and its work environment to thrive. **Why did you become involved in your profession or industry:** Mrs. Powell's involvement in long-term care began as many others do, through a deep personal connection brought about by a loved one's experience. At a young age, Mrs. Powell's grandmother became a resident of a local nursing home, where she recalls being very comfortable in an environment that many of her peers seemed to shy away from. Her comfort level was so much so that she began volunteering there, as both a way to see her grandmother, as well as pursue her burning interest in helping others. In typical Mrs. Powell fashion, she soon became a resident of the resident council and that is where she truly realized that this was a space that she wanted to dedicate her professional life to. **Religion:** Catholic **Thoughts on Life:** Mrs. Powell truly believes that you get back what you put out.

Fred Titus Pregger, EdD

Title: Professor Emeritus **Industry:** Education/Educational Services **Company Name:** College of New Jersey **Date of Birth:** 5/14/1924 **Place of Birth:** Paterson **State/Country of Origin:** NJ/USA **Parents:** Herman Pregger; Lena Emma (Schwaeble) Pregger **Marital Status:** Widowed **Spouse Name:** Betty Mayhew (4/18/1953, Deceased 2007) **Children:** Brian H.; Bruce A. (Deceased 2017) **Education:** EdD, Columbia University (1956); MA, Montclair State University, New Jersey (1950); BA, Montclair State University, New Jersey (1948) **Certifications:** Certified 5-12 Science Teacher, New Jersey **Career:** Consultant, Science Education (1991-Present); Professor Emeritus, Trenton State College (Now The College of New Jersey), New Jersey (1989-Present); Lecturer, Astronomy, Georgian Court College, Lakewood, NJ (1988-Present); Professor, Physics, Trenton State College (Now The College of New Jersey), New Jersey (1962-1988); Chairman, Physics Department, Trenton State College (Now The College of New Jersey), New Jersey (1968-1980); Associate Professor, Trenton State College (Now The College of New Jersey), New Jersey (1958-1962); Assistant Professor of Science, Trenton State College (Now The College of New Jersey), New Jersey (1955-1958); Teacher, Physics, West Orange High School, New Jersey (1952-1955); Teacher, Science, Wayne Junior-Senior High School, New Jersey (1948-1952) **Career Related:** Education Committee, Public Service Electric and Gas Company, Newark, NJ (1982-Present); Research Advisory Council (RAC) (1988-1991) **Civic:** Radiation Coordinator, Mercer County CD, Trenton, NJ (1957-1964) **Military Service:** Corporal, Radio Instructor, U.S. Army Air Force, World War II (1944-1946); U.S. Army Air Force, World War II (1943-1946) **Creative Works:** Contributor, Articles, Professional Journals **Awards:** Plaque, American Association of Physics Teachers (2002); Award, Public Service Electric and Gas Company, Jersey Central Power & Light Company (1981-1989); Grantee, National Science Foundation (1969-1980) **Memberships:** Executive Board, New Jersey Section, American Association of Physics Teachers (1974-Present); President, New Jersey Section, American Association of Physics Teachers (1975-1977); National Science Teachers Association; New Jersey Science Teachers Association; Trenton Torch Club; Masons **Marquis Who's Who Honors:** Albert Nelson Marquis Lifetime Achievement Award **Avocations:** Model railroading; Train travel; Photography; Antiques; Railfan **Religion:** Presbyterian

August B. Pust, PhD

Title: Multicultural and International Relations Specialist (Retired); Artist **Industry:** Government Administration/Government Relations/Government Services **Date of Birth:** 02/22/1938 **Place of Birth:** Ljubljana, Slovenia **State/Country of Origin:** Slovenia **Parents:** Franz Pust; Angela Terskan-Pust **Marital Status:** Married **Spouse Name:** Gloria Pust **Children:** Adriana A. Pust **Education:** Dr. Honoris Causa, Valahia University of Tãrgovi?te, Romania (1999); International Fellow, International Leadership Development Institute, Colorado College (1990); Diploma, Commercial Art, Cooper School of Art, (1961); Architectural Design, Ljubljana Technical School, Slovenia (1955-1957) **Career:** Director, Multicultural Affairs & International Relations, State of Ohio (1999-2002); Special Assistant to the Governor of Ohio (1991-1999); Project Director of Ethnic Affairs & International Relations, Executive Assistant to the Mayor, Cleveland, OH (1982-1991); Office of Community & Economic Development, Cleveland, OH (1974-1985); Supervisor, Premier Industrial, Cleveland, OH (1970-1974); Art Director, Penton Pub. Co., Cleveland, OH (1964-1970) **Civic:** US Commission for the Preservation of American Heritage Abroad (2001-2005); Ohio Delegate, Republican National Convention, New York (2004); International Children's Games, Cleveland, OH (2004); Ohio Bicentennial Commission, Columbus, OH (1997-1998); Greater Cleveland Ethnographic Museum (1974-1976) **Creative Works:** Sel. Participant, International Fine Arts Colonies in Hungarian/Italian/Slovenian Region (2003, 2010); Plaque, Commemorative Ellis Island Poster, "Our American Mosaic" (2008); Group Shows, Slovenia (1985); Published Postcard Portfolio, "I Remember Slovenia" (1974); Numerous Exhibits, Cleveland, OH **Awards:** Honorary Medal for Liberty and Independence of Slovenia (2010); Inductee, Cleveland International Hall of Fame (2010); Ellis Island Medal of Honor (2008); Slovenian Man of the Year (2008); Citizen Diplomat, National Council for International Visitors (2002); DSM, Ohio National Guard (1996); Martin Luther King Award (1991); Key of the City of Cleveland (1989, 1991); Vitez-Hungarian Knightly Order (1990); Honorary Mayor, Cleveland, OH (1986) **Memberships:** Ohio Refugee & Immigrant Council (1995-Present); International Visitors Council, Ohio (1991-Present); UNA-USA, Col./New York (1992); All-Nations Festival Foundation (1985-1989); American Nationalities Movement, Cleveland, OH (1974-1976); Federation of Asian Indian Association of Central Ohio **Marquis Who's Who Honors:** Albert Nelson Marquis Lifetime Achievement Award

David Racich

Title: President, Chief Executive Officer **Industry:** Financial Services **Company Name:** Brokers Alliance **Education:** BS in Network and Global Communication Management, DeVry University (2003); BS in Business Management, Entrepreneurship and Electrical Engineering, Arizona State University (2001) **Career:** President, Chief Executive Officer, Life's Best Insurances, Fountain Hills, AZ (2015-Present); Founder, BDR Holding Group (2012-Present); Founder, Emerson Art Gallery (2012-Present); Founder, Chief Executive Officer, Integrated IO (2010-Present); President, Chief Executive Officer, Brokers Alliance (1999-Present); Founder, Outlook Life (2002-2014); Software Developer, Project Manager, Sourcing Analyst, BimSym eBusiness Solutions (2005-2008) **Civic:** Sponsor, Multiple Organizations **Awards:** Listee, Most Admired Leaders, Phoenix Business Journal; Listee, Best Small Companies to Work for in Arizona, Brokers Alliance **Memberships:** Acrylic Financial **Why did you become involved in your profession or industry:** Mr. Racich became involved in his profession because of his early experiences in the field. When he was 19 years old, he started his own company and built two custom servers for a local company and taught himself coding. During the rise of online marketing, he taught himself once more. Upon his father falling ill, he further fostered his businesses in order to ensure a lasting legacy for his family.

Bernard T. Reed

Title: President **Industry:** Manufacturing **Company Name:** Reeds Metals, LLC **Career:** President, Owner, Reeds Metals, LLC (1998-Present) **Civic:** Donor, Free Roof to a Person in Need the Month before Christmas **Awards:** Top CEOs of 2016 Award (2016); Top 50 CEOs of Mississippi **To what do you attribute your success:** Mr. Reed likes to listen to audible books, he really enjoys motivation books. Especially, Think and Grow Rich by Napoleon Hill. He believes that these books helped him and sharpened him. **Why did you become involved in your profession or industry:** Mr. Reed grew up in a family that moved about every six months. He moved out around 20 years old. He just wanted to settle down and do something on his own. He learned a lot of different things and realized that hard work pays off.

Emily Ann Reed

Title: Criminal Justice Analyst, Systems and Database Administrator, Adjunct Professor, Photographer, Artist **Industry:** Other **Date of Birth:** 09/05/1941 **Place of Birth:** South Bend **State/Country of Origin:** IN/USA **Parents:** Richard Edward; Leona Marie (Kochanowski) Fabrycki **Marital Status:** Married **Spouse Name:** Thomas James Reed (12/29/1962) **Children:** Valerie Romer **Education:** PhD, University of Massachusetts (1982); MPA, University of Hartford (1978); BA in Political Science, Philosophy and French, Marquette University (1963); Coursework, St. Mary's College **Career:** Adjunct Professor of Criminal Justice, University of Delaware (1994-2001); Management Analyst, Criminal Justice Council, State of Delaware (1985-1995); Teacher, La Salle University (1989); Management Analyst, Division of Corporations, State of Delaware (1983-1984); Assistant Professor, Ursinus College (1982-1983); Lecturer, University of Saint Joseph (1978-1981); Instructor, Western New England University (1979); Assistant Planner, Enfield, CT (1979); Professor, Osher Lifelong Learning Institute, University of Delaware **Creative Works:** Multimedia Artist Working in Watercolors, Oils, Pastels and Photography (2003-Present); Artist, "Rehoboth Bay 4th" (2018); Artist, "Cape Henlopen" (2017); Artist, "African American Medal of Honor Winners Memorial" (2016); Artist, "Great Blue Heron in Winter" (2014); Artist, "Delaware Breakwater East End Lighthouse, Cape Henlopen" (2013); Artist, "Cardinal Brothers" (2012); Artist, "Walker's Mill" (2011); Artist, "Urn and Waterlilies at Gilbralter Garden" (2010); Artist, "Dewey Beach Sunset" (2009); Author, "UD Right to Take Drinking Seriously," Sunday News Journal (1996) **Memberships:** APSA; The American Society for Public Administration; Delaware Association for Public Administration; Justice Research and Statistics Association; Newark Arts Alliance; Gibby Center for the Arts, The Everett Theatre, Inc. **Marquis Who's Who Honors:** Albert Nelson Marquis Lifetime Achievement Award; Marquis Who's Who Top Professional **Why did you become involved in your profession or industry:** Dr. Reed became involved in her profession because she was inspired by her mother, a grade school teacher. **Avocations:** Writing books and articles; Swimming; Piano playing; Visiting oceans and beaches; Playing bridge

Rose Marie Reich, MA

Title: Art Educator (Retired) **Industry:** Education/Educational Services **Date of Birth:** 12/24/1937 **Place of Birth:** Milwaukee **State/Country of Origin:** WI/USA **Parents:** Valentine John Kosmatka; Mary Jane (Grochowski) Kosmatka **Marital Status:** Widowed **Spouse Name:** Kenneth Pierce Reich (07/13/1968) **Education:** MA, University of Wyoming (1967); BA, Milwaukee-Downer College, Lawrence University (1959) **Career:** Retired (1993); Art Teacher, Oconomowoc Area School District, WI (1959-1993) **Memberships:** Vice President, AAUW (1989-Present); Oconomowoc Education Association; Lifetime Member, National Education Association; Wisconsin Educational Association Council; Former President, DKGSI **Marquis Who's Who Honors:** Albert Nelson Marquis Lifetime Achievement Award **Why did you become involved in your profession or industry:** Ms. Reich became involved in her profession because she descends from a creative family. **Avocations:** Designing stationery; Paper cutting; Doing crafts; Newfoundland dogs; Restoring old church statues and mannequins **Religion:** Roman Catholic

Adam J. Resmini

Title: Attorney **Industry:** Law and Legal Services **Company Name:** Law Office of Ronald J. Resmini, Ltd. **Education:** JD, School of Law, Roger Williams University (2009); Degree in Political Science, Furman University **Career:** Partner, Law Office of Ronald J. Resmini, Ltd. (2014-Present); Attorney, Law Office of Ronald J. Resmini, Ltd. (2009-Present) **Awards:** Rising Star, Super Lawyers (2016-2020) **Memberships:** Rhode Island Association for Justice **To what do you attribute your success:** Mr. Resmini attributes his success to his work ethic, the drive to succeed and be the best that he can be and his desire to do right by his clients. **Why did you become involved in your profession or industry:** Mr. Resmini became involved in his profession because he was inspired by his father, a practicing lawyer of more than 45 years.

Reynaldo Rey Fernandez

Title: General Manager **Industry:** Leisure, Travel & Tourism **Company Name:** Highgate Hotels, Inc. **Parents:** Elisa **Marital Status:** Married **Spouse Name:** Enid **Children:** Dened **Education:** Bachelor's in Health and Physical Education/Fitness, University School, Cuba (1988); Technical Diploma in Physical Education Teacher, Cuba (1983) **Career:** General Manager, Highgate Hotels, Inc., San Juan, Puerto Rico (2016-Present); Director of Operations, San Juan Marriott Resort & Stellaris Casino, Marriott International, Inc. (2012-2016); Assistant Front Office Manager, Hilton Worldwide (2012); General Manager, Courtyard by Marriott Bridgetown, Barbados, Marriott International, Inc. (2010-2011); Teacher, Sport History, Judo, Taekwondo, Cuban University (1988-1996); International Referee, Taekwondo Federation (Now World Taekwondo) **Career Related:** Technical Board, Cuban Taekwondo Federation; Teacher, Martial Arts; Teacher, Private Taekwondo **Civic:** Speaker/Lecturer, Hospitality, Tourism, University of Puerto Rico; Volunteer Lecturer, Boys & Girls Clubs of America; Volunteer, Painting and House Restoration, Habitat for Humanity; Volunteer, Beach Cleaning **Awards:** Named American Leader of the Year, General Manager, Highgate Hotel, Highgate Hotels, Inc. (2018); J. Willard Marriott Award of Excellence (2009) **Memberships:** Marriott International Training Network, Caribbean, Latin America (2006-Present) **To what do you attribute your success:** Mr. Rey Fernandez attributes his success to his dedication and understanding that you are not alone in what you do. He believes in dedicating and pushing yourself to grow in the business and including others in the decisions you make everyday; that is what got him the success he has had so far. **Why did you become involved in your profession or industry:** When Mr. Rey Fernandez came to America in 1996, he came with a background in sports and education, but when he saw the opportunity to work in the hospitality industry, he saw a lot of synergy in managing people's relations. For him it was all about building those relationships; that is the key point in hospitality, making people feel welcome and have a good experience. When he got involved with this industry, there was a moment that his background in sports and the offerings he was getting in hospitality started to compete. He had to decide which role he should follow and he went with hospitality. For him it has been the most rewarding job he could ask for; it has given him opportunities to meet people from different cultures and backgrounds.

Robert Joel Reynolds

Title: Principal Emeritus, Economist; Consultant **Industry:** Financial Services **Company Name:** The Brattle Group, Inc. **Date of Birth:** 05/13/1944 **Place of Birth:** Indianapolis **State/Country of Origin:** IN/USA **Parents:** Joel Burr Reynolds; Betty (Schimpf) Reynolds **Marital Status:** Married **Spouse Name:** Lucinda Margaret Lewis (1979) **Children:** Joel; Sarah **Education:** PhD in Economics, Northwestern University, Evanston, IL (1970); BSBA in Finance, Northwestern University (1965) **Career:** Principal Emeritus, The Brattle Group, Inc. (2016-Present); Principal, The Brattle Group, Inc. (2004-2016); Chairman, Competition Economics, Inc., Washington, DC (1997-2007); Chairman, Executive Vice President, Econsult of DC, Inc., Washington, DC (1997); Executive Vice President, Principal, Econsult Corporation, Washington, DC (1991-1996); Senior Vice President, ICF Incorporated (Now ICF International, Inc.), Washington, DC (1987-1991); Senior Economist, Vice President, ICF Incorporated (Now ICF International, Inc.) (1981-1987); Assistant Director, Senior Economist, Economic Policy Office, U.S. Department of Justice, Washington, DC (1973-1981); Associate Professor, University of Idaho (1973-1975); Assistant Professor, Economics, University Idaho (1969-1973) **Career Related:** Visiting Associate Professor, Cornell University (1981); Visiting Associate Professor, University of California Berkeley (1976-1977) **Creative Works:** Reviewer, "National Science Foundation, Revised"; Member, Editorial Board, Managerial and Decision Economics; Contributor, Articles to Professional Journals **Awards:** AT&T Grantee (1971-1972); Brookings Institution Grantee (1968-1969); National Defense Education Act Fellow (1965-1969); Dow Jones Award, The Wall Street Journal (1965) **Memberships:** American Association for the Advancement of Science; Computer Section, IEEE; Society for Industrial and Applied Mathematics; American Math Association; American Economic Association; Royal Economic Society; American Statistical Association; Mathematical Association of America (MAA) **Marquis Who's Who Honors:** Albert Nelson Lifetime Achievement Award **Religion:** Congregationalist

James Jennings "Jim" Rhyne, PhD

Title: Research Physicist (Retired) **Industry:** Sciences **Date of Birth:** 11/14/1938 **Place of Birth:** Oklahoma City **State/Country of Origin:** OK/USA **Parents:** Jennings Jefferson Rhyne; Clyde Margaret (Russell) Rhyne **Marital Status:** Married **Spouse Name:** Susan Margaret Rhyne (05/26/1990) **Children:** Nancy Marie (1966); Edward Paxton (1969) **Education:** Doctor of Philosophy in Physics, Iowa State University of Science and Technology (1965); Master of Science in Physics, University of Illinois (1961); Bachelor of Science in Physics, University of Oklahoma (1959) **Career:** Guest Scientist, National Institute of Standards and Technology (2018-Present); Program Manager, Department of Energy (2013-2018); Deputy Director, Science, Lujan Neutron Scattering Center, Los Alamos National Laboratory (2003-2012); Professor, Physics, University of Missouri, Columbia, MO (1991-2003), Director, Research Reactor, (1991-1996); First Director, NSF/NIST Center for High-Resolution Neutron Scattering, National Institute of Standards and Technology (1988-1990), Research Physicist, (1975-1990); Research Scientist, Naval Ordnance Laboratory, White Oak, MD (1965-1975) **Civic:** Advisory Editor, Journal of Magnetism and Magnetic Materials (1990-2008); Editorial Board, Journal of Applied Physics (1986-1989) **Creative Works:** 42 Invited Talks, National/International Conferences (1973–2019); Editor, 11 Published Conference Proceedings (1970–2005); Author, Over 230 Publications, 12 Book Chapters **Awards:** Distinguished Career Service Award, Office of Science, Department of Energy (2018); Outstanding Referee, American Physical Society (2008); Doctor Honoris Causa, University of Lorraine (1995); Department of Commerce Gold Metal (1987); Fellow, American Physical Society, Neutron Scattering Society of America **Memberships:** Chair, American Physical Society Topical Group on Magnetism (2006-2007); Chair, American Physical Society Insurance Trust (2000-2004); President, Neutron Scattering Society of America (1999-2002) **Marquis Who's Who Honors:** Albert Nelson Marquis Lifetime Achievement Award **Why did you become involved in your profession or industry:** Dr. Rhyne first became involved in education due to the encouragement of his parents, who spurred him to take an interest in science and engineering. **Avocations:** Travel; Photography; Model trains

Joan Ribley-Borck, BSN, RN

Title: Medical/Surgical Rehabilitation Nurse **Industry:** Medicine & Health Care **Date of Birth:** 01/05/1939 **Place of Birth:** Schenectady **State/Country of Origin:** NY/USA **Parents:** Harry Jacob Ribley; Lillian Josephine (Cheney) Ribley **Marital Status:** Married **Spouse Name:** Walter Carl Borck Jr. (10/24/1964) **Children:** Constance Maria **Education:** BSN, Russell Sage College, Troy, NY (1981); Diploma, Ellis Hospital School of Nursing (Now The Belanger School of Nursing), Ellis Medicine, Schenectady, NY (1960) **Certifications:** RN, New York **Career:** Staff Nurse, Gentiva Health Services, Schenectady, NY (2006-Present); Substitute Staff Nurse, South Colonie Central School District (1996-Present); Staff Nurse, Apria Healthcare Group Inc. (Formerly Homedco Home Care) (1984-Present); Substitute Staff Nurse, Wildwood Program, NY (1989-1996, 2001-2002, 2002-2003); Staff Nurse, Evening Charge Nurse, St. Peter's Hospital, Albany, NY (1968-1989); Staff Nurse, Cardiovascular Operating Room, University of Maryland Medical Center, Baltimore, MD (1965-1966); Staff Nurse, Rusk Rehabilitation, Columbia Memorial Hospital, Hudson, NY (1963-1964); Staff Nurse, Operating Room, Columbia Memorial Hospital (1960-1963) **Career Related:** Independent Provider in Nursing, Medicaid Management Information System (MMIS), NY (2004) **Memberships:** American Nurses Association; New York State Nurses Association; Albany Council of Catholic Nurses **Marquis Who's Who Honors:** Albert Nelson Marquis Lifetime Achievement Award **Why did you become involved in your profession or industry:** Mrs. Ribley-Borck became involved in her profession because she felt all her life that being a nurse was who she was supposed to be. **Religion:** Roman Catholic

Michael H. Ricca

Title: Member **Industry:** Law and Legal Services **Company Name:** The Law Offices of Michael H. Ricca PC **Education:** Doctor of Jurisprudence in Criminal Law, Touro College Jacob D. Fuchsberg Law Center (2012); Master of Business Administration in Management and Human Resources, Adelphi University (2008); Bachelor of Arts in Political Science, Binghamton University (2005) **Career:** Attorney, The Law Offices of Michael H. Ricca PC (2013-Present); Attorney, Neil Greenberg and Associates (2012-2013); Attorney, Federal Defenders of New York (2012-2013); Law Library Research Assistant, Touro Law Center (2011) **Awards:** Super Lawyers Rising Stars List (2016-Present); Listee, Top 10 Under 40 Attorney's, National Academy of Criminal Defense Attorneys (2017); Young Lawyer of the Month, Nassau County Bar Association (2015); Executive Member, American Association of Premier DUI Attorneys **Memberships:** New Lawyers Committee, Nassau County Bar Association; Federal Bar Council; New York State Bar Association; The National Association of Criminal Defense Attorneys; New York Association of Criminal Defense Lawyers; The New York State Defenders Association **Bar Admissions:** State of New York; United States District Court for the Eastern and Southern Districts; Supreme Court of the United States **Marquis Who's Who Honors:** Marquis Who's Who Top Professional **To what do you attribute your success:** Mr. Ricca attributes his success on the passion he has for the law, as well as his drive to achieve positive outcomes for his clients. He thrives on advocating for underrepresented people. **Why did you become involved in your profession or industry:** Having always held a passion for law, Mr. Ricca's background in construction and business enabled him to excel in the legal profession, specializing in construction litigation. **Avocations:** Working on classic automobiles; Traveling

Mary E. Rice, PhD

Title: Senior Research Scientist Emeritus; Biologist **Industry:** Sciences **Company Name:** Smithsonian Marine Station, Smithsonian Institution **Date of Birth:** 08/03/1926 **Place of Birth:** Washington, DC **State/Country of Origin:** DC/USA **Parents:** Daniel Gibbons Rice; Florence Catharine (Pyles) Rice **Education:** PhD, University of Washington (1966); MA, Oberlin College and Conservatory (1949); AB, Drew University (1947) **Career:** Senior Research Scientist Emeritus, Smithsonian Marine Station, Smithsonian Institution, Washington, DC (2002-Present); Director, Curator, Invertebrate Zoology, Smithsonian Marine Station, Smithsonian Institution (1966-2002); Research Assistant, National Institutes of Health (1953-1961); Research Associate, Columbia University (1950-1953); Instructor, Biology, Drew University (1949-1950) **Career Related:** Overseers Committee on Biology, Harvard University (1982-1988); Advisory Panel on Systematic Biology, National Science Foundation (1977-1978); Committee on Marine Invertebrates, National Academy of Sciences (1976-1981) **Creative Works:** Editor, Invertebrate Biology (1995); Co-editor with F.W. Harrison, "Microscopic Anatomy of Invertebrates, Volume 12" (1993); Associate Editor, Journal of Morphology (1985-1991); Co-editor, Books; Contributor, Articles to Professional Journals **Awards:** Leadership and Achievement Award, Harbor Branch Oceanographic Institute, Florida Atlantic University (2016); Named Conservationist of the Year, St. Lucie Conservation Alliance, FL (2001); Drew University Alumni Achievement Award in Science (1980) **Memberships:** President, American Microscopical Society (1999); President, American Society of Zoologists (Now Society for Integrative and Comparative Biology (SICB)) (1979); Fellow, American Association for the Advancement of Science; The Phi Beta Kappa Society; Sigma Xi, The Scientific Research Honor Society **Marquis Who's Who Honors:** Albert Nelson Marquis Lifetime Achievement Award **Why did you become involved in your profession or industry:** Dr. Rice became involved in her profession because she grew up in a rural area, and had an aunt who was an artist and did a lot of paintings of wild flowers and trees, which did much to awaken her fascination with the natural world. After school, she secured a scholarship to Drew University. She pursued a program involving a marine biology lab during the summer months. The experience inspired her to work exclusively on marine organisms, particularly invertebrates. **Avocations:** Birdwatching

Norma Jane Richards, RN, BSN, MS

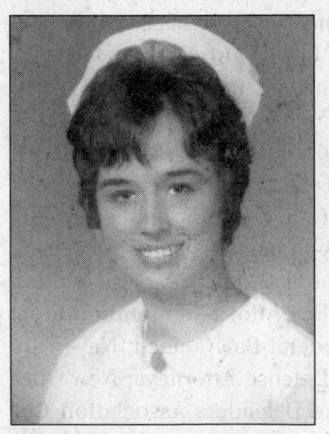

Title: Medical/Surgical Nurse, Educator (Retired) **Industry:** Education/ Educational Services **Date of Birth:** 03/29/1947 **Place of Birth:** New Orleans **State/Country of Origin:** LA/USA **Parents:** Benjamin Ammon Richards; Norma Agnes Richards (Deceased) **Marital Status:** Single **Education:** MS, Texas Woman's University; BSN, Louisiana State University **Certifications:** Board Certified, American Nurses Credentialing Center, American Nurses Association **Career:** Instructor of Advanced Medical-Surgical Nursing, Mississippi Gulf Coast Community College; Staff Nurse, Intensive Care Unit, Howard Memorial Hospital; Staff Nurse, Female Surgical Unit, Charity Hospital **Awards:** Instructor of the Year Award, Mississippi Gulf Coast Community College **Memberships:** American Nurses Association; American Heart Association; American Association of Critical-Care Nurses; Former President, District Five, Mississippi Nurses Association **Marquis Who's Who Honors:** Albert Nelson Marquis Lifetime Achievement Award **To what do you attribute your success:** Ms. Richards attributes her success to her dedication and always believing in the impossible. **Why did you become involved in your profession or industry:** Ms. Richards became involved in her profession because of her lifelong desire to become a nurse. **Avocations:** Reading; Gardening **Religion:** Methodist

Florence Mae "See See" Rigney

Title: Nurse **Industry:** Medicine & Health Care **Company Name:** MultiCare Tacoma General Hospital **Date of Birth:** 05/08/1925 **Place of Birth:** Tacoma **State/Country of Origin:** WA/USA **Marital Status:** Widowed **Children:** Doralyn Long **Education:** Diploma, Tacoma General School of Nursing, MultiCare (1946); Coursework, College of Puget Sound (Now University of Puget Sound) **Career:** Nurse, MultiCare Tacoma General Hospital, Tacoma, WA (1946-Present);Nurse, Baptist Memorial Hospital, Cheyenne Memorial (Now Cheyenne Regional Medical Center), Cheyenne WY; Nurse, San Antonio, Texas; Nurse, Nix Hospital, Nix Health, Atlanta, GA; Nurse, Georgia Baptist Hospital (Now Atlanta Medical Center) **Creative Works:** Featured, "The Dr. Oz Show," "Nightly News with Lester Holt," and Many Television News Networks **Awards:** Accolades for Long Career in Nursing **Memberships:** Former Member, American Operating Room Nurses (Now Association of periOperative Registered Nurses (AORN)); American Nurses Association; Washington State Nurses Association **To what do you attribute your success:** Mrs. Rigney attributes her success to the love of her profession and her willingness to learn. **Why did you become involved in your profession or industry:** Mrs. Rigney knew that she wanted to be a nurse ever since she was a child. At age 6 she had a mastoidectomy, and grew an appreciation for the nurses. She recalls paying her tuition in 1946 as only around $175 dollars. Her father did not want her to be a nurse, instead he wanted her to go to business school. Mrs. Rigney ignored her father's wishes and went to nursing school. In 1943, America had entered World War II and transitioned the hospital to the Cadet's Nursing program where she became a nurse cadet. She chose nursing because she really wanted to help people. In addition, what inspired her to go into nursing goes back to when she was young and she made it her goal since graduating from high school to go to nurse training. She took courses, and at that time, she had to take foreign language, so she took two years of Latin and two years of Spanish. Then, she had to take biology and chemistry in order to get into the nurses' training. **Thoughts on Life:** Mrs. Rigney's motto is, "Count your blessings."

Kenneth William Ritchey

Title: Human Services Administrator/Trainer **Industry:** Professional Training & Coaching **Company Name:** Workforce Performance Group **Date of Birth:** 06/07/1947 **Place of Birth:** Washington **State/Country of Origin:** WA/USA **Parents:** Conrad Monroe Ritchey; Katherine Costance (Sheris) Ritchey **Marital Status:** Married **Spouse Name:** Nancy Jayne Kirk (08/22/1970) **Children:** Kirk Damon; Erin Kathryn (Deceased 04/1988) **Education:** Graduate Diploma, Senior Executives in State and Local Government Program, Harvard University (1992); MS, Leadership Dayton (1991); MS in Educational Administration, University of Dayton (1980); MEd in Special Education, University of Virginia (1972); BS in Education, Shippensburg University (1969) **Career:** Part-time Human Service Administrator/Trainer, Workforce Performance Group (2015-Present); Senior Partner, Public Policy Impacts (2011-2016); Assistant Commissioner, Division of Developmental Disabilities, New Jersey Department of Human Services (2007-2011); Director, Governor's Cabinet, Ohio Department of Developmental Disabilities (1999-2007); Superintendent Board, Montgomery County Board of Mental Health/Developmental Disabilities, Ohio (1983-1999); Assistant Superintendent, Management Services, Montgomery County Board of Developmental Disabilities (1977-1983); Adult Education Teacher, Franklin County Jail, PA (1972-1976); Master Teacher, Coordinator, Work Experience Program, Lincoln Intermediate Unit, PA (1971-1976); Head, Cross Country and Track Coach, Shippensburg University (1970-1974); Special Education Teacher, Shippensburg Area School District, PA (1969-1971) **Career Related:** Trustee, Ohio Political Action Committee, Brighter Tomorrow Foundation (1990-2000); Member, Needs and Priorities Committee, Human Services Levy Council (1982-1984, 1987-1999); County Corporation (1992-1998); Faculty, University of Dayton (1983-1997); Consultant in Field **Civic:** Volunteer, CASA County (2011-Present); Member, Governor's Cabinet and Governor's Vision Committee, IL (1997-2000); Volunteer, Member, Community and Agencies Resources Council, United Way (1986-1998); President, Vice President, HelpLink Board; Past President, Board of Directors, Ohio Public Images, Inc. **Creative Works:** Former Editor, Newsletter for Teachers and Profiles in Work Experience **Marquis Who's Who Honors:** Albert Nelson Marquis Lifetime Achievement Award; Marquis Who's Who Top Professional **Why did you become involved in your profession or industry:** Mr. Ritchey was offered a position in special education, which he knew nothing about. He decided he wanted to give it a try, so he took it with no concept of what special education was. He liked it so much that he got a masters in it. **Avocations:** Reading; Collecting posters from presidential campaigns in the 1800s **Political Affiliations:** Democrat **Religion:** Methodist

Lewis Allen Rivlin

Title: Entrepreneur, Former Lawyer **Industry:** Business Management/Business Services **Date of Birth:** 10/15/1929 **Place of Birth:** Brooklyn **State/Country of Origin:** NY/USA **Parents:** Benjamin Rivlin; Lena (Levy) Rivlin **Marital Status:** Married **Spouse Name:** Dianne M. Farrington (10/07/1977); Alice Mitchell Rivlin (06/28/1955, Divorced 09/1977) **Children:** Catherine Amy; Allan Mitchell; Douglas Gray; Benjamin Farrington Rivlin; Leigh Farrington Rivlin **Education:** JD, Harvard Law School (1957); BA, Swarthmore College (1951) **Career:** Chairman, Chief Executive Officer, New Venture Capital Corp., Bethesda, MD (1981-2010); Founding Partner, Peabody, Rivlin, Gore, Cladouhos & Lambert, Washington, DC (1969-1981); Campaign Coordinator, Humphrey-Muskie Presidential Campaign Pennsylvania for Democratic National Committee, Harrisburg, PA (1968); Delegate Coordinator, Hubert H. Humphrey for President Campaign, Washington, DC (1968); Partner, O'Connor, Green, Thomas, Walters & Kelly, Washington, DC (1965-1968); Advance Man, Hubert H. Humphrey for Vice President Campaign (1964); Senior Trial Attorney, Antitrust Division, United States Department of Justice, Washington, DC (1957-1964) **Career Related:** Advisor, Consultant, Ex Royal Ownership Families of Brazil (2010-Present); **Military Service:** Commanding Officer, First Place Naval Reserve Division, Fifth Naval District, United States Naval Reserve (1967); Commander, United States Naval Reserve; Aide & Flag Lieutenant to Commander, United States Naval Forces, Germany (1953-1954) **Creative Works:** Co-author, "Regulating Prices in Competitive Markets," Yale Law Journal, Volume 82, Issue 7 (1973) **Bar Admissions:** Supreme Court of the United States (1960); District of Columbia (1957); United States Court of Appeals for the District of Columbia Circuit (1957) **Marquis Who's Who Honors:** Albert Nelson Marquis Lifetime Achievement Award; Marquis Who's Who Top Professional **Avocations:** Tennis; Classical music; Travel; Flying; Sailing **Political Affiliations:** Democrat

Brian L. Roberts

Title: Chairman, Chief Executive Officer **Industry:** Business Management/Business Services **Company Name:** Comcast Corporation **Date of Birth:** 06/28/1959 **Place of Birth:** Philadelphia **State/Country of Origin:** PA/USA **Parents:** Ralph J. Roberts; Suzanne F. Roberts **Marital Status:** Married **Spouse Name:** Aileen Kennedy (12/28/1985) **Children:** Sarah; Tucker; Amanda **Education:** BS, University of Pennsylvania (1981) **Career:** Chairman, President, Chief Executive Officer, Comcast Corporation (2004-Present); President, Chief Executive Officer, Comcast Corporation (1997-2004); President, Comcast Corporation (1992-1997); Executive Vice President, Comcast Corporation (1986-1992); Vice President of Operations, Comcast Cable Communications, Inc. (Now Comcast Corporation), Philadelphia, PA (1985-1986) **Career Related:** Director, Executive Committee, CableLabs (1999); Chairman, Board Director, CableLabs; Board of Directors, The Bank of New York (Now The Bank of New York Mellon Corporation); Board of Trustees, Simon Wiesenthal Center; Founding Co-chair, Philadelphia 2000 **Civic:** Vice Chairman, The Walter Katz Foundation **Awards:** Legend of the Maccabiah, Maccabi USA (2012); Ambassador for Humanity Award, USC Shoah Foundation (2011); Named One of the Business People of the Year, Fortune Magazine (2010); Named One of the 50 Most Influential People in Sports Business, Street & Smith's SportsBusiness Journal (2009); Silver Medal, U.S. Squash Team, Maccabiah Games, Israel (1981, 1985, 1997, 2009); Named One of the Most Influential People in the World of Sprts, Bloomberg Businessweek (2007); Named to Cable Hall of Fame (2006); Gold Medal, U.S. Squash Team, Maccabiah Games, Israel (2005); Named One of America's Top CEOs, Institute Investor Magazine (2004-2007); Humanitarian Award, Simon Wiesenthal Center (2004); Steven J. Ross Humanitarian Award, UJA Federation of New York (2003); Named to List of Politically Influential Individuals, PoliticsPA (2003) **Memberships:** Chairman, National Cable & Telecommunications Association (Now NCTA) (2005-Present, 1995-1996) **Avocations:** Squash (All-American Player)

Michael A. Robinson, Esq.

Title: Founder/Owner **Industry:** Law and Legal Services **Company Name:** Robinson Law, PLLC **Marital Status:** Married **Spouse Name:** Nicole **Children:** Three Children **Education:** Coursework, National College for DUI Defense (2013); Coursework, National Trial Advocacy College, University of Virginia School of Law (2012); JD, Regent University (2006); BS in Political Science, English, Radford University (2001) **Career:** Founder, Owner, Managing Attorney, Robinson Law, PLLC (2008-Present); Assistant Commonwealth's Attorney, Fauquier County Government (2008); Assistant Commonwealth's Attorney, Newport News, VA (2006-2008) **Awards:** Listee, Virginia Rising Stars, Super Lawyers (2016-2018); Listee, Washington DC Rising Stars, Super Lawyers (2016-2018); Top Lawyer, Northern Virginia Magazine (2014, 2016, 2017); Clients Choice, AVVO (2013, 2017); AV-Rated, Martindale-Hubbell (2017); Listee, Top 100 Trial Lawyers, National Trial Lawyers Association (2014, 2015, 2016); Clients Choice DUI (2013, 2016); Listee, Top 40 Under 40, National Trial Lawyers Association (2013-2016); A+ Rating, Better Business Bureau (2015); Listee, Best DUI Cases in Virginia, Legal Elite (2015) **Memberships:** National College for DUI Defense; National Academy of DUI Attorneys; American Bar Association; Fairfax Bar Association; Virginia Trial Lawyers Association **To what do you attribute your success:** Mr. Robinson attributes his success to his mindset. For all of his life, he has focused on his end goal and worked backward from it. He has always done whatever it takes to provide for his family; he never wants to let anyone down. **Why did you become involved in your profession or industry:** Inspired by a high school teacher, Mr. Robinson decided to pursue a career in law at a young age. He was additionally inspired by his wife, who is a successful businesswoman. She served as a great mentor, and Mr. Robinson knows he would not be where he is today without her. **Avocations:** Playing sports; Golfing; Spending time with family; Traveling

Rosalie Robles

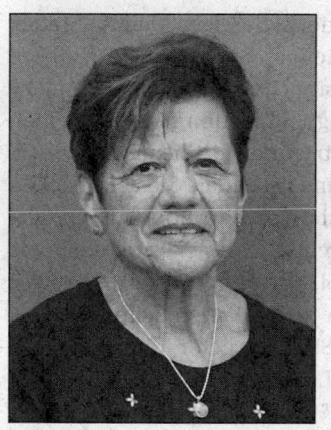

Title: Elementary School Educator **Industry:** Education/Educational Services **Date of Birth:** 10/30/1942 **Place of Birth:** Los Angeles **State/Country of Origin:** CA/USA **Parents:** Richard Miranda; Carmen (Garcia) Miranda **Marital Status:** Widow **Spouse Name:** Ralph Rex Robles (07/12/1986, Deceased) **Children:** Gregory; Eric; Karen; Cassandra; Logan (Grandson); Benjamin (Grandson); Amaya (Granddaughter); Adrian Steven (Grandson) **Education:** Postgraduate Coursework, Northridge State College; BA, California State College, Los Angeles, CA (1964) **Career:** School Site Representative, Faculty Club Chair, PTA, La Merced Elementary (2006-Present); Elementary Teacher, Montebello Unified Schools, California (1964-Present); Playground Supervisor, L.A. City Schools (1961-1964) **Career Related:** Union Representative, Montebello Unified Schools (2000-2009); Member, School Site Council (1989-1992); Bilingual Committee, Montebello Credit Union (1983-1988); Chairman, School Site Council (1980-1983); Representative, Montebello Credit Union (1973-1975); **Awards:** Golden Oak Award (1995); Honorary Service Continuing Award (1982); Honorary Service Award, PTA (1979); Awarded, 45 Year Pin upon Retirement, Montebello Unified School District **Memberships:** Secretary, Recording Secretary, President, Delta Kappa Gamma (2004-Present); Vice President, Program, American Association of University Women (2003-Present); President, American Association of University Women (2001-2003); Cultural Chair, American Association of University Women; Faculty Club Chair, Montebello Teachers Association **Marquis Who's Who Honors:** Albert Nelson Marquis Lifetime Achievement Award **Avocations:** Antique clock collector; Oil painting; Lladro; Rockwell Hummel collector **Religion:** Roman Catholic

David Roemer, PhD

Title: Educator (Retired) **Company Name:** Edward R. Murrow High School **Date of Birth:** 09/15/1942 **Place of Birth:** Bronx **State/Country of Origin:** NY/ USA **Parents:** David Henry Roemer; Madeline Eleanor (Stangenberg) Roemer **Marital Status:** Single **Education:** MBA, Pace University, Lubin School of Business (1980); PhD in Physics, New York University (1971); BS in Physics, Fordham University (1964) **Career:** High School Teacher, Science and Physics, Edward R. Murrow High School, New York City Department of Education (1984-1998); Product Specialist, Siemens Corporation (1977-1983); Manager of Radiation Therapy Products, Litton Medical Systems (1972-1977); High School Teacher, Science and Physics, Erasmus High School; High School Teacher, Science and Physics, Midwood High School **Creative Works:** Coordinator, Website about Science and Religion **Why did you become involved in your profession or industry:** Dr. Roemer became involved in his profession because he was inspired by W. Norris Clarke, his metaphysics teacher, who impressed everybody by the end of his class. Father Clarke even got a standing ovation at the end of the class, which Dr. Roemer never saw before. Additionally, he was extremely logical and rational and made everything clear, so Dr. Roemer learned a lot from him. **Avocations:** Watching movies; Reading novels; Reading science related to religion **Thoughts on Life:** Dr. Roemer publishes his articles at: https://www. academia.edu/25681124/Science_Metaphysics_Philosophy_Theology_History_and_the_Holy_Shroud Additional information can be found at: http://www.newevangelization.info; http://www.holyshroud. info; http://www.pseudoscience123.com; http://www.newevangelist.me/

Susan Haley Rogers, EdD

Title: Secondary School Educator **Industry:** Education/Educational Services **Marital Status:** Married **Spouse Name:** Doug Rogers **Education:** EdD in Curriculum and Instruction, Texas A&M University (2014); MS in Biology, Louisiana Tech University (1999); MEd in Secondary Education, Centenary College of Louisiana (1994); BS in Biology Education, Louisiana Tech University (1990) **Certifications:** Certified in Biology, Chemistry and AP Chemistry Education, National Board for Professional Teaching Standards; Online Essentials Master Teacher, Intel **Career:** Supervisor of Science, Caddo Parish Public Schools, Shreveport, LA (2008-2013); Advanced Placement Chemistry Teacher, Airline High School, Bossier Parish Schools (2004-2008); Honors Science Teacher, Southwood High School, Shreveport, LA (1991-2004); Honors Science Teacher, Broadmoor High School, East Baton Rouge Parish School System (1990-1991); Teaching Assistant, Louisiana Tech University (1989); Instructor, Department of Education, Centenary College of Louisiana **Career Related:** Louisiana Teacher Assistance **Creative Works:** Co-Author, "Students Teaching and Reaching" **Awards:** Teacher of the Year in Caddo Parish (2000); Teaching Award, Salle Mae Bank (1990); Most Outstanding First Year Teacher Award, LA (1990) **Marquis Who's Who Honors:** Albert Nelson Marquis Lifetime Achievement Award; Marquis Who's Who Top Professional **To what do you attribute your success:** Dr. Rogers attributes her success to her love of science, her mentors and the students that challenged her to do her best. **Why did you become involved in your profession or industry:** Dr. Rogers became involved in her profession because of her lifelong love of science, her desire to share those interests with others and her former chemistry teacher, Mrs. Donna White, who invited her to teach a lesson, which is when she fell in love with teaching.

Barry Rooth

Title: Owner **Industry:** Education/Educational Services **Company Name:** Theodoros & Rooth, PC **Place of Birth:** , **Marital Status:** Married **Children:** Two Daughters **Education:** Doctor of Jurisprudence, Valparaiso University (1982); Bachelor of Arts, Indiana University Bloomington (1979) **Career:** Founder, Owner, Theodoros & Rooth (1988-Present); Director, Quantum Immunologics Inc. (2007-2012) **Civic:** Past President, Congregation Beth Israel, Munster; Past Vice-President, Jewish Federation of Northwest Indiana; With, Indiana Chapter, Multiple Sclerosis Foundation; Director, Quantum Immunologic Inc.; With, Food Bank Northwest Indiana **Creative Works:** Featured, Attorney Seminar, "Indiana Trial Lawyers Lifetime Achievement Seminar" in Indianapolis, Indiana (2014) **Awards:** AV Preeminent, Martindale Hubbell (2017-2018); Best Lawyers in America (2017-2018); Top 50 Super Lawyers (2014-2018); Best Lawyer, Medical Malpractice (2008-2018); Indiana Super Lawyer (2006-2018) **Memberships:** Lake County Bar Association; Indiana State Bar Association; Illinois State Bar Association; American Bar Association; Indiana Trial Lawyers Association; American Association for Justice **Bar Admissions:** Indiana (1982); Illinois (1982); U.S. District Court of the Northern and Southern Districts of Indiana (1982); United States Court of Appeals for the Seventh Circuit **Marquis Who's Who Honors:** Marquis Who's Who Top Professional **To what do you attribute your success:** Mr. Rooth attributes his success to his passion and drive. **Avocations:** Cyclist

Jeffrey Allen Rouze

Title: President; Real Estate Executive **Industry:** Business Management/Business Services **Company Name:** Creative Aspirations, Inc. **Date of Birth:** 02/05/1952 **Place of Birth:** Rockford **State/Country of Origin:** IL/USA **Parents:** Robert Lloyd Rouze; Ellen Erma (Korpi) Rockford **Marital Status:** Divorced **Children:** Mirabel; Sophia **Education:** MS in Business–Real Estate Appraisal and Investment Analysis, University of Wisconsin-Madison (1977); BBA in Real Estate Finances, University of Wisconsin-Madison (1974) **Certifications:** Notary Public, State of Wisconsin (1980); Licensed Real Estate Broker, State of Wisconsin (1972); Certified Property Manager, Institute of Real Estate Management; Certified Commercial Investment Member, Certified Commercial; Investment Management Institute; Master of Corporate Real Estate, International Association of Corporate Real Estate Executives **Career:** President, Creative Aspirations, Inc. (2007-Present); Partner, Hollywood Development LLC, Los Angeles, CA (2001-2007); President, Hollywood Economic Alliance (2002-2003); Senior Asset Manager, CUNA Mutual Insurance Society, Madison, WI (1994-2001); Real Property and Mortgage Manager, CUNA Mutual Insurance Society, Madison, WI (1984-1993); Real Estate Consultant, CUNA Mutual Insurance Society, Madison, WI (1979-1984); Executive Management Trainee, Grootemaat Corporation, Milwaukee, WI (1977-1979) **Civic:** Board of Directors, Treasurer, Palisades Preschool (2004-Present); Hollywood Heritage (2003-Present); Landmark Communities LLC (2005-2009); Board of Directors, Hollywood Entertainment District, CA (1998-1999, 2005-2008); Board of Directors, Hollywood Neighborhood Council (2003-2007); Treasurer, St. Paul's Lutheran Church, Santa Monica, CA (2002-2007); Hollywood Historic Trust (2000-2006); Treasurer, Strollers Theater, Limited, Madison, WI (1985-1989) **Creative Works:** Featured, "Hooray for Hollywood," Update Magazine, School of Business, University of Wisconsin-Madison (2006); Featured, "Mr. Fix-It and his Work on El Capitan Helped Spark Rebirth," Los Angeles Business Journal (2005); Featured, "El Capitan Courageous," Los Angeles Times (1998); Featured, "The Inside Track to Careers in Real Estate," Urban Land Institute **Awards:** Named, Real Estate Pioneer, Los Angeles Business Journal (2005) **Marquis Who's Who Honors:** Albert Nelson Marquis Lifetime Achievement Award **Avocations:** Downhill skiing **Thoughts on Life:** Mr. Rouze resurrected the famous El Capitan Theater in downtown Hollywood and helped turn the area into a family-friendly and entertaining venue.

Alfonso Rueda, PhD

Title: Physics Researcher; Professor Emeritus **Industry:** Education/Educational Services **Date of Birth:** 04/17/1940 **Place of Birth:** Bucaramanga, Santander **State/Country of Origin:** Colombia **Parents:** Genaro Rueda; Emma (Acevedo) Rueda **Marital Status:** Widowed **Spouse Name:** Silvia Gaviriat (08/15/1970) **Children:** Cristina; Andres; Monica **Education:** PhD in Applied Mathematics, Cornell University (1973); MA in Applied Physics, Cornell University (1968); MEE, Massachusetts Institute of Technology (1963); BEE, Massachusetts Institute of Technology (1963) **Career:** Professor Emeritus, California State University (2010-Present); Professor, California State University (1993-2010); Associate Professor, California State University (1989-1993); Associate Professor, Professor, University of Puerto Rico (1984-1989); Professor, Researcher, University de Los Andes, Bogota, Colombia (1973-1984); Dean, Arts and Sciences, University de Los Andes (1980-1982); Chairman, Physics Department, University de Los Andes (1974-1976); Organization of American States Fellow, Cornell University (1970-1972); Instructor, University de Los Andes (1963-1966) **Creative Works:** Contributor, Articles, Professional Journals **Awards:** Associateship, Senior Associateship, International Centre for Theoretical Physics, Trieste, Italy (1980-1986, 1987-1993) **Memberships:** IEEE; American Physical Society; The New York Academy Sciences; The Planetary Society; Bogota Gun Club; IEEE-Eta Kappa Nu; The Tau Beta Pi Association, Inc.; The Honor Society of Phi Kappa Phi **Marquis Who's Who Honors:** Albert Nelson Marquis Lifetime Achievement Award; Marquis Who's Who Top Professional **Why did you become involved in your profession or industry:** Dr. Rueda became involved in his profession because his father's friend was an astronomer and he was inspired by him. When he was in high school, his teacher, Jose Maria Venegas, was a physicist and he inspired him to do physics. **Avocations:** Investigating extraterrestrial life; Traveling; Reading history, history of science and mathematics

Darin L. Rumer

Title: Partner **Company Name:** Joseph Greenwald & Laake, PA **Date of Birth:** 01/29/1970 **Marital Status:** Married **Spouse Name:** Cindy (10/15/2004) **Children:** Reese; Lauren **Education:** JD, Regent University, VA (2000); BS in Psychology, Sociology (Criminal Justice), Clemson University, SC (1997) **Career:** Partner, Joseph, Greenwald & Laake, PA (2011-Present) **Civic:** Pro Bono, Maryland Volunteer Legal Services (Now Maryland Volunteer Lawyers Service); Pro Bono, Bar Association of Montgomery County, MD; Volunteer, MountainView Community Church **Awards:** Named One of the 10 Best Attorneys for Exceptional Client Service, American Institute of Family Law Attorneys (2016-2019); Nationally Ranked Top 10, National Academy of Family Law Attorneys (2016-2019); Named Top 10 Attorney for Excellence in the Field of Family Law; Counselor at Law Award, Clemson University **Memberships:** Maryland State Bar Association; Montgomery County Bar Association; Fredrick's County Bar Association **To what do you attribute your success:** Mr. Rumer attributes his success to the good mentors that he had at good firms, that taught him the focus of the law and good trial skills. **Why did you become involved in your profession or industry:** Mr. Rumer initially was in school with aspirations to become a therapist counselor, and worked in a youth treatment center and a psych hospital for a total of six years. Through one of his friends becoming wrongfully arrested due to a race issue, a college advisor talked him into law school. He then applied, and went to law school. He interned with a criminal defense attorney, and did an externship with the US Attorney's office in the eastern district of Virginia. His fiancé was working with the FDA in Washington, DC, and so he applied for jobs and moved to the area. He started out doing many types of law but after a while, he realized he had a niche for family law. Due to his past work at a group home, he believes that is what helped him to do so well in family law. **Thoughts on Life:** "Psalm 68:5 says, "Father of the fatherless and protector of widows, is God in his holy habitation." He who numbers the hairs on our head will certainly not turn away from the children living as orphans, and this should inspire us to act..."

Tara Ryan

Title: President/Owner **Industry:** Architecture & Construction **Company Name:** Ryan Young Interiors **Date of Birth:** 10/08/1954 **Place of Birth:** Staten Island **State/Country of Origin:** NY/USA **Marital Status:** Married **Children:** Mackenzie **Education:** BS in Fine/Studio Arts, School of Design and Construction, Washington State University **Career:** President, Owner, Ryan Young Interiors (1991-Present); Designer, Vice President of Design, McMillin Company (1984-1989) **Creative Works:** Speaker, Pacific Coast Conference; Speaker, Various National Conferences **Awards:** Finalist, The Nook East Village, Best Interior Merchandising of a Multi-Family Home Plan, Icon Awards (2019); Finalist, Anden Plan, Best Interior Merchandising of a Multi-Family Home Plan, Icon Awards (2019); Finalist, Stones Throw, Best Interior Design of a Detached Home, Northstate BIA Awards (2019); Finalist, The Ridge at Paradiso, Best Interior Design of a Detached Home, Northstate BIA Awards (2019); Winner, Cascada, Best Design of a Multifamily Project, Excellence in Homebuilding Awards (2019); Winner, Origin Apartments, Best Design of a Multifamily Project, Tribute Awards (2018); Silver Award Winner, Lenah Mill Carolinas (Plan Ahrens), Best Interior Merchandising of a Home; Winner, Rosehaven, Best Interior Merchandising of a Model; Recipient, Over 250 Best Interior Design Awards **Memberships:** Building Industry Association; Sales and Marketing Council; National Association of Building Industries **Marquis Who's Who Honors:** Marquis Who's Who Top Professional **To what do you attribute your success:** Ms. Ryan attributes her success to working hard. **Why did you become involved in your profession or industry:** After proving her skills while working with McMillian, Ms. Ryan was offered a design position with the team. Though she had little experience, she took on the role immediately and ran the design division with ease. Two years later, she became the vice president of McMillian. This established her as a well-respected individual in the design industry.

Eva Marie Rzucidlo, MD

Title: Director and Chief of Vascular Surgery **Company Name:** Mcleod Regional Medical Center **Date of Birth:** 11/21/1966 **Place of Birth:** Jersey City **State/Country of Origin:** NJ/USA **Parents:** Gene Rzucidlo; Marianne Rzucidlo **Marital Status:** Married **Spouse Name:** Greg Henderson (01/2009) **Education:** Fellowship, Dartmouth-Hitchcock Medical Center, NH (2002); Residency, New England Deaconess Hospital, MA (2000); MD, Robert Wood Johnson Medical School, New Brunswick, NJ (1993); BA in Biological Chemistry, Wellesley University, Wellesley, MA, with Honors (1988) **Certifications:** Licensure, State of South Carolina (2016); Vascular Surgery Certification (2013, 2004); General Surgery Certification (2002); Licensure, State of New Hampshire (2002); Licensure, State of Massachusetts (1999) **Career:** Clinical Associate Professor, Dartmouth-Hitchcock Clinic (2016-Present); Staff Surgeon, McLeod Vascular Associates (2016-Present); Associate Program Director, Vascular Surgery Training Clinical Associate Professor of Surgery, Dartmouth Hitchcock Medical Center (2016-Present); Staff Surgeon, Mary Hitchcock Memorial Hospital (2002-Present); Associate Professor of Surgery, Vascular Surgery, Dartmouth Medical School (2013-2016); Associate Professor, Cheshire Medical Center (2008-2016); Vascular Surgeon, Dartmouth-Hitchcock Clinic (2002-2016); Associate Professor, White River Junction VA Medical (2002-2016); Assistant Professor of Surgery, Vascular Surgery, Dartmouth Medical School (2002-2008) **Career Related:** Tri-Vascular Advisory Board, American Heart Association (2014-2016); Associate Program Director, Department of Vascular Surgery, Dartmouth-Hitchcock Medical Center (2013-2016); Program Director, Medical Student Vascular Surgery Elective, PEMM Graduate Course, Vascular Biology (2006-2016) **Creative Works:** Editorial Board, Journal of Vascular Surgery (2012-Present); Author, Contributor, Numerous Articles, Professional Journals (1999-2016); Author, Contributor, Numerous Invited Articles; Presenter, Numerous Invited Presentations **Awards:** Student Research Fellowship Award, Dartmouth Medical School (2015); Inductee, Thomas Almay Chapter, Gold Humanism Honor Society Dartmouth Medical School (2014); Inductee, Distinguished Fellow Society for Vascular Surgery (2013) **Memberships:** Southern Vascular Society (2017); Eastern Vascular Society (2010) **To what do you attribute your success:** Dr. Rzucidlo attributes her success to her parents, who raised her right and taught her to push herself to succeed in life. **Why did you become involved in your profession or industry:** Dr. Rzucidlo became involved in her profession due to her mentor, Dr. Frank Logerfo. She admired his practice and how he handled his patients. **Avocations:** Spending time with family; Driving race cars; Autocross racing; Painting; Cooking

Lawrence C. Sager, PhD, PMP

Title: Human Systems Integration Consultant; Psychologist **Industry:** Consulting **Company Name:** The Lockwood Group, LLC **Date of Birth:** 1/15/1952 **Place of Birth:** Manhattan **State/Country of Origin:** KS/USA **Parents:** Roderick Cooper Sager; Ruth Regina (Ross) Sager **Marital Status:** Widowed **Spouse Name:** Stephanie Kulak (1/8/1999, Deceased 4/2009); Lynn Whaley (4/29/1978, Divorced 2/1994) **Children:** Lauren M.; Mackenzie M. **Education:** PhD, Johns Hopkins University (1978); MA, Johns Hopkins University (1976); BA, Hamilton College, Clinton, NY (1974) **Certifications:** Masters Certificate in Project Management, The George Washington University (1997); Project Management Professional (PMP) **Career:** Human Systems Integration Consultant, The Lockwood Group LLC, Spring Lake, NJ (2015-Present); Human Factors Consultant, CSMI, Lawrence, MA (2012-2015); Human Factors Consultant, Hi-Tec Systems, Egg Harbor Township, NJ (2009-2012); Lead Research Engineer, BAE Systems, Arlington, VA (2009); Senior Scientist, Aptima, Inc., Washington, DC (2004-2008); Technical Consultant, CGS Technology Associates Inc, Iselin, NJ (2002-2004); Director, Business Development, Masterson Technology, Inc., New York, NY (2002); Director, System Engineering, Vonage Holdings, Inc., Edison, NJ (2001-2002); Director, Project Management, VocalTec Communications Inc., Fort Lee, NJ (1998-2001); Principal Technical Staff Member, AT&T Communications Services, Holmdel, NJ (1991-1998); Distinguished Member, Technical Staff, AT&T Bell Laboratories, Holmdel, NJ (1984-1991); Technical Staff, AT&T Bell Laboratories, Holmdel, NJ (1978-1984) **Civic:** Elder, Vice President, Lincroft Presbyterian Church, Lincroft, NJ (2012-2018) **Creative Works:** Contributor, Articles, Professional Journals and Symposia **Awards:** Nominee, IEEE Engineer of the Year Award (2010); Quality Excellence Award, AT&T Inc. (1997); Distinguished Technical Staff Award, Bell Laboratories (1984); Graduate Fellow, National Institute of Mental Health (1974-1978) **Memberships:** Administrative Controls Management, Inc., Project Management Institute; Human Factors and Ergonomic Society; Sigma Xi **Marquis Who's Who Honors:** Albert Nelson Marquis Lifetime Achievement Award **Why did you become involved in your profession or industry:** Dr. Sager was inspired by several professors he met in college and graduate school to pursue his chosen career. **Avocations:** Golf; Sailing; Music; Travel **Religion:** Presbyterian

Angelique Salazar

Title: Vice President **Industry:** Business Management/Business Services **Company Name:** Central Street Capital, Inc. **Education:** BA, University of Colorado Denver (2007) **Career:** Owner, The Crafty Fox Taphouse & Pizzeria (2016-Present); Owner, U Lucky Dog Daycare & Dog Boarding (2010-Present); Vice President, Central Street Capital, Inc. (2005-Present) **Civic:** Board of Directors, Latino Donor Collaborative (2009-Present); Board of Directors, Metropolitan State University; President, Colorado Association of Dog Daycares; Board of Directors, Mile High Business Alliance; Creator, Christmas at Crafty **Awards:** Listee, Top 10 Leaders, Hispanic Executive Magazine (2019) **To what do you attribute your success:** Ms. Salazar attributes her success to her paternal grandfather, an ATD bus driver for 20 years, and her grandma, who was a smart woman with a PhD. Neither one of Ms. Salazar's parents was born with money but she saw the success her father found as a businessman, and all of his hard work inspired her to achieve her own success. **Thoughts on Life:** Ms. Salazar's ambition is to live her best life.Additional information: https://hispanicexecutive.com/2018/angelique-salazar-moyer/

J. Frank Sampson

Title: 1) Professor Emeritus 2)Artist **Industry:** Education/Educational Services **Company Name:** 1) University of Colorado Boulder 2) Sandra Phillips Gallery **Date of Birth:** 03/24/1928 **Place of Birth:** Edmore **State/Country of Origin:** ND/USA **Parents:** Silas Abner Sampson; Mabel Elizabeth (Trimble) Sampson **Marital Status:** Single **Education:** Postgraduate Coursework, University of Iowa, Iowa City, Iowa (1956-1959); Master of Fine Arts, University of Iowa, Iowa City, IA (1952); Bachelor of Arts, Concordia College, Moorhead, MN (1950) **Career:** Professor Emeritus of Fine Arts, University of Colorado Boulder, Boulder, CO (1990-Present); Professor of Fine Arts, University of Colorado Boulder, Boulder, CO (1972-1990); Associate Professor of Fine Arts, University of Colorado Boulder, Boulder, CO (1968-1972); Assistant Professor of Fine Arts, University of Colorado Boulder, Boulder, CO (1961-1967) **Career Related:** Artist, Several Art Galleries **Military Service:** With, United States Army (1954-1956) **Creative Works:** Artist, Boulder Museum of Contemporary Arts, CO (2018); Artist, Arvada Center of the Arts, CO (2003); One Man Show, Denver Art Museum, CO (1975); One Man Show, Walker Art Center, Minneapolis, MN (1954); Represented in Permanent Collection, Colorado Springs Fine Arts Center; Represented in Permanent Collection, Des Moines Art Center, Iowa; Represented in Permanent Collection, Dulin Gallery of Art, Knoxville, TN; Represented in Permanent Collection, Joslyn Art Museum, Omaha, NE; Represented in Permanent Collection, Library of Congress; Represented in Permanent Collection, Littleton Museum; Represented in Permanent Collection, Minnesota Museum of Art, Saint Paul, MN; Represented in Permanent Collection, Mulvane Art Center, Washburn University, Topeka, KS; Represented in Permanent Collection, Sheldon Memorial Art Center, University of Nebraska-Lincoln; Represented in Permanent Collection, Springfield Art Museum, MO; Represented in Permanent Collection, Walker Art Museum, Minneapolis, MN; Represented in Permanent Collection, Boston Public Library; Represented in Permanent Collection, Nelson Gallery-Atkins Museum, Kansas City, MO; Artist, Sandra Phillips Gallery, CO **Awards:** Fulbright Fellow, Belgium (1959-1961) **Marquis Who's Who Honors:** Albert Nelson Marquis Lifetime Achievement Award; Marquis Who's Who Top Professional; Marquis Who's Who Humanitarian Award **Avocations:** Exercise; Classical music **Religion:** Lutheran

Charles W. Sasser

Title: Journalist, Educator, Writer **Industry:** Writing and Editing **Company Name:** Self-Employed Freelance Writer, Journalist **Date of Birth:** 01/03/1942 **Place of Birth:** Sallisaw **State/Country of Origin:** OK/USA **Parents:** Ben Garland; Mary Louise Sasser **Marital Status:** Married **Spouse Name:** Donna Sue Sasser (10/07/1995); Katherine Renee Pitts (02/02/1979, Divorced 10/1986); Dianne Carol Reilly (10/08/1965, Divorced 1978) **Children:** David Charles Sasser; Michael Wayne Sasser; Joshua Dale Sasser; Darren Cagle (Stepson); Michael Haworth (Stepson); DeAnn Schisler (Stepdaughter) **Education:** Postgraduate Coursework, Oklahoma State University (1977-1978); BA, Florida State University (1969); AA, Miami Dade Junior College (1968) **Certifications:** Pilots License; SCUBA Certified; Special Forces Medic; Navy Journalist; Police Officer; Detective, Florida, Oklahoma **Career:** Freelance Journalist (1979-Present); College Instructor, Tulsa Junior College (1976-Present); Homicide Detective, Tulsa Police Department (1970-1979); Police Officer, Miami Police Department (1965-1968) **Career Related:** President, Chief Executive Officer, Fly High Inc. (2000-Present); Horse Rancher, Trainer, Chouteau, OK (1996-Present); Instructor, Creative Writing, Tulsa Community College (1986-Present) **Civic:** Member, 1st Baptist Church, Wagoner, OK **Military Service:** U.S. Army Reserves Combat Instructor (1983-1995); U.S. Army Special Forces (1966-1967, 1973-1983); Oklahoma Army National Guard (1970-1973); Navy Journalist, U.S. Navy (1960-1964) **Creative Works:** Actor, Wagoner Playhouse Dinner Theater (1997-Present); Author, "Blood in The Hills" (2017); Author, "Six: Blood Brothers" (2017); Author, "Six: End Game" (2017); Author, "Crushing the Collective" (2017); Author, "The Night Fighter" (2016); Author, "Two Fronts, One War" (2014) **Awards:** Tulsa Authors Award, City of Tulsa (1992); Numerous Awards for Military Leadership; Numerous Awards for Journalism; Numerous Awards as a Police Officer and Detective **Memberships:** President, Tulsa Nightwriters (2002, 2003-2006); Oklahoma Writers Federation **Marquis Who's Who Honors:** Albert Nelson Marquis Lifetime Achievement Award **To what do you attribute your success:** He taught himself to read and told his mom that he was going to live many lives and write about it. She built him a desk in the three-room shack where they lived in the hills when he was about 7 and he has been writing ever since. He learned the value early of hard work and self-reliance. **Avocations:** Martial arts; Steer roping; Scuba diving; Parachuting; Horses **Political Affiliations:** Republican **Religion:** Protestant

Robert L. Sawyer, MD

Title: Physician **Company Name:** Arizona Digestive Health **Marital Status:** Married **Children:** Two Children **Education:** Fellowship in Gastroenterology, University of Arizona VA Medical Center (1987-1989); Residency in Internal Medicine, The University of Kansas School of Medicine, The University of Kansas Medical Center (1984-1987); MD in Internal Medicine, The University of Kansas School of Medicine, The University of Kansas Medical Center (1984); BS, MidAmerica Nazarene University, Olathe, KS **Career:** Owner/ Physician, Arizona Digestive Health (1989-Present) **Awards:** Named to Best Doctors in America (2015-2016); Recipient, 25 Year Pin, American College of Gastroenterology **Memberships:** American College of Gastroenterology **Marquis Who's Who Honors:** Marquis Who's Who Top Professional **To what do you attribute your success:** Dr. Sawyer attributes his success to hard work and effort. **Why did you become involved in your profession or industry:** When Dr. Sawyer was young his father nearly bled out with a bleeding ulcer and had to have surgery. He was interested in medicine then gravitated towards internal medicine and gastroenterology. You don't have to be a surgeon, which he is not, but you were able to do some procedures which is nice. He liked internal medicine because of the thought process and he wanted to do something with his hands but he wasn't quite surgical. **Avocations:** Reading; Gun Club; Looking at and driving exotic cars

Subhash Chandra Saxena, PhD

Title: Mathematics Professor, Researcher, Academic Administrator **Industry:** Education/ Educational Services **Place of Birth:** Etawah **State/Country of Origin:** India **Parents:** Prem Narain Saxena; Hansmukh (Rani) Saxena **Marital Status:** Married **Spouse Name:** Pushpa Rani Kudesia **Children:** Anita; Anil **Education:** PhD, University of Delhi (1958); MA, University of Delhi (1954); BA, University of Delhi, India, with Honors (1952) **Career:** Distinguished Professor Emeritus, University of South Carolina (Now Coastal Carolina University), Conway, SC (2000-Present); Distinguished Professor, Coastal Carolina University (1999-2000); Professor, Coastal Carolina University (1977-2000); Professor, Chair, Coastal Carolina University (1987-1993); Associate Professor, Coastal Carolina University (1973-1977); Associate Professor, The University of Akron, Ohio (1968-1973); Associate Professor, North Illinois University, DeKalb, IL (1963-1968); Associate Professor, Atlanta University (Now Clark Atlanta University) (1960-1963); Assistant Professor of Mathematics, Atlanta University (1959-1960); Senior Postdoctoral Fellow, Council of Science & Industrial Research, Delhi, India (1958-1959); Instructor, National Defense Academy, Khadakvasla, India (1958) **Career Related:** Advisor, Consultant, Ansal Institute of Technology, New Delhi, India (2000); Consultant, ETS (1997) **Civic:** The American National Red Cross; Hands Across the Sand; Environmentalist **Creative Works:** Author, "Theory of Real Variables" (1972); Biographer, Contributor, Biographical Encyclopedia of Mathematicians, Numerous Articles, Professional Journals **Awards:** Outstanding Teacher Award, Amoco Foundation (1985); Distinguished Teaching Award, University of South Carolina (1985); Recipient, Awards **Memberships:** State Director, Mathematical Association of America (MAA), SC (2000-2003); Section Lecturer, Mathematical Association of America (MAA) (1997-1998); American Mathematical Society; Member, Several Organizations **Marquis Who's Who Honors:** Albert Nelson Marquis Lifetime Achievement Award **Avocations:** Bridge **Thoughts on Life:** For more information on Dr. Saxena, please visit: www.coastal.edu/endowment/donorstories/subhashandpushpasaxena/ and www.indiawest.com/news/global_indian/coastal-carolina-establishes-dr-subhash-saxena-math-suite-at-college/article_7675ee8a-690b-11e8-a89a-7f435a8dcd4f.html

Robert A. Schemmel

Title: Electronics Engineering Technician **Industry:** Engineering **Company Name:** Wrightspeed **Date of Birth:** 04/24/1949 **State/Country of Origin:** CA/USA **Marital Status:** Married **Spouse Name:** Guadalupe **Children:** Carla; Renee **Education:** BS in Electronics Engineering Technology, DeVry University (1995) **Certifications:** IPC/WHMA-A-620; IPC J-STD-001 Training and Certification; Small Crane Certification **Career:** Electronics Engineering Technician, Wrightspeed (2019-Present); Electronics Engineering Technician, Google (2019); Electronics Engineering Laboratory Technician, Apple Inc. (2017-2018); Harness Technician, Tesla (2017-2018); Power Electronic Research and Development and Production Technician, Varentec (2012-2016); Electronic Engineering Technician, Tesla (2011); Research and Development Electronics Engineering Technician (2010-2011); Electronics Engineering Technician, Xyratex (Now Seagate Technology LLC) (2006-2008); Engineering Technician, Reflectivity (2005-2006); Engineering Technician, Applied Materials, Inc. (2003-2004); Electronics Engineering Technician (2000-2002); Production Technician, Magellan (1999-2000); Electronics Engineering Technician, Joslyn Electronic Systems (1998) **Military Service:** Sergeant, U.S Air Force (1969-1971) **Creative Works:** YouTube Video, "Benchmark USMC Diamond Pushup" **Awards:** Who's Who in Technology Today (1980) **To what do you attribute your success:** Mr. Schemmel attributes his success to his humble nature and hard work. **Why did you become involved in your profession or industry:** Mr. Schemmel became involved in his profession because of his lifelong fascination with technology. **Avocations:** Mountain biking; Motorcycle riding **Thoughts on Life:** Mr. Schemmel states, "try to be the best you can."

W. Joseph "Joe" Schlitt III, PhD, PE

Title: Metallurgical Engineer **Industry:** Engineering **Company Name:** Hydrometal Inc. **Date of Birth:** 06/12/1942 **Place of Birth:** Columbus **State/Country of Origin:** OH/USA **Parents:** William Joseph Schlitt Junior; Florence (McCall) Schlitt **Marital Status:** Married **Spouse Name:** Anne Marie Ritchie (4/1/1994) **Education:** PhD in Metallurgy, Pennsylvania State University (1968); BSMetE, Carnegie Institute Technology, Pittsburgh, PA (1964) **Certifications:** Professional Engineer, State of Texas; Qualified Professional, Mining & Metallurgical Society of America **Career:** Metallurgical Engineer, President, Hydrometal Inc. (2005-Present); Private Practice Consultant (2004-2005); Principal Consulting Metallurgist, Aker-Kvaerner (2003-2004); Director, Metallurgy, Aker-Kvaerner (1999-2003); Manager, Process Technical Metals Engineering and Construction Division, Aker-Kvaerner (1994-1999); Product Line Manager, Chemicals, Brown & Root, Inc. (1993-1994); Manager, Technology, Brown & Root, Inc. (1983-1993); Process Staff Manager, Brown & Root, Inc. (1982-1983); Principal Program Manager, Kennecott Minerals Company (1981-1982); Manager, Hydrometallurgy Department, Kennecott Minerals Company (1977-1981); Senior Scientist, Kennecott Minerals Company (1975-1976); Scientist, Kennecott Minerals Company (1968-1975) **Career Related:** International Advisory Board, Situ Journal, New York, NY (1988-2004); Oversight Committee, Smelter Flue Dust, Environmental Protection Agency (1978-1979); Oversight Committee, Solution Mining, National Science Foundation, Socorro, NM (1977-1979) **Civic:** President, Fort Bend County Kennel Club, Richmond, TX (1988-1990) **Creative Works:** Associate Editor, SME Mining Engineering Handbook (1992); Editor, Salts and Brines (1985); Publication Board Commendation, Interfacing Technologies in Solution Mining (1983); Contributor, Over 60 Technical Articles, Professional Journals, Trade Publications **Awards:** Milton E. Wadsworth Award (2009); Arthur F. Taggart Award (1998, 2006) **Memberships:** Board of Directors, Navajo-Churro Sheep Association (2001-2009); Board of Directors, Metallurgy and Exploration (1984-1995) **Marquis Who's Who Honors:** Albert Nelson Marquis Lifetime Achievement Award; Marquis Who's Who Top Professional **Why did you become involved in your profession or industry:** Growing up, Mr. Schlitt was expected to follow in the footsteps of his grandfather, who was a construction professional. He was not gifted in mathematics, though, which was necessary to pursue the field; however, he excelled in chemistry. This prompted his decision to pursue metallurgical engineering. **Avocations:** Ranching

Alexander W. Schneider Jr., PE, F-IEEE

Title: Reliability Engineer (Retired) **Industry:** Engineering **Date of Birth:** 11/25/1945 **Place of Birth:** Kalamazoo **State/Country of Origin:** MI/USA **Parents:** Alexander William Schneider; Jennylouise Standish (Lockwood-White) Schneider **Marital Status:** Married **Spouse Name:** Lauretta Ann Gerretse (09/18/1971) **Children:** Alexander W. III; James A. **Education:** MBA, The University of Chicago, Chicago, IL (1972); MS, Northwestern University, Evanston, IL (1968); BSEE, Northwestern University, Evanston, IL (1967) **Certifications:** Registered Professional Engineer, State of Illinois **Career:** Consultant, Quanta Technology (2012-2016); Consultant, TRC Solutions Power Systems (2006-2012); Reliability Engineer, Mid-America Interconnected Network (MAIN), Lombard, IL (1992-1996, 1998-2005); Various Engineer and Statistical Positions, Commonwealth Edison Company, Chicago, IL (1968-1992) **Career Related:** Consulting, Cognition with TRC (2006-2012) **Civic:** Elder, Presbyterian Church in the United States (PC(USA)); Volunteer, Illinois Railway Museum, Union, IL **Creative Works:** Contributor, "Handbook of Electric Power Calculations, Fourth Edition" (2015); Contributor, Articles to Professional Journals **Awards:** District Award of Merit, Boy Scouts of America (1992); First Use Award, Electrical Power Research Institute, Inc. (1985) **Memberships:** Life Fellow, IEEE (2018); Chair, IEEE Power & Energy Society, Analytic Methods for Power Systems (AMPS) Committee (2017-2018) **Marquis Who's Who Honors:** Albert Nelson Marquis Lifetime Achievement Award **Why did you become involved in your profession or industry:** Mr. Schneider became involved in his profession because of family expectations, as his father and his grandfather were both civil engineers. **Avocations:** Model Railroads **Religion:** Presbyterian

Suzanne Scott

Title: Chief Executive Officer **Industry:** Media & Entertainment **Company Name:** Fox News Media **Marital Status:** Married **Children:** One Daughter **Education:** Bachelor's Degree in Political Science, American University **Career:** Chief Executive Officer, Fox News and Fox Business Network (Fox News Media) (2017-Present); Executive Vice President, Programming, Fox News (2016-2017); Senior Vice President, Programming and Development, Fox News (2009-2016); Vice President, Programming, Fox News (2007-2009); Network Executive Producer, Fox News (2005-2007); Senior Producer, Producer, Associate Producer, "On the Record with Greta Van Susteren," Fox News (2002-2005); Programming Assistant, Fox News (1996); Executive Assistant to Chet Collier, CNBC **Awards:** Named One of the Women of the Year, Police Athletic League, Inc. (2019); Named One of the Most Powerful Women in New York, Crain's New York Business (2019); Named to the Variety 500 (2019); Named One of the Most Powerful Women in Cable, Cablefax Magazine (2017, 2018, 2019); Named One of the Most Powerful Women in New York Media, The Hollywood Reporter (2018, 2019); Named One to the New Power of New York, Variety (2018); Named One of the Wonder Women, Multichannel News (2006)

Akhil K. Seth

Title: Doctor **Company Name:** NorthShore University HealthSystem **Date of Birth:** 12/15/1981 **Place of Birth:** Los Angeles **State/Country of Origin:** CA/USA **Children:** Daughter; Son **Education:** Fellowship in Plastic and Reconstructive Surgery, Microsurgery, Memorial Sloan Kettering Cancer Center (2017-2018); Resident in Plastic Surgery, Harvard Medical School, Brigham and Women's Hospital (2014-2017); Resident in General Surgery, McGaw Medical Center, Northwestern University, Feinberg School of Medicine (2007-2014); MD, Johns Hopkins School of Medicine (2007); BS in Biomedical Engineering, Minor in Computer Science, The Johns Hopkins University (2003) **Career:** Attending Physician, Plastic Surgery, NorthShore University HealthSystem, Evanston, IL (2018-Present) **Career Related:** Clinical Assistant Professor, Surgery, Pritzker School of Medicine, University of Chicago **Civic:** Mentor, High School Students; Volunteer, Community Outreach Programs, Breast Cancer Awareness **Creative Works:** Presenter, More Than 60 Presentations, National Meetings; Author, More Than 50 Peer-Reviewed Journal Articles **Awards:** Outstanding Paper Presentation, American Society of Plastic Surgeons Annual Meeting, Los Angeles, CA (2016); General Surgery Resident as Teacher Award (2014); Kanaval Surgical Scholar Award, General Surgery (2013-2014); Goldberg Family Trust Award, Northwestern Memorial Foundation (2011); Northwestern University Physician-Scientist Training Program Scholar (2011); Scientific Presentation Award, Best Presentation by a Resident or Fellow, American Society of Breast Surgeons Annual Meeting, Washington, DC (2011); Wound Biotechnology Foundation Award, Wound Healing Society (2011); Northwestern Memorial Hospital SICU Partner in Care Award (2009-2010); Resident Teacher Award, Outstanding Teaching; Best Paper Award, American Society of Plastic Surgeons; Best Paper Award, American Society of Breast Surgery; Service Award, Outstanding Service to Patients, NorthShore University HealthSystem **Memberships:** National Society of Collegiate Scholars; Golden Key International Honors Society for Undergraduate Students; Alpha Epsilon Delta National Honorary Society for Premedical Students; Alpha Eta Mu Beta National Honorary Society in Biomedical Engineering; Tau Beta Pi National Honorary Society in Engineering; American Medical Association; American Medical Student Association; Member, American College of Surgeons; Member, Plastic Surgery Research Council; Candidate Member, American Society of Plastic Surgeons; Candidate Member, American Society for Reconstructive Microsurgery **Avocations:** Family time; Sports; Traveling; Culture in the city; Arts and food; City life

Dina Maria Sevayega, EdD

Title: Associate in Education (Retired) **Industry:** Education/Educational Services **Date of Birth:** 08/05/1936 **Place of Birth:** Rio Hondo **State/Country of Origin:** TX/USA **Parents:** Manuel B. Garza; Sara (Flores) Garza **Children:** Reginald Brandon (Deceased); Mario Antonio **Education:** EdD, Indiana University (1983); MS, Youngstown University (1976); Postgraduate Coursework, Miami University, Oxford, Ohio (1975-1976); BS, The Ohio State University (1964) **Certifications: Career:** Retired (2019); Associate, College and University Evaluation, New York State Education Department, Albany, NY (1986-2019); Director, Educational Opportunity Program, Ithaca College, NY (1982-1986); With, Indiana University Bloomington (1979-1982); Assistant Director, Developmental Education, Miami University, Oxford, Ohio (1976-1979); Teacher, Youngstown Board of Education (1967-1976); Teacher, Columbus Board of Education (1964-1967) **Career Related:** Ontario College of Teachers; National University of Patagonia, San Juan Bosco; National Commission Evaluation & Accreditation, Buenos Aires, Argentina; Regents Accreditation, New York State Representative, TEAC and NCATE **Civic:** Board Member, Harvest of Hope Foundation (2002-2005); Wellness Alliance Foundation **Marquis Who's Who Honors:** Albert Nelson Marquis Lifetime Achievement Award; Marquis Who's Who Top Professional; Marquis Who's Who Humanitarian Award **Why did you become involved in your profession or industry:** Dr. Sevayega grew up in the Rio Grande Valley of Texas, the oldest of 12 children; they migrated from the valley of Texas to Michigan, following crops, picking cotton, fruits and vegetables, doing farm work. She graduated high school and completed a two-year degree in business. She wanted to be an accountant. After two years of working as a bookkeeper, she attended Ohio State University to complete a four-year degree in business. She wondered who would hire a female in accounting? She decided to become a teacher after tutoring her roommate in Spanish. She figured that would be one way to utilize her business degree and native language, and became a certified business and Spanish teacher.

Harshad Shah

Title: Founder **Industry:** Nonprofit & Philanthropy **Company Name:** Vegetarian Vision **Marital Status:** Married **Children:** Dennis; Eva **Education:** Bachelor of Arts in Economics (1953) **Career:** Founder, Chairperson, Vegetarian Vision (1992-Present); Owner, Chambord Prints **Memberships:** Various Indian Committees **To what do you attribute your success:** Mr. Shah attributes his success to his hard work. **Why did you become involved in your profession or industry:** Mr. Shah became involved in his profession after excelling as a successful printing executive for several years. Additionally, he is a strong believer in veganism, and decided to advocate in a nonprofit capacity.

Zhenhua Shao

Title: Electrical Engineer, Consultant **Industry:** Engineering **Parents:** Jinrui Shao; Rujing Hua **Children:** Xinyue **Education:** Doctor of Philosophy in Electrical Engineering, University of Kansas (1994); Master of Science in Mechanical Engineering, Shanghai Jiao Tong University (1989) **Certifications:** Registered Professional Engineer, California **Career:** Advanced Electronics Engineer, California Institute of Technology; Circuit Design Manager L.A. Division, Ibiden USA Inc., Torrance, CA; Electrical Design Engineer, Eastman Kodak, Kansas City, KA; Visiting Scholar, Department of Electrical and Computer Engineering, University Of Southern California **Career Related:** Reviewer, Institute of Electrical and Electronics Engineers **Creative Works:** Contributor, Articles to Professional Journals **Awards:** Member of Engineering and Research Group that Won a Nobel Prize in Physics (2017); Paul F. Forman Team Engineering Excellence Award (2016); Breakthrough Prize Award, Breakthrough Prize Foundation, Washington, DC (2001); Named, Top 50 Pairs in Open Pair Game, North America Bridge Championships, American Contract Bridge League (1999); Named, Top 50 Pairs in Open Pair Game, North America Bridge Championships (1998) **Marquis Who's Who Honors:** Albert Nelson Marquis Lifetime Achievement Award **Why did you become involved in your profession or industry:** Mr. Shao became involved in his profession due to his interest in mathematics and engineering.

Judith Susan "Judge Judy" Sheindlin

Title: Television Personality; Judge **Industry:** Law and Legal Services **Date of Birth:** 10/21/1942 **Place of Birth:** Brooklyn **State/Country of Origin:** NY/USA **Parents:** Murray Blum; Ethel Blum **Marital Status:** Married **Spouse Name:** Gerald "Jerry" Sheindlin (1991, 1977-1990); Ronald Levy (1964, Divorced 1976) **Children:** Jamie; Adam; Gregory (Stepchild); Jonathan (Stepchild); Nicole (Stepchild) **Education:** Honorary LLD, Elizabethtown College; Honorary LLD, University at Albany, State University of New York; JD, New York Law School (1965); BA, American University, Washington, DC (1963) **Career:** Supervising Judge, New York City Family Court (1986-1996); Judge, New York City Family Court, Bronx, NY (1982-1986); Prosecution Attorney, New York City Family Court (1978-1982) **Career Related:** Launched whatwouldjudysay.com (2012-Present) **Civic:** International Spokesperson, North Shore Animal League America **Creative Works:** Television Personality, "Judge Judy" (1996-Present); Author, "You're Smarter Than You Look: Uncomplicating Relationships in Complicated Times" (2001); Author, "Judge Judy Sheindlin's You Can't Judge a Book By Its Cover: Cool Rules for School" (2001); Author, "Keep It Simple, Stupid: You're Smarter Than You Look: Uncomplicating Families in Complicated Times (2000); Author, "Judge Judy Sheindlin's Win or Lose by How You Choose" (2000); Author, "Beauty Fades, Dumb is Forever: The Making of a Happy Woman" (1999); Appearance, "ChiPs '99" (1998); Author, "Don't Pee on My Leg and Tell Me It's Raining: America's Toughest Family Court Judge Speaks Out" (1996) **Awards:** Lifetime Achievement Emmy, Television Academy (2019); Mary Pickford Award, Hollywood Chamber Community Foundation (2014); Inductee, Broadcasting & Cable's Hall of Fame (2012); Named One of the 100 Most Powerful Women in Entertainment, The Hollywood Reporter (2011-2012); Named One of the 100 Most Powerful Celebrities, Forbes.com (2007, 2008); Recipient, Star, Hollywood Walk of Fame (2006); Gracie Allen Tribute Award, American Women in Radio and TV (Now Alliance for Women in Media and Foundation) **Memberships:** Vice President, UCD Law Society (2013) **Bar Admissions:** New York (1965)

Jon Hardy Shirley

Title: Physicist **Industry:** Research **Company Name:** National Institute of Standards and Technology **Date of Birth:** 02/24/1936 **Place of Birth:** Minneapolis **State/Country of Origin:** MN/USA **Parents:** Hardy Lomax; Mary Hayward (Connard) S. **Marital Status:** Married **Spouse Name:** Lou Ann Wulf (05/10/1975) **Children:** Ann (Deceased); Christine; Andrew; Jespersen **Education:** Doctor of Philosophy, California Institute of Technology (1963); Bachelor of Arts, Middlebury College (1957) **Career:** Consultant, National Institute of Standards and Technology (1983-Present); Consultant, Joint Institute for Laboratory Astrophysics, Boulder, CO (1978-1980); Research Associate, University of Helsinki, Finland (1975-1976); Research Associate, University of Colorado, Boulder, CO (1974); Physicist, National Institute of Standards and Technology, Boulder, CO (1963-1973) **Creative Works:** Contributor, 30-40 Articles to Professional Journals; Patentee of Modulation Transfer Spectroscopy **Awards:** I. I. Rabi Award, Institute of Electrical and Electronics Engineers (2002) **Memberships:** American Physical Society; Colorado Mountain Club; Phi Beta Kappa; Sigma Xi **Marquis Who's Who Honors:** Albert Nelson Marquis Lifetime Achievement Award; Marquis Who's Who Top Professional **Why did you become involved in your profession or industry:** Dr. Shirley became involved in his profession due to his lifelong enjoyment of mathematics. Upon attending college, he found that the field was more aimed toward proving theorems than the utilization of mathematics itself, which led to his specialization. In addition, he drew inspiration from his family, who encouraged him to enter the field of physics. **Avocations:** Hiking; Square and round dancing

Joshua Shuval

Title: Director of Operations and Risk Management **Industry:** Financial Services **Company Name:** KEV Group **Marital Status:** Married **Spouse Name:** Mariam **Children:** Two children **Education:** BACS, Finance and Administration (2003) **Certifications:** Chartered Account, Chartered Accountants of Ontario (2006) **Career:** Director, Operations and Risk Management, KEV Group (2010-Present); Associate, Corporate Restructuring Division, RSM Richter (2009-2010); Senior Accounting, Soberman LLP (2007-2009); Senior Associate, PricewaterhouseCoopers LLP (2003-2007) **Civic:** Advisory Board Chair, Western Hillel (2012-Present); Chair, UJA Young Leaders, UJA Federation of Greater Toronto (2010-2012); Volunteer, Associated Hebrew Schools of Toronto **Memberships:** Chartered Professional Accountants of Canada **To what do you attribute your success:** Being part of a great team, he has learned a lot from the CEO and the management of the business. **Why did you become involved in your profession or industry:** Mr. Shuval saw the opportunity to be a part of a growing company. Part of a company that has a ton of opportunity for growth and investment. He wanted to be a part of something growing then sitting on the sidelines.

Stanley S. Siegelman, MD

Title: Radiologist, Educator **Industry:** Medicine & Health Care **Date of Birth:** 06/18/1932 **Place of Birth:** Brooklyn **State/Country of Origin:** NY/USA **Parents:** Charles Siegelman; Kate (Guttenplan) Siegelman **Marital Status:** Married **Spouse Name:** Merle Ann Beck Siegelman (05/16/1999); Doris Franklin Siegelman (1956, Deceased 1995) **Children:** Bryan; Evan; Jonathan; Sharon; Betty **Education:** Residency in Radiology, Montefiore Medical Center (1961-1964); Internship, Walter Reed Army Medical Center (1957-1958); MD, SUNY (1957); BA, Cornell University (1953) **Certifications:** Certified, American Board of Radiology (1965) **Career:** Professor Emeritus, Johns Hopkins University, Baltimore, MD (2017-Present); Professor of Radiology, Johns Hopkins University (1973-2017); Director of Diagnostic Radiology, Johns Hopkins University (1973-1986) **Military Service:** Captain, Fort Meade Army Hospital, Medical Service Corps, U.S. Army (1958-1961) **Creative Works:** Editor, "Radiology" (1986-1998); Co-Author, "Computed Tomography of the Thorax" (1984); Author, "The Lungs in Systemic Disease" (1969); Contributor, Nine Monographs, 350 Scientific Papers **Awards:** Teacher of the Year, Department of Pulmonary Medicine, Johns Hopkins University (2018); Harry Z. Mellins Teaching Award, SUNY Downstate Health Sciences University (2017); Gold Medal, Society of Computed Body Tomography and Magnetic Resonance (Now Society for Advanced Body Imaging) (2015); Gold Medal, Radiological Society of North America (2002); Gold Medal, American Roentgen Ray Society (2001); Grubbe Memorial Award, Chicago Radiological Society (1986) **Memberships:** Honorary Member, German Radiological Society (2001); French Society of Radiology (1998); European Society of Radiology (1995); Society of Computed Body Tomography and Magnetic Resonance (Now Society for Advanced Body Imaging) (1988); Chairman, Executive Committee, American Roentgen Ray Society (1986); Founding Member, International Skeletal Society; Alpha Omega Alpha Honor Medical Society **Marquis Who's Who Honors:** Albert Nelson Marquis Lifetime Achievement Award **Avocations:** Sports; Reading **Political Affiliations:** Independent **Religion:** Jewish

Carol Ann Sigmond

Title: Attorney, Chair; Construction Law Team **Industry:** Law and Legal Services **Company Name:** Porzio Bromberg & Newman, P.C. **Place of Birth:** Philadelphia, PA **State/Country of Origin:** United States **Parents:** Irwin Sigmond; Mary Florence (Vollmer) Sigmond **Education:** JD, The Catholic University of America (1975); BA, Grinnell College (1972) **Career:** Attorney, Porzio Bromberg & Newman, P.C. (2020-Present); Private Practice, New York, NY (1989-2020); (1986-1989); Assistant General Counsel, Washington Metropolitan Area Transit Authority (1978-1985) **Career Related:** Lawyers Council, Citizens Crime Commission of New York (2019-Present); Vice President, First Judicial District, NYSBA (2017-Present); President, NYCLA (2015-2017); Member, ABA House of Delegates 2014-2017), Member, House of Delegates NYSBA (2007-2015) **Creative Works:** Member, Construction Editorial Advisory Board, Law360 (2019-Present); Columnist, The Mann Report Residential, The Condo-Coop Help Line, (2013- Present) **Awards:** Real Estate Section Award for Professionalism, New York State Bar Association (2020); Named to New York Super Lawyers List, Construction Litigation (2018); Named Mann Foundation Residential Real Estate Attorney of the Year (2009) **Memberships:** New York County Lawyers Association; New York State Bar Association; Lawyers Council, Citizens Crime Commission of New York City; Association of the Bar of the City of New York; American Bar Association; Fellow American Bar Association Foundation; Fellow New York State Bar Association Foundation **Bar Admissions:** Court of International Trade (2006); Federal Claims Court (2002); United States Court of Appeals for the Second Circuit (2000); United States District Court for the Southern District of New York (1991); United States District Court for the Eastern District of New York (1991); United States District Court for the District of Maryland (1990); New York State Bar (1990); Maryland State Bar (1988); United States Court of Appeals for the Federal Circuit (1987); United States District Court for the District of Columbia Circuit (1984); District of Columbia (1980); United States Court of Appeals for the Fourth Circuit (1976); Virginia Bar (1975); United States District Court for the Eastern District of Virginia (1975) **Marquis Who's Who Honors:** Albert Nelson Marquis Lifetime Achievement Award; Marquis Who's Who Top Professional

Adam Silver

Title: Commissioner **Industry:** Athletics **Company Name:** National Basketball Association (NBA) **Date of Birth:** 04/26/1962 **Place of Birth:** Rye **State/Country of Origin:** NY/USA **Marital Status:** Married **Spouse Name:** Maggie Silver (2015) **Children:** Louise Burns Silver **Education:** JD, University of Chicago Law School (1988); BA in Political Science, Duke University (1984) **Career:** Commissioner, National Basketball Association (NBA) (2014-Present); Chief Operating Operator, Deputy Commissioner, National Basketball Association (NBA) (2006-2014); Chief Operating Officer, NBA Entertainment (2000-2006); President, NBA Entertainment, National Basketball Association (NBA) (1997-2006); Senior Vice President, Chief Operating Officer, NBA Entertainment, National Basketball Association (NBA) (1995-1997); Chief of Staff, National Basketball Association (NBA) (1993-1995); Special Assistant to Commissioner, National Basketball Association (NBA) (1992-1993); Associate, Cravath, Swaine & Moore LLP, New York, NY (1989-1992); Clerk, Judge Kimba Wood, U.S. District Court for the Southern District of New York, New York, NY (1988-1989); Legislative Aide to Rep. Les AuCoin, U.S. House of Representatives, Washington, DC (1984-1985) **Civic:** Member, Board of Trustees, Duke University; Board Member, Lustgarten Pancreatic Cancer Foundation; Board Member, New York City Sports Development Corporation (2003-Present); Member, Visiting Committee, University of Chicago Law School; Member, Special Presidential Council on Campus Life and Culture, Duke University; Board Member, Duke University Library; Board Member, Partnership for a Drug-Free America; Board Member, Hands on Network Corporation Service Council; Board Member, PENCIL **Creative Works:** Himself, "What Men Want" (2019); Executive Producer, Documentary, "The Year of the Yao" (2004); Executive Producer, "Like Mike" (2002); Executive Producer, Documentary, "Michael Jordan to the Max" (2000); Executive Producer, Documentary, "Whatever Happened to Michael Ray?" (2000) **Awards:** Distinguished Alumnus Award, University of Chicago Law School (2016); Ranked #1, 50 Most Influential People in Sports Business, Sports Business Journal (2016); Executive of the Year, Sports Business Journal (2015); Named Among "100 most Influential People," Time (2015); Named Among "50 Greatest Leaders," Fortune (2015); Executive of the Year, Sports Illustrated (2014); Named One of "The Most Influential People in the World of Sports," Business Week (2008, 2007); Named Among the "50 Most Influential People in Sports Business," Street and Smith's Sports Business Journal (2007-2009); Named Among "The Most Powerful People in Sports," The Sporting News (2005) **Religion:** Jewish

Robert Morris Skaler

Title: Forensic Architect, Architect; Educator **Industry:** Architecture & Construction **Company Name:** Robert M. Skaler Forensic Architect **Place of Birth:** Philadelphia **State/Country of Origin:** PA/USA **Parents:** Louis Skaler; Minnie Skaler **Marital Status:** Single **Education:** BArch, University of Pennsylvania (1959) **Certifications:** Registered Architect (1963); Certified Architect, Commonwealth of Pennsylvania, States of New Jersey, Maryland and Delaware; Certified, NCARB - National Council of Architectural Registration Boards **Career:** Principal, Robert M. Skaler Forensic Architect (1970-Present); Staff Architect, Vincent G. Kling (1966-1970); Staff Architect, H2L2 Architects, (1965-1966); Staff Architect, Wolfgang Rapp Architect (1964-1965); Designer, Vincent G. Kling Architect (1960-1964) **Career Related:** Expert Witness, Forensic Architecture (1984-Present); Adjunct Professor, Architecture, Philadelphia University (Now Thomas Jefferson University) (1988-1994); Adjunct Professor, Architecture, Spring Garden College (1985-1991) **Civic:** Cheltenham Township Historical (1982-1988) **Military Service:** Honorable Discharge, Pennsylvania National Guard (1959) **Creative Works:** Author, "Philadelphia's Rittenhouse Square" (2008); Author, "Society Hill and Old City" (2005); Author, "Philadelphia's Broad Street: South and North" (2003); Author, "West Philadelphia-University City to 52nd Street" (2002); Featured, Robert M. Skaler Postcard Collection, The Athenaeum **Awards:** Certificate of Appreciation, Germantown Historical Society (2004); Preservation Initiative Award, University City Historical Society (2003); Stokes Book Lecturer Award (2002); Commendation for Restoration, Victorian Society in America (1994); Certificate of Merit, Penna Historical & Museum Commission (1985); John McArthur Prize, Restore Philadelphia, Habitat for Humanity Philadelphia, Inc. (1984-1985); First Prize, Lighting Competition (1961); T-Square Club, Philadelphia, PA (1960); Inductee, Tau Sigma Delta Honor Society (1959) **Memberships:** The Athenaeum; Old York Road Historical Society; The Union League of Philadelphia; Maxwell Mansion; President, Victorian Society, Philadelphia, PA; BOCA Code; National Fire Protection Association (NFPA) **Marquis Who's Who Honors:** Albert Nelson Marquis Lifetime Achievement Award **To what do you attribute your success:** Mr. Skaler attributes his success to working. **Why did you become involved in your profession or industry:** Mr. Skaler became involved in his profession because he saw the need for restoration. **Avocations:** Deltiology; Philadelphia architectural books **Political Affiliations:** Republican **Religion:** Jewish

Adam D. Smith

Title: Managing Attorney **Industry:** Law and Legal Services **Company Name:** Adam Smith Law **Education:** JD, Northwestern University School of Law, IL (2005); BS, Accounting, University of Illinois at Urbana-Champaign (2000) **Career:** Managing Attorney, Adam Smith Law (2018-present); Partner, Smith Carbajal (2017-2018); Managing Attorney, Adam Smith Law (2016-2017); Attorney, Glen Lerner Injury Attorneys (2010-2016); Attorney, Glaser Weil Fink Jacobs Howard & Shapiro, LLP (2008-2010); Attorney, Lionel Sawyer & Collins (2005-2008) **Awards:** Super Lawyer (2019); Top 100, National Trial Lawyers; High Stakes Litigators; Nevada Legal Elite **Bar Admissions:** Nevada (2005) **To what do you attribute your success:** Mr. Smith attributes his success to a lot of hard work and genuinely caring about his clients. Mr. Smith treats his clients the way that they want to be treated. **Why did you become involved in your profession or industry:** Mr. Smith was inspired by a desire to help others and help his community. He had the desire to take care of people through some of the hardest times in their lives.

James Marshall Smith

Title: Author, Physicist **Industry:** Research **Date of Birth:** 09/28/1942 **Place of Birth:** Charleston **State/Country of Origin:** WV/USA **Parents:** Louis Benton Smith; Edna Christine (Norman) Smith **Spouse Name:** June Wright (07/26/1961) **Children:** James Jr. (Deceased); Timothy; Kym **Education:** PhD, West Virginia University (1969); MS, West Virginia University (1966); BS, West Virginia University (1964) **Certifications:** Certified, American Board of Health Physics (1981-1995) **Career:** Chief, Radiation Studies Branch, Centers for Disease Control and Prevention (1991-2006); Chief, Physical Agents Effects Branch, The National Institute for Occupational Safety and Health (1983-1990); Research Associate Professor, School of Medicine, The University of Utah (1974-1983); Senior Research Fellow, Institute of Molecular Biophysics, Florida State University (1971-1974); Physicist, Industry Space Center, Princeton, NJ (1969-1971); Author; Physicist **Career Related:** Distinguished Scientist and Consultant, Centers for Disease Control and Prevention **Creative Works:** Author, "Hybrid" (2017); Author, "Silent Source" (2016); Co-Author, 100 Scientific Publications and Reports **Awards:** Superior Service Award, U.S. Public Health Service (1994); Finalist, Clive Cussler Grand Master Award; Semi-Finalist, William Faulkner Wisdom Award; Nominee, Charles C. Shepard Science Award, Centers for Disease Control and Prevention **Memberships:** Health Physics Society; Radiation Research Society; Authors Guild **Marquis Who's Who Honors:** Albert Nelson Marquis Lifetime Achievement Award **Why did you become involved in your profession or industry:** Dr. Smith became involved in his profession because he read the biography of Albert Einstein at the age of 12, which sparked his interest in theoretical physics. **Avocations:** Writing; Fly-fishing; Traveling

Karla Smith

Title: Executive Vice President **Industry:** Business Management/Business Services **Company Name:** AEI Consultants **Education:** MBA in Business Administration, Southern Methodist University-Cox School of Business (2002); MS in Geoscience, University of Louisiana at Monroe (1990); BS in Geology, Millsaps College (1982) **Career:** Executive Vice President, AEI Consultants (2017-Present); National Division Lead, Site Mitigation and Remediation, AEI Consultants (2015-Present); Senior Vice President, Midwest Regional Director, Vice President, AEI Consultants (2012-2015); Principal Geologist, LFR Inc./ARCADIS (2008-2012); Vice President of National Accounts, Nova Consulting (2006-2008); Vice President, National Client Group, Professional Service Industries, Inc. (2003-2006); Vice President, Operations Manager, Reed Engineering Group (1995-2003) **Civic:** Senior Warden, Episcopal Church of Atlanta **Awards:** Women of influence, Real Estate Forum; Divisional Excellence Award, Site Mitigation Division, AEI Consultants Corporate **Memberships:** Environmental Bankers Association (EBA); Women of Renewable Industries and Sustainable Energy (WRISE); American Wind Energy Association (AWEA); Solar Energy Industries Association (SEIA) **To what do you attribute your success:** Ms. Smith attributes her success to her strong educational background. Likewise, she is experienced in the scientific and technical sides of the business industry. She additionally credits the endless love and support of her family. **Why did you become involved in your profession or industry:** Growing up, Ms. Smith always loved being outside in nature. She enjoyed picking up and examining rocks and fossils. In middle school, she took her first geology class and passed with perfect grades. From there, she continued to love geology and excelled in the field. Initially, upon entering college, she thought that she would end up becoming a chemistry major and going into the medical field. However, she quickly found out she had no interest in chemistry. She then took a geology class, and everything came full circle for her. She realized she was exactly where she belonged. Since then, she has continued to live her passion.

Madison H. Smith

Title: Senior Vice President **Company Name:** JESCO, Inc. **Date of Birth:** 07/29/1951 **Place of Birth:** Opp **State/Country of Origin:** AL/USA **Parents:** M. H. Smith; Mattie Merle Sumblin Smith **Marital Status:** Widowed **Spouse Name:** Debra Lynn Middleton Smith **Children:** Amelia Smith Lawrence; Wade Smith **Education:** BS, Auburn University, AL (1972) **Certifications:** Master Plumbing License, MI, AR, GA, TN, NC, FL and VA; Master Mechanical License, MI, AL, LA, AR, FLNC, VA, TN; Master Gasfitter License, AL, NC, VA; Master Boiler Contractor License, GA, AR, KY; Master Electrical License, MI; Total of 27 Different Licenses and Certifications **Career:** Assistant Project Manager, Project Manager, Manager of Estimating, Vice President of Estimating, Vice President, Senior Vice President, Mechanical & Electrical Process Division, JESCO, Inc. (1976-Present) **Career Related:** Project Experience, PACCAR Engine Plant; Project Experience, Mueller Casting; Project Experience, Caterpillar, Inc.; Project Experience, Volvo Automotive (Volvo Car Corporation) **Civic:** The Salvation Army USA; Quail Unlimited; Duck Unlimited; Rocky Mountain Elk Foundation; Friends of NRA **Memberships:** Past President, Northern Mississippi Chapter, American Society of Refrigeration Heating and Air Conditioning Engineers (ASHRAE); Mississippi Chapter, Associated Builders and Contractors, Inc.; Electrical Representative, Mississippi State Board of Contractors **Marquis Who's Who Honors:** Marquis Who's Who Top Professional **To what do you attribute your success:** Mr. Smith attributes his success to hard work and determination. **Why did you become involved in your profession or industry:** Mr. Smith became involved in his profession because he grew up in a mechanical contracting firm that was family-owned in Northwest Florida. He went to school for aerospace engineering and actually wanted to get out of construction. When he was graduating, there was not a lot of people or openings in aircraft development, so, by default, he came back to construction. **Avocations:** Hunting; Fishing; Enjoying the outdoors; Spending time with his family and friends **Political Affiliations:** Republican **Religion:** Baptist **Thoughts on Life:** Mr. Smith always takes others into consideration, whatever their needs and requirements are, in conjunction with his company.

Margaret Smith

Title: Owner **Industry:** Business Management/Business Services **Company Name:** Scout & Molly's Boutique **Career:** Owner, Scout & Molly's Boutique, Alpharetta, GA (2016-Present);Manager of Student Financial Aid, Interactive Learning Systems (2011-2015); Occupational Admissions Counselor, Interactive Learning Systems (2010-2015); Director of Financial Aid, Interactive Learning Systems (2010-2013); Data Quality Specialist, Houston Independent School District (1997-2010) **Civic:** Volunteer, Various Church and Charity Organizations **Awards:** Best Boutique, Alpharetta, GA **Why did you become involved in your profession or industry:** Mrs. Smith started her adult life by being a stay-at-home mom. Quickly, she became driven to open her own boutique. Fashion was her passion and she enjoyed being social, so when Mrs. Smith noticed her town needed a wider variety of fashion choices, she knew it was the right time to open a boutique. She found success and has held onto it since 2016. Mrs. Smith hopes to be an example for her children that they can achieve every one of their dreams. **Thoughts on Life:** Mrs. Smith lives by the quote, "Strive each day as if it is your last." Mrs. Smith would like to use her story to show people, especially women, that regardless of their current circumstances, they can still achieve what they desire through focus, determination and hard work.

Sheila Robertson Smith

Title: Hematology Technician (Retired) **Industry:** Medicine & Health Care **Date of Birth:** 01/04/1945 **Place of Birth:** Washington **State/Country of Origin:** DC/USA **Parents:** Philip Franklin Smith; Emelyn Fiske Smith **Education:** AS, Penn Hall College (1965); Coursework in Physical Education, University of Miami **Career:** Hematology Technician, Anne Arundel Medical Center, Annapolis, MD (1973-1993); Hematology Technician, North Arundel Hospital, Glen Burnie, MD (1972-1973); Hematology Technician, Duke University Medical Center, Durham, NC (1966-1972) **Career Related:** Representative, Employees Council, Duke University Medical Center, Durham, NC (1968-1972) **Civic:** Board of Directors, Port Tobacco Courthouse (1997-Present); Board of Directors, Society for the Restoration of Port Tobacco (1997-2017); Board of Directors, Smallwood Foundation, LaPlata, MD (1997-1998) **Awards:** Charles County Historic Trust Preservation Award (2007); Mrs. Frank J. Fletcher Award, Charles County Garden Club (2007); Numerous Awards for Sportsmanship, High School, College; Numerous Blue Ribbons, Best in Show **Memberships:** Charles County Historical Society; Charles County Garden Club; Smallwood Foundation **Marquis Who's Who Honors:** Albert Nelson Marquis Lifetime Achievement Award; Marquis Who's Who Humanitarian Award **Why did you become involved in your profession or industry:** Ms. Smith became involved in her profession by happy circumstance. Originally, she was a physical education major at the University of Miami. However, she ended up leaving her junior year and went to visit a friend. During her visit, they went to the employment office at Duke University, which led to a job at the medical center and a decades' long career in hematology. **Avocations:** Gardening; Needlepoint; Traveling **Political Affiliations:** Republican **Religion:** Episcopalian

Will Carroll Smith Jr.

Title: Actor; Rap Artist **Date of Birth:** 09/25/1968 **Place of Birth:** Philadelphia **State/Country of Origin:** PA/USA **Parents:** Willard Smith; Caroline Smith **Marital Status:** Married **Spouse Name:** Jada Pinkett Smith (12/31/1997); Sheree Smith (05/09/1992, Divorced 1995) **Children:** Willard III; Jaden Christopher Syre; Willow Camille Reign **Career:** Partner, Overbrook Entertainment, Beverly Hills, CA; Co-owner, Treyball Development Inc., Beverly Hills, CA **Creative Works:** Actor, Producer, "Bad Boys for Life" (2020); Rap Artist with Joyner Lucas, "Will (Remix)" (2020); Actor, "Gemini Man" (2019); Voice Actor, "Spies in Disguise" (2019); Actor, Producer, "Aladdin" (2019); Producer, "Bright" (2017); Actor, "Collateral Beauty" (2016); Actor, Producer, "Suicide Squad" (2016); Producer, "Collateral Beauty" (2016); Producer, "Focus" (2015); Actor, Producer, "Concussion" (2015); Actor, "Focus" (2015); Actor, "Winter's Tale" (2014); Producer, "Annie" (2014); Producer, "The Queen Latifah Show" (2013); Actor, Writer, Producer, "After Earth" (2013); Actor, "Men in Black 3" (2012); Executive Producer, "Free Angela and All Political Prisoners" (2012); Producer, "This Means War" (2012); Producer, "The Karate Kid" (2010); Actor, "Hancock" (2008); Producer, "The Secret Life of Bees" (2008); Producer, "Lakeview Terrace" (2008); Actor, "Seven Pounds" (2008); Actor, "I Am Legend" (2007); Producer, "ATL" (2006); Actor, "The Pursuit of Happyness" (2006); Actor, Producer, "Hitch" (2005); Solo Rap Artist, "Lost and Found" (2005); Actor, Executive Producer, "I, Robot" (2004); Executive Producer, "The Seat Filler" (2004); Producer, "Saving Face" (2004); Actor, Writer, Executive Producer, "All of Us" (2003); Executive Producer, "Showtime" (2002); Voice Actor, "Shark Tale" (2004); Actor, "Bad Boys II" (2003) **Awards:** Image Award for Outstanding Actor in a Motion Picture, NAACP (2009); People's Choice Award for Favorite Male Action Star, Favorite Male Movie Star (2009); Named One of the 100 Most Powerful Celebrities, Forbes.com (2007, 2008); Best Male Performance, MTV Movie Awards (2008); Choice Movie Actor: Horror/Thriller, Teen Choice Awards (2008); Named One of Barbara Walters' Ten Most Fascinating People (2008); Named to Power 150, Ebony Magazine (2008); Named One of the Top 25 Entertainers of Year, Entertainment Weekly (2007); Choice Movie Actor: Drama, Teen Choice Awards (2007); Named One of the 50 Smartest People in Hollywood (2007); Named One of the 100 Most Influential People, TIME Magazine (2006); American Music Award for Favorite Male Artist (1999, 2005)

Adrienne Charlene Smyth

Title: Program Executive **Industry:** Government Administration/Government Relations/ Government Services **Date of Birth:** 02/16/1965 **Place of Birth:** Baltimore **State/Country of Origin:** MD/USA **Parents:** Nobile Guy Costantine **Marital Status:** Married **Spouse Name:** Dr. David Ralph Smyth (05/24/1985) **Education:** BA in Psychology and Early Childhood Education, Shippensburg University; AA in Liberal Arts, Hillsborough Community College **Career:** Program Executive, Office of Child Development and Early Learning, Commonwealth of Pennsylvania (2007-Present); Office of Income Maintenance, Department of Human Services, Commonwealth of Pennsylvania (2003-2007); Youth Development Program Manager, Center for Schools and Communities (1998); Executive Director, Fulton County Family Partnership (1995); Group Supervisor, Mount Rock Care & Share, Shippensburg, PA (1991-1995); Parent Educator Childcare, Migrant Child Development, Chambersburg, PA (1993); Instructor, Pennsylvania State College of Technology, Wellsboro, PA (1989); Lead Teacher, Hand in Hand, Lambertville, NJ (1989-1991); Site Manager, Latchkey Services for Children, Pasco County, FL (1988-1989); Group Leader, Lutz Baptist Daycare, FL (1983-1986) **Awards:** Above and Beyond Award, Office for Child Development and Early Learning (2011, 2013, 2014); Treasure Award, Office for Child Development and Early Learning (2009); Leader Designation, Office for Child Development and Early Learning (2008); Golden Apple Award (2002); Human Services Provider of the Year, Fulton County, PA (1998); Center Award, Latchkey Services for Children, Pasco County, FL (1988) **Marquis Who's Who Honors:** Albert Nelson Marquis Lifetime Achievement Award **Why did you become involved in your profession or industry:** Ms. Smyth became involved in her profession because she has always loved working with children. As a teenager, she worked at Chuck E. Cheese as a character performing for children. **Thoughts on Life:** Ms. Smyth states, "Children are everything that is good in the world."

Richard G. Soper

Title: Chief Executive Officer, Medical Director **Company Name:** Center for Behavioral Wellness **Date of Birth:** 03/12/1960 **Place of Birth:** Shirley **State/Country of Origin:** MA/USA **Year of Passing:** 2015 **Parents:** Berry C. Soper; Mary T. Soper **Marital Status:** Widow **Spouse Name:** Sherry Ruth Soper **Children:** Vanessa; Larissa; Cordell; Ashley **Education:** JD, Vanderbilt University Law School, Nashville, TN; Fellowship, University of North Carolina-Chapel Hill; Residency, St. Jude Hospital, University of Tennessee; MD, University of Tennessee College of Medicine, Memphis, TN; MA in Addiction Psychology, Capella University; BA in Philosophy/Psychology, University of Michigan, Ann Arbor **Certifications:** Diplomate, American Board of Addiction Medicine; Distinguished Fellow, American Society of Addiction Medicine; American Academy of Addiction Psychology; American Psychological Association **Career:** Chief Executive Officer, Medical Officer, Center for Behavioral Wellness, PLLC; Indian Health Services, Navajo Preservation, Albuquerque NM **Career Related:** Professor, University of Tennessee (2017-Present); Consulting Physician, Drug Court, 21st Judicial District (2006-2011) **Civic:** Director, National Association of Drug Court Professionals (2016-Present); Councilor, Tennessee Medical Association (2015-Present); Opioid Task Force, American Medical Association (2014-Present); Board of Directors, Nashville Academy of Medicine (2014-Present); Diplomat, American Board of Addiction Medicine (2009-Present); President, Tennessee Society of Addiction Medicine, (2006-2008); Secretary/Treasurer, Nashville Academy of Medicine **Creative Works:** "Opioid Use Disorders in Pregnancy," Cambridge Medicine (2018); Editor-in-Chief, ASAM Weekly, American Society of Addiction (2011-2015); Associate Editor, Journal of Addiction and Addictive Disorders **Awards:** Distinguished Fellow, American Society of Addiction Medicine (2002-Present); Top Doctor, Findatopdoc.com; Fellow, Johns Hopkins University School of Medicine; Fellow, University of North Carolina at Chapel Hill **Memberships:** Co-Chair, Patient Advocacy Task Force, American Society of Addiction Medicine (2011-Present); National Association of Alcohol and Drug Abuse Counselors (2009-Present) **Marquis Who's Who Honors:** Marquis Who's Who Top Professional **To what do you attribute your success:** Dr. Soper believes that being able to help individuals reestablish their self-esteem and find stable functional behavior is a blessing. Patients are the driving factor behind his success. **Why did you become involved in your profession or industry:** Dr. Soper is an empath; he is affirmed by being part of the healing path for his patients. He feels there is no greater reward in life than to assist someone in actualizing their potential.

Sonia Maria Sotomayor

Title: Associate Justice **Company Name:** Supreme Court of the United States **Date of Birth:** 06/25/1954 **Place of Birth:** South Bronx **State/Country of Origin:** NY/USA **Parents:** Juan Sotomayor; Celina (Baez) Sotomayor **Marital Status:** Divorced **Spouse Name:** Kevin Edward Noonan (08/14/1976, Divorced, 1983) **Education:** Honorary LLD, Yale University (2013); Honorary LLD, New York University (2012); Honorary LLD, St. Lawrence University (2010); Honorary LLD, Howard University (2010); Honorary LLD, Northeastern University School of Law (2007); Honorary LLD, Hofstra University (2006); Honorary LLD, Pace University (2003); Honorary LLD, Princeton University (2001); Honorary LLD, Brooklyn Law School (2001); Honorary LLD, Lehman College, City University of New York (1999); JD, Yale Law School, New Haven, CT (1979); BA, Princeton University, Summa Cum Laude (1976) **Career:** Associate Justice, Supreme Court of the United States, Washington, DC (2009-Present); Judge, United States Court of Appeals for the Second Circuit, New York, NY (1998-2009); Judge, United States District Court for the Southern District of New York, New York, NY (1992-1998); Partner, Pavia & Harcourt, LLP, New York, NY (1988-1992); Associate, Pavia & Harcourt, LLP, New York, NY (1984-1987); Assistant District Attorney, New York County, New York, NY (1979-1984) **Career Related:** Lecturer of Law, Columbia Law School (1999-Present); Adjunct Professor, New York University School of Law (1998-2007) **Civic:** Trustee, Princeton University (2006-2011); New York State Advisory Panel of Inter-Group Relations (1990-1992); Board of Directors, New York City Campaign Finance Board, New York, NY (1988-1992) **Creative Works:** Author, "Turning Pages: My Life Story" (2018); Author, "My Beloved World: A Memoir" (2013) **Awards:** Listee, 100 Most Powerful Women in DC, Washingtonian Magazine (2009, 2011); Listee, World's 100 Most Powerful Women, Forbes Magazine (2009, 2010); Listee, 10 Most Powerful Women in Washington, Fortune Magazine (2010); Listee, Washington's Most Influential Women Lawyers, National Law Journal (2010); Listee, 100 Most Influential People in the World, Time Magazine (2010); Outstanding Latino Professional Award, Latino/a Law Students Association (2006) **Memberships:** American Bar Association; American Philosophical Society; Association of Hispanic Judges; New York Women's Bar Association; Puerto Rican Bar Association of New York; Hispanic National Bar Association; The Phi Beta Kappa Society **Bar Admissions:** United States District Court for the Eastern District of New York (1984); United States District Court for the Southern District of New York (1984); New York (1980) **Religion:** Roman Catholic

Lisa D. Sparks

Marquis Who's Who
18 98
Biographee

Title: Owner **Industry:** Food & Restaurant Services **Company Name:** Lisa's Pie Shop **Marital Status:** Married **Spouse Name:** Jim **Career:** Owner, Lisa's Pie Shop **To what do you attribute your success:** Ms. Sparks attributes her success to God and learning to run her business rather than letting her business run her. **Why did you become involved in your profession or industry:** Ms. Sparks became involved in her profession because her mother-in-law was one of the best cooks in the entire world and she wanted to impress her husband. She experimented with pie recipes, but many didn't turn out the way she wanted. Her best friend's mom gave her the secret ingredient to making the best pie crust and she has never looked back. **Avocations:** Quilting; Gardening

Nicholas Charles Sparks

Title: Author; Screenwriter **Industry:** Writing and Editing **Date of Birth:** 12/31/1965 **Place of Birth:** Omaha **State/Country of Origin:** NE/USA **Parents:** Patrick Michael Sparks; Jill Emma Marie (Thoene) Sparks **Marital Status:** Divorced **Spouse Name:** Catherine Cote (07/22/1989, Divorced 2015) **Children:** Miles; Ryan; Landon; Lexie; Savannah **Education:** BBA, University of Notre Dame, with High Honors (1988) **Career:** Salesman, Pharmaceuticals (1992-1995); Real Estate Appraiser; Waiter; Salesman, Dental Products; Owner, Manufacturing Business **Career Related:** Contributor, Creative Writing Program (MFA), University of Notre Dame **Civic:** Founder, Nicholas Sparks Foundation (2011-Present); Co-founder, The Epiphany School, New Bern, NC **Creative Works:** Author, "The Return" (2020); Author, "Every Breath" (2018); Author, "Two by Two" (2016); Author, "See Me" (2015); Author, "The Longest Ride" (2013); Author, "The Best of Me" (2011); Author, "Safe Haven" (2010); Author, "The Last Song" (2009); Author, "The Lucky One" (2008); Author, "The Choice" (2007); Author, "Dear John" (2006); Author, "True Believer" (2005); Author, "At First Sight" (2005); Co-author with Micah Sparks, "Three Weeks with My Brother" (2004); Author, "The Guardian" (2003); Author, "The Wedding" (2003); Author, "Nights in Rodanthe" (2002); Author, "A Bend in the Road" (2001); Author, "The Rescue" (2000); Author, "A Walk to Remember" (1999); Author, "Message in a Bottle" (1998); Author, "The Notebook" (1996); Co-author with Billy Mills, "Wokini: A Lakota Journey to Happiness and Self-Understanding (1990); Producer, Screenwriter, Film Adaptations

Michael A. Stein, MD

Title: Vice President; Cardiologist; Medical Educator; Medical Researcher **Industry:** Medicine & Health Care **Company Name:** Bayer Healthcare Pharmaceuticals **Date of Birth:** 05/31/1958 **Place of Birth:** Chicago **State/Country of Origin:** IL/USA **Parents:** Harold Marc Stein; Carlyne Mae (Skirow) Stein **Marital Status:** Married **Spouse Name:** Patricia Michelle Barrette (05/19/2016); Ann Palmer Coe (06/09/1984, Divorced 2007) **Children:** Sarah Elizabeth; David Benjamin; Kathryn Marie **Education:** Fellow in Cardiology, Interventional Cardiology, University of Iowa, Iowa City, Iowa (1987-1991); Resident in Medicine, Intern, University of Illinois, Chicago, IL (1984-1987); MD, University of Illinois (1984); BA, Lawrence University, Magna Cum Laude (1980) **Certifications:** Diplomate in Internal Medicine, Cardiovascular Diseases and Interventional Cardiology, American Board of Internal Medicine **Career:** Vice President, Head, Medical Experts & Medical Standards, Bayer HealthCare Pharmaceuticals (2016-Present); Executive Director, Bayer HealthCare Pharmaceuticals (2013-2016); Senior Director, Ikaria Biopharmaceuticals (2011-2013); Senior Director, Novo Nordisk (2009-2011); Senior Director, Daiichi Sankyo Pharmaceuticals (2007-2009); Associate Director, Astra Zeneca (2005-2007); Clinical Assistant Professor, University of Wisconsin-Madison (1998-2005); Director, Cardiology Department, Lower Florida Keys Health Systems (1997-1998); Assistant Professor, Emory University, Atlanta, GA (1991-1995) **Career Related:** Medical Director, Cardiac Catheterization Laboratory, Dunwoody Medical Center, Atlanta, GA (1994-1995); Medical Director, CCU Atlanta VA Medical Center, Decatur, GA (1991-1995) **Civic:** Board Member, Brodhead Watershed Association (2018-Present); Vice President, Fond du Lac City Council (2000-2001) **Awards:** Clinical Investigator Award, NIH (1990-1995); Clinical Scientist Award, American Heart Association (1990-1995), National Research Service Award, NIH (1987-1990) **Memberships:** Fellow, American College of Cardiology; Fellow, American Heart Association; Fellow, Society for Cardiovascular Angiography and Intervention **Marquis Who's Who Honors:** Albert Nelson Marquis Lifetime Achievement Award **Avocations:** Hiking; Adventure Travel; Photography; Outdoors

George Robert Stephanopoulos

Title: News Anchor, Political Correspondent **Date of Birth:** 02/10/1961 **Place of Birth:** Fall River **State/Country of Origin:** MA/USA **Parents:** Robert George Stephanopolous; Nickolitsa Gloria (Chafos) Stephanopolous **Marital Status:** Married **Spouse Name:** Ali Wentworth (11/20/2001) **Children:** Elliott Anastasia Stephanopoulos; Harper Andrea Stephanopoulos **Education:** Honorary LLD, St. John's University (2007); MA in Theology, Balliol College, University of Oxford (1984); BA in Political Science, Columbia University, Summa Cum Laude (1982) **Career:** Host, "This Week with George Stephanopoulos," ABC News (2012-Present, 2002-2010); Co-Anchor Good Morning America, ABC News (2009-Present); Chief Political Correspondent, ABC News (2009-Present); Political Analyst, Correspondent, ABC News (1997-Present); Chief Washington Correspondent, ABC News (2005-2009); Senior Adviser to the President for Policy and Strategy, The White House, Washington, DC (1993-1996); Communications Director, The White House, Washington, DC (1992-1996); Communications Director, Clinton/Gore Presidential Campaign, Little Rock, AR (1992); Deputy Communications Director, Dukakis/Bentsen Presidential Campaign (1988); Legislative Assistant, Chief of Staff to Congressman Edward Feighan, U.S. House of Representatives, Washington, DC; Executive Floor Manager to House Majority Leader Dick Gephardt, U.S. House of Representatives, Washington, DC **Civic:** Founding Member, Next Generation Initiative (2003) **Creative Works:** Himself, "'Agents of S.H.I.E.L.D."; Himself, "House of Cards" (2013); Author, "All Too Human: A Political Education" (1999); Himself, "Spin City" (1996); Himself, Documentary, "The War Room" (1993) **Awards:** Daytime Emmy Award for Outstanding Morning Program, "Good Morning America" (2014); News & Documentary Emmy Award for Outstanding Live Coverage of a Current News Story – Long Form, "ABC News Special Events" (2010); Walter Cronkite Award for Excellence in TV Political Journalism, USC Annenberg School for Communication and Journalism, University of Southern California (USC) (2009, 2007); Named One of "50 Most Powerful People in D.C.," GQ (2009); Named a Maverick, Details Magazine (2007); Medal of Excellence, Columbia University (1993); Harry S. Truman Scholarship, Columbia University; Rhodes Scholar, Oxford University **Memberships:** Phi Beta Kappa **Political Affiliations:** Democrat **Religion:** Greek Orthodox

Sylvia Ann Stetz

Title: Small Business Owner **Industry:** Apparel & Fashion **Company Name:** Sylvia Ann LLC **Date of Birth:** 01/03/1941 **Place of Birth:** Dearborn Heights **State/Country of Origin:** MI/USA **Parents:** John Hlasny; Eleanore Hlasny **Marital Status:** Married **Spouse Name:** Donald N. Stetz (08/29/1964) **Children:** Karyn Elaine; Julie Renee **Education:** Coursework, Pfaff School of Creative Sewing, Las Vegas, NV (1993); Postgraduate Coursework, Eastern Michigan University (1987-1989); Postgraduate Coursework, University of Michigan (1965); BS, Wayne State University, Detroit, MI (1963) **Career:** Owner, President, Sylvia Ann, LLC, Pinckney, MI (1994-Present); With, Custom Decorating Department, JC Penney, JCP Media, Inc. (1996-2003); Service Representative, Manpower, Howell, MI (1994-1996); Demonstrator, Instructor, Dralle Brothers, Pfaff and New Home Sewing Machine Sales (1992-1993); Part-time Sewing-Sales Educator, Dralle Brothers, Waterloo, Iowa (1992-1993); Owner, President, Sylvia Ann, Cedar Falls, Iowa (1989-1993); Business Office Manager, Waverly Hospital (Now Waverly Health Center) (1990-1991); Office, Branch Manager, E.H. Rowley Company, Detroit, MI (1986-1989); Personnel Coordinator, Uniforce Temporary Services, Southfield, MI (1985-1986); Manager, Major Accounts, International Calculator Sales, Southfield, MI (1984-1985); Salesperson, Saks Fifth Avenue, Dearborn, MI (1982-1984); Teacher, Crestwood School District, Dearborn Heights, MI (1964-1966); Salesperson, Sears Roebuck & Corp., Lincoln Park, MI (1963) **Civic:** Trustee, Secretary, Plymouth-Canton Board of Education (1979-1983); Chair, Helping Hand District Program, Plymouth-Canton Community Schools (1977-1982); Representative, Vice President, Plymouth-Canton Community School Council (1975-1979); President, Plymouth PTO (1973-1979); Volunteer, Helped Organize to Pass Equal Rights Amendment, National Organization for Women, State and National Level **Creative Works:** Writer, Presenter, Workshop on a Ballot Proposal, P.E.O. State Convention (2018); Custom Designer, From Bridal Wear to Home Décor **Awards:** First Place Award Winning Designer for Pfaff Sewing Machines and Vogue Patterns in Formal Wear, Vogue-Pfaff Fashion Show Contest (1993); Woman of the Year Award, Jaycettes, Plymouth, MI and Michigan District 30 (1977) **Memberships:** P.E.O. International (2009-Present); Ann Arbor City Club (2005-2009); Board of Directors, American Association of University Women (AAUW); Board of Directors, Chair, Ways and Means Committee; Bylaws; Secretary, Chapter President, Chair, Writer and Presenter, Workshop to Pass Amendment to State Bylaws, Michigan State Level, Amendments and Recommendations Committee **Marquis Who's Who Honors:** Marquis Lifetime Achievement Award **Avocations:** Sewing; Reading

LaTanya Stewart

Title: Payroll Manager, Owner **Industry:** Financial Services **Company Name:** 1) Ellie Mae 2) 3B Financial **Children:** One Child **Education:** MAFM, Keller Graduate School of Management, DeVry University, Fremont, CA (2012); BS in Accounting, University of Phoenix, AZ (2008) **Certifications:** Notary Public, California (2013-2021) **Career:** Payroll Manager, Ellie Mae, Pleasanton, CA (2019-Present) Small Business Owner, 3B Financial, Oakland, CA (2019-Present); Payroll Manager, OSIsoft, San Leandro, CA (2018-2019); Payroll Administrator, OSIsoft, San Leandro, CA (2017-2019); Payroll Analyst, OSIsoft, San Leandro, CA (2017-2018); Accounts Payable, Payroll Manager, Livescribe, Inc., Oakland, CA (2010-2016); Payroll Manager (Contract), Tesla Motors, Inc., San Carlos, CA (2009); Payroll Administrator (Contract), Equinox, Inc., Foster City, CA (2009); Payroll Manager, Westin San Francisco Market Street, San Francisco, CA (2008-2009); Payroll Supervisor (Contract), Innovative Technical Solutions, Inc., Walnut Creek, CA (2007-2008); Financial Director, The Mentoring Center, Oakland, CA (2005-2007); Payroll Supervisor, Exploratorium, San Francisco, CA (2001-2005); Payroll Supervisor, The American Red Cross, Oakland, CA (1997-2001); Billing/Payroll Supervisor, Alert Staffing, Pleasanton, CA (1998-1999) **Civic:** Financial Literacy Teacher, Institute For the Advanced Study of Black Family Life & Culture **Memberships:** American Payroll Association (APA); National Association of Professional Women **Marquis Who's Who Honors:** Marquis Who's Who Top Professional **To what do you attribute your success:** Ms. Stewart attributes her success to having a strong family foundation, which was provided by both her mother and grandmother. **Why did you become involved in your profession or industry:** Ms. Stewart became involved in her profession because she always wanted to be able to help others. People go to work to do a job and forget that they are paid for the services they offer, so she wanted to provide customer service for those employees and help reward them through their paychecks for what they do. She said, "Employees are the backbone of many organizations and people take for granted what they do." **Thoughts on Life:** Ms. Stewart's motto is, "Live in the moment and do not live with regret."

Marlana K. Stoddard-Hayes

Title: Artist, Educator **Industry:** Fine Art **Date of Birth:** 11/05/1957 **Place of Birth:** Ottumwa **State/Country of Origin:** IA/USA **Parents:** Roy Keables Stoddard Junior (Adoptive Father); Joyce Ellen McNeight (Adoptive Mother); Sally Werner Schmidt (Biological Mother); Dr. Wallace Hi, MD (Biological Father) **Education:** MA in Interdisciplinary Studies, Maryhurst University (2002); Coursework, Marchutz School, Aix-En-Provance, France (1989); MFA in Painting, Wichita State University (1983); BFA in Painting, Colorado State University (1980); Institute of European Studies, Vienna, Austria (1978); Foundations, Kansas City Art Institute (1975-1977) **Career:** Instructor, Sitka Center of Art & Ecology (1991-2020); Adjunct Professor, Art, Portland Community College (2001-2015); Faculty, School of Graduate Studies, Marylhurst University, Portland, OR (2013); Adjunct Professor, Drawing, Clark College (2000-2003); Professor, Art, Dodge City Community College (1995-2000); Artist-in-Residence, Kansas Arts Commission (1983-1995); Artist-in-Residence, Neskowin Coast Foundation, Cascade Head, OR (1990-1991) **Career Related:** Presenter, Stanford University (2008); Presenter, National Academy of Religion Conference, Marylhurst University (2013); Thesis Advisor, Oregon College of Art and Craft (2010); Advisor Sitka Center of Art & Ecology (2006-2010); Invited Lecturer, Numerous Universities **Civic:** St. Micheals Episcopal Parish, Portland, OR; Thesis Advisor, Oregon College of Art and Craft; PEO Sisterhood, Women's Cottey College **Creative Works:** Solo Exhibition, Butters Gallery, Portland, OR (2013, 2015, 2016, 2018); Group Show, Makeshift Museum, Los Angeles, CA (2016); Group Show, Scope Miami (2015); Exhibition, Port Angeles Fine Arts Center (2013); Exhibition, Chehalem Cultural Center, Newberg, OR (2012); Solo Exhibition, Beppu Wiarda Gallery, Portland, OR (2008, 2009); Group Show, Red Dot Fair (2008); Solo Exhibition, RC Gallery (2005-2006) **Awards:** Oregon Arts Commission and Ford Family Foundation Grant for Professional Development (2019); Regional Arts and Cultural Council Grant for Professional Development (2019); Professional Development Grant, Regional Arts and Cultural Council (2011) **Marquis Who's Who Honors:** Albert Nelson Marquis Lifetime Achievement Award **To what do you attribute your success:** Ms. Stoddard-Hayes attributes her success to her parents and grandparents; they inspired and encouraged her to succeed. **Why did you become involved in your profession or industry:** Ms. Stoddard-Hayes' field of work is an area that she always enjoyed exploring, which led to her involvement. **Avocations:** Gardening; Researching philosophy and history **Political Affiliations:** Democrat **Religion:** Episcopalian

Donald Arthur Stork

Title: Advertsing Executive (Retired) **Industry:** Advertising & Marketing **Date of Birth:** 06/17/1939 **Place of Birth:** Walsh **State/Country of Origin:** IL/USA **Parents:** Arthur William Stork, Katherine Frances Young **Marital Status:** Married **Spouse Name:** Joanna Gentry (06/09/1962) **Children:** Brian Wesley Stork **Education:** Postgraduate Coursework, St. Louis University, St. Louis, MO (1968-1969); BS, Southern Illinois University, Carbondale, IL (1961) **Career:** President Emeritus, PHD Unit Omnicom Group; President, Advanswers Unit, Omnicom; President, Advanswers Division, Wells Rich Greene; Senior Vice President, Marketing, Advanswers; Media Executive, Gardner Advertising; Media Executive, Naegele Outdoor Advertising; Media Executive, Commercial Letter Inc. **Civic:** Board of Governors, Missouri Athletic Club (2009-2012), Board of Directors, St. Clair Country Club (2001-2003); Member, Corporate Development Council, St. Louis Art Museum **Military Service:** Captain, Missouri Air National Guard (1961-1968) **Awards:** Inductee, Advertising Hall of Fame-St Louis Advertising Club; Journalism Alumnus of the Year, Alumni Achievement Award, Dean's National Industry Council, Southern Illinois University; Aid to Advertising Education Award, Alpha Delta Sigma **Marquis Who's Who Honors:** Albert Nelson Marquis Lifetime Achievement Award (2019) **To what do you attribute your success:** Mr. Stork attributes his success to all of the individuals who contributed to the creation of Advanswers Media/Programming and its success. His clients were of equal importance, whose belief and conviction in his business was vital to its survival. **Why did you become involved in your profession or industry:** Mr. Stork became interested in advertising at an early age while working in his father's general retail store, particularly in how to compete with larger establishments and franchises.

Dulce Suarez-Resnick

Title: Vice President **Industry:** Insurance **Company Name:** NCF Insurance Associates/Acentria Insurance **Place of Birth:** Miami Beach **State/Country of Origin:** FL/USA **Parents:** Farrah Figuirado **Education:** Associate of Science in Insurance Services, Insurance Institute of America (1994) **Career:** Vice President, Sales & Marketing, NCF Insurance Associates/Acentria Insurance (2009-Present); Assistant Vice President, Personal Lines, Sales and Marketing, HPA Insurance **Career Related:** Chairman, Co-Chair of Legislation, Political Committee, Latin Agents Association **Awards:** Rookie of The Year, Insurance Women Association; Recognition, Elite Women in Insurance (Choice 95 Women Throughout the United States) **Memberships:** Florida Residential Property and Casualty Joint Underwriting Association; Florida Windstorm Underwriting Association; Latin Agents Association; Florida Association of Insurance Agents **To what do you attribute your success:** Ms. Suarez-Resnick attributes her success to the people who helped her along the way. She knew the technical aspect to her studies, and benefited from the tutelage of good mentors. **Why did you become involved in your profession or industry:** Ms. Suarez-Resnick became involved in her profession because she was a science honor student in middle school and high school, and in the 10th grade she served as a medical explorer for six weeks at a local hospital, but became very anxious when it came to needles. She realized that her dream of becoming a pediatrician was over. So, in the 11th grade, she had no direction. She worked at a condominium after school and met several insurance agents. One particular agent came in and spoke to Ms. Suarez-Resnick and asked her to interview for a clerk position, since her school was nearby, which launched her career in insurance. **Thoughts on Life:** Always look forward and never look back.

Jennifer Sutton

Title: Partner, President **Industry:** Veterinary Care **Company Name:** Gulf Coast Veterinary Services **Date of Birth:** 09/20/1970 **Place of Birth:** Washington **State/Country of Origin:** DC/USA **Parents:** Jeffrey Sutton, DVM **Children:** Connor; Ashleigh; Taylor; Ava **Education:** Master of Business Administration, Louisiana State University, Shreveport, LA (2019); Doctor of Veterinary Medicine, Louisiana State University School of Veterinary Medicine, Baton Rouge, LA (1998); BS in Biology, Millsaps College, Jackson, MS (1992) **Certifications:** Graduate Certificate, Teaching in the Healthcare Professions, Louisiana State University, Baton Rouge, La (2020); Professional Coach with International Coach Federation Credentialing, Emphasis in Generative Coaching Techniques (2020); Veterinary Practice Manager Certification, Veterinary Hospital Manager's Association (2020); Emergency Healthcare Professional (CEHP) (2019); Emergency Disaster Professional (CEDP) (2019); Licensed, Mississippi Board of Veterinary Medicine; Licensed, Louisiana Board of Veterinary Medicine; U.S. Department of Agriculture Animal Health and Inspection Service National Accreditation; ARRL Amateur Radio Licensure; U.S. Government Interim Secret Clearance **Career:** Partner, Veterinarian, Beach View Veterinary Hospital, LLC, Biloxi, MS (2015-Present); President, Partner, Veterinarian, Gulf Coast Veterinary Emergency Hospital, Biloxi, MS (2002-Present); Interim Executive Director, Hancock County Court Appointed Special Advocate (CASA) Program, Bay St. Louis, MS (2013) **Civic:** Mississippi Animal Rescue Team; USDA National Animal Emergency Response Corps; Volunteers in Preparedness Registry; Member, Various Philanthropic Organizations in Field **Creative Works:** Lecturer, "Dogs Vs. Cats: Their Amazing Sense of Smell" (2016-Present); Lecturer, USM-Office of Lifelong Learning Institute (2015-Present); Lecturer, "Emergency Medical Assessment and Care of Animals in Disasters" (2013-Present); Lecturer, "Top 5 Small Animal Emergencies Encountered in Disasters" (2013-Present); Lecturer, Canine First Aid for Search and Rescue Dog Handlers (2013-Present); Lecturer, "Hug a Tree and Survive" (2010-Present) **Awards:** NSLS State of Mind Award, Mississippi (2019); "Director's Coin of Excellence," Mississippi Emergency Management Agency (2019); Listee, "100 Successful Women to Know," Gulf Coast Woman's Magazine Success Showcase (2019, 2018) **Memberships:** American Veterinarian Medical Association; American Animal Hospital Association; Member, Various Field Organizations **Marquis Who's Who Honors:** Marquis Who's Who Top Professional; Distinguished Humanitarian **To what do you attribute your success:** Dr. Sutton attributes her success to her mentors.

Angela Mae "Angel Mae" Svoboda

Title: Coordinator, Business Education Department Chair (Retired) **Industry:** Education/Educational Services **Place of Birth:** Central City **State/Country of Origin:** IA/USA **Parents:** Frank Joseph Svoboda; Annie Marie (Vrba) Svoboda **Marital Status:** Single **Education:** MS in Education, University of Michigan (1961); BSc in Commerce, The University of Iowa (1956); Diplomate, Coe College (1955); Postgraduate Coursework, Rackham College of Education, Appalachian State University; Postgraduate Coursework, The University of Iowa; Postgraduate Coursework, University of Northern Iowa **Career:** Business Teacher, Washington High School, Cedar Rapids Community School District, Cedar Rapids, Iowa (1959-1994); Office of Education Coordinator, Washington High School, Cedar Rapids Community School District, Cedar Rapids, Iowa (1959-1994); Business Education Department Chair, Washington High School, Cedar Rapids Community School District, Cedar Rapids, Iowa (1959-1994); Business Teacher, Burlington Community High School, Iowa (1956-1959); Departmental Assistant to Head of Business Education Department, Coe College, Cedar Rapids, Iowa (1954-1955); Executive Secretary, Iowa Organic Association, Foods, Cedar Rapids, Iowa (1947-1953); Public Speaker **Career Related:** Clerk, The Quaker Oats Company (1955); Secretary, Zachar and Fries Real Estate (1954); Secretary, Shea & Lillios Attorneys (1953) **Awards:** Sophomore Honors, Coe College (1954); Valedictorian, High School Graduating Class, Central City, Iowa (1947) **Memberships:** First Vice President, Cedar Rapids Chapter, Quota Club (Now Quota International, Inc.) (1976-1977); Secretary-treasurer, District Quota Club (Now Quota International, Inc.) (1975-1976); Life Member, National Education Association; Czech Heritage Foundation; Past President, Cedar Rapids Chapter, Daughters of Isabella; Past State Vice President, Daughters of Isabella; Professional Secretaries Inc. (Now International Association of Administrative Professionals); Iowa State Education Association; Secretary, Cedar Rapids Education Association; Iowa Business Education Association; American Vocational Association (Now Association for Career & Technical Education) **Marquis Who's Who Honors:** Albert Nelson Marquis Lifetime Achievement Award **To what do you attribute your success:** Ms. Svoboda attributes her success to her mother, Annie Marie Svoboda. **Why did you become involved in your profession or industry:** Ms. Svoboda became involved in her profession because she has always been interested in learning and education. **Avocations:** Dance; World Traveler; Casinos **Political Affiliations:** Democrat **Religion:** Roman Catholic

Bernard Francis "Bernie" Sweener

Title: Clinician-Licensed Master Social Worker **Industry:** Social Work **Company Name:** Vanderheyden Hall Inc. **Date of Birth:** 10/08/1956 **Place of Birth:** Pittsfield **State/Country of Origin:** MA/USA **Parents:** Ulysses F. Sweener, Jr.; Roseanna R. Sweener **Marital Status:** Married **Children:** Dustin Hector Sweener **Education:** MSW, University at Albany, State University of New York, Albany, NY (2004); AAS in Human Services, Hudson Valley Community College (1995) **Certifications:** Licensed Master Social Worker **Career:** LMSW, Vanderheyden Hall Inc., Wynantskill, NY (2014-Present); Medical Social Worker, Seton Health (2005-2006); BSW Case Manager, St. Anne's Institute (1999-2004) **Memberships:** National Association of Social Workers; National Coalition Building Institute **Marquis Who's Who Honors:** Marquis Who's Who Top Professional **To what do you attribute your success:** Mr. Sweener attributes his success to his parents, Ulysses and Roseanna. His mother was a sensitive and caring person, and his father's kind-hearted nature, combined with his great work ethic, had the biggest influence on Mr. Sweener's career. **Why did you become involved in your profession or industry:** Mr. Sweener started his career as a construction worker for 30 years. However, he soon felt called to pursue social work, which is how he began working at a nearby hospital. There, he encountered a man who was told he would never walk again. This man was incoherent but eventually provided the hospital workers with his name. Mr. Sweener was able to find this man's sister, who was elated to hear of her brother surfacing. They had not been in contact for 10 years. This experience inspired Mr. Sweener to continue his career as a social worker. **Avocations:** Golfing

Margot Swetman

Title: Self Development and Executive Leadership Life Coach **Industry:** Other **Company Name:** Margot M.J. Swetman **Place of Birth:** Hattiesburg **State/Country of Origin:** MS/USA **Parents:** Glenn R. Swetman; Margertia Swetman **Children:** Glenn Quave; William Quave; Kathryn Smith Evans **Education:** MS in Counseling Psychology (2007); MBA (1998); BS in Economics, William Carey University (1998); MEd in English Education, William Carey University (1997); BS in Economics, Nicholls State University (1996) **Certifications:** Life Coach in Transition and Executive Leadership Coaching, Institute for Professional Excellence in Coaching; Certified Energy Leadership Index Master Practitioner **Career:** Life Coach (2017-Present); Case Manager, Catholic Diocese of Biloxi; Assistant Dean of Students, Adjunct Professor, William Carey University **Civic:** Officer, Board Member, Sea and Sun Camp, Inc.; Board Member, Ohr-O'Keefe Museum of Art; Vice President, Band Booster Club, Saint Stanislaus; Vice President, Bay St. Louis Lions Club; Volunteer, Society of St. Vincent de Paul-Biloxi **Creative Works:** Author, "The 9 Questions of English" **Memberships:** International Association for Counseling **Marquis Who's Who Honors:** Marquis Who's Who Top Professional; Marquis Who's Who Humanitarian Award **To what do you attribute your success:** Ms. Swetman attributes her success to hard work, patience and faith. She took advantage of opportunities as they came up. **Why did you become involved in your profession or industry:** Ms. Swetman became involved in her profession because William Carey University wasn't building dorms on the beach in the aftermath of Hurricane Katrina so there was no need for her position. She decided to pursue a career helping others and became a life coach. **Thoughts on Life:** Ms. Swetman states, "Love all, trust a few, and do wrong to none."

Debora Taylor Swisher, BSN, RN-BC

Title: Registered Nurse, Complex Care Manager **Industry:** Medicine & Health Care **Company Name:** OSF Healthcare System Western Region **Date of Birth:** 04/05/1959 **Place of Birth:** Canton **State/Country of Origin:** IL/USA **Parents:** Richard Jean Taylor; Barbara Elaine (Bump) Taylor **Marital Status:** Married **Spouse Name:** Duane E. Swisher (08/08/1998) **Education:** BSN, University of Illinois Chicago (1990); AAS, Carl Sandburg College (1980) **Certifications:** Board Certified in Case Management (2018-2023); Certified in Pediatric Advanced Life Support, American Heart Association (2008-2019); Certified in Basic Life Support, American Heart Association (1990-2019) **Career:** Registered Nurse, Complex Care Manager, OSF Healthcare System Western Region (2015-Present); Staff Nurse, Medical-Surgical Pediatric Oncology Unit, St. Mary Medical Center (2006-2015); Home Health Nurse Case Manager (2004-2006); Performance Improvement and Education Coordinator, Home Health Aide Supervisor, St. Mary Medical Center (2000-2004); Operational Support Nurse, St. Mary Medical Center (1998-2000); Home Health Staff Nurse, St. Mary Medical Center (1994-1998); Pediatrics Staff Nurse, St. Mary Medical Center (1980-1994) **Career Related:** Pediatric Advanced Life Support Instructor, American Heart Association (2008-2020); Basic Life Support Instructor, American Heart Association (1990-2019); Clinical Instructor, Licensed Practical Nursing Program, Carl Sandburg College; Co-Chairman, Unit Based Council, Medical-Surgical Pediatric Oncology Unit, OSF St. Mary Medical Center **Civic:** Choral Dynamics (2015-Present); Superintendent, Sunday School, First United Methodist Church, Henderson, TX (1986-1992) **Awards:** Daisy Award, OSF St. Mary Medical Center (2015); Award, Board of Directors, Nursing Alumni Association, University of Illinois (1990) **Memberships:** Board Member, Quad Cities Chapter, Nursing Alumni Association, University of Illinois (1990-1998); Alpha Lambda Chapter, Sigma Theta Tau International Honor Society of Nursing; American Nurses Association **Marquis Who's Who Honors:** Albert Nelson Marquis Lifetime Achievement Award **Why did you become involved in your profession or industry:** Ms. Swisher became involved in her profession because she was inspired by her mother, an aide in a mental hospital.

Carmen Tafolla

Title: Professor Emerita, President **Industry:** Other **Company Name:** Carmen Tafolla **Date of Birth:** 07/29/2019 **Place of Birth:** San Antonio **State/Country of Origin:** TX/USA **Marital Status:** Married **Spouse Name:** Ernesto Bernal **Children:** Three Children **Education:** PhD in Bilingual and Foreign Education, The University of Texas at Austin (1981); MA in Mexican American Education, Austin College (1974); BA in Spanish and French, Austin College (1973); Honorary Doctorate in Humanities, Austin College **Career:** Associate Professor Education, The University of Texas at San Antonio (2006-Present); Director, Mexican-American Studies Center, Texas Lutheran University (1973-1976, 1978-1979); Special Assistant to President, Northern Arizona University; Associate Professor of Women's Studies, California State University, Fresno; Head Writer, National Council for Children's Television; Coordinator, Parent Training Packages, SEDL **Civic:** President, Texas Institute of Letters (2019-Present); Member, Texas Institute of Letters (2009-Present) **Creative Works:** Commissioned to Write Poem, "Child's Faith"; Commissioned to Write Poem, 50th Anniversary of the Founding of the University of Texas, San Antonio **Awards:** Poet Laureate of San Antonio (2012-2014) **Memberships:** Academy of American Poets **To what do you attribute your success:** Ms. Tafolla attributes her success to her creativity, optimism and commitment to helping others accept and celebrate each other. **Why did you become involved in your profession or industry:** Ms. Tafolla became involved in her profession because of her lifelong love of writing. She became involved in writing for children after having her own daughter in the 1980s.

Desi Tahiraj

Title: Business Consultant; Life Coach **Industry:** Consulting **Company Name:** Desi Tahiraj Consulting **Children:** Arthur **Education:** Coursework, Leading Organizational Change Executive Program, Columbia University (2019-2020); Coursework, University of Navarra IESE Business School (2016-2018); LLB in Civil Administration and Property, European University of Tirana, Albania (1996) **Certifications:** Licensed, Business Trainer Jack Canfield Success Training Institute, The Canfield Training Group, Self Esteem Seminars, L.P.; Licensed Life Coach, Life Mastery Institute; Leading Organizational Performance and Change Executive Management, Columbia University **Career:** Business Consultant (2018-Present); With, University of Navarra IESE Business School (2016-2018); With, Human Resources and Academic Affairs, Columbia University (2000-2016) **Civic:** Volunteer, Fundraiser, St. Jude's Children's Research Hospital **Awards:** Awards of Excellence, Columbia University (2010, 2011); Named Top Transformational Coach, IAOTP **Marquis Who's Who Honors:** Albert Nelson Marquis Lifetime Achievement Award **To what do you attribute your success:** Ms. Tahiraj attributes her success to being a compassionate person; she feels people's pain and wants to help them in every way possible. **Why did you become involved in your profession or industry:** Since Ms. Tahiraj was 9 years old, she has felt the calling to serve and help people. Born in a communist country and because her family was not communist, they killed 27 people from her family. They wanted to kill her father as well, but he was a great professional and educated. He saved the life of the prime minister so the prime minister saved her father's life. Living in such a harsh environment they were not allowed to go to school, get a job, love someone, build anything, or go anywhere. Living that hell, she promised herself and prayed to God to help her help everyone she came across. When communism was over, she went and completed law school. People voted for her to become attorney of the city and she helped everyone with no question. Upon traveling to the U.S., she worked as a trusted HR and Academic Affairs Professional at Columbia University in New York. Her areas of expertise include, but are not limited to, coaching, leadership and development, team building, management, and culture change.

Rongjia Tao, PhD

Title: Professor **Industry:** Medicine & Health Care **Company Name:** Temple University **Date of Birth:** 01/28/1947 **Place of Birth:** Shangai **State/Country of Origin:** China **Parents:** Yun Tao; Xiao-Mei Zou **Marital Status:** Married **Spouse Name:** Hong Guo **Children:** Han; Jing; Henry; James **Education:** PhD, Columbia University (1982), MA, Columbia University (1980); BS, University of Science and Technology of China (1970) **Career:** With, Cardiovascular Research Center (2016-Present); Professor, Physics, Temple University (2000-Present); Chairman, Temple University (2007-2014); Chairman, Physics, Southern Illinois University, Carbondale, IL (1994-1999); Professor, Temple University (1989-1999); Assistant Professor, Physics, Northeastern University (1985-1989); Research Assistant Professor, University of Southern California, Los Angeles, CA (1984-1985); Research Associate, University of Washington (1982-1984) **Career Related:** Consultant, United Nations Development Programme (1992) **Creative Works:** Chief Editor, Modern Physics Letter B and International Journal of Modern Physics B. (2010-Present); Author, 150 Research Publications and 10 Patent Inventions with Distinguished Contributions to Quantum Hall Effect, Topological Quantization, ER and MR Fluids, Oil, Energy, and Cardiovascular Health Science **Awards:** Outstanding Research Award, Temple University (2014); Fellow, American Physical Society (2004); Outstanding Scholar Award, Southern Illinois University, Carbondale, IL (1998); Omni Prize for Solving a Mathematical Puzzle, "Vicious Neighbor Problem" (1987) **Memberships:** Life Member, Fellow, American Physical Society **Marquis Who's Who Honors:** Albert Nelson Marquis Lifetime Achievement Award; Marquis Who's Who Top Professional **Why did you become involved in your profession or industry:** Dr. Tao has always been fascinated with the nature of science and wanted science to make a difference for mankind.

Jake Tapper

Title: News Correspondent, Journalist **Date of Birth:** 03/12/1969 **Place of Birth:** New York **State/Country of Origin:** NY/USA **Parents:** Theodore S. Tapper; Anne Tapper **Marital Status:** Married **Spouse Name:** Jennifer Marie Brown (09/03/2006) **Children:** Alice Paul Tapper; One Son **Education:** BA in History, Dartmouth College, Magna Cum Laude (1991); Coursework, University of Southern California School of Cinematic Arts **Career:** Host, "State of the Union with Jake Tapper," CNN (2015-Present); Host, "The Lead with Jake Tapper," CNN (2013-Present); Chief White House Correspondent, CNN (2013-Present); Chief White House Correspondent, ABC News (2008-2012); National/Senior Political Correspondent, Washington, DC Bureau, ABC News (2003-2008); Washington Correspondent, Salon.com (1999-2002); Senior Writer, Washington City Paper (1998-1999); With, Handgun Control, Inc. (Now the Brady Center to Prevent Gun Violence) (1997); Campaign Press Secretary, Representative Marjorie Margolies-Mezvinsky, U.S. House of Representatives (1992); Publicist, Powell Tate, Washington, DC **Career Related:** Interim Anchor, "This Week," ABC News (2010); Host, Sundance Channel (2003); Host, Entertainment News Specials, VH1 (2002); Host, "Take Five," CNN (2001); Contributing Anchor, "Good Morning America," "Nightline," "World News with Diane Sawyer"; Contributor, ABCNews.com, ABC NewsNOW **Creative Works:** Author, "The Hellfire Club" (2018); Guest Illustrator, "Dilbert" (2016); Author, "The Outpost: The Untold Story of American Valor" (2012); Creator, "Capitol Hell," Roll Call (1994-2003); Author, "Down & Dirty: The Plot to Steal the Presidency" (2001); Author, "Body Slam: The Jesse Ventura Story" (1999); Contributor, Cartoons, Various Publications; Guest, "Jimmy Kimmel Live!", "The Colbert Report," "Late Night with Seth Meyers," "Conan," "The View," "Real Time with Bill Maher"; Contributing Writer, Various Publications; Columnist, TALK Magazine; Contributor, "All Things Considered," National Public Radio (NPR) **Awards:** LHD (Honorary), University of Massachusetts Amherst (2018); Veterans Award (Vetty) (2018); Merriman Smith Memorial Award (2010, 2011, 2012, 2018); LHD (Honorary), Dartmouth College (2017); Walter Cronkite Award for Excellence in Political Journalism (2017); John F. Hogan Distinguished Service Award, Rdio Television Digital News Association (RTDNA) (2017); Tribute Award, CJF (2017); Robert S. Greenberger Journalism Award, Moment Magazine (2017); President's Award for Impact on Media, Los Angeles Press Club (2017) **Memberships:** Phi Beta Kappa

Nell Cochrane Taylor

Title: Nonprofit Association Executive (Retired) **Industry:** Nonprofit & Philanthropy **Date of Birth:** 12/25/1929 **Place of Birth:** Brooklyn **State/Country of Origin:** NY/USA **Parents:** Zeddie Marshall Cochrane; Eunice Hamilton Cochrane **Marital Status:** Divorced **Spouse Name:** Timothy M. Taylor Senior (06/11/1955, Divorced 06/1988) **Children:** Timothy; Stuart; Blair; Scott; Marshall **Education:** MA, Yale University (1952); BA, Smith College, Cum Laude (1951) **Career:** Educational Consultant, Scarborough, NY (1998-2001); Executive Director, White Plains Child Day Care Associates (1990-1997); Director of Administrative Services, Sheltering Arms Children and Family Services (1988-1990); Manager, Research Commissions, CJ Lawrence (1985-1986); Manager of Community College Relations, Assistant to the Vice President of Human Resources, The Continental Group (1980-1984); Program Administrator for Training, Westchester County (1979-1980); Instructor of Language Arts, Purchase College, State University of New York (1978-1979); English Teacher, Guidance Counselor, Hunter College High School (1953-1959) **Career Related:** Board of Directors, Child Care Council of Westchester, Inc. (1992-1998); Advisory Board Member, Not-for-Profit Management Center (1995-1997); Vice President, Child Care Council of Westchester, Inc. (1994-1995); Development Consultant, Department of Community Mental Health, Westchester County (1987-1988); Member, Commerce and Industry Council, National Urban League (1981-1984) **Civic:** Board of Directors, Scarborough Manor Owners Corporation (1999-2002); Elder, Presbyterian Church of Mount Kisco (1999-2001); Women's Advisory Board Member, Westchester County (2000); Trustee, Northern Westchester Hospital, Northwell Health (1987-1999); Board of Directors, Planned Parenthood Federation of America Inc. (1989-1993) **Creative Works:** Co-Author, "Social Aspects of Education" (1962) **Awards:** Jan Silverman Award, White Plains Child Day Care Associates (1998); John M. Greene Award, Smith College (1994); Paul Harris Fellow, Westchester Club (1994); Black Achiever in Industry, Harlem YMCA (1982) **Memberships:** Board of Directors, Westchester Club (1995-1998); Member, Rotary International **Marquis Who's Who Honors:** Albert Nelson Marquis Lifetime Achievement Award **Why did you become involved in your profession or industry:** Ms. Taylor became involved in her profession because her family stressed the importance of education. **Avocations:** Reading; Writing; Playing piano **Political Affiliations:** Democrat

Patricia Marie Tesar, PhD

Title: Special Education Administrator **Industry:** Education/Educational Services **Company Name:** Gallaudet University **Date of Birth:** 10/07/1955 **Place of Birth:** Cleveland **State/Country of Origin:** OH/USA **Parents:** John Joseph; Florence Louise Tesar **Education:** PhD in Special Education Administration, Summa Cum Laude, Gallaudet University (2002); MA in Rehabilitation Counseling, Summa Cum Laude, Gallaudet College (1986); BA in Interpersonal Communications, Cleveland State University (1982) **Career:** Part Time, Community Colleges (2019-Present); Director, Coordinator, Office for Students with Disabilities, Gallaudet University, Washington, DC (1990-2007, 2007-2019); Career Counselor, Career Center, Gallaudet University, Washington, DC (1984-1990) **Career Related:** National Conference Presenter, Association for Higher Education and Disability and Postsecondary Training Institute, University of Connecticut (2003, 2004, 2014-2018); President-Elect, Board Member, C-AHEAD (2013-2015); White House Keynote Presenter, National Disability Awareness Month (2003) **Civic:** Co-Chair, Sub-Committee, Adult Employment Development Disabilities State Planning Council DC (1997-Present) **Awards:** Who's Who Among Students in American Universities and Colleges (1992, 1998-2002, 2018-2019); U.S. Congressional Award of Achievement (1986, 1992); National Distinguished Service Registry Counseling Award (1990) **Memberships:** Association for Supervision and Curriculum Development; President, Metropolitan Washington Chapter, American Deafness and Rehabilitation Association (1988-1990, 1990-1992); American Association Counseling and Development; National Rehabilitation Association; National Association for Deaf; American Association for Deaf-Blind; Maryland Career Development Association; Maryland Rehabilitation Counseling Association; Washington Consortium of Universities Career Development Group; Washington Consortium of Universities Student Support Services Coalition (Regional Conference Coordinator); Metropolitan Washington Association Deaf-Blind; College Placement Council; Registry of Interpreters for the Deaf; Association Higher Education **Marquis Who's Who Honors:** Albert Nelson Marquis Lifetime Achievement Award (2019) **Religion:** Baptist

Ronald L. Thune

Title: Professor **Industry:** Education/Educational Services **Company Name:** Louisiana State University **Marital Status:** Married **Spouse Name:** Lynette **Children:** Carrie; Leanne **Education:** PhD, Auburn University; MS, Western Illinois University; BS, Colorado State University **Certifications:** Certified, Fish Pathologist, Fish Health Section of the AFS **Career:** Professor, School of Veterinary Medicine, Louisiana State University (1980-Present); Head, Department of Pathobiological Sciences (2000-2019) **Career Related:** Educator, Animal Health Courses, Turkey, China (1997 to 2015) **Creative Works:** Editor, "Journal of the World Aquaculture Society" (1986-1994); Contributor, Professional Journals **Awards:** Best Paper Award, Journal of Aquatic Animal Health (2005); S.F. Snieszko Distinguished Service Award, AFS Fish Health Section (2002); Exemplary Service Award from the World Aquaculture Society (2001); Award of Excellence for Outstanding Research, Triad Nitrogen, Inc. (2001); Best Paper Award, Journal of Aquatic Animal Health (1999); Pfizer Animal Health Award for Research Excellence (1999); Merit Award, Research, LSU Chapter, Gamma Sigma Delta (1992); Distinguished Scholar Award, School of Veterinary Medicine, Louisiana State University (1990) **Memberships:** The American Society for Microbiology; Fish Health Section of the American Fisheries Society; President, Fish Health Section (1993-1994) **To what do you attribute your success:** Dr. Thune attributes his success to a little bit of luck and a lot of hard work. **Why did you become involved in your profession or industry:** Dr. Thune became involved in his profession because of his general love for science. He was particularly interested in microbiology, aquatic animal health, and aquaculture, topics from which he has made a rewarding career. **Avocations:** Fishing; Golfing; Baseball; Soccer; Travel **Thoughts on Life:** Life is wonderful.

Burton L. Tillman, Esq.

Title: Founder & Attorney **Industry:** Law and Legal Services **Company Name:** Burton L. Tillman PC dba Tillman and Associates **Place of Birth:** Valdosta **State/Country of Origin:** GA/USA **Parents:** Burton L. Tillman; Gladys Stump Tillman **Marital Status:** Married **Education:** JD, School of Law, University of Georgia, Athens, GA (1979); BA, Emory University, Atlanta, GA (1971) **Certifications:** Registered Mediator, Georgia Office of Dispute Resolution (2007-Present); Registered Arbitrator, Georgia Office of Dispute Resolution (2007-Present) **Career:** Founder, Attorney, Mediated Resolutions LLC (2017-Present); Founder, Attorney, Mediated Dispute Resolutions, LLC (2008-2017); Founding Partner, Burton L. Tillman, PC, Tillman & Associates (1991-Present); Partner, Buchanan and Tillman (1987-1991); Attorney, Insurance Defense Litigation; Defense Practice, Bovis, Kyle, Burch & Medlin, LLC **Career Related:** Teacher, Shambhala Meditation Center of Atlanta **Civic:** Contributor, Volunteer, kidschancega.org; Volunteer, Chairman, Board of Directors, The Atlanta Boy Choir; Board Member, Open Hand, Atlanta, GA **Creative Works:** Featured Presenter and Speaker, Annual Seminar, State Workers' Compensation Law Institute, State Bar of Georgia, St. Simons Island, GA; Featured Presenter and Speaker, Seminars, Atlanta Claims Association **Awards:** Lifetime Achievement Award, America's Top 100 Attorneys® America's Top 100 LLC (2019); Workers' Compensation Attorney of the Year (2019); The National Trial Lawyers: Top 100, The National Trial Lawyers (2019); Top 100 Diplomate, Registry, National Academy of Distinguished Neutrals (2019); Certificate of Achievement, Roundtable Magazine (2019); Mediator of the Year, Roundtable Magazine (2019); Howard Osofsky Award (2019) **Memberships:** Chairman, Vice-Chairman, Board of Directors, Workers' Compensation Section, Atlanta Bar Association; State Bar of Georgia; Georgia Trial Lawyers Association **Bar Admissions:** State of Georgia (1979) **To what do you attribute your success:** Mr. Tillman attributes his success to his credibility, knowledge and people skills. He is uniquely able to persuade others to hear him and participate with him, and he is proud of his advocacy. **Why did you become involved in your profession or industry:** Mr. Tillman became involved in his profession with inspiration from his father, who was also a lawyer. Apart from having the right skill set, he was attracted to the idea of being in the position to master his own faith. Upon graduating from law school, Mr. Tillman worked for a few big firms before launching his own practice.

Robert Wilson Timmerman, PE, CEM, LEED AP

Title: Engineering Executive, Researcher **Industry:** Engineering **Date of Birth:** 06/27/1944 **Place of Birth:** Abington **State/Country of Origin:** PA/USA **Parents:** Clarence Arthur Timmerman; Mildred Wilson (Slack) Timmerman **Marital Status:** Married **Spouse Name:** Nancy Jean Spinka (09/28/1974) **Children:** Robert Jr; Elizabeth Jane **Education:** ME, Cornell University, Ithaca, NY (1966); BS, Cornell University, Ithaca, NY (1965); Graduate Coursework, Northwestern University and University of Pennsylvania **Certifications:** Certified Energy Manager, Association of Energy Engineers (2002); LEED Accredited Professional, U.S. Green Building Council (2002); PE, Pennsylvania, Massachusetts, New Jersey **Career:** Self-Employed HVAC and Energy Consultant (2012-Present, 1977-1993); Various Engineering Firms (1968-2012); Project Engineer, Monsanto Co. (1966-1968); With, Stone and Webster Engineering Corp **Civic:** Community Member, Boston University Institutional Biosafety Committee (2013-Present); Community Member, Member, Community Liaison Committee, Boston University New Emerging Infectious Diseases Laboratory (2012-Present); City of Boston Biosafety Committee; Volunteer and Trustee, Charles River Museum of Industry and Innovation, Waltham, MA **Creative Works:** Author, Six Papers on District Heating/Cooling; 3 Patents on Use of Power Plant Waste Heat **Memberships:** Chairman, Boston Section, American Society of Mechanical Engineers (1979-1989) **Marquis Who's Who Honors:** Albert Nelson Marquis Lifetime Achievement Award; Marquis Who's Who Top Professional **Why did you become involved in your profession or industry:** Mr. Timmerman started out as a Liberal Arts student at Wesleyan University but soon discovered he would make a better engineer than physicist, and transferred to Cornell University. After his first course in Thermodynamics, he found his calling. **Avocations:** Designing theater lighting for 75 performances; Broadcast audio and recording **Religion:** Presbyterian

Michael Tomkies

Title: Partner **Industry:** Law and Legal Services **Company Name:** Dreher Tomkies LLP **Place of Birth:** , **Education:** Doctor of Jurisprudence, Harvard Law School (1986); Bachelor of Arts in Managerial Economics, Summa Cum Laude (1983) **Career:** Partner, Dreher Tomkies LLP (1995-Present); Partner, Zeiger Dreher & Carpenter (1994-1995); Associate, Jones Day (1986-1994) **Career Related:** Chair, Interstate Telemarketing and Debt Collection, American Bar Association Annual Meeting (1994) **Creative Works:** Author, Co-author, Numerous Articles on Consumer Finance to Legal Publications (1989-2019); Chair, Co-Chair, Speaker or Presenter, Numerous Conferences and Symposia on Business Law **Awards:** Listee, Ohio Super Lawyers (2019); Listed, People to Know in Banking and Finance, Columbus Business First (2013); President's Award for Excellence, Social Sciences; Fellow, American College of Consumer Financial Services Lawyers **Memberships:** Former Chair, Business Law Section, Consumer Financial Services Committee, American Bar Association; Ohio State Bar Association; Columbus Bar Association; Former Vice-Chair, Retail Banking Subcommittee of the Banking Law Committee, American Bar Association; Former Vice-Chair, Publications Subcommittee of the Consumer Financial Services Committee, American Bar Association; Founding Former Chair; Joint Task Force on Preemption, American Bar Association; Law Committee, American Financial Services Association **Marquis Who's Who Honors:** Marquis Who's Who Top Professional **To what do you attribute your success:** Mr. Tomkies attributes his success to his academic years at Hampden-Sydney College, which bestowed him with a wonderful liberal arts background and a degree in economics. **Why did you become involved in your profession or industry:** Mr. Tomkies became involved in his profession due to the influence of his father and grandfather, who were both attorneys. **Avocations:** Kids; Pets; Travel; Camping

Gayle S. Tuch

Title: Attorney, Certified Mediator **Industry:** Law and Legal Services **Company Name:** The Law Office of Gayle Goldsmith Tuch, P.C. **Marital Status:** Single **Children:** Rose; Hal **Education:** LLM in Environmental Law, Vermont Law School, Summa Cum Laude (2015); JD, College of Law, The University of Toledo (1989); Master's Degree in Environmental Science, Miami University (1986); BS in Geography, University of Cincinnati (1983) **Career:** Attorney, Certified Mediator, The Law Office of Gayle Goldsmith Tuch, P.C. (2002-Present); Attorney, Goldsmith & Goldsmith (1989-2002) **Civic:** Board Member, The Climate Times (2016-Present); Board Member, Yadkin Riverkeeper Inc. (2009-2016); Board Member, Piedmont Environmental Alliance (2008-2010); Chair of the Board, North Carolina Climate Solutions Coalition; Sierra Club; Dogwood Alliance; Volunteer, Various Environmental Initiatives **Awards:** Outstanding Women in Business Award, Triad Business Journal (2018); Legacy Award, Yadkin Riverkeeper Inc. (2016); Conservation Award, National Society Daughters of the American Revolution (2014) **Memberships:** Member, Environmental Movement, Temple Emanuel (2007-Present); North Carolina Advocates for Justice; North Carolina Bar Association; Forsyth County Bar Association; Environmental Law Institute; Cincinnati Bar Association; Ohio State Bar Association; Sierra Club **Marquis Who's Who Honors:** Marquis Who's Who Top Professional **To what do you attribute your success:** Ms. Tuch attributes her success to her passion for the field. **Why did you become involved in your profession or industry:** Ms. Tuch became involved in her profession because she wanted to help people and was inspired by her father. **Avocations:** Spending time with her dogs, Zen and Brownie; Socializing; Traveling

Elvin Leroy Turner

Title: School System Administrator (Retired) **Date of Birth:** 01/09/1938 **Place of Birth:** Springfield **State/Country of Origin:** OH/USA **Parents:** Willie Turner; Jinada (Lawson) Turner **Marital Status:** Widowed **Spouse Name:** Carrie Johnson (08/03/1972, Deceased 03/24/2013) **Children:** Anthony; Brenetta Bell **Education:** Postgraduate Coursework, Kensington University, Glendale, CA (1993-2005); Postgraduate Coursework, Nova University, Fort Lauderdale, FL (1973); MEd, University of Cincinnati (1968); BS in Biology and Chemistry, Knoxville College, TN (1962) **Certifications:** Permanent Certificate, Secondary Principal, Teacher, State of Ohio **Career:** Assistant Principal, Cincinnati Public Schools (1972-1978, 1990-1993); Principal, Cincinnati Public Schools (1978-1990); Coordinator of Special Education, Cincinnati Public Schools (1969-1972); Special Education Teacher, Cincinnati Public Schools (1965-1969) **Career Related:** Speaker, Rotary Club of Pike County, Waverly, Ohio (1998); Ombudsman, Professional-Services, Waverly, Ohio (1997-1999); Bus Driver, Bristol Village Retirement Community, National Church Residences (1997-1999); Secretary, Bristol Village Residents Association (1997); Speaker, Bristol Retirement Village Vesper Service (1997) **Civic:** Volunteer, Ohio Department of Aging, DNN Corp, Columbus, Ohio (2002-2005); Volunteer, Radio, TV and Newspaper Coverage, Independence, Ohio (2001); Bible Study Course Instructor, Asbury North United Methodist Church, Columbus, Ohio (2000-2001); Elected Secretary of Executive Advisory Council, Bristol Village National Church Residencies, Waverly, Ohio (1997) **Creative Works:** Author, Various Non-published Poems & Books (1993, 1995, 2004-2012, 2014-2015); Author, Poetry Book **Awards:** Named to Wall of Tolerance, Southern Poverty Law Center, Montgomery, AL (2004); Plaque for One of 20 Statewide Outstanding Senior Volunteers, State of Ohio (2001); Named Outstanding Young Man (1966) **Memberships:** President, Kiwanis Club, Kiwanis International (1978-1979); President, University of Cincinnati Chapter, Phi Delta Kappa International (1970); Alpha Phi Alpha; Southern Poverty Law Center; Knoxville College Alumni Association **Marquis Who's Who Honors:** Marquis Who's Who Top Professional **To what do you attribute your success:** Mr. Turner attributes his success to those who encouraged him in diverse multi-disciplines, as well as personal friends. **Why did you become involved in your profession or industry:** Mr. Turner became involved in his profession because it was an excellent opportunity for him to persevere as an educator and make a difference in the children and public schools. **Avocations:** Bowling; Golf; Reading; Travel; Writing

James E. Tyrrell Jr., Esq.

Title: Member **Industry:** Law and Legal Services **Company Name:** Sills, Cummis & Gross P.C. **Parents:** James E. Tyrrell **Marital Status:** Married **Spouse Name:** Kathleen A. (Gilvey) Tyrrell **Children:** Four Children **Education:** JD, Harvard Law School (1974); BSFS, Walsh School of Foreign Service, Georgetown University, Summa Cum Laude (1971) **Career:** Member, Sills Cummis & Gross P.C.; Partner, New Jersey Office of Locke Lord; Managing Partner, New Jersey Office of Latham & Watkins; Regional Managing Partner, Member, Executive Committee, New York and New Jersey Offices of Patton Boggs (Now Squire Patton Boggs); Attorney, Townley & Updike; Associate Attorney, Sullivan & Cromwell LLP; Clerk, Honorable Leonard I. Garth, U.S. Court of Appeals for the Third Circuit **Career Related:** Speaker in the Field, Symposiums and Seminars **Civic:** Chairman of the Board, Reflex Sympathetic Dystrophy Syndrome Association (RSDSA) **Military Service:** Lieutenant, U.S. Navy JAG Corps **Awards:** Benchmark Litigation: America's Leading Litigation Firms and Attorneys (2019); The Best Lawyers in America 2007-2019, Commercial Litigation (2007-2019); Chambers USA Guide to America's Leading Lawyers for Business 2006-2019, New Jersey Litigation: Products Liability (2006-2019); New Jersey Super Lawyers ®* 2005-2019, Class Action/Mass Torts (2005-2019); Lawyer of the Week, American Lawyer (2011); Super Lawyers, "Master of Disaster" (2007); Civil Litigation: Defense; Lawdragon 500 - Leading Lawyers in America **Memberships:** American Bar Association; New Jersey State Bar Association; New York State Bar Association **Bar Admissions:** U.S. District Court for the Southern District of New York (1976); U.S. District Court for the District of New Jersey (1974) **Why did you become involved in your profession or industry:** Mr. Tyrrell became involved in his profession because he was the first member of his family to go to college, but he knew that he wanted to be a lawyer in grammar school. He did a great deal of public speaking and debate starting in grammar school and was privileged to get some nice honors. In high school, he competed for the National Debate Championship, debated for Georgetown in college, and was the top speaker in law school at the Harvard Law School Moot Court competition. All of those things made him realize he was better with his mouth than his hands. **Avocations:** Spending time at the New Jersey Shore; Boating; Playing golf; Spending time with family

Ufot Frank Umana Sr.

Title: Counselor Educator **Company Name:** Texas Rehabilitation Commission **Date of Birth:** 06/14/1942 **Place of Birth:** Ikot Akpan Afaha **State/Country of Origin:** Nigeria **Year of Passing:** 1988 **Parents:** Frank Umana; Mary Ekpu **Marital Status:** Married **Spouse Name:** Mfon Ufot Umana (09/05/1970) **Children:** Ufot Frank Umana Jr.; Unyime Umana Udosen; Mfonobong Ufot Umana; Ekaete Ufot Umana **Education:** Doctor of Education in Counselor Education (1988); Master of Education (1983); Bachelor of Science (1980); Master of Science (1980); Teachers' Grade 11 Certificate (1972); Teachers' Grade Three Certificate (1964); First School Leaving Certificate (1954) **Certifications:** The Arc of Austin (1995); Adult Vocational Program on Skill Presentation (1991); National Board For Certified Counselors Inc. (1988); Texas Commission on Alcohol and Drug Abuse (1972) **Career:** Financial Monitoring Specialist (1977-2013); Vocational Rehabilitation Counselor (1989-1997); Vocational Rehabilitation Counselor, Texas Southern University, Houston, TX (1989); Counselor, Richmond State School, Texas (1982-1983); Counselor, Mental Health and Retardation, Terrell, TX (1979-1981); Instructor Assistant, East Texas State University (1977-1980); Headmaster, Government Schools, Nigeria (1970-1976) **Career Related:** Secretary, Village Council, Ikot Akpan Afaha, Nigeria (1975-1976) **Civic:** National Council of Nigeria and Cameroon Party, Cross River State, Nigeria (1969); Director, Young Farmers Club **Military Service:** None **Awards:** Excellence on Education and Leadership Award, The Nigerian Foundation (2017); 30-Year Certificate of Service, State of Texas (2013); Outstanding Patronage Award, Houston Chapter, Akwa Ibom State Association of Nigeria (1999); Texas Rehabilitation Commission Award, State of Texas (1998); Recognition, Ibibio Group (1988); Nigerian Federal Education Scholarship (1983-1988); Cross River State Education Scholarship (1977-1980); Golden Eagle Award **Memberships:** American College Personnel Association; American Association of Counseling and Development; Phi Delta Kappa; Akwa Ibom State Association of Nigeria, Houston Chapter; The Nigerian Foundation **To what do you attribute your success:** Dr. Umana credits his success on his mother, his spouse, and his propensity for determination and hard work. **Why did you become involved in your profession or industry:** Dr. Umana became involved in his profession due to the educational scholarships he received to study in the United States, particularly in the areas of special education and counseling. **Avocations:** Photography; Jogging **Political Affiliations:** Democracy of America Party; Akwa Ibom State PDP Party

Susan Unterberg

Title: Photographer, Philanthropist **Industry:** Fine Art **Children:** Two Daughters **Education:** MA, New York University (1985); BFA, Sarah Lawrence College (1977) **Career:** Visiting Artist, American Academy in Rome (1996) **Civic:** Co-Chairwoman, Yaddo (2013); Founder, Sole Benefactor, Anonymous Was a Woman Award (1996-2018) **Creative Works:** Photographer, Human and Animal Portraiture, Prints, Books, and Video Installations; Artist, Permanent Collection, The Museum of Modern Art, NY; Artist, Permanent Collection, The Metropolitan Museum of Art, NY; Artist, Permanent Collection, Los Angeles County Museum of Art; Artist, Permanent Collection, Jewish Museum; Artist, Permanent Collection, The Nelson-Atkins Museum of Art **Awards:** Distinguished Alumni Award, New York University (2019); Honoree, Skowhegan Awards Dinner (2019); Fellow, MacDowell Colony (1995); Fellow, New York Foundation for the Arts (1992)

Magda Van Hoyweghen, MD

Title: Surgeon **Industry:** Medicine & Health Care **Date of Birth:** 10/21/1934 **Place of Birth:** Temse **State/Country of Origin:** Belgium **Parents:** Hendrik Van Hoyweghen; Maria Amelberga Servotte **Marital Status:** Single **Education:** European Master's Degree in Bioethics, Université Catholique de Louvain (2004); Master of Science in Bioethics, Antwerp, Belgium (1998); Fellowship, International College of Surgeons (1980); Fellowship, American College of Surgeons (1975); Fellowship, John L. Madden Surgical Society (1972); Surgical Resident, New York, NY (1967-1971); Surgical Residency, New York, NY (1966-1970); Doctor of Medicine, Utrecht University, Netherlands (1966); Diploma, Onze-Lieve-Vrouw-Presentatie, Sint Niklaas, Belgium (1953) **Career:** General Surgeon, Medical Mission Sisters, Government of Holland, Netherlands and Belgium (1998-Present); Elected, Sector Africa Coordinator (1992-1998); General Government, Medical Mission Sisters, Nairobi, Kenya (1992-1998); Senior Surgeon, Local Government, Lilongwe, Malawi (1981-1992); General Surgeon, Terre des Hommes, Serabu, Sierra Leone (1978); General Surgeon, Medical Mission Sisters, Attat, Ethiopia (1978); General Surgeon, Caritas, Juba, South Sudan (1977-1978); General Surgeon, Local Government, Mwanza, Tanzania (1973-1977) **Career Related:** Fellow, East African College of Surgeons (1996-Present); Fellow, American College of Surgeons (1975-Present); Pediatric Surgery, Cape Town, South Africa (1981) **Civic:** Member, Diocesan Committee for Peace and Justice, Antwerp, Belgium **Memberships:** John L. Madden Surgical Society Inc. (1972); Member, International Organization, Medical Mission Sisters **Marquis Who's Who Honors:** Albert Nelson Marquis Lifetime Achievement Award; Marquis Who's Who Top Professional; Marquis Who's Who Humanitarian Award **To what do you attribute your success:** Dr. Van Hoyweghen attributes her success to loving what she does and being active. **Why did you become involved in your profession or industry:** In 1972, Dr. Van Hoyweghen began 25 years of service as a missionary doctor in Africa. In the years that followed, she held a number of general surgeon roles, including with the local governments in Tanzania, South Sudan, Malawi and Kenya, and as a member of the general government for Medical Mission Sisters in the whole of Africa.

Antonio Velasquez

Title: Owner **Industry:** Retail/Sales **Company Name:** Tortillas Velasquez & Son **Date of Birth:** 03/27/1981 **Place of Birth:** Boise City **State/Country of Origin:** OK/USA **Spouse Name:** Erica **Children:** Nathanial; Cindy **Education:** Bachelor of Arts, Oklahoma Panhandle State University (2007) **Career:** Owner, Tortillas Velasquez & Son (2005-Present) **Civic:** Volunteered, Community Service **To what do you attribute your success:** Mr. Velasquez attributes his success to his parents, who established the business as a small investment and developed it into an empire.

Seema Verma

Title: Administrator **Industry:** Medicine & Health Care **Company Name:** Centers for Medicare & Medicaid Services **Date of Birth:** 09/27/1970 **Place of Birth:** Portsmouth **State/Country of Origin:** VA/USA **Marital Status:** Married **Spouse Name:** Sanjay Mishra **Children:** Maya; Shaan **Education:** MPH in Health Policy and Management, Johns Hopkins School of Public Health (Now Johns Hopkins Bloomberg School of Public Health) (1996); BA in Life Sciences, University of Maryland, College Park, MD (1993) **Career:** Administrator, Centers for Medicare and Medicaid Services (2017-Present); President, Chief Executive Officer, Founder, SVC; Association of State and Territorial Health Officials, Washington, DC; Vice President of Planning, Health & Hospital Corporation of Marion County **Civic:** White House Coronavirus Task Force (2020-Present)

Valentine Marie Villa, PhD

Title: Professor **Industry:** Education/Educational Services **Company Name:** 1) UCLA 2) Cal State LA **Date of Birth:** 02/14/1961 **Parents:** Edward Villa; Martha "Billie" Villa **Marital Status:** Married **Spouse Name:** Robert Martus **Education:** PhD in Gerontology, University of Southern California (1993); MS in Gerontology, University of Southern California (1985); MA in Public Administration, University of Southern California (1985); BA in Communication Arts and Sciences, University of Southern California (1983) **Career:** Professor of Social Work, Cal State LA; Adjunct Professor of Public Health, UCLA **Civic:** Volunteer, City, County and National Programs **Creative Works:** Author, 60 Manuscripts **Awards:** Goldman Excellence in Research Award, U.S. Department of Veterans Affairs; Commendations, Los Angeles Mayor Antonio Villaraigosa and Mayor Eric Garcetti **Memberships:** Fellow, The Gerontological Society of America **To what do you attribute your success:** Dr. Villa attributes her success to the professors at the University of Southern California, as well as her colleagues, family and friends. Her professors taught her the importance of critical thinking and maintaining the highest ethical standards in teaching and research.

Mary F. Voce, Esq.

Title: Former Chair of the Cross Border Tax Planning Practice **Industry:** Law and Legal Services **Company Name:** Greenberg Traurig LLP **Date of Birth:** 02/04/1944 **Place of Birth:** Flint **State/Country of Origin:** MI/USA **Marital Status:** Married **Spouse Name:** Stephen D. Gardner (9/19/1973) **Children:** Benjamin Joseph Voce-Gardner; Daniel Alexander Voce-Gardner **Education:** LLM, New York University (1975); LLB, University of Virginia (1969); BA, University of Michigan (1966) **Certifications:** **Career:** Shareholder and Chair International Tax, Greenberg Traurig LLP (2003-2019); Partner, Coudert Brothers (1996-2003); Partner, Whitman Breed Abbott & Morgan, New York, NY (1993-1996); Partner, Breed, Abbott & Morgan, New York, NY (1977-1993); Associate, Breed, Abbott & Morgan, New York, NY (1969-1977) **Awards:** Listee, Tax Law, Best Lawyers in America (2007-Present); Listee, New York Metro Super Lawyers, Super Lawyers Magazine (2006-2020); Listee, Best of the Best in Tax, Euromoney's Expert Guide (2019); Listee, International Tax, The Legal 500 in the United States (2007, 2009, 2014-2019); Listee, U.S Taxes- Non-Contentious, The Legal 500 in the United States (2018); Shortlisted, Best in Tax, America's Women in Business Law Awards, Euromoney Legal Media Group (2016-2017); Listee, Guide to the Worlds Leading Women in Business Law, Euromoney's Expert Guides: Women in Business Law (2014, 2017); Best in Tax, America's Women in Business Law Awards, Euromoney Legal Media Group (2014-2015); Listee, Guide to the Worlds Leading Women in Business Law, Euromoney Institutional Investors Expert Guides (2012); Listee, Legal Elite, Real Estate, AVENUE Magazine (2011); Listee, Top 50 Female Attorneys in the New York Metropolitan Area (2009); Leading Practitioner, Guide to the World's Leading Tax Advisors, International Tax Review (2004); AV Preeminent Rating, Martindale-Hubbell **Memberships:** New York State Bar Association; Association of the Bar of the City of New York; Phi Beta Kappa; The Tax Club, Fellow, American Bar Association; International Tax Institute **Bar Admissions:** New York **Marquis Who's Who Honors:** Marquis Who's Who Top Professional

John Vranish

Title: Electrical Engineer, Researcher **Industry:** Engineering **Date of Birth:** 05/20/1939 **Place of Birth:** Brainerd **State/Country of Origin:** MN/USA **Parents:** John Paul Vranish (Deceased); Louise Ann (Jenkins) Vranish **Marital Status:** Married **Spouse Name:** Dorothy Jean Ward (6/27/1980) **Children:** John Christopher; Anthony Brian **Education:** MSEE, George Washington University (1973); BS, U.S. Military Academy (1962) **Career:** Electrical Engineer, Researcher; President, Vranish Innovative Techs. (2006-Present); Emeritus, Goddard Space Flight Center (2006-2019); Staff Engineer, Space Mechanisms and Space Robotics, Goddard Space Flight Center, Greenbelt, MD (1986-2006); Staff Engineer, Robotics Research, National Bureau Standards, Gaithersburg, MD (1982-1986); Staff Engineer, Robotics Research, Naval Surface Weapons Center, White Oak, Silver Spring, MD (1971-1982) **Career Related:** Consultant, U.S. Congress (1983, 1987, 1996); Member, Technical Task Force, Office of Secretary Defense (1981-1982); Member, Fact Finding Committee, Office of Secretary Defense (1981); Speaker in Field **Military Service:** Captain U.S. Army (1962-1970) **Creative Works:** Most Patents in the History of Goddard Space Flight Center; Contributor Articles, Professional Publications **Awards:** NASA Administrator Daniel Golden Award, Goddard Space Flight Center (2004-Present); 100 Award, R&D Magazine (2006, 1997); Named Inventor of the Year, Goddard Space Flight Center (2004-2005, 1992-1996); Bose Award, Design News Magazine (1997); Award, Robotics International of Society Manufacturing Engineers (1981); Grantee, Productivity Enhancement Program, Department of Defense (1979); Outstanding Service as Mentor, NASA Robotics Academy Program; Exceptional Service Medal, NASA; Exceptional Achievement Technology Medal; Exceptional Engineering Achievement Medal; Nominee, National Inventors Hall of Fame, NASA, Goddard Space Flight Center **Memberships:** Charter Member, Robotics International of Society Manufacturing Engineers **Marquis Who's Who Honors:** Albert Nelson Marquis Lifetime Achievement Award; Marquis Who's Who Top Professional **Why did you become involved in your profession or industry:** Mr. Vranish became involved in his profession because he was a failure as an army officer. He went to West Point and they were interested in an infantry commander and he did not fit that role. He was forced to go back and reevaluate himself and he came to the conclusion that his mind was a research mind that looked into things deeply beneath the surface. He was forced into mentoring kids and although he was not a people person, he did it, and that was the reason why he went into the technology side of it. **Avocations:** Sports; Physical fitness; Military history

Sharon Rose Wallen

Title: Elementary School Teacher **Company Name:** Wallen's Global Learners **Parents:** Leslie Wallen; Myrtle Wallen **Marital Status:** Married **Education:** Coursework, Equity and Social Justice in Education Plenary (2020); Coursework, Core Connections: Blended and Virtual Learning (2020); MS in Elementary Education, Nova Southeastern University (1988); Bachelor's in Psychology and Sociology, Brooklyn College, NY (1982) **Certifications:** Certificate in Early Childhood, National Board of Certified Teachers; Licensed, Elementary Education Certificate with Additional Endorsements in Gifted Education, ESOL (English for Speakers of Other Languages) and Reading, FL **Career:** Educator with Miami-Dade County Public Schools, Miami, FL; Curriculum Support Specialist; Reading Coach; Founder, Wallen's Global Learners **Civic:** Participant, Class Pet Blanket Drive, Methods to Make Pet Ownership Less Expensive (2019) **Creative Works:** Published, "TLC Tender Loving Care" (2019); Published, "Intentions of Fifth Graders" (2018); Published, "Vive Moi! Hooray for Me" (2017); Published, "Make Your Mark" (2016); Published, "Live Meaningfully Today" (2015) **Awards:** Spirit of Service-learning Certificate of Appreciation for "Dedication to the Growth of Her Students Academically and as Engaged Citizens Through Incorporating Service-learning into Her Curriculum" (2019); Best and Brightest Highly Effective Teacher Designee for Student Curricular Achievement Growth (2017-2018, 2018-2019) **Memberships:** Delta Kappa Gamma Society International; International and National Travel Club; Florida Association of the Gifted; National Alliance on Mental Illness (NAMI) **Marquis Who's Who Honors:** Marquis Who's Who Top Professional **To what do you attribute your success:** Mrs. Wallen attributes her success as a beginning teacher to the great mentors who encouraged her to attend professional development, seminars, and workshops pertinent to professional and personal growth. She also attained her National Board Certification early in her career because that process propelled the internal classroom work, intertwined with her personality and abilities. **Why did you become involved in your profession or industry:** Mrs. Wallen became involved in her profession because teaching was of interest to her since childhood. Once she began working in the field as a substitute teacher, principals liked her, her personality, and her work ethics, so they requested for her to be placed as permanent substitute teacher at their schools. **Religion:** Christian

Diane Eve Warren

Title: Songwriter **Industry:** Media & Entertainment **Date of Birth:** 09/07/1956 **Place of Birth:** Van Nuys **State/Country of Origin:** CA/USA **Parents:** David Warren; Flora Warren **Marital Status:** Single **Education:** Diploma, California State University, Northridge (1978); Coursework, Los Angeles Pierce College **Career:** Founder, Owner, Realsongs, Los Angeles, CA (1987-Present); Staff Writer, Jack White (1983) **Civic:** Honorary Committee Member, PETA; Donor, Lange Foundation; Donor, Tenth Life Foundation; Donor, Wildlife Waystation, Inc.; Founder, David S. Warren Weekly Entertainment Series, Jewish Home for the Aging **Creative Works:** Songwriter, More Than 100 Top-Ten Pop Songs Including "I'll Never Get Over You (Getting Over Me)," "How Do I Live," "I Don't Want to Miss a Thing," "If You Asked Me To," "Don't Turn Around," "Set The Night to Music," "I'll Still Love You More," "Because You Loved Me," "Rhythm of the Night," "Nothing's Gonna Stop Us Now," "Unbreak My Heart," "Music of My Heart," "My First Night with You," "I Will Get There," "There You'll Be" and "You Haven't Seen the Last of Me" **Awards:** Primetime Emmy Award for Outstanding Original Music and Lyrics, Academy of Television Arts & Sciences (2016); Golden Globe Award for Best Original Song in a Motion Picture, Hollywood Foreign Press Association (2011); 100 Most Powerful Women in Entertainment, The Hollywood Reporter (2006); Telly Award, The Foundation for a Better Life (2003); Star, Hollywood Walk of Fame (2001); Inductee, Songwriters Hall of Fame (2001); Musician's Adviser Award, American Society of Young Musicians (2001); Angel Award, Angels on Earth (2000); Lifetime Achievement Award, Bill Gavin Heritage Foundation (2000); Dream Maker's Circle Award, Dream Foundation (2000); Two-Time Recipient, Award for Superior Creativity in the Words and Music of a Song, Nashville Songwriters Association International (2000); Songwriter of the Year, Nashville Songwriters Association International (2000); Songwriter of the Year, ASCAP (1990-1991, 1993, 1998-2000); Songwriter of the Year, Billboard Awards (1997-1999); Legacy Award, Organization for the Needs of the Elderly (1999); New Millennium Visionary Award, American Cinema Awards Foundation (1999); George and Ira Gershwin Award for Outstanding Musical Achievement (1998); Number One Pop Songwriter of the Year, American Song Writing Awards (1997); Grammy Award for Song Written Specifically for a Motion Picture or TV, Recording Academy (1997); Songwriter of the Year, National Academy of Songwriters (1996)

Daniel H. Weiss, PhD

Title: President, Chief Executive Officer, Art Historian **Industry:** Fine Art **Company Name:** The Metropolitan Museum of Art **Marital Status:** Married **Spouse Name:** Sandra Jarva **Children:** Teddy; Joel **Education:** Honorary Degree, Ithaca College (2018); PhD in Western Medieval and Byzantine Art, Johns Hopkins University (1992); MBA, Yale School of Management (1985); MA in Medieval and Modern Art, Johns Hopkins University (1982); BA in Psychology and Art History, Columbian College of Arts & Sciences, The George Washington University (1979) **Career:** Chief Executive Officer, The Metropolitan Museum of Art (2017-Present); President, The Metropolitan Museum of Art (2015-Present); President, Haverford College (2013-2015); President, Lafayette College (2005-2013); Dean, Zanvyl Krieger School of Arts & Sciences, Johns Hopkins University (2002-2005); Dean, Johns Hopkins University (2001-2002); Chair, Department of Art History, Johns Hopkins University (1998-2001); Booz Allen Hamilton Inc. **Civic:** Board Member, Samuel H. Kress Foundation; Member, Board of Directors, The Posse Foundation; Member, Board of Directors, Library of America; Member, Advisory Board, Yale School of Management; Trustee, The Park School, Baltimore, MD; Board Member, Shriver Hall Concert Series; Board Member, The Walters Art Museum, Johns Hopkins University; Trustee, The Institute of Fine Arts, New York University **Creative Works:** Author, "In That Time: Michael O'Donnell and the Tragic Era of Vietnam" (2019); Author, "Art and Crusade in the Age of St. Louis"; Author, "The Book of Kings: Art, War & the Morgan Library's Medieval Picture Bible"; Author, "France and the Holy Land: Frankish Culture at the End of the Crusades"; Author, "Remaking College: Innovation and the Liberal Arts"; Contributor, Articles, Professional Journals; Author, Books **Awards:** Centennial Medal, Foreign Policy Association (2018); Leadership and Society Award, Yale School of Management (2018); Distinguished Alumni Achievement Award, George Washington University (2016)

Ryan J. Weissmueller, CPA

Title: President **Industry:** Financial Services **Company Name:** Fintrepid Solutions **Children:** Two Children **Education:** BSBA in Finance and Accounting, The University of Arizona Eller College of Management (2000) **Career:** President, Fintrepid Solutions, Scottsdale, AZ (2016-Present); President, Signature Analytics, Scottsdale, AZ (2015-2016); Chief Investment Officer, Solterra Holdings, LLC, Scottsdale, AZ (2009-2013); Managing Partner, Balance Capital Partners, LLC, Scottsdale, AZ (2007-2009); Managing Director, Franchise Capital Advisors, Scottsdale, AZ (2005-2007); Assistant Vice President, GE Commercial Finance, General Electric, Scottsdale, AZ (2001-2005); Staff Accountant, Assurance and Advisory Services, Deloitte, Phoenix, AZ (2000-2001) **Civic:** Board of Directors, Shepard of the Desert Lutheran Church **Memberships:** AICPA **To what do you attribute your success:** Mr. Weissmueller attributes his success to being very creative, and having an experienced group of employees that help their clients come up with creative solutions to their problems, leveraging their knowledge and experience. **Why did you become involved in your profession or industry:** Mr. Weissmuller has always been passionate about becoming an entrepreneur. His father and grandfather were both successful entrepreneurs while he was growing up. He always enjoyed the excitement of being a part of other people's success; it is also a pleasure to be involved in other people's ideas. He applied his passion and achieved success. **Avocations:** Gym; Swimming; Running; Hiking; Playing sports; Golf; Family time

Arthur Stellhorn Welch

Title: Association Executive (Retired); Consultant **Industry:** Military & Defense Services **Date of Birth:** 08/15/1930 **Place of Birth:** Sewanee **State/Country of Origin:** TN/USA **Parents:** James Tracy Welch; Rachel Catherine (Stellhorn) Welch **Marital Status:** Widowed **Spouse Name:** Ingrid Beeken Welch (1954, Deceased 2010) **Children:** Suzanne Tracy Welch Hulse; Christine Anne Welch **Education:** MCS, Benjamin Franklin University (1953); BCS, Benjamin Franklin University (1952); Coursework, George Washington University (1948-1950) **Certifications:** Certified Administrative Manager (1972); Fellow, Institute of Administrative Management, Great Britain (1997) **Career:** Vice President Finance and Administration, Chief Financial Officer, Association of the United States Army (1992-2000); President, The Silver Thistle, Ltd. (1987-1997); Treasurer, Chief Financial Officer, Association of the United States Army, Arlington, VA (1954-1992); Accountant, Lamon & Henderson, Washington, DC (1952-1954) **Career Related:** Chairman, Washington Association Financial Management Roundtable, Inc. (1989-1990); **Civic:** Chairman, Board Directors, Arlington Committee 100 (1997); Chairman, Administrative Management Society Foundation (1988-1992); Founding President, Administrative Management Society Foundation (1980-1981) **Military Service:** Captain, United States Army (1961-1962) **Awards:** Decorated, Armed Forces Reserve Medal **Memberships:** Member Administrative Managment Society 1972-1990, Director, Academy of Certified Administrative Managers–Administrative Management (1974-1976); Former Member, Institute Administrative Management Great Britain; Greater Washington Society Association Executives; American Society Association Executives; Member, Arlington Committee of 100 **Marquis Who's Who Honors:** Albert Nelson Marquis Lifetime Achievement Award; Marquis Who's Who Top Professional; Marquis Who's Who Humanitarian Award **To what do you attribute your success:** Mr. Welch attributes his success to a combination of factors. Military contact identified a position with the Associate of the United States Army where he worked for 46 years and 18 years following as a consultant. **Why did you become involved in your profession or industry:** He became involved in his profession because he was provided an opportunity to use a variety of skills. **Political Affiliations:** Republican **Religion:** Episcopalian

Charles L. Welling

Industry: Retail/Sales **Date of Birth:** 06/10/1950 **Place of Birth:** Morristown **State/Country of Origin:** TN/USA **Parents:** Dr. Arthur Welling; Mary W. Welling **Marital Status:** Widowed **Spouse Name:** Margaret (07/04/1999) **Education:** Diploma, South Knoxville High School (1969); Coursework, The University of Tennessee, Knoxville **Career:** Retired (2011) Tailor, Rider's Men's & Women's Clothing, Elizabethtown, KY (1999-2011); Ministry Worker (1998); WJCR Radio, KY (1994); Tailor, Owner, Watson's Department Store (1991); Tailor, Owner, Welling Fine Tailoring (1981-1991); Tailor, Owner, Men's World (1973-1981) **Career Related:** Official Tailor, Canadian Pavilion, World's Fair (1982) **Civic:** St. Jude Children's Research Hospital (1991-Present); Volunteer, Food Bank, KY (1998); Volunteer Lay Preacher, Jail Ministry; Boys & Girls Club of America; The Salvation Army USA; PETA; American Society for the Prevention of Cruelty to Animals **Awards:** Speaker of the Year for Best Program, Hardin County AM Rotary Club (2007); Donor of the Year, DAV **Memberships:** Local Chapter, Alcoholics Anonymous; The Navigators; Wycliffe Bible Translators **To what do you attribute your success:** Mr. Welling attributes his success to his faith and sobriety through God's grace. **Why did you become involved in your profession or industry:** Mr. Welling became involved in his profession because he wanted to help others recover from addiction to drugs and alcohol and help them see a better life for themselves. **Political Affiliations:** Conservative **Religion:** Christian **Thoughts on Life:** Mr. Welling states, "It would solve so many problems in this world, if people would just treat others the way they, themselves, want to be treated."

Robert G. Wellon

Title: Lawyer **Industry:** Law and Legal Services **Company Name:** Robert G. Wellon Attorney & Counselor at Law **Date of Birth:** 04/18/1948 **Place of Birth:** Port Jervis **State/Country of Origin:** NY/USA **Parents:** Frank Lewis Wellon; Alice (Stevens) Wellon **Marital Status:** Married **Spouse Name:** Jan Montgomery (08/12/1972) **Children:** Robert F.; Alice Wynn **Education:** JD, Stetson University College of Law (1974); AB, Emory University (1970) **Career:** Lawyer, Robert G. Wellon Attorney & Counselor at Law, GA (2000-Present); Of Counsel, Wilson, Strickland & Benson, GA (1987-2000); Partner, Ridley, Wellon, Schweiger & Brazier, GA (1978-1986); Associate, Turner, Turner & Turner, GA (1974-1978); Fellow, American Bar Foundation **Career Related:** Adjunct Professor of Law, Emory University School of Law (1995-Present); Adjunct Professor, Atlanta Law School (1981-1994) **Civic:** Chairman, Governor's Task Force, GA (2000); Administrative Board, Northside United Methodist Church (1996-1999); Second Vice President, Treasurer, Executive Committee, Atlanta East Seals Society (Easterseals) (1983-1988); Representative, Neighborhood Planning Unit (NOU) (1981-1983); Active Stephen Minister, Atlanta Sports Council **Military Service:** With, United States Army Reserve (1970-1976) **Creative Works:** Course Material, Emory Law School **Awards:** Honoree, Super Lawyer and Atlanta Magazine (2004-2018); Named One of the Top Lawyers, Georgia Trend Magazine (2007-2012, 2016); Named to Top Lawyers, Georgia Trend Magazine (2014); Chief Justice Thomas O. Marshall Professionalism Award, State Bar of Georgia (2012); Distinguished Service Award, Atlanta Bar Association (2005); Charles E. Watkins Service Award, Atlanta Bar Association (1995) **Memberships:** Executive Committee, Atlanta Foundation for Psychoanalysis, Inc. (1997-Present); Board of Directors, Atlanta Bar Foundation (1996-Present); Board of Directors, Atlanta Foundation for Psychoanalysis, Inc. (1994-Present); President, Greenlaw (2013-2014); Member, Numerous Organizations **Marquis Who's Who Honors:** Albert Nelson Marquis Lifetime Achievement Award; Marquis Who's Who Top Professional **To what do you attribute your success:** Mr. Wellon attributes his success to luck and his first and only boss, Jack Turner, who was also his mentor. **Why did you become involved in your profession or industry:** Mr. Wellon always wanted to be a lawyer ever since high school. He can best contribute to society by being a lawyer.

John V. Wemlinger

Title: Author **Industry:** Publishing **Company Name:** Michigan Writers Association **State/Country of Origin:** MI/USA **Parents:** Victor W. Wemlinger; Josephine E. Wemlinger **Marital Status:** Married **Spouse Name:** Diane **Children:** Brynn Catherine Monetsanti **Education:** MA in National Security Strategy and Leadership, U.S. Naval War College (1993); MS in Education, St. John's University, New York (1983); BS in Secondary School Education and Teaching, The Ohio State University (1968) **Career:** Commanding Officer, MTMC, Pacific, Honolulu, HI (1991-1993); Commanding Officer, MTMC Terminal, Okinawa, Japan (1988-1990); Commanding Officer, MTMC Outport, Cape Canaveral, FL (1984-1987); Commanding Officer, Co A&HHC, 394th Trans BN, 2nd SUPCOM, Germany (1978-1979); Commanding Officer, Co. E, 1st Student BN, School BDE, Fort Eustis, VA (1975-1976) **Military Service:** Colonel, Officer, U.S. Army (1968-1995) **Creative Works;** Author, Novel, "Before the Snow Flies" (2019); Author, Novel, "Operation Light Switch" (2017); Author, Novel, "Winter's Bloom" (2016) **Awards:** Decorated, Defense Superior Service Medal; Decorated, Legion of Merit; Decorated, Bronze Star Medal; Decorated, Defense Meritorious Service Medal with Two Oak Leaf Clusters; Decorated, Army Meritorious Service Medal with Three Oak Leaf Clusters; Decorated, Army Commendation Medal with Four Oak Leaf Clusters; Decorated, Meritorious Unit Commendation; Decorated, Second Award, National Defense Service Medal; Decorated, Vietnam Service Medal; Decorated, Army Service Ribbon; Finalist, Independent Book of the Year Contest, Foreword Reviews; Third Place Winner, Colorado Independent Publishers' Association Book of the Year **Memberships:** Michigan Writers Association **Marquis Who's Who Honors:** Who's Who Lifetime Achievement Award (2020-2021) **To what do you attribute your success:** Mr. Wemlinger attributes his success to education, hard work, and the help of those around him. **Why did you become involved in your profession or industry:** Mr. Wemlinger became involved in his profession because he wanted to serve his country. He writes now because of the inspiration of those with whom he served. **Avocations:** Playing golf; Gardening; Reading; Driftwood art **Political Affiliations:** Independent **Religion:** Episcopalian **Thoughts on Life:** Mr. Wemlinger said, "Ask yourself 'What would you attempt if you knew you could not fail?'"

Gary Bernard Wetterberg

Title: International Forestry Support Program Manager (Retired) **Company Name:** U.S. Forest Service, U.S. Department of Agriculture **Place of Birth:** Denver **State/Country of Origin:** CO/USA **Parents:** Frances Rita Weisbeck Wetterberg; Bernard Frederick Wetterberg **Marital Status:** Married **Spouse Name:** Page Anderson Manning Wetterberg **Children:** Heidi-Hakone Wetterberg Jovanovic; Cristi-Cara Wetterberg; Tammy-Tayrona Wetterberg Wonnacott; Sean-Sarek Wetterberg; Larry A. Manning Jr. (Stepson); Von Edward Manning (Stepson) **Education:** PhD in Forestry, University of Washington, Seattle, WA (1974); Master of Forest Resources, University of Washington, Seattle, WA (1974); MSc in Forestry, Colorado State University, Fort Collins, CO; BSc in Forestry, Colorado State University, Fort Collins, CO **Certifications:** Certification, Society of American Foresters **Career:** Retired (2003); International Forestry Support Program Manager, U.S. Forest Service, U.S. Department of Agriculture, Washington DC (1993-2003) **Career Related:** Featured Speaker, XI World Forestry Congress, Antalya, Turkey (1997); Participant, Speaker, International Seminar on Planning and Management of Wild Areas Held in Asuncion, Paraguay at Ybycuí National Park (1982); Conference Speaker, First Seminar on Administration of Natural Areas and Wildlife, Republic of Ecuador Ministry of Agriculture of and Livestock, Guascan, Ecuador (1978); United Nations Food and Agriculture Organization, South America; Food and Agriculture Organization Department (FAOD), United Nations (10 Years) **Military Service:** U.S. Air Force ROTC **Creative Works:** Contributor, "Protected Area System Based on Pleistocene Refuges," Analysis of Nature Conservation Priorities in the Amazon, Brazilian National Congress on Conservation Units (2003); Contributor, Numerous Articles, Professional Publications (1967-2003) **Awards:** Certificate of Appreciation for Support to International Forestry the Forestry Support Program, and Leadership as Latin American Branch Chief (1995); United States Forest Service Award of Recognition of Contributions Made to National Forest System (1991); Certificate of Merit for Outstanding Performance in Developing and Implementing Forest Service Programs in Russia, Brazil and Latin America (1990); International Honor Award for Outstanding Performance in the Delivery of Professional and Technical Services (1990); Technical Services in Forestry and Natural Resource Management to Developing Countries throughout the World (1990); Letter of Recognition, National Park Service Director, Russell Dickenson (1984); Quality Performance Award, United States Department of Interior, National Park Service (1984) **Political Affiliations:** Democrat **Religion:** Roman Catholic

Gary Eugene Wiedle

Title: Real Estate Broker **Industry:** Real Estate **Date of Birth:** 07/28/1944 **Place of Birth:** San Antonio **State/Country of Origin:** TX/USA **Parents:** Eugene Wiley; Melba Frances (Keeney) Wiedle **Marital Status:** Married **Spouse Name:** Regena Zokosky (7/7/1977, Divorced 1983) **Children:** Ana Lauren; Aric Brandt **Education:** Associate of Arts, College of the Desert, Palm Desert, CA (1975); Master of Arts, University of Southern California (1973); Bachelor of Arts, California State University Long Beach (1967) **Career:** Owner, Fortune West Management, Palm Desert, CA (1990-2002); Professor of Political Science, College of the Desert, Palm Desert, CA (1987-1990); Manager, The Springs Country Club, Rancho Mirage, CA (1984-1987); Executive Director, Coachella Valley Association of Governments, Palm Desert, CA (1974-1984); Assistant City Manager, City of Inglewood, California (1970-1974); Administrative Assistant, City of Inglewood, California (1967-1968) **Career Related:** Consultant, Political Organizations, Business and Community Groups, Riverside County, CA (1984-2010) **Civic:** Volunteer, Bible Study for Seniors, Indio, CA (2013-2019); State Commander, Disabled American Veterans, California (1982); President, Palm Desert Rotary Club (1981) **Military Service:** First Lieutenant, United States Army (1968-1970) **Awards:** Decorated Bronze Star for Valor; Purple Heart; Army Commendation for Valor **Memberships:** President, Community Associations Institute (1986-1989); American Institute of Certified Planners; California Association of Community Managers; American Planning Association; Western Governmental Research Association; Gideons International **Why did you become involved in your profession or industry:** Mr. Wiedle initially became involved in city management, having first gained experience in civil service as a student body treasurer. As a city manager, he specialized in federal grants. Following this period of his vocational journey, he entered real estate and led a successful career. Finally, after leaving real estate, he decided to immerse himself fully in his Christian faith and become a deacon. **Political Affiliations:** Republican **Religion:** Christian

Edward Starsmeare Wilkinson Jr.

Title: Retired **Industry:** Military & Defense Services **Date of Birth:** 08/17/1948 **Place of Birth:** Norfolk **State/Country of Origin:** VA/USA **Parents:** Edward Starsmeare Wilkinson; Marguarite Pricilla (Adams) Wilkinson **Marital Status:** Single **Education:** MS, National Defense University, Washington, DC (1995); MA, Sam Houston State University (1974); BS, Sam Houston State University (1973) **Career:** Senior Intelligence Service, Central Intelligence Agency (1975-2003) **Military Service:** Commissioned Officer, Enlisted Non-Commissioned Officer, U.S. Army Infantry (1967-1971) **Awards:** Distinguish Career Intelligence Medal, Central Intelligence Agency; Bronze Star for Valor, U.S. Army; Bronze Star for Service, U.S. Army; Two-Time Recipient, Army Commendation for Valor, U.S. Army; Two-Time Recipient, Purple Heart for Wounds, U.S. Army; Vietnamese Honor Medal, U.S. Army; Vietnamese Air Force Honor Medal, U.S. Army; Vietnamese General Staff Medal, U.S. Army; Combat Infantry Badge, Senior Parachutist Badge, U.S. Army **Memberships:** Associate, Criminal Justice Research Society; Industrial College of Armed Forces Association; Military Order of the Purple Heart; Phi Theta Kappa; Lambda Alpha Epsilon **Marquis Who's Who Honors:** Albert Nelson Marquis Lifetime Achievement Award **Avocations:** Auto racing **Religion:** Baptist

Terry Williams

Title: President **Industry:** Financial Services **Company Name:** Terry A. Williams Accountants Inc. **Parents:** Romey Williams; Wanita (Hall) Williams **Marital Status:** Married **Children:** Four Children **Education:** BS in Accounting, Minnesota State University (1971) **Career:** President/CPA, Terry A. Williams Accountants Inc. (1992-Present); Accounting Manager, Treasury Assitant, Financial Controller, Accountant, Technip USA (1998-2009) **Civic:** Treasurer, Several Nonprofit Organizations, Churches; Mary Taylor Foundation **To what do you attribute your success:** Mr. Williams attributes his success to treating others how he would want to be treated. He is happy to go the extra mile to help others achieve success. He reminds himself every day of his journey to success, as well as his family roots and history. **Why did you become involved in your profession or industry:** Mr. Williams decided to study accounting in college. He loves interacting with people and finds it rewarding to watch investments grow, which is why it is the perfect field for him.

Bertina Iolia Wilson

Title: Elementary Educator, School Administrator (Retired) **Industry:** Education/Educational Services **Company Name:** Newark Public Schools **Date of Birth:** 08/17/1938 **Place of Birth:** Southampton **State/Country of Origin:** VA/USA **Parents:** Purcell Lee; Clarine Branch **Marital Status:** Divorced **Spouse Name:** (08/25/1963, Divorced 05/1977) **Children:** Brian Keith; Linda Elizabeth **Education:** MA, Kean College (Now Kean University) (1981); BA, Newark State College (Now Kean University) (1960) **Certifications:** Certified Elementary Education Teacher, NJ; Certified Principal, Supervisor, NJ **Career:** Vice Principal, Newark Public Schools, NJ (1995-1997); Project Coordinator, Newark Board of Education (1977-1995); Teacher, Newark Board of Education (1960-1977) **Career Related:** Church Organist, Choir Director, Zion Hill Baptist Church, Newark, NJ (1974-2014) **Civic:** Teacher, Sunday School, Zion Hill Baptist Church, Newark, NJ (2007-2014); Former Member, Executives Board, Newark Chapter, The Project Coordinators Association (1981) **Awards:** Outstanding Church Musician Award, Order of the Eastern Star (1986); Living Legend Award, Zion Hill Baptist Church; Community Service Award, Essex County Civic Association **Memberships:** Public Relations Director, PDK International (1987-1989); Newark Teachers Union; PDK International **Marquis Who's Who Honors:** Albert Nelson Marquis Lifetime Achievement Award; Marquis Who's Who Top Professional; Marquis Who's Who Humanitarian Award **To what do you attribute your success:** Ms. Wilson attributes her success to her parents and other relatives, who instilled in her at an early age the importance of education. She, in turn, focused on these same values as she taught her students over the years. **Why did you become involved in your profession or industry:** Ms. Wilson believed her parents when they continually stressed the importance of excelling in school. Even as a child, she enjoyed helping others with their school work. Her parents also emphasized the importance of being fair and honest with her fellow man. This led her to choose teaching as her profession. **Avocations:** Singing; Playing the organ **Political Affiliations:** Democrat **Thoughts on Life:** Ms. Wilson's feelings are expressed in the words of her favorite song: "If I can help somebody as I pass along, then my living will not be in vain."

Daniel Winstead

Title: Professor (Retired) **Company Name:** Tulane Univeristy **Parents:** Daniel Sebastian Winstead; Betty Jane (Kirsch) Winstead **Marital Status:** Married **Spouse Name:** Jennifer Reiner (6/15/1968) **Children:** Laura Suzanne; Nathaniel Scott **Education:** MD, Vanderbilt University (1970); BA, University of Cincinnati (1966) **Certifications:** Diplomate, American Board of Psychiatry and Neurology **Career:** Staff Psychiatrist, VA Medical Center, New Orleans, LA (1987-2018); Chairman, Department of Psychiatry and Neurology, Tulane University (1987-2018); Professor, Tulane University (1987-2018); Director, Psychiatric Education and Residency Training, Tulane University (1983-1987); Associate Chief Staff for Education, VA Medical Center, New Orleans, LA (1979-1987); Associate Professor, Tulane University (1979-1984); Director, Consultation/Liaison Psychiatric Training, Tulane University (1979-1983); Chief, Psychiatric Service, VA Medical Center, New Orleans, LA (1976-1980); Chief, VA Medical Center Psychiatric Service, Tulane University (1976-1979); Fellow, University of Cincinnati (1972-1973); Resident, University of Cincinnati (1970-1972) **Career Related:** Visiting Physician, Psychiatry, Charity Hospital, New Orleans, LA (1979-1990); Consultant, E.R. Squibb and Sons (1985-1986); Medical Director, Jefferson Parish Substance Abuse Clinic (1980-1981) **Military Service:** Major, U.S. Army (1973-1976) **Creative Works:** Contributor, Articles, Professional Journals **Memberships:** President, Louisiana Psychiatric Association (1991-1992, 2009-2010); President, Board of Directors, American Board Psychiatric and Neurology (2006); American Medical Association; American College of Psychiatrists; American Academy of Psychiatry and Law; American Psychiatric Association; Louisiana State Medical Society; Southern Association for Research in Psychiatry; President, Academy of Psychosomatic Medicine; President-Elect, American Association Chairmen Departments Psychiatry; American Association of Directors of Psychiatric Residency Training; Association Academy of Psychiatry; Society of Biological Psychiatry; New Orleans Area Psychiatric Association; New Orleans Neurological Society; Orleans Parish Medical Society **Marquis Who's Who Honors:** Marquis Who's Who Top Professional **To what do you attribute your success:** Mr. Winstead attributes his success to hard work. He was inspired by his father, who was a pharmacist, as he encouraged Mr. Winstead to further his education. **Why did you become involved in your profession or industry:** Mr. Winstead decided when he was in medical school that he wanted to work in academics. **Avocations:** Winemaking; Traveling; Supervising assisted living residents **Political Affiliations:** Republican **Religion:** Presbyterian

Norbert Rolf Wirsching

Title: Electronics Company Executive (Retired) **Industry:** Technology **Date of Birth:** 05/26/1937 **Place of Birth:** Rotenfels **State/Country of Origin:** Germany **Parents:** Victor; Anna (Gieringer) Wirsching **Marital Status:** Married **Spouse Name:** Elizabeth Pyle Valdez Wirsching **Children:** Elizabeth V. del Alamo; Margaret G. Still; Earlene Welch **Education:** High School, Stuttgart Germany **Career:** Trustee, Wooster School, Danbury, CT (2005-2009); Independent Director, Emerson Radio Corp. (2006-2008); Chairman, Chief Executive Officer, Capetronic Group Ltd, Hong Kong, China, New York, NY (1981-1994); Director, Polly Peck International PLC, London, England (1989-1991); Director, BSR PLC, London, England (1982-1986); Chief Operating Officer, Capetronic Group Ltd, Hong Kong, China, (1974-1981) General Manager, Transworld Electronic Limited, Hong Kong, China (1967-1974); Manager, Engineering, Radio Electronics Headquarters Inc., Manila, Philippines (1958-1967); Tool & Die Maker, Mercedes Benz AG, Stuttgart, Germany (1953-1958) **Creative Works:** Quoted in "The Turquoise Conspiracy," by Bilge Nevzat, with Gill Fraser (1999); Quoted in "Who Killed Polly Peck?" by Elizabeth Forsyth (1996); Quoted in "Asil Nadir and the Rise and Fall of Polly Peck" by David Barchard of the Financial Times (1992); Quoted in "Asil Nadir, Fugitive From Injustice?" by Tim Hindle (1991); Quoted in "The Sultan of Berkley Square, Asil Nadir and the Thatcher Years" by Tim Hindle (1991) **Awards:** S. David Feir Humanitarian Award, Anti-Defamation League (1991); Award, Manila Philippines Jaycees (1965); Award of Merit, Manila Philippines Chapter, American Society of Tool Manufacturing Engineers (1965); Award of Merit, Society of Manufacturing Engineers (1964); Macintosh Team-1 Award **Memberships:** Chairman, Manila Philippines Chapter 165, American Society of Tool Manufacturing Engineers; Chairman, Manila Jaycees **Marquis Who's Who Honors:** Albert Nelson Marquis Lifetime Achievement Award **Why did you become involved in your profession or industry:** Mr. Wirsching became involved in his profession because he realized very early in his life, in the 1950s, that in order to be able to succeed in business, he had to get involved in finance, sales and marketing, as opposed to his prior technical work. **Avocations:** Collecting art **Political Affiliations:** Republican

Marcia H. Wishengrad

Title: Lawyer **Industry:** Law and Legal Services **Date of Birth:** 02/10/1936 **Place of Birth:** Hudson **State/Country of Origin:** NY/USA **Parents:** Joseph Wishengrad; Jessie (Diamond) Wishengrad **Marital Status:** Married **Spouse Name:** Robert J. Metzger (09/03/1961) **Children:** Jocelyn M. **Education:** JD, Cornell University (1960); BA, Cornell University (1957) **Career:** Lawyer, Private Practice, Rochester, NY (1963-2013); Deputy County Attorney, Monroe County, NY (1974-1993); Senior Urban Renewal Attorney, City of Rochester, NY (1971-1974); Attorney, Monroe County, The Legal Aid Society (1965-1967); Attorney, Monroe County Family Court (1963-1965) **Civic:** Board of Directors, Monroe County Chapter, The American National Red Cross (1983-2000); Vice President, Association for Retarded Children (Now The Arc of the United States), Monroe Foundation (1990-1999); President, Board of Visitors, State School Industry, Rochester, NY (1991-1998); Board of Visitors, State School Industry, Rochester, NY (1983-1998); President, Board of Directors, Monroe County Chapter, The American National Red Cross (1991-1993) **Awards:** Excellence in Law Award, The Daily Record (2012); Paul Harris Award, Rotary International (2008); Paul Harris Award, Rotary International (1990) **Memberships:** Monroe County Bar Association; Judiciary Committee, Greater Rochester Association for Women Attorneys; Rochester/Monroe County Domestic Violence Consortium; World Affairs Council of Hilton Head; South Carolina Chapter, The Women's National Republican Club, Inc.; Beaufort County Disabilities and Special Needs Board; Women's Association of Hilton Head Island **Bar Admissions:** Supreme Court of the United States (1964); United States District Court for the Southern District of New York (1962); United States District Court for the Eastern District of New York (1962); New York (1960) **Marquis Who's Who Honors:** Albert Nelson Marquis Lifetime Achievement Award; Marquis Who's Who Humanitarian Award **Why did you become involved in your profession or industry:** Ms. Wishengrad's father wanted to be a lawyer but couldn't afford it and she feels he influenced her to be independent. By the time she was 10, she knew she wanted to be a lawyer. Ms. Wishengrad always enjoyed anything about the law; her dad had a great influence on her. He said, 'if you want to go to law school and you do well, I want you to be capable in doing something you want to do.' **Avocations:** Boating; Tennis; Reading **Political Affiliations:** Republican **Religion:** Jewish

Aaron C. Witmer

Title: Chief Operating Officer **Industry:** Architecture & Construction **Company Name:** GCI Slingers **Education:** Coursework in Mass Media Communications, Cornerstone University **Career:** Operations Manager, GCI Slingers LLC (2015-Present); Department Manager, GCI Slingers LLC (2014-2015) **Civic:** Community Volunteer, YMCA of Greater Indianapolis **Memberships:** Concrete Foundations Association (CFA); Business Fleet; World of Concrete; CONEXPO-CON/AGG **To what do you attribute your success:** Mr. Witmer attributes his success to working with good mentors and a great upbringing. He additionally credits the abundance of hard work he put into his career. **Why did you become involved in your profession or industry:** Mr. Witmer originally was going to school at Cornerstone University when an amazing opportunity presented itself. He was given a salary that he could not pass up as a construction director, which lead him to GCI Slingers. **Thoughts on Life:** Mr. Witmer's motto is, "Every minute, every mile, every day."

Maryalice Witzel, RN, BSN, MA

Title: Paramedic Educator, Emergency Trauma Nurse **Industry:** Medicine & Health Care **Date of Birth:** 01/25/1947 **Place of Birth:** North Bend **State/Country of Origin:** NE/USA **Children:** Lakisha **Education:** MS in Bioethics, Midwestern University, Glendale, AZ (2008); BSN, Excelsior College (2003); Student, Phoenix Community College (Now Phoenix College) (1991); Student, Grand Canyon College (Now Grand Canyon University) (1982-1983); Student, University of Nebraska Omaha (1976-1977); Student, Creighton University (1976-1977); Student, Iowa Western Community College (1973-1975); Diploma in Nursing, Lincoln General Hospital, Illinois (1966-1968) **Certifications:** Certified Paramedic Instructor, Adult Learning Technique; Instructor, Basic Life Support; Instructor, Trainer, Basic Life Support, Nebraska Heart Association; Instructor, Advanced Cardiovascular Life Support; Instructor, Advanced Cardiovascular Life Support, American Heart Association; Certified, Emergency Nurse; Wilderness Emergency Medical Trainer **Career:** Retired (2014); Disaster Chairman, Good Samaritan Medical Center (1992-2014); South Central Area Coordinator, Good Samaritan Regional Medical Center, Phoenix (1987-2000); Disaster Coordinator, Good Samaritan Medical Center (1991-1992); Staff Nurse, Maricopa Medical Center, Phoenix (1988-1990); Staff Nurse, Emergency Department, Good Samaritan Regional Medical Center, Phoenix (1982-1987); Paramedic Instructor, Clinical Coordinator, Creighton University, Omaha (1976-1980); Charge Nurse, Emergency Department, Creighton St. Joseph's Hospital, Omaha (1975-1976); School Nurse, Council Bluffs Public School System (1974-1975); Charge Nurse, Emergency Department, Mercy Hospital, Council Bluffs, IA (1974-1975); Staff Float Nurse, Lincoln General Hospital (1968-1969) **Career Related:** Guest Reviewer, Moby Publishing Company (1995); National Registry Testing (1992); Instructor, Advanced Trauma Care for Nurses, Phoenix (1984); Instructor, Emergency Medical Technician Refresher, State of Nebraska Metropolitan Technical Community College, Omaha (1976-1980); Instructor, Coordinator, Emergency Medical Skills Education Department, Creighton University, Secondary Teachers of Omaha Public School Systems (1977-1979); Instructor, Basic CPR, Northwestern Bell Telephone Company, Omaha (1977-1979); Instructor, CPR, CPR-IT, Advanced Cardiovascular Life Support, American Heart Association, Nebraska, Arizona (1977) **Memberships:** Affiliate Faculty, American Heart Association, Inc. (1995-Present); Emergency Nurses Association **Marquis Who's Who Honors:** Albert Nelson Marquis Lifetime Achievement Award; Marquis Who's Who Top Professional **Avocations:** Music; Crocheting; Running **Religion:** Methodist

Dale Edward Wolf, PhD

Title: Former Governor of Delaware **Date of Birth:** 09/06/1924 **Place of Birth:** Kearney **State/Country of Origin:** NE/USA **Marital Status:** Widowed **Spouse Name:** Clarice Wolf (Deceased 2/26/2018) **Children:** Janet; Glenda; Thomas; Jim **Education:** Honorary PhD, University of Delaware (2019); PhD in Agronomy and Weed Control, Rutgers, the State University of New Jersey (1949); BSc, University of Nebraska (1945) **Career:** Group Vice President, Agricultural Products, Wilmington, DE (1983-Present); Vice President, Biochemistry, Endo Pharmaceuticals Inc., Wilmington, DE (1979-Present); With, E.I. DuPont de Nemours and Company, Inc. (1950-Present); Governor, State of Delaware, Dover, DE (1992-1993); Lieutenant Governor, State of Delaware, Dover, DE (1989-1993); Director, Delaware Development Office, Dover, DE (1987-1989); Director, Agrichemical Marketing, E.I. DuPont de Nemours and Company, Inc. (1972-1979); General Manager, Biochemical Department, E.I. DuPont de Nemours and Company, Inc. (1972-1979); Associate Professor of Agronomy, Rutgers, the State University of New Jersey (1949); Department of Agriculture (1946) **Career Related:** Trustee, Christiana Care Healthy System (2002-Present); Vice Chairman, Wilmington Savings Fund Society, FSB (1998-2005) **Civic:** Advisory Board, Department of Hospitality Business Management, Alfred Lerner College of Business & Economics, University of Delaware (1993-Present); Chairman, Subsidiary Board, Endo Pharmaceuticals Inc., Wilmington, DE (1979-Present); Chairman, Stand Up for What is Right and Just (SURJ) (2003-2007); Chairman, Literacy Delaware (1993-1998); General Campaign Chairman, Board of Directors, Boys & Girls Clubs of Delaware Inc. (1987) **Military Service:** First Lieutenant, U.S. Army (1943-1946) **Creative Works:** Co-Author, "Principles of Weed Control" (1951) **Awards:** Brooman Award, Delaware Criminal Justice Council (2017-Present); Named to Hall of Fame, Fort Sill Artillery OCS, OK (2008); Liberty Bell Award, Delaware State Bar Association (2007); Josiah Marvel Award, Delaware State Chamber of Commerce, Inc. (2005); Brooman Exemplar of Justice Award, Delaware Center for Justice; Decorated Purple Heart; Decorated Bronze Star **Memberships:** Chairman, National Agricultural Chemicals Association (1981-1983); Director, Pharmaceutical Research and Manufacturers of America; Freemasons; FarmHouse Fraternity, Inc.; Sigma Xi, the Scientific Research Honor Society; Alpha Zeta **Marquis Who's Who Honors:** Albert Nelson Marquis Lifetime Achievement Award **Political Affiliations:** Republican **Thoughts on Life:** Mr. Wolf would like to dedicate this award to his family. He was asked to be governor and wanted to give back to the State of Delaware that was always good to him.

Lynn Worley

Title: IT Director, Licensed Practical Nurse **Industry:** Health, Wellness and Fitness **Company Name:** Gastroenterology of the Rockies **Children:** Two Sons **Certifications:** Medical Billing and Coding, Ultimate Medical Academy (2015-2016); Medical Office Billing Specialist, Ultimate Medical Academy (2015-2016); Licensed Nurse Practitioner (LPN), Trinidad State Junior College (1996) **Career:** IT Director, Gastroenterology of the Rockies (2017-Present); Licensed Practical Nurse, Gastroenterology of the Rockies (2017-Present); Account Technology Manager, Miraca Life Sciences (Now Inform Diagnostics) (2013-2017); Licensed Practical Nurse, Office Manager, EMR Systems Manager, Rocky Mountain Gastroenterology, Thornton, CO (2003-2013); Licensed Practical Nurse/Medical Nurse, Bear Creek Center (2001-2003) **Career Related:** Owner, President, Northern Colorado Integrated Technology **Civic:** Benefactor, Denver Scholarship Foundation (2016); Former President, Western Allscripts Regional User Group **Awards:** Appearance, Top 100 National Executive Magazine (2013); Outstanding Recognition, Allscripts Healthcare, LLC **Why did you become involved in your profession or industry:** Ms. Worley has always loved computers. Her passion for programming began when computers looked like big boxes; she remembers when it would take two entire pages just to print a smiley face. As computer programming became more complex, Ms. Worley changed direction in pursuit of nursing. She had dreams of becoming a nurse as a young girl but struggled to find confidence. Ms. Worley credits her mom for giving her the courage and strength to become the nurse she'd always wanted to be. **Avocations:** Spending time with her family; Hiking; Disc golfing; Crocheting

Halina Wyss

Title: Associate Professor **Company Name:** University of Portland **Marital Status:** Married **Children:** Two Sons **Education:** PhD in Nursing Science, University of Washington (2013); MSN, Nursing University of Portland (2004); BSN, Registered Nurse, University of Portland, Cum Laude (2002); BS in Biology, Lewis and Clark College (1993) **Certifications:** RN, State of Oregon (2020); American Heart Association CPR Certification, BLS for Healthcare Providers (2020); Certified Simulation Specialist; RN, Oregon State Board of Nursing; RN, Washington State Board of Nursing **Career:** Clinical Documentation Integrity Specialist, Oregon Health and Science University (2016-Present); Clinical Documentation Specialist Nurse, Providence Health & Services (2011-2016); Assistant Nurse Manager, Charge Nurse, Providence Milwaukee Hospital (2008-2011); Senior Research Assistant, Department of Medicine, Division of Infectious Diseases, Oregon Health and Science University (2007); Staff Registered Nurse, Cardiac, Providence St. Vincent Medical Center (2002-2007); Research Assistant III, Oregon Medical Laser Center, Providence St. Vincent Medical Center (1999-2002); Research Assistant, Oregon Medical Laser Center (1998-2000); Surgical Pathology Assistant, Providence St. Vincent Medical Center (1997-1999); Research Assistant, Epitope, Inc. (1997); Senior Research Assistant, Veterans' Administration Medical Center (1994-1996); Research Associate, Laboratory of Tumor and Molecular Immunology, Earle A. Chiles Research Institute (1994) **Career Related:** Associate Professor, School of Nursing, University of Portland (2020-Present); Assistant Professor, School of Nursing, University of Portland (2014-2020) **Civic:** Green Dot Faculty Member, University of Portland (2019-Present) **Creative Works:** Co-Author, Numerous Publications, Peer-Reviewed Journals; Speaker, Presenter, Numerous Refereed Presentations; Speaker, Numerous Invited Presentations **Awards:** Corps Loan Repayment Recipient, United States Department of Health Resources and Services Administration (2014-2015); Kitty Powell Innovation Fellow, Providence Health Services, Oregon Region (2014-2015) **Memberships:** Academic Network for Mental Health, University of Portland (2019-Present); Art Committee, University of Portland School of Nursing (2019-Present); Quality and Safet Education for Nurses (QSEN) (2019-Present) **To what do you attribute your success:** Dr. Wyss attributes her success to loving her job. **Why did you become involved in your profession or industry:** Dr. Wyss never planned on teaching. However, she found nursing school to be incredibly stressful, and, unfortunately, she had a lot of traumatic experiences, which inspired her to become a teacher.

Stuart Young

Title: Allergist, Immunologist, Medical Legal Consultant **Industry:** Medicine & Health Care **Company Name:** Stuart H. Young, MD, PC **Parents:** John Young; Sylvia Young **Marital Status:** Married **Spouse Name:** Ronnian J. Young **Education:** Doctor of Medicine, State University of New York Downstate Medical Center, Brooklyn, NY (1963); Bachelor of Arts, Colgate University, Hamilton, NY (1959) **Certifications:** Diplomate, American Board of Allergy and Immunology (1972); Diplomate, American Board of Pediatrics (1968) **Career:** Clinical Assistant Professor of Medicine and Clinical Immunology, Icahn School of Medicine at Mount Sinai, New York (2012-Present); Clinical Associate Professor of Pediatrics, Icahn School of Medicine at Mount Sinai, New York (1983-Present); Private Practice, Allergy for Adults and Children (1970-2013); Chief of Allergy, Department of Internal Medicine and Pediatrics, Mount Sinai Medical Center, New York (1975-1988); President, New York Pediatric Society (1985-1986) **Career Related:** Associate Clinical Professor of Medicine, Icahn School of Medicine at Mount Sinai, New York (1989-2011); Assistant Clinical Professor of Medicine, Icahn School of Medicine at Mount Sinai, New York (1975-1988); Assistant Clinical Professor of Pediatrics, Icahn School of Medicine at Mount Sinai, New York (1973-1983) **Military Service:** Captain, Medical Corps, Amarillo Air Force Base, Texas (1966-1968) **Creative Works:** Co-Author, "Allergies: The Complete Guide to Diagnosis, Treatment, and Daily Management (2011)"; Co-Author, "The Psychobiological Aspects of Allergic Disease" (1985); Co-Author, "The Asthma Handbook: A Complete Guide for Patients and Their Families" (1985) **Awards:** Named, One Of Top Doctors, New York Magazine; Recipient, 10 Years Top Doctor Award, Castle Connolly Guide **Memberships:** Fellow Emeritus, American College of Allergy, Asthma and Immunology (2012-Present); Fellow Emeritus, American Academy of Allergy, Asthma and Immunology (2012-Present); Fellow, American College of Chest Physicians (1980-Present); Fellow, American College of Allergy, Asthma and Immunology (1972-2012) **Marquis Who's Who Honors:** Albert Nelson Marquis Lifetime Achievement Award; Marquis Who's Who Top Professional

Anthony Ziccardi

Title: Founder **Industry:** Fine Art **Company Name:** Anthony Ziccardi Studios **Place of Birth:** Denville **State/Country of Origin:** NJ/USA **Parents:** James Ziccardi; Debora **Marital Status:** Married **Spouse Name:** Sarah (04/06/2010) **Children:** Zachary; Mason **Education:** Bachelor of Arts in Visual Communications **Certifications:** Certified Teacher, Ramapo College (2002) **Career:** Owner, Founder, Anthony Ziccardi Studios, Sparta, NJ (2002-Present); Teacher, Graphic Design and Photography (2002-2012) **Creative Works:** Author, "The Wedding Guide"; Published, 201 Bride; Published, Manhattan Bride; Published, Temporary Wedding Magazine; Published, The Not.Com **Awards:** Best Photographers, Manhattan Brides (2019); The Best of Weddings, The Knot (2010-2019); Couple's Choice Award, Wedding Wire (2010-2019); Best of Weddings Hall of Fame, The Knot; Sussex Count, New Jersey Best Photographers, New Jersey Herald **To what do you attribute your success:** Mr. Ziccardi attributes his success to hard work and perseverance, as well as the influence of his wife, who shares in his desire to meet new challenges. **Why did you become involved in your profession or industry:** Mr. Ziccardi has always been passionate about photography. He recalls, as a child, when everyone wanted video game consoles, he wanted a camera. He always loved art and decided to attend design school, where he majored in photography and graphic design, after which he became a high school teacher, where he taught graphic design and photography between 2002 and 2012. During this time, Mr. Ziccardi built up his own independent company to the point where he could finally dedicate himself to it on a full-time basis. **Avocations:** Motorcycles; Travel **Thoughts on Life:** "Believe in yourself and you can do anything."

ESTEEMED LISTEES

73rd Edition

AAGAARD, EVA, MD, T: Senior Associate Dean for Education **I:** Education/Educational Services **CN:** Washington University School of Medicine in St. Louis **ED:** MD, Joan and Sanford I. Weill Medical College of Cornell University (1995); BA in Medical Microbiology, University of California Santa Barbara (1991) **C:** Senior Associate Dean for Education, Washington University School of Medicine in St. Louis, MO (2017-Present); Associate Dean for Educational Strategy, University of Colorado School of Medicine (2014-2017); Director, Academy of Educators, University of Colorado (2010-2017); Vice Chair for Education, University of Colorado (2006-2012); Assistant Professor, University of California San Francisco (2000-2006); Resident to Assistant Professor, University of California San Francisco (1995-2006) **AW:** Named Carol B. and Jerome T. Loeb Professor of Medical Education, Washington University School of Medicine in St. Louis (2018) **MEM:** Alpha Delta Pi

AARON, HENRY, "HANK" LOUIS, T: Former Professional Baseball Player; Entrepreneur **I:** Athletics **DOB:** 02/05/1934 **PB:** Mobile **SC:** AL/USA **YOP:** 2021 **PT:** Herbert Aaron Sr.; Estella A. Aaron **MS:** Married **SPN:** Billye Suber (Williams) Aaron (11/13/1973); Barbara Lucas (1953, Divorced 1971) **CH:** Gary (Deceased); Lary; Dorinda; Gaile; Hank Jr.; Ceci (Adopted) **ED:** Honorary HHD, Princeton University (2011) **C:** Founder, Chairman, 755 Restaurant & Lounge, Atlanta, GA (1995-Present); Senior Vice President, Assistant to President, Atlanta National League Baseball Club, Inc.(Now Atlanta Braves), MLB (1989-Present); President and Chief Executive Officer, Hank Aaron Automotive Group (1999-2007); Vice President, Player Development, Atlanta National League Baseball Club, Inc. Now Atlanta Braves), MLB (1976-1989); Outfielder, Designated Hitter, Milwaukee Brewers, MLB (1975-1976); Outfielder, Atlanta Braves, MLB (1966-1975); Outfielder, Milwaukee Braves, MLB (1954-1965); Shortstop, Jacksonville Braves (1953); Shortstop, Eau Claire Bears (1952); Shortstop, Indianapolis Clowns (1951); Player, Mobile Black Bears (1951); Corporate Vice President, Community Relations, TBS, Turner Broadcasting System, Inc.; Vice President, Business Development, CNN Airport Network, Turner Broadcasting System, Inc. **CR:** Board of Directors, Atlanta Braves (2007-Present); Board of Advisors, Atlanta Falcons Football Club (2004-Present); Board of Directors, Medallion Financial Corp. (2004-Present); Board of Directors, Retail Ventures, Inc. (2003-2011); Board of Directors, Atlanta Technical College **CIV:** Georgia Trustee, Georgia Historical Society (2010-Present); Co-founder, Hank Aaron Chasing the Dream Foundation (1994-Present); Co-founder, Honorary Director, World Children's Baseball Fair, Japan (1992-Present); Benefactor, The Dreamchaser Scholarship, Hank Aaron Chasing the Dream Foundation; Founder, Hank Aaron Rookie League; Board of Selectors, Jefferson Awards for Public Service, Multiplying Good; Board of Governors, Boys & Girls Clubs of America; Board of Councilors, The Carter Center **CW:** Author, "I Had a Hammer: The Hank Aaron Story" (1991) **AW:** Named to Order of the Rising Sun, Gold Rays with Rosette, Akihito, Emperor of Japan (2016); Inductee, International Civil Rights Walk of Fame, Atlanta, GA (2005); Featured, "100 Greatest African Americans," Molefi Kete Asante (2002); Lombardi Award of Excellence, Vince Lombardi Cancer Foundation (2002); Presidential Medal of Freedom, George W. Bush (2002); Presidential Citizens Medal, Bill Clinton (2001); Inductee, Miller Park Walk of Fame, Milwaukee, WI (2001); Inductee, Ivan Allen Jr. Braves Museum and Hall of Fame (1999); Named to All-century Team, MLB (1999); Named One of the 100 Greatest Baseball Players, Sporting News

(1999); Inductee, Wisconsin Athletic Hall of Fame (1988); Inductee, National Baseball Hall of Fame (1982); Golden Plate Award, American Academy of Achievement (1977); Springarn Medal, NAACP (1976); Named American League All-star (1975); Named National League All-star (1955-1974); Lou Gehrig Memorial Award, MLB (1970); Named Player of the Year, Sporting News (1956, 1963); Rawlings Gold Glove Award, National League, MLB (1958-1960); National League Batting Title, MLB (1956, 1959); Named MVP, National League, MLB (1957) **AV:** Fishing; Playing tennis; Golfing

ABBOTT, DAVID H., T: Manufacturing Executive **I:** Manufacturing **DOB:** 07/06/1936 **PB:** Milton **SC:** KY/USA **PT:** Carl Abbott; Rachael (Miles) Abbott **MS:** Married **SPN:** Joan Shefchik (08/14/1976) **CH:** Kristine; Gina; Beth; Linsey **ED:** MBA, University of Kentucky (1961); BS, University of Kentucky (1960) **C:** Retired (2002); President, Chief Executive Officer, Director, E.D. Etnyre & Co. (1998-2002); President, Chief Operating Officer, Portec, Inc. (1981-1987); Executive Vice president of Worldwide Construction Equipment, J.I. Case Collectors' Association, Inc. (1979-1981); Vice President, General Manager, Drott Division, J.I. Case Collectors' Association, Inc. (1977-1979); Vice President, General Manager, Construction Equipment Division, J.I. Case Collectors' Association, Inc. (1975-1977); Vice President, J.I. Case Collectors' Association, Inc. (1975); General Manager, Service Parts Supply Division, J.I. Case Collectors' Association, Inc. (1973-1975); Division Controller, J.I. Case Collectors' Association, Inc. (1970-1973); Various Positions, Ford Motor Company (1961-1969); Director, Portec, Inc. **CR:** Director, Oak Brook Bank & Trust (1982-1988) **MIL:** U.S. Army (1958) **MEM:** Board of Directors, Construction Industry Manufacturers Association (1979-1981, 1982-2002); Director, American Road & Transportation Builders Association (1988-2002); Chairman, Construction Industry Manufacturers Association (1992) **MH:** Albert Nelson Marquis Lifetime Achievement Award **B/I:** Mr. Abbott became involved in his profession because after graduating from college he went into a graduate program at Ford. **AV:** Water skiing; Riding motorcycles **PA:** Republican **RE:** Methodist

ABBOTT, GREGORY, "GREG" WAYNE, T: Governor of Texas **I:** Government Administration/ Government Relations/Government Services **DOB:** 11/13/1957 **PB:** Wichita Falls **SC:** TX/USA **PT:** Calvin Roger Abbott; Doris Lacristia (Jacks) Abbott **MS:** Married **SPN:** Cecilia Therese Phalen (1982) **CH:** Audrey **ED:** JD, Vanderbilt University Law School, Nashville, TN (1984); BBA in Finance, The University of Texas at Austin (1981) **C:** Governor, State of Texas (2015-Present); Attorney General, State of Texas (2002-2015); Associate Justice, Texas Supreme Court, Austin, Texas (1996-2001); Trial Judge, 129th State District Court, Houston, Texas (1992-1996); Attorney, Butler & Binion, Houston, Texas (1984-1992) **CR:** Member, Governor's Committee to Promote Adoption **CIV:** Honorary State Chairman, Big Brothers Big Sisters of Lone Star (2004); Member, Advisory Board, Career and Recovery Resources, Inc.; Board of Trustees, Goodwill Industries of Central Texas; Board of Directors, Maywood Children & Family Services; Board of Directors, Texas Institute Rehabilitation & Research Foundation (Now TIRR Foundation) **AW:** Outstanding Trial Judge, Texas Association of Civil Trial and Appellate Specialists (1995); Named an Outstanding Young Texan, Texas Jaycees (1995); Named Outstanding Young Lawyer, Houston Bar Association (1994); American Jurisprudence Award (1983); Named Appellate Judge of the Year, American Board of Trial Advocates, Texas Chapter; Jurist of the Year, Texas Review of Law & Politics

MEM: Texas Association of State Judges; Houston Young Lawyers Association, Houston Bar Association; State Bar of Texas; Supreme Court Liaison Committee on Judicial Ethics, State Bar of Texas **BAR:** United States District Court for the Southern District of Texas (1985); State of Texas (1985) **PA:** Republican **RE:** Roman Catholic

ABDEL-LATIF, ATA A., PHD, T: Professor Emeritus **I:** Education/Educational Services **CN:** Medical College Of Georgia **DOB:** 01/22/1933 **PB:** Beitunia **SC:** Ramallah/Palestine **PT:** Abdel-Hafez Latif; Aysha Abdel-Latif **MS:** Married **SPN:** Iris K. Graham (09/10/1957, Deceased 2018) **CH:** Rhonda; David; Joseph; Rhadi **ED:** Postgraduate in Neurochemistry, University of Illinois College of Medicine (1963-1965); PhD in Biochemistry, Mount Sinai Medical Research Foundation, Illinois Institute of Technology (1963); MS in Chemistry, DePaul University, Chicago, IL (1958); BS in Biology and Chemistry, DePaul University, Chicago, IL (1955) **C:** Retired (2004); Emeritus, Medical College of Georgia, Augusta University (2000-Present); Regents Professor, Medical College of Georgia, Augusta University (1987-2004); Professor, Medical College of Georgia, Augusta University (1974-1987); Associate Professor, Biochemistry and Molecular Biology, Medical College of Georgia, Augusta University (1967-1974); Medical Research Scientist V, Department of Mental Health, State of Illinois (1963-1967); Research Associate, Department of Psychiatry, University of Illinois (1963-1967) **CR:** Visiting Professor University of Nottingham (1975-1976); Researcher and Speaker in Field **AW:** Grantee, National Institutes of Health (1965-2004); Award for Outstanding Contribution to Vision Research, Alcon Research Institute (1990); Merit Award National Institutes of Health (1989) **MEM:** American Society of Biological Chemists; American Physiological Society; American Society for Pharmacology and Experimental Therapeutics; American Society for Neurochemistry; Society for Experimental Biology and Medicine; International Society for Eye Research; American Association for the Advancement of Science; Association for Research in Vision and Ophthalmology **MH:** Albert Nelson Marquis Lifetime Achievement Award **AS:** Dr. Abdel-Latif attributes his success to perseverance, curiosity, hard work and good work ethic. **B/I:** Dr. Abdel-Latif became involved in his profession because he was born in a small town near Ramallah, West Bank, 20 miles from Jerusalem. He came to the United States from Palestine in 1951 at the age of 18, with only $15 in his pocket, and wound up in Chicago. However, he still managed to become successful and make it on his own. He began studying chemistry and English in a Catholic high school in Palestine. His parents were farmers who worked very hard and wanted him to go to school. The driving factor behind him coming to America was to help make the lives of his parents better. While living in Palestine, he had a hard life. He had to walk five miles to school and five miles back through the mountains. When he finished high school, he passed the London Matriculation Examination in England, which was a certificate to pass what would be equivalent to a regents exam in the United States. At the time, Palestine was under British rule. It was a major accomplishment to him, and when he applied to the University of Illinois in Chicago, he was accepted. When he arrived to the United States, he stayed with a great uncle for about six months before moving out on his own. It was hard to work and go to school but he still managed to get his bachelor's degree in three years. **AV:** Going to the gym; Reading; Taking courses; Gardening; Planting vegetables **RE:** Muslim **THT:** Dr. Abdel-Latif advised others to "set your goals, work hard to achieve them, and this will give you a happy life."

ABDELSAMAD, MOUSTAFA H., DBA, T: Finance Professor **I:** Education/Educational Services **PT:** Hassan **MS:** Married **CH:** Dina; Omar **ED:** DBA, The George Washington University (1970); MBA, The George Washington University (1965); Bachelor in Commerce, Cairo University, with Honors (1961) **C:** Professor of Finance, Texas A&M University-Corpus Christi (1991-2013);Dean, Texas A&M University-Corpus Christi College Business (1991-2013); Dean, Finance Professor, University of Massachusetts Dartmouth, Dartmouth, MA (1988-1991); Assistant Dean, Virginia Commonwealth University, Richmond, VA (1977-1988) **CR:** Consultant in Field **CW:** Editor-in-chief, SAM Advanced Management Journal (1985-Present) **AW:** Taylor Key Award, Society for Advancement of Management (2000); Management Excellence Award, Society for Advancement of Management (1991, 1998); President's Excellence Award, Society for Advancement of Management (1996); Phil Carroll Advancement Management Finance Award, Society for Advancement of Management (1989) **MEM:** Financial Management Associate, Society for Advancement of Management President, ECEO, Society for Advancement of Management (1997-Present);International President, Society for Advancement of Management (1983-1986, 1996-Present); Texas Council, College of Business Education; Southern Business Administration Association **MH:** Albert Nelson Marquis Lifetime Achievement Award **B/I:** When Dr. Abdelsamad first entered college at Cairo University, he admired the work of his professors. They were kind of independent contractors and did their own research. They taught, consulted and practiced whatever they have learned in different fronts. **THT:** Dr. Abdelsamad's father was a math teacher and principal at an elementary school in Egypt.

ABDUL-JABBAR, KAREEM, T: Former Professional Basketball Player **I:** Athletics **DOB:** 04/16/1947 **PB:** New York **SC:** NY/USA **PT:** Ferdinand Lewis; Cora Alcindor **MS:** Divorced **SPN:** Habiba (Janice Brown) (05/28/1971, Divorced 1978) **CH:** Habiba Alcindor; Kareem Jr.; Sultana; Amir; Adam **ED:** Honorary Doctorate, School of Education, Loyola Marymount University (2019); Honorary Doctorate in Public Service, University of Central Florida (2017); Honorary HHD, Princeton University (2017); Honorary LHD, Drew University (2016); Honorary LHD, New York Institute of Technology (2011); Honorary LHD, McDaniel College (2007); BA in History, University of California Los Angeles (1969) **C:** Special Assistant Coach, Los Angeles Lakers, NBA, Los Angeles, CA (2005-2011); Consultant, Scout, New York Knicks, NBA, New York, NY (2004-2005); Head Coach, Oklahoma Storm, United States Basketball League, Enid, OK (2002); Consultant, Indiana Pacers, NBA, Indianapolis, IN (2001-2002); Assistant Coach, Los Angeles Clippers, NBA, Los Angeles, CA (1999-2000); Center, Los Angeles Lakers, NBA, Los Angeles, CA (1975-1989); Center, Milwaukee Bucks, NBA, Milwaukee, WI (1969-1975) **CR:** With, CCAC (2017-2018); Global Cultural Ambassador, United States Department of State (2012) **CIV:** Founder, Skyhook Foundation (2009-Present); With, President's Council on Sports, Fitness & Nutrition (2017); Volunteer Coach, Alchesay High School, Whiteriver USD, Fort Apache Reservation, Whiteriver, AZ (1998) **CW:** Columnist, Guardian News & Media Limited (2017-Present); Contributing Editor, Columnist, The Hollywood Reporter (2017-Present); Executive Producer, "Black Patriots: Heroes of the Revolution" (2020); Co-producer, Writer, "Veronica Mars" (2019); Co-author with Anna Waterhouse, "Mycroft and Sherlock: The Empty Birdcage" (2019); Appearance, "iZombie" (2019); Appearance, "The Big Bang Theory" (2019); Appearance, "The Comedy Get Down" (2018); Co-author with Anna Waterhouse, "Mycroft and Sherlock" (2018); Co-author with Raymond Obstfeld, "Becoming Kareem: Growing Up On and Off the Court" (2017); Co-author with Raymond Obstfeld, "Mycroft Holmes and the Apocalypse Handbook" (2017); Author, "Coach Wooden and Me: Our 50-Year Friendship On and Off the Court" (2017); Contributor, TIME USA, LLC (2014-2016); Co-author with Raymond Obstfeld, "Writings on the Wall: Searching for a New Equality Beyond Black and White" (2016); Co-author with Raymond Obstfeld, "The Magnificent Severn" (2016); Subject, "Kareem: Minority of One" (2015); Co-author with Raymond Obstfeld, "Stealing the Game" (2015); Contributor, "College Athletes of the World, Unite," "Jacobin" (2014); Appearance, "The Crazy Ones" (2014); Co-author with Raymond Obstfeld, "Sasquatch in the Paint" (2013); Appearance, "Guys with Kids" (2012); Author, "What Color Is My World?: The Lost History of African-American Inventors" (2012); Executive Producer, Writer, "On the Shoulders of Giants: The Story of the Greatest Team You Never Heard Of" (2010); Co-author with Raymond Obstfeld, "On the Shoulders of Giants: My Journey Through the Harlem Renaissance" (2007); Actor, "Whitepaddy" (2006); Appearance, "Scrubs" (2006); Co-author with Anthony Walton, "Brothers in Arms: The Epic Story of the 761st Tank Battalion, WWII's Forgotten Heroes" (2004); Co-author with Stephen Singular, "A Season on the Reservation: My Sojourn with the White Mountain Apache" (2000); Appearance, "The Brian Benben Show" (2000); Appearance, "Saved by the Bell: The New Class" (1998); Actor, "BASEketball" (1998); Appearance, "Living Single" (1997); Appearance, "Boston Common" (1997); Appearance, "Martin" (1996); Appearance, "Everybody Loves Raymond" (1996); Co-author with Alan Steinberg, "Black Profiles in Courage: A Legacy of African-American Achievement" (1996); Actor, "Forget Paris" (1995); Appearance, "Fresh Prince of Bel-Air" (1995); Appearance, "Full House" (1995); Appearance, "The Critic" (1994); Actor, "The Stand" (1994); Executive Producer, "The Vernon Johns Story" (1994); Appearance, "Matrix" (1993); Appearance, "Good Sports" (1991); Appearance, "Uncle Buck" (1991); Appearance, "Amen" (1991); Appearance, "21 Jump Street" (1990); Co-author with Mignon McCarthy, "Kareem" (1990); Producer, "All-Star Tribute to Kareem Abdul-Jabbar" (1989); Appearance, "Stingray" (1987); Actor, "Fletch" (1985); Appearance, "Tales from the Darkside" (1985); Appearance, "Pryor's Place" (1984); Co-author with Peter Knobler, "Giant Steps: The Autobiography of Kareem Abdul-Jabbar" (1983); Appearance, "Diff'rent Strokes" (1982); Actor, "Airplane!" (1980); Actor, "The Fish That Saved Pittsburgh" (1979); Actor, "Game of Death" (1978); Appearance, "The Man from Atlantis" (1977); Appearance, "Dinah!" (1977); Appearance, "The Way It Was" (1977); Appearance, "Emergency!" (1974); Appearance, "Mannix" (1971); Columnist, The Washington Post **AW:** Named Columnist of the Year, National Arts & Entertainment Journalism Awards, Los Angeles Press Club (2019); Named One of President Barack Obama's Favorite Books (2017); Named One of the Best Books of 2017, Boston Globe (2017); Presidential Medal of Freedom (2016); Named Best Documentary, NAACP Image Awards (2013); Named Best Children's Book, NAACP Image Awards (2013); Double Helix Medal, Cold Spring Harbor Laboratory (2011); Lincoln Medal, Ford's Theatre Society (2011); Inductee, National Collegiate Basketball Hall of Fame (2006); Named to 50th Anniversary All-time Team, NBA (1996); Inductee, Naismith Memorial Basketball Hall of Fame (1995); Named Western Conference All-star (1976-1989); Named to All-NBA First Team (1971-1974, 1976, 1977, 1980, 1981, 1984, 1986); Named Sportsman of the Year, Sports Illustrated (1985); Named NBA Finals MVP (1971, 1985); Named to NBA All-Defensive First Team (1974, 1975, 1979-1981); Named to NBA 35th Anniversary Team (1980); Named NBA MVP (1971, 1972, 1974, 1976, 1977, 1980); Named Eastern Conference All-star (1970-1975); Named Rookie of the Year, NBA (1970); Named Naismith Men's College Player of the Year Award, Atlanta Tipoff Club (1969); College Basketball Player of Year, The Associated Press (1967, 1969); Named to First Team All-American, USBWA, NABC, United Press International, Inc. and The Associated Press (1967-1969); Named NCAA Basketball Tournament Most Outstanding Player (1967-1969) **AV:** Jazz **RE:** Muslim

ABDULMAJID, ZARA, "IMAN" MOHAMED, T: Model; Actress; Entrepreneur **I:** Media & Entertainment **DOB:** 07/25/1955 **SC:** Mogadishu/Somalia **PT:** Mohamed Abdulmajid; Marian Abdulmajid **MS:** Widowed **SPN:** David Bowie (04/24/1992, Deceased 2016); Spencer Haywood (1977, Divorced 02/1987); Hassan (1973, Divorced 1975) **CH:** Two Daughters; One Stepson **ED:** Coursework in Political Science, University of Nairobi (1975) **C:** Founder, Spokesperson, Iman Cosmetics (1994-Present); Launched, Clothing Line, Global Chic, Home Shopping Network (2007); Model, Vogue (1976); Model, Magazine Covers; Model, Prominent Designers Including Halston, Gianni Versace, Calvin Klein, Issey Miyake, Donna Karen, Yves Saint-Laurent; Actress, Television and Film **CIV:** Global Advocate, CARE; Spokesperson, Keep a Child Alive; Children's Defense Fund; Enough Project **CW:** Co-Host, "The Fashion Show" (2010); Host, Judge, "Project Runway Canada" (2007-2009); Author, "The Beauty of Color" (2005); Author, "One Love Lost: A True Story" (2005); Author, "I Am Iman" (2001); Appearance, "Omikron: The Nomad Soul," Quantic Dream (1999); Actress, "Exit to Eden" (1994); Appearance, "Remember the Time" (1992); Actress, "Star Trek VI: The Undiscovered Country" (1991); Actress, "Lies of the Twins" (1991); Actress, "The Linguini Incident" (1991); Actress, "L.A. Story" (1991); Actress, "227" (1990); Actress, "House Party 2" (1991); Actress, "In the Heat of the Night" (1988); Actress, "Miami Vice" (1985, 1988); Actress, "No Way Out" (1987); Actress, "Surrender" (1987); Actress, "The Cosby Show" (1985); Actress, "Out of Africa" (1985); Actress, "The Human Factor" (1979) **AW:** Inspiration Award, DVF Awards (2020); Fashion Icon Award, Council of Fashion Designers of America (CFDA) (2010) **RE:** Muslim

ABELS, ZACH, T: HEAD Golf Professional **I:** Athletics **CN:** Canyon Springs Golf Course **ED:** BS in Psychology, Montana State University, Billings, MT (2008) **C:** Director of Instruction, Assistant Golf Professional, Canyon Springs Golf Course, Twin Falls, ID (2011-Present); Twin Falls Golf Club, Twin Falls, ID (2009-2010); Blue Lakes Country Club, Twin Falls, ID (2004-2009) **CIV:** Board Member, United Way **MEM:** Professional Golf Association of America (PGA) **AS:** Mr. Abels attributes his success to the people with whom he surrounds himself. His mother has always been the most supportive. Likewise, he is consistently looking to become the best version of himself. **B/I:** When he was 7, Mr. Abels started playing golf. Though he was not immediately talented, he was always inspired to become a better golfer. This is how he got involved in his field. **AV:** Watching college basketball; Traveling; Spending time with friends

ABNEY, DAVID PHILLIP, T: Executive Chairman **I:** Government Administration/Government Relations/Government Services **CN:** United Parcel Service of America, Inc. **PB:** Greenwood **SC:** MS/USA **MS:** Married **SPN:** Sherry **CH:** Valerie; Matt **ED:** Honorary Doctorate, Delta State University (2015); BBA in Marketing, Delta State University (1976) **C:** Executive Chairman, United Parcel Service of America, Inc. (2014-Present); Chief Executive Officer, United Parcel Service of America, Inc. (2014-2020); Chief Operating Officer, United Parcel Service of America, Inc., Atlanta, GA (2007-2014); President, UPS Airlines (2007-2008); Senior Vice President, United Parcel Service of America, Inc., Atlanta, GA (2003-2007); President, UPS International, United Parcel Service of America, Inc. (2002-2007); Integration Manager, Fritz Companies Merger, United Parcel Service of America, Inc., Atlanta, GA (2001-2002); Manager, President and Chief Operating Officer, SonicAir, Inc., United Parcel Service of America, Inc., Atlanta, GA (1995-2000); Various Positions, United Parcel Service of America, Inc., Atlanta, GA (1974-1995) **CR:** Board of Directors, United Parcel Service of America, Inc. (2014-Present); Board of Directors, Johnson Controls, Inc. (2009-Present); Board, Coalition of Service Industries; Board, Southern Center for International Studies; Board, U.S.-Japan Business Council, The U.S. Chamber of Commerce; Board of Directors, Air Courier Conference of America; Chairman, Air Transportation Liaison Committee; Board, Cargo Network Services, International Air Transport Association (IATA); Board, Macy's, Inc.; Board, Catalyst **CIV:** Trustee, UPS Foundation, United Parcel Service of America, Inc; Board of Directors, Delta State University Foundation, University Advancement and External Relations, Delta State University; Co-Founder, Sponsor, International Business Symposium, College of Business, Delta State University; Board of Trustees, Annie E. Casey Foundation **AW:** Horatio Alger Award, The Horatio Alger Association of Distinguished Americans, Inc. (2019); Most Admired CEO Lifetime Achievement Award, Atlanta Business Chronicle, American City Business Journals (2018); Alumnus of the Year, Delta State University (2007) **MEM:** Chairman, Metro Atlanta Chamber (2019); The Horatio Alger Association of Distinguished Americans, Inc.; World Affairs Council of Atlanta; Business Roundtable **B/I:** Mr. Shapiro became involved in his profession after graduating from UCLA. He decided to supplement his business ambitions with a legal background, and pursued law school. There, he won a moot court competition, during which he was inspired by several judges to become a trial lawyer. Afterward, he found work with the Los Angeles County District Attorney's Office.

ABRAHAM, KATY K., T: Chief Executive Officer, President, Owner **I:** Business Management/Business Services **CN:** Construction Cost Management Inc. (CCM) **PT:** Keith Kothmann; Ann Kothmann **MS:** Married **SPN:** Joe Abraham **ED:** BA in Business, University of North Texas (1998) **C:** Chief Executive Officer, President, Owner, Construction Cost Management (CCM) (2012-Present); District Manager of Retail, Royal Canin (2014-2017); Account Executive, Lynden International (2012-2014); Territory Manager, Stallion Oilfield Services (2010-2012); Account Manager, Stallion Oilfield Services (2008-2012); Associate Buyer, Tuesday Morning (2006-2008); Key Accounts, Old World Design (2002-2006); Associate Buyer, Bombay Co. (1998-2002) **CIV:** Saving Hope; The Humane Society of North Texas; Texas Sporting Breed Rescue; Fort Worth Syndicate **AW:** Listee, 100 List, #20 Ranking, Initiative for a Competitive Inner City (2018); Fort Worth Small Business Excel-lence Award, Small Business Excellence (2017); Nominee, Fort Worth Chambers Small Business of the Year; Nominee, Halsey Award **MEM:** Society of American Military Engineers; Association for Professional Women in Construction; Consulting Estimators Round Table; Women's Business Council - Southwest **AS:** Ms. Abraham attributes her success to surrounding herself with amazing people. **B/I:** Ms. Abraham entered her profession because she was inspired by her father, Keith, to buy the family business and continue to grow the company even though she never worked for him. Her very first job there was as the owner. Inspired to run her own company, Ms. Abraham wanted to offer the industry a real value to complete government projects. Her clients in government are important to her because of their certification clearances. Ms. Abraham brings value to the clients on the large government contracts. Under her leadership, the business has grown over 600%. **AV:** Playing with dogs

ABRAHAM, RALPH LEE JR., MD, T: U.S. Representative from Louisiana **I:** Government Administration/Government Relations/Government Services **CN:** U.S. House of Representatives **DOB:** 09/16/1954 **PB:** Alto **SC:** LA/USA **PT:** Ralph Abraham Sr.; Marlene Posey **MS:** Married **SPN:** Dianne Abraham (1977) **CH:** Three Children **ED:** Doctor of Medicine, Louisiana State University School of Medicine (1994); Doctor of Veterinary Medicine, Louisiana State University School of Veterinary Medicine (1980); Bachelor of Arts, Louisiana State University (1980) **C:** Member, U.S. House of Representatives from Louisiana's Fifth Congressional District (2015-Present); Member, Veterans Affairs Committee (2015-2016); Member, Committee on Agriculture; Member, Committee on Science, Space, and Technology; Member, Committee on Veterans Affairs **MIL:** Advanced through Ranks to First Lieutenant, United States Coast Guard Auxiliary; With, Mississippi National Guard **PA:** Republican

ABRAMS, JEFFREY, "J.J." JACOB, T: Director, Producer, Screenwriter, Musician, Composer, Actor, Comic Book Writer **I:** Media & Entertainment **DOB:** 06/27/1966 **PB:** New York **SC:** NY/USA **PT:** Gerald W.; Carol Ann Abrams **MS:** Married **SPN:** Sarah McGrath (1996) **CH:** Henry; Gracie; August **ED:** Bachelor's Degree, Sarah Lawrence College (1988) **CW:** Executive Producer, "Lovecraft Country" (2020); Executive Producer, "The Wrong Mans" (2019); Producer, Director, Writer, Voice Actor, "Star Wars: Episode IX-The Rise of Skywalker" (2019); Executive Producer, Writer, "Castle Rock" (2018-2019); Executive Producer, "Glare" (2018); Producer, "Overlord" (2018); Producer, "The Cloverfield Paradox" (2018); Producer, "Mission: Impossible-Fallout" (2018); Executive Producer, Writer, "Westworld" (2016-2018); Executive Producer, "Star Wars: Episode VIII-The Last Jedi" (2017); Executive Producer, "100 Years" (2017); Actor, "The Disaster Artist" (2017); Actor, "Nightcap" (2017); Actor, "Tour de Pharmacy" (2017); Appearance, "The Magic History of Cinema" (2017); Executive Producer, "Moon Shot" (2016); Producer, "Valencia" (2016); Executive Producer, Composer, "11.22.63" (2016); Executive Producer, Writer, "Roadies" (2016); Producer, "Star Trek Beyond" (2016); Producer, "10 Cloverfield Lane" (2016); Executive Producer, Writer, Composer, "Person of Interest" (2011-2016); Producer, Writer, Director, "Star Wars: Episode VII-The Force Awakens" (2015); Producer, "Mission: Impossible-Rogue Nation" (2015); Executive Producer, Writer, "Dead People" (2015); Executive Producer, Writer, "Believe" (2014); Executive Producer, "Infinitely Polar Bear" (2014); Appearance, "Showrunners: The Art of Running a TV Show" (2014); Executive Producer, Writer, Composer, "Almost Human" (2013-2014); Executive Producer, Writer, Composer, "Revolution" (2012-2014); Co-Author, "S." (2013); Producer, Director, "Star Trek Into Darkness" (2013); Creator, Executive Producer, Writer, Composer, "Fringe" (2008-2013); Executive Producer, Writer, Composer, "Alcatraz" (2012); Executive Producer, Writer, "Shelter" (2012); Voice Actor, "Family Guy" (2012); Creator, Executive Producer, Director, Writer, "Undercovers" (2010-2012); Producer, "Mission: Impossible-Ghost Protocol" (2011); Producer, Director, Writer, "Super 8" (2011); Producer, "Morning Glory" (2010); Creator, Executive Producer, Director, Writer, "Lost" (2004-2010); Executive Producer, Director, Writer, "Anatomy of Hope" (2009); Co-Producer, "The People Speak" (2009); Producer, Director, "Star Trek" (2009); Executive Producer, "Boundaries" (2008); Producer, "Cloverfield" (2008); Director, "The Office" (2007); Executive Producer, "Six Degrees" (2006-2007); Executive Producer, "What About Brian" (2006-2007); Creator, Executive Producer, Director, Writer, Composer, Actor, "Alias" (2001-2006); Digital Artist, Director, Writer, "Mission: Impossible III" (2006); Creator, Executive Producer, Director, Writer, Composer, "Felicity" (1998-2002); Producer, Writer, "Joy Ride" (2001); Actor, "The Suburbans" (1999); Producer, Writer, "Armageddon" (1998); Writer, "Gone Fishin'" (1997); Producer, "The Pallbearer" (1996); Actor, "Diabolique" (1996); Composer, "Future Shock" (1994); Actor, "Six Degrees of Separation" (1993); Executive Producer, Writer, "Forever Young" (1992); Co-Producer, Writer, Actor, "Regarding Henry" (1991); Writer, Actor, "Taking Care of Business" (1990); Composer, Sound Effects, "Nightbeast" (1982) **AW:** Jupiter Award, Best International Film (2016); Empire Award, Best Sci-Fi/Fantasy Film (2016); Empire Award, Best Director (2016); Saturn Award, Best Writing (2016); Norman Lear Achievement Award in TV, Producers Guild of America (2013); Saturn Award, Best Director (2012); BAM Award, Best Screenplay (2011); Scream Award, Best Scream-Play (2011); SFX Awards, Best Director (2010); Agent of Change, RS 100 List, Rolling Stone, LLC (2009); Scream Award, Best Director (2009); 50 Smartest People in Hollywood, Entertainment Weekly (2007); The Celebrity 100, Forbes Media LLC (2007); Time 100, Time USA, LLC (2006); PGA Award, Best Drama (2006); Writers Guild of America Award, Dramatic Series (2006); Film and Television Music Award, Top TV Series, ASCAP (2006); Best TV Series, Drama, Producers Guild of America (2006); 100 People in Hollywood You Need to Know, Fade In (2005); Emmy Award for Outstanding Directing for a Drama Series (2005); Emmy Award for Outstanding Directing for a Drama Series-Pilot (2005) **MEM:** Creative Council, Represent.Us **RE:** Jewish

ACCAD, AILA, MSN, RN, T: Nurse; Speaker; Author; Health Coach **I:** Professional Training & Coaching **CN:** LifeQuest International, LLC **DOB:** 10/06/1947 **PB:** Brooklyn **SC:** NY/USA **PT:** Robert Cuccioli; Ann (Amalfitano) Cuccioli **MS:** Single **CH:** Aaron Joseph; Beth Rose **ED:** Master of Science in Nursing, West Virginia University; Bachelor of Science in Nursing, Villanova University **CT:** Reiki Master (2002); Certified Comprehensive Life Coach; AAMET Certification in Energy Meridian Therapies; (EQI) Emotional Intelligence Certification; Certification in Critical Incident Stress Debriefing, Healing Touch Levels 1, 2A, 2B, American Holistic Nurses Association **C:** Executive Director, Future of Nursing Action Coalition (2014-Present); Founder and President, LifeQuest International LLC (1996-Present); President, Peoplework Solutions Corp. (1992-1995); Founder and Executive Director, Nurse Care Network (1985-

1995); President, Chief Executive Officer, Banonis Associates, South Charleston, WV (1982-1992); Director, Limen House, Inc., Wilmington, DE (1979-1981); Consultant, Writer, Freelance Contracts, Newark, NJ (1978); Faculty of Nursing, Delaware Technical Community College, Newark, NJ (1976-1978); Occupational Health Consultant, Division of Mental Health, New Castle, DE (1972-1975); Public Health Nurse, State of Delaware, Wilmington, DE (1972); Coordinator, Autistic Children's Research Unit, Eastern State School and Hospital, Trevose, PA (1969-1971) **CR:** Adjunct Faculty, West Virginia College of Graduate Studies, University of Charleston (1991-1993); Adjunct Faculty, West Virginia University (1991); Adjunct Faculty, West Virginia University School of Nursing; Emotional Freedom Techniques Advanced Practitioner and Trainer, Employee Assistance Professional, Cornell University School of Industrial Relations; Occupational Health Consultant, National Occupational Alcoholism Training Institute, East Carolina University; Employee Assistance Professional, East Carolina University and University of Delaware; Group Counseling, Rutgers School of Alcohol Studies, Alcoholism Institute, Delaware Institute of Alcoholism Studies, Eastern Pennsylvania Psychiatric Institute, Family Systems Therapy **CIV:** Board of Directors, United Way of Central West Virginia (1986-1989); Allocations Volunteer, United Way of Kanawha Valley (Now United Way of Central West Virginia), Charleston, WV (1984-1989); Allocations Panel Chairman, United Way of Central West Virginia (1985); Co-founder, Board of Directors, Task Force on Women and Chemical Dependency, Wilmington, DE (1976-1983); Commissioner, Council on Family Services, Governor of Delaware, Pierre Dupont, Wilmington, DE (1978); Chair, Women's Conference (10 Years) **CW:** Author, "Quick Tips to De-Stress Fast with No Extra Time or Money," Flowing Owl Press (2013); Author, "The Call of the Soul: A Path to Knowing Your True Self and Your Life's Purpose," Career Press, New Page Books (2013); Author, "34 Instant Stress Busters" (2009); Author, "Empowerment for Nurses," In Burkhardt, M.A. & Nathaniel, A.K., "Ethics & Issues in Contemporary Nursing" (1998); Author, "Metaphors in the Practice of the Human Becoming Theory," In Parse, R. "Illuminations: The Human Becoming Theory in Practice and Research," National League for Nursing Press, NY (1989); Author, "The Lived Experience of Recovering from Addiction," Nursing Science Quarterly (1988); Author, "Networking a Nurse Consulting Business," Nurses Network (1987); Author, "The Occupational Health Nurse and the Vietnam Veteran: Integrating Theory into Practice," AAOHN Journal (1981); Author, "Grounded Research Study on Factors of Family Strength," In "Family Strengths 3, Roots of Well-being," University of Nebraska Press (1978); Publisher, Flowing Owl Press (1977); Author, Six Guided Meditations CDs, "A Breaking the Perfection Myth, CD & DVD with Guide Book"; Author, "The Community Health Nurse as an Agent in Primary Prevention," In "National Center for Alcohol Education"; Author, "The Community Health Nurse and Alcohol Related Problems," Rockville, MD; Author, Publications Including NIAAA **AW:** Named Alumna of the Year, Rockefeller Award, West Virginia School of Nursing (2020); Golden Graduate Award, West Virginia School of Nursing (2010); Business Woman of the Year Award, Business and Professional Women, WV (2005) **MEM:** Founding Member, Charleston Chapter, Women for Economic Leadership and Development (WELD) (2017); President, West Virginia Nurses Association (1999-2001, 2012-2014); Board of Directors, Charleston Metro Chamber of Commerce (1998); President, Charleston Women's Forum (1985-1986); American Nurses Association; American

Holistic Nurses Association; West Virginia Nurses Association; Sigma Theta Tau Nursing Honor Society (Now Sigma Theta Tau International Honor Society of Nursing); National Speakers Association (NSA); National Nurses in Business Association; Charleston Women's Forum; Toastmasters International; Charleston Metro Chamber of Commerce; DHHS Health Innovation Collaborative; West Virginians for Affordable Health Care (WVAHC); West Virginians for a Healthy Future **MH:** Albert Nelson Marquis Lifetime Achievement Award **AS:** Ms. Accod attributes her success to reading on a wide range of subjects, especially on the cutting edge of physics, and having exceptional mentors and role models. **B/I:** Ms. Accad became involved in her profession because her mother encouraged her to be a nurse and her father encouraged her to go to college. **AV:** Reading; Photography; Being with friends; Sharing interesting information **PA:** Independent **RE:** Non-Denominational **THT:** Ms. Accad says, "Life is a precious gift. Each person has something to offer the world. The key to a happy life is fulfilling your potential and purpose." Ms. Accad was formerly known as Barbara Ann Cucioli. She is Non-Denominational, but has studied comparative religions and philosophies.

ACKMAN, WILLIAM, "BILL" ALBERT, T: Founder, Chief Executive Officer; Philanthropist **I:** Financial Services **CN:** Pershing Square Capital Management, L.P. **DOB:** 05/11/1966 **PT:** Lawrence David Ackman; Ronnie I. (Posner) Ackman **MS:** Married **SPN:** Neri Oxman (01/2019); Karen Herskovitz (07/10/1994, Divorced 2018) **CH:** Four Children **ED:** MBA, Harvard Business School (1992); BA, Harvard College, Magna Cum Laude (1988) **C:** Founder, Chief Executive Officer, Managing Partner, Pershing Square Capital Management, L.P., New York, NY (2003-Present); Chairman, Imperial Parking Corp. (Impark), REEF Technology Inc. (2000-2010); Co-founder, Gotham Partners Management Co., LLC, New York, NY (1992-2002) **CR:** Chairman, Howard Hughes Corporation (HHC) (2010-Present); Board of Directors, Canadian Pacific Railway (2012-Present); Board of Directors, J.C. Penney Co., Inc. (2011-2013); Board of Directors, General Growth Properties, Inc. (2009-2010); Board of Directors, GiftCertificates.com Corporation (1999-2019) **CIV:** Trustee, The Pershing Square Foundation (2006-Present); Advisory Board, Harvard Business School; Supporter, Center for Jewish History, Innocence Project, Centurion Ministries **CW:** Author, "Who Wants to be a Millionaire?" (2014) **AW:** Named to the Billionaires List, Forbes (2019); Named One of the Forbes' 400 (2015); Named One of the Highest-earning Hedge Fund Managers, Forbes (2015); Named to the Philanthropy 50, The Chronicle of Philanthropy (2011); Named One of the 40 Under 40 Rising Stars, Crain's New York Business (1998) **RE:** Jewish

ACOSTA, RENE, "ALEX" ALEXANDER, T: Former United States Secretary of Labor **I:** Government Administration/Government Relations/Government Services **DOB:** 01/16/1969 **PB:** Miami **SC:** FL/USA **MS:** Married **SPN:** Jan Williams **ED:** JD, Harvard Law School (1994); BA, Harvard University **C:** United States Secretary of Labor, United States Department of Labor, Washington, DC (2017-2019); Dean, Florida International University Law School, Miami, FL (2009-2017); U.S. Attorney, Southern District of Florida, United States Department of Justice, Miami, FL (2006-2009); Interim U.S. Attorney, Southern District of Florida, United States Department of Justice, Miami, FL (2005-2006); Assistant Attorney General, Civil Rights Division, United States Department of Justice, Washington, DC (2003-2005); Principal Deputy Assistant Attorney General, Civil Rights Division, United States Depart-

ment of Justice, Washington, DC (2001-2002); Senior Fellow, Ethics and Public Policy Center (1997-2000); Associate, Kirkland & Ellis LLP (1995-1997); Law Clerk, United States Court of Appeals for the Third Circuit **CR:** Member, National Labor Relations Board (2002-2003) **AW:** Named One of the 100 Most Influential People in Business Ethics, Ethisphere Institute (2008); Friend in Government Award, American-Arab Anti-Discrimination Committee (2005); Distinguished Leadership Award, Arab American Anti-Discrimination Committee, MI (2004); Hugh A. Johnson Jr. Memorial Award, Hispanic Bar Association of the District of Columbia (2003); Excellence in Government Service Award, Mexicana American Legal Defense and Education Fund (2003); Twice Named One of the Nation's 50 Most Influential Hispanics, Hispanic Business Magazine

ACTON, BRIAN, T: Executive Chairman **CN:** Signal **DOB:** 02/17/1972 **SC:** MI/USA **MS:** Married **SPN:** Tegan **CH:** One Child **ED:** BS in Computer Science, Stanford University (1994); Coursework, University of Pennsylvania **C:** Co-Founder, Executive Chairman, Signal Foundation (2017-Present); Co-Founder, WhatsApp Inc. (2009-2017); Vice President of Engineering, Yahoo! Inc. (2006-2007); Director of Engineering, Yahoo! Inc. (2002-2006); Software Engineer, Yahoo! Inc. (1996-2002); Quality Assurance Tester, Adobe (1994); Software and Hardware Engineer, Apple Inc. (1993-1996); Systems Administrator, Rockwell International (1992-1993) **CIV:** Co-Founder, Sunlight Giving (2014-Present) **AW:** The Forbes 400 (2019); Billionaires List, Forbes (2019); One of the Richest in Tech, Forbes (2017)

ADAMCZYK, DARIUS, T: Chairman and Chief Executive Officer **I:** Technology **CN:** Honeywell International Inc. **DOB:** 02/08/1966 **SC:** Poland **ED:** MBA, Harvard Business School, Harvard University (1995); Master's in Computer Engineering, Syracuse University (1991); BS in Electrical and Computer Engineering, Michigan State University (1988) **C:** Chairman and Chief Executive Officer, Honeywell International Inc. (2017-Present); President and Chief Operating Officer, Honeywell International Inc. (2016-2017); President and Chief Executive Officer, Honeywell Performance Materials and Technologies, Honeywell International Inc. (2014-2016); President and Chief Executive Officer, Honeywell Process Solutions, Honeywell International Inc., Houston, Texas (2012-2014); President, Honeywell Scanning and Mobility, Honeywell International Inc. (2008-2012); Chief Executive Officer, Metrologic Instruments, Blackwood, NJ (2007-2008); Vice President, Business Development and President, Air Solutions, Heavy Industrial Business, Ingersoll Rand plc (2001-2007); Senior Associate, Booz Allen Hamilton Inc. (1995-1999); Electrical Engineer, General Electric (1988) **CR:** Board of Directors, Honeywell International Inc. (2016-Present) **AW:** Great Immigrants Honoree, Carnegie Corporation of New York (2019); Corporate Social Responsibility Award, Foreign Policy Association (2018); Corporate Visionary Award, Latino Corporate Directors Association (2018); John D. Ryder Electrical and Computer Engineering Alumni Award, Michigan State University (2018)

ADAMO, JOSEPH A., PHD, T: Biologist, Educator, Researcher (Retired) **I:** Sciences **DOB:** 10/22/1938 **PB:** Hoboken **SC:** NJ/USA **PT:** Anthony Adamo; Helen Annamarie (Hornfeck) Adamo **MS:** Married **SPN:** Connie **CH:** Thomas Anthony; Jo Anne; Samantha; Connie **ED:** PhD, Rutgers, The State University of New Jersey (1975); Postgraduate Coursework, University of the Philippines

Los Baños (1973-1974); MS, Fairleigh Dickinson University (1967); BA, New Jersey City University (1964) **C:** Retired (2010); Professor, Georgian Court University (1990-2010); Director, Environmental Center, Ocean County College (1978-2007); Co-Director, Auto-Tutorial Units in Biology, Ocean County College (1968-2007); Professor, Ocean County College (1967-2007); Professor, Monmouth University (1997-1998); Chairman, Department of Science, Ocean County College (1981-1991); Assistant Professor of Biology, New Jersey City University (1966-1967); Instructor of Botany, Fairleigh Dickinson University (1965-1966) **CR:** Visiting Professor, Drexel University (1992-1994); Visiting Professor, Rutgers, The State University of New Jersey (1986-1988, 1994) **CIV:** Lieutenant Colonel, Commander, Aerospace Education Officer, Civil Air Patrol (2009-Present) **MIL:** U.S. Air Force (1955-1961) **CW:** Contributor, Articles, Professional Journals **AW:** Fulbright-Hayes Fellowship (1973-1974); University Fellowship (1967); Hammond Science Award, New Jersey City University (1964) **MEM:** American Society of Microbiology; Society of Nematologists; The American Phytopathological Society; Sigma Xi, The Scientific Research Honor Society; Iota Mu Pi; Phi Theta Kappa **MH:** Albert Nelson Marquis Lifetime Achievement Award **B/I:** Dr. Adamo became involved in his profession because as a high school student he was very interested in science and aviation.

ADAMS, ALMA, T: U.S. Representative from North Carolina **I:** Government Administration/Government Relations/Government Services **DOB:** 05/27/1946 **PB:** High Point **SC:** NC/USA **PT:** Benjamin Shealey; Mattie Stokes **MS:** Divorced **CH:** Two Children **ED:** PhD in Art Education/Multicultural Education, Ohio State University (1981); MS in Art Education, North Carolina Agricultural and Technical State University (1972); BS in Art Education, North Carolina Agricultural and Technical State University (1969) **C:** Member, U.S. House of Representatives from North Carolina's 12th Congressional District (2015-Present); State Representative, District 58, State of North Carolina (2003-2015); Former State Representative, District 26, State of North Carolina; Administrator, Professor of the Arts, Bennett College, Greensboro, SC **CR:** Member, Committee on Education and the Workforce; Member, Committee on Small Business; Member, Joint Economic Committee; Member, Committee on Agriculture; Chairman, Appropriations Committee; Vice Chairman, Commerce, Small Bus and Entrepreneurship Committee; Member, Health Committee; Member, Education Subcommittee on Universities; Member, Education Committee; Member, Aging Committee **CIV:** Co-founder, African American Atelier (1990); Director, Steele Hall Art Gallery, Bennett College; Chair, North Carolina Legislative Black Caucus Foundation **PA:** Democrat

ADAMS, CLAUDINE, T: Board President, Chief Executive Officer **I:** Engineering **CN:** Bravura, Inc. **MS:** Married **SPN:** Charles **CH:** Two Daughters **ED:** Master of Theology, Calvary Christian College (2000); Bachelor in Psychology, University of Pennsylvania (1982) **CT:** ISO 9001 Quality Management Certification (2008) **CR:** Board President, Chief Executive Officer, Bravura, Inc., Aberdeen, MD (Present) **CIV:** Board Member, Northeastern Maryland Technology Council (NMTC); County Education; Board Member, Harford County Education Foundation; Board Member, Harford County Community College Board **AW:** Visionary Award, Northeastern Maryland Technology Council (NMTC) (2019); Best of Bell Camp Award for Computer Support and Services (2015, 2016); Named Renaissance Woman of the Year (2016); Athena

Leadership Award Nominee (2016); Top Honoree Award (2015); Presidential Volunteer Service Award (2009); Named Charles County Business of the Year (2009); Named One of the Top 100 Minority-Owned Businesses, State of Maryland (2008); Named One of the Top 500 Minority-Owned Businesses, United States (2008) **AS:** Mrs. Adams attributes her success to her hard work. **B/I:** Mrs. Adams became involved in her profession because of her desire to own a business. **AV:** Reading; Cardiovascular exercising; Traveling **THT:** Mrs. Adams operates a woman-owned, minority-owned, small, disadvantaged business with a wealth of Department of Defense, U.S. Army, and Intel-community experience. She is also a member of the Harford County Education Foundation, an organization designed to help under privileged children in the county to get the right resources for their education (K-12).

ADAMS, JERRY L., T: Owner **I:** Agriculture **DOB:** 11/04/1946 **PB:** Cape Girardeau **SC:** MO/USA **PT:** Julius Jefferson; Sarah Jean Adams **MS:** Married **SPN:** Marilyn G. Adams (03/03/1973) **CH:** Lori; Darren; Brian **ED:** BS, Southeast Missouri State University (1968) **C:** Retired (2011); Crop Specialist, Bayer AG (2006-2011); Agricultural Specialist, Aventis Crop Science (Now Bayer AG) (1999-2006); Agricultural Specialist, Rhone Poulenc Agricultural Company (1986-1999); Sales Representative, Union Carbide Company (1972-1986) **CR:** Founder, JLA Consulting Service Inc. (2011-Present) **MIL:** U.S. Navy (1968-1972) **AW:** Agrinaut Award **MEM:** Industry Representative, South Carolina Aviation Association (1974-1991); President, South Carolina Pest Control Association (1983); VFW; The American Legion **MH:** Albert Nelson Marquis Lifetime Achievement Award; Marquis Who's Who Top Professional **B/I:** Mr. Adams became involved in his profession because his grandfather and father were farmers and he fell in love with the industry. **AV:** Hunting; Playing baseball; Gardening **PA:** Republican **RE:** Presbyterian

ADAMS, JOHN COOLIDGE, T: Composer, Conductor **I:** Fine Art **DOB:** 02/15/1947 **PB:** Worcester **SC:** MA/USA **PT:** Carl John; Elinore Mary (Coolidge) A. **MS:** Married **SPN:** Deborah O'Grady **CH:** Samuel Carl Adams (Composer); Emily (Painter) **ED:** Honorary MusD, Royal Academy of Music, London, United Kingdom (2015); Honorary MusD, Yale University (2013); Honorary MusD, Harvard University (2012); Honorary MusD, The Juilliard School (2011); Honorary MusD, Duquesne University (2009); Honorary ArtsD, Northwestern University (2008); Honorary Degree, University of Cambridge, Cambridge, United Kingdom (2003); MA, Harvard University (1971); BA, Harvard University, Magna Cum Laude (1969) **C:** Composer (1968-Present); Composer-in-Residence, Conductor, San Francisco Symphony (1979-1985); Faculty, San Francisco Conservatory of Music (1972-1983) **CR:** Creative Chair, Los Angeles Philharmonic Association (2009-Present); Artistic Adviser, San Francisco Symphony (1978-Present); Richard and Barbara Debs Composer's Chair, Carnegie Hall (2003-2007); Director, New Music Ensemble, San Francisco Conservatory of Music (1972-1981); Composer-in-Residence, Marlboro Music Festival (1970); Creative Chair, The Saint Paul Chamber Orchestra; Musical Director, Cabrillo Festival of Contemporary Music; Founder, New and Unusual Music Series, San Francisco Symphony; Founder, In Your Ear Festival; Conductor, New York Philharmonic; Conductor, New World Symphony; Conductor, London Symphony Orchestra; Contributor, The New York Times Book Review; Contributor, The New Yorker; Contributor, The Times, London, United Kingdom **CIV:** Co-Founder, President, Pacific Harmony

Foundation **CW:** Composer, "Must the Devil Have All the Good Tunes?" (2018); Composer, "I Still Play" (2017); Contributing Composer, "Call Me by Your Name" (2017); Composer, "Girls of the Golden West" (2017); Composer, "Second Quartet" (2014); Composer, "Scheherazade.2" (2014); Composer, "The Gospel According to the Other Mary" (2013); Composer, "Saxophone Concerto" (2013); Composer, "Absolute Jest" (2012); Composer, "City Noir" (2009); Author, "Hallelujah Junction: Composing an American Life" (2008); Composer, "First Quartet" (2008); Composer, "String Quartet" (2008); Composer, "Fellow Traveler" (2007); Composer, "Son of Chamber Symphony" (2007); Composer, "Doctor Atomic Symphony" (2007); Composer, "A Flowering Tree" (2006); Composer, "Doctor Atomic" (2005); Composer, "The Dharma at Big Sur" (2003); Composer, "My Father Knew Charles Ives" (2003); Composer, "On the Transmigration of Souls" (2002); Composer, "Nancy's Fancy" (2001); Composer, "American Berserk" (2001); Composer, "El Niño" (2000); Composer, "American Tapestry" (1999); Composer, "Naïve and Sentimental Music" (1998); Composer, "Century Rolls" (1997); Composer, "Slonimsky's Earbox" (1996); Composer, "Gnarly Buttons" (1996); Composer, "Scratchband" (1996); Composer, "Hallelujah Junction" (1996); Composer, "Todo Buenos Aires" (1996); Composer, "Lollapalooza" (1995); Composer, "I Was Looking at the Ceiling and Then I Saw the Sky" (1995); Composer, "Road Movies" (1995); Composer, "La Mufa" (1995); Composer, "John's Book of Alleged Dances" (1994); Composer, "Le Livre de Baudelaire" (1994); Composer, "Six Songs by Charles Ives" (1989-1993); Composer, "Violin Concerto" (1993); Composer, "Hoodoo Zephyr" (1993); Composer, "Chamber Symphony" (1992); Composer, "El Dorado" (1991); Composer, "Choruses from The Death of Klinghoffer" (1991); Composer, "The Death of Klinghoffer" (1991); Composer, "Eros Piano" (1989); Composer, "The Wound-Dresser" (1989); Composer, "The Black Gondola" (1989); Composer, "Berceuse Élégiaque" (1989); Composer, "Wiegenlied" (1989); Composer, "Fearful Symmetries" (1988); Composer, "The Nixon Tapes" (1987); Composer, "Nixon in China" (1987); Composer, "Short Ride in a Fast Machine" (1986); Composer, "Tromba Lontana" (1986); Composer, "The Chairman Dances" (1985); Composer, "Harmonielehre" (1985); Composer, "Light Over Water" (1983); Composer, "Shaker Loops (for string orchestra)" (1983); Composer, "Matter of Heart" (1982); Composer, "Grand Pianola Music" (1982); Composer, "Harmonium" (1980); Composer, "Common Tones in Simple Time" (1979); Composer, "Shaker Loops (for string septet)" (1978); Composer, "Phrygian Gates" (1977); Composer, "China Gates" (1977); Composer, "Studebaker Love Music" (1976); Composer, "Onyx" (1976); Composer, "Grounding" (1975); Composer, "Ktaadn" (1973); Composer, "American Standard" (1973); Composer, "Heavy Metal" (1970); Composer, "Piano Quintet" (1970); Composer, "Electric Wake" (1968) **AW:** Erasmus Prize, Praemium Erasmianum Foundation (2019); Gold Medal in Biography and Music, American Academy of Arts and Letters (2018); BBVA Foundation Frontiers of Knowledge Award, Music and Opera, BBVA USA Bancshares, Inc. (2018); Chevalier dans l'Ordre des Arts et des Lettres, Ministère de la Culture, Paris, France (2015); Opera Honors, The National Endowment for the Arts (2009); Northern California Book Award, Creative Nonfiction (2009); Distinguished Composer Award, American Composers Orchestra (ACO) (2007); Harvard Arts Medal, Harvard University (2007); Michael Ludwig Nemmers Prize in Music Composition, Henry and Leigh Bienen School of Music Northwestern University (2004); Centennial Medal, Graduate School of Arts and Sciences, Harvard University (2004); Grammy Award, Best Classical Album (2004); Grammy Award, Best Orchestral Performance (2004); Grammy Award, Best Classical Contemporary Composition (2004); Pulitzer Prize, Music (2003); Grammy Award, Best Contemporary Composition (1998); Grawemeyer Award for Music Composition, University of Louisville (1995); Best Chamber Composition, Royal Philharmonic Society, London, United Kingdom (1994); Grammy Award, Best Contemporary Composition (1989); Cyril Magnin Award for Outstanding Achievement in the Arts; California Governor's Award for Lifetime Achievement in the Arts **MEM:** American Academy of Arts and Letters (1997-Present); American Academy of Arts and Sciences (1997) **AV:** Attending Oakland A's games; Reading Spanish language books **THT:** Mr. Adams had the privilege of studying with Leon Kirchner, Earl Kim and Roger Sessions at Harvard University.

ADAMS, STEVEN FUNAKI, T: Professional Basketball Player **I:** Athletics **CN:** Oklahoma City Thunder **DOB:** 7/20/1993 **PB:** Rotorua **SC:** New Zealand **PT:** Sid Adams **ED:** Coursework, University of Pittsburgh (2012) **C:** Professional Basketball Player, Oklahoma City Thunder, NBA (2013-Present) **CW:** Author, "Steven Adams: My Life, My Fight" (2018) **AW:** Named, NBL Rookie of the Year (2011) **AV:** Video games

ADDISON REID, BARBARA JEAN, EDD, T: Management Educator, Human Resources Consultant **I:** Education/Educational Services **DOB:** 06/16/1943 **PB:** Rendville **SC:** OH/USA **PT:** Isaac Norman Reid; Mary (Addison) Reid **MS:** Divorced **SPN:** Leon Noel Brathwaite (01/20/1973, Divorced 1987) **CH:** Leon Philip Addison Brathwaite; Sonia Yvette Brathwaite **ED:** DEd, University of Massachusetts Amherst (1992); MEd, Northeastern University, Boston, MA (1985); BS, Northeastern University, Boston, MA (1974) **C:** Director of Equal Opportunity and Inclusion, Massachusetts Title IX Coordinator, Lesley University, Cambridge, MA (2008-2016); Executive Director of Human Resources, Bentley College, Waltham, MA (1997-2008); Assistant Professor of Management, Consultant of Human Resources, Bentley College, Waltham, MA (1994-2008); Director of Human Resources, Automatic Data Processing, Waltham, MA (1986-1994); Director of Personnel, Tufts University, Medford, MA (1978-1986); Assistant Manager of Staffing, Harvard University, Cambridge, MA (1969-1978) **CR:** Senior Lecturer in Business Administration, Northeastern University, Boston, MA (1980-1994); Consultant, Businesses in Massachusetts and Rhode Island **CIV:** Town Meeting Member, Town of Burlington, MA (1992) **CW:** Author, "Everyday Artist: Creating the Life You Want to Live" (2018) **AW:** Named, Boston's Most Influential Women, Leadership Committee, Women of the Harvard Club (2017); Martin Luther King Scholarship, Northeastern University (1973-1974); Recognition for Strong Leadership Influence, Governor Charles D. Baker, Lieutenant Governor Karyn E. Polite **MEM:** Harvard Club of Boston (2007-2016); Leadership Committee Chair, Women of the Harvard Club (2010-2012); Board of Directors, Northeast Human Resources Association (1989-1998); President, Northeast Human Resources Association (1994-1997); Vice President, Northeast Human Resources Association (1993-1994); Kappa Delta Pi Honorary Society (1985); Sigma Epsilon Rho Honor Society (1974); National Forensic League (1959) **MH:** Albert Nelson Marquis Lifetime Achievement Award; Marquis Who's Who Humanitarian Award **AS:** Dr. Addison Reid attributes her success to love and guidance from Mrs. Helen Paxton, owner of Paxey's Play School in Columbus, Ohio, who taught her a lot between the ages of three and five, such as the alphabet and how to read words. Mrs. Paxton

taught her to eat different foods and take naps in the afternoon, the joys of hearing stories, learning poems, and singing songs. She also taught her to be a leader and work hard, and that hard work always brings success. Dr. Addison Reid learned to continue to be lovely, nice, kind, obedient, honest, cooperative, and beautiful within as well as without. Mrs. Paxton also told her to obey and love her parents, that they are her best friends on earth, to never be unkind or hate anyone, to never forget God and that anything she asked of Him, He would grant to her. Mrs. Paxton's guidance, as well as her parents' love and affection, taught Dr. Addison Reid how to self-motivate and become successful in anything in which she endeavored. **B/I:** Dr. Addison Reid became involved in her profession at an early age, and her quest for learning continued throughout her life. After a year at Ohio State University, she decided that she would select another school, and she moved from Columbus, Ohio to Boston, Massachusetts, and entered Northeastern University in 1968. With guidance from Northeastern faculty, Dr. Addison Reid learned she could apply for an application to pay for courses and she became a Dr. Martin Luther King Jr. Scholarship recipient at Northeastern University. As luck prevailed, Barbara also earned a scholarship award from Harvard University, which supported her continued education at Northeastern, where she earned a bachelor's degree in business administration in 1974. To earn a bachelor's degree without any loan repayment was outstanding. As evidence shows, Dr. Addison Reid had continued her education and earned a Master's degree and a Doctorate degree with the support of academic institutions. Dr. Addison Reid's decisions made around education and what she wanted to accomplish professionally are a result of a letter that Mrs. Paxton wrote to Barbara when she was 5 years old. What she wanted to do professionally in human resources, and being able to teach undergraduate and graduate students and work with managers in corporations, was all founded in the very beginning to understand. She was determined from an early age to learn and teach others what they needed to do to be complete people. **AV:** Exercising; Treadmilling; Bicycling; Stepping; Reading; Journal writing **PA:** Democrat **RE:** Episcopalian **THT:** In April 2016, Dr. Addison Reid abruptly left her position at Lesley University; after two weeks, the president of the university advised her to see a counselor, or they would accept her absence as a resignation. Dr. Addison Reid saw her physician, who ordered further testing. She was hospitalized within days of her doctor's visit; Dr. Addison Reid had a brain tumor that was 1/4 the size of her head which had been growing for 10 years or more. Even with its massive size, she never had a headache. The surgeon removed the tumor and monitored her healing. Dr. Addison Reid had to relearn tasks, such as how to interpret words. She decided to write a book to push herself toward higher thinking abilities. Her surgeon said he had never had a patient who had written a book about their brain surgery and experiences in her life about dreams, goals, decisions, action steps, and results. The past three years have taught Dr. Addison Reid lessons that she'd like to share with others. First, she is in charge of herself. Second, her illness made her realize that she must continue to focus on her intellectual development by everyday work. Third, she exercises on a daily basis to stimulate her body to last longer in her lifetime. "You are the center for who you really are; You are in charge of you; You decide what is important to you;You decide what you must do to stimulate your brain;You decide what you must do to exercise your body; You decide to pursue goals, make decisions, create action steps, and evaluate your results! Be blessed!"

ADELSON, SHELDON GARY, T: Chairman, Chief Executive Officer **I:** Leisure, Travel & Tourism **CN:** Las Vegas Sands Corp. **DOB:** 08/04/1933 **PB:** Boston **SC:** MA/USA **YOP:** 2021 **PT:** Arthur Adelson; Sarah (Tonking) Adelson **MS:** Married **SPN:** Miriam Farbstein Orchshorn (1991); Sandra Adelson (Divorced 1988) **CH:** Adam Arthur; Matan Sarel; Mitchell (Adopted); Gary (Adopted); Shelley (Adopted) **ED:** Coursework, City College of New York **C:** Founder, Chairman, Chief Executive Officer, Sands China Ltd. (2009-Present); Founder, Chairman, Chief Executive Officer, Treasurer, Las Vegas Sands Corp. (1989-Present); Chairman, Chief Executive Officer, Interface Group Inc., Needham, MA (1974); Finance Consultant; Investment Adviser; Mortgage Broker **CR:** Founder, The Palazzo Tower, The Venetian Resort Las Vegas (2008); Founder, The Venetian Macao, Macau, China (2007); Founder, Sands Macao, Sé, Macau, China (2004); Founder, The Venetian Resort Las Vegas (1997); Founder, Sands Expo and Convention Center (1988) **CIV:** Founder, Adelson Family Foundation (2007); Benefactor, Yad Vashem (2006); Chairman, Benefactor, Adelson Educational Campus; Benefactor, Birthright Israel; Co-Founder, Dr. Miriam and Sheldon G. Adelson Research Clinic; United States Holocaust Memorial Council, United States Holocaust Memorial Museum, Washington, DC **CW:** Guest Speaker, Colleges and Universities **AW:** World's Richest People, Forbes Media LLC (2005-Present); Forbes 400, Forbes Media LLC (2019); Billionaires, Forbes Media LLC (2019); World's Richest People, Business Insider, Insider Inc. (2019); Powerful People, Forbes Media LLC (2016); CNBC First 25 (2014); 25 Most Influential Republicans, Newsmax (2008); Woodrow Wilson Award for Corporate Citizenship, Wilson Center (2008); Presidential Delegation, 60th Anniversary Celebrations, Israel (2008); Chairman's Award, Nevada Policy Research Institute **PA:** Republican **RE:** Jewish

ADERHOLT, ROBERT BROWN, T: U.S. Representative from Alabama, Lawyer **I:** Government Administration/Government Relations/Government Services **CN:** U.S. House of Representatives **DOB:** 07/22/1965 **PB:** Haleyville **SC:** AL/USA **PT:** Bobby Ray Aderholt; Mary Frances Aderholt **MS:** Married **SPN:** Caroline McDonald **CH:** Mary Elliot; Robert Hayes **ED:** Doctor of Jurisprudence, Cumberland School of Law, Samford University (1990); Bachelor of Arts, Birmingham-Southern College (1987); Coursework, University of North Alabama **C:** Member, Alabama's Fourth Congressional District, United States Congress, Washington, DC (1997-Present); Assistant Legal Advisor to Governor, State of Alabama, Montgomery, AL (1995-1996); Municipal Judge, Haleyville, AL (1992-1996); Delegate, Republican National Convention (1992); Member, Committee on Foreign Affairs **CR:** Member, U.S. Helsinki Commission on Security and Cooperation in Europe **AW:** Commander, Order of the Star of Romania (2017) **MEM:** Kappa Alpha Order **PA:** Republican

ADKERSON, RICHARD C., T: President, Vice Chairman and Chief Executive Officer **I:** Financial Services **CN:** Freeport-McMoRan **ED:** Honorary DSc, Mississippi State University (2010); Advanced Management Program, Harvard Business School, Harvard University (1988); MBA, Mississippi State University (1970); BS in Accounting, Mississippi State University, with Honors (1969) **C:** President, Freeport-McMoRan (1997-2007, 2008-Present); Chief Executive Officer, Freeport-McMoRan (2003-Present); Chief Financial Officer, Freeport-McMoRan (2000-2003); Executive Vice President, Freeport-McMoRan (1995-1997); Various Financial Management Positions, Freeport-McMoRan, New Orleans, LA (1989-1995); Partner,

Managing Director, Head, Worldwide Oil and Gas Industry Practice, Arthur Anderson & Co. (1978-1989) **CR:** Vice Chairman of the Board, Freeport-McMoRan (2013-Present); Board of Directors, Freeport-McMoRan (2006-Present); Executive Board, International Copper Association, Ltd. **CIV:** Trustee, National WWII Museum; Board of Directors, Alumni Association, Mississippi State University; Board of Directors, Bulldog Club, Mississippi State University; Advisory Board, The Crosby Arboretum; President's Council, Xavier University of Louisiana; Executive Board of Advisors, E.J. Ourso College of Business, Louisiana State University; Development Board, Fellowship Christian Athletes, New Orleans, LA; Business Council of New Orleans and the River Region; Advisory Board, College of Business, Mississippi State University; Vice President, President, Board Director, Executive Committee, Mississippi State University Foundation, Mississippi State University; Honorary Chair, Pride Campaign, Phoenix Zoo; Chair, "State of the Future" Capital Campaign, Mississippi State University **AW:** Inductee, National Mining Hall of Fame (2012); National Alumnus of the Year, Mississippi State University (2011); Charles F. Rand Memorial Gold Medal, American Institute of Mining, Metallurgical, and Petroleum Engineers (2011); Executive of the Year, Dean's Council, W.P. Carey School of Business, Arizona State University (2011); Ankh Award, The Copper Club (2009); Best CEO in Metals and Mining, Institutional Investor LLC (2008, 2009); Outstanding Alumnus, College of Business and Industry, Mississippi State University (1991); Outstanding Accounting Alumnus, Mississippi State University (1989); Dean's Council of 100, W.P. Carey School of Business, Arizona State University **MEM:** Chairman, International Council on Mining and Metals (2008-2011); Professional Accounting Fellow, U.S. Securities and Exchange Commission (1976-1978); Council on Foreign Relations; The Business Council; Business Roundtable; Advisory Council, Kissinger Institute on China and the United States, The Wilson Center; Clinton Global Initiative, Clinton Foundation; Board of Directors, Arizona Commerce Authority; Board of Directors, Greater Phoenix Leadership, Inc.; Board of Directors, Greater Phoenix Economic Council; Vice Chairman, National WW II Museum, New Orleans, LA; Board of Visitors, The University of Texas MD Anderson Cancer Center, Houston, Texas; Board of Directors, Mississippi State University Foundation, Mississippi State University

ADKINS, ADELE LAURIE BLUE, T: Singer-Songwriter **I:** Media & Entertainment **DOB:** 05/05/1988 **PB:** London **SC:** United Kingdom **PT:** Penny Adkins; Marc Evans **MS:** Separated **SPN:** Simon Konecki (Separated 2019) **CH:** Angelo (10/19/2012) **ED:** Diplomate, The BRIT School, London, United Kingdom (2006) **C:** Singer-Songwriter, Columbia Records, Sony Music Entertainment (2008-Present); Singer-Songwriter, XL Recordings (2006-Present) **CIV:** Benefactor, Victims of Grenfell Tower Fire (2017); Performer, Pride London (2011); Performer, Red Nose Day, Comic Relief, Charity Projects (2011); Performer, Little Noise Sessions, Union Chapel Project, London, United Kingdom (2007-2008); Performer, Black Ball, Keep a Child Alive, London, United Kingdom and New York, NY (2008); Contributor, MusiCares, Recording Academy; Contributor, Sands (Stillbirth and Neonatal Death Society) **CW:** Subject, "Adele Live in New York City" (2015); Subject, "Adele: Live in London" (2015); Musical Guest, "Saturday Night Live" (2008, 2015); Singer-Songwriter, "25" (2015); Subject, "Adele Live at the Royal Albert Hall" (2011); Singer-Songwriter, "21" (2011); Musical Guest, "Later... With Jools Holland" (2007, 2008, 2011); Actress, "Ugly Betty" (2009); Subject, "Adele 20" (2008); Singer-Songwriter, "19" (2008) **AW:** APRA Award for International Work of the Year, APRA AMCOS (2017); Brit Award for Global Success, BPI (2017); Grammy Award for Album of the Year, The Recording Academy (2017); Grammy Award for Best Pop Vocal Album, The Recording Academy (2017); Grammy Award for Record of the Year, The Recording Academy (2017); Grammy Award for Song of the Year, The Recording Academy (2017); Grammy Award for Best Pop Solo Performance, The Recording Academy (2017); iHeartRadio Music Award for Female Artist of the Year, iHeartRadio (2017); iHeartRadio Music Award for Pop Album of the Year, iHeartRadio (2017); Music Business Association Award for Artist of the Year, Music Business Association – Music Biz (2017); NME Award for Best Festival Headliner, NME (2017); AIM Independent Music Award for Independent Track of the Year, Association of Independent Music (2016); American Music Award for Favorite Adult Contemporary Artist, Dick Clark Productions, LLC (2016); BBC Music Award for BBC Radio 2 Album of the Year, BBC (2016); BBC Music Award for BBC Song of the Year, BBC (2016); BBC Radio 1 Teen Award for Best British Solo Artist, BBC (2016); Billboard Music Award for Top Selling Song, Billboard (2016); Billboard Music Award for Top Billboard 200 Album, Billboard (2016); Billboard Music Award for Top Billboard 200 Artist, Billboard (2016); Billboard Music Award for Top Female Artist, Billboard (2016); Billboard Music Award for Top Artist, Billboard (2016); Billboard Touring Award for Breakthrough Artist, Billboard (2016); Brit Award for British Female Solo Artist, BPI (2016); Brit Award for Global Success, BPI (2016); Brit Award for British Album of the Year, BPI (2016); Brit Award for British Single of the Year, BPI (2016); Echo Music Prize for Best International Rock/Pop Female Artist, ECHO Awards (2016); Edinburgh TV Award for TV Moment of the Year, The Edinburgh International Television Festival (2016); Guinness World Record for Fastest Time for a Video to Reach One Billion Views on YouTube, Guinness World Records Limited (2016); IFPI Global Recording Artist of 2015, IFPI (2016); iHeartRadio Music Award for Song of the Year, iHeartRadio (2016); Ivor Novello Award for Songwriter of the Year, The British Academy of Songwriters, Composers and Authors (2016); Juno Award for International Album of the Year, The Canadian Academy of Recording Arts and Sciences (CARAS) (2016); Juno Award for Video of the Year, The Canadian Academy of Recording Arts and Sciences (CARAS) (2016); Nickelodeon Kids' Choice Award for Favorite Song of the Year, Viacom International Inc. (2016); Pollstar Award for Major Tour of the Year, Pollstar (2016); Premios Juventud Award for Favorite Hitmaker, Univision Communications Inc. (2016); Premios Juventud Award for Favorite Hit, Univision Communications Inc. (2016); Shorty Award for Arts & Entertainment: Musician, Shorty Awards LLC (2016); Space Shower Music Award for Best International Artist, Space Shower Networks Inc. (2016); TIME 100, TIME USA, LLC (2012, 2016); BBC Music Award for British Artist of the Year, BBC (2015); BBC Music Award for BBC Live Performance of the Year, BBC (2015); Gaffa-Prisen for Best Foreign Female Act, Gaffa, Denmark (2015); Gaffa-Prisen for Best Foreign Album, Gaffa, Denmark (2015); Artist of Honor, NRJ (2015); Grammy Award for Best Song Written for Visual Media, The Recording Academy (2014); MBE (2013); Academy Award for Best Original Song, Academy of Motion Picture Arts and Sciences (2013); Billboard Music Award for Top Pop Album, Billboard (2012, 2013); BMI Film & TV Award for Academy Award Winners, Broadcast Music, Inc.® (2013); BMI London Award for Pop Songs, "Rumour Has It," "Skyfall," Broadcast Music, Inc.® (2013); BMI London Award for Academy Award, Broadcast Music, Inc.® (2013); BMI Pop Award for Award-Winning Songs, "Rumour Has It," "Someone Like You," "Set Fire to the Rain," Broadcast Music, Inc.® (2013); Brit Award for British Single of the Year, BPI (2013); Critics' Choice Movie Award for Best Song, The Critics Choice Association (2013); Golden Globe Award for Best Original Song-Motion Picture, Hollywood Foreign Press Association (2013); Grammy Award for Best Pop Solo Performance, The Recording Academy (2013); Award for Best Original Song, Houston Film Critics Society (2013); Nickelodeon UK Kids' Choice Award for Best UK Female, Viacom International Media Networks (2013); Premios Oye! Award for Álbum en Inglés, Academia Nacional de la Música en México (2013); World Soundtrack Award for Best Original Song Written Directly for a Film, World Soundtrack Academy (2013); AIM Independent Music Award for Most Played Independent Act, Association of Independent Music (2012); American Music Award for Favorite Adult Contemporary Artist, dick clark productions, llc (2012); Arqiva Commercial Radio Award for Most Played UK Artist on Commercial Radio, Arqiva (2012); Billboard Music Award for Top Billboard 200 Album, Billboard (2012); Billboard Music Award for Top Alternative Song, Billboard (2012); Billboard Music Award for Top Streaming Song (Audio), Billboard (2012); Billboard Music Award for Top Pop Artist, Billboard (2012); Billboard Music Award for Top Digital Media Artist, Billboard (2012); Billboard Music Award for Top Digital Songs Artist, Billboard (2012); Billboard Music Award for Top Radio Songs Artist, Billboard (2012); Billboard Music Award for Top Hot 100 Artist, Billboard (2012); Billboard Music Award for Top Billboard 200 Artist, Billboard (2012); Billboard Music Award for Top Female Artist, Billboard (2012); Billboard Music Award for Top Artist, Billboard (2012); BMI London Award for Award-Winning Songs, "Set Fire to the Rain," "Someone Like You," "Rolling in the Deep," Broadcast Music, Inc.® (2012); BMI London Award for Song of the Year, Broadcast Music, Inc.® (2012); BMI Pop Award for Award-Winning Songs, "Rolling in the Deep," Broadcast Music, Inc.® (2012); Brit Award for British Female Solo Artist, BPI (2012); Brit Award for British Album of the Year, BPI (2012); Echo Music Prize, Best International Rock/ Pop Female Artist, ECHO Awards (2012); Echo Music Prize for Album of the Year, ECHO Awards (2012); Fryderyk Award for International Album, ZPAV (2012); Grammy Award for Album of the Year, The Recording Academy (2012); Grammy Award for Best Pop Vocal Album, The Recording Academy (2012); Grammy Award for Record of the Year, The Recording Academy (2012); Grammy Award for Song of the Year, The Recording Academy (2012); Grammy Award for Best Short Form Music Video, The Recording Academy (2012); Grammy Award for Best Pop Solo Performance, The Recording Academy (2012); Grammis Award for Best International Album, Grammisgalan, Sweden (2012); Guinness World Record for First Album in UK Chart History to Reach Sales of Three Million in a Calendar Year, Guinness World Records Limited (2012); Guinness World Record for Most Consecutive Weeks with UK No. 1 Album by a Solo Female, Guinness World Records Limited (2012); Guinness World Record for Most Cumulative Weeks with UK No. 1 Album by a Solo Female, Guinness World Records Limited (2012); Guinness World Record for Biggest-Selling Digital Album in the UK, Guinness World Records Limited (2012); Guinness World Record for Biggest-Selling Digital Album in the US, Guinness World Records Limited (2012); Guinness World Record for Biggest-Selling Digital Track in a Calendar Year in the US, Guinness World Records Limited (2012); Guinness World Record for First Female Artist to Reach Digital Sales of One Million in the US, Guinness World Records Limited (2012); Guinness World Record for First UK Artist to Reach Digital Sales of One Million in the US, Guinness World Records Limited (2012); Ivor Novello Award for Songwriter of the Year, The British Academy of Songwriters, Composers and Authors (2012); Ivor Novello Award for PRS for Music Most Performed Work, The British Academy of Songwriters, Composers and Authors (2012); Juno Award for International Album of the Year, The Canadian Academy of Recording Arts and Sciences (CARAS) (2012); Los Premios 40 Principales Award for Best International Song, Prisa Radio (2012) **MEM:** Order of the British Empire (2013-Present) **PA:** Labour

ADLER, STEPHEN J., T: President, Editor-in-Chief **I:** Media & Entertainment **CN:** Reuters **PT:** Norman Adler; Mildred Adler **MS:** Married **SPN:** Lisa Grunwald **ED:** Doctor of Jurisprudence, Harvard Law School (1983); Bachelor of Arts in Social Studies, Harvard University (1977) **C:** President, Editor-in-Chief, Reuters (2013-Present); Editor-in-Chief, Reuters News (2009-Present); Executive Vice President, Reuters News (2010-2012); Editor-in-Chief, Bloomberg Businessweek, McGraw-Hill (2005-2009); Editor-in-Chief, Bloomberg Businessweek (2005-2009); Deputy Managing Editor, The Wall Street Journal (1988-2004); Editor, American Lawyer Magazine (1983-1988); Reporter, Capital Bureau, Tallahassee Democrat (1978-1980); Reporter, Tampa Times (1977-1978) **CR:** Speaker, Journalism Conferences, Universities and Public Forums **CIV:** Board Member, Thomson Reuters Foundation; Board Member, Columbia Journalism Review; Board Member, International Media Council, World Economic Forum; Board Member, Committee to Protect Journalists; Board Member, Council on Foreign Relations; Board of Final Judges, Gerald Loeb Awards **CW:** Author, "The Jury: Trial and Error in the American Courtroom"; Co-editor, "Letters of the Century: America 1900-1999"; Co-editor, "Women's Letters: America from the Revolutionary War to the Present"; Co-author, "The Marriage Book"; Executive Editor, Harvard Independent **AW:** Silver Gavel Award, American Bar Association

ADRA, HALA, ASSOCIATE BROKER, T: Real Estate Adviser **I:** Real Estate **CN:** Compass **DOB:** 11/08/1959 **PB:** Beirut **SC:** Lebanon **MS:** Divorced **CH:** Rania; Danny; Aya **ED:** BA in Business Management, Lebanese American University, New York, NY (1981) **CT:** Real Estate Salesperson (Residential); Real Estate Associate Broker; Relocation Specialist; Luxury Specialist **C:** Realtor, Associate Broker, Compass (2019-Present); Associate Broker, Long & Foster Real Estate (1994-2019); Marketing and Sales Consultant, "3 Beirut" (2010-2011); Sales Associate, AGS Realty, Inc. (1989-1994); Insurance Consultant, Cedars Brokerage Consultants (1983-1985); Marketing Manager, La Phenicienne Insurance Company S.A.L. (1981-1983) **CR:** Specialties as a Luxury Specialist, Relocation Specialist, Residential New Homes & Resale, Sellers & Buyers Representation, International Clients; Areas of Coverage in the Washington, D.C. Metro Area, Including Arlington, McLean, Vienna, Chevy Chase, Bethesda, and Potomac **CIV:** Supporter, Numerous Charity Organizations Focused on Education, Children's Health, Children's Health and Development in the U.S. and Lebanon; Supporter, Save the Children, Red Cross, Food Bank, American University of Beirut Medical Center **AW:** Best of Washingtonian (2015, 2018, 2019, 2020); Lifetime Top Producer, Masters Club, Multi-Million Dollars Club, Top 10 Individual Office Top Produc-

ers, Top 1% Realtors Nationwide **MEM:** Greater Capital Area Association of REALTORS®; Northern Virginia Association of REALTORS®; National Association of REALTORS® **AS:** Ms. Adra attributes her success to her invested time and hard work. She was a single parent and did not have any family or friends when she was starting in America. She had three children to take care of and she told herself she had to make it work. She survived the civil war in Lebanon so everything else is manageable considering the hardship she went through. **B/I:** Ms. Adra became involved in her profession because, coming from Lebanon, her specialty was business management and marketing. She wanted to pick a profession that combines the world that she lived in. Her dad was a builder and her brother was an architect. She wanted to combine what she saw and loved with her marketing professional. When she came to the United States, she saw that real estate is a regulated profession that requires much more than regular sales skills. **AV:** Traveling; Relaxing on the beach; Listening to live music; Watching shows on Broadway **THT:** Ms. Adra said, "Life is a journey for one to enjoy, accomplish and give back."She speaks Arabic, French, and English.

ADRIAN, OLIVIA, T: President **I:** Business Management/Business Services **CN:** Federal Asian Pacific American Council (FAPAC) **MS:** Married **CH:** Two Daughters **ED:** MA, Troy State University, Troy, AL (1989) **CT:** Master Certification in Program Management (2013); Certified Professional Contracts Manager (CPCM), National Contract Management Association (NCMA) (2012); Certified Functional Contracts Manager (CFCM), National Contract Management Association (NCMA) (2004); Certified Diversity Change Agent, U.S. Department of Interior (DOI), Bureau of Safety and Environmental Enforcement (BSEE) **C:** Committee Chair, Lifetime Member, Executive Board, Federal Asian Pacific American Council (FAPAC) (2005-Present); Chief, Contract Support Section, Senior Supervisory Program Manager, U.S. Department of Interior (DOI), Bureau of Safety and Environmental Enforcement (BSEE), Office of Offshore Regulatory Programs (OORP) **CR:** President, Federal Asian Pacific American Council (FAPAC) (2014-Present) **CIV:** Volunteer, Diversity Change Agent; Volunteer, Sunrise Retirement Home, Reston, VA; Lay Eucharistic Minister, Local Church **AW:** Excellence Leadership Award, San Francisco, National Conference (2014); Distinguished Toastmasters (DTM) Award (2010); Presidential Distinguished Division and the Area Governor Distinguished Award, District 27; Individual Leadership Award **AS:** Ms. Adrian attributes her success to her empathy, honesty, and genuine desire to give back. **B/I:** Ms. Adrian became involved in her profession because she grew up with her grandmother in the Philippines. They had a better house than some of the surrounding homes, and during typhoons, some people in the neighborhood would be left homeless. Ms. Adrian's grandmother took these people in, gave them shelter, and fed them soup. This is what encouraged Ms. Adrian to give back.

AFSHAR-MOHAJER, KAMBIZ, DMD, MSD, T: Clinical Professor **I:** Health, Wellness and Fitness **CN:** New York University College of Dentistry **DOB:** 10/04/1947 **PB:** Tehran **SC:** Iran **MS:** Married **SPN:** Nahid **CH:** Roya Afshar-Mohajer; Ramin Afshar-Mohajer **ED:** DMD, Tehran University College of Dentistry; MSD, Certificate of Specialty in Periodontology, New York University, NY (1976) **CT:** Specialty in Periodontology; Diplomat, Board, International Congress of Oral Implantologists (ICOI) **C:** Dentist (1976-Present); Private Practice, Periodontology and Implant Surgery, NY; Clinical Professor, New York University College of Den-

tistry, NY **AW:** Best Faculty Teaching Award of Periodontology and Implant Dentistry, New York University College of Dentistry (2019); Alumni Award to Best Faculty, New York University College of Dentistry (2017); Outstanding Teaching Award, American Academy of Periodontology (2013); Award for Faculty of the Year, Residents Over Many Years of Graduating Residents **MEM:** American Academy of Periodontology; American Dental Association; International College of Oral Implantologists (ICOI) **AS:** Dr. Afshar-Mohajer attributes his success to his self dependence and his responsibility to provide for his family. He says, "You have to be the best in the field that you are in...but you have to like it as well..." **B/I:** Dr. Afshar-Mohajer's grandfather was a dentist. So since childhood, he was exposed to the profession and loved it from a young age.

AGEE, EARLEEN HEINER, T: Business Owner, Sales Executive **I:** Retail/Sales **CN:** Leigh-Hi-Enterprises **DOB:** 01/07/1933 **PB:** Huntington **SC:** WV/USA **PT:** Earl Wesley Heiner; Florence Heiner **MS:** Widowed **SPN:** Robert Walter Agee (06/14/1952, Deceased 08/03/2017) **CH:** Wesley; Brian; Kimberly; Katherine **ED:** BA, Marshall University (1975); AA, Stephens College (1952) **C:** Owner, Vice President, Leigh-Hi-Enterprises, Huntington, WV (1978-Present); Sales Executive, C.F. Reuschlein Jewelers, Huntington, WV (1977) **CIV:** Member, Graduate School Advisory Board, Marshall University (1990-Present); Board of Directors, Hospice of Huntington (1989-Present); The American National Red Cross, Huntington, WV (1989-Present); Member, Marshall University Foundation (1989-Present); Board of Directors, President, The American National Red Cross, Huntington, WV (1975-1981); American Red Cross Blood Services; Member, Board of Directors, Foundation Board, Cabell Huntington Hospital **MEM:** Junior League of Huntington **MH:** Albert Nelson Marquis Lifetime Achievement Award **AV:** Tennis; Travel; Knitting; Walking; Golf **PA:** Republican **RE:** Presbyterian

AGNEW, JANET BURNETT, T: Secondary School Educator **I:** Education/Educational Services **DOB:** 08/29/1936 **PB:** Spartanburg **SC:** SC/USA **PT:** James Agnew; Ruby Evelyne (Burnett) Agnew **CH:** James Gilmour **ED:** Postgraduate Coursework, University of South Carolina, Columbia, SC (1990-1997); Postgraduate Coursework, Clemson University, South Carolina (1970-1972); MA in Teaching, Converse College, Spartanburg, SC (1966); BA, University of North Carolina, Greensboro, NC (1958) **CT:** Certified Teacher, Principal, Mathematics Supervisor, General Science, Physics **C:** Teacher, General Mathematics for Technicals II, Algebra I and II, Pacolet and Broome High School, Spartanburg School #3 (1976-1998); Substitute Teacher, Spartanburg Schools #7 (1975-1976); Instructor, Mathematics, Spartanburg Methodist College (1968-1975); Corporate Secretary, Delagrave Company, Spartanburg, SC (1963-1975); Teacher, Mathematics, Algebra, Spartanburg Schools #7 (1965-1968); Teacher, General Physical, Science Campobello School, Spartanburg Schools #1 (1962-1963); Teacher, General Mathematics, Algebra, Roebuck High School, Spartanburg Schools #6 (1962); Teacher, College Preparatory Mathematics, Air Force Dependent High School, Stevenville, Newfoundland, Canada (1960-1961); Teacher, General Mathematics, Algebra I and II, Greensboro Schools, Aycock (1958-1960) **CR:** Consultant in Field **CIV:** Resolution Chairman, General Federation Women's Clubs (2018-2020); Chairman, Trustee, General Federation Women's Clubs (1978-2003); Vice President, Southern Region, General Federation Women's Clubs (1992-1999); Chairman, Scholarship Committee, General Federation Women's Clubs (1995-

1997); President, Southern Region, General Federation Women's Clubs (1994-1996); Chairman, Scholarship Committee, General Federation Women's Clubs (1991-1993); Secretary-Treasurer, Southern Region, General Federation Women's Clubs (1990-1992) **CW:** Contributor, Articles, Professional Journals **AW:** Service Award, Spartanburg March of Dimes (1967-1968) **MEM:** President, General Federation Women's Clubs Jubilee Club (1996-2000, 2019-Present); By-Law Chairman, Alpha Eta State (2005-Present); President, South Carolina Education Association (2005-Present); Treasurer, Spartanburg County Retired Educators Association (2005-Present); Spartanburg Council of Federated Women's Clubs (2000-Present); Delegate Assembly, South Carolina Education Association (1999-Present); President, Spartanburg County Retired Educators Association (2003-2005); President, Delta Kappa Gamma (2002-2004); Vice President, Spartanburg County Retired Educators Association (2000-2003); Secretary, General Federation Women's Clubs Jubilee Club (2000-2002); Chapter Vice President, Delta Kappa Gamma (2000-2002); Representative, District Director, South Carolina Education Association (1999-2001); Chairman, By-Laws and Politics Committee, South Carolina Education Association (1999-2001); Representative, Delegate Assembly, Spartanburg County Association Educators (1987-1998); Representative Assembly, National Education Association, Spartanburg County Association Educators (1989-1997); President, Spartanburg County Association Educators (1992-1993); Vice President, President Elect, Spartanburg County Association Educators (1991-1992); President, Piedmont Junior Woman's Clubs (1974-1976); National Council of Teachers of Mathematics; Lifetime Member, South Carolina of Teachers of Mathematics; Lifetime Member, National Education Association **AV:** Crafts; Traveling **PA:** Democrat **RE:** Presbyterian

AGUIAR, ARTUR, T: Owner **I:** Business Management/Business Services **CN:** Arm Strong Home Improvement **DOB:** 04/14/1971 **SC:** Brazil **PT:** Artur Aguiar; Maria Aguiar **MS:** Married **CH:** Four Children **C:** Carpenter, Arm Strong Home Improvement, Cape Cod, MA (2007-Present) **AW:** Featured, New England Home Magazine (2019) **AS:** Mr. Aguiar attributes his success to hard work and dedication to the high quality of his work. **B/I:** When Mr. Aguiar came to America from Brazil 15 years ago, he began working in construction. His boss in America, who he regards as "a great guy," took him under his wing, despite his language barrier. His boss owned a condo in Cape Cod that he was working on. One day, he came to Mr. Aguiar and said "Artur...I know you don't speak English, and I don't speak Portuguese either, but watch me, and copy what I do." For six months, Mr. Aguiar followed him and watched his every move. After those six months passed, Mr. Aguiar became the first man in his business. **THT:** Mr. Aguiar likes to be clear and honest with his customer. He delivers what he can to meet their desires.

AGUILAR, PETER, "PETE" REY, T: U.S. Representative from California **I:** Government Administration/Government Relations/Government Services **DOB:** 06/19/1979 **PB:** Fontana **SC:** CA/USA **MS:** Married **SPN:** Alisha Aguilar **CH:** Evan; Palmer **ED:** BA in Government and Business Administration, University of Redlands (2001) **C:** Member, U.S. House of Representatives from California's 31st Congressional District, United States Congress, Washington, DC (2015-Present); Mayor, City of Redlands, CA (2010-2014); Councilman, City of Redlands, CA (2006-2010); Deputy Director, Interim Director, Inland Empire Regional Office of Governor (2001-

2006); Vice-Chair, Committee on Appropriations; Committee on House Administration; Committee on Energy and Commerce **PA:** Democrat

AGUIRRE, MARIA G., MD, FAAP, T: MD Emerita **I:** Medicine & Health Care **CN:** Kaiser Permanente **DOB:** 08/22/1948 **PB:** San Antonio **SC:** TX/USA **MS:** Married **SPN:** David A. Johnson, PhD **CH:** Marisol; Zachary D. **ED:** Doctor of Medicine, University of California San Francisco, San Francisco, CA (1976); Master of Science in Health and Medical Sciences, University of California Berkeley, Berkeley, CA (1974); Bachelor of Science in Nursing, Biology, Incarnate Word College, San Antonio, TX (1972) **CT:** Board-Certified, American Academy of Pediatrics **C:** Pediatrician Emerita, Kaiser Permanente Fontana Medical Center, Fontana, CA (2014-Present); Pediatrician, Redlands Family Clinic, Redlands, CA (2009-2013); Physician in Charge, Coachella Valley - Kaiser Permanente (2006-2008); Regional Chief of Pediatrics (2004-2005); Chief of Pediatrics, Kaiser Permanente, Riverside, CA (1993-2005); Member, Voluntary Clinical Staff, Keck School of Medicine of USC, Los Angeles, CA (1990-2005); Staff Pediatrician, Kaiser Permanente, Riverside, CA (1989-1993); Staff Pediatrician, San Bernardino County Medical Center, San Bernardino, CA (1986-1989); Assistant Clinical Professor, Department of Pediatrics, University of California Irvine, Irvine, CA (1986-1989); Chief of Pediatrics, Scripps Hospital, Vista, CA (1984-1985); Clinical Instructor, Department of Community Medicine, Division of Health Care Sciences, University of California San Diego, San Diego, CA (1980-1985); Private Practice, San Diego, CA (1979-1985); Pediatric Resident, Moffitt Hospital, University of California San Francisco, San Francisco, CA (1977-1979); Pediatric Resident, San Francisco General Hospital (1976-1977); With, Family Care Center, Kaiser, Fontana, CA; NICU, Ontario, California, CA **CR:** Member, Executive Committee, KP (1993-Present); Balloting Committee Membership (2003-2006); Member, Regional Immunization Practice Committee (2002-2006); Member, Institutional Review Board (2002-2004); Chairman, Credential and Privileges Committee (2002-2004); Clinical Sub-Investigator, Kaiser-UCLA Vaccine Study (1999-2002); President, Executive Committee, KP (1997-1998); Member, Quality Assurance Committee, San Bernardino County Medical Center (1988-1989); Member, Infectious Disease Control Committee, San Bernardino County Medical Center (1987-1989); Member, Fetus and Newborn Committee, San Diego Chapter, American Academy of Pediatrics (1983-1985); Member, Pediatric Bi-national Conference, Coordinator, San Diego Chapter, American Academy of Pediatrics (1983) **AW:** Physician Exceptional Contribution Award, Kaiser Permanente, Riverside, CA (2000); Chief of the Year Award, Kaiser Permanente, Riverside, CA (1995) **MEM:** Hinterland Pediatric Society (1986-1997); San Diego Woman Physicians (1983-1985); San Diego Pediatric Society (1979-1985); Fellow, American Academy of Pediatrics; Flying Samaritans; LIGA; American Board of Pediatrics **AS:** Dr. Aguirre attributes her success to her curiosity. She doesn't feel that she is any more or less bright than anyone. She simply has the desire to figure things out and cannot rest until she does so. **B/I:** Dr. Aguirre became involved in her profession because, while studying biology as an undergraduate, a school guidance counselor advised her that she would never be accepted into medical school because she was Mexican and a woman. From there, she decided to go into nursing. **THT:** Don't be afraid to leave an unhappy situation. Life is short - enjoy it to the fullest!

AHRENDTS, ANGELA JEAN, T: Former Senior Vice President **I:** Technology **CN:** Apple Inc. **DOB:** 06/07/1960 **PB:** New Palestine **SC:** IN/USA **PT:** Richard Ahrendts; Jean Ahrendts **MS:** Married **SPN:** Gregg Couch **CH:** Jennings; Summer; Angelina **ED:** Honorary LHD, Ball State University, Muncie, IN (2010); BA in Merchandising and Marketing, Ball State University, Muncie, IN (1981) **C:** Senior Vice President, Retail and Online Stores, Apple Inc., Cupertino, CA (2014-2019); Chief Executive Officer, Burberry Group Plc, London, England (2006-2014); Executive Vice President, Liz Claiborne, Inc., New York, NY (2002-2006); Senior Vice President, Corporate Merchandising, Liz Claiborne, Inc., New York, NY (2000-2002); Group President, Liz Claiborne, Inc., New York, NY (2000-2002); Vice President, Corporate Merchandising and Design, Liz Claiborne, Inc., New York, NY (1998-2000); Vice President, General Merchandise Manager, Henri Bendel (1996-1998); President, Donna Karan Collection, Donna Karan International, Donna Karan Company (1992-1996); Vice President, Merchandising, Donna Karan Company (1992); President, Carmelo Pomodoro Ltd. (1990-1991); Vice President, Marketing and Sales, Carmelo Pomodoro Ltd. (1989-1990); National Sales Manager, Warnaco, Inc. (1985-1987); Account Executive, Warnaco, Inc. (1983-1985); Account Executive, Damon Creations (1981-1983); Senior Vice President, Valentino Intimate Apparel and Ungaro Intimate Apparel, Warnaco, Inc.; President, Pringle of Scotland Division, Warnaco, Inc.; Vice President, Sales, Geoffrey Beene Knitware, Warnaco, Inc. **CR:** Member, Prime Minister's Business Advisory Group (2010-Present); Board of Directors, Burberry Group Plc. (2006-2014) **CIV:** Co-founder, Burberry Foundation (2008-Present) **AW:** Named One of the 50 Most Powerful Women in Business, Fortune Magazine (2007, 2008, 2001-2015); Named Dame Commander of the Most Excellent Order of the British Empire, Her Majesty Queen Elizabeth II (2014); Named One of the Most Creative People in Business, Fast Company (2014); Named One of the Women of 2013, Financial Times (2013); Distinguished Alumni Award, Ball State University (2012); Medal of Honor, St. George's Society of New York (2011); Outstanding Leadership Award, Oracle World Retail Awards (2010); Named One of the Business People of the Year, Fortune (2010, 2011, 2013); Named European Business Leader of Future, CNBC (2010); Named One of the International Power 50 (2008-2013); Named One of the 100 Most Powerful Women, Forbes Magazine (2006-2013); Named One of the 50 Women to Watch, The Wall Street Journal (2005, 2006); Named to the Women in Fashion Power List, Time Style & Design Magazine (2004); Alumni Achievement Award, Ball State University (2003); Named One of the Rising Stars 40 Under 40, Crain's New York (2000) **MEM:** Honorary Fellow, Shenkar College of Engineering, Design and Art (2011) **RE:** Christian

AIELLO, FRANCESCO, T: Chef, Owner **I:** Food & Restaurant Services **CN:** Francesco's Ristorante & Pizzeria **CH:** Isabella; Francesco **ED:** Culinary Degree, Italy **C:** Chef, Owner, Francesco's Ristorante & Pizzeria (2011-Present); Chef, Various Restaurants, Central Florida **AW:** Hall of Fame Man of the Year; Best Italian Restaurant; Two-Time Nominee, Best Chef **MH:** Marquis Who's Who Top Professional **AS:** Mr. Aiello attributes much of his success to his partner, John Markowitz. He believed in Mr. Aiello and what he could accomplish, which motivated him to invest money in Mr. Aiello's services. Mr. Aiello is who he is today because of John. **B/I:** Mr. Aiello has loved food since he was young. Growing up in Italy, his family hosted a feast every Sunday. Watching his grandmother, mother, and father cook fostered his love for the kitchen. Mr. Aiello knew he wanted to operate a restaurant so he could share his favorite dishes with his customers. **AV:** Traveling; Driving and listening to music; Spending time with family; Going to the beach

AIKINS, ALISTINE SIMONS, RN, T: Medical and Surgical Nurse **I:** Medicine & Health Care **DOB:** 11/02/1933 **PB:** New York **SC:** NY/USA **PT:** Herbert Simons; Genevieve Simons **MS:** Married **SPN:** Samuel C. Aikins (02/26/1966) **CH:** Catherine G.; Jeanne L. **ED:** Bachelor's Degree in Professional Studies, SUNY Empire State College (1997); RN, Bellevue School of Nursing (1956) **C:** Site Director, Early Lung Cancer Action Program, Weill Cornell Medicine (2001-2002); Retired (1998); Head Nurse, King's County Hospital (1990-1998); Director of Childcare Provider Program, College of Health Related Professions, SUNY Downstate Health Sciences University (1995-1996); Nursing Care Instructor, College of Health Related Professions, SUNY Downstate Health Sciences University (1992-1995); Assistant Head Nurse, King's County Hospital (1987-1990); Staff Nurse, King's County Hospital (1977-1987); Private Duty Nurse, New York State Employment Service (1958-1975); IV Nurse, Brooklyn Jewish Hospital (1965-1968); Staff Nurse, Surgical Floor, Bellevue Hospital (1956-1958) **CR:** Religious Educator **CIV:** Trustee, Parish Girl Scout Leader (1973); Lector; Minister of Holy Communion **AW:** Service Awards, Diocese of Brooklyn; Ghanaian Apostolate, Diocese of Brooklyn **MEM:** American Nurses Association; New York State Nurses Association; Council of Nurses, King's County Hospital **MH:** Albert Nelson Marquis Lifetime Achievement Award **AS:** Ms. Aikins attributes her success to taking advantage of the opportunities presented to her and surrounding herself with successful people. **B/I:** Ms. Aikins became involved in her profession because she was inspired by her great aunt, Gertrude Simons, the matriarch of the family. She worked as a home health aide and furthered her education by taking classes at night. **AV:** Serving as a Girl Scout leader; Spending time with her family; Practicing golf, tennis and fencing **PA:** Democrat

AJALAT, SOL P., ESQ., T: Lawyer **I:** Law and Legal Services **CN:** Ajalat & Ajalat, LLP **DOB:** 07/12/1932 **PB:** Chicago **SC:** IL/USA **PT:** Peter S. Ajalat; Tesbina (Shahadie) Ajalat **MS:** Married **SPN:** Lily Mary Roum (08/21/1960) **CH:** Stephen; Gregory; Denise; Lawrence **ED:** JD, University of California Los Angeles (1962); BS in Public Health and Health Administration, University of California Los Angeles (1958) **C:** Partner, Ajalat & Ajalat, LLP, Burbank, CA, North Hollywood, CA (1993-Present); Practicing Attorney, Sole Practitioner, Burbank, CA, Los Angeles, CA (1965-1993); Referee, State Bar Court of California (1984-1990); Private Practice, Los Angeles, CA (1965); Practicing Attorney in General Civil and Civil Litigation, Millikan and Montgomery, LLP, Pasadena, CA (1964-1965); Personal Legal Assistant to the Chief Judge, United States District Court for the Central District of California (1962-1964) **CR:** Chairman, Senior Lawyers Committee, The State Bar Court of California (2006); Member, LA Superior Court Bench and Bar Committee, Los Angeles County Bar Association (1991-1994); Media Bench and Bar Committee, Los Angeles County Bar Association (1987-1994); Referee, The State Bar Court of California (1984-1990); Trustee, Los Angeles County Bar Association (1987-1988); resident, Lawyers Club of LA County (1985-1986); Chairman, Municipal Courts Committee, Los Angeles County Bar Association (1985-1986); Assistant Athletic Director, Hollywood YMCA (1951-1953); Assistant Secretary of Boy's Affairs, Hollywood YMCA (1950-1951) **CIV:** Director, The Arab-American Educational Foundation (1986-Present); Participant, Numerous Organizational Committees, Functions and Activities, Toluca Lake, CA (1963-Present); Participant, Numerous Organizational Committees, Functions and Activities, St. Nicholas Antiochian Orthodox Cathedral (1953-Present); Participant, RAND Institute for Civil Justice, RAND Corporation (2007-2017); Hollywood Community Hospital (2004-2012); Chairman, Toluca Lake Neighborhood Council (2002-2004); Angels of the Year Awards (1996-2003); Life Services, Inc. (1997-2001); Member, Improvement Advisory Committee, Burbank City Media District, CA (1997-2000); Trustee, Medical Center of North Hollywood (1991-1999); Board of Directors, Medical Center of North Hollywood (1991-1998); President, Toluca Lake Chamber of Commerce (1997); President, Advisory Council, Providence High School, Los Angeles, CA (1985-1986); President, Advisory Council, Los Angeles Unified School District Area I (1980-1981); President, Advisory Council, Toluca Lake Elementary, Los Angeles, CA (1979); President, William A. Neima Republican Club (1978-1979); President, Board of Directors, St. Nicholas Orthodox Catholic Church, Los Angeles, CA (1976-1978) **MIL:** Instructor in Emergency Medical Care, United States Army Medical Corps. and Brooke Army Medical Center (BAMC), Fort Sam, Houston, Texas (1955-1957) **AW:** Certificate for Fifty Years of Service, California Supreme Court and State Bar (2013); Outstanding Legal Service Award, Arab American Lawyers Association (2011); Good Neighbor Award, Toluca Lake Chamber of Commerce (2009); Business of the Year Award, Toluca Lake Chamber of Commerce (2008); Distinguished Service Award, St. Nicholas Antiochian Orthodox Cathedral (2005); Community Service Award, Toluca Lake Chamber of Commerce (2005); Distinguished Service Award, Toluca Lake Chamber of Commerce (2002); Distinguished Service Award, Lawyers Club of Los Angeles County (2002) **MEM:** Delegate, Conference of Bar Delegates (1985-Present); Board Member, Lawyers Club of Los Angeles County (1975-2017); President, North Hollywood Kiwanis (2002-2003); Consumer Attorneys Association of California (1975-1998); Consumer Attorneys Association of Los Angeles (CAALA) (1975-1998); President, Toluca Lake Chamber of Commerce (1997); Los Angeles Superior Court Bench and Bar Committee, Los Angeles County Bar Association (1987-1996); Media Branch and Bar Committee, Los Angeles County Bar Association (1987-1994); Trustee, Los Angeles County Bar Association (1987-1988); President, Board of Directors, Lawyers Club of Los Angeles County (1985-1986); Chair, Municipal Court's Committee, Los Angeles County Bar Association (1985-1986); Founder, Arab-American Lawyers Association (Now Arab American Lawyers Association of Southern California (AALASC)); California Bar Association (The State Bar of California); Los Angeles County Bar Association; California Trial Lawyers Association (Now Consumer Attorneys Association of California); Conference of Bar Delegates; Los Angeles Trial Lawyers Association; Lawyers Club of Los Angeles County; Toluca Lake Chamber of Commerce; William A. Neima Republican Club; Masons; Shriners International; North Hollywood Kiwanis Club **BAR:** United States Court of Appeals for the Federal Circuit, Washington, DC (2014-Present); United States Court of Claims (1992-Present); California (1963-Present); California Supreme Court (1963-Present); United States Court of Appeals for the Ninth Circuit (1963-Present); United States Court of Claims (1990); United States District Court for the District of California; United States District Court for the Northern District of California; United States District Court for the Central District of California; United States District Court for the Eastern District of California; United States District Court for the Southern District of California **AS:** Mr. Ajalat attributes his success to hard work, determination, honesty and fairness. **B/I:** Mr. Ajalat became involved in his profession because he was thinking medicine first, but he was taking a graduate course in the public health field and one of the topics had to do with the legal aspect of medicine. He said, "hey, this sounds interesting." So, it was a calling. **AV:** Photography; Physical fitness; Extensive family and community involvement; Continuing education in legal, healthcare and historical fields of study **RE:** Eastern Orthodox Catholic **THT:** Mr. Ajalat follows the need always to be active and productive in life as a giver and not as a taker.

AKINS, NICHOLAS, "NICK" K., T: President, Chairman and Chief Executive Officer **I:** Oil & Energy **CN:** American Electric Power Company, Inc. **SC:** LA/USA **MS:** Married **SPN:** Donna **ED:** MS in Electrical Engineering, Louisiana Tech University, Ruston, LA (1986); BS in Electrical Engineering, Louisiana Tech University, Ruston, LA (1982); Reactor Technology Course for Utility Executives, Department of Nuclear Science & Engineering, Massachusetts Institute of Technology; Coursework in Executive Management, Louisiana State University; Coursework in Executive Management, University of Idaho **CT:** PE (Professional Engineer), State of Texas **C:** President, Chairman and Chief Executive Officer, American Electric Power Company, Inc. (2010-Present); Executive Vice President, Generation, American Electric Power Company, Inc. (2006-2010); President, Chief Operating Officer, Southwestern Electric Power Company, American Electric Power Company, Inc. (2004-2006); Vice President, Energy Marketing Services, American Electric Power Company, Inc. (2002-2004); Vice President, Industry Restructuring, American Electric Power Company, Inc.; Director, Restructuring Readiness, Central and South West Corporation; Director, Mergers and Acquisitions, Central and South West Corporation; Director, Solid Fuels, Central and South West Corporation; Director, Fuels, West Texas Utilities Company (Now WTU Retail Energy L.P.) **CR:** Board of Directors, American Electric Power Company, Inc.; Board of Directors, CDDC; Board of Directors, Nuclear Electric Insurance Limited; Board of Directors, Fifth Third Bank, National Association; Board of Directors, OhioHealth; Board, America's Power; Board, INPO; Board, Global Sustainable Electricity Partnership; Executive Committee, Columbus Partnership; Former Board of Directors, Nuclear Energy Institute; Former Board of Directors, National Association of Manufacturers; Former Chairman, Energy & Environment Committee, Business Roundtable; Former Chairman, Board of Directors, Edison Electric Institute; Former Chairman, Board of Directors, EPRI **CIV:** Former Board of Trustees, Greater Columbus Arts Council; Former Board of Trustees, Wexner Center for the Arts; Former Board of Trustees, Mid-Ohio Foodbank; Donor, Rock and Roll Hall of Fame and Museum **MEM:** National Society of Professional Engineers; Texas Society of Professional Engineers; Eta Kappa Nu, IEEE; The Tau Beta Pi Association, Inc.

ALAJAJIAN, HAGOP JACK, T: Chiropractor **I:** Medicine & Health Care **CN:** Alajajian Chiropractic Corp. **ED:** Chiropractic Degree, Southern California University of Health Sciences **C:** Chiropractor, Alajajian Chiropractic Corporation **CIV:** Volunteer, Patriot Project **AS:** Dr. Alajajian attributes his success on hard work, good education and a wealth of experience. **B/I:** Dr. Alajajian became involved in his profession due to a positive experience he had with a chiropractor, which inspired him to help people in a similar fashion.

ALBA, JESSICA MARIE, T: Actress; Co-Founder **I:** Media & Entertainment **CN:** The Honest Company, Inc. **DOB:** 04/28/1981 **PB:** Pomona **SC:** CA/USA **PT:** Mark David Alba; Catherine Louisa (Jensen) Alba **MS:** Married **SPN:** Cash Warren (05/19/2008) **CH:** Honor Marie; Haven Garner; Hayes Alba **C:** Launched, Honest Beauty, The Honest Company, Inc. (2015-Present); Co-Founder, The Honest Company, Inc. (2012-Present); Actress, Television and Film (1992-Present) **CIV:** Clothes Off Our Back; Habitat for Humanity; National Center for Missing and Exploited Children; Project HOME; RADD; Revlon Run/Walk for Women; SOS Children's Villages; Soles4Souls; Step Up; Baby2Baby **CW:** Actress, "L.A.'s Finest" (2019-Present); Actress, "Killers Anonymous" (2019); Actress, "No Activity" (2018); Actress, "El Camino Christmas" (2017); Actress, "Dear Eleanor" (2016); Actress, "The Veil" (2016); Actress, "Mechanic: Resurrection" (2016); Appearance, "Entourage" (2015); Actress, "Baby, Baby, Baby" (2015); Actress, "Bad Blood," Taylor Swift (2015); Appearance, "Finding Your Roots" (2014); Actress, "Sin City: A Dame to Kill For" (2014); Actress, "How to Make Love Like an Englishman" (2014); Actress, "Stretch" (2014); Actress, "Some Kind of Beautiful" (2014); Actress, "Barely Lethal" (2014); Actress, "Dear Eleanor" (2014); Actress, "The Spoils of Babylon" (2014); Author, "The Honest Life: Living Naturally and True to You" (2013); Actress, "A.C.O.D." (2013); Voice Actress, "Escape from Planet Earth" (2013); Actress, "Spy Kids: All the Time in the World in 4D" (2011); Actress, "I Just Had Sex," Lonely Island (2010); Actress, "Valentine's Day" (2010); Actress, "Machete" (2010); Actress, "Little Fockers" (2010); Actress, "The Eye" (2008); Actress, "The Love Guru" (2008); Actress, "The Ten" (2007); Actress, "Fantastic Four: Rise of the Silver Surfer" (2007); Actress, "Good Luck Chuck" (2007); Actress, "Bill" (2007); Actress, "Awake" (2007); Host, MTV Movie Awards (2006); Actress, "Sin City" (2005); Actress, "Fantastic Four" (2005); Actress, "Into the Blue" (2005); Guest Appearance, "Entourage" (2004); Actress, "The Sleeping Dictionary" (2003); Actress, "Honey" (2003); Actress, "Dark Angel" (2000-2002); Actress, "Paranoid" (2000); Actress, "P.U.N.K.S." (1999); Actress, "Never Been Kissed" (1999); Actress, "Idle Hands" (1999); Guest Appearance, "Beverly Hills 90210" (1998); Actress, "Brooklyn South" (1998); Guest Appearance, "The Love Boat: The Next Wave" (1998); Actress, "Too Soon for Jeff" (1996); Guest Appearance, "Chicago Hope" (1996); Actress, "Flipper" (1995-1996); Actress,"Venus Rising" (1995); Guest Appearance, "The Secret World of Alex Mack" (1994); Actress, "Camp Nowhere" (1994) **AW:** Listee, Most Beautiful at Every Age, People Magazine (2012); Listee, 100 Hottest Women of All-Time, Men's Health (2011); Fashion Icon Award, ALMA Awards (2009); Favorite Movie Actress, Nickelodeon Kids Choice Awards (2008); Choice Movie Actress Award for Horror/Thriller, Teen Choice Awards (2008); Listee, 100 Most Beautiful People, People Magazine (2007); Listee, 25 Sexiest Celebrities, Playboy (2006); Choice Red Carpet Fashion Icon Award (Female), Teen Choice Awards (2006); Listee, 50 Most Beautiful People, People Magazine (2005); Superstar of Tomorrow, Young Hollywood Awards (2005); Listee, Hot 100 List, Maxim Magazine (2001-2014); Breakthrough Actress of the Year, ALMA Awards (2001); Listee, FHM's Sexiest Women; Fifth-Sexiest Female Star, Hollywood.com

ALBRIGHT, CHERYL, T: Owner/Therapist **I:** Health, Wellness and Fitness **CN:** Soul to Soul Yoga LLC **DOB:** 01/23/1980 **PB:** Columbus **SC:** OH/USA **MS:** Married **SPN:** Jeremy Gorzynski **ED:** BS in Occupational Therapy, East Carolina University, NC (2003) **CT:** Registered and Licensed Occupational Therapist; Certified International Yoga Therapist; Yoga Teacher **C:** Founder and Secretary, Removing Obstacles, Incorporated, FL (2018-Present); Owner, Soul to Soul Yoga, LLC (2016-Present); Occupational Therapist, Doctors Hospital of Sarasota, C-HCA, Inc. (2015-Present); Licensed Practitioner, Yoga for the Special Child (2009-Present) **CIV:** Family Network on Disabilities of Florida, Inc.; Leadership Manatee Alumni Association **CW:** Contributor, Special Needs Sibling, www.specialsib.com; Author, Article, Bradenton Harold; Author, Article, Sarasota Magazine; Mention, Forbes Magazine; Featured, Podcast Interviews **AW:** Healthcare Award Nominee, Manatee Chamber of Commerce **MEM:** Florida Occupational Therapy Association; American Occupational Therapy Association, Inc.; International Association of Yoga Therapists **AS:** Mrs. Albright attributes her success to the mentors she has had in her career. **B/I:** Mrs. Albright looks at it from a neurological approach to guide the therapeutic process. Mrs. Albright had a large amount of health issues growing up. Within about a week of starting yoga, her symptoms began to subside. Eventually she was off all of her medications together. She also has a special needs sibling, and her level of understanding with her clients is more than many other therapists.

ALBRIGHT, ROBERT LEE, T: Chemist **I:** Sciences **DOB:** 01/28/1932 **PB:** Leola **SC:** PA/USA **PT:** Martin Albright; Ida (Wolgemuth) Albright **MS:** Married **SPN:** Wanda Cardella Sprow (09/20/1959) **CH:** Rhonda Fae; Colleen Dawn **ED:** Doctor of Philosophy in Organic Chemistry, University of Illinois (1958); Bachelor of Science in Chemistry, Elizabethtown College, Summa Cum Laude (1954) **C:** Consultant, Albright Consulting (1994-2016); Rohm and Haas (1994); Senior Research Fellow, Rohm and Haas Co., Spring House, PA (1991-1993); Research Fellow, Rohm and Haas Co., Spring House, PA (1982-1991); Senior Consultant, Rohm and Haas Co., Philadelphia, PA (1970-1982); From Consultant to Director of Technology, Philadelphia Plant Development Laboratory (1970-1982); Ion Exchange Product Development Laboratory (1964-1970); Senior Scientist, Rohm and Haas Co., Philadelphia, PA (1958-1970); Process Development Laboratory (1958-1964) **CR:** Chairman, Gordon Research Conference, Newport, RI (1991); Chairman, Thermal Analysis Forum, Wilmington, DE (1980); Lecturer, Elizabethtown College, Pennsylvania (1959); Consultant, 62 Companies, United States, Europe, Asia, South Africa and Japan **CIV:** Teacher, Bible Class, Sunday Mornings **CW:** Contributor, Articles, 20 Technical Journals; Lecturer, Conferences, Symposia, Corporations, and Universities; Contributor, Articles to Publications in Field **AW:** Oscar F. Stambaugh Award, Chemistry Department, Elizabethtown College (1974) **MEM:** American Association for the Advancement of Science; American Chemical Society; Former Member, Philadelphia Catalyst Club; Philadelphia Chemist Club; International Adsorption Society; Organic Chemistry Division, American Chemical Society **MH:** Albert Nelson Marquis Lifetime Achievement Award **B/I:** Dr. Albright first became involved in his profession due to the encouragement of Mr. Evans, a high school chemistry teacher. **AV:** Reading Christian literature **RE:** Christian

ALDER, DOUGLAS DEXTER, T: College President, Historian (Retired) **I:** Education/Educational Services **DOB:** 11/10/1932 **PB:** Salt Lake City **SC:** UT/USA **PT:** Linden Benson Adler; Georgia (Payzant) Alder **MS:** Married **SPN:** Elaine Reiser **CH:** Scott; Elise; Nathan; Linden **ED:** PhD, University of Oregon (1966); MA, The University of Utah (1959); BA, The University of Utah (1957) **C:** Professor of History, Dixie College, St. George, Utah (1993-Present); Past President, Dixie College, (Now Dixie State University) St. George, Utah (1986-1993); Founder, Colleagues of the Dixie College Faculty (1988); Director of Honors Program, Utah State University, Logan, Utah (1974-1986); Professor of History, Utah State University, Logan, Utah (1970-1986); Associate Director for Instructional Development, Utah State University, Logan, Utah (1969-1974); Director, Experienced Teacher Fellowship Program, Utah State University, Logan, Utah (1967-1970); Instructor, Assistant Professor, Associate Professor of History, Utah State University, Logan, Utah (1963-1970); Director, National Defense Education Act History Institute, Utah State University, Logan, Utah (1965-1967); Monthly Lecture Series for Local Residents from Major Scholars; Founder, "Historic St. George LIVE!" Reenactment of Pioneer Life at Six Different Historical Venues in Town; Tours for Visitors and Residents; Instructor and Tour Guide, Road Scholars Program; Three-hour Historical and Scenic Tour for Retirees, Pioneer Buildings, 40 Times per Year, U.S. Road Scholars Part of National Organization (Formerly Elderhostel) **CR:** Member, National Advisory Board, History Teacher (1976-1985); Danforth Associate (1971-1983); Former Member, Committee, National Council for Social Studies; Former Member, Task Groups, Social Science Education Consortium, Boulder, CO; Member, Board of Directors, Member of Accreditation Teams, National Council for Accreditation of Teacher Education (NCATE); Teaching History, Journal of Methods **CIV:** Chairman, Utah Endowment for the Humanities, Salt Lake City, UT (1984-1986); Director, Utah Endowment for the Humanities, Salt Lake City, UT (1981-1986); Board of Directors, Utah Endowment for the Humanities, Salt Lake City, UT (1981); Chairman for Logan City, U.S. Bicentennial (1976); Board, Qwest; Chairman, Washington County Library Board; Fundraising for Dixie College (Now Dixie University), Udver-Hazy Building, Val A. Browning Building, Science Building, Library and Science Building Extensions, Completion of Dixie Center on Campus and The Mesa Creativity Center in Springdale, UT **MIL:** With, United States Army; With, Utah National Guard (Six Years) **CW:** Member, Editorial Board, Dialogue: A Journal of Mormon Thought (1967-1970, 1983-1993); Member, Editorial Board, Sunstone; Contributor, Numerous Articles to Professional Publications Including Utah Historical Quarterly, Journal of Mormon History, The University of Portland Review, The Sunstone Review **AW:** Governor's Award in Humanities, State of Utah (1991); Outstanding Faculty Award, Associated Students at Utah State University (1981); Award, University of Bonn, Germany (1980); Named Professor of the Year, Utah State University (1967); Fulbright Scholar to University of Vienna, Austria (1962-1963) **MEM:** Chairman, Awards Committee, Mormon History Association (1981-1984); Awards Committee, Western Association for German Studies (1981); President, Mormon History Association (1977-1978); Board of Directors, Utah State Historical Society; Western Association for German Studies; Mormon History Association; Celebrity Concert Series Board, Washington County Historical Society; The Mesas Governing Board **MH:** Albert Nelson Marquis Lifetime Achievement Award **B/I:** Dr. Adler had a wonderful history teacher in high school, however, he was determined to be a dentist. In his freshmen year at the University of Utah, calculus made a decision that he was not going to be a dentist. So he quickly dropped that and stayed with history all the time. Dr. Adler received a fellowship from the University of Oregon to do his doctorate and that is when he received a Fulbright to go to Vienna to do his dissertation. After receiving the Fulbright, he was hired by Utah State University and he was there for 23 years teaching history. **AV:** Choir singing; Writing; Public speaking **PA:** Republican **RE:** Church of Jesus Christ of Latter-day Saints

ALEXANDER, ANDREW, "LAMAR" LAMAR JR., **T:** U.S. Senator **I:** Government Administration/Government Relations/Government Services **DOB:** 07/03/1940 **PB:** Maryville **SC:** TN/ USA **PT:** Andrew Lamar Alexander; Geneva Floreine (Rankin) Alexander **MS:** Married **SPN:** Leslee Kathryn "Honey" Buhler (01/04/1969) **CH:** Andrew; Leslee; Kathryn; Will **ED:** JD, New York Law School (1965); BA in Latin American History, Vanderbilt University, Nashville, TN (1962) **C:** Chairman, U.S. Senate Commission on Health, Education, Labor, & Pensions (2015-Present); U.S. Senator, State of Tennessee (2003-Present); Chairman, U.S. Senate Republican Conference (2007-2011); Private Practice Attorney, Nashville, TN (1999-2001); Counsel, Baker, Donelson, Bearman, Caldwell & Berkowitz, PC, Nashville, TN (1993-1998); Secretary, U.S. Department of Education, Washington, DC (1991-1993); President, University of Tennessee (1988-1991); Chairman, Leadership Institute, Belmont College, Nashville, TN (1987-1988); Governor, State of Tennessee, Nashville, TN (1979-1987); Partner, Dearborn & Ewing, Nashville, TN (1970-1976); Executive Assistant to Bryce Harlow, Congressional Liaison Office, The White House (1969-1970); Legislative Assistant to Senator Howard Baker, U.S. Senate (1967-1968); Law Clerk to Honorable John Minor Wisdom, United States Court of Appeals for the Fifth Circuit, New Orleans, LA (1965-1966); Associate, Fowler, Rountree, Fowler & Robertson, Knoxville, TN (1965) **CR:** Goodman Visiting Professor, Practice of Public Service, Harvard University (2001-2002); Co-Director, Empower America (1994-1995); Chairman, President's Commission on Americans Outdoors (1985-1987); Chairman, National Governors Association (1985-1986) **CIV:** Republican Presidential Candidate (1995-1996, 2000); Chairman, Republican Exchange Satellite Network (1993-1995); Republican Nominee for Tennessee Governor (1974); Chief, Transition Team (1970-1971); Campaign Manager, Winfield Dunn for Governor (1970) **CW:** Author, "Lamar Alexander's Little Plaid Book" (1998); Co-Editor, "The New Promise of American Life" (1995); Author, "We Know What to Do" (1995); Author, "Six Months Off" (1988); Co-Editor "Friends, Japanese and Tennesseans: A Model of U.S.-Japan Cooperation" (1986); Author, "Steps Along the Way" (1986) **AW:** Spirit of Enterprise Award, United States Chamber of Commerce (2005, 2006, 2008, 2010); Thomas Jefferson Award, International Foodservice Distributors Association (2006, 2010); Charles Dick Medal of Merit Award, United States National Guard (2008); National Geographic Legislator Award (2008); Gold Medallion Award, Tennessee Independent Colleges and Universities Association (2008); Public Affairs Leadership Award, March of Dimes Foundation (2007); Horst G. Denk Legislative Service Award (2007); George E. Brown Junior Science, Engineering and Technology Leadership Award, Science, Engineering and Technology Work Group (2007); William Penn Mott Junior Park Leadership Award, National Parks Conservation Association (2007); Distinguished Friend of Science Award, Southwestern Universities Research Association (2006); Dale E. Kildee Civitas Award, We the People, Center for Civic Education (2005); Congressional Leadership Award, Center for the Study of the Presidency (Now Center for the Study of the Presidency and Congress) (2005); National Congressional Award, National Recreation and Park Association (2005); Krieble Freedom & Democracy Award, Free Congress Foundation (2004); Distinguished Congressional Award, National League of Cities (2003); Teddy Roosevelt Award, National College Athletic Association (1993); Distinguished State Leadership Award, American Association of State Colleges and Universities (1989); James B. Conant Award, Education Commission of the States (1988) **MEM:** The Phi Beta Kappa Society **BAR:** Tennessee Bar Association (1965) **PA:** Republican **RE:** Presbyterian

ALEXANDER, EDWARD HARRISON, PHD, T: Mathematician, Educator **I:** Education/Educational Services **PT:** Edward Harrison; Muriel Corliss Alexander **MS:** Divorced **SPN:** Betty Lynn Zorn (05/05/1965, Divorced 12/23/1995) **CH:** Christopher; Benjamin; Holly (Adopted) **ED:** PhD in Mathematics, The University of Arizona, Tucson, AZ (1997); MS in Mathematics, The University of Arizona, Tucson, AZ (1994); MA in International Relations, Salve Regina College (Now Salve Regina University), Newport, RI (1990); BA in Mathematics, Tufts University, Cum Laude, with Honors (1961) **C:** Member, Adjunct Faculty, Mathematics Department, The University of Arizona, Tucson, AZ (1997-2019); Graduate Teaching Assistant, Mathematics Department, The University of Arizona, Tucson, AZ (1991-1997); Charles A. Lockwood Chair, Submarine Warfare, U.S. Naval War College, Newport, RI (1987-1991); Strategic Plans and Programs Officer, Office of Chief Naval Operations, Pentagon, Washington, DC (1985-1987); Representative, U.S. Commander in Chief, Atlantic, Strategic Air Command, Offutt Air Base, Omaha, NE (1982-1985); **CIV:** Volunteer, Church; Volunteer, Literacy Connects; Active Member, Retired Submarine Groups; Former Volunteer, After School Programs, Church; Former Member, Explorer Scouts **MIL:** Captain, Numerous Positions, United States Navy (1961-1991); Commanding Officer, USS John Marshall SSBN/SSN, United States Navy (1979-1982); Staff Officer, Missile Patrol Scheduling, Commander of a Submarine Force, United States Pacific Fleet (1976-1978); Executive Officer, USS Theodore Roosevelt, U.S. Navy (1976); Executive Officer, U.S. Ship Robert E. Lee, United States Navy (1973-1976); Navigator, U.S. Ship Patrick Henry, United States Navy (1969-1973); Division Officer, U.S. Ship Theodore Roosevelt, United States Navy (1966-1969); Staff, Commander Submarine Flotilla Two, United States Navy, New London, CT (1965-1966) **AW:** Meritorious Service Medal, United States Navy **MEM:** Mathematical Association of America (MAA); American Mathematical Society (AMS); Navy League of the United States; U.S. Naval Institute **MH:** Albert Nelson Marquis Lifetime Achievement Award; Marquis Who's Who Top Professional **B/I:** Dr. Alexander became involved in his profession when he was in Explorer Scouts in high school. The scoutmaster, Mr. Bartnik, took the group onto ships in the Boston Harbor (Navy Yard), and Dr. Alexander thought driving a ship sounded fun. So at that point, he decided that he wanted to be in the Navy on a ship and command a ship if he could, but he got a submarine, and that was close enough. He enjoyed the work he did, even the more intense moments. Dr. Alexander achieved his dream of driving a ship at 21-years-old, which he found to be pretty amazing. After this, Dr. Alexander was drafted into nuclear power by Admiral Rickover. He decided to focus on submarines because he thought it would be the only way he could command a ship. **RE:** Episcopalian

ALEXANDER, ROGER E. DDS, T: Oral and Maxillofacial Surgeon, Educator **I:** Health, Wellness and Fitness **DOB:** 09/15/1940 **PB:** Wichita **SC:** KS/ USA **PT:** John Denzil Alexander JD; Bonnie Jean (Moore) Alexander **MS:** Widower **SPN:** Barbara Frances Wehrle BSN (1941-2016, Deceased) **CH:** Daniel Adam (Deceased, 1972-2003); Matthew Scott (Deceased, 1967-2000); Marc Alan **ED:** DDS, Marquette University School of Dentistry, Milwaukee, WI (1964); Residency in Oral and Maxillofacial Surgery, U.S.Naval Hospital, Philadelphia, PA (1972-1975); Pre-Med Coursework, University of Wisconsin, Milwaukee **CT:** Diplomate, American Board Oral and Maxillofacial Surgery; Licensed Dentist, States of Texas, Wisconsin; Emeritus Professor, Texas A&M University Health Science Center **C:** Professor Emeritus (2009-Present); Professor, Texas A&M University Health Science Center, Baylor College of Dentistry, Dallas, TX (2000-2009); Associate Professor, Texas A&M University Health Science Center, Baylor College of Dentistry, Dallas (1994-2000); Assistant Professor, Department of Oral-Maxillofacial Surgery, Pharmacology, Texas A&M University, Baylor College of Dentistry, Dallas, TX (1990-1994) **CR:** Medico-Legal Consultant (1994); National Lecturer, Numerous Dental Organizations; Consultant, Lecturer, U.S.Army and U.S.Navy Dental Corps Training Programs **CIV:** First Presbyterian Church of Rockwall, TX (2015-Present); Forensic Identification Disaster Team, Dallas County Medical Examiner's Office (1994-2000); Board of Directors, Dallas Division, American Heart Association (1996-1998); Chairman, Dallas/Fort Worth Coalition Uniformed Services Academies (1994); President, Naval Academy Parents Club of North Texas, Dallas, Fort Worth (1992-1993); Trained Ambassador, Veteran Coordination Office Volunteer, Patriot Paws Service Dogs, Rockwall, TX **MIL:** Retired, United States Navy (1962-1990); Oral and Maxillofacial Surgeon, United States Navy Dental Corps, San Diego, CA (1972-1990); Exodontist, United States Navy Dental Corps (1967-1972); General Dentist, United States Navy Dental Corps (1964-1967); Commissioned Lieutenant, United States Navy (1964); Ensign, United States Naval Reserves (1962-1964) **CW:** Contributor, Chapters, Books; Contributor, Articles, Professional Journals; Author, Over 80 Peer-Reviewed Articles, Professional Journals **AW:** Invited Speaker, Veteran's Day City Ceremony, Rowlett, TX (2018); Invited Speaker, Wreaths Across America (2017); President's Award for Exceptional Service, Dallas County Dental Society (2010); 3rd Place Award, William J. Gies Foundation, American Association of Dental Editors award (2009); Golden Pen Award, International College of Dentists, American Association of Dental Editors (2008); Master Delt Degree, Delta Sigma Delta International Dental Fraternity (2008); Daniel M. Laskin Award, American Association of Oral and Maxillofacial Surgeons (2007); Literacy Award, International College of Dentists (2005); Faculty of the Year, Dallas Dental Society (2004); Meritorious Service Medal, United States Navy; United States Navy Commendation Medal; National Defense Service; Sea Service Deployment Ribbon; Invited Fellow, International College of Dentists; Invited Fellow, American College of Dentists **MEM:** Diplomate, American Board of Oral and Maxillofacial Surgery (1978); Life Member, American Dental Association; Life Member, Texas Dental Association; Life Member, Dallas Dental Society; Marquette University Alumni Association; Delta Sigma Delta; Fellow, International College of Dentists; Fellow, American College of Dentists; Fellow, American Association of Oral and Maxillofacial Surgeons; Fellow, Academy of Dentistry International; Omicron Kappa Upsilon **MH:** Albert Nelson Marquis Lifetime Achievement Award

AS: Dr. Alexander attributes his success to a work ethic that enabled him to exceed his God-given talents. Likewise, he credits his sense of humor, as it allowed him to become a military leader and educator. **B/I:** In high school, Dr. Alexander wanted to be a dentist. It was a profession that called to him. He worked hard in high school and completed his pre-dental coursework at the University of Wisconsin -Milwaukee; he then chose Marquette University for his professional training. Before Dr. Alexander graduated into dentistry, he made the decision to join the U.S. Navy; however, he did not expect to maintain a full career. He initially was not excited about oral surgery but, as he worked, he became more interested and involved in the specialty. It became his career. **AV:** Researching computer-based multimedia; Public speaking; Historical coin collecting; Shooting rifles **PA:** Independent **RE:** Presbyterian

ALI, MAHERSHALA, T: Actor **I:** Media & Entertainment **DOB:** 02/16/1974 **PB:** Oakland **SC:** CA/USA **PT:** Willicia (Goines) Gilmore; Phillip F. Gilmore **MS:** Married **SPN:** Amatus-Sami Karim (06/27/2013) **CH:** Bari Najma Ali **ED:** MFA, Tisch School of the Arts, New York University (2000); BA in Mass Communication, Saint Mary's College of California (1996) **CIV:** Benefactor, Moonlight Scholarship, St. Mary's College of California (2018-Present); Appearance, WE Day California, WE Charity (2019); Benefactor, Elton John AIDS Foundation; Benefactor, City Year; Benefactor, Stand Up to Cancer, Entertainment Industry Foundation; Benefactor, Vital Voices **CW:** Executive Producer, "We Are the Dream: The Kids of the Oakland MLK Oratorical Fest" (2020); Appearance, "TV's Black Renaissance: Reggie Yates in Hollywood" (2019); Actor, "True Detective" (2019); Actor, "Alita: Battle Angel" (2019); Actor, "Room 104" (2018); Voice Actor, "Spider-Man: Into the Spider-Verse" (2018); Actor, "Green Book" (2018); Actor, "Comrade Detective" (2017); Actor, "Roxanne Roxanne" (2017); Actor, "Hidden Figures" (2016); Actor, "Luke Cage" (2016); Actor, "The Realest Real" (2016); Actor, "Moonlight" (2016); Actor, "Free State of Jones" (2016); Actor, "Gubagude Ko" (2016); Actor, "Kicks" (2016); Actor, "House of Cards" (2013-2016); Actor, "The Hunger Games: Mockingjay - Part 2" (2015); Actor, "The Hunger Games: Mockingjay - Part 1" (2014); Actor, "Supremacy" (2014); Actor, "Go for Sisters" (2013); Actor, "Alphas" (2011-2012); Actor, "Treme" (2011-2012); Actor, "The Place Beyond the Pines" (2012); Actor, "Alcatraz" (2012); Actor, "Lights Out" (2011); Actor, "All Signs of Death" (2010); Actor, "Predators" (2010); Actor, "The Wronged Man" (2010); Actor, "Law & Order: Special Victims Unit" (2009); Actor, "Lie to Me" (2009); Actor, "Crossing Over" (2009); Actor, "The Curious Case of Benjamin Button" (2008); Actor, "Umi's Heart" (2008); Rapper, "Curb Side Service" (2007); Actor, "The 4400" (2004-2007); Actor, "Threat Matrix" (2003-2004); Actor, "The Handler" (2003); Actor, "Making Revolution" (2003); Actor, "CSI: Crime Scene Investigation" (2003); Actor, "NYPD Blue" (2002); Actor, "Haunted" (2002); Actor, "Crossing Jordan" (2001-2002) **AW:** Academy Award for Best Supporting Actor, Academy of Motion Picture Arts and Sciences (2017, 2019); Award for Best Film Actor in a Supporting Role, British Academy of Film and Television Arts (2019); Golden Globe Award for Best Supporting Actor-Motion Picture, Hollywood Foreign Press Association (2019); Award for Outstanding Performance by a Male Actor in a Supporting Role in a Motion Picture, SAG-AFTRA (2017, 2019); Australian Academy of Cinema and Television Arts Award for Best Supporting Actor, Australian Film Institute (2019); Critics' Choice Award for Best Movie Supporting Actor, The Critics Choice Association (2017, 2018); BET Award for Best Actor, BET Interactive, LLC (2017); Critics' Choice Award for Best Movie Cast, The Critics Choice Association (2017); Award for Outstanding Performance by an Ensemble in a Motion Picture, SAG-AFTRA (2017); Award for Best Supporting Actor, African American Film Critics Association, Inc. (2016); Award for Best Supporting Actor, Alliance of Women Film Journalists (2016); Award for Best Supporting Actor, Austin Film Critics Association (2016); Award for Outstanding Supporting Actor, Black Reel Awards (2016); Award for Best Supporting Actor, Boston Society of Film Critic (2016); Award for Best Supporting Actor, Chicago Film Critics Association (2016); Award for Best Supporting Actor, Dallas-Fort Worth Film Critics Association (2016); Independent Spirit Robert Altman Award, Film Independent (2016); IndieWire Critics Poll Award for Best Supporting Actor, Penske Business Media, LLC (2016); London Film Critics' Circle Award for Supporting Actor of the Year, Critics' Circle (2016); Award for Best Supporting Actor, The Los Angeles Film Critics Association (2016); Best Actor Award, Mar del Plata International Film Festival (2016); Award for Outstanding Supporting Actor in a Motion Picture, NAACP Image Awards (2016); Award for Best Supporting Actor, National Society of Film Critics (2016); Award for Best Supporting Actor, New York Film Critics Circle (2016); Award for Best Supporting Actor, Online Film Critics Society (2016); Breakthrough Performance Award, Palm Springs International Film Society (2016); Award for Best Supporting Actor, San Diego Film Critics Society (2016); Award for Best Supporting Actor, San Francisco Bay Area Film Critics Circle (2016); Satellite Award for Best Cast in a Motion Picture, International Press Academy (2016); Award for Best Supporting Actor, St. Louis Film Critics Association (2016); Award for Best Supporting Actor, The Toronto Film Critics Association (2016); Award for Best Supporting Actor, Vancouver Film Critics Association (2016); Village Voice Film Poll Award for Best Supporting Actor, Village Voice, LLC (2016); Award for Best Supporting Actor, The Washington DC Area Film Critics Association (2016) **RE:** Ahmadi Muslim

ALI, SHAMREZ ESQ., T: Attorney **I:** Law and Legal Services **CN:** Ramji Law Group **ED:** JD in Litigation, Western Michigan University (2013); BA in Criminal Justice, The University of Texas at San Antonio (2009); Legal Intern, The Schaezler Law Firm, PLLC (2007-2008); Legal Intern, The Laird Law Firm (2006-2007); Associate in Criminology, St. Mary's University (2006) **C:** Attorney, Ramji Law Group (2015-Present); Lecturer, Personal Injury Seminars (2015-Present); Regional Director, Reed Law Group (2015-2017); Law Clerk, De Mott, McChesney, Curtright & Armendariz, LLP (2013-2014); Law Clerk, The Law Offices of Rudy Vasquez (2013) **CR:** Teacher, Personal Injury Seminar, Chiropractic Courses **AW:** Named One of the Top Ten Best in San Antonio for Client Satisfaction, Personal Injury **MEM:** American Bar Association (ABA); San Antonio Trial Lawyers Association (SATLA) **AS:** Mr. Ali attributes his success to hard work; he doesn't give up. **B/I:** When Mr. Ali was a kid, he saw a lawyer argue in a trial and it impressed him how he fought for his case, even though he lost. It was inspiring to see him at work and the respect he received; it was something he wanted to have for himself. He wanted to help people with his life. What sets him apart from other lawyers is a lot of people do things by the books, a lot of lawyers don't use chess tactics like he does. He is a big chess player, he likes to think of himself as someone that looks at the case and sees all the holes as soon as he sees the case. He knows every little issue that he has to overcome, he likes to think of every case as a challenge. He has the ability to flip cases.

ALITO, SAMUEL ANTHONY JR., T: Associate Justice **I:** Law and Legal Services **CN:** Supreme Court of the United States **DOB:** 04/01/1950 **PB:** Trenton **SC:** NJ/USA **PT:** Samuel A. Alito Sr.; Rose (Fradusco) Alito **MS:** Married **SPN:** Martha-Ann (Bomgardner) Alito (1985) **CH:** Philip; Laura **ED:** Doctor of Jurisprudence, Yale Law School (1975); Bachelor of Arts, Princeton University Woodrow Wilson School of Public and International Affairs, Summa Cum Laude (1972) **C:** Associate Justice, Supreme Court of the United States, Washington, DC (2006-Present); Judge, United States Court of Appeals for the Third Circuit, Newark, NJ (1990-2006); U.S. Attorney, U.S. Department of Justice, Newark, NJ (1987-1990); Deputy Assistant to Attorney General Edwin Meese, Office of Legal Counsel, U.S. Department of Justice, Washington, DC (1985-1987); Assistant to Solicitor General Rex E. Lee, U.S. Department of Justice, Washington, DC (1981-1985); Assistant U.S. Attorney, U.S. Department of Justice, Newark, NJ (1977-1981); Law Clerk to Honorable Leonard I. Garth, United States Court of Appeals for the Third Circuit, Newark, NJ (1976-1977) **CR:** Visiting Professor, Duke University School of Law (2011, 2012); Adjunct Professor, Seton Hall University (1999-2004); Editor, Yale Law Journal (1974-1975) **MIL:** Advanced through Grades to Captain, United States Army Reserve (1972-1980) **AW:** St. Thomas More Award, Diocese of Trenton, St. Thomas More Society (2006) **MEM:** Fellow, American Bar Foundation; Essex County Bar Association, American Judicature Society; The Federalist Society; Association of the Federal Bar of New Jersey; The American Law Institute; Advisory Committee on Appellate Rules **BAR:** State of New Jersey (1975); State of New York (1970) **RE:** Roman Catholic

ALLEN, DAVID, MS, T: Director, Officer and Principal Engineer **I:** Technology **CN:** Propulsor Technology, Inc. **DOB:** 09/20/1944 **PB:** Hampton **SC:** IA/USA **PT:** Edward DeWalt Allen; Julia Woodroffe (Lamb) Allen **MS:** Married **SPN:** Barbara Ann Schneider (9/15/1973) **ED:** MS, University of Pittsburgh (1974); BA, Grinnell College, Iowa (1967) **C:** Director, Officer, Principal Engineer, Propulsor Technology, Inc., Pittsburgh, PA (1996-Present); Fellow Engineer, Westinghouse Electric Corporation, Pittsburgh, PA (1994-1996); Principal Engineer, Westinghouse Electric Corporation, Pittsburgh, PA (1990-1994); Senior Computer Scientist, Westinghouse Electric Corporation, Pittsburgh, PA (1984-1990); Senior Engineer, Westinghouse Electric Corporation, Sharon, PA (1979-1984); Engineer, Westinghouse Electric Corporation, Sharon, PA (1970-1979); Associate Engineer, Westinghouse Electric Corporation, Sharon, PA (1967-1970) **CW:** Author, "Small-Scale Feature Removal in Propeller Inspection," Journal of Electronic Imaging (2012); Author, "Scan Image Registration in Industrial Inspection of Propeller Blades," Proceedings of the SPIE (2009); Author, "Propeller Geometric Parameter Extraction from Inspection Data Clouds," Journal of Ship Production (2005); Author, "Computer-Aided Marine Propeller Inspection Data Analysis," Naval Engineers Journal (1995); Author, "New Methods in Marine Propeller Inspection," ASNE Technical Innovation Symposium (1990); Author, "Computer Aided Design Methods for Propeller Fillet Gages," Naval Engineers Journal (1990); Author, "EGRID: an Automatic Mesh Generator for Transformer Designs," IEEE Transactions on Magnetics (1985); Author, "The Short Circuit Radial Response of Core Form Transformer Coils," IEEE Transactions on Power Apparatus and Systems (1985); Author, "Basic research on transformer life characteristics" (1982); Speaker, "Power Transformer Noise Abatement," ESEERCO Seminar, Power Transformer Noise Abatement (1982); Speaker, "Determination of Current Transformer Transient Performance," Minnesota Power Systems Conference (1982); Speaker, "Current Transformer Output During a Transient," Conference for Protective Relay Engineers (1982); Author, "Help for the Relay Engineer in Dealing with Transient Currents," IEEE Transactions on Power Apparatus and Systems (1982); Author, "Transient Performance of Current Transformers," IEEE Special Report (1976); Author, "Methods for Estimating Transient Performance of Practical Current Transformers for Relaying," IEEE Transactions on Power Apparatus and Systems (1975); Author, "The Effects of Paralleling Current Transformers on Metering Performance," Missouri Valley Electrical Association (1972); Contributor, Articles, Professional Journals **AW:** James S. Cogswell Award, Outstanding Industrial Security Achievement (1998); George Westinghouse Innovation Award (1993); George Westinghouse Signature Award of Excellence (1992); George Westinghouse Signature Award of Excellence (1989) **MEM:** Treasurer, Silicon Graphics Users Group of Western Pennsylvania, Association for Computing Machinery (1991-1994); Section Secretary-Treasurer, Life Member, Institute of Electrical and Electronics Engineers (IEEE); Referee, Technical Papers for IEEE Computer Magazine **MH:** Albert Nelson Marquis Lifetime Achievement Award; Marquis Who's Who Top Professional **AS:** Mr. Allen attributes his success to his ability to learn and take on work in new technological areas. He additionally credits his ability to work with people and solve problems. **B/I:** Mr. Allen became interested in computer programming while studying mathematics in college. He expressed this interest when he interviewed with Westinghouse. He was then hired into the instrument transformer engineering department; his first job was to take over a computer program for designing current transformers. He later became proficient in writing programs for designing and analyzing instruments and power transformers. **PA:** Democrat

ALLEN, RICHARD, "RICK" WAYNE, T: U.S. Representative from Georgia **I:** Government Administration/Government Relations/Government Services **DOB:** 11/07/1951 **PB:** Augusta **SC:** GA/USA **MS:** Married **SPN:** Robin (Reeve) Allen (1975) **CH:** Jennifer; Andy; Molly; Robin Anne **ED:** Diploma in Building Construction, Auburn University **C:** Member, U.S. House of Representatives from Georgia's 12th Congressional District, United States Congress, Washington, DC (2014-Present); Founder, President, Chief Executive Officer, R.W. Allen & Associates, Inc., Augusta, GA (1976); Committee on Agriculture; Committee on Education and the Workforce; Republican Study Committee **PA:** Republican

ALLEN, SAMUEL R., T: Chairman and Chief Executive Officer (Retired) **I:** Business Management/Business Services **CN:** Deere & Company **PB:** Sumter **SC:** SC/USA **ED:** Honorary Doctorate in Management, Purdue University (2017); BS in Industrial Management, Purdue University (1975) **C:** Chairman, Chief Executive Officer, Deere & Company (2010-2019); President, Chief Executive Officer, Deere & Company (2009-2010); President, Chief Operating Officer, Deere & Company (2009); President, Worldwide Construction & Forestry Division, Deere & Company (2005-2009); Senior Vice President, Deere & Company (2001-2009); President, Global Financial Services, Deere & Company (2003-2005); Senior Vice President, Global Human Resources, Deere & Company (2001-2002); Vice President, Region I, Worldwide Agricultural Equipment Division, Deere & Company (1999-2001); Manager, Worldwide Engine Manufacturing Operations, Deere Power Systems, Deere & Company (1998-1999); Manager, Engine Manufacturing Operations, Deere & Company (1995-1998); Staff, Consumer Products Division, Deere & Company, Iowa and Horicon, WI (1975-1995) **CR:** Board of Directors, The Dow Chemical Company (2019-Present); Chairman Emeritus, Council on Competitiveness (2017-Present); Presiding Director, Chairman, Corporate Governance and Nominating Committee, Whirlpool Corporation (2010-Present); Human Resources Committee, Board of Directors, Whirlpool Corporation (2010-Present); Chairman, Board of Directors, Deere & Company (2010-Present) **AW:** CEO of the Year Award, Thurgood Marshall College Fund, Inc. (2015); Evans Scholar, Western Golf Association, Evans Scholars Foundation

ALLEN, THOMAS WESLEY, DO, MPH, T: Physician **I:** Health, Wellness and Fitness **CN:** Oklahoma State University **DOB:** 09/13/1938 **PB:** Chicago **SC:** IL/USA **PT:** Thomas Allen; Helen Irene (Spitler) Allen **MS:** Married **SPN:** Keith Mayo Capen (10/16/1988); Annette Faye Power (06/23/1962, Divorced 1988) **CH:** Roderick Nelson; Andrea Jane; Hilary (Stepchild) **ED:** MPH, University of Oklahoma, Oklahoma City, OK (2010); Honorary DHL, University of New England, Biddeford, ME (1989); DO, Midwestern University Chicago College of Osteopathic Medicine, Downers Grove, IL (1964); BA in Biology, Ottawa University, Ottawa, KS (1960) **CT:** Medical License, Oklahoma; Board Certified Diplomate, American Osteopathic Board of Internal Medicine; BLS; ALS; Basic Disaster Life Support; ADLS; Advanced Trauma Life Support **C:** Clinical Professor of Family Medicine, Oklahoma State University College of Osteopathic Medicine, Stillwater, OK (2005-Present); Professor of Medicine & Vice President Emeritus, Oklahoma State University College of Osteopathic Medicine, Stillwater, OK (2003-Present); Clinical Professor, Volunteer Faculty, University of Oklahoma School of Community Medicine, Tulsa, OK (2019); Adjunct Professor of Biostatistics and Epidemiology, College of Public Health, University of Oklahoma, Tulsa, OK (2012-2019); Adjunct Professor of Emergency Medicine, University of Oklahoma School of Community Medicine, Tulsa, OK (2010-2019); Clinical Professor, Center for Exercise & Sports Medicine, Department of Family Medicine, University of Oklahoma School of Community Medicine, Tulsa, OK (2005-2019); Director, Human Performance Laboratory, University of Oklahoma School of Community Medicine, Tulsa, OK (2005-2019); Interim Program Director, Primary Sports Medicine Residency, Oklahoma State University College of Osteopathic Medicine, Stillwater, OK (2005); Program Director, Primary Sports Medicine Residency, Oklahoma State University College of Osteopathic Medicine, Stillwater, OK (2002-2003); Southwestern Bell Professor of Telemedicine, Oklahoma State University College of Osteopathic Medicine, Stillwater, OK (1998-2003); Vice President for Health Affairs, Oklahoma State University College of Osteopathic Medicine, Stillwater, OK (1991-2003); Professor of Internal Medicine, Oklahoma State University College of Osteopathic Medicine, Stillwater, OK (1991-2003); Dean, Oklahoma State University College of Osteopathic Medicine, Stillwater, OK (1991-2002); Associate Dean for Academic and Clinical Affairs, University of Medicine and Dentistry of New Jersey School of Osteopathic Medicine (1987-1991); Professor of Clinical Medicine, University of Medicine and Dentistry of New Jersey School of Osteopathic Medicine (1987-1991); Director of Sports Medicine, University of Medicine and Dentistry of New Jersey School of Osteopathic Medicine (1987-1991); Director, New Jersey Area Health Education Center (AHEC), University of Medicine and Dentistry of New Jersey School of Osteopathic Medicine (1988-1989); Vice President for Academic Affairs, Midwestern University/Chicago College of Osteopathic Medicine (1981-1987); Clinical Assistant in Medicine, Northwestern University Medical School (1973-1978); Chief, Pulmonary Disease Section, Department of Medicine, Midwestern University/Chicago College of Osteopathic Medicine (1970-1978); Instructor in Medicine, Northwestern University Medical School (1970-1973) **CR:** Oklahoma Genetics Advisory Council (2000-2002); Special Emphasis Panel, National Center for Complementary and Alternative Medicine (2000); National Advisory Council on the National Health Service Corps, Washington, DC (1994-1997); Oklahoma Committee on Violence and Public Health (1994); National Advisory Council on Health Professions Education, Washington, DC (1986-1990); Special Assistant to the Director, Bureau of Health Professions, Department of Health and Human Services (1987); Bureau of Health Professions, Bureau of Maternal Child Health, Resource Development Coordinating Committee on AIDS (1987) **CIV:** Health Unit Chair, Tulsa Area United Way (2000); Civic Unit Chair, Tulsa Area United Way (1995); Trustee, Elected Official, Village of Western Springs, IL (1981-1985) **MIL:** Colonel, Medical Corps, U.S. Army Reserve (1990-2005); Major, Medical Corps, U.S. Army Reserve (1988-1990); Consultant, 85th Medical Battalion in Hyperthermia, U.S. Army (1987) **CW:** Co-Author, "Exercise Prescription for Healthy Living" (2019); Co-Author, "Disaster Medicine, Current Diagnosis and Treatment Emergency Medicine" (2011); Author, "Flexibility: A Concise Guide to Conditioning, Performance Enhancement, Injury Prevention, and Rehabilitation" (2009); Author, "Exercise Physiology: People and Ideas" (2005); Editor-in-Chief, Journal of the American Osteopathic Association (1987-1998); Author, "Sports Medicine," "Foundations for Osteopathic Medicine" (1997); Co-Author, "Exercise Science: foundations and applications"; Actor, "The Great Gatsby"; Actor, "As You Like It"; Actor, "The Drunkard"; Actor, "All The Way"; Actor, "Caine Mutiny Court-Martial"; Actor, "Amadeus"; Actor, "Jade Black"; Actor, "Children of the Corn: Runaway"; Contributor, Numerous Editorials, 100 Publications **AW:** Inductee, Oklahoma Chapter, National Wrestling Hall of Fame (2012); Legion of Merit, U.S. Army (2005); Meritorious Service Medal, U.S. Army (1995, 2004); Outstanding Service Award, Rural Health Association of Oklahoma (2002); Bob Dellinger Award for Service to OSU Wrestling (2002); Military Outstanding Volunteer Service Medal, U.S. Army (2002); The Phillips Medal of Public Service, Ohio University (2001); Dale Dodson, D.O. Award, American Association of Colleges of Osteopathic Medicine (1997); Citation, Doctor of the Day, Oklahoma House of Representatives (1996); Outstanding Achievement Award, Chicago College of Osteopathic Medicine Alumni Association (1993); A.T. Still Award of Excellence, Oklahoma Osteopathic Association (1992); Army Achievement Medal, U.S. Army (1992); Army Commendation Medal, U.S. Army (1991); "Faculty Member of the Year," Chicago College of Osteopathic Medicine (1972); "Outstanding Young Man of America Year," National Junior Chamber of Commerce (1971) **MEM:** American College of Chest Physicians; American Association of Colleges of Osteopathic Medicine; American College of Osteopathic Internists; Fellow, American College of Physicians (FACP); American College of Sports Medicine; American Heart Association; American Medical Society for Sports Medicine; American

Osteopathic Association; National Osteopathic Foundation; American Osteopathic Board of Internal Medicine; American Thoracic Society; Chicago Lung Association; Chicago Thoracic Society; Council of Medical Deans of Illinois; Institute of Medicine of Chicago; International Sports Hall of Fame; North American Academy of Manipulative Medicine; Oklahoma Rural Research and Demonstration Center; Phi Kappa Phi **MH:** Marquis Who's Who Top Professional **AS:** Dr. Allen attributes his success to staying on course, setting goals, and working to accomplish them. **B/I:** Dr. Allen became involved in his profession because he knew from a young age that he wanted to pursue medicine. As a boy, he received medical care for an injured leg. His doctors were so caring that he was immediately inspired to become a doctor. He was driven to become a pulmonologist because a professor in medical school hired him as a summer research fellow working on pulmonology physiology. Dr. Allen then decided that was the specialty he wanted to pursue. He had always been an active runner, which inspired him to work with athletes. **AV:** Running; Wrestling; Reading; Writing; Researching **RE:** Episcopalian

ALLEN, WOODY, T: Filmmaker, Writer, Actor **I:** Media & Entertainment **DOB:** 12/01/1935 **PB:** Brooklyn **SC:** NY/USA **PT:** Nettie (Cherry) Konigsberg; Martin Konigsberg **MS:** Married **SPN:** Soon-Yi Previn (12/23/1997); Mia Farrow (Partner, 1980-1992); Louise Lasser (1966-1970); Harlene Susan Rosen (1956-1959) **CH:** Ronan Farrow; Moses Farrow (Adopted); Dylan Farrow (Adopted); Bechet Dumaine Allen (Adopted); Manzie Tio Allen (Adopted) **ED:** Honorary Doctorate, Universitat Pompeu Fabra, Barcelona, Spain (2008); Coursework in Film, City College of New York (1954); Coursework in Communication and Film, New York University (1953) **CR:** Former Faculty Member, The New School **CW:** Writer, Director, Actor, "Rifkin's Festival" (2020); Appearance, "Very Ralph" (2019); Writer, Director, "A Rainy Day in New York" (2019); Director, "Gianni Schicchi," La Scala, Milan, Italy (2019); Appearance, "Always at the Carlyle" (2018); Appearance, "This Is Bob Hope" (2017); Appearance, "AFI Life Achievement Tribute: Diane Keaton" (2017); Writer, Director, "Wonder Wheel" (2017); Writer, Director, Narrator, "Café Society" (2016); Actor, "Crisis in Six Scenes" (2016); Writer, Director, "Irrational Man" (2015); Director, "Gianni Schicchi," Teatro Real, Madrid, Spain (2015); Writer, Director, "Magic in the Moonlight" (2014); Writer, "Bullets Over Broadway," St. James Theatre, New York, NY (2014); Writer, Director, "Blue Jasmine" (2013); Actor, "Fading Gigolo" (2013); Appearance, "AFI Life Achievement Tribute: Mel Brooks" (2013); Appearance, "Marvin Hamlisch: What He Did for Love" (2013); Contributor, "Now, Where Did I Leave That Oxygen Tank?," The New Yorker (2013); Writer, Director, Actor, "To Rome with Love" (2012); Actor, "Paris-Manhattan" (2012); Subject, "Woody Allen: A Documentary American," "American Masters" (2011); Writer, "Honeymoon Motel," Brooks Atkinson Theatre, New York, NY (2011); Writer, Director, "Midnight in Paris" (2011); Writer, Director, "You Will Meet a Tall Dark Stranger" (2010); Writer, Director, "Whatever Works" (2009); Writer, Director, "Vicky Cristina Barcelona" (2008); Director, "Gianni Schicchi," Dorothy Chandler Pavilion, Los Angeles, CA (2008); Author, "The Insanity Defense: The Complete Prose" (2007); Author, "Mere Anarchy" (2007); Writer, Director, "Cassandra's Dream" (2007); Writer, Director, Actor, "Scoop" (2006); Appearance, "Home" (2006); Author, "Woody Allen: Interviews" (2006); Co-Author, with Stig Björkman, "Woody Allen on Woody Allen: In Conversation with Stig Björkman" (2005); Writer, Director, "Match Point" (2005); Appearance, "The Outsider" (2005); Appearance, "The Ballad of Greenwich Village" (2005); Writer, Director, "Melinda and Melinda" (2004); Appearance, "François Truffaut, une Autobiographie" (2004); Writer, Director, "A Second Hand Memory," Atlantic Theater Company, New York, NY (2004); Writer, Director, "Old Saybrook," Atlantic Theater Company, New York, NY (2003); Writer, Director, "Riverside Drive," Atlantic Theater Company, New York, NY (2003); Appearance, "Charlie: The Life and Art of Charles Chaplin" (2003); Writer, Director, Actor, "Anything Else" (2003); Appearance, "100 Years of Hope & Humor" (2003); Actor, "Last Laugh" (2003); Appearance, "The Magic of Fellini" (2002); Subject, "Woody Allen: A Life in Film" (2002); Writer, Director, Actor, "Hollywood Ending" (2002); Appearance, "Stanley Kubrick: A Life in Pictures" (2001); Writer, Director, Actor, "The Curse of Jade Scorpion" (2001); Writer, Director, "Sounds from a Town I Love" (2001); Actor, "Picking Up the Pieces" (2000); Actor, "Light Keeps Me Company" (2000); Writer, Director, "Small Time Crooks" (2000); Actor, "Company Man" (2000); Writer, Director, Actor, "Sweet and Lowdown" (1999); Writer, Voice Actor, "Antz" (1998); Writer, Director, "Celebrity" (1998); Actor, "The Impostors" (1998); Performer, "Wild Man Blues" (1998); Appearance, "AFI's 100 Years... 100 Movies" (1998); Subject, "Wild Man Blues" (1997); Writer, Director, Actor, "Deconstructing Harry" (1997); Actor, "The Sunshine Boys" (1996); Writer, Director, Actor, "Everyone Says I Love You" (1996); Writer, Director, Actor, "Mighty Aphrodite" (1995); Writer, "Death Defying Acts: Central Park West," Variety Arts Theatre, New York, NY (1995); Writer, Director, "Don't Drink the Water" (1994); Writer, Director, "Bullets over Broadway" (1994); Writer, Director, Actor, "Manhattan Murder Mystery" (1993); Writer, Director, Actor, "Husbands and Wives" (1992); Writer, Director, Actor, "Shadows and Fog" (1991); Actor, "Scenes from a Mall" (1991); Writer, Director, "Alice" (1990); Writer, Director, Actor, "Crimes and Misdemeanors" (1989); Writer, Director, "Another Woman" (1988); Writer, Director, "September" (1987); Actor, "King Lear" (1987); Writer, Director, Actor, "Radio Days" (1987); Writer, Director, Actor, "Hannah and Her Sisters" (1986); Writer, Director, "The Purple Rose of Cairo" (1985); Subject, "Meeting Woody Allen" (1986); Writer, Director, Actor, "Broadway Danny Rose" (1984); Writer, Director, Actor, "Zelig" (1983); Writer, Director, Actor, "A Midsummer Night's Sex Comedy" (1982); Writer, "The Floating Light Bulb," Vivian Beaumont Theater, New York, NY (1981); Author, "Side Effects" (1980); Subject, "To Woody Allen from Europe with Love" (1980); Writer, Director, Actor, "Stardust Memories" (1980); Writer, Director, Actor, "Manhattan" (1979); Writer, Director, "Interiors" (1978); Performer, "Standup Comic" (1978); Writer, Director, Actor, "Annie Hall" (1977); Writer, Director, Actor, "Love and Death" (1975); Author, "Without Feathers" (1975); Writer, "God" (1975); Writer, "Death" (1975); Writer, Director, Actor, "Sleeper" (1973); Writer, Director, Actor, "Everything You Always Wanted to Know About Sex* (*But Were Afraid to Ask)" (1972); Performer, "The Nightclub Years 1964-1968" (1972); Writer, Actor, "Play It Again, Sam" (1972); Writer, Director, Actor, "Bananas" (1971); Director, Writer, "Men of Crisis: The Harvey Wallinger Story" (1971); Author, "Getting Even" (1971); Writer, Performer, "Play It Again, Sam," Broadhurst Theatre, New York, NY (1969); Writer, Subject, "The Woody Allen Special" (1969); Writer, Director, Actor, "Take the Money and Run" (1969); Performer, "The Third Woody Allen Album" (1968); Actor, "Casino Royale" (1967); Writer, "Don't Drink the Water," Coconut Grove Playhouse, Miami, FL and Morosco Theatre, New York, NY (1966); Writer, Director, Actor, "What's Up, Tiger Lily?" (1966); Writer, Actor, "What's New Pussycat?" (1965); Performer, "Woody Allen Vol. 2" (1965); Performer, "Woody Allen" (1964); Writer, "The Laughmakers" (1962); Writer, "The Garry Moore Show" (1961-1962); Writer, "From A to Z," Plymouth Theatre, New York, NY (1960); Writer, "Candid Camera" (1960); Writer, "General Electric Theater" (1960); Writer, "Hooray for Love" (1960); Writer, "At the Movies" (1959); Writer, "The Sid Caesar Show" (1958); Writer, "Stanley" (1956) **AW:** Cecil B. DeMille Award, Hollywood Foreign Press Association (2014); Golden Globe Award for Best Screenplay, Hollywood Foreign Press Association (1986, 2012); Grammy Award for Best Compilation Soundtrack for Visual Media, The Recording Academy (2012); Academy Award for Best Original Screenplay, Academy of Motion Picture Arts and Sciences (1978, 1987, 2012); Writers Guild of America Award for Best Original Screenplay, Writers Guild of America West (1977, 1984, 1986, 1989, 2011); Academy Fellowship, British Academy of Film and Television Arts (1997); Award for Best Original Screenplay, British Academy of Film and Television Arts (1985-1987, 1993); Lifetime Achievement Award in Comedy, American Comedy Awards (1987); American Comedy Award for Funniest Actor in a Motion Picture, American Comedy Awards (1987); Award for Best Direction, British Academy of Film and Television Arts (1978, 1987); Laurel Award for Screenwriting Achievement, Writers Guild of America West (1987); Award for Best Film, British Academy of Film and Television Arts (1980, 1986); President's Award, The Saturn Awards (1986); Award for Best Screenplay, British Academy of Film and Television Arts (1978, 1980); Academy Award for Best Director, Academy of Motion Picture Arts and Sciences (1978); Directors Guild of America Award for Outstanding Achievement-Feature Film, DGA (1977); Silver Bear for Outstanding Artistic Contribution, Berlin Film Festival (1975) **AV:** Playing clarinet; Doing magic tricks **PA:** Democrat **RE:** Jewish

ALLISON, ADRIENNE AMELIA, MA, MPA, T: Senior FP/RH Consultant **I:** Nonprofit & Philanthropy **DOB:** 11/02/1940 **PB:** Toronto **SC:** Ontario/Canada **PT:** Harold Whitfield Hedley; Emmeline Amelia (Banister) Hedley **MS:** Divorced **SPN:** Armin U. Kuder (08/26/1989, Divorced, 2002); Stephen Vyvyan Allison, (01/02/1960, Divorced 1982) **CH:** Mark Hedley Allison; Myles Stephen Allison; Alexander Andrew Allison **ED:** MPA, Harvard University (1986); MA, Georgetown University (1980); BA, The George Washington University (1978) **C:** Consultant, Senior Technical Advisor of Family Planning/Reproductive Health, World Vision US (2007-2018); Director, Maternal and Neonatal Health Program, Jhpiego Johns Hopkins Jhpiego, Baltimore, MD (1998-2002); Vice President, Center for Development and Population Activities (1989-1999); Vice President, Centre for Development and Population Activities (1988-1998); Office of Global Health, United States Agency for International Development (1980-1989); Advisor, Presidential Commission on the HIV Virus Epidemic (1988) **CR:** Adjunct Professor, Johns Hopkins Bloomberg School of Public Health (1998-2005); Adjunct Professor, Milken Institute School of Public Health, George Washington University (1991-1997) **CIV:** Vestry Member, St. Alban's Parish, Washington, DC (2017-2020); Chair of Peace Commission, Episcopal Diocese of Washington, DC (2002-2006); Vestry Member, St. Alban's Parish (1984-1988) **CW:** Co-Author, "Vegetable Gardening in Bangladesh" (1975) **AW:** Scholarship, Georgetown University; Scholarship, Harvard Kennedy School of Government **MEM:** St. Alban's Episcopal Church; Washington National Cathedral Association; Harvard Alumni

Association; USAID Alumni Association; American Public Health Association; Women's Club of Chevy Chase; Cognashene Cottagers' Association **MH:** Albert Nelson Marquis Lifetime Achievement Award **AS:** Ms. Allison attributes her success to the many great and generous teachers with whom she has worked. **B/I:** Ms. Allison entered her profession as a result of an unplanned pregnancy while living in Malawi. Due to complications from malaria, her son was born with brain damage. Consequently, Ms. Allison studied demography and reproductive health, devoting her career to designing and implementing family planning programs around the world. **AV:** Researching archaeology; Antiquing; Exploring history **PA:** Democrat **RE:** Episcopalian **THT:** Ms. Allison is grateful to the many wonderful people who have so generously enriched her life and inspired her to pay it forward.

ALLMON, MICHAEL, CPA, T: Certified Public Accountant & Financial Consultant **I:** Financial Services **CN:** Allmon, DiBernardo & Associates, CPAs and Wealth Strategists, LLP **DOB:** 07/14/1951 **PB:** Oceanside **SC:** CA/USA **PT:** William Bryan Allmon; Cecelia Audrey (Wright) Allmon **MS:** Married **SPN:** Monika Ann (Arth) Allmon **CH:** Stefanie Michele Pace; Danika Audrey Allmon, CPA (Deceased) **ED:** Master in Business Taxation, University of Southern California, Los Angeles, CA (1986); BBA in Accounting, The University of Texas at Austin, Austin, Texas (1975) **CT:** Certified Public Accountant, State of California (1978) **C:** Partner, Allmon, DiBernardo & Associates, CPAs and Wealth Strategists, LLP (Formerly Michael B. Allmon & Associates LLP, CPAs), Manhattan Beach, CA (1988-Present); Director, Tax & Financial Planning Services, Zusman, Cameron and Allmon, CPAs (1985-1988); CPA, Laventhol & Horwath, CPAs, Los Angeles, CA (1977-1985); CPA, Alexander Grant & Co., Los Angeles, CA (1976-1977) **CR:** Member, Finance & Investment Committee, Group Insurance Trust (2013-Present); Member, Board of Directors, CalCPA Health (2011-Present); Chairman, MBA Advisers, Inc., Manhattan Beach, CA (1999-Present); Chair, Finance & Investment Committee, CalCPA Health (2015-2019); Member, Executive Committee, Group Insurance Trust (2015-2019); Member, Audit Committee, Group Insurance Trust (2012-2014); Member, Claims & Plan Design Committee, Group Insurance Trust (2008-2012); Associate Member, Taxation Section, The State Bar of California (2001-2009); President, MBA Group, Inc., Marina Del Rey, CA (1991-2004); Chief Executive Officer, Director, Essential Professional Services, Inc. (1985-1986) **CW:** Author, Numerous Articles to Professional Journals **AW:** Saul Braverman Award, California Society of CPAs (CalCPA) **MEM:** Founding Chair, Mentor and Intern Program, California Society of CPAs (2007-Present); Appointed Committee Member, Group Insurance Trust, California Society of CPAs (2008-2011); Statewide Board of Directors, California Society of CPAs (1995-1997); Board of Directors, Los Angeles Chapter, California Society of CPAs (1992-1999); American Institute of Certified Public Accountants (AICPA); President, Los Angeles Chapter, Association for Financial Professionals; Wall-Nuts Track Club; Manhattan Beach Country Club; Associate Member, The State Bar of California **MH:** Albert Nelson Marquis Lifetime Achievement Award **B/I:** Mr. Allmon became involved in his profession because he was a psychology and philosophy major putting himself through college. He needed a summer job and was told that the only jobs were in the School of Business. There were so many jobs available that he realized he should take some businesses classes. Accounting is the language of business, so he learned to speak "business" and he remained on that path for his full career. He learned to "marry" his background in psychology with that of accounting; his expertise is in personal finance. **AV:** Distance running; Horticulture **THT:** For more information on Mr. Allmon's written work, please see: www.mbamdcpas.com/articles/

ALLRED, COLIN ZACHARY, T: U.S. Representative from Texas **I:** Government Administration/ Government Relations/Government Services **DOB:** 04/15/1983 **PB:** Dallas **SC:** TX/USA **MS:** Married **SPN:** Alexandra Eber (03/25/2017) **CH:** Jordan **ED:** JD, University of California Berkeley School of Law (2014); BA in History, Baylor University (2005) **C:** Member, U.S. House of Representatives from Texas's 32nd Congressional District, United States Congress, Washington, DC (2019-Present); Linebacker, Tennessee Titans, NFL (2006-2010); Attorney, Perkins Coie LLP; Special Assistant, Office of General Counsel, U.S. Department of Housing and Urban Development; Member, Committee on Foreign Affairs; Member, Committee on Transportation and Infrastructure; Member, Committee on Veterans' Affairs **PA:** Democrat

ALLRED, GLORIA RACHEL, T: Partner, Lawyer **I:** Law and Legal Services **CN:** Allred, Maroko & Goldberg **DOB:** 07/03/1941 **PB:** Philadelphia **SC:** PA/USA **PT:** Morris Bloom; Stella Bloom **MS:** Divorced **SPN:** William Allred (12/31/1969, Divorced 10/1987); Peyton Bray (1960, Divorced 1962) **CH:** Lisa **ED:** Honorary LLD, University of West Los Angeles (1981); JD, Loyola Law School, Los Angeles, CA (1974); MA, New York University (1966); BA in English, University of Pennsylvania, with Honors (1963) **C:** Partner, Allred, Maroko, Goldberg & Ribakoff (Now Allred, Maroko & Goldberg), Los Angeles, CA (1976-Present) **CR:** Lecturer, University of Southern California; Former Host, 790 KABC Talk Radio, Los Angeles, CA; Teacher, Jordan High School, Los Angeles, CA; With, Los Angeles Teachers Association; Teacher, Fremont High School, Los Angeles, CA; Teacher, Benjamin Franklin High School, Philadelphia, PA **CIV:** President, Women's Equal Rights Legal Defense and Education Fund, Los Angeles, CA (1978-Present); President, Women's Movement Inc., LA. **CW:** Featured, "Seeing Allred" (2018); Appearance, "Graves" (2016); Host, "We the People with Gloria Allred" (2011); Co-Author, "Fight Back and Win: My Thirty-Year Fight Against Injustice - and How You Can Win Your Own Battles" (2006); Appearance, "Rat Race" (2001); Panelist, "To Tell the Truth" (1990); Contributor, Articles to Professional Journals **AW:** Southern California Super Lawyer, Law & Politics, LA Magazine (2004, 2007, 2009, 2010, 2011); The Judy Jarvis Memorial Award (2001); Inductee, Millennium Hall of Fame, National Association of Women Business Owners, Los Angeles Chapter, CA (2000); One of 50 Most Powerful Women in Law (1998); Women of Distinction Award, National Council on Aging (1994); Commendation Award, City of Los Angeles, CA (1986); Commendation Award, Mayor of Los Angeles, CA (1986); Public Service Award, National Association of Federal Investigators (1986); Volunteer Action Award, President of the United States (1986) **MEM:** American Bar Association; The State Bar of California; The District of Columbia Bar; National Association of Women Lawyers; California Women Lawyers; Women Lawyers Association of Los Angeles; Friars Club, New York, NY; Magic Castle Club, Hollywood, CA **BAR:** Supreme Court of the United States (1979); United States Court of Appeals for the Ninth Circuit (1976); United States District Court Central District of California (1975); The State Bar of California (1975)

ALLYN, JAMES, T: Retired Medical Research Scientist **I:** Sciences **DOB:** 11/25/1930 **PB:** Gowen **SC:** OK/USA **PT:** Charles Lyman Allyn; Barbara M. (Hague) Allyn **MS:** Widower **SPN:** Katy Stickelmayer (Deceased 10/04/1954) **CH:** Barbara Jean Buldt; Cindy Allyn; Linda Ruffin **ED:** BS, Fairleigh Dickinson University (1964) **CT:** St. Simmons School Laboratory Technician (1952); Payne Hall School of Laboratory Technicians (1951) **C:** President, Allyn Enterprises (1993-2002); Chairman, Protocol Committee, Lederle Laboratory (1990-1991); Database Coordinator, Nutritional Advisor, Lederle Laboratory (1986-1991); Assistant Administrator, New Product Evaluator Pharmaceutical Research and Development Stability Group, Lederle Laboratory (1975-1988); Specifications Writer and Laboratory Supervisor, Quality Control, Lederle Laboratory (1970-1975); Analytical Microbiologist, Lederle Laboratory (1964-1967); Technician, Biochemistry, Lederle Laboratory, Pearl River, NY (1960-1964); Medical Technician, Valley Hospital, Ridgewood, NJ (1957-1960); Bacteriology Technician, St. Joseph Hospital, Paterson, NJ (1952) **CR:** Vice President, Treasurer, Lenrow Allergy Inc., Passaic, NJ (1955-1968); Buyer and Seller, Antiques, Hawthorne, NJ (1950-1960) **MIL:** United States Army (1952-1954); New Jersey National Guard (1950-1952) **MEM:** Committee Member, Bibliolator, American Society Quality Control; Metropolitan Section, American Statistical Association **MH:** Albert Nelson Marquis Lifetime Achievement Award **PA:** Republican

ALMÁNZAR, BELCALIS, "CARDI B", T: Rapper, Songwriter **I:** Media & Entertainment **DOB:** 10/11/1992 **PB:** New York **SC:** NY/USA **MS:** Married **SPN:** Kiari "Offset" Cephus **CH:** Kulture Kiari Cephus **ED:** Coursework, Borough of Manhattan Community College **CR:** Designer, Cardi B Collection, Fashion Nova, Inc. (2018-Present) **CW:** Actress, "F9" (2020); Actress, "Hustlers" (2019); Appearance, "Rhythm + Flow" (2019); Musical Guest, "Saturday Night Live" (2018); Rapper, Songwriter, "Invasion of Privacy" (2018); Panelist, "Hip Hop Squares" (2017); Actress, "Being Mary Jane" (2017); Actress, "Love & Hip Hop: New York" (2015-2017); Rapper, Songwriter, "Gangsta Bitch Music, Vol. 2" (2017); Rapper, Songwriter, "Gangsta Bitch Music, Vol. 1" (2016) **AW:** Guinness World Record for Most Simultaneous Billboard US Hot 100 Entries by a Female, Guinness World Records Limited (2020); Guinness World Record for First Solo Female Artist to Win Best Rap Album at the Grammy Awards, Guinness World Records Limited (2020); American Music Award for Favorite Artist-Rap/Hip Hop, dick clark productions, llc (2019); ASCAP Pop Music Awards for Winning Songs, "I Like It (feat. Bad Bunny and J Balvin)," "Finesse" (with Bruno Mars), "Girls Like You" (with Maroon 5), "No Limit" (with G Eazy and ASAP Rocky), ASCAP (2019); ASCAP Rhythm & Soul Music Award for Songwriter of the Year, ASCAP (2019); ASCAP Rhythm & Soul Music Awards for Winning Songs, "Be Careful," "I Like It (feat. Bad Bunny and J Balvin)," "MotorSport" (with Migos and Nicki Minaj), "No Limit" (with G Eazy and ASAP Rocky), "Bartier Cardi (feat. 21 Savage)," "Bodak Yellow," "Finesse" (with Bruno Mars), "Ring (feat. Kehlani)," ASCAP (2019); El Premio ASCAP Award for Song of the Year, ASCAP (2019); El Premio ASCAP Awards for Winning Songs, "La Modelo" (with Ozuna), "Taki Taki" (with DJ Snake, Selena Gomez & Ozuna), ASCAP (2019); BET Award for Best Female Hip-Hop Artist, BET Interactive, LLC (2019); BET Award for Album of the Year, BET Interactive, LLC (2019); BET Hip Hop Award for Best Hip-Hop Video, BET Interactive, LLC (2019); Made-You-Look Award, BET Hip Hop Awards, BET Interactive, LLC (2017, 2019); BET Social Award for Best Celebrity Follow, BET Interactive, LLC (2019); Billboard Latin Music Award for Crossover Artist of the Year, Billboard (2019); Billboard Music Award for Top Hot

100 Song, Billboard (2019); Billboard Music Award for Top Collaboration, Billboard (2019); Billboard Music Award for Top Radio Song, Billboard (2019); Billboard Music Award for Top Selling Song, Billboard (2019); Billboard Music Award for Top Rap Song, Billboard (2019); Billboard Music Award for Top Rap Female Artist, Billboard (2018, 2019); BreakTudo Award for International Female Artist, BreakTudo (2019); BreakTudo Award for International Hit, BreakTudo (2019); Bravo Otto Award for Hip-Hop International, BRAVO (2019); Gaffa-Prisen for Best Foreign New Act, Gaffa, Denmark (2019); Grammy Award for Best Rap Album, The Recording Academy (2019); Guinness World Record for Most Streamed Album on Apple Music in One Week by a Female Artist, Guinness World Records Limited (2019); Guinness World Record for Most Simultaneous Billboard US Hot R&B/Hip-Hop Top 10 Entries by a Female, Guinness World Records Limited (2019); Guinness World Record for Most Simultaneous Billboard US Hot 100 Entries by a Female, Guinness World Records Limited (2019); iHeartRadio Music Award for Hip-Hop Artist of the Year, iHeartRadio (2019); iHeartRadio Music Award for Best Collaboration, iHeartRadio (2019); iHeartRadio Remix Award for Best Remix in Latin, iHeartRadio (2019); Titanium Award for Winning Songs, "I Like It," "Finesse (Remix)" (with Bruno Mars), "Girls Like You" (with Maroon 5), iHeartRadio (2019); Latin American Music Award for Song of the Year, Telemundo (2019); Latin American Music Award for Favorite Song – Urban, Telemundo (2019); Latin Music Italian Award for Best Latin Female Artist of the Year, Latin Music Official (2019); Lo Nuestro Award for Crossover Collaboration of the Year, Univision Communications Inc. (2019); MTV Europe Music Award for Best Hip-Hop, Viacom International Media Networks (2019); MTV Video Music Award for Best Hip Hop, Viacom International Inc. (2019); Rhythm & Bars Award, Soul Train Music Awards, BET Interactive, LLC (2019); Teen Choice Award for Choice Artist: R&B/Hip-Hop, Fox Media LLC (2018, 2019); American Music Award for Favorite Artist-Rap/Hip Hop, dick clark productions, llc (2018); American Music Award for Favorite Song-Soul/R&B, dick clark productions, llc (2018); American Music Award for Favorite Song-Rap/Hip Hop, dick clark productions, llc (2018); Apple Music Award for Song of the Year, Apple Inc. (2018); ASCAP Pop Music Award for Winning Songs, ASCAP (2018); ASCAP Rhythm & Soul Music Award for Winning Songs, ASCAP (2018); BBC Radio 1 Teen Award for Most Entertaining Celeb, BBC (2018); BET Award for Best Female Hip-Hop Artist, BET Interactive, LLC (2018); Coca-Cola Viewers' Choice Award, BET Awards, BET Interactive, LLC (2018); MVP of the Year, BET Hip Hop Awards, BET Interactive, LLC (2018); BET Hip Hop Award for Sweet 16: Best Featured Verse, BET Interactive, LLC (2018); Bravo Otto Award for Hip-Hop, BRAVO (2018); People's Icon, Break the Internet Awards, PAPER Magazine (2018); Break the Internet Award for Meme of the Year, PAPER Magazine (2018); Honoree, Entertainment & Arts, Ebony Power 100, Ebony (2018); Entertainer of the Year, Entertainment Weekly, Meredith Corporation (2018); HipHopDX Award for Comeup of the Year, HipHopDX (2017, 2018); iHeartRadio Music Award for Best New Artist, iHeartRadio (2018); iHeartRadio Music Award for Best New Hip-Hop Artist, iHeartRadio (2018); iHeartRadio Remix Award for Best Remix in Rap, iHeartRadio (2018); Latin Music Italian Award for Best Look, Latin Music Official (2018); MTV Europe Music Award for Best New Act, Viacom International Media Networks (2018); MTV Video Music Award for Best New Artist, Viacom International Inc. (2018); MTV Video Music Award for Best Collaboration, Viacom International Inc. (2018); MTV Video Music Award for Song of Summer, Viacom International Inc. (2018); NRJ Music Award for Song of the Year, NRJ (2018); Star of the Year, People en Español, Meredith Latino Network, Meredith Corporation (2018); Soul Train Music Award for Video of the Year (2018); BET Hip Hop Award for Best New Hip-Hop Artist, BET Interactive, LLC (2017); BET Hip Hop Award for Hustler of the Year, BET Hip Hop Awards, BET Interactive, LLC (2017); BET Hip Hop Award for Single of the Year, BET Interactive, LLC (2017); BET Hip Hop Award for Best Mixtape, BET Interactive, LLC (2017); HipHopDX Award for Hottest Song of the Year, HipHopDX (2017) **RE:** Catholic

ALPERN, ROBERT J., MD, T: Medical Educator, Former Dean **I:** Education/Educational Services **CN:** Yale School of Medicine **DOB:** 11/03/1950 **PB:** New York **SC:** NY/USA **MS:** Married **SPN:** Patricia Ann Preisig **CH:** Rachelle; Kyle **ED:** Fellowship, Nephrology and Renal Physiology, Cardiovascular Research Institute, San Francisco, CA (1979-1982); Residency, Internal Medicine, Columbia University, New York, NY (1977-1979); Internship, Internal Medicine, Columbia University, New York, NY (1976-1977); Doctor of Medicine, Pritzker School of Medicine, The University of Chicago, with Honors (1976); Bachelor of Arts in Chemistry, Northwestern University, with Honors (1972) **CT:** Diplomate, American Board of Internal Medicine; Certified, Nephrology, American Board of Internal Medicine **C:** Ensign Professor of Medicine of Nephrology, Professor of Cellular and Molecular Physiology, Yale School of Medicine, New Haven, CT (2004-Present); Dean, Yale School of Medicine, New Haven, CT (2004-2019); Atticus James Gill, M.D. Chair in Medical Science, The University of Texas Southwestern Medical Center, Dallas, TX (2000-2004); Dean, The University of Texas Southwestern Medical Center, Dallas, TX (1998-2004); Ruth W. and Milton P. Levy Senior Chair in Molecular Nephrology, The University of Texas Southwestern Medical Center, Dallas, TX (1994-2004); Professor of Medicine, The University of Texas Southwestern Medical Center, Dallas, TX (1990-2004); Chief, Division of Nephrology, The University of Texas Southwestern Medical Center, Dallas, TX (1987-1998); Associate Professor of Medicine, The University of Texas Southwestern Medical Center, Dallas, TX (1987-1990); Assistant Professor of Nephrology, Cardiovascular Research Institute, San Francisco, CA (1982-1987) **CR:** Board of Directors, AbbVie Inc. (2013-Present); Director, Abbott (2008-Present); Board of Trustees, Yale New Haven Health (2005-Present); Chairman, Scientific Advisory Board, Board of Directors, Tricida Inc., South San Francisco, CA (2013-2018); Committee on the Review of Clinical Guidance for the Care of Health Conditions Identified by the Camp Lejeune Legislation, Health and Medicine Division, National Academy of Sciences (2015); Scientific Advisory Board, Relypsa Inc. (2007-2014); Scientific Advisory Board, Ilypsa Inc. (2004-2007); Council, American Society of Nephrology (1995-2002); President, American Society of Nephrology (2000-2001); Chair, School Admissions Committee, The University of Texas Southwestern Medical Center (1996-1998); Search Committee for Chief of Hematology/Oncology, The University of Texas Southwestern Medical Center (1997); Search Committee for Chief of Infectious Diseases, The University of Texas Southwestern Medical Center (1994-1996); School Admissions Committee, The University of Texas Southwestern Medical Center (1994-1996); Max Martin Salick Visiting Professor, School of Medicine, University of California Los Angeles (1994); Search Committee for Chairman of Urology, The University of Texas Southwestern Medical Center (1993); Chairman, Advisory Committee, General Clinical Research Center, The University of Texas Southwestern Medical Center (1987-1991); Search Committee for Chief of Cardiology, The University of Texas Southwestern Medical Center (1989); Admissions Committee, School of Medicine, University of California, San Francisco (1985-1987); Advisory Council, National Institute of Diabetes and Digestive and Kidney Diseases, U.S. Department of Health and Human Services; Presenter, Lecturer in Field **CIV:** Visionary Circle, American Society of Nephrology **CW:** Contributor, The American Journal of Medicine, Alliance for Academic Internal Medicine (1997-Present); Contributor, Kidney and Blood Pressure Research, S. Karger AG (1996-Present); Contributor, The American Journal of the Medical Sciences, The Southern Society for Clinical Investigation (1996-Present); Contributor, Seminars in Nephrology, Elsevier B.V. (1990-Present); Consultant Editor, Kidney International, International Society of Nephrology (1990-Present); Section Editor, Current Opinion in Nephrology and Hypertension (1997-1999); Consultant Editor, The Journal of Clinical Investigation, American Society for Clinical Investigation (1993-1999); Section Editor, Annual Review of Physiology (1993-1997); Contributor, American Journal of Kidney Diseases, National Kidney Foundation Inc. (1991-1996); Contributor, Renal Physiology and Biochemistry, S. Karger AG (1989-1995); Contributor, American Journal of Physiology, American Physiological Society (1992-1994); Associate Editor, Hospital Practice: Physiology in Medicine (1991-1994); Editorial Committee, The Journal of Clinical Investigation, American Society for Clinical Investigation (1988-1993); Contributor, International Yearbook of Nephrology (1989-1992); Associate Editor, American Journal of Physiology, American Physiological Society (1989-1992); Contributor, Kidney International, International Society of Nephrology (1989-1990); Contributor, Papers, Chapters, Articles, Professional Publications **AW:** John P. Peters Award, American Society of Nephrology (2008); Merit Award, National Institutes of Health, U.S. Department of Health and Human Services (1995); Award for Research in Developmental Biology, National Science Foundation (1971) **MEM:** Health and Medicine Division, National Academy of Sciences (2007-Present); Association of American Physicians (1993-Present); The American Society of Clinical Investigation (1987-Present); Alpha Omega Alpha Honor Medical Society (1976-Present); Phi Beta Kappa Society (1972-Present); National Kidney Foundation Inc.; American Society of Nephrology; ISN; American Physiological Society; American Heart Association Inc.; Sigma Xi, The Scientific Research Honor Society

ALPERT, JONATHAN EDWARD, T: Chair **I:** Education/Educational Services **CN:** Albert Einstein College of Medicine and Montefiore Medical Center **PB:** Brooklyn **SC:** NY/USA **PT:** Harold Alpert; Alice Lila (Goldman) Alpert **MS:** Married **SPN:** Wendy Lee (09/03/1989) **CH:** Samuel Jeremy; Anthony Lee **ED:** PhD, University of Cambridge, Cambridge, England (1987); Intern, Pediatrics, Children's Hospital Medical Center, Boston, MA (1986-1987); MD, Yale University, New Haven, CT, Cum Laude (1986); BA, Yale College, New Haven, CT, Summa Cum Laude (1977) **CT:** Certification in Psychiatry, American Board of Psychiatry and Neurology (1993-Present); Permanent Physician and Surgeon License, Commonwealth of Massachusetts (1990-Present); Diplomate, American Board Psychiatry and Neurology **C:** Professor, Pediatrics, Albert Einstein College of Medicine, Bronx, NY (2017-Present); Professor, Neuroscience, Albert Einstein College of Medicine, Bronx, NY (2017-Present); Dorothy and Marty Silverman Professor, Psychiatry, Albert Einstein College of Medicine, Bronx, NY (2017-Present); Joyce R. Tedlow Associate Professor, Psychiatry, Harvard Medical School, Boston, MA (2009-2017); Associate Professor, Psychiatry, Harvard Medical School, Boston, MA (2005-2017); Assistant Professor, Psychiatry, Harvard Medical School, Boston, MA (1997-2005); Instructor, Psychiatry, Harvard Medical School, Boston, MA (1992-1997); Chief Resident, Psychiatry, Psychopharmacology Program, McLean Hospital, Belmont, MA (1991-1992); Clinical Fellow, Psychiatry, Harvard Medical School, Boston, MA (1989-1992); Resident, Psychiatry, Psychopharmacology Program, McLean Hospital, Belmont, MA (1989-1992); Resident, Pediatrics, Children's Hospital Medical Center, Boston, MA (1987-1989); Clinical Fellow, Pediatrics, Harvard Medical School, Boston, MA (1986-1989) **CR:** University Chair, Department of Psychiatry and Behavioral Sciences, Albert Einstein College of Medicine and Montefiore Medical Center (2017-Present); Non-Clinical Staff, Psychiatry, Massachusetts General Hospital, Boston, MA (2017-Present); Department Chair, Psychiatry, Montefiore Medical Center, Bronx, NY (2017-Present); Psychiatrist, Psychiatry, Massachusetts General Hospital, Boston, MA (2003-Present); Teacher, Courses, Numerous Hospitals and Facilities (1991-Present); Director, Depression Clinical and Research Program, Massachusetts General Hospital, Boston, MA (2014-2017); Associate Chief of Psychiatry for Clinical Services, Department of Psychiatry, Massachusetts General Hospital, Boston, MA (2009-2017); Holmes Society Faculty Liaison, Harvard Medical School, Boston, MA (2005-2017); Senior Mentor, Principal Clinical Experience, Massachusetts General Hospital, Boston, MA (2008-2015); Chair, Course and Clerkship Review and Evaluation Committee, Harvard Medical School, Boston, MA (2010-2014); Director, Medical Student Education in Psychiatry, Harvard Medical School, Boston, MA (2004-2014); Associate Director, Depression Clinical and Research Program, Massachusetts General Hospital, Boston, MA (1992-2014); Clinical Director, Department of Psychiatry, Massachusetts General Hospital, Boston, MA (2007-2009); Assistant, Psychiatry, Massachusetts General Hospital, Boston, MA (1995-2003); Clinical Assistant, Psychiatry, Massachusetts General Hospital, Boston, MA (1992-1995); Staff Psychiatrist, McLean Hospital, Belmont, MA (1991-1992) **CIV:** Incoming Chair, Council on Research, American Psychiatric Association (2019-Present); Research Leadership Council, Albert Einstein College of Medicine, Bronx, NY (2019-Present); Philanthropy Leadership Council, Albert Einstein College of Medicine, Bronx, NY (2018-Present); Senate Council, Albert Einstein College of Medicine (2018-Present); Co-Chair, Neurosurgery-Psychiatry Working Group, Montefiore Medical Center, Bronx, NY (2018-Present); Dean's Search Committee, Albert Einstein College of Medicine, Bronx, NY (2017-Present); Medical Executive Committee, Montefiore Medical Center, Bronx, NY (2017-Present); Faculty Senate, Albert Einstein College of Medicine, Bronx, NY (2017-Present); Chair, Executive Leadership Committee, Department of Psychiatry and Behavioral Sciences, Montefiore Medical Center (2017-Present); Founding Member, Psychiatry and Nutrition, Academy of Psychosomatic Medicine (2016-Present); Steering Committee, MoodNetwork (PCORI), National Coordinating Center (2014-2019); Chair, Older Adult Psychiatry Task Force, Massachusetts General Hospital, Boston, MA (2016-2017); Undergraduate Medical Education Leadership Committee, Massachusetts General Hospital, Boston, MA (2015-2017); Chair, Psychology Strategic Planning Committee and Psychology Chief Search Committee, Massachu-

setts General Hospital, Boston, MA (2014); Board of Directors, National Network of Depression Centers (NNDC) (2012-2017); Office of Clinical Careers Council, Massachusetts General Hospital, Boston, MA (2010-2017); Psychiatry Research Committee, Massachusetts General Hospital, Boston, MA (2004-2017); Chair, Outpatient Division Executive Committee, Department of Psychiatry, Massachusetts General Hospital, Boston, MA (2012-2016); Mentor, Education Scholars Program, Association of Directors of Medical Student Education in Psychiatry (ADMSEP); Chair, Task Force on Research and Scholarship, Association of Directors of Medical Student Education in Psychiatry (ADMSEP); Co-Chair, HMS Academy Interest Group on Feedback and Evaluation, Harvard Medical School, Boston, MA (2010-2014); Quality and Safety Committee, department of Psychiatry, Massachusetts General Hospital, Boston, MA (2009-2017); Clinical Care Committee, National Network of Depression Centers (NNDC) (2009-2014); Chair, Search Committee, Director of Acute Psychiatry Service, Department of Psychiatry, Massachusetts General Hospital, Boston, MA (2008); Education Assessment Committee, Harvard Medical School, Boston, MA (2004-2007); Task Force on Educator Interactions with Pharma, Association of Directors of Medical Student Education in Psychiatry (ADMSEP) **CW:** Member, Editorial Board, Psychiatric Research and Clinical Practice (2017-Present); Member, Editorial Board, Psychosomatics (2016-Present); Consulting Editor, Overcoming Depression, Belvoir Publications, Inc. (2012-Present); Member, Editorial Advisory Board, Neuropsychiatry (2010-Present); Member, Editorial Board, MGH Mind, Mood and Memory Newsletter, Belvoir Publications, Inc. (2004-2017); Reviewer, "Practice Guidelines for the Treatment of Patients with Major Depressive Disorder" (2008); Member, Editorial Advisory Board, The Medical Psychiatry Series, Marcel Dekker, Inc. (2003-2006); Editor, Academic Psychiatry, American Journal of Psychiatry, Archives of General Psychiatry, Biological Psychiatry, BioMed Central Psychiatry, BMJ Open, Clinical Nutrition, Clinical Psychiatry, CNS Spectrums, European Journal of Child and Adolescent Psychiatry, General Hospital Psychiatry, Journal of Affective Disorders, Journal of American College Health, Journal of Clinical Psychiatry, Journal of Clinical Psychopharmacology, Journal of Psychiatric Research, Psychosomatics, and Psychotherapy and Psychosomatics; Contributor, Numerous Articles to Professional Journals; Author, Contributor, Numerous Peer-Reviewed Publications in Print or Other Media; Author, Co-Author, Numerous Book Chapters; Contributor, Numerous Research Investigations; Presenter, Contributor, Numerous Abstracts, Poster Presentations and Exhibits Presented at Professional Meetings **AW:** Irene Jakab MD Award, Depression and Bipolar Support Alliance (2017); Psychiatrist Education Award, Massachusetts Psychiatric Society (2015); Partners in Excellence Award, Massachusetts General Hospital (2013); Compassionate Caregiver Certificate, The Schwartz Center (2011); Clinical Mentor Award, MGH Department of Psychiatry (2010); Psychopharmacology Supervision Award, MGH/McLean Psychiatry Residency Training Program (2008); Cynthia N. Kettyle Teaching Award, Harvard Medical School, Boston, MA (2006); Psychopharmacology Supervision Award, MGH/McLean Psychiatry Residency Training Program (2006); Nancy C.A. Roeske Certificate of Recognition for Excellence in Medical Student Education, American Psychiatric Association (2005); Partners in Excellence Award, Massachusetts General Hospital (2002, 2003, 2004); Young Investigator Award, National Alliance for Research on Schizophrenia and Depression (1996); Travel Award, American

College of Neuropsychopharmacology/Mead Johnson (1994); Paul M. Howard Prize, McLean Adult Psychiatry Residency Program (1992); Merit Award, Dr. Henry P. and M. Page Durkee Laughlin Foundation (1992); Yale Medical Scientist Training Program Award, Yale University School of Medicine (1986); Arthur Twining Hadley Prize, Yale College (1977); Andrew D. White Prize in European History, Yale College (1974) **MEM:** Anxiety and Depression Association of America (2017-Present); American Association of Chairs of Departments of Psychiatry (2017-Present); Society of Biological Psychiatry (2017-Present); Academy of Psychosomatic Medicine (2016-Present); American Society of Clinical Psychopharmacology (1997-Present); American Psychiatric Association (1992-Present); Massachusetts Psychiatric Society (1992-Present); Association for Academic Psychiatry (2004-2016); Association of Directors, Medical Student Education in Psychiatry (ADMSEP) (2004-2016) **AV:** Piano; Reading; Travel

ALSOP, MARIN, T: Music Director, Conductor, Violinist **I:** Education/Educational Services **DOB:** 10/16/1956 **PB:** New York **SC:** NY/USA **PT:** Ruth Alsop; LaMar Alsop **CH:** One Son **ED:** Honorary MusD, Yale (2016); Honorary MusD, Bournemouth University, Bournemouth, United Kingdom (2007); MusM in Violin, The Julliard School, New York, NY (1978); MusB in Violin, The Julliard School, New York, NY (1977); Coursework, Yale University, New Haven, CT (1972-1975) **C:** Chief Conductor, ORF Vienna Radio Symphony Orchestra, Vienna, Austria (2019-Present); Director, Graduate Conducting, Peabody Institute, Johns Hopkins University (2015-Present); Music Director, Baltimore Symphony Orchestra (2007-Present); Conductor Laureate, Music Director, Colorado Symphony, Denver, CO (1993-Present); Principal Conductor, Music Director, São Paulo Symphony Orchestra (2012-2019); Music Director, Conductor, Cabrillo Festival of Contemporary Music, Santa Cruz, CA (1991-2016); Principal Conductor, Bournemouth Symphony Orchestra, Poole, United Kingdom (2002-2008); Music Director Designate, Baltimore Symphony Orchestra (2006-2007); Principal Conductor, Music Director, Colorado Symphony Orchestra, Denver, CO (1993-2005); Music Director, Long Island Philharmonic (1989-1996); Music Director, Eugene Symphony Orchestra, OR (1989-1996); Associate Conductor, Richmond Symphony, Richmond, VA (1989); Founder, Music Director, Concordia Chamber Orchestra, New York, NY (1984) **CR:** Artist in Residence, Southbank Centre, London, United Kingdom (2011-2012); Guest Conductor, New York Philharmonic (2004); Principal Guest Conductor, City of London Sinfonia (1999); Guest Conductor, Philadelphia Orchestra (1990); Guest Conductor, LA Phil, Los Angeles Philharmonic Association (1990); Freelance Violinist, New York, NY (1976); Principal Guest Conductor, Royal Scottish National Orchestra; Guest Conductor, Tokyo Philharmonic Orchestra; Guest Conductor, Pittsburgh Symphony Orchestra; Guest Conductor, Boston Symphony; Guest Conductor, Bavarian Radio Symphony; Guest Conductor, Orchestre de Paris; Guest Conductor, Tonhalle-Gesellschaft Zürich; Guest Conductor, Concertgebouworkest, Amsterdam, The Netherlands **CIV:** Rusty Musicians, Baltimore Symphony Orchestra, Baltimore, MD (2010-Present); Founder, OrchKids, Baltimore Symphony, MD (2008-Present); Founder, Taki Concordia Conducting Fellowship **AW:** Conductor of Honor, São Paulo Symphony Orchestra (2020-Present); Crystal Award, World Economic Forum (2019); Association of British Orchestras Award (2018); Ditson Conductor's Award, Columbia University (2017); Luise Vosgerchian Teaching Award, Harvard University (2015); Honorary Membership,

Royal Philharmonic Society (2014); Champion of New Music Award, American Composers Forum (2014); Honorary Membership, Royal Academy of Music, London, United Kingdom (2012); Top 100 Women, Guardian News & Media Limited (2011); Grammy Award for Best Classical Contemporary Composition, The Recording Academy (2010); Conductor of the Year, Musical America (2009); John S. Edwards Award for Strongest Commitment to New American Music, ASCAP (2009); European Woman of Achievement Award (2007); BBC Radio 3 Listeners Award, Royal Philharmonic Society (2006); MacArthur Fellow, John D. and Catherine T. MacArthur Foundation (2005); Classic Brit Award, Female Artist of the Year (2005); Artist of Year, Gramophone Magazine, MA Business and Leisure Ltd. (2003); Conductor's Award, Royal Philharmonic Society (2003); Koussevitzky Conducting Prize, Tanglewood Music Center, Boston Symphony Orchestra, Boston, MA (1989); Leonard Bernstein Conducting Fellowship, Tanglewood Music Center, Boston Symphony Orchestra (1989) **MEM:** Fellow, American Academy of Arts & Sciences (2008-Present) **THT:** Ms. Alsop made history as the first woman to head a major American orchestra and is the first and only conductor (thus far) to receive the prestigious MacArthur Fellowship. In 2013, she became the first woman to conduct the BBC's renowned Last Night of the Proms.

ALSTON, ALEX ARMSTRONG JR., T: Lawyer **I:** Law and Legal Services **DOB:** 07/22/1936 **PB:** Cleveland **SC:** MS/USA **PT:** Alex Armstrong Alston; Elizabeth (Davidson) Alston **MS:** Married **SPN:** Sarah Jane Givens (06/28/1959) **CH:** Alex Armstrong; Alice Carolyn; Sheldon Givens **ED:** LLB, University of Mississippi (1964); BA, Millsaps College (1958) **C:** Partner, Alston, Rutherford & Van Slyke, Jackson, MS (1968-2009); Brunini (1968-1971); Associate, Partner, Wells, Thomas & Wells, Jackson, MS (1964-1968) **CIV:** Scoutmaster, Troop 302, Andrew Jackson Council, Boy Scouts of America (1965-1980) **MIL:** U.S. Marine Corps **CW:** Editor-in-Chief, Mississippi Law Journal (1963-1964) **AW:** Silver Beaver Award, Boy Scouts of America (1981) **MEM:** President, Mississippi State Bar Association (1991-1992); American Bar Association; Hinds County Bar Association; Defense Research Institute; American Law Institute; American College of Trial Lawyers; American Board of Trial Advocates; Phi Delta Phi; Omicron Delta Kappa **BAR:** Mississippi (1964) **MH:** Albert Nelson Marquis Lifetime Achievement Award **B/I:** Mr. Alston always wanted to help others. He could do so by being a lawyer. **RE:** Presbyterian

ALTON, KEVIN, T: Chief Executive Officer, Founder **I:** Business Management/Business Services **CN:** The Way Organization **DOB:** 06/02/1980 **PB:** Pittsburgh **SC:** PA/USA **PT:** Renee Alton; Stanley Alton **MS:** Married **SPN:** Charis Alton **CH:** Nyla Alton; Kevin Alton II **ED:** Indiana University of Pennsylvania (2000); Perry Traditional Academy, Pittsburgh, PA (1999) **C:** Chief Executive Officer, Founder, President, The Way Organization (2015-Present);President, Bears Youth Athletic Association (2010 - Present); Behavioral Specialist, Brashear High School (2009-Present) **CIV:** The Way Organization; South Side Bears Youth Athletic Association; Camp F.U.N, BMe Vanguard **MIL:** U.S. Army Reserve (2000-2008) **AW:** Listed, "50 Men of Excellence in Pittsburgh" (2019); Neighborhood Superstar Award (2018); Coro Leadership Award (2017); South Pittsburgh Community Leader Award (2018) **AS:** Mr. Alton attributes his success to his family and community. He has a tremendous support system starting with his wife, Charis Alton, without whom none of this would be possible. **B/I:** Mr. Alton became involved in his profession because

in 2008, his younger brother, Brandon, was a fatal victim of gun violence at the hands of a 15-year-old boy. For months, he had trouble accepting and coping with the tragic loss of his brother. A year later, he had a daughter and needed to find the strength needed to get up and provide for his daughter. He first received a job at a summer camp and continued to build and branch off until finally forming his own organizations. Mr. Alton chose his career due to the experiences he had during his upbringing. He understood the difficulties for many kids like himself who needed guidance, navigating through high school and the education system. He decided to offer not only his experiences but his skills and education to help students reach their goals through patience and unconditional love. Mr. Alton feels that all students deserve a chance and that it is part of his duty to provide them with one. He was attracted to his career because his mother was a school teacher and she was involved in community development.Furthermore, what inspired him to get involved in his profession is that the kids in his neighborhood had a lack of mentoring, and he grew up in that area. So, they increased GPA and more than 100 boys graduated high school and went on to secondary schools, as well as armed forces, which they probably would not have been able to do without the program. **RE:** The Way **THT:** Mr. Alton said, "The way, there is no wrong way..."

AMASH, JUSTIN, T: U.S. Representative from Michigan **I:** Government Administration/Government Relations/Government Services **DOB:** 04/30/1980 **PB:** Grand Rapids **SC:** MI/USA **PT:** Attallah Amash; Mimi Amash **MS:** Married **SPN:** Kara Amash **CH:** Alexander; Anwen; Evelyn **ED:** JD, University of Michigan Law School (2005); BA in Economics, University of Michigan, Magna Cum Laude (2002) **C:** Member, U.S. Representative from Michigan's Third Congressional District, United States Congress (2011-Present); Member, United States House Committee on Oversight and Reform (2011-Present); Member, United States House Budget Committee (2011-2012); Member, District 72, Michigan House of Representatives (2009-2010) **AW:** Named One of the Politics 40 Under 40, TIME Magazine (2010) **MEM:** National Rifle Association of America; State Bar of Michigan; Right to Life of Michigan; Grand Rapids Bar Association; The Economic Club of Grand Rapids **PA:** Republican **RE:** Eastern Orthodox

AMELIO, WILLIAM, "BILL" J., T: Chief Executive Officer **I:** Business Management/Business Services **CN:** Avnet, Inc. **MS:** Married **SPN:** Jamie Amelio **CH:** Six Children **ED:** Honorary Doctorate in Engineering, Lehigh University (2008); MBA, Stanford Graduate School of Business, Stanford, CA (1989); BS in Chemical Engineering, Lehigh University, Bethlehem, PA (1979) **C:** Chief Executive Officer, Avnet, Inc. (2016-Present); Partner, Daylight Partners (2009-Present); Chief Executive Officer, CHC Helicopter (2010-2015); President and Chief Executive Officer, Lenovo (2005-2010); President, Asia-Pacific and Japan Region, Senior Vice President, Dell Inc. (2001-2005); Executive Vice President, Chief Operating Officer, Retail and Financial Group, NCR Corporation (2000-2001); President, Transportation, Power Systems, Honeywell International Inc (1997-2000); Various Management Positions, General Manager, Personal Computing Division, IBM Corporation (1979-1997) **CR:** Board of Directors, S&P Global (2019-Present); Board of Directors, Avnet, Inc. (2014-Present); Former Board of Directors, National Semiconductor **CIV:** Chairman of the Board, Caring for Cambodia (2003-Present) **AW:** Sloan Fellow, Stanford Graduate School of Business

AMIRNOVIN, RAMIN, MD, FAANS, T: Neurosurgeon **I:** Medicine & Health Care **CN:** Inland Neurosurgery Institute (INI) **ED:** Neurosurgery Residency, Massachusetts General Hospital, Boston, MA (2001-2006); Functional/Stereotactic Neurosurgery Fellowship, Harvard Medical School Center for CNS Regeneration, Boston, MA (2003-2005); General Surgery Internship, Massachusetts General Hospital (2000-2001); MD in Pathology, New York University School of Medicine, New York, NY, with Honors (2000); BS in Chemistry, Revelle College, University of California San Diego, San Diego, CA, with Honors and Highest Distinction (1996) **CT:** Certification, Medical Board of California (2007-Present); Diplomat, American Board of Neurological Surgery (2010); Former Certification, Massachusetts Board of Medicine (2002-2007) **C:** Trauma Neurosurgery Liaison, Pomona Valley Hospital Medical Center (2016-Present); Adjunct Assistant Professor, Touro College and University System, New York, NY (2014-Present); Partner, Inland Neurosurgery Institute (INI) (2010-Present); Chair, Surgery Department, Pomona Valley Hospital Medical Center (2019-2021); Vice-Chair, Surgery Department, Pomona Valley Hosptial Medical Center (2017-2019); Clinical Instructor in Neurosurgery, Western University of Health Sciences, Pomona, CA (2008-2013); Clinical Instructor in Neurosurgery Rotations, Western University Physicians Assistant School (2008-2013); Neurosurgical Associate, LDR Neurosurgery Group, Pomona, CA (2007-2010); Medical Director, Neuro-Science Program, San Dimas Community Hospital (2008); Clinical Instructor in Neurosurgery, Director of North Neurosurgery Service, Massachusetts General Hospital (MGH), Boston, MA (2006-2007) **CR:** Information Systems Advisory Committee, San Antonio Community Hospital (2008-2010); Researcher, "Neurophysiology of the Primate (Human & Non-Human) Basal Ganglia," Department of Neurosurgery, Massachusetts General Hospital, Boston, MA (2003-2005); Researcher, "Angiogenesis in Brain Tumors," Department of Neuropathology, New York University School of Medicine (1998-2000); Researcher, "The Origin of the Genetic Code," Department of Chemistry, University of California San Diego (1999); Researcher, "The Organic Synthesis of Corranulene and its Derivatives," Department of Chemistry, University of California San Diego (1994-1996) **CW:** Speaker, Presenter, Numerous Oral Presentations (1996-2017); Speaker, Presenter, Numerous Poster Presentations (1999-2014); Author, Contributor, Numerous Peer-Reviewed Publications (1997-2014); Author, "Deep Brain Stimulation for Parkinsons," The Journal of Southern California Clinicians (2012); Author, "Trigeminal Neualgia (TN): An Overview," The Journal of Southern California Clinicians (2010); Author, "Treating Epilepsy with Vagus Nerve Stimulation," Physicians Today (2007); Co-Author, Book Chapter, "Neurosurgical Pain Management," Massachusetts General Hospital: Handbook of Pain Management (2006) **AW:** "Rising Star" (Top 2.5%) in Neurological Surgery, SuperDoctors.com (2013, 2014); "Patient's Choice Award," "Compassionate Doctor Award, Vitals.com (2010, 2014); PVMC Guardian Angel Recognition (2011); Neurosurgery Research and Education Foundation (NREF) Grant (2003-2005); Lucien J. Rubinstein Award (1999); Second Place, Student Research Competition, NYU School of Medicine (1999); Mention for Innovative Research, Angiogensis Foundation (1998); Research Scholar Award (1994-1996); California Assembly Scholastic Achievement Award (1996); Outstanding Academic and Leadership Service Award (1996); Harold C. Urey Award (1996) **MEM:** NorthAmerican Spine Society (2009-Present); American Society of Stereotactic and Functional Neurosurgery

(ASSFN) (2008-Present); California Association of Neurological Surgeons (CANS) (2008-Present); American Association of Neurological Surgeons (AANS) (2000-Present); Congress of Neurosurgeons (CNS) (2000-Present); North American Spine Society (NASS) (2009-2016); Golden Key National Honor Society; Alpha Omega Alpha; Phi Beta Kappa **AS:** Dr. AmirNovin attributes his success to hard work, focus, and dedication to helping others. **B/I:** Dr. AmirNovin became involved in his profession because he witnessed his first surgery while volunteering at a San Diego Hospital. He saw the surgeon save a patient's life; it was inspiring. From that moment, he knew he wanted to become a neurosurgeon. **AV:** Playing backgammon; Bicycling; Playing chess; Researching computers; Practicing digital photography; Rollerblading; Swimming; Scuba diving; Skiing; Weightlifting **THT:** Dr. AmirNovin said, "It is important for patients and colleagues to know that I take my work very seriously and believe in evidence-based medicine. I muster the courage on a daily basis to offer both aggressive surgeries or tell the patient that nothing can be done."

AMODEI, MARK EUGENE, T: U.S. Representative from Nevada **I:** Government Administration/ Government Relations/Government Services **DOB:** 06/12/1958 **PB:** Carson City **SC:** NV/USA **PT:** Donald Mark Amodei; Joy (Longero) Amodei **MS:** Married **SPN:** Michelle Brooks **CH:** Ryanne; Erin; Brian; Melissa Welch **ED:** JD, McGeorge School of Law, University of the Pacific (1983); BA, University of Nevada, Reno (1980) **C:** Member, U.S. Representative from Nevada's Second Congressional District, U.S. Congress, Washington, DC (2011-Present); Member, U.S. House Committee on Natural Resources (2011-Present); Member, Committee on Appropriations (2011-Present); Member, U.S. House Judiciary Committee (2011-Present); Member, U.S. House Committee on Veterans' Affairs (2011-Present); Sole Practitioner (2009-Present); Chairman, Nevada State Republican Party, Carson City, NV (2010-2011); Member, Nevada State Senate, Carson City, NV (1999-2010); Attorney, Kummer Kaempfer Bonner Renshaw and Ferrario (Now Kummer Kaempfer), Reno, NV (2004-2007); Chairman, Judiciary Committee, Nevada State Senate, Carson City, NV (2003-2007); President Pro Tempore, Nevada State Senate, Carson City, NV (2003-2007); Attorney, Allison MacKenzie, Carson City, NV (1987-2004); Member, District 40, Nevada State Assembly, Carson City, NV (1997-1998) **CR:** President, Nevada Mining Association (2007-2008) **MIL:** Captain, U.S. Army Judge Advocate General's Corps (1983-1987) **AW:** Named Outstanding Freshman Legislator, Nevada Assembly (1997); Decorated Meritorious Service Medal; Army Commendation Medal; Army Achievement Medal **MEM:** American Bar Association (ABA); Clark County Bar Association; State Bar of Nevada; Reserve Officers Association of the United States (ROA); Washoe County Bar Association **PA:** Republican

AMOS, DANIEL, "DAN" PAUL, T: Chairman, President, Chief Executive Officer **I:** Insurance **CN:** Aflac Incorporated **DOB:** 08/13/1951 **PB:** Pensacola **SC:** FL/USA **PT:** Paul Shelby; Mary Jean (Roberts) Amos **MS:** Married **SPN:** Mary Shannon Landing (09/12/1972) **CH:** Paul Shelby; Lauren Alyse **ED:** BS in Risk Management and Insurance, University of Georgia, Athens, GA (1973) **C:** President, Aflac Incorporated (2017-Present); Chairman, Aflac Incorporated (2001-Present); Chief Executive Officer, Aflac Incorporated, Columbus, GA (1990-Present); President, American Family Life Insurance Company of Columbus (Now Aflac Incorporated), Columbus, GA (1983-1996); Chief Operating Offi-

cer, American Family Life Insurance Company of Columbus (Now Aflac Incorporated) (1987-1990); Salesperson, American Family Life Insurance Company of Columbus (Now Aflac Incorporated), Columbus, GA (1973-1983) **CR:** Chair, Board of Directors, Aflac Incorporated (2001-Present); Director, Synovus Financial Corp. (2001-2011); Director, Southern Company (2000-2006) **CIV:** Board of Trustees, House of Mercy, Columbus, GA; Board of Trustees, Children's Healthcare of Atlanta Inc.; Former Chairman of the Board, The Japan-America Society of Georgia, Inc.; Former Chairman of the Board, University of Georgia Foundation, University of Georgia **AW:** Salute to Greatness Award, The King Center, Atlanta, GA (2013); Stuart Lewengrub Torch of Liberty Award, Anti-Defamation League (2004) **AV:** Playing bridge **RE:** Methodist

ANDERSEN, JUDITH ALTENHEIN FULLER, T: Special Education Educator **I:** Education/Educational Services **DOB:** 09/05/1940 **PB:** Battle Creek **SC:** MI/USA **PT:** Emmett Barnard; Wilmuth Alice (Lichty) Altenhein **MS:** Married **SPN:** David Leroy Fuller (07/29/1967, Deceased 2001); Ronald Philip Crable Andersen (03/29/2002) **CH:** Karen; Daniel; Christine; Sheila; Eric; Erin **ED:** MA, Michigan State University (1980); BA in Elementary Education, Michigan State University (1970); Learning Disability Certificate, Central Michigan University **CT:** Certified Learning Disabilities Teacher, Teacher Consultant **C:** High School Consultant, Resource Room Teacher, Olivet School (1986-1994); Learning Disabilities Teacher Consultant, Olivet School (1980-1986); Development/Regular Kindergarten Teacher, Olivet School (1975-1980); Fifth Grade Teacher, Olivet School (1973-1975); Second Grade Teacher, Olivet School (1971-1972); Numerous Teaching Positions, Olivet School (1967-1971); Kindergarten Teacher, Interlochen School (1965-1966); Kindergarten Teacher, Howell School (1964-1965); Kindergarten Teacher, Pennfield School, Battle Creek, MI (1962-1964) **CR:** Kid's Care America **CW:** Editor, Publication Newsletter, Learning Disabilities Association of America (1990-1991); Author, "Handbook for Learning Disabilities"; Author, "2C Hymn Ministries" **AW:** Co-Exemplary Leadership Award, Statewide Communication and Dissemination System, Michigan (1990); Award for Contributions as Educator to 1989 Michigan Discovery Science Fair, Governor of Michigan (1989); Award of Excellence, Learning Disabilities Association of America (1989); Appreciation Award, Michigan Association of Learning Disabilities Educators (1988) **MEM:** Former Member, National Education Association; Michigan Education Association; Olivet Education Association; Executive Board, Michigan Association of Learning Disabilities Educators; Michigan Occupational Special Needs Association; Science Educators for Exceptional Children; Learning Disabilities Association of America **MH:** Albert Nelson Marquis Lifetime Achievement Award **B/I:** Ms. Andersen became involved in her profession because she was inspired by her high school principal, Fern Persons, whom the elementary school is named after, and her English teacher Louise Boucher. When she first moved there at the age of 12, she didn't know all the mechanics of English and had some problems with math. Mr. and Mrs. Boucher took her home after school every day for two months and taught her the skills of English and math. They took her under their wings when she went to high school. Her principal also taught the math classes and was the one who filled out all her papers and inspired her to go onto school. Both her parents wanted her to go to college. The way she became a teacher was she got married after two years of college; her husband was a grand mal epileptic and

his mother took him out of the state and would not let her have any contact with him. By this time, they had two children. So Mrs. Persons called her and said "Judith, I think you would be a good teacher. I want you to work under Ronda Powell in third grade for the rest of the semester." At this time, she only had two years of college and was working at a bank. The superintendent called her at the bank and gave her a half-day kindergarten job. The principal and superintendent came in for a month and took turns mentoring her on how to teach kids. They showed her how to discipline and do lesson plans; she had 40 students at 19 years old. They showed her how to work. She doesn't know how she did it but it was the most rewarding experience. **AV:** Traveling **PA:** Republican **RE:** Olivet First Assembly of God Church

ANDERSON, BELINDA CHILDRESS, T: Academic Administrator, Dean (Retired) **I:** Education/Educational Services **DOB:** 06/21/1954 **PB:** Roanoke **SC:** VA/USA **PT:** Irvin Daniel; Mary Davis (Flippen) Childress **MS:** Married **SPN:** Eugene Anderson, (7/12/1980) **ED:** EdD, Virginia Polytechnic Institute and State University (1986); MS, Radford University (1977); BS, Radford University (1976) **CT:** Certified Collegiate Professional Teacher and Secondary Education Teacher, State of Virginia **C:** Dean, College of Liberal Arts, Norfolk State University (2011-2018); President, Virginia Union University (2003-2009); Vice President for Academic Affairs, Virginia Union University (2000-2003); Director of Student Affairs, Academic Affairs Coordinator, State Council of Higher Education for Virginia (1998-2000); Dean, School of General and Continuing Education, Norfolk State University (1990-1998); Acting Dean, Norfolk State University (1989-1990); Assistant Professor, Administrator, Radford University (1988-1989); Director of Academy Advisory Services, Radford University (1984-1988); Director of Student Transition, Radford University (1983-1988); Social Studies Teacher, Norfolk City Schools (1981-1982); Instructor, Jefferson Community and Technical College (1980-1981); Social Sciences Teacher, Portsmouth Public Schools (1977-1980) **CIV:** Task Force on Pluralism Member, Girl Scouts of the Colonial Coast (1990-Present); Better Information Project (1984-Present) **CW:** Contributor, Articles, Professional Journals **AW:** Outstanding Woman Award for Education, YWCA USA (2007); Richmond Stars Award (2006); Outstanding Alumnus Award, Radford University (2001); Pluralism Committee Award, Girl Scouts of the Colonial Coast (1991); Young Educator Award, Virginia Jaycees (1990) **MEM:** Secretary, AABHE (1989-Present); NACADA (1987); Association for Continuing Education; National Association for Women in Education; American Association for Higher Education; Phi Alpha Theta **MH:** Albert Nelson Marquis Lifetime Achievement Award **B/I:** Ms. Anderson became involved in her profession because her parents stressed the importance of education. **AV:** Reading historical novels; Traveling

ANDERSON, DONALD A., T: Utilities Executive (Retired) **I:** Utilities **DOB:** 05/25/1931 **PB:** New Britain **SC:** CT/USA **PT:** Harold Anderson; Sara I. (Lundin) Anderson **MS:** Married **SPN:** Helene L. Friedlander (01/13/1958, Divorced 1978); Linda Hillquist Anderson **CH:** Steven; David; Thomas; Leslie; Jason **ED:** Master of Science, Columbia University (1958); Bachelor of Science, University of Connecticut (1957); Advanced Management Program, Harvard Graduate School **C:** Vice President, Information System and Corporate Services, Public Service Electric and Gas Company, Newark, NJ (1977-1993); Director, Auditing, Southern Company, Atlanta (1976-1977); Director, Systems and Data Processing, Northeast Utilities, Berlin, CT

(1970-1975); Treasurer, Northeast Utilities, Berlin, CT (1962-1969); Accountant, Connecticut Light and Power Company, Berlin, CT (1958-1962) **CIV:** Jr. Worden, St. Paul's Episcopal Church, Naples, FL (2019-Present); Active, Bradley Memorial Hospital, Southington (1970-1975); Member Board Education, Southington, CT (1970-1973); Trustee, Former Board Chairman, YMWCH of Newark; Trustee, Kessler Rehabilitation Institute; Trustee, Bergen Community College **MIL:** U.S. Air Force (1951-1955) **AW:** Arthur Young Scholar, Columbia University (1957) **MEM:** Masons Lodge (1980); Chairperson, Information Systems Committee, Edison Electric Institute (1975); Society for Information Management; Institute Internal Auditors; Institute Internal Auditors; National Management Association; Board of Directors, Association for System Management **MH:** Albert Nelson Marquis Lifetime Achievement Award **B/I:** Mr. Anderson became an accountant because of the basic education he received in the Air Force. When he left the military, he attended the University of Connecticut and earned a degree in accounting, and received his master's at Columbia. The information systems industry was just beginning to take shape in the late 1950s. He tested well for it, and when they were looking for people he went from accounting to the information systems industry. He enjoyed this and made a career out of it. **PA:** Republican **RE:** Episcopalian

ANDERSON, JOEL D., T: President, Chief Executive Officer **I:** Business Management/Business Services **CN:** Five Below **ED:** MBA, Harvard Business School; BA in Political Science and Speech Communications, St. Olaf College **C:** President, Chief Executive Officer, Five Below (2015-Present); Chief Operating Officer, Five Below (2014-2015); President, Chief Executive Officer, Walmart.com (2011-2014); Senior Vice President, Divisional Operations, Walmart (2007-2011); President, Lenox Group/Department 56 (2005-2007); Senior Vice President, Marketing, Babies R Us (2004-2005); Vice President, New Ventures, Toys R Us (2001-2004); Vice President, ToyRUs.com (1998-2001); Various Positions, Toys R Us (1993-2005); Sales Manager, DHL (1986-1991) **CIV:** Board Member, Sprouts Farmers Markets (SFM LLC) (2019-Present); Board Member, Five Below (2015-Present)

ANDERSON, JULIE, T: Editor-in-Chief **I:** Publishing **CN:** Sun Sentinel Media Group; Orlando Sentinel Media Group **ED:** Master's Degree in Political Science, University of Central Florida (1989); BA in Journalism, University of Central Florida (1984) **C:** Editor-in-Chief, Sun Sentinel Media Group and Orlando Sentinel Media Group (2018-Present); Editor-in-Chief, South Florida Sun Sentinel (2018-Present); Senior Vice President, Content and Business Development, Orlando Sentinel Media Group (2016-Present); Senior Vice President, Digital Publishing, Sun Sentinel Media Group and Orlando Sentinel Media Group (2016); Vice President, Digital Publishing, Tribune Publishing (2013-2016); Senior Vice President, Content Services, Tribune Publishing Company (2010-2013); Vice President, Content and Integration, Tribune Interactive (2009-2010); Vice President, New Markets, Tribune Interactive (2007-2008); Director, Local Market Operations, Tribune Interactive (2006-2007); Vice President, Marketing and Interactive, Orlando Sentinel Communications (2005-2007); General Manager, Tribune Interactive (1999-2007); Online Business and Product Development Manager, Orlando Sentinel Interactive (1997-1999); General Manager, Destination Florida LLC (1995-1997); Assistant Business Editor, Copy Chief, Business News, Orlando Sentinel Communications (1992-1994); Copy Chief, Copy Editor, Orlando Sentinel Communications (1990-1994); News Editor, Special Sections Editor, Orlando Business Journal (1986-1989); Reporter, Daytona Beach News-Journal (1984-1985) **CIV:** University of Central Florida Nicholson School of Communications and Media; Boys & Girls Club of Central Florida **CW:** Editor-in-Chief, Managing Editor, News Editor, Central Florida Future **AW:** Pulitzer Prize for Public Service (2019) **MEM:** Alpha Chi Omega

ANDERSON, LLOYD PHD, T: Professor Emeritus, Charles F. Curtis Distinguished Professor Agriculture & Life Sciences **I:** Education/Educational Services **CN:** Iowa State University **CH:** Mark; James **C:** Professor Emeritus, Charles F. Curtis Distinguished Professor Agriculture & Life Sciences, Iowa State University **MH:** Albert Nelson Marquis Lifetime Achievement Award **B/I:** Mr. Anderson became involved in his profession because he has been in education all his life in terms of faculty and in the area of physiology; that's applied to animal physiology not a medical doctor. Teaching and researching has been his whole career in the university system. With that, he just received some recognition for that, which is how this came about. He has always been interested in animal biology. He is in a university system, where the agriculture is very important. They are focused on animal models that represent that industry. Mr. Anderson has been retired for a few years now.

ANDERSON, RHONDA VALERIE, RN, T: Registered Nurse **I:** Medicine & Health Care **DOB:** 05/08/1962 **PB:** Vansant **SC:** VA/USA **PT:** Ronnie Andrew Daniels; Myrtle (Rife) Daniels **MS:** Married **SPN:** Billy Victor Anderson Jr. **CH:** Sara Elizabeth; Rhea Kaye **ED:** Diploma, Cancer Chemotherapy Course (2005); Associate's Degree in Nursing, Southwest Virginia Community College (1992); Coursework, East Tennessee State University (1983-1984); Licensed Practical Nurse, Buchanan County School (1983) **CT:** Certification in Chemotherapy Administration, Massey Cancer Center (1992); Registered Nurse, Virginia **C:** Substitute Instructor, Buchanan County School of Practical Nursing (1996-Present); Oncology Nurse Coordinator, Buchanan General Hospital Home Health Agency, Grundy, VA (1992-1996); Oncology Nurse Coordinator, Buchanan General Hospital, Grundy, VA (1992-1996); Staff Nurse, Buchanan General Hospital Home Health Agency, Grundy, VA (1991-1992); Charge Nurse, Buchanan General Hospital, Grundy, VA (1990-1991); Licensed Practical Nurse, Obstetrics Unit, Buchanan General Hospital, Grundy, VA (1987); Licensed Practical Nurse, Buchanan General Hospital, Grundy, VA (1983, 1984-1986); Licensed Practical Nurse, Private Practice Physician's Office, Grundy, VA (1984); Nursing Assistant, Private Practice Obstetrics Office, Grundy, VA (1982-1983); Nursing Assistant, Private Practice Pediatrics Office, Grundy, VA (1982); Clinical Auditor, Corporate Compliance and Integrity, Pikeville Medical Center, Pikeville, KY; Clinical Documentation Improvement Specialist, Clinch Valley Medical Center, Richlands, VA; Emergency Department Care Coordinator, Clinch Valley Medical Center, Richlands, VA; Intensive Care Unit, Acute Care Charge Nurse, Buchanan General Hospital, Grundy, VA; Performance Improvement Coordinator, Safety and Risk Management Coordinator, Richlands Home Care Inc., Richlands, VA; Patient Care Coordinator, Oncology Nurse Coordinator, Performance Improvement Coordinator, Safety and Risk Management Coordinator, Field Nurse PRN, Home Health and Hospice, Total Home Care, Medical Services America, Grundy, VA; Obstetric Nurse, Buchanan General Hospital, Grundy, VA; Private Duty Nurse, Preferred Home Health Services, Richlands, VA; Hospice Choice Inc., Big Stone Gap, VA; Carilion Home Care Services, Private Duty Nurse; Office Nurse, General Practice, Grundy, VA **CR:** Advisory Board, Women's Health Coalition on Breast and Cervical Cancer, Grundy, VA (1994-Present); Presenter in Field **CIV:** Member, Grundy Woman's Club (2000-2007); Member, Friends of the Library (2000-2007); Advisory Board Member, Women's Health Coalition on Breast and Cervical Cancer (1994-1997); Volunteer, American Cancer Society **MEM:** American Cancer Society Member, Retention and Recruitment Committee, Buchanan General Hospital (1992-1996) **MH:** Albert Nelson Marquis Lifetime Achievement Award; Marquis Who's Who Top Professional **AS:** Ms. Anderson attributes her success to hard work and dedication. **B/I:** Ms. Anderson became involved in her profession due to her innate compassion for people. She chose to focus on oncology because those services were not available to people in rural Virginia, where she lived. **AV:** Music; Painting; Drawing; Sewing; Crocheting; Cross-stitch **RE:** Christian

ANDERSON, ROGER C., PHD, T: Biology Educator **I:** Education/Educational Services **DOB:** 10/30/1941 **PB:** Wausau **SC:** WI/USA **PT:** Jerome Alfred Anderson; Virginia Stella (Hoffman) Anderson **SPN:** Mary Rebecca Blocher (08/05/1967) **CH:** John Allen; Nancy Lynn **ED:** PhD, University of Wisconsin (1968); MS, University of Wisconsin (1965);BS, University of Wisconsin, La Crosse, Magna Cum Laude (1963) **C:** Distinguished Professor Emeritus, Illinois State University (1976-2008); Associate Professor, Central State University (1973-1976); Associate Professor, University of Wisconsin (1970-1973); Arboretum Director, University of Wisconsin (1970-1973); Assistant Professor, Southern Illinois University (1968-1970) **CR:** Chairman, Parknet Physics Advisory Committee, Fermilab (1986-1993); Illinois Nature Preserves Commission (1985-1990) **CIV:** President, ParkLands Foundation (1987-Present); Midwest Great Lakes Chapter, Society for Ecological Restoration; Illinois Natures Preserve Commission **CW:** Co-Editor, "Savannas, Barrens, and Rock Outcrop Plant Communities of North America" (1999); Editorial Board Member, Journal of Restoration Ecology (1992); Co-Author, "Fire in North American Tallgrass Prairies" (1990); Author, "Grasses and Grasslands Systematics and Ecology" (1982); Author, "Phenology and Seasonality Modeling" (1974); Author, "Environmental Biology" (1970); Contributor, Chapters in Books, Articles in Professional Journals **AW:** Named McMullen Lecturer, Monmouth College (1983) **MEM:** Fellow, Vice President of Meetings, Illinois State Academy of Science; Ecological Society of America, Society for Ecological Restoration; The Botanical Society of America; Kappa Delta Pi, International Honor Society in Education **MH:** Albert Nelson Marquis Lifetime Achievement Award **B/I:** Dr. Anderson became involved in his profession because he grew up in Central Wisconsin and frequently went hunting, fishing and hiking. Due to these experiences, he became interested in the ecology of plants.

ANDRETTI, MARIO GABRIELE, T: Race Car Driver (Retired) **I:** Athletics **DOB:** 02/28/1940 **PB:** Motovun **SC:** Croatia **PT:** Alvise Andretti; Rina (Benvegnu) Andretti **MS:** Married **SPN:** Dee Ann Hoch (11/25/1961) (Deceased 07/02/2018) **CH:** Michael; Jeffrey; Barbra **AW:** Honorary Citizen, Lucca, Italy (2016); America Award, Fondazione Italia USA (2015); Inductee, Diecast Hall of Fame (Now Model Car Hall of Fame) (2012); Spirit of Competition Award, Simeone Foundation Automotive Museum (2008); Lombardi Award of Excellence, Vince Lombardi Cancer Foundation (2007); Honorary Mayor, Libero Comune di Montona in Esilio (2007); Commendatore dell'Ordine al Merito della Repubblica Italiana (2006); Inductee, Automotive Hall of Fame (2005); Inductee, International Motorsports Hall of Fame (2001); Driver of the Century, RACER Magazine (2000); Inductee, National Sprint Car Hall of Fame & Museum (1996); Driver of the Quarter Century, United States (1992); Inductee, Motorsports Hall of Fame of America (1990); Inductee, Hall of Fame, Indianapolis Motor Speedway Museum (1986); Driver of the Year, United States (1967, 1978, 1984); Inductee, Hoosier Auto Racing Hall of Fame (1970); Indianapolis 500 Rookie of the Year (1965) **THT:** In 1993, aged 53 years and 34 days, Mr. Andretti made history as the oldest race winner in IndyCar history. He is the only driver to win IndyCar races in four different decades. Through his illustrious career, Mr. Andretti recorded 12 Formula One victories and 18 Formula One pole positions.

ANDREWS, GROVER J., EDD, T: Interim Director **I:** Education/Educational Services **CN:** University of Georgia Center for Continuing Education & Hotel **DOB:** 06/01/1930 **PB:** Batesville **SC:** AR/USA **PT:** Grover Jones Andrews; Ruth Burlie (Ruble) Andrews **ED:** EdD, North Carolina State University (1972); MA, Vanderbilt University (1964); BA, Vanderbilt University (1963) **C:** Interim Director, University of Georgia Center for Continuing Education & Hotel (1998-Present); Interim Director, The University of Georgia Center for Continuing Education & Hotel (1998-2008); Researcher on Georgia Leads, Board of Regents, University Systems of Georgia (2002-2005); Associate Vice President, Public Service and Outreach, University of Georgia Center for Continuing Education & Hotel (1999-2001); Adjunct Associate Professor, Adult Education, University of Georgia Center for Continuing Education & Hotel (1989-2001); Senior Public Service Associate, University of Georgia Center for Continuing Education & Hotel (1989-2001); Chair, Senior Public Service Faculty, University of Georgia Center for Continuing Education & Hotel (1989-2001); Associate Director for Instruction, University of Georgia Center for Continuing Education & Hotel (1989-2001); Assistant Vice President, Public Service and Outreach, University of Georgia Center for Continuing Education & Hotel (1998-1999); Associate Director for Instruction, University of Georgia Center for Continuing Education & Hotel (1989-1999); Associate Vice Chancellor for Extension, North Carolina State University, Raleigh, NC (1979-1989); Associate Professor, Adult Education, North Carolina State University, Raleigh, NC (1979-1989); Associate Executive Director, Commission on Colleges, Southern Association Colleges and Schools, Atlanta, GA (1968-1979); Assistant to Dean of Extension, North Carolina State University, Raleigh, NC (1967-1968); Director of Development, Meredith College, Raleigh, NC (1966-1967); Assistant Professor of English, University of Arkansas, Little Rock, AK (1964-1966); Assistant Academy Dean, University of Arkansas, Little Rock, AK (1964-1966); Assistant to President, Peabody College, Vanderbilt University, Nashville, TN (1961-1964); Director, University Relations, Baylor University, Waco, TX (1955-1961) **CR:** President, International Association for Continuing Education and Training, Washington, DC (1992-1996); Director of Research, International Association for Continuing Education and Training, Washington, DC (1987-1992); Board of Directors, American Technical Institute, Memphis, TN (1985-1998); Trustee, Council for Adult and Experimental Learning, Chicago, IL (1985-1991) **CIV:** Raleigh Lions (1979-1989); Patron, Atlanta Arts Center (1968-1979); Raleigh Lions (1967-1968); Chair, Christmas Pageant Waco Jaycees (1956-1960) **MIL:** U.S. Navy (1948-1950) **AW:** Meritorious Service Award, Southern Association of Colleges and Schools (2003); Pinnacle Award for Outstanding Leadership, International Association for Continuing Education and Training (1996); International Hall of Fame for Adult and Continuing Education (1996); Grover J. Andrews Research Endowment, International Association for Continuing Education and Training (1996); M. Nolte Award, National University Continuing Education Association (1995); Gruman Award, North Carolina Adult Education Association (1985); National Leadership Award, Association for Continuing Higher Education (1984); Educator of the Year, Federation of Women's Clubs (1966) **MEM:** Chair, Accrediting Committees, Southern Association of Colleges and Schools (1980-Present); Chair Elect, Research Division, National University Continuing Education Association (1996-1999); Georgia Adult Education Association; Pi Kappa Alpha; Sigma Tau Delta; Phi Delta Kappa **MH:** Albert Nelson Marquis Lifetime Achievement Award **B/I:** Mr. Andrews became involved in his profession through an inspiring experience at Vanderbilt University. He was very impressed with the Peabody College, the institution, what they did, and what they taught him to do. Mr. Andrews met President Kennedy because the Kennedy family granted endowments to programs his daughter was a part of. The Kennedy family hired the best faculty in the world that they could find and continued to help people. They weren't just teaching in the classroom, they were teaching people how to serve others, the community, and beyond. **AV:** Gardening; Arts; Antiques **PA:** Democrat **RE:** Baptist

ANDREWS, JULIE, T: Actress **I:** Media & Entertainment **DOB:** 10/11/1935 **PB:** Walton-on-Thames **SC:** United Kingdom **PT:** Barbara Ward Wells; Edward Charles "Ted" Wells **MS:** Widowed **SPN:** Blake Edwards (11/12/1969, Deceased 12/15/2010); Tony Walton (05/10/1959, Divorced 11/14/1968) **CH:** Emma Katherine Walton; Amy (Adopted); Joanna (Adopted); Jennifer Edwards (Stepdaughter); Geoffrey Edwards (Stepson) **ED:** Honorary LittD, Stony Brook University (2012); Honorary DFA, Yale University (1999); Honorary DFA, University of Maryland (1970) **CW:** Voice Actress, "Minions: The Rise of Gru" (2020); Voice Actress, "Bridgerton" (2020); Co-author with Emma Walton Hamilton, "Home Work: A Memoir of My Hollywood Years" (2019); Voice Actress, "Aquaman" (2018); Voice Actress, "Despicable Me 3" (2017); Actress, "Julie's Greenroom" (2017); Host, Performer, "Great Performances" (1989-2014); Co-author with Emma Walton Hamilton, "The Very Fairy Princess Follows Her Heart" (2013); Voice Actress, "Despicable Me" (2010); Voice Actress, "Shrek Forever After" (2010); Actress, "Tooth Fairy" (2010); Co-author with Emma Walton Hamilton, "The Very Fairy Princess" (2010); Co-author with Emma Walton Hamilton, "Julie Andrews' Collection of Poems, Songs, and Lullabies" (2009); Author, "Home: A Memoir of My Early Years" (2008); Co-author with Emma Walton Hamilton, "Thanks to You: Wisdom from Mother & Child" (2007); Narrator, "Enchanted" (2007); Voice Actress, "Shrek the Third" (2007); Co-author with Emma Walton Hamilton, "The Great American Mousical" (2006); Featured Subject, "My Favorite Things: Julie Andrews Remembers" (2005); Co-author with Emma Walton Hamilton, "Dragon: Hound of Honor" (2005); Actress, "The Princess Diaries 2: Royal Engagement" (2004); Voice Actress, "Shrek 2" (2004); Actress, "Eloise at Christmastime" (2003); Actress, "Eloise at the Plaza" (2003); Co-author with Emma Walton Hamilton, "Simeon's Gift" (2003); Actress, "Unconditional Love" (2002); Actress, "The Princess Diaries" (2001); Actress, "On Golden Pond" (2001); Actress, "Relative Values" (2000); Co-author with Emma Walton Hamilton, "Dumpy the Dumptruck" (2000); Author, "Little Bo: The Story of Bonnie Boadicea" (1999); Actress, "One Special Night" (1999); Actress, "Victor/Victoria," New York, NY (1995-1997); Featured Subject, "The Sound of Julie Andrews" (1995); Actress, "Victor/Victoria" (1995); Actress, "Putting it Together," New York, NY (1993); Singer, "The King and I" (1992); Actress, "Julie" (1992); Actress, "A Fine Romance" (1992); Actress, "Our Sons" (1991); Performer, "Julie Andrews: The Sound of Christmas" (1987); Actress, "Duet for One" (1986); Actress, "That's Life!" (1986); Actress, "The Man Who Loved Women" (1983); Actress, "Victor Victoria" (1982); Actress, "S.O.B." (1981); Actress, "Little Miss Marker" (1980); Actress, "10" (1979); Host, "Julie Andrews: One to One" (1975); Actress, "The Tamarind Seed" (1974); Author, "The Last of the Really Great Whangdoodles" (1974); Host, "Julie's Christmas Special" (1973); Performer, "Julie on Sesame Street" (1973); Host, "The Julie Andrews Hour" (1972-1973); Featured Subject, "Julie" (1972); Author, "Mandy" (1971); Performer, "Julie and Carol at Lincoln Center" (1971); Actress, "Darling Lili" (1970); Actress, "Star!" (1968); Actress, "Thoroughly Modern Millie" (1967); Actress, "Hawaii" (1966); Actress, "Torn Curtain" (1966); Actress, "The Sound of Music" (1965); Actress, "The Americanization of Emily" (1964); Actress, "Mary Poppins" (1964); Performer, "Julie and Carol at Carnegie Hall" (1962); Guest Appearance, "The Garry Moore Show" (1961-1962); Actress, "Camelot," New York, NY (1960-1962); Performer, "The Ed Sullivan Show" (1956-1961); Actress, "My Fair Lady," New York, NY and London, United Kingdom (1956-1960); Host, "The Julie Andrews Show" (1959); Actress, "The Gentle Flame" (1959); Actress, "Cinderella" (1957); Actress, "Ford Star Jubilee" (1956); Actress, "The Boy Friend," New York, NY (1954-1955); Voice Actress, "The Singing Princess" (1949); Singer, Hippodrome, London, United Kingdom (1947-1948) **AW:** Golden Lion, La Biennale di Venezia (2019); Lifetime Achievement Award, HamptonsFilm (2017); Grammy Award for Lifetime Achievement, Recording Academy (2011); Grammy Award for Best Spoken Word Album for Children, Recording Academy (2011); Prince Rainier III Award, Princess Grace Foundation-USA (2011); George and Ira Gershwin Award, UCLA Alumni (2009); Screen Actors Guild Award for Life Achievement, SAG-AFTRA (2007); Primetime Emmy Award for Outstanding Nonfiction Series, Television Academy (2005); William Holden Lifetime Achievement Award, Las Vegas Film Critics Society (2005); Golden Plate Award, American Academy of Achievement (2004); Named, 100 Greatest Britons, BBC (2002); Honoree, The Kennedy Center, John F. Kennedy Center for the Performing Arts, Washington, DC (2001); Award for Life Achievement, Society of Singers (2001); Donostia Award, San Sebastián International Film Festival (2001); Named Dame Commander (DBE), Order of the British Empire (2000); Drama Desk Award for Outstanding Actress in a Musical (1996); Crystal Award, Women in Film (1993); Inductee, Film, Disney Legends (1991); Golden Globe Award for Best Actress-Motion Picture Comedy or Musical, Hollywood Foreign Press Association (1965, 1966, 1983); David di Donatello Award for Migliore Attrice Straniera, Accademia del Cinema Italiano (1966, 1983); Hasty Pudding Theatrical Award for Woman of the Year, The Hasty Pudding - Institute of 1770, Inc. (1983); People's Choice Award for Favorite Movie Actress (1983); Award for Best Actress, Kansas City Film Critics Circle (1982); Recipient, Star, Hollywood Walk of Fame (1979); Primetime Emmy Award for Outstanding Variety Musical Series, Television Academy (1973); Henrietta Award for World Film Favorite-Female, Hollywood Foreign Press Association (1967, 1968,

1970); Laurel Award for Best Female Comedy Performance, Motion Picture Exhibitor Magazine (1968); Laurel Award for Female Star, Motion Picture Exhibitor Magazine (1967); Laurel Award for Best Female Musical Performance, Motion Picture Exhibitor Magazine (1965, 1966); Academy Award for Best Actress, Academy of Motion Picture Arts and Sciences (1965); Award for Most Promising Newcomer to Leading Film Roles, BAFTA Awards (1965); Grammy Award for Best Recording for Children, Recording Academy (1965); Theatre World Award for Outstanding Broadway Debut, Theatre World Awards, Inc. (1955) **MEM:** Order of the British Empire

ANDREWS, MASON, T: Associate Professor of Architecture **I:** Architecture & Construction **CN:** Hampton University **PT:** Mason Cooke Andrews, Sabine Alston Goodman Andrews **CH:** Alston Cooke Underwood **ED:** MArch, Princeton University (1982); BA in English and History, University of Virginia (1976) **C:** Co-Director, The Coastal Community Design Collaborative (2014-Present); Associate Professor of Architecture, Hampton University (2009-Present); President, Sweetwater Construction Corporation (1986-Present); Principal, Archipelago (1984-2009); President, Sturgeon Creek Development Corporation (1986-1998); Planning and Design Coordinator, Saudi Arabia Plan, John Carl Warnecke & Associates (1982-1984) **CR:** Principal Investigator, "Charting a Path to Transdisciplinary Collaboration," National Science Foundation (2019-Present); Co-Author, Chapter Six, "Adaptation to Sea Level Rise," Handbook of Environmental Engineering (2018); Collaborator, "Cross-Municipal Adaptation Strategies for Shared Watershed," Blue Moon Fund (2018); Director, National Resilience Initiative (2016-2018); Coordinator of Student Staffing, Dutch Dialogues Virginia: Life at Sea Level (2015); Collaborator, Virginia Sea Grant (2014-2015); Co-Investigator, Solar Decathlon Team Tidewater, U.S. Department of Energy (2009-2011); Architectural Designer, Neighborly Houses, National Endowment for the Arts and Habitat for Humanity International (2006-2008); Speaker, U.S. Army Corp of Engineers; Speaker, Society of Military Engineers; Speaker, AIAVA; Speaker, ASEE **CIV:** Consortium to Educate Coastal Virginia (2015); Chair, Design Review Committee, City of Norfolk (2008-2014); Chair, Hampton Roads Chamber (2009); President, Ghent Neighborhood League (2005-2008); Director, Architectural Review Board, City of Norfolk; Coastal Virginia Coalition; Marilyn and Ray Gindroz Foundation; United Way of South Hampton Roads; Five Points Community Farm Market **CW:** Aldo Rossi Buildings and Projects, Rizzolli (1986); Frank Gehry Buildings and Projects, Rizzolli (1986); Architect, Lafayette Square (1983); Architect, Saks House, NY; Architect, Maison Andrews, VA; Architect, New Jersey National Bank, NJ; Architect, The Hearing Lab; Architect, Connor House, CA; Architect, Tribute Showroom, NY; Architect, Sturgeon Creek, VA; Architect, Model Duplex for Traditional Neighborhood, Habitat for Humanity **AW:** Climate, Architecture, and Society Course Development Prize, ACSA, The Temple Hoyne Buell Center for the Study of American Architecture (2020); Outstanding Woman in Flood Risk Architecture and Academic Leader in Graduate Studies, InBuild (2017); Innovation in Teaching Award, Hampton University (2015); Resilience Builder, City of Norfolk (2015); Environmental Stewardship Award, City of Norfolk (2015); Outstanding Service to the City of Norfolk, City Council (2014, 2015); Medal for Outstanding Teaching of Architecture, Tau Sigma Delta (2012); Andy Award, Advertising Club of New York (1985); Thesis Prize, Princeton University (1982); Fellowship, Princeton University, 1978-1982; Howard

Crosby Butler Travel Fellowship (1980) **MEM:** Ghent Neighborhood League; Chesterfield Heights Civic League; Park Place Civic League; Urban Land Institute; Society of Architectural Historians; Congress for the New Urbanism **MH:** Marquis Who's Who Top Professional **AS:** Ms. Andrews attributes her success to her hard work and her openness to learning from others. **B/I:** Ms. Andrews became involved in her profession because of a desire to be creative.

ANGEL, DENNIS, T: Lawyer **I:** Law and Legal Services **DOB:** 02/14/1947 **PB:** Brooklyn **SC:** NY/USA **PT:** Morris; Rosalyn (Sobiloff) Angel **MS:** Married **SPN:** Linda Marlene Lobel (5/15/1977) **CH:** Stephanie Lee; Michele Bari; Rebecca Jo **ED:** Doctor of Jurisprudence, Washington and Lee University (1972); Bachelor of Arts, Saint Lawrence University (1968); Diplôme d'études en langue française, University of Rouen, France (1967) **C:** Sole Practice, New York, NY (1978-Present); Associate, Johnson & Tannenbaum, New York, NY (1972-1977) **MIL:** U.S. Army Reserve (1969-1975) **CW:** Contributor, Articles to Professional Journals **MEM:** Subcommittee Chairperson, American Bar Association (1977-1982); New York State Bar Association; Copyright Society of the USA; Phi Alpha Delta **MH:** Albert Nelson Marquis Lifetime Achievement Award; Marquis Who's Who Top Professional **B/I:** Mr. Angel became involved in his profession out of a longstanding interest in not only music, but history and the law. He read a book by Louis Nizer, "My Life in Court," and the passages he found on music copyright infringement fascinated him. **AV:** Trumpet **RE:** Jewish

ANGEL PAYNE, PHYLLIS J., T: Business Owner **I:** Business Management/Business Services **DOB:** 08/10/1947 **PB:** North Platte **SC:** NE/USA **PT:** Ralph Henry; Lucille (Bussell) Shinn **MS:** Married **SPN:** Lewis Worth Angel, 01/11/1969 (Divorced, 1975); Stanley Stephen Payne (1997) **CH:** Stepson, Joshua S. Payne **ED:** Student, Cosmetology, Mile Hi Beauty School (1969); AA, North Eastern Junior College (1967) **C:** Owner, Rocky Mountain Hair Design, Littleton, Colorado, (1996-Present); Owner, American Hairways, Littleton, CO (1989-1996); Financial Administrator, Martin Marietta, Denver, CO (1978-1989); Owner, Stylist, Phyl's Styling Salon, Sedalia, CO (1976-1977); Secretary, Prudential Insurance Co., Denver, CO (1973-1976); Secretary, King Soopers Bakery, Denver, CO (1973); Information Operator, Mountain Bell, Denver, CO (1967); Office Representative, Standard Quarter Horse Association, Lakewood, CO (1967-1969) **CR:** Owner, Shaklee Product Distribution, Denver, CO (1982-Present); A & B Enterprises, Denver, CO (1974-1976); Consultant, Frisbie & Frisbie, Denver, CO (1973-1980); Self Images, Denver, CO (1973-1979) **CIV:** Sponsor, Little League Baseball Team (1976); Active, Multiple Sclerosis Ride-A-Thon (1975); Active, Muscular Dystrophy Telethon (1974); Coach, Wagon Wheel Softball Team (1963-1965) **CW:** Author, "Grandma" (1984); Author, "Wax Doll" (1984); Author, "A Wolf Pup Was Born" (1983) **AW:** Recipient, Golden Poet and Silver Poet Awards (1985-1986); Grand Cross of Colors, Rainbow Girls (1965) **MEM:** Career Women's Association; International Platform Association; National Museum Women in Arts; Rodeo Club, 4-H Club; Square Dance Club; Eastern Star **MH:** Albert Nelson Marquis Lifetime Achievement Award **B/I:** Ms. Payne became involved in her profession in high school, where she had her first experience as a hairdresser. She was the person in her family to pursue a career in cosmetology. **RE:** Methodist

ANGLIN, JOHN EDSON, T: Theatre and Television Director, Educator **I:** Media & Entertainment **DOB:** 09/15/1946 **PB:** Arlington **SC:** VA/USA **PT:** Murray Edson Anglin; Bernice Marie (McGhee) Anglin **MS:** Married **SPN:** Vivian Moira Poole (06/08/1968) **CH:** Sean Murray; Andrew Benjamin; Matthew Jeremy; Adam Mongomery **ED:** Postgraduate Coursework, University of Illinois (1980); MA, University of Wyoming (1971); BS, James Madison University (1969) **C:** Fine Arts Division Chair, East Central College, Union, MO (1997-Present); Director, Two Rivers Community Television, Union, MO (1990-Present); Director, Theatre, Teacher, East Central College, Union, MO (1971) **CR:** Theatre Consultant, Videotechnilites, Union, MO (1971-Present); Teacher, Tele Course/Mitco (1983); Accepted, National Institute of Staff and Organizational Development (NISOD), Austin, TX; Appointed Chairman, Division of Fine Arts, East Central College **CIV:** Selected Participant, Great Teachers Seminar (1991, 1994); Councilman, City of Washington, MO (1980-1986) **CW:** Author, Producer, Director, "Aristophanes' The Birds' (1994); Actor, "Waiting For Godot" (1991); Actor, "Mornings At Seven" (1988); Actor, "Superman" (1970); Actor, "Antigone"; Actor, "The Subject Was Roses"; Actor, "Deathtrap"; Actor, "Dracula"; Actor, "Children of Eden"; Actor, "You Can't Take it With You"; Director, "Fiddler On the Roof"; Director, "My Fair Lady"; Director, "Quilters"; Director, "Little Shop of Horrors"; Director, "The Lion in Winter"; Director, "Antigone"; Director, "A Sleep of Prisoners"; Director, "Arsenic and Old Lace"; Director, "Mousetrap"; Director, "Crimes of the Heart"; Director, "Mame, 1776"; Director, "Two by Two"; Director, "Wind in the Willows" **AW:** Governor's Award for Excellence in Teaching, State of Missouri (1999); Meritorious Achievement Award, American College Theatre Festival, Washington, DC (1990); Outstanding Educator of America (1975); Eponym, John Edson Anglin Performing Arts Center **MEM:** American Theatre in Higher Education; Speech Communication Association; U.S. Institute of Theatre Technology; Speech & Theatre Association of Missouri **MH:** Albert Nelson Marquis Lifetime Achievement Award **B/I:** Mr. Anglin started his career at James Madison University, planning to be a music minister. One of his professors noticed his natural performing abilities, asking him to audition for the play. He did, and the rest is history. Mr. Anglin changed his major to theater, proceeding to progress naturally in his career. **AV:** Reading; Golfing; Acting **PA:** Democrat

ANSARI, MOHAMMED R., T: General and Vascular Surgery **I:** Medicine & Health Care **DOB:** 10/10/1935 **PB:** Gokaram **SC:** India **PT:** Mohammed Mahboob Ali Ansari; Abbas (Bibi) Ansari **MS:** Widowed **SPN:** Raoof Yasmin Ansari, (6/2/1962, Deceased 7/2004) **CH:** Farrah Yasmin **ED:** MB, BChir, Osmania University (1962); BS, Osmania University (1957) **CT:** Fellow of American College of Surgeons, (F.A.C.S.) (1975); Certified, American Board of Surgery & Vascular Surgery (1974) **C:** Clinical Assistant Professor, University of Michigan, Detroit (1980-Present);Consultant, Blue Cross Blue Shield (2001-2009); Retired (2000); Staff Surgeon, Henry Ford Hospital, Detroit, MI (1973-2000); Clinical Assistant Professor, Surgery, University of Michigan (1980-1996); Clinical Instructor, Surgery, University of Michigan, Detroit, MI (1976-1980); Resident, Henry Ford Hospital, Detroit, MI (1968-1973); Intern, St. Luke Hospital, St. Paul (1967-1968); Assistant Surgeon, District Hospital, Karimnagar, India (1963-1967) **CR:** Researcher, Laboratory Animal Research Work on Development of Atherosclerosis in Implanted Vascular Grafts; Developer, Kidney Cooling Jacket for Hypothermia of Transplant Kidney during Vascular

Anastomosis, so as to Preserve its Function. **CIV:** Founding Member, Islamic Association of Greater Detroit in Michigan (1978); Detroit Chirurgie Association **CW:** Contributor, Five Articles and 12 Journal Publications **AW:** Roy D. McClure Surgical Award, Henry Ford Hospital-McClure Surgical Society (1971) **MEM:** American Medical Association; Fellow, American College of Surgeons; Midwest Surgical Association; Michigan State Medical Society; Academy of Surgery Detroit; Society International de Chirurgie **MH:** Albert Nelson Marquis Lifetime Achievement Award **B/I:** Dr. Ansari became involved in his profession because his father was a farmer and he came from a small village. He saw his father have asthma attacks quite often and he died from asthma in his middle 60s. That was his fuel to get into medicine. He was sent to live with his sister in the city to get his education and until he graduated and both his sister and his brother-in-law helped him in his career. Most of his education was based on scholarships. **AV:** Reading **PA:** Republican **RE:** Muslim

ANTHONY-SMITH, MARYANNE, T: Professor Emeritus of Mathematics **I:** Education/Educational Services **CN:** Santa Ana College **DOB:** 10/19/1952 **PB:** New York **SC:** NY/USA **PT:** Harry Antoniades Anthony; Anne (Skoufis) Anthony **MS:** Married **SPN:** John LeRoy Smith **CH:** Alexander Chousmith; Anastastia Lewis; Jeannette Chan **ED:** MS in Educational Computing, Pepperdine University, Malibu, CA (1984); MS in Statistics, San Diego State University (1975); BS in Math, University of California San Diego (1973) **C:** Community College Coordinator, Mathematics Diagnostic Testing Project, University of California/California State University (2003-2018);Member, Mathematics Diagnostic Testing Project, University of California/California State University (1988-2018); Professor of Mathematics, Santa Ana College (1976-2015); Acting Dean, Science and Mathematics, Santa Ana College (1996); Chair, Mathematics Department, Santa Ana College (1993-1996) **CIV:** Member, Woodbridge Village Association Architectural Committee (2014-Present); Sunday School Teacher, Board Member, Saint Paul's Greek Orthodox Church, Irvine, CA (1987-Present); Member, School Site Council, Stone Creek Elementary, Irvine Unified School District, Irvine, CA (1991-2000) **CW:** Senior Contributing Author, "Prealgebra," OpenStax (2017); Senior Contributing Author, "Elementary Algebra," OpenStax (2017); Co-author, "Foundations of Algebra," OpenStax (2015); Co-author, "Strategies for Success: Study Skills for the College Math Student, Second Edition," Pearson (2014); Co-author, "Strategies for Success, Study Skills for the College Math Student," Pearson (2012); Co-author, "Developing Mathematically Promising Students" (1999); Author, Producer, Video, "Classroom Voices" (1993) **AW:** Professional Achievement Award, Santa Ana College (2015); Curriculum Development Award, Santa Ana College (2008); Distinguished Faculty Award, Rancho Santiago Community College District, Santa Ana, CA (1993); Professional Development Award, Santa Ana College (1993) **MEM:** National Council of Teachers of Mathematics; California Mathematics Council Community Colleges (CMC3); American Mathematical Association of Two-Year Colleges **MH:** Albert Nelson Marquis Lifetime Achievement Award **AS:** Mrs. Anthony-Smith's role models were her father and her husband. She saw how they truly cared about their students. They both encouraged her to pursue her career. **B/I:** Mrs. Anthony-Smith became involved in her profession because she always wanted to be a teacher and knew she would be one day. Her father was a professor and her paternal grandfather was a teacher. She went into mathematics because it

was something she was interested in. She was the first female full-time mathematics teacher hired at Santa Ana College. **AV:** Gardening; Quilting; Reading **PA:** Democrat **RE:** Greek Orthodox **THT:** Mrs. Anthony-Smith motto is, "Always do your best. Don't wait to make a change until you can fix the world for everyone; fixing the world for one person at a time puts you on the right path."

APPALARAJU, RAM V., T: Executive Analyst **I:** Technology **DOB:** 08/24/1960 **PB:** Madras **SC:** Tamil Nadu **PT:** Ambados Appalaraju (Father); Sarojini Devi Appalaraju (Mother) **MS:** India **SPN:** Asha Appalaraju **CH:** Monisha Appalaraju; Megy Appalaraju **ED:** Coursework in Advanced Executive Management, Stanford University; MSEE in Computer Engineering, Northeastern University, Boston, MA (1985); Bachelor of Engineering, University of Madras (1982) **C:** Executive Advisor, Rainq Strategies (2019-Present); President and Chief Executive Officer, 8kpc Inc. (2015-2019); Strategic Advisor, ON.Lab (2014-2015); Vice President, Product Marketing, Business Development Solutions for Engineering, Data Center Group, Cisco Systems Inc. (2012-2014); Vice President and Chief Marketing Officer, Corporate and Product Marketing, Siemens Enterprise Communications (Now Unify Atos SE), Enterasys Networks (Now Extreme Networks) (2011-2012); Senior Vice President and Chief Marketing Officer, Meru Networks (2009-2011); Senior Vice President, Isilon Systems (2008-2009); Vice President of Marketing, Azul Systems (2006-2008); Vice President, Enterprise Business, Hewlett Packard (Now Hewlett Packard Enterprise Development LP) (1995-2006); With, Digital Equipment Corporation (1987-1995); With, General Electric (1984-1987) **CR:** Delivering Innovative Solution Concepts on Artificial Intelligence and Quantum Computing: Data Sciences, Algorithm Development, Business Outcomes, etc.; Conceived and Delivered Products in All Aspects of Cloud/Data Center Technologies; Engaged and Consulted to Chief Executive Officers, Chief Technology Officers, and Chief Security Officers Worldwide in All Major Industries: Financial Services, Health Care, Telco Service Providers, Retail, Hospitality, etc. **CIV:** Volunteer, Homeless Shelter, San Jose, CA **CW:** Contributor, Articles to Professional Journals and Magazines **AW:** Named Most Valuable Employee, Hewlett Packard (2004); Numerous Awards and Recognition for Products and Services Conceived Under His Leadership **MEM:** IEEE; IEEE Computer Society **MH:** Albert Nelson Marquis Lifetime Achievement Award **AS:** Mr. Appalaraju attributes his success to perseverance, ability to work with people of all backgrounds, and bringing a sense of gratitude to God and people in his life. He has a profound interest in managing time efficiently to achieve goals and objectives. He is an excellent communicator and treats people fairly and equitably. He strongly believes in being humble and is influenced by books by Jim Collins, particularly "Good to Great." Mr. Appalaraju has keen interest in constantly learning on new technology areas and management sciences and engages with several thought leaders and is grateful for their mentorship. Mr. Appalaraju also credits his success to support and love from his wife Asha and his daughters, Monisha and Megy. He is also grateful to his parents for instilling work ethic, excellent guidance and love from his brother and sister through his life. **B/I:** Mr. Appalaraju came to the USA as a graduate student aided by support from his parents and his brother for the first few months in 1982. After graduating with MSEE in Computer Engineering, he saw a great opportunity in the industry to embrace innovative technology in several areas of Information technology. He quickly capitalized on technology boom of the eighties by

learning and contributing to several technology areas. He is grateful for several good mentors at different companies who worked with him to convert opportunities into technology solutions and businesses. **AV:** Amateur photographer with over 30,000 (and growing) in his collection all taken on Nikon prosumer cameras; Traveling to historic sites (visited 50 countries); Avid fan of Boston area sports teams (Celtics, Patriots, Red Sox and Bruins); Avid reader of nonfiction in several areas including history, science, law, and philosophy **PA:** Independent **RE:** Practitioner of Mindfulness; Hindu by Birth **THT:** Mr. Appalaraju believes that complexities in life are best addressed not by looking at life (or work) as a list of tasks but by empowering and supporting people who are all capable of achieving extraordinary things. He passionately believes in capitalizing on opportunities with timely perseverance and to do the right thing aided by moral compass. He believes in constantly searching and looking for greater purpose in life beyond a professional role. Ram is building on his 30 years of technology experience by conceiving and delivering products and solutions related to all aspects of computing solutions. Mr. Appalaraju contributed to technology in the areas of digital transformation as a product and business manager and marketing lead for several innovative areas such as parallel computing, distributed computing, cloud computing, storage architectures, networking, application development, etc. He also led all aspects of product business: product management, solution engineering, marketing, and go-to market execution worldwide. He brings a broad expertise in startups, midsize companies and large corporations in successfully delivering sustained growth and profitability. He has engaged extensively with chief executive officers, chief information officers and chief technology officers of global 1000 enterprises in over 50 countries. Mr. Appalaraju is a rational Independent and supports equally capitalism and social causes.

APPLEGATE, H. REED, T: Graphic Designer, Advertising Executive **I:** Advertising & Marketing **DOB:** 03/26/1943 **PB:** Chico **SC:** CA/USA **PT:** Michael Applegate; Jean (Shear) Applegate **ED:** BFA, California State University, Chico (1967) **C:** Business Owner (1977-1993); Retired Graphic Designer, Chico Enterprise-Record (1983-1987); Advertising Account Executive, Butte County Bugle Newspaper (1971-1977) **CR:** Visual Arts Committee, Annie Awards (1995-Present); Research Librarian, Annie Awards Visual Arts Committee, Chico (1995-Present); Research Librarian, Janet Turner Print Museum, California State University, Chico (1995-Present); Adviser, North State Symphony (1994-1996) **CW:** Controller, Articles on Area Artist, Local Newspaper (1993-Present) **AW:** The Janet Turner Prize for Excellence in the Arts (2012) **MEM:** Chico Art Center; Founding Member, The Museum of Northern California Art **MH:** Albert Nelson Marquis Lifetime Achievement Award **B/I:** Mr. Applegate became involved in his profession because at the time he started it was just a job, and he thought that he could succeed doing his own graphic work. When the newspaper opportunity came along he decided to try that. **AV:** Collecting the works of Northern California artists; Attending art receptions and concerts

ARANDA, JACOB V., T: Professor of Pediatrics, Director **I:** Education/Educational Services **CN:** SUNY Downstate Health Sciences University **DOB:** 12/29/1942 **SC:** Philippines **PT:** Anacleto T. Aranda; Gorgonia S. (Velasco) Aranda **MS:** Widowed **SPN:** Betty I. Sasyniuk (12/28/1974, Deceased) **CH:** Two sons **ED:** PhD in Pharmacology, McGill University (1975); Fellowship in Neonatology, School of

Medicine, Case Western Reserve University (1968-1969); Residency in Pediatrics, SUNY Downstate Health Sciences University (1966-1968); Internship, Washington Hospital Center, George Washington University (1965-1966); Internship, U.S. Naval Hospital (1964-1965); MD, Manila Central University (1965) **CT:** Diplomate, The American Board of Pediatrics **C:** Director of Developmental Pharmacology and Perinatal Research, Montreal Children's Hospital (1979-Present); Acting Director of Neonatal Research, Montreal Children's Hospital (1974-1979); Research Fellow in Neonatology, McGill University (1969-1971); Director of Neonatology, Professor of Pediatrics and Ophthalmology, SUNY Downstate Health Sciences University; Consulting Pediatrician, St. Mary's Hospital; Attending Neonatologist, Montreal Children's Hospital **CR:** Professor, School of Medicine, McGill University (1984-Present); Associate Professor, School of Medicine, McGill University (1977-1984); Assistant Professor of Pediatrics, Pharmacology and Therapeutics, School of Medicine, McGill University (1974-1977); Fellow, Medical Council of Canada (1971-1974) **CIV:** Chair, National Steering Committee, Pediatric Developmental Pharmacology Research Network, National Institutes of Health **CW:** Co-Author, Five Books; Contributor, 250 Articles, Professional Journals; Co-Author, "Neonatal and Pediatric Pharmacology"; Editor-in-Chief, "Developmental Pharmacology and Therapeutics" **MEM:** Fellow, American College of Clinical Pharmacology; Fellow, American Academy of Pediatrics; American Federation for Medical Research; American Thoracic Society; Federation Medical Specialists Quebec; Canadian Paediatric Society; STC; Canadian Thoracic Society; Canadian Society of Pharmacology and Therapeutics; New York Academy of Sciences; Society for Pediatric Research; Canadian Society for Clinical Investigation **MH:** Marquis Who's Who Top Professional **AS:** Dr. Aranda attributes his success to his hard work, imagination and curiosity. **B/I:** Dr. Aranda became involved in his profession because of his wonderful mentors, including Mary Ellen Avery and Leo Stern. **RE:** Methodist

ARCHIBALD, PATRICIA A., PHD, T: Biology Educator, College Director **I:** Education/Educational Services **DOB:** 07/18/1931 **PB:** Olney **SC:** IL/USA **PT:** Stanley Ray Archibald; Mable Ellen (Seed) Archibald **ED:** PhD in Botany, The University of Texas (1969); MA, Ball State University (1961); BS, Ball State University (1953) **C:** Director, Office of Academy Grants, Slippery Rock University, PA (1987-1994); Professor of Biology, Slippery Rock University, PA (1969-1994); Teacher of Biology, Elkhart Senior High School, IN (1958-1964) **CR:** Leader, Seminar Group, China Science and Technology Exchange Center (1989); Science Administrator, U.S. Environmental Protection Agency (EPA), Washington, DC (1980-1982); Secretary, Marine Science Consortium of PA Space Schools, Pennsylvania's State System of Higher Education (1979); Co-director, Marine Consortium at Wallops Island, VA **CW:** Contributor, Chapters to Books, Articles to Professional Journals **AW:** Collection Expedition Award, New York Botanical Garden (1984); Bronze Medal of Achievement, U.S. Environmental Protection Agency (EPA) (1982); Award, The National Academy of Sciences (1978); Research Exchange Award, IREX (1977); Fulbright Teaching Exchange Award (1962-1963) **MEM:** Secretary, Psychological Society America (1982-1984); Sigma Xi, The Scientific Research Honor Society **MH:** Albert Nelson Marquis Lifetime Achievement Award **AS:** Dr. Archibald attributes his success to the idea of being comfortable and satisfied with what you've done with your life. What's best for one person may not be for another.

B/I: Dr. Archibald grew up with a family of teachers and she always liked the subject of biology. In her generation, a women probably taught or went into nursing. People in her generation had a chance to see women start to do more because it was during World War II; men were at war, and you had women teaching in science and math that probably before had not as much because those field were for men not women. She had a woman biology teacher and a woman chemistry teacher that she really respected and admired their work. **AV:** Gardening; Reading; Traveling

ARGUIROVA, BORIANA D., T: Consultant; Strategic Manager/Lead Electrical Engineer **I:** Engineering **CN:** Morrison Hershfield **MS:** Married **ED:** MSEE, Technical University of Sofia (1993); MS in Accounting and Estimating; MBA, ABD **C:** Strategic Manager, ABD Consulting, Inc. (2018-Present); Mechanical/Electrical Department Manager, Lead Electrical Engineer, Morrison Hershfield (2014-Present); Business Development Manager, Senior Electrical Engineering Lead for British Columbia, Morrison Hershfield (2013-Present); Senior Project Manager, Applied Engineering Solutions, Inc. (2010-2013); Senior Associate, Project Manager, Stantec (2003-2010) **CIV:** The National Children's Cancer Society **MEM:** IEEE (Institute of Electrical and Electronics Engineers); Canadian Healthcare Engineering Society (CHES); Illumination Engineering Society **MH:** Albert Nelson Marquis Lifetime Achievement Award; Marquis Who's Who Top Professional **AS:** Mrs. Arguirova attributes her success to the challenge to create and build something, and actually see it completed. **B/I:** Mrs. Arguirova became involved in her profession because of the magic of light and how one sees things. It was a pure professional choice to pursue electrical design as a career. **AV:** Tennis; Reading **THT:** The biggest challenge Mrs. Arguirova has overcome is gender bias. This is a man's field, and she has to fight those men who don't know what she is capable of. She enjoys this challenge. Mrs. Arguirova believes she has many accomplishments over the years. She is proud of every project that she has achieved. This includes working with the government, secret service, prisons, and hospitals.

ARISON, MICKY, T: Chairman; Owner **I:** Business Management/Business Services **CN:** Carnival Corporation & PLC; Miami Heat **DOB:** 06/29/1949 **SC:** Tel Aviv/Israel **PT:** Ted Arison; Mina Wasserman Arison **MS:** Married **SPN:** Madeleine Arison **CH:** Two Children **ED:** Honorary Doctorate in Naval Architecture, University of Genoa;Coursework, University of Miami **C:** Owner, Managing General Partner, Miami Heat, NBA (1995-Present); Chairman, Carnival Corporation & PLC (1990-Present); Chief Executive Officer, Carnival Corporation & PLC (1990-2013); President, Chief Executive Officer, Carnival Corporation & PLC (1979-1990); Vice President, Passenger Traffic, Carnival Corporation & PLC (1976-1979); Reservations Manager, Carnival Corporation & PLC (1974-1976) **CR:** Chairman, Board of Governors, NBA (2005-Present); Managing General Partner, Miami Heat, FL (1995-Present); Board of Directors, Carnival Corporation & PLC (1987-Present) **AW:** Listee, Forbes 400: Richest Americans (1999-Present); Listee, World's Richest People, Forbes Magazine (1999-Present); Listee, Forbes Billionaires List (2019); Listee, Most Influential People in the World of Sports, Business Week (Now Bloomberg Businessweek) (2007); Officer of the French Legion of Honor, French President Jacques Chirac; Decoration of Commander, First Class of the Order of the Lion of Finland, President

of Finland; Onorificenza al Merito della Repubblica Italiana, President of Italy **MEM:** Chairman, Florida-Caribbean Cruise Association **RE:** Jewish

ARKING, LUCILLE MUSSER, RN, MSN, T: Nurse, Epidemiologist, Consultant **I:** Medicine & Health Care **DOB:** 01/26/1936 **PB:** Centre County **SC:** PA/USA **PT:** Boyd Albert; Marion Anna (Merryman) Musser **MS:** Married **SPN:** Dr. Robert Arking (05/08/1958) **CH:** Henry David (Spouse Deanne); Jonathan Jacob (Spouse Carolyn) **ED:** Doctoral Studies in Evaluation Statistics, Wayne State University, Detroit, MI (1991-1996); Master of Science in Nursing, Wayne State University (1986); Bachelor of Science in Nursing, University of Pennsylvania (1968) **C:** With, Arking Consultant Associates (2003-Present); With, Office of International Affairs, Pusan National University, South Korea (2001, 2011); With, St. James Nursing Center, Detroit, MI (2002-2003); Executive Director, St. Anthony Nursing Care Center, Warren, MI (1999-2001); Administrator, Cadillac Nursing Center, Detroit, MI (1997-1999); Vice President of Clinical Services, Great Lakes Rehabilitation Hospital, Southfield, MI (1994-1996); Senior Clinical Epidemiologist, Henry Ford Hospital, Detroit, MI (1990-1994); Director, Hospital Epidemiology, Henry Ford Hospital, Detroit, MI (1984-1989); Nurse Epidemiologist, Henry Ford Hospital, Detroit, MI (1975-1984); Director of Nursing, Bellwood Hospital, Bellflower, CA (1974-1975); Assistant Director of Nursing Education, Rio Hondo Hospital, Downey, CA (1973-1975); Assistant Director of Nursing, University of Kentucky, Lexington, KY (1968-1970); Head Nurse, University of Virginia, Charlottesville, VA (1967-1968); Director of Nursing, Green Acres Nursing Center, Philadelphia, PA (1966-1967); Public Health Nurse, Community Nursing Service, Philadelphia, PA (1961-1964); Hospital Supervisor, Philadelphia Psychiatric Center, Pennsylvania (1959-1961); Psychiatric Research Nurse, Boston City Hospital, Massachusetts (1958) **CR:** Lecturer on Drug Abuse, Fountain Valley, CA (1970-1975); Instructor, Santa Ana College (1971-1973) **CIV:** Member, Troy Democratic Club (2011-Present); Board Member, Troy Democratic Club (2011-2018); Senior Commissioner, Oakland County, Michigan (2007-2010); Chairperson, Religious Affiliation Social Action Committee, Michigan Medical Society AIDS Task Force (1984-1990); Member, Michigan Governor AIDS Task Force (1985-1986); Founding Member, Board of Directors, Wellness Networks, Detroit, MI (1982-1986); Den Leader, Cub Scouts, Fountain Valley and Troy, MI (1968-1975); Co-founder, Parents and Friends Learning Disabilities Organization (1968-1970) **CW:** Contributor, Articles to Professional Journals **AW:** Florence Nightingale Award, Oakland University (2009); Nursing Trainee, U.S. Public Health Service (1965); Education Grant, Philadelphia Community Nursing Service (1963-1964); Scholar, Women's Club of Centre County (1954-1958) **MEM:** Epidemiology Section, American Public Health Association (1975-1999); HIV Advisory Committee, Michigan Nurse's Association (1989-1990); AIDS Task Force, Michigan Nurse's Association (1987-1989); American Nurses Association; Association of Practitioners of Infection Control; Science Research Society; Association of Women in Science; Sigma Xi **MH:** Albert Nelson Marquis Lifetime Achievement Award **B/I:** Ms. Arking became involved in her field due to growing up with a speech defect, which led her to attend speech therapy classes at Pennsylvania State University. She became inspired by her nurse, who drove her to these sessions. **AV:** Gardening; Cooking; Genealogy **PA:** Democrat **RE:** Jewish

ARKING, ROBERT, PHD, T: Geneticist, Gerontologist; Educator **I:** Medicine & Health Care **CN:** Wayne State University **DOB:** 07/01/1936 **PB:** Brooklyn **SC:** NY/USA **PT:** Henry Arking; Mollie (Levinson) Arking **MS:** Married **SPN:** Lucille Mae Musser (05/08/1958) **CH:** Henry David; Jonathan Jacob **ED:** PhD in Biology, Developmental Genetics, Temple University (1967); BS in Biology, Dickinson College (1958) **C:** Undergraduate Officer, Wayne State University (1997-Present); Professor, Wayne State University (1993-Present); Associate Professor, Wayne State University (1981-1983); Assistant Professor, Biology, Wayne State University (1975-1981); Research Biologist, Development Biology Center, University of California Irvine (1970-1975); Assistant Professor, Zoology, University of Kentucky, Lexington, KY (1968-1970); Science Teacher, Philadelphia Public Schools (The School District of Pennsylvania) (1959-1961) **CR:** Fulbright Foundation (2006-Present); Grant Reviewer, AFAR (American Federation for Aging Research) Review Board (2004-Present); Expert Visiting Professor, Pusan National University (2001, 2013); Fulbright Distinguished Chair, Natural Science, University of Salzburg, Austria (2006); Faculty Associate, Institute of Gerontology, Wayne State University **CW:** Author, "Biology of Aging: Observations and Principles, Fourth Edition" (2019); Author, "Biology of Aging: Observations and Principles, Third Edition" (2006); Author, "Biology of Aging: Observations and Principles, Second Edition" (1998); Author, "Biology of Aging: Observations and Principles" (1991); Contributor, Articles to Professional Journals **AW:** Fellowship, National Institutes of Health (1967-1968); Fellowship, National Science Foundation (1964-1966) **MEM:** Fellow, The Gerontology Society of America; American Association for the Advancement of Science; Sigma Xi, The Scientific Research Honor Society **MH:** Albert Nelson Marquis Lifetime Achievement Award **B/I:** Dr. Arking always wanted to teach and started as a high school teacher. **AV:** History buff; Reading; Gardening **THT:** Dr. Arking's son, Henry David, is married to Deanne, and his son, Jonathan Jacob is married to Carolyn.

ARMOUR, DAVID, T: President, Chief Executive Officer; Executive Producer **I:** Business Management/Business Services **CN:** 79th & York Entertainment **ED:** Diploma, Columbia University (1992) **C:** President, 501 East Entertainment (2017-Present); President, 79th & York Entertainment (2005-Present); Executive Vice President, Youtoo Technologies (2012-2014); Vice President, Development, Programming and Sales, Digital Media, Endemol USA (2008-2012); Executive Producer, Endemol USA (2006-2008); Executive Producer, MySpace (2006-2007); Creative Consultant, GO TV (2005-2007); Consulting Producer, Game Show Network, LLC (GSN) (2005-2006); Executive Producer, FOX/Twentieth Television, Twentieth Century Fox Film Corporation (2002-2005); Executive Producer, King World (2001-2002); Executive Creative Consultant, Traffix, Inc. (2000-2002); Executive Producer, Telepictures, Warner Bros. Entertainment Inc. (1999-2000); AP/Co-Executive Producer, "Ricky Lake," Sony Television (1993-1999) **CW:** Creator, Executive Producer, "Paternity Court"; Creator, Executive Producer, "Couples Court"; Creator, Executive Producer, "Personal Injury Court" **AW:** Outstanding Legal/Courtroom Program, Emmy Awards (2019)

ARMSTRONG, DANIEL W., CHD, T: R.A. Welch Distinguished Professor **I:** Education/Educational Services **CN:** University of Texas at Arlington **DOB:** 11/02/1949 **PB:** Fort Wayne **SC:** IN/USA **PT:** Robert Eugene Armstrong; Nila Louise (Koeneman) Armstrong **MS:** Married **SPN:** Linda Marilyn Todd (6/11/1972) **CH:** Lincoln Thomas; Ross Alexander; Colleen Victoria **ED:** Doctor Honoris Causa, Slovak University of Technology, Bratislava, Slovakia (2018); ChD, Texas A&M University, College Station, TX (1977); MS in Chemical Oceanography, Texas A&M University, College Station, TX (1974); BS, Washington and Lee University, Lexington, VA (1972) **C:** President, Chief Executive Officer, AZYP, LLC, Arlington, TX (2010-Present); Robert A. Welch Professor, Chemistry and Biochemistry, University of Texas at Arlington, Arlington, TX (2006-Present); P.W. West Lecturer, Louisiana State University, Baton Rouge, LA (2014); Caldwell Professor of Chemistry, Iowa State University, Ames, IA (2000-2006); Head, Department of Analytical Chemistry, Missouri University of Science and Technology, Rolla, MO (1987-2000); Professor, Texas Technical University, Lubbock, TX (1983-1987); Professor, Georgetown University, Washington, DC (1980-1983); Professor, Bowdoin College, Brunswick, ME (1978-1979); Curators' Distinguished Professor, Head, Center for Environmental Science and Technology **CR:** Lecturer, Columbia University (2003); Dow Lecturer (2003); R.A. Welch Distinguished Professor, University of Texas at Arlington (2002); Moreton Lecturer, Millsaps College, Jackson, MS (2001); Board of Directors, Advanced Separation Technologies, Inc., Whippany, NJ **CW:** Writer, Host, Weekly Radio Show, "We're Science National Public Radio" (1993-Present); Host, University Forum Radio Show, Washington, DC (1981-1983); Author, Film, Radio Shows; Contributor, Numerous Articles, Professional Journals; Author, Contributor, More Than 700 Publications **AW:** Supelco Grant (2008-Present); Named, Power List Top 10 Analytical Scientist in the World (2019); UTA Excellence in Doctoral Mentoring Award (2018-2019); Dow Chemical WesTEC Award for "Distinguished Leader in Science and Technology" (2018); National Institutes Of Health (1986, 1991, 1995, 2000, 2003, 2005, 2010, 2014, 2016, 2018); Analytical Scientist Separations Power List Top 10 and Mentor Power List Top 10 (2017); Named, Analytical Scientist's Power List Top 10 (2015); Wilfred T. Doherty Research and Service Award, DFW Section of American Chemical Society (2015); American College of Surgeons Award (2014); Separation Science & Technology Award (2014); M.J.E. Golay Award (2014); Academy Distinguished Scholar (2014); American Chemical Society Award (2013); Distinguished Record Research Creative Activity Award, University of Texas (2012); Department of Agriculture Award (2012); Slovak Medical Society Medal (2007); Dal Nogre Award For Separation Science (2005); Honorary Vladimir J. Zuffu Medal, Slovak Pharmaceutical Society (2004); Chirality Medal (2003); Kenneth A. Spencer Award, Agriculture And Food Chemistry (2002); CLDG Merit Award (2001); Weber Medal (2001); Chromatography Award, American Chemical Society (1999); Named, Distinguished Scholar, Hope College (1999); Helen M. Free Award, American College Of Surgeons (1998); Benedetti-Pichler Award, American Microchemical Society (1996); R&D 100 Award, R&D Magazine (1995); EPA Award (1995); Teaching Excellence Award, University of Missouri (1985, 1988-1989, 1992, 1994); Department of Energy (1984, 1987, 1991, 1994); Perkin Elmer Award (1994); Presidential Award (1993); 49th Midwest Award for Chemistry, American Chemical Society (1993); Isco Award (1992); Shell Company (1989-1992); Martin Medal (1991); Petroleum Research Fund (1979, 1991); EAS Chromatography Award (1990); Faculty Excellence Award, University of Missouri (1988-1989); Research Grantee, Whatman Corp. (1981); National Science Foundation Award (1981); Grantee, Research Corp. (1979); University of Texas Excellence in Doctoral Mentoring Award; LCGC Lifetime Achievement Award **MEM:** Fellow, National Academy of Inventors (2014); Fellow, Royal Society of Chemistry (2009); Fellow, American Association of Pharmaceutical Scientists; American Chemical Society; Royal Society of Chemistry; Sigma Xi; Phi Lambda Upsilon **MH:** Albert Nelson Marquis Lifetime Achievement Award; Marquis Who's Who Top Professional **B/I:** Dr. Armstrong became involved in his profession because he likes doing research and teaching. He has a theory that you can quantify your existence on Earth by the following questions: "Do you add anything to society that would not have been done if you did not exist?" "Did you inspire or save the life of someone who has completed the first thing?" "Have your children done anything worthwhile?" **AV:** Snow and water skiing; Hiking; Spending time with grandchildren

ARMSTRONG, GREG L., T: Chairman and Chief Executive Officer (Retired) **I:** Business Management/Business Services **CN:** Plains All American Pipeline, L.P. **ED:** BS in Accounting and Management, Southeastern Oklahoma State University (1980) **CT:** CPA (Certified Public Accountant) **C:** Co-Founder, Chairman and Chief Executive Officer, Plains All American Pipeline, L.P., Houston, Texas (1998-2019); Director, President and Chief Executive Officer, Plains Resources, Inc. (Now Plains All American Pipeline, L.P.) (1992-2001); President, Chief Operating Officer, Plains Resources, Inc. (Now Plains All American Pipeline, L.P.) (1992); Executive Vice President, Chief Financial Officer, Plains Resources, Inc. (Now Plains All American Pipeline, L.P.) (1984-1992); Corporate Secretary, Plains Resources, Inc. (Now Plains All American Pipeline, L.P.) (1981-1988); Treasurer, Plains Resources, Inc. (Now Plains All American Pipeline, L.P.) (1984-1987); With, Price Waterhouse **CR:** Director, PAA GP Holdings LLC (2019-Present); Chairman, Board of Directors, Federal Reserve Bank of Dallas (2015-Present); Board of Directors, National Oilwell Varco (2004-Present); Advisory Board, Maguire Energy Institute, Cox School of Business, Southern Methodist University; Former Chairman, National Petroleum Council; Board of Directors, Petroleum Club of Houston; Board of Trustees, Texas Southeast Region, IPAA **CIV:** Board of Trustees, The Council on Recovery, Houston, Texas;

ARMSTRONG, JEANETTE, T: Realtor **I:** Real Estate **CN:** RE/MAX Four Corners **MS:** Married **SPN:** Brian Armstrong **CH:** Corinne; Chelsea; Brendan **CT:** ABR, GRI, New Homes Sales Certification, Collin College, TX (2000); Licensed Cosmetologist, Barber/Styling, & Nail Instructor, Graham Webb International Academy of Hair (1990) **C:** Realtor, RE/MAX Four Corners, Texas (2011-Present); Real Estate Consultant, Harmon Props (2008-2011); Real Estate Consultant, Keller Williams Realty (2000-2008) **CIV:** Youth Leader President, Church Group (2007-2011); Scout Leader, Church Group; President of Woman's Organization, Church Group; The MS Society of America; The American Cancer Society **AW:** D Magazine's Best Realtors, Texas Monthly; 5 Star Agent Top 10 Dallas **MEM:** National Association of Realtors; Texas Association of Realtors; Collin County Association of Realtors; RE/MAX Hall of Fame; The Relief Society Organization **AS:** Ms. Armstrong attributes her success to how hard she works for each person. She puts all of her clients in places that she would want to live. She was raised with a high standard of ethics and believes that has had a major role in her success. **B/I:** Ms. Armstrong became involved in her profession due to the influence of her sister-in-law, who had also distinguished herself in the field. After discussing the possibility with her husband, both she and her mother-in-law enrolled in real estate school in order to obtain their licenses together.

ARMSTRONG, JENNIFER A., MD, T: Chief Executive Officer **I:** Medicine & Health Care **DOB:** 01/17/1977 **PB:** Orange County **SC:** CA/USA **PT:** Robert Armstrong **ED:** Doctor of Medicine in Dermatology, John A. Burns School of Medicine at the University of Hawaii; Residency, University of California Los Angeles; Master of Arts in Biophysics and Physiology, Georgetown University; Bachelor of Arts in Psychology, Concordia University **CT:** Fellowship, Trained Aesthetic Medicine Physician and Surgeon **C:** President, Chief Executive Officer, Jennifer Armstrong, MD (2018-Present); Chief Executive Officer, Advanced Skincare Dermatology and Plastic Surgery (2016-Present); Physician, Urgent Care of Newport Beach (2016-Present); Medical Director, Synergy Med (2017-2018); President, Managing Member, Pacific Coast Medical Group LLC (2013-2018); President, Skin Cancer Rx (2014-2016); President, Managing Member, OC Brachytherapy LLC (2013-2016); President, Managing Member, Photon Finance LLC (2013-2016) **CR:** Peer Reviewer in Optical Engineering, SPIE (2006-Present) **CIV:** FHT Foundation **AW:** Top Doctor in Aesthetic Medicine (2020); Named, Top Doctor (2019, 2020); Top Doctor in Aesthetic Medicine (2019); First Place Outstanding Presentation, Best Clinical Vignette, Society of General Internal Medicine, California Regional Meeting, University of California Irvine (2009); Nominated, Excellence In Entrepreneurship Awards, Orange County Business Journal, Orange County, CA; Best Young Investigator International Award; Award, Most Innovative Research; International Award, Best Research in Critical Care, Scientific Presentations and Awards Committee, American College of Chest Physicians; Best Young Investigators, Scientific Presentations and Awards Committee, American College of Chest Physicians; Inductee, Psi Chi; National Dean's List Undergraduate Honor Society; The Chancellor's List Graduate Honor Society; First Place, Wyoming State Art Ceramics Competition; Third Place in Wyoming State Art Sculpture Competition; Recognized, Expert in Horsemanship, State of Utah **MEM:** American Academy of Esthetic Medicine; American Medical Association **AS:** Ms. Armstrong attributes her success to her father. As a successful businessman, he inspired her to be confident enough to follow her dreams. **B/I:** Ms. Armstrong became involved in her profession because she was unable to watch people suffer. She has long been dedicated to the ideal of helping others. **THT:** Diamond is a chunk of coal that does well under pressure.

ARMSTRONG, KELLY MICHAEL, T: U.S. Representative from North Dakota **I:** Government Administration/Government Relations/Government Services **DOB:** 10/08/1976 **PB:** Dickinson **SC:** ND/USA **MS:** Married **SPN:** Kjertsi Hoiby **CH:** Two Children **ED:** JD, University of North Dakota School of Law (2003); BA, University of North Dakota (2001) **C:** Member, U.S. House of Representatives, North Dakota's At-large District (2019-Present); Chair, North Dakota Republican Party (2015-2018); Member, North Dakota Senate, 36th District, ND (20012-2018); Member, Committee on the Judiciary; Member, Committee on Oversight and Reform; Member, Select Committee on the Climate Crisis **PA:** Republican

ARNOLD, ROBERT JAMES, SLPD, MS, CCC-SLP, BCS-S, T: Chief Clinical Officer **I:** Other **CN:** Southeastern Biocommunication Associates, LLC **DOB:** 05/25/1966 **PB:** Birmingham **SC:** AL/USA **PT:** Harry Lynn Arnold; Julie (Crandall) Arnold **MS:** Divorced **SPN:** Maria Angela Pimentel (03/12/1993, Divorced) **CH:** Larissa; Karol; Esteban Tomas **ED:** Doctor of Speech-Language Pathology, Nova Southeastern University (2010); Coursework, The University of Alabama at Birmingham (1994); MS, The University of Mississippi (1990); BA, The University of Mississippi (1988) **CT:** Board Certified Specialist in Swallowing and Swallowing Disorders, American Board of Swallowing and Swallowing Disorders **C:** Chief Clinical Officer, Southeastern Biocommunication Associates, LLC, Birmingham, AL (2010-Present); Vice President of Clinical Services, Restore Therapy, Birmingham, AL (1995-2010); Direct Care Provider, Developer of Endoscopy Program, NovaCare, Rehabilitation, Birmingham, AL (1991-1995); Staff Speech Pathologist, New Medico, West Palm Beach, FL (1990) **CR:** Teacher of Continuing Education, NovaCare Rehabilitation, Birmingham, AL (1991-1995); Conductor, Workshops in Field on Medical Speech Pathology, United States and Canada **CW:** Author, Doctoral Dissertation (2010) **AW:** Distinguished Clinical Achievement Award, Speech and Hearing Association of Alabama (1995, 2010); Grant, NovaCare (1991-1992) **MEM:** American Speech-Language-Hearing Association; Speech and Hearing Association of Alabama; Associate Member, Dysphagia Research Society; The Voice Foundation **MH:** Albert Nelson Marquis Lifetime Achievement Award; Marquis Who's Who Top Professional **B/I:** Dr. Arnold became involved in his profession because he believed there was a better way to diagnose and treat physiological disorders of the upper digestive tract. **AV:** Composing music for guitar, piano and flute; Flying

ARNOLD, SIR ROBERT LLOYD MICHAEL, T: Director **I:** Environmental Services **CN:** Club Earth **DOB:** 06/18/1952 **PB:** Seattle **SC:** WA/USA **PT:** Vern Lloyd Arnold; Ruth Francis (Bruty) Arnold **MS:** Married **SPN:** Pamela **ED:** MS, Yale University (1977); BS, University of Washington, Magna Cum Laude (1975); Coursework, Bellevue College, WA (1971-1972) **CT:** Licensed Federal Securities Agent; Certified Financial Planner; IRS Enrolled Agent **C:** Founder, Club Earth, Ltd. (2016-Present); Director of Financial Services, 1st Global Advisors, Inc. (2002-Present); Owner, Fairfields, Seattle, WA (1982-Present); Senior Financial Advisor, Waddell & Reed, Inc., Bellevue, WA (1983-2001); Transportation Manager, Northwest Hydra-Line, Inc., Seattle, WA (1981-1983); General Manager, Full Value Roofing, Bellevue, WA (1979-1981); Economist, U.S. Government, Walla Walla, WA (1978-1979); Group Leader, U.S. Government, Miramonte, CA (1977-1978) **CR:** Adjunct Faculty, Professor, Graduate Courses, Financial Statement Analysis and Certified Financial Planner Program, Undergraduate Course Advertising, City University of Seattle (2007-2009); Coordinator, Charles Givens Foundation, Seattle, W (1984-1985, 1988-1990); Lecturer, Community School, Seattle, WA (1984-1991); Guest Speaker, Puyallup Kiwanis, WA (1985); Seminar Leader, Chicago Title Insurance Co., Seattle, WA (1985-1990) **CIV:** Chairman, Financial Committee, Unity Church of Seattle (Now Seattle Unity) (1988-1990); Fundraiser, The American National Red Cross, Seattle, WA (1984-1985) **CW:** Guest Speaker, Financial Strategies, KVI AM Radio (2002-Present); Contributing Author, "More Than" (2008) **AW:** Fellow, Yale University (1975-1977); Grantee, Bishop Society, Society of Teachers of Family Medicine (1974-1975); Grantee, Bloedel Foundation (1973-1974) **MEM:** Trustee, Rolls-Royce Owners Club, Pacific Northwest Region (2002-Present); Treasurer, Rolls-Royce Owners Club, Pacific Northwest Region (2002-Present); Reciprocity Committee, Rainier Club (1994-Present); Trustee, Inglewood Beach Club (1996-2000); President, Inglewood Beach Club (1995-2000); Arts and Library Committee, Rainier Club (1996-1998); President, Bellevue Mastermind Group (1996-1997); Vice President, Letip International, Inc., Eastside (1996); Vice President, Inglewood Beach Club (1996); President, Letip International, Inc., Eastside (1996); Young Rainier's Committee, Rainier Club (1994-1995); Life Member, Chairman, Seattle Delta Group (1985-1987); Treasurer, Xi Sigma Pi (1974-1975); Rainier Club; Seattle Delta Group; Letip International, Inc., Eastside; Inglewood Beach Club; Bellevue Mastermind Group; Rolls-Royce Owners Club, Pacific Northwest Region; Rotary International; Xi Sigma Pi **MH:** Albert Nelson Marquis Lifetime Achievement Award **B/I:** Mr. Arnold became involved in his profession because one of his first positions was as a junior economist for the federal government in the 70s. It was a government office, so they did not have their own space, and they had to share offices. His desk was in the corner of the office and in the other corner another economist. There were about 600 people working there and they would all come back and ask the senior economist for financial advice and he hated it. He did not like being interrupted and did not like people telling him what to do with their money, and the people sensed that and never came back. Meanwhile, he would be at his desk studying investment and thinking to himself, "ask me," so that was what inspired him to get into financial services. **AV:** Fishing; Exploring ghost towns; Classic cars **PA:** Green **RE:** Christian

ARQUETTE, PATRICIA, T: Actress, Executive Director **I:** Media & Entertainment **CN:** GiveLove **DOB:** 04/08/1968 **PB:** Chicago **SC:** IL/USA **PT:** Lewis Arquette; Brenda Olivia "Mardi" (Nowak) Arquette **MS:** Divorced **SPN:** Thomas Jane (06/25/2006-07/01/2011); Nicolas Cage (04/08/1995-05/18/2001) **CH:** Enzo Rossi; Harlow Olivia Calliope Jane **C:** Actress **CIV:** Co-Founder, Executive Director, GiveLove (2010-Present); Participant, Women's March (2017); Fundraiser, The Heart Truth, National Heart, Lung, and Blood Institute, U.S. Department of Health and Human Services (2009); Participant, Speaker, Race for the Cure, Susan G Komen (2005); Spokesperson, Lee National Denim Day (1999); Supporter, Louis Gossett, Jr.'s Eracism Foundation; Fundraiser, The Libby Ross Foundation; Supporter, The Art of Elysium **CW:** Actress, "Otherhood" (2019); Voice Actress, "Toy Story 4" (2019); Actress, "The Act" (2019); Actress, "Escape at Dannemora" (2018); Actress, "Permanent" (2017); Actress, "CSI: Cyber" (2015-2016); Actress, "Inside Amy Schumer" (2015); Actress, "The Wannabe" (2015); Actress, "CSI: Crime Scene Investigation" (2014); Actress, "Boyhood" (2014); Actress, "Electric Slide" (2014); Actress, "The Wannabe" (2014); Actress, "Boardwalk Empire" (2013-2014); Actress, "A Glimpse Inside the Mind of Charles Swan III" (2013); Actress, "Vijay and I" (2013); Actress, "Law & Order: Special Victims Unit" (2012); Actress, "Girl in Progress" (2012); Actress, "Medium" (2005-2011); Actress, "A Single Woman" (2008); Actress, "Fast Food Nation" (2006); Actress, "Deeper than Deep" (2003); Actress, "Holes" (2003); Actress, "Tiptoes" (2003); Actress, "The Badge" (2002); Actress, "Human Nature" (2001); Actress, "Little Nicky" (2000); Actress, "Stigmata" (1999); Actress, "Bringing Out the Dead" (1999); Actress, "Goodbye Lover" (1998); Actress, "The Hi-Lo Country" (1998); Actress, "Toby's Story" (1998); Actress, "Lost Highway" (1997); Actress, "Nightwatch" (1997); Actress, "Flirting with Disaster" (1996); Actress, "The Secret Agent" (1996); Actress, "Infinity" (1996); Actress, "Beyond Rangoon" (1995); Actress, "Holy Matrimony" (1994); Actress, "Ed Wood" (1994); Actress, "Wildflower, Betrayed by Love" (1994); Actress, "Trouble Bound" (1993); Actress, "Ethan Frome" (1993); Actress, "True Romance" (1993); Actress, "Inside Monkey Zetterland" (1992); Actress, "Dillinger"

(1991); Actress, "The Indian Runner" (1991); Actress, "Prayer of the Rollerboys" (1991); Actress, "Especially on Sunday" (1991); Actress, "The Girl with the Crazy Brother" (1990); Actress, "thirtysomething" (1990); Actress, "Tales From the Crypt" (1990); Actress, "Time Out" (1988); Actress, "Far North" (1988); Actress, "Daddy" (1987); Actress, "A Nightmare on Elm Street 3: Dream Warriors" (1987); Actress, "Pretty Smart" (1986) **AW:** Golden Globe Award for Best Supporting Actress – Series, Limited Series, or Television Film, Hollywood Foreign Press Association (2020); Primetime Emmy Award for Outstanding Supporting Actress in a Limited Series or Movie, Television Academy (2019); Screen Actors Guild Award for Outstanding Performance by a Female Actor in a Miniseries or Television Movie, SAG-AFTRA (2019); Critics' Choice Television Award for Best Actress in a Movie/Miniseries, The Critics Choice Association (2019); Golden Globe Award for Best Actress – Miniseries or Television Film, Television Academy (2019); Academy Award for Best Supporting Actress, Academy of Motion Picture Arts and Sciences (2015); BAFTA Award for Best Actress in a Supporting Role, British Academy of Film and Television Arts (2015); Golden Globe Award for Best Supporting Actress – Motion Picture, Hollywood Foreign Press Association (2015); Screen Actors Guild Award for Outstanding Performance by a Female Actor in a Supporting Role, SAG-AFTRA (2015); Critics' Choice Award for Best Supporting Actress, The Critics Choice Association (2015); Eyegore Award (2007); Primetime Emmy Award for Outstanding Lead Actress in a Drama Series, Television Academy (2005); CableACE Award for Actress in a Movie or Miniseries, National Cable Television Association (1993)

ARRIETA, JACOB, "JAKE" JOSEPH, T: Professional Baseball Player **I:** Athletics **CN:** Philadelphia Phillies **DOB:** 03/06/1986 **PB:** Farmington **SC:** MO/USA **PT:** Lou Arrieta; Lynda Arrieta **MS:** Married **SPN:** Brittany **CH:** Two Children **ED:** Diploma, Texas Christian University (2008); Coursework, Weatherford Junior College (2005) **C:** Pitcher, Philadelphia Phillies, MLB (2018-Present); Pitcher, Chicago Cubs, MLB (2013-2017); Pitcher, Baltimore Orioles, MLB (2010-2013); United States National Baseball Team (2006) **CW:** Appearance, "Chicago Fire" (2017); Appearance, "Veep" (2012) **AW:** First-Team All-Mountain West (2007); Pitcher of the Year Award, Mountain West Conference (2006); Second-Team College Baseball All-American

ARRINGTON, JODEY COOK, T: U.S. Representative from Texas **I:** Government Administration/Government Relations/Government Services **CN:** U.S. House of Representatives **DOB:** 3/9/1972 **PB:** Kansas City **SC:** MO/USA **PT:** Gene Arrington; Betty Arrington **MS:** Married **SPN:** Annie Arrington **ED:** Certificate of International Business Management, McDonough School of Business, Georgetown University, Washington, DC (2004); Master of Public Administration, Texas Tech University (1997); Bachelor of Arts in Political Science, Texas Tech University (1994) **C:** Member, U.S. Representative from Texas' 19th Congressional District, United States Congress, Washington, DC (2017-Present); Member, Committee on Agriculture (2017-Present); Member, Committee on Budget (2017-Present); Member, Committee on Veterans' Affairs (2017-Present); President, Scott Laboratories (2014-2017); Administrator, Texas Tech University (2007-2014); Deputy Federal Coordinator, Chief Executive Officer, Office of the Federal Coordinator for Gulf Coast Rebuilding (2005-2006); Staff, Chairperson, Federal Deposit Insurance Corporation (2001-2005); Special Assistant to President George W. Bush (2001) **AW:** Distinguished Public Service Award, 22nd Annual Center for Public Service Symposium, Lubbock, TX (2003) **MEM:** Phi Delta Theta

ARSHT, ADRIENNE, T: Founding Chairman, Chairman Emerita, Lawyer **I:** Other **CN:** The Adrienne Arsht Center **DOB:** 02/04/1942 **PB:** Wilmington **SC:** DE/USA **PT:** Samuel Arsht; Roxana (Cannon) Arsht **MS:** Widowed **SPN:** Myer Feldman (09/28/1980, Deceased 2007) **ED:** JD, Charles Widger School of Law, Villanova University (1966); BA, Mount Holyoke College (1963) **C:** Chairman Emerita, TotalBank Corporation of Florida (Now City National Bank of Florida), Miami, FL (2007-Present); Vice President, Ardman Broadcasting Corporation, Washington, DC (1984-Present); Chairman, Board, TotalBank Corporation of Florida (Now City National Bank of Florida), Miami, FL (1996-2007); President, Chairman, Board, Land Title & Escrow Corporation, Washington, DC (1981-1986); Director, Government Affairs, TWA, New York, NY (1969-1979); Associate, Bregman, Abel and Kay, Washington, DC (1979-1984); Associate, Morris, Nichols, Arsht & Tunnell LLP, Wilmington, DE (1966-1969) **CR:** Chairman, Eve Stillman Corporation, New York, NY (1989-1999); Board of Directors, Ardman, Inc., Washington, DC; Board of Directors, Capital Broadcasting, Inc., Kansas City, MO; Board of Directors, Trade National Bank, Miami, FL; Board of Directors, Eve Stillman Corporation, New York, NY; Board of Directors, Totalbank Corporation of Florida (Now City National Bank of Florida), Miami, FL; Board of Directors, Ardman Broadcasting Corporation, Washington, DC **CIV:** Founding Member, Adrienne Arsht Center Foundation (2008-Present); Founder, Arsht-Cannon Fund (2004-Present); Chairman, Board of Directors, John F. Kennedy Center for the Performing Arts (1982-Present); Board of Directors, Fit and Fabulous, Washington, DC (1992-1993); Member, Executive Committee, Georgetown Lombardi Comprehensive Cancer Center, Washington, DC (1988-1992); Founder, Chairman, Van Guard Foundation, Washington, DC (1987-1994); Board of Directors, American Ballet Theatre, Ballet Theatre Foundation, Inc., New York, NY (1984-1990); Board of Directors, Washington Opera Company (1982-1984); Member, Committee of 200, Council on Foreign Relations; U.S. Advisory Board, WIF; Member, Executive Committee, Dare to Dream Foundation; Secretary, Performing Arts Foundation, Miami, FL; Board Member, Lincoln Center; Executive Vice Chair, Atlantic Council; Member, Trustees Council, National Gallery of Art; Board Member, Blair House Restoration Fund; Member, Fine Arts Committee, United States Department of State **AW:** Distinguished Service Award, Atlantic Council (2019); Medal of Excellence, Carnegie Hall (2017); Woman of the Year, American Ballet Theatre, Ballet Theatre Foundation, Inc. (1989) **MEM:** Delaware State Bar Association; WIF; Greater Miami Chamber of Commerce; Founder, Rana Society **BAR:** Delaware State Bar Association (1966) **RE:** Jewish

ARTHUR, JOHN SCRIPTURE, MD, FACS, T: Thoracic and Vascular Surgeon **I:** Medicine & Health Care **DOB:** 11/30/1942 **PB:** Rome **SC:** NY/USA **PT:** William Maurice Arthur Jr.; Ruth Priscilla Scripture Arthur **MS:** Divorced **CH:** Kelly Allison; Rachael Kimberly; Jason Andrew; Rebecca Susan; Benjamin Douglas; Sara Gamble; Luke William; Jesse Richard **ED:** Degree in Cardio-Thoracic Surgery, University of Washington (1975); Degree in General Surgery, University of Washington (1974); Degree in Straight Surgery, University of Washington (1969); Doctor of Medicine, Albany Medical College (1968); Bachelor of Arts, Dartmouth College (1964) **CT:** Physician and Surgeon License, Washington State (1971-Present); Diplomate, American Board Surgery **C:** Clinical Associate Professor of Surgery, Department of Surgery, Vascular Division, Director of Surgical Skills and Simulation Training, University of Washington (2016-Present); Clinical Assistant Professor, Department of Surgery, Vascular Division, University of Washington (2013-2016); Clinical Assistant Professor, Department of Surgery, University of Washington (1986-2012); Surgical Private Practice, Thoracic and Vascular Surgery, Bremerton, Washington (1977-2012); Attending Staff, Department of Surgery, Thoracic & Vascular Surgeon, Harrison Memorial Hospital (1977-2010); Attending Staff, University of Washington at Harborview Medical Center, Cardio-Thoracic Surgery (2004); Attending Staff, University of Washington at Harborview Medical Center, Vascular Surgery (2003-2004); Chief of Surgery, Harrison Memorial Hospital, Bremerton (1984-1986); Attending Staff, Department of Surgery, Thoracic & Vascular Surgeon, NRMC Camp Pendleton (1975-1977) **CR:** Director, Surgical Skills and Simulation Training, Department of Surgery, Vascular Division, University of Washington, (2016-Present); Founder, Kitsap Vein Center (2003); Founder, Kitsap Vascular Laboratory (2002); Founder, Kitsap Thoracic & Vascular (2002); Founder, Narrows Vascular Laboratory (1982); Founding Member, Olympic Radiology (1981); Founder, Thoracic & Vascular Center of Kitsap County (1981) **CIV:** Board of Directors, Kitsap Community Foundation; Board of Directors, Hood Canal Environmental Council; Board of Directors, Bremerton Symphony Association **MIL:** U.S. Navy Medical Corps, Reserves (1965-1969, 1977-1987); U.S. Navy Medical Corps, Active Duty (1975-1977) **MEM:** Fellow, American College of Surgeons; Member, American Medical Association; Member, Washington State Medical Association; Founding Member, Pacific Northwest Vascular Society; Founding Member, Puget Sound Vascular Society; Founding Member, Personal Care Physicians; Member, Kitsap Medical Society; Member, University Washington Surgical Society; Member, Columbia Tower Club; Member, Bremerton Tennis and Swim Club; Brother, Kappa Sigma; Epsilon Chapter, Dartmouth College **MH:** Albert Nelson Marquis Lifetime Achievement Award; Marquis Who's Who Top Professional **AS:** Dr. Arthur attributes his success to family values and the influence of his parents, as well as the surgical wisdom and technical ability of William F. Tracy, Thomas L. Marchioro, Eugene Strandness and James R. Cantrell. Likewise, he benefited from preparation and more than a bit of good luck. **B/I:** Dr. Arthur became familiar with surgery after a childhood injury, and was constantly exposed to health-related issues through his father, a dentist. He became even more fascinated after his physics teacher, Joseph Palombi, encouraged his participation in a science fair. Finally, when faced in college with the choice to focus on football or medicine, he chose to become a doctor. **AV:** History; Americana; Classical music; Opera patron; Classic automobile collector; Amateur rugby **PA:** Independent **RE:** Baptist

ASENCIO, DIEGO C., JD, T: State Agency Administrator, Former Federal Commission Administrator, Consultant, Business Executive **I:** Government Administration/Government Relations/Government Services **DOB:** 07/15/1931 **PB:** Nijar **SC:** Spain **PT:** Manuel Asencio; Dolores Cortes **MS:** Married **SPN:** Nancy Rodriguez Asencio **CH:** Manuel; Diego Carlos; Anne Frances (Deceased); Maria; Francis Xavier **ED:** Georgetown Graduate School (1957-1958); BS in Foreign Service Degree, Georgetown Law School (1952-1953); Georgetown University School of Foreign Service (1949-1952); Georgetown University (1952); Mexico City College (1951) **C:** U.S. Ambassador, Brazil (1983-1986); Assistant Secretary for Consular Affairs, U.S. Department of

State (1980-1983); Ambassador, Colombia (1977-1980); Ambassador, American Embassy Colombia (1977-1980); Deputy Chief of Mission, American Embassy, Caracas, Venezuela (1975-1977); Political Counsellor, American Embassy Brazil (1972-1975); Political Officer Promoted to Deputy Chief of Mission, American Embassy Lisbon, Portugal (1967-1972);Special Assistant to Assistant Secretary for Interamerican Affairs, U.S. Department of State (1964-1967); Political Officer, American Embassy, Panama (1962-1964); Vice Consul in American Mexico City, Mexico (1959-1962); Underwriter, Prudential Insurance Company, Newark, NJ (1952-1955) **CR:** Executive Director, US-Spain Council (1994-1999); Latin American Adviser for McDonald's Corporation (1991-1999); Becker and Poliakoff (1994-1996); Member, Academy of Diplomacy Florida International Affairs Commission (1991-1993); Chairman, Commission of International Migration (1988-1991); Executive Director, Una Chapman Cox Foundation (1986-1987) **MIL:** Sergeant E-5, G-1, Fourth Army Headquarters, Fort Sam Houston, TX (1955-1957) **CW:** Co-Author, "Our Man Is Inside; The Joys and Perils of Serving Abroad; How I Survived The 61-Day Cocktail Party" **AW:** Department of State Director General's Cup (1990); Department of State Award for Valor (1980); Georgetown University Constantine Maguire Gold Medal **MEM:** US-Spain Council; Council on Foreign Relations; The American Academy of Diplomacy (AAD); Americas Society / Council of the Americas **B/I:** Mr. Asencio became involved in his profession because he always had it in his mind that he wanted to do diplomatic work. He went to Georgetown Foreign Service Graduate School on diplomatic matters, but that was after he was already in the foreign service. He had a professor of international law school at Georgetown, who thought of him as his protégé. When he applied for the foreign service, his professor took him aside and told him that he would do much better studying law, and that would be the way to go in particularly in international matters. He did not say anything to him and then applied to the state department and got that job. They investigated him and an agent went to see the professor and the professor was shocked that he went into the foreign service and then proceeded to kick the agent out. However, he got through that and decided that after a year of doing law that it was not for him. He wanted to do foreign service work directly. **AV:** Philately; Archeology; History; Crossword puzzles **PA:** Democrat **RE:** Roman Catholic

ASHLEY, KRISTEN, "KIT", T: Author **I:** Publishing **CN:** Rock Chick LLC **DOB:** 04/08/1968 **PB:** Gary **SC:** IN/USA **ED:** Bachelor of Arts, Purdue University (1990) **C:** Owner, Rock Chick LLC (2013-Present); Author **CIV:** Rock Chick Nation **AW:** Multiple Goodreads Choice Awards, Nominee for Best Romance; Best Romantic Suspense, RT Book Reviews; Multiple Bestseller, New York Times, USA Today and Wall Street Journal **AS:** Ms. Ashley attributes her success to her transparency in writing. People connect with her work because of how real her writing is. She does not put up a facade. **B/I:** Ms. Ashley became involved in her profession due to the influence of her mother, whom she describes as "a lioness." After attending Purdue University, she enrolled in several women's studies classes and recognized the importance of her relationships with her female friends. As a young novelist, she initially struggled to find publishers or agents who were interested in her work, and eventually decided to publish independently. Her works have been published in 15 different languages, and she has sold over three million copies. **THT:** "If women stop tearing each other down, we would rule the world, and do it a lot better than men."

ASSEO, LAUREEN, T: Founder, Chief Executive Officer **I:** Food & Restaurant Services **CN:** Fresh n' Lean **ED:** Bachelor's Degree in Apparel Manufacturing and Business Management, Fashion Institute of Design & Merchandising (2011) **C:** Founder, Chief Executive Officer, Fresh n' Lean, Chino Hills, CA (2012-Present) **CIV:** Founder, Feeding Friends (2014) **AW:** One of the 30 Under 30, Forbes (2019)

ATKINS, GENE, "GENO" REYNARD JR., T: Professional Football Player **I:** Athletics **CN:** The Cincinnati Bengals **DOB:** 03/28/1988 **PB:** Pembroke Pines **SC:** FL/USA **PT:** Gene Atkins **MS:** Married **SPN:** Kristen Merritt (06/25/2016) **ED:** Coursework, University of Georgia **C:** Professional Football Player, Defensive Tackle, The Cincinnati Bengals, National Football League (NFL) (2010-Present) **AW:** Named Eight-times, Pro Bowl (2011, 2012, 2014-2019); Twice-Named, All-Pro (2012, 2015); Invited, Second-Team All-Pro (2011); Most Valuable Defensive Player, University of Georgia (2009); John A. Addison Jr. Family Football Scholarship, University of Georgia (2007, 2009); First-team All-SEC (2007); Defensive Newcomer of the Year, University of Georgia (2006)

ATKINSON, ALANNA BETH, T: Music Educator; Church Pianist/Organist **I:** Education/Educational Services **DOB:** 07/04/1952 **PB:** Mobile **SC:** AL/USA **PT:** John Walter Atkinson; Mildred Dalton Atkinson **MS:** Single **ED:** Bachelor of Science in Music Education, University of South Alabama, Mobile, AL (1974) **C:** Piano Teacher, St. Mark Methodist School, Mobile, AL (2003-Present); Piano Teacher, Kate Shepard Elementary School, Mobile, AL (2003-Present); Private Piano Teacher, At-Home, Mobile, AL (1973-Present); Piano Teacher, Indian Springs Elementary School, Mobile, AL (1975-2003); Piano Teacher, Morningside Elementary School, Mobile, AL (1987-2001) **CIV:** Organist, Westminster Presbyterian, Mobile, AL (2002-Present); Volunteer, Music Leader, Bible School, Fulton Heights Methodist, Mobile, AL (1998-Present); Tenor Recorder, West Minister Consort, Dulcimer Player, Church, Community and Nursing Home Programs, Mobile, AL (1996-Present); Clarinetist, Mobile Pops Band (1995-Present); Member, University Southern Alabama Guitar Ensemble (2004); Member, Southern Alabama Presbyterian Cursillo (2004); Soprano, Gloria Dei Chorale (1999-2002);Organist, Forest Hill United Methodist, Mobile, AL (1984-2002); Soprano, Springhill Consort (1992-1997); Organist, Kingswood United Methodist, Mobile, AL (1974-1983); Organist, Our Savior Lutheran, Mobile, AL (1973); Crestview Community Action Group **CW:** Organ Recital, Our Savior Lutheran Church (2014) **AW:** United Methodist Women Mission Pin, Forest Hill United Methodist Church, Concord, NC (1985); United Methodist Women Mission Pin, Kingswood Methodist (1983) **MEM:** Board of Directors, American Organist Guild (1984, 1990); Treasurer, Mobile Music Teachers Association (1988-1989); Second Vice President, Mobile Music Teachers Association (1978, 1982) **MH:** Albert Nelson Marquis Lifetime Achievement Award **B/I:** Ms. Atkinson became involved in her profession due to her childhood passion for playing the piano, as well as the influence of her family. **AV:** Sewing; Cats; Dogs; Photography; Decorating; Studying local history; Travel **PA:** Democrat **RE:** Presbyterian

ATWOOD, MARGARET ELEANOR, CH CC OONT FRSC, T: Novelist, Poet **I:** Writing and Editing **DOB:** 11/18/1939 **PB:** Ottawa **SC:** ON/CA **PT:** Carl Edmund Atwood; Margaret Dorothy (Killam) Atwood **MS:** Partnered **SPN:** Graeme Gibson (1973-2019) (Deceased 2019); Jim Polk (1968-1973) **CH:** Eleanor Jess Atwood Gibson; Two stepchildren **ED:** Doctora Honoris Causa, Universidad Autónoma de Madrid, Madrid, Spain (2017); Honorary LittD, The University of Edinburgh, Edinburgh, United Kingdom (2014); Doctor Honoris Causa, School of Philosophy, National and Kapodistrian University of Athens, Athens, Greece (2013); Honorary LLD, Royal Military College of Canada, Kingston, Ontario, Canada (2012); Honorary LittD, Ryerson University, Toronto, Ontario, Canada (2012); Honorary Doctorate in Literature, National University of Ireland, Galway, Galway, Ireland (2011); Honorary LittD, Ontario College of Art & Design (Now OCAD University) (2009); Honorary Doctorate, Literary and Historical Society, University College Dublin, Dublin, Ireland (2005); Docteur Honoris Causa, Sorbonne Nouvelle, Paris, France (2005); LittD, Harvard University (2004); Honorary LittD, Dartmouth College (2004); Honorary LittD, Algoma University, Sault Ste. Marie, Ontario, Canada (2001); Honorary LittD, University of Cambridge, Cambridgeshire, United Kingdom (2001); Honorary LittD, University of Oxford, Oxford, Oxfordshire, United Kingdom (1998); Honorary LittD, Lakehead University, Thunder Bay, Ontario Canada (1998); Honorary LittD, McMaster University, Hamilton, Ontario, Canada (1996); Honorary Doctorate, University of Leeds, Leeds, West Yorkshire, United Kingdom (1994); Honorary Doctorate in Littérature Canadienne, Université de Montréal (1991); Honorary LittD, Mount Holyoke College (1985); Honorary LittD, College of Arts, University of Guelph, Guelph, Ontario, Canada (1985); Honorary LittD, University of Waterloo, Waterloo, Ontario, Canada (1985); Honorary LittD, Victoria College, University of Toronto (1983); Honorary LTD, Smith College, Northampton, MA (1982); Honorary LLD, Concordia University, Montreal, Quebec, Canada (1979); Honorary LLD, Queen's University, Kingston, Ontario, Canada (1974); Honorary LittD, Trent University, Peterborough, Ontario, Canada (1973); Coursework, Harvard University (1962-1963, 1965-1967); MA, Radcliffe College (Now Radcliffe Institute for Advanced Study), Harvard University (1962); BA in English, Minors in Philosophy and French, Victoria College, University of Toronto, with Honors (1961) **C:** Writer-in-Residence, Trinity University, San Antonio, TX (1989); Writer-in-Residence, Macquarie University, Sydney, Australia (1987); Berg Professor of English, New York University (1986); MFA Honorary Chair, The University of Alabama, Tuscaloosa, AL (1985); Writer-in-Residence, University of Toronto (1972-1973); Assistant Professor of English, York University, Toronto, Ontario, Canada (1971-1972); Faculty, University of Alberta, Edmonton, Canada (1969-1970); Instructor of English, Sir George Williams University, Montreal, Quebec, Canada (1967-1968); Lecturer in English, The University of British Columbia, Vancouver, Canada (1964-1965) **CR:** Co-Founder, President, PEN Canada, PEN International (1984-1986); President, The Writers' Union of Canada (1981-1982); Co-Founder, Writers' Trust of Canada (1976); Vice President, PEN International **CIV:** Tribute Committee, Toronto Arts Foundation; Founding Trustee, Griffin Poetry Prize **CW:** Author, "The Testaments" (2019); Author, "War Bears", Volumes 1-3 (2018); Author, "Angel Catbird," Volumes 2-3 (2017); Author, "Angel Catbird," Volume 1 (2016); Editor, "Hag-Seed" (2016); Editor, "The Heart Goes Last" (2015); Author, "Stone Mattress: Nine Tales" (2014); Author, "MaddAddam" (2013); Author, "I Dream of Zenia with the Bright Red Teeth" (2012); Author, "In Other Worlds: SF and the Human Imagination" (2011); Author, "Wandering Wenda and Widow Wallop's Wunderground Washery" (2011); Author, "The Year of the Flood" (2009); Author, "Payback: Debt and the Shadow Side of Wealth" (2008); Writer, "The Penelopiad: The Play" (2007);

Author, "The Door" (2007); Author, "Up in the Tree" (2006); Author, "Moral Disorder" (2006); Author, "Bashful Bob and Doleful Dorinda" (2006); Author, "The Tent" (2006); Author, "Writing with Intent: Essays, Reviews, Personal Prose 1983-2005" (2005); Author, "Curious Pursuits: Occasional Writing" (2005); Author, "The Penelopiad" (2005); Author, "Moving Targets: Writing with Intent 1982-2004" (2004); Author, "Bottle" (2004); Author, "Rude Ramsay and the Roaring Radishes" (2003); Author, "Oryx and Crake" (2003); Author, "Negotiating with the Dead: A Writer on Writing" (2002); Author, "The Blind Assassin" (2001); Author, "Eating Fire: Selected Poetry" (1998); Author, "Alias Grace" (1996); Author, "Princess Prunella and the Purple Peanut" (1995); Co-Editor, with Robert Weaver, "The New Oxford Book of Canadian Short Stories in English" (1995); Author, "Morning in the Burned House" (1995); Author, "Strange Things: The Malevolent North in Canadian Literature" (1995); Author, "The Robber Bride" (1993); Author, "Good Bones" (1992); Author, "Wilderness Tips" (1991); Author, "Margaret Atwood Poems 1976-1986" (1991); Author, "For the Birds" (1990); Author, "Selected Poems 1966-1984" (1990); Co-Editor, with Shannon Ravenel, "The Best American Short Stories" (1989); Editor, "The Canlit Foodbook" (1987); Author, "Selected Poems II: Poems Selected and New, 1976-1986" (1987); Co-Editor, with Robert Weaver, "The Oxford Book of Canadian Short Stories in English" (1986); Author, "The Handmaid's Tale" (1985); Author, "Interlunar" (1984); Author, "Bluebeard's Egg" (1983); Author, "Murder in the Dark" (1983); Author, "Snake Poems" (1983); Author, "Unearthing Suite" (1983); Author, "Encounters with the Element Man" (1982); Editor, "The New Oxford Book of Canadian Verse in English" (1982); Author, "Second Words: Selected Critical Prose" (1982); Author, "Bodily Harm" (1981); Author, "True Stories" (1981); Author, "Notes Towards a Poem That Can Never Be Written" (1981); Co-Author, with Joyce Barkhouse, "Anna's Pet" (1980); Author, "Life Before Man" (1979); Author, "Two-Headed Poems" (1978); Author, "Dancing Girls" (1977); Author, "Days of the Rebels 1815-1840" (1977); Author, "Marsh, Hawk" (1977); Author, "Lady Oracle" (1976); Author, "Selected Poems, 1965-1975" (1976); Author, "You Are Happy" (1974); Author, "Surfacing" (1973); Author, "Survival: A Thematic Guide to Canadian Literature" (1972); Author, "Power Politics" (1971); Author, "The Edible Woman" (1970); Author, "The Journals of Susanna Moodie" (1970); Author, "The Animals in That Country" (1968); Author, "Speeches for Doctor Frankenstein" (1966); Author, "Talismans for Children" (1965); Author, "Kaleidoscopes Baroque: A Poem" (1965); Author, "The Circle Game" (1964); Author, "Double Persephone" (1961) **AW:** On-Screen Award, The Center for Fiction, Brooklyn, NY (2019); Lifetime Achievement Award, Glamour Women of the Year Awards, Glamour, Condé Nast (2019); Burke Medal for Outstanding Contribution to Discourse Through the Arts, College Historical Society, Trinity College Dublin (2019); Booker Prize for Fiction, Booker Prize Foundation (2000, 2019); Honoree, VH1 Trailblazer Honors, Viacom International Inc. (2019); LARB/UCR Creative Writing Lifetime Achievement Award, University of California, Riverside (2019); Lorne Pierce Medal, Royal Society of Canada (2018); Adrienne Clarkson Prize for Global Citizenship, Institute for Canadian Citizenship (2018); Ulysses Medal, University College Dublin (2018); Academy Board of Directors' Tribute, Academy of Canadian Cinema & Television (2018); Order of the Companions of Honour (2018); Raymond Chandler Award, Courmayeur Noir Film Festival, Courmayeur, Italy (2017); Luminary Award, The Daughters for Life Foundation (2017); Aurora Award for Best Graphic Novel, Canadian Science Fiction and Fantasy Association (2017); Lifetime Achievement Award, PEN Center USA, PEN International (2017); Franz Kafka International Literary Prize, Spolecnost Franze Kafky (2017); Friedenspreis des Deutschen Buchhandels, Börsenverein des Deutschen Buchhandel, Germany (2017); Carl Sandburg Literary Award, Chicago Public Library (2017); St. Louis Literary Award, Saint Louis University Library Associates, Saint Louis University (2017); Ivan Sandrof Award for Lifetime Achievement, National Book Critics Circle (2017); Pinter Prize, English PEN (2016); Golden Wreath Award, Struga Poetry Evenings, Macedonia (2016); Kitschies Red Tentacle Award for Most Progressive, Intelligent and Entertaining Novel of the Year, Blackwell's Ltd (2016); Gold Medal of Honorary Patronage, University Philosophical Society, Trinity College Dublin, Ireland (2016); Gold Medal, The Royal Canadian Geographical Society (2015); Arthur C. Clarke Award for Imagination in Service to Society, The Arthur C. Clarke Foundation (2015); Arthur Ellis Award for Best Short Story, Crime Writers of Canada (2015); Barnes & Noble Writers for Writers Award, Poets & Writers (2015); Library Lion Honoree, The New York Public Library (2014); Medal for Distinguished Achievement, Institute for the Arts and Humanities, The Pennsylvania State University (2014); Aster Award, Toronto Botanical Garden (2014); Orion Book Award, Orion Magazine (2014); Harvard Arts Medal, Office for the Arts, Harvard University (2014); President's Medal, BirdLife International (2013); Heart & Vision Award, Toronto United Church Council (2013); Innovator's Award, L.A. Times Book Prizes, Festival of Books (2013); Literary Award, Nashville Public Library Foundation (2012); Lifetime Achievement Award, Canadian Booksellers Association (2012); Queen Elizabeth II Golden Jubilee Medal, The Governor General of Canada (2012); Sun Life Financial Arts and Communications Award, Canada's Most Powerful Women: Top 100, Women's Executive Network (2011); Nelly Sachs Prize, Dortmund, Germany (2010); Dan David Prize for Literature, Dan David Foundation (2010); Crystal Award, World Economic Forum (2010); Prince of Asturias Award for Literature, Fundación Princesa de Asturias, Spain (2008); Kenyon Review Award for Literary Achievement Award, The Kenyon Review (2007); Blue Metropolis International Literary Grand Prize, Metropolis Bleu, Montreal, Canada (2007); Order of the Forest, Markets Initiative (Now Canopy) (2006); Chicago Tribune Literary Prize, Chicago Tribune (2005); Enlightenment Award, The Edinburgh International Book Festival Ltd (2005); National Arts Award, Banff Centre (2005); Harold Washington Literary Award, Near South Planning Board (2003); Radcliffe Medal, Harvard University (2003); People's Choice Award, Canadian Booksellers Association (2001); Hammett Prize, International Crimewriters Association (2001); Peggy V. Helmerich Distinguished Author Award, Tulsa City County Library (1999); Best Fiction of the Year, Salon Magazine (1997); Premio Letterario Internazionale Mondello, Italy (1997); Medal of Honor for Literature, The National Arts Club (1996); Author of the Year, Canadian Booksellers Association (1989, 1996); Giller Prize (1996); Norwegian Order of Literary Merit (1996); Trillium Book Award, Province of Ontario (1992, 1994, 1995); Sunday Times Award for Literary Excellence, Times Newspapers Limited, London, United Kingdom (1994); Chevalier dans l'Ordre des Arts et des Lettres, Government of France (1994); Novel of the Year, Canadian Authors Association (1993); 125th Anniversary of the Confederation of Canada Medal, The Governor General of Canada (1992); Book of the Year Award, Periodical Marketers of Canada (Now The Book and Periodical Council) (1992); John Hughes Prize, Welsh Development Board (1992); Centennial Medal, Harvard University (1990); Order of Ontario (1990); Outstanding Canadian Award, Armenian Community Centre of Toronto (1989); Book of the Year, Foundation for the Advancement of Canadian Letters, Periodical Marketers of Canada (Now The Book and Periodical Council) (1983, 1989); Coles Book of the Year (1989); Toronto Book Award, City of Toronto (1977, 1989); Torgi Award, CNIB (1989); National Magazine Award for Environmental Journalism, NMAF, Ontario Arts Council (1988); Women of Distinction Award, YWCA Toronto (1988); Fellow, Royal Society of Canada (1987); Prometheus Award, Libertarian Futurist Society (1987); Humanist of the Year Award, American Humanist Association (1987); Regional Winner, Commonwealth Writers' Prize for Best Book, Commonwealth Foundation (1987); Arthur C. Clarke Award for Best Science Fiction, The Arthur C. Clarke Foundation (1987); Woman of the Year, Ms. Magazine (1986); Los Angeles Times Book Prize for Fiction, Festival of Books (1986); Governor General's Award for English-Language Fiction, The Governor General of Canada (1986); Toronto Arts Award (1986); Ida Nudel Humanitarian Award (1986); National Magazine Award for Travel Writing, NMAF, Ontario Arts Council (1983); International Writer's Prize, Art Council of Wales (1982); Companion of the Order of Canada (1981); Fellowship in Fiction, John Simon Guggenheim Memorial Foundation (1981); Molson Prize, Canada Council for the Arts (1981); Radcliffe Graduate Society Medal, Harvard University (1980); St. Lawrence Award for Fiction (1978); Award for Short Fiction, Periodical Distributors of Canada (1977); CBA Award, Canadian Booksellers Association (1977); Bess Hoskins Prize for Poetry, Chicago, IL (1974); Officer, Order of Canada (1973); Union Poetry Prize, Chicago, IL (1969); Winner, Centennial Commission Poetry Competition (1967); Governor General's Award for Literary Merit, The Governor General of Canada (1966); President's Medal, University of Western Ontario (Now Western University) (1965); E.J. Pratt Medal in Poetry, University of Toronto (1961) **MEM:** Order of the Companions of Honour (2018-Present); Honorary Member, American Academy of Arts and Letters (2015-Present); Companion, Royal Society of Literature, London, United Kingdom (2012-Present); Honorary Fellow, The Royal Canadian Geographical Society (2007-Present); Order of Ontario (1990-Present); Foreign Honorary Member, Literature, American Academy of Arts and Sciences (1988-Present); Fellow, Royal Society of Canada (1987-Present); Honorary Co-President, Rare Bird Club, BirdLife International

AULL, ELIZABETH BERRYMAN, T: Chair, Hazardous Waste Management Commission **I:** Government Administration/Government Relations/Government Services **CN:** State of Missouri **PB:** Independence **SC:** MO/USA **PT:** Homer Aull; Mary Aull **ED:** Diploma, American Economic Development Institute, University of Oklahoma (1992); Coursework, Northwestern University, Evanston, IL (1991); MBA Coursework, Drury College (1985-1988); BS, University of Missouri (1973); AA, Christian College (1971) **CT:** Real Estate License, State of Missouri (1973-2002) **C:** Chair, Hazardous Waste Management Commission, State of Missouri (2016-2020); Recycling Coordinator, Nestle Purina PetCare, North America (2002-2018); Department of Natural Resources, Hazardous Waste Commission, State of Missouri (2007-2008); Consultant, Real Estate Development (1996-2001); Industrial and Market Development Manager, Burlington Northern Railroad, Fort Worth, TX (1991-1995);

Industrial Development Manager, Burlington Northern Railroad, Omaha, NE (1989-1991); Director of Property Management, Glacier Park Company Subsidiary, Burlington Northern, Inc. (1987-1988); Senior Property Management Specialist, Burlington Northern Inc., Springfield, MO (1984-1987); Industrial Development Representative, Springfield, Saint Louis, MO (1980-1984); Industrial Development/Real Estate Agent, Saint Louis-San Francisco Railway Co. (1978-1980); Rate Routing Analyst, Missouri Pacific Railroad, Saint Louis, MO (1976-1978); Administrative Assistant, Bingham Sketches, Inc., Saint Louis, MO (1976); Administrative Assistant, Executive Director's Office, Bi-State Development Agency, Saint Louis, MO (1974-1976); Missouri Senate Staff (1974); Missouri Department of Revenue (Senior Citizen Property Tax Relief Program, Public Information), Jefferson City, MO (1973) CR: Author, "Target Marketing as an Economic Development Tool" CIV: Master Gardener, University of Missouri Extension, Columbia, MO (1996-2015); Greeting Card Chairman, UNICEF Committee, Southwest Missouri (1997); Vision 20/20, Springfield-Greene County (1995-1996); Junior League, Fort Worth, TX (1992); Junior League, Omaha, NE (1989-1992); Chairman, Building Subcommittee, Ozark Food Harvest, Springfield Council of Churches (1987-1988); Junior League, Springfield, MO (1984-1988); Mental Health Association of Ozarks, Springfield, MO (1983-1987); Board Member, Mental Health Associations, State of Missouri (1982-1986); Board of Directors, Independence Center, Saint Louis, MO (1982-1983); President, Greater Saint Louis Area Christian College Alumni Association (1981-1983); Junior League, Saint Louis, MO (1980-1983); Chair, Junior League Project for Independence Center; Missouri State Historical Society CW: Author, Presenter, "The Beginning of Our Country in Jamestown, Virginia, and the Creation of Williamsburg, Virginia" (2000-2005); Presenter, Developer, Symposium on Mental Health Issues (1982) AW: Waste District Award for Recycling Education (2003); Who's Who in America (2001); Listee, Outstanding Young Women of America (1980-1981, 1978) MEM: Daughters of the American Revolution; National Society of Daughters of the American Colonists; Colonial Dames of the 17th Century; German, Austrian and Swiss Society; Lifetime Member, Northern Neck of Virginia Historical Society; Missouri Historical Society; Pachyderms MH: Albert Nelson Marquis Lifetime Achievement Award AS: Ms. Aull attributes her success to having excellent Christian parents who encouraged her to succeed. Likewise, her mother's and father's genes combined to give her a ruthless curiosity, for which she is ever thankful. B/I: Ms. Aull liked to ride trains as a child. Her parents took her on vacations every summer. Ms. Aull's parents taught her to garden and recycle when she was quite young. She read Rachel Carson's "Silent Spring" when it was first published, which has served as an inspiration to her ever since. She has always been passionate about the environment. In school, she worked on an environmental study with a group in order to complete a research paper. This experience strengthened her knowledge and her acumen in dealing with business issues. AV: Researching genealogy; Participating at local church; Studying colonial English history; Herb gardening PA: Republican RE: Anglican Church of North America THT: Ms. Aull believes in being kind and helping others to make the world a better place.

AURNER, ROBERT RAY, T: President, Chief Executive Officer **I:** Real Estate **CN:** Aurner and Associates Retail Land Development Consultants **DOB:** 03/24/1927 **PB:** Madison **SC:** WI/USA **PT:** Robert Ray Aurner; Kathryn (Dayton) Aurner

MS: Divorced **SPN:** Deborah Marion Lucas (01/31/1976, Divorced 1999); Phyllis Barrett (1951, Divorced 1966) **CH:** Sheryl; Roxanne; Kathryn; Suzanne; Robert III; Lucas; Christopher **ED:** BA, California State University, Fresno, CA (1950); BA, Occidental College, Eagle Rock, CA (1950); AA, Monterey Peninsula College (1949); Postgraduate Coursework, Duquesne University, Pittsburgh, PA; Postgraduate Coursework, University of California Berkeley, CA **CT:** Licensed in Real Estate, State of California; Licensed in Real Estate, Commonwealth of Pennsylvania; Licensed in Real Estate, State of New York; Registered Investment Advisor **C:** National Director of Real Estate, Consultant of Store Development, Nathan's Famous Coney Island Hot Dog Restaurants, Inc. (Now Nathan's Famous, Inc.), New York, NY (1990-1991); Real Estate Manager, Kentucky Fried Chicken and Pizza Hut Divisions (Now Yum! Brands RSC), PepsiCo Metro Standard Metropolitan Statistical Area (1987-1990); Restaurant Division, Pillsbury Companies (Now General Mills), NY, NJ, PA and CT (1977-1987); Manager, Real Estate Store Development, Pittsburgh Division, Supermarkets, Atlantic and Pacific Tea Company (A&P) (1974-1977); Manager, Site Development, Milex Auto Diagnostic Tune-Up and Brakes, Inc. (Milex Complete Auto Care), Plymouth Meeting, PA (1972-1974); Manager of Operations, Eastern Division, Sunray DX Oil Company (Sunmarks, LLC), Tulsa, OK (1967-1972); Director of Development, Central California Coast Service Station, Gulf Oil Corporation (Gulf Oil L.P.) (1960-1967); Senior Sales Supervisor, Shell Oil Company (Now Shell Global), San Francisco, CA (1952-1960); Announcer, Radio Station WSUI, Iowa City, Iowa (1946-1948); Real Estate Administrator, Store Development, Northeast Region, Steak and Ale, Bennigan's Restaurant Division, Pillsbury Companies (Now General Millls); Real Estate Manager, New York and Philadelphia Regions, Burger King Corporation **CR:** Chairman, Board of Directors, Aurner and Associates, Retail Land Development Consultants, Carmel, CA (1990-Present); President and Chief Executive Officer, Aurner and Associates, Retail Land Development Consultants, Carmel, CA (1987-Present); Founder, Trader Bob Fashions, Inc., Carson City, NV (1997); Tower Development Consultant, Nextel Wireless Telecommunications Corporation (Now Sprint), NJ (1994-1995); Supervisor, Shell Oil Companies (Now Shell Global), San Francisco, CA; Career Counselor, United States Coast Guard Academy and Public Affairs; Founder, Chairman, Board of Directors, President, Chief Executive Officer, Bristlecone Trading and Development, Inc. (Now Bristlecone, Inc.), Carmel, CA **CIV:** District Chairman, Nominating Committee, District 25, Boat Show (2006-Present); Elected Member, District 25 Bridge (2010); Squadron Commander, Monterey Bay Sail & Power Squadron, United States Power Squadrons Headquarters, Raleigh, NC (2005-2007); Division Chairman, National Safe Boating Week, United States Coast Guard Auxiliary (2001-2008); Officer and Flotilla Commander, Flotilla 6-4, United States Coast Guard Auxiliary, Coast Guard Station, Monterey, CA (2000-2009); Staff Administrative Officer, United States Power Squadrons, San Francisco, CA **MIL:** Plans and Tactics Officer, United States Navy (1944-1946); With, United States Naval Reserve, WWII **AW:** Named to Honorable Order of Kentucky Colonels, Governor of Kentucky; Named Commodore in Oklahoma Navy, Governor Johnston Murray **MEM:** Secretary, Board of Directors, Carmel Valley Chamber of Commerce, Carmel, CA (1999-2003); Moss Landing Harbor Safe Boating Committee; Moss Landing Chamber of Commerce; Navy League of the United States, Monterey Peninsula, CA; U.S. Ship Yellowstone Association; Compari Club, Monterey Peninsula; Monterey Peninsula Yacht Club, CA; President, Buccaneer Club, NY and

CT; Rotary Club of Monterey, CA; Pacheco Club, Monterey Peninsula, CA; Elkhorn Yacht Club; Monterey Elks Club; Sigma Alpha Epsilon Fraternity **MH:** Albert Nelson Marquis Lifetime Achievement Award; Marquis Who's Who Top Professional **AS:** Mr. Aurner attributes his success to his drive and focus. **PA:** Republican **RE:** Episcopalian **THT:** Mr. Aurner has spoken at city councils, supervisory boards, and attorney groups. Mr. Aurner's grandparents, father, and uncle were all PhD recipients.

AUSTIN, NEIL, T: Lighting Designer **I:** Media & Entertainment **DOB:** 07/22/1972 **SC:** London/United Kingdom **PT:** Anthony Charles Austin; Patricia Anne (Daly) Austin **ED:** Diploma, Guildhall School of Music & Drama, London, United Kingdom; Diploma, St. Paul's School, London, United Kingdom **C:** Lighting Designer (1992-Present) **AW:** Tony Award for Best Lighting Design in a Play, "Ink," American Theatre Wing Inc. (2019); Knight of Illumination Award for Best Lighting Design (Musical Theatre), "Company" (2019); Helpmann Award for Best Lighting Design, "Harry Potter and the Cursed Child" (2019); Tony Award for Best Lighting Design in a Play, "Harry Potter and the Cursed Child," American Theatre Wing Inc. (2018); Drama Desk Award for Outstanding Lighting Design for a Play, "Harry Potter and the Cursed Child" (2018); Outer Critics Circle Award for Outstanding Lighting Design, "Harry Potter and the Cursed Child" (2018); Laurence Olivier Award for Best Lighting Design, "Harry Potter and the Cursed Child," Society of London Theatre (2017); WhatsOnStage Award for Best Lighting Design, "Harry Potter and the Cursed Child" (2017); Falstaff Award for Best Lighting Design, "The Winter's Tale" (2015); Falstaff Award for Best Lighting Design, "Macbeth" (2013); Knight of Illumination Award for Best Lighting Design (Musical Theatre), "Company" (2012); Laurence Olivier Award for Best Lighting Design, "The White Guard," Society of London Theatre (2011); Tony Award for Best Lighting Design in a Play, "Red," American Theatre Wing Inc. (2010); Drama Desk Award for Outstanding Lighting Design for a Play, "Red" (2010); LDI Award for Excellence in Lighting Design, "Red" and "Hamlet" (2010); Backstage Garland Award for Lighting Design, "Parade" (2010); Knight of Illumination Award for Best Lighting Design (Musical Theatre), "Parade" (2008)

AVALLONE, ANTHONY F., T: Retired Lawyer **I:** Law and Legal Services **DOB:** 11/05/1926 **PB:** Mount Vernon **SC:** NY/USA **PT:** Frank P. Avallone; Mary T. (Anechiarico) Avallone **MS:** Widowed **SPN:** Edith M. Tese (Deceased) **CH:** Mary; Camille; Elizabeth; Claire; Frank; Anthony; Michael; Joseph **ED:** LLB, Columbia University (1952) **C:** Retired (1999); Private Practice, West Nyack, NY (1968-1999); Private Practice, Las Cruces, NM (1958-1967); Private Practice, Mount Vernon (1956-1958) **MIL:** Captain, U.S. Army Reserve (1947) **MEM:** New Mexico Bar Association **BAR:** United States District Court for the District of New Mexico (1968); New Mexico (1968); United States District Court for the District of New York (1960); New York (1956) **MH:** Albert Nelson Marquis Lifetime Achievement Award; Marquis Who's Who Top Professional **AS:** He attributes his success to dedication to doing the best possible job he could, nothing less than that. **B/I:** Mr. Avallone's goal pursuit came from his father's encouragement and the challenge of law. In addition, Mr. Avallone chose to become a lawyer because it was a challenge, and he met that challenge in so many ways. He told his father he wanted to be a lawyer, then he inquired and he found out that in order to be a lawyer when he got out of the army he would have to go to school. He only had five semesters in college that meant he would have to be in college another year and a half. He checked out the GI bill and he would have to have money in order to finish law school. He complained about the circumstances to his father, his father said he needed advise and advised him to go see a friend of his who attended Columbia. Mr. Avallone went to visit his father's friend, he asked how well his grades were, he was an A student. This gentleman gave him a letter introducing him to the Dean of Columbia. He went down to Columbia and met with the dean, he was asked to come back the following day to take a six hour intelligence exam. The following week he received a letter stating that he was admitted to Columbia without an undergraduate degree. This was based on simple determination. **AV:** Philosophy; Gardening; Cooking; Talking **PA:** Democrat **RE:** Catholic

AVANT, CLARENCE, "THE BLACK GODFATHER" ALEXANDER, T: Music Producer; Entrepreneur; Film Producer **I:** Media & Entertainment **DOB:** 02/25/1931 **PB:** Climax **SC:** NC/USA **ED:** Coursework, Dudley High School, Greensboro, SC **C:** Founder, Tabu Productions, Los Angeles, CA (1975-1991); Owner, Avant Garde Broadcasting Inc. (1971-1975); Founder, Sussex Records, Los Angeles, CA (1966-1975); Founder, Venture Records (1967-1969); Owner, Avant Garde Enterprises Inc., CA (1962); Consultant, PlayTape, MGM Records; Manager, Teddy P's Lounge, Newark, NJ; Manager, Several Artists Including Little Willie John, Sarah Vaughan, Kim Weston, Luiz Bonfa, Wynton Kelly, Freddie Hubbard, Curtis Fuller, Pat Thomas, Tom Wilson, Creed Taylor, Jimmy Smith and Lalo Schifrin **CR:** Law Directory; Stock Clerk, Macy's **CIV:** Advisor, Board Member and Executive, National Association of Radio Announcers (NARA)/National Association of Television and Radio Announcers (NATRA) (Now National Association of Broadcasters); Consultant, PlayTape; Fundraiser, Democratic Campaigns **CW:** Executive Producer, "Save the Children" (1973); Associate Producer, "The Reckoning" (1969) **AW:** President's Merit Award as a Grammy Icon, The Recording Academy (2018); Star, Hollywood Walk of Fame (2016); Trustees Award, National Association of Recording Arts and Sciences (Now The Recording Academy) (2008); Featured, Billboard Magazine (2006)

AXNE, CYNTHIA, "CINDY" LYNNE, T: U.S. Representative from Iowa **I:** Government Administration/Government Relations/Government Services **DOB:** 04/20/1965 **PB:** Grand Rapids **SC:** MI/USA **PT:** Terry Wadle; Joanne Wadle **MS:** Married **SPN:** John Axne **CH:** Two Sons **ED:** MBA, Northwestern University Kellogg School of Management; BA in Journalism, University of Iowa **C:** Member, U.S. House of Representatives from Iowa's Third Congressional District (2019-Present); Service Delivery, Government of Iowa (2005-2014); Leadership Development and Strategic Planning, Tribune Company (Now Nexstar Media Group), Chicago, IL; Member, Committee on Agriculture; Member, United States House Committee on Financial Services **PA:** Democrat **RE:** Catholic

AYERS, RENDALL P., T: Public Relations Consultant **I:** Advertising & Marketing **DOB:** 08/25/1937 **PB:** Wichita Falls **SC:** TX/USA **PT:** Richard Kelly Ayers; Gertrude Christine (Paul) A. Ayers **MS:** Married **SPN:** Sara Lee Ayers (08/27/1960) **CH:** Sydney Lynn; Reed A. **ED:** BA in Journalism, University of Colorado (1961) **C:** Owner, Ayers Public Relations (2009-2010); President, Ayers Communications, Inc., Denver, CO (1997-2009); Chairman, Darcy Communications, Inc., Denver, CO (1988-1996); Partner, Ayers, Grimm, Starzel & Associates, Denver, CO (1985-1987); Principal, Rendall Ayers Public Relations, Denver, CO (1980-1987);

President, William Kostka & Associates Public Relations, Denver, CO (1975-1980); Public Relations Manager, Denver Division, Safeway Stores, Inc. (1970-1974); District Manager, Insurance Information Institute, Denver, CO (1968-1969); Assistant City Editor, Denver Post (1962-1967); Assistant Bureau Chief, Associated Press, Helena, MT (1960-1961) **CR:** Lecturer in Field **CIV:** Board of Directors, Ronald McDonald House Charities, Colorado (2010-2011); Board of Directors, Design Council of the Denver Art Museum (2006); Colorado Humanities (1998-2003); Director, Colorado Chapter, American Parkinson Disease Association (1993-1996); Vice President, Hope for the Children (1987-1988); Kempe Center for the Prevention and Treatment of Child Abuse and Neglect (1984-1987); Board of Directors, Goodwill Industries Denver (1970-1984); Board of Directors, Men's Assistance Center (1970-1982); Board of Directors, Colorado Retail Council (1972-1974); Board of directors, Colorado Heart Association (1970-1980); Chairman, Colorado Heart Fund Campaign (1971-1973) **MIL:** With, U.S. Army Reserve (1960-1968) **AW:** Lifetime Achievement Award, Colorado Chapter, Public Relations Society of America, Inc. (2002); Outstanding Volunteer Award Colorado Heart Association (1973); Award for Outstanding Reporting, Denver Newspaper Guild (1966) **MEM:** President, Colorado Chapter, Public Relations Society of America, Inc. (1978); Fellow, Public Relations Society of America, Inc.; Mount Vernon Country Club; Meadow Creek Racquet Club (Denver); Sigma Delta Chi; Alpha Delta Sigma **MH:** Albert Nelson Marquis Lifetime Achievement Award **B/I:** Mr. Ayers became involved in his profession because his father was involved in public relations so he knew of the job at a fairly young age. The newspaper aspect was something he truly loved because every day was new, different and extremely interesting. But, he also realized, being a journalist, you have a great obligation to be reflecting a true and accurate picture of everything you observed and reported to your readers. You could not/should not distort the image of what you say and what you write in the newspaper. He felt very strict about that. He also realized the world kind of went by and he wasn't doing anything about the world as it went by. He felt that in public relations he had an opportunity to change the direction or things, whether it was for the better or the worse based ones ethics/morals. **AV:** Playing tennis; Global traveling all continents; Photography; Hiking **PA:** Democrat **RE:** Episcopal

AYOUB, ELSA, T: Lawyer **I:** Law and Legal Services **CN:** Law Offices Elsa Ayoub, PLLC **DOB:** 09/24/1978 **PB:** Beirut **SC:** Lebanon **PT:** H.E. Gharamy Ayoub; Marcelle Ayoub **MS:** Married **CH:** Three Children **ED:** LLM in International Legal Studies, American University, Washington College of Law (2002); JD and Master's Degree, International Private Law, Universite Paris II, Pantheon-Assas Droi International Prive, Paris, France (2001); Licence en droit, Universite Pantheon Assas (2000); Baccalaureate in French Literature, Academy of Paris (1996) **C:** Attorney at Law, The Law Offices of Elsa Ayoub, PLLC (2012-Present); Of Counsel, Mccormick & O'Brien LLP (2009-2011); Of Counsel, Gleason & Koatz LLP (2004-2009); Attorney at Law, Schulte Roth & Zabel, LLP, New York, NY (2004); Attorney at Law, Shamy & Shamy Law Offices, New Brunswick, NJ (2003-2004) **CR:** Consultant Embassy, Consulate General of Lebanon, New York, NY (2003-Present); 1010 WINS Town Hall on Immigration Panel of Experts (2018); Lead, CRE Class, The EB-5 Program CRE Lecture (2014); Sharon Barnes Waters Host of City Views **CW:** Author, "The EB-5 Program and its Relevancy to Purchasing Real Estate" Article, Immigration Law Expert Guide,

United Kingdom (2019); Author, "The EB-5 Program and its Relevancy to Purchasing Real Estate" Article, Mann Report (2013) **AW:** Top Immigration Attorney, IAOTP International Association of Top Professionals (2019); Top 3% of Lawyers in the Nation; Lawyers of Distinction (2019); Super Lawyers (2013-2019); Crain's New York Business Leading Women in NYC, Top 100 Lawyers (2018); American Institute of Legal Counsel 10 Best Immigration Attorneys (2016-2018); Corporate LiveWire – Global Awards Immigration Law (2016, 2017); Distinguished Lawyer Designation©, Expert Network (2016) **MEM:** American Immigration Lawyers Association; International Association of Top Professionals; New York State Bar **BAR:** New York (2003) **AS:** Mostly because she went through the immigration process herself as a foreign student so she knows what people expect. You have to be competent and knowledgeable in what you do, but what she feels what sets her apart is that she tries to find a solution always. Creativity and the fact that she knows how personal and how much it matters to people. **B/I:** Mrs. Ayoub was inspired to become an attorney because of her father. Before he retired he was a diplomat so she grew up in embassy's all over Europe and the world. So even though she wanted to go into international commercial arbitration people wanted her to help. One thing lead to another she ended up working and specializing in the field because of her childhood. She developed an interest by chance and not something she had anticipated when she was still in school. **AV:** Travel; Politics **RE:** Maronite

AYRES, STEVEN D., T: Real Estate Broker; Investor **I:** Real Estate **DOB:** 07/06/1948 **PB:** Atlanta **SC:** GA/USA **PT:** Thelbert Grenoble Ayres; Blanche (Seignious) Ayres **MS:** Married **SPN:** Elizabeth Ann Hill (07/01/1978) **CH:** Heather; Stephanie; Benjamin **ED:** Postgraduate Coursework, Mercer University (1970-1971); BBA, Emory University (1970); AA, Oxford College of Emory University (1968) **CT:** Real Estate Broker, State of Georgia; Licensed Private Pilot **C:** Broker, Owner, Ayres Realty Co., Lithia Springs, GA (1971-Present); With, King & Spalding Law Firm, Atlanta, GA (1968-1970); Owner, Ayresouth Aviation, Inc. **CIV:** President, Lithia Springs Ruritan Club (1974); President, Douglas County Chamber of Commerce (1974) **MIL:** With, United States Air Force ROTC, Emory University **CW:** Author, Illustrator, Publisher, "The Glory Road" (2019); Author, Illustrator, Publisher, "Under the Wedding Tree" (2012); Author, Illustrator, Publisher, "We Danced Until Dawn" (2008); Author, Illustrator, Publisher, "Fallow are the Fields" (2004); Author, Illustrator, Publisher, Historical Novels – Trilogy **AW:** Audio/Visual Promotional Presentation Award, "Welcome to Douglas County Georgia," Douglas County Chamber of Commerce (1975); Recipient, Various Civic Awards and Recognitions **MEM:** President, West Georgia Board of Realtors (1978); Aircraft Owners and Pilots Association; Experimental Aircraft Association; Ercoupe Owners Club; Vintage Aircraft Association; Antique Aircraft Association; Masons, Battle Hill Lodge #523; EAA Chapter 976 West Georgia **MH:** Albert Nelson Marquis Lifetime Achievement Award **AS:** Mr. Ayres attributes his success to hard work, tenacity, a spirit of adventure and helping his fellow man. He also credits his loving parents, who taught him the value and meaning of life and a dollar, and a good wife and family, in addition to a good education. **B/I:** Mr. Ayres became involved in his profession because he was in law school studying to be a lawyer and he felt he was going to school all his life and was interested in working instead. His family was in the real estate business at the time, and by default, he went into the business. Within three years, he got his broker's license, and eventually took over the family business. He has been in the business for over 50 years and has found it to be very fulfilling. The business is over 60 years old. **AV:** Civil war history; Flying; Music; Art; Swimming; Horseback riding; Farming; Motorcycle riding and touring **PA:** Republican **RE:** Baptist by Faith **THT:** Mr. Ayres' 1975 award, the Audio/Visual Promotional Presentation Award, "Welcome to Douglas County Georgia," from the Douglas County Chamber of Commerce was used at the opening of the Atlanta Georgia World Congress Center and other venues in promotion of Douglas County, Georgia.

AZARPAY, GUITTY, T: Education, Educator (Retired) **I:** Education/Educational Services **DOB:** 10/28/1939 **PB:** Teheran **SC:** Iran **PT:** Rahim Azarpey; Shekar Dowlatshahi **MS:** Widowed **SPN:** Ralph Werner Alexander (12/18/1963, Deceased 1998); Ronald Antonioli **CH:** Vesa Alexander Becam **ED:** PhD, University of California Berkeley (1964) **C:** Retired (1994); Professor, University of California Berkeley Graduate School (1994); Professor, University of California Berkeley (1963-1994) **CW:** Member, Editorial Board, Encyclopaedia Iranica (1994-Present); Author, "Sasanian Sealstone: An Electronic Cataloging Project" (2002); Author, "Sogdian Painting" (1981); Author, "Urartian Art & Artifacts" (1969) **AW:** Award, National Endowment for the Humanities (1970-1971, 1971-1972); Travel Grants, American Philosophical Society, and UCLA Center for Near Eastern Studies (1967); Award, AIA, University of California Press **MEM:** American Institute of Archaeology (Archaeological Institute of America); American Oriental Society; Bulletin of the Asia Institute **MH:** Albert Nelson Marquis Lifetime Achievement Award **B/I:** Dr. Azarpay first went to the University of California when she finished high school in England. She was always interested in art and so on, but she didn't know about the history of art. She had a very helpful instructor by the name of Author Maenchen-Helfen. He was a professor of the history of Chinese art, in the art history department. He never had a PhD student; she was his first and last PhD student because he retired. **AV:** Chess; Hiking

AZIZ, EMAD, T: Director of Cardiac Electrophysiology **I:** Medicine & Health Care **CN:** Mount Sinai St. Luke's Hospital (Now Mount Sinai Morningside) **CH:** One Child **ED:** MB, CHB in Medicine, Columbia University, NY (2007); MD in Osteopathic Medicine, New York Institute of Technology College of Osteopathic Medicine, NY (2004); MB, CHB in Medicine, Alexandria University (1987) **C:** Chief of Cardiac Electrophysiology, Director of Arrhythmia Institute, Rutgers New Jersey Medical School (2019-Present); Clinical Cardiac Electrophysiologist, St. Luke's-Roosevelt Hospital (Now Mount Sinai Morningside) and Mount Sinai West Hospital (2010-Present); Director, ACAP Cardiac Research Group, St. Luke's-Roosevelt Hospital (Now Mount Sinai Morningside), NY (2004-Present) **MEM:** President, Executive Board, Egyptian American Medical Society **AS:** Dr. Aziz is very dedicated. He also has a great support system around him. He is a man of faith and he believes his faith has led him through many tough situations to continue moving forward in life. He says, "I plan to help anyone who seeks my help....rich or poor.." **B/I:** At age 6, Dr. Aziz had a fatal illness that nearly took his life. His mother rushed him to a special physician, Dr. Neiman, who was an elderly gentleman that at the time, to him, resembled Santa Claus. It was around December, and Dr. Aziz thought his mother had in fact taken him to Santa Claus to be cured. Dr. Neiman cured him from the disease that he had. He became so fascinated by the doctor and never forgot him. He remembers

being home one day, and his father had a plaque on his desk. Dr. Aziz carved his name in it as "Dr. Emad Aziz" and that was the beginning of his path to becoming the doctor he is today.

BABBIN, DONALD FRANCIS JR., T: Lieutenant **I:** Other **CN:** Brunswick Police Department **PB:** Boston **SC:** MA/USA **PT:** Donald F. Babbin Sr.; Theresa Mary Babbin **MS:** Married **SPN:** Juanita Babbin **CH:** Isabella Sophia Babbin **ED:** Bachelor's Degree in Public Administration (2020) **CT:** Certified Marijuana Examiner; Certified Glock Armorer; Certified Sig Armorer; Certified Management, Supervisor, FBI-LEEDA **CIV:** State Board of Police Benevolent Association; President, Brunswick Police Association; Advisory Board, Bank of America; Senior Vice President, Southern States Police Benevolent Association, Inc. **AW:** Named, Officer of the Year, Exchange Club Brunswick (2014); Named, Officer of the Year, Brunswick Police (2012, 2013) **MEM:** National Association of Policeman; FBI; NAACP; NRA; Knights of Columbus; International Association of Chief of Police; The National Society of Leadership and Success; The National Society of Collegiate Scholars **AS:** Lt. Babbin attributes his success to hard work and dedication. He advises others to never stop learning because things constantly change. **B/I:** Lt. Babbin became involved in his profession because his father was a police officer from the Massachusetts Port Authority Police and every day he would come home in a uniform, which he found very impressive. So, since the age of five, he knew he wanted to become a police officer. **AV:** Hunting; Fishing; Traveling; Traveling in Europe; Spending time in his cabin **PA:** Independent **THT:** Lt. Babbin follows the motto: "Do what's right every time."

BABIN, BRIAN PHILIP, DDS, T: U.S. Representative from Texas **I:** Government Administration/Government Relations/Government Services **DOB:** 3/23/1948 **PB:** Port Arthur **SC:** TX/USA **MS:** Married **SPN:** Roxanne Babin (1972) **CH:** Marit; Leif; Kirsten; Lucas; Laura **ED:** DDS, The University of Texas Health Science Center School of Dentistry (1976); BS in Biology, Lamar University, Texas (1975) **C:** Member, U.S. Representative from Texas' 36th Congressional District, United States Congress (2015-Present); Dentist, Woodville, Texas (1979-Present); Chairman, Tyler County Republican Party, Texas (1990-1995); Councilman, City of Woodville, Texas (1984-1989); Mayor, City of Woodville, Texas (1982-1984); County coordinator, Regional Coordinator, Ronald Reagan's Presidential Campaign (1980); Member, Committee on Science, Space and Technology; Member, Committee on Transportation and Infrastructure **CR:** Member, Lower Neches Valley Authority (1999-Present); Board Member, Woodville Independent School District (1992-1995); Board Member, Texas Historical Commission (1989-1995); President, Texas State Board of Dental Examiners (1981-1987); Board Member, Deep East Texas Council of Governments (1982-1984) **MIL:** Advanced through Ranks to Captain, United States Air Force (1975-1979) **PA:** Republican

BABROWSKI, TRISSA A., T: Physician **I:** Medicine & Health Care **CN:** University of Chicago **ED:** MD, University of Illinois College of Medicine, Chicago, IL **MEM:** American College of Surgeons; Midwestern Vascular Surgical Society; Society for Vascular Surgery; American Medical Association **B/I:** Dr. Babrowski became involved in her profession because she developed an interest in science over time; it gave her the opportunity to pursue a career in which she could be interactive with people and provide positive change.

BACHELDER, JOSEPH ELMER III, T: Lawyer **I:** Law and Legal Services **CN:** McCarter & English, LLP **DOB:** 11/13/1932 **PB:** Fulton **SC:** MO/USA **PT:** Joseph Elmer Jr.; Frances Evelyn (Gray) **MS:** Married **SPN:** Louise Este Mason (6/12/1955) **CH:** Louise "Lisa" Stewart Bachelder Alcock; Christina "Cary" Cathryn Bachelder Dufresne; Hilary Houston Bachelder **ED:** Harvard Law School Yale University; Pullman High School; Phillips Exeter Academy **C:** Special Counsel, McCarter & English, LLP (2012-Present); Chairman, The Bachelder Group, Inc. (1989-2012); Founder, Senior Partner, Law Offices of Joseph E. Bachelder, New York, NY (1980-2012); Partner, Leboeuf, Lamb, Lieby & MacRae, New York, NY (1972-1980); Partner, Satterlee and Stephens, New York, NY (1969-1972); Associate, McKinsey and Co., Inc., New York, NY (1967-1969); Associate, Mudge, Rose, Guthrie & Alexander, New York, NY (1958-1967) **CR:** Member, Advisory Board, Harvard Law School Forum on Corporate Governance, Speaker, Academic Symposia (1999-2006); Lecturer, The Conference Board (1986, 2004-2006); Lecturer, Practicing Law Institute (1977-1980, 2000); Lecturer, American Law Institute (1980, 1997, 1999); Lecturer, New York University Ann. Institute on Federal Taxation (1972-1974) **CIV:** Trustee, Concord Academy, Massachusetts (1986-1992); Member, Princeton Township Zoning Board, New Jersey (1981-1982) **CW:** Columnist, New York Law Journal (1977-Present); Co-Author, Editor, "Employee Stock Ownership Plans" (1979) **AW:** Patterson Prize, Yale University (1955); Social Science Research Foundation Award (1954) **MEM:** Fellow, American of College Tax Counsel; American Bar Association; New York State Bar Association; Association of Bar of New York; Clubs: The Down Town Association, New York; Yale Club of New York; Bedens Brook Club (Princeton); Nassau Club (Princeton); Springdale Golf Club (Princeton); Siasconset Casino, Nantucket, MA **BAR:** New York (1959) **B/I:** Mr. Bachelder had an uncle, Byron Gray, who practiced law in Topeka, Kansas and was a significant factor in Mr. Bachelder's choice to go into law. Another influence was Mr. Bachelder's great grandfather, George B. Swift, who was mayor of Chicago. **PA:** Republican **RE:** Christian (Congregationalist Church)

BACON, DONALD JOHN, T: U.S. Representative from Nebraska **I:** Government Administration/Government Relations/Government Services **CN:** U.S. House of Representatives **DOB:** 8/16/1963 **PB:** Momence **SC:** IL/USA **PT:** Don Bacon; Joan Bacon **MS:** Married **SPN:** Angie Hardison **CH:** Four Children **ED:** Master of Arts, National War College, National Defense University (2004); Master of Business Administration, University of Phoenix (1996); Bachelor of Arts, Northern Illinois University (1984) **C:** Member, U.S. Representative from Nebraska's Second Congressional District (2017-Present); Assistant Professor, University of Bellevue (2014-2017); Staff, U.S. Representative Jeff Fortenberry of Nebraska (2014-2015); Director, ISR Strategy, Plans, Doctrine, and Force Development (2012-2014); Member, Committee on Agriculture; Member, Committee on Armed Services; Member, Committee on Small Business **MIL:** With, United States Air Force (1985-2014) **AW:** Europe's Top Air Force Wing Commander (2009); Distinguished Service Medal; Two Legion of Merits; Two Bronze Stars

BACON, KEVIN NORWOOD, T: Actor **I:** Media & Entertainment **DOB:** 07/08/1958 **PB:** Philadelphia **SC:** PA/USA **PT:** Edmund Bacon; Ruth Bacon **MS:** Married **SPN:** Kyra Sedgwick (09/03/1988) **CH:** Travis; Sosie Ruth **ED:** Diploma, Julia R. Masterman Laboratory and Demonstration School (1976) **CIV:** Founder, SixDegrees.org (2007) **CW:** Actor, "North Star" (2020); Actor, "You Should Have

Left" (2020); Actor, Co-Executive Producer "City on a Hill" (2019); Actor, "SMILF" (2019); Musician, "The Bacon Brothers" (2018); Actor, Executive Producer, "Tremors" (2018); Actor, Director, "Duck: A Film by Kevin Bacon" (2018); Actor, "Tour de Pharmacy" (2017); Actor, "Story of a Girl" (2017); Actor, Co-Executive Producer, "I Love Dick" (2016-2017); Actor, "Patriots Day" (2016); Actor, "The Darkness" (2016); Actor, "Black Mass" (2015); Producer, Director, Writer, Star, "Free the Bacon" (2015); Actor, Producer, "The Following" (2013-2015); Actor, Executive Producer, "Cop Car" (2015); Musician, "36¢" (2014); Actor, "Tough Day" (2014); Actor, "R.I.P.D." (2013); Actor, "8" (2012); Actor, "Jayne Mansfield's Car" (2012); Musician, "Philadelphia Road - Best of the Bacon Brothers" (2011); Actor, "Crazy, Stupid, Love" (2011); Actor, "X-Men: First Class" (2011); Actor, "Elephant White" (2011); Actor, "Super" (2010); Actor, "The Bellamy Brothers: Guilty of the Crime" (2009); Actor, "Beyond All Boundaries" (2009); Actor, "These Vagabond Shoes" (2009); Actor, "My One and Only" (2009); Actor, "Taking Chance" (2009); Director, "The Closer" (2006-2009); Actor, "Frost/Nixon" (2008); Musician, "New Years Day" (2008); Actor, "Saving Angelo" (2007); Actor, "Rails & Ties" (2007); Actor, "Death Sentence" (2007); Actor, "The Air I Breathe" (2007); Actor, "Where the Truth Lies" (2005); Musician, "White Knuckles" (2005); Actor, "Beauty Shop" (2005); Actor, Producer, Director, "Loverboy" (2005); Actor, "Cavedweller" (2004); Actor, Executive Producer, "The Woodsman" (2004); Musician, "The Bacon Brothers Live - No Food Jokes Tour" (2003); Actor, "Mystic River" (2003); Actor, "Trapped" (2002); Musician, "Can't Complain" (2001); Actor, "Novocaine" (2001); Actor, "Hollow Man" (2000); Actor, "My Dog Skip" (2000); Musician, "Getting There" (1999); Actor, "Stir of Echoes" (1999); Actor, Executive Producer, "Wild Things" (1998); Actor, "Telling Lies in America" (1997); Actor, "Digging to China" (1997); Actor, "Picture Perfect" (1997); Musician, "Forosoco" (1997); Actor, "Sleepers" (1996); Director, "Losing Chase" (1996); Voice Actor, "Balto" (1995); Actor, "Apollo 13" (1995); Actor, "Murder in the First" (1995); Actor, "The River Wild" (1994); Actor, "The Air Up There" (1994); Actor, "A Few Good Men" (1992); Actor, "JFK" (1991); Actor, "Pyrates" (1991); Actor, "He Said, She Said" (1991); Actor, "Queens Logic" (1991); Actor, "Flatliners" (1990); Actor, "Tremors" (1990); Actor, "The Big Picture" (1989); Actor, "Criminal Law" (1988); Actor, "She's Having a Baby" (1988); Actor, "Lemon Sky" (1988); Actor, "Planes, Trains & Automobiles" (1987); Actor, "End of the Line" (1987); Actor, "White Water Summer" (1987); Actor, "Quicksilver" (1986); Actor, "Mister Roberts" (1984); Actor, "Footloose" (1984); Actor, "Enormous Changes at the Last Minute" (1983); Actor, "The Demon Murder Case" (1983); Actor, "Forty Deuce" (1982); Actor, "Diner" (1982); Actor, "Guiding Light" (1980-1981); Actor, "Only When I Laugh" (1980); Actor, "Friday the 13th" (1980); Actor, "Hero at Large" (1980); Actor, "The Gift" (1979); Actor, "Starting Over" (1979); Actor, "National Lampoon's Animal House" (1978) **AW:** Saturn Award for Best Actor on Television, Academy of Science Fiction, Fantasy and Horror Films (2013); Golden Globe Award for Best Actor in a Miniseries or Motion Picture Made for Television, Hollywood Foreign Press Association (2010); Screen Actors Guild Award for Outstanding Performance by a Male Actor in a Television Movie or Miniseries, SAG-AFTRA (2010); Joel Siegel Award, The Critics Choice Association (2010); Career Achievement in Acting Award, SIFF (2010); American Rivera Award, Santa Barbara International Film Festival (2005); John Cassavetes Award, Denver Film (2004); Star, Motion Picture Category, Hollywood Walk of Fame, Hollywood Chamber of Commerce (2003); Award for Best Ensemble Cast, Boston Society of Film Critics (2003); Blockbuster Entertainment Award for Favorite Actor-Science Fiction, Blockbuster LLC (2001); Award for Best Actor, Giffoni International Film Festival, Ente Autonomo Giffoni Experience (1997); Critics' Choice Movie Award for Best Actor, The Critics Choice Association (1996); Screen Actors Guild Award for Outstanding Performance by a Cast in a Motion Picture (1996)

BADALAMENTI, FRED, T: Artist, Educator **I:** Education/Educational Services **DOB:** 06/25/1935 **PB:** Long Island City **SC:** NY/USA **PT:** Leopoldo Badalamenti; Concetta (Vitale) Badalamenti **MS:** Married **SPN:** Barbara Badalamenti (06/14/1959) **CH:** Katherine; Alexander; Frederick **ED:** MFA, Brooklyn College (1967); BS, SUNY New Paltz (1961); Student, University of Alaska (1957-1958); Student, Pratt Institute (1953-1955) **C:** Professor Emeritus, Brooklyn College (1967-1992); Art Teacher, Deer Park High School, Deer Park, NY (1963-1965); Art Teacher, Newburgh Public Schools, New York (1960-1963) **CR:** Adjunct Faculty, Art Department, Stony Brook University (1993-1999); Adjunct Faculty, Art Department, Brooklyn College (1992-1993); Deputy Chairman, Studio Art, Brooklyn College (1990-1992); Visiting Professor of Art, Lecturer, Stony Brook University (1977-1978, 1980, 1981, 1983); Director, First Street Gallery, New York, NY (1978); Jurist, Art Exhibition **MIL:** U.S. Air Force (1955-1958) **CW:** Artist, Exhibited Paintings, Drawings, Representational Art, Numerous Cities and Galleries (1967, 2012, 2017, 2018, 2019); Artist, One-Man Shows, Suffolk County Community College, Selden, NY (1971, 2007); Artist, One-Man Show, Alfred Van Loen Gallery, South Huntington, NY (1998); Artist, One-Man Shows, First Street Gallery (1973, 1976, 1980, 1989); Artist, One-Man Show, Nassau County Museum of Fine Arts (1987) Artist, One-Man Show, St. Joseph's College (1987) **AW:** Honoree, Gallery North, Setauket, NY (2018); "Artist of the Month," Long Island Museum of Art, Stony Brook, NY (2018); Graduate Fellow, Brooklyn College (1965-1967) **MEM:** College Art Association; Gallery North, East Setauket, NY; Artist Advisory Board, Gallery North, East Setauket, NY; American Association of University Professors **AV:** Traveling; Playing tennis; Gardening **PA:** Democratic Party **RE:** Catholic

BADAWY, SHAWKY Z.A., MD, T: Gynecologist **I:** Medicine & Health Care **DOB:** 07/30/1935 **PB:** Cairo **SC:** Egypt **PT:** Zaki A. Badway; Katifa A. Kandil **MS:** Married **SPN:** Lauren F. Badway (10/3/1972) **CH:** Rami; Tarek; Shareef; Zaki **ED:** Senior Resident in Obstetrics and Gynecology, SUNY Upstate Medical University (1972-1973); Fellowship in Reproductive Endocrinology and Physiology, Rockefeller University (1968-1970); Postdoctoral Fellow in Reproductive Physiology and Endocrinology, The Rockefeller University (1968-1970); Master's in Surgery, AinShams University (1963); Research Fellow, Department of Ob/Gyn, Ain Shams University, Cairo, Egypt (1962-1963); Resident in Obstetrics and Gynecology, AinShams University (1960-1962); Intern, AinShams University (1959-1960); MB, Ain-Shams University (1958); Bachelor's Degree in Surgery, AinShams University (1958); Residency, University Hospital, SUNY Health Science Center at Syracuse **CT:** Diplomate in Reproductive Endocrinology, American Board of Obstetrics and Gynecology, Inc. (1979); Diplomate, American Board of Obstetrics and Gynecology, Inc. (1975); Licensed to Practice Medicine, State of New York; Licensed to Practice Medicine, Washington, DC **C:** Professor, Department of Pathology, SUNY Upstate Medical University (1993-Present); Professor, Department of Obstetrics and Gynecology, SUNY Upstate Medical University (1981-Present); Director, Division of Reproductive Endocrinology, SUNY Upstate Medical University (1975-Present); Chairman, Residency Program, SUNY Upstate Medical University (1998-2011); Director, Residency Program, SUNY Upstate Medical University (1998-2011); Chief, Department of Obstetrics and Gynecology, Crouse Hospital (1997-2011); Interim Chairman, Residency Program, SUNY Upstate Medical University (1997-1998); Associate Professor, Department of Obstetrics and Gynecology, SUNY Upstate Medical University (1978-1981); Assistant Professor, Department of Obstetrics and Gynecology, SUNY Upstate Medical University (1973-1978); Assistant Professor, Department of Obstetrics and Gynecology, AinShams University (1971-1972); Lecturer, Department of Obstetrics and Gynecology, AinShams University (1965-1971); Clinical Instructor, Department of Obstetrics and Gynecology, AinShams University (1963-1965) **CR:** Member, Laser Safety Committee, SUNY Upstate Medical University (2013-Present); Chairman, Search Committee for Chairman of Family Medicine, SUNY Upstate Medical University (2005); Chairman, Search Committee for the Chairman of Orthopedic Surgery SUNY Upstate Medical University (2000); Quality Assurance Board, SUNY Upstate Medical University (1988-2009); Member, Faculty Appointments and Promotion for Committee of the Medical School, SUNY Upstate Medical University (1988-2003); Chairman, Quality Assurance Committee, SUNY Upstate Medical University (1986-2009); Chairman, Reproductive Biology Course, SUNY Upstate Medical University (1985-1986); Search Committee for Chairman of Department of Family Practice, SUNY Upstate Medical University (1985-1986); Quality Assurance Committee, SUNY Upstate Medical University (1983-1986); Operating Room Committee, SUNY Upstate Medical University (1982-1984); Chairman, Tissue Committee, SUNY Upstate Medical University (1980-1986); Speaker in Field **CW:** Editorial Board Member, Journal of Gynecology and Infertility (2017-Present); Editorial Board Member, Journal of Pediatric and Adolescent Gynecology (2012-Present); Editorial Board Member, Journal of Gynecologic Surgery (2011-Present); Editorial Board Member, Dataset Papers in Medicine; Editorial Board Member, BioMed Research International; Editorial Board Member, Applied Scientific Reports; Contributor, 177 Articles, Professional Journals; Contributor, 25 Chapters, Books; Author, 75 Abstracts **AW:** Inductee, Leading Physicians of the World (2014); Award, Association of Professors of Gynecology and Obstetrics (2002); President's Award for Excellence in Faculty Service (2001); The Berlex Award (1990); Military Academy of Medicine (1981-1982); National Scientific Merit Award, Egypt (1959); Grants in Field **MEM:** American Academy of Family Physicians (1978-Present); The North American Menopause Society (2007); Fellow, Royal Society of Medicine (1975-1992); Society of Adolescent and Pediatric Gynecology (1988); Fallopius International Society (1984); Society of Reproductive Surgeons (1984); Society for the Advancement of Contraception (1983); Society for Reproductive Endocrinology and Infertility (1983); President, Co-Founder, Fertility Society of Upstate New York (1983); American Society of Immunology of Reproduction (1982); Military Academy of Medicine (1981-1982); Fellow, American College of Surgeons (1977); Fellow, American College of Obstetricians and Gynecologists (1976); Society of the Study of Reproduction (1975); American Fertility Society (Now American Society for Reproductive Medicine) (1975); OB/GYN Associates of Central New York (1975); Association of Planned Parenthood Physicians (1974); Fellow, International College of Surgeons (1970) **MH:** Albert Nelson Marquis Lifetime Achievement

Award; Marquis Who's Who Humanitarian Award **B/I:** Dr. Badawy became involved in his profession because he was really impressed during his educational years. Having a doctor who asked questions, gives thorough examinations and a diagnosis along with a cure, just fascinated him since he was a young person. **AV:** Travel; Tennis

BADDOUR, ANNE BRIDGE, T: Pilot **I:** Aviation **PB:** Royal Oak **SC:** MI/USA **PT:** William George Bridge; Esther Rose (Pfiester) Bridge **MS:** Widowed **SPN:** Raymond F. Baddour (09/25/1954) **CH:** Cynthia Anne; Frederick Raymond; Jean Bridge **ED:** Coursework, Detroit Business School (1948-1950); BA, Pine Manor College, Chestnut Hill, MA **CT:** Airline Transport Pilot **C:** Research Test Pilot, Lincoln Laboratory Flight Test Facility, Massachusetts Institute of Technology, Lexington, MA (1977-1997); Manager, Pilot, Baltimore Airways, Inc., Bedford, MA (1976-1977); Administrative Assistant, Ferry Pilot, Jenney Beechcraft, Bedford, MA (1976); Flight Dispatcher, Ferry, Pilot, Comerford Flight School, Bedford, MA (1974-1976); Co-pilot, Flight Attendant, Raytheon Company, Bedford, MA (1958-1963); Aeronautical Instructor, Powers School, Boston, MA (1958); Stewardess, Eastern Airlines, Boston, MA (1952-1954) **CR:** Board of Advisors, Massachusetts Air & Space Museum (2010-Present); Board Advisor Member, Aero Club of New England (2010-Present); Board of Visitors, Pine Manor College (2009-2013); Aviation Consultant, Corporate Pilot, Energy Resources, Inc., Cambridge, MA (1974-1984) **CIV:** Board of Directors, Monadnock Community Hospital (2015-Present); Board of Trustees, Fairchild Tropical Botanic Garden (2015-Present); Trustee, Vizcaya Museum & Gardens (2002-Present); Board of Directors, Florida Maritime Museum, Key West, FL (2004-2013); Trustee, Daniel Webster College, Nashua, NH (1995-2009); Board of Directors, National Air and Space Museum, Smithsonian Institution (1998-2005); Vice President, Trustee, Friends of the Library Special Collections, Boston University (1999-2002); Trustee, Board of Administration, Amelia Earhart Birthplace Museum (1992-1993); Commissioner, Massachusetts Aeronautics Commission (1979-1983); Board of Directors, Cambridge City Opera (1977-1979); Commissioner, Commonwealth of Massachusetts; Member, Council Associates, French Library in Boston; Member, Campaign Council, Museum of Transportation, Boston, MA **AW:** Katherine Wright Trophy, NAA (2018); DAR Award for Women in American History (2014); Award, Fairchild Tropical Botanic Garden (2013); Inductee, Women in Aviation International Pioneer Hall of Fame (2005); Pilot of the Year, New England Section, The Ninety-Nines, Inc., International Organization of Women Pilots (1992); Listee, International Aviation Forest of Friendship, Atchison, KS (1991); Special Recognition Award, FAA (1990); Clifford B. Harmon Trophy, International Aviatrix (1988); New England Safety trophy 1986, The Ninety-Nines, Inc. (1986); Trophy, New England Air Race (1957); First Place Trophy, Philadelphia Transcontinental Air Race (1954) **MEM:** Director, Aero Club of New England (1978-2002); Vice President, Aero Club of New England (1978-1980); National Society Daughters of the American Revolution (NCDAR); The Barnacle Society, Coconut Grove, FL; Women in Aviation International; Friends of Switzerland; Sea Plane Pilots Association; Association of Women Transcontinental Air Race; The Bostonian Society; The Society of Experimental Test Pilots; Aircraft Owners and Pilots Association; Federation Aeronautique Internationale; National Apartment Association; The Ninety-Nines, Inc.; Boston Women's Travel Club; Fairchild Tropical Botanical Garden; Harvard

Travellers Club; Chilton Club; Belmont Hill Club **MH:** Albert Nelson Marquis Lifetime Achievement Award; Marquis Who's Who Top Professional

BADEN, SHERI L, T: Kindergarten Teacher **I:** Education/Educational Services **CN:** All Saints School **C:** Retired, Citizens in Action **B/I:** When she was a kid, Ms. Baden and her neighbor used to play school in their garages, and they would have the neighborhood kids come and they would teach them to read. They just had fun doing it and she decided to become a teacher.

BADER, TROY, T: President, Chief Executive Officer **I:** Business Management/Business Services **CN:** International Dairy Queen, Inc. **DOB:** 07/28/1964 **SC:** MN/USA **MS:** Married **ED:** JD, University of Minnesota Law School (1988); BBA in Banking and Finance, University of North Dakota (1985) **C:** President, Chief Executive Officer, International Dairy Queen, Inc. (2018-Present); Various Positions Including Chief Operating Officer, Chief Development and Legal Officer, EVP Franchise Department, EVP Mail Division, International Dairy Queen, Inc. (2001-2018) **PA:** Republican

BADRA, ROBERT GEORGE, T: Professor **I:** Education/Educational Services **CN:** Kalamazoo Valley Community College **DOB:** 12/08/1933 **PB:** Lansing **SC:** MI/USA **PT:** Razouk Anthony; Anna (Paul) Badra **SPN:** Kristen Lillie Stuckey (12/30/1977, Divorced 2001); Maria Theresa Beer (10/25/1968, Divorced 1973) **CH:** Rachal Jennifer (Deceased 2012); Danielle Elizabeth Jane **ED:** Master of Divinity, St. John's Provincial Seminary, Detroit, MI (1985); Master of Arts, Western Michigan University, Kalamazoo, MI (1968); Bachelor of Arts, Sacred Heart Seminary, Detroit, MI (1957) **CT:** Ordained Priest, Roman Catholic Church (1961-1968) **C:** Adjunct Professor of Philosophy, Religion and the Humanities, Siena Heights University, Adrian, MI (1993-2018); Professor of Philosophy, Religion and the Humanities, Kalamazoo Valley Community College, Kalamazoo, MI (1968-2018) **CR:** Adjunct Professor, Siena Heights University, Adrian, MI (1993-2018); Member, Faculty, Ministry Formation, Diocese of Kalamazoo, Kalamazoo, MI (1999-2003); Nazareth College, Rochester, NY (1985-1991) **CIV:** Vice President, Van Buren Youth Camp (2002-2007); Board of Directors, Van Buren Youth Camp (1993-2007); Kalamazoo Council for the Humanities (1983-1986) **CW:** Author, Book, "Meditations for Spiritual Misfits" (1987) **AW:** Solid Glass Obelisk for Teaching Excellence, Kalamazoo Valley Community College (1996); Grantee, National Endowment for the Humanities (1991-1993); Education Reward, Exxon (1986); Innovation Award for his Paper, "The Genetics Revolution," Exxon Education Foundation **MH:** Albert Nelson Marquis Lifetime Achievement Award; Marquis Who's Who Humanitarian Award **B/I:** Mr. Badra became involved in his profession because he is a truth seeker; he is a seeker of beautiful landscapes; and he is an inner beauty seeker. He delights in finding this in others. **AV:** Books; Travel; Writing; Enjoying the company of his daughter, Danielle, and her partner, Holly, in Fairfax, Virginia

BAEZ, JOAN CHANDOS, T: Singer-songwriter; Activist **I:** Media & Entertainment **DOB:** 01/09/1941 **PB:** Staten Island **SC:** NY/USA **PT:** Albert Vinicio Baez; Joan (Bridge) Baez **MS:** Divorced **SPN:** David Victor Harris (1968-1973) **CH:** Gabriel Earl **ED:** Honorary LHD, Antioch University (1980); Honorary LHD, Rutgers, The State University of New Jersey (1980) **CR:** Lecturer, 92nd Street Young Men's and Young Women's Hebrew Association, New York, NY (2008-2009) **CIV:** Participant, Catalan Independence Movement, Catalonia, Spain

(2017-Present); Supporter, Performer, Bread & Roses (1974-Present); Performer, Four Voices Benefit Concerts (1991, 2017); Performer, Death Penalty Abolition Campaign, Amnesty International (2011); Performer, Benefit Concert for Occupy Wall Street, New York, NY (2011); Participant, Tree Sit, South Central Farm, Los Angeles, CA (2006); Participant, Anti-war Protest, Texas (2005); Performer, Slacker Uprising Tour (2004); Performer, Concert for a Landmine-Free World, London, United Kingdom (2003); Performer, Anti-war Protest Concerts, San Francisco, CA (2003); Performer, Benefit Concert, Bread & Roses, Alcatraz Island, CA (1993, 1996); Performer, Fight the Right, National LGBTQ Task Force (1994); With, Refugees International, Bosnia-Herzegovina (1993); Performer, Death Penalty Protest Vigil, San Quentin State Prison (1992); Founder, Director, Humanitas International Human Rights Committee (1979-1992); National Advisory Council, United States, Amnesty International (1974-1992); Performer, Anti-war Protest Concerts (1991); Performer, Conspiracy of Hope Tour, Amnesty International (1986); Performer, Live Aid (1985); Participant, United Nations Humanitarian Conference on Kampuchea, United Nations, Cambodia (1981); Founder, Conductor, Fact-Finding Mission to Refugee Camps, Southeast Asia (1979); Participant, Memorial Marches for Harvey Milk (1978); Participant, Marches, Irish Peace People, Northern Ireland (1978); With, Peace Delegation, Vietnam (1972); Participant, Moratorium to End the War in Vietnam (1969); Numerous Anti-war Television Appearances and Speaking Engagements (1967-1968); Performer, Anti-war Benefit Concert, Washington Monument, Washington, DC (1967); Participant, Delano Grape Strike, Agricultural Workers Organizing Committee (Now United Farm Workers), Delano, CA (1966); Participant, Numerous Protests, Fifth Avenue Vietnam Peace Parade Committee (1966); Co-founder, Vice President, Institute for the Study of Nonviolence, Carmel Valley, CA (1965); Participant, Stars for Freedom Rally, Montgomery, AL (1965); Participant, Selma to Montgomery Marches (1965); Participant, Free Speech Movement, University of California Berkeley (1964); Performer, Participant, March on Washington for Jobs and Freedom (1963); Participant, Numerous Civil Rights, Anti-war, Human Rights and Environmental Marches; Supporter, Innocence Project; Supporter, The Innocence Network; Supporter, Human Rights Watch; Supporter, Hard Miles Music; Supporter, Circle of Life **CW:** Appearance, "The Glance of Music" (2020); Appearance, "Rolling Thunder Revue: A Bob Dylan Story by Martin Scorsese" (2019); Appearance, "Don't Get Trouble in Your Mind: The Carolina Chocolate Drops' Story" (2019); Singer-songwriter, "Live at Woodstock" (2019); Singer-songwriter, "Whistle Down the Wind" (2018); Appearance, "Hugh Hefner's After Dark: Speaking Out in America" (2018); Appearance, "King in the Wilderness" (2018); Artist, "Mischief Makers," Seager Gray Gallery, Mill Valley, CA (2017); Singer-songwriter, "75th Birthday Celebration" (2016); Subject, "Joan Baez: Rebel Icon" (2015); Singer-songwriter, "Diamantes" (2015); Appearance, "The March" (2013); Appearance, "For the Love of the Music: The Club 47 Folk Revival" (2012); Performer, "American Masters" (1994-2012); Appearance, "Welcome to Eden" (2009); Appearance, "Hugh Hefner: Playboy, Activist and Rebel" (2009); Singer-songwriter, "Day After Tomorrow" (2008); Appearance, "The Power of Their Song: The Untold Story of Latin America's New Song" (2008); Appearance, "Fierce Light: When Spirit Meets Action" (2008); Appearance, "Pete Seeger: The Power of Song" (2007); Singer-songwriter, "Bowery Songs" (2005); Singer-songwriter, "Dark Chords on a Big Guitar"

(2003); Appearance, "Tree Sit: The Art of Resistance" (2001); Singer-songwriter, "Gone from Danger" (1997); Singer-songwriter, "Live at Newport" (1996); Singer-songwriter, "Ring Them Bells" (1995); Performer, "The Kennedy Center Honors: A Celebration of the Performing Arts" (1994); Appearance, "Woodstock Diary" (1994); Appearance, "Kris Kristofferson: His Life and Work" (1993); Singer-songwriter, "Play Me Backwards" (1992); Singer-songwriter, "Speaking of Dreams" (1989); Appearance, "We Shall Overcome" (1989); Singer-songwriter, "Diamonds & Rust in the Bullring" (1988); Author, "And a Voice to Sing With: A Memoir" (1987); Appearance, "The Return of Bruno" (1987); Singer-songwriter, "Recently" (1987); Appearance, "In Remembrance of Martin" (1986); Appearance, "An All-Star Celebration Honoring Martin Luther King Jr." (1986); Appearance, "Live Aid" (1985); Singer-songwriter, "Live Europe '83" (1984); Appearance, "Woody Guthrie: Hard Travelin'" (1984); Appearance, "In Our Hands" (1984); Singer-songwriter, "European Tour" (1980); Singer-songwriter, "Honest Lullaby" (1979); Actress, "Renaldo and Clara" (1978); Singer-songwriter, "Blowin' Away" (1977); Appearance, "The Memory of Justice" (1976); Singer-songwriter, "Gulf Winds" (1976); Singer-songwriter, "From Every Stage" (1976); Appearance, "Hard Rain" (1976); Singer-songwriter, "Diamonds & Rust" (1975); Subject, "A War Is Over" (1975); Singer-songwriter, "Gracias a la Vida" (1974); Singer-songwriter, "Where Are You Now, My Son?" (1973); Singer-songwriter, "Come from the Shadows" (1972); Appearance, "Earl Scruggs: The Bluegrass Legend - Family & Friends" (1972); Singer-songwriter, "Blessed Are…" (1971); Appearance, "Dynamite Chicken" (1971); Singer-songwriter, "One Day at a Time" (1970); Subject, "Carry It On" (1970); Singer-songwriter, "Joan Baez in Italy" (1969); Singer-songwriter, "David's Album" (1969); Singer-songwriter, "Any Day Now" (1968); Author, "Daybreak: An Intimate Journal" (1968); Singer-songwriter, "Baptism: A Journey Through Our Time" (1968); Appearance, "Bob Dylan: Don't Look Back" (1967); Singer-songwriter, "Joan" (1967); Appearance, "Festival" (1967); Singer-songwriter, "Noël" (1966); Singer-songwriter, "Farewell, Angelina" (1965); Singer-songwriter, "Joan Baez/5" (1964); Appearance, "The March" (1964); Singer-songwriter, "Joan Baez in San Francisco" (1964); Appearance, "The March in Washington" (1963); Singer-songwriter, "Joan Baez in Concert, Part 2" (1963); Singer-songwriter, "Joan Baez in Concert" (1962); Singer-songwriter, "Joan Baez, Vol. 2" (1961); Singer-songwriter, "Joan Baez" (1960); Singer-songwriter, "Folksingers 'Round Harvard Square" (1959) **AW:** Latin Grammy Lifetime Achievement Award, The Latin Recording Academy, The Recording Academy (2019); Justice in the Arts Award, Death Penalty Focus (2017); Inductee, Rock & Roll Hall of Fame (2017); Award for Best Cover Song, The Independent Music Awards (2016); Ambassador of Conscience Award, Amnesty International (2015); Centennial Award, ASCAP (2014); Courage of Conscience Award, The Peace Abbey Foundation, Boston, MA (2011); Elaine Weissman Lifetime Achievement Award, Folk Alliance International (2011); Inductee, Grammy Hall of Fame, The Recording Academy (2011); Joan Baez Award for Outstanding Inspirational Service in the Global Fight for Human Rights, Amnesty International (2011); Humanitarian Award, Children's Health Fund (2010); Named to Orden de las Artes y las Letras de España, Spain (2010); eChievement Award, eTown (2008); "Spirit of Americana" Free Speech Award, First Amendment Center and Americana Music Association (2008); Grammy Lifetime Achievement Award, The Recording Academy (2007); Distinguished Leadership Award, Legal Community Against Violence (Now Giffords: Courage to Fight Gun Violence) (2006); Josephine and Frank Duveneck Humanitarian Award (2003); Governors Award, San Francisco Chapter, The Recording Academy (2003); John Steinbeck Award, Martha Heasley Cox Center for Steinbeck Studies, San Jose State University (2003); International Bluegrass Award for Recorded Event of the Year, International Bluegrass Music Association (2002); Golden Achievement Award, WXPN-FM, Philadelphia, PA (1996); BAMMY Award for Top Female Vocalist, San Francisco Bay Area Music Awards (1978, 1979, 1995); Achievement Award, The Gleitsman Foundation (1994); Death Penalty Focus of California Award, Death Penalty Focus (1992); Leadership Award, ACLU of Southern California (1989); Award for Best Live Album, Académie Charles Cros, Chézy-sur-Marne, France (1983); Named Chevalier, Legion d'Honneur, France (1983); Peace Award, SANE Education Fund (1983); A.D.A. Award, Americans for Democratic Action (1982); Lennon Peace Tribute Award (1982); Jefferson Award for Public Service, American Institute for Public Service (Now Multiplying Good) (1980); Earl Warren Civil Liberties Award, American Civil Liberties Union (ACLU) (1978); Public Service Award, Rock Music Awards (1977); Thomas Merton Award, Thomas Merton Center (1976); Award for Service, Chicago Chapter, Business Executives Move for Vietnam Peace (1971) **MEM:** Member, National Academy of Songwriters; Member, National Academy of Popular Music; Member, The Recording Academy; Member, Rock & Roll Hall of Fame

BAGWILL, JOHN W., T: Retired Pension Fund Executive **I:** Financial Services **DOB:** 08/09/1930 **PB:** Seattle **SC:** WA/USA **PT:** John Williams Bagwill; Amy (Munday) Bagwill **MS:** Married **SPN:** Emily Bend Sedgwick (12/28/1953) **CH:** John Williams III; David Sedgwick; Elizabeth Bagwill Komjathy **ED:** MBA, Harvard University (1958); BA, Hamilton College (1952) **CT:** Certified Financial Planner **C:** Retired (1994); President, Pentegra Services, White Plains, NY (1987-1994); Executive Vice President, Financial Institutions Retirement Fund, White Plains, NY (1985-1987); Vice President, Financial Institutions Retirement Fund, White Plains, NY (1964-1985); Assistant to President, George O. Muir, Inc., New York, NY (1961-1964) **CR:** Consultant, Long-term Care Issues, Newport Health Care Corp. (1999-Present); Governor, Newport Health Care Corp. (1997) **CIV:** Trustee, Treasurer, Newport Art Museum (1997-2006); President, Hamilton College (1980-1982); Alumni Council, Hamilton College (1977-1982); President, Town Club New Castle, Chappaqua, NY (1978-1979); Board of Directors, Town Club New Castle, Chappaqua, NY (1975-1979); Member, Pension Fund Investment. com, Middletown, RI **MIL:** Lieutenant J.G., Supply Corps., U.S. Navy (1953-1957) **MEM:** Newport Reading Room; Quindecim Club; Ida Lewis Yacht Club **MH:** Albert Nelson Marquis Lifetime Achievement Award **B/I:** Mr. Bagwill became involved in his profession because a good friend of his was president of a pension business with 14 employees. He was looking for someone who would be president number two and would succeed him and he liked him and decided why not. He was in his 30s and it looked like a good opportunity and liked to work where he could make a difference. **AV:** Gardening; Fishing; Sailing **PA:** Independent **RE:** Episcopalian

BAILEY, CHARLES WILLIAM, T: Management Consultant, Researcher **I:** Other **DOB:** 05/26/1932 **PB:** Minneapolis **SC:** MN/USA **PT:** Charles Nelson Bailey; Ruth Elthleen (Brower) Bailey **MS:** Divorced **SPN:** Anne G. Stultz (Divorced 1979) **CH:** Charles R.; George L.; Dana R.; William W.; Jonathan D.; Margaret R. **ED:** BBA in Industrial Relations and Psychology, University of Minnesota (1955) **C:** President, Bailey and Associates (1986-Present); Director of Safety, Duluth, Missabe and Iron Range Railway (1967-1986); Supervisor of Organization Planning, Duluth, Missabe and Iron Range Railway (1960-1967); Organization Analyst, Duluth, Missabe and Iron Range Railway (1958-1960); Teacher, Inclusion Safety Program, University of Minnesota **CIV:** Adviser, Minnesota Safety Council (1982-1986); Treasurer, Duluth Public Schools (1967-1971) **MIL:** U.S. Army (1955-1957) **CW:** Inventor, System for Digital Computer Recording of Petroglyphs (1991); Author, "Using Behavioral Techniques to Improve Safety Program Effectiveness" (1989) **MEM:** Secretary, Treasurer, Northern Lakes Archaeological Society (1988-1991); Chairman, Safety Research Committee, Association of American Railroads (1976-1986); General Chairman, Railroad Section, National Safety Council (1973-1974); Researcher, Institute for Study of American Cultures; The Epigraphic Society; American Rock Art Research Association **MH:** Albert Nelson Marquis Lifetime Achievement Award **B/I:** Mr. Bailey became involved in his profession because the industry provided a vast sea of opportunities. **PA:** Republican **RE:** Presbyterian

BAILEY, F. LEE, T: Chairman, Chief Executive Officer **I:** Other **CN:** IMPAC Control Systems Inc. **DOB:** 06/10/1933 **PB:** Waltham **SC:** MA/USA **ED:** LLB, Boston University (1960); Coursework, Harvard University (1950-1952, 1957) **CT:** U.S. District Court Eastern District of Wisconsin (1991); U.S. Court of Appeals for the Fifth Circuit (1985); U.S. Court of Appeals for the Eighth Circuit (1984); U.S. Court of Appeals for the Eleventh Circuit (1984); United States Court of Appeals for the Armed Forces (1981); U.S. District Court Western District of Texas (1980); U.S. District Court Northern District of Texas (1980); U.S. Court of Appeals for the Fourth Circuit (1971); U.S. Court of Appeals for the Seventh Circuit (1971); U.S. Court of Appeals for the Ninth Circuit (1970); U.S. Court of Appeals for the Third Circuit (1969); U.S. Court of Appeals for the Tenth Circuit (1968); U.S. Court of Appeals for the Second Circuit (1967); Supreme Court of the United States (1964); U.S. Court of Appeals for the Sixth Circuit (1964); United States Tax Court (1964); U.S. Court of Appeals for the First Circuit (1963); U.S. District Court District of Massachusetts (1961) **C:** Chairman, Chief Executive Officer, IMPAC Control Systems, Inc.; Principal, Law Offices of F. Lee Bailey, West Palm Beach, FL; Interstate Chemical, Inc., Mobile, AL; Interstate Chemical, Inc., West Palm Beach, FL; Palm Beach Roamer, Inc., West Palm Beach, FL; Murray Chris Craft Industries, Inc., Sarasota, FL; Fairchild Aircraft, San Antonio, TX; TelShare Publishing Company, Chelsea, MA; Enstrom Helicopter Manufacturing Company, Menominee, MI **MIL:** Lieutenant, United States Marine Corps (1952-1956) **CW:** Author, "To Be a Trial Lawyer" (1983); Author, "How to Protect Yourself Against Cops in California and Other Strange Places" (1982); Author, "Novel Secrets" (1979); Author, "Cleared for the Approach" (1977); Co-Author, "For the Defense" (1976); Co-Author, "The Defense Never Rests" (1971); Co-Author, Numerous Works in Criminal Law **MEM:** Association of Trial Lawyers of America (Now American Association for Justice); American Bar Association

BAILOWITZ, ANNE, T: Pediatrician **I:** Medicine & Health Care **DOB:** 08/27/1951 **PB:** New York **SC:** NY/USA **PT:** Paul **MS:** Married **CH:** Gabe; Lyle **ED:** MPH, John Hopkins School of Hygiene (1983); Resident in Pediatrics, Johns Hopkins Hospital, Baltimore, MD (1980-1982); Intern in Pediatrics, Stanford

Hospital, Palo Alto, CA (1979-1980); MD, Stanford University (1979); BA in Biology, Harvard College, Magna Cum Laude (1974); Coursework, University College Hospital, London, UK (1972-1973); Fellowship in Infectious Disease Epidemiology, National Institute of Allergy and Infectious Diseases **CT:** Diplomate, American Board of Pediatrics **C:** Founder, Principal, Consultants in Public Health, Baltimore, MD (2013-Present); Commissioner, Maryland Statewide Advisory Committee on Immunization, Baltimore City Health Department, Baltimore, MD (2011-2012); Chief Medical Officer, Baltimore City Health Department, Baltimore, MD (2009-2011); Director, Medical Services, Baltimore City Health Department, Baltimore, MD (2009-2010); Bureau Chief, Children's Health, Baltimore City Health Department, Baltimore, MD (2001-2010); Private Practice, Baltimore, MD (1991-2001); Director, Pediatrics and Quality Assurance, Jai Medical Systems Managed Care Organization (1991-2000); Director, Medical Services, Baltimore County Health Department, Towson, MD (1988-1991); Pediatric Epidemiologist, Maryland Department of Health and Mental Hygiene, Baltimore, MD (1986-1988); Assistant Professor, Preventive Medicine, Johns Hopkins School of Hygiene, Baltimore, MD (1985-1986); Fellow, Infectious Disease, National Institutes of Health, Bethesda, MD (1982-1985) **CR:** Mentor, Johns Hopkins Bloomberg School of Public Health (2012-Present); Associate, Department of International Health, Johns Hopkins School of Hygiene and Public Health (1989-Present); Clinical Assistant Professor Pediatrics University Maryland, Baltimore (1987-Present); Chair, Committee on Infectious Diseases, American Academy of Pediatrics, Maryland Chapter (2013-2019); Chair, Maryland Statewide Advisory Commission on Immunization (2013-2018); Lecturer in Field **CIV:** Neighborhood Beautification Projects, Oakenshawe Garden Club (1985-1991); Board of Directors, Harvard-Radcliffe; Board of Directors, Stanford University School of Medicine **CW:** Contributor, Articles, Professional Journals **AW:** Special Achievement Award, HPV Education, American Academy of Pediatrics (2015); Certificate of Appreciation, Maryland Department of Health and Mental Hygiene Secretary (2012); Baltimore's Mayoral Certificate of Recognition (2012); Baltimore City Health Department Commissioner's Commendation for Citizen Health Improvement (2012); Baltimore's Mayoral Commendation, Swine Flu (2010); RAND Certificate of Appreciation for Contributions to "Prepare for Pandemic Influenza" Collaborative (2007); "Most Improved Immunization Rates in US Metro Area 2001-2004," Centers for Disease Control and Prevention (2006); Certificate of Appreciation, Government of Honduras (2003); California State Fellow (1974); Josephine Murray Traveling Fellow (1972) **MEM:** Fellow, American Academy of Pediatrics; AAP Section on Infectious Disease; Phi Beta Kappa **MH:** Albert Nelson Marquis Lifetime Achievement Award **B/I:** Dr. Balowitz has always loved biology and change. The field of pediatrics is all about change and development. Growing up in New York City, she would be riding the subway and reading books on infectious disease. When she went to Stanford University, she enjoyed, admired, and respected the teachers who taught her pediatrics. Being a pediatrician allows Dr. Balowitz to continue to maintain her human side in medicine. The ability to give what one can give mentally and physically is what was most attractive to her about the field. **AV:** Practicing equestrian sports; Swimming; Hiking

BAINUM, STEWART WILLIAM JR., T: Chairman **I:** Leisure, Travel & Tourism **CN:** Choice Hotels International, Inc. **DOB:** 03/25/1946 **PB:** Takoma Park **SC:** MD/USA **PT:** Stewart William Bainum Sr.; Jane Loretta (Goyne) Bainum **MS:** Married

SPN: Sandra Ann Yarish (09/26/1987) **CH:** Two children **ED:** Postgraduate Coursework in Theology, Andrews University (1971-1972); MBA, Anderson School of Management, UCLA (1970); BA, Pacific Union College (1968) **C:** Manager, Artis Senior Living (2017-Present); Chief Executive Officer, HCR ManorCare USA, Inc., Silver Spring, MD (1987-Present); Member, Maryland State Senate, Annapolis, MD (1983-1987); Member, Maryland House of Delegates, Annapolis, MD (1979-1983); With, Quality Inns (Now Choice Hotels International, Inc.) (1977); Senior Vice President, Manor Care Inc. (Now HCR ManorCare USA, Inc.), Silver Spring, MD (1974-1979); Director, Manor Care Inc. (Now HCR ManorCare USA, Inc.), Silver Spring, MD (1972-1974) **CR:** Member, Advisory Board, SunBridge Capital Management, LLC (2017-Present); Chairman, Choice Hotels International, Inc. (2017-Present); Chairman, HCR ManorCare USA, Inc., Silver Spring, MD (2001-2002); Vice Chairman, Manor Care Inc. (Now HCR ManorCare USA, Inc.), Silver Spring, MD (1982-1987); Board of Directors, HCR ManorCare USA, Inc., Silver Spring, MD **CIV:** Participant, The Giving Pledge (2018); Board of Directors, Invest in America, Washington, DC (1987); Co-Chairman, Democratic Forum, Montgomery County, MD (1987); Alternate Delegate, Democratic National Convention, San Francisco, CA (1984); Board of Advisers, Anderson School of Management, UCLA; Board of Trustees, University of Maryland Medical System; Board of Trustees, St. Mary's College of Maryland; Board of Trustees, Baltimore Symphony Orchestra; Board of Trustees, Johns Hopkins University; Board of Trustees, Bowdoin College; Honorary Co-Chair, Marylanders Against Handgun Use **AW:** Certificate of Merit, Common Cause Maryland, Annapolis, MD (1982, 1985); Torch of Liberty Award, Washington Region, Anti-Defamation League (1984); Outstanding State Official of the Year, Young Democrats of Maryland (1981) **AV:** Playing tennis; Maintaining physical fitness; Reading

BAIRD, JAMES, "JIM" RICHARD, T: U.S. Representative from Indiana **I:** Government Administration/Government Relations/Government Services **DOB:** 06/04/1945 **PB:** Covington **SC:** ID/USA **MS:** Married **SPN:** Denise Baird **CH:** Three Children **ED:** PhD, University of Kentucky; MS, Purdue University; BS, Purdue University **C:** Member, U.S. House of Representatives from Indiana's Fourth Congressional District (2019-Present); Member, District 44, Indiana House of Representatives (2011-2018); Commissioner, Putnam County, IN; Owner, Operator, Home Health Care Agency; Program Director and Monogastric Nutritionist, Multi-state Cooperative; Livestock Specialist and Extension Agent; Owner, Operator, Baird Family Farms **MIL:** First Lieutenant, United States Army (1969-1972) **AW:** Bronze Star; Two Purple Hearts **PA:** Republican

BAIRD, SCOTT JAMES, PHD, T: English Language Educator **I:** Education/Educational Services **DOB:** 05/16/1939 **PB:** Shelby **SC:** NE/USA **PT:** Hugh Vance Baird; Faye Maureen (Roberts) Baird **MS:** Married **SPN:** Kay Johnson (04/09/2016); Renee Smith Baird (06/18/1966, Deceased 06/09/2014) **CH:** Nicole Simon; Tania Uribe **ED:** PhD, The University of Texas at Austin (1969); MA, The University of Texas at Austin (1968); BA, Midland College (1961) **C:** Professor Emeritus, Trinity University (2009-Present); Professor, Trinity University (1974-2009); Professor, International Christian University (1969-1974); Adjunct Professor, Japan Lutheran Theological Seminary (1969-1974); High School Teacher, Kyushu Gakuin, Kumamoto, Japan (1961-1964) **CR:** Associate Member, Bexar County Historical Commission (2013-Present); Consultant, ETS (1980-2005); Commissioner, Accrediting Council

for Continuing Education & Training (1991-1994); Lecturer, Fulbright Association, Japan (1970, 1972) **CIV:** Co-Director, Origin of Names Booth, Texas Folklife Festival, San Antonio, TX (1985-2009); Member, Cemetery Conservation, Alamo Area Council of Governments, San Antonio, TX (1994-1999); Board of Directors, Good Samaritan Center, San Antonio, TX (1977-1985); Board of Directors, Tokyo Woman's Christian University, Tokyo, Japan (1970-1974) **CW:** Contributor, Articles, Professional Journals **AW:** Equipment Grantee, Educational Training, Incorporated (1992); Writing Program Grantee, National Endowment of the Humanities (1984-1985); Research Grantee, The American Folklife Center at the Library of Congress, Washington, DC (1982) **MEM:** Chair, Non-English Section, American Dialect Society (1969-2000); Regional Secretary, American Dialect Society (1981-1989); Teachers of English to Speakers of Other Languages (Now TESOL International Association); Linguistic Society of America; American Name Society; Association for Gravestone Studies; American Culture Association; Officer, San Antonio RoadRunners **MH:** Albert Nelson Marquis Lifetime Achievement Award; Marquis Who's Who Top Professional **B/I:** Dr. Baird became involved in his profession because he was inspired by his parents, Vance and Faye. They were both born and raised in Nebraska and attended the same church college, where Dr. Baird eventually attended. His father was a Lutheran minister and his mother was a kindergarten educator. **AV:** Running marathons; Singing

BAKER, CHARLES DUANE JR., T: Governor of Massachusetts **I:** Government Administration/Government Relations/Government Services **DOB:** 11/13/1956 **PB:** Elmira **SC:** NY/USA **MS:** Married **SPN:** Lauren Cardy Schadt (1987) **CH:** Charlie Baker; Andrew "AJ" Baker; Caroline Baker **ED:** MBA, Northwestern University School of Management (1986); BA in English, Harvard College (1979) **C:** Governor, Commonwealth of Massachusetts (2015-Present); Executive-in-residence, General Catalyst Partners, Cambridge, MA (2011-Present); Republican Candidate for 2010 Massachusetts Gubernatorial Race (2009-2010); President, Chief Executive Officer, Harvard Pilgrim Health Care, Inc., Quincy, MA (1999-2009); President, Chief Executive Officer, Harvard Vanguard Medical Associates (Now Atrius Health) (1998); Secretary of Administration and Finance, Commonwealth of Massachusetts (1994-1998); Secretary of Health and Human Services, Commonwealth of Massachusetts (1991-1994); Under Secretary for Health and Human Services, Commonwealth of Massachusetts, Boston, MA (1991-1992); Co-founder, Pioneer Institute for Public Policy Research (1988-1991); corporate communications director for the Massachusetts High Technology Council **CR:** Board of Directors, MedVentive Inc. (2010-Present); Board Trustee, Natixis Funds (2005-Present); Board of Directors, Athenahealth, Inc. (2012); Board of Directors, Tremont Credit Union (2010) **CIV:** Board Selectman, Swampscott, MA (2004-2007); Board Member, Greater Boston Chamber of Commerce; Board Trustee, Rose Fitzgerald Kennedy Greenway Conservancy **AW:** Distinguished Service Award, National Governors Association (NGA) (1998) **MEM:** Board Chair, Massachusetts Association of Health Plans (MAHP) **PA:** Republican

BAKER, EARL H., PHD, T: Medical Psychologist, Educator, Academic Administrator **I:** Education/Educational Services **DOB:** 08/03/1946 **PB:** Amarillo **SC:** TX/USA **PT:** Benjamin Harold Baker; Narcesia (Cranmer) Baker **MS:** Married **SPN:** Ambia Jane Campbell (02/17/1973) **CH:** Douglas; Caroline; James; Steven **ED:** MS in Clinical Psychopharmacology, California School of Professional Psychology (1999); PhD, University of Rhode Island (1984); MS, University of Rhode Island (1979); BS, Boise State University (1971) **CT:** Licensed, Louisiana State Board of Medical Examiners (2010); Licensed Medical Psychologist (2006); Licensed Psychologist, Louisiana State Board of Examiners of Psychologists (1989) **C:** E. H. Baker, PhD, MP & Associates (1996-Present); Director of School Psychology, Northeast Louisiana University (1986-1996); School Psychologist, Coventry Public Schools (1980-1986) **MIL:** Sergeant, US Army (1967-1969) **CW:** Contributor, Articles, Professional Journals **MEM:** President, Louisiana School Psychological Association (1993); President Elect, Louisiana School Psychological Association (1992); American Psychological Association; Louisiana Academy of Medical Psychologists, Inc.; Louisiana Psychological Association **MH:** Albert Nelson Marquis Lifetime Achievement Award **B/I:** Dr. Baker became involved in his profession after taking his first psychology class in college. **AV:** Traveling; Fishing; Hunting **PA:** Conservative **RE:** Christian

BAKER, ERICA JOY, T: Principal Group Engineering Manager; Co-Founder **I:** Business Management/Business Services **CN:** Microsoft; Project Include **ED:** AAS in Information Technology Support, University of Alaska (2001); Coursework, University of Miami **C:** Principal Group Engineering Manager, Microsoft (2019-Present); Senior Engineering Manager, Infrastructure, Patreon (2017-2019); Build and Release Engineer, Slack Technologies, Inc. (2015-2017); Site Reliability Engineer, Google (2014-2015); Corporate Operations Engineer, Google (2012-2014); Trial Programs Manager, Google TV, Google (2009-2012); Executive Support Technician II, Google (2008-2009); IT Field Technician, Google (2006-2008); Desktop Support Technician, Scientific Games Corporation (2005-2006); Network Operations and Mobile Desktop Support, Home Depot (2004-2005); Windows Domain Administrator, University of Alaska System (2001-2004) **CR:** Featured Speaker, Bond Conference (2018); Featured Speaker, Berkeley Center for New Media Panel (2018); Featured Speaker, Women in the Workplace Forum, The Wall Street Journal (2018); Keynote Speaker, Women of Color in Computing Conference, Mills College (2017) **CIV:** Co-Founder, Project Include (2016-Present); Advisory Board, Hack the Hood (2015-Present); Diversity Council Member, Code.org (2017-2019); Board of Directors, Girl Develop It (2016-2019); Technology Mentor, Black Girls Code **CW:** Writer, Creator, Numerous Websites **AW:** Crunchies Award for Fastest Rising Startup (for Slack Technologies, Inc.), TechCrunch (2016) **AV:** Researching genealogy

BAKER, FRANK, T: Psychologist, Educator **I:** Education/Educational Services **DOB:** 02/28/1936 **PB:** Dallas, Texas **SC:** USA **PT:** Dave; Estelle Portnoy Baker **MS:** Widower **SPN:** Adrienne Polland Baker **CH:** Steven; David; Julie **ED:** PhD in Social Psychology, Northwestern University; MA in Social Psychology, Northwestern University; BA in Psychology, Vanderbilt University, Cum Laude **CT:** Licensed Psychologist, Commonwealth of Massachusetts **C:** Senior Program Evaluation Consultant, Conneticut Department of Corrections, Wethersfield, CT (2015-Present); Research Professor, University of Conneticut, Director of Research Division, Connecticut Department of Mental Health and Addiction Services (2011-2015); Adjunct Professor of Medicine, Director, Center for Medical Outcomes Research (2010-2011); Professor, Epidemiology and Community Health (2009-2010); School of Public Health, New York Medical College (2006-2009); Professor of Behavioral Sciences

and Health Education, Department of Behavioral Sciences and Health Education (1997-2008); Vice President for Behavioral Research, Founding Director, Behavioral Research Center (1995-2005); Professor, Director, Health Psychology, Division of Occupational Health (1987-1995); Professor, Chairman, Department of Behavioral Sciences and Health Education, Johns Hopkins University (1985-1987); Visiting Lecturer, Psychiatry, Harvard Medical School (1981-1982); Professor, Psychiatry, Psychology and Social Preventative Medicine (1974-1985); Director, Organizational Systems Research, Harvard Medical School (1973-1974); Assistant Professor, Psychology, Psychiatry, Harvard Medical School (1965-1974); Assistant Professor, Social Relations, Lehigh University (1963-1965) **CW:** Contributor, Articles in Professional Journals **AW:** Listee, Who's Who in Science and Engineering (1996-1997); Listee, Who's Who in the World (1995-1996); Listee, Men of Achievement (1990); Inductee, Delta Omega (1985); Listee, Who's Who in Frontier Science and Technology (1983); Listee, Who's Who in Healthcare (1977); Listee, Who's Who in the East (1973-2010) **MEM:** American Association for the Advancement of Science; Academy of Health; American Psychological Association; American Public Health Association; American Society of Clinical Oncology; American Sociological Association; International Society for Quality of Life Research; Society of Behavioral Medicine **MH:** Albert Nelson Marquis Lifetime Achievement Award **B/I:** In his efforts as a premed student of Vanderbilt, Dr. Baker took psychology courses, which piqued his interest significantly. He was also lucky to have a professor who took an active interest in his students. He performed excellently in psychology, and received several offers of being financially supported as a graduate student in psychology. In the interest of not depending on his parents to help him pay for attending medical school, he decided to continue his graduate education in psychology. He was accepted as doctoral student in social psychology at Northwestern University and as a research assistant for Dr. Donald T. Campbell, who was making a national name for himself as a professor at the school.

BAKER, JAMES, "JIM" ADDISON III, T: Former White House Chief of Staff; Partner **I:** Law and Legal Services **CN:** Baker Botts L.L.P. **DOB:** 04/28/1930 **PB:** Houston **SC:** TX/USA **PT:** James Addison Baker Jr.; Ethel Bonner (Means) Baker **MS:** Married **SPN:** Susan Garrett Winston (08/06/1973); Mary Stuart McHenry (1953, Deceased 1970) **CH:** Eight Children **ED:** Honorary LLD, University of Pennsylvania (2007); LLB, University of Texas (1957); BA, Princeton University (1952) **C:** Senior Partner, Baker Botts LLP, Washington, DC and Houston, TX (1993-Present); Member, Iraq Study Group (2006); Chief of Staff, Senior Counselor to President, The White House (1992-1993); Secretary, U.S. Department of State (1989-1992); Chairman, George H.W. Bush Presidential Campaign (1988); Secretary, U.S. Department of the Treasury (1985-1988); Chief of Staff to President, The White House (1981-1985); Under Secretary, U.S. Department of Commerce, Washington, DC (1975-1976); Attorney, Andrews Kurth Campbell & Jones, Houston, Texas (1957-1975) **CR:** Chairman, The B.P. Refineries Independent Safety Review Panel (2005-2007); Co-Chair, Iraq Study Group (2006); With, Personal Envoy of Secretary-General for Western Sahara, United Nations (1997-2004); Senior Counselor, The Carlyle Group (1993-2005); With, Special Presidential Envoy to Iraqi for Debt Reduction, The White House (2003); Member, Board of Directors, Electronic Data Corporation (1996-2003); Gulf Coast Regional Chairman, President Richard Nixon's Re-Election Campaign (1972); Finance Chairman,

Republican Party (1971) **CIV:** Honorary Chairman, Rice University Baker Institute for Public Policy, Houston, Texas (1993-Present); Member, Board of Trustees, Smithsonian Institution; Member, Board of Trustees, Woodrow Wilson International Center for Scholars (The Wilson Center); Member, World Justice Project; Member, Climate Leadership Council **MIL:** With, U.S. Marine Corps (1952-1954) **CW:** Appearance, Documentary, "Reagan" (2011); Author, "Work Hard, Study...and Keep Out of Politics!: Adventures and Lessons from an Unexpected Political Life" (2006); Author, "The Politics of Diplomacy: Revolution, War and Peace, 1989-1992" (1995) **AW:** Named Grand Cordon, Order of the Rising Sun (2015); Named One of America's Best Leaders, U.S. News & World Report (2007); Lifetime Achievement Award, American Lawyer Magazine (2007); Woodrow Wilson Award for Public Service, Princeton University (2000); Presidential Medal of Freedom, The White House (1991); John Heinz Award for Greatest Public Service to an Elected or Appointed Official (1985); George F. Kennan Award; Hans J. Morgenthau Award; Alexander Hamilton Award, U.S. Department of the Treasury; Distinguished Service Award, U.S. Department of State; Jefferson Award, American Institute for Public Service **MEM:** Fellow, American Academy of Arts and Sciences; American Bar Association; American Judicature Society; Houston Bar Association; State Bar of Texas; The International Legal Honor Society of Phi Delta Phi **AV:** Hunting; Fishing; Playing tennis; Playing golf **PA:** Republican **RE:** Episcopalian

BAKER, JILL WITHROW, T: Artist **I:** Fine Art **CN:** Jill Baker's Artist's Studio **DOB:** 10/12/1942 **PB:** Ilion **SC:** NY/USA **PT:** Alfred Seiders Withrow; Rosalee (Wilson) Withrow **MS:** Divorced **SPN:** Samuel T. Smith (07/11/2006); Patrick Halvorson (10/18/1981, Divorced); James T. Baker (08/23/1963, Divorced 1978) **CH:** Virginia; Elizabeth **ED:** Master of Fine Arts in Painting, Pratt Institute, Brooklyn, NY (1981); Bachelor of Arts in Fine Arts and English, Baylor University, Waco, TX (1964) **CT:** Kentucky Colonel, Commercial Driver's License **C:** Adjunct Professor of Art, University of Southern Indiana, Evansville, IN (2008-2017); Visiting Adjunct Professor of Art History, University of Evansville, Evansville, IN (2011); Adjunct Professor of Humanities, University of Southern Indiana, Evansville, IN (2008-2011); Reporter, Photographer, Posey County News, New Harmony, IN (2006-2007); Adjunct Professor of Studio Art, Art Institute of Tennessee, Nashville, TN (2005-2006); Adjunct Professor of Humanities, Composition/Communication, Ground and Online Courses, Donelson and Franklin Campuses, Phoenix University, Nashville, TN (2001-2006); Professor of Drawing, Composition and Studio Courses, Success Strategies, Computer, Nossi College of Art, Nashville, TN (1995-2004); Editor, West Coast, Women Artists News, New York (1984-1989); Arts Review Writer, Downtown News, Los Angeles, California (1985-1986); Professor, Studio Art, Pierce College, Woodland Hills, CA (1984-1985); Intern Professor, Drawing, Pratt Institute, Brooklyn, NY (1979) **CR:** Owner, Winchester Cottage Gallery and Print (1997-Present); Interpretive Museum Aide (2009-2011); Reporter, Women Artist News (1978-2006); Officer, Manager, and Web Designer, Vanderbilt University, Nashville, TN (2001-2002); Visiting Artist to the Republic of South Korea, U.S. Information Services (1977); Editor, Phoenix Magazine, Baylor University, Waco, TX (1962-1963); Editor, Youth Weekly, First Baptist Church, Waco, TX (1962-1963) **CIV:** Founder, President, ART-Sumner, Sumner County, TN (1997-2006); Coordinator, Co-Founder, Southern KY Guild of Artists and Craftsmen (1971) **CW:** Exhibition, Saatchi Gallery,

London, England (2018-Present); Artist, Jill Baker Artist's Studio (2012-Present); Sole Proprietor, Artist's Studio (2012-Present); Artist, Artist's Studio (2012-Present); Exhibition, New Harmony/University of Southern Indiana Gallery of Contemporary Art (2006-Present); Gallery Artist, Ward-Nasse Gallery (1979-Present); Numerous Group Exhibitions (1975-2019); Author, Book, "Elba Journal" (2009); Author, Book, "My Turn" (2009); Author, Book of Poetry, "Poems of Accord and Satisfaction" (2009); Contributor, Numerous Published Articles (1973-2009); Art Editor, Tale Trader (1976-2000); Numerous Cover Articles for Discover E-Magazine, Vanderbilt University, Nashville, TN (1990-1995); Arts Review Writer, Downtown News, Los Angeles, CA (1985-1986); Editor, West Coast, Women Artists News (1984-1989); One-Woman Show, U.S. Embassy, Seoul, South Korea (1978); One-Woman Show, Palazzo Strozzi, Florence, Italy (1975); Judge, Art Consultant, At Least Five Exhibitions, Los Angeles, CA and Nashville, TN; Exhibition, Merton Gallery, Bellarmine College, "Thomas Merton from Life"; Author, Many Works on Writing and Hundreds of Research Articles on Ancient Art **AW:** Jerry's Artarama Award from Michael Marchetta (2016); Artavita Certificate of Excellence, 11th Online Contest (2015); Award of Excellence, for "Grand Canal," Manhattan Arts Gallery, New York, NY (2013); Purchase Award, Jefferson Jubilee, Jefferson Community and Technical College, Louisville, KY (2012); Honorable Mention at Hoosier Salon, New Harmony (2011); Honorable Mention for "Running Horses," in "Working Together" (2009); 2D Honorable Mention, Art In The City, Arts Council of Southwestern Indiana (2009); Purchase Award, for "Red House" Field to Finish Plein Air Show at Hoosier Salon, New Harmony, IN (2008); Exhibition, 2D Awards, Evansville Museum of Arts, Evansville, Indiana; Featured Artist, Bower-Suhrheinrich Foundation Gallery **MEM:** Regional Vice President, Northeastern U.S., National Artists Equity Association, Washington, DC (1988-1995); Regional Vice President, Southwestern U.S. Artists Equity Association, Washington, DC (1988-1995); President, Executive Board Member, Los Angeles Chapter, Artists Equity Association (1982-1991); Board of Directors, Nonprofit Arm of Artists Equity, Los Angeles, CA; President, New York State Chapter, National Artists Equity Association; Board Member, Visual Artists Guild; Graphics Committee, L.A. County Museum of Contemporary Art; New York Artists Equity; Women's Caucus for the Arts; Women Artists Association; Foundation for Community of Artists; National Association of Women Artists; Louisville Visual Arts Association; College Art Association; National Association of Professional Women; Ward-Nasse Gallery; Americans for the Arts Action Fund; Manhattan Arts, The Artists Registry **AS:** Ms. Baker attributes her success to hard work and motivation. She was fortunate enough to have had great teachers, including Karl Zerbe (at Florida State University) and Silvio LoFreddo (at the Academia di Belle Arti in Florence) She attributes her ethics to her father, Alfred Seiders Withrow, a daring and strong-willed individual. **B/I:** Ms. Baker became involved in her profession due to her lifelong interest in drawing and art. **AV:** Yoga **PA:** Democrat **RE:** Unitarian

BAKER, KRISTI A., DMA, T: Pianist, Church Musician, Composer **I:** Media & Entertainment **DOB:** 12/10/1957 **PB:** Topeka **SC:** KS/USA **PT:** J. Roland Williams; Lila Ann (Kern) Williams **MS:** Widowed **SPN:** Charles Burton Baker **CH:** Barbara Baker McCall; Elizabeth Baker Emery **ED:** Doctor of Musical Arts, University of Kansas (2012); MusM, Kansas State University (1984); BS, Kansas State University (1979) **CT:** Nationally Certified Teacher

of Music (2008); K-12 Music Teacher, Kansas (1979) **C:** Choral Director, Osawatomie Schools (2005-2010); Choral Director, Abilene High School (2003-2005); Choral Director, Junction City Middle School, Junction City, KS (1988-2003); Elementary Music Teacher, Ware Elementary School, Fort Riley, KS (1984-1988); Band, Choral Director, Wakefield Public Schools (1981-1984); Graduate Teaching Assistant, Kansas State University Department of Music (1979-1981); Private Piano Instructor, Topeka, KS (1972-1975); Pianist, Church Musician, Composer; Freelance Recitalist, Master Clinician; Owner, Operator, KB Piano, Topeka, KS **CR:** Adjunct Instructor, Applied Piano, Ottawa University (2006-Present); Commission on Music, Liturgy Episcopalian Diocese of Kansas (2001-Present); Church Organist, Choir Master, Various Churches (1988-Present); Private Piano and Voice Instructor, Junction City, KS (1981-Present) **CW:** Performer, 6 European Tours, St.David's Psalm Project (2017); Composer, "St. John's Mass" (2006); Composer, "The Magic of Your Dreams" (2000); Composer, "A Song for Advent" (1988) **AW:** Superior Plus Ratings, National Piano Teachers Guild (1968-1975); Winner, Youth Talent Auditions, Topeka Symphony Orchestra (1974) **MEM:** Grand Director of Music, Job's Daughters of Kansas (2000-2007); American Choral Directors Association; Order of the Eastern Star (2005-2006); Chair, North Central District, Kansas Music Educators Association (1995-2005); Commission Liturgy; Art and Music; Episcopal Diocese of Kansas; Music Educators' National Conference; Music Teachers National Association; Music Teachers National Association **MH:** Albert Nelson Marquis Lifetime Achievement Award; Marquis Who's Who Top Professional **B/I:** Dr. Baker became involved in her profession because she started playing the piano when she was 7 years old, as did a lot of her friends. Most of her friends quit but she stuck with it because she really liked it. Honing in on her talent, she ultimately received a lot of scholarships to attend college in pursuit of a music degree, which is how she made a career out of it. She also knew she always wanted to teach. **AV:** Practicing needlepoint; Sewing; Water sports **PA:** Democrat **RE:** Episcopalian

BAKER, MARC, T: President, Chief Executive Officer **I:** Other **CN:** 1) Combined Jewish Philanthropies of Greater Boston 2) Gann Academy **ED:** MA in Jewish Education, The Hebrew University of Jerusalem (2002); Coursework, Pardes Institute of Jewish Studies (1999-2002); BA in Religious Studies, Yale University (1997) **C:** President, Chief Executive Officer, Combined Jewish Philanthropies (2018-Present); Head, Gann Academy (2007-Present); Director, Jewish and Student Life, The Weber School (2002-2006); Assistant Director, Camp Bauercrest (2000)

BALDERRAMA, CELEDONIA, "CELIA" I., T: Attorney **I:** Law and Legal Services **CN:** Balderrama Law Firm, LLC **DOB:** 08/12/1983 **PB:** Albuquerque **SC:** NM/USA **PT:** Jose Munoz; Michele Rael **MS:** Married **SPN:** Frank V. Balderrama **CH:** One Son; Two Stepsons; One Stepdaughter **ED:** JD, University of New Mexico, Albuquerque, NM (2014); BS in Criminology/Sociology, University of New Mexico, Albuquerque, NM (2010) **C:** Attorney, Balderrama Law Firm, LLC (2018-Present); Prosecutor, Attorney General's Office (2014-2018) **MEM:** Kappa Alpha Delta; Phi Alpha Delta **BAR:** U.S. District Court of New Mexico (2018); New Mexico Bar (2015) **AS:** Ms. Balderrama was raised in a household where doing the bare minimum was not acceptable. Her parents raised her family to have pride in what they did and to never give up just because something was difficult. Her dad is very creative, smart, and talented. He taught her that there is always

a solution, even if one has to take a step back and re-evaluate the situation. Her mom is a compassionate hard worker. She taught her to never give up, even when she felt like nothing mattered because in the end, it all matters. **B/I:** Ms. Balderrama became involved in her profession because, during her undergraduate years, she was working at a law firm. Initially, she was only looking for a part-time job as a file clerk but was promoted to receptionist and then legal secretary. Her interest blossomed while she was at the personal injury law firm. She really liked how the attorneys were able to help people. While Ms. Balderrama was in law school, she clerked at the district attorney's office, which triggered her interest in criminal law. **AV:** Attending church and children's sporting events; Exercising; Reading; Crocheting; Cooking **RE:** Christian **THT:** Ms. Balderrama's motto is, "Take it one day at a time."

BALDERSON, DIANE K. BROWN, RN, T: Business Owner **I:** Retail/Sales **CN:** Carl's Pawn Shop, Inc. **DOB:** 09/26/1952 **PB:** Parkersburg **SC:** WV/USA **PT:** Ray H. Brown; Lorraine M. (Gwynn) Brown **MS:** Widowed **SPN:** Carl W. Balderson Jr. **ED:** BSN, West Virginia University (1989); Diploma, St. Mary's Hospital (St. Mary's Medical Center), Huntington, WV (1974) **CT:** RN; Former Instructor, ACLS, BLS, Critical Care **C:** Owner, D.B. Balderson Rentals, LLC, and Carl's Pawn Shop, Inc.; Administrative Director of Physicians Services, Administrative Director of Emergency/Trauma Services, St. Joseph's Hospital, Parkersburg, West Virginia University Health System, WV; Trauma Nurse Coordinator, Assistant Director of Nursing Emergency Medical Service, St. Joseph's Hospital, Parkersburg, West Virginia University Health System, WV; With, Open Heart Intensive Care Unit, Milton S. Hershey Medical Center, Penn State Health, Hershey, PA; Staff Nurse, Timken Mercy Hospital, Canton, Ohio; With, Dr. M. Homer Cummings Jr., Huntington, WV **CR:** Consultant in Field, Emergency and Trauma **CIV:** Board Member, Parkersburg Country Club, Parkersburg, WV; Teacher, Sunday School (25 Years); Board Member, Parkersburg Area Community Foundation, Parkersburg, WV; Member, Various Church Committees, Trinity United Methodist Church, Parkersburg, WV; Singer, Church Choir, Trinity United Methodist Church, Parkersburg, WV **MEM:** Former Member, West Virginia State Trauma Nurse Coordinators; American Trauma Society, WV; Board of Directors, Southern Emergency Medical Services; Board of Directors, Mid Ohio Valley Emergency Medical Services Incorporated **MH:** Albert Nelson Marquis Lifetime Achievement Award **AS:** Mrs. Balderson attributes her success to God and her parents. **B/I:** Mrs. Balderson has always liked taking care of people. **PA:** Republican **RE:** Christian **THT:** Mrs. Balderson's motto is, "Be thankful for every day God has given you and live it to fullest. Think before you speak and use kind words when speaking to others. Always be truthful, honest, kind, thoughtful, and ready to help others."

BALDERSON, WILLIAM, "TROY" TROY, T: U.S. Representative from Ohio **I:** Government Administration/Government Relations/Government Services **DOB:** 01/16/1962 **PB:** Zanesville **SC:** OH/USA **MS:** Divorced **SPN:** Angela Mattingly (1985, Divorced 2014) **CH:** Joshua **ED:** Coursework, The Ohio State University; Coursework, Muskingum College (Now Muskingum University) **C:** Member, U.S. House of Representatives from Ohio's 12th Congressional District, United States Congress, Washington, DC (2018-Present); Member, District 20, Ohio State Senate (2011-2018); Member, District 94, Ohio House of Representatives (2009-2011); Co-owner, Balderson Motor Sales; Operation Assistant, Family-owned Farm, Salem, OH; Member, U.S. Senate Committee on Energy and Natural Resources; Member, U.S. Senate Committee on Finance **CIV:** Member, First Christian Church, Zanesville, OH **AV:** Running; Cycling **PA:** Republican **RE:** Christian

BALDWIN, TAMMY SUZANNE, T: U.S. Senator from Wisconsin **I:** Government Administration/ Government Relations/Government Services **DOB:** 02/11/1962 **PB:** Madison **SC:** WI/USA **PT:** Joseph Edward Baldwin; Pamela (Green) Baldwin **ED:** JD, University of Wisconsin Law School, Madison, WI (1989); AB in Government and Mathematics, Smith College, Northampton, MA (1984) **C:** Secretary, Senate Democratic Conference (2017-Present); U.S. Senator, State of Wisconsin (2013-Present); Member, U.S. Senate Special Committee on Aging (2013-Present); Member, U.S. Senate Committee on Health, Education, Labor & Pensions (2013-Present); Member, U.S. Senate Homeland Security and Governmental Affairs (2013-Present); Member, U.S. Senate Committee on the Budget (2013-Present); Member, U.S. Representative from Wisconsin's Second Congressional District, United States Congress, Washington, DC (1999-2013); Member, U.S. House Judiciary Committee (2007-2011); Member, District 78, Wisconsin State Assembly (1993-1999); Private Law Practice, WI (1989-1992); Supervisor, Dane County Board of Supervisors (1986-1994); Councilwoman, Madison City Council (1986) **MEM:** American Civil Liberties Union; National Organization for Women; State Bar of Wisconsin; International Network of Lesbian & Gay Officials **PA:** Democrat

BALDWIN, WILLIAM, "BILL" EDWARD, T: Owner **I:** Architecture & Construction **CN:** The Baldwin Group **PB:** Evergreen Park **SC:** IL/USA **MS:** Married **SPN:** Sarah **CH:** Five Children **ED:** Coursework, University of Illinois (1964) **CT:** Architect License, NCARB - National Council of Architectural Registration Boards, IL, IN, and FL; General Contractor's License, FL **C:** Owner, The Baldwin Group, Inc. (1970-Present); Owner, Future Environment (1970-1983) **CIV:** Volunteer, County Zoning Board, DuPage County, IL; Chair, Architectural Committee, Downers Grove, IL; Member, Ad-hoc Committee for New Sign Ordinance, Downers Grove, IL; Volunteer, Beautification Committee, Clearwater, FL; Board of Directors, Bent Tree Community, Inc., Jasper, GA **AW:** Award, Best Overall Site Plan; Award, Best Architectural Design; Award, Best Overall Landscape Plan for La Villita Condominium Villas Development, Clearwater, FL **MEM:** SARA; AIA **AS:** Mr. Baldwin attributes much of his success to studying hard, as well as understanding his client's needs in developing a well designed successful project. He also credits his success to volunteering, by giving of his time and expertise to the community and civic organizations and committees. **B/I:** Mr. Baldwin became involved in his profession because of his general interests in architecture and construction, which he developed while still in high school in Chicago. Above all, he was influenced by the beautiful architecture of the city around him; he took up drafting courses in high school and was encouraged by his instructors to move ahead into the profession. Mr. Baldwin entered the architectural engineering program at the University of Illinois, where he drew on inspiration from Frank Lloyd Wright, Ludwig Mies van der Rohe and other giants of the industry. Later, he was lucky enough to meet some of the most prominent architects in the world through the AIA.

BALE, CHRISTIAN CHARLES PHILIP, T: Actor **I:** Media & Entertainment **DOB:** 01/30/1974 **PB:** Haverfordwest **SC:** Wales/United Kingdom **PT:** David Bale; Jenny (James) Bale; Gloria Steinem (Stepmother) **MS:** Married **SPN:** Sandra "Sibi" Blažic (01/29/2000) **CH:** Emmaline; Joseph **CIV:** Supporter, Sea Shepherd Conservation Society; Supporter, Greenpeace; Supporter, World Wildlife Fund; Supporter, Redwings Horse Rescue & Sanctuary; Supporter, The Ark Trust, Inc., The Humane Society of the United States; Supporter, HCI; Board of Trustees, Dian Fossey Gorilla Fund International, Inc. **CW:** Actor, "Ford v Ferrari" (2019); Actor, "Vice" (2018); Voice Actor, "Mowgli: Legend of the Jungle" (2018); Actor, "Hostiles" (2017); Actor, "The Promise" (2016); Actor, "The Big Short" (2015); Actor, "Knight of Cups" (2015); Actor, "Exodus: Gods and Kings" (2014); Actor, "American Hustle" (2013); Actor, "Out of the Furnace" (2013); Actor, "The Dark Knight Rises" (2012); Actor, "The Flowers of War" (2011); Actor, "The Fighter" (2010); Actor, "Public Enemies" (2009); Actor, "Terminator Salvation" (2009); Actor, "The Dark Knight" (2008); Actor, "I'm Not There" (2007); Actor, "3:10 to Yuma" (2007); Actor, "The Prestige" (2006); Actor, "Rescue Dawn" (2006); Actor, "The New World" (2005); Actor, Executive Producer, "Harsh Times" (2005); Actor, "Batman Begins" (2005); Voice Actor, "Howl's Moving Castle" (2004); Actor, "The Machinist" (2004); Actor, "Equilibrium" (2002); Actor, "Reign of Fire" (2002); Actor, "Laurel Canyon" (2002); Actor, "Captain Corelli's Mandolin" (2001); Actor, "Shaft" (2000); Actor, "American Psycho" (2000); Actor, "Mary, Mother of Jesus" (1999); Actor, "A Midsummer Night's Dream" (1999); Actor, "All the Little Animals" (1998); Actor, "Velvet Goldmine" (1998); Actor, "Metroland" (1997); Actor, "The Secret Agent" (1997); Actor, "The Portrait of a Lady" (1996); Voice Actor, "Pocahontas" (1995); Actor, "Little Women" (1994); Actor, "Royal Deceit" (1994); Actor, "Swing Kids" (1993); Actor, "Newsies" (1992); Actor, "A Murder of Quality" (1991); Voice Actor, "The Dreamstone" (1990); Actor, "Treasure Island" (1990); Actor, "Henry V" (1989); Actor, "Empire of the Sun" (1987); Actor, "Mio in the Land of Faraway" (1987); Actor, "Heart of the Country" (1987); Actor, "Anastasia: The Mystery of Anna" (1986) **AW:** Satellite Award for Best Actor – Motion Picture Drama, International Press Academy (2020); Critics' Choice Award for Best Actor in a Comedy, The Critics Choice Association (2016, 2019); Critics' Choice Award for Best Actor, The Critics Choice Association (2019); Golden Globe Award for Best Actor – Motion Picture Musical or Comedy, Hollywood Foreign Press Association (2019); Satellite Award for Best Supporting Actor – Motion Picture, International Press Academy (2010, 2015); Critics' Choice Award for Best Acting Ensemble, The Critics Choice Association (2011, 2014); Screen Actors Guild Award for Outstanding Performance by a Cast in a Motion Picture, SAG-AFTRA (2014); Academy Award for Best Supporting Actor, Academy of Motion Picture Arts and Sciences (2011); Critics' Choice Award for Best Supporting Actor, The Critics Choice Association (2011); Golden Globe Award for Best Supporting Actor – Motion Picture, Hollywood Foreign Press Association (2011); Screen Actors Guild Award for Outstanding Performance by a Male Actor in a Supporting Role, SAG-AFTRA (2011); Award for Best Supporting Actor, National Board of Review (2010); Empire Award for Best Actor, Empire Magazine, Bauer Media Group (2009); Award for Best Superhero, The Scream Awards (2008); Independent Spirit Robert Altman Award, Film Independent (2007); Saturn Award for Best Actor, Academy of Science Fiction, Fantasy and Horror Films (2006); Award for Outstanding Juvenile Performance, National Board of Review (1987)

BALL, SHERI BETH, T: Senior Vice President **I:** Financial Services **CN:** Global Corporate Trust Services **DOB:** 06/12/1963 **PB:** Montebello **SC:** CA/USA **PT:** Chester Bert; Shirley Ann (Winnemore) Dickason **MS:** Married **SPN:** Andrew Ball (5/23/1987) **CH:** Michael; Victoria **CT:** Certified Corporate Trust Specialist (1991) **C:** Senior Vice President, Team Manager, Administration, US Bank (1995-Present); Vice President, Team Manager, Administration, Bank of America, Los Angeles, CA (1989-1995); Assistant Vice President and Manager, Corporate Trust Operations, Security Pacific National Bank, Glendale, CA (1987-1989); Corporate Trust Officer, Security Pacific National Bank, Los Angeles, CA (1985-1987); Supervisor Trust Securities, First Interstate Bank, Los Angeles, CA (1981-1985); Assistant Manager, Van's Tennis Shoes, Anaheim, CA (1978-1981) **CR:** Work Improvement Coordinator, First Interstate Bank, Los Angeles, CA (1984-1985) **CIV:** Board of Directors, Pasadena Playhouse **CW:** Choreographer, "Behold the Man" (1987); Choreographer, "In His Light" (1988) **MEM:** Western Stock Transfer Association; Treasurer, Sacred Dance Guild (1987-1989) **MH:** Albert Nelson Marquis Lifetime Achievement Award **B/I:** Ms. Ball became involved in her profession because it was an opportunity that presented itself. She applied for a job at UCB when she was 17 years old. **AV:** Theater; Dancing; Gourmet cooking; Wine tasting; Reading **RE:** Presbyterian

BALLARD, ROBERT DUANE, PHD, T: Professor; Oceanographer **I:** Education/Educational Services **CN:** University of Rhode Island **DOB:** 07/30/1942 **PB:** Wichita **SC:** KS/USA **PT:** Chester Patrick Ballard; Harriet Nell (May) Ballard **MS:** Married **SPN:** Barbara Earle (01/1991); Marjorie C. Jacobsen (07/01/1966, Divorced) **CH:** Todd (Deceased); Doug; Benjamin; Emily **ED:** Honorary DSc, University of Bath (1988); PhD in Marine Geology and Geophysics, University of Rhode Island (1974); Postgraduate Coursework, University of Southern California (1966-1967); MA in Geophysics, Hawaii Institute of Geophysics & Planetology, University of Hawaii (1965-1966); BS in Chemistry and Geology, University of California Santa Barbara, CA (1965) **C:** Professor, Graduate School of Oceanography, University of Rhode Island (2001-Present); Director, Institute of Archaeological Oceanography, University of Rhode Island (2001-Present); Explorer-in-Residence, National Geographic Society (1999-Present); Scientist Emeritus, Woods Hole Oceanographic Institution (1997-Present); Senior Scientist, Woods Hole Oceanographic Institution (1983-1997); Associate Scientist, Woods Hole Oceanographic Institution (1976-1983); Assistant Scientist, Woods Hole Oceanographic Institution (1974-1976) **CR:** Founder, President, Institute for Exploration, Mystic Aquarium, CT (1995-Present); Founder, Director, Deep Submergence Laboratory (1983-Present); Consultant Professor, Stanford University (1980-1981); Visiting Scholar, Stanford University (1979-1980) **CIV:** Board of Directors, Founder, The Jason Foundation, Inc.; Trustee, Sea Research Foundation, Inc. **MIL:** Commander, United States Navy Reserve (1970-1995); United States Navy (1967-1970); United States Army (1965-1967) **CW:** Co-Author, "Return to Titanic: A New Look at the World's Most Famous Lost Ship" (2004); Author, "Explorations" (1995); Author, "Exploring the Lusitania" (1995); Technical Consultant, "SeaQuest DSV" (1993-1994); Author, "The Lost Ships of Guadalcanal" (1993); Author, "The Wreck of the ISIS" (1990); Author, "Discovery of the Bismarck" (1990); Author, "Discovery of the Titanic" (1989); Author, "Exploring Our Living Planet" (1983) **AW:** National Humanities Medal (2003); Caird Medal, National Maritime Museum (2002); Lone Sailor Award, U.S. Navy

Memorial Foundation (1996); U.S. Navy Robert Dexter Conrad Award for Science Achievement (1992); Golden Plate Award, American Academy of Achievement (1990); Westinghouse Award, American Association for the Advancement of Science (1990); Centennial Award, National Geographic Society (1988); Cutty Sark Science Award (1982); Newcomb Cleveland Prize, American Association for the Advancement of Science (1981); Compass Distinguished Achievement Award (1977); Scientific Award, Underwater Society of America (1976); Hubbard Medal **MEM:** Geological Society of America; Marine Technology Society; American Geophysical Union; The Explorers Club; Sigma Alpha Epsilon Fraternity

BALLMER, STEVEN, "STEVE" ANTHONY, T: Professional Sports Team Executive **I:** Athletics **CN:** Los Angeles Clippers **DOB:** 03/24/1956 **PB:** Detroit **SC:** MI/USA **PT:** Frederick Ballmer; Beatrice (Dworkin) Ballmer **MS:** Married **SPN:** Connie Snyder (1990) **CH:** Three Sons **ED:** Coursework, Stanford Graduate School of Business (1980); AB in Applied Mathematics and Economics, Harvard University (1977) **C:** Owner, Los Angeles Clippers (2014-Present); Chief Executive Officer, Microsoft, Redmond, WA (2000-2014); Director, Accenture (2001-2006); President, Microsoft, Redmond, WA (1998-2001); Executive Vice President, Sales and Support, Microsoft, Redmond, WA (1992-1998); Vice President of Marketing, Vice President of Corporate Staffs, Senior Vice President of System Software, Microsoft, Redmond, WA (1980-1992); Assistant Product Manager, Procter & Gamble (1977-1979) **CR:** Board of Directors, Microsoft (2000-2014); Board of Directors, Accenture (2001-2006); Member, Advisory Council, Stanford Graduate School of Business; Board of Overseers, Harvard University **CIV:** Founder, USAFacts.org (2017-Present) **AW:** Forbes 400: Richest Americans, Forbes Media LLC (2009-Present); World's Richest People, Business Insider, Insider Inc. (2006-Present); World's Most Powerful People, Forbes Magazine, Forbes Media LLC (2012); Legion d'honneur, France (2011); TIME 100, TIME USA, LLC (2008) **MEM:** World Chairman's Council, Jewish National Fund **AV:** Exercising; Jogging; Basketball **RE:** Jewish

BAND, DAVID M., T: Artist, Conservator, Collector, Dealer **I:** Fine Art **DOB:** 10/16/1947 **PB:** Portland **SC:** ME/USA **PT:** Benjamin Band; Priscilla Maybelle Band **ED:** Coursework, Summer Art Program, University of Maine, Orono, ME **C:** Artist, The Baker Gallery, Lubbock, Texas; Medical Illustrator, School of Health Sciences, Sheppard Air Force Base, Wichita Falls, TX; Art Restoration; Art Framing **CIV:** Juror, Annual Exhibition, Red River Valley Museum, Vernon, TX (2004, 2006, 2008-2018); Juror, Lubbock Arts Alliance Studio Tour, Lubbock, TX (2014); Juror, East Texas Regional Exhibition, Longview Museum of Fine Art, Longview, TX (2004); Juror, 90th Annual Exhibition, Allied Artists of America, The National Arts Club, NY (2003); Juror, Annual Exhibition, Red River Valley Museum, Vernon, TX (2003); Juror, Annual Exhibition, Lubbock Arts Alliance, Lubbock, TX (2002) **MIL:** U.S. Air Force (1967-1987); Langley Air Force Base, Hampton, VA; Hospital Squadron, Sheppard Air Force Base, Wichita Falls, TX **CW:** Artist, 98th Annual Exhibition, Allied Artists of America, The National Arts Club, New York, NY (2011); Artist, 127th Annual Members' Exhibition, Salmagundi Club, New York, NY (2010); Artist, 96th Annual Exhibition, Allied Artists of America, The National Arts Club, New York, NY (2009); Artist, Annual Juried Exhibition, Watercolor USA, Springfield Art Museum, MO (2008); Artist, Allied Artists of America Inc. Invitational, Bennington Art Center, Bennington, VT (2007); Artist, Annual Combined Members Exhibition, Salmagundi Club, New York, NY (2007); Artist, Annual Thumb Box Exhibition, Salmagundi Club, New York, NY (2006-2007); Artist, 70th Annual Exhibition, The Butler Institute of American Art, Youngstown, Ohio (2006); Artist, 107th Annual Exhibiting Artist Member Exhibition, The National Arts Club (2005-2006); Artist, All-Members Exhibition, National Watercolor Society, San Pedro, CA (2005); Artist, Group Show, 85th-92nd Annual Exhibitions, Allied Artists of America, The National Arts Club, New York, NY (1998-2005); Artist, Exhibition, Watercolor USA, Springfield Art Museum, Springfield, MO (2004); Artist, Invitational Exhibition of Contemporary American Art, 179th Annual Exhibition, National Academy of Design (2004); Artist, Group Show, 63rd-68th Annual Midyear Exhibitions, The Butler Institute of American Art, Youngstown, Ohio (1999-2004); Artist, 83rd Annual Exhibition, National Watercolor Society, CA (2003); Artist, National Watercolor Society Travel Show (2003); Contributor, "Getting Greenery Right," The Artist's Magazine (2003); Author, "Bathed in Light," Art Clinic Critique, The Artist's Magazine (2003); Artist, 60th-61st Annual Exhibitions, Audubon Artists Inc., Salmagundi Club, New York, NY (2002-2003); Artist, Solo Exhibition, Cole Pratt Gallery, New Orleans, LA (2002); Artist, "Side by Side," Works on Paper, National Watercolor Society, Philadelphia Water Color Society, Philip and Muriel Berman Museum of Art, Collegeville, PA (2002); Artist, Group Show, Watercolor USA, Springfield Art Museum (2002); Contributor, "Splash VII," "A Celebration of Light, the Best in Watercolor," North Light Publications (2002); Artist, 42nd Annual Invitational Exhibit, Longview Museum of Fine Arts, Longview, Texas (2002); Artist, 103rd Annual Exhibiting Artist Members' Exhibition, The National Arts Club, New York, NY (2001-2002); Featured, "Master Painters of the World," International Artist's Magazine (2001); Author, "Growing with Grass," Landscape Basics, The Artist's Magazine (2001); Author, "Layers of Distance," Landscape Basics, The Artist's Magazine (2001); Author, "Right from the Start," Landscape Basics, The Artist's Magazine (2001); Contributor, Special Issue from the Editors, Watercolor Magic Magazine, Watercolor Magic Handbook, A to Z Watercolor Reference (2001); Author, "The Laws of Light," Landscape Basics, The Artist's Magazine (2000); Author, "Harnessing Nature's Elements," Landscape Basics, The Artist's Magazine (2000); Artist, Group Show, Watercolor USA, Springfield Arts Museum, MO (2000); Artist, Group Show, 175th Annual Exhibition, National Academy of Design, New York, NY (2000); Artist, Exhibition, National Watercolor Society Membership, Glendale, CA (2000); Artist, Group Show, 58th Annual Exhibition, Audubon Artists Inc., Salmagundi Club, New York, NY (2000); Artist, Group Show, Springfield Arts Museum, MO (1999); Author, "Clearing the Way to Clouds," Landscape Basics, The Artist's Magazine (1999); Author, "Shaping Realistic Rocks," Landscape Basics, The Artist's Magazine (1999); Contributor, "Splash IV," "America's Best Contemporary Watercolors, The Splendor of Light" (1996); Artist, Group Show, Retrospective Exhibition, Wichita Falls Museum of Art at MSU, Texas (1995); Feature Article, 10th Anniversary Issue, The Artist's Magazine (1995); Artist, Group Show, 81st Annual Exhibition, Allied Artists of America, The National Arts Club, New York, NY (1994); Contributor, "Splash III," "America's Best Contemporary Watercolors, Ideas and Inspirations" (1994); Artist, Group Show, 169th Annual Exhibition, National Academy of Design, New York, NY (1994); Feature Article, The Artist's Magazine (1994); Author, "Enrich Your Paintings with Texture," North Light Publications (1993); Contributor, "Splash II," "America's Best Contemporary Watercolors, Watercolor Breakthroughs" (1993); Artist, Group Show, 79th Annual Exhibition, Allied Artists of America, The National Arts Club, New York, NY (1992); Represented in Permanent Collections, The Butler Institute of American Art, Youngstown, Ohio, Museum of Texas Tech University, Lubbock, Texas, Davis Museum, Wellesley College, The Dunnegan Gallery of Art, Bolivar, MO, United States Air Force, Washington, DC, Salmagundi Club, NY, Springfield Art Museum, MO, Wichita Falls Teachers FCU; Contributor, Books; Contributor, Articles to Professional Journals **AW:** Loring W. Coleman Award for Watercolor, Annual Exhibition, Allied Artists of America Inc. (2011); John N. Lewis Memorial Award, 127th Annual Members' Exhibition, Salmagundi Club (2010); Grumbacher Gold Medallion, 111th Annual Members' Exhibition, The National Arts Club, NY (2010); Martin Hannon Memorial Award, Annual Thumb Box Exhibition, Salmagundi Club (2009); SCNY Purchase Award, Salmagundi Club, NY (2009); Samuel O. King Cash Award, Prints USA, Springfield Art Museum (2009); Samuel O. King Award, Watercolor USA, Springfield Art Museum (2009); Macowin Tuttle Memorial Award, Annual Members Exhibition, Salmagundi Club, NY (2008); Robert L. Johnson Memorial Award, Watercolor USA, Springfield Art Museum (2008); Ogden Pleissner Memorial Award, Annual Combined Members Exhibition, Salmagundi Club, New York, NY (2007); D. Wu and Elsie Ject-Key Memorial Award for Oil or Watercolor, Salmagundi Club (2006); Genevieve Cain Award for Watercolor, 107th Annual Exhibiting Artist Members' Exhibition, The National Arts Club (2006); Audubon Artists Gold Medal of Honor, 63rd Annual Exhibition, Salmagundi Club (2005); Kent Day Coes Memorial Award for Watercolor, 91st Annual Exhibition, Allied Artists of America (2004); Cash Award, Watercolor USA, Springfield Museum (2004); William A. Paton Prize for Watercolor, 179th Annual Exhibition, National Academy of Design (2004); Exhibition Committee Award, 105th Annual Exhibiting Artist Members' Exhibition, The National Arts Club (2003); John Young-Hunter Memorial Award, 90th Annual Exhibition, Allied Artists of America (2003); The Connecticut Academy of Fine Arts Graphic Award, 89th Annual Exhibition, Allied Artists of America (2002); Patron Purchase Award, Watercolor USA, Springfield Art Museum (2002); Museum Cash Award, Watercolor USA, Springfield Art Museum (2002); Committee Award, 103rd Annual Exhibiting Artist Members' Exhibition, The National Arts Club (2001); Adolph and Clara Obrig Prize for Watercolor, 175th Annual Exhibition, National Academy of Design (2000); Third Place Cash Award, Annual Members Exhibition, National Watercolor Society (2000); Robert E. Wood Memorial Award, Watercolor USA, Springfield Art Museum (2000) **MEM:** Allied Artists of America; Audobon Artists Inc.; The National Arts Club; Salmagundi Club; Associate Member, American Watercolor Society Inc.; Signature Member, National Watercolor Society; Associate Member, Southwest Watercolor Society; Signature Member, Watercolor USA Honor Society; Member, Baker Gallery of Fine Art, Lubbock, TX **B/I:** Mr. Band became involved in his profession because he drew constantly as a child. His eye for detail drew the attention of his teachers, who gave him artistic clay to sculpt with.

BANGA, AJAYPAL, "AJAY" SINGH, T: President, Chief Executive Officer **I:** Business Management/ Business Services **CN:** Mastercard **PB:** Khadki, Pune **SC:** Maharashtra/India **PT:** Harbhajan Singh Banga **ED:** MBA, Indian Institute of Management, Ahmedabad (1981); BA in Economics, Delhi University **C:** President, Chief Executive Officer, MasterCard, Purchase, NY (2010-Present); President, Chief Operating Officer, MasterCard, Purchase, NY (2009-2010); Chief Executive Officer, Citi Asia Pacific, Citigroup, Inc. (2008-2009); Citigroup, Inc. (1996-2009); Chairman, Chief Executive Officer, Global Consumer Group, Citigroup, Inc. (2005-2008); Executive Vice President, Global Consumer Group, President, Retail Banking, North America Organization, Citigroup, Inc. (2002-2005); Head, CitiFinancal, U.S. Consumer Assets Division, Citigroup, Inc. (2000-2002); Management Trainee, Various Positions in Marketing, General Management and Sales, Nestle, India (1981-1994); Head of Marketing, Sales and Business Development of Europe, Middle East, African Region, Citigroup, Inc., Brussels, Belgium; Division Executive, Consumer Bank of Central and Eastern Europe, Middle East, Africa, India, Citigroup, Inc. **CR:** Board of Directors, The Dow Chemical Co. (2013-Present); Board of Directors, MasterCard (2010-Present); Keynote Speaker, Graduation Convocation, Indian Institute of Management, Ahmedabad (2015); Keynote Speaker, Graduation Convocation, Leonard N. Stern School of Business, New York University (2014); Board of Directors, Kraft Foods Inc. (2007-2012); Speaker, Financial Technology, Leadership Conferences **CIV:** Board of Trustees, Asia Society; Board of Trustees, National Urban League; Board of Trustees, Enterprise Foundation; Board of Directors, National Council on Economic Education (Now Council for Economic Education); Board of Directors, New York Hall of Science; Chairman, U.S.-India Business Council **AW:** Padma Shri Civilian Honor, Government of India (2016) **MEM:** Executive Committee, Business Roundtable; The Economic Club of New York; Financial Services Roundtable; Council on Foreign Relations; International Business Council, World Economic Forum

BANKS, JAMES, "JIM" EDWARD, T: U.S. Representative from Indiana **I:** Government Administration/Government Relations/Government Services **DOB:** 07/16/1979 **PB:** Columbia City **SC:** IN/USA **MS:** Married **SPN:** Amanda Banks **CH:** Three Daughters **ED:** MBA, Grace College & Seminary School of Business; BA in Political Science, Indiana University Bloomington **C:** Member, U.S. House of Representatives from Indiana's Third Congressional District, United States Congress, Washington, DC (2017-Present); Member, District 17, Indiana State Senate (2010-2017); Councilman, Whitley County Council, IN (2009-2010); Member, Committee on Armed Services; Member, Committee on Science, Space, and Technology; Member, Committee on Veterans' Affairs; Director of Business Development, The Hagerman Group **MIL:** Lieutenant, United States Navy Reserve (2012-Present) **MEM:** The Delta Chi Fraternity **PA:** Republican **RE:** Presbyterian

BANNON, STEPHEN, "STEVE" KEITH, T: Senior Counselor to the President, Media Executive, Former Investment Banker **I:** Media & Entertainment **DOB:** 11/27/1953 **PB:** Norfolk **SC:** VA/USA **PT:** Martin J. Bannon Jr.; Doris (Herr) Bannon **MS:** Divorced **SPN:** Diane Clohesy (2006, Divorced 2009); Mary Louise Piccard (04/1995, Divorced 1997); Cathleen Suzanne Houff (Divorced) **CH:** Emily; Grace; Maureen **ED:** Master of Arts in Business Administration, Harvard Business School, with Honors (1985); Master of Arts in National Security Studies, Georgetown University School of Foreign Service (1983); Bachelor of Arts in Urban Planning, Virginia Polytechnic Institute and State University College of Architecture (1976) **C:** Executive Chairperson, Breitbart News (2012-2018); Senior Counselor, Donald J. Trump (2017); Chief Strategist, White House (2017) **CR:** Chair, Chief Executive Officer, Affinity Media (2007-2011); Partner, Film and

Television Management Company, The Firm Inc. (2002-2003); Acting Director, Biosphere 2, Oracle, AZ (1993-1995); Co-founder, Bannon & Co. (1990-1998); Vice President, Entertainment, Goldman Sachs, Los Angeles, CA (1987-1989); Investment Banker, Mergers and Acquisitions Department, Goldman Sachs, NY (1983-1987); Vice President, Board, Cambridge Analytica; Founding Board Member, Breitbart News **CIV:** Co-founder, Executive Chair, Government Accountability Institute (2012-2016) **MIL:** Lieutenant, United States Navy (1976-1983) **CW:** Co-host, Radio Show and Podcast, "War Room: Impeachment" (2019); Producer, Film, "Trump @ War" (2018); Producer, Film, "Clinton Cash" (2016); Producer, Film, "Torchbearer" (2016); Producer, Film, "Rickover: The Birth of Nuclear Power" (2014); Producer, Film, "The Birth of Nuclear Power" (2014); Producer, Film, "The Hope and the Change" (2012); Producer, Film, "District of Corruption" (2012); Producer, Film, "Sweetwater" (2012); Producer, Film, "Occupy Unmasked" (2012); Producer, Film, "Still a Turning World: Ronald Reagan and His Ranch" (2011); Producer, Film, "The Undefeated" (2011); Producer, Film, "Generation Zero" (2010); Producer, Film, "Battle for America" (2010); Producer, Film, "Fire from the Heartland" (2010); Producer, Film, "The Chaos Experiment" (2009); Producer, Film, "Border War: The Battle Over Illegal Immigration" (2006); Producer, Film, "Cochise County USA: Cries from the Border" (2005); Producer, Film, "In the Face of Evil: Reagan's War in Word and Deed" (2004); Producer, Film, "Titus" (1999); Producer, Film, "The Indian Runner" (1991); Host, Radio Show, "Breitbart News Daily," SiriusXM Patriot **AW:** Named, One of the 100 Most Influential People, TIME Magazine (2017); Named, One of the 25 Most Influential in Political News Media, Medialite (2015) **PA:** Republican

BAPTIST, JEREMY EDUARD, T: Allergist, Clinical Immunologist, Educator **I:** Medicine & Health Care **DOB:** 03/22/1940 **PT:** Arthur Henry Baptist; Margaret Jane (Beck) Baptist **MS:** Married **SPN:** Avis Garret Baptist; Sylvia Evelyn Bonin (07/21/1962, Deceased 1999) **CH:** Sarah; Margaret; Catherine **ED:** Internship in Medicine, Northwestern University (1978-1979); MD, University of Missouri-Kansas City (1978); PhD in Biophysics, The University of Chicago (1966); BS in Physics, The University of Chicago (1960) **C:** Clinical Assistant Professor of Internal Medicine, School of Medicine, University of Kansas Medical Center (1994-2002); President, Allergy Link (1999-2019); Vice President, Speer Allergy & Asthma Clinic, Shawnee Mission, KS (1985-1990, 1996-1999); Allergist, Speer Allergy & Asthma Clinic, Shawnee Mission, KS (1979-1999); President, Speer Allergy & Asthma Clinic, Shawnee Mission, KS (1991-1995); Vice President, Multiple Data Services, Leawood, KS (1992-1994); Claims Authorizer, United States Social Security Administration (1974-1975); Assistant Professor of Radiation Biophysics, The University of Kansas (1966-1973) **CIV:** Member, Ethnic Enrichment Commission of Kansas City, MO (1988-2004); Community of Christ **CW:** Editor, "Allergy Letters," International Correspondence Society of Allergists and Clinical Immunologists (1991-1999); Associate Editor, "Allergy Letters," International Correspondence Society of Allergists and Clinical Immunologists (1985-1990); Assistant Editor, "Allergy Letters," International Correspondence Society of Allergists and Clinical Immunologists (1984-1985); Editorial Board Member, "Topics in Allergy and Clinical Immunology" (1982-1983); Co-Author, "Handbook of Clinical Allergy" (1982); Contributor, "Britannica Yearbook of Science and the Future" (1973-1974) **AW:** Grantee, Brown-Hazen (1970); Pre-Doctoral Fellowship, U.S. Public Health Service (1964-1966) **MEM:** Executive Director, Inter-

national Correspondence Society of Allergists and Clinical Immunologists (1991-Present); Secretary, American Scandinavian Association (1997-1999); Chairman, Armenian Society of Greater Kansas City (1995-1999); Chairman of Kansas City Club (1986-1990, 1992-1993, 1996-1997); Board of Directors, Scandinavian Club (1994-1997); President, Armenian Society of Greater Kansas City (1993-1995); Vice President, Armenian Society of Greater Kansas City (1989-1993); Committee on Adverse Reactions to Foods, American College of Allergy, Asthma & Immunology (1989-1993); International for Association Aerobiology; Pan-American Aerobiology Association; American Medical Association; American Association for the Advancement of Science; Southern Medical Association; Kansas Medical Society; Johnson County Medical Society; The New York Academy of Sciences; Sigma Xi, The Scientific Research Honor Society **MH:** Albert Nelson Marquis Lifetime Achievement Award **B/I:** Dr. Baptist became involved in his profession because his daughter developed asthma and food allergies at a young age, which spurred his interest in the field. **RE:** Christian

BAQUET, DEAN PAUL, T: Executive Editor, Journalist **I:** Writing and Editing **CN:** The New York Times Company **DOB:** 09/21/1956 **PB:** New Orleans **SC:** LA/USA **PT:** Edward Joseph Baquet; Myrtle (Romano) Baquet **MS:** Married **SPN:** Dylan F. Landis (09/06/1986) **CH:** Ari Theogene Landis **ED:** Honorary LittD, Tulane University (2019); Honorary Doctorate, Loyola University New Orleans (2013); Coursework in English, Columbia University (1974-1978) **C:** Executive Editor, The New York Times Company (2014-Present); Managing Editor, The New York Times Company (2011-2014); Washington Bureau Chief, National Editor, Assistant Managing Editor, The New York Times Company (2007-2011); Editor, Los Angeles Times (2005-2006); Managing Editor, Los Angeles Times (2000-2005); National Editor, The New York Times Company (1995-2000); Deputy Metropolitan Editor, The New York Times Company (1995); Special Projects Editor, Business Desk, The New York Times Company (1992-1995); Metropolitan Reporter, The New York Times Company (1990-1992); Associate Metropolitan Editor, Investigations, Chief Investigative Reporter, Chicago Tribune (1987-1990); Investigative Reporter, Chicago Tribune (1984-1987); Investigative Reporter, The Times-Picayune (Now The Times-Picayune/The New Orleans Advocate, NOLA.com), New Orleans, LA (1978-1984) **CR:** Board of Directors, Committee to Protect Journalists (2003-Present) **AW:** Missouri Honor Medal for Distinguished Service, Missouri School of Journalism, University of Missouri (2019); Distinguished Journalist Award, Center for Journalism Integrity & Excellence, DePaul University (2019); Larry Foster Award, Arthur W. Page Center, Donald P. Bellisario College of Communications, The Pennsylvania State University (2019); Fourth Estate Award, The National Press Club (2018); Freedom of the Press Award, Reporters Committee for Freedom of the Press (2018); Excellence Honoree, Klein College of Media and Communication, Temple University (2017); Zenger Award for Press Freedom, School of Journalism, The University of Arizona (2017); William H. Jones Award for Investigative Reporting, Chicago Tribune (1987-1989); Pulitzer Prize for Investigative Reporting (1988); Peter Lisagor Award, Chicago Headline Club, Society of Professional Journalists (1988) **MEM:** Fellow, American Academy of Arts and Sciences (2006-Present) **THT:** Mr. Paquet is the first Black executive editor in the history of The New York Times.

BARBANO, FRANCES ELIZABETH, T: Writer, Photographer, Columnist **I:** Writing and Editing **DOB:** 05/28/1944 **PB:** Corry **SC:** PA/USA **PT:** Francis Joseph Dufresne; Mercy Elizabeth (Quinn) Dufresne **MS:** Married **SPN:** Duane Louis Barbano (10/1974); Robert Lee Harkins (1967, Divorced); John W. Moyle (1961, Divorced) **CH:** Matthew Scott; Sheila Marie; Lisa Jane; Terri Lyn; Jeffrey Scott **ED:** Coursework, Phoenix Union Area Vocational School (1977); Coursework, Cecil Lawter Real Estate School, Inc., Phoenix, AZ (1973); Coursework, New York Institute of Photography **CT:** Licensed Cosmetologist, State of Arizona (1977-Present); Licensed Reflexologist (1977-Present) **C:** Freelance Writer, Photographer, Numerous National and Regional Publications (1984-Present); Owner, Editor, Ad Director, Carefree Enterprise Magazine (1991-2003); Editor, U.S. Bass Magazine, Mesa, AZ (1988); Editor, Lady Bass Magazine, West Monroe, LA (1987-1988); Owner, Manager, Professional Images, Cave Creek, AZ (1985-1994); Advertising Director, Arizona Hunter Magazine, Cottonwood, AZ (1985); Feature Writer, Columnist, Carefree Enterprise Magazine, Scottsdale, AZ, Carefree, AZ (1983-2003); Cosmetologist, Owner, Operator, Carefree Hair Designs, Carefree, AZ (1979-1984); Cosmetologist, Stylist, Sandra's Isle of Beauty, Carefree, AZ (1977-1979) **CR:** Adjunct Faculty, Prescott College, Prescott, AZ (1993); Assistant Manager, Palo Verde Restaurant, The Boulders Resort, Carefree, AZ (1989-1990); Supervisor, Boulders Club Restaurant, Carefree, AZ (1985-1988) **CIV:** Started "Prayer Watch," Prayer Ministry to Support Pastors, and Ministry Leadership within Church (2019-Present); Writer, "Olive Branch," AJ First Assembly of God (2013-Present); Involved with Prayer Chain in Praying for Those with Needs in Congregation; Praying for Government Leaders in this Nation, State and Federal **CW:** Columnist, Olive Branch Column (2014-Present); Columnist, Column, "Spiritual Perspectives", The Gallup Independent Newspaper (2011-Present); Contributor, More Than 100 Nonfiction Articles and Photos, Various National and International Magazines (1983-Present) **AW:** First Place in Writing and Photography Statewide, Arizona Press Women (2002); Award for Excellency in Writing, Arizona Newspapers Association (2002); Second Place, Various Categories for Writing and Photography Statewide, Arizona Press Women (2001) **MEM:** American Association of Christian Counselors; Arizona Press Women/Arizona Professional Writers; New Mexico Press Women; National Federation of Press Women; National Association of Female Executives (NAFE); Outdoor Writers Association of America **MH:** Albert Nelson Marquis Lifetime Achievement Award **AS:** Mrs. Barbano attributes her success to her supportive husband, editors who purchased her work, and others who provided encouraging words when they didn't purchase. Last but not least, she attributes it to the nudging she felt to write and the God-given perseverance and persistence He built into her. **B/I:** Mrs. Barbano became involved in her profession because she began writing poetry as a child, as it was easier to express herself in words. Her writing career did not begin until 1983 when she attended a half-day writer's class where she learned the basics, beginning terminology, and how to present oneself to an editor. Stopping at the library on the way home, she discovered the Writer's Market and found three publications to try and sent out three queries the following week. One came back with a go-ahead on speculation, meaning that the editor was interested and would "take a look," but that he wasn't obligated to buy it if it didn't live up to his expectations. That first article languished a few months as the publication was sold but the new editor liked her work, published that article, and gave her assignments for future articles. That began her writing career, which today spans nearly four decades. In the beginning, freshwater tournament bass fishing was in its heyday. The first years of writing included covering various bass fishing tournaments, primarily in the southwest. She writes for various general interest publications with topics including fishing, camping, hiking, health, home, parenting, elder care, and spiritual perspectives. Mrs. Barbano's first religious/spiritual article was published in Billy Graham's Decision Magazine in 1986. **AV:** Reading; Gardening; Oil and watercolor painting; Sewing; Quilting; Teaching Bible study **PA:** Conservative **RE:** Christian **THT:** Mrs. Barbano says, "We are only here on earth for a short time, and are in this life together. I do not believe in coincidence and believe God put us here for a purpose. We must do what we can, where we are, with what we have, and help those we can while there is time. Someday, time will end for each of us."

BARBE, DAVID O., MD, MHA, T: Doctor; Vice President **I:** Health, Wellness and Fitness **CN:** Mercy **PB:** St. Louis **SC:** MO/USA **MS:** Married **SPN:** Debbie Barbe **CH:** Two Children **ED:** MHA, University of Missouri, Columbia, MO (2005); Residency in Family Medicine, Ascension Via Christi, The University of Kansas, Wichita, KS (1980-1983); MD, University of Missouri, Columbia, MO (1980); BS in Microbiology, University of Missouri, with Honors Columbia, MO (1976) **CT:** Family Medicine Certification, American Board of Family Medicine, Inc. **C:** Vice President, Regional Operations, Mercy, Springfield, MO (2016-Present); Physician, Family Medicine, Mountain Grove, MO (1997-Present); President, Regional Division, Mercy, Springfield, MO (1999-2015); Medical Director, Department of Obstetrics, Texas County Memorial Hospital (1983-2006); President, Managing Partner, Southwest Missouri Family Health Care, Inc., Mountain Grove and Houston, MO (1987-1997); Chief, Medical Staff, Texas County Memorial Hospital (1994-1995); Chief, Medical Staff, Mercy Hospital, Mansfield, MO; (1986-1991); Private Practice, Family Medicine and Obstetrics, Mountain Grove, MO (1983-1987) **CR:** Missouri Medical Political Action Committee, Missouri State Medical Association (1999-Present); President, South Central Medical Society (1985-1987, 1990-Present); World Medical Association Council (2016-2019); Board of Trustees, American Medical Association (2009-2019); Executive Committee, American Medical Association (2011-2015, 2016-2019); President, American Medical Association (2017-2018); Presiding Officer, WMA General Assembly, Chicago, IL (2017); Chair, Board of Trustees, American Medical Association (2013-2014); Chair, Council on Medical Service, American Medical Association (2008-2009); Board, Executive Committee, URAC (2006-2009); Council on Medical Service, American Medical Association (2003-2009); Delegate, Missouri, American Medical Association (1996-2009); President, Missouri State Medical Association (2005-2006); Quality Assurance Committee, Texas County Memorial Hospital (1990-2006); Administrative Board, Missouri Patient Care Review Foundation (1987-2005); Budget and Finance Committee, Missouri State Medical Association (1994-1998, 2002-2005); Board, Missouri State Medical Association (1987-2004); Chair, Missouri State Medical Association (2003); Vice President, Missouri State Medical Association (1999-2000); Clinical Instructor, School of Medicine, University of Missouri, Columbia, MO **CIV:** Worship Leader, Sunday School Teacher, First Christian Church; President, Mountain Grove High School Alumni Association; President, Mountain Grove Area Community Foundation **AW:** Missourian Award, The Missourian Award Inc. (2015); Distinguished Service Award, School of Medicine, University of Missouri (2013); Missouri Family Physician of the Year Award, Missouri Academy of Family Physicians (1993) **MEM:** American Medical Association; American Academy of Family Physicians; Missouri Academy of Family Physicians; Missouri State Medical Association **AV:** Traveling; Gourmet cooking

BARCELONA, ISAAC G.D., T: President & Chief Executive Officer **I:** Government Administration/Government Relations/Government Services **DOB:** 06/24/1949 **PB:** Mexico City **SC:** Mexico **PT:** Isaac Guerrero Corona; Rebecca Cristina Garcia-Nevarez-Padilla-Fuentes; Ramiro S. Diaz (Stepfather) **MS:** Married **SPN:** Shawny May Sherman Barcelona **CH:** Isaac L.; Rebecca L.; Eddy; Jeremy J.; Nicole Noel; Diamond Ryan-Shawn; Rachel Valdez; Taylor **ED:** Doctor of Metaphysics, Dr. Clark Wilkerson Institute, Los Angeles, CA (1972); Doctor of Metaphysics, Dr. Clark Wilkerson Institute, Honolulu, Hawaii (1972); Doctor of Hypnosis, Dr. Clark Wilkerson Institute, Los Angeles, CA (1971); Doctor of Hypnosis, Dr. Clark Wilkerson Institute, Honolulu, Hawaii (1971); PhD, Dr. Clark Wilkerson Institute, Los Angeles, CA (1970); PhD, Dr. Clark Wilkerson Institute, Honolulu, Hawaii (1970); Diploma, Marian High School (Now Mater Dei, Chula Vista), Imperial Beach, CA (1967) **C:** District Director, Senior Field Representative, California State Assembly (2015-2018); Congressional District Liaison Officer, United States House of Representatives (2015-2018); President, Chief Executive Officer, Palmdale Chamber of Commerce (2003-2006, 2012-2014); District Director, 21st State Senate (2008-2012); Palmdale School District Spokesman, Translator, Public Relations Director (1991-2003); United States Representative, Congressman, Steve Knight, California's 25th Congressional District **CR:** Producer, Singer, Songwriter, Guitarist, Actor, Canada, Mexico and South America (1970-2018); Leadership, Management, Media, Public Relations; Chair Emeritus, Commissioner, Citizens' Economy & Efficiency Commission, County of Los Angeles, CA (19 Years) **CIV:** Commissioner, Chair Emeritus, Antelope Valley Hispanic Chamber of Commerce (2001-2019); Co-founder, Palmdale-Yeoncheon Sister City Project (2016-2017); Founding Committee Chairman, Palmdale-Yeoncheon Sister City Project (2016-2017); President Emeritus, Palmdale-Yeoncheon Sister City Project (1999-2013, 2014-2015); Board of Directors, United Way; Organization President, Antelope Valley Public Relations Officials (2003, 2004, 2014); Public Relations Director (1998-2012); "Plazas Comunitarias" Educational Program, Mexico City, Mexico (2001-2002); Founder, Antelope Valley Hispanic Chamber of Commerce (1997); Citizens' Economy & Efficiency Commission, Los Angeles County, CA; Elected, Public Official; President, Chief Executive Officer, Nonprofit Organizations **CW:** Recorded, "3 Worlds/3 Mundos" (2018-2019); Author, "Songs for the Gypsy/Canciones para el Gitano" (1988-2019); Recorded, "Could Be My Age" (1990); Author, "Perfectly Imperfect (This Could Be You) & Imperfectly Perfect" (1990); Author, "Barcelona Bandits ARMADA (Champions & Friends... Forever); Reflection: Love is Us-You and I" (1988); Author, "Messages from the Soul" (1988); Author, "Time and Pain-Why?" (1988); Author, "The Beast" (1988); Author, "In My Words, Things We Crave" (1987); Author, "Dressings on the Sculpture" (1987); Co-author, Recorded "Ayudemos" (1985); Recorded, Released, "Espejo de Amor" (1979); Recorded, Released, "Amandote Amada" (1979); Recorded, Released "Rika Y Sus Piratas" (1979); Recorded with Toto, David Foster, Robert Lamm & Bill Champlin (Chicago), Kenny Rogers Jr., and Humberto Gatica, "Hands Across America";

Singer, "Voices of America"; Publisher, Opinion Columns; Editor, Publisher, Magazines; Program Host, Radio, Television **AW:** Inductee, Rock and Roll Hall of Fame, Mexico (2011); Southern California Chamber of the Year (2010) **MEM:** American Federation of Musicians, Local 47 (AFM Local 47) **MH:** Albert Nelson Marquis Lifetime Achievement Award; Marquis Who's Who Top Professional **AS:** Above all else, Dr. Barcelona attributes his success to God, his parents, Rebecca and Isaac, his Catholic school education, (San Ysidro Academy/Our Lady of Mount Carmel and Marian High, Imperial Beach, CA/Mater Dei Chula Vista Catholic High School), friends and family, and sports and music. He also credits his early, formative years, growing up in Tijuana, his native Mexico, and his amazing journey once he arrived in "my beloved Land of Liberty and Opportunity...(Declaration of Independence, U.S. Constitution, Bill of Rights, American exceptionalism and Trinity...In God We Trust, E Pluribus Unum & Liberty) the United States of America." **B/I:** Dr. Barcelona became involved in his profession because he wanted to help people. Dr. Barcelona believes that everyone has a purpose and the ability to fulfill it. **AV:** World travel; Cruises; Reading; Making new friends; Collecting artwork; Collecting stamps; Sports; Theater; Photography **PA:** Conservative Republican **RE:** Roman Catholic **THT:** Dr. Barcelona says, "I've been a prolific, creative force, musically, poetically, and with the written word, for the past 45+ years. I have traveled and visited lands and cultures beyond my own and I have grown and prospered from all of it. My life has been full, yet I am not finished, not even close. Too much yet unfinished and pending. That is what my life is about now... completing that which has yet to be completed. My journey has taken many turns, and I have enjoyed and survived all of them. As Yogi Berra once said, "I came to a fork in the road, and I took it!" 2007-2008 brought yet another turn, and it was magical. United with siblings I didn't know I had, Ismael & Nancy (Ivette & Isaac), Ivan, Patricia, Belinda & Daniel, & Rene, while bonding closer to my brothers Hijolee Art & Elsa, Laura & Chuy, my wife Shawny (who has grown to be the perfect mate and partner for me) our sisters Shelley, her husband Rick & our beautiful and talented Larissa, our children (Isaac & Irma, Rebecca & Craig, Eddy & Norma, Jeremy, Nicole, Joel Isaac & Karen, Rachel & Manny, Diamond & Adriana (little Jaden and Mama Grace), and Taylor). I dedicate my time and this thought to them, and to those who I consider have affected my life and continue to do so. You know who you are (Knights; Cachos; Johnsons; Wards; Camachos; Campanos; Toni & Oscar Aleman; Matt Lindsey; Jimbo Ledford; Venegas; Nancy Smith; Stephan Q; Windi, Robin, Cristina; Midori; Dr. Chiu; Juan Carlos; Juvenal & Chabe "Las Cazuelas"; Leo's Catering; Nick "Splash"; Lic. Jorge Flores; Rigoberto "Encantoz"; Sarah & Dymitri La Fonda; Don Juan; Juan & Felipe M "Primos"; Las Leyendas Musicales de Tijuana; Al McKay; Ed Wynn; Rick Zahariades; Jorge "Piteco"; Raul Felix; Ray Briz; Tavo Valdez; Clayton; Daniel & Seco Tello; Jorge "Chino" V; Los Lupillos; Rudy C; Nahuatl; Joe Ganem; Alfredo Rubalcava; Jimmy Espinoza/ Thee Midniters; Chuy G; Derek W; Sammy; TIERRA; El Chicano; Randy Seol; Charlie & Alberto Rivera; Pako Diaz; Pablito; Dr. J. Ramos; Garcia-Padillas & Guerreros). Dr. Barcelona has many grandchildren, Joel Isaac, Jazzie, Ethyn, Eddie, Nicole, Isaac Gordo, Vanessa, Isabel, Alyssa, Anthony, Sean, Elvia, Karen Fuentes, Junior, Genica, Samantha and Diamond Santana. He has six great-grandchildren, Ciara, Kash, Eddy III, Isaac Ezequiel, Rome, Victor "Moose," and Gabby, and one Goddaughter, Santana Hallberg.

BARKER, FRED, PHD, T: Research Geologist, Scientific Editor **I:** Research **DOB:** 11/04/1928 **PB:** Seekonk **SC:** MA/USA **PT:** Reuben; Eleanor Regina (Mead) Barker **MS:** Widowed **SPN:** Margaret Walsh (05/07/1961, Deceased 2016) **CH:** Matthew F.; Thomas A.; Aileen M. **ED:** Postdoctoral Coursework, Harvard University (1956-1957); PhD, California Institute Technology (1954); MS, California Institute Technology (1952); BS, Massachusetts Institute of Technology (1950) **C:** Retired Geologist Emeritus (1993); Research Geologist, U.S. Geological Survey, Denver, CO (1962-1993); Research Geologist, U.S. Geological Survey (1957-1962); Research Geologist, U.S. Geological Survey, Menlo Park, CA (1955-1956); Research Geologist, U.S. Geological Survey, Juneau, AK (1954-1955) **CR:** Editorial Adviser, Elsevier (1974-1993) **CW:** Author, "The 50 Ma Granodiorite of the Eastern Gulf of Alaska: Melting in an Accretionary Prism in the Forearc," (1992); Author, "Trondhjemites, Dacites, and Related Rocks" (1979); Contributor, Articles, Professional Journals **AW:** Visiting Research Fellow, University of the Witwatersrand, Johannesburg (1974); Research Grant, GSAF (1972) **MEM:** Guest Editor, American Geophysical Union (1981); Fellow, Editorial Adviser, The Geological Society of America, Inc. (1974-1978); Mineralogical Society of America **MH:** Albert Nelson Marquis Lifetime Achievement Award **B/I:** Mr. Barker became involved in his profession because when he was in high school he read a book on geology that his uncle left in the house where he grew up. His uncle was a graduate of Brown University in 1923 and he eventually went to California where he designed bridges for the state of California. **AV:** Nontechnical writing; Taking photographs; Skiing; Shooting rifles **PA:** Republican

BARKLEY, CHARLES WADE, T: Analyst, Professional Basketball Player (Retired) **I:** Athletics **CN:** Warner Media, LLC **DOB:** 02/20/1963 **PB:** Leeds **SC:** AL/USA **MS:** Married **SPN:** Maureen Blumhardt (02/09/1989) **CH:** Christiana **ED:** Coursework, Auburn University, Auburn, AL (1981-1984) **C:** Analyst, "Inside the NBA," NBA on TNT, Turner Sports, Warner Media, LLC (2001-Present); Forward, Houston Rockets (1996-2000); Forward, Phoenix Suns (1992-1996); Forward, Philadelphia 76ers (1984-1992) **CR:** United States Men's National Basketball Team (1992, 1996) **CIV:** Benefactor, Miles College (2020); Benefactor, The Obama Presidential Center (2020); Benefactor, Hoops2O, Waterboys (2019); Benefactor, Community Foundation of Northwest Mississippi (2018); Benefactor, Morehouse College (2017); Benefactor, Alabama A&M University (2016); Benefactor, Clark Atlanta University (2016); Benefactor, Angora Fire Victims, El Dorado County, CA (2007-2009); Participant, Ante Up for Africa, Las Vegas, NV (2008); Benefactor, Hurricane Katrina Victims (2005); Numerous Charitable Donations **CW:** Actor, "The Goldbergs" (2019); Voice Actor, "We Bare Bears" (2018); Actor, "Modern Family" (2017); Voice Actor, "The Simpsons" (2017); Actor, "With a Kiss" (2016); Actor, "Suits" (2015); Actor, "Thunderstruck" (2012); Actor, "The Bernie Mac Show" (2005); Author, "Who's Afraid of a Large Black Man?" (2005); Author, "I May Be Wrong But I Doubt It" (2002); Voice Actor, "Clerks" (2000-2001); Actor, "Jackie's Back!" (1999); Actor, "Arli$$" (1999); Actor, "V.I.P." (1998); Actor, "He Got Game" (1998); Actor, "Space Jam" (1996); Actor, "Forget Paris" (1995); Co-Author, "Sir Charles: The Wit and Wisdom of Charles Barkley" (1995); Actor, "Hangin' with Mr. Cooper" (1992); Co-Author, "Outrageous!: The Fine Life and Flagrant Good Times of Basketball's Irresistible Force" (1992) **AW:** Inductee, National Collegiate Basketball Hall of Fame (2008); Inductee, Naismith Memorial Basketball Hall of Fame (2006); Inductee, Ring of Honor,

Phoenix Suns (2004); Inductee, Alabama Sports Hall of Fame (2001); Western Conference All-Star (1993-1997); 50th Anniversary All-Time Team, NBA (1996); NBA MVP (1993); Eastern Conference All-Star (1987-1992); NBA All-Star Game MVP (1991); SEC Player of the Decade, Birmingham Post-Herald (1990); IBM Award, NBA and IBM (1986-1988); SEC Player of the Year, The Associated Press (1984) **PA:** Democrat

BARKLEY, SAQUON RASUL QUEVIS, T: Professional Football Player **I:** Athletics **CN:** New York Giants **DOB:** 02/03/1997 **PB:** Bronx **SC:** NY/USA **PT:** Alibay Barkley; Tonya Johnson **CH:** One Daughter **ED:** Coursework, The Pennsylvania State University **CR:** Professional Football Player, Running Back, New York Giants, National Football League (NFL) (2018-Present) **AW:** Invited, Pro Bowl (2018); Rookie of the Year, Pepsi NFL (2018); FedEx Ground Player of the Year (2018); Offensive Rookie of the Year, NFL (2018); Invited, All-Rookie Team, Pro Football Writers of America (2018); Fiesta Bowl Champion (2017); Six-time Big Ten Offensive Player of the Week (2016, 2017); Midseason All American, ESPN and Sporting News (2017); Two-time Big Ten Special Teams Player of the Week (2017); Paul Hornung Award (2017); Consensus All-American (2017); All-American First Team, Sporting News (2017); First Team All-American, ESPN (2017); First Team All-American, Football Writers Association of America (2017); First Team All-American, Associated Press (2017); First Team All-American, Walter Camp (2017); Big Ten Return Specialist of the Year (2017); Big Ten Offensive Player of the Year (2016, 2017); Big Ten Champion (2016); Third Team All-American, Associated Press (2016); Second Team All-American, Sporting News (2016); All-Big Ten First Team (2016); All-Big Ten Second Team (2015)

BARNES, HARRISON BRYCE JORDAN, T: Professional Basketball Player **I:** Athletics **CN:** Sacramento Kings **DOB:** 03/30/1992 **PB:** Ames **SC:** IA/USA **MS:** Married **SPN:** Brittany Johnson (07/29/2017) **ED:** Coursework, University of North Carolina at Chapel Hill (2010-2012) **C:** Professional Basketball Player, Sacramento Kings (2019-Present); Dallas Mavericks, NBA (2016-2019); Golden State Warriors, NBA (2012-2016) **AW:** Invited, United States National Team, FIBA World Cup (2019); Gold Medal, United States National Team, Summer Olympics, Rio, Brazil (2016); Invited, United States National Team, Summer Olympics, Rio, Brazil (2016); Winner, NBA Chamionship, Golden State Warriors (2015); Invited, Second Team All-American, National Association of Basketball Coaches (NABC) (2012); Invited, First Team All-ACC, Atlantic Coast Conference (2012); Rookie of the Year, Atlantic Coast Conference (2011); Invited, All-ACC Freshmen Team, Atlantic Coast Conference (2011); Invited, Second Team All-ACC, Atlantic Coast Conference (2011); Invited, Preseason All-American Team (2010, 2011); 2010 Morgan Wootten Player of the Year Award (2010); Invited, McDonald's All-America Team (2010); Invited, Jordan Brand High School All-American Team (2010); Invited, First Team All-American, Parade (2010); Iowa Mr. Basketball Award (2010); Invited, Second Team All-American Parade (2009) **RE:** Christian

BARNETT, FRANKLIN DEWEES, MD, T: Obstetrician/Gynecologist **I:** Medicine & Health Care **DOB:** 08/01/1935 **PB:** Fort Thomas **SC:** KY/USA **PT:** Harry Barnett; Elizabeth (McKeny) Barnett **MS:** Married **SPN:** Louise Baillod (10/23/1976) **CH:** Julie; Brian; Kelly; Colin; Robert; Shelley (Kelly Deceased 2019) **ED:** MD, The University of Kansas (1961); BS, Asbury College (Now Asbury University) (1957) **CT:** Board Certificate, OB-GYN (1969)

C: Retired (2000); Obstetrician-gynecologist, Private Practice, Midwest City, OK (1967-2000); Resident, OB-GYN, The University of Oklahoma, Oklahoma City, OK (1964-1967); Intern, Wesley Medical Center, C-HCA, Inc., Wichita, KS (1961-1962); Chief of Staff, Midwest City Memorial Hospital, AllianceHealth Midwest & Seminole **CR:** Board of Directors, Oklahoma Blood Institute, Oklahoma City, OK (1980-Present); Covering Doctor, OB-GYN, During Iraq War, Substituting for Dr. In Enid, OK (14 Months); Clinical Associate Professor, The University of Oklahoma College of Medicine; President, Oklahoma City Obstetrics and Gynecology Society **CIV:** Councilman, Midwest City, OK (1988-1992); Board, Oklahoma Blood Institute; YMCA; Church Leadership Roles, St. Matthew United Methodist Church, Midwest City, OK **MIL:** With, United States Air Force (1962-1964) **AW:** Named to Personalities of the South **MEM:** Midwest City Chamber of Commerce; Member, Rotary Club of Midwest City (1970-Present); President, Rotary Club of Midwest City (1994-1995); American Medical Association; American Association of Gynecologic Laparoscopists (AAGL); American Fertility Society; American College of Obstetricians and Gynecologists **MH:** Albert Nelson Marquis Lifetime Achievement Award **AS:** The attributes that Dr. Barnett possesses that have contributed to him being a doctor is God's gift to him of helping and caring for people. That is his strongest; even now he is currently involved with the Rotary Club (50 years of perfect attendance) dealing with many Rotary projects. and being very active with his church. So, he believed that is his attribute loving and helping people with whom he came in contact and being a friend to all of them. **B/I:** Dr. Barnett at age 12 felt a calling for his medical career after cutting his knee on a broken whiskey bottle upon jumping out of a tree back in Kentucky. After jumping out of a tree, his knee hit the ground where the broken whiskey bottle laid. This was during WWII, but his mother was able to take him to their family physician and as the doctor sewed up the laceration, Dr. Barnett was so fascinated by watching him sew up the wound, that from that moment on, he felt his calling was for a career into medicine. At that time he no idea how many mountains he would have to climb, but God always opened the doors for him. Being poor (but not feeling poor) his parents were not able to help financially and he received no scholarship or grants to help with his education, but God helped him along the way. For example, he worked his way through Asbury College (now Asbury University) delivering 300 to 500 papers daily by walking and using his bicycle (he had no car). Dr. Barnett was blessed to care for his patients. He also loved doing things with his hands, which lead him into his obstetrical and surgical career. So, it all fit together for him. **AV:** Motor homing; Photography; Skiing; Traveling **PA:** Republican or Best Candidate **RE:** Methodist **THT:** Dr. Barnett believes that especially with God's help and with hard work and dedication, one can accomplish one's goal and God's calling.

BARNETT, GEORGE, "BO" REX IV, T: President **I:** Architecture & Construction **CN:** KB Custom Pools **DOB:** 12/31/1978 **PB:** Lewisville **SC:** TX/USA **PT:** George Rex Barnett III; Delores Barnett **MS:** Married **SPN:** Amber Barnett **CH:** Brooklyn; George Rex Barnett V; London **CT:** Certified Building Professional, American Pool and Spa Association (2016); Certified Pool Builder, Residential and Commercial Pool Construction, Association of Pool and Spa Professionals (2015) **C:** President, KB Custom Pools (2007-Present); Senior Designer, Blue Haven Pools (2003-2007) **CIV:** Supporter, The East Austin Lion's Club; Sponsor, South Austin Optimist Little League Baseball Team; Supporter, Colins Hope; Supporter, Dell Children's Medical Center **CW:** Featured, "Pool and Spa News"; Featured, "Aqua Magazine" **AW:** Listee, Top 50 Builders in the Nation, Association of Pool and Spa Association (2019); Aqua News Young Professional of the Year (2018); Luxury Builder of the Year, Central Texas (2012, 2015, 2018) **MEM:** Pool and Hot Tub Alliance; Tributary Revelation; The Aqua Group; Genesis 3Inc **AS:** Mr. Barnett attributes his success to hard work and education. Likewise, he is thankful for his family, as they allow him to put in the time he needs to succeed in his professional ventures. **B/I:** The design aspect of his work has always led Mr. Barnett's choices. It inspired him to continue working, growing, and finding success. **AV:** Spending time with family; Practicing faith **PA:** Conservative **RE:** Christian

BARNETT, MICHELE SZMANIA, T: Salon Owner, Hair Stylist **I:** Business Management/Business Services **CN:** MB Salon **ED:** AS, Business; Hair School, BOTEX School; **CT:** Redken Certified; Certified in Board of Color; Certified in Design and Finishing; Certified in Balayge; Certified in Hair Extension **C:** Business Owner, Stylist, MB Salon (2018-Present) **CIV:** Cut-A-Thon; Days of Beauty with Local Hospitals; Free Education Classes **AS:** Ms. Barnett attributes her success to her education. You need to constantly learn, the hair industry is constantly changing. **B/I:** Ms. Barnett told her parents at the age of 4 that she wanted to do hair. Both of her aunts did hair. She loves making other women feel beautiful.

BARNETT, SARAH A., T: Controller **I:** Education/Educational Services **CN:** Washington College **ED:** MBA, Webster University (2006); Bachelor's Degree in Business Administration, Southern Illinois University (1977) **CT:** Certified Public Accountant (1981) **C:** Expertise in Banking and Law Industries **AV:** Crafting; Jewelry making

BARNEY, TRENT, T: Chief Executive Officer **I:** Real Estate **CN:** Keller Williams Signature Partners **MS:** Married **SPN:** Jendy **CH:** Brody; Bristol; Blaine **ED:** Bachelor of Business Administration, Friends University (2007) **C:** Chief Executive Officer, Team Leader, Keller Williams Signature Partners (2016-Present); Real Estate Agent, Keller Williams Signature Partners (2015-Present); President, Front Porch Management (1997-Present) **CR:** First Head Basketball Coach, Classical School of Wichita; Head Assistant Basketball Coach, Friends University; Basketball Coach, Maize High School **CIV:** Committee Member, Team Challenge; RED Day; Habitat for Humanity; Red Cross; Executive Leadership Board, Leukemia Lymphoma Society; Light the Night **AW:** Wichita Top Residential Real Estate Firm (2016, 2017, 2018, 2019); 40 under 40, Wichita Business Journal (2018); Emerging Leader, Wichita Business Journal (2016, 2017); Barry Sanders Athlete of the Year, Greater Sports Commission (2013) **MEM:** National Association of Realtors; Kansas Association of Realtors; Realtors of South Central Kansas **AS:** Mr. Barney attributes his success to the influence of his mother and her real estate career. He also drew inspiration from his father, whose work ethic and longevity served as an excellent role model. **B/I:** Mr. Barney was inspired to go into the real estate industry because he thinks it is one of the best industries to be a part of, through which one can serve their community and clients everyday.

BARON, MARTIN, "MARTY", T: Executive Editor **I:** Writing and Editing **CN:** The Washington Post **DOB:** 10/24/1954 **PB:** Tampa **SC:** FL/USA **PT:** Howard Naftali (Heinz) Baron; Rebecca Zimerman **ED:** Honorary Doctorate in Public Service, The George Washington University (2017); Honorary LHD, George Mason University (2017); Honorary LHD, Lehigh University (2014); MBA, Lehigh University, Bethlehem, PA (1976); BA in Journalism, Lehigh University, Bethlehem, PA (1976) **C:** Executive Editor, The Washington Post (2013-Present); Executive Editor, Boston Globe Media Partners, LLC (2001-2012); Executive Editor, Miami Herald (2000-2001); Associate Managing Editor, Nighttime News Operations, The New York Times Company (1997-1999); Various Editorial Positions, The New York Times Company (1996-1997); Editor, Orange County Edition, Los Angeles Times (1993-1996); Assistant Managing Editor, Los Angeles Times (1991-1993); Business Editor, Los Angeles Times (1983-1991); Various Editorial Positions, Los Angeles Times (1979-1983); State Reporter, Business Writer, Miami Herald, Miami, FL (1976-1979) **CR:** Advisory Board, Reuters Institute for the Study of Journalism, University of Oxford, Oxford, United Kingdom **CIV:** Board of Trustees, John S. and James L. Knight Foundation (2016-Present) **AW:** First Amendment Award, Ford Hall Forum, Suffolk University (2019); ICFJ Founders Award for Excellence in Journalism, International Center for Journalists (2019); Goldsmith Career Award, Shorenstein Center (2019); Special Citation Award, The Canadian Journalism Foundation (2019); Damon Runyon Award, The Denver Press Club (2018); Fourth Estate Award, The National Press Club (2018); Gabe Pressman Truth to Power Award, NY Press Club (2018); Benton Medal for Distinguished Public Service, The University of Chicago (2018); Pulitzer Prize for Investigative Reporting (2018); Pulitzer Prize for National Reporting (2016, 2018); Freedom of the Press Award, Reporters Committee for Freedom of the Press (2017); Al Neuharth Award for Excellence in the Media, University of South Dakota (2017); Gerald Sass Award for Distinguished Service to Journalism and Mass Communication, AEJMC (2016); Carr Van Anda Award for Excellence in Journalism, E.W. Scripps School of Journalism, Ohio University (2016); Award for Public Leadership, Fels Institute of Government, College of Liberal and Professional Studies at The University of Pennsylvania (2016); Hitchens Prize, The Dennis and Victoria Ross Foundation (2016); Pulitzer Prize for Public Service (2003, 2014); Stephen Hamblett First Amendment Award, New England First Amendment Coalition (2012); Benjamin C. Bradlee Editor of the Year Award, National Press Foundation (2004); Editor of the Year, Editor & Publisher Magazine (2001); Pulitzer Prize for Breaking News Coverage (2001) **MEM:** Fellow, American Academy of Arts & Sciences (2012-Present); American Society of News Editors; Phi Beta Kappa Society

BARR, GARLAND, "ANDY" HALE IV, T: U.S. Representative from Kentucky **I:** Government Administration/Government Relations/Government Services **DOB:** 07/24/1973 **PB:** Lexington **SC:** KY/USA **PT:** Garland Hale Barr III; Donna R. (Faulkoner) Barr **MS:** Married **SPN:** Eleanor Carol Leavell (2008) **CH:** Eleanor Dumont; Mary Clay **ED:** JD, University of Kentucky College of Law (2001); BA in Government and Philosophy, University of Virginia (1996); Intern to Senator Mitch McConnell, United State Senate **C:** Member, U.S. Representative from Kentucky's Sixth Congressional District, United States Congress, Washington, DC (2013-Present); Member, United States House Committee on Financial Services (2013-Present); Associate, Kinkead & Stilz, PLLC, Lexington, KY (2008-2012); Deputy General Counsel to Governor Ernie Fletcher, Commonwealth of Kentucky, Frankfort, KY (2007-2008); General Counsel, Governor's Office of Local Development, Commonwealth of Kentucky, Frankfort, KY (2004-2007); Associate,

Stites & Harbison, PLLC, Lexington, KY (2002-2004); Legislative Assistant to Representative Jim Talent, U.S. House of Representatives (1996-1998); Republican Study Committee **CR:** Governor-Elect Ernie Fletcher's Transition Team (2003-2004); Vice-President, Fayette County Republican Party; Part-Time Instructor, Constitutional Law, Morehead State University; Part-Time Instructor, Constitutional Law, University of Kentucky College of Law **CIV:** Board of Directors, Friends of the Isaac Murphy Memorial Art Garden **MEM:** President, Prevent Child Abuse Kentucky (2008-2009); Vice President, Prevent Child Abuse Kentucky (2007); Fayette County Bar Association; Kentucky Bar Association **PA:** Republican **RE:** Episcopalian

BARR, JON-HENRY, T: Managing Member **I:** Law and Legal Services **CN:** J.H. Barr & Associates, LLC **DOB:** 09/01/1970 **PB:** Livingston **SC:** NJ/USA **PT:** Gary Barr; Susan Barr **MS:** Married **SPN:** Lauren Barr **CH:** Ainsley; Leah; Elizabeth; Gregory **ED:** JD, Seton Hall University School of Law, Newark, NJ (1995); BA in Government, Lehigh University, Bethlehem, PA (1992) **CT:** State-Certified EMT (2003-Present) **C:** Municipal Prosecutor, Township of Clark (2001-Present); Founder, Managing Member, J.H. Barr & Associates, LLC, Clark, NJ (1998-Present); Municipal Prosecutor, Borough of Kenilworth (2008-2014); Associate, Law Offices of Robert B. Blackman, Edison, NJ (1996-1998); Law Clerk, Honorable Paul F. Chaiet, JSC, Freehold, NJ (1995-1996); Councilman, Township of Clark, Clark, NJ (1993-1994) **CIV:** Clark Republican Civic Association (1996-Present); President, Clark Volunteer Emergency Squad (2006); Clark Volunteer Emergency Squad **CW:** Contributor, "Get Ready to Meet a Sovereign Citizen," New Jersey Municipalities (2015); Contributor, "Why Municipal Prosecutors Now Favor Pot Legalization" (2014); Guest Appearance, "Due Process," WNET Channel 13/NJTV Public Television (2014); Contributor, "Comptroller Has It Wrong On Pensions," New Jersey Law Journal (2012); Media Appearances, Various Television Networks **AW:** New Jersey State Bar Association Municipal Court Practice Award (2014); Service to the Community Award, Young Lawyers' Division, New Jersey State Bar Association (2005) **MEM:** Vice-President, Board of Education, Union County Vocational-Technical Schools (2019); Secretary, New Jersey State Municipal Prosecutors Association (2016-2017); President, Union County Bar Association (2016); President, New Jersey State Municipal Prosecutors Association (2008-2015); New Jersey State Bar Association; District of Columbia Bar Association **BAR:** U.S. Supreme Court (2006); District of Columbia (1998); U.S. Court of Appeals for the Third Circuit (1997); U.S. District Court for the District of New Jersey (1996); New Jersey (1996) **MH:** Albert Nelson Marquis Lifetime Achievement Award **B/I:** Mr. Barr always knew wanted to be a lawyer. **AV:** Research in politics; Traveling **RE:** Jewish

BARR, MARLENE JOY, T: Volunteer **I:** Nonprofit & Philanthropy **DOB:** 02/25/1935 **PB:** Grosse Pointe Farms **SC:** MI/USA **PT:** Max John Bielenberg; Viola Christina (Funke) Bielenberg **MS:** Married **SPN:** John Monte Barr Sr. (12/17/1954) **CH:** John Monte Jr.; Karl Alexander; Elizabeth Marie Letter **ED:** MA, Eastern Michigan University (1959); BA, Michigan State University (1956); Coursework, Mexico City College (1955) **CT:** Certified Elementary Teacher **C:** Block Coordinator, Ypsilanti Recycling (1990-1995); Receptionist, Barr, Anhut & Associates, P.C., Ann Arbor, MI (1989-1995); Volunteer, Thrift Shop Association of Ypsilanti (1969-Present); Chair, Fifth Grade Teachers, Secretary, Curriculum Council, Ypsilanti Public Schools (Now Ypsilanti Community Schools), YCS (1961-1966); Teacher,

A.G. Erickson School, Ypsilanti, MI (1956-1966) **CIV:** Chancel Choir, Emmanuel Lutheran Church (1980-1996, 1998-Present); Scheduling Chairman, Thrift Shop Association of Ypsilanti (1993-1996, 2000-Present); Treasurer, Troop 290, Boy Scouts of America (2000-2018); Board of Directors, Ypsilanti Community Choir (1984-2010); President, Thrift Shop Association of Ypsilanti (2002, 2009-2010); Chairman, Church Nominating Committee, Emmanuel Lutheran Church (1999-2000, 2007-2009); Scheduling Chairman, Thrift Shop Association of Ypsilanti (2007); Chairman, Nominating Committee, Thrift Shop Association of Ypsilanti (1998-1999); Secretary, Endowment Committee, Emmanuel Lutheran Church (1995-1996); Active, Endowment Board, HighScope Educational Research Foundation (1993-1996); Secretary, Troop 290, Boy Scouts of America (1989-1995); Church Council, Emmanuel Lutheran Church (1986-1990); Youth Coordinator and Secretary, Youth Standing Committee, Emmanuel Lutheran Church (1983-1989); Assistant Leader, Girl Scouts of the United States of America (1978-1988); Room Mother, Fletcher Elementary School, Ypsilanti, MI (1982-1983); President, Thrift Shop Association of Ypsilanti (1981-1983); Advisory Council, Fletcher Elementary School (1980-1981); Vice President, Thrift Shop Association of Ypsilanti, (1979-1981) **CW:** Author, "Grandpa We Never Knew You! Maximilian Johannas Bielenberg 1857-1907" (2011); Author, "Our Swedish Ancestors: Written for Granddaughter Olivia Marie Barr for Our Trip to Scandinavia July, 2007" (2007); Editor, Law Wives of Washtenaw County (1970-1972); Author, "Memories of the U.P.," Author, "Then and Now, Memories of India" **AW:** Women of Merit Award, Celebrating Women in Scouting (2019); 50-Year Service Award, Thrift Shop Association of Ypsilanti (2019); Certificate of Appreciation, Troop 290, Boy Scouts of America (2018); Community Service Award, Kiwanis Club of Ypsilanti, MI (2017); Honorary Life Member, AAUW (2016); Golden Sister Award, Michigan Chapter, Alpha Delta Kappa (2015); Life Membership, Ladies' Literary Club of Ypsilanti (2010) **MEM:** Board Member, Ypsilanti Heritage Festival Committee (2017-Present); Chairman, Altruistic Committee, Alpha Delta Kappa, Beta Zeta Chapter (2010-Present); Treasurer, Ann Arbor Chapter, United States Power Squadron (2008-Present); Gourmet Arts Study Group (1968-Present); Chapter President, Chapter DL; PEO (1997-1999, 2019-2021); Social Chair, Farmington Genealogical Society (2014-2019); Chairman, Program Committee, PEO (2004-2005, 2009-2010, 2014-2018); Vice President, Chapter DL, PEO (2005); Co-historian, Alpha Delta Kappa, Beta Zeta Chapter (2002-2004); Treasurer, PEO (2001-2003); Chairman, Membership Committee, PEO (1999-2000, 2001-2002); Nominating Committee, Ann Arbor Women's City Club (Now Ann Arbor City Club) (2000, 2002); Chairman, Home Tour, Ann Arbor Women's City Club (Now Ann Arbor City Club) (2001); Assistant Membership and Chairman, Ann Arbor Women's City Club (Now Ann Arbor City Club) (1998-1999); Treasurer, Board of Trustees, Ladies' Literacy Club (1992-1997); Chairman, Home Tour, Ann Arbor Women's City Club (Now Ann Arbor City Club) (1996-1997); Chairman, Ways and Means Committee, Ann Arbor Women's City Club (Now Ann Arbor City Club) (1995-1997); Chairman, Ways and Means Committee, Alpha Delta Kappa, Beta Zeta Chapter (1994-1996); Co-chair, "One Helluva Ride!", Ann Arbor Bicycle Touring Society (1995); Chaplain, PEO (1991-1993); President, Ladies Literacy Club (1990-1992); Treasurer, Chandler Birthday Club (1990); Vice President, Ladies Literacy Club (1986-1990); Historian, Alpha Delta Kappa, Beta Zeta Chapter (1986-1988); Secretary, Board of Trustees, Ladies Literacy Club (1982-1986);

Corresponding Secretary, Ladies Literacy Club (1976-1978); President, Area X President Council of Michigan, Alpha Delta Kappa (1966-1968); First President, Beta Zeta Chapter, Alpha Delta Kappa (1965-1968); The Genealogical Society of Washington County; Life Member, Depot Town Association, Ypsilanti Historical Society; Life Member, Marquette County Historical Society; Friends of the Ypsilanti District Library; Life Member, Ann Arbor Women's City Club **B/I:** Mrs. Barr became involved in teaching because of her mother, who encouraged her. She took an aptitude test and met with her counselor, who told her that if she were a male, she would encourage her to go into engineering, but since she was a female, she should go into education or nursing. She also had two aunts who were teachers. **AV:** Skiing; Bicycling; Hiking; Boating; Genealogy; Foreign travel **RE:** Lutheran

BARR, MICHAEL, T: Executive Administrator, Lawyer **I:** Law and Legal Services **DOB:** 11/2/1947 **PB:** White Plains **SC:** NY/USA **PT:** Charles Yerger Barr; Joan Tames (Biggar) Barr **MS:** Married **SPN:** Helen June Rumsey (3/17/1973) **ED:** MBA, Columbia University (1980); JD, Columbia University (1972); BA, Rutgers, the State University of New Jersey, Summa Cum Laude (1969); Coursework, Columbia University; Coursework, Washington and Lee University **C:** Executive Director, Harold Rivkin Art Associates (2015-Present); Research Director, H. Rivkin & Company, Incorporated, Princeton, NJ (2006-2015); Principal, Barr & Company, Far Hills, NJ (2003-2006); Corporate Bond Correspondent, Dow Jones and Company, New York, NY (2001-2003); Financial Consultant, Axa Advisors, Incorporated, New York, NY (2000); Emerging Markets Specialist, Hp Capital Markets Group, New York, NY (1999-2000); Russian Securities Specialist, H. Rivkin & Company, Incorporated, New York, NY (1998-1999); Securities Analyst, Standard & Poor's Corporation, New York, NY (1993-1998); Corporate Secretary, Director, H. Rivkin & Company, Incorporated, New York, NY (1992-1993); Vice President, A-L Associates, New York, NY (1990-1992); Vice President, Manufacturers Hanover Trust Company, New York, NY (1982-1990); Investment Banker, Kidder, Peabody & Company, Incorporated, New York, NY (1980-1982); Associate, Conboy, Hewitt, O'Brien & Boardman, New York, NY (1977-1978); Associate, McCarter & English, Newark, NY (1976-1977) **CR:** Guest Commentator, Russia CNN, Bloomberg News (1998-2000) **CIV:** 50th Reunion Committee, Rutgers Class of 1969 (2019); Secretary, Rutgers Alumni Class of 1969 (2009-2019); Reunion Committee, Columbia Business School Class of 1980 (2010, 2015); 30th Reunion Planning Committee, Columbia Law School Class Of 1972 (2002); Advisory Board, Washington and Lee Alumni College (1996-1998) **MIL:** Lieutenant, U.S. Navy (1972-1976) **CW:** Actor, TV Series, "Law & Order: Trial By Jury" (2005); Actor, Film, "The Interpreter" (2004) **AW:** Loyal Son Award, Rutgers Alumni Association (1976) **MEM:** U.S. Polo Association; Phi Beta Kappa **BAR:** State of New York (1978); State of New Jersey (1976); Supreme Court of the United States (1976) **MH:** Albert Nelson Marquis Lifetime Achievement Award

BARR, WILLIAM PELHAM, T: United States Attorney General; Lawyer **I:** Law and Legal Services **CN:** U.S. Department of Justice **DOB:** 05/23/1950 **PB:** New York **SC:** NY/USA **PT:** Donald Barr; Mary (Ahern) Barr **MS:** Married **SPN:** Christine Moynihan (06/23/1973) **CH:** Meg; Patricia; Mary **ED:** JD, School of Law, The George Washington University (1977); MA, Columbia University (1973); AB, Columbia University (1971) **C:** Attorney General, U.S. Department of Justice, Washington, DC (1991-

1993, 2019-Present); Of Counsel, Kirkland & Ellis LLP, Washington, DC (2009-2019); Vice President, General Counsel, Verizon Communications Inc., New York, NY (2000-2008); Executive Vice President, Government and Regulatory Advocacy, GTE Corporation (1997-2000); General Counsel, GTE Corporation, Washington, DC (1994-2000); Partner, Shaw, Pittman, Potts & Trowbridge (Now Pillsbury Winthrop Shaw Pittman LLP), Washington, DC (1985-1989, 1993-1994); Deputy Attorney General, U.S. Department of Justice, Washington, DC (1990-1991); Assistant Attorney General, Office of Legal Counsel, U.S. Department of Justice, Washington, DC (1989-1990); Associate, Shaw, Pittman, Potts & Trowbridge (Now Pillsbury Winthrop Shaw Pittman LLP), Washington, DC (1978-1982, 1983-1984); Deputy Assistant Director, Domestic Policy Staff, The White House, Washington, DC (1982-1983); Private Law Practice (1978-1979); Law Clerk to the Honorable Malcolm Wilkey, United States Court of Appeals for the District of Columbia Circuit, Washington, DC (1977-1978); Assistant, Office of Legislative Counsel, Central Intelligence Agency (1975-1977); Analyst, Intelligence Directorate Division, Central Intelligence Agency, Washington, DC (1973-1977) **CR:** Board of Directors, Dominion Resources, Inc. (Now Dominion Energy) (2009-Present); Board of Directors, Time Warner Inc. (Now Warner Media, LLC) (2009-Present); Board of Directors, Holcim US (2008-Present); Board of Directors, The Selected Funds (1994-Present); Board Member, Davis Selected Advisers (Now Davis Advisers) **CIV:** Board of Visitors, College of William & Mary (2001-2004); City of Washington Pipe Band **MEM:** American Bar Association; The Virginia Bar Association; The Bar Association of DC; Knights of Columbus **BAR:** The District of Columbia (1978); Commonwealth of Virginia (1977); State of New York **AV:** Playing bagpipe **PA:** Republican **RE:** Roman Catholic

BARRA, MARY, T: Chair, Chief Executive Officer; Automotive Executive **I:** Automotive **CN:** General Motors **DOB:** 12/24/1961 **PB:** Royal Oak **SC:** MI/USA **MS:** Married **SPN:** Tony Barra (08/03/1985) **CH:** Two Children **ED:** Honorary Doctorate, Duke University (2018); MBA, Stanford Graduate School of Business (1990); BSEE, Kettering University, Flint, MI (1985) **C:** Chairman, Chief Executive Officer, General Motors, Detroit, MI (2016-Present); Chief Executive Officer, General Motors, Detroit, MI (2014-2016); Executive Vice President, Global Product Development, Senior Vice President, Global Products Development, General Motors, Detroit, MI (2011-2014); Vice President, Human Resources, General Motors, Detroit, MI (2009-2011); Vice President, Global Manufacturing Engineering, General Motors, Detroit, MI (2008-2009); Executive Director, Vehicle Manufacturing Engineering, General Motors, Detroit, MI (2004-2008); Plant Manager, General Motors, Detroit, MI (2003-2004); Executive Director, Competitive Operations Engineering, North American Vehicle Systems, General Motors (2001-2003); General Director, Internal Communications of North America, General Motors (1999-2001); Business Manager, Corporate Staffs, General Motors (1996-1999); Manager, Manufacturing Planning, Midsize Car Division, General Motors (1993-1996); Senior Staff Engineer to Manager, Manufacturing Planning, General Motors, Warren, MI (1990-1996); Associate Plant Engineer to Senior Supervisor, Maintenance, Tooling Fiero Assembly Plant, General Motors, Pontiac, MI (1985-1988); Kettering University Co-op Student, Pontiac Motor Division, General Motors (1980-1985) **CR:** Board of Directors, General Motors (2014-Present); Board of Directors, General Dynamics Corporation (2011-Present) **CIV:** Board, Disney (2017-Present); Board of

Trustees, Kettering University; Board of Directors, Inforum Center for Leadership **AW:** First Place in All-American Executive Team Survey, Institutional Investor (2019); Legend in Leadership Award, Yale Chief Executive Institute (2018); Listee, Top 50 Best CEOs of Large Companies, Comparably (2018); Listee, Most Powerful Women, Fortune (2015, 2017); Listee, Most Powerful Women, Forbes (2017); Listee, 100 Most Influential People in the World, Time Magazine (2014); Listee, 50 Most Influential People in Global Finance, Bloomberg Markets (2014); Listee, World's Most Powerful People, Forbes Magazine (2014); Listee, 50 Most Powerful Women in Business, Fortune Magazine (2012-2015); Listee, 100 Most Powerful Women, Forbes Magazine (2011-2014); Kettering Alumni Association Management Achievement Award (2010); Listee, 100 Leading Women in North American Auto Industry, Automotive News (2005, 2010); GM Fellowship **MEM:** Institute of Electrical and Electronics Engineers (IEEE); Eta Kappa Nu; The Tau Beta Pi Association, Inc. **AV:** Practicing aerobics; Cooking; Skiing; Windsurfing

BARRAGAN, NANETTE DIAZ, T: U.S. Representative from California **I:** Government Administration/Government Relations/Government Services **DOB:** 09/15/1976 **PB:** Harbor City **SC:** CA/USA **ED:** JD, University of Southern California Gould School of Law (2005); BA in Political Science, Minor in Public Policy, University of California Los Angeles (2000) **C:** Member, U.S. House of Representatives from California's 44th Congressional District (2017-Present); Member, Hermosa Beach City Council (2013-2015); Member, Committee on Homeland Security; Member, Committee on Natural Resources **CIV:** Executive Director, The Gillian S. Fuller Foundation (2000-2003) **CW:** Contributor, Interdisciplinary Law Journal **PA:** Democrat

BARRAN, LINDA MARI, T: Lawyer **I:** Law and Legal Services **DOB:** 04/18/1954 **PB:** Scranton **SC:** PA/USA **PT:** Emil George Barran; Marion Barbara (Dranshak) Barran **ED:** JD, Georgetown University (1993); MA, University of Cincinnati (1982); MusEd, Susquehanna University (1976) **C:** Associate Attorney, Brock & Scott PLC (2019-2020); Stern & Eisenberg Mid-Atlantic P.C (2016-2019); Counsel, Attorney Contractor, Various Law Firms, Washington, DC (2003-2016); Intellectual Property Attorney, Levy & Grandinetti, Washington, DC (2001-2003); Associate, Oliff & Berridge, PLC, Alexandria, VA (2001); Associate, Levy & Grandinetti, Washington, DC (1997-2001); Counsel, Various Law Firms, Washington, DC (1994-1996); Department Head, Development Associate, American Symphony Orchestra League (1980-1984); Master Class Administrator, Wolf Trap Foundation, Vienna, VA (1980); Instructor, Music, Indian River School District, Frankford, DE (1976-1979) **CR:** Volunteer Counsel, Veterans Consortium, Pro Bono Program, Washington, DC (1997-2003) **BAR:** U.S. District Court for the Eastern District of Virginia (2003); Virginia (2002); U.S Court of Appeals for the 4th Circuit (2002); Court of Appeals of the Federal Circuit (1998); U.S. Court of Appeals for Veterans Claims (1998); U.S. Supreme Court (1997); District of Columbia (1993) **MH:** Albert Nelson Marquis Lifetime Achievement Award **B/I:** Ms. Barran became interested in law and politics at an early age. Likewise, her family encouraged her to pursue a career in law all throughout her childhood.

BARRAN, THOMAS, T: Emeritus Professor **I:** Education/Educational Services **CN:** Brooklyn College **DOB:** 07/08/1946 **PB:** Warren **SC:** OH/USA **PT:** Paul Thomas Barran; Sophia Catherine Barran **MS:** Married **SPN:** Barbara Caplan (06/05/1983) **ED:** PhD, Columbia University (1984); AB, Columbia College

(1968) **C:** Professor, Russian, Brooklyn College, New York, NY (1986-Present); Preceptor, Columbia University, New York, NY (1978-1979) **CR:** Visiting Professor, Hunter College, New York, NY (1991); Board of Directors, Classic Rug Collection, Inc., New York, NY; Lecturer in Field; Expert Witness in Field; Consultant in Field **CIV:** Board of Directors, ROSAS Neighborhood Association, Brooklyn, NY (1998-2002) **CW:** Author, "Russia Reads Rousseau: 1762-1825" (2002); Contributor, Articles, Professional Journals **AW:** Fellow, International Research & Exchanges Board (1976-1977); United States State Department (1972-1974) **MEM:** New York Public Library; Slavic Language Professional Association; Modern Language Association of America; Bigelow Society **MH:** Albert Nelson Marquis Lifetime Achievement Award **B/I:** Dr. Barran's father was an interpreter in Iran during World War II. He spoke many Slavic languages, but Mr. Barran had not learned the languages himself at the time. He then studied Russian at Columbia College and continued to read in Russian. He was accepted into graduate school but took a four-year hiatus to teach elementary school. Then, in 1972, he began graduate school at Columbia University, studying Slavic languages. The more he became involved, the more trips he made to Russia. Dr. Barran became enthralled in the culture. He was always interested in literature as well, but when he began studying foreign languages, like Russian, he discovered how rich the literature of the culture truly was. **AV:** Deep-sea fishing; Researching archaeology; Traveling

BARRASSO, JOHN ANTHONY, T: U.S. Senator from Wyoming **I:** Government Administration/Government Relations/Government Services **DOB:** 07/21/1952 **PB:** Reading **SC:** PA/USA **PT:** John A. Barraso; Louise M. (DeCisco) Barrasso **MS:** Married **SPN:** Bobbi Brown (01/01/2008); Linda D. Nix (05/06/1978, Divorced) **CH:** Peter; Emma; Hadley **ED:** Resident, Yale New Haven Hospital, Yale New Haven Health (1978-1983); MD, Georgetown University School of Medicine, Washington, DC (1978); BS, Georgetown University, Washington, DC (1974) **CT:** Diplomate, American Board of Orthopaedic Surgery **C:** Chairman, U.S. Senate Republican Conference (2019-Present); Chairman, U.S. Senate Republican Policy Committee (2013-Present); U.S. Senator, State of Wyoming (2007-Present); Chairman, U.S. Senate Environment Committee (2017); Chairman, U.S. Senate Committee on Indian Affairs (2015-2017); Vice Chairman, U.S. Senate Committee on Indian Affairs (2009-2015); Vice Chairman, U.S. Senate Republican Conference (2010-2012); Chairman, Transportation, Highways & Military Affairs Committee, Wyoming State Senate (2005-2007); Member, District 27, Wyoming State Senate (2003-2007); Orthopedic Surgeon, Casper Orthopedic Associates, WY (1983-2007); Member, Minerals, Business & Economic Development Committee, Wyoming State Senate (2003-2005); Member, Labor, Health & Social Services Committee, Wyoming State Senate (2003-2005); Chief of Staff, Wyoming Medical Center (2003-2005) **CR:** Delegate, Republican National Convention (1992, 2004); Leader, Delegation to Republic of China, Republican National Convention (1994); Treasurer, Republican National Committee (1991-1992) **CIV:** Emcee, "Jerry Lewis MDA Labor Day Telethon," K2TV, WY; President, Wyoming Health Fairs/Wellness Health Fairs; President, United Way of Natrona County **AW:** Named One of the 10 Members to Watch in the 112th Congress, Roll Call (2011); Friend of Farm Bureau Award, Wyoming Farm Bureau Federation (2010); Congressional Award, Small Business Council of America (SBCA) (2010); Ken Alvord Community Service Award, National Association of Medical Communicators (NAMC) (1992); Legislature Service Award, Veterans of Foreign Wars (VFW); Medal of Excellence, Wyoming National Guard; Wyoming Physician of the Year Award **MEM:** President, National Association of Physician Broadcasters (1988-1989); Wyoming Medical Society **PA:** Republican

BARRINGTON, MARTIN, "MARTY" JOSEPH, T: Chairman and Chief Executive Officer (Retired) **I:** Law and Legal Services **CN:** Altria Group, Inc. **DOB:** 07/16/1953 **PB:** Albany **SC:** NY/USA **ED:** JD, Albany Law School (1980); BA in History, The College of Saint Rose (1977) **C:** President, Altria Group, Inc. (2015-2018); Chairman and Chief Executive Officer, Altria Group, Inc. (2012-2018); Vice Chairman, Altria Group, Inc. (2011-2012); Executive Vice President, Chief Administrative Officer, Chief Compliance Officer, Altria Group, Inc. (2003-2011); Senior Vice President, General Counsel, Philip Morris USA, Inc. and Philip Morris International, Philip Morris Products S.A., New York, NY (1993-2003); Partner, Hunton & Williams (1990-1993); Associate, Hunton & Williams (1982-1989); Law Clerk, United States Court of Appeals for the Fourth Circuit (1980-1982) **CR:** Chairman, Board of Directors, Anheuser-Busch InBev (2019-Present); Adjunct Instructor, Discrimination Law, University of Richmond (1988-1989); Labor and Employment Law Section, Committee on the Development of the Law Under the NLRA, American Bar Association **CIV:** Board of Trustees, The College of Saint Rose (2009); Founding Chairman, NextUp RVA, Inc.; Board of Directors, Richmond Performing Arts Alliance; Board of Directors, Navy Hill Foundation, NH District Corp.; Former Commissioner, Virginia Port Authority; Board of Trustees, Virginia Museum of Fine Arts **CW:** Contributor, "Albany Law Review," Albany Law School (1979-1980) **MEM:** American Bar Association; Justinian Society of Lawyers **BAR:** State of Virginia (1982); State of New York (1981)

BARRIS, MICHAEL CRAIG, PHD, T: Neurophysiologist **I:** Sciences **CN:** Nova Southeastern University **DOB:** 02/19/1944 **PB:** Dunkirk **SC:** NY/USA **PT:** W. Record Barris; Thelma M. (Snow) Barris **MS:** Divorced **SPN:** Rhoda Lee Seidlin (06/30/1968, Divorced 12/1974) **ED:** PhD, City University of New York (1976); AB, University of Rochester (1966) **C:** Assistant Professor of Optometry, Nova Southeastern University, Davie, FL (1995-1998); Visiting Assistant Research Professor of Biochemistry, Michigan State University, East Lansing, MI (1994); Assistant Professor of Internal Medicine, Michigan State University, East Lansing, MI (1990-1992); Research Assistant in Psychology, Queens College, Flushing, NY (1989); Assistant Professor of Optometry, Inter American University of Puerto Rico, Metropolitan Campus, San Juan, Puerto Rico (1983-1988); Fellow in Ophthalmology, University of Florida, Gainesville, FL (1976-1979) **CR:** Adjunct Instructor of Ophthalmology, Mount Sinai School of Medicine, New York, NY (1980-1981); Adjunct Lecturer of Psychology, Queens College, Flushing, NY (1971-1976) **CIV:** Trustee, Village of Fredonia, NY (2018-2019) **CW:** Contributor, 43 Papers, Articles to Professional Journals Including Vision Research, Investigative Ophthalmology and Vision Science, Documenta Ophthalmologica, Annals of Neurology, Electroencephalography and Clinical Neurophysiology, Journal of Physiology, American Journal of Physiology, Journal of the Acoustical Society of America and Optometry and Vision Science **AW:** Postdoctoral Research Fellowship, Fight for Sight (1981); Grantee-in-aid, Research National Society to Prevent Blindness (1981); Institutional Research Grantee, American Cancer Society, Inc. (1976); National Research Service Fellowship, National Eye Institute (1976) **MH:** Albert Nelson Marquis Lifetime Achievement Award; Marquis Who's Who Top Professional **B/I:** Dr. Barris was inspired to go into his profession by the time he spent working in a psychiatric hospital during junior year of his undergraduate education. He decided he wanted to go into research because he felt that would help people more. In addition, his great-grandfather was a physician and had a great influence on his profession. His father, W. Record Barris, was an art teacher so it skipped two good generations. **AV:** Opera fan **PA:** Democrat

BARSNESS, RICHARD, "DICK" W. PHD, T: Management Educator, Academic Administrator **I:** Education/Educational Services **CN:** Lehigh University **DOB:** 04/26/1935 **PB:** Elbow Lake **SC:** MN/USA **PT:** Russel E.; Joanna (Warga) B. **MS:** Married **SPN:** Dorothea L. Gother (8/22/1964) **CH:** Karen Louise; Erik Richard **ED:** Doctor of Philosophy in American Economic History, University of Minnesota (1963); Master in Public Administration, University of Minnesota (1960); Master of Arts in History, University of Minnesota (1958); Bachelor of Science, University of Minnesota (1957) **C:** Emeritus Professor, Lehigh University (2004-Present); Professor, Prague, Lehigh University (2000-2015); Director, Office of Fellowship Advising (2011-2013); Distinguished Service Professor of Management, Lehigh University (1995-2004); Professor, Lehigh University, Bethlehem, PA (1978-2004); Executive Director, Iacocca Institute, Lehigh University, Bethlehem, PA (1992-1995); Professor of Business, Iacocca Institute, Lehigh University, Bethlehem, PA (1992-1993); Dean, Professor, Lehigh University, Bethlehem, PA (1978-1992); Associate Dean, Northwestern University, Evanston, IL (1972-1978); Associate Professor, Northwestern University, Evanston, IL (1969-1978); Instructor, Assistant Professor, Northwestern University, Evanston, IL (1962-1969); Budget Analyst, United States Bureau Budget, Washington, DC (1960-1961) **CR:** With, Lexington Group Inc. (1997-2005); Visiting Professor, Sasin Graduate, Institute of Business Administration, Chulalongkorn University, Bangkok (1983-1992); Executive Secretary, Lexington Group in Transport History (1969-1989); Lecturer, Transportation Center, Evanston, IL (1964-1984); President, Business History Conference (1981-1982) **CIV:** Chair, Third Millennium Fund, Cathedral Church Nativity (2009-2014); Board of Directors, Episcopal House, Allentown, PA (1999-2007); President, Episcopal House (2003-2005); General Chairman, United Way, Lehigh University (1981); Governor's Advisors Council, State of Illinois (1969-1972) **CW:** Contributor, Articles to Professional Journals; Editor, Lexington Newsletter **AW:** R.R. and E.C. Hillman Award, Lehigh University (1991) **MEM:** President, Business History Conference (1981-1982); Trustee, Business History Conference (1978-1981); International Association for Business and Society; Academy of International Business; Transportation Research Forum; Academy of Management; Phi Beta Kappa; Beta Gamma Sigma **MH:** Albert Nelson Marquis Lifetime Achievement Award **B/I:** Mr. Barsness became involved in his profession due to the influence of his mother, who served as a teacher and librarian. His initial interest was in economic history, a subject in which he received a doctorate. **PA:** Republican **RE:** Episcopalian

BARSTOW, DAVID, T: Professor; Journalist, Investigative Reporter (Retired) **I:** Education/Educational Services **CN:** University of California Berkeley Graduate School of Journalism **DOB:** 01/21/1963 **PB:** Boston **SC:** MA/USA **MS:** Married **CH:** Two Children **ED:** MA in International Journalism, University of Southern California (1996); Degree in Journalism, Media, Integrated Marketing Communications, Medill School of Journalism, Northwestern University, Evanston, IL (1986) **C:** Reva and David Logan Distinguished Chair, Professor, Investigative Journalism, University of California Berkeley Graduate School of Journalism (2019-Present); Investigative Reporter, The New York Times Company (2002-2019); Metropolitan Desk Reporter, The New York Times, New York, NY (1992-2002); Staff Writer, St. Petersburg Times (1989-1999); Staff, Rochester Times-Union **AW:** Co-Recipient, Pulitzer Prize for Explanatory Reporting (2019); Inductee, Hall of Achievement, Medill School of Journalism, Northwestern University (2015); Co-Recipient, Pulitzer Prize for Investigative Reporting (2013); George Polk Award for National Reporting (2007, 2012); Distinguished Alumni Award, Medill School of Journalism, Northwestern University (2010); Pulitzer Prize for Investigative Reporting (2009); Goldsmith Award for Investigative Reporting, Joan Shorenstein Center Press, Politics & Public Policy (2004); Pulitzer Prize for Public Service (2004); Pulitzer Prize for Explanatory Journalism (1998); George Polk Award; Alfred I. duPont Silver Baton; Barlett and Steele Gold Medal; Loeb Award; Sidney Hillman Award; Daniel Pearl Award for Investigative Reporting; Two-time Winner, Sigma Delta Chi Awards for Distinguished Service; Peabody Award; Award, Investigative Reporters & Editors Award, Mirror Award; Citation, Overseas Press Club of America; Two-time Award Winner, Society of American Business Editors and Writers (Now Society for Advancing Business Editing and Writing); Gold Keyboard Award

BARTELS, ALOYSIA JEANNE MARIE, T: Food Scientist, Mariculturist **I:** Sciences **DOB:** 08/11/1923 **PB:** Victoria **SC:** British Columbia/Canada **PT:** Jean Marie de Hedouville; Aloysia Theresa van Goidtsoven (Sant Anna) **MS:** Married **SPN:** Jay Murray Bartels; George P. Meade III (Divorced); Karl L. Agricola (Divorced) **CH:** Joseph W.; William L. **ED:** Convent Marat Immaculate Classical Education, Girls Boarding School **C:** President, Director, West Indies Sea Farms Ltd., Carriacore, Grenada (1986-1992); Owner, Five Shrimp Fishing Boats, Florida, Texas (1972-1986) **CR:** Teacher, Art & Oil Paint **CW:** Author, Poem, "Navaho" (1993); Co-author, "Pageant of Eight Flags" (1993); Publisher, Poetry **AW:** Best of Award, NY Poets Society (1993) **MEM:** Past President, Head of Restoration Commission, Fernandina Beach Florida Historical Society **MH:** Albert Nelson Marquis Lifetime Achievement Award **B/I:** Ms. Bartels worked at the Navy Yard during WWII in Key West. During that time she also had a daily radio show, WKIZ Key West. She spoke to a man at the radio station and told him that she felt that they should have a radio show for women, because all they did was rock and roll music and sports. He gave her a half an hour on Saturdays, and she had to get her own sponsors. She ended up with an hour show everyday. **AV:** Travel; History; Painting; Writing; Poetry **PA:** Republican

BARTELS, ANN-MARIE, AAP, T: Chief Executive Officer Emeritus **I:** Nonprofit & Philanthropy **CN:** EPCOR **DOB:** 12/15/1954 **PB:** Alton **SC:** IL/USA **PT:** Norman William Bartels; Betty L. (Pruessing) Bartels Julian **MS:** Married **SPN:** Anthony E. Cowell **ED:** Coursework, Southern Illinois University, Carbondale, IL (1972-1976) **CT:** Accredited ACH Professional **C:** Chief Executive Officer Emeritus, EPCOR, (2020-Present); Chief Executive Officer, EPCOR (2009-2020); President, Chief Executive Officer, Mid-America Payment Exchange (2000-2009); President, Mid-America Payment Exchange (1998-2000); Vice President, Mid-America Payment Exchange (1995-1998); Communications Director, Mid-America Payment Exchange (1989-1995);

Owner, The Amber Group (1987-1990); Public Relations Director, Mid-America Payment Exchange, St. Louis, MO (1987-1988); Deputy, Director Conferences (1984-1987); Marketing Manager, American Federation of Information Processing Societies (1982-1984); Public Relations Consultant (1981-1982); Public Relations Director, Ringling Brothers and Barnum & Bailey (1979-1981); Public Relations Coordinator, Ringling Brothers and Barnum & Bailey (1978); Public Relations Director, Showtime Inc. (1976-1978) **CR:** Board of Directors, EPCOR (2009-Present); Chair, Payments Executives Leadership Forum (2003-2005, 2015-2017); Federal Reserve Faster Payment Task Force (2015-2017); Chair, Communications & Marketing Advisory Group, NACHA (2010-2014); Board of Directors, Mid-America Payments Exchange (1998-2009); Corporate Payments Council, NACHA (2004-2006); Board of Directors, NACHA (1998-2006); Chair, Banker's Institute (2000-2002); ACH Committee, American Payroll Association (1995-2001) **CW:** Contributor, Numerous Regional and National Speaking Engagements; Contributor, Numerous Articles and Publications **AW:** Excellence Certificates, Association Trends (1983); Merit Certificate, Printing United Alliance (1982) **MEM:** American Federation of Information Processing Societies; American Society of Association Executives **MH:** Albert Nelson Marquis Lifetime Achievement Award **AS:** Ms. Bartels attributes her success to ensuring that the association is serving the best interests of its members. **B/I:** Ms. Bartels became involved in her profession because of her expertise in public relations and the opportunity she was presented with the American Federation of Information Processing Societies, where she fell in love with association management. **AV:** Traveling; Gardening; Taking photographs

BARTIROMO, MARIA SARA, T: Anchor, Columnist, Author **I:** Media & Entertainment **CN:** FOX Business Network **DOB:** 09/11/1967 **PB:** Brooklyn **SC:** NY/USA **PT:** Vincent Bartiromo; Josephine Bartiromo **MS:** Married **SPN:** Jonathan Laurence Steinberg (06/13/1999) **ED:** Certificate in Screenwriting, New York University (1990); Bachelor of Arts in Journalism, New York University (1989) **C:** Anchor Global Markets Editor, FOX Business Network, FOX News Network LLC (2014-Present); Freelance Columnist, Independent Investor Magazine, New York, NY (1991-Present); Journalist, USA Today (2015); Journalist, FOX News Channel (2014-2015); Anchor, "Closing Bell with Maria Bartiromo," CNBC (2006-2013); Host, Managing Editor, "Wall Street Journal Report," CNBC (2000-2013); Television Journalist, CNBC (1993-2013); Host, "Market Wrap," CNBC (1998-2000); Host, CNBC's "Business Center," CNBC (1997-1999); Correspondent, CNBC, New York, NY (1993-1997); Producer, CNN Business News, Cable News Network, New York, NY (1989-1993); Associate Producer, "Barry Farber Show," New York, NY **CR:** Columnist, Reader's Digest Magazine (2004-Present); Adjunct Professor, New York University Leonard N. Stern School of Business (2010-2012); Columnist, Bloomberg Businessweek (2005-2009); Controller, Newsweek, Town & Country, Registered Rep, New York Post **CIV:** Board Director, Girl Scout Council of Greater New York, Girl Scouts of the United States of America; Member, Wharton Leadership Advisory Board; Board of Governors, Columbus Citizens Foundation; Board of Trustees, New York University; Board of Directors, Public Education Needs Civic Involvement and Leadership; Board of Directors, New York City Ballet **CW:** Appearance, "Arbitrage" (2012); Appearance, "Wall Street: Money Never Sleeps" (2011); Appearance, "Inside Job" (2010); Author, "The Weekend That Changed Wall Street: And How the Fallout

is Still Impacting Our World" (2010); Co-author, with Catherine Whitney, "The 10 Laws of Enduring Success" (2010); Appearance, "The Taking of Pelham 123" (2009); Appearance, "Risk/Reward" (2003); Author, "Use the News: How to Separate the Noise from the Investment Nuggets and Make Money in Any Economy" (2001) **AW:** Lifetime Achievement Award, National Italian American Foundation (2019); Inductee, Cable Hall of Fame (2011); Grand Marshal, Columbus Day Parade, NY (2010); Named, One of the Top 25 Market Movers, U.S. News & World Report (2009); Emmy Award for Outstanding Business and Economic Reporting, Television Academy (2009); Emmy Award for Outstanding Coverage of a Breaking News Story, Television Academy (2008); Named, One of the 100 Most Influential Business Journalists in the US, Newbios.com (2007); Lincoln Statue Award, The Union League of Philadelphia (2004); Excellence in Broadcast Journalism Award, Coalition of Italo-American Associations (1997) **MEM:** New York Financial Writers' Association; Council on Foreign Relations; The Economic Club of New York

BARTOLOMEI, JOAN MARIE, T: Elementary School Educator **I:** Education/Educational Services **DOB:** 10/24/1943 **PB:** Chicago **SC:** IL/USA **PT:** Gordon Richard Kennerley; Florence Mary (Gundry) Kennerley **MS:** Widow **SPN:** Roland Bartolomei (06/25/1966, Deceased 1995) **CH:** Gordon Richard; Elizabeth Marie **ED:** MEd, National Louis University (1990); BEd, Northern Illinois University (1965) **C:** Teacher, District 105 (1980-Present); Delegate to Representative, Assembly National Education Association (1999-2004); Substitute Teacher, District 105 (1975-1980); Teacher, District 105, LaGrange, Illinois (1965-1970); Member Committee, School District #105 **CIV:** Cub Scout Leader, Countryside (1978-1979); Representative, Library Committee, Countryside, Illinois (1978-1979); Sunday School Teacher, Grace Episcopal Church, Hinsdale (1977-1978) **MEM:** Secretary, Illinois Education Association (1980-Present); National Education Association; Alpha Delta Pi; Staff Development Committee; Mathematics Committee; Technology Committee; Literacy Committee; Behavior Committee; Writing Committee

BARTON, WILLIAM, "BILL," ARNOLD, T: Lawyer, Educator **I:** Law and Legal Services **CN:** Barton Trial Attorneys **DOB:** 03/15/1948 **PB:** Morton **SC:** WA/USA **PT:** Marvin Buryl Barton; Jo Ellen (Wilson) Barton **MS:** Married **SPN:** JoAnn Barton **CH:** Monique Barton; Almine Barton; Brent Barton **ED:** JD, Willamette University (1972); BS, Pacific University (1969) **CT:** Oregon State Bar (1972) **C:** Private Practice, Newport, OR (1973-Present) **CR:** Adjunct Professor, College of Law, Willamette University (1983-Present) **CW:** Author, "Recovering for Psychological Injuries, Third Edition" **AW:** Dale Haralson Fallout Award, Western Trial Lawyers Association (2018); Award of Merit, Oregon State Bar (2015); Owen M. Panner Professionalism Award, Oregon State Bar (2013); Distinguished Trial Lawyer Award, Oregon Trial Lawyers Association (2005); **MEM:** Vice President, Oregon State Bar (1986-Present); Board of Governors, Association of Trial Lawyers of America (Now American Association for Justice) (1988-1991); President, Western Trial Lawyers Association (1985); President, Oregon Trial Lawyers Association (1983); Fellow, The International Academy of Trial Lawyers; International Society of Barristers; American Board of Trial Advocates; American College of Trial Lawyers **MH:** Albert Nelson Marquis Lifetime Achievement Award; Marquis Who's Who Top Professional **AV:** Traveling; Writing; Running a boot camp for lawyers

BARYSHNIKOV, MIKHAIL, "MISHA" NIKOLA-YEVICH, T: Dancer; Actor; Artistic Director **I:** Media & Entertainment **DOB:** 01/27/1948 **PB:** Riga **SC:** Latvia **PT:** Alexandra (Kiselyova) Baryshnikov; Nikolay Baryshnikov **MS:** Married **SPN:** Lisa Rinehart (2006); Jessica Lange (1976, Divorced 1982) **CH:** Aleksandra Lange "Shura" Baryshnikov; Peter Andrew Baryshnikov; Anna Katerina Baryshnikov; Sofia-Luisa Baryshnikov **ED:** Honorary Doctorate, University of Southern California (2019); Honorary Doctorate, Northwestern University (2013); Honorary Doctorate, The Juilliard School (2010); Honorary Doctorate, Montclair State University (2008); Honorary Doctorate, Shenandoah Conservatory, Shenandoah University (2007); Honorary DFA, New York University (2006); Honorary LHD, University of Toronto (1999); Honorary DFA, Yale University (1979); Coursework, Vaganova Academy of Russian Ballet (Now Vaganova Ballet Academy), St. Petersburg, Russia (1964-1967) **C:** Founder, Artistic Director, Baryshnikov Arts Center (BAC), New York, NY (2005-Present); Artistic Director, White Oak Dance Project (1990-2002); Artistic Director, American Ballet Theater, Ballet Theatre Foundation, Inc. (1980-1989); Principal Dancer, New York City Ballet, Inc. (1978-1979); Principal Dancer, American Ballet Theatre, Ballet Theatre Foundation, Inc. (1974-1978) **CIV:** Baryshnikov Dance Foundation Inc. **CW:** Actor, "Doll & Em" (2015); Actor, "Man in a Case" (2013-2014); Actor, "In Paris," Santa Monica College Performing Arts Center (2012); Actor, Dancer, "Place" (2009); Actor, "Beckett Shorts," New York Theatre Workshop, New York, NY (2007); Actor, "Forbidden Christmas or The Doctor and the Patient," Lincoln Center Theater, New York, NY (2004); Actor, "Sex and the City" (2003-2004); Appearance, "The Babilée Mystery" (2001); Appearance, "Betty Oliphant: A Life in Dance" (2001); Performer, "Babilée '91" (1991); Actor, "Company Business" (1991); Actor, "The Cabinet of Dr. Ramirez" (1991); Actor, "Metamorphosis" (1989); Actor, "Dancers" (1987); Actor, "White Nights" (1985); Performer, "American Ballet Theatre at the Met" (1984); Performer, "Don Quixote (Kitri's Wedding), a Ballet in Three Acts" (1984); Performer, "Baryshnikov: The Dancer and the Dance" (1983); Performer, "Baryshnikov in Hollywood" (1982); Performer, "Carmen" (1981); Host, "IBM Presents Baryshnikov on Broadway" (1980); Performer, "Baryshnikov at the White House" (1979); Dancer, Actor, "The Nutcracker" (1977); Actor, "The Turning Point" (1977); Performer, "Live from Lincoln Center" (1977); Appearance, "Making Television Dance" (1977); Performer, "Baryshnikov: Live at Wolf Trap" (1976); Actor, "Fiesta" (1971); Dancer, "Gorod i Pesnya" (1968) **AW:** Praemium Imperiale Award for International Arts, Japan Arts Association (2017); Honorary Citizenship, Republic of Latvia (2017); Vilcek Prize in Dance, Vilcek Foundation (2012); Named Officier, Légion d'Honneur, France (2010); George and Judy Marcus Prize for Lifetime Achievement (2006); National Arts Award, Americans for the Arts (2005); Jerome Robbins Award, Jerome Robbins Foundation (2005); Chubb Fellowship, Yale University (2003-2004); Prix Benois de la Danse for Lifetime Achievement, International Dance Association, Moscow, Russia (2003); National Medal of Arts, President of the United States (2000); Honoree, Kennedy Center Honors (2000); Special Award, Outer Critics Circle (1989); Theatre World Special Award, Theatre World Awards, Inc. (1989); Hasty Pudding Theatrical Award for Man of the Year, The Hasty Pudding - Institute of 1770, Inc. (1987); Nijinsky Prize, The Opéra de Paris, Paris, France (1969); Commonwealth Award **MEM:** Fellow, American Academy of Arts & Sciences (1999-Present)

BASHSHUR, RASHID L., T: Professor Emeritus of Health Management and Policy **I:** Education/Educational Services **CN:** University of Michigan **PT:** Lutfallah M. Bashshur; Yamna D. Bashshur **MS:** Married **SPN:** Naziha S. Sima'an (9/15/1957) **CH:** Ramona R.; Noura R. **ED:** PhD, University of Michigan (1962) **C:** Emeritus Professor, University of Michigan (2012-Present); Director, Telemedicine, University of Michigan Health Systems, Ann Arbor, MI (1998-Present); Professor, Health Management and Policy, University of Michigan (1977); Retired, Senior Advisor for E-Health **CR:** Staff Associate, Institute of Medicine, National Academy of Sciences, Washington, DC (1970-1972) **CIV:** President, President Emeritus, American Telemedicine Association, Washington, DC (2000-2002) **CW:** Editor in Chief, Telemedicine and Health (1995-2005) **AW:** Grantee, Effects of Telemedicine on Cost, Quality and Access, Health Care Financing Administration (1996-1998) **MH:** Albert Nelson Marquis Lifetime Achievement Award; Marquis Who's Who Top Professional **AV:** Watercolor painting; Swimming

BASINGER, KIMILA, "KIM" ANN, T: Actress **I:** Media & Entertainment **DOB:** 12/08/1953 **PB:** Athens **SC:** GA/USA **PT:** Ann Lee Basinger; Donald Wade Basinger **MS:** Divorced **SPN:** Alec Baldwin (08/19/1993-12/03/2002); Ron Snyder-Britton (10/12/1980-12/01/1988) **CH:** Ireland Eliesse Baldwin **ED:** Coursework, University of Georgia **C:** Model, IMG Worldwide, Inc. (2013-Present); Model, Ford Models, New York, NY (1972-1976) **CIV:** Spokesperson, PETA; Spokesperson, Farm Sanctuary, Inc. **CW:** Actress, "Fifty Shades Freed" (2018); Actress, "Comrade Detective" (2017); Actress, "Fifty Shades Darker" (2017); Actress, "The Nice Guys" (2016); Actress, "The 11th Hour" (2014); Actress, "4 Minute Mile" (2014); Actress, "Grudge Match" (2013); Actress, "Third Person" (2013); Actress, "Black November" (2012); Actress, "Charlie St. Cloud" (2010); Actress, "The Informers" (2008); Actress, Executive Producer, "While She Was Out" (2008); Actress, "The Burning Plain" (2008); Actress, "The Mermaid Chair" (2006); Actress, "The Sentinel" (2006); Actress, "Even Money" (2006); Actress, "Cellular" (2004); Actress, "Elvis Has Left the Building" (2004); Actress, "The Door in the Floor" (2004); Actress, "People I Know" (2002); Actress, "8 Mile" (2002); Actress, "Bless the Child" (2000); Actress, "I Dreamed of Africa" (2000); Voice Actress, "The Simpsons" (1998); Actress, "L.A. Confidential" (1997); Actress, "Ready to Wear" (1994); Actress, "The Getaway" (1994); Actress, "Wayne's World 2" (1993); Actress, "The Real McCoy" (1993); Actress, "Cool World" (1993); Actress, "Final Analysis" (1992); Actress, "The Marrying Man" (1991); Actress, "Batman" (1989); Actress, "My Stepmother Is an Alien" (1988); Actress, "Nadine" (1987); Actress, "Blind Date" (1987); Actress, "No Mercy" (1987); Actress, "9½ Weeks" (1986); Actress, "Fool for Love" (1985); Actress, "The Natural" (1984); Actress, "The Man Who Loved Women" (1983); Actress, "Never Say Never Again" (1983); Actress, "Mother Lode" (1982); Actress, "Killjoy" (1981); Actress, "Hard Country" (1981); Actress, "From Here to Eternity" (1979-1980); Actress, "Vega$" (1978); Actress, "Katie: Portrait of a Centerfold" (1978); Actress, "The Ghost of Flight 401" (1978); Actress, "Dog and Cat" (1977); Actress, "McMillan & Wife" (1977); Actress, "The Six Million Dollar Man" (1977); Actress, "Charlie's Angels" (1976); Actress, "Gemini Man" (1976) **AW:** Award for Best Actress, Boston Society of Film Critics (2004); Academy Award for Best Supporting Actress, Academy of Motion Picture Arts and Sciences (1997); Golden Globe Award for Best Supporting Actress - Motion Picture, Hollywood Foreign Press Association (1997); Screen Actors Guild Award for Outstanding Performance by a Female Actor in a Supporting Role (1997); Award for Best Actress in a Supporting Role, Southeastern Film Critics Association Awards (1997); Award for Best Acting by an Ensemble, National Board of Review (1994); Star, Motion Picture Category, Hollywood Walk of Fame, Hollywood Chamber of Commerce (1992); Jupiter Award for Best International Actress (1987)

BASS, KAREN RUTH, T: U.S. Representative from California **I:** Government Administration/Government Relations/Government Services **DOB:** 10/03/1953 **PB:** Los Angeles **SC:** CA **PT:** DeWitt Talmadge Bass; Wilhelmina (Duckett) Bass **MS:** Divorced **SPN:** Jesus Lechuga (1980, Divorced 1986) **CH:** Emilia (Deceased); Four Stepchildren **ED:** Master's in Social Work, University of Southern California (2015); BS in Health Services, California State University, Dominguez Hills, CA (1990); Coursework in Philosophy, San Diego State University (1971-1973) **CT:** Certified Physician Assistant, Keck School of Medicine of University of Southern California **C:** Member, U.S. House of Representatives from California's 35th Congressional District, United States Congress, Washington, DC (2015-Present); Member, U.S. House Judiciary Committee (2013-Present); Member, U.S. Representative from California's 37th Congressional District, United States Congress, Washington, DC (2013-Present); Member, U.S. House Foreign Affairs Committee (2011-Present); Speaker Emeritus, California State Assembly (2010-Present); Member, United States House Budget Committee (2011-2013); Member, U.S. Representative from California's 33rd Congressional District, United States Congress, Washington, DC (2011-2013); Speaker, California State Assembly (2008-2010); Member, District 47, California State Assembly (2005-2010); Majority Floor Leader, California State Assembly (2007-2008); Majority Whip, California State Assembly (2005-2006); Member, Committee on Foreign Affairs; Member, Committee on Natural Resources **CR:** Adjunct Instructor, California State University (1989-1996); Project Director, Health Careers Opportunity Program (1986-1990); Clinical Instructor, Keck School of Medicine of University of Southern California (1986) **CIV:** Chair, Black Congressional Caucus; Member, Congressional Progressive Caucus **PA:** Democrat **RE:** Christian

BASSETT, ANGELA EVELYN, T: Actress **I:** Media & Entertainment **DOB:** 08/16/1958 **PB:** New York **SC:** NY/USA **PT:** Daniel Benjamin Bassett; Betty Jane (Gilbert) Bassett **MS:** Married **SPN:** Courtney B. Vance (10/12/1997) **CH:** Bronwyn Golden Vance; Slater Josiah Vance **ED:** Honorary ArtsD, Morehouse College (2019); Honorary DFA, Yale University (2018); MFA, Yale School of Drama (1983); BA in African-American Studies, Yale University (1980) **CIV:** Spokesperson, Know Diabetes by Heart Initiative, American Diabetes Association® and American Heart Association, Inc. (2019-Present); Ambassador, UNICEF (2003-Present); Supporter, Royal Theater Club, Boys & Girls Clubs of America, St. Petersburg, FL **CW:** Executive Producer, "9-1-1: Lone Star" (2020-Present); Narrator, "The Imagineering Story" (2019-Present); Actress, Executive Producer, "9-1-1" (2018-Present); Voice Actress, "Soul" (2020); Actress, "Gunpowder Milkshake" (2020); Actress, "Attorneys at Love" (2020); Actress, Executive Producer, "Otherhood" (2019); Actress, "A Black Lady Sketch Show" (2019); Actress, "Avengers: Endgame" (2019); Voice Actress, "Bumblebee" (2018); Actress, "Mission: Impossible - Fallout" (2018); Actress, "Black Panther" (2018); Voice Actress, "BoJack Horseman" (2015-2018); Actress, Director, "American Horror Story" (2013-2018); Actress, "Master of None" (2017); Actress, "Underground" (2017); Executive Producer, "Remand" (2017); Actress, "Close to the Enemy" (2016); Voice Actress, "The Snowy Day" (2016); Actress, "London Has Fallen" (2016); Actress, "Chi-Raq" (2015); Voice Actress, "Curious George 3: Back to the Jungle" (2015); Actress, "Survivor" (2015); Director, "Breakthrough" (2015); Director, "Whitney" (2015); Actress, "White Bird in a Blizzard" (2014); Actress, "Black Nativity" (2013); Actress, "Olympus Has Fallen" (2013); Actress, "Betty and Coretta" (2013); Actress, "Rogue" (2012); Actress, "This Means War" (2012); Actress, "The Mountaintop," Bernard B. Jacobs Theatre, New York, NY (2011); Actress, "Identity" (2011); Actress, "Green Lantern" (2011); Actress, "Jumping the Broom" (2011); Voice Actress, "The Simpsons" (2010); Actress, "Notorious" (2009); Actress, "ER" (2008-2009); Actress, "Gospel Hill" (2008); Actress, "Nothing But the Truth" (2008); Actress, "Meet the Browns" (2008); Actress, "Of Boys and Men" (2008); Voice Actress, "Meet the Robinsons" (2007); Co-author with Courtney B. Vance and Hilary Beard, "Friends: A Love Story" (2007); Actress, "Time Bomb" (2006); Actress, "Akeelah and the Bee" (2006); Actress, "Fences," Pasadena Playhouse, Pasadena, CA (2006); Actress, "Alias" (2005); Actress, "His Girl Friday," Guthrie Theater, Minneapolis, MN (2005); Actress, "Mr. 3000" (2004); Actress, "The Lazarus Child" (2004); Voice Actress, "Freedom: A History of Us" (2003); Actress, "The Bernie Mac Show" (2003); Actress, "Masked and Anonymous" (2003); Actress, "Sunshine State" (2002); Actress, Executive Producer, "The Rosa Parks Story" (2002); Executive Producer, "Our America" (2002); Actress, Producer, "Ruby's Bucket of Blood" (2001); Actress, "The Score" (2001); Actress, "Boesman and Lena" (2000); Voice Actress, "Whispers: An Elephant's Tale" (2000); Actress, "Supernova" (2000); Actress, "Music of the Heart" (1999); Voice Actress, "Our Friend, Martin" (1999); Actress, "How Stella Got Her Groove Back" (1998); Actress, "Macbeth," Joseph Papp Public Theater, New York, NY (1998); Actress, "Contact" (1997); Actress, "Waiting to Exhale" (1995); Actress, "Vampire in Brooklyn" (1995); Actress, "Strange Days" (1995); Actress, "Panther" (1995); Actress, "What's Love Got to Do with It" (1993); Actress, "Malcolm X" (1992); Actress, "The Jacksons: An American Dream" (1992); Actress, "Innocent Blood" (1992); Actress, "Passion Fish" (1992); Actress, "Critters 4" (1992); Actress, "Nightmare Café" (1992); Actress, "One Special Victory" (1991); Actress, "Locked Up: A Mother's Rage" (1991); Actress, "The Heroes of Desert Storm" (1991); Actress, "Boyz n the Hood" (1991); Actress, "Stat" (1991); Actress, "Fire: Trapped on the 37th Floor" (1991); Actress, "City of Hope" (1991); Actress, "The Flash" (1991); Actress, "Line of Fire: The Morris Dees Story" (1991); Actress, "Kindergarten Cop" (1990); Actress, "In the Best Interest of the Child" (1990); Actress, "Perry Mason: The Case of the Silenced Singer" (1990); Actress, "Equal Justice" (1990); Actress, "Challenger" (1990); Actress, "Family of Spies" (1990); Actress, "Alien Nation" (1990); Actress, "Thirtysomething" (1989); Actress, "227" (1989); Actress, "Tour of Duty" (1989); Actress, "A Man Called Hawk" (1989); Actress, "HeartBeat" (1989); Actress, "Joe Turner's Come and Gone," Yale Repertory Theatre, New Haven, CT and Ethel Barrymore Theatre, New York, NY (1986, 1988); Actress, "The Cosby Show" (1985, 1988); Actress, "Leg Work" (1987); Actress, "Guiding Light" (1987); Actress, "Liberty" (1986); Actress, "Black Girl," Second Stage Theatre, New York, NY (1985); Actress, "F/X" (1986); Actress, "Doubletake" (1985); Actress, "Spenser: for Hire" (1985); Actress, "Search for Tomorrow" (1985); Actress, "Ma Rainey's Black Bottom," Yale Repertory Theatre, New Haven, CT (1984); Actress, "Colored

People's Time" (1984) **AW:** NAACP Image Award for Outstanding Actress in a Drama Series, NAACP Image Awards (2020); AAFCA TV Honors Award for Best Performance - Female, African American Film Critics Association, Inc. (2019); Icon Award, Black Girls Rock Awards, BGR!FEST (2019); Screen Actors Guild Award for Outstanding Performance by a Cast in a Motion Picture, SAG-AFTRA (2019); DOC LA Icon Award, Los Angeles Documentary Film Festival (2017); Gracie Award for Outstanding Director – Entertainment, Alliance for Women in Media Foundation (2016); Diamond Award for Lifetime Achievement, CineRockom International Film Festival (2015); NAACP Image Award for Outstanding Lead Actress in a Motion Picture, NAACP Image Awards (1995, 1999, 2014); WIN Award for Outstanding Actress in a Made for Television Movie/Mini-Series, Women's Image Network (2013); Pioneer Award, LA Femme Film Festival (2010); NAACP Image Award for Outstanding Supporting Actress in a Drama Series, NAACP Image Awards (1995, 2000, 2002, 2009); Recipient, Star, Motion Picture Category, Hollywood Walk of Fame, Hollywood Chamber of Commerce (2008); Black Movie Award for Outstanding Performance by an Actress in a Supporting Role, American Black Film Festival, ABFF Ventures, LLC (2006); Susan B. Anthony 'Failure Is Impossible' Award, High Falls Women's Film Festival (2005); Black Reel Award for Outstanding Actress in a Motion Picture, Black Reel Awards (2003); Christopher Award for Television & Cable, The Christophers (2003); Black Reel Award for Outstanding Actress in a Television Movie or Limited Series, Black Reel Awards (2002, 2003); NAACP Image Award for Outstanding Actress in a Miniseries, Television Movie, or Dramatic Special, NAACP Image Awards (2002, 2003); Lena Horne Award for Outstanding Career Achievement in the Field of Entertainment, Soul Train Lady of Soul Awards (2002); Black Film Award for Best Actress, Acapulco Black Film Festival (Now American Black Film Festival, ABFF Ventures, LLC) (1999); Crystal Award, Women In Film Los Angeles (1996); Saturn Award for Best Actress, Academy of Science Fiction, Fantasy and Horror Films (1996); Muse Award, New York Women in Film & Television (1995); Golden Apple Award for Female Discovery of the Year, Women's Press Club (1994); Golden Globe Award for Best Actress – Motion Picture Musical or Comedy, Hollywood Foreign Press Association (1994) **MEM:** Honorary Member, Delta Sigma Theta Sorority, Inc. (2013-Present) **PA:** Democrat

BASSIM, BEHROOZ, MD, T: Pathologist **I:** Medicine & Health Care **DOB:** 11/28/1934 **PB:** Ashkabad **SC:** Russia **PT:** Esmail Bassim; Goharieh (Hosainov) Bassim **MS:** Widowed **SPN:** Patricia Oliva Bassim (11/26/1967, Deceased 2014) **CH:** Darian; Parisa **ED:** Resident in Pathology, New York Medical College, New York, NY (1965-1979); Intern, Barberton Citizens Hospital, Summit Health, Ohio (1964-1965); MD, University of Tehran (1961) **CT:** American Board of Anatomical Pathology; American Board of Clinical Pathology **C:** Private Practice in Medicine, Potsdam, NY (1980-1991); Director, Healthcare Laboratory, Potsdam, NY (1979-1991); Director of Laboratories, Central St. Lawrence Health Services, Potsdam, NY (1973-1979); Associate Pathologist, Paterson General Hospital, NJ (1969-1972) **CIV: CW:** Author, "Human, Human Being, Sub-Human (People Rated According to How They Behave)" (2019); Author, "Beyond Communism, Beyond Capitalism"; Author, "The Absolute Proof"; Author, "About God" **MEM:** Former Member, Secretary, St. Lawrence County Medical Society; Former Member, The Medical Society of the State of New York; Past Membership, 350.org **MH:** Albert Nelson Marquis Lifetime Achievement

Award; Marquis Who's Who Top Professional **AS:** Dr. Bassim is a driven person; once he thinks to do something, he never rests until it is done. **B/I:** When Dr. Bassim was 4 1/2 years old, his father was running a high fever. He and his mother were putting cool clothes on him to bring his fever down. In the middle of the night, two Army officers knocked on the door to take his father to Siberia. He was one of the last men to be sent to Siberia. It felt good trying to bring his father's fever down. His father said to him, "someday you are going to be a doctor." Then they released his father from prison after being there for six months, so he went to Iran with them. When he was in the fifth grade, his father was overseeing a building project for the medical school for University of Tehran. He took Dr. Bassim there and asked an engineer to show him around to show him what they were building. The engineer took him around and he remembers a room that had no door; it was cement and had a hole in the top. The engineer said they drop the dead bodies there and leave them there six months to a year so the students can learn using them. That was impressive to him. His father said that he was doing his best to make the best building at the university in hopes that one day Dr. Bassim would go to school there and learn medicine in a building he built. He wrote his first book in the fifth grade, and his second book in the ninth grade, which he still has. Growing up having attended institutes thinking about medical school, he couldn't help but think about all the problems going on around the world, so he decided he was going to become a physician for all the ills around the world. Beyond communism, beyond capitalism, it is only about this idea, and most of all, we live on one Earth and we have to take care of it. **AV:** Writing symphonies; Composer (classical music); Listening to 18th and 19th century European classical music **RE:** Atheist **THT:** Dr. Bassim says, "I am not a person, I am the personification of my genome that I have inherited. I am the continuation of my ancestral lives; I am a reincarnation of lives before us as we all are." He also says, "World peace, peace with nature, universal human rights including equal rights between men and women, and among all gender varieties, universal economic justice...These would amount to Paradise on Earth. We can accomplish these within a decade if peace lovers join us." Dr. Bassim is pro climate and pro peace.

BASTIAN, EDWARD, "ED" H., T: Chief Executive Officer **I:** Leisure, Travel & Tourism **CN:** Delta Air Lines, Inc. **DOB:** 06/06/1957 **PB:** Poughkeepsie **SC:** NY/USA **MS:** Married **SPN:** Anna Bastian **CH:** Four Children **ED:** BBA, St. Bonaventure University, Allegany, NY (1979) **CT:** CPA (Certified Public Accountant) **C:** Chief Executive Officer, Delta Air Lines, Inc., Atlanta, GA (2016-Present); President, Delta Air Lines, Inc., Atlanta, GA (2010-2016); President, Chief Executive Officer, NWA, Delta Air Lines, Inc., Eagan, MN (2008-2010); President, Chief Financial Officer, Delta Air Lines, Inc., Atlanta, GA (2007-2008); Executive Vice President, Chief Financial Officer, Delta Air Lines, Inc., Atlanta, GA (2005-2007); Senior Vice President, Finance, Controller, Delta Air Lines, Inc., Atlanta, GA (2000-2005); Vice President, Controller, Delta Air Lines, Inc., Atlanta, GA (1998-2000); Financial Manager, Frito-Lay North America, Inc. (1990-1998); Audit Partner, Price Waterhouse (Now PwC), New York, NY (1979-1990) **CIV:** Chair, Metro Atlanta Chamber (2021); Board of Advisers, Rally Foundation for Childhood Cancer Research; Board of Trustees, The Woodruff Arts Center, Atlanta, GA; Former International Board of Directors, Habitat for Humanity® International **AW:** Inducted Georgia Trustee, Georgia Historical Society (2018-Present); Listee, "50 Greatest Leaders," Fortune Media IP Limited (2018); Listee,

"Atlanta's Most Admired CEOs," Atlanta Business Chronicle, American City Business Journals (2017) **AV:** Playing golf; Traveling; Reading

BASTIYALI, TARKAN, T: Founder, President **I:** Events Services **CN:** Midtown Loft & Terrace **DOB:** 11/14/1977 **PB:** Düsseldorf **SC:** Germany **SPN:** Viktroiya (2005) **CH:** Aryanna; Adryan **ED:** BA in History and Economics, New York University, New York, NY, With Honors (2000) **C:** Owner, Founder, President, Midtown Loft & Terrace, New York, NY (2006-Present) **CR:** Host, Events, Fortune 500 Companies Including Google, Yelp, IBM, Facebook and Samsung **CIV:** Donor, Several Charities **MIL:** Turkish Army **CW:** Patentee, Patent for the Auto Industry, "Smart Safe" (2019); Featured, "The Apprentice"; Featured, "The Girl on the Train"; Featured, TV Shows, Bravo and Netflix; Featured, Home Textiles Today; Patentee, Seven Total Patents; Creator, www.Bastiyaliinventions.com **AW:** Bridal Choice Award, Wedding Wire **AS:** Mr. Bastiyali attributes his success to being very self-motivated and having things come naturally to him. He likes to give back to the world through his creative ideas and abilities. **AV:** Traveling; Boating; Playing tennis; Playing basketball **THT:** The low point in Mr. Bastiyali's life was when he was diagnosed with tinnitus after an international flight. Tinnitus is an incurable disease and from that point on, he has had a loud tea kettle sound in his right ear almost 24/7. At the beginning of 2018, he came up with the idea of streaming crickets and other sounds through an iPad via Bluetooth to get through the day, which he recommends to others in need of help. Since he was able to get relief with that idea, in the summer of 2018, he came up with seven more revolutionary ideas, all of which he filed a patent for. In 2019, he received an approved patent for the auto industry. The product is called the "Smart Safe" and will save lives by preventing drivers from texting, and is currently being marketed to the automobile industry. The main objective is that the car won't start unless the smartphone is in the console and will only reopen once the car's engine is shut off. This product prevents texting while the driver is operating the vehicle by securing the smartphone, Apple Watch and Google Glasses in the "Smart Safe."

BATEMAN, JASON KENT, T: Actor **I:** Media & Entertainment **DOB:** 01/14/1969 **PB:** Rye **SC:** NY/USA **PT:** Kent Bateman; Victoria Elizabeth Bateman **MS:** Married **SPN:** Amanda Anka (07/03/2001) **CH:** Francesca Nora; Maple Sylvie **CR:** Co-Founder, DumbDumb Productions (2010) **CW:** Producer, "Scarlet" (2021); Actor, Executive Producer, Director, "The Outsider" (2020-Present); Executive Producer, "A Teacher" (2020-Present); Actor, Executive Producer, Director, "Ozark" (2017-Present); Actor, Director, "Arrested Development" (2003-2019); Executive Producer, "Kidding" (2018); Producer, Actor, "Game Night" (2018); Actor, "Nobodies" (2017); Actor, "Office Christmas Party" (2016); Actor, "Central Intelligence" (2016); Voice Actor, "Zootopia" (2016); Actor, "The Muppets" (2015); Actor, Producer, Director, "The Family Fang" (2015); Actor, "The Gift" (2015); Narrator, "Beyond the Brick: A LEGO Brickumentary" (2014); Executive Producer, "Two to Go" (2014); Actor, "Horrible Bosses 2" (2014); Actor, "This Is Where I Leave You" (2014); Actor, "The Longest Week" (2014); Executive Producer, Narrator, "Growing Up Fisher" (2014); Actor, Producer, Director, "Bad Words" (2013); Actor, Producer, "Identity Thief" (2013); Executive Producer, "Mansome" (2012-2013); Actor, "Disconnect" (2012); Actor, "Hit and Run" (2012); Executive Producer, "Always Open" (2011); Actor, "The Change-Up" (2011); Actor, "Horrible Bosses" (2011); Actor, "Paul" (2011); Actor, "The

Switch" (2010); Actor, "Sit Down Shut Up" (2009); Actor, "Couples Retreat" (2009); Actor, "The Invention of Lying" (2009); Actor, "Up in the Air" (2009); Actor, "Extract" (2009); Actor, "State of Play" (2009); Director, "Do Not Disturb" (2008); Actor, "Tropic Thunder" (2008); Actor, "Hancock" (2008); Actor, "Forgetting Sarah Marshall" (2008); Actor, "The Promotion" (2008); Actor, "Mr. Magorium's Wonder Emporium" (2007); Actor, "Juno" (2007); Actor, "The Kingdom" (2007); Actor, "The Ex" (2006); Actor, "Smokin' Aces" (2006); Voice Actor, "Arthur and the Invisibles" (2006); Actor, "The Jake Effect" (2006); Actor, "The Break-Up" (2006); Actor, "Scrubs" (2006); Host, "Saturday Night Live" (2005); Voice Actor, "The Fairly OddParents" (2005); Voice Actor, "Justice League Unlimited" (2005); Voice Actor, "King of the Hill" (2005); Actor, "Dodgeball: A True Underdog Story" (2004); Actor, "Starsky & Hutch" (2004); Actor, "The Twilight Zone" (2003); Actor, "Sol Goode" (2003); Actor, "One Way Out" (2002); Actor, "The Sweetest Thing" (2002); Actor, "Some of My Best Friends" (2001); Director, "For Your Love" (1999-2001); Actor, "Rude Awakening" (2000); Director, "Two of a Kind" (1999); Director, "Brother's Keeper" (1999); Actor, "Love Stinks" (1999); Actor, "George & Leo" (1997-1998); Director, "Family Matters" (1997); Actor, "Chicago Sons" (1997); Actor, "Simon" (1995-1996); Actor, "Ned and Stacey" (1996); Actor, "Burke's Law" (1995); Actor, "An Affection Look at Fatherhood" (1995); Actor, "Hart to Hart: Secrets of the Hart" (1995); Actor, "Black Sheep" (1994); Actor, "This Can't Be Love" (1994); Actor, "Confessions: Two Faces of Evil" (1992); Actor, "How Can I Tell If I'm Really in Love" (1992); Actor, "Breaking the Rules" (1992); Actor, "A Taste for Killing" (1992); Actor, "Necessary Roughness" (1991); Actor, Director, "Valerie" (1986-1991); Actor, "Crossing the Mob" (1988); Actor, "Our House" (1988); Actor, "Moving Target" (1988); Actor, "Matlock" (1987); Actor, "Teen Wolf Too" (1987); Actor, "Bates Motel" (1987); Actor, "The Magical World of Disney" (1986); Actor, "St. Elsewhere" (1986); Actor, "Can You Feel Me Dancing?" (1986); Actor, "Mr. Belvedere" (1986); Actor, "Right to Kill?" (1985); Actor, "It's Your Move" (1984-1985); Actor, "Robert Kennedy and His Times" (1985); Actor, "Knight Rider" (1984); Actor, "Silver Spoons" (1982-1984); Actor, "The Fantastic World of D.C. Collins" (1984); Actor, "Just a Little More Love" (1983); Actor, "Little House on the Prairie" (1981-1982) **AW:** Primetime Emmy Award for Outstanding Directing for a Drama Series, Television Academy (2019); Screen Actors Guild Award for Outstanding Performance by a Male Actor in a Drama Series, SAG-AFTRA (2019); Star, Motion Picture Category, Hollywood Walk of Fame, Hollywood Chamber of Commerce (2018); Screen Actors Guild Award for Outstanding Performance by an Ensemble in a Comedy Series (2006); Satellite Award for Best Actor in a Musical or Comedy, International Press Academy (2005); Golden Globe Award for Best Actor in a Television Series - Musical or Comedy, Hollywood Foreign Press Association (2005) **PA:** Democrat

BATES, BEVERLY B., T: Lawyer **I:** Law and Legal Services **DOB:** 01/23/1938 **PB:** Atlanta **SC:** GA/USA **PT:** Fred Eugene Bates; Justine Elizabeth (Marques) Bates **MS:** Married **SPN:** Betty C. Bates **CH:** Barbra Bates Gardner (Deceased); Benjamin K. Bates **ED:** LLB, Mercer University (1961); AB, Mercer University (1959) **C:** Co-Founder, Bates & Baum, Atlanta, GA (1974); Assistant U.S. Attorney, Northern District of Georgia, U.S. Department of Justice, Atlanta, GA (1966-1974); Lawyer, Private Practice **CR:** Vice Chair, Fulton County Personnel Board (2017-2019); Special Master, Georgia Commission on Equal Employment (1986-1995) **CIV:** Representative, Buckhead Neighborhood Plan-

ning Unit, Atlanta, GA (1982-1985); Vice President, Board Director Pine Hills Civic Club, Atlanta, GA (1982-1985) **MIL:** Served as Defense Appellate Council Under the Judge Advocate General, U.S. Army Trial Judiciary (1962-1966, Honorably Discharged); Served to Captain, U.S. Army (1961-1966) **CW:** Contributor, Articles, Journal of Southern Legal History **AW:** Younger Federal Lawyer of Year, Atlanta Chapter, Federal Bar Association (1972) **MEM:** President, Downtown Council, Atlanta Chamber of Commerce (1982-1983); Board Director, Downtown Council, Atlanta Chamber of Commerce (1982-1983); President, Resurgens Atlanta, GA (1981-1982); President, Atlanta Chapter, Mercer University Alumni Society (1974-1975); President, Atlanta Chapter, Federal Bar Association (1971-1972); President, Mercer University Law School Alumni Society (1971-1972); American Bar Association; Atlanta Lawyers Club **BAR:** U.S. District Court for the Middle District of Georgia (1985); U.S. Court of Appeals for the Federal Circuit (1984); U.S. Court of Appeals for the Eleventh Circuit (1981); U.S. District Court for the Northern District of Georgia (1966); District of Columbia (1965); Supreme Court of the U.S. (1965); U.S. Court of Appeals for the Armed Forces (1963); Georgia (1961) **MH:** Albert Nelson Marquis Lifetime Achievement Award **B/I:** Mr. Bates became involved in his profession because his father, Fred, enrolled in law school three times but due to work schedule changes, he was unable to complete his schooling. Due to his father's inability to complete law school, he felt compelled to do so, and his father wanted him to pursue it as well. **PA:** House District 55 Republican Chair (2014-2019)

BATES, KATHLEEN, "KATHY" DOYLE, T: Actress **I:** Media & Entertainment **DOB:** 06/28/1948 **PB:** Memphis **SC:** TN/USA **PT:** Langdon Doyle Bates; Bertye Kathleen (Talbot) Bates **MS:** Divorced **SPN:** Anthony Campisi (1991-1997) **ED:** BFA in Theatre, Southern Methodist University (1969) **CIV:** Spokesperson, Lymphatic Education & Research Network **CW:** Actress, "American Horror Story" (2013-Present); Actress, "Richard Jewell" (2019); Actress, "The Highwaymen" (2019); Actress, "On the Basis of Sex" (2019); Actress, "The Big Bang Theory" (2018); Actress, "The Death and Life of John F. Donovan" (2018); Voice Actress, "Moose" (2018); Actress, "Disjointed" (2017-2018); Actress, "Krystal" (2017); Actress, "Feud: Bette and Joan" (2017); Actress, "Bad Santa 2" (2016); Actress, "The Boss" (2016); Actress, "Complete Unknown" (2016); Actress, "The Great Gilly Hopkins" (2016); Actress, "Mike & Molly" (2014-2015); Voice Actress, "American Dad!" (2015); Actress, "Boychoir" (2014); Voice Actress, "When Marnie Was There" (2014); Actress, "Tammy" (2014); Actress, "Harry's Law" (2011-2012); Actress, "Two and a Half Men" (2012); Actress, "Cadaver" (2012); Actress, "The Office" (2010-2011); Actress, "Midnight in Paris" (2011); Actress, "You May Not Kiss the Bride" (2011); Actress, "A Little Bit of Heaven" (2011); Actress, "Valentine's Day" (2010); Actress, "Alice" (2009); Actress, "The Blind Side" (2009); Actress, "Personal Effects" (2009); Actress, "Chéri" (2009); Actress, "Revolutionary Road" (2008); Actress, "The Day the Earth Stood Still" (2008); Actress, "The Family That Preys" (2008); Actress, "P.S. I Love You" (2007); Voice Actress, "The Golden Compass" (2007); Actress, "Fred Claus" (2007); Voice Actress, "Bee Movie" (2007); Actress, "Guilty Hearts" (2006); Actress, Director, "Have Mercy" (2006); Voice Actress, "Charlotte's Web" (2006); Actress, "Bonneville" (2006); Actress, "Relative Strangers" (2006); Actress, "Failure to Launch" (2006); Actress, "Solace" (2006); Actress, Director, "Ambulance Girl" (2005); Actress, "Warm Springs" (2005); Actress, Direc-

tor, "Six Feet Under" (2003-2005); Actress, "The Bridge of San Luis Rey" (2004); Actress, "Little Black Book" (2004); Actress, "Around the World in 80 Days" (2004); Actress, Executive Producer, "The Ingrate" (2004); Narrator, "American Experience" (1993, 2004); Director, "Fargo" (2003); Director, "Everwood" (2002); Actress, "Unconditional Love" (2002); Actress, "About Schmidt" (2002); Actress, "Dragonfly" (2002); Actress, "My Sister's Keeper" (2002); Actress, "Love Liza" (2002); Voice Actress, "King of the Hill" (2001); Actress, "American Outlaws" (2001); Actress, "Possessed" (2000); Actress, "MADtv" (2000); Actress, "Bruno" (2000); Actress, "Annie," "The Wonderful World of Disney" (2000); Director, "Dash and Lilly" (1999); Actress, "Baby Steps" (1999); Actress, "3rd Rock from the Sun" (1999); Director, "Oz" (1998); Actress, "A Civil Action" (1998); Actress, "The Waterboy" (1998); Voice Actress, "The Effects of Magic" (1998); Actress, "Primary Colors" (1998); Director, "NYPD Blue" (1997); Actress, "Titanic" (1997); Actress, "Swept from the Sea" (1997); Actress, "Adventures from the Book of Virtues" (1997); Director, "Homicide: Life on the Street" (1996); Actress, "The War at Home" (1996); Actress, "Diabolique" (1996); Actress, "The Late Shift" (1996); Actress, Director, "Great Performances" (1995); Actress, "The West Side Waltz" (1995); Actress, "Angus" (1995); Actress, "Dolores Claiborne" (1995); Actress, "Curse of the Starving Class" (1994); Actress, "North" (1994); Actress, "Living and Working in Space: The Countdown Has Begun" (1993); Actress, "A Home of Our Own" (1993); Actress, "Used People" (1992); Actress, "Hostages" (1992); Actress, "Prelude to a Kiss" (1992); Actress, "Fried Green Tomatoes" (1991); Actress, "At Play in the Fields of the Lord" (1991); Actress, "Shadows and Fog" (1991); Actress, "The Road to Mecca" (1991); Actress, "Misery" (1990); Actress, "White Palace" (1990); Actress, "Dick Tracy" (1990); Actress, "Men Don't Leave" (1990); Actress, "No Place Like Home" (1989); Actress, "L.A. Law" (1989); Actress, "High Stakes" (1989); Actress, "Roe vs. Wade" (1989); Actress, "Signs of Life" (1989); Actress, "China Beach" (1989); Actress, "Arthur 2: On the Rocks" (1988); Actress, "The Road to Mecca," Promenade Theatre, New York, NY (1988); Actress, "My Best Friend Is a Vampire" (1987); Actress, "Summer Heat" (1987); Actress, "Murder Ordained" (1987); Actress, "Frankie and Johnny in the Clair de Lune," Manhattan Theatre Club and Westside Theatre, New York, NY (1987); Actress, "St. Elsewhere" (1986-1987); Actress, "The Morning After" (1986); Actress, "Cagney & Lacey" (1986); Actress, "Johnny Bull" (1986); Actress, "Curse of the Starving Class," Promenade Theatre, New York, NY (1985); Actress, "One Life to Live" (1984); Actress, "'night, Mother," Cambridge, MA and New York, NY (1983-1984); Actress, "Two of a Kind" (1983); Actress, "Come Back to the 5 & Dime Jimmy Dean, Jimmy Dean" (1982); Actress, "Fifth of July," New Apollo Theatre, New York, NY (1980); Actress, "Goodbye Fidel," New Ambassador Theatre, New York, NY (1980); Actress, "The Art of Dining," The Public Theater, New York, NY (1979); Actress, "The Doctors" (1978); Actress, "Straight Time" (1978); Actress, "The Love Boat" (1978); Actress, "Vanities" (1977); Actress, "Vanities," Playwrights Horizons, New York, NY (1976); Actress, "Taking Off" (1971); Actress, "All My Children" (1970) **AW:** Honoree, 19th Annual Broadway Gala, The 24 Hour Plays, New York, NY (2019); Award for Best Supporting Actress, National Board of Review (2002, 2019); Star, Motion Picture Category, Hollywood Walk of Fame, Hollywood Chamber of Commerce (2016); Primetime Emmy Award for Outstanding Supporting Actress in a Limited Series or Television Movie, Television Academy (2013); Primetime Emmy Award for Outstanding Guest Actress in a

Comedy Series, Television Academy (2012); PSIFF Award for Best Ensemble Cast, Palm Springs International Film Society (2009); Mary Pickford Award, International Press Academy (2007); François Truffaut Award, Giffoni International Film Festival, Ente Autonomo Giffoni Experience (2006); DFWFCA Award for Best Supporting Actress, Dallas-Fort Worth Film Critics Association (2002); WAFCA Award for Best Supporting Actress, The Washington DC Area Film Critics Association (2002); CFCA Award for Best Supporting Actress, Chicago Film Critics Association (1999); Critics' Choice Award for Best Supporting Actress, The Critics Choice Association (1999); Screen Actors Guild Award for Outstanding Performance by a Female Actor in a Supporting Role in a Motion Picture, SAG-AFTRA (1999); LVFCS Award for Best Supporting Actress, Las Vegas Film Critic Society (1998); SDFCS Award for Best Supporting Actress, San Diego Film Critics Society (1998); Golden Globe Award for Best Supporting Actress – Series, Miniseries or Television Film, Hollywood Foreign Press Association (1997); Satellite Award for Best Supporting Actress – Series, Miniseries or Television Film, International Press Academy (1997); Screen Actors Guild Award for Outstanding Performance by a Female Actor in a Television Movie or Miniseries, SAG-AFTRA (1997); Women of Vision Award, Women in Film & Television International (1995); Academy Award for Best Actress, Academy of Motion Picture Arts and Sciences (1991); CFCA Award for Best Actress, Chicago Film Critics Association (1991); UFCA Award for Best Actress, Utah Film Critics Association (1990); DFWFCA Award for Best Actress, Dallas-Fort Worth Film Critics Association (1991); Golden Globe Award for Best Actress in a Motion Picture – Drama, Hollywood Foreign Press Association (1991); Obie Award for Distinguished Performance by an Actress, Village Voice (1988) **MEM:** Alpha Delta Pi

BATES, SHARON, T: Chief Executive Officer, Founder **I:** Nonprofit & Philanthropy **CN:** Anthony Bates Foundation **ED:** BBA in Management, Marketing **C:** Founder, Event Coordinator, Chief Executive Officer, Board President, Anthony Bates Foundation (2000-Present); Computer Program, Product/Program Manager, Anthony Bates Foundation (1996-2001) **CIV:** Parent Heart Watch **AW:** Named Woman of the Year **MEM:** Women Society of Business (Now Society of Women in Business) **B/I:** Ms. Bates was a single parent for most of Anthony's life and their relationship was exceptionally close. In any case, the death of a child is a tragedy. The only thing making it more tragic is when it could be prevented through early detection. Within one year of Anthony's death from undiagnosed HCM, Ms. Bates began volunteering with the HCMA, Hypertrophic Cardiomyopathy Association. Working tirelessly alongside Lisa Salberg, President and Founder, Ms. Bates learned a great deal about HCM and the dangers of this hidden heart ailment in young people. Anthony's mom believes the work of all the passionate grassroots programs worldwide will spare thousands of parents the pain that she suffered so needlessly.

BAUER, RAYMOND G., T: Sales Professional (Retired) **I:** Retail/Sales **CN:** Ray Bauer Associates **DOB:** 06/19/1934 **PB:** Merchantville **SC:** NJ/USA **PT:** Joseph Bauer; Florence Winifred (Guyer) Bauer **MS:** Life Partner **SPN:** Mary Eileen Ott (2002); Jayne Whitehead (02/15/1955, Deceased 2000) **CH:** Linda Joan Bauer Ulschafer **ED:** BBA, University of Miami (1958); AA, Monmouth College (Now Monmouth University) (1955) **C:** Owner, Ray Bauer Associates, Manufacturers Representatives, Haddonfield, NJ (1975-2000); Division Sales Manager, Eastern Tablet Corporation, Albany, NY

(1974-1975); Manager, Mid-Atlantic, United States Envelope Company, Springfield, MA (1968-1974); Division Manager, R.J. Reynolds Tobacco Company, Winston-Salem, NC (1959-1968) **MIL:** Staff Sergeant, United States Air Force Reserve (1959-1964); Officer, United States Air Force Auxiliary **AW:** Camden County Military Service Medal for Honorable Service **MEM:** Friends of Haddonfield Library; Haddonfield Civic Association; Smithsonian Association; University of Miami Alumni Association; Monmouth University Alumni Association; National Philatelic Society; American Security Council Foundation; Air Force Association; American Conservative Union; American Management Association; The International Platform Association; School and Home Office Products Association; Haddonfield Republican Club; U.S. Senatorial Club; Arrowhead Racquet Club; Iron Rock Swim and Country Club; President, Lambda Sigma Alpha; American Legion Post #38, Haddonfield, NJ; Lambda Sigma Tau, Monmouth University; Honor Society Pledge Class President, Lambda Chi Alpha Social Fraternity, University of Miami **MH:** Albert Nelson Marquis Lifetime Achievement Award; Marquis Who's Who Top Professional **B/I:** Mr. Bauer became involved in his profession after taking exams to help him pick a career path in high school. He scored quite high in the area of "persuasion," which directed him to take up law or sales. From there, he pursued sales and immediately loved the field. **AV:** Stamp collecting; Gardening; Baseball **PA:** Republican **RE:** Protestant-Methodist **THT:** Mr. Bauer played baseball with The American Legion Championship team. He also played baseball for Monmouth University and had a tryout with the New York Yankees.

BAUMANN, LARRY, T: Partner **I:** Law and Legal Services **CN:** Kelley, Scritsmier & Byrne P.C. L.L.O. **DOB:** 02/19/1946 **PB:** Chadron **SC:** NE/USA **PT:** Robert R. Baumann; Mary Nadine (Simpson) Baumann **MS:** Married **SPN:** Marcia Lynn Bliefernich **CH:** Brenda Sue; Andrea Lynn; Abigail Lynn; Jeffrey Scott; Jennifer Lynn; Chele Joyce **ED:** JD, University of Nebraska (1974); BA in Business Administration, Chadron State College (1968) **C:** Owner, Kelley, Scritsmier & Byrne (1981-Present); Partner, Fillman & Baumann, Attorneys (1974-2000) **CIV:** Nebraskaland Days, Inc. (1994-1998); Board of Directors, Chamber of Commerce (1992-1994); President, York Jaycees (1976) **MIL:** U.S. Army (1968-1971) **AW:** Top 10 Attorney, Family Law Attorneys, State of Nebraska, NAFTA (2018) **MEM:** President, Nebraska Council School Attorneys (1988-1989); Council of School Attorneys; NAFTA; Nebraska Bar Association; Lincoln County Bar Association **BAR:** U.S. Court Appeals for the 8th Circuit (1989); U.S. Tax Court (1983); Nebraska (1974); U.S. District Court of Nebraska (1974) **MH:** Albert Nelson Marquis Lifetime Achievement Award; Marquis Who's Who Top Professional **AS:** Mr. Baumann attributes his success to hard work and focusing on helping people in the most compassionate way he could. He loves to make a difference in the lives of others. **B/I:** In high school, Mr. Baumann scored high in the engineering section of an aptitude test. However, engineering scared him. He was always intrigued by legal studies, which is how he became a lawyer.

BAUMBACH, NOAH, T: Screenwriter; Film Director **I:** Media & Entertainment **DOB:** 09/03/1969 **PB:** Brooklyn **SC:** NY/USA **PT:** Jonathan Baumbach; Georgia Brown **MS:** Divorced **SPN:** Jennifer Jason Leigh (09/03/2005, Divorced 09/2013) **CH:** Harold; Rohmer Emmanuel **ED:** BA in English, Vassar College (1991) **C:** Screenwriter, Film Director, Various Films (1995-Present) **CW:** Writer, Producer, Director, "Marriage Story" (2019); Writer, Direc-

tor, "The Meyerowitz Stories" (2017); Co-director, Producer, "De Palma" (2015); Co-writer, Director, Producer, "Mistress America" (2015); Writer, Director, Producer, "While We're Young" (2014); Director, Co-writer, Producer, "Frances Ha" (2013); Co-writer, "Madagascar 3: Europe's Most Wanted" (2012); Writer, "The Corrections" (2012); Director, Writer, "Greenberg" (2010); Co-writer, "Fantastic Mr. Fox" (2009); Director, Writer, "Margot at the Wedding" (2007); Director, Writer, "The Squid and the Whale" (2005); Actor, Co-writer, "The Life Aquatic with Steve Zissou" (2004); Writer, "Thirty" (2000); Actor, Director, Writer, Producer, "Mr. Jealousy" (1997); Actor, Director, Writer, "Highball" (1997); Actor, Director, Writer, "Kicking and Screaming" (1995) **AW:** Best Screenplay, Independent Spirit Award (2019); Robert Altman Award for Ensemble, Independent Spirit Award (2019); Named Best Screenplay, National Society of Film Critics (2006); Named Best Original Screenplay, National Board of Review (2005)

BAYLIS, WILLIAM ERIC, T: 1) Science Centre Director 2) Distinguished University Professor Emeritus **I:** Education/Educational Services **CN:** 1) Canada South Science City 2) University of Windsor **PT:** Charles Augustus Baylis; Ruth Woodruff Baylis **MS:** Married **SPN:** Bobbye Kaye Whitenton (06/10/1961) **CH:** Evelyn Marie Somer; Katherine Ruth **ED:** DSc, Technical University of Munich, Germany (1967); MS, University of Illinois, Champaign-Urbana (1963); BS, Duke University, Durham, NC (1961) **C:** President, Board of Directors, Canada South Science City, Windsor, ON (2009-Present); Distinguished University Professor Emeritus, University of Windsor(2005-Present); Acting Department Head, University of Windsor, Canada (2005-2006); Physics Department Head (1993-96), Physics Professor, University of Windsor, Canada (1969-2005) **CR:** Visiting Scientist, Cavendish Lab, Cambridge University (1999-2000); Visiting Scientist, Institut de Recherche Fondamentale (1985); Visiting Scientist, MPI for Fluid Dynamics, Göttingen, Germany (1976-1977) **CIV:** President, Unitarian-Universalist Church Olinda (2010); Volunteer, Canada South Science City, Windsor, ON (2001-2009); Choir Director, Sunday Service Director **CW:** Author, "Electrodynamics: A Modern Geometric Approach" (1999, 2001); Author, "Theoretical Methods in the Physical Sciences" (1994); Author, Over 100 Articles, Professional Journals; Author, 28 Book Chapters; Editor, Four Books **MEM:** Honorary President, Royal Astronomical Society of Canada-Windsor Branch (1995-Present); Fellow, American Physical Society (1989); Canadian Association of Physicists; American Association of Physics Teachers **MH:** Albert Nelson Marquis Lifetime Achievement Award; Marquis Who's Who Top Professional **B/I:** He was always interested in science, especially astronomy, physics and chemistry. **AV:** Music; Astronomy **RE:** Unitarian Universalist

BAZZY, NAJAH, T: Founder, Chief Executive Officer, Interfaith Leader, Nurse **I:** Nonprofit & Philanthropy **CN:** Zaman International **SC:** MI/USA **MS:** Married **SPN:** Allie Bazzy **CH:** Four Children **ED:** Nursing Degree, Madonna University **CT:** Registered Nurse **C:** Host, Transcultural Leadership Workshops on Bereavement and Medical Ethics, Bayan Claremont Theological School; Adjunct Professor, Institute of International Health, Michigan State University; Chief Executive Officer, Diversity Specialists; With, DMC Sinai Grace Hospital, TH Medical; With, Harper-Hutzel Hospital, Detroit Michigan Center, TH Medical; With, Oakwood Hospital (Now Beaumont Health), Dearborn, MI **CIV:** Co-Founder, Senior Adviser, Young Muslim Association (Now Muslim Youth Connection)

(1997-Present); Founder, Director, Zaman International (1996-Present); Supporter, Sips of Hope Well Campaign **CW:** Author, "The Beauty of Ramadan"; Featured, Documentary, "Muhammad: Legacy of a Prophet," PBS; Featured, "Eye On The Future: The Power of Women," CBS; Featured, Billboard, United Way of Southeastern Michigan **AW:** One of the Top Ten CNN Heroes, Cable News Network (CNN) (2019) **AV:** Reading **RE:** Muslim

BEAL, BRADLEY EMMANUEL, T: Professional Basketball Player **I:** Athletics **CN:** Washington Wizards **DOB:** 06/28/1993 **PB:** St. Louis **SC:** MO/USA **PT:** Bobby Beal; Besta Beal **CH:** Two sons **ED:** Coursework, University of Florida (2011-2012) **C:** With, Washington Wizards, NBA (2012-Present) **AW:** Two-Time NBA All-Star (2018, 2019); All-Rookie First Team, NBA (2013); First Team All-SEC (2012); Gatorade National Player of the Year (2011); First Team All-American, Parade (2011); McDonald's All-American Team (2011); Mr. Show-Me Basketball, Missouri Basketball Coaches Association (2011); FIBA Under-17 World Cup MVP (2010)

BEARD, CHRIS, T: Former Chief Executive Officer **I:** Business Management/Business Services **CN:** Mozilla Corporation **ED:** MBA in International Business, University of Edinburgh Business School (2004); Coursework in International Business, ESADE Business School (2003); Coursework in Economics and Biochemistry, University of Ottawa (1996) **C:** Chief Executive Officer, Mozilla Corporation (2014-2019); Executive-in-Residence, Greylock Partners (2013-2014); Chief Marketing Officer, Mozilla Corporation (2010-2013); Chief Innovation Officer, Mozilla Corporation (2007-2010); Senior Vice President, Products and Marketing, Mozilla Corporation (2004-2007); Vice President, Corporate Development, Cluster File Systems, Inc. (2003-2004); Linux and Open Source Product Management, Hewlett Packard (2001-2002); General Manager, Emerging Services, Linuxcare, Inc. (1999-2001); Co-Founder, Chief Executive Officer, The Puffin Group, Inc., Ottawa, Canada (1998-1999); Systems Analyst, Government of Canada (1996-1998); Field Service Engineer, General Dynamics Corporation (1993-1994) **CIV:** National Association of Corporate Directors (2019-Present); YPO Golden Gate (2017-Present); Board Member, Mozilla Corporation (2014-2019); Board Member, Make-A-Wish Foundation of America (2014-2019) **AW:** John McFarlane Prize for Leadership

BEARD, VICTORIA, "VICKY" FRANCES, T: Director of Forensics, Fine Arts Chair **I:** Education/Educational Services **CN:** Spring Woods High School **PT:** Frank Beard; Berta Beard **SPN:** Cecil Trent **ED:** MA in Theater, University of Houston (1982); BA in Speech and Theater, Houston Baptist University (1980) **CT:** Lifetime Provisional Teaching Certificate at the Secondary Level in Speech, Theater, and English, State of Texas **C:** Director of Forensics, Fine Arts Chair, Spring Woods High School (2005-Present); Teacher, English, Speech, and Drama, Northbrook High School (1985-2005); Teacher, Speech and Drama, Landrum Junior High School (1984-1985); Teacher, English, Speech/Drama, Paul Revere Middle School, Houston Independent School District (1982-1984); Acting Teacher, School for Theater Arts, Houston, TX (1982-1983); Actor, Management and Industrial Training Films (1981) **CR:** Coach, Champions and Finalists, State Tournament, The Texas Forensic Association, The Interscholastic League, The Tournament of Champions, The National Individual Events Tournament of Champions, and the National Speech and Debate Association; Coach, Finalists, Yale University's Debate Tournament, Harvard University's Debate Tournament, University of Texas; Caucus Leader, Hispanic/Latinx, National Speech & Debate Association **CIV:** Weekly Volunteer, Houston's First Baptist Church **CW:** Director, Actress, Volunteer, Numerous Community Theaters, Houston, TX, including Theatre Southwest, Country Playhouse, Playhouse 1960, Theatre Suburbia, and Dos Chicas Productions **AW:** Semi-Finalist, Educator of the Year, H-E-B, LP (2020); Excellence in Education Award, Spring Woods High School (2016); Second Diamond Award, National Speech and Debate Association (2016); Secondary Educator of the Year, Texas Speech and Communication Association (2013); One of Three District Finalists for Spring Branch Independent School District Teacher of the Year (2013); Stars in the Classroom, The Texans and the First Community Credit Union (2012); Jim Moore Memorial Award for Outstanding Education, Spring Woods High School (2012); First Diamond Award, National Speech and Debate Association (2011); Fired-Up Tiger Teaching Award, Spring Woods High School (2005); Teacher of the Year, Northbrook High School (2001); Selected, "Inspiring Youth in the Quest for Success," Northbrook High School **MEM:** Texas Speech Communication Association; Secretary, Texas Forensic Association; National Speech & Debate Association; National Debate Coaches Association; Vice President, Spring Branch Chapter, American Federation of Teachers **MH:** Marquis Who's Who Top Professional; Marquis Who's Who Professional Women; Fifth and Eighth Edition, Who's Who Among America's Teachers **AS:** Ms. Beard attributes her success to hard work, a competitive spirit, and sheer determination. She enjoys seeing her students being successful and it is highly rewarding to know that she has helped them achieve their goals. **B/I:** Ms. Beard became involved in her profession because in her own education, she had the privilege to have some wonderful teachers who have inspired her. In turn, this encouraged her to become an educator to inspire the youth of today. **AV:** Plays at theater; Opera; Debate tournaments **THT:** Ms. Beard said, "Throughout my 38 years of teaching career, I have taught a variety of subjects, such as English, Theatre, Public Speaking, Communication Applications, Speech, and Debate. I have truly loved every subject; however, I feel that teaching and coaching speech and debate at Spring Woods High School has been the most rewarding and is where I have made the most impact. It is not the trophies or accolades my program has received over the years, but helping my all debaters to obtain full-ride scholarships to attend college and earn a degree is the one major accomplishment of which I am most proud. I teach at a Title I school, where being on free and reduced lunch is the norm on my team. Out of 62 debaters, only four are not on free lunch. Not only did these students' parents not attend college but some didn't even finish middle or high school. In fact, most of my students' parents don't speak English as their native tongue. In my debate program, I impart the value of higher education and make sure all of them attend college. I tell them that by taking debate in high school, maintaining good grades, and volunteering in their communities, they can earn scholarships, and go to college. For all my debaters, I serve as their academic adviser and interview them on what their goals are and where they should be throughout their junior and senior year. Every week at lunch, I meet with each senior individually to check on their progress and to see what they need to graduate and apply to college. For example, I ensure they sign up and take the SAT or ACT, proofread their college essays, and serve as one of their recommenders for the colleges of their choice. I also help them with applying for FAFSA or TAFSA as well. I periodically send out reminds of testing deadlines, recommendation or application deadlines. I am proud to say that all my seniors do attend college. The first student on my team to receive a full-ride was 15 years ago, who is currently working on her Master's. Some of my debaters attend colleges and university in Texas, but many have graduated or are attending college out-of-town. Two of my former debaters received the Gates Millennium Scholarship and were the only students at my high school to receive them. Three of my former debaters received a full academic scholarship from George Washington University. Others have received full academic scholarships to Yale, Rice, Trinity, University of Texas at Austin, or are currently enrolled at Smith, Clark, Brandeis, Colby, and Colgate. I am so proud to see my former students become successful leaders. I have a former debater who works for a think tank in DC, another portrays Tina in 'Tina Turner The Musical' in Hamburg, Germany, several who are now attorneys, and most importantly, and two who are public school teachers in my own school district. I look forward to helping more students in the future."

BEASLEY, JAMES W., T: Attorney **I:** Law and Legal Services **PB:** Atlanta **SC:** GA/USA **ED:** LLB, Harvard University, Cambridge, MA, Cum Laude (1968); BA, Davidson College, Davidson, NC, Cum Laude (1965) **C:** Attorney, James W. Beasley Jr., P.A., West Palm Beach, FL, (2019-Present); With, Beasley Kramer & Galardi, P.A., West Palm Beach, FL (1997-2019); With, Tew & Beasley LLP, West Palm Beach, FL (1995-1997);With, Cadwalader, Wickersham & Taft, Palm Beach, FL (1989-1994); With, Miami Law Firms (1976-1989); With, Wilmer, Cutler & Pickering, Washington, DC (1970-1972); With, Sullivan & Cromwell, New York, NY (1968) **CR:** **CIV:** Past President, Harvard Law School Association of Florida; Past President, South Florida Alumni Chapter, Davidson College; Past Member, Urban Land Institute; Past Chairman, England Delegation, South Florida Initiative; Past Member, Board of Directors, Channel 2 Public Television; Past Member, Board of Directors, Vice Chairman, Greater Miami Chamber of Commerce; New World Center Action Committee; Past Member, Downtown Transportation Policy Committee, Dade County; Past Member, Board of Patrons, Greater Miami Opera Association; Chairman, Advisory Board, Palm Beach County Convention Center; Past President, Palm Beach Opera; Board of Governors, Historical Society of Palm Beach County **MIL:** Captain, U.S. Army (1968-1970) (Two years in the Pentagon) **CW:** Subject, Article, South Florida Legal Guide (2017); Subject, Book Chapter, "The Money Lawyers" by Joseph C. Goulden (2006); Subject, Article, Washington & Lee Law Review (1997) **AW:** Ranked, Best Lawyers, U.S. News & World Report (2010-Present); Florida Trend's Legal Elite (2007-Present); Listed, Florida Super Lawyers (2006-Present); Firm Recognized as a "Top Law Firm," South Florida Legal Guide (2004-Present); Ranked, Best Lawyers in America (1983-Present); AV Preeminent Peer Review Rated, Martindale-Hubbell (34 Years); Firm Ranked as a Best Law Firm, U.S. News & World Report **MEM:** Federal Bar Association (2013-Present); Palm Beach County Bar Association (2013-Present); Master of the Bench, Craig S. Barnard American Inn of Court (2017-2018); Chairman, Securities Regulation Committee (1975 - 1977); Florida Bar, Business and Corporate Litigation Section **BAR:** Supreme Court of the United States (1973); Florida (1972); New York (1969); U.S Court of Appeals for the Second, Fifth, and 11th Circuits; U.S. District Court for the Southern District of Florida; U.S. District Court for the Middle District of Florida; U.S. District Court for the Northern District of Florida **MH:** Albert Nelson Marquis Lifetime Achievement Award; Marquis Who's Who **B/I:** Mr. Beasley became involved in his profession because he grew up in a little town in North Alabama. There was one circuit judge in the entire county and he was a good friend of his father as they were golfing buddies. So he had a great respect for him and when he was a senior in high school he allowed him to go into the courtroom and would let him sit at the table with other lawyers with their permission of course. He remembers that vividly and his dad also had a few other good friends that were lawyers. It was a natural progression for him and at one point he almost went to Harvard business school instead of Harvard law school. He stuck with law because he felt he could always do business but he could not always practice law without a license. **AV:** Ocean racing sailing; Playing golf; Practicing yoga; Exercising

BEASLEY, JOHN S. II, T: University Administrator (Retired) **I:** Education/Educational Services **CN:** Vanderbilt University **DOB:** 10/02/1930 **PB:** Franklin **SC:** TN/USA **PT:** Thomas Earl Beasley; Elsie (Eggleston) Beasley **MS:** Married **SPN:** Allison Tidman Beasley (09/04/1958) **CH:** John S. Beasley, III; Eleanor Christensen Beasley Nahley **ED:** JD, Vanderbilt University (1954); BA, Vanderbilt University (1952) **C:** Vice-Chancellor Emeritus, Counselor to Chancellor, Vanderbilt University, Nashville, TN (2000-2018); Vice-Chancellor Emeritus, Special Assistant to Chancellor, Vanderbilt University, Nashville, TN (1999-2000); Vice Chancellor for Alumni and Development, Vanderbilt University (1983-1999); Special Assistant to Chancellor, Vanderbilt University (1981-1983); National Alumni Director, Centennial Campaign, Vanderbilt University (1980-1981); Vice Chairman, Trust Board, Commerce Union Bank, Nashville, TN (1978-1980); Executive Vice President, Commerce Union Bank, Nashville, TN (1974-1978); Senior Vice President, Commerce Union Bank, Nashville, TN (1971-1974); Associate Dean, Professor, Vanderbilt Law School (1970-1971); Associate Dean, Associate Professor, Vanderbilt Law School (1966-1970); Associate Dean, Assistant Professor, Vanderbilt Law School (1964-1966); Assistant Dean, Assistant Professor, Vanderbilt Law School (1962-1964); Executive Secretary, Alumni Association, Vanderbilt University (1958-1961); Attorney, Franklin, TN (1957-1958) **CR:** Co-Founder, Pebblestone Court, Franklin, TN (1965-1985); Chairman, The Harpeth Hall School (1977-1981); Trustee, The Harpeth Hall School (1975-1981); President, Alumni Association, Vanderbilt University (1979-1980); Board, Alumni Association, Vanderbilt University (1974-1980); President, Tennessee Botanical Gardens and Fine Arts Center at Cheekwood (Now Cheekwood Estate & Gardens), Nashville, TN (1973-1975); Board, Tennessee Botanical Gardens and Fine Arts Center at Cheekwood (Now Cheekwood Estate & Gardens), Nashville, TN (1969-1975); President, Nashville Symphony Association (1962-1964); Board, Nashville Symphony Association (1958-1964) **CIV:** Advisory Board, Junior League of Nashville (2000-2003); Board of Directors, Tennessee Performing Arts Center (1986-1992); Board of Directors, Franklin Special School District (1974-1976); Trustee, Battle Ground Academy, Franklin, TN (1970-1974); Founding President, Heritage Foundation of Franklin and Williamson County (1965-1968) **MIL:** Air Intelligence Officer, Fleet Air Intelligence Augmentation Unit (1957); Lieutenant, United States Navy Reserve (1958-1962); Air Intelligence Officer to Commander, Task Force 72, Commander Fleet Air Wing One, Commander Taiwan Patrol Force, United States Navy (1955-1956) **MEM:** Vice President, Belle Meade Country Club (1979-

1980); Board of Directors, Belle Meade Country Club (1974-1980); University Club of New York City; University Club of Nashville; Order of the Coif; Phi Beta Kappa; Omicron Delta Kappa; Sigma Chi; Pi Delta Epsilon; Phi Delta Phi **BAR:** Tennessee (1954) **MH:** Albert Nelson Marquis Lifetime Achievement Award **AS:** Mr. Beasley attributes his success to the grace of God. **AV:** Playing piano **PA:** Republican **RE:** Episcopalian **THT:**

BEATTY, JOYCE BIRDSONG, T: U.S. Representative from Ohio **I:** Government Administration/Government Relations/Government Services **DOB:** 03/12/1950 **PB:** Dayton **SC:** OH/USA **MS:** Married **SPN:** Otto Beatty Jr. **CH:** Laural; Otto III (Stepchild) **ED:** Honorary PhD, Ohio Dominican University (2003); PhD Coursework, University of Cincinnati (1997); MS in Counseling Psychology, Wright State University, Dayton, OH (1974); BA in Speech, Central State University, Wilberforce, OH (1972) **C:** U.S. Representative from Ohio's Third Congressional District, United States Congress, Washington, DC (2013-Present); Member, U.S. House Financial Services Committee, Washington, DC (2013-Present); Assistant Minority Leader, Ohio House of Representatives, Columbus, OH (2007-2009); Member, District 27, Ohio House of Representatives, Columbus, OH (1999-2008) **CR:** Senior Vice President, Outreach and Engagement, The Ohio State University, Columbus, Ohio (2008-2012); Delegate, Democratic National Convention (1996, 2000, 2004, 2008, 2012) **AW:** Listee, Power 150, Ebony Magazine (2008); Women of Achievement Award, YWCA (2002); Linden Pride Grand Marshall (2000); Legislator of the Year, The Ohio Credit Union Association; Legislator of the Year, Ohio Nurses Association; Legislator of the Year, PCSAO; Service Award, Ohio Legislative Black Caucus **MEM:** National Association for the Advancement of Colored People (NAACP); American Society for Training & Development; Chairman, Board of Directors, Columbus Urban League; Ohio Legislative Black Caucus; Democratic Women's Caucus, National Endowment Chair, The Links, Incorporated; United Negro College Fund, Inc. (UNCF); Life Member, Delta Sigma Theta Sorority, Inc.; The Links, Incorporated; Columbus Urban League; American Heart Association, Inc. **AV:** Writing; Boating; Traveling **PA:** Democrat **RE:** Baptist

BEAUFAIT, FREDERICK, "FRED" WILLIAM, PHD, T: Engineering Educator (Retired) **I:** Education/Educational Services **DOB:** 11/28/1936 **PB:** Vicksburg **SC:** MS/USA **PT:** Frank W. Beaufait; Eleanor Chambliss (Haynes) Beaufait **MS:** Married **SPN:** Lois Erdman (11/27/1964) **CH:** Paul Frederick Beaufait; Nicole Beaufait **ED:** PhD in Structural Engineering, Virginia Polytechnic Institute and State University (1965); MSc in Structural Engineering, University of Kentucky (1961); BSc in Civil Engineering, Mississippi State University (1958) **C:** President, New York City College of Technology (1999-2004); Director, Greenfield Engineering Education Coalition, National Science Foundation (1996-1998); Dean, College of Engineering, Wayne State University, Detroit, MI (1986-1995); Associate Dean, College of Engineering, West Virginia University, Morgantown, WV (1983-1986); Professor, Chairman, Department of Civil Engineering, West Virginia University, Morgantown, WV (1979-1983); Professor, Civil Engineering, Vanderbilt University, Nashville, TN (1965-1979); Visiting Lecturer, Civil Engineering, University of Liverpool, England (1960-1961); Engineer, L.E. Gregg Associates (1959-1960); Structural Engineer, U.S. Army Corps of Engineers, Vicksburg, MS (1958-1959) **CR:** Board of Directors, Ford Design Institute (1991-1996); Consultant in Field, Member, ABET (1988-1993); Engineering Manpower Commission (1988-1992);

Visiting Professor, Civil and Structural Engineering, Cardiff University, Wales (1975-1976) **CIV:** Deputy Mayor of Lewes (2015-Present); Elected Mayor, Elected City Council Member, Lewes (2011-Present); Active, Lewes Presbyterian Church (2006-Present); Elder, Sanctuary Restoration Committee, Lewes Presbyterian Church (2008-2013, 2015-2017); Session Clerk, Sanctuary Restoration Committee, Lewes Presbyterian Church (2010-2017); Co-Chair, Sanctuary Restoration Committee, Lewes Presbyterian Church (2006-2009); Board of Directors, Independence Community Bank Foundation, Brooklyn, NY (2001-2004); Member, Long-Range Planning Committee (1985-1986); Elder, Stewardship Committee, First Presbyterian Church, Morgantown, WV (1983-1985); Vice Chairman, Stewardship Committee, First Presbyterian Church, Morgantown, WV (1982); Elder, Southminster Presbyterian Church, Nashville, TN (1971-1973, 1978-1979); Member, Citizens Advisory Committee, Metropolitan School System, Nashville, TN (1978-1979); President, Presbyterian Campus Ministry, Nashville, TN (1976-1978); Board of Directors, Presbyterian Campus Ministry, Nashville, TN (1972-1978); Treasurer, Presbyterian Campus Ministry, Nashville, TN (1972-1975); Clerk of Session, Southminster Presbyterian Church, Nashville, TN (1971-1973); Deacon, Southminster Presbyterian Church, Nashville, TN (1968-1969) **CW:** Co-Editor, "Behavior of Building Systems and Building Components" (1979); Author, "Basic Concepts in Structural Analysis" (1977); Editor, "Tall Buildings: Planning, Design and Construction" (1974); Co-Author, "Computer Methods of Structural Analysis" (1970); Contributor, 40 Articles, Professional Journals; Contributor, Numerous Papers; Presenter, Numerous Presentations and Lectures; Guest Lecturer **AW:** Academy Distinguished Alumni, Department of Civil And Environmental Engineering, Virginia Technical Institute (2004); Gold Award, The Engineering Society of Detroit (1997); Outstanding Engineer in Education, MSPE (1994); George K. Wadlin Award, Civil Engineering Division (1994); Centennial Medallion (1993); Distinguished Engineering Fellow, Mississippi State University (1992); Outstanding Volunteer of the Year, Michigan Center For High Technology (1991); Decorated Chevalier Ordre Des Palmes Academiques **MEM:** Vice President, MSPE (1997-1998); Treasurer, State Board of Directors, MSPE (1995-1997); Board of Governance, Order of Engineers (1989-1997); Chairman, MSPE (1993); Chairman, Civil Engineering Division, ASEE (1992-1993); President, Professionals in Engineering Education Division, MSPE (1990-1993); Chairman-Elect, MSPE (1992); Board of Directors, Detroit Metro Chapter, MSPE (1987-1990); Distinguished Member, The National Society of Collegiate Scholars; National Society of Professional Engineers; College of Fellows, The Engineering Society of Detroit; Chi Epsilon, Inc.; Tau Alpha Pi; The Tau Beta Pi Association, Inc. **MH:** Albert Nelson Marquis Lifetime Achievement Award **AS:** Dr. Beaufait attributes his success to Thomas West at Mississippi State University, Hans Gesund at the University of Kentucky, and Dr. George Gray at Virginia Polytechnic Institute. **B/I:** Dr. Beaufait became involved in his profession because he of his father, Frank, who never finished high school and urged his son to continue his studies after his undergraduate was completed. When Dr. Beaufait arrived at the University of Kentucky to get his master's degree, he was asked to teach a freshman slide rule class; he was then asked to teach at a higher level structural engineering course, during which time he realized he liked to teach. **AV:** Painting; Reading **PA:** Republican **RE:** Presbyterian

BEAVER, LAURA E., T: Attorney **I:** Law and Legal Services **CN:** Beaver Law Firm **ED:** JD, Norman Adrian Wiggins School of Law, Campbell University (2008); BA, NC State University (2004) **C:** Attorney, Beaver Law Firm (2016-Present); Attorney, Hatch Little & Bunn, LLP (2013-2016); Attorney, DeMent Askew & Johnson (2010-2013); Attorney, Fannie & Jackson (2008-2010) **CIV:** Kiwanis Club **AW:** Client Distinction Award, Lawyers.com; Martindale Hubbell **AS:** Ms. Beaver attributes her success to loads of hard work and a great team of attorneys who work hard alongside her. **B/I:** Ms. Beaver became involved in her profession because she was inspired by her father, a criminal defense attorney. He believed so passionately in his work that she too learned to be just as passionate about her work. She would ask to be checked out of school so that she could watch some of his biggest cases. She watched him argue in the Supreme Court and became so moved by it that she pursued a similar path.

BECCHETTI, FREDERICK D., PHD, T: Physicist, Researcher **I:** Sciences **DOB:** 03/03/1943 **PB:** Minneapolis **SC:** MN/USA **PT:** Frederick Daniel Becchetti; Olga Maxine Becchetti **MS:** Married **CH:** Two Children **ED:** PhD, University of Minnesota (1969); MS, University of Minnesota (1968); BS, University of Minnesota (1965) **C:** Professor of Physics, Emeritus, University of Michigan (2013-Present); Professor of Physics, University of Michigan (1982-2013); Associate Professor, University of Michigan (1976-1982); Assistant Professor, University of Michigan, Ann Arbor, MI (1973-1976); Research Associate, Lawrence Berkeley Laboratory (1971-1973); Research Associate, Niels Bohr Institute (1969-1971) **CW:** Contributor, Articles, Professional Journals; Cited, "Physics Today" **AW:** Fellow, National Science Foundation (1970-1971); Fellow, American Physical Society; Citations Award **MEM:** Fellow, American Physical Society; Institute of Electrical and Electronics Engineers (IEEE); American Association of Physicists Teachers; American Association of Physicists in Medicine **MH:** Albert Nelson Marquis Lifetime Achievement Award **B/I:** Dr. Becchetti's father was a steel and dye maker. He worked with complicated machinery and raised Dr. Becchetti to be mechanically inclined. Ever since then, Dr. Becchetti was always curious about new discoveries. He grew up as an amateur astronomer. Growing up in Minneapolis, he could always clearly see the northern lights, the galaxy, and the Milky Way galactic center. In October of 1957, he saw a little blinking light come across the sky; it was Sputnik. This moment inspired Dr. Becchetti to become enamored with physics. **PA:** Democrat **RE:** Roman Catholic

BECK, DEBORAH BERMAN, T: Industry Association Executive **I:** Business Management/Business Services **DOB:** 05/21/1938 **PB:** Boston **SC:** MA/USA **PT:** Charles Arthur Berman; Eve (Cohen) Berman **MS:** Married **SPN:** Bertram M. Beck (02/21/1965) **CH:** Rachel V.; Melissa M. **ED:** MBA in Corporate Finance, Adelphi University, Garden City, NY, With Honors (1982); MSW, Columbia University, New York, NY (1963); BA, Smith College, Northampton, MA, With Honors (1960) **C:** Executive Vice President, Real Estate Board of New York, Inc., New York, NY (1988-2003); Senior Vice President, Government Affairs, Real Estate Board of New York, Inc., New York, NY (1986-1988); Managing Director, Div. Owners and Builders, Real Estate Board of New York, Inc., New York, NY (1981-1986); Research Analyst, Real Estate Board of New York, Inc., New York, NY (1981); Construction Consultant, Owners' Representative, Various Facilities, New York, NY (1981-Present) **CR:** Mayor's Building Industry Advisory Council, New York, NY (1981-Present); Gov-

ernor's Advisory Committee, New York City Construction Industry; Mayor's Construction Advisory Committee; Commissioner's Task Force; Participant, Various Industry-Government Forums **MEM:** New York Building Congress; Women in Housing and Finance, Inc.; Urban Land Institute; Board of Directors, Commercial Real Estate Women; Board of Directors, Association of Real Estate Women; Board of Directors, Women's City Club of New York **MH:** Albert Nelson Marquis Lifetime Achievement Award **B/I:** Ms. Beck became involved in her profession after rising as an owner's representative for the construction of a community building.

BECKER, BORIS FRANZ, T: Tennis Executive, Analyst, Coach, Professional Tennis Player (Retired) **I:** Athletics **CN:** Deutscher Tennis Bund **DOB:** 11/22/1967 **PB:** Leimen **SC:** Germany **PT:** Karl-Heinz Becker; Elvira Becker **MS:** Divorced **SPN:** Sharlely "Lilly" Kerssenberg (06/12/2009-2018); Barbara Feltus (12/17/1993-01/15/2001) **CH:** Noah Gabriel; Elias Balthasar; Amadeus Benedict Edley Luis; Anna **C:** Head, Men's Tennis, Deutscher Tennis Bund (2017-Present); Analyst, Fox Sports Australia (2017-Present); Commentator, BBC (2013-Present); Owner, Völkl Int. GmbH (2000-Present); Coach, Novak Djokovic (2013-2016); Professional Tennis Player, ATP Tour, Inc. (1985-1999) **CIV:** Patron, Elton John AIDS Foundation **CW:** Appearance, "Top Gear" (2014); Founder, "Boris Becker TV" (2009); Contestant, "They Think It's All Over" (2005-2006); Author, "The Player: An Autobiography" (2003); Actor, "Steiners Sketchparade - Lachen ist die beste Medizin" (1997) **AW:** Inductee, International Tennis Hall of Fame (2003); Player of the Year, International Tennis Federation (1989); Player of the Year, ATP Tour, Inc. (1989); Most Improved Player, ATP Tour, Inc. (1985) **MEM:** Laureus World Sports Academy, Laureus World Sports Awards Ltd. **AV:** Poker

BECKHAM, ODELL CORNELIOUS JR., T: Professional Football Player **I:** Athletics **CN:** Cleveland Browns **DOB:** 11/05/1992 **PB:** Baton Rouge **SC:** LA/USA **PT:** Odell Cornelious Beckham, Sr.; Heather (Van Norman) Beckham **ED:** Coursework, Louisiana State University (2011-2013) **C:** Wide Receiver, Cleveland Browns, Cleveland, OH (2019-Present); Wide Receiver, New York Giants, East Rutherford, NJ (2014-2018) **CIV:** Benefactor, Make-A-Wish Foundation of America (2016-Present); Benefactor, Americares (2017); Benefactor, Samaritan's Purse (2017); Benefactor, Victims of Louisiana Floods (2016) **CW:** Actor, "Ballers" (2019); Subject, "I Am More: OBJ" (2018); Actor, "Code Black" (2016); Subject, "Catching Odell" (2015) **AW:** NFL Pro Bowl (2014-2016); NFL Offensive Rookie of the Year, The Associated Press (2014); Rookie of the Year, Pro Football Writers of America (2014); All-Rookie Team, Pro Football Writers of America (2014); Paul Hornung Award, Louisville Sports Commission (2013); First-Team All-American, NCAA (2013); First-Team All-SEC, The Associated Press (2013)

BEE, SAMANTHA ANNE, T: Comedian, Actress **I:** Media & Entertainment **CN:** Samantha Bee **DOB:** 10/25/1969 **PB:** Toronto **SC:** ON/CA **PT:** Debra Bee; Ronald Bee **MS:** Married **SPN:** Jason Jones (2001) **CH:** Piper; Fletcher; Ripley **ED:** BA in Theatre and English, University of Ottawa, with Honours (2015); Coursework, George Brown Theatre School, George Brown College, Toronto, Ontario, Canada **C:** Founder, Swimsuit Competition (2018-Present); Host, "Full Frontal with Samantha Bee," TBS, Turner Broadcasting System, Inc. (2016-Present); Correspondent, "The Daily Show," Comedy Central, Comedy Partners (2003-2015) **CR:** Co-Founder, The Atomic Fireballs (1999)

CIV: Fundraiser, Planned Parenthood Federation of America Inc.; Supporter, Karam Foundation; Supporter, Distributing Dignity®, Inc.; Supporter, Fundraiser, Committee to Protect Journalists; Supporter, Hispanic Federation; Benefactor, Khazir Kurdish Displaced Persons Camp, Iraq; Supporter, NAACP; Supporter, RAICES; Supporter, TIME'S UP™ Now; Supporter, Me Too; Supporter, Life After Hate Inc.; Supporter, Floridians for a Fair Democracy; Supporter, New Brunswick Today LLC; Supporter, Girl Scouts of the United States of America; Supporter, Women's March **CW:** Executive Producer, "It's Personal with Amy Hoggart" (2020-Present); Writer, Executive Producer, "Full Frontal with Samantha Bee" (2016-Present); Co-Creator, Writer, Producer, "The Detour" (2016-Present); Voice Actress, "BoJack Horseman" (2020); Voice Actress, "Elliot the Littlest Reindeer" (2018); Voice Actress, "Creative Galaxy" (2013-2017); Voice Actress, "Bob's Burgers" (2012-2017); Actress, "Game On" (2015-2016); Actress, "Sisters" (2015); Voice Actress, "A.C.O.R.N.S.: Operation Crackdown" (2015); Actress, "Halal in the Family" (2015); Actress, "Learning to Drive" (2014); Actress, "Deadbeat" (2014); Actress, "The Michael J. Fox Show" (2014); Actress, "Bounty Hunters" (2013); Voice Actress, "Phineas and Ferb" (2013); Actress, "Good God" (2012); Actress, "Sesame Street" (2010-2012); Co-Writer, "Eating Over the Sink," Babble.com (2011); Actress, "Michael: Every Day" (2011); Actress, "Bored to Death" (2009-2011); Actress, "Furry Vengeance" (2010); Actress, "Love Letters" (2010); Actress, "Law & Order" (2010); Author, "I Know I Am, But What Are You?" (2010); Actress, "Whatever Works" (2009); Actress, "Motherhood" (2009); Actress, "Coopers' Camera" (2008); Actress, "The Love Guru" (2008); Actress, "Two Families" (2007); Actress, "Little Mosque on the Prairie" (2007); Actress, "Rescue Me" (2007); Actress, "Underdog" (2007); Actress, Writer, Co-Producer, "Not This But This" (2007); Actress, "Love Monkey" (2006); Actress, "Odd Job Jack" (2005); Actress, "Ham & Cheese" (2004); Actress, "Jasper, Texas" (2003); Actress, "Ham I Am" (2001); Actress, "The Endless Grind" (2001); Actress, "Real Kids, Real Adventures" (2000) **AW:** WGA Award for Comedy/Variety – Specials, Writers Guild of America West (2020); GLAAD Media Award for Outstanding variety or Talk Show Episode, GLAAD (2019); Dorian Award for TV Current Affairs Show of the Year, GALECA (2016-2019); Honoree, Television Academy Honors, Television Academy (2018); Gracie Award for Special, Alliance for Women in Media Foundation (2018); Primetime Emmy Award for Outstanding Writing for a Variety Special, Television Academy (2017); Gracie Award for On-Air Talent – Entertainment or Sports, Alliance for Women in Media Foundation (2017); Gold Derby Award for Best Variety Performer, Gold Derby (2016); TCA Award for Outstanding Achievement in News & Information, Television Critics Association Awards (2016); History Making Award, Women's Media Center (2016); CCA Award for Canadian Comedy Person of the Year, Canadian Comedy Awards (2015); CCA Award for Best Performance by a Female – Film, Canadian Comedy Awards (2009); CCA Award for Television – Pretty Funny Female Performance, Canadian Comedy Awards (2005)

BEEBE, ABIGAIL, T: Managing Partner **I:** Law and Legal Services **CN:** The Law Office of Abigail Beebe, P.A. **ED:** JD, Nova Southeastern University Shepard Broad Law School, Cum Laude (2006); BS, Florida Atlantic University **CT:** Board Certified Specialist in Martial & Family Law, The Florida Bar **C:** Managing Owner, The Law Office of Abigail Beebe, PA (2014-Present); Associate Attorney, Sasser, Cestero & Sasser, PA (2011-2014); Staff Attorney, Legal

Aid Society of Palm Beach County, Inc. (2006-2010) **CIV:** Board of Directors, Cancer Alliance of Help and Hope's (2016-Present); Executive Committee, The Susan B. Greenberg Family Law American Inn of Court of the Palm Beaches (2015-2016); Founding Member, The Susan B. Greenberg Family Law American Inn of Court of the Palm Beaches; Chair, Family Law CLE Committee; Past Chair, Unified Family Practice Committee for the Palm Beach County Bar Association; Past Chair, Family Law Section of the Palm Beach County Bench Bar Conference; Chair, the Fourth Annual Princess and Pirate Ball, Pat Reeves Village Shelter for The Center for Family Services of Palm Beach County, Kids Helping Kids; Chair, Luncheon, Shop the Day Away; Chair, Family Picnic, Hanely Foundation; Historical Society of Palm Beach County; Lea gal Aid Society of Palm Beach County **AW:** Pro Bono Attorney of the Year, Florida Children's First (2015); Pro Bono Attorney of the Year, Legal Aid Society of Palm Beach County (2013); Best Lawyer; Florida Super Lawyer; Rising Star; Top 100 Lawyer by The National Advocates **MEM:** Chair, Legislation, Family Law Section, Florida Bar Association (2018-2019); American Institute of Family Law Attorney **AS:** She attributes her success to the type of work that she does, it requires a fine balance between listening to the clients while properly counseling them so they dont have unreasonable expectations. **B/I:** Ms. Beebe realized she had an interest in the law while attending college. She decided on family law prior to going to law school.

BEHLMER, RUDY H. JR., T: Director, Writer, Film Educator (Retired) **I:** Media & Entertainment **DOB:** 10/13/1926 **PB:** San Francisco **SC:** CA/USA **YOP:** 2019 **PT:** Rudy H. Behlmer; Helen Mae (McDonough) Behlmer **SPN:** Stacey Michele Behlmer (1992-2019); Sandra Lee Wightman (1959, Divorced 1966) **CH:** Curt Randolph Behlmer **ED:** Coursework, Los Angeles City College (1949-1950); Coursework, Pasadena Playhouse College (1946-1949) **C:** Lecturer of Film, University of California Los Angeles (1988); Lecturer of Film, California State University, Northridge, CA (1984-1992); Lecturer of Film, Art Center College of Design, Pasadena, CA (1967-1992); Vice President, Television Commercial Producer-Director, Leo Burnett USA, Hollywood, CA (1963-1984); Executive Producer-Director, KCOP-TV, Hollywood, CA (1960-1963); Television Commercial Producer-Director, Executive, Grant Advertising, Hollywood, CA (1957-1960); Network Television Director, ABC-TV, Hollywood, CA (1956-1957); Director, Station KLAC-TV, Hollywood, CA (1952-1956) **CR:** Special Collection of Rudy Behlmer Papers, Margaret Herrick Library, Academy of Motion Picture Arts and Sciences **MIL:** Served, Air Corps, United States Naval Reserve (1944-1946) **CW:** Author, Special DVD Packages, Production Book, "Singin' in the Rain" (2012); Author, Blu-ray Digibook, "King Kong" (2010); Author, "Shoot the Rehearsal!: Behind the Scenes with Assistant Director Reggie Callow" (2010); Author, Production Book, "Gone With the Wind" (2009); Author, Photo Book, "Casablanca" (2008); Author, "Henry Hathaway: A Directors Guild of America Oral History" (2001); Author, "W.S. Van Dyke's Journal: White Shadows in the South Seas (1927-1928) and Other Van Dyke on Van Dyke" (1996); Author, "Memo from Darryl F. Zanuck" (1993); Author, "Behind the Scenes: The Making of . . ." (1989); Author, "Inside Warner Bros. (1935-1951)" (1985); Editor, Annotator, "The Sea Hawk" (1982); Author, "America's Favorite Movies: Behind the Scenes" (1982); Editor, Annotator, "The Adventures of Robin Hood" (1979); Co-author with Tony Thomas, "Hollywood's Hollywood: The Movies About the Movies" (1975); Author, "50 Years of Film Music," Warner Brothers (1973); Author,

"Memo from David O. Selznick" (1972); Co-author with Tony Thomas and Clifford McCarty, "The Films of Errol Flynn" (1969); Editor, Annotator, Wisconsin/Warner Bros. Screenplay Series; Author, Magazine Articles on Film History, Booklets and Liner Notes, Film Music CDs, LPs, and Laserdiscs; Writer, Narrator and On Camera Participant, DVDs, Laserdiscs, and Video Documentaries and Commentary Tracks **MEM:** Directors Guild of America (DGA) **MH:** Albert Nelson Marquis Lifetime Achievement Award

BEIK, WILLIAM, "BILL" HUMPHREY, T: Historian, Editor, Writer **I:** Education/Educational Services **DOB:** 06/28/1941 **PB:** New York **SC:** NY/USA **YOP:** 08/31/2017 **PT:** Paul H. Beik; Doris Humphrey Beik **MS:** Married **SPN:** Mildred Allen (08/15/1975) **CH:** John Eric Kauffman (Stepson, Deceased); Carl Vincent Kauffman (Stepson) **ED:** PhD, Harvard University (1968); MA, Harvard University (1966); BA, Haverford College (1963) **C:** Retired, Professor Emeritus, Emory University (2007-2017); Professor, Emory University (1997-2007); Associate Professor, Emory University (1990-1997); Associate Professor, Northern Illinois University, DeKalb, IL (1984-1990); Assistant Professor, Northern Illinois University (1968-1984) **CR:** Senior Editor, "New Approaches to European History," Cambridge University Press (1994-2016) **CIV:** Supporter, Progressive Causes **CW:** Author, "Absolutism and Society in Seventeenth-Century France: State Power and Provincial Aristocracy in Languedoc" (1986); Author, "Urban Protest in Seventeenth-Century France: the Culture of Retribution"; Author, "Louis XIV and Absolutism: a Brief Study with Docs"; Author, "A Social and Cultural History of Early Modern France"; Contributor, Articles, Professional Journals **AW:** Mellon Emeritus Fellowship (2009); Senior Fellow, Center for Humanistic Inquiry, Emory University (2005-2006); Fellow, American Philosophical Society (1987); Herbert Baxter Adams Prize, American Historical Association (1986); Summer Fellow, American Council Of Learned Societies (1974, 1984); National Endowment of The Humanities Fellow (1974-1975); Fellow, Shelby Cullom Davis Center, Princeton University (1974); Woodrow Wilson Dissertation Fellowship, Woodrow Wilson Foundation (1966-1967); Woodrow Wilson Fellow (1963-1964) **MEM:** Battle of Homestead Foundation Society (2007-2017); Co-President, Board Member, Society for French Historical Studies (1994-1996); American Historical Association; Phi Beta Kappa **MH:** Albert Nelson Marquis Lifetime Achievement Award **AS:** Dr. Beik often attributed his success to a fortunate upbringing, the support of family and friends, and good luck. **B/I:** Dr. Beik's father, Paul H. Beik, was a professor of French history at Swarthmore College from 1946 until 1980. From early childhood on, Dr. Beik and his family periodically went to France during his father's sabbaticals and other research trips. As a result, Dr. Beik spent a couple of his early years in French schools, traversed the streets of Paris as a teen, and learned to appreciate the French people, French culture, and history. He was naturally oriented toward teaching as a profession. After pursuing artistic interests, as well as history, at Haverford College, he decided to specialize in seventeenth-century French history. **AV:** Maintaining historical website; Gardening; Listening to music **PA:** Independent **THT:** Dr. Beik appreciated the joy of being alive and lead a meaningful life. Although he suffered greatly during the last 20 years of his life due to Parkinson's disease, he retained admirable good spirits and modestly continued his interest in French history.

BEKEY, IVAN, T: Space Systems Engineer **I:** Military & Defense Services **CN:** The Aerospace Corporation **DOB:** 11/21/1931 **PB:** Prague **SC:** Czechoslovakia **PT:** Andrew Bekey; Elizabeth (Magyar) Bekey **MS:** Married **SPN:** Marlene Ann (Woodbury) Bekey (05/30/1968) **CH:** Lisa Ann; Suzanne Jeanine **ED:** Program for Senior Managers in Government, Harvard University (1986); MSE, UCLA (1959); BSE, UCLA (1954) **C:** Advanced Space System Concepts, The Aerospace Corporation (2018-Present); Space Systems Consultant, Bekey Designs, Inc. (1997-2018); Director of Advanced Concepts, NASA (1994-1997); Special Assistant to the Deputy Administrator, NASA, Washington, DC (1992-1993); Director of Advisory Programs, The National Space Council, The White House, Washington, DC (1990-1991); Special Assistant for Exploration, NASA, Washington, DC (1989-1990); Director of Advanced Programs, NASA, Washington, DC (1978-1987); Group Director, The Aerospace Corporation, Los Angeles, CA (1975-1978); Director of Advanced Mission Planning, The Aerospace Corporation, Los Angeles, CA (1964-1975); Head, Advanced Communications Techniques Section, The Aerospace Corporation (1960-1964); Section Head, Space Technology Laboratories, Los Angeles, CA (1959-1960); Senior Engineer, RCA, Los Angeles, CA (1957-1959); Section Leader, Douglas Aircraft Company, Santa Monica, CA (1954-1957) **CR:** President, Bekey Designs, Inc., Annandale, VA (1983-Present); Adviser, Defense Science Board (2006); Adviser, Scientific Advisory Board, U.S. Air Force (1995-2005); Adviser, US Army Future Studies Group (1995); Member, Naval Studies Board/Space, Washington, DC (1988-1993); Technical Director and Partner, Mountain Venture, Monrovia, CA (1989-1992) **CIV:** Board of Directors, Community Organization Council, Annandale, VA (1979, 1982, 1987) **CW:** Author, "Advanced Space System Concepts and Technologies" (2003); Editor, "Space Stations and Space Platforms" (1987); Contributor, "Exploring the Unknown" (1999); Author, Articles, Professional Journals **AW:** Group Achievement Award, Lunar and Mars Exploration Initiative Team, NASA (1990); Group Achievement Award-Space Station Task Force, NASA (1984); Exceptional Service Medal, NASA (1982); Group Achievement Award, Space Policy Task Team, NASA (1982); Charter Member, Senior Executive Service, US Government (1979); Group Public Service Achievement Award, Mission Analysis Group, NASA (1977); Member, Tau Beta Pi Honorary Fraternity (1953); Group Achievement Award on the National Commission on Space, NASA **MEM:** Fellow, American Institute of Aeronautics and Astronautics; Fellow, Washington Academy of Sciences; Full Member, International Academy of Astronautics; American Astronautical Society; The Cosmos Club; Sigma Phi Delta Fraternity; Tau Beta Pi Fraternity **MH:** Albert Nelson Marquis Lifetime Achievement Award **AS:** Mr. Bekey attributes his success to his loving childhood and the unconditional love and support of his wife. **B/I:** Mr. Bekey became involved in his profession because of his family background. Many of his family members are engineers. **AV:** Sailing; Skiing; Hiking; Camping; Listening to classical music; Collecting and restoring radios and phonographs **PA:** Republican

BELAFONTE, HARRY GEORGE JR., T: Singer, Songwriter, Actor **I:** Media & Entertainment **DOB:** 03/01/1927 **PB:** Harlem **SC:** NY/USA **PT:** Harold George Bellanfanti Sr.; Melvine (Love) Bellanfanti **MS:** Married **SPN:** Pamela Frank (2008); Julie Robinson (03/08/1957, Divorced 2004); Marguerite Byrd (1948, Divorced 1957) **CH:** Adrienne; Shari; David; Gina **ED:** Honorary Doctor of Law, Princeton University (2015); Honorary Doctorate, Berklee College of Music, Boston, MA (2014); Honorary

Doctor of Humane Letters, Brooklyn College (1998); Honorary Doctor of Civil Law, University of Newcastle, England, United Kingdom (1998); Honorary Doctor of Law, McMaster University, Hamilton, Ontario, Canada (1996); Honorary Degree, University of Massachusetts (1996); Honorary Doctor of Letters, University of the West Indies, Kingston, Jamaica (1996); Honorary Doctor of Arts, Bard College (1993); Honorary Doctor of Humane Letters, Columbia University (1993); Honorary Doctor of Science, Long Island University (1991); Honorary Doctor of Science, Brandeis University (1991); Honorary Doctor of Science, Tufts University (1991); Honorary Doctor of Fine Arts, City College of New York (1990); Honorary Doctor of Fine Arts, Spelman College (1990); Honorary Doctor of Fine Arts, Purchase College, State University of New York (1987); Honorary Doctor of Music, Morehouse College (1987); Honorary Doctor of Humane Letters, Park University, Missouri (1968); Honorary Doctorate in Liberal Arts, The New School for Social Research, NY; Honorary Degree, Park University, Missouri **C:** President, Belafonte Enterprises Inc., New York, NY (1957-Present); Singer, RCA Victor (1953-1974); Singer, Roost Records (1949); Club Singer, Charlie Parker Band, NY; Singer, Various Arenas, Including The Village Vanguard, NY and the Sands Hotel and Casino, Las Vegas, NV **CIV:** Board of Directors, New York State Martin Luther King Jr. Institute for Nonviolence (1989-Present); Honorary Co-chair, Women's March on Washington (2017); Grand Marshal, New York City Pride Parade (2013); Participant, Voices of the Arts, John F. Kennedy Center for the Performing Arts, Washington, DC (2006); Chairperson, Martin Luther King Jr. Holiday Commission (1987); Goodwill Ambassador, UNICEF (1987); Performer, Live Aid (1985); Bankroller, Student Nonviolent Coordinating Committee (1964); Member, New York State Employees Brotherhood Committee; Cultural Advisor, Peace Corps; Chairperson, International Symposium of Artists and Intellectuals for African Children, Dakar, Senegal; Ambassador, The Bahamas; Board of Directors, Advancement Project; Advisory Council, Nuclear Age Peace Foundation; Master of Ceremonies, African National Congress, American Committee on Africa, The Africa Fund, Roosevelt House, Hunter College, New York, NY; Board Member, TransAfrica Forum; Board Member, Institute for Policy Studies; Ambassador of Conscience, Amnesty International; Founder, Sankofa Justice & Equity Fund **MIL:** With, United States Navy, World War II **CW:** Actor, "BlacKkKlansman" (2018); Interviewer, "Speakeasy" (2015); Appearance, Documentary, "Hava Nagila: The Movie" (2013); Author, "My Song," Knopf Books (2011); Appearance, Documentary, "Sing Your Song" (2011); Appearance, Documentary, "Motherland" (2009); Actor, "Bobby" (2006); Actor, "When the Levees Broke: A Requiem in Four Acts" (2006); Actor, "That's What I'm Talking About" (2006); Appearance, Documentary, "Mo & Me" (2006); Narrator, Documentary, "Ladders" (2004); Actor, "Tanner on Tanner" (2004); Appearance, Documentary, "Conakry Kas" (2003); Appearance, Documentary, "XXI Century" (2003); Appearance, Documentary, "Fidel" (2001); Featured Musician, "The Long Road to Freedom: An Anthology of Black Music" (2001); Actor, "PB&J Otter 'The Ice Moose'" (1999); Actor, "Swing Vote" (1999); Appearance, Documentary, "Scandalize My Name: Stories from the Blacklist" (1998); Appearance, "An Evening with Harry Belafonte and Friends" (1997); Actor, "Kansas City" (1996); Actor, "Jazz '34" (1996); Actor, "White Man's Burden" (1995); Actor, "Hank Aaron: Chasing the Dream" (1995); Appearance, "Ready to Wear" (1994); Featured Musician, "Falling in Love Again: Two Duets with Nana Mouskouri" (1993); Appearance, "The

Player" (1992); Narrator, Documentary, "We Shall Overcome" (1989); Appearance, "After Dark" (1989); Musician, "Paradise in Gazankulu" (1988); Producer, "Asinamali!" (1987); Actor, "Don't Stop the Carnival" (1985); Organizer, Musician, "We Are the World" (1985); Appearance, Documentary, "Der Schonste Traum" (1984); Appearance, Documentary, "Sag Nein" (1983); Actor, Short Film, "Drei Lieder" (1983); Featured Musician, "Kunstler fur den Frieden" (1982); Actor, "A Veces Miro Mi Vida" (1982); Appearance, Documentary, "Fundi: The Story of Ella Baker" (1981); Actor, "Grambling's White Tiger" (1981); Musician, "Loving You is Where I Belong" (1981); Appearance, "The Muppet Show" (1978); Musician, "Turn the World Around" (1977); Musician, "Belafonte's Christmas" (1976); Actor, "Uptown Saturday Night" (1974); Actor, "Free to Be... You and Me" (1974); Appearance, "The Flip Wilson Show" (1973); Actor, "Play Me" (1973); Actor, "Buck and the Preacher" (1972); Musician, "Calypso Carnival" (1971); Musician, "The Warm Touch" (1971); Musician, "Belafonte by Request" (1970); Musician, "This is Harry Belafonte" (1970); Actor, "The Angel Levine" (1970); Narrator, Documentary, "King: A Filmed Record... Montgomery to Memphis" (1970); Featured Musician, "Harry & Lena, For the Love of Life" (1970); Musician, "Homeward Bound" (1970); Actor, "A World in Love" (1970); Actor, "A World in Music" (1969); Appearance, "The Tonight Show" (1968); Appearance, "The Smothers Brothers Comedy Hour" (1968); Actor, "Petula" (1968); Musician, "Belafonte on Campus" (1967); Musician, "Calypso in Brass" (1966); Musician, "In My Quiet Room" (1966); Featured Musician, "An Evening with Belafonte/Mouskouri" (1966); Featured Musician, "An Evening with Belafonte/Makeba" (1965); Musician, "Ballads, Blues and Boasters" (1964); Musician, "Streets I Have Walked" (1963); Appearance, "1963 Round Table" (1963); Musician, "The Many Moods of Belafonte" (1962); Musician, "Midnight Special" (1962); Musician, "Jump Up Calypso" (1961); Musician, "Swing Dat Hammer" (1960); Musician, "My Lord What a Mornin'" (1959); Actor, "Odds Against Tomorrow" (1959); Appearance, "Belafonte at the Palace" (1959); Producer, "Moonbirds" (1959); Actor, "The World, the Flesh and the Devil" (1959); Musician, "Love is a Gentle Thing" (1959); Featured Musician, "Porgy and Bess" (1959); Performer, "Tonight with Belafonte" (1959); Appearance, "The Steve Allen Show" (1958); Musician, "Belafonte Sings the Blues" (1958); Musician, "To Wish You a Merry Christmas" (1958); Musician, "Belafonte Sings of the Caribbean" (1957); Actor, Short Film, "The Heart of Show Business" (1957); Actor, "Island in the Sun" (1957); Musician, "An Evening with Belafonte" (1957); Musician, "Calypso" (1956); Musician, "Belafonte" (1956); Actor, "3 for Tonight" (1955); Musician, "Mark Twain and Other Folk Favorites" (1954); Actor, "Carmen Jones" (1954); Actor, "Bright Road" (1953); Actor, "John Murray Anderson's Almanac" (1953); Actor, "Sugar Hill Times" (1949-1950); Musician, Video Album, "Listen to the Man" **AW:** Jean Hersholt Humanitarian Award, Academy of Motion Picture Arts and Sciences (2014); Named CineCause ChangeMaker Icon, Hollywood Film Festival (2014); Spingarn Medal, NAACP (2013); Keynote Speaker, Honoree, MLK Celebration Series, Rhode Island School of Design, Providence, RI (2013); Berlinale Camera, Berlin International Film Festival (2011); Pioneer Award, Black Film Critics Circle Awards (2011); Chief Justice Earl Warren Civil Liberties Award, Keynote Speaker, Bill of Rights Day Celebration, ACLU of Northern California (2007); Co-recipient, Impact Award, AARP the Magazine (2006); Award for Ensemble of the Year, Hollywood Film Awards (2006); BET Humanitarian Award (2006); Domestic Human Rights

Award, Global Exchange, San Francisco, CA (2004); Bishop John T. Walker Distinguished Humanitarian Service Award, Africare (2002); Freedom in Film Award, Nashville Film Festival (2000); Lifetime Achievement Award, Grammy Awards, The Recording Academy (2000); Lifetime Achievement Award, Jamerican International Film Festival (1999); Award, New York Film Critics Circle Awards (1996); National Medal of Arts (1994); Benjamin Potocker Brotherhood Award, New York State Employees Brotherhood Committee (1993); Honoree, Kennedy Center Honors, John F. Kennedy Center for the Performing Arts (1989); President's Merit Award, Grammy Awards, The Recording Academy (1986); Grammy Award for Best Folk Recording, The Recording Academy (1965); Primetime Emmy Award for Outstanding Individual Performance in a Variety or Music Program, Academy of Television Arts & Sciences (1960); Grammy Award for Best Performance - Folk, The Recording Academy (1960); Star, Hollywood Walk of Fame (1960); Number One Album, Billboard Year-End Charts (1956); Tony Award for Best Performance by a Featured Actor in a Musical (1954) **MEM:** Honorary Member, Phi Beta Sigma Fraternity Inc. (2014); Fellow, The Sanders Institute **PA:** Democrat

BELL, CONSTANCE CONKLIN, T: Administrator (Retired) **I:** Other **DOB:** 06/02/1934 **PB:** Columbus **SC:** OH/USA **PT:** John Brevoort; Josephine (Suttles) Conklin **MS:** Married **SPN:** Robert Kilborne Hudnut (09/12/1957, Divorced 06/1975); Gerald Duane Bell (Deceased) **CH:** Heidi A.; Robert K. Junior; Heather E.; Matthew C. **ED:** Postgraduate Coursework, Union Theological Seminary (1956-1957); BA, Ohio Wesleyan University (1956) **C:** Executive Director, Greater Minneapolis Day Care Association (1991-1995); Associate Director, Greater Minneapolis Day Care Association (1982); Assistant Director, Greater Minneapolis Day Care Association (1977); Center Coordinator, Greater Minneapolis Day Care Association (1973); Teacher, Center Presbyterian Church (1956-1959) **CR:** Member, Success by Six, United Way of Central Florida (1989-1995); Minneapolis Early Intervention Committee (1987-1994); President, Education Minnesota (1991-1992); Minnesota Child Care Licensing Committee (1985-1987) **CIV:** Management Member, Success by Six, United Way of Central Florida (1988-2002); Strategic Planning Communications Committee, GMCC (1993-Present); Board of Directors, GMCC (1988-1992); Member, Social Ministries Committee, GMCC (1983-1988); Member, Priorities Committee, Greater Twin Cities United Way (1984-1988); Minneapolis Community Business Employment Alliance (1984-1985); Project Self-Sufficiency (1984); Elder, St. Luke's Presbyterian Church (1978-1981) **CW:** Author, "Sick Child Care, A Problem for Working Parents and Employers (1983); Author, "How to Start a Child Care Center (1977, 1983); Co-Author, "Business and Childcare Handbook" (1981) **AW:** Resolution of Commendation, Hennepin County Commissioner (1995); Ruth Hathaway Jewson Distinguished Service to Families Award, Council of Family Relations (1995); Special Recognition for Service to the Community, City of Minneapolis (1995) **MEM:** Co-Director, Child Care Works Steering Committee, Minnesota Children's Lobby (1983-Present); Board Member, Congregations Concerned for Children, Minnesota Council of Churches (1990-1995); President, Minnesota Association for the Education of Young Children (1990-1993); Member, Minnesota Association for the Education of Young Children (1987); President, Gamma Deuteron Chapter, Kappa Alpha Theta (1955-1956) **MH:** Albert Nelson Marquis Lifetime Achievement Award **AS:** Ms. Bell attributes her success to her desire to make a difference in the lives of families and children.

B/I: Ms. Bell became involved in her profession because of the need for quality child care for inner city children. **AV:** Social activism **PA:** Democrat **RE:** Protestant

BELL, DARRIN, T: Editorial Cartoonist **I:** Publishing **CN:** King Features Syndicate **DOB:** 01/27/1975 **PB:** Los Angeles **SC:** CA/USA **ED:** BA in Political Science, University of California Berkeley (1999) **C:** Editorial Cartoonist, King Features Syndicate (2018-Present); Creator, Cartoonist, "Candorville,", The Washington Post Writers Group (2003-2018); Writer, Cartoonist, "Rudy Park," United Features Syndicate, The Washington Post Writers Group (2012-2018); Cartoonist, "Rudy Park," United Features Syndicate, The Washington Post Writers Group (2001-2012); Cartoonist, "Lemont Brown," The Daily Californian, University of California Berkeley (1993-2003); Editorial Cartoonist, The Daily Californian (1995); Contributor, Los Angeles Times, San Francisco Chronicle, Bay Area News Group **CW:** Author, "Does the Afterlife Have Skittles? - The Sixth Candorville Collection" (2013); Author, "Run! Vampires, Werewolves, the One That Got Away, and Other Demons: The 5th Candorville Collection" (2011); Author, "The Starbucks at the End of the World: The Fourth Candorville Collection" (2011); Author, "Katrina's Ghost: The Third Candorville Collection" (2006); Author, "Another Stereotype Bites the Dust: A Candorville Collection" (2006); Author, "Candorville: Thank God for Culture Clash" (2005); Author, "Peace, Love, and Lattes: A Rudy Park Collection" (2004); Author, "Rudy Park: The People Must Be Wired" (2003); Creator, Cartoonist, Comic Strip, "Candorville" and "Rudy Park" **AW:** Pulitzer Prize for Editorial Cartooning (2019); Clifford K. & James T. Berryman Award for Editorial Cartoons (2016); Robert F. Kennedy Journalism Award for Editorial Cartooning (2015); Mark of Excellence Awards, Society of Professional Journalists; Numerous California Intercollegiate Press Association Awards **RE:** Jewish

BELL, TIFFANI ASHLEY, T: Founder, Executive Director **I:** Business Management/Business Services **CN:** The Human Utility, Inc. **ED:** BA in Science in Systems and Computer Science, Howard University (2008); User Interface Design Intern, Hewlett-Packard (2007); SMB Intern, Hewlett-Packard (2006) **C:** Founder, Executive Director, The Human Utility, Inc. (2014-Present); Technology and Democracy Fellow, Harvard Kennedy School, John F. Kennedy School of Government (2017-2018); Fellow, Code for America (2014); Founder, Chief Executive Officer, Pencil You In (2009-2014); Web Developer, R4 Incorporated (2009-2011); Part-time Web Content Manager, Council of Institutional Investors (2006-2007) **AW:** Listee, Grist 50, Grist Magazine, Inc.; Grantee, Shuttleworth Foundation; Honoree, The Root 100; Listee, Mic 50

BELLAS, ALBERT C., T: Founder, Managing Director **I:** Business Management/Business Services **CN:** Solaris Group, LLC **DOB:** 09/15/1942 **PB:** Steubenville **SC:** OH/USA **PT:** Constantine Michael Bellas; Kiki (Michalopoulos) Bellas **MS:** Married **SPN:** Kay Mazzo (12/21/1978) **CH:** Andrew James; Kathryn Kiki **ED:** MBA, Columbia University, New York, NY (1968); JD, The University of Chicago (1967); BA, Yale University, New Haven, CT (1964) **C:** Founder, Managing Director, Solaris Group, LLC (2004-Present); Chairman, Chief Executive Officer, Neuberger Berman Trust Co., New York, NY (2000-2003); Managing Director, Neuberger Berman, LLC, New York, NY (2000-2003); Managing Director, Offitbank, New York, NY (1992-2000); Board of Directors, Lehman Brothers, New York, NY (1981-1991); Senior Executive Vice President, Shearson Lehman Brothers,

New York, NY (1979-1991); General Partner, Loeb Rhoades & Co., New York, NY (1976-1978); Vice President, Goldman Sachs & Co., New York, NY (1973-1976); Associate, Dillon, Read & Co. Inc., New York, NY (1968-1972) **CR:** Allied Member, New York Stock Exchange (1976-1992) **CIV:** Regent Emeritus, Mercersburg Academy (2018-Present); Board of Directors, English Concert of America (2018-Present); Member, Investment Committee, Library of America (2017-Present); Chairman of the Board, Statue of Liberty-Ellis Island Foundation (2015-Present); Board of Directors, American Friends of the Royal Ballet School (2009-Present); Chairman, Investment Committee, Statue of Liberty-Ellis Island Foundation (2008-Present); Chairman Emeritus, School of American Ballet (2004-Present); Trustee, Statue of Liberty-Ellis Island Foundation (2002-Present); Member, Rockefeller University Committee on Trusts and Estates (1999-Present); Board of Directors, Guild Hall (1998-Present); Chairman, Investment Committee, Guild Hall (1998-Present); Member, Finance Committee, Guild Hall (1998-Present); Board of Regents, Mercersburg Academy (2017, 1992-Present); Board of Directors, Partnership for Children's Rights (2006-2018); Chairman, Finance Committee, Mercersburg Academy (1994-2017); Member, Executive Committee, Mercersburg Academy (1993-2017); Member, Investment Committee, Society for Neuroscience (2005-2015); Member, Yale School of Management Campaign Committee (2007-2012); Member, Audit Committee, Lincoln Center for the Performing Arts (1989-2011); Board of Directors, Lincoln Center for the Performing Arts (1987-2011); Board of Management, Century Association (2002-2006); Treasurer, Century Association (2002-2006); Chairman, School of American Ballet (1987-2004); School of American Ballet (1975-2004); Board of Trustees, Lenfest Foundation (2000-2003); Board of Directors, St. Mary's Foundation for Children (1999-2002); Member, Day School Committee, Brick Church, New York, NY (1985-1988); Board of Directors, School of American Ballet **CW:** Author, "Copyright: Comprehensive Nonprofit Financial Management"; Author, Copyrighted Article in Endowment and Financial Management **AW:** McKinsey Scholar (1968) **MEM:** American Bar Association (ABA); Ohio Bar Association; Economic Club of New York; Brook Club; University Club; Maidstone Club **BAR:** State of Ohio **MH:** Albert Nelson Marquis Lifetime Achievement Award; Marquis Who's Who Top Professional **B/I:** Mr. Bellas became involved in his profession because he always wanted to be in finance-law and have a great background. **AV:** Tennis; Travel **PA:** Independent **RE:** Orthodox

BELLE ISLE, ALBERT PIERRE, PHD, T: Independent Investor **I:** Financial Services **DOB:** 08/11/1943 **PB:** Newburgh **SC:** NY/USA **PT:** Albert Joseph Belle Isle; Marguerite Anna (Durick) Belle Isle **MS:** Married **SPN:** Mary Jean Rogers (08/20/1966) **CH:** Paul Philippe; Nicole Ghislaine **ED:** PhD in Engineering and Applied Mathematics, Polytechnic Institute of Brooklyn (Now NYU Tandon School of Engineering) (1971); MS, Polytechnic Institute of Brooklyn (Now NYU Tandon School of Engineering) (1968); BEE, Rensselaer Polytechnic Institute (1965) **CT:** 50 Ton Master License, U.S. Coast Guard **C:** Chairman, Nominating and Governance Committee, Mercury Computer Systems, Inc., Lowell, MA (1998-2010); Audit Committee, Mercury Computer Systems, Inc., Lowell, MA (1993-2010); Board of Directors, Mercury Computer Systems, Inc., Lowell, MA (1986-2010); President, Cerberus Systems, Inc., Andover, MA (1994-2000); Investor, Mercury Computer Systems, Inc., Lowell, MA (1992-1993); Chairman, Compensation Com-

mittee, Mercury Computer Systems, Inc., Lowell, MA (1988-1992); President, Emusil Corporation, Andover, MA (1989-1991); President, Custom Silicon, Inc., Lowell, MA (1983-1989); Vice President, Wang Laboratories, Inc., Lowell, MA (1981-1983); Director, Corporate Technology Center, Wang Laboratories, Lowell, MA (1980-1983); Manager, Information and Circuit Technologies, General Electric Electronics Laboratory, Syracuse, NY (1975-1980); Manager, Advanced Weapon Control Development Engineering, General Electric, Pittsfield, MA (1973-1975); Engineer, Ordnance Systems Department, General Electric, Pittsfield, MA (1965-1973) **CR:** Adjunct Faculty, Boston University (1982-1985); Adjunct Faculty, Syracuse University (1976-1980); Chairman, Architecture Session (1979); Adjunct Faculty, Union College (1974); Consultant, National Lab Defense Industry Association (Formerly National Security Industrial Association) (1972-1974); Adjunct Faculty, Massachusetts Institute of Technology (1969-1974); National Science Foundation Special Research Fellow, Polytechnic Institute of Brooklyn (Now NYU Tandon School of Engineering) (1969-1970); Director, NetClarity, Inc; Chairman, Board, PredatorWatch, Inc.; Chairman, Computers in Aerospace Conference **CIV:** Andover Computer Advisory Committee, MA (1985-1987); Andover Industry Education Collaborative, MA (1982-1986); Massachusetts State Microelectronics Center Task Force (1982); Loaned Executive, United Way of Central Berkshire (1974); Pittsfield Republican City Committee (1972-1974) **CW:** Contributor, Articles, Professional Journals; Contributor, Automatica Journal, International Federation of Automatic Control; Transactions on Automatic Control, Institute of Electrical and Electronics Engineers; Patentee, Digital Circuits and Computer Architectures **AW:** Award to Inventors, General Electric (1971, 1974) **MEM:** Executive Committee, New England Council, American Electronics Association (1987-1988); American Association for the Advancement of Science; Senior Member, Institute of Electrical and Electronics Engineers; New York Academy of Sciences; American Electronics Association; Association for Computing Machinery; Sigma Xi, the Scientific Research Honor Society; Pi Lambda Phi **MH:** Albert Nelson Marquis Lifetime Achievement Award **B/I:** Dr. Belle Isle became involved in his profession because as a child, he salvaged old shortwave radios to listen to foreign radio stations and became the neighborhood's television repair man, which inspired him to become an electrical engineer. **AV:** Sailing; Cruising the New England coast **THT:** Dr. Belle Isle said, "Fortune favors the bold; but you have to have opportunities, in order to grasp them. Learning from the mistakes of others is better than having to learn from one's own."

BELLO, BROOK PARKER, PHD, T: Founding Chief Executive Officer **I:** Business Management/Business Services **CN:** More Too Life, Inc. **MS:** Married **ED:** PhD in Pastoral Clinical Counseling, Covenant Theological Seminary (2017); Master in Pastoral Clinical Counseling, Covenant Theological Seminary; Bachelor's Degree in Biblical Studies, Covenant Theological Seminary **CT:** Master's Series of Distinguished Leader Fellow, Skinner Leadership **C:** Founding Chief Executive Officer, International Consultant on Human Trafficking & Sexual Violence Prevention, More Too Life, Inc. (2000-Present); Founder, YOUTHIASM®, Brook Bello Ministries (1996-Present) **CR:** Motivational Speaker **CW:** Author, "Living Inside the Rainbow" (2013) **AW:** Department of Justice/ATF Victim Advocate of the Year (2019); Google Next-Gen Policy Leader/Fellow (2018-2019); Advocate of the Year Award, AG Pam Bondi and Governor Rick Scott (2017-2018); Hero Award via Hero Effect, United Way Worldwide

(2017); Lifetime Achievement Award, President Barack Obama and the White House (2016); Scarlet Thread Award, Beverly Bam Crawford the Company (2016); Humanitarian Award, Progressive Baptist International Convention (2013); First Survivor Keynote, White House and Human Trafficking Summit (2013) **AS:** Dr. Bello believes her success is a direct result of her faith and her mentors. She has been lucky to work with extraordinary mentors from all walks of life who took the time to teach her what they understood. She is consistently inspired by her experience getting a book signed by Maya Angelou before she died; it was an incredible encounter. **B/I:** As a child, Dr. Bello had big dreams which were extorted by violence; it crippled her life, and, when she found her wings again, she couldn't just fly away. Ever since then, she has dedicated herself to helping others find their wings.

BELT, DAVID LEVIN, LLB, T: Lawyer **I:** Law and Legal Services **CN:** Jacobs, Grudberg, Belt Dow & Katz Professional Corporation **DOB:** 01/13/1944 **PB:** Wheeling **SC:** WV/USA **PT:** David Homer Belt; Mae Jean (Duffy) Belt **MS:** Married **SPN:** Caroline Annmarie (07/22/1967) **CH:** David Clifford; Amy Elizabeth **ED:** LLB, Yale University (1970); BA, Yale University, Magna Cum Laude (1965) **C:** Lawyer, Hurwitz, Sagarin, Slossderg & Knuff LLC, Milford, CT (2001-Present); Partner, Jacobs, Grudberg, Belt Dow & Katz Professional Corporation, New Haven, CT (1974-Present); Partner, Jacob, Grudberg, Belt and Katz Firm, New Haven, CT (2011); Associate, Jacobs, Grudberg, Belt & Dow Professional Corporation, New Haven, CT (1970-1974) **CR:** Adjunct Professor, Quinnipiac University School of Law, North Haven, CT (2004-Present) **MIL:** U.S. Army, Vietnam (1966-1967); First Lieutenant, U.S. Army Reserve (1965-1967) **CW:** Senior Topical Editor, Antitrust/Trade Regulation, Connecticut Bar Journal (2012-Present); Co-Author, "Connecticut Unfair Trade Practices, Business Torts and Antitrust," (2015-2016); Author, "Should the FTC's Current Criteria for Determining Unfair Acts or Practices Be Applied to Little FTC Acts?" (2010); Author, "Unresolved Issues Under the Unfair Trade Practices Act" (2008); Author, Numerous Books and Articles Concerning Antitrust and Trade Regulations; Contributor, Articles, Professional Journals **AW:** Local Ligation Star, Benchmark Ligation (2009-2016); Named, Connecticut Super Lawyer (2006-2016); Named, Best Lawyers of America (2003-2016); Listee, America's Leading Lawyers for Business, Chambers USA (2003-2016); Bronze Star Medal for Meritorious Achievement **MEM:** Fellow, The Connecticut Bar Foundation (2016); Connecticut Bar Association; The Phi Beta Kappa Society; Omicron Delta Epsilon **BAR:** U.S. District Court for the District of Rhode Island (1981); U.S. District Court for the Southern District of New York (1975); U.S. District Court for the Eastern District of New York (1975); Supreme Court of the United States (1975); U.S. Court of Appeals for the Second Circuit (1971); U.S. District Court for the District of Connecticut (1970); Connecticut (1970) **MH:** Albert Nelson Marquis Lifetime Achievement Award; Marquis Who's Who Top Professional

BENCH, JOHNNY LEE, T: Former Professional Baseball Player **I:** Athletics **DOB:** 12/07/1947 **PB:** Oklahoma City **SC:** OK/USA **PT:** Ted Bench **MS:** Divorced **SPN:** Lauren Baiocchi (2004, Divorced 2017); Elizabeth Benton (1997, Divorced 2000); Laura Cwikowski (1987, Divorced 1995); Vickie Chesser (1975) **CH:** Bobby Singer; Justin; Josh **ED:** Diplomate, Binger-Oney High School, Binger, OK **C:** Speaker, Sports, Keppler Speakers (1998-Present); Golfer, PGA TOUR, Inc. (1998-2004); Special Consultant to General Manager, Cincinnati

Reds, MLB (1999); Field Reporter, Major League Baseball on NBC, NBC Universal (1994); Color Commentator, CBS Sports Radio, CBS Interactive (1989-1993); Commentator, Major League Baseball on ABC, ABC Entertainment (1986); Catcher, Cincinnati Reds, MLB (1967-1983) **CR:** Board of Directors, Cincinnati Reds Hall of Fame & Museum **CIV:** Benefactor, Johnny Bench Scholarship Fund (1983-Present); Former Head, Athletes' Division, American Cancer Society, Inc. **CW:** Co-author with Paul Daugherty, "Catch Every Ball: How to Handle Life's Pitches" (2008); Actor, "Married... with Children" (1993); Actor, "Mr. Belvedere" (1989); Actor, "Damn Yankees," Cincinnati, Ohio (1985); Host, "The Baseball Bunch" (1982-1985); Co-author with William Brashler, "Catch You Later" (1979); Actor, "The Partridge Family" (1973); Actor, "Mission: Impossible" (1971) **AW:** Living Legend Award, Louisville Slugger Museum & Factory (2011); Named to All-time Gold Glove Team, Rawlings and MLB (2007); Named to All-century Team, MLB (1999); Named to 100 Greatest Baseball Players, Sporting News (1999); Named to All-time Team, MLB (1997); Inductee, Oklahoma Sports Hall of Fame (1990); Inductee, National Baseball Hall of Fame (1989); Inductee, Cincinnati Reds Hall of Fame (1986); Named All-star, National League, MLB (1968-1980, 1983); Hutch Award, Fred Hutchinson Cancer Research Center (1981); Rawlings Gold Glove Award, National League, MLB (1968-1977); Named World Series MVP (1976); Named MVP, National League, MLB (1975, 1976); Babe Ruth Award, New York Chapter, BBWAA (1976); Lou Gehrig Memorial Award, MLB (1975); Named Rookie of the Year, National League, MLB (1968)

BENDER, RICHARD, T: Dean, Architect, Educator **I:** Architecture & Construction **DOB:** 01/19/1930 **PB:** New York **SC:** NY/USA **PT:** Edward Bender; Betty (Okun) Bender **MS:** Married **SPN:** Sue Rosenfeld (08/09/1956) **CH:** Michael; David **ED:** MArch, Harvard University (1956); BCE, City College of New York (1951) **C:** Private Practice, Berkeley, CA (1966-Present); Principal, Town Planning Associates (1966); Partner, Town Planning Associates (1961-1966); With Paul Lester Wiener, Town Planning Associates, New York, NY (1960-1966); Architect, William Lescaze (1958-1960); Architect, Walter Gropius (1951-1953) **CR:** Roppongi Hills Urban Plan (2005); New Town Cergy Pontoise, France (1993-2000); Master Plan, MediaPolis, Taipei, Taiwan (1997-2000); Master Plan, Benesse Institute of Arts, Naoshima Island, Japan (1993-2000); Consultant, University Campus Planning, University of California Merced (2000-2003); Consultant, University Campus Planning, University of California Santa Cruz (1992-1996); Consultant, University Campus Planning, University of California Davis (1989-1993); Visiting Professor, Harvard University, Massachusetts Institute of Technology (MIT), American Academy in Rome, ETH Zurich, Visiting Professor, Urban Design and Construction, Endowed Visiting Chair, University of Tokyo (1989); Consultant, University Campus Planning, University of California San Diego (1987-1990); Dean, College of Environmental Design, University of California Berkeley (1976-1989); Founder, Director, Campus Planning Study Group, University of California Berkeley (1976); Director, Building Research Board, National Academy of Sciences (1974-1980); Chairman, Department, University of California Berkeley (1974-1976); Consultant, University Campus Planning, University of California Berkeley (1972-1995); Professor (Now Professor Emeritus), Architecture, University of California Berkeley (1969); Assistant Professor, Cooper Union (1961); Lecturer, Columbia University, New York, NY (1957-1960); Member, Advisory Board on the Built Environment Advisory Panels, HUD,

National Endowment for the Arts, Member, Design Review Board, City of San Francisco, University of California, J.P. Getty Trust **CIV:** Member, Board of Directors, Bridge Housing, San Francisco, CA (1980) **MIL:** U.S. Army (1954-1955) **CW:** Author, "Reflections: An Architect's Journey: Living, Teaching and Practice in a World Without Walls" (2012); Author, "A Crack in the Rearview Mirror" (1973) **AW:** The Bender Fellowship: For Graduate Students of Housing: Community Planning, Established in the CED (2013) **MH:** Albert Nelson Marquis Lifetime Achievement Award **B/I:** Mr. Bender became involved in his profession because he grew up in a house where his grandfather was a builder, watching and learning during the Depression. He had no work so did minor repairs and built bookcases in his basement. He got interested in building because it seemed that by working together, people could make things out of nothing. He wanted to be an architect before he knew what it was. **AV:** Writing; Drawing

BENÉ, THOMAS L., T: Chairman, President, Chief Executive Officer **I:** Food & Restaurant Services **CN:** Sysco Corporation **ED:** BS in Business Administration, The University of Kansas (1984) **C:** Chairman, President, Chief Executive Officer, Sysco Corporation (2018-2020); President, Chief Operating Officer, Sysco Corporation (2016-2017); President of Foodservice Operations, Executive Vice President, Sysco Corporation (2015); Executive Vice President, Chief Commercial Officer, Sysco Corporation (2013-2014); Executive Vice President, Chief Merchandising Officer, Sysco Corporation (2013); President, Foodservice (2010-2013); President, Beverages Division, PepsiCo North America (2009-2010); Senior Vice President of Sales and Franchise Development, PepsiCo North America (2006-2009); President, Beverages & Food Division, PepsiCo Canada, Mississauga, Ontario, Canada (2004-2005); With, PepsiCo (1989-2003); Regional Sales Manager, American Scientific (1987-1989); Sales Representative, American Scientific (1984-1987) **CR:** Chairman, Board of Directors, Sysco Corporation (2018-2020); Dean's Advisory Board, The University of Kansas; Board of Directors, Greater Houston Partnership; Former Member, Board of Directors, WFF **CIV:** United Way of Greater Houston; National MS Society **AW:** Industry Titan Award, WFF (2019); SigEp Citation, Sigma Phi Epsilon (2019) **MEM:** Sigma Phi Epsilon

BENING, ANNETTE CAROL, T: Actress **I:** Media & Entertainment **DOB:** 05/29/1958 **PB:** Topeka **SC:** KS/USA **PT:** Arnett Grant Bening; Shirley Katherine (Ashley) Bening **MS:** Married **SPN:** Warren Beatty (03/03/1992); James Steven White (1984-1991) **CH:** Stephen; Benjamin; Isabel; Ella **ED:** MFA, American Conservatory Theater (1986); BA in Drama, San Francisco State University (1980) **CR:** Board of Governors, Academy of Motion Picture Arts and Sciences (2008-2017); Co-Chair, Academy Museum of Motion Pictures **CW:** Actress, "Turn of Mind" (2020); Actress, "Death on the Nile" (2020); Actress, "All My Sons," American Airlines Theatre, New York, NY (2019); Actress, "Hope Gap" (2019); Actress, "Georgetown" (2019); Actress, "Captain Marvel" (2019); Actress, "The Report" (2019); Actress, "Life Itself" (2018); Actress, "The Seagull" (2018); Actress, "Film Stars Don't Die in Liverpool" (2017); Actress, "Rules Don't Apply" (2016); Actress, "20th Century Women" (2016); Actress, "Danny Collins" (2015); Actress, "The Search" (2014); Actress, "King Lear," Delacorte Theater, New York, NY (2014); Actress, "The Face of Love" (2013); Actress, "Girl Most Likely" (2012); Actress, "Ginger & Rosa" (2012); Actress, "Ruby Sparks" (2012); Actress, "The Kids Are All Right" (2010); Actress, "The Female of the Species," Los Angeles,

CA (2010); Actress, "Mother and Child" (2009); Actress, "Medea," Ralph Freud Playhouse, UCLA, Los Angeles, CA (2009); Actress, "The Women" (2008); Host, "Saturday Night Live" (2006); Actress, "Running with Scissors" (2006); Actress, "Mrs. Harris" (2005); Actress, "Being Julia" (2004); Actress, "The Sopranos" (2004); Actress, "Open Range" (2003); Voice Actress, "Liberty's Kids" (2002-2003); Actress, "What Planet Are You From?" (2000); Actress, "American Beauty" (1999); Actress, "In Dreams" (1999); Actress, "Hedda Gabler," The Geffen Playhouse, Los Angeles, CA (1999); Actress, "The Siege" (1998); Actress, "Mars Attacks!" (1996); Actress, "The American President" (1995); Actress, "Richard III" (1995); Actress, "Love Affair" (1994); Actress, "Bugsy" (1991); Actress, "Regarding Henry" (1991); Actress, "Guilty by Suspicion" (1991); Actress, "Postcards from the Edge" (1990); Actress, "The Grifters" (1990); Actress, "Valmont" (1989); Actress, "The Great Outdoors" (1988); Actress, "Spoils of War," McGinn-Cazle Theatre, New York, NY (1988);Actress, "Coastal Disturbances," McGinn-Cazale Theatre and Circle in the Square Theatre, New York, NY (1986-1988); Actress, "Wiseguy" (1987); Actress, "Miami Vice" (1987); Actress, "Manhunt for Claude Dallas" (1986) **AW:** Movies for Grownups Career Achievement Award, AARP (2020); Gregory Peck Award for Cinematic Excellence, San Diego Film Foundation (2016); Actress Defying Age and Ageism Award, Alliance of Women Film Journalists (2016); DFCS Award for Best Ensemble, Detroit Film Critics Society (2016); Women in Hollywood Award, Elle, Hearst Magazine Media, Inc. (2014); Lifetime Achievement Award, American Conservatory Theater (2012); Dorian Award for Film Performance of the Year, GALECA (2011); IFTA Award for Best International Actress, The Irish Film & Television Academy (2011); London Film Critics' Circle Award for Actress of the Year, Critics' Circle (2000, 2011); SBIFF Award for Best Actress, Santa Barbara International Film Festival (2005, 2011); Golden Globe Award for Best Actress – Motion Picture Musical or Comedy, Hollywood Foreign Press Association (2005, 2011); AWFJ Award for Best Actress, Alliance of Women Film Journalists (2010); Women's Image Award, Alliance of Women Film Journalists (2010); NYFCC Award for Best Actress, New York Film Critics Circle (2010); WFCC Award for Best Comedic Actress, Women Film Critics Circle (2010); Board of Governors Award, American Society of Cinematographers (2008); Ibsen Centennial Commemoration Award, Government of Norway (2006); Star, Motion Picture Category, Hollywood Walk of Fame, Hollywood Chamber of Commerce (2006); Award for Best Actress, National Board of Review (2005); Golden Kinnaree Award for Best Actress, Bangkok International Film Festival, Tourism Authority of Thailand (2005); Hollywood Film Award for Best Actress of the Year, Hollywood Film Festival (2004); Satellite Award for Best Actress - Musical or Comedy, International Press Academy (2004); BAFTA Award for Best Actress in a Leading Role, British Academy of Film and Television Arts (2000); Screen Actors Guild Award for Outstanding Performance by a Female Actor in a Leading Role, SAG-AFTRA (2000); Screen Actors Guild Award for Outstanding Performance by a Cast in a Motion Picture, SAG-AFTRA (2000); SDFCS Award for Best Actress, San Diego Film Critics Society (2000); London Film Critics' Circle Award for Newcomer of the Year, Critics' Circle (1992); NSFC Award for Best Supporting Actress, National Society of Film Critics (1991); Theatre World Award, Theatre World Awards, Inc. (1987); Clarence Derwent Award, Actors' Equity Association (1987)

BENIOFF, DAVID, T: Screenwriter, Producer, Director **I:** Media & Entertainment **DOB:** 09/25/1970 **PB:** New York **SC:** NY/USA **PT:** Stephen Friedman; Barbara (Benioff) Friedman **MS:** Married **SPN:** Amanda Peet (09/30/2006) **CH:** Frances Pen; Molly June; Henry Peet Friedman **ED:** MFA in Creative Writing, University of California Irvine (1999);Coursework in Irish Literature, Trinity College, Dublin, Ireland (1995); BA in English, Dartmouth College, Hanover, NH (1992) **C:** Screenwriter, Producer, Director (2002-Present) **CR:** Disc Jockey, Radio **CW:** Actor, "Games of Thrones" (2019); Writer, Executive Producer, Director, "Game of Thrones" (2011-2019); Actor, "It's Always Sunny in Philadelphia" (2017); Co-Screenwriter, "Gemini Man" (2019); Screenwriter, "Brothers" (2009); Co-Screenwriter, "X-Men Origins: Wolverine" (2009); Author, "City of Thieves: A Novel" (2008); Screenwriter, "The Kite Runner" (2007); Screenwriter, "Stay" (2005); Author, "When the Nines Roll Over (And Other Stories)" (2004); Screenwriter, "Troy" (2004); Author, "The Kite Runner" (2003); Author, "The 25th Hour" (2001); Screenwriter, "The 25th Hour" (2002) **AW:** Norman Felton Award for Outstanding Producer of Episodic TV - Drama, Producers Guild of America (2016); Emmy Award for Outstanding Writing for a Drama Series, Television Academy (2015, 2016); Listee, America's Top 50 Most Eligible Bachelors, People Magazine (2001)

BEN-MEIR, MARC J., T: Psychologist, Substance Abuse Counselor, Author **I:** Medicine & Health Care **DOB:** 06/23/1946 **PB:** Bronx **SC:** NY/USA **PT:** Murray Norman; Shirley Lenora (Fox) Friedman **MS:** Divorced **SPN:** Tina Ellen White (09/08/1996); Candace Jo Drinnon (06/05/1983, Divorced 04/1994); Aliza Assulin (06/22/1971, Divorced 04/1983) **CH:** Neil; Ron; Jonathan; Stepsons, Christopher; Daniel **ED:** PhD in Organizational Psychology, La Salle University (1992); MA in Organizational Behavior, Norwich University, Cum Laude (1990); BA in Humanities, Thomas Edison State University, Trenton, NJ (1984); AA in Human Cultural Development, Brookdale Community College, Lincroft, NJ (1979) **CT:** Ordained, Rabbi (1995); Licensed Chemical Dependency Counselor; Certified Clinical Hypnotherapist; Certified Addictions Counselor; Licensed Social Work Associate **C:** Owner, Springhaven Addictions Clinic, Fort Worth, TX (1992-1998); Director, Training Coordinator, National Veterans Outreach, American GI Forum (1990-1991) **CR:** Adjunct Professor, La Salle University **CIV:** Diplomat, American Jewish Congress; Texas National Guard **MIL:** Major, U.S. Army (1997); Counselor, U.S. Air Force, Carswell Air Force Base (1986-1991); Counselor, U.S. Army (1976-1985); U.S. Army, Vietnam (1968-1969) **CW:** Author, "Phoenix Rising From A Savage Time: Book Three of the Savage Time Trilogy" (2017); Author, "Ashes of a Savage Time" (2015); Author, "Witness of a Savage Time" (2015); Author, "The Sons of Joshua: The Story of the Jewish Contribution to the Confederacy" (2012); Author; "The Frozen Mountain: How to Counsel Native Americans" (1994); Author, "Concepts in Prisoner Rehabilitation" (1991) **AW:** Tudor Philip Benjamin Award for Excellence in Historical Research, United Daughters of the Confederacy **MEM:** American Society of Clinical Hypnosis; 32nd Degree Masons **MH:** Albert Nelson Marquis Lifetime Achievement Award **B/I:** Mr. Ben-Meir became involved in his profession by accident. People would often seek his advice and that led to him pursuing psychology professionally. **AV:** Camping; Shooting black powder primitive guns; Historical re-enacting **PA:** Democrat **RE:** Jewish

BENNET, MICHAEL FARRAND, T: U.S. Senator from Colorado **I:** Government Administration/Government Relations/Government Services **DOB:** 11/28/1964 **PB:** New Delhi **SC:** India **PT:** Douglas Joseph Bennet; Susanne Christine (Klejman) Bennet **MS:** Married **SPN:** Susan Diane Daggett (10/25/1997) **CH:** Three Daughters **ED:** Doctor of Jurisprudence, Yale Law School, New Haven, CT (1993); Bachelor of Arts in History, Wesleyan University, CT **C:** Member, U.S. Senate Finance Committee (2013-Present); U.S. Senator, State of Colorado (2009-Present); Member, U.S. Senate Committee on Health, Education, Labor and Pensions, Washington, DC (2009-Present); Member, U.S. Senate Committee on Agriculture, Nutrition and Forestry, Washington, DC (2009-Present); Candidate for Democratic Nomination, 2020 Presidential Election (2019-2020); Chairperson, Democratic Senatorial Campaign Committee (2013-2015); Member, U.S. Senate Committee on Banking, Housing and Urban Affairs, Washington, DC (2009-2013); Member, U.S. Senate Special Committee on Aging, Washington, DC (2009-2013); Superintendent, Denver Public Schools (2005-2009); Chief of Staff to Mayor John Hickenlooper, City of Denver, CO (2003-2005); Managing Director, Anschutz Investment Co., Denver, CO (1997-2003); Counsel to Deputy Attorney General, U.S. Department of Justice, Washington, DC (1995-1997); Law Clerk to Honorable Francis D. Murnaghan, United States Court of Appeals for the Fourth Circuit (1993-1994) **CR:** Board of Visitors, United States Air Force Academy (2011-Present); Chairman, Democratic Senatorial Campaign Committee (2013-2015); National Campaign Co-chair, Obama for America (2012) **PA:** Democrat **RE:** Episcopalian

BENNETT, CAROLINE, "CAROL" ELISE, T: Retired Librarian, Reporter, Actress **I:** Media & Entertainment **DOB:** 12/27/1938 **PB:** New Orleans **SC:** Louisiana/USA **PT:** Gerald Clifford Graham Kerr; Edna Doris (Toennies) Kerr **MS:** Married **SPN:** Ralph Decker Bennett, Jr (2/27/1966) **CH:** Ralph Decker Bennett III; Katherine Elise Bennett **ED:** BLS, McGill University, Montreal, Quebec, Canada (1962); BA, University of British Columbia, Vancouver, Canada (1960) **C:** Reporter, Radio, Washington-Alabama News Report, Washington DC (1981-2001); Librarian, Various Locations (1962-1976) **CR:** Member, History Committee, National Press Club; Interviewer, Broadcast Pioneers, Broadcast Pioneer Archive, Hornbake Library, University of Maryland **CW:** Co-author, "How to Move to Canada, A Primer for Americans" (2006); Actor, Film, "Prime Risk" (1984); Actor, Film, "Kennedy" (1983); Actor, Play, "There's a Girl in My Soup" (1978); Host, TV Series, American Association of Retired Persons' Modern Maturity, PBS (1986-1988); Author, Half a Dozen People's Life Stories; Extra, Numerous Films **AW:** Award for Best Coverage of a Scheduled Event, Alabama Associated Press Broadcasters Association (1983); Awarded to the ALANET News Team **MEM:** American Association of University Women; SAG-AFTRA; Older Womens League; National Press Club History and Heritage Committee; Society of Professional Journalists **MH:** Albert Nelson Marquis Lifetime Achievement Award **AS:** Showing up and "the kindness of strangers." **B/I:** Having been an English and Theatre major in college, Ms. Bennett found herself at an employment agency when she graduated. The agency sent her to a library job in the Reference Department at the Howard-Tilton Memorial Library at Tulane University in New Orleans. Her immediate boss had traveled extensively working with U.S. Army Libraries and encouraged her to get a degree and do the same. Ms. Bennett did that and subsequently traveled to Germany where she was responsible for several army libraries in the Mainz area and where she met her husband. Ms. Bennett holds a Bachelor of Arts degree from the University of British Columbia in Vancouver and a Bachelor of Library Science from McGill University in Montreal. Her BA prepared her for acting and she worked in theatre as well. **AV:** Reading; Genealogy research **THT:** Friends are treasures and all of us are vulnerable; we need to be careful with each other. Tennessee Williams had it right when he had Blanche say deliberate cruelty is the one unforgivable thing.

BENNETT, JANET, T: Legislative Staff Member **I:** Government Administration/Government Relations/Government Services **DOB:** 10/06/1932 **PB:** Portland **SC:** OR/USA **PT:** Stephen Loren Huff; Melba Sperry (Stout) Huff **MS:** Married **SPN:** Michael Jesse Bennett (12/30/1968); Gerald Randolph Petrey (10/11/1950, Divorced 1968) **CH:** Mark Randall; Karee M. Petrey Cannon; Creighton Petrey **ED:** University of Washington **C:** Deputy State Director, Senator Robert Bennett (1993-2005); Assistant State Director, Senator Orrin Hatch (1979-1992); Office Manager, Promised Valley Theater (1977-1979); Various Positions, ZCMI (1975-1977) **CIV:** Coalition for Utah Families (1995-Present); Board of Directors, Utah Chamber Artists (1995-Present); Government Commission on Women and Families (1993-Present); Advisory Board Member, Utah Symphony (1990-Present); Utah Council for Crime Prevention (1989-Present); Chair, Governor's Conference on Marriage (1997-1998); Chair, Women's Legislative Council of Utah (1996-1997); Co-Chair for Legislative Issues, Women's Legislative Council of Utah (1989-1997); Third District Judicial Nominating Commission (1992-1994); President, Utah Symphony Guild (1992-1993); Chair, Utah Women's Conference (1985-1992); Chair, Board of Directors, Discovery Gateway (1989-1990) **MEM:** First Vice President, Utah Federation of Republican Women (2000-Present); Associate Member, Board of Directors, National Association of Commissions for Women (2000-Present); Board of Directors, National Association of Commissions for Women (1995-2000) **MH:** Albert Nelson Marquis Lifetime Achievement Award **AV:** Painting **PA:** Republican **RE:** Church of Jesus Christ of Latter-Day Saints

BENNETT, JOHN MICHAEL, PHD, T: Poet; Professor; Librarian **I:** Education/Educational Services **CN:** Luna Bisonte Productions **DOB:** 10/12/1942 **PB:** Chicago **SC:** IL/USA **PT:** John William Bennett; Kathryn (Goldsmith) Bennett **MS:** Married **SPN:** C. Mehrl (07/04/1980); Janifer Holley (09/1964, Divorced 1980) **CH:** William E.; Benjamin K.; John A. **ED:** PhD in Latin American Literature, University of California Los Angeles (1970); MA in Spanish, Washington University in St. Louis (1966); BA in Spanish and English, Washington University in St. Louis, with Honors (1964) **C:** Founding Curator, Avant Writing Collection, The Ohio State University (1998-2011); Latin American Bibliographical Assistant, Editor, The Ohio State University (1976-1998); Assistant Professor of Spanish, The Ohio State University (1969-1976) **CIV:** Volunteer Poetry Therapist, Central Ohio Psychiatric Hospital (1979-1986) **CW:** Publisher, Editor, Luna Bisonte Productions (1974-Present); Author, "OJI-JETE," Luna Bisonte Productions (2020); Author, "Leg Mist," Luna Bisonte Productions (2019); Author, "Sesos Extremos," Luna Bisonte Productions (2018); Author, "Olas Cursis," Luna Bisonte Productions (2018); Author, "The Sweating Lake," Luna Bisonte Productions (2017); Co-author with Osvaldo Cibils, "Poemas Visuales, con Movimientos con Ruidos con Combinaciones/Deep White Sound" (2017); Author, "The World of Burning," Luna Bisonte Productions (2017); Author, "Select Poems," Poetry Hotel Press/Luna Bisonte Pro-

ductions (2016); Editor, Lost and Found Times (1975-2005); Co-editor with Geoffrey D. Smith, "Everything Lost: The Latin American Notebook of William S. Burroughs" and "The Revised Boy Scout Manual: An Electronic Revolution," by William S. Burroughs, The Ohio State University Press; Collections, Several Major Institutions Including Washington University in St. Louis, University at Buffalo, The Ohio State University, The Museum of Modern Art, and Other Major Libraries; Publisher, Over 400 Books and Chapbooks of Poetry and Other Materials; Publisher, Performer, Exhibits, Word Art, Publications and Venues, Worldwide **AW:** Grantee, Ohio Arts Council (1979-1980, 1982, 1985, 1988-1996) **MEM:** Certified Member, National Association for Poetry Therapy (1985) **MH:** Albert Nelson Marquis Lifetime Achievement Award **B/I:** Dr. Bennett, as a young child, had been writing before he knew it was writing. It was something very basic he has always done. He did not know anything about poetry or narrative, later he realized that people call that poetry. In junior high school, he started reading other poets and at the same time he had begun writing. He does visual and textual poetry. What attracted Dr. Bennett to his profession as a poet, professor, and librarian is that it is something that he felt he had to do. He had done it before he knew what it was. **AV:** Art; Gardening **THT:** Dr. Bennett work is in Spanish and Latin American literature; he writes in Spanish as well as English. Richard Kostelanetz has called him, "the seminal American poet of my generation." For more information on his work, please see: http://www.johnmbennettpoetry.blogspot.com/ and http://www.lulu.com/spotlight/lunabisonteprods

BENNETT, THOMAS, "TOM" JERMAN, PHD, T: Engineer (Retired) **I:** Engineering **DOB:** 04/25/1940 **PB:** Sioux City **SC:** IA/USA **PT:** Crane Delbert Bennett; Janie (Jerman) Bennett **SPN:** Mary Ann Bennett **CH:** David Robert; Michelle; James **ED:** PhD in Civil Engineering, Washington State University (1988); MS in Nuclear Engineering, University of Washington (1967); BS in Engineering, University of California Los Angeles (1964); AS, Long Beach City College (1983) **CT:** Completed Summer Science Institute, Washington State University (1997); Registered Professional Engineer, Washington State License # 12571 **C:** Full-time Engineering Instructor, Big Bend Community College, Moses Lake, WA (18 Years); Senior Engineer, The Boeing Company, Everett, WA (Two Years); Pre-doctoral Associate, Washington State University (Two Years) **CR:** Research Scientist, Hanford Nuclear Reservation, Richland, WA (Six Years); Teacher, College Courses to Gifted High School Students, WA (7 Years) **CIV:** Trustee, Vestry, St. Martin Episcopal Church (2017-2018); Chairman, Major Political Party, Grant County, WA (1974-1975); Trustee, Free Moses Lake United Methodist Church, Moses Lake, WA (1970-1980); Member, Rose Bowl Team, University of California Los Angeles (1962); Member, Junior Rose Bowl Team, Long Beach City College (1960) **MIL:** With, United States Air Force Reserve (Six Years) **CW:** Contributor, Articles on Nuclear Power to Professional Journals (Seven Years) **AW:** Certificate of Achievement, Participation in Difficult Students Continuing Education (1996); Certificate of Attendance, Helping All Students Achieve Success (1996); Outstanding Teacher's Award (1996); Excellence in Education Award (1996); Named One of the Outstanding Educators of America; Recipient, Key to City of Long Beach, CA; Fellow, Atomic Energy Commission (AEC) **MEM:** President, Big Bend College Faculty Association; Elks Club (BPO Elks); The Tau Beta Pi Association, Inc.; Toastmasters International **MH:** Albert Nelson Marquis Lifetime Achievement Award **AS:**

Dr. Bennett attributes his success to concentration, hard work, and fortunately being at the right place at the right time. **B/I:** Dr. Bennett went into engineering because he was good in math. He had a real good math teacher in high school, and he notices a continual parade of university students coming back to thank her. Teaching those really smart kids in high school and the college level was really fun and enjoyable. **AV:** Reading **PA:** Democrat **RE:** Free Methodist/Episcopal **THT:** Dr. Bennett really enjoyed political cartoons drawn by Bill Watterson and Paul Conrad. Dr. Bennett's motto is, "Don't forget - we are here to help others."

BENNETT, TONY DOMINICK, T: Singer, Artist **I:** Media & Entertainment **DOB:** 08/03/1926 **PB:** Astoria **SC:** NY/USA **PT:** John Benedetto; Anna (Suraci) Benedetto **MS:** Married **SPN:** Susan Crow (2007); Sandra Grant (1971, Divorced 2007); Patricia Beech (1952, Divorced 1971) **CH:** Danny; Daegal; Joanna; Antonia **ED:** Honorary Doctorate, Fordham University (2012); Honorary Doctorate, The Juilliard School (2010); Honorary Doctorate, Cleveland Institute of Music (2010); Honorary Doctorate, The George Washington University (2001); Honorary Doctorate, Chicago College of Performing Arts (1995); Honorary Doctorate, The Art Institute of Boston (1994); Honorary Doctor of Music, Berklee College of Music (1974); Coursework, American Theatre Wing, New York, NY **CR:** Official Artist, Kentucky Derby (2001); Commissioned Artist, United Nations **CIV:** Co-founder, with Susan Crow, Frank Sinatra School of the Arts High School, Queens, NY (2001); Fundraiser, Juvenile Diabetes Foundation **MIL:** With, Infantry Unit and Special Services Band, Army of the United States, World War II (1944-1946) **CW:** Singer with Diana Krall, "Love is Here to Stay" (2018); Author, "Just Getting Started" (2016); Singer with Bill Charlap, "The Silver Lining: The Songs of Jerome Kern" (2015); Singer with Lady Gaga, "Cheek to Cheek" (2014); Singer, "Viva Duets" (2012); Author, "Life is a Gift: The Zen of Bennett" (2012); Singer, "Duets II" (2011); Singer, "Tony Bennett Sings the Ultimate American Songbook, Volume One" (2007); Co-author, "Tony Bennett in the Studio: A Life of Art & Music" (2007); Singer, "Duets: An American Classic" (2006); Performer, "Tony Bennett: An American Classic" (2006); Singer, "The Art of Romance" (2004); Singer with k.d. lang, "A Wonderful World" (2002); Singer, "Christmas with Tony Bennett and the London Symphony Orchestra" (2002); Singer, "The Essential Tony Bennett" (2002); Singer, "Playin' With My Friends: Bennett Sings The Blues" (2001); Singer, "The Ultimate Tony" (2000); Singer, "Bennett Sings Ellington: Hot & Cool" (1999); Appearance, "Analyze This" (1999); Co-author, "The Good Life: The Autobiography of Tony Bennett" (1998); Singer, "Tony Bennett on Holiday" (1997); Performer, "Tony Bennett on Holiday: A Tribute to Billy Holiday" (1997); Appearance, "Suddenly Susan" (1997); Appearance, "Muppets Tonight" (1996); Author, "Tony Bennett: What My Heart Has Seen" (1996); Appearance, "Sinatra: 80 Years My Way" (1995); Singer, "Here's to the Ladies" (1995); Appearance, "The Scout" (1994); Appearance, "Space Ghost Coast to Coast" (1994); Appearance, "Men, Movies & Carol" (1994); Exhibited Art, Butler Institute of American Art, Youngstown, Ohio (1994); Singer, "MTV Unplugged" (1994); Singer, "In Person! With Count Basie and His Orchestra" (1994); Singer, "Steppin' Out" (1993); Singer, "The Essence of Tony Bennett" (1993); Singer, "Perfectly Frank" (1992); Singer, "Forty Years: The Artistry of Tony Bennett" (1991); Singer, "Astoria" (1990); Singer, "The Movie Song Album" (1989); Appearance, "The Simpsons" (1989); Singer, "Bennett/Berlin" (1987); Singer, "The Art of Excellence" (1986);

Singer, "16 Most Requested Songs" (1986); Singer, "Sunrise, Sunset" (1973); Singer, "Summer of '42" (1972); Singer, "Love Story" (1971); Appearance, "The Jackie Gleason Show" (1969); Singer, "Snowfall: The Tony Bennett Christmas Album" (1968); Appearance, "The Andy Williams Show" (1966); Singer, "I Wanna Be Around" (1963); Singer, "I Left My Heart in San Francisco" (1963); Singer, "Bennett and Basie Strike Up the Band" (1961); Singer, "To My Wonderful One" (1960); Singer, "Blue Velvet" (1959); Singer, "Count Basie Swings, Tony Bennett Sings" (1958); Singer, "Tony" (1957); Singer, "Treasure Chest of Songs" (1955); Exhibited Art, National Arts Club, New York, NY; Painting, "Homage to Hockney", Butler Institute of American Art; Singer, Songs and Albums; Appearances, Television Shows; Artist, Paintings **AW:** Grammy Award for Best Traditional Pop Vocal Album, The Recording Academy (1995, 2003, 2004, 2006, 2007, 2012, 2015, 2016, 2018); Grammy Award for Best Pop Performance by a Duo or Group, The Recording Academy (2012); Inductee, New Jersey Hall of Fame (2011); Inductee, Long Island Music Hall of Fame (2011); Grammy Award for Pop Collaboration with Vocals, The Recording Academy (2007); Inductee, International Civil Rights Walk of Fame (2007); Primetime Emmy Award for Outstanding Individual Performance in a Variety or Music Progressive, Academy of Television Arts & Sciences (1996, 2007); Billboard Century Award (2006); National Endowment for the Arts Jazz Masters Award (2006); UN High Commissioner for Refugees Humanitarian Award (2006); Honoree, Kennedy Center Honor, John F. Kennedy Center for the Performing Arts (2005); Best Traditional Pop Vocal, "Steppin' Out", Grammy Awards (2003); Lifetime Achievement Award, ASCAP (2002); Society of Singers Lifetime Achievement Award (2000); Inductee, Big Band and Jazz Hall of Fame (1997); Grammy Award for Album of the Year, The Recording Academy (1962, 1995); Grammy Award for Best Traditional Vocal Performance, The Recording Academy (1992); Bronze Medallion, City of New York (1969); Best Male Vocalist Award, Cash Box Magazine (1951); Grammy Lifetime Achievement Award; Salute to Greatness Award, Martin Luther King Center, Atlanta, GA; Gold Record; Star, Hollywood Walk of Fame; Numerous Awards

BENTLEY, WILLIAM ROSS, PHD, T: Forestry Educator **I:** Education/Educational Services **DOB:** 01/29/1938 **PB:** Oakland **SC:** CA/USA **PT:** Jay R. Bentley; Olive (Manson) Bentley **MS:** Married **SPN:** Ann Wilhelm (12/01/1990) **CH:** Michael; Anne; Andrew; Russell; Frederick **ED:** MF, University of Michigan, Ann Arbor, MI (1961); PhD, University of California Berkeley, Berkeley, CA (1965); BS, University of California Berkeley, Berkeley, CA (1960) **C:** Co-owner, Wilhelm Farm, North Granby, CT (2003-Present); Professor Emeritus, Professor of Forest Policy and Management, State University of New York (SUNY) College of Environmental Science and Forestry, Syracuse, NY (1997-Present); Principal, Salmon Brook Associates, Granby, CT (1994-2010); Member, Adjunct Faculty, Yale School of Forestry & Environmental Studies (Now Yale School of the Environment), Yale University, New Haven, CT (1990-1997); Senior Program Officer, Director, Winrock International, Morrilton, AR (1985-1994); Program Officer, Ford Foundation, India (1983-1985); Professor, University of Connecticut, Storrs, CT (1980-1984); Manager, Forest Research, Crown Zellerbach Corp., Wilsonville, OR (1976-1980); Professor, University of Michigan, Ann Arbor, MI (1974-1976); Associate Professor, University of Michigan, Ann Arbor, MI (1969-1974); Associate Professor, University of Wisconsin - Madison, Madison, WI (1966-1969); Assistant Professor, Iowa State University, Ames, Iowa

(1963-1966) **CR:** Consultant, Connecticut Forest & Park Association, Middletown, CT (2003-2010); Consultant, Secretary of Agriculture, Forestry Research Advisory Council (FRAC) (1991-1993, 2000-2003); Consultant, U.S. Department of Justice (1981-1985); Consultant, George Banzhaf & Company, Milwaukee, WI (1968-1969) **CIV:** Volunteer, Granby 4-H, Holcomb Farm, and McLean Game Refuge (2003-2012); Board of Directors, Nitrogen Fixing Tree Association, Maui, Hawaii (1992-1994) **CW:** Co-author, "Hotelling's Theory, Enhancement, and the Taking of the Redwood National Park," American Journal of Agricultural Economics (1997); Co-author, "Rural Resource Managers: Problem-solving Tools for the Long Term," Iowa State University Press, Ames, Iowa (1994); Co-author, "Management of Agroforestry Research" (1990) **AW:** Fellow, Society of American Foresters (2007); Fulbright Fellow (1991-1994); Charles Bullard Fellowship in Forest Research (1975-1976); Schoen-Rene Fellow (1960-1961) **MEM:** Society of American Foresters (1957-Present) **MH:** Albert Nelson Marquis Lifetime Achievement Award **AS:** Dr. Bentley attributes his success to liking people. As a manager and a leader, this gregariousness lends itself very well to his responsibilities. **B/I:** Dr. Bentley became involved in his teaching profession because of the good teachers he had. Both of his parents were educated but were non-educators; however, they both felt that education was the route to a better life. He went into forestry because his father was a range grassland ecologist for the United States Forest Service, so he was exposed from early on. A day after he graduated from high school, he got a job as a forest firefighter and did that for a couple of years. He then moved to working under a wonderful and strange man in ecology and while he was doing that, one day on the Fourth of July, he climbed Mt. Mammoth and found it all wonderful. The district ranger was sitting on his front porch and he called him over, offered him a drink, they started talking, and he asked him where he went to school, to which Dr. Bentley said Stanford. So he told him he should transfer to the University of California Berkeley as it was free and when he was done, there would be jobs available. Dr. Bentley then did that, got a transfer into forestry, and never looked back. **AV:** Farming; Watercolor painting; Cooking **PA:** Democrat **RE:** Congregational

BENTZ, GREGORY M., T: Partner **I:** Law and Legal Services **CN:** Polsinelli PC **MS:** Married **SPN:** Nancy (Murphy) Bentz **CH:** Elizabeth Cornell; Jeffrey **ED:** JD, University of Nebraska-Lincoln, Lincoln, NE, with Distinction (1983); BS in Business Administration, University of Nebraska-Lincoln, Lincoln, NE, with Distinction (1980) **C:** Shareholder, Polsinelli PC (1989-Present); Senior Partner, Polsinelli PC (1983-Present); Shareholder, Polsinelli Shughart PC (Now Polsinelli PC) (1983-2012); Associate, Polsinelli PC (1983-1989) **CR:** Committee on Governance, American Hospital Association (2019-Present); Board of Directors, St. Luke's Physician Group, St. Luke's University Health Network (2017-Present); Board of Directors, St. Luke's Health System, St. Luke's University Health Network (2014-Present); Board of Directors, Saint Luke's South Hospital (2008-Present); Board Leadership Fellow, National Association of Corporate Directors (2019); Board of Directors, Saint Luke's Cardiovascular Consultants (2010-2017); Board of Directors, Co-chair, Ethics Committee, St. Luke's Hospital (2005-2018); Senior Warden, St. Andrew's Episcopal Church (2003-2004); Trustee, Interest on Lawyer Trust Account (IOLTA) Board (2002-2008) **CIV:** Senior Warden, St. Andrew's Episcopal Church (2003-2004, 2015-2018); Chancellor, St. Andrew's Episcopal Church (2005-2014)

CW: Executive Editor, Nebraska Law Review **AW:** Named Antitrust Lawyer of the Year, Best Lawyers in America, Kansas City (2020); NACD Board Leadership Fellow, National Association of Corporate Directors (2019); Named Trustee of the Year, Kansas Hospital Association (2018); Named One of the Best of the Bar in Business Litigation, Kansas City Business Journal (2018); Named Super Lawyer, Super Lawyers (2011-2018) **MEM:** American Hospital Association; American Health Lawyers Association; National Association of Corporate Directors; Saint Luke's Health System; Saint Luke's South Hospital; Kansas City Metropolitan Bar Foundation; Kansas City Metropolitan Bar Association; Kansas Bar Association; American Health Law Association; Lawyers Association of Kansas City; Nebraska State Bar Association; President, Beta Theta Pi; Beta Gamma Sigma; Omicron Delta Epsilon The International Economics Honor Society **BAR:** Kansas (2007); Nebraska (1983); Missouri (1983); Supreme Court of the United States; Supreme Court of Missouri; Kansas Supreme Court; United States District Court for the Western District of Missouri; United States District Court for the District of Kansas; United States Court of Appeals for the Fifth Circuit; United States Court of Appeals for the Eighth Circuit; United States Court of Appeals for the Ninth Circuit; United States Court of Appeals for the Tenth Circuit **MH:** Marquis Who's Who Top Professional **AS:** Mr. Bentz attributes his success to hard work and intellectual curiosity. Resolving people's problems and applying the law to do that has always interested him. It makes each case new and interesting, and it allows him to use his skills to help people within the parameters of the law. **B/I:** Mr. Bentz became involved in his profession because he always knew he was going to be an attorney. When he was in high school, he made the decision that that is what he was going to do. He had seen that lawyers were the leaders in the community and was motivated by having the ability to help others. **THT:** Mr. Bentz is very active within the committee on governance for the American Hospital Association on the national level.

BERA, AMERISH, "AMI" BABULAI, MD, T: U.S. Representative from California; Physician **I:** Medicine & Health Care **DOB:** 03/02/1965 **PB:** Hollywood **SC:** CA/USA **PT:** Babular Bera; Kanta Bera **MS:** Married **SPN:** Janine Bera (1991) **CH:** Sydra **ED:** MD, University of California Irvine (1991); BS in Biological Sciences, University of California Irvine (1983) **C:** U.S. Representative from California's Seventh Congressional District, United States Congress, Washington, DC (2013-Present); Member, U.S. House Committee on Space, Science and Technology (2013-Present); Member, U.S. House Foreign Affairs Committee (2013-Present); Clinical Professor of Medicine, University of California Davis School of Medicine (2005-2012); Associate Dean for Admissions, University of California Davis School of Medicine (2004-2007); Chief Medical Officer, Sacramento County Department of Health & Human Services (1999-2004); Director, Care Management, Mercy Healthcare (1998-1999); Assistant Medical Director, MedClinic Medical Group (1997-1998); Chief, Internal Medicine Department, MedClinic Medical Group (1996-1997); Committee on Ways and Means **CIV:** American Sikh Congressional Caucus; New Democrat Coalition; Congressional Asian Pacific American Caucus; Climate Solutions Caucus; U.S.-Japan Caucus **PA:** Democrat

BERENBEIM, RONALD E., SENIOR FELLOW, T: Business Writer, Educator **I:** Education/Educational Services **CN:** The Conference Board Inc. **DOB:** 05/05/1944 **PB:** Denver **SC:** CO/USA

PT: Samuel Leonard Berenbeim; Joan Madelon (Goodney) Berenbeim **MS:** Married **SPN:** Jane Susan Rosen (03/25/1979) **CH:** Jessica Lucy; Sarah Katherine (Deceased 2013) **ED:** JD, Harvard University (1971); MA, University of Oxford (1971); BA, University of Oxford (1968); BA, Cornell University, Cum Laude (1966) **C:** Director, Working Group on Business Ethics Principles, New York, NY (1997-Present); Senior Fellow, The Conference Board Inc. (2010); Principal Researcher, The Conference Board Inc. (1998-2010); Senior Research Associate, The Conference Board Inc. (1980-1997); Director, Guaranty National Corporation (1977-1988); Research Associate, The Conference Board Inc. (1977-1980); Business Representative, Motion Picture and Television Union, New York, NY (1975-1977); Attorney, National Labor Relations Board, Seattle (1971-1973) **CR:** Professor, Stern School of Business Administration, New York University, New York, NY (1990-Present); Teacher, Business Ethics and Anti-Corruption Courses, PAS Program, Prudens, Shanghai (2019); Teacher, Business Ethics and Anti-Corruption Courses, IASE, Buenos Aires (2016); Co-Facilitator, Global Compact Principles for Responsible Management Education Anti-Corruption Working Group, United Nations (2011-2016); Teacher, Business Ethics and Anti-Corruption Courses, ISCTE-University Institute of Lisbon (2014); Executive Advisory Panel, Open Compliance and Ethics Group (2002-2006); Project Director, East Asia Pacific Private Sector, Anti-Corruption Project, The World Bank Group (2001); Visiting Fellow, New Zealand Center for Business Ethics (2000); Director, The Conference Board Working Group on Global Business Ethnics Principles, New York, NY (1997) **CW:** Co-Author, "Fighting Corruption in East Asia, Solutions from the Private Sector" (2003); Contributor, Articles, Professional Journals; Contributor, Chapters, Books **AW:** Top 100 Thought Leaders in Trustworthy Business Behavior, Trust Across America (2010-2011); Keasbey Memorial Scholar, University of Oxford (1966) **MEM:** Business Principles Steering Committee, Transparency International (2000-Present); Tenth Principle for Countering Bribery Group, United Nations Global Compact (2010); Ethics Committee, Institute of Management Consultants of the United States (2002-2005); Blue Ribbon Commission Report, National Association of Corporate Directors (1996) **BAR:** Massachusetts Bar Association (1974); Washington State Bar Association (1973) **MH:** Albert Nelson Marquis Lifetime Achievement Award; Marquis Who's Who Top Professional **B/I:** Mr. Berenbeim became involved in his profession because he was inspired by his father and grandfather. **THT:** Mr. Berenbeim states, "Not being able to complete the task does not relieve you of the responsibility to undertake it."

BERENDT, JOHN LAWRENCE, T: Author, Writer **I:** Writing and Editing **DOB:** 12/05/1939 **PB:** Syracuse **SC:** NY/USA **PT:** Ralph Sidney; Carol (Deschere) B. **ED:** Bachelor of Arts, Harvard University, Cambridge, MA (1961) **C:** Columnist, Esquire Magazine, New York, NY (1982-1994); Editor, New York Magazine, New York, NY (1977-1979); Writer, Dick Cavett Show, New York, NY (1973-1975); Associate Producer, David Frost Show, New York, NY (1969-1971); Senior Staff Editor, Holiday Magazine, New York, NY (1969); Associate Editor, Esquire Magazine, New York, NY (1961-1969) **CIV:** Board of Directors, Theatre for a New Audience **MIL:** U.S. Army National Guard (1963-1969) **CW:** Author, "The City of Falling Angels" (2005); Author, "Midnight in the Garden of Good and Evil" (1994) **AW:** Finalist, Pulitzer Prize in General Nonfiction (1995); Nonfiction Award, Southern Book Critics Circle (1994) **MEM:** PEN International; Century

Association **MH:** Marquis Lifetime Achievement Award **AV:** Collecting American art, paintings and drawings

BERG, JANICE, T: Elementary School Educator (Retired) **I:** Education/Educational Services **CN:** Allegheny-Clarion Valley School District **DOB:** 02/18/1953 **PB:** Painesville **SC:** OH/USA **PT:** Kenneth White Edds; Audrey Helen Nelson **CH:** Peter James; Steven Alan **ED:** MEd, Slippery Rock University of Pennsylvania (1987); BS in Elementary Education, Slippery Rock University of Pennsylvania (1975) **CT:** Certified in Early Childhood Education, Slippery Rock University of Pennsylvania (1995); Certified Reading Specialist, Clarion University of Pennsylvania (1994) **C:** Retired (2017); Reading Specialist, Allegheny-Clarion Valley School District (1996-2017); Reading Specialist, Punxsutawney Area School District (1994); First-Grade Teacher, Seoul Foreign School (1978-1979); Fifth-Grade Teacher, Seoul Foreign School (1977-1978); Third-Grade Teacher, Brookville Area School District (1975-1976) **CR:** Private Tutor, Brookville, PA (1993); Substitute Teacher, Derry Township School District (1990) **CIV:** Committee Chairman, Boy Scouts of America (1987-1994); Room Mother, Parent-Teacher Organization, Elizabethtown, PA (1985); Director, Vacation Bible School; Sunday School Teacher **AW:** Who's Who Among America's Teachers; Who's Who in American Education; Who's Who in America **MEM:** Secretary, Butler Outdoor Club (2004-2005); Conference Membership Committee, Keystone State Literacy Association (2002); President, Correspondence Secretary, Seneca Reading Council (2001-2002); PSEA; Allegheny-Clarion Valley Education Association **MH:** Albert Nelson Marquis Lifetime Achievement Award, Marquis Who's Who Top Educators **AS:** Ms. Berg attributes her success to her hard work and continuing education. **B/I:** Ms. Berg became involved in her profession because of her long-standing desire to be a teacher. After working in the field for many years, she returned to school to become a certified reading specialist. **AV:** Swimming; Hiking; Bicycling; Reading; Playing table tennis

BERG, JANICE CAROL, T: Elementary School Educator **I:** Education/Educational Services **CN:** Allegheny-Clarion Valley Elementary School **DOB:** 02/18/1953 **PB:** Painesville **SC:** OH/USA **PT:** Kenneth White Edds; Audrey Helen Nelson **CH:** Peter James; Steven Alan **ED:** MEd, Slippery Rock University (1987); BS in Elementary Education, Slippery Rock State College (Now Slippery Rock University) (1975) **CT:** Certified in Early Childhood Education, Slippery Rock University (1995); Certified Reading Specialist, Clarion University (1994); Certified Elementary Teacher, Commonwealth of Pennsylvania **C:** Reading Specialist, Allegheny-Clarion Valley Elementary School, Allegheny-Clarion Valley School District, Foxburg, PA (1996-2017); Reading Specialist, Punxsutawney Area School District, PA (1994); First Grade Teacher, Seoul Foreign School, Republic of Korea (1977-1979); Third Grade Teacher, Brookville Area School District, PA (1975-1976) **CR:** Private Tutor, Brookville, PA (1993); Substitute Teacher, Derry Township School District, Hershey, PA (1990) **CIV:** Den Leader, Chairman of Committee, Boy Scouts of America, Elizabethtown, PA (1987-1994); Room Mother, Elizabethtown, PA (1985); Vacation Bible School Director, Teacher, Sunday School Teacher, Chairman, Christian Education Committee **MEM:** Secretary, Butler Outdoor Club (2004-2005); Conference Membership Committee, Keystone State Reading Association (Now Keystone State Literacy Association) (2002); President, Correspondence Secretary, Seneca Reading Council (2001-2002);

President, Butler Outdoor Club; Pennsylvania State Education Association (PSEA); Allegheny-Clarion Valley Education Association **MH:** Albert Nelson Marquis Lifetime Achievement Award; Marquis Who's Who Top Professional **B/I:** Ms. Berg wanted to be a teacher her whole life. **AV:** Swimming; Hiking; Bicycling; Reading; Table tennis

BERGGRUEN, NICOLAS, T: Founder, President **I:** Financial Services **CN:** Berggruen Holdings **DOB:** 08/10/1961 **PB:** Paris **SC:** France **PT:** Heinz Berggruen; Bettina Moissi **CH:** Two children **ED:** BS in Finance and International Business, New York University (1981) **C:** Founder, President, Berggruen Institute (2010-Present); Founder, President, Berggruen Holdings (1984-Present); Co-Founder, Alpha Investment Management (1984-2004); Associate, Jacobson & Company, Inc. (1983-1987); Analyst, Bass Brothers Enterprises **CR:** Board Member, Los Angeles County Museum of Art; Board Member, Museum Berggruen, Berlin, Germany **CIV:** Leadership Council, Center for Public Leadership, Harvard Kennedy School (2014); Global Advisory Council, Harvard University (2014); Trustee, Asia Society; Member, World Economic Forum; Advisory Council, The Brookings Institution; President's Global Council, New York University; Member, The Museum of Modern Art, NY; Member, Fondation Beyeler; Member, International Council, Serpentine Gallery; Member, International Advisory Board, Sotheby's; Participant, The Giving Pledge; Member, Nicolas Berggruen Charitable Trust **CW:** Co-Author, "Intelligent Governance for the 21st Century: A Middle Way Between West and East" (2012) **AW:** Ellis Island Medal of Honor (2018); Honoree, Haskins Giving Society Award Dinner, New York University (2016); Senior Fellow, Center for European Studies, Harvard University (2013); Richest Americans, Forbes 400 (2009) **MEM:** Pacific Council on International Policy; YPO; International Council, Tate Museum; Council on Foreign Relations; Foro Iberoamericano de Organismos Reguladores Radiológicos y Nucleares; Helena Group; Commission on Global Ethics and Citizenship

BERGMAN, JOHN, "JACK" WARREN, T: U.S. Representative from Michigan; Military Officer **I:** Government Administration/Government Relations/Government Services **DOB:** 02/02/1947 **PB:** Savage **SC:** MN/USA **MS:** Married **SPN:** Cindy Bergman **ED:** MBA, University West Florida College of Business (1975); BA in Business Administration, Gustavus Adolphus College (1969) **C:** U.S. Representative from Michigan's First Congressional District, United States Congress, Washington, DC (2017-Present); Commander, Marine Forces North, United States Marine Forces Reserve (2005-2009); Director, Reserve Affairs, Quantico, VA (2003-2005); Commander, Fourth Marine Aircraft Wing, New Orleans, LA (2000-2002); Commander, II Marine Expeditionary Force Augmentation Command Element, Camp Lejeune (2000); Chief of Staff, Marine Expeditionary Force Augmentation Command Element, Camp Pendleton, CA (1996-1999); Commander, Marine Corps Mobilization Station, Chicago, IL (1991-1995); Commanding Officer, Stewart ANGB, Newburgh, NY (1988-1990); Logistics Officer, Marine Corps Mobilization Station, Chicago, IL (1988); Pilot Training Officer, National Academy of Sciences, Glenview, United States Marine Corps Reserve (1978-1981); Flight Instructor, National Academy of Sciences, Whiting Field, Milton, FL (1972-1975); Squadron Pilot, Marine Corps Air Station, New River, NC (1970-1972); Member, Committee on the Budget; Member, Committee on Natural Resources; Member, Committee on Veterans' Affairs **CR:** Chairman, Marine Corps Reserve Policy Board, Secretary of the Navy (2001-

2003) **MIL:** Advanced through Grades to Brigadier General, United States Marine Corps (1969-2009); Commissioned Second Lieutenant, United States Marine Corps (1969) **AW:** Distinguished Service Medal, United States Navy; Defense Meritorious Service Medal; Air Medal with Valor Device and Strike/Flight Numeral "1"; Joint Meritorious Unit Award; Navy Unit Commendation; Navy Meritorious Unit Commendation with Two Bronze Service Stars; Selected Marine Corps Reserve Medal with One Silver Service Star; National Defense Service Medal with Two Bronze Service Stars; Vietnam Service Medal with Three Bronze Campaign Stars; Global War on Terrorism Service Medal; Navy and Marine Corps Overseas Service Ribbon with One Bronze Service Star; Armed Forces Reserve Medal with Gold Hourglass Devices; Vietnam Gallantry Cross with Bronze Star; Vietnam Gallantry Cross Unit Citation with Bronze Laurel Leaf Palm Emblem; Vietnam Civil Actions Unit Citation with Bronze Laurel Leaf Palm Emblem; Vietnam Campaign Medal with Silver Date Bar; Office of the Secretary of Defense Identification Badge **PA:** Republican

BERKLEY, ROBERT, "BOB" JOHN, T: Retired Federal Agency Professional **I:** Aviation **CN:** Federal Aviation Administration **DOB:** 10/02/1933 **PB:** Albion **SC:** MI/USA **PT:** Paul Clifford Berkley; Ina Muriel (Burroughs) Berkley **MS:** Married **SPN:** Sharon Irene Haynes (9/9/1955, Divorced 1965); Jacquelyn Jane (Lewis) Ballou **CH:** Thomas Alan; Richard Jon; Luann Michele **ED:** BS in Police Administration, California State University (1962); AA, Jackson Community College (1953) **C:** Retired, Federal Aviation Administration, Seattle, WA (1999); Office Manager, Federal Aviation Administration, Seattle, WA (1973-1999); Special Agent, Federal Aviation Administration, Seattle, WA (1972-1999); Investigator, U.S. Civil Service Commission (1962-1963, 1966-1972); Police Officer, Claremont, CA (1959-1962, 1963-1966) **CIV:** Local Chairman, Selective Service Board, Washington, DC (1981-2001) **MIL:** Sergeant, U.S. Marine Corps (1953-1956) **MEM:** President, Local Area Genealogical Society (2006-2009); State Representative, Region 8, Washington State Genealogical Society (2004-2009); Patron, American Legion, Eastern Star (1989-1990); President, State Secretary, Sons of the American Revolution (1989-1992); Master, Masons (1984); Scottish Rite, Shriners **MH:** Albert Nelson Marquis Lifetime Achievement Award; Marquis Who's Who Top Professional **AV:** Researching computers; Practicing photography; Camping; Traveling **RE:** Methodist

BERLIN, KENNETH DARRELL, T: Regents Professor, Consultant, Researcher, Instructor **I:** Education/Educational Services **DOB:** 06/12/1933 **PB:** Quincy **SC:** IL/USA **PT:** Kenneth Marion Fischer; Mary Esther (Beckley) Berlin **MS:** Married **SPN:** Grace Frances Berlin (4/3/1937) **CH:** Grace Esther; James Darrell **ED:** Post-Doctoral Fellow, University of Florida (1958-1960); PhD, University of Illinois (1958); BA, North Central College, Naperville, IL, Cum Laude (1955) **C:** Regents Professor, Oklahoma State University (1971-Present); Professor, Oklahoma State University (1966-1971); Associate Professor, Oklahoma State University (1963-1966); Assistant Professor of Chemistry, Oklahoma State University (1960-1963); Postdoctoral Fellow, University of Florida, Gainesville, FL (1958-1960) **CR:** Arizona Disease Control Commission (1989-Present); Special Consultant, National Cancer Institute, Bethesda, MD (1969-Present); American Heart Association (1983-1986); Consultant, E.I. DuPont Co., Wilmington, DE (1969-1970) **CW:** Co-Author, "Phosphorous Stereochem" (1977); Co-Author, "Organic Chemistry" (1972);

Contributor, Research Journal of Organic Chemistry (1960); Contributor, Articles, Professional Journals; Author, 347 Published Papers, Peer-Reviewed Journals; Patentee, 27 Patents **AW:** Elected Member, National Academy of Inventors (2015, 2016); Outstanding Professor Award, College of Arts and Science (2014); Listee, Top 20 Scientists and Engineers in Oklahoma (2013); Rall Medal (2011); Fellow, American Chemical Society (2011); International Golden Torch Award (2008); Oklahoma Medallion (2003); Regents Distinguished Research Award (2003); Eminent Faculty Award (1998); Regents Distinguished Teaching Award (1998); Burlington Northern Faculty Achievement Award (1988); Oklahoma Chemist of the Year Award (1977); Scientist of the Year, Oklahoma Academy of Science (1976); Sigma Xi Research Award, Oklahoma State University (1969) **MEM:** International Society of Heterocyclic Chemists; Alpha Chi Sigma; Senior Member, Royal Society of London; American Chemical Society **MH:** Albert Nelson Marquis Lifetime Achievement Award **AS:** Dr. Berlin attributes his success to hard work and perseverance. **B/I:** Dr. Berlin became involved in his profession because of some of his college and graduate mentors. In addition, he became involved in education because it appealed to him when he was in college. Prior to this discovery, Dr. Berlin was unsure if he could attend college because of his financial situation. Luckily, he was offered an assistantship, which changed his entire career course. **AV:** Playing tennis; Coin collecting/numismatics; Traveling **RE:** Assembly of God Church **THT:** Dr. Berlin is helpful and forgiving.

BERLIND, ROGER S., T: Stage and Film Producer **I:** Media & Entertainment **DOB:** 06/27/1930 **PB:** New York **SC:** NY/USA **PT:** Peter Sydney Berlind; Mae (Miller) Berlind **MS:** Married **SPN:** Brook Wheeler (05/19/1979); Helen Polk Clark (07/07/1962, Deceased) **CH:** William Polk Berlind **ED:** AB, Princeton University, Princeton, NJ (1952) **C:** Vice-Chairman of the Board, Shearson Lehman Brothers, New York, NY (1974-1975); Chief Executive Officer, Shearson Lehman Brothers, New York, NY (1969-1973); Chairman, Executive Committee, Cogan, Berlind, Weill & Levitt, Inc., New York, NY (1965-1969); General Partner, Carter, Berlind & Weill, New York, NY (1960-1965); Account Executive, Eastman Dillon, Union Securities & Co., New York, NY (1956-1960) **CR:** Board of Directors, Lehman Brothers Holdings, Inc. (1985-Present) **CIV:** Honorary Trustee, American Academy of Dramatic Arts **MIL:** Counter Intelligence Corps, United States Army (1952-1954) **CW:** Producer, "Beyond Therapy" (1987); Producer, "The Merchant"; Producer, "Rex"; Producer, "Music Is"; Producer, "Diversions and Delights"; Producer, "The 1940s Radio Hour"; Producer, "Passione"; Producer, "The Lady from Dubuque"; Producer, "Amadeus"; Producer, "Sophisticated Ladies"; Producer, "Lydie Breeze"; Producer, "Nine"; Producer, "All's Well That Ends Well"; Producer, "The Real Thing"; Producer, "The Rink"; Producer, "Joe Egg"; Producer, "After the Fall"; Producer, "Precious Sons"; Producer, "Big Deal"; Producer, "Long Day's Journey Into Night"; Producer, "Ain't Misbehavin"; Producer, "Jerome Robbins' Broadway"; Producer, "City of Angels"; Producer, "Artist Descending a Staircase"; Producer, "Lettice and Lovage"; Producer, "Death and the Maiden"; Producer, "Guys and Dolls"; Producer, "Passion"; Producer, "Indiscretions"; Producer, "Hamlet"; Producer, "Getting Away With Murder"; Producer, "A Funny Thing Happened on the Way to the Forum"; Producer, "Skylight"; Producer, "Steel Pier"; Producer, "The Life"; Producer, "A View From The Bridge"; Producer, "The Judas Kiss"; Producer, "The Blue Room"; Producer, "Closer"; Producer, "Amy's View"; Pro-

ducer, "Kiss Me Kate"; Producer, "Copenhagen"; Producer, "Proof"; Producer, "Dance of Death"; Producer, "Medea"; Producer, "The Wild Party"; Producer, "Anna in the Tropics"; Producer, "Wonderful Town"; Producer, "Caroline or Change"; Producer, "Who's Afraid of Virginia Woolf"; Producer, "Doubt"; Producer, Play, "Well"; Producer, "Faith Healer and History Boys"; Producer, "The Vertical Hour"; Producer, Play, "The Year of Magical Thinking"; Producer, "Deuce"; Producer, Play, "Curtains"; Producer, "The Caine Mutiny Court Martial"; Producer, "Rock'n'Roll"; Producer, "Is He Dead?"; Producer, "Gypsy 13"; Producer, "Curious Incident of the Dog in the Nighttime"; Producer, "Book of Mormon"; Producer, "Dear Evan Hanson"; Producer, "Hello, Dolly!"; Producer, "Mean Girls" **AW:** Winner, 25 Tony Awards **MEM:** Former Governor, League of American Theatres and Producers; Former Member, Princeton Club; University Club; Century Association; Knickerbocker Club **MH:** Albert Nelson Marquis Lifetime Achievement Award

BERLY, ALICE ANNE, T: Financial Administrator (Retired) **I:** Financial Services **DOB:** 08/18/1935 **PB:** Portland **SC:** OR/USA **PT:** John Joseph (1910-2001); Curtiss Roxanne (Hottel) Pearl (1908-1999) **MS:** Widowed **SPN:** Thomas E. Berly (09/16/1979, Died 03/23/2016); Arthur Raymond Woods (10/16/1979, Died 12/25/1980); Tommy Joe Pressley (12/12/1954, Divorced 06/1963) **CH:** Diana Lynn Pressley Covington (1960) **ED:** MBA, UNLV (1987); BSBA, UNLV (1985); AA, Clark County Community College (1983) **C:** Retired (1997); Financial Administrator, U.S. District Court District of Nevada (1987-1997); Instructor, 55 Alive Mature Driving, Las Vegas, NV (1987-1993) **MEM:** Institute of Management Accountants, Inc.; Retired Member, The Honor Society of Phi Kappa Phi **MH:** Albert Nelson Marquis Lifetime Achievement Award **B/I:** Ms. Berly became involved in her profession because she took a safe driving class in her 50s and felt that she could do a better job of teaching than her teacher at the time. **AV:** Writing; Swimming; Whitewater rafting; Riding horses **RE:** Christian **THT:** Ms. Berly believes older students shouldn't be discredited. When she finished high school, she did not feel that she was ready for college. She felt that if she was to go straight to college she would waste her time and her parents' money. At the time, she worked at the Hotel Tropicana, which eventually burned in a fire and closed for seven months. Her husband then suggested she go back to school and so she did.

BERNARD, SHARON E., ESQ., T: Lawyer **I:** Law and Legal Services **DOB:** 04/19/1943 **PB:** Detroit **SC:** MI/USA **PT:** John Robert Bernard; Dorothea Cleo (Graves) Bernard **MS:** Single **CH:** Cylenthia Latoya Miller; Sharon Gayle Miller **ED:** BSL, JD, University of Arkansas (1969) **C:** First Vice President, Director of Community Relations, Michigan National Bank (1995-Present); Staff Attorney, Michigan National Bank (1975-Present); Vice President, Senior Business Development and Community Relations Officer, Michigan National Bank (1982-1994); Various Administrative Positions, Michigan National Bank (1977-1982); Private Practice (1974-1974); President, Chief Executive Officer, Plaza Theater & Miller Enterprises (1961-1974) **CR:** Member, Advisory Board, Wayne County Neighborhood Legal Services **CIV:** Vice Chair of Community Services (1995-Present); Vice Chair, United Way for Southeastern Michigan (1988-Present); Chair, Ennis Center for Children (1988-Present); President, Neighborhood Service Organization (1984-1994); Vice President, United Way for Southeastern Michigan (1989); Vice Chair, United Community Services (1989); Board of Directors, Detroit

Branch, NAACP (1986-1989); Chair, Urban League of Detroit and Southeastern MI (1986-1989); Board of Directors, National Committee for Prevention Child Abuse; Board of Directors, Boys Hope **MEM:** Kappa Beta Pi **BAR:** State Bar of Michigan (1975); Arkansas Bar Association (1970) **MH:** Albert Nelson Marquis Lifetime Achievement Award **B/I:** Ms. Bernard became involved in her profession because she was a junior in college and went to a law school that had only three women. She was the president of the legal sorority and has never looked back. **PA:** Democrat **RE:** Roman Catholic

BERNHARDT, DAVID LONGLY, T: United States Secretary of the Interior **I:** Government Administration/Government Relations/Government Services **DOB:** 08/17/1969 **PB:** Rifle **SC:** CO/USA **MS:** Married **SPN:** Gena Rae Bernhardt **CH:** William; Katherine **ED:** JD, National Law Center, The George Washington University, with Honors (1994); BA in Political Science, University of Northern Colorado, Greeley, CO (1990) **C:** United States Secretary of the Interior, U.S. Department of the Interior (2019-Present); Acting United States Secretary of the Interior, U.S. Department of the Interior (2019); Deputy Secretary, U.S. Department of the Interior (2017-2019); Head, Energy, Environment & Resource Strategies Department, Brownstein Hyatt Farber Schreck, LLP (2013-Present); Shareholder, Brownstein Hyatt Farber Schreck, LLP, Washington, DC (2009-Present); Solicitor, U.S. Department of the Interior (2006-2009); Deputy Solicitor, U.S. Department of the Interior (2005-2006); Deputy Chief of Staff, Counselor to Secretary, U.S. Department of the Interior (2004-2005); Director, Congressional Affairs, Counselor to Secretary, U.S. Department of the Interior, Washington, DC (2001-2004); Associate, Brownstein, Hyatt & Farber, Professional Corporation (Now Brownstein Hyatt Farber Schreck, LLP), Denver, CO (1998-2001); Legislative Director to Representative Scott McInnis, U.S. House of Representatives, Washington, DC (1992-1998) **CR:** Chairman, International Boundary Commission on United States and Canada (2007-2009) **BAR:** Colorado Bar Association **AV:** Hunting; Angling

BERNSTEIN, CARL, T: Jewelry Designer; Artist **I:** Fine Art **DOB:** 12/11/1930 **PB:** Botosani **SC:** Romania **PT:** Shalom Bernstein; Deborah Bernstein **MS:** Married **SPN:** Sylvia Dorfman (08/10/1983); Lena Goldstein (11/12/1951, Divorced 06/1978) **CH:** Shlomo; Selma; Rony **ED:** Coursework, Art School, Bat Yam, Israel (1965-1970); Coursework, Laurian, Romania (1948) **C:** Owner, Gold Styles Inc., New York, NY (1982-Present); Teacher, Arts, Art History, Art School, Bat Yam, Israel (1972-1975) **CR:** Chairman, Jewelers Organization, Tel-Aviv, Israel (1970-1975); Chairman, Arts Students Association **CW:** Artist, Flecher Gallery, Woodstock, NY (2000); Artist, 4 West Gallery, Piermont, NY (2000); Artist, Arts Forum, New York, NY (1999-2000); Artist, Exhibition, New York Institute of Technology (1999); Artist, Exhibition, World Art Gallery, New York, NY (1998) **AW:** Zahal Award, Israeli Army (1953-1958) **AV:** Painting; Travel; Camping; Archaeology **PA:** Democrat **RE:** Jewish

BERNSTEIN, CARL, T: Investigative Journalist; Author **I:** Writing and Editing **DOB:** 02/14/1944 **PB:** Washington, DC **SC:** DC/USA **PT:** Alfred David Bernstein; Sylvia (Walker) Bernstein **MS:** Married **SPN:** Christine Kuehbeck (2003); Nora Ephron (04/14/1976, Divorced 1980); Carol Ann Honsa (04/28/1968, Divorced 1972) **CH:** Jacob Walker; Max Ephron **ED:** LLD, Boston University (1975); Coursework, University of Maryland (1961-1964) **C:** Guest Lecturer, Stony Brook University, NY (2013-Present); Contributing Editor, Vanity Fair (1997-Present); Corresponding Contributor, TIME

Magazine (1990-1991); Correspondent, ABC News, NY (1981-1984); Washington Bureau Chief, ABC News (1979-1981); Reporter, The Washington Post (1966-1976); Reporter, Elizabeth Journal, NJ (1965-1966); From Copyboy to Reporter, Washington Star (1960-1965); Political Commentator, CNN **CR:** Visiting Professor, New York University (1992); Executive Editor, Voter.com **CIV:** With, Army of the United States (1968) **CW:** Author, "A Woman in Charge: The Life of Hillary Rodham Clinton" (2007); Co-author with Marco Politi, "His Holiness: John Paul II and the History of Our Time" (1996); Author, "Loyalties: A Son's Memoir" (1989); Co-author with Bob Woodward, "The Final Days" (1976); Co-author with Bob Woodward, "All The President's Men" (1974); Contributor, Articles to Professional Journals **AW:** Gold Medal, University of Missouri School of Journalism (1972); Pulitzer Prize (1972); Drew Pearson Prize for Investigative Reporting of Watergate (1972); First Prize for Feature Writing (1966); First Prize for General Reporting, New Jersey Press Association (1966) First Prize for Investigative Reporting (1966); George Polk Memorial Award; Worth Bingham Prize; Heywood Broun Award, International Newspaper Guild; Sigma Delta Chi Distinguished Service Award; Sidney Hillman Foundation Award

BERNSTEIN, PHYLISS LOUISE, PHD, T: Psychologist **I:** Health, Wellness and Fitness **DOB:** 11/27/1940 **PB:** Baltimore **SC:** MD/USA **PT:** Samuel Wilfred Wilke; Helen Dorothy (Gerson) Wilke **MS:** Married **SPN:** Robert **CH:** Steve; Susan; David **ED:** Doctor of Philosophy in Counseling Psychology, University of Missouri, Kansas City, MO, Summa Cum Laude (1986); Master of Science in Psychology, Avila College, Summa Cum Laude (1981); Bachelor of Arts in Psychology, Avila College, Summa Cum Laude (1980) **CT:** Licensed Psychologist, Missouri **C:** Semi-Retired (2006); Psychologist in Private Practice, Kansas City, MO (1986-2006); Associate Psychologist, Counseling and Human Development Services, Kansas City, MO (1985-1986); Psychotherapist, Community Counseling Center, Kansas City, MO (1983-1985) **CR:** With, Jewish Vocational Services, Kansas City, MO (1988-1991); Director, Jewish Community Foundation; With, Jewish Family and Children Services; With, Department of Education, University of Missouri, Kansas City, MO **CIV:** Vice President, Board of Directors, Advertising Icon Museum, Kansas City, MO (2006-Present); Advisory Board Member, Friendship House (2001-Present); Lifetime Member, National Council of Jewish Women, Kansas City, MO; Involved, Ronald McDonald House Charities; Involved, Children's Mercy Hospital; Board of Counselors, Avila University; Eponym, Numerous Scholarships, University of Missouri–Kansas City; Involved, Jewish Federation; Board Member, Jewish Family Services; Board Member, Jewish Community Foundation; Involved, Genesis School Board; Involved, Jewish Vocational Services; Education Division Board, University of Missouri–Kansas City **CW:** Contributor **AW:** Outstanding Alumni Award, Avila College (1995); Up and Comers Award, Kansas City Business Journal **MEM:** American Psychological Association; Greater Kansas City Psychological Association; Psi Chi; Pi Lambda Theta; Phi Kappa Phi **MH:** Albert Nelson Marquis Lifetime Achievement Award **B/I:** After working at a bank and striving throughout her college studies, Dr. Bernstein became involved in her profession after receiving a master's degree in psychology at Avila College, and her doctorate at the University of Missouri-Kansas City. **AV:** Scuba diving; Bungee jumping; Skiing; Horseback riding; Reading; Playing with

grandchildren; Hiking; Walking; Passionate about music from classical to rap; Avid all sports fan **RE:** Jewish

BERRY, DEAN G., T: Chief Executive Officer **I:** Manufacturing **CN:** Sterling Distributors **CH:** Taylor; Dean Jr.; Lauren **ED:** BSBA, McDonough School of Business, Georgetown University (1999) **C:** Owner, Sterling Distributors (2001-Present); Chief Executive Officer, President, Denled Holdings (2004-Present); Financial Planner **CIV:** Founder, Florida Flight Elite **AS:** Mr. Berry attributes his success to his selfless nature, discipline and focus. **B/I:** Mr. Berry became involved in his profession because of his desire to help others.

BERRY, HALLE MARIA, T: Actress **I:** Media & Entertainment **DOB:** 08/14/1966 **PB:** Cleveland **SC:** OH/USA **PT:** Jerome Berry; Judith Ann (Hawkins) Berry **MS:** Divorced **SPN:** Olivier Martinez (07/13/2013-12/2016); Eric Benét (01/24/2001-01/03/2005); David Christopher Justice (12/31/1992-06/24/1997) **CH:** Nahla Ariela Aubry; Maceo Robert Martinez **ED:** BA, Cuyahoga Community College, Cleveland, OH (1986) **CW:** Director, Actress, "Bruised" (2020); Executive Producer, "Boomerang" (2019); Actress, "John Wick: Chapter 3 – Parabellum" (2019); Actress, "Kingsman: The Golden Circle" (2017); Actress, "Kings" (2017); Actress, Producer, "Kidnap" (2017); Actress, Executive Producer, "Extant" (2014-2015); Actress, "X-Men: Days of Future Past" (2014); Actress, "The Call" (2013); Actress, "Movie 43" (2013); Actress, "Cloud Atlas" (2012); Actress, "Dark Tide" (2012); Actress, "New Year's Eve" (2011); Voice Actress, "The Simpsons" (2011); Actress, Producer, "Frankie & Alice" (2010); Actress, "Things We Lost in the Fire" (2007); Actress, "Perfect Stranger" (2007); Actress, "X-Men: The Last Stand" (2006); Executive Producer, "Lackawanna Blues" (2005); Voice Actress, "Robots" (2005); Actress, "Their Eyes Were Watching God" (2005); Actress, "Catwoman" (2004); Actress, "Gothika" (2003); Actress, "X2: X-Men United" (2003); Actress, "Die Another Day" (2002); Actress, "Monster's Ball" (2001); Actress, "Swordfish" (2001); Actress, "X-Men" (2000); Actress, Executive Producer, "Introducing Dorothy Dandridge" (1999); Actress, "Welcome to Hollywood" (1998); Actress, "Why Do Fools Fall in Love" (1998); Actress, "Bulworth" (1998); Actress, "The Wedding" (1998); Actress, "B*A*P*S" (1997); Actress, "The Rich Man's Wife" (1996); Actress, "Race the Sun" (1996); Actress, "Executive Decision" (1996); Actress, "Losing Isaiah" (1995); Actress, "Solomon & Sheba" (1995); Actress, "The Flintstones" (1994); Actress, "The Program" (1993); Actress, "Father Hood" (1993); Actress, "Queen" (1993); Actress, "Boomerang" (1992); Actress, "Knots Landing" (1991); Actress, "The Last Boy Scout" (1991); Actress, "Strictly Business" (1991); Actress, "Jungle Fever" (1991); Actress, "They Came from Outer Space" (1991); Actress, "A Different World" (1991); Actress, "Amen" (1991); Actress, "Living Dolls" (1989) **AW:** NAACP Image Award for Outstanding Actress in a Motion Picture (2002, 2011); Sherry Lansing Leadership Award, The Hollywood Reporter (2009); BET Award for Best Actress, BET Interactive, LLC (2002, 2004, 2008); Star, Motion Picture Category, Hollywood Walk of Fame, Hollywood Chamber of Commerce (2007); NAACP Image Award for Outstanding Supporting Actress in a Motion Picture, NAACP (2003); Academy Award for Best Actress, Academy of Motion Picture Arts and Sciences (2002); Screen Actors Guild Award for Outstanding Performance by a Female Actor in a Leading Role in a Motion Picture, SAG-AFTRA (2002); Award for Best Actress, National Board of Review (2002); Black Reel Award for Best Actress,

Black Reel Awards (2002); AFI Award for Actress of the Year, American Film Institute (2001); Berlinale Award for Best Actress, Berlin International Film Festival (2001); Primetime Emmy Award for Outstanding Lead Actress in a Limited Series or Television Movie, Television Academy (2000); Golden Globe Award for Best Actress in a Miniseries or Motion Picture – Television, Hollywood Foreign Press Association (2000); Screen Actors Guild Award for Outstanding Performance by a Female Actor in a Television Movie or Miniseries, SAG-AFTRA (2000); NAACP Image Award for Outstanding Actress in a Television Movie, Mini-Series, or Dramatic Special, NAACP (1995, 2000)

BERRYHILL, MARY FINLEY, RN, BSN, T: Emergency Nurse **I:** Medicine & Health Care **DOB:** 12/11/1944 **PB:** Miami Beach **SC:** FL/USA **PT:** Clyde A. Finley; Alice J. (White) Finley **MS:** Married **SPN:** Robert L. Snyder (07/18/1996); Michael W. Berryhill (Divorced 11/1977) **CH:** Jennifer Ann (Clairemarie); John Michael **ED:** BSN, University of Florida (1967) **CT:** Registered Nurse; Certified Emergency Nurse; Emergency Nursing Pediatric Course Instructor; Trauma Nurse Core Course Instructor **C:** Student Health Service Nurse, Berkshire School, Sheffield, MA (2001-2012); Educator, Fairview Hospital, Berkshire Health System, Great Barrington, MA (1998-2010); Shift Director, Fairview Hospital, Great Barrington, MA (1992-1999); Nurse, Emergency Department, Fairview Hospital, Great Barrington, MA (1984-2003); Student Health Service Nurse, Berkshire School, Sheffield, MA (1978-1990); State Coordinator, American Society for Psychoprophylaxis in Obstetrics, Ocala, FL (1974-1978); Childbirth Educator, Ocala, FL (1970-1978); Outpatient Obstetrics Nurse, Keith H. Knorr, MD, PA, Ocala, FL (1970-1972); Research Associate, University of Florida College of Nursing, Gainesville, FL (1968-1970); Staff Nurse, Nurse Clinician, UF Health Shands Hospital, University of Florida Health, Gainesville, FL (1967-1968) **CR:** Teacher of Emergency Childbirth, Pediatric Emergency Care and Child Abuse Recognition and Care to EMTs **CIV:** Emergency Childbirth Instructor, Southern Berkshire Volunteer Ambulance Squad, Great Barrington, MA (1983-1993, 2004-Present); Appalachian Trail Volunteer (1994); Member, Vice President, Southern Berkshire Volunteer Ambulance Squad (1984-1985) **AW:** Named OGYN Nurse of the Year, Florida Nurses Association, American College of Obstetricians and Gynecologists (1977) **MEM:** Emergency Nurse Pediatrics Curriculum Instructor, Emergency Nurses Association (1993-2012); Massachusetts State Pediatrics Committee, Emergency Nurses Association (1994-2010); Trauma Nurse Core Curriculum Instructor, Emergency Nurses Association (1992-2008); President, Emergency Nurses Association (1998, 1999); Treasurer, Emergency Nurses Association, Berkshire Chapter, MA (1993); Emergency Nurses Association **MH:** Albert Nelson Marquis Lifetime Achievement Award **B/I:** Mrs. Berryhill became involved in her profession because she came from a medical family. Her daughter was a nurse, her paternal grandfather was a surgeon, and her grandmother was also a nurse. **AV:** Cross country skiing; Hiking; Backpacking; White water canoeing; Birding

BERTINELLI, VALERIE ANNE, T: Actress; Television Personality **I:** Media & Entertainment **CN:** Food Network **DOB:** 04/23/1960 **PB:** Wilmington **SC:** DE/USA **PT:** Andrew Bertinelli; Nancy (Carvin) Bertinelli **MS:** Married **SPN:** Tom Vitale (01/01/2011); Eddie Van Halen (04/11/1981, Divorced 12/20/2007) **CH:** Wolfgang Van Halen **ED:** Coursework, Tami Lynn School of Artists, CA **CR:** Spokesperson, Jenny Craig (2009-2013) **CW:** Host, "Family Food Showdown," Food Network

(2019-Present); Host, "Family Restaurant Rivals," Food Network (2019-Present); Co-Host, "Kids Baking Championship," Food Network (2015-Present); Host, "Valerie's Home Cooking," Food Network (2015-Present); Actress, "Hot in Cleveland" (2010-2015); Author, "One Dish at a Time: Delicious Recipes and Stories from My Italian-American Childhood and Beyond" (2012); Author, "Finding It: And Satisfying My Hunger for Life without Opening the Fridge" (2009); Appearance, "Valerie Bertinelli: Losing It and Keeping Fit" (2009); Author, "Losing It... And Gaining My Life Back One Pound at a Time" (2008); Actress, "True Confessions of a Hollywood Starlet" (2008); Actress, "Claire" (2007); Actress, "One Day at a Time Reunion" (2005); Actress, "Crazy Love" (2003); Actress, "Finding John Christmas" (2003); Actress, "Touched by an Angel" (2001-2003); Guest Appearance, "Who Wants to be a Millionaire" (2001); Voice Actress, "Family Guy" (2001); Actress, "Personally Yours" (2000); Actress, "Night Sins" (1997); Actress, "A Case for Life" (1996); Actress, "Two Mothers for Zachery" (1996); Actress, "The Haunting of Helen Walker" (1995); Actress, "Cafe Americain" (1993-1994); Actress, "Aladdin and His Magic Lamp, Murder of Innocence" (1993); Actress, "What She Doesn't Know" (1992); Actress, "In a Child's Name" (1991); Actress, "Sydney" (1990); Actress, "Taken Away" (1989); Actress, "Pancho Barnes" (1988); Actress, "Number One with a Bullet" (1987); Actress, "I'll Take Manhattan" (1987); Actress, "Rockabye" (1986); Actress, "Ordinary Heros" (1986); Actress, "Silent Witness" (1985); Actress, "The Seduction of Gina" (1984); Actress, "Shattered Vows" (1984); Actress, "I Was a Mail Order Bride" (1982); Actress, "The Princess and the Cabbie" (1981); Actress, "The Promise of Love" (1980); Actress, "One Day at a Time" (1975-1984); Actress, "Young Love, First Love" (1979); Actress, "The Secret of Charles Dickens" (1979); Actress, "C.H.O.M.P.S." (1979); Guest Appearance, "The Hardy Boys/Nancy Drew Mysteries" (1978); Guest Appearance, "Apple's Way" (1974); Actress, "The Magic of David Copperfield" **AW:** Emmy Award for Outstanding Culinary Program, Television Academy (2019); Emmy Award for Outstanding Culinary Host, Television Academy (2019); Star, Hollywood Walk of Fame (2012)

BERTKA, SARA, T: Art Director, Business Analyst II **I:** Financial Services **CN:** BOK Financial **ED:** AA, The School of Advertising Art (Now The Modern College of Design), Kettering, OH (2018); Diploma, Bluffton High School, Bluffton, OH (2016) **C:** Business Analyst II, Art Director, BOK Financial, Tulsa, OK (2018-Present); Intern, Digital Solutions Group, BOK Financial, Tulsa, OK (2018); Intern, Design, TotallyPromotional.com, Coldwater, OH (2017); Contract Graphic Designer, United Desert Gateway, El Centro, CA (2017); Designer, Marybeth's Cottage, Inc., Jacksonville, FL (2016-2017); Graphic Designer, Contract, BMoore Connected, Bluffton, OH (2016-2017) **CIV:** Photographer, Guns & Ribbons, Pink Ribbon Girls (2017); Children's Leader, AWANA, Cable Road Alliance Church (2012-2016); Volunteer, Media Team Member, Cable Road Alliance Church, Lima, OH (2011-2016); Small Group Leader, Youth For Christ/USA Inc., Tulsa, OK; Teacher, Sunday School, Bible Study, Fellowship Bible Church, Tulsa, OK **AW:** American Graphic Design Award, Graphic Design USA (2018); Daniel E. Johnson Memorial Scholarship, The School of Advertising Art (Now The Modern College of Design) (2016) **AS:** Ms. Bertka attributes her success to her faith in God, who has blessed her with talent and opportunity. In taking advantage of her circumstances, she has worked hard and taken risks. In fact, Ms. Bertka had never been to Oklahoma before working for BOK Financial, but was

brave enough to take the chance on an unfamiliar place. **B/I:** Ms. Bertka became involved in her profession because of her enjoyment of art and her natural talents. She credits her high school's well-developed art program for exposing her to an array of mediums and career options; initially a fine arts student, Ms. Bertka saw a career path in graphic and digital design. **AV:** Cooking; Baking

BERTOLINI, MARK T., T: Chairman and Chief Executive Officer (Retired) **I:** Medicine & Health Care **CN:** Aetna Inc. **ED:** MBA in Finance, Cornell University; BS in Business Administration, Wayne State University **C:** Chairman, Chief Executive Officer, Aetna Inc., Hartford, CT (2011-2018); President, Chief Executive Officer, Aetna, Inc., Hartford, CT (2010-2011); President, Aetna, Inc., Hartford, CT (2007-2010); Executive Vice President, Business Operations, Aetna, Inc., Hartford, CT (2007); Executive Vice President, Regional Business, Aetna, Inc., Hartford, CT (2006-2007); Senior Vice President, Regional Business, Aetna, Inc., Hartford, CT (2005-2006); Senior Vice President, Specialty Group, Aetna, Inc., Hartford, CT (2005); Senior Vice President, Specialty Products, Aetna, Inc., Hartford, CT (2003-2005); Senior Vice President, Regional & Middle Market, Cigna Corp., (2002-2003); Senior Vice President, National Sales & Delivery, Cigna Corp., (2000-2002); Child Executive Officer, SelectCare (1992-1995; Executive Vice President, NYLCare Health Plans **CR:** Board of Directors, Aetna Inc. (2010-Present) **CIV:** Advisory board, Cornell University School Human Ecology; Chairman, Operations Committee, Association Health Insurance Plans; Board of Directors, The Connecticut Business & Industry Association; Board of directors, University of Connecticut Health Center

BERTRAM, CHRISTOPHER D., T: Engineer **I:** Engineering **DOB:** 11/17/1963 **PB:** Colorado Springs **SC:** CO/USA **PT:** David Frederick Bertram; Carmen Bertram **ED:** AAS in Network Technologies, Heald Institute of Technology (1997); AAS in Electronics Technology, Heald Institute of Technology (1996); AS, American River College (1994); AA in Social and Behavioral Science, Merritt College (1990); AS in Mathematics, Merritt College (1990) **C:** Engineer, Perkin Elmer (2000-Present); With, TYN Research, San Francisco, CA (1994-Present); Engineer, Programmer, Applied Surfaces Technology, Inc., San Carlos, California (1996-2001); Numistic Die Finisher, Treasury Department, San Francisco, CA (1991-1994) **CR:** Chief Executive Officer, Analog Data Enterprises **MIL:** With, U.S. Navy (1985-1990) **CW:** Editor, Publisher, Bay Area Rock Magazine (1989-1992); Inventor, Passive Prosthetic Bionic Light Interpreter **MEM:** IEEE; American Society of Composers, Authors and Publishers (ASCAP); Association for Computing Machinery **MH:** Albert Nelson Marquis Lifetime Achievement Award **AV:** Computer science

BESHEAR, ANDREW, "ANDY" GRAHAM, T: Governor of Kentucky **I:** Government Administration/Government Relations/Government Services **DOB:** 11/29/1977 **PB:** Louisville **SC:** KY/USA **PT:** Steve Beshear; Jane Beshear **MS:** Married **SPN:** Britainy Beshear **CH:** Two children **ED:** JD, School of Law, University of Virginia; BA, Vanderbilt University, Magna Cum Laude **C:** Governor, Commonwealth of Kentucky (2019-Present); Attorney General, Commonwealth of Kentucky (2016-2019); With, Stites & Harbison, PLLC (2005) **PA:** Democrat **RE:** Christian

BETH, RICHARD SPRAGUE, PHD, T: Retired **I:** Civil Service **DOB:** 06/29/1944 **PB:** Princeton **SC:** NJ/USA **PT:** Richard Alexander; Hettie (Sprague) B. **MS:** Married **SPN:** Claire Emma

(Kreymborg) B. (05/08/1982); Janet McFerren (05/24/1975, Divorced 1981) **CH:** Hettie Jeanette B. (Deceased); Erika Anne B.; Two Grandchildren **ED:** Doctor of Philosophy in Political Science, Yale University (1976); Master of Philosophy in Political Science, Yale University (1970); Bachelor of Arts in Public Affairs, Princeton University, Magna Cum Laude (1966); Diploma, Bellport High School, New York (1962) **C:** Specialist on Congress & the Legislative Process, Congressional Research Service, Library of Congress, Washington, DC (1993-2017); Specialist Legislative Process & Head Legislative & Budget Process Secretary, Congressional Research Service (1988-1993); Analyst, American National Government, Congressional Research Service (1980-1988); Assistant Professor of Political Science, Southwest Missouri State University, Springfield, MO (1978-1980); Instructor to Assistant Professor of Political Science, Boston University (1974-1978) **CIV:** Citizens Advisory Committee, School Board, Prince George's County, Maryland (1993-1997); Democratic Socialists of America (1982-1992); Boston Food Cooperative (1974-1978); Active, Various Election Campaigns, Wisconsin, Connecticut, New York (1967-1972) **MIL:** First Lieutenant to Captain, Adjutant General Corps, U.S. Army, Fort Bragg, NC (1970-1972) **CW:** Author, Numerous Congressional Research Service Reports, Including "Implementing Bills for Trade Agreements: Statutory Procedures Under Trade Promotion Authority", "Lame Duck Sessions of Congress," "Procedures for Considering Changes in Senate Rules," "Sessions, Adjournments & Recesses of Congress," "Supreme Court Nominations: Senate Floor Procedure & Practice" and Many More; Author, Professional Conference Papers, Including "The Senate's Nuclear Precedent: Implications for Efforts to Control the Filibuster," ""Leadership Tools for Managing US Senate," "On Recent German Reception of Peirce," "Is the Committee of the Whole the House? Implications of Michel v. Anderson," "What We Don't Know About Filibusters," ""How Transformationalists Think About Transformation" and More; Author, Contributor to Professional Journals, Including Book Reviews, Review Articles and Research on the House of Representatives **AW:** Inducted, Bellport High School Wall of Fame, New York (2017); Lifetime Achievement CRS Directors Award (2011); Distinguished Service Award, Congressional Research Employees Association (1984, 1986); Grantee, National Endowment for the Humanities (1979); Army Commendation Medal (1972); Graduate Fellow, National Science Foundation (1966-1970); Valedictorian, Bellport High School, New York (1962) **MEM:** Secretary, Congressional Research Employees Association (2002-2003); Vice President, Congressional Research Employees Association (1984-1985); Phi Beta Kappa (1966); Transformational Politics Section, American Political Science Association; Conference Group on Interpretive Methods, American Political Science Association; Qualitative & Multi-Method Research Section, American Political Science Association; Legislative Studies Section, American Political Science Association **MH:** Albert Nelson Marquis Lifetime Achievement Award **AV:** Legislative process and procedure; Community action; Political group dynamics; Theorizing on political interaction; Interpretive methods in political science; Poetry

BEURET, KEVIN PAUL, T: Secondary School Educator **I:** Education/Educational Services **DOB:** 07/01/1945 **PB:** Garrett **SC:** IN/USA **PT:** Jules Wayne Beuret; Patricia Louise (Benton) Beuret **ED:** MS, Indiana University, Fort Wayne, IN (1974); Postgraduate Coursework, Monash University, Clayton, Victoria, Australia (1968); Postgraduate Coursework, Pontificia Universidad Javeriana, Bogota, Colombia (1967); BA, University of Saint Francis (Formerly St. Francis College), Fort Wayne, IN (1967) **CT:** Certified Secondary English Teacher, State of Indiana **C:** Coordinator, English as a New Language, Westview Jr-Sr High School, Westview School Corporation, Topeka, IN (2002-Present); Master of Religious Instruction, Howe Military Academy, Howe, IN (2009-2010); Teacher of English, Latin Enrichment, Cultural Enrichment, Lakeland School Corporation, Lagrange, IN (1970-2002); Staff Announcer, C.P. Broadcasting, Inc., Auburn, IN (1969-1970); Teacher, Fifth Grade, Saint Joseph's School, IN (1967-1969) **CW:** Featured, Editorial Writer, Nixon Newspapers (1970) **AW:** Fellow, Lilly Endowment, Inc. (1992); Fellow, Rotary Foundation, Rotary International (1967); Hoosier Teacher of English Award, Indiana Council of Teachers of English (ICTE) (1985); College Editorial of the Year Award, State of Indiana (1967) **MEM:** Indiana Council of Teachers of English (ICTE) **MH:** Albert Nelson Marquis Lifetime Achievement Award; Marquis Who's Who Top Professional **B/I:** Mr. Beuret received an award from the Rotary Foundation, and he knew there would be study in Australia. But the school year there doesn't start untill March, and it was June where he was at the time. He went to South America for about 10 weeks, and when he got back, his father had the idea that he should work until he went to Australia. The only job offer he had was to teach fifth grade, which is not what he wanted to do. He found out to his great surprise that he really liked teaching; he was able to spot the kids who were struggling and help them. That is what brought him back to teaching. **AV:** Music; Civil War history; French cuisine; Travel; Photography; Writing; Politics; Bridge **RE:** Roman Catholic **THT:** Mr. Beuret is currently volunteering at a used book store that assists a no-kill animal shelter.

BEWLEY, BRIAN ANTHONY, T: President, Chief Executive Officer **I:** Military & Defense Services **CN:** Tactical Solutions International, Inc. **DOB:** 12/23/1958 **SC:** WY/USA **PT:** Patricia A. Aragon **MS:** Married **SPN:** S. Jessica Bewley **CH:** Jason A. Bewley; Jessica M. Bewley; Ryan A. Bewley; Cole J. Miller; Warren Johnson **ED:** MBA in Global Management, University of Phoenix (1999); BA in Liberal Arts, Concentration on Foreign Language and Management, University at Albany, State University of New York (1997); AS in Diving Business and Technology, Florida Keys Community College (Now College of the Florida Keys) (1990) **C:** President, Chief Executive Officer, Tactical Solutions International, Inc. (2003-Present); General Manager, Al Tuff International LLC (2003-2011); ATFP Plans, Lockheed Martin/SYTEX (2002-2003); Military Program Manager, High Energy Access Tools (HEAT) (2001-2002); Military Advisor, SOC, Abu Dhabi, United Arab Emirates (1997-2001); SFODA Assistant Commander/SFODA Commander/SF Company XO, First Special Forces Group (Airborne), Okinawa, Japan (1991-1997); Senior Instructor/Writer-Combat Driver, First Special Forces Group (Airborne), Key West, FL (1987-1990); SF Weapons/Intel NCO (CIF/Combat Dive/Military Freefall), First Special Forces Group (Airborne), Republic of Panama (1980-1987) **CIV:** Volunteer Medical Technician, EMT, Local Community; Volunteer, Fire Department; Runs Civics Program, Local School "Lights On" Program **MIL:** Retired Chief Warrant Officer, United States Army Special Forces (1976-1997) **AW:** Named Instructor of the Year, National Association of Underwater Instructors (NAUI); Multiple Military Awards **MEM:** American Society of Industrial Security (Now ASIS International); National Association of Underwater Instructors (NAUI); Special Forces Association **MH:** Marquis Who's Who Top Professional **AS:** Mr. Bewley attributes his success to having great mentors throughout his life which provided him with the tools of success. **B/I:** Mr. Bewley, as a member of the United States Army Special Forces, consistently pushed for excellence of self, family and his military organization. Upon retirement from the military, he carried his desire for excellence back into the defense industry to assist the war-fighter from a commercial vantage point. **PA:** Libertarian/Constitutionalist **THT:** Mr. Bewley's motto is, "Never be satisfied with your physical state and knowledge...constantly train and learn. Strive to set the example in honesty, courage and ethical behavior. Love your family, friends and God without conditions."

BEYER, DONALD, "DON" STERNOFF JR., T: U.S. Representative **I:** Government Administration/Government Relations/Government Services **DOB:** 06/20/1950 **PB:** Trieste **SC:** Free Territory of Trieste **PT:** Donald Sternoff Beyer Sr.; Nancy Prew (McDonald) Beyer **MS:** Married **SPN:** Megan Caroll Beyer (09/19/1987); Carolyn Anne (McInerney) Beyer (07/15/1972, Divorced) **CH:** Donald III; Stephanie; Clara; Grace **ED:** BA in Economics, Williams College, Magna Cum Laude (1972) **C:** U.S. Representative, Virginia's Eighth Congressional District, United States Congress (2015-Present); Owner, Don Beyer Volvo, Falls Church, VA (1974-Present); United States Ambassador to Switzerland and Liechtenstein, U.S. Department of State, Bern, Switzerland (2009-2013); Lieutenant Governor, Commonwealth of Virginia, Richmond, VA (1990-1998); Member, Committee on Natural Resources; Member, Committee on Science, Space and Technology; Member, Joint Economic Committee **CR:** Transportation and Land Use Group, Virginia Commission on Climate Change (2008); Chairman, Virginia Poverty and Welfare Reform Commission (1994-1995); Urban-at-Large Member, Commonwealth Transportation Board, VA (1987-1990) **CIV:** Democratic Nominee, Governor of Virginia (1998); Bill Clinton for President, Commonwealth of Virginia (1992); Member, 11th District, Democratic Committee, Vienna, VA (1992); Paul Simon for President, Commonwealth of Virginia (1988); Chairman, Baliles for Governor, Northern VA (1985) **AW:** Quality Dealer of Year, Time (1991); Dealer of Excellence Award; Grand Award for Highway Safety, National Safety Federation; James Wheat Award for Service to Virginians with Disabilities; Earl Williams Leadership in Technology Award **MEM:** American International Automobile Dealers Association (2006-2007); President, Land Rover Alexandria (1997); Northern Virginia Business Roundtable; Co-Founder, Northern Virginia High Technology Council; American International Automobile Dealers Association; Board Member, Youth for Tomorrow; Washington Community Foundation; The American National Red Cross **AV:** Golfing; Skiing; Climbing **PA:** Democrat **RE:** Episcopalian

BEZOS, JEFF, T: Chief Executive Officer **I:** Internet **CN:** Amazon.com, Inc. **DOB:** 01/12/1964 **PB:** Albuquerque **SC:** NM/USA **PT:** Miguel Bezos; Jacklyn (Gise) Bezos **MS:** Divorced **SPN:** MacKenzie Scott (1993, Divorced 2019) **CH:** Four Children **ED:** Honorary Doctor in Science and Technology, Carnegie Mellon University, Pittsburgh, PA (2008); BS in Electrical Engineering and Computer Science, Princeton University, NJ, Summa Cum Laude (1986) **C:** Owner, The Washington Post (2013-Present); Founder, Blue Origin, Seattle, WA (2000-Present); Chief Executive Officer, Amazon.com, Inc., Seattle, WA (1996-Present); President, Amazon.com, Inc., Seattle, WA (2000-Present); Founder, Chairman, Amazon.com, Inc., Seattle, WA (1994-Present); President, Amazon.com, Inc., Seattle, WA (1994-1999); Treasurer, Secretary, Amazon. com, Inc., Seattle, WA (1996-1997); Senior Vice President, D.E. Shaw & Co., New York, NY (1992-1994); Vice President, D.E. Shaw & Co., L.P., New York, NY (1990-1992); With, Bankers Trust Co., New York, NY (1988-1990); With, FITEL, New York, NY (1986-1988) **CR:** Chairman, The Business Council (2014-Present); Board of Directors, Amazon. com, Inc. (1994-Present); Board of Directors, Drugstore.com (1998-2004) **AW:** Named One of the World's Richest People, Forbes (2006-Present); Named One of the Forbes 400: Richest Americans (2005-Present); Named One of the 10 Most Fascinating People of 2015, Barbara Walters' Special (2015); Named One of the World's Most Powerful People, Forbes Magazine (2010-2014); Named One of the 100 Most Influential People in the World, TIME Magazine (2008-2009, 2014); Named One of the 50 Most Influential People in Global Finance, Bloomberg Markets (2013); Named Business Person of the Year, Fortune Magazine (2012); Innovation Award, The Economist (2011); Named One of the Business People of Year, Fortune Magazine (2010); Named One of the 100 Agents of Change, Rolling Stone Magazine (2009); Named America's Best Leaders, US News & World Report (2008); Named to The Global Elite, Newsweek Magazine (2008); Named Person of the Year, Publishers Weekly (2008); Named One of the 50 Who Matter Now, CNNMoney.com Business 2.0 (2006, 2007); Named One of the 50 Most Important People on the Web, PC World (2007); Named One of the 40 Under 40 (2003); Named Person of the Year, TIME Magazine (1999) **MEM:** The Tau Beta Pi Association, Inc.; The Phi Beta Kappa Society

BHALLA, VINOD K., T: Endocrinologist, Biochemist, Educator (Retired) **I:** Education/Educational Services **CN:** Augusta University **DOB:** 08/04/1940 **PB:** Lahore **SC:** India **PT:** Lal C.; Shanti (Punga) Bhalla **MS:** Widow **SPN:** Madhu Bhalla, MD **CH:** Niti Bhalla Carlson; Jyoti Bhalla Ramsey; Varun Bhalla **ED:** Doctor of Philosophy, National Chemical Laboratory, Poona, India (1968); Master of Science, St. John's College, Agra, India (1964); Bachelor of Science, St. John's College, Agra, India (1962) **C:** Professor of Endocrinology, Medical College of Georgia (1982-Present); Faculty Member, Medical College of Georgia (1974-Present); With, Endocrine Study Section, National Institutes of Health (1985-1989); Research Associate, Emory University, Atlanta, GA (1972-1974); Research Associate, University of Georgia, Athens, GA (1969-1972) **CR:** Speaker in Field **CIV:** Donations to the Department of Physiology in Augusta University, Cancer institute in Augusta University and to the department of Obgyn in Augusta University **CW:** Reviewer, Alcoholism: Clinical and Experimental Research (1982-Present); Reviewer, Endocrinology Journal (1980-Present); Editorial Board, Biology of Reproduction (1978-1983); Reviewer, Andrology Journal (1982) **AW:** Grantee, National Institutes of Health (1976-1982); Grantee, National Science Foundation (1976-1979) **MEM:** American Chemical Society; American Fertility Society; New York Academy of Sciences; Society for the Study of Reproduction; Endocrine Society; Endocrine Study Section, American Society of Biological Chemists **AS:** Mr. Bhalla attributes his success to those who have inspired him. **B/I:** Mr. Bhalla became involved in his profession due to his early interest in the field of reproduction while working in endocrinology. **AV:** Reading **PA:** Republican **RE:** Hindu

BHARGAVA, MANOJ, T: Founder, Chief Executive Officer **I:** Other **CN:** Living Essentials, LLC **PB:** Lucknow **SC:** India **MS:** Married **CH:** One child **ED:** Coursework, Princeton University (1972) **C:** Founder, Chief Executive Officer, Inno-

vation Ventures LLC (DBA Living Essentials LLC) (2003-Present); Launched, 5-hour Energy Drink, Innovation Ventures LLC (DBA Living Essentials LLC) (2003-Present); Financier, Bleeker Street (2014); Owner, Prime PVC Inc. (1990-2006); Founder, MicroDose Life Sciences, Stage 2 Innovations LLC, ETC Capital LLC, Plymouth Real Estate Holdings LLC and Oakland Energy and Water Ventures; Owner, Chemicalpartners.com; With, Bhar Incorporated, New Haven, IN; Various Office and Construction Jobs **CIV:** Participant, The Giving Pledge; Member, The Hans Foundation; Member, Rural India Supporting Trust **CW:** Featured, Documentary, "Billions in Change" (2015) **AW:** Forbes' Billionaires (2013)

BHUSRI, ANEEL, T: Co-Founder, Chief Executive Officer **I:** Business Management/Business Services **CN:** Workday, Inc. **DOB:** 02/14/1966 **PB:** Pittsford **SC:** NY/USA **MS:** Married **SPN:** Allison Thoreson **CH:** One Daughter; One Son **ED:** MBA, Stanford Graduate School of Business (1993); BS in Electrical Engineering, Brown University (1988); BA in Economics, Brown University (1988) **C:** Advisory Partner, Greylock Partners (2015-Present); Chief Executive Officer, Co-Founder, Workday, Inc. (2014-Present); Partner, Greylock Partners (1999-2015); Chairman, Co-Chief Executive Officer, Co-Founder, Workday, Inc. (2012-2014); Co-Chief Executive Officer, Co-Founder, Workday Inc. (2009-2012); President, Co-Founder, Workday Inc. (2007-2009); Chairman, Data Domain Inc. (2007-2009); Vice Chairman, Peoplesoft Inc. (1999-2004); President, Chief Executive Officer, Data Domain Inc. (2002-2003); Senior Vice President, Peoplesoft Inc. (1993-1999); Corporate Finance Analyst, Morgan Stanley **AW:** Entrepreneur of the Year Award, EY (2013)

BIANCHINI, JAMIE, T: Chief Visionary Officer **I:** Consumer Goods and Services **CN:** LuDela Technologies, Inc. **DOB:** 02/10/1972 **PB:** San Mateo **SC:** CA/USA **MS:** Married **SPN:** Cristina **CH:** Luca; Candela; Sol **ED:** BA in Entrepreneurship, University of Southern California-Marshall School of Business, CA (1995) **C:** Founder, Profit & Purpose (2020-Present); Chief Visionary Officer, LuDela Technologies LLC (2019-Present); Author, Speaker, "A Bicycle Built for Two Billion," LuDela Press (2014-Present); Co-Founder, Chief Executive Officer, LuDela Technologies LLC (2015-2019); Co-Founder, President, Amber's RV Rentals, Santa Cruz, CA (2013-2016); Field Sales and Operations Manager, Nordic Naturals (2011-2014); Co-Founder, Expedition Leader, The Peace Pedalers; The Worldwide Invitation to Ride (2002-2010) **AW:** Winner of Best Business Plan, Entrepreneur Program, University of Southern California (1995) **AS:** Mr. Bianchini attributes his success to blending passion, purpose and hard work. When he stopped focusing on just financial success and started adding purpose and passion into his goals, things really started to take off. This philosophy kicked off while in Africa on the Peace Pedalers expedition where he created the motto "Live Big. Give Big," to signify a balance of personal and contribution goals. This led to the completion of 11 charity projects in health, education, and mobility. This philosophy also gave Mr. Bianchini the strength and persistence to complete the challenging 81-country intercultural expedition. Since this realization, Mr. Bianchini has become a passionate social entrepreneur, dedicating his gifts, experience and education to creating ventures that blend both Profit & Purpose. **B/I:** Mr. Bianchini became involved in his profession because of a near-death experience he had in Burkina Faso, West Africa. The event inspired him to invent and patent the LuDela tech-enabled candle. Since he had already helped to found the

Good Hope School for AIDS orphans and the needy in Africa he decided to make LuDela a public benefit corporation to support literacy and education in Africa, where the product was inspired. For every LuDela candle product sold, the company donated a book to bring libraries to underserved communities. By 2019, LuDela helped create four libraries in East Africa.

BIDEN, JOSEPH, "JOE" ROBINETTE JR., T: President-Elect of the United States, 47th Vice President of the United States, Professor **I:** Government Administration/Government Relations/Government Services **DOB:** 11/20/1942 **PB:** Scranton **SC:** PA/USA **PT:** Joseph Robinette Biden Sr.; Catherine Eugenia (Finnegan) Biden **MS:** Married **SPN:** Jill Tracy Jacobs (06/17/1977); Neilia Hunter (08/27/1966, Deceased 1972) **ED:** JD, Syracuse University College of Law (1968); BA in History and Political Science, University of Delaware (1965) **C:** President-Elect of the United States (2020); Democratic Candidate, Presidential 2020 Campaign (2019-2020); Chairman, Middle Class Working Families Task Force (MCWFTF), The White House (2009-2017); Vice President of the United States (2009-2017); Chairman, International Narcotics Caucus (2007-2009); Chairman, U.S. Senate Committee on Foreign Relations (2001-2003, 2007-2009); U.S. Senator from Delaware (1973-2009); U.S. Representative to General Assembly, United Nations (2000); Chairman, U.S. Senate Judiciary Committee (1987); Private Law Practice, Wilmington, DE (1968-1972) **CR:** Benjamin Franklin Professor, University of Pennsylvania (2017); U.S. Democratic Vice Presidential Nominee (2008); Adjunct Professor, Widener University Delaware Law School, Wilmington, DE (1991); Member, New Castle County Council, DE (1970-1972) **CW:** Author, "Promises to Keep: On Life and Politics" (2007) **AW:** Named One of the 100 Most Influential People in the World, TIME Magazine (2011, 2013); Named to the Peter J. McGovern Little League Hall of Excellence (2009); Harry S. Truman Award, Democratic Leadership Council (2005); National Leadership Award, Coalition for Juvenile Justice (2004); Rail Spike Award, Delmarva Rail Passenger Association (2003); Balkan Peace Award, Albanian American Civic League (2002); Charles Dick Medal of Merit, United States National Guard Association, Delaware Chapter (2002); Named Senator of the Year, National Association of Police Organizations (2000); Silver Medal of Appreciation, Czech Republic (1999); Spirit of Enterprise Award, United States Chamber of Commerce (1998); Friend of Zion Tribute Award, Jerusalem Fund (1998) **BAR:** State of Delaware (1968) **PA:** Democrat **RE:** Roman Catholic

BIEBER, JUSTIN DREW, T: Musician **I:** Media & Entertainment **DOB:** 03/01/1994 **PB:** London **SC:** ON/CA **PT:** Jeremy Jack Bieber; Patricia Lynn Mallette **MS:** Married **SPN:** Hailey Baldwin (2018) **ED:** Diplomate, St. Michael Catholic Secondary School, Stratford, Ontario, Canada (2012) **CIV:** Supporter, Active Minds (2020); Fundraiser, Victims of Typhoon Haiyan (2013); Spokesperson, PETA; Spokesperson, Pencils of Promise; Supporter, It Gets Better Project; Supporter, Children's Miracle Network Hospitals; Supporter, Alzheimer's Association® **CW:** Executive Producer, Voice Actor, "Cupid" (2021); Subject, Executive Producer, "Justin Bieber: Seasons" (2020); Singer, Songwriter, "Changes" (2020); Actor, "Killing Hasselhoff" (2017); Actor, "Zoolander 2" (2016); Singer, Songwriter, "Purpose" (2015); Singer, Songwriter, "Journals" (2013); Subject, Producer, "Justin Bieber's Believe" (2013); Voice Actor, "The Simpsons" (2013); Singer, Songwriter, "Believe" (2012); Singer, "Under the Mistletoe" (2011); Subject, Producer,

"Justin Bieber: Never Say Never" (2011); Actor, "CSI: Crime Scene Investigation" (2010-2011); Actor, "Cubed" (2010); Singer, Songwriter, "My World 2.0" (2010); Actor, "School Gyrls" (2009); Actor, "True Jackson, VP" (2009); Singer, Songwriter, "My World" (2009) **AW:** Billboard Latin Music Award for Crossover Artist of the Year, Billboard (2018); Billboard Latin Music Award for Hot Latin Song of the Year, Billboard (2018); Billboard Latin Music Award for Hot Latin Song of the Year-Vocal Event, Billboard (2018); Billboard Latin Music Award for Airplay Song of the Year, Billboard (2018); Billboard Latin Music Award for Digital Song of the Year, Billboard (2018); Billboard Latin Music Award for Streaming Song of the Year, Billboard (2018); Billboard Latin Music Award for Latin Pop Song of the Year, Billboard (2018); Billboard Music Award for Top Latin Song, Billboard (2018); Billboard Music Award for Top Collaboration, Billboard (2018); Billboard Music Award for Top Selling Song, Billboard (2018); Billboard Music Award for Top Streaming Song (Video), Billboard (2018); Billboard Music Award for Top Hot 100 Song, Billboard (2018); ASCAP Award for Song of the Year, ASCAP (2017); ASCAP Awards for Winning Songs, "Sorry," "Cold Water," "Let Me Love You," ASCAP (2017); Latin Grammy Award for Best Urban Fusion/Performance The Latin Recording Academy, The Recording Academy (2017); Los Premios 40 Principales Award for Best International Song, Prisa Radio (2017); Golden Music Award, Prisa Radio (2017); Teen Choice Award for Choice R&B/Hip-Hop Song, Fox Media LLC (2017); Teen Choice Award for Choice Summer Song, Fox Media LLC (2017); Teen Choice Award for Choice Latin Song, Fox Media LLC (2017); iHeartRadio Music Award for Best Lyrics, iHeartRadio (2017); iHeartRadio Music Award for Male Artist of the Year, iHeartRadio (2016, 2017); American Music Award for Favorite Pop/Rock Song, Dick Clark Productions, LLC (2016, 2017); American Music Award for Collaboration of the Year, Dick Clark Productions, LLC (2015, 2017); American Music Award for Favorite Rap/Hip-Hop Song, Dick Clark Productions, LLC (2017); CRMA Award for SOCAN Song of the Year, Canadian Music Week (2017); Music Award for International Song of the Year, NRJ (2016, 2017); MMVA Award for Fan Fave Artist or Group, Bell Media (2012-2017); Brit Award for International Male Solo Artist, BPI (2016); Danish Music Award for Årets Internationale Udgivelse, IFPI (2016); Grammy Award for Best Dance Recording, The Recording Academy (2016); iHeartRadio Music Award for Dance Song of the Year, iHeartRadio (2016); iHeartRadio Music Award for Best Fan Army, iHeartRadio (2016); Latin American Music Award for Favorite Crossover Artist, Telemundo (2016); Latin American Music Award for Favorite Crossover Song, Telemundo (2016); American Music Award for Video of the Year, Dick Clark Productions, LLC (2016); MTV Europe Music Award for Best Song, Viacom International Media Networks (2016); Music Award for International Male Artist of the Year, NRJ (2016); Teen Choice Award for Choice Break-Up Song, Fox Media LLC (2016); Teen Choice Award for Choice Male Single, Fox Media LLC (2012, 2013, 2016); Teen Choice Award for Choice Twitter Personality, Fox Media LLC (2011, 2013, 2016); Teen Choice Award for Choice Male Artist, Fox Media LLC (2010-2013, 2016); MTV Europe Music Award for Biggest Fans, Viacom International Media Networks (2015, 2016); MTV Europe Music Award for Best Canadian Act, Viacom International Media Networks (2013-2016); American Music Award for Favorite Pop/Rock Album, Dick Clark Productions, LLC (2010, 2012, 2016); American Music Award for Favorite Pop/Rock Male Artist, Dick Clark Productions, LLC (2010, 2012, 2016); Billboard Music Award for Top Male Artist, Billboard (2013, 2016); Billboard Music Award for Top Social Artist, Billboard (2011-2016); Juno Award for Pop Album of the Year, The Canadian Academy of Recording Arts and Sciences (2011, 2016); MTV Video Music Award for Best Special Effects, Viacom International Media Networks (2015); MTV Europe Music Award for Best Collaboration, Viacom International Media Networks (2015); MTV Europe Music Award for Best North American Act, Viacom International Media Networks (2015); MTV Europe Music Award for Best Look, Viacom International Media Networks (2015); MTV Europe Music Award for Best Male, Viacom International Media Networks (2010-2015); Artist of Honor, NRJ (2012, 2015); Fan Choice Award, Juno Awards, The Canadian Academy of Recording Arts and Sciences (2011-2015); ASCAP Awards for Most Performed Songs, "As Long As You Love Me" (with Big Sean), "Beauty and a Beat (feat. Nicki Minaj)," ASCAP (2013, 2014); Milestone Award, Billboard (2013); Star, Eastwood City Walk of Fame, Quezon City, Philippines (2013); Queen Elizabeth II Diamond Jubilee Medal, The Governor General of Canada (2012); ASCAP Award for Top Box Office Films, ASCAP (2012); MTV Europe Music Award for Best World Stage Performance, Viacom International Media Networks (2012); Disruptive Innovation Award, Tribeca Disruptive Innovation Awards (2012); Teen Choice Award for Choice Male Summer Music Star, Fox Media LLC (2010, 2012); MTV Europe Music Award for Best Pop, Viacom International Media Networks (2011, 2012); American Music Award for Artist of the Year, Dick Clark Productions, LLC (2010, 2012); MMVA Award for International Video of the Year by a Canadian, Bell Media (2010-2012); Diamond Award, RIAA (2011); Brit Award for International Breakthrough Act, BPI (2011); Billboard Music Award for Top Pop Album, Billboard (2011); Billboard Music Award for Top Digital Media Artist, Billboard (2011); Billboard Music Award for Top New Artist, Billboard (2011); Billboard Music Award for Top Streaming Artist, Billboard (2011); Billboard Music Award for Fan Favorite, Billboard (2011); CMT Music Award for Collaborative Video of the Year, Country Music Television, Inc. (2011); Voices Award, MTV Europe Music Awards, Viacom International Media Networks (2011); MTV Video Music Award for Best Male Video, Viacom International Media Networks (2011); MMVA Award for Fave Artist, Bell Media (2011); Music Award for International Revelation of the Year, NRJ (2011); Star, Avon Theatre, Stratford, Ontario, Canada (2011); American Music Award for New Artist of the Year, Dick Clark Productions, LLC (2010); Time 100, TIME USA, LLC (2011); MTV Europe Music Award for Best Push Act, Viacom International Media Networks (2010); MTV Video Music Award for Best New Artist, Viacom International Media Networks (2010); MMVA Award for Fave New Artist, Bell Media (2010); MMVA Award for Fave Video, Bell Media (2010); Teen Choice Award for Choice Pop Album, Fox Media LLC (2010); Teen Choice Award for Choice Male Breakout Artist, Fox Media LLC (2010); Power of Youth Philanthropy Award, Variety Media, LLC (2010) **RE:** Christian

BIENENSTOCK, ARTHUR, T: Physicist, Educator, Federal Official **I:** Education/Educational Services **CN:** Stanford University **DOB:** 03/20/1935 **PB:** New York **SC:** NY/USA **PT:** Leo Bienenstock; Lena Bienenstock **MS:** Married **SPN:** Roslyn Doris Goldberg (04/14/1957) **CH:** Eric Lawrence; Amy Elizabeth (Deceased); Adam Paul **ED:** Honorary Doctor of Philosophy, Lund University (2006); Honorary Doctor of Philosophy, New York University Tandon School of Engineering (1998); Doctor of Philosophy, Harvard University (1962); Master of Science, Poly New York University Tandon School of Engineering (1957); Bachelor of Science, New York University Tandon School of Engineering (1955) **C:** Member, National Science Board (2012-Present); Associate Director, Wallenberg Research Link, Stanford University, California (2006-Present); Special Assistant to the President, Stanford University, California (2006-Present); Professor of Applied Physics, Stanford University, California (1972-2010); Faculty Member, Stanford University, California (1967-2010); Vice Provost, Dean of Research and Graduate Policy, Stanford University, California (2003-2006); Director, Laboratory for Advanced Materials, Stanford University, California (2002-2003); Associate Director of Science, Office of Science and Technology Policy, Washington (1997-2001); Director, Synchrotron Radiation Laboratory, Stanford University, California (1978-1997); Vice Provost, Faculty Affairs, Stanford University, California (1972-1977); Assistant Professor, Harvard University, Cambridge, MA (1963-1967) **CR:** Board on Chemical Sciences and Technology, National Research Council (2001-2003); Committee on Condensed Matter and Materials Physics, National Research Council (1996-1997); Science Advisory Committee, European Synchrotron Radiation Facility (1988-1990, 1993-1996); U.S. National Committee on Crystallography (1983-1988) **CIV:** With, National Science Board (2005-Present); Chairman, Council of Scientific Society Presidents (2010); Trustee, Associate Director for Science, White House Office of Science and Technology Politics (1997-2001); With, Cystic Fibrosis Foundation (1982-1988); President's Advisory Council, Cystic Fibrosis Research Foundation (1980-1982); Board Director, California Chapter, Cystic Fibrosis Research Foundation (1970-1973) **CW:** Contributor, Scientific Papers to Professional Journals **AW:** Phillip Hague Abelson Award, American Association for the Advancement of Science (2017); Cuthbertson Award, Stanford University (2009); Distinguished Service Award, U.S. Department of Energy (2005); Distinguished Contribution to Research Administration Award, Society Research Administrator (2000); Distinguished Alumnus Award, Poly Technical Institute New York (1977); Sidhu Award, Pittsburgh Diffraction Society (1968); National Science Foundation Fellow (1962-1963) **MEM:** President-Elect, American Physical Society (2007-Present); President, American Physical Society (2008); Vice President, American Physical Society (2006); General Councilor, American Physical Society (1993-1996); Fellow, American Association for the Advancement of Science; Foreign Member, Royal Swedish Academy of Engineering Science; Materials Research Society; American Crystallographic Association **MH:** Albert Nelson Marquis Lifetime Achievement Award; Marquis Who's Who Top Professional **AS:** Mr. Bienenstock attributes his success on hard work and valuable mentors. **B/I:** Mr. Bienenstock became involved in his profession while attending college, and greatly enjoyed engineering, physics and mathematics. Having come of age in a very socially conscientious family, he had the opportunity to deal heavily with both the advancement of women and minorities in the student body and faculty, which became the second theme in his career. The third theme is simple science and higher education policy. **AV:** Ballet; Music; Movies; Books; Theater; Swimming;Travel **RE:** Jewish

BIGGERS, R. LEE LEE JR., T: Structural Engineer **I:** Engineering **DOB:** 12/23/1941 **PB:** Charlotte **SC:** NC/USA **PT:** Ralph Lee Biggers; Sara Wilma (Kidd) Biggers **MS:** Married **SPN:** Sally Anne (Miller) Biggers (06/21/1969) **CH:** Lee Anne; Sara Katherine (Deceased); Katie Grace; Seven Grandchildren **ED:** MS, San Diego State University (1973); BS, North Carolina State University (1964) **CT:** Registered

Structural Engineer, California (1973); Registered Civil Engineer, California (1968) **C:** Principal Structural Engineer, Brady Engineers (2002-Present); President, R.L. Biggers & Associates, La Mesa, CA (1991-2002); Executive Vice President, Atkinson, Johnson & Spurrier, Inc., San Diego, CA (1986-1991); Board of Directors, Atkinson, Johnson & Spurrier, Inc., San Diego, CA (1980-1991); Corporate Secretary, Atkinson, Johnson & Spurrier, Inc., San Diego, CA (1977-1991); Senior Engineer, Atkinson, Johnson & Spurrier, Inc., San Diego, CA (1974-1991); Senior Engineer, Inter-City Engineers, Inc., San Diego, CA (1971-1973); Project Manager, Scott Memorial, San Diego, CA (1970-1971); Design Engineer, Whitman-Atkinson, San Diego, CA (1969-1970); Construction Foreman, Roanoke Construction Co., Roanoke Rapids (1964-1965) **CR:** Lecturer, Civil Engineering, San Diego State University (1982, 1976-1977) **CIV:** Trustee, Christian Heritage College (1992-1993); Trustee, Scott Memorial Baptist Church, El Cajon, CA (1986-1989); Vice President, Christian Unified Schools, San Diego, CA (1983-1984); President, Christian Heritage Retirement Center, San Diego, CA (1980-1982); Trustee, Shadow Mountain Community Church **MIL:** Captain, U.S. Naval Reserve (Retired) **AW:** ACI Award of Merit, San Diego, CA (1988); ASCE Project of the Year Award, San Diego, CA (1976) **MEM:** Board Member, Structural Engineers Association of California (1994-1995); President, Structural Engineers Association, San Diego, CA (1993-1994); Director, San Diego Post, Society of American Military Engineers (1990-1991); American Concrete Institute; American Society of Civil Engineers; Naval Reserve Association **MH:** Albert Nelson Marquis Lifetime Achievement Award **AS:** God's gracious gifts. **B/I:** Mr. Biggers became involved in his profession because his uncle worked for the Southern Railway for 44 years starting as a survey crewman and and became a civil engineer. He was his inspiration and also his dad was a small time contractor. The construction industry always had his attention. When he was 10 or 11 years old he saw a movie called "The Fighting Seabees" with John Wayne and that inspired him to go into the Navy's Civil Engineer Corps. He served 4 1/2 years of active duty and 22 years as a reservist. **AV:** Travel **PA:** Republican **RE:** Evangelical Christian

BIGGS, ANDREW, "ANDY" STEVEN, T: U.S. Representative from Arizona **CN:** U.S. House of Representatives **DOB:** 11/07/1959 **PB:** Tucson **SC:** AZ/USA **MS:** Married **SPN:** Cindy Biggs **CH:** Six Children **ED:** Doctor of Jurisprudence, University of Arizona James E. Rogers College of Law; Master of Arts in Political Science, Arizona State University; Bachelor of Arts in Asian Studies, Brigham Young University **C:** U.S. Representative from Arizona's Fifth Congressional District (2017-Present); Member, District 22, Arizona State Senate (2011-2017); Member, District 22, Arizona House of Representatives (2003-2011); Member, Ways and Means Committee, Arizona House of Representative; Vice Chair, Appropriations Committee, Arizona House of Representatives; Chair, Transportation and Infrastructure Committee, Arizona House of Representatives; Retired Attorney **AW:** Named, Friend of Liberty, Goldwater Institute; Named, #1 Friend of Taxpayer, Arizona Federation of Taxpayers **BAR:** Arizona; District of Columbia; New Mexico **PA:** Republican **RE:** Church of Jesus Christ of Latter-day Saints

BIGGS, WILLIAM C., MD, FACE, T: Endocrinologist, Chief Medical Information Officer, Managing Partner **I:** Medicine & Health Care **CN:** Amarillo Medical Specialists, LLP **DOB:** 11/16/1956 **PB:** Merced **SC:** CA/USA **PT:** Everett Eugene; Betty Louise (Allanach) **MS:** Married **SPN:** Grace Emily

Archer **CH:** Richard; William; Sarah; Grace **ED:** Fellowship in Endocrinology, Joslin Diabetes Center, Harvard Medical School (1985-1986); Residency in Internal Medicine, Beth Israel Deaconess Medical Center, Harvard Medical School (1983-1985); Internship in Medicine, UC San Diego (1982-1983); MD, The University of Texas Southwestern Medical Center (1982); BA in Chemistry, UC San Diego (1978) **CT:** Diplomate, American Board of Internal Medicine; Diplomate, American Board of Preventive Medicine **C:** Private Practice, Amarillo Medical Specialists (1986-Present); Manager, CBLF Partners, LLC (1999-2013) **CR:** Chief Executive Officer, Amarillo Legacy Medical ACO (2012-Present); Assistant Clinical Professor, School of Medicine, TTUHSC (1986-Present); Board of Governors, Northwest Texas Healthcare System (1996-2004); President, Medical Staff, Northwest Texas Healthcare System (1994-1996); Chairman, Department of Internal Medicine, Northwest Texas Healthcare System (1989-1993) **CIV:** Vice Chairman, Board of Manager, Amarillo Hospital District (2017-Present); Honorary Chairman, Walktoberfest (1994); Board of Directors, Amarillo Chapter, American Diabetes Association (1992-1993); Refugee Camp Volunteer, American Red Cross (1975) **AW:** Texas Monthly Super Doctor (2005-2019) **MEM:** Board of Directors, Potter-Randall CMS (2020-Present); President, Texas Chapter, American Association of Clinical Endocrinology (2009-2010); American Medical Association; American Diabetes Association; Texas Medical Association; Panhandle Amateur Radio Club; Potter-Randall CMS **MH:** Albert Nelson Marquis Lifetime Achievement Award; Marquis Who's Who Top Professional **B/I:** Mr. Biggs became involved in his profession because he liked the challenge behind it all as far as the integration of science and working with people.

BILIRAKIS, GUS MICHAEL, T: U.S. Representative, Lawyer **I:** Government Administration/Government Relations/Government Services **DOB:** 02/08/1963 **PB:** Gainesville **SC:** FL/USA **PT:** Michael Bilirakis; Evelyn (Miaoulis) Bilirakis **MS:** Married **SPN:** Eva Lialios **CH:** Michael; Theodore; Emmanuel; Nicholas **ED:** JD, College of Law, Stetson University, DeLand, FL (1989); BA, University of Florida (1986) **C:** U.S. Representative, Florida's 12th Congressional District, United States Congress (2013-Present); U.S. Representative, Florida's Ninth District, United States Congress, Washington, DC (2007-2013); Senior Whip, Florida's Ninth Congressional District, United States Congress (2006-2008); Member, District 48, Florida House of Representatives (1999-2006); Member, Committee on Energy and Commerce; Member, Committee on Veterans' Affairs; Attorney, Bilirakis Law Group, Holiday, FL; Intern to President Ronald Reagan, The White House **CR:** Member, Pinellas County Republican Executive Committee (1996-Present); Adjunct Professor, St. Petersburg Junior College (Now St. Petersburg College) (1997); Staff Member, Representative Don Sundquist, U.S. House of Representatives **MEM:** West Pasco Chamber of Commerce; Tarpon Springs Chamber of Commerce; Palm Harbor Chamber of Commerce; Clearwater Bar Association; American Hellenic Educational Progressive Association; Rotary Club of Tarpon Springs; Masons; Elks, Moose Lodge **PA:** Republican **RE:** Greek Orthodox

BINEY, ISAAC NOBLE, MD, T: Physician **I:** Medicine & Health Care **CN:** The University of Tennessee Graduate School of Medicine **DOB:** 11/01/1983 **PB:** Burmingham **SC:** England **PT:** Noble Biney; Georgina Biney **MS:** Married **SPN:** Genevieve **CH:** Micah; Nathan **ED:** Bachelor of Medicine and Bachelor of Surgery, University of Ghana Medical School (2009); Residency in Internal Medicine,

Howard University; Fellowship, University of Tennessee Graduate School of Medicine **CT:** Diplomate in Pulmonary Disease, American Board of Internal Medicine (2019); Diplomate in Internal Medicine, American Board of Internal Medicine (2015) **C:** Pulmonary Critical Care Fellow, University of Tennessee, Knoxville, TN (2017-Present); IPC Hospitalist, Bristol Regional Medicine Center (2015-2017); Internal Medicine Resident, Howard University Hospital (2012-2015) **AW:** Fellow of the Year, University of Tennessee Graduate School of Medicine (2020); Diversity Travel Grant, CHEST Foundation (2019); Overall Most Outstanding Resident, Howard University Hospital, Department of Internal Medicine (2014-2015); Outstanding Leadership Award, Howard University Hospital, Department of Internal Medicine (2014-2015); Akuaba Prize, Primary Health Care Community Pediatrics (2009); Professor H. H. Philips Prize in Physiology (2006) **MEM:** American Thoracic Society (2019-Present); American College of Chest Physicians (2016-Present); Society of Critical Care Medicine (2014-Present) **AS:** Dr. Biney attributes his success on his ability to relate to his patients. **B/I:** Despite having long been interested in mathematics and physics, Dr. Biney resolved to become a doctor after watching an episode of "ER." He subsequently specialized in cardiology, and gradually shifted his focus to pulmonary disease and critical care medicine. **RE:** Christian **THT:** Always pursue excellence and always strive to be your best in every situation.

BING, STEPHEN, "STEVE" LEO, T: Chief Executive Officer **I:** Media & Entertainment **CN:** Shangri-La Entertainment **DOB:** 03/31/1965 **PT:** Peter S. Bing; Helen Bing **CH:** Damian Hurley; Kira Bonder **ED:** Coursework, Stanford University **C:** Founder, Shangri-La Entertainment **CR:** Investor, "Beowulf" (2007); Investor, "The Polar Express" (2004) **CIV:** Participant, The Giving Pledge (2012-Present) **CW:** Producer, "Shine a Light" (2008); Producer, "Last Man Standing" (2006); Producer, "The Big Bounce" (2004); Writer, "Kangaroo Jack" (2003); Producer, "Night at the Golden Eagle" (2002); Producer, "Without Charlie" (2001); Executive Producer, "Get Carter" (2000); Writer, "Married...with Children" (1987-1997); Actor, "The Dark Backward" (1991); Writer, "Missing in Action 2: The Beginning" (1985); Writer, "Missing in Action" (1984) **AW:** Wealthiest Angelenos, Los Angeles Business Journal (2010); 50 Most Powerful People in Hollywood, Premiere Magazine (2005)

BIPPUS, DAVID P., T: Manufacturing Financial Executive (Retired) **I:** Manufacturing **DOB:** 11/29/1949 **PB:** Evansville **SC:** IN/USA **PT:** James Paul Bippus; Mary Louise (Elder) Bippus **MS:** Married **SPN:** Kohnne Susann Heikens (08/28/1971) **CH:** Laura **ED:** MSBA, Boston University, with Honors (1975); BS, Iowa State University (1971) **CT:** Certified Chartered Property and Casualty Underwriter (1982) **C:** Treasurer and Chief Financial Officer, Rockford Process Control, LLC (2008-2018); Vice President of Finance and Information Technology, Haldex (1999-2008); Chief Financial Officer, Reliant Industries (1995-1999); Corporate Controller, Reliant Industries (1994); Vice President of Operations, Secretary, Treasurer, Suntec Industries (1989-1994); Vice President of Finance, Secretary, Treasurer, Suntec Industries (1984-1989); Controller, Hydraulics Division, Sundstrand Corporation (1982-1984); Manager of Financial Planning, Hydro-Transmission Division, Sundstrand Corporation (1979-1982); Assistant Director of Planning, Horace Mann (1976-1979); Technology Manager, Illinois Department of Education (1976) **CR:** Instructor, Lincoln Land Community College (1976-1978) **CIV:** Chairman, Boone County Planning Commission (2015-2017); Member, Boone County Planning Commission (2011-2017); President, Zion Evangelical Lutheran Church (2000-2001, 2010-2012); Church Council, Zion Evangelical Lutheran Church (1998-2001, 2009-2012); Board of Directors, The New American Theater (1991-1997); President, The New American Theater (1993-1995); Board of Directors, Parents for Gifted Children (1989-1991); Board of Directors, Rockford Civic New Comers (1982-1985); Member, Story County Planning and Zoning Commission; Volunteer, Former President, Local Church **MIL:** First Lieutenant, U.S. Army (1972-1976) **MEM:** Board of Directors, Local Chapter, Financial Executives Institute (1989-Present); President, Local Chapter, Financial Executives Institute (1993-1994); Society of ; Property and Casualty Underwriters; National Society of Accountants; The American Legion; Forest Hills Country Club **MH:** Albert Nelson Marquis Lifetime Achievement Award **B/I:** Mr. Bippus became involved in his profession because he followed in his father's footsteps. **AV:** Taking photographs; Woodworking **PA:** Republican

BIRD, LARRY JOE, T: Professional Sports Team Executive, Professional Basketball Player (Retired) **I:** Athletics **CN:** Indiana Pacers **DOB:** 12/07/1956 **PB:** West Baden Springs **SC:** IN/USA **PT:** Claude Joseph "Joe" Bird; Georgia (Kerns) Bird **MS:** Married **SPN:** Dinah Mattingly (10/01/1989); Janet Condra (1975-1976) **CH:** Corrie; Conner (Adopted); Mariah (Adopted) **ED:** Honorary Doctor of Letters, Boston University (2009); Bachelor of Science, Indiana State University (1979) **C:** Advisor, Indiana Pacers (2017-Present); President, Basketball Operations, Indiana Pacers (2003-2012, 2013-2017); Head Coach, Indiana Pacers (1997-2000); Special Executive Assistant, Boston Celtics (1992-1997); Forward, Boston Celtics (1979-1992) **CR:** United States Men's National Basketball Team (1992); United States Men's Universiade Team (1977) **CW:** Appearance, "Celtics/Lakers: Best of Enemies," "30 for 30" (2017); Appearance, "The Doctor" (2013); Appearance, "The Dream Team" (2012); Appearance, "The Announcement" (2012); Subject, "Magic & Bird: A Courtship of Rivals" (2010); Co-Author, with Magic Johnson and Jackie MacMullan, "When the Game Was Ours" (2009); Actor, "Celtic Pride" (1996); Actor, "Space Jam" (1996); Actor, "Blue Chips" (1994); Co-Author, with Bob Ryan, "Drive: The Story of My Life" (1989) **AW:** Executive of the Year, NBA (2012); Inductee, National Collegiate Basketball Hall of Fame (2009); Coach of the Year, NBA (1998); Inductee, Naismith Memorial Basketball Hall of Fame (1998); 50th Anniversary All-Time Team, NBA (1996); Eastern Conference All-Star (1980-1988, 1990-1992); All-NBA First Team (1980-1988); NBA MVP (1984-1986); NBA Finals MVP (1984, 1986); NBA All-Star Game MVP (1982); NBA All-Rookie First Team (1980); Rookie of the Year, NBA (1980); NCAA Player of Year, Associated Press, United Press International, National Association Coaches (1979); Naismith Men's College Player of the Year Award, Atlanta Tipoff Club (1979); John R. Wooden Award, Los Angeles Athletic Club (1979); First Team All-American, NABC, United Press International, Inc. and The Associated Press (1978, 1979)

BIRD, PHILIP, "BRAD" BRADLEY, T: Film Director, Producer, Screenwriter, Animator **I:** Media & Entertainment **CN:** Disney/Pixar **DOB:** 09/11/1957 **PB:** Kalispell **SC:** MT/USA **PT:** Phillip Cullen Bird; Marjorie A. (Cross) Bird **MS:** Married **SPN:** Elizabeth Canney (1988) **CH:** Michael; Jack; Nicholas **ED:** BFA, California Institute of the Arts **C:** Director, Pixar Animation Studios, Disney/Pixar (2000-Present); Director, Screenwriter, Warner Bros. Entertainment, Inc.; With, Walt Disney Company **CW:** Director, Writer, Voice Actor, "The Incredibles 2" (2018); Executive Producer, Voice Actor, "Auntie Edna" (2018); Voice Actor, "Jurassic World" (2015); Director, Producer, "Tomorrowland" (2015); Director, "Mission: Impossible - Ghost Protocol" (2011); Director, Screenwriter, Voice Actor, "Ratatouille" (2007); Executive Producer, "Your Friend the Rat" (2007); Executive Producer, "One Man Band" (2006); Screenwriter, Director, "Jack-Jack Attack" (2005); Executive Producer, "More Making of 'The Incredibles'" (2005); Executive Producer, "One-Man Band" (2005); Director, Screenwriter, Executive Producer, "Mr. Incredible and Pals" (2005); Executive Producer, "Vowellet: An Essay by Sarah Vowell" (2005); Executive Producer, "The Making of 'The Incredibles'" (2005); Director, Screenwriter, Voice Actor, "The Incredibles" (2004); Director, Screenwriter, Voice Actor, "The Iron Giant" (1999); Executive Consultant, "King of the Hill" (1997); Executive Consultant, "The Critic" (1994); Writer, Creator, "Family Dog" (1993); Animator, "Rugrats" (1991); Director, "Do the Bartman" (1990); Executive Consultant, "The Simpsons Christmas Special" (1989); Director, Executive Consultant, "The Simpsons" (1989); Screenwriter, "*batteries not included" (1987); Director, Writer, Animation Producer, "Amazing Stories" (1985); Animator, "The Black Cauldron" (1985); Animator, "Mickey's Christmas Carol" (1983); Animator, "Winnie the Pooh and a Day for Eeyore" (1983); Animator, "Garfield on the Town" (1983); Animator, "The Plague Dogs" (1982); Animator, "The Fox and the Hound" (1981); Animator, "Animalympics" (1980); Voice Actor, "Doctor Doom" (1979) **AW:** Named to Variety's 500 (2019); Best Writing, Saturn Award (2005, 2012); Lifetime Achievement Award, Venice Film Festival (2009); Outstanding Individual Achievement for Directing in an Animated Feature Production, Annie Award, ASIFA - Hollywood (1999, 2005, 2008); Outstanding Individual Achievement for Writing in an Animated Feature Production, Annie Award, ASIFA - Hollywood (1999, 2005, 2008); Best Animated Feature, Annie Award, ASIFA - Hollywood (1999, 2005, 2008); Best Animated Feature, Academy Award, Academy of Motion Picture Arts and Sciences (2005, 2008); Award for Best Animated Film, Producers Guild of America (2008); Award for Best Animated Film, BAFTA (2008); Best Animated Feature Film, Golden Globe Award, Hollywood Foreign Press Association (2008); Best Animation Award, Los Angeles Film Critics Association (1999, 2004, 2007); Award for Best Screenplay, Boston Society Film Critics (2007); Named One of the 50 Smartest People in Hollywood, Entertainment Weekly (2007); Outstanding Individual Achievement for Voice Acting in an Animated Feature Production, Annie Award, ASIFA - Hollywood (2005); Best Dramatic, Hugo Award (2005); Best Feature Film, Children's Award, BAFTA (2000); Disney Scholarship, California Institute of the Arts

BIRD, WENDELL R., PHD, JD, T: Legal Historian **I:** Law and Legal Services **ED:** DPhil, University of Oxford; JD, Yale Law School (1978); BA, Vanderbilt University, Summa Cum Laude (1975) **C:** Visiting Scholar, Emory Law School (2012-Present); Senior Partner and Senior Counsel, Bird, Loechl, Brittain & McCants, Atlanta, GA (1986-Present) **CR:** Lecturer, Washington Non-Profit Tax Conference (1982-2018); Adjunct Professor, Emory University School of Law, Atlanta, GA (1985-1990); Law Clerk to Judge Robert S. Vance, U.S. Court of Appeals for the Fifth Circuit, Birmingham, AL (1979-1980); Law Clerk to Judge J. Dickson Phillips, U.S. Court of Appeals for the Fourth Circuit, Durham, NC (1978-1979) **CW:** Author, "The Revolution in Freedoms of Press and Speech," Oxford University Press (2020); Author, "Criminal Dissent," Harvard University Press (2020); Author, "Press and Speech Under Assault," Oxford University Press (2016); Co-Author of Section, "CCH Federal Tax Service" (1988-2000); Co-Author, "Federal and State Taxation of Exempt Organizations," Warren Gorham & Lamont (1994); Contributor, Articles, Professional Journals **AW:** Egger Prize, Yale Law School (1978) **MEM:** Litigation Section, American Bar Association (1982-2020); Taxation Section, American Bar Association, Committee on Exempt Organizations, American Bar Association (1982-2020); Co-Chairman, Subcommittee on Charitable Contributions, American Bar Association (2002-2019); Past Chairman, Subcommittee on Religious Organizations, American Bar Association; Past Chairman, Subcommittee on State and Local Taxes, American Bar Association; American Bar Foundation; The American Law Institute **MH:** Albert Nelson Marquis Lifetime Achievement Award

BIRDSONG, JAMES CHARLES JR., T: Founder, President & Executive Director **I:** Nonprofit & Philanthropy **CN:** Birdsong Association of Broadcasting & Arts, Inc. **DOB:** 05/16/1980 **PB:** Richmond **SC:** CA/USA **PT:** Belinda Germany-Birdsong (1947); Rev. James C. Birdsong, Sr. (1938-1997) **MS:** Single **ED:** Graduate Certificate in Marketing, University of Phoenix (2020); BA in Biblical Education, Beulah Heights University, Atlanta, GA (2010); Diploma, Fairfield High School, Fairfield, CA (1998) **CT:** Pastor Ordination Credentials, Covenant Covering Christian Fellowship, Santa Rosa, CA (2015); Standard Teachers Diploma, Evangelical Training Association, Calumet City, IL (2010); Ministers License, World Christianship Ministries, Fresno, CA (2002) **C:** Musician; Religious Services **CIV:** College Internship, Albert T. Mills Enrichment Center, Atlanta, GA; Chairperson, National Association for the Advancement of Colored People Cobb County Branch Religious Affairs Committee, Marietta, GA; Volunteer, Gods Resting Place Community Outreach, Richmond, CA; Election/Poll Worker, Alameda County Registrar of Voters, Oakland, CA **CW:** Author, "One Marriage, Many Tales, And a Separation: A Message of Hope"; Author, "The Best is Yet to Come: A Testimony of One Young Mans Redemption" **AW:** Nominee, Gulf Coast Gospel Music Awards, Gulfport, MS; Shining Star Awards Gala Honoree, Preach the World Worldwide Network TV, Roswell, GA; Proclamation, City of Atlanta, Atlanta, GA; Proclamation, City of Bossier City, Bossier City, LA; Proclamation, City of Compton, Compton, CA; Proclamation, City of Fairfield, Fairfield, CA; Proclamation, City of Los Angeles, Los Angeles, CA; Proclamation, City of Marietta, Marietta, GA; Proclamation, City of Pinole, Pinole, CA; Proclamation, City of Richmond, Richmond, CA; Proclamation, City of Shreveport, Shreveport, LA; Proclamation, City of Vallejo, Vallejo, CA; Proclamation, Caddo Parish, Caddo Parish, LA; Proclamation, Clayton County, Clayton County, GA; Proclamation, Cobb County, Cobb County, GA; Proclamation, Contra Costa County, Contra Costa County, CA; Proclamation, Fulton County, Fulton County, GA; Proclamation, Solano County, Solano County, CA; Resolution, California State Assembly, Sacramento, CA; Resolution, California State Senate, Sacramento, CA; Resolution, Georgia State Senate, Atlanta, GA; Resolution, Georgia House of Representatives, Atlanta, GA; Resolution, Louisiana House of Representatives, Baton Rouge, LA; Resolution, Louisiana State Senate, Baton Rouge, LA; Resolution, Texas State Senate, Austin, TX; Commendation, State of California, Sacramento, CA; Congressional Record, United States House of Representatives, Washington, DC; Congressional Recognition, United States House of Representatives, Washington, DC; Congratulatory Letter, United States Senate, Washington, DC; Award of Honor, Fairfield High School,

Fairfield, CA; Blue Ribbon Honoree, Nystrom Elementary School, Richmond, CA; Wall of Tolerance Induction, Civil Rights Memorial Center, Montgomery, AL; Certificate of Appreciation, Albert T. Mills Enrichment Center, Atlanta, GA; Certificate of Appreciation, Booker T. Washington Revisited Student Conference, Fairfield, CA; Certificate of Appreciation, United Negro College Fund, Fairfax, VA; Certificate of Membership, Gospel Music Association, Nashville, TN; Certificate of Recognition, Alpha Kappa Alpha Sorority, Fairfield, CA; Gospel Music Industry Award, Black Essence Awards, Benton Harbor, MI; Family & Friends Award, Macedonia Church of God in Christ, Suisun City, CA; Outstanding Georgia Citizen Award, State of Georgia, Atlanta, GA; Commendation, State of California, Sacramento, CA; Commendation, State of Louisiana, Baton Rouge, LA; Commendation, State of Georgia, Atlanta, GA MEM: Global United Fellowship, Nassau, Bahamas; National Association for the Advancement of Colored People, Baltimore, MD; Gospel Music Workshop of America, Atlanta, GA; Gospel Music Association, Nashville, TN; Stellar Awards Gospel Music Academy, Chicago, IL; Gulf Coast Gospel Music Awards, Gulfport, MS MH: Albert Nelson Marquis Lifetime Achievement Award AS: Mr. Birdsong attributes his success to his faith and trust in God, as well as the motivation his family, friends, and teachers instilled in him alongside his journey to success. B/I: Mr. Birdsong always desired a career in the gospel music industry and entertainment arena. Prior to being educated on the business side of the music industry, he sang in his local choir as a child and oftentimes around the house. In 11th grade, he wrote a research paper about the gospel music industry, which required research consisting of visiting the websites of national gospel artists and record companies. As a high school senior, he subscribed to Gospel Today Magazine, which allowed him to read articles on how to pursue a career in the field. AV: Singing; Performing; Writing; Public speaking PA: Independent RE: Pentecostal THT: James C. Birdsong Jr. is an aspiring Gospel vocalist, songwriter, motivational speaker, entrepreneur, advocate for our children and author of "The Best is Yet to Come: A Testimony of One Young Man's Redemption", an inspirational memoir published nationally and to this date, received positive reviews and appearances on multiple television, radio and print media platforms nationwide and globally. A native of Richmond, CA, his efforts have caught the attention and respect of politicians, community, media, and entertainment leaders and luminaries. A member of the famed Birdsong family, his lineage includes R&B legend Cindy Birdsong, a former member of Patti LaBelle and the Bluebells and the Supremes, former four-time NBA All-Star pro basketball player Otis Birdsong and the late Edwin Birdsong, a Grammy-Award winner and legendary 1970s era funk keyboardist, whose music has been sampled by Kanye West, Snoop Dogg, and Dalf Punk. Mr. Birdsong was the great-nephew of the late Rev. Sidney Birdsong, Sr., a respected icon who served as the pastor of the historical Solid Rock Baptist Church in Los Angeles from 1959 to his death in 1976. A graduate of Fairfield High School in Fairfield, CA, Mr. Birdsong earned his Bachelor of Arts in Biblical Education at Beulah Heights University in Atlanta, GA. He is currently pursuing a graduate certificate in marketing at the University of Phoenix. The recipient of the Albert Nelson Marquis Lifetime Achievement and Marquis Who's Who Top Artist Award, a three-time listee in Who's Who in America, the Outstanding Georgia Citizen Award, the Congressional Record (United States Congress), the Black Essence Award in Gospel Music, numerous citations, honors, nominations,

proclamations and resolutions and an inductee on the Wall of Tolerance at the Civil Rights Memorial Center in Montgomery, AL. His memberships of major music organizations include the Gospel Music Workshop of America Atlanta Chapter (GMWA), the Stellar Awards Gospel Music Academy (SAGMA), and the Gospel Music Association (GMA Dove Awards). He is working on his next book for youth as a discussion of various topics they face today from dating and relationships to the hip-hop culture and advice on how to enroll in college. The book is scheduled for publication in 2021.

BIRKENHEAD, THOMAS BRUCE, PHD, T: Theater Producer, Educator **I:** Education/Educational Services **DOB:** 12/19/1931 **PB:** New York **SC:** NY/USA **PT:** Thomas A. Birkenhead; Florence (Morison) Birkenhead **MS:** Married **SPN:** Maria Martins (05/26/1999) **CH:** Peter Lawrence; David Andrew; Richard James; Alison Jane; Leila Alessandra **ED:** PhD, The New School (1963); MA, Brooklyn College (1958); BA, Brooklyn College (1954) **C:** Professor Emeritus, Brooklyn College (1975-Present); Dean School of Social Sciences (1972-1975); Professor, Brooklyn College (1972-1975); Lecturer to Professor of Economics, Brooklyn College (1957-1972) **CR:** Management Consultant, Keystone Musical Arts Center (1999-Present); Business Manager, Theatre II, Glen Cove, New York (1970-1974) **CIV:** Member, Negotiating Committee, Broadway Contract, ATPAM (2006-Present); ATPAM (2007-2008); Sponsor, Founding Member, Shooting Team, Brooklyn College; United States Holocaust Memorial Museum; IWM; United States Navy Memorial **CW:** General Manager, "Duke and the Duchess" (2001-Present); General Manager, "Dream a Little Dream" (1994-1995); General Manager, Honky Tonk Highway (1994-1996); General Manager, "Fresh Air Taxi" (1993) **AW:** Teaching Award, City University of New York (1999); Eponym, T. Bruce Birkenhead Scholarship, Performing Arts Management Program, Brooklyn College **MEM:** National Rifle Association of America; United States Naval Institute; Marine Corps Heritage Foundation; Habitat for Humanity International; World Jewish Congress; The Groucho Club; Friends of the Israel Defense Forces **MH:** Albert Nelson Marquis Lifetime Achievement Award **AV:** Collecting British antique weapons **PA:** Democrat

BISANZ, ANNETTE KAY, T: Nurse **I:** Medicine & Health Care **CN:** University of Texas **DOB:** 07/03/1942 **PB:** Kalamazoo **SC:** MI/USA **PT:** Frank John Bisanz; Arlowyne Biddle (Fisher) Bisanz **MS:** Single **ED:** MPH, University of Michigan, Ann Arbor, MI (1972); BSN, Marquette University, Milwaukee, WI (1966); Diploma in Nursing, Borgess Hospital School of Nursing (1964) **C:** Bowel Management Clinical Nurse Specialist (2003-2012); Clinical Nurse Specialist, M.D. Anderson Cancer Center, University of Texas (1983-2012); Case Manager, M.D. Anderson Cancer Center, University of Texas (1999-2003); Clinical Practice Coordinator, M.D. Anderson Cancer Center, University of Texas (1996-1999); Discharge Planning Nurse, M.D. Anderson Cancer Center, University of Texas (1983-1994); Director, Education and Training, St. Lawrence Hospital, Lansing, Michigan (1979-1981); Supervisor, Lansing Visiting Nurses Association, Michigan (1969-1979); Staff Nurse, Project Hope, Sri Lanka (1968-1969) **CR:** Co-Founder, Volunteer Interfaith Care Givers, BNA Senior Rides and More (1994-Present); Scientific Advisory Board Member, Colon Cancer Alliance (1991-1995) **CIV:** Hospice Volunteer, Facilitator of Bereavement Support Groups (2000-Present); Senior Rides and More **CW:** Contributor, Chapters to Various Books; Contributor, Articles to Various Professional Journals **AW:** Staff Educator of the Year, University of Texas M.D. Anderson Cancer Center (2006); Ethics Career Development Award, Oncology Nursing Foundation (1996); Ethel Fleming Arceneaux Outstanding Nurse Oncology Award, Brown Foundation (1995); Honoree for Outstanding Contribution to Clinical Nursing Practice, Texas Nurses Association (1993) **MEM:** Oncology Nursing Society **MH:** Albert Nelson Marquis Lifetime Achievement Award; Marquis Who's Who Top Professional **AS:** Ms. Bisanz's parents instilled a good work ethic, the importance of high integrity and the need to always to be true to herself in her. Her faith has guided her into the path of service in nursing, and her professors instilled in her the need to pave the way to meet unmet needs of patients through problem solving and innovation in her nursing practice. **B/I:** Ms. Bisanz received a calling to be helpful to others with health problems. **AV:** Swimming; Reading; Music; Flower arranging **RE:** Roman Catholic **THT:** God gave us one life and Ms. Bisanz wanted to make it beneficial to those whom she was privileged to share the journey with.Fulfillment is the joy of seeing others succeed as a result of my intervention in their life.

BISHOP, BRYAN EDWARDS, JD, T: Attorney **I:** Law and Legal Services **CN:** Locke Lord LLP **DOB:** 11/29/1945 **PB:** Providence **SC:** RI/USA **PT:** Charles Frederick Bishop, Junior; Emma Kirtley (Edwards) Bishop **MS:** Married **SPN:** Martha Jo Maben (06/21/1970) **ED:** JD, Harvard University (1972); BSME, University of Texas, Arlington, TX, with High Honors (1968) **C:** Of Counsel, Locke Lord LLP, Dallas, TX (2007-Present); Partner, Of Counsel, Locke Liddell & Sapp LLP, Dallas, TX (1999-2007); Partner, Locke Purnell Rain Harrell, Dallas, TX (1987-1998); Partner, Rain, Harrell, Emery, Young & Doke, Dallas, TX (1972-1987) **CW:** Author, "The New Texas Business Organizations Code" **AW:** Listed, Best Lawyers in America (2003-Present); Texas Super Lawyer, Texas Monthly Magazine **MEM:** American Bar Association; Corporate Law Committee, Corporate Banking and Business Law Section, State Bar of Texas; Board of Directors, Texas Business Law Foundation; Dallas Petroleum Club; Delta Tau Delta; Tau Beta Pi; Pi Tau Sigma; Alpha Chi **BAR:** Texas (1972); U.S. Court Appeals of the Fifth Circuit (1972) **MH:** Albert Nelson Marquis Lifetime Achievement Award **B/I:** Mr. Bishop had a general interest in the law, which initially attracted him to the field. Later, he had a particular mentor who sparked his fascination with the industry and encouraged him to pursue a career as a lawyer. **AV:** Volunteering with the Special Olympics

BISHOP, JAMES, "DAN" DANIEL, T: U.S. Representative from North Carolina **I:** Government Administration/Government Relations/Government Services **DOB:** 07/01/1964 **PB:** Charlotte **SC:** NC/USA **MS:** Married **SPN:** Jo Bishop **CH:** One Child **ED:** JD, University of North Carolina School of Law (1990); BS in Business Administration, University of North Carolina at Chapel Hill (1986) **C:** Member, U.S. House of Representatives from North Carolina's Ninth Congressional District (2019-Present); Member, North Carolina Senate (2017-2019); Member, U.S. House of Representatives from North Carolina's 104th Congressional District (2015-2017); Member, Fifth District, Mecklenburg County Commission (2004-2008) **PA:** Republican

BISHOP, ROBERT W., ESQ., T: Lawyer **I:** Law and Legal Services **DOB:** 01/07/1949 **PT:** James Clarence Bishop; Dorothy Davis Whitsitt Bishop **MS:** Married **SPN:** Cynthia Graham Bishop (08/26/1970) **CH:** Jessica Levesque; Joshua Davis

Bishop; Amanda Joyce Bishop; Alexandra Kelt Bishop **ED:** JD, Order of the Coif, University of Kentucky College of Law (1976); Coursework, George Washington University, National Law Center, Washington, DC; BA, University of Kentucky, with High Distinction, Dean's List **C:** President, Founder, Bishop Friend, P.S.C (2000-Present); President/Founder, Bishop & Associates, P.S.C. (1993-2000) **CIV:** Kentucky Bar Association; Louisville Bar Association; Bar of the United States Supreme Court; Federal Bar Association; Phi Beta Kappa; Past Chairman, Federal Practice Section, Louisville Bar Association; Former Board Member, Louisville Central Community Centers, Inc.; Founder, Owner, Director, Louisville Thunder Professional Indoor Soccer Team Officer; Director, Greater Louisville Soccer League **AW:** Lifetime Member, Multi-Million Dollar Advocates Forum, Kentucky Super Lawyers (2012-Present) **BAR:** Kentucky Bar Association; Louisville Bar Association; United States Supreme Court; Federal Bar Association; U.S. Court of Appeals for the 3rd Circuit; U.S. Court of Appeals for the 4th Circuit; U.S. Court of Appeals for the 6th Circuit; U.S. Court of Appeals for the 7th Circuit; U.S. Court of Appeals for the 9th Circuit; U.S. District Courts for the Eastern District of Kentucky; U.S. District Courts for the Western District of Kentucky; U.S. District Court for the Northern District of Ohio Commonwealth of Kentucky **MH:** Albert Nelson Marquis Lifetime Achievement Award; Marquis Who's Who Top Professional **B/I:** Mr. Bishop was inspired by his mother to pursue law school. Likewise, his brother, James Clarence Bishop, attended law school. He served as an inspiration as well. **AV:** Climbing; Rowing; Sailing; Cycling; Hiking; Reading; Exercising with German Shepherd rescue on Whidbey Island, Washington **PA:** Democrat **RE:** Jeffersonian Theist

BISHOP, ROBERT, "ROB" WILLIAM, T: U.S. Representative from Utah; Ranking Member of the U.S. House Committee on Natural Resources; Former Educator **I:** Government Administration/Government Relations/Government Services **DOB:** 07/31/1951 **PB:** Kaysville **SC:** UT/USA **MS:** Married **SPN:** Jeralynn (Hansen) Bishop **CH:** Shule; Jarom; Jashon; Zenock; Maren **ED:** BA in Political Science, The University of Utah, Salt Lake City, UT (1974) **C:** Ranking Member, House Committee on Natural Resources (2019-Present); Member, U.S. House of Representatives from Utah's First Congressional District, United States Congress, Washington, DC (2003-Present); Chairman, U.S. House Committee on Natural Resources (2015-2019); Teacher, Government and History, Box Elder High School (1985-2002); Chairman, Utah Republican Party (1997-2001); Speaker, Utah House of Representatives (1992-1994); Member, District Two, Utah House of Representatives (1982-1994); Minority Leader, Utah House of Representatives (1990-1992); Teacher, Debate Coach, Ben Lomond High School, Ogden, Utah (1980-1985); Member, District 61, Utah House of Representatives (1978-1982); Teacher, Civics, Box Elder High School, Brigham City, Utah (1974-1980) **CR:** Co-Founder, Member, Executive Board, Coalition of Western States (1994); Chair, Utah State Convention (1990); Member, Utah Speech Arts Association (1975-1987); Chairman, Utah Speech Arts Association (1981-1984) **CIV:** Mormon Missionary, Germany (1970-1972); Chairman, Brigham City Community Theater (Heritage Theatre); Brigham City Heritage Alliance Committee; Brigham City Historic Preservation Committee **AW:** Third Best-Dressed Congressman, Washingtonian (2012) **PA:** Republican **RE:** Church of Latter-Day Saints

BISHOP, SANFORD DIXON JR., T: U.S. Representative from Georgia; Lawyer **I:** Government Administration/Government Relations/Government Services **DOB:** 02/04/1947 **PB:** Mobile **SC:** AL/USA **PT:** Sanford Bishop; Minnie Bishop **MS:** Married **SPN:** Vivian Creighton **CH:** Aayesha J. Reese **ED:** JD, Emory University School of Law (1971); BA in Political Science, Morehouse College (1968) **C:** U.S. Representative from Georgia's Second Congressional District, United States Congress (1993-Present); Member, Georgia State Senate (1991-1992); Partner, Bishop & Buckner, Professional Corporation, Columbus, GA (1972-1992); Member, 94th District, Georgia House of Representatives (1977-1990); Member, Appropriations Committee **CR:** Delegate, Democratic National Convention (1980, 1984, 1988) **AW:** Listee, Power 150, Ebony Magazine (2008); Listee, Most Influential Black Americans, Ebony Magazine (2006); Legislative Service Award, Georgia Municipal Association (1984, 1986); Outstanding Legislative Award, National Organization for Women, Georgia Chapter (1983-1984); Black Georgian of the Year (1983); Man of the Year, Men's Progressive Club, Columbus, GA (1977); Earl Warren Fellow (1971-1972); Most Influential Black Men in Georgia; Friend of the Children Award, Child Advocacy Coalition; Distinguished Eagle Scout Award **MEM:** American Bar Association; National Bar Association; Georgia Bar Association; Alabama Bar Association; American Judicature Society; Shriners; 32 Degree Member, Masons; The International Legal Honor Society of Phi Delta Phi; Pi Sigma Alpha; Kappa Alpha Psi Fraternity, Inc.; Sigma Pi Phi **PA:** Democrat **RE:** Baptist

BISTRIAN, BRUCE RYAN MD, MPH, PHD, T: Internist, Educator **I:** Medicine & Health Care **CN:** Harvard Medical School **DOB:** 10/22/1939 **PB:** Southampton **SC:** NY/USA **PT:** Peter Bistrian; Mary Laura (Ryan) Bistrian **MS:** Married **SPN:** Eleanor Alice Dix (09/03/1964) **CH:** Tennille Ryan; Jordan Brooke; Britton Perry **ED:** AM (Honorary), Harvard University, Cambridge, MA (1990); PhD, Massachusetts Institute of Technology, Cambridge, MA (1975); MPH, Johns Hopkins University, Baltimore, MD (1971); Resident in Medicine, University of Vermont, Burlington, VT (1969-1970); Metabolism Fellow, University of Vermont, Burlington, VT (1968-1969); Intern, Cornell University, New York, NY (1965-1966); MD, Cornell University, Ithaca, NY (1965); BA, New York University, New York (1961) **CT:** Critical Care Medicine (1987-2007); Diplomate in Internal Medicine (1972); American Board Internal Medicine **C:** Professor of Medicine, Harvard Medical School, Harvard University, Boston, MA (1990-Present); From Assistant Clinical Professor to Associate Professor, Harvard University School Medicine, Boston, MA (1975-1990) **CR:** Lecturer, Massachusetts Institute of Technology (1981-1984); Clinical Associate, Physician Research Resources Division, National Institutes of Health (1975-1978) **MIL:** Captain, U.S. Army (1966-1968) **CW:** Member, Editorial Board, "Critical Care Medicine" (1994-2016); Member, Editorial Board, "European Journal of Clinical Nutrition" (2007-2012); Member, Editorial Board, "Harvard Health Letter" (1999-2012); Member, Editorial Board, "Women's Health Watch" (1997-2012); Member, Editorial Board, "Journal of Parenteral and Enteral Nutrition" (1985-2007); Member, Editorial Board, "Journal of Nutrition" (1990-1995); Member, Editorial Board, American Journal of Clinical Nutrition (1978-1981); Contributor, More Than 500 Science Articles, Professional Publications **AW:** Outstanding Mentor Award, American Society of Parenteral and Enteral Nutrition (2018); Lifetime Mentoring Award, Medical School (2013); Goldberger Award in Clinical Nutrition American, Medical Association (2004); National Institute of Arthritis, Diabetes, Diges-

tive and Kidney Diseases (1985-1995); Grantee, National Cancer Institute (1984-1987); Grantee, National Institute of Arthritis, Metabolism and Digestive Disease (1979-1983); Grantee, National Institute of General Medical Sciences (1977-1980); Army Commendation Medal (1968) **MEM:** Surgeon, Massachusetts Society of Mayflower Descendants (2008-Present); Board Assistant, Massachusetts Society of Mayflower Descendants (2007-Present); Committee on Military Nutrition Research, Institute of Medicine (2001-2013); Board of Directors, Federation of American Society for Experimental Biology (2001-2007); President, Federation of American Society for Experimental Biology (2005-2006); President, American Society for Clinical Nutrition (2000); Vice President, American Society for Clinical Nutrition (1999); Secretary, American Society for Clinical Nutrition (1993-1996); President, American Society Parenteral & Enteral Nutrition (1989-1990); Sigma Xi (1975); Phi Beta Kappa (1961); Fellow, American College of Physicians; Fellow, American Society of Nutritional Sciences; Massachusetts Medical Society; Society of Critical Care Medicine **MH:** Albert Nelson Marquis Lifetime Achievement Award **B/I:** Dr. Bistrian became involved in his profession because he always liked sciences and medicine, and doing research. He started out as an engineering major and decided that he wanted to pursue "engineering that helped people" and, with a family farming background, pursued training and a career in clinical nutrition. **AV:** Spending time with grandchildren; Hunting; Fishing **RE:** Presbyterian

BIVENS, VICKI STIVER, T: Public Services Librarian (Retired) **I:** Library Management/Library Services **DOB:** 07/09/1952 **PB:** Madison **SC:** IN/USA **PT:** William Earl Stiver; Norma Cull Stiver **MS:** Married **SPN:** Douglas Maxwell Bivens III (08/10/1974) **CH:** Douglas Maxwell IV; Darren Matthew **ED:** BS, Towson University (1974) **CT:** Library Associate Training Institute (2011) **C:** Public Services Librarian, Calvert Library (2010-2020); School Librarian, Aftercare Group Leader, Summer Day Camp Registrar, The Calverton School (2006-2010); Home School Group Leader, Activity Coordinator, Educator, Advocate, Consultant, Portfolio Reviewer, Baltimore, MD (1990-2010); Consultant, Tupperware (1989-1991); Child Care Provider (1985-1988); Preparation Department Supervisor, The Milton S. Eisenhower Library, Johns Hopkins University (1978-1985); Recreational Therapy Assistant, Manor Care Nursing Home (1977-1978); Clerk, Treasurer's Office, Johns Hopkins University (1974-1978); Summer Playground Leader and Supervisor, The Maryland-National Capital Park and Planning Commission (1970-1974) **CR:** Leadership Positions, Community Outreach Programs, Calvert Library; MLA Paraprofessional Committee Member, The Milton S. Eisenhower Library, Johns Hopkins University **CIV:** Financial Secretary, Olivet United Methodist Church (2016-2019); Facilitator, Church and Community Bible Studies (1996-2010) **MEM:** Friends of Calvert Library (2010-Present); Maryland Library Association **MH:** Albert Nelson Marquis Lifetime Achievement Award **AS:** Ms. Bivens attributes her success to her respect for others. **B/I:** Ms. Bivens became involved in her profession because of her love of people, information, books and libraries. **AV:** Doing arts and crafts; Reading; Writing; Taking photographs **PA:** Independent **RE:** Christian

BIZZI, EMILIO, MD, T: Neuroscientist, Educator **I:** Education/Educational Services **DOB:** 02/22/1993 **PB:** Rome **SC:** Italy **PT:** Vittorio Bizzi; Anna (Galeazzi) Bizzi **MS:** Married **SPN:** Maureen K. (Holden) Bizzi **ED:** MD, University of Rome, Summa Cum Laude with Highest Honors (1958) **C:** Institute

Professor, Massachusetts Institute of Technology, Cambridge, MA (2002-Present); Eugene Mcdermott Professor, Brain Sciences and Human Behavior, Massachusetts Institute of Technology, Cambridge, MA (1980-2002); Chairman, Department of Brain and Cognitive Sciences, Massachusetts Institute of Technology, Cambridge, MA (1986-1997); Director, Whitaker College, Massachusetts Institute of Technology, Cambridge, MA (1983-1988); Professor, Massachusetts Institute of Technology, Cambridge, MA (1972-1980); Associate Professor, Neurophysiology, Massachusetts Institute of Technology, Cambridge, MA (1969-1972); Lecturer, Department of Psychology, Massachusetts Institute of Technology, Cambridge, MA (1967-1968); Research Associate, Department of Psychology, Massachusetts Institute of Technology, Cambridge, MA (1966-1967); Visiting Associate, Section of Physiology, Laboratory of Clinical Science, National Institute of Mental Health, Bethesda, MD (1964-1966); Research Associate, Neurophysiological Laboratory, Department of Zoology, Washington University, St. Louis, MO (1963-1964); Postdoctoral Trainee, Institute of Physiology, University Pisa, Italy (1960-1963); Postdoctoral Trainee, Institute of Medical Pathology, University of Siena, Italy (1958-1960) **CW:** Editorial Board, Journal of Motor Behavior (1981-Present); Editorial Board, Journal of Neurobiology (1981-Present); Editorial Board, Brain Theory Newsletter (1980-Present); Contributor, Articles, Professional Journals; Contributor, Chapters, Books **AW:** Fellow, Foundation of Research Psychiatry (1978-Present); Hermann von Hlmholtz Award (1992); Alden Spencer Award, Columbia University College of Physicians and Surgeons (1978) **MEM:** President, American Academy of Arts and Sciences (2006-Present); National Academy of Sciences; Institute of Medicine (National Academy of Medicine); American Academy of Clinical Neurophysiology; Academy dei Lincei; International Brain Research Organization **MH:** Albert Nelson Marquis Lifetime Achievement Award **B/I:** While studying medicine in pursuit of his degree, Dr. Bizzi began to take an interest in neurological diseases. After graduating and practicing as a general physician for a few years, Dr. Bizzi decided to start his medical career all over again by leaving his practice and fully enthralling himself into the study of neurological sciences. Upon completion of his studies in Italy, in 1963, Dr. Bizzi relocated to the United States, where his career in neurosciences began to flourish.

BJORKLUND, VICTORIA B., PHD, T: Chair, Lawyer **I:** Law and Legal Services **CN:** Doctors Without Borders **DOB:** 2/20/1952 **PB:** Glen Cove **SC:** NY/USA **ED:** Doctor of Jurisprudence, Columbia Law School (1983); Doctor of Philosophy in Medieval Studies, Yale University (1977); Bachelor of Arts, Princeton University, Magna Cum Laude (1973) **C:** Co-chair, Pro Bono Committee, Simpson Thacher & Bartlett LLP, New York, NY; Head, Exempt Organizations Group, Simpson Thacher & Bartlett LLP, New York, NY; Partner, Simpson Thacher & Bartlett LLP, New York, NY **CR:** Instructor, Law of Nonprofit Organizations, Harvard Law School (2008-2017); Director, Secretary, Pro Bono Legal Counsel, Doctors Without Borders (1989-2001); Director, Pro Bono Legal Counsel, Robin Hood Foundation **CIV:** Chair, Board of Advisors, Doctors Without Borders; Director, Friends of Fondation de France, Institute for Advanced Study, Princeton University, Nutrition Science Initiative and Lawyers' Committee for Civil Rights Under Law; Former Trustee, American Friends of the Louvre, Louvre Endowment, and Princeton University **CW:** Co-author, "New York Nonprofit Law and Practice" (1997) **AW:** Commissioner's Award, Commissioner of the IRS (2003); Named, Pro Bono

Lawyer of the Year, American Bar Association (2002) **MEM:** Co-chair, Subcommittee, Private Foundation, American Bar Association (2003-Present); Chair, American Bar Association (2001-2003); Vice Chair, American Bar Association (1999-2001); Subcommittee, Private Foundation, American Bar Association (1997-1999); Co-chair, Subcommittee, Precedential Guidance, American Bar Association (1995-1997); Committee of Nonprofit Organizations, The Association of the Bar of the City of New York (1991-1997); Co-chair, Subcommittee of International Philanthropy, American Bar Association; Co-chair, Tax Section Committee for Exempt Organizations, American Bar Association; The Phi Beta Kappa Society **BAR:** State of New York (1984)

BLACK, CLINT PATRICK, T: Singer, Songwriter, Actor **I:** Media & Entertainment **DOB:** 2/4/1962 **PB:** Long Branch **SC:** NJ/USA **PT:** G.A. Black; Ann Black **MS:** Married **SPN:** Lisa Hartman (1991) **CH:** Lily Pearl **CR:** Founder, Equity Music Group (2003-2008) **CW:** Singer, Songwriter, "Still Killin' Time" (2019); Singer, Songwriter, "On Purpose" (2015); Appearance, "History Detectives" (2012); Actor, "Flicka: Country Pride" (2012); Voice Actor, "The Adventures of Chuck & Friends" (2011); Actor, "Flicka 2" (2010); Contestant, "Celebrity Apprentice" (2009); Singer, Songwriter, "The Long Cool EP" (2008); Singer, Songwriter, "The Love Songs" (2007); Actor, "Hot Properties" (2005); Singer, Songwriter, "Drinkin' Songs and Other Logic" (2005); Singer, Songwriter, "Christmas with You" (2004); Singer, Songwriter, "Spend My Time" (2004); Appearance, "Nashville Star" (2003); Actor, "Hope & Faith" (2003); Actor, "Anger Management" (2003); Actor, "Going Home" (2000); Voice Actor, "King of the Hill" (1999); Singer, Songwriter, "D'lectrified" (1999); Actor, "Still Holding On: The Legend of Cadillac Jack" (1998); Actor, "The Larry Sanders Show" (1994, 1998); Singer, Songwriter, "Nothin' but the Taillights" (1997); Singer, Songwriter, "Looking for Christmas" (1995); Actor, "Maverick" (1994); Singer, Songwriter, "One Emotion" (1994); Singer, Songwriter, "No Time to Kill" (1993); Singer, Songwriter, "The Hard Way" (1992); Singer, Songwriter, "Put Yourself in My Shoes" (1990); Singer, Songwriter, "Killin' Time" (1989) **AW:** ACM Award for Vocal Event of the Year, Academy of Country Music (1999); Grammy Award for Best Country Collaboration with Vocals (1998); CMA Award for Male Vocalist of the Year, CMA Country Music Association Inc. (1990); American Music Award for Favorite Country New Artist, Dick Clark Productions LLC (1990); ACM Award for Album of the Year, Academy of Country Music (1989); ACM Award for Top Male Vocalist, Academy of Country Music (1989); ACM Award for Top New Male Vocalist, Academy of Country Music (1989); ACM Award for Single of the Year, Academy of Country Music (1989); CMA Horizon Award, CMA Country Music Association Inc. (1989) **MEM:** Grand Ole Opry (1991-Present)

BLACK, RECCA M., T: Elementary School Educator **I:** Education/Educational Services **DOB:** 02/04/1964 **PB:** Marion **SC:** IN/USA **PT:** Charles Lee Barbour (Deceased 2019); Jerry Ann Barbour **MS:** Single **ED:** MEd, Marion College (Now Indiana Wesleyan University); BA in Elementary Education, Marion College (Now Indiana Wesleyan University) (1987); Pursuing Doctorate, Postgraduate Coursework, Indiana Wesleyan University **CT:** Daycare Provider Certificate (2009); Certified Paralegal, Stratford Career Institute (2007); Certified Principal, Indiana Wesleyan University (2006) **C:** Teacher, Marion Community Schools, IN (25 Years); Audio-visual Assistant, VA Medical Center; Casual Clerk, Cashier, Secretary, U.S. Post Office USPS; Food Service Worker, Marion College Bald-

win Food Service; Librarian, Marion Public Library **CR:** Reporter, Marion Newspaper; Camp Counselor for Church; Tutor for Development Center; Mentor for College Students **CIV:** Board of Directors, YWCA; Board of Directors, Community Foundation, Secretary, Neighborhood Association; Secretary, Trustee Board, Secretary for Steward Board, and Secretary for Quarterly Conference, Missionary President, and Stewardist **CW:** Contributor, Numerous Articles to Professional Journals **AW:** Named, Freshman Scholar, Sugar Scholar, National Honor Society **MEM:** Board of Directors, American Association of University Women (AAUW); National Education Association, American Association of University Women (AAUW) **MH:** Albert Nelson Marquis Lifetime Achievement Award; Marquis Who's Who Top Young Professional, Who's Who in America, Who's Who in the World **AS:** Ms. Black attributes her success to great parents. **B/I:** Ms. Black became involved in her profession because it is something that she always wanted to do. She started out by babysitting her nieces and nephews (over 20 plus) and teaching them while babysitting. **AV:** Reading; Shopping; Talking; Being with family and friends; Traveling **THT:** Ms. Black's motto is, "Believe in yourself."

BLACKBURN, MARSHA, T: U.S. Senator from Tennessee **I:** Government Administration/Government Relations/Government Services **CN:** U.S. Senate **DOB:** 06/06/1952 **PB:** Laurel **SC:** MS/USA **PT:** Hillman Wedgeworth; Mary Jo (Morgan) Wedgeworth **MS:** Married **SPN:** Chuck Blackburn **CH:** Two Children **ED:** Bachelor of Science in Home Economics, Mississippi State University (1974) **C:** U.S. Senator, State of Tennessee (2019-Present); Member, U.S. House of Representatives from Tennessee's Seventh Congressional District (2003-2019); Member, Tennessee Senate, 23rd District (1999-2003); Executive Director, Tennessee Film, Entertainment, and Music Commission (1995-1997); Chair, Williamson County Republican Party (1989-1991); Chair, Williamson County Republican Party (1989-1991); Director, Retail Fashion and Special Events, Castner Knott Division, Mercantile Stores Inc. (1975-1978) **CIV:** Founding Member, Williamson County Young Republicans **MEM:** Chi Omega **PA:** Republican **RE:** Presbyterian

BLACKWELL, MARY LOUISE, T: Nurse **I:** Medicine & Health Care **DOB:** 07/05/1942 **PB:** Benton **SC:** KY/USA **PT:** William Burnett; Katie Lee (Raburn) Kendall Burnett **MS:** Married **SPN:** Royce M. Blackwell (01/09/1965) **CH:** Roberta Christine; Catherine Lynn **ED:** AA in Sciences, Elgin Community College (1984); MS, Northern Illinois University (1970); BS, Murray State University (1960) **CT:** Certification in Pediatric Advanced Life Support **C:** Charge Nurse, Sherman Hospital, Elgin, IL (1989-1994); Staff Nurse, Sherman Hospital, Elgin, IL (1984-1989); Teacher, Carpentersville, IL (1969-1982) **CR:** Volunteer, Pain Clinic, Advocate Sherman Hospital (2004); Patient Acuity Committee, Elgin, IL (1986-1993) **AW:** Nursing Excellence Award, Sherman Hospital (2002) **MH:** Albert Nelson Marquis Lifetime Achievement Award **B/I:** Ms. Blackwell became involved in her profession because she wanted to be a teacher from a young age. Unfortunately, though, as a teacher, she was challenged daily when her students would not cooperate in doing their work; it became a frustration for her, so she decided to find something else to do. She then went back to summer school and consequently pursued nursing. **AV:** Reading; Traveling; Listening to music **PA:** Independent **RE:** Presbyterian

BLACKWOOD, KARLA RENÉE, APRN-NP, T: Nurse Practitioner **I:** Medicine & Health Care **DOB:** 08/08/1954 **PB:** Meade **SC:** SD/USA **PT:** Glona Knight; James Melville **MS:** Single **CH:** James Blackwood; Joan Blackwood **ED:** Master of Science in Nursing, University of Nebraska (1998); Bachelor of Science in Nursing, University of Nebraska (1992); Diploma, Riverside Hospital School of Nursing, Newport News, VA (1984); Bachelor of Arts, University of North Carolina, Chapel Hill, NC (1978) **CT:** Family Nurse Practitioner, Community General Hospital, Syracuse, NY (1989) **C:** Family Nurse Practitioner, Papillion, NE (1998-Present); Nurse of Cardiology, New York; Nurse, Patient-Centered Care, Michigan **CIV:** Den Leader, Assistant, Boy Scouts of America (1986-1992); Caseworker, Assistant, American Red Cross (1980-1986) **AW:** Certificate of Achievement, Sigma Theta Tau; Honors; Clinical Honors **MEM:** American Academy of Nurse Practitioners; Nebraska Nurse Practitioners **MH:** Albert Nelson Marquis Lifetime Achievement Award **AV:** Crafts; Reading; Music

BLAIR, THERESA LUCILLE, T: Records Manager, Electrical Contractor, Court Recorder, Customer Service and Sales **I:** Retail/Sales **DOB:** 06/27/1943 **PB:** Hernandez **SC:** NM/USA **PT:** Ben Lovato; Lucy (Roybal) Lovato **MS:** Married **SPN:** Roger Charles Blair **CH:** Darrell; Yvette; Sean; DeVonne **ED:** MBA, Highlands University, Las Vegas, NV (1982); BS in Business Administration, University of Albuquerque (1979) **CT:** Court Recorders of New Mexico (1988) **C:** Sales Agent, Southwest Airlines (1993-Present); Electrical Contractor, Owner, Operator, T. L Blair Electric, Albuquerque, NM (1981-Present); Director's Representative, Employee Contributor Program (1981-Present); Court Recorder (1988-1992); Staff Member, Records Manager, Sandia National Laboratories, Albuquerque, NM (1980-1987); Office Secretary, Sandia National Laboratories, Albuquerque, NM (1964-1979) **CR:** Planning and Allocations Panel, United Way of Greater Albuquerque (1981) **CIV:** Fundraiser, Volunteer, Ronald McDonald House; Volunteer, Hispanic Chamber of Commerce; Volunteer, Senior Olympics **CW:** Author, Several Published Articles **MEM:** Association of Record Managers and Administrators **B/I:** Ms. Blair became involved in her profession after accepting a job at Sandia National Laboratories. After having her children, Ms. Blair decided to return to school, acquiring a master's degree and a bachelor's degree. She then got involved in electrical contracting and, later, court recording. **AV:** Collecting dolls; Collecting Native American art and pottery; Reading; Watching movies **PA:** Democrat **RE:** Roman Catholic

BLAKELY FORBES, JOSEPH, T: Founder, President **I:** Fine Art **CN:** Scenic Art Studios, Inc. **SC:** VA/USA **MS:** Married **SPN:** Debra **CH:** Emma; Colin **ED:** Coursework, Lester Polakov's Studio and Forum of Stage Design; BFA in Scene Design, University of North Carolina, Greensboro, NC; AA in Journalism, Chowan College **C:** Founder, President, Charge Artist, Scenic Art Studios, Inc. (1994-Present); Scenic Artist, Nolands Scenery Supplier **CR:** Scene Painting and Rendering Teacher, State University of New York at Purchase **CIV:** Founder, Studio and Forum of Scenic Arts (2004) **MEM:** United Scenic Artists Local 829 (1979) **AV:** Canoeing; Whitewater rafting

BLANKENSHIP, JAMES, "JIMMY" LYNN JR., SR. STAFF MEMBER, T: Research Professor (Physicist) **I:** Sciences **CN:** Oak Ridge National Labratory (Retired) **DOB:** 03/26/1931 **PB:** Knoxville **SC:** TN/USA **PT:** James Lynn Blankenship Sr.; Louise Franklin Toole Blankenship **MS:** Married **SPN:** Jamie Marguerite Gillenwaters **CH:** Sylvia; Maria; Bruce; James III **ED:** PhD in Physics, University of Tennessee (1973); MS in Physics, University of Tennessee (1955); BS in Engineering Physics, University of Tennessee (1954) **CT:** State Certified Emergency Medical Technician; State Certified Fire Department Instructor; CPR Instructor **C:** Research Professor, Joint Institute Heavy Ion Research, Oak Ridge, TN (1991-2012); Development Engineer, Senior Staff Member, Physics Division, Lockheed Martin Energy Systems (Formerly Union Carbide), Oak Ridge, TN (1955-1991) **CIV:** Volunteer Fire Department Communications Officer **CW:** Patentee in Field; Contributor, Articles, Professional Journals **AW:** Inductee, Central High School Alumni Associations Wall of Fame **MEM:** Former Member, American Physical Society; Senior Member, Institute of Electrical and Electronics Engineers (IEEE) **MH:** Albert Nelson Marquis Lifetime Achievement Award **AS:** Dr. Blakenship attributes his success to hard work and good genes. **B/I:** After exploring chemistry in college, Dr. Blakenship found that he was better sought to pursue a career in physics. It was on this journey that he found his interest in electrical engineering. **AV:** Practicing photography; Practicing carpentry **RE:** Presbyterian

BLANKFEIN, LLOYD CRAIG, T: Senior Chairman, Investment Banker **I:** Financial Services **CN:** Goldman Sachs **DOB:** 09/20/1954 **PB:** Bronx **SC:** NY/USA **PT:** Seymour Blankfein **MS:** Married **SPN:** Laura Jacobs **CH:** Alexander; Jonathan; Rachel **ED:** JD, Harvard Law School (1978); AB in History, Harvard College (1975) **C:** Senior Chairman, Goldman Sachs (2019-Present);Chairman and Chief Executive Officer, Goldman Sachs, New York, NY (2006-2018); President and Chief Operating Officer, Goldman Sachs, New York, NY (2003-2006); Vice Chairman, Goldman Sachs, New York, NY (2002-2003); Co-head, Fixed Income, Currency and Commodities Division, Goldman Sachs, London, United Kingdom and New York, NY (1997-2002); Co-head, J. Aron Currency and Commodities Division, Goldman Sachs, New York, NY (1994-1997); Partner, J. Aron Currency and Commodities Division, Goldman Sachs, New York, NY (1988-1994); Salesman, Precious Metals, J. Aron Currency and Commodities Division, Goldman Sachs, New York, NY (1982-1988) **CR:** Board of Directors, Goldman Sachs (2003-Present); Board of Directors, FIA (1992-1995); Advisory Board, Tsinghua University School of Economics and Management, Beijing, China; Governing Board, Indian School of Business, Telangana, India; Board of Overseers, Weill Cornell Medicine; Executive Committee on University Resources, Harvard University; Co-chair, Financial Aid Task Force, Harvard University **CIV:** Board of Trustees, New-York Historical Society (2004-2007); Emeritus Board of Directors, Robin Hood; Board of Directors, Partnership for New York City; Co-founder, Lloyd and Laura Blankfein Foundation **AW:** Named One of the World's Most Powerful People, Forbes (2018); Named One of the 50 Most Influential People in Global Finance, Bloomberg Markets, Bloomberg L.P. (2011-2016); Person of the Year, The Financial Times LTD (2009); Named to TIME 100, TIME Magazine (2008); Listee, 25 Most Powerful People in Business, Fortune Magazine (2007); Inductee, Futures Hall of Fame, FIA (2005) **PA:** Democrat **RE:** Jewish

BLAYDES, JEFFREY, T: Attorney **I:** Law and Legal Services **CN:** Blaydes Law, PLLC **MS:** Married **CH:** Three Children **CT:** Elements of Renewable Energy (2017); Electrical Engineer (2009); IOSH Managing Safely **C:** Senior Process Technician, Amey (2016-Present); Electrical Engineer, Maintenance/Operations, ITI Energy (2011-2015); Inivotive Engineering & Research, ITI Energy (2011-2015); Inivotive Engineering & Research, ITI Energy (2009-2013); Electrical Control and Instrumental Engineer (2009-2011) **CIV:** Coach, Middle School Teams, Little League Baseball **MEM:** West Virginia State Bar; Pennsylvania State Bar **BAR:** West Virginia; Pennsylvania **AS:** Mr. Blaydes has a desire for favorable outcomes, as well as a strong work ethic to provide individuals the representation that he believes they deserve. **B/I:** Mr. Blaydes enjoys providing assistance where people need it. This inspired him to become a lawyer.

BLECHARCZYK, NATHAN, "NATE", T: Co-Founder, Chief Strategy Officer **I:** Leisure, Travel & Tourism **CN:** Airbnb, Inc. **PB:** Boston **SC:** MA/USA **PT:** Paul Steven Blecharczyk; Sheila (Underwood) Blecharczyk **MS:** Married **SPN:** Elizabeth Morey Blecharczyk **CH:** Two children **ED:** BS in Computer Science, Harvard University (2005) **C:** Chief Strategy Officer, Airbnb, Inc. (2017-Present); Co-Founder, Chief Technology Officer, Airbnb, Inc. (2008-2017); Software Engineer, Batiq (2007-2008); Owner, Consult Mavens, LLC (2006-2008); Engineer, OPNET Technologies, Inc. (Now Riverbed Technology) (2005-2006); Research Assistant, Teaching Fellow, Harvard Kennedy School, Harvard University (2003-2005); Intern, Program Management, Microsoft (2004); Programmer, Bioinformatics, Brigham and Women's Hospital, Boston, MA (2003) **CR:** Chairman, Aibiying, Airbnb, Inc., China (2017-Present) **CIV:** Philanthropist, The Giving Pledge (2016-Present) **CW:** Contributor, "Airbnb Co-Founder: Why Fathers Need Parental Leave Too," Fortune Media IP Limited (2017) **AW:** Listee, America's Richest Entrepreneurs Under 40, Forbes Media LLC (2016)

BLEDSOE, GARY L., ESQ., T: Owner, Attorney **I:** Law and Legal Services **CN:** Cotton Bledsoe Tighe & Dawson, P.C. **ED:** JD, School of Law, The University of Texas at Austin (1976) **C:** Attorney, Cotton Bledsoe Tighe & Dawson, P.C. (1994-Present) **CIV:** Board of Directors, ACLU of Texas; National Board of Directors, NAACP; Board of Directors, TIEER **CW:** Contributor, Journal of African American Life and History **AW:** Man of the Year Award, Houston Business Women (2018); Educator of the Year, Houston Lawyers Association; Virgil Lott Award, School of Law, The University of Texas at Austin; Estate President of the Year Award, NAACP; Civil Rights Advocate of the Year Award, NAACP **MEM:** National Bar Association; American Bar Association; Austin Black Lawyers Association; Houston Lawyers Association **AS:** Mr. Bledsoe attributes his success to encountering great people who made smart decisions. **B/I:** Mr. Bledsoe became involved in his profession because he wanted to serve others and make a difference.

BLEIER, ROBERT, "ROCKY" PATRICK, T: Former Professional Football Player **I:** Athletics **DOB:** 03/05/1946 **PB:** Appleton **SC:** WI/USA **PT:** Bob Bleier; Ellen Bleier **MS:** Married **SPN:** Jan Gyurina; Aleta Giacobine Whitaker (Divorced 1996) **CH:** Four Children **ED:** Bachelor in Business Management, University of Notre Dame, South Bend, IN (1968) **C:** Dallas Cowboys, NFL (1975-1980); Halfback, Pittsburgh Steelers, NFL (1968, 1970-1980) **CR:** Co-Founder, Bleier Zagula Financial, Pittsburgh, PA (2011); Author, Speaker in Field, Retirement and Financial Management **MIL:** United States Army, Vietnam War (1968-1969) **CW:** Co-Host, "The Rock on Retirement," 104.7 FM WPGB, iHeartMedia, Inc.; Author, "Don't Fumble Your Retirement"; Author, "Fighting Back: The Rocky Bleier Story" **AW:** Inductee, International Sports Hall of Fame (2019); Bronze Star; Purple Heart; Combat Infantryman Badge

BLIGE, MARY J., T: Singer, Songwriter, Actress **I:** Media & Entertainment **DOB:** 01/11/1971 **PB:** Bronx **SC:** NY/USA **PT:** Thomas Blige; Cora Blige **MS:** Divorced **SPN:** Martin "Kendu" Isaacs (12/07/2003-06/21/2018) **CH:** Briana Latrise Isaacs (Stepdaughter); Jordan Isaacs (Stepdaughter); Nas Isaacs (Stepdaughter) **ED:** Honorary Diploma, Roosevelt High School, Yonkers, NY (2014); General Educational Diploma **CR:** Founder, Matriarch Records (2004) **CIV:** Founder, Chief Executive Officer, The Mary J. Blige Foundation for the Advancement of Women Now Inc. (2007-Present); Judge, Love Ball III, CFDA (2019); Spokesperson, M·A·C AIDS Fund, Make-Up Art Cosmetics (2000, 2002, 2019); Performer, "We Are the World 25 for Haiti" (2010); Performer, Million Family March, Washington, DC (2000); Performer, B.I.G. Night Out, Christopher Wallace Memorial Foundation Inc. (2000); Spokesperson, Partnership for Drug-Free Kids **CW:** Actress, "Power Book II: Ghost" (2020-Present); Actress, "Respect" (2020); Actress, "The Violent Heart" (2020); Actress, "Body Cam" (2020); Actress, "Pink Skies Ahead" (2020); Voice Actress, "Trolls World Tour" (2020); Actress, "Scream: The TV Series" (2019); Actress, "The Umbrella Academy" (2019); Voice Actress, "Sherlock Gnomes" (2018); Actress, "Mudbound" (2017); Singer-Songwriter, "Strength of a Woman" (2017); Actress, "How to Get Away with Murder" (2016); Performer, "The Wiz Live!" (2015); Actress, "Black-ish" (2015); Singer-Songwriter, "The London Sessions" (2014); Singer, "A Mary Christmas" (2013); Actress, "Black Nativity" (2013); Actress, Executive Producer, "Betty and Coretta" (2013); Appearance, "The X Factor" (2013); Appearance, "The Voice" (2012); Appearance, "American Idol" (2010, 2012); Singer-Songwriter, "My Life II... The Journey Continues (Act 1)" (2011); Voice Actress, "Chico & Rita" (2010); Singer-Songwriter, "Stronger with Each Tear" (2009); Actress, "I Can Do Bad All by Myself" (2009); Actress, "30 Rock" (2009); Singer-Songwriter, "Growing Pains" (2007); Appearance, "America's Next Top Model" (2007); Actress, "Entourage" (2007); Actress, "Ghost Whisperer" (2007); Singer-Songwriter, "The Breakthrough" (2005); Actress, "The Exonerated," 45 Bleecker Theatre, New York, NY (2004); Singer-Songwriter, "Love & Life" (2003); Actress, "Strong Medicine" (2001); Actress, "Prison Song" (2001); Singer-Songwriter, "No More Drama" (2001); Singer-Songwriter, "Mary" (1999); Actress, "Moesha" (1999); Actress, "The Jamie Foxx Show" (1998); Singer-Songwriter, "Share My World" (1997); Actress, "New York Undercover" (1995); Singer-Songwriter, "My Life" (1994); Musical Guest, "Saturday Night Live" (1993); Actress, "Out All Night" (1992); Singer, "What's the 411?" (1992) **AW:** Lifetime Achievement Award, BET Awards, BET Interactive LLC (2019); BET Her Award, BET Awards, BET Interactive LLC (2018); BFCC Award for Best Supporting Actress, Black Film Critics Circle (2018); BFCC Award for Best Ensemble, Black Film Critics Circle (2018); Black Reel Award for Outstanding Original Song, Black Reel Awards (2018); ASCAP Rhythm & Soul Awards for Award Winning R&B/Hip Hop Songs, "U + Me (Love Lesson)," "Thick of It," ASCAP (2018); HMMA Award for Original Song – Animated Film, Hollywood Music in Media Awards™ (2018); Independent Spirit Robert Altman Award, Film Independent (2018); IndieWire Award for Breakthrough Performance, Penske Business Media LLC (2018); PSIFF Award for Breakthrough Performance, Palm Springs International Film Society (2018); SDFCS Award for Best Ensemble, San Diego Film Critics Society (2018); Virtuoso Award, Santa Barbara International Film Festival (2018); Icon Award, Black Girls Rock Awards, BGR!FEST (2009, 2018); Icon of the Year, Billboard Women in Music, Billboard (2017); Gotham Independent Film Award for Best Ensemble, IFP (2017); Hollywood Film Award for Breakout Performance Actress, Hollywood Film Festival (2017); NAACP Image Award for Outstanding Female Artist, NAACP (2007, 2010, 2011, 2017); Hollywood Film Award for Breakthrough Ensemble, Hollywood Film Festival (2016); NAACP Image Award for Outstanding Duo, Group or Collaboration, NAACP (2012, 2015); Listee, 500 Greatest Albums of All Time, Rolling Stone LLC (2012); Black Reel Award for Best Original or Adapted Song, Black Reel Awards (2012); Critics' Choice Award for Best Song, The Critics Choice Association (2007, 2012); Listee, ALL-TIME 100 Albums, TIME USA LLC (2010); Listee, 100 Greatest Artists of All Time, VH1 (2010); NAACP Image Award for Outstanding Album, NAACP (2010); Grammy Award for Best Contemporary R&B Album, The Recording Academy (2009); ASCAP Rhythm & Soul Award for Award Winning R&B/Rap Songs, ASCAP (2008); Grammy Award for Best Gospel Performance, The Recording Academy (2008); Grammy Award for Best R&B Vocal Performance by a Duo or Group, The Recording Academy (2008); Voice of Music Award, ASCAP Pop Music Awards, ASCAP (2007); ASCAP Pop Music Award for Songwriter of the Year, ASCAP (2007); ASCAP Pop Music Award for Song of the Year, ASCAP (2007); Award for Pop Music, ASCAP Pop Music Awards, ASCAP (2007); BET Award for Best Collaboration, BET Interactive LLC (2007); Grammy Award for Best R&B Album, The Recording Academy (2007); Grammy Award for Best R&B Song, The Recording Academy (2007); NAACP Image Award for Outstanding Music Video, NAACP (2007); Soul Train Award for Best R&B/Soul Album – Female, Soul Train Music Awards (2007); World Music Awardd for World's Best Selling R&B Artist, World Music Awards (2007); Grammy Award for Best Female R&B Vocal Performance (2003, 2007); ASCAP Pop Music Award for Most Performed Songs, ASCAP (2003, 2007); American Music Award for Favorite Soul/R&B Artist, dick clark productions llc (2006); BET Award for Video of the Year, BET Interactive LLC (2006); Billboard Music Award for Video Clip of the Year, Billboard (2006); Billboard Music Award for Hot 100 Airplay of the Year, Billboard (2006); Billboard Music Award for R&B/Hip-Hop Song Airplay of the Year, Billboard (2006); Billboard Music Award for R&B/Hip-Hop Song of the Year, Billboard (2006); Billboard Music Award for R&B/Hip-Hop Albums Artist of the Year, Billboard (2006); Billboard Music Award for R&B/Hip-Hop Songs Artist of the Year, Billboard (2006); Billboard Music Award for Female Artist of the Year, Billboard (2006); Legend Award: For Outstanding Contribution to R&B Music, World Music Awards (2006); Billboard Music Award for R&B/Hip-Hop Artist of the Year, Billboard (2006); BET Award for Best Female R&B Artist, BET Interactive LLC (2001, 2006); American Music Award for Favorite Soul/R&B Album, dick clark productions llc (1998, 2006); Billboard Music Award for R&B/Hip-Hop Album of the Year, Billboard (1995, 2006); VLegend Award, Vibe Awards, Vibe Magazine (2005); Grammy Award for Best Pop Collaboration with Vocals, The Recording Academy (2004); American Music Award for Favorite Hip-Hop/R&B Female Artist, dick clark productions llc (2003); MTV Video Music Award for Best R&B Video, Viacom International Inc. (2002); Patrick Lippert Award, Rock the Vote (2001); Do Something Award, Rolling Stone LLC (2000); Lady of Soul Award for Best R&B/Soul Album, Soul Train Lady of Soul Awards (2000); Sammy Davis Jr. Award for Entertainer of the Year – Female, Soul Train Music Awards (2000); Soul Train Award for Best R&B/ Soul Album – Female, Soul Train Music Awards (1993, 1996, 2000); Source Award for R&B Artist of the Year, Source Magazine (1994, 1995, 2000); Hero Award, New York Chapter, The Recording Academy (1999); ASCAP Rhythm & Soul Awards for Award Winning R&B/Rap Songs, "Love Is All We Need," "I Can Love You," with Lil' Kim, ASCAP (1998); ASCAP Rhythm & Soul Award for Most Performed Songs (1996); Soul Train Award for Best R&B/Soul or Rap New Artist, Soul Train Music Awards (1993); New York Music Award for Best R&B Album, New York Music Awards (1993)

BLISS, CORWIN, "CORRY" ALBERT, T: Political Consultant **I:** Consulting **CN:** FP1 Strategies **DOB:** 02/26/1981 **PB:** Westchester **SC:** NY/USA **MS:** Married **SPN:** Kim Fanok **CH:** Two Children **ED:** JD, The City University of New York School of Law; Bachelor's Degree, Boston University **C:** Partner, FP1 Strategies (2018-Present); Executive Director, Congressional Leadership Fund (2016-2018); Executive Director, American Action Network (2016-2018); Partner, PLUS Communications **CR:** Campaign Manager, U.S. Senator Pat Roberts, KS (2014); Campaign Manager, Linda McMahon, CT (2012); Campaign Manager, Lt. Gov. Brian Dubie, VT (2010) **PA:** Conservative

BLISS, MARIAN JACKSON, MBA, MS, T: Information Systems Professional **I:** Information Technology and Services **CN:** Pacific Bell/AT&T **DOB:** 02/15/1943 **PB:** Burlington, Wisconsin **SC:** WI/USA **PT:** Charles Homer Jackson; Mabel Alice (Mantz) Jackson **MS:** Married **SPN:** Erlan Shelly Bliss (1982); Robert L. McDill (1965-1979, Divorced, Deceased) **CH:** Kimberly Ann Parker; Scott Daniel McDill **ED:** MS in Systems Management, University of Denver (1991); MBA, Golden Gate University (1985); BA in Zoology, University of Colorado (1965) **CT:** Certificate, Implementing Business Process Re-engineering, University of California Berkeley (1993); Certificate of Completion, Stanford University Program on Managing Innovation (1989); Certified Computing Professional Institute for Certification of Computing Professionals; Project Management Professional, Project Management Institute **C:** Program Management, Software Development and Implementation Consultant, Management Consultant, Program and Project Management, Strategic System Engineering, Managing Consultant Interim Technology (1997-2002); Project Manager, Pacific Bell/AT&T (1996); Program Manager, Pacific Bell/AT&T (1994-1995); Senior Systems Analyst, Manager of Software Configuration Management (1990-1992); Senior Systems Analyst, Pacific Bell/AT&T (1989-1990); Staff Analyst, Pacific Bell/AT&T (1988-1989); Systems Design Analyst, Pacific Bell/AT&T (1986-1988); Account Executive Telemarketing, Pacific Bell/AT&T, San Jose, CA (1985); Marketing Consultant, Pacific Bell/AT&T, Concord, CA (1980-1985); Pulmonary Technologist, Dallas County Hospitals (1967-1968); Cardiology Technologist, William Beaumont Hospital, Royal Oak, MI (1966-1967); Cardiopulmonary Technician, Rancho Los Amigos Hospital, Downey, CA (1965-1966) **CR:** Part-time Professional Photographer, Professional Photographers of California **CIV:** Member, Board of Directors, Registrar, The National Society of The Colonial Dames of America in California (2015-Present); Member, AAUW (1976-Present); President, Role Players Ensemble (2017-2019); Treasurer, Role Players Ensemble (2015-2019); Member, Board, Role Players Ensemble (2014-2019); Board of Directors, President, AAUW Danville-Alamo-Walnut Creek, CA (2009-2010); Board of Directors, Treasurer, Greenbrook Homes Association (2002-2006); Board of Directors, Greenbrook Elementary School, Danville, CA (1980); Treasurer, Greenbrook Elementary School, Danville, CA (1979); President, Greenbrook Elementary School PTA, Danville, CA **CW:** Author, "Software Configuration Management, Information Systems Management," Volume 10, No. 3 (1993); Author, "Keeping Managers Abreast of State of the Art Software Development" (1993); Author, "Software Configuration Management Guidelines," Pacific Bell (1992); Author, "Software Configuration Management: Delivering Quality Software Products," Soft Watch; Author, "Photographs of the Role Players Ensemble, The Danville Community Band, AAUW Home and Garden Tours" **AW:** Certificate of Achievement, Pacific Bell Information Systems Best Practices, Project Management (1995); Pacific Bell Winner's Circle Award (1992); University of Denver Certificate in Information Systems, Decision Support and Expert Systems, Managing Information Systems, and Teleprocessing and Computer Networks (1991); Singular Achievement Award for Developing the Pacific Bell Software Configuration Management Guidelines **MEM:** American Association of University Women (AAUW); The National Society of The Colonial Dames of America in California; San Ramon Valley Genealogical Society; Professional Photographers of California; Advisory Board, Eugene O'Neill Foundation, Tao House, Danville, CA; Danville - Alamo Garden Club **MH:** Albert Nelson Marquis Lifetime Achievement Award **AS:** The keys to Mrs. Bliss' success were being able to successfully work with people. This included being able to work with those in the company wanting new and/or enhanced information systems capability to effectively manage their area of the business and simultaneously being able to successfully communicate with and support those building the proposed and agreed on systems. This included frequent conversations with all parties involved and honest assessments about development capabilities and deployment time frames. And it included clear assessments of requested changes and impacted development time frames. **B/I:** Following graduation from the University of Colorado, Mrs. Bliss began working at Los Angeles County Rancho Los Amigos Hospital. She had a degree in zoology and the position offered her was an opportunity to work in medical research. She accepted the position and enjoyed her work at "Rancho". Medical technology was an evolving field. Mrs. Bliss became involved in setting up and managing patient monitoring equipment used during heart catherizations. Following the procedures, she completed and prepared study data for the physicians working with patients. She and her husband moved several times in succeeding years and following each move she was able to find an opportunity to utilize and enhance her skills working in hospital cardiac and respiratory laboratories. These positions were in William Beaumont Hospital in Royal Oak, MI, and Parkland Hospital in Dallas, Texas. After having children and subsequent family moved to the Chicago area and then to the San Francisco Bay area, Mrs. Bliss went to work at Pacific Bell in 1980. She enjoyed the challenging and ever changing work in the world of information systems development. **AV:** Golf; Photography; Genealogy **PA:** Independent **RE:** Episcopalian

BLOCK, STEPHANIE JANETTE, T: Actress, Singer **I:** Media & Entertainment **DOB:** 09/19/1972 **PB:** Brea **SC:** CA/USA **PT:** Steven Block; Rosemarie (Garritano) Block **MS:** Married **SPN:** Sebastian Arcelus (10/25/2007) **CH:** Vivienne Helena **ED:** Diploma, Orange County High School of the Arts; Coursework, Rosary High School, Fullerton, CA; Coursework, St. Angela Merici Parish School **CW:** Actress, "The Bedwetter" (2020); Actress, "The Cher Show" (2018-2019); Actress, "Rise" (2018); Actress, "Falsettos: Live from Lincoln Center" (2017); Actress, "Madam Secretary" (2017); Actress, "Brigadoon" (2017); Actress, "Falsettos" (2016-2017); Actress, "Orange is the New Black"

(2016); Actress, "It Could Be Worse" (2014); Actress, "Homeland" (2013); Actress, "Little Miss Sunshine" (2013); Actress, "The Mystery of Edwin Drood" (2012-2013); Actress, "Anything Goes" (2011-2012); Actress, "By the Way, Meet Vera Stark" (2011); Actress, "Cats" (2010); Actress, "They're Playing Our Song" (2010); Singer, "This Place I Know" (2009); Actress, "9 to 5" (2008-2009); Actress, "Wicked" (2003, 2005-2008); Actress, "The Pirate Queen" (2006-2007); Narrator, "James Marshall's Cinderella" (2006); Actress, "The Tonight Show with Jay Leno" (2005); Actress, "The Boy from Oz" (2003-2004); Actress, "Let Me Sing" (2003); Actress, "The Grass Harp" (2002); Actress, "Fiddler on the Roof" (2002); Actress, "I Love a Piano" (2002); Actress, "Triumph of Love" (2001); Actress, "Oliver!" (2001); Actress, "Haven" (2001); Actress, "Crazy for You" (1997, 2001); Actress, "Call Me Madam" (2000); Actress, "James Joyce's The Dead" (2000); Actress, "Funny Girl" (2000); Actress, "Bye Bye Birdie" (1999); Actress, "Bells are Ringing" (1999); Actress, "Guys and Dolls" (1998); Actress, "Damn Yankees" (1997); Actress, "South Pacific" (1997); Actress, "Godspell" (1995); Actress, "The Will Rogers Follies" (1994); Actress, "Life Goes On"; Singer, Various Concerts; Singer, Various Broadway Cast Recordings **AW:** Outstanding Actress in a Musical, "The Cher Show," Outer Critics Circle Awards (2019); Outstanding Actress in a Musical, "The Cher Show," Drama Desk Awards (2019); Best Actress in a Musical, "The Cher Show," Tony Awards (2019); Favorite Diva Performance, "The Mystery of Edwin Drood," Broadway.com Audience Awards (2013); Best Actress in a Non-Resident Production, "Wicked," Carbonell Awards (2007); Best Leading Actress – Non-Resident Production, "Wicked," Helen Hayes Awards (2006); Best Supporting Actress, "Triumph of Love," Robby Awards (2002); Best Actress, "Oliver!," Austin Critics Table Awards (2001); Best Actress, "Funny Girl," Robby Awards (2000)

BLOOMBERG, MICHAEL, "MIKE" RUBENS, T: Financial News Services Company Executive; Publishing Executive; Former Mayor **I:** Financial Services **CN:** Bloomberg Finance L.P. **DOB:** 02/14/1972 **PB:** Boston **SC:** MA/USA **PT:** William Henry Bloomberg; Charlotte (Rubens) Bloomberg **MS:** Divorced **SPN:** Diana Taylor (Domestic Partner) (2000); Susan Elizabeth Barbara Brown-Meyer (1975, Divorced 1993) **CH:** Emma; Georgina **ED:** Honorary Degree, Washington University in St. Louis (2019); Honorary Degree, Villanova University (2017); Honorary Degree, University of Michigan (2016); Honorary LLD, Harvard University (2014); Honorary Degree, Williams College (2014); Honorary Doctor, Fordham University (2009); Honorary LLD, University of Pennsylvania, Philadelphia, PA (2008); Honorary Degree, Rockefeller University (2007); Honorary LHD, Bard College (2007); Honorary Doctor in Public Service, Tufts University (2007); MBA, Harvard Business School (1966); BEE, Johns Hopkins University (1964) **CT:** Licensed Commercial Pilot **C:** Candidate, Democratic Nominee, 2020 Presidential Election (2019-2020); President, Chief Executive Officer, Bloomberg Finance L.P. (2015-2019); Founder, Bloomberg Associates (2014); Mayor, New York, NY (2002-2013); President, Chief Executive Officer, Bloomberg Finance L.P., New York, NY (1981-2001); Founder, Bloomberg Finance L.P., New York, NY (1981); General Partner, Salomon Brothers, New York, NY (1972-1981); Processing Clerk, Salomon Brothers (1966-1972) **CR:** United Nations Special Envoy on Cities and Climate Change (2014); Chairman, World Trade Center Memorial Foundation (2006) **CIV:** Chairman, Serpentine Gallery, London, England (2013-Present); Chairman, Board of Trustees, Johns Hopkins Univer-

sity (1966-1972); Participant, The Giving Pledge; Founder, Chairman, Bloomberg Philanthropies; Trustee, United States Ski Team Educational Foundation; Trustee, S.L.E. Foundation; Trustee, Prep for Prep; Trustee, Spence School; Trustee, New York Police/Fire Widows' and Children's Benefit Fund; Trustee, The Jewish Museum; Trustee, Lincoln Center for the Performing Arts; Trustee, High School of Economics and Finance, Institute for Advanced Study; Trustee, Metropolitan Museum of Art; Trustee, Central Park Conservancy; Trustee, Big Apple Circus **CW:** Co-Author, "Climate of Hope: How Cities, Businesses, and Citizens Can Save the Planet" (2017); Appearance, "The Adjustment Bureau" (2011); Appearance, "New Year's Eve" (2011); Co-Author, "Bloomberg by Bloomberg" (1997); Appearance, "30 Rock"; Appearance, "Curb Your Enthusiasm"; Appearance, "The Good Wife"; Appearance, "Law & Order"; Contributor, Articles, The New York Times **AW:** Listee, World's Richest People, Business Insider (2001-Present); Listee, Forbes 400: Richest Americans (1999-Present); Honorary Knight Commander, The Most Excellent Order of the British Empire, Her Majesty Queen Elizabeth II (2014); Listee, World's Most Powerful People, Forbes Magazine (2010-2014); William Penn Mott Junior Park Leadership Award, National Parks Conservation Association (2013); Library Lion Medal, New York Public Library (2013); Genesis Prize, Genesis Prize Foundation (2013); Listee, Vanity Fair 100 List of Influential Figures, Vanity Fair (2010); U.S. Senator John Heinz Award for Greatest Public Service by an Elected or Public Official (2010); Mary Woodward Lasker Award for Public Service, Lasker Foundation (2009); Leadership for Healthy Communities' Healthy Communities Leadership Award, Robert Wood Johnson Foundation (2009); Board of Directors Award, Council of Fashion Designers of America (CFDA) (2008); Barnard Medal of Distinction (2008); Listee, Global Elite, Newsweek Magazine (2008); Listee, 100 Most Influential People in the World, TIME Magazine (2007, 2008); New Yorker of the Year, Daily News (2006); Listee, 50 Most Generous Philanthropists, Fortune Magazine (2005); Golden Plate Award, Academy of Achievement (2004); Distinguished Leadership in Global Capital Markets Award, Yale School of Management (2003) **MEM:** Fellow, American Academy of Arts & Sciences; Trustee, U.S. Chamber of Commerce; Phi Kappa Psi Fraternity; Kappa Beta Phi **PA:** Democrat **RE:** Jewish

BLOOMFIELD, SUZANNE L., T: Artist **I:** Fine Art **DOB:** 06/23/1934 **PB:** Cleveland **SC:** OH/USA **PT:** Norman Latin; Francis Latin **MS:** Married **SPN:** Nathaniel Bloomfield (06/17/1956) **CH:** Miriam; Andrew; Rachel **ED:** MEd, The University of Arizona (1975); BS in Education, Ohio University (1955) **CW:** Exhibit, Group Show, Omma Center of Contemporary Art, Santa Barbara, CA (2005-2006); Exhibit, Group Show, Omma Center, Greece (2006); Exhibit, Group Show, Chopin Society, Tucson, AZ (2006); Exhibit, Group Show, Tucson Museum of Art (2005); Exhibit, Group Show, Texas A&M University (2004); Exhibit, Group Show, The University of Alabama (2003); Exhibit, Group Show, National Association of Women Artists Printmaking USA Tour (1998-2000); Exhibit, Group Show, College of Business and Public Administration, The University Arizona (1998); Exhibit, Group Show, Museum of Art (Now Los Angeles County Museum of Art), Los Angeles, CA (1997); Exhibit, Group Show, Galeria Berta Armas, Ensenada, Mexico (1997); Exhibit, Group Show, Global Focus UN Fourth World Conference on Women, Beijing, China (1995); Exhibit, Group Show, City of Tucson, AZ (1992-1994); Exhibit, Group Show, Arizona State Capitol, AZ (1994); Exhibit, Group Show, San Francisco Women Artists Gallery (1990); Exhibit,

Group Show, National Museum of Women in the Arts, WA (1990); Exhibit, Group Show, National Association of Women Artists, Inc., New York, NY (1988); Exhibit, Group Show, UN World Conference on Women, Nairobi, Kenya (1987); Exhibit, Group Show, The Pennsylvania State University (1987); Exhibit, Group Show, University of Portland (1987); Exhibit, Group Show, Alfred State College of Technology, State University of New York (1986); Exhibit, Group Show, Grove Gallery, University of California San Diego (1985); Exhibit, Group Show, Idaho State University (1984); Exhibit, Group Show, Iowa State University (1983); Exhibit, Group Show, University of Innsbruck, Austria (1982); Exhibit, Group Show, University of South Dakota (1981); Exhibit, Group Show, Ohio University (1981); Exhibit, Group Show, Arizona Invitational, Flagstaff, AZ (1980); Exhibit, Group Show, Walker Art Institute (Now Walker Art Center), New York, NY (1976); Exhibit, Group Show, Ford Foundation (1976); Exhibit, Group Show, Fordham University (1976); Exhibit, Group Show, The New School for Social Research (1976); Exhibit, Group Show, Cleveland Museum of Art, 1950; Exhibit, Group Show, The University of Arizona (1968, 1972); Exhibit, Group Show, Northern Arizona University (1968) **AW:** Irwin Zlowe Memorial Award for Printmaking, National Association of Women Artists, Inc., New York, NY **MH:** Albert Nelson Marquis Lifetime Achievement Award **AS:** Mrs. Bloomfield has always had an interest in art; the women in her family worked with porcelain. Mrs. Bloomfield was always interested in painting and drawing ever since she was a child.

BLUE, MONTE EDD, T: Chairman of the Board of Regents **I:** Education/Educational Services **CN:** Texas Chiropractic College **DOB:** 02/25/1945 **PB:** Fort Worth **SC:** TX/USA **PT:** Bert Leonard Blue; Mary Lee (Cooper) Blue **MS:** Married **SPN:** Sheryl Doris O'Connor (7/1/1966) **CH:** Michelle Denea; Laura Lynn **ED:** EdD, Administration of Higher Education, University of Houston (1979); MA in Art, North Texas State University (1972); BA in Advertising Art, North Texas State University (1967) **C:** Chairman of the Board of Regents, Texas Chiropractic College (2014-Present); President, San Jacinto Junior College, Pasadena, TX (1983-2008); Dean, Student Services, Central Campus, San Jacinto Junior College, Pasadena, TX (1981-1983); Dean, Student Services, South Campus, San Jacinto Junior College, Pasadena, TX (1979-1981); District Director, Instructor of Media, San Jacinto Junior College, Pasadena, TX (1975-1979); Instructor, Advertising Art, Central Campus, San Jacinto Junior College, Pasadena, TX (1971-1974); Illustrator, General Dynamics, Fort Worth, TX (1967-1971) **CR:** Board of Directors, Southeast Economic Development Council (1995-Present); Board of Directors, Deer Park Educational Foundation (1996-2007); Board of Directors, Moderator, Board of Southmore Medical Center Consumer Credit Counselor Service (1999-2000) **CIV:** Vice-Chairman, Board of Directors, San Jacinto YMCA, Pasadena, CA (1986-1987) **CW:** Contributor, Articles, Professional Journals; Speaker, Numerous Presentations, Various Community, Civic and Professional Groups **AW:** Outstanding Alumni, Fort Worth Independent School District (1984) **MEM:** Board of Directors, President, LaPorte/Bayshore Chamber of Commerce (1987-1989); Local President, Rotary (1986-1987); Honorable Member, Phi Theta Kappa (1985); Texas Public Community Junior College Association; Association of Texas Colleges and Universities; National Organization on Legal Problems in Education; American Association Higher Education; American Association Community Junior Colleges **MH:** Albert Nelson Marquis Lifetime Achievement Award **B/I:** Dr. Blue

always had an interest in art. Upon entering high school, he made the choice to go to technical high school and study commercial art. Art has always been one of the most important parts of his life. **AV:** Painting **PA:** Republican **RE:** Baptist

BLUMENAUER, EARL FRANCIS, T: U.S. Representative from Oregon **I:** Government Administration/Government Relations/Government Services **DOB:** 08/16/1948 **PB:** Portland **SC:** OR/USA **MS:** Married **SPN:** Margaret Kirkpatrick (2004) **CH:** Two Children **ED:** JD, Lewis & Clark Law School, Portland, OR (1976); BA in Political Science, Lewis & Clark College, Portland, OR (1970) **C:** Member, U.S. House of Representatives from Oregon's Third Congressional District, United States Congress, Washington, DC (1996-Present); Commissioner of Public Works, Portland City Council (1987-1996); Commissioner, Member, Governor Board, Multnomah County Board of Commissioners (1979-1987); Member, District 11, Oregon House of Representatives (1973-1979); Assistant to President, Portland State University (1971-1977); Member, Committee on Ways and Means **CR:** Member, Governor's Commission on Higher Education (1990-1991); Board of Directors, Portland Community College (1975-1981) **AW:** Ralph Lowell Award for Outstanding Contributions to Public Television (2010); Named Humane Legislator of the Year, American Humane Society (2008); Public Official's Award, Water Environment Federation (2006); Named One of the Top 25 Change Agents in Bicycling History, The League of American Bicyclists (2005); Global Sustainability Award, ITDP (2005); Public Radio Leadership Award, NPR (2005); National Distinguished Service Award, American Public Transit Association (2004); Community Health Super Hero Award, National Association of Community Health Centers, Inc. (2002); Apgar Award, National Building Museum, Washington, DC (2000); Named Legislator of the Year, APA (1999); Grantee, German Marshall Fund of the United States (1995) **MEM:** Honorary Member, American Society of Consulting Engineers; Honorary Member, American Institute for Architects (AIA); Honorary Member, The American Society of Landscape Architects; Honorary Member, Amalgamated Transit Union **AV:** Bicycling; Running **PA:** Democrat

BLUMENTHAL, RICHARD, T: U.S. Senator from Connecticut; Lawyer **I:** Government Administration/Government Relations/Government Services **DOB:** 02/13/1946 **PB:** New York **SC:** NY/USA **PT:** Martin Blumenthal; Jane (Rosenstock) Blumenthal **MS:** Married **SPN:** Cynthia Allison Malkin (06/27/1982) **CH:** Four Children **ED:** JD, Yale Law School (1973); BA, Harvard College (1967) **C:** Member, U.S. Senate Committee on Veterans' Affairs, Washington, DC (2013-Present); Member, U.S. Senate Committee on Commerce, Science and Transportation, Washington, DC (2013-Present); U.S. Senator, State of Connecticut, Washington, DC (2011-Present); Member, U.S. Senate Armed Services Committee, Washington, DC (2011-Present); Member, U.S. Senate Judiciary Committee, Washington, DC (2011-Present); Member, U.S. Senate Special Committee on Aging, Washington, DC (2011-Present); Member, U.S. Senate Health, Education, Labor and Pensions, Washington, DC (2011-2013); Attorney General, State of Connecticut, Hartford, CT (1991-2011); Member, District 27, Connecticut State Senate, Hartford, CT (1987-1990); Member, District 145, Connecticut House of Representatives, Hartford, CT (1984-1987); Partner, Silver Golub & Teitell LLP, Stamford, CT (1984-1990); Partner, Cummings & Lockwood LLC (1981-1984); United States Attorney, District of Connecticut, U.S. Department of Justice, Hart-

ford, CT (1977-1981); Administrator Assistant to Representative Abraham Ribicoff, U.S. Senate, Washington, DC (1975-1976); Law Clerk to Justice Harry A. Blackmun, Supreme Court of the United States, Washington, DC (1974-1975); Law Clerk to Honorable Jon O. Newman, United States District Court for the District of Connecticut (1973-1974) **CR:** Founder, Citizens Crime Commission of Connecticut (1982); Volunteer Counsel, NAACP Legal Defense and Educational Fund, Inc. (1981-1986) **MIL:** Sergeant, United States Marine Corps Reserve (1970-1976) **AW:** Raymond E. Baldwin Award for Public Service, Quinnipiac University School of Law (2002) **PA:** Democrat **RE:** Jewish

BLUNT, EMILY OLIVIA LEAH, T: Actress **I:** Media & Entertainment **DOB:** 2/23/1983 **PB:** London **SC:** United Kingdom **PT:** Oliver Simon Peter Blunt, QC; Joanna Blunt **MS:** Married **SPN:** John Krasinski (07/10/2010) **CH:** Hazel; Violet **ED:** Diplomate, Hurtwood House, Dorking, Surrey, United Kingdom (1999) **CIV:** Board of Directors, American Institute for Stuttering; Fundraiser, Malala Fund; Volunteer, Family Reach **CW:** Actress, "Wild Mountain Thyme" (2021); Actress, "Jungle Cruise" (2020); Actress, "A Quiet Place Part II" (2020); Singer, "Mary Poppins Returns: Original Motion Picture Soundtrack" (2018); Actress, "Mary Poppins Returns" (2018); Voice Actress, "Sherlock Gnomes" (2018); Actress, "A Quiet Place" (2018); Voice Actress, "Animal Crackers" (2017); Actress, "The Girl on the Train" (2016); Actress, "The Huntsman: Winter's War" (2016); Host, "Saturday Night Live" (2016); Actress, "Sicario" (2015); Singer, "Into the Woods: Original Motion Picture Soundtrack" (2014); Actress, "Into the Woods" (2014); Actress, "Edge of Tomorrow" (2014); Voice Actress, "The Wind Rises" (2013); Actress, "Arthur Newman" (2012); Actress, "Looper" (2012); Actress, "The Five-Year Engagement" (2012); Actress, "The Muppets" (2011); Actress, "Your Sister's Sister" (2011); Actress, "Salmon Fishing in the Yemen" (2011); Actress, "The Adjustment Bureau" (2011); Voice Actress, "Gnomeo & Juliet" (2011); Actress, "Gulliver's Travels" (2010); Actress, "Wild Target" (2010); Actress, "The Wolfman" (2010); Actress, "The Young Victoria" (2009); Voice Actress, "The Simpsons" (2009); Actress, "Sunshine Cleaning" (2008); Actress, "The Great Buck Howard" (2008); Actress, "Charlie Wilson's War" (2007); Actress, "Dan in Real Life" (2007); Actress, "The Jane Austen Book Club" (2007); Actress, "Wind Chill" (2007); Actress, "The Devil Wears Prada" (2006); Actress, "Irresistible" (2006); Actress, "Gideon's Daughter" (2005); Actress, "The Strange Case of Sherlock Holmes & Arthur Conan Doyle" (2005); Actress, "Empire" (2005); Actress, "My Summer of Love" (2004); Actress, "Poirot" (2004); Actress, "Foyle's War" (2003); Actress, "Henry VIII" (2003); Actress, "Warrior Queen" (2003); Actress, "Boudica" (2003); Actress, "Romeo and Juliet," Chichester Festival Theatre, West Sussex, United Kingdom (2002); Actress, "Vincent in Brixton," Royal National Theatre, London, United Kingdom (2002); Actress, "The Royal Family," Haymarket Theatre, London, United Kingdom (2001) **AW:** Screen Actors Guild Award for Outstanding Performance by a Female Actor in a Supporting Roles, SAG-AFTRA (2019); Critics' Choice Award for Best Actress in an Action Movie, The Critics Choice Association (2015); Kick Ass Award for Best Female Action Star, Alliance of Women Film Journalists (2015); Satellite Award for Best Ensemble – Motion Picture, International Press Academy (2015); Gotham Independent Film Award for Best Ensemble, IFP (2012); Saturn Award for Best Supporting Actress, Academy of Science Fiction, Fantasy and Horror Films (2012); Jupiter Award for Best International Actress, TV Spielfilm, Germany (2011); Award for Best Actress in a Canadian Film, Vancouver Film Critics Circle (2010); Britannia Award for British Artist of the Year, BAFTA Los Angeles, British Academy of Film and Television Arts (2009); Golden Globe Award for Best Supporting Actress – Series, Miniseries or Television Film, Hollywood Foreign Press Association (2007); London Film Critics' Circle Award for Supporting Actress of the Year, Critics' Circle (2007); Face of the Future Award, Women in Film Los Angeles (2007); Award for Most Promising Newcomer, Evening Standard British Film Awards (2005)

BLUNT, ROY DEAN, T: U.S. Senator from Missouri **I:** Government Administration/Government Relations/Government Services **DOB:** 01/10/1950 **PB:** Niangua **SC:** MO/USA **PT:** Leroy Blunt; Neva (Letterman) Blunt **MS:** Married **SPN:** Abigail Perlman (2003); Roseann Blunt (Divorced, 2003) **CH:** Matthew Roy; Amy Roseann; Andrew Benjamin; Charlie (Adopted) **ED:** MA in History and Government, Southwest Missouri State University (Now Missouri State University) (1972); BA in History, Southwest Baptist University (1970) **C:** Chair, Senate Rules Committee (2015-2017, 2018-Present); Vice Chairman, U.S. Senate Republican Conference (2012-Present); U.S. Senator, State of Missouri, Washington, DC (2011-Present); Member, U.S. Senate Committee on Rules and Administration, Washington, DC (2011-Present); Member, U.S. Senate Committee on Commerce, Science and Transportation, Washington, DC (2011-Present); Member, U.S. Senate Select Committee on Intelligence, Washington, DC (2011-Present); Member, U.S. Senate Appropriations Committee, Washington, DC (2011-Present); Assistant Minority Leader (Minority Whip), United States Congress from Missouri's Seventh Congressional District (2007-2009); Interim Majority Leader, United States Congress from Missouri's Seventh Congressional District (2005-2006); Assistant Majority Leader (Majority Whip), United States Congress from Missouri's Seventh Congressional District (2002-2007); Chief Deputy Majority Whip, United States Congress from Missouri's Seventh Congressional District (1999-2002); U.S. Representative from Missouri's Seventh Congressional District, United States Congress (1997-2011); President, Southwest Baptist University (1993-1996); Secretary of State, State of Missouri (1985-1993); Clerk, Greene County, MO (1973-1985); Instructor, Drury College, Springfield, MO (1973-1982); Teacher, Marshfield High School, MO (1970-1973) **CR:** Delegate, Atlantic Treaty Association Conference (1987) **CIV:** Missouri Mental Health Advocacy Council (1998-1999); Executive Board, American Council of Young Political Leaders (1998-1999); Co-Chairman, Missouri Opportunity 2000 Commission (1985-1987); Chairman, Missouri Housing Development Commission, Kansas City, MO (1981); Chairman, Republican State Convention, Springfield, MO (1980); Republican Candidate for Lieutenant Governor of Missouri (1980); Chairman, Governor's Advisory Council on Literacy **CW:** Co-Author, "Jobs Without People: The Coming Crisis for Missouri's Workforce" (1989); Co-Author, "Missouri Election Procedures: A Layman's Guide" (1977) **AW:** Community Health Defender Award, National Association of Community Health Centers, Inc. (2005); Arthur T. Marix Congressional Leadership Award, Military Officers Association of America (2004); Health Leadership Award, American Association of Nurse Anesthetists (2003); Distinguished Member of Congress Award, American Wire Producers Association (2002); Missouri Republican of the Year (2002); Listee, 10 Outstanding Young Americans, US Jaycees (1986); Listee, Missouri's Outstanding Young Civic Leaders (1981); Outstanding Young Man, Springfield Jaycees (1980)

MEM: Vice President, National Association of Secretaries of State (NASS) (1990); American Council of Young Political Leaders (ACYPL); Kiwanis International; Masons **PA:** Republican **RE:** Baptist

BLYTH, MYRNA, T: Senior Vice President, Editorial Director **I:** Nonprofit & Philanthropy **CN:** AARP **DOB:** 03/22/1939 **PB:** New York **SC:** NY/USA **PT:** Benjamin Greenstein; Betty (Austin) Greenstein **MS:** Widowed **SPN:** Jeffrey Blyth (11/25/1962, Deceased 2013) **CH:** Jonathan; Graham **ED:** Bachelor of Science, Bennington College, Vermont (1960) **C:** Senior Vice President, Editorial Director, AARP (2012-Present); Editor-in-Chief, ThirdAge.com (2010-2012); Editor-in-Chief, BettyConfidential. com (2009-2010); With New Product Development, Meredith Corporation (2002-2003); Vice President, Editorial Director, More Magazine (2002-2003); Editor-in-Chief, Publishing Director, More Magazine (1998-2002); Publishing Director, Senior Vice President, Ladies' Home Journal (1987-2002); Editor-in-Chief, Ladies' Home Journal (1981-2002); Executive Editor, Family Circle Magazine (1978-1981); Book and Fiction Editor, Then Associate Editor, Family Circle Magazine, New York, NY (1972-1978); Book Editor, Family Health Magazine (1968-1971); Senior Editor, Ingenue Magazine, New York, NY (1963-1968); Senior Editor, Datebook magazine, New York, NY (1960-1962); Freelance Writer **CR:** Chairperson, Take Your Kids 2 Vote **CIV:** Chairperson, President's Commission on White House Fellows (2002-2009); Delegate, White House Conference on Aging; Board Member, Goddess Fund; Member, National Advisory Board, Susan G. Komen Breast Cancer Foundation **CW:** Author, "How to Raise an American" (2007); Author, "Spin Sisters" (2004); Author, "For Better and For Worse" (1978); Author, "Cousin Suzanne" (1975); Columnist, National Review Online and The New York Sun; Contributor, Articles to New Yorker Magazine, New York Magazine, Redbook Magazine, Cosmopolitan Magazine, Reader's Digest **AW:** Henry Johnson Fisher Award (1999); Matrix Award, New York Women in Communications Inc. (1998); Human Relations Award, American Jewish Commitee's Publishing Division (1992); Headliner Award, Women in Communications Inc. (1992); Named, Publishing Executive of the Year, Advertising Age **MEM:** Women's Forum Inc.; Women's Media Group; Past President, New York Women in Communications Inc.; Ambassador of Excellence, New York Women in Communications Inc.; American Society of Magazine Editors; Overseas Press Club of America; Authors League Fund

BOAL, DEAN, T: Arts Center Administrator, Educator (Retired) **I:** Education/Educational Services **DOB:** 10/20/1931 **PB:** Longmont **SC:** CO/USA **PT:** Elmer C. Boal; L. Mildred (Snodgrass) Boal **MS:** Married **SPN:** Ellen Christine TeSelle (08/23/1957) **CH:** Brett; Jed **ED:** Doctor of Musical Arts, University of Colorado (1959); MusM, Indiana University (1956); MusB in Education, University of Colorado (1953) **C:** President Emeritus, Interlochen Center for the Arts (1995-Present); President, Interlochen Center for the Arts (1989-1995); Director of Arts and Performance Programs, National Public Radio (NPR), Washington, DC (1982-1989); Vice President, General Manager, Station WETA-FM, Washington, DC (1978-1983); Director, Radio Station KWMU, St. Louis Public Radio (1976-1978); President, St. Louis Conservatory (1973-1976); Professor of Piano, Chair of Music, State University of New York at Fredonia (1970-1973); Dean, Pianist, Peabody Conservatory, Baltimore, MD (1966-1970); Head, Piano Department, Bradley University, Peoria, IL (1960-1966); Member, Faculty, Hastings College, NE (1958-1960) **CIV:** With, Frasier Meadows Retirement Community (2012-

2017); Board of Directors, Chairman, Peak Association of the Arts (1998-2000); Member, Advisory Board, University of Colorado College of Music (1987-2000); Trustee, Alma College (1992-1995) **MIL:** Served, United States Army (1953-1955) **CW:** Author, "Interlochen, A Home for the Arts" (1998); Author, "Concepts and Skills for the Piano, Book II" (1970); Author, "Concepts and Skills for the Piano, Book I" (1969); Contributor, Articles to Professional Journals **AW:** George Norlin Award, University of Colorado (2011); Woodrow Wilson Teaching Fellow (1983-1989); Distinguished Alumnus Award in Professional Music, University of Colorado (1987) **MEM:** Chairman, Eastern Public Radio Network (1979-1982); The College Music Society; The Society of Pi Kappa Lambda; Mu Phi Epsilon; Phi Mu Alpha (Now Phi Mu Alpha Sinfonia Fraternity of America) **MH:** Albert Nelson Marquis Lifetime Achievement Award **B/I:** Dr. Boal became involved in his profession because of his childhood interest in piano. In high school, he had two fantastic colleagues, Vance Brand, an astronaut, and the other was a famous mathematician at Princeton university, Robert Gunnine. They grew up in a small town in Colorado together so the inspiration came from growing up with those people and their families. In addition to academic influence, there was also family influence. His mother, L. Mildred (Snodgrass) Boal, played piano at the movie theaters and inspired him to start playing the piano. **RE:** Presbyterian

BOBZIEN, DAVID PAUL JR., T: Director **I:** Government Administration/Government Relations/Government Services **CN:** Nevada Governor's Office of Energy **DOB:** 12/11/1972 **PB:** Washington **SC:** DC/USA **MS:** Married **SPN:** Lisa Bobzien **CH:** Luca; Finnegan **ED:** Master of Public Affairs in Natural Resources and Public Lands, Boise State University; Bachelor of Arts in Government and Politics, George Mason University **C:** Director, Nevada Governor's Office of Energy (2019-Present); Member, Reno City Council, At-Large District, State of Nevada (2014-2019); Member, District 24, Nevada Assembly (2006-2014); Former Staff Member, University of Nevada, Reno (1997); Member, Former Chairperson, Washoe County School District; Former Member, Council Career and Technical Education; Former Management Analyst Classified System; Former Staff Member, Budget and Analysis Office; Former Staff Member, Program of Assistant Planning; Former Staff Member, Office of the State Controller, State of Idaho; Former Summer Staff, Montana Wildlife Federation **CR:** Vice Chairperson, Committee on Government Affairs, Nevada Assembly; Member, Committee on Natural Resources, Nevada Assembly; Member, Committee on Agriculture and Mining, Nevada Assembly; Member, Committee on Education, Nevada Assembly; Member, Committee on Transportation, Nevada Assembly **AW:** Named, Assemblyman of the Year, Nevada Conservation League (2009); Highest-Rated Freshman Legislator of the 2007 Session, Las Vegas Review-Journal (2007); Named, Freshman of the Year, Peace Officers Research Association of Nevada (2007); Leadership in Energy Efficiency Award, Southwest Energy Efficiency Project; Award for Distinguished Deed, Nevada Conservation League; Golden Pinecone Award for Environmental Excellence as a Public Servant, Nevada EcoNet **MEM:** Representative, Greenway Plan Working Group; Former Chair, Wildlife Planning Subcommittee; Chairperson, Reno Recreation & Parks Commission **PA:** Democrat

BOCCHINO, ROBERT LOUIS, T: Communications Professional; Actor; Singer; Writer **I:** Media & Entertainment **DOB:** 05/28/1936 **PB:** Philadelphia **SC:** PA/USA **PT:** Daniel Bocchino; Gertrude

Rita (LaBattaaglia) Bocchino **MS:** Married **SPN:** Nancy L. Bocchino **CH:** Robert L. Bocchino Jr.; Steven R. Bocchino **ED:** Coursework in Acting and Musical Theater, HB Studios (1996-1998); Private Coaching with David Brunetti and Michael Warren, New York, NY; MBA, Temple University (1973); BA, Temple University (1964); Diploma, St. Joseph's Preparatory School (1955) **C:** Director, Alumni Board, Temple University College of Liberal Arts (1994-Present); Director, Marketing Programs (1978-1979); Director, Marketing Programs, Philadelphia Electric Company (Now PECO Energy Company) (1977); Audio Visual Public Relations Programs, Bryn Mawr, PA (1975-1977); Principal, Executive Communications Consultant, Robert L. Bocchino, Haverford, PA (1973); Past Member, Energy Advisory Committee, Economic Advisory Committee, Penjerdel; Audio Visual Public Relations Programs, Shipley School Audio Visual Public Relations Programs, Wills Eye Hospital, Philadelphia, PA; Audio Visual Public Relations Programs, Professional Photographers of America, Chicago, IL **CIV:** Treasurer, Mansard House Condominiums Association (2004-2007); President, Mansard House Condominiums Association (2006); Board Member, Mansard House Condominiums Association (1980s, 1990s, 2004); Treasurer, Haverford Civic Association (1997-1999); President, Treasurer, Mansard House Condominiums Association, Haverford, PA (1981-1982); Member, Board of Directors, Main Line YMCA, Ardmore, PA (1980); Past Member, New York Public Library Museum of Broadcasting **CW:** Producer, Announcer, Radio, TV Spots, The Haverford School (1996); Producer, Announcer, Radio, TV Spots, Woodford Mansion (1986); Producer, Announcer, Radio, TV Spots, Bartram's Garden (1984); Freelance Reporter, Voice of America (1979); Freelance TV Commercial and Movie Actor, "The Adams Chronicles," Bicentennial Productions (1976); Freelance Reporter, NBC Radio Network (1975-1976); Freelance TV Commercial and Movie Actor, Bicentennial Productions, Independence (1975); General Assignment Reporter, News Writer, Westinghouse Broadcasting Company, Philadelphia, PA; Vocal Artist, "Songs to Remember," and "Songs to Remember, Volume II," Easy Listening Standards Available on Most Internet Streaming Services **AW:** Inductee, Hall of Fame The Chamber of Commerce for Greater Philadelphia (1978) **MEM:** Broadcast Pioneers of Philadelphia (2014-Present); SAG-AFTRA (1967-Present); New York Chapter, The National Academy of Television Arts & Sciences (1994); Board of Directors, John Bartram Association (1986-1989); Chairman, Communications Committee, John Bartram Association (1986-1987); The Metropolitan Museum of Art, NY; Pennsylvania Horticultural Society; Past Member, New York Local On-Camera Commercial Performers Committee, SAG-AFTRA; Past Member, New York National Telecommunications Committee, SAG-AFTRA; Past Member, Philadelphia Museum of Art; Past Member, Standing Committee - The Membership Committee, The National Academy of Television Arts & Sciences; Past Member, National Trust for Historical Preservation; Past Member, Independence National Historic Park, The Franklin Institute; Philadelphia Orchestra Association; Life Member, The Chamber of Commerce for Greater Philadelphia **MH:** Albert Nelson Marquis Lifetime Achievement Award **B/I:** Mr. Bocchino became involved in his profession because he was always interested in communications since he was young, as well as singing, but he never really worked on it until an opportunity presented itself in 1996. He basically followed the talent aspect of it rather than the business part, and after earning an MBA, he became interested in the business side. He has both analytical business and performance skills.

AV: Gardening; Photography **PA:** Independent **RE:** Christian **THT:** For more information about Mr. Bocchino and his work, see the following link: http://www.robertbocchino.com/aboutartist/aboutartist.htm

BOECKMANN, JACOB OTTO, T: MD **I:** Medicine & Health Care **CN:** Pacific Coast Facial Plastic Surgery **MS:** Married **SPN:** Jessie **CH:** Mary Josephine **ED:** MD, University of Arkansas for Medical Sciences (2008) **CT:** Double-Board Certified Facial Plastic Surgeon **C:** Founder, Pacific Coast Facial Plastic Surgery (2019-Present); Facial Plastic Surgeon, Facial Aesthetic Concepts (2014-2019) **CW:** Contributor, "Aesthetic and Functional Outcomes in 100 Patients" (2014-Present); Author, "Le Fort I and Le Fort II Fractures," Master Techniques in Otolaryngology-Head and Neck Surgery: Facial Plastic Surgery, Wolters Kluewer, Philadelphia, PA (2018); Co-Author, "Facial Plastic and Reconstructive Surgery Study Guide" (2016); Author, "Rhinoplasty, Facial Plastic and Reconstructive Surgery Study Guide," Springer, New York, NY (2016); Co-Author, "Evidence-Based Medicine, Facial Plastic and Reconstructive Surgery Study Guide," Springer, New York, NY (2015); Contributor, "Lateral Neck Dissection for Well-Differentiated Thyroid Carcinoma: A Systematic Review Laryngoscope" (2014); Contributor, "Focal Thyroid Uptake on (18)f-fluorodeoxyglucose positron emission tomography: interpreting the data" (2013); Contributor, "Can the Pathology of a Thyroid Nodule Be Determined by Positron Emission Uptake?" Otolaryngol Head Neck Surgery (2012); Contributor, "Survival Following Free Flap Reconstruction for Primary and Salvage Surgery for Head and Neck Carcinoma" (2012); Contributor, "Impact on quality of life after mastoid obliteration," Laryngoscope (2008); Contributor, "Assessing Subjective Visual Vertical in Patients with Posterior Canalithiasis Before and After Canalith Repositioning with On-Axis Yaw Rotation," University of Arkansas for Medical Sciences (2005-2006); Contributor, "Thyroid incidentalomas in FDG PET/CT: prevalence and clinical impact," Eur Arch Otorhinolaryngol **AW:** Southern California Super Doctor Rising Star (2016-2018); Jack R. Anderson Award for Scholastic Excellence, American Board of Facial Plastic and Reconstructive Surgery (2014); Highest Excellence in Scientific Research, J. Floyd Kyser, MD, 18th Annual Resident Research and Alumni Conference, University of Arkansas for Medical Science (2011); Ryan Gibson Scholarship for Excellence in Medical Education, University of Arkansas for Medical Science, Little Rock, AR (2007) **MEM:** American Board of Facial Plastic Reconstructive Surgery; American Academy of Facial Plastic Surgery; California Society of Facial Plastic Surgeons; Alpha Omega Alpha; American Board of Facial Plastic Surgery Examination Development Committee **AS:** Dr. Boeckmann attributes his success to hard work. **B/I:** Dr. Boeckmann really wanted to make an impact on the lives of his patients. He looks at plastic surgery as a practice between art and science. It's a creative field that allows him to make an impact. He had many mentors who were influential and inspired his interest in the field. In addition, his involvement developed over time, starting with reconstruction procedures and, now, he is seeing the huge impact of what a single procedure can do for someone. **AV:** Spending time with family; Practicing fitness; Spending time outdoors; Maintaining physical health

BOGUCKI, RAYMOND SPENCER, ATTORNEY, T: Lawyer **I:** Law and Legal Services **CN:** The Raymond S. Bogucki Law Offices, P.S.C. **DOB:** 08/14/1951 **PB:** Hammond **SC:** IN/USA **PT:** Raymond L. Bogucki; Bette J. (Spencer) Bogucki **MS:** Married **SPN:**

Stephanie (Hendrix) Bogucki (2003); Vickie Kincheloe **CH:** Chant Graham; Anthony Dean; Justin Hendrix; John Ross Hendrix; Lyle Hendrix **ED:** JD, Northern Kentucky University, Highland Heights, KY (1980); BA in Communications, University of Kentucky (1976) **C:** Lawyer, Private Practice, Maysville, KY (1994-Present); Lawyer, Private Practice, Augusta, KY (1981-Present); Lawyer, Private Practice, Florence, KY (1980) **CR:** Professor, Northern Kentucky University, Highland Heights, KY (1981-1994) **CIV:** Attorney, Robinson County School Board; Robinson County Historic Society; Hands, LLC **MIL:** With, United States Navy (1969-1971) **CW:** Contributor, "Yearbook for Poetry," University of Kentucky; Contributor, Articles to Professional Journals **AW:** Named, Best of the Best in Maysville, KY (2006); AV Rating, Martindale-Hubbell **MEM:** Former Member, ABA; Former Member, Association of Trial Lawyers of America (Now American Association for Justice); Kentucky Justice Association **BAR:** Kentucky (1980); United States District Court for the Eastern District of Kentucky; United States Court of Appeals for the Sixth Circuit **MH:** Albert Nelson Marquis Lifetime Achievement Award; Marquis Who's Who Top Professional **B/I:** Mr. Bogucki is one of seven children and his father was a petroleum worker. He had the desire to become a lawyer when he was 7 years old. Then, he changed paths and left home when he was 12 and went into a seminary to pursue priesthood. Mr. Bogucki did that for three years, decided that was not for him, so he worked at the steel mills for a year. He then went into the United States Navy to receive the GI Bill of Rights to put himself through college and law school and finally achieved being a lawyer in 1980. Mr. Bogucki began his law career in 1979 as an intern with the Boone County prosecutor's office. **AV:** Farm

BOHANNON, CAMILLE, T: National Network Radio News Correspondent **I:** Media & Entertainment **DOB:** 05/30/1946 **PB:** Las Vegas **SC:** NV/USA **PT:** George W. Skora; Lillian Marie Guffey **MS:** Divorced **SPN:** James E. Bohannon (09/26/1970, Divorced 07/1987) **ED:** BA, New Mexico Highlands University (1968) **C:** News Anchor, Associated Press (1992-2008); News Anchor, NBC/Mutual Radio Networks (1987-1992); News Anchor, Station WRC Radio (1984-1987); News Anchor, United Press International Radio Network (1983-1984); News Anchor, WCFL Radio Chicago (1980-1983); News Anchor, Station WRC Radio (1977-1980); News Anchor, Station WTOP Radio (1975-1977); Classical Music Announcer, Station WETA Radio (1970-1972); News Anchor, Assistant Program Director, Clear Sight Cable Television (1967-1968); Disc Jockey, Station KFUN Radio (1967-1968) **CR:** Founder, Local Chapter, American Women in Radio and Television, The George Washington University (1978-1980); Speaker, 100 Events; Stars TV Fundraiser for Cerebral Palsy; Super Walk, March of Dimes; Bike-a-Thon, American Cancer Society **CIV:** Gaithersburg Chorus (2000-Present); Choir Member, Lay Leader, Covenant United Methodist Church (1984-Present) **AW:** Hackes Memorial Award, Radio Television Digital News Association (2011); Distinguished Alumni Award, New Mexico Highlands University (2008); Edward R. Murrow Award, Radio Television News Directors Association (2002); Outstanding Public Service Program Award, Chesapeake Associated Press Broadcasters (1987); Best Newscast Award, Illinois Associated Press Broadcasters (1983); Spot News Reporting Award, Chesapeake Associated Press Broadcasters (1977) **MEM:** The National Press Club; Society of Professional Journalists; National Capital Radio & Television Museum **MH:** Albert Nelson Marquis Lifetime Achievement Award **AS:** Ms. Bohannon attributes her success to her drive, patience and ambitious goals. **B/I:** Ms. Bohannon became involved in her profession because she is the daughter of a U.S. Foreign Service Officer and was always interested in diversity among people and nations. **AV:** Reading; Traveling; Watching sports **RE:** Methodist

BOHBOT, ALYZA, T: Owner, Chief Executive Officer **I:** Food & Restaurant Services **CN:** Alakef Coffee Roasters **PB:** Duluth **SC:** MN/USA **PT:** Nessim; Deborah **ED:** Master of Education in School Counseling, University of Massachusetts, Boston, MA (2013); Bachelor of Arts in Retail Management, Syracuse University (2008) **CT:** Certified, Women's Business Enterprise National Council **C:** Owner, Chief Executive Officer, Alakef Coffee Roasters (2015-Present); Owner, Chief Executive Officer, City Girl Coffee (2014-Present); Server, Anthem (2010-2013); Account Manager, The Boston Beer Company, Sam Adams (2008-2010) **CIV:** With, Women in Business Leadership Counsel; With, Minnesota Business Journal; Board of Directors, International Women's Coffee Alliance **AW:** Wavemaker Award, Team Minnesota Women (2018); Listee, 40 under 40, Minneapolis Business Journal (2017); Women Who Lead, Minnesota Business Journal (2017); Future Forward Award, Women's Business Development Council (2017); Manufacturing Sustainability Award, Minnesota Business Journal (2017) **MEM:** CEO Roundtable; Women Presidents Organization **AS:** Ms. Bohbot attributes her success on being knowledgeable of her greatest strengths, as well as knowing where to look for the greatest opportunities. Likewise, she credits her propensity for integrity and ability to allow more educated people to take the lead. **B/I:** Ms. Bohbot initially became involved in her profession out a desire to not see the wealth and success of her parents go to waste. The City Girl brand came about when she became aware of the inequities women in the coffee industry are routinely faced with. She wanted to bring awareness and educate consumers on what those challenges are and how solutions can be reached.

BOHN, ROBERT HERBERT, T: Lawyer **I:** Law and Legal Services **DOB:** 09/02/1935 **PB:** Austin **SC:** TX/USA **PT:** Herbert Bohn; Alice Bohn **MS:** Married **SPN:** Gay P. Maloy (06/04/1957) **CH:** Rebecca Shoemaker; Katherine Bernat; Robert H. John Jr. **ED:** LLB, University of Texas (1963); BBA, University of Texas (1957) **C:** Partner, Bohn & Bohn LLP (1998-Present); Partner, Bohn, Bennion & Niland (1992-1997); Partner, Alexander & Bohn, San Jose, CA (1987-1991); Partner, Boccardo Law Firm, San Jose, CA (1965-1987) **CR:** Speaker, California Continuing Education of Bar, Judge Pro Tempore, Superior Court of California, San Jose, CA (1975-2006) **MIL:** U.S. Air Force **AW:** Lifetime Achievement Award, Santa Clara County Trial Lawyers Association (2010); Named One of the Best Lawyers Silicon Valley, San Jose Magazine, (1995-2007); Super Lawyers of Northern California, San Francisco Magazine (2005, 2006); Best Lawyers in America (1995, 2006) **MEM:** President, Santa Clara County Trial Lawyers Association (1999); American Association for Justice; American College Master Barristers and Advisers; Consumer Attorneys of California; American Board of Trial Advocates; Santa Clara County Bar Association; California State Bar Association; Trial Lawyers for Public Justice; Roscoe Pound Foundation; Million Dollar Advocates Forum; Silicon Valley Capital Club; Commonwealth Club; Texas Cowboys Association; Phi Gamma Delta; Saratoga Rotary Club; Saratoga Men's Club; Saratoga Federated Church **BAR:** California (1965); Texas (1963) **MH:** Albert Nelson Marquis Lifetime Achievement Award **B/I:** Mr. Bohn became involved in his profession because

he always thought he would pursue a career in business. He joined the Reserve Officer Training Corps (ROTC) in college and later enlisted in the U.S. Air Force. After leaving the Air Force, he attended law school and finished in two years. Mr. Bohn then worked as a law clerk in Austin, Texas, before starting his own practice in California.

BOITANO, BRIAN ANTHONY, T: Professional Figure Skater **I:** Athletics **DOB:** 10/22/1963 **PB:** Mountain View **SC:** CA/USA **PT:** Donna; Lew **ED:** Diplomate, Marian A. Peterson High School, Sunnyvale, CA **CR:** Co-Founder, White Canvas Productions (1995); United States Men's National Figure Skating Team (1984, 1988, 1994) **CIV:** Founder, Youth Skate, San Francisco, CA (1998) **CW:** Host, "The Brian Boitano Project" (2014); Appearance, "Rise" (2011); Performer, "Brian Boitano Skating Specatacular" (2010); Appearance, "Be Good Johnny Weir" (2010); Host, "What Would Brian Boitano Make?" (2009-2010); Performer, "Frankie Valli & the Four Seasons: Tribute on Ice" (2008); Performer, Executive Producer, "Brian Boitano Skating Spectacular Starring Barry Manilow" (2007); Actor, "Blades of Glory" (2007); Actor, "Ice Princess" (2005); Co-Author (with Suzanne Harper), "Boitano's Edge: Inside the Real World of Figure Skating" (1997); Performer, "Skating Romance" (1996); Actor, "Nutcracker on Ice" (1995); Performer, "Super Bowl XXVI Halftime Show" (1992); Actor, "Carmen on Ice" (1990); Subject, "Brian Boitano: Canvas of Ice" (1988) **AW:** Inductee, U.S. Olympic & Paralympic Hall of Fame, United States Olympic & Paralympic Committee (2008); Gustave Lussi Award, Professional Skaters Association (PSA) (1999); Role Model of the Year, ProSkaters (1998);Inductee, World Figure Skating Museum and Hall of Fame (1996); Inductee, U.S. Figure Skating Hall of Fame (1996); Inductee, National Italian American Sports Hall of Fame (1996); Primetime Emmy Award for Outstanding Classical Music-Dance Program, Television Academy (1990) **MEM:** United States Delegation, Winter Olympics, Sochi, Russia (2014) **AV:** Cooking

BOLLINGER, LEE CARROLL, T: President, Lawyer, Educator **I:** Education/Educational Services **CN:** Columbia University **DOB:** 04/30/1946 **PB:** Santa Rosa **SC:** CA/USA **PT:** Patricia Mary Bollinger; Lee C. Bollinger **MS:** Married **SPN:** Jean Magnano Bollinger **CH:** Carey Jean; Lee Carroll **ED:** JD, Columbia Law School, Columbia University (1971); BS in Political Science, University of Oregon (1968) **C:** President, Columbia University (2002-Present); President, University of Michigan (1997-2001); Provost, Professor, Government, Dartmouth College (1994-1997); Dean, The University of Michigan Law School, Ann Arbor, MI (1987-1994); Professor, The University of Michigan Law School, Ann Arbor, MI (1979-1994); Associate Professor, The University of Michigan Law School, Ann Arbor, MI (1976-1979); Assistant Professor, The University of Michigan Law School, Ann Arbor, MI (1973-1976); Law Clerk, Chief Justice Warren Burger, Supreme Court of the United States (1972-1973); Law Clerk, Judge Wilfred Feinberg, U.S. Court of Appeals for the Second Circuit (1971-1972) **CR:** Board, The Pulitzer Prizes (2003-Present); Board of Directors, Graham Holdings Company (2007-Present); Chairman, Federal Reserve Bank of New York (2007-2012); Governor, Royal Shakespeare Company; Founder, Zuckerman Institute, Columbia University **CIV** Board of Trustees, The Kresge Foundation (2001-2017); Board of Trustees, Institute of International Education, Inc. **CW:** Co-Editor (with Geoffrey R. Stone), "The Free Speech Century" (2018); Author, "Uninhibited, Robust, and Wide-Open" (2010); Co-Editor (with Geoffrey R. Stone), "Eternally Vigilant: Free Speech in the Modern Era" (2001); Author, "Images of a

Free Press" (1991); Author, "The Tolerant Society: Freedom of Speech and Extremist Speech in America" (1986); Co-Author (with Jackson), "Contract Law in Modern Society" (1980) **AW:** Giving Back Award, INSIGHT Into Diversity (2016); Clark Kerr Award, University of California, Berkeley (2005); Medal of Excellence, Columbia Law School Association (2002); National Equal Justice Award, Legal Defense and Educational Fund, Inc.; National Humanitarian Award, National Conference for Community and Justice **MEM:** Honorary Fellow, Clare Hall, Cambridge University; Fellow, American Academy of Arts and Sciences **RE:** Catholic

BOLTON, JOHN ROBERT, T: Former United States National Security Advisor; Lawyer **I:** Law and Legal Services **DOB:** 11/20/1947 **PB:** Baltimore **SC:** MD/USA **PT:** Edward Jackson Bolton; Virginia Clara (Godfrey) Bolton **MS:** Married **SPN:** Gretchen Louise Brainerd; Christine Bolton (1972, Divorced 1983) **CH:** Jennifer Sarah **ED:** JD, Yale Law School (1974); BA, Yale University, Summa Cum Laude (1970) **C:** Of Counsel, Kirkland & Ellis LLP, Washington, DC (2008-Present); Senior Fellow, American Enterprise Institute, Washington, DC (2007-Present); United States National Security Advisor, Washington, DC (2018-2019); Senior Advisor, Freedom Capital Investment Management (2015); Permanent U.S. Representative to United Nations, U.S. Department of State, New York, NY (2005-2006); Under Secretary for Arms Control and International Security Affairs, U.S. Department of State, Washington, DC (2001-2005); Of Counsel, Kutak Rock LLP, Washington, DC (1999-2001); Senior Vice President, American Enterprise Institute, Washington, DC (1997-2001); Partner, Lerner, Reed, Bolton & McManus (and Predecessor Firms), Washington, DC (1993-1999); Assistant Secretary for International Organization Affairs, U.S. Department of State, Washington, DC (1989-1993); Assistant Attorney General, Civil Division, U.S. Department of Justice, Washington, DC (1988-1989); Assistant Attorney General for Legislative Affairs, U.S. Department of Justice, Washington, DC (1985-1988); Partner, Covington & Burling LLP, Washington, DC (1983-1985); Executive Director, Committee on Resolutions, Republican National Committee, Washington, DC (1983-1984); Assistant Administrator for Progressive and Policy Coordination, U.S. Agency for International Development (USAID), Washington, DC (1982-1983); General Counsel, U.S. Agency for International Development (USAID), Washington, DC (1981-1982); Legal Consultant, The White House, Washington, DC (1981); Associate, Covington & Burling LLP, Washington, DC (1974-1981) **CR:** EMS Technologies, Inc. (2009-Present); Board of Directors, Diamond Offshore Drilling, Inc. (2007-Present); Commissioner, U.S. Commission on International Religious Freedom (1999-2001); Member, Subcommittee on International Law, The Federalist Society (1999-2001); Board of Directors, Project for a New American Century (1989-2001); President, National Policy Forum, Washington, DC (1995-1996); Adjunct Professor, George Mason University Antonin Scalia Law School, Arlington, VA (1994-1996); Senior Fellow, Manhattan Institute, New York, NY (1993) **MIL:** United States Army Reserve (1974-1976); Maryland Air National Guard (1970-1974) **CW:** Author, "The Room Where it Happened: A White House Memoir" (2020); Author, "How Barack Obama Is Endangering Our National Sovereignty" (2010); Author, "Surrender is Not an Option: Defending America at the United Nations" (2007); Contributor, Articles, Professional Journals **AW:** Edmund J. Randolph Award, U.S. Department of Justice (1998); Tree of Life Award, Hadassah Northern Region and Hadassah Southern New England Region (1990);

Distinguished Service Award, U.S. State Department **MEM:** Pi Sigma Alpha; The Phi Beta Kappa Society **BAR:** United States Court of Appeals for the Second Circuit (1989); United States Court of Appeals for the Ninth Circuit (1988); United States Court of Appeals for the Eighth Circuit (1988); United States Court of Appeals for the Seventh Circuit (1988); United States Court of Appeals for the Sixth Circuit (1988); United States Court of Appeals for the First Circuit (1988); United States Court of Appeals for the Tenth Circuit (1983); United States Court of Appeals for the Eleventh Circuit (1981); United States Court of Appeals for the Fifth Circuit (1981); Supreme Court of the United States (1978); United States Court of Appeals for the Third Circuit (1978); United States Court of Appeals for the Fourth Circuit (1977); The District of Columbia (1975); United States District Court for the District of Columbia (1975); United States Court of Appeals for the District of Columbia Circuit (1975) **PA:** Republican **RE:** Lutheran

BOLY, LILLIAN, T: Language Educator (Retired) **I:** Education/Educational Services **DOB:** 02/25/1929 **PB:** St. Louis **SC:** MO/USA **PT:** Joseph Robert Boly; Mary Pearl (Park) Boly **ED:** MA in Education, Washington University in St. Louis, MO (1964); BS in Education, Southeast Missouri State University, Cape Girardeau, MO (1955); Postgraduate Coursework, University of Oregon; Postgraduate Coursework, Washington University in St. Louis, MO **CT:** Certified in Elementary Education, Secondary English, and Social Studies **C:** Teacher, English, Riverview Gardens School District, St. Louis, MO (1963-1990); Teacher, Fourth Grade, Riverview Gardens School District, St. Louis, MO (1954-1963); Teacher, Third and Fourth Grades, Naylor School District, MO (1949-1954); Teacher in One-Room Schools, Butler County, MO (1945-1948); Sponsor, Future Teachers of America and Spectrum Literary Publication, Riverview Gardens School District, St. Louis, MO **CR:** Member, National Council of Teachers of English (NCTE) and the Missouri Association of Teachers of English (Missouri English Teachers) (1963-1993); Member, Board of Directors, St. Louis Suburban Teachers of English (1970-1978); President, St. Louis Suburban Teachers of English (1971-1972); Vice President, St. Louis Suburban Teachers of English (1970-1971); Member, Convention Delegate, Treasurer, President, Riverview Gardens NEA **CIV:** Friendship International (30 Years) **CW:** Newsletter Editor, American Association of University Women (AAUW) (2004-2010) **MEM:** Treasurer, American Association of University Women (AAUW) (2010-2015); President, American Association of University Women (AAUW) (1991-1995, 1998-1999, 2001-2002, 2004-2006); Program Vice President, St. Louis Chapter, Phi Delta Kappa (PDK International) (2003-2004); Secretary, St. Louis Chapter, Phi Delta Kappa (PDK International) (1992-1994, 2001-2003, 2003-2004); Cultural Interest Chair, American Association of University Women of Missouri (AAUW of Missouri) (1993-1995); National Education Association; Missouri NEA-Retired; American Association of University Women (AAUW) **MH:** Albert Nelson Marquis Lifetime Achievement Award **AS:** Ms. Boly attributes her success to loving to read and liking school. **B/I:** Ms. Boly became involved in her profession because her dad was a student teacher before she was born. Her elementary school teacher, Charlotte Gray, was also an inspiration. **AV:** Traveling (41 countries); Photography of travels

BON JOVI, JON, T: Musician **I:** Media & Entertainment **DOB:** 03/02/1962 **PB:** Perth Amboy **SC:** NJ/USA **PT:** John Francis Bongiovi, Sr.; Carol (Sharkey) Bongiovi **MS:** Married **SPN:** Dorothea Hurley (1989) **CH:** Stephanie Rose; Jesse James Louis; Jacob Hurley; Romeo Jon **ED:** Diplomate, Sayreville War Memorial High School (1980) **C:** Singer-Songwriter (2004-2011) **CIV:** Founder, JBJ Soul Kitchen, Jon Bon Jovi Soul Foundation, Red Bank, NJ (2011-Present); Foudnder, Phase V Homeownership Project, Jon Bon Jovi Soul Foundation, Philadelphia, PA (2007); Performer, Live Earth (2007); Benefactor, Oprah's Angel Network (2005) **CW:** Singer-Songwriter, Guitarist, "Bon Jovi: 2020" (2020); Singer-Songwriter, Guitarist, "This House Is Not for Sale" (2016); Singer-Songwriter, Guitarist, "Burning Bridges" (2015); Singer-Songwriter, Guitarist, "What About Now" (2013); Actor, "New Year's Eve" (2011); Actor, "30 Rock" (2010); Singer-Songwriter, Guitarist, "The Circle" (2009); Singer-Songwriter, Guitarist, "Lost Highway" (2007); Actor, "The West Wing" (2006); Actor, "National Lampoon's Pucked" (2006); Actor, "Cry Wolf" (2005); Singer-Songwriter, Guitarist, "Have a Nice Day" (2005); Actor, "Ally McBeal" (2002); Actor, "Vampires: Los Muertos" (2002); Singer-Songwriter, Guitarist, "Bounce" (2002); Actor, "Pay It Forward" (2000); Actor, "U-571" (2000); Singer-Songwriter, Guitarist, "Crush" (2000); Actor, "Sex and the City" (1999); Actor, "Row Your Boat" (1998); Actor, "Homegrown" (1998); Actor, "No Looking Back" (1998); Actor, "Destination Anywhere: The Film" (1997); Singer-Songwriter, Instrumentalist, Producer, "Destination Anywhere" (1997); Actor, "Little City" (1997); Actor, "The Leading Man" (1996); Actor, "Moonlight and Valentino" (1995); Singer-Songwriter, Guitarist, "These Days" (1995); Singer-Songwriter, Guitarist, "Keep the Faith" (1992); Singer-Songwriter, Instrumentalist, Producer, "Blaze of Glory" (1990); Singer-Songwriter, Guitarist, "New Jersey" (1988); Singer-Songwriter, Guitarist, "Slippery When Wet" (1986); Singer-Songwriter, Guitarist, "7800° Fahrenheit" (1985); Singer-Songwriter, Guitarist, "Bon Jovi" (1984) **AW:** Inductee, Rock & Roll Hall of Fame (2018); Billboard Music Award for Top Touring Artist, Billboard (2014); Inductee, New Jersey Hall of Fame (2009); Inductee, Songwriters Hall of Fame (2009); Diamond Award, World Music Awards (2005); Award of Merit, American Music Awards, dick clark productions, llc (2004); Brit Award for International Male Solo Artist, British Phonographic Industry (1998); American Music Award for Favorite Pop/Rock Song, dick clark productions, llc (1991); Golden Globe Award for Best Original Song, Hollywood Foreign Press Association (1991); **MEM:** White House Council for Community Solutions (2010) **PA:** Democrat

BONAMICI, SUZANNE MARIE, T: U.S. Representative from Oregon **I:** Government Administration/Government Relations/Government Services **DOB:** 10/14/1954 **PB:** Detroit **SC:** MI/USA **MS:** Married **SPN:** Michael Howard Simon (06/16/1985) **CH:** Andrew David; Sara **ED:** JD, University of Oregon School of Law (1983); BA in Journalism, University of Oregon (1980); AA, Lane Community College (1978) **C:** U.S. Representative from Oregon's First District, United States Congress (2012-Present); Member, District 17, Oregon State Senate (2008-2011); Member, District 34, Oregon House of Representatives (2007-2008); Legislative Assistant, Oregon House of Representatives (2001-2006); Member, Committee on Science, Space and Technology; Member, Committee on Education and the Workforce; Attorney, Stoll & Stoll, Portland, OR; Legal Assistant, Law Clerk, Lane County Legal Aid Service; Attorney, Bureau of Consumer Protection, Federal Trade Commission (FTC) **CIV:** Board of Directors, Northwest Children's Theater and School (NWCT) **MEM:** Citizens for Beaverton Schools; Beaverton Education Foundation **PA:** Democrat

BOND, JOSEPH, T: Retail Manager **I:** Retail/Sales **CN:** Zac Posen **PB:** Queens **SC:** NY/USA **ED:** BFA in Theater & Costume Design, Long Island University, C.W. Post Campus (2005) **C:** VIP Services, Zac Posen, New York, NY (2016-Present); Senior Sales Associate, Carolina Herrera, New York, NY (2015-2016); Sales Associate, Carolina Herrera, New York, NY (2013-2015); Junior Sales Associate, Carolina Herrera, New York, NY (2012-2013); Sales & Operations Assistant, Carolina Herrera, New York, NY (2010-2012); Sales Coordinator, Akris (2007-2010) **CIV:** Volunteer, Imperial Court of New York (ICNY) (2010-Present); God's Love We Deliver; Gay & Lesbian Alliance Against Defamation (GLAAD); Gay Men's Health Crisis (GMHC); Former Student-Body President, Flushing High School **AW:** Student Medal, Metropolitan Museum of Art (2000); New York State Lottery Scholarship **AS:** Mr. Bond attributes his success to his friends and family, all of whom allowed him to be creative and pursue his dreams. He also has a strong drive, which caused him to set goals in his life that he consistently worked toward achieving. **B/I:** Mr. Bond was first inspired to pursue fashion as a career when he was a child because he was always involved in the arts. He went to school for costume design and theater. He loved the history of fashion. He recalled making and designing clothes for Barbie dolls while playing with his sister as a child. He always felt that playing with Barbie dolls gave him a creative world to create beautiful things; he felt fortunate to have that in his early life. After college, he worked in advertising for a brief time before moving into fashion merchandising and wholesale. He then received a job with a luxury brand called Akris. He was later hired by the president of the company to work for Carolina Herrera, where he stayed for 10 years and became one of the top salesmen in the world. **THT:** Mr. Bond treats other people how he wants to be treated. He is kind and generous.

BONDS, BARRY LAMAR, T: Professional Baseball Player (Retired) **I:** Athletics **DOB:** 07/24/1964 **PB:** Riverside **SC:** CA/USA **PT:** Bobby Bonds; Patricia (Howard) Bonds **MS:** Divorced **SPN:** Liz Watson (01/10/1998, Divorced 2011); Susann ("Sun") Margreth Branco (02/05/1988, Divorced 12/1994) **CH:** Nikolai; Shikari; Aisha **ED:** BA in Criminology, Arizona State University (1986) **C:** Special Advisor to Chief Executive Officer San Francisco Giants, MLB (2017-Present); Hitting Coach, Miami Marlins, MLB (2015-2016); Outfielder, San Francisco Giants, MLB (1992-2007); Outfielder, Pittsburgh Pirates, MLB (1986-1992) **CR:** With, United States National Baseball Team (1984) **CIV:** Founder, Barry Bonds Family Foundation (1993-Present) **CW:** Subject, "Bonds on Bonds" (2006) **AW:** Inductee, San Francisco Giants Wall of Fame (2017); Named All-star, National League (1990, 1992-1998, 2000-2004, 2007); Named National League MVP (1990, 1992, 1993, 2001-2004); Named Major League Player of the Year, Baseball America Enterprises (2001, 2003, 2004); Hank Aaron Award, National League (2001, 2002, 2004); Named Major League Player of the Year (1990, 2001, 2004); Named All-star, Baseball America Enterprises (1993, 1998, 2000-2004); Silver Slugger Award (1990-1994, 1996, 1997, 2000-2004); Babe Ruth Home Run Award (2001); MLB Athlete of the Decade, 1990s, Sporting News (1999); Philanthropist of the Year Award, National Conference for Black Philanthropy, Inc. (1999); Rawlings Gold Glove Award (1990-1994, 1996-1998) **AV:** Golfing; Photography; Music

BONE, HENRY G., MD, MACP, FRCP, FACE, T: Physician, Clinical Researcher **I:** Medicine & Health Care **DOB:** 04/04/1947 **PB:** Seattle **SC:** WA/USA **PT:** Henry Grady Bone Jr.; Mary Isabel

(Sheehan) Bone **ED:** Postdoctoral Fellow, Clinical Instructor, University of California San Diego, La Jolla, CA (1977-1978); Clinical Research Fellow, The University of Texas Southwestern Medical School and Affiliated Hospitals, Dallas, Texas (1974-1977); Intern, Resident, Parkland Memorial Hospital, Parkland Health & Hospital System, The University of Texas Southwestern Medical Schools & Affiliated Hospitals, Dallas, Texas (1972-1974); MD, University of Washington, with Honors (1972); AB in Biology, Princeton University (1968) **CT:** Diplomate, American Board of Internal Medicine; American Board of Endocrinology and Metabolism **C:** Chief of Endocrinology and Metabolism, St. John Hospital (2002-Present); Staff Physician, St. John Hospital (1997-Present); Staff Physician, WM Beaumont Hospital, Grosse Pointe, MI (2007-Present); Senior Staff Physician, Henry Ford Hospital, Henry Ford Health System, Detroit, MI (1987-1997); Director of Clinical Research, Ciba-Geigy Pharmaceuticals, Summit, NJ (1984-1987); Research Associate, Veterans Affairs Medical Center, La Jolla, CA (1980-1983); Assistant Professor of Medicine, University of California San Diego, La Jolla, CA (1978-1984); National Institutes of Health Clinical Investigator, University of California San Diego, La Jolla, CA (1978-1980) **CR:** Adjunct Professor of Medicine, University of Michigan (2007-Present); Consultant, U.S. Food and Drug Administration (1991-Present); Consultant, Pharmaceutical Industry (1988-Present); Lecturer, Various Medical Centers (1977-Present) **CIV:** Chairman, Endocrine and Metabolic Drugs Advisory Committee (1995-2000); Endocrine and Metabolic Drugs Advisory Committee (1994-2000); Chair, Medical Advisory Panel, Paget Foundation (1988-2017); Member, Board of Directors, Former Secretary-treasurer, U.S. Food and Drug Administration; Ad-hoc Chairman, Endocrine and Metabolic Drugs Advisory Committee; President, Michigan Consortium for Osteoporosis **CW:** Contributor, Reviewer, Medical Articles to Professional Journals **AW:** Great Internist of Michigan Award, American College of Physicians (2016); Laureate Award, American College of Physicians, MI, (2012); Dr. Boy Frame Memorial Award (1989); Boeing Merit Scholarship, Princeton University (1964-1968) **MEM:** Fellow, Royal College of Physicians, London, England, United Kingdom; Fellow, American Society for Bone and Mineral Research (ASBMR); Master, American College of Physicians; Fellow, American College of Endocrinology, American Association of Clinical Endocrinology (AACE); Alpha Omega Alpha Honor Medical Society); American Medical Association; The Endocrine Society; Detroit Institute of Arts; Seattle Tennis Club; The Princeton Club New York **MH:** Albert Nelson Marquis Lifetime Achievement Award **RE:** Roman Catholic

BONE, PAMELA WEAVER JEAN, T: Elementary School Educator **I:** Education/Educational Services **CN:** U.S. Department of Education **DOB:** 02/12/1965 **PB:** Trujillo **SC:** Peru **PT:** Donald Grove Weaver; Barbara Ann (Geil) Weaver **MS:** Married **SPN:** David F. Bone (10/07/2000) **CH:** Melinda W. Bone **ED:** MEd, University of Maryland, Cum Laude (1995); BS, Eastern Mennonite College (Now Eastern Mennonite University), Cum Laude (1988) **CT:** Certified Teacher, Reading Specialist, State of Maryland (1989) **C:** Contracting Officer, U.S. Department of Education (2003-Present); Contract Specialist, U.S. Department of Education (1997-2003); Reading Specialist, Montgomery County Public Schools (1995-1997); Teacher, Bethesda Community School, MD (1988-1995) **CIV:** Counselor, Stephen Ministries, Bethesda, MD (1989-1992); Sunday School Teacher, Immanuel Bible Church **CW:** Author, "Parents and Educators Opinions and Practices of Parental Involvement,"

Literacy Issues and Practices (1996) **MEM:** International Reading Association (Now International Literacy Association) **MH:** Albert Nelson Marquis Lifetime Achievement Award **B/I:** Mrs. Weaver Bone grew up being teased as a child. She was average and never felt that she was particularly smart. She remembers one year the teacher was trying to explain something to her and she just looked at her and thought, 'why doesn't she stop that and just show me?'. Mrs. Weaver Bone is a visual learner. She recalls her third grade teacher; she was excellent. She would read them "Charlotte's Web," changing her voice for each of the characters, which made it fun. In seventh grade, she took Russian history, and during the first part of the semester, the teacher would pretend to be a czar and the class had to bow to him and call him such. In the second half of the semester, everyone wore red to every class to make themselves feel equal. He made learning fun and was also an excellent teacher. **AV:** Reading; Aerobics; Badminton; Tennis; Hiking **PA:** Democrat **RE:** Presbyterian

BONNETT, AUBREY W., PHD, T: Professor Emeritus **I:** Education/Educational Services **DOB:** 02/01/1942 **PB:** Georgetown **SC:** Guyana **PT:** Julius S. Bonnett; Olivia (Pile) Bonnett **MS:** Married **CH:** Mark; Pierre **ED:** Doctor of Philosophy, City University of New York (1976); Master of Arts, University of Alberta, Edmonton, Alberta, Canada (1969); Bachelor of Arts in Sociology, Inter American University of Puerto Rico, Magna Cum Laude (1966) **C:** Dean, School of Social and Behavioral Sciences, California State University, San Bernardino, CA (1987-Present); Vice President of Academic Affairs, State University of New York College at Old Westbury, New York (1994-1997, 1999-2003); Chairman, Department of Sociology, Hunter College, New York, NY (1985-1987); Faculty, Fellow in Academy Administration, City University of New York (1983-1984); President, Administration Intern, Hunter College, New York, NY (1982-1983); Deputy Executive Officer, Graduate Center, City University of New York, New York, NY (1980-1982) **CR:** Seminar Associate, Columbia University, New York, NY (1982-1985) **CIV:** Board of Directors, Home of Neighborly Service, San Bernardino, CA (1987-1989) **CW:** Co-Author, "Continuing Perspectives on the Black Diaspora" (2007); Co-Author, "Emerging Perspectives on the Black Diaspora" (1990); Author, "Institutional Adaptation of West Indian Immigrants to America: An Analysis of Rotating Credit Associations" (1981); Author, "Group Identification Among Negroes: An Examination of the Soul Concept in the U.S.A." (1980); Contributor, Chapters to Books and Articles to Professional Journals **AW:** Postdoctoral Grantee, Social Sciences, Research Council, New York, NY (1977); Honor Scholar, Jessie Smith Noyes Foundation, New York, NY (1966) **MEM:** American Association for Higher Education; American Sociological Association; Council of Colleges of Arts and Sciences; Caribbean Studies Association **MH:** Albert Nelson Marquis Lifetime Achievement Award; Marquis Who's Who Humanitarian Award **B/I:** Dr. Bonnett became involved in his profession after he received his master's degree. He originally had intentions of being a lawyer before immigrating to the United States with his parents. At the time of his arrival, the Attica Rebellion was a major social topic of the time and Dr. Bonnett was not pleased with the way the governor handled the situation, causing him to change his mind about working in law. After attaining his degree, he decided to take up teaching instead, through which he benefited from the mentorship of Congresswoman Donna Shalala. **AV:** Theater; Black history; Spectator sports **PA:** Republican **RE:** Episcopalian

BONOMO, DONALD, T: Attorney, Partner **I:** Law and Legal Services **CN:** Law Offices of Perez and Bonomo **DOB:** 01/01/2050 **ED:** JD, Rutgers Law School (2001); BS in Criminal Law, St. John's University (1998) **C:** Founding Member, Senior Partner, The Law Offices of Perez and Bonomo (2002-Present); Judicial Clerk to Honorable Joseph Yannotti, Appellate Division (2002) **CIV:** Pro Bono Work; Bankruptcy Courses, Northeast New Jersey of Legal Service **CW:** Quoted, Wall Street Journal; Quoted, Bergen Record; Quoted, The Jersey Journal; Contributor, Several Publications Regarding Bankruptcy and Foreclosure Law; Lectures, St. Peters University and New Jersey City University **AW:** Equal Justice Medal, Outstanding Legal Services (2017); **MEM:** National Association of Consumer Bankruptcy Attorneys; Northeast New Jersey Legal Services; North American Consumer Bankruptcy Association; New Jersey State Bar Association; Bergen County Bar Association; Consumer Protection Attorney **AS:** Mr. Bonomo attributes his success to his late mother. She pushed him to go into law school. **B/I:** Mr. Bonomo really wanted to help people. He wanted to help people get into their own homes. **THT:** Mr. Bonomo's motto is to have good, clear communication with his clients. He is always honest.

BONVILLIAN, WILLIAM B., T: Lecturer **I:** Education/Educational Services **DOB:** 03/07/1947 **PB:** Honolulu **SC:** HI/USA **PT:** William Doughty Bonvillian; Florence Elizabeth (Boone) Bonvillian **MS:** Married **SPN:** Janis Ann Sposato (04/12/1980) **CH:** Raphael William Boone; Marcus Doughty **ED:** JD, Columbia University (1974); MA in Religion, Yale University (1972); AB, Columbia University (1969) **C:** Lecturer, Senior Director, MIT Office of Open Learning (2017-Present); Director, Washington Office, Massachusetts Institute of Technology, Washington, DC (2006-2017); Chief Counsel, Legislative Director to Senator Joseph Lieberman, United States Senate, Washington, DC (1989-2006); Partner, Jenner & Block, Washington, DC (1985-1989); Partner, Brown, Roady, Bonvillian & Gold, Washington, DC (1981-1985); Deputy, Assistant Secretary, Director, Conglomerate Affairs, Liaison Officer, United States Department of Transportation, Washington, DC (1977-1981); Associate, Steptoe & Johnson, Washington, DC (1975-1977); Law Clerk, Honorary Jack B. Weinstein, United States District Court for the Eastern District of New York (1974-1975) **CIV:** Board Member, (ITIF) Information Technology & Innovation Foundation **CW:** Co-author, "Advanced Manufacturing, The New American Innovation Policies" (2018); Co-author, "Technological Innovation in Legacy Sectors" (2015); Co-author, "Structuring an Energy Technology Revolution" (2009); Board of Editors, Columbia Law Review (1973-1974); Contributor, Articles, Scientific Policy Journals **AW:** IEEE Public Service Award (2007); Two Outstanding Performance Awards, United States Secretary of Transportation, Washington, DC (1979-1980) **MEM:** Chair, Standing Committee on Science Engineering and Public Policy, American Association for the Advancement of Science (2017-Present); Fellow, American Association for the Advancement of Science; Standing Committee, Innovation Policy Forum, National Academy of Sciences **BAR:** Supreme Court of the United States (1983); District of Columbia (1976); Connecticut (1975) **MH:** Albert Nelson Marquis Lifetime Achievement Award **B/I:** Mr. Bonvillian became involved in his profession because he really wanted to work in the government policy area and law was a good background for that. **PA:** Democrat **RE:** Episcopalian

BOOHER, CHARLES FOREST, T: Business Executive **I:** Business Management/Business Services **DOB:** 12/02/1944 **PB:** Columbus **SC:** OH/USA **PT:** Charles Henry; Ruth (Wood) C **MS:** Married **SPN:** RuthAnn Shisler **CH:** Cynthia Lynn; Stephanie Kaye; Melissa; Leslie Ann; Jennifer **ED:** Diploma, High School, Millersport, OH **C:** Owner, Charles Booher & Associates Inc., Ohio (1974-Present); Founder, President, American Benefit Life Assurance Co. (1998); Owner, Simplified Business Solutions, Inc. (1993); Owner, Benefits International, Inc., Ohio (1990-1992); Owner, National Benefit Managers, Inc., Sarasota, FL (1986-1988); Owner, Health Administrators of America, Powell, OH (1978-1992); Assistant Manager, Mutual of New York, Columbus, OH (1973-1974); Sales Director, New England Life, Columbus, OH (1971-1973); Insurance Agent, Great West Life, Columbus (1969-1971); Insurance Agent, John Hancock Life Insurance Co., Columbus, OH (1967-1969); Electronic Technician, Battelle Memorial Institute, Columbus, OH (1966-1967) **CR:** Speaker, Various Civic and Trade Organizations **CIV:** Board of Directors, Six Pence School for the Learning Disabled, Columbus, OH (1980); Johnstown Presbyterian Church **MIL:** U.S. Navy (1962-1966); Vietnam Veteran **AW:** National Sales Achievement and National Quality Awards **MEM:** Member, National Association of Life Underwriters; Million Dollar Round Table; Top of the Table; Society of Professional Benefit Administrators; Columbus Life Underwriters Association **MH:** Albert Nelson Marquis Lifetime Achievement Award **B/I:** Mr. Booher became involved in his profession because he needed money. He worked for a research center in Columbus Ohio at first and had a child that was born while he was in Vietnam. He needed to make money quickly and he was not making enough at the research center so he answered an ad for an insurance salesman and got the job and started selling insurance door to door. **AV:** Golf; Hunting **PA:** Republican **RE:** Christian

BOOKER, CORY ANTHONY, T: U.S. Senator from New Jersey **I:** Government Administration/Government Relations/Government Services **DOB:** 04/27/1969 **PB:** Washington, DC **SC:** DC/USA **PT:** Cary Alfred Booker; Carolyn Rose (Jordan) Booker **ED:** Honorary Doctorate, Fairleigh Dickinson University (2012); Honorary LLD, Bard College (2012); Honorary LLD, Washington University in St. Louis (2013); Honorary LHD, Williams College (2011); Honorary LHD, Yeshiva University (2010); Honorary LHD, New Jersey Institute of Technology (2009); JD, Yale Law School (1997); BA, University of Oxford, with Honors (1994); MA in Sociology, Stanford University (1992); BA, Stanford University, with Honors (1991) **C:** Democratic Nominee, Presidential 2020 Campaign (2019); U.S. Senator, State of New Jersey (2013-Present); U.S. Senate Small Business Committee (2013-Present); U.S. Senate Committee on Environment and Public Works (2013-Present); U.S. Senate Commerce Committee (2013-Present); Mayor, Newark, NJ (2006-2013); Partner, Booker, Rabinowitz, Trenk, Lubetkin, Tully, DiPasquale & Webster, PC, West Orange, NJ (2002-2013); Councilman, Central Ward, Newark, NJ (1998-2002); Program Coordinator, Newark Youth Project (1998); Staff Attorney, Urban Justice Center (1997) **CR:** Board of Trustees, Bloomberg Family Foundation (2010-Present); Skadden Fellow, University of Oxford (1997); Co-founder, Board Member, Waywire (2012); Board Member, International Longevity Center (ILC); Board Member, Integrity Inc.; Board Member, North Star Academy; Board Member, Black Alliance for Educational Options (BAEO); Board of Trustees, Stanford University; Board of Trustees, Columbia University Teacher's College; Executive Committee, Yale Law School; Honorary Public Interest Fellow, University of Pennsylvania Carey Law School; Senior Fellow, Rutgers University Eugene J. Bloustein School **CIV:** Founder, Director, Newark Now **CW:** Author, "United: Thoughts on Finding Common Ground and Advancing the Common Good" (2016); Appearance, "Parks and Recreations" (2015); Appearance, "Miss Representation" (2011); Appearance, "The Lottery" (2010); Featured, "Brick City" (2009); Featured, "Street Fight" (2002); Contributor, Articles, Law Journals **AW:** Named One of the 100 Most Influential People in the World (2011); John Heinz Award for Greatest Public Service by an Elected or Appointed Official (2010); Named One of America's Best Leaders, U.S. News & World Report (2009); Named to Power 150, Ebony Magazine (2008); Named to America's Most Powerful Players Under 40, Black Enterprise (2005); Named One of the Country's 40 Best and Brightest, Esquire Magazine (2002); Named Savior of Newark, TIME Magazine (2000); Named to New Jersey Top 40 Under 40, New Jersey Monthly **BAR:** State of New Jersey (1998) **PA:** Democrat **RE:** Christian

BOOTH, DAVID GILBERT, T: Co-founder, Executive Chairman **I:** Business Management/Business Services **CN:** Dimensional Fund Advisors **MS:** Married **ED:** MBA, The University of Chicago Booth School of Business (1971); MS, The University of Kansas (1969); BA in Economics, The University of Kansas (1968) **C:** Co-founder, Executive Chairman, Dimensional Fund Advisors (1981-Present); Research Assistant, Eugene Fama **CIV:** Participant, The Giving Pledge (2018); Trustee, The University of Chicago Booth School of Business **CW:** Co-author, "Diversification Returns and Asset Management"; Contributor, Articles, Professional Journals **AW:** Listee, Billionaires List, Forbes (2019); Listee, 50 Top American Givers, BusinessWeek (Now Bloomberg Businessweek) (2008); Graham and Dodd Award of Excellence, Financial Analysts Journal (1992)

BOOZMAN, JOHN NICHOLS, T: U.S. Senator from Arkansas; Optometrist **I:** Government Administration/Government Relations/Government Services **DOB:** 12/10/1950 **PB:** Shreveport **SC:** LA/USA **PT:** Fay Winford Boozman Jr.; Marie E. (Nichols) Boozman **MS:** Married **SPN:** Cathy Marley **CH:** Three Daughters **ED:** OD, Southern College of Optometry (1977); Coursework, University of Arkansas, Fayetteville, AR (1969-1972) **C:** U.S. Senator, State of Arkansas, Washington, DC (2011-Present); Member, U.S. Senate Committee on Veterans' Affairs, Washington, DC (2011-Present); Member, U.S. Senate Committee on Agriculture, Nutrition and Forestry, Washington, DC (2011-Present); Member, U.S. Senate Committee on Environment and Public Works, Washington, DC (2011-Present); Member, U.S. Senate Committee on Commerce, Science and Transportation, Washington, DC (2011-Present); U.S. Representative from Arkansas' Third Congressional District, United Sates Congress, Washington, DC (2001-2011) **CR:** Co-founder, BoozmanHof Regional Eye Clinic, P.A., Rogers, AR (1977) **CIV:** Member, Board of Education of Rogers, AR (1994-2001); Founder, Low Vision Program, Arkansas School for the Blind and Visually Impaired, Little Rock, AR **AW:** A in English Award, U.S. English, Inc. (2010); Award for Manufacturing Legislative Excellence, National Association of Manufacturers (2010); Brighter Vision Award, Age Related Macular Degeneration Alliance International (AMD Alliance) (2006); Small Business Advocate Award, Small Business Survival Committee (2004); Hero of the Taxpayer Award, Americans for Tax Reform (2001, 2002, 2003); Spirit of Enterprise Award, United States Chamber of Commerce (2001, 2002, 2003); Distinguished Advocate Award, Association for Education and Rehabilitation of the Blind and Visually Impaired (AER), Arkansas Chapter **MEM:** International Academy of Sports Vision; Arkansas Optometric Association; American Optometric Association; Fellowship of Christian Athletes **PA:** Republican **RE:** Baptist

BORAS, SCOTT DEAN, T: Sports Agent **I:** Athletics **CN:** Boras Corporation **DOB:** 11/2/1952 **PB:** Sacramento **SC:** CA/USA **MS:** Married **SPN:** Jeanette Boras **CH:** Natalie; Shane; Trent **ED:** JD, McGeorge School of Law, University of the Pacific (1982); PharmD, University of the Pacific (1976); BS in Chemistry, University of the Pacific (1974) **CT:** State of Washington **C:** Sports Agent (1981-Present); Baseman, Arkansas Travelers, Midland Cubs and St. Petersburg Cardinals (1977); Baseman, St. Petersburg Cardinals (1975-1976); Baseman, Gulf Coast League Cardinals (1974); President, Owner, Boras Corporation **AW:** 50 Most Influential People in Sports Business, Street & Smith's Sports Business Journal, American City Business Journals, Inc. (2007-2009); Most Influential People in the World of Sports, Businessweek (2007, 2008); Inductee, Athletics Hall of Fame, University of the Pacific (1995)

BORDEN, RICHARD CRAIG, T: President, Chief Executive Officer **I:** Business Management/Business Services **CN:** Sigma Affiliates, Ltd **DOB:** 08/11/1936 **PB:** Minneapolis **SC:** MN/USA **PT:** Thomas Walton Borden; Elaine Fern (Bardill) Borden **MS:** Married **SPN:** Joyce Mary Seaberg (08/18/1962) **CH:** Christopher J. Borden; Eric C. Borden **ED:** MS in Statistics & Mathematics, University of Minnesota (1968); BA in Mathematics & Psychology, University of Minnesota (1962); Coursework, U.S. Military Academy (1957) **CT:** Exemplar Global Master Auditor; Lean Six Sigma Black Belt, American Society for Quality; Commercial Pilot, Federal Aviation Agency **C:** President, Sigma Affiliates, LTD (1994-Present); Quality Manager, 3M Co., St. Paul, MN (1974-1987); Principal Engineer, MTS Systems Corp. (1971-1974); Senior Analyst, 3M Co., St. Paul, MN (1968-1971); Senior Scientist, University of Minnesota (1966-1968); Programmer Analyst, Control Data Co., Minneapolis, MN (1963-1966); Assistant Mathematician, Sperry Univac Co., St. Paul, MN (1959-1962) **CR:** Exemplar Global Master Auditor **CIV:** Blue and Gold Officer, U.S. Naval Academy (1970-1990);Mt. Olivet Lutheran Church, Minneapolis, MN **MIL:** Captain, U.S. Naval Reserve (1965-1992); Retired, Reserve Intelligence Area Ten Commander **CW:** "Numerical Inversion of Four Statistical Functions," MS Paper; "Algebra of Correlation," MS Paper; Probability Analysis of Promotional Mail Units **AW:** Quality Achievement Award, 3M; First Quality Improvement Team, 3M **MEM:** National Science Foundation Register of Science and Technology Personnel; Association of Graduates of the U.S. Military Academy; Naval Reserve Association; U.S. Naval Institute; Reserve Officers Association; Twin Cities Navy Flying Club **MH:** Albert Nelson Marquis Lifetime Achievement Award **AS:** Mr. Borden attributes his success to great university education. **B/I:** Mr. Borden became involved in his profession because of his experience at Univac. He was never enthusiastic about anything in college until he started working there; he realized he had a talent in mathematics, and so, at that point, he was encouraged to explore that direction. **AV:** Golfing; Biking; Practicing fitness **RE:** Lutheran **THT:** Mr. Borden lives life to the fullest.

BORG, BJÖRN RUNE, T: Fashion Designer, Professional Tennis Player (Retired) **I:** Apparel & Fashion **CN:** Björn Borg **DOB:** 06/06/1956 **PB:** Stockholm

SC: Sweden **PT:** Rune Borg; Margaretha Borg **MS:** Married **SPN:** Patricia Östfeld (06/08/2002); Loredana Bertè (09/04/1989, Divorced 1992); Mariana Simionescu (07/24/1980, Divorced 1984) **CH:** Robin; Leo **C:** Founder, Designer, Björn Borg (1984-Present) **CW:** Co-Author (with Eugene L. Scott), "My Life and Game" (1980) **AW:** Top Swedish Sportsperson of All Time, Dagens Nyheter (2014); Lifetime Achievement Award, BBC (2006); Inductee, International Tennis Hall of Fame (1987); ATP Player of the Year (1976-1980); Overseas Sports Personality of the Year, BBC (1979)

BORGES, WANDA, T: Attorney, Owner **I:** Law and Legal Services **CN:** Borges & Associates, LLC **DOB:** 08/29/1950 **PB:** Bronx **SC:** NY/USA **PT:** Jaime Nemesio Borges; Ada C. (Pujadas) Borges Mady **MS:** Married **ED:** BA in Modern Foreign Languages, Mercy College, Dobbs Ferry, NY (1972) **C:** Member, Borges & Associates, LLC, Syosset, NY (2000-Present); Partner, Teitelbaum, New York, NY (1985-2000); Associate, Teitelbaum, New York, NY (1982-1984); Associate, Teitelbaum, New York, NY (1979-1982); Law Clerk, Teitelbaum, New York, NY (1972-1979); Legal Secretary, Teitelbaum, New York, NY (1972) **CR:** Adjunct Professor, Elizabeth Seton College, Yonkers, NY (1986-Present); Lecturer, National Association of Credit Management, NJ (1983-Present); Lecturer, American Management Association (1982-Present) **CIV:** Volunteer Director, Youth Music Ministry, Leader of Song, Adult Choir Member, Lector, Our Lady Star of the Sea, Stamford, CT **CW:** Contributor, "Hidden Liens: Who is Entitled to What?" Commercial Law Journal (1998); Contributor, "Capsized Businesses: Don't Be Swamped by Bankruptcy," Broadcast Cable Financial Journal (1995); Contributor, "The Difference Between Civil and Criminal Credit Fraud," National Association of Credit Management, Fraud Watch (1986); Contributor, Numerous Articles, Professional Journals **AW:** Top Attorneys in New York Metro Area, Super Lawyers (2009-Present); Inductee, Alumni Hall of Fame, Mercy College (2010); Robert P. Caine Award for Leadership, Commercial Law League of America, Commercial Collection Agency Association (2010); Excellence Award, Indiana Association of Credit Management (2008); Top 25 Most Influential Collection Professionals, Collection Advisor Magazine (2006); Strength in Numbers Recognition Certificate, National Association of Credit Management (2004); Career Achievement Award, Broadcast Cable Credit Association (2001); 50 Outstanding Alumni, Mercy College (2000); Trustee's Medal, Mercy College (1996); Professional Achievement Award, Alumni Association, Mercy College (1991); Human Valor Award (1985); Woman of Distinction Award **MEM:** ABA; Federal Bar Council; New York State Bar Association; Bankruptcy Lawyers Bar Association; Vice President, Director, Alumni Association, Mercy College; The Fairfield County Chorale; United States Power Squadron; American Bankruptcy Institute **BAR:** United States District Court Eastern District of Michigan (2007); United States Circuit Court of Appeals for the Second Circuit (2004); United States District Court Western District of New York (1985); United States District Court District of Connecticut (1984); Supreme Court of the United States (1984); United States District Court Northern District of New York (1982); New York State Bar Association (1979); United States District Court Southern District of New York (1979); United States District Court Eastern District of New York (1979) **AS:** Ms. Borges attributes her success to the following motto: "In service consumed." She has lived that throughout her whole life. Ms. Borges serves her clients, as well as her church and community. She believes that being of service brings great things and

success back to her life. **B/I:** Ms. Borges became involved in her profession because she wanted to stand up for the rights of others. From a young age, she knew she wanted to be a lawyer. For some reason, between high school and college, she lost her interest in becoming a lawyer. In her junior year of college, Ms. Borges found a job working for a company that published children's books. Shortly after, the company went bankrupt. Jules Teitelbaum was the attorney for the business during the time that the company's doors were being locked by the sheriff. Ms. Borges was the only one present in the office and quickly called the lawyer. Mr. Teitelbaum instructed Ms. Borges to pay the sheriff $25 to not lock the door. The company ended up filing for bankruptcy and she found herself out of a job. The following day, Ms. Borges' former boss called her and told her that Mr. Teitelbaum wanted to meet with her. The following Tuesday, she met with her and was offered a job. Ms. Borges stayed with the job throughout college until she was presented with the question of what she would do next after graduation. She initially thought she would become a teacher, but was offered to stay at the law firm and become a legal secretary. **RE:** Roman Catholic

BORNSTEIN, CARL M., ESQ, T: Principal **I:** Law and Legal Services **CN:** Law Office of Carl M. Bornstein, PLLC **ED:** JD, Brooklyn Law School (1968); BA, Washington Square College, New York University (1965) **C:** Principal, Law Office of Carl M. Bornstein, PLLC, New York, NY; Adjunct Assistant Professor, Masters in Public Administration - Oversight & Inspection (IG) Program, John Jay College of Criminal Justice (2005-Present); Instructor, National Institute for Trial Advocacy, Northeast Region, Hofstra University Law School (1982-Present); Co-founder, Chief Operating Officer, Fortress Monitoring Group JV (2007-2014); Instructor, Investigative Techniques for the IG Certification Course of the Association of Inspectors General) (2005); Instructor Intensive Trial Advocacy Program, Widener University School of Law (1997-2004); Inspector General, New York City School Construction Authority (SCA-IG) (1999-2002); Executive Special Assistant Attorney General, NYC Criminal Justice System, Office of the NYS Special Prosecutor for Corruption (1976-1980); Special Attorney, United States Department of Justice, Organized Crime and Racketeering Section, Southern and Eastern Districts of New York (1974-1976); Deputy Chief Assistant District Attorney, Queens County, NY (1973-1974); Chief, Rackets Bureau (1972-1973); Assistant District Attorney, Bronx County, NY (1968-1973); Instructor, ABA National Trademark Trial Advocacy Institute **CR:** Panel's Successor, the Mayoral Building Safety Oversight Board (2015); Appointed to a Mayoral Special Independent Advisory Commission (SIAC) to Evaluate the Philadelphia Department of Licensing & Inspection (2013-2014); Co-presenter, Monitoring Large Construction Projects, Fall Conference of the Association of Inspectors General (2012); Panel Moderator, First Conference on Democracy and Global Security, Istanbul, Turkey (2005); Invited Speaker, Serbian Public Officials, U.S. Department of States New York Office **MIL:** Military Police Corps, United States Army Reserve (Honorable Discharge) **CW:** Articles Editor, Senior Editor, Brooklyn Law Review **AW:** AV Rated, Martindale-Hubbell (1985-Present); Who's Who in America (2020) **MEM:** Association Delegate, New York County Democratic Party Independent Screening Panel, New York Bar Association (2007); Judiciary Committee, New York State Bar Association; Sub-committee, Executive Committee to Evaluate a Nominee for Chief Justice of the U.S. Supreme Court, New York State Bar Association; Criminal

Courts Committee, New York State Bar Association; Committee on Federal Legislation, New York State Bar Association; Criminal Justice Operations and Budget Committee, New York State Bar Association; American Bar Association; Association of Inspectors General **BAR:** Supreme Court of the United States (1980); U.S. Court of Appeals for the Second Circuit (1975); United States District Court for the Eastern District of New York (1971); United States District Court for the Southern District of New York (1971); New York State Supreme Court (1968) **MH:** Marquis Who's Who Top Professional

BORST, WILLIAM ADAM, T: Radio Personality, Educator, Writer **I:** Publishing **DOB:** 09/06/1943 **PB:** New York **SC:** NY/USA **PT:** Adam Stiehl Borst; Helen (Moyse) Borst **MS:** Married **SPN:** Anna Maria Bommarito (01/06/2018); Judith Carol O'Rourke (08/27/1966, Deceased 2016) **CH:** Three Children **ED:** Doctor of Philosophy, St. Louis University (1972); Master of Arts, St. John's University (1969); Bachelor of Science, Holy Cross College (1965) **C:** Talk Show Host, Station WGNU-Radio (1984-2006); Founder, St. Louis Browns Historical Society (1984) **CR:** Columnist, catholicjournal.org (2014-2019); Featured Editor, Mindszenty Foundation (2003-2013); Social Science Instructor Maryville University (1991-1997); Continuing Education Instructor, Maryville University (1994-1995); Appeared on NBC Radio Today Show (1974) **CIV:** Board of Directors, Birthright (1991-2000); Foundation for Special Education (1990-2000); Treasurer, Archdiocesan Pro Life Executive Committee (1992-1994); YMCA, Brentwood, MO (1981-1984); Chalfonte-Hannon Hall Co. (1973-1976) **CW:** Essayist, Catholic Journal (2014-Present); Author, "The Anniversary of the 1944 World Series between the St. Louis Browns and the St. Louis Cardinals" (2019); Author, "The St. Louis Browns: The Story of a Beloved Team" (2017); Contributor, The Scorpion and the Frog: A Natural Conspiracy (2004); Co-author, "Liberalism: Fatal Consequences" (1999); Co-author, "The North American Encyclopedia" (1996); Co-author, "The Biographical Dictionary of American Sports" (1987-1996); Author, "The Best of Seasons: The 1944 St. Louis Cardinals & St. Louis Browns" (1995); Contributor, Dugout Magazine" (1994); Author, "Still Last in the American League: The St. Louis Browns" (1993); Co-author, "The Baseball Chronology" (1991); Co-author, "The Ball Players" (1990); Self Published Memoirs, "Laughter among the Thorns: A vintage Catholic's Coming of Age"; Unpublished Memoir, "Staying Alive: A Memoir of the Brownie Boys of Winter and Their Fans" **AW:** Mindszenty Foundation Freedom Award (2011); James Hartnett, Birthright (1997); Named, Man of the Year, Vatterott Foundation (1995); Staunder Graduate School Alumni Merit Award, St. Louis University (1995) **MEM:** Founder and Member, St. Louis Brown Historical Society (1984-2020) **MH:** Albert Nelson Marquis Lifetime Achievement Award **AS:** Mr. Borst attributes his success on his quality education and an inquisitive mind. **B/I:** Mr. Borst became a writer after having spent almost a decade as an educator. **RE:** Roman Catholic

BORUM, RODNEY, T: Corporate Financial Executive **I:** Financial Services **CN:** Pearl of Virginia **DOB:** 09/30/1929 **PB:** High Point **SC:** NC/USA **PT:** Carl Macy Borum; Etta (Sullivan) Borum **MS:** Married **SPN:** Helen Marie Rigby (06/27/1953) **CH:** Richard Harlan; Sarah Elizabeth **ED:** BS, United States Naval Academy (1953); Coursework, University of North Carolina (1947-1949) **C:** Vice President, Chief Financial Officer, Pearl of Virginia (1995-Present); Associate, Financial Services Organization, Cocoa, FL (1987-1989); Executive Vice President, Amasek Inc., Cocoa, FL (1986-1987); President, W.H. Rigby Consultants (1985-1986); Staff Consultant, Printing Industries of America, Arlington, VA (1985-1986); Director, Executive Committee, Printing Industries of America, Arlington, VA (1969-1985); President, Printing Industries of America, Arlington, VA (1968-1985); Administrator, Business and Defense Services Administration-Department of Commerce (1966-1968); Manager, Eastern Test Range Engineering, GE, Cape Kennedy, FL (1961-1965); Manager, Ground Equipment Engineer, GE, Cape Kennedy, FL (1960-1961); Missile Test Conductor, GE, Cape Kennedy, FL (1958-1960); Design-Development Engineer, GE, Cape Kennedy, FL (1957-1958); Design-Development Engineer, GE, Syracuse, NY (1956-1957) **CR:** Operations Manager, COVIX Corporation (1990-Present); Republican Candidate, 11th District of the United States Congress (1988-1990); Secretary, Graphic Arts Show Corporation; Director; Inter-Comprint Limited; Strangers Cay; Limited Member, Governing Board, Comprints International **CIV:** Education Council, Board of Directors, Graphic Arts Technical Foundation, Pittsburgh, PA (1970-1986); Trustee, Founder, Graphic Arts Education and Research Trust Fund, Arlington, VA (1978-1985); Executive Council, Cub Scouts of America (1965); Board of Directors, Brevard Beaches Concert Association (1965); Board of Directors, Vice President, Brevard County United Fund (1964-1965) **MIL:** 1st Lieutenant, United States Air Force (1953-1956) **AW:** Boss of the Year, Chamber of Commerce (1965); Guggenheim Jet Propulsion Fellowship (1954); American Legion Award (1952); Archibald Henderson Medal (1949); Bausch and Lomb Science Award (1947) **MEM:** Board of Directors, Graphic Arts Council of North America (1977); United States Naval Institute; United States Naval Academy Alumni Association; Phi Eta Sigma **MH:** Albert Nelson Marquis Lifetime Achievement Award **B/I:** Mr. Borum began his career in the United States Naval Academy. From there, he took advantage of his available opportunities, leading him to the highly diverse and successful career he has had.

BOSEMAN, CHADWICK AARON, T: Actor **I:** Media & Entertainment **DOB:** 11/29/1977 **PB:** Anderson **SC:** SC/USA **PT:** Carolyn Boseman; Leroy Boseman **MS:** Married **SPN:** Taylor Simone Ledward **ED:** Honorary LHD, Howard University (2018); BFA in Directing, Howard University (2000); Diplomate, Digital Film Academy, New York, NY; Coursework, British American Drama Academy, Oxford, United Kingdom **CR:** Instructor of Drama, Schomburg Junior Scholars Program, Schomburg Center for Research in Black Culture, The New York Public Library **CW:** Actor, "The Black Child" (2020); Actor, "Ma Rainey's Black Bottom" (2020); Actor, "Da 5 Bloods" (2020); Actor, Producer, "21 Bridges" (2019); Actor, "Avengers: Endgame" (2019); Actor, "Avengers: Infinity War" (2018); Actor, "Black Panther" (2018); Actor, Co-producer, "Marshall" (2017); Actor, Executive Producer, "Message from the King" (2016); Actor, "Captain America: Civil War" (2016); Actor, "Gods of Egypt" (2016); Actor, "9 Kisses" (2014); Actor, "Get on Up" (2014); Actor, "Draft Day" (2014); Actor, "42" (2013); Executive Producer, Director, "Heaven" (2012); Actor, "The Kill Hole" (2012); Actor, "Fringe" (2011); Actor, "Justified" (2011); Actor, "Detroit 1-8-7" (2011); Actor, "Castle" (2011); Actor, "The Glades" (2010); Actor, "Persons Unknown" (2010); Executive Producer, "In Retrospect..." (2009); Actor, "Lincoln Heights" (2008-2009); Actor, "Lie to Me" (2009); Executive Producer, Writer, Director, Editor, "Blood Over a Broken Pawn" (2008); Actor, "Cold Case" (2008); Actor, "ER" (2008); Actor, "The Express" (2008); Actor, "The Appointment" (2007); Actor, "CSI: NY" (2006); Actor, "LadyLike" (2006); Actor, "Date" (2004); Actor, "Third Watch" (2003) **AW:** Best Actor Award, Los Angeles Film Critics Association

(2020); Best Supporting Actor Award, New York Film Critics Association (2020); Best Ensemble Cast, Boston Society of Film Critics (2020); Named Outstanding Actor in a Motion Picture, NAACP Image Awards (2019); Screen Actors Guild Award, Outstanding Cast in a Motion Picture, SAG-AFTRA (2019); Black Reel Award for Outstanding Actor (2019); Named Male Movie Star of the Year, People's Choice Awards (2018); BET Award for Best Actor (2018); Named Best Hero, Best Performance in a Movie, MTV Movie & TV Awards (2018); Virtuosos Award, Santa Barbara International Film Festival (2018); Best Short Film Award, Hollywood Black Film Festival (2008); Best Supporting Actor in a Drama, AUDELCO Awards (2002) **RE:** Christian

BOST, MICHAEL, "MIKE" JOSEPH, T: U.S. Representative from Illinois **I:** Government Administration/Government Relations/Government Services **DOB:** 12/30/1960 **MS:** Married **SPN:** Tracy Bost **CH:** Stephen; Kasey; Kaitlin **ED:** Coursework, University of Illinois; Certified Firefighter II Academy **CT:** Certified Firefighter, Murphysboro Fire Department, Murphysboro, IL (1992) **C:** Member, U.S. House of Representatives from Illinois' 12th Congressional District (2015-Present); Township Trustee, Murphysboro, IL (1993-Present); Co-owner, White House Beauty Salon, Murphysboro, IL (1989-Present); Member, District 115, Illinois House of Representatives (1999-2015); Treasurer, Murphrysboro, IL (1989-1992); Truck Manager (1982-1992); Firefighter, Murphysboro Fire Department, IL (1992); Committeeman, Precinct 4, Murphysboro, IL (1985-1989); Member, Jackson County Board (1984-1988); Driver, Bost Trucking Service (1979); Member, Jackson County Super Max Prison; Member, Patriots Bravo Country; Member, Transportation and Motor Vehicles Committee; Member, Veterans' Affairs Committee; Member, Steering Committee; Member, Local Government Committee; Member, Elementary, Secondary and Higher Education; Member, Committee on Agriculture; Member, Committee on Small Business; Member, Committee on Veterans' Affairs; Member, Republican Study Committee **CIV:** Youth Minister, Elm Street Baptist Church (1985-1991); Deacon **MIL:** With, U.S. Marine Corps (1979-1982) **MEM:** Treasurer, Jackson County Young Republicans (1986); President, Jackson Country Republican Boosters (1986); Murphysboro Rotary Club (1986); Member, 32 Degree, Mason **PA:** Republican

BOSTON, BRUCE O., PHD, T: Writer, Editor, Publications Consultant **I:** Writing and Editing **CN:** Wordsmith, Inc. **DOB:** 08/11/1940 **PB:** New Castle **SC:** PA/USA **PT:** John Ormand Boston; Williamina (Loudon) Boston **MS:** Married **SPN:** Jean Nelson (12/23/1989); Sandra Waymer (06/08/1963, Divorced 1973) **CH:** Aaron Clark; Nathan Waymer; Kyle Richard **ED:** PhD, Princeton Theological Seminary (1973); BDiv, Princeton Theological Seminary (1968); BA, Muskingum University (1962) **C:** President, Wordsmith Inc., Reston, VA (1976-2004); Associate, Colloquy of Reston (1973-1978); Instructor of Theology, St. Joseph's College, Philadelphia, PA (1972-1973) **CR:** Communications Counsel, Reston Association (1986-1989); Assistant Chief Clerk, Committee on Veterans Affairs, United States Senate, Washington, DC (1976); Publications Developer, Council for Exceptional Children, Reston, VA (1973-1975) **CIV:** Docent, Washington National Cathedral (2000-Present); General Editor, "Habits of the Heart Project," Independent Humanities Council (1999-2001); Faculty Learning in Retirement Institute, George Mason University (1999); Community Service Learning Center, Springfield, MA (1992-1996); Senior Warden, St. Anne's Episcopal Church, Reston, VA (1990-1992); Reston Task Force on Town Governance (1988-

1989); Board of Directors, Episcopal Awareness Center on Handicaps, Washington, DC (1986-1989); Lay Preacher, Episcopal Diocese Virginia (1984); President, Fairfax Farms Community Association (1980-1981) **CW:** Author, "All The Company of Heaven: A Guide to the Few Tera Sanctus Reredos", Washington National Cathedral (2008); Author, "No Dream Denied" (2003); Author, "Every Student a Citizen" (2000); Author, "Before It's Too Late" (2000); Author, "Their Best Selves" (1997); Author, "Connections: Integrating the High School Curriculum through the Arts" (1996); Author, "The Arts and Education: Partners in Achieving Our National Education Goals" (1995); Author, "Perspectives on Implementation: Arts Education Standards for America's Students" (1994); Author, "Arts Education for the 21st Century American Economy" (1994); Author, "The Cutting Edge of Common Sense" (1993); Author, "Language on a Leash" (1988); Author, "STET! Tricks of the Trade for Writers and Editors" (1986); Co-Author, with Cox and Daniel, "Educating Able Learners" (1985); Author, "Preparing to Teach the Gifted and Talented, Two Volumes" (1980); Author, "The Sorcerer's Apprentice" (1976); Co-Author, "Testing the Gifted Child (1976); Editor, "A Resource Manual on Educating the Gifted and Talented" (1975); Author, "Gifted and Talented: Developing Elementary and Secondary School Programs" (1975); Author, Numerous Articles and Scripts **AW:** Achievement Award, Education Press Association (1991); Second Place Award, Editor's Forum (1991); Achievement Award, Education Press Association (1986); First Place Award, Editor's Forum (1986); Golden Eagle Award, Council for International Non-Theatrical Events (1984); Golden Eagle Award, Council for International Non-Theatrical Events (1977); Graduate Fellow, United Presbyterian (1968-1973); Fellowship, Danforth Foundation (1962-1964); Kent Fellowship in Religion **MEM:** Board of Directors, Reston Chapter, Rotary (1988-1990); Board of Directors, Washington Independent Writers (1982-1984) **MH:** Albert Nelson Marquis Lifetime Achievement Award **B/I:** Dr. Boston entered his profession because he was always drawn to writing; he learned how to write term papers through three different graduate schools by the time he was finished with his studies, consequently making a living from his passion. He enrolled at the graduate school of Princeton University in the fall of 1962 and left less than a year later. He then spent some time at Union Seminary in New York, though he also inevitably to study at Princeton Theological Seminary in 1964. **AV:** Collecting books of quotations **PA:** Democrat **RE:** Episcopalian

BOTANA, DERRICK, T: Vice President **I:** Business Management/Business Services **CN:** BayWater Boat Club **PT:** Omar Botana; Sherry Botana **ED:** Some College **C:** Vice President, BayWater Boat Club (2014-Present); BayWater Boat Club (2009-Present); Verizon Wireless, South Carolina **CIV:** Chairman, Astero Council of Leaders; Vice President, Benita Springs Historical Society; Board Member, Lovers Key State Park **AW:** Guest Designer and 50th year in Business; Honorary Acknowledgement, Junior Achievement **AS:** Mr. Botana attributes his success to his strong work ethic that he got from his father who was a Cuban immigrant who came to America with nothing. His example, and the life he made for his family instilled the value of hard work into Mr. Botana's life. **B/I:** Mr. Botana began his profession due to it being a family business. His parents owned the business and began planning for retirement. They asked Mr. Botana would he want to be a part of the business and take over in their retirement and he accepted.

BOUDREAUX, GAIL, T: President, Chief Executive Officer **I:** Medicine & Health Care **CN:** Anthem, Inc. **PB:** Chicopee **SC:** MA/USA **MS:** Married **SPN:** Terry Boudreaux **CH:** Two sons **ED:** MBA in Finance and Health Care Administration, Columbia Business School, Columbia University, with Honors, New York, NY (1989); BS in Psychology, Dartmouth College, Cum Laude, Hanover, NH (1982) **CT:** Certified Employee Benefit Specialist **C:** President, Chief Executive Officer, Anthem, Inc. (2017-Present); Founder, Chief Executive Officer, GKB Global Health, LLC (2015-2017); Chief Executive Officer, UnitedHealthcare Services, Inc. (2011-2014); Executive Vice President, UnitedHealth Group (2008-2014); President, United HealthCare Services, Inc. (2008-2011); Executive Vice President, External Operations, Health Care Service Corporation (2006-2008); President, Illinois Division, Blue Cross Blue Shield, Health Care Service Corporation (2002-2005); General Manager, Vice President, Senior Vice President, Aetna, Inc. (1982-2002) **CR:** Board of Directors, Anthem, Inc. (2017-Present); Board of Directors, Zimmer Biomet (2012-Present); Board of Directors, Novavax, Inc. (2015-2017); Board of Directors, Xcel Energy Inc. (2012-2017); Senior Fellow, Tuck School of Business, Dartmouth College **CIV:** Board of Trustees, Dartmouth College (2011-2019); President's Advisory Council, YWCA USA; The Chicago Network **AW:** Listee, The World's 100 Most Powerful Women, Forbes Media LLC (2019); Listee, Most Powerful Women, Fortune Media IP Limited (2019); Billie Jean King Leadership Award, Women's Sports Foundation (2018); Listee, Most Influential People in Healthcare, Modern Healthcare, Crain Communications, Inc. (2018); Inaugural Class, Legends of Ivy League Basketball, Ivy League (2017); Honoree, Outstanding Directors Awards, Twin Cities Business Magazine, Key Enterprises LLC (2016); Listee, 50 Most Powerful Women in American Business, Fortune Media IP Limited (2008-2014); Listee, Top 25 Women Leaders in Healthcare, Modern Healthcare, Crain Communications, Inc. (2011, 2013); Honoree, Women in Business, Minneapolis/St. Paul Business Journal, American City Business Journals (2009); Silver Anniversary Award, NCAA (2007); Inductee, New England Basketball Hall of Fame (2003); 25-Year Anniversary Team, Women's Basketball, Ivy League (1999); 25-Year Anniversary Team, Women's Basketball, Dartmouth College (1999); 25-Year Anniversary Team, Women's Track & Field, Dartmouth College (1999); All-American, Women's Track & Field (1982); Ivy League Women's Basketball Player of the Year, NCAA (1980-1982)

BOUMAN, KATHERINE LOUISE, PHD, T: Assistant Professor; Computer Scientist **I:** Education/Educational Services **CN:** California Institute of Technology **DOB:** 05/09/1989 **PB:** West Lafayette **SC:** IN/USA **PT:** Charles Bouman; Cristina Bouman **MS:** Married **SPN:** Joe Leong (09/02/2018) **ED:** PhD in Electrical Engineering and Computer Science, Massachusetts Institute of Technology (2017); MS in Electrical Engineering and Computer Science, Massachusetts Institute of Technology (2013); BS in Electrical Engineering, University of Michigan, Ann Arbor, MI, Summa Cum Laude (2011) **C:** Assistant Professor, California Institute of Technology (2019-Present); Visiting Associate, California Institute of Technology (2018-2019); Event Horizon Telescope Imaging Team (2013) **CR:** Haystack Observatory, Massachusetts Institute of Technology **AW:** Breakthrough Prize for Fundamental Physics (2020); Rosenberg Scholar (2019); Ernst Guillemin Award for Best Master's Thesis in Electrical Engineering; Graduate Fellowship, National Science Foundation

BOURLA, ALBERT, DVM, PHD, T: Chairperson and Chief Executive Officer **I:** Pharmaceuticals **CN:** Pfizer Inc. **ED:** Doctor of Veterinary Medicine, Aristotle University of Thessaloniki (1985); Doctor of Philosophy in Biotechnology of Reproduction, Aristotle University of Thessaloniki **C:** Chief Executive Officer, Pfizer Inc. (2019-Present); Chief Operating Officer, Pfizer Inc. (2018-2019); President, Pfizer Innovative Health, Pfizer Inc. (2016-2017); President, Global Vaccines, Oncology and Consumer Healthcare, Pfizer Inc. (2014-2016); President and General Manager, Established Products, Pfizer Inc. (2010-2013); President, Zoetis, Europe, Africa and the Middle East Group, Pfizer Inc. (2006-2009); Vice President, Business Development and New Products Marketing, Zoetis, Pfizer Inc. (2004-2006); Marketing Director, U.S. Group, Zoetis, Pfizer Inc. (2001-2004); With, Zoetis, Pfizer Inc., Greece and Europe (1993-2001) **CR:** Chairperson, Board of Directors, Pfizer Inc. (2020-Present); Executive Committee, BIO (2017-Present); Founder, Patient and Health Impact Group (2016); Board of Directors, Pharmaceutical Research and Manufacturers of America® **CIV:** Board of Directors, Catalyst (2019-Present); Board of Directors, The Pfizer Foundation, Pfizer Inc.; Board of Directors, Partnership for New York City **MEM:** Board of Trustees, United States Council for International Business (2019-Present); Business Roundtable; The Business Council

BOWDEN, A. BRUCE, T: Equity Partner **I:** Law and Legal Services **CN:** Leech Tishman Fuscaldo & Lampl LLC. **ED:** JD, Stanford University (1966); BA in English Language and Literature, Amherst College (1963) **C:** Partner, Leech Tishman Fuscaldo & Lampl LLC (2012-Present); Partner, Duane Morris LLP (2003-2012); Partner, Buchanan Ingersoll & Rooney PC (1966-2003) **CIV:** Solicitor, Tax Collector, Borough of Fox Chapel; Board of Directors, Avrio Advocati **MIL:** Colonel, General Staff, U.S. Army Reserve (Retired) **CW:** Speaker, "The Best Exit Strategy; Options for VC-Funded Companies in 2011," ExecuSense (2011); Author, Local Government and Community Development Topics, "What About Pittsburgh?" Pittsburgh Post-Gazette (2010); Author, International Business Law Topics, "GAAP and IFRS: The Convergence and Transition of International Accounting Standards," New Jersey Lawyer (2010); Author, International Business Law Topics, "Rules and Recommendations for Doing Business Under NAFTA," U.S. Department of Commerce; Author, Chapter, Business Law Topics, "Public Procurement," Legalink; Author, Healthcare Topics, "Negotiating a System Purchase: 8 Principles for Protecting Your Institution's Interests," Healthcare Executive; Speaker, Presentation, "Supply and Distribution Agreements," Pennsylvania Bar Institute; Speaker, Presentation, "What Every Employment Agreement Should Contain," Pro Arts Workshop; Speaker, Numerous Speeches and Presentations **AW:** Volunteer of the Year Award, National Kidney Foundation; Peer Review Rated Attorney, Martindale-Hubbell **MEM:** Secretary, General Counsel, Accuracy Incorporated; President, Executive Committee, Associates Program, Katz Graduate School of Business; Secretary, General Counsel, Aurora Imaging Technology, Inc.; Avrio Advocati, Eurocentric Network of International Business Lawyers; Board of Directors, Center for Organ Recovery and Education; Deacon, Elder, East Liberty Presbyterian Church; President, Family Services of Western Pennsylvania; Chairman, Legalink; Chairman, Executive Committee, Mattress Factory Limited; Chairman, National Kidney Foundation; President, Pittsburgh Ballet Theater; Pittsburgh Cultural Trust; Compensation Committee, Board Medical Staff Planning Committee, Shadyside Hospital; Secretary, General Counsel, Tinplate Partners International, Inc.; Executive Committee, Membership Committee, Professional Standards Committee, Finance Committee, United Network for Organ Sharing; Chair, Entertainment Committee, House Committee, University Club; Board of Directors, Beckwith Institute for Innovation in Patient Care; Ducane Club; Golf Club; American Bar Association; Pennsylvania Bar Association; Allegheny County Bar Association **BAR:** Pennsylvania Bar Association; United States District Court Eastern District of Pennsylvania; United States District Court Western District of Pennsylvania; United States Court of Appeals for the Third Circuit; Supreme Court of the United States **MH:** Marquis Who's Who Top Professional **AS:** Mr. Bowden attributes his success to preparation and hard work. **B/I:** Mr. Bowden became involved in his profession because he didn't want to follow in his father's footsteps and become a banker. He enjoyed learning about how to analyze problems and was compelled to pursue a career in law. **THT:** Mr. Bowden's motto is, "Do the right thing."

BOWER, SHELLEY A., ESQ., T: Attorney **I:** Law and Legal Services **DOB:** 01/31/1954 **PB:** Catskill **SC:** NY/USA **PT:** Edward Philip Bower; Antoinette (Post) Bower **MS:** Married **SPN:** Paul Allan Benfatto (10/02/1999); Richard D. Connors (08/28/1976, Divorced 1984) **ED:** JD, Detroit College (Now School of Law, Michigan State University) (1984); BA, Michigan Technological University (1977) **C:** Private Practice (2016-Present); Director of Strategy and Planning, GPJ (2014-2015); Program Director for Software, IBM (2005-2013); Offering Manager, Lotus Division, IBM (2002-2005); Consultant, IBM Global Consultant Service Manufacturing Industries, White Plains, NY (2001-2003); Customer Relationship Management Principal, Executive, IBM, White Plains, NY (2001-2002); Principal, IBM Global Consultant Service Manufacturing Industries, White Plains, NY (1998-2000); Principal, Oracle (1996-1997); Director of Planning and Development, Corporate Counsel, C.T. Male Associate, PC, Latham, NY (1995-1996); Consultant, Electronic Data Systems, Southfield, MI (1992-1995); Engineering Technology, Director, Corporate Training and Program Administration, Troy, MI (1988-1992); General Motors (1986); Division Manager, Property Professionals, Saugerties, NY (1986-1988); Supervisor, Equal Employment Opportunity, Cadillac, Detroit, MI (1985-1986); Employee in Training, Cadillac, Detroit, MI (1984-1985) **CIV:** Corresponding Secretary, Board of Directors, Catskill Education Foundation (2018-Present); President, Board of Directors, Catskill Education Foundation (2013); Founding Member, Board of Directors, Catskill Education Foundation (2005) **MEM:** National Association of Female Executives; New York State Bar Association **BAR:** New York State Bar Association **MH:** Albert Nelson Marquis Lifetime Achievement Award **AS:** Ms. Bower attributes her success to her desire to find an approach that works for everyone. **B/I:** Ms. Bower became involved in her profession because it was something she always wanted to do. **AV:** Skiing; Hiking

BOWIE, SYRETTA, CCP, T: Vice President of Executive Compensation **I:** Human Resources **CN:** R.R. Donnelley & Sons Company **MS:** Married **CH:** One Son **ED:** MA in Industrial Organizational Psychology, Elmhurst College (Now Elmhurst University), Elmhurst, IL (2011); BA in Interdepartmental Communications, Elmhurst College (Now Elmhurst University), Elmhurst, IL (1998) **CT:** Certified Compensation Professional (CCP), WorldatWork (2004); Certified Executive Compensation, WorldatWork (2004) **C:** Vice President, Executive

Compensation, Global Mobility and Analytics, R.R. Donnelley & Sons Company, Warrenville, IL (2018-Present); Senior Director, Compensation, HR Systems and Analytics, MEDNAX Health Solution Partners (Now MEDNAX Services, Inc.), Sunrise, FL (2013-2018); Director, Compensation and Benefits, Carnival Cruise Lines, Carnival Corporation, Miami, FL (2011-2013); Director, International Compensation and Benefits, Office Depot, LLC, Boca Raton, FL (2007-2011); Senior Manager, Compensation, Hillshire Brands (Now Tyson Foods, Inc.), Downers Grove, IL (2005-2007); Manager II, Compensation, Zimmer Inc., Warsaw, IN (2001-2004) **CIV:** Volunteer, Loaves and Fishes Food Pantry **MEM:** Society for Human Resource Management (SHRM); WorldatWork; National Association of Stock Plan Professionals (NASPP) **B/I:** Mrs. Bowie became involved in her profession because she went to college on a computer science scholarship, but realized she hated it. She then decided to take a year off and went to work for a great company doing data entry. She saw this compensation job come across the board and knew she could do it. She went to talk to them but they said that she didn't have a degree. She asked for a chance to interview for the job so they could see what her ideas would be for the position. They gave her the chance to interview and lowered the job by a grade so she could apply for it. **THT:** The Global Mobility part of Mrs. Bowie's job is working with relocation companies trying to move people all across the world; they have people who move from country to country, there has to be someone that coordinates their move, but also makes sure all their taxes are paid. The Workforce Analytics is her looking at all HR data and interpreting to give the business information to give the business strategy. Then the executive compensation piece is the fun piece. Mrs. Bowie is responsible not just for base compensation, but also the incentive compensation and any long term incentive compensation. She works very closely with the board of directors.

BOWMAN, GEORGIANNE G., T: Historian **I:** Government Administration/Government Relations/Government Services **PB:** Buffalo **SC:** NY/USA **PT:** George J. Miller; Lota M. Miller **MS:** Married **SPN:** Neil V. Bowman (01/04/1964) **CH:** Jenifer A. Stanley; Maureen A. O'Beirne; Deborah A.; Candice A. Soles **ED:** Regents Diploma, Immaculata Academy, Hamburg, NY, With Honors (1960) **C:** Historian, Village of North Collins, NY (2003-Present); Historian, Town of North Collins, NY (2001-Present); Local Newspaper Reporter, H & K Publication (1985-2007); Executive Secretary, Baillie Lumber Co., Inc., Hamburg, NY (1961-1964); Secretary, Clarke & Rapuana, Blasdell, NY (1960-1961) **CR:** History Club Advisor, North Collins Central Schools (2001-2002) **CIV:** Secretary, Museum Director, North Collins Historical Society (1995-Present); Secretary, Collection Committee, Schoolhouse #8 History Center and Museum, Inc. (2000-2010); Project Leader, Lawtons Progressors 4-H Club, Lawtons, NY (1974-2000); Secretary, Publicity Chairman, Newsletter Editor, Immaculate Conception School Catholic School Parents, Eden, NY (1986-1996); Secretary, Publicity Chairman, Event Chairman, Federation of Catholic School Parents, Diocese of Buffalo (1984-1996); Committee Member, Middle States Accreditation Committee, Immaculate Conception School, Eden, NY (1994-1995); Publicity Chairman, New York State Federation of Catholic School Parents, Binghamton, NY (1987-1994); Committee Member, Regionalization Task Force, Immaculate Conception School (1993); Secretary, President, Publicity Chairman, Events Chairman, Newsletter Editor, Holy Spirit School Home School Association (1968-1985); Quaker Meeting House

Restoration Grantee **CW:** Author, "Around North Collins"; Author, "1860s Foods: Union, Confederate & on the Frontier"; Editor, "Lawtons Progressors 4-H Club - 75th Anniversary Cookbook"; Editor, "Holy Spirit School - Still Cookin'"; Editor, "Immaculate Conception School - 35th Anniversary Cookbook"; Editor, "The Dole Family - Still Cookin', A Taste of North Collins Traditions" **AW:** Registered Historian Award, Association of Public Historians of New York State (2011); Spring Conference Scholar, Small Museum Association (2003); Federation of Catholic School Parents, Diocese of Buffalo (1995); Parent Volunteer of the Year, Immaculate Conception Home School Association (1994); Catholic School Volunteer of the Year, Today's Catholic Teacher Magazine (1989); School Parent Organization Service Award, National Catholic Education Association (1988); Catherine Aungst Parent Volunteer of Year Award **MEM:** Association of Living History & Agriculture Museum; Civil War Preservation Trust; American Association of Museum Volunteers; Colonial Williamsburg Foundation; Museum Wise; Erie County Historical Federation of New York; National Council of Public Historians; Government Appointed Historians of Western New York; Buffalo Historical Society; New York State Archives Partnership Trust; Association of Public Historians of New York State; Association of State and Local History; Director, North Town Historical Society Museum; Director, 1851 Hicksite Quaker Meeting House Museum **MH:** Albert Nelson Marquis Lifetime Achievement Award **AS:** Ms. Bowman attributes her success to a willingness to learn, as well as her persistence. **B/I:** Ms. Bowman has always been passionate about genealogy and learning about history. She was also inspired by her grandmother, Catherine Dole, who would often tell Ms. Bowman stories about her early life and memories. **AV:** Sewing; Practicing needlework; Creating ceramics; Completing word puzzles; Researching genealogy

BOYLE, BRENDAN FRANCIS, T: U.S. Representative from Pennsylvania **I:** Government Administration/Government Relations/Government Services **DOB:** 02/06/1977 **PB:** Philadelphia **SC:** PA/USA **PT:** Francis Boyle; Eileen Boyle **MS:** Married **SPN:** Jennifer Boyle **CH:** One Child **ED:** MPP, Harvard Kennedy School, John F. Kennedy School of Government, Cambridge, MA (2005); BA in Government, Hesburgh Program in Public Service, University Notre Dame, Notre Dame, IN (1999) **C:** Member, U.S. House of Representatives from Pennsylvania's Second Congressional District (2019-Present); Member, U.S. House of Representatives from Pennsylvania's 13th Congressional District (2015-2019); Member, District 170, Pennsylvania House of Representatives (2009-2015); Member, Committee on Foreign Affairs; Member, Committee on Oversight and Government Reform; Consultant, U.S Department of Defense; Former Sportscaster, 640 WVFI-AM, South Bend, IN **AW:** Legislator of the Year, Pennsylvania School Counselor Association (PSCA) (2013); Rodel Fellow, The Aspen Institute (2011); Named One of the Top 10 Rising Stars, Philadelphia Daily News (2008) **PA:** Democrat

BRACY, CATHERINE, T: Co-Founder, Executive Director **I:** Technology **CN:** TechEquity Collaborative **ED:** MPP, The University of Texas at Austin (2011); BA in Communication, Boston College (2002) **C:** Co-Founder, Executive Director, TechEquity Collaborative (2016-Present); Consultant, Event Curator, Google (2012-2013); Program Manager, Tech4Obama, Obama Administration (2012); Co-Director, Technology Field Office, Obama Administration, San Francisco, CA (2011-2012); Product Manager, Obama Administration, Chicago, IL (2011-2012); Administrative Director,

Berkman Klein Center for Internet & Society, Harvard University (2002-2010) **CR:** Speaker in Field **CIV:** Board Member, Public Lab (2013-Present); Senior Director, Partnerships and Ecosystems, Code for America (2015); Director, Community Organizing, Code for America (2013-2015); International Program Director, Code for America (2013); Consultant, Manager, News Challenge, John S. and James L. Knight Foundation (2010-2011); Board of Directors, Data & Society Research Institute and the Public Lab **CW:** Speaker, "Why Good Hackers Make Good Citizens," TED Talk (2017)

BRADLEY, MARILYNNE G., T: Advertising Executive, Educator **I:** Education/Educational Services **DOB:** 04/12/1938 **PB:** Rockford **SC:** IL/USA **PT:** Sherwin S. Gersten; Lillian (Leopold) Gersten **MS:** Married **SPN:** Charles S. Bradley (1954, Divorced 02/1994) **CH:** Suzanne; Scott **ED:** Postgraduate Coursework, St. Louis Teachers Academy (1990); MFA, Syracuse University (1981); MAT, Webster University, St. Louis, MO (1975); BFA, Washington University at St. Louis (1960) **C:** Professor Emeritus (2018-Present); Supervisor, Webster University (2002-Present); Instructor, University of Missouri (1980-Present); Instructor, Webster University, Webster Groves, MO (1973-1982, 1997-Present); Instructor, St. Louis University (1978-1999); Instructor, Washington University at St. Louis (1984-1987); Teacher, Webster Groves High School (1970-1998); With, Essayons Studio, St. Louis, MO (1968-1969); Artist, Architectural Illustration (1960) **CR:** Presenter, National Art Education Association (1980-1998); Member, Teachers Academy (1990-1992); Secretary, Missouri Art Education, State of Missouri (1986-1987) **CIV:** Active, Arts Commission (2005-Present); Commissioner, City of Webster Groves (1995-Present); Board of Governors, Webster Groves Historical Society (1965-1972, 1994-Present); Vice President, Historical Preservation Committee (2002-2006); Co-chairman, Historical Preservation Committee (2002); Member, St. Louis Philharmonic Society (1956-1972) **CW:** Editor, Video, "Once upon a time in St. Louis; Geometric Transition" (2019); Editor, Video, "St. Louis in Watercolor" (2009); Editor, Video, "Borrowed Ideas and Famous Firsts - St. Louis Architecture" (2008); Editor, Video, "I Love St. Louis" (2007); Editor, Video, "World Travels" (2006); Editor, Video, "Sidewalks of St. Louis" (2005); Editor, Video, "The Mathematics of Moorish Mosaics" (2004); Editor, Video, "St. Louis World's Fair" (2004); Editor, Video, "It's Somewhere in St. Louis" (2002); Editor, Video, "Lewis and Clark Trail" (2001); Editor, Video, "Apre's Paris" (2001); Editor, Video, "Art Along the Katy Trail" (2000); Editor, Video, "The Katy Trail Series" (2000); Editor, Video, "Molas, Snip and Sew: The Kuna Indians; Molas: Panamanian Traditions" (1999); Editor, Video, "Line, Shape, Value" (1998); Editor, Video, "Drawing and Painting Techniques" (1997); Editor, Video, "Aboriginal Art - Past, Present and Future" (1996); Editor, Video, "Australian Dreamings" (1996); Editor, Video, "City of Century Homes" (1995); Editor, Video, "Aboriginal Art Techniques" (1994); Editor, Video, "Over Gauguin's Shoulder" (1994); Editor, Video, "The Santa Fe Trail Series" (1993); Editor, Video, "Techniques of American Watercolor" (1990); Editor, Video, "12 Water Color Lessons" (1987); Author, Illustrator, "Packets on Parade" (1980); Illustrator, "St. Louis Silhouettes" (1977); Author, Illustrator, "Arpens and Acres" (1976) **AW:** Lifetime Achievements of the Arts (2014); Best of American Water Colors (2010); The St. Louis Book Award (2014); Purchase Award, Washington (2010); Citizen of Year, Webster Groves (2010); Humana Foundation Award (2006); Educator of Year Award, Missouri Art Education Association (2006); Best of Show, Missouri

Watercolor Society (2000); Named Teacher of the Year (1987); Distinguished Woman, St. Louis Artist Guild (1987); Silver Brush Award, Southern Watercolor Society; Exceptional Salute to the Masters Award, Southern Watercolor Society **MEM:** President, Southern Watercolor Society (2004-Present); Board Member, Missouri Watercolor Society (2001-Present); Vice President, President's Council, St. Louis Artist Guild (1995-Present); Treasurer, St. Louis Artist Guild (2004); Vice President, Southern Watercolor Society (2002-2004); President, St. Louis Artist Guild (1989-1992); Secretary, St. Louis Artist Guild (1985-1986); Chairman, Monday Club (1979-1983); Secretary, Southern Watercolor Society (1978-1980); St. Louis Woman Artists; Life Member, Southern Watercolor Society; Chair, 26th Annual Exhibit, Chair, 28th Annual Exhibit, Southern Watercolor Society **MH:** Albert Nelson Marquis Lifetime Achievement Award **B/I:** Her first position, which was Architectural Illustration taught her to paint. She started out as an illustrator and she was competing with her husband and she did not want to compete anymore so she went into teaching. She went on to get her certification for teaching and she taught for 28 years. **AV:** Music; Art; Travel; Historian; Painting

BRADLEY, ROGER WILLIAM, T: Attorney **I:** Law and Legal Services **CN:** Melvin & Melvin PLLC **DOB:** 09/25/1944 **PB:** New York **SC:** NY/USA **PT:** Joseph Wilson Bradley; Alyce (Halferty) Bradley **MS:** Married **SPN:** Ann Marie Cummings (08/27/1977) **CH:** Daniel; Brendan **ED:** JD, Syracuse University, Magna Cum Laude (1969); BA in Political Science, Colgate University (1966) **CT:** U.S. District Court for the Western District of New York (1979); U.S. Court Appeals for the 2nd Circuit (1975); U.S. District Court for the Southern District of New York (1975); U.S. District Court for the Northern District of New York (1974); New York State Bar (1970) **C:** Partner, Melvin & Melvin, PLLC, Syracuse, NY (1973-Present); Special Assistant Attorney General, State of New York (1971-1973); Law Assistant, Appellate Division, 3rd Judicial Department, New York Supreme Court, Binghamton, NY (1969-1971) **CR:** Presenter, National Construction Webinars (2020); Presenter, Construction Lawyers Society of America at both the Yale and Harvard Club (2017-2018); Judge, Competitions at the Syracuse University College of Law and Yale University; Member, Alternate Dispute Resolution Panel, U.S. District Court for the Northern District of New York **CIV:** Member, U.S. Green Building Council; Former Director, Syracuse Boys Club **AW:** Albert Nelson Marquis Lifetime Achievement Award (2017) **MEM:** Forum of Construction Industry, American Bar Association (1989-Present); Litigation Section, American Bar Association (1989-Present); Panel of Arbitrators, American Arbitration Association (1980-Present); American Bar Association; Tort and Insurance Practice Sections, American Bar Association; Business Law Section, American Bar Association; Environment, Energy & Resources Section, American Bar Association; American Arbitration Association; Construction Specifications Institute; New York State Bar Association; Onondaga County Bar Association **MH:** Albert Nelson Marquis Lifetime Achievement Award; Marquis Who's Who Top Professional **B/I:** He became involved in his profession because it represented a professional area involving both thoughtful analysis and contribution to other people. **AV:** Classical music; Weight training; Fine red wines **PA:** Republican **RE:** Roman Catholic

BRADSHAW, CAROL, T: Executive Director **I:** Media & Entertainment **CN:** The Laugh Makers **DOB:** 10/23/1959 **PB:** Alliance **SC:** OH/USA **PT:** Charles C. Eynon; Susan H. Eynon **MS:** Single **ED:** Coursework in Dramatics/Theatre Arts, University of North Carolina School of the Arts; Coursework, American Academy of Dramatic Arts **CT:** Certification in Hospice, Long Beach, CA **C:** Executive Director, The Laugh Maker (1997-Present); Producer, Creative Consultant (1984-Present); Director, Coach, The Actors Group (1987-1990) **CR:** American Scenes Awards Committee, Screen Actors Guild **CIV:** Trauma Room Specialist, Hospice Care, Long Beach Memorial Medical Center (1981-1984); Lobbied, International MS Society; Volunteer, Meals on Wheels; Volunteer, Gay Men's Health Crisis; Activist, Wildlife Care; Activist, Environmental Awareness **CW:** Producer, "Carol Bradshaw's Production of Brevities," Proctors Theater, Schenectady, NY (2015); Producer, "George Washington Dinner," Old Dutch Church, Kingston, NY (2007); Producer, Director, Writer, "A Night of Burly's Bits and Pieces," Players Club of Gramercy Park, New York, NY (2000); Producer, "The Joey Faye Memorial Tribute," Friends at the Friars Club, New Victory Theater, New York, NY (1997); Producer, "An Afternoon at the Palace with the Vitaphone Group," The Actors Fund of America (1996); Producer, "A Tribute Night for Allan Jones," Snug Harbor Cultural Center (1994); Director, Writer, Story Editor, "The Fatigued Goddess of Frankfurt Filmmuseum," Frankfurt, Germany **MEM:** Women in Film; National Association of Professional Women; Screen Actors Guild; American Federation of Television and Radio Artists; Writers Guild of America; The Episcopal Actors Guild; The Players Club of Gramercy Park; The Comedy Hall of Fame; Museum of Modern Art; The Museum of Television and Radio; Roundabout Theater Company; Carnegie Hall; Art Society of Kingston; Los Angeles Conservancy **AS:** Ms. Bradshaw attributes her success to her scholarship, passion, and a strong sense of ethics. She additionally credits her determination in bringing out the best in her collaborative creative efforts through finding reliable, supportive performers. **B/I:** Ms. Bradshaw always had a love for music and classic comedy. Starting at the early age of 6 years old, she collected memorabilia and made up shows for her neighbors and community clubs. Later, she went on to meet many of the legends of stage and screen. She got the opportunity to partake in filmed interviews with these icons, writing published articles about their careers and contributions to American popular culture. **AV:** Rescuing animals; Talking politics; Collecting rare theater and film memorabilia; Researching astrology and genealogy; Maintaining health and fitness **PA:** Independent **RE:** Christian

BRADSHER, HENRY ST. AMANT, T: Journalist, Foreign Affairs Analyst **I:** Writing and Editing

BRADWAY, ROBERT, "BOB" A., T: Chairman and Chief Executive Officer **I:** Biotechnology **CN:** Amgen Inc. **ED:** MBA, Harvard Business School, Harvard University (1990); BS in Biology, Amherst College (1985) **C:** Chairman, Amgen Inc., Thousand Oaks, CA (2013-Present); Chief Executive Officer, Amgen Inc., Thousand Oaks, CA (2012-Present); President and Chief Operating Officer, Amgen Inc., Thousand Oaks, CA (2010-2012); Chief Financial Officer, Amgen Inc., Thousand Oaks, CA (2007-2010); Vice President, Operations Strategy, Amgen Inc., Thousand Oaks, CA (2006-2007); Managing Director, International Activities, Morgan Stanley, London, United Kingdom (2001-2006); Investment Banker, Morgan Stanley, New York, NY and London, United Kingdom (1985-2001) **CR:** Board of Directors, Boeing (2016-Present); Board of Trustees, University of Southern California (2014-Present); Board of Directors, Amgen Inc. (2011-Present); Advisory Board, USC Schaeffer Center (2011-Present); Board of Directors, Norfolk Southern Corporation (2011-2017); Board of Directors, Pharmaceutical Research and Manufacturers of America® **CIV:** Chairman, CEO Roundtable on Cancer, Inc. (2015-Present)

BRADY, KEVIN PATRICK, T: U.S. Representative from Texas **I:** Government Administration/Government Relations/Government Services **DOB:** 04/11/1955 **PB:** Vermillion **SC:** SD/USA **MS:** Married **SPN:** Cathy Patronella Brady **CH:** Will; Sean **ED:** BS in Mass Communications, University of South Dakota, Vermillion, SD (1990) **C:** Chairman, U.S. House Committee of Ways and Means (2015-Present); U.S. Representative from Texas' Eighth Congressional District, United States Congress (1997-Present); Member, District 15, Texas House of Representatives (1991-1997); President, South Montgomery County-Woodlands Chamber of Commerce (1985-1996); Deputy Whip, Texas' Eighth Congressional District, United States Congress **CIV:** Active, Saints Simon and Jude Catholic Church **AW:** Named Legislative Standout, Dallas Morning News; Named Outstanding Young Texan, Texas Jaycees; Named One of the 10 Best Legislators for Families and Children, State Bar of Texas; Victims Rights Equalizer Award, Texans for Equal Justice Center; Support for Family Issues Award, Texas Extension Homemakers Association; Scholars Achievement Award for Excellence in Public Service, North Harris Montgomery Community College District (Now Lone Star College System); Achievement Award, Texas Conservative Coalition; Named Hometown Hero, The Woodlands, Texas; Spirit of Enterprise Award; Guardian of Small Business Award; Savior of Gnomes Award; Golden Bulldog Award, Watchdogs of the Treasury; Special Recognition, Citizens Against Government Waste **MEM:** Rotary International **AV:** Baseball **PA:** Republican **RE:** Roman Catholic

BRADY, THOMAS, "TOM" EDWARD PATRICK JR., T: Professional Football Player **I:** Athletics **DOB:** 08/03/1977 **PB:** San Mateo **SC:** CA/USA **PT:** Thomas Brady; Galynn (Johnson) Brady **MS:** Married **SPN:** Gisele Bündchen (02/26/2009) **CH:** Benjamin Rein; Vivian Lake; John Edward Moynahan **ED:** BA in Organizational Studies, University of Michigan (2000) **C:** Quarterback, Tampa Bay Buccaneers (2020-Present); Quarterback, New England Patriots, NFL (2000-2020) **CR:** Co-founder, TB12, Inc. (2016-Present) **CIV:** Co-founder, TB12 Foundation (2016-Present) **CW:** Author, "The TB12 Method: How to Achieve a Lifetime of Sustained Peak Performance" (2017); Appearance, "Ted 2" (2015); Appearance, "Entourage" (2009); Voice Actor, "Family Guy" (2006); Host, "Saturday Night Live" (2005); Voice Actor, "The Simpsons" (2005) **AW:** Named One of the 100 Most Influential People, TIME Magazine (2017); Named to the Pro Bowl (2017); Super Bowl Champion, New England Patriots (2002, 2004, 2005, 2015); Named Super Bowl XLIX MVP (2015); Named to the American Football Conference Pro Bowl Team, NFL (2001, 2004, 2005, 2007, 2009-2014); Ed Block Courage Award, New England Patriots (2010); Named to the First Team All-Pro, The Associated Press (2007, 2010); Named NFL MVP (2007, 2010); Named NFL Offensive Player of the Year (2007, 2010); Named NFL Comeback Player of the Year, The Associated Press (2009); ESPY Award, Best NFL Player, ESPN (2008); Named One of the Most Influential People in the World of Sports, Business Week (Now Bloomberg Businessweek) (2007, 2008); Named Sportsman of the Year, The Sporting News (2004, 2007); Named NFL Player of the Year, The Sporting News (2007); Named Male Athlete of the Year (2007); Named Sportsman of the Year, Sports Illustrated (2005); Named Super Bowl XXXVIII MVP (2004); Named to Junipero Serra High School Hall of Fame (2003); Named Super Bowl XXXVI MVP (2002); ESPY Award, Best Breakthrough Athlete, ESPN (2002)

BRAID, RALPH M., T: Professor of Economics **I:** Education/Educational Services **CN:** Wayne State University **DOB:** 10/01/1953 **PB:** Princeton **SC:** NJ/USA **PT:** Thomas H. Braid; Mary D. Braid **MS:** Divorced **SPN:** Ann D. Harrison (06/01/1991, Divorced 2002) **CH:** Julia M. Braid **ED:** PhD in Economics, Massachusetts Institute of Technology (MIT), Cambridge, MA (1979); AB in Physics, University of Chicago, Chicago, IL, Honors Degree (1975); Completed AB in Mathematics, University in Chicago (But the School Did Not Officially Award Double Majors) **C:** Professor of Economics, Wayne State University, Detroit, MI (1993-Present); Associate Professor of Economics, Wayne State University, Detroit, MI (1988-1993); Assistant Professor of Economics, Columbia University, New York, NY (1979-1988); Visiting Assistant Professor of Economics, Princeton University, Princeton, NJ (1986) **CR:** Member, Editorial Board, American Economic Review (2006-2011); Associate Editor, Regional Science and Urban Economics (1991-2004); Journal of Regional Science (1990-2011); Member, Editorial Board, Journal of Urban Economics (1989-2007) **CW:** Contributor, 48 Articles, Professional Journals **AW:** President's Award for Excellence in Teaching, Wayne State University; Graduate Fellow, National Science Foundation **MEM:** American Economic Association; Phi Beta Kappa **MH:** Albert Nelson Marquis Lifetime Achievement Award **AS:** Dr. Braid attributes his success to his father, Thomas H. Braid, who was a physicist for a national laboratory, and his mother, Mary D. Braid, a math teacher who went on to become a computer programmer. He attributes much of his success and abilities to them. **B/I:** Dr. Braid became involved in his profession because as an undergraduate, he took a lot of courses in physics, economics, and mathematics. He applied to graduate schools in physics and economics and was accepted everywhere he applied. He then decided to go for economics. He always wanted to be a teacher and researcher.

BRAIS, KEITH S., ESQ., T: Attorney **I:** Law and Legal Services **CN:** Brais & Associates, PA **ED:** JD, New England Law (1990); BS in Marine Engineering, Massachusetts Maritime Academy (1981) **CT:** Driller Level Certificate in Well Control, Surface Stack and Subsea Stack (1984) **CR:** Speaker, "Florida Marina Storage Agreements at a Glance," Marine Underwriters (2008); Speaker, "Covered Losses, Exclusions and Burdens of Proof," Marine Underwriters (2008); Speaker, "Ship's Medical Negligence: Respondeat Superior or Strict Liability?" Marine Underwriters (2008); Speaker, International Council of Cruise Lines, Legal and Insurance Seminar, Washington, DC (2006); Speaker, "Plowing Your Way into Environmental Liabilities in South Florida," Legal and Insurance Seminar, International Council of Cruise Lines, Washington, DC (2006); Speaker, "The Shipowner's Limitation of Liability Act: Pitfalls for the Unwary," Seminar, Fort Lauderdale Mariners Club (2006); Speaker, "To Deny Coverage or Not Deny Coverage: Questions Underwriters Must Ask When Deciding to Accept a Marine Claim," Seminar, Southeastern Admiralty Law Institute, Savannah, GA (2006); Presenter, Fort Lauderdale Mariners Club (2002) **AW:** Top Attorneys in Florida, Florida's Legal Elite (2015-Present); Member, Multi-Million Dollar Advocates Forum (2015-Present); 10/10 Superb Rating, Avvo.com (2010-Present); Super Lawyer (2008-Present); AV Preeminent Rating, Martindale-Hubbell (1997-Present); Board Certified Admiralty and Maritime Attorney, The Florida Bar

(1996-Present) **BAR:** The Florida Bar; Massachusetts Bar Association; United States District Court District of Massachusetts; United States District Court Northern District of Texas; United States District & Bankruptcy Courts of Southern District of Texas; United States District Court Eastern District of Texas; United States District Court Southern District of Florida; United States District Court Middle District of Florida; United States District Court Northern District of Florida; United States Court of Appeals for the Fifth Circuit; United States Court of Appeals for the Eleventh Circuit; Supreme Court of the United States **AS:** Mr. Brais attributes his success to a real desire to help clients and his empathetic nature. **B/I:** Mr. Brais became involved in his profession because he got hurt while working in the oil field and that ended one of his careers. He decided to go to law school and when he finished, a firm in Miami, Florida took a look at his background in law and told him he was perfect for their maritime department. **AV:** Fishing; Camping; Enjoying and preserving nature; Spending time with family

BRANAGH, KENNETH CHARLES, T: Actor, Director, Producer, Writer **I:** Media & Entertainment **DOB:** 12/10/1960 **PB:** Belfast **SC:** United Kingdom **PT:** William Branagh; Frances (Harper) Branagh **MS:** Married **ED:** Honorary LittD, Shakespeare Institute, University of Birmingham, Stratford upon Avon, United Kingdom (2001); Honorary DLitt, Queen's University Belfast, Belfast, United Kingdom (1990); Diplomate, Royal Academy of Dramatic Art, London, United Kingdom (1981) **CR:** President, Royal Academy of Dramatic Art (2015-Present); Founder, Actor-Manager, Kenneth Branagh Theatre Company (2015-2016); Co-Founder, Renaissance Theatre Company (1987-1992) **CIV:** Honorary President, NICVA (2001-Present) **CW:** Actor, Producer, Director, "Death on the Nile" (2020); Actor, "Tenet" (2020); Producer, Director, "Artemis Fowl" (2020); Narrator, "Twisted Tales of Love" (2019); Actor, "Upstart Crow" (2018); Actor, Producer, Director, "All Is True" (2018); Actor, Producer, Director, "Murder on the Orient Express" (2017); Actor, "Dunkirk" (2017); Actor, "Branagh Theatre Live: The Entertainer" (2016); Actor, "The Entertainer," Garrick Theatre, London, United Kingdom (2016); Actor, "Romeo and Juliet," Garrick Theatre, London, United Kingdom (2016); Actor, Director, "The Painkiller," Garrick Theatre, London, United Kingdom (2016); Actor, Director, "Harlequinade," Garrick Theatre, London, United Kingdom (2015); Actor, Director, "The Winter's Tale," Garrick Theatre, London, United Kingdom (2015); Director, "Cinderella" (2015); Actor, "Branagh Theatre Live: The Winter's Tale" (2015); Actor, Executive Producer, "Wallander" (2008-2015); Actor, Director, "Jack Ryan: Shadow Recruit" (2014); Co-Director, "Macbeth," Manchester International Festival, Manchester, United Kingdom and Park Avenue Armory, New York, NY (2013-2014); Producer, "Thor: The Dark World" (2013); Director, "Thor" (2011); Actor, "My Week with Marilyn" (2011); Actor, "Prodigal" (2011); Actor, "Masterpiece Mystery" (2010); Actor, "Pirate Radio" (2009); Actor, "Ivanov," Wyndham's Theatre, London, United Kingdom (2008); Actor, "Valkyrie" (2008); Actor, "10 Days to War" (2008); Actor, "Alien Love Triangle" (2008); Director, "Sleuth" (2007); Voice Actor, "The Bible Revolution" (2007); Director, Writer, "The Magic Flute" (2006); Narrator, "American Experience" (2006); Executive Producer, Director, Writer, "As You Like It" (2006); Actor, "Warm Springs" (2005); Actor, "Five Children and It" (2004); Director, "The Play That I Wrote," Lyceum Theatre, New York, NY (2003); Actor, "Edmond," Royal National Theatre, London, United Kingdom (2003); Executive Pro-

ducer, Writer, "Listening" (2003); Actor, "Richard III," Crucible Theatre, Sheffield, United Kingdom (2002); Actor, "Shackleton" (2002); Actor, "Harry Potter and the Chamber of Secrets" (2002); Actor, "Rabbit-Proof Fence" (2002); Director, "The Play That I Wrote," Liverpool Playhouse Theatre, Liverpool, United Kingdom and Wyndham's Theatre, London, United Kingdom (2001); Actor, "Conspiracy" (2001); Actor, "Schneider's 2nd Stage" (2001); Actor, "How to Kill Your Neighbor's Dog" (2000); Voice Actor, "The Road to El Dorado" (2000); Actor, Producer, Director, Writer, "Love's Labour's Lost" (2000); Voice Actor, "The Periwig-Maker" (1999); Actor, "Wild Wild West" (1999); Actor, "The Dance of Shiva" (1998); Actor, "The Theory of Flight" (1998); Actor, "Celebrity" (1998); Actor, "The Proposition" (1998); Actor, "The Gingerbread Man" (1998); Actor, Director, Writer, "Hamlet" (1996); Director, Writer, "A Midwinter's Tale" (1995); Actor, "Othello" (1995); Actor, "Performance" (1995); Actor, Co-Producer, Director, "Mary Shelley's Frankenstein" (1994); Narrator, "Omnibus" (1994); Actor, Producer, Director, Writer, "Much Ado About Nothing" (1993); Director, "Swan Song" (1992); Actor, Producer, Director, "Peter's Friends" (1992); Actor, Director, "Dead Again" (1991); Actor, "Look Back in Anger" (1989); Actor, Director, Writer, "Henry V" (1989); Actor, "Renaissance Shakespeare on the Road," United Kingdom (1988); Actor, "Thompson" (1988); Actor, "Coming Through" (1988); Actor, "American Playhouse" (1988); Actor, "Lorna" (1987); Actor, "The Lady's Not for Burning" (1987); Actor, "Fortunes of War" (1987); Actor, "High Season" (1987); Actor, "A Month in the Country" (1987); Actor, "Theatre Night" (1987); Actor, "Play for Today" (1982-1984); Actor, "Boy in the Bush" (1984); Actor, "Maybury" (1983); Actor, "To the Lighthouse" (1983); Actor, "Play for Tomorrow" (1982) **AW:** Freedom of the City, Belfast, Northern Ireland, United Kingdom (2018); Albert R. Broccoli and, BAFTA Los Angeles, British Academy of Film and Television Arts (2017); International Emmy Award for Best Performance by an Actor, Television Academy (2017); Laurence Olivier Award for Society of London Theatre Special Award, Society of London Theatre (2017); Pragnell Prize (2015); Knight Bachelor (2012); London Film Critics' Circle Award for Supporting Actor of the Year, Critics' Circle (2011); Lifetime Achievement Award, RomaFictionFest (2009); Award for Best Actor, British Academy of Film and Television Arts (2009); Award for Best Drama Series, British Academy of Film and Television Arts (2008); BPG Award for Best Actor, Broadcasting Press Guild (2008); London Film Critics' Circle Award for British Supporting Actor of the Year, Critics' Circle (2002); Primetime Emmy Award for Outstanding Lead Actor in a Miniseries or a Movie, Television Academy (2001); Award for Best Actor, San Diego Film Critics Society (1996); Golden Osella, La Biennale di Venezia (1995); Michael Balcon Award for Outstanding British Contribution to Cinema Award, British Academy of Film and Television Arts (1993); London Film Critics' Circle Award for Supporting Actor of the Year, Critics' Circle (1993); European Film Award for European Actor of the Year, European Film Academy (1990); European Film Award for Best Director, European Film Academy (1990); European Film Award for Young European Film of the Year, European Film Academy (1990); Award for Best Direction, British Academy of Film and Television Arts (1989); Olivier Award for Best Newcomer, Society of London Theatre (1982)

BRANDT, PAMELA A., MAED, T: Art and Art Special Education Educator **I:** Education/Educational Services **DOB:** 09/13/1962 **PB:** Manitowoc **SC:** WI/USA **PT:** Jerome Nicholas; Patricia Ann

Gresenz MS: Married SPN: Robert Martin Brandt (06/18/1988) CH: Adam Jerome; Eric Robert; Elise Patricia ED: Master in Education, National Louis University (2010); BA, Alverno College (1984) CT: Certificate, Art and Art Special Education Teacher, Department of Public Instruction, State of Wisconsin (1984) C: Art, Art Special Education Teacher, Hartford Joint No. 1 School District (HJT1), WI (1984) CR: Chairperson, Art Department Curriculum, Hartford Joint No. 1 School District (HJT1) (1994-Present); Chair, Applied and Fine Arts Curriculum (2015) CIV: Leader, Girl Scouts of the United States of America, Slinger, WI (2002-Present); Mentor, Day Camp Directors, Girl Scouts of the United States of America, Fall (2019); Volunteer Day Camp Director, Girl Scouts of the United States of America (2004-2019); Troop Committee Member, Boy Scouts of America, Slinger, WI (1999-2009) AW: Herb Kohl Fellowship (2008); Arrowhead Honor Award, Boy Scouts of America (2002); Recipient, Scouter's Key, Boy Scouts of America (2002); Scouter's Training Award, Boy Scouts of America (2002) MEM: National Education Association; Wisconsin Education Association; Hartford Elementary Education Association; Wisconsin Association for Middle Level Educators; American Art Therapy Association; Wisconsin Art Therapy Association; National Art Education Association; Wisconsin Art Education Association; Delta Kappa Gamma (DKGSI) MH: Albert Nelson Marquis Lifetime Achievement Award; Marquis Who's Who Top Professional; Marquis Who's Who Humanitarian Award B/I: Mrs. Brandt became involved in her profession because she was always fascinated with working in the Girls Scouts with the special needs groups. She decided that she wanted to be an art teacher and she had an art teacher that she was very impressed with. Also, in high school she was told not to go into education because she would never find a job and she felt crushed about that. So she started researching and found art therapy which still gave her the chance to teach and work with handicapped people and incorporate the art. Ironically enough she got a job teaching back at her school district that she had also passed through. They happened to have an art opening and she was selected for the job and had been there for over 35 years. AV: Crafts; Camping; Hiking; Swimming; Fishing

BRANDYS, PAUL, T: Computer Programmer (Retired) I: Other CN: Convergys MS: Married CH: One son; One daughter ED: MS in Chemistry, DePaul University; BS in Computer Programming, University of Illinois C: Retired (2011); Discover (2007-2011); Computer Programmer, Convergys (1995-2007); Chicago Northwestern (1987-1995); Specialty Product Unit, PPG Industries; Quaker Oats; Chemist; Contract Employee, United Stationers CIV: Cold Calls, Democratic Party B/I: Mr. Brandys became involved in his profession because of his experiences as a chemist. After fellow employees passed away due to being exposed to chemicals, he went back to night school during the dawn of the computers, which changed the course of his life. PA: Democrat

BRANSON, HARLEY KENNETH, T: Attorney at Law, Retired; Venture Capital, Retired I: Law and Legal Services CN: Flying Palms LLC DOB: 06/10/1942 PB: Ukiah SC: CA/USA PT: Harley Branson; Clara Branson CH: Erik Jordan ED: JD, Santa Clara University (1968); BS in Accounting and Finance, San Jose State University (1965) C: President, Flying Palms LLC, San Diego, CA (1995-2000); Chief Executive Officer, Flying Palms LLC, San Diego, CA (1995-2000); Executive Vice President, General Counsel, Corporate Secretary, Bumble Bee Seafoods, San Diego, CA (1985-1989); Group

General Counsel, Castle & Cooke, Inc., San Diego, CA (1983-1985); Division Counsel, Ralston Purina Company (Now Nestle Purina Petcare Company), San Diego, CA (1978-1983); Private Practice, San Diego, CA (1969-1978); Law Clerk for Judge James M. Carter, United States Court of Appeals for the Ninth Circuit, San Diego, CA (1968-1969) AW: Articles Editor, "Santa Clara Lawyer, Vol. 8" BAR: California (1969-1998) MH: Albert Nelson Marquis Lifetime Achievement Award

BRASSARD, JANICE A., T: Owner, Instructor, Educational Consultant, and Retired Secondary School Educator I: Education/Educational Services CN: Miz B's Tutorials and Educational Consulting DOB: 10/07/1949 PB: Harlingen SC: TX/USA PT: Gaston Paul Junior; Jewel Aline (Davis) Jennet MS: Widowed SPN: Raymond Maurice Brassard (06/03/1972) CH: Brenden Eugene; Bryan Edward; Britten Elliott ED: MEd in Supervision, Lamar University (1975); BS in Secondary Education, University of Texas (1971) CT: Dyslexia Practitioner (2018); Certified Teacher, Texas C: Owner, Instructor, Educational Consultant, Miz B's Tutorials and Educational Consulting, Beaumont, TX (2005-Present); Teacher, English, High School, South Park/Beaumont Independent School District, Texas (1973-2005); Teacher, 8th Grade, Our Mother of Mercy Catholic School, Houston, TX (1972-1973); Teacher, English and Language Arts, Silsbee Independent School District, Texas (1971-1972) CR: Member, School Improvement Division, Texas Education Agency, Austin, TX (1996-1997); In-Service Trainer, Beaumont Independent School District (1980, 1994, 1996) CIV: Swim Coach, Beaumont Independent School District (1996-2004); Troop Leader, Girl Scouts of the USA, Beaumont, TX (1979-1995); Delegate, Democratic State Convention, Beaumont, TX (1976, 1982, 1992); Board of Trustees, Beaumont Independent School District; Founder, Swim Program, Beaumont Independent School District CW: Co-Author, 10th Grade Gifted and Talented Curriculum (1997); Author, High School Basic Curriculum (1975) AW: Named Outstanding Teacher, Beaumont Independent School District (1993); Named One of 10 Outstanding Teachers, Quality Education Beaumont (1986); Named Outstanding Teacher of Year, South Park Independent School District (1980) MEM: Legislative Advisory Committee (2008-Present); Fellow, Center for Reform of School Systems (2007); National Education Association; Retired Texas State Teachers Association; Master Trustee, TASB-Leadership; National Teachers Organization MH: Albert Nelson Marquis Lifetime Achievement Award; Marquis Who's Who Top Professional B/I: Ms. Brassard became involved in her profession because it was providence. She went to the University of Texas with the intention of becoming a pediatrician. Back in the 1960s, that door was not wide open for women and, at one point, after a year and a half, she went to the dean and asked how could she get out within a year and a half and he suggested that she could teach. After much back and forth on the topic of what to teach, she finally settled on becoming an English teacher. For the next three semesters, she completed 21 hours of training to become a teacher. In addition, what led Ms. Brassard to go from teaching to opening up her own consulting business was that she injured herself, and when she returned to teaching, she couldn't stand on her feet all day. She had been teaching long enough to retire, so she retired with teachers retirement. She was staying home, but she wasn't busy, so she knew there were kids that needed help with their school work, so she decided to open her own tutoring business. She started out with herself, one certified math teacher

and one certified reading specialist and now she has eight people on staff and a part-time worker. AV: Reading; Cooking; Swimming RE: Lutheran

BRASWELL, JACKIE BOYD, T: State Agency Administrator I: Real Estate CN: Rayner Real Estate DOB: 02/15/1938 PB: Leon County SC: FL/USA PT: Chalmer Parks Boyd; Kathryn Iris (Johnson) Boyd MS: Married SPN: Fletcher Braswell (11/28/1957) CH: Flecia Lori; Carmen Ethelee ED: Master's Degree in Educational Administration (1976); BS, Florida State University (1964) CT: Licensed Real Estate Sales Associate, State of Florida (2005); Certified Educator, Valdosta State University (1968); Certified in Rayner Real Estate, Tallahassee, FL; Licensed Administrator, State of Florida C: Real Estate Associate, Rayner Real Estate (2005-Present); Director of Educational Affairs and Policy, Florida Lottery (1999-2005); Chairman, Business-Vocational Teacher, Department of Career Education, Lincoln High School (1975-1999); Teacher of Business Education, James S. Rickards High School, Tallahassee, FL (1970-1975); Teacher of Business Education, Berrien High School, Berrien County Board of Education, Nashville, GA (1966-1969); Single Manager, U.S. Air Force, Moody Air Force Base (1958-1961) CR: Co-Owner, Financial Manager, Rundown Farms, Tallahassee, FL (1969-Present); Governor's Mentoring Initiative Lottery Mentoring Program (1999-2005); President, Eight Out Investment Group (1993-2003) CIV: Annual Fundraiser Committee, PACE Center for Girls, Inc (2005-2008); Fundraising Committee, Boys & Girls Clubs of the Big Bend (2005-2006); Sponsorship Chairman, Capital Cultural Center, Chukker Challenge (1997-1998); Fundraising Chairman, District School Superintendents Campaign (1996); Invited Delegate to China, Citizens Ambassador Program, People International (1995); Chairman, Appointed Member, Representatives to Florida Commission on Education Reform and Accountability, Speaker of the Florida House of Representatives (1991-1993); Vice Chairman, Florida Department of Education, Governor Bob Martinez (1990-1991); Appointee, Florida Department of Education, Governor Bob Martinez (1987-1990) CW: Editor, In Touch (1979-1980); Contributor, Articles, Professional Journals AW: Selectee, Harvard Institute for Higher Education (1991); Merit Award, National FFA Organization (1974) MEM: Gold-Sustaining Member, Political Action Committee, Florida Realtors (2008-2015); Treasurer, Capital Gains Club (2000); Governmental Relations, Parliamentarian, Luzerne County Transportation Authority (1991); President, President-Elect, Leon Vocational Association (1987-1989); Secretary-Treasurer, Luzerne County Transportation Authority (1987-1988); Charter Member, National Museum of Women in the Arts; National Business Education Association; Florida Vocational Association (Now FACTE); Florida Business Education Association; Dance Arts Guild; Leon County Farm Bureau; Quill and Scroll; The Honor Society of Phi Kappa Phi MH: Albert Nelson Marquis Lifetime Achievement Award PA: Republican

BRATCHER, CARLA, T: Obstetrician and Gynecologist I: Medicine & Health Care DOB: 09/18/1942 PB: Wichita SC: KS/USA PT: Carl E Dillon; Armilda Elizabeth Dillon MS: Married SPN: Carl E. Bratcher III (04/09/1982, Deceased 2019) ED: Doctor of Medicine, University of Pennsylvania (1979); Bachelor of Science, University of Florida (1966); Coursework, University of Washington (1960-1962) CT: Diplomate, American Board Obstetrics-Gynecology C: Retired (1999); Chief Obstetrics Department, Central Oregon District Hospital (1990-1995, 1997-1999); Private Practice, Obstetrics-Gynecology., Redmond, OR (1990-1999); Private Practice,

Grand Prairie, TX (1988-1989); Chief, Ambulatory Care Service, Obstetrics-Gynecology, Second General Hospital, Landstuhl, Germany (1984-1987); Resident in Obstetrics-Gynecology, Madigan Army Medical Center, Tacoma, WA (1980-1983); Obstetrics-Gynecology Intern, Madigan Army Medical Center, Tacoma, WA (1979-1980); Research Technician, Wistar Institute, Philadelphia, PA (1973-1975); Research Technician, National Cancer Institute, National Institutes of Health, Bethesda, MD (1967-1973) **CR:** Volunteer, Instructor Department, Obstetrics-Gynecology, Dallas-Ft. Worth Medical Center (1988-1989) **MIL:** Major, Medical Corps, U.S. Army (1979-1987) **MEM:** American Association of University Women; Oregon Medical Association **MH:** Albert Nelson Marquis Lifetime Achievement Award **B/I:** Dr. Bratcher had the inclination to become an obstetrician before and during medical school, having always wanted to help people. **PA:** Democrat

BRAUN, MICHAEL, "MIKE" K., T: U.S. Senator from Indiana **I:** Government Administration/Government Relations/Government Services **CN:** U.S. Senate **DOB:** 03/24/1954 **PB:** Jasper **SC:** IN/USA **MS:** Married **SPN:** Maureen Braun **CH:** Four Children **ED:** Master of Business Administration, Harvard University; Bachelor of Arts in Economics, Wabash College, Summa Cum Laude **C:** U.S. Senator, State of Indiana (2019-Present); President, Chief Executive Officer, Meyer Distributing (1995-Present); Member, Indiana House of Representatives, 63rd District (2014-2017) **CIV:** Member, Jasper School Board (2004-2014) **MEM:** Phi Delta Theta **PA:** Republican **RE:** Roman Catholic

BREAZEALE, HELENE, T: Arts Administrator, Educator **I:** Education/Educational Services **DOB:** 09/14/1937 **PB:** Baltimore **SC:** MD/USA **PT:** Harry Saille Cohen; Sophia Himmelfarb Cohen **MS:** Divorced **CH:** Gregory A. Breazeale **ED:** PhD in Dance Education, Union Institute and University (1976); MA in Dance Education, Columbia University (1972); BS/MA in Dance, The Juilliard School (1959) **C:** Executive Director, World Music Congresses, Towson University, Baltimore, MD (1995-2005); Producer/Director, World Cello Congress III, Towson University (2000); Producer/Director, World Cello Congress II, St. Petersburg, Russia (1997); Associate Dean, Towson University College of Fine Arts and Communication, Baltimore, MD (1990-1996); Professor, Chair, Department of Dance, Towson University, Baltimore, MD (1972-1990); Faculty, Cleveland State University (1969-1972); Faculty, Case Western Reserve University, Cleveland, OH (1965-1969) **CR:** Baltimore Mayor's Advisory Committee (1988-1994); Consultant, Maryland State Arts Council, Baltimore, MD (1972-1980) **CIV:** Baltimore Symphony Associates (2015-Present); Jewish Museum of Maryland (1986-1998); Volunteer, Baltimore Museum of Art (1987-1991) **CW:** Contributor, Articles, Professional Journals **AW:** Living Legacy Award, Maryland Dance Education Association (2017); Two-Time Recipient, Towson University Merit Award; Maryland Council for Dance Award for Outstanding Service to Dance in the State of Maryland **MEM:** National Association of Schools of Dance; American Association of University Administrators; Baltimore Symphony Associates; Baltimore Symphony Orchestra Governing Members **B/I:** Dr. Breazeale became involved in her profession because, when she was 5 years old, her mother took her to see Peter and the Wolf at the Ballet Theater. She was transfixed by it all. She then announced to her mother that she wanted to be a ballerina, which is where her journey to success began. Her mother contacted the head of the dance department at the Peabody Institute of Music in an effort to enroll Dr. Breazeale. From there, her career progressed naturally.

BRECHER, HOWARD, T: Lawyer; Publishing Executive **I:** Law and Legal Services **CN:** Value Line, Inc. **DOB:** 10/18/1953 **PB:** New York **SC:** NY/USA **PT:** Milton Brecher; Dorothy (Zahler) Brecher **MS:** Married **SPN:** Ellen R. Brecher **CH:** Emma Brecher **ED:** LLM, New York University (1984); JD, Harvard University, Cum Laude (1979); MBA, Harvard University (1979); AB, Harvard University, Magna Cum Laude (1975) **C:** Chairman, Chief Executive Officer, Value Line, Inc. (2011); Acting Chairman, Chief Executive Officer, Value Line, Inc. (2009); Vice President, Secretary, Value Line Funds, Value Line, Inc. (2008-2010); Vice President, Chief Legal Officer, Secretary, Value Line, Inc. (1996); Vice President, Secretary, Treasurer, General Counsel, AB&Co. (1991-1996); Attorney, Legal Department, New York Telephone Co. (Now Verizon), New York, NY (1984-1991); Associate, Chadbourne, Parke, Whiteside & Wolff, New York, NY (1982-1984); Associate, Roberts & Holland, LLP, New York, NY (1979-1982) **CR:** Member, Tax Committee, NYC Chamber of Commerce (1985-1988, 1994-Present) **MEM:** Tax Section, American Bar Association (ABA); Tax Section, New York State Bar Association; Committee of Taxation of Affiliated Corps., New York State Bar Association; Trusts and Estates Section, New York State Bar Association; Harvard Business School Club of Greater New York; Harvard Club of New York; Harvard Club of Boston **BAR:** United States District Court for the Southern District of New York (1983); United States Tax Court (1981); New York (1980) **PA:** Democrat **RE:** Jewish

BREEDIN, B. BRENT, T: Historian **I:** Law and Legal Services **CN:** White House Weekly **DOB:** 11/03/1925 **PB:** Beaufort **SC:** SC/USA **PT:** Berryman Brent Breedin; Jane Cunningham Dixon **MS:** Married **SPN:** Catherine McCuen Muller (2006); Allain Crenshaw (1959, Divorced 1978) **CH:** David Singleton; Sarah Breedin Chase; Amelia Breedin Twarogowski **ED:** BA, Washington and Lee University (1947) **C:** Private Practice, Brent Breedin and Associates, Columbia, SC (1988-Present); Historian, White House Weekly, Washington, DC (1998-2003); Resident Manager, Hunt Energy and Mineral Company Australia (1996-1997); Director of Public Relations, Rice University, Houston, TX (1981-1987); Director of Public Relations, Georgetown University, Washington, DC (1977-1979); Editor, Council on Library and Information Resources, Washington, DC (1972-1975); Editor, American College Public Relations Association, Washington, DC (1966-1971); Editor, Clemson University (1964-1966); Information Specialist, DuPont Company (1960-1963); Press Secretary, U.S. Senator Strom Thurmond (1958-1959); Resident Manager, Hunt International Oil Company, Pakistan (1955-1958); Publicist, Clemson University (1952-1955); Sports Editor, Columnist, Daily Mail, Anderson, SC (1949-1952); Reporter, Caller-Times, Corpus Christi, TX (1947-1948) **CR:** Adviser, Houston Zoo (1981-1987); Adviser, Washington DC Library (1972-1976) **CIV:** Field School, Washington, DC (1972); Founding Member, Capital Hill Montessori, Washington, DC (1964) **MIL:** U.S. Navy (1944-1945) **MEM:** National Press Club; Sigma Delta Chi **MH:** Albert Nelson Marquis Lifetime Achievement Award; Marquis Who's Who Top Professional; Marquis Who's Who Humanitarian Award **AV:** Sports history; Movie history **RE:** Episcopalian

BREEN, EDWARD DEVEAUX, T: Executive Chairman **I:** Sciences **CN:** DuPont **DOB:** 03/14/1956 **SC:** PA/USA **MS:** Married **SPN:** Lynn (Branster) Breen **CH:** Three Children **ED:** BS in Economics and Business, Grove City College (1978) **C:** Chief Executive Officer, DuPont (2020-Present); Executive Chairman, DuPont (2019-2020); Chief Executive Officer, DowDuPont (2015-2019); Chairman and Chief Executive Officer, Tyco International (Now Johnson Controls), Portsmouth, NH (2002-2012); President and Chief Operating Officer, Motorola Mobility LLC, Schaumburg, IL (2002); President, Broadband Communications Sector and Executive Vice President, Motorola Mobility LLC (2000-2002); President, Chairman and Chief Executive Officer, General Instrument (1997-2000); President, Broadband Networks Group and Eastern Operations, Communications Division, General Instrument (1994-1997); With, General Instrument (1978-1994) **CR:** Board of Directors, DuPont (2015-Present); Lead Independent Director, Comcast Corporation (2005-2011, 2014-Present); Board of Directors, Corteva (2017-2020); Board of Directors, McLeod USA (2004-2005); Advisory Board, New Mountain Capital, LLC **CIV:** Grove City College Board of Trustees (2001-Present) **AW:** Leadership Award for Historic Corporate Reinvention, Chemical Marketing and Economics Group, New York Section, American Chemical Society (2018); Listee, 100 Most Influential People in Cable, Cablefax Magazine (1999); Vanguard Award, NCTA (1998)

BREES, ANDREW, "DREW" CHRISTOPHER, T: Professional Football Player **I:** Athletics **CN:** New Orleans Saints **DOB:** 1/15/1979 **PB:** Austin **SC:** TX/USA **PT:** Eugene Wilson "Chip" Brees; Mina Ruth (Atkins) Brees **MS:** Married **SPN:** Brittany Dudchenko (02/2003) **CH:** Rylen Judith; Baylen Robert; Bowen Christopher; Callen Christian **ED:** Bachelor of Arts in Industrial Management and Manufacturing, Purdue University, West Lafayette, IN (2001) **C:** Quarterback, New Orleans Saints, NFL (2006-Present); Quarterback, San Diego Chargers, NFL (2001-2006) **CR:** Owner, Walk-On's Restaurant, Midland, TX (2019-Present); Owner, Several Jimmy John's Restaurants **CIV:** Co-founder, The Brees Dream Foundation (2003-Present); Co-chair, President's Council on Fitness, Sports and Nutrition (2010) **CW:** Co-author with Chris Fabry, "Coming Back Stronger: Unleashing the Hidden Power of Adversity" (2010); Appearance, "Entourage" (2010) **AW:** Bart Starr Man of the Year Award (2011); Named, NFL Offensive Player of the Year, The Associated Press (2008, 2011); Inductee, National Football Conference Pro Bowl Team, NFL (2006, 2008-2011); Winner, Super Bowl XLIV, New Orleans Saints (2010); Named, Male Athlete of the Year, The Associated Press (2010); Named, Sportsman of the Year, Sports Illustrated (2010); Named Super Bowl XLIV MVP, NFL (2010); Bert Bell Award, Maxwell Football Club (2009); Named, Offensive Player of the Year, National Football Conference (2006, 2008, 2009); Named, NFL Offensive Player of the Year, The Sporting News (2008, 2009); Named, FedEx Air NFL Player of the Year (2008); Grand Marshal, Bacchus Parade (2007); Co-recipient, Walter Payton Man of the Year Award (2006); Inductee, First Team All-Pro (2006); Named, Most Improved Player of the Year, FoxSports.com (2004); Named, Most Improved Player of the Year, CBSSportsline.com (2004); Named, Most Improved Player of the Year, Pro Football Writers of America (2004); Named, Most Improved Player of the Year, Pro Football Weekly (2004); Named, NFL Comeback Player of the Year, Dallas Morning News (2004); Named, NFL Comeback Player of the Year, Sports Illustrated (2004); Named, NFL Comeback Player of the Year, The Associated Press (2004); Inductee, American Football Conference Pro-Bowl Team (2004); Maxwell Award (2000); Named, Big Ten Player of the Year (1998, 2000) **MEM:** Sigma Chi Fraternity **PA:** Republican

BREGSTEIN, HENRY, T: Partner **I:** Law and Legal Services **CN:** Katten Muchin Rosenman LLP **ED:** JD, Benjamin N. Cardozo School of Law, Yeshiva University, Magna Cum Laude (1993); BA, University of Pennsylvania (1970) **C:** Partner, Global Co-chair of Financial Services, Katten Muchin Rosenman LLP (1996-Present); Attorney, Moses & Singer (1994-1996) **AW:** Named to Best Lawyers in America, Private Funds/Hedge Funds Law (2018-2020); Named to Chambers Global, Investment Funds: Hedge Funds, USA (2010, 2012-2019); Named to Chambers USA, Leading Individual (2009-2019); Named to The Legal 500 United States Recommended Attorney (2008-2019); Named to Who's Who Legal Private Funds Regulatory (2016) **MEM:** Committee on Commodities and Futures Law, Association of the Bar of the City of New York; New York State Bar Association **AS:** Mr. Bregstein attributes his success to his hard work and luck. **B/I:** Mr. Bregstein was in business, and it was a very difficult business that was in direct competition with China. With all the legal competition that he fought, he thought law might be a good idea to study. There was a family member that was in law. But Mr. Bregstein did not know about him until about a decade after graduating law school. A relative of his was a heroic figure in Dutch legal history. He married a non-Jewish Dutch woman, (you were not allowed to be sent to the camps if you married non-Jewish). After World War II was over, he was put in-charge of returning property to those who lost their property.

BRELJE, MICHAEL, T: Senior Attorney **I:** Law and Legal Services **CN:** Rogers, Sheffield & Campbell, LLP **DOB:** 10/25/1981 **ED:** JD, Santa Barbara College of Law (2008); BA in Communication, University of California Santa Barbara (2003) **C:** Senior Attorney, Rogers, Sheffield & Campbell, LLP (2018-Present); Senior Associate Attorney, Grokenberger & Smith (2010-2017); Law Clerk, Grokenberger & Smith (2009-2010); Legal Assistant, Garrison Law Corporation (2003-2009) **CIV:** Settlement Master, Santa Barbara Superior Court (2017-Present); Board of Directors, Events Chair, MCLE Chair, Mandatory Fee Arbitration Committee, Santa Barbara County Bar Association (2016-2017); President, Vice President, Santa Barbara Barristers (2011-2012) **AW:** Rating of 10, Avvo **MEM:** Associate, Inns of Court, William L. Gordon Chapter (2011) **BAR:** United States Supreme Court (2018); United States District Court for the Eastern District of California (2018); United States District Court for the Central District of California (2010); California State Bar (2010) **AS:** Mr. Brelje attributes his success to his mentors and his hard-working nature. **B/I:** Mr. Brelje did not know what he wanted to do with his life. Someone who he respected told him that he had the demeanor and the skill for a career in law. He was inspired by his mentors and he eventually realized it was his passion. **THT:** Mr. Brelje's motto is, "Work harder than the other person."

BRENNAN, ROBERT L., T: Educational Director, Psychometrician **I:** Education/Educational Services **DOB:** 05/31/1944 **PB:** Hartford **SC:** CT/USA **PT:** Irene V. Brennan; Robert J. Brennan **MS:** Married **SPN:** Cicely E. Brennan **CH:** One Child **ED:** EdD, Harvard University (1970); Master of Art in Teaching, Harvard University (1968); BA, Salem State College (1967) **C:** Distinguished Research Scientist, American College Testing Program, Iowa City, IA (1990-1994); Assistant Vice President, Measurement Research, American College Testing Program, Iowa City, IA (1984-1992); Director, Measurement Research Department, American College Testing Program, Iowa City, IA (1979-1984); Senior Research Psychologist, American College Testing Program, Iowa City, IA (1976-1979); Assistant Pro-

fessor, Education, Stony Brook University (1971-1976); Research Associate, Lecturer, Graduate School Education, Harvard University, Cambridge, MA (1970-1971) **CR:** Emeritus Professor, University of Iowa (2017); E.F. Lindquist Professor, Education Measurement, School of Education University of Iowa (1994-2017); Director, Center for Advanced Studies in Measurement and Assessment, University of Iowa (2002-2016); Director, Iowa Testing Programs (1994-2002); Adjunct Faculty, School of Education University of Iowa (1979-1994) **CW:** Associate Editor, Journal of Educational Measurement (1978-1983, 1996-Present); Associate Editor, "Applied Psychological Measurement" (1982-Present); Editor, "Educational Measurement, 4th Edition" (2006); Author, "Test Equating, Scaling and Linking Methods and Practices" (2004); Author, "Generalizability Theory" (2001); Editor, "Cognitively Diagnostic Assessment" (1995); Author, "Test Equating Methods and Practices" (1995); Editor, "Methodology Used in Scaling the Act Assessment and P-ACT" (1989); Author, "Elements of Generalizability Theory" (1983); Contributor, Articles, Professional Journals **AW:** Robert. L. Linn Distinguished Address Award, Association of Test Publishers (2019); Career Achievement Award (2011); E.F. Lindquist Career Contribution Award, American Educational Research Association (2004); Career Contribution Award, National Council of Measurement Education (2000); Technology Contribution Award, National Council of Measurement Education (1997); Division D Award, American Educational Research Association (1980); Harvard University Prize Fellow (1967); Eponym, Robert L. Brennan Chair of Psychometric Research Award **MEM:** President, Iowa Academy Education (1996-1999); President, National Council of Measurement Education (1997-1998); Vice President, American Educational Research Association (1994-1996); Vice President, National Council of Measurement Education (1995); Board of Directors, National Council of Measurement Education (1987-1990); Midwestern Educational Research Association (1987-1988); Fellow, American Psychological Association; Fellow, American Education Research Association; Psychometric Society; American Statistical Association **MH:** Albert Nelson Marquis Lifetime Achievement Award **AS:** He attributes his success to accomplishing a fair number of his most important objectives. **B/I:** Mr. Brennan was a graduate student at Harvard University and received a research assistance-ship to do testing. He taught himself measurement because at the time there were no courses at Harvard. The assistance position is what created his interest for the field he is in. Mr. Brennan claims it wasn't a direct path. In his case, he got into it primarily because he had a research assistance-ship at Harvard which required him to do some evaluation and testing research and so he actually principally taught himself methods in order to do that work and then he continued with that the rest of his career in a point but that was the beginning point.

BRENT-CHESSUM, TRACEY, PHD, T: Assistant Professor of Musical Theatre Techniques **I:** Education/Educational Services **CN:** Point Park University **ED:** PhD in Theatre and Performance Studies, University of Maryland, College Park (2012); MA in Humanities, California State University, Dominguez Hills (2007); MM in Music Performance and Conducting, Azusa Pacific University (2004); BA in Communications and Theater, The Master's University (2000) **C:** Assistant Professor of Musical Theater Techniques, Point Park University (2016-Present); Founder, Artistic Director, Pallas Theater Collective (2010-2019); Assistant Professor of Theater, Ball State University (2014-2016);

Adjunct Assistant Professor of Theater, Point Park University (2013-2015); Online Adjunct Professor, Southern New Hampshire University (2014); Adjunct Instructor, College of Southern Medicine (2011-2013); Adjunct Instructor, Westwood College (2005-2009); Performing Arts Teacher, Maranatha High School (2003-2005); Graduate Conducting Assistant, Azusa Pacific University (2003-2004); Fine Arts Director, Pacific Christian on the Hill (2000-2003); Theater Arts Coordinator, The Master's University (1998-2002) **CR:** Instructor, Audition Workshop, "God, I Hope I Get In!" (2019); Instructor, Continuing Education Workshop, "God, I Hope I Get In!" (2019); Adjudicator, "Sing, DC!" Musical Theater Audition Competition (2019); External Reviewer, Journal of American Music (2018); Instructor, Parent Workshop, "Navigating College BFA Auditions" (2018); Instructor, Various Adventure Theater, MTC Pre-College Program Workshops (2018); Speaker, "Selling Americanism: Musicals as Patriotic Opportunists," Point Park University Faculty Colloquium (2018); Panelist, "#MeToo: What's Next?" Point Park University (2018); Instructor, Children's Theater Audition Workshop (2017); Instructor, Audition Workshop Series, Pittsburgh Cultural Trust (2017); Small Theater Producers Panel, The Shakespeare Theater Company Apprentice Program, Washington, DC (2016); Chair, Organizer, Graduate Student Pre-Conference, American Theater and Drama Society, Chicago, IL (2016); Co-Organizer, Song, Stage, and Screen IV International Conference (2009); Faculty Mentor, Student Disability Services, Ball State University; Graduate Faculty, Ball State University; Mentor Instructor, Faculty Mentoring Program, College of Southern Maryland **CW:** Speaker, Presentation, "The In Series Director's Salon: Victor Herbert & Early American Operetta," (2018); Director, Musical, "Buried in Prosperity," Kennedy Center Page-to-Stage Festival (2017); Director, Musical, "Crazy Mary Lincoln," Pallas Theater Collective (2017); Director, Musical, "Crazy Mary," Kennedy Center Page-to-Stage Festival (2016); Director, Musical, "Lost In Wonderland," Pallas Theater Collective (2016); Director, Musical, "As You Like It," Ball State University Mainstage (2015); Director, Musical, "Code Name: Cynthia," Kennedy Center Page-to-Stage Festival, Pallas Theater Collective, The International Spy Museum (2015); Director, Musical, "Oneida: A New Musical," Pallas Theater Collective (2015); Director, Musical, "Carrie: The Musical," Muncie Civic Theater (2015); Director, Musical, "The Fall of the House of Usher: A New Musical," Pallas Theater Collective (2014); Director, Musical, "The Yellow Wallpaper: A New Musical," Pallas Theater Collective (2014); Director, Musical, "The Tempest: Such Stuff Dreams are Made of," Pallas Theater Collective (2013); Director, Musical, "The Comedy of Mirrors," Pallas Theater Collective (2012); Director, Musical, "The Many Women of Troy," Pallas Theater Collective (2011); Director, Musical, "The Fantasticks," School of Music, University of Maryland (2011); Director, Musical, "Agnes Under the Big Top," Arena Stage (2011); Speaker, Presentation, "The Politics of Politicizing Sousa's Marches," University of Illinois, American Music Month (2011); Speaker, Presentation, "Theatrical Exploitation of John Sousa as 'Salesman of Americanism,'" University of Illinois, Urbana-Champaign (2011); Assistant Director, Musical, "Cymbeline," Center for Renaissance & Baroque Studies, University (2010); Director, Musical, "Come and Meet Those Dancing Feet," Ambassador Auditorium (2005); Director, Musical, "Hamlet," Pacific Community Theater (2002); Director, Musical, "Out of the Frying Pan," The Master's University Theater Arts (2001); Director, Musical, "Much Ado About Nothing," The Master's University Theater Arts (2001); Director,

Musical, "See How They Run," The Master's University Theater Arts (2000); Director, Musical, "The Secret Garden," The Master's University Theater Arts (2000) **AW:** Faculty Development Grant, Point Park University (2018-2019); Best Musical, "Crazy Mary Lincoln," Small Professional Theater, BroadwayWorld Awards (2017); Nominee, John Ainello Award, Outstanding Emerging Theater (2016); Ball State University, iLearn Course Development Grant (2015); Best Director of a Musical, D.C. Metro Theater Arts (2015); Best Musical, "Code Name: Cynthia," D.C. Metro Theater Arts (2015); Best Production Design, D.C. Metro Theater Arts (2015); Best Actor, Actress, "Code Name: Cynthia," D.C. Metro Theater Arts (2015); Runner Up, New Musical Theater Company, Pallas Theater Collective, Washington City Paper (2015); Best Director of a Musical, D.C. Metro Theater Arts (2014); Best Actor, Actress, Supporting Actor, "The Fall of the House of Usher," D.C. Metro Theater Arts (2014); Best Play, "The Taming of the Shrew," D.C. Metro Theater Arts (2014); Graduate Teaching Award, University of Maryland, College Park (2007-2011); Best Musical, Theater International Initiatives Grant, University of Maryland (2010); Summer Grant, University of Maryland (2008-2010); Listee, Who's Who Among American High School Teachers (2005); National Exemplary School Program Award, Association of Christian Schools International (2003); Honor Choir Award, Association of Christian Schools International (2003) **MEM:** Chair, Secretary, University Core and Assessment Committee, Point Park University (2018-Present); Chair, Theater Department Curriculum Committee, Point Park University (2016-Present); Theater Department Artistic Committee, Point Park University (2016-Present); Associate Member, Stage Directors and Choreographers Society (2013-Present); Association for Theater in Higher Education (2010-Present); Board Member, External Reviewer (2019); Faculty Search Committee, Point Park University (2018); Treasurer, American Theater and Drama Society (2013-2017); American Theater and Drama Society (2011-2017); Production Season Selection Committee, Ball State University (2014-2016); Technology Committee, Ball State University (2014-2016); Diversity Committee, Ball State University (2015); Faculty Search Committee, Design, Ball State University (2015); American Choral Directors Association (2011-2013); Chair, Undergraduate Programs, Middle States Commission, Higher Education Accreditation Committee, Point Park University

BRETSCHNEIDER, BARRY, T: Attorney **I:** Law and Legal Services **CN:** Baker & Hostetler LLP **CH:** Two Daughters **ED:** Master of Laws, The George Washington University Law School, Washington, DC (1974); Doctor of Jurisprudence, University of Iowa College of Law, With Distinction (1971); Bachelor of Arts in Classics, Princeton University, Princeton, NJ (1968) **CT:** Registered Patent Attorney **C:** Partner, Baker & Hostetler LLP (2012-Present); Partner, Morrison and Foerster LLP (1997-2012); Partner-then-Principal, Fish & Richardson PC, Washington, DC (1990-1997); Founding Partner, Later Shareholder, Wegner & Bretschneider PC, Washington, DC (1980-1990); Associate, Stevens, Davis, Miller & Mosher, Arlington, VA (1980); Associate, Keil & Witherspoon, Washington, DC (1978-1980); Associate, Arnold, White & Durkee PC, Houston, TX (1976-1978); Technical Adviser to the late Hon. Giles S. Rich, Associate Judge, U.S. Court of Customs and Patent Appeals, Later Circuit Judge, U.S. Court of Appeals for the Federal Circuit (1974-1976); Attorney-Adviser, Trial Counsel, Office of the General Counsel, U.S. Department of the Navy (1971-1974) **CR:** Lecturer on Patent Law, Osaka Institute of Technology, Intellectual Property Faculty, Osaka, Japan (2005-2016); Lecturer on Interference Practice and International Patent Litigation, Center for Advanced Study and Research in Intellectual Property, University of Washington School of Law, Seattle, WA (1999-2008); Visiting Professor of Law, Acting Director, Patent Law Program, George Washington University National Law Center (1988-1989) **CW:** Co-Author, Book, "How to Win Interferences" **AW:** Best Lawyers in America (2009-Present); AV Rated, Martindale-Hubbell (1981-Present); Listed in IAM 250 World's Leading Patent Litigators (2011, 2013, 2015); Enduring Leadership Award, Federal Circuit Bar Association **MEM:** Federal Circuit Bar Association; American Intellectual Property Lawyers Association; American Bar Association; State Bar of Texas; Virginia State Bar; District of Columbia Bar **BAR:** U.S. District Court for the Eastern District of Texas (2008); U.S. District Court for the Eastern District of Virginia (2004); U.S. District Court for the Western District of Virginia (2004); Virginia (2004); U.S. District Court for the District of Arizona (1994); U.S. Court of Appeals for the Federal Circuit (1982); Texas (1976); U.S. Court of Appeals for the District of Columbia Circuit (1975); District of Columbia (1975); U.S. Supreme Court (1974); Iowa (Inactive) (1971) **AS:** Mr. Bretschneider attributes his success to a willingness to do more than the job appears to call for. **B/I:** Mr. Bretschneider became involved in his profession after leaving the U.S. Department of the Navy, after which he worked in several different fields of legal service before settling on patent law. Despite having little experience in this field, he excelled and eventually clerked under a judge at the U.S. Court of Customs and Patent Appeals.

BREWER, NEVADA NANCY, T: Teacher Supervisor **I:** Education/Educational Services **CN:** Maryland State Department of Education **DOB:** 01/21/1949 **PB:** Baltimore **SC:** MD/USA **PT:** Leo Brewer; Rebecca (Johnson) Brewer **MS:** Single **ED:** Postgraduate Coursework, Coppin State University (2006-2007); Postgraduate Coursework, Community College of Baltimore County (1985); MEd in Special Education, Coppin State University (1981); MEd in Correctional Education, Coppin State University (1974); BS, Coppin State University (1973) **CT:** Certified Elementary/Middle School Teacher; Certified Special Education Teacher **C:** Teacher Supervisor, Charles H. Hickey Jr. School (2013-Present); Teacher Supervisor and Special Education Coordinator, Department of Juvenile Services, William Donald Schaefer House (2005-2012); Teacher Supervisor, Department of Juvenile Services, Baltimore City Juvenile Justice Center (2004 -2005); Coordinator, Mathematics Elementary Laboratory, Baltimore City School Systems (Now Baltimore City Public Schools) (2003-2004); Academic Coach, Mathematics and Science, Baltimore City School Systems (Now Baltimore City Public Schools) (2002-2003); Coordinator of the Discipline Center (2001-2002); Manager, Summer School, Baltimore City School Systems (Now Baltimore City Public Schools) (2000-2002); Teacher, Baltimore City School Systems (Now Baltimore City Public Schools) (1973 - 2003); Teacher, Baltimore County Adult Education, Towson, MD (1977-1984); Coordinator, Just Say No to Drugs Program, Baltimore City School Systems (Now Baltimore City Public Schools) (1986-1988) **CR:** Teacher Supervisor, Maryland State Department of Education (2013-Present); Resource Teacher, Maryland State Department of Education (2012-2013); Elementary Mathematics Laboratory (2003-2004); Advisory Board, Echo Hill Outdoor School (2003-2004); Coordinator, 24 Challenge Mathematics Tournament (1996-2003); Coordinator, Math-a-thon Program, St. Jude Children's Research Hospital (1993-2003); Supervisor Teacher for Student Teachers, Towson University, University of Notre Dame, Coppin State University (1989-2003); Academic Coach, Math and Science, Grades Pre-K-5 (2002-2003); Coordinator, Echo Hill Outdoor School (1988-2003); Leadership Teacher, STARS Science Program (1995); Write to Learn Program, Baltimore City School Systems (Now Baltimore City Public Schools) (1990-1991); Coordinator, Heads Up Program (1980); Participant, Project Future Search Phone-a-thon to Recruit Minority Students, University of Maryland, College Park, MD (1980) **AW:** Named Teacher of the Year (1994); Recognized, Teacher of the Year (1994); Named Outstanding Teacher, Iota Phi Lambda Sorority, Inc. (1993); Freedoms Foundation National Award (1974) **MH:** Albert Nelson Marquis Lifetime Achievement Award; Marquis Who's Who Top Professional **AS:** Ms. Brewer attributes her educational success to her cousin, who was the principal of a special education school. When Ms. Brewer started teaching, her cousin would give her advice, look over her evaluations, and give her constructive criticisms. She was a great influence in Ms. Brewer's life. **B/I:** Ms. Brewer became involved in her profession because she always enjoyed school as a child growing up. When she was in the classroom as a school teacher in the public school system, they always gave her the kids that had problems. She enjoyed working with those children because she saw progress with them from September to June. Though she is skilled at working with students with problems, she is happy to work with any child, whether they have problems or not. Ms. Brewer's love of school dates back to the first grade, when she demonstrated learning beyond her years. For example, she knew her ABCs, time telling, and writing her name. This initial leg-up was partially due to her mother, who would teach her in place of kindergarten. Because of her positive experiences, she always enjoyed school and helping others. **AV:** Art; Decorating **PA:** Democrat **RE:** Baptist **THT:** Ms. Brewer feels that it is better to say, "I am glad I did, instead of I wish I had." She believes that if she can help someone, then her living will not have been in vain.

BREWER, ROSALIND GATES, T: Chief Operating Officer, Group President **I:** Food & Restaurant Services **CN:** Starbucks Corporation **MS:** Married **SPN:** John Brewer **CH:** Two children **ED:** BS in Chemistry, Spelman College, Atlanta, GA (1984); Diploma, Director's College, Executive Education Program, Booth School of Business, The University of Chicago; Diploma, Advanced Management Program, The Wharton School, The University of Pennsylvania **C:** Chief Operating Officer, Group President, USA Division, Starbucks Corporation (2017-Present); President, Chief Executive Officer, Sam's Club Division, Wal-Mart Stores, Inc., Bentonville, AR (2012-2017); Executive Vice President, President, Wal-Mart East, Wal-Mart Stores, Inc. (Now Walmart Inc.), Atlanta, GA (2011-2012); Executive Vice President, President, Wal-Mart South, Wal-Mart Stores, Inc. (Now Walmart Inc.) (2010-2011); President, Southeast Operating Division, Wal-Mart Stores, Inc. (Now Walmart Inc.) (2007-2010); Regional Vice President of Operations, Wal-Mart Stores, Inc. (Now Walmart Inc.), GA (2006); President, Global Nonwovens Division, Kimberly-Clark Corporation (2004-2006); Chemist, Various Senior Management Positions, Kimberly-Clark Corporation (1984-2004) **CR:** Former Member, Board of Directors, Lockheed Martin Corporation (2011); Former Member, Board of Directors, Molson Coors Beverage Company (2006-2011) **CIV:** Board Director, Amazon (2019-Present); Chair, Spelman College (2011-Present); Board of Trustees, Spelman

College (2006-Present) **AW:** One of the 100 Most Powerful Women, Forbes Magazine (2012-2014, 2019); One of the 50 Most Powerful Women in Business, Fortune Magazine (2010-2015); Woman of Achievement Award, YWCA of Atlanta (2013); One of the Most Powerful Black Women, Forbes Magazine (2013); One of the 25 Power Women to Watch, Atlanta Women Magazine (2005); Legacy of Leadership Award, Spelman College (2005); Millennium Pacesetter Award, Atlanta Business League

BREYER, JAMES, "JIM" WILLIAM, T: Chief Executive Officer **I:** Financial Services **CN:** Breyer Capital **DOB:** 07/26/1961 **PB:** New Haven **SC:** CT/USA **PT:** John Paul Breyer; Eva Breyer **MS:** Married **SPN:** Angela Chao; Susan Zaroff (1987-2004) **ED:** MBA, Harvard University (1987); BS in Interdisciplinary Studies, Stanford University, with Distinction (1983) **C:** Founder, Chief Executive Officer, Breyer Capital (2006-Present); Founder, Strategic Partner, IDG Capital (2005-Present); Managing Partner, Accel Partners, San Francisco, CA (1995-2006); Partner, Accel Partners, San Francisco, CA (1990-1995); Venture Capitalist, Accel Partners, San Francisco, CA (1987-1990); Management Consultant, McKinsey & Company, New York, NY (1983-1985) **CR:** Board of Directors, The Blackstone Group Inc. (2016-Present); Co-Board, Harvard Corporation (2013-2019); Board of Directors, 21st Century Fox (2011-2019); Board of Directors, Etsy, Inc. (2008-2016); Board of Directors, News Corporation (2011-2013); Board of Directors, Dell (2009-2013); Board of Directors, Facebook (2005-2013); Board of Directors, Wal-Mart Stores, Inc. (Now Walmart Inc.) (2001-2013); Board of Directors, Marvel (2006-2009); Board of Directors, RealNetworks, Inc. (1995-2008); Board of Advisers, Pacific Community Ventures Inc. (2000-2007); Honorary Professor, Yuelu Academy, Hunan University (2005); Advisory Board, Tsinghua University School of Economics and Management; Minority Owner, Boston Celtics; Board of Dean's Advisers, Harvard Business School, Harvard University; Board of Associates, TechNet; Former Chairman, Board of Associates, Stanford Technology Ventures Program, Stanford University **CIV:** Co-Founder, FWD. us (2013); Board of Trustees, Menlo School; Board of Trustees, San Francisco Museum of Modern Art **AW:** Listee, Forbes 400, Forbes Media LLC (2019); Listee, Midas List: Top Tech Investors, Forbes Media LLC (2018); Listee, Richest in Tech, Forbes Media LLC (2017); Business Leader of the Year Award, Harvard Business School Association of Northern (2016); Lifetime Achievement Award, Venture Capital Journal (2014); Listee, 10 Smartest People in Tech, Forbes Media LLC (2010); Baker Scholar, Harvard Business School, Harvard University (1987) **MEM:** Co-Founder, Global Advisory Council, Harvard University (2012); Harvard Business School Association of Northern California; Former Chairman, Board of Directors, National Association of Venture Capitalists; Former President, Western Association of Venture Capitalists **AV:** Art; Film

BREYER, STEPHEN GERALD, T: Associate Justice **I:** Law and Legal Services **CN:** Supreme Court of the United States **DOB:** 08/15/1938 **PB:** San Francisco **SC:** CA/USA **PT:** Irving Gerald Breyer; Anne A. (Roberts) Breyer **MS:** Married **SPN:** Joanna Freda Hare (09/04/1967) **CH:** Chloe; Nell; Michael **ED:** Honorary LLD, University of Rochester (1983); LLB, Harvard University, Magna Cum Laude (1964); BA in Philosophy, Politics and Economics, Magdalen College, University of Oxford, with Honors (1961); AB in Philosophy, Stanford University, with Honors (1959) **CT:** State of Massachusetts (1971); District of Columbia (1966); State of California (1966) **C:** Associate Justice, Supreme Court of the

United States, Washington, DC (1994-Present); Chief Judge, United States Court of Appeals for the First Circuit, Boston, MA (1990-1994); Lecturer, Harvard Law School, Harvard University (1980-1994); Judge, United States Court of Appeals for the First Circuit, Boston, MA (1980-1990); Commissioner, U.S. Sentencing Commission, Washington, DC (1985-1989); Chief Counsel, United States Senate Committee on the Judiciary (1979-1981); Professor, Harvard Kennedy School, Harvard University (1977-1980); Professor, Law, Harvard Law School, Harvard University (1970-1980); Special Counsel, Administrative Practices Subcommittee, United States Senate Committee on the Judiciary (1974-1975); Assistant Special Prosecutor, Watergate Special Prosecution Force, U.S. Department of Justice, Washington, DC (1973); Assistant Professor, Law, Harvard University (1967-1970); Special Assistant to Assistant Attorney General for Antitrust Donald F. Turner, U.S. Department of Justice, Washington, DC (1965-1967); Law Clerk to Justice Arthur J. Goldberg, Supreme Court of the United States, Washington, DC (1964-1965) **CR:** Judicial Conference of the United States (1990-1994); Judicial Conference Representative, Administrative Conference of the United States (1981-1994); Visiting Professor, Sapienza Università di Roma, Rome, Italy (1993); Lecturer, Economics and Law, Salzburg Global Seminar, Salzburg, Austria (1978, 1993); Oliver Wendell Holmes Lecturer, Harvard Law School, Cambridge, MA (1992); Board of Directors, Dia Art Foundation (1985-1986); Visiting Lecturer, Antitrust Law, The College of Law, Sydney, Australia (1975) **CIV:** Board of Overseers, Dana-Farber Cancer Institute, Boston, MA (1977-1994); Trustee, University of Massachusetts (1974-1981) **MIL:** U.S. Army (1957) **CW:** Author, "The Court and the World: American Law and the New Global Realities" (2015); Author, "Making Our Democracy Work: A Judge's View" (2010); Author, "Active Liberty: Interpreting Our Democratic Constitution" (2005); Author, "Breaking the Vicious Circle: Toward Effective Risk Regulation" (1993); Co-Author, "Teacher's Manual: Administrative Law and Regulatory Policy," (1992); Author, "Regulation and Its Reform" (1982); Co-Author, "Administrative Law and Regulatory Policy" (1979); Co-Author, "The Federal Power Commission and the Regulation of Energy" (1974); Contributor, Articles, Professional Journals **AW:** Fordham-Stein Prize, Fordham University (2008); Distinguished Eagle Scout Award, Boy Scouts of America (2007); Annual Award for Scholarship in Administrative Law, American Bar Association (1987); Marshall Scholar, University of Oxford (1959-1961) **MEM:** Chair, Jury, Pritzker Architecture Prize, The Hyatt Foundation (2018-Present); Académie des Sciences Morales et Politiques (2012-Present); American Academy of Arts & Sciences (1982-Present); American Bar Association; Council on Foreign Relations; The American Law Institute; American Bar Foundation **RE:** Jewish

BRIDENSTINE, JAMES, "JIM" FREDERICK, T: Administrator **I:** Sciences **CN:** National Aeronautics and Space Administration **DOB:** 06/15/1975 **PB:** Ann Arbor **SC:** MI/USA **MS:** Married **SPN:** Michelle Ivory (2004) **CH:** Walker; Sarah; Grant **ED:** MBA, Cornell University (2009); BS in Economics, Psychology, and Business, Rice University (1998) **C:** Administrator, National Aeronautics and Space Administration (2018-Present); Member, United States House of Representatives, Oklahoma's 1st Congressional District, Washington, DC (2013-2018); Executive Director, Tulsa Air and Space Museum (2008-2010); Defense Consultant, Wyle Laboratories (Now KBR Inc.) (2007-2008) **CR:** United States House Committee on Science, Space, and Technology (2013-2018); United States House

Committee on Armed Services (2013-2018) **MIL:** Oklahoma Air National Guard (2015-Present); U.S. Navy Reserve (2010-2015); U.S. Navy (1998-2007) **AW:** Battle Efficiency Ribbon, U.S. Navy; Marksmanship Medal, U.S. Navy; Sea Service Ribbon, U.S. Navy; Global War on Terrorism Expeditionary Medal; Iraq Campaign Medal; Armed Forces Expeditionary Medal; National Defense Service Medal; Two-Time Recipient, Navy and Marine Corps Achievement Medals, U.S. Navy and U.S. Marine Corps; Commendation Medal with Combat "V", U.S. Navy; Air Medal; Eagle Scout, Boy Scouts of America **PA:** Republican **RE:** Southern Baptist

BRIDGES, JEFFREY, "JEFF" LEON, T: Actor, Musician **I:** Media & Entertainment **DOB:** 12/04/1949 **PB:** Los Angeles **SC:** CA/USA **PT:** Lloyd Vernet Bridges; Dorothy (Simpson) Bridges **MS:** Married **SPN:** Susan Geston (06/05/1977) **CH:** Isabelle Annie; Jessica Lily; Haley Roselouise **CIV:** Spokesperson, No Kid Hungry Campaign, Share Our Strength (2010-Present); Co-founder, End Hunger Network (1983-2019); Supporter, Amazon Conservation Team **CW:** Producer, Narrator, "Living in the Future's Past" (2018); Actor, "Bad Times at the El Royale" (2018); Actor, "Only the Brave" (2017); Actor, "Kingsman: The Golden Circle" (2017); Actor, Executive Producer, "The Only Living Boy in New York" (2017); Actor, "Hell or High Water" (2016); Artist, "Sleeping Tapes" (2015); Voice Actor, "The Little Prince" (2015); Actor, "Seventh Son" (2014); Actor, Producer, "The Giver" (2014); Actor, "R.I.P.D." (2013); Co-author with Bernie Glassman, "The Dude and the Zen Master" (2013); Narrator, "Pablo" (2012); Singer, Songwriter, "Jeff Bridges" (2011); Actor, "True Grit" (2010); Actor, "TRON: Legacy" (2010); Host, "Saturday Night Live" (1983, 2010); Actor, Executive Producer, "Crazy Heart" (2009); Actor, "The Men Who Stare at Goats" (2009); Actor, "A Dog Year" (2009); Actor, "The Open Road" (2009); Actor, "How to Lose Friends and Alienate People" (2008); Actor, "Iron Man" (2008); Voice Actor, "Surf's Up" (2007); Actor, "Stick It" (2006); Actor, "Tideland" (2005); Actor, "The Amateurs" (2005); Actor, "The Door in the Floor" (2004); Photographer, "Pictures: Photographs by Jeff Bridges" (2003); Actor, "Seabiscuit" (2003); Actor, "Masked and Anonymous" (2003); Narrator, "Lewis & Clark: Great Journey West" (2002); Narrator, "Lost in La Mancha" (2002); Actor, "K-PAX" (2001); Actor, "Scenes of the Crime" (2001); Narrator, "Raising the Mammoth" (2000); Actor, "The Contender" (2000); Singer, Songwriter, "Be Here Soon" (2000); Actor, "Simpatico" (1999); Actor, "The Muse" (1999); Actor, "Arlington Road" (1999); Actor, "The Big Lebowski" (1998); Actor, Executive Producer, "Hidden in America" (1996); Actor, "The Mirror Has Two Faces" (1996); Actor, "White Squall" (1996); Actor, "Wild Bill" (1995); Actor, "Blown Away" (1994); Actor, "Fearless" (1993); Actor, "The Vanishing" (1993); Actor, Producer, "American Heart" (1992); Actor, "The Fisher King" (1991); Actor, "Texasville" (1990); Actor, "The Fabulous Baker Boys" (1989); Actor, "See You in the Morning" (1989); Actor, "Tucker: The Man and His Dream" (1988); Actor, "Nadine" (1987); Actor, "The Morning After" (1986); Actor, "8 Million Ways to Die" (1986); Actor, "Jagged Edge" (1985); Actor, "Starman" (1984); Actor, "Against All Odds" (1984); Actor, "Faerie Tale Theatre" (1983); Actor, "Kiss Me Goodbye" (1982); Actor, "TRON" (1982); Voice Actor, "The Last Unicorn" (1982); Actor, "Cutter's Way" (1981); Actor, "Heaven's Gate" (1980); Actor, "The American Success Company" (1980); Narrator, "Heroes of Rock and Roll" (1979); Actor, "Winter Kills" (1979); Actor, "Somebody Killed Her Husband" (1978); Actor, "The Yin and the Yang of Mr. Go" (1978); Actor, "King Kong" (1976); Actor, "Stay Hungry" (1976);

Actor, "Hearts of the West" (1975); Actor, "Rancho Deluxe" (1975); Actor, "Thunderbolt and Lightfoot" (1974); Actor, "The Iceman Cometh" (1973); Actor, "The Last American Hero" (1973); Actor, "Lolly-Madonna XXX" (1973); Actor, "Bad Company" (1972); Actor, "Fat City" (1972); Actor, "The Last Picture Show" (1971); Actor, "In Search of America" (1971); Actor, "The Most Deadly Game" (1970); Actor, "Halls of Anger" (1970); Actor, "Silent Night, Lonely Night" (1969); Actor, "Lassie" (1969); Actor, "The F.B.I." (1969); Actor, "The Loner" (1965); Actor, "The Lloyd Bridges Show" (1962-1963); Actor, "Sea Hunt" (1958-1960) **AW:** Cecil B. DeMille Award, Hollywood Foreign Press Association (2019); Satellite Award for Best Supporting Actor in a Motion Picture (2016); Saturn Award for Best Actor, Academy of Science Fiction, Fantasy and Horror Films (1984, 2011); Academy Award for Best Actor, Academy of Motion Picture Arts and Sciences (2010); Golden Globe Award for Best Actor in a Motion Picture – Drama, Hollywood Foreign Press Association (2010); Critics' Choice Award for Best Movie Actor, The Critics Choice Association (2010); Desert Palm Achievement Award, Palm Springs International Film Festival (2010); Screen Actors Guild Award for Outstanding Performance by a Male Actor in a Leading Role in a Motion Picture, SAG-AFTRA (2009); Independent Spirit Award for Best Male Lead, Film Independent (1992, 2009)

BRIDGES, R. BARTON, T: Medical Doctor (Retired) **I:** Medicine & Health Care **DOB:** 12/15/1940 **PT:** A. Frank Bridges; LaDaw (Waynescott) **MS:** Married **SPN:** Glenda B. Bridges **CH:** Mark; Trisha Freely; Rebecca Combs **ED:** Doctor of Medicine, St. Louis University School of Medicine (1968); CMEA, Contemporary Diagnostic Radiology, Wolters Kluwer;Bachelor of Science in Mathematics, Southern Illinois University, Carbondale, IL **CT:** Diplomate in Radiology, American Board of Radiology (1973) **C:** Retired (2001); Radiologist, Mid America Radiology LTD (1974-2001); Residency, St. Louis University, St. Louis City Hospital, Missouri (1969-1972); Internship, St. Joseph's Hospital, Phoenix, AZ (1968-1969) **CIV:** Former School Board Member, Single Hill School; Former Board Member, St. Claire Country Club; Former Board Member, St. Claire Medical Society **MIL:** Major, U.S. Army, 101st Airborne Medical Service Corps (1972-1974) **MEM:** St. Claire County Medical Society; American Medical Association; American College of Radiology; Radiology Society or North American **AS:** Dr. Bridges attributes his success to the influence of his parents, who both taught at Southern Illinois University, and were fantastically well-educated in their own right. **B/I:** Dr. Bridges became involved in his profession due his family and friends, many of whom were medical doctors as well. He spent quite a bit of time at St. Louis University Hospital and at the children's hospital in radiology. When he left the main hospital the radiologist, who he spend a lot of time with, asked what he planned on doing. Dr. Bridges said he wasn't sure at the time, and the radiologist suggested he look into radiology.

BRIENZA, KRISTIN L., T: Team Leader **I:** Leisure, Travel & Tourism **CN:** Liberty Travel **ED:** Associate Degree in Photography, Art Institute of Pittsburgh (2008) **CT:** Certification in Graphic Communications, Eastern Center for Arts and Technology (2005) **C:** Team Leader, Liberty Travel (2013-Present); Retail Agent, AAA Mid-Atlantic (2009-2011) **MEM:** Blue Comets **AS:** Ms. Brienza attributes her success to being human and caring about others. **B/I:** Ms. Brienza became involved in her profession because of her desire to help others make

memories. **THT:** Ms. Brienza states, "We're never the best version of ourselves. You can't grow until you step outside of your comfort zone."

BRIGGS-KRULL, SHARON LEE, T: Owner **I:** Retail/Sales **CN:** A Stitch In Time Bridal Boutique **MS:** Married **CH:** Two Children **ED:** AA, Bishop Sewing Institute (1970) **C:** Owner, A Stitch In Time Bridal Boutique (1999-Present); Owner, The Humpty-Dump (1974-1999); Office Worker (1974); Saleswoman, Stanley Home Products; Adult Educator, Bishop Style Method of Sewing **CIV:** Volunteer, Local Church **AW:** Recipient, Various 4H Awards; Various Gold Cup Awards, Stanley Home Products **AS:** Mrs. Briggs-Krull attributes her success to the grace of God. Had it not been for the health that he granted her, she would not have been able to achieve her various accomplishments. **B/I:** Mrs. Briggs-Krull began doing alterations for clothing when she was a little girl. Over the past 40 years as a seamstress, she has opened various businesses. She enjoys being busy and insists that she must stay that way. She appreciates everything that she learned from her mother and grandmother; she carries on their legacy every day. **THT:** Ms. Briggs-Krull wants people to know that she cares.

BRIGHT, CHRISTOPHER PATRICK, T: Chief **I:** Infrastructure **CN:** Revere Fire Department **DOB:** 02/03/1961 **PB:** Everett **SC:** MA/USA **PT:** Paul; Katherine **MS:** Married **SPN:** Mary **CH:** Fallon; Aidan **ED:** JD, New England Law (1990); Degree in Public Administration, Suffolk University (1985) **CT:** Certified Fire Officer III and IV; Certified Hazardous Materials Technician; Certified Fire Instructor I, Firefighter I and II **AW:** Horses and Heroes Foundation Award (2019); Revere Journal Man of the Year Award (2019); Massachusetts Department of Fire Services Firefighter of the Year (2016); Individual Medal of Valor Award **MEM:** Massachusetts Bar Association; Metro Fire Chiefs Association; Fire Chiefs of Massachusetts; International Association of Fire Chiefs; Box 52 Association **BAR:** Massachusetts (1991) **AS:** Mr. Bright attributes his success to his parents Paul and Kay, his wife Mary, and his children Fallon and Aidan. **B/I:** He became interested because his father Paul was a Revere Fire Fighter and he remembers how much he loved his job. **AV:** Music; Collecting vinyl records; Reading books **PA:** Progressive Democrat **RE:** Catholic

BRIN, SERGEY MIHAILOVICH, T: Information Technology Executive, Computer Scientist **I:** Information Technology and Services **CN:** Alphabet Inc. **DOB:** 08/21/1973 **PB:** Moscow **SC:** Russia **PT:** Michael Brin; Eugenia Brin **MS:** Divorced **SPN:** Anne Wojcicki (2007, Divorced 2015) **CH:** One Son; One Daughter **ED:** Honorary Master of Business Administration, IE Business School, Madrid, Spain (2003); Master of Science, Stanford University, CA (1995); Bachelor of Science in Mathematics and Computer Science, University of Maryland, with Honors, College Park, MD (1993) **C:** Chief Executive Officer, Alphabet Inc. (2017-Present); Director of Special Projects, Google Inc., Mountain View, CA (2011-Present); President of Technology, Google Inc., Mountain View, CA (2001-2011); Co-president, Google Inc., Mountain View, CA (1998-2001); Co-founder, Google Inc., Mountain View, CA (1998) **CR:** Board of Directors, Google Inc. (1998-Present); Speaker, Technological, Entertainment & Design Conference, World Economic Forum **CIV:** Co-founder, The Brin Wojcicki Foundation **CW:** Author, "Extracting Patterns and Relations from the World Wide Web" (1998); Author, "Scalable Techniques for Mining Causal Structures" (1998); Co-author with Larry Page, "Dynamic Data Mining: A New Architecture for Data with High

Dimensionality" (1998); Author, "Dynamic Itemset Counting and Implication Rules for Market Basket Data" (1997); Author, "Beyond Market Baskets: Generalizing Association Rules to Correlations" (1997); Author, Published Academic Papers; Guest Appearances, Television Including "Charlie Rose Show", CNBC, CNNfn **AW:** Named, One of the World's Richest People, Forbes Magazine (2007-Present); Named, One of the Forbes 400: Richest Americans (2006-Present); Named, One of the World's Richest People, Business Insider (2019); Named, One of the World's Most Powerful People, Forbes Magazine (2009-2014); Named, One of the 40 Under 40, Fortune Magazine (2009-2012); Named, Power Player, Advertising Age (2009); Named, One of the 100 Agents of Change, Rolling Stone Magazine (2009); Named, One of the 25 Most Powerful People in Business, Fortune Magazine (2007); Named, One of the 50 Most Important People on the Web, PC World (2007); Named, One of the 50 Who Matter Now, CNNMoney.com Business 2.0 (2006, 2007); Named, One of the 100 Most Influential People in the World, TIME Magazine (2005); Named, Business Leader of the Year, Scientific American Magazine (2005); Co-recipient, with Larry Page, Marconi Prize (2004); Named, Persons of Week, with Larry Page, "ABC World News Tonight" (2004); National Science Foundation Graduate Fellowship (1993-1995) **MEM:** Fellow, American Academy of Arts & Sciences **RE:** Jewish

BRINDISI, ANTHONY JOSEPH, T: U.S. Representative from New York; Lawyer **I:** Government Administration/Government Relations/Government Services **DOB:** 11/22/1978 **SC:** NY/USA **PT:** Louis T. Brindisi; Jacqueline Brindisi **MS:** Married **SPN:** Erica (McGovern) Brindisi **CH:** Two Children **ED:** JD, Albany Law School (2004); BA in History, Siena College (2000); Coursework, Mohawk Valley Community College **C:** Member, U.S. House of Representatives from New York's 22nd Congressional District, United States Congress, Washington, DC (2019-Present); Member, District 119, New York State Assembly, Utica, NY (2011-Present); Partner, Brindisi, Murad, Brindisi, Pearlman, Julian & Pertz, LLP (Now Brindisi, Murad & Brindisi Pearlman), Utica, NY (2004) **CR:** Member, Million Dollar Advocates Forum, LLC (2008-Present); Member, New York State Academy of Trial Lawyers (2008-Present); Member, Legal Aid Society of Mid-New York, Inc. (2008-Present) **CIV:** Member, Utica School Board **MEM:** ABA; Oneida County Bar Association; Northern District of New York Federal Court Bar Association, Inc.; New York State Bar Association **BAR:** United States District Court for the Northern District of New York (2004); State of New York (2004)

BRINDLE, LEWIS CARVER, T: Arts Administrator **I:** Fundraising **DOB:** 06/26/1953 **PB:** DuBois **SC:** PA/USA **PT:** Louis Young Brindle; Etta Lorraine Carver **MS:** Single **ED:** MM, Boston University (1978); BS in Education, Indiana University of Pennsylvania, Magna Cum Laude (1975) **CT:** Expert Fundraiser **C:** Founding Director, Lewis Carver Brindle Arts Consultants, New York, NY (2004-2018); Director, George H. Heyman Jr. Center for Philanthropy and Fundraising, New York University (2006-2009); Founding Director, Alberto Vilar Global Fellows in the Performing Arts, New York University (2001-2006); Associate Director of Development for Major Gifts, Faculty of Arts and Science, New York University (1996-2001); Director of Development, Parrish Art Museum, Southampton, NY (1995-1996); Associate Director, Foundation Relations, Office of University Development, New York University (1992-1995); Executive Assistant to the President, Secretary to the Board of Directors, Union Theological Seminary (1988-1992);

Assistant to the Vice President for Development, Union Theological Seminary (1987-1988) **CR:** Adjunct Faculty, New York University (2005-2009) **CIV:** Accompanist, Kiwanis Club (1965-1971) **CW:** Freelance Opera Singer (1978-1987) **MEM:** Alumni Board of Directors, Indiana University of Pennsylvania, Indiana, PA (2002-2010) **MH:** Albert Nelson Marquis Lifetime Achievement Award **AS:** Mr. Brindle was interested in music since childhood. By the time he entered high school, he had developed some proficiency on the piano. He often used his talents in the school's productions. Later, during his college years, Mr. Brindle auditioned and was selected to perform the leading tenor roles in each of the operas presented every semester by the department of music. He continued to perform as a soloist in operas and choral works during graduate school and as a freelance musician. He was then selected to continue his studies during summers at the Chautauqua Institute, the Banff Centre for the Arts, and the Lake George Opera. These experiences predisposed him to the life of a freelancer. Its very lack of structure can be thrilling but at the same time frightening. In New York, one learns early on never to turn down a job offer, whether it be as a chorister, soloist, or catering waiter because one knows that several others, who may be equally if not more talented, are awaiting the same call. Faced with this constant array of pitfalls, Mr. Brindle grew to dread freelancing and began searching for a permanent position. **B/I:** Mr. Brindle was interested in fundraising because of how welcoming the field appeared. His entry role as the assistant to the vice president for fundraising brought together the best parts of each sector of fundraising. It encompassed all aspects of the profession while situated at the center of institutional power. **AV:** Cooking; Swimming; Gardening; Singing **RE:** Episcopalian

BRITTON, RUTH ANN, T: Educator **I:** Education/Educational Services **CN:** Cochise College **DOB:** 04/04/1943 **PB:** Fort Smith **SC:** AR/USA **PT:** Ralph M. Wright; Margaret E. (Reising) Wright **MS:** Widowed **SPN:** Joseph D. Britton (9/25/1965, Deceased 5/2017) **CH:** Beth; Meg; Jo **ED:** MS, Kansas State University (1978); BA in Elementary Education, Concordia Teachers College (Now Concordia Chicago), River Forest, IL (1965) **CT:** Certification in Reading, K-12 Education; Certification in Elementary Education; Certification in Developmental Reading; Certification in Developmental Education **C:** Faculty Emeritus, Cochise College (2012-Present); Instructor, Department Head, Cochise College, Douglas, AZ (1993-2006); Director, Junior High School Reading Laboratory, Hillsborough County Public Schools, Tampa, FL (1986-1992); Chapter I Reading Teacher, Montgomery County Public Schools, Christianburg, VA (1982-1986); Second and Fifth Grade Teacher, Manhattan City Schools, Manhattan, KS (1969, 1977-1978); Teacher, Fifth Grade, School District of Pickens County (1966-1968) **CIV:** Secretary, Board of Directors, Legacy Foundation of South East Arizona (2012-Present); Philanthropy Committee Chair, Legacy Foundation of South East Arizona (2010-Present); Governance Chair, Cochise County Education Foundation (2010-2017); Sierra Vista Regional Health Center **CW:** Co-Author, "Reading Handbook for Parents"; Co-Author, "Making Connections" **AW:** Inductee, Hall of Fame, Cochise College (2017); Outstanding Instructor, Cochise College (1999-2000); Excellence in Education, National Institute for Staff and Organizational Development (1997-1998); Teacher of the Year, Texas Commission on Jail Standards (1989-1990); Helping Hands Award for Volunteer Service, Seventh Corps, U.S. Army (1980); Arizona Governor's Lifetime Achievement Award for Volunteerism **MEM:** Chair, Governor's Commission for

Service Learning and Volunteerism (2002-2015); International Reading Association; Literacy Volunteers; College Reading and Learning Association **MH:** Albert Nelson Marquis Lifetime Achievement Award; Marquis Who's Who Top Professional **B/I:** Ms. Britton entered her profession because she had very good teachers all throughout her time in school. She also had two babysitters when she was growing up, both of whom were women who were studying to becoming teachers. Each of these individuals served as a great role model for Ms. Britton.

BROAD, EDYTHE LOIS, T: Philanthropist **I:** Nonprofit & Philanthropy **CN:** The Eli and Edythe Broad Foundation **MS:** Married **SPN:** Eli Broad (12/09/1964) **CH:** Jeffrey Alan; Gary Stephen **ED:** Honorary Degree, University of Southern California (2019) **C:** Co-Founder, The Eli and Edythe Broad Foundation; Co-Founder, The Broad Art Foundation **CIV:** Participant, The Giving Pledge (2010-Present); Supporter, Los Angeles County Museum of Art; Supporter, UCLA; Supporter, The Edye, The Broad Stage; Benefactor, Eli and Edythe Broad Art Museum, Michigan State University; Benefactor, Broad Institute; Benefactor, The Eli and Edythe Broad Center for Regenerative Medicine and Stem Cell Research, University of Southern California; Benefactor, Eli and Edythe Broad Center of Regenerative Medicine and Stem Cell Research, UCLA; Benefactor, Eli and Edythe Broad Center of Regenerative Medicine and Stem Cell Research, University of California San Francisco **AW:** Co-Recipient, Distinguished Philanthropist, John F. Kennedy Center for the Performing Arts, Washington, DC (2018); Cultural Leadership Award, American Federation of the Arts (2018); Power 100, ArtReview (2018); William E. Simon Prize for Philanthropic Leadership, Philanthropy Roundtable (2013); Eli Broad College of Business and Eli Broad Graduate School of Business Named in her Honor, Michigan State University (1991); Eli and Edythe Broad Art Center Named in her Honor, UCLA **AV:** Collecting contemporary Art

BROAD, ELI, T: Philanthropist, Entrepreneur **I:** Nonprofit & Philanthropy **CN:** The Eli and Edythe Broad Foundation; KB Home **DOB:** 06/06/1933 **PB:** New York **SC:** NY/USA **PT:** Leon Broad; Rebecca (Jacobson) Broad **MS:** Married **SPN:** Edythe Lois Lawson (12/09/1954) **CH:** Jeffrey Alan; Gary Stephen **ED:** Honorary Degree, University of Southern California (2019); Honorary HHD, Michigan State University (2002); Honorary LLD, Southwestern University (2000); BA in Accounting, Michigan State University, Cum Laude (1954) **CT:** CPA, State of Michigan (1956) **C:** Founder, Chairman, Kaufman and Broad Home Corp. (Now KB Home), Los Angeles, CA (1993-Present); Chairman, SunAmerica Inc. (Formerly Kaufman & Broad, Inc., Now AIG Retirement Services Inc.) (2001-2005); Co-Founder, Chairman, President, Chief Executive Officer, SunAmerica Inc. (Formerly Kaufman & Broad, Inc., Now AIG Retirement Services Inc.), Los Angeles, CA (1957-2001); Chairman Executive Committee, Kaufman and Broad Home Corp. (Now KB Home), Los Angeles, CA (1993-1995); Chairman, Kaufman and Broad Home Corp. (Now KB Home), Los Angeles, CA (1989-1993); Assistant Professor, Detroit Institute of Technology (1956); Certified Public Accountant (1954-1956) **CR:** Active Member, California Business Roundtable (1986-2000); Co-Owner, Sacramento Kings & Arco Arena (1992-1999); Trustee, Committee for Economic Development (1993-1995); Member, Real Estate Advisory Board, Citibank, NY (1976-1981); Member, Executive Committee, Advisory Board, Federal National Mortgage Association (Now Fannie Mae) (1972-1973); Board of Directors, Sacramento Kings and

Arco Arena **CIV:** Signatory, The Giving Pledge (2010-Present); Trustee, The Museum of Modern Art, NY (2004-Present); Board of Regents, Smithsonian Institute (2004-Present); Honorary Governor, Music Center, Los Angeles County, CA (1998-Present); Executive Committee, Board of Visitors, School of the Arts and Architecture, University of California Los Angeles (1997-Present); Honorary Member, Board of Directors, DARE America (1995-Present); Trustee, Los Angeles County Museum of Art (1995-Present); California Institute of Technology (1993-Present); Life Trustee, Pitzer College (1982-Present); Trustee Emeritus, California State University (1982-Present); Chancellor's Associate, University of California Los Angeles (1971-Present); Co-founder, Board Member, The Eli and Edythe Broad Foundation (1999-2017); Member, Board of Directors, Los Angeles World Affairs Council (1988-2003); Member, Contemporary Art Committee, Harvard University Art Museum, Cambridge, MA (1992-2004); Leland Stanford Mansion Foundation (1992-2000); Board of Directors, Armand Hammer Museum of Art and Cultural Center, University of California Los Angeles (1994-1999); Member, Board of Governors, Music Center, Los Angeles County, CA (1996-1998); Member, International Directors Council, Guggenheim Museum, NY (1993-1998); Archives of American Art, Smithsonian Institution, Washington, DC (1985-1998); Chairman, Los Angeles World Affairs Council (1994-1997); Trustee, Democratic National Committee Victory Fund (1988, 1992, 1996); Trustee, UCLA Foundation (1986-1996); DARE America (1989-1995); Mayor's Special Advisory Committee on Fiscal Administration, Los Angeles, CA (1993-1994); The Museum of Contemporary Art, Los Angeles, CA (1980-1993); Board of Overseers, Music Center, Los Angeles County, CA (1991-1992); Chairman, Advisory Board, ART/LA (1989); American Federation of the Arts (1988-1991); National Trustee, Baltimore Museum of Art (1985-1991); Member, Painting and Sculpture Committee, Whitney Museum of American Art, NY (1987-1989); Los Angeles Business Journal (1986-1988); Member, Advisory Council, Town Hall of California (1985-1987); Member, Advisory Board, Boy Scouts of America (1982-1985); Life Trustee, California State University (1978-1982); Board of Trustees, Acquisitions Committee, Los Angeles County Museum of Art (1978-1981); Founding Chairman, The Museum of Contemporary Art, Los Angeles, CA (1980); Vice Chairman, Board of Trustees, California State University (1979-1980); Maeght Foundation, St. Paul de Vence, France (1975-1980); Board Fellows, Member, Executive Committee, Claremont Colleges, CA (1974-1979); Chairman, Board of Trustees, Pitzer College (1973-1979); Member, Contemporary Council, Los Angeles County Museum of Art (1973-1979); Founding Trustee, Windward School, Santa Monica, CA (1972-1977); Associate Chairman, United Crusade, Los Angeles, CA (1973-1976); Chairman, Mayor's Housing Policy Committee, Los Angeles, CA (1974-1975); Delegate, Speaker, Federal Economic Summit Conference (1974); Delegate, Speaker, State Economic Summit Conference (1974); Active Member, National Industrial Pollution Control Council (1970-1973); President, California Non-partisan Vote Registration Foundation (1971-1972) **CW:** Author, "The Art of Being Unreasonable: Lessons in Unconventional Thinking" (2012) **AW:** Listee, World's Richest People, Forbes Magazine (1999-Present); Listee, Forbes 400: Richest Americans (1999-Present); Listee, Power 100, ArtReview (2018); Co-recipient, Distinguished Philanthropist Award, John F. Kennedy Center for the Performing Arts, Washington, DC (2018); Co-recipient, Cultural Leadership Award, American Federation of the Arts (2018); Listee, 100 Most Influential People,

Time Magazine (2016, 2018); William E. Simon Prize for Philanthropic Leadership, Philanthropy Roundtable (2013); Listee, Top 200 Collectors, ARTnews (2004-2012); Louise T. Blouin Foundation Award (2006); Frederick R. Weisman Award, Americans for the Arts (2005); Service to the Community Award, AIA, Los Angeles Chapter (2005); Civic Medal of Honor, Los Angeles Area Chamber of Commerce (2004); Earl Warren Outstanding Public Service Award, American Society for Public Administration, LA Metro Chapter (2004); Brass Ring Award, United Friends of the Children (2003); Exemplary Leadership in Management Award, University of California Los Angeles Anderson School of Management (2002); Alexis de Tocqueville Award, United Way (2002); Educational Leadership Award, Teach for America (2001); Julius Award, University of Southern California School of Policy, Planning and Development (Now Sol Price School of Public Policy) (2001); Chairman's Award, Asia Society, Southern California (2000); Lifetime Achievement Award, Los Angeles Area Chamber of Commerce (1999); Visionary Award, HBS Association of Southern California (1999); Visionary Award, KCET (1999); Knighted Chevalier, National Order Legion of Honor, France (1994); Eli Broad College of Business and Eli Broad Graduate School of Business Named in His Honor, Michigan State University (1991); Honors Award, Visual Arts, L.A. Arts Council (1989); Public Affairs Award, Coro Foundation (1987); American Heritage Award, Anti-Defamation League (1984); Housing Man of the Year Award, National Housing Council (1979); Humanitarian Award, National Conference of Christians and Jews (1977); Golden Plate Award, American Academy of Achievement (1971); Man of the Year Award, City of Hope (1965) MEM: Fellow, American Association for the Advancement of Science; The California Club; Hillcrest Country Club, Los Angeles, CA; Regency Club; Beta Alpha Psi; Fellow, American Academy of Arts and Sciences AV: Collecting contemporary art

BROADUS, CALVIN, "SNOOP DOGG" CORDOZAR JR., T: Rapper, Actor I: Media & Entertainment DOB: 10/20/1972 PB: Long Beach SC: CA/USA PT: Vernall Varnado; Beverly (Tate) Broadus MS: Married SPN: Shante Taylor (06/12/1997-2004, 2008-Present) CH: Cordé; Cordell; Julian Corrie; Cori C: Founder, Doggy Style Records (1995-Present) CR: Investor, Outstanding Foods, Inc. (2020-Present); Ambassador, Beyond Meat (2018-Present); Founder, Merry Jane (2015); Founder, Leafs by Snoop (2015); Chairman, Priority Records (2009) CIV: Leader, Protest March, Operation H.U.N.T., Los Angeles, CA (2016); Founder, Snoop Youth Football League, California (2005) CW: Voice Actor, "Utopia Falls" (2020-Present); Host, "Martha & Snoop's Potluck Dinner Party" (2016-Present); Actor, "Blood Pageant" (2020); Actor, "Unbelievable!!!!!" (2020); Voice Actor, "The SpongeBob Movie: Sponge on the Run" (2020); Voice Actor, "Modern Family" (2020); Voice Actor, "The Addams Family" (2019); Appearance, "Untold Stories of Hip Hop" (2019); Actor, "Dolemite Is My Name" (2019); Voice Actor, "Trouble" (2019); Voice Actor, "American Dad!" (2019); Appearance, "Law & Order: Special Victims Unit" (2019); Actor, "The Beach Bum" (2019); Rapper, Songwriter, "I Wanna Thank Me" (2019); Actor, "Redemption of a Dogg" (2018); Voice Actor, "Ask the StoryBots" (2018); Actor, "Future World" (2018); Actor, "GGN: Snoop Dogg's Double G News Network" (2011-2018); Rapper, Songwriter, "Bible of Love" (2018); Rapper, Songwriter, "220" (2018); Host, "The Joker's Wild" (2017); Rapper, Songwriter, "Neva Left" (2017); Rapper, Songwriter, "Make America Crip Again" (2017); Voice Actor, "The Simpsons" (2017); Actor, "Grow House" (2017); Actor, "Trailer Park Boys" (2016-2017); Actor, "Empire" (2015-2017); Actor, "Popstar: Never Stop Never Stopping" (2016); Rapper, Songwriter, "Coolaid" (2016); Actor, "Meet the Blacks" (2016); Actor, "What Are the Chances?" (2016); Actor, "Pitch Perfect 2" (2015); Rapper, Songwriter, "Bush" (2015); Actor, "Scary Movie 5" (2013); Actor, "Turbo" (2013); Rapper, Songwriter, "Reincarnated" (2013); Actor, "One Life to Live" (2008, 2010, 2013); Rapper, Songwriter, "Stoner's EP" (2012); Actor, "Mac & Devin Go to High School" (2012); Actor, "We the Party" (2012); Rapper, Songwriter, "Doggumentary" (2011); Actor, "The Big Bang" (2011); Voice Actor, "The Boondocks" (2010); Subject, "Dogg After Dark" (2009); Rapper, Songwriter, "Malice n Wonderland" (2009); Actor, "Brüno" (2009); Actor, "Falling Up" (2009); Subject, "Snoop Dogg's Father Hood" (2007-2009); Rapper, Songwriter, "Ego Trippin'" (2008); Actor, "Singh Is Kinng" (2008); Voice Actor, "Arthur and the Invisibles" (2007); Actor, "Monk" (2007); Rapper, Songwriter, "Tha Blue Carpet Treatment" (2006); Actor, "Weeds" (2006); Actor, "Boss'n Up" (2005); Voice Actor, "Racing Stripes" (2005); Actor, "The Tenants" (2005); Actor, "Soul Plane" (2004); Rapper, Songwriter, "R&G (Rhythm & Gangsta): The Masterpiece" (2004); Actor, "Starsky & Hutch" (2004); Actor, "Chappelle's Show" (2004); Actor, "Las Vegas" (2004); Actor, "The L Word" (2004); Actor, "Playmakers" (2003); Voice Actor, "Malibu's Most Wanted" (2003); Actor, "Old School" (2003); Host, "Doggy Fizzle Televizzle" (2002-2003); Rapper, Songwriter, "Paid tha Cost to Be da Boss" (2002); Actor, "The Wash" (2001); Actor, "Bones" (2001); Actor, "Baby Boy" (2001); Actor, "Training Day" (2001); Actor, "Hot Boyz" (2000); Rapper, Songwriter, "Tha Last Medal" (2000); Actor, "The Wrecking Crew" (1999); Rapper, Songwriter, "No Limit Top Dogg" (1999); Actor, "Ride" (1998); Actor, "Half Baked" (1998); Rapper, Songwriter, "Da Game Is to Be Sold, Not to Be Told" (1998); Actor, "The Steve Harvey Show" (1997); Actor, "A Thin Line Between Love and Hate" (1996); Rapper, Songwriter, "Tha Doggfather" (1996); Actor, "Murder Was the Case" (1994); Rapper, Songwriter, "Doggystyle" (1993) AW: Star, Music Category, Hollywood Walk of Fame, Hollywood Chamber of Commerce (2018); Inductee, WWE Hall of Fame (2016); MTV Video Music Award for Best Art Direction, Viacom International Inc. (2015); APRA Music Award for International Work of the Year, APRA AMCOS (2011); MTV Australia Award for Best Hip Hop Video, Viacom International Inc. (2006, 2007); Billboard R&B/Hip-Hop Award for Hot Rap Track, Billboard (2005); MOBO Award for Best Video, MOBO Organisation Ltd. (2005); MTV Europe Music Award for Best Hip Hop Act, Viacom International Media Networks (2005); Soul Train Award for Best R&B/Soul or Rap Dance Cut, Soul Train Music Awards (2005); BET Award for Best Collaboration, BET Interactive, LLC (2003); Source Award for New Artist of the Year (with Tha Eastsidaz), Source Magazine (2000); American Music Award for Favorite Rap/Hip-Hop Artist, Dick Clark Productions, LLC (1995); Soul Train Award for Best Rap Album, Soul Train Music Awards (1995); Source Award for Video of the Year, Source Magazine (1995); Billboard Year-End Chart Award for Top Billboard 200 Album Artist – Male, Billboard (1994); Billboard Year-End Chart Award for Top R&B Album Artist, Billboard (1994); Billboard Year-End Chart Award for Top R&B Album Artist – Male, Billboard (1994); MTV Video Music Award for Best Rap Video, Viacom International Inc. (1994); Source Award for New Artist of the Year (Solo), Source Magazine (1994); Source Award for Lyricist of the Year, Source Magazine (1994); Source Award for Artist of the Year (Solo), Source Magazine (1994)

BROCAGLIA, JOYCE, T: Chief Executive Officer I: Human Resources CN: Alta Associates SC: USA ED: B.S. in Accounting and Law, Montclair State University (1982) C: Chief Executive Officer, BoardSuited (2018-Present); Chief Executive Officer, Executive Women's Forum on Information Security, Risk Management & Privacy (2002-Present); Chief Executive Officer, Alta Associates (1986-Present) CIV: Creator, Cybersecurity Women on Capitol Hill Private-Public Symposium; Established the Joyce Brocaglia Fellowship, Carnegie Melon University; Creator, Cybersecurity School Challenge Educating over 100k Students AW: Named, Top 50 Women Entrepreneurs in NJ (2020); Named, Top 100 Women in Cybersecurity (2020); Alta Associates Named, Top 100 Trusted Company in Cybersecurity (2020); New York University Women Leaders in Cybersecurity Award (2019); Named, NJBizTop 50 Women in Business (2018); SmartCEO Award (2016); CSO Compass Award for Outstanding Achievement in Security and Risk Management Leadership (2015); Named, Best 50 Women in Business in NJ (2015); Compass Award for Outstanding Achievement in Security and Risk Management Leadership (2015); SANS Person Who Made a Difference in Cybersecurity Award (2014); Named, Top 25 Women Entrepreneurs in New Jersey (2014); Named, CIOReview 20 Most Promising Enterprise Security Companies CSO's (2014); Ranked One of Forbes Best Executive Recruiting Firms; Named, Top 20 Firm in Enterprise Security, CIOReview; Cybersecurity Recruiting Pioneer, Hunt Scanlon's Executive Search Review MEM: Board of Directors, Cybercrime Support Network (2020); Board of Advisors, Women's Technology Council of New York Institute of Technology (NYIT) (2019); Board of Trustees, Drew University (2018); Strategic Advisory Board, International Consortium of Minority Cybersecurity Professionals (2015); Board of Advisors, Shared Assessments (2012); New York University (NYU) Cybersecurity Advisory Council; Board of Advisors, RSA Conference

BROCCHINI, RONALD, T: Architect (Retired) I: Architecture & Construction DOB: 11/06/1929 PB: Oakland SC: CA/USA PT: Gino Mario Brocchini; Yoli Louise (Lucchesi) Brocchini MS: Married SPN: Myra Mossman (02/03/1957) CH: Christopher Ronald ED: MA in Architecture, University of California Berkeley, with Honors (1957); BA in Architecture, University of California Berkeley, with Honors (1953) CT: Registered Architect, State of California C: Retired (2014); Principal Architect, Brocchini Architects, Berkeley, CA (1987-2014); Principal Architect, Worley K. Wong, Ronald G. Brocchini & Associates, San Francisco, CA (1968-1987); Principal Architect, Ronald G. Brocchini, Berkeley, CA (1964-1967); Associate Architect, Campbell & Wong, San Francisco, CA (1961-1963); Designer, Associate, SMP, Inc., San Francisco, CA (1956-1960); Architect, Designer, SMP, Inc., San Francisco, CA (1948-1953) CR: Commissioner, California Board Architectural Examiners (Now California Architects Board) (1961-1989); Member, Examiner Committee, NCARB - National Council Architectural Registration Boards (1983-1985); Lecturer, California College of Arts and Crafts (Now California College of the Arts), Oakland, CA (1981-1983) MIL: With, United States Army (1953-1955) CW: Author, "Long Range Master Plan for Bodega Marine Biology," University of California (1982); Principal Works Include San Simeon Visitor Center, Hearst Castle, CA, Mare Island Medical-Dental Facility, IBM Educational and Data Processing Headquarters, San Jose, CA, Simpson Fine Arts Gallery, California College of the Arts, Ceramics and Metal Crafts, Emery Bay Public Market Complex, Analytical Measurement Facility, University of California Berkeley, Bodega Marine Biology Campus, University of California Berkeley, Fromm & Sichell (Christian Brothers) Headquarters, The Nature Co., Corporate Offices, Berkeley, Merrill College, Athletic Facilities, University of California Santa Cruz, College III Housing, University of California San Diego, Center Pacific Rim Studies, University of San Francisco, Married Student Housing Escondido II, III, IV, Stanford University, CA **AW:** Design Award, California Department of Rehabilitation (DOR), CA (1995); Alumni Citation (1988); Bear of the Year Award, University of California Berkeley (1987); Design Honor Awards for Architecture **MEM:** President, San Francisco Chapter, American Institute of Architects (AIA) (1982); Fellow, American Institute of Architects (AIA); Board of Directors, California Council, American Institute of Architects (AIA); Bear Backers Club; Board of Directors, University of California Berkeley Athletic Council, Bear Backers; Berkeley Breakfast Club; Board of Governors, Berkeley Breakfast Club; Order of the Golden Bear **MH:** Albert Nelson Marquis Lifetime Achievement Award **AS:** Mr. Brocchini attributes his success to an excellent eye for design, and also because he started his career during the late 40s and 50s, when there was an explosion in architectural projects. **B/I:** Mr. Brocchini became involved in his profession because he became interested in drawing plans when he was in high school; he took two years of architecture drafting in high school and the rest was history. His parents, Gino Mario and Yoli Louise (Lucchesi) Brocchini, also encouraged his career and were always supportive of what he was trying to do. **AV:** Auto restoration; Photography; Sports; Art **PA:** Republican **RE:** Roman Catholic

BROCK, D. HEYWARD, T: English Literature Educator, University Official **I:** Education/Educational Services **DOB:** 06/02/1941 **PB:** Greenville **SC:** SC/USA **PT:** Dewey Calhoun Brock; Sarah Edith (Moose) Brock **MS:** Married **SPN:** Patricia Lee Farmer (08/25/1963) **CH:** Sarah Michelle; Paul Heyward; David Patrick **ED:** PhD, The University of Kansas (1969); MA, The University of Kansas (1965); BA, Newberry College (1963) **C:** Instructor, Professor, University of Delaware, Newark, DE (1968-2019); Senior Associate Dean of Arts and Sciences, University of Delaware, Newark, DE (1987-2001); Associate Chair, Department of English, University of Delaware, Newark, DE (1985-1987); Professor, Department of Literature, University Essex, Colchester, England, United Kingdom (1981-1982); Director, Center of Science and Culture, University of Delaware, Newark, DE (1977-1979); Assistant Dean of Arts and Sciences, University of Delaware, Newark, DE (1969); Assistant Instructor, The University of Kansas, Lawrence, KS (1963-1968) **CR:** General Manager, PLFB Enterprises, LLC (2018-Present); TSD Bioservices, Newark, DE (1991-2010); Vice President, Waves Council Owners, Ocean City, MD (1990-2005); Member, Animal Welfare Committees, DuPont Co., Wilmington, DE (1990-1995); Member, Professional Consultation Committee, Medical Center of Delaware, Stanton, DE (1989-1994); Member, National Board Consultant, Washington, DC (1979-1984); National Endowment of the Humanities (1979-1984) **CW:** Co-author, "The Ben Jonson Encyclopedia" (2016); Author, Pseudonym Jon Benon, "Elsburg, USA" (2013); Author, Pseudonym Jon Benon, "Sign of Jonah" (2010); Author, "A Ben Jonson Companion" (1983); Co-author, "Ben Jonson: A Quadricentennial Bibliography, 1947-72" (1974); Editor, Numerous Books on Science and Culture, Literature and Medicine; Contributor, Articles to Professional Journals **AW:** Grantee, American Philosophical Society (1981-1982); Grantee, National Science Foundation and National Endowment of the

Humanities (1980); Institute of Humanistic Computation Fellow, National Science Foundation (1979) **MH:** Albert Nelson Marquis Lifetime Achievement Award; Marquis Who's Who Top Professional **B/I:** When Dr. Brock was an undergraduate, he was a pre-ministry student because he went to Newberry College which is a small Lutheran college. He was asked by others why he was going into seminary and he said that was what you have to do to become a minister, in which they responded that he should go on to graduate school which he did. **AV:** Sports; Carpentry **PA:** Independent **RE:** Lutheran

BROCKMEIER, NORMAN, T: President (Retired) **I:** Consulting **CN:** Oakwood Consulting, Inc **DOB:** 09/05/1937 **PB:** Montclair **SC:** NJ/USA **PT:** Norman Henry; Catherine Carol (Weidmann) Brockmeier **MS:** Married **SPN:** Sharon Helen Olson (07/02/1992); Marilyn Irene Ellman, (09/10/1960, Divorced 4/1979) **CH:** Linda; Elaine; Frederick **ED:** PhD, Massachusetts Institute of Technology (1966); BSChemE, Cornell University (1960) **CT:** Registered Professional Engineer, Texas **C:** President, Oakwood Consulting, Inc., Wheaton, IL (1992-Present); Research Associate, Amoco Chemical Co., Naperville, IL (1971-1992); Assistant Professor, University of Texas, Austin (1966-1971); Research Engineer, Minnesota Mining & Manufacturing Co., St. Paul, MN (1960-1963) **CR:** Adjunct Professor, Energy Systems Division, Argonne National Laboratory (1993-2000); Adjunct Professor, Chemical Engineering, The Ohio State University, Columbus, OH (1993); Chairman, Steering Committee for Polymer Solution Handbook, American Institute of Chemical Engineers (1988-1991) **CIV:** Member, Faith Lutheran Church, Glen Ellyn, IL (1971-Present); Vice President, Glenbard High School District 87 Board of Education, Glen Ellyn, IL (1983-1991); Master, School Board Member, Illinois Association of School Boards (1990); Vice President, District 89 Elementary School Board Education, Glen Ellyn, IL (1980-1983); Board of Directors, Kiwanis Club, Austin, TX (1969-1971); Lay Delegate to Illinois Synod, Lutheran Church in America Convention; Secretary, Illinois Synod Peace Task Force; Adult Bible Class Facilitator, Past Vice Chairman, West Suburban Interfaith Peace Initiative **CW:** Publications and Presentations, Technical Assemblies Written & Oral Presentations (1963-2018); Author, "A Process to Recover Plastics from Obsolete Automobiles" (1995); Author, "Scoping Economics for the Commercial Manufacture of Metallocene Catalysts" (1994); Author, "The Amoco/Chisso Gas Phase Polypropylene Copolymer Technology" (1991); Author, "Comparison of Latest Processes for Polypropylene Manufacture" (1989); Co-author, "Encyclopedia of Polymer Science and Engineering" (1987); Contributor, Over 60 Articles, Refereed Journals, Contributor, 23 Seminars; Holder of Two Key U.S. Patents for Comm. Olefin Polymerization Processes **AW:** Fellow of the American, American Institute of Chemical Engineers (1999); Area Quality Award-Recognition on Targeted Selection Communications (1990); Best Articles on Process Control, Instrument Society of America (1970) **MEM:** Creation Research Society (1972-Present); American Chemical Society (1967-Present); Various Committees, American Institute Chemical Engineers (1966-Present); American Scientific Affiliation (1972); Educators for Social Responsibility **B/I:** Mr. Brockmeier became involved in his profession because he chose his parents very well. His mother was valedictorian of her class and went on to graduate with honors from Columbia university and spoke four languages. Her family valued accomplishments in science and also

christian faith. **AV:** Snow skiing; NASTAR trophies for slalom; Model railroading; Golf; Bicycling **PA:** Progressive **RE:** Lutheran

BRODERICK, MATTHEW JOHN, T: Actor **I:** Media & Entertainment **DOB:** 03/21/1962 **PB:** New York **SC:** NY/USA **PT:** James Broderick; Patricia (Biow) Broderick **MS:** Married **SPN:** Sarah Jessica Parker (05/19/1997) **CH:** James Wilkie; Marion Loretta; Tabitha Hodge **ED:** Diplomate, Walden School, New York, NY (1980) **CW:** Actor, "Plaza Suite," Hudson Theatre, New York, NY (2020); Actor, "Lazy Susan" (2020); Voice Actor, "Rick and Morty" (2019); Actor, "Daybreak" (2019); Actor, "Better Things" (2019); Actor, "Love Is Blind" (2019); Actor, "At Home with Amy Sedaris" (2019); Actor, "The Starry Messenger," Wyndham's Theatre, London, United Kingdom (2019); Actor, "The Conners" (2018-2019); Actor, "To Dust" (2018); Actor, "Celebrity Autobiography," Marquis Theatre, New York, NY (2018); Actor, "The Closet," Williamstown Theatre Festival, Williamstown, MA (2018); Actor, "A Christmas Story Live!" (2017); Voice Actor, "BoJack Horseman" (2017); Actor, "Evening at the Talk House," Signature Theatre, New York, NY (2017); Actor, "Rules Don't Apply" (2016); Actor, "The American Side" (2016); Actor, "Manchester by the Sea" (2016); Actor, "Shining City," Irish Repertory Theatre, New York, NY (2016); Actor, "Oh, Hello on Broadway," Lyceum Theatre, New York, NY (2016); Actor, "The Jim Gaffigan Show" (2015); Actor, "Trainwreck" (2015); Actor, "Dirty Weekend" (2015); Actor, "Sylvia," Cort Theatre, New York, NY (2015); Actor, "Louie" (2010, 2015); Actor, "It's Only a Play," Gerald Schoenfeld Theatre, New York, NY (2014-2015); Actor, "Untitled Tad Quill Project" (2013); Actor, "Nice Work If You Can Get It," Imperial Theatre, New York, NY (2012-2013); Actor, "Modern Family" (2012); Actor, "30 Rock" (2008, 2012); Actor, "Tower Heist" (2011); Actor, "Margaret" (2011); Actor, "Beach Lane" (2010); Actor, "Wonderful World" (2009); Actor, "The Starry Messenger," Theatre Row, New York, NY (2009); Actor, "The Philanthropist," American Airlines Theatre, New York, NY (2009); Voice Actor, "The Tale of Desperaux" (2008); Actor, "Finding Amanda" (2008); Actor, "Diminished Capacity" (2008); Voice Actor, "Bee Movie" (2007); Actor, "Then She Found Me" (2007); Actor, "Deck the Halls" (2006); Actor, "The Producers" (2005); Actor, "Strangers with Candy" (2005); Actor, "The Odd Couple," Brooks Atkinson Theatre, New York, NY (2005); Actor, "The Last Shot" (2004); Actor, "The Stepford Wives" (2004); Actor, "Marie and Bruce" (2004); Actor, "The Foreigner," Laura Pels Theatre, New York, NY (2004); Voice Actor, "The Lion King 3: Hakuna Matata" (2003); Voice Actor, "Freedom: A History of Us" (2003); Voice Actor, "Good Boy" (2003); Actor, "The Music Man" (2003); Actor, "Short Talks on the Universe," Longacre Theatre, New York, NY (2002); Actor, "The Producers," St. James Theatre, New York, NY (2001-2002); Actor, "You Can Count on Me" (2000); Actor, "Taller Than a Dwarf," Longacre Theatre, New York, NY (2000); Actor, "Inspector Gadget" (1999); Actor, "Election" (1999); Actor, "Night Must Fall," Helen Hayes Theatre, New York, NY (1999); Voice Actor, "The Lion King 2: Simba's Pride" (1998); Actor, "Walking to the Waterline" (1998); Actor, "Godzilla" (1998); Actor, "Addicted to Love" (1997); Actor, Producer, Director, "Infinity" (1996); Actor, "The Cable Guy" (1996); Actor, "How to Succeed in Business Without Really Trying," Richard Rogers Theatre, New York, NY (1995); Actor, "The Road to Wellville" (1994); Voice Actor, "The Lion King" (1994); Actor, "Mrs. Parker and the Vicious Circle" (1994); Actor, "A Life in the Theater" (1994); Actor, "The Night We Never Met" (1993); Actor, "Out on a Limb" (1992); Actor, "The Freshman" (1990); Actor,

"Glory" (1989); Actor, "Family Business" (1989); Actor, "Torch Song Trilogy" (1988); Actor, "Biloxi Blues" (1988); Actor, "Project X" (1987); Actor, "The Widow Claire," Circle in the Square Theatre, New York, NY (1986-1987); Actor, "Ferris Bueller's Day Off" (1986); Actor, "On Valentine's Day" (1986); Actor, "'Master Harold' ... and the Boys" (1985); Actor, "Cinderella," "Faerie Tale Theatre" (1985); Actor, "Ladyhawke" (1985); Actor, "1918" (1985); Actor, "Biloxi Blues," Neil Simon Theatre, New York, NY (1985); Actor, "WarGames" (1983); Actor, "Max Dugan Returns" (1983); Actor, "Brighton Beach Memoirs," 46th Street Theatre, New York, NY (1983); Actor, "Lou Grant" (1981); Actor, "Torch Song Trilogy," Village Actors' Playhouse, New York, NY (1981) **AW:** Audience Award, Tribeca Film Festival (2018); Recipient, Star, Motion Picture Category, Hollywood Walk of Fame, Hollywood Chamber of Commerce (2006); Tony Award for Best Actor in a Musical, American Theatre Wing (1995); Outer Critics Circle Award for Best Actor in a Musical, Outer Critics Circle (1995); Tony Award for Best Featured Actor in a Play, American Theatre Wing (1983) **MEM:** Actors' Equity Association; SAG-AFTRA

BROG, DAVID, T: Executive Director **I:** Military & Defense Services **CN:** Air Warrior Courage Foundation **DOB:** 08/11/1933 **PB:** Manchester **SC:** CT/USA **PT:** Israel Brog; Pesha (Blonstein) Brog **MS:** Married **SPN:** Verda Anna Raney (11/09/1959) **CH:** Kai Ling; Tov Binyamin **ED:** MS, University of Southern California (1967); BA, University of Pittsburgh (1955) **C:** President, IRD, Inc., Silver Spring, MD (1982-Present); Domestic and International Consultant, IRD, Inc., Silver Spring, MD (1982-Present) **CIV:** Executive Director, Air Warrior Courage Foundation **MIL:** Deputy Chief of Staff, Operations, Command Control and Communications Countermeasures, U.S. Air Force (1981-1982); Director, Readiness and Electronic Combat, Headquarters, U.S. Air Force (1981); Advanced Through Grades to Colonel, U.S. Air Force (1978); Commissioned 2nd Lieutenant, U.S. Air Force (1956) **CW:** Contributor, Articles, Professional Journals **AW:** Distinguished Flying Cross; Two Legions of Merit; Air Medal with 12 Oak Leaf Clusters; Named Distinguished Graduate, Air War College, U.S. Air Force **MEM:** President, Red River Valley Fighter Pilots Association; Association of Old Crows; Air Force Association **MH:** Albert Nelson Marquis Lifetime Achievement Award **AS:** Mr. Brog attributes his success to understanding problems and finding the best solutions without outside biases. **B/I:** Mr. Brog became involved in his profession because he wanted to give back to those that have defended their country. **RE:** Jewish **THT:** Mr. Brog has said, "Never think old. Always look to the future to make it better for those who follow."

BRONFMAN, CHARLES ROSNER, T: Philanthropist; Former Distillery Executive **I:** Nonprofit & Philanthropy **CN:** The Andrea & Charles Bronfman Philanthropies, Inc. **DOB:** 06/27/1931 **PB:** Montreal, Quebec **SC:** Canada **PT:** Samuel Bronfman; Saidye (Rosner) Bronfman **MS:** Married **SPN:** Rita Mayo (2012); Bonita Roche (2008, Divorced 2011); Andrea Brett Morrison (1982, Deceased 01/23/2006); Barbara Baerwald (1961, Divorced 1982) **CH:** Stephen Rosner Bronfman; Ellen Jane Bronfman Hauptman **ED:** Honorary LLD, University of Toronto (2000); Honorary LLD, University of Waterloo (1995); Honorary LLD, Concordia University (1992); Honorary LHD, Brandeis University (1992); Honorary LLD, McGill University (1990); Honorary PhD, Hebrew University of Jerusalem (1990); Coursework, McGill University (1948-1951) **C:** Chairman, Koor Industries Ltd. (1997-2002); Co-chairman, Seagram Co., Ltd. (1986-1997);

Chairman, Executive Committee, Seagram Co., Ltd. (1975-1997); With, Seagram Co., Ltd. (1951-1997); Co-owner, Cemp Investments (1951-1987); Department Chairman, Seagram Co., Ltd. (1979-1986); President, Seagram Co., Ltd. (1975-1979); Executive Vice President, Seagram Co., Ltd. (1971-1975); Vice President, Director, Seagram Co., Ltd. (1958-1971) **CR:** Chairman, CRB Foundation (The Andrea & Charles Bronfman Philanthropies, Inc.) (1986-2016); Owner, Montreal Expos, MLB (1968-1990); Chairman, Board, Claridge Israel Inc.; Board of Directors, Power Corporation of Canada; Trustee, Brandeis University; Trustee, Mount Sinai Medical Center, Inc. (Now Icahn School of Medicine at Mount Sinai), New York, NY **CIV:** Co-founder, The Charles Bronfman Prize (TCBP) (2002-Present); Co-founder, Vice-chairman, Birthright Israel (2000-Present); Co-founder, Chairman, The Andrea & Charles Bronfman Philanthropies, Inc. (1986-Present); Past President, Allied Jewish Community Services (Federation CJA), Montreal, Canada; Life Member, Board of Governors, Jewish General Hospital; Board of Directors, Canadian Council for Christians and Jews (Canadian Centre for Diversity); Honorary Chairman, Canadian-Israel Securities Ltd. (State of Israel Bonds Canada); Participant, The Giving Pledge **CW:** Co-author, "The Art of Doing Good: Where Passion Meets Action" (2012); Co-author, "The Art of Giving: Where the Soul Meets a Business Plan" (2010) **AW:** Named Honorary Citizen, City of Montreal, Canada (2019); Named One of the New York Influentials, New York Magazine (2006); Co-recipient with Andrea Brett Morrison, Honorary Citizenship of Jerusalem (2002); Promoted to Companion, Order of Canada (1992); Named to Queen's Privy Council for Canada (1992); Inductee, Canadian Baseball Hall of Fame and Museum (1985); Named Officer, Order of Canada (1981) **MEM:** Montefiore Club, Montreal, Canada; The Mount Royal Club, Montreal, Canada; Club Saint-Denis, Montreal, Canada; Elm Ridge Golf and Country Club, Montreal, Canada; Palm Beach Country Club **RE:** Jewish

BROOKS, GARTH, T: Musician **I:** Media & Entertainment **DOB:** 02/07/1962 **PB:** Tulsa **SC:** OK/USA **PT:** Troyal Raymond Brooks Jr.; Colleen McElroy Carroll **MS:** Married **SPN:** Trisha Yearwood (12/10/2005); Sandy Mahl (05/24/1986, Divorced 12/17/2001) **CH:** Taylor Mayne Pearl; August Anna; Allie Colleen **ED:** MBA, Oklahoma State University (2011); BS in Advertising and Journalism, Oklahoma State University, Stillwater, OK (1984) **CIV:** Co-founder, Board of Directors, Teammates for Kids Foundation (1999-Present); Performer, Benefit Concert for Hospital de Câncer de Barretos, Barretos, Brazil (2015); Performer, Oklahoma Tornado Victims Benefit Concert (2013); Performer, Benefit Concerts for Victims of Tennessee Floods (2010); Performer, Benefit Concerts for Victims of California Wildfires (2007); Performer, "Shelter from the Storm: A Concert for the Gulf Coast" (2005); Performer, Equality Rocks, Millennium March on Washington, Washington, DC (2000); Supporter, Jimmy & Rosalynn Carter Work Project, Habitat for Humanity International **CW:** Singer-Songwriter, "Fun" (2020); Singer-Songwriter, "Gunslinger" (2016); Singer-Songwriter with Trisha Yearwood, "Christmas Together" (2016); Singer-Songwriter, "Man Against Machine" (2014); Singer-Songwriter, "The Lost Sessions" (2005); Singer-Songwriter, "Scarecrow" (2001); Singer, "Garth Brooks and the Magic of Christmas" (1999); Singer-Songwriter, "The Life of Chris Gaines" (1999); Singer-Songwriter, "Sevens" (1997); Singer-Songwriter, "Fresh Horses" (1995); Singer-Songwriter, "In Pieces" (1993); Singer-Songwriter, "The Chase" (1992); Singer-Songwriter, "Beyond the Season" (1992); Singer-Songwriter, "Ropin' the Wind" (1991); Sing-

er-Songwriter, "No Fences" (1990); Singer-Songwriter, "Garth Brooks" (1989) **AW:** CMA Award for Entertainer of the Year, CMA Country Music Association Inc. (1991, 1992, 1997, 1998, 2016, 2017, 2019); iHeartRadio Music Award for Best Tour, iHeartRadio (2016); Inductee, Musicians Hall of Fame (MHOF) and Museum (2016); ACM Award for Entertainer of the Year, Academy of Country Music (1990-1995, 1997, 1998, 2001, 2016); Named Arkansas Traveler (2014); Milestone Award, Academy of Country Music (2014); Centennial Award, ASCAP (2014); American Music Award for Favorite Country Album, dick clark productions, llc (1992-1994, 1996-1999, 2008, 2014); Billboard Music Award for Top Country Album, Billboard (1991, 1992, 1998, 2014); Inductee, Country Music Hall of Fame and Museum (2012); Inductee, Songwriters Hall of Fame (2011); Cliffie Stone Pioneer Award, Academy of Country Music (2010); Inductee, Hall of Fame, Cheyenne Frontier Days (2010); GRAMMYs on the Hill Award for Solo Artist of the Century, Recording Academy (2010); American Music Award for Favorite Country Male Artist, dick clark productions, llc (1991, 1993-1995, 1997-1999, 2008); Crystal Milestone Award, Academy of Country Music (2007); 40th Anniversary Milestone Award, Academy of Country Music (2005); Award of Merit, American Music Awards, dick clark productions, llc (2002); Howie Richmond Hitmaker Award, Songwriters Hall of Fame (2002); Billboard Music Award for Country Songs Artist of the Year, Billboard (1998, 2002); ACM Award for Vocal Event of the Year, Academy of Country Music (1998, 2001); ACM Award for Artist of the Decade, Academy of Country Music (1999); Founder Award, ASCAP (1999); Billboard Music Award for Country Album Artist of the Year, Billboard (1998, 1999); Billboard Music Award for Album Artist of the Year, Billboard (1991, 1992, 1999); Billboard Music Award for Male Album of the Year, Billboard (1998); Billboard Music Award for Male Album Artist of the Year, Billboard (1998); Billboard Music Award for Top Country Artist, Billboard (1992, 1993, 1996, 1998); ACM Award for Album of the Year, Academy of Country Music (1990-1992, 1994, 1997, 1998); Gene Weed Special Achievement Award, Academy of Country Music (1997); Billboard Music Artist Achievement Award, Billboard (1997); Grammy Award for Best Country Collaboration with Vocals, Recording Academy (1997); Founders Award, NAACP (1996); ACM Award for Video of the Year, Academy of Country Music (1990, 1991, 1993, 1994, 1996); Billboard Music Award for Top Billboard 200 Album, Billboard (1995); Jim Reeves Memorial Award, Academy of Country Music (1994); ACM Award for Top Male Vocalist, Academy of Country Music (1990-1994); Songwriter of the Year Award, ASCAP (1993); GLAAD Media Award for Outstanding Recording, GLAAD (1993); Billboard Music Award for Top Pop Artist, Billboard (1992, 1993); Billboard Music Award for Top Artist, Billboard (1992, 1993); American Music Award for Favorite Country Single, dick clark productions, llc (1992, 1993); Juno Award for International Entertainer of the Year, The Canadian Academy of Recording Arts and Sciences (CARAS) (1992, 1993); ACM Award for Single of the Year, Academy of Country Music (1989-1993); ACM Award for Top Vocal Duet, Academy of Country Music (1992); CMA Award for Album of the Year, CMA Country Music Association Inc. (1991, 1992); Grammy Award for Best Male Country Vocal Performance, Recording Academy (1991); CMT Music Award for Entertainer of the Year, Country Music Television, Inc. (1991); CMT Music Award for Video of the Year, Country Music Television, Inc. (1991); CMA Award for Single of the Year, CMA Country Music Association Inc. (1991); CMA Award for Music Video of the Year, CMA Country Music Association Inc. (1990, 1991); ACM

Award for Song of the Year, Academy of Country Music (1990); CMA Horizon Award, CMA Country Music Association Inc. (1990); ACM Award for Top New Male Vocalist, Academy of Country Music (1989); ACM Award for Song of the Year – Artist, Academy of Country Music (1989); ACM Award for Song of the Year – Composer, Academy of Country Music (1989)

BROOKS, MORRIS, "MO" JACKSON JR., T: U.S. Representative, Lawyer **I:** Government Administration/Government Relations/Government Services **DOB:** 04/29/1954 **PB:** Charleston **SC:** SC/USA **PT:** Morris Jackson "Jack" Brooks; Betty J. (Nolan) Brooks **MS:** Married **SPN:** Martha Jenkins (1976) **CH:** Two Sons; Two Daughters **ED:** JD, School of Law, The University of Alabama (1978); BA in Political Science and Economics, Duke University **C:** U.S. Representative, Alabama's Fifth Congressional District, United States Congress, Washington, DC (2011-Present); Private Law Practice (2002-Present); Commissioner, Madison County Commission (1996-2010); Special Assistant Attorney General, State of Alabama (1995-2002); Counselor to Partner, Leo & Brooks LLC (1993); District Attorney, Madison County, AL (1991-1992); Member, District 10, Alabama House of Representatives (1984-1992); Member, District 18, Alabama House of Representatives (1982-1984); Law Clerk, Circuit Court Judge John David Snodgrass (1980-1982); Attorney, Tuscaloosa District Attorney Office (1980); Member, Committee on the Budget; Member, Committee on Oversight and Government Reform; Member, Committee on Science, Space and Technology; Member, Republican Study Committee **PA:** Republican

BROOKS, SUSAN LYNN, T: U.S. Representative (Retired), Chairwoman (Retired), Lawyer **I:** Law and Legal Services **DOB:** 08/25/1960 **PB:** Fort Wayne **SC:** ID/USA **PT:** Robert Wiant; Marilyn Wiant **MS:** Married **SPN:** David Brooks **CH:** Two children **ED:** JD, Robert H. McKinney School of Law, Indiana University (1985); BA, Miami University, OH (1982); Honorary Doctorate of Public Service, Marian University, Indianapolis, IN; Honorary JD, Indiana University Robert H. McKinney School of Law; Honorary Degree, Wabash College; Honorary Associate of Science, College and Community Service, Ivy Tech Community College **C:** Chairwoman, House Committee on Ethics (2017-2019); Member, U.S. House Select Committee on the Events Surrounding the 2012 Terrorist Attack in Benghazi (2014-2019); U.S. Representative, Indiana's Fifth Congressional District, United States Congress, Washington, DC (2013-2019); Member, U.S. House Homeland Security Committee (2013-2019); Member, U.S. House Committee on Education and Labor (2013-2019); Member, U.S. House Committee on Ethics (2013-2017); Senior Vice President of Workforce and Economic Development, General Counsel, Ivy Tech Community College (2007-2011); U.S. Attorney, Southern District of Indiana, The U.S. Department of Justice (2001-2007); Of Counsel, Ice Miller LLP, Indianapolis, IN (2000-2001); Deputy Mayor, City of Indianapolis, IN (1998-1999); Partner, McClure, McClure & Kammen (1985-1997) **CIV:** Protocol Chair, World Police and Fire Games, Indianapolis, IN (2001); Chair, Violence and Safety Impact Council, United Way; Board Member, Network of Women in Business; Board Member, MCCOY; Board Member, Little Red Door Cancer Agency; Board Member, Junior League of Indianapolis; Board Member, Indiana Federal Community Defenders; Nominating Committee, Hoosier Capitol Girl Scouts Council (Now Girl Scouts of Central Indiana); Board Member, Greater Indianapolis Progress Committee **AW:** Government Leader of the Year, CADCA

(2014); Alumnae of the Year, Robert H. McKinney School of Law, Indiana University (2006); Influential Woman of Indianapolis, Indianapolis Business Journal (1999); Congressional Biosecurity Champion, Alliance for Biosecurity; Congressional Leadership Award, CADCA; Nancy A. Maloley Outstanding Public Servant Award, Richard G. Lugar Excellence in Public Service Series; Spirit of Enterprise Award, U.S. Chamber of Commerce; Nathan Hale Award, Indiana Reserve Officers Association **PA:** Republican **RE:** Catholic

BROUILLETTE, DANNY, "DAN" RAY, T: United States Secretary of Energy **I:** Government Administration/Government Relations/Government Services **CN:** U.S. Department of Energy **DOB:** 09/18/1962 **PB:** Paincourtville **SC:** LA/USA **MS:** Married **SPN:** Adrienne Brouilette **CH:** Nine Children **ED:** BA, University of Maryland, College Park, MD **C:** United States Secretary of Energy, U.S. Department of Energy, Washington, DC (2019-Present); United States Deputy Secretary of Energy, U.S. Department of Energy, Washington, DC (2017-2019); Board of Directors, Public Affairs Council (2010-2011); Senior Vice President, Government and Industry Relations, U.S. Automobile Association (USAA) (2006); Vice President, Ford Motor Company (2004-2006); Staff Director, U.S. House Committee on Energy and Commerce, Washington, DC (2003-2004); Chief of Staff, U.S. Representative Billy Tallzin, United States Congress, Washington, DC (2003-2004); Partner, Alpine Group, Inc. (2000-2001, 2003); Assistant Secretary, Congressional and Intergovernmental Affairs, U.S. Department of Energy, Washington, DC (2001-2003); Senior Vice President, R. Duffy Wall & Associates (1997-2000); Legislative Director to U.S. Representative Billy Tallzin, United States Congress, Washington, DC (1989-1997) **CR:** Mineral and Energy (2013-2016); North American Operating Committee, Ford Motor Company **MIL:** United States Army

BROUS, THOMAS R., T: Lawyer **I:** Law and Legal Services **DOB:** 01/07/1943 **PB:** Fulton **SC:** MO/USA **PT:** Richard Pendleton; Augusta (Gilpin) B. **MS:** Married **SPN:** Mary Lou Brous; Patricia Catlin (09/12/1964, Deceased 1999) **CH:** Anna Catlin Brous; Joel Pendleton Brous; Brad; Reed **ED:** Doctor of Jurisprudence, University of Michigan, Cum Laude (1968); Bachelor of Science in Business Administration, Northwestern University (1965) **C:** Partner, Stinson Morrison Hecker LLP, Kansas City, MO (2002-2016); Shareholder, Stinson, Mag & Fizzell PC, Kansas City, MO (1996-2002); Partner, Watson & Marshall L.C., Kansas City, MO (1978-1996); Managing Partner, Watson & Marshall L.C., Kansas City, MO (1992-1994); Associate, Watson & Marshall L.C., Kansas City, MO (1968-1978) **CR:** Adjunct Faculty, University of Kansas School of Law (2006-2016); With, Central Mountain Tax Exempt and Governmental Entities Council IRS (1997-2005); Steering Committee, University of Missouri Kansas City School of Law Employee Benefits Institute (1990-2001); Chairman, University of Missouri Kansas City School of Law Employee Benefits Institute (1992-1993) **CIV:** Trustee, Kansas City Public Library Foundation (2009-Present); Grace & Holy Trinity Cathedral (1994-Present); Trustee, Kansas City Repertory Theatre, Incorporated (1990-Present); Visiting Committee, University of Chicago Divinity School (2006-2015); Director, Metropolitan Organization to Counter Sexual Abuse, Kansas City, KS (1992-1995); Vice President, Treasurer, Barstow School, Kansas City, KS (1982-1986); Vestry, Saint Andrews Episcopal Church, Kansas City, KS (1974-1977) **MIL:** Captain, U.S. Army Judge Advocates General Corps (1968-1972) **CW:** Author, "Why Read Four Quartets?" (2017); Author, "Chapter 10, Missouri

Specialized Business Entities" (2006); Author, "Chapter 26, III Missouri Business Organizations" (1998); Assistant Editor, Michigan Law Revised (1966-1968) **AW:** Named, Super Lawyers of Missouri **MEM:** Vice Chairman, Employee Benefits Committee, The Missouri Bar Association (1997-2000); President, University Club (1988-1989); Missouri Society of Hospital Attorneys; Heart of America Employee Benefit Conference; Kansas City Metropolitan Bar Association; Greater Kansas City Society of Hospital Attorneys; American Bar Association; Delta Upsilon; Beta Gamma Sigma **BAR:** Missouri (1968) **MH:** Albert Nelson Marquis Lifetime Achievement Award **B/I:** Mr. Brous became involved in his profession due to the influence of his father, Richard Pendleton, who was also a lawyer. **AV:** Reading **RE:** Episcopalian

BROUSSARD, BRUCE DALE, T: President and Chief Executive Officer **I:** Medicine & Health Care **CN:** Humana **ED:** MBA, C.T. Bauer College of Business, The University of Houston (1989); BBA, Mays Business School, Texas A&M University (1984) **CT:** CPA (Certified Public Accountant) **C:** President, Chief Executive Officer, Humana (2013-Present); President, Humana, Louisville, KY (2011-2013); Chairman, The US Oncology Network, McKesson Corporation (2009-2011); Chief Executive Officer, The US Oncology Network, McKesson Corporation (2008-2011); President, The US Oncology Network, McKesson Corporation, Houston, Texas (2006-2008); Executive Vice President, Pharmaceutical Services, The US Oncology Network, McKesson Corporation, Houston, Texas (2003-2005); Chief Financial Officer, The US Oncology Network, McKesson Corporation, Houston, Texas (2000-2003); Chief Executive Officer, Harbor Dental (1997-2000); Executive Vice President, Chief Financial Officer, Regency Health Services, Inc. (1996-1997); Chief Financial Officer, Sun Healthcare Group, Inc. (1993-1996); Vice President, Finance, Continental Medical Systems (1990-1993); Manager, PwC (1987-1990) **CR:** Board of Directors, Sun Healthcare Group, Inc. (1993-1996); Board of Directors, U.S. Physical Therapy, Inc.

BROWN, ANTHONY GREGORY, T: U.S. House of Representatives from Maryland; Military Officer; Lawyer **I:** Government Administration/Government Relations/Government Services **DOB:** 11/21/1961 **PB:** Huntington **SC:** NY/USA **PT:** Roy Hershel Brown; Lilly Ida (Berlinger) Brown **MS:** Married **SPN:** Karmen Walker Bailey (05/27/2012); Patricia Arzuaga (01/29/1993, Divorced 2009) **CH:** Rebecca; Jonathan (Adopted); Anthony Michael (Stepchild) **ED:** JD, Harvard Law School (1992); AB in Government, Harvard College, Cum Laude, Cambridge, MA (1984) **C:** Member, U.S. House of Representatives from Maryland's Fourth Congressional District (2017-Present); Member, Committee on Armed Services (2017-Present); Member, Committee on Ethics (2017-Present); Member, Committee on Natural Resources (2017-Present); Lieutenant Governor, State of Maryland (2007-2015); Attorney, Gibbs & Haller, Lanham, MD (1998-2007); Majority Whip, Maryland House of Delegates (2004); Representative, District 25, Maryland House of Delegates (1999-2004); Attorney, Wilmer Cutler Pickering Hale and Dorr LLP, Washington, DC (1994-1998); Law Clerk, United States Court of Appeals for the Armed Forces, Washington, DC (1992-1994) **CR:** Member, Legislative Black Caucus of Maryland (1999-Present); Member, Governor's Task Force, Medical Malpractice and Health Care Access (2004); Member, Committee on Higher Education, Maryland House of Delegates (2003-2004); Member, Committee on Affordability and Accessibility, Maryland House of Delegates (2003-2004); Co-chair, Judiciary Committee (2003-2004); Member, Article 27 Revision Committee (2003-2004); Member, Joint Committee on Administrative, Executive and Legislative Review (2003-2004); Member, Economic Matters Committee (1999-2003); Member, Law Enforcement and State-appointed Board Committee (1999-2002); Member, Technology and Business Division Task Force (2000); Lecturer, Legal Assistant Program, Georgetown University, Washington, DC (1996-1997) **CIV:** Board of Directors, Adoptions Together, Inc., Silver Spring, MD (2001); Board of Directors, Prince George's County Law Foundation (Now Community Legal Services of Prince George's County, Inc.), Hyattsville, MD (2000); Chairman, Prince George's Community College, Largo, MD (1998-1999); Member, Board of Trustees, Prince George's Community College, Largo, MD (1995-1999) **MIL:** Colonel, Judge Advocate General's Corps, United States Army Reserve (2014); Senior Consultant, Iraqi Ministry of Displacement and Migration, 353rd Civil Affairs Command (2004-2005) **AW:** Distinguished Community Service Award, Prince George's County Educators' Association (PGCEA) (2005); Medal of Civic Honor, National Conference of State Legislatures (2005); Leadership Award, Maryland Justice Coalition (2004); Adoption Visionary Award, Maryland Social Services Administration (2003); Legislative Award, Medical and Chirurgical Faculty of Maryland (Now MedChi, The Maryland State Medical Society) (2003); Army Achievement Medal; Decorated Armed Forces Reserve Medal; Military Outstanding Volunteer Service Medal; Global War on Terrorism Service Medal; National Defense Service Medal; Army Reserve Component Achievement Medal; Army Commendation Medal; Meritorious Service Medal; Bronze Star **MEM:** President, Lake Pointe Homeowners' Association (1996-1998); J. Franklyn Bourne Bar Association, Inc.; Real Property, Planning and Zoning Section, Maryland State Bar Association, Inc. **BAR:** Washington, DC (1994); State of Maryland (1994); State of New York (1993) **PA:** Democrat **RE:** Roman Catholic

BROWN, ANTONIO TAVARIS SR., T: Professional Football Player **I:** Athletics **DOB:** 07/10/1988 **PB:** Miami **SC:** FL/USA **PT:** Adrianne Moss; Eddie Brown **CH:** Five Children **ED:** Coursework, Central Michigan University (2007-2010) **C:** Wide Receiver, New England Patriots (2019); Wide Receiver, Pittsburgh Steelers (2010-2018) **AW:** Pro Bowl (2011, 2013-2018); First-Team All-Pro (2014-2017); Second-Team All-Pro (2013); First-Team All-American (2008, 2009); First-Team All-MAC (2008, 2009); Special Teams Player of the Year, MAC (2008, 2009); Second-Team All-MAC (2007); Freshman Player of the Year, MAC (2007)

BROWN, BETTY JANE, T: Elementary School Educator (Retired) **I:** Education/Educational Services **PB:** Red Bluff **SC:** CA/USA **PT:** Hugh Jerry Moran; Leana Belle (Dobkins) Moran **MS:** Widowed **SPN:** Richard Owen Brown (11/26/1958, Deceased 2013) **CH:** Karen; Gretchen; Heidi (Deceased 2013) **ED:** BA in Education, California State University, Chico (1956) **CT:** Certified Teacher, State of California **C:** Teacher, Richfield Elementary District (1970-2003); Substitute Reading Teacher, Richfield Elementary District, Corning, CA (1968-1970); Reading Teacher, Richfield Elementary District, Corning, CA (1968); Teacher, Gridley Elementary District, California (1956-1961) **CR:** Clinical Supervisor, Western Governors University, Glen County, Town of Willow (2019-Present); Board of Directors, School Site Council, Corning (1990-2000); Secretary Learning Council, Red Bluff (1995-1999); County Language Arts Committee, Red Bluff (1987-1999) **CIV:** President, Tehama County School Board, (2014-Present); Area Director, DKG, Tehama

County School Board (2008-Present); President, Kelly-Griggs House Museum (2002-Present); Volunteer, Shrine Hospital, Sacramento (1998-2000); Home Town Christmas, Corning (1996-2000); Writing Contest Coordinator, Tehama County (1992-2006); Advisory Board, Deputy, Rainbow Girls, Corning (1975-1987) **AW:** Service to the Area of Public Service Award, Delta Lambda Chapter, Beta Lambda Chapter (2019); Literacy Award, Tehama County Reading Council (1995-2001); National Educator Award, Milken Family Foundation (1994); Service to the Chapter Award, Beta Lambda Chapter, Delta Kappa Gamma **MEM:** President, Delta Kappa Gamma, Beta Lamdba Chapter (2004-2006); Legislation Chair, Delta Kappa Gamma, Beta Lambda (2003-2004); Treasurer, Tehama County Shrine Club Wives (1989-2004); California Reading Council, Tehama County (1972-2003); President, Tehama County Shrine Club Wives (2001-2002); President, Tehama County Shrine Club Wives (1996); Two-Time President, Tehama County Reading Council (1991-1993); President, Tehama County Shrine Club Wives (1990); American Association of University Women (1959-1968); Order Eastern Star; Maywood Women's Club **MH:** Albert Nelson Marquis Lifetime Achievement Award; Marquis Who's Who Top Professional **B/I:** Ms. Brown became involved in her profession because she had two aunts; one was a teacher and the other spent her time as a housewife. This aunt mentored her tremendously and really encouraged her to further her education. She was the first woman in her family to finish her education. **AV:** Reading; Biking; Skiing; Traveling; Spending time with family, friends, and cats **PA:** Republican **RE:** Presbyterian

BROWN, CARRIE, T: Editor **I:** Writing and Editing **CN:** Politico LLC **PB:** York **SC:** PA/USA **ED:** BA in Political Science and Government, Rutgers University (1998) **C:** Editor, Politico LLC (2016-Present); Managing Editor, Politico Europe, Politico SPRL, Brussels, Belgium (2014-2016); White House Correspondent, Politico LLC (2009-2014) **AW:** Listee, 50 Most Powerful People In Trump's Washington, GQ, Condé Nast (2019); Listee, Most Powerful Women in Washington, Washingtonian Media Inc. (2019); Merriman Smith Award for Excellence in Presidential News Coverage Under Deadline Pressure, WHCA (2012)

BROWN, DAVID H., T: Author **I:** Other **DOB:** 01/15/1926 **PB:** Cleveland **SC:** OH/USA **PT:** Joseph M. Brown; Rose (Wolchok) Brown **MS:** Married **SPN:** Rose Sanker Brown (07/10/1994); Marilyn Nathan (01/29/1951, Deceased 1990) **CH:** Holly; Mark **ED:** MS in Public Relations, American University (1980); BA in Journalism and Speech, Cleveland College (1950) **C:** Media Columnist, Montgomery Journal (1998-2000); Adjunct Professor, Speech, Montgomery College, Rockville, MD (1991-1998); Public Information Officer, U.S. Government Publishing Office (1974-1991); Public Information Officer, U.S. Department of Transportation (1971-1974); Public Information Officer, Federal Aviation Administration, U.S. Department of Transportation (1969-1971); Assistant Director of Public Information, U.S. Department of Justice (1967-1969); Reporter, Cleveland Press (1950-1951, 1959-1967); State Editor, Columbus Citizen (1956-1959); Reporter, Circleville Herald (1954-1956); Sales Correspondent, Serbin, Incorporated, Miami, FL (1951-1954) **CR:** President, Brown Speak Communications, Rockville, MD (1994-Present); Presenter and Consultant in the Field **CIV:** Member, Advisory Board, Lifelong Learning Society, Florida Atlantic University (2003-2006); Co-Chair, Political Action Community Engagement, Montgomery County Education Association (1999-2001); Board

of Directors, Chairman, Board of Appeals, Montgomery College Foundation, Rockville, MD (1976-1979); Member, Planning Commission, Board of Zoning Appeals, City Councilman, University Heights, OH (1962-1967) **MIL:** Lieutenant Colonel, U.S. Army Reserve (1950-1978, Retired); Private, First Class, U.S. Army (1944-1946) **CW:** Author, "Still Coming of Age into my 90s" (2020); Author, "The Condo Board" (2019); Author, "Harry" (2018); Author, "Air Force One Has Vanished" (2013); Author, "Next in Line to the Oval Office" (2011); Author, "Full-Body Scam" (2011); Author, "Life Is Just a Bowl of Memories" (2010); Author, "Murder at 250 Center Street" (2009); Author, "The Decoration Day War" (2008); Author, "Operation Red Herring" (2007); Author, "Airline Passenger Screening Has Become a Fema-Type Snafu: The Screening System Developed During 1969-70 Holds the Key to Refocusing on Modern Day Terrorism" (2004); Co-Author, "Nine/Eleven: Could The Federal Aviation Administration Alone Have Deterred The Terrorist Skyjackers? You Will Find The Answer Here, But Not In The 9/11 Commission Report" (2004); Columnist, Sun Sentinel (2003-2004); Columnist, Montgomery Journal (1998-1999); Author, "I Would Rather Be Audited By the IRS Than Give a Speech" (1995) **AW:** Community Hero Award, Montgomery County Civic Federation (2002); Dalton Pen Award (1997); Decorated Meritorious Service Medal, Combat Infantry Badge, Bronze Star, U.S. Army Reserve; Excellence Award, NISOD **MEM:** Founding President, National Association of Government Communicators **MH:** Albert Nelson Marquis Lifetime Achievement Award **B/I:** Mr. Brown became involved in his profession after World War II, when he finished his term in the U.S. Army and enrolled at Cleveland College under the GI Bill. A childhood friend of his worked for the college newspaper as an advertiser, and as Brown had always liked to write at his own leisure, he joined the publication as a reporter. The biggest influence on his career was a class he had taken, which was taught by a reporter. It was in that class where Mr. Brown discovered that journalism was the career for him. **THT:** Mr. Brown has always been curious about people both professionally and personally.

BROWN, DOLORES CONNOR, T: Medical Association Administrator **I:** Medicine & Health Care **DOB:** 03/07/1937 **PB:** Cumberland **SC:** MD/USA **PT:** George Conrad Connor; Sara Regina (Sidaway) Connor **MS:** Married **SPN:** Timothy C. Brown Junior (08/02/1958) **CH:** Thomas Charles; Sara Ann; Teresa Lynn **ED:** MBA, University of Southern California (1988); BS, University of Southern California (1983) **C:** Administrative Director, Richland Member Hospital, Columbia, SC (1989-1999); Assistant Chief Technologist, Richland Member Hospital, Columbia, SC (1985-1989); Supervisor Technologist, Richland Memorial Hospital, Columbia, SC (1974-1985); Head Instructor, Atlanta College of Medical Assistants (1973-1974); Medical Technologist, Hendon, Blodgett, Minish, Graves & Ward (1965-1973); Medical Technologist, Kentucky Medical Society (1965); Medical Technologist, Gerald Greenfield, Louisville, KY (1960-1965); Chief Technologist, Hazelwood TB Hospital, Louisville, KY (1958-1959) **CR:** Advisor, Midland Technical College (1987) **CIV:** Volunteer, AARP Women's Group; Volunteer, Local Library **MEM:** American Society of Medical Technology; South Carolina American Society of Medical Technology; ASMT; American Clinical Society **MH:** Albert Nelson Marquis Lifetime Achievement Award **B/I:** Ms. Brown became involved in her profession because she had gotten a scholarship to Ursuline College in Kentucky. After completing her studies, she found a job in which she could comfortably travel with her husband.

BROWN, EDWARD L., T: Cultural Arts Teacher **I:** Education/Educational Services **CN:** Katherine Dunham Center For the Performing Arts **PT:** Rebecca Brown James **MS:** Married **SPN:** Jone Renee **CH:** Katherine Kine; Arama Mara **ED:** Bachelor of Fine Arts in Theater and Dance, Southern Illinois University (1975) **C:** Cultural Arts Teacher, Better Family Life Inc. (2014-Present); Teacher Aide, St. Louis Public School District (2005-2014); Teacher, Performer, Performing Arts Training Center, Southern Illinois University (1975-2005) **CR:** Drummer, Performer, Black Dance USA; Yearly Festival, Better Family Life Inc. **AW:** Award, 40 Years of Community Work with Youth; Humanitarian Fine Arts Award; Community Development Award, New Age Truth of Missouri; Certificate of Appreciation **AS:** Mr. Brown attributes his success to being the best in his field, as well as his propensity for dedication and persistence.

BROWN, ETHAN, T: President, Chief Executive Officer **I:** Food & Restaurant Services **CN:** Beyond Meat **ED:** Master of Business Administration, Columbia Business School; Master's Degree, University of Maryland **C:** President, Chief Executive Officer, Founder, Beyond Meat (2018-Present); President, Chief Executive Officer, Founder, Savage River Inc. (2009-2018) **CR:** Board Member, Beyond Meat (2018-Present); Board Member, Savage River Inc. (2009-2018); Vice Chairperson, National Hydrogen Association **AW:** Beyond Meats Named Company of the Year, People for the Ethical Treatment of Animals (2013)

BROWN, JAMES, "JIM" NATHANIEL, T: Professional Football Player (Retired), Actor **I:** Media & Entertainment **DOB:** 02/17/1936 **PB:** St. Simon's Island **SC:** GA/USA **PT:** Swinton Brown; Theresa Brown **MS:** Married **SPN:** Monique Gunthrop Brown (1997); Sue Jones (1959-1972) **CH:** Kim; Kevin; James Jr.; Aris; Morgan **ED:** BA in Physical Education, Syracuse University (1957) **C:** Special Adviser, Cleveland Browns (2013-Present); Executive Adviser, Cleveland Browns (2008-2010); Running Back, Cleveland Browns (1957-1965) **CR:** Co-Owner, New York Lizards (2012-Present) **CIV:** Founder, Amer-I-Can (1988); Executive Director, Vital Issues (1986); Co-Founder, Negro Industrial and Economic Union (1966) **CW:** Actor, "Draft Day" (2014); Executive Producer, "Frontliners" (2010); Actor, "Dream Street" (2010); Actor, "Sideliners" (2006); Actor, "Animal" (2005); Actor, "Sucker Free City" (2004); Actor, "She Hate Me" (2004); Actor, "Soul Food" (2004); Subject, "Jim Brown: All-American" (2002); Actor, "On the Edge" (2002); Director, "Keeping the Music Alive" (1999); Actor, "New Jersey Turnpikes" (1999); Voice Actor, "Any Given Sunday" (1999); Actor, "Small Soldiers" (1998); Actor, "He Got Game" (1998); Actor, "Mars Attacks!" (1996); Actor, "Original Gangstas" (1996); Actor, "The Divine Enforcer" (1992); Actor, "Hammer, Slammer, & Slade" (1990); Actor, "Twisted Justice" (1990); Co-Author, "Out of Bounds" (1989); Actor, "Crack House" (1989); Actor, "L.A. Heat" (1989); Actor, "Killing American Style" (1988); Actor, "I'm Gonna Git You Sucka" (1988); Actor, "The Running Man" (1987); Actor, "The A-Team" (1986); Actor, "Lady Blue" (1985); Actor, "Cover Up" (1984); Actor, "Knight Rider" (1984); Executive Producer, "Richard Pryor...Here and Now" (1983); Actor, "T.J. Hooker" (1983-1984); Actor, "CHiPs" (1979-1984); Actor, "One Down, Two to Go" (1982); Actor, Executive Producer, "Pacific Inferno" (1979); Actor, "Fingers" (1978); Producer, "The Magnificent Magical Magnet of Santa Mesa" (1977); Actor, "Vengeance" (1977); Actor, "Police Story" (1977); Actor, "Take a Hard Ride" (1975); Actor, "Three the Hard Way" (1974); Actor, "I Escaped from Devil's Island" (1973); Actor, "The Slams" (1973); Actor, "Slaughter's Big Rip-Off" (1973); Actor, "Black Gunn" (1972); Actor, "Slaughter" (1972); Actor, "El Condor" (1970); Actor, "The Grasshopper" (1970); Actor, "...tick...tick..." (1970); Actor, "100 Rifles" (1969); Actor, "Riot" (1969); Actor, "The Split" (1968); Actor, "Ice Station Zebra" (1968); Actor, "Kenner" (1968); Actor, "Dark of the Sun" (1968); Actor, "The Dirty Dozen" (1967); Actor, "I Spy" (1967); Actor, "Rio Conchos" (1964); Co-Author, "Off My Chest" (1964) **AW:** Blanton Collier Award, NFL Players Association (2010); Player of the Century, Sports Illustrated (1999); Inductee, College Football Hall of Fame (1995); Inductee, Lacrosse Hall of Fame (1983); Inductee, Football Hall of Fame (1971); Pro Bowl MVP (1961-1962, 1965); NFL Pro Bowl (1958-1965); NFL MVP Award (1957-1958, 1965); First Team NFL All-Pro (1957-1965); Hickock Belt Professional Athlete of the Year (1964); Bert Bell Memorial Award (1964); Jim Thorpe Trophy (1959); NFL Rookie of the Year Award, The Associated Press (1957)

BROWN, KATHERINE, "KATE", T: Governor of Oregon **I:** Government Administration/Government Relations/Government Services **DOB:** 06/21/1960 **PB:** Torrejon de Ardoz, Madrid **SC:** Spain **MS:** Married **SPN:** Dan Little **CH:** Dylan (Stepchild); Jessie (Stepchild) **ED:** JD in Environmental Law, Northwestern School of Law of Lewis & Clark College (1985); BA in Environmental Conservation, University of Colorado Boulder (1981) **C:** Governor, State of Oregon (2015-Present); Secretary of State, State of Oregon, Salem, OR (2009-2015); Majority Leader, Oregon State Senate (2004-2009); Member, District 21, Oregon State Senate (1997-2009); Member, District 13, Oregon House of Representatives (1991-1997); Attorney, Tennyson, Winemiller & Lavalle (1991-1994) **CR:** Adjunct Professor, Administration Justice, Portland State University (1994) **AW:** Profiles in Courage Award, Basic Rights Oregon (2012); Named One of 24 Rising Stars in American Politics, Rodel Fellowship (2009); President's Award of Merit, Oregon State Bar (2007); National Public & Community Service Award, American Mental Health Counselors Association (2004); Woman of Achievement Award, Oregon Commission for Women (1995); Outstanding Young Oregonian Award, Oregon Jaycees (1993) **MEM:** Multnomah Bar Association; Oregon Trial Lawyers Association (OTLA) **PA:** Democrat

BROWN, KC, T: Executive Chef, Owner **I:** Food & Restaurant Services **CN:** Bistro49 Culinary Laboratory **ED:** Coursework in Culinary Arts, Institute of Technology (2003); Apprenticeship, American Culinary Federation **CT:** Certified Sous Chef, American Culinary Federation **C:** Executive Chef, Owner, Bistro49 Culinary Laboratory, CA (2019-Present); Executive Chef, The National Hotel, CA (2017-2019); Executive Chef, Cactus Creek Prime Steakhouse, NV (2015-2017); Chef, JW Marriot Desert Springs Resort & Spa (2013-2015); Sous Chef, Parker Palm Spring, CA (2011-2013); Line Cook, Embassy Suites (2004-2005); Line Cook, Esquire Grill (2003-2004) **AW:** Chef of the Year, Ledger Dispatch (2019); Best New Business, Ledger Dispatch (2019); Chef of the Year, High Sierra Chefs Association (2017) **MEM:** American Culinary Federation **AS:** Mr. Brown attributes his success to his great mentors and the support of his wife. **B/I:** Mr. Brown became involved in his profession because he was involved in the food industry for many years. After his mother passed away, he became inspired to open his own restaurant.

BROWN, LAWRENCE, "LARRY" HARVEY, T: Professional Basketball Coach (Retired) **I:** Professional Training & Coaching **DOB:** 09/14/1940 **PB:** Brooklyn **SC:** NY/USA **PT:** Milton Brown; Ann Brown **MS:** Married **SPN:** Shelly Brown (1993) **CH:** Madison; Alli; Kristen; L.J. **ED:** Bachelor's Degree, The University of North Carolina at Chapel Hill (1963) **C:** Head Coach, Auxilium Torino (2018); Head Coach, Men's Basketball, Southern Methodist University, Dallas, Texas (2012-2016); Head Coach, Charlotte Bobcats, Charlotte, NC (2008-2010); Executive Vice President, Philadelphia 76ers, NBA, Philadelphia, PA (2007-2008); Head Coach, New York Knicks, NBA, New York, NY (2005-2006); Head Coach, Detroit Pistons, NBA, Detroit, MI (2003-2005); Head Coach, Philadelphia 76ers, NBA, Philadelphia, PA (1997-2003); Head Coach, Indiana Pacers, NBA, Indianapolis, IN (1993-1997); Head Coach, Los Angeles Clippers, NBA, Los Angeles, CA (1992-1993); Head Coach, San Antonio Spurs, NBA, San Antonio, Texas (1988-1992); Head Coach, Men's Basketball, The University of Kansas, Lawrence, KS (1983-1988); Head Coach, New Jersey Nets, NBA, East Rutherford, NJ (1981-1983); Head Coach, Men's Basketball, University of California Los Angeles (1979-1981); Head Coach, Denver Nuggets, NBA, Denver, CO (1974-1979); Head Coach, Carolina Cougars (1972-1974); Point Guard, Denver Rockets. Denver, CO (1971-1972); Point Guard, Virginia Squires (1970-1971); Point Guard, Washington Caps (1969-1970); Point Guard, Oakland Oaks (1968-1969); Point Guard, New Orleans Buccaneers (1967-1968); Assistant Coach, Men's Basketball, The University of North Carolina at Chapel Hill (1965-1967); Point Guard, Akron Goodyear Wingfoots, Akron, Ohio (1963-1965) **CR:** Head Coach, United States Men's National Basketball Team (2004); Assistant Coach, United States Men's National Basketball Team (2000); With, United States Men's National Basketball Team (1964) **AW:** Inductee, National Collegiate Basketball Hall of Fame (2006); Inductee, Naismith Memorial Basketball Hall of Fame (2002); Named Coach of Year, NBA (2001); Named Head Coach, NBA All-star Game (1977, 2001); Named Naismith College Coach of the Year (1988); Named Coach of the Year, American Basketball Association (ABA) (1973, 1975, 1976); Named ABA All-star, American Basketball Association (ABA) (1968-1970); Named All-star Game MVP, American Basketball Association (ABA) (1968)

BROWN, MILLIE BOBBY, T: Actress **I:** Media & Entertainment **DOB:** 02/19/2004 **PB:** Marbella **SC:** Andalusia/Spain **PT:** Robert Brown; Kelly Brown **C:** Model, IMG, Endeavor Operating Company, LLC (2017-Present); Actress, Television and Film **CIV:** Ambassador, Together #WePlayStrong Campaign, UEFA (2019); UNICEF Goodwill Ambassador (2018) **CW:** Actress, "Stranger Things" (2016-Present); Actress, "Godzilla: King of the Monsters" (2019); Appearance, "Happy Anniversary, All I Want for Christmas is You," Mariah Carey (2019); Appearance, "Girls Like You," Maroon 5 Featuring Cardi B (2018); Appearance, "In My Feelings," Drake (2018); Actress, "I Dare You," The xx (2017); Actress, "Find Me," Sigma featuring Birdy (2016); Actress, "Grey's Anatomy" (2015); Actress, "Modern Family" (2015); Actress, "NCIS" (2014); Actress, "Intruders" (2014); Actress, "Once Upon a Time in Wonderland" (2013) **AW:** Choice Summer TV Actress, Teen Choice Award (2019); Favorite TV Actress, Kids' Choice Awards (2018); Best Performance in a Show, MTV Movie & TV Awards (2018); Listee, 100 Most Influential People, Time Magazine (2018); Choice Sci-fi/Fantasy TV Actress, Teen Choice Awards (2018); Outstanding Performance by an Ensemble in a Drama Series, Screen Actors Guild Awards (2017); Best TV Actress, Fangoria Chainsaw Awards (2017); Best Younger Actor in a Television Series, Saturn Awards (2017); Best Actor in a TV Show, MTV Movie & TV Awards (2017);

Breakthrough Performer of the Year, Gold Derby TV Awards (2017); Best Dramatic TV Performance, IGN People's Choice Awards (2017)

BROWN, OMER, T: Lawyer **I:** Law and Legal Services **DOB:** 03/04/1947 **PB:** Somerville **SC:** NJ/USA **PT:** George Alvin Brown; Frances (Schnitzler) Brown **MS:** Married **SPN:** Sandra Cannon-Brown (4/3/1982) **ED:** JD, Cornell University (1972); AB, Rutgers University, the State University of New Jersey (1969) **C:** Partner, Omer F. Brown II Law Office (2008-Present); Partner, Harmon Wilmot Brown LLP, Washington, DC (1997-2008); Partner, Davis Wright Tremaine, Washington, DC (1987-1996); Senior Trial Attorney, U.S. Department of Energy, Washington, DC (1979-1983); Deputy Attorney General, Department of Law and Public Safety, State of New Jersey, Trenton, NJ (1972-1975) **CR:** International Expert Group on Nuclear Liability, International Atomic Energy Agency (2003-Present); G-7 Joint Task Force on Ukrainian Nuclear Legislation (1996-Present); Organization of European Cooperation, Development Contact Group on Nuclear Safety Assistance for Eastern Europe (1994-Present); Board Directors, Secretary VideoTakes, Inc., Washington, DC (1986-Present); Civilian International Nuclear Trade Advisory Communications, U.S. Department of Commerce (2014-2018); Visiting Lecturer, Cornell University Law School (1993-1995, 2002); Nuclear Law Committee, Nuclear Energy Agency, Organisation for Economic Co-operation and Development **MIL:** Captain, U.S. Army Reserve (1969-1975) **CW:** Editorial Board, Atoms for Peace (2004-Present); Editorial Board, International Journal of Nuclear Law (2004-Present); Contributor, Articles, Professional Journals **AW:** Loyal Son of Rutgers Award (1980); Class of 1931 Award, Rutgers University Alumni Association (1979) **MEM:** Various Offices, American Bar Association (1981-1999); Department of Energy Contractor Attorney's Association; University Club of Washington DC **BAR:** U.S. Supreme Court (1976); District of Columbia (1974); New Jersey (1972) **MH:** Albert Nelson Marquis Lifetime Achievement Award **PA:** Democrat **RE:** Roman Catholic

BROWN, PATRICK, "PAT" O'REILLY, T: Founder, Chief Executive Officer; Professor Emeritus **I:** Business Management/Business Services **CN:** Impossible Foods Inc. **DOB:** 09/23/1954 **PB:** Washington **SC:** DC/USA **MS:** Married **SPN:** Sue Klapholz **CH:** Zach; Ariel; Isaac **ED:** Postdoctoral Fellowship, University of California San Francisco (1985-1988); Pediatrics Resident, Children's Memorial Hospital (Now Ann & Robert H. Lurie Children's Hospital of Chicago), Chicago, IL (1982-1985); MD, The University of Chicago Pritzker School of Medicine (1982); PhD, The University of Chicago (1980); BA, The University of Chicago, With Honors (1976) **C:** Founder, Chief Executive Officer, Impossible Foods Inc. (2011-Present); Professor, Biochemistry, Stanford University School of Medicine, CA (2000-2009); Associate Professor, Biochemistry, Stanford University School of Medicine, CA (1995-2000); Assistant Professor, Biochemistry and Pediatrics, Stanford University School of Medicine, CA (1988-1995) **CR:** Board Director, Co-Founder, Public Library of Science (PLOS) (2001-Present); Investigator, Howard Hughes Medical Institute (1988-Present) **CW:** Contributor, Scientific Papers and Articles, Professional Journals **AW:** Technology Pioneer, World Economic Forum (2016); Award, Association of Biomolecular Resource Facilities (2010); Medal of Honor for Basic Research, American Cancer Society, Inc. (2006); Award for Media and Journalism, The World Technology Network (2005); Curt Stern Award, American Society of Human Genetics, Incoporated

(2005); BioTech Helsinki Prize (2003); Takeda Award, The Takeda Foundation (2002); Millennium Pharmaceutical Senior Award for Genomics Research in Clinical Immunology (2001); Award in Molecular Biology, National Academy of Sciences (2000); Listee, America's Best in Science and Medicine, Time Magazine **MEM:** Fellow, The World Technology Network; Fellow, American Association for the Advancement of Science; National Academy of Sciences

BROWN, SHERROD CAMPBELL, T: U.S. Senator from Ohio **I:** Government Administration/Government Relations/Government Services **DOB:** 11/09/1952 **PB:** Mansfield **SC:** OH/USA **PT:** Charles Gailey Brown, MD; Emily (Campbell) Brown **MS:** Married **SPN:** Connie Schultz; Larke Recchie (1979, Divorced 1987) **CH:** Emily; Elizabeth; Caitlin; Andy **ED:** Honorary Doctorate in Public Service, Otterbein University (2014); Honorary Doctorate, Capital University (2007); MPA, The Ohio State University (1981); MEd, The Ohio State University (1979); BA in Russian Studies, Yale University, New Haven, CT (1974) **C:** Ranking Member, Senate Banking Committee (2015-Present); U.S. Senator, State of Ohio, Washington, DC (2007-Present); Vice Chairman, Joint Pensions Committee (2018-2019); Member, U.S. Representative from Ohio's 13th Congressional District, United States Congress, Washington, DC (1993-2007); Secretary of State, State of Ohio, Columbus, Ohio (1983-1991); Member, Ohio House of Representatives, Columbus, Ohio (1975-1982) **CR:** Faculty Associate, Mershon Center, The Ohio State University (1991-1993); Political Science Instructor, The Ohio Sate University (1979-1980) **CIV:** Eagle Scouts (1967) **CW:** Author, "Desk 88: Eight Progressive Senators Who Changed America" (2019); Author, "Myths of Free Trade" (2004); Author, "Congress from the Inside: Observations from the Majority and the Minority" (1999) **AW:** Named Distinguished Public Health Legislator of the Year, American Public Health Association (2002); Friend of Education Award (1978) **MEM:** National Association of Secretaries of State (NASS) **PA:** Democrat **RE:** Lutheran

BROWN, SUSAN ELIZABETH, T: Secondary School Educator **I:** Education/Educational Services **DOB:** 02/25/1940 **PB:** Niagara Falls **SC:** NY/USA **PT:** Harold Marvin Sonnichsen; Thelma A. (Lowenberg) Sonnichsen **MS:** Single **SPN:** Robert Goodell Brown (06/23/1988); Edward J. Hehre Jr. (06/22/1963, Divorced 04/1977) **CH:** Nancy Elizabeth; Edward James III **ED:** MA in Liberal Studies, Dartmouth College, Hanover, New Hampshire, 1986); Coursework, University of Geneva, Switzerland; Coursework, Long Island University (1970-1973); BA, Cornell University, Ithaca, NY (1963) **CT:** Certificate. Professional Educator Level II, State of Vermont; Librarian/Media Specialist Level I, State of Vermont **C:** Latin, French Teacher, Thetford Academy, VT (1988-2003); Telecommunications Coordinator, Thetford Academy, VT (1993-1994); Latin, French, Journalism Teacher, Woodsville High School, NH (1974-1988);French Teacher, Shelter Island High School, NY (1972); Administrative Secretary, New England Board of Higher Education, New England Council of Higher Education for Nurses, Durham, NH (1968); Latin, French Teacher, Pinkerton Academy, Derry, NH (1964-1967) **CR:** Adjunct Professor, English Composition, New Hampshire Community Technical College, Woodsville, NH (2002, 2003); Adjunct Professor, English Composition, New Hampshire Community Technical College, Littleton, NH (2000); Advisor, Committee, The National Latin Exam (NLE) (1999); Member, Advisory Council, New Hampshire Humanities (1999); Adjunct Professor, English Composition, New Hampshire Community

Technical College, Claremont, NH (1998, 1999); Alternative Certified Boards, NH and VT; Member, Teacher, OSHER Institute for Lifelong Education, Continuing Education, Dartmouth College; Broom Squire, Enfield Shaker Museum **CIV:** Volunteer, La Casa, OSHER, Dartmouth College (2004-Present); Town Library Trustee, Haverhill Library Association, NH (2003-2009); Trustee Chair, Haverhill Library Association, NH (1978-1988, 2002-2004); Treasurer, Latham Library, Thetford Libraries, VT (1992-1998); Moderator, Haverhill United Church of Christ (1985) **CW:** Contributor, Articles to Professional Journals **AW:** Matthew I. Wiencke Teaching Award for Excellence for Secondary School Teachers, Classical Association of New England (2000) **MEM:** Executive Board, Classics Association of New England (1981-1987, 1992-1993, 2000-2002, 2008); Treasurer, New Hampshire Classical Association (1977-1987); Honorary Member, New Hampshire Classical Association (1970); President, New Hampshire Classical Association (1966-1968); New Hampshire Classical Association; Classics Association of New England Sigma Tau Delta **MH:** Albert Nelson Marquis Lifetime Achievement Award **B/I:** Ms. Brown became involved in her profession because she liked teaching and she learned a lot from it. She taught English at Claremont Community College and loved the kids and was appreciative of the fact that she also learned from them. **AV:** Singing; Sewing; Reading; Travel; Kayaking ·

BROWN, WILLIAM FERDINAND, T: Artist, Writer **I:** Fine Art **DOB:** 04/16/1928 **PB:** Jersey City **SC:** NJ/USA **PT:** Douglas Brown; Dorothy (Ferrett) Brown **MS:** Married **SPN:** Ann Elizabeth Distler (Divorced 1979); Christina Eller Tippit (10/03/1981) **CH:** Debra Susan; William Todd **ED:** BA in Psychology, Princeton University, Cum Laude (1950) **C:** Freelance Artist; Writer **CR:** Agency TV Producer, Batten, Barton, Durstine, and Osborn (1954-1962); Talent Agent, MCA (1952-1954); Staff Writer, Look Magazine (1950-1951) **CIV:** Trustee, Princeton Tiger (1950-2007) **MIL:** Served to 1st Lt., U.S. Army, Korea (1951-1952) **CW:** Freelance Writer, Artist (1962-Present); Writer, Cabarets, Night Club Acts, Industrial Shows (1962-Present); Author, "The Nutley Papers" (2001); Co-Author, Co-Artist, Comic Strip, Boomer, Syndicated by United Features (1972-1981); Author, "Damon's Song" (1979); Author, "A Broadway Musical" (1978); Author, "The Wiz" (1975); Sketch and Lyric Writer, Julius Monk Revs. (1960-1969); Sketch Writer, "New Faces of 1968" (1968); Author, "How to Steal an Election" (1968); Author, "The Girl in the Freudian Slip" (1967); Writer, "That Was the Week That Was" (1964-1965); Author, Illustrator, "The World is My Yo-Yo" (1963); Writer, "Jackie Gleason Show" (1962); Writer, "Max Liebman Spectaculars" (1960-1961); Author, Illustrator, "The Abominable Snowmen" (1960); Associate Producer, "Silents Please" (1959-1960); Author, Illustrator, "Beat Beat Beat" (1959); Author, Illustrator, "The Girl in the Freudian Slip" (1959); Author, Illustrator, "Tiger, Tiger" (1950); Contributing Writer, "Love, American Style"; Illustrator, Other Books; Contributor, Articles, Fiction and Cartoons, Popular Magazines **AW:** Tony Award, Nomination League New York Theatres and Producers (1975); Drama Desk Award (1975) **MEM:** American Society of Composers; National Cartoonists Society; Writers Guild of America, East; Dramatists Guild of America; Artists and Writers; Theatre Artists Workshop (Connecticut); Phi Beta Kappa **MH:** Albert Nelson Marquis Lifetime Achievement Award; Marquis Who's Who Top Professional **B/I:** Mr. Brown became involved in his profession because when he was in prep school he started drawing and eventually got to the point where he started thinking that he could sell his work. He sent one of them to

King Features, which published it and paid him 25 dollars. They bought some more and so he started sending his drawing to other magazines. The Julius Monk show was where he began writing as he would write for the theater. He saw what they did there and liked it, submitted his writing, and Mr. Monk bought it. **AV:** Playing golf; Playing tennis; Coin collecting/numismatics **PA:** Republican **THT:** William Ferdinand Brown, born April 16, 1928 in Jersey City, New Jersey, was an American playwright best known for writing the book of the musical "The Wiz" in 1974, an adaptation of L. Frank Baum's "The Wonderful Wizard of Oz" with music and lyrics by Charlie Smalls, for which he received a nomination for the Tony Award for Best Book of a Musical."

BROWNLEY, JULIA ANDREWS, T: U.S. Representative from California **I:** Government Administration/ Government Relations/Government Services **CN:** U.S. House of Representatives **DOB:** 08/28/1952 **PB:** Aiken **SC:** SC/USA **MS:** Divorced **CH:** Hannah; Fred **ED:** Master of Business Administration, American University (1979); Bachelor of Arts in Political Science, The George Washington University (1975) **C:** Member, U.S. Representative from California's 26th Congressional District, United States Congress, Washington, DC (2013-Present); Member, U.S. House Committee of Veterans' Affairs (2013-Present); Member, U.S. House Committee on Science, Space and Technology (2013-Present); Member, District 41, California State Assembly (2006-2012); Member, Santa Monica-Malibu Unified School Board (1994-2006) **AW:** Named, YWCA Woman of the Year (2005) **PA:** Democrat **RE:** Episcopalian

BRUSCH, JOHN, T: Physician **I:** Medicine & Health Care **CN:** Cambridge Health Alliance **DOB:** 11/03/1943 **PB:** Boston **SC:** MA/USA **PT:** Charles Brusch; Margaret Agnes (Lynch) Brusch **C:** Senior Consultant, Youville Hospital (2007-Present);Attending Physician, Division of Infectious Diseases, Cambridge Health Alliance, Cambridge, MA (1976-Present); Medical Director, Somerville Hospital (2001-2015); Chief of Medicine, Somerville Hospital (1999-2009); Clinical Associate in Medicine, Massachusetts General Hospital, Boston, MA (1996-2009); Director of Community Medicine, Youville Hospital (1995-2007); Chief of Medicine, Youville Hospital, Cambridge, MA (1991-2007); Assistant Chief of Medicine, Brighton Public Health Service Hospital, Boston, MA (1974-1976); Resident in Infectious Disease, New England Medical Center, Boston, MA (1971-1974); Resident in Medicine, New England Medical Center, Boston, MA (1970-1971); Intern, New England Medical Center, Boston, MA (1969-1970) **CR:** Staff, Community Health Advisory Council, Cambridge Health Alliance (2012-Present); Cambridge Bio-Safety Committee, Cambridge Health Alliance (2011-Present); Board of Directors, North Cambridge Coop Bank; Assistant Professor, Medicine, Harvard Medical School (2001-Present); Associate Chief of Medicine, Cambridge Health Alliance (1999-Present); Director, Primary Care Unit, Cambridge Hospital (2015); Senior Consultant, Spaulding Hospital (2011); Director, Hospital Board, Cambridge Health Alliance (2003-2012); Chief Editor, Infectious Disease Section, Medscape Medical **CIV:** Board of Directors, Council on Aging (2000-2009) **CW:** Chief Editor, "Infectious Disease" (2014); Managing Editor, "Emedicine Medscape" (2001-2014); Editor, "Endocarditis Essentials" (2011); Co-Author, Editor, "Infective Endocarditis: Management in the Era of Intravascular Devices" (2007); Co-Author, "Infective Endocarditis" (1996); Contributor, Articles, Professional Journals **MEM:** Fellow, American College of Physicians; Knight Commander Equestrian Order of Holy Sepulchre;

Infectious Disease Society of America; American Society of Microbiology **AS:** Dr. Brusch attributes his success to all of the people who have been a teacher to him throughout his career. He specifically credits Dr. Louis Weinstein, the chief of infectious diseases at Tufts University, as his mentor. **RE:** Roman Catholic

BRUSCH, JOHN, T: Medical Director **I:** Medicine & Health Care **CN:** Cambridge Health Alliance **ED:** MD, Tufts University School of Medicine, MA (1969); BS in Biochemistry, Medicine, Tufts Medical School, MA (1969) **C:** Regional Medical Director, Cambridge Health Alliance (2015-Present); Chief Editor, Infectious Disease Section, Medscape (2014-Present); Specialty Editor, Medscape (2000-Present); Medical Director, Somerville Hospital, Cambridge Health Alliance (1996-Present); Associate Chief of Medicine, Cambridge Health Alliance (1976-Present) **CR:** Member, Cambridge Bio-safety Committee, Cambridge, MA (2011-Present); President, John L. Brusch, MD, PC (1976-Present); Assistant Chief of Medicine, USPHS Hospital, Brighton, MA (1974-1976) **MEM:** Infectious Disease Society of America (IDSA) **AS:** Dr. Brusch attributes his success to his parents. **B/I:** Dr. Brusch's father was a doctor, so growing up it was expected of him to do the same. Luckily for him, it worked out that way. **THT:** Dr. Brusch's motto is, "To whom much is given, much is expected..."

BRUTGER, JAMES H., T: Art Educator **I:** Education/Educational Services **CN:** University of Minnesota **DOB:** 10/23/1932 **PB:** Minneapolis **SC:** MN/USA **PT:** Phil Brutger; Madaline Berg **MS:** Married **SPN:** Marjorie Ann (Theisen) **CH:** Stephen; Mary; Diane; Brian; Joseph; Ray; Peggy **ED:** Certificate, Zhejiang Academy Fine Arts, China (1990); Master of Arts, University of Minnesota (1960); Bachelor of Arts, St. John's University (1954); Postgraduate, University of Minnesota **CT:** Teacher, State of Minnesota (1956-1967) **C:** Director, Study in England Program, University of Minnesota, Duluth, MN (1994-1995); Associate Professor, University of Minnesota, Duluth, MN (1984-1998); Head, Art Department, University of Minnesota, Duluth, MN (1974-1984); Instructor of Art Education, University of Minnesota, Duluth, MN (1967-1974); Instructor of Oil Painting, St. Paul Adult Education Programs (1959-1967); Teacher of Art, St. Paul Public Schools (1956-1967); Teacher of Art and History, St. John's Preparatory School, Collegeville, MN (1953-1954) **CR:** Faculty Member, University of Birmingham, England (1987-1988, 1990-1991, 1994-1995); Group Leader, Travel Agency, China (1992); Trip Supervisor, University Students to China (1990, 1991) **CIV:** Vice President, Duluth Art Institute (1990-1992); Board of Directors, Duluth Art Institute (1988-1992); Board of Directors, Chisholm Museum, Duluth, MN (1978-1983); Planning Committee, Chisholm Museum, Duluth, MN (1982) **MIL:** U.S. Army (1954-1956) **CW:** Photographer, Sights and Sounds of China (1992); Photographer, Editor of Videotapes, Fu Hsing Kang College, China (1991); Artist, Paintings in Oil and Acrylic, Water Color Wood Block Prints **AW:** Faculty Member, 11th Year of Study in England Program, University of Birmingham, Barber Institutes of the Fine Arts (1990-1991); Horace T. Morse Bronze Sculpture for Outstanding Contributions for to Undergraduate Education, AMOCO Foundation (1982); Art Educators Minnesota Award (1981); National Art Education Award for Contributions to Art Education, National Art Education Association Conference, Atlanta, GA (1980); Leadership Award from the States Assembly of the National Art education Association (1979); Nominated and Installed in the Duluth Chapter of Phi Delta Kappa, Duluth, MN (1978); Listed in Outstanding Educators of

America (1975); Horace T. Morse Award, AMOCO Foundation (1974); National Art Education Western Regional Award (1970); Army of Occupation Medal, Germany, U.S. Army; Good Conduct Medal, U.S. Army **MEM:** National Art Education Association; American Association of Colleges for Teacher Education; University Education Association; Art Educators of Minnesota; Phi Delta Kappa; Duluth Art Institute; Tweed Museum **AS:** Mr. Brutger attributes his success to his propensity for voicing his thoughts wherever he went, which led to him being elected to positions of high authority. **B/I:** Mr. Brutger became involved in his profession due to the influence of his family, which was deeply involved in the arts. Likewise, he enjoyed the mentorship of several teachers, who encouraged him as well. **AV:** Computer art; Reading; Fishing; Travel; Woodworking; Photography **RE:** Roman Catholic

BRYANT, DEWEY, "PHIL" PHILLIP, T: Governor of Mississippi **I:** Government Administration/Government Relations/Government Services **DOB:** 12/09/1954 **PB:** Moorhead **SC:** MS/USA **PT:** Dewey C. Bryant; Estelle R. Bryant **MS:** Married **SPN:** Deborah Hays **CH:** Katie; Patrick **ED:** Master of Science in Political Science, Mississippi College, Clinton, MA (1988); Bachelor of Science in Criminal Justice, University of Southern Mississippi, Hattiesburg, MS (1977); Associate of Arts, Hinds Community College, Raymond, MS **C:** Governor, State of Mississippi, Jackson, MS (2012-Present); President, Mississippi State Senate, Jackson, MS (2007-2012); Lieutenant Governor, State of Mississippi, Jackson, MS (2008-2012); Auditor, State of Mississippi, Jackson, MS (1996-2008); Member, Mississippi House of Representatives, Jackson, MS (1991-1996); Insurance Fraud Investigator (1981-1991); Deputy Sheriff, Hinds County, MS (1976-1981) **CR:** Part-time Faculty, Mississippi College (2008-Present) **CIV:** Member, Law Enforcement & Fire Fighter Relief Fund; Member, Governor's Commission on Recovery, Rebuilding and Renewal; Active Member, Mission Mississippi; Active Member, The MENTOR Network, MS; Active Member, Habitat for Humanity; Active Member, St. Mark's United Methodist Church **CW:** Contributing Author, "21st Century Government: Digital Promise, Digital Reality"; Contributing Author, "Leadership Secrets of Government Financial Officials"; Contributing Author, "Best Case Practices" **AW:** Kirk Fordice Freedom Award, National Rifle Association of America, Central MS (2005); Named, Statesman of the Year, American Family Radio (2004); Crime Victims Advocate of the Year Award (2003); Mississippian of the Year Award, Association of Information Technology Professionals (2003); Inductee, Southern Miss Alumni Association Hall of Fame (1999); Henry Toll Fellow (1998); Distinguished Alumnus Award, Department of History & Political Science, Mississippi College (1997); In the Arena Award, Center for Digital Government **MEM:** National Rifle Association of America; Past President, Mississippi Republican Elected Officials Association; President, Greater Jackson Law Enforcement Officers Association; Mississippi Republican Elected Officials Association; National Associations of State Auditors, Comptrollers and Treasurers; Chairperson, Bylaws Committee, National Associations of State Auditors, Comptrollers and Treasurers; Executive Committee, National Associations of State Auditors, Comptrollers and Treasurers; Mississippi Fire Investigators Association; International Association of Arson Investigators; Leadership 2000; Ducks Unlimited; Greater Jackson Law Enforcement Officers Association; Jaycees; Lions Club Reservoir **PA:** Republican **RE:** Methodist

BRYANT, WILLIAM LLOYD, T: Retired Air Force Officer, Classical Music Recording Engineer, Radio Broadcaster **I:** Media & Entertainment **CN:** Lloyd Bryant Productions **DOB:** 01/07/1941 **PB:** Dalton **SC:** GA/USA **PT:** James C. Bryant; Lucy H. Bryant **MS:** Married **SPN:** (Carol) Ann Bryant **CH:** Kathryn; Timothy; Kristin; Selena; Kerry Beth;Christopher (Grandchild); Jeffrey (Grandchild); Kathleen (Grandchild); Kimberly (Grandchild); Lacy (Grandchild); Joel (Grandchild); Sarah (Grandchild); Connor (Grandchild); Joseph (Grandchild); William (Grandchild); Caitlyn (Grandchild); James (Grandchild); Sarah (Grandchild); Casey (Grandchild); Kendall (Grandchild); Julia (Great-Grandchild); Evelyn (Great-Grandchild); Margot (Great-Grandchild) **ED:** MS in Electrical Engineering, Georgia Institute of Technology (1975); BS in Electrical Engineering, Georgia Institute of Technology (1975); Distinguished Graduate, U.S. Air Force Officer and Navigator Flight School (1964); Coursework in Liberal Arts, LaGrange College (1959-1960); Coursework in Liberal Arts, University of Georgia (1960-1962) **C:** Radio Broadcaster, Audio Recording Engineer (1955-Present); United States Air Force Officer (1963-1985) **CIV:** Judges Committee, Advisory Committee, Dayton Area Walk of Fame; Board of Directors, Kettering Children's Choir; Founding Board of Directors, Dayton Public Radio **MIL:** United States Air Force (1963-1985) **CW:** Recorder, Editor, Narrator, Over 100 Concerts, Operas, Numerous Radio Programs; Narrator, Master of Ceremonies, Over 100 Live Military Events; Voice, Dayton Philharmonic Orchestra; Voice, Dayton Opera; Voice, Society of Dayton; Voice, The Bach **AW:** Electrical Engineering Academic Honorary, Eta Kappa Nu, Georgia Institute of Technology; Recipient, Numerous Awards, United States Air Force; Top Gun Award, DaNang Air Base; Person of the Year, Dayton Women's Club **MEM:** The Engineers Club, Dayton, OH **AS:** Mr. Bryant attributes his success to good genes and his parents' influence. He was fortunate to have the love and guidance of great, caring people. He additionally was influenced by several Godsent people who he encountered in every stage of his life. **B/I:** At 14, Mr. Bryant started working on the radio. Throughout his life, this passion has endured. However, he was additionally always passionate about airplanes and aviation. This led to his interests in military service, which eventually motivated him to enlist. During his time with the United States Air Force, Mr. Bryant flew B-52 bombers and F-4 Phantom fighters. He feels lucky to have had such experiences in his life. **PA:** Conservative **RE:** Protestant

BRYANT, YVONNE, T: Educator (Retired) **I:** Education/Educational Services **CN:** Douglas County Schools **PT:** Sanford N. Holliway; Thelma M. Holliway **MS:** Married **SPN:** Dr. Gregory Alexander Bryant **ED:** Master of Education in Urban Teacher Leadership, Georgia State University (2003); Bachelor of Science in Education, University of West Georgia College (1973); Postgraduate Coursework, Georgia State University **CT:** Certified in Teaching K-8 **C:** Teacher, Douglas County Schools (1989-2014); Administrative Assistant, IBM; Teacher, Atlanta Public School System **CR:** Owner, Vonde's Wraps LLC **CIV:** Mentor, Adults in Continuing Education **AW:** Esther Award; Named, First Lady, A Place of Destiny Inc., The More Than Concourse Fellowship International Inc.; Women of Worth Award, Deborah's Daughters **MEM:** Former Member, Georgia Association of Educators **AS:** Ms. Bryant attributes her success to her Christian faith. Moreover, her husband was very supportive while she continued her education. After they married, he encouraged her to get a master's degree. Ms. Bryant had some of the greatest supporters. She

feels she would have never made it without them and appreciates them very much. **B/I:** Ms. Bryant entered her profession because her mother and father were both educators in their own right, and she drew inspiration from them in following her own career path.

BUBLÉ, MICHAEL STEVEN, T: Singer; Songwriter; Record Producer; Actor **I:** Media & Entertainment **DOB:** 09/09/1975 **PB:** Burnably **SC:** Canada **PT:** Lewis Bublé; Amber (Santaga) Bublé **MS:** Married **SPN:** Luisana Loreley Lopilato de la Torre (04/07/2011) **CH:** Vida; Elias; Noah **C:** Co-owner, Vancouver Giants (WHL) (2008-Present); Signed to 143 Records (Reprise) (2001) **CW:** Singer, "Love" (2018); Appearance, "Tour Stop 148" (2016); Singer, "Nobody But Me" (2016); Appearance, "Michael Bublé's Day Off" (2013); Singer, "To Be Loved" (2013); Singer, "Christmas" (2011); Author, "Onstage, Offstage" (2011); Singer, "Hollywood" (2010); Appearance, Singer, "Michael Bublé Meets Madison Square Garden" (2009); Singer, "Crazy Love" (2009); Singer, "Call Me Irresponsible" (2007); Singer, "It's Time" (2005); Appearance, "Michael Bublé: Caught in the Act" (2005); Singer, "Caught in the Act" (2005); Singer, "Spider-Man 2 Original Motion Picture Soundtrack" (2004); Appearance, Singer, CD/DVD, "Come Fly with Me" (2004); Appearance, "Las Vegas (Catch of the Day)" (2004); Singer, Producer, "Michael Bublé" (2003); Singer, "Down with Love Soundtrack" (2003); Singer, "Let It Snow" (2003); Appearance, "The Snow Walker" (2003); Singer, "Dream" (2002); Appearance, "Totally Blonde" (2001); Singer, "BaBalu" (2001); Appearance, "Duets" (2000) **AW:** Juno Award, Adult Contemporary Award (2018, 2019); Juno Award, Fan Choice Award (2007, 2010, 2015); Grammy Award for Best Traditional Pop Vocal Album, The Recording Academy (2014); Juno Award, Album of the Year (2004, 2006, 2009, 2012); Grammy Award for Best Traditional Pop Vocal Album, The Recording Academy (2011); Named Favorite Adult Contemporary Artist, American Music Awards (2010); Grammy Award for Best Traditional Pop Vocal Album, The Recording Academy (2010); Juno Award, Single of the Year (2006, 2009); Juno Award, Pop Album of the Year (2006, 2009); Grammy Award for Best Traditional Pop Vocal Album, The Recording Academy (2008); Juno Award, Artist of the Year (2006); World Music Award, World's Best Selling Artist (Canada) (2005); Juno Award, Breakthrough Artist of the Year (2004)

BUCHANAN, LOUISE, T: Political Organization Worker, Consultant **I:** Government Administration/Government Relations/Government Services **PT:** James Ellis Buchanan; May (Hall) Buchanan **MS:** Single **ED:** MA, Carver School of Missions and Social Work (1960); BA, Blue Mountain College (1958) **C:** Executive Board President, Life Pieces to Masterpieces, Washington, DC (1997-Present); Consultant, Child Advocacy, Washington, DC (1993-Present); Member, Advisory Board, Efforts from Ex-Convicts, Inc., Washington, DC (1978-1996); Executive Assistant to Republican Joe Early, US House of Representatives, Washington, DC (1976-1993); Executive Assistant to Republican Jack Kemp, US House of Representatives, Washington, DC (1974-1976); Supervisor, Community Resources, Kentucky Department of Child Welfare, Louisville and Frankfort, KY (1971-1974); Neighborhood Coordinator, Community Action Commission, Louisville, KY (1966-1971); Community Organizer, Inner City Methodist Council, Louisville, KY (1965-1966); Executive Director, Baptist Goodwill Center, Charleston, SC (1960-1965) **CR:** Task Force: Arlington (VA) County Democrats (2008-2019); Volunteer Leader: American Youth Chorus (2009-2019); Hillary Clinton for President (2015); Cam-

paign Teams, Obama for President, (2008, 2011); Campaign Chairperson, Berta Seitz for Congress (1994); Team Member, Health Care Reform (1993) **CIV:** Common Cause (1989-Present); Member, Vice President, Park Spring Board, Park Spring Condo Association (1999-2019); Arlingtonians for a Better County (1997); Organizer, Capitol Hill Staffers for Hungry and Homeless, Washington, DC (1976-1993); Trainer, Benefit Walks, For Love of Children, Washington, DC (1988); Founding Member, Advisory Board, Congressional Chorus, Washington, DC (1989); Coordinator, Capitol Hill Women's Political Caucus, Washington, DC (1976-1983) **CW:** Article: Lessons Our Children Teach Us **AW:** Exceptional Philanthropist Award (2005); Leadership Award, Life Pieces to Masterpieces (2002); Outstanding Service Award, Efforts from Ex-Convicts (1992); Recipient, Keys to City of Worcester, Worcester City Council, MA (1986, 1988); Certificate of Appreciation, Hillary Clinton **MEM:** Kennedy Center (2009-2019); Steering Committee, Interfaith Alliance (2000); Love Tennis Benefit to End World Hunger (1999); Southern Poverty Law Center (SPLC); NAACP; Interfaith Alliance **MH:** Albert Nelson Marquis Lifetime Achievement Award **AV:** Music; Writing; Travel; Tennis; Being a loyal friend; Civil rights; Human rights; Voting rights; Justice for children; Low income housing units to rent **RE:** Presbyterian: Elder; Baptist Deacon

BUCHANAN, VERN GALE, T: U.S. Representative from Florida **I:** Government Administration/Government Relations/Government Services **DOB:** 05/08/1951 **PB:** Detroit **SC:** MI/USA **MS:** Married **SPN:** Sandy Buchanan **CH:** James; Matt **ED:** MBA, University of Detroit Mercy (1986); BBA, Cleary University, MI (1975) **C:** U.S. Representative from Florida's 16th Congressional District, United States Congress (2013-Present); Member, Ways and Means Committee (2013-Present); Chairman, Buchanan Enterprises, Inc. (1994-Present); U.S. Representative from Florida's 13th Congressional District, United States Congress, Washington, DC (2007-2013); Owner, Car Dealerships (1992-2005); Founder, Chairman, American Speedy Printing (1976-1991); Owner/Co-owner, Reinsurance Companies **CR:** State Finance Chair, Mel Martinez's Election Campaign (2004) **CIV:** Active Member, Community Foundation of Sarasota County; Active Member, Boys & Girls Clubs of America **MIL:** With, Michigan Air National Guard (1969-1975) **MEM:** Executive Committee, Board of Directors, United States Chamber of Commerce; Past Chairman, Greater Sarasota Chamber of Commerce; Chairman, Board of Directors, Florida Chamber of Commerce **PA:** Republican **RE:** Baptist

BUCK, KENNETH, "KEN" ROBERT, T: U.S. Representative **I:** Government Administration/Government Relations/Government Services **DOB:** 02/16/1959 **PB:** Ossining **SC:** NY/USA **MS:** Divorced **SPN:** Perry Lynn Buck (1996, Divorced 2018); Dayna Roane (1984, Divorced 1994) **CH:** Kaitlin; Cody James **ED:** JD, College of Law, University of Wyoming (1985); BA, Princeton University (1980) **C:** U.S. Representative, Colorado's Fourth Congressional District, United States Congress (2014-Present); District Attorney, Weld County, CO (2005-Present); Construction Executive, Hensel Phelps, Greeley, CO (2002-2005); Prosecutor, United States Attorney's Office (1990-2002); Trial Attorney, The U.S. Department of Justice (1987-1990); Staff Attorney, Iran-Contra Investigation (1986-1987) **CR:** Instructor, Sturm College of Law, University of Denver; Instructor, National Institute for Trial Advocacy **CW:** Author, "Drain the Swamp: How Washington Corruption is Worse Than You Think" (2017) **PA:** Republican

BUCSHON, LARRY DEAN, MD, T: U.S. Representative, Surgeon **I:** Government Administration/Government Relations/Government Services **DOB:** 05/31/1962 **PB:** Taylorville **SC:** IL/USA **PT:** Ronald Bucshon; Barbara Bucshon **MS:** Married **SPN:** Kathryn Bucshon **CH:** Luke; Alexander; Blair; Zoe **ED:** MD, University of Illinois College of Medicine, Chicago, IL (1988); Bachelor's Degree, University of Illinois at Urbana-Champaign (1984); Residency, Milwaukee VA Medical Center; Fellowship in Cardiothoracic Surgery, Medical College of Wisconsin; Chief Residency in Surgery, Medical College of Wisconsin **CT:** Certified in Cardiothoracic Surgery, American Board of Thoracic Surgery **C:** Committee on Transportation and the Workforce, U.S. House of Representatives, Washington, DC (2011-Present); Member, Committee on Energy and Commerce (2011-Present); Member, Republican Study Committee (2011-Present); Member, Committee on Education and the Workforce, U.S. House of Representatives, Washington, DC (2011-Present); U.S. Representative, Indiana's Eighth Congressional District, United States Congress, Washington, DC (2011-Present); Cardiothoracic Surgeon, President, Ohio Valley Heart Care, Evansville, IN (1998-2010); Surgeon, Private Medical Practice, Wichita, KS (1995-1998); Chief of Cardiothoracic Surgery, St. Mary's Hospital, Evansville, IN; Medical Director, Open Heart Recovery Intensive Care Unit, St. Mary's Hospital, Evansville, IN **CIV:** Coach, Youth Hockey; Our Redeemer Lutheran Church, Evansville, IN **MIL:** Lieutenant Commander, Medical Corps, U.S. Navy Reserve (1994-1998); Lieutenant, Medical Corps, U.S. Navy Reserve (1989-1994) **AW:** Physician of the Year, St. Mary's Medical Staff (2007) **PA:** Republican **RE:** Lutheran

BUCY, ERWIN, T: Principal **I:** Real Estate **CN:** Paragon Commercial Group **PT:** Richard Snowden Bucy **MS:** Married **CH:** 2 Children **ED:** MBA, Finance, Loyola Marymount University, College of Business Administration (1994); BS, Finance, University of Southern California, Marshall School of Business (1989) **C:** Principal, Paragon Commercial Group (2010-Present); Senior Vice President, Investments, Regency Centers (1998-2010) **CIV:** Lights of Literacy; Loyola Marymount University Real Estate Advisory Committee; Deans Council, Loyola Marymount University **AW:** Martin E. Stein Senior Award, Regency Centers **MEM:** International Council of Shopping Centers **AS:** Mr. Bucy attributes his success to his tenacity, stubbornness and the desire to succeed. **B/I:** Mr. Bucy became interested in retail shopping centers because that industry is in a constant state of change. There are always unique opportunities to provide social spaces for the retailer that generate revenue and assist in developing a great community as well. **THT:** Mr. Bucy believes in the idea, "Straight at the gate, narrow is the way that leads to righteousness."

BUDANO, VINNY, T: General Manager **I:** Engineering **CN:** Scott Shafiroff Race Engines **CH:** Five Children **ED:** High School Diploma **C:** General Manager, Scott Shafiroff Race Engines (2002-Present); Owner, Car Palace Automotive (1986-2002) **CIV:** Korean Days/Nights **MEM:** National Hot Rod Association; The Official Northeast Outlaw Pro Mod Association **AS:** Mr. Budano attributes his success to the people he works with, and his family. It has been a labor of love and friendship. **B/I:** Mr. Budano's passion for mechanical things started when he was child and he saw his father open the hood of his car. He remembers looking inside the hood and would study and was amazed by the car. He built a go cart from a lawn mower at age 14. **THT:** Treat people the right way, and don't pretend to be something you're not.

BUDD, PATRICIA, "PAT" J., PHD, T: Psychologist **I:** Medicine & Health Care **CN:** Patricia J. Budd, PhD **DOB:** 05/06/1947 **PB:** Phillipsburg **SC:** NJ/USA **PT:** Joseph Lewis Budd; Josephine (Lesko) Budd **ED:** PhD, Lehigh University (1991); MEd, Lehigh University (1974); BS, Bloomsburg University (1969) **CT:** Licensed Psychologist, Pennsylvania **C:** Psychologist, Private Practice, Patricia J. Budd, PhD, (2000-Present); Secondary School Counselor, Whitehall High School (1974-2004); Secondary English Teacher, Phillipsburg High School (1969-1973) **CR:** Part-time Instructor, Carbon-Lehigh Intermediate Unit (1989-2000); Psychotherapist Alliance for Creative Development, Allentown, PA (1987-2000); Adjunct Assistant Professor, Department of Counseling Psychology, Lehigh University (1994-1998); Colonial-Northampton Intermediate Unit (1990-1998); Schuylkill Intermediate Unit (1997-1998); Pennsylvania Student Assistance Professionals Convention (1994, 1996, 1998); Kutztown University Art Conference (1997); Workshop Presenter, Kutztown University (1997); Pennsylvania State Counselors Convention, Hershey, PA (1986, 1994); American Counseling Association (1993); Allied Health Staff, Department of Psychiatry, Quakertown Community Hospital (1987-1991); Pennsylvania State Association of Student Councils, Allentown, PA (1986, 1988); National Education Association, Northeast Regional Leadership Conference, Portland, ME (1988) **CIV:** Family Violence Task Force, Pennsylvania Attorney General (1998-1999); Guest Speaker, Whitehall Exchange Club (1995, 1986); Advisory Board, Northampton County Children, Youth and Families Division (1996-1999) **CW:** Collaborator, Production of a CD to Benefit the 1-800 National Suicide Hotline, "Who's Better Than You?" **AW:** William W. Purkey Professional Development Award (1992); Gratitude Award, Northampton County Children and Youth Family Division (1992); National Distinguished Service Registry, Counseling and Development (1990); President, Chi Sigma Iota, Lehigh University (1988-1990) **MEM:** Lehigh University College of Education Alumni Council (1994-1999); Executive Board, (1997-1999); President, Alpha Tau Chapter, Chi Sigma Iota (1988-1990); American Counseling Association; National Education Association; American Psychological Association; Pennsylvania School Counselors Association; Pennsylvania Association of Student Assistance Professionals; Phi Delta Kappa **MH:** Albert Nelson Marquis Lifetime Achievement Award; Who's Who Among America's Teachers; Who's Who in America; Who's Who in American Women; Who's Who in the East **AS:** Dr. Budd attributes her success to a desire to make a meaningful difference in the lives of others. **B/I:** Dr. Budd became involved in her profession while she was a high school English teacher. Dr. Budd was inspired by a student with serious mental health problems and she decided to become a counselor so that she could help students like this boy. **AV:** Photography; Writing; Music; Reading; Theater; Travel **THT:** Think positive

BUDD, THEODORE, "TED" PAUL, T: U.S. Representative from North Carolina **I:** Government Administration/Government Relations/Government Services **CN:** U.S. House of Representatives **DOB:** 10/21/1971 **PB:** Winston-Salem **SC:** NC/USA **MS:** Married **SPN:** Amy Kate Budd **CH:** Three Children **ED:** Bachelor of Science in Business, Appalachian State University (1994); Master of Business Administration, Wake Forest University School of Business; Master of Arts, Dallas Theological Seminary **C:** U.S. Representative from North Carolina's 13th Congressional District, United States Congress (2017-Present); Member, Committee on Financial Services **CR:** Owner, Gun Store, Rural Hall, NC **PA:** Republican

BUETTNER, RUSS, T: Investigative Reporter **I:** Writing and Editing **CN:** The New York Times Company **ED:** Coursework, University of Missouri School of Journalism; Diploma, California State University **C:** Investigative Reporter, The New York Times Company (2006-Present); Member, Investigation Teams, New York Daily News; Member, Investigation Teams, Newsday **AW:** Co-Recipient, Pulitzer Prize (2019); Polk Award (2019); Scripps Howard Award for Investigative Reporting (2018)

BUFE, NOEL C., PHD, T: Program Director **I:** Education/Educational Services **CN:** Northwestern University **DOB:** 12/25/1933 **PB:** Wyandotte **SC:** MI/USA **PT:** Carl Frederick Bufe; Alcha D. (Brumfield) Bufe **MS:** Married **SPN:** Mary (10/2001); Nancy Carolyn Sinclair (03/23/1957) **CH:** Kevin; Lynn; Bruce; Carol **ED:** Doctor of Philosophy, Michigan State University (1974); Master of Science in Criminal Justice, Michigan State University (1971); Bachelor of Science, Michigan State University (1956) **C:** Howard L. Willett Jr. Professor, The Traffic Institute, Northwestern University (1998-2001); Director, The Traffic Institute, Northwestern University (1978-2000); Administrator, Office of Criminal Justice Program, Michigan Department of Management and Budget (1975-1978); Deputy Administrator, National Highway Traffic Safety Administration, United States Department of Transportation (1974-1975); Executive Director, Office of Highway Safety Planning, Michigan Governors' Highway Safety Representative (1967-1974); Executive Secretary, Michigan Law Enforcement Officers Training Council, Lansing, MI (1966-1967); Management Consultant, International Association of Chiefs of Police, Highway Safety Division, Washington, DC (1964-1966); Procedures Analyst, Board of Police Commissioners, Metropolitan Police Department, St. Louis, MO (1963-1964); Research Assistant, Board of Police Commissioners, Metropolitan Police Department, St. Louis, MO (1962-1963); Research Investigator, Wayne State University, Detroit, MI (1962-1963); Office Manager, J.L. Hudson Company, Detroit, MI (1960-1962); Security Investigator, J.L. Hudson Company (1960); Executive Trainee, Security Investigation, J.L. Hudson Company (1956-1957) **CR:** Past Chairperson, Board of Directors, National Safety Council (1998-2002); Chairperson-Elect, Board of Directors, National Safety Council (1996-1998); Member, Center for Disease Control (CDC), U.S. Department of Human Services (1997-2001); Board Member, Project Safety Illinois Inc. (1994-2000); Vice President, Traffic Safety, National Safety Council (1987-1998); Chairperson, Board of Directors, Finance Committee (1995-1996); Board Member, Illinois Governor's Council on Workplace Safety and Health (1994-1996); Board Member, Illinois Secretary of State's License Plate Task Force (1994-1996); Board Member, Committee for a Strategic Transportation Research Study, Highway Safety, National Research Council (1989-1991); Chairperson, Vice-Chairperson, Injury Research Grant Review Committee, Center for Disease Control (1986-1991); Chairperson, Traffic Division, National Safety Council (1984-1987) **CIV:** Chairperson, Board of Elders, Community Christian Church, Lincolnshire, IL (1983-1985); President, Okemos School Board, Michigan (1975-1978); Chairperson, Okemos Community Recreation Program (1971-1974) **MIL:** Lieutenant, Air Police Officer, United States Air Force (1957-1960) **CW:** Contributor, Articles, Professional Journals **AW:** Wyandotte, Michigan Sports Hall of Fame (1995); Distinguished Graduates Hall of Fame (1993); Inductee, Football Hall of Fame Roosevelt High School (1992) **MEM:** President, Michigan State University School Criminal Justice Alumni Association (1984-1986); Highway Safety Committee,

National Sheriffs Association; Lifetime Member, Michigan State University S. Club **B/I:** During his time in college, Dr. Bufe thought about coaching and ran a parallel career field between that field and criminal justice. He felt the two were integrated in terms of working with people. Following this period, he decided to enter law enforcement. He went on to work for Michigan Governor George Romney, and became the first director in the state-wide law enforcement training program. **AV:** Golf; Boating; Cross-country skiing; Professional and college sports

BUFFETT, WARREN EDWARD, T: Chief Executive Officer **I:** Real Estate **CN:** Berkshire Hathaway **DOB:** 08/30/1930 **PB:** Omaha **SC:** NB/USA **PT:** Howard Homan; Leila (Stahl) Buffett **MS:** Married **SPN:** Susan Thompson **ED:** MS in Economics, Columbia Business School (1951); BS in Economics, University of Nebraska (1950); Coursework, University of Pennsylvania **C:** Chairman, Chief Executive Officer, Berkshire Hathaway, Inc. (1970-Present); General Partner, Buffett Partnership, Ltd. (1956-1969); Security Analyst, Graham-Newman Corporation, New York, NY (1954-1956); Investment Salesman, Buffett-Falk & Company, Omaha, NE (1951-1954) **CR:** Board of Directors, The Kraft Heinz Company (2015-Present); Board of Directors, The Lubrizol Corporation (2012-Present); Board of Directors, MidAmerican Energy Holdings Company (2011-Present); Board of Directors, Berkshire Hathaway, Inc. (1965-Present); Board of Directors, H.J. Heinz Company (2013-2015); Board of Directors, Graham Holdings Company (1996-2011); Board of Directors, The Coca-Cola Company (1989-2006); Board of Directors, The Washington Post Company (1974-1986, 1996-2011) **CIV:** Lifetime Trustee, Grinnell College (1968-Present); Life Trustee, Urban Institute **CW:** Author, "The Essays of Warren Buffet: Lessons for Corporate America (2008); Author, "The Essays of Warren Buffet Second Edition" (2008); Actor, "All My Children" (2008); Author, "The Essays of Warren Buffet" (2001) **AW:** The World's Richest People (2001-Present); The Richest People in America, The Forbes 400 (1982-Present); The World's Most Powerful People (2009-2015); One of the 50 Most Influential People in Global Finance, Bloomberg Markets (2011-2014); Lifetime Philanthropy Award (2013); The 100 Most Influential People in the World, Time (2007, 2012); Business People of the Year, Fortune Magazine (2010); Presidential Medal of Freedom, The White House (2010); The Top 25 Market Movers, U.S. News & World Report (2009); The Global Elite, Newsweek Magazine (2008); The 25 Most Powerful People in Business (2007) **MEM:** American Academy of Arts and Sciences **PA:** Democrat

BUFORD, ROBERT, "R.C." CANTERBURY, T: Chief Executive Officer **I:** Athletics **CN:** Spurs Sports & Entertainment LLC **MS:** Married **SPN:** Beth Boozer Buford (1987) **CH:** C.C.; Chase **ED:** Bachelor's Degree, Friends University (1987); Coursework, Oklahoma State University; Coursework, Texas A&M University **C:** Chief Executive Officer, Spurs Sports & Entertainment LLC (Now ATT Center) (2019-Present); President, Spurs Sports & Entertainment LLC (Now ATT Center) (2008-2019); General Manager, Spurs Sports & Entertainment LLC (Now ATT Center) (2002-2019); Assistant General Manager, Spurs Sports & Entertainment LLC (Now ATT Center) (1999-2002); Director, Scouting, Spurs Sports & Entertainment LLC (Now ATT Center) (1997-1999); Head Scout, Spurs Sports & Entertainment LLC (Now ATT Center) (1994-1994); Assistant Coach, Men's Basketball, University of Florida (1993-1994); Assistant Coach, Los Angeles Clippers, NBA (1992-1993); Assistant Coach, San Antonio Spurs, NBA (1988-1992); Assistant Coach,

Men's Basketball, The University of Kansas (1983-1988) **CIV:** Advisory Board, Center on Leadership & Ethics (COLE), The Fuqua School of Business, Duke University (2015-Present); Board of Directors, PeacePlayers International; Director, Basketball Without Borders (BWB) Africa, NBA **AW:** Named Executive of the Year, NBA (2014, 2016)

BULL, REBECCA D., MED, T: Music Educator, Musician **I:** Media & Entertainment **DOB:** 05/11/1962 **PB:** Baltimore **SC:** MD/USA **PT:** Elmer Leon Ledford; Nova Neavie Sherlock **MS:** Married **SPN:** Donald Cylburn Bull Jr. (1/15/1983) **ED:** Postgraduate Coursework, New York University (2002); Master of Education, Towson State University (1993); Bachelor of Arts in Music Education, Towson State University (1987) **CT:** Certification in Violin, Music Teachers National Association (2003); Certification in Violin, Maryland State Music Teachers Association (1993); State of Tennessee Endorsement for Music Education **C:** Orchestra Director, Children Of Crossville Chamber Orchestra (1996-Present); Music Teacher, Cumberland County, Crossville, TN (1993-Present); Orchestra Director, Westminster Youth Orchestra, Westminster, MD (1988-1993); String Teacher, Western Maryland College, Westminster, MD (1986-1993); String Teacher, Hereford Zone Music Program, Baltimore, MD (1988-1992) **CIV:** Community Orchestra Director Children of Crossville (1996-Present); Westminster Youth Orchestra, Maryland (1986-1993) **CW:** Instrumental Anthology (2000-Present); Author, Vocal Work, "Anthology" (1997-1999); Author, Orchestral Work, "Kumon" (1993) **AW:** Nominated, Elizabeth A.H, Green School Educator Award (2015-2017); Woman of the Year, Business and Professional Women's Association (2000); Teacher of the Year, Crossville Elementary School (1998); Butterfly Award, Music In Motion (1997) **MEM:** Treasurer, Plateau Area Music Teachers Association (1997-Present); National Education Association; Nashville Songwriters Association; American String Teachers Association; Middle Tennessee State Band and Orchestra Association; East Tennessee State Band and Orchestra Association; National Association of Music Educators; National Wildlife Federation; Papayago Rescue House Inc. **MH:** Albert Nelson Marquis Lifetime Achievement Award; Marquis Who's Who Top Professional **AS:** Ms. Bull attributes her success to the work ethic instilled in her by her parents, alongside her belief that if one works hard enough, one will succeed. Talent and hard work make a clear path to success. **B/I:** Over the years, Ms. Bull had amazing teachers that acted as major influences in her life. She grew up in a bad area where, unfortunately, her younger brother and many friends died of a drug overdoses. Music became her outlet. If it was not for music, Ms. Bull would not have stayed in school. It was her relief - she feels her students need something beyond academics to carry them through their day. **AV:** Songwriting; Painting; Reading; Crafts; Nature enthusiast **RE:** Christian

BULLOCK, SANDRA ANNETTE, T: Actress **I:** Media & Entertainment **DOB:** 07/26/1964 **PB:** Arlington **SC:** VA/USA **PT:** Helen Mathilde Meyer; John W. Bullock **MS:** Divorced **SPN:** Jesse James (07/16/2005, Divorced 2010) **CH:** Louis; Laila **ED:** BFA in Drama, East Carolina University (1987) **C:** Founder, Owner, Fortis Films (1995-Present) **CR:** Founder, Owner, Walton's Fancy and Staple (2009-Present); Founder, Owner, Bess Bistro (2006-2016) **CIV:** Donor, Victims of California Wildfires (2018); Donor, Victims of Hurricane Harvey, Texas (2017); Donor, Victims of Tohoku Earthquake and Tsunami (2011); Donor, Victims of Haiti Earthquake (2010); Supporter, Kindred Life Foundation, Inc. (Now NPCC Inc.) (2008);

Donor, Victims of Hurricane Katrina (2005); Donor, Victims of Indian Ocean Earthquake and Tsunamis (2004); Donor, Liberty Disaster Relief Fund (2001); Donor, The American National Red Cross; Donor, Humane Society of Ventura County **CW:** Actress, Executive Producer, "Bird Box" (2018); Actress, "Ocean's Eight" (2018); Actress, Executive Producer, "Our Brand Is Crisis" (2015); Voice Actress, "Minions" (2015); Voice Actress, "Aningaaq" (2013); Actress, "Gravity" (2013); Actress, "The Heat" (2013); Actress, "Extremely Loud & Incredibly Close" (2011); Actress, "The Blind Side" (2009); Actress, Producer, "All About Steve" (2009); Actress, Executive Producer, "The Proposal" (2009); Actress, "Premonition" (2007); Executive Producer, "George Lopez" (2002-2007); Actress, "Infamous" (2006); Actress, "The Lake House" (2006); Actress, Producer, "Miss Congeniality 2: Armed & Fabulous" (2005); Actress, "Loverboy" (2005); Executive Producer, "Sudbury" (2004); Actress, "Crash" (2004); Actress, "Two Weeks Notice" (2002); Actress, "Divine Secrets of the Ya-Ya Sisterhood" (2002); Actress, "Murder by Numbers" (2002); Actress, Producer, "Miss Congeniality" (2000); Actress, "Lisa Picard Is Famous" (2000); Actress, "28 Days" (2000); Actress, Producer, "Gun Shy" (2000); Actress, "Action" (1999); Actress, "Forces of Nature" (1999); Producer, "Trespasses" (1999); Voice Actress, "The Prince of Egypt" (1998); Actress, "Welcome to Hollywood" (1998); Actress, "Practical Magic" (1998); Actress, Director, Writer, "Making Sandwiches" (1998); Actress, Executive Producer, "Hope Floats" (1998); Actress, "Speed 2: Cruise Control" (1997); Producer, "Our Father" (1996); Executive Producer, "Mailman" (1996); Actress, "In Love and War" (1996); Actress, "A Time to Kill" (1996); Actress, "Two If by Sea" (1996); Actress, "The Net" (1995); Actress, "While You Were Sleeping" (1995); Actress, "Who Do I Gotta Kill?" (1994); Actress, "Speed" (1994); Actress, "Wrestling Ernest Hemingway" (1993); Actress, "Fire on the Amazon" (1993); Actress, "Demolition Man" (1993); Actress, "The Thing Called Love" (1993); Actress, "When the Party's Over" (1993); Actress, "The Vanishing" (1993); Actress, "Love Potion No. 9" (1992); Actress, "Working Girl" (1990); Actress, "Lucky Chances" (1990); Actress, "A Fool and His Money" (1989); Actress, "The Preppie Murder" (1989); Actress, "Who Shot Pat?" (1989); Actress, "Starting from Scratch" (1989); Actress, "Bionic Showdown: The Six Million Dollar Man and the Bionic Woman" (1989); Actress, "Hangmen" (1987) **AW:** Critics' Choice Award for Best Actress in an Action Movie, The Critics Choice Association (2014); Desert Palm Achievement Award, Palm Springs International Film Festival (2014); Saturn Award for Best Actress, Academy of Science Fiction, Fantasy and Horror Films (1995, 2014); AAFCA Award for Best Actress, African American Film Critics Association, Inc. (2013); Kick Ass Award for Best Female Action Star, Alliance of Women Film Journalists (2013); AWFJ Award for Actress Defying Age and Ageism, Alliance of Women Film Journalists (2013); Award for Actress of the Year, Hollywood Film Festival (2013); Invisible Woman Award, Women Film Critics Circle (2013); Inductee, Hall of Fame, Warren Easton Charter High School, New Orleans, LA (2012); Humanitarian Activism Award, Alliance of Women Film Journalists (2011); Academy Award for Best Actress, Academy of Motion Picture Arts and Sciences (2010); Golden Globe Award for Best Actress – Motion Picture Drama, Hollywood Foreign Press Association (2010); Screen Actors Guild Award for Outstanding Performance by a Female Actor in a Leading Role, SAG-AFTRA (2010); Critics' Choice Award for Best Actress, The Critics Choice Association (2010); American Riviera Award, Santa Barbara

International Film Festival (2010); WIN Award for Outstanding Actress in a Feature Film, Women's Image Network (2009); Screen Actors Guild Award for Outstanding Performance by a Cast in a Motion Picture, SAG-AFTRA (2006); Critics' Choice Award for Best Acting Ensemble, The Critics Choice Association (2006); Award for Supporting Actress of the Year, Hollywood Film Festival (2006); Crystal Award, Women In Film Los Angeles (2005); Star, Motion Picture Category, Hollywood Walk of Fame, Hollywood Chamber of Commerce (2005); Award for Ensemble of the Year, Hollywood Film Festival (2005); Hasty Pudding Theatrical Award for Woman of the Year, The Hasty Pudding - Institute of 1770, Inc (2004); Virginia Film Award, Virginia Film Festival (2004); Raul Julia Award for Excellence, National Hispanic Foundation for the Arts (2002); Female Star of the Year, National Association of Theatre Owners (1996, 2001); Joseph Plateau Award of Honor, Film Fest Gent, Ghent, Belgium (1999); Career Excellence Award, Montreal World Film Festival (1998)

BULLOCK, STEPHEN CLARK, T: Governor of Montana **I:** Government Administration/Government Relations/Government Services **DOB:** 04/11/1966 **PB:** Missoula **SC:** MT/USA **PT:** Mike Bullock; Penny Clark **SPN:** Lisa Bullock **CH:** Caroline; Alexandria; Cameron **ED:** JD, Columbia Law School, with Honors, New York, NY (1994); BA, Claremont McKenna College, CA (1988) **C:** Governor, State of Montana, Helena, MT (2013-2020); Candidate, Democratic Nominee, 2020 Presidential Campaign (2019); Chair, National Governors Association (NGA) (2018-2019); Attorney General, State of Montana, Helena, MT (2009-2013); Private Law Practice, Helena, MT (2004-2008); Attorney, Steptoe & Johnson LLP, Washington, DC (2001-2004); Executive Assistant Attorney General to Acting Chief Deputy, State of Montana, Helena, MT (1997-2001); Chief Legal Counsel to Secretary of State, State of Montana, Helena, MT (1996) **CR:** Adjunct Professor, George Washington University Law School (2001-2004) **PA:** Democrat

BUMPAS, STUART M., T: Lawyer **I:** Law and Legal Services **CN:** Locke Lord LLP **DOB:** 10/07/1944 **PB:** Little Rock **SC:** AR/USA **PT:** Hubert Wayne Bumpas; Martha Conway (Maryman) Bumpas **MS:** Married **SPN:** Diane Ellen DeWare (10/01/1977) **CH:** Joseph Stuart Bumpas **ED:** LLM, The George Washington University (1973); JD, The University of Texas at Austin (1969); BA, Brown University (1966) **C:** Partner, Locke Lord LLP (2008-Present); Partner, Locke, Liddell & Sapp (Now Locke Lord LLP), Dallas, Texas (1999-2007); Partner, Locke, Purnell, Rain, Harrell (Now Locke Lord LLP), Dallas, Texas (1974-1998); Assistant to Commissioner, Internal Revenue Service, Washington, DC (1973-1974); Attorney Advisor, Office of the Chief Counsel, Washington, DC (1969-1972) **CR:** Adjunct Professor, Employee Benefits, Southern Methodist University, Dallas, Texas (1975); Lecturer, Washington Non-Profit Legal & Tax Conference; Lecturer, The American Law Institute; Annual Lecturer, Nonprofit Organizations Institute, Philosophy Southwest **CIV:** Board of Directors, Callier Center for Communication Disorders, Dallas, Texas (1984-Present); National Counsel, American Heart Association, Inc., Dallas, Texas (1979-Present); Board of Directors, Dallas Grand Opera Association (1984); Vice President, Dallas Grand Opera Association (1984); Executive Committee, Southern Methodist University Meadows School of Arts, Dallas, Texas; Board of Directors, Friends of Alzheimer's Disease Center, The University of Texas Southwestern Medical Center; Board of Directors, Goodwill Industries of Dallas, Inc.; Member, Mayor's Commission on International Development;

Member, Task Force on Arts and Culture, Dallas, Texas; Trustee, The Lamplighter School; General Counsel, The Hockaday School; General Counsel, Dallas Museum of Art; Trustee, Dallas Museum of Art; Member, Executive Committee, Dallas Museum of Art; Trustee, Southwestern Medical Foundation; Member, The Chancellor's Council, The University of Texas System; Member, Advisory Committee, Meadows Museum **CW:** Contributor, Articles, Professional Journals **MEM:** Exempt Organizations Committee, ABA; Former Chairman, Legal Aspects of Arts Committee, State Bar of Texas; Dallas Bar Association; Business Advisory Committee; American Council on Germany; Council on Foreign Relations; The Dallas Petroleum Club; Brook Hollow Golf Club; The Idlewild Club; The Society of the Cincinnati; Coral Beach & Tennis Club **BAR:** The District of Columbia Bar (1972); State Bar of Texas (1969) **MH:** Marquis Who's Who Top Professional **RE:** Episcopalian

BUNN, DOROTHY I., T: International Conference Reporter **I:** Writing and Editing **DOB:** 04/30/1948 **PB:** Trinidad **SC:** CO/USA **CH:** Kristy Lynn; Wade Allen; Russell Ahearn **ED:** Student, University of Virginia, Fairfax, VA (1971-1972); Student, Northern Virginia Community College (1970-1971); Student, University of Wyoming **CT:** Certified Shorthand Reporter; Registered Professional Reporter **C:** President, Chief Executive Officer, Bunn & Associates, Lusk, WY (2000-2018); President, Chief Executive Officer, Bunn & Associates, Glenrock, WY (1981-1999); Co-Manager, Bixby Hereford Co. (1989-1997); Consultant, Bixby Hereford Co., Glenrock, WY (1981-1989);President, Chief Executive Officer, Ahearn Ltd., Springfield, VA (1970-1971) **CIV:** Member, Wyoming Advisory Council, Small Business Administration (1994-1996); State Chair, White House Conference on Small Business, Washington, DC (1995); Delegate, White House Conference on Small Business, Washington, DC (1995); Delegate, White House Conference on Small Business, Washington, DC (1986) **MEM:** President, National Federation of Business and Professional Women (1995-1996); Vice President, National Federation of Business and Professional Women (1994-1995); Public Relations Chair, Choices Chair, National Federation of Business and Professional Women; National Association of Female Executives; Association Advancement CAT Tech.; National Federation of Independent Business; Wyoming Shorthand Reporters Association; National Federation of Independent Business; National Court Reporters Association; American Indian Society of Washington, DC **B/I:** Ms. Bunn became involved in her profession because she thought of it as another language and also taught herself Mandarin Chinese. She was in the process of learning sign language and felt that it was just another language that might be fun to learn. A friend of hers encouraged her to do it and loaned her one of his steno machines and study books and two years later she passed the exams. **AV:** Photography

BUOLAMWINI, JOY ADOWAA, T: 1) Computer Scientist 2) Founder **I:** Education/Educational Services **CN:** 1) Massachusetts Institute of Technology Media Lab 2) Algorithmic Justice League **PB:** Edmonton **SC:** AL/CAN **ED:** Master's Degree in Algorithmic Bias, Massachusetts Institute of Technology (2017); Master's Degree in Education, University of Oxford, with Distinction (2014); BS in Computer Science, Georgia Institute of Technology, with Highest Honors (2012) **C:** Founder, Algorithmic Justice League (2016-Present); Ambassador to Africa, Georgia Institute of Technology (2013-Present); Adams House Resident Tutor, Harvard University (2015-2017); Founder, Code4Rights

(2014-2016); Founder, Jovial Designs, Memphis, GA (2007-2015); Co-Founder, Executive Director, Zamrize, Lusaka, Zambia (2013-2014); Co-Founder, Chief Technology Officer, Techturized, Inc., Atlanta, GA (2012-2013); Founding Chief Technology Officer, Excelgrade, Atlanta, GA (2012); Technical Consultant, Volunteer Director of Global Mobile Surveying Tools, The Carter Center, Ethiopia and United States (2011-2014); Research Assistant, Computational Perception Lab, Georgia Institute of Technology (2011); Software Engineering Intern, Yahoo!, Sunnyvale, CA (2011); Mentor, College of Computing, Georgia Institute of Technology (2010-2011); Research Assistant, Everyday Computing Lab, Georgia Institute of Technology (2009); Intern, Profounder, Atlanta, GA (2009) **CR:** Graduate Researcher, Center for Civic Media, Massachusetts Institute of Technology Media Lab (2015-Present); Board Member, College of Computing OMS, Georgia Institute of Technology (2013-Present) **CIV:** Co-Founder, Zamrize Indiegogo Campaign (2013) **MIL:** Co-Author, "Gender Shades: Intersectional Accuracy Disparities in Commercial Gender Classification," Proceedings of Machine Learning Research (2018); Co-Author, "A Novel Electronic Data Collection System for Large-Scale Surveys of Neglected Tropical Diseases," PLOS One (2013) **AW:** One of the 100 Next Honoree, Time Magazine (2019); One of the World's Greatest Leaders, Fortune Magazine (2019); One of the 30 Under 30 in Enterprise Technology, Forbes (2018); One the Top 50 Women in Technology, Forbes (2018); One of the Bloomberg 50 People Who Shaped Global Business (2018); One of the 35 Under 35, MIT Tech Review (2018); Grand Prize Winner, Search for Hidden Figures, 21 Century and PepsiCo (2017); NCWIT Collegiate Award Winner, Hewlett Packard Enterprise and Qualcomm (2016); Young Africans Committed to Excellence , Face2Face Africa (2015); Rhodes Scholar (2012); Fulbright Fellow (2012); Google Anita Borg Scholar (2011); Astronaut Scholar, Astronaut Scholarship Foundation (2010); Stamps Scholar, Stamps Family Charitable Foundation (2008)

BURAKOVSKY, LEONID, PHD, T: Physicist, Researcher **I:** Sciences **CN:** Los Alamos National Laboratory **DOB:** 01/14/1964 **PB:** Kiev **SC:** Ukraine **PT:** Nahum Burakovsky; Polina Burakovsky **MS:** Married **SPN:** Maya Derechin (11/19/1989) **CH:** Arik; Naftali **ED:** Doctor of Philosophy in Theoretical Physics, Tel-Aviv University, Tel-Aviv, Israel (1996); Master of Science in Theoretical Physics, Kiev State University, Ukraine (1990); Bachelor of Science in Engineering, Moscow Institute of Steel and Alloys, Moscow, Russia (1984) **C:** Scientist, Theoretical Division, Los Alamos National Laboratory, Triad National Security, Los Alamos, NM (2018-Present); Scientist, Theoretical Division, Los Alamos National Laboratory, LANS LLC, Los Alamos, NM (2006-2018); Staff Member, Theoretical Division, Los Alamos National Laboratory, Los Alamos, NM (1999-2006); Postdoctoral Fellow, Theoretical Division, Los Alamos National Laboratory, Los Alamos, NM (1995-1999) **CR:** Teaching Associate, General Physics, Preparatory Division, Tel Aviv University, Tel Aviv, Israel (1993-1995) **MIL:** Armed Forces, Former USSR (1984-1986) **CW:** Author, Co-Author, Contributor, More Than 150 Peer-Reviewed Papers, Preprints, and Conference Presentations **MH:** Albert Nelson Marquis Lifetime Achievement Award; Marquis Who's Who Top Professional **B/I:** Dr. Burakovsky became involved in his profession because he started developing an interest in science as a child. He was born in the Soviet Union and studied in Moscow and Kiev, where he fully developed this interest and taste for excelling in the field of science. **AV:** Reading; Walking; Traveling; Spending time with family

BURCHETT, TIMOTHY, "TIM" FLOYD, T: U.S. Representative **I:** Government Administration/Government Relations/Government Services **DOB:** 08/25/1964 **PB:** Knoxville **SC:** TN/USA **MS:** Married **SPN:** Kelly Kimball (2014); Allison Beaver (2008, Divorced 2012) **ED:** BS in Education, The University of Tennessee, Knoxville **C:** U.S. Representatives, Tennessee's Second District, U.S. House of Representatives (2019-Present); Mayor, Knox County, TN (2010-2018); Member, District Seven, Tennessee State Senate (1999-2010); Former Member, District 18, Tennessee House of Representatives (1995-1999); Businessman **MEM:** West Hill Estates Home Owners Association; Knox County Young Republicans; Knoxville Chamber; West Knoxville Republican Club **PA:** Republican **RE:** Presbyterian

BURCK, JOSEPH RUSSELL, PHD, T: Medical Educator, Consultant, Minister, Travel Blogger **I:** Education/Educational Services **DOB:** 12/28/1937 **PB:** Roswell **SC:** NM/USA **PT:** William Joseph Burck; Leta Gladys (Menefee) Burck **MS:** Married **SPN:** Dorothy Antoinette Pilc (08/06/1960) **CH:** Peter Warren; Elisabeth Varner **ED:** PhD, Princeton Theological Seminary (1976); World Council of Churches Fellowship (1971-1972); Doctoral Fellowship in Theology and Personality, Princeton Theological Seminary (1964-1967); BD, Princeton Theological Seminary (1964); AB, Princeton University (1959) **CT:** Board-Certified Chaplain, Association of Professional Chaplains (1998); Certified Chaplain Supervisor, Association for Clinical Pastoral Education (1981); Pastoral Counselor, American Association of Pastoral Counselors (1977); Ordained, Presbytery of Philadelphia (1970); Certified Finger and Hand Analyst; Certified Energy Healer **C:** Associate Professor Emeritus, Religion, Health, and Human Values, Rush University Medical Center (Formerly Rush-Presbyterian, St. Luke's Medical Center), Chicago, IL (2008-Present); Director, Program in Ethics and Ethics Consultation Service, Rush University Medical Center (Formerly Rush-Presbyterian, St. Luke's Medical Center), Chicago, IL (1988-2005); Associate Professor, Religion, Health, and Human Values, Rush University Medical Center (Formerly Rush-Presbyterian, St. Luke's Medical Center), Chicago, IL (1985-2008); Assistant Professor, Religion and Health, Rush University Medical Center (Formerly Rush-Presbyterian, St. Luke's Medical Center), Chicago, IL (1978-1985); Director, Chaplaincy Services, Larned State Hospital, Kansas (1976-1978); Educator, Pastoral Care, Seminaries, Tuebingen University, Innere Mission, Berlin, Germany (1972-1974); Associate Editor, Bibliography, Political Science, Princeton Information Technology (1967-1969); Educator, Pastoral Care, Seminaries, Lueckendorff; Educator, Pastoral Care, Seminaries, Herborn; Educator, Pastoral Care, Seminaries, Stuttgart, Germany **CR:** Board of Directors, Representing Rush College of Health Sciences, Rush Geriatric Interdisciplinary Team Training Program, Chicago, IL (1997-Present); Course Director, Clerkship, Medical Ethics, Rush Medical College, Chicago, IL (1993-Present); Member, Illinois Task Force on Preparedness for Avian Flu Pandemic (2006-2007); Chair, Faculty Council, College of Health Sciences, Rush University Medical Center (2005-2007); Course Co-director, Ethics in Medicine, Rush Medical College, Chicago, IL (1998-2005); Marshal, Rush University Graduation, Representing College of Health Sciences (2004); Peer Reviewer, Articles, Critical Care Medicine, Des Plaines, IL (1999-2003); Lay Member, National Ethics and Peer Review Committee, American Association of Electrodiagnostic Medicine (1993-2000); Chair, Ethics Grand Rounds, Rush University Medical Center (Formerly Rush-Presbyterian, St. Luke's Medical Center)

(1980-1999); Consultant to Author, Book, "Ethical Issues, and Patient Rights Joint Commission on the Accreditation of Health Care Organizations", Chicago, IL (1997-1998); Vice-chair, Work Group on Governance and Administration, NCA Accreditation Review, Rush University, Chicago, IL (1997); Course Director, Spiritual Dimensions of Health Care Teleconference Network of Texas, Austin, Texas (1992-1997); President, Chicago Clinical Ethics Programs (1994-1995); Member, National Task Force to Prepare Brief Course in Ethics, Association of Professional Chaplains (1993-1995); Editor, Rush Ethics Reporter, Rush University Medical Center (Formerly Rush-Presbyterian, St. Luke's Medical Center) (1991-1994); Outside Member, Animal Care and Use Committee, University of Illinois at Chicago (1988-1993); Chairperson, Committee on Senior Faculty Appointments and Promotions, College of Health Sciences, Rush University (1988-1992); Chairperson, Ethics Advisory Committee, Institute of Medicine of Chicago, Chicago, IL (1990-1991); Project Director, Clergy Ethics Study Group (1988-1990); U.S. Delegate, International Congress on Pastoral Care and Counseling, San Francisco, CA (1983); U.S. Delegate International Congress on Pastoral Care and Counseling, Edinburgh, Scotland (1979); Interpreter, Arnoldshain, Germany (1973); Intuitive Consulting; Energy Healer **CIV:** Instructor, Courses, Adult Christian Education, Faith and Illness, Theology of Genetics, Medical Ethics, Faith and Money, Numerous Churches, Chicago, IL (1980-Present) **CW:** Co-Editor, "Clergy Ethics in a Changing Society: Mapping the Terrain"; Author, E-book, "Is it OK to Have Money and Still Go to Church?"; Contributor, Articles, Columns, Essays to Professional Journals; Contributor, Book Chapters **AW:** Grantee, Greenwall Foundation (1999-2000); Professional Service Award, Teleconference Network of Texas (1993); Named One of the Ten Best Books in Ministry for "Clergy Ethics in a Changing Society: Mapping the Terrain" (1991); Research Award, Joint Council on Research in Pastoral Counseling (1988) **MEM:** Board of Governors, Institute of Medicine of Chicago (1990-1991); Presbytery of Chicago; Association for Clinical Pastoral Education; Association of Professional Chaplains; Institute of Medicine of Chicago; Association for Bioethics and the Humanities **MH:** Albert Nelson Marquis Lifetime Achievement Award **AV:** Traveling; Photography; Hiking; Opera; Films **RE:** Presbyterian

BURGESS, MICHAEL CLIFTON, MD, T: U.S. Representative from Texas; Physician **I:** Government Administration/Government Relations/Government Services **DOB:** 12/23/1950 **PB:** Rochester **SC:** MN/USA **PT:** Harry Meredith Burgess; Norma (Crowhurst) Burgess **MS:** Married **SPN:** Laura Burgess **CH:** Three Children **ED:** Honorary Doctor of Public Service, University of North Texas Health Science Center (2009); Resident, Parkland Memorial Hospital, Dallas, Texas; MA in Medical Management, The University of Texas at Dallas (2000); MD, The University of Texas Health Science Center at Houston (1977); MS, North Texas State University (Now University of North Texas) (1976); BS, North Texas State University (Now University of North Texas) (1972) **C:** Chair, Congressional Health Care Caucus, Texas' 26th Congressional District, United States Congress (2009-Present); U.S. Representative from Texas' 26th Congressional District, United States Congress (2003-Present); Member, Committee on Energy and Commerce; Chief of Obstetrics, Chief of Staff, Medical Center of Lewisville; Private Practice, Ob-Gyn Associates, Lewisville, Texas **AW:** Named House Legislator of the Year, National Multiple Sclerosis Society (2008); Named Legislator of the Year, American Academy of Nurse Practitioners (2005); Taxpayer Hero Award, Council

for Citizens Against Government Waste (CCAGW); Guardian of Small Business Award, National Federation of Independent Business **MEM:** Past President, Denton County Medical Society **PA:** Republican **RE:** Anglican

BURGOS-SASSCER, RUTH, T: Chancellor Emeritus **I:** Education/Educational Services **DOB:** 09/05/1931 **PB:** New York **SC:** NY/USA **PT:** Carmelo Burgos; Maria (Lebron) Burgos (Deceased) **MS:** Married **SPN:** Donald Sasscer (06/14/1958) **CH:** Timothy; James; Julie; David **ED:** PhD in High Education Administration, Florida State University (1987); MA in Religion, Columbia University (1956); BA in Sociology, Maryville College, TN (1953); Coursework, Iowa State University; Coursework, InterAmerican University; Coursework, University of Salamanca; Coursework, Harvard University **C:** Chancellor Emeritus (2000-Present); Senior Fellow, University of Houston Law Center Institute for Higher Education Law and Governance (2001-2003); Adjunct Professor, University of Texas (1996-2000); Chancellor, Houston Community College Systems (1996-2000); President, San Antonio College (1993-1996); Vice President, Faculty and Instruction, Harry S. Truman College, Chicago, IL (1988-1993); Director, Dean, Chief Executive Officer, University of Puerto Rico, Aguadilla, Puerto Rico (1981-1985); Director, Non-traditional Programs, Central Administration Regional College, University of Puerto Rico (1976-1981); Instructor to Associate Professor, University of Puerto Rico (1972-1981); Department Chair, University of Puerto Rico, Aguadilla, Puerto Rico (1972-1976); Member, Faculty, InterAmerican University, Puerto Rico (1968-1971) **CR:** Accreditation Evaluator, Middle States, North Central Association of Colleges and Schools (NCA) and Southern Association of Colleges and Schools (Now Southern Association of Colleges and Schools Commission on Colleges) (1981-Present); Educational Consultant (2000-2011); Research Association, Postsecondary Education Planning Commission, Florida Board of Education (1986-1987); Association of Community College Trustees (ACCT); Hispanic Association of Colleges & Universities (HACU); Kaleidoscope; President, Women's Affairs Commission, Office of the Governor of Puerto Rico (1979-1981) **CIV:** Board of Directors, National Postsecondary Education Cooperative (NPEC), Maryville College; Second Chair, National Advisory Council, Montgomery County Coalition for Adult Literacy and ESOL **CW:** Author, 15 Articles/Monographs; Author, Contributor, Editor, 10 Books; Over 200 Speeches and Papers Presented in Field **AW:** Recipient, Numerous Awards, Recognitions; Honorary Doctorate **MEM:** Treasurer, International Consortium for Economic Development (1993-1996); American Association of Community College; Montgomery Coalition for Literacy and English for Speakers of Other Languages (ESOL); National Postsecondary Education Cooperative (NPEC) **MH:** Albert Nelson Marquis Lifetime Achievement Award **B/I:** Dr. Burgos-Sasscer's first goal was to be a minister at Union Theological Seminary but her denomination did not ordain women and they were struggling with that. So she transferred to Columbia University to get an academic degree rather than a theological degree. She transferred to the department of philosophy and religion and got her master's degree. She then went to Iowa State University to work but also started a doctoral program in sociology of religion. She quit after a year to get married and her husband was offered a job in Puerto Rico and so she moved there with him. They stayed in Puerto Rico for 24 years and she began teaching and eventually became an administrator, and then the chief executive of one of the community colleges. Her children had grown up and she decided to finish her doctorate so she went back to Florida State University and finished her doctorate with her husband's support. She moved to the city colleges of Chicago to work and later became president of San Antonio College and Chancellor of the Houston system; she retired from there. **AV:** Reading; Traveling **PA:** Democrat **RE:** Presbyterian

BURGUM, DOUGLAS, "DOUG" JAMES, T: Governor of North Dakota **I:** Government Administration/Government Relations/Government Services **DOB:** 08/01/1956 **PB:** Arthur **SC:** ND/USA **MS:** Married **SPN:** Kathryn Helgaas (2016); Karen Stoker (1991, Divorced 2003) **CH:** Three Children **ED:** Honorary PhD, University of Mary, ND (2006); Honorary PhD, North Dakota State University (2000); MBA, Stanford Graduate School of Business (1980); BA, North Dakota State University (1978) **C:** Governor, State of North Dakota (2016-Present); Senior Vice President, Microsoft Business Solutions Group, Microsoft Business Division, Microsoft Corporation (2005-2007); Joined, Microsoft Corporation (2001); Chairman, Chief Executive Officer, Great Plains Software Inc. (Acquired by Microsoft Corporation) (1984-2001); Consultant, McKinsey & Company (1980-1983) **CR:** Board of Directors, SuccessFactors, Inc. (2007-Present); Founder, Kilbourne Group **CIV:** Founder, Doug Burgum Family Fund (2008-Present); Board Member, Stanford Graduate School of Business

BURKE, CLEMENT, "CLEM" ANTHONY, T: Musician **I:** Media & Entertainment **CN:** Blondie **DOB:** 11/24/1955 **PB:** Bayonne **SC:** NJ/USA **C:** Drummer, with Blondie (1998-Present); Co-Founder, The International Swingers (2011); Co-Founding Member, The Split Squad (2011); Drummer, with Nancy Sinatra (2004-2005); Drummer, with The Romantics (1990-2004); Drummer, with Blondie (1975-1982); Drummer, Various Acts Including Pete Townshend, Bob Dylan, Eurythmics, Dramarama, the Fleshtones, Iggy Pop and Joan Jett; Co-Founding Member, Total Environment and Sweet Willie Jam Band **CW:** Musician, with Blondie, "Best Live" (2005); Musician, with Blondie, "The Curse of Blondie" (2004); Musician, with Blondie, "Livid" (2000); Musician, with Blondie, "Live in New York" (1999); Musician, with Blondie, "No Exit" (1999); Musician, with Blondie, "The Hunter" (1982); Musician, with Blondie, "Autoamerican" (1980); Musician, with Blondie, "Eat to the Beat" (1979); Musician, with Blondie, "Parallel Lines" (1978); Musician, with Blondie, "Plastic Letters" (1977); Musician, with Blondie, "Blondie" (1976); Drummer, Various Artists, Various Albums **AW:** Co-Recipient, Golden Note Award, ASCAP (2019); Inductee, Rock & Roll Hall of Fame (2006)

BURKE, DAVID, T: Owner **I:** Food & Restaurant Services **CN:** David Burke Hospitality Group **ED:** Culinary Arts and Chef Training, Culinary Institute of America (1982); Pastry Chef Coursework, France **C:** President, Esquared Hospitality, New York, NY (1995-Present); Principal, Founder/Owner, David Burke Hospitality Group (2003-2015); President, DB Global **CW:** Author, "David Burke's American Classics"; Author, "Cooking with David Burke" **AW:** Best Chef in New York, James Beard Foundation; M.O.F. Award, Meilleurs Ouvriers de France; Japanese Medal of Skill & Technique; Chef Magazine's Chef of the Year **MEM:** American Culinary Federation; Table to Table; James Beard Foundation **MH:** Albert Nelson Marquis Lifetime Achievement Award; Marquis Who's Who Top Professional **AS:** Mr. Burke attributes his success to a lack of fear of failure. He additionally embraces curiosity, hard work, and luck, and tries to surround himself with great people. **B/I:** Mr. Burke fell in love with

the energy and the dynamic environment of the kitchen while he was in high school. There were no two days alike in the kitchen, and he was intrigued by that nature of the profession. **THT:** Mr. Burke stands by the statement, "Failure is not an option."

BURKE, MICHAEL S., T: Chairman and Chief Executive Officer **I:** Financial Services **CN:** AECOM **ED:** JD, Southwestern Law School; BS in Accounting, The University of Scranton **CT:** CPA (Certified Public Accountant) **C:** Chairman and Chief Executive Officer, AECOM (2014-Present); President, AECOM (2011-2014); Chief Financial Officer, AECOM (2006-2011); Partner, KPMG LLP (1995-2005); With, KPMG LLP (1990-1995) **CR:** Board of Directors, Business Roundtable (2018); Board of Directors, KPMG LLP (2000-2005); Co-chair, Steering Committee, Infrastructure and Urban Development Industries, World Economic Forum; Board of Directors, ADM; Board of Directors, LA 2028; Board of Directors, Rentech, Inc. **CIV:** Board of Directors, Children's Bureau; Trustee, Neighborhood Youth Association **AW:** Listee, Top 300 Architecture Firms, Architectural Record, BNP Media (2019) **MEM:** Association of International Certified Professional Accountants; California Society of CPAs; The State Bar of California **BAR:** State of California

BURKE, TARANA J., T: Activist **I:** Civil Service **DOB:** 09/12/1973 **PB:** Bronx **SC:** NY/USA **ED:** BA in Political Science, Auburn University at Montgomery (1996) **C:** Founder, Me Too Movement (2006-Present); Founder, Just Be Inc. (2003-Present); Senior Director, Girls for Gender Equity, Brooklyn, NY **CR:** Contributor, "Tarana Burke on What We Can Learn From Cyntoia Brown's Story," TIME USA, LLC (2019); Speaker in Field **CIV:** With, Art Sanctuary Philadelphia, PA (2008) **CW:** Consultant, "Selma" (2014) **AW:** Trailblazer Award, VH1 Trailblazer Honors (2019); Listee, Power 100, ArtReview (2018); VOTY Catalyst Award, She Media (2018); Ridenhour Prize for Courage (2018); Named One of the TIME 100, TIME USA, LLC (2018); Named Person of the Year, TIME USA, LLC (2017)

BURLESON, LYNN, T: Lawyer **I:** Law and Legal Services **DOB:** 07/19/1948 **PB:** Albermarle **SC:** NC/USA **PT:** Ira Pierce Burleson; Hazel (Austin) Burleson **CH:** Jennifer Hinkle **ED:** JD, Wake Forest University (1980); MPA, University of North Carolina at Chapel Hill (1974); BA, University of North Carolina at Chapel Hill (1970) **C:** Partner, Tharrington Smith LLP, Raleigh, NC (2001-Present); Associate, Tharrington Smith LLP, Raleigh, NC (1999-2000); Partner, Kilpatrick, Stockton LLP, Winston-Salem, NC (1987-1999); District Court Judge, State of North Carolina, Winston-Salem, NC (1984-1987); Assistant District Attorney, State of North Carolina (1981-1984); Associate, Yokley & Teeter, Winston-Salem, NC (1980-1981) **CR:** Adjunct Professor, High Point University (1986-1999); Adjunct Professor, Wake Forest University School of Law (1982-1984) **CW:** "There's Money on the Table: Issues in High End Family Law Cases: High Alimony and Child Support Awards," Family Law Intensive Seminar, North Carolina Bar Foundation (2016); "Family Law Arbitration," Indiana State Bar Association Annual Meeting (2015); Course Planner, It's a Small World After All, Family Law Section Annual Meeting, North Carolina Bar Foundation (2012); "Family Law Arbitration: Third Party ADR," Campbell Law Symposium (2008); "Family Law Arbitration," Family Law Issues, Wake County Bar Association (2007); "Arbitrating Under the North Carolina Family Law Arbitration Act," Family Law Section of Mecklenburg County Bar Association, North Carolina Chapter of the American Acad-

emy of Matrimonial Lawyers (2006); "Codifying Marital Torts," Family Law Specialists Meeting (2006); "Family Law Arbitration From The Court Perspective," North Carolina District Court Judges Conference (2006); Presenter, Course Planner, "Arbitrating Family Law Cases," American Academy of Matrimonial Lawyers Regional Workshops (2001-2006); "Amendments to the N.C. Family Law Arbitration Act," North Carolina Bar Foundation (2005); Presenter, Course Planner; "Arbitration – A New Concept in Family Law", Family Law in Our Changing World, American Academy of Matrimonial Lawyers (2005); Course Planner, Basics of Family Law, North Carolina Bar Foundation (2004); "Matrimonial Law Arbitration", American Academy of Matrimonial Lawyers Annual Meeting (2004); Arbitration Training Institute, American Academy of Matrimonial Lawyers (2004); "Hot Tips for Matrimonial Arbitration," American Academy of Matrimonial Lawyers Annual Meeting (2003); "Professionalism", Equitable Distribution, Wake Forest University School of Law (2003); "Family Law Arbitration," Family Law Specialists Seminar, North Carolina State Bar (2003); Course Planner, Family Law Specialists Seminar, North Carolina State Bar (2003); "Professional Responsibility," Practical Family Law (2002); "Arbitration for the Family Lawyer," Mecklenburg County Family Law Section (2002); "Ethics and Professionalism in Custody Cases," North Carolina Bar Foundation (2002); "History and Overview of Family Law Arbitration," Arbitration of Marital Issues, American Academy of Matrimonial Lawyers (2002); "Professionalism," Family Law, Wake Forest University School of Law (2002); "North Carolina Family Law Arbitration Act," Family Law Section Annual Meeting, North Carolina Bar Association (2000); Course Planner, Family Law Section Annual Meeting, North Carolina Bar, Association (2000) **MEM:** Uniform Laws Commission Family Law Arbitration Act Drafting Committee, Observer-Member (2013-Present); Wake County Bar Association (1999-Present); 10th Judicial District Bar (1999-Present); American College of Family Trial Lawyers, Diplomate (2008); Forsyth County Bar Association (1980-1999); American Academy of Matrimonial Lawyers, Fellow (1993); Board of Governors, Family Law Chair (1991-1992); Twenty-First Judicial District Bar Member (1980); North Carolina State Bar (1980); North Carolina Bar Association (1980); Family Law Section (1980); United States District Court for the Eastern District of North Carolina; United States District Court for the Middle District of North Carolina; United States District Court for the Western District of North Carolina; North Carolina Chapter of the American Academy of Matrimonial Lawyers **BAR:** State of North Carolina (1980) **MH:** Albert Nelson Marquis Lifetime Achievement Award **B/I:** Mr. Burleson had initially hoped to build on a master's degree and become a city attorney; however, he could not find a job right after law school. To make ends meet, he became an assistant district attorney for several years and then he became a state district court judge. The state district judge hears a lot of family court cases, so it became a logical step for Mr. Burleson to pursue that field after he came off the bench. **AV:** Cycling; Exercising; Reading; Admiring musical theatre

BURNET, GEORGE V, T: Engineering Educator **I:** Education/Educational Services **DOB:** 01/30/1924 **PB:** Fort Dodge **SC:** IA/USA **PT:** George Burnet; Myrtle Violet (Hutchinson) Burnet **MS:** Married **SPN:** Martha Anderson (2015); Betty Arlene Riggs (10/08/1944, Deceased 02/1993) **CH:** Kathryn Ann; Betty Jo; Dolores Unalee; Joan Marie; Elaine Kaye; George **ED:** PhD, Iowa State University (1951); MS, Iowa State University (1949); BSChemE, Iowa State University (1948) **CT:** Registered Professional

Engineer, State of Iowa **C:** Dean Emeritus, Iowa State University, Ames, IA (1995-Present); Interim Dean of Engineering, Iowa State University, Ames, IA (1994-1995); Associate Dean of Engineering for Outreach and External Affairs, Iowa State University, Ames, IA (1990-1994); Coordinator, Engineering Education Projects Office, Iowa State University, Ames, IA (1978-1990); Chairman, Department of Nuclear Engineering, Iowa State University, Ames, IA (1978-1983); Anson Marston Distinguished Professor, Iowa State University, Ames, IA (1975-1995); Professor, Chemical Engineering, Iowa State University, Ames, IA (1958-1995); Head, Department of Chemical Engineering, Iowa State University, Ames, IA (1961-1978); Faculty Member, Iowa State University, Ames, IA (1956-1995, 1949-1951) **CR:** Associate, U.S. Department of Energy (1956-Present); Advisory Committee, Science and Engineering Education Directorate, National Science Foundation (1984-1986); President's Task Force on Energy Research and Development, U.S. Atomic Energy Commission (1973); Phillips Lecturer, Oklahoma State University (1970); Consultant, Agency for International Development in Higher Education to India (1967); Process Design Engineer, Commercial Solvents Corp. (1952-1956); Senior Engineer, Division Chief, Ames Laboratory **CIV:** National Science Board Commission on Pre-college Education (1982-1983); Trustee, Chairman of the Board, Iowa State University Alumni Achievement Fund (1973-1974); Boy Scouts of America **MIL:** Army Reserve (1948-1968); Lieutenant Colonel, U.S. Army (1944-1948) **CW:** Contributor, Articles, Professional Journals **AW:** Unsung Hero Award (2003); Centennial Medallion, American Society Engineering Education (1993); Leighton Collins Award, American Society Engineering Education (1991); Ronald Schmitz Award, American Society Engineering Education (1987); Edward Mikol Award, American Society Engineering Education (1984); Grinter Award, Accreditation Board of Engineering and Technology (1984); Lamme Medal, American Society Engineering Education (1982); Founders Award, American Institute of Chemical Engineers (1981); Iowa Citizen Chemical Engineer Award (1970); Faculty Citation, Iowa State University (1969) **MEM:** Charter Fellow, Accreditation Board of Engineering and Technology (1988); U.S. Representative, Committee on Education and Training World Federation of Engineering Organizations (1984-1988); National Representative to Engineers Council for Professional Development, American Institute of Chemical Engineers (1969-1984); Executive Committee, Accreditation Board of Engineering and Technology (1981-1983); Director, Accreditation Board of Engineering and Technology (1977-1983); Chairman, Educational Affairs Council, American Association Engineering Societies (1980-1981); President, American Society Engineering Education (1976); Chairman, Engineering Education and Accreditation Committee, Accreditation Board of Engineering and Technology (1975-1977); National Director, American Society Engineering Education (1972-1974); National President, Omega Chi Epsilon (1970); Chairman, Division of Fertilizer and Soil Chemistry, American Chemical Society (1969); Chairman, Iowa Section, American Institute of Chemical Engineers (1967); Honorary Member, American Society Engineering Education (1964); Chairman, Chemical Engineering Division, American Society Engineering Education (1964); Charter, American Institute of Chemical Engineers (1956); Chairman, Terre Haute Section, American Institute of Chemical Engineers (1956); Fellow, American Association for the Advancement of Science; Distinguished Fellow, Iowa Academy Science; American Society of Engineering Education; Sigma Xi; Tau Beta Pi; Phi Lambda Upsilon; Phi Kappa Phi; Alpha Chi Sigma; Tau Kappa Epsilon **MH:** Albert Nelson Marquis Lifetime Achievement Award **B/I:** Mr. Burnet's father was a civil engineer, and he always admired his work and lifetime achievements. While Mr. Burnet was in high school, he worked with his father's land surveying crew and became very interested in engineering. During his senior year in high school, he had an outstanding chemistry teacher, who was a true inspiration. This teacher inspired Mr. Burnet to pursue chemical engineering. **RE:** Methodist

BURNETT, MARK, T: Television Producer; Chairman **I:** Media & Entertainment **CN:** MGM Television Worldwide Group and Digital **DOB:** 07/17/1960 **PB:** London **SC:** England **PT:** Archie Burnett; Jean Burnett **MS:** Married **SPN:** Roma Downey (04/28/2007); Diane J. (Valentine) Burnett (1992, Divorced 2003) **CH:** James; Cameron; Reilly Marie Anspaugh (Stepdaughter) **C:** President, MGM Television and Digital Group (2015-2018); Founder, President, Mark Burnett Productions, Inc. **CR:** Chairman, MGM Television and Digital Group (2018-Present) **CIV:** Ambassador, Operation Smile; Board of Directors, Elizabeth Glaser Pediatric Aids Foundation **MIL:** Section Commander, Parachute Regiment, British Army (1978-1982) **CW:** Creator, Executive Producer, "Survivor" (2000-Present); Executive Producer, "Beat Shazam" (2017); Executive Producer, "Steve Harvey's Funderdome" (2017); Executive Producer, "Coupled" (2016); Executive Producer, "Ben Hur" (2016); Executive Producer, "A.D. The Bible Continues" (2015); Executive Producer, "Woodlawn" (2015); Executive Producer, "The Dovekeepers" (2015); Executive Producer, "Shark Tank" (2009-2015); Executive Producer, "Are You Smarter Than a 5th Grader?" (2007-2015); Executive Producer, "Son of God" (2014); Executive Producer, "Little Boy" (2014); Executive Producer, "The Bible" (2013); Creator, Writer, "Diili" (2005-2013); Executive Producer, "Stars Earn Stripes" (2012); Creator, Executive Producer, "Celebrity Apprentice Australia" (2011-2012); Executive Producer, "The Voice" (2011-2012); Creator, Writer, "Bully Beatdown" (2009-2012); Creator, Writer, "O Aprendiz" (2004-2011); Creator, Executive Producer, "The Apprentice" (2003-2011); Executive Producer, "Expedition Africa" (2009); Executive Producer, "Wedding Day" (2009); Executive Producer, "How'd You Get So Rich?" (2009); Executive Producer, "StarMaker" (2009); Executive Producer, "The Contender" (2006-2009); Executive Producer, "On the Lot" (2007); Executive Producer, "The Restaurant" (2003-2004); Executive Producer, "Rock Star: INXS" (2005); Executive Producer, "Apprentice: Martha Stewart" (2005); Author, "Jump In! Even if You Don't Know How to Swim" (2005); Executive Producer, "The Casino" (2004); Executive Producer, "Are We There Yet?" (2003); Executive Producer, "Boarding House: North Shore" (2003); Executive Producer, "Combat Missions" (2002); Author, "Dare to Succeed: How to Survive and Thrive in the Game of Life" (2002); Creator, "Eco-Challenge" (1995-2002); Producer, Television Shows and Award Shows **AW:** Outstanding Producer of Competition TV Award, Producers Guild of America (2014, 2016); Entertainment Industry Award, Anti-Defamation League (2014); Norman Lear Achievement Award in Television, Producers Guild of America (2010); Star, Hollywood Walk of Fame (2009); Inductee, Broadcast & Cable Hall of Fame (2008); Maverick, Details Magazine (2007); People's Choice Award for Favorite Reality-Based Television Program (2001, 2002, 2003, 2004); Listee, 100 Most Influential People, Time Magazine (2004); Philanthropist of the Year, Reality Cares Foundation (2004); Special Recognition Award, Gay & Lesbian Alliance Against Defamation (GLAAD) (2001); Emmy Award for Outstanding Nonfiction Program, Academy of Television of Arts & Sciences (2001); Sports Emmy Award for Outstanding Program Achievement for Eco-Challenge: Morocco, National Academy of Television Arts and Sciences (2000); Banff Rockie Award in the Sports Program Category, Banff Rockie Awards Festival (2000); Recipient, Numerous Awards **MEM:** National Academy of Television Arts & Sciences; Two Elected Terms, Board of Directors, British Academy of Film and Television Arts (BAFTA) **AV:** Scuba diving; Skydiving

BURNS, CHRISTINE, DR., T: Program Manager, Acquisition Task Lead **I:** Information Technology and Services **CN:** The MITRE Corporation **DOB:** 03/15/1968 **PB:** Flint **SC:** MI/USA **PT:** Robert Burns; Sharon D. Burns (Deceased); Hattie t. Burns **MS:** Single **ED:** PhD in Business Management, Capella University, Minneapolis, MN (2018); MBA in Business Administration, University of Phoenix, Phoenix, AZ (2012); MS in Computer Information Systems, University of Phoenix, Phoenix, AZ (2004); BS in Information Systems Management, University of Maryland University College, Adelphi, MD, Magna Cum Laude (2002) **CT:** Certified Project Management Professional (2007); Masters Certificate, Project Management for Information Systems (2006) **C:** MITRE Corporation (2010-Present); Senior Intelligence Officer, Defense Intelligence Agency (2008-2010); Senior Information Systems Specialist, Electronic Data Systems (2006-2008); Information Systems Specialist, Electronic Data Systems (2006); Information Systems Chief, U.S. Army Human Resources Command (2004-2006); Telecommunications Center Duty Officer, Office of the Administrative Assistant to the Secretary of the Army (2002-2004); MITRE Project Work: Army Central Command (ARCENT) FWD/335th Signal Command Theater (T) Provisional (P) Task Lead, MITRE Corporation; National Leadership Command Capability (NLCC) Services and Infrastructure Office Program Management and Acquisition, Support, and Center for Medicare and Medicaid Services (CMS) End Stage Renal Disease Quality Incentive Program (ESRD-QIP) Systems Lead) **MIL:** U.S. Army Signal Corps (1986-2006, Retired) **AW:** Trailblazer Award, MITRE Corporation **MEM:** Project Management Institute, Inc.; Honor Society of Phi Kappa Phi; Delta Mu Delta International Honors Society **AS:** Dr. Burns attributes her success to her faith and her upbringing. She believes in herself and never believed that she couldn't overcome a challenge. She believes in the quote from Philippians 4:13, "I can do all things through Christ, who strengthens me..." **B/I:** Dr. Burns became involved in her profession because she initially joined the U.S. Army with goals of funding her college education. When she was presented with a second enlistment, she was inspired to stay and serve her country. Once she retired from the Army, going into the IT-profession was simply a natural progression of the work that she did in the Army. She never planned it, she was simply presented with opportunities and continued to take advantage and progress. **THT:** Dr. Burns' motto is, "Although things are not always easy, they are still achievable..."

BURNS, JEFFREY, T: Founder/Partner **I:** Law and Legal Services **CN:** Dollar, Burns & Becker, L.C. **MS:** Married **CH:** Four Sons; Two Daughters **ED:** JD, University of Missouri School of Law, Columbia, MO, Cum Laude (1983); Coursework, Visiting Student, University of Leicester Faculty of Law (Leicester Law School), Leicester, England, United Kingdom (1980-1981); Coursework, Visiting Student, Saint Louis University School of Law (1979-1980); Coursework, Universidad Complutense de Madrid, Madrid, Spain (1978-1979); BS in Industrial Education, Northeast Missouri State University (Now Truman State University, Kirksville, MO, Summa Cum Laude (1978) **CT:** Board Certified in Truck Accident Law, National Board of Trial Advocacy **C:** Founding Partner, Dollar, Burns & Becker, L.C. (2005-Present); Attorney, Shook, Hardy & Bacon, P.C. and Shook, Hardy & Bacon, L.L.P. (1985-2004); Law Clerk, Honorable Elmo B. Hunter, United States District Judge, Western District of Missouri (1983-1985) **CIV:** Board Member, Truck and Bus Safety Committee, National Academy of Sciences; Appointed Member, National Freight Advisory Committee, Secretary of Transportation **CW:** Contributor, Articles, Professional Journals; Featured, Missouri Law Review **AW:** Named to Top 100 Trial Lawyers in America, American Trial Lawyers Association (2008-Present); Named to Super Lawyers (2005-Present); Named Best Lawyers in America (2005-Present); Distinguished Service Award, Truck Safety Coalition, Sorrow to Strength Conference (2005); Lifesaver Award, Parents Against Tired Truckers (1998); Unsung Hero Award, Missouri Lawyers Weekly (1996); West Publishing Award for Highest Scholastic Average, University of Missouri, Columbia; Second Prize for Comments, G.A. Thompson Prize; University of Missouri School of Law Scholarship; Listee, Who's Who Among Students in American Universities **MEM:** Transportation Research Board; Vice-Chair, Commercial Transportation Litigation Committee, Tort Trial & Insurance Practice Section, American Bar Association (ABA); Truck Litigation Group, American Association for Justice; Citizens for Reliable and Safe Highways (CRASH), Truck Safety Coalition; Parents Against Tired Truckers (P.A.T.T.); National Transportation Counsel, Parents Against Tired Truckers (P.A.T.T.), Truck Safety Coalition; The Missouri Bar; American Bar Association (ABA); Kansas City Metropolitan Bar Association; Chair, Truck Litigation Group, American Association for Justice; Missouri Association of Trial Attorneys; Former Member, National Freight Advisory Committee; Former Director, Alliance for Safe Highways, Coalition Against Bigger Trucks, MO and KS; Former Director, Center for Truck Safety (C.T.S.); Former Director, Brain Injury Association of Kansas; Order of the Coif; Life Member, National Registry of Who's Who **BAR:** Missouri **AS:** Mr. Burns attributes his success to believing in trying to make the roads safer and always keeping that as the primary goal. **B/I:** Mr. Burns knew of two little girls that were killed in an accident. One of his kids was the same age as one of the girls. It hit home; he would have nightmares about losing those two girls. He promised the girls' grandfather that their deaths would make a difference. His entire career has been a mission to make the road safer. **THT:** Mr. Burns' motto is "Have fun, be careful, help others."

BURNS, LYLE D., T: Organic Chemist **I:** Sciences **DOB:** 12/15/1951 **PB:** Maryville **SC:** MO/USA **PT:** Rex Lavern Burns; Margaret Jane (Dougherty) Burns **MS:** Married **SPN:** Carolyn Louise Eck (08/12/1972) **CH:** Michael Aaron Burns; Marcus Sean Burns **ED:** MS in Organic Chemistry, Iowa State University, Ames, IA (1977); BS in Chemistry, Northwest Missouri State University, Maryville, MO (1974) **C:** President, Terra Environmental Products Co., Bartlesville, OK (1994-Present); General Manager, Biorecovery Systems, Inc., Church Point, LA (1993); Environmental Tech. Planning Team Leader, Phillips Petroleum Co., Bartlesville, OK (1991-1992); Special Projects Director, Crude Oil, Phillips Petroleum Co., Bartlesville, OK (1988-1990); Marketing Manager, Phillips Petroleum Co., Bartlesville, OK (1986-1988); Senior Product Development Specialist, Phillips Petroleum Co., Bartlesville, OK (1982-1986); Market Research Analyst, Phillips Petroleum Co., Bartlesville, OK (1981); Fuel Additives Chemist, Phillips Petroleum Co., Bartlesville, OK (1979-1981); Polymer Chemist, Phillips Petroleum Co., Bartlesville, OK (1977-1979); President, Clean Tech Innovations, Bartlesville, OK **CIV:** Judge, Annual Bartlesville Science Fair (1978-Present); Teacher, OSHAA HAZWOPER Safety Course for Workers Exposed to Hazardous Environments **CW:** Contributor, Numerous Articles, Professional Publications; Patentee in the Field, 30 Patents **AW:** IR-100 Award, Industrial R&D Magazine (1986) **MEM:** Treasurer, Northeast Oklahoma Chapter, American Chemical Society (1979-1981); Society of Petroleum Engineers (SPE); Phi Kappa Upsilon; Elks Lodge **MH:** Albert Nelson Marquis Lifetime Achievement Award **B/I:** Mr. Burns became involved in his profession because chemistry and music were his subjects of interest in high school. He pursued chemistry in graduate school. Though he loved music, he figured he could make more money as a scientist. **AV:** Golfing; Worldwide traveling; Gardening

BURNS, MARIAN M., T: Lawyer **I:** Law and Legal Services **DOB:** 04/18/1931 **PB:** Burlingame **SC:** KS/USA **PT:** Victor S. Mussatto; Janet (Hotchkiss) Mussatto **MS:** Married **SPN:** Clyde M. Burns **CH:** Janet C. Walsh; Richard Burns **ED:** LLB, Kansas University (1954); AB, Kansas University (1952) **C:** Municipal Judge, Osage City (1967-Present); Attorney, Burns Burns Walsh & Walsh PA (1954-Present); Republican Party Candidate, State Senate 17th District (1984); Court Attorney, Osage County, Kansas (1955-1961) **CR:** Past President, Lincoln Day Club, Independence, KS; President, U.S. District 421 School Board, Lyndon, KS; Co-owner, Lyndon Bank **CIV:** Pro Bono Work, Kansas Bar Association; President, Economic Development, Osage County; Kansas Calvary State Organization **AW:** President's Circle, Top Attorneys of North America (2018-2019); Distinguished Service Award; Judges Award, Osage County **MEM:** American Legion Auxiliary; Osage County Bar Association; Kansas Bar Association; Masons **BAR:** Kansas **MH:** Albert Nelson Marquis Lifetime Achievement Award; Marquis Who's Who Top Professional **B/I:** Ms. Burns' major in college was political science, she has always been interested in the field. There was a husband and wife team in town when she was in high school and she thought that was nifty, and feels they had some influence on her choice.

BURR, RICHARD MAUZE, T: U.S. Senator from North Carolina **I:** Government Administration/Government Relations/Government Services **DOB:** 11/30/1955 **PB:** Charlottesville **SC:** VA/USA **PT:** David Horace White Burr; Martha (Gillum) Burr **MS:** Married **SPN:** Brooke Fauth (1984) **CH:** Tyler; William **ED:** BA in Communications, Wake Forest University, Winston-Salem, NC (1978) **C:** Chairman, U.S. Senate Select Committee on Intelligence (2015-Present); U.S. Senator, State of North Carolina (2005-Present); U.S. Representative from North Carolina's Fifth Congressional District, U.S. Congress (1995-2005); State Co-Chairman, North Carolina Taxpayers United (1993-1998); National Sales Manager, Carswell Distributing, Winston-Salem, NC (1978-1994) **CIV:** Co-Chairman, Partnership for a Drug-free North Carolina, Inc.; Member, Forsyth County Earning by Learning; Board of Directors, Brenner Children's Hospital, Winston-Salem, NC **AW:** Named Legislator of the Year, Biotechnology Industry Organization (Now Biotechnology Innovation Organization (BIO)) (2002); Jefferson Award, Citizens for a Sound Economy (2001); Ground Water Protector Award, National Ground Water Association (2000); Manufacturing Legislative Excellence Award, National Association of Manufacturers (1999); Alfred & Alma Hitchcock Tribute Award, Cystic Fibrosis Foundation (1999) **MEM:** Optimist Soccer League; Rotary International **PA:** Republican

BURRIS, KEITH C., T: Executive Editor **I:** Publishing **CN:** Pittsburgh Post-Gazette **C:** Executive Director, Pittsburgh Post-Gazette (2019-Present); Vice President, Editorial Director, Block Newspapers **AW:** Pulitzer Prize (2019)

BURROW, DEBORAH JETT, T: Class Teacher **I:** Education/Educational Services **CN:** Claude Thompson Elementary School **PT:** Leanna Jett **ED:** Master of Arts in Education, George Mason University, Fairfax, VA; Bachelor of Science in Education, Virginia State University **C:** Classroom Teacher, Claude Thompson Elementary School **CIV:** Treasurer, Auxiliary of Churches, Northern Virginia Baptist Sunday School **AW:** Teacher of the Year; Martin Luther King Education Award **MEM:** Various Educational Associations **AS:** Ms. Burrow credits her success to her first grade teacher, Mrs. Boyd, who helped her to succeed. Learning has always been very important to her. **B/I:** Having long held a desire to support others in their education, Ms. Burrow wanted to become a teacher since the age of seven. Even as a second grade student, she can recall a great motivation to help her peers succeed. **THT:** "Children are the future."

BURROW, JOSEPH LEE, T: Collegiate Football Player **I:** Athletics **DOB:** 12/10/1996 **PB:** Athens **SC:** OH/USA **PT:** Jim Burrow **ED:** Coursework, Louisiana State University (2018-2019); Diploma in Consumer and Family Financial Services, The Ohio State University (2017); Diplomate, Athens High School, The Plains, Ohio (2014) **C:** Quarterback, Louisiana State University, Baton Rouge, LA (2018-2019); Quarterback, The Ohio State University, Columbus, Ohio (2015-2017); Quarterback, Athens High School, The Plains, Ohio (2011-2014) **AW:** Offensive MVP, College Football Playoff National Championship (2020); Heisman Trophy (2019); Maxwell Award (2019); Water Camp Award (2019); College Football Player of the Year, The Associated Press (2019); Johnny Unitas Golden Arm Award (2019); Davy O'Brien Award (2019); Named Consensus All-American (2019); SEC Offensive Player of the Year (2019); Invited, First Team All-SEC (2019); SEC Champion (2019); Mr. Football Award (2014); James A. Rhodes Award (2014)

BURSTYN, ELLEN, T: Actress **I:** Media & Entertainment **DOB:** 12/07/1932 **PB:** Detroit **SC:** MI/USA **PT:** John Austin Gillooly; Correine Marie (Hamel) Gillooly **MS:** Divorced **SPN:** Neil Nephew (1964, Divorced 04/1972); Paul Roberts (09/14/1958, Divorced 1962); William Alexander (1950, Divorced 09/1955) **CH:** Jefferson (Adopted) **ED:** Honorary LHD, Dowling College; Honorary DFA, School of Visual Arts **C:** Artistic Director, The Actor's Studio, New York, NY (1982-1988); Dancer; Model **CIV:** Member, Individual Artists Grants and Policy Overview Panels, National Endowment for the Arts; Member, Theater Advisory Council, City of New York, NY **CW:** Actress, "Lucy in the Sky" (2019); Actress, "American Woman" (2019); Actress, "The Tale" (2018); Actress, "Nostalgia" (2018); Actress, "The House of Tomorrow" (2017); Actress, "A Little Something for Your Birthday" (2017); Actress, "Wiener-Dog" (2016); Actress, "Custody" (2016); Actress, "House of Cards" (2016); Actress, "The Age of Adeline" (2015); Actress, "About Scout" (2015); Actress, "Mom" (2015); Actress, "The Calling" (2014); Actress, "Interstellar" (2014); Actress, "Old Soul" (2014); Actress, "Flowers in the Attic" (2014); Actress, "Petals on the Wind" (2014); Actress, "Wish You Well" (2013); Actress, "Political Animals" (2012); Actress, "Coma" (2012); Actress,

"Another Happy Day" (2011); Actress, "Someday This Pain Will Be Useful" (2011); Actress, "Main Street" (2010); Actress, "The Velveteen Rabbit" (2009); Actress, "According to Greta" (2009); Actress, "The Mighty Macs" (2009); Actress, "Possible Side Effects" (2009); Actress, "Law & Order: Special Victims Unit" (2009); Actress, "The Loss of a Teardrop Diamond" (2008); Actress, "Lovely Still" (2008); Actress, "W." (2008); Actress, "The Little Flower of East Orange" (2008); Actress, "Big Love" (2007-2011); Actress, "Mitch Albom's For One Day" (2007); Actress, "The Elephant King" (2006); Actress, "The Wicker Man" (2006); Actress, "30 Days" (2006); Actress, "The Fountain" (2006); Author, "Lessons in Becoming Myself" (2006); Actress, "Our Fathers" (2005); Actress, "Mrs. Harris" (2005); Actress, "Down in the Valley" (2005); Actress, "The Madam's Family: The Truth About the Canal Street Brothel" (2004); Actress, "The Five People You Meet in Heaven" (2004); Actress, "Brush with Fate" (2003); Actress, "Picnic" (2003); Actress, "Oldest Living Confederate Widow Tells All" (2003); Actress, "Divine Secrets of the Ya-Ya Sisterhood" (2002); Actress, "Distance" (2002); Voice Actress, "Red Dragon" (2002); Actress, "Within These Walls" (2001); Actress, "Dodson's Journey" (2001); Actress, "Mermaid" (2000); Actress, "Walking Across Egypt" (1999); Actress, "Requiem for a Dream" (1999); Actress, "The Yards" (1999); Actress, "Night Ride Home" (1999); Actress, "You Can Thank Me Later" (1998); Actress, "Flash" (1998); Actress, "The Patron Saint of Liars" (1998); Actress, "Playing by Heart" (1998); Actress, "A Will of Their Own" (1998); Actress, "Deceiver" (1997); Actress, "A Deadly Vision" (1997); Actress, "The Spitfire Grill" (1996); Actress, "Our Son, The Matchmaker" (1996); Actress, "Murder in the Mind" (1996); Actress, "Roommates" (1995); Actress, "The Baby-Sitters Club" (1995); Actress, "How to Make an American Quilt" (1995); Actress, "My Brother's Keeper" (1995); Actress, "Follow the River" (1995)' Actress, "Timepiece" (1995); Actress, "Sacrilege" (1995); Actress, "The Color of Everything" (1994); Actress, "Getting Out" (1994); Actress, "Getting Gotti" (1994); Actress, "Trick of the Eye" (1994); Narrator, Presenter, "Choosing One's Way: Resistance in Auschwitz/Birkenau" (1994); Actress, "When a Man Loves a Woman" (1994); Actress, "The Cemetery Club" (1993); Actress, "Shattered Trust: The Shary Karney Story" (1993); Actress, "Taking Back My Life: The Nancy Ziegenmeyer Story" (1992); Actress, "Shimada" (1992); Actress, "Grand Isle" (1991); Actress, "Mrs. Lambers Remembers Love" (1991); Actress, "Dying Young" (1991); Actress, "When You Remember Me" (1990); Actress, "Shirley Valentine" (1989); Actress, "Hanna's War" (1988); Actress, "Hello Actors Studio" (1987); Voice Actress, "Dear America: Letters Home from Vietnam" (1987); Actress, "Pack of Lies" (1987); Host, "The Ellen Burstyn Show" (1986-1987); Actress, "Something in Common" (1986); Actress, "Act of Vengeance" (1986); Actress, "Twice in a Lifetime" (1985); Actress, "Surviving" (1985); Actress, "Into Thin Air" (1985); Actress, "In Our Hands" (1984); Actress, "The Ambassador" (1984); Actress, "84 Charing Cross Road" (1982-1983); Actress, Lee Strasberg/The Actors Studio (1981); Actress, "Silence of the North" (1981); Actress, "The People versus Jean Harris" (1981); Actress, "Resurrection" (1980); Actress, Film, "Same Time, Next Year" (1978); Actress, Broadway, "Same Time, Next Year" (1975-1978); Actress, "Thursday's Game" (1974); Actress, "Harry and Tonto" (1974); Actress, "Alice Doesn't Live Here Anymore" (1974); Actress, "The Exorcist" (1973); Actress, "The King of Marvin Gardens" (1972); Actress, "The Last Picture Show" (1971); Actress, "Alex in Wonderland" (1970); Actress, "Tropic of Cancer" (1970);

Actress, "The Bold Ones: The Lawyers" (1969); Actress, "The Time Tunnel" (1966); Actress, "The Big Valley" (1965); Actress, "Gunfight in Black Horse Canyon" (1961); Actress, "Fair Game" (1957-1958); Actress, "Maverick" (1957); Dancer, "The Jackie Gleason Show" (1955-1956); Actress, "Cheyenne" (1955); Actress, "Gunsmoke" (1955) **AW:** Primetime Emmy Award for Outstanding Supporting Actress in a Mini-Series or a Movie, Television Academy (2013); Named to American Theater Hall of Fame (2013); Primetime Emmy Award for Outstanding Guest Actress - Drama Series, Television Academy (2009); Named to Michigan Women's Hall of Fame (1997); Golden Globe Award for Best Actress - Motion Picture Musical or Comedy, Hollywood Foreign Press Association (1979); Academy Award for Best Actress, Academy of Motion Picture Arts and Sciences (1975); BAFTA Award for Best Actress in a Leading Role (1975); Numerous Awards **MEM:** President, Actors' Equity Association (1982-1985) **PA:** Democrat **RE:** Sufist

BURTON, BARBARA A., T: Psychotherapist **I:** Medicine & Health Care **PB:** Columbia **SC:** SC/USA **PT:** Eugene Walter Able Cantelou; Mary Louise (Chadwick) Cantelou **CH:** Stacia Louise Burton Farr **ED:** MSW, University of Alabama (1970); BA in Psychology, Georgia State University **CT:** Diplomate, American Board of Examiners in Clinical Social Work; Certification, International Academy of Behavioral Medicine, Counselling and Psychotherapy (IABMCP) **C:** Psychotherapist, Private Practice, New Orleans, LA (1983-2000); Program Manager and Clinical Consultant, Alabama Goodwill Industries, Birmingham, AL (1977-1981); Director, School Social Work, Miles College, Birmingham, AL (1977-1978); Miles College, Birmingham, AL (1977-1978); Director, Ensley Outpatient Drug Abuse Clinic, Birmingham, AL (1975-1977); Member, Adjunct Faculty, University of Alabama, Tuscaloosa, AL (1975-1977); Director, Ensley Outpatient Drug Abuse Clinic, Birmingham, AL (1975-1977); Member, Adjunct Faculty, University of Alabama, Tuscaloosa, AL (1975-1977); Associate Executive Director, Positive Maturity, Inc., Birmingham, AL (1970-1977); Communications Organization Planner, Community Service Council, Inc., Birmingham, AL (1972-1975); Communications Organization Planner, Community Service Council, Inc., Birmingham, AL (1972-1975); Associate Executive Director, Positive Maturity, Inc., Birmingham, AL (1970-1972) **CR:** Consultant, Omega International Institute, New Orleans, LA (1988-1994) **CIV:** Past Chairman, Policy and Program Committee, Birmingham Urban League; Alabama Advisory Committee on Social Services; Alabama Committee for Development Higher Education; Alabama Conference of Social Work **CW:** Author, "Love Me, Love Me Not, and Other Matters That Matter" (1990) **AW:** Fellow, Institute on Human Sexuality, University of Hawaii (1976); National Institute of Mental Health (NIMH), National Institutes of Health (NIH) **MEM:** Diplomate in Clinical Social Work, National Association of Social Workers; American Association of Sex Educators, Counselors and Therapists (AASECT); Academy of Certified Social Workers; International Platform Committee; Psi Chi, the International Honor Society in Psychology **MH:** Albert Nelson Marquis Lifetime Achievement Award **B/I:** Ms. Burton became involved in her profession because she took a psychology course in high school and immediately knew that was the right choice for her. Initially, she ended up choosing different majors at various colleges. It wasn't until she became the legal guardian of her little brother that she knew she needed a job, so she went to Emory University and received a position as the secretary to chairman of pediatrics. She spent a great deal of time using med-

ical dictionaries. She then traveled and became a secretary to psychologists. There were hospitals funded by Kennedy grants that were for the mentally retarded. Ms. Burton spent much time working in institutions and with people with special needs. After getting her brother out of school, she decided she would need to go back to school for herself. She went to Georgia State University, and she had already completed some coursework in the past. She was notified by an adviser that it would be wiser for her to pick a major with course work that she had already completed. The adviser gave her choices, and one of them happened to be psychology. Ms. Burton decided on psychology. **AV:** Creative writing; Reading; Interior design; Rescuing animals **PA:** Liberal

BURTON, LAUREN G., T: Attorney **I:** Law and Legal Services **ED:** Doctor of Jurisprudence, Southwestern University Law School (2014); Bachelor of Arts in Organizational Studies, University of California Davis (2011) **C:** Associate, Boucher LLP (2015-Present); Legal Extern, IMAX (2013-2014); Communications Intern, Office of Governor Arnold Schwarzenegger, California (2010-2011); Legislative intern, United States Senator Barbara Boxer's Office (2008-2009) **AW:** CALI Excellence in Academic Achievement Award, Southwestern Law School (2012); Dean-Merit Scholar, Southwestern Law School **BAR:** State Bar of California (2015) **AS:** Ms. Burton attributes her success to her family, which let her go in her own direction and celebrated her successes wherever she chose to go. **B/I:** Ms. Burton became involved in her profession due to the influence of her sister, who attended law school but unfortunately succumbed to cancer. Driven to follow her example, she aspired to make a difference in people's lives.

BURTON, TIM, T: Director **I:** Media & Entertainment **DOB:** 08/25/1958 **PB:** Burbank **SC:** CA/USA **PT:** Bill Burton; Jean (Erickson) Burton **MS:** Divorced **SPN:** Lena Gieseke (Divorced, 1991) **CH:** Billy Ray; Indiana Rose **ED:** Coursework, California Institute Arts (Disney Fellowship) (1979-1980) **C:** Apprentice Animator, Disney Production; Cartoon Artist, Disney Production **CW:** Director, "Dumbo" (2019); Producer, "Alice Through the Looking Glass" (2016); Director, "Miss Peregrine's Home for Peculiar Children" (2016); Director, Producer, "Big Eyes" (2014); Director, Producer, "Frankenweenie" (2012); Director, "Dark Shadows" (2012); Producer, "Abraham Lincoln: Vampire Hunter" (2012); Director, "Alice in Wonderland" (2010); Director, "Sweeney Todd: The Demon Barber of Fleet Street" (2007); Director, "Charlie and the Chocolate Factory" (2005); Director, "Corpse Bride" (2005); Director, "Big Fish" (2003); Director, "Planet of the Apes" (2001); Executive Producer, "Lost in Oz" (2000); Director, Producer, "The World of Stainboy" (2000); Director, "Sleepy Hollow" (1999); Author, "The Melancholy Death of Oyster Boy and Other Stories" (1997); Director, Producer, "Mars Attacks!" (1996); Director, "James and the Giant Peach" (1996); Producer, "Batman Forever" (1995); Director, Producer, "Ed Wood" (1994); Producer, "Cabin Boy" (1994); Author, "My Art & Films" (1993); Producer, "The Nightmare Before Christmas" (1993); Executive Producer, "Family Dog" (1992); Director, Producer, "Batman Returns" (1992); Executive Producer, "Beetlejuice" (Television Series) (1989-1991); Director, Producer, "Edward Scissorhands" (1990); Director, "Batman" (1989); Director, "Beetlejuice" (1988); Director, "Pee-Wee's Big Adventure" (1984); Director, "Hansel and Gretel" (1982); Director, "Vincent" (1982); Director, Producer, "Stalk of the Celery" (1979) **AW:** Officer Ordre des Arts et de Lettres, Government of France (2010); Golden

Lion Award, Venice International Film Festival (2007); Listee, 50 Greatest Directors of All Time, Entertainment Weekly

BUSCH, KURT FREDERICK, T: Founder, Chief Executive Officer **I:** Technology **CN:** Syntiant Corp **MS:** Married **SPN:** Amy Busch **CH:** Dominick; Bridget; Vincent **ED:** MBA in Business Administration, Santa Clara University (1998); BS in Biological Science, University of California, Irvine (1993); BS in Electrical Engineering, University of California, Irvine (1993) **C:** Founder, Chief Executive Officer, Syntiant Corp, Irvine, CA (2017-Present); Chief Executive Officer, Busch Toschi, LLC (2015-Present); Chief Executive Officer, Lantronix, Irvine, CA (2011-2015); Senior Vice President, General Manager, High-Performance Analog, Mindspeed Technologies (2006-2011); Business Development Manager, Analog Devices (2003-2006); Vice President, Sales & Marketing, TeraCross (2001-2003); President, United States Subsidiary, Switchcore Corporation (1998-2001); Strategic Marketing Manager, Intel, Santa Clara, CA (1998); Strategic Marketing Manager, Digital Equipment Corporation (1995-1998); Project Design Engineer, Standard Microsystems (1990-1995) **CIV:** Assistant Scout Master, Boy Scouts of America **CW:** Patent, Print Server for a Portable Device; Author, "Is Time Ripe for Fabric on a Chip?"; Author, "Is Standardization Impeding on the Deployment of Switch Fabric Chip Sets"; Creator, Full-Custom Silicon Design **AW:** Inductee, Samueli School of Engineering Hall of Fame (2015); OC 500, Orange County Business Journal **MEM:** Chief Executive Officer, Round Table, University of California, Irvine; Young Presidents' Organization **MH:** Marquis Who's Who Top Professional **AS:** Mr. Busch attributes his success to his ability to build successful teams that compliment what he can bring to the table and address the market at the right time. He says, "It is not the critic that counts." **B/I:** Mr. Busch became interested in sciences and engineering when he read books by Carl Sagan as a teenager. One in particular, titled "Contact," prompted him to go into sciences and engineering.

BUSH, GEORGE WALKER, T: 43rd President of the United States **I:** Government Administration/Government Relations/Government Services **DOB:** 07/06/1946 **PB:** New Haven **SC:** CT/USA **PT:** George Herbert Walker Bush; Barbara (Pierce) Bush **MS:** Married **SPN:** Laura Lane (Welch) Bush (11/05/1977) **CH:** Barbara; Jenna **ED:** MBA, Harvard Business School (1975); BA in History, Yale University (1968) **C:** 43rd President, United States, Washington, DC (2001-2009); Governor, State of Texas, Austin, Texas (1994-2000); Managing General Partner, Texas Rangers, MLB (1989-1994); Senior Advisor, George Herbert Walker Bush Presidential Campaign (1988); Board of Directors, Harken Energy Corp. (Formerly Spectrum 7 Energy Corp.), Midland, TX (1986-1999); Chairman, Spectrum 7 Energy Corp. (Formerly Bush Exploration), Midland, TX (1984-1986); Founder, Chief Executive Officer, Bush Exploration (Formerly Arbusto Energy Inc.), Midland, TX (1982-1984); Founder, Chief Executive Officer, Arbusto Energy Inc., Midland, TX (1977-1982) **CR:** Board of Directors, Caterair International, Inc. (1990-1994) **CIV:** Pilot, Texas Air National Guard (1968-1970) **CW:** Author, "41: A Portrait of My Father" (2014); Author, "Decision Points" (2010); Co-author with Karen Hughes, "A Charge to Keep" (1999) **AW:** Named One of the 50 Highest-earning Political Figures, Newsweek (2010); Named One of the 100 Most Influential People in the World, TIME Magazine (2004, 2005, 2006, 2008); Named Person of the Year, TIME Magazine (2004); Big D Award, Dallas All Sports Associ-

ation (1989) **MEM:** President, Delta Kappa Epsilon (1965-1968); Delta Kappa Epsilon **PA:** Republican **RE:** Methodist

BUSH, JOHN, "JEB" ELLIS, T: Governor of Florida (Retired), Consulting Firm Executive **I:** Other **DOB:** 02/11/1953 **PB:** Midland **SC:** TX/USA **PT:** George Herbert Walker Bush; Barbara (Pierce) Bush **MS:** Married **SPN:** Columba Garnica Gallo (02/23/1974) **CH:** George; Noelle; John, Jr. **ED:** BA in Latin American Affairs, The University of Texas at Austin, Magna Cum Laude (1974) **C:** Founder, President, Jeb Bush & Associates LLC, Miami, FL (2007-Present); Candidate, Republican Nominee, 2016 Presidential Election (2015-2016); Senior Adviser, Barclays PLC (2008-2014); Governor, State of Florida, Tallahassee, FL (1999-2007); President, Chief Operating Officer, Codina Partners, Miami, FL (1995-1998); Secretary of Commerce, State of Florida, Tallahassee, FL (1987-1988); Co-Founder, Codina Bush Group, Miami, FL (1981-1993); Vice President, Texas Commerce Bank, Caracas, Venezuela (1974-1979) **CR:** Chairman, National Constitution Center (2013-Present); Board of Directors, CorMatrix Cardiovascular, Inc. (2010-2014); Board Member, Bloomberg Family Foundation (2010-2014); Board of Directors, Swisher Hygiene, Inc. (2010-2013); Board of Directors, Rayonier, Inc. (2008-2014); Board of Directors, Angelica Corp. (2008-2014); Board of Directors, TH Medical (2007-2014); Board of Directors, CNL Bancshares, Inc. (Now Valley National Bank) (2007-2014); Board of Directors, Safecard Services (1995-1996); Chairman, Miami-Dade County Republican Party (1984-1986) **CIV:** Founder, Foundation for Florida's Future (1995); Co-Founder, Liberty City Charter School (1995); Trustee, The Heritage Foundation (1995); Chairman, Miami-Dade Beacon Council (1990-1991); Volunteer, Miami Children's Hospital (Now Nicklaus Children's Hospital); Volunteer, United Way of Miami-Dade; Volunteer, Miami-Dade County Homeless Trust **CW:** Co-Author, "Profiles in Character" (1996) **MEM:** The Phi Beta Kappa Society **PA:** Republican **RE:** Roman Catholic

BUSH, LAURA WELCH, T: Former First Lady of the United States; Educator **I:** Government Administration/Government Relations/Government Services **DOB:** 11/04/1946 **PB:** Midland **SC:** TX/USA **PT:** Harold Bruch Welch; Jenna Louise (Hawkins) Welch **MS:** Married **SPN:** George Walker Bush (11/05/1977) **CH:** Jenna; Barbara Pierce **ED:** Honorary LittD, Wayland Baptist University (2015); MLS, The University of Texas at Austin (1973); BS in Education, Southern Methodist University (1968) **C:** First Lady of the United States, Washington, DC (2001-2009); First Lady of the State of Texas (1995-2000); Librarian, Dawson Elementary School, Austin, Texas (1974-1977); Librarian, Houston Public Librarian (1973-1974); Teacher, John F. Kennedy Elementary School, Houston, Texas (1969-1972); Teacher, Longfellow Elementary School, Dallas, Texas (1968-1969) **CR:** Founder, George W. Bush Presidential Center (2013-Present); Chair, Bush Institute's Women's Initiative (2013-Present); Speaker, Republican National Convention, New York, NY (2004); Co-creator, The Heart Truth Campaign (2003); Co-creator, Red Dress Project (2003); Creator, National Book Festival (2001); Creator, Texas Book Festival, Austin, Texas (1996) **CIV:** Volunteer, Hurricane Help for Schools **CW:** Co-author, Children's Book, "Our Great Big Backyard" (2016); Co-author, Children's Book, "Read All About It!" (2011); Author, Memoir, "Spoken from the Heart" (2010) **AW:** Award, Women Making History Awards, Washington, DC (2017); Prevent Blindness Person of Vision Award (2015); Named Distinguished Alumnus, The University of Texas at Austin (2012); Named One of the 100 Most

Powerful Women, Forbes (2004-2008); President's Crystal Apple Award, American Association of School Librarians (2006); Award, Kuwait-America Foundation (2006); Award, American Library Association (2005); Award, Elie Wiesel Foundation for Humanity (2002); Named the Most Fascinating Person of the Year, Barbara Walters' Special (2002) **MEM:** Honorary Ambassador, United Nations Literacy Decade (2003-Present); U.S.-Afghan Women's Council (USAWC) **PA:** Republican **THT:** Mrs. Bush and her husband, George W. Bush, co-founded the George W. Bush Presidential Center in Dallas, Texas. The facility, which also houses the Bush Presidential Museum and Library and the George W. Bush Institute, was created to advance human freedom, economic growth, education reform, and global health. Mrs. Bush's main focuses are literacy, women's health, women's rights, and education. As the chair of the Bush Institute's Women's Initiative, she works to promote health and human freedom for women and girls around the world. Notably, Mrs. Bush delivered the president's weekly radio address in 2001 to bring attention to the Taliban's oppression of women. This was the first time a First Lady had delivered the address. With regards to literacy and education, Mrs. Bush was instrumental in creating the National Book Festival and the Texas Book Festival, which continue to this day. She also visited numerous international schools, including ones in Afghanistan and Zambia. On the health spectrum, Mrs. Bush developed The Heart Truth campaign and the Red Dress Project with the National Heart, Lung, and Blood Institute to help raise awareness of the risk of heart disease in women. Then, a few years later, she expanded on the idea and launched international initiatives. She continues her work today through Pink Ribbon Red Ribbon, a subsidiary of the Bush Institute that adds cervical and breast cancer to PEPFAR in sub-Saharan Africa.

BUSH, WESLEY G., T: Chairman **I:** Technology **CN:** Northrop Grumman Corporation **ED:** BS in Electrical Engineering, Massachusetts Institute of Technology (1983); MSEE, Massachusetts Institute of Technology **C:** Chairman, Northrop Grumman Corporation (2018-Present); Chairman, Chief Executive Officer, Northrop Grumman Corporation (2018-2019); President, Chief Executive Officer, Chairman, Northrop Grumman Corporation, Los Angeles, CA (2017-2018); President, Chief Executive Officer, Northrop Grumman Corporation, Los Angeles, CA (2010-2017); President, Chief Operating Officer, Northrop Grumman Corp., Los Angeles, CA (2007-2009); President, Chief Financial Officer, Northrop Grumman Corp., Los Angeles, CA (2006-2007); Corporate Vice President, Chief Financial Officer, Northrop Grumman Corporation, Los Angeles, CA (2005-2006); Corporate Vice President, President, Space Tech., Northrop Grumman Corporation, Los Angeles, CA (2003-2005); President, Chief Executive Officer, Global Aeronautical System, TRW-United Kingdom (2001-2003); President, Chief Executive Officer, TRW Aeronautical Systems (2001-2003); Vice President, General Manager, TRW Ventures (2000-2001); Advanced from System Engineer to Vice President, General Manager, Telecommunications Programs Division, TRW Aeronautical Systems (1987-1999); Corporate Vice President, President, Space Tech., Comsat Labs; With, Engineering Staff, Aerospace Corporation **CR:** Board of Directors, Northrop Grumman Corporation (2009-Present); Member, National Infrastructure Advisory Council (2008-Present) **CIV:** Board Member, Conservation International; Board Member, National Air and Space Museum, Smithsonian Institution; Board Member, Business-Higher Education Forum (BHEF); Board Director, National Action Council for Minorities in Engineering, Inc. (NACME)

BUSQUETS, MIGUEL A., T: Ophthalmologist **I:** Medicine & Health Care **DOB:** 07/14/1971 **PB:** Hyannis **SC:** MA/USA **PT:** Miguel Salvador Busquets; Anne Healy Busquets **MS:** Married **SPN:** Gretchen Elizabeth Gruener **CH:** Talia; Marisa **ED:** Doctor of Medicine, Duke University School of Medicine, Duke University, Durham, NC (1996); Bachelor of Arts in Biological Anthropology, Harvard University, Cambridge, MA, Magna Cum Laude (1992) **CT:** Certification, American Board of Ophthalmology (2002-Present); Licensures, Pennsylvania, West Virginia, Kentucky **C:** Specialty in Vitreoretinal Surgery, Associates in Ophthalmology Ltd., Wheeling, WV (2010-Present); Specialty in Vitreoretinal Surgery, Associates in Ophthalmology Ltd., Butler, PA (2008-Present); Private Practice, Specialty in Vitreoretinal Surgery, Associates in Ophthalmology Ltd., Meadville, PA (2007-Present); Private Practice, Specialty in Vitreoretinal Surgery, Associates in Ophthalmology, Ltd., West Mifflin, PA (2006-Present); Private Practice, Specialty in Vitreoretinal Surgery, Associates in Ophthalmology, Greensburg, PA (2004-Present); Private Practice, Specialty in Vitreoretinal Surgery, Associates in Ophthalmology Ltd., Monroeville, PA (2002-Present); Private Practice, Specialty in Vitreoretinal Surgery, Associates in Ophthalmology Ltd. (2002-Present); Private Practice, Specialty in Vitreoretinal Surgery, Associates in Ophthalmology, West Mifflin, PA (2002-2006); Fellowship, Barnes Retina Institute, Washington University School of Medicine, St. Louis, MO (2000-2002); Resident, Department of Ophthalmology, Washington University School of Medicine, St. Louis, MO (1997-2000); Transitional Residency/Medical Surgical Intern, Carilion Health System, Roanoke Memorial Hospital, Roanoke, VA (1996-1997) **CR:** Member, Courtesy Staff, Ophthalmology, Western Pennsylvania Hospital, Pittsburgh, PA (2013-Present); Consulting, Ophthalmology, Wheeling Hospital, Wheeling, WV (2010-Present); Active Member, Ophthalmology, Associates Surgery Centers LLC, West Mifflin, PA (2006-Present); Director, Vitreoretinal Fellowship Program, Associates in Ophthalmology, Pittsburgh, PA (2007-2019); Clinical Instructor, University of Pittsburgh School of Medicine, Pittsburgh, PA (2002-2019); Clinical Instructor, Pennsylvania College of Optometry, Pittsburgh, PA (2002-2019); Researcher, Investigator, Numerous Studies for Facilities (1994-2019); Participant, Iluvien/Alimera Sciences Advisory Board, Chicago, IL (2016); Clinical Instructor, Ophthalmology, Lake Erie College of Osteopathic Medicine, Erie, PA (2010-2012); Participant, Allergan U.S. Retina Advisory Board Meeting, Fort Lauderdale, FL (2009); Participant, Macugen Clinical Roundtable Meeting, Eyetech, Washington, DC (2009); Participant, Retina Advisory Meeting, Alcon, Dallas, TX (2008); Participant, Lucentis Advisory Board, Genentech, New York, NY (2007); Participant, Macugen Advisory Board, Eyetech, New Orleans, LA (2007); Participant, Lucentis Advisory Board, Genentech, Chicago, IL (2007); Participant, Macugen Advisory Board, Eyetech, Los Angeles, CA (2006); Member, Committee on Admissions, Duke University School of Medicine, Duke University, Durham, NC (1994-1995); Teaching Fellow, Harvard University, Cambridge, MA (1991); Consultant, Vortex Surgical; Vitroretinal Consultant, Allergan Pharmaceuticals; Advisory Board Member, Alcon; Advisory Board Member, Genentech; Advisory Board Member, Eyetech OSI Pharmaceuticals; Member, Novartis Pharmaceutical Ophthalmic Division, Novartis National Speakers Bureau; Member, ISTA Pharmaceuticals National Speakers Bureau; Member,

Pfizer National Speakers Bureau; Member, Eyetech OSI National Speakers Bureau; Member, Allergan National Speakers Bureau; Member, Genetech National Speakers Bureau; Faculty Adviser, "Ophthalmology Times"; Faculty Adviser, "Ocular Surgery News"; Lecturer in the Field **CIV:** Pro Bono Surgery for Hurricane Maria Victims via Airlift **CW:** Reviewer, Retina, The Journal of Retinal and Vitreous Diseases (2007-Present); Author, Contributor, Articles to Professional Journals (2006-2018); Presenter, Numerous Presentations and Lectures (1999-2018); Author, Contributor, Articles for Numerous Peer-Reviewed Publications (2003-2017); Author, Contributor, Numerous Published Abstracts (1999-2016) **AW:** Grantee, Retina Research Foundation Joseph M. and Eula C. Lawrence Grant, Association for Research in Vision and Ophthalmology (1999); Rosenbaum Research Award for "Best Ophthalmological Research by a Resident," Washington University School of Medicine (1998); Pediatric Ophthalmology Grant Award, Knights Templar Eye Foundation, Foundation for Retinoblastoma Research (1998) **MEM:** Pittsburgh Chapter, Young Presidents Organization (2010-2013); American Academy of Ophthalmology; Fellow, American Society of Retina Specialists; Fellow-in-Training Section, Education and Training, Committee Member, American Society of Retina Specialists; Pittsburgh Ophthalmology Society; Research to Prevent Blindness, Ophthalmological Associate; American College of Surgeons; Association for Research in Vision and Ophthalmology; Pennsylvania Academy of Ophthalmology; Allegheny County Medical Society; Pennsylvania Medical Society; Outpatient Ophthalmic Surgery Society; Fellow, American Academy of Ophthalmology; Fellow, American College of Surgeons **MH:** Albert Nelson Marquis Lifetime Achievement Award; Marquis Who's Who Top Professional **B/I:** Dr. Busquets became involved in his profession because of his grandfather, who served as a physician in rural Puerto Rico during the 1940s. He was the first pediatrician in the area and that level of care and dedication inspired Dr. Busquets to become a physician. He became attracted to ophthalmology and the sub specialty of vitro retinal surgery. **AV:** Marathon running; swimming

BUSTOS, CHERYL, "CHERI" LEA, T: U.S. Representative from Illinois **I:** Government Administration/Government Relations/Government Services **DOB:** 10/17/1961 **PB:** Springfield **SC:** IL/USA **PT:** Gene Callahan; Ann Callahan **MS:** Married **SPN:** Gerry Bustos **CH:** Nick; Tony; Joey **ED:** MA in Journalism, University of Illinois Springfield (1985); BS in Political Science and History, University of Maryland, College Park, MD (1983); Coursework, Illinois College (1981) **C:** Chair, House Democratic Steering Committee (2021-Present); Chair, Democratic Congressional Campaign Committee (2019-Present); U.S. Representative from Illinois' 17th Congressional District, United States Congress, Washington, DC (2013-Present); Member, U.S. House Committee on Transportation and Infrastructure (2013-Present); Member, U.S. House Committee on Agriculture (2013-Present); Member, Democratic Policy and Communications Committee (2017-2019); Alderman City Council, City of East Moline, IL (2007-2011); Vice President, Public Relations and Communications, Iowa Health System (Now UnityPoint Health) (2008-2010); Senior Director, Corporate Communications, Trinity Regional Health System (Now UnityPoint Health) (2001-2007); Reporter, Editor, Quad-City Times, Davenport, Iowa (1985-2001) **AW:** Athena Business Women's Award (2009); Named to the Illinois College Sports Hall of Fame (1994) **MEM:** Blue Dog Coalition **PA:** Democrat **RE:** Roman Catholic

BUTCHER, EDWARD BERNIE, T: Retired State Legislator/Business Consultant **I:** Consulting **DOB:** 07/20/1943 **PT:** Milton H. Butcher; Louise Wildung Butcher **MS:** Married **SPN:** Pamela Ward Butcher **CH:** Trevis M. Butcher; Ross W. Butcher; Rebecca Butcher **ED:** Post-Graduate Coursework, Study University of Colorado (1969); Post-Graduate Coursework, North Dakota State University (1968); MA, University of Montana (1967); BS, Eastern Montana College (1966) **C:** Senior Regional Manager (2000-Present); Aftco Associate, Senior Consultant (1988-Present); Owner, Butchers Rolling Hills Ranch (1972-Present); National Sales Director, Evans Biocontrol (1986-1988); Lecturer, University of Great Falls (1974-1980); Assistant Professor, Valley City State University (1968-1971); High School Government Teacher (1967-1968) **MEM:** Life Membership, National Rifle Association; State President, National Farmers Organization; Gideons International **MH:** Albert Nelson Marquis Lifetime Achievement Award **B/I:** Senator Butcher became involved in his profession because his mother was active in the democratic party, so he grew up as an activist. When he went to college, he organized a young Democratic organization and got involved in a lot of state-wide campaigns. Later, at the University of North Dakota, he was teaching several political science courses and found that he loved being an educator. **PA:** Republican **RE:** Lutheran

BUTKUS, DICK MARVIN, T: Former Professional Football Player **I:** Athletics **DOB:** 12/09/1942 **PB:** Chicago **SC:** IL/USA **MS:** Married **SPN:** Helen (Essenberg) Butkus (1963) **CH:** Nicole; Richard; Matthew **ED:** Coursework, University of Illinois **C:** Broadcaster, Station WGN-Radio, Chicago, IL (1986-Present); Broadcaster, "The NFL Today," CBS, New York, NY (1988-1989); Middle Linebacker, Chicago Bears, NFL (1965-1973) **CIV:** Founder, The Butkus Foundation; Founder, Dick Butkus Center for Cardiovascular Wellness, Orange County, CA **CW:** Co-author, "The OC Cure for Heart Disease" (2006); Appearance, "Teddy Bears' Picnic" (2002); Appearance, "Any Given Sunday" (1999); Appearance, "Necessary Roughness" (1991); Appearance, "Spontaneous Combustion" (1990); Appearance, "Gremlins 2: The New Batch" (1990); Appearance, "The Stepford Children" (1987); Appearance, "Hamburger: The Motion Picture" (1986); Appearance, "Blue Thunder" (1984); Appearance, "Johnny Dangerously" (1984); Appearance, "Cracking Up" (1983); Appearance, "The Legend of Sleepy Hollow" (1980); Appearance, "Superdome" (1978); Appearance, "Rich Man, Poor Man" (1977); Appearance, "Mother, Jugs & Speed" (1976); Appearance, "Gus" (1976); Appearance, "Cry, Onion!" (1975); Appearance, "The Longest Yard" (1974); Appearance, "Brian's Song" (1971); Appearances, Television and Movies; Numerous Television Commercials **AW:** Named to the NFL 100th Anniversary All-time Team (2019); Award, Order of Lincoln, The Lincoln Academy of Illinois (2018); Named One of the Best Players in the NFL, New York Daily News (2014); Named to National Lithuanian American Hall of Fame (2013); Named One of the Top 100: NFL's Greatest Players, NFL Network (2010); Named to Chicagoland Sports Hall of Fame (2008); Named One of the Best Players in NFL History, Sporting News (1999); Named to the NFL 75th Anniversary All-time Team (1994); Named to Pro Football Hall of Fame (1979); Named Six-times to First-team All-Pro (1965, 1967–1970, 1972); Named Eight-times to Pro Bowl (1965–1972); Named Two-times to Second-team All-Pro (1966, 1971); Named Two-time NFL Defensive Player of the Year (1969, 1970); Named UPI Lineman of the Year (1964); Named Two-time Consensus All-American (1963, 1964); Named Big Ten Most Valuable Player (1963);

Named to the NFL 1960s All-Decade Team; Named to the NFL 1970s All-Decade Team; Named One of the Greatest Athletes of the 20th Century, ESPN

BUTLER, WILLIAM L. SR., T: Business Owner (Retired) **I:** Retail/Sales **CN:** Butler Sales Associates **DOB:** 01/26/1939 **PB:** Indianapolis **SC:** IN/USA **PT:** Edward Morris Butler Jr; Louise Hughes (Dyer) Butler **MS:** Widowed **SPN:** Grace Caroline (Gage) **CH:** Mary Dyer; William Langdon Jr. **ED:** BA, Middlebury College (1962) **C:** President, Owner, Butler Sales Associates (1998-2014); Vice President, General Merchandise Division, Trina Incorporated, Fall River, MA (1987-1997); Vice President Sales, Trina Incorporated, Fall River, MA (1982-1987); Regional Sales Manager, Trina Incorporated, Fall River, MA (1980-1982); Chief Executive Officer, Owner, Butler Sales & Marketing Incorporated, Summit, NJ (1967-1980); Regional Manager, Hi-Fashion Incorporated, Atlanta, GA (1966-1967); Owner, Butler Sales Associates, Summit, NJ (1965-1966); With, J.J. Newberry Company, New York, NY (1961-1963) **CIV:** Trustee, Summit Jaycee Foundation (1970); Coach, Junior Raider Football League, Fanwood, NJ (1968) **MIL:** First Lieutenant, United States Army, Air Defense Artillery (1963-1965); With, United States Army ROTC, Middlebury College (1957-1961) **AW:** Named, Outstanding Young Man, American Jaycees (1971); Outstanding Director Award, Summit Jaycees (1970); Key Man Award, Summit Jaycees (1970) **MEM:** Board of Directors, Society for the Preservation and Encouragement of Barber Shop Quartet Singing in America, Inc. (SPEBSQSA) (Now Barbershop Harmony Society), Westfield, NJ (1972-1974); New Jersey NG Association (National Guard Association of New Jersey); Summit Jaycees; Sigma Phi Epsilon Fraternity **MH:** Albert Nelson Marquis Lifetime Achievement Award **B/I:** Mr. Butler began working in the business due to joining the family company, Butler Sales Associates, with his father, Edward and brother, Edward. Butler's father and brother worked in the cosmetic sales industry. When Mr. Butler got out of the Army, he knew he wanted to do sales as well. Between the three men, they went around to cosmetic companies to see if they would be allowed to sell their cosmetic accessory products, which ultimately kickstarted the family business that lasted over 50 years. **AV:** Barbershop quartet singing; Stamp collecting/philately; Spectator sports **PA:** Republican **RE:** Presbyterian

BUTNER, ROBERT WESTBROOK, MD, T: Ophthalmologist, Educator **I:** Medicine & Health Care **DOB:** 07/05/1942 **PB:** Fort Oglethorpe **SC:** GA/USA **PT:** Wendell Boise Butner; Helen Salkeld (Taylor) Butner **MS:** Married **SPN:** Mary Carol Steib (1966) **ED:** MD, Johns Hopkins University (1968); BA, Rice University, Cum Laude (1964) **CT:** Diplomate, National Board of Medical Examiners; Diplomate, American Board of Ophthalmology; Fellow, American College of Surgeons; Fellow, International College of Surgeons **C:** Clinical Assistant Professor, University of Texas-Houston School of Medicine (2002-Present); Clinical Associate Professor, Baylor College Medicine, Houston, TX (1992-2002); Clinical Assistant Professor, Baylor College of Medicine, Houston, TX (1983-1992); Clinical Instructor, Baylor College of Medicine, Houston, TX (1977-1983); Retinal Surgery Fellowship, Baylor College of Medicine, Houston, TX (1975-1976); Ophthalmology Residency, Baylor College of Medicine, Houston, TX (1972-1975); Internship, Charity Hospital, Tulane University, New Orleans, LA (1968-1969) **MIL:** Colonel, Medical Corps; Group Surgeon, 1st and 20th Special Forces Groups **CW:** Contributor, Articles, Professional Journals **AW:** Inductee, Order of St. John of Jerusalem (2015); Outstanding Teacher Award, University of Texas Health Science

Center at Houston, Department of Ophthalmology and Visual Science (2014); Honorary Membership, Union of Bulgarian Ophthalmologists (2013); Basic, Belarusian Army (2011); Distinguished Medical Alumnus Award, Johns Hopkins University School of Medicine (2011); Special Diploma, Ophthalmological Society of the Federation of Bosnia and Herzegovina (2009); Basic, Israeli Army (2008); Basic, Spanish Air Force (2008); Basic, Russian Army (2003); Basic, Argentine Army (2003); International Public Service Award, Foundation of the American Academy of Ophthalmology (2002); Basic, Tunisian Army (2001); Basic, Nepalese Army (2001); Outstanding Humanitarian Service Award, American Academy of Ophthalmology (2001); Basic, Italian Army (1987); Master, United States Army (1986); Rough Terrain, Republic of China Army (1972); Senior, United States Army (1972); Basic, United States Army (1970); Eagle Scout Award, Boy Scouts of America; God and Country Award; Explorer Silver Award; Order of the Arrow; Master Parachutist Badge, U.S. Army; Flight Surgeon Badge, U.S. Army; Special Forces Tab, U.S. Army; Meritorious Service Medal, U.S. Army **MEM:** Special Forces Association; American Society of Retinal Specialists; Texas Medical Association; Houston Ophthalmological Society; Harris County Medical Society; Phi Beta Kappa; National Rifle Association; Texas Rifle Association; Lay Reader, St. Thomas Episcopal Church, Houston, TX **MH:** Albert Nelson Marquis Lifetime Achievement Award **AV:** Running; Researching Civil War history; Traveling **RE:** Anglican

BUTT, CHARLES CLARENCE, T: Chairman, Chief Executive Officer **I:** Food & Restaurant Services **CN:** H.E. Butt Grocery Company (H-E-B, LP) **DOB:** 02/03/1938 **PB:** Houston **SC:** TX/USA **PT:** Howard Edward Butt Sr.; Mary Elizabeth Holdsworth **ED:** BS in Economics, The Wharton School, The University of Pennsylvania (1959); MBA, Harvard Business School; Diploma, Graduate Advanced Management Program, Harvard University **C:** Chairman, Chief Executive Officer, H.E. Butt Grocery Company (H-E-B, LP), San Antonio, TX (1984-Present); President, H.E. Butt Grocery Company (H-E-B, LP), San Antonio, TX (1971-1984) **CR:** Director, Texas Commerce Bancshares, Inc. (1974-1989) **CIV:** Participant, The Giving Pledge (2018); Chairman, Advisory Council, The University of Texas at Austin Marine Science Institute (1976-1986); Member, Coordinator, Board, Texas College and University Systems (1978-1983); Chairman, Annual Campaign, M.D. Anderson Cancer Hospital (Now The University of Texas MD Anderson Cancer Center) (1981); Member, Board of Overseers, The Wharton School, The University of Pennsylvania; Member, Board of Directors of Associates, Harvard Business School; Chairman, Faculty Salaries Committee **AW:** Named to Forbes List of Billionaires (2015); Named One of Forbes 400: Richest Americans (2006-2014); Mr. South Texas Award, Washington's Birthday Celebration Association (1996); Conservation Award, Winedale Historical Complex, The Dolph Briscoe Center for American History, The University of Texas at Austin; Amanda Cartwright Taylor Award, Conservation Society of San Antonio **MEM:** San Antonio German Club; Order of the Alamo; New York Yacht Club; Nantucket Yacht Club; Corpus Christi Yacht Club; The Argyle **AV:** Sailing; Historical preservation; Photography

BUTTERFIELD, GEORGE KENNETH JR., T: U.S. Representative from North Carolina; Former State Supreme Court Justice **I:** Graphic Design **DOB:** 04/27/1947 **PB:** Wilson **SC:** NC/USA **PT:** G. K. Butterfield; Addie (Davis) Butterfield **SPN:** Jean Farmer (1971, Divorced 1991) **CH:** Valeisha

Monique; Jenetta Lenai; Tunya Michelle **ED:** JD, NCCU School of Law (1974); BS in Political Science and Sociology, North Carolina Central University (1971) **C:** Second Vice Chair, Congressional Black Caucus (2011-Present); U.S. Representative from North Carolina's First District, United States Congress (2004-Present); Chair, Congressional Black Caucus (2015-2017); Judge, North Carolina Special Superior Court (2002-2004); Justice, North Carolina Supreme Court (2001-2002); Judge, North Carolina Resident Superior Court, District 7BC (1989-2001); Senior Partner, Butterfield, Fitch & Wynn (1974-1988); Member, Committee on Energy and Commerce **MIL:** Specialist, U.S. Army (1968-1970) **AW:** Named to the Power 150 (2008); Named One of the Most Influential Black Americans, Ebony Magazine (2006); Lawyer of the Year Award, North Carolina Association of Black Lawyers **MEM:** Vice President, North Carolina Bar Association (2003-Present) **BAR:** State of North Carolina (1975) **PA:** Democrat **RE:** Baptist

BUTTIGIEG, PETER, "PETE" PAUL MONTGOMERY, T: Mayor **I:** Government Administration/Government Relations/Government Services **DOB:** 1/19/1982 **PB:** South Bend **SC:** IN/USA **PT:** Joseph Buttigieg; Jennifer Anne (Montgomery) Buttigieg **MS:** Married **SPN:** Chasten Glazmen Buttigieg (2018) **ED:** Bachelor of Arts in Philosophy, Politics and Economics, Pembroke College, University of Oxford, with First Class Honors (2007); Bachelor of Arts in History and Literature, Harvard University, Magna Cum Laude (2004) **C:** Mayor, South Bend, IN (2012-Present); Nominee, Democratic Candidate, 2020 Presidential Election (2019-2020); Consultant, McKinsey & Company (2007-2010); Conference Director, U.S. Secretary of Defense William Cohen, The Cohen Group (2004-2005) **MIL:** Lieutenant, United States Navy Reserve (2014-2017); Ensign, United States Navy Reserve (2009) **CW:** Author, "Shortest Way Home: One Mayor's Challenge and a Model for America's Future" (2019); Editor, Oxford International Review **AW:** Listee, Pride50, Queerty (2019); Named, Mayor of the Year, GovFresh.com (2013); Rhodes Scholarship (2004); First Prize, John F. Kennedy Presidential Library and Museum's Profiles in Courage Essay Conte (2000) **MEM:** The Phi Beta Kappa Society **PA:** Democrat **RE:** Christian

BUTTON, LEWIS A. III, T: Attorney **I:** Law and Legal Services **CN:** Office of the Secretary of the State **PT:** Lewis Button; Mildred Button **MS:** Single **ED:** JD, University of Connecticut School of Law (1999); BA in English Language and Literature, University of Connecticut (1993) **C:** Attorney, Office of the Secretary of State (2004-Present) **CIV:** Chief Negotiator/Officer, A & R Employees Union 4200 **AS:** Mr. Button attributes his success to his parents. He success stems from what they taught him and how they raised him. **B/I:** Mr. Button believes he was a teacher before he became a lawyer. He was trying to teach civic education and began to see and feel how important the law was in shaping our lives. And even though teaching is important, he wanted to have a more direct impact on shaping the law. **THT:** Mr Buttons motto is, "Some men see things as they are, and ask why. I dream of things that never were, and ask why not?"

BYRD, JOSEPH, MUSB, MA, T: Composer, Musician (Retired) **I:** Fine Art **DOB:** 12/19/1937 **PB:** Louisville **SC:** KY/USA **PT:** J. H. Byrd; Dian Nall Byrd **MS:** Married **SPN:** Angela Blackthorne; Beni Bennett (1984) (Deceased 2015) **CH:** Clarissa Elizabeth **ED:** Postgraduate Coursework, UCLA (1963-1966); MA in Music and Composition, Stanford University (1960); MusB, University of Arizona (1959) **C:** Associate Professor of Music, College of the Redwoods

(1996-2015); Founder, The New Music Workshop (1963-1966); Staff Arranger, Composer, Capital Records (1963); Secretary, Virgil Thomson (1961-1963) **CR:** Scholar, American Popular Music **CIV:** Eureka Chamber Music Series **CW:** Arranger, "A Christmas Yet to Come" (1970); Arranger, "Yankee TranscenDoodle" (1970); Arranger, "Joe Byrd and the Field Hippies" (1969); Arranger, "The United States of America" (1969); Solo Concert Performance, Fluxus (1962); Arranger, CBS Evening News with Dan Rather; Composer, Film, "Lions Love"; Composer, Film, "The Long Riders"; Composer, First National Campaign, Dr. Pepper **AW:** National Endowment for the Arts (1982); National Endowment for the Humanities (1982); Grantee, Ford Foundation (1962) **MH:** Albert Nelson Marquis Lifetime Achievement Award **B/I:** Mr. Byrd became involved in his profession because of his childhood experiences. At the age of 12, he had his first heartbreak and his mother rented an accordion for him to help take his mind off things. His love of music has grown ever since.

BYRD, LIDIA M., T: Language Educator **I:** Education/Educational Services **PT:** Geremar Valverde; Natalia Vega **MS:** Married **SPN:** Eddie Ray Byrd (03/01/1986) **CH:** Walter Joseph **ED:** Master's Degree, Louisiana State University (2002) **C:** Instructor, Louisiana State University (2003-Present); Instructor, Southeastern Louisiana University (2002) **CR:** Co-Chair, Social Events Committee, Friends of Spanish Studies, Louisiana State University (2011-2012); Founding Adviser, Spanish Club, Louisiana State University (2005-2010); Teacher, Courses in Elementary and Intermediate Spanish, Textual Commentary, Advanced Grammar and Composition, and Advanced Oral Communication **CIV:** Volunteer Food Server, Spanish Resource Center Open House and Concert (2009, 2011); Participant, Student Organization Fair (2007-2008, 2010); Coordinator, Movies Series (2009); Organizer, Spanish Movie Night in Conjunction with the Mathematics Club (2009); General Coordinator, "Day of the Dead" Altar, Spanish Club Table, Music, Dance Performance (2007-2009); Volunteer, Fall Festival (2005-2006); Consul, Baton Rouge International Heritage Festival **AW:** Recognition Certificates, Baton Rouge Center for World Affairs (2009-2011); Recognition Certificate, Spanish Club, Louisiana State University; Appreciation Letter, Baton Rouge Mayor's Office **MEM:** Spanish Undergraduate Studies Committee (2006); Costa Rican Representative, Baton Rouge International Heritage Celebration, Baton Rouge Center for World Affairs; Costa Rican Representative, Global Community Day; Sigma Delta Pi **MH:** Albert Nelson Marquis Lifetime Achievement Award **AS:** Ms. Byrd attributes her success to her parents, who taught her discipline, gratitude, honesty and hard work. **B/I:** Ms. Byrd became involved in her profession because of her love of other languages and cultures. **RE:** Catholic

BYRD, LORENDA SUE, RN, BSN, MSN, T: Vice President of Patient Care **I:** Medicine & Health Care **DOB:** 01/31/1941 **PB:** Eureka **SC:** IL/USA **PT:** Denver C. Aucutt; Sadie M. (Van Sickle) Aucutt **MS:** Married **SPN:** Larry L. Byrd **CH:** Scott; Ellen; Leslie; Brian **ED:** MSN, Southern Illinois University (1990); BSN, McKendree University (1981) **CT:** Certification in Nursing Administration, American Nurses Credentialing Center, American Nurses Association; Registered Nurse, States of Illinois and Missouri **C:** Retired (2008); Chief Nursing Officer, Jefferson Memorial Hospital, Festus, MO (2001-2008); Chief Nursing Officer, Three Rivers Healthcare (2000-2001); Chief Nursing Officer, Lucy Lee Healthcare System (1998-2000); Vice President of Patient Services, St. Joseph Hospital, St. Charles,

MO (1996-1997); Director of Nursing, St. Joseph Hospital-West, St. Louis, MO (1991-1996); Associate Director of Patient Services, Alexian Brothers Medical Center, AMITA Health (1988-1991); Marketing Employee, International Clinical Laboratories, Nashville, TN (1986-1987); Nurse Manager, Medical-Surgical and Oncology Development, St. Elizabeth Medical Center, Granite City, IL (1980-1986); Head Nurse, Emergency Room, Memorial Hospital, Bellevue, IL (1976-1980); Faculty Member, Mennonite College of Nursing, Illinois State University (1965-1976); Staff Nurse, Charleston Community Hospital (1962-1965) **CR:** Advisory Board, Jefferson College (2001-2002) **CIV:** We Can 2000, Wentzville, MO (1992-1995); Business and Professional Women (1993-1994) **AW:** Who's Who Among Human Services Professionals; Who's Who in America in American Nursing; Who's Who in the Midwest **MEM:** Secretary, Lake St. Louis Chamber of Commerce (1994-Present); Sigma Theta Tau International Honor Society of Nursing (1980-Present); Board of Directors, Lake St. Louis Chamber of Commerce (1994, 1996); Former President-Elect, Local Chapter, Rotary International (1996); Former Secretary, Local Chapter, Rotary International (1995); Former President, Greater St. Louis Region, Council of Nurse Leaders (1994); Former President-Elect, Greater St. Louis Region, Council of Nurse Leaders (1993); Former Member, Missouri Organization of Nurse Leaders; Former Member, American Organization for Nursing Leadership; Former Member, Twin City Area Optimist Club **MH:** Albert Nelson Marquis Lifetime Achievement Award; Marquis Who's Who Top Professional **AS:** Ms. Byrd attributes her success to electing the right people to carry out the organization's mission. **B/I:** Ms. Byrd became involved in her profession because she always wanted to help people. Through numerous nursing opportunities, her experience grew, which led to a long and notable career in the field. **AV:** Traveling; Spending time with grandchildren; Remaining affiliated with the church **RE:** Presbyterian

BYRNE, BRADLEY ROBERTS, T: U.S. Representative from Alabama; Lawyer **I:** Government Administration/Government Relations/Government Services **DOB:** 02/16/1955 **PB:** Mobile **SC:** AL/USA **PT:** Arthur LaCoste Byrne; Elizabeth Patricia (Langsdale) Byrne **MS:** Married **SPN:** Rebecca Dow Dukes (05/16/1981) **CH:** Patrick MacGuire; Kathleen Roberts; Laura Ann; Colin Arthur **ED:** JD, The University of Alabama School of Law (1980); BA, Duke University (1977) **C:** U.S. Representative from Alabama's First Congressional District, Washington, DC (2014-Present); Member, U.S. House Committee on Natural Resources (2014-Present); Member, U.S. House Armed Services Committee (2014-Present); Chancellor, Alabama Department of Postsecondary Education (2007-2009); Member, District 32, Alabama State Senate (2003-2007); Member, Jackson Myrick Chambers & Byrne, Mobile, AL (1995-2013); Partner, Member, Management Committee, Miller, Hamilton, Snider & Odom, Mobile, AL (1989-1995); Partner, Miller, Hamilton, Snider & Odom, Mobile, AL (1985-1995); Associate, Miller, Hamilton, Snider & Odom, LLC, Mobile, AL (1980-1985) **CIV:** Active Member, Alabama State Board of Education (1994-2002); Secretary, Mobile City Planning Commission (1990-1994); Honorary Life Member, Alabama PTA **AW:** Leadership Award, Alabama Civil Justice Reform Committee (2007); South Alabama Literacy Champion Award (2006); Legislator of the Year Award, Alabama Wildlife Federation (2005); Champion for Children Award, Alabama Association of School Boards (2004); Legislative Leadership Award, Council for Leaders in Alabama Schools (2004); Phi Delta Phi Outstanding Lay Person Award (1998); Named One

of the Outstanding Young Men of America (1981, 1982) **MEM:** Vice Chairman, Mobile Area Chamber of Commerce (1989-1991); Litigation Section, ABA; Alabama Bar Association; Alabama State Bar; Mobile Bar Association; Mobile Area Chamber of Commerce; Leadership Alabama; ABA **BAR:** Supreme Court of the United States (1987); United States District Court for the Northern District of Alabama (1986); United States Court of Appeals for the Eighth Circuit (1985); United States District Court for the Middle District of Alabama (1985); United States Court of Appeals for the Fifth Circuit (1981); United States Court of Appeals for the Eleventh Circuit (1981); The State of Alabama (1980); United States District Court for the Southern District of Alabama (1980) **RE:** Episcopalian

CABRERA, MIGUEL, T: Professional Baseball Player **I:** Athletics **CN:** Detroits Tigers **DOB:** 04/18/1983 **PB:** Maracay **SC:** Venezuela **PT:** Miguel Cabrera; Gregoria Cabrera **MS:** Married **SPN:** Rosangel Cabrera **CH:** Three Daughters; Two Sons **C:** Infielder, Detroit Tigers, MLB (2008-Present); Infielder, Florida Marlins, MLB (2003-2007) **CR:** Member, Venezuelan National Team World Baseball Classic (2009) **AW:** Silver Slugger Award, American League (2005, 2006, 2010, 2012, 2013, 2015, 2016); Inductee, American League All-Star Team, MLB (2004-2007, 2010-2016); Named, American League's Most Valuable Player, Baseball Writers' Association of America (2012, 2013); Hank Aaron Award, American League (2012, 2013); Named, Player of the Year, Major League Baseball Players Association (2012); American League Triple Crown Award (2012); Named, American League's Outstanding Player (2012); Inductee, National League All-Star Team (2004-2007); Silver Slugger Award, National League (2005, 2006); Winner, Florida Marlins, World Series Champion (2003)

CAFARO, RENEE, T: U.S. Editor **I:** Writing and Editing **CN:** SLiNK Magazine **DOB:** 01/14/1984 **PB:** Youngstown **SC:** OH/USA **PT:** John Cafaro; Janet Cafaro **C:** U.S. Editor, SLiNK Magazine, New York, NY and London, England, United Kingdom (2016-Present); Freelance Writer, Self-employed (2014-Present); Treasurer, Community Board Five - Manhattan, NY (2009-Present); Advocacy Ambassador, Chair, NYC Walk to Cure Arthritis, Arthritis Foundation (2015-2016); Freelance Consultant/ Fundraiser (2009-2016); Deputy Political Director, Scott Stringer for Comptroller, NY (2013); Vice President, Villa Firenze Foundation (2009-2012); Special Assistant to the Secretary, NY State Executive Chamber - Governor David A. Paterson (2008-2010); Deputy Director of External Affairs, Office of Manhattan Borough President (2006-2008); Campaign Manager/Strategist, Capri Cafaro for Congress (2004-2006); Research of Political Action, 1199 SEIU (2005) **CIV:** Chair of Advocacy, New York Arthritis Foundation; Public Safety & Quality of Life; Board Member, The Creative Coalition **AW:** Named Activist of the Year (2018); National Adult Honoree (2015); NYC Honoree (2013); National Youth Leadership Award, Arthritis Foundation **AS:** Ms. Cafaro attributes her success to never taking anything for granted as well as her mentality to work like she is always the underdog. **B/I:** Ms. Cafaro spent 14 years in government working on campaigns, and in labor union political action departments. While living in New York, she worked for the Manhattan Borough president's office and then was approached to work in the governor of New York's administration team following the Elliot Spitzer scandal. Ms. Cafaro continued to work in government for years before starting her own fundraising company and then going back into political campaigns. She even worked on the finance committee for Hillary Clinton's 2016 presidential campaign. Also in 2016, she ran for delegate, as well as was asked to run for New York City Council. **THT:** Ms. Cafaro was homeschooled until she was in high school and began when she was only 12. She wanted to attend the London School of Economics but was too young to receive a visa. She then decided to change course. She was able to take college courses while in high school in the state of Ohio. She transferred to Stanford University at age 16. She nearly completed her education but could not due to an illness that caused her chronic pain and was constantly misdiagnosed. She had intentions of going back and completing her education but received her first job as her career and continued with her career instead. She found out that the condition she suffered from was arthritis, which in result, she became a big advocate for finding a cure. She also became the national honoree for the Arthritis Foundation.

CAFORIO, GIOVANNI, T: Chairperson, Chief Executive Officer **I:** Pharmaceuticals **CN:** Bristol-Myers Squibb Company **ED:** Doctor of Medicine, Sapienza University of Rome **C:** Chairperson, Chief Executive Officer, Bristol-Myers Squibb Company (2017-Present); Chief Executive Officer, Bristol-Myers Squibb Company (2015-2017); Chief Operating Officer, Bristol-Myers Squibb Company (2014-2015); Executive Vice President, Chief Commercial Officer, Bristol-Myers Squibb Company (2013-2014); President of Pharmaceuticals, Bristol-Myers Squibb Company (2011-2013)

CAIN, WILLIAM HOWARD, T: Private Piano Teacher, Organist, Music Educator **I:** Fine Art **CN:** Centenary United Methodist Church **DOB:** 09/19/1949 **PB:** Terre Haute **SC:** IN/USA **PT:** Rush M. Cain; Mary Margaret (Shepard) Cain **ED:** MS in Music Education, Indiana State University, Terre Haute, IN (1976); BS in Music Education, Indiana State University, Terre Haute, IN (1971) **CT:** State of Indiana Public School Teacher's Certificate (1977) **C:** Private Teacher of Piano, Centenary United Methodist Church, Terre Haute, IN (1977-Present); Church Organist, Centenary United Methodist Church, Terre Haute, IN (1974-Present); Choral Teacher, Paul C. Schulte High School, Terre Haute, IN (1973-1975); Choral Teacher, Attica School System (Now Attica Consolidated School Corp.), IN (1971-1973) **CR:** Organist, Winter and Spring Commencements, Part-time Musician, Indiana State University (1999-Present); Piano Player, Private Events **CW:** Author, Book, "Veggie Carols and Crazy Carols," BookLocker.com, Inc. (2018) **AW:** Lawrence Eberly Organ Award, Indiana State University (1971) **MEM:** Dean, American Guild of Organists (1974-1984); Music Teachers National Association **MH:** Albert Nelson Marquis Lifetime Achievement Award; Marquis Who's Who Top Professional **AS:** Mr. Cain attributes his success to hard work and determination. **B/I:** When Mr. Cain was a young person in grade school, his parents purchased two pump organs and had them rebuilt into one good pump organ. His mother would play it in the living room and he enjoyed listening. He was fascinated by having many sounds on one keyboard, so he decided to learn the organ. His mother died when he was in sixth grade, and his father hired a housekeeper to help him and his three siblings. He didn't have a private teacher at the time, so he taught himself the notes on the organ from a church hymnal. He knew he really wanted to take organ lessons, but at that time, the only way to start was with piano. Thus, he studied piano a few years, including study with a university piano teacher during high school. Then he went on to earn two degrees in music with an emphasis on piano and organ. **AV:** Songwriting; Walking; Exercise; Fossil collecting; YouTube channel: "Veggie Carols and Crazy Carols" **RE:** Free Thinker **THT:** Mr. Cain's personal fossil collection was exhibited in the Cordell Collection at the Indiana State University Library, in the summer of 2019. Mr. Cain's motto is, "Think for yourself and use your best judgement."

CAINE, EDWARD P., T: Managing Partner **I:** Financial Services **CN:** EP Caine & Associates CPA, LLC **DOB:** 03/05/1951 **PB:** New York **SC:** NY/USA **PT:** Stuart Caine; Doris Caine **MS:** Married **SPN:** Jill Barbara Winkleman (09/10/1978) **CH:** Ilysse Brooke; Jennifer Anne **ED:** MBA, Temple University, Philadelphia, PA (1977); BA in History, Lehigh University, Bethlehem, PA (1973); BS in Engineering, Lehigh University, Bethlehem, PA (1973) **CT:** CPA; CFF; CITP; CGMA **C:** Managing Partner, EP Caine & Associates CPA, LLC (2005-Present); Chief Administrative Officer, Union for Reform Judaism, New York, NY (2002-2005); Senior Manager, Maximus, Reston, VA (1996-2002); Chief Financial Officer, Chief Administrative Officer, ECC Management Services, PA (1990-1996); Vice President of Finance, Treasurer, Berger Holdings, PA (1985-1990); Second Vice President, Chase Manhattan (Now JPMorgan Chase & Co.), NY (1981-1983); Senior Manager, Arthur Andersen & Company, PA (1983-1985); Manager, Arthur Andersen & Company, PA (1977-1981); Chief Financial Analyst, Girard Bank, PA (1973-1977) **CR:** With Leadership Group, Business Network International (BNI); Main Line II Chapter, Executive Committee, Business Connectors President; Delaware Valley Chapter, National Conference of CPA Practitioners (NCCPAP) **CIV:** Board Member, Treasurer, BNI International Foundation (2019-Present); Audit Chair, Radnor Township, PA; Board Member, Past President, Golden Slipper Club & Charities; Past President, Temple University Fox School of Business Alumni Association; Business Consultant, RJ Magazine, New York, NY; Past Regional Vice President, Union of American Hebrew Congregations (Now Union for Reform Judaism), Philadelphia, PA; Past President, Main Line Reform Temple, Wynnewood, PA; Past Board of Directors, Reform Pension Board, New York, NY; Board of Directors, Union for Reform Judaism Press Board, New York, NY; Past Board of Directors, 633 Condo Board, New York, NY; Adviser, RJ Health and Welfare Trust; Past Treasurer, Ithan Mills Homeowners Association, Bryn Mawr, PA; Member, President Bill Clinton's Round Table on Race Relations **AW:** Named One of the 100 Most Influential CPAs in Accounting Today (2013) **MEM:** Council Member, American Institute of Certified Public Accountants (AICPA); NPL Committee; IRS Committee, Main Line Chamber of Commerce; BNI Business Connectors; National Conference of CPA Practitioners; Past Chairman, BGE Committee, Council Member, Pennsylvania Institute of Certified Public Accountants (PICPA); Beta Alpha Psi **MH:** Albert Nelson Marquis Lifetime Achievement Award; Marquis Who's Who Top Professional **B/I:** Mr. Caine became involved in his profession because he has always enjoyed numbers and explaining them to other people. It was an interest and strength that he took and decided to make a career out of and use it to help others. **PA:** Democrat **RE:** Jewish **THT:** Mr. Caine's in-laws are Arthur and Elaine Gold.

CAINE, MICHAEL, T: Actor **I:** Media & Entertainment **DOB:** 03/14/1933 **PB:** London **SC:** United Kingdom **PT:** Maurice Micklewhite; Ellen Frances Marie Micklewhite **MS:** Married **SPN:** Shakira Baksh (01/08/1973); Patricia Haines (1955, Divorced 1962) **CH:** Dominique; Natasha **C:** Actor, Theatre Workshop, London, England, United Kingdom (1955); Actor, The Seagull Lowestoft (1953-1955); Assistant Stage Manager, Westminster Repertory, Horsham, England, United Kingdom (1953) **CW:** Actor, "Come Away" (2020); Actor, "Four Kids and It" (2020); Author, "Blowing the Bloody Doors Off: And Other Lessons in Life" (2018); Actor, "King of Thieves" (2018); Actor, "Dear Dictator" (2018); Voice Actor, "Sherlock Gnomes" (2018); Actor, "Going in Style" (2017); Actor, "Dunkirk" (2017); Actor, "Now You See Me 2" (2016); Actor, "Youth" (2015); Actor, "The Last Witch Hunter" (2015); Actor, "Stonehearst Asylum" (2014); Actor, "Interstellar" (2014); Actor, "Kingsman: The Secret Service" (2014); Executive Producer, "The Double" (2013); Actor, "Now You See Me" (2013); Actor, "Last Love" (2013); Actor, "Journey 2: The Mysterious Island" (2012); Actor, "The Dark Knight Rises" (2012); Voice Actor, "Gnomeo & Juliet" (2011); Voice Actor, "Cars 2" (2011); Actor, "Inception" (2010); Author, "The Elephant to Hollywood" (2010); Actor, "Flawless" (2008); Actor, "The Dark Knight" (2008); Actor, "Is Anybody There?" (2008); Actor, "The Prestige" (2007); Actor, "Children of Men" (2006); Actor, "The Weatherman" (2005); Actor, "Batman Begins" (2005); Actor, "Bewitched" (2005); Actor, "Around the Bend" (2004); Actor, "The Actor" (2003); Actor, "Secondhand Lions" (2003); Actor, "Freedom: A History of Us" (2003); Actor, "The Statement" (2003); Actor, "The Quiet American" (2002); Actor, "Austin Powers 3" (2002); Actor, "Last Orders" (2001); Executive Producer, "Forever After" (2001); Actor, "Quicksand" (2001); Actor, "Sleuth" (1971, 2000); Actor, "Shiner" (2000); Actor, "Miss Congeniality" (2000); Actor, "Debtors" (1999); Actor, "Cider House Rules" (1999); Actor, "Quills" (1999); Actor, "Little Voice" (1998); Actor, "Mandela and De Kleerk" (1997); Actor, "20,000 Leagues Under the Sea" (1997); Actor, "Curtain Call" (1997); Actor, "Blood and Wine" (1996); Actor, "Bullet to Beijing" (1995); Actor, "World War II: When Lions Roared" (1994); Actor, "On Deadly Ground" (1994); Actor, "Blue Ice" (1993); Author, "What's It All About?: An Autobiography" (1993); Actor, "The Muppet Christmas Carol" (1992); Actor, "Noises Off" (1991); Actor, "Bullseye!" (1990); Actor, "Mr. Destiny" (1990); Actor, "Jekyll and Hyde" (1990); Actor, "A Shock to the System" (1989); Actor, "Without a Clue" (1988); Actor, "Dirty Rotten Scoundrels" (1988); Actor, "Jack the Ripper" (1988); Actor, "Jaws: The Revenge" (1987); Actor, "Surrender" (1987); Actor, "The Fourth Protocol" (1987); Executive Producer, "The Fourth Protocol" (1987); Actor, "Hannah and Her Sisters" (1986); Actor, "Sweet Liberty" (1986); Actor, "Mona Lisa" (1986); Actor, "Half Moon Street" (1986); Actor, "The Whistle Blower" (1985); Actor, "Water" (1985); Actor, "The Jigsaw Man" (1984); Actor, "The Holcroft Covenant" (1984); Actor, "Blame It On Rio" (1984); Actor, "Educating Rita" (1983); Actor, "Beyond the Limit" (1983); Actor, "Deathtrap" (1982); Actor, "The Hand" (1981); Actor, "Victory" (1981); Actor, "Dressed to Kill" (1980); Actor, "The Island" (1980); Actor, "Beyond the Poseidon Adventure" (1979); Actor, "California Suite" (1978); Actor, "The Swarm" (1977); Actor, "The Eagle Has Landed" (1976); Actor, "A Bridge Too Far" (1976); Actor, "Silver Bears" (1976); Actor, "Peeper" (1975); Actor, "The Romantic Englishwoman" (1975); Actor, "The Man Who Would Be King" (1975); Actor, "Harry and Walter Go to New York" (1975); Actor, "The Black Windmill" (1974); Actor, "Marseilles Contract" (1974); Actor, "The Wilby Conspiracy" (1974); Actor, "Zee & Co." (1972); Actor, "Kidnapped" (1972); Actor, "Pulp" (1972); Actor, "The Last Valley" (1971); Actor, "Too Late the Hero" (1970); Actor, "The Italian Job" (1969); Actor, "The Magus" (1968); Actor, "Battle of Britain" (1968); Actor, "Play Dirty" (1968); Actor, "Woman Times Seven" (1967); Actor, "Deadfall" (1967); Actor, "Hurry Shutdown" (1967); Actor, "Gambit" (1966); Actor, "The Wrong Box" (1966);

Actor, "Alfie" (1966); Actor, "The Ipcress File" (1965); Actor, "Zulu" (1964); Actor, "Next Time I'll Sing for You" (1963); Actor, "How to Murder a Rich Uncle" (1958); Actor, "A Hill in Korea " (1956) **AW:** Variety Club Award for Outstanding Contribution to Show Business (2008); Honorary Knight Commander, Most Excellent Order of the British Empire (2000); Academy Award for Best Supporting Actor, Academy of Motion Picture Arts & Sciences (1986, 1999); SAG Award for Outstanding Performance by a Male Actor in a Supporting Role, SAG-AFTRA (1999); Golden Globe Award for Best Performance by an Actor in a Motion Picture - Comedy or Musical, Hollywood Foreign Press Association (1983, 1998); Golden Globe Award for Best Actor – Miniseries or Television Film, Hollywood Foreign Press Association (1988); Commander, Most Excellent Order of the British Empire, Her Majesty Queen Elizabeth II (1993); BAFTA Award for Best Actor in a Leading Role (1983); Numerous Awards

CAIRL, STEPHAN D., T: Owner **I:** Automotive **CN:** Lonsbury Garage **DOB:** 09/09/1986 **PB:** Auburn **SC:** IN/USA **PT:** Daniel Cairl; Cindy Cairl **MS:** Married **SPN:** Jessica Cairl **CH:** Abriella; Bennett; Molly **ED:** AS in Diesel Management, Lincoln Technical Institute, Indianapolis, IN (2006) **CT:** Cummins ISX Certified; Navistar Master Certified; ASE Certification **C:** Business Owner, Lonsbury Garage, Angola, IN (2017-Present); General Manager, Lonsbury Garage, Angola, IN (2015-Present); Diesel Technician, Lonsbury Garage, Angola, IN (2015-2016); Shop Foreman/Mechanic, Rush Enterprises, Inc., Indianapolis, IN (2007-2015); Shop Supervisor/Mechanic, Ryder System, Inc. (2005-2007) **AW:** Nominee, Small Business of the Year (2018); Nominee, Best Customer Service (2017); Half-Century Award, State of Indiana **MEM:** Shopfix Academy; Automotive Training Institute; Board Member, Angola Area Chamber of Commerce; Fairview Missionary Church **AS:** Mr. Cairl attributes his success to a lot of hard work and dedication. It has been a long road and hard journey. However, he set goals and constantly worked on achieving them. **B/I:** Mr. Cairl was inspired to pursue his career from his childhood hobby of riding 4-wheelers and dirtbikes. In high school, he began technical schooling when he received an apprenticeship at Lonsbury Garage. He then moved away to Indianapolis and received an opportunity to work at a truck dealership. An opportunity at Lonsbury Garage then arose and inspired Mr. Cairl to move back home. He eventually bought the garage and he remains the owner today. **RE:** Christian

CALANTZOPOULOS, ANDRÉ, T: Chief Executive Officer **I:** Other **CN:** Philip Morris International Inc. **PB:** Pyrgos **SC:** Greece **ED:** MBA, INSEAD; Degree in Electrical Engineering, Swiss Federal Institute of Technology Lausanne (École Polytechnique Fédérale de Lausanne) **C:** Chief Executive Officer, Philip Morris International, Inc. (2013-Present); Chief Operating Officer, Philip Morris International, Inc., Lausanne, Switzerland (2008-2013); President, Chief Executive Officer, Philip Morris International (Subsidiary Altria Group), Lausanne, Switzerland (2002-2008); President, Eastern European Region, Philip Morris (1999-2002); Managing Director, Philip Morris, Poland (1996-1999); Manager, PMI Affiliate, Philip Morris (1993-1996); Area Director, Central Europe, Philip Morris (1992-1993); General Manager, Philip Morris, Czech Republic (1991-1992); General Manager, Philip Morris, Finland (1990-1991); With, Area Operations Department, Philip Morris (1987-1990); Business Development Analyst, Philip Morris (1985-1987)

CALDWELL, BILLY RAY, PHD, T: Geologist **I:** Education/Educational Services **CN:** Tarrant County College **DOB:** 04/20/1932 **PB:** Newellton **SC:** LA/USA **PT:** Leslie Richardson Caldwell; Helen Merle (Clark) Caldwell **MS:** Widowed **SPN:** Carolyn Marie Heath (Deceased 01/12/2018) **CH:** Caryn; Jeana; Craig **ED:** PhD, University of Cambridge (2004); MA, Texas Christian University (1970); BA, Texas Christian University (1954) **CT:** Certified Petroleum Geologist No. 2476, American Association of Petroleum Geologists; Certified Professional Geologist No. 7464, American Institute of Professional Geologists (AIPG); Licensed Professional Geoscientist No. 3112, State of Texas **C:** Adjunct Geology Professor, Tarrant County College, Fort Worth, Texas (1971-Present); Independent Geological Consultant, Fort Worth, Texas (1971-Present); Manager, Outdoor Living Inc. (1963-1971); Science Teacher, Lake Worth ISD (1960-1963); Geologist, Geological Engineering Services, Inc., Fort Worth, Texas (1954-1960) **CR:** Petroleum and Environmental Geology Consultant, Fort Worth, Texas (1971-Present) **CIV:** Board of Directors, Greater Fort Worth Builders Association (1973); Past Chairman, Environmental Management, City of Fort Worth, Texas; Director, Fort Worth Jaycees **CW:** Author, "The History of the Fort Worth Basin," The Professional Geologist (2012); Author, "Geology in the Bible," Exposure Publishing (2005); Author, "Barnett Shale Production Potentials" (2000); Author, "Geological Investigations in Environmental Studies," The Professional Geologist (1991) **AW:** Buster Kirkpatrick Award for the Director of the Year, Fort Worth Jaycees (1966-1967) **MEM:** American Institute of Professional Geologists (AIPG); American Association of Petroleum Geologists; The Geological Society of America, Inc.; FWGS; Texas Association for Environmental Education **MH:** Albert Nelson Marquis Lifetime Achievement Award; Marquis Who's Who Top Professional **AS:** Dr. Caldwell attributes his success to trying to do the best he could in every job he ever had, struggling, hoping, hard work, and enjoying what he does. **B/I:** Dr. Caldwell became involved in his profession after taking a course in geology and loving it. He didn't know it existed when he went to college until he was told about it. He thought it sounded like something he would like, so he took the course. **AV:** Travel; Cruise ship lectures **PA:** Republican **RE:** Baptist

CALIFANO, JOSEPH ANTHONY JR., T: Chairman Emeritus, Lawyer **I:** Law and Legal Services **CN:** National Center on Addiction and Substance Abuse **DOB:** 05/15/1931 **PB:** Brooklyn **SC:** NY/USA **PT:** Joseph Anthony Califano; Katherine (Gill) Califano **MS:** Married **SPN:** Hilary Paley Byers (1983) **CH:** Mark Gerard; Joseph Anthony III; Claudia Frances; Brooke A. Byers (Stepdaughter); John (Stepson) **ED:** LLB, Harvard University (1955); BA, Holy Cross College (1952) **C:** Chairman Emeritus, National Center on Addiction and Substance Abuse, Columbia University, New York, NY (2012-Present); Professor of Public Health Policy, School Medicine and Public Health, Columbia University, New York, NY (1992-Present); Chairman, National Center on Addiction and Substance Abuse, Columbia University, New York, NY (1992-2012); Senior Partner, Dewey Ballantine LLP, Washington, DC (1983-1992); Partner, Califano, Ross & Heineman, Washington, DC (1980-1982); Secretary, U.S. Department of Health, Education, and Welfare (Now U.S. Department of Health and Human Services), Washington, DC (1977-1979); Partner, Williams, Connolly & Califano, Washington, DC (1971-1977); General Counsel, Democratic National Committee (1971-1972); Partner, Arnold & Porter LLP, Washington, DC (1969-1971); Special Assistant to President, The White House (1965-1969); General Counsel, U.S. Department of the Army (1963-1964); Special Assistant to Secretary, U.S. Department of the Army (1962-1963); Special Assistant to Secretary and Deputy Secretary, U.S. Department of Defense (1964-1965); Special Assistant to General Counsel, U.S. Department of Defense (1961-1962); Attorney, Dewey Ballantine LLP, New York, NY (1958-1961) **CR:** Board of Directors, CBS Corporation (2006-Present); Board of Directors, Midway Games Inc. (2004-2009); Board of Directors, Willis Group Holdings, Ltd. (2004-2013); Board of Directors, Viacom Inc. (2003-2005); Board of Directors, Automatic Data Processing, Inc. (1982-2005) **CIV:** Chairman, Institute of Social and Economic Policy in Middle East, Harvard University (1983-1998); Trustee, Urban Institute, The American Ditchley Foundation, The Century Foundation, LBJ Foundation, National Museum of Health and Medicine; Board of Governors, NewYork-Presbyterian Hospital; Trustee Emeritus, John F. Kennedy Center for the Performing Arts; Member, Advisory Council, American Foundation for AIDS Research; Member, Council on Foreign Relations **MIL:** Lieutenant, U.S. Navy (1958); With, Office of the Judge Advocate General (1955-1958); Officer Candidate, U.S. Navy (1955) **CW:** Author, "How to Raise a Drug-Free Kid - The Straight Dope for Parents" (2009); Author, "High Society: How Substance Abuse Ravages America and What to Do About It" (2007); Author, Memoir, "Inside: A Public and Private Life" (2004); Author, "Radical Surgery: What's Next for America's Health Care" (1995); Author, "The Triumph and Tragedy of Lyndon Johnson: The White House Years" (1991); Author, "The 1982 Report on Drug Abuse and Alcoholism, America's Health Care Revolution: Who Lives, Who Dies, Who Pays" (1986); Author, "Governing America: An Insiders Report from the White House and the Cabinet" (1981); Co-Author, "The Media and Business" (1978); Co-author with Howard Simons, "The Media and the Law" (1976); Author, "A Presidential Nation" (1975); Author, "The Student Revolution: A Global Confrontation" (1969); Editor, Harvard Law Review **AW:** Gustav O. Lienhard Award, Institute of Medicine, National Academy of Sciences (2010); One of the 10 Outstanding Young Men of America (1966); Man of the Year Award, Justinian Society of Lawyers (1966); Distinguished Public Service Medal, U.S. Department of Defense (1965); Distinguished Civilian Service Award, U.S. Department of the Army (1964) **MEM:** New York State Bar Association; The District of Columbia Bar; The Metropolitan Club of the City of Washington; The Century Association; The University Club of New York; Harvard Legal Aid Bureau **BAR:** The District of Columbia Bar (1969); Supreme Court of the United States (1966); New York State Bar Association (1955) **PA:** Democrat **RE:** Roman Catholic

CALKINS, KEITH G., PHD, T: Computational Physical Scientist **I:** Education/Educational Services **DOB:** 02/01/1958 **PB:** Cadillac **SC:** MI/USA **PT:** James Fred Calkins; LaFern Elvira Elaine (Bloomquist) Calkins **MS:** Married **SPN:** Terri Lou (Fivash) Calkins **CH:** Theron; Jared **ED:** PhD in Physics, University of Notre Dame, Notre Dame, IN (2005); MAT in Secondary Education, Andrews University, Berrien Springs, MI (2002); MS in Physics, University of Notre Dame, Notre Dame, IN (1996); MS in Physics/Mathematics, Andrews University, Berrien Springs, MI (1991); BS in Physics, Andrews University, Berrien Springs, MI, with Honors (1988); MS in Computer Information Science, Andrews University, Berrien Springs, MI (1982); BS in Mathematics, Andrews University, Berrien Springs, MI (1981) **CT:** Secondary Teaching, Math, Physics, Computer Science, Chemistry, Michigan **C:** Contingent Faculty, Physical Sciences, Ferris State University, Big Rapids, MI (2011-2019);

Consultant, XDX, Berrien Springs (1981-Present); Associate Professor, Mathematics and Science, Andrews University, Berrien Springs, MI (1993-2011); Assistant Director, Technology Support, Andrews University Computing Center, Berrien Springs, MI (1978-1993) **CR:** CP-V and Xerox Sigma Consultant, Living Computer Museum, Seattle, WA (2012-2015) **CIV:** Board, Calkins Family Association **CW:** Co-Author, Book, "Euclidean Geometry and its Subgeometries" (2015); Contributor, Articles, Various Professional Journals **AW:** Honored Teacher Many Times **MEM:** National Speleological Society; American Physical Society; American Mathematics Society; Sons of the American Revolution Chapter; Sigma Xi; Phi Kappa Phi; Sigma Pi Sigma; Pi Mu Epsilon **MH:** Albert Nelson Marquis Lifetime Achievement Award; Marquis Who's Who Top Professional **AS:** He attributes his success to hard work to overcome dyslexia and high functioning autism. **B/I:** Dr. Calkins became involved in his profession because he has always been interested in computers, math, and physics. **AV:** Genealogy; Caving **RE:** Seventh-day Adventist

CALLAHAN, THOMAS JAMES, T: Lawyer **I:** Law and Legal Services **CN:** Thompson Hine LLP **ED:** JD, Case Western Reserve University, Cleveland, Ohio, Cum Laude (1985); BS in Accounting, Duke University, Durham, NC, Cum Laude (1979) **CT:** Certified Public Accountant, Ohio (1981) **C:** Partner, Thompson Hine LLP, Cleveland, Ohio (1997-Present); Associate, Thompson Hine LLP, Cleveland, Ohio (1986-1996); Manager, PricewaterhouseCoopers (PwC), Cleveland, Ohio (1985-1986); Accountant, PricewaterhouseCoopers (PwC), Cleveland, Ohio (1979-1982); Leader, Tax Practice, Thompson Hine LLP, Cleveland, Ohio **CW:** Presenter in the Field; Contributor, Articles to Professional Journals **MEM:** Section Chair, Section Officer, Section Past Council Member, Past Chair of the Administrative Practice Committee, American Bar Association (ABA);American College of Tax Counsel (2003-Present); President, American College of Tax Counsel (2013-2015); Vice President, American College of Tax Counsel (2012); Executive Committee, Cleveland Tax Institute (2011-2014); Secretary Treasurer, American College of Tax Counsel (2011); Regent, American College of Tax Counsel (2004-2010); President, Tax Club of Cleveland (2004-2005); Chair, Cleveland Tax Institute (2001, 2004); Vice President, Tax Club of Cleveland (2002-2003); Treasure, Tax Club of Cleveland (2001); Board Director, Tax Club of Cleveland (2000); Chairman, General Tax Committee, Cleveland Metropolitan Bar Association (1999); American Institute of Certified Public Accountants (AICPA); Tax Advisory Board, Thomson West Publishers (Thomas Reuters) **BAR:** Supreme Court of the United States (2000); United States Court of Appeals for the Federal Circuit (2000); United States Court of Federal Claims (1987); United States District Court for the Northern District of Ohio (1987); United States Tax Court (1987); United States Court of Appeals for the Sixth Circuit (1987); Ohio (1985)

CALVERT, KENNETH, "KEN" STANTON, T: U.S. Representative from California **I:** Government Administration/Government Relations/Government Services **DOB:** 06/08/2963 **PB:** Corona **SC:** CA/USA **PT:** Ira D. Calvert Jr.; Marceline Hamblen Calvert **ED:** BS in Economics, San Diego State University (1975); AA, Chaffey College (1973) **C:** U.S. Representative from California's 42nd Congressional District, United States Congress, Washington, DC (2013-Present); Member, Committee on Appropriations (2013-Present); U.S. Representative from California's 44th Congressional District, United States Congress, Washington, DC (2003-2013); U.S.

Representative from California's 43rd Congressional District, United States Congress, Washington, DC (1992-2003); President, General Manager, Calvert Real Properties, Inc., Corona, CA (1980-1991); General Manager, Marcus W. Meairs Co., Corona, CA (1979-1981); General Manager, Jolly Fox Restaurant, Corona, CA (1975-1979); Congressional Aide to U.S. Representative Vitor Veysey, U.S. House of Representatives, CA (1975-1979) **CR:** Reagan-Bush Campaign Worker (1980); Corona/Norco Youth Chairman for Nixon (1968) **MEM:** President, Corona Rotary Club (1991); President, Corona Chamber of Commerce (1990); Monday Morning Group; Elks; Founder, Chair, Riverside County Lincoln Club of Riverside County; Corona Rotary Club; Corona Chamber of Commerce **PA:** Republican

CAMERON, JAMES FRANCIS, T: Film Director, Screenwriter, Producer **I:** Media & Entertainment **DOB:** 8/16/1954 **PB:** Kapuskasing, Ontario **SC:** Canada **PT:** Philip Cameron; Shirley (Lowe) Cameron **MS:** Married **SPN:** Suzy Amis (2000); Linda Hamilton (07/26/1997, Divorced 1999); Katheryn Bigelow (08/17/1989, Divorced 1991); Gale Ann Hurd (1985, Divorced 1989); Sharon Williams (02/14/1974, Divorced 1984) **CH:** Three Daughters; One Son **ED:** Honorary Doctorate, University of South Hampton (2004); Honorary Doctor of Fine Arts, California State University, Fullerton (1999); Honorary Doctor of Fine Arts, Carelton University, Ottawa, Canada (1998); Honorary Doctorate, Brock University, St. Catherines, Ontario, Canada (1998); Coursework, Fullerton College (1973-1974) **C:** Founder, Head, Lightstorm Entertainment, Burbank, CA (1992-Present); Board of Directors, Digital Domain, Los Angeles, CA (1993-1998); Co-founder, Earthship Productions; Explorer-in-residence, National Geographic **CIV:** Member, Advisory Board, Science Fiction Museum & Hall of Fame **CW:** Writer, Executive Producer, "Terminator: Dark Fate" (2019); Writer, Producer, "Alita Battle Angel" (2018); Executive Producer, Host, "James Cameron's Story of Science Fiction" (2018); Executive Producer, Appearance, "Years of Living Dangerously" (2014); Appearance, "A New Age of Exploration: National Geographic at 125" (2013); Appearance, "James Cameron: Voyage to the Bottom of the Earth" (2012); Executive Producer, "Sanctum" (2011); Director, Writer, Producer, Co-editor, "Avatar" (2009); Writer, "Terminator: The Sarah Connor Chronicles" (2008-2009); Executive Producer, "The Lost Tomb of Jesus" (2007); Executive Producer, "The Lost Tomb of Jesus" (2007); Executive Producer, "The Exodus Decoded" (2006); Appearance, "Entourage" (2005-2006); Co-director, Producer, Editor, Appearance, "Aliens of the Deep" (2005); Appearance, "Titanic Adventure" (2005); Director, Producer, Appearance, "Last Mysteries of the Titanic" (2005); Director, "Terminator 3: Rise of the Machines" (2003); Executive Producer, "Volcanoes of the Deep Sea" (2003); Director, Producer, "Ghosts of the Abyss" (2002); Director, "Expedition Bismarck" (2002); Writer, Executive Producer, "Dark Angel" (2000-2002); Director, "Earthship" (2001); Director, Writer, Producer, Editor, "Titanic" (1997); Director, "Terminator 2 3-D" (1996); Writer, Producer, "Strange Days" (1995); Director, Writer, Producer, "True Lies" (1994); Executive Producer, "Point Break" (1991); Director, Producer, Writer, "The Terminator 2: Judgement Day" (1991); Director, "The Abyss" (1989); Director, "Aliens" (1986); Co-writer, "Rambo: First Blood Part II" (1985); Director, "The Terminator" (1984); Production Designer, "Galaxy of Terror" (1981); Creator, Special Effects, "Escape from New York" (1981); Director, Co-writer, "Piranha II: The Spawning" (1981); Art Director, "Battle Beyond the Stars" (1980); Co-director, Co-writer,

Producer, Editor, "Xenogenesis" (1978); Director, Writer, Producer, Editor, Appearance, Numerous Television Shows, Films and Documentaries **AW:** Named, Companion of the Order of Canada (2019); Nierenberg Prize for Science in the Public, Scripps Institution of Oceanography (2013); Inductee, Science Fiction Hall of Fame, Museum of Pop Culture (2012); Milestone Award, Producers Guild of America (2011); Named, One of the 10 Smartest People in Tech, Forbes Magazine (2010); Named, One of the 100 Most Influential People in the World, TIME Magazine (2010); Lifetime Achievement Award, Visual Effects Society (2010); Golden Globe Award for Best Motion Picture - Drama and Best Director, Hollywood Foreign Press Association (2010); Critics' Choice Award for Best Action and Best Editing, Broadcast Film Critics Association (2010); Named, One of the 100 Agents of Change, Rolling Stone Magazine (2009); Recipient, Star, Hollywood Walk of Fame (2009); Recipient, Star, Canada's Walk of Fame (2008); Named, One of the 50 Smartest People in Hollywood, Entertainment Weekly (2007); Academy Awards for Best Picture, Best Director, and Best Film Editing, Academy of Motion Picture Arts & Sciences (1997); Golden Globe Awards for Best Motion Picture - Drama and Best Director, Hollywood Foreign Press Association (1997); Saturn Awards for Best Director and Best Science Fiction Film (1992); MTV Movie Award for Best Movie (1992); People's Choice Award for Favorite Dramatic Motion Picture (1992); Inaugural Ray Bradbury Award for Dramatic Screenwriting, Science Fiction and Fantasy Writers of America (1992); Numerous Awards **MEM:** American Cinema Editors

CAMMACK, CAROLYN A., T: Secondary School Educator **I:** Education/Educational Services **DOB:** 11/21/1944 **PB:** Japser **SC:** TX/USA **PT:** Bernard Ardean Cammack; Ettie Lee (Minton) Cammack **MS:** Married **SPN:** Jack Blanton Matthews (05/25/1997, Divorced) **CH:** Twyla Carter **ED:** MBA, Sam Houston State University (1975); BBA, Lamar University (1966) **CT:** Professional Teaching Certificate, Texas **C:** Part-time Supervisor of Student Teachers, Steven F. Austin State University (2006-2014); Retired from School System (1997); Business Teacher, Klein Independent School District (Klein ISD) (1990-1997); Business Professor, University of Wisconsin-Eau Claire (1987-1989); Business Teacher, Spring Independent School District, Texas (1970-1987); Business Teacher, Bastrop Independent School District, Texas (1969-1970); Business Teacher, West Sabine Independent School District, Pineland, Texas (1967-1969); Secretary, Exxon, Houston, Texas (1966-1967) **CR:** Member, CATE Advisory Board, Career and Technical-Consumer Sciences, Nacogdoches Independent School District (2001-2002) **CIV:** Lineage Groups; Community Service; With, Cum Concilio Study Club **AW:** Named Teacher of the Year Spring High School (1986); Named Secondary Teacher of the Year, Texas Business & Technology Educators Association (TBTEA) (2003); Named Business Teacher of the Year, Texas Business & Technology Educators Association (TBTEA) (1994); Named Business Teacher of the Year, Secondary Level, Texas Business & Technology Educators Association (TBTEA) (1986) **MEM:** Treasurer, West Sabine High School Alumni Association (2002); President, Zeta Tau Alpha Fraternity, Nacogdoches, Texas (2000-2002); Cum Concilio Study Club (2001); Region President, Texas Business & Technology Educators Association (TBTEA) (1992-1993); President-elect, Texas Business & Technology Educators Association (TBTEA); National Business Education Association; West Sabine High School Alumni Association **MH:** Albert Nelson Marquis Lifetime Achievement Award; Marquis Who's Who

Top Professional **AS:** Ms. Cammack attributes her success to the initiative and drive she had to want to work and do well. She loved college; she was ready to spread her wings and see what she could do. **B/I:** When Ms. Cammack graduated from high school, that is where her interest was; she enjoyed her business classes, so she decided that is what she would pursue. **AV:** Volunteering; Knitting; Gardening; Traveling **RE:** Baptist **THT:** The Cum Concilio Study Club was organized in 1894; in 2019, they celebrated 125 years. It started out with 15 women, there are 20 now. They are responsible for starting the public library and their group of women tore down a fort that was in downtown Nacogdoches. Their group of women back then had it moved to the campus of Stephen F. Austin State University and it's still there today. In honor of their 125th anniversary, they had two chairs made out of the original wood, reupholstered and put into the museum. The group of women put the rod iron fence up across the front of the cemetery, a foundation helped repair it with them in 2019. They put statues of famous women there.

CAMPBELL, SAMUEL, T: Commander, General Manager **I:** Nonprofit & Philanthropy **CN:** American Legion Post 86 **MS:** Married **CH:** 7 Children **ED:** Business Administration Degree **C:** Commander, General Manager, American Legion Post 86, Indiana (2012-Present); With, American Legion Post 86 (1957-2012) **CIV:** Administrator, Governor, Moose Lodge **MIL:** U.S. Air Force **AW:** American Legion Service Award; Son's of the American Legion, Service Award **MEM:** American Legion Post 86 **AS:** Mr. CampBell attributes his success to hands on experience and hard work. He believes that, while one can learn much from reading, practical experience is a superior teacher. **B/I:** Mr. CampBell has been involved in public service since attending high school, and used his practical experience to save his local chapter of the American Legion of bankruptcy. **AV:** Fishing

CAMPOS, LEONARD PETER, PHD, T: Clinical Psychologist **I:** Health, Wellness and Fitness **DOB:** 12/24/1932 **PB:** Arecibo **SC:** PR/USA **PT:** Joseph Gervasio Campos; Emma (Roman) Crespi **MS:** Partner **SPN:** Patricia Tocher; Lee Barrett (06/13/1986-1992); Mary Lois Cole (10/01/1961-1976) **CH:** David; Elizabeth (Deceased); Barbara **ED:** PhD in Clinical Psychology, Michigan State University, East Lansing, MI (1963); Predoctoral Research Fellowship, National Institute of Mental Health, Michigan State University, East Lansing, MI (1962-1963); Internship in Psychology, Veteran's Administration Hospitals of Palo Alto and Battle Creek, MI (1960-1962); U.S. Public Health Research Fellowship in Psychology, Michigan State University, East Lansing, MI (1958-1960); BA in Psychology, City College of New York, New York, NY, Cum Laude (1955) **CT:** Diplomate, American Board of Forensic Psychology (1984-Present); Diplomate, American Board of Professional Psychology (1983-Present); Certified Teaching Member, ITAA (1970-Present); Licensed Psychologist, State of California (1967-Present); Diplomate, Redecision Therapy **C:** Consultant, Sacramento Institute for Redecision Therapy (2000-Present); Staff Psychologist, Northern Reception Center-Clinic (1995-1999); Psychologist, Short-Term Family Counselor, Victim Witness Program, Sacramento County District Attorney (1990-1997); Director, Sacramento Institute for Redecision Therapy (1982-2000); Founder, Director, Child Treatment Program, El Hogar Community Services, Inc., Sacramento, CA (1982-1987); Consultant, California Youth Authority of Stockton and Sacramento (1972-1994); Psychologist, Private Practice (1970-1994); Director, San Joaquin Transactional Analysis Institute,

Stockton, CA (1970-1981); Staff Psychologist, O.H. Close School for Boys, Northern California Youth Center (Now N. A. Chaderjian Youth Correctional Facility), Stockton, CA (1966-1970); Assistant Professor of Psychology, University of the Pacific, Stockton, CA (1963-1966) **CR:** Medical Expert, Social Security Administration; Special Consultant, California State Personnel Board of Appeals Panel **MIL:** Personnel Psychologist, U.S. Army (1955-1957) **CW:** Author, "Introduce Your Relationship to Transactional Analysis" (1994); Author, "Introduce Yourself to Transactional Analysis" (1969); Author, More Than 30 Professional Journal Articles and Several Books **AW:** Certification of Appreciation, Northern Youth Correctional Reception Center and Clinic, California Youth Authority (Now Division of Juvenile Justice), California Department of Corrections & Rehabilitation (1999); Certificate of Commendation, Health Care Services Division, California Youth Authority (Now Division of Juvenile Justice), California Department of Corrections & Rehabilitation (1999); Certificate of Appreciation, Task Force on Fairness, Juvenile Detention Alternatives Initiative, Annie E. Casey Foundation (1997); Service Award, Sacramento Valley Psychological Association (1993); Silver Psi Award, California Psychological Association (1993); Helen Margulies Mehr, Ph.D. Award, California Psychological Association (1993); In Appreciation for Service as President, Forensic Division, Sacramento Valley Psychological Association (1992); Certificate of Appreciation, El Hogar Community Services, Inc. (1991); Certificate of Appreciation, Management Development Center, ITAA, Taipei, Taiwan (1978); Numerous Commendations **MEM:** President, Division II, Sacramento Valley Psychological Association (1992); President, Division I, Sacramento Valley Psychological Association (1988-1989); Life Member, American Psychological Association; Teaching Member, ITAA **MH:** Albert Nelson Marquis Lifetime Achievement Award **AV:** Golfing; Playing tennis; Swimming; Camping; Traveling; Songwriting **PA:** Democrat **RE:** Unitarian-Universalist

CANDIDO, KENNETH DAVID, MD, T: Anesthesiologist, Educator **I:** Medicine & Health Care **DOB:** 11/21/1957 **PB:** East Orange **SC:** NJ/USA **PT:** Albert Babbits Candido; Rose Marie Candido **CH:** Rosemarie C.; Albert J.; Farrin, Jannah R. **ED:** MD, New York State Board of Regents (1991); Chief Resident, University of Illinois at Chicago (1988-1989); Residency, University of Illinois at Chicago (1988-1989); Fellowship in Pain and Regional Anesthesia, University of Illinois at Chicago (1987-1988); Internship in Internal Medicine, New York Medical College (1986-1987); Residency in Anesthesiology CA1-2, New York Medical College (1985-1986); Fifth Pathway, New York Medical College (1984); MD, Universided del Noreste, Mexico (1983); BA, Rutgers College, The State University of New Jersey, New Brunswick, NJ (1979) **CT:** Certification in Pain Management, American Board of Anesthesiology (1994); Diplomate, American Board Anesthesiology (1989); Instructor, American Heart Association (1987); Medical License, New Jersey (1988); Medical License, Illinois (1987); Medical License, New York (1985) **C:** Clinical Professor of Surgery, University of Illinois at Chicago (2016-Present); Clinical Professor, Anesthesiology, University of Illinois College of Medicine, Chicago, IL (2008-Present); Chairman, Department of Anesthesiology, Advocate Illinois Masonic Medical Center (2008-Present); Director, Pain Management Fellowship Program, Loyola University Chicago (2007-2008); Professor, Anesthesiology, Loyola University Chicago (2006-2008); Director, Division of Pain Management, Loyola University Chicago (2005-2008); Associate Professor,

Anesthesiology, Loyola University Chicago (2005-2006); Director, Division of Acute Pain Management, Northwestern University Feinberg School of Medicine, North-Western Memorial Hospital (2002-2005); Associate Professor, Anesthesiology, Northwestern University Feinberg School of Medicine, North-Western Memorial Hospital (2001-2005); Assistant Professor, Anesthesiology, Rush Medical College (1998-2002); Attending Physician, Department of Anesthesiology and Pain Management, Cook County Hospital (1997-2001); Assistant Clinical Professor, Anesthesiology, University of Illinois at Chicago (1989-1995); Assistant Adjunct Attending, Anesthesiology, Regional Anesthesia, Pain Management, Lenox Hill Hospital (1989-1992) **CR:** Medical Director, City of Chicago Police and Fire Death Benefit Fund (2018-Present); Procedural Sedation Committee, Advocate Illinois Masonic Medical Center (2010-Present); Gaston Labat Award Committee, American Society of Regional Anesthesia (2007-Present); Society for Pain Practice Management, Leawood, KS (2006-Present); Subcommittee on Regional Anesthesia and Acute Pain, American Society of Anesthesiologists (2009-2010); Subcommittee on Chronic and Cancer Pain, American Society of Anesthesiologists (2007-2009); Committee Member, Institutional Review Board, Loyola University (2005); Conductor, Over 100 Clinical Trials **CIV:** Chair, Veterans Affairs Initiative (2016-Present) **CW:** Contributor, Articles, Professional Publications **AW:** Academic Achievement Award, American Society of Interventional Pain Physicians (2016); Alon P. Winnie Honorary Lecture Award, Dannemiller (2013); Favorite Physician, Illinois People's Choice Award (2008-2012); First Place Award, AHC Research Day, Advocate Illinois Masonic Medical Center (2011); Physician MVP Award, Advocate Illinois Masonic Medical Center (2009); Elected Member, Association of University Anesthesiologists (2008); Program Chairman Plaque, American Society of Regional Anesthesia and Pain Medicine (2008); Elected Fellow, Institute of Medicine of Chicago (2003); Golden Apple Award, Outstanding Teacher, Northwestern University, Department of Anesthesiology (2002-2003); Outstanding Attending Physician and Teacher, Anesthesiology, Cook County Hospital (2000-2001); Outstanding Researcher, University of Illinois at Chicago, Anesthesiology (1987-1989) **MEM:** Fellow, Institute of Medicine Chicago; American Medical Association; American Academy of Pain Medicine; American Society of Anesthesiologist; American Academy of Pain Management; American Society of Regional Anesthesia; American Society of Interventional Pain Physicians; Illinois State Society of Anesthesiology; Chicago Society of Anesthesiologists; New York State Society of Anesthesiology; New York State Medical Society; New York County Medical Society; International Anesthesia Research Society; International Trauma Anesthesia and Critical Care Society **MH:** Albert Nelson Marquis Lifetime Achievement Award; Marquis Who's Who Top Professional **B/I:** Dr. Candido was attracted to the medical profession because of his desire to confront his deepest and darkest fears: pain and death. Rather than run and hide from them, he wanted to challenge and conquer them by learning about both respective situations that every human being faces at one point in their lives. He wanted to be active in his confrontation, but he knows it does not mean he would solve each patient's dilemma. However, he finds solace in having a chance to know he is trying. **AV:** Traveling; Weightlifting; Playing sports; Watching movies and theater **PA:** Libertarian **RE:** Roman Catholic

CANTWELL, MARIA ELAINE, T: U.S. Senator from Washington **I:** Government Administration/Government Relations/Government Services **DOB:** 10/13/1958 **PB:** Indianapolis **SC:** IN/USA **PT:** Paul Cantwell; Rose Cantwell **ED:** BA in Public Administration, Miami University (1981) **C:** Ranking Member, U.S. Senate Committee on Commerce (2019-Present); U.S. Senator, State of Washington (2001-Present); Ranking Member, U.S. Senate Committee on Energy and Natural Resources (2015-2019); Chair, U.S. Senate Committee on Small Business and Entrepreneurship (2014-2015); Chair, U.S. Senate Committee on Indian Affairs (2013-2014); Senior Vice President, Consumer & E-commerce, Real Networks (Formerly Progressive Networks), Seattle, WA (1997-2000); Vice President, Marketing, Progressive Networks, Seattle, WA (1995-1997); U.S. Representative from Washington's First Congressional District (1993-1995); Member, District 44, Washington House of Representatives, Olympia, WA (1987-1992); Public Relations Consultant, Cantwell & Associates (1981-1987) **CIV:** Board of Directors, Washington Economic Development Finance Authority **AW:** Inductee, Indianapolis Public Schools Hall of Fame (2006); Friend of Blues Award, Experience Music Project, Vulcan, Inc. (2003); Cyber Champion Award, BAS, The Software Alliance (2003); Woman of the Year, KING-TV Evening Magazine (2001) **PA:** Democrat **RE:** Roman Catholic

CAO, YOUFANG, PHD, T: Senior Scientist **I:** Sciences **CN:** Merck & Co., Inc. **ED:** PhD in Biomedical Engineering, Shanghai Jiao Tong University (2011); MSc in Biochemistry, Molecular Biology, Shanxi University, China (2002); BSc in Computational Mathematics, China (1999) **C:** Senior Scientist, Quantitative Sciences, Quantitative Pharmacology and Pharamcometrics, Merck & Co., Inc., PA (2018-Present); Postdoctoral Research Associate, Los Alamos National Laboratory, NM, (2015-2018); Research Assistant Professor, The University of Chicago, IL (2012-2015); Postdoctoral Research Associate, IL (2011-2012); Assistant Research Scientist, Shanghai Center for Systems, Biomedicine, Shanghai Jiao Tong University, China (2002-2011); Visiting Scholar, Department of Bioengineering, The University of Chicago, IL (2009-2010) **AS:** Dr. Cao attributes his success to his hard work and passion for his job. He is confident in his education and the tools available for his work. **B/I:** Dr. Cao was always fascinated about things that he could control. To him, biology became an interest in high school, but as a child, he was fascinated by rockets, and the precision of mathematics in computers.

CAPITO, SHELLEY WELLONS, T: U.S. Senator from West Virginia **I:** Government Administration/Government Relations/Government Services **DOB:** 11/26/1953 **PB:** Glen Dale **SC:** WV/USA **PT:** Arch Alfred Moore Jr.; Shelley (Riley) Moore **MS:** Married **SPN:** Charles L. Capito **CH:** Charles; Moore; Shelley **ED:** MEd, University of Virginia Curry School of Education and Human Development (1976); BS in Zoology, Duke University, Durham, NC (1975) **C:** U.S. Senator, State of West Virginia (2015-Present); Member, U.S. Senate Committee on Rules & Administration (2015-Present); Member, U.S. Senate Appropriations Committee (2015-Present); Member, U.S. Senate Committee on Environment and Public Works (2015-Present); Member, U.S. Senate Committee on Energy and Natural Resources (2015-Present); U.S. Representative from West Virginia's Second District, United States Congress (2001-2015); Member, District 30, West Virginia House of Delegates (1996-2000); Director, Educational Information Center, West Virginia Board of Regents (1978-1981); Career Counselor, West Virginia State College (Now West Virginia State University) (1976-1978) **MEM:** Kappa Kappa Gamma **PA:** Republican **RE:** Presbyterian

CAPLAN, JUDITH, T: Genealogist; Poet; Editor; Educator; Sewist **I:** Education/Educational Services **DOB:** 02/03/1945 **PB:** Brooklyn **SC:** NY/USA **PT:** Rabbi Samuel Langer (1905-1996); Gladys Surnamer Langer (1907-1983) **MS:** Married **SPN:** Neil Howard Caplan, MD (06/28/1970) **CH:** Hillel N.; Baruch I. **ED:** Master's Degree in Mass Communication/Television, Syracuse University, Syracuse, NY (1967-1968); BA in English, Brooklyn College, Brooklyn, NY (1966) **CT:** Temporary New York City Teachers License (1966) **C:** Genealogist, Up, Roots! Genealogy Research Services, Long Beach, NY (1995-Present); English Teacher, Springfield Gardens High School, Springfield Gardens, NY (1985-2001); Hebrew School Teacher, Temple Israel, Long Beach, NY (1983-1985); Hebrew Teacher, Merrick Jewish Centre, Merrick, NY (1982-1985); English Teacher, Far Rockaway High School, Far Rockaway, NY (1983); Hebrew Teacher, Congregation Sherith Israel, Atlanta, GA (1978-1979); Hebrew Teacher, Congregation Beth Jacob, Atlanta, GA (1975-1977); English Teacher, George W. Wingate High School, Brooklyn, NY (1969-1972); English Teacher, Andries Hudde Middle School, Brooklyn, NY (1966-1967) **CR:** Sewist Present) **CW:** Editor Emerita, LitvakSIG Online Journal (2009-Present); Author, Genealogy Article, "My Hashava Experience," Avotaynu (2017); Editor, LitvakSIG Online Journal, NY (1997-2009); Author, Genealogy Article, "Introduction to Database," The Rabbi Samuel Langer Database; Author, "Database Introduction to the Bialystoker Children's 1943 Transport Database," Internet Online (2002); Contributor, Book of Poetry, Jewish Women's Literary Annual (2001); Author, Genealogy Article, "1946 Medingen Mystery-and Miracle," Avotaynu (2001); Talk, "How to Read a Hebrew Tombstone" (2000); Author, Genealogy Article, "What Does a Litvak Look Like?," LitvakSIG (1999); Author, Genealogy Article, "Another Surnamer Surfaces," Avotaynu (1997); Author, Genealogy Article, "Following the Weber Trail: of Genealogical Haystacks and Cakes" (1994); Contributor, "Poetry and Memoirs Filtered Images: Women Remembering Their Grandmothers" (1992); Contributor, Book of Poetry, "Sarah's Daughters Sing" (1990) **AW:** Award, Outstanding Contributions to Student Editing and Writing (1988, 1989) **MEM:** Jewish Genealogy Society of Long Island (JGSLI); Jewish Genealogy Society of New York (Jewish Genealogical Society, Inc.); Association of Professional Genealogists (APG) **MH:** Albert Nelson Marquis Lifetime Achievement Award **B/I:** Mrs. Caplan became involved in her profession because when she was growing up her father was a rabbi and in high school she would teach a Sunday school class. Back then, in 1962, there weren't many options for women and teaching was the best choice so she taught English in high school. She also taught Hebrew school in a synagogue in Atlanta where she had moved to with her husband. When she moved back to New York she went back to teaching English and then she got interested in genealogy. Her son suggested to her that she should do a genealogy program and do her family tree and he would help her. She sent out a questionnaire to both her side and her husband's side of the family to get the information. She found it to be very enjoyable especially when she had retired from teaching. **AV:** Sewing; Gardening **RE:** Jewish

CAPPELLAZZO, AMY, T: Chairperson, Executive Vice President **I:** Retail/Sales **CN:** Sotheby's **SPN:** Joanne Cappellazzo (Life Partner) **CH:** Marina (Adopted); Benjamin (Adopted) **ED:** Master of Arts in Urban Design and City Planning, Pratt Institute, New York, NY; Bachelor of Fine Arts, New York University **C:** Chairperson, Executive Vice President, Sotheby's (2016-Present); Co-founder, Art Agency, Partners (2014-Present); Head, Global Fine Arts Division, Sotheby's (2009-Present); International Co-Head, Post-War and Contemporary Art Department, Christie's, New York, NY (2001-2014); Deputy Chairperson, Christie's Americas (2008-2009); Director, Rubell Family Collection & Foundation, Miami, FL **CR:** Lecturer in Field; Board of Directors, Los Angeles Contemporary Exhibitions **CIV:** Board Director, Miami Light Project **CW:** Co-editor, "In Company: The Collaborations of Robert Creeley" (1999) **AW:** Named, One of the 40 Under 40, Crain's New York Business Journal (2006)

CARBAJAL, SALUD ORTIZ, T: U.S. Representative from California **I:** Government Administration/Government Relations/Government Services **DOB:** 10/18/1964 **PB:** Moroleon **SC:** Mexico **MS:** Married **SPN:** Gina Carabajal **CH:** Natasha; Michael **ED:** Master's in Organizational Management, Fielding Graduate University; Diploma, University of California Santa Barbara **C:** Member, U.S. House of Representatives from California's 24th Congressional District (2017-Present); Member, Committee on Armed Services (2017-Present); Member, Committee on the Budget (2017-Present); Member, House Committee on Agriculture (2017-Present); Member, House Committee on Transportation and Infrastructure (2017-Present); Member, Board of Supervisors, Santa Barbara County, CA (2004-2016) **CR:** Member, Congressional Hispanic Caucus; Member, Congressional Asian Pacific American Caucus; Member, Climate Solutions Caucus; Member, Congressional Solar Caucus; Member, House Baltic Caucus; Member, New Democrat Coalition **MIL:** With, United States Marine Corps

CARBONARA, ROBERT STEPHEN, PHD, T: Discipline Lead, Materials Scientist **I:** Sciences **CN:** SEA Limited **DOB:** 03/14/1937 **PB:** Pittsburgh **SC:** PA/USA **PT:** Stephen E. Carbonara; Lena G. (Pujia) Carbonara **MS:** Married **SPN:** Marilyn B. Hensley (11/22/1993); Elizabeth S. Keegan (11/27/1965, Divorced 1989) **CH:** Matthew; Stephen; Nathan; Christopher (Stepson) **ED:** PhD in Materials Science, University of Cincinnati (1970); BS in Physics, University of Pittsburgh (1959) **CT:** Certified Private Investigator, State of Ohio **C:** Discipline Lead, Materials Sciences, SEA, Ltd. (2019-Present); Senior Analyst, S.E.A. Inc., Columbus, OH (1998-2019); Group Manager, S.E.A. Inc., Columbus, OH (1988-1998); Associate Manager, Battelle Memorial Institute, Columbus, OH (1977-1988); Research Scientist, Battelle Memorial Institute, Columbus, OH (1968-1977); NASA Trainee, University of Cincinnati (1964) **CR:** Consultant, Battelle Development Corporation, Columbus, OH (1983-1987) **CIV:** National Board of Directors (1998-1999); Chairman, Board of Directors, American Heart Association, Ohio Valley Affiliate (1980-1998) **CW:** Casting, "Near Net Shape Products" (1988); Editor, "Surface Analysis Techniques" (1976); Patentee in Field; Presenter in field **AW:** President's Award, ASM International; Battelle Intellectual Achievement Award **MEM:** Chapter Chairman, American Society of Metals International (1981); Phi Eta Sigma; Phi Lambda Upsilon **MH:** Albert Nelson Marquis Lifetime Achievement Award; Marquis Who's Who Top Professional **AS:** Dr. Carbonara attributes his success to being a non-conventional thinker. He has solved problems for many people, which is the main source of his success. He believes non-conventional thinking is the key to solving those seemingly difficult problems. **B/I:** Dr. Carbonara became involved in his profession because he transitioned from a chemistry major to a physics major as an undergraduate at the University of Pittsburgh. He was working at the Mellon Institute part-time and the gentleman he was working for was a fairly well-known materials scientist named Dr. Thaddeus Massalski. He advised Dr. Carbonara to go into materials science, which he did and make a career out of. He subsequently started taking courses part-time at Carnegie Tech. He later left Pittsburgh and went to school at the University of Cincinnati, where he earned his PhD. **AV:** Fishing; Boating; Gardening **THT:** Growing up in the small suburb of Dormont, just south of Pittsburgh, contributed to Dr. Carbonara in very significant ways. Being a middle-class community, the culture in Dormont was working hard to succeed. His father, whose education ended in the sixth grade as he had to work to support his younger brothers and sisters, was adamant about his son getting a good education. He was also a role model in that he was clever and a hard worker. He never let his lack of formal education stop him from solving a problem or getting ahead. His mother, a stay at home mom, kept a neat and clean house and made sure he was always neat and clean and taught me to be organized. Having good parents is important for one's future. Being the first in his father's family to go to college was eye opening for him. He had no idea what he would encounter. In order to pay for his education, he worked at two jobs, one, between classes, at the University of Pittsburgh Cyclotron and the other at a grocery chain at night. The remainder of his time was devoted to his studies, as failure was not an option. Raising three boys was not an easy task, but it taught him that life is a process and that things can change in unexpected ways. In the long run raising a family was one of the most rewarding experiences of his life.

CARDARELLA, C. JOANN FOUST, MSN, ARNP, T: Nursing Administrator **I:** Medicine & Health Care **DOB:** 02/27/1931 **PB:** Fayetteville **SC:** NC/USA **PT:** George Francis Foust; Maude Ernestine (White) Foust **MS:** Widowed **SPN:** Louis Cardarella (Deceased); Herman H. Brown **ED:** MSN, University of North Carolina (1970);BSN, University of Miami (1968); Diploma, The McLeod Infirmary (Now McLeod Health) (1952) **C:** Retired (1998); Nurse Manager of Mental Health, Lake Placid Medical Center (Now AdventHealth Lake Placid), FL (1992-1998); Staff Nurse, Jackson Memorial Hospital, Jackson Health System, Miami, FL (1957-1998); Owner, The Chocolate Strawberry, Marco Island, FL (1984-1989); Director of Nursing, Jackson Memorial Hospital, Jackson Health System, Miami, FL (1970-1984);Staff Nurse, VA Hospital (Durham VA Health Care System), Durham, NC (1953-1957); Staff Nurse, The McLeod Infirmary (Now McLeod), Florence, SC (1952-1953); Head Nurse, Jackson Memorial Hospital, Jackson Health System, Miami, FL; Associate Head Nurse, Jackson Memorial Hospital, Jackson Health System, Miami, FL **MIL:** First Lieutenant, United States Air Force Reserves (1960-1962); Captain, United States Air Force Reserves **MEM:** American Nurses Association, Florida Nurses Association **MH:** Albert Nelson Marquis Lifetime Achievement Award; Marquis Who's Who Top Professional **B/I:** Mrs. Cardarella had an aunt who was a nurse and her mannerism intrigued her. She always knew that she was going to be a nurse. Although finances was involved in a decision to be nurse, Mrs. Cardarella's motivation and encouragement from her family helped her solidify her decision. She has always had a passion for caring for people. **AV:** Needlepoint; Movies; Sailing; Reading

CÁRDENAS, ANTONIO, "TONY", T: U.S. Representative from California **I:** Government Administration/Government Relations/Government Services **DOB:** 3/31/1963 **PB:** Los Angeles **SC:** CA/USA **PT:** Andres Cárdenas; Maria (Quezada) Cárdenas **MS:** Married **SPN:** Norma Cárdenas **CH:** Cristian; Andres; Alina; Vanessa (Stepchild) **ED:** Bachelor of Electrical Engineering, University of California Santa Barbara (1986) **C:** U.S. Representative from California's 29th Congressional District, United States Congress, Washington, DC (2013-Present); Member, U.S. House Committee on Oversight and Government Reform (2013-Present); Member, U.S. House Committee on Natural Resources (2013-Present); Member, U.S. House Budget Committee (2013-Present); Member, Committee on the Judiciary (2013-Present); Member, Committee on Small Business (2013-Present); Councilman, District Six, Los Angeles City Council (2003-2013); Member, District 39, California State Assembly (1996-2002); Owner, President, Our Community Real Estate Co.; Engineering Specialist, Hewlett Packard Co. **CIV:** Commissioner, El Pueblo de Los Angeles Historical Monument; Member, Coalition Against Pipeline; Member, Los Angeles Business Advisory Committee **MEM:** San Fernando Valley Association of Realtors **PA:** Democrat **RE:** Christian

CARDIN, BENJAMIN LOUIS, T: U.S. Senator from Maryland **I:** Government Administration/Government Relations/Government Services **DOB:** 10/05/1943 **PB:** Baltimore **SC:** MD/USA **PT:** Meyer M. Cardin; Dora (Green) Cardin **MS:** Married **SPN:** Myrna Edelman (11/24/1964) **CH:** Michael (Deceased); Deborah **ED:** Honorary LLD, Villa Julie College (Now Stevenson University), Stevenson, MD (2007); Honorary LLD, Goucher College, Baltimore, MD (1996); Honorary LLD, Baltimore Hebrew University (Now Baltimore Hebrew Institute, Towson University) (1994); Honorary LLD, University of Maryland, Baltimore (1993); Honorary LLD, University of Baltimore (1990); JD, University of Maryland Francis King Carey School of Law (1967); BA, University of Pittsburgh, Cum Laude (1964) **C:** Ranking Member, U.S. Senate Committee on Small Business and Entrepreneurship (2015, 2018-Present); U.S. Senator, State of Maryland (2007-Present); Ranking Member, U.S. Senate Committee on Foreign Relations (2015-2018); Member, U.S. House Committee on Ways and Means, Washington, DC (1999-2005); Chairman, U.S. House Committee on Organization and Study Review (1997-2006); Member, U.S. House Subcommittee on Human Resources and Social Security, Washington, DC (1991-2006); Member, U.S. House Committee on Standards Official Conduct, Washington, DC (1991-1997); U.S. Representative from Maryland's Third Congressional District, United States Congress, Washington, DC (1987-2006); Speaker, Maryland House of Delegates (1979-1986); Chairman, Committee on Ways and Means, Maryland House of Delegates (1974-1979); Private Practice Attorney, Baltimore, MD (1967-1987); Member, Maryland House of Delegates (1967-1986) **CR:** Chairman, Commission on Security and Cooperation in Europe (U.S. Helsinki Commission) (2009-Present); Commissioner, Commission on Security and Cooperation in Europe (U.S. Helsinki Commission) (1993-Present); Vice President, Organization for Security and Co-Operation in Europe Parliamentary Assembly (OSCE PA); Member, National Security Working Group **CIV:** Board of Visitors, United States Naval Academy (2007-Present); National Advisory Board, Johns Hopkins University Institute for Policy Studies (2003-Present); Baltimore Council on Foreign Affairs (1999-Present); Board of Visitors, University of Maryland (1998-Present); Board of Visitors, University of Maryland Francis King Carey School of Law (1991-Present); Trustee,

Goucher College (1999-2008); Trustee, St. Mary's College of Maryland (1988-1999); Chairman, Maryland Legal Services Corporation (1988-1995) **CW:** Contributor, Articles, Professional Journals **AW:** Commander, Order of the Star of Romania (2017); Congressional Voice Children Award, National PTA (2009); Maryland Affordable Housing Coalition Leadership Award (2009); Elizabeth & David Scull Metropolitan Public Service Award, Metropolitan Council of Government (2008); Congressional Champion Award, National Association of Psychiatric Health Systems (Now National Association for Behavioral Healthcare (NABH)) (2008); Leadership Law Award, Daily Record (2008); Inductee, Welfare Advocates Wall of Fame (2005); Small Business Council of America (SBCA) Congressional Award (1993, 1999, 2005); Legislator of the Year, American Association of Health Plans (2003); Congressional Champion Award, National Coalition for Cancer Research (2002); Congressional Leadership Award, American College of Emergency Physicians (2001); Congressional Advocate of the Year Award, Child Welfare League of America (CWLA) (2000); National Leadership Award for Service to Children and Families, Casey Family Service (2000); Jacob K. Javits Award, American Psychiatric Association (1999); Dr. Nathan Davis Award for Public Service, American Medical Association (1999); Listee, Concord Coalition's Deficit Hawk Honor Roll (1998, 1999); Representative of the Year Award, National Association of Police Organizations (1998); Living Stream Award, Maryland Save Our Streams (1996); Public Policy Leadership Award, Digestive Disease National Coalition (1996); Vernon Eney Award, Maryland Bar Foundation (1996); Hunting S. Williams Award (1995); H. John Heinz III National Leadership Award, Coalition for a Lead-Safe Environment, Alliance to End Childhood Lead Poisoning (1994); National Multiple Sclerosis Society Representative of the Year Award (1993); Israel Freedom Award (1992); Cardin Pro Bono Award, University of Maryland Francis King Carey School of Law Alumni Association (1990); Pro Bono Publico Award, American Bar Association (1989); Friend of Psychiatry Award, Maryland Psychiatric Society (1988); Ann Hogan Memorial Award, Common Cause of Maryland (1987) **MEM:** Maryland State Bar Association; American Bar Association; The Bar Association of Baltimore City **BAR:** The State of Maryland (1967) **PA:** Democrat **RE:** Jewish

CARELL, STEVE JOHN, T: Actor, Comedian **I:** Media & Entertainment **DOB:** 08/16/1963 **PB:** Concord **SC:** MA/USA **PT:** Edwin A. Carell; Harriet Theresa (Koch) Carell **MS:** Married **SPN:** Nancy Walls (08/05/1995) **CH:** Elizabeth Anne; John **ED:** BA in History, Denison University (1984) **CR:** Performed with Theater Groups including Wisdom Bridge, The Goodman, Second City, Chicago, IL **CW:** Actor, Executive Producer, "Space Force" (2020-Present); Actor, "The Morning Show" (2019-Present); Actor, "Irresistible" (2020); Appearance, "The Kelly Clarkson Show" (2019); Appearance, "The Kelly Clarkson Show" (2019); Guest Host, "Saturday Night Live" (2005, 2008, 2018); Actor, "Beautiful Boy" (2018); Actor, "Welcome to Marwen" (2018); Actor, "Backseat" (2018); Actor, "Despicable Me 3" (2017); Actor, "Battle of the Sexes" (2017); Actor, "Too Funny to Fail" (2017); Actor, "Last Flag Flying" (2017); Actor, Executive Producer, Writer, "Angie Tribeca" (2016-2019); Actor, "Café Society" (2016); Voice Actor, "Minions" (2015); Actor, "The Big Short" (2015); Actor, "Freeheld" (2015); Actor, "Foxcatcher" (2014); Actor, "Alexander and the Terrible, Horrible, No Good, Very Bad Day" (2014); Appearance, "The Tonight Show Starring Jimmy Fallon" (2014); Actor, "Web Therapy" (2013); Actor, "The Incredible Burt Wonderstone" (2013); Actor,

"Anchorman 2: The Legend Continues" (2013); Voice Actor, "Despicable Me 2" (2013); Actor, "The Way, Way Back" (2013); Actor, "Hope Springs" (2012); Actor, "Seeking a Friend for the End of the World" (2012); Voice Actor, "The Simpsons" (2012); Actor, "Life's Too Short" (2011); Actor, Producer, "Crazy, Stupid, Love" (2011); Actor, "The Office" (2005-2011); Actor, "Dinner for Schmucks" (2010); Voice Actor, "Despicable Me" (2010); Actor, "Date Night" (2010); Actor, "Get Smart" (2008); Voice Actor, "Horton Hears a Who" (2008); Actor, "The Naked Trucker and T-Bones Show" (2007); Actor, "Evan Almighty" (2007); Actor, "Dan in Real Life" (2007); Voice Actor, "Over the Hedge" (2006); Actor, "Little Miss Sunshine" (2006); Actor, Writer, Producer, "The 40-Year-Old Virgin" (2005); Actor, "Bewitched" (2005); Actor, "Melinda and Melinda" (2004); Actor, "Anchorman" (2004); Actor, "Come to Papa" (2004); Actor, "Sleepover" (2004); Actor, "The Daily Show with Jon Stewart" (1999-2004); Actor, "Bruce Almighty" (2003); Actor, "Watching Ellie" (2002-2003); Actor, "Street of Pain" (2002); Voice Actor, "Saturday Night Live" (1996-2002); Actor, "H.U.D." (2000); Actor, "Suits" (1999); Actor, "Tomorrow Night" (1998); Actor, "Over the Top" (1997); Actor, "Over the Top" (1997); Actor, Writer, "The Dana Carvey Show" (1996); Actor, "Curley Sue" (1991); Actor, "Life as We Know It" (1991) **AW:** Honoree, Star, Hollywood Walk of Fame (2016); Named Favorite TV Comedy Actor, People's Choice Awards (2010); Named One of the 100 Most Powerful Celebrities, Forbes.com (2008); SAG Awards for Outstanding Performance by an Ensemble in a Comedy Series, SAG-AFTRA (2007, 2008); Teen Choice Award for Choice TV Actor: Comedy (2007, 2008); SAG Award for Outstanding Performance by an Ensemble in a Motion Picture, SAG-AFTRA (2007); Award for Episodic Comedy, Comedy Series, Writers Guild of America (2007); Named One of the 50 Most Powerful People in Hollywood, Premiere Magazine (2006); Golden Globe Award for Best Performance by an Actor in TV Series-Musical or Comedy, Hollywood Foreign Press Association (2006); MTV Movie Award for Best Comedic Performance (2006); Numerous Awards

CAREY, MARIAH, T: Singer, Songwriter **I:** Media & Entertainment **DOB:** 03/27/1970 **PB:** Huntington **SC:** NY/USA **PT:** Alfred Roy Carey; Patricia (Hickey) Carey **MS:** Divorced **SPN:** Nick Cannon (04/30/2008, Divorced 2016); Thomas Mottola (06/05/1993, Divorced 03/05/1998) **CH:** Moroccan Scott; Monroe **ED:** Coursework, 500 Hours, Beauty School; Diploma, Harborfield High School, Greenlawn, NY (1987) **CR:** Global Ambassador, Jenny Craig (2011-2013); Launched, Collection of Jewelry, Fragrances and Shoes, HSN, Inc. (2010); Launched, Fragrance, Mariah Carey's Luscious Pink (2008); Launched, Fragrance, M by Mariah Carey Gold Deluxe Edition (2008); Launched, First Fragrance, M by Mariah Carey (2007); Launched, Jewelry Line, Glamorized by Mariah Carey (2006); Backup Singer to Brenda K. Starr; Various Positions Including Waitress and Coat Check Girl **CIV:** Hunger Ambassador, World Hunger Relief Movement (2008); Co-founder, Camp Mariah/The Fresh Air Fund; Supporter, Make-A-Wish Foundation, NewYork-Presbyterian Hospital; Performer, Numerous Benefit Concerts **CW:** Performer, "The Butterfly Returns," Caesars Palace, Las Vegas, NV (2018-2020); Singer, "Caution" (2018); Voice Actress, Featured, "Mariah Carey's All I Want for Christmas Is You" (2017); Actress, "The Lego Batman Movie" (2017); Actress, "Girls Trip" (2017); Appearance, "The Star" (2017); Performer, The Colosseum, Caesars Palace, Las Vegas, NV (2015-2017); Appearance, "Popstar: Never Stop Never Stopping" (2016); Actress, "Empire" (2016); Reality TV Personality, "Mariah's World" (2016);

Author, "All I Want for Christmas is You" (2015); Appearance, "A Christmas Melody" (2015); Singer, "#1 to Infinity" (2015); Singer, "Me. I Am Mariah... The Elusive Chanteuse" (2014); Judge, "American Idol" (2013); Voice Actress, "American Dad!" (2013); Actress, "The Butler" (2013); Singer, "Merry Christmas II You" (2010); Singer, "Memoirs of an Imperfect Angel" (2009); Actress, "Precious" (2009); Actress, "Tennessee" (2008); Singer, "E=MC2" (2008); Actress, "State Property 2" (2005); Singer, "Emancipation of Mimi" (2005); Singer, "Through the Rain" (2003); Singer, "The Remixes" (2003); Singer, "Charmbracelet" (2002); Actress, "WiseGirls" (2002); Appearance, "Ally McBeal" (2002); Singer, "Greatest Hits" (2001); Appearance, "The Bachelor" (1999); Singer, "Rainbow" (1999); Actress, "Glitter" (1998); Singer, "#1's" (1998); Singer, "Butterfly" (1997); Singer, "Daydream" (1995); Singer, "Merry Christmas" (1994); Singer, "Music Box" (1993); Singer, "Mariah Carey MTV Unplugged" (1992); Singer, "Emotions" (1991); Singer, "Mariah Carey" (1990) **AW:** Inductee, Songwriters Hall of Fame (2020); Billboard Icon Award (2019); Angel for Animals Award, PETA (2017); Ally Award, GLAAD Media Awards (2016); Recipient, Star, Hollywood Walk of Fame (2015); Named Favorite R&B Artist, People's Choice Awards (2010); Honorable Award, American Music Awards (2008); Named One of the 50 Most Powerful Women in New York City, New York Post (2008); Named One of the 100 Most Influential People in the World, TIME Magazine (2008); Special Achievement Award, World Music Awards (2008); Grammy Awards for Best R&B Song, Best Female R&B Vocal Performance, Best Contemporary R&B Album, Recording Academy (2006); Award for Outstanding Album, NAACP Image Awards (2006); Award for Female Entertainer of Year, World Music Awards (2005); Awards for Best-Selling R&B Artist, Best-Selling Pop Female Artist, Female Billboard 200 Album Artist of the Year, Billboard Music Awards (2005); Awards for Female R&B/Hip-Hop Artist of Year, Favorite Female R&B Artist, American Music Awards (2005); Award for Song of the Year, Radio Music Awards (2005); Awards for Hot 100 Song of the Year, Rhythmic Top 40 Title of the Year, Hot 100 Airplay of the Year, Billboard Music Awards (2005); Horizon Award, Congressional Foundation Awards (1999); Award for Artist of the Decade, Billboard Music Awards (1999); Award for Outstanding Duo or Group, NAACP Image Awards (1999); Named Woman of the Year, Glamour Magazine (1998); Grammy Awards for Best Pop Vocal Performance by a Female, Best New Artist, Recording Academy (1990); Numerous Awards

CAREY, ROBERT, T: Chief Executive Officer **I:** Financial Services **CN:** Carey Secure Money Management & Financial Services **DOB:** 08/06/1940 **PB:** Huntington **SC:** WV/USA **MS:** Married **SPN:** Deborah Carey **CT:** LUTCF; Million Dollar Round Table **C:** Chief Executive Officer, Carey Secure Money Management & Financial Services (1989-Present) **MIL:** U.S. Army (1958-1964) **MEM:** National Association of Insurance and Finical Advisers **MH:** Marquis Who's Who Top Professional **AS:** Mr. Carey attributes his success to a lot of hard work, a supportive family and clients. He treats all clients with honor and integrity. Most of his business comes from referrals and he treats his clients how he would like to be treated. **B/I:** Mr. Carey became involved in his profession because after being approached by people who had previously retired and lost a big portion of their retirement dollars in the market, he wanted to show them a better and safer way to protect their retirement money. In addition, what attracted him to his profession was just looking for a job and then he found out he liked it, cared about people, and what happened

to them. He started out as a debt company where they went around to peoples homes and collected premiums every month. How people would retire and put their money in the market wasting their money and having to go back to work, and he was always concerned about how they could jeopardize that money that is supposed to last them the rest of their lives. His philosophy is that you don't take your money out of your 401k and invest in the market because that has to last you the rest of your life, but instead to put it in secure funds, products that are guaranteed, where they won't lose their principal. **AV:** Golf; NASCAR races; Fishing **PA:** Independent **RE:** Protestant **THT:** "Do on to others as you would have them do on to you."

CARL, JOAN STRAUSS, T: Sculptor, Painter **I:** Fine Art **DOB:** 03/20/1926 **PB:** Cleveland **SC:** OH/USA **PT:** Dr. Abraham Strauss; Marion Halle Strauss **ED:** Coursework, New School of Art, Los Angeles; Coursework, Chicago Art Institute; Coursework, Cleveland School Art **C:** Teacher, University of Judaism; Lecturer, Federal Visual Arts Program, Title Three (1961-1964); Faculty, Valley Center of the Arts (1960-1964) **CW:** Solo Exhibitor, Paideia Gallery, Los Angeles, Bel Air Extension Gallery, Beverly Hills, California, Laguna Beach Art Museum, Courtney Collins Gallery, Raleigh, NC, Linden-Kicklighter Gallery, Cleveland, Muskegon Community College, Bakersfield College, Fresno Art Center Museum, Brand Library Gallery, Glendale, California, Thinking Eye, Los Angeles, Courtright Gallery, Los Angeles; Exhibitor, Group Shows, Cerritos College, Los Angeles. Art Association, Southern California Exposition, San Diego, Santa Cruz Art Show, West End Gallery, New York City, Stuart Kingston Galleries, Naples, FL, Laguna Beach Art Museum, Mint Museum, Charlotte, NC, Paideia Gallery, Oborn Gallery, Kansas City, KS, Gallery Judaica, Los Angeles, Feldheim Library Gallery, San Bernardino, CA, Feingood Gallery, Milkin Center, Northridge, CA, Judson Gallery, Los Angeles, CA, Lankershim Gallery, North Hollywood, CA; Exhibitor, Commission and Collections, Zinkal Limited, Tel Aviv, Raleigh Museum, Northern Ohio Museum, Cleveland, Sinai Memorial Park, Los Angeles, CA, Government of Japan, International Cultural Center Youth, Jerusalem **AW:** Design Award, Ceramic Tile Institute **MEM:** Founding Member California Confederation of Arts; Past President, Los Angeles Chapter, Artists Equity Association; Past President, Los Angeles Art Association **MH:** Albert Nelson Marquis Lifetime Achievement Award **AS:** Ms. Carl's parents were incredibly supportive of her career as an artist despite her father, Dr. Abraham Strauss, being a surgeon and her mother Marion Halle Strauss, being and English major and writer. It was a blessing that her parents didn't push her to do something they may have thought would be a better profession during World War II times. Instead they heavily encouraged her career pursuits. **B/I:** Ms. Carl says, "the world was there, and I wanted to make the things that I saw, mine. So the way to do that for me was to draw..." Ever since a girl it was natural for me to "touch things with my eyes and your hand moves..." That is all she has known to do her whole life.

CARLINI, JAMES MBA, T: Management Consultant **I:** Technology **CN:** Carlini & Associates, Inc. **DOB:** 08/27/1954 **PB:** Berwyn **SC:** IL/USA **PT:** Harvey Reno Carlini; Helen Dorothy (Stan) Carlini **MS:** Married **SPN:** Holly R. Haupin (09/29/1979) **ED:** MBA in Management Information Systems and Marketing, DePaul University (1982); BS in Computer Science, Roosevelt University (1978); MusB, Roosevelt University (1976) **C:** President, Carlini & Associates, Inc., East Dundee, IL (1986-Present); Director, Telecommunications and Computer Hardware Consultant, Arthur Young & Co., Chicago, IL (1983-1986); Manager, Illinois Bell, Chicago, IL (1981-1983); Software Engineer, Motorola, Schaumburg, IL (1979-1981); Information Systems Designer, Western Electric Division Bell Laboratories, Naperville, IL (1977-1979) **CR:** Guest Panelist, Public Policy Radio FM 104.1, Milwaukee, WI (2017-2019); Elected Chairman, Rolls-Royce Owners Club, Lake Michigan Region (2014-2017); International Business Columnist, Alrroya Dubai (2010-2011); Adjunct Professor, Stuart School of Business, Illinois Institute Technology (2010); Adjunct Professor, Technological Institute School of Speech, Northwestern University, Evanston, IL (1986-2006); Adjunct Professor, Graduate School of Business, DePaul University, Chicago, IL (1986-1989) **CIV:** Appointed Member, Fox Valley Cable Commission; East Dundee Liquor Commission (2007-2009); Village Trustee, East Dundee, IL (2005-2009); President, Mental Health Board, Berwyn, IL (1983) **MIL:** United States Army Reserve (1972-1985) **CW:** Contributing Author, Whitepapers, Military Intelligence Topics, American Intelligence Journal (2017-Present); Contributor, Articles, Professional Journals (1986-Present); Contributing Editor, Electrical Contractor Magazine (2016-2019); Author, "Location Location Connectivity" (2014); Author, "Intelligent Infrastructure: Securing Regional Sustainability," U.S. Department of Homeland Security (2009); Editorial Columnist, MidwestBusiness.com (2000-2009); Editorial Advisory Board Member, Cabling Business Magazine **AW:** Bentley Drivers Club, John Julien Award (2019); Shoup Award, National Rolls-Royce Owners Club (2013, 2014, 2015); Chairman's Award, Rolls-Royce Owners Club, Lake Michigan Region (2010); Distinguished Teaching Award, Northwestern University (1996); Alumni Professors Award, Northwestern University (1995); Certificate of Appreciation, Association of Information Technology (1993) **MEM:** American Legion (1972-Present) **MH:** Albert Nelson Marquis Lifetime Achievement Award **AS:** Mr. Carlini attributes his success to consistent learning throughout his entire career. While moving into new areas, he has kept an eye on current cutting-edge technologies and their creative applications in the next generation of real estate. Further, Mr. Carlini's multi-faceted career has been made up of consulting, teaching, litigation support, and writing, all of which have provided him with a unique perspective from which to work. Because of this, he is often sought after by many clients, as they are confident in his strategic abilities to keep their organizations competitive and present in today's global economy. **B/I:** Mr. Carlini graduated with a bachelor's degree in music education from Roosevelt University in 1976. However, he struggled to find a teaching position. After seeing that Bell Laboratories was hiring, he took a chance and applied for work. It ended up being a great opportunity, as Mr. Carlini became familiar with real-time software within the mission-critical infrastructure. He learned a lot as an information systems designer. Seeking to further his career, he enrolled at DePaul University in pursuit of an MBA. Later, he was recruited by Arthur Young (now known as Ernst & Young), becoming a practice area director. This experience provided him with many of the necessary skills to venture out on his own. **AV:** Yachting; Golfing; Collecting vintage posters; Participating in Rolls-Royce and Bentley car clubs **RE:** Roman Catholic

CARLSON, ERIK, T: Chief Executive Officer, President **I:** Technology **CN:** Dish Network Corporation **ED:** BA, Bradley University **C:** President, Chief Executive Officer, Dish Network Corporation (2017-Present); President, Chief Operating Offi-cer, Head of Sling, TV Dish Network Corporation (2017); President, Chief Operating Officer, Dish Network Corporation (2015-2017)

CARMICHAEL, JAMES V. JR., T: Library and Information Science Educator **I:** Library Management/Library Services **DOB:** 11/27/1946 **PB:** Atlanta **SC:** GA/USA **PT:** James Vinson Carmichael; Frances Elizabeth (McDonald) Carmichael **SPN:** Karen Bryce Powers (06/18/1969, Divorced 1973) **CH:** Gerald; Christina; Jason **ED:** PhD, University of North Carolina (1988); MLN, Emory University (1977); BA, Emory University (1969) **C:** Professor, University of North Carolina (2000-Present); Associate Professor of Library and Information Science, University of North Carolina (1995-2000); Assistant Professor of Library and Information Sciences, University of North Carolina (1989-1995); Instructor, University of North Carolina (1988-1989); Instructor, The University of North Carolina at Chapel Hill (1988-1989); Reference Instruction Librarian, Georgia College (1977-1981); Trust Administrative Assistant, Trustco Bank (1970-1976); Logistics Assistant, Lockheed Martin Aircraft (1969-1970); Inventory Control Clerk, Lockheed Martin Aircraft (1969) **CW:** Editor, "Daring to Find Our Names: The Search for Lesbigay Library History" (1998); Contributor, Articles, Professional Journals **AW:** Edmund Pearson Award (2001); Distinguished Alumni Award, University of North Carolina (1995); Franklin M. Garrett Award, Atlanta History Center (1990); Louis Round Wilson Award, Southeastern Library Association (1988) **MEM:** Chair, College and University Secretary, North Carolina Library Association (2001-2003); Library History Roundtable, American Library Association (1995-1996); Member, Committee Status of Women, American Library Association (1993-1996); ALISE **MH:** Albert Nelson Marquis Lifetime Achievement Award **B/I:** Mr. Carmichael became involved in his profession because of his cousin. He mentioned wanting to become more involved with the library and they guided him on the right path. **AV:** Reading

CARNES, EDWARD EARL, T: Chief Judge **I:** Law and Legal Services **CN:** United States Court of Appeals for the Eleventh Circuit **DOB:** 06/03/1950 **PB:** Albertville **SC:** AL/USA **ED:** JD, Harvard Law School, Cum Laude (1975); BS, University of Alabama, Tuscaloosa, AL (1972) **C:** Chief Judge, United States Court of Appeals for the Eleventh Circuit (2013-Present); Judge, United States Court of Appeals for the Eleventh Circuit (1992-2013); Chief, Capital Punishment and Post-conviction Litigation Division, State of Alabama (1981-1992); Assistant Attorney General, State of Alabama, Montgomery, AL (1975-1992) **MEM:** Chairman, Advisory Committee on Criminal Rules, Judicial Conference (2001-2004)

CARNEY, JOHN CHARLES JR., T: Governor of Delaware **I:** Government Administration/Government Relations/Government Services **DOB:** 05/20/1956 **PB:** Wilmington **SC:** DE/USA **PT:** John Charles "Jack" Carney; Ann Marie (Buckley) Carney **MS:** Married **SPN:** Tracey Quillen **CH:** Sam; James **ED:** Bachelor of Arts in English, Dartmouth College (1978); Master of Public Administration, University of Delaware **C:** Governor, State of Delaware (2017-Present); Member, United States House Committee of Financial Services, Washington, DC (2011-Present); Member at-Large, United States Congress from Delaware, Washington, DC (2011-2017); Lieutenant Governor, State of Delaware, Dover, DE (2001-2009); Secretary of Finance, State of Delaware, Dover, DE (1997-2000); Deputy Chief of Staff to Governor, State of Delaware (1994-1997); Deputy Chief Administrative Officer, New Castle County, DE (1989-1994); Staff Assistant to Senator Joseph R. Biden, United States Senate (1986-1989); Acting Director of Public Works, New Castle County, DE **CR:** President, Chief Operating Officer, Transformative Technologies **CIV:** Board of Directors, Catholic Youth Organization, Wilmington, DE **PA:** Democrat **RE:** Roman Catholic

CARPENTER, ADELBERT, "BUZ" W., T: Air Force Officer (Retired) **I:** Military & Defense Services **DOB:** 07/31/1943 **PB:** Darby **SC:** PA/USA **PT:** Adelbert Carpenter; Maxine (Wall) Carpenter **MS:** Married **SPN:** Nancy Ann Jackson (06/24/1967) **CH:** Kristin L.; Kimberly L.; Kelli L. **ED:** MS in Systems Management, University of Southern California, Los Angeles, CA (1974); BS in International Affairs, U.S. Air Force Academy (1967) **CT:** U.S. Air Force Command Pilot **C:** Vice President, Business Development L-3 Communications, ComCept Div, Arlington, VA (2000-2013); Director, Program, Dev Raytheon, Washington DC Office (1998-2000); Director, Program Development, Falls Church Division E-Sys. Co., Virginia (1995-1997); Vice Commander, 2nd Air Force, Beale AFB, California (1991-1995); Commander, 377th Combat Support Wing, Ramstein AB (1990-1991); Director, Programs, Headquarters, U.S. Air Force in Europe, Ramstein AB, Germany (1987-1990); Commander, 70th Tactical Fighter Squadron, Moody AFB, Georgia (1985-1987) **CR:** Saw Combat in Vietnam (1971) **CIV:** Smithsonian Air & Space Museum Docent (2003-Present) **MIL:** Advanced Through Grades to Colonel, U.S. Air Force (1988); Commissioned Second Lieutenant, U.S. Air Force (1967); Colonel & Command Pilot (Retired) **CW:** Smithsonian Documents, Data References, Videos on SR-71 History **AW:** Inductee into the Virginia Aviation Hall of Fame (2017); Two Decorated Legions of Merit; Five Air Medals **MEM:** Life Member, Air Force Association; Life Member, Air Force Academy Association of Graduates; Daedalians **MH:** Albert Nelson Marquis Lifetime Achievement Award; Marquis Who's Who Humanitarian Award **AS:** Col. Carpenter attributes his success to a wonderful nurturing family upbringing, and having a plan and the dedication to stick with it. He had a vision of his future and pursued it the best he could. He also attributes it to excellent mentors along the way. **B/I:** Col. Carpenter became involved in his profession because his father and two uncles were aeronautical engineers, and early on, he was fascinated with flying and becoming a military pilot. He wanted a career serving his nation. Col. Carpenter became fascinated with U.S. Air Force Academy after he saw a film of its dedication in the late 1950s. **AV:** Exercising; Investing; Theater; Travel **PA:** Conservative **RE:** Presbyterian

CARPENTER, JOHN T., MD, T: Professor Emeritus **I:** Education/Educational Services **CN:** University of Alabama at Birmingham **DOB:** 09/25/1942 **PB:** Shreveport **SC:** LA/USA **PT:** John Topham Carpenter; Anna Belle (Thomas) Carpenter **MS:** Married **SPN:** Sandra Ann Moore (06/02/1984) **CH:** Claire Elizabeth **ED:** MD, Tulane University (1968);BA, Johns Hopkins University, (1964) **CT:** Diplomate, American Board of Internal Medicine (ABIM); Diplomate, Medical Oncology; Diplomate, Hematology; Diplomate, Hematology, American Board of Pathology **C:** Professor of Medicine, University of Alabama at Birmingham (1986-Present); From Assistant Professor of Medicine to Associate Professor of Medicine, University of Alabama at Birmingham (1973-1986) **CR:** Member, UAB Institutional Review Board for Human Use (1995-Present); Member, Oncologic Drugs Advisory Committee, FDA (2000-2004); Professor of Clinical Oncology, American Cancer Society (1987-1991); Member, Clinical Fellowship Committee, American

Cancer Society (1979-1989); Chair, Breast Cancer Committee, Southeastern Cancer Study Group (1984-1985) **CIV:** Board of Directors, Alabama Division, American Cancer Society (1987-1991); Volunteer Community of Hope Clinic **CW:** Author, Contributor, 62 Articles, Peer-Reviewed Journals **AW:** Outstanding Teacher, Division of Hematology/Oncology, University of Alabama at Birmingham (2005-2006) **MEM:** Fellow, American College of Physicians; American Society of Clinical Oncology; American Society of Hematology **MH:** Albert Nelson Marquis Lifetime Achievement Award; Marquis Who's Who Top Professional **B/I:** Dr. Carpenter became involved in his profession because he was interested in medicine from as far back as high school, and as someone who had health problems himself from an early age, he had more insight into the medical world than most people at that stage in life got.He had a passion to be a medical doctor since he was a teenager. He chose the field of oncology as a medical student, which turned out to be developing as a subspecialty when he was in training. By chance, he got into some breast cancer research that he really liked so he shifted his focus, but he did oncology for a long time. **AV:** Cooking; Travel **RE:** Episcopalian **THT:** Dr. Carpenter's daughter, Claire Elizabeth, is a nurse. His wife, Sandra, is a nutritionist.

CARPENTER, JUNE EVANS, T: Retired Educator **I:** Education/Educational Services **DOB:** 06/19/1952 **PB:** Montgomery **SC:** AL/USA **PT:** Aubrey L. Evans; Voncile M. Evans **MS:** Married **SPN:** Jerry Carpenter **CH:** Leslie; Lynlee; Lauren **ED:** MS in Education, Troy State University, Montgomery, AL (1989); Postgraduate Coursework, Auburn University, Montgomery, AL (1976-1977); BS in Education, Auburn University (1974); Coursework, University of Montevallo (1970-1972) **CT:** Certified Class A Elementary Teacher, Alabama **C:** Title I Reading Laboratory Teacher, Title I Building Chair, Elmore County Board of Education (2001-2008); Reading Teacher, Elmore County Board of Education (1999-2008); Chairman, Accreditation Steering Committee, Southern Association of Colleges and Schools Elmore County Board of Education (1997-2008); Coordinator, Writing to Read, Elmore County Board of Education (1995-2002); Elementary Teacher, Chapter I Reading and Mathematics, Elmore County Board of Education, Wetumpka, AL (1989-1995); Teacher, First United Methodist Church Kindergarten, Montgomery, AL (1981-1982, 1986-1989); Assistant Director, First United Methodist Church Kindergarten, Montgomery, AL (1982-1983); Elementary Teacher, Elmore County Board of Education, Wetumpka, AL (1974-1980) **CR:** Judge, Science Fair, Wetumpka Elementary School (2015-2017); Judge, Science Fair, Wetumpka Junior High School (1989) **CIV:** Cathedral Bells, Charles Forester Sunday School Class, First United Methodist Church of Montgomery (2015-Present); Board of Trustees, Alabama-West Florida UMC Conference (2011-2019); President, Three Seasons Arts League Wetumpka (2001-2002, 2016-2018); History Committee, Bell Choir, Adult Choir, Chair, Worship Committee (2005-2015); Chair, Altar Guild (2001-2015); Wedding Director (1995-2015); Treasurer, Troop 93, Girl Scouts of the United States, Wetumpka, AL (1992-1996); Wetumpka High School Band of Parents (1990-1995); Sunday School Teacher, Jane Blair Class (1992); Chairman, Council on Ministries (1989-1992); Director, Bible School (1990); Education Committee, First United Methodist Church of Wetumpka (1989); Chairman, Fall Bazaar First United Methodist Church of Montgomery (1985-1986); Charter Member, The Kelly Fitzpatrick Memorial Gallery **CW:** Author, "The Kelly Canvas," The Kelly Fitzpatrick Memorial Gallery, Wetumpka, AL **AW:** Elmore County

School System Teacher of the Year (1999-2000); Cooperation in Teaching Award, Elmore County Board of Education (1990); Excellence in Leadership Award, Alpha Delta Kappa (1990); Award for Outstanding Volunteer Work, Wetumpka Elementary School (1989); Volunteer Appreciation Award, Girl Scouts of the USA (1989) **MEM:** International Mentor, Chairman, Gulf Region (2014-2018); International Executive Board Chairman (2011-2013); Board of Directors, International Executive Board (2009-2013); International Vice President, Gulf Region (2005-2007); Alpha Delta Kappa (1980-2000); National Education Association; Alabama Education Association; Elmore County Education Association; Auburn Alumni Association Life Member, Kappa Delta Pi; Gamma Beta Phi **MH:** Albert Nelson Marquis Lifetime Achievement Award; Marquis Who's Who Top Professional; Distinguished Humanitarian **AS:** Ms. Carpenter attributes her success to working with wonderful mentors, especially Doris P. Beatty, her sixth-grade teacher. **B/I:** Ms. Carpenter got the opportunity to work with elementary-age children through the Future Teachers of America. This experience inspired her to become an educator. **AV:** Playing piano; Smocking; Decorating; Reading; Cooking; Playing handbells **RE:** United Methodist Church **THT:** Ms. Carpenter believes life is a gift.

CARPER, THOMAS, "TOM" RICHARD, T: U.S. Senator **I:** Government Administration/Government Relations/Government Services **DOB:** 01/23/1947 **PB:** Beckley **SC:** WV/USA **PT:** Wallace Richard Carper; Mary Jean (Patton) Carper **MS:** Married **SPN:** Martha Ann Stacy (01/01/1986); Diane Beverly Isaacs (1978, Divorced 1983) **CH:** Christopher Thomas; Benjamin Michael **ED:** MBA, Lerner Business and Economics, University of Delaware (1975); BA in Economics, The Ohio State University (1968) **C:** Ranking Member, U.S. Senate Committee on Environment and Public Works (2017-Present); Chairman, U.S. Senate Committee on Homeland Security and Governmental Affairs (2013-Present); Member, U.S. Senate Committee on Finance (2009-Present); U.S. Senator, State of Delaware (2001-Present); Member, U.S. Senate Committee on Commerce, Science and Transportation (2007-2009); Governor, State of Delaware (1993-2001); U.S. Representative, Delaware's At-Large Congressional District, United States Congress, Washington, DC (1983-1993); State Treasurer, State of Delaware, Dover, DE (1977-1983); Industrial Development Specialist, Delaware Economic Development, Dover, DE (1975-1976) **CR:** Board of Directors, AMTRAK, National Railroad Passenger Corporation (1994-1997) **CIV:** Honorary Chair, Delaware Special Olympics (1987-Present); Fundraising Chairman, Big Brothers, Big Sisters of Delaware (1985, 1993) **MIL:** Commander, U.S. Navy Reserve (1973-1991); Lieutenant, U.S. Navy (1968-1973) **AW:** George Falcon Golden Spike Award, National Association of Railroad Passengers (2004); Early Stage East Founders' Award (2003); Rookie of the Year Award, Rehoboth Beach-Dewey Beach, Delaware State Chamber of Commerce (2002); Magnificent Mentor Award, Delaware Mentoring Council (2002); American Financial Leadership Award, Financial Services Roundtable (2002); Decorated Commendation Medal; Air Medal **MEM:** Chairman, NGA (1998-1999); Vice Chairman, NGA (1997-1998) **PA:** Democrat **RE:** Presbyterian

CARR, EILEEN A., T: President **I:** Other **CN:** Phoenix Philosophies, Inc. **DOB:** 07/26/1960 **PB:** Syracuse **SC:** NY/USA **PT:** Larry McCafferty; Rosemary McCafferty **CH:** Sean; Matthew; Lisa **ED:** MS, Keuka College (2012) **C:** President, Phoenix Philosophies, Inc., Syracuse, NY (2010-Present) **CIV:** Organizer, Salt City BBQ Festival, Syracuse, NY (Three Years)

MH: Marquis Who's Who Top Professional **B/I:** Ms. Carr became involved in her profession because she has always had a place in her heart for military veterans, particularly those who were homeless. Her boyfriend was an ex-Army Ranger and made her aware that when soldiers are discharged from the military, they are technically homeless and unemployed because the military provides it for them. **AV:** Horseback riding; Hiking; Visiting family a lot; Exercising; Volunteering with other local organizations

CARRANZA, JOVITA, T: Administrator; Former Treasurer of the United States **I:** Government Administration/Government Relations/Government Services **CN:** U.S. Small Business Administration **DOB:** 06/29/1949 **PB:** Chicago **SC:** IL/USA **MS:** Married **SPN:** Joel Roque **CH:** Klaudene **ED:** MBA, University of Miami; BA, University of Miami; Undergraduate Coursework, California State University, Los Angeles; Undergraduate Coursework, University of Miami; Coursework in Executive Management and Financial Training, INSEAD, University of Michigan; Coursework, The University of Chicago **C:** Administrator, U.S. Small Business Administration, Washington, DC (2020-Present); Treasurer of the United States, Washington, DC (2017-2020); Acting Administrator, U.S. Small Business Administration, Washington, DC (2008); Deputy Administrator, U.S. Small Business Administration, Washington, DC (2006-2009); Vice President, Air Operations, United Parcel Service of America, Inc. (UPS), Louisville, KY (2003-2006); Region Manager, International Operations, United Parcel Service of America, Inc. (UPS), Miami, FL (2000-2003); Manager of American Regions (Including Mexico, Puerto Rico, Dominican Republic, Virgin Islands), United Parcel Service of America, Inc. (UPS) (1999-2000); Division Manager, Hub, Packer, and Feeder Operations, United Parcel Service of America, Inc. (UPS), WI (1996-1999); District Manager, United Parcel Service of America, Inc. (UPS), Central FL (1993-1996); Division Manager, Hub, Packer, and Feeder Operations, United Parcel Service of America, Inc. (UPS), IL (1991-1993); District Human Resources Manager, United Parcel Service of America, Inc. (UPS), IL (1990-1991); District Human Resources Manager, United Parcel Service of America, Inc. (UPS), Texas (1987-1990); Business Manager, United Parcel Service of America, Inc. (UPS), Los Angeles, CA (1987); Workforce Planning Manager, United Parcel Service of America, Inc. (UPS), Los Angeles, CA (1985-1987); Human Resources Supervisor, United Parcel Service of America, Inc. (UPS), Los Angeles, CA (1979-1985); Supervisor, United Parcel Service of America, Inc. (UPS), Los Angles, CA (1976-1979); Night-shift Hub Clerk, United Parcel Service of America, Inc. (UPS), Los Angeles, CA (1976) **CR:** Member, Women's Suffrage Centennial Commission; Lecturer, Johns Hopkins University; Founder, President, The JCR Group **CIV:** Women for Rauner Campaign (2014); Volunteer, Habitat for Humanity International; Board Member, The Library Foundation, Louisville, KY; The National Center for Families Learning; United Way **CW:** Contributor, Articles, Professional Publications **AW:** Woman of Distinction, American Association of University Women (2008); Woman of Distinction, NASPA, National Conference for College Women Student Leaders (2008); Award, The Latino Coalition, Washington, DC (2008); Listee, 50 Most Important Hispanics in Technology and Business, Hispanic Engineer & Information Technology Magazine (2005); Woman of the Year, Hispanic Business Magazine (2004); Honorary Alumna, Alverno College; Albert Schweitzer Leadership Award, Hugh O'Brian Youth Leadership **MEM:** National Council of La Raza (Now UnidosUS)

CARRERAS, JOSÉ, T: Opera Singer **I:** Fine Art **DOB:** 12/05/1947 **PB:** Barcelona **SC:** Spain **PT:** José Carrerasi Soler; Antònia Coll i Saigi **MS:** Divorced **SPN:** Jutta Jager (2006, Divorced 2011); Mercedes Perez (1971, Divorced 1992) **CH:** Alberto; Julia **ED:** Honorary Doctorate, University of Saarland (2012); Honorary Doctorate, Philipps-Universität Marburg, Germany (2006); Honorary Doctorate, Rutgers, the State University of New Jersey; Honorary Doctorate, University of Coimbra, Portugal; Honorary Doctorate, National University of Music Bucharest, Romania; Honorary Doctorate, University of Pécs, Hungary; Honorary Doctorate, Kyunghee University; Honorary Doctorate, University of Porto, Portugal; Doctor Honoris Causa, University of Camerino, Italy; Doctor Honoris Causa, Mendeleev University of Chemical Technology, Russia; Doctor Honoris Causa, The University of Sheffield, United Kingdom; Doctor Honoris Causa, Loughborough University, United Kingdom; Doctor Honoris Causa, University of Barcelona, Spain; Coursework in Chemistry, University of Barcelona, Spain **CIV:** Museum Director, Opening Ceremonies, Olympics, Barcelona, Spain (1992); Founder, José Carreras Medical Research Foundation; President, José Carreras International Leukemia Foundation; Honorary Member, Leukemia Support Group; Grand Official, Republic of Italy; Goodwill Ambassador, United Nations Educational, Scientific and Cultural Organization **CW:** Author, "Singing from the Soul" (1991); Appearance, "TV Great Performances: West Side Story" (1985); Appearance, "Don Carlos" (1980); Performer, La Scala Debut, Riccardo, "Un Ballo in Maschera" (1975); Performer, Metropolitan Opera Debut, "Cavaradossi" (1974); Performer, "Rigoletto," Vienna Staatsoper, Austria (1974); Performer, "Traviatta," London's Royal Opera House, United Kingdom, New York Metropolitan Opera House (1974); Performer, "Tosca," Oper of Munich, Germany (1974); Performer, American Debut, Pinkerton, "Madame Butterfly," New York City Opera, NY (1972); Performer, "La Bohème," "Un Ballo in Maschera," and "I Lombardi alla Prima Crociata," Teatro Regio, Parma, Italy (1972); Performer, Professional Opera Debut, Gennaro, "Lucrezia Borgia," Liceo Opera House, Barcelona, Spain (1970-1971); Performer, "La Bohème," San Francisco Opera, CA; Performer, Appearances, Numerous Venues Worldwide Including Carnegie Hall, NY, Barbican and Royal Albert Hall, London, England, United Kingdom, Salle Pleyel, Paris, France, Teatro Colón, Buenos Aires, Argentina, Covent Garden, London, England, United Kingdom, Vienna Staatsoper, Austria, Easter Festival, Summer Festival, Salzburg, Austria, Aix en Provence, Edinburgh, Scotland, United Kingdom, Verona, Italy, Austria, Lyric Opera of Chicago, IL, Musikverein and Konzerthaus, Vienna, Austria, Suntory Hall and NHK Hall, Tokyo, Japan; Performer, Recitals Including "Otello," Rossini, "Un Ballo in Maschera," "La Battaglia di Legnano," "Il Corsaro," "Un Giorno," "I Due Fuscari," "Simone Boccanegra," "Macbeth," "Don Carlo," "Tosca," "Thais," "Aida," "Cavalleria," "Turandot," "Pagliacci," Lucia di La Mmermoor," "Elisabetta d'Inghilterra," "Amigos para Siempre," "Cabellé and Carreras in Paris," "Hollywood Golden Classics," "My Barcelona," and "With a Song in My Heart"; Performer with Placido Domingo and Luciano Pavarotti, PBS Special, Videotape, "Tenorissimi" and "The Three Tenors," Los Angeles, CA; Performer, Repertoire of Over 60 Operas Including "Andrea Chenier," "La Bohème," "Tosca," "Werther," "Carmen," "La Forza del Destino," "I Pagliacci," "L'Elisir d'Amore," "Un Ballo in Maschera"; Performer, Leading Role, Operatic Films Including "La Bohème," "I Lombardi," "Andrea Chnier," "Turandot," "Carmen," "Requiem," Verdi, "Don Carlo," "La Forza del Destino," "Stiffelio," "Fedora" and "Jerusalem"; Performer, Leading Roles, Numerous Operatic Films for Television, Cinema **AW:** Brit Award for Outstanding Contribution to Music (2009); Honorary Medal, City of Leipzig, Germany (2009); Golden Plate Award, Academy of Achievement (2004); Albert Schweizer Music Award (1996); International Award, St. Boniface Hospital Research Foundation (1996); Emmy Award, Academy of Television Arts & Sciences (1992); Grammy Award, The Recording Academy (1991); Prince of Asturias Award (1991); Grand Prix du Disque, Académie Charles Cros; Luigi Illica Prize; Sir Lawrence Olivier Award; Gold Medal, Spanish Institute, NY and City of Vienna, Austria; Gold Medal in Fine Arts, His Majesty the King of Spain, City of Barcelona, Spain; Award, Autonomous Government of Catalonia; Honorary Award, Republic of Austrian; Commandeur, Ordre des Arts et des Lettres, Republic of France; Chevalier, Ordre de la Légion d'Honneur, Republic of France; Gran Croce di Cavaliere, Republic of Italy; Numerous Awards **MEM:** Honorary Member, Royal Academy of Music; Honorary Member, European Society of Medicine; Kammersänger, Lifetime Honorary Member, Vienna Staatsoper; Honorary Patron, European Society for Medical Oncology

CARREY, JIM EUGENE, T: Actor; Comedian **I:** Media & Entertainment **DOB:** 01/17/1962 **PB:** Newmarket **SC:** Ontario/Canada **PT:** Percy Carrey; Kathleen (Oram) Carrey **MS:** Divorced **SPN:** Lauren Holly (09/23/1996, Divorced 07/29/1997); Melissa Womer (03/28/1987, Divorced 12/11/1995) **CH:** Jane Erin **ED:** Honorary DFA, Maharishi University of Management (Now Maharishi International University) (2014) **C:** Stand-up Comedian, "The Tonight Show" (1983); Stand-up Comedian, "An Evening at the Improv" (1982); Stand-up Comedian, The Comedy Store; Opening Act, Rodney Dangerfield Tour; Stand-up Comedian, Numerous Night Clubs **CW:** Actor, Executive Producer, "Kidding" (2018-Present); Actor, "Sonic the Hedgehog" (2020); Co-Author, "Memoirs and Misinformation" (2020); Featured, "The Zen Diaries of Garry Shandling" (2018); Executive Producer, "I'm Dying Here" (2017-2018); Featured, "Jim & Andy: The Great Beyond - Featuring a Very Special, Contractually Obligated Mention of Tony Clifton" (2017); Actor, "The Bad Batch" (2016); Actor, "True Crimes" (2016); Producer, "Rubbie Kings" (2015); Actor, "Dumb and Dumber To" (2014); Author, "How Roland Rolls" (2013); Actor, "The Incredible Burt Wonderstone" (2013); Actor, "Kick-Ass 2" (2013); Actor, "Anchorman 2: The Legend Continues" (2013); Actor, "Mr. Popper's Penguins" (2011); Actor, "I Love You Phillip Morris" (2009); Voice Actor, "A Christmas Carol" (2009); Voice Actor, "Horton Hears a Who!" (2008); Actor, "Yes Man" (2008); Actor, "The Number 23" (2007); Actor, Producer, "Fun with Dick and Jane" (2005); Actor, "Eternal Sunshine of the Spotless Mind" (2004); Actor, "Lemony Snicket's A Series of Unfortunate Events" (2004); Actor, Producer, "Bruce Almighty" (2003); Actor, "The Majestic" (2001); Actor, "How the Grinch Stole Christmas" (2000); Actor, "Me, Myself and Irene" (2000); Actor, "Man on the Moon" (1999); Actor, "Simon Birch" (1998); Actor, "The Truman Show" (1998); Actor, "The Mask's Revenge" (1996); Actor, "Liar, Liar" (1996); Actor, "The Cable Guy" (1996); Actor, "Batman Forever" (1995); Actor, "Ace Ventura: When Nature Calls" (1995); Actor, "The Mask" (1994); Actor, "Dumb and Dumber" (1994); Actor, "High Strung" (1991); Actor, "In Living Color" (1990-1994); Actor, Writer, "Ace Ventura: Pet Detective" (1994); Actor, "Doing Time on Maple Drive" (1992); Actor, "Earth Girls are Easy" (1989); Actor, "Mike Hammer: Murder Takes All" (1989); Actor, "Pink Cadillac" (1989); Actor, "The Dead Pool" (1988); Actor, "Peggy Sue Got Married" (1986); Actor, "Once Bitten" (1985); Actor, "Finders Keepers" (1984); Actor, "The Duck Factory" (1984); Actor, Producer, Television Shows and Films; Artist, Paintings **AW:** Webby Award for Best Celebrity or Fan Website, International Academy of Digital Arts and Sciences (2011); Award for Favorite Comedic Star, People's Choice Awards (2010); Award for Best Comedic Performance, MTV Movie Awards (2009); Award for Favorite Funny Male Star, People's Choice Awards (2008); Muhammad Ali Celebrity Entertainer Award (2006); Listee, 50 Most Powerful People in Hollywood (2004-2006); Award for Favorite Motion Picture Star in a Comedy, People's Choice Awards (2001); Golden Globe Award for Best Performance by an Actor in a Motion Picture Musical or Comedy, Hollywood Foreign Press Association (2000); Star, Hollywood Walk of Fame (2000); Golden Globe Award for Best Performance by an Actor in a Motion Picture Drama, Hollywood Foreign Press Association (1999); Award for Favorite Actor in a Comedy Motion Picture, People's Choice Awards (1996); Recipient, Numerous Awards

CARRIER, SANDRA L., RN, COHN/CM, ABDA, FAAOHN, T: President (Retired) **I:** Consulting **CN:** Carrier Associates Consulting **DOB:** 05/02/1945 **MS:** Married **SPN:** Joseph Carrier (2012) **ED:** BSN, Gwynedd Mercy University, Gwynedd Valley, PA (1982); RN, Bucks County Community College, Newtown, PA (1975) **CT:** Re-entry Certificate in Clinical Nursing, Bucks County Community College and Nazareth Hospital (Now Trinity Health Mid Atlantic) (2004); CPR/AED for Healthcare Providers Certification (2004); Situational Leadership®, Leadership Studies, Inc. (2002); Management Development Certificate (2002); Senior Disability Analyst and Diplomate, American Board of Disability Analysts (ABDA) (1998); CCM (Certified Case Manager) (1997); COHN-S (Certified Occupational Health Nurse-Specialist) (1984); Registered Professional Nurse, Pennsylvania (1975) **C:** President, Workforce Management Solutions (2004-Present); Principal, Carrier Associates Consulting (1997-Present); Vice President, Sales and Marketing, EarthMark Companies (2004-2006); National Practice Leader, Occupational Health, Aon plc, Chicago, IL (2002-2004); Senior Vice President, Practice Leader, Claim Consulting and Risk Control, Aon plc, Chicago, IL (1999-2002); Vice President, Integrated Health and Disability, Aon plc, Chicago, IL (1997-1999); Consultant, Occupational Health, Professional Health Services, Havertown, PA (1994-1997); Vice President, Ocean Reef Club Sotheby's International Realty (1980-1996); Account Executive, Consultant, Mediq Inc., Pennsauken Township, NJ (1992-1994); Marketing Director, Occupational Health Consultant, Health Examinetics, Inc., Pennsauken Township, NJ (1992-1994); Consultant, Occupational Health and Safety and Casualty Loss Control, Mutual of Wausau Insurance Corporation, Philadelphia, PA (1987-1992); Manager, Medical Department, Henkel Corporation, Union Carbide Corporation and Amchem Products Inc., Ambler, PA (1976-1987) **CIV:** Foundation Trustee, AAOHN, Inc. (2001-2003); Volunteer, BARC Developmental Services; Volunteer, Doylestown Junior Women's Club **AW:** Occupational Health Nurse of the Year, AAOHN, Inc. (2000); Dorothy M. Saller Nursing Award (1992); Medique Leadership Award, MediqueProducts (1989) **MEM:** Fellow, American Association of Occupation Health Services (1979-Present); Chair-elect, AAOHN, Inc. (2003-2005); Treasurer, AAOHN, Inc. (1999-2003); Board of Directors, AAOHN, Inc., Atlanta, GA (1988, 1992, 1994-1998); President, Pennsylvania Association of Occupational Health Nurses (1993-1996); Editorial Review Board, AAOHN, Inc. (1991-1993); American Board of Disability Analysts (ABDA) **MH:** Marquis Who's Who

Top Professional **B/I:** Mrs. Carrier has wanted to pursue nursing since the age of 5, and has always loved people. Her biggest influence was her father, who was tough but fair, and always had a smile on his face.

CARRISON, DALE MITCHELL, DO, MS, FACEP, FACOEP, T: Professor Emeritus **I:** Medicine & Health Care **CN:** University of Nevada, Reno **DOB:** 09/24/1939 **PB:** Macomb **SC:** IL/USA **MS:** Married **SPN:** Laurie Bisch Carrison **CH:** Catherine Louise Carrison, PhD; Kelley Lynne Simpson; Michelle Marie DiMauro; Michael Dale Carrison **ED:** Resident in Emergency Medicine, Cook County Hospital (Now John H. Stroger, Jr. Hospital of Cook County), Cook County Health, Chicago, IL (1988-1991); Rotating Intern, Flint Osteopathic Hospital (1987-1988); DO, Western University of Health Sciences College of Osteopathic Medicine of the Pacific (1987); MS in Biology, California State University, San Bernardino, CA (1983); BS in Criminology, California State University, Long Beach, CA (1968); AA in Police Science, Santa Ana College (1966) **CT:** ATLS Instructor/Provider; ACLS Instructor/Provider; Diplomate, American Board Emergency Medicine (ABEM); Certified Medical Review Officer; Fellow, American College of Emergency Physicians; Fellow, American College of Osteopathic Emergency Physicians; Basic/Advanced Disaster Life Support Provider/Instructor; Course Director, National Disaster Life Support Foundation, Inc. **C:** Professor Emeritus, University of Nevada, Reno, NV (2018-Present); Medical Director, Las Vegas Motor Speedway, Speedway Motorsports, LLC, Las Vegas, NV (1995-Present); Assistant Professor of Emergency Medicine, Department of Family Medicine, Western University of Health Sciences College Osteopathic Medicine of the Pacific (1993-Present); Certified Medical Review Officer, Las Vegas Metropolitan Police Department (LVMPD) (2011-2019); Chief of Staff, University of Nevada Medical Center (2011-2018); Professor, Chairman, Emergency Medicine, University of Nevada Las Vegas School of Medicine, Las Vegas and Reno, NV (2007-2018); Medical Director, Clark County Fire Department, Las Vegas, NV (2003-2018); Member, Medical Advisory Board, Southern Nevada Health District (2003-2018); Director, Attending Physician, Department of Emergency Medicine, Emergency Physicians' Medical Group, University Medical Center, Las Vegas, NV (1995-2018); Chairman, Medical Advisory Board, Southern Nevada Health District (2015-2017); Commissioner, Chairman, Nevada Commission on Homeland Security (2003-2011); Medical Director, Mercy Air, Las Vegas, NV (2003-2010); Medical Director, Motorsports Medical Services, Las Vegas, NV (1998-2010); Medical Director, EMS Training Center of Southern NV, Las Vegas, NV (2000-2006); Clinical Professor of Surgery, University of Nevada Las Vegas School of Medicine, Las Vegas, NV (1994-2006); Assistant Director, Attending Physician, Department of Emergency Medicine, Emergency Physicians' Medical Group, University Medical Center of Southern Nevada, Las Vegas, NV (1992-1994); Assistant Director, Attending Physician, Department of Emergency Medicine, University Medical Center of Southern Nevada, Las Vegas, NV (1991-1992); President, General Manager, Carrison Enterprises, Inc., Southern CA (1976-1983); Special Agent, FBI, Los Angeles, CA and Portland, OR (1971-1976); Deputy Sheriff, Orange County Sheriff's Department, CA (1964-1971) **CR:** Medical Director, EMS Program, Western Nevada College (2018-Present); Instructor, Heckler & Koch International Training Division for Tactical Emergency Medicine, Sterling, VA (1995-Present); Member, Council, Reviewer, Health Insight, Las Vegas, NV (1995-Present); Medical Director, Emergency Medical Services, Lake Mead National Recreational Area, Henderson, NV (1993-Present); Medical Director, Emergency Medical Services, National Park Service, Death Valley, CA (1992-Present); Medical Director, Electric Daisy Carnival, Las Vegas, NV (2011-2019); Medical Director, SWAT and Tactical Emergency Medicine Las Vegas Metropolitan Police Department (LVMPD) (1995-2019); Medical Director, Sexual Assault Nurse Examiner, University Medical Center of Southern Nevada (1994-2019); Member, Health Alert Nevada, Southern Nevada Health District (2008-2018); Member, Disease Prevention and Control Advisory Committee, Southern Nevada Health District (2006-2018); Executive Medical Director, Burning Man (2015-2016); Member, Governor's Ebola Task Force (2015-2016); Member, Governor's Health and Wellness Council (2014-2016); Nevada Regional Director, Emergency Physicians' Medical Group, San Francisco, CA (1996-2013); Member, Board of Directors, Emergency Physicians' Medical Group, San Francisco, CA (1994-2004); Member, Sheriff's Mental Health Task Force (2000-2003); Medical Director, Nevada Region Sports Car Club of America, Las Vegas, NV (1993-1998); Staff Physician, Emergency Department, Gottlieb Memorial Hospital, Loyola Medicine, Melrose Park, IL (1990-1991); With, Aurora Lakeland Medical Center, Aurora Health, Elkhorn, WI (1989-1991); With, Westlake Community Hospital, Melrose Park, IL (1989-1991); Presenter, Researcher in Field **MIL:** Major, United States Army Reserve Medical Corps (1987-1995); With, United States Navy, United States Naval Reserve (1956-1961) **CW:** Contributor, Multiple Articles to Professional Publications **AW:** Named Best University Medical Center Hospital Physician (2018); Las Vegas Heals Award (2017); Las Vegas Motor Speedway Infield Care Center Renamed to "Carrison Care Center" (2016); Recognition for 20 Years of Service, Las Vegas Metropolitan Police Department (LVMPD) (2015); Named Citizen of the Month, City of Las Vegas, NV (2015); "Dale Carrison Day" Named in His Honor, Clark County, NV (2015); Lifetime Achievement Award, American College of Osteopathic Emergency Physicians (2013); Most Valuable Person Award, Tactical Physician Team, Las Vegas Metropolitan Police Department (LVMPD) (2011); Emergency Medicine Research Award Established in His Name (2011); Life Saving Award, Las Vegas Metropolitan Police Department (LVMPD) (2007); Named Ambassador of the Year, Nevada Osteopathic Medical Association (2003); Established an Annual Award in His Name, Nevada Osteopathic Medical Association (2003); Named Nevada Emergency Physician of the Year (1998); Finalist for the Professional of the Year Award, Las Vegas Chamber of Commerce (1998, 1999); Nurse's Choice Award, March of Dimes (1997); Founder's Distinguished Alumnus Award, Western University of Health Sciences College of Osteopathic Medicine (1996); Named Intern of the Year, Flint Osteopathic Hospital (1983-1987, 1988); Dean's Student Government Award, Western University of Health Sciences College of Osteopathic Medicine of the Pacific; CIBA Award; President's Award, Merck Scholarship Award; Sigma Sigma Phi; Who's Who in American Colleges and Universities **MEM:** Fellow, American College Emergency Physicians; Fellow, American College of Osteopathic Emergency Physicians; American Osteopathic Association (AOA); Nevada Delegate, Bureau Student Affairs, AOA; Nevada Osteopathic Medical Association; Vice President, President, Nevada Osteopathic Medical Association; Western University of Health Sciences College of Osteopathic Medicine of the Pacific; International Council of Motorsports Sciences; Council on International Osteopathic Medical Education **B/I:** Dr. Carrison became involved in his profession as a physician because when he got out of the FBI, he decided to go into business with his father. He had a number of NAPA auto parts stores with his father, however, he got into a scuba diving accident and was totally paralyzed on one side and that was an eye opener for him. He decided to start over and went back to college and got an equivalent to a bachelor's degree and then got a masters degree in biology in 2 1/2 years. He went into law enforcement because he wanted to put the bad guys in jail. He always took care of other people all throughout his life and it was an opportunity to do that. His first father-in-law was a first deputy sheriff reserve so he started talking to him and when he got out of the Navy academy, he was searching as to what he should do, so he looked into law enforcement. He took the test and was selected and that was how it got started. In addition, the biggest thing that prompted him to go for his DO at the College of Osteopathic Medicine, was he started enjoying law enforcement and was recruited as special agent at the FBI, Los Angeles, CA and Portland, OR in 1971-1976. He was with the Los Angeles FBI SWAT Team and went to the California Highway Patrol Motorcycle Academy. He rode the motorcycle on different cases, such as for kidnappings. His father-in-law wanted him out of law enforcement, which he didn't realize at the time. However, his father asked him to come run the business. The scuba diving accident was his wake up call, and he went back to school in San Bernardino. His college counselor thought he was too old to go to medical school. However, he was tested at UCLA, and there they have an excellent counseling system for individuals having mid-life crisis, kids who couldn't figure out what they want to do, etc. After 56 hours of counseling and testing, his highest correlations were biomedical, engineer, geophysicist, and emergency physician. So, he was asked, "what do you want to do?" He replied, "Medical school," and was excepted. **AV:** Working out four days a week; Lifting weights; Riding his bike; Raising Bees; Gardening

CARROLL, ANTIONETTE D., T: Owner **I:** Nonprofit & Philanthropy **CN:** Creative Reaction Lab **ED:** Master of Arts in Communication, University of Missouri-St. Louis (2009-2012); Bachelor of Science, University of Missouri-St. Louis, Magna Cum Laude (2005-2009) **C:** President, Chief Executive Officer, Founder, Creative Reaction Lab (2014-Present); Chair Emerita, American Institute of Graphic Arts (2016-2018); President of the Board, American Institute of Graphic Arts Saint Louis (2016-2017); International Speaker, Facilitator, Conversationalist (2015-2017); Founding Chair, Diversity and Inclusion Task Force, American Institute of Graphic Arts (2014-2016); Adjunct Lecturer, Saint Louis University (2014-2016); Marketing and Communications Manager, Diversity & Communications Manager (2013-2014); Communications Manager, Copy Editor, Rodgers Townsend/DDB (2012-2013); Student Conference Co-Chair, American Institute of Graphic Arts (2011-2013); Marketing Coordinator, STAGES St. Louis (2011-2012); Marketing Analyst, DNI Properties, INC (2011); Katherine Dunham Fellow of Grants Management and Arts Administration, Regional Arts Commission (2011); Advertising and Marketing Coordinator, Judicial Officer, Marketing Assistant, University of Missouri (2008-2011) **CR:** Co-Organizer, Online Producer, National Town Hall, Racial Justice by Design Program, American Institute of Graphic Arts (2016); President Emerita, American Institute of Graphic Arts St. Louis; Co-Founder, Design and Diversity Conference, American Institute of Graphic Arts St. Louis; Speaker, Microsoft, NASA, TEDxHerndon/ TEDxGatewayArch, Harvard University, American Institute of Graphic Art National Conference and

The Ohio State University **CIV:** Steering Committee Member, Office Resiliency City of St. Louis (2016-Present); Dialogues on Race Advisory Board Member, Design Ignites Change, The Worldstudio Foundation (2015-Present); Founding Chair, Diversity & Inclusion Task Force, American Institute of Graphic Arts Design (2014-Present); Katherine Dunham Fellowship Selection Committee Member, Regional Arts Commission (2012-Present); President, St. Louis American Institute of Graphic Arts (2011-2017); Committee Member, Anti-Bias/Anti Racism Committee, City Garden Montessori School (2015); Former Chair, Focus St. Louis Connect with St. Louis Young Professionals Group (2013-2015); Grants Panelist, Regional Arts Commission (2012-2015); Mentor, The Marcus Graham Project (2014); What's Right with the Region Judge, FOCUS St. Louis (2014); Member, Graphic Designer, Let's Talk About it Mental Health Committee (2013); Visionary Awards for Women in the Arts Host, Committee Member, Grand Center, Inc. (2012-2013); Communications Director, Co-Founder, Emerging Leaders in the Arts (2011-2013); Assistant Volunteer Coordinator, St. Louis Cultural Engagement Conference, Gitana Productions (2012); National Convention Planning Committee Member, Phi Kappa Phi Honor Society (2010-2012) **CW:** Contributor, "Design Humbly," Communication Arts (2016); Contributor, "Three Tips to Transform Designers Into Agents of Social Change," Core77.com (2016); Contributor, "Diversity and Inclusion in Design: Why Do They Matter?" (2014); Contributor, "Case Study: Come Out Swinging Integrated Campaign," American Institute of Graphic Arts Design (2012) **AW:** Fellowship, Camelback Ventures Fellow (2018); Global Fellowship, Echoing Green (2018); Fellowship, TED (2018); Community Impact Artist Honoree, Saint Louis Visionary Awards (2017); Named, Next City Vanguard, Next City (2017); Named, AMEX/Ashoka Emerging Innovator, Ashoka Changemakers, American Express (2016); Social Entrepreneurship Scholarship, Social Capital Markets (2016); Power 100 Spirit of the Entrepreneurs Award, DELUX Magazine (2015); Fellowship, StartingBloc, Washington, DC (2015); Named, 20 Under 40 Artists to Watch, Alive Magazine (2015); Community Arts Training Fellowship, Regional Arts Commission (2014); Named, Amethyst Award Honoree, Sue Shear Institute of Public Policy (2013); Silver ADDY Award, Ad Club of Saint Louis, American Advertising Federation (2013); Certificate of Achievement, Design Show, St. Louis American Institute of Graphic Arts (2012); Katherine Dunham Fellowship, Regional Arts Commission (2011); Future Influential Leader Award, Kawame Foundation (2010); Named, Most Promising Minority Student, Class of 2009, American Advertising Federation (2009); Named, Trailblazer in the Arts, Office of Equal Opportunity, University of Missouri-St. Louis (2008); Fellowship, Sue Shear, Sue Shear Institute of Public Policy, University of Missouri-St. Louis (2007) **MEM:** American Institute of Graphic Arts: The Professional Association of Design **AS:** Ms. Carroll attributes her success to being able to admit her failures and being vulnerable to others and having them being vulnerable with her. She is extremely concerned and shares her stories a lot. Ms. Carroll takes her hardships and turns them into positives and shares them with others to make an impact in other people's lives. **B/I:** Ms. Carroll entered her profession because saw inequities within her community. She was the first one within her family to attend college. Ms. Carroll saw what the American Institute of Graphic Art was doing and wanted to support them.

CARROLL, DIAHANN, T: Actress **I:** Media & Entertainment **DOB:** 07/17/1935 **PB:** New York **SC:** NY/USA **PT:** John Johnson; Mabel (Faulk) Johnson **MS:** Divorced **SPN:** Vic Damone (Divorced, 1996); Robert DeLean (Divorced, 1977); Fredde Glusman (Divorced, 1973); Monte Kay (Divorced, 1963) **CH:** Suzanne Kay **ED:** Coursework, New York University **CW:** Actor, "The Masked Saint" (2014); Actor, "Peeples" (2013); Actor, "A Raisin in the Sun" (2014); Actor, "White Collar" (2009-2013); Guest Star, "Diary of a Single Mom" (2010-2011); Actor, "At-Risk" (2010); Actor, "The Front" (2010); Guest Star, "Grey's Anatomy" (2006-2007); Guest Star, "The 4th Annual TV Land Awards: A Celebration of Classic TV" (2006); Guest Star, "Soul Food" (2004); Actor, "Bubbling Brown Sugar" (2004); Guest Star, "Strong Medicine" (2003); Guest Star, "Whoopi" (2003); Actor, "The Courage to Love" (2000); Actor, "Sally Hemmings: An American Scandal" (2000); Actor, "Livin' for Love: the Natalie Cole Story" (2000); Actor, "Jackie's Back!" (1999); Actor, "Having Our Say: The Delany Sisters' First 100 Years" (1999); Actor, "Motown 40: The Music is Forever" (1998); Actor, "The Sweetest Gift" (1998); Actor, "Motown 40: The Music is Forever" (1998); Actor, "Eve's Bayou" (1997); Singer, "The Time of My Life" (1997); Guest Star, "Touched By An Angel" (1995); Actor, "Sunset Boulevard" (1995); Actor, "The Colbys" (1986); Actor, "Lonesome Dove" (1994-1995); Guest Star, "Evening Shade" (1994); Actor, "A Perry Mason Mystery: The Case of the Lethal Lifestyle" (1994); Guest Star, "Different World" (1991-1993); Actor, "Sunday in Paris" (1991); Actor, "The Five Heartbeats" (1991); Actor, "Murder in Black and White" (1990); Actor, "Love Letters" (1990); Actor, "Dynasty" (1984-1987); Actor, "Agnes of God" (1983); Actor, "Sister, Sister" (1982); Actor, "I Know Why the Caged Bird Sings" (1979); Actor, "Roots: The Next Generations" (1979); Actor, "Same Time, Next Year" (1977); Actor, "Death Scream" (1975); Singer, "A Tribute to Ethel Waters" (1978); Singer, "Diahann Carroll" (1974); Actor, "Claudine" (1974); Actor, "Julia" (1968-1971); Guest Star, "Julia" (1970-1971); Actor, "The Split" (1968); Singer, "A You're Adorable: Love Songs for Children" (1967); Singer, "Nobody Sees Me Cry" (1967); Actor, "Hurry Sundown" (1967); Singer, "The Fabulous Diahann Carroll" (1963); Singer, "Modern Jazz Quartet - The Comedy" (1962); Actor, "No Strings" (1962); Singer, "Showstopper!" (1962); Singer, "Fun Life" (1961); Actor, "Paris Blues" (1961); Singer, "Diahann Carroll and the Andre Previn Trio" (1960); Singer, "The Persian Room Presents Diahann Carroll" (1959); Actor, "Porgy and Bess" (1959); Singer, "Best Beat Forward" (1958); Singer, "Diahann Carroll Sings Harold Arlen Songs" (1957); Actor, "House of Flowers" (1954); Actor, "Carmen Jones" (1954); Actor, "Same Time, Next Year"

CARROLL, ROSEMARY F., T: Historian; Educator; Lawyer **I:** Education/Educational Services **DOB:** 10/15/1935 **PB:** Providence **SC:** RI/USA **PT:** Francis Edward Carroll; Katherine Loretta (Graham) Carroll **MS:** Single **ED:** JD, University of Iowa, Iowa City, Iowa (1983); PhD, Rutgers, The State University of New Jersey, New Brunswick, NJ (1968); MA, Wesleyan University, Middletown, CT (1962); AB, Brown University, Providence, RI (1957) **C:** Henry and Margaret Haegg Distinguished Professor of History Emerita, Coe College, Cedar Rapids, Iowa (2001-Present); Henry and Margaret Haegg Distinguished Professor of History, Coe College, Cedar Rapids, Iowa (2000-2001); Chair, Department of History, Coe College, Cedar Rapids, Iowa (1988-2000); Professor of History, Coe College, Cedar Rapids, Iowa (1984-2000); Faculty Representative, British Marshal Scholarship, Coe College, Cedar Rapids, Iowa (1996-1998); Faculty Representative, Rhodes Scholarship Trust, Coe College, Cedar Rapids, Iowa (1993-1998); Faculty Representative, Truman Foundation, Coe College, Cedar Rapids, Iowa (1988-1998); Pre-law Advisor, Coe College, Cedar Rapids, Iowa (1988-1998); Affirmative Action Officer, Coe College, Cedar Rapids, Iowa (1973-1998); Associate Professor of History, Coe College, Cedar Rapids, Iowa (1975-1984); Assistant Professor of History, Coe College, Cedar Rapids, Iowa (1971-1975); Visiting Assistant Professor of History, Denison University, Granville, Ohio (1970-1971); Assistant Professor of History, Notre Dame College (1968-1970) **CIV:** Member, Advisory Council, Legal Services Corporation, Cedar Rapids, Iowa (1985-2001); Volunteer Lawyer, Legal Services Corporation, Cedar Rapids, Iowa (1984-2001) **CW:** Contributor, Articles to Professional Journals **AW:** Grantee, Herbert W. Hoover Foundation (1992-1994); Grantee, National Endowment for the Humanities (1992-1993); Olmsted Fellow, Herbert Hoover Presidential Library and Museum (1987-1992) **MEM:** Board of Directors, Brown University Club of the Treasure Coast (2007-Present); Board of Directors, Hanson's Landing Association (2008-2010); Public Policy Chair, American Association of University Women (AAUW) (2002-2006, 2008-2010); Branch President, American Association of University Women (AAUW), Stuart, FL (2006-2008); Taylor Prize Committee, Southern Association for Women Historians (2005); Continuing Legal Education Committee, Linn County Bar Association (1990-2002); Legal Heritage Committee, The Iowa State Bar Association (1988-2001); Membership Committee, Southern Association for Women Historians (1987-1988, 1989-1990, 1996-1998); Membership Committee, Southern Historical Association (1986-1987, 1988-1989, 1996-1998); Treasurer, Linn County Women Attorneys (1990-1991); Membership Committee, Organization of American Historians (1978); President, Southern Association for Women Historians (1975-1976); American Bar Association (ABA); American Association of University Women (AAUW); The Iowa State Bar Association; Linn County Bar Association; Linn County Women Attorneys; Organization of American Historians; Southern Historical Association; Southern Association for Women Historians; American Historical Association; The Honor Society of Phi Kappa Phi **MH:** Albert Nelson Marquis Lifetime Achievement Award **B/I:** Dr. Carroll had loved history for as long as she could remember. Growing up in Providence, Rhode Island, history was all around her growing up. Going back, her mother and as far back as her grandparents, Dr. Carroll recalled all had a love for history. As a child, her and her parents would take trips to visit various historical places. She moved to Newport when she was 5 years old, where there were historical homes built in the Gilded Age from 1743. She moved to the capital, Providence, which her grandfather always spoke about. **AV:** Bicycling; Swimming **RE:** Roman Catholic

CARSON, ANDRÉ D., T: U.S. Representative from Indiana; Marketing Specialist **I:** Government Administration/Government Relations/Government Services **DOB:** 10/16/1974 **PB:** Indianapolis **SC:** IN/USA **MS:** Married **SPN:** Mariama Shaheed **CH:** Salimah **ED:** MA in Business Management, Indiana Wesleyan University (2005); BA in Criminal Justice and Management, Concordia University Wisconsin (2003) **C:** Member, U.S. House Committee on Intelligence (2015-Present); Whip, Congressional Black Caucus (2011-Present); U.S. Representative from Indiana's Seventh Congressional District, United States Congress (2008-Present); Member, Indianapolis City-County Council, 15th District (2007-2008); Member, Armed Services Committee; Member, Committee on Transportation and Infrastructure; Committeeperson, Center Township of Marion County, IN; Marketing Specialist, Cripe Architects & Engineers; Local Board Officer, Investigator, Indiana State Excise Police **CR:** Board Member, Citizens Neighborhood Coalition; Member, Advisory Board, IndyParks Kennedy/King Park **AW:** Named to the Power 150, Ebony Magazine (2008) **PA:** Democrat **RE:** Muslim

CARSON, BENJAMIN SOLOMON SR., T: United States Secretary **I:** Government Administration/Government Relations/Government Services **CN:** U.S. Department of Housing and Urban Development **DOB:** 09/18/1951 **PB:** Detroit **SC:** MI/USA **PT:** Robert Solomon Carson; Sonya (Copeland) Carson **MS:** Married **SPN:** Lacena Beatrice Rustin (07/06/1975) **CH:** Murray Nedlands; Benjamin Solomon Jr.; Rhoeyce Harrington **ED:** Honorary DSc, College of William & Mary (1998); Honorary DSc, University of Delaware (1997); Honorary DSc, Medical University of South Africa (1997); Honorary DSc, Delaware State University (1996); Honorary DSc, Yale University (1996); Honorary DSc, Tuskegee University (1995); Honorary DSc, North Carolina State University (1994); Honorary DSc, Long Island University (1994); Honorary DSc, Western Maryland College (1994); Honorary DSc, Spalding University (1994); Honorary DSc, University of Detroit Mercy (1994); Honorary DSc, Marygrove College (1993); Honorary DSc, University of Massachusetts, Boston, MA (1992); Honorary DSc, Southwestern Adventist College (1992); Honorary DSc, Jersey City State College (1990); Honorary DSc, Shippenburg University (1990); Honorary DSc, Sojourner-Douglas College (1989); Honorary DSc, Andrews University (1989); Honorary DSc, Gettysburg College (1988); Chief Resident, Fellow Neurological Surgery, Johns Hopkins Hospital, Baltimore, MD (1982-1983); Neurosurgical Resident, Johns Hopkins Hospital, Baltimore, MD (1978-1982); Surgical Intern, Johns Hopkins Hospital, Baltimore, MD (1977-1978); MD, University of Michigan Medical School, Ann Arbor, MI (1977); BA, Yale University, New Haven, CT (1973); Numerous Other Honorary Degrees **CT:** Diplomate, American Board of Neurological Surgery; Diplomate, American Board of Pediatrics Neurological Surgery; Diplomate, National Board of Medical Examiners **C:** United States Secretary of Housing and Urban Development, United States Department of Housing and Urban Development, Washington, DC (2017-Present); Chairman, Vaccinogen, Inc. (2014-2017); Professor, Neurological Surgery of Oncology, Plastic Surgery and Pediatrics, Johns Hopkins School of Medicine (1999-2013); Director, Division of Pediatric Neurosurgery, Johns Hopkins Hospital (1984-2013); Associate Professor, Neurological Surgery of Oncology, Plastic Surgery and Pediatrics, Johns Hopkins School of Medicine (1991-1999); Assistant Professor, Pediatrics, Johns Hopkins School of Medicine, Baltimore, MD (1987-1996); Assistant Professor of Neurological Surgery, Assistant Professor of Oncology, Johns Hopkins School of Medicine, Baltimore, MD (1984-1991); Senior Registrar, Sir Charles Gairdner Hospital, Perth, Western Australia (1983-1984) **CR:** Member, Advisory Board, Vaccinogen, Inc. (2014-Present); Weekly Opinion Columnist, The Washington Times (2013-Present); Board of Directors, Costco Wholesale Corporation (1999-Present); Board of Directors, Kellogg Co. (1997-Present); Candidate for the 2016 Republican Party Presidential Nomination (2016); Contributor, FOX News (2013-2014); Co-director, Johns Hopkins Cleft & Craniofacial Center (1991-2013); Served on President's Council on Bioethics (2004); Senior Neurosurgical Resident, Baltimore City Hospitals (1981); Senior Neurosurgical Resident, Loch Raven VA Hospital, Baltimore, MD (1980) **CIV:** Member, Medical Advisory Board, The Children's Cancer

Foundation, Inc. (1987-Present); Honorary Chair, Maryland Red Cross, The American National Red Cross (1987); Emeritus Fellow, Yale Corporation; Co-founder, Carson Scholars Fund **CW:** Author, "A More Perfect Union: What We the People Can Do to Reclaim Our Constitutional Liberties" (2015); Author, "One Nation: What We Can All Do to Save America's Future" (2014); Author, "America the Beautiful: Rediscovering What Made This Nation Great" (2011); Author, "Take the Risk: Learning to Identify, Choose, and Live with Acceptable Risk" (2008); Author, "The Big Picture" (1999); Author, "Think Big" (1996); Author, "Gifted Hands" (1989); Contributor, Articles, Professional Journals; Contributor, Chapters, Books **AW:** Named, One of America's Best Leaders, U.S. News & World Report (2008); Presidential Medal of Freedom, The White House (2008); The Lincoln Medal, Ford's Theatre Society (2008); Named to Society of World Changers, Indiana Wesleyan University (2007); Spingarn Award, NAACP (2006); Ralph Metcalfe Award, Congressional Black Caucus (2003); Medical Award of Excellence, Ronald McDonald House Charities (2003); Distinguished Service to Children Award, National Association of Elementary School Principals (2002); Named, One of America's Top 20 Physicians & Scientists, CNN/TIME Magazine (2001); Named, One of the Top 100 Black Physicians in America, Black Enterprise Magazine (2001); Living Legend Award, Library of Congress (2000); Public Service Award, American Institute of Public Service (2000); Making a Difference Award, NAACP, Baltimore Chapter, MD (1998); Tree of Life Award, Jewish National Fund (1998); Award, Congress of Racial Equality (CORE) (1996); Outstanding Achievement Award, Anheuser-Busch Companies, LLC (1996); Golden Plate Award, American Academy of Achievement (1995); Horatio Alger Award (1994); Excellence in Medicine Award, National Medical Association (1994); Martin Luther King Jr. Award for Community Service, Johns Hopkins Hospital (1994); George Washington Carver Award (1993); John Conley Scholar, American Academy of Otolaryngology-Head & Neck Surgery (1993); Essence Award (1993); Living Legend Award, National Medical Association (1992); William E. Matory Award, National Medical Association (1992); Benjamin E. Mays Memorial Award, North Carolina State University (1991); Special Recognition Award, National Council Negro Women, Inc. (1991); Appreciation Award, National Association of Equal Opportunity in Higher Education (NAFEO) (1991); Booker T. Washington Award, Baltimore Business League (1990); Achievement Award, Maryland Department of Health & Mental Hygiene (1989); Dr. Daniel Hale Williams Award, Jefferson Medical College (Now Sidney Kimmel Medical College), Philadelphia University + Thomas Jefferson University, Philadelphia, PA (1989); Outstanding Service & Excellence in Medicine Award, Medical Society of Eastern Pennsylvania (1989); Andrew White Medal, Loyola College, Baltimore, MD (1989); Leonard F. Swain Esteemed Alumni Award, University of Michigan (1989); Partner in Health Award, Maryland Health Convocation (1988); Outstanding Achievements in Medicine Award, Howard University, Baltimore, MD (1988); American Black Achievement Award, Ebony Magazine (1988); Clinical Practitioner of Year Award, National Medical Association (1988); Paul Harris Fellow, Rotary International (1988); Howard L. Cornish Humanitarian Award, Omega Psi Phi Fraternity Inc. (1987); Achievement Award, Detroit Medical Society (1987); Memorial Award for Outstanding Service to Underprivileged Children, Continental Societies, Inc. (1987); Liberty Bell Award, City of Philadelphia, PA (1987); Citation for Excellence, Detroit City Council (1987); Citation for Excellence, Philadelphia City Council

(1987); Citation for Excellence, Michigan State Senate (1987); Cum Laude Award, Radiological Society of North America (1982) **MEM:** American Medical Association; American Association for the Advancement of Science; Institute of Medicine (Now the National Academy of Medicine); American Cleft Palate-Craniofacial Association (ACPA); Maryland Neurological Society; Congress of Neurological Surgeons; American Association of Neurological Surgeons; National Medical Association; National Pediatric Oncology Group; Monumental Medical Society; Honorary Life Member, PTA Maryland Congress of Parents & Teachers, Inc.; Alpha Omega Alpha Honor Medical Society

CARSON CARRUTH, ZANE, T: President **I:** Business Management/Business Services **CN:** Carson Marketing, LLC **DOB:** 06/07/2019 **PB:** Seguin **SC:** TX/USA **MS:** Married **SPN:** Brady **CH:** Britney Clark; Chad Reagor (Deceased) **CT:** Certified Business Etiquette and Protocol Professional **C:** President, Owner, Carson Marketing, LLC, Houston, TX (2010-Present); President, Etiquette to Excel; Former Vice President of Marketing, Hard-to-Place Insurance Risks **CIV:** Board Member, Discovery Green Conservancy (2015-Present); Board Member, Houston SPCA (2013-Present); Board Member, Houston Grand Opera (2016); Donor, Books, Young Children; Sponsor, Storybook Opera, Northland Christian School **CW:** Author, "The Legend Begins" (2020); Author, "Abella and the Tooth Fairy School" (2020); Author, "The World's First Tooth Fairy...Ever" (2017); Author, "The Adventures of Abella and Her Magic Wand"; Contributor, Articles on Etiquette, Numerous Regional Magazines **AW:** Impact Maker, CKW Luxe Magazine (2020); Woman of Distinction, ABC13 Houston (2019); Fundraising Honor, SPCA; Story Monsters Award **MH:** Marquis Who's Who Top Professional **AS:** Ms. Carruth attributes her success to the grace of God, luck, and having people around her who want to help her succeed and grow in life. She believes that having "no quit in you" is important when one decides to self publish. **B/I:** Ms. Carruth became involved in her profession because she has had a lifelong passion for etiquette; she loved beautiful manners and she loved to write. Ms. Carruth earned her certification for etiquette, which enabled her to be published in quite a few magazines. People then asked her to write articles on the subject. Ms. Carruth wrote her first book about 25 years ago but didn't know how to get it published. She discovered the act of self-publishing shortly after and decided to do so. Ms. Carruth has always loved sales; her career is an accumulation of everything she is passionate about. **AV:** Thoroughbred horse racing; Spending time with her children and grandchildren

CARTER, DWAYNE, "LIL WAYNE" MICHAEL JR., T: Rap Artist **I:** Media & Entertainment **DOB:** 09/27/1982 **PB:** New Orleans **SC:** LA/USA **PT:** Dwayne Michael Turner Carter; Jacida Carter **MS:** Divorced **SPN:** Antonia Johnson (02/14/2004, Divorced 2006) **CH:** Reginae; Dwayne III; Lennox Samuel Ari; Neal Carter **ED:** Coursework, University of Houston (2005); Coursework, University of Phoenix **C:** Solo Artist (1999-Present); Founder, Chief Executive Officer, Young Money Entertainment (2005-2007); Founding Member, Rap Group, Hot Boys (1997-2001) **CW:** Rap Artist, "Funeral" (2020); Appearance, "The Masked Singer" (2020); Appearance, "Growing Up Hip Hop: Atlanta" (2017); Rap Artist, "In Tune We Trust" (2017); Author, "Gone Til' November: A Journal of Rikers Island" (2016); Rap Artist, "Free Weezy Album" (2015); Rap Artist, "Tha Carter V" (2015); Rap Artist, "I am Not a Human Being II" (2013); Rap Artist, "Tha Carter IV" (2011); Rap Artist,

"Rebirth" (2010); Rap Artist, "I am Not a Human Being" (2010); Actor, "Hurricane Season" (2010); Actor, "Freaknik: The Movie" (2010); Rap Artist with Young Money Entertainment, "We Are Young Money" (2009); Rap Artist with Young Money Featuring Lloyd, "Bedrock" (2009); Rap Artist, "Tha Carter III" (2008); Rap Artist Featuring Static Major, "Lollipop" (2008); Rap Artist, "A Milli" (2008); Rap Artist with Jay-Z, T.I. and Kanye West, "Swagga Like Us" (2008); Rap Artist with Keri Hilson, "Turnin' Me On" (2008); Actor, "Who's Your Caddy?" (2007); Rap Artist, Extended Plays, "The Leak" (2007); Rap Artist with Birdman, "Like Father, Like Son" (2006); Rap Artist, "Tha Carter II" (2005); Rap Artist, "Tha Carter" (2004); Rap Artist with Hot Boys, "Let Em Burn" (2003); Rap Artist, "500 Degreez" (2002); Rap Artist, "Lights Out" (2000); Actor, "Baller Blockin'" (2000); Rap Artist, "Tha Block is Hot" (1999); Rap Artist with Hot Boys, "Guerilla Warfare" (1998); Rap Artist with Hot Boys, "Get It How U Live" (1997); Contributor, ESPN The Magazine; Appearances, Television Shows; Rap Artist, Solo and Collaboration Albums **AW:** Grammy Award for Best Rap Song, The Recording Academy (2017); Awards for Top Rap Album, Top Rap Artist, Top Male Artist, Billboard Music Awards (2012); Grammy Awards for Best Rap Solo Performance, Best Rap Song, Best Rap Performance by a Duo or Group, The Recording Academy (2009); Awards for Best Collaboration, Best Male Hip Hop Artist, BET Awards (2009); Named One of the 100 Agents of Change, Rolling Stone Magazine (2009); Awards for Track of the Year, Lyricist of the Year, BET Hip-Hop Awards (2008); Award for Best Hip Hop Video, MTV Video Music Awards (2008); BET Viewer's Choice Award (2008); Named Choice Rap Artist, Teen Choice Awards (2008); Named Hottest MC in the Game, MTV Music Awards (2007); Award for Best Rapper, Vibe Music Awards (2007); Numerous Awards

CARTER, EARL, "BUDDY" LEROY, T: U.S. Representative from Georgia **I:** Government Administration/Government Relations/Government Services **DOB:** 09/06/1957 **PB:** Savannah **SC:** GA/USA **MS:** Married **SPN:** Amy (Coppage) Carter (1978) **CH:** Joel; Barret; Travis **ED:** BS in Pharmacy, University of Georgia (1980); Associate Degree, Young Harris College (1977) **C:** Member, U.S. House of Representatives from Georgia's First Congressional District (2015-Present); State Senator, District One, Georgia State Senate (2009-2015); State Representative, District 159, Georgia House of Representatives (2004-2009); Mayor, Pooler, GA (1996-2004); Member, Committee on Energy and Commerce; Member, Republican Study Committee; Secretary, Committee on Health and Human Services; Member, Committee on Appropriations, Economic Development and Tourism **PA:** Republican

CARTER, ELEANOR, "ROSALYNN" ROSALYNN, T: Former First Lady **DOB:** 08/18/1927 **PB:** Plains **SC:** GA/USA **PT:** Edgar Smith; Allie (Murray) Smith **MS:** Married **SPN:** James Earl Carter Jr. (07/07/1946) **CH:** John William; James Earl III; Donnel Jeffrey; Amy Lynn **ED:** Honorary Degree, Queens University (2012); Honorary Doctor of Law, Regis College (2002); Honorary Doctor of Humane Letters, Georgia Southwestern State University (2001); Honorary Doctor of Letters, Emory University (1991); Honorary Doctor of Law, University of Notre Dame (1987); Honorary Doctor of Humane Letters, Morehouse College (1980); Coursework, Georgia Southwestern State University (1944-1946) **C:** Distinguished Fellow, Women's Studies Department, Emory University, Atlanta, GA (1990-Present); Co-founder, The Carter Center (1982-Present); Distinguished Centennial Lecturer, Agnes Scott College, Decatur, GA (1988-1992); First Lady of the United States, Washington, DC (1977-1981) **CIV:** Deacon, Maranatha Baptist Church, Plains, GA (2006-Present); Founder, Rosalynn Carter Fellowships for Mental Health Journalism (1996); Co-founder with Jimmy Carter, The Carter Center (1982); Honorary Chair, President's Commission on Mental Health (1977-1978); Member, Georgia Governor's Commission to Improve Services for Mentally and Emotionally Handicapped (1971); Co-founder, Every Child by Two/Vaccinate Your Family; Trustee, Founder, Chair, Mental Health Task Force; Annual Host, Rosalynn Carter Symposium on Mental Health Policy; Chair, International Committee of Women Leaders for Mental Health; Advisory Board Member, Habitat for Humanity; President, Board Director, Rosalynn Carter Institute for Caregiving, Georgia Southwestern State University **CW:** Co-author, with Susan Golant and Kathryn E. Cade, "Within Our Reach: Ending the Mental Health Crisis" (2010); Appearance, Documentary, "Jimmy Carter: Man from Plains" (2007); Co-author, with Susan Golant, "Helping Someone with Mental Illness: A Compassionate Guide for Family, Friends and Caregivers" (1998); Co-author, with Susan Golant, "Helping Yourself Help Others: A Book for Caregivers" (1994); Co-author, with Jimmy Carter, "Everything to Gain: Making the Most of the Rest of Your Life" (1987); Author, "First Lady from Plains" (1984) **AW:** Inductee, National Women's Hall of Fame (2001); U.S. Surgeon General's Medallion, Presidential Medal of Freedom (1999); Jefferson Award, American Institute for Public Service (1996); National Caring Award, The Caring Institute (1995); Kiwanis World Service Medal, Kiwanis International Foundation (1995); Notre Dame Award for International Humanitarian Service (1992); Eleanor Roosevelt Living World Award, Peace Links (1992); Dean's Award, Columbia University Vagelos College of Physicians and Surgeons (1991); Dorothea Dix Award, Mental Illness Foundation (1988); Distinguished Alumnus Award, American Association of State Colleges and Universities (1987); Nathan S. Kline Medal of Merit, International Committee Against Mental Illness (1984); Presidential Citation, American Psychological Association (1982); Volunteer of the Decade Award, National Mental Health Association (1980); Georgia Woman of the Year Award, Georgia Commission on Women; Rhoda and Bernard Sarnat International Prize in Mental Health, Institute of Medicine **MEM:** Fellow, American Psychiatric Association; Honorary Member, American Psychiatric Association **AV:** Fly fishing; Birdwatching; Swimming; Bicycling **PA:** Democrat

CARTER, JAMES, "JIMMY" EARL JR., T: 39th President of the United States **I:** Government Administration/Government Relations/Government Services **DOB:** 10/1/1924 **PB:** Plains **SC:** GA/USA **PT:** James Earl Carter; Lillian (Gordy) Carter **MS:** Married **SPN:** Rosalynn (Smith) Carter (07/07/1946) **CH:** John William; James Earl III; Donnel Jeffrey; Amy Lynn **ED:** Honorary PhD, University of Haifa (1987); Honorary LLD, Creighton University (1987); Honorary DHL, Central Connecticut State University (1985); Honorary LLD, School of Law, New York University (1985); Honorary LLD, Bates College (1985); Honorary PhD, Tel Aviv University (1983); Honorary LLD, Kwansei Gakuin University, Japan (1981); Honorary LLD, Georgia Southwestern College (Now Georgia Southwestern State University) (1981); Honorary PhD, Weizmann Institute of Science (1980); Honorary DEng, Georgia Institute of Technology (1979); Honorary LLD, Emory University (1979); Honorary LLD, University of Notre Dame (1977); Honorary LLD, Morris Brown College (1972); Honorary LLD, Morehouse College (1972); BS, United States Naval Academy (1947); Coursework, Georgia Institute of Technology; Coursework, Georgia Southwestern College (Now Georgia Southwestern State University) **C:** University Distinguished Professor, Founder, Carter Presidential Center, Emory University, Atlanta, GA (1982-Present); 39th President of the United States, Washington, DC (1977-1981); Founder, Jimmy Carter Presidential Library and Museum, Atlanta, GA (1977-1981); Governor, State of Georgia, Atlanta, GA (1971-1975); Member, District 14, Georgia State Senate (1963-1967); Farmer, Warehouseman, Plains, GA (1953-1977) **CR:** Chairman, Congressional Campaign Committee, Democratic National Committee (1974) **CIV:** Trustee, Mercer University (2012-Present); Founding Member, The Elders (2007-Present); Board of Directors, Habitat for Humanity (1984-1987); Chairman, Sumter County School Board, GA (1960-1962); Member, Sumter County School Board, GA (1955-1962); Active Volunteer, Habitat for Humanity; Sunday School Teacher, Maranatha Baptist Church, Plains, GA **MIL:** With, U.S. Navy Reserve (1953-1961); Advanced through Grades to Lieutenant, U.S. Navy (1946-1953) **CW:** Author, "A Full Life: Reflections at Ninety" (2015); Author, "A Call to Action: Women, Religion, Violence, and Power" (2014); Author, "NIV Lessons from Life Bible: Personal Reflections with Jimmy Carter" (2012); Author, "White House Diary" (2010); Author, "We Can Have Peace in the Holy Land: A Plan That Will Work" (2009); Author, "A Remarkable Mother" (2008); Author, "Beyond the White House: Waging Peace, Fighting Disease, Building Hope" (2007); Author, "Palestine Peace Not Apartheid" (2006); Author, "Our Endangered Values: America's Moral Crisis" (2005); Author, "Sharing Good Times" (2004); Author, "The Hornet's Nest: A Novel of the Revolutionary War" (2003); Author, "The Nobel Peace Prize Lecture" (2002); Author, "An Hour Before Daylight: Memories of a Rural Boyhood" (2001); Author, "Christmas in Plains: Memories" (2001); Author, "The Virtues of Aging" (1998); Author, "Sources of Strength: Meditations on Scripture for a Living Faith" (1997); Author, "Living Faith" (1996); Author, "Always a Reckoning" (1995); Author, "Talking Peace: A Vision for the Next Generation" (1993); Author, "Turning Point: A Candidate, a State, and a Nation Come of Age" (1992); Author, "An Outdoor Journal" (1988); Author, "Everything to Gain: Making the Most of the Rest of Your Life" (1987); Author, "The Blood of Abraham" (1985); Author, "Negotiation: The Alternative to Hostility" (1984); Author, "Keeping Faith: Memoirs of a President" (1982); Author, "A Government as Good as its People" (1977); Author, "Why Not the Best?" (1975) **AW:** Grammy Award for Best Spoken Word Album (2007, 2016); International Advocate for Peace Award, Benjamin N. Cardozo School of Law, Yeshiva University (2013); International Catalonia Award (2010); Mahatma Gandhi Global Nonviolence Award, Mahatma Gandhi Center for Global Nonviolence, James Madison University (2009); American Peace Award (2009); Berkeley Medal, University of California Berkeley (2007); Nobel Peace Prize, Norwegian Nobel Committee (2002); Zayed International Prize for the Environment, Zayed International Foundation for the Environment (2001); Herbert Hoover Humanitarian Award, Boys & Girls Clubs of America (2001); William Penn Mott Junior Park Leadership Award, National Parks Conservation Association (2000); International Child Survival Award, Atlanta Chapter, UNICEF USA, GA (1999); Human Rights Award, United Nation (1998); Hoover Medal (1998); Indira Gandhi Prize for Peace, Disarmament and Development (1997); Bishop John T. Walker Distinguished Humanitarian Award, Africare (1996); Humanitarian of the Year, GQ Magazine (1996); Félix Houphouët-Boigny Peace Prize,

United Nations Educational Center (1994); Freedom Award, National Civil Rights Museum (1994); Spark M. Matsunaga Medal of Peace, United States Institute of Peace (1993); Humanitarian Award, CARE International (1993); Conservationist of the Year Medal, National Wildlife Federation (1993); W. Averell Harriman Democracy Award, National Democratic Institute for International Affairs (1992); Physicians for Social Responsibility Award (1991); Aristotle Prize, Alexander S. Onassis Public Benefit Foundation (1991); Liberty Medal, National Constitution Center (1990); Spirit of America Award, National Council for the Social Studies (1990); Jefferson Award, American Institute for Public Service (1990); Edwin C. Whitehead Award, National Center for Health Education (1989); Albert Schweitzer Prize for Humanitarianism (1987); World Methodist Peace Award (1985); Human Rights Award, International League for Human Rights (1983); Ansel Adams Conservation Award, The Wilderness Society (1982); Harry S. Truman Public Service Award (1981); Gold Medal, International Institute of Human Rights (1979); International Mediation Medal, American Arbitration Association (1979); Martin Luther King Junior Peace Prize (1979); International Human Rights Award, Synagogue Council of America (1979); Silver Buffalo Award, Boy Scouts of America (1978); American Campaign Medal; World War II Victory Medal; China Service Medal; National Defense Service Medal **MEM:** Honorary Member, The Phi Beta Kappa Society **PA:** Democrat

CARTER, JOHN L., T: Lawyer **I:** Law and Legal Services **DOB:** 10/02/1948 **PB:** Clayton **SC:** NM/USA **PT:** John Allen Carter; Ruth (Laughlin) Carter **MS:** Widowed **SPN:** Dorel Susan Payne (09/20/1975, Deceased 2017) **CH:** Matthew; Caroline; Susan **ED:** JD, Southern Methodist University, Cum Laude (1973); BA, Southern Methodist University (1970) **C:** Partner, Vinson & Elkins LLP, Houston, Texas (1980-2012); Associate, Vinson & Elkins LLP, Houston, Texas (1973-1980) **CIV:** Treasurer, Board of Directors, TIRR Foundation **CW:** Editor-in-chief, Southwestern Law Review (1972-1973) **MEM:** Fellow, American College of Trial Lawyers; American Bar Foundation; Life Member, Texas Bar Foundation; Houston Bar Foundation; Order of the Coif; Barristers **BAR:** United States Court of Appeals for the District of Columbia Circuit (2004); United States District Court for the Western District of Texas (1999); United States District Court for the Eastern District of Texas (1985); United States District Court for the Northern District of Texas (1978); Supreme Court of the United States (1976); United States Court of Appeals for the Fifth Circuit (1975); United States Court of Appeals for the Eleventh Circuit (1975); United States District Court for the Southern District of Texas (1974); Texas (1973) **MH:** Albert Nelson Marquis Lifetime Achievement Award **B/I:** Mr. Carter's parents both had degrees in science related fields. His father was an agronomist and his mother was a home economics teacher. When Mr. Carter was a teenager, he began to think the skills that he had at the time would make him a great lawyer. He enjoyed public speaking but had not learned much about lawyers until he became one. **THT:** As Mr. Carter looks back on his legal career, the thing that made his career the "richest" was the people within his work, (inside and outside his firm) that he worked hard on cases with. The teamwork aspect of his work was gratifying.

CARTER, JOHN RICE, T: U.S. Representative from Texas; Lawyer **I:** Government Administration/Government Relations/Government Services **DOB:** 11/06/1941 **PB:** Houston **SC:** TX/USA **PT:** John James Carter; Elizabeth (Rice) Carter **MS:** Married

SPN: Erika Theodora Van Bruegel (06/15/1968) **CH:** Gilianna; John; Theodore; Danielle **ED:** JD, The University of Texas at Austin School of Law (1969); BA in History, Texas Tech University (1965) **C:** U.S. Representative from Texas' 31st Congressional District, United States Congress, Washington, DC (2003-Present); Secretary, U.S. House Republican Conference, Washington, DC (2007-2013); District Judge, 277th District Court, Williamson County, Texas (1982-2002); Judge, 277th District Court, Williamson County, Texas (1981-1982); Private Practice Attorney, Round Rock, Texas (1973-1981); Municipal Judge, Round Rock, Texas (1978-1980); Counsel, Texas House of Representatives, Austin, Texas (1969-1972); Member, Committee on Appropriations **CR:** Chairman, Round Rock Planning Committee (1975-1978) **AW:** Named Jaycee of the Year, Round Rock Jaycees (1975) **MEM:** President, Williamson County Bar Association (1976); Round Rock Jaycees (1975) **BAR:** State of Texas (1969) **PA:** Republican

CARTER, LISA, T: Horse Ranch Owner; AKC Yorkie Breeder **I:** Agriculture **CN:** Carter Yorkies **CH:** Two Children **ED:** BS in Anthropology and Sociology, Valdosta State University, GA (1978) **CT:** Horse Show Judge, University of North Carolina **C:** Owner, Carter Yorkies (1973-Present) **CIV:** Board of Directors, Southern Artist League (1995) **AW:** Two-time Quality Breeder Award (2017, 2018) **MEM:** Order of Diana; Tau Kappa Epsilon **B/I:** Ms. Carter has always had a love of animals, especially Yorkshire terriers.

CARTER, SHAWN, "JAY-Z" COREY, T: Rapper; Music Company Executive **I:** Media & Entertainment **CN:** Roc Nation **DOB:** 12/04/1969 **PB:** Brooklyn **SC:** NY/USA **PT:** Adnis Reeves; Gloria Carter **MS:** Married **SPN:** Beyoncé Giselle (Knowles) Carter (04/04/2008) **CH:** Blue Ivy Carter; Rumi Carter; Sir Carter **C:** Licensed Agent, Roc Nation Sports (2013-Present); Co-founder, Roc Nation, LLC (2008-Present); Principal, Owner, 40/40 Club, Atlantic City, NJ (2005-Present); Principal, Owner, 40/40 Club, New York, NY (2003-Present); Co-founder, Chief Executive Officer, Rocawear (1999-Present); Co-founder, StarRoc (2008); President, Def Jam Recordings (2005-2007); Co-owner, Brooklyn Nets (2004-2013); Co-founder, Roc-A-Fella Records, New York, NY (1996) **CIV:** Founder, Shawn Carter Scholarship Fund (2002-Present); Founder, Annual Jay-Z Santa Claus Toy Drive; Founder, Team Roc **CW:** Rap Artist, Album, "4:44" (2017); Rap Artist, Song with Justin Timberlake, "Holy Grail" (2014); Actor, Film, "Annie" (2014); Actor, Film, "Made in America" (2013); Rap Artist, Album, "Magna Carta...Holy Grail" (2013); Executive Producer, Video Game, "NBA2K13" (2012); Rap Artist, Collaboration Album with Kanye West, "Watch the Throne" (2011); Rap Artist, Song with Kanye West, "Otis" (2011); Rap Artist, Song, "Niggas in Paris" (2011); Rap Artist, Song with Kanye West, Frank Ocean, The-Dream, "No Church in the Wild" (2011); Author, Memoir, "Decoded" (2010); Rap Artist, Album, "The Blueprint 3" (2009); Rap Artist, "D.O.A. (Death of Auto-Tune)" (2009); Rap Artist, Song with Rihanna & Kanye West, "Run This Town" (2009); Rap Artist, Song with Alicia Keys, "Empire State of Mind" (2009); Rap Artist, Song with Swizz Beatz, "On to the Next One" (2009); Rap Artist, Song with T.I., Kanye West & Lil Wayne, "Swagga Like Us" (2008); Rap Artist, Album, "American Gangster" (2007); Rap Artist, Song with Rihanna, "Umbrella" (2007); Rap Artist, Album, "Kingdom Come" (2006); Rap Artist, Collaboration Album with Linkin Park, "Collision Course" (2004); Rap Artist, Collaboration Album with R. Kelly, "Unfinished Business" (2004); Rap Artist, Song, "99 Problems" (2004); Rap Artist, Song with Linkin

Park, "Numb/Encore" (2004); Actor, Film, "Fade to Black" (2004); Producer, "Fade to Black" (2004); Rap Artist, Song with Beyoncé, "Crazy in Love" (2003); Rap Artist, Album, "The Black Album" (2003); Rap Artist, Album, "Blueprint 2.1" (2003); Rap Artist, Album, "The Blueprint, Vol. 2: The Gift & The Curse" (2002); Rap Artist, Collaboration Album with R. Kelly, "The Best of Both Worlds" (2002); Rap Artist, Song, "Excuse Me Miss" (2002); Producer, "Paid in Full" (2002); Actor, Film, "State Property" (2002); Actor, Film, "Paper Soldiers" (2002); Rap Artist, Album, "The Blueprint" (2001); Rap Artist, Album, "MTV Unplugged" (2001); Rap Artist, Album, "The Dynasty: Roc la Familia" (2000); Rap Artist, Song, "I Just Wanna Love U (Give It 2 Me)" (2000); Rap Artist, Album, "In My Lifetime, Vol. 3: Life and Times of S. Carter" (1999); Rap Artist, Album, "In My Lifetime, Vol. 2: Hard Knock Life" (1998); Rap Artist, Song, "Hard Knock Life (Ghetto Anthem)" (1998); Actor, Producer, Writer, "Streets is Watching" (1998); Rap Artist, Album, "In My Lifetime, Vol. I" (1997); Rap Artist, Album, "Reasonable Doubt" (1996) **AW:** Listee, Power 100, Billboard (2019); Best Rap/Sung Collaboration, Grammy Awards (2014); Named, One of the 100 Most Influential People in the World, TIME Magazine (2005, 2013); Best Rap/Sung Collaboration, Grammy Awards (2013); Best Rap Performance, Best Rap Song, Grammy Awards (2013); Best Rap Performance, Grammy Awards (2012); Video of the Year, BET Awards (2012); Best Group, BET Awards (2012); Best Rap Performance by a Duo or a Group, Grammy Awards (2011); Best Rap/Sung Collaboration, Best Rap Song, Grammy Awards (2011); Best Collaboration, BET Awards (2010); Named, Favorite Male Singer, Nickelodeon Kids' Choice Awards (2010); CD of Year, BET Hip Hop Awards (2010); Best Rap Solo Performance, Grammy Awards (2010); Best Rap/Sung Collaboration, Best Rap Song, Grammy Awards (2010); Favorite Rap/Hip Hop Artist, American Music Awards (2004, 2009); Favorite Rap/Hip Hop Album, American Music Awards (2009); Best Rap Performance by a Duo or a Group, Grammy Awards (2009); Named, One of the 40 Under 40 Rising Stars, Fortune Magazine (2009); Named, One of the 100 Most Powerful Celebrities, Forbes.com (2008); Best Rap/Sung Collaboration, Grammy Awards (2008); Listee, Power 150, Ebony Magazine (2008); Best Rap/Sung Collaboration, Grammy Awards (2006); Named, One of the 10 Most Fascinating People, Barbara Walters Special (2006); Best Rap Solo Performance, Grammy Awards (2005); Best Rap/Sung Collaboration, Best R&B Song, Grammy Awards (2004); Best Collaboration, BET Awards (2004); Best Male Hip Hop Artist, BET Awards (2001, 2004); Sammy Davis Junior Entertainer of the Year, Soul Train Music Awards (2001); Best Rap Album, Grammy Awards (1999)

CARTWRIGHT, MATTHEW ALTON, T: U.S. Representative from Pennsylvania; Legal Services **I:** Government Administration/Government Relations/Government Services **DOB:** 05/01/1951 **PB:** Erie **SC:** PA/USA **PT:** Alton S. Cartwright; Adelaide Cartwright **MS:** Married **SPN:** Marion Munley (1985) **CH:** Jack; Matthew **ED:** JD, University of Pennsylvania Carey Law School (1986); BA in History, Hamilton College, Magna Cum Laude (1983); Coursework, London School of Economics (1981) **C:** U.S. Representative from Pennsylvania's Eighth Congressional District, United States Congress, Washington, DC (2019-Present); Member, U.S. House Committee on Oversight and Government Reform (2013-Present); Member, U.S. House Committee on Natural Resources (2013-Present); U.S. Representative from Pennsylvania's 17th Congressional District, United States Congress, Washington, DC (2013-2019); Partner, Munley, Munley

& Cartwright (Now Munley Law), Scranton, PA (1988-2012); Associate, Montgomery McCracken Walker & Rhoads LLP (1986-1989); Committee on Appropriations; Committee on Steering and Policy **CR:** Delegate, Democratic National Convention (1992) **CW:** Co-Author, "Litigating Commercial and Business Tort Cases" (2011); On-Air Legal Analyst, "The Law & You," WBRE-TV, Nexstar Broadcasting Group (2005-2011) **AW:** Silver Beaver Award, Boy Scouts of America, Northeastern Pennsylvania Council (2010) **MEM:** Board of Governors, American Association for Justice (2009-2011); District Governor, District 7410, Rotary International (2001-2002); International Society of Barristers; New York State Bar Association; Pennsylvania Bar Association; The Phi Beta Kappa Society **BAR:** New York (2005); Commonwealth of Pennsylvania (1986) **PA:** Democrat **RE:** Roman Catholic

CARVEL, ROBERT, "BERTIE" HUGH, T: Actor **I:** Media & Entertainment **DOB:** 09/06/1977 **PB:** London **SC:** United Kingdom **PT:** John Carvel **MS:** Married **SPN:** Sally Scott (2019) **ED:** Diploma, Royal Academy of Dramatic Art (2003); Coursework, University of Sussex; Coursework, University College School **CW:** Actor, "Doctor Foster" (2015-Present); Actor, "The Pale Horse" (2020); Actor, "Big Cats" (2018); Actor, "Ink" (2017-2019); Actor, "The Crown" (2017); Actor, "Revolting Rhymes" (2016); Actor, "Splendid's" (2016); Actor, "Bakkhai" (2015); Actor, "The Hairy Ape" (2015); Actor, "Coalition" (2015); Actor, "Jonathan Strange & Mr. Norell" (2015); Actor, "Babylon" (2014); Actor, "The Wrong Mans" (2014); Actor, "Matilda" (2010-2013); Actor, "Les Misérables" (2012); Actor, "Restless" (2012); Actor, "The Secret World" (2012); Actor, "The Crimson Petal and the White" (2011); Actor, "Dr. Dee" (2011); Actor, "Star Wars: The Old Republic" (2011); Actor, "Damned by Despair" (2011); Actor, "Hidden" (2011); Actor, "Sherlock" (2010); Actor, "Just William" (2010); Actor, "Rope" (2009); Actor, "Primeval" (2009); Actor, "Waking the Dead" (2009); Actor, "Midsomer Murders" (2009); Actor, "Haze" (2008); Actor, "The Pride" (2008); Actor, "Parade" (2008); Actor, "The Circle" (2008); Actor, "John Adams" (2008); Actor, "The Man of Mode" (2007); Actor, "Doctor Who" (2007); Actor, "Bombshell" (2006); Actor, "Holby City" (2006); Actor, "The Life of Galileo" (2006); Actor, "Coram Boy" (2005-2007); Actor, "Rose Bernd" (2005); Actor, "Faustus" (2005); Actor, " Professor Bernhardi" (2005); Actor, "Beethoven" (2005); Actor, "Victory? A Musical Drama for Peace" (2004); Actor, "Hawking" (2004); Actor, "Agatha Christie: A Life in Pictures" (2004); Actor, "Revelations" (2003) **AW:** Tony Award for Best Performance by a Featured Actor in a Play (2019); Laurence Olivier Award for Best Supporting Actor (2018); Drama Desk Award for Outstanding Featured Actor in a Musical (2013); Named Best Performance in a Musical, TMA Awards (Now UK Theatre Awards) (2012); Laurence Olivier Award for Best Actor in a Musical (2012)

CARVER, JAMES, T: Theatre Director and Consultant **I:** Media & Entertainment **DOB:** 01/30/1932 **PB:** Kalamazoo **SC:** MI/USA **PT:** Norman F. Carver; Helen Louise (Blackaller) Carver **MS:** Married **SPN:** Nancy Ann Organ (03/05/1955) **CH:** Scott Vaughan; Stephen Caleb **ED:** Master of Arts, Michigan State University (1965); Bachelor of Arts, Michigan State University (1954) **C:** Managing Director, Kalamazoo Civic Players (1974-1997); Business Manager, Kalamazoo Civic Players (1968-1974); Production Assistant, Kalamazoo Civic Players (1959-1968); Film Director, Station WNEM-TV, Bay City, MI (1954-1955) **CR:** Manager, Civic Auditorium, Kalamazoo, MI (1968-Present); Conductor, Workshop for Theatre Organizations throughout U.S.

(1959-Present); Consultant, Armed Forces, Germany (1990); Guest Instructor, Western Michigan University Theatre, Kalamazoo, MI (1977-1978); Chairman, Theatre Department, Nazareth College, Kalamazoo, MI (1960-1977); Director, Longmont Theater Company **CIV:** Trustee, Community Theatre Foundation, Kalamazoo, MI (1986-Present); Vice President, Save Our Roadside Environmental (1985-Present); Board of Directors, Mad Hatters, Kalamazoo, MI (1985-Present); Member, Advisory Committee, Kalamazoo, MI (1980, 2000); Vice President, Kalamazoo Arts Council (1980-1986) **MIL:** Captain, U.S. Army (1955-1957) **CW:** Author, "Penalty for Early Withdrawal" (1988); Author, "The Exchange" (1969); Author, "Carver's Manual for Directing Community Theatre"; Author, "Carver's Advice to the Players" **AW:** Distinguished Merit Award, American Association of Community Theatres (1989); Dionysis Award, American Association of Community Theatres (1980); AACT's Art Cole Award for a Lifetime of Leadership in Community Theatre **MEM:** President, American Association of Community Theatres (1987-1989); President, Community Theatre Association of Michigan (1964-1966) **MH:** Albert Nelson Marquis Lifetime Achievement Award **AS:** Mr. Carver credits his success on his ability to listen to his imagination and act on his creative impulses. **B/I:** Mr. Carver became involved in his profession due to his upbringing, having enjoyed the influence of parents who encouraged his participation in the arts. **AV:** Golf; Bicycling **PA:** Republican **RE:** Presbyterian

CASAGRANDE, GREG F., T: Founder, President **I:** Financial Services **CN:** SPBD Microfinance Network **DOB:** 08/20/1963 **PB:** Passaic **SC:** NJ/USA **PT:** Francis J. Casagrande; Rebecca Lynn Casagrande **CH:** Two daughters **ED:** MBA in Finance and Marketing, Kellogg School of Management, Northwestern University (1990); MS in Accounting, Leonard N. Stern School of Business, New York University (1987); BA in Economics, Colgate University (1985) **CT:** Certified Public Accountant **C:** Executive Chairman, Chief Executive Officer, WaterHealth International Inc. (2020-Present); Founder, Managing Director, Transformative Ventures LLC (2009-Present); Founder, Menlo Park Capital, MP Solutions, Auckland, New Zealand (2004-Present); Director, Cumulo9 Limited, Auckland, New Zealand (2004-Present); Chairman, English-To-Go, Auckland New Zealand (2003-Present); Chairman, Biomatters, Auckland, New Zealand (2003-Present); Founder, Managing Director, The MicroDreams Foundation, Newark, NJ (2002-Present); Founder, Chairman, President, SPBD Microfinance Network (1999-Present); Director, WaterHealth International Inc. (2012-2020); Lecturer, Kellogg School of Management, Northwestern University (2012); Executive Committee, The International Association of Microfinance Investors, New York, NY (2008-2012); Fund Adviser, Plebys, Irvine, CA (2007-2009); Director, Planet Finance, Paris, France (2004-2008); Co-Founder, ICE Angels, Auckland, New Zealand (2003-2007); Board of Patrons, Global Advisers Group, United Nations International Year of MicroCredit (2004-2005); Various Financial and General Management Positions, Ford Motor Company (1990-2005); Summer Associate, Overseas Private Investment Corporation (1989); Analyst, Colgate Palmolive (1985-1987); Auditor, CPA, Coopers & Lybrand (1985-1987) **CIV:** Global Board of Advisers, International Year of Microcredit, United Nations (2005) **AW:** President's Club Impact Award, Colgate University **MEM:** Mensa Society **MH:** Marquis Who's Who Top Professional **AS:** Mr. Casagrande attributes his success to his strong foundation through schooling and work, as well as his problem solving skills, hard work

and passion for what he does. **B/I:** Mr. Casagrande became involved in his profession because of his significant background in finance. During the early years of his career, he became interested in third-world economic development. Through a series of opportunities, he began working in microfinance, specifically empowering female entrepreneurs. **AV:** Jogging; Skiing; Playing tennis

CASE, EDWARD, "ED" ESPENETT, T: U.S. Representative from Hawaii; Lawyer **I:** Government Administration/Government Relations/Government Services **DOB:** 09/27/1952 **PB:** Hilo **SC:** HI/USA **MS:** Married **SPN:** Audrey Nakamura (2001) **CH:** James; David; David (Stepchild); Megan (Stepchild) **ED:** JD, University of California Hastings College of the Law (1981); BA in Psychology, Williams College (1975) **C:** Member, U.S. House of Representatives from Hawaii's First District, United States Congress (2019-Present); From Associate to Managing Partner, Carlsmith Ball LLP, Honolulu, Hawaii (1983-Present); U.S. Representative from Hawaii's Second Congressional District, United States Congress, Washington, DC (2002-2007); Member, Committee on Education and Labor (2002-2007); Member, Committee on Agriculture (2002-2007); Member, Small Business Committee (2002-2007); Member, Hawaii House of Representatives (1994-2002); Majority Leader, Hawaii House of Representatives (1999-2000); Clerk to Honorable William S. Richardson, Hawaii Supreme Court (1981-1982); Aide to U.S. Representative Spark Matsunaga, United States Congress, Washington, DC (1975-1978); Clerk, Hawaii Department of Labor **CIV:** Member, Manoa Neighborhood Board, Honolulu, Hawaii (1985-1989) **AW:** Named New Economy Legislator of the Year, Hawaii Technology Trade Association (2000); Named Legislator of the Year, Small Business Hawaii (2000); Named Legislator of the Year, Honolulu Weekly (1995) **PA:** Democrat

CASE, JEAN, T: 1) Chairman 2) Chief Executive Officer **I:** Other **CN:** 1) National Geographic Society 2)The Case Foundation **MS:** Married **SPN:** Steve Case (1998) **ED:** Honorary LHD, George Mason University (2016); Honorary LHD, Lilly Family School of Philanthropy, Indiana University (2014); Diploma, Westminster Academy, FL (1978) **C:** Chairman of the Board, National Geographic Society (2016-Present); Chief Executive Officer, The Case Foundation (1997-Present); Vice President of Corporate Communications, America Online, Inc., Verizon Media (1993-1996); Vice President of Marketing, America Online, Inc., Verizon Media (1989-1993); Director of Marketing, America Online, Inc., Verizon Media (1988-1989); Various Positions, Information Services Division, GE; Marketing Manager, The Source **CR:** Speaker in Field **CIV:** Co-Chair, U.S. Palestinian Partnership (2007); Chair, President's Council on Service and Civic Participation (2006); Board Member, White House Historical Association; Advisory Board, Brain Trust Accelerator Fund, Smithsonian American Women's History Initiative, Georgetown University Beeck Center for Social Impact and Innovation; Member, Advisory Council, Women's Initiative Policy, George W. Bush Presidential Center; Board Member, Accelerate Brain Cancer Cure; Participant, The Giving Pledge **AW:** Co-Recipient, One of the Nine Most Generous Tech Entrepreneurs, Fast Company (2013); Excellence in Entrepreneurship Award, Wake Forest University (2013); Co-Recipient, One of the 25 Best Givers, Barron Magazine (2011); Philanthropist of the Year, Washington Business Journal (2011); Co-Recipient, Citizen of the Year, National Conference on Citizenship (2011); Lifetime of Idealism Award, City Year (2009); Woodrow Wilson Award for Corporate Citizenship, Woodrow Wilson International Center for Scholars, Smithsonian Institution, Washington, DC (2001) **MEM:** American Academy of Arts and Sciences

CASE, KAREN A., BS, JD, LLM IN TAXATION, T: Attorney: Tax Law **I:** Law and Legal Services **CN:** Fonhe Inc. **DOB:** 04/07/1944 **PB:** Milwaukee **SC:** WI/USA **PT:** Alfred F. Case; Hilda M. (Tomich) Case **ED:** LLM in Taxation, New York University (1973); JD, Marquette University (1966); BS, Marquette University (1963) **C:** Lawyer, Fonhe Inc. (2009-Present); CoVac (1997-2009); Partner, Case, Drinka & Diel, Milwaukee, WI (1989-1996); Secretary of Revenue, State of Wisconsin (1987-1988); Partner, Meldman, Case & Weine Division, Mulcahy & Wherry, Milwaukee, WI (1985-1986); Partner, Meldman, Case & Weine, Milwaukee, WI (1973-1985); Teacher, Milwaukee Public School System, Milwaukee, WI (1968-1972) **CR:** Instructor, Ringling School of Art, Longboat Key, FL (2003-2008); Guest Lecturer, Marquette University Law School (1974-1978); Instructor, University of Wisconsin, Milwaukee, WI, School of Business (1974-1978) **CIV:** President's Council, Alverno College (1988-1994); Wisconsin Governor's Economic Advisory Commission (1989-1991); Wisconsin Governor's Commission on Taliesin (1988) **CW:** Contributor, Articles, Legal Journals **MEM:** Therapy Dogs International (1999-Present); Former Director, Wisconsin Breast Cancer Coalition (1996-Present); Florida CraftArt in St. Petersburg (1995-Present); Tempo Professional Women's Organization (1985-Present); Founding Member, Former President, Friends of Boerner Botanical Gardens of Milwaukee County (1984-Present); Founding Member, Association of Women Lawyers (1975-Present); American Rose Society (1970-Present); Former President, Milwaukee Rose Society (1970-Present); State Bar of Wisconsin (1966-Present); Art Uptown Gallery, Sarasota, FL (1999-2015); Director, Coalition for Vaccines Against Cancer (1996-2004); Peer-Reviewer, California Breast Cancer Research Program (1999-2000); Peer-Reviewer, Department of Defense Breast Cancer Research Program (1998, 1999); Professional Dimensions Organization (1984-1995); Chapter Director, American Academy of Matrimonial Lawyers (1980-1995); American Bar Association (1973-1995); State Bar Taxation Committee (1981-1994); Director, Treasurer, Wisconsin Bar Foundation (1974-1994); State Bar Board of Governors (1981-1991); Director, Park People of Milwaukee County (1982-1987); Wisconsin Delegate, National Association of Women Lawyers (1980-1987); Board of Directors, Office Management Committee, Milwaukee Bar Association (1966-1997) **BAR:** United States Court of Appeals for the Seventh Circuit (1973); United States Tax Court (1973); United States Court of Federal Claims (1973); Wisconsin Bar (1966) **MH:** Albert Nelson Marquis Lifetime Achievement Award; Marquis Who's Who Top Professional **AS:** Ms. Case attributes her success to the hard-working mindset instilled in her by her parents. **B/I:** Ms. Case always had a mathematical mind and found her passion in taxation and the internal revenue code. When she graduated from law school, women weren't accepted in many law firms and government positions. Many female lawyers who did manage to get hired in law were treated as paralegals, rather than lawyers. Ms. Case was fortunate to be accepted by a firm that viewed women as equals and allowed her to practice as any male lawyer in her field at that time. **AV:** Surviving breast cancer **THT:** Ms. Case believes in taking the time to do what one is passionate about, as well as delegating tasks when one is able. She is passionate about nourishing one's soul.

CASE, STEPHEN, "STEVE" MCCONNELL, T: Former Chairperson and Chief Executive Officer **I:** Internet **CN:** American Online **DOB:** 8/21/1958 **PB:** Honolulu **SC:** HI/USA **PT:** Daniel Case; Carol Case **MS:** Married **SPN:** Jean (Villanueva) Case (1998); Joanne Barker (1985, Divorced 1996) **CH:** One Son; Four Daughters **ED:** Bachelor's Degree in Political Science, Williams College, Williamstown, MA (1980) **C:** Chairperson, Startup America Partnership (2011-Present); Chairperson, Accelerate Brain Cancer Cure (2008-Present); Chairperson, Chief Executive Officer, Revolution, Washington, DC (2005-Present); Chairperson, The Case Foundation (1997-Present); Chairperson, America Online Inc. (1995-2003); Chief Executive Officer, America Online Inc. (1991); Executive Vice President, Marketing, Quantum Computer Services (1987-1991); Vice President, Marketing, Quantum Computer Services (1985-1987); Marketing Consultant, Control Video Corporation (1983-1985); Manager, New Pizza Marketing, Pizza Hut Inc., Wichita, KS (1982-1983); Assistant Brand Manager, Procter & Gamble, Cincinnati, OH (1980-1981) **PA:** Independent

CASEY, DANIEL L., EDD, T: School Counselor **I:** Education/Educational Services **DOB:** 09/19/1942 **PB:** Litchfield **SC:** MN/USA **PT:** Thomas Austin Casey; Beatrice Lucille (Christie) Casey **CH:** Jeffrey; Jennifer; Danielle **ED:** EdD, University of Minnesota (1999); MA, Bemidji State University (1991); BS, Bemidji State University (1988) **CT:** Certified Traumatologist; Board Certified in Expert School Crisis Response **C:** Executive Director, Green Cross Academy of Traumatology (GCAT) (1999-2014); Counselor, St. John's University, Collegeville, MN (1994-1998); Professor of Psychology, Bemidji State University (1993-1994); Firefighter, Forester, DNR/U.S. Forest Service (1968-1993); Crisis Management Counseling and Consultation, Clear Lake, MN **CR:** Advisory Committee, International Critical Incident Stress Foundation, Inc. (ICISF), Baltimore, MD (1987-Present) **MIL:** Sergeant, United States Air Force, Hawaii (1960-1963) **CW:** Author, "Rural Emergency Response" (2001); Author, "Crisis in Colleges and Universities" (1996); Contributor, Articles to Professional Journals **AW:** Lifetime Achievement Award, Green Cross Academy of Traumatology (GCAT) (2018); Lifetime Achievement Award, International Critical Incident Stress Foundation, Inc. (ICISF) (2013); Unsung Hero Award, International Critical Incident Stress Foundation, Inc. (ICISF) (2009); Award, Government's Council, St. Paul, MN (1991) **MEM:** The American Legion **MH:** Albert Nelson Marquis Lifetime Achievement Award **B/I:** Dr. Casey, once a fireman, was fighting the wild fires and was burned over twice being on the front lines. It prompted him to return back to school to work in psychiatry. He received calls from wildlife firefighters from all over the U.S. The state bought his master's degree for him to help wildlife firefighters **AV:** Raising paso fino horses; Hunting; Fishing; Motorcycle riding **PA:** Republican **RE:** Catholic **THT:** Dr. Casey went to fire camps all over the west and he took two summers off. He went to Ireland to qualify for his licenses in alcoholic treatments centers in Ireland.

CASEY, ROBERT, "BOB" PATRICK JR., T: U.S. Senator from Pennsylvania **I:** Government Administration/Government Relations/Government Services **DOB:** 04/13/1960 **PB:** Scranton **SC:** PA/USA **PT:** Robert Patrick Casey; Ellen Theresa (Harding) Casey **MS:** Married **SPN:** Terese Foppiano (1985) **CH:** Elyse; Caroline; Julia; Marena **ED:** JD, The Catholic University of America Columbus School of Law, Washington, DC (1998); BA, College of the Holy Cross, Springfield, MA (1982) **C:** Ranking Member, Senate Aging Committee (2017-Present); U.S. Senator, Commonwealth of Pennsylvania (2007-Present); Member, U.S. Congressional Joint Economic Committee (JEC) (2007-Present); State Treasurer, Commonwealth of Pennsylvania, Harrisburg, PA (2005-2007); Auditor General, Commonwealth of Pennsylvania, Harrisburg, PA (1997-2005); Private Practice Attorney, Scranton, PA (1991-1996) **BAR:** Commonwealth of Pennsylvania (1991) **PA:** Democrat

CASIANO, FERNANDO R., T: Financial Analyst **I:** Financial Services **CN:** F.R.C. Enterprises, Inc. **ED:** BS in Managerial Accounting, Fordham University; Diploma in Public Accounting, International Correspondence Schools; Coursework, Estate, Gift, Trust Tax Course, The Sobelsohn School **C:** Financial Analyst, F.R.C. Enterprises, Inc. (1996-Present) **CIV:** Presidential Business Commission Appointee, National Republican Congressional Committee; Honorary Co-chairman, Business Advisory Council, National Republican Congressional Committee **AW:** Republican Congressional Leadership Certificate of Honor (2018); Majority Gold Member, National Republican Congressional Committee (2018); Presidential Commission Award, National Republican Congressional Committee (2008); Congressional Order of Merit, National Republican Congressional Committee (2007); Listed, Cambridge Who's Who (2006); Ronald Reagan Gold Medal Award, National Republican Congressional Committee (2004, 2005); Businessman of the Year Award, National Republican Congressional Committee (2003); National Leadership Award, National Republican Congressional Committee **MEM:** American Institute of Professional Bookkeepers (AIPB) **PA:** Republican

CASPER, MARC NOLAN, T: Chief Executive Officer and President **I:** Business Management/Business Services **CN:** Thermo Fisher Scientific, Inc. **DOB:** 03/10/1963 **PB:** New York **SC:** NY/USA **PT:** Herman Casper; Betty Casper **ED:** MBA, Harvard University, With High Distinction (1995); BA in Economics, Wesleyan University (1990) **C:** President, Chief Executive Officer, Thermo Fisher Scientific, Inc., Waltham, MA (2009-Present); Executive Vice President, Chief Operating Officer, Thermo Fisher Scientific, Inc., Waltham, MA (2008-2009); President, Analytical Technologies Group (Subsidiary of Thermo Fisher Scientific, Inc.) (2007-2009); Executive Vice President, Thermo Fisher Scientific, Inc., Waltham, MA (2007-2008); Executive Vice President, Thermo Electron Corporation (Subsidiary of Thermo Fisher Scientific, Inc.) (2006-2007); President, Life & Laboratory Sciences, Thermo Electron Corp. (Subsidiary of Thermo Fisher Scientific, Inc.) (2001-2005); Senior Vice President, Thermo Electron Corporation (Subsidiary of Thermo Fisher Scientific, Inc.) (2003); President, Chief Executive Officer, Kendro Laboratory Products, Newton, CT (2000-2001); President, Americas, Dade Behring Inc., Deerfield, IL (1997-2000); Associate, Bain Capital, Boston, MA (1995-1996); Strategy Consultant, Bain & Co., Inc., Boston, MA (1992-1993); Associate Consultant, Bain & Co., Inc., Boston, MA (1990-1992) **CR:** Board of Directors, Zimmer, Inc. (2009-Present) **AW:** Listee, Top 50 Healthcare Technology CEO, The Healthcare Technology Report (2019) **MEM:** The Phi Beta Kappa Society

CASSAR, GEORGE, HARRIS, PROFESSOR EMERITUS, T: Historian, Educator **I:** Education/Educational Services **DOB:** 10/31/1938 **PB:** Sherbrooke **SC:** Quebec/Canada **PT:** Michael Cassar; Nazareth Cassar **MS:** Married **SPN:** Mary Louise Breutzman (05/11/1984) **CH:** Alexandra; Michael; Jarrod **ED:** PhD, McGill University, Montreal, Quebec, Canada

(1968); MA, University of New Brunswick (1963); BA, University of New Brunswick (1962) **C:** Professor Emeritus, Eastern Michigan University, Ypsilanti, MI (2018-Present); Professor, Eastern Michigan University, Ypsilanti, MI (1977-2018); Associate Professor, Eastern Michigan University, Ypsilanti, MI (1972-1977); Assistant Professor, Eastern Michigan University, Ypsilanti, MI (1968-1972); Lecturer, Northern Michigan University, Marquette, MI (1966-1968) **CW:** Author, "Reluctant Partner: The Complete Story of the French Participation in the Dardanelles Campaign of 1915" (2019); Author, "Kitchener as Proconsul in Egypt 1911-1914" (2016); Author, "Trial By Gas: The 2nd British Army's Defense of Ypres, April/May 1915" (2014); Author, "Hell in Flanders Fields: Canadians at the Second Battle of Ypres" (2010); Author, "Lloyd George at War, 1916-1918" (2009); Author, "Kitchener's War: British Strategy from 1914 to 1916" (2004); Co-Author, "A Survey of Western Civilization" (2002); Author, "The Forgotten Front" (1998); Author, "Asquith as War Leader" (1994); Author, "Beyond Courage" (1985); Author, "The Tragedy of Sir John French" (1985); Author, "Kitchener: Architect of Victory" (1977); Author, "The French and the Dardanelles" (1971); Author, Contributor, Papers, Academic Conferences, Dozens of Articles, Book Reviews, and Chapters for Three Books; Interviewee, Canadian Radio Program on the Second Battle of Ypres; Interviewee, UK TV Program on "The Forgotten Front" **AW:** Named Honorary Colonel, Reserve Officer Training Corps (ROTC) Department University Award for Publication (1985); Listed, "Kitchener: Architect of Victory," "One of the 10 Best Books in History" (1977) **MH:** Albert Nelson Marquis Lifetime Achievement Award **AS:** Mr Cassar attributes his success to hard work and love of his profession. Throughout his career he looked forward to going to the university every morning, often working on weekends in his office. **B/I:** Mr. Cassar became involved in his profession by accident. As an indifferent student in high school, he was not planning to go to college as his hope was to join the air force after graduation. He grew up in Canada and he wanted to see the world so he crossed over to the United States to enroll in the air force. Attracted to their pilot program, he (fortunately) flunked the physical as he did not have 20/20 vision. Returning to Quebec he drifted from one low paying job to another, eventually realizing that in the interest of a stable future he would be required to get a college education. He entered the university of New Brunswick, settled down and became a good student. Instantly attracted to history he entered the honors program in his junior year and graduated second in the class. The head of the department was sufficiently impressed to offer him a scholarship to return to the university in the fall for an MA. As Mr Cassar had no idea of the type of career he intended to pursue, he accepted and, once he had completed his graduate degree, a close fiend urged him to acquire a PhD, arguing that he was "already half way home." As it happened his friend was wrong, but Mr. accepted his advice. and enrolled at McGill University in Montreal. As soon as Mr Cassar completed his course work he obtained his first teaching post at Northern Michigan in Marquette and two years later with the PhD in hand he moved to Eastern Michigan University in Ypsilanti where he taught for fifty years. He came to love his profession , often saying that he had the best job in the world. Although he no longer teaches, he continues to write. **PA:** Republican **RE:** Lutheran

CASSIDY, KEVIN ANDREW, T: Engineering Company Executive (Retired) **I:** Engineering **DOB:** 05/20/1931 **PB:** New York **SC:** NY/USA **PT:** Joseph Aloyisius Cassidy; Norine Beatrice (Mangan) Cassidy **MS:** Widowed **SPN:** Mary Elizabeth Hennessey (01/16/1954) **CH:** Kevin Andrew Jr.; Mark Robert; Karen Marie; Richard Joseph **ED:** BCE, Manhattan College (1953) **CT:** Registered Professional Engineer, State of New Jersey **C:** Director, Foster Wheeler Energy Ltd., Perryville, NJ (1985-1996); Director, Foster Wheeler Energy Ltd., Reading, England, United Kingdom (1982-1996); Director, Hi-Tech, Moscow, Russia (1989-1994); Division Vice President, Foster Wheeler Energy Corp., Livingston, NJ (1978-1982); Project Manager, Foster Wheeler Energy Corp., Livingston, NJ (1969-1978); Project Engineer, Foster Wheeler International Corp., New York, NY (1959-1969); Engineer, Standard Oil, Whiting, IN (1953-1959); Vice President, Foster Wheeler International Corp. **CR:** Director, Foster Wheeler Eastern Private Ltd., Singapore **MIL:** Combat Engineer, United States Army (1954-1956) **MH:** Albert Nelson Marquis Lifetime Achievement Award **B/I:** A colleague of Mr. Cassidy went to the same high school as he did, and he had a cousin that was an engineer as well. Mr. Cassidy's friend was going to get involved with engineering and he and his friend had a lot in common, so he thought perhaps that would be a good profession to pursue. When he finished high school, they both went to Manhattan College. **AV:** Golf; Skiing **PA:** Republican **RE:** Roman Catholic

CASSIDY, WILLIAM, "BILL" MORGAN, MD, T: U.S. Senator from Louisiana **I:** Government Administration/Government Relations/Government Services **DOB:** 09/28/1957 **PB:** Highland Park **SC:** IL/USA **PT:** James F. Cassidy; Elizabeth Cassidy **MS:** Married **SPN:** Laura Layden **CH:** Will, Meg, Kate **ED:** MD, Louisiana State University School of Medicine (1983); BS in Biochemistry, Louisiana State University (1979) **C:** U.S. Senator, State of Louisiana (2015-Present); Member, U.S. House of Representatives from Louisiana's Sixth District, United States Congress (2009-2015); Member, District 16, Louisiana State Senate (2006-2009); Associate Professor of Medicine, Louisiana State University Health Sciences Center **CIV:** Sunday School Teacher, Chapel on the Campus **MEM:** President, East Baton Rouge Parish Medical Society (1998); American College of Physicians; Board of Directors, Louisiana State Medical Society; American Association for the Study of Liver Diseases; Gastroenterology Society; Rotary Club of Baton Rouge; East Baton Rouge Parish Medical Society **PA:** Republican

CASTAN, FREDERIC, T: Executive Chef **I:** Food & Restaurant Services **CN:** Mix Restaurant & Lounge at Hilton Anaheim **SC:** Avignon/France **MS:** Married **SPN:** Maria Castan **CH:** Georges; Brian **ED:** Degree, Culinary School, Marseille, France (1970); EFAA, CAP, BM, Conservatoire National des Arts et Metiers (1970) **CT:** Master Chef, France **C:** Executive Chef, Hilton Anaheim (2015-Present); Executive Chef, St. Regis Hotel (2006-2015); Executive Chef, Starwood Hotels & Resorts Worldwide, Inc. (2006-2013); Executive Chef, Sofitel Chicago Water Tower (2002-2006); Executive Chef, Ritz Carlton (1991) **CIV:** Volunteer, Fundraiser for the Homeless; Volunteer, Chefs Table Foundation **MIL:** French Navy **AW:** Chef of the Year, White Toques Southern California (1995); Chef of the Year, Maitre Cuisiniers de France **MEM:** MCF; Academie Culinaire de France (ACF); Chaîne des Rôtisseurs; Les Amis d'Escoffier Society of New York **AS:** Mr. Castan attributes his success to his passion, tenacity, and the goals and objectives he sets and constantly meets. He sets the bar high and never gives up. **B/I:** Mr. Castan became involved in his profession because he was born and raised on a farm in Southern France, and was always surrounded by beautiful produce, fruits, vegetables, chickens, pigs, and horses. He would frequently help his grandmother cook and create recipes for the family. The smell and the touching of the produce was always something that excited him about cooking. His mother, who was also a good cook, would have guests from the church come to eat from time to time. He was only 11 or 12 years old but asked his mother if she would let him make the cake instead. She accepted and that was the beginning for him. He continued to be a better and better cook and baker. When he was 14, he decided he wanted to pursue a career as a chef. **AV:** Restoring classic cars; Riding bicycles

CASTEN, SEAN THOMAS, T: U.S. Representative from Illinois **I:** Government Administration/Government Relations/Government Services **CN:** U.S. House of Representatives **DOB:** 11/23/1971 **PB:** Dublin **SC:** Ireland **MS:** Married **SPN:** Kara Casten **CH:** Two Daughters **ED:** Master of Science in Engineering Management, Dartmouth College (1998); Master of Science in Biochemical Engineering, Thayer School of Engineering at Dartmouth (1998); Bachelor of Arts in Molecular Biology and Biochemistry, Middlebury College (1993) **C:** Member, U.S. House of Representatives, Illinois' Sixth Congressional District (2019-Present); Founder, Chief Executive Officer, Recycled Energy Development (2006-2016); President, Chief Executive Officer, Turbosteam Corporation (2000-2006) **CIV:** Chairperson, Northeast Clean Heat and Power Initiative **CW:** Contributor, Articles, Professional Journals **AW:** Named to Chicago Council on Global Affairs' Emerging Leaders Class of 2011 (2011) **PA:** Democrat

CASTOR, KATHERINE ANNE, T: U.S. Representative from Florida **I:** Government Administration/Government Relations/Government Services **DOB:** 08/20/1966 **PB:** Miami **SC:** FL/USA **PT:** Don F. Castor; Betty Elizabeth (Bowe) Castor **MS:** Married **SPN:** William Lewis **CH:** Julia; Chrissy **ED:** JD, Florida State University College of Law (1991); BA in Political Science, Emory University, Atlanta, GA (1988) **C:** Chair, House Climate Crisis Committee (2019-Present); U.S. Representative from Florida's 14th Congressional District, United States Congress, Washington, DC (2013-Present); U.S. Representative from Florida's 11th Congressional District, United States Congress, Washington, DC (2007-2013); Member, Hillsborough County Board of Commissioners, FL (2003-2007); Practicing Attorney, FL (1994-2000); Assistant General Counsel, Florida Department of Community Affairs (1991-1994); Member, Committee on the Budget; Member, Committee on Energy and Commerce **AW:** Named Woman of the Year, Tampa Bay Business Journal **MEM:** Past President, Florida Association for Women Lawyers, Inc.; Delta Delta Delta Fraternity (Tri Delta) **PA:** Democrat **RE:** Presbyterian

CASTRO, JOAQUÍN, T: U.S. Representative **I:** Government Administration/Government Relations/Government Services **DOB:** 09/16/1974 **PB:** San Antonio **SC:** TX/USA **PT:** Jesse Guzman; Maria Castro **MS:** Married **SPN:** Anna Flores (11/02/2013) **CH:** Andrea Elena; Roman Victor **ED:** JD, Harvard Law School (2000); BA in Communications and Political Science, Stanford University, with Honors (1996) **C:** U.S. Representative, Texas' 20th Congressional District, United States Congress, Washington, DC (2013-Present); Member, U.S. House Committee on Foreign Affairs (2013-Present); Member, U.S. House Armed Services Committee (2013-Present); Co-Founder, Law Offices of Julián Castro, PLLC, San Antonio, Texas (2005-2013); Member, District 125, Texas House of Representatives, Austin, Texas (2003-2013); Associate, Akin Gump Strauss Hauer & Feld LLP, San Antonio, TX (2001-2005); Member, Permanent Select Committee on Intelligence **CR:** Adjunct Professor, Trinity University, San Antonio, TX; Visiting Professor of Law, St. Mary's University **CIV:** Member, National College Advising Corps; Member, Mission and Identity Task Force, St. Mary's University; Member, President's Advisory Board, St. Philip's College; Member, Texas Family Impact Seminar; Member, Achieving the Dream; Member, Task Force on Education, NALEO Educational Fund **PA:** Democrat **RE:** Roman Catholic

CASTRO, JULIÁN, T: Former Secretary; Lawyer **I:** Government Administration/Government Relations/Government Services **CN:** U.S. Department of Housing and Urban Development **DOB:** 09/16/1974 **PB:** San Antonio **SC:** TX/USA **PT:** Jessie Guzman Castro; Maria Castro **MS:** Married **SPN:** Erica Lira Castro (2007) **CH:** Carina **ED:** Doctor of Jurisprudence, Harvard Law School (2000); Bachelor of Arts in Political Science and Communications, Stanford University (1996) **C:** Co-founder, Law Offices of Julián Castro PLLC (2005-Present); Candidate, Democratic Nominee, 2020 Presidential Election (2019-2020); Secretary, U.S. Department of Housing and Urban Development, Washington, DC (2014-2017); Mayor, San Antonio, Texas (2009-2014); City Councilman, San Antonio, Texas (2001-2005); Associate, Akin Gump Strauss Hauer & Feld LLP, San Antonio, Texas (2001-2005) **CR:** Keynote Speaker, Democratic National Convention (2012) **CIV:** Board Member, Family Services Association; Advisory Board Member, San Antonio National Bank, San Antonio, Texas; Advisory Board Member, iHeartMedia Inc. **CW:** Author, "An Unlikely Journey: Waking Up from My American Dream" (2018) **AW:** Dean's Distinguished Fellow, LBJ School of Public Affairs, The University of Texas at Austin (2018); Fellow, Dávila Chair in International Trade Policy, LBJ School of Public Affairs, The University of Texas at Austin (2018); Named, One of the Politics 40 Under 40, TIME Magazine (2010); Named to Young Global Leaders, World Economic Forum (2010) **PA:** Democrat **RE:** Roman Catholic

CATCHINGS, YVONNE, PHD, T: Artist, Educator **PT:** Andrew Walter Parks; Hattie Marie Parks **MS:** Widowed **SPN:** James A. Catchings (Deceased) **CH:** Andrea (Deceased); Wanda; James **ED:** MA in Art therapy, Wayne State University (1994); PhD in Education, University of Michigan (1970); MA in Museum Practice, University of Michigan (1970); MA in Art Education, Columbia University (1958); AB in Art, Spelman College (1955) **CT:** Board Certified Art Therapist, Art Therapy Credentials Board, Inc. (1995) **C:** Reading Specialist, Detroit Board of Education (1987-1992); Art Specialist, Detroit Board of Education (1976-1977); Teacher of Art, Detroit Board of Education (1959-1975); Teacher of Art, Atlanta Board of Education (1955-1959); Instructor of Art, Spelman College (1956-1957) **CR:** Assistant Professor of Art, Valdosta State College (Now Valdosta State University) (1987-1988); Lecturer, Marygrove College (1970-1972) **CIV:** Chairman, Reception Committee, United Negro College Fund, Inc., Detroit, MI (1980); Chairman, Art and Craft National Auxiliary, National Dental Association (1976); Program Chairman, National Auxiliary, National Dental Association (1966); Tuskegee Afro-American Museum (Now Tuskegee Airmen, National Museum of African American History & Culture), Smithsonian (1970-1972); Plymouth United Church of Christ; Volunteer, Links Club (The Links) **CW:** Featured, "Creating Their Own Image: The History of African American Women Artists by Lisa Farrington" (2005); Featured, "St. James Guide to Black Artists" (1997); Featured,

"Gumbo Ya Ya: Anthology of Contemporary African American Women Artists" (1995); Featured, "The Art of Black American Women," Robert Henkes (1993); Featured, Traveling Show, Westbeth Gallery, NY (1993); Featured, Group Show, NCA Michigan Gallery (1993); Featured, "Builders of Detroit by Anne Russell" (1978); One-woman Show, "Black Artist South," Alabama Museum, Huntsville, AL (1978); Author, "You Ain't Free Yet: Notes from a Black Woman" (1976); Featured, "Black Personalities of Detroit" (1975); Featured, "Black Artist on Vol. 2," Samella Lewis (1970); Subject, "American Negro Art," Cedric Dover (1960); Featured, Group Show, "Forever Free: Art by African American Women (1862-1980)"; Exhibit, Paintings, "Say it Loud: Art History, Rebellion," Charles H. Wright Museum of African American History **AW:** Black Achievement Award (2009); Blue Diamond Award, Spelman College (2007); Alumnae Achievement Award (2001); Fulbright Hayes Grant for Study, Zimbabwe (1982); Mayor's Award of Merit, City of Detroit (1980); James D. Parks Art Award, National Conference Art (1979); Spirit of Detroit Award, Detroit Common Council (1978) **MEM:** American Art Therapy Association; Past Member, Michigan Art Therapist Association; Past Member, Your Heritage House Museum; National Conference of Artists; Past member, National Art Education Association; Carousels Club; Links Club (The Links); Smart Set Club; Moles Club; National Chairman, Executive Activities, National Executive Board, Moles Club; Delta Sigma Theta Sorority, Inc.; Phi Delta Kappa (PDK International) **B/I:** Dr. Catchings became involved in her profession because she was always an artist, even at elementary school, and they would use her to paint pictures at Christmas on the windows. People would ask her to draw things on wedding invitations, as this was before the invention of computers. She liked teaching and when she was a child, she would use her dolls and friends as her students. She organized a spring dance for the community and wrote a Christmas play.

CATES, LINDLEY A., T: Professor (Retired) **I:** Education/Educational Services **DOB:** 11/20/1932 **PB:** Chicago **SC:** IL/USA **PT:** Lindley Addison Cates Sr.; Alice Jewett Gilbert **MS:** Married **SPN:** Ruth Elizabeth Gammell (1957) **CH:** Douglas Addison Cates, PhD; Catherine Sue Johnson, BS **ED:** PhD in Medicinal Chemistry, University of Colorado Boulder, Boulder, CO (1961); MS in Medicinal Chemistry, University of Colorado Boulder, Boulder, CO (1958); BS in Pharmacy, University of Minnesota, Minneapolis, MN (1954) **CT:** Registered Pharmacist, States of Minnesota, Colorado, and Texas; Junior College Teaching Certification **C:** Retired (1998); Professor, University of Houston (1968-1998); Associate Dean, University of Houston (1985-1990); Associate Professor, University of Houston (1964-1968); Assistant Professor, Medicinal Chemistry, University of Houston (1961-1964) **CR:** Chairman, Board of Directors, Great Southern Laboratory, Incorporated, Houston, Texas (1989-2015) **CIV:** Community Pharmacist (1961-1973); Staff Hospital Pharmacist (1956) **MIL:** Resigned (1956); Captain, United States Air Force, Guam (1954-1956) **CW:** Patentee, Phosphorothiomide (2), Organophosphorus Anticonvulsants **AW:** Grantee, Robert A. Welch Foundation (1969-1973, 1982-1988); Men of Achievement Award (1971, 1983); National Institute of Neurological and Communicative Disorders and Stroke (Now National Institute of Neurological Disorders and Stroke) (1980-1983); Five Grant Awards, National Cancer Institute, National Institute of Health (1963-1966, 1966-1966, 1972-1975, 1976-1979, 1978-1981); Fellow, American Association of Pharmaceutical Scientists; American Academy for Pharmaceutical Scientists; American Foundation

for Pharmaceutical Education; The Rho Chi Society; Phi Lambda Upsilon; Professional Resources in Cancer; American Men of Science; Listee, Who's Who in the South and Southwest; Listee, Who's Who in the Frontiers of Science and Technology; Inductee, Freemasonry **MEM:** Founder, Chair, Section of Medicinal Chemistry (1987); American Association of Pharmaceutical Scientists (1987); Academy of Pharmaceutical Sciences (1980-1986); Secretary, Vice President, Chair, Section of Medicinal Chemistry; American Foundation for Pharmaceutical Education; Chair, American Association of Colleges of Pharmacy; Chair, Section of Teachers of Chemistry; American Chemical Society; Order of the Eastern Star **MH:** Albert Nelson Marquis Lifetime Achievement Award; Marquis Who's Who Top Professional **AS:** Dr. Cates attributes his success to his thesis director, Dr. Tony Jones and his father, Lindley Sr. Dr. Jones encouraged him to excel; he set an excellent example, not only in the laboratory but as a person. His father set many examples for him as well by encouraging and financing the pursuit of a college education, his interest in scientific subjects and his protestant work ethic. **B/I:** Dr. Cates became involved in his profession when he received a chemistry set as a child. He was always curious about the content and makeup of things. Growing up, he was an only child with no father figure for the formative years of 6 to 12 years of age, so he spent much of his free time alone. Although barely living above the poverty line during the Great Depression, he still would often use what little money he had to send for scientific materials, such as a metal cup for measuring dew points. While living with his mother, he was constantly moving, so he attended eight different elementary schools, a situation that was not conducive to proper social development. He was then inspired a bit later by his high school chemistry teacher during a demonstration of explosive properties featuring sodium metal and water. His doctorate advisor, Dr. Jones, was a consultant for a pharmaceutical company, which allowed Dr. Cates an opportunity to learn firsthand that additional productive work was available in the industrial world. He considered Dr. Jones a role model as well as respecting a marvelous individual from Texas. Dr. Cates also consulted for one pharmaceutical company (Comatic Laboratories of Houston, TX) and worked some 20 years as a 25% owner of Great Southern Lab while at the University of Houston. Finally, his father set many examples he endeavored to emulate. He attended only one semester of college, leaving due to financial restraints, but as a self-educated man, he had few peers with as high an intellect. He had an interest in many scientific subjects, but he mostly concentrated on electronics. He worked on one of the first television sets in the country and built education electronic kits for a mail order company to have sent out to aspiring trainees in this field. At the same time, he taught mathematics for a few night classes at a junior college while doing repair work on televisions and radios. So, following this example, Dr. Cates acquired a protestant work ethic which remained with him all his life. He recalls one of his father's projects on which he was constantly working was an attempt to convert torque into thrust. He also invented a hand device to trace electrical circuits in electronic apparatuses. **AV:** Traveling; Bicycling; Swimming **PA:** Republican **RE:** Methodist **THT:** Dr. Cates obtained a Junior College Teaching Certificate, which required a sufficient amount of education courses for which to qualify. His purpose in doing so was to improve his teaching abilities in classrooms. He takes pride in his ability to teach as well as conduct research. While stationed in Guam, Dr. Cates would hitch rides to Japan, Thailand and

India. An avid traveler and biker, he would participate in frequent excursions with his wife and family. This includes visits to Italy, Greece, France, Austria, England, Wales, Scotland, Switzerland, Scandinavia, Ireland and Iceland. He has also visited and biked in the Caribbean Islands, South American countries, Hawaii, Tahiti, Bora Bora, and all of the United States except West Virginia and North Dakota. Dr. Cates was inducted into Freemasonry over 60 years ago as a graduate student. His induction occurred in Littleton, CO, at Weston Lodge No. 22. After moving to Houston, acclimating with a new job in a new city, and raising a family, Dr. Cates didn't have a chance to get reactivated with the organization. However, masonic ideals are still very important to him. The same applies to another of his previous organizations, the Order of DeMolay, a excellent group for teenage boys which often leads into Freemasonry. Boy scouting was also important to him and, although he did not obtain a high rank like his son did with an Eagle Scout award, he profited from the activities and camaraderie. Of course, some opportunities fall through the cracks. One such past negligent event occurred regarding the awarding of emeritus status as a professor. When he retired, a new administration was taking over the college with many other things on its mind and he also was busy working at Great Southern Laboratories, Inc., of which he was a 25% owner. He spent many part-time hours over 20 years with this organization and then for less time involved, or two years prior to moving to the Woodlands, TX. So it also wasn't on his mind to make reference to the oversight but, in any case, he had, and still has, no great interest in the subject. Dr. Cates' 38.5 years tenure and lengthy sponsored research activities at UH more than warrants being qualified for this award. A few years after he moved 40 miles out of the city, he was not present on a regular basis at GSL, which was mismanaged so badly they were forced to sell it. Over twenty years of hard work went for almost naught and he felt worse about the more than 50 employees that had lose their jobs. Dr. Cates' motto is, "Deo Fidens Proficio," (go forward trusting in God).

CATTELAN, MAURIZIO, T: Artist **I:** Fine Art **DOB:** 11/21/1960 **PB:** Padua **SC:** Italy **ED:** Honorary Degree in Sociology, University of Trento, Italy **C:** Co-curator, Fourth Berlin Biennale, Germany (2006); Co-founder, The Wrong Gallery, New York, NY (2002); Co-curator, Caribbean Biennial (1999); Designer, Producing, Wooden Furniture **CW:** Artist, Solo Exhibit, Hôtel des Monnaies, Paris (2017); Artist, "America" (2017); Featured, Documentary, "The Art World's Prankster: Maurizio Cattelan," BBC (2016); Artist, Solo Exhibit, "Not Afraid of Love," Monnaie de Paris (2016); Artist, Solo Exhibit, "All," Solomon R. Guggenheim Museum (2011); Artist, "Turisti," Venice Biennale (2011); Featured, "60 Minutes" (2011); Artist, "L.O.V.E." (2011); Artist, "Daddy, Daddy" (2008); Co-author, "Of Mice and Men" (2006); Artist, Solo Exhibit, "Untitled," The Nicola Trussardi Foundation (2004); Artist, Solo Exhibit, Museum Ludwig, Cologne, Germany (2003); Artist, Solo Exhibit, Museum of Contemporary Art, Los Angeles, CA (2003); Co-author, Sixth Caribbean Biennal (2001); Artist, "Him" (2001); Artist, Solo Exhibit, Migros Museum für Gegenwartskunst, Zurich, Switerzerland (2000); Artist, Solo Exhibit, Project 65 at the Museum of Modern Art, New York, NY (1999); Artist, Solo Exhibit, The Kunsthalle Basel, Basel, Switzerland (1999); Artist, Solo Exhibit, Skulptur Projekte Münster (1997); Artist, Solo Exhibit, Wiener Secession, Vienna, Austria (1997); Artist, Solo Exhibit, Castello di Rivoli, Turin, Itlay (1997); Artist, "Working is a Bad Job" (1993); Artist, Solo Exhibit, Le Consortium, Dijon, France; Artist, Solo Exhibit, Centre Georges Pompidou, Paris, France; Co-editor, Charley Magazine; Contributor, Articles, Professional Journals **AW:** Gold Medal, 15th Rome Quadriennale (2009); Arnold Bode Prize, Kunstverein Kassel, Germany (2004)

CELL, EDWARD CHARLES, T: Philosophy Educator **I:** Education/Educational Services **DOB:** 10/05/1928 **PB:** Elizabeth **SC:** NJ/USA **PT:** Samuel Wesley Cell; Clara Matilda (Magnuson) Cell **MS:** Widowed **SPN:** Marjorie Louise Braswell (01/15/1981); Mary Evelyn Cashman (12/03/1955, Divorced 06/1975) **CH:** Kathryn Mendez; Robin Hart; Terryn Dwyer; Kristin Cell **ED:** PhD in Philosophy of Religion, Princeton University (1964); MA in Philosophy of Religion, Princeton University (1959); BD in Philosophy of Religion, Andover Newton Theological School, Newton Center, MA (1956); BA in Philosophy, Boston University (1954) **C:** Chairman, Professor, Department of Philosophy, University of Illinois, Springfield, IL (1975-1999); Chairman, Division of Comparative World Studies, U.S. International University, San Diego, CA (1971-1975); Program Officer, National Endowment for the Humanities, Washington, DC (1967-1970); Professor of Philosophy, Albion College, MI (1963-1967); Associate Professor of Philosophy and Religion, Simpson College, Indianola, Iowa (1959-1965) **CR:** Member, Executive Committee, Faculty Union, University of Illinois, Springfield (1984-1988) **CIV:** Member, Habitat, Springfield, IL (1989-Present); Volunteer, San Diego Hospice, CA (2001-2017); Board of Directors, Sangamon-Menard Alcoholism and Drug Council, Springfield, IL (1976-1979) **CW:** Editor, "Organizational Life, Learning to be Self-Directed" (1997);Editor, "Bringing Life to Completion" (2012) **AW:** Albion Fellow, Albion College (1969); Danforth Associate, Danforth Foundation (1963-1965); Chair, Humanities Council, The Great Lakes Colleges Association (1960); University Fellow, Princeton University (1957-1959); Danforth Fellow, Danforth Foundation (1958); Andover Fellow, Andover Newton Theological School (1955) **MEM:** Executive Committee, Springfield Chapter, American Civil Liberties Union (1976-1979); American Civil Liberties Union; Chair, School of the Humanities, U.S. International University **B/I:** Dr. Cell became involved in his profession because it was always something he wanted to do from an early age which led to him pursuing higher academia as a professor of philosophy and a scholar. **PA:** Democrat **RE:** Christian

CERERE, ANDREW, T: Chief Executive Officer, Vice Chairperson **I:** Financial Services **CN:** U.S. Bancorp **ED:** Bachelor of Arts, University of Saint Thomas; Master of Business Administration in Finance, University of Minnesota **C:** Chief Executive Officer, U.S. Bancorp (2017-Present); Vice Chairperson, U.S. Bank (2015-Present); Independent Director, Donaldson Company (2013-Present)

CERVERIS, MICHAEL, T: Actor **I:** Media & Entertainment **DOB:** 11/06/1960 **PB:** Bethesda **SC:** MD/USA **PT:** Michael Cerveris; Marsha (Laycock) Cerveris **ED:** Diploma in Theater Studies, Yale University, Cum Laude (1983); Diploma, Phillips Exeter Academy (1979) **CR:** Founder, Loose Cattle (2011); Solo Artist (2004); Guitarist, Bob Mould's Touring Band (2002) **CW:** Actor, "The Plot Against America" (2020); Actor, "Prodigal Son" (2019); Actor, "Mindhunter" (2019); Actor, "Elementary" (2018); Actor, "Mosaic" (2018); Actor, "Ant-Man and the Wasp" (2018); Actor, "The Tick" (2017); Actor, "Gotham" (2017); Musician, "Piety" (2016); Actor, "Detours" (2016); Actor, Broadway, "Fun Home" (2015-2016); Actor, "The Good Wife" (2013, 2014-2015); Actor, "Leaving Circadia" (2014); Actor, Off-Broadway, "Fun Home" (2013); Actor, "Nikolai and the Others" (2013); Actor, "Evita" (2011-2013); Actor, "Fringe" (2008-2013); Actor, "Treme" (2011-2012); Actor, "Meskada" (2010); Actor, "Stake Land" (2010); Actor, "Cirque du Freak: The Vampire's Assistant" (2009); Actor, "Road Show" (2008); Actor, "Brief Interviews with Hideous Men" (2007); Actor, "King Lear" (2007); Actor, "Lovemusik" (2007); Actor, "Sweeney Todd" (2005-2006); Actor, "The Apple Tree" (2005); Actor, "Children and Art" (2005); Actor, "Passion" (2004); Actor, "Assassins" (2004); Actor, "The Temptation" (2004); Solo Artist, "Dog Eared" (2004); Actor, "Fifth of July" (2003); Actor, "The Mexican" (2001); Actor, "Hedwig and the Angry Inch" (2000); Actor, "Titanic" (1997-1999); Actor, "Lulu on the Bridge" (1998); Actor, "The Who's Tommy" (1993-1995); Actor, "A Woman, Her Men, and Her Futon" (1992); Actor, "Steel and Lace" (1991); Actor, "Rock 'n' Roll High School Forever" (1990); Actor, "Tokyo Pop" (1988); Actor, "Fame" (1986); Actor, "Blood Sports" (1986); Actor, "Abingdon Square" (1986); Actor, "Green Fields" (1985); Actor, "Total Eclipse" (1985); Actor, "Life is a Dream" (1984); Actor, "The Games" (1984); Actor, "MacBeth" (1983); Actor, Plays, Television Shows and Films; Musician, Albums **AW:** Tony Award for Best Performance by an Actor in a Leading Role in a Musical (2015); Award for Outstanding Actor in a Musical, Outer Critics Circle Awards (2014); Tony Award for Best Featured Actor in a Musical (2004); Award for Outstanding Featured Actor in a Musical, Outer Critics Circle Awards (2004); Theatre World Award (1993)

CÉSPEDES, YOENIS, T: Professional Baseball Player **I:** Athletics **CN:** New York Mets **DOB:** 10/18/1985 **PB:** Campechuela, Granma Province **SC:** Cuba **PT:** Cresencio Céspedes; Estela (Milanés) Céspedes **CH:** Yoenis Jr. **C:** Outfielder, New York Mets, MLB (2015-Present); With, Detroit Tigers (2015); With, Boston Red Sox (2014); With, Oakland Athletics (2012-2014) **AW:** Silver Slugger Award at Outfield (2016); Two-Time MLB All-Star (2014, 2016); Rawlings Gold Glove Award at Left Field (2015); National League Champion (2015); Two-Time MLB Player of the Week (2012, 2015); Two-Time Home Run Derby Champion (2013, 2014); Rookie of the Month, American League (2012); Gold Medal, Cuba National Team, International Cup (2010); Gold Medal, Cuba National Team, World University (2010); All-World Baseball Classic Team (2009); Gold Medal, Cuba National Team, Pan Am Games (2007)

CHA, SE DO, MD, FACP, FSCAI, T: Invasive and Interventional Cardiologist **I:** Medicine & Health Care **CN:** Deborah Heart and Lung Center **DOB:** 12/17/1942 **PB:** Seoul **SC:** Republic of Korea **PT:** Young Sun Cha; Hee Joo (Chang) Cha **MS:** Married **SPN:** Elsa Jane Greene (12/21/1974) **CH:** Elizabeth Anne **ED:** Chief Medical Resident, Roger William General Hospital, Providence, RI (1971-1972); Resident in Medicine, Harrisburg Hospital (1967-1970); Intern, Presbyterian University, Pennsylvania Medical Center (1966-1967); MD, Yonsei University (1966) **CT:** Diplomate, American Board of Internal Medicine **C:** Retired (2009-Present); Cardiologist, Deborah Heart and Lung Center, Browns Mills, NJ (1975-2009); Director of Adult Cardiac Catheterization Laboratory, Deborah Heart and Lung Center, Browns Mills, NJ (1975-2003); Cardiologist, Roger Williams General Hospital, Providence, RI (1973-1975); Fellow in Cardiology, Deborah Heart and Lung Center, Browns Mills, NJ (1971-1973); Chief Resident in Medicine, Roger Williams General Hospital, Providence, RI (1970-1971) **CR:** Clinical Assistant Professor, UMDNJ (1980-1990); Instructor, Brown University (1973-1975); Fellow, American College of Physicians; Fellow,

Society for Cardiovascular Angiography and Interventions **CW:** Contributor, Numerous Medical Articles, Professional Journals; Presenter in Field **AW:** Albert Nelson Marquis Lifetime Achievement Award **MEM:** American Medical Association; Federation of Clinical Research; American Heart Association **AS:** Dr. Cha studied and worked hard. **B/I:** Dr. Cha liked to cure diseases for people and help them to a healthier life. **AV:** Fishing; Hunting; Photography; Reading books **RE:** Presbyterian

CHALIF, RONNIE, T: 1) Co-Founder 2) Artist **I:** Medicine & Health Care **CN:** 1) Neuropathy Association **DOB:** 04/14/1933 **PB:** New York **SC:** NY/USA **MS:** Married **SPN:** Seymour Chalif (06/13/1954) **CH:** John Lewis; Peter Adley; Four Stepchildren **ED:** BS in Art Education, New York University (1954); Diploma, Parsons School of Design, with Honors (1953) **C:** Honorary President, Neuropathy Association (2009-Present); Artist, Sculptor, Painter (1968-Present); President, Neuropathy Association (2005-2009); Co-Founder, Director, Honorary President, Neuropathy Association (1995-2009); Buyer, I. Magnin & Co. (1954-1959) **CW:** Exhibitor, Group Show, Southampton Cultural Center, NY (2012-2013); Exhibitor, Group Show, Ashawagh Hall, East Hampton, NY (1987-2008); Exhibitor, Group Show, Arlene Bujese Gallery (1995-2006); Solo Exhibitor, Arlene Bujese Gallery (2006); Solo Exhibitor, Gayle Willson Gallery (2003); Exhibitor, Group Show, Benson Gallery (2000-2002); Author, Illustrator, "Exercising with Neuropathy" (2001); Exhibitor, Group Show, Atelier 14, NY (2000); Solo Exhibitor, Gayle Willson Gallery (2000); Solo Exhibitor, Arlene Bujese Gallery (1996); Exhibitor, Group Show, Guild Hall Museum (1992-1993); Solo Exhibitor, Garrison Arts Center, NY (1989); Solo Exhibitor, Benton Gallery, Southampton, NY (1989); Solo Exhibitor, Marymount Manhattan College Gallery (1986); Solo Exhibitor, Jacob K. Javits Federal Building (1986); Solo Exhibitor, Federal Court House, NY (1984-1985); Exhibitor, Group Show, GE Co., Fairfield, CT (1983); Solo Exhibitor, Benson Gallery, Bridghampton, NY (1975); Solo Exhibitor, Benson Gallery, Bridghampton, NY (1972); Solo Exhibitor, Guild Hall Museum, East Hampton, NY; Exhibitor, Permanent Collection, Guild Hall Museum; Exhibitor, Permanent Collection, Continental Telephone Co., Washington, DC; Exhibitor, Permanent Collection, McGraw-Hill, Inc. (Now McGraw-Hill Education); Exhibitor, Permanent Collection, Cadillac-Fairview (Now The Cadillac Fairview Corporation Limited), Dallas, Texas; Exhibitor, Permanent Collection, GE International Headquarters; Exhibitor, Permanent Collection, Grey Advertising Inc. (Grey Group); Exhibitor, Permanent Collection, United States Home Corporation, Houston, Texas; Exhibitor, Permanent Collection, Zimmerli Art Museum, New Brunswick, NJ; Exhibitor, Permanent Collection, World Trade Center; Exhibitor, Permanent Collection, Sculpture Garden of the Gus & Judith Leiber Museum, East Hampton, NY **MEM:** Women's Caucus for Art; Women in the Arts Foundation; National Association of Women Artists; New York Society of Women Artists **MH:** Albert Nelson Marquis Lifetime Achievement Award; Marquis Who's Who Top Professional

CHAMBERLAIN, STEVEN CRAIG, PHD, T: Mineralogist, Neuroanatomist, Bioengineer **I:** Engineering **DOB:** 12/13/1946 **PB:** Everett **SC:** PA/USA **PT:** Carl Eugene Chamberlain; D. Suzanne (Rearick) Chamberlain **MS:** Married **SPN:** Helen Haritou Chamberlin (04/29/1972) **ED:** PhD, Syracuse University (1978); BSEE, Massachusetts Institute of Technology (1968) **C:** Retired; Coordinator, New York State Museum Center Mineralogy (2001-Present); Consultant Editor, Rocks and Minerals, Wash-

ington (1980-Present); Chairman, Department of Bio-engineering, Neuroscience, Institute of Sensory Research, Syracuse University (1998-2001); Dean, College of Engineering, Institute of Sensory Research, Syracuse University (1992-1995); Professor, Institute of Sensory Research, Syracuse University (1988-2006); Chairman, Department of Bio-engineering, Institute of Sensory Research, Syracuse University (1986-1992); Associate Director, Institute of Sensory Research, Syracuse University (1985-1986); American Editor, Jour Russell Society (1984-1994); Associate Professor, Institute of Sensory Research, Syracuse University (1982-1988); Curator, Minerals, Hamilton College, Clinton, NY (1981-2002); Assistant Professor, Institute of Sensory Research, Syracuse University (1978-1982); Instructor, Institute of Sensory Research, Syracuse University (1977-1978); Electrical Engineer, United States Army, CDAASG-EUR, Augsburg, Germany (1970-1973) **CR:** Scientific Editor, The Hosta Journal (2000-Present); Consultant, Editor, Visual Neuroscience (1991-1993); Chairman, Rochester Mineralogical Symposium (1986-2018) **CIV:** Parks Commission, Village of Manlius, NY (2003-2011); Editorial Board, Visual Neuroscience (1991-1993); Advisory Panel Member, National Science Foundation, Sensory Physiology and Perception; Chairman, Bioengineering, Neuroanatomist **MIL:** United States Army (1970-1973) **CW:** Scientific Editor, Hosta Journal (2000-Present); Contributor, Articles, Professional Journals; Co-Author, Three Mineralogy Books **AW:** Faculty Research Award, Sigma Xi (1993); Best Paper Award, Friends Mineralogy (1984); President Award, Eastern Federal Mineral Lapidary Society (1978); Grass Foundation Fellow (1977); Meritorious Service Medal; Army Commendation Medal **MEM:** Fellow, Rochester Academy of Science; Association of Research Vision and Ophthalmology; Tau Beta Pi; Sigma Xi **MH:** Albert Nelson Marquis Lifetime Achievement Award; Marquis Who's Who Top Professional **AS:** Dr. Chamberlain has from the time he got out of the Army he was drafted, from 1972 on he's woke up every morning excited about getting on with the day and a lot of people don't get that in their career he thinks he's been successful by that measure, he doesn't take himself very seriously his work very seriously and he enjoys it. **B/I:** Dr. Chamberlain started collecting minerals at age 11. He started working on a PhD at Syracuse University in 1968. The same year, he was granted a 7-year NASA doctoral fellowship. He finished two years of it before the draft board of Pennsylvania called him to serve during the Vietnam War. He was in the Army for three years, and when he was discharged, he returned to pursing his doctorate. **AV:** Photography; Opera; Collecting minerals and hostas

CHAN, JACKIE, T: Actor; Martial Artist **I:** Media & Entertainment **DOB:** Apr 7 1954 12:00AM **SC:** Hong Kong **PT:** Chi-Ping "Charles" Chan; Lee-Lee Chan **MS:** Married **SPN:** Lin Fong Chiao (12/01/1982) **CH:** Jaycee **ED:** Honorary PhD, University of Cambodia (2009); Honorary Doctorate in Social Science, Hong Kong Baptist University (1996); Trained, Peking Opera School **C:** Dean, Jackie Chan Film and Television Academy (2015-Present); Owner/ Co-owner, Jackie and Willie Productions (Now JCE Movies Limited) (2004-Present); Owner, Founder, Film Company, JCE Movies Ltd. (2004-Present); Owner/Co-owner, Jackie & JJ Productions; Owner/ Co-owner, JC Group China **CIV:** Founder, Dragon's Heart Foundation (2005); Goodwill Ambassador, UNICEF (2004); Founder, Jackie Chan Charitable Foundation (1988) **CW:** Actor, "Vanguard" (2020); Actor, "The Climbers" (2019); Actor, "The Knights of Shadows: Walker Between Halfworlds" (2019); Actor, "Viy 2" (2018); Actor, "Kung Fu Yoga" (2017);

Actor, "The Nut Job 2: Nutty by Nature" (2017); Actor, "The Lego Ninjago Movie" (2017); Actor, "The Foreigner" (2017); Actor, "Bleeding Steel" (2017); Actor, "Namiya" (2017); Voice Actor, "Kung Fu Panda 3" (2016); Actor, "The Master: A Lego Ninjago Short" (2016); Actor, "Railroad Tigers" (2016); Actor, Executive Producer, "Skiptrace" (2016); Actor, Executive Producer, "Dragon Blade" (2015); Producer, "Gambling on Extinction" (2015); Actor, "As the Light Goes Out" (2014); Actor, "Personal Tailor" (2013); Actor, "Police Story: Lockdown" (2013); Actor, Director, Executive Producer, Writer, "Chinese Zodiac" (2012); Voice Actor, "Kung Fu Panda 2" (2011); Actor, "Shaolin" (2011); Actor, "1911" (2011); Producer, "Legendary Amazons" (2011); Actor, "The Spy Next Door" (2010); Actor, "The Karate Kid" (2010); Actor, "The Legend of Silk Boy" (2010); Actor, "Looking for Jackie" (2009); Actor, Executive Producer, "The Shinjuku Incident" (2009); Actor, "The Forbidden Kingdom" (2008); Voice Actor, "Kung Fu Panda" (2008); Actor, "Rush Hour 3" (2007); Actor, "San Wa" (2005); Actor, "Around the World in 80 Days" (2004); Actor, "Fa Dou Daai Jin" (2004); Actor, "San Gin Chaat Goo Si" (2004); Actor, "Shanghai Knights" (2003); Actor, "Vampire Effect" (2003); Actor, "The Medallion" (2003); Actor, "The Tuxedo" (2002); Actor, "Rush Hour 2" (2001); Actor, Producer, "The Accidental Spy" (2001); Actor, "Shanghai Noon" (2000); Actor, Producer, Writer, "Gorgeous" (1999); Actor, "The King of Comedy" (1999); Actor, "Gen-X Cops" (1999); Actor, "Rush Hour" (1998); Actor, "Who Am I?" (1998); Actor, "Mr. Nice Guy" (1997); Actor, "Police Story IV: First Strike" (1996); Actor, Executive Producer, "Thunderbolt" (1995); Actor, "Drunken Master II" (1994); Actor, "Rumble in the Bronx" (1994); Actor, "City Hunter" (1993); Actor, "Crime Story" (1993); Actor, "Twin Dragons" (1992); Actor, Executive Producer, "Police Story 3: Supercop" (1992); Producer, "Center Stage" (1991); Actor, "Amour of God II: Operation Condor" (1991); Actor, "Island of Fire" (1991); Actor, "Mr. Canton and Lady Rose" (1989); Actor, "Armour of God" (1987); Actor, "Project A Part 2" (1987); Actor, "Dragons Forever" (1987); Actor, "Police Story II" (1987); Actor, Director, Executive Producer, Writer, "Police Story" (1985); Actor, "My Lucky Stars" (1985); Actor, "The Protector" (1985); Actor, "Twinkle Twinkle Lucky Stars" (1985); Actor, "Heart of the Dragon" (1985); Actor, "The Fearless Hyena Part 2" (1984); Actor, "Cannonball Run II" (1984); Actor, "Wheels on Meals" (1984); Actor, "Winners and Sinners" (1983); Actor, Director, Writer, "Project A" (1983); Actor, Director, Writer, "Dragon Strike" (1982); Actor, "Marvelous Fists" (1982); Actor, "The Cannonball Run" (1981); Actor, "The Young Master" (1980); Actor, "Half a Loaf of King Fu" (1980); Actor, "Battle Creek Brawl" (1980); Actor, Director, Executive Producer, Writer, "The Fearless Hyena" (1979); Actor, "Dragon Fist" (1979); Actor, "Snake in the Eagle's Shadow" (1978); Actor, "Snake and Crane Arts of Shaolin" (1978); Actor, "Magnificent Bodyguards" (1978); Actor, "Drunken Master" (1978); Actor, "Spiritual Kung Fu" (1978); Actor, "To Kill with Intrigue" (1977); Actor, "New Fist of Fury" (1976); Actor, "Shaolin Wooden Men" (1976); Actor, "Little Tiger of Guangdong" (1975); Actor, "Little Tiger from Canton" (1975); Actor, "Hand of Death" (1975); Actor, Numerous Films; Featured, Documentaries **AW:** Albert R. Broccoli Britannia Award, Britannia Awards (2019); Academy Honorary Award for Extraordinary Achievements in Film, Academy of Motion Picture Arts and Sciences (2016); Hong Kong Film Awards for Best Action Choreography (1990, 1996, 1999, 2005, 2013); Named Favorite Action Star, People's Choice Awards (2011); Taurus Honorable Award, Outstanding Achievement for Acting in Action Films, World Stunt Awards (2002); Innovator Award,

American Choreography Awards (2002); Recipient, Star, Hollywood Walk of Fame (2002); International Lifetime Achievement Award, International Leadership Foundation (2000); PETA Humanitarian Award (1999); Lifetime Achievement Award, MTV Movie Awards (1995); Numerous Awards

CHAN, WENDY, T: Lawyer **I:** Law and Legal Services **CN:** Chan & Associates **DOB:** 07/26/1975 **SC:** Taiwan **MS:** Married **SPN:** Joseph **CH:** Catherine; Joseph **ED:** JD, Brooklyn Law School, Brooklyn, NY (2001); BA, Pace University, NY, Cum Laude (1998) **C:** Adjunct Professor, Paralegal Studies Courses such as Legal Research & Writing and Ethics, Harrisburg Area Community College **CIV:** Member, Women's Republican Club of Lancaster County; Volunteer, Sacred Heart of Jesus School, Lancaster, PA; Volunteer, Pennsylvania Immigration Resource Center (PIRC); Volunteer, Wills for Heroes; Volunteer, MidPenn Legal Services; Volunteer, American Legal Defense; Volunteer, Education Fund; Volunteer, YMCA; Volunteer, Local Church; Volunteer, Catholic School **AW:** Named People's Favorite Lawyer Firm, Lancaster Newspaper **MEM:** Lancaster Bar Association; Pennsylvania Bar Association; American Immigration Lawyers Association **BAR:** Pennsylvania (2008) **AS:** Mrs. Chan attributes her success to her willingness to make mistakes. **B/I:** Mrs. Chan's first career was in human resources in state government in Harrisburg. She did not have the interest in law at first. She didn't take the bar until 2008. She was in between jobs and she went to a commissioner's office public meeting. There she heard dads talking about how they lost contact with their children after being abused; they ran out of money because they needed to find a place to live and they couldn't get their things. They also they needed to get an attorney for child support and divorce. So many things pile up. They were pleading to the commissioners that the system was broken because by the time someone heard that they were innocent, it was three months later. She went up to these men at the meeting and told them that she just recently passed the bar and that she doesn't know much but she wanted to help and that's truly how she got started. **THT:** Mrs. Chan only takes on cases when they are in the best interest in the children.

CHANG, CHIA-HWA LYDIA CHU, T: Artist **I:** Fine Art **PB:** Shanghai **SC:** China **SPN:** M.H. Chang **CH:** Victor Chang; Mona Chang **ED:** BS in Economics, Utopia University, Shanghai, China **C:** Lecturer, Chinese Calligraphy, Hunter College, New York, NY; Lecturer, Painting, Continuing Education Program, Columbia University, New York, NY; Tutor, Chinese Calligraphy, Columbia University, New York, NY; Instructor, Chinese Language, United Nations International School's After School Program, New York, NY; Instructor, Chinese Classical Literature, United Nations, New York, NY; **CR:** Invited Lecturer, China Institute, New York, NY; Invited Lecturer, Asia Society, New York, NY; Invited Lecturer, Metropolitan Museum of Art, New York, NY; Invited Lecturer, Massachusetts Institute of Technology, Cambridge, MA; Invited Lecturer, United Nations; Invited Lecturer, Long Island University, Brookville, NY; Invited Lecturer, Riverside Church, New York, NY **CW:** Featured Artist, Greeting Card, "Golden Fish," UNICEF International Art Committee, United States National Committee; Artist, "New Year's Offering," "Gold Fish," "Spring," UNICEF International Art Committee; Artist, "Hermitage in Autumn"; Exhibiting Artist, Annual Art Exhibitions of the United Nations; Exhibiting Artist, United States People for the United Nations Gallery; Exhibiting Artist, Community Art Gallery; Exhibiting Artist, Aspen Institute for Humanist

Studies; Exhibiting Artist, Fairfield University; Exhibiting Artist, School of Chinese Brushwork; Exhibiting Artist, Wustum Museum of Fine Arts; Exhibiting Artist, Riverside Church Arts Gallery; Exhibiting Artist, RAA Art Gallery; Exhibiting Artist, Hunter Arts Gallery; Exhibiting Artist, Ziegfeld Gallery; Exhibiting Artist, Massachusetts Institute of Technology; Exhibiting Artist, Columbia University; Featured Artist, Cover of United Nations Secretariat News **MH:** Albert Nelson Marquis Lifetime Achievement Award (2017) **AS:** Ms. Chang attributes her success to her study of Chinese painting and calligraphy under leading artists Xu Bang-Da, Chi Shao-Chen, and Chang Da-Chien. **THT:** Ms. Chang specialized in landscape painting and drew inspiration from paintings in the Ming and Ching dynasties. Her paintings showed clarity of perception, exquisite colors, meticulous brushwork and majesty in design and composition. In 1973, Henry S. Evans, National Director for United States People for the United Nations, wrote to Ms. Chang that he was impressed with her painting "Hermitage in Autumn," saying "It is a rare example of artistic originality within the traditional Chinese landscape technique."

CHANG, EMILY, T: Journalist **I:** Writing and Editing **CN:** Bloomberg Technology **DOB:** 08/11/1980 **PB:** Kailua, Honolulu County **SC:** HI/USA **PT:** Laban Lee Bun Chang; Sandra Galeone Chang **MS:** Married **SPN:** Jonathan DeWees Stull (2010) **CH:** Four Children **CW:** Author, "Brotopia: Breaking Up the Boys' Club of Silicon Valley" (2018); Appearance, "Morning Joe" (2018); Anchor, "Bloomberg Technology" (2016); Anchor, "Bloomberg West," San Francisco, CA (2011-2016); With, Bloomberg Television (2010); International Correspondent, Cable News Network (CNN), Beijing, China and London, United Kingdom (2007-2010); Reporter, KNSD; News Producer, NBC, NY; Host, "Studio 1.0"; Appearance, "Silicon Valley"; Appearance, "Good Morning America," "This Morning" and "Marketplace"; Contributor, Articles to Professional Journals **AW:** Salesforce Equality Award (2018); Named One of the Top 50 Journalists Followed by CEOs on Twitter, Rational360 Influencer Index (2018); Named One of the 100 Most Influential Tech People on Twitter, The Business Insider (2014); Five Emmy Awards, Television Academy

CHANG, JIN SOOK, T: Co-founder, Chief Merchandising Officer **I:** Apparel & Fashion **CN:** Forever 21 Inc. **MS:** Married **SPN:** Do Won Chang **CH:** Linda; Esther **C:** Co-founder, Chief Merchandising Officer, Forever 21 Inc., Los Angeles, CA (1984) **AW:** Named to America's Self-made Women List, Forbes Magazine (2019); Named One of the 100 Most Powerful Women, Forbes Magazine (2011)

CHANG, MONA MEI-HSUAN, I: Medicine & Health Care **PB:** New York **SC:** NY/USA **PT:** Meng-Hsiu Chang; Chia-Hwa (Lydia) Chu Chang **ED:** MPhil in Medical Informatics, Columbia University (1999); MA in Medical Informatics, Columbia University (1997); BA in Computer Science and Biochemistry, Columbia University (1985) **C:** Research Data Coordinator, Memorial Sloan-Kettering Cancer Center, New York, NY (2002-2006); Trainee in Medical Informatics, National Library of Medicine, Columbia University, New York, NY (1999-2001); Computer Programmer Analyst, New York Hospital, Cornell University Medical Center, New York, NY (1992-1996); Data Manager, New York Hospital, Cornell University Medical Center, New York, NY (1990-1992) **MEM:** Chairman, Computer Committee for Data Managers, Cancer and Leukemia Group B (1990-1992); Iota Sigma Pi **MH:** Albert Nelson Marquis Lifetime Achievement Award (2017) **B/I:** Ms. Chang was inspired to join

her profession when she read about the INTERNIST program by Drs. Jack Meyers and Harry Pople that combined computer programming and medical diagnosis. In college, she majored in both biochemistry and computer science. **AV:** Chinese butterfly harp; Chinese watercolor painting

CHANG, WILLIAM, PHD, T: Research Scientist **I:** Sciences **DOB:** 06/06/1955 **PB:** Shanghai **SC:** China **PT:** Yinfang Chang; Shanlin Chen Chang **MS:** Married **SPN:** Sandra Schlachter (08/1987) **CH:** Caroline Dagmar **ED:** PhD, University of Southern California (1992); MS, University of Southern California (1985); BS, University of Southern California (1984) **C:** Senior Scientist, Rapiscan Systems Inc., Fremont, CA (1996-Present); Research Scientist, Max Planck Society X-Ray Optics Group, Friedrich-Schiller University, Jena, Germany (1993-1996); Research Associate, University of Southern California (1992-1993) **CW:** Contributor, Articles, Professional Journals; Contributor, Chapters, Books **AW:** Distinguished Scholar, Microbeam Analysis Society, San Jose, CA (1991) **MH:** Albert Nelson Marquis Lifetime Achievement Award **AV:** Watching opera; Practicing calligraphy

CHAO, ELAINE LAN, T: United States Secretary of Transportation **I:** Government Administration/ Government Relations/Government Services **DOB:** 03/26/1953 **PB:** Taipei **SC:** Taiwan **PT:** James S. C. Chao; Ruth Mulan L. (Chu) Chao **MS:** Married **SPN:** Mitch McConnell (1993) **ED:** Honorary LittD, Shanghai Jiao Tong University (2012); Honorary LittD, St. Catharine College (2011); Honorary Doctor in Public Service, Western Kentucky University (2011); Honorary LittD, Nyack College and Alliance Theological Seminary (2008); Honorary DHL, Murray State University (2008); Honorary Doctor in Public Service, Sweet Briar College (2007); Honorary LLD, Marquette University (2006); Honorary LLD, Elmira College (2006); Honorary LLD, Agnes Scott College (2006); Honorary Doctor in Public Administration, Northern Kentucky University (2004); Honorary DHL, Wingate University (2004); Honorary LLD, Catholic University of America (2004); Honorary Doctor in Organizational Leadership, Regent University (2003); Honorary DHL, Centre College (2003); Honorary DHL, Northern Alabama University (2003); Honorary LLD, Fu Jen Catholic University (2003); Honorary Doctor in Public Service, DePauw University (2002); Honorary Doctor in Public Administration, Campbellsville University (2002); Honorary LLD, St. Mary's College (2002); Honorary Doctor in Arts and Letters, Miami-Dade College (2001); Honorary DHL, University of South Carolina (2001); Honorary HHD, Kentucky Wesleyan College (1998); Honorary LLD, University of Notre Dame (1998); Honorary DHL, University of Louisville (1996); Honorary DHL, Goucher College (1996); Honorary DHL, University of Toledo (1995); Honorary DHL, Bellarmine University (1995); Honorary HHD, Thomas More College (1994); Honorary HHD, Drexel University (1992); Honorary DHL, Niagara University (1992); Honorary LLD, Sacred Heart University (1991); Honorary LLD, St. John's University (1991); Honorary LLD, Villanova University (1989); MBA, Harvard Business School (1979); BA in Economics, Mount Holyoke College (1975) **C:** United States Secretary of Transportation, Washington, DC (2017-Present); United States Secretary of Labor, United States Department of Labor, Washington, DC (2001-2009); Deputy Secretary, United States Department of Transportation, Washington, DC (1989-1991); Chairman, Federal Maritime Commission, Washington, DC (1988); Deputy Maritime Administrator, United States Department of Transportation, Washington, DC (1986-1988); Vice President, Capital Markets Group, Bank of America Corporation, San Francisco, CA (1984-1986); Senior Lending Officer, Citicorp, New York, NY (1979-1983); Associate, Gulf Oil Corporation, Pittsburgh, PA (1978) **CR:** Board of Directors, News Corporation (2012-Present); Board of Directors, Protective Life Corporation (2011-Present); Board of Directors, Wells Fargo & Company (2011-Present); Distinguished Fellow, Heritage Foundation, Washington, DC (1996-2001, 2009-2017); Board of Directors, Dole Food Company, Inc. (2009-2013); Adjunct Assistant Professor, St. John's University Graduate School of Business Administration (Now The Peter J. Tobin College of Business), NY (1984); White House Fellow (1983-1984) **CIV:** President, United Way of America, Alexandria, VA (1992-1996); Director, Peace Corps (1991-1992); Board Member, The National World War II Museum; Board Member, Harvard Kennedy School, John F. Kennedy School of Government; Board Member, Ford's Theatre **AW:** Woodrow Wilson Award for Public Service (2011); Outstanding Alumni Award, Harvard Business School (1993); Young Achiever Award, National Council of Women of the United States, Inc. (1986); Fellow, Eisenhower Association (1984) **MEM:** Council on Foreign Relations; Harvard Club of New York **PA:** Republican **RE:** Southern Baptist

CHAPMAN, KENNETH MAYNARD, T: Science Education Consultant **I:** Education/Educational Services **CN:** Cardinal Workforce Developers, LLC **DOB:** 09/30/1938 **PB:** Corinth **SC:** KY/USA **PT:** Leonard N. Chapman; Rachel (Howard) Chapman **MS:** Married **SPN:** Virginia L. Robinson (06/04/1976); Patricia L. Gross Barnhill (07/15/1960, 1976) **CH:** Kenneth L.; Karen L. **ED:** MA in Adult Education, The George Washington University, Washington, DC (1969); BS in Chemical Engineering, Massachusetts Institute of Technology (1961); AAS in Chemical Technology, Ohio College of Applied Science (Now College of Engineering and Applied Science, University of Cincinnati), OH (1958) **CT:** Professional Engineer in Pennsylvania (1966, Elapsed 1973) **C:** Principal Partner, Cardinal Workforce Developers, LLC (2001-Present); Teacher, Science, The Carmel School, Ruther Glen, VA (2006-2017); President, CWD Informatics, Inc. (2002-2007); Consultant, College Chemistry Consultants Service, American Chemical Society (1999-2006); Head, Technology Resources and Education, American Chemical Society, Washington, DC (1993-1999); Special Assistant to Director, Education Division, American Chemical Society, Washington, DC (1990-1999); Head, Research and Development, Education Division, American Chemical Society, Washington, DC (1982-1990); Manager, Special Programs, American Chemical Society, Washington, DC (1973-1982); Vice President, Computer-Based Instructional Systems, San Antonio, TX (1972-1973); Associate Director, Chemical Technology Curriculum Project, American Chemical Society, Berkeley, CA (1969-1972); Assistant Secretary, Education for Two-Year Colleges, American Chemical Society, Washington, DC (1967-1969); Head, Chemical Engineering Technology, Temple University, Philadelphia, PA (1963-1967); Acting Head, Chemical Technology, Ohio College of Applied Sciences (Now College of Engineering and Applied Science, University of Cincinnati), Cincinnati, OH (1961-1963); Engineer, Williamstown Manufacturing Company, Williamstown, KY (1960-1963); Lab Technician, Chemist, The DuBois Chemical Company, Cincinnati, OH (1956-1959) **CIV:** President, Caroline County Agricultural Fair Board (2002-2007) **CW:** Creator, Website, Model STEM System (2018); Co-Author, "Foundations for Excellence in the Chemical Process Industries: Voluntary Industry Standards for Chemical Process Industries Technical Workers" (1997); Co-Author, Co-Editor,

"Gaining the Competitive Edge: Critical Issues in Science and Engineering Technician Education" (1993); Co-Author, "Chemical Technology Handbook: Guidebook for Industrial Chemical Technologists and Technicians" (1973); Co-Author, Co-Editor, "Modern Chemical Technology," (1970) **AW:** Alumni of the Year, Ohio College of Applied Science (Now College of Engineering and Applied Science, University of Cincinnati) (1995) **MEM:** Board of Directors, National Technical Honor Society (1998-2001); Board of Directors, Triangle Coalition for Science and Technology Education (1985-1999); Secretary, Vice-President, Triangle Coalition for Science and Technology Education (1990-1997) **MH:** Albert Nelson Marquis Lifetime Achievement Award **AS:** Mr. Chapman attributes his success to persistence and spending many extra hours to get the details right. **B/I:** Mr. Chapman became involved in his profession because a combination of a desire to expand markets for American agriculture through chemical applications and an interest in teaching that started in late elementary school led to his current activities on behalf of STEM education that continue in retirement. **PA:** Independent **RE:** Christian **THT:** Mr. Chapman said, "Technology is a servant to be used as fully as possible in service to humankind. Step back, and examine all aspects of a complex problem. Only then, create a reasonable path to achieve the real objective."

CHAPPELL, DOROTHY, PHD, T: Biologist, Cell Biologist; Educator, Dean of Natural and Social Sciences, Senior Scholar **I:** Education/Educational Services **CN:** Wheaton College **DOB:** 08/12/1947 **PB:** Farmville **SC:** VA/USA **PT:** William Cabot; Helen (Morris) Cabot **MS:** Single **ED:** PhD, Miami University, Ohio (1977); MS, The University of Virginia (1973); BS, Longwood College (Now Longwood University) (1969) **C:** Biologist, Cell Biologist, Educator, Dean of Natural and Social Sciences, Senior Scholar and Professor of Biology, Wheaton College, IL (1977-1994); Dean, Natural and Social Sciences, Wheaton College, IL (2000-2019); Evaluator, Consultant, North Central Association- Higher Learning Commission (1978-1999, 2000-2006); Academic Dean, Gordon College, Wenham, MA (1994-2000); Consultant, Evaluator, New England Association of Colleges and Universities (1994-1999); Chair, Professor, Biology, Wheaton College, IL (1977-1994) **CR:** Consultant, Evaluator, North Central Association, Chicago (1980-1994, 2000- 2006); Evaluator, Higher Learning Commission, Chicago (1978-1994, 2000-2006); Fellow, American Science Affiliation (1992) **CIV:** Board of Trustees, Gordon College, (2016-Present); Advisory Board, for SCIO (Scholarship & Christianity), Oxford, England, United Kingdom (2014- Present); Board of Advisors, John Templeton Foundation (2002, 2005-2010); President, American Scientific Affiliation (2002); Board of Trustees, Phycological Society of American (1991-2001); Board of Trustees, Wheaton College (1995-1999) **CW:** Associate Editor, Various Biology Textbooks (1987); Contributor, Chapters, Books; Contributor, Articles, Professional Journals **AW:** Listee, "One of 50 Women You Should Know," Christianity Today (2012); Named Outstanding Alumnus, Alumni Achievement Award, Longwood College (Now Longwood University) (1995); Named Outstanding Educator, Chicago Region, IL (1994); Fulbright Research Grantee, New Zealand, Australia, Fiji (1989-1990); Named Member of the Year, Midwest Society of Electron Microscopists (MSEM) (1988); Named Junior Teacher of the Year, Wheaton College (1981-1982); Named Outstanding Young Woman of America, Farmville, VA (1972) **MEM:** American Association for the Advancement of Science; American Scientific Affiliation; Fulbright Association; Sigma XI,

The Scientific Research Honor Society **MH:** Albert Nelson Marquis Lifetime Achievement Award **AS:** Dr. Chappell's success is attributed to the grace of God who has redeemed her and equipped her to do His will in teaching, research, administration, and church life, and has provided family and friends' support. That grace included being well mentored by her parents, who opened many opportunities for their children and saw women as excellent participants in various career paths, including academia and research. They believed that their four female children would be effective in any career they entered, and they admonished them to pursue their dreams, including being leaders. The early studies of liberal arts in college, opened many doors of thought and opportunity, including the admonition by her advisor to define her interests, seek entry into graduate school and initiate specialization. She was often the only female in most graduate school classes and had great experiences with excellent advisors and peers. She gained much confidence in graduate school and continued her desire to be an educator in various roles as they emerged. Serving at Wheaton College was a great training ground for faith and science integration discussions and studies which have readily informed Dr. Chappell's work with students and peers. Being a faculty member provided many opportunities for her to conduct research, publish and teach. Part of her mentorship of students and peers has included performing science as a Christian and inspiring them to be excellent scientists, as well as holding to their Christian faith. **B/I:** Dr. Chappell became involved in her career as a result of her basic love for education. She loves to watch individuals grow and mentally develop. Her parents raised her and her four sisters to do whatever they wanted, despite the limits of the 1950s and 1960s. She taught for over 20 years. Prior to pursuing administration, she had a love for teaching. She has additionally never regretted her decision to explore science, as her Christian calling includes her administrative work and the sciences. **AV:** Writing; Reading; Photography; Hiking; Music; Playing piano and clarinet; Travel **RE:** Christian **THT:** Dr. Chappell says, "Among many other people who are Christians, I enjoy encounters with the Triune God directly and through revelations in his word and his creation. I had wonderful Christian parents and siblings, and my life exemplifies commitment to excellence in life, service, study and worship. I had no female mentors teaching any class I took in my natural science training. I have enjoyed the liberal arts disciplines and my specialization in the natural sciences been productive. My studies have involved organisms from, as well as travel to, many places on Earth. During my career, I have attempted to mentor and increase the number of female faculty and students into academic roles. During my leadership roles as a department chair and dean, I have successfully increased the number of female hires. While being a faculty member and also serving in leadership roles, I have had the privilege of continuing to publish. I have attempted to be just and righteous while being civil, pure and productive in all of my work, communication, worship and recreation. My life has been blessed through the Lord's provision of family, friends, a wonderful career, fellowship and worship in many venues."

CHAPPELLE, DAVE KHARI WEBBER, T: Actor, Comedian **I:** Other **DOB:** 08/24/1973 **PB:** Washington, DC **PT:** William David Chappelle III; Yvonne K. (Reed) Chappelle **MS:** Married **SPN:** Elaine Mendoza Erfe (12/05/2004) **CH:** Sulayman; Ibrahim; Sonal **ED:** Diploma in Theater Arts, Duke Ellington School of the Arts (1991) **CW:** Performer, "Dave Chappelle: 8:46" (2020); Performer, "Dave Chappelle: Sticks & Stones" (2019); Actor, "A Star is Born" (2018); Appearance, "Comedians in Cars Getting Coffee" (2018); Writer, Producer, "Deep in the Heart of Texas: Dave Chappelle Live at Austin City Limits" (2017); Writer, Producer, "The Age of Spin: Dave Chappelle Live at the Hollywood Palladium" (2017); Performer, "Dave Chappelle: Equanimity" (2017); Performer, "Dave Chappelle: The Bird Revelation" (2017); Host, "Saturday Night Live" (2016); Actress, "Chi-Raq" (2015); Writer, Executive Producer, "Dave Chappelle: Killin' Them Softly" (2000); Writer, Producer, "Dave Chappelle's Block Party" (2006); Writer, Producer, "Dave Chappelle: For What It's Worth" (2004); Actor, Writer, Executive Producer, "Chappelle's Show" (2003-2006); Actor, "Undercover Brother" (2002); Voice Actor, "Crank Yankers" (2002); Actor, "Screwed" (2000); Actor, "200 Cigarettes" (1999); Actor, "Blue Streak" (1999); Actor, "Woo" (1998); Actor, "You've Got Mail" (1998); Actor, "Con Air" (1997); Actor, "The Real Blonde" (1997); Actor, "Bowl of Pork" (1997); Actor, Co-writer, and Producer, "Half Baked" (1998); Writer, Executive Producer, "The Dave Chappelle Project" (1997); Actor, "The Nutty Professor" (1996); Actor, "Joe's Apartment" (1996); Actor, "Buddies" (1996); Actor, "Getting In" (1994); Actor, "Comedy: Coast to Coast" (1994); Actor, "Robin Hood: Men in Tights" (1993); Actor, "Undercover Blues" (1993) **AW:** Grammy Award for Best Comedy, The Recording Academy (2018, 2019, 2020); Mark Twain Prize for American Humor, John F. Kennedy Center for the Performing Arts (2019); Emmy Award for Outstanding Variety Special (Pre-Recorded), Academy of Television Arts & Sciences (2018); Emmy Award for Outstanding Guest Actor, Academy of Television Arts & Sciences (2017)

CHASDI, RICHARD J., PHD, T: Professorial Lecturer **I:** Education/Educational Services **CN:** The George Washington University **DOB:** 01/21/1958 **PB:** Boston **SC:** MA/USA **PT:** Simon Chasdi; Eleanor (Hollenberg) Chasdi **MS:** Married **SPN:** Sharon M. Applebaum (2003) **ED:** PhD in Political Science, Purdue University (1995); MA in Political Science, Boston College (1985); BA in Politics, Brandeis University (1981) **C:** Professorial Lecturer, The George Washington University, Washington, DC (2018-Present); Adjunct Senior Fellow, International Centre for Political Violence and Terrorism Research, S. Rajaratnam School of International Studies, Nanyang Technological University, Singapore (2018-Present); Visiting Fellow, International Centre for Political Violence and Terrorism Research, S. Rajaratnam School of International Studies, Nanyang Technological University, Singapore (2017); Special Term Appointment, Homeland and National Security Advisor Position, Argonne National Laboratory, The University of Chicago (2015); Professor of Management, Walsh College, Troy, MI (2015-2018); Associate Professor of Management, Walsh College, Troy, MI (2013-2015); Adjunct Associate Professor, Department of Management, Walsh College, Troy, MI (2012-2013); Adjunct Research Fellow, Center for Technology and National Security Policy, National Defense University, Washington, DC (2012); Adjunct Associate Professor, Department of Political Science, University of Windsor, Windsor, Ontario, Canada (2010-2013); Adjunct Assistant Professor, CAENSIS, Wayne State University (2010-2011); Affiliate Assistant Professor of Policy Fellow, Schar School of Policy and Government, George Mason University, Arlington, VA (2010-2011); Distinguished Fellow, Project on National Security Reform (2010-2011); Deputy Team Leader, Vision Working Group, Project on National Security Reform, Washington, D.C (2009-2011); Sessional Instructor, Department of Political Science, University of

Windsor, Windsor, Ontario, Canada (2008-2009); Adjunct Faculty Member, Center of Academic Excellence in National Security Intelligence Studies, Wayne State University (2007-2009); Adjunct Faculty Member, Master of Arts Dispute Resolution Program, Department of Communications, Wayne State University (2005-2008); Fellow, Center for Peace and Conflict Studies, Wayne State University (2003-2013); Adjunct Assistant Professor, Center for Peace and Conflict Studies, Wayne State University (2003-2013); Scholar-in-Residence, Department of Political Science, Eastern Michigan University, Ypsilanti, MI (2003); Visiting Assistant Professor of History, Department of History, The College of Wooster (2002); Visiting Assistant Professor of International Relations in Political Science, Department of Political Science, The College of Wooster (2001-2002); Adjunct Faculty Member, Interdisciplinary Studies Program, Wayne State University (1999); Adjunct Lecturer of Political Science, Department of Social Sciences, University of Michigan-Dearborn (1997); Adjunct Faculty Member, Department of Political Science, Center for Peace and Conflict Studies, Wayne State University (1996-2001); Policy Consultant, Lt. Governor Evelyn F. Murphy, Commonwealth of Massachusetts (1989-1990); Legislative Aide, State Senator Royal L. Bolling, Boston, MA (1985-1987); Research Assistant, State Senator Royal L. Bolling, Boston, MA (1985) **CR:** Presenter, "A 'Mini-Max' Counterterror Framework for Iraq and Afghanistan," Society for the Advancement of Socio-Economics, Temple University, Philadelphia, PA (2010); Presenter, "Tapestry of Terror: A Portrait of Middle East Terrorism," Muskingum College, Ohio (2002); Presenter, "Middle East Terrorism," Lunch Hour Seminars, Center for Peace and Conflict Studies, Wayne State University, Detroit, MI (1996); Contributor, Academic Presentations in Field; Consultant in field **CW:** Member of Editorial Board, "Armed Forces and Society," Texas State University (2015-Present); Member of the Editorial Board, "Perspectives on Terrorism: A Journal of the Terrorism Research Initiative" (2011-Present); Contributor, "Tackling Horizontal and Vertical Supply Chain Vulnerabilities: Risks from Interstate Conflict and Terrorism," The Journal of Counterterrorism and Homeland Security International (2019); Author, "Counterterror Offensives for the Ghost War World: The Rudiments of Counterterrorism Policy" (2010); Consultant Writer, Alon Ben-Meir Institute (2008-2010); Author, "Tapestry of Terror: A Portrait of Middle East Terrorism" (2002); Author, "Serenade of Suffering: A Portrait of Middle East Terrorism" (1999); Author, "Tapestry of Terror: A Portrait of Middle East Terrorism" (1994-1999); Author, "Serenade of Suffering: A Portrait of Middle East Terrorism" (1968-1993); Editorial Board Member, "Perspectives on Terrorism," Terrorism Research Initiatives; Contributor, Articles, Professional Journals; Contributor, Chapters, Books **AW:** Named, Fulbright Specialist, Singapore (2017); Honorable Mention, Ralph Cowan Fellowship Program, ROTC, Department of Military Science and Leadership, Eastern Michigan University (2003); Outstanding Academic Title Award, Field of International Relations, Choice Magazine (2000); Great Decisions Grant, Foreign Policy Association, Detroit Council for World Affairs (1998); Grant, Program on Mediating Theory and Democratic Systems, Wayne State University (1998); Grant, Purdue Research Foundation (1992-1993); Grant, Project on North American Terrorism, Canadian Consulate General, Detroit, MI, Canadian Studies Program, Wayne State University **MEM:** Member of the International Advisory Board, "Terrorism: An Electronic Journal" (2012-Present); Fellow, Inter-University Seminar on Armed Forces and

Society; Standing Group in Extremism and Democracy, European Consortium for Political Research; American Political Science Association

CHASE, ANDY, T: Utility Relationship Manager **I:** Utilities **CN:** American Water Works Association **ED:** BA in Political Science, Fort Lewis College (1992) **C:** Utility Relationship Manager, American Water Works Association (2015-Present); Account Executive, Leisure Trends, A NPD Group Company (2013-2014); National Account Manager, Mercury Payment Systems (2011-2013); President, Board of Directors, Fort Lewis College Alumni Association, Fort Lewis College (2007-2011); National Accounts Manager, American Century Investments (1998-2008); Retirement Education Consultant, JP Morgan Retirement Plan Services (1998-2004) **CIV:** Big Brother/Mentor, Big Brothers Big Sister of Colorado (2012-Present);Advisory Board Member, Best Buddies International (2015-2016); President, Board of Directors, Foundation Board Member, Fort Lewis College Alumni Association (2007-2012) **AW:** Citation for his Work with the Alumni Association, State of Colorado; Citation for Placing Graduates with Alumnus that are in the Fields that are aspiring to get into, State of Colorado; Value Award, American Century Investments **MEM:** American Water Works Association **AS:** He attributes his success to the passion for his work, his background in sales and business development. The feedback he receives is that he is very positive and very well received. **B/I:** Right before Mr. Chase started his career with American Water works, he took some time off. He stumbled upon the American Water Works Association and a gentleman that he had met at one of the Alumni events that he sponsored worked at the association and they became close friends and recommending him for a job offer.

CHASE, WILLIAM J., PHD, T: History Educator **I:** Education/Educational Services **DOB:** 09/04/1947 **PB:** Glen Cove **SC:** NY/USA **PT:** William J. Chase; Frances S. (Storen) Chase **MS:** Widowed **SPN:** Donna M. Schaefer (1972, Deceased 05/10/2010) **CH:** Matthew; Alexander (Deceased 2012) **ED:** PhD in Russian and Modern European History, Boston College, with Highest Distinction (1979); MA in Russian Studies, Boston College, with Highest Distinction (1973); BA in History, Lafayette College (1969); Coursework, Universidad de Madrid (1967) **C:** Professor Emeritus of History, University of Pittsburgh (2018-Present); Member, Committee, Center for Russian, East European and Eurasian Studies, University of Pittsburgh (1979-Present); Director, Urban Studies Program, University of Pittsburgh (2011-2018); Professor, History, University of Pittsburgh (2000-2018); Chair, Department of History, University Pittsburgh (2000, 2002-2006, 2009); Director, Center for Russian, East European and Eurasian Studies, University of Pittsburgh (1989-1991, 2007); Associate Professor, History, University of Pittsburgh (1985-2000); Assistant Professor, History, University of Pittsburgh (1979-1985); Member, Advisory Board, University Honors College, University of Pittsburgh (1980-1982); History Instructor, Boston College (1976-1979) **CR:** Director, The Russian Publications Project (1991-2002); Co-director, The Russian Archive Series (1991-2002); Conference Organizer, The Spanish Civil War's Impact on Spanish and Soviet Political Cultures (2011); Conference Organizer, Restructuring USA/USSR, University of Pittsburgh (1991); Co-director, The Soviet Data Bank, Data Archive on the History of Soviet Society and State (1989); Historical Consultant, Pittsburgh-Donetsk Oral History Project, Film, "Perestroika from Below" (1989); Presenter in Field **MIL:** Sergeant, United States Marine Corps Reserve (1969-1975) **CW:** Presenter, "The Opportunities and Challenges of the Popular Front, Anti-Fascism and 'Bourgeois Democratic' Revolutions: The Comintern in Spain and Mexico, 1935-1940" (2017); Co-presenter, "The Many Faces of Antifascism: The Fractured Antifascist Movement During the Spanish Civil War and the Stalinist Mass Repression," Trajectories of Antifascism Conference, Rutgers, The State University of New Jersey (2017); Co-editor, "The Carl Beck Papers in Russian and East European Studies" (1982-2017); Author, "Scapegoating One's Comrades in the USSR, 1934-1937," Anatomy of Terror, Political Violence Under Stalin (2013); Member, Editorial Board, "Annals of Communism Series," Yale University Press (1993-2012); Author, "The Socialist Experiment: A Companion to European History, 1900-1945" (2006, 2010); Author, "The Comintern," Encyclopedia of Russia History (2004); Member, Editorial Board, "Russkoe Proshoe" (1991-2002); Author, "Enemies Within the Gates?: The Comintern and the Stalinist Repression, 1934-1939" (2001); Author, "Stalinism," Encyclopedia of Social History (1994); Co-editor, "Rossiiskii Gosudarstvennyi Arkhiv Ekonomiki. Putevoditel. Tom 1. (Guide to the Russian State Archive of the Economy, Vol. 1)" (1994); Co-author, "Research Guide to the Russian State Archive of the Economy" (1993); Author, "Voluntarism, Mobilization and Coercion" Subbotniki, 1919-1921," Soviet Studies (1989); Author, "Workers, Society and the Soviet State: Labor and Life in Moscow, 1918-1929" (1987); Author, "The Dialectics of Production Meetings, 1923-1929," Russian History (1986); Author, "Towards an Understanding of Soviet Labor: A Review Essay," International Labor and Working Class History (1982); Presenter, "The Dialectics of the Drive for Productivity, 1921-1929," Annual Meeting of the American Association for the Advancement of Slavic Studies (1982); Author, "The Moscow Bolshevik Cadres of 1917: A Prosopographic Analysis," Russian History (1978); Presenter, "The Revolution and Pre-Revolution in Moscow," New England Slavic Conference (1977); Contributor, Articles to Professional Journals **AW:** Recipient, Awards, National Council for Soviet and East European Research (1983-1984, 1985-1986, 1995-1996); Hewlett Research, University of Pittsburgh (1993); Grantee, Social Science Research Council (SSRC) (1991); Grantee, U.S. Department of Education (1991); Award, American Council of Learned Societies (ACLS) (1990); Award, International Research and Exchanges Board (IREX) (1990); Award, Kennan Institute for Advanced Russian Studies, The Wilson Center (1990); Award, National Endowment for the Humanities (1985-1986); Chancellor's Distinguished Teaching Award (1984); W. Averell Harriman Institute for Advanced Study of the Soviet Union, Columbia University (1982); Fellow, American Council of Learned Societies (1981) **MH:** Albert Nelson Marquis Lifetime Achievement Award **AS:** Dr. Chase attributes his success to being in the right places at the right times, good fortune, and hard work. **B/I:** Dr. Chase became involved in his profession because he was inspired as a student of the 1960s. The Vietnam War was going on, and it raised many questions in him. He started studying Marxism and communist history so as to understand why so many people were being killed. He taught at a high school for more than two years, but he did not want to continue because teaching high school requires a great deal of time, emotional energy, and constant work demands that took away from his desire to continue his studies. Dr. Chase went back to school for a master's degree in Russian studies, and then his PhD. His career took off from there.

CHASTAIN, JACK KESSLER, AA, DMD, FICD, T: Dentist **I:** Medicine & Health Care **CN:** Jack Kessler Chastain, DMD - General Dentist in Louisville, KY **DOB:** 04/12/1933 **PB:** Berea **SC:** KY/USA **PT:** Homer Lee Chastain; Rosella Maria (Kessler) Chastain **MS:** Married **SPN:** Irene Elizabeth Sample (06/17/2000) **CH:** Jack Kessler Junior; Richard Lee; Martha Ann **ED:** DMD, University of Louisville (1957); AA, University of Louisville (1953) **CT:** Diplomate, American Board of Forensic Dentistry (Now American Board of Forensic Odontology); FAA Commercial License, Aircraft Owners and Pilots Association **C:** Retired (2007); Private Practice, Jack Kessler Chastain, DMD - General Dentist in Louisville, KY (1957-2007) **CR:** Former Member, Advisory Board, Watterson College (1974-1977); Former Member, Staff, Louisville Jewish Hospital, UofL Health; Presenter in Field **CIV:** Member Emeritus, Louisville Jaycees President, Fraternal Order of Police; Associate Lodge # 14, Fraternal Order of Police; Chairman, Board of Directors, Fraternal Order of Police **AW:** Named Honored Great, North Stafford Shine Society of Dental Surgeons: Lecture, Dentistry in the U.S.A.; Invited by Dr. Eduardo Calderon to Lecture to His Graduate Students, Santiago, Chile **MEM:** Committee of Forensic Dentistry, Louisville Dental Society (1977-1978); Advisor to President, Louisville Dental Society (1972-1973); Fellow, Counselor, International College of Dentists; Life Member, American Dental Association; Board of Directors, Secretary-treasurer, Program Director, President, Association of American Dentists; Association of American Dentists; Life Member, American Equilibration Society (AES); The American Prosthodontic Society; Life Member, Charter Member, American Academy of Craniomandibular Orthopedics (Now American Academy of Orofacial Pain); American College of Forensic Examiners; Kentucky Dental Association; Life Member, Kentucky Academy of Dental Research Founding Member, First Director, President, Kentucky Academy of Dental Research; Life Member, Louisville Dental Society; Secretary-treasurer, Louisville Dental Study Club; Chicago Dental Society (CDS); Aircraft Owners and Pilots Association; Single and Multi-engine Land, with Instrument Endorsement, Aircraft Owners and Pilots Association; Colonel, Honorary Order, Kentucky Colonels; Lambda Chi Alpha; Past Alumni Vice President, Lambda Chi Alpha; Psi Omega Dental Fraternity; Board of Directors, Senior Member, Psi Omega Dental Fraternity, University of Louisville; Senior Member, Letter Winners (L) Club **MH:** Albert Nelson Marquis Lifetime Achievement Award **B/I:** Dr. Chastain became involved in his profession because he decided on dentistry when he was 15 or 16 years old. It probably had a lot to do with an uncle, and cousin-in-law, both who were also on the faculty of Louisville, School of Dentistry. There was a distant relative who was an MD and another distant relative who was a dentist. **AV:** International monetary affairs; Travel; Writing; Flying

CHAVEZ, JAVIER JR., T: President **I:** Food & Restaurant Services **CN:** Cerveza Zolupez Beer Company **SC:** Utah **MS:** Married **SPN:** June **ED:** Coursework, Craft Beer Classes, UCLA Extension Program; JD, Boston College (2006); MBA, Boston College; BA in History, University of Utah **C:** President, Founder, Cerveza Zolupez Beer Company (2017-Present); Attorney, Dwayne Morris LLP (2012-2017); Arthur Gallagher; Edward Jones **CIV:** Give Me a Chance Youth **AW:** Empire State Counsel Award; Stephenson Canyon Scholar Award; College of Humanities Graduation Speaker **MEM:** Utah Hispanic Chamber of Commerce; Brewers Association **BAR:** New York; Utah **AS:** His parents were really good role models and encouraged him to be the best he could be. **B/I:** Mr. Chavez's parents are in the restaurant business and he saw how much lawyers helped businesses. They had so much help from good lawyers for his family. He wanted to do the same for other families with small businesses remain successful, as well as his own.

CHAVKIN, RACHEL, T: Stage Director, Artistic Director **I:** Fine Art **CN:** The TEAM **DOB:** 07/20/1980 **PB:** Washington, DC **SC:** DC/USA **MS:** Married **SPN:** Jake Heinrichs (2011) **ED:** MFA, School of the Arts, Columbia University (2008); BFA, Tisch School of the Arts, New York University **C:** Artistic Director, The TEAM, Brooklyn, NY; Stage Director, Numerous Theater Productions **CW:** Director, "Moby-Dick" (2019); Director, "Lempicka" (2018); Director, "Natasha, Pierre & the Great Comet of 1812" (2013-2014, 2016); Director, "Hadestown" (2016); Director, "The Royale" (2016); Director, "Anything That Gives Off Light" (2016); Director, "Three Pianos" (2010-2011); Director, "The American Clock"; Director, "Light Shining in Buckinghamshire"; Director, "Small Mouth Sounds"; Director, "I'll Get You Back Again"; Co-Director, "The Lily's Revenge, Act 2 (HERE)"; Co-director, "Confirmation"; Co-Director, "Status"; Director, Many Works Including "Roosevelvis," "Mission Drift," and "Architecting," The TEAM **AW:** Outer Critics Circle Award, Outstanding Director of a Musical (2019); Drama Desk Award, Outstanding Director of a Musical (2017, 2019); Tony Award, Best Direction of a Musical (2019); American Ingenuity Award (2017); Eliot Norton Award, Outstanding Director - Large Theater (2016); Obie Award, Best Director (2016); Obie Award, Special Citations (2013)

CHEADLE, DONALD, "DON" FRANK JR., T: Actor **I:** Media & Entertainment **DOB:** 11/29/1964 **PB:** Kansas City **SC:** MO/USA **PT:** Donald Frank Cheadle Sr.; Bettye Garner (North) Cheadle **MS:** Partner **SPN:** Bridgid Coulter **CH:** Two Children **ED:** BFA, California Institute of Arts **CIV:** Goodwill Ambassador, UN Environmental Programme (2010) **CW:** Actor, "Black Monday" (2019-Present); Actor, "Ratched" (2020); Host, "Saturday Night Live" (2019); Actor, "Avengers: Endgame" (2019); Actor, "Captain Marvel" (2019); Voice Actor, "DuckTales" (2018-2020); Actor, "Avengers: Infinity War" (2018); Actor, "Captain America: Civil War" (2016); Actor, "Kevin Hart: What Now?" (2016); Actor, Producer, Director, Writer, "Miles Ahead" (2015); Actor, "Avengers: Age of Ultron" (2015); Actor, "Iron Man 3" (2013); Actor, "House of Lies" (2012-2016); Actor, "Flight" (2012); Actor, Executive Producer, "The Guard" (2011); Actor, "Iron Man 2" (2010); Actor, "Hotel for Dogs" (2009); Actor, "Brooklyn's Finest" (2009); Producer, "Crash" (2008); Actor, "Traitor" (2008); Actor, "Reign Over Me" (2007); Actor, "Ocean's Thirteen" (2007); Actor, "Talk to Me" (2007); Co-author with John Prendergast, "Not on Our Watch: The Mission to End Genocide in Darfur and Beyond" (2007); Actor, "The Other Side of Simple" (2006); Actor, "The Dog Problem" (2006); Actor, Producer, "Crash" (2004); Actor, "The Assassination of Richard Nixon" (2004); Actor, "Hotel Rwanda" (2004); Actor, "Ocean's Twelve" (2004); Actor, "The United States of Leland" (2003);Actor, "The Hire: Ticker" (2002); Actor, "ER" (2002); Actor, "The Bernie Mac Show" (2001); Actor, "Manic" (2001); Actor, "Swordfish" (2001); Actor, "Rush Hour 2" (2001); Ator, "Ocean's Eleven" (2001); Actor, "Mission to Mars" (2000); Actor, "The Family Man" (2000); Actor, "Traffic" (2000); Actor, "Things Behind the Sun" (2000); Actor, "Fail Safe" (2000); Actor, "A Lesson Before Dying" (1999); Actor, "The Rat Pack" (1998); Actor, "Bulworth" (1998); Actor, "Out of Sight" (1998); Actor, "Rosewood" (1997); Actor, "Volcano" (1997); Actor, "Boogie Nights" (1997); Actor, "Rebound: The Legend of Earl the Goat Manigault" (1996); Actor, "Things to Do in Denver When You're Dead" (1995); Actor, "Devil in a Blue Dress" (1995);

Actor, "Lush Life" (1993); Actor, "The Meteor Man" (1993); Actor, "Roadside Prophets" (1992); Actor, "Colors" (1988); Actor, "Hamburger Hill" (1987); Actor, "The Bronx Zoo" (1987); Actor, "Punk" (1986); Actor, "L.A. Law" (1986); Actor, "Moving Violations" (1985); Actor, "3 Days" (1984); Actor, "Fame" (1982); Actor, "Hill Street Blues" (1981); Actor, "Hooperman" (1988); Actor, "Night Court" (1984); Actor, "Booker" (1989); Actor, "China Beach" (1988); Voice Actor, "The Simpsons" (1989); Actor, "The Fresh Prince of Bel-Air" (1990); Actor, "Picket Fences" (1992); Actor, "The Golden Palace" (1992); Actor, "Hangin' with Mr. Cooper" (1992); Actor, Appearances, Television Shows, Films, Video Games and Music Videos **AW:** Grammy Award for Best Compilation Soundtrack for Visual Media, The Recording Academy (2017); Award for Outstanding Directing in a Comedy Series, NAACP Image Awards (2016); Golden Globe Award for Best Performance by an Actor in a TV Series-Comedy or Musical, Hollywood Foreign Press Association (2013); Award for Outstanding Actor in a Comedy Series, NAACP Image Awards (2013); Award for Outstanding Literary Work - Nonfiction, NAACP Image Awards (2008); Named to Power 150, Ebony Magazine (2008); Summit Peace Award (2007); Award for Best Actor, African American Film Critics Association (2007); Humanitarian of the Year Award, BET Awards (2007); Satellite Award for Best Actor (1999, 2004); SAG Award for Outstanding Performance by a Cast in Motion Picture, SAG-AFTRA (2000, 2005); Golden Globe Award for Best Performance in a Supporting Role, Hollywood Foreign Press Association (1999)

CHEN, FEN, T: Mathematician **I:** Education/Educational Services **DOB:** 11/28/1939 **PB:** Lutsao Village/Chia-Yi Shien **SC:** Taiwan **PT:** Shin-Ting Chen; Susan Liaw **MS:** Married **SPN:** Ann-Hua Shieh (08/10/1966) **CH:** Chu-Yi Chen; Chu-Wen Chen **ED:** Advanced Graduate Specialist, University of Maryland (1984); Postgraduate Coursework, University of Wisconsin (1979-1980); Postgraduate Coursework, University of Michigan (1978-1979); Diploma in Mathematics, University of Tokyo (1977); MEd, University of Tokyo (1977); BS, National Taiwan Normal University, Taipei, Taiwan (1968) **C:** Math Adjunct Professor, Prince George's Community College, Largo, MD (2015-2017); Mathematics Professor, Northern Virginia Community College, Annandale, VA (2013-2015); Teacher, Mathematics, Prince George County Public Schools (2006-2012); Substitute Teacher, Mathematics, Alexandria City Public Schools, VA (2005-2006); Substitute Teacher, Mathematics, Arlington Public Schools, VA (1999-2005); Substitute Teacher, Mathematics, Fairfax County Public Schools, MD (1990-1998); Substitute Teacher, Mathematics, Prince George County Public Schools and Montgomery County Public Schools (1984-1990); Volunteer Instructor, University of Maryland (1982-1986); Private Instructor, Montgomery College, MD (1985); Teaching Assistant, University of Maryland, College Park, MD (1981-1983); Instructor, Mathematics, Education Research, Japanese Education, University of Tokyo (1974-1977); Instructor, Mathematics, Tainan Pharmacy University, Tainan Shien, Taiwan (1970-1974); Teacher, Mathematics, Taichung First Senior High School, Taichung City, Taiwan (1966-1970); Teacher, Mathematics, Pekung Senior High School, Pekung, Iling Shien, Taiwan (1963-1966); Teacher, Mathematics, Tailin Junior Hugh School, Tailin, Chia-Yi, Taiwan (1961-1963) **CIV:** Mathematics Education Delegate, People to People Ambassador Program, India (2010); Mathematics Education Delegate, People to People Ambassador Program, China (2009); Mathematics Education Delegate, People to People Ambassador Program, Cambodia (2008); Mathematics Education Delegate, People

to People Ambassador Program, Vietnam (2008); Mathematics Education Delegate, People to People Ambassador Program, Egypt (2007) **CW:** Author, "Regular Polygons, Volume II," People to People Ambassador (2009); Author, "Regular Polygons, Volume I" (2001); Author, "New Theory of Trisection" (1999); Author, "Elementary Calculus" (1972) **AW:** Fellow, Kyo-Dai-Ken Mathematics Study Group (1975-1978) **MEM:** Mathematics Education Research Group, Tokyo, Japan; National Council of Teachers of Mathematics; American Mathematical Society; Mathematical Association of America (MAA); Association of Mathematics Teacher Educators **MH:** Albert Nelson Marquis Lifetime Achievement Award

CHENEY, ELIZABETH, "LIZ" LYNNE, T: U.S. Representative from Wyoming **I:** Government Administration/Government Relations/Government Services **DOB:** 07/28/1966 **PB:** Madison **SC:** WI/USA **PT:** Richard Bruce Cheney; Lynne Anne (Vincent) Cheney **MS:** Married **SPN:** Philip J. Perry (1993) **CH:** Kate; Elizabeth; Grace; Philip; Richard **ED:** JD, University of Chicago Law School (1996); BA, Colorado College (1988) **C:** Chair, House Republican Conference (2019-Present); Member, U.S. House of Representatives from Wyoming's at-large District (2017-Present); Co-founder, Board Member, KeepAmericaSafe.com (2009-Present); Principal Deputy Assistant Secretary, U.S. Department of State (2005-2006); Deputy Assistant Secretary, Bureau Near Eastern Affairs, U.S. Department of State, Washington, DC (2002-2004); International Law Attorney, Consultant, International Finance Corporation (IFC) (1999-2002); Associate, White & Case LLP (1996-1999); Associate, Armitage Associates (1993-1996); With, United States Agency for International Development (USAID); Special Assistant to Deputy Secretary for Assistance to Former Soviet Union, U.S. Department of State; Member, Committee on Natural Resources; Member, Committee on Armed Services; Member, Committee on Rules **CR:** Contributor, FOX News (2012-Present) **CIV:** Senior Foreign Policy Adviser, Mitt Romney Presidential Campaign (2008); National Co-Chair, Fred Thompson Presidential Campaign (2007-2008); Member, W Stands for Women Initiative, Bush-Cheney Re-Election Campaign (2003-2004); Member, International Board of Visitors, University of Wyoming **CW:** Co-Author (with Dick Cheney), "In My Time: A Personal and Political Memoir" (2011) **PA:** Republican

CHENEY, RICHARD, "DICK" BRUCE, T: 46th Vice President of the United States **I:** Government Administration/Government Relations/Government Services **DOB:** 01/30/1941 **PB:** Lincoln **SC:** NE/USA **PT:** Richard Herbert Cheney; Marjorie Lorraine (Dickey) Cheney **MS:** Married **SPN:** Lynne Anne (Vincent) Cheney (08/29/1964) **CH:** Elizabeth; Mary Claire **ED:** MA in Political Science, University of Wyoming (1966); Intern, Wyoming State Legislature, Cheyenne, WY (1965); BA in Political Science, University of Wyoming (1965); Coursework, Casper Community College (1963); Coursework, Yale University (1959-1962); Coursework, University of Wisconsin-Madison (1966-1968) **C:** 46th Vice President of the United States, Washington, DC (2001-2009); Chairman, Chief Executive Officer, Halliburton Co., Dallas, Texas (1995-2000); Senior Fellow, American Enterprise Institute, Washington, DC (1993-1995); Secretary, U.S. Department of Defense, Washington, DC (1989-1993); Minority Whip, United States Congress from Wyoming, Washington, DC (1988-1989); Chairman, U.S. House Republican Policy Committee, Washington, DC (1981-1988); Member, United States Congress, Washington, DC (1979-1989); Partner, Bradley Woods & Co. (1973-1974,

1977-1978); Chief of Staff to President, The White House, Washington, DC (1975-1977); Deputy Assistant to President for Operations, The White House, Washington, DC (1974-1975); Assistant Director for Operations Cost of Living Council, The White House, Washington, DC (1971-1973); Deputy to Presidential Counselor, The White House, Washington, DC (1970-1971); Special Assistant to Director, Office of Economic Opportunity, The White House, Washington, DC (1969-1970); Congressional Fellow, Staff Member to Representative William A. Steiger, U.S. House of Representatives, Washington, DC (1968-1969); Staff Aide to Governor Warren Knowles, State of Wisconsin, Madison, WI (1966) **CIV:** United Methodist Church; Board of Advisers, Jewish Institute for National Security of America **CW:** Author, "Exceptional: Why the World Needs a Powerful America" (2015); Co-Author, with Jonathan Reiner, "Heart: An American Medical Odyssey" (2013); Appearance, Documentary, "The World According to Dick Cheney" (2013); Co-Author, with Liz Cheney, "In My Time: A Personal and Political Memoir" (2011); Co-Author, with Lynne V. Cheney, "Kings of the Hill: Power and Personality in the House of Representatives" (1983) **AW:** Reagan Award, National Republican Congressional Committee (2011); One of the 50 Highest-earning Political Figures, Newsweek (2010); Conservative of the Year, Human Events Magazine (2009); One of the 50 Most Powerful People in DC, GQ Magazine (2009); Presidential Medal of Freedom, The White House (1991); J.E. Davies Congressional Fellowship Award (1968) **MEM:** Alumni Association, University of Wyoming **PA:** Republican **RE:** Methodist

CHENG, DORIS, ESQ., T: Shareholder **I:** Law and Legal Services **CN:** Walkup, Melodia, Kelly & Schoenberger **ED:** JD, School of Law, University of San Francisco (1998); Judicial Externship, Honorable Saundra B. Armstrong, Northern District of California (1997); Summer Abroad Studies, Trinity College, Dublin, Ireland (1996); BA in English, Emphasis in Creative Writing, UC Davis (1994) **C:** Shareholder, Walkup, Melodia, Kelly & Schoenberger (1998-Present) **CR:** Fellow, Litigation Counsel of America (2012-Present); Board of Counselors, School of Law, University of San Francisco (2011-Present); Executive Committee, Faculty, School of Law, University of San Francisco (1999-Present); Faculty, Kessler-Eidson Trial Techniques Program, School of Law, Emory University, Atlanta, GA (2011); Adjunct Professor, Boalt Hall, University of California, Berkeley (2010-2011); Advocacy Training, United States Agency for International Development Grant, School of Law, University of San Diego, Mexicali, Mexico (2010); Co-director, Intensive Advocacy Program, School of Law, University of San Francisco (2005); Coach, Thomas Tang Moot Court Competition, School of Law, University of San Francisco (2004); Faculty, Kessler-Eidson Trial Techniques Program, School of Law, Emory University, Atlanta, GA (2003-2008); Board of Governors, School of Law, University of San Francisco (2003-2006); Speaker, Fellows of the American College of Trial Lawyers; Lecturer in Field, Speaker in Field **CIV:** Coach, Mock Trial Team, Lowell High School, San Francisco, CA (2010-Present); Volunteer, Log Cabin Ranch Gardening Project, San Francisco Youth Guidance Center (2014); Girls Basketball Coach, Fifth Through Seventh Grade, St. Patrick Catholic Youth Organization (2007-2009); Girls Basketball Coach, Fifth and Sixth Grade, BCSFYAO (2004-2006); Girls Basketball Coach, Junior Varsity, Varsity, Summer Clinic, Lowell High School, San Francisco, CA (2003); Girls Basketball Coach, Fifth Through Eighth Grade, Notre Dame des Victoires (1999-2002); Cooperative Restraining Order Clinic (1997-2000); Girls Basketball Coach, Eighth Grade,

Cornerstone Academy (1995); Trainer, Rule of Law Initiative, U.S. Department of Justice, Mexico, Kosovo, Macedonia; Collaborator, Civil Practitioners, Belfast, Northern Ireland, Singapore; Program Director, Western Region Advocacy Teacher Training Program, National Institute for Trial Advocacy **CW:** Co-Author, "Rutter Group California Practice Guide on Personal Injury"; Co-Author, "Mastering the Mechanics of Civil Jury Trials"; Contributor, Articles, Professional Journals; Presenter in Field **AW:** Top 50 Women Lawyers in Northern California (2011-Present); Best Lawyers in America (2010-Present); California Super Lawyers (2010-Present); San Francisco's Top Attorneys (2010-Present); Professional Achievement Award, School of Law, University of San Francisco (2015); Justice & Diversity Center Volunteer Award, The Bar Association of San Francisco (2013, 2015); Robert E. Keeton Award for Outstanding Service, National Institute for Trial Advocacy (2012); Bar Register of Preeminent Lawyers (2012); Merit Award, The Bar Association of San Francisco (2008); Finalist, Trial Lawyer of the Year, San Francisco Trial Lawyer Association (2008); John J. Meehan Alumni Fellow Award, School of Law, University of San Francisco (2007); Public Interest Law Scholar, School of Law, University of San Francisco(1998); Dean's Honor List, UC Davis (1993-1994); Top Women Lawyers in Northern California; Minority 40 Under 40, National Law Journal; Hon. Robert Keeton Faculty Award, National Institute for Trial Advocacy; Top 100, National Trial Lawyers **MEM:** Secretary, The Bar Association of San Francisco (2016-Present); Executive Committee, National Representative, San Francisco Chapter, American Board of Trial Advocates (2015-Present); Fellowship Committee, American College of Trial Lawyers (2015-Present); National Trial Competition Committee, American College of Trial Lawyers (2015-Present); State Committee, American College of Trial Lawyers (2015-Present); National Trial Lawyers (2012-Present); American Board of Trial Advocates (2011-Present); Board Member, Kaiser Arbitration Oversight Board (2010-Present); Committee on Directors, San Francisco Trial Lawyers Association (2009-Present); Finance Committee, San Francisco Trial Lawyers Association (2009-Present); Resource Board, National Association of Women Judges (2007-Present); President-Elect, San Francisco Trial Lawyers Association (2014); Vice President, San Francisco Trial Lawyers Association (2013); Chair, Civility Matters Programs, Law School Division, American Board of Trial Advocates (2012-2014); Conference of Delegates, The Bar Association of San Francisco (2012); Secretary, San Francisco Trial Lawyers Association (2012); Early Settlement Panelist, The Bar Association of San Francisco (2010-2012); Counselor, University of San Francisco Chapter, American Inns of Court (2009-2011); Board of Directors, The Bar Association of San Francisco (2009-2011); Educational Programs Chair, San Francisco Trial Lawyer Association (2009); Conference of Delegates, The Bar Association of San Francisco (2009); Chair, Judiciary Committee, The Bar Association of San Francisco (2008); Judiciary Committee, The Bar Association of San Francisco (2006-2008); Educational Programs Chair, San Francisco Trial Lawyers Association (2006); Women's Caucus Chair, San Francisco Trial Lawyers Association (2004); Mock Trial Committee, San Francisco Trial Lawyers Association (2003-2011); Chair, Barrister Club Newsletter, The Bar Association of San Francisco (2003); Secretary-Treasurer, University of San Francisco Chapter, American Inns of Court (2002-2003); Vice Chair, Barrister Club Newsletter, The Bar Association of San Francisco (2002); Program Chair, University of San Francisco Chapter, American Inns of Court (2001-2002); Membership Chair, University of San Francisco Chapter, American Inns of Court (2000-2001); Executive Committee, University of San Francisco Chapter, American Inns of Court (1999-2011); Treasurer, Parliamentarian, San Francisco Trial Lawyers Association **BAR:** The State Bar of California; United States District Court Northern District of California; United States District Court Eastern District of California; United States Court of Appeals for the Ninth Circuit **MH:** Albert Nelson Marquis Lifetime Achievement Award; Marquis Who's Who Top Professional **B/I:** Ms. Cheng became involved in her profession because of the opportunities with which she was presented.

CHENOWETH, KRISTIN DAWN, T: Actress; Singer **I:** Machinery **DOB:** 07/24/1968 **PB:** Broken Arrow **SC:** OK/USA **PT:** Jerry Morris Chenoweth; Junie (Smith) Chenoweth **ED:** Honorary LHD, Oklahoma City University (2013); Honorary Doctorate in Performing Arts, University of North Carolina School of the Arts (2009); MA in Opera Performance, Oklahoma City University (1992); BA in Musical Theater, Oklahoma City University (1990) **CW:** Performer, "Kristin Chenoweth: For the Girls" (2019); Singer, "For the Girls" (2019); Actress, "A Christmas Love Story" (2019); Voice Actress, "Harvey Girls Forever!" (2019); Performer, "A Very Wicked Halloween" (2018); Actress, "Mom" (2018); Appearance, "Rupaul's Drag Race: All Stars" (2018); Actress, "American Gods" (2017); Actress, "Younger" (2017); Actress, "Class Rank" (2017); Actress, "My Little Pony: The Movie" (2017); Actress, "The Star" (2017); Performer, "My Love Letter to Broadway" (2016); Author, "The Art of Elegance" (2016); Actress, "The Boy Next Door" (2015); Voice Actress, "Strange Magic" (2015); Voice Actress, "BoJack Horseman" (2015); Actress, "On the Twentieth Century" (2015); Voice Actress, "The Peanuts Movie" (2015); Actress, "Descendants" (2015); Actress, "Hard Sell" (2015); Actress, "The Muppets" (2014-2015); Singer, "Coming Home" (2014); Voice Actress, "Rio 2" (2014); Actress, "The Opposite Sex" (2014); Actress, "Glee" (2009-2014); Actress, "The Dames of Broadway...All of 'Em!" (2013); Actress, "Family Weekend" (2013); Actress, "Family Weekend" (2012); Actress, "Hit and Run" (2012); Actress, "Lovin' Lakin" (2012); Actress, "Hot in Cleveland" (2012); Actress, "The Good Wife" (2012); Actress, "GCB" (2012); Singer, "Some Lessons Learned" (2011); Actress, "Legally Mad" (2010); Actress, "You Again" (2010); Actress, "Promises Promises" (2010); Actress, "Sit Down Shut Up" (2009); Author, "A Little Bit Wicked: Life, Love, and Faith in Stages" (2009); Actress, "Love, Loss, and What I Wore" (2009); Actress, "12 Men of Christmas" (2009); Singer, "A Lovely Way to Spend Christmas" (2008); Voice Actress, "Space Chimps" (2008); Actress, "Four Christmases" (2008); Actress, "Pushing Daisies" (2007-2009); Actress, "Stairway to Paradise" (2007); Actress, "Ugly Betty" (2007); Actress, "The Pink Panther" (2006); Actress, "RV" (2006); Actress, "Stranger than Fiction" (2006); Actress, "Running with Scissors" (2006); Actress, "Deck the Halls" (2006); Actress, "The West Wing" (2004-2006); Actress, "Bewitched" (2005); Singer, "As I Am" (2005); Actress, "The Apple Tree" (2005); Actress, "Wicked" (2003-2004); Actress, "The Music Man" (2003); Appearance, "Sesame Street" (2003); Actress, "Topa Topa Bluffs" (2002); Actress, "Funny Girl" (2002); Actress, "Baby Bob" (2002); Singer, "Let Yourself Go" (2001); Actress, "Kristin" (2001); Actress, "Epic Proportions" (1999-2000); Actress, "You're a Good Man, Charlie Brown" (1999); Actress, "Steel Pier" (1999); Actress, "Paramour" (1999); Actress, "Annie" (1999); Actress, "LateLine" (1998); Actress, "A New Brain" (1998); Actress, "Strike Up the Band" (1998); Actress, "Scapin," (1997); Actress, "The Fantasticks" (1995); Actress, "Box Office of the Damned" (1994); Actress, "Dames at Sea" (1994); Actress, "Phantom" (1994); Actress, "Frasier" (1993); Guest Soloist, "West Side Story Suite of Dances"; Performer, Leading Roles, Goodspeed Opera House, Guthrie Theatre, Paper Mill Playhouse, North Shore Music Theatre; Guest Soloist, National Symphony Orchestra, New York Philharmonic, "London's Divas at Donmar" Series, Carnegie Hall, Lincoln Center, John F. Kennedy Center for the Performing Arts; Performer with Placido Domingo, Paul Newman, Joshua Bell and Harvey Fierstein; Actress, Theater, Television, Films; Singer, Solo and Collaborations **AW:** Recipient, Star, Hollywood Walk of Fame (2015); Drama Desk Award for Outstanding Actress in a Musical (2015); GLAAD Vanguard Award (2011); Named to the Oklahoma Hall of Fame (2010); Primetime Emmy Award for Outstanding Supporting Actress in a Comedy Series, Academy of Television Arts & Sciences (2009); Tony Award for Best Featured Actress (1999); Drama Desk Award (1999); Clarence Derwent Award (1999); Outer Critics Circle Award (1999); Theatre World Award (1999); Metropolitan Opera Award **MEM:** Honorary Member, Sigma Alpha Iota International Music Fraternity, Eastman School of Music, University of Rochester (2015); Gamma Phi Beta

CHERIAN, JOY, PHD, T: President; Former Consulting Company Executive **I:** Consulting **DOB:** 05/18/1942 **PB:** Kochi **SC:** Kerala/India **PT:** T. Chandy Herian Cherian; Mariam (Paul) Cherian **MS:** Married **SPN:** Alice Paul (08/15/1970) **CH:** Sheela; Saj **ED:** Master's Degree in Comparative Law, George Washington University, Washington, DC (1978); PhD in International Law, Catholic University, Washington, DC (1974); MA in International Law, Catholic University, Washington, DC (1970); BL, University of Kerala, India (1965); BS, University of Kerala, India (1963) **C:** President, J. Cherian Consultant, Incorporated, Washington, DC (1993-2005); Commissioner, United States Equal Employment Opportunity Commission, Washington, DC (1987-1993); Director, International Insurance Law, American for Council Life Insurance, Washington, DC (1982-1987); Director, Legal Research, American Council for Life Insurance, Washington, DC (1979-1982); Editor, Law Publications, American Council for Life Insurance, Washington, DC (1973-1979) **CIV:** National Chairman, Asian American Voters Coalition, Washington, DC (1986-1987); Founder, National President, Indian-American Forum for Political Education, Washington, DC (1983-1986); President, Association of Americans For Civic Responsibility (AACR) **CW:** Author, "Investment Contracts and Arbitration" (1975); Contributor, Articles, Professional Journals **AW:** Pravasi Bharatiya Saman Award, Government of India (2008); India Abroad Lifetime Achievement Award (2008); Community Leadership Award, LEAP, Los Angeles, CA (1992); Award, Council of Asian Indian Organizations (1989); Distinguished Service Award, Asian American Coalition of Chicago (1988); Community Service Award, National Federation of Asian Indian Organizations (1986) **MEM:** President, American Council for Trade in Services (1994-Present); International Law Section, Chairman, Committee on International Insurance Law, American Bar Association (1982-1992) **BAR:** Council of Kerala (1966) **MH:** Albert Nelson Marquis Lifetime Achievement Award **AS:** Dr. Cherian attributes her success to working hard, as well as God's blessings. **B/I:** Dr. Cherian got involved in her work to serve the people. **AV:** Reading; Gardening **PA:** Independent **RE:** Roman Catholic

CHERNG, PEGGY, PHD, T: Co-Chief Executive Officer **I:** Food & Restaurant Services **CN:** Panda Restaurant Group, Inc. **SC:** Myanmar/Burma **MS:** Married **SPN:** Andrew Cherng (1975) **CH:** Three Daughters **ED:** PhD in Electrical Engineering, University of Missouri (1974); MS in Computer Science, University of Missouri (1971); BS in Mathematics, Oregon State University (1970); Coursework, Baldwin University **C:** Co-Chair, Co-Chief Executive Officer, Panda Restaurant Group, Inc. (2004-Present); President, Chief Executive Officer, Panda Restaurant Group, Inc. (1997-2003); Operations Manager, Panda Restaurant Group, Inc. (1982-1997); Technical Engineer, Software Department Manager, Comtal Corporation, 3M (1977-1982); Engineering Specialist, McDonnell Douglas (1975-1977) **CIV:** Co-Founder, Cherng Family Trust; Board Member, Los Angeles Branch, Federal Reserve Bank of San Francisco; Board Member, United Way of Los Angeles; Board Member, Methodist Hospital of Arcadia; Board Member, Peter F. Drucker School of Management, Claremont Graduate University **AW:** Listee, America's Self-Made Women, Forbes Magazine (2019)

CHERTOW, MARIAN RUTH, T: Industrial Ecologist; Educator **I:** Environmental Services **DOB:** 04/14/1955 **PB:** Syracuse **SC:** NY/USA **PT:** Bernard Chertow; Doris (Saltzman) Chertow **MS:** Married **SPN:** Matthew L. Nemerson (11/10/1985) **CH:** Elana; Joy **ED:** PhD in Environmental Studies, Yale University (2000); MA in Public and Private Management, Yale School of Management (1981); BA, Barnard College, Columbia University, Magna Cum Laude (1978) **C:** Tenured Associate Professor, Industrial Environmental Management, Yale School of Forestry & Environmental Studies (Now Yale School of the Environment) (2011-Present); Associate Professor, Yale School of Management (2009-Present); Visiting Associate Professor for MSc in Environmental Management Programme, School of Design and Environment, National University of Singapore (2001-Present); Director of Industrial Environmental Management Program, Yale University School of Forestry and Environmental Studies (Now Yale School of the Environment) (1991-Present); Director of Program on Solid Waste Policy, Yale University School of Forestry & Environmental Studies (Now Yale School of the Environment (1990-Present); Associate Professor, Industrial Environmental Management, Yale University School of Forestry & Environmental Studies (2007-2011); Assistant Professor of Industrial Environmental Management, Yale University School of Forestry & Environmental Studies (Now Yale School of the Environment (2002-2007); Chair, Founder, Corporate Environmental Leadership Seminar, Yale University School of Forestry & Environmental Studies (Now Yale School for the Environment (1992-2002); Director of Environmental Reform: The Next Generation Project, Yale Center for Environmental Law and Policy, Yale University (1995-1999); Visiting Fellow, Institution for Social and Policy Studies, Yale University (1989-1990); Senior Fellow, The United States Conference of Mayors (1988-1989); Connecticut Resources Recovery Authority (CRRA) (1986-1988); Assistant Town Manager, Assistant to Town Manager, Town of Windsor, CT (1983-1986); Financial Manager of Solid Waste Management Program, Assistant to the Chief Administrative Officer, City and County of San Francisco, CA (1981-1983); Director of Marketing and Development, Resource Recovery Systems, Inc., Essex, CT (1978-1979) **CR:** Speaker in Field **CW:** Contributor, "Quantity, Components, and Value of Waste Materials in the United States," Journal of Industrial Ecology (2018); Co-author, "Long Term Socio-Ecological Research: Studies in Society-Nature Interactions Across Spatial and Temporal Scales," Springer (2013); Contributor, "Environmental Pollution," World Book Encyclopedia (1993-1996); Member, Editorial Board, BioCycle Magazine; Contributor, Journal of Industrial Ecology; Contributor, Numerous Articles to Professional Journals **AW:** Selected, Science to Achieve Results Research Grants Program (2016-2017); Selected, Representative of Unites States, Launch of G7 Alliance for Resource Efficiency, Berlin Germany (2015); Honoree, Connecticut Women's Hall of Fame (2014); Connecticut's Distinguished Environmental Fellowship, Briarwood College (2000); Clyde O. Fisher Award, Environmental Law Section, Connecticut Bar Association (2000); Teresa Heinz Scholarship for Environmental Research (1999-2000); Environmental Merit Award, United States Environmental Protection Agency, Region 1 (1997) **MEM:** Board of Directors, Alliance for Research on Corporate Sustainability (2011-Present); Selected Member, Board of Directors, Terracycle U.S. Inc. (2018); President, International Society of Industrial Ecology (2013-2014); Elected Council Member, International Society for Industrial Ecology (2008-2011); Founding Advisory Board Member, Connecticut Clean Energy Fund (2000-2007); Past President, Connecticut Council, The American Society for Public Administration; Air & Waste Management Association; National Council for Science and the Environment; World Business Council for Sustainable Development; The New York Academy of Sciences; Chautauqua Institution, Chautauqua, NY **MH:** Albert Nelson Marquis Lifetime Achievement

CHESHIRE, WILLIAM POLK, T: Newspaper Columnist, Editor **I:** Writing and Editing **DOB:** 02/02/1931 **PB:** Durham **SC:** NC/USA **PT:** James Webb Cheshire; Anne Ludlow (McGehee) Cheshire **MS:** Married **SPN:** Judith Ann Keel Tunstall; Lucile Geoghegan (08/01/1959) **CH:** William Polk Jr.; Helen Wood; James Webb; **ED:** AB, University of North Carolina at Chapel Hill (1958) **C:** Newspaper Columnist, The Arizona Republic, Phoenix, AZ (1996); Editor, The Arizona Republic, Phoenix, AZ (1996); Senior Editorial Columnist, The Arizona Republic, Phoenix, AZ (1993-1996); Editor, Editorial Pages, The Arizona Republic, Phoenix, AZ (1987-1993); Editor, Editorial Pages, The Washington Times (1984-1987); Editor-in-chief, The Charleston Daily Mail, West Virginia (1978-1984); Editorial Page Editor, Greensboro Record, North Carolina (1975-1978); Editorial Director, Capital Broadcasting Co., Raleigh, North Carolina (1972-1975); Associate Editor, The State, Columbia, South Carolina (1968-1972); Associate Editor, Charleston Evening Post, South Carolina (1963-1968); Associate Editor, Canton Enterprise, North Carolina (1961-1962); General Assignment Reporter, Deputy State Editor, State Capital Reporter, Richmond News Leader, Virginia (1958-1961) **CR:** Commentator, Voice of America, Washington Suns, Washington DC (1986-1987); Professor of Journalism, University of Charleston (1979-1983) **CIV:** Board of Directors, Charleston United Way (1978-1984); Director of Communications, North Carolina U.S. Senate Campaign (1972); Admiral, Great Kanawah River Navy, Charleston, WV; Board of Directors, Sunrise Museum, Charleston, WV **MIL:** United States Coast Guard (1952-1956) **CW:** Articles, National Review **AW:** Washington-Lafayette Eagle, Society of the Cincinnati (2016); Media Fellow, Hoover Institution (1991); Distinguished Fellow in Journalism, Heritage Foundation (1987); Council for the Defense of Freedom Award (1980); George Washington Honor Medal, Freedoms Foundation (1975) **MEM:** President, North Carolina Society of the Cincinnati (1988-1991); President, Piedmont Chapter, Sigma Delta Chi (1978); Philadelphia Society; National Press Club; Phoenix Country Club; Washington Yacht and Country Club **MH:** Albert Nelson Marquis Lifetime Achievement Award **B/I:** Mr. Cheshire initially planned to go into law, but after getting out of the service he decided to change his major to journalism. He excelled at journalism and graduated at the top of his class from Chapel Hill. **AV:** Reading **RE:** Methodist

CHESNEY, KENNY ARNOLD, T: Singer, Songwriter, Musician **I:** Media & Entertainment **DOB:** 03/26/1968 **PB:** Knoxville **SC:** TN/USA **PT:** David Chesney; Karen Chandler **SPN:** Renee Zellweger (05/09/2005, Annulled 12/20/2005) **ED:** Diploma in Advertising, East Tennessee State University (1991) **C:** Creator, Owner, Blue Chair Bay Rum (2013-Present); With, Capricorn, TN (1993); With, Publication Deal, Acuff-Rose (1992); With, RCA, Subsidiary BNA, TN; Resident Performer, The Turf, Nashville, TN; Performer, Chuckie's Trading Post and Quarterback's Barbecue, Johnson City, TN **CIV:** Founder, Love For Love City (2017) **CW:** Singer, Musician, "Here and Now" (2020); Singer, Musician, "Live in No Shoes Nation" (2017); Singer, Musician, "Some Town Somewhere" (2016); Singer, Musician, "Cosmic Hallelujah" (2016); Singer, Musician, "The Big Revival" (2014); Singer, Musician, "Life on a Rock" (2013); Singer, Musician, "Welcome to the Fishbowl" (2012); Singer with Tim McGraw, "Feel Like a Rock Star" (2012); Singer with Grace Potter, "You and Tequila" (2011); Producer, Co-director, "Boys of Fall" (2010); Singer, Musician, "Hemingway's Whiskey" (2010); Singer, Musician, "Lucky Old Sun" (2008); Singer with Tracy Lawrence and Tim McGraw, "Find Out Who Your Friends Are" (2007); Singer, Musician, "Just Who I Am: Poets & Pirates" (2007); Singer, Musician, "The Road & the Radio" (2005); Singer, Musician, "You Save Me" (2005); Singer, Musician, "I Go Back" (2004); Singer, Musician, "When the Sun Goes Down" (2004); Singer, Musician with Willie Nelson and Leon Russell, "Last Thing I Needed First Thing This Morning" (2003); Singer, Musician, "All I Want for Christmas is a Real Good Tan" (2003); Singer, Musician, "The Good Stuff" (2002); Singer, Musician, "No Shirt, No Shoes, No Problem" (2002); Singer, Musician, "Everywhere We Go" (1999); Singer, Musician, "I Will Stand" (1997); Singer, Musician, "Me & You" (1996); Singer, Musician, "All I Need To Know" (1995); Singer, Musician, "In My Wildest Dreams" (1993); Singer, Songwriter, Musician, Solo and Collaboration, Songs and Albums **AW:** Touring Award, Billboard Music Awards (2005-2000, 2011, 2017, 2019); Milestone Award (2015); CMA Award for Musical Event of the Year, CMA Country Music Association Inc. (2012); CMA Award for Music Video of the Year, CMA Country Music Association Inc. (2011); Award, Vocal Event of the Year, Academy of Country Music (2008); CMA Awards for Entertainer of the Year, CMA Country Music Association Awards Inc. (2004, 2006-2008); Awards for Entertainer of the Year, Academy of Country Music Awards (2005-2008); Award for Male Video of Year, Country Music TV (2005, 2007); CMA Award for Musical Event of the Year, CMA Country Music Association Inc. (2007); Award for Favorite Male Singer, People's Choice Awards (2007); Award for Country Songs Artist of the Year, Billboard Music Awards (2006); CMA Award for Album of the Year, CMA Country Music Association Inc. (2004); Award for Single of the Year, Academy of Country Music (2003); Award for Top Male Vocalist, Academy of Country Music Awards (2002); Award for Top New Male Vocalist, Academy of Country Music Awards (1997); Numerous Awards **MEM:** Lambda Chi Fraternity

CHICAGO, JUDITH, "JUDY CHICAGO" SYLVIA, T: Artist **I:** Fine Art **DOB:** 07/20/1939 **PB:** Chicago **SC:** IL/USA **PT:** Arthur M. Cohen; May (Levenson) Cohen **MS:** Married **SPN:** Donald Woodman (1985); Lloyd Hamrol (1965, Divorced 1979); Jerry Gerowitz (1961, Deceased) **ED:** Honorary Doctorate, Duke University (2003); Honorary Doctorate, Smith College (2000); Honorary Doctorate, Lehigh University (2000); Honorary Doctorate, Russell Sage College (1992); MA, University of California (1964); BFA, UCLA (1962) **CR:** Visiting Artist, California Polytechnic Institute, Pomona, CA (2003); Professor-in-Residence, Western Kentucky University (2001); Visiting Artist, Duke University (2000); Visiting Artist, University of North Carolina (2000); Visiting Artist, Indiana University (1999); Co-Founder, Through the Flower Corporation (1977); Co-Founder, Feminist Studio Workshop, Los Angeles, CA (1973); Teacher, Fresno State College (Now California State University, Fresno) (1970); Teacher, California Institute for the Arts **CW:** Author, "Institutional Time: A Critique of Studio Art Education" (2014); Author, "Frida Kahlo: Face to Face" (2010); Author, "Through the Flower: My Struggle as a Woman Artist," Lincoln: Authors Choice Press (2006); Author, "Kitty City: A Feline Book of Hours" (2005); Artist, One-Woman Show, American Counseling Association Galleries, New York, NY (1984, 1985, 1986, 2004, 2005); Author, "Fragments from the Delta of Venus" (2004); Artist, One-Woman Show, National Museum of Women in the Arts (2002); Artist, One-Woman Show, Brooklyn Museum (1980, 2002); Author, "Women and Art: Contested Territory" (1999); Author, "Beyond the Flower: The Autobiography of a Feminist Artist" (1996); Author, "The Dinner Party" (1996); Author, "Holocaust Project: From Darkness into Light" (1993); Author, "The Birth Project" (1985); Artist, One-Woman Show, Musee d'Art Contemporain, Montreal, Canada (1982); Artist, One-Woman Show, Fine Arts Gallery, Irvine, CA (1981); Artist, One-woman Show, Parco Galleries, Japan (1980); Author, "Embroidering Our Heritage: The Dinner Party Needlework" (1980); Author, "The Dinner Party: A Symbol of Our Heritage" (1979); Artist, One-Woman Show, San Francisco Museum of Modern Art (1979); Artist, One-Woman Show, Quay Ceramics, San Francisco, CA (1976); Author, "Through the Flower: My Struggle as a Woman Artist" (1975); Artist, One-Woman Show, JPL Fine Arts, London, United Kingdom (1975); Artist, Group Exhibit, Winnipeg Art Gallery (1975); Artist, One-Woman Show, Jack Glenn Gallery, Corona del Mar, CA (1972); Artist, Group Exhibit, Whitney Museum (1972); Artist, One-Woman Show, Pasadena Museum of California Art (1969); Artist, Group Exhibit, Jewish Museum, New York, NY (1966, 1967); Artist, Solo and Group Exhibits, Numerous Museums; Represented in Permanent Collections, Brooklyn Museum, San Francisco Museum of Modern Art, Oakland Museum of Art, Pennsylvania Academy of Fine Arts, Los Angeles County Museum of Art and Numerous Private Collections **AW:** One of the 100 Most Influential People, Time Magazine (2018) **THT:** Between May 9, 2020 and September 6, 2020, The Fine Arts Museum of San Francisco will celebrate pioneering feminist artist Judy Chicago with a retrospective spanning from her early engagement with the Californian Light and Space Movement in the 1960s to her current body of work, a searing investigation of mortality and environmental devastation, begun in 2015. The exhibition will include around 150 works and related archival material that chart the boundary-pushing path of the artist named Cohen by birth and Gerowitz by marriage, who, after trying to fit into the patriarchal structure of the Los Angeles art world, decided to change her name and the course of history. Organized on the heels of the 40th anniversary of The Dinner Party's first San Francisco presentation and opening in conjunction with the 100th anniversary of wom-

en's right to vote across the United States, Judy Chicago: A Retrospective pays homage to an artist whose lifelong fight against the suppression and erasure of women's creativity has finally come full circle.

CHILES, ROBERT S. SR., T: President, Chief Executive Officer **I:** Financial Services **CN:** Greensboro National Bank (now merged) **CH:** Two Children **ED:** MBA in Business Administration, Wake Forest University, NC (1973); BS in Accounting, North Carolina Central University (1956) **C:** President, Chief Executive Officer, Chiles Dunnings Incorporated, Greensboro, NC (1982-Present); Greensboro National Bank, NC (1979-1994; President, Greensboro National Bank, NC (1981); Wachovia Bank & Trust Company (1969-1979) **CIV:** Greensboro Merchants Association; Haze Taylor YMCA Fundraiser **AW:** Chester's Merit Award, North Carolina Central University; Three Time Alumnus of the Year, North Carolina Central University **MEM:** Minority MBA's; National Society of Public Accountants **AS:** Mr. Chiles atributes his success to hard work and keeping his eyes on the goal. "Build relationships in life... people respond to others whether it's fundraising, or friend-raising..." **B/I:** Mr. Chiles believes that he was inspired by his grandparents who were not very highly educated but made successes out of themselves. His grandfather became a successful business man in the construction industry. He always aspired to be like him. After his grandfather passed away, his grandmother continued to push and inspire him to strive to be the best that he could be. Mr. Chiles began his career in baking in 1969 with the Wachovia Banking & Trust Company. He began working with the general loan administration department, where he was in charge of the responsibility of developing small business loans with an interest in minority lending. Prior to that he worked with the small business administration, where he was responsible for getting banking loans for small businesses in North Carolina. Mr. Chiles first charge with Wachovia Bank was from the request of Floyd McKissick who was developing a new city in North Carolina named Soul City. This opportunity allowed Mr. Chiles to fly around the United States and learn from other American city developers, useful techniques he can apply to his assignment.

CHIN, CHEN OI, T: Scholar **I:** Education/Educational Services **SC:** Singapore **MS:** Married **SPN:** Chang Jang Hsieh, PhD **CH:** Chih-Mao Hsieh, PhD **ED:** PhD, The Ohio State University, Columbus, Ohio (1976); MA, Yale University, New Haven, CT (1968); BA, National Taiwan University, Taipei, Taiwan (1966) **C:** President, Chinese American Educational and Cultural Center of Michigan (CAECC), Ann Arbor, MI (2017-Present); Advisor, Chongqing University, China (1982-Present); Executive Director, Chinese American Educational and Cultural Center of Michigan (CAECC), Ann Arbor, MI (1976-2016); Dean, Center for Cultural Diversity, Services Performed Between USA-Singapore; Professor, Lawrence Technological University, Southfield, MI; Assistant Professor, University of Detroit Mercy, Detroit, MI; Lecturer, National Diversity of Singapore **CR:** Cultural and Arts Consultant on China, Singapore and Several Asian Regions for General Motors, Ford Motor Company, Berlitz International, Oriental Resources International, Prudential (Prudential Financial, Inc.), GMAC, International Orientation Resources, and Langua Tutor; Vice Presidents and Senior Executive, McDonald's, Coca Cola (The Coca-Cola Company), Northwest Airlines, Delphi, Daimler Chrysler (Daimler AG), Lear Corporation, Federal Mogul (Tenneco Inc.) and Johnson Controls, National Endowment for the Arts, Chinese Music

Society of North America, Michigan State Department of Education, Eastern Michigan University, Bilingual Department, HEW, Washington; Michigan Council for the Arts and Cultural Affairs (Michigan Economic Development Corporation), Advisory Board, University of Michigan Musical Society (University Musical Society); Founder, Chinese American Educational and Cultural Center of Michigan (CAECC) **CIV:** Funding Reviewer, Michigan Council for Arts and Cultural Affairs (Michigan Economic Development Corporation), National Endowment for the Arts, and Cultural Grants Funding; Funding Reviewer, Michigan Council for the Humanities (Michigan Humanities Council); Project Director, Michigan Chinese Americans Archives Collection; Teachers-in-service Training on Chinese Arts and Culture; Curriculum Development on Chinese Culture; Chinese Arts and Culture Symposia/Seminars; Presenter, Numerous Annual Arts and Cultural Activities in Michigan Statewide Public Places, Chinese Folk Art Festival, The Moon Festival, Early Chinese Settlers in Michigan Archival Exhibits, Works on Chinese American Artists Exhibits; Chinese Instrumental Training and Musical Presentations, Workshops for Teachers and Students on Chinese Painting, Calligraphy and Chinese Culture; Invited Distinguished Speaker, Eastern Michigan University Business School; Chair, Michigan Statewide Conference, "Leadership and Culture: Experiences Sharing with Profit and Nonprofit Organizations" **CW:** Author, "Yuan Ming Tsachu Ch'uan-kuan Kao" ("The Costumes and Props of the Yuan Dynasty : Drama"); Author, "The Concept of Imitation"; Author, Numerous Articles on Global Leadership; Author, "Private Collections of Chinese Arts in Michigan"; Author, "Private Collections of Calligraphy in Michigan"; Author, "Twelve Years of Harvest"; Author, "Twenty Years of Harvest"; Author, "Early Michigan Chinese Settlers (1872-1950s); Producer, Video, "Vision, Courage, Action" **AW:** Named Confucian Scholar, Singapore "International Conference on Confucianism on World Civilization"; Grantee, National Education Association; Adviser, Chongqing University, China; Grantee, The Asia Foundation; Six National Taiwan University Academic Annual Awards; Six Overseas Chinese Students Annual Awards; Yale University Fellowship; Distinguished Community Service Award, Michigan; Best Paper Award, Midwest Academy of Management Conference **MEM:** Academy of Management; Midwest Academy of Management; Concerned Citizens for the Arts in Michigan; Yale Alumni Association **MH:** Albert Nelson Marquis Lifetime Achievement Award **AS:** Dr. Chin attributes his success to constantly holding a positive attitude. **B/I:** Dr. Chin became involved in his profession because of interests and challenges. **RE:** Christian **THT:** Dr. Chin said, "Let nature take its course." He also believes all humans are equal.

CHITTENDEN, SHERRY DIANNE, T: Special Education Educator **I:** Education/Educational Services **DOB:** 08/12/1950 **PB:** Springfield **SC:** MO/USA **PT:** John Jacob; Mary Ethel (Bozarth) Cavin **MS:** Married **SPN:** Ted Anthony Chittenden (08/18/1972) **CH:** Kimberly Dianne; Carolyn Jean **ED:** MEd, Southwest Missouri State University (Now Missouri State University), Springfield, MO (1986); BS, Southwest Missouri State University (Now Missouri State University), Springfield, MO (1972); Diploma, Central High School Springfield, MO (1968) **CT:** Teacher's Certificate in Elementary Education K-8; Teacher's Certificate in Mentally Handicapped K-12; Teacher's Certificate in Learning Disabilities K-12; Teacher's Certificate in Behavioral Disorders K-12; Teacher's Certificate in Educational Resource K-12 **C:** Substitute Teacher, Fordland R-III School District and New Covenant Christian Academy (2018-2020); Special Education

Teacher, Fordland R-III School District (2002-2016); Special Education Teacher, Ozark R-VI School District (1987-2002); Substitute Teacher, Springfield Public School (1984-1987); Substitute Teacher, Greene Valley State School (Now Greene Valley School for the Severely Disabled), Springfield, MO (1980-1981); Teacher, Fifth Grade, Sixth Grade, Halfway School District R-III (1978-1979); Substitute Teacher, Morrisville School District (1977-1978); Substitute Teacher, Pleasant Hope R-VI School District (1977-1978); Teacher, Fourth Grade, Pleasant Hope R-VI School District (1972-1973) **CR:** Autism Consultant **CIV:** Ridgecrest Baptist Church **CW:** Board Newsletter Editor, Missouri CEC Federation (Now Missouri Council for Exceptional Children (CEC)) (2004-2005); Presenter, Conferences, Council for Exceptional Children; Contributor, Numerous Project Access Workshops **MEM:** Secretary, Delta Kappa Gamma (DKGSI), Epsilon Chapter (2008-2010, 2014-2020); Treasurer, Springfield Council for Exceptional Children (CEC), Chapter 164 (2012-2020); Missouri Council for Exceptional Children (CEC) (1987-2020); Missouri CEC Federation Board (Now Missouri Council for Exceptional Children (CEC)) of the Subdivision on the Division on Autism and Developmental Disabilities (DADD) Board Representative (2010-2016); President, Missouri Council for Exceptional Children (CEC) Subdivision of the Division on Autism and Developmental Disabilities (2011-2014); Vice President, Missouri Council for Exceptional Children (CEC) Subdivision of the Division on Autism and Developmental Disabilities (2009-2011); Vice President, Springfield Council for Exceptional Children (CEC), Chapter 164 (2009-2011); Missouri Federation Council for Exceptional Children (Now Missouri Council for Exceptional Children (CEC)) of the Subdivision on Mental Retardation and Developmental Disabilities Board Representative (1996-2010); President-elect, Missouri CEC Federation (Now Missouri Council for Exceptional Children (CEC) Council on Behavioral Disorders (Now Council for Children with Behavioral Disorders) (2007-2009); CAN Coordinator, Springfield Council for Exceptional Children (CEC), Chapter 164 (2007-2009); President, Delta Kappa Gamma (DKGSI), Alpha Kappa Chapter (2004-2006); President, CAN Coordinator, Springfield Council for Exceptional Children (CEC), Chapter 164 (2001-2003); Member-at-large, Missouri CEC Federation (Now Missouri Council for Exceptional Children (CEC) Council on Behavioral Disorders (Now Council for Children with Behavioral Disorders) (1997-1998, 2001-2002); CAN Coordinator, Missouri CEC Federation (Now Missouri Council for Exceptional Children (CEC) Council on Behavioral Disorders (Now Council for Children with Behavioral Disorders) (2000-2001); Missouri CEC (Now Missouri Council for Exceptional Children (CEC)) Subdivision of the Division on Mental Retardation and Disabilities (1999-2001); Past President, Missouri CEC Federation (Now Missouri Council for Exceptional Children (CEC) Council on Behavioral Disorders (Now Council for Children with Behavioral Disorders) (1999-2000); President, Missouri CEC Federation (Now Missouri Council for Exceptional Children (CEC) Council on Behavioral Disorders (Now Council for Children with Behavioral Disorders) (1998-1999); Past President, Missouri CEC (Now Missouri Council for Exceptional Children (CEC)) Subdivision of the Division on Mental Retardation and Disabilities (1996-1999); Missouri Council for Exceptional Children (CEC) Subdivision of the Division on Mental Retardation and Developmental Disabilities Vice President (1994-1996); President, Missouri CEC (Now Missouri Council for Exceptional Children (CEC)) Subdivision of the Division on Mental Retardation and Disabilities (1993-1996); Secretary, Springfield Council for

Exceptional Children (CEC), Chapter 164 (1993-1996); Missouri State Teachers Association; Ozark Teachers Association **MH:** Albert Nelson Marquis Lifetime Achievement Award; Marquis Who's Who Top Professional **AS:** Mrs. Chittenden attributes her success in education through the guidance of her Christian parents and of course, teachers who inspired her to achieve a degree in education. Without God's grace, help, and guidance, none of the above would have been accomplished. **B/I:** Mrs. Chittenden became involved in the education profession when she graduated from college. During that time, she had planned to become either a secretary or a teacher. She decided it would be best for her to become a teacher so that she could spend time with her family when school was out and would have time to take care of them. **AV:** Sewing; Quilting; Cooking; Nature walking **PA:** Republican **RE:** Southern Baptist **THT:** Mrs. Chittenden says, "A good life is what you make of it and the choices we make. It has a foundation of truth that never wavers. My foundation is the Bible and it's teachings from the inspired word of God of where we came from and why we are here on earth. I thank God as stated in the Bible for the gift of Jesus Christ (God's Son) who gave His life for the sacrifice of our sins if we only trust and believe in Him. God gives us every thing we have, even the next breath we take, and the strength to go the next step in life."

CHMIELEWSKI, DAWN M., T: Attorney **I:** Law and Legal Services **CN:** Neblett, Beard & Arsenault **PB:** Cleveland **SC:** OH/USA **ED:** JD, Cleveland-Marshall College of Law, Cleveland State University, Ohio, Magna Cum Laude (2004); BSN, The University of Akron, Akron, Ohio (1996) **C:** Attorney, Neblett, Beard & Arsenault (2013-Present); Department Head, Department of Pharmaceuticals and Defective Medical Devices, Climaco, Wilcox, Peca, Tarantino & Garofoli, Co. LPA (2003-2013); Registered Nurse, The Cleveland Clinic Foundation (1996-2003) **CR:** Active Member, Actos (Pioglitazone) Products Liability Litigation Trial Team; Active Member, Pinnacle Hip Implant Products Liability Litigation Trial Teams, Dallas, Texas **CIV:** Participant, Fundraising, Crohn's & Colitis Foundation, Northeast Ohio Chapter and Ovarian Cancer Coalition of Ohio **MEM:** Ohio State Bar Association **BAR:** United States District Court for the Northern District of Ohio; United States District Court for the Southern District of Ohio; United States Court of Appeals for the Sixth Circuit; United States District Court for the Eastern District of Arkansas; United States District Court for the Western District of Arkansas **AS:** Ms. Chmielewski attributes her success to hard work; she puts in serious hours when taking pharmaceutical and drug companies to trial. All six of her recent trials were lengthy, lasting 12 weeks or more. She often travels to other states. **B/I:** Ms. Chmielewski became involved in her profession because she has always been interested in the law. Her mother was a registered nurse so she wanted to follow in her footsteps. As a nurse, she enjoyed the work, but she felt she had to give being a lawyer a shot because it was what she originally wanted to do. She didn't realize in the beginning that she would still be able to use her nursing, but as she was going through law school learning about different areas of the law, that's when it first clicked for her. She could continue doing what she loves from a medical standpoint, while also reaching for the goal she had to work in the legal profession. Ms. Chmielewski enjoys utilizing both her science and law backgrounds. **AV:** Reading; Traveling; Cheering on her favorite teams, including Ohio State football and every Cleveland sports team **THT:** Ms. Chmielewski's motto is, "Be dedicated to your

cause, go after the things you care about. The things that are important you have to prioritize and dedicate your time to and get it done."

CHO, AUSTINA, T: Psychiatrist **I:** Medicine & Health Care **CN:** Harbor Psychologists **ED:** MD, Louisiana State University, New Orleans, LA (1995); BS in Biochemistry, Louisiana State University, Baton Rouge, LA (1990) **CT:** Board Certified, Adult Psychiatry **C:** Psychiatrist, Harbor Psychologists (2018-Present); Psychiatrist, Excess Urgent Care, University of California Los Angeles (UCLA); Psychiatrist, Los Angeles County; Psychiatrist, Orange County Mental Health; Residency, University of California Irvine; Internship, Riverside General Hospital **CR:** Behavioral Health Director, Korean Community Services (2013-Present) **CIV:** Former Board Member, Domestic Violence Agencies; Former Board Member, Asian Rehabilitation Services; Member, Family Mental Health Mission, Orange County; Volunteer, Working with the Homeless in Downtown Los Angeles **AW:** Numerous Awards, Healthcap **MEM:** Fellow, American Psychological Association (APA); Southern California Psychiatric Society; American Board of Psychiatry and Neurology (ABPN) **MH:** Marquis Who's Who Top Professional **AS:** Dr. Cho attributes her success to perseverance, despite any kind of challenges or obstacles that came along the way, and dedication, believing in the vision and the mission to help mentally ill persons. Helping to relieve suffering has been the driving motivating force for her. **B/I:** Dr. Cho became involved in her profession because she felt that personality disorders weren't really understood. She saw so many patients suffering severely with untreated personality disorders, some had attempted suicide multiple times. It has really had a negative impact on their lives. She wanted to see if there were better choices as far as treatment options. She also thinks tat a lot of people in jail have anti social personality disorder and have probably not had the best upbringing and opportunities in life. Dr. Cho believes that instead of writing these people off, giving them hope for rehabilitation and changing the decisions they have made in their life is better for society as whole and them as an individual.

CHOI, HYONGGUN, PHD, T: Chief Executive Officer, President, Owner **I:** Education/Educational Services **CN:** Elite Academy Inc. **DOB:** 11/28/1957 **PB:** Gyeongju **SC:** Korea **PT:** Tae-sik Choi; Young-ae Jeong **MS:** Married **SPN:** Sylvia Hsiahua Choi **CH:** Michael Sung-gyu Choi **ED:** PhD in Philosophy, Kangwon National University, Chuncheon, South Korea (2015); MLS, University at Albany, Albany, NY (1990); MA in Journalism, National Chengchi University, Taipei, Taiwan (1987); BA in Chinese Language and Literature, Sungkyunkwan University, Seoul, South Korea (1981) **C:** Executive Director, Bridge to Humanity (2009-Present); President, Elite Academy Inc., Glenview, IL (1997-Present); Head, Public Services and Korean Studies, Joseph Regenstein Library, The University of Chicago, Chicago, IL (1993-2003); Librarian, Joseph Regenstein Library, The University of Chicago, Chicago, IL (1993-2003); Specialist, Korean Bibliography, Class/ASIA Department of Education, Los Angeles, CA (1991-1993) **CIV:** Executive Director, Founder, Bridge to Humanity **MIL:** Served, Korean Army (1981-1983); With United States Army, Camp Red Cloud, Uieongbu, Korea **CW:** Author, "Korean Collections Development in North America Libraries," Journal of Asian Studies (2007); Author, "Hyonggun Choi Essay Collection: I Miss My Mother"; Contributor, Articles, Professional Journals **AW:** Tung-Hsien-Guang Journalism Scholarship, Graduate School of Journalism, National Chengchi University (1984); Suseon Scholarship, Sungkyunkwan University (1978-1980) **MEM:** Former Member, CEAL: Council on East Asian Libraries **AS:** Dr. Choi attributes his success to trying to be sincere to himself. **B/I:** Dr. Choi became involved in his profession with inspiration from great teachers who pointed him in the right direction. **THT:** Dr. Choi values sincerity and selflessness. As Executive Director of Bridge to Humanity, he organizes a team of high school students on charitable trips to Haiti, Colombia and Nicaragua. In addition to English, Dr. Choi is fluent in Chinese and Korean.

CHOMSKY, AVRAM NOAM, PHD, T: Philosopher, Political Activist, Historian, Professor **I:** Education/Educational Services **CN:** The University of Arizona **DOB:** 12/07/1928 **PB:** Philadelphia **SC:** PA/USA **PT:** William Chomsky; Elsie (Simonofsky) Chomsky **MS:** Widowed **SPN:** Carol Doris Schatz (12/24/1949, Deceased 12/19/2008) **CH:** Aviva; Diane; Harry Alan **ED:** Honorary DHL, Uppsala University, Sweden (2007); Honorary DHL, University de la Frontera, Temuco, Chila (2006); Honorary DHL, University de Chile (2006); Honorary DHL, University of Bologna (2005); Honorary DHL, University of Ljubljana (2005); Honorary DHL, National and Kapodistrian University of Athens (2004); Honorary DHL, Central Connecticut State University (2004); Honorary DHL, University Florence (2004); Honorary DHL, Central Connecticut State University (2003); Honorary DHL, Vrije Universiteit Brussel (2003); Honorary DHL, Universidad Nacional de Colombia (2002); Honorary LittD, University of Calcutta (2001); Honorary DHL, National University of Comahue, Argentina (2001); Honorary DHL, University of Western Ontario (2000); Honorary DHL, University of Toronto (2000); Honorary LLD, Harvard University (2000); Honorary DHL, University of Connecticut (1999); Honorary Doctorate, Scuola Normale Superiore, Pisa, Italy (1999); Honorary DHL, Columbia University (1999); Honorary DHL, University Guelph, Canada (1999); Honorary DHL, McGill University (1998); Honorary DHL, Universitat Rovira i Virgili, Catalonia, Spain (1998); Honorary LLD, University Buenos of Aires (1996); Honorary DHL, Amherst College (1995); Honorary LittD, University of Cambridge, England, United Kingdom (1995); Honorary DHL, Gettysburg College (1992); Honorary DHL, University of Maine (1992); Honorary DHL, University of Pennsylvania (1984); Honorary LittD, Visva-Bharati University, Santiniketan, West Bengal, India (1980); Honorary DHL, University of Massachusetts (1973); Honorary LittD, Delhi University, India (1972); Honorary DHL, Bard College (1971); Honorary DHL, Swarthmore College (1970); Honorary DHL, Loyola University Chicago (1970); Honorary DHL, The University of Chicago (1967); Honorary LittD, University of London (1967); PhD, University of Pennsylvania (1955); MA, University of Pennsylvania (1951); BA, University of Pennsylvania (1949) **C:** Laureate Professor of Linguistics, Agnese Nelms Haury Chair, The University of Arizona (2017-Present); Institute Professor Emeritus, Massachusetts Institute of Technology (2017-Present); Institute Professor, Massachusetts Institute of Technology (1976-2017); Ferrari P. Ward Professor, Modern Language and Linguistics, Massachusetts Institute of Technology (1966-1976); Professor, Modern Languages, Massachusetts Institute of Technology (1961-1976); Faculty Member, Massachusetts Institute of Technology (1955-1961) **CR:** Pauling Memorial Lecturer, Oregon State University (1995); Jeanette K. Watson Distinguished Visiting Professor, Syracuse University (1982); Kant Lecturer, Stanford University (1979); Woodbridge Lecturer, Columbia University (1978); Huizinga Lecturer, Leiden University (1977); Nehru Memorial Lecturer, New Dehli, India (1972); Bertrand Russell Memorial Lecturer, Cambridge, England,

United Kingdom (1971); John Locke Lecturer, University of Oxford (1969); Beckman Professor, University of California Berkeley (1966-1967); Linguistic Society of America Professor, University of California Los Angeles, Summer (1966); Member, Institute for Advanced Study, Princeton University (1958-1959); Visiting Professor, Columbia University, NY (1957-1958) **CW:** Author, "Requiem for the American Dream" (2017); Author, "Global Discontents: Conversation on the Rising Threats to Democracy" (2017); Author, "Who Rules the World" (2016); Author, "Masters of Mankind: Essays and Lectures, 1969-2013" (2015); Author, "What Kind of Creatures are We?" (2015); Author, "Because We Say So" (2015); Author, "Masters of Mankind: Essays and Lectures" (2014); Author, "Democracy and Power: The Delhi Lectures" (2014); Author, "The Quotable Chomsky" (2014); Author, "Occupy: Reflections on Class War, Rebellion and Solidarity" (2013); Author, "Nuclear War and Environmental Catastrophe" (2013); Author, "On Anarchism" (2013); Author, "On Western Terrorism: From Hiroshima to Drone Warfare" (2013); Author, "The Science of Language" (2012); Author, "Making the Future: Occupations, Interventions, Empire and Resistance" (2012); Author, "Power Systems: Conversations on Global Democratic Uprisings and the New Challenges to the U.S. Empire" (2012); Author, "9-11: Was There an Alternative?" (2011); Author, "Hopes and Prospects" (2010); Author, "New Worlds of Indigenous Resistance" (2010); Author, "Making the Future: The Unipolar Imperial Moment" (2010); Co-Author, with Ilan Pappe, "Gaza in Crisis: Reflections on Israel's War Against the Palestinians" (2010); Author, "The Essential Chomsky" (2008); Author, "Interventions" (2007); Author, "What We Say Goes: Conversations on U.S. Power in a Changing World" (2007); Author, "Inside Lebanon: Journey to a Shattered Land with Noam and Carol Chomsky" (2007); Author, "Failed States: The Abuse of Power and the Assault on Democracy" (2006); Co-Author, with Gilbert Achcar, "Perilous Power: The Middle East and U.S. Foreign Policy" (2006); Author, "Imperial Ambitions: Conversations with Noam Chomsky on the Post-9/11 World" (2005); Author, "Middle East Illusions" (2003); Author, "Hegemony or Survival: America's Quest for Global Dominance (The American Empire Project)" (2003); Author, "Understanding Power: The Indispensable Chomsky" (2002); Author, "On Nature and Language" (2002); Author, "Pirates and Emperors, Old and New" (2002); Author, "9-11" (2001); Author, "Propaganda and the Public Mind" (2001); Author, "New Horizons in the Study of Language and Mind" (2000); Author, "Rogue States" (2000); Author, "A New Generation Draws the Line" (2000); Author, "Architecture of Language" (2000); Author, "The New Military Humanism" (1999); Author, "The Common Good" (1998); Author, "Profits Over People" (1998); Author, "Powers and Prospects" (1996); Author, "The Minimalist Program" (1995); Author, "Language and Thought" (1994); Author, "World Orders, Old and New" (1994); Author, "Year 501" (1993); Author, "Rethinking Camelot" (1993); Author, "Letters from Lexington" (1993); Author, "The Prosperous Few and the Restless Many" (1993); Author, "Chronicles of Dissent" (1992); Author, "What Uncle Sam Really Wants" (1992); Author, "Deterring Democracy" (1991); Author, "Necessary Illusions" (1989); Co-Author, with Edward Herman, "Manufacturing Consent" (1988); Author, "Language and Politics" (1988); Author, "Culture of Terrorism" (1988); Author, "On Power and Ideology" (1987); Author, "Language and Problems of Knowledge" (1987); Author, "Language in a Psychological Setting" (1987); Author, "Generative Grammar" (1987); Author, "Barriers" (1986); Author, "Knowledge of

Language" (1986); Author, "Pirates and Emperors" (1986); Author, "Turning the Tide" (1985); Author, "Fateful Triangle" (1983); Author, "Concepts and Consequences of the Theory of Government and Binding" (1982); Author, "Towards a New Cold War" (1982); Author, "Radical Priorities" (1982) **AW:** Sean Macbride Peace Prize (2017); Neil and Saras Smith Medal for Linguistics (2011); Sydney Peace Prize (2011); Carl-von-Ossietzky Prize, Oldenburg, Germany (2004); Award, United Nations Society of Writers (2004); Award, Kurdistan Human Rights Association, Diyarbakir, Turkey (2002); Peace Award, Turkish Publishers Association, Istanbul, Turkey (2002); Adela Dwyer St. Thomas Villanova Peace Award, Villanova University, Philadelphia, PA (2002); Rising Sun of Mehgarh Award, Dawn Islamabad (2001); Kyoto Prize, Kyocera Foundation (1988, 2001); Rabindranath Tagore Centenary Award, The Asiatic Society, Calcutta, India (2000); Benjamin Franklin Institute Award (1999); Helmholtz Medal, Berlin-Brandenburgische Akademie der Wissenschaften (1996); Loyola Mellon Humanities Award, Loyola University Chicago (1994); Homer Smith Award, New York University School of Medicine (1994); Joel Seldin Peace Award, Psychologists for Social Responsibility (1993); Lannan Literature Award for Nonfiction (1992); James Killian Faculty Award, Massachusetts Institute of Technology (1992); Professional Excellence Award, Association for Education in Journalism and Mass Communications (1991); George Orwell Award, NCTE (1989, 1987); Distinguished Science Contribution Award, American Psychological Association (1984); Junior Fellow, Society of Fellows, Harvard University (1951-1955); Recipient, Honorary Doctorates, Numerous Universities **MEM:** William James Fellow, American Psychological Association (1990); Fellow, Correspondent Member, American Association for the Advancement of Science; Fellow, Correspondent Member, British Academy; Honorary Member, The British Psychological Society; Royal Anthropological Institute, Great Britain, United Kingdom; Royal Anthropological Institute, Ireland; Honorary Member, Utrecht University Arts and Sciences Society; Honorary Member, Gesellschaft für Sprachwissenschaft; American Academy of Arts & Sciences; American Academy of Philosophy; Foreign Member, Royal Society of Canada; he American Philosophical Society; American Psychological Association; National Academy of Sciences; Linguistic Society of America; Deutsche Akademie der Naturforscher Leopoldina; Association for Education in Journalism and Mass Communications

CHOPRA JONAS, PRIYANKA, T: Actress **I:** Media & Entertainment **DOB:** 07/18/1982 **PB:** Jamshedpur, Bihar **SC:** India **PT:** Ashok Chopra; Madhu Chopra **MS:** Married **SPN:** Nick Jonas (12/01/2018) **CR:** Founder, Purple Pebble Pictures (2015-Present) **CIV:** With, UNICEF (2006-Present); Goodwill Ambassador, UNICEF (2010, 2016); Founder, The Priyanka Foundation **CW:** Appearance, "Happiness Continues" (2020); Appearance, "Chasing Happiness" (2019); Actress, "Isn't It Romantic" (2019); Actress, Producer, "The Sky is Pink" (2019); Actress, "A Kid Like Jake" (2018); Producer, "Pahuna" (2018); Producer, "Bhoga Khirikee" (2018); Producer, "Firebran" (2018); Producer, "Paani" (2018); Producer, "Sarvann" (2017); Producer, "Kay Re Rascalaa" (2017); Producer, "Kaashi Amarnath" (2017); Actress, "Baywatch" (2017); Actress, "Jai Gangaajal" (2016); Actress, "Ventilator" (2016); Producer, "Bam Bam Bol Raha Hai Kashi" (2016); Producer, "Ventilator" (2016); Actress, "Gunday" (2014); Actress, "Mary Kom" (2014); Actress, "Dil Dhadakne Do" (2014); Actress, "Dewana Main Deewana" (2013);

Actress, "Girl Rising" (2013); Actress, "Shootout at Wadala" (2013); Actress, "Planes" (2013); Actress, "Krrish 3" (2013); Actress, "Goliyon Ki Raaslella Ram-Leela" (2013); Actress, "Agneepath" (2012); Actress, "Teri Meri Kahaani" (2012); Actress, "Barfi" (2012); Actress, "7 Khoon Maaf" (2011); Actress, "Ra. One" (2011); Actress, "Don 2" (2011); Actress, "Pyaar Impossible!" (2010); Actress, "Anjaana Anjaani" (2010); Actress, "Kaminey: The Scoundrels" (2009); Actress, "What's Your Raashee" (2009); Actress, "Dostana" (2008); Actress, "Love Story 2050" (2008); Actress, "God Tussi Great Ho" (2008); Actress, "Chamku" (2008); Actress, "Drona" (2008); Actress, "Fashion" (2008); Actress, "Salaam-E-Ishq" (2007); Actress, "Big Brother" (2007); Actress, "Taxi No. 9 2 11: Nau Do Gyarah" (2006); Actress, "36 China Town" (2006); Actress, "Alag: He is Different... He is Alone..." (2006); Actress, "Krrish" (2006); Actress, "Don" (2006); Actress, "Blackmail" (2005); Actress, "Karam" (2005); Actress, "Wagt: The Race Against Time" (2005); Actress, "Yakeen" (2005); Actress, "A Sublime Love Story: Barsaat" (2005); Actress, "Plan" (2004); Actress, "Kismat" (2004); Actress, "Asambhav" (2004); Actress, "Mujhse Shaadi Karogi" (2004); Actress, "Aitraaz" (2004); Actress, "The Hero: Love Story of a Spy" (2003); Actress, "Andaaz" (2003); Actress, "Thamizhan" (2002); Columnist, Hindustan Times and Elle; Actress, Appearances, Music Videos, Television Shows, Films **AW:** Named One of the Most Beautiful Women in the World, People Magazine (2017, 2019); Named One of the 50 Most Powerful Women in Entertainment, USA Today (2019); Named One of the 100 Most Influential People in the World, TIME Magazine (2017, 2018); Named One of the 500 Most Influential Leaders, Variety (2017, 2018); Named One of India's 50 Most Powerful People, India Today (2017, 2018); Named One of the World's Eight-highest-paid Television Actresses, Forbes Magazine (2016, 2017); Mother Teresa Memorial Award for Social Justice (2017); Named One of the Most Powerful Indian Women, Verve Magazine (2009, 2010, 2013, 2015, 2016); Padma Shri Award, Government of India (2016); Neilsen Box Office Star of Asia Award, Asian Film Awards (2009); Award for Best Actress, Screen Weekly Awards (2009); Award for Best Actress, Filmfare Awards (2009); Award for Best Performance in a Negative Role, Screen Weekly Awards (2005): Award for Best Actor in a Villainous Role, Filmfare Awards (2005); Award for Best Debut - Female, Filmfare Awards (2004); Named Winner, Beauty Pageants Including Miss World, Miss India World and Miss World Continental Queen of Beauty - Asia & Oceania (2000); Named One of the Most Intriguing People of the Year, People Magazine; Numerous Awards

CHORNEY, MICHAEL, T: Musician, Music Producer **I:** Fine Art **C:** Musician, Composer, Hollar General (2011-Present); Guitarist, Arranger, Band Leader, "Hadestown" Orchestra (2007-Present); Musician, Composer, Magic City (2005-Present); Guitarist, Producer, Arranger, Collaborations with Anais Mitchell (2004-Present); Solo Musician, Composer (2004-Present); Musician, Collaborations with Miriam Bernardo (2003-Present); Musician, Composer, Orchid (2001-Present); Musician, MC6 (2009-2010); Musician, Seven Deadly Sins (2004); Band Leader, Composer, ViperHouse (1995-2000); Band Leader, Composer, So-called Jazz Sextet (1990-1995); Guitarist, Saxophonist, Sun Dog (1988-1990); Musician, Feast or Famine (1980-1985); Producer, Artists Including David Moss, Iain Morrison, Adrian Roye, Round Mountain, Seth Eames, the Dupont Brothers, Maryse Smith and Others **CW:** Musician, Producer, "Shameless Light" (2015); Musician, Producer, "Reclaimed" (2013); Musician, Producer, "Young Man in Amer-

ica" (2012); Musician, Producer, "Wonder" (2010); Musician, Producer, "Hadestown" (2010); Musician, Producer, "It Disappears" (2009); Musician, Producer, "Songs in Secret Ink" (2008); Musician, Producer, "Dispensation of the Ordinary" (2012); Musician, Producer, "Oom Pah of the Ghost Parade" (2010); Producer, "The Brightness" (2007); Musician, Producer, "Glossolalia" (2007); Musician, Producer, "Mother Tongue" (2006); Producer, "Hymns for the Exiled" (2004); Musician, Producer, "Orchid" (2002); Musician, Producer, "Lap Hen" (1999); Musician, Producer, "Tribute to Mingus" (1999); Musician, Producer, "Shed" (1997); Musician, Producer, "Ottawa" (1997); Musician, Producer, "Viperhouse" (1995); Musician, Producer, "Vermont Avenue" (1993); Musician, Producer, "Songs and Music of Paul Bowles" **AW:** Co-Recipient, Tony Award, Best Orchestrations, "Hadestown" (2019)

CHOU, GRACE I., T: Assistant Controller **I:** Business Management/Business Services **CN:** Logan Bus Company **ED:** Bachelor of Science in Business Administration, Tan Kang University (1980) **AS:** Ms. Chou attributes her success to her work experience. **AV:** Listening to music; Singing in choirs

CHOUCAIR, BECHARA, MD, T: Senior Vice President, Chief Health Officer **I:** Medicine & Health Care **CN:** Kaiser Permanente **ED:** Doctor of Medicine, American University of Beirut (1997); Bachelor of Science, American University of Beirut (1993); Master's Degree in Healthcare Management, The University of Texas at Dallas **C:** Chief Health Officer, Kaiser Permanente (2020-Present); Chief Community Health Officer, Kaiser Permanente (2016-2020); Senior Vice President, Safety Net and Community Health, Trinity Health (2015-2016); Commissioner, Chicago Department of Public Health (2009-2014); Executive Director, Medical Director, Heartland Health Centers, Chicago, IL (2005-2009); Medical Director, Crusader Clinic (2001-2005) **CW:** Contributor, Articles to Professional Journals **AW:** Named, One of the 100 Most Influential People in Healthcare, Modern Healthcare (2019); Housing Champion Award, Metropolitan Tenants Organization (2014); Named, One of Chicago's 40 Under 40, Crain's Chicago Business (2012); Friend for Life Award, Howard Brown Health Center (2012); Healthcare Community Leadership Award, The Chicago Health Executives Forum (2011); Community Leadership Award, Midwest Asian Health Association (2010)

CHOYKE, WOLFGANG JUSTUS, PHD, T: Research Professor Emeritus **I:** Education/Educational Services **CN:** University of Pittsburgh **DOB:** 07/24/1926 **PB:** Berlin **SC:** Germany **PT:** Frederick Samuel Choyke; Alice Sophia Amalia (Dessauer) Choyke **MS:** Widowed **SPN:** Helen Ruth Rubenfeld (06/19/1949, Deceased 05/2007) **CH:** Alice Mathea; Peter Lyle **ED:** PhD in Nuclear Physics, The Ohio State University (1952); BSc, The Ohio State University (1948); Diploma, The Bronx High School of Science (1943) **C:** Research Professor Emeritus, University of Pittsburgh (2018-Present); Research Professor in Physics, University of Pittsburgh (1988-2018); Consultant Physicist, Westinghouse Research Laboratories, Pittsburgh, PA (1978-1988); Adjunct Professor of Physics, University of Pittsburgh (1974-1988); Advisory Physicist, Westinghouse Research Laboratories, Pittsburgh, PA (1963-1978); Physicist Fellow, Westinghouse Research Laboratories, Pittsburgh, PA (1960-1963); Research Physicist, Westinghouse Research Laboratories, Pittsburgh, PA (1952-1960) **CR:** Visiting Professor, University of Erlangen-Nuremberg (1990-2004); Chairman, Committee on Large Band Gap Semiconductor Devices, National Research

Council (1993-1995); Consultant, Northrup-Grumman and Westinghouse Science & Technology Center, Pittsburgh, PA (1988-1998) **MIL:** With, United States Army Signal Corps (1944-1946) **CW:** Contributor, "Silicon Carbide Recent Major Advances," Springer (2004); Contributor, "Fundamental Aspects of SiC in Handbook of Semiconductor Technology," Wiley-VCH (2000); Contributor, "The Physics and Chemistry of Carbides, Nitrides and Borides," Series E Applied Sciences (1989); Contributor, "Volume I and II Silicon Carbide: A Review of Fundamental Questions and Applications to Current Device Technology," Academie Verlag (1977); Contributor, Articles to Professional Journals; Contributor, Edited Books **AW:** Humboldt Research Prize, Alexander von Humboldt Foundation, Bonn, Germany (1990); Recipient, Westinghouse Order of Merit (1983) **MEM:** Committee on Applications Physics, American Physical Society (1977-1986); Fellow, American Physical Society; Fellow, American Association for the Advancement of Science; Material Research Society **MH:** Albert Nelson Marquis Lifetime Achievement Award **AS:** Dr. Choyke attributes his success to luck and hard work. **B/I:** As a child, Dr. Choyke was interested in painting, particularly with watercolors. Then, he met a friend who lived in his apartment-house in New York who was interested in science. That's how he got interested in astronomy. Since then, this same friend has won a Nobel Prize for physics. **AV:** Research

CHRISTENSEN, BARBARA JEAN, RN, BS, MS, T: Nurse Educator, Medical and Surgical Nurse **I:** Medicine & Health Care **DOB:** 09/08/1935 **PB:** Sioux Rapids **SC:** IA/USA **PT:** Nels; Mabel (Johnson) Lauritsen **MS:** Widowed **SPN:** Gerald Christensen (Deceased) **CH:** Jennifer Holly, MD; Jessica Heather, BA; Jason Heath, PhD **ED:** MS, The University of Nebraska at Kearny (1988); BS, The University of Nebraska at Kearny (1978); Diploma, St. Joseph Mercy School of Nursing, Sioux Falls, IA (1956) **CT:** Registered Nurse **C:** Retired (2008); Medical Surgical Nurse, Great Plains Regional Medical Center (1991-2002); Medical Surgical Nurse Educator, Mid-Plains Community College (1972-2008); Nurse Educator, El Paso County Education Association (1964-1967); Nurse Educator, St. Francis Hospital (1964-1967); Nurse Educator, St. Joseph Mercy Hospital School of Nursing (1958-1963) **CR:** Nurse Representative, Nebraska Board of Health (1992-1994) **CIV:** Board of Directors, North Platte Swim Team (1979-1985); President, Washington Parent-Teacher Association (1979-1980); Board Member, North Platte Opportunity Center **CW:** Nurse Reviewer, "Comprehensive Review of Practical Nursing, Tenth Edition" (1990); Co-Editor, "Foundations of Nursing"; Co-Editor, "Adult Health Nursing" **AW:** Women of Achievement Award (1998, 2016); Lifetime Membership, Local Parent-Teacher Association **MEM:** National League for Nursing **MH:** Albert Nelson Marquis Lifetime Achievement Award **B/I:** Ms. Christensen became involved in her profession because she came from a small town and wanted to pursue a career in which she could help others.

CHRISTENSEN, RAYMOND G., MD, FAAFP, T: Physician **I:** Medicine & Health Care **CN:** Gateway Family Health Clinic, Ltd. **DOB:** 04/03/1944 **PB:** Valley City **SC:** ND/USA **PT:** Irvin Arthur Christensen; Phyllis Ione (Myers) Christensen **SPN:** Joan Johnson **CH:** Kari Rae; Anna Marie **ED:** Intern, St. Mary's Medical Center, Essentia Health, Duluth, MN (1971-1972); MD, University of Wisconsin (1971); BS in Agriculture, Wisconsin State University (Now University of Wisconsin-River Falls) (1966) **CT:** Diplomate, American Academy of Family Physicians **C:** Physician, Gateway Family Health Clinic LTD, Moose Lake, MN (1972-Present) **CR:** Preceptor, Rural Physician Program, University of Minnesota Medical School, Duluth, MN (1972-Present); Medical Advisor, Minnesota Department of Health, Minneapolis, MN (1991-1995); Rural Consultant, Medical Outreach Department, University of Minnesota, Minneapolis, MN (1992); Airman Medical Examiner, Federal Aviation Administration (FAA), U.S. Department of Transportation, Moose Lake, MN **CIV:** Trustee, Minnesota Hospital Association, Minneapolis, MN (1989-Present); President, Northern Lakes Health Care Consortium, Duluth, MN (1984-Present); Chair, Foundation Health Care Evaluation (1992); Founder, Rural Access Clinic, Cromwell, MN (1992); Director, Lake Superior Chapter, Duluth, MN (1989-1991); Arrowhead Emergency Medical Services, Duluth, MN (1984-1991); Chairman, National Rural Health Resource Center, Duluth, MN; Vice Chairman, World Health Innovations, Duluth, MN; Associate Dean for Rural Health, National Rural Health Resource Center; Association Professor of Family Medicine, National Rural Health Resource Center; Associate Director, Rural Physician Associate Program, National Rural Health Resource Center; Director, Rural School Leadership Academy **AW:** Community Service Award, Minnesota Medical Association (1992); Louis Goren Award, National Rural Health Association (1989); Merit Award, Minnesota Academy of Family Physicians; Recipient, Various Awards, North Lakes Health, North Lakes Consortium, Arrowhead EMS Association, Lake Superior Medical Society **MEM:** President-elect, Minnesota Medical Association (1995-1996); Vice President, Minnesota Medical Association (1993-1995); President, Minnesota Academy of Family Physicians (1993-1994); President-elect, Minnesota Academy of Family Physicians (1992); President, Lake Superior Medical Society (1991); Fifth District Representative, Grand Lodge, Masons (1991); Chairman, Board of Directors, Minnesota Academy of Family Physicians (1990-1991); Past Master, Solomon's Lodge, Masons (1987); American Medical Association; American Hospital Association; American Academy of Family Physicians; American Geriatrics Society; Civil Aviation Medical Association; Scottish Rite, Shriners International; Past President, National Rural Health Association; Past President, Minnesota Rural Health Association (MRHA) **MH:** Albert Nelson Marquis Lifetime Achievement Award **AS:** Dr. Christensen attributes his success to his mission to provide healthcare access to rural citizens and our visitors. **B/I:** As the oldest of six from a small, poor farm, Dr. Christensen did not see himself following the path of a doctor. What brought him over, however, was the observation of lapses of care in the people he grew up with. He saw a great injustice in the way people around him were neglected in their health, which stayed with him and inspired him to become a doctor himself. **AV:** Biking; Running; Canoeing; Tennis; Fishing **RE:** Lutheran

CHU, JONATHAN MURRAY, T: Director **I:** Media & Entertainment **DOB:** 11/02/1979 **PB:** Palo Alto **SC:** CA/USA **PT:** Lawrence Chu; Ruth Chu **MS:** Married **SPN:** Kristin Hodge (2018) **CH:** Jonathan Heights; Willow **ED:** University of Southern California School of Cinematic Arts (2003) **CW:** Director, Executive Producer, "Good Trouble" (2019-Present); Director, "In the Heights" (2020); Producer, "Step Up: Year of the Dance" (2019); Director, "Crazy Rich Asians" (2018); Director, "Now You See Me 2" (2016); Director, Producer, "Jem and the Holograms" (2015); Executive Producer, "Step Up: All In" (2014); Director, "Justin Bieber's Believe" (2013); Director, "G.I. Joe: Retaliation" (2013); Executive Producer, "Step Up Revolution" (2012); Director, "Justin Bieber: Never Say Never" (2011);

Director, Executive Producer, Writer, Editor, "The Legion of Extraordinary Dancers" (2010-2011); Director, "Step Up 3D" (2010); Director, "Step Up 2: The Streets" (2008); Director, Producer, "When the Kids Are Away" (2002); Director, Producer, Writer, "Silent Beats" (2001) **AW:** Princess Grace Award; Dore Schary Award, Anti-Defamation League; Jack Nicholson Directing Award; Honoree, IFP/West Program, Project: Involve

CHU, JUDY MAY, T: U.S. Representative from California **I:** Government Administration/Government Relations/Government Services **DOB:** 07/07/1953 **PB:** Los Angeles **SC:** CA/USA **PT:** Judson Chu; May Chu **MS:** Married **SPN:** Mike Eng (1978) **ED:** PhD, California School of Professional Psychology, Alliant International University (1979); MA in Clinical Psychology, California School of Professional Psychology, Alliant International University (1977); BA in Mathematics, University of California Los Angeles (1974) **C:** Member, U.S. House of Representatives from California's 27th Congressional District, United States Congress (2013-Present); Member, Committee on Armed Services (2013-Present); Member, Committee on Science, Shape and Technology (2013-Present); Member, Committee on Small Business (2013-Present); Member, U.S. House Committee on Education and Labor (2009-Present); Member, U.S. House of Representatives from California's 32nd Congressional District, United States Congress (2010-2013); Vice Chair, California State Board of Equalization (2009); Chair, California State Board of Equalization (2008); Member, District 4, California State Board of Equalization (2007-2009); Member, District 49, California State Assembly (2001-2006); Monterey Park City Council (1988-2001); Professor, East Los Angeles College, Monterey Park, CA (1988-2001); Mayor, Monterey Park City Council (1995-1995); Mayor, Monterey Park City Council (1990-1991); Associate Professor, Los Angeles City College, CA (1981-1988); Lecturer, University of California Los Angeles (1980-1986) **CIV:** Board of Directors, Garvey School District (1985-1988); Chair, Los Angeles Unified School District (1984-1985); Chair, Commission for Sex Equity **CW:** Author, Editor, "Linking Our Lives: Chinese American Women in Los Angeles" (1984); Contributor, Articles, Professional Journals **AW:** Named Los Angeles' Outstanding Founder (1995); Award for Excellence in Public Service, UCLA Alumni (1991); Volunteer of the Year, San Gabriel Valley Chapter, United Way (1989); Democrat of the Year, 59th Assembly District Democratic Committee (1989); Public Service Award, Pacific Legal Center (1989); Listee, 88 Leaders for 1988, Los Angeles Times (1988); Achievement Award, Asian Pacific Family Center (1980); Leadership Award, West San Gabriel Valley Chapter, The American National Red Cross **MEM:** Soroptimists **PA:** Democrat **RE:** Unitarian Universalist

CHUKWU, CHINONYE, T: Director **I:** Media & Entertainment **PB:** Port Harcourt **SC:** Nigeria **ED:** Bachelor's in English, DePauw University; Coursework, Temple University **CW:** Director, Writer, "Clemency" (2019); Director, "Alaska-Land" **AW:** U.S. Dramatic Grand Jury Prize, Sundance (2019)

CICALA, ROGER STEPHEN, T: Entrepreneur **I:** Medicine & Health Care **CN:** Lensrentals **DOB:** 08/21/1956 **PB:** Parkersburg **SC:** WV/USA **PT:** Edmond D. Cicala; Ann (Pettit) Cicala **MS:** Divorced **SPN:** Shari Lee Miller (03/17/1982, Divorced 12/1989) **CH:** Kristin Cicala Beckman; Paul Andrew Cicala **ED:** Chief Resident, The University of Tennessee (1985); MD, The University of Tennessee Health Science Center, Memphis, TN (1982); BS in Biology, Christian Brothers College

(Now Christian Brothers University), Memphis, TN (1978) **CT:** Diplomate, The American Board of Anesthesiology; American Board of Independent Medical Examiners (ABIME); American Board of Pain Medicine **C:** Staff Physician, Semmes Murphey Clinic (2003-2011); Founder, Lensrentals.com (2007); Associate Professor of Anesthesiology, The University of Tennessee (1990-1994); Director of Pain Center, The University of Tennessee (1988-1994); From Instructor to Assistant Professor, The University of Tennessee (1987-1990) **CR:** Chief Executive Officer, Olaf Optical Testing (2013-2019); Chief Executive Officer, Lensrentals. com (2011-2018); Director, Methodist Hospitals Comprehensive Pain Treatment Center (1998); Eastwood Medical Center, Memphis, TN (1991-1994); Director of Trauma Anesthesia, Elvis Presley Trauma Center, Regional One Health, Memphis, TN (1988-1992); Member, Staff, Elvis Presley Trauma Center, Regional One Health, Memphis, TN (1987-1994); Member, Staff, Methodist Hospital Memphis (1986-1994); Anesthesiology Staff, Memphis Neuroscience Center (1986-1987); Presenter in Field **CIV:** **CW:** Medical Author, Illustrator (1994-1997); Co-author, "The Heart Disease Handbook" (1996); Co-author, "Handbook of Trauma Surgery" (1993); Co-author, "Manual of Trauma Anesthesia" (1993); Co-editor, "Textbook of Trauma Anesthesia and Critical Care" (1992); Co-author, "Geriatric Anesthesiology" (1992); Co-author, "Textbook of Trauma Anesthesia and Critical Care" (1992); Co-author, "Headache: Diagnosis and Interdisciplinary Treatment" (1992); Co-author, "Refresher Course in Anesthesiology, Volume 20" (1992); Co-author, "Courtroom Medicine: Pain and Suffering" (1991); Co-editor, Books; Contributor, Published Papers for Optics **MEM:** Board of Directors, Society for Pain Practice Management (1991-1994); Co-chairman, Task Force, International Trauma Anesthesia and Critical Care Society (1991-1993); American Association for the Advancement of Science; American Medical Association; American Society of Anesthesiologists (ASA); American Pain Society; International Association for the Study of Pain; International Trauma Anesthesia and Critical Care Society; International Anesthesia Research Society, Tennessee Medical Association; Tennessee Society Anesthesiologists; Shelby County Medical Society; Shelby County Anesthesia Society; Society of Cardiovascular Anesthesiologists; Society for Pain Practice Management; Association of University Anesthetists **MH:** Albert Nelson Marquis Lifetime Achievement Award **B/I:** Dr. Cicala's hobby was photography and he bought too much equipment, so he started renting some of his equipment out and he did the rental online; business took off and he was the first one to do online rentals. He became the founder of Lens Rental. His company grew 100 percent every three months for two years. **AV:** Computer programming; Photography

CICILLINE, DAVID NICOLA, T: U.S. Representative from Rhode Island **I:** Government Administration/Government Relations/Government Services **DOB:** 07/15/1961 **PB:** Providence **SC:** RI/USA **PT:** John Francis Cicilline; Sabra (Peskin) Cicilline **ED:** JD, Georgetown University Law Center, Washington, DC, Cum Laude (1986); BA in Political Science, Brown University, Providence, RI, Magna Cum Laude (1983) **C:** Co-chair, Democratic Policy and Communications Committee (2017-Present); Member, U.S. House Committee on Foreign Affairs (2011-Present); Member, U.S. House Small Business Committee (2011-Present); Member, U.S. House of Representatives from Rhode Island's First Congressional District, United States Congress (2011-Present); Private Practice, Providence, RI (1987-Present); Mayor, City of Providence, RI

(2003-2011); Member, District Four, Rhode Island House of Representatives (1995-2003); Staff Attorney, Public Defender Service, Washington, DC (1986-1987); Member, Committee on the Judiciary **CR:** President, National Conference of Democratic Mayors (2008); Adjunct Professor of Law, Roger Williams University School of Law, Bristol, RI **CIV:** Volunteer Attorney, ACLU, Providence, RI (1990-Present); Member, Rhode Island Criminal Justice Commission; Board of Directors, Nickerson Community Center; Board of Directors, Mount Hope Neighborhood Association; Board of Directors, Langston Hughes Center for Arts; Board of Directors, Aids Project Rhode Island; Board of Directors, Center for Individualized Teaching and Education; Chairman, Board of Directors, Very Special Arts Rhode Island **CW:** Contributing Author, "Criminal Practice Institute Trial Manual" (1987) **MEM:** Rhode Island Association of Criminal Defense Lawyers; Rhode Island Bar Association; Bar Association of DC; Public Defender Alumni Association; National Association of Criminal Defense Lawyers **PA:** Democrat **RE:** Jewish

CIFU, DOUGLAS A., T: Chief Executive Officer, Co-Founder **I:** Financial Services **CN:** VIRTU Financial Inc. **ED:** JD, Columbia Law School (1990); BA in Political Science, Columbia University, Magna Cum Laude (1987) **C:** Chief Executive Officer, Co-Founder, VIRTU Financial Inc. (2013-Present); Vice Chairman, Partner, Alternate Governor, Florida Panthers, NHL (2013-Present); Partner, Paul, Weiss, Rifkind, Wharton & Garrison LLP (1990-2008) **CR:** Member, Management Committee, Paul, Weiss, Rifkind, Wharton & Garrison LLP; Deputy Chairman, Corporate Department, Paul, Weiss, Rifkind, Wharton & Garrison LLP; Lead Independent Director, Board of Directors, Independent Bank Group, Inc. **CIV:** Board of Directors, U.S. Chamber of Commerce; Board of Visitors, Columbia College, Columbia University **MEM:** The Phi Beta Kappa Society

CIMERA, RICHARD F., T: Senior Director of Aerospace Engineering (Retired) **I:** Engineering **DOB:** 04/25/1934 **PB:** Clifton **SC:** NJ/USA **PT:** Rudolph Frank Cimera; Genevieve Cimera **MS:** Married **SPN:** Joyce Carol Pranio Cimera (10/06/1956) **CH:** Renee Lynn Cimera McFadden; Keith Bryan; Glenn Robert (Deceased) **ED:** Professional Diploma of Mechanical Engineering, New Jersey Institute of Technology (1976); MME, Newark College of Engineering (1970); MS, Stevens Institute of Technology, Hoboken, NJ (1958); Diploma in Mechanical Engineering, Stevens Institute of Technology, Hoboken, NJ, with Honor (1955) **CT:** Registered Professional Engineer, State of New Jersey **C:** Director, Inertial Component Development, Kearfott Guidance & Navigation Corporation (Now Kearfott Corporation), Wayne, NJ (1984-2015); Manager, Special Gyro Products, Kearfott Division, The Singer Company Limited, Wayne, NJ (1978-1984); Supervisor, Special Gyros, Kearfott Division, The Singer Company Limited, Wayne, NJ (1966-1978); Senior Staff Engineer, Kearfott Division, The Singer Company Limited, Little Falls, NJ (1963-1966); Product Manager, Kearfott Division, General Precision Corporation, Little Falls, NJ (1961-1963); Unit Head, Kearfott Division, General Precision Corporation, Little Falls, NJ (1960-1961); Project Engineer, Kearfott Division, General Precision Corporation, Clifton, NJ (1958-1960); Junior Project Engineer, Kearfott Division, General Precision Corporation, Clifton, NJ (1956-1958); Equipment Engineer, Standard Oil Company of New Jersey, Bayonne, NJ (1955-1956) **CIV:** Little League Baseball Manager, Fairfield, NJ (10 Years); Co-founding Member, Saint Thomas More R.C. Church, Fairfield, NJ **CW:** Published, Numerous Technical Papers on Gyroscope Design and Application; Contributor, Articles to Professional Journals; Inventor, Seven U.S. Patents **AW:** Named Engineer of the Year, Kearfott Division, The Singer Company Limited (1982); Outstanding Patent Award, Research and Development, Council of New Jersey (1973); Ranked Fifth in Class of 125, Stevens Institute of Technology, Hoboken, NJ (1955) **MEM:** The American Society of Mechanical Engineers; Past President, Stevens Alumni Association, Stevens Institute of Technology **MH:** Albert Nelson Marquis Who's Who 2020 Albert Nelson Marquis Lifetime Achievement Award 2020Albert Nelson Marquis Who's Who in Science and Engineering 3rd Edition 1996-1997 **AS:** Mr. Cimera attributes his success to a great college education in mechanical engineering. He also credits having a great mentor at Kearfott, Walter J. Krupick, and working for a great company, Kearfott Guidance and Navigation Corporation. **B/I:** Mr. Cimera had always had a love for technology. When he started working at Kearfott, he realized the work that he did was exactly what he prepared for in college. It was the perfect job for him and he knew it would be. His first job out of college was for an oil company. He was a mechanical engineer and he found a company, Kearfott Division, General Precision Corporation, that made products that he wanted to work on, so he wanted to work for them. **AV:** Photography; Stamp collecting; Playing billiards/pool; Ping pong; Bridge (at the Parsippany Community Center); Played semi-pro baseball after college **PA:** Republican **RE:** Roman Catholic **THT:** Prior to the launch of Apollo 11, that landed the first man on the moon (Neil Armstrong), Mr. Cimera's company had to give his phone number to President Nixon in case there was trouble. At a management dinner, he sat next to Jim Lovell, Commander of the Apollo 13, since he worked on the Rate Gyro Package intended to guide the LEM vehicle. But when the Apollo 13 Guidance System was destroyed, Commander Lovell had to use the Rate Gyro Package to safely return to Earth. He asked Commander Lovell if he was ever worried about returning home. He said, "Every second of every minute of every hour."

CIOCHETTY, JOHN, T: Protective Services Site Supervisor **I:** Other **CN:** Aegis Protective Services **DOB:** 06/17/1955 **PB:** Parkersburg **SC:** WV/USA **PT:** John Joseph Ciochetty; Mary Ann Ciochetty **CH:** Amanda Raye Bodkin **ED:** MS, Marshall University, Huntington, WV (1988); BA, Marshall University, Huntington, WV (1980) **CT:** Certification in NIM-SICS (National Incident Management Systems, Incident Command System), Incident Command Course EMA (Emergency Management Associates) (2013); Certification, Crisis International Training Officer, Delaware-Morrow Mental Health & Recovery Services, Delaware Police Department (2008); Certification, Campus Law Enforcement, Purdue University, West La Fayette, IN (2003); Certification in Crisis Prevention Non-Violent Intervention, West Virginia Department of Corrections (1984); Certification, Terrorist Education Course, Denison University, U.S. Department of Homeland Security (2003); Certification, FEMA (Federal Emergency Management Agency); Certification, Homeland Security and Delaware County, Ohio **C:** Site Security Supervisor, Aegis Protective Services (2020); Site Security Supervisor, Garda World (2019-2020); Patrol Officer, Ohio Dominican University, Columbus, OH (2018-2019); Custom Protection Officer, G4S Global Solutions-USA, Columbus, OH (2017-2019); Public Safety Campus Police, Ohio Wesleyan University, Delaware, OH (2001-2017); Loss Prevention Investigator, Meijer Corporation, Columbus, OH (1995-2000); Instructor, Sociology and Criminology, West Virginia University, Parkersburg, WV (1990-1991); Judicial Officer, Probation Services, West Virginia Supreme Court, Charleston, WV (1988-1990); Correctional Deputy Sheriff, Wood County Sheriff's Department, Parkersburg, WV (1986-1988); Instructor, Political Science, Marshall University, Huntington, WV (1976-1986) **CR:** Custom Protection Officer, Investigator, Wackenhut Corporation, Columbus, OH (1992-1995); Adult Probation Officer, Marysville Municipal Court, Ohio (1991-1992); Vice President, Management Development, Junior Chamber of Commerce, Parkersburg, WV (1986-1992); Patrolman, Investigator, Statewide Bureau Investigations, Parkersburg, WV (1975-1983) **CIV:** Member, National Performance Review Office of U.S. Vice President Al Gore (1993-2000); Advisory Board Member, Big Brothers Big Sisters of America, Parkersburg, WV (1980-1983) **MIL:** Lt., U.S. Army Reserve (1980-1988) **CW:** Author, "The Ghosts of Historic Delaware Ohio" (2010); Author, "The Ghosts of Stuyvesant Hall and Beyond," Volume 1" (2007); Author, "Nuclear Biological and Chemical Defense" (1986) **AW:** Professional of the Year Award, Campus Safety & Law Enforcement-National Recognition (2010); Letter of Commendation, Ohio Police Department, Delaware, OH (2006); Military Order of World Wars Citation, U.S. Army (1979) **MEM:** Delaware County Historical Society **MH:** Albert Nelson Marquis Lifetime Achievement Award; Marquis Who's Who Top Professional **AS:** Mr. Ciochetty attributes his success to being compassionate toward people. **B/I:** Mr. Ciochetty became involved in his profession because he was inspired while he was in college. During breaks from school, he would work as an investigator. He has a family history of law enforcement. His third cousin was Don Knotts, the actor who, ironically, played a sheriff on "The Andy Griffith Show." **AV:** Horseback riding; Writing; Computers; Traveling; Karate; Aikido

CIPOLLONE, PAT, T: White House Counsel **I:** Law and Legal Services **ED:** BA in Economics and Political Philosophy, Fordham University (1988) **C:** Counsel, White House (2018-Present); Litigation Partner, Kirkland and Ellis LLP, Washington, DC; Assistant to Hon. William P. Barr, U.S. Department of Justice; Judicial Clerk to Judge Danny J. Boggs, United States Court of Appeals for the Sixth Circuit **CW:** Managing Editor, The University of Chicago Law Review **AW:** Attorney General's Award for Excellence in Management **BAR:** District of Columbia (1995); Illinois (1993) **PA:** Republican

CISNEROS, GILBERT RAY JR., T: U.S. Representative **I:** Government Administration/Government Relations/Government Services **DOB:** 02/12/1971 **PB:** Los Angeles **SC:** CA/USA **MS:** Married **SPN:** Jacki Cisneros **CH:** Two children **ED:** MBA, Regis University; MA in Urban Education Policy, Brown University; BA in Political Science, The George Washington University **C:** U.S. Representative, California's 39th District (2019-Present); Member, U.S. House Committee on Armed Services (2019-Present); Member, U.S. House Committee on Veterans' Affairs (2019-Present); Shipping and Manufacturing Manager, Frito-Lay (2010); Member, Congressional Hispanic Caucus; Member, Congressional Asian Pacific American Caucus; Member, Bipartisan for Country Caucus **CIV:** Founder, The Gilbert & Jacki Cisneros Foundation **MIL:** Supply Officer, U.S. Navy **AW:** Navy Commendation Medal; Navy Achievement Medal; National Defense Medal; Armed Forces Expeditionary Medal **PA:** Democrat

CLANCY, MICHELE, T: Resource Room Educator **I:** Education/Educational Services **CN:** Lacey Township School District **PT:** Robert Valenza; Josephine Valenza **MS:** Married **SPN:** Joseph Clancy **CH:** Meghan Curso; Erin Rebello; One Son **ED:**

PhD in Educational Research, Capella University, Summa Cum Laude; MS in Education, University of South Carolina, Summa Cum Laude; BS in Education, Columbia College **C:** Resource Room Educator, Lacey Township School District (1991-Present); Teacher, Orthopedic School (1987-1991) **CIV:** Lacey Parent Teacher Association **MEM:** Alumni Association, University of South Carolina; Alumni Association, Columbia College; Alumni Association, Capella University **AS:** Dr. Clancy attributes her success to "intrinsic motivation" and her desire to make a difference in a child's life. Ms. Clancy also attributes her success to her parents, Robert and Josephine Valenza, both of whom worked very hard and never retired. Also, her grandparents, Elizabeth and Nunzio Gangi, were instrumental to her success. They were immigrants from Italy who learned English in the United States. Likewise, they promoted life-learning and the importance of education. Further, Dr. Clancy's husband, Joseph, who is an MD, encouraged her to pursue a PhD. **B/I:** When Dr. Clancy was a teenager, she volunteered to work with children with down syndrome, which was where she found her comfort zone. She grew up with a cousin who had down syndrome and became inspired to work in education. She continued to work in the field, working with children who were orthopedically handicapped and terminally ill.

CLAPTON, ERIC PATRICK, T: Guitarist, Singer **I:** Media & Entertainment **DOB:** 3/30/1945 **PB:** Ripley **SC:** England **PT:** Edward Walter Fryer; Patricia Molly Clapton **MS:** Married **SPN:** Melia McEnery (2002); Patricia Anne Boyd (1979, Divorced 1989) **CH:** Julie Rose; Ella May; Sophie Belle; Ruth Kelly; Conor (Deceased 1991) **ED:** Diploma, Hollyfield School, Surbiton, England (1961); Coursework, Kingston School of Art, Kingston University London **C:** Solo Artist (1970-Present); Guitarist, Singer, Derek and the Dominos (1970-1971); Guitarist, Delaney and Bonnie and Friends (1969-1970); Guitarist, Singer, Blind Faith (1969); Guitarist, Singer, Cream (1966-1968); Guitarist, Eric Clapton and the Powerhouse (1966); Guitarist, Singer, John Mayall and the Bluesbreakers (1965-1966); Member, The Glands (1965); Guitarist, The Yardbirds (1963-1965); Guitarist, Casey Jones and the Engineers (1963); Guitarist, The Roosters (1963); Busker, Kingston, Richmond and West End, England **CR:** Sponsor, West Bromwich Albion FC, UEFA Cup (1978-1979) **CIV:** Founder, Crossroads Centre (1998-Present); Donor, Aid Still Required (2008); Board of Directors, Chemical Dependency Centre (1994-1999); Director, Board Member, Clouds House (1993-1997); Organizer, Crossroads Guitar Festival; Collaborator, The Prince's Trust **CW:** Musician, "Happy Xmas" (2018); Musician, "I Still Do" (2016); Musician, "The Breeze: An Appreciation of JJ Cale" (2014); Musician, "Old Sock" (2013); Musician, "Clapton" (2010); Featured Musician with J.J. Cale, "The Road to Escondido" (2006); Musician with Cream, "Royal Albert Hall London May 2-3-5-6, 2005" (2005); Musician, "Back Home" (2005); Musician, "Sessions for Robert J" (2004); Musician, "Me and Mr. Johnson" (2004); Musician with Cream, "BBC Sessions" (2003); Musician with The Yardbirds, "Live! Blueswailing July '64" (2003); Musician, "Reptile" (2001); Featured Musician with B.B. King, "Riding with the King" (2000); Featured Musician with Beatchuggers, "Forever Man (How Many Times?)" (2000); Musician, "Pilgrim" (1998); Featured Musician with Cher, Chrissie Hynde, and Neneh Cherry, "Love Can Build a Bridge" (1995); Musician, "From the Cradle" (1994); Musician with as Derek and the Dominos, "Live at the Fillmore" (1994); Musician, "Rush" (1992); Featured Musician with Sting, "It's Probably Me" (1992); Featured Musician with Elton John, "Runaway Train" (1992); Featured Musician with Zuccero, "Wonderful World" (1991); Musician with Derek and the Dominos, "The Layla Sessions: 20th Anniversary Edition" (1990); Musician, "Journeyman" (1989); Musician, "August" (1986); Musician, "Behind the Sun" (1985); Musician, "Money and Cigarettes" (1983); Musician with The Yardbirds, "London 1963: The First Recordings!" (1981); Musician, "Another Ticket" (1981); Musician, "Backless" (1978); Musician, "Slowhand" (1977); Musician, "No Reason to Cry" (1976); Musician, "Knockin' on Heaven's Door" (1975); Musician, "There's One for Every Crowd" (1975); Musician, "461 Ocean Boulevard" (1974); Musician with Derek and the Dominos, "In Concert" (1973); Musician with Cream, "Live Cream Volume II" (1972); Musician with Delaney and Bonnie and Friends, "On Tour with Eric Clapton" (1970); Musician with Cream, "Live Cream" (1970); Featured Musician with Vivian Stanshall and the Sean Head Showband, "Labio-Dental Fricative" and "Paper Round" (1970); Musician with Derek and the Dominos, "Layla and Other Assorted Love Songs" (1970); Musician, "Eric Clapton" (1970); Featured Musician with John Lennon and the Plastic Ono Band, "Live Peace in Toronto 1969" (1969); Musician with Blind Faith, "Blind Faith" (1969); Musician with Cream, "Goodbye" (1969); Musician with Cream, "Wheels of Fire" (1968); Musician with Cream, "Disraeli Gears" (1967); Musician with Cream, "Fresh Cream" (1966); Musician with John Mayall and the Bluesbreakers, "Blues Breakers with Eric Clapton" (1966); Musician with Powerhouse, "What's Shakin'" (1966); Musician with The Yardbirds, "Sonny Boy Williamson and the Yardbirds" (1965); Musician with The Yardbirds, "Having a Rave Up" (1965); Musician with The Yardbirds, "For Your Love" (1965); Musician with The Yardbirds, "Five Live Yardbirds" (1964); Musician, Several Solo and Compilation Live Albums; Featured Musician, Several Albums, Soundtracks, and Tribute Albums **AW:** Honorary Plaque for Over 2000 Shows, Royal Albert Hall (2018); Award for Over 175 Shows, Royal Albert Hall (2017); Named, Commandeur, Ordre des Arts et des Lettres (2017); Inductee, Blues Hall of Fame (2015); Plaque, Le Disque a Go! Go! (2014); Sold Out Award, SAP Arena (2014); Two IFMCA Awards (2013-2014); Lifetime Achievement Award, Baloise Session Awards (2013); Bestseller of the Year - Echo Jazz, Echo Music Prize (2012); Ranked, Best Guitar Albums of 1992, Guitar World (2011); Named, One of the 100 Greatest Artists of All Time, Rolling Stone (2011); Star, Yasayan Efsaneler, Istanbul, Turkey (2010); Award for Over 150 Shows, Royal Albert Hall (2009); Grammy Award for Best Contemporary Blues Album, The Recording Academy (2008); Primetime Emmy Award for Outstanding Special Class - Variety, Music, Comedy Program, Academy of Television Arts & Sciences (2008); Grammy Lifetime Achievement Award, The Recording Academy (2006); Award for Best Engineered Album, Grammy Participation Awards (2006); Primetime Emmy Award for Outstanding Picture Editing for a Special, Academy of Television Arts & Sciences (2005); Award, with Cream, for Significant Contribution to the History of Music, Rock Walk Awards (2004); Named, Commander, Order of the British Empire (2004); Named to 500 Greatest Songs of All Time, Rolling Stone (2004); Awards for Historical/Lasting Rock Single, Grammy Hall of Fame (1998, 2003); Twice Named to 500 Greatest Albums of All Time, Rolling Stone (2003); Grammy Award for Best Pop Instrumental Performance, The Recording Academy (2002); Named, Best Live Act in Mexico, Lunas del Auditorio Awards (2002); Best Traditional Blues Album, Grammy Awards (1995, 2001); Inductee, Songwriters Hall of Fame (2001); Award for Contemporary Album of the Year, W.C. Handy Awards (2001); Ranked, Songs of the Century, RIAA (2001); Awards for Historical/Lasting Rock Album, Grammy Hall of Fame (1999, 2000); Grammy Awards for Best Rock Instrumental Performance, The Recording Academy (1997, 2000); Named, One of the Best British Albums of All Time, Q Magazine (2000); Star, Rock and Roll Walk (2000); Inductee, Rock and Roll Hall of Fame (2000); Grammy Awards for Best Male Pop Vocal Performance, The Recording Academy (1997, 1999); Awards for Favorite Pop/Rock Male Artist, American Music Awards (1994, 1997, 1999); BMI Film Music Award, BMI Film & TV Awards (1988, 1990, 1993, 1999); Stevie Ray Vaughan Award, Music Assistance Program (1999); Man of the Year Award for Music, GQ Awards (1999); Most Performed Song of the Year, Robert Musel Awards (1999); Award, with The Yardbirds, for Significant Contribution to the History of Music, Rock Walk Awards (1998); Grammy Awards for Song of the Year, Record of the Year, The Recording Academy (1997); Best Male Solo Song, OFTA Film Awards (1996); Named, Officer, Order of the British Empire (1995); Evian Health Award (1995); Crossover Artist of the Year, W.C. Handy Awards (1995); Merit Award, Q Awards (1995); Special Award for Artistic Excellence, Billboard Music Awards (1994); Bestselling British Recording Artist of the Year, World Music Awards (1994); Bestselling Rock Artist of the Year, Bestselling British Recording Artist of the Year, World Music Awards (1993); Grammy Awards for Best Male Pop Vocal Performance, Song of the Year, Album of the Year, Record of the Year, Best Rock Song, The Recording Academy (1993); Best Film Theme or Song, Ivor Novello Awards (1993); Composer's Gold Award (1993); Inductee with Cream, Rock and Roll Hall of Fame (1993); Sold Out Award, Royal Albert Hall (1993); Engraving, Cavern Club (1992); Inductee with The Yardbirds, Rock and Roll Hall of Fame (1992); Lifetime Achievement Award, Ivor Novello Awards (1992); Award for Best Male Video, MTV Video Music Awards (1992); Grammy Award for Best Male Rock Vocal Performance, The Recording Academy (1991); Key to a Box Award, Royal Albert Hall (1991); Music Therapy Award (1991); Sold Out Award, Alpine Valley Music Theater, East Troy, WI (1990); Sold Out Award, Birmingham NEC, Royal Albert Hall (1990); #1 Album Rock Tracks Artist, Billboard Music Awards (1990); Living Legend Award, International Rock Awards (1990); Best Guitarist Award, International Rock Awards (1989); Best Historical Album, Best Album Notes, Grammy Participation Awards (1989); Royal Honour for 25 Years in the Music Industry, Prince Charles (1988); Concert Award, Palace of Auburn Hills, Auburn Hills, MI (1988); Lifetime Achievement Award, BPI Awards (1987); Best Original Television Music, BAFTA Awards (1986); Best Theme from a Television or Radio Production, Ivor Novello Awards (1986); Outstanding Achievement in the World of British Music, Silver Clef Awards (1983); Music Life Popularity Award (1975); Grammy Award for Album of the Year, The Recording Academy (1973); Outstanding Contribution to Music, Ivor Novello Awards (1971); Music Life Magazine Award (1970); Best International Musician, Melody Maker Awards (1969); Numerous Awards **MEM:** Countryside Alliance **AV:** Collecting cars; West Bromwich Albion FC

CLARIDGE, DAVID E., T: Engineering Educator, Consultant **I:** Education/Educational Services **DOB:** 05/01/1943 **PB:** Walla Walla **SC:** WA/USA **PT:** John A.; Earlene Jane C. **MS:** Married **SPN:** Joanne Marie Kirsch Girtz (05/1992); Karen Elaine Parmley (Divorced 1990) **CH:** Shelley Ann; Jonathon Lee; Kelly Girtz (Stepchild); Britta (Stepchild); Christopher (Stepchild) **ED:** PhD in Physics, Stanford University, Stanford, CA (1976); MS in Physics, Stanford University, Stanford, CA (1966); BS in Engineering Physics, Walla Walla College (Now Walla Walla University), College Place, WA, Cum Laude (1964) **CT:** Professional Engineer (Mechanical), State of Texas (1991) **C:** Senior Fellow, Texas Engineering Experiment Station, College Station, TX (1999-Present); Professor, Mechanical Engineering, Texas A&M University, College Station, TX (1995-Present); Dresser Industries Professor, Dwight Look College of Engineering, Texas A&M University, College Station, TX (1996-1997); Associate Professor, Mechanical Engineering, Texas A&M University, College Station, TX (1986-1995); Associate Professor, Civil and Architectural Engineering, University of Colorado, Boulder (1982-1986); Research Group Manager, Solar Energy Research Institute, Golden, CO (1980-1982); Project Director, Office Technology Assessment, U.S. Congress, Washington, DC (1979-1980); Member, Staff, Office Technology Assessment, U.S. Congress, Washington, DC (1977-1979); Science Fellow, Office Technology Assessment, U.S. Congress, Washington, DC (1976-1977) **CR:** Director, Energy Systems Laboratory, Texas A&M Engineering Experiment Station, College Station, TX (2007-Present); Consultant, Various Organizations (1980-Present); Leland Jordan Professor of Mechanical Engineering, Texas A&M University, College Station, TX (2005-2018); Visiting Erskine Fellow, Canterbury University, Christchurch, New Zealand (2000); Director, Symposium of Improving of Building Efficiency in Hot and Humid Climates, Texas (1988-1992) **CIV:** Board of Directors, Brazos Valley Emmaus Community (Church); Board of Directors, Southwest Partnership for Energy Efficiency as a Resource; Board, Local Homeowners Association **CW:** Deputy Editor, International Journal Energy Research (1988-1997); Co-Author, Three Books; Contributor, Numerous Articles, Professional Journals **AW:** E.K. Campbell Award of Merit for Outstanding Service and Achievement in Teaching, American Society of Heating, Refrigerating and Air Conditioning Engineers (1998); Service Award, Department of Civil, Environmental and Architectural Engineering, University of Colorado (1985); Appreciation Award, American Society of Heating (1985); Numerous Research Grants; Honorary International Member, American Society of Heating, Refrigeration, and Air Conditioning Engineers; Honorary International Member, Society of Heating, Air-Conditioning And Sanitary Engineers of Japan; Three Best Paper Awards; Asian/American Who's Who; Lexington Who's Who Registry; Who's Who in the South and Southwest **MEM:** Secretary, Chair, Numerous Committees, American Society of Heating (1982-Present); Committee Member, Chair, American Society of Mechanical Engineers (1989-2008); Congressional Science Fellow, American Association for the Advancement of Science (1971); American Solar Energy Society **MH:** Albert Nelson Marquis Lifetime Achievement Award **B/I:** Dr. Claridge became involved in his profession in 1973 while he was sitting in gas lines during the shortage, which sparked his interest in both energy and energy efficiency. That is what led him to make a career change because he then ended up getting involved with an individual that wrote a proposal for a summer study on energy efficiency that was held in the summer of 1974 at Princeton University. He was one of two graduate students there; most of the attendees were senior professors, so he met a number of people who later became major mentors for him, including Art Rosenfield, who is the most influential person in energy efficiency in the United States over the past 40 years. They remained in close contact until he passed away several years ago. It was a real privilege to know him. He initially planned to become a physics professor, which is why he has all those degrees in physics. **AV:** Gardening; Cooking; Jogging **RE:** Methodist

CLARK, CHRIS SAINT, T: Owner/Artist **I:** Fine Art **CN:** Kustom Thrills Tattoo **PB:** Atlanta **SC:** GA/USA **ED:** Bachelor of Arts in Art Instruction, Minnesota (1992) **C:** Owner and Artist, Kustom Thrills Tattoo, Nashville, TN (2007-Present); Apprentice Tattoo Artist, Sacred Heart, Atlanta, GA (1997-2011) **MIL:** Second Lieutenant, Military Police **CW:** Developer, Comic Book, The Devil Walks Among Us (2015); Developer, Comic Book, Race with the Devil (2014); Featured, Ink Masters **AW:** Winner, Over 100 Awards for Artwork and Tattooing **MEM:** Alliance of Professional Tattooists; National Tattoo Association; Freemason **MH:** Marquis Who's Who Top Professional; Marquis Who's Who Humanitarian Award **AS:** Mr. Clark attributes his success to hard work and determination. **B/I:** Before he was a full-time tattoo artist, Mr. Clark was a bartender. He then received an apprenticeship to study under the famous tattoo artist Tony Olivas, in Atlanta, who gave him the opportunity to learn how to tattoo. After 9/11, Mr. Clark moved to Savannah, Georgia and joined the State Guard, where he became a second lieutenant in the Georgia State Guard. He subsequently moved to Nashville, Tennessee, where his daughter was born and opened up his own tattoo shop, where he has remained since.

CLARK, DONALD LEWIS, T: Minister, Psychologist, Educator **I:** Education/Educational Services **DOB:** 08/31/1926 **PB:** Lynchburgh **SC:** VA/USA **PT:** Myron L. Clark; Edis Clark **MS:** Married **SPN:** M. Sue Stocks (01/06/1937) **CH:** Rebecca A.; Donna J. (Deceased); Michael W.; Edward Taylor **ED:** EdD, University of Florida (1962); MA, Appalachian State Teachers College (1958); BD, Southeastern Baptist Theological Seminary (1956); BA, The George Washington University (1950) **CT:** Ordained to Ministry Anglican Church in America (2019); Licensed Psychologist, State of North Carolina (1994); Ordained Priest to Ministry, Episcopal Church (1986); Diplomate, American Board of Professional Psychology (1978); Ordained to Ministry, Baptist Church (1954) **C:** Professor Emeritus in Psychology, Appalachian State University (2001); Counselor, Cooperative Christian Counseling Center, Hickory, NC (1979-1985); Instructor, Psychology, Universidad Centroamericano Managua, Nicaragua (1974-1975); Professor of Psychology, Appalachian State University (1969-2001); Director, Honduras Peace Corps Education Program (1967-1969); Director, National Defense Counseling and Guidance Training Institutes, University of Kentucky (1965-1967); Associate Professor of Psychology, University of Kentucky (1964-1967); Associate Professor of Psychology, Mississippi College(1962-1964) **CR:** Priest St Matthews Episcopal Chuch, Todd, NC (2014-2017); Priest, St. Stephen's Episcopal Church, Morganton, NC (1989-1990); Priest, Church of Our Saviour (Episcopal-Lutheran), Newland, NC (1988-1989); Chaplain, North Carolina Baptist Hospital (1957-1959); Pastor, Kittrell Baptist Church, North Carolina (1953-1956); Pastor, Middleburg Baptist Church, North Carolina (1953-1956); Crew Member, Marjorie Merriweather Post's Four-Masted Yacht, Sea Cloud, Bush piloting in own plane, Laurentian Mountains, Canada (1947-1949) **CIV:** Secretary The Academy of Counseling Psychology (1995-1997); Commissioner, North Carolina Commission on Mental Health, Substance Abuse and Developmental Disabilities, Raleigh, NC (1989-1991); Established, Local Chapter, National Alliance of Mental Illness; Chair, North Carolina National Alliance of Mental Illness; Board Member, Local Mental Health, Developmental Disabilities, Addiction Substance Abuse Services; Chair, North Carolina Mental Health Planning Council; Advisory Board, Psychiatric Section, Frye Hospital, Hickory, NC **MIL:** U.S. Merchant Marines (1946); U.S. Army Air Corps (1944-1945) **CW:** Author, "Modern Divorce Began With the Curse, Overcomer Vol LXXVII No 2" (1996); Author, "Wordly Sorrow That Brings Death, Overcomer Vol LXXVII No 2" (1995); Author, "Here They Come, A Response to Aldorf, Journal of Psychology and Theology Vol 17 No 3" (1989); Author, "Theory of Personality, Illness and Cure In the Writings of Agnes Sanford and Those Acknowledging Her Influence, Journal of Psychology and Theology Vol 17 No 3" (1989); Author, "An Implicit Theory of Personality, Illness and Cure Found in the Writings of Neo Pentecostal Faith Teachers, Journal of Psychology and Theology, Vol 12 No 4" (1984); Author, "Interpret Your Dreams with George Wesley," Kendall/Hunt Publisher (1973); Author, Blog, "A Watauga Conservative"; Author, Blog, Spirit Filled Life" **AW:** Lifetime Achievement Award in Counseling, Division of Counseling Psychology, American Psychology Association (2000); Fellowship, Psychology Univeridad Centroamericano, Managua, Nicaragua (1973); Fellowship, Academy of Counseling Psychology; Danforth Scholarship, Graduate School **MEM:** Secretary, Academy of Counseling Psychology (1995-1997); American Psychological Association; North Carolina Psychological Association; Fellow, Academy of Counseling Psychology; Society for the Scientific Study of Religion **MH:** Albert Nelson Marquis Lifetime Achievement Award; Marquis Who's Who Top Professional **AS:** He is the one who people describe as "highly favored by God" as illustrated by the following: In every level of his training, he was the student selected to either stay on in the team or be recommended to a choice position later. Therefore, those who selected him remained his mentors. Next, every position in higher education he wanted, he received. Every church he wanted to minister, he did. **B/I:** He began in the Baptist ministry, after receiving a call from God. His love for psychology started after reading books from Freud on psychoanalysis such as "Introduction to Psycho Analysis." He was hooked ever since and never got bored or tired of the study. **AV:** Tai Chi **PA:** Republican **RE:** Christian **THT:** From early childhood, having intimacy with God, the Father of Jesus, made life a wonderful adventure.

CLARK, KATHERINE MARLEA, T: U.S. Representative from Massachusetts **I:** Government Administration/Government Relations/Government Services **DOB:** 07/17/1963 **PB:** New Haven **SC:** CT/USA **PT:** Harrison C. Clark **MS:** Married **SPN:** Rodney Scott Dowell (1992) **CH:** Addison; Jared; Nathaniel **ED:** MPA, Harvard Kennedy School, John F. Kennedy School of Government, MA; JD, Cornell Law School, Ithaca, NY (1989); BA, St. Lawrence University, Canton, NY (1985); Coursework, Nagoya, Japan (1983) **C:** Member, U.S. House Committee on Natural Resources (2014-Present); Member, U.S. House of Representatives from Massachusetts' Fifth Congressional District, United States Congress, Washington, DC (2013-Present); Member, House Appropriations Committee (2017-2019); Member, Middlesex and Essex District, Massachusetts Senate (2011-2013); Member, 32nd Middlesex District, Massachusetts House of Representatives (2008-2011); Prosecutor, Colorado Attorney General's Office (1991-1993); Clerk, Federal Judge Alfred Albert Arraj, United States District Court for the District of Colorado (1990-1991); Chief, Policy Division, Office of Massachusetts Attorney General; General Counsel, Massachusetts Office of Childcare Services; Private Practice Attorney; Attorney, Colorado District Attorney's Council **CR:** Member,

Melrose School Committee, MA (2001-2007); Chair, Melrose School Committee, MA (2001-2003); Member, Congressional Progressive Caucus; Member, Congressional Asian Pacific American Caucus **AW:** Named Legislator of the Year, Citizens Public Schools (2010) **PA:** Democrat

CLARK, MARCIA RACHEL, T: Lawyer **I:** Law and Legal Services **DOB:** 8/31/1953 **PB:** Berkeley **SC:** CA/USA **PT:** Abraham I. Kleks; Rozlyn (Masur) Kleks **SPN:** Gordon Clark (1980-1995); Gabriel Horowitz (1976-1980) **CH:** Two Children **ED:** Doctor of Jurisprudence, Southwestern University (1979); Bachelor of Arts in Political Science, University of California Los Angeles (1974) **C:** Prosecutor, LA County District Attorney's Office, Los Angeles, CA (1981-1997); Attorney, Brodey and Price, Los Angeles, CA (1979-1981) **CR:** Legal Analyst and Expert Commentator, NBC, CNBC and MSNBC (1998-2000); Host, "Judge and Jury," MSNBC; Host, "Equal Time," CNBC; Substitute Host, "Rivera Live"; Legal Correspondent, "Entertainment Tonight" **CW:** Author, "Snap Judgement" (2017); Author, "Moral Defense" (2016); Author, "Blood Defense" (2016); Author, "The Competition" (2014); Author, "Killer Ambition" (2013), Author, "If I'm Dead" (2013); Author, "Trouble In Paradise" (2013); Author, "Guilt By Degrees" (2012); Author, "Guilt By Association" (2011); Executive Consultant, Co-writer, "For the People," Lifetime TV (2002); Host, "Lie Detector," FOX (1998); Co-author, with Teresa Carpenter, "Without a Doubt" (1997); Contributor, The Daily Beast; Guest, "Oprah Winfrey Show"; Guest, "Larry King Show"; Guest, "The Today Show"; Guest, "The Early Show"; Guest, "Good Morning America"; Guest, "Anderson Cooper 360"; Guest, "Issues with Jane Velez Mitchell" **BAR:** The State Bar of California (1979)

CLARK, RICHARD L. MD, T: Radiologist, Educator **I:** Education/Educational Services **DOB:** 06/01/1940 **PB:** Mount Vernon **SC:** NY/USA **PT:** Kenneth Fenton; Gertrude Lathrop (Dezendorf) C. **MS:** Married **SPN:** Linda Lenore Horne (8/27/1963) **CH:** Jonathan Kenneth; Jennifer Lee **ED:** Graduate Coursework, Manager, Leadership Institute of North Carolina Memorial Hospital, University of North Carolina School Business Administration (1987); Doctor of Medicine, Johns Hopkins University (1966); Bachelor of Arts, Oberlin College, Magna Cum Laude (1962) **CT:** Diplomate, American Board of Radiology (1971) **C:** Professor Emeritus, University North Carolina, Chapel Hill, NC (2005-Present); Professor, University of North Carolina, Chapel Hill, NC (1983-2005); Associate Professor Radiology, University of North Carolina, Chapel Hill, NC (1973-1983); Advisor to Medical Class, University of North Carolina, Chapel Hill, NC (1981); Director, Diagnostic Radiological Research, University of North Carolina, Chapel Hill, NC (1973-1979); Chief Resident, Instructor, Johns Hopkins Hospital, Baltimore, MD (1970-1971); Resident in Radiology, Johns Hopkins Hospital, Baltimore, MD (1967-1970); Intern, University of Kentucky Medical Center, Lexington, KY (1966-1967) **CR:** Consultant to Chief Medical Examiner, North Carolina Memorial Hospital (1973-Present); Director of Genitourinary Radiology, University of North Carolina School of Medicine (1999-2005); Science Integrity Officer, University of North Carolina School of Medicine (1993-2001); Vice Chairman of Research, North Carolina Memorial Hospital (1991-1999); Associate Chairman, North Carolina Memorial Hospital (1987-1991); Acting Chairman, Department of Radiology, North Carolina Memorial Hospital (1987); Director, Division of General Radiology, North Carolina Memorial Hospital (1979-1986) **CIV:** Past Trustee, Past President, Eno River Unitarian Universalist Fellowship; Board

of Directors, Mallarme Youth Chamber Orchestra, Community Coach Myco; Board of Directors, Raleigh Chamber Music Guild; Past President, Board of Directors, Chapel Hill Philharmonia **MIL:** With, U.S. Public Health Service (1971-1973) **AW:** Pollack Gold Medalist, Society of Agdominal Radiology (2013); National Institutes of Health Research Grantee (1976-1994, 1999-2004); James Picker Foundation Scholar (1975-1979); Faculty Research Grantee, North Carolina (1974-1975); Henry Strong Denison Research Award, Johns Hopkins Medical School (1965-1966); Departmental Teaching Award, Radiology **MEM:** Co-President, Oberlin Alumni of North Carolina (1975-1977); Fellow, American College of Radiology; Association of University Radiologists; Past President, Society of Uroradiology; Past President, American College of Radiology; American Roentgen Ray Society; Radiological Society of North America; North Carolina Medical Society; Johns Hopkins Medical Association; Johns Hopkins University Alumni Association; Durham Orange County Medical Society; Chapel Hill Chamber Players; Chapel Hill Philharmonia; Doctoral Themes Chamber Music Group; Sigma Xi; Chapel Hill Philharmonica Cello Quartet **MH:** Albert Nelson Marquis Lifetime Achievement Award **AV:** Music; Woodworking; Gardening; Paws4ever animal shelter; Resale store; Technical advisor; Education philanthropy **PA:** Democrat **RE:** Unitarian Universalist

CLARK, SANDRA, T: Geologist **I:** Sciences **DOB:** 07/27/1938 **PB:** Kansas City **SC:** MO/USA **PT:** LuVern John; Mildred (File) Becker **MS:** Divorced **SPN:** Allen LeRoy Clark (11/10/1955, Divorced 1976) **CH:** Ken Allen (Deceased); Brett Harlan (Deceased); Holly Lin Clark Gray **ED:** PhD in Geology, University of Idaho (1968); MS in Geology, University of Idaho (1964); BS in Geology, University of Idaho (1963); Coursework, Iowa State University (1956-1960) **C:** Scientist Emeritus, U.S. Geological Survey, Reston, VA (2001-Present); Geologist, Eastern Mineral Resource Survey Team, U.S. Geological Survey, Reston, VA (1996-2001); Deputy Chief, Mineral Resource Assessments Office of Mineral Resources, U.S. Geological Survey, Reston, VA (1995-1996); Geologist, Commodity Specialist, Eastern Mineral Resources Branch, U.S. Geological Survey, Reston, VA (1980-1995); Equal Employment Opportunity Officer, U.S. Geological Survey, Reston, VA (1976-1980); Participant, Departments Manager, Development Program, U.S. Department Interior, Washington, DC (1975-1976); Alaska Gas Pipeline Task Force, U.S. Department Interior, Washington, DC (1974-1975); Staff Geologist, Office of Mineral Resources, U.S. Geological Survey, Washington, DC (1972-1974); Geologist, Alaskan Mineral Resources Branch, U.S. Geological Survey, Menlo Park, CA (1967-1972); Geologist, Cominco Am., Inc., Spokane, WA (1966-1967); Teaching Assistant, College of Mines, University of Idaho (1964-1966); Field Assistant, Bear Creek Mining Co., Spokane, WA (1965); Field Assistant, Idaho Bureau of Mines and Geology (1963-1964) **CW:** Contributor, Maps and Articles, Professional Publications (1964-Present) **AW:** Gold World Medal, New York Festivals Film and Video Competition (2003); Gold Screen Award, National Association of Government Communicators (2002); Silver Screen Award, International Film and Video Festival (2002); Stewardship Award (1996); Meritorious Service Award, Department of the Interior (1995); Graduate Fellow, National Science Foundation (1963-1964) **MEM:** Vice President, Geologic Division Retires (2002-2009); Chairman, Commission on Fluorite and Barite, International Association of Genesis Ore Deposits (1996-2000); Delegate, American Association of Petroleum Geologists (1992-1996); Vice President, Potomac Chapter, Associa-

tion of Women Geologists (1989-1990); President, Camera Club (1986); Fellow, Geological Society of America; Society of Economic Geologists; Toastmasters International; Association of Geologists for International Development **MH:** Albert Nelson Marquis Lifetime Achievement Award; Marquis Who's Who Top Professional **B/I:** Dr. Clark became involved in her profession because she wanted to help her then-husband. In school, he changed his major to geology and began struggling. Though she was studying economics at the time, Dr. Clark saw no future there. She consequently changed her major to geology; the rest is history. **AV:** Scuba diving; Snorkeling; Practicing photography; Camping; Figure skating; Cross country skiing; Painting; Jewelry making

CLARK, TRENT L., T: Owner, President, Chief Executive Officer **I:** Consumer Goods and Services **CN:** Customalting LLC **DOB:** 07/12/1961 **PB:** Jackson Hole **SC:** WY/USA **PT:** Richard L. Clark; Carolyn T. Clark **MS:** Married **SPN:** Rebecca Lee **CH:** Brittany (Deceased 2009); Kathleen; Christin; Alexander **ED:** Bachelor of Arts, Brigham Young University (1984); Associate of Science, Ricks College (1980) **CT:** Certified in Public Health, Harvard University (1995) **C:** Owner, President, Chief Executive Officer, Customalting LLC (2019-Present); Director, Government and Public Affairs, Bayer U.S., Soda Springs, ID (2018-2019); Director, Government and Public Affairs, Monsanto Co., Soda Springs, ID (1999-2017); Federal Affairs Manager, Solutia Inc., Soda Springs, ID (1998-1999); Senior Commissions Specialist, Monsanto Co., Soda Springs, ID (1993-1998); State Director, Idaho Farm Services Administration, Boise, ID (1991-1993); Chief Environmental Economist, Joint Economic Committee Congress, Washington, DC (1990-1991); Legislative Staff, U.S. Senate, Washington, DC (1983-1990) **CIV:** Chair, Idaho Workforce Development Council (2019-Present); Vice-Chairperson, Idaho Humanities Council, Boise, ID (2018-2020); Chairperson, Idaho Rural Development Council, Boise, ID (1997, 2003); Chairperson, Idaho Republican Party (1999-2002) **AW:** Governor's Safety Conference Award, Governor of Idaho (1998); Merit Award, U.S. Department of Agriculture (1992) **MEM:** Chairperson, Idaho Council on Industry and the Environment (2010); Chairperson, Idaho Association of Commerce & Industry (2008); Chairperson, Rotary (2008); President, Soda Springs Chamber of Commerce (1998-1999) **MH:** Albert Nelson Marquis Lifetime Achievement Award **B/I:** Mr. Clark came of age in a rural community in Wyoming, where he developed an interest in barley farming and associated products. Most of his career has involved dealing with how the government approaches rural communities and burgeoning businesses. He first became involved after graduating from college, having undertaken an internship at the Supreme Court in Washington, DC. He observed a wide range of issues that impact rural communities, including recycling programs and water quality protection. **AV:** Fencing; Back country horse packing **RE:** The Church of Jesus Christ of Latter-day Saints

CLARK, WESLEY GLEASON, PHD, T: Pharmacologist, Educator (Retired) **I:** Pharmaceuticals **DOB:** 07/01/1933 **PB:** Wadsworth **SC:** OH/USA **PT:** Alfred William Clark; Mary June (Starn) Clark **MS:** Married **SPN:** Yvonne Lee Stanfield (04/16/1964) **CH:** David Lee; Rebecca Lynne Catlett; Roger Dale **ED:** PhD, The University of Utah (1962); MS, University of Colorado (1958); BA, University of Colorado (1955) **C:** Retired Pharmacologist, Educator (2000); Associate Professor, The University of Texas Southwestern Medical Center, Dallas, Texas (1972-2000); Assistant Professor, The University of Texas Southwestern Medical Center, Dallas,

Texas (1963-1972); Instructor, The University of Texas Southwestern Medical Center, Dallas, Texas (1962-1963) **CW:** Editor, Textbook, "Goth's Medical Pharmacology, 13ᵗʰ Revised Edition" (1992); Editor, Textbook, "Goth's Medical Pharmacology, 12ᵗʰ Revised Edition" (1988); Contributor, Over 50 Research Articles and Over 20 Reviewed Articles to Professional Journals **AW:** Grantee, National Institute on Drug Abuse, National Institutes of Health (1979-1981); Grantee, National Institutes of Health (1964-1966,1970-1978) **MEM:** American Society for Pharmacology and Experimental Therapeutics (ASPET) **MH:** Albert Nelson Marquis Lifetime Achievement Award; Marquis Who's Who Top Professional

CLARK, WILLIAM N., T: Lawyer, Retired Military Officer **I:** Law and Legal Services **CN:** Redden Mills Clark & Shaw, LLP **DOB:** 01/19/1941 **PB:** Meridian **SC:** MS/USA **PT:** Oliver Watson Clark; Mildred Catherine (Northington) Clark **MS:** Married **SPN:** Faye Virginia Baker (02/01/1964) **CH:** Helen Catherine Smith; William Northington Junior **ED:** JD, University of Alabama (1971); BS, U.S. Military Academy (1963) **C:** Partner, Redden Mills & Clark (now Redden Mills Clarks Show LLP) (1972-Present); Partner, Rogers Howard Redden & Mills, Birmingham, AL (1974-1979); Associate, Rogers Howard Redden & Mills, Birmingham, AL (1972-1974); Law Clerk, Judge Walter P. Gewin, U.S. Court Appeals for the 5ᵗʰ Circuit (1971-1972) **CR:** Alabama Supreme Court Advisory Committee on Criminal Procedure (1979-1994); Adjunct Professor, Business Fraud, University of Alabama School of Law (2001); Adjunct Professor, Criminal Procedure (2000); Adjunct Professor, Evidence (1979) **CIV:** Teacher, Adult Sunday School, Highlands United Methodist Church (1993-Present); President, University of Alabama Law School Foundation (2000-2002); Birmingham Bar Foundation (1995); Metro YMCA Birmingham (1989); Chair, Vulcan District Boy Scouts of America (1987-1989); Board of Directors, Boys and Girls Club of Central Alabama (1987); Chairman, Board of Directors, Kiwanis Club Birmingham (1984-1986) **MIL:** Major General, U.S. Army Reserve (1968-2000); Captain, U.S. Active Army (1963-1968) **AW:** Lifetime Achievement Award, Birmingham Bar Association (2017); Lifetime Achievement Award, Birmingham Criminal Defense Lawyers Association (2017); Parachute Badge; Combat Infantryman Badge; Vietnamese Cross of Gallantry Bronze Star; Army Commendation Medal; Meritorious Service Medal; Air Medal; Bronze Star Medal; Legion of Merit; Distinguished Service Medal; Listee, Super Lawyers; Listee, Best Lawyers in America; Roderick P. Beddow Distinguished Service Award, Alabama Criminal Defense Lawyers Association **MEM:** Chairman, President, President-Elect, Alabama State Bar Association (1983-2004); Secretary, Treasurer, President, Birmingham Bar Association (1987-1993); Chairman, Children's Code Committee, Alabama Law Institute (1986-1993); Fellow, American College Trial Lawyers; National Association of Criminal Defense Lawyers; American Law Institute **BAR:** Alabama (1971); U.S. Court of Appeals for the 5ᵗʰ and 11ᵗʰ Circuits; U.S. Supreme Court **MH:** Albert Nelson Marquis Lifetime Achievement Award; Marquis Who's Who Top Professional **B/I:** Mr. Clark was introduced to the legal industry at West Point. As he took more law classes, he became increasingly interested in the career. He later became an advisor in Vietnam, which solidified his decision to become an attorney. **RE:** Methodist

CLARKE, EMILIA OSOBEL EUPHEMIA ROSE, T: Actress **I:** Media & Entertainment **DOB:** 10/26/1986 **PB:** London **SC:** United Kingdom **ED:** Diploma, Drama Centre, University Arts London (2009)

CW: Actress, "The Seagull" (2020); Actress, "Last Christmas" (2019); Actress, "Above Suspicion" (2019); Appearance, "Saturday Night Live" (2019); Actress, "Game of Thrones" (2011-2019); Actress, "Solo: A Star Ways Story" (2018); Voice Actress, "Animals" (2017); Featured, Cover, Rolling Stone (2017); Voice Actress, "Thunderbirds are Go" (2017); Voice Actress, "Robot Chicken" (2016); Actress, "Voice from the Stone" (2016); Actress, "Me Before You" (2016); Actress, "Terminator Genisys" (2015); Appearance, Video Game, "Game of Thrones" (2015); Actress, "Dom Hemingway" (2013); Voice Actress, "Futurama" (2013); Actress, "Breakfast at Tiffany's" (2013); Actress, "Shackled" (2012); Actress, "Spike Island" (2012); Actress, "Triassic Attack" (2010); Actress, "Lisa's Story" (2009); Actress, "Sense" (2009); Actress, Many Plays, Drama Centre, University Arts London **AW:** Named One of the 100 Most Influential People in the World, TIME Magazine (2019); Named Sexiest Woman Alive, Esquire (2015); Named Most Desirable Woman in the World, AskMen (2014); Named One of the UK Stars of Tomorrow, Screen International (2010)

CLARKE, YVETTE DIANE, T: U.S. Representative **I:** Government Administration/Government Relations/Government Services **DOB:** 11/21/1964 **PB:** Brooklyn **SC:** NY/USA **PT:** Lesley Clarke; Una S.T. Clarke **ED:** Coursework, Oberlin College and Conservatory (1982-1986); Coursework, Medgar Evers College **C:** U.S. Representative, New York's Ninth Congressional District, United States Congress (2013-Present); Secretary, Congressional Black Caucus (2011-Present); U.S. Representative, New York's 11ᵗʰ Congressional District, United States Congress (2007-2013); Councilwoman, District 40, New York City Council (2002-2007); Director of Youth Programs, 1199SEIU Funds (1991); Legislative Aide to Senator Velmanette Montgomery, New York State Senate (1986); Child Care Specialist, Erasmus Neighborhood Federation (1985); Member, Committee on Energy and Commerce; Member, Committee on Small Business; Director of Business Development, Bronx Empowerment Zone; Executive Assistant to Assemblywoman Barbara Clark, New York State Assembly **AW:** Power 150, Ebony Magazine (2008) **PA:** Democrat **RE:** African Methodist Episcopal

CLARKSON, LAWRENCE, T: Air Transportation Executive **I:** Aviation **DOB:** 04/29/1938 **PB:** Grove City **SC:** PA/USA **PT:** Harold William Clarkson; Jean Henrietta (Jaxtheimer) Clarkson **SPN:** Barbara Louise Stevenson (08/20/1960) **CH:** Michael (Deceased); Elizabeth (Deceased); Jennifer **ED:** JD, University of Florida (1962); BA, DePauw University (1960) **C:** Senior Vice President, Project 2000, Seattle, WA (2000-Present); President, Boeing Enterprises, Seattle, WA (1997-1999); Senior Vice President, Boeing Enterprises, Seattle, WA (1994-1999); Corp. Vice President, Planning and International Development, Boeing Co., Seattle, WA (1992-1993); Senior Vice President, Boeing Commercial Airplanes Group, Seattle, WA (1988-1991); President, Commercial Products Division, Pratt & Whitney, Hartford, CT (1982-1987); Vice President, Contracts, Pratt & Whitney, Hartford, CT (1980-1982); Vice President, Marketing, Pratt & Whitney, West Palm Beach, FL (1978-1980); Vice President, Managing Director, Pratt & Whitney, Brussels (1975-1978); Program Manager, Pratt & Whitney, West Palm Beach, FL (1974-1975); Program Deputy Director, Pratt & Whitney, West Palm Beach, FL (1972-1975); Counsel, Pratt & Whitney, West Palm Beach, FL (1967-1972) **CR:** Hitco Carbon (2002-Present); Chairman, Interturbine NV (2000-2002); Board of Directors, Avnet Inc., Atlas Air, Washington, DC (1988-1991) **CIV:** Trustee, Seat-

tle Opera (1990-Present); Trustee, Interlochen Center Arts, Michigan (1988-Present); Trustee, DePauw University, Greencastle, IN (1987-Present); Vice-Chairman, DePauw University, Greencastle, IN (1996-2002); Chairman, Seattle Opera (1991-2002); Chairman, Interlochen Center Arts, Michigan (1996-2001); Chairman, United States-Pacific Economic Corporate Council (1993-2000); Overseer, Tuck School Dartmouth, Hanover, NH (1993-1999); President, Japan-American Society, Washington (1993); President, Washington State China Relations Committee (1992-1993); Corp. Counsel, Interlochen Center Arts, Michigan (1987); Trustee, Embry-Riddle Aeronautical University, Daytona Beach, FL; Chairman, Council Foreign Relations; Chairman, National Bureau of Asia Research; Overseer, Tuck School of Business at Dartmouth University **MIL:** United States Air Force (1960-1971) **CW:** Article Feature, Newsweek, "Boeing's Secretary of State" **MEM:** Board of Directors, American Institute Contemporary German Studies (1997-1999); National Association of Manufacturers (1993-1999); Board of Governors, The Pilgrims of the United States, Wings Club (1987-1991); Metropolitan Club of DC; New York Yacht Club; Knight, Order of St. John; Board Member, Metropolitan Opera **BAR:** Florida **MH:** Albert Nelson Marquis Lifetime Achievement Award; Marquis Who's Who Top Professional **B/I:** Mr. Clarkson served in the United States Air Force as a lawyer; when he left, he joined a law firm in Palm Beach, Florida, called Pratt & Whitney. They had a research and development center in West Palm Beach, for which they were looking for a new corporate lawyer. He took the opportunity with open arms and excitement. Mr. Clarkson got involved with general management, working as the director of contracts. He later became the deputy program manager for the engine F15 and, later, the vice program manager for the F16 engine. In the subsequent years, he was once again relocated to commercial work where he ended up as the vice president of the commercial division. Later in his career, he was recruited by Boeing, where he found much success. Mr. Clarkson's natural love of airplanes is what drew him to explore a career in the United States Air Force. **RE:** Episcopalian

CLARKSON, ROBERT, "BOB" NOEL, T: Commercial Photographer; Magician **I:** Media & Entertainment **DOB:** 03/02/1950 **PB:** Clinton **SC:** MO/USA **PT:** Arthur W. Clarkson; Vivian (Noel) Clarkson **MS:** Single **ED:** BA in Economics, Carroll College, Helena, MT (1973) **CT:** Private Pilot; Open Water SCUBA; Food Service Manager; Ordained Minister **C:** Owner, Sleepy Senator Bed and Breakfast, Helena, MT (2003-Present); Drama Coach, Helena High School, Helena Public Schools, MT (2009-2014); Substitute Teacher, Helena Public Schools (2003-2014); Owner, Founder, Clarkson Studio, Helena, MT (1973) **CR:** Innkeeper/Property Manager (2002-Present); Professional Magician (1987-2001); Montana House of Representatives (1983-1985); Photographer, Montana Senate, Helena, MT (1981-1985); Press Officer, Montana Army National Guard, Helena, MT (1977-1981) **CIV:** Public Elected Officer, Helena Citizens' Council (1999-2001); Moderator, Christian Church, Disciples of Christ Church (1996); Secretary, Lewis and Clark County Disaster and Emergency Services Council (1982) **MIL:** With, United States Army (1981-1991); With, Montana Army National Guard (1975-1980); With, Montana Air National Guard (1970-1974) **CW:** Author, Contributor, Numerous Articles and Photographs in M-U-M, Linking Ring, and Genii Magic Magazines; Magic and Illusion Shows **AW:** Service Award, Montana Exchange Club (1986, 1987); Distinguished Club Secretary Award, Montana Exchange Club (1983-1987); Life Member Award,

The Society of American Magicians; Award of Achievement, The Society of American Magicians; Named Convention Show Emcee, The Society of American Magicians International Conventions; Alliance of Harry Houdini Award Silver Tier, The Society of American Magicians; Wizard's Award, The International Brotherhood of Magicians **MEM:** World Clown Association (1990-1994); Secretary, Yellowstone District, Montana Exchange Club (1988); Secretary, Montana Exchange Club (1983-1988); President, Helena Chapter, Reserve Officers Association (Now Reserve Organization of America) (1983); Magician Member, The Magic Castle/Academy of Magical Arts, Hollywood CA; American Society of Media Photographers, Inc.; The Society of American Magicians; Past Regional Vice President, Former National Deputy, Past Assembly President, Society of American Magicians; The International Brotherhood of Magicians; Masons; Shriners International **MH:** Who's Who in the World; Who's Who in America; Albert Nelson Marquis Lifetime Achievement Award **B/I:** Mr. Clarkson became involved in his photography profession because of his father. He was an enthusiastic amateur photographer and filmmaker, who took pictures to show his family of the places he traveled to while working as a professional engineer for the state. Mr. Clarkson's mother and grandmother were both college graduates in the fine arts. When he was in high school, he befriended the local radio and television on-air hosts; they encouraged and mentored him and made him a station intern. The editor-in-chief and photographer at the local newspaper also mentored him in press photography technique. One of his teachers, Ray Chaplin, taught him dark room technique and a local photographer, Clarence Dewalt, took him under his wing and showed him how to do lightning and general portrait photography. **AV:** Flying; Scuba diving; Skiing; Auto racing; Computer programming; Woodworking **THT:** Mr. Clarkson says, "Our purpose here is to have a strong faith belief, not judge others, help out those truly in need, and strive to become a good example for others."

CLAY, WILLIAM, "LACY" LACY JR., T: U.S. Representative from Missouri **I:** Government Administration/Government Relations/Government Services **DOB:** 07/27/1956 **PB:** St. Louis **SC:** MO/USA **PT:** William Lacy Clay; Carol Ann (Johnson) Clay **MS:** Married **SPN:** Ivie Lewellen (01/24/1992) **CH:** Carol; Will **ED:** BS in Government and Politics, University of Maryland, College Park, MD (1983); Honorary LLD, Harris-Stowe State University; Honorary LLD, Lincoln University; Coursework, Harvard Kennedy School, John F. Kennedy School of Government **CT:** Certified Paralegal; Licensed Real Estate Salesman, State of Missouri **C:** Member, U.S. House of Representatives from Missouri's First Congressional District, United States Congress (2001-Present); Member, District Four, Missouri State Senate (1991-2001); Member, District 59, Missouri House of Representatives, Jefferson City, MO (1983-1991); Assistant Doorman, U.S. House of Representatives (1978-1983); Member, Committee on Financial Services; Member, Committee on Oversight and Government Reform **CIV:** Chairman, Jesse Jackson 1988 Presidential Campaign, MO (1988); Delegate, Democratic National Convention (1988); Committeeman, Democratic National Committee; Board of Directors, William L. Clay Scholarship and Research Fund (WLCSRF); Member, Congressional Black Caucus Foundation **AW:** Award for Political Leadership, National Newspaper Publishers Association Foundation (2011); Health Care Advocate Award, Missourians for Single Payer (2006); Outstanding Legislator, Americans for Democratic Action, Missouri Chapter (1985, 1986) **MEM:** Americans for Democratic

Action **AV:** Reading; Researching history; Playing sports; Listening to music **PA:** Democrat **RE:** Roman Catholic

CLAYTON, JAMIE, LE, T: President, Owner **I:** Cosmetics **CN:** Bare Medical Spa + Laser Center **CH:** Two Sons **CT:** Laser Technician, State of Vermont; Makeup Artist, State of Vermont; Medical Esthetician, Electrologist, State of Vermont **C:** Founder, Owner, Bare Medical Spa + Laser Center (2008-Present) **AW:** Named Best Medical Spa, State of Vermont **AS:** Ms. Clayton attributes her success to her training. She and her staff are training and traveling around the United States and Canada to learn. **B/I:** Ms. Clayton was working for a corporate business prior to starting the medical spa. She decided she wanted to do something more satisfying and different for her and her family. **AV:** Traveling with family **THT:** Ms. Clayton is the owner and founder of Bare Medical Spa + Laser Center. She is licensed in the state of Vermont as a medical esthetician, electrologist, certified laser technician and makeup artist. She has been working in the skincare industry since 2008. Her passion is to help people feel self-confident and find their inner-beauty. She has focused her business around providing a warm and inviting atmosphere to all her clients, enabling them to learn more about caring for their skin. She believes skin health determines the overall health of the body, especially one's emotional well being. She regularly travels throughout the United States and Canada to continue her education in medical skincare and laser technology in order to best serve her clients. Ms. Clayton resides in Essex with her two beautiful boys. When she is not working at Bare, she enjoys traveling with her family.

CLAYTON, WILLIAM, T: Utilities Executive (Retired) **I:** Oil & Energy **DOB:** 02/10/1930 **PB:** Sugarland **SC:** TX/USA **PT:** Jessie W. Clayton; Ruth (Pitts) Clayton **MS:** Widowed **SPN:** Vivian Adele Davis (08/20/1952) **CH:** Mark; Susan; Larry **ED:** BSEE, University of Houston (1950) **C:** Retired (1992); Senior Vice President of Engineering, Operations and Data Processing, Entex, Incorporated, Houston, Texas (1987-1992); Vice President of Engineering Operations and Data Processing, Entex, Incorporated, Houston, Texas (1985-1987); Vice President of Engineering, Operations and Administration, Entex, Incorporated, Houston, Texas (1983-1985); Vice President of Administration, Entex, Incorporated, Houston, Texas (1976-1983); Chief Engineer, Entex, Incorporated, Houston, Texas (1972-1976); Assistant Chief Engineer, Entex, Incorporated, Houston, Texas (1968-1972); Various Engineering Positions, Entex, Incorporated, Houston, Texas (1950-1968) **CIV:** President, Fonn Villas Civic Association, Inc., Houston, Texas (1984-1992) **MIL:** With, United States Army, Korea (1952-1954) **MEM:** Chairman, Operating Section, American Gas Association (1987-Present); National Society of Professional Engineers; The American Society of Mechanical Engineers; Houston Engineering and Science Society; Texas Society of Professional Engineers; Southern Gas Association; American Gas Association; The Houstonian Club; Houston Club; Masons **MH:** Albert Nelson Marquis Lifetime Achievement Award; Marquis Who's Who Top Professional **B/I:** Mr. Clayton read about a venture where there was an effort to make a tunnel from Alaska to Russia. To him, it sounded like an operation he would love to be in charge of. **RE:** Presbyterian

CLEAVER, EMANUEL II, T: U.S. Representative from Missouri; Minister **I:** Government Administration/Government Relations/Government Services **DOB:** 10/26/1944 **PB:** Waxahachie **SC:** TX/USA **PT:**

Lucky G. Cleaver; Marie (McKnight) Cleaver **MS:** Married **SPN:** Dianne Donaldson (06/1970) **CH:** Evan Donaldson; Emanuel III; Emiel Davenport; Marissa Dianne **ED:** Honorary DD, Baker University (1988); MDiv, Saint Paul School of Theology, Kansas City, MO (1974); BS in Sociology, Prairie View A&M University, Texas (1968) **CT:** Ordained to Ministry, United Methodist Church **C:** Member, U.S. House of Representatives from Missouri's Fifth Congressional District, United States Congress (2005-Present); Senior Pastor, St. James United Methodist Church, Kansas City, MO (1969-Present); Chairman, Congressional Black Caucus (2011-2013); Special Advisor to Secretary Andrew Cuomo, U.S. Department of Housing and Urban Development (HUD) (1999-2000); Mayor, City of Kansas City, MO (1991-1999); Mayor Pro-tem, City of Kansas City, MO (1987-1991); Council Member, City of Kansas City, MO (1979-1991); Member, Committee on Financial Services **CR:** Lecturer, Churches, Schools, Civic and Social Organizations, Nationwide **CIV:** Member, Policy and Rules Committee (1987-1991); Chairman, Kansas City Council Plans and Zoning Committee (1984-1987); Mid-central Regional Vice President, Southern Christian Leadership Conference; Founder, Co-chair, Harmony in a World of Difference, Kansas City, MO **CW:** Host, "Under the Clock," KCUR-FM Public Radio, Kansas City, MO (2000-2004) **AW:** Named to the Power 150, Ebony Magazine (2008); Named One of the Most Influential Black Americans, Ebony Magazine (2006); Governor Award for Local Elected Official of the Year, State of Missouri (1994); Distinguished Graduate Award, Saint Paul School of Theology (1993); Kansas City Anti-Apartheid Award (1993); James C. Kirkpatrick Excellence for Government Award (1993); Distinguished Citizen of the Midwest Award, NCCJ (1993); Named One of the 100 Most Influential Kansas Citizens, Kansas City Globe (1991, 1992, 1993); Rainbow Award (1992); Bridge Builders Award, Kansas City Globe (1992); Harold L. Holiday Senior Civil Rights Award, NAACP (1992); Public Service Award, American Jewish Committee (AJC) (1991); Junteenth Man of the Year Award, Black Archives of Mid-America Inc., Kansas City, MO (1991); Distinguished Citizen Award, Greater Kansas City Urban Affairs Council (1991); Community Service/Leadership Award, Webster University (1991); Distinguished Service Award, Park College (1991); Friend of Youth Award, Boys & Girls Clubs of America (1991); Outstanding Contributions to the Black Community Award, Concerned Citizens Black Clergy of Atlanta (1991); Drum Major for Justice Award, Southern Christian Leadership Conference (1991); William Yates Distinguished Service Medallion, William Jewell College (1987); Centurions Leadership Award, Greater Kansas City Chamber of Commerce (1987) **MEM:** NAACP; Greater Kansas City Chamber of Commerce; Alpha Phi Alpha Fraternity, Inc. **PA:** Democrat

CLEMENS, ROGER, T: Retired Baseball Pitcher **I:** Athletics **DOB:** 08/04/1962 **PB:** Dayton **SC:** OH/USA **PT:** Bess Clemens; Woody Booher (Stepfather) **MS:** Married **SPN:** Debra Lynn Godfrey (11/24/1984) **CH:** Koby Aaron; Kory Allen; Kacy Austin; Kody Alec **ED:** Coursework, University of Texas at Austin (1982-1983); Coursework, San Jacinto Junior College, Pasadena, TX (1981) **C:** Pitcher, Sugar Land Skeeters, Atlantic League, Texas (2012); Pitcher, New York Yankees (2007); Pitcher, Houston Astros (2004-2006); Pitcher, New York Yankees (1999-2003); Pitcher, Toronto Blue Jays (1997-1998); Pitcher, Boston Red Sox (1984-1996) **CR:** Pitcher, Team USA, World Baseball Classic (2006) **CIV:** Co-Founder, Roger Clemens Foundation (1992) **AW:** ERA Leader (1986, 1990-1992, 1997, 1998, 2005); Invited, National League All-

Star Team (2004-2005); Cy Young Award, National League (2004); American League All-Star Team (1986, 1988, 1990-1992, 1997-1998, 2001, 2003); Sportsman of the Year, March of Dimes (2001); Cy Young Award, American League (1986-1987, 1991, 1997-1998, 2001); Pitcher of the Year (1986, 1991, 1997-1998, 2001); World Series Champion (1999, 2000); All-Century Team, MLB (1999); AL Strikeout Leader (1988, 1991, 1996-1998); Triple Crown (1997-1998); Major League Player of Year, Sporting News (1986); All-Star Game MVP (1986); American League MVP (1986); Thomas A. Yawkey Award, Boston Red Sox (1986); Rookie of the Year, Boston Red Sox (1984)

CLEMENTI, STEVE, T: Software architect **I:** Information Technology and Services **CN:** StorageCraft **ED:** MS in Geophysics, University of Wisconsin-Milwaukee (1991) **C:** Software Architect, StorageCraft Technology, Corp. (2016-Present); Chief Technology Officer, Software Architect, Gillware Data Services (2006-2016) **AS:** Mr. Clementi attributes his success to curiosity, a lot of diligence, and constantly learning. **B/I:** Mr. Clementi has always been fascinated by computers. It started as a hobby and turned into a job. After graduating he went into geophysics, but did a lot of software development there, and eventually the software was more interesting then the geophysics. **AV:** Camping; Kayaking; Cross country skiing; Playing the guitar

CLINE, BENJAMIN, "BEN" LEE, T: U.S. Representative from Virginia **I:** Government Administration/Government Relations/Government Services **DOB:** 02/29/1972 **PB:** Stillwater **SC:** OK/USA **PT:** Philip L. Cline; Julie Cline **MS:** Married **SPN:** Elizabeth (Rocovich) Cline **CH:** Catherine; Sarah **ED:** JD, University of Richmond School of Law (2007); BA, Bates College, Lewiston, ME (1994) **C:** Member, U.S. House of Representatives from Virginia's Sixth Congressional District (2019-Present); Member, District 24, Virginia House of Delegates, VA (2002-Present); President, NDS Corporation, VA (2002-2007); Policy Advisor, Chief of Staff, Bib Goodlatte, U.S. House of Representatives, Washington, DC (1994-2002); Assistant Commonwealth Attorney, City of Harrisburg, VA **PA:** Republican **RE:** Roman Catholic

CLINGER, WILLIAM F., T: Former United States Representative from Pennsylvania **I:** Government Administration/Government Relations/Government Services **DOB:** 04/04/1929 **PB:** Warren **SC:** PA/USA **PT:** William Floyd; Lelia May Clinger **MS:** Widowed **SPN:** Julia Whitla (08/02/1952, Deceased) **CH:** Eleanore Miller; William F. Clinger III; James B. Clinger; Julia B. Clinger **ED:** LLB, University of Virginia (1965); BA, Johns Hopkins University (1951) **C:** Senior Fellow, Johns Hopkins University Center for the Study of American Government, Baltimore, MD (1997-Present); Chairman, U.S. House of Oversight & Government Reform Committee (1995-1997); Member, U.S. Congress from 5th Pennsylvania District, Washington DC (1993-1997); Member, U.S. Congress from 23rd Pennsylvania District, Washington DC (1979-1993); Partner, Harper, Clinger & Eberly (formerly Stone & Harper), Warren, PA (1965-1978); Advertising Executive, New Process Co., Warren, PA (1955-1962) **CR:** Chairman, Board of Directors, Chautauqua Institution (2000-Present); Senior Fellow, Institute of Politics, Harvard University (1998); Chief Counsel, Economic Development Administration (1975-1977); Delegate, Pennsylvania Constitutional Convention (1968); Chairman, Board of Directors, Ripon Educational Fund, Inc. **CIV:** Delegate, Republican National Convention (1972, 1988, 1996); President, Warren Hospital Board (1971-1975); President, Warren Library

Association (1957-1962, 1967-1970); Chairman, Kinzua Dam Dedication Committee (1966); Chairman, Ripon Society **MIL:** Served to Lieutenant, U.S. Navy (1951-1955) **CW:** Member, Editorial Board, University of Virginia Law Review (1964-1965) **AW:** Named, Man of the Year, Pennsylvania Jaycees (1960); Decorated Spirit of Honor Medal **MEM:** President, Warren Jaycees (1959-1960); American Bar Association; Warren County Bar Association; Pennsylvania Bar Association; Former Chairman, House Wednesday Group; Association Reformers Caucus **BAR:** Supreme Court of the United States (1975); Pennsylvania (1965); Virginia **MH:** Albert Nelson Marquis Lifetime Achievement Award **B/I:** At one point, Mr. Clinger was chief counsel at the department of commerce in the economic development administration which was a program that was designed to assist areas that were having trouble with economic development. The government would select areas that would be assisted with federal grants. That got him interested in the idea of doing a better job, he couldn't change that where he was. The only way he could really do anything about reforming it was to be a member of congress. So he ran for congress to reform economic development in the country. **AV:** Sailing; Travel **PA:** Republican **RE:** Presbyterian

CLINGERMAN, BRYCE, T: Chief Operating Officer **I:** Architecture & Construction **CN:** FODS LLC **C:** Chief Operating Officer, FODS LLC (2016-Present); Partner, FODS LLC (2011-Present); Superintendent, Construction; New Home Foundation Construction **MEM:** International Erosion Control Association; Association of General Contractors **AS:** Mr. Clingerman attributes his success to his father and the work ethic he learned.

CLINTON, BILL, T: 42nd President of the U.S. **I:** Government Administration/Government Relations/Government Services **DOB:** 08/19/1946 **PB:** Hope **SC:** AR/USA **PT:** William Jefferson Blythe II; Virginia (Dell Cassidy) Blythe Clinton; Roger Clinton Sr. (Stepfather) **MS:** Married **SPN:** Hillary Diane (Rodham) Clinton (10/11/1975) **CH:** Chelsea Victoria **ED:** Honorary Doctorate, The University Edinburgh (2013); Honorary LHD, University of Central Florida (2013); Honorary Doctorate, Mediterranean University (2011); Honorary LHD, University of Central Missouri (2011); Honorary LHD, Icahn School of Medicine at Mount Sinai (2010); Honorary LHD, West Virginia University (2010); Honorary LLD, McGill University (2009); Honorary LLD, The University of Hong Kong (2008); Honorary LHD, University of New Hampshire (2007); Honorary LHD, Pace University (2006); Honorary Doctorate in Public Service, Northeastern University (1993); JD, Yale Law School (1973); BS in International Affairs, Georgetown University (1968); Postgraduate Coursework, University of Oxford (1970) **C:** Special Envoy to Haiti, United Nations (2009-2013); Co-Chairman, Interim Haiti Recovery Commission (2010-2011); Special Envoy for Tsunami Recovery, United Nations (2005-2007); 42nd President of the United States, Washington, DC (1993-2001); Of Counsel, Wright Lindsey Jennings, Little Rock, AR (1981-1982); Governor, State of Arkansas, Little Rock, AR (1979-1981, 1983-1992); Attorney General, State of Arkansas, Little Rock, AR (1977-1979); Private Law Practice (1973-1976); Professor of Law, University of Arkansas School of Law, Fayetteville, AR (1973-1976) **CR:** Chairman, Advisory Board, Teneo Holdings, LLC (2011-Present); Chairman, National Constitution Center, Philadelphia, PA (2009-2013); Chairman, Southern Growth Policies Board (1985-1986) **CIV:** Founder, American India Foundation (2001); Chairman, Democratic Leadership Council (1990-1991); Chairman, Education Commission of the States (1986-1987);

Member, Task Force on Adolescent Education, Carnegie Foundation; Honorary Co-Chair, Club of Madrid; Co-Chair, Families of Freedom Scholarship Fund; Chairman, Global Fairness Initiative; Advisory Board Co-Chair, International AIDS Trust **CW:** Author, "Back to Work: Why We Need Smart Government for a Strong Economy" (2011); Author, "Giving: How Each of Us Can Change the World" (2007); Author, "My Life" (2004); Author, "Between Hope and History: Meeting America's Challenges for the 21st Century" (1996) **AW:** Happy Heart Fund Lifetime Achievement Award (2014); Advocate for Change GLAAD Media Award (2013); Presidential Medal of Freedom, The White House (2013); Father of the Year, The Father's Day/Mother's Day Council Inc. (2013); One of the World's Most Powerful People, Forbes Magazine (2009, 2011-2014); One of the 100 Most Influential People in the World, Time Magazine (2004-2006, 2010); Distinguished International Leadership Award, Atlantic Council (2010); Person of the Year, PETA (2010); One of the 50 Highest Earning Political Figures (2010); Global Elite, Newsweek Magazine (2008); Co-Recipient, Liberty Medal, National Constitution Center (2006); Citizen of World Award, UN Correspondents Association (UNCA) (2006); Fellow, The World Technology Network (2006); Jimmy and Rosalynn Carter Award for Humanitarian Contributions to the Health of Humankind, National Foundation Infectious Diseases (2005); Pasteur Foundation Award (2005); Knight Commander of the Most Courteous Order of Lesotho (2005); Grammy Award for Spoken Word Album (2005); Biography of the Year, British Book Awards (2005); Audiobook of the Year, Audio Publication Association (2005); Medal for Distinguished Public Service, U.S. Department of Defense (2001); James Madison Award for Distinguished Public Service, The American Whig Cliosophic Society, Princeton University (2000); Rhodes Scholar, University of Oxford University College (1968-1970) **MEM:** Co-Chairman, Task Force for Education, NGA (1990-1992); Chairman, NGA (1986-1987); Vice Chairman, NGA (1986); American Bar Association; Arkansas Bar Association; NGA; Fellow, American Association for the Advancement of Science **PA:** Democrat **RE:** Baptist

CLINTON, LOTTIE D.E., T: State Agency Administrator (Retired) **I:** Government Administration/Government Relations/Government Services **DOB:** 07/26/1937 **PB:** Wilmington **SC:** NC/USA **PT:** King Solomon Dry; Bessie Theresa Mouzon **MS:** Married **SPN:** Robert Clinton (6/24/1993); Edmund Russell Edwards, III (8/30/1954, Deceased 8/29/1969) **CH:** Desireé; Vickie; Edmonia; Cheryl; Michele; Kevin **ED:** Coursework, Central Piedmont Community College (1984); Coursework, University of North Carolina, Wilmington, NC (1974-1975); Associate of Applied Science in Business Administration, Cape Fear Community College (1972) **CT:** Certified, Notary Public, State of North Carolina **C:** Retired (1998); Administrative Supervisor, North Carolina State Port Authority, Wilmington, NC (1985-1998); Administrator Supervisor, Charlotte Intermodal Terminal, North Carolina State Port Authority, Wilmington, NC (1983-1985); Administrative Supervisor, North Carolina State Port Authority, Wilmington, NC (1980-1983); Supervisor, Open Dock, North Carolina State Port Authority, Wilmington, NC (1980); Accounting Clerk to Supervisor, Shipping and Receiving, North Carolina State Port Authority, Wilmington, NC (1976-1980) **CR:** Member, Wilmington Race Riot Commission (2006); Appointed Member, 1898 Wilmington Race Riot Commission, State of North Carolina (2002-2006) **CIV:** Board of Directors, New Hanover Community Health Center, Wilmington, NC (1997-2005); Chairman, Committee on

African American History, Wilmington, NC (1980-1990); Deaconess, Saint Luke Consecrated (1980); Chairman, Service to Disabled, Wilmington, NC (1970-1980); Treasurer, Community Boy's Club, Wilmington, NC; Advisory Board, Business Curriculum, Child and Family Care Coordination; Board of Advisors, Cape Fear Museum of History and Science **AW:** Albert Nelson Marquis Lifetime Achievement Award (2019); Community Service Award, Elderhaus (2007); Named Outstanding Citizen, Winston-Salem Alumni Association (1995); Named Woman of the Year, North Carolina Liberty Light Chapter, American Business Women's Association (1979) **MEM:** Delta Nu Alpha (1984-1985); American Legion Women's Auxiliary; Lifetime Member, Disabled American Veterans Auxiliary **MH:** Albert Nelson Marquis Lifetime Achievement Award **AS:** Ms. Clinton attributes her success to hard work, prayer and opportunities to make decisions within guidelines of the federal, state and local governments, as well as the shipping community. **B/I:** Ms. Clinton became involved in accounting due to an opportunity that arose when her manager asked her to put various import and export operations on paper for its transfer to a computer database. She took great pride in moving water-borne, rail and inter-modal containers as efficiently and quickly as possible, without errors. **AV:** Reading; Sewing; Gardening; Music; Beach **PA:** Democrat **RE:** African Methodist Episcopal Zionite

CLONINGER, CLAUDE ROBERT, MD, PHD, T: Psychiatrist, Epidemiologist, Educator, Researcher, Geneticist **I:** Sciences **DOB:** 04/04/1944 **PB:** Beaumont **SC:** TX/USA **PT:** Morris Sheppard; Marie Concetta (Mazzagatti) Cloninger **MS:** Married **SPN:** Sharon Lee Cloninger (07/11/1969) **CH:** Kevin Michael Cloninger; Bryan Joseph Cloninger **ED:** Honorary PhD, University of Gothenburg (2012); Honorary MD, PhD, Umeå University (1983); MD, Washington University in St. Louis (1970); BA, University of Texas (1966) **CT:** Diplomate, American Board of Psychology and Neurology **C:** Professor Emeritus, Washington University in St. Louis (2019-Present); Director, Anthropedia (2008-Present); Director, Center for Child and Family Well-Being, Washington University in St. Louis (2002-2019); Director, Center for Psychobiology of Personality, Washington University in St. Louis (1994-2019); Wallace Renard Professor of Psychiatry, Washington University in St. Louis (1991-2019); Professor of Genetics, Washington University in St. Louis (1978-2019); Head, Department of Psychiatry, Washington University in St. Louis (1989-1994); Professor of Psychology, Washington University in St. Louis (1989-1991); Associate Professor, Washington University in St. Louis (1978-1981); Assistant Professor, Washington University in St. Louis (1974-1978); Instructor of Psychiatry, Washington University in St. Louis (1973-1974) **CR:** World Health Organization (1981-Present); American Psychiatric Association (1978-Present); Taskforce Member, World Psychiatric Association (2006-2010); National Institute on Alcohol Abuse and Alcoholism (1984-1999); Chairman, Genetics Initiative, National Institute of Mental Health (1989-1997); Mental Health Commissioner, State of Missouri (1990-1995); Psychiatrist-in-Chief, Barnes and Renard Hospitals 1989-1994); Consultant, Institute of Medicine (1986); Chairman, Psychopathology Review Committee, National Institute of Mental Health (1980-1984); Visiting Professor, Umea University (1980); Visiting Professor, University of Hawaii, Honolulu (1978-1979) **CIV:** Director, Anthropedia (2008-Present); National Academy of Medicine (1989-Present) **CW:** Author, "Origins of Altruism and Cooperation" (2011); Author, "Feeling Good, The Science of Well-Being" (2004); Author, "Human Heredity" (1989-2000); Associate

Editor, Genetic Epidemiology (1983-1992); Associate Editor, Journal of Clinical Genetics (1981-1987); Editor, Journal of Behavior Genetics (1980-1986); Editor, American Journal of Human Genetics (1980-1983); DVD Series, "Know Yourself," Anthropedia; Member, Editorial Board, Journal of Comprehensive Psychiatry; Member, Editorial Board, Journal of Psychiatric Research; Member, Editorial Board, Journal of Medical Genetics **AW:** Tournier Award, The International College of Person-centered Medicine (2018); Distinguished Alumnus Award, School of Medicine, Washington University in St. Louis (2015); Oscar Pfister Award (2014); Judd Marmor Award, American Psychiatric Association (2009); Lifetime Achievement Award, International Society of Psychiatric Genetics (2003); Lifetime Achievement Award, American Society of Addiction Medicine (2000); Adolf Meyer Award, American Psychiatric Association (1993); Samuel Hamilton Award, APPA (1993); James D. Isaacson Award, International Society for Biomedical Research on Alcoholism (1992); Strecker Award, Institute of the Pennsylvania Hospital (1988); Research Scientist Award, National Institute of Mental Health (1975, 1980, 1985); Award, American Psychological Association **MEM:** Editorial Board, Behavior Genetics Association (1980-Present); Secretary, APPA (1994-1996); President, APPA (1991-1993); Vice President, APPA (1990); Board of Directors, Research Society on Alcoholism (1987-1990); Treasurer, APPA (1984-1989); American Society of Human Genetics, Incorporated (1980-1983); Fellow, American Association for the Advancement of Science; Alpha Omega Alpha Honor Medical Society; The Phi Beta Kappa Society; National Academy of Medicine **MH:** Albert Nelson Marquis Lifetime Achievement Award **AS:** Dr. Cloninger attributes his success to his loving family, mentors, a love of learning and the grace of God. **B/I:** Dr. Cloninger became involved in his profession because he wanted to be a doctor since he was 10 years old. He was very impressed with the family doctor and decided to pursue a similar path. **AV:** Gardening; Reading; Traveling **PA:** Independent **RE:** Christian

CLOONEY, GEORGE, T: Actor **I:** Media & Entertainment **DOB:** 05/06/1961 **PB:** Lexington **SC:** KY/USA **PT:** Nick Clooney; Nina Clooney **SPN:** Amal Alamuddin (09/27/2014); Talia Balsam (December 15, 1989, Divorced 1993) **CH:** Alexander; Ella **ED:** Student, Northern Kentucky University (1979-1981) **C:** Messenger of Peace, United Nations (2008-Present); Co-Founder, Not On Our Watch (2007) **CIV:** Organizer, Hope for Haiti Telethon (2010) **CW:** Actor, "The Midnight Sky" (2020); Actor, "Catch-22" (2019); Actor, "Suburbicon" (2017); Actor, "Hail, Caesar!" (2016); Actor, Producer, "Money Monster" (2016); Producer, "Our Brand Is Crisis" (2015); Actor, "A Very Murray Christmas" (2015); Actor, "Tomorrowland" (2015); Actor, Producer, Director, Writer, "The Monuments Men" (2014); Actor, "Text Santa 4" (2014); Actor, "Gravity" (2013); Producer, "Argo" (2012); Actor, "The Descendants" (2011); Actor, Director, "The Ides of March" (2011); Actor, "The American" (2010); Actor, "Fail Safe" (2000, 2010); Actor, "Hope for Haiti Now" (2010); Actor, "The Men Who Stare at Goats" (2009); Actor, "Fantastic Mr. Fox" (2009); Actor, "Up in the Air" (2009); Actor, Director, "Leatherheads" (2008); Actor, "Burn After Reading" (2008); Actor, "Ocean's Thirteen" (2007); Actor, Executive Producer, "Michael Clayton" (2007); Actor, Director, Writer, "Good Night and Good Luck" (2005); Actor, Executive Producer, "Syriana" (2005); Director, "Unscripted" (2005); Executive Producer, "The Jacket" (2005); Actor, Executive Producer, "Ocean's Twelve" (2004); Producer, "Criminal" (2004); Actor, "Spy Kids 3-D: Game Over" (2003); Executive Producer, "K Street" (2003); Actor, "Intolerable Cru-

elty" (2003); Actor, "Solaris" (2002); Executive Producer, "Far From Heaven" (2002); Executive Producer, "Insomnia" (2002); Actor, Director, "Confessions of a Dangerous Mind" (2002); Executive Producer, "Welcome to Colinwood" (2002); Actor, "Ocean's Eleven" (2001); Executive Producer, "Rock Star" (2001); Actor, "Spy Kids" (2001); Actor, "O Brother, Where Art Thou" (2000); Actor, "The Perfect Storm" (2000); Actor, Executive Producer, "Fail Safe" (2000); Actor, "Three Kings" (1999); Producer, Writer, "Kilroy" (1999); Actor, "South Park: Bigger, Longer and Uncut" (1999); Actor, "E/R" (1994-1999); Actor, "The Thin Red Line" (1998); Actor, "Murphy Brown" (1998); Actor, "Out of Sight" (1998); Actor, "Batman & Robin" (1997); Actor, "The Peacemaker" (1997); Actor, "South Park" (1997); Actor, "One Fine Day" (1996); Actor, "From Dusk Till Dawn" (1996); Actor, "Friends" (1995); Actor, "Sisters" (1993-1994); Actor, "Without Warning: Terror in the Towers" (1993); Actor, "The Building" (1993); Actor, "Bodies of Evidence" (1992-1993); Actor, "Unbecoming Age" (1992); Actor, "Baby Talk" (1991); Actor, "Rewrite for Murder" (1991); Actor, "Sunset Beat" (1990); Actor, "Red Surf" (1990); Actor, "Knights of the Kitchen Table" (1990); Actor, "Roseanne" (1988-1989); Actor, "Return of the Killer Tomatoes" (1988); Actor, "Grizzly II: The Predator" (1987); Actor, "Return to Horror High" (1987); Actor, "Bennett Brothers" (1987); Actor, "Hunter" (1987); Actor, "Murder, She Wrote" (1987); Actor, "The Golden Girls" (1987); Actor, "The Facts of Life" (1985-1986); Actor, "Combat High" (1986); Actor, "Hotel" (1986); Actor, "Throb" (1986); Actor, "E/R" (1984-1985); Actor, "Street Hawk" (1985); Actor, "Crazy Like A Fox" (1985); Actor, "Riptide" (1984) **AW:** Cecil B. DeMille Award, Hollywood Foreign Press (2015); Darryl F. Zanuck Award for Outstanding Producer of Theatrical Motion Pictures, Producers Guild of America (2013); Critics' Choice Award for Best Actor (2012); Golden Globe Award for Best Performance by an Actor in a Motion Picture-Drama (2012); National Board Review Award for Best Actor (2011); Chairman Award, Palm Springs International Film Festival (2011); Hope Humanitarian Award, Primetime Emmy Awards, Academy of TV Arts and Sciences (2010); National Board Review Award for Best Actor (2009); New York Film Critics Circle Award for Best Actor (2009); The 100 Most Influential People in the World, TIME Magazine (2006, 2007, 2008, 2009); Favorite On Screen Match-Up (with Brad Pitt), People's Choice Awards (2008); National Board Review Award for Best Actor (2007); One of 50 Smartest People in Hollywood (2007); Top 25 Entertainers of the Year, Entertainment Weekly (2007); Chevalier des Arts et Lettres Medal, Government of France (2007); 100 Most Powerful Celebrities, Forbes.com (2007); George Selvin Award, Writers Guild of America (2006); American Cinematheque Award (2006); Freedom Award, Broadcasting Film Critics Association (2006); Golden Globe Award for Best Performance by an Actor in a Supporting Role in a Motion Picture (2006); Academy Award for Best Supporting Actor, Academy of Motion Picture Arts & Sciences (2006); Named a WIRED Renegade, WIRED Rave Awards (2006); Sexiest Man Alive, People Magazine (1997, 2006); National Board Review Award for Best Film (2005); Golden Globe Award for Best Performance by an Actor in a Motion Picture (2001); SAE Award (1998, 1999)

CLOSE, GLENN, T: Actress **I:** Media & Entertainment **DOB:** 03/19/1947 **PB:** Greenwich **SC:** CT/USA **PT:** William Taliaferro Close; Bettine (Moore) Close **MS:** Single **SPN:** David Shaw (02/03/2006, Divorced 2015); James Marlas (1984-1987); Cabot Wade (1969-1971) **CH:** Annie Maude Starke **ED:** BA in Drama and Anthropology, College of

William and Mary (1974) **C:** Joined, New Phoenix Repertory Company (1974) **CR:** Co-Owner, The Leaf and Bean Coffee House, Bozeman, MT (1993-1994) **CIV:** Founder and Chairman, BringChange-2Mind **CW:** Actress, "Wireless" (2020); Actress, "Sunset Boulevard" (2020); Actress, "Hillbilly Elegy" (2020); Actress, "Four Good Days" (2020); Voice Actress, "The Simpsons" (1995-2019); Actress, "3Below: Tales of Arcadia" (2018-2019); Actress, "Let's Dance" (2018); Actress, "Father Figures" (2017); Actress, "The Wife" (2017); Actress, "What Happened to Monday?" (2017); Actress, "The Wilde Wedding" (2017); Actress, "Crooked House" (2017); Actress, "Father Figures" (2017); Actress, "Sea Oak" (2017); Actress, "Warcraft" (2016); Actress, "The Girl with All the Gifts" (2016); Actress, "Family Guy" (2016); Actress, "Anesthesia" (2015); Actress, "The Great Gilly Hopkins" (2015); Actress, "Louie" (2015); Actress, "Low Down" (2014); Actress, "5 to 7" (2014); Actress, "Guardians of the Galaxy" (2014); Actress, "A Delicate Balance" (2014); Actress, "Damages" (2007-2012); Actress, Producer, Writer, "Albert Nobbs" (2011); Actress, "Hoodwinked Too! Hood VS. Evil" (2010); Actress, "Evening" (2007); Actress, "Nine Lives" (2005); Actress, "Heights" (2005); Actress, "The Chumscrubber" (2005); Actress, "Hoodwinked" (2005); Actress, "Tarzan II" (2005); Actress, "The Shield" (2005); Actress, "Strip Search" (2004); Actress, "The Stepford Wives" (2004); Actress, "The Lion in Winter" (2003); Actress, "Le Divorce" (2003); Actress, "Pinocchio" (2002); Actress, "The Safety of Objects" (2001); Actress, Executive Producer, "The Ballad of Lucy Whipple" (2001); Actress, Executive Producer, "South Pacific" (2001); Actress, "Things You Can't Tell Just by Looking at Her" (2000); Actress, "102 Dalmatians" (2000); Actress, Executive Producer, "Baby" (2000); Actress, "Cookie's Fortune" (1999); Actress, "Tarzan" (1999); Actress, Executive Producer, "Sarah, Plain and Tall: Winter's End" (1999); Actress, "The Vagina Monologues" (1998); Actress, "Paradise Road" (1997); Actress, "Air Force One" (1997); Actress, "In the Gloaming" (1997); Actress, "Mary Reilly" (1996); Actress, "101 Dalmatians" (1996); Actress, "Mars Attacks!" (1996); Actress, Executive Producer, "Serving in Silence: The Margarethe Cammermeyer Story" (1995); Executive Producer, "Journey" (1995); Actress, "Sunset Boulevard" (1994-1995); Actress, "The Paper" (1994); Actress, "Sunset Boulevard (LA)" (1993-1994); Actress, "The House of the Spirits" (1993); Actress, Executive Producer, "Skylark" (1993); Actress, "Death and the Maiden" (1992); Actress, "Meeting Venus" (1991); Actress, Executive Producer, "Sarah, Plain and Tall" (1991); Actress, "Hook" (1991); Actress, "She'll Take Romance" (1990); Actress, "Reversal of Fortune" (1990); Actress, "Hamlet" (1990); Actress, "Immediate Family" (1989); Actress, "Gandahar" (1988); Actress, "Dangerous Liaisons" (1988); Actress, "Stones for Ibarra" (1988); Actress, "Fatal Attraction" (1987); Actress, "Benefactors" (1985-1986); Actress, "Jagged Edge" (1985); Actress, "Maxie" (1985); Actress, "The Real Thing" (1984-1985); Actress, "Childhood" (1985); Actress, "Joan of Arc at the Stake" (1985); Actress, "Greystoke: The Legend of Tarzan, Lord of the Apes" (1984); Actress, "The Natural" (1984); Actress, "The Stone Boy" (1984); Actress, "Something About Amelia" (1984); Actress, "The Big Chill" (1983); Actress, "The Elephant Man" (1982); Actress, "Uncommon Women and Others, The Singular Life of Albert Nobbs" (1982); Actress, "The World According to Garp" (1982); Actress, "Barnum" (1980-1981); Actress, "Too Far to Go" (1979); Actress, "Orphan Train" (1979); Actress, "Rex" (1976); Actress, "The Member of the Wedding" (1975); Actress, "The Rules of the Game" (1975); Actress, "Love for Love" (1974); Actress, "Rules of the Game" (1974) **AW:** Screen Actors Guild Award, Best Lead Actress (2018); Emmy Award for Outstanding Lead Actress in a Drama Series (2008, 2009); Golden Globe Award for Best Performance by an Actress in a TV Series - Drama (2008); Sherry Lansing Leadership Award, Sherry Lansing Foundation (2008); Top 25 Entertainers of the Year, Entertainment Weekly (2007); Golden Globe Award for Best Actress in a Mini-series or TV Movie (2005); Screen Actors Guild Award for Best Actress in a TV Movie or Miniseries (2005); Emmy Award for Best Actress in a Miniseries or Special (1995); Tony Award for Best Actress in a Musical (1995); Tony Award for Best Actress in a Play (1992); Woman of Year Award, Hasty Pudding Theatricals, Harvard University (1990); Dartmouth Film Award (1990); Tony Award for Best Actress in a Play (1984) **MEM:** The Phi Beta Kappa Society

CLOUD, MICHAEL JONATHAN, T: U.S. Representative from Texas **I:** Government Administration/Government Relations/Government Services **DOB:** 05/13/1975 **PB:** Baton Rouge **SC:** LA/USA **MS:** Married **SPN:** Rosel Cloud **CH:** Three Children **ED:** BS in Communications, Oral Roberts University **C:** Member, U.S. House of Representatives from Texas' 27th Congressional District, United States Congress, Washington, DC (2018-Present); Member, House Committee on Oversight and Reform, United States Congress; Member, House Committee on Science, Space and Technology, United States Congress **CR:** Chair, Victoria County Republican Party (2010-2017) **PA:** Republican

CLOWE, KELLEY A., CFP, CHFC, T: Certified Financial Planner, Registered Investment Adviser **I:** Financial Services **CN:** Capital West Financial Advisers **DOB:** 09/27/1942 **PB:** Tulsa **SC:** OK/USA **PT:** Kendall Dean Clowe; Clare Curry (Abington) Clowe **MS:** Married **SPN:** Patricia Clowe (1986); Virginia Sue Carroll (03/21/1964) **CH:** Sean; Douglas; Malinda; Richard (Stepson); Michelle (Stepdaughter) **ED:** MBA, The Wharton School, The University of Pennsylvania (1966); BA, Central Methodist College (Now Central Methodist University), Fayette, MO (1964) **C:** Certified Financial Planner, Registered Investment Adviser, Capital West Financial Advisors (2002-Present); Senior Vice President, Branch Development, Bank of America Corporation (1995-2002); Vice President, BankUnited, Inc., Houston, Texas (1992-1995); Vice President of Marketing, Associates Corporation of North America, Dallas, Texas (1983-1992); Vice President of Marketing, People's National Bank of Washington, Seattle, WA (1981-1983); Senior Vice President, Cashier, Dominion Banker, Denver, CO (1980-1981); Assistant Vice President of Marketing, First National Bank of Denver (1974-1980); President, Clowe Mather Research Associates, Inc., Lakewood, CO (1972-1974); Marketing Research Manager, Ralston Purina Co., St. Louis, MO (1969-1972); Marketing Research Analyst, Anheuser Busch, Inc. (Now Anheuser-Busch Companies, LLC), St. Louis, MO (1967-1969); Research Assistant, General Foods Corp., White Plains, NY (1966-1967) **CR:** Instructor, University of Puget Sound (1982-Present); Bank Marketing Association (1975-1981); School of Bank Marketing (1975-1976); Institute of Marketing Research **CIV:** Past President, Rotary International; Elder, The Hills Church; Teacher, Sunday School **CW:** Co-author with Anthony N. Diina, "The Basics of Bank Marketing Research" (1978) **MEM:** Chairman, Financial Services Marketing Conference, American Marketing Association (1985); Chairman, Marketing Planning Conference, Bank Marketing Association (1979); Chairman, Research and Planning Council, Bank Marketing Association (1977-1978); President, Col-orado Chapter, American Marketing Association (1976-1977); Bank Marketing Association; American Marketing Association **MH:** Marquis Who's Who Top Professional **AS:** Mr. Clowe attributes his success to hard work and a good personality. **B/I:** Mr. Clowe became involved in his field with the desire to run his own company and to financially serve the citizens of his community. He was living in Fort Worth but he was working in Houston. He had an apartment and every night he would go home and turn on the television on CNBC; they paraded these three guys on there and they had the initials behind their name and he didn't know what they stood for. He went to the library to find out and the more he listened to them and understood what it was they did, the more he decided that's what he wanted to do. **AV:** Travel; Scuba; Spending time with family

CLUSIN, WILLIAM THOMAS, T: Physician, Neuroscientist, Cardiologist, Educator **I:** Research **CN:** Stanford University School of Medicine **DOB:** 03/31/1949 **PB:** Chicago **SC:** IL/USA **PT:** Edward M. Clusin; Lorena M. Clusin **MS:** Single **CH:** Jonathan A.; Daniel P.; Joshua D.; Audrey A. **ED:** Resident in Medicine, Stanford Medical School, California (1976-1981); PhD, Albert Einstein College Medicine, Bronx, NY (1976); MD, Albert Einstein College Medicine, Bronx, NY (1976); BS, Massachusetts Institute of Technology, Cambridge, MA (1970) **CT:** Diplomate, Cardiovascular Disease, American Board of Internal Medicine (1995); American Board of Internal Medicine (1981); National Board of Medical Examiners (1977) **C:** Associate Professor of Medicine With Tenure, Stanford University (1989-Present); Assistant Professor of Medicine, Stanford University; Attending Physician, Stanford Hospital; Fellow in Cardiology, Stanford Medical School **CR:** Member, Editorial Board, Cardiology Plus (2020-Present); Member, Editorial Board, Journal of Cardiovascular Disorders (2014); Member, Editorial Board, Heart Rhythm Case Reports (2014); Member, Editorial Board, Circulation Research (1989-1994); Associate Editor, Journal of Clinical Investigation (1988-1992) **CIV:** With, Dem. National Committee, 2014 **CW:** Contributor, Book; Contributor, Articles, Professional Journals **AW:** National Merit Scholar (1970) **MEM:** American Society for Clinical Investigation (1988-Present); Fellow, American College of Physicians; Fellow, Royal Society of Medicine; Fellow, American Heart Association; National Institutes of Health Study Section; Biophysical Society; Society of General Physiologists; Alpha Omega Alpha **MH:** Albert Nelson Marquis Lifetime Achievement Award **AS:** Dr. Clusin attributes his success to excellent mentorship at all stages of training, as well as outstanding colleagues who were co-investigators on research projects. He also received scholarship and grant support from private foundations and the federal government. **B/I:** Dr. Clusin became involved in his profession because he wanted to be a scientist since he was young. He had excellent role models. Biology was a good fit for her academic strengths. **AV:** Genealogy **PA:** Democrat

CLYBURN, JAMES, "JIM" ENOS, T: U.S. Representative from South Carolina **I:** Government Administration/Government Relations/Government Services **DOB:** 07/21/1940 **PB:** Sumter **SC:** SC/USA **PT:** Enos Lloyd Clyburn; Almeta (Dizzley) Clyburn **MS:** Widowed **SPN:** Emily England (1961, Deceased 2019) **CH:** Mignon; Jennifer; Angela **ED:** Honorary LLD, Voorhees College (1996); Honorary LHD, South Carolina State University (1995); Honorary LLD, Claflin College (Now Claflin University) (1995); Honorary LHD, St. Augustine College (1994); Honorary DSc, Medical University of South Carolina (1993); Honorary DSc, College of Charleston (1992); Honorary LHD, Winthrop College (Now Winthrop University) (1987); BA in History, South Carolina State College (Now South Carolina State University), Orangeburg, SC (1962) **C:** House Majority Whip, United States Congress (2019-Present); Member, U.S. House of Representatives from South Carolina's Sixth Congressional District, United States Congress (1993-Present); Assistant Minority Leader (Minority Whip), United States Congress from South Carolina's Sixth District (2011-2019); Member, Joint Select Committee on Deficit Reduction (2011); Assistant Majority Leader (Majority Whip), United States Congress from South Carolina's Sixth District (2007-2011); Chairman, U.S. House Democratic Caucus (2006-2007); Commissioner, South Carolina Human Affairs Commission (1974-1992); Staff Member, Governor John C. West, Charleston, SC (1971-1974); Executive Director, South Carolina Commission for Farm Workers, Inc. (1968-1971); Director, Charleston County Neighborhood Youth Corps/ New Careers Projects (1966-1968); Employment Counselor, South Carolina Employment Security Commission (1965-1966); Teacher, Charleston County Public School Systems, SC **CIV:** President, International Association of Official Human Rights Agencies (1985-1987); President, The National Association of Human Rights Workers (1980-1981); Board of Directors, South Carolina Literacy Association; Board of Directors, James R. Clark Memorial Sickle Cell Foundation **AW:** Named One of the Most Influential Black Americans, Ebony Magazine (2006); Public Administrator of the Year Award, The American Society for Public Administration **MEM:** Life Member, NAACP; Shriners International; Masons; Omega Psi Phi Fraternity, Inc. **PA:** Democrat

COATES, ARTHUR DONWELL, MA, T: Chemist; Consultant **I:** Sciences **DOB:** 06/14/1928 **PB:** Steubenville **SC:** OH/USA **PT:** Arthur Raymond Coates; Margaret June (Thompson) Coates **MS:** Married **SPN:** Marie Maslin Silver (04/06/1957) **CH:** Arthur Donwell Jr.; Randolph Silver; Dr. Stephen Thompson Coates **ED:** MS in Chemistry, University of Delaware (1961); BS in Chemistry, College, Steubenville, Ohio (1950) **C:** President, Silver Farms, Inc., Aberdeen, MD (1979-Present); Special Assistant to Director, Terminal Ballistics Research Laboratory (TBRL) (1978-1986); Technical Assistant to Chief, Terminal Ballistics Research Laboratory (TBRL) (1975-1978); Chief, Methodology Section, Terminal Ballistics Research Laboratory (TBRL) (1970-1975); Chief, Radiation Damage Section, Terminal Ballistics Research Laboratory (TBRL) (1960-1970); Chief, Ignition Section, Terminal Ballistics Research Laboratory (TBRL) (1955-1960); Chemist, Research Chemist, Terminal Ballistics Research Laboratory (TBRL), Aberdeen Proving Ground, MD (1951-1955); Practice Engineer, Wheeling Steel Corp., Steubenville, Ohio (1950-1951); President, Swan Crest, LLC **CR:** Retired CY (2006); Consultant in Fields of Applied Chemistry and Ballistic Technology; Chairman, Silver Farms, Inc., Chairman, Swan Crest, LLC **CIV:** Board of Directors, The Historical Society of Harford County, MD (2002-Present) **MIL:** With, United States Army (1951-1953) **MEM:** Board of Directors, Aberdeen Area Chamber of Commerce (1994-Present); President, Friends of Harford County Public Library, Aberdeen Branch; Fellow, American Institute of Chemists; American Association for the Advancement of Science; American Chemical Society; Aberdeen Area Chamber of Commerce; Friends of Harford County Public Library; Sigma Xi, The Scientific Research Honor Society **MH:**

Albert Nelson Marquis Lifetime Achievement Award; Marquis Who's Who Top Professional **AV:** Architecture; Finance **RE:** Methodist

COATES, TA-NEHISI, T: Author **I:** Writing and Editing **DOB:** 09/30/1975 **PB:** Baltimore **SC:** MD/ USA **ED:** Howard University **CW:** Author, "Black Panther #1" (2018); Author, "Captain America" (2018); Author, "We Were Eight Years in Power: An American Tragedy" (2017); Author, "Black Panther and the Crew" (2017); Author, "Black Panther #1" (2016); Author, "Black Panther: World of Wakanda" (2016); Author, "Between the World and Me: Notes on the First 150 Years in America" (2015); Author, "The Beautiful Struggle: A Father, Two Sons, and an Unlikely Road to Manhood" (2008); Author, "Asphalt Sketches" (1990) **AW:** Eisner Award (2018); Dayton Literary Peace Prize in Nonfiction (2018); Listee, Time 100 Most Influential (2016); Kirkus Prize in Nonfiction (2015); Harriet Beecher Stowe Center Prize for Writing to Advance Social Justice (2015); George Polk Award (2014); National Magazine Award (2013); Hillman Prize (2012)

COATS, DANIEL RAY, T: United States Director of National Intelligence (Retired) **I:** Government Administration/Government Relations/Government Services **DOB:** 05/16/1943 **PB:** Jackson **SC:** MI/USA **PT:** Edward R. Coats; Vera E. Coats **MS:** Married **SPN:** Marcia Ann Crawford (09/04/1965) **CH:** Laura; Lisa; Andrew **ED:** JD, Indiana University School of Law (Now Indiana University Robert H. McKinney School of Law), Cum Laude (1971); BA in Government and Economics, Wheaton College, IL (1965) **C:** Director of National Intelligence, Washington DC (2017-2019); Chair, Joint Economic Committee, Washington, DC (2015-2017); Senator, State of Indiana, Washington, DC (1989-1999, 2011-2017); Member, Congressional Joint Economic Committee, Washington, DC (2011-2017); Member, Select Committee on Intelligence, United States Senate, Washington, DC (2011); Member, Energy and Natural Resources Committee, United States Senate, Washington, DC (2011); Member, Appropriations Committee, United States Senate, Washington, DC (2011); Senior Counsel, Co-Chairman, Government Relations Group, King & Spalding LLP, Washington, DC (2005-2009); United States Ambassador to Germany, United States Department of State, Berlin, Germany (2001-2005); Special Counsel, Verner, Liipfert, Bernhard, McPherson & Hand (1999-2001); Member, United States Congress, Indiana's Fourth District, Washington, DC (1981-1989); District Representative for Representative Dan Quayle, United States House of Representatives (1976-1980); Assistant Vice President, Counsel, Mutual Security Life Insurance Company, Fort Wayne, IN (1969-1975) **CIV:** President, Big Brothers Big Sisters of America **MIL:** U.S. Army (1966-1968) **CW:** Associate Editor, Indiana Law Review **AW:** Benjamin Harrison Presidential Site Award, Advancing American Democracy (2015); Charles G. Berwind Lifetime Achievement Award, Big Brothers Big Sisters of America (2012) **BAR:** Illinois State Bar Association (1972) **PA:** Republican **RE:** Presbyterian

COBLE, JOHN, T: Partner **I:** Law and Legal Services **CN:** Albrechta & Coble, Ltd. **DOB:** 07/31/1956 **PB:** Toledo **SC:** OH/USA **PT:** Richard Alan May; Nancy Lee (Marquardt) May **MS:** Married **SPN:** Karin Coble (2007); Cynthia Lou Rundquist (03/10/1979, Divorced) **CH:** Richard; Owen; Forrest; Kira **ED:** JD, University of Toledo, Toledo, OH (1984); PhB in Interdisciplinary Studies, Miami University, Oxford, OH (1974) **C:** Lawyer, Albrechta & Coble, Toledo, OH (1995-Present); Lawyer, Britz & Zemmelman, Toledo, OH (1987-1995); Lawyer, Gallon, Kalniz & Iorio, Toledo, OH (1987); Lawyer, Toledo Legal Aid Society (1985-1987); Mort-

gage Representative, Northern Ohio Investment Company, Toledo, OH (1980-1984); Community Organizer, Covington Neighborhood Action Committee, Kentucky (1979-1980); Laborer, Square D Company, Oxford, OH (1978-1979) **CIV:** Treasurer, Harbor House Homeless Shelter, Toledo, OH (1985-1996); President, Fair Housing Center, Toledo, OH (1990-1994); Greater Toledo Housing Coalition (1987-1990); Board Member, Teamsters Local 20 Legal Defense Fund; Trustee, Toledo Women's Bar Association **AW:** Order of the Sole, Toledo Junior Bar Association (2018); Trustees Award, Toledo Bar Association (2001) **MEM:** Trustee, Toledo Bar Association (1994-Present); President, Toledo Junior Bar Association (1993-1994); Committee Chairmanships, Toledo Bar Association (1987-1994); Executive Committee, Toledo Junior Bar Association (1987-1994); Lucas County Bar Association; Sandusky County Bar Association **BAR:** U.S. Supreme Court (1987); U.S. District Court for the Northern District of Ohio (1985); Ohio (1984) **MH:** Marquis Who's Who Top Professional **AS:** Mr. Coble attributes his success to his partner, Joe AlBrecta, the legal community in Northwest Ohio, and his clients, who have recommended him to other clients over the years. **B/I:** Mr. Coble became involved in his profession because he saw law as a good way to assist families and people with their lives; he wanted to use the law to protect them and make a positive impact. He always had a great interest in law and social policy, as both his father and grandfather were lawyers. However, when he was younger, he actually fought against the expectation that he would go down that professional route and tried for a few years to pursue other things. Mr. Coble later decided that law was, ultimately, what he was best suited for and went into it. **AV:** Researching history and theology; Writing poetry; Playing tennis **PA:** Democrat

COCHRAN, BRENT HARTMAN, T: Professor **I:** Education/Educational Services **DOB:** 04/02/1956 **PB:** Greenville **SC:** TN/USA **PT:** Gene B Cochran; Patricia (Hartman) Cochran **MS:** Married **SPN:** Angela C. Reffrel (04/06/1989) **CH:** Anton; Kara **ED:** PhD, Harvard University (1984); BS, Massachusetts Institute of Technology (1978) **C:** Professor, School of Medicine, Tufts University (2002-Present); Associate Professor of Physiology, School of Medicine, Tufts University (1993-2002); Assistant Professor of Biology, Massachusetts Institute of Technology (1985-1992) **CR:** Teacher of Endocrinology and Molecular Genetics **AW:** Pfizer Career Development Professorship, Massachusetts Institute of Technology (1988-1991); Searle Scholarship (1987-1990); Rita Allen Scholarship (1985-1990) **MEM:** American Association for the Advancement of Science; Society for NeuroOncology; The International Society for Stem Cell Research; American Association for Cancer Research **MH:** Albert Nelson Marquis Lifetime Achievement Award; Marquis Who's Who Top Professional **B/I:** Dr. Cochran became involved in his profession because of his lifelong interest in science, his curiosity regarding cancer research and his desire to make a difference. **AV:** Playing basketball; Learning to play the guitar; Reading; Watching movies

COCHRAN, RICH, T: President, Chief Executive Officer **I:** Environmental Services **CN:** Western Reserve Land Conservancy **MS:** Married **SPN:** Jennifer **CH:** Sophie; Isabelle; Josie **ED:** BA in English Literature and Economics, Middlebury College (1991) **C:** Manager, WRLC Properties, Ltd. (2006-Present); President, Chief Executive Officer, Western Reserve Land Conservancy (1996-Present); Director, Rivers Unlimited (1997-1999); Director of Development, Case Western Reserve University School of Law (1994-1996)

CIV: National Leadership Council, Land Trust Alliance (2011-Present); Trustee, Natural Areas Land Conservancy (2006-Present); Board of Directors, Healing Our Waters, Great Lakes Coalition (2013-2015); Chairman, Officer, Cleveland Chapter, Young Presidents' Organization (YPO) (2008-2015); Trustee, Western Reserve Conservation Education Fund (2008-2014); Board of Directors, Kendal Northern Ohio (2005-2010); Board of Directors, Holimont, Inc. (2005-2008); Alumnus, Leadership Cleveland (2005-2006); Founding Trustee, Chagrin River Watershed Partners (1996-1998) AW: Conservation Award, Cleveland Museum of Natural History (2010); CEO of the Year, Crain's Cleveland Business Magazine AS: Mr. Cochran attributes his success to working hard and being a life-long learner. B/I: After graduating from college, Mr. Cochran went backpacking. Through this experience, he learned about the importance of preserving nature. He believes nature makes people healthier, happier, and more productive. Once he returned from backpacking, he began working with conservation groups. In the years since then, Mr. Cochran has continued to work toward improving communities. He is inspired by seeing nature thrive.

COEN, ETHAN, T: Filmmaker **I:** Media & Entertainment **DOB:** 09/21/1957 **PB:** Saint Louis Park **SC:** MN/USA **PT:** Edward Coen; Rena Coen **MS:** Married **SPN:** Tricia Cooke (10/02/1990) **CH:** Dusty; Buster **ED:** Coursework in Philosophy, Princeton University **C:** Former Statistical Typist, Macy's, New York, NY **CW:** Executive Producer, "Fargo" (2014-Present); Executive Producer, "The Ballad of Buster Scruggs" (2018); Writer, Director, Producer, "Suburbicon" (2017); Writer, Director, Producer, "Hail, Caesar!" (2016); Writer, Director, Producer, "Inside Llewyn Davis" (2013); Writer, "Gambit" (2012); Writer, Director, Producer, "True Grit" (2010); Writer, Director, Producer, "A Serious Man" (2009); Writer, Director, Producer, "Burn After Reading" (2008); Writer, Director, Producer, "No Country for Old Men" (2007); Writer, Director, "Paris, I Love You" (2006); Writer, "Romance & Cigarettes" (2005); Writer, Director, Producer, "The Ladykillers" (2004); Writer, "Bad Santa" (2003); Writer, Director, Producer, "Intolerable Cruelty" (2003); Writer, "A Fever in the Blood" (2002); Writer, Director, Producer, "The Man Who Wasn't There" (2001); Executive Producer, "Down From the Mountain" (2000); Writer, Director, Producer, "O Brother, Where Art Thou?" (2000); Producer, "The Big Lebowski" (1998); Producer, "The Naked Man" (1998); Producer, "Fargo" (1996); Producer, "The Hudsucker Proxy" (1994); Producer, "Barton Fink" (1991); Producer, "Miller's Crossing" (1990); Producer, "Raising Arizona" (1987); Writer, "Crime Wave (formerly XYZ Murders)" (1985); Producer, "Blood Simple" (1984) **AW:** Nominee, Academy Award for Best Adapted Screenplay (2019); The David L. Wolper Award for Outstanding Producer of Long-Form TV, Producers Guild of America (2016); National Board Review Award for Best Original Screenplay (2013); National Society Film Critics Award for Best Screenplay (2010); National Board Review Award for Best Original Screenplay (2009); Boston Society Film Critics Award for Best Screenplay (2009); Critics' Choice Award, Broadcast Film Critics Association (2008); Golden Globe Award for Best Screenplay/Motion Picture (2008); Directors Guild of America Award for Outstanding Directorial Achievement in Feature Film (2008); Producers Guild of America Award for Best Feature Film (2008); British Academy Film and TV Arts Award for Best Director (2008); Writers Guild of America Award for Best Adapted Screenplay (2008); Academy Awards for Best Adapted Screenplay, Best Directing, Best Picture (2008); Listee,

The 100 Most Influential People in the World, Time Magazine (2008); National Board Review Award for Best Adapted Screenplay (2007); New York Film Critics Circle Awards for Best Screenplay, Best Director, Best Picture (2007); Boston Society Film Critics Award for Best Picture (2007); Academy Award for Best Screenplay (1997); Cannes International Film Festival award for Best Director (1996); Palme D'Or Award for Best Director Award, Cannes International Film Festival (1996) **MEM:** Fellow, American Academy of Arts & Sciences

COEN, JOEL, T: Filmmaker **I:** Media & Entertainment **DOB:** 11/29/1954 **PB:** Saint Louis Park **SC:** MN/USA **PT:** Ed Coeh; Rena Coen **MS:** Married **SPN:** Frances McDormand (04/01/1984) **CH:** Pedro **ED:** Coursework in Film, New York University; Coursework, Simon's Rock College **CW:** Executive Producer, "Fargo" (2014-Present); Executive Producer, "The Ballad of Buster Scruggs" (2018); Writer, Producer, Director, "Suburbicon" (2017); Writer, Producer, Director, "Hail, Caesar!" (2016); Writer, "Bridge of Spies" (2015); Writer, Producer, Director, "Inside Llewyn Davis" (2013); Writer, "Gambit" (2012); Writer, Producer, Director, "True Grit" (2010); Writer, Producer, Director, "A Serious Man" (2009); Writer, Producer, Director, "Burn After Reading" (2008); Writer, Producer, Director, "No Country for Old Men" (2007); Writer, Director, "Paris, I Love You" (2006); Executive Producer, "Romance & Cigarettes" (2005); Writer, Producer, Director, "The Ladykillers" (2004); Writer, Director, "Intolerable Cruelty" (2003); Executive Producer, "Bad Santa" (2003); Writer, Director, "The Man Who Wasn't There" (2001); Writer, Director, "O Brother, Where Art Thou?" (2000); Executive Producer, "Down From the Mountain" (2000); Writer, Director, "The Big Lebowski" (1998); Writer, Director, "Fargo" (1996); Writer, Director, "The Hudsucker Proxy" (1994); Writer, Director, "Barton Fink" (1991); Writer, Director, "Miller's Crossing" (1990); Writer, Director, "Raising Arizona" (1987); Writer, "Crime Wave (formerly XYZ Murders)" (1985); Writer, Director, "Blood Simple" (1984) **AW:** Nominee, Academy Award for Best Adapted Screenplay (2019); The David L. Wolper Award for Outstanding Producer of Long-Form TV, Producers Guild of America (2016); National Board Review Award for Best Original Screenplay (2013); National Society Film Critics Award for Best Screenplay (2010); National Board Review Award for Best Original Screenplay (2009); Boston Society Film Critics Award for Best Screenplay (2009); Critics' Choice Award, Broadcast Film Critics Association (2008); Golden Globe Award for Best Screenplay/Motion Picture (2008); Directors Guild of America Award for Outstanding Directorial Achievement in Feature Film (2008); Producers Guild of America Award for Best Feature Film (2008); British Academy Film and TV Arts Award for Best Director (2008); Writers Guild of America Award for Best Adapted Screenplay (2008); Academy Awards for Best Adapted Screenplay, Best Directing, Best Picture (2008); The 100 Most Influential People in the World, TIME Magazine (2008); National Board Review Award for Best Adapted Screenplay (2007); New York Film Critics Circle Awards for Best Screenplay, Best Director, Best Picture (2007); Boston Society Film Critics Award for Best Picture (2007); Academy Award for Best Screenplay (1997); Cannes International Film Festival award for Best Director (1996); Palme D'Or Award for Best Director Award, Cannes International Film Festival (1996) **MEM:** Fellow, American Academy Arts & Sciences

COHEN, HERMAN JAY, T: Diplomat, Consultant to U.S. investors in Africa **I:** Government Administration/Government Relations/Government Services

DOB: 02/10/1932 **PB:** New York **SC:** NY/USA **PT:** Morris Cohen; Fannie (Zauzner) Cohen **MS:** Married **SPN:** Suzanne (Karpman) Cohen (04/04/1957) **CH:** Marc; Alain **ED:** Honorary Doctorate, Southeastern University, Lakeland, FL (1990); Honorary Doctorate, St. Augustine's College, Raleigh, NC (1990); Graduate Coursework, American University, Washington, DC (1962); BA in Liberal Arts, City University of New York, New York, NY (1953) **C:** Founder, Consultant, Cohen & Woods International (1993-Present); Assistant Secretary for African Affairs, U.S. Department of State, Washington, DC (1989-1993); Special Assistant to the President, Senior Director for Africa, National Security Council, Washington, DC (1987-1989); Principal Deputy, Assistant Secretary, Deputy Director-General, Bureau Personnel, Department State (1984-1986); Principal Deputy Assistant Secretary, Bureau of Intelligence and Research, U.S. Department of State, Washington, DC (1980-1984); Ambassador to Republics of Senegal and Gambia, Dakar, Senegal (1977-1980); Political Counselor, American Embassy, Paris (1974-1977); Director, Bureau of African Affairs, U.S. Department of State, Washington, DC (1969-1974); Deputy Chief of Mission, American Embassy, Kinshasa, Zaire (1966-1969); Economic Commercial Officer, American Embassy, Lusaka, Zambia (1965-1966); Foreign Service, U.S. Department of State, Washington, DC (1955) **CR:** Senior Advisor, Global Coalition for Africa (1994-2000); Career Ambassador (1991) **CIV:** President, French International School, Washington, DC (1984-1995) **MIL:** Army Service, Germany (1953-1955) **CW:** Author, "US Policy Toward Africa: Eight Decades of Realpolitik" (2020); Author, "the Mind of the African Strongman: Conversations with Dictators, Statesmen, and Father Figures" (2015); Author, "Intervening in Africa: Superpower Peacemaking in a Troubled Continent" (2000); Blogger, "Hank Cohen's Africa Blog" **AW:** Lifetime Contribution to Diplomacy, American Foreign Service Association (2019); Distinguished Honor Award (1993); Presidential Meritorious Rank Award (1989); Senior Foreign Service Award (1984, 1987); Christian A. Herter Award, U.S. Department of State (1982); Decorated Legion of Honor, Order of Leopold II **MEM:** Council on Foreign Relations (CFR); American Academy of Diplomacy (AAD); Phi Beta Kappa **MH:** Albert Nelson Marquis Lifetime Achievement Award; Marquis Who's Who Humanitarian Award **B/I:** Mr. Cohen became involved in his profession because, during his university studies, he took a special interest in international relations; he knew he wanted to pursue an international and philanthropic career. His professor of international relations suggested that he take an exam to be accepted into the U.S Foreign Service. He accomplished this and was also accepted into Harvard Business School. The state advised Mr. Cohen to attend Harvard, telling him they would hold his position. He decided that he did not want to wait, so he joined the U.S. Foreign Service directly.

COHEN, STEPHEN, "STEVE" IRA, T: U.S. Representative from Tennessee **I:** Government Administration/Government Relations/Government Services **DOB:** 05/24/1949 **PB:** Memphis **SC:** TN/USA **PT:** Morris David Cohen; Genevieve (Goldsand) Cohen **ED:** JD, The University of Memphis Cecil C. Humphreys School of Law (1973); BA, Vanderbilt University, Nashville, TN (1971) **C:** Member, U.S. House of Representatives from Tennessee's Ninth Congressional District, United States Congress (2007-Present); Deputy Speaker, Tennessee State Senate (2000-2007); Member, District 30, Tennessee State Senate (1983-2007); Commissioner, Shelby County Board of Commissioners (1978-1980); Legal Advisor, Memphis Police

Department (1975-1978); Member, Committee on the Judiciary; Member, Committee on Transportation and Infrastructure **CR:** Member, Executive Committee, National Conference State Legislatures (1998-2005); Member, Shelby County Charter Commission (1984); Interim Judge, Shelby County General Sessions Court (1980) **CIV:** Delegate, Democratic National Convention (1980, 1992, 2004-2016); Board of Trustees, Memphis College of Art (1988-2002); Chairman, Shelby County Legislative Delegation (1988-1990); Delegate, Japan Study Mission, American Council of Young Political Leaders (1986); Vice President, Tennessee Constitutional Convention (1977) **AW:** Legislator of the Year, Boys & Girls Clubs in Tennessee (2003); Public Leadership Award, Tennessee The Human Rights Campaign (2002) **MEM:** Memphis Bar Association **BAR:** State of Tennessee (1974) **PA:** Democrat **RE:** Jewish

COHEN, TIM, T: Editor **I:** Writing and Editing **CN:** Daily Maverick **SC:** South Africa **ED:** BA in Literature and African Politics, University of KwaZulu-Natal (1983); Diploma/Matric, Pretoria Boys High School (1977) **CT:** Open Water One (Sailing); Padi Certified Diver; Basic Programming; Intermediate Wine Certificate **C:** Editor, Business Maverick, Daily Maverick, South Africa (2019-Present); Editor, Business Day, Johannesburg, South Africa (2016-2018); Editor, Financial Mail, Johannesburg, South Africa (2013-2016); Contributing Editor, Business Day (2010-2013) **CW:** Author, "A Piece of the Pie: The Battle Over Nationalisation" (2012)

COHN, GARY DAVID, T: Director (Retired) **I:** Business Management/Business Services **CN:** National Economic Council **DOB:** 08/27/1960 **PB:** Cleveland **SC:** OH/USA **PT:** Victor Cohn; Ellen Cohn **MS:** Married **SPN:** Lisa Pevaroff-Cohn **CH:** Three Daughters **ED:** BSBA in Finance, American University Kogod School of Business (1982) **C:** Director, National Economic Council, Office of the White House, Washington, DC (2017-2018); Chief Economic Adviser to President Trump, Washington, DC (2017-2018); President, Chief Operating Officer, Goldman Sachs Group, Inc. (Formerly Goldman Sachs & Co.) (2009-2017); Management Committee, Goldman Sachs & Co. (2002-2017); Managing Director, Goldman Sachs & Co. (1996-2017); President, Co-Chief Operating Officer, Goldman Sachs Group, Inc. (2006-2009); Co-head global securities, Goldman Sachs Group, Inc, 2004-2006); Co-Head, Equities Division, Goldman Sachs Group, Inc. (2003-2004); Head, Fixed Income, Currency and Commodities Division, Goldman Sachs & Co. (2002-2006); Co-Chief Operating Officer, Fixed Income, Currency and Commodities Division, Goldman Sachs & Co., (2002); Co-Head, Commodities Division, Goldman Sachs & Co. (1996-1999); Partner, Goldman Sachs & Co. (1994-1996); Senior Trader, J. Aron Futures Unit, Goldman Sachs & Co., London, England (1990); Silver Trader; Salesman, Home Products Division, United States Steel Corporation **CR:** Board of Directors, Goldman Sachs Group, Inc. (2006-Present); Board of Directors, New York Mercantile Exchange (CME Group, Inc.) (1998-2000); Board of Directors, London Medal Exchange (1994); Treasurer, Commodity Exchange Inc. (1990); Visiting Professor, Harvard Kennedy School, John F. Kennedy School of Government **CIV:** Trustee, New York University School of Medicine Foundation; Trustee, American University; Trustee, Gilmour Academy, Cleveland, OH; Trustee, New York University Child Study Center, NYU Langone Hospitals; Trustee, New York University Hospital, NYU Langone Hospitals; Trustee, Harlem's Children Zone; Treasury Borrowing Advisory Committee, Securities Industry, and Financial Markets Association **AW:** Effecting Change Award, 100 Women in Hedge Funds (Now 100 Women in Finance) (2005) **PA:** Democrat

COLANDUONI, BERNADETTE L. CONNELLY RN. MED, RN, MED, T: School Nurse **I:** Medicine & Health Care **DOB:** 12/03/1942 **PB:** Somerville **SC:** NJ/USA **PT:** Woodrow Wilson Connelly; Anna Elizabeth (Poltorak) Connelly **MS:** Married **SPN:** Donald John Colanduoni (5/12/1965) **CH:** Bernadette Marie Colanduoni-Danner Nina (Granddaughter); Benjamin Scott Kish (Great-Grandson); Donald John (Grandchild); Breanna Colanduoni (Grandchild); Lewis (Grandchild) **ED:** Master of Education, Trenton State University (1984); Bachelor of Arts, Jersey City State (1976); Registered Nurse, St. Francis School Nursing, Trenton, NJ (1963) **CT:** Certified School Nurse and Teacher, New Jersey **C:** Covering Staff Nurse, Dr. Lawrence Gross, Somerset, NJ (2002-2013); Substitute School Nurse, Middlesex Board of Education, New Jersey (1998-2002); Retired, Middlesex Board Education, New Jersey (1998); School Nurse, Middlesex (New Jersey) Board Education (1971-1998); Occupational Nurse, Art Color Printing Co., Dunellen, NJ (1965-1969); Staff Nurse, Muhlenberg Hospital, Plainfield, NJ (1963-1965) **CIV:** Middlesex Borough Board of Health Commission (1995-Present); Co-leader Middlesex Borough, Girl Scouts of the U.S.A. (1973-1979); Life Member, Bound Brook Chapter, Deborah Heart and Lung Hospital **CW:** Quilts of Valor; Quilts for Kids; Quilts for Veterans; Quilts for Battered Women **AW:** Governor Teacher Recognition Award, State of New Jersey (1991); Meritorious Award, Deborah Heart and Lung Hospital (1969) **MEM:** Liaison, Middlesex Borough Drug Alliance, Middlesex Education Association (1991-Present); Negotiating Team, Middlesex Education Association (1989-1998); Recording Secretary, Middlesex County School Nurses (1980-1984); National Education Association; New Jersey Education Association; National Association School Nurses; New Jersey State School Nurses; Monday Morning Quilters, Bridgewater, NJ; Pieced Together Quilters, Bridgewater, NJ, Stitchers in the Snow, Kingfeld, ME; Pine Tree Quilters, Maine **MH:** Albert Nelson Marquis Lifetime Achievement Award **B/I:** Ms. Colanduoni became involved in her career due to her lifelong fascination with becoming a nurse. She grew up across the street from two schools, and was eventually approached by one of the nurses, who asked her to join the school faculty. **AV:** Travel; Swimming; Crafts; Family activities **PA:** Republican **RE:** Roman Catholic.

COLARESI, LINDA ANN, T: Senior Industrial Engineer (Retired) **I:** Manufacturing **DOB:** 10/23/1945 **PB:** New Britain **SC:** CT/USA **PT:** Quinto Adam Colaresi; Lucy Alice (DiMauro) Colaresi **MS:** Single **ED:** BS in Industrial Technology, Central Connecticut State University (1987) **CT:** Certification in Applied Industrial Ergonomics, Joyce Institute; Certification in Value Stream Mapping, Connstep **C:** Senior Industrial Engineer, Colt's Manufacturing Company, LLC (2000-2011); Industrial Engineer, Kaman Corporation (1999-2000); Industrial Engineer, GE (1998-1999); Senior Industrial Engineer, Doncasters Group (1997-1998); Senior Industrial Engineer, U.S. Repeating Arm Company (1995-1997); Senior Industrial Engineer, Colt's Manufacturing Company, LLC (1981-1995); Industrial Engineer, Gould Inc. (1978-1981); Industrial Engineer, Burndy Corporation (1978); Industrial Engineer, Philips Medical Systems (1977-1978); Work Measurement Technician, Stanley Works (Now Stanley Black & Decker, Inc.) (1966-1977) **MEM:** Treasurer, Institute of Industrial Engineers (1996-2001); President, Institute of Industrial Engineers (1994-1996); Vice President, Institute of Industrial Engineers (1992-1994) **MH:** Albert Nelson Marquis Lifetime Achievement Award; Marquis Who's Who Top Professional **B/I:** Ms. Colaresi became involved in her profession because she dropped out of college and started working in the hospital and did not like it. She then worked at Stanley Works and did clerical work but she wanted to learn more, so they trained her and she stayed there for 11 years and began moving onward and upward. It was just something she liked to do. **AV:** Computers; Rug hooking; Collecting hats **RE:** Roman Catholic

COLBERT, STEPHEN, T: Talk Show Host, Comedian, Actor **I:** Media & Entertainment **DOB:** 05/13/1964 **PB:** Washington **SC:** DC/USA **PT:** James Colbert, Lorna (Tuck) Colbert **MS:** Married **SPN:** Evelyn McGee (October 9, 1993) **CH:** Madeleine; Peter; John **ED:** Honorary DFA, Knox College (2006); Graduate Coursework, Northeastern University (1986) **C:** Performer, Annoyance Theatre, Chicago, IL; Performer, Second City, Chicago, IL **CW:** Host, Writer, Executive Producer, "Late Show with Stephen Colbert" (2015-Present); Host, 69th Primetime Emmy Awards (2017); Voice Actor, "Mr. Peabody & Sherman" (2014); Host, Writer, "The Colbert Report" (2005-2014); Author, "America Again: Re-becoming the Greatness We Never Weren't" (2012); Author, "I Am a Pole (And So Can You!)" (2012); Actor, "Company" (2011); Voice Actor, "Monsters versus Aliens" (2009); Performer, "A Colbert Christmas: The Greatest Gift of All!" (2008); Actor, "The Love Guru" (2008); Author, "I Am America (And So Can You!)" (2007); Featured Entertainer, White House Correspondents' Association Dinner (2006); News Voice Actor, "Harvey Birdman, Attorney at Law" (2001-2005); Correspondent, "The Daily Show with Jon Stewart" (1997-2005); Actor, "Bewitched" (2005); Actor, "Nobody Knows Anything" (2003); Co-Author, "Wigfield: The Can Do Town That Just May Not" (2003); Voice Actor, "Crank Yankers" (2002); Actor, Writer, Co-Producer, "Strangers with Candy" (1999-2000); Actor, "Snow Days" (1999); Actor, "Strangers with Candy: Retardation, a Celebration" (1998); Actor, Writer, "Exit 57" (1995-1996); Actor, Writer, "The Dana Carvey Show" (1996); Voice Actor, "Saturday Night Live" (1996) **AW:** Producers Guild Outstanding Producer of Live Entertainment and Competition Television (2008-2015); Emmy Award for Outstanding Variety Series (2013, 2014); People's Choice Award for Favorite Late-Night Talk Show Host (2014); Grammy Award for Best Spoken Word Album (2014); Producers Guild of America Award for Outstanding Producer of Live Entertainment & Talk TV (2013, 2014); Co-Recipient, Emmy Award for Outstanding Writing for a Variety, Music or Comedy Program (2004, 2005, 2006, 2008, 2010, 2013, 2014); Emmy Award for Outstanding Writing for a Variety Series (2013); Listee, The 100 Most Influential People in the World, Time Magazine (2006, 2012); The 50 Highest-Earning Political Figures, Newsweek (2010); Grammy Award for Best Comedy Album (2010); Producers Guild of America Award for Live Entertainment/Competition (2009, 2010); Listee, 100 Agents of Change, Rolling Stone (2009); Best Comedy/Variety - Series, Writers Guild America (2008); Emmy Award for Outstanding Writing for a Variety, Music or Comedy Program, Academy TV Arts & Sciences (2008); Webby Person of Year, International Academy Digital Arts & Sciences (2008); Celebrity of the Year, Associated Press (2007); Person of the Year, US Comedy Arts Festival (2007); Peabody Award (2007); Listee, The Men of the Year, GQ (2006); New York Times Bestseller; Publishers Weekly Bestseller; Co-Recipient, Peabody Awards

COLBURN, NANCY DOUGLAS, LCSW, T: Social Worker; Educator **I:** Social Work **PT:** Cleaveland Fisher Colburn; Virginia Bahrs **ED:** MDiv, McCormick Theological Seminary, (1971); MSW, University of Illinois at Chicago (1971); BA, Rutgers, The State University of New Jersey (1963) **CT:** Certified Addictions Treatment Counselor IV, CA (2017); Ordained to Ministry Vineyard Christian Fellowship (1990); LCSW, CA (1982); Certified Teacher/Administrator in Child Development Programs, CA **C:** Special Education Technician, San Diego Unified School District (2007-2009); Social Worker, Family Advocacy, U.S. Department of Defense, United States Navy, San Diego, CA (1992-1997); Social Worker, Department of Social Services, County of San Diego, CA (1979-1992); Social Worker, California Department of Corrections & Rehabilitation **AW:** Recipient, Various Scholarship and Grants **MEM:** Former Member, National Association of Social Workers **MH:** Albert Nelson Marquis Lifetime Achievement Award **B/I:** Although Ms. Colburn had a difficult childhood, she recognized at an early age that adversity sometimes produces very determined and motivated people. She studied and worked hard. Her high grades and extra curricular activities resulted in Ms. Colburn receiving a scholarship to Rutgers University. Ms. Colburn interacted with Christian believers along the way in her life who pointed out the benefits of a relationship with God, who could redeem the hard places in life and turn it to good. As a result of those influences, when Ms. Colburn attended Rutgers, she joined inter-varsity Christian fellowship and they helped Ms. Colburn experience the love and the salvation of the Lord. She earned a BA in Biological Sciences, thinking to work in a science research laboratory but after she became a Christian, her spiritual awakening gave her compassion for other people and a strong desire to help others in difficult situations. **AV:** Gardening; Pets

COLE, GERRIT ALAN, T: Professional Baseball Player **I:** Athletics **CN:** New York Yankees **DOB:** 09/08/1990 **PB:** Newport Beach **SC:** CA/USA **PT:** Mark Cole; Sharon Cole **MS:** Married **SPN:** Amy Crawford **CH:** One Son **ED:** Diploma, University of California Los Angeles **C:** Pitcher, New York Yankees, MLB (2019-Present); Pitcher, Houston Astros, MLB (2018-2019); Pitcher, Pittsburgh Pirates, MLB (2013-2017) **AW:** Three-time All-star (2015, 2018, 2019); Named to All-MLB First Team (2019); Named ERA Leader, American League (2019); Named MLB Strikeout Leader (2019); Named Pitcher of the Month, National League (2015); Named Rookie of the Month, National League (2013)

COLE, RANSEY GUY JR., T: Chief Judge **I:** Government Administration/Government Relations/Government Services **CN:** U.S. Court of Appeals for the Sixth Circuit **DOB:** 05/23/1951 **PB:** Birmingham **SC:** AL/USA **PT:** Ransey Guy Cole; Sarah Nell (Coker) Cole **MS:** Married **SPN:** Kathleine Kelley (11/26/1983) **CH:** Justin Robert Jefferson; Jordan Paul; Alexandra Sarah **ED:** JD, Yale Law School (1975); BA, Tufts University (1972) **C:** Chief Judge, U.S. Court of Appeals for the Sixth Circuit, Cincinnati, OH (2014-Present); Judge, U.S. Court of Appeals for the Sixth Circuit, Cincinnati, OH (1995-Present); Partner, Vorys, Sater, Seymour and Pease LLP, Columbus, Ohio (1993-1995); Judge, U.S. Bankruptcy Court, Columbus, OH (1987-1993); Partner, Vorys, Sater, Seymour and Pease LLP, Columbus, OH (1980-1986); Trial Attorney, U.S. Department of Justice, Washington, DC (1978-1980); Associate, Vorys, Sater, Seymour and Pease LLp, Columbus, Ohio (1975-1978) **CIV:** Board Trustee, Children's Hospital (1990-Present); Board Trustee, Columbus Area International Progressive (1986-1994); Board Trustee, March of Dimes, Ohio

(1985-1988); Board Trustee, Neighborhood House (1985-1988); Board Trustee, YMCA (1984-1988) **MEM:** American Bar Association; Columbus Bar Association; National Bar Association **BAR:** The District of Columbia (1982); The State of Ohio (1975)

COLE, THOMAS, "TOM" JEFFERY, T: U.S. Representative from Oklahoma **I:** Government Administration/Government Relations/Government Services **DOB:** 04/28/1949 **PB:** Shreveport **SC:** LA/USA **PT:** John D. Cole; Helen Gale Cole **MS:** Married **SPN:** Ellen Decker **CH:** Mason **ED:** PhD in British History, The University of Oklahoma, Norman, OK (1984); MA in British History, Yale University, New Haven, CT (1974); BA in History, Grinnell College, Grinnell, IA (1971) **C:** Member, U.S. House of Representatives from Oklahoma's Fourth Congressional District, U.S. Congress (2003-Present); Founding Partner, President, Cole Hargrave Snodgrass & Associates, Oklahoma City, OK (1989-Present); Secretary of State, State of Oklahoma, Oklahoma City, OK (1995-1999); Member, Oklahoma State Senate (1988-1991); Instructor, Oklahoma Baptist University (1981); Lecturer, Grinnell College (1977-1979); Instructor, History and Politics, The University of Oklahoma (1975-1978); Member, Committee on Appropriations; Member, Committee on the Budget; Member, Committee on Rules **CR:** Chairman, National Republican Congressional Committee (2006-2008); Executive Director, National Republican Congressional Committee (1999-2000) **CIV:** Chairman, Oklahoma Republican Party (1985-1989); Executive Director, Reagan-Bush Presidential Campaign, OK (1984); Executive Director, Oklahoma Republican Committee (1980-1981); Member, National Board of Directors, Fulbright Association; Enrolled Member, The Chickasaw Nation, OK; Board of Regents, Smithsonian Institution **AW:** Congressional Lifetime Achievement Award, National Center for American Indian Enterprise Development (2009); Named to the Chickasaw Nation Hall of Fame (2004); Fulbright Fellow (1977-1978); Guardian Small Business Award, National Federation of Independent Business; Robert A. Taft Award, Oklahoma Republican Party; Thomas J. Watson Fellow **MEM:** Oklahoma Chamber of Commerce; Society for the Study of Labor History; American Historical Association; Institute of Historical Research; Phi Alpha Theta National History Honor Society **PA:** Republican **RE:** Methodist

COLE, WALTER, T: Owner, Founder **I:** Business Management/Business Services **CN:** Darcelle XV Showplace **DOB:** 12/01/1930 **PB:** Linton **SC:** OR/USA **MS:** Divorced **CH:** Two Children **ED:** Diploma, Lincoln High School, Portland, OR (1950) **C:** Owner, Founder, Darcelle XV Showplace, Portland, OR (1969-Present) **CR:** Owner, Caffe Espresso Bar; Owner, Floral Shop; Owner, After Hours Jazz Club; Owner, Ice Cream Parlor, Portland, OR **MIL:** U.S. Army **CW:** Exhibitor, "Many Shades of Being Darcelle: 52 Years of Fashion, 1967-2019," Oregon Historical Society (2019); Creator, "Darcelle the Musical," Portland, OR (2019); Featured, "Queens of Heart: Community Therapists in Drag"; Featured, "Oregon Experience... Darcelle XV"; Author, "Just Call Me Darcelle" **AW:** Listee, 100 Greatest Oregonians Ever, The Oregonian (2019); Oldest Working Drag Queen, Guinness World Records (2018); Emmy Award **B/I:** After completing his service during the Korean War, Mr. Cole returned home to work in a grocery store. He decided that he would rather go into business for himself, and he did just that. He went on to start the first coffee shop in Portland, Oregon, eventually opening an ice cream bar before landing on the property where he began Darcelle XV in 1967. He has remained there since.

He had never dressed in drag before until he met his partner Roxy Neuhardt, who convinced him to wear drag for the first time. He learned on the job how to become a drag queen. He has had major success in the industry ever since then. **THT:** Mr. Cole is an author, playwright, actor, costume designer, owner, and headliner of the Darcelle XV Showplace. It is the oldest continuously running cabaret in the United States. His motto is, "Be who you are and be happy with it."

COLELLA, ALEXANDRA, T: Attorney **I:** Law and Legal Services **CN:** Marc J. Bern & Partners LLP **ED:** Doctor of Jurisprudence, Pace University School of Law (2016); Bachelor of Arts in Political Science and Government, James Madison University (2013) **C:** Associate, Marc J Bern & Partners LLP (2015-Present); Legal Assistant, Clark, Gagliardi and Miller (2014-2015); Legal Assistant, Barasch McGarry Salzman & Penson (2014); Intern, U.S. Congress (2012) **CIV:** Intern, Pace Land Use Law Center (2015); Pro Bono Work, New Jersey **AW:** Nominee, Super Lawyers **BAR:** New York; New Jersey **AS:** Ms. Colella attributes her success on her propensity for determination and working hard. **B/I:** Ms. Colella became involved in her profession due to a lifelong interest in legal services.

COLEMAN, CARINA E., CFA, T: Director, Pension & Trust Investments **I:** Oil & Energy **CN:** Sempra Energy **CH:** Three Children **ED:** MA in International/Global Studies, University of Pennsylvania, The Lauder Institute (2004); MBA in Finance, University of Pennsylvania, The Wharton School (2004); BA in Economics/German Studies, University of California Los Angeles (1996) **CT:** CFA (Chartered Financial Analyst) **C:** Director, Pension & Trust Investments, Sempra Energy; Finance Manger, Sempra Energy (2010-2013); Manger, Disney (2004-2009); Summer Associate, Merrill Lynch (2003); Research Associate, Bradford & Marzec (1999-2002) **CIV:** Board of Administration, San Diego City Employees' Retirement System (2016-Present); Investment Committee Member, San Diego City Employees' Retirement System (2015-Present); Vice Chair, Local Diversity and Inclusion Council (2019); Finance Council Member, Diocese of San Diego (2016); Member, Finance Advisory Committee, City of Rancho Palos Verdes, (2007-2010) **AW:** Co-Chair, Pensions & Investments, West Coast Defined Contribution Conference (2016); Co-Chair of the local diversity and inclusion counsel for Sempra energy, HQChair of the investment committee for San Diego city employee retirement systemVice President of the Board of Administrations **MEM:** The CFA institute (2003-Present) **AS:** She attributes her success to her work ethics. You have to take on challenge with courage and hard work and if you are diligent you would reach your goal. **B/I:** Ms. Coleman was the first to go to college in her family. Her dad had an interest in the stock market and as a child she would watch it on the television with him so initially that's where her interest in finance was developed. When she got to UCLA having a major in economics made the most sense and she did her MBA in finance when she went to grad school. When she was a child, her dad was investing on the side as sort of a small time investor. It's really the opportunity her parents provided to her as really as a first generation to go to college in her town. Her mom was a waitress, her dad a refinery worker. He's a blue collar refinery worker. He actually worked 47 years at the same plant. Neither of them went to college and provided her that opportunity. She felt very responsible to make the most out of it. What inspires her is that early introduction to the ability to make money on your money and understanding the time value of money from her Dad. He is a very conservative person, not to be frivolous in her spending but to think about tomorrow and save for tomorrow. Those were engraved early on. **AV:** Writing; Walking; Traveling; Reading

COLEMAN, MARSHALL, T: Psychiatrist, Psychoanalyst **I:** Medicine & Health Care **DOB:** 12/27/1925 **PB:** Utica **SC:** NY/USA **PT:** Jacob Coleman; Lucille (Smith) Coleman **MS:** Married **SPN:** Beverly Sitrin (06/28/1949) **CH:** Charles Theodore; Jacqueline Sue; Rachel Coleman Noah; Daniel Coleman; Jacqueline Sue Coleman-Frict **ED:** Teaching Fellow, Harvard Medical School, Boston, MA (1953-1956); Resident, Boston Psychopathic Hospital, Boston (1953-1956); Intern, Massachusetts Memorial Hospitals, Boston, MA (1952-1953); MD, Harvard Medical School (1952); BA, Harvard College (1947) **CT:** Diplomate, American Board of Psychiatry and Neurology, Inc. **C:** Private Practice, Mamaroneck, NY (1968-2011); Assistant Clinical Professor, Albert Einstein College of Medicine, Bronx, NY (1963-2009); Senior Visiting Staff, Jacobi Hospital (Now NYC Health + Hospitals/Jacobi), Bronx, NY (1962-2009); Assistant Professor, Albert Einstein College of Medicine, Bronx, NY (1957-1963); Instructor, Albert Einstein College of Medicine, Bronx, NY (1956-1957) **CR:** President, New York State Psychoanalytic Coordinating Committee (1988-2005); Director, Walk-in Psychiatric Clinic, Albert Einstein College of Medicine (1956); Faculty of Newly Founded Albert Einstein College of Medicine (1956) **CIV:** Chairman Emeritus, Mental Health Professionals New York Area, United Jewish Appeal (2003); Co-chairperson, Mental Health Professionals New York Area, United Jewish Appeal (1990-2003); ETO, Lifetime Zionist Supporter **MIL:** With. United States Army (1944-1946); With, United States Army, Unit German Battle Star **CW:** Contributing Editor, "Generations of Holocaust" (1982); Author, Unpublished, "Winston S. Churchill: Character Shapes History"; Editor, Articles on Psychiatric Walk-in Clinics, Brief Psychotherapy and Agoraphobia **AW:** M. Jucovy Lifetime Achievement Award (2000) **MEM:** President, Westchester Psychoanalytic Society (1978-1979); Fellow, Life Member, American Psychiatric Association; New York Psychoanalytic Society & Institute; International Psychoanalytical Society; Westchester Psychoanalytic Society **MH:** Albert Nelson Marquis Lifetime Achievement Award **B/I:** Dr. Coleman became involved in his profession because of medicine in general but primarily in understanding the human heart. **RE:** Jewish

COLEMAN, ZENDAYA, "ZENDAYA" MAREE STOERMER, T: Actress; Singer **I:** Media & Entertainment **DOB:** 09/01/1996 **PB:** Oakland **SC:** CA/USA **PT:** Samuel David "Kazembe Ajamu" Coleman; Claire Marie (Stoermer) Coleman **ED:** Coursework, CalShakes Conservatory Program, American Conservatory Theater; Coursework, Oakland School of the Arts **C:** Launched, Shoe Line, Daya (2015); Model, Macy's, Mervyns and Old Navy **CW:** Actress, "Dune" (2020); Actress, "Spider-Man: Far from Home" (2019); Actress, "The OA" (2019); Actress, "Euphoria" (2019); Voice Actress, App, "Spider-Man: Far from Home" (2019); Actress, "Duck Duck Goose" (2018); Actress, "Smallfoot" (2018); Actress, Producer, "K.C. Undercover" (2015-2018); Actress, "Spider-Man: Homecoming" (2017); Actress, "The Greatest Showman" (2017); Appearance, "Walk the Plank" (2017); Appearance, "Lip Sync Battle" (2017); Actress, "Black-ish" (2015); Actress, "Zapped" (2014); Appearance, "The Making of SWAY" (2014); Appearance, "SWAY: A Dance Trilogy" (2014); Appearance, "Dancing with the Stars" (2013); Appearance, "The Story of Zendaya" (2013); Voice Actress, "Super Buddies"

(2013); Singer, "Zendaya" (2013); Actress, "Shake It Up" (2010-2013); Actress, "A.N.T. Farm" (2012); Actress, "Frenemies" (2012); Actress, "Good Luck Charlie" (2011); Actress, "PrankStars" (2011); Actress, "Pixie Hollow Games" (2011); Singer, Various Singles **AW:** Satellite Award, Best Actress - Television Series Drama (2020); People Choice Award, The Drama TV Star of 2019 (2019); People Choice Award, The Female Movie Star of 2019 (2019); Teen Choice Award, Choice Summer Movie Actress (2017, 2019); Co-recipient, Teen Choice Award, Choice Collaboration (2018); Co-recipient, Teen Choice Award, Choice Movie Ship (2018); Teen Choice Award, Choice Movie Actress: Drama (2018); Nickelodeon Kids' Choice Award, Favorite Movie Actress (2018); Nickelodeon Kids' Choice Award, Favorite TV Actress (2016); Teen Choice Award, Candie's Style Icon (2014); Radio Disney Music Award, Best Style (2014) **AV:** Singing; Dancing; Designing Clothes

COLEMAN RADEWAGEN, AMATA, "AUMUA AMATA" CATHERINE, T: Delegate to the U.S. House of Representatives from American Samoa **I:** Government Administration/Government Relations/Government Services **DOB:** 12/29/1947 **PB:** Pago Pago **SC:** American Samoa **PT:** Peter Tali Coleman; Nora (Stewart) Coleman **MS:** Married **SPN:** Fred Radewagen (12/04/1971) **CH:** Erika; Mark; Kristen **ED:** BS in Psychology, University of Guam (1975) **C:** Member, President's Commission for Asian Americans and Pacific Islanders (2019-Present); Delegate, U.S. House of Representatives from American Samoa's At-large District (2015-Present); Deputy Director, Pacific Islands, Washington Office (1984-Present); Member, Executive Committee, Chairman's Transition Committee, Republican National Committee (2017); Member, Executive Committee, Presidential Transition Team, Republican National Committee (2016-2017); Staff, House Republican Conference (1999-2005); Staff, U.S. Representative J.C. Watts Jr., United States Congress (1999-2003); White House Commissioner, Asian Americans and Pacific Islanders (2001); Staff, U.S. Representative Phil Crane, Unites States Congress (1997-1999); Government Affairs Advisor, American Samoa Power Authority, Washington, DC (1995-1996); Deputy Director, Washington Pacific Associates (1975-1982); Assistant to Undersecretary, U.S. Department of Health, Education and Welfare, Washington, DC (1973-1975); Assistant to Associate Director, Office of Economic Opportunity, Washington, DC (1972-1973); Executive Secretary, Office of Delegate-at-Large for American Samoa, Washington, DC (1971-1972); Scheduling Director, U.S. House of Representatives Majority Leadership **CR:** Chief Diplomatic Correspondent, Washington Pacific Report, Washington, DC, Pago Pago, American Samoa (1984-1997); Chair, Community Security Committee, Asian Americans and Pacific Islanders **CIV:** Spokesperson, Samoan Women's Health Fund, Pago Pago, American Samoa (1993-Present); Member, Republican National Committee, Pago Pago, American Samoa (1986-Present); Republican Congressional Nominee, American Samoa (1994, 1996); Delegate, Samoan Women's Health Fund, Pago Pago, American Samoa (1992, 1996); Assistant Sergeant at Arms, Republican National Convention, Houston, Texas (1992); Founding Board of Directors, Washington Roundtable Asian Pacific Press (1987-1990) **MEM:** International Women's Media Foundation; American Samoa Society, Washington; Hawaii State Society; Life Member, Capitol Hill Club; Guam Society of America; Women's Foreign Policy Group; Independent Women's Forum (IWF); Pan-Pacific & Southeast Asia Women's Association **PA:** Republican **RE:** Roman Catholic

COLLINS, CHRISTOPHER CARL, T: U.S. Representative from New York (Retired) **I:** Government Administration/Government Relations/Government Services **DOB:** 05/20/1950 **PB:** Schenectady **SC:** NY/USA **PT:** Gerald Edward Collins; Constance (Messier) Collins **MS:** Married **SPN:** Mary Sue Kuhn (01/09/1988); Margaret Elizabeth Busby Cox (05/20/1972, Divorced 04/1978) **CH:** Carly Elizabeth; Caitlin Christine; Cameron Christopher **ED:** MBA, Culverhouse College of Business, The University of Alabama (1975); BS in Mechanical Engineering, North Carolina State University (1972) **C:** U.S. Representative, New York's 27th Congressional District, United States Congress (2013-2019); Member, U.S. House Committee on Agriculture (2013-2018); Member, U.S. House Small Business Committee (2013-2018); Member, U.S. House Committee on Science, Space and Technology (2013); County Executive, Erie County, NY (2007-2011); Vice President, Easom Automation Systems (Now The Lincoln Electric Company), Detroit, MI (2003); Treasurer, Volland Electric Equipment Corp., Buffalo, NY (2001-2007); Vice President of Corporate Development, Wilson Greatbatch Ltd., Clarence, NY (1999); Chairman, Board, ZeptoMetrix Corporation, Buffalo, NY (1999); Chairman, Board, Chief Executive Officer, Bloch Industries LLC, Rochester, NY (1999); President, Nuttall Gear, LLC, Altra Industrial Motion Corp., Niagara Falls, NY (1997-1998); Chairman, President, Chief Executive Officer, Nuttall Gear Corp., Altra Industrial Motion Corp., Niagara Falls, NY (1983-1997); Manager, Gearing Division, Westinghouse Electric Corporation, Buffalo, NY (1980-1982); Manager, Market Planning, Westinghouse Electric Corporation, Buffalo, NY (1978-1979); Market Research Analyst, Westinghouse Electric Corporation, Buffalo, NY (1976-1977); Sales Engineer, Westinghouse Electric Corporation, Birmingham, AL (1972-1976) **CR:** Chairman, Starboard Sun Corp., Buffalo, NY (2007-2008); Vice President, Board of Directors, Innate Therapeutics Ltd., Auckland, New Zealand (2006); President, Chief Executive Officer, Buckler Biodefense Corporation, Buffalo, NY (2006); Treasurer, Niagara Ceramics Corp., Buffalo, NY (2004-2012); Treasurer, Lang & Washburn Electric, Buffalo, NY (2004); Chairman, Chief Executive Officer, Oxygen Generating Systems International, Buffalo, NY (2004); Chairman, Bio Clinical Partners, Boston, MA (2004); Chairman, Chief Executive Officer, Audubon Machinery Corporation, Buffalo, NY (2004); Chairman, Niagara Machinery Corporation, Wilson, NY (2003-2004); Treasurer, Mead Supply, Inc., Buffalo, NY (2002); Treasurer, Frontier Industrial Supply Company, Inc., Buffalo, NY (2001) **CIV:** Mentor, Center for Entrepreneurial Leadership, State University of New York (1999); Vice President of Administration, Executive Board of Directors, Greater Niagara Frontier Council, Boy Scouts of America (1998); Republican and Conservative Candidate for United States Congress (1998); Member, Buffalo Financial Planning Committee (1994); Member, Small Business Advisory Council, Federal Reserve Bank, NY (1992-1995); Member, House of Delegates, United Way, Buffalo, NY (1986-2003); Board of Directors, Kenmore Mercy Hospital, Catholic Health (1986-1993); Treasurer, Small Business Advisory Council, Federal Reserve Bank, NY **AW:** Inductee, Mechanical and Aerospace Engineering Department Hall of Fame, North Carolina State University (2015) **MEM:** Chairman, Executive Committee, YPO (1991-1996); Chairman Membership, YPO (1990-1991); Chapter Chairman, YPO (1989-1990); Chairman, Education Committee, YPO (1988-1989); Sigma Pi Fraternity (1972); Chief Executives Organization; World President's Organization; YPO; Brookfield Country Club; Holimont Ski Club **AV:** Golfing; Skiing; Flying **PA:** Republican **RE:** Roman Catholic

COLLINS, DENNIS GLENN, PHD, T: Mathematics Professor (Retired) **I:** Education/Educational Services **DOB:** 06/26/1944 **PB:** Gary **SC:** IN/USA **PT:** Glenn Collins; Irene Martha (Richman) Collins **MS:** Married **SPN:** Barbara Jean Hamilton (07/14/1979) **CH:** Glenn H. **ED:** PhD, Illinois Institute of Technology (1975); MS, Illinois Institute of Technology (1970); BA, Valparaiso University (1966) **C:** Chairman, Personnel Committee, University of Puerto Rico, Mayaguez, Puerto Rico (1994-1995); Assistant Professor to Professor of Mathematics, University of Puerto Rico, Mayaguez, Puerto Rico (1982-2009); Assistant Professor, Valparaiso University, Valparaiso, IN (1979-1982); Instructor, University of New Orleans (1976-1979); Temporary Instructor, Michigan State University, East Lansing, MI (1975-1976) **CR:** Blog, Quantum History Institute (2013); Detection of Some Malignant 2-D Tumors, Purdue Northwest - North Central, Purdue University (2010); Continuous Symmetry of Wedge and Other Shapes, University of Notre Dame, IN (2010); Toward a Mathematical Origin of Species, 7th Biennial Emergy Research Conference (2010); Moral Codes III, Department of Mathematical Sciences, University of Puerto Rico, Mayaguez, Puerto Rico (2009); Architecture Case Study in Transformative Factorization, Annual ISSS Meeting, Madison, WI (2008); Visiting Scholar, University of Puerto Rico, Mayaguez, Puerto Rico (2003-2004); Visiting Scholar, Michigan State University (1988-1989, 1996-1997); Judge, Computer Science, International Science and Engineering Fair, San Juan, Puerto Rico (1987); Presenter, Lectures in Field **CIV:** Book Talk, "Code Red for Democracy," Pulaski County Public Library (2020) **CW:** Lecturer, "Toward Thermodynamics and Emergy of Picture and Other Puzzle Solving", Tri-State MAA, Valparaiso University (2018); Number Blocks Talk, Trine University, Angola, IN (2014); Energy-Simplicity Talk, Gainesville, FL (2014); Talk, "Approximating Continuous Symmetry of Some Systems & Solids," Akron, Ohio (2012); Speaker, Founding Fathers Postcards (2012); Talk, "Measuring Symmetry of a Finite Group," University of Indianapolis (2011); Author, "Conflict in History Measuring Symmetry, Thermodynamic Modeling and Other Work" (2011); Author, "Some Continuous Empower -Z Models Political Spectrum Models," University of Florida, Gainesville, FL (2010); Composer, "Meditation" (2010); Author, Examples of Measuring Continuous Symmetry (2008); Composer, "Amadis Lullaby" (2007); Composer, "New Orleans Serenade" (2006); Composer, Short Columbus Cantata and Short Spaceship Cantata, Short Cosmic Cantata, "One Size Fits All," (2001); Creator, Postcards of 120 Mathematicians and Physicists (1983-2001); Author, Three Papers on the Topic of Emergy Synthesis 9, Center for Environmental Policy, Gainesville, FL; Author, "Toward Max and Min Symmetry of Order 24 Groups," Butler University, Indianapolis, IN; Meetings, Mathematical Association of America **AW:** Fellow, National Science Foundation (1966-1967) **MEM:** St. Louis Chapter, American Mathematical Society (2013); Talk on Symmetry, American Mathematical Society (2007); Fourth Energy Conference, American Mathematical Society (2006); President, Sigma Xi, The Scientific Research Honor Society (2003-2004); Dialog Committee to Rector, American Mathematical Society (1997-2003); Informatics and Cybernetics, American Mathematical Society (1990); Conflict in History, American Mathematical Society (1971); American Mathematical Society; Mathematical Association of America (MAA); American Chemical Society; The New York Academy of Sciences; Society for Industrial and Applied Mathematics; SPIE; International Society for the Systems Sciences **MH:** Albert Nelson Marquis Lifetime Achievement Award **RE:** Lutheran

COLLINS, DOUGLAS, "DOUG" ALLEN, T: U.S. Representative from Georgia; Lawyer **I:** Government Administration/Government Relations/Government Services **DOB:** 08/16/1966 **PB:** Gainesville **SC:** GA/USA **MS:** Married **SPN:** Lisa Collins (1988) **CH:** Jordan; Copelan; Cameron **ED:** Diploma, Georgia Legislative Leadership Institute; JD, UIC John Marshall Law School (2007); MDiv, New Orleans Baptist Theological Seminary (1996); BA in Political Science and Criminal Law, North Georgia College & State University (Now University of North Georgia) (1988) **C:** Member, U.S. House of Representatives from Georgia's Ninth Congressional District, United States Congress, Washington, DC (2013-Present); Member, U.S. House Committee on Oversight and Government Reform (2013-Present); Member, U.S. House Judiciary Committee (2013-Present); Member, U.S. House Committee on Foreign Affairs (2013-Present); Managing Partner, Collins and Csider, LLC (2010-Present); Vice Chairman, House Republican Conference (2017); Member, District 27, Georgia House of Representatives (2007-2013); Senior Pastor, Chicopee Baptist Church (1994-2005); Member, Committee on Rules **MIL:** Major-chaplain, Lieutenant Colonel, 94th Airlift Wing, U.S. Air Force Reserve (2002-Present); With, 94th Airlift Wing, U.S. Air Force Reserve, Iraq War; Chaplain, U.S. Navy **AW:** Named One of Georgia's Most Influential Citizens, James Magazine **PA:** Republican **RE:** Southern Baptist

COLLINS, PHIL, T: Drummer **I:** Media & Entertainment **DOB:** 01/30/1951 **PB:** London **SC:** England **PT:** Greville Collins; June Collins **SPN:** Orianne Cevey (1999-2008); Jill Collins (1984-1996); Andrea Collins (1975-1982) **CH:** Simon; Lily Jane; Joely (Stepchild); Nicholas; Matthew **C:** Lead Singer and Songwriter, Genesis (1975-Present); Drummer, Genesis (1971-1975) **CW:** Artist, "Remixed Sides" (2019); Artist, "Other Sides" (2019); Solo Artist, "Hello, I Must be Going" (1982), Remastered Deluxe Edition (2016); Solo Artist, "Both Sides" (1993), Remastered Deluxe Edition (2016); Solo Artist, "Face Value" (1981), Remastered Deluxe Edition (2016); Solo Artist, "Dance into the Light" (1996), Remastered Deluxe Edition (2016); Solo Artist, "Take a Look At Me Now Collector's Edition" (2016); Composer, "Going Back" (2010); Composer, Lyricist, "Tarzan" (2006); Solo Artist, "The Platinum Collection" (2004); Solo Artist, "Love Songs: A Compilation...Old and New" (2004); Composer, "Brother Bear" (2003); Composer, "The Jungle Book 2" (2003); Solo Artist, "Testify" (2002); Composer, "Moulin Rouge!" (2001); Composer, "Tarzan" (1999); Solo Artist, "Big Band-A Hot Night in Paris" (1999); Solo Artist, "Hits" (1998); Composer, "Balto" (1995); Artist, "The Way That We Walk Volume Two: The Longs" (1993); Composer, "Frauds" (1993); Composer, "Calliope" (1993); Composer, "And the Band Played On" (1993); Artist, "The Way That We Walk Volume One: The Shorts" (1992); Composer, "Hook" (1991); Artist, "We Can't Dance" (1991); Solo Artist, "Serious Hits-Live" (1990); Solo Artist, "...But Seriously" (1989); Composer, "Buster" (1988); Solo Artist, "12"Ers" (1987); Artist, "Invisible Touch" (1986); Composer, "White Nights" (1985); Solo Artist, "No Jacket Required (1985); Composer, "Against All Odds" (1984); Artist, "Genesis" (1983); Artist, "Three Sides Live" (1982); Artist, "Abacab" (1981); Artist, "Duke" (1980); Artist, "And Then There Were Three" (1978); Artist, "Wind and Wuthering" (1977); Artist, "Seconds Out" (1977); Artist, "Spot the Pigeon" (1977); Artist, "Trick of the Tail" (1976); Artist, "The Lamb Lies Down on Broadway" (1974); Artist, "Selling England by the Pound" (1973); Artist, "Genesis Live" (1973); Artist, "Foxtrot" (1972); Artist, "Nursery Cryme" (1971) **AW:** Honorary Doctorate of Jazz and Pop Music, University of Music and Performing Arts Graz (2019); Johnny Mercer Award, Songwriters Hall of Fame (2010); Inductee, with Genesis, Rock and Roll Hall of Fame (2010); City of Life Award (2002); Academy Award (2000); Golden Globe Award (1989, 2000); Diamond Award, RIAA (1999); Star, Hollywood Walk of Fame (1999); Grammy Award (1985, 1986, 1989); Elvis Award; Two Awards, Variety Club of Great Britain; Two-Time Winner, Silver Clef Award; Nominee, Academy Award

COLLINS, SUSAN MARGARET, T: U.S. Senator **I:** Government Administration/Government Relations/Government Services **DOB:** 12/07/1952 **PB:** Caribou **SC:** ME/USA **PT:** Donald F. Collins; Patricia (McGuigan) Collins **MS:** Married **SPN:** Thomas Daffron (08/11/2012) **ED:** Honorary LHD, Bates College (2017); BA in Government, St. Lawrence University, Canton, NY, Magna Cum Laude (1975) **C:** Chairwoman, Senate Aging Committee (2015-Present); Member, U.S. Senate Appropriations Committee (2009-Present); Member, U.S. Senate Homeland Security and Governmental Affairs Committee (1997-Present); U.S. Senator from Maine (1997-Present); Chairman, U.S. Senate Homeland Security and Governmental Affairs Committee (2003-2007); Executive Director, Center for Family Business, Husson College, Bangor, Maine (1993-1996); Director, New England Operations, U.S. Small Business Administration (1992-1993); Commissioner, Maine Department of Professional and Financial Regulation (1987-1992); Staff Director, U.S. Senate Subcommittee on Oversight Government Management (1981-1987); Principal Adviser, Business Affairs to Representative William S. Cohen, U.S. House of Representatives (1975-1978) **CR:** Special Inspector General, Hurricane Katrina Relief (2005-Present) **CIV:** Republican Candidate for Governor, Maine (1994) **CW:** Co-Author, "Nine and Counting: The Women of the Senate" (2000) **AW:** Congressional Award, Veterans of Foreign Wars (2017); One of the 10 Most Powerful Women in DC, Elle Magazine (2014); Publius Award, Center for the Study of the Presidency and Congress (2014); Thought Leader Award, Corporation for Public Broadcasting (2014); Legislator of the Year Award, Congressional Fire Services Institute (2013); Spirit of Enterprise Award, U.S. Chamber of Commerce (2013); Congressional Sea Services Award, Navy League of the United States (2012); One of the 10 Most Powerful Women in Washington, Fortune Magazine (2009, 2010); Port Person of the Year, American Association of Port Authorities (2006); Congressional Leadership Award, National Urban League (2006); Outstanding Legislative Award, Triangle Coalition for Science and Technology Education (2005); Public Service Award, Emergency Nurses Association (2004); Teacher Leader Award, Reading Recovery Council of North America (2004); Outstanding Alumni Award, St. Lawrence University (1992); National Public Policy Leadership Award, American Diabetes Association **MEM:** The Rotary Club of Bangor; The Phi Beta Kappa Society **PA:** Republican **RE:** Roman Catholic

COLLIS, STEVEN H., T: Chairman, Chief Executive Officer, and President **I:** Medicine & Health Care **CN:** AmerisourceBergen Corporation **SC:** South Africa **ED:** Bachelor of Commerce, University of the Witwatersrand, Johannesburg, with Honors **CT:** Licensed Chartered Accountant (1986) **C:** President, Chief Executive Officer, Chairman, AmerisourceBergen Corporation, Valley Forge, PA (2011-Present); President, Chief Operating Officer, AmerisourceBergen Corporation, Valley Forge, PA (2010-2011); President, AmerisourceBergen Drug Corp. (2009-2010); Executive Vice President, AmerisourceBergen Corporation, Valley Forge, PA

(2007-2010); President, AmerisourceBergen Specialty Group, Dallas (2001-2009); Senior Executive Vice President, President, ASD Specialty Healthcare, Inc. (2000-2001); Executive Vice President, ASD Specialty Healthcare, Inc. (1996-2000); General Manager, ASD Specialty Healthcare, Inc. (1994-1996); Principal and General Manager, Sterling Medical, Irvine, California; Member, Johannesburg Stock Exchange **CR:** Board of Directors, Thoratec Corporation (2008-Present) **CIV:** Active, American Cancer Society, Inc.

COLLOPY, LIAM THOMAS, T: Publicist **I:** Corporate Communications & Public Relations **CN:** Harden Communications Partners **MS:** Married **SPN:** Alexandra Camarillo **ED:** MBA, Notre Dame de Namur University, Belmont, CA (1997); BLA, California State University, East Bay, Hayward, CA **C:** Executive Vice President, Harden Communications Partners, Oakland, CA (2013-Present); President, Levine Communications Office, Beverly Hills, CA (2004-2013); With, Longs Drugstores Inc. (Now CVS) **CIV:** Volunteer, Local Church **AW:** Best General Business Campaign of the Year, Bulldog Awards for Excellence in Media Relations and Publicity (2014); Best Crisis Communications Campaign of the Year, Bulldog Awards for Excellence in Media Relations and Publicity (2014); Arts and Entertainment Campaign of the Year, Bulldog Awards for Excellence in Media Relations and Publicity (2010-2011); Arts and Entertainment Campaign of the Year, Bulldog Awards for Excellence in Media Relations and Publicity (2006) **MEM:** Public Relations Society of America, Inc.; California Scholarship Federation **AS:** Mr. Collopy attributes his success to his mother and father, who instilled in him a great work ethic, as well as his wonderful mentors. **B/I:** Mr. Collopy became involved in his profession because one day while working in retail, which he had done for many years, a friend who worked for Apple computers approached him and told him he was wasting his time at the store and that he could get him an internship at a public relations firm. That night, he went home and looked up what the internship entailed and was hooked right away. After years of working in the industry, he realized his true passion was working with entertainers in the field of public relations. **AV:** Swimming; Traveling **THT:** Mr. Collopy's mantra comes from the Franki Valli song, "My Eyes Adored You," in which he sang: "Worked my fingers to the bone, made myself a name..."

COLLUM, LISA, T: Chief Executive Officer **I:** Education/Educational Services **CN:** Top Score Writing, Inc.; Coastal Middle and High School, Inc. **MS:** Married **SPN:** (08/06/2004) **CH:** Four Children **ED:** MS in Education, Nova Southeastern University, Broward County, FL (2011); BA in Elementary Education, Florida Atlantic University, Boca Raton, FL (2004) **CT:** K-12 Teaching, Florida Department of Education **C:** Owner and Principal, Coastal Middle and High School, Lake Park, FL (2014-Present); Owner and Founder, Top Score Writing, Inc., West Palm Beach, FL (2010-Present); Fourth Grade Teacher, Connections Academy (Now Connections Education, LLC), West Palm Beach, FL (2012-2014); Writing Resource Specialist, North Area Support Team, The School District of Palm Beach County, West Palm Beach, FL (2010-2012); Reading Coach, Grades 3-8, Village Academy Elementary School/Howell L. Watkins Middle School, West Palm Beach, FL (2007-2010); Fourth Grade Teacher, Village Academy Elementary School, Delray Beach, FL (2004-2007); Brotherhood/Sisterhood Program Planner/Instructor, Village Academy Elementary School, Delray Beach, FL (2003-2006) **CR:** Travels the Country Helping Students, Teachers, Administrators and District Leaders Create Individualized

Action Plans and Delivers Energetic Presentations Incorporating Strategic Approaches to Improve Writing Using her Cutting-Edge Print and Digital Curriculum **CIV:** Volunteer, Place of Hope **AS:** Mrs. Collum attributes her success to a combination of her experience and the people she has met along the way. She had experience as a teacher, before she began her own business. She began her career in a Title I, low performing district. She had first-hand experience working with some of the best educators which prepared her for her future endeavors. She worked with a great principal who pushed her, supported and encouraged her to do something with her writing. She attributes much of her success to meeting the right people and putting her into position to continue to progress. **B/I:** Mrs. Collum became involved in her profession because she knew that she wanted to be a teacher since the age of 5. She began her career as a teacher where she spent 10 years before opening her own business. She started out teaching fourth grade writing, then became a writing coach and eventually a writing specialist. When she first worked in a classroom, she didn't have intentions on doing so initially, but she had such great results with teaching, people wanted her to share her ideas. That is when she decided to begin a business, to share her ideas and make a positive contribution to the education system. She not only would make the job of the teacher easier but also create a way for students to be more engaged in what they are learning. **THT:** Mrs. Collum always wanted to be a teacher. She grew both businesses although she is an educator at heart. She has four children and is married, so she is active in sports with her children. Her motto is, "Being happy with what you do every day." She's written four books from 2nd-12th grade. Mrs. Collum is a chief executive officer, author, educator, and mother of four with a remarkable history of working to improve students' lives both inside and outside the classroom. She owns and operates two educational companies, Top Score Writing, Inc. and Coastal Middle and High School. Top Score Writing, Inc. is a company that specializes in writing curriculum for grades 2nd-12th and is the one and only program specifically designed to prepare students for the state writing assessment. During her time working in a Title I school, where most of the students struggled with basic writing skills, she knew there was an immediate need to create a structured writing curriculum that had daily lessons built in such a way that each day had its own progressive sections. Knowing the common errors made by students in the classroom, she developed lessons that were user-friendly for teachers and super easy to follow and understandable for students. Year after year, students that are taught using this curriculum show a significant improvement in their writing skills. She says, "It is the most simple and effective approach to learning basic writing skills that you will ever find." As a result of the significant increase in student achievement using Top Score Writing, this curriculum has been adopted nationally by hundreds of public, private, and charter schools and several homeschool organizations positively impacting tens of thousands of students. Due to the trailblazing success of the Top Score Writing curriculum, Mrs. Collum is now sought out across the nation as an expert in writing and a dynamic professional development speaker. She travels the country helping students, teachers, administrators and district leaders create individualized actions plans and delivers energetic presentations incorporating strategic approaches to improving writing using her cutting-edge print and digital curriculum. She has the unique experiences of achieving a 100% pass rate with her students on the state writing assessment

two years in a row, speaking at educational conventions and conferences, leading professional development in some of the largest school districts in the nation, and continuously providing teachers with the direction they need to successfully teach writing to students.

COLMAN, SARAH, "OLIVIA" CAROLINE OLIVIA, T: Actress **I:** Media & Entertainment **DOB:** 01/30/1974 **PB:** Norwich, Norfolk **SC:** England **PT:** Keith Colman; Mary Colman **MS:** Married **SPN:** Ed Sinclair (08/2001) **CH:** Three children **ED:** Diploma in Drama, Bristol Old Vic Theatre School (1999); Coursework in Primary Teaching, Homerton College, Cambridge, England **C:** Actress (2000-Present) **CW:** Actress, "Fleabag" (2016-Present); Actress, "Thomas & Friends" (2014-Present); Actress, "Them That Follow" (2019); Actress, "The Crown" (2019); Actress, "Les Miserables" (2019); Actress, "The British Airways Safety Video" (2018); Actress, "The Favourite" (2018); Actress, "Watership Down" (2018); Actress, "The Super Squirrels" (2018); Actress, "Murder on the Orient Express" (2017); Actress, Theater, "Mosquitoes" (2017); Actress, "Inside Dior" (2017); Actress, "Flowers" (2016-2018); Actress, "We're Going on a Bear Hunt" (2016); Actress, "The Night Manager" (2016); Actress, "Drunk History" (2016); Actress, "London Road" (2015); Actress, "Thomas & Friends: Sodor's Legend of the Lost Treasure" (2015); Actress, "The Lobster" (2015); Actress, "Thomas & Friends: Tale of the Brave" (2014); Actress, "Pudsey the Dog: The Movie" (2014); Actress, "Cuban Fury" (2014); Actress, "This is Jinsy" (2014); Actress, "Mr. Sloane" (2014); Actress, "The Secrets" (2014); Actress, "W1A" (2014); Actress, "The 7.39" (2014); Actress, "Big Ballet" (2014); Actress, "Broadchurch" (2013-2017); Actress, "The Five(ish) Doctors Reboot" (2013); Actress, "The Thirteenth Tale" (2013); Actress, "Run" (2013); Actress, "The Suspicions of Mr. Whicher: The Murder in Angel Lane" (2013); Actress, "Locke" (2013); Actress, "I Give It a Year" (2013); Actress, "Hyde Park on Hudson" (2012); Actress, Theater, "Hay Fever" (2012); Actress, "Bad Sugar" (2012); Actress, "Accused" (2012); Actress, "Twenty Twelve" (2011-2012); Actress, "The Iron Lady" (2011); Actress, "Exile" (2011); Actress, "Arrietty" (2011); Actress, "Tyrannosaur" (2011); Actress, "Rev" (2010-2014); Actress, "Doctor Who" (2010); Actress, "Mister Eleven" (2009); Actress, "Midsomer Murders" (2009); Actress, "Skins" (2009); Actress, Theater, "England People Very Nice" (2009); Actress, "Le Donk & Scor-zay-zee" (2009); Actress, "Beautiful People" (2008-2009); Actress, "Consuming Passion" (2008); Actress, "Hancock and Joan" (2008); Actress, "Love Soup" (2008); Actress, "Dog Altogether" (2007); Actress, "I Could Never Be Your Woman" (2007); Actress, "Grow Your Own" (2007); Actress, "Hot Fuzz" (2007); Actress, "The Time of Your Life" (2007); Actress, "The Grey Man" (2007); Actress, "That Mitchell and Webb Look" (2006-2008); Actress, "Confetti" (2006); Actress, "One Day" (2005); Actress, "Zemanovaload" (2005); Actress, "ShakespeaRe-Told" (2005); Actress, "Murder in Suburbia" (2005); Actress, "The Robinsons" (2005); Actress, "Look Around You" (2005); Actress, "Angell's Hell" (2005); Actress, "Green Wing" (2004-2005); Actress, "Terkel in Trouble" (2004); Actress, "Coming Up" (2004); Actress, "NY-LON" (2004); Actress, "Swiss Toni" (2004); Actress, "Black Books" (2004); Actress, "Peep Show" (2003-2015); Actress, "The Strategic Humour Initiative" (2003); Actress, "Eyes Down" (2003); Actress, "Gash" (2003); Actress, "The Office" (2002); Actress, "Holby City" (2002); Actress, "Rescue Me" (2002); Actress, "Comedy Lab" (2001); Actress, "Mr Charity" (2001); Actress, "People Like Us" (2001); Actress, "The Mitchell and Webb Situation"

(2001); Actress, "Bruiser" (2000) **AW:** Best Actress, Academy Awards (2019); Best Actress in a Leading Role, BAFTA Film Award (2019); Best Actress in a Motion Picture, Musical or Comedy, Golden Globe Awards, Hollywood Foreign Press Association (2019); Best International Lead Actress, AACTA Awards (2019); Best Actress, British Independent Film Awards (2018); Best Actress in a Comedy Movie, Critics' Choice Awards (2018); Best Supporting Actress in a Series, Miniseries or Television Film, Golden Globe Awards, Hollywood Foreign Press Association (2017); Best Supporting Actress, British Independent Film Awards (2015); Best Actress, BAFTA TV Award (2014); Two TV Awards for Best Supporting Actress, British Academy of Film and Television Arts (2013); Best Female Comedy Performance, BAFTA TV Award (2012); Best Supporting Actress, British Independent Film Awards (2012); Best Actress, British Independent Film Awards (2011)

COLON-NAVARRO, FERNANDO, T: Professor of Law **I:** Law and Legal Services **CN:** Thurgood Marshall School of Law **PB:** Arroyo **SC:** Puerto Rico **PT:** Fernando Colon; Hilda Navarro **MS:** Married **SPN:** Carol Jeane Johnson **CH:** Annikah Mercedes; Daniel Zakai **ED:** LLM, Harvard Law School, Cambridge, MA (1991); EdM, Harvard Graduate School of Education, Harvard Law School, Cambridge, MA (1990); JD, University of Minnesota Law School, Minneapolis, MN (1981); BA, St. John's University, Collegeville, MN (1974) **C:** Professor of Law and Director of LL.M. & Immigration Development (2012-Present); Visiting Professor, Escuela de Derecho Universidad de Puerto Rico, San Juan, Puerto Rico (2005-Present); Associate Dean (2003-2012); Associate Professor, Thurgood Marshall School of Law, Texas Southern University, Houston, TX (1991-2008); Visiting Associate Professor, Texas Wesleyan University School of Law, Fort Worth, TX (1999-2000); Clinical Director, Thurgood Marshall School of Law, Texas Southern University, Houston, TX (1992-1995); Director, Clinical Instructor, Harvard Law School Immigration Clinic, Cambridge, MA (1987-1991); Assistant Attorney, Chicago Board of Education, Chicago, IL (1986-1987); Staff Attorney, Mexican American Legal Defense and Educational Fund (MALDEF), Chicago, IL (1983-1986); Staff Attorney, Legal Aid Society of Minneapolis, Minneapolis, MN (1981-1983); Law Clerk, Trial Assistant, Hennepin County Public Defenders Office, Minneapolis, MN (1979-1980) **CW:** Author, "Technology and Assessment in the Legal Classroom: An Empirical Study, in The Legal Profession: Education and Ethics in Practice 7" (2013); Author, "Technology and Assessment in the Legal Classroom: An Empirical Study, in Inted 2011 Proceedings" (2011); Co-Author, "Racial Profiling as a Means of Thwarting the Alleged Latino Security Threat," Thurgood Marshall Law Review (2011); Author, "Lead Counsel in Matter of Edwards," Immigration Law and Procedure (1999); Author, "Thinking Like a Lawyer, Expert Novice Differences in Simulated Client Interviews" (1997); Author, "Political Asylum and Judicial Review: The Rise and Fall of Imputed Political Opinion," Thurgood Marshall Law Review (1994) **AW:** Professor of the Year Award, 2013 Class (2013); Professor of the Year, Outstanding Adviser, Hispanic Law Student Association, Thurgood Marshall School of Law (2001-2002); Named Outstanding Visiting Professor, Student Bar Association, Wesleyan University School of Law (1999-2000); Named 1L Outstanding Evening Professor, Student Bar Association, Wesleyan University School of Law (1999-2000); Professor of the Year, Chicano Law Association (1997-1998); Professor of the Year, Chicano Law Association (1996-1997); Achievement Award, Chicano Law Student Association (1995-1996); Pro-

fessor of the Year, Chicano Law Association (1994-1995); Lex Justa Award, Thurgood Marshall School of Law (1991-1992) **MEM:** Co-Founder, Thurgood Marshall School of Law Institute for International and Immigration Law; American Bar Association; Hispanic Bar Association **BAR:** Seventh Circuit Court of Appeals, Massachusetts (1988); Illinois State and Federal Court (1983); Minnesota State and Federal Court (1982) **MH:** Albert Nelson Marquis Lifetime Achievement Award; Marquis Who's Who Top Professional **B/I:** Mr. Navarrao became involved in his profession because he was working at a social services agency in Detroit. There was a desegregation case ordering the desegregation and integration of schools in the area. He was appointed by the court to be a committee member to supervise this, because the court cannot supervise agencies. Every time people would come in dissatisfied with something, they would use "statutes" to support their claim, but Mr. Navarro wasn't familiar with all of the statues. He decided it was necessary for him to get a degree in law, to be more well versed in his line of work.

COMANECI, NADIA, T: Professional Gymnast **I:** Athletics **DOB:** 11/12/1961 **PB:** Onesti **SC:** Romania **ED:** Coursework, College Physical Education and Sports, Bucharest, Romania **C:** Junior Team Coach (1984) **AW:** Great Immigrant Honoree, Carnegie Corporation (2016); The Olympic Order (2004); Flo Hyman Award (1998); Marca Leyen, International Gymnastics Hall of Fame (1993); Champion, World University Games, Bucharest (1981); Gold Medal for Vault, Bars, Floor and Team Title World University Games, Bucharest (1981); Gold Medal for Beam and Floor, Moscow (1980); Individual All-round and Team Title, Moscow (1980); Overall European Champion, Copenhagen (1979); Gold Medal for Vault and Floor World Cup, Tokyo (1979); Silver Medal for Vault World Championships, Strasbourg (1978); Individual All-round and Team Title for Beam World Coup, Tokyo (1979); Gold Medal for Vault and Floor Exercises, Copenhagen (1979); Team Title, Fort Worth (1979); Gold Medal for Beam World Championships, Strasbourg, France (1978); Gold Medal for Bars, Prague (1977); Silver Medal for Vault, Prague (1977); Overall European Champion, Prague, Czechoslovakia (1977); Olympic Champion, Montreal, Quebec, Canada (1976); Gold Medal for Bars and Beam Olympic Games, Montreal (1976); Team Title Olympic Games, Montreal (1976); Bronze Medal for Floor Olympic Games, Montreal (1976); Silver Medals for Floor European Championships, Skien (1975); Gold Medal for Vault, Asymmetric Bars and Beam, European Championships, Skien (1975); Overall European Champion, Skien (1975)

COMBS, SEAN, T: Record Company Executive, Producer, Actor, Entrepreneur **I:** Media & Entertainment **DOB:** 11/04/1969 **PB:** Harlem **SC:** NY/USA **PT:** Melvin Combs; Janice Combs **SPN:** Misa Hylton-Brim (Partner); Kimberly Porter (Partner); Cassie Ventura (Partner) **CH:** Justin; Christian; D'Lila Star; Jessie James **ED:** Coursework, Howard University, Washington, DC (1988-1990) **C:** Launched Clothing Line, Sean John (1998-Present); Founder, Chief Executive Officer, Bad Boy Entertainment (1993-Present); Owner, Justin, Atlanta (1997-2012); Launched Fragrance, Unforgivable, I Am King (2008); Acquired, Enyce (2008); Launched Fragrance, Unforgivable (2006); Various Positions including Intern and Head of A&R Department, Uptown Records (1990-1993) **CW:** Actor, "Can't Stop Won't Stop: A Bad Boy Story" (2017); Performer, Producer, "MMM" (2014); Actor, "Muppets Most Wanted" (2014); Actor, "Draft Day" (2014); Executive Producer, "Undefeated" (2012); Actor, "It's Always Sunny in Philadelphia" (2012);

Actor, "Hawaii Five-0" (2011); Actor, "Get Him to the Greek" (2010); Actor, "Entourage" (2010); Executive Producer, "I Want to Work for Diddy" (2010); Executive Producer, "StarMaker" (2009); Actor, "CSI: Miami" (2009); Executive Producer, Actor, "A Raisin in the Sun" (2008); Executive Producer, "Making the Band 4" (2007); Executive Producer, "Taquita & Kaui" (2007); Executive Producer, "Making the Band III" (2005-2006); Executive Producer, "The Making of 'Press Play'" (2006); Executive Producer, "Diddy Makes an Album" (2006); Executive Producer, "Run's House" (2005); Actor, "A Raisin in the Sun" (2004); Executive Soundtrack Producer, "Bad Boys II" (2003); Actor, "Death of a Dynasty" (2003); Executive Producer, "Making the Band II" (2002); Actor, "Monster's Ball" (2001); Actor, "Made" (2000) **AW:** Outstanding Actor in a Television Movie (2009); The Power 150 (2008); The 100 Most Powerful Celebrities, Forbes.com (2007, 2008); BET Best Male Hip Hop Artist (2007); The 100 Most Influential People in the World, TIME Magazine (2006); The Most Influential Black Americans, Ebony Magazine (2006); The 50 Most Influential African-Americans (2004); Named Menwear Designer of Year, Council of Fashion Designers of America (2004); Alumni Award for Distinguished Postgraduate Achievement, Howard University (1999); Songwriter of the Year, American Society of Composers (1996)

COMER, BRENDA WARMEE, T: Elementary School Educator; Real Estate Company Officer **I:** Education/Educational Services **DOB:** 05/14/1938 **PB:** Lakewood **SC:** OH/USA **PT:** Walter Byron; Annabelle (Broderick) Warmee **MS:** Married **SPN:** Gerald Edmund Comer (6/30/1962) **CH:** Brian; James; David; Kristen **ED:** Reading Certificate, Baldwin Wallace College (1987); Postgraduate, Bowling Green State University (1981, 1982, 1983-1984); BS, Kent State University (1961) **CT:** Certified Reading Specialist **C:** Private Practice Tutor, Lorain, OH (2004-Present); Teacher, Chapter I Reading Program, Lorain Board Education (1987-2004); Teacher, Auxiliary Services, Remedial Reading and Mathematics, Lorain Board Education (1979-1987); Elementary Teacher, Lorain Board Education (1961-1963) **CR:** Reading Recovery, Ohio State University (2001-2002); Vice President Warmee, Inc. **CIV:** Scholarship Chairman (1973-1976); Vice President, Lakeland Woman's Club, Lorain, OH (1972) **AW:** Grantee, National Education Association (2004-2005) **MEM:** National Education Association; Ohio Education Association; Loraine Education Association; International Reading Association; Daniel T. Gardner Reading Council; American Association of University Women **B/I:** Ms. Comer became involved in her profession because she always wanted to be a teacher. Some of the teachers she had all throughout elementary and high school were the ones who inspired her. She always liked working with children.

COMER, JAMES RICHARDSON JR., T: U.S. Representative from Kentucky **I:** Government Administration/Government Relations/Government Services **DOB:** 08/19/1972 **PB:** Carthage **SC:** TN/USA **MS:** Married **SPN:** Tamara Jo Comer (2003) **CH:** Reagan; Harlan; Aniston **ED:** BA in Agriculture, Western Kentucky University, Bowling Green, KY, Magna Cum Laude (1993) **C:** Member, U.S. House of Representatives from Kentucky's First Congressional District (2016-Present); Commissioner, Kentucky Department of Agriculture (2012-2016); Member, District 53, Kentucky House of Representatives (2001-2012); Director, South Central Bank, Monroe County, KY; Co-Owner, Comer Land and Cattle Company, Inc., KY; Founder, Owner, James Comer Jr. Farms, Monroe County, KY **CR:** President, Monroe County Chamber of Commerce (1999-2000) **MEM:** Monroe County Farm Bureau; President, Future Farmers of America (Now National FFA Organization) **PA:** Republican **RE:** Baptist

COMER, JODIE MARIE, T: Actress **I:** Media & Entertainment **DOB:** 03/11/1993 **PB:** Liverpool **SC:** United Kingdom **CW:** Actress, "Killing Eve" (2018-Present); Actress, "The Last Duel" (2020); Actress, "Free Guy" (2020); Actress, "Star Wars: The Rise of Skywalker" (2019); Actress, "Either Way" (2019); Actress, "Snatches: Moments from Women's Lives" (2018); Actress, "The White Princess" (2017); Actress, "England is Mine" (2017); Actress, "Rillington Place" (2016); Actress, "Thirteen" (2016); Actress, "Doctor Foster" (2015-2017); Actress, "Lady Chatterley's Lover" (2015); Actress, "Remember Me" (2014); Actress, "Inspector George Gently" (2014); Actress, "My Mad Fat Diary" (2013-2015); Actress, "Vera" (2013); Actress, "Law & Order: UK" (2013); Actress, "Coming Up" (2012, 2013); Actress, "Casualty" (2012); Actress, "Good Cop" (2012); Actress, "Silent Witness" (2012); Actress, "In T'Vic" (2013); Actress, "Doctors" (2012); Actress, "The Last Bite" (2012); Actress, "Justice" (2011); Actress, "Waterloo Road" (2010); Actress, "Holby City" (2010); Actress, "The Price of Everything" (2010); Actress, "The Royal Today" (2008) **AW:** Broadcasting Press Guild Award, Best Actress (2019); Gold Derby Award, Drama Actress (2019); Royal Television Society Award Best Actor (Female) (2019); Stylist Remarkable Women Award, Best Entertainer (2019); British Academy Television Award, Best Actress (2019); TV Choice Award, Best Actress (2019); Primetime Emmy Award, Outstanding Lead Actress in a Drama Series, Television Academy (2019); Broadcast Digital Award, Best Short-Form Drama (2019); Female First Award, Television Actress of the Year (2018); Marie Claire Future Shaper Award, Acting High Flyer (2018)

COMEY, JAMES BRIEN JR., T: Director (Retired) **I:** Government Administration/Government Relations/Government Services **CN:** Federal Bureau of Investigation **DOB:** 12/14/1960 **PB:** Yonkers **SC:** NY/USA **PT:** J. Brien Comey; Joan Marie (Herald) Comey **MS:** Married **SPN:** Patrice Failor (1987) **CH:** Five Children **ED:** JD, University of Chicago Law School (1985); BS in Chemistry and Religion, William & Mary (1982) **C:** Director, Federal Bureau of Investigation, U.S. Department of Justice, Washington, DC (2013-2017); Senior Research Fellow, Hertog Fellow in National Security Law, Columbia Law School, New York, NY (2013); General Counsel, Bridgewater Associates, LP, Westport, CT (2010-2013); Senior Vice President, General Counsel, Lockheed Martin Corporation, Bethesda, MD (2005-2010); Deputy Attorney General, U.S. Department of Justice, Washington, DC (2003-2005); U.S. Attorney, U.S. District Court for the Southern District of New York, U.S. Department of Justice, New York, NY (2002-2003); Managing Assistant U.S. Attorney, U.S. District Court for the Eastern District of Virginia, U.S. Department of Justice, Richmond, VA (1996-2002); Partner, McGuire Woods, LLP, Richmond, VA (1993-1996); Assistant US Attorney, U.S. District Court for the Southern District of New York, U.S. Department of Justice, New York, NY (1987-1993); Associate, Gibson, Dunn & Crutcher LLP, New York, NY (1986-1987); Law Clerk to the Honorable John M. Walker, United States District Court for the Southern District of New York, New York, NY (1985-1986) **CR:** Board of Directors, HSBC Holdings plc (HSBC Group) (2013); Member, Defense Legal Policy Board (2012-2013); Chairman, National Chamber Litigation Center, U.S. Chamber of Commerce (2009-2013); Carter O. Lowance Fellow, William & Mary Law School (2011-2012) **CW:** Author, "A Higher Loyalty: Truth, Lies and Leadership" (2018) **AW:** Named One of the 100 Most Influential, TIME Magazine (2017); Henry L. Stimson Medal, New York Bar Association (1993) **AV:** Squash; Bicycling; New York Giants; New York Knicks; Teaching Sunday school **PA:** Independent

COMMA, LEONARD, "LENNY" A., T: Chairperson, Chief Executive Officer **I:** Food & Restaurant Services **CN:** Jack in the Box Inc. **ED:** Master of Business Administration, Nova Southeastern University, Fort Lauderdale, FL; Bachelor of Arts in Finance, Drexel University, Philadelphia, PA **C:** Chairperson, Chief Executive Officer, Jack in the Box Inc. (2014-Present); President, Chief Operating Officer, Jack in the Box Inc. (2012-2014); Senior Vice President, Chief Operating Officer, Jack in the Box Inc. (2010-2012); Vice President, Operations, Division II, Jack in the Box Inc. (2007-2010); Vice President, Southern California Region, Jack in the Box Restaurants, Jack in the Box Inc. (2006-2007); Director, Convenience Store and Fuel Operations, Quick Stuff Convenience Stores, Subsidiary, Jack in the Box Inc. (2001-2006); Numerous Positions, Including Regional Manager, Exxon Mobil Corporation (1989-2001) **CIV:** Board Member, Big Brothers Big Sisters of America (2012-Present)

CONAWAY, KENNETH, "MIKE" MICHAEL, T: U.S. Representative from Texas; Ranking Member, House Committee on Agriculture **I:** Government Administration/Government Relations/Government Services **DOB:** 06/11/1948 **PB:** Borger **SC:** TX/USA **PT:** Louis Denton Conaway; Helen Jean (McCormick) Conaway **MS:** Married **SPN:** Suzanne (Kidwell) Conaway (1991) **CH:** Two Sons; Two Daughters **ED:** BBA, Texas A&M University-Commerce (1970) **CT:** CPA; Ordained Deacon, Baptist Church **C:** Ranking Member, House Committee on Agriculture (2019-Present); Member, U.S. House of Representatives from Texas' 11th District, United States Congress, Washington, DC (2005-Present); Leader, House Intelligence Committee (2017-2019); Chairman, U.S. House Committee on Agriculture (2015-2019); Chairman, U.S. House Committee on Ethics (Formerly House Standards of Official Conduct Committee) (2013-2015); Chief Financial Officer, Arbusto Energy Inc., Midland, Texas (1981-1986); Accountant, Price Waterhouse (Now PwC), Midland, Texas; Member, House Armed Services Committee; Member, Permanent Select Committee on Intelligence **CIV:** Chairman, Texas State Board Public Accountancy (1997-2005); Member, Texas State Board of Public Accountancy (1995-2002); Member, Midland Independent School District (1985-1988) **MIL:** With, United States Army (1970-1972) **AW:** Named Volunteer of the Decade, Midland YMCA (1990) **PA:** Republican **RE:** Baptist

CONDE, MARILYN T., MAOM, FCSP, T: Material Manager **I:** Medicine & Health Care **DOB:** 12/04/1947 **PB:** Los Angeles **SC:** CA/USA **PT:** Paul Conde; Edith G. (Sherman) McHugh Conde **MS:** Single **CH:** Joshua; Paul **ED:** Master of Arts in Organizational Management, University of Phoenix (1999); Bachelor of Science in Business Administration, University of Phoenix (1995); Licensed Vocational Nurse, El Camino College, Torrance, CA (1970) **CT:** Certified Gastrointestinal Technician; Certified Registered Central Service Technician **C:** Instructor, Central Service Technician Course; Manager, Sterile Processing Department, Saint Francis Medical Center, Lynwood, CA; Manager, Central Service, Saint Jude Hospital and Rehabilitation Center, Fullerton, CA; Supervisor, Emergency Room Staff, Central Service, Gastrointestinal Laboratory, Chino Community Hospital; Gastrointestinal Laboratory Technician, Infection Control, Costa Mesa Memorial Hospital **AW:** Instructor of the Year, California Central Service Association; Employee of the Year, Costa Mesa Memorial Hospital **MEM:** International Association of Healthcare Central Service Personnel; California Central Service Association **MH:** Albert Nelson Marquis Lifetime Achievement Award **B/I:** Ms. Conde served as a nurse until a superior asked her to switch into central service, the hospital department that ensures that all medical equipment is clean and sanitized. **AV:** Reading; Writing **RE:** Catholic

CONLON, JAMES E., T: Professor Emeritus **I:** Education/Educational Services **DOB:** 12/09/1935 **PB:** Cincinnati **SC:** OH/USA **PT:** Ralph Leroy Conlon; Elvera Ann Conlon **MS:** Widowed **SPN:** Joanne Lois Kuhns (6/12/1959, Deceased 11/13/2018) **CH:** Kevin; Kathleen; Kristopher **ED:** MFA, Ohio State University (1962); BS in Art Education, Ohio State University (1959) **C:** Professor Emeritus, University of South Alabama, Mobile, AL (1998-Present); Professor, University of South Alabama, Mobile, AL (1980-1997); Associate Professor, University of South Alabama, Mobile, AL (1972-1980); Assistant Professor Art, University of South Alabama, Mobile, AL (1965-1972); Lecturer, Indiana University Bloomington (1962-1965); Graduate Assistant, Ohio State University, Columbus, OH (1961-1962); Art Teacher, Cincinnati Public Schools (1960-1961) **CIV:** Board of Directors, Habitat for Humanity, Mobile, AL (1995-1997); Volunteer, Teaching Drawing Classes, Ahavas Cheled, Mobile, AL; Volunteer, Art Courses, Connie Hudson Senior Center **CW:** Designer, Mobile Terrace Playground (1971-1972) **AW:** Grantee, Samuel H. Kress Foundation (1969-1978) **MEM:** Watercolor and Graphic Arts Society, Mobile, AL **MH:** Albert Nelson Marquis Lifetime Achievement Award; Marquis Who's Who Top Professional **B/I:** Mr. Conlon has always been drawn to the arts even as a child, which started in grade school. He had an excellent High School teacher by the name of Robert Fister just very encouraging and genuine critique suggestions to help you improve your work. **AV:** Photography; Numismatics

CONNERY, SEAN, T: Actor **I:** Media & Entertainment **DOB:** 08/25/1930 **PB:** Edinburgh **SC:** Scotland **YOP:** 2020 **PT:** Joseph Connery; Euphamia Connery **SPN:** Micheline Roquebrune (1975); Diane Cilento (12/06/1962-09/06/1973) **CH:** Jason; One stepdaughter **ED:** Honorary PhD, Edinburgh Napier University (2009); Honorary DLitt, St. Andrews University (1988); Honorary DLitt, Heriot-Watt University (1981) **C:** Founder, Fountainbridge Films, Los Angeles, CA (1992-2002) **MIL:** With, British Royal Navy **CW:** Actor, "Sir Billi" (2012); Author, "Being a Scot" (2008); Actor, "Blitz" (2006); Voice Actor, "James Bond 007: From Russia with Love" (2005); Actor, Executive Producer, "The League of Extraordinary Gentlemen" (2003); Actor, "Finding Forrester" (2000); Narrator, "Macbeth" (1999); Actor, Producer, "Entrapment" (1999); Actor, "Playing By Heart" (1998); Actor, Executive Producer, "The Avengers" (1998); Producer, "Something Like the Truth, Playing by Heart" (1998); Actor, "A Good Man in Africa" (1994); Actor, "Rising Sun" (1993); Actor, Co-Executive Producer, "Medicine Man" (1992); Actor, "Highlander 2: The Quickening" (1991); Actor, "Robin Hood: Prince of Thieves" (1991); Actor, "The Hunt for Red October" (1990); Actor, "The Russia House" (1990); Actor, "Indiana Jones and the Last Crusade" (1989); Actor, "Family Business" (1989); Actor, "The Presidio" (1988); Actor, "The Untouchables" (1987); Actor, "Highlander" (1986); Actor, "The Name of the Rose" (1986); Actor, "Never Say Never Again" (1983); Actor, "Sword of the Valiant" (1982); Actor, "Wrong is Right" (1982); Actor,

"Five Days One Summer" (1982); Actor, "Outland" (1981); Actor, "Time Bandits" (1981); Actor, "The Great Train Robbery" (1979); Actor, "Cuba" (1979); Actor, "Meteor" (1979); Actor, "A Bridge Too Far" (1977); Actor, "Robin and Marian" (1976); Actor, "The Next Man" (1976); Actor, "The Wind and the Lion" (1975); Actor, "The Man Who Would be King" (1975); Actor, "Zardoz" (1974); Actor, "The Terrorists" (1974); Actor, "Murder on the Orient Express" (1974); Actor, "The Offence" (1973); Actor, "The Red Tent" (1971); Actor, "The Anderson Tapes" (1971); Actor, "Diamonds are Forever" (1971); Actor, "The Molly Maguires" (1970); Actor, "Male of the Species" (1969); Actor, "Shalako" (1968); Actor, "You Only Live Twice" (1967); Actor, "A Fine Madness" (1966); Actor, "The Hill" (1965); Actor, "Thunderball" (1965); Actor, "Marnie" (1964); Actor, "Woman of Straw" (1964); Actor, "Goldfinger" (1964); Actor, "From Russia With Love" (1963); Actor, "The Longest Day" (1962); Actor, "Dr. No." (1962); Actor, "Without the Grail" (1961); Actor, "MacBeth" (1961); Actor, "Anna Karenina" (1961); Actor, "The Frightened City" (1961); Actor, "Operation Snafu" (1961); Actor, "Colombe" (1960); Actor, "Tarzan's Greatest Adventure" (1959); Actor, "Darby O'Gill and the Little People" (1959); Actor, "The Square Ring" (1959); Actor, "The Crucible" (1959); Actor, "Another Time, Another Place" (1958); Actor, "Action of the Tiger" (1957); Actor, "Hell Drivers" (1957); Actor, "Time Lock" (1957); Actor, "Requiem For a Heavyweight" (1957); Actor, "Women in Love" (1957); Actor, "No Road Back" (1956); Actor, "Let's Make Up" (1955); Actor, "Lilacs in the Spring" (1954); Actor, "Macbeth, Judith" (1953) **AW:** Campidoglia Prize (2006); Life Achievement Award, American Film Institute (2005); Commander of Arts, France, Knight Commander of the Most Excellent Order of the British Empire, Queen Elizabeth II (2000); Lifetime Achievement Award, ShoWest Convention (1999); Cecil B. DeMille Golden Globe Award, Hollywood Foreign Press Association (1996); Career Achievement Award, National Board of Review (1993); Tribute Award, British Academy of Film and Television Arts (1990); Star of the Year, National Association Theater Owners (1987); Academy Award for Best Supporting Actor

CONNOLLY, GERALD, "GERRY" E., T: U.S. Representative from Virginia **I:** Government Administration/Government Relations/Government Services **DOB:** 10/20/1950 **PB:** Boston **SC:** MA/USA **MS:** Married **SPN:** Cathy Connolly **CH:** Caitlin **ED:** MPA, Harvard University (1979); BA in Literature, Maryknoll College, Glen Ellyn, IL (1971) **C:** Member, U.S. House of Representatives from Virginia's 11th Congressional District, United States Congress, Washington, DC (2009-Present); Providence District Supervisor, Fairfax County Board of Supervisors (1995-2003); Vice President, SRI International, Washington, DC (1989-1997); Senior Professional Staff Member, U.S. Senate Committee on Foreign Relations, Washington, DC (1979-1989); Executive Director, U.S. Committee of Refugees, Arlington, VA (1975-1978); Associate Executive Director, American Freedom from Hunger Foundation (1972-1974); Development Associate, Heifer Project International, Little Rock, AR (1971-1972); Director of Community Relations, Science Applications International Corp. (SAIC); Member, Committee on Foreign Affairs, United States Congress; Member, Committee on Oversight and Government Reform, United States Congress **CR:** Chairman, Fairfax County Board of Supervisors (2003-2008); Chairman, Northern Virginia Transportation Commission (NVTC); Chairman, Northern Virginia Regional Commission; Chairman, Metropolitan Washington Council of Governments **CIV:** Member, U.S. Delegate to 14th Annual Conference Soviet

Academy of Sciences (Now Russian Academy of Sciences), Moscow, Russia (1990); Delegate, Democratic National Convention (1984, 1988); Member, Fairfax County Democratic Committee (1984); Congressional Advisor, United Nations Conference on New and Renewable Sources of Energy (1981); Member, U.S. Delegate to World Population Conference, Bucharest, Romania (1974); Past President, Mantua Citizens Association; Past President, Fairfax County Federation of Citizens Associations (FCFCA); Board of Trustees, Greater Washington Initiative; Board of Directors, Virginia Institute of Government; Board of Directors, Institute for Regional Excellence; Board of Directors, Medical Care for Children Partnership (MCCP); Board of Directors, Fairfax County Chamber of Commerce; Board of Directors, The American National Red Cross, National Capital Area; Board of Directors, Fairfax Partnership for Youth; Member, Providence Players of Fairfax **MEM:** Virginia Association of Counties; Washington International Trade Association (WITA) **PA:** Democrat

CONNOLLY, SEAN, T: Chief Executive Officer and President **I:** Business Management/Business Services **CN:** Conagra Brands Inc. **ED:** MBA, University of Texas; BA in Economics, Vanderbilt University **C:** Chief Executive Officer, President, Conagra Brands Inc., Chicago, IL (2015-Present); Chief Executive Officer, Sara Lee North American Retail (2012-Present); Chief Executive Officer, President, Conagra Foods Inc. (2014-2016); Chief Executive Officer, The Hillshire Brands Company (2012-2014); President North America Soup, Sauces and Beverages Division, Campbell Soup Company, Camden, NJ (2010-2012); President, Campbell USA, Camden, NJ (2008-2010); President, North American Foodservice, Campbell Soup Company, Camden, NJ (2007-2008); Vice President, General Manager U.S. Soup, Campbell Soup Company, Camden, NJ (2004-2006); Vice President, General Manager Beverages & Mexico-Latin Am., Campbell Soup Company, Camden, NJ (2003-2004); Vice President Food Brands, Campbell Soup Company, Camden, NJ (2002-2003); Food & Beverage Brand Management Positions, Procter & Gamble Co. (1992-2002)

CONNOLLY-O'NEILL, BARRIE JANE, T: Owner, Interior Designer **I:** Other **CN:** Barrie Connolly and Associates **DOB:** 12/22/1943 **PB:** San Francisco **SC:** CA/USA **PT:** Harry Wallach Jr.; Jane Isabelle (Barr) Wallach **MS:** Married **SPN:** Peter Smith O'Neill (11/27/1983) **ED:** BFA in Environmental Design, California College of Arts and Crafts (California College of the Arts) (1978); Certificate of Design, New York School of Interior Design (1975) **C:** Interior Designer, Barrie Connolly & Associates, Boise, ID (1978-Present); TV Personality, KGO TV, San Francisco, CA (1969-1972); Professional Model, Brebner Agency, San Francisco, CA (1963-1972) **CR:** Board of Directors, Zoo Boise; Board of Directors, Idaho Humane Society; Interior Designer, Alumni and Friends Center, Boise State University; Interior Designer, Morrison Center for Performing Arts; Interior Designer, Cottonwood Drill Restaurant; Interior Designer, Angel's Bar & Grill; Interior Designer, The Rocks, Scottsdale, AZ; Interior Designer, Inn at 500 Capital Hotel, Boise, ID **AW:** BCA Awards (1999); National Sales & Marketing Award for Best Interior Merchandising, Portland, ME (1995, 1998); Gold Nugget Award (1997); National Merit Award (1992); Best Interior Design Award for Marketing and Merchandising Excellence, (1981, 1984, 1991); People's Choice Award, Street of Dreams (1991); Silver Award, Institute of Residential Marketing (IRM) (1991); Award for Best Interior, Merchandising Manufacturers Association of Maine (MAME), Portland, ME (1991);

National Silver Award for Best Interior Design, National Association of Home Builders (1991); Two Gold Nugget Merit Awards (1990); Grand Award, Best in American Living, National Association of Home Builders (1986, 1989); Best Interior Design Award, Sales and Marketing Council (1985, 1986); Best Residential Design Award, Boise Design Revue Committee (1983); Honoree, The Living Room of the Boise State Alumni & Friends Building Named after Barrie Connolly & Association for Designing the Interiors **MEM:** National Association of Home Builders; Affiliate, American Society of Interior Designers (ASID); Institute of Residential Marketing (IRM); Allied Member, American Society of Interior Designers (ASID) **MH:** Albert Nelson Marquis Lifetime Achievement Award **AS:** Ms. Connolly-O'Neill attributes her success to the work ethic her parents instilled in her and her desire to help the community, which was in large part due to her husband. **B/I:** Ms. Connolly-O'Neill became involved in her profession because she began modeling organically, starting with runway photography and then received a full time modeling job with a show called "The Anniversary Game," which was filmed seven days a week. After finishing her time at the game show, she moved to New York in search of new opportunities. Inspired by her aunt, who was known as a great interior designer, she wanted to follow her footsteps and began her education and career in interior design. **AV:** Playing tennis; Skiing; Gardening; Art **THT:** Ms. Connolly-O'Neill receives a great deal of motivation from her clients. Her clients influence her to keep going with her career and to continue to do the best work she can. She enjoys creating environments clients can be comfortable in and enjoy.

CONRAD, MARIAN, "SUSIE", T: Special Education Educator (Retired) **I:** Education/Educational Services **DOB:** 05/03/1946 **PB:** Columbus **SC:** OH/USA **PT:** Harold Marion Griffith; Susie Belle (House) Goheen **MS:** Married **SPN:** Richard Lee Conrad (01/23/1971) **ED:** BS, The Ohio State University (1967) **C:** Work-Study Coordinator, Special Education, Briggs High School, Columbus, OH (1980-1997); Work-Study Coordinator, Special Education, West High School, Columbus, OH (1970-1997); Work-Study Coordinator, Special Education, Whetstone High School, Columbus, OH (1979-1980); Work-Study Coordinator, Special Education, North High School, Columbus, OH (1974-1979); Teacher, Special Education, West High School, Columbus, OH (1967-1970) **CR:** Chairman, Hall of Fame Committee, West High School (2005-2007) **CIV:** Board of Directors, Chair Committees, Junior League of Columbus, Inc., Columbus, OH (1982-1999); Vice Chairman, Development Committee, Dublin Counseling Center (Now Syntero), Dublin, OH (1987-1997); Vice Chairman, Zoofari, Columbus Zoo and Aquarium, Columbus, OH (1978-1997); Trustee, Columbus Zoo and Aquarium (1991); Board of Directors, Wazoo, Columbus, OH (1974-1987); Board of Directors, Junior Division, The Columbus Symphony Club (Now Columbus Symphony Orchestra Inc) (1972-1979); Life Member, Wazoo, Columbus, OH **AW:** Educator of the Year, Council for Exceptional Children (CEC) (1989); Mayor's Award for Volunteer Service, Columbus, OH (1988); Woman of the Year, ABWA Management LLC (1980) **MEM:** President, Council for Exceptional Children (CEC) (1988-1989); Board of Directors, ABWA Management LLC (1980); Vice President, ABWA Management LLC (1979-1980); ABWA Management LLC; Council for Exceptional Children (CEC); Ohio ASCD; Dublin Women in Business and Professions; The Country Club at Muirfield Village; Dublin Women's Philanthropic Club; Iota Lambda Sigma Chapter of Sigma Gamma Rho Sorority, Inc. **MH:** Albert Nelson Marquis Lifetime Achievement Award **B/I:** Ms. Conrad became involved in her profession because of the flexibility of her bachelor's degree. After graduating from the Ohio State University, she was invited by the principal of West High School to teach special education, her minor area of study, at age 20. She took the job, and also assumed advising responsibilities for the National Honor Society, girls' athletics, student council and the future teachers of America. She stayed in her position until she married four years later. **AV:** Golfing; Gardening; Traveling; Cooking **PA:** Republican **RE:** Methodist

CONRAD, T. CHARLES III, CPA, T: Partner **I:** Financial Services **CN:** Conrad & Company CPA's **PT:** Ted Conrad, Jr.; Patty B. Conrad **MS:** Married **SPN:** Susan Hines (1990) **CH:** Stephen; Laura; Marianna **ED:** BA in Political Science, University of South Carolina (1984) **CT:** Certified Public Accountant **C:** Partner, Tax Specialist, Conrad & Company CPA's (1989-Present); Account Administrator, IBM (1984-1989) **CIV:** Hospitality Tax Advisory Board, Spartanburg County, SC (2019-Present); Spartanburg County Board for Higher Education (2012-2018); Former President, United Methodist Men **MEM:** Eagle Scout, Boy Scouts of America (1977-Present); American Institute of Certified Public Accountants; South Carolina CPA's; The Phi Beta Kappa Society **MH:** Marquis Who's Who Top Professional **AS:** Mr. Conrad attributes his success to hard work and his love of serving others. He enjoys helping clients achieve their planning and tax strategy goals. **B/I:** Mr. Conrad became involved in his profession because he is a fourth generation accountant. Right out of college, he began working for IBM. Some time after that, Mr. Conrad's father told him he had a great opportunity at his firm, and after four years at IBM, he decided to take his father up on his offer; he has remained there since.

CONTINO, RICHARD MARTIN, ESQ., T: Lawyer, Leasing Executive, Consultant **I:** Law and Legal Services **DOB:** 03/31/1940 **PB:** Richmond **SC:** VA/USA **PT:** Samuel Contino; Theresa Contino **MS:** Married **SPN:** Penelope **CH:** May-Lynne; Matthew **ED:** LLM, New York University (1972); JD, University of Maryland (1965); Bachelor in Aeronautical Engineering, Rensselaer Polytechnic Institute (1962) **C:** President, Captive Lease Advisors (2019-Present); Managing Director, Fairfield Capital Group, LLC (2014-Present); President, First Lease Advisors (2000-Present); Partner, Contino & Partners, Rye Brook, NY (1986-Present);General Counsel, De Lage Financial Services Inc., Wayne, PA (1999-2000); Partner, Contino Ross & Benedict, New York, NY (1978-1986); Vice President, Marketing, Gatx Capital Corporation, New York, NY (1976-1978); Eastern Regional Counsel, Gatx Capital Corporation, New York, NY (1974-1976); Associate, Fried, Frank, Harris, Shriver & Jacobson, New York, NY (1972-1974); Associate, Winthrop, Stimson, Putnam & Roberts, New York, NY (1969-1972) **CR:** Chairman, Founder ELM Corporation (1986-Present); Attorney, Consultant, Businessman, Lecturer, Equipment Lease Business (1987-2002) **MIL:** Captain, U.S. Air Force (1968-1971) **CW:** Revision Editor, "Equipment Leasing and Financing, A Product Marketing and Sale Strategy" (2019); Revision Editor, "Getting The Best Equipment Lease Deal, An Equipment Leasing Guide For Business Leases" (2019); "Equipment Leasing and Financing, A product sales and business profit strategy" (2019); Revision Editor, New York Commercial Law (2012); Revision Editor, Commercial Law and Practice Guide (2008); Revision Tax Editor, Asset-Based Financing (2006); "The Complete Handbook of Equipment Leasing" (2002, 2006); Revision Editor, Negotiating Business Equipment Leasing:

1995 (1998); "The Complete Book of Equipment Leasing Agreements, Worksheets and Checklists" (1997); "Trust Your Gut" (1997); Revision Editor, The Franchising Handbook (1993); "Handbook for Equipment Leasing-The Deal Makers Guide" (1989); "Business Emotions" (1988); "Legal and Financial Aspects of Equipment Leasing Transactions" (1979); Revision Editor, The Handbook of Equipment Leasing **MEM:** American Bar Association; New York State Bar Association; Former Member, Association of the Bar of the City of New York **BAR:** New York (1969); Maryland (1965); District of Columbia (1965) **MH:** Albert Nelson Marquis Lifetime Achievement Award **B/I:** Starting his career as an engineer, Mr. Contino quickly found he wanted to work with people. This was how he became a lawyer. **AV:** Practicing karate

CONWAY, KELLYANNE ELIZABETH, T: Former Senior Counselor to the President **I:** Government Administration/Government Relations/Government Services **DOB:** 01/20/1967 **PB:** Atco **SC:** NJ/USA **MS:** Married **SPN:** George T. Conway **CH:** Claudia; George IV; Charlotte; Vanessa **ED:** JD, George Washington University, with Honors; Coursework, University of Oxford; BA, Trinity College, Magna Cum Laude **C:** Senior Counselor to the President, United States (2017-2020); President and Chief Executive Officer, The Polling Co., Inc./WomanTrend, Washington, DC (1995) **CR:** Board Member, National Journalism Center; Former Adjunct Professor, George Washington University Law Center **CIV:** Board Member, Men Against Breast Cancer; Board Member, National Women's History Museum **CW:** Co-author, "What Women Really Want: How American Women Are Quietly Erasing Political, Racial, Class, and Religious Lines to Change the Way We Live" (2005); Editor, WomanTrends **MEM:** Qualitative Research Consultants Association (QRCA); American Association for Public Opinion Research (AAPOR); The Phi Beta Kappa Society **BAR:** The District of Columbia Bar; Pennsylvania Bar Association; New Jersey State Bar Association; Maryland State Bar Association, Inc.

CONWAY, KEVIN, T: Actor, Director **I:** Media & Entertainment **DOB:** 05/29/1942 **PB:** New York **SC:** NY/USA **PT:** James John C.; Margaret O'Brien **MS:** Divorced **SPN:** Mila Quiros (4/5/1966, Divorced); Geraldine Newman **CIV:** Board of Directors, Second Stage Company **MIL:** U.S. Navy (1960-1962) **CW:** Director, Play, "Other Peoples Money" (1990); Actor, Play, "Other People's Money" (1988); Director, Actor, "The Sun and the Moon" (1985); Actor, Play, "Dinner at Eight"; Actor, Play, "Elephant Man"; Actor, Play, "Of Mice and Men"; Actor, Play, "Moonchildren"; Actor, Play, "Red Ryder"; Actor, Play, "One Flew Over the Cuckoo's Nest"; Actor, Play, "Life Class"; Actor, Play, "Other Places"; Actor, Play, "King John"; Actor, Play, "On the Waterfront"; Actor, Play, "Lawyers"; Actor, Film, "Slaughterhouse Five"; Actor, Film, "Portnoy's Complaint"; Actor, Film, "FIST"; Actor, Film, "Paradise Alley"; Actor, Film, "The Funhouse"; Actor, Film, "Flashpoint"; Actor, Film, "Homeboy"; Actor, Film, "Jesse"; Actor, Film, "One Good Cop"; Actor, Film, "Ramblin Rose"; Actor, Film, "Jennifer 8"; Actor, Film, "Gettysburg"; Actor, Film, "Lawnmower Man II"; Actor, Film, "Whipping Boy"; Actor, Film, "The Quick and the Dead"; Actor, Film, "Rage of Angels"; Actor, Film, "The Scarlet Letter"; Actor, Film, "The Deadliest Season"; Actor, Film, "The Lathe of Heaven"; Actor, Film, "Elephant Man"; Actor, Film, "Something About Amelia"; Actor, Film, "When Will I Be Loved"; Actor, Film, "Breaking the Silence"; Actor, Film, "Train Wreck"; Actor, Film, "Gun in Pocket"; Actor, Miniseries, "Mark Twain"; Actor, Miniseries, "Gettysburg"; Actor, Miniseries,

"Streets of Laredo"; Actor, Miniseries, "Flamingo Rising"; Actor, Miniseries, "Calm at Sunset"; Actor, Miniseries, "Sally Hemmings"; Actor, Miniseries, "Oz"; Actor, Miniseries, "Brotherhood"; Actor, Film, "Black Knight"; Actor, Film, "Gods and Generals"; Actor, Film, "13 Days"; Actor, Film, "Looking for Richard"; Actor, Film, "Mercury Rising"; Actor, Film, "The Confession"; Actor, Film, "Person of Interest"; Actor, Film, "Mystic River"; Actor, Film, "Invincible"; Actor, TV Miniseries, "The Bronx Is Burning"; Actor, TV Miniseries, "The Good Wife"; Actor, TV Miniseries, "Person of Interest"; Actor, TV Miniseries, "Miami Vice"; Actor, TV Miniseries, "Law and Order"; Actor, TV Miniseries, "Jag"; Actor, TV Miniseries, "Equalizer"; Actor, TV Miniseries, "Law and Order: Criminal Intent"; Actor, TV Miniseries, "The Black Donnellys"; Actor, TV Miniseries, "Life on Mars"; Actor, TV Miniseries, "Lights Out"; Actor, TV Miniseries, "Gotham TV"; Voice Actor, Ken Burns Documentary on Mark Twain; Director, Play, "The Milk Train Doesn't Stop Here Anymore"; Director, Play, "Chicago" **AW:** Outer Critics Circle Award (1990); Outer Critics Circle for Best Actor, Other People's Money (1989); Drama Desk Award (1973-1974); Village Voice Obie Award (1973) **MEM:** Board of Directors, Screen Actors Guild (1979-1981); National Academy of Television Arts and Sciences **MH:** Albert Nelson Marquis Lifetime Achievement Award **B/I:** Mr. Conway became involved in acting after serving in the navy, and at IBM, which was his first real job. During a chance encounter at a bar, he helped a woman, who later took him to see a play "Stop the World, I Want to Get Off," which inspired him to pursue acting lessons.

COOK, IAN M., T: Chairman, President, and Chief Executive Officer **I:** Consumer Goods and Services **CN:** Colgate-Palmolive Company **ED:** Coursework, University of London; Graduate, London Guildhall University (Now London Metropolitan University) **C:** Chairman, President, Chief Executive Officer, Colgate-Palmolive Company (2009-Present); Director, Colgate Holdings (2003-Present); President, Chief Executive Officer, Colgate-Palmolive Company (2007-2008); President, Chief Operating Officer, Colgate-Palmolive Company (2005-2007); Chief Operating Officer, Colgate-Palmolive Company (2004-2005); Executive Vice President, Colgate-Palmolive Company (2000-2004); President Colgate-North America, Colgate-Palmolive Co. (1997-2002); Executive Vice President Marketing, Colgate North America, Colgate-Palmolive Co., New York, NY (1994-1997); With, Colgate, United Kingdom (1976); General Manager, Colgate's Nordic Group, Copenhagen; General Manager, Colgate, Dominican Republic; Marketing Director, Colgate, Philippines **CR:** Board of Directors, PepsiCo, Inc. (2008-Present); Colgate-Palmolive Company (2007-Present); Director, Catalyst; Director, The Consumer Goods Forum

COOK, PAUL JOSPEH JR., T: 1) U.S. Representative from California 2) Military Officer (Retired) **I:** Government Administration/Government Relations/Government Services **CN:** 1) U.S. House of Representatives 2) U.S. Marine Corps **DOB:** 3/3/1943 **PB:** Meriden **SC:** CT/USA **MS:** Married **SPN:** Jeanne Cook **ED:** Master of Arts in Political Science, University of California Riverside (2000); Master of Public Administration, California State University, San Bernardino, CA (1996); Bachelor of Science in Teaching, Southern Connecticut State University (1966) **C:** Member, U.S. House of Representatives from California's Eighth Congressional District, United States Congress, Washington, DC (2013-Present); Member, U.S. House Committee on Foreign Affairs (2013-Present); Member, U.S. House Committee on Veterans' Affairs (2013-Present);

Member, U.S. House Armed Services Committee (2013-Present); Member, District 65, California State Assembly (2006-2012); City Councilman, City of Yucca Valley, CA (1998-2006); Member, Committee on Energy and Commerce **CR:** Instructor, Political Violence and Terrorism, University of California Riverside (2002-Present); Professor, Copper Mountain College (1998-2002); Director, Yucca Valley Chamber of Commerce (1993-1994) **MIL:** Advanced to the Rank of Colonel, United States Marine Corps (1966-1992); Infantry Officer, United States Marine Corps, Vietnam **AW:** Two Decorated Purple Hearts; Bronze Star **MEM:** Disabled American Veterans; Yucca Valley Chamber of Commerce; United Way, Local Chapter; The American National Red Cross, Local Chapter; Veterans of Foreign Wars; The American Legion **PA:** Republican **RE:** Roman Catholic

COOK, RENAY, T: Elementary School Educator **I:** Education/Educational Services **PB:** Cleveland, Ohio **SC:** Ohio / USA **PT:** Luke Owens Sr.; Marjorie Redmond **MS:** Married **SPN:** Stanley Rephael Cook (08/13/1994) **ED:** MEd, Ashland University, OH (2002); BA, University Akron, OH (1979) **C:** Educator, East Cleveland City School, OH (1979-2010) **CIV:** Volunteer, Lifeline, East Mount Zion Baptist Church **MEM:** National Education Association; Ohio Education Association; Delta Sigma Theta Sorority, Incorporated **MH:** Albert Nelson Marquis Lifetime Achievement Award **B/I:** Ms. Cook became inspired to pursue the education career path by a 3rd grade teacher she had growing up. As she recalls, her favorite grade to teach was the 2nd grade. During her career, she was offered a job as a principal, but she turned it down. Ms. Cook genuinely loved being around children and "seeing those light bulbs go on" when they learned something new. She felt as if children needed someone that they could count on will support them, and she felt that was the best way to do so. **AV:** Reading; Walking; Cooking; Traveling; Theater; Concerts; Festivals; Museums **RE:** Baptist Christian

COOK, SCOTT DAVID, T: Co-Founder **I:** Business Management/Business Services **CN:** Intuit Inc. **DOB:** 07/26/1952 **PB:** Glendale **SC:** CA/USA **MS:** Married **SPN:** Signe Ostby **CH:** David; Karl; Annie **ED:** MBA, Harvard University; BA in Economics and Mathematics, University of Southern California **C:** Independent Director, The Proctor and Gamble Company (2000-Present); Board of Directors, Intuit, Inc., Menlo Park, CA (1984-Present); Co-founder, Intuit, Inc., Menlo Park, CA (1983-Present); Independent Director, eBay (1998-2015); Founder, Center for Brand and Product Management, University of Wisconsin–Madison School of Business (2002); Chairman, Intuit, Inc., Menlo Park, CA (1993-1998); President, Chief Executive Officer, Intuit, Inc., Menlo Park, CA (1984-1994); Consultant, Bain & Co., Inc. **CR:** Board of Directors The Procter & Gamble Co. (2000-Present); Various Marketing Positions, including Brand Manager and Board of Directors eBay (1998-Present) **CIV:** Board of Visitors, Intuit Scholarship Foundation; Board of Visitors, Center Brand and Product Management, University of Wisconsin; Board of Visitors, Harvard Business School; Board of Trustees, Asia Foundation **AW:** Forbes 400 Richest Americans (2006-Present); Lifetime Achievement Award, PC Magazine (2003); Software Publishers Association (1994) **MEM:** Phi Beta Kappa

COOK, TIMOTHY, "TIM" DONALD, T: Chief Executive Officer **I:** Technology **CN:** Apple Inc. **DOB:** 11/01/1960 **PB:** Mobile **SC:** AL/USA **PT:** Donald D. Cook; Geraldine Cook **ED:** MBA, Duke University's Fuqua School of Business (1988); BS in Industrial Engineering, Auburn University Samuel Ginn College of Engineering (1982) **C:** Chief Executive Officer, Apple Inc. (2011-Present); Chief Operating Officer, Apple Inc., Cupertino, CA (2005-2011); Interim Chief Executive Officer, Apple Computer Inc. (Now Apple Inc.) (2009); Executive Vice President, Worldwide Sales and Operations, Apple Computer Inc. (Now Apple Inc.) (2002-2005); Senior Vice President, Worldwide Operations, Sales and Support, Apple Computer Inc. (Now Apple Inc.) (2000-2002); Senior Vice President, Worldwide Operations, Apple Computer Inc. (Now Apple Inc.), Cupertino, CA (1998-2000); Vice President, Corporate Materials, Compaq Computer Corporation, Harris County, Texas (1997-1998); Chief Operating Officer, Reseller Division, Intelligent Electronics (1996-1997); Senior Vice President, Fulfillment, Intelligent Electronics (1994-1996); With, IBM Corporation, Research Triangle Park, NC (1982-1994) **CR:** Board of Directors, Apple Inc. (2011-Present); Board of Directors, National Football Foundation & College Hall of Fame, Inc. (2011-Present); Board of Directors, Nike, Inc. (2005-Present) **CIV:** Board of Trustees, Duke University (2015-Present) **AW:** Courage Against Hate Award, Anti-Defamation League (2018); Named One of the 100 Most Influential People in the World, TIME Magazine (2012, 2015, 2016); Named One of the 50 Most Influential People in Global Finance, Bloomberg Markets (2012, 2014, 2015); Visibility Award, Human Rights Campaign (2015); Inductee, Alabama Academy of Honor (2015); Named the World's Greatest Leader, Fortune Magazine (2015); Ripple of Change Award (2015); Person of the Year, Financial Times (2014); Named One of the World's Most Powerful People, Forbes Magazine (2011-2015); Fuqua Scholar, Duke University **AV:** Hiking; Cycling

COOKE, JESSICA, T: Founder **I:** Consumer Goods and Services **CN:** Yuppy Puppy Pet Spa **ED:** AS, Hickey College; Coursework, St. Charles Community College **CT:** Pet Technician, ABKA; Canine Skin and Coat, National Dog Groomers Association of America, Inc. (NDGAA); Animal First Aid, The American Red Cross; Infectious Disease Certified; Women Entrepreneur Certification Class **C:** Owner, Yuppy Puppy Pet Spa (2003-Present); Facilities Manager, Kennelwood Village (Kennelwood Pet Resorts) (1998-2003); Reception Manager, ITHR (1997-1998); Dog Groomer, Lucky Critters (1993-1998); Veterinary Technician, Shackleford Animal Hospital (Shackleford Vet Clinic) (1995-1997) **AW:** Named Champion for Children, United Services, Inc. (2019); Named Best Training, St. Charles Country (2017); Named One of the Top Local Pet Businesses in Missouri **MEM:** Pet Boss Club; AKC Pet Grooming; IPG; The Dog Gurus; Women in the Pet Industry **AS:** Ms. Cooke attributes her success to her great staff. She believes it takes a village. She had 50 employees and a great team of managers, who are women with great passion. She also credits a lot of her community involvement and wanting to better herself. She believes you can not keep stagnate and you have to keep growing to achieve greatness and more business. **B/I:** When Ms. Cooke was 13 years old, she worked at a local dog grooming company. She continued to work for them throughout high school and college, and this is where her passion started. She tried to be in the business world and wanted to become a recruiter but hated it. She always went back to the dog. She became a vet tech; she liked it but did not like the sadness that came along with the profession. She wanted to be more involved with the care and the holding of animals. She worked for another local grooming company that shamed her and she was passed up for a job opportunity. That is when she quit and decided to start her own business. **THT:** Ms. Cooke's company mainly focuses on dogs who have deceased owners. She takes those dogs in because of those animals have a lot of emotions challenges and trust issues. She also takes dogs who have been in the pound for too long.

COONS, CHRISTOPHER, "CHRIS" ANDREW, T: U.S. Senator **I:** Government Administration/Government Relations/Government Services **DOB:** 09/09/1963 **PB:** Greenwich **SC:** CT/USA **PT:** Ken Coons; Sally Coons **MS:** Married **SPN:** Annie Lingenfelter (1996) **CH:** Michael; Jack; Maggie **ED:** MA in Ethics, Yale Divinity School (1992); JD, Yale Law School (1992); BA in Chemistry and Political Science, Amherst College (1985); Coursework, University of Nairobi, Kenya **C:** Vice Chair, U.S. Senate Select Committee on Ethics (2017-Present); Member, U.S. Senate Committee on Appropriations (2013-Present); Member, Committee on the Judiciary, U.S. Senate (2010-Present); Member, U.S. Senate Committee on Foreign Relations (2010-Present); Member, U.S. Senate Committee on the Budget (2010-Present); Senator, State of Delaware (2010-Present); Member, Senate Committee on Energy and Natural Resources (2010-2013); County Executive, New Castle County (2005-2010); President, New Castle County Council, DE (2001-2005); In-House Counsel, W.L. Gore & Associates, Inc. (1996-2004) **CIV:** Active Member, South African Council of Churches; Active, Council for Homeless; Honorary Life Member, Minquadale Fire Company; Member, Advisory Board, Hearts and Minds Film Organization; Member, Advisory Board, DCAD; Member, Advisory Board, First State Innovation; Member, Advisory Board, Better Business Bureau; Member, Advisory Board, Riverfront Development Corporation, Riverfront Wilmington, DE; Member, Advisory Board, Boys & Girls Clubs of Delaware Inc.; Board of Directors, "I Have a Dream" Foundation **AW:** Rodel Fellow in Public Leadership, The Aspen Institute (2009); Governor's Outstanding Volunteer Award (1999); Honorary Commander, 166th Air Wing of Delaware Air National Guard **MEM:** Honorary Life Member, Minquadale Fire Company; Kiwanis Club of Wilmington, DE **PA:** Democrat **RE:** Presbyterian

COOPER, JAMES, "JIM" HAYES SHOFNER, T: U.S. Representative from Tennessee; Lawyer **I:** Government Administration/Government Relations/Government Services **DOB:** 06/19/1954 **PB:** Nashville **SC:** TN/USA **PT:** William Prentice Cooper Jr.; Hortense (Powell) Cooper **MS:** Married **SPN:** Martha Bryan Hayes (1985) **CH:** Mary Argentine Adams; John James Audubon; Hayes Hightower **ED:** JD, Harvard Law School (1980); MA in Politics and Economics, University of Oxford (1977); BA in Politics and Economics, University of Oxford (1977); BA in History and Economics, University of North Carolina at Chapel Hill (1975) **C:** Member, U.S. House of Representatives from Tennessee's Fifth Congressional District, United States Congress (2003-Present); Co-founder, Partner, Chairman, Board of Directors, Brentwood Capital Advisors LLC, Nashville, TN (1999-2002); Managing Director, Equitable Securities Corp., Nashville, TN (1995-1999); Member, U.S. House of Representatives from Tennessee's Fourth Congressional District, United States Congress (1983-1995); Attorney, Waller Lansden Dortch & Davis, Nashville, TN (1980-1982); Member, Committee on Armed Services; Member, Committee on Oversight and Government Reform **CR:** Adjunct Professor, Vanderbilt University Owen Graduate School of Management, Nashville, TN (1995-Present) **AW:** Rhodes Scholar (1975); Morehead-Cain Scholar (1972) **MEM:** Chi Psi Fraternity, Alpha Sigma Chapter **PA:** Democrat **RE:** Episcopalian

COOPER, KENNETH R., PHD, T: Professor **I:** Education/Educational Services **DOB:** 11/21/1942 **PB:** Ridley Park **SC:** PA/USA **PT:** Earl Kenneth Cooper; Catherine (Owens) Cooper **MS:** Married **SPN:** Marilyn J. Clore (08/04/1963) **CH:** Kevin; Corey **ED:** PhD, Louisiana Baptist University, Shreveport, LA (2009); MA, The University of Texas at Arlington (1974); BA, The University of Texas at Arlington (1970); BD, Bible Baptist Seminary, Arlington, Texas (1963) **C:** Professor, Bible and Theology, Tyndale Theological Seminary, Hurst, TX (2014-Present); Thesis/Dissertation Advisor (2014-Present); Conference Speaker, Bible Teacher, Writer for Biblical Faith Ministries, Abilene, TX (1984-Present); Senior Editor, Tyndale Seminary Press (2009-2010); Professor of Communications (2009-2010); President, Institute of Judaic-Christian Research, Arlington, TX (1985-1992); Field Representative, Institute of Judaic-Christian Research, Arlington, TX (1974-1985) **CR:** Human Services Specialist, Texas Department of Human Services, Arlington, TX (1974-2003); Educational Director, Temple Baptist Church, Fort Worth, TX (1963-1965) **CIV:** Chaplain, Troop 83, Boy Scouts of America, Fort Worth, Texas (1980-1992); Active Program Committee, YMCA, Fort Worth, Texas (1975-1979) **CW:** Author, Book, "Candle Drippings: Musings from My Mind and Other Itinerant Places" (2014); Contributor, Articles on Biblical, Theological, and Religious Themes to Professional Journals **AW:** Listee, Who's Who in Religion (1992); Listee, Who's Who in Biblical Studies and Archaeology (1987); Good Shepherd Award, Association of Baptists for Scouting (1984); Phi Alpha Theta National History Honor Society (1970); Sigma Tau Delta National English Honor Society (1969); Alpha Chi Honor Society (1968); Phi Kappa Theta Scholastic Honor Society (Now Phi Kappa Theta Fraternity), The University of Texas at Arlington (1968) **MEM:** Society of Biblical Literature; The Evangelical Theological Society; Near Eastern Archaeological Society; Charter Member, United States Holocaust Memorial Museum; Associates for Biblical Research; Society of Dispensational Theology **MH:** Albert Nelson Marquis Lifetime Achievement Award **AS:** Any success Mr. Cooper has achieved resulted from God's strength, to support from family, to encouragement from friends, and determination to grow and achieve goals. **B/I:** Mr. Cooper became involved in his profession because when he was growing up in Pennsylvania, he did not appear to be very good at anything else. He loved history, English, and the Bible, in particular. He grew up in a strong fundamentalist Bible-believing church and everyone encouraged him to go into the ministry initially. He was a bit too shy for this and so he took the second best choice and decided to be a teacher. However, that did not work out either. He then went to work as a case worker, a task in which he succeeded for 12 years, until he was promoted to Supervisor and finally to Regional Policy Specialist for an entire region of North Texas. At the same time, he managed to teach at his church, which he began to enjoy. After retiring in 2003, he continued to volunteer at the Biblical Faith Ministries, and went on to become a teacher at Tyndale Theological Seminary and Bible Institute. **AV:** Reading; Writing; Working out **PA:** Republican **RE:** Baptist **THT:** Dr. Cooper says, "For this, I borrow a few thoughts from others who have impacted my life. The thoughts are mine as well, but these persons said it better at the time. First, John Wooden, a great basketball coach said, "Talent is God given. Be humble. Fame is man-given. Be grateful. Conceit is self-given. Be careful." John Wooden also said, "Be more concerned with your character than your reputation, because your character is what you really are, while your reputation is merely what others think you are." One from John Bunyan,

"You have not lived today until you have done something for someone who can never repay you." And to wind up these few significant thoughts, one from J.R.R. Tolkien's, Lord of the Rings, "All we have to do is decide what to do with the time that is given to us." Finally, one of my own, "Nothing less than the best for the Lord."

COOPER, ROY ASBERRY III, T: Governor of North Carolina **I:** Government Administration/Government Relations/Government Services **DOB:** 07/13/1957 **PB:** Nashville **SC:** NC/USA **PT:** Roy Asberry Jr.; Beverly (Batchelor) Cooper **MS:** Married **SPN:** Kristin Bernhardt (03/28/1992) **CH:** Hilary Godette; Natalie Rose; Claire Kristin **ED:** JD, University of North Carolina School of Law (1982); BA, University of North Carolina at Chapel Hill (1979) **C:** Governor, State of North Carolina (2017-Present); Attorney General, State of North Carolina (2001-2017); Democratic Majority Leader, North Carolina Senate (1997-2001); Partner, Fields & Cooper, PLLC, Rocky Mount, NC (1982-2001); Member, North Carolina Senate (1991-2001); Chairman, Judicial Committee, North Carolina House of Representatives (1989-1991); Member, North Carolina House of Representatives (1987-1991) **AW:** Kelley-Wyman Award, National Association of Attorneys General (NAAG) (2013); Morehead Scholar, University of North Carolina at Chapel Hill (1975-1979) **MEM:** President, National Association of Attorneys General (NAAG) (2010-2011) **BAR:** State of North Carolina (1982) **PA:** Democrat **RE:** Presbyterian

COOPERMAN, LEON, "LEE" G., T: Former Chairperson, Chief Executive Officer (Retired) **I:** Financial Services **CN:** Omega Advisors Inc. **DOB:** 4/25/1943 **PB:** New York **SC:** NY/USA **PT:** Harry Cooperman; Martha (Rothenstein) Cooperman **MS:** Married **SPN:** Toby Cooperman **CH:** Wayne M.; Michael S. **ED:** Master of Business Administration, Columbia Business School (1967); Bachelor of Arts, Hunter College, City University of New York (1964); Honorary Doctorate, Roger Williams University **CT:** Certified Financial Analyst **C:** Founder, Chairperson, Chief Executive Officer, Omega Advisors Inc., New York, NY (1992-2016); Chairperson, Chief Executive Officer, Goldman Sachs Asset Management, New York, NY (1989-1990); Partner, Goldman Sachs & Co., New York, NY (1967-1990); Quality Control Engineer, Xerox Corporation, Webster, NY (1965-1967) **CR:** Co-owner, American Media Inc. (2014-Present); Board of Directors, Automatic Data Processing Inc. (1991-2011) **CIV:** Signatory, The Giving Pledge (2010); Trustee, United Jewish Appeal, NJ (1980); Trustee, St. Barnabas Hospital, SBH Health System, Livingston, NJ; Board of Overseers, Columbia Business School; Board of Directors, Vice Chairman of Finance, Treasurer, Damon Runyon Cancer Research Foundation; Member, Global Leadership Council, buildOn Inc.; Founder, Leon and Toby Cooperman Family Foundation; Member, Songs of Love Foundation **AW:** Named to the Forbes 400: Richest Americans (2009-Present); Named, One of the 50 Most Influential People in Global Finance, Bloomberg Markets (2012, 2014) **MEM:** Director, CFA Institute (1980-Present); President, CFA Society of New York (1980); Atlantis Yacht Club, Monmouth Beach, NJ **RE:** Jewish

COPPOLA, SABRINA L., T: Founder **I:** Medicine & Health Care **CN:** Social Butterfly Counseling **DOB:** 12/21/1982 **SC:** NJ/USA **MS:** Married **SPN:** Matt **CH:** Olivia; Alexander **ED:** MSW, Fordham University (2005-2008); BA, Ramapo College Of New Jersey (2001-2004) **CT:** Licensed Social Worker, State of New Jersey **C:** Assistant Professor, Ramapo College of New Jersey (2015- Present); Founder, Clinical Director, Social Butterfly Counseling (2013-

Present); Clinical Consultant, Case Conference Model, Care Plus NJ, Inc. (2013- Present); Director of Therapeutic Visitation Services, Care Plus NJ, Inc. (2015); Assistant Director of Operations for Outpatient Services, Care Plus Innovations, Care Plus NJ, Inc. (2004-2015); Executive Director, Care Plus Foundation (2011-2012) **MEM:** National Association of Social Workers; The Honor Society of Phi Kappa Phi; Working Mother's Networking Group, The Third Shift; Small Business Network of Bergen County New Jersey; Young Professionals of Bergen County New Jersey; Bergen Volunteer Center; Therapists Linked **AS:** Ms. Coppola attributes her success to her family's support, empowerment and encouragement, as well as her supportive husband who she has been with for the last 20 years. **B/I:** Ms. Coppola became involved in her profession because of the events of September 11, 2001. Originally, she was studying to become a doctor, but in those moments after those horrific events, she was inspired to do her part in other ways. **THT:** Ms. Coppola states, "If at first you don't succeed, try, and try again" and "don't sweat the small stuff."

COPPOLA, SOFIA CARMINA, T: Film Director, Film Producer, Scriptwriter **I:** Media & Entertainment **DOB:** 05/14/1971 **PB:** New York **SC:** NY/USA **PT:** Francis Ford Coppola; Eleanor Coppola **MS:** Married **SPN:** Thomas Mars (August 27, 2011); Spike Jonze (June 26, 1999-December 9, 2003) **CH:** Romy; Lil' Cosimo **C:** Designer, Milk Fed; Intern with Karl Lagerfield, Chanel **CW:** Director, Producer, Screenwriter, "Somewhere" (2010); Director, Producer, Screenwriter, "The Beguiled" (2017); Director, Producer, Screenwriter, "A Very Murray Christmas" (2015); Director, Producer, Screenwriter, "The Bling Ring" (2013); Director, Producer, Screenwriter, "Marie Antoinette" (2006); Creator, Writer, Executive Producer, "Platinum" (2003); Director, Producer, Screenwriter, "Lost in Translation" (2003); Actor, "CQ" (2001); Actor, "Star Wars: Episode I-The Phantom Menace" (1999); Director, Producer, Screenwriter, "Lick the Star" (1998); Director, Screenwriter "The Virgin Suicides" (1999); Host, "Hi-Octane" (1994); Actor, "Inside Monkey Zetterland" (1992); Actor, "The Godfather: Part III" (1990); Costume Designer, "The Spirit of '76" (1990); Segment Writer, Costume Designer, "New York Stories" (1989); Actor, "Anna" (1987); Actor, "Peggy Sue Got Married" (1986); Actor, "The Cotton Club" (1984); Actor, "Frankenweenie" (1984); Actor, "The Outsiders" (1983); Actor, "Rumble Fish" (1983); Actor, "The Godfather: Part II" (1974); Actor, "The Godfather" (1972) **AW:** Award for Special Filmmaking Achievement, National Board of Review (2010); Golden Globe for Best Screenplay (2004); Academy Award for Best Screenplay (2004); Award for Best Director, Boston Society of Film Critics (2003); Award for Special Achievement, National Board of Review (2003); Award for Best Director, New York Film Critics Circle (2003)

CORBAT, MICHAEL LOUIS, T: Chief Executive Officer **I:** Financial Services **CN:** Citigroup, Inc. **DOB:** 05/02/1960 **PB:** Bristol **SC:** CT/USA **PT:** Deanne Corbat **MS:** Married **SPN:** Donna D. Corbat **CH:** Brian; Allison **ED:** BA in Economics, Harvard University, Cambridge, MA (1983) **C:** Chief Executive Officer, Citigroup, Inc. (2012-Present); Chief Executive Officer, Citi Holdings (2009-2012); Chief Executive Officer, Europe, Middle East and Africa Region, Citigroup, Inc. (2012); Interim Chief Executive Officer, Citi Holdings (2009); Chief Executive Officer, Citi Global Wealth Management (2008-2009); Managing Director, Head of Fixed Income Sales Department, Salomon Brothers (1993-1998); With, Fixed Income Sales Department, Salomon

Brothers, Atlanta (1983-1993); Managing Director, Head of Global Corporate/Global Commercial Banks, Citigroup, Inc.; Head of Global Emerging Markets, Citigroup, Inc.; Various Advisory/Structuring Positions, Citigroup, Inc., London, New York, NY **CR:** Board of Directors, Citigroup, Inc. (2012-Present) **CIV:** Board of Trustees, Salisbury School **MEM:** Board of Directors, Swedish American Chamber of Commerce **AV:** Fly fishing; Golfing; Skiing

CORBIN, RICHARD, "DICK" H., T: Business Development Consultant **I:** Consulting **CN:** Westport Consulting Associates **DOB:** 12/21/1936 **PB:** Cleveland **SC:** OH/USA **PT:** Milford H.; Miriam (Eshner) Corbin **MS:** Married **SPN:** Eileen R. Corbin **CH:** Peter; Caroline; Philip **ED:** BA, Lehigh University (1958) **C:** Lecturer, Frost & Sullivan, England (1986-Present); Lecturer, Business Week, New York, NY (1984-Present); Managing Director, Principal, Westport Consultant Group, Inc. (1986-1991); Lecturer, American Management Association, New York, NY (1983-1987); Vice President, Partner, Glendinning Associates, LLC, Westport, CT (1982-1986); Partner, Glendining Consultants (1986); Senior Vice President, Innotech Corporation, Trumbull, CT (1977-1982); Consultant, Richard Corbin Associates, Westport, CT (1975-1977); Member, Senior Management Staff, Helena Rubinstein/Faberge, New York, NY (1967-1975); Director, New Products, Kayser-Roth Corporation, New York, NY (1965-1967); Project Manager, St. Regis Paper Company, New York, NY (1963-1965) **CIV:** President, Westport Sunrise Rotary; Mentor, Bedford Middle School, Westport, CT **MIL:** Lt. (Junior Grade), U.S. Naval Reserve (1959-1962) **CW:** Contributor, Articles, Business Journals **MH:** Albert Nelson Marquis Lifetime Achievement Award **AS:** Mr. Corbin attributes his success to honesty and sincere interest in people and their success. **B/I:** Mr. Corbin became involved in his profession because his father was a great inspiration. He became ambitious because of the naval work he did and the responsibility the Navy gave him at a very young age. He felt inspired to make something of himself. **AV:** Playing golf; Public speaking **THT:** Mr. Corbin has always had interest in people and giving back to society.

CORBITT, JOHN H., REV. DR., T: Former Pastor **I:** Religious **CN:** Springfield Baptist Pastor Chruch **PB:** Salley **SC:** SC/USA **MS:** Widower **SPN:** Betty Starks Corbitt (Deceased) **CH:** Bruce; Terry (Deceased) **ED:** Postgraduate Coursework, Vanderbilt University; Postgraduate Coursework, Yale University; DMin, McCormick Theological Seminary, Chicago, IL; MDiv, Interdenominational Theological Center, Atlanta, GA; BA, South Carolina State University, Orangeburg, SC **C:** Pastor of Monks, Grove Baptist Church (2014-2015); Former Pastor, Springfield Baptist Church, Greenville, SC (1974-2011); National Director, National Baptist Student Union Retreat (1973-1996); Former Pastor, Bells Chapel Baptist Church, Bells, TN; Former Pastor, Mount Pleasant Baptist Church, Little Rock, AR; Former College Minister, Owen College, Memphis, TN; Former College Minister, Arkansas Baptist College, Little Rock, AR; Former College Minister, Professor of Religion, Philander Smith College, Little Rock, AR; Former Dean, National Baptist Congress of Christian Education; Former President, South Carolina Baptist Congress of Christian Education; Former President, Greater Greenville Ministerial Association; Former President, Baptist Ministers Fellowship of Greenville and Vicinity **CR:** Elected, Trustee Board, South Carolina State University (2003, 2007, 2011); Appointed, Trustee Board, South Carolina State University (2001) **CIV:** Board of Directors, Urban

League, Greenville, SC; Board of Directors, Urban League of Little Rock Arkansas **CW:** Author, "Black Churches Reaching College Students," National Baptist Sunday School Board (1995) **AW:** Arkansas Traveler's Award, Governor Bill Clinton (1992); Order of the Palmetto, Governor of South Carolina (1988); Alumnus of the Year, McCormick Theological Seminary **MEM:** Life Member, National Association for the Advancement of Colored People (NAACP); International Association of Christian Educators; Baptist World Alliance; Baptist Youth Congress; Former Chapter President, Phi Beta Sigma Fraternity, Inc. **B/I:** Dr. Corbitt feels that, about 50 years ago, he was called to the ministry. His great-grandfather organized his home church in Aiken County, South Carolina, in 1900. He was born in 1856, seven years before the Emancipation Proclamation. After his family received their freedom, they bought land in South Carolina and eventually started a church, which has been in his family ever since. At age 7, Dr. Corbitt was baptized. His faith has never strayed.

CORDANI, DAVID M., T: Chief Executive Officer and President **I:** Medicine & Health Care **CN:** Cigna **ED:** MBA in Marketing, University Hartford, CT (1994); BS, Texas A&M University, College Station, TX (1988) **CT:** Certified Public Accountant (CPA); Chartered Financial Consultant (ChFC) **C:** President, Chief Executive Officer, Cigna (2010-Present); President, Chief Operating Officer, Cigna (2008-2009); President, CIGNA HealthCare (2005-2008); President, Health Segments, Cigna HealthCare (2004-2005); Senior Vice President, Chief Financial Officer, Cigna HealthCare (2002-2004); Senior Vice President Transformation and Progressive Management, Cigna HealthCare (2002); Vice President of Corporate Accounting and Planning, Cigna (2000-2002); Chief Financial Officer of Field Operations, Cigna HealthCare; President, Southeast Region, CIGNA HealthCare; Controller, Cigna; With, Coopers & Lybrand **CR:** Board of Directors, National Association of Manufacturers

CORDEN, JAMES, T: Actor, Television Personality **I:** Media & Entertainment **DOB:** 08/22/1978 **PB:** Buckinghamshire **SC:** England/United Kingdom **PT:** Malcolm Corden; Margaret (Collins) Corden **MS:** Married **SPN:** Julia Carey (09/15/2012) **CH:** Max; Charlotte; Kimberley; Carey **C:** Television Personality, Actor, Comedian (1996-Present) **CW:** Host, "The Late Late Show with James Corden" (2015-Present); Voice Actor, "Superintelligence" (2020); Voice Actor, "Trolls World Tour" (2020); Actor, "Cats" (2019); Appearance, "Yesterday" (2019); Voice Actor, "Ralph Breaks the Internet: Wreck-It Ralph 2" (2018); Voice Actor, "Peter Rabbit" (2018); Voice Actor, "Ocean's 8" (2018); Voice Actor, "Smallfoot" (2018); Voice Actor, "The Emoji Movie" (2017); Host, "59th Annual Grammy Awards" (2017); Voice Actor, "Norm of the North" (2016); Voice Actor, "Trolls" (2016); Host, "70th Tony Awards" (2016); Actor, "Matilda and the Ramsay Bunch" (2016); Actor, "John Bishop: In Conversation With..." (2016); Actor, "Kill Your Friends" (2015); Actor, "The Lady in the Van" (2015); Actor, "Very British Problems" (2015); Actor, Writer, "The Wrong Mans" (2013-2014); Actor, "The Guess List" (2014); Actor, "Into the Woods" (2014); Narrator, "Ronald Dahl's Esio Trot" (2014); Actor, "Can a Song Save Your Life?" (2013); Actor, "One Chance" (2013); Actor, "One Man, Two Guvnors" (2012); Actor, "Stella" (2012); Actor, "National Theatre Live" (2011); Voice Actor, "The Gruffalo's Child" (2011); Actor, "The Three Musketeers" (2011); Actor, "Gulliver's Travels" (2010); Actor, "Beast Hunters" (2010); Actor, "The One Ronnie" (2010); Actor, Writer, Associate Producer, "Gavin & Stacey" (2007-2010); Actor, "Horne & Corden" (2009); Voice

Actor, "The Gruffalo" (2009); Actor, "Vampire Killers" (2009); Actor, "How to Lose Friends & Alienate People" (2008); Actor, "Telstar: The Joe Meek Story" (2008); Actor, "The History Boys" (2006); Actor, "Heroes and Villains" (2006); Actor, "Starter for 10" (2006); Actor, "Pierrepoint: The Last Hangman" (2005); Actor, "Fat Friends" (2000-2005); Actor, "Teachers" (2001-2003); Actor, "Heartlands" (2002); Actor, "Cruise of the Gods" (2002); Actor, "Jack and the Beanstalk: The Real Story" (2001); Actor, "Boyz Unlimited" (1999); Actor, "Whatever Happened to Harold Smith" (1999) **AW:** Primetime Emmy Award for Outstanding Variety, Music, or Comedy Special, The Television Academy (2016-2017); Primetime Emmy Award for Outstanding Special Class Program, The Television Academy (2017); Primetime Emmy for Outstanding Interactive Program, The Television Academy (2016); Tony Award for Best Performance by an Actor in a Leading Role in a Play (2012)

CORHAN, ALBERT, T: Director of Academy Operations **I:** Education/Educational Services **CN:** Adelphi Academy of Brooklyn **PB:** Brooklyn **SC:** NY/USA **ED:** Coursework, St. John's University, Staten Island, NY; Coursework, Upper School College Preparatory Program, Adelphi University **C:** Director of Academy Operations, Adelphi Academy, Brooklyn, NY (2000-Present); Director of Academy Advancement, Adelphi Academy, Brooklyn, NY (2000) **CIV:** Member, Board of Directors, Kiwanis Club; Donator, St. Jude Children's Research Hospital; Donator, Wounded Warriors; Donator, American Society for the Prevention of Cruelty to Animals; Producer, Adelphian Players Community Theater Organization **AW:** Philip David Stone '65 Dedication to the Adelphi Student Award (2018); Shel Silverstein "Put Something in the World That Ain't Been There Before" Award (2017); Russell E. Bonanno Dedication to the Adelphi Spirit Award, Adelphi University (2017); Above and Beyond Award, Adelphi University (2015); Outstanding Service Award, Adelphi University (2013); Dr. Edwin N. Beery '27 Alumni Award for Distinguished Service, Adelphi University; Man of the Year, Adelphi University; Pioneer of Bay Ridge, 3rd Avenue Merchants Association **MEM:** Ben-Bay Kiwanis Club; Committee Member, Hugh O'Brian Youth Leadership; Association of Fundraising Professionals, Society for Human Resource Management; Adelphi Alumni Association; National Association of Student Activity Advisors; Juvenile Diabetes Research Foundation; Arab-American Christian Coalition; Salaam Club of New York; Community Emergency Response Team; Merchants of Third Avenue Civic Improvement Association, Inc; Steering Committee, Business Improvement District **AS:** Mr. Corhan attributes his success to the many great people he has met, as well as great mentors he has had over the course of his career. He also studied very hard because he has a genuine passion for the work that he does. He believes that "no matter who you are or what you've done, you can always learn new things..." His number one philosophy in life is to treat everyone the way he would want to be treated. **B/I:** Mr. Corhan became involved in his profession as a promoter and in marketing. He is an alum of Adelphi Academy, and began doing a lot of fundraising and volunteer work for the school after graduation. Based on his experience and expertise he was asked to become involved with different fundraisers over the years. Finally an opportunity presented itself for a position as a director of advancement. It fit the criteria of the way he had made a living for the last few years, so he decided to take the position. That position naturally evolved into more of the operations management of the school.

CORLETT, TREVOR, T: Chief Executive Officer, President **I:** Other **CN:** Madcap Coffee Company **C:** Certified Lead Instructor, Specialty Coffee Association of America (2010-Present); Chief Executive Officer, Founder, Madcap Coffee Company (2009-Present); Subject Matter Expert in the Area of Espresso (2010-2017); Chair/Executive Council Member, Barista Guild of America (2010-2015); Owner, Moon Monkey Coffee Company (2005-2008); Music Program Manager, The House Cafe + Music (2002-2003); Assistant Store Manager, Blockbuster Video (1998-2002) **CIV:** Board Member, Local First West Michigan (2017-Present) **AW:** Grand Rapids Best Barista - Grand Rapids Magazine (2016); Eastern Conference Barista Champion, Specialty Coffee Association (2016); Current Vice Chair of Local First, Service to the Association Award (2014); Named One of the Most Influential People in the Beverage Industry, Imbibe Magazine (2013); Triple Bottom Line Award, Local First (2011); First annual TNT Latte art Champion, Specialty Coffee Association (2010) **MEM:** Board of Directors, Specialty Coffee Association (2016); Past Chair, Barista Guild of America **AS:** Mr. Corlett attributes his success to the relentless pursuit of exhaustively understanding the product that he works with. He also has surrounded himself with the right people who share similar vision and values that he has. **B/I:** Mr. Corlett became involved in his profession because he was interested in the impact coffee shops had in their local communities. From there, he learned a great deal about coffee and realized that it is a commodity and has a large global impact. He realized that a small local coffee shop could have a large global impact on a product that isn't locally available is what drew him to pursue it full time.

CORNELL, BRIAN CHRISTIAN, T: Chairman and Chief Executive Officer **I:** Retail/Sales **CN:** Target Corporation **PB:** New York **SC:** NY/USA **CH:** Two Children **ED:** Coursework, UCLA Anderson School of Management; BA, University of California Los Angeles (1981) **C:** Chairman, Chief Executive Officer, Target Corporation (Target Brands, Inc.), Minneapolis, MN (2014-Present); President, Chief Executive Officer, Sam's Club Division, Wal-Mart Stores, Inc. (Walmart), Bentonville, AR (2009-2012); Chief Executive Officer, Michaels Stores, Inc., Irving, Texas (2007-2009); Executive Vice President, Chief Marketing Officer, Safeway, Inc., Pleasanton, CA (2004-2007); Senior Vice President of Sales and President, North American Food Service Division, PepsiCo, Inc. (2002-2004); Senior Vice President of Marketing, European Regional President, PepsiCo Beverages International (2001-2002); President, Tropicana International, Tropicana Products, Inc. (1999-2001); Senior Vice President, General Manager Tropicana North America, Tropicana Products, Inc. (1998-1999); Management Positions, Joseph E. Seagram Co. (1984-1991); Management Positions, Gallo Wine Co. (Now E. Gallo Winery) (1981-1984) **CR:** Board of Directors, Target Corporation (Target Brands, Inc.) (2014-Present); Polaris Industries, Inc. (2012-Present); Centerplate, Inc. (2010-Present); The Home Depot, Inc. (Home Depot Product Authority, LLC) (2008-2009); OfficeMax Inc. (OfficeDepot, LLC) (2004-2007) **CIV:** Board of Visitors, UCLA Anderson School of Management **AW:** Retailer of the Year, "Grocery Headquarters" (2006); Marketer of the Year, "Supermarket News" (2005)

CORNYN, JOHN III, T: U.S. Senator from Texas **I:** Government Administration/Government Relations/Government Services **DOB:** 02/02/1952 **PB:** Houston **SC:** TX/USA **PT:** John Cornyn II; Atholene Gale (Danley) Cornyn **MS:** Married **SPN:** Sandy Hansen (1979) **CH:** Danley; Haley **ED:** LLM, University of Virginia (1995); JD, St. Mary's School of Law (1977); BA in Journalism, Trinity University, San Antonio, TX (1973) **CT:** Certified in Personal Injury Trial Law, Texas Board of Legal Specialization **C:** Chair, Senate Narcotics Caucus (2019-Present); Assistant Majority Leader (Majority Whip) (2015-Present); Member, U.S. Senate Committee on Finance (2009-Present); U.S. Senator, State of Texas (2002-Present); Senate Majority Whip (2015-2019); Assistant Minority Leader (Minority Whip) (2013-2015); Member, U.S. Senate Armed Services Committee (2011-2013); Chairman, National Republican Senatorial Committee (NRSC) (2009-2013); Member, U.S. Senate Committee on Agriculture, Nutrition & Forestry (2009-2011); Vice Chairman, U.S. Senate Republican Conference (2007-2009); Vice Chairman, U.S. Senate Select Committee on Ethics (2007-2009); Attorney General, State of Texas (1999-2002); Partner, Thompson & Knight LLP (1997-1999); Justice, Supreme Court of Texas, Austin, TX (1991-1997); Presiding Judge, Fourth Administrative Judicial Region (1989-1992); Judge, 37th District Court, Bexer County, TX (1985-1990); Attorney, Groce, Locke & Hebdon, San Antonio, TX (1977-1984) **CR:** Chairman, James Madison Memorial Fellowship Foundation (2009-Present); Texas Supreme Court Liaison, Gender Bias Task Force (1993-1995) **AW:** Border Texan of the Year Award (2005); Champion for Healthcare in Rio Grande Valley, Valley Baptist Medical Center, Texas (2004); Manufacturing Legislative Excellence Award, National Association of Manufacturers (2004); Congressional Partnership Award, National Association of Development Organizations (2004); Friend of the Farm Bureau Award, American Farm Bureau Federation (2004); Friend of Rural Water Award, Texas Rural Water Association (2004); Hero of Taxpayer Award, Americans for Tax Reform (2004); Statesman of the Year Award, Texas Asian Republican Conference (2004); James Madison Award, Freedom of Information Foundation of Texas (2001); Distinguished Alumnus Award, Trinity University (2001); Outstanding Texas Leader Award, John Ben Shepperd Public Leadership Forum (2000); Children's Champion Award, National Child Support Enforcement Association; Fighter of Free Enterprise Award, Texas Association Business; Guardian of Small Business Award, National Federation of Independent Business; Latino Leadership Award, National Coalition of Latino Clergy and Christian Leadership; International Leadership Legislative Award, United States-Mexico Chamber of Commerce **MEM:** President, Robert W. Calvert Inn of Court (1994-1995); President, William S. Sessions Inn of Court (1989-1990); Master Bencher, William S. Sessions Inn of Court (1988-1990); Fellow, San Antonio Bar Foundation; Fellow, Texas Bar Foundation; American Bar Association; Texas Bar Association; Robert W. Calvert Inn of Court; William S. Sessions Inn of Court; American Law Institute; Chi Delta Tau **BAR:** United States District Court of the Western District of Texas (1980); State of Texas (1977) **PA:** Republican **RE:** Church of Christ

CORREA, JOSE, "LOU" LUIS, T: U.S. Representative from California **I:** Government Administration/Government Relations/Government Services **CN:** U.S. House of Representatives **DOB:** 1/24/1958 **PB:** Anaheim **SC:** CA/USA **MS:** Married **SPN:** Esther Correa **CH:** Alex; Andres; Adan; Emilia **ED:** Doctor of Jurisprudence, University of California Los Angeles School of Law; Master of Business Administration, University of California Los Angeles; Bachelor of Arts in Economics, California State University, Fullerton **C:** Member, U.S. House of Representatives from California's 46th Congressional District (2017-Present); Member, District 34, California State Senate (2006-2017); Member,

District 69, California State Assembly (1998-2004); Board Member, California Small Business Association; Board Member, Orange City Community Development Council; Member, Banking, Finance and Insurance Committee, California State Senate; Member, Business, Professions and Economic Development Committee, California State Senate; Vice Chair, Committee on Veterans' Affairs, California State Senate; Chair, Public Employees and Retirement Committee, California State Senate; Board Supervisor, District One, Orange City, CA **CIV:** Board Member, Boy Scouts of America, Orange City, CA **AW:** Named, Legislator of the Year, Orange County Area Council; Named, Legislator of the Year, California Hispanic Chambers of Commerce; Named, Legislator of the Year, Boys & Girls Clubs of America; Award, California Optometric Association; Award, Crime Victims United of California, California Sexual Assault Investigators Association; Award, California Association for Nurse Practitioners; Award, Golden State Mobile Home Owners League; Award, Peace Officers Research Association of California; Named, High Technology Legislator of the Year, American Electronics Association; Superintendent's Bravo! Award, Santa Ana Unified School District; Hunger Fighter Award, California Hunger Action Coalition **MEM:** California Real Estate Board; The State Bar of California **PA:** Democrat **RE:** Roman Catholic

CORRIGAN, HELEN GONZALEZ, T: Cytologist (Retired) **I:** Biotechnology **DOB:** 09/30/1922 **PB:** San Diego **SC:** TX/USA **PT:** Rodrigo Simon Gonzalez; Eva Ruby (Corrigan) Gonzalez **ED:** BS, Our Lady of Lake, San Antonio, Texas (1943) **CT:** Registered Cytologist, International Academy of Cytology; Associate Registered Cytologist, American Society of Clinical Pathologists; Registered Medical Technologist, American Society of Clinical Pathologists **C:** Retired (1997); Owner, Corrigan Enterprises, San Diego, CA (1981-1991); Instructor, Trouble Shooters, Quality Control Analyst, Cytology Section, Brooks Medical Center, Fort Sam, Houston, Texas (1978-1981); Cytologist in Charge, Cytology Section, Pathology Laboratory, Fourth and Fifth United States Army Reference Area Laboratory, Fort Sam, Houston, Texas (1964-1978); Cytologist in Charge, Jackson-Todd Cancer Detection Center, San Antonio, Texas (1961-1964); Medical Technologist, Tucson Medical Center (1959-1960); Microbiologist, Nix Hospital Professional Laboratory, San Antonio, Texas (1952-1959); Teacher, San Diego High School (1943-1945) **CR:** Head Cytologist, Dr. R. Garza & Associates, Weslaco, Texas (1992-Present); Cytologist, International Cancer Screening Laboratory, San Antonio, Texas (1990-1991); National Health Laboratory, San Antonio, Texas (1989-1990); Waco Medical Laboratory Service, Waco, Texas (1988-1989) **CIV:** Advisory Board Member, Equal Employment Opportunity, Fort Sam, Houston, TX (1972-1974) **MEM:** National Association of Female Executives; American Society of Clinical Pathologists; Greater San Antonio Women's Chamber of Commerce **MH:** Albert Nelson Marquis Lifetime Achievement Award **AV:** Fishing; Hunting; Tennis; Skiing; Dancing **PA:** Republican **RE:** Roman Catholic

CORTEZ MASTO, CATHERINE MARIE, T: U.S. Senator from Nevada **I:** Government Administration/Government Relations/Government Services **DOB:** 03/29/1964 **PB:** Las Vegas **SC:** NV/USA **PT:** Manny Cortez; Joanna (Musso) Cortez **MS:** Married **SPN:** Paul E. Masto **ED:** JD, Gonzaga University School of Law, Spokane, WA, Cum Laude (1990); BS in Business Administration in Finance, University of Nevada (1986) **C:** Chair, Democratic Senatorial Campaign Committee (2019-Present); U.S. Senator, State of Nevada (2017-Present); Attorney General, State of Nevada (2007-2015); Attorney General, State of Nevada, Carson City, NV (2007-2015); Assistant County Manager, Clark County, NV (2002-2006); Assistant U.S. Attorney, U.S. Department of Justice, Washington, DC (2000-2002); Chief of Staff to Governor Bob Miller, State of Nevada, Carson City, NV (1998-2000); Legislative Assistant to Governor Bob Miller, State of Nevada, Carson City, NV (1995-1998); Associate, Raleigh, Hunt & McGarry, PC, Las Vegas, NV (1991-1995); Law Clerk to the Honorable Michael J. Wendell, Eighth Judicial District Court, Clark County, NV (1990-1991) **CR:** Member, Supreme Court of Nevada; Member, Court Funding Commission; Member, Southern Nevada Domestic Violence Court Task Force **BAR:** United States Court of Appeals for the Ninth Circuit (1994); United States District Court for the District of Nevada (1991); Nevada (1990) **AV:** Hiking; Appreciating nature **PA:** Democrat

CORYELL, DANIEL CAROLL, T: Minister **I:** Religious **DOB:** 12/25/1951 **PB:** Oakland **SC:** CA/USA **PT:** Carroll Clifford Coryell; Carmel Juanita (Loggins) Coryell **MS:** Single **ED:** Teaching Credential, University of California Berkeley, CA (1979); BA, Patten College (now Patten University) (1976) **CT:** Ordained Minister, Evangelical Church Alliance (1989); Commercial Radio-Telephone License; Licensed Radio Amateur, Federal Communications Commission **C:** Deputy Sheriff (1995-2000); Chaplain, Alameda County Sheriffs Department (1990-2000); Volunteer, Protestant Chaplain San Quentin State Prison (1988-1990); Consultant Firm; Guest Lecturer, Instructor, Martial Arts, YMCA; Owner, President, Dan Coryell Associates; President, Chief Financial Officer, Corporate Operations, CWE Systems, Inc., Oakland, CA (1980-1990); Corporate Director, CWE Systems, Inc., Oakland, CA (1979-1990); Instructor, Broadcast Arts, TV Production Services, Patten College (1979-1990); Chief Engineer, TV Production Services, Patten College (1973-1990); Disk Jockey, Station KFMR-FM (1972-1973) **CR:** Director, Church Television Ministry **CIV:** Salvation Army Emergency Disaster Services **MIL:** Captain, Civil Air Patrol, Para-military Organization; United States Air Force Auxiliary (1996) **CW:** Technical Director, Film, "The Impossible Dream," Filmed on Location in Israel (1975) **AW:** Recipient, Black Belt, TaeKwonDo (1981); Founders Medal, CECA (1980); Heart Award, Patten College (1978); Recipient, Black Belt, Ju-Jitsu (1970) **MEM:** Society of Professional Journalists; National Sheriffs Association; National Association of Evangelists; American Protestant Correctional Chaplains Association; American Correctional Association; Society of Broadcast Engineers; Society of Motion Picture & TV Engineers; American Entrepreneurs Association; National Academy of Arts & Sciences; American Judo & Ju Jitsu Federation; World Taekwondo Federation **MH:** Albert Nelson Marquis Lifetime Achievement Award **AS:** He attributes his success to his faith in God and his father and mothers examples of selfless service to others. **B/I:** His first major in college was journalism and television production arts, he was always interested in writing. His father, Carroll Clifford Coryell, an ordained minister as well as an electronics engineer, was a great influence on Mr. Coryell, which encouraged him to get into technical fields around media, which he found he had a natural aptitude for.

CORZO, JUAN JR., T: Vice President **I:** Business Management/Business Services **CN:** South Florida Tissue Paper Co. **DOB:** 11/14/1987 **PB:** Guatemala City **SC:** Guatemala **PT:** Juan Corzo; Maria Spillari **ED:** Degree in Production Management, New York City College of Technology (2013); The City College of New York (2008) **C:** Vice President, South

Florida Tissue Paper Co. (2015-Present) **AW:** Top 5000 Fastest Growing Companies in the United States (2016-2018); Recognition, Article, Business Journal; Recognition, Article, Miami Herald Newspaper; Recognition, Forbes Magazine **AS:** Mr. Corzo attributes his success to his education, availability and reliability. **B/I:** Mr. Corzo became involved in his profession because he has an infatuation with manufacturing and, from a young age, wanted to know how things worked. **RE:** Christian

COSTA, JAMES, "JIM" MANUEL, T: U.S. Representative from California **I:** Government Administration/Government Relations/Government Services **DOB:** 04/13/1952 **PB:** Fresno **SC:** CA/USA **ED:** BA in Political Science, California State University, Fresno, CA (1974) **C:** Member, U.S. House of Representatives from California's 16th Congressional District (2013-Present); Member, U.S. House of Representatives from California's 20th Congressional District, Washington, DC (2005-2013); Chief Executive Officer, Costa Group (2002-2004); Member, District 16, California State Senate (1994-2002); Member, District 30, California State Assembly (1978-1994); Administrative Assistant to Representative Richard Lehman, California State Assembly (1976-1978); Special Assistant to Representative John Krebs, U.S. House of Representatives (1975-1976); Committee on Intelligence; Committee on Armed Services **CR:** Senate Representative, California World Trade Commission (1995-2004); President, National Conference of State Legislatures (2000-2001); Co-Founder, Co-Chair, Congressional Victims' Rights Caucus; Co-Founder, Congressional Water Caucus; Blue Dog Coalition **CIV:** Board Member, Fresno-Madera Agency on Aging **MEM:** Board of Directors, Fresno Historical Society; Steering Committee, Fresno County Farm Bureau; Fresno Cabrillo Club **PA:** Democrat **RE:** Roman Catholic

COSTNER, KEVIN MICHAEL, T: Actor **I:** Media & Entertainment **DOB:** 1/18/1955 **PB:** Lynwood **SC:** CA/USA **PT:** William Costner; Sharon Rae (Tedrick) Costner **MS:** Married **SPN:** Christine Baumgartner (2004); Cindy Silva (1978, Divorced 1994) **CH:** Annie; Lily; Joe; Liam; Cayden Wyatt; Hayes Logan; Grace Avery **ED:** Bachelor of Arts in Marketing and Finance, California State University, Fullerton (1978) **C:** Owner, Midnight Star Casino, Deadwood, SD; Singer, Guitarist, Modern West; Owner, TIG Productions **CW:** Actor, Executive Producer, "Yellowstone" (2018-Present); Actor, "Let Him Go" (2020); Voice Actor, "The Art of Racing in the Rain" (2019); Actor, "The Highwaymen" (2019); Actor, "Molly's Game" (2017); Actor, "Criminal" (2016); Actor, "Batman v Superman: Dawn of Justice" (2016); Actor, "Hidden Figures" (2016); Actor, "McFarland, USA" (2015); Actor, Producer, "Black or White" (2014); Actor, "Jack Ryan: Shadow Recruit" (2014); Actor, "Draft Day" (2014); Actor, "3 Days to Kill" (2014); Actor, "Man of Steel" (2013); Actor, "Three Days to Kill" (2013); Actor, "Hatfields & McCoys" (2012); Actor, "The Company Men" (2010); Actor, "The New Daughter" (2009); Actor, "Swing Vote" (2008); Singer, Guitarist, "Untold Truths" (2008); Actor, "Mr. Brooks" (2007); Actor, "The Guardian" (2006); Actor, "The Upside of Anger" (2005); Actor, "Rumor Has It..." (2005); Actor, Director, Producer, "Open Range" (2003); Actor, "Dragonfly" (2002); Actor, "3,000 Miles to Graceland" (2001); Actor, Producer, "Thirteen Days" (2000); Actor, Producer, "Message in a Bottle" (1999); Actor, "For Love of the Game" (1999); Actor, "Play It to the Bone" (1999); Actor, Director, Producer, "The Postman" (1997); Actor, "Tin Cup" (1996); Actor, Producer, "Waterworld" (1995); Executive Producer, "Rapa Nui" (1994); Actor, Producer, "Wyatt Earp" (1994); Actor, "The War" (1994); Actor, "A Perfect World"

(1993); Co-producer, "China Moon" (1993); Actor, "The Bodyguard" (1992); Actor, "JFK" (1991); Actor, Producer, "Robin Hood: Prince of Thieves" (1991); Actor, Producer, "Revenge" (1990); Actor, Director, Producer, "Dances with Wolves" (1990); Actor, "Field of Dreams" (1989); Actor, "Bull Durham" (1988); Actor, "The Untouchables" (1987); Actor, "No Way Out" (1987); Actor, Producer, "Amazing Stories" (1985); Actor, "American Flyers" (1985); Actor, "Fandango" (1985); Actor, "Silverado" (1985); Actor, "Testament" (1983); Actor, "Table for Five" (1983); Actor, "Stacy's Knights" (1983); Actor, "The Gunrunner" (1983); Actor, "The Big Chill" (1983); Actor, "Frances" (1982); Actor, "Night Shift" (1982); Actor, "Shadows Run Black" (1981); Actor, "Chasing Dreams" (1981); Actor, "Sizzle Beach U.S.A." (1974); Host, Executive Producer, "500 Nations"; Actor, Television Shows, Films **AW:** Inductee, Hall of Great Western Performers, National Cowboy & Western Heritage Museum, Oklahoma City, OK (2019); Golden Globe Award for Best Performance by an Actor in a Miniseries or Motion Picture Made for Television, Hollywood Foreign Press Association (2013); Screen Actors Guild Award for Outstanding Performance by a Male Actor in a TV Movie or Miniseries, Screen Actors Guild - American Federation of Television and Radio Artists (2013); Emmy Award for Outstanding Lead Actor in a Miniseries or Movie, Academy of Television Arts & Sciences (2012); Star, Hollywood Walk of Fame (2003); Inductee, World of Little League Hall of Excellence (2000); Academy Awards for Best Director, Best Picture, Academy of Motion Picture Arts and Sciences (1991); Award for Best Director of a Feature Film, Directors Guild of America (1991); Screen Actors Guild Award for Outstanding Performance by a Cast, Screen Actors Guild - American Federation of Television and Radio Artists (1991); Named, Hasty Pudding Man of the Year, Hasty Pudding Theatricals, Harvard University (1990); Star of Tomorrow Award, National Association Theatre Owners (1987) **MEM:** The Delta Chi Fraternity

COTILLARD, MARION, T: Actress **I:** Media & Entertainment **DOB:** 09/30/1975 **PB:** Paris **SC:** France **PT:** Jean-Claude Cotillard; Niseema Theillaud **CH:** Marcel **CR:** Spokesperson, Greenpeace International **CW:** Actress, "Ismael's Ghosts" (2017); Actress, "It's Only the End of the World" (2016); Actress, "From the Land of the Moon" (2016); Actress, "Allied" (2016); Actress, "Assassin's Creed" (2016); Voice Actress, "The Little Prince" (2015); Actress, "Macbeth" (2015); Voice Actress, "April and the Extraordinary World" (2015); Actress, "Castings" (2015); Actress, "Comedy Central's All- Star Non-Denominational Christmas Special" (2014); Actress, "Two Days, One Night" (2014); Actress, "Blood Ties" (2013); Actress, "The Immigrant" (2013); Actress, "Anchorman 2: The Legend Continues" (2013); Actress, "Le Debarquement" (2013); Actress, "Jeanne d'Arc au Bûcher" (2012); Actress, "Rust & Bone" (2012); Actress, "The Dark Knight Rises" (2012); Actress, "Midnight in Paris" (2011); Actress, "Contagion" (2011); Actress, "Inception" (2010); Actress, "Little White Lies" (2010); Actress, "Nine" (2009); Actress, "La Vie en Rose" (2007); Actress, "Toi et Moi" (2006); Actress, "Dikkenek" (2006); Actress, "Fair Play" (2006); Actress, "A Good Year" (2006); Actress, "Cavalcade" (2005); Actress, "Edy" (2005); Actress, "Ma vie en l'air" (2005); Actress, "Mary" (2005); Actress, "Burnt Out" (2005); Actress, "La Boîte Noire" (2005); Actress, "Innocence" (2004); Actress, "A Very Long Engagement" (2004); Actress, "Taxi 3" (2003); Actress, "Love Me If You Dare" (2003); Actress, "Big Fish" (2003); Actress, "A Private Affair" (2002); Actress, "Heureuse" (2001); Actress, "Boomer" (2001); Actress, "Une Femme

Piégée" (2001); Actress, "Lisa" (2001); Actress, "Pretty Things" (2001); Actress, "Quelques Jours de Trop" (2000); Actress, "Le Marquis" (2000); Actress, "Taxi 2" (2000); Actress, "War in the Highlands" (1999); Actress, "Furia" (1999); Actress, "L'Appel de la cave" (1999); Actress, "Blue Away to America" (1999); Actress, "Taxi" (1998); Actress, "Interdit de Vieillir" (1998); Actress, "My Sex Life... Or How I Got Into an Argument" (1996); Actress, "La Belle Verte" (1996); Actress, "Snuff Movie" (1995); Actress, "The Story of a Boy Who Wanted to Be Kissed" (1994) **AW:** Chevalier, Order of Arts and Letters, French Government (2010); Best Performance by an Actress in a Motion Picture-Musical or Comedy, Golden Globe Awards (2008); Best Leading Actress, British Academy of Film and TV Awards (2008); Best Actress in a Leading Role, Academy Awards (2008); Best Actress, LA Film Critics Association (2007); Best Actress, Boston Society Film Critics (2007); Best Actress, African American Film Critics Association (2007); Chopard Trophy, Cannes Film Festival (2004)

COTTON, THOMAS, "TOM" BRYANT, T: U.S. Senator from Arkansas **I:** Government Administration/Government Relations/Government Services **DOB:** 05/13/1977 **PB:** Dardanelle **SC:** AK/USA **PT:** Thomas Leonard Cotton; Avis (Bryant) Cotton **MS:** Married **SPN:** Anna Peckham (03/15/2014) **CH:** Two Children **ED:** JD, Harvard Law School (2002); BA in Government, Harvard College (1999); Coursework, Claremont Graduate University **C:** U.S. Senator, State of Arkansas (2015-Present); Committee on Foreign Affairs (2013-Present); U.S. House Committee on Foreign Services (2013-2015); U.S. House Committee on Financial Services (2013-2015); U.S. House of Representatives from Arkansas' Fourth Congressional District, United States Congress, Washington, DC (2013-2015); Management Consultant, McKinsey & Company (2010-2011); Associate, Gibson, Dunn & Crutcher LLP (2003-2005); Law Clerk to Honorable Jerry Edwin Smith, United States Court of Appeals for the Fifth Circuit (2002-2003) **MIL:** Captain, United States Army (2013); United States Army Reserve (2009-2013); 101st Airborne Division, United States Army (2005-2009); 101st Airborne Division, United States Army, Afghanistan (2008); 101st Airborne Division, United States Army, Iraq (2006) **AW:** Decorated Army Commendation Medal; Combat Infantryman Badge; Ranger Tab; Bronze Star, U.S. Army; Parachutist Badge; Air Assault Badge; Afghanistan Campaign Medal; Iraq Campaign Medal **PA:** Republican **RE:** Methodist

COUCH, JOHN ALEXANDER, PHD, T: Research Biologist **I:** Sciences **DOB:** 02/12/1938 **PB:** Washington **SC:** DC/USA **PT:** Raymond Carl Couch; Rubye Frances (Wates) Couch **MS:** Married **SPN:** Carolyn Barrett Couch (1963) **CH:** Catherine Couch Brooks; John Alexander Couch, Jr. **ED:** PhD, Florida State University, Tallahassee, FL (1971); MS, Florida State University, Tallahassee, FL (1964); BS, University of Alabama, Tuscaloosa, AL (1961) **CT:** Certificate of Aquanaut Training, Department of Interior (1970) **C:** Senior Research Scientist, U.S. Environmental Protection Agency (EPA), Gulf Breeze, FL (1987-1996); Branch Chief, Pathobiology, U.S. Environmental Protection Agency (EPA), Gulf Breeze, FL (1985-1990); Research Biologist, U.S. Environmental Protection Agency (EPA), Gulf Breeze, FL (1971-1987); Coordinator, Interagency Research Program, NCI/Environmental Protection Agency (EPA) (1978-1982); Research Biologist, National Oceanic and Atmospheric Administration (NOAA), Oxford, MD (1964-1971) **CR:** Speaker, "The Use of Small Fishes in Carcinogenicity Testing," National Cancer Institute, Bethesda, MD (1981), Speaker, "Phyletic Approaches to Cancer," Princess Taka-

matsu Research Fund and National Cancer Center, Tokyo, Japan (1980), Speaker, National Academy of Sciences Symposium's "Pathobiology of Environmental Pollutants," Storrs, CT (1977); Speaker, III International Congress of Virology, Madrid, Spain (1975); Speaker, International Union Against Cancer, Special Symposium, Cork, Ireland (1974); Speaker, VI International Meeting of Society for Invertebrate Pathology, Oxford, England (1973); Speaker, Man-in-the-Sea Symposium, Marshal Space Flight Center, NASA, Huntsville, AL (1971); Speaker, Symposium on Tumors in Lower Animals, National Cancer Institute, Washington, DC (1968); Expert Witness, Court Trial on Mass Mortality of Marine Organisms, Santa Rosa County Court, FL (1972); Expert Witness, Numerous Court Trials **CW:** Author, Major Review of Known Penaeid Shrimp Diseases, Both Infectious and Non-Infectious (1978); Invited Speaker, Symposium on Diseases of Crustacea, AIBS-SIP, Amherst, MA (1973); Invited Speaker, Silver Anniversary Symposium, AIBS-Society for Invertebrate Pathology, Minneapolis, MN (1972); Invited Speaker, Mississippi State NSF Teacher's Summer Course, Southern Mississippi University, Hattiesburg, MS (1972); Invited Speaker, Man-in-the-Sea Symposium, Marshal Space Flight Center, NASA, Huntsville, AL (1971); Invited Speaker, Symposium on Tumors in Lower Animals, National Cancer Institute, Washington, DC (1968); Invited Speaker, Chairman, Organizer, Expert Witness, Numerous International, National, Regional Meetings; Contributor, Numerous Articles, Professional Journals; Associate Editor, Journal of Aquatic Animal Health; Reviewer, Aquatic Toxicology; Reviewer, Journal of Parasitology; Reviewer, Journal of the National Cancer Institute; Reviewer, Journal of Toxicology and Environment Health; Reviewer, Cancer Research **AW:** Sustained Superior Performance Award (1992); Recipient, Numerous Scientific and Technological Awards for Scientific Writing (1981-1982, 1968-1987, 1989, 1991-1993); Recipient, Numerous U.S. Environmental Protection Agency (EPA) Awards for Scientific Publications **MEM:** Trustee, Society for Invertebrate Pathology (1985); Editorial Board, Journal of Invertebrate Pathology (1980-1983); International Union of Biological Sciences Advisory Board; Steering Committee for Program on Bioindicators (Physiology and Biochemistry); American Men and Women of Science; Board of Editors, Diseases of Aquatic Organisms; Gulf Estuarine Research Society; Southeastern Electron Microscopy Society; American Fisheries Society; Society of Sigma Xi **MH:** Albert Nelson Marquis Lifetime Achievement Award **B/I:** Dr. Couch became involved in his profession because, as a youth, he had a keen interest in nature, as he spent time exploring the woods and fields of his grandfather's Alabama farm. He became interested in biological science studies because of this early childhood curiosity and especially so after his family relocated to the Gulf Coast of Florida. He had opportunities to explore the Gulf Coast's boundless sea life, both along the shore and under the gulf waters. He became an experienced self-taught snorkeler and scuba diver, later exploring underwater caves and springs near Tallahassee, Florida when studying for his master's degree in biological science at Florida State University. While he was a student there, he was trusted to use his scuba gear to dive in Wakulla Springs to clean the water filters at the mouth of the underwater cave. From the beginning of his college studies, Dr. Couch was fortunate to take mentorship from excellent teachers and professors. When starting his full-time professional career at Oxford Maryland Laboratory (NOAA), he had great opportunities to collaborate with high-quality scientists in his related fields of interest, including parasitology, marine biology,

pathology of aquatic organisms, and underseas research. Having been an experienced scuba diver, he was selected as a scientist aquanaut for the Man-in-the-Sea experiment, Tektite II, sponsored by NASA, the Department of the Interior, the U.S. Navy, and other federal agencies. General Electric built the habitat. After transferring to the U.S. Gulf Breeze Environmental Research Lab, Dr. Couch became involved in environmental research with toxicology and pathologies of aquatic organisms. **AV:** Reading; Fishing; Family boating; Traveling; Visiting American History sites

COULTER, ANN HART, T: Writer, Political Columnist, Lawyer **I:** Law and Legal Services **DOB:** 12/08/1961 **PB:** New York **SC:** NY/USA **PT:** John Vincent Coulter; Nell Husabands (Martin) Coulter **ED:** JD, University of Michigan Law School (1988); BA in History, Cornell University, Cum Laude (1985) **C:** Political Commentator, MSNBC (1996); With, Senator Spencer Abraham, US Senate Judiciary Committee, Michigan (1994-1996); Law Clerk to Hon. Pasco Bowman II, Eighth Circuit, US Court Appeals, Kansas City (1989); Legal Affairs Correspondent, Human Events; Litigator, Center for Individual Rights, Washington, DC; Corporate Lawyer, Private Practice, New York, NY; Attorney, US Department Justice Honors Program for Outstanding Law School Graduates **CR:** Writer, Weekly to Occasional Columns, Human Events (1998-2003); Contributing Editor, Syndicated Columnist, National Review Online (2001); Regular Columnist, George Magazine (1999); Guest, "The Today Show, Piers Morgan"; Guest, "The Early Show"; Guest, "The Tonight Show with Jay Leno"; Guest, "Entertainment Tonight"; Guest, "Hannity"; Guest, "Fox & Friends"; Guest, "Dr. Drew"; Guest, "The Glen Beck Show"; Guest, "Real Time with Bill Maher"; Guest, "The Leeza Show"; Guest, "Good Morning America"; Guest, "This Week", ABC"; Guest, "Crossfire"; Guest, "American Morning with Paula Zahn"; Guest, "The O'Reilly Factor"; Guest, "Hannity and Colmes"; Guest, "Larry King Live"; Legal Correspondent, "Politically Incorrect"Syndicated Column Writer, Universal Press Syndicate **CW:** Author, "Adios America: The Left's Plan to Turn Our Country into a Third World Hellhole" (2015); Author, "Never Trust a Liberal Over Three-Especially a Republican" (2013); Author, "Mugged: Racial Demagoguery from the Seventies to Obama" (2012); Author, "Demonic: How the Liberal Mob is Endangering America" (2011); Author, "Guilty: Liberal 'Victims' and Their Assault on America" (2009); Author, "If Democrats Had Any Brains, They'd Be Republicans" (2007); Author, "Godless: The Church of Liberalism" (2006); Author, "How to Talk to a Liberal (If You Must): The World According to Ann Coulter" (2004); Author, "Treason: Liberal Treachery From the Cold War to the War on Terrorism" (2003); Author, "Slander: Liberal Lies About the American Right" (2002); Author, "High Crimes and Misdemeanors: The Case Against Bill Clinton" (1998) **AW:** 50 Highest-Earning Political Figures, Newsweek (2010); The 100 Most Influential People in the World, "TIME" (2005); Top 100 Public Intellectuals (2001) **PA:** Republican

COURIC, KATIE ANNE, T: Broadcast Journalist **I:** Media & Entertainment **DOB:** 01/07/1957 **PB:** Arlington **SC:** VA/USA **PT:** John Martin Couric; Elinor Tullie (Hene) Couric **MS:** Married **SPN:** John Molner (2014); John Paul (Jay) Monahan III (1989, Deceased 1998) **CH:** Elinor Tully Monahan; Caroline Couric Monahan **ED:** Honorary Doctor of Humane Letters, Boston University (2011); Honorary Doctor of Science, Case Western Reserve University, Cleveland, Ohio (2010); Bachelor of Arts in American Studies, University of Virginia (1979) **C:** Founder, Katie Couric Media (2017-Present); Global Anchor, Yahoo News and ABC News, Sunnyvale, CA (2014-2017); Host, "Katie" (2012-2014); Guest Co-host, "Good Morning America" (2012); Special Correspondent, ABC News (2011-2013); Correspondent, "60 Minutes," CBS Evening News (2006-2011); Anchor, Managing Editor, CBS Evening News, New York, NY (2006-2011); Co-host, "Today," NBC News (1991-2006); National Political Correspondent, Substitute Anchor, "The Today Show," NBC News (1989-1991); Deputy Pentagon Correspondent, NBC News, Washington, DC (1989); Reporter, WRC-TV, Washington, DC (1987-1989); General Assignment Reporter, WTVJ, Miami, FL (1984-1986); Desk Assistant, ABC News, Washington, DC (1979); Assignment Editor, Cable News Network, Atlanta, GA **CR:** Contributing Anchor, "Dateline NBC" (1994-2006); Co-host, Live Coverage, Macy's Thanksgiving Day Parade, NBC (1991-2005); Substitute Anchor, Sunday Edition, "NBC Nightly News" (1989-1993) **CIV:** Co-founder, National Colorectal Cancer Research Alliance (1999); Goodwill Ambassador, UNICEF **CW:** Executive Producer, "Flint" (2017); Executive Producer, "Gender Revolution" (2017); Executive Producer, "Fed Up" (2014); Appearance, "General Hospital" (2013); Appearance, "Glee" (2011); Author, "The Best Advice I Ever Got: Lessons from Extraordinary Lives" (2011); Author, "The Blue Ribbon Day" (2004); Voice Actress, "Shark Tale" (2004); Appearance, "Will & Grace" (2002); Appearance, "Austin Powers in Goldmember" (2002); Author, "The Brand New Kid" (2000); Appearance, "Cheers" (1993); Appearance, "Murphy Brown" (1992); Appearances, Television Shows, Films **AW:** Shorty Award for Best Journalist (2016); Emmy Award, National Academy of Television Arts & Sciences (1999-2000, 2004, 2014); Named, One of the 100 Most Powerful Women in Entertainment, The Hollywood Reporter (2012); Named, One of the 100 Most Powerful Women, Forbes Magazine (2010); Walter Cronkite Award for Journalism Excellence (2009); Gracie Allen Award, Alliance for Women in Media and Foundation (2009); Emmy Governor's Award (2009); Named, One of the 100 Most Powerful Women, Forbes Magazine (2005-2008); Named, One of the 100 Most Influential People in the World, TIME Magazine (2006); Golden Plate Award, Academy of Achievement (2006); Inductee, Television Hall of Fame (2005); Julius B. Richmond Award, Harvard School of Public Health (2003); Named, Wow Woman of the Year, Glamour Magazine (2002); Named, One of the 25 Most Intriguing People, People Magazine (2001); Named, News Person of the Year, TV Guide (2001); Peabody Award (2001); Named, Woman of the Year, Glamour Magazine (1992); Sigma Delta Chi Award, National Society Professional Journalists; Award, The Associated Press; Matrix Award; National Headliner Award; Numerous Awards

COURTNEY, JOSEPH, "JOE" DARREN, T: U.S. Representative **I:** Government Administration/Government Relations/Government Services **DOB:** 04/16/1953 **PB:** Hartford **SC:** CT/USA **PT:** Robert Edward Courtney; Dorothy (Kane) Courtney **MS:** Married **SPN:** Audrey Courtney **CH:** Robert; Elizabeth **ED:** JD, University of Connecticut School of Law (1978); BA, Tufts University (1975) **C:** U.S. Representative, Connecticut's Second Congressional District, United States Congress (2006-Present); Member, 56th District, Connecticut General Assembly (1987-1994); Assistant Public Defender, Rockville Superior Court (1979-1981); Member, Armed Services Committee; Member, Committee on Energy and Labor, Connecticut's Second Congressional District, United States Congress; Town Attorney, Vernon, CT; Partner, Courtney, Boyan & Foran, LLC **CR:** Connecticut Coordinator, John Edwards Campaign (2004) **AW:** Democrat Most Admired by Republicans, Connecticut Magazine (1994) **PA:** Democrat

COUTINHO, CHARLES PHD, T: Managing Director **I:** Real Estate **CN:** Coutinho Properties **DOB:** 06/03/1963 **PB:** New York **SC:** NY/USA **PT:** Maria Coutinho; J. D. Coutinho **MS:** Married **SPN:** Anna **CH:** Alexander **ED:** PhD in History, New York University (1997); MA in History, New York University (1989) **C:** Managing Director, Coutinho Properties (1997-Present) **CR:** President, Sutton Area Community (2017-Present) **CIV:** Board, Sutton Area Community; Real Estate Board of New York **CW:** "International Affairs of Aurelie Basha i Novosejt's 'I made mistakes': Robert McNamara's Vietnam policy, 1960-1968" (2020); "Jonathan Fennell's 'Fighting the Peoples War: British and Commonwealth Armies and the Second World War'" (2020)'; "International Affairs of Kori Schake's 'Safe Passage': the Transition from British to American Hegemony" (2019); "Peter Hitchen's 'The Phoney Victory: the World War II Illusion'" (2019); "Christopher Lee's 'Carrington: An Honorable Man'" (2019); "The Lion and the Eagle: The interaction of the British and American Empires" (2019); "The Failure to Prevent World War I: the unexpected Armageddon" (2018); "Neil Ferguson's biography of Henry Kissinger" (2018); "Simon Kerry's 'Lansdowne: the last Great Whig'" (2018); Contributor, "David Cannadeine: The Victorious Century," "Cercle" (2018); Contributor, "Cercle" (2013); Contributor, "Reviews in History" (2013); "The Perfect Diplomat", Joaquim Nabuco e o Novo Brasil (2011) **AW:** 'Our Town Thanks You' Award, Our Town Newspaper (2020) **MEM:** Metropolitan Opera Club; The Amateur Comedy Club; The Royal United Services Institute; The National Arts Club; The Royal Historical Society; The Royal Institute of International Affairs; The Lotos Club **AS:** Dr. Coutinho attributes his success to talent, ingenuity, and circumstances. **B/I:** Dr. Coutinho's father was an academic for a portion of his life, so his interests came from that. Likewise, his property management company was a family-owned business in which he took a great interest, which inspired his career. **AV:** Podcasting on "New Book Network"; Watching opera and ballet; Writing book reviews; Reading **RE:** Roman Catholic **THT:** Dr. Coutinho maintains his faith in God, as, to him, it is the clearest duty of man.

COX, DAVID BRUMMAL, T: Accounting Firm Executive **I:** Consulting **DOB:** 03/29/1940 **PB:** Campbellsville **SC:** KY/USA **PT:** Henry Alfred Cox; Jennye Elizabeth (Penick) Cox **MS:** Married **SPN:** Mary Jennings Randolph (06/30/1962) **CH:** Stephen Brooke; Tyler Randolph; Sarah Wakefield **ED:** MBA, University of Michigan (1962); BBA, University of Michigan (1961) **CT:** Certified Public Accountant, State of Kentucky (1965) **C:** Retired (2018); Consultant, David B. Cox CPA (1989-2018); Partner, Energy Tax Services, National Tax Department, Ernst & Whinney (Now EY) Washington, DC (1981-1989); Ernst & Whinney, (Now EY), Louisville KY (1969-1980); Ernst & Whinney, (Now EY), Washington, DC (1968-1969); Ernst & Ernst, Louisville, KY (1962-1967) **CR:** Frequent Speaker, Various Tax Institutes and Energy Resources Tax Meetings; Testimony on Proposed Regulations, IRS National Office; Continuing Professional Education Instructor, Various State CPA Societies; Lecturer, Adjunct Instructor, MBA Program, The University of Tennessee; Lecturer, Adjunct Instructor, Undergraduate and Graduate Programs, Tusculum University; Advisory Board, International Oil and Gas Educational Center, Southwestern Legal Foundation; Editorial Board, Oil and Gas Tax Quarterly **MIL:** U.S. Army Reserve (1967-1975) **CW:** Author, Editor, "The Coal Industry" (1988); Author, Editor, "Energy Resources Tax Reporter" (1983); Contributor, Articles, Professional Journals; Concertmaster, University Symphony Orchestra, University of Louisville; Concertmaster, Orchestras, University of Michigan; Concertmaster, Cincinnati Conservatory Summer Orchestra; Music Teachers National Association **AW:** Highest Score, Kentucky Society of Certified Public Accountants (1964) **MEM:** Current: American Institute of Certified Public Accountants; Prior: Officer, Board of Directors, Committee Chairman, Kentucky Society of Certified Public Accountants; Knoxville Tax Committee, Tennessee Society of Certified Public Accountants **MH:** Albert Nelson Marquis Lifetime Achievement Award **AS:** Faith, family, friends, good teachers, and the desire and competitive drive to become the very best in his chosen fields. **B/I:** Mr. Cox's father, a successful Certified Public Accountant, encouraged him to major in business and seriously consider an accounting career. **AV:** Hunting; Shooting; Fishing **PA:** Republican **RE:** Methodist **THT:** Your family and friends are blessings from God. They are more important than anything else you do or have.

COX, JEROME, "JERRY" JR., T: Electrical Engineer, Cybersecurity Provider **I:** Telecommunications **CN:** Q-Net Security, Inc. **DOB:** 05/24/1925 **PB:** Washington **SC:** DC/USA **PT:** Jerome R. Cox; Jane (Mills) Cox **MS:** Widowed **SPN:** Barbara Jane Lueders Cox (09/02/1951) **CH:** Nancy Battersby; Jerome M. Cox; Randall A. Cox **ED:** Honorary ScD, Washington University in St. Louis, MO (2001); ScD, Massachusetts Institute of Technology (1954); MS, Massachusetts Institute of Technology (1949); BS, Massachusetts Institute of Technology (1947) **C:** Co-founder, MultiEars, LLC, St. Louis, MO (2015-Present); Founder, President, Q-Net Security, Inc. (2015-Present); Founder, Chief Executive Officer, Blendics (2007-Present); Senior Professor, Computer Science, Washington University in St. Louis (1999-Present); Vice President, Growth Networks (1999-2000); Professor, Bio-Medicine, Institute for Biomedical Computing, Washington University in St. Louis (1983-2000); Professor, Biomedical Engineering, Physiology and Biophysics, Washington University School of Medicine (1965-2000); Professor, Electrical Engineering, Washington University, St. Louis (1961-1999); Harold B. and Adelaide G. Welge Professor of Computer Science, Washington University in St. Louis (1989-1998); Director, Applied Research Laboratory, Washington University in St. Louis (1991-1995); Faculty, Washington University in St. Louis (1955-1991); Chairman, Department of Computer Science, Washington University in St. Louis (1975-1991); Chairman, Computer Laboratories, Washington University in St. Louis (1967-1983); Program Director, Training Program in Technology, Health Care, Washington University in St. Louis (1970-1978); Director, Biomedical Computer Laboratory, Washington University in St. Louis (1964-1975); Assistant Professor, Electrical Engineering, Washington University in St. Louis (1955-1958); With, Liberty Mutual Research Laboratory, Hopkington, MA (1952-1955); Consultant, Acoustics, Bolt Beranek and Newman, Inc. (Now Raytheon Company) (1949-1952) **CR:** Consultant, Gateway Venture Partners, L.P., St. Louis, MO (1985-1991); Computer Science and Engineering Research, Panel on Applications (1975-1977); Epidemiology, Biostatistics, and Bioengineering Cluster, President's Biomedical Research Panel (1975-1976); Chairman, Founder, Computers in Cardiology Conference (1974-1976) **CIV:** Board of Directors, Central Institute for the Deaf (1993-Present); Board of Directors, Mass Sensors, Inc. (2000-2004) **MIL:** With, United States Army (1943-1944) **CW:** Editorial Board, Applied

Mathematics Letters (1987-2005); Editorial Board, Computers and Biomedical Research (1967-1998); Editorial Board, IEEE Computer Society Press (1982-1984); Associate Editor, IEEE Transactions on Biomedical Engineering (1969-1971); Editorial Board, Noise Control (1955-1961); Inventor, Patents, Air Traffic Control; Inventor, Patent, Computerized Tomography; Inventor, Patents, Medical Display Technology; Inventor, Patents, Network Traffic Pacing; Designer, Cybersecurity Systems **AW:** Lifetime Achievement Award, Academy of Science of St. Louis (2001); William Greenleaf Eliot Society Search Award, Washington University in St. Louis (1997); William Phillips Technology and Development Award, St. Louis County Economic Council (1995); Distinguished Faculty Award, Washington University in St. Louis (1987); Fellow, National Academy of Inventors **MEM:** Board of Advisors, Appistry, Inc., St. Louis, MO (2003-2006); Technical Advisory Board, Cernium, Inc., St. Louis, MO (2001-2006); Board of Trustees, St. Louis Academy of Science (1998-1999); Board of Directors, Academy of Science of St. Louis (1997-1999); PROPHET Advisory Panel, National Institutes of Health (1983-1998); Member-at-large, Senate Council, Washington University in St. Louis (1997); National Advisory Council, Human Genome Research, National Institutes of Health (1990-1995); Fellow, Evaluation Committee, Computer Society, IEEE (1994); Computer Center Peer Review Panel, National Institutes of Health (1989-1992); Advisory Committee, Harvard-MIT Division of Health Sciences and Technology, Cambridge, MA (1988-1992); Co-chairman, Demonstrations, IEEE Computer Society (1990-1991); National Neural Circuitry Database Committee, Institute of Medicine, National Academy of Sciences (1989-1991); Treasurer, Association for Advanced Technology in the Biomedical Sciences (1981-1991); Genome Database Scientific Advisory Committee, Howard Hughes Medical Institute (1989-1990); Committee on Study of Patient Record, Technology Subcommittee, Institute of Medicine, National Academy of Sciences (1989); Consultant, Human Gene Mapping, Howard Hughes Medical Institute, Bethesda, MD (1988); Chairman, Division of Computer Research and Technology Review Committee, National Institutes of Health (1983-1984); Tri-Services Medical Information Systems Review Group (1978-1979); CLINFO Ad Hoc Review Group, National Institutes of Health (1976-1979); Chairman, Biomedical Engineering Panel, National Institutes of General Medical Sciences (NIGMS) (1977-1978); Cardiology Advisory Committee, National Heart and Lung Institute (Now Heart, Lung, and Blood Institute) (1975-1978); Research Evaluation Committee, Veterans Administration (1969-1972); Member National Academy of Medicine (1971); Advisory Committee, Jet Propulsion Laboratory (1969-1971); Engineering in Biology and Medicine Training Committee, National Institute of General Medical Sciences (NIGMS) (1969-1971); National Advisory Research Resources Committee, National Institutes of Health (1965-1969); Study Section on Computer Research, National Institutes of Health (1962-1965); Advisory Panel, Specialized Biological Facilities, National Science Foundation (1961-1969); Chairman, Sectional Committee, S1, Physical Acoustics, American Standards Association (Now American National Standards Institute (ANSI)) (1960-1962); Committee on Hearing and Bio-Acoustics, Armed Forces, National Research Council (1955-1961); Institute of Medicine; The Tau Beta Pi Association, Inc.; IEEE - Eta Kappa Nu; Sigma Xi, The Scientific Research Honor Society; American College of Medical Informatics; Acoustical Society of America; National Academy of Sciences; Institute of Electrical and Electronics Engineers (IEEE) **MH:** Albert Nelson Marquis Lifetime Achievement Award **AS:** Dr. Cox attributes his success to persistence and a thirst for adventure. **B/I:** Dr. Cox became involved in his profession because when he was 11 years old, he took a radio apart and was fascinated by the parts inside. He wanted to know more about them. He then decided to go to a ham radio store and bought an American Radio Relay League handbook, which taught him about electronics. Again, he was fascinated, which resulted in that crucial moment that guided his path to success; Dr. Cox decided to pursue electrical engineering. Additionally, his geometry teacher, Miss Kitner, opened his mind to mathematics and guided him along the way. **THT:** Dr. Cox's motto is, "Work hard and be kind."

COX, LAVERNE, T: Actress **I:** Media & Entertainment **PB:** Mobile **SC:** AL/USA **ED:** Coursework, Alabama School of Fine Arts; Coursework, Marymount Manhattan College **CW:** Actress, "Freak Show" (2017); Actress, "Doubt" (2017); Actress, "The Rocky Horror Picture Show: Let's Do the Time Warp Again" (2016); Actress, "Lip Sync Battle" (2016); Actress, "The Mindy Project" (2015); Actress, "Grandma" (2015); Actress, "Faking It" (2014); Actress, "Girlfriends Guide to Divorce" (2014); Actress, "Grand Street" (2014); Actress, "Laverne Cox Presents: The T Word" (2014); Actress, "Orange is the New Black" (2013); Actress, "36 Saints" (2013); Actress, "Migraine" (2012); Actress, "The Exhibitionists" (2012); Actress, "Carla" (2011); Actress, "Musical Chairs" (2011); Actress, "Bronx Paradise" (2010); Actress, "TRANSform Me" (2010); Actress, "Uncle Stephanie" (2009); Actress, "Bored to Death" (2009); Actress, "Law & Order: Special Victims Unit" (2008); Actress, "I Want to Work for Diddy" (2008); Actress, "Law and Order" (2008); Actress, "All Night" (2008); Actress, "The Kings of Brooklyn" (2004); Actress, "Betty Anderson" (2000) **AW:** Listee, Time 100 Most Influential (2015); Daytime Emmy for Outstanding Special Class Special (2015)

COX, TERRANCE, "TJ" J., T: U.S. Representative from California **I:** Government Administration/Government Relations/Government Services **CN:** U.S. House of Representatives **DOB:** 7/18/1963 **PB:** Walnut Creek **SC:** CA/USA **SPN:** Kathleen Murphy **CH:** Four Children **ED:** Master of Business Administration, Southern Methodist University; Bachelor of Science in Chemical Engineering, University of Nevada, Reno **C:** Member, U.S. House of Representatives from California's 21st District (2019-Present); Founder, Two Nut Processing Companies; Manager, Community Development Enterprise **CR:** Member, Congressional Asian Pacific American Caucus **PA:** Democrat

CRAIG, ANGELA, "ANGIE" DAWN, T: U.S. Representative **I:** Government Administration/Government Relations/Government Services **DOB:** 02/14/1972 **PB:** West Helena **SC:** AK/USA **MS:** Married **SPN:** Cheryl Greene **CH:** Four children **ED:** BA in Journalism, The University of Memphis **C:** U.S. Representative, Minnesota's Second Congressional District (2019-Present); Vice President of Corporate Relations, St. Jude Medical, Inc., Abbott (2006-2017); Vice President of Communications, St. Jude Medical, Inc., Abbott (2005-2006); Vice President of U.S. Public Relations, Investor Relations, Smith + Nephew, London, MN (2003-2005); Director of Corporate Affairs, Smith + Nephew, London, MN (2002-2003); Reporter, The Commercial Appeal **CIV:** Liaison, Advanced Medical Technology Association; President, St. Jude Medical Foundation **PA:** Democrat

CRAIG, DAVID R., T: State Legislator (Retired) **I:** Government Administration/Government Relations/Government Services **DOB:** 06/12/1949 **PB:** Havre de Grace **SC:** MD/USA **PT:** J. Emerison Craig; Mary Elizabeth (Foard) Craig **MS:** Married **SPN:** Melinda Lee (Blevins) Craig **CH:** Randolph; Courtney; P.J (Pamela Joyce) **ED:** MS, Morgan State University (1983); BS, Towson State College (1971) **C:** Secretary, Maryland Department of Planning (2015-2016); Executive, Hartford County, MD (2005-2014); Mayor, Havre de Grace, MD (1985-1989, 2001-2005); Senator District 34, Maryland State Senate, Annapolis, MD (1995-1999); Delegate District 34, Maryland State Delegation (1991-1994); Assistant Principal, Teacher, Hartford County School District **CR:** Executive Director, Maryland World War I Centennial Commission (2019-2020) **CIV:** Delegate, Republican National Convention (1992); Mayor, City of Havre de Grace (1985-1989); Councilman, City of Havre de Grace (1979-1985); Boy Scouts of America; Lifetime Member, Susquehanna Art Museum; Friends of Concord Point Lighthouse **CW:** Author, "Greetings from Gettysburg"; Author, "Greetings from Havre de Grace" **AW:** Virginia Scotten Award, Harford County Republican Party (1987); Soccer Coach of the Year (1986); National Citation **MEM:** Vice Commander, Sons of American Legion (2019-Present) **MH:** Albert Nelson Marquis Lifetime Achievement Award **AS:** Mr. Craig attributes his success to the lessons that his mother and father taught him. **B/I:** Mr. Craig became involved in his profession because of experiences in education at a young age. **AV:** Enjoying puzzles and sudoku; Spending time with grandchildren **RE:** Methodist

CRAIG, FORD MORRIS, EDD, T: Educational Administrator, Researcher **I:** Education/Educational Services **DOB:** 11/03/1948 **PB:** Omaha **SC:** NE/USA **PT:** Norman John Craig; Betty (Tuma) Craig **MS:** Married **SPN:** Doris Craig (08/15/1970) **CH:** Jody Jane; Jill Diane **ED:** EdD in Higher Education, Nova University (Now Nova Southeastern University), Fort Lauderdale, FL (1991); EdS in Educational Administration, University of Nebraska Kearney (1988); MS in English Education, Kearney State College (Now University of Nebraska Kearney) (1974); BA in English Education, Wayne State College, Cum Laude (1970) **CT:** Certified Lay Pastor, Presbyterian Church in America (2011) **C:** Adjunct Faculty, Concordia University (2017-Present); Commission Lay Pastor, PCUSA, Stapleton, NE (2013-2015); Doctoral Faculty Member, University of Phoenix (2006-2013); Educational Consultant (2004-2006); Institutional Research Person, Mid-Plains Community College Area, North Platte, NE (1991-2004); Instructor of English, Administrative Assistant, McCook Community College, NE (1988-1992); Instructor of English, McCook Community College, NE (1978-1992); Teacher, North Platte Public Schools, NE (1974-1978); Teacher of English and Speech, St. Paul Public Schools, NE (1971-1974); Teacher of English and Speech, Palmer Public Schools, NE (1970-1971) **CR:** Consultant, Evaluator, North Central Accrediting Association (Now North Central Association of Colleges and Schools (NCA)) (1995-Present); Manuscript Evaluator, Teaching English in Two-year College Journal (1992-Present); Member, Midwest Regional Conference on English in Two-year College (1980-Present); Book Reviewer, Great Plains Chautauqua, North Platte, NE (1993); Recording Secretary, McCook, NE (1990) **CIV:** Elder, First Presbyterian Church, North Platte, NE (1995-Present); Chair, New Church Continuation Committee (1997); Deacon, First Presbyterian Church, North Platte, NE (1992-1995); Chairman, Board of Missions, First Congregational Church, McCook, NE (1991); Moderator, First Congregational Church, McCook,

NE (1989); Presbyterian Church of North Platte; Pulpit Supply Pastor, Presbyterian; United Church of Christ; Congregational Member, American Baptist; Evangelical Lutheran Church in America; Disciples of Christ **CW:** Contributor, Poetry, Essays, Articles **AW:** Scholarship, Nebraska Council for Humanities (1989) **MEM:** Kiwanis International (1992-2015); Lifetime Member, National Education Association; Presbyterian Church in America **MH:** Albert Nelson Marquis Lifetime Achievement Award **B/I:** Dr. Craig had a history teacher and an English teacher in high school that inspired him to go into his profession. The history teacher was Ralph Stout; the English teacher was Tom Barret. He believes that in many instances, a high percentage of people that get into the ministry felt the calling. Dr. Craig came from a family that didn't attend church. He calls his journey toward ministry his dot-to-dot story. There was a series of events that lead him to his calling. **AV:** Fishing; Reading; Travel **PA:** Democrat **RE:** Presbyterian

CRAIG, HURSHEL, "GENE" EUGENE, T: Retired Agronomist **I:** Advertising & Marketing **DOB:** 05/18/1932 **PB:** Chrisman **SC:** IL/USA **PT:** Thomas Hurshel Craig; Letha Mae (Short) Craig **MS:** Married **SPN:** Zada Pauline Honnold (12/29/1954) **CH:** Toni Jane; Tina Jean (Deceased) **ED:** Postgraduate Coursework, University of Illinois (1974); MS, University of Illinois (1970); BS, University of Illinois (1958); Coursework, Illinois State University (1956); Coursework, Eastern Illinois University (1951) **C:** Commissioned Sales Role, Cal-Mar Soil Testing Laboratory (1990-2015); Retired, Cal-Mar Soil Testing Laboratory (2003); Soil and Plant Tissue Analysis Sales, Cal-Mar Soil Testing Laboratory, West Lafayette, IN (1990-2003); Self-Employed Agronomy Consultant (1987-2003); Freelance Soil Sampler (1985-1987); Agronomy Consultant, Ag-Vantage, Westerville, OH (1980-1985); Agronomy Consultant, Partner, C & S Pro-Farm Services, Ridge Farm (1977-1980); Instructor, Agriculture, Danville Area Community College (1970-1980); Partner, Agronomist, Harris Fertilizer, Inc., Farmer City, IL (1967-1969); Home Office Manager, Remole Soil Service, Inc., Potomac, IL (1966-1967); Farm Consultant, Gifford State Bank (1964-1966); Branch Manager, Remole Soil Service, Inc., Gifford, IL (1961-1964); Manager, Lime Service Co. (1959-1961); Partner, Hurshel Craig & Sons (1954-1958) **CIV:** Chairman, Administrative Council, Bismarck United Methodist Church (1989-1991) **MIL:** U.S. Army (1952-1954) **CW:** Co-Author, "Career Awareness Test for Agriculture Students and Prospective Spouses" (1974) **MEM:** Former Charter Member, Treasurer, Vice President, President, Professional Crop Consultants of Illinois **MH:** Albert Nelson Marquis Lifetime Achievement Award **B/I:** Mr. Craig is the oldest of four boys. He grew up on a farm, which made it a natural progression for him to turn to a career in crops and soils. Mr. Craig was a senior in high school when he was offered a teacher's college scholarship and accepted it. He attended Eastern Illinois University in 1951. **AV:** Reading; Gardening; Collecting rifles and guns

CRAIG, SUSANNE, T: Investigative Reporter **I:** Writing and Editing **CN:** The New York Times Company **PB:** Calgary **SC:** Alberta/Canada **ED:** Summer Intern, Windsor Star (1991); BA in Political Science and Government, University of Calgary (1991); Intern, Calgary Herald (1990) **C:** Investigative Reporter, New York City Hall Bureau Chief, The New York Times Company (2015-Present); Reporter, The New York Times Company (2010-2015); Staff Writer, Wall Street Journal; Reporter, The Globe and Mail; Reporter, Windsor Star, Windsor, Ontario, Canada **AW:** Co-Recipient, Pulitzer Prize for Explanatory Reporting (2019); George

Polk Award for Political Reporting (2018); Gerald Loeb Award for Breaking News for "The Day That Changed Wall Street" (2009); Gerald Loeb Award for Beat Writing for "Breakdown at Bear Stearns" (2008); Pulitzer Prize (2008); Gerald Loeb Award for Deadline Writing for "The Day Grasso Quit as NYSE Chief" (2004); National Newspaper Award (1999)

CRAMER, KEVIN JOHN, T: U.S. Senator from North Dakota **I:** Government Administration/Government Relations/Government Services **CN:** U.S. Senate **DOB:** 1/21/1961 **PB:** Rolla **SC:** ND/USA **PT:** Richard Cramer; Clarice Cramer **MS:** Married **SPN:** Kris Cramer **CH:** Ian; Isaac; Rachel; Annie **ED:** Master of Arts in Management, University of Mary, Bismarck, ND (2003); Bachelor of Arts in Social Work, Concordia College, Moorhead, MN (1983) **C:** U.S. Senator, State of North Dakota (2019-Present); Member, U.S. House of Representatives from North Dakota's At-Large Congressional District (2013-2019); Member, U.S. House Committee on Science, Space, and Technology (2013-2019); Member, U.S. House Committee on Natural Resources (2013-2019); Member, U.S. House of Representatives from North Dakota's At-Large Congressional District, United States Congress, Washington, DC (2013-2019); Commissioner, North Dakota Public Service Commission (2003-2012); Director, Harold Schafer Leadership Foundation, Bismarck, ND (2001-2003); State Economic Development Director, State of North Dakota (1997-2000); State Tourism Director, State of North Dakota (1993-1997); Member, Committee on Energy and Commerce **CR:** Committee Member, Growing North Dakota III (1994); Supporter, Member, Growing North Dakota Programs **CIV:** Chairperson, Executive Director, North Dakota Republican Party (1991-1993) **PA:** Republican

CRANDALL, ROGER W., T: Chairman, President, Chief Executive Officer **I:** Insurance **CN:** Massachusetts Mutual Life Insurance Company **ED:** MBA, University of Pennsylvania; BA in Economics, The University of Vermont; **CT:** Chartered Financial Analyst **C:** Chairman, President, Chief Executive Officer, MassMutual Financial Group (2010-Present); President, Chief Executive Officer, MassMutual Financial Group (2010); President, Chief Operating Officer, MassMutual Financial Group (2008-2009); Co-Chief Operating Officer, Massachusetts Mutual Life Insurance Company, MassMutual Financial Group (2007-2008); Executive Vice President, Chief Investment Officer, Massachusetts Mutual Life Insurance Company, MassMutual Financial Group (2005-2007); President, Chief Executive Officer, Babson Capital Management LLC, MassMutual Financial Group (2006-2008); Chairman, Babson Capital Management LLC, MassMutual Financial Group (2005-2008); Vice Chairman, Managing Director, Head of Corporate Securities, Babson Capital Management LLC, MassMutual Financial Group (2000); Joined, MassMutual Financial Group (1988); Head of Corporate Bond Management, Public Bond Trading and Institutional Fixed Income Units, Babson Capital Management LLC, MassMutual Financial Group

CRANE, CHRISTOPHER MARK, T: Chief Executive Officer and President **I:** Oil & Energy **CN:** Exelon Corporation **ED:** Coursework, New Hampshire Technical College **CT:** Certified Senior Reactor Operator **C:** President, Chief Executive Officer, Exelon Corporation (2012-Present); President, Chief Operating Officer, Exelon Corporation (2008-2012); President, Exelon Generation Corporation, LLC (2008-2012); Executive Vice President, Chief Operating Officer, Exelon Generation Company, LLC (2007-2008); President, Chief Executive Offi-

cer, AmerGen, Exelon Corporation; President, Chief Nuclear Officer, Exelon Nuclear (2004-2007); Chief Operating Officer, Exelon Nuclear (2003-2007); Senior Vice President of Nuclear Operations, Exelon Corporation (1999-2003); Vice President, Boiling Water Reactor Operations, Exelon Corporation (1998-1999); Site Vice President, Tennessee Valley Authority Browns Ferry Nuclear Plant, Athens, AZ (1997-1998) **CR:** Board of Directors, Exelon Corporation (2012-Present)

CRANE, ELIZABETH, "BETSY", T: Professor (Retired) **I:** Education/Educational Services **CN:** Widener University **DOB:** 08/06/1949 **PB:** Ithaca **SC:** NY/USA **PT:** George I. Crane; Doris Spencer Crane **MS:** Married **SPN:** Robert Heasley **CH:** Jesse Crane-Seeber, Nathanael Heasley, Rachel-Storm Heasley **ED:** PhD in Human Service Studies with Concentration in Program Evaluation and Planning, Cornell University, Ithaca, NY (2000); MA in Communications with Concentration in Mental Health Information, University of Texas at Austin, Austin, TX (1972); Fellowship, National Institute of Mental Health (1971-1972); BS in Sociology, Nazareth College, Rochester, NY (1971) **C:** Professor, Center for Human Sexuality Studies, Widener University, Chester, PA (2012-Present); Professor and Director, Graduate Programs in Human Sexuality, Center for Education, Widener University, Chester, PA (2009-2012); Associate Professor and Director, Graduate Programs in Human Sexuality, Center for Education, Widener University, Chester, PA (2007-2012); Adjunct Assistant Professor, Department of Psychiatry, State University of New York Upstate Medical University, Binghamton, NY (2007-2012); Associate Professor, Department of Sociology, Director, PhD Program in Administration and Leadership Studies in Nonprofit and Public Sectors, Indiana University of Pennsylvania, Harrisburg, PA (2001-2007); Extension Faculty, Cornell University, Department of Human Development, College of Human Ecology (1994-2000); Lecturer, Human Sexuality, Department of Human Service Studies, Cornell University, Ithaca, NY (1995); Training Coordinator, New York State Family development Training and Credentialing Program (1994); Lecturer, Women and Health, Sociology Department, Ithaca College, Ithaca, NY (1989-1990) **CR:** Executive Director, Planned Parenthood of Tompkins County, Ithaca, NY (1990-1994); Director of Community Education, Planned Parenthood of Tompkins County, Ithaca, NY (1979-1990); Co-Creator, AIDS Task Force, Tompkins County, Ithaca, NY (1984); Outreach Worker & Teen Counselor, Family Planning Program, Cortland County Health Department, Cortland, NY (1978-1979); News Reporter, Cortland Standard, Cortland, NY (1976-1977); Program Communication Director, River Region Mental Health-Mental Retardation Board, Inc., Louisville, KY (1974-1975); Media Liaison Specialist, River Region Mental Health-Mental Retardation Board, Inc., Louisville, KY (1973-1974); Public Information Internships, Austin State School, Austin, TX, Rochester Mental Health Center, Rochester, NY, and Human Opportunities Corporation, Austin, TX (1971-1972); Attendant, Rochester State Hospital, Rochester, NY (1970-1971) **CIV:** Fund Drive Co-Chair, Unitarian-Universalist Church of Delaware County, Media, PA (2009-2010); Co-Leader for Workshop on Raising Boys, Unitarian-Universalist Church of Delaware County, Media, PA (2009); Member, Indiana County Children's Roundtable, appointed by Family Court Judge Carol Hanna (2006-2007); Founding Member, Steering Committee Member, Indiana Cares Campaign to End Homophobia (2002-2007); Religious Education Teacher, First Unitarian-Universalist Church of Indiana, PA (2001-2007); President, Downtown Business Women's Association, Ithaca, NY (1992-

1994); Member, Ithaca Rotary Club (1990-1994); Founder, Safe Space Allies Program, Widener University **CW:** Interviewee, TV Series, "Sexish" (2016); Interviewee, SFGate.com, San Francisco Forty Niners Reporter Kevin Lynch Regarding the First "Out" NCAA Division 1 College Football Player and the NFL Draft (2014); Quoted, Article, "New Study: Teen Girls Report Sexual Violence as Normal," Shape.com (2014); Interviewee, Feature Article, "Sex after 50? After 75? But of course," Philadelphia Inquirer (2013); Author, Book, "Forever Sexual," CBS Talk Philly (2012); Guest, Online Radio Show, Sex Talk With Lou, "How Bright is Your Future in Sex?" (2012); Presenter, DVD, "Transgender Student Athletes," National Collegiate Athletic Association (2011); Co-Editor, "Sexual lives: A reader on the theories and realities of human sexualities" (2003); Author, Co-Author, Contributor, Numerous Peer-Reviewed Journal Articles, Professional Articles, Books, Chapters, and Monographs; Speaker, Presenter, Numerous International and National/Regional Academic Presentations; Speaker, Presenter, Numerous Invited Professional and Academic Presentations; Reviewer, Numerous Publications; Author, 49 Academic and Professional Publications **AW:** Distinguished University Professor Award, Widener University (2014); 2007 Woman of the Year, Indiana, PA Chapter, American Association of University Women (AAUW) (2007); Certificate of Appreciation "for service and contributions towards creating a more inclusive and affirming campus community," Indiana University of Pennsylvania Commission on Gay, Lesbian, Bisexual and Transgender Issues **MEM:** Society for the Scientific Study of Sexuality; American Association of Sexuality Educators, Counselors & Therapists (AASECT); American Men's Studies Association (AMSA); Association for the Study of Women in Mythology (ASWM); Foundation for the Scientific Study of Sexuality (FSSS); Society for Scientific Study of Sexuality (SSSS); World Association for Sexual Health (WAS); Presidents Diversity Issues Response Team, Widener University; Gender & Women's Studies Board, Widener University; Co-Chair, LGBT Task Force, Widener University; Gamma Eta Rho National Honor Society in Human Sexuality; Kappa Delta Pi (KDP), International Honor Society in Education **AS:** Dr. Crane attributes her success to her love of learning and her high level of enthusiasm. She also has strong social justice values that she thinks have been very important. Dr. Crane recommends to her students, "Do well at whatever you are doing and opportunities that you never imagined will emerge." **B/I:** Dr. Crane became involved in her profession in part because she was raised in a very Catholic family in the 1950s and sexuality was never talked about. She believes that her personal lack of sex education growing up, and growing awareness of sexism, racism, homophobia, and other societal oppressions, inspired and compelled her to pursue her career path. **PA:** Progressive Democrat **THT:** The seventh of eight children in a Catholic family, Dr. Crane was raised to be a traditional woman, wife, and mother. She is aware of her white privilege, being an 11th generation immigrant from England on her mother's side, being a descendant of Gerald Spencer who came to what is now Cambridge in 1630. As well, her paternal great-grandmother Lucy Updike was descended from Dutch fur traders who came to New Amsterdam about that same time. The Updikes were Revolutionary War soldiers who acquired land near Ithaca, NY around 1800s after the native Cayuga peoples were driven from their land. Her paternal grandmother Katheryn McNiff was the daughter of Irish immigrants who escaped conditions created by British oppression by emigrating to the U.S. in 1871. All of her ancestors

lived in the central New York area since the mid-late 1800s.She credits the social change occurring during the late 1960s when she was in high school, continuing into the 1970s with providing opportunities for her to work for causes she has believed in throughout her career. She is thankful for her higher education, financed in large part by state and federal tuition assistance, and advocates for greater government investment in education. She did become a mother, then a stepmother, and now cherishes being a grandmother. She will continue to work for needed systemic change to reduce social inequality.

CRANIN, MARILYN, T: Landscape Designer **I:** Architecture & Construction **CN:** London Landscape **DOB:** 08/01/1932 **PB:** New York **SC:** NY/USA **PT:** William Sunners; Rebecca (Yates) Sunners **MS:** Widowed **SPN:** Dr. A. Norman Cranin (1953, Deceased 2011) **CH:** Jonathan Blake; Andrew Ross; Elizabeth S. **ED:** Honorary LHD, Arcadia University, Glenside, PA (1996); Honorary LLD, Arcadia University, Glenside, PA (1996); Honorary DHL, Arcadia University, Glenside, PA (1996); Coursework, Harvard University (1981-1982); BA, Arcadia University, Glenside, PA (1954) **C:** Landscape Designer, London Landscape, Massapequa, NY (1984-2006); Master Gardener, Cornell Cooperative Extension of Nassau County, New York, NY (1976-1980); Horticultural Therapist, New York Botanical Gardens, New York, NY (1976-1978); Horticultural Therapist, Beth Abraham Center (1975-1985); Landscape Designer, New York Botanical Gardens, New York, NY (1974-1976) **CR:** Horticultural Therapist, Zucker Hillside Hospital, Northwell Health, Five Towns Premier Rehabilitation and Nursing Center **CIV:** Secretary, Board of Trustees, Arcadia University (1987-Present); Waldorf School of Garden City, NY (1985-Present); The American Chamber Ensemble (1981-Present); President, Board of Trustees, Hewlett-Woodmere Public Library (1977-Present); Vice President, Board of Directors, Five Towns Music and Arts Foundation, Woodmere, NY (1962-Present); Board Member, Nassau Land Trust (2015); Trustee, Nassau Library Systems, Uniondale, NY (1980-1986); Board, Arcadia University Alumni Association (1979-1986); Trustee, Deputy Mayor, Village of Hewlett Bay Park, NY (1974-1984); Vice President, Board Member, Center of Adult Learning Experience **CW:** Columnist, South Shore Record (1975-1982) **AW:** Alumni of the Year Golden Disc Award, Arcadia University (1994); Named Woman of the Year, Hewlett-Woodmere Merchants Association (Now Hewlett Woodmere Business Association)(1994); Silver Award for Excellence in Design, Long Island Nursery & Landscape Association (1992) **MEM:** American Horticultural Society; Cornell Cooperative Extension of Nassau County; New York State Association of Library Boards; New York Botanical Garden; Wave Hill; Woodmere Bay Yacht Club; Woodmere Club **MH:** Albert Nelson Marquis Lifetime Achievement Award **B/I:** Mrs. Cranin got into horticulture and landscape design because she enjoyed observing things grow. As a young girl, she and her grandmother grew corn for the World War II effort. The U.S. Army would come to pick up the corn for the soldiers. **AV:** Gardening; Reading; Skiing

CRANSTON, BRYAN LEE, T: Actor **I:** Media & Entertainment **DOB:** 03/07/1956 **PB:** San Fernando Valley **SC:** CA/USA **PT:** Joseph Louis Cranston; Annalisa (Sell) Cranston **MS:** Married **SPN:** Robin Dearden (07/08/1989); Mickey Middleton (11/10/1977, Divorced 04/08/1982) **CH:** Taylor Dearden **ED:** Associate Degree in Police Science, Los Angeles Valley College (1976) **CW:** Actor, "The One and Only Ivan" (2020); Appearance, "Jeopardy!

The Greatest of All Time" (2020); Appearance, "Last Week Tonight with John Oliver" (2019); Actor, "El Camino: A Breaking Bad Movie" (2019); Actor, Executive Producer, "SuperMansion" (2015-2019); Co-creator, Executive Producer, Actor, "Sneaky Pete" (2015-2019); Co-creator, Writer, Executive Producer, "The Dangerous Book for Boys" (2018); Actor, "Isle of Dogs" (2018); Voice Actor, "Robot Chicken" (2011, 2016, 2018); Actor, "The Disaster Artist" (2017); Actor, "Power Rangers" (2017); Actor, "The Upside" (2017); Actor, "Last Flag Flying" (2017); Actor, Executive Producer, "Philip K Dicks Electric Dreams" (2017); Actor, "Curb Your Enthusiasm" (2017); Actor, "The Infiltrator" (2016); Actor, Executive Producer, Film, "All the Way" (2016); Author, "A Life in Paris" (2016); Voice Actor, "Kung Fu Panda 3" (2016); Actor, "The Masterpiece" (2016); Actor, "In Dubious Battle" (2016); Actor, "Why Him?" (2016); Actor, "Wakefield" (2016); Actor, "Get a Job" (2016); Host, "Saturday Night Live" (2010, 2016); Actor, "Trumbo" (2015); Actor, Broadway Play, "All the Way" (2014); Actor, "Godzilla" (2014); Actor, "Cold Comes the Night" (2013); Narrator, "Big History" (2013); Actor, Producer, "Breaking Bad" (2008-2013); Actor, "How I Met Your Mother" (2006-2007, 2013); Voice Actor, "The Cleveland Show" (2012-2013); Voice Actor, "The Simpsons" (2012-2013); Actor, "30 Rock" (2012); Actor, "Archer" (2012); Actor, "Red Tails" (2012); Actor, "John Carter" (2012); Voice Actor, "Madagascar 3: Europe's Most Wanted" (2012); Actor, "Rock of Ages" (2012); Actor, "Argo" (2012); Actor, "Total Recall" (2012); Actor, "The Lincoln Lawyer" (2011); Actor, "Detachment" (2011); Actor, "Contagion" (2011); Actor, "Larry Crowne" (2011); Actor, "Drive" (2011); Actor, "Glenn Martin, DDS" (2010-2011); Actor, "Love Ranch" (2010); Actor, "Get a Job" (2008); Actor, "The Hollywood Quad" (2008); Actor, "Hard Four" (2007); Actor, "Thank God You're Here" (2007); Actor, "Fallen" (2007); Actor, "Intellectual Property" (2006); Actor, "Little Miss Sunshine" (2006); Actor, "Malcolm in the Middle" (2000-2006); Voice Actor, "Magnificent Desolation: Walking on the Moon 3D" (2005); Actor, "Seeing Other People" (2004); Actor, "Illusion" (2004); Actor, "Thanksgiving Family Reunion" (2003); Actor, "'Twas the Night" (2001); Actor, "The Santa Claus Brothers" (2001); Actor, "The King of Queens" (1999-2001); Actor, "The Big Thing" (2000); Actor, "The Prince of Light" (2000); Actor, "Terror Tract" (2000); Actor, Writer, Director Producer, "Last Chance" (1999); Actor, "Saving Private Ryan" (1998); Actor, "From the Earth to the Moon" (1998); Actor, "Strategic Command" (1997); Actor, "Eagle Riders" (1996); Actor, "The Rockford Files: Punishment and Crime" (1996); Actor, "Time Under Fire" (1996); Actor, "That Thing You Do!" (1996); Actor, "Street Corner Justice" (1996); Actor, "Extreme Blue" (1995); Actor, "Kissing Miranda" (1995); Actor, "Seinfeld" (1994-1997); Actor, "Teknoman" (1994); Actor, "Clean Slate" (1994); Actor, "Erotique" (1994); Actor, "Men Who Hate Women & the Women Who Love Them" (1994); Actor, "Days Like This" (1994); Actor, "The Companion" (1994); Actor, "Moldiver" (1993); Voice Actor, "Mighty Morphin' Power Rangers" (1993); Actor, "The Disappearance of Nora" (1993); Actor, "Prophet of Evil: The Ervil LeBaron Story" (1993); Actor, "Dead Silence" (1991); Actor, "Dead Space" (1991); Actor, "Corporate Affairs" (1990); Actor, "I Know My First Name is Steven" (1989); Actor, "The Big Turnaround" (1988); Actor, "Raising Miranda" (1988); Actor, "Wings of Honneamise" (1987); Actor, "Amazon Women on the Moon" (1987); Actor, "The Return of the Six-Million-Dollar Man and the Bionic Woman" (1987); Actor, "North and South, Book II" (1986); Actor, "One Life to Live" (1985); Actor, "Loving" (1983); Actor, "KidSmartz"; Actor, Numerous Television Shows and Movies

AW: Tony Award for Best Leading Actor in a Play (2014, 2019); Screen Actors Guild Award for Outstanding Performance by a Male Actor in a Television Movie or Miniseries, SAG-AFTRA (2017); Golden Globe for Best Television Series - Drama, Hollywood Foreign Press Association (2014); Golden Globe for Best Actor in a Television Series - Drama, Hollywood Foreign Press Association (2014); Primetime Emmy Award for Outstanding Lead Actor in a Drama Series, Television Academy (2014); Screen Actors Guild Award for Outstanding Performance by an Ensemble in a Drama Series, SAG-AFTRA (2014); Drama Desk Award for Outstanding Actor in a Play (2014); Primetime Emmy Award for Outstanding Drama Series, Television Academy (2013, 2014); Screen Actors Guild Award for Outstanding Performance by a Male Actor in a Drama Series, SAG-AFTRA (2013, 2014); Named One of the 100 Most Influential People in the World, TIME Magazine (2013); Screen Actors Guild Award for Outstanding Performance by an Ensemble in a Motion Picture, SAG-AFTRA (2013); Primetime Emmy Award for Outstanding Lead Actor in a Drama Series, Television Academy (2008-2010)

CRAPO, MICHAEL, "MIKE" DEAN, T: U.S. Senator from Idaho **I:** Government Administration/ Government Relations/Government Services **CN:** U.S. Senate **DOB:** 05/20/1951 **PB:** Idaho Falls **SC:** ID/USA **PT:** George Lavelle Crapo; Melba (Olsen) Crapo **MS:** Married **SPN:** Susan Diane Hasleton (06/22/1974) **CH:** Michelle; Brian; Stephanie; Lara; Paul **ED:** Doctor of Jurisprudence, Harvard Law School, Cum Laude (1977); Bachelor of Arts in Political Science, Brigham Young University, Provo, UT, Summa Cum Laude (1973); Coursework, University of Utah **C:** Chairperson, Senate Banking Committee (2017-Present); U.S. Senator, State of Idaho (1999-Present); Member, U.S. House of Representatives from Idaho's Second Congressional District, United States Congress, Washington, DC (1993-1999); Member, District 32A, Idaho State Senate (1985-1993); President, Pro-tempore, Idaho State Senate (1989-1992); Partner, Holden, Kidwell, Hahn & Crapo PLLC, Idaho Falls, ID (1983-1992); Attorney, Holden, Kidwell, Hahn & Crapo PLLC, Idaho Falls, ID (1979-1992); Assistant Majority Leader, Idaho State Senate (1987-1989); Associate, Gibson, Dunn & Crutcher, Los Angeles, CA (1978-1979); Law Clerk to Honorable James M. Carter, United States Court of Appeals for the Ninth Circuit, San Diego, CA (1977-1978) **CR:** Member, State Affairs Committee (1987-1992); Member, Resources and Environmental Committee (1985-1990); Representative, President Task Force (1989); Member, Health and Welfare Committee (1985-1989); Vice Chairperson, Legislative District 29 (1984-1985); Precinct Committeeman, District 29 (1980-1985) **CIV:** Active Member, Boy Scouts of America, CA and Idaho (1977-1992) **AW:** Named, One of the 10 Members to Watch in the 112th Congress, Roll Call (2011); Best and Brightest Award, American Conservative Union (2003); Ground Water Protector Award, National Ground Water Association (2002); Watchdogs of Treasury Golden Bulldog Award, American Frozen Food Institute (2000); Distinguished Eagle Scout Award (2000); Thomas Jefferson Award, National American Wholesale Grocers Association-Independent Food Distributors Association (1996); Golden Bulldog Award, Watchdogs of the Treasury (1996); Spirit of Enterprise Award, United States Chamber of Commerce (1993, 1994, 1995, 1996); Guardian of Small Business Award, National Federation of Independent Business (1990, 1994); National Legislator of the Year Award, National Republican Legislators Association (1991); Certificate of Recognition, American Cancer Society Inc. (1990); Award, Idaho Housing Agency (1990); Certificate of Merit,

Republican National Committee (1990); Friend of Agricultural Award, Idaho Farm Bureau (1989-1990); Medal of Merit, Republican Presidential Task Force (1989); Award, American Lung Association, Idaho (1985, 1986, 1989); Named, One of the Outstanding Young Men of America (1985) **MEM:** American Bar Association; Idaho Bar Association; Rotary International **BAR:** State of Idaho (1979); State of California (1977) **AV:** Sports; Backpacking; Hunting; Skiing **PA:** Republican **RE:** The Church of Jesus Christ of Latter-day Saints

CRAWFORD, ERIC, "RICK" ALAN RICK, T: U.S. Representative **I:** Government Administration/ Government Relations/Government Services **DOB:** 01/22/1966 **PB:** Homestead AFB **SC:** FL/USA **PT:** Donny J. Crawford; Ruth Anne Crawford **MS:** Married **SPN:** Stacy Crawford **CH:** Will; Delaney **ED:** BA in Agriculture Business and Economics, Arkansas State University, Jonesboro, AR (1996) **C:** Member, The House Committee on Transportation and Infrastructure, U.S. House of Representatives (2011-Present); Member, Committee on Agriculture, U.S. House of Representatives (2011-Present); U.S. Representative, Arkansas' First Congressional District (2011-Present); Owner, Operator, AgWatch Network; Dealer Group Marketing Manager, John Deere; Syndicated Producer, Anchor, Delta Farm Roundup TV, Greenville, MS; Syndicated Producer, Anchor, Delta Farm Roundup TV, Jonesboro, AR; Syndicated Producer, Anchor, Delta Farm Roundup TV, Cape Girardeau, MO; Farm Director, Station KFIN-FM, Jonesboro, AR; Agri-Reporter, News Anchor, Station KAIT-TV, Jonesboro, AR **CIV:** First Vice-Chairman, Craighead County Republican Committee; Member, 4-H Foundation Board of Arkansas **MIL:** Advanced through Grades to Sergeant, U.S. Army (1985-1989) **CW:** Featured Columnist, Northeast Arkansas Business Today **AW:** Newscast Award, National Association of Farm Broadcasting (2006, 2008); Announcer of the Year, National Federation of Professional Bullriders (1996-1998) **MEM:** National Association of Farm Broadcasting **PA:** Republican

CRAWFORD, KATE, ABR, T: Co-Founder, Director **I:** Education/Educational Services **CN:** New York University **SC:** Australia **ED:** PhD, University of Sydney **C:** Inaugural Holder, AI & Justice Visiting Chair, École Normale Superieure and Fondation Abeona, Paris, France (2019); Co-Founder, AI Now Institute, Tandon School of Engineering, New York University (2017) **CR:** Former Musician, B(if)tek (1998-2003); Co-Founder, Deluxe Mood Recordings; Clan Analogue; Fellow, Centre for Policy Development **CIV:** Participant, Australia 2020 Summit (2008); Deep Lab **CW:** Writer, The Sydney Morning Herald **AW:** Co-Author, "Understanding the Internet: Language, Technology, Media, Power" (2014); Speaker, DataEDGE Conference, University of California Berkeley School of Information (2013); Speaker, O'Reilly Strata Conference (2013); Biennial Medal for Outstanding Scholarship, Australian Academy of the Humanities (2008); Manning Clark National Cultural Award

CRAWFORD, KATHERINE, "KITTY" E., RN, BSN, MSN, T: Pediatrics and Neonatal Nurse; Nursing Educator; Case Manager **I:** Medicine & Health Care **DOB:** 11/13/1945 **PB:** New Orleans **SC:** LA/USA **PT:** Donald Aden Eskridge Sr.; Alma Marie (O'Dowd) Eskridge **MS:** Married **SPN:** Jack Andrew Crawford (09/09/1967) **CH:** Timothy Andrew; Rebecca Elizabeth; Jenifer Aimee Marie **ED:** MSN, Northwestern State University, Natchitoches, LA (1975); BSN, Northwestern State University, Natchitoches, LA (1968); Diploma, Charity Hospital School of Nursing, New Orleans, LA (1966) **CT:** RN, State of Louisiana; Notary Caddo Parish, LA **C:** Retired (2011);

Neonatal ICU Nurse, Pediatric Case Manager, Christus Schumpert Medical Center, Shreveport, LA; Neonatal Coordinator, Christus Schumpert Medical Center, Shreveport, LA; Clinical Instructor, Christus Schumpert Medical Center, Shreveport, LA; Instructor, Northwestern State University College of Nursing, Shreveport, LA **CR:** Presenter, Various Professional Conferences; Member, Professional Advisory Boards **MEM:** Nurses' Association of the American College of Obstetricians and Gynecologists; National Association Neonatal Nurses; Sigma Theta Tau International Honor Society of Nursing; The Honor Society of Phi Kappa Phi **MH:** Albert Nelson Marquis Lifetime Achievement Award; Marquis Who's Who Top Professional **B/I:** Mrs. Crawford chose her profession for no reason other than that she simply liked it. She always wanted to know where the ambulance was going when she would see one pass. She always wanted to follow it. Also, growing up, she always loved children and babies. She wanted her mother to open an orphanage just so she would always be around them. In addition, she chose nursing not knowing what she was going to do when she got out of high school. Anyway, she had gotten a scholarship from the March of Dimes to go to college, and a girl named Barbara, who was not in one of her groups but they counseled at a camp together one summer, said that she was going to go to "Charity" (Charity Nursing Hospital School, New Orleans, 1966), and they were having an open house. She asked Mrs. Crawford if she wanted to go with her. Mrs. Crawford said, "I don't know", but Barbara kept on saying, "come on, come on" and so she went. She saw the building, and some of her upper classmates were there too, but then Barbara said that she was going to take the test and asked Mrs. Crawford if she would take the test too, but Mrs. Crawford wasn't sure. Later, she did take the test. However, Mrs. Crawford believes it was God leading her there. She took the test and passed. The nuns said she did well and asked if she wanted to go to Charity, but Mrs. Crawford had a scholarship already to go to college. But the nun asked if she could get Mrs. Crawford a scholarship to go to Charity would she go? Mrs. Crawford said she would. That was it; she went to Charity, and she loved it. It was no longing or nothing, but her mother said to her, her whole life, that God takes care of babies, drunks, and fools; that God would take care of her, too. In addition, she was always willing to try something new. **AV:** Puzzles; Cross stitch; Reading; Football (going to all of her grandbabies' games); Family time (with grandbabies) **THT:** Mrs. Crawford grew up in the 50's. Her father was a lawyer, as was his father. When her grandfather passed away, her father left his law practice to become a newspaper delivery man. He wanted to be a doctor but his father didn't want him to be one.

CRAWFORD, MARK H., T: Analyst **I:** Financial Services **CN:** United States Department of Commerce **DOB:** 08/02/1950 **PB:** Washington **SC:** DC/USA **PT:** Sterling Lee; Patricia (Moore) Lee **MS:** Married **SPN:** Jean Burke (02/02/1974) **CH:** Emily Lee **ED:** BA in Political Science and Communications, The American University (1973) **C:** Senior Trade and Industry Analyst, Office of Technology Evaluation, U.S. Department of Commerce (2006-2020); Senior Trade and Industry Analyst, Office Strategic Industries & Economic Security, United States Department of Commerce (1999-2006); Correspondent, The Energy Daily, Washington, DC (1991-1999); Senior Reporter, New Technology Week, Washington, DC (1991-1999); Freelance Reporter, Washington, DC (1990); Senior Writer, Science Magazine, Washington, DC (1985-1990); Correspondent, McGraw Hill World News, Washington, DC (1983-

1985); Associate Editor, Inside Energy, Washington, DC (1981-1983); Managing Editor, Coal Week, Washington, DC (1978-1981); Associate Editor, Fairfax Journal, Springfield, VA (1975-1977); Reporter, Suffolk Life, Westhampton, NY (1974-1975) **CIV:** Board Member, Hillbrook-Tall Oaks Civic Association (2016-2020); Vice President, Hillbrook-Tall Oaks Civic Association (2011); President, Hillbrook-Tall Oaks Civic Association (2008-2010) **CW:** Co-Editor, Developer, "Federal Coal Leases" (1981) **AW:** Gold Medal Award, Department of Commerce (2018); Bronze Medal Award, Department of Commerce (2011); Silver Medal Award, Department of Commerce (2004); National Press Club Award, Best Exclusive Story, National Press Foundation (1998); First Place, Investigative Reporting, Virginia Press Association (1977); Commendation Letter, Fairfax Police Department, Virginia (1976) **MEM:** Vice President, Board of Directors, Washington Chapter, Society of Professional Journalists (1989-1996) **MH:** Albert Nelson Marquis Lifetime Achievement Award

CREAMER, JACK MAJOR, T: Marketing Executive **I:** Advertising & Marketing **CN:** Square D by Schneider Electric **DOB:** 02/15/1954 **PB:** Detroit **SC:** IL/USA **PT:** Cary Rowland Creamer; Virginia (Major) Creamer **MS:** Married **SPN:** Zane Creamer **CH:** Troy; Cary; Mont **ED:** MBA, Rensselaer Polytechnic Institute (RPI), Troy, NY (1976); BS in Industrial Engineering, Syracuse University, Syracuse, NY (1975) **C:** Segment Marketing Manager, Knightdale, NC (2008-Present); Marketing Executive, Marketing Manager, Component Products, Knightdale, NC (1991-2007); Original Equipment Manufacturers Marketing Manager, Square D Co. (Now Square D by Schneider Electric, Knightdale, NC (1990-1991); Original Equipment Manufacturers Marketing Development Manager, General Electric, Bloomington, IL (1988-1990); National Sales Manager, General Electric, Bloomington, IL (1986-1988); Regional Sales Manager, General Electric, Bloomington, IL (1986-1987); Manager, Market Development, General Electric, Bloomington, IL (1984-1986); Area Sales Manager, General Electric, Bloomington, IL (1981-1984); Sales Engineer, General Electric, Pittsburgh, PA, Louisville, KY (1979-1981); Sales Trainee, General Electric, Milwaukee, WI and Cleveland, Ohio (1976-1979) **CIV:** Member, Board of Directors, Blooming Grove Academy, Normal, IL (1986); Member, New Building Committee, College Park Christian Church **CW:** Contributor, Numerous Articles to Technical Journals, White Papers, Sales Tool Creation **MEM:** President, Elfun Society (1988-1989); Vice President, Elfun Society (1987-1988); Hydraulic Institute; Submersible Wastewater Pump Association (SWPA) **MH:** Albert Nelson Marquis Lifetime Achievement Award; Marquis Who's Who Top Professional **AS:** Mr. Creamer attributes his success to the methodology of being a team leader plus knowing how to use teams to be effective. Also, getting good feedback and taking action from the feedback. **B/I:** Mr. Creamer became involved in his profession because his father worked at General Electric and was in sales. He saw what he did and liked what he did and decided that he would follow his path. **AV:** Traveling; Playing and spending time with his dog (Cavalier King Charles Spaniel mixed with poodle); Former golfer/volleyball/basketball (over the course of his life) **PA:** Republican **RE:** Christian

CREASMAN, CARL E. SR., I: Education/Educational Services **DOB:** 01/28/1938 **PB:** Riceville **SC:** TN/USA **PT:** J. W. Creasman; Ollie Womac Creasman **MS:** Married **SPN:** Roberta Jean Lamkin **CH:** Christina Denise Creasman Mason; Carl E Creasman Jr. **ED:** EdS, University of Tennessee; MSEE, University of Tennessee; BSEE, Auburn University

CT: Licensed Parliamentarian; Ordained Baptist Minister **C:** Retired State Director, SkillsUSA, Tennessee Postsecondary Association (2012); Retired Vocational Electronics/Computer Instructor, McMinn County Career and Technology Center (2001); Senior Engineer, Clinch River Nuclear Breeder Reactor Project, Oak Ridge, TN; Manufacturing Engineer, Westinghouse Electric, Athens, TN; Senior Computer Design Engineer, Pershing Missile Control Computer, Martin Mariette Corporation, Orlando, FL **CR:** Parliamentarian, Tennessee Baptist Convention (1999-2017); State Director, SkillsUSA (2005-2012); Consultant, Tennessee Secondary Association of SkillsUSA (2002-2005); Bi-Vocational Baptist Minister; Trainer of Delegates, State and National VICA/SkillsUSA Conventions **CIV:** State Director, SkillsUSA, TN **MIL:** Tennessee National Guard **AW:** Honorary Life Membership, National SkillsUSA (2014); Honorary Life Membership, Tennessee SkillsUSA (2005); Lifetime Achievement in Education Award, Optimist Club, Athens, TN (2001); Tennessee Distinguished Classroom Teacher (2000); McMinn County Teacher of the Year (1988, 1998); Advisor of the Year, Tennessee SkillsUSA (1993, 1996) **MEM:** Institute of Electrical and Electronics Engineers (IEEE); National Education Association (NEA); Tennessee Education Association (TEA); National Association of Parliamentarians (NAP); Tennessee Association of Parliamentarians (TAP); Vocational Industrial Clubs of America/SkillsUSA **MH:** Marquis Who's Who Top Professional **AS:** Mr. Creasman attributes his success to determination and work ethic, which were instilled by his parents and family. **B/I:** Mr. Creasman's love for electronics and computers led to his career in the field. Likewise, his love for working with young people led him to become a teacher, which eventually got him the role of state director for Tennessee Postsecondary SkillsUSA. His love for God inspired him to become a minister. **PA:** Republican **RE:** Baptist **THT:** In addition to being a teacher and electrical engineer, Mr. Creasman also is a licensed parliamentarian and Baptist Minister. He taught computer electronics and computer programming and repair for 27 years. He was involved with SkillsUSA for over 50 years, serving as the Tennessee State Postsecondary Director for eight years and retired in 2012. He remains active with SkillsUSA as a volunteer and participates in Baptist Church activities as a parliamentarian and Pulpit Supply.

CREATH, CURTIS J., DMD, MS, T: Owner **I:** Medicine & Health Care **CN:** Milford Pediatric Dentistry, Inc **DOB:** 03/10/1958 **PB:** Lynwood **SC:** CA/USA **PT:** Ronald J. Creath; Madelyn W. (Chryst) Creath **MS:** Married **SPN:** Deborah Ann Lipari (06/23/1990) **CH:** Andrew **ED:** MS, University of Alabama (1988); DMD, Oral Roberts University (1985); Student, UCLA (1976-1981) **C:** Private Practice, Milford, OH (1995-Present);Staff Pediatric Dentist, Family Central Care Associates, Cincinnati, OH (1994-1995);Assistant Professor, UAB School of Dentistry (1991-1994); Assistant Professor, Stony Brook School of Dental Medicine (1988-1991) **CR:** Team Leader, Dental Mission Trips to Mexico, Jamaica, Peru (1982-1984) **CIV:** Team Leader, Dental Mission Trips to Mexico, Jamaica and Peru (1982-1984); Elder, Grace Bible Presbyterian Church; Teacher, Adult Secondary School; Teacher, Men's Bible Study; Music Leader, Worship Services **CW:** Contributor, Chapter, "Clark's Clinical Dentistry, Vol. 2" (1994); Contributor, Chapter, "Special and Medically Compromised Patients in Dentistry" (1989); Contributor, Articles, Reviews on Tobacco Control, Pediatric Dentistry, and Preventive Medicine, Professional Journals **AW:** Omicron Kappa Upsilon National Dental Honor Society **MEM:** Secretary-Treasurer, Alabama Society Pedi-

atric Dentistry (1992-1994); Vice President, American Association of Dental Schools (Now American Dental Education Association) (1986-1988); American Dental Association; Education Committee, American Academy of Pediatric Dentistry; Christian Medical & Dental Associations; Omicron Kappa Upsilon **MH:** Albert Nelson Marquis Lifetime Achievement Award; Marquis Who's Who Top Professional; Marquis Who's Who Humanitarian Award **AS:** Dr. Creath attributes his success to trying to be personable and explain things. He has always had a teacher mentality. **B/I:** Dr. Creath became involved in his profession because he has always loved science and was inspired by his grandmother, who suggested he be a dentist. It was his experiences while in dental school that made him choose pediatrics; he did not start out with pediatric dentistry; it was his experiences while training that he decided to specialize in pediatric dentistry. **AV:** Vocal music; Preaching; Missionary work; Woodworking; Gardening; Reading; Traveling **PA:** Republican **RE:** Presbyterian **THT:** Dr. Creath has participated in dental mission trips to Mexico, Peru, and Jamaica. He has published more than 25 articles and book chapters in professional journals and textbooks, many having been reprinted in other languages. He was selected to the Omicron Kappa Upsilon National Honorary Dental Society and is included in Marquis' Who's Who in America. He is a member of the American Academy of Pediatric Dentistry, the American Dental Association, and the Ohio Dental Association, among others.

CRENN, DOMINIQUE, T: Chef **I:** Food & Restaurant Services **C:** Chef/Owner, Bar Crenn (2016-Present); Chef/Owner, Petit Crenn (2015-Present); Chef/Owner, Atelier Crenn (2011-Present); Luce (2009-2011) **AW:** Best Female Chef, Worlds 50 Best Restaurant Awards (2016); Two Michelin Stars (2009, 2010)

CRENSHAW, BEN, T: Professional Golfer **I:** Athletics **DOB:** 01/11/1952 **PB:** Austin **SC:** TX/USA **MS:** Married **SPN:** Julie Ann **CH:** Katherine Vail; Claire Susan; Anna Riley **ED:** Graduate, University of Texas **C:** Professional Golfer (1973-Present); Team Captain, Ryder Cup Team (1999); Member, U.S. Ryder Cup (1981, 1983, 1987, 1995); U.S. Team Captain, Kirin Cup (1988); Member, U.S. World Amateur Cup Team (1972) **AW:** Winner, Wendy's Champions Skins Game (2009); World Golf Hall of Fame (2002); Winner, Ryder Cup (1999); Masters Winner, Augusta National Golf Club (1995); Champion, Masters Tournament (1984, 1995); Winner, Western Open (1992); Winner, Doral Ryder Open (1988); Winner, World Cup (1988); Winner, Ryder Cup (1981, 1983, 1987); Winner, USF&G (1987); Winner, Buick Open (1986); Winner, Vantage Championship (1986); Winner, PGA Senior Event, Jeremy Ranch Shoot-Out (1985); Winner, Byron Nelson Classic (1983); Winner, Texas State Open (1980); Winner, Anheuser-Busch Classic (1980); Winner, Walt Disney World Team Championship (1980); Winner, Phoenix Open (1979); Winner, Colonial National Invitational (1977); Winner, Irish Open (1976); Winner, Bing Crosby National Pro-Am., Ohio Kings Island Open, Hawaiian Open (1976); Winner, NCAA Championship (1971, 1972, 1973); Winner, San Antonio Open (1973); Western Amateur Open Match and Medal Plan Champion (1973) **MEM:** PGA of America

CRENSHAW, DANIEL, "DAN" REED, T: U.S. Representative from Texas **I:** Government Administration/Government Relations/Government Services **DOB:** 03/14/1984 **PB:** Aberdeen **SC:** Scotland, United Kingdom **MS:** Married **SPN:** Tara Blake (2013) **ED:** MPA, Harvard Kennedy School,

John F. Kennedy School of Government (2017); BA in International Relations, Tufts University **C:** Member, U.S. House of Representatives from Texas' Second Congressional District (2019-Present) **MIL:** Advanced through Grades to Lieutenant Commander, United States Navy (2006-2016) **AW:** Purple Heart; Bronze Star; Navy Commendation Medal **PA:** Republican **RE:** Methodist

CREWS, MARA, T: Writer **I:** Writing and Editing **DOB:** 08/12/1957 **PB:** Shreveport **SC:** LA/USA **PT:** Marlin E. Crews; Velma L. Branno **MS:** Single **ED:** Diploma, Institute of Children's Literature, Institute for Writers LLC (2008); Diploma, Institute of Children's Literature, Institute for Writers LLC (2007) **C:** Private Childcare Provider (2005-Present); Assistant, The Complete Mortgage Company, Ltd. (2002-2005); Preschool Teacher, Children's Learning Center (2001-2002); Direct Service Worker II, Evergreen Presbyterian Ministry, Bossier City, LA (1994-1996); Job Coach, Job Boost-Bossier Parish Community College, Bossier City, LA (1992-1994); Production Technician, City of Shreveport, LA (1977-1991) **CIV:** Captain, Givens St. Neighborhood Watch, Bossier City, LA (1993-1995); Member, Northwest Louisiana Brain Injury Support Group, Shreveport, LA (1989-1996) **CW:** Author, "Best Poems of the 90s" (1998); Author, "Dimensions of Thought" (1997); Author, "American Poetry Anthology" (1995); Author, Anthologies, "A Break in the Clouds" (1993) **AW:** Editors' Choice Award, The Poetry Guild (1998) **MEM:** Charter Member, National Women's History Museum (2010-Present); Academy of American Poets **MH:** Albert Nelson Marquis Lifetime Achievement Award **AV:** Reading; Embroidery; Latch hook pillow; Floral arrangements; Container gardening; Collecting dolls **THT:** Ms. Crews' motto is, "Life happens everyday, it just depends on what you do with it. Wrong things make you strong."

CRIM, LORETTA GRACE, T: Music Educator **I:** Education/Educational Services **DOB:** 07/24/1930 **PB:** Joplin **SC:** MO/USA **PT:** Herbert William Gullette; Mary (Munzuris) Gullette; **SPN:** William T. Crim (04/04/1954) **CH:** William T. Crim Jr; Sabrina Lee **ED:** Bachelor of Music, Master of Education, Hardin-Simmons University, Abilene, TX (1952); Coursework in Music, Joplin Junior College (1950) **C:** Retired (1991); Music Director, South Junior High School, R-VIII Systems, Joplin, MO (1967-1991); Music Director, Sun Oil Company, Silver, TX (1952-1954) **CIV:** Youth Choir Director, St. Paul Methodist Church, Joplin (1983-1988); Music Director, Joplin Little Theater (1976-1988); Board of Directors, Youth for Christ, Texas (1952-1959) **CW:** Author, "Anthology of Poems" (1948); Director, Choreographer, Various Musicals **AW:** Friend of Music Award (2006); Theater Award, Joplin Little Theater (1989); Outstanding Teacher of the Year, Clay Cowgill Blair Memorial (1989); Nominated, Golden Apple Award, Joplin Chamber of Commerce (1988-1989) **MEM:** Vocal Director, Music Educators of America (1983-1989); Joplin Community of Teachers; Joplin Education Association; International Professional and Business Women; Alpha Delta Kappa **MH:** Albert Nelson Marquis Lifetime Achievement Award **AS:** Ms. Crim attributes her success to hard work and her Christian faith. **B/I:** Ms. Crim became involved in her profession out of a lifelong passion for music and dance. **AV:** Sewing; Crafts; Cooking, Poetry; Decorating **PA:** Republican **RE:** Christian

CRISCUOLO, NICOLE, T: Special Education Teacher **I:** Education/Educational Services **CN:** West Haven Public School **PT:** Linda Criscuolo **ED:** Master of Arts in Early Childhood, St. Joseph College; Bachelor of Arts in Child Psychology, East-

ern Connecticut State University **CT:** Certificate in Autism; State Teacher Certificate in Integrated Pre-Kindergarten through Grade 3; State Teacher Certificate in Special Education Pre-Kindergarten through Grade 12 **C:** Special Education Pre-Kindergarten Teacher, West Haven Public Schools, Connecticut (2014-Present); Special Education Teacher, Derby Public Schools, Connecticut (2011-2014) **CR:** Presenter, Workshops on Children with Autism, West Haven, CT **CW:** Comprehensive List of Autism Resources **AS:** Ms. Criscuolo attributes her success to her mother. Her mother was her cheerleader her entire life. She always instilled in her that she can do whatever she put her mind to. **B/I:** Ever since she was in kindergarten, Ms. Criscuolo knew that she would become a teacher. When she was in undergraduate studies, she initially had plans to become a second grade teacher. Looking back, she began to notice that nearly all of her placement assignments were to assist students with special needs. That is when she discovered her niche. While trying to get her foot in the door, she was placed in a special education classroom and fell in love with it. She felt that it was meant to be.

CRISP, POLLY LENORE, PHD, T: Psychologist (Retired) **I:** Medicine & Health Care **DOB:** 05/20/1952 **PB:** Atlanta **SC:** GA/USA **PT:** John Pershing Crisp; Dorotha Amelia (Hogan) Crisp **ED:** BFA in Studio Arts (Sculpture), The University of Tennessee, Knoxville (2004); PhD in Clinical Psychology, Michigan State University, East Lansing, MI (1984); MA in Clinical Psychology, Michigan State University, East Lansing, MI (1981); BA, Liberal Arts, The University of Tennessee, Knoxville (1976) **C:** Clinical Psychologist, North Knox Health Center, Cherokee Health Systems (1993-1998); Private Practice, Psychology, Knoxville, TN (1992-1998); Clinical Psychologist, Overlook Mental Health Center, Maryville, TN (1990-1993); Adjunct Assistant Professor, The University of Tennessee, Knoxville (1990-1991); Clinical Psychologist, Kennebec Valley Mental Health Center, Augusta, ME (1987-1990); Psychotherapist, Arbours Centre, London, England, United Kingdom (1983-1985) **MEM:** Membership Committee, Division on Clinical Psychology, American Psychological Association (1990-1992); The British Psychological Society; Society for Psychotherapy Research; The New York Academy of Sciences; The Phi Beta Kappa Society; The Honor Society of Phi Kappa Phi; Alpha Lambda Delta **MH:** Albert Nelson Marquis Lifetime Achievement Award **AS:** Dr. Crisp attributes her success to hard work. **B/I:** Dr. Crisp became involved in her profession because psychology is an integration of art and science and that fascinated her. She wanted to better understand and help people. **AV:** Woodworking; Stained glass; Sculpture; Stone carving; Glass; Iron work

CRIST, CHARLES, "CHARLIE" JOSEPH JR., T: U.S. Representative from Florida, Lawyer **I:** Government Administration/Government Relations/Government Services **CN:** U.S. House of Representatives **DOB:** 7/24/1956 **PB:** Altoona **SC:** PA/USA **PT:** Charles Joseph Crist; Nancy (Lee) Crist **MS:** Married **SPN:** Carole Rome (12/12/2008); Amanda Morrow (1979, Divorced 02/15/1980) **CH:** Jessica (Stepchild); Skylar (Stepchild) **ED:** Doctor of Jurisprudence, Samford University Cumberland School of Law, Birmingham, AL (1981); Bachelor of Arts in Government, Florida State University (1978); Coursework, Wake Forest University, Winston-Salem, NC **C:** Member, U.S. House of Representatives from Florida's 13th Congressional District (2017-Present); Partner, Morgan & Morgan, St. Petersburg, FL (2011-Present); Governor, State of Florida (2007-2011); Attorney General, State of

Florida (2003-2007); Education Commissioner, State of Florida (2000-2002); Deputy Secretary, Florida Department of Business and Professional Regulation (1999-2000); Attorney, Wood & Crist (1987-1999); Member, Florida State Senate, Tallahassee, FL (1992-1998); General Counsel, National Association of Professional Baseball Leagues (1982-1987) **CIV:** Member, Advisory Committee, Muscular Dystrophy Association Inc., Tampa Bay, FL; Member, Pinellas County Republicans Executive Committee; Member, Administrative Board, First United Methodist Church; Board of Directors, Police Athletic League; Board of Directors, Foundation for Florida's Future **AW:** Legislative Award, Florida Sheriffs Association (1994, 1996); Distinguished Legislator Award, Florida Police Benevolent Association (1996); Legislative Conservation Award, Florida Conservation Association (1996); Senatorial Leadership Award, Florida Professional Attorneys Association (1995); Government Award, Urban League (1995); Named, Honorary Sheriff, Police Benevolent Association (1995); Named, Conservationist Legislator of the Year, Florida Wildlife Federation (1995); Award, Florida Association of School Administrators Inc. (1993); Award, Pinellas School Administrators (1993); Roll Call Award, Florida Chamber of Commerce (1993); Phil Piton Award for Service to MLB, Leadership St. Petersburg; True Grit Award, Suncoast Tiger Bay Club **MEM:** Fellow, American Swiss Association; American Bar Association; Board of Governors, Republican National Lawyers Association; St. Petersburg Bar Association; Hillsborough County Bar Association; Pinellas Park/Gateway Chamber of Commerce; St. Petersburg Chamber of Commerce; Florida Conservation Association; Pinellas County President's Council, American Lung Association; Rotary International; Board of Directors, Suncoast Tiger Bay Club; Suncoaster Civic Club **AV:** Water-skiing; Reading; Jogging **PA:** Democrat **RE:** Methodist

CRIST, WILLIAM GARY, T: Professor Emeritus **I:** Fine Art **CN:** Warren Piece and Creative Concepts **DOB:** 01/17/1937 **PB:** Pocatello **SC:** ID/USA **PT:** Margaret Alice (Zimmerman) Crist; Norman Benjamin Crist **MS:** Married **SPN:** Mary Ruth Crist **CH:** Julie Ann Crist Cantu **ED:** Coursework in Sculpture, Staatliche Kunstakademie (1981, 1983); MFA in Sculpture, Cranbrook Academy of Art (1971); Postgraduate Coursework in Art Education, University of Washington (1966-1969); BA in Arts Education, University of Washington (1966); Coursework in Art, Olympic College (1955-1957) **CT:** Certified Teacher, State of Washington; Founding Sponsor Certificate, National Museum of the United States Army; Achievement Certificate, The Leadership Institute, OSBA **C:** Adjunct Instructor of Art, Portland Community College (2002); Emeritus Professor of Art, University of Missouri, Kansas City (2000); Visiting Professor of Art, Hochschule Augsburg (1995); Director of 2D and 3D Computer Graphics, Video Instructional Network, Distance Learning Group, University of Missouri, Kansas City (1990); Professor of Art, University of Missouri, Kansas City (1988); Faculty Adviser, College Credit Program, Troost High School (1988); Associate Professor of Art, University of Missouri, Kansas City (1978); Graduate Faculty, Principal Graduate Adviser, University of Missouri, Kansas City (1977); Assistant Professor of Art, University of Missouri, Kansas City (1974); Instructor of Art, Cameron University (1972); Assistant Professor of Art, Wesleyan College (1971); Adjunct Instructor of Art, Bellevue Community College (1966); Arts and Crafts Teacher, Mount Si High School (1966); Engineering Illustrator, Boeing (1962); Technical Illustrator, Boeing (1957) **CR:** Strategic Educational Planning Committee, St. Helens

School Board (2004); Appointed, Chairman, Arts & Cultural Commission, City of St. Helens (2003); Consultant, Wayne State University (1984); Consultant, University of Detroit; Consultant; Spelman College **CIV:** Elected Member, School Board, St. Helena's School District (2007-2011); Elected Head Elder, St. Helen's Christian Church (2005) **MIL:** Post Art and Publicity Department, Fort Lewis, WA (1961); H-21 Helicopter Crew Chief, 57th Transportation Company (1961); Promoted, Specialist Fourth Class (1961); Helicopter Crew Chief, 55th Aviation Company (1960); Helicopter Crewman, 57th Transportation Company (1959); Aviation School (1959); Enlisted, Basic Training, US Army (1959) **CW:** Rotating Exhibition, Local Church (2020); Mural Commission, City of St. Helens (2008); Sculpture, City of St. Helens (2006); One-Man Exhibition, Cusick Gallery (2004); One-Man Exhibition, Campenella Gallery (1997); Juried Exhibition, Spring National Exhibition, Bridge Fine Arts Gallery (1993); Juried Exhibition, Fifth Annual National Computer Art Invitational, Eastern Washington University (1993); Juried Exhibition, Fifth International Open Exhibition, Sacramento Fine Arts Center (1992); Juried Exhibition, Hearst Art Gallery (1992); Juried Exhibition, "Points of View," Pleiades Gallery (1992); Juried Exhibition, Third Annual National Juried Competition, Eleven Art Ashland Independent Art Space (1992); Juried Exhibition, Poudre Valley Art League Art Exhibition, Lincoln Center (1992); Juried Exhibition, 13th Annual Paper in Particular National Exhibition, Columbia College (1992); Juried Exhibition, Fourth National Computer Art Invitational, Art Gallery, Eastern Washington University (1991); Juried Exhibition, "Oppression/Expression," Contemporary Arts Center (1986); One-Man Exhibition, Staatloiche Kunstakademie (1981); One-Man Exhibition, Noho Gallery (1980); One-Man Exhibition, Noho Gallery (1979); One-Man Exhibition, 7E7 Gallery (1978); One-Man Exhibition, University of Central Missouri (1976); One-Man Exhibition, University of Missouri, Kansas City (1975); One-Man Exhibition, Contemporary Arts Foundation (1974); Sculpture Commission, Cameron University (1974); One-Man Exhibition, Southern Oregon College (1972); One-Man Exhibition, Henry Gallery, University of Washington (1972); One-Man Exhibition, Wesleyan College (1971); One-Man Exhibition, Cranbrook Academy of Art (1971); One-Man Exhibition, Valley Gallery (1969) **AW:** Research Grants, University of Missouri (1982, 1992, 1999); Grant, Visiting Professor, Hochschule Augsburg (1995); Grant, Southwestern Bell Company (1993); Elected Chairman, Department of Art and Art History, University of Missouri, Kansas City (1987); Interdisciplinary Arts Fellow, National Endowment for the Arts (1986) Awarded Sabbatical for Research (1981, 1983); Who's Who in America; Who's Who in the Midwest; Who's Who in American Art; Who's Who in American Education **MEM:** St. Helen's Christian Church; Emeritus Club, University of Missouri; Retirees Association, University of Missouri; Alumni Association, Cranbrook Academy of Art; VFW; The American Legion; BPO Elks; Northwest Association of Corvette Clubs; National Rifle Association of America; OSWA **MH:** Albert Nelson Marquis Lifetime Achievement Award **AS:** Mr. Crist attributes his success to God, his wife, parents, daughter, teachers and mentors. **B/I:** Mr. Crist became involved in his profession because he has always been his happiest while creating. **AV:** Maintaining Warren Piece Farm; Corvette racing; Sailing **PA:** Constitutional Conservative **RE:** Christian

CRITES, MARSHA SMITH, BS, MSW, T: Owner, Social Worker **I:** Social Work **CN:** Harvest Moon Gardens **DOB:** 06/28/1952 **PB:** Greer **SC:** SC/USA **YOP:** 2019 **PT:** Donald Newton Smith; Mildred Lou (Kelly) Smith **MS:** Divorced **SPN:** Lee (Kern) Crites (06/20/1974) **CH:** Savannah Noel; Emily Harrison; Lillian Walker **ED:** MSW, San Diego State University (1978); BS in Human Services, University of Tennessee (1974) **CT:** Facilitation for Child Protective Services, Sylva Department of Social Services **C:** Owner, Harvest Moon Gardens Landscape Design Rental Property (1985-Present); Senior Associate, North Carolina Community Foundation (1992-2009); Program Director, Save The Children, Asheville, NC (1990-1992); Human Resource Director, Center for Improving Mountain Living, Western Carolina University, Cullowhee, NC (1987-1990); Project Director, Center for Improving Mountain Living, Western Carolina University, Cullowhee, NC (1984-1987); Instructor, Southwestern Community College (1983-1984); Medical Social Worker, Home Health Service Agency, Sylva, NC (1978-1980); Social Work Director, Golden Age Convalescent Center, Vista, CA (1974-1975) **CR:** Consultant, Mountain View Manor, Bryson City, NC (1983-1985); Consultant, Western Carolina University, Cullowhee, NC (1979-1983); Private Practice, Social Work, Marsha Smith Crites MSW; Associate, NC Community Foundation; Staff, Harris Hospital Home Health Social Worker; Staff, Western Carolina University; Moonshadow Learning Services; Facilitator, Social Worker, Child Protective Services, Save the Children **CIV:** President, United Christian Ministries (1989-1992); Jackson County Council on Aging (1988-1990); Jackson Village Retirement Village (1988-1990); Co-Founder, Clean Slate Coalition **CW:** Co-Author, "Walking Up to Poverty in Western North Carolina" (1990); Author, "Intergenerational Programs, Imperatives, Strategies, Trends" (1989) **AW:** NAACP Humanitarian Award (2017, 2019); Nancy Susan Reynolds Award for Personal Service, Z. Smith Reynolds Foundation (1991); Best Practice Showcase Winner, American Society on Aging (1987); Rural Aging Award (1987); Listee, Outstanding Young Women of America (1987) **MEM:** Secretary, National Society of Fundraising; Western North Carolina Association of Fundraising Profiles **MH:** Albert Nelson Marquis Lifetime Achievement Award; Distinguished Humanitarian **AS:** Mrs. Crites' parents believed in sharing wealth and assistance. Her father was the mayor of Greer, South Carolina; he additionally owned and operated Greer Gas Company, which inspired her to long for success. **B/I:** Mrs. Crites grew up in South Carolina, and her parents were public servants. She spent some time working for South Carolina Peaches, where she was exposed to the plight of migrant farm workers. She became interested in their story and the United Methodist Church sent her to an area to work with these workers. **AV:** Landscaping; Flower arranging; Painting water colors **PA:** Democratic **RE:** United Methodist **THT:** Mrs. Crites chooses to age in peace as the future nears.

CRIVELLI, CHAD, T: Farmer **I:** Agriculture **MS:** Married **CH:** Two Children **ED:** BS in Plant Sciences, California State University, Fresno, CA (2001) **C:** Farmer (1995-Present) **CIV:** Board Member, California Certified Organic Farmers; Merced County Agribusiness Committee; San Joaquin Political Academy; Board Member, Cotton Pest Control; California Tomato Research Institute; National Cotton Council **AW:** High Cotton Award, Western Farm Press (2013); National Fiber Crop Proficiency, National FFA Organization **AS:** Mr. Crivelli attributes his success to his drive that is fueled by the fear of failure. His grandfather and father were both great inspirations who instilled a strong work ethic in him. His motto is, "Just keep digging." **B/I:** Mr. Crivelli was featured in a famous traveling art exhibit. The quote that he used to describe himself in the feature was, "I always loved farming, and I always loved dirt." He doesn't know how else to describe his passions. Mr. Crivelli feels that he's always had a connection with the sight, the smell, and the feel of the farms. The connection is indescribable.

CROCKER, CHARLES ALLAN, T: Lawyer **I:** Law and Legal Services **CN:** Charles A. Crocker Attorney at Law **DOB:** 05/26/1940 **PB:** Waco **SC:** TX/USA **PT:** Wiley Vernon; Edith Mae Crocker **MS:** Married **SPN:** Mary Ann Herndon (09/01/1962) **CH:** Cathryn Ann; Amy Lynn **ED:** LLB, University of Texas (1965); BBA, Texas Technical University (1962) **CT:** Certified, Estate Planning and Probate (40 Years) **C:** Private Practice, Houston, TX (1987-Present); Attorney, Hendricks Management Company, Houston, TX (1986-1987); Attorney, Baker & Botts, Houston, TX (1974-1986); Accountant, Peat, Marwick, Mitchell, Houston, TX (1972-1974); Estate Tax Examiner, IRS, Houston, TX (1965-1972) **CR:** Director, Salient Trust Company, Houston, TX (1996-2018); Director, Houston Estate and Financial Forum (HEFF) (1976-1980) **AW:** 40 Year Award, Board Certified, Estate Planning & Probate; AV Preeminent, Martindale Hubbell **MEM:** American Bar Association; Probate Section, Houston Bar Association **BAR:** U.S. Court of Appeals for the Federal Circuit (1984); U.S. Claims Court (1981); U.S. District Court for the Southern District of Texas (1980); U.S. Tax Court (1979); Texas (1965) **MH:** Albert Nelson Marquis Lifetime Achievement Award; Marquis Who's Who Top Professional **B/I:** Mr. Crocker became involved in his profession because he was somewhat influenced by his brother, who was a lawyer. **AV:** Playing golf; Skiing **THT:** Mr. Crocker's areas of practice are estate planning, probate and estate, administration, trusts, wills, tax law, certifications and specialties, and estate planning and probate, among others.

CROCKETT, WEBB WEBB, T: Lawyer (Retired) **I:** Law and Legal Services **CN:** Fennemore Craig, P.C. **DOB:** 02/16/1934 **PB:** Preston **SC:** ID/USA **PT:** Frank Lee Crockett; Alta (Webb) Crockett **MS:** Married **SPN:** Nan Marie Mattice (6/27/1958). **CH:** Jeffrey Webb; Nicole; Karen; Cynthia **ED:** LLB, The University of Arizona (1962); MBA, Northwestern University (1959); BS, Brigham Young University (1958) **C:** Partner, Director, Fennemore Craig, P.C., Phoenix, AZ (1968-2017); Law Clerk, Arizona Supreme Court (1962-1963); **CR:** Instructor, Evening Division, Mesa Community College, AZ; Board of Directors, Southwest Airlines Co.; Board of Directors, East Valley Partnership; Board of Directors, Arizona Chamber of Commerce and Industry **CIV:** Chairman, Member, Board of Adjustment, City of Mesa, AZ (1996-Present); Member, Chairman, Valley Forward Association (1998); Mesa Crime Commission (1980-1982); Board of Directors, Maricopa Mental Health Association (Now Maricopa Integrated Health System (MIHS)) (1976-1978); Chairman, Board of Adjustment (1971-1973); Member, Board of Adjustment, Scottsdale, AZ (1968-1973); Member, Charter Review Committee, Scottsdale, AZ (1966-1967); Phoenix Community Alliance; Valley Forward Association; Member, Social Services Advisory Board, The Church of Jesus Christ of Latter-day Saints; Vice Chair, Governor's Regulatory Review Council, State of Arizona; Bishop, The Church of Jesus Christ of Latter-day Saints, Utah, Tempe, Scottsdale, AZ; Precinct Committeeman, Legislative District 19; Maricopa County Republican Committee Parliamentarian; Chairman, Bylaws Committee, State Republican Party; Member-at-large, Arizona's First Congressional District **MIL:** United States Army Reserves **CW:** Member, Editorial Board, Arizona Law Review (1961) **AW:** Best Lawyers in America (1991-Present); Jesse A. Lindall Distinguished

Service Award **MEM:** Commission on Salaries for Elective State and Judicial Officers (Now Arizona Commission on Salaries for Elective State Officers (CSESO)) (1998, 2002, 2006, 2008); ABA; State Bar of Arizona; Maricopa County Bar Association; American Judicature Society; Phoenix Chamber of Commerce (Now Greater Phoenix Chamber of Commerce); Arizona Academy; Mesa United Way **BAR:** Supreme Court of the United States (1970); State Bar of Arizona (1962); Arizona Supreme Court; Mississippi Supreme Court; United States District Court for the District of Arizona; North Circuit Court of Appeals **MH:** Albert Nelson Marquis Lifetime Achievement Award **B/I:** Mr. Crockett attended Brigham Young University. He ran for student body president at BYU and won that position, serving as president during his senior year. That experience piqued his interest in politics, but he was also very interested in business and he had a grant to go to Northwestern to get an MBA. He decided while he was at Northwestern working on his MBA that he would take the LSAT and apply to law school. He went on to law school at that point. He had a great interest in business throughout his life but most of his activity in the practice of law has been with major corporations within the country. Mr. Crockett has represented almost all of the major corporations, such as General Motors, Southwest Airlines, and a number of others. He later decided to run for public office. **AV:** Political activities: events and campaigns **PA:** Republican **RE:** Church of Jesus Christ of Latter-Day Saints

CROFUT, DONALD MERWIN, BS, T: Senior Buyer (Retired) **I:** Other **CN:** IBM **DOB:** 01/26/1931 **PB:** Ossining **SC:** NY/USA **PT:** Charles Merwin Crofut; Florence Grace (Martin) Crofut **MS:** Divorced **CH:** Mark Merwin (Deceased); Karin Joyce **ED:** BS, The University of Vermont (1954) **C:** Staff, Senior Buyer, Purchasing Department, IBM (1954-1992) **CR:** Verger, Pastoral Care Community Memorial Garden (2000-Present); Community Chairman, Pastoral Care Community Memorial Garden (2000-Present); All Saints Episcopal Church, South Burlington, VT (1977-Present); Pledge Treasurer, Verger, Pastoral Care Community Memorial Garden (1977-Present); Group, All Saints Episcopal Church, South Burlington, VT (1972-Present); Lay Reader, Teacher, Verger, Pledge Treasurer, All Saints Episcopal Church, South Burlington, VT (1970-Present); Teacher, Pastoral Care Community Memorial Garden (1988-2018); Lay Reader, Pastoral Care Community Memorial Garden (1988-2018); Verger, Pastoral Care Community Memorial Garden (1988-2018); Pledge Treasurer, Pastoral Care Community Memorial Garden (1988-2018); Chairman, Memorial Garden (2001-2017); Committee Chairman, Diocesan Congregational Support and Resources (2006-2016); Council Education Committee, Alcohol and Drug Abuse Council, Burlington, VT (1983-1985); Families Anonymous (1982-1987); Various Committees, Green Mountain Council, Boy Scouts of America (1974-1978); Co-President, South Burlington PTA (1976-1977); Cost Review Subcommittee, Burlington School District (1968-1970); Christian Education Teacher, Middle School and High School **CIV:** Chair, Episcopal Diocese Congregational Services and Resource Community (2006-2016); Chairman, Fire District, South Burlington (1964-1967) **MEM:** The Phi Beta Kappa Society (1954); Masons **MH:** Albert Nelson Marquis Lifetime Achievement Award; Marquis Who's Who Top Professional **B/I:** Mr. Crofut became involved in his profession because it fit his personality. **AV:** Canoeing; Hiking; Bicycling; Skiing; Fishing; Kayaking; Studying history and his family genealogy **PA:** Republican **RE:** Episcopalian

CROMARTIE, ROBERT SAMUEL III, MD, FACS, T: Thoracic Surgeon **I:** Medicine & Health Care **DOB:** 12/25/1943 **PB:** Fayetteville **SC:** NC/USA **PT:** Robert Samuel Cromartie Jr.; May Hunter Cook Cromartie **MS:** Married **SPN:** Mary Elaine Collier **CH:** Robert Samuel Cromartie IV; Judge David Alan Cromartie; Kimberly Elaine Cromartie, Esq. **ED:** Resident in Thoracic Surgery, Medical University of South Carolina, Charleston, SC (1976-1978); Resident in General Surgery, Louisiana State University School of Medicine, New Orleans, LA (1974-1976); Resident in General Surgery, University of Miami, Miami-Dade County, FL (1972-1974); Intern in Surgery, University of Miami, Miami-Dade County, FL (1969-1970); MD, University of North Carolina School of Medicine, Chapel Hill, NC (1969); AB in Chemistry, University of North Carolina, Chapel Hill, NC (1965); Diploma, Fayetteville Senior High School, Fayetteville, NC (1962) **CT:** Diplomate, American Board Surgery; American Board of Thoracic Surgery; American Board of Laser Surgery **C:** Chief of Thoracic and Cardiovascular Surgery, Halifax Hospital, Daytona Beach, FL (1984-2006); Thoracic and Cardiovascular Surgeon, Memorial Hospital, Ormond Beach, FL (1981-2006); Thoracic and Cardiovascular Surgeon, Columbia Medical Center, Daytona Beach, FL (1981-1999); Chief of Surgery, Columbia Medical Center, Daytona Beach, FL (1996-1997); Thoracic and Cardiovascular Surgeon, Tampa General Hospital, Tampa, FL (1980-1981); Assistant Professor of Cardiac and General Thoracic Surgery, Indiana University School of Medicine, Indianapolis, IN (1978-1980); Thoracic and Cardiovascular Surgeon, Memorial Hospital Flager, Palm Coast, FL **CIV:** Delegate, Florida Medical Association (1992-1994); Tiger Bay Club of Volusia County; Chairman, Environmental Committee of the Volusia County Medical Society **MIL:** Captain, U.S. Army Medical Corps (1970-1972) **CW:** Author, "The Weather Girl's Assassin" (2018); Author, "Romanov Curse" (2017); Author, "Romanov Quest" (2017); Author, "Himmler's Mistress" (2017); Author, "Ultimate Duty" (2017); Author, "Good Fortune's Curse" (2017); Author, "An Innocent Lie" (2017); Author, "Family Survival Guide" (2012); Author, "Creating a Kindle Ebook on the Mac" (2012); Co-Author, "High-Tech Terror: Recognition, Management, and Prevention of Biological, Chemical, and Nuclear Injuries Secondary to Acts of Terrorism" (2009); Contributor, Multiple Articles, Medical Journals **AW:** Finalist, Beverly Hills Thriller Screenplay Contest (2017); Runner Up, Best Dramatic Short Screenplay, Hollywood Dreamz and Action on Film, International Film Festival in Las Vegas (2017); Second Place, Feature Thriller, Horror, Woods Hole Film Festival Screenplay Competition (2012); Fifth Honorable Mention, Writers-Editors Network International Writing Competition (2012); Sci-Fi Horror Honorable Mention, Woods Hole Film Festival Screenplay Competition (2010); Runner-Up, Feature Screenplay Competition, 11th Annual Bare Bones International Film Festival (2010); Finalist, Screenplay Competition, Las Vegas International Film Festival (2010); Honorable Mention, Television/Movie Script Category, 78th Annual Writer's Digest Writing Competition (2009); Finalist, Screenwriting Category, Literary Contest, Pacific Northwest Writers Association (2009); Third Place in Fiction, Novel, Josiah W. Bancroft Senior Novel Contest, Florida First Coast Writers Festival (2009); Second Place for Fiction, Novel Chapter, Writers-Editors Network International Writing Competition (2009); Finalist, Writers' League of Texas Manuscript Contest (2008); Third Place for Fiction, Novel Chapter, CNW/FFWA Florida State Writing Competition (2008); Semifinalist, Rupert Hughes Prose Writing Award, Maui Writers Conference (2007) **MEM:** President, Coastal Cardiovascular and Thoracic Society (2006); Fellow, American College of Surgeons; American College of Chest Physicians; International College of Surgeons; American Medical Association; Southern Thoracic Surgical Association; Society of Thoracic Surgeons; James D. Rives Surgical Society; American Heart Association; Society of Critical Care Medicine **MH:** Albert Nelson Marquis Lifetime Achievement Award **B/I:** Dr. Cromartie became involved in his profession because of a book he read when he was 16 years old, "Hiroshima Diary: The Journal of a Japanese Physician," which sparked his interest in medicine. **AV:** Snow skiing; Playing racquetball; Writing novels

CRONIN, ROBERT HILLSMAN, T: Musical Instrument Manufacturer (Retired) **I:** Manufacturing **DOB:** 02/09/1943 **PB:** Houston **SC:** TX/USA **PT:** Thomas Dillon Cronin; Anne Catherine (Heyck) Cronin **MS:** Single **ED:** PhD in Applied Mechanics, Stanford University, Stanford, CA (1972); MS in Applied Mechanics, Stanford University, Stanford, CA (1966); BSME, Rice University, Houston, Texas (1965); BA, Rice University, Houston, Texas (1964) **C:** Owner, Robert H. Cronin (RHC) Historical Instruments, Menlo Park, CA (1981-Present); Technical Staff, KLA Instruments, Santa Clara, CA (1981-1986); Research and Development Engineer, Stanford University, Stanford, CA (1978-1980); Research Engineer, SRI International, Menlo Park, CA (1972-1977) **CIV:** Member, Bicycle Advisory Committee (1990-1996) **CW:** Author, "Understanding the Operation of Auxiliary Fingerings on the Modern Bassoon" (1996); Author, Article, Rice University Publication (1995); Author, "Evolution of the Bassoon Bore" (1981); "Evolution of the Bassoon Bore," Presented, Meeting, American Musical Instrument Society, Vancouver, Canada, British Columbia; Author, Published Paper, Journal of the International Double Reed Society, Number 24 **MEM:** International Double Reed Society; Historical Brass Society, Inc.; American Musical Instrument Society; San Francisco Early Music Society **MH:** Albert Nelson Marquis Lifetime Achievement Award **B/I:** Mr. Cronin became involved in his profession because while he was a graduate student at Stanford University, he was satisfied with the instruments he was playing but thought he could make them better. He began his interest in music in the 1970s but did not sell them until the 1980s. He taught himself how to play the ancestors of the oboe and bassoon. **AV:** Sailing; Bicycling; Music; Travel

CROSWELL, BEVERLY ANN, T: Newborn Screening Nurse, Specialty Case Manager **I:** Medicine & Health Care **DOB:** 01/07/1954 **PB:** Wilkes-Barre **SC:** PA/USA **PT:** George Margitish; Mary (Cahoot) Margitish **MS:** Married **SPN:** David Croswell **CH:** Ryan Croswell **ED:** BSN, Wilkes University (1976) **CT:** RNC, Nurses Association of the American College of Obstetrics and Gynecology; Certified Lamaze Instructor **C:** Lead Newborn Screening Nurse Coordinator, Southern California Kaiser Permanente 14 Hospital System; Regional Nurse Coordinator, Preterm Birth Prevention Program, Kaiser Permanente, Southern California Region, Pasadena, CA (1988-Present); Perinatal Nurse Educator, Hollywood Presbyterian Medical Center, Los Angeles, CA (1986-1988); Perinatal Staff Nurse, LAC-USC Medical-Center, Women's Hospital (1985-1986); Director, Obstetrics-Gynecology, California Hospital Medical Center (1983-1985); Birthing Center, Nurse Manager, LAC-USC Medical-Center, Women's Hospital (1977-1983); Perinatal Clinical Nurse Specialist, LAC-USC Medical-Center, Women's Hospital (1977-1983); Perinatal Nurse Educator, LAC-USC Medical-Center, Women's Hospital (1977-1983); Staff Nurse, LAC-USC Medical-Center, Women's Hospital (1977-1983); Staff Nurse, Sibley

Memorial Hospital, Washington, DC (1976-1977) **CR:** Chairperson, March of Dimes-Visual Professionals in Nursing (1991-Present); Perinatal Nurse Educator (1990-Present); Lamaze Instructor, California Hospital (1983-1994); Committee Member, State Steering Committee for Pre-Term Birth (1991-1993) **MEM:** Nurses Association of the American College of Obstetrics and Gynecology; Perinatal Advisory Council, One-C. **MH:** Albert Nelson Marquis Lifetime Achievement Award; Marquis Who's Who Top Professional **B/I:** Ms. Croswell started off working in premed but she wanted to work in research in oncology and pediatrics. In her second year in college, the nursing program was starting up and it gave her an opportunity. As a nurse, Ms. Croswell could work different shifts and not be on call for so many hours a week. She pursued a career in the field, working in a unit that delivered 17-thousand babies a year. Ms. Croswell hoped to learn as much as possible, getting a fantastic clinical experience. She then became a clinical educator, clinical nurse specialist, and then a head nurse. She opened one of the first birthing centers, which was early on in her career, and, at the time, they were not common but she knew it would become an important part of her work. **AV:** Gardening; Biking; Traveling; Kayaking **PA:** Conservative **RE:** Christian

CROW, JASON A., T: U.S. Representative from Colorado **I:** Government Administration/Government Relations/Government Services **CN:** U.S. House of Representatives **DOB:** 03/15/1979 **PB:** Madison **SC:** WI/USA **MS:** Married **SPN:** Deserai Anderson **CH:** Two Children **ED:** Doctor of Jurisprudence, University of Denver Sturm College of Law (2009); Bachelor of Arts, University of Wisconsin-Madison **C:** Member, U.S. House of Representatives from Colorado's Sixth Congressional District (2019-Present); Member, Colorado Board of Veterans' Affairs (2009-2014); Partner, Holland and Hart LLP **MIL:** Captain, United States Army (2002-2006) **AW:** Bronze Star **PA:** Democrat

CROWE, RUSSELL, T: Actor **I:** Media & Entertainment **DOB:** 04/07/1964 **PB:** Wellington **SC:** New Zealand **PT:** John Alexander Crowe; Jocelyn Yvonne (Wemyss) Crowe **MS:** Divorced **SPN:** Danielle Spencer (04/07/2003, Divorced 10/2018) **CH:** Charles Spencer; Tenyson Spencer **CW:** Actor, "True History of the Kelly Gang" (2019); Actor, "Unhinged" (2020); Actor, "Boy Erased" (2018); Actor, "War Machine" (2017); Actor, "The Mummy" (2017); Actor, "The Nice Guys" (2016); Actor, Executive Producer, "Fathers and Daughters" (2015); Actor, "Winter's Tale" (2014); Actor, Director, "The Water Diviner" (2014); Actor, "Noah" (2014); Actor, "Broken City" (2013); Actor, "Man of Steel" (2013); Director, "Sydney Unplugged" (2013); Actor, "The Man with the Iron Fists" (2012); Actor, "Republic of Doyle" (2012); Actor, "Les Misérables" (2012); Actor, "The Next Three Days" (2010); Actor, Producer, "Robin Hood" (2010); Actor, "State of Play" (2009); Actor, "Tenderness" (2008); Actor, "Body of Lies" (2008); Actor, "3:10 to Yuma" (2007); Actor, "American Gangster" (2007); Actor, "Cinderella Man" (2005); Singer, "Soundstage" (2004); Actor, "Master and Commander: The Far Side of the World" (2003); Director, "60 Odd Hours in Italy" (2002); Director, Producer, "Texas" (2002); Actor, "A Beautiful Mind" (2001); Actor, "Gladiator" (2000); Actor, "Proof of Life" (2000); Actor, "Mystery Alaska" (1999); Actor, "The Insider" (1999); Actor, "Heaven's Burning" (1997); Actor, "Breaking Up" (1997); Actor, "L.A. Confidential" (1997); Actor, "The Quick and the Dead" (1995); Actor, "Proof" (1995); Actor, "Romper Stomper" (1995); Actor, "Rough Magic" (1995); Actor, "Virtuosity" (1995); Actor, "Under the Gun" (1995); Actor, "The

Crossing" (1993); Actor, "Brides of Christ" (1991); Actor, "Neighbours" (1987); Actor, "Grease"; Actor, "Rocky Horror Picture Show" **AW:** Named One of 50 Most Powerful People in Hollywood, Premiere Magazine (2004-2006); Golden Globe Award for Best Actor in a Drama, Hollywood Foreign Press Association (2002); Screen Actors Guild Award for Best Actor, SAG-AFTRA (2002); BAFTA Film Award for Best Actor (2002); Academy Award for Best Actor, Academy of Motion Picture Arts and Sciences (2001); Global Achievement Award, Australian Film Institute (2001); Award for Best Actor, National Society of Film Critics (2000)

CRUISE, TOM, T: Actor **I:** Media & Entertainment **DOB:** 07/03/1962 **PB:** Syracuse **SC:** NY/USA **PT:** Thomas C. Cruise III; Mary Lee Mapother **SPN:** Katie Holmes (11/18/2006, Divorced 2012); Nicole Kidman (12/24/1990, Divorced 2001); Mimi Rogers (05/09/1987, Divorced 1990) **CH:** Isabella Jane; Connor Antony; Suri **C:** Co-Owner (with Paula Wagner), United Artists Entertainment, LLC (2006-Present); Co-Founder (with Paula Wagner), Cruise/Wagner Productions (1993-2006); Producer, Partner, Cruise/Wagner Productions **CW:** Actor, Producer, "Top Gun: Maverick" (2021); Actor, Producer, "Mission: Impossible-Fallout" (2018); Actor, "The Mummy" (2017); Actor, "American Made" (2017); Actor, Producer, "Jack Reacher: Never Go Back" (2016); Actor, "Jack Reacher Never Go Back" (2016); Actor, Producer, "Mission: Impossible-Rogue Nation" (2015); Actor, "Edge of Tomorrow" (2014); Actor, "Oblivion" (2013); Actor, "Rock of Ages" (2012); Actor, Producer, "Jack Reacher" (2012); Actor, Producer, "Mission: Impossible-Ghost Protocol" (2011); Actor, "Knight and Day" (2010); Actor, Producer, "Valkyrie" (2008); Actor, "Tropic Thunder" (2008); Actor, Executive Producer, "Lions for Lambs" (2007); Producer, "Ask the Dusk" (2006); Actor, Producer, "Mission: Impossible III" (2006); Producer, "Elizabethtown" (2005); Actor, "War of the Worlds" (2005); Actor, "Collateral" (2004); Actor, Producer, "The Last Samurai" (2003); Executive Producer, "Shattered Glass" (2003); Actor, "Minority Report" (2002); Executive Producer, "Narc" (2002); Actor, Producer, "Vanilla Sky" (2001); Executive Producer, "The Others" (2001); Actor, Producer, "Mission: Impossible II" (2000); Actor, "Magnolia" (1999); Actor, "Eyes Wide Shut" (1999); Producer, "Without Limits" (1998); Actor, "Jerry McGuire" (1996); Actor, Producer, "Mission: Impossible" (1996); Actor, "Interview with the Vampire" (1994); Actor, "The Firm" (1993); Actor, "Far and Away" (1992); Actor, "A Few Good Men" (1992); Actor, Writer, "Days of Thunder" (1990); Actor, "Born on the Fourth of July" (1989); Actor, "Cocktail" (1988); Actor, "Rain Man" (1988); Actor, "Top Gun" (1986); Actor, "The Color of Money" (1986); Actor, "Legend" (1985); Actor, "The Outsiders" (1983); Actor, "Losin' It" (1983); Actor, "Risky Business" (1983); Actor, "All the Right Moves" (1983); Actor, "Endless Love" (1981); Actor, "Taps" (1981) **AW:** Ten Most Fascinating People of 2008 (2009); Barbara Walters, The 100 Most Powerful Celebrities, Forbes.com (2006-2007, 2008); Museum of the Moving Image Salute (2007); The 10 Most Fascinating People of 2005 (2006); Barbara Walters Special, 50 Most Powerful People in Hollywood, "Premiere" (2004-2006); Golden Globe Award for Best Supporting Actor in a Motion Picture (2000); John Huston Award for Artists Rights, The Artists Rights Foundation (1998); Golden Globe Award for Best Actor (1997); Co-recipient, Nova Award for Outstanding Achievement by New or Emerging Producer in Theatrical Motion Pictures, Producer's Guild (1997); Golden Globe Award for Best Actor in a Motion Picture Drama (1990); Star on the Hollywood Walk of Fame

CRUZ, PENÉLOPE, T: Actress **I:** Media & Entertainment **DOB:** 04/28/1974 **PB:** Madrid **SC:** Spain **PT:** Eduardo Cruz; Encarna Cruz **MS:** Married **SPN:** Javier Bardem (07/2010) **CH:** Leonardo Encinas Cruz; Luna Encinas Cruz **ED:** Coursework in Classical Ballet, National Conservatory, Madrid **CIV:** Founder, Sabera Foundation **CW:** Actress, "355" (2021); Actress, "Wasp Network" (2019); Actress, "El Hormiguero: Vacaciones en el Titanic" (2019); Actress, "Pain and Glory" (2019); Actress, "Everybody Knows" (2018); Actress, "The Assassination of Gianni Versace" (2018); Actress, "Loving Pablo" (2017); Actress, "Murder on the Orient Express" (2017); Actress, Producer, "The Queen of Spain" (2016); Actress, Producer, "Layover" (2016); Actress, "The Brothers Grimsby" (2016); Actress, "The Queen of Spain" (2016); Actress, "Zoolander 2" (2016); Actress, Producer, "Ma Ma" (2015); Actress, "I'm So Excited" (2013); Actress, "The Counselor" (2013); Co-producer, "Twice Born" (2012); Actress, "To Rome with Love" (2012); Actress, "Venuto al mondo" (2012); Actress, "Pirates of the Caribbean: On Stranger Tides" (2011); Actress, "Sex and the City 2" (2010); Actress, "Los abrazoz rotos" (2009); Actress, "Nine" (2009); Actress, "Elegy" (2008); Actress, "Vicky Cristina Barcelona" (2008); Actress, "The Good Night" (2007); Actress, "Bandidas" (2006); Actress, "Volver" (2006); Actress, "Sahara" (2005); Actress, "Chromophobia" (2005); Actress, "Noel" (2004); Actress, "Head in the Clouds" (2004); Actress, "Masked and Anonymous" (2003); Actress, "Fanfan la tulipe" (2003); Actress, "Gothika" (2003); Actress, "Waking Up in Reno" (2002); Actress, "Blow" (2001); Actress, "Captain Corelli's Mandolin" (2001); Actress, "Sin noticias de Dios" (2001); Actress, "Vanilla Sky" (2001); Actress, "Woman on Top" (2000); Actress, "All the Pretty Horses" (2000); Actress, "Todo sobre mi madre" (1999); Actress, "Volavèrunt" (1999); Actress, "Don Juan" (1998); Actress, "The Man with Rain in His Shoes" (1998); Actress, "Talk of Angels" (1998); Actress, "La Niña de tus ojos" (1998); Actress, "The Hi-Lo Country" (1998); Actress, "Et Hjørne af paradis" (1997); Actress, "Carne trémula" (1997); Actress, "Abre los ojos" (1997); Actress, "La Celestina" (1996); Actress, "Más que amor, frenesí" (1996); Actress, "La Ribelle" (1993); Actress, "Belle époque" (1992); Actress, "Framed" (1992); Actress, "Jamón, jamón" (1992); Actress, "El Laberinto griego" (1991) **AW:** Sexiest Woman Alive, "Esquire" (2014); Best Supporting Actress, British Academy Film and TV Arts (2009); Best Actress in a Supporting Role, Academy Awards (2009); Outstanding Actress - Motion Picture, ALMA Awards (2009); World's Most Influential People, "TIME" (2009); Best Supporting Actress, National Board of Review (2008); Best Supporting Actress, New York Film Critics Circle (2008); Best Supporting Actress, Boston Society Film Critics (2008); Recipient, Best Film Award "Elle" (2007); Knight, Order of Arts and Letters, France (2006)

CRUZ, RAFAEL, "TED" EDWARD, T: U.S. Senator from Texas; Lawyer **I:** Government Administration/Government Relations/Government Services **DOB:** 12/22/1970 **PB:** Calgary **SC:** Alberta/Canada **PT:** Rafael Bienvenido Cruz; Eleanor Elizabeth (Darragh) Cruz **MS:** Married **SPN:** Heidi Suzanne Nelson (05/27/2001) **CH:** Caroline; Catherine **ED:** JD, Harvard Law School, Magna Cum Laude (1995); AB, Princeton University, Cum Laude (1992) **C:** U.S. Senator, State of Texas (2013-Present); Vice Chairman, Grass Roots Outreach, National Republican Senatorial Committee (NRSC) (2013-Present); Member, U.S. Senate Special Committee on Aging (2013-Present); Member, U.S. Senate Judiciary Committee (2013-Present); Member, U.S. Senate Committee on Rules and

Administration (2013-Present); Member, U.S. Senate Committee on Commerce, Science and Transportation (2013-Present); Member, U.S. Senate Armed Services Committee (2013-Present); Partner, Morgan, Lewis & Bockius LLP, Houston, TX (2008-2012); Solicitor General, State of Texas, Austin, TX (2003-2008); Director, Office Policy Planning, Federal Trade Commission, Washington, DC (2001-2003); Associate Deputy Attorney General, U.S. Department of Justice, Washington, DC (2001); Domestic Policy Advisor, Bush-Cheney 2000, Austin, TX(1999-2000); Associate, Cooper, Carvin, & Rosenthal PLLC, Washington, DC (1997-1999); Law Clerk to Justice William Rehnquist, Supreme Court of the United States, Washington, DC (1996-1997); Law Clerk to Honorable J. Michael Luttig, United States Court of Appeals for the Fourth Circuit, Washington, DC (1995-1996) **CR:** Candidate, 2016 Republican Party Presidential Nomination (2016); Adjunct Professor, United States Supreme Court Litigation, The University of Texas School of Law (2004-2009); U.S Department of Justice Coordinator, Bush-Cheney Transition Advisory Committee (2000-2001); Team Member, Bush-Cheney 2000, Inc. (1999-2000) **CIV:** Attorney, Bush-Cheney Presidential Recount, FL (2000); Foundation Director, Texas Mavericks; Board of Advisors, Hispanic Alliance for Progress; Board of Advisors, Texas Review of Law & Politics **CW:** Author, "A Time for Truth: Reigniting the Promise of America" (2015); Primary Editor, Harvard Law Review (1995); Executive Editor, Harvard Journal of Law and Public Policy (1995); Co-Founding Editor, Harvard Latino Law Review **AW:** Listee, 100 Most Influential People in the World, TIME Magazine (2016); Listee, America's Leading Lawyers for Business, Chambers USA (2009, 2010); Listee, 25 Greatest Texas Lawyers of the Past Quarter Century, Texas Lawyer (2010); Listee, Appellate Hot List, The National Law Journal (2010); Listee, 50 Most Influential Minority Lawyers in America, The National Law Journal (2008); Listee, Litigation's Rising Stars, The American Lawyer (2007); Best United States Supreme Court Merits Brief Award, National Association of Attorney Generals (2003-2007); Listee, 50 Most Influential People in Politics, George Magazine (2001); Listee, 100 Most Influential Hispanics, Hispanic Business Magazine (1999, 2000); Listee, 20 Young Hispanics to Watch, Newsweek Magazine (1999); John M. Olin Fellow, Harvard Law School; Traphagen Distinguished Alumnus, Harvard Law School **MEM:** The American Law Institute; Philosophical Society of Texas; Past Vice President, Director, The Texas Lyceum **BAR:** Supreme Court of the United States, Washington, DC (1998); State of Texas (1997); United States District Court for the District of Texas; United States Court of Appeals for the Fourth Circuit; United States Court of Appeals for the Fifth Circuit; United States Court of Appeals for the District of Columbia Circuit **PA:** Republican **RE:** Baptist

CRUZ-ALVAREZ, RAUL, T: Chief Executive Officer **I:** Business Management/Business Services **CN:** Landing Gears Technologies **DOB:** 05/11/1967 **PB:** Havana **SC:** Cuba **PT:** Raul Cruz-Alvarez; Maria (Bustio) Cruz-Alvarez **MS:** Married **SPN:** Ibis Cruz-Alvarez **CH:** Rolando Raul Estrada; Daniella Espinosa; Alexis Estrada; Estefania Cruz-Alvarez **ED:** Coursework, Dade County Community College (1984-1986); Coursework, George T. Baker Aviation Technical College (1983-1985) **CT:** Certified Aircraft Technician; Certified Private Pilot **C:** President, Transcontinental Asset Management (1995-Present); President, Diversified Aeronautics, Incorporated, Miami, FL (1994-1996); General Manager, Castle Precision Industries, Van Nuys, CA (1990-1994); Director of Operations, Associate Director, Director of Production, AAR Corporation

(Formerly Dixie Aircraft Corporation), Miami, FL (1987-1989); Director of Operations, Dixie Aircraft Corporation, Miami, FL (1986-1987); Technician/Inspector, Cleveland Pneumatics, Corporation (1984-1986); Accountable Manager, Chief Executive Officer, Landing Gear Technologies **CR:** Director, Miami Racing Team **CIV:** Manager, Director, Disaster Relief, Hurricane Andrew, South Miami, Florida (1992); Associate Director, Kids in Distress, Miami, FL (1989-1991); Registered Director, American Red Cross, Miami, FL (1988-1989) **CW:** Author, "FAA Procedure Manual" (1987, 1990, 2006, 2009) **AW:** New Member Award, PAMA **MEM:** Vice President, PAMA (1988) **MH:** Albert Nelson Marquis Lifetime Achievement Award **B/I:** Mr. Cruz-Alvarez's friend suggested he look into a career in aviation after seeing his interest in the field. Mr. Cruz-Alvarez took the advice and never looked back; he quickly discovered he loved the work. **PA:** Republican **RE:** Roman Catholic

CRYSTAL, BILLY, T: Actor **I:** Media & Entertainment **DOB:** 03/14/1948 **PB:** Long Beach **SC:** NY/USA **PT:** Jack Crystal; Helen Crystal **MS:** Married **SPN:** Janice Goldfinger (06/04/1970) **CH:** Jennifer; Lindsay **ED:** BFA in Television and Film Direction, New York University (1970); Coursework, Nassau Community College; Coursework, Marshall University, Huntington, WV **CW:** Actor, "Standing Up, Falling Down" (2019); Appearance, "Sammy Davis Jr.: I've Gotta Be Me" (2019); Appearance, "Robin Williams: Come Inside My Mind" (2018); Appearance, "Andre the Giant" (2018); Actor, "Untogether" (2018); Narrator, "This Is Bob Hope" (2017); Actor, "Modern Family" (2017); Actor, "Untogether" (2017); Actor, "The Comedian" (2016); Host, "Saturday Night Live" (1984-1985, 2015); Actor, "Party Central" (2014); Actor, "700 Sundays" (2005, 2013); Voice Actor, "Monsters University" (2013); Author, "65: Where I've Been, Where I'm Going, and Where the Hell Are My Keys?" (2013); Author, "Still Foolin' 'Em" (2013); Actor, "Small Apartments" (2012); Actor, Producer, "Parental Guidance" (2012); Host, Academy Awards (1990-1993, 1996-1998, 2000, 2004, 2012); Voice Actor, "Cars" (2006); Author, "Grandpa's Little One" (2006); Author, "700 Sundays" (2005); Author, "I Already Know I Love You" (2004); Voice Actor, "Howl's Moving Castle" (2004); Voice Actor, "Mike's New Car" (2002); Actor, "Analyze That" (2002); Director, Producer, "61" (2001); Actor, "America's Sweethearts" (2001); Voice Actor, "Monsters, Inc. (2001); Actor, "The Adventures of Rocky & Bullwinkle" (2000); Host, "AFI's 100 Years, 100 Laughs: America's Funniest Movies" (2000); Host, "Saturday Night Live: 25th Anniversary" (1999); Actor, "Analyze This" (1999); Actor, "My Giant" (1998); Actor, "Father's Day" (1997); Actor, "Deconstructing Harry" (1997); Actor, "Hamlet" (1996); Actor, "Forget Paris" (1995); Actor, "Sessions" (1991); Comedian; Executive Producer, Writer, "Midnight Train to Moscow" (1989); Actor, "When Harry Met Sally..." (1989); Actor, Producer, Co-screenwriter, "Memories of Me" (1988); Actor, "The Princess Bride" (1987); Actor, "Goodnight Moon" (1987); Actor, "Throw Momma from the Train" (1987); Actor, "Running Scared" (1986); Host, "Comic Relief" (1986); Co-author with Dick Schaap, "Absolutley Mahvelous" (1986); Artist, "You Look Mahvelous" (1985); Actor, "This Is Spinal Tap" (1984); Actor, "Rabbit Test" (1978); Voice Actor, "Animalympics" (1979); Actor, "City Slickers II: The Legend of Curley's Gold" (1994); Actor, "Mr. Saturday Night" (1992); Actor, Director, Producer, Writer, "City Slickers" (1991); Host, Grammy Awards" (1988, 1989); Host, "The Billy Crystal Comedy Hour" (1982); Director, Producer, "Soap" (1977-1981); Actor, Producer, "Enola Gay, the Men, the Mission, the Atomic Bomb" (1980); Actor, Producer, "Breaking Up Is Hard to Do"

(1979); Actor, Producer, "Human Feelings" (1978); Actor, Producer, "SST-Death Flight" (1977); House Manager, "You're a Good Man Charlie Brown" (1971) **AW:** Mark Twain Prize for American Humor, Kennedy Center (2007); Outer Critics Circle Award for Outstanding Solo Performance (2005); Tony Award for Best Special Theatrical Event (2005); Drama Desk Award for Outstanding Solo Performance (2005); Emmy Award for Outstanding Individual Performance, Television Academy (1991, 1998); Emmy Award for Outstanding Writing, Television Academy (1989, 1991); American Comedy Award (1991); Emmy Award for Outstanding Performance in Special Events, Television Academy (1989)

CUBAN, MARK, T: Owner; Co-owner; Sports Team Executive; Entrepreneur; Television Personality; Investor **I:** Athletics **CN:** Dallas Mavericks; 2929 Entertainment; Brondell **DOB:** 07/31/1958 **PB:** Pittsburgh **SC:** PA/USA **PT:** Norton Cuban; Shirley Cuban **MS:** Married **SPN:** Tiffany Stewart (09/21/2002) **CH:** Alexis Sofia; Alyssa; Jake **ED:** BS in Management, Indiana University Kelley School of Business, Bloomington, IN (1981); Coursework, University of Pittsburgh **C:** Principal Owner, Professional Futsal League (PFL) (2016-Present); Co-owner, 2929 Entertainment (2002-Present); Co-founder, President, Chairman, HDNet LLC and HDTV Cable Network (Now AXS TV) (2001-Present); Owner, Managing Partner, Dallas Mavericks, NBA (2000-Present); Chairman, Co-owner, Landmark Theaters (2003); Co-founder, Audionet (Broadcast.com) (Acquired by Yahoo!) (1995-1999); Founder, MicroSolutions (Acquired by CompuServe) (1983-1990); Chairman, Majority Owner, Rysher Entertainment; Chairman, Co-owner, Magnolia Pictures; President, Radical Computing **CR:** Panelist, MIT Sloan Sports Analytics Conference (2009-Present); Co-investor, Veldskoen Shoes USA (2019); Investor, Unikrn (2015); Founder, BailOutSleuth.com (2008); Investor, Goowy Media Inc. (Acquired by AOL, Verizon Media); Investor, Brondell, Inc.; Investor, Weblogs, Inc. (Acquired by AOL, Verizon Media); Financed, ShareSleuth.com; Partner, Red Swoosh; Owner, IceRocket (Acquired by Meltwater); Partner, Synergy Sports Technology; Speaker in Field **CIV:** Founder, Fallen Patriot Fund (2003-Present); Donor, Indiana University Mark Cuban Center for Sports Media and Technology (2015); Founder, Mark Cuban Foundation **CW:** Panel Member, "Shark Tank" (2011-Present); Appearance, "Trailer Park Boys: The Animated Series" (2020); Appearance, "Brooklyn Nine-Nine" (2020); Appearance, "Billions" (2017, 2019); Appearance, "Grace and Frankie" (2019); Appearance, "The Rookie" (2019); Appearance, "What Men Want" (2019); Appearance, "Game Over, Man!" (2018); Appearance, "Bar Rescue" (2018); Appearance, "Fast N' Loud" (2013, 2017); Appearance, "The Clapper" (2017); Appearance, "Girl Meets World" (2016); Appearance, "Entourage" (2015); Actor, "Sharknado 3: Oh Hell No!" (2015); Appearance, "Cristela" (2014); Appearance, "The League" (2014); Appearance, "Bad Teacher" (2014); Voice Appearance, "American Dad!" (2014); Appearance, "Necessary Roughness" (2013); Appearance, "The Neighbors" (2013); Appearance, "Dallas" (2013); Voice Actor, "Kick Buttowski: Suburban Daredevil" (2012); Appearance, "The Men Who Built America" (2012); Appearance, "Trust Us with Your Life" (2012); Executive Producer, "Tim and Eric's Billion Dollar Movie" (2012); Actor, "Entourage" (2010, 2011); Author, "How to Win at the Sport of Business: If I Can Do It, You Can Do It" (2011); Executive Producer, "Rejoice and Shout" (2010); Executive Producer, "Casino Jack and the United States of Money" (2010); Appearance, "NBA All-Star Weekend Celebrity Game" (2010); Executive

Producer, "The Girlfriend Experience" (2009); Executive Producer, "The Road" (2009); Appearance, "WWE Raw" (2009); Executive Producer, "Conquering Kilimanjaro with Angie Everhart" (2009); Appearance, "Real Time with Bill Maher" (2008-2015); Executive Producer, "What Just Happened" (2008); Voice Appearance, "The Simpsons" (2008); Executive Producer, "Quid Pro Quo" (2008); Executive Producer, "Two Lovers" (2008); Executive Producer, "The Burning Plain" (2008); Executive Producer, "Gonzo: The Life and Work of Dr. Hunter S. Thompson" (2008); Actor, "One, Two, Many" (2008); Executive Producer, "Broken English" (2007); Executive Producer, "We Own the Night" (2007); Executive Producer, "Redacted" (2007); Executive Producer, "The Life Before Her Eyes" (2007); Executive Producer, "Geek to Freak with Dennis Rodman" (2007); Performer, "Dancing with the Stars" (2007); Actor, "20 on 20" (2007); Author, "Let's Go Mavs!" (2007); Appearance, "The Loop" (2007); Executive Producer, "Akeelah and the Bee" (2006); Executive Producer, "The Architect" (2006); Executive Producer, "Diggers" (2006); Executive Producer, "Fay Grim" (2006); Executive Producer, "Turistas" (2006); Executive Producer, "Black Christmas" (2006); Executive Producer, "Fast Track" (2006); Executive Producer, "Herbie Hancock: Possibilities" (2006); Actor, "Like Mike 2: Streetball" (2006); Appearance, "All In" (2006); Executive Producer, "The War Within" (2005); Executive Producer, "One Last Thing..." (2005); Executive Producer, "Bubble" (2005); Executive Producer, "Good Night and Good Luck" (2005); Appearance, "Colbert Report" (2005); Executive Producer, "The Jacket" (2005); Executive Producer, "Enron: The Smartest Guys in the Room" (2005); Executive Producer, "Godsend" (2004); Host, Producer, "The Benefactor" (2004); Appearance, "The Cookout" (2004); Executive Producer, "Criminal" (2004); Actor, "WWE Survivor Series" (2003); Co-executive Producer, "Star Search" (2002-2004); Executive Producer, "Searching for Debra Winger" (2002); Executive Producer, "The Mark Cuban Show" (2002); Actor, "Walker, Texas Ranger" (2000); Actor, "Lost at Sea" (1995); Actor, "Talking About Sex" (1994); Founder, Blog Site, BlogMaverick.com **AW:** Named One of the Forbes 400: Richest Americans (2000-Present); Named One of World's Richest People, Forbes Magazine (2018); Named CEO of the Year, D Magazine (2011); Winner (as Owner), Dallas Mavericks, NBA Championships (2011); Winner (as Owner), Dallas Mavericks, Outstanding Team ESPY Award (2011); Named One of the Most Influential People in the World of Sports, Business Week (Now Bloomberg Businessweek) (2007, 2008); Named One of the 50 Most Influential People in Sports Business, Street & Smith's SportsBusiness Journal (2007, 2008); Named Webby Entrepreneur of the Year, The International Academy of Digital Arts and Sciences (IADAS) (2006); Named a WIRED Renegade, WIRED Rave Awards (2006); Kelley School of Business Alumni Award - Distinguished Entrepreneur, Indiana University (1998) **MEM:** Pi Lambda Phi Fraternity **RE:** Jewish

CUDNEY, GERALD, "JERRY" EDWARD, T: Minister; Real Estate Professional **I:** Religious **DOB:** 02/28/1941 **PB:** Tacoma **SC:** WA/USA **PT:** Henry Edward Cudney; Lucille Ellen (Ward) Cudney **MS:** Married **SPN:** Donna Jo Stowell Cudney **CH:** Carin Cudney; Jerilynn Cudney Beattie; Amy Cudney Miller; Jill Cudney Parsons **ED:** BA, Western Baptist College (Now Corban University) (1963) **CT:** Ordained to Ministry, General Association of Regular Baptist Churches (GARBC) (1965) **C:** Retired from Ministry After Serving 55+ Years, CA, MI, WA, PA (2016); Assistant to the Pastor, Eastgate Baptist Church, Bellevue, WA (2006-2016); West Coast Representative, Association of Baptists for World Evangelism (ABWE), Harrisburg, PA (1995-2005); Senior Pastor, Maranatha Baptist Church, Issaquah, WA (1986-1992); Senior Pastor, South Center Baptist Church (1984-1986); Senior Pastor, First Baptist Church, Woodland, CA (1982-1984); Senior Pastor, Eastgate Baptist Church, Bellevue, WA (1972-1982); Minister Education, Northland Baptist Church, Grand Rapids, MI (1966-1972); Minister Education, Cedar Avenue Baptist Church, Fresno, CA (1963-1966) **CR:** Real Estate Broker, RSVP Real Estate, Bellevue, WA (2009-2019); Real Estate Broker, Executive Real Estate, Bellevue, WA (1999-2009); Sales Associate, Heritage West Properties, Bellevue, WA (1986-1998) **CIV:** Trustee Emeritus, Corban University (2017); Trustee, Western Baptist College (Now Corban University), Salem, OR (1975-1995); Advisory Board, Association Baptists for World Evangelism (ABWE), Cherry Hill, NJ and Harrisburg, PA (1975-1995); Chairman, Board of Directors, Baptist Family Agency, Seattle, WA (1975-1982); Chairman, Board, Gilead Baptist Camping Association, Carnation, WA (1975-1982) **CW:** Author, "Administering the Ministry" (1980) **AW:** Outstanding Service Award, Corban University, Salem, OR (2014); Named Real Estate Sales Person of the Year (1990, 1992, 1994, 1995, 1997); Named One of the Outstanding Young Men of America, Outstanding Americans Foundation, Chicago, IL (1968); Recognition, Master Builders & Heritage West Properties **MH:** Albert Nelson Marquis Lifetime Achievement Award **B/I:** Minister Cudney became involved in his profession because his Christian life began in bible camp in 1950 when he received Christ as his savior at he was 9 years old. He got involved in real estate because God led them to Issaquah, which was a suburb outside of Bellevue and they ended up with 13 people. Those 13 people said they wanted to be a part of things and made a commitment that they would plant a church. When he went home, he had a discussion with his wife and he thought that they may not eat well with the offerings of 13 people and wondered what he could do. He decided to be a pastor realtor. **AV:** Golf (Hole in One at Buck Hill Falls Golf Club, PA on July 17, 2002) **PA:** Conservative **RE:** Evangelical Baptist

CUELLAR, HENRY ROBERTO, PHD, T: U.S. Representative from Texas; Lawyer **I:** Government Administration/Government Relations/Government Services **DOB:** 09/19/1955 **PB:** Laredo **SC:** TX/USA **PT:** Martin Siller Cuellar Sr.; Odilia (Perez) Cuellar **MS:** Married **SPN:** Imelda Rios **CH:** Christina Alexandra; Catherine Ann **ED:** PhD in Government, The University of Texas at Austin, Texas (1998); MA in International Trade, Texas A&M International University, Laredo, Texas (1982); JD, The University of Texas School of Law, Austin, Texas (1981); BS in Foreign Service, Georgetown University, Washington, DC, Cum Laude (1978); AA, Laredo College (1976) **CT:** Licensed Customs Broker (1983) **C:** Member, U.S. House of Representatives from Texas' 28th Congressional District, United States Congress (2005-Present); U.S. Secretary of State, State of Texas (2001); Member, District 42, Texas House of Representatives (1993-2001); Member, District 43, Texas House of Representatives (1987-1993); Private Practice Attorney, Laredo, Texas; Member, Committee on Appropriations; Member, Committee on Homeland Security **CR:** Adjunct Professor, International Commercial Law, Texas A&M International University (1984-1986); Instructor, Laredo College (1982-1986) **CIV:** State Legal Advisor, American GI Forum of Texas (1986-1988); President, Board of Directors, International Good Neighbor Council (1984-1985); President, Board of Directors, Laredo Legal Aid Society Inc. (1982-1984); Board of Directors, Treasurer, Stop Child Abuse and Neglect (SCAN, Inc.) (1982-1983); President, Board of Directors, Laredo Volunteer Lawyers Program Inc. (1982-1983) **AW:** Named Laredo Pro Bono Attorney of the Year (1985) **MEM:** President, Laredo Young Lawyers Association (1982-1983); Board of Directors, Kiwanis International (1982-1983); ABA; Inter-American Bar Association (IABA), Texas Bar Association, Laredo Young Lawyers Association; Kiwanis International **BAR:** United States Court of International Trade; United States Court of Appeals for the Fifth Circuit; United States District for the Southern District of Texas; State of Texas **PA:** Democrat **RE:** Roman Catholic

CULP, HENRY LAWRENCE JR., T: Chief Executive Officer, Chairman **I:** Business Management/Business Services **CN:** General Electric **MS:** Married **CH:** Three Children **ED:** MBA, Harvard Business School (1990); BA in Economics, Washington College (1985) **C:** Chief Executive Officer, Chairman, General Electric (2018-Present); Chief Executive Officer, President, Danaher Corporation (2001-2014); Chief Operating Officer, Danaher Corporation (2000-2001); Executive Vice President, Danaher Corporation (1999-2000); Group Executive, Corporate Officer, Danaher Corporation (1995-1999); President, Veeder-Root (1993-1995); Vice President, Marketing and Sales, Veeder-Root; Product Manager, Veeder-Root (1990); Senior Advisor, Bain Capital Private Equity **CR:** Board of Directors, General Electric (2018-Present)

CUMBERBATCH, BENEDICT, T: Actor **I:** Media & Entertainment **DOB:** 08/19/1976 **PB:** London **SC:** England **PT:** Timothy Carlton Cumberbatch; Wanda Ventham Cumberbatch **MS:** Married **SPN:** Sophie Hunter (02/14/2015) **CH:** Christopher Carlton **ED:** MA in Classical Acting, London Academy of Music and Dramatic Art; BA in Drama, University of Manchester **C:** Co-founder, SunnyMarch Ltd. (2013) **CIV:** Ambassador, Motor Neurone Disease Association **CW:** Actor, "Sherlock" (2010-Present); Actor, "Magik" (2018); Actor, "Avengers Infinity War" (2018); Actor, "Mowgli" (2018); Voice Actor, "Dr. Seuss How the Grinch Stole Christmas" (2018); Actor, "The Current War" (2017); Actor, "Thor Raganrok" (2017); Actor, "The Child in Time" (2017); Actor, "The Hollow Crown" (2016); Host, "Saturday Night Live" (2016); Actor, "Zoolander 2" (2016); Actor, "Doctor Strange" (2016); Actor, "Black Mass" (2015); Voice Actor, "Cristiano Ronaldo: World at His Feet" (2014); Actor, "The Imitation Game" (2014); Voice Actor, "Penguins of Madagascar" (2014); Voice Actor, "The Hobbit: The Battle of the Five Armies" (2014); Actor, "Hamlet" (2014); Actor, "Star Trek into Darkness" (2013); Actor, "12 Years a Slave" (2013); Actor, "The Fifth Estate" (2013); Actor, "August: Osage County" (2013); Voice Actor, "The Hobbit: The Desolation of Smaug" (2013); Actor, "50 Years on Stage" (2013); Actor, "Neverwhere" (2013); Actor, "Copenhagen" (2013); Voice Actor, "The Hobbit: An Unexpected Journey" (2012); Actor, "Parade's End" (2012); Voiceover, "Girlfriend in a Coma" (2012); Actor, "Frankenstein" (2011); Actor, "Tinker Tailor Soldier Spy" (2011); Actor, "War Horse" (2011); Actor, "Wreckers" (2011); Actor, "Four Lions" (2010); Actor, "Third Star" (2010); Actor, "The Whistleblower" (2010); Actor, "Hedda Gabler, The Children's Monologues" (2010); Actor, "Burlesque Fairytales" (2009); Actor, "Creation" (2009); Actor, "Rumpole and the Penge Bungalow Murders" (2009); Actor, "Van Gogh: Painted with Words" (2010); Actor, "Small Island" (2009); Actor, "The Last Enemy" (2008); Actor, "The Other Boleyn Girl" (2008); Actor, "Atonement" (2007); Actor, "Stuart: A Life Backwards" (2007); Actor, "Amazing Grace" (2006); Actor, "Starter for 10" (2006); Actor,

"To the End of the Earth" (2005); Actor, "Hawking" (2004); Actor, "Cambridge Spies" (2003); Actor, "To Kill a King" (2003); Actor, "Fortysomething" (2003); Actor, "Fields of Gold" (2002); Actor, "Tipping the Velvet" (2002); Actor, "Cabin Pressure"; Audiobook Narrator, "Casanova"; Audiobook Narrator, "The Tempest"; Audiobook Narrator, "The Making of Music"; Audiobook Narrator, "Death in a White Tie"; Audiobook Narrator, "Artists in Crime"; Audiobook Narrator, "Shelock Holmes: The Rediscovered Railway Mysteries and Other Stories" **AW:** Emmy Award for Outstanding Lead Actor in a Miniseries or a Movie (2014); Named Hollywood's Hottest Star, Critics' Choice Awards (2013); Laurence Olivier Award for Best Actor

CUMMINGS, ANNE MARIE, T: Logistics Manager **I:** Manufacturing **DOB:** 01/30/1952 **PB:** Cleveland **SC:** OH/USA **PT:** Eugene Patrick Cummings; Mary Agnes (Callahan) Cummings **MS:** Single **ED:** Coursework, Chemistry Major, Cleveland State University (1970-1972) **C:** Retired Logistics Manager (2000); Manager, ADC Kentrox, Portland, OR (1984-2000); Inventory Control Supervisor, Harris Calorific, Cleveland, Ohio (1974-1983); Cashier, Lane Bryant, Cleveland, Ohio (1970-1974) **CR:** Vice Chairman, Board of Directors, Sunset Science Park Federal Credit Union, Portland, OR (1989-1999); Cashier, Lane Bryant, Westlake, Ohio (1970-1974) **CIV:** Auxiliary Volunteer, Tualatin Valley Fire & Rescue, Portland, OR (2002-2012) **AW:** Recipient, 3000 ADC Stock Shares for Successful Computer System Implementation Across Four Subdivisions; Recipient, Other Awards and Certificates **MEM:** Former Member, American Society of Production & Inventory; Material Handling Society **MH:** Albert Nelson Marquis Lifetime Achievement Award **AS:** Ms. Cummings attributes her success to learning from a very young age to listen, learn and continually push herself. It is also very important to be able to work with multicultural and multinational people of all ages. Most of all, never quit trying! **B/I:** After growing up in Cleveland, Ohio, jobs became scarce, and she decided to move to Oregon in 1983. Oregon drew her into its beautiful countryside after a vacation there. Ms. Cummings became involved in her profession because she had some wonderful mentors and bosses, like Jim Faraudo, Willa Ralston and Alex Blanock, who encouraged her to take classes along the way which broadened her horizons. She continually became involved with other management professionals who helped her advance her knowledge of other areas of interest, such as computer software and accounting. **AV:** Golf; Reading; Travel; Fishing; Gardening; Painting; Genealogy **PA:** Republican **RE:** Roman Catholic **THT:** Ms. Cummings says, "When life hands you lemons, you make lemonade.' When I was diagnosed with multiple sclerosis in 2000, I had to retire from working because of health reasons. However, I found myself very useful volunteering at a pace I could do."

CUMMINGS, BILL, T: Philanthropist, Real Estate Developer **I:** Real Estate **PB:** Medford **SC:** MA/USA **MS:** Married **SPN:** Joyce Cummings **CH:** Four Children **ED:** BA in Economics, Tufts University (1958) **C:** Owner, United Shoe Machinery Corporation, Beverly, MA (1996); Founder, Cummings Properties, Woburn, MA (1970) **CIV:** Founder, $100K for 100 Program, Cummings Foundation, Boston, MA (2012); Participant, The Giving Pledge (2011); Donor, Tufts University Cummings School of Veterinary Medicine (2004); Co-founder, Cummings Foundation (1986); Co-founder, University of Global Health Equity, Rwanda; New Horizons **CW:** Author, "Starting Small and Making it Big" (2018)

AW: Lifetime Achievement Award, New England Real Estate Journal (2019); Named to Top Givers List, Forbes Magazine (2018)

CUMMINGS, LAUREEN, I: Medicine & Health Care **CT:** LPN, Lackawanna County Vocational-Technical (1984) **C:** Chief Executive Officer, President, Owner, Lorimar Home Care & Staffing Services, Inc. (1999-Present) **CIV:** Elected, State Committee Commissioner; Active, Conservation District **AW:** Business Woman of the Year, National Republican Business Council Advisory Board (2001); Awarded for Marsy's Law, Women in Domestic Violence **AS:** Ms. Cummings attributes her success to her faith in God. She was raised in foster care and she found her family through the system. **B/I:** Ms. Cummings has twin daughters, one of whom was hospitalized at a young age because of an ailment in her leg. They did not know what it was at first, and her daughter had to go for testing. In the pediatric ward, Ms. Cummings saw a lot of children in need of emotional support. Through this realization, she decided to become a nurse. **THT:** Ms. Cummings has always worked with geriatric patients. She loves caring for the elderly, and she believes that, as a society, we can learn so much from these individuals.

CUMMINGS, RICHARD J., MD, FACS, T: Otologist (Retired) **I:** Medicine & Health Care **DOB:** 11/18/1932 **PB:** Topeka **SC:** KS/USA **PT:** John Edward Cummings; Mary J. (Harrington) Cummings **MS:** Married **SPN:** Laura Roberta Herring (12/21/1956) **CH:** Thomas; Anne; William; John **ED:** Honorary LLD, Newman University, Wichita, KS (2000); Resident, University Oklahoma Medical Center, Oklahoma City, OK (1959-1962); Intern, St. Benedict Hospital, Ogden, UT (1957-1958); MD, University of Kansas (1957); BA, University of Kansas (1954) **CT:** MD, FACS **C:** Practice Medicine, Specializing in Otology, Wichita (Kansas) Ear Clinic (1962-2002); Practice Medicine, Specializing in Ear, Nose, Throat, Colorado Springs Medical Clinic, Colorado (1961-1962) **CR:** President, Medical Staff, St. Joseph Hospital, Wichita, KS (1990-1991); Host, MD Radio Program, Wichita, KS (1978-1979); President, Medical Staff, St. Francis Hospital, Wichita, KS (1974-1975) **CIV:** Newman University (1995-Present); Member, University of Kansas Athletic Board (1991-1995); Member, Kansas Tissue Transplantation Committee, American Red Cross (1990-1994); Kansas Commission for the Deaf and Hard of Hearing (1988-1991); Physician's Group Chairman, United Way Campaign (1984, 1977, 1969, 1968); Board of Directors, Kansas State Board of Healing Arts (1981-1983); Chairman, St. Joseph Charity Classic Tournament (1981) **MIL:** U.S. Public Health Service (1958-1959) **CW:** Contributor, Articles, Medical Journals **AW:** Fred Ellsworth Medallion Award, University of Kansas (1998); Kansas Certificate of Recognition, Kansas State (1990); Spirit of the Plains Award, St. Mary's of the Plains College (1988) **MEM:** Sedgwick County Medical Society (2004); Chairman, University of Kansas National Alumni Association (1995-1996); Vice Chairman, University of Kansas National Alumni Association (1994-1995); President, Wichita Surgical Society (1989); Board of Directors, University of Kansas National Alumni Association (1979-1984); Board of Directors, Wichita Chapter, Rotary (1978-1979); President, Sedgwick County Medical Society (1978); President, Kansas Ear, Nose, and Throat Society (1975); Fellow, American College of Physicians; American College of Surgeons; American Academy Otolaryngology; American Medical Association; American Audiology Society; Kansas Medical Society; Otosclerosis Study Group; Hearing Conservation Association; Pan American Society Otolaryngol-

ogy; Board of Directors, Wichita Cochlear Implant Program **MH:** Albert Nelson Marquis Lifetime Achievement Award **B/I:** Dr. Cummings became involved in his profession because he was born with hearing loss, and he wanted to learn more about it and help others with the same issue. **AV:** Golf **PA:** Independent **RE:** Roman Catholic

CUMMINGS, RULON, T: Financial Counselor (Retired) **I:** Financial Services **DOB:** 11/04/1925 **PB:** Salt Lake City **SC:** UT/USA **PT:** James R. Cummings; Gwendolyn M. (Caine) Cummings **MS:** Married **SPN:** Jeannine Mae Astler Cummings (8/14/1947) **CH:** Craig; Kent; Douglas; Cynthia; Celia; Annalisa **ED:** BS, Northwestern College of Allied Sciences (1980); Diploma, Associate in Business, LaSalle Extension University (1960) **C:** Member, Clearfield City Council (1982-1992); Director of Installation Services, Defense Depot Ogden (1982-1986); Chairman of Executive Committee, Federal Safety Council (1979-1980); Instructor, National Safety Council (1970-1986); Safety and Health Director, Defense Depot Ogden (1970-1982); Assistant Chief of Methods and Standards Branch, Defense Depot Ogden (1966-1970); Management Analyst, Defense Depot Ogden (1959-1966); Administrative Assistant of Engineer Supply Section, Utah Army Depot (Defense Depot Ogden), Ogden, UT (1953-1959); Chief of Administration Section, Utah Army Depot (Defense Depot Ogden), Ogden, UT (1950-1953) **CIV:** Coach, Community Softball, Volleyball and Basketball Teams, Clearfield, UT (1964-1986); President, Wasatch Little League Football (1959-1960); Coach, Little League Football (1958-1962); Counselor in Stake Presidency, High Councilor, Bishop, Clerk, President Stake, The Church of Jesus Christ of Latter-Day Saints **MIL:** U.S. Army (1944-1946) **AW:** Exceptional Civilian Service Award, Defense Logistics Agency (1986); Certificate of Appreciation, Assistant Secretary of Labor (1980); Supply Agency Meritorious Civilian Service Award (1973); Superior Performance Award, Defense Depot Ogden (1968-1980) **MEM:** Methods Time Measurement Association for Standards and Research (Now MTM Association); Society of American Military Engineers; Association of Quartermasters; Armed Forces Management Association; American Society of Safety Engineers (Now American Society of Safety Professionals); Kiwanis International **MH:** Albert Nelson Marquis Lifetime Achievement Award **B/I:** Mr. Cummings always wanted to serve people and help them out. When they work with people, they care about them as individuals, not only just a servant or employee. They're a person that has a life, husbands, wives, children, and working is only an important part of providing for a family. A family is something that it grows with you and stays with you. **PA:** Republican

CUNNINGHAM, BETTY, T: Adult Education Educator **I:** Education/Educational Services **DOB:** 04/11/1942 **PB:** Venice **SC:** IL/USA **PT:** John Wells; Anna DeBow **MS:** Single **SPN:** Langford Allen Cunningham (07/18/1967, Divorced 12/1976) **CH:** Langford Allen Jr. **ED:** Master in Secondary Education and Adult Education, University of Missouri-St. Louis (1991); BS in Elementary Education, Southern Illinois University (1967) **C:** Reading Teacher, Venice Lincoln Technical Center (1968-Present); Director, Madison County Equal Opportunity Center (1966-1967) **CR:** Member, Metro East Literacy Advisory Council, East St. Louis, IL (1989-1994) **CIV:** Volunteer, Des Peres Hospital (Now St. Luke's Des Peres Hospital), St. Louis, MO (1993-1995) **AW:** Recipient, Steward of Records, Bethel AME Church (2003) **MEM:** Senior Director, Region V, Illinois Adult and Continuing Educators Association, Inc. (IACEA) (1997-1998); Junior Director, Region V, Illinois Adult and Continuing Educators

Association, Inc. (IACEA) (1996-1997); Illinois Adult and Continuing Educators Association, Inc. (IACEA) **MH:** Albert Nelson Marquis Lifetime Achievement Award; Marquis Who's Who Top Professional **AS:** Ms. Cunningham is a people person and her personal attribute to success goes back to her being in high school and wanting to become an airline stewardess but ended up taking a different direction into teaching. **B/I:** Ms. Cunningham became involved in her profession because she graduated in 1960 and she knew she did not want to go into nursing and teaching was all that was left. So that's what she did. She also came from a family of educators. Her older sister, Patricia Anne DeBow Hunter, father, John Wells DeBow, her son, Langford Allen Jr., and maternal grandfather, Frank M. Gray, were teachers. **AV:** Bowling

CUNNINGHAM, JOSEPH, "JOE", T: U.S. Representative from South Carolina **I:** Government Administration/Government Relations/Government Services **DOB:** 05/26/1982 **PB:** Caldwell County **SC:** KY/USA **MS:** Married **SPN:** Amanda Cunningham (2014) **CH:** Boone **ED:** JD, Northern Kentucky University Salmon P. Chase College of Law; BS in Ocean Engineering, Florida Atlantic University (2005); Coursework, College of Charleston **C:** Member, U.S. House of Representatives from South Carolina's First District, United States Congress (2019-Present); Ocean Engineer, Naples, FL **CIV:** Eagle Scouts **PA:** Democrat

CUNNINGHAM, LANGFORD JR., T: Deputy Juvenile Officer **I:** Civil Service **CN:** St. Louis County **DOB:** 01/10/1968 **PB:** St. Louis **SC:** MO/USA **PT:** Betty Cunningham; Langford Cunningham **MS:** Single **CH:** Tyree Granneman; Aubrey Cunningham Bell **ED:** Bachelor's Degree in Criminal Justice, Stanford Brown University (2013) **CT:** Broadcasting Certificate, Illinois Broadcast Center, Aurora, IL (2002) **C:** Deputy Juvenile Officer, St. Louis County (2013-2018); Counselor, SWICC (2014-2016); In-School Suspension Monitor, Blow Middle School and Mullanphy Elementary (2002-2008); Psychiatric Aide, St. Louis State Hospital (1997-2000) **CR:** Volunteer Mentor, Americorps; Mentor, At-Risk Youth; Gang Interventionist, YDS **CIV:** Founder, Blind City Podcast; Founder, Redemption Academy; Participant, Community Affairs **AS:** Mr. Cunningham attributes his success to his life experiences and ability to learn important life lessons. He witnessed the deaths of some friends at an early age, which motivated him to make good choices. **B/I:** Mr. Cunningham became involved in his profession because he felt that something was missing from the urban community. He saw that he had the ability to provide important lessons from his own experiences to point youths in the right direction and break the cycle of criminal behavior. **AV:** Producing a podcast; Motivational speaking through his nonprofit organization **PA:** Independent **RE:** Spiritual

CUNNINGHAM, SHARON M., CFP, T: Morgan Stanley Wealth Management **I:** Financial Services **CN:** Executive Director, Senior Portfolio Management Director **MS:** Married **CH:** Two Children **ED:** BBA in Management, Specializing in Finance and Marketing, Adelphi University (1990) **CT:** Nationwide Mortgage Licensing System (2015-Present); Certified Financial Planner, CFP Board of Standards (1998-Present); Financial Planning, New York University **C:** Executive Director, Senior Portfolio Management Director and Financial Advisor, Morgan Stanley (1991-Present) **CIV:** Board Member, NEXT for AUTISM; Investment Committee, Girls Scouts of Greater New York **AW:** Forbes Top Women Advisor Award (2018, 2019); Forbes Best in State Advisors Award (2018, 2019); Named to Working Mothers

Magazine Top Advisors; Named to The Makers **AS:** Mrs. Cunningham attributes her success to being very determined in helping other people and being self motivated as a person. She wants to be a valuable resource to others. **B/I:** Mrs. Cunningham was inspired by her course of study in finance and marketing. This was a field that she could utilize both skill sets and work with people in which she enjoys. Her specialty in working with women came from an experience she had as a young adult when her stepfather died suddenly and her mother was widowed at age 43. Her mother was very good at running the household finances but she struggled with other financial matters. This made a real impression on Mrs. Cunningham and she felt that at that time no one should be left so vulnerable and should have a sense of security of their own finances. Being a financial advisor and teaching people the things that will keep them financial stable and growing their wealth for their ambitions is very satisfying for her. Over the years, she just wanted to surround herself with people who were the best that they can be. She wanted to always have a competitive drive with very high standards to be able to deliver the best self that she could produce. In the beginning, it was coming from a family and watching them struggle where things didn't come so easily, having some hardships, just learning those tough lessons of not to fear adversity, but to understand that when one door closes another may open. She learned to remain positive and do the hard work and not to be afraid to do it. She also learned to be good to other people along the way, be supportive when you can and again, just be the best person that's within your potential. **THT:** Mrs. Cunningham's motto is, "Think big but stay humble."

CUNNINGHAM, STACEY, T: President **I:** Financial Services **CN:** New York Stock Exchange **ED:** BS in Industrial Engineering, Lehigh University (1996) **C:** President, New York Stock Exchange (2018-Present); Chief Operating Officer, New York Stock Exchange (2015-2018); President, Governance Services, New York Stock Exchange (2014-2015); Head of Sales and Relationship Management, New York Stock Exchange (2013-2014); Vice President, Sales and Relationship Management, New York Stock Exchange (2012-2013); Head of Sales, Transaction Services U.S., NASDAQ OMX (2011-2012); Managing Director, Transaction Services U.S., NASDAQ OMX (2008-2011); Director, Capital Markets, NASDAQ OMX (2007-2008); Vice President, Specialist, Banc of America Specialist, Inc. (1996-2005) **AW:** Listee, BBC's 100 Women (2018)

CUNNINGTON, RICO, T: Owner, Chef **I:** Food & Restaurant Services **CN:** Rico's World Kitchen **MS:** Married **SPN:** Kathleen **CH:** Isabelle; Ella; Noah **ED:** Degree, Community College **C:** Owner, Chef, The Brunch Apothecary (2015-Present); Owner, Chef, Rico's World Kitchen (2008-Present) **AS:** An understanding of teamwork and collaboration with his fellow chefs got him to where he is today. He also credits his mother for her outsize influence on the style and substance of his cooking. **B/I:** His mother, Proserpina Cunnington, also a chef, introduced him to the restaurant business, and Filipino food in particular. He also picked up a lot of techniques while he studied at community college, rubbing elbows with chefs and professionals in the food industry.

CUOMO, ANDREW MARK, T: Governor of New York **I:** Government Administration/Government Relations/Government Services **DOB:** 12/06/1957 **PB:** Queens **SC:** NY/USA **PT:** Mario Matthew Cuomo; Matilda (Raffa) Cuomo **MS:** Divorced **SPN:** Kerry Kennedy (06/09/1990, Divorced 2005) **CH:**

Cara Ethel Kennedy-Cuomo; Mariah Matilda Kennedy-Cuomo; Michaela Andrea Kennedy-Cuomo **ED:** JD, Albany Law School (1982); BA, Fordham University, Bronx, NY (1979) **C:** Governor, State of New York, Albany, NY (2011-Present); Attorney General, State of New York, Albany, NY (2007-2010); Secretary, U.S. Department of Housing and Urban Development (HUD), Washington, DC (1997-2001); Assistant Secretary, Community Planning and Development, U.S. Department of Housing and Urban Development (HUD), Washington, DC (1993-1997); Chairman, New York City Commission on Homeless (1991-1993); Partner, Blutrich, Falcone & Miller, New York, NY (1985-1988); Assistant District Attorney, Manhattan District Attorney's Office, New York, NY (1984-1985); Special Assistant to Governor Mario Cuomo, State of New York, Albany, NY (1983) **CR:** Visiting Fellow, Harvard Kennedy School Institute of Politics; Public Speaker, The Allen Agency **CIV:** Candidate for Governor, New York (2002); Founder, Housing Enterprise for Less Privileged (HELP USA) (1986); Campaign Manager, Mario M. Cuomo Gubernatorial Campaign, NY (1982) **CW:** Author, Memoir, "All Things Possible: Setbacks and Success in Politics and Life" (2014); Editor, "Crossroads: The Future of American Politics" (2003) **AW:** Named One of the 100 Most Influential People in the World, TIME Magazine (2012); Innovation Award, Harvard Kennedy School John F. Kennedy School of Government (1998); Distinguished Community Service Award, New York University (1991); Public Service Award, Council of Jewish Organizations (1989); Ed Sulzberger Award, Our Town - Manhattan Media LLC (1989); Man of the Year Award, Coalition of Italian-American Organizations (1988) **PA:** Democrat **RE:** Roman Catholic

CUPP, DARREN, T: Entrepreneur **I:** Other **CN:** Darren's Ballroom Dance Studios **ED:** BA in Psychology, University of Phoenix (2008) **C:** Owner, Darren's Ballroom Dance Studios (2009) **CW:** Producer, Actor, "Ballroom Revolution" (2015); Actor, "Dracula Now" (2015); Performer, Madonna, Halftime Show, Super Bowl 46 (2012); Himself, "Dance Dream" **AW:** Best of Carmel for Dance Instruction (2014, 2015, 2016, 2017, 2018, 2019); Top Studio, Superstars Dancesport Championships (2019); Top Instructor, Superstars Dancesport Championships (2019); Top Instructor, Grand Nationals (2016); Nominated for a Star, Latin American Walk of Fame, Mexico City, Mexico (2015) **MEM:** National Dance Council of America **AS:** Mr. Cupp attributes his success to never taking "no" for an answer. He does not rely on the doors of other people; he would rather create his own. **B/I:** Mr. Cupp became involved in his profession because he had been a performer since he was a child. At age 14, he was inspired to become a dancer after seeing Paula Abdul perform live in concert. **THT:** "Darren Lee Cupp is a dancer, singer and actor that was born in the United Kingdom and began his ballroom dance career at a very young age. He has trained all over the world and been coaching, competing, and teaching dance for over 20 years. He has worked with some of the biggest names in the industry including some of the professionals you see on Dancing with the Stars. Turning to the entertainment industry he began singing, acting, and modeling and worked on the promotion of many motion pictures. He has done extensive work on stage and even choreographed the musical version of 'Legally Blonde' while playing the principle role of Emmett on stage. When Liz Claiborne launched the perfume Mambo, Darren and his studio were chosen to promote the perfume. In 2012 he performed with Madonna in the Emmy-nominated halftime show at Super Bowl 46. Darren has also starred on the big screen as

Dracula in the independent film 'Dracula Now' and was the subject and star of the international reality television show 'Dance Dream,' which aired in 47 countries and earned him a nomination for a star on the Latin American walk of fame in Mexico City.In 2015 Darren produced and starred in the reality show called Ballroom Revolution which is currently out on Demand at Vimeo.com. In Spring 2016 he launched his first music EP that was produced by the legendary Warren McRae. Warren not only plays bass for Tina Turner but he has produced albums for Tina, Patti LaBelle, Nona Hendrix, and Joe Cocker to name a few. His first single, 'Dance Like Nobody's Watching,' has been downloaded, streamed and heard in over 12 countries. As well as a music EP Darren also launched his own bracelet line called 'The Ballroom Collection.'Watch for him on Netflix this summer playing Ethan in the post-apocalyptic thriller 'HAVEN.'He owns and runs Darren's Ballroom Dance Studios in Carmel, Indiana."

CURIEL, HERMAN F., T: Social Worker; Educator, Professor Emeritus **I:** Education/Educational Services **DOB:** 08/27/1934 **PB:** Corpus Christi **SC:** TX/USA **PT:** Hermerejildo Curiel; America (Fernandez) Ramirez **MS:** Single **ED:** PhD, Texas A&M University (1979); MSW, Our Lady of the Lake University, San Antonio, Texas (1962); BA, St. Mary's University, San Antonio, Texas (1960); AA, Del Mar College, Corpus Christi, Texas (1956) **CT:** Oklahoma State Board of Licensed Social Workers; Licensed Clinical Social Worker (LCSW); National Association of Social Workers; Academy of Certified Social Workers (ACSW) **C:** Professor Emeritus, University of Oklahoma Anne and Henry Zarrow School of Social Work (2008-2014); Associate Professor of Social Work, The University of Oklahoma, Norman, OK (1981-2008); Assistant Professor of Social Work, University of Houston, Texas (1972-1981); Program Developer, Harris County Mental Health Mental Retardation Center (Now Harris Center for Mental Health), Houston, Texas (1967-1972); Counseling Supervisor, Harris County Community Action, Houston (1966-1967); Family Counselor, Family Service Center, Houston, Texas (1962-1966) **CR:** Consultant, Oklahoma City Public Schools (1990-Present); Three Feathers Associates, Norman, OK (1989-Present); Research Associate, Brasman Health and Business Research, Silver Spring, MD (1988-1989); Part-time Family Counselor, Sunbeam Family Services, Oklahoma City, OK (1985-1988); Intern-coordinator, National Hispanic Council on Aging (NHCA), Washington, DC (1987); Clinical Instructor, Baylor College of Medicine (1978-1981) **CIV:** Board of Directors, Consortium of AIDS Resources and Education, CarePoint Inc. of Oklahoma City (1994-Present); Social Work Affiliate, Treasurer, Southwestern Social Science Association (1982-2007); Secretary, Consortium of AIDS Resources and Education, CarePoint Inc. of Oklahoma City (1997); Board of Directors, Urban League of Greater Oklahoma City, Inc. (1992-1994); Appointee, Advisory Board on Foster Care and Adoptions (1983-1988); Advisory Board on Cultural Diversity, Oklahoma Department of Commerce **CW:** Consultant Editor, Journal of Social Work Education (1996-Present); Contributor, U.S. Department of Health & Human Services (2008); Co-editor with H. Land, "Outreach & Care Approaches to HIV/AIDS Along US/Mexico Border," Haworth Press (2006); Senior Editor, Papers on Substance Abuse Prevention and Social Work with Minority Populations (1996); Contributor, Pan American University (1996); Member, Editorial Board, Social Work (1989-1992); Co-editor with M. Sotomayor, "Hispanic Elderly: A Cultural Signatures" (1988); Author, Editor, "Growing Innovative Care: Strategies for HIV/AIDS Prevention & Care

Along US/Mexico Border, Washington, DC; Editor, Select Papers in Substance Abuse Prevention and Family Practice with Minority Populations; Contributor, Articles to Professional Journals, Chapters to Books **AW:** Recognition as NASW Pioneer, National Association of Social Workers (2011); Lifetime Achievement Award, National Association of Social Workers (NASW), OK Chapter (2008); Named to Hall of Honor, Social Work Educator, National Association of Social Workers (NASW) (2005-2006); Elected Member-at-Large, National Association of Social Workers (NASW) (1984-1987) **MEM:** Appointee, Commission on Certification Competence, National Association of Social Workers (NASW) (1998-2000); Treasurer, Oklahoma Hispanic Professors Association (1989-1991); Chairman, Oklahoma Chapter, Nominations and Leadership Committee, National Association of Social Workers (NASW) (1989-1991); Chairman, Oklahoma Chapter, Fundraising Committee, National Center for Social Policy and Practice, National Association of Social Workers (NASW) (1989-1991); Board of Directors, National Association of Social Workers (NASW) (1984-1987); President, Oklahoma Hispanics in Higher Education (1985); National Association of Social Workers (NASW); Chairman, Oklahoma Chapter, M.K. Ho Memorial Fund, National Association of Social Workers (NASW); Oklahoma Hispanic Professors Association; Oklahoma Hispanics in Higher Education; Board of Visitors, National Association of Social Workers (NASW); National Board of Directors, National Association of Social Workers (NASW) **MH:** Albert Nelson Marquis Lifetime Achievement Award; Marquis Who's Who Top Professional **AS:** Dr. Curiel was fortunate to have had good health, a caring family, and many caring teachers. He had sufficient intelligence to not fail in his school work. Feeling different due to his poor economic background and minority status, (Mexican American in a majority White high school), motivated me to become like his non-Hispanic peers. **B/I:** Dr. Curiel started working at age 9 to support his grandmother. He worked nights in a laundry which led to deprived sleep and falling asleep in class. The teacher assumed he was neglected and made a referral to Child Welfare at the Department of Human Services. This became his first and only contact with a social worker. The young male social worker was caring and helped Dr. Curiel find a job with fewer work hours. He was a positive role model and probably led him to choose social work as a profession. **AV:** Physical fitness; Reading; Writing; Travel **PA:** Democrat **RE:** Roman Catholic **THT:** Dr. Curiel says, "We only have one life and I have been blessed to have had a rich life with great memories of places and friends all over the world. In era COVID19, I feel blessed to have lived at a time when we could touch and be close. I feel very fortunate to have had a career in academia for 45-plus years. My grandmother, who had no formal education, had modest educational goals for me. Get enough education to protect me from the weather. I have been pleased with roofs at Ryne Hall and Anne and Henry Zarrow Hall.

CUROL, HELEN BROUSSARD, MLIS, T: Library Consultant **I:** Library Management/Library Services **CN:** Calcasieu Parish Public Schools **DOB:** 05/30/1944 **PB:** Grayson **SC:** LA/USA **PT:** Alfred John Broussard; Ethel Lea (McDaniel) Broussard **MS:** Single **SPN:** Kenneth Arthur Curol (06/25/1967, Divorced 1988) **CH:** Edward; Bryan **ED:** MLIS, Louisiana State University (1987); Postgraduate Coursework, Long Island University (1969-1970); BA, McNeese State University (1966) **CT:** Lifetime Certification in English and Library Science, Louisiana Department of Education (1995) **C:** Library Consultant, Calcasieu Parish Public Schools, LA

(2004-Present); Media Library Technician, Technical Representative, LaGrange High School, Lake Charles, LA (1997-2004); Owner, Curol Consulting, Lake Charles, LA (1995-2002); Head of Adult Services, Laman Public Library, Laman Library System, North Little Rock, AK (1996); Reference Librarian, McNeese State University (1976-1996); Manager, Circulation Department, McNeese State University (1976-1996); Assistant Professor, McNeese State University (1989-1995); Test Administrator, Education Testing Service, Princeton, NJ (1987-1995); School Librarian, Patchogue High School (Now Patchogue-Medford High School), NY (1969-1971); Media Specialist, Brentwood Union Free School District, NY (1967-1969); Teacher, Cameron Parish Schools, Grand Lake, LA (1966-1967); Librarian, Cameron Parish Schools, Grand Lake, LA (1966-1967) **CR:** Teacher, Online Library Courses, Northwestern State University (2013-2018); Reference Librarian, Calcasieu Parish Public Library (1990-1995); Project Manager, Community Housing Resource Board, Lake Charles, LA (1988-1993); Researcher, Vidtron, Dallas, Texas (1990-1992); Development Consultant, Calcasieu Women's Shelter (1988-1992); Consultant, Louisiana Public Broadcasting, LETA, Baton Rouge, LA (1989); Researcher, National Archives, Washington, DC (1989); Research Consultant, Boyce International Engineers, Houston, Texas (1988-1989); Researcher, Boise Cascade, DeRidder, LA (1987-1988); Presenter at Conferences **CIV:** Multicultural Wine Down Women Planning Board for SW LA (2018-Present); Appointed Member, Alcohol Review Board, City of Lake Charles (2003-Present); Representative, Louisiana's Virtual Library Study Commission (2000-Present); Member, Advisory Board, Ethel Precht HOPE Breast Cancer Foundation, Inc. (2018-2019); Member, I-10 Petrochemical Industry's Citizen Advisory Panel (2003-2016); Vice President, Louisiana Library Association (2013); Secretary, Southwest Louisiana Region, League of Women Voters (2008-2012); Member, Southwest Louisiana Delegate Distance Learning Committee (2007); Representative, National Taxpayer Advocacy Panel (2002-2005); Board of Directors, United Way of Southwest Louisiana, Lake Charles (1995-1996); Senior Arbitrator, Lake Charles Better Business Bureau, Council of Better Business Bureaus, Inc. (1986-1995); Chairperson, Budget Panel Committee, United Way of Southwest Louisiana, Lake Charles, LA (1992-1994); Program Speaker, Region IV Training Conference, United States Department of Housing and Urban Development, El Paso, Texas (1992); Judge, Louisiana Region IV Social Studies Fair (1979-1989); Local Facilitator, Louisiana Committee for Fiscal Reform, Lake Charles, LA (1988); Member, State Board of Directors, PTA, Baton Rouge, LA (1981-1985) **CW:** Author, "The Power of Collaboration & Content Curation with your Librarian," Region V, Louisiana Association of Computer Using Educators (2017); Contributor, Articles, Professional Journals **AW:** Inducted into Advisory Board, Friends of the Calcasieu Parish Public Library (2018); Honoree, Librarian of the Year, Louisiana Reading Association (2015); USA Freedom Corp Silver Medal of Appreciation (2000); Grantee, Louisiana Center for Women in Government and Business, Nicholls State University (1993); Grantee, United States Department of Housing and Urban Development (1992); Honoree, Mardi Gras Court Duchess, Krewe du Feteurs (1992); Grantee, Fair Housing Initiative Program (1990); Grantee, Louisiana Division of the Arts (1989); Grantee, Louisiana Endowment for the Humanities (1987); Honoree, Named Citizen of the Day, Station KLOU (1978) **MEM:** LACUE: Louisiana Association of Computer Using Educators (2000-Present); LSU Alumni Association (1988-Present); Beta Phi Mu -

The International Library and Information Studies Honor Society (1988-Present); Ad & Press Club of Southwest Louisiana (2000-2012); Speaker, Annual State Convention, Louisiana Library Association (2006); Arkansas Library Association (1996); Chairperson, Louisiana Association of College and Research Librarians (ACRL) (1995-1996); Mardi Gras Court Duchess, Krewe du Feteurs (1992); Legislative Committee, Southwest Louisiana Chamber of Commerce (Now SWLA Chamber-Economic Alliance) (1992); Chairperson, Council, American Library Association (1990-1991); Chairperson, Reference Group, Louisiana Library Association (1988-1990); Secretary, Council, American Library Association (1988-1990); Chairperson, Intellectual Freedom Committee, American Association of University Women (AAUW) (1988-1989); President, Lake Charles Chapter, Beta Sigma Phi (1983-1984); McNeese State University Alumni Association **MH:** Albert Nelson Marquis Lifetime Achievement Award **AS:** Ms. Curol attributes her success to one of her high school teachers, Mrs. Nelson, who taught Spanish, as well as Richard Reid, the library director at McNeese State University. He inspired her to get a master's degree. **B/I:** Ms. Curol became involved in her profession because her father owned a small business, which he and her mother worked tirelessly at. They always told her that she needed to get a good career to avoid 24/7 on-call status. She needed to get a college degree and, so, she was the first one in her family to go to college. **AV:** Political campaigns; Traveling; Collecting cups and saucers **PA:** Republican **RE:** Lutheran **THT:** According to Ms. Curol: "An independent thinker with an ability to discuss reasons for and respect for differing opinions are imperative for success. Stress is relieved by exercise, work, and reading. Travel to different cultures (whether in your town or abroad) is a mandate in the 21st Century. Education that promotes respectful discussion of opposing viewpoints is essential for civilization to reach its pinnacle."

CURRY, STEPHEN, "STEPH" II, T: Professional Basketball Player **I:** Athletics **CN:** Golden State Warriors **DOB:** 03/15/1988 **PB:** Akron **SC:** OH/USA **PT:** Dell Curry; Sonya Curry **MS:** Married **SPN:** Ayesha Alexander (07/30/2011) **CH:** Cannon W.; Jack; Ryan Carson; Riley Elizabeth **ED:** Coursework in Sociology, Davidson College, NC (2006-2009) **C:** Professional Basketball Player, Guard, Golden State Warriors, NBA (2009-Present) **CR:** Founder, Unanimous Media (2018-Present); Member, U.S. National Team, FIBA World Championships, Turkey (2010); Investor, Active Faith; Investor, Palm **CW:** Executive Producer, Resident Golf Pro, "Holey Moley" (2019-Present); Executive Producer, "Breakthrough" (2019); Executive Producer, "Emanuel" (2019) **AW:** Named Sportsman of the Year, BET Awards (2015, 2019); Teen Choice Award for Choice Male Athlete (2019); Named to All-NBA First Team (2015, 2016, 2019); Named NBA All-star (2014-2019); NBA Champion, Golden State Warriors (2015, 2017, 2018); Named to All-NBA Third Team (2018); Named to All-NBA Second Team (2014, 2017); Named NBA Scoring Champion (2016); Named NBA Steals Leader (2016); Named to the 50-40-90 Club (2016); Named NBA Most Valuable Player (2015, 2016); Named NBA Three-Point Contest Champion (2015); Named Athlete of the Year, The Associated Press (2015); Recipient, Hickok Belt (2015); Named Best Male Athlete, ESPY Awards (2015); Named Best NBA Player, ESPY Awards (2015); Gold Medal, FIBA World Championship (2010, 2014); NBA Sportsmanship Award (2011); Jefferson Award for Outstanding Public Service in Professional Sports (2011); Named to First Team NBA All-rookie (2010); Named to First Team All-American, The Associ-

ated Press (2009); Named to First Team All-American, Sporting News (2009); Named to First Team All-American, National Association of Basketball Coaches (2009); Named NCAA Season Scoring Leader (2009); Named SoCon Player of the Year (2008, 2009) **AV:** Golfing **RE:** Christian

CURTIS, JAMIE LEE, T: Actress **I:** Media & Entertainment **DOB:** 11/22/1958 **PB:** Los Angeles **SC:** CA/USA **PT:** Tony Curtis; Janet Leigh Curtis **MS:** Married **SPN:** Christopher Guest (December 18, 1984) **CH:** Annie; Thomas **ED:** Coursework, University of the Pacific, Stockton, CA (1976) **CW:** Actress, "Halloween Kills" (2020); Actress, "Knives Out" (2019); Actress, "An Acceptable Loss" (2018); Actress, "Halloween" (2018); Actress, "Scream Queens" (2015-2016); Actress, "New Girl" (2012-2015); Actress, "Spare Parts" (2015); Actress, "Veronica Mars" (2014); Actress, "Only Human" (2014); Actress, "NCIS" (2012); Voice Actress, "From Up on Poppy Hill" (2011); Voice Actress, "The Little Engine That Could" (2011); Author, "My Mommy Hung the Moon: A Love Story" (2010); Actress, "You Again" (2010); Actress, "Beverly Hills Chihuahua" (2008); Author, "Big Words for Little People" (2008); Author, "Is There Really a Human Race?" (2006); Actress, "The Kid and I" (2005); Actress, "Christmas with the Kranks" (2004); Author, "It's Hard to Be Five: Learning How to Work My Control Panel" (2004); Actress, "Freaky Friday" (2003); Actress, "Halloween: Resurrection" (2002); Author, "I'm Gonna Like Me: Letting Off a Little Self-Esteem" (2002); Actress, "The Tailor of Panama" (2001); Actress, "Daddy and Them" (2001); Voice Actress, "Rudolf the Red-Nosed Reindeer and the Island of Misfit Toys" (2001); Actress, "Drowning Mona" (2000); Voice Actress, "Pigs Next Door" (2000); Author, "Where Do Balloons Go? An Uplifting Mystery" (2000); Actress, "Virus" (1999); Actress, "Homegrown" (1998); Actress, "Halloween H2O" (1998); Actress, "Nicolas' Gift" (1998); Author, "Today I Feel Silly and Other Moods That Make My Day" (1998); Actress, "Fierce Creatures" (1997); Actress, "The Drew Carey Show" (1996); Author, "Tell Me Again About the Night I Was Born" (1996); Actress, "House Arrest" (1996); Actress, "Ellen's Energy Adventure" (1996); Actress, "The Heidi Chronicles" (1995); Actress, "My Girl 2" (1994); Actress, "Mother's Boys" (1994); Actress, "True Lies" (1994); Author, "When I Was Little: A Four-Year-Old's Memoir of Her Youth" (1993); Actress, "Anything but Love" (1989-1992); Actress, "Forever Young" (1992); Actress, "Queens Logic" (1991); Actress, "My Girl" (1991); Actress, "Blue Steel" (1990); Director, "Anything But Love" (1990); Actress, "Dominick and Eugene" (1988); Actress, "A Fish Called Wanda" (1988); Actress, "A Man in Love" (1987); Actress, "Amazing Grace and Chuck" (1987); Actress, "Welcome Home" (1986); Actress, "As Summers Die" (1986); Actress, "Perfect" (1985); Actress, "Love Letters" (1984); Actress, "Grandview USA" (1984); Actress, "The Adventures of Buckaroo Banzai: Across the 8th Dimension" (1984); Actress, "Trading Places" (1983); Actress, "Money on the Side" (1982); Actress, "Halloween II" (1981); Actress, "Road Games" (1981); Actress, "Death of a Centerfold: The Dorothy Stratten Story" (1981); Actress, "She's in the Army Now" (1981); Actress, "The Fog" (1980); Actress, "Prom Night" (1980); Actress, "Terror Train" (1980); Actress, "Buck Rogers in the 25th Century" (1979); Actress, "Charlie's Angels" (1978); Actress, "The Love Boat" (1978); Actress, "Halloween" (1978); Actress, "Operation Petticoat" (1977-1978); Actress, "Quincy" (1977); Actress, "Hardy Boys/Nancy Drew Mysteries" (1977); Actress, "Colombo: Bye-Bye Sky-High I.Q. Murder Case" (1977) **AW:** Golden Globe Award (1989); Golden Globe Award for Best Actress - Musical or Comedy

CURTIS, JOHN R., T: U.S. Representative from Utah **I:** Government Administration/Government Relations/Government Services **CN:** U.S. House of Representatives **DOB:** 5/10/1960 **PB:** Salt Lake City **SC:** UT/USA **PT:** Jesse Duckworth Curtis; Hazel Dawn Curtis **MS:** Married **SPN:** Sue Snarr (1982) **CH:** Six Children **ED:** Bachelor of Science in Management, Brigham Young University **C:** Member, U.S. House of Representatives from Utah's Third Congressional District (2017-Present); Mayor, Provo, UT (2010-2017); Small Business Owner, Action Target, Provo, UT (2000); With, OC Tanner; With, Citizen Watch Company **AW:** Community Hero Award, Silicon Slopes (2017); Civic Innovator of the Year Award, Office of New Urban Mechanics, Utah Valley University (2017); Outstanding Citizen Award, Office of Civic Engagement Leadership, Brigham Young University (2017); Named, Freedom Festival Grand Marshal (2017); Named, Person of the Year, Utah Clean Air (2017); Named, Person of the Year Award, Utah Valley Magazine (2017); Named, Top Elected Official on Social Media, Government Social Media (2015); The Star Award, SCERA Center for the Arts (2015); Ranked, Number One in the Nation for Business and Careers, Forbes Ranked Number One in the Nation for Well-being, Gallup **PA:** Republican

CURTIS, THOMAS, "TOM" PELHAM II, T: Artist, Small Business Owner **I:** Fine Art **CN:** Curtis Studio **DOB:** 06/10/1938 **PB:** Manhattan **SC:** NY/USA **PT:** Thomas James Curtis; Elizabeth Longfellow Curtis **MS:** Married **SPN:** Denise Willman Curtis (11/18/1972) **CH:** Elizabeth L.; Thomas J.; Andrew W.; Anna C.; Margarete W. (Deceased 2007) **ED:** Degree, U.S. Army Command and General Staff College (1979); Coursework in Art, Corcoran School of Art (1966); BA in Architecture, Harvard College (1960) **C:** Private Practice, Curtis Studio, Milwaukee, WI (1985-Present); Retired (2009); Teacher, Art and History of Art, Brookfield Academy, Wisconsin (1986-2009); Editorial Cartoonist, Milwaukee Sentinel (1969-1983); Private Practice, Washington (1966-1969) **MIL:** U.S. Army Reserves (1960-1987); Advanced through Grades to Lieutenant Colonel, U.S. Army (1979); Active Duty, Corps of Engineers, U.S. Army, United States, Germany (1960-1965); Commissioned Lieutenant, U.S. Army (1960) **CW:** Author, Artist, "Clouds of Witness, Portraits by Thomas P. Curtis II" (2019); Author, Artist, "A Retrospective, Thomas P. Curtis" (2018); Author, Cartoonist, "Curtis In Profile" (1983); Author, Cartoonist, "The Turn of A Decade" (1970) **AW:** Distinguished Service Award, SMOTJ, Inc. (2001); Knight Grand Cross, SMOTJ, Inc. (1983); Decorated Knight, The Military and Hospitaller Order of Saint Lazarus of Jerusalem; Knight Commander, Order St. Gregory The Great; Knight Grand Cross, Imperial Ethiopian Order St. Mary of Zion; U.S. Army Meritorious Service Medal with Oak Leaf Cluster; U.S. Army Commendation Medal; OSMTH Companionate of Honor-Gold **MEM:** Commander-in-Chief, Northern Masonic Jurisdiction Scottish Rite (2019); President, The New York State Society of the Cincinnati (2005-2008); Governor General, The Order of the Founders and Patriots of America (1995-1996); President, The Association of American Editorial Cartoonists (1977-1978); American Society Portrait Artists; Philadelphia Society; Free and Accepted Masons of Wisconsin; Deputy Governor, General Society of Colonial Wars **MH:** Albert Nelson Marquis Lifetime Achievement Award **AS:** Mr. Curtis attributes his success to his God-given talent, parental support, optimism, personal drive and a joy for life. **B/I:** Mr. Curtis became involved in his profession because of mother, Elizabeth Curtis, a nationally-recognized portrait artist. In the early years, he chose to follow a different path and went into political cartooning, inspired by his undergraduate activities at the Harvard Lampoon. However, when his mother ceased her painting in the 1980s, he became active in that art form. **AV:** Studying genealogy and history; Playing bagpipes; Collecting coins **RE:** Episcopalian

CUSTER, JOHN C, T: Portfolio Manager **I:** Business Management/Business Services **DOB:** 08/30/1934 **PB:** Chicago **SC:** IL/USA **PT:** John Howard Custer; Irene Lillian (McGovern) Custer **MS:** Widowed **SPN:** Barbara Ann Welcher (09/05/1959, Deceased 1996) **CH:** John Thomas; Kaitlin Mary **ED:** Graduate, Advanced Management Program Harvard Business School (1975); MHA, University of Minnesota (1966); AB, Indiana University (1956) **C:** Partner, Heritage Wealth Advisers, Lemoyne, PA (2006-Present); Investment Broker, Smith Barney (2006); Investment Broker, Legg Mason Wood Walker, Inc. (1992-2006); President, Chief Executive Officer, Custer & Associates, Hummelstown, PA (1987-1992); President, Chief Executive Officer, Keystone Health Plan, Camp Hill, PA (1984-1987); Vice President, Kaiser Permanente Adv. Services, Oakland, CA (1979-1984); Vice President, Health Plan Manager, Kaiser Permanente Medical Care Program, Oakland CA (1974-1979); Manager, Health Plan, Kaiser Permanente Medical Care Program, Cleveland, OH (1970-1974); Director, Materials, Kaiser Permanente Medical Care Program, Oakland, CA (1969-1970); Clinical Administrator, Kaiser Permanente Medical Care Program, Oakland, CA (1967-1969); Assistant Administrator, Johns Hopkins Hospital, Baltimore, MD (1966-1967) **CR:** Member, Board of Advisers, Harrisburg Area Salvation Army (2012-2017); Lecturer, University of Minnesota School of Public Health, Minneapolis, MN (1979-1984); Lecturer, Harvard T.H. Chan School of Public Health, Boston, MA (1980-1983); Technology Consultant, U.S. Department of Health and Human Services (1979-1983); Executive Board Member, Easter Seal Society, Oakland, CA (1969-1970); Mid-County Chairman, American Cancer Society, Alameda County, CA (1967-1969) **CIV:** Chairman, Pennsylvania Association of HMOs, Harrisburg, PA (1984-1986) **MIL:** Col., U.S. Army Reserve (1958-1984); 1st Lt., U.S. Army (1956-1958) **MEM:** Trustee, Hershey Golf Club (2004-2010); American Public Health Association; American College of Healthcare Executives; American Hospital Association; Medical Group Management Association; International Federation of Employee Benefit Plans; Chairman, Health Care Cost Containment Committee, Pennsylvania Chamber of Commerce; Pennsylvania State Department of Public Welfare (Pennsylvania Department of Human Services); President, Oakmont Homeowners Association; Cosmos Club; Army-Navy Club; Harvard Club; Elks; Delta Upsilon **B/I:** Mr. Custer became involved in his profession because of the need to eat and have a roof over his head. **AV:** Playing golf; Traveling; Reading **PA:** Independent **RE:** Episcopalian

CUSTODIO, BRENDA KAY, PHD, T: English Language Educator **I:** Education/Educational Services **CN:** Newcomer and ELL Services **DOB:** 12/27/1948 **PB:** Mansfield **SC:** OH/USA **PT:** Charles C. Mabry; Geraldine (Payton) Mabry **MS:** Divorced **CH:** Jeremy K. Borden; Vanessa Kay (Borden) O'Dee **ED:** PhD, The Ohio State University (2001); MA, The Ohio State University (1991); BA in English and History, Spring Arbor College (Now Spring Arbor University) (1970) **CT:** English and History Teacher, Secondary Level; TESOL, K-12; Building Administrator **C:** Adjunct Professor, The Ohio State University (2002-Present); Adjunct Professor, Ohio Dominican University (2006-Present); Building Administrator, Columbus City Schools, Ohio (2007-2012); Coordinator, English as Second

Language Department, Columbus Public Schools (1999-2006); Teacher, English as Second Language, Columbus Public Schools, Ohio (1985-1999); Teacher, English, Knox County JVS, Mount Vernon, Ohio (1970-1973) **CR:** Educational Consultant (2012-Present); President, Owner, Lotus House Publications, Columbus, Ohio (1992-2005) **CIV:** Board of Directors, Dayspring Church of Nazarene, Ohio (1985-Present) **CW:** Author, "Supporting the Journey of English Learners after Trauma" (2020); Author, "Students with Interrupted Formal Education" (2017); Author, "How to Design & Implement a Newcomer Program" (2011); Author, "Tonight, by Sea" (1997); Co-author, "Franklinton, History and Heritage" (1997); Author, "Shadow of the Dragon" (1995); Author, "New Kids in Town," "Journey of the Sparrows," "The Return" (1994); Author, "Shabanu," "The Good Earth," "A Woman of Her Tribe," "Year of Impossible Goodbyes" (1993); Author, "Pocket Guide to Columbus" (1992); Author, "Study Guides for: Children of the River" (1992) **AW:** Traveling Fellow, Winston Churchill Memorial Trust (1998); National Excellence in English Award, The English-Speaking Union of the United States, Columbus, Ohio (1997); Recipient, McKenzie Literacy Grant (1996); Ingram-White Castle Grantee, The Columbus Foundation (1994); Impact II Teaching Award, Ameritech/Ohio Department of Education, Columbus, Ohio (1990-1994) **MEM:** President, Ohio Teachers of English as a Second Language (ESL) (2010); Founder, President, Columbus Christian Writers Association (1989-1996) **MH:** Albert Nelson Marquis Lifetime Achievement Award **AV:** Reading; Writing; Star Trek; Soccer **PA:** Democrat **RE:** Church of the Nazarene **THT:** Dr. Custodio has one grandchild, Avieana O'Dee.

CYNAR, SANDRA JEAN, PHD, T: Electrical Engineering Educator **I:** Education/Educational Services **DOB:** 08/07/1941 **PB:** Chicago **SC:** IL/USA **PT:** Lionel Thomas Bowers; Dorothy Adeline (Swain) Bowers **MS:** Widowed **SPN:** Raymond John Cynar (03/06/1965) (Deceased 2018) **CH:** Mark Jon **ED:** PhD in Electrical Engineering, University of California, Irvine (1986); MSEE, California State University, Long Beach (1978); BSEE, California State University, Long Beach (1963) **C:** Professor of Engineering and Computer Engineering, California State University, Long Beach (1977-Present); Chairman, Computer Engineering and Computer Science Department, California State University, Long Beach (1995-2006); Science Programmer, McDonnell Douglas (1968-1970); Science Programmer, North American Rockwell (1965-1968); Manager Trainee, Pacific Telephone (1964-1965); Controls Engineer, General Dynamics (1963-1964) **CR:** Faculty Adviser, IEEE Computer Society, California State University (1988-1994); Society of Women Engineers (1988-1994) **CW:** Creator, Animated Film, "Solution Of Ode's" (1989); Creator, Animated Film, "Tuned Pendulum" (1988); Author, "Numerical Methods for Engineers"; Contributor, Articles, Professional Journals **AW:** Excellence in Teaching Award, TRW (1992) **MEM:** Senior Member, IEEE; Society for Modeling & Simulation International; National Computer Graphics Association; ASEE; Society of Women Engineers; ACM, Inc. **MH:** Albert Nelson Marquis Lifetime Achievement Award **B/I:** Dr. Cynar became involved in her profession because she was inspired by another women in the STEM fields. **AV:** Gardening; Reading; Building computers; Traveling **PA:** Republican **RE:** Methodist

CYRUS, MILEY, T: Singer, Actress **I:** Media & Entertainment **DOB:** 11/23/1992 **PB:** Franklin **SC:** TN/USA **PT:** Billy Ray Cyrus; Leticia Cyrus **MS:** Divorced **SPN:** Liam Hemsworth (December

23, 2018) **CW:** Judge, "The Voice" (2016-Present); Performer, "Younger Now" (2017); Actress, "Guardians of the Galaxy Vol. 2" (2017); Actress, "A Very Murray Christmas" (2016); Actress, "Crisis in Six Scenes" (2016); Actress, "The Night Before" (2015); Host, MTV Video Music Awards" (2015); Performer, "Miley Cyrus and Her Dead Petz" (2015); Host, "Billboard Music Awards" (2014); Performer, "Bangerz" (2013); Performer, "Wrecking Ball" (2013); Guest, "Two and a Half Men" (2012); Actress, "LOL" (2012); Actress, "So Undercover" (2012); Actress, "Hannah Montana" (2006-2011); Performer, "Can't Be Tamed" (2010); Actress, "The Last Song" (2010); Performer, "Hannah Montana Forever" (2010); Performer, "The Time of Our Lives" (2009); Voice Actor, "Hannah Montana: The Movie" (2009); Host, "MTV Movie Awards" (2009); Performer, "Hannah Montana: The Movie" (2009); Voice Actress, "Bolt" (2008); Performer, "Breakout" (2008); Performer, "Hannah Montana/ Miley Cyrus: Best of Both Worlds Concert Tour" (2008); Performer, "Hannah Montana: One in a Million" (2008); Performer, "Hannah Montana, Vol. 2: Meet Miley Cyrus" (2007); Performer, "Home at Last" (2007); Guest, "The Emperor's New School" (2007); Guest, "High School Musical 2" (2007); Performer, "Hannah Montana" (2006); Performer, "Wanna Be Your Joe" (2006); Guest, "The Suite Life of Zack and Cody" (2006); Voice Actress, "Big Fish" (2003); Guest, "Doc" (2003) **AW:** Video of the Year, "MTV Video Music Awards" (2014); 10 Most Fascinating People of 2013 (2014); Top Streaming Artist, Billboard Music Awards (2014); The 100 Most Influential People in the World, "TIME" (2008, 2014); The 100 Most Powerful Women in Entertainment, Hollywood Reporter (2008, 2013); Favorite Breakout Movie Actress, People's Choice Awards (2010); Barbara Walters Special, The 10 Most Fascinating People of 2008 (2009); Choice Music: Single, "Teen Choice Awards" (2009); Choice TV Actress: Comedy, "Teen Choice Awards" (2007, 2008, 2009); Choice Movie Actress Music/Dance, "Teen Choice Awards" (2009); Favorite Female Singer, Kids Choice Awards (2008); Favorite TV Actress (2008); Choice Music Female Artist, Teen Choice Awards (2008); The 100 Most Powerful Celebrities, Forbes. com (2008); Choice Summer Artist (2007); Favorite TV Actress, Nickelodeon Kids' Choice Awards (2007); The Top 25 Entertainers of Year, "Entertainment Weekly" (2007); Best Song from a Movie; Top Streaming Song

DAFOE, WILLEM, T: Actor **I:** Media & Entertainment **DOB:** 07/22/1995 **PB:** Appleton **SC:** WI/USA **PT:** William Dafoe; Muriel (Sprissler) Isabel Dafoe **MS:** Married **SPN:** Giada Colagrande (03/25/2005) **CH:** Jack **CR:** Co-founder, The Wooster Group Theatrical Company, New York, NY (1977-Present); Member, Theatre X Theatrical Company (1975) **CW:** Appearance, "Sportin' Life" (2020); Actor, "Siberia" (2020); Actor, "The Last Thing He Wanted" (2019); Actor, "Togo" (2019); Actor, "Tommaso" (2019); Actor, "The Lighthouse" (2019); Actor, "Motherless Brooklyn" (2019); Actor, "Aquaman" (2018); Actor, "At Eternity's Gate" (2018); Narrator, "Piigs" (2017); Actor, "Do Donkeys Act?" (2017); Actor, "The Florida Project" (2017); Actor, "What Happened to Monday" (2017); Actor, "Mountain" (2017); Voice Actor, "Death Note" (2017); Actor, "Justice League" (2017); Actor, "Murder on the Orient Express" (2017); Actor, "Opus Zero" (2017); Actor, "Dog Eat Dog" (2016); Actor, "Finding Dory" (2016); Actor, "The Headhunter's Calling" (2016); Actor, "Sculpt" (2016); Actor, "The Great Wall" (2016); Actor, "My Hindu Friend" (2015); Actor, "The Old Women" (2014); Voice Actor, "The Simpsons" (1997, 2014); Actor, "The Grand Budapest Hotel" (2014); Actor, "A Most Wanted Man" (2014); Actor, "Bad Country" (2014); Actor, "The Fault in Our Stars" (2014);

Actor, "Pasolini" (2014); Actor, "John Wick" (2014); Actor, "Odd Thomas" (2013); Actor, "Out of the Furnace" (2013); Actor, "Nymphomaniac: Vol. 1" (2013); Actor, "Nymphomaniac: Vol. 2" (2013); Actor, "John Carter" (2012); Actor, "Tomorrow You're Gone" (2012); Actor, "Miral" (2011); Actor, "Fireflies in the Garden" (2011); Actor, "4:44 Last Day on Earth" (2011); Actor, "The Hunter" (2011); Actor, "American Experience" (2010); Actor, "Farewell" (2010); Actor, "Daybreakers" (2010); Actor, "A Woman" (2010); Voice Actor, "Fantastic Mr. Fox" (2009); Actor, "Idiot Savant" (2009); Actor, "Family Guy" (2007); Actor, "Inside Man" (2006); Actor, "American Dreamz" (2006); Actor, Writer, "Before It Had a Name" (2005); Actor, "Ripley Under Ground" (2005); Actor, "Control" (2005); Actor, "xXx: State of the Union" (2005); Actor, "The Reckoning" (2004); Actor, "The Clearing" (2004); Actor, "Spider-Man 2" (2004); Actor, "The Life Aquatic with Steve Zissou" (2004); Actor, "The Aviator" (2004); Voice Actor, "Finding Nemo" (2003); Actor, "Once Upon A Time in Mexico" (2003); Voice Actor, "Camel Cricket City" (2003); Actor, "Spider-Man" (2002); Actor, "Auto-Focus" (2002); Actor, "Pavillion of Women" (2001); Actor, "Edges of the Lord" (2001); Actor, "Bullfighter" (2000); Actor, "The Animal Factory" (2000); Actor, "Shadow of the Vampire" (2000); Actor, "The Gangs of New York" (2000); Actor, "American Psycho" (1999); Actor, "The Boondock Saints" (1999); Actor, "North Atlantic" (1999); Actor, Co-producer, "New Rose Hotel" (1998); Actor, "The Hairy Ape" (1997); Actor, "Speed 2: Cruise Control" (1997); Actor, "Affliction" (1997); Actor, "The English Patient" (1996); Actor, "Basquiat" (1996); Actor, "Lulu on the Bridge" (1998); Actor, "eXisten Z" (1998); Actor, "Tom and Viv" (1995); Actor, "Victory" (1995); Actor, "The Night and the Moment" (1994); Actor, "Clear and Present Danger" (1994); Actor, "Far Away So Close!" (1993); Actor, "White Sands" (1992); Actor, "Light Sleeper" (1992); Actor, "Body of Evidence" (1992); Actor, "Flight of the Intruder" (1991); Actor, "Cry-Baby" (1990); Actor, "Wild at Heart" (1990); Actor, "Triumph of the Spirit" (1989); Actor, "Born on the Fourth of July" (1989); Actor, "The Last Temptation of Christ" (1988); Actor, "Off Limits" (1988); Actor, "Mississippi Burning" (1988); Actor, "Platoon" (1986); Actor, "To Live and Die in LA" (1985); Actor, "The Hitchhiker" (1985); Actor, "Roadhouse 66" (1984); Actor, "Streets of Fire" (1984); Actor, "New York Nights" (1984); Actor, "The Hunger" (1983); Actor, "The Loveless" (1982) **AW:** Named Best Supporting Actor in a Motion Picture, Satellite Awards (2000, 2019); Best Supporting Actor Award, Seattle Film Critics Society (2017, 2019); Named Best Actor in a Motion Picture, Drama, Satellite Awards (2018); Volpi Cup for Best Actor, Venice Film Festival (2018); Green Drop Award, Venice Film Festival (2018); Fondazione Mimmo Rotella Award, Venice Film Festival (2018); Best Supporting Actor Award, National Board of Review (2017); Crystal Globe for Outstanding Contribution to World Cinema, Karlovy Vary International Film Festival (2016); Recipient, Numerous Awards

DAGUM, ALEXANDER, MD, T: Professor of Surgery and Orthopaedic Surgery, Chief of Plastic Surgery, Executive Vice Chair of Surgery **I:** Medicine & Health Care **CN:** Stony Brook Medicine **MS:** Married **SPN:** Isabelle Von Althen **CH:** Erika; Camilla; Conrad **ED:** Surgical Intern, Ottawa Civic Hospital (Now The Ottawa Hospital) (1987-1988); MD, University of Ottawa, Ontario, Canada, Magna Cum Laude (1987); BSc in Mathematics and Engineering, Queen's University Kingston, Ontario, Canada (1982) **CT:** Certificate of Added Qualification in Surgery of the Hand, The American Board of Plastic Surgery (2004, 2014-Present); Diplomate, The American Board of Plastic

Surgery (2003, 2013-Present); New York State Medical License (2003-Present); Certification in Plastic Surgery, Royal College of Physicians and Surgeons of Canada (1993); General License, The College of Physicians and Surgeons of Ontario (1988); Diplomate, National Board of Medical Examiners (NBME) (1988); Certificate, Advance Cardiac Life Saving, University of Ottawa (1987); Certified, American Advance Life Saving Training Program, The American National Red Cross, Bethesda, MD (1978) **C:** Plastic Surgery Fellowship Program Site Supervisor for LIPSG Fellows (2014-Present); Professor of Surgery with Tenure (2013-Present); Executive Vice Chair, Department of Surgery, SUNY at Stony Brook (Now Stony Brook University), NY (2013-Present); Director and Secretary, Stony Brook Surgical Associates, LLC (2013-Present); Clinical Professor of Orthopaedic Surgery, SUNY at Stony Brook (Now Stony Brook University), NY (2009-Present); Clinical Professor of Surgery, SUNY at Stony Brook (Now Stony Brook University), NY (2009-Present); Chief, Division of Plastic Surgery, SUNY at Stony Brook (Now Stony Brook University), NY (2000-Present); President, Stony Brook Surgical Associates, LLC (2012-2013); Interim Chairman, Department of Surgery, SUNY at Stony Brook (Now Stony Brook University), NY (2012-2013); Associate Professor of Clinical Surgery and Orthopaedic Surgery, SUNY at Stony Brook (Now Stony Brook University), NY (2000-2009); ACE Site Supervisor, Lakeridge Health, University of Toronto, Canada (1999-2000); Lecturer, University of Toronto, Ontario, Canada (1995-2000); Joint Director of Research, University Hand Program, University of Toronto, Canada (1995-1998); Research Consultant, Department of Physiology, Queens University, Kingston, Ontario, Canada (1983-1985) **CR:** Active Staff Privileges, Mather and St. Charles Hospitals, Port Jefferson, NY (2012-Present); Active Staff Privileges, Facebook, St. Catherine's of Siena Hospital (St. Catherine of Sienna), Smithtown, NY (2011-Present); Attending Plastic Surgeon, SUNY at Stony Brook (Now Stony Brook University), NY (2000-Present); Active Staff Privileges, Lakeridge Health Oshawa, Ontario, Canada (1997-2001); Section Chair, Plastic Surgery, Ontario Medical Association (1999-2000); President, The Canadian Society of Plastic Surgeons (1999-2000); Consultant, Plastic Surgeon, The Hospital for Sick Children (SickKids), Toronto, Canada (1996-2000); Associate Plastic Surgeon, North York General Hospital, Toronto, Canada (1995-1998); Trauma Team Leader, St. Michael's Hospital, Toronto, Canada (1993-1994) **CIV:** Board of Directors, Blanca's House (2013-Present); Member, Board of Directors, The Smile Rescue Fund for Kids (2011-Present); Volunteer Surgeon, Blanca's House, Babahoyos Ecuador (2010-2014); Volunteer Surgeon, Smile Train Medical Exchange, Nairobi, Kenya (2010); Volunteer Surgeon, EMAS, Kunming, China (2005-2012); Co-director, Stony Brook University Craniofacial-Cleft Palate Multidisciplinary Team **CW:** Author, Book Chapter, "Soft Tissue Coverage Elbow," Operative Techniques: Shoulder & Elbow Surgery Elsevier (2018); Contributor, Peer-reviewed Publication, "Comparison of the Basal View and a Previously Standardized Cleft Lip Rating Scale" (2018); Author, Book Chapter, "Replantation," Principles of Hand Surgery and Therapy (2017); Contributor, Peer-reviewed Publication, "Utilizing Indocyanine Green Dye Angiography to Detect Simulated Flap Venous Congestion in a Novel Experimental Rat Model," Journal of Reconstructive Microsurgery (2015); Author, Book Chapter, "Fingertip Amputation: Replantation and Supermicrosurgery," Fingertip Injuries: Diagnosis, Management, and Reconstruction (2015); Contributor, "Waltzing a Facial Artery Musculomucosal Flap: A Novel Approach for Repair of Recurrent

Palatal Fistula: A Case Report," Cleft Palate Craniofacial Journal (2011); Faculty Reviewer, "Surgical Subspecialties," First Aid for the ABSITE (2008); Contributor, Peer-reviewed Publication, "Non-equivalent Cylinder Models of Neurons: Interpretation of Voltage Transients Generated by Somatic Current Injection," Journal of Neurophysiology (1988); Author, Book Chapter, "The Natural History of Obstetrical Brachial Plexus Paralysis," Plastic Surgical Forum (1991); Contributor, Peer-reviewed Publication, "Digital Image Speckle Correlation (DISC) to Optimize Botulinum Toxin Type A Injection: A Prospective Randomized Cross-Over Trial"; Contributor, Peer-reviewed Papers Read at Scientific Meetings; Contributor, Numerous Publications, Presentations, Lectures, Poster Presentations, Scientific Exhibits, and Movie Presentations **AW:** Mentorship Award, Long Island Plastic Surgery Group (2018); University of Toronto Alumni Chairman's Medal in Recognition of Contribution to the Specialty of Plastic Surgery (2016); Excellence in Surgical Education Award, Long Island Plastic Surgery Group (2016); Attending of the Year Award, Stony Brook University Hospital Medical Center (Stony Brook Medicine) (2010); Listee, Guide to America's Top Plastic Surgeons (2006); Certificate of Recognition for Participating in the Education of Medical Students Health, Illness and the Community Course (1997); A.W. Harrison Resident Teaching Award, Sunnybrook Health Science Centre, Toronto, Canada (1992); Named Best Surgical Teacher of Undergraduate Students, St. Michael's Hospital, Toronto, Canada (1991); Upjohn Plaque for Highest Standing in Fourth Year Subjects, University of Ottawa, Canada (1987); Sandoz Prize for Highest Standing in Clinical Medicine, University of Ottawa, Canada (1987); Gold Medalist for Graduating First in His Class, University of Ottawa (1987); Book Award for Highest Standing in the Final Year, University of Ottawa (1987); Arthur Richard Prize for Highest Standing Throughout the Entire Medical Course, University of Ottawa, Canada (1987); Mosby Book Award for Highest Class Standing in the 1985-1986 Year, University of Ottawa, Canada (1986); Fourth Place, Canadian Karate Championship (1977) **MEM:** Fellow, American College of Surgeons; Fellow, Royal College of Physicians and Surgeons of Canada; New York Regional Society of Plastic Surgery; American Association of Plastic Surgeons; New York Society for Surgery of the Hand; Northeastern Society of Plastic Surgeons; Groupe pour L'Avancement de la Microchirurgie Canada; American Cleft Palate-Craniofacial Association; The Canadian Society of Plastic Surgeons; The Canadian Society of Plastic Surgeons; Gold Humanism Honor Society; Alpha Omega Alpha Honor Medical Society; Omicron Kappa Upsilon **MH:** Albert Nelson Marquis Lifetime Achievement Award

DAHL, DEBORAH A., PHD, T: Principal **I:** Technology **CN:** Conversational Technologies **DOB:** 06/01/1953 **PB:** Columbus **SC:** OH/USA **PT:** Robert Eugene Dahl; Marilyn Anne (Turner) Dahl **MS:** Married **SPN:** Richard Anthony Schranz (08/20/1977) **CH:** Sarah Montrey Schranz Oliveira; Peter Wakeman Schranz **ED:** PhD, University of Minnesota (1984); MA, University of Minnesota (1980); BS, University of Illinois (1975) **C:** Co-Program Chair, SpeechTEK Conference (2019-Present); Principal, Conversational Technologies (2002-Present); Visiting Scientist, Research Institute for Advanced Computer Science, Universities Space Research Association (2016-2020); Manager of Advanced Development, Natural Language Understanding Group, Unisys, Malvern, PA (1995-2002); Manager of Symbolic Processing and Analysis, Paramax Corporation, Paoli, PA (1992-1995); Senior Staff

Scientist, Unisys, Paoli, PA (1989-1995); Manager of Spoken Language Systems, Unisys, Paoli, PA (1990-1992); Staff Research Scientist, Unisys, Paoli, PA (1987-1989); Manager, Natural Language Processing, Unisys, Paoli, PA (1987-1989); Project Engineer, Burroughs Corporation, Paoli, PA (1984-1987) **CR:** Co-Chair, Voice Interaction Community Group, W3C (2017-Present); Board of Directors, The Applied Voice Input-Output Society (2008-Present); Chair, Multimodal Interaction Working Group, W3C (2002-2016); Member, DARPA Spoken Language Coordinating Committee (1990-1995) **CIV:** Plymouth Meeting Historical Society **CW:** Author, "Multimodal Interaction with W3C Standards" (2016); Author, "Speech and Language Technology for Language Disorders" (2016); Co-Editor, "Multimodal Architecture and Interfaces", W3C (2012); Co-Editor, "EMMA: Extensible Multimodal Annotation", W3C (2009); Author, "Practical Spoken Dialog Systems" (2005); Patentee, "Task Oriented Dialog Manager and Model (2003); Patentee, "System and Method for Creating a Language Grammar using a Spreadsheet or Table Interface" (1999); Patentee, "Robust Language Processor for Segmenting and Parsing Language Containing Multiple Instructions" (1997); Author, Thesis, "The Structure and Function of One-Anaphora in English" (1984) **AW:** Group Achievement Award, Autonomy Operating System, Unmanned Aerial Vehicle Team, NASA (2018); Speech Luminary, Speech Technology Magazine (2012, 2014); Fellow in Cognitive Science, Alfred P. Sloan Foundation, University of Pennsylvania (1983-1984); Graduate Fellow, National Science Foundation (1976-1979) **MEM:** Association for Computational Linguistics; Linguistic Society of America; ACM, Inc.; The Applied Voice Input-Output Society; The Phi Beta Kappa Society **MH:** Albert Nelson Marquis Lifetime Achievement Award **B/I:** Dr. Dahl became involved in her profession after she discovered her passions for the scientific study of language and computing. She was able to combine those interests to pursue a career in computational linguistics, with an emphasis on practical applications. Her interest in practical applications led to her 2005 book, "Practical Spoken Dialog Systems."

DAIGLE, LAUREN ASHLEY, T: Singer, Songwriter **I:** Media & Entertainment **DOB:** 09/09/1991 **PB:** Lafayette **SC:** LA/USA **ED:** Diploma in Child and Family Studies, Louisiana State University **CR:** Member, "Outcry Tour" (2015, 2017); Solo Tour, "A Night with Lauren Daigle" (2016); Member, "Winter Jam Tour" (2016) **CW:** Singer, National Anthem, College Football Playoff National Championship (2020); Performer, Austin City Limits (2019); Solo Artist, "Look Up Child" (2018); Co-Writer, Artist, "Almost Human" (2017); Solo Artist, "Behold: A Christmas Collection" (2016); Solo Artist, "How Can It Be" (2015); Artist, "It is Well" (2015); Contestant, "American Idol" (2010, 2012); Artist, "Close"; Artist "You Alone" **AW:** Grammy Award, Best Contemporary Christian Music Album, The Recording Academy (2019); Grammy Award, Best Contemporary Christian Music Performance/ Song, The Recording Academy (2019); Billboard Music Award, Top Christian Song (2019); Billboard Music Award, Top Christian Album (2017, 2019); Billboard Music Award, Top Christian Artist (2017, 2019); Dove Award, Pop/Contemporary Album of the Year, Gospel Music Association (2019); Dove Award, Artist of the Year, Gospel Music Association (2016, 2019); Dove Award, Song of the Year, Gospel Music Association (2015, 2019); American Music Award, Contemporary Inspirational (2017, 2018); Dove Award, Rock/Contemporary Recorded Song of the Year, Gospel Music Association (2017); Dove Award, Pop/Contemporary Recorded Song of the Year, Gospel Music Association (2016); Dove

Award, Songwriter of the Year, Gospel Music Association (2016); Dove Award, Pop/Contemporary Song of the Year, Gospel Music Association (2015); Dove Award, New Artist of the Year, Gospel Music Association (2015)

DAINES, STEVEN, "STEVE" DAVID, T: U.S. Senator from Montana **I:** Government Administration/ Government Relations/Government Services **DOB:** 08/20/1962 **PB:** Van Nuys **SC:** CA/USA **PT:** Clair W. Daines; Sharon R. Daines **MS:** Married **SPN:** Cindy Daines **CH:** Michael; David; Caroline; Ann **ED:** BS in Chemical Engineering, Montana State University (1984) **C:** U.S. Senator, State of Montana (2015-Present); Member, U.S. House Committee on Transportation and Infrastructure (2013-2015); Member, U.S. House Committee on Natural Resources (2013-2015); Member, U.S. House Committee on Homeland Security (2013-2015); Member, U.S. House of Representatives from Montana's At-large District, United States Congress, Washington, DC (2013-2015); Various Positions Including Vice President of Customer Service, Vice President of Asia-Pacific, and Vice President of North American Sales, RightNow Technologies, Bozeman, MT (2000-2012); Private Construction Business, Bozeman, MT (1997-2000); Management Roles, Procter & Gamble, Hong Kong, China (1991-1997); Management Roles, Procter & Gamble (1984-1991) **CR:** Montana Chairman, Governor Mike Huckabee for President (2008); Delegate, Republican National Convention (1984); Co-founder, Giveitback.com **PA:** Republican **RE:** Presbyterian

DALE, ADRIANNE MARIE, T: Information Technology Executive, Consultant (Retired) **I:** Information Technology and Services **PT:** Almore Marcus; Marie Antoinette (Howard) Dale **MS:** Single **ED:** Coursework in Computer Technology, Professional Development Program, George Washington University (1998-1999); Bachelor of Science, Howard University, Washington, DC (1961); Web Design Degree, Westlake Internet, Washington, DC **CT:** A+ Certified Computer Specialist, CompTIA (2002); Computer Technology Certificate, George Washington University, Washington, DC (1999); Medical Technology Certificate, Providence Hospital, Washington DC (1967); Certified Medical Technologist, American Society for Clinical Pathology (1967) **C:** Retired (2016); Founder, Chief Executive Officer, Mouse Calls LLC (2000-2016); Program Officer, Episcopal Diocese of Washington (1990-1999); Administrative Assistant, Episcopal Church Women Diocese of Washington (1989-1990); Consultant, D.C. Commission on Women, Washington, DC (1987-1987); Associate Professor of Medical Technology, Prince Georges Community College, Largo, MD (1972-1987); Instructor of Medical Technology, D.C. General Hospital (1971-1972); Medical Technologist, Providence Hospital, Washington, DC (1967-1971) **CIV:** Co-chair, Vespers Guiding Team, All Souls Church Unit (2012-Present); Bell ringer, All Souls Church, Unitarian (2011-Present); Akoma Drummers (2014, 2008-Present); Member, All Souls Unitarian Choir (2003-Present); Volunteer, Arena Stage (2003-Present); With, Fort Washington Community Chorus (2009-2011, 2009-2018); Steering Committee, Hiroshima Peace Pilgrimage to Japan with All Souls Church (2014); With, Washington Humane Society (2012-2013); Webmaster, Oracle Set Foundation (2008-2013); Webmaster, Oracle Set Foundation (2008-2013); With, Chorister Heritage Signature Chorale (2009-2011); Archive Committee, Friends of the Woodridge Library (2008-2009); Member, Oracle Set Foundation (1999-2009); Board of Directors, ByteBack Community Computer Center (2005); Lay Leader, Trinity Episcopal Church, Washington, DC (1987-

2003); Secretary, Episcopal Senior Ministries (1993-1999); Diocesan, Parish Consultant, Episcopal Diocese of Washington (1985-1999); Volunteer, DC Crisis Hotline, Washington (1995); Archive Committee, All Souls Church **CW:** Author, "Earl Neil: Black Civil Rights Reformer" (2006); Editor, "People of the Promise" **AW:** Volunteer of the Year, ByteBack Community Computer Center (2005) **MH:** Albert Nelson Marquis Lifetime Achievement Award; Marquis Who's Who Top Professional **AV:** Classical and jazz piano; Yoga; Crossword puzzles; Reading; Travel; Dance; Bicycling; Choral singing **RE:** Episcopalian and Unitarian Universalist

DALEY, SANDY DAKOTA, T: Artist (Retired), Filmmaker, Photographer **I:** Media & Entertainment **DOB:** 02/28/1940 **PB:** Fargo **SC:** ND/USA **PT:** Cecil Raymond Daley; Margaret (Anderson) Daley **ED:** MFA, California College of the Arts, With High Distinction, Oakland, CA (1965); AB, Oberlin College, Cum Laude, Ohio (1961) **CW:** Director, "Cine Portraits," (featuring Leonard Cohen, Edie Sedgwick, Gregory Corso, Incredible String Band, Lucy Colella, Arthur C. Clarke, Harry Smith, Syd Barrett, et al.), The Hotel Chelsea, and London (1965-1975); Director, Producer, Featuring Patti Smith, Vali, Sam Shepard, "Patti Having Her Knee Tattooed" (1971); Director, Producer, "Cine Probe," Featuring Alan Lanier, Patti Smith, The Museum of Modern Art (1971); Director, Producer, Featuring Robert Mapplethorpe and David Croland, "Robert Having His Nipple Pierced" (1970); Proposal "Floating Landscape" (in collaboration with Nicholas Quennell), "Experiments in Art and Technology," Osaka World's Fair, 1970; Photo album, "Backstage with the Rolling Stones," the Civic Auditorium, California, 1965; Photographer and Filmmaker, backstage with The Beatles, at Cow Palace, San Francisco and Hollywood Bowl, Los Angeles, California, 1964; Director(with Sally Potter), Producer, "London Mysteries" (1964); Co-Art Editor, With Geoffrey C. Ward, "Contemporary Photographer Magazine" (1960); Artist(in collaboration with Nicholas Quennell) exhibited with Andy Warhol, Roy Lichtenstein, Robert Rauschenberg **AV:** Writing; Drawing

DALTREY, ROGER, T: Singer **I:** Media & Entertainment **DOB:** 03/01/1944 **SC:** London/England **PT:** Harry Daltrey; Irene Daltrey **MS:** Married **SPN:** Heather Taylor (07/19/1971); Jacqueline (1964-1968) **CH:** Simon; Rosie Lea; Willow Amber; Jaimie **ED:** Honorary Degree, Middlesex University (2012) **C:** Lead Singer, The Who (1964-Present) **CW:** Actor, "Going Back Home" (2014); Actor, "Pawn Stars" (2013); Actor, "Once Upon a Time" (2012); Voice Actor, "Mango's Big Dog Parade" (2008); Singer, "Amazing Journey: The Story of The Who" (2007); Actor, "The Last Detective" (2007); Actor, "Actor, "Once Upon a Time on the Westway" (2006); Actor, "Johnny Was" (2006); Singer, "Live from Toronto" (2006); Singer, "Endless Wire" (2006); Actor, "CSI: Crime Scene Investigation" (2006); Voice Actor, "Wheels on the Bus Series: Mango & Papaya's Animal Adventure" (2005); Voice Actor, "Mango Helps the Moon Mouse" (2005); Actor, "Trafalgar's Battle Surgeon" (2005); Singer, "The Who: Then & Now" (2004); Singer, "Live at the Royal Albert Hall" (2003); Singer, "The Ultimate Colllection" (2002); Actor, ".com for Murder" (2002); Actor, "That 70's Show" (2002); Actor, "Witchblade" (2001-2002); Actor, "Strange Frequency 2" (2001); Actor, "Chasing Destiny" (2001); Actor, "Chasing Destiny" (2001); Actor, "Rude Awakening" (1999-2000); Actor, "Best" (2000); Actor, "Dark Prince: The True Story of Dracula" (2000); Singer, "The BBC Sessions" (1999); Singer, "The Blues to the Bush" (1999); Actor, "The Magical Legend of the Leprechauns" (1999); Actor, "The Bill" (1999);

Actor, "Fitzcairn" (1997-1998); Actor, "Highlander" (1998); Actor, "Scrooge" (1998); Actor, "Like It Is" (1998); Actor, "Sliders" (1997); Actor, "Pirate Tales" (1997); Singer, "Message to Love: The Isle of Wight Festival" (1997); Singer, "Martyrs & Madmen: The Best of Roger Daltrey" (1997); Singer, "The Rolling Stones Rock 'N' Roll Circus" (1996); Actor, "Lois & Clark: The New Adventures of Superman" (1996); Actor, "Bad English I: Tales of a Son of a Brit" (1995, 1996); Singer, "Live at the Isle of Wight Festival 1970" (1996); Singer, "My Generation: The Very Best of The Who" (1996); Actor, "The Wizard of Oz in Concert: Dreams Come True" (1995); Actor, "Lightning Jack" (1994); Singer, "Thirty Years of Maximum R&B" (1994); Actor, "Tales from the Crypt" (1993); Singer, "Rocks in the Head" (1992); Voice Actor, "The Real Story of Happy Birthday to You" (1992); Actor, "Midnight Caller" (1991); Actor, "If Looks Could Kill" (1991); Singer, "Join Together" (1990); Actor, "Buddy's Song" (1990); Actor, "Forgotten Prisoners: The Amnesty Files" (1990); Actor, "Cold Justice" (1989); Actor, "Mack the Knife" (1989); Actor, "Three Penny Opera" (1988); Actor, "How to Be Cool" (1988); Singer, "Who's Better, Who's Best" (1988); Actor, "The Hunting of the Snark" (1987); Singer, "Can't Wait to See the Movie" (1987); Actor, "The Little Match Girl" (1987); Actor, "Crossbow" (1987); Actor, "Gentry" (1987); Singer, "Two's Missing" (1987); Actor, "Buddy" (1986); Singer, "Under a Raging Moon" (1985); Singer, "Who's Missing" (1985); Singer, "Parting Should Be Painless" (1984); Actor, "Pop Pirates" (1984); Actor, "Murder: Ultimate Grounds for Divorce" (1984); Singer, "Who's Greatest Hits" (1983); Singer, "Who's Last" (1983); Actor, "Bitter Cherry" (1983); Actor, "The Beggar's Opera" (1983); Actor, "The Comedy of Errors" (1983); Singer, "The Who Rocks America" (1982); Singer, "It's Hard" (1982); Singer, "Face Dances" (1981); Singer, "Hooligans" (1981); Singer, "McVicar" (1980); Actor, Producer, "McVicar" (1980); Singer, "The Kids Are Alright" (1979); Singer, "The Kids Are Alright" (1979); Actor, "The Legacy" (1979); Executive Producer, "Quadrophenia" (1979); Singer, "Quadrophenia" (1979); Singer, "Who Are You" (1978); Singer, "One of the Boys" (1977); Actor, "One of the Boys" (1977); Actor, "Tommy" (1975); Actor, "Lisztomania" (1975); Singer, "Ride A Rock Horse" (1975); Singer, "The Who By Numbers" (1975); Singer, "Odds & Sods" (1974); Singer, "Quadrophenia" (1973); Singer, "Daltrey" (1973); Singer, "Meaty Beaty Big & Bouncy" (1971); Singer, "Who's Next" (1971); Singer, "Live At Leeds" (1970); Performer, "Woodstock" (1970); Singer, "Tommy" (1969); Performer, "Monterrey Pop" (1968); Singer, "The Magic Bus: The Who on Tour" (1968); Singer, "The Who Sell Out" (1967); Singer, "Happy Jack" (1966); Singer, "The Who Sings My Generation" (1965); Featured, Numerous Documentaries) AW: Steiger Award (2012); James Joyce Award (2009); Kennedy Center Honors, John F. Kennedy Center for the Performing Arts (2008); Inductee, UK Music Hall of Fame (2005); Honorary Knight Commander of the Most Excellent Order of the British Empire (2005); Grammy Lifetime Achievement Award (2001); Inductee, Rock & Roll Hall of Fame (1990); BRIT Award for Outstanding Contribution to British Music (1988); Ivor Novello Award for Contribution to British Music (1982); Best Blues Award, British Blues Awards

DAMICO, JAMES A., T: Library Director **I:** Library Management/Library Services **DOB:** 05/22/1932 **PB:** Syracuse **SC:** NY/USA **PT:** Stephen Alfonso Damico; Astrid (Nyman) Damico **MS:** Married **SPN:** Kathryn Elizabeth Briwa (10/13/1962) **CH:** Andrew; Mark; Matthew **ED:** MLS, Rutgers, The State University of New Jersey (1961); BSBA, C.W. Post College (Now LIU Post), Greenvale, NY

(1959) **C:** Director of Libraries, University of South Alabama, Mobile, AL (1986-1999); Director, Cook Library, The University of Southern Mississippi, Hattiesburg, MS (1981-1986); Associate Director, Rice University, Houston, Texas (1977-1981); Science Librarian, Head Reference, Brown University, Providence, RI (1972-1977); Head, Reference and Systems, University of Dayton, Ohio (1967-1972); Manager, Technology Information Center, General Precision, Inc., Little Falls, NJ (1964-1967); Technology Librarian, Thiokol Chemical Corp., Denville, NJ (1963-1964); Acting Index Editor), American Institute of Aeronautics and Astronautics, New York, NY (1961-1963) **CR:** Consultant in Field **MIL:** With, United States Navy (1951-1955) **MEM:** Board of Directors, Southeastern Library Network (1985-1988); American Library Association; Alabama Librarian Association; Special Libraries Association; Southeastern Library Association; Southeastern Library Network; Italian American Cultural Society; Lions Clubs International **MH:** Albert Nelson Marquis Lifetime Achievement Award **B/I:** Mr. Damico started working part-time at the University Library and he became interested in it. He was asked to apply at Rutgers University; he did and was accepted. Mr. Damico has always incorporated reading into his family circle. **AV:** Private Pilot (Retired)

DAMON, MATT, T: Actor **I:** Media & Entertainment **DOB:** 10/08/1970 **PB:** Cambridge **SC:** MA/USA **PT:** Kent Telfer Damon; Nancy Carlsson-Paige Damon **MS:** Married **SPN:** Luciana Barroso (12/09/2005) **CH:** Isabella; Gia Zavala; Stella Zavala; Alexa **CR:** Member, ONEXONE Foundation **CW:** Actor, "Jay and Silent Bob Reboot" (2019); Actor, "Deadpool 2" (2018); Actor, "Ocean's 8" (2018); Actor, "Bending the Arc" (2017); Actor, "Downsizing" (2017); Actor, "Suburbicon" (2017); Actor, "Thor: Ragnarok" (2017); Actor, Producer, "Jason Bourne" (2016); Executive Producer, "The Runner" (2016); Producer, "Manchester-by-the-Sea" (2016); Actor, "The Great Wall" (2016); Actor, "The Runner" (2016); Actor, "Incorporated" (2016); Actor, "The Martian" (2015); Executive Producer, "The Leisure Class" (2015); Actor, "The Leisure Class" (2015); Executive Producer, "More Time with Family" (2014); Actor, "Years of Living Dangerously" (2014); Actor, "The Monuments Men" (2014); Actor, "Interstellar" (2014); Actor, "Journey to Planet Earth" (2003-2014); Actor, "House of Lies" (2013); Actor, "Behind the Candelabra" (2013); Actor, "Elysium" (2013); Actor, "The Zero Theorem" (2013); Actor, Screenwriter, Producer, "Promised Land" (2012); Actor, "The Adjustment Bureau" (2011); Actor, "Contagion" (2011); Actor, "Margaret" (2011); Voice Actor, "Happy Feet Two" (2011); Actor, "We Bought a Zoo" (2011); Actor, "30 Rock" (2010-2011); Actor, "Cubed" (2010); Actor, "Green Zone" (2010); Actor, "Hereafter" (2010); Actor, "True Grit" (2010); Narrator, "Inside Job" (2010); Actor, "Entourage" (2009); Actor, "Invictus" (2009); Actor, "The Informant!" (2009); Actor, "The People Speak" (2009); Voice Actor, "Arthur" (2007); Actor, "Ocean's Thirteen" (2007); Actor, "The Bourne Ultimatum" (2007); Actor, "The Departed" (2006); Actor, "The Good Shepherd" (2006); Executive Producer, "Feast" (2005); Actor, "The Brothers Grimm" (2005); Actor, "Syriana" (2005); Executive Producer, "Project Greenlight" (2001-2005); Actor, "Eurotrip" (2004); Actor, "The Bourne Supremacy" (2004); Actor, "Ocean's Twelve" (2004); Actor, "Stuck on You" (2003); Executive Producer, "The Battle of Shaker Heights" (2003); Actor, Executive Producer, "The Third Wheel" (2002); Executive Producer, "Speakeasy" (2002); Producer, "Stolen Summer" (2002); Producer, "Push, Nevada" (2002); Host, "Saturday Night Live" (2002); Actor, "The Bernie Mac Show" (2002); Actor, "Will and

Grace" (2002); Actor, "Gerry" (2002); Actor, "The Bourne Identity" (2002); Voice Actor, "Spirit: Stallion of the Cimarron" (2002); Actor, "Confessions of a Dangerous Mind" (2002); Actor, "Jay and Silent Bob Strike Back" (2001); Actor, "The Majestic" (2001); Actor, "Oceans Eleven" (2001); Voice Actor, "Titan A.E." (2000); Actor, "The Legend of Bagger Vance" (2000); Actor, "The Talented Mr. Ripley" (1999); Actor, "Dogma" (1999); All the Pretty Horses" (1999); Actor, "Rounders" (1998); Actor, "Saving Private Ryan" (1998); Actor, "Chasing Amy" (1997); Actor, "The Rainmaker" (1997); Actor, Screenwriter, "Good Will Hunting" (1997); Actor, "Courage Under Fire" (1996); Actor, "Glory Daze" (1996); Actor, "Geronimo: An American Legend" (1993); Actor, "School Ties" (1992); Actor, "Mystic Pizza" (1988) **AW:** Golden Globe Award for Best Performance by an Actor in a Motion Picture - Musical or Comedy (2016); Award for Best Actor, National Board of Review (2015); 100 Most Influential People in the World, "TIME" (2011); Named Favorite Male Action Star, People's Choice Awards (2008); The 100 Most Powerful Celebrities, Forbes.com (2007, 2008); Star on the Hollywood Walk of Fame (2007); Sexiest Man Alive, "People" (2007); Top 25 Entertainers of Year, "Entertainment Weekly" (2007); 50 Most Powerful People in Hollywood, "Premiere" (2005-2006); Golden Globe Award for Best Screenplay-Motion Picture (1998); Academy Award for Best Writing, Screenplay Written Directly for Screen (1998)

DANGERMOND, JACK, T: President, Co-founder **I:** Information Technology and Services **CN:** Environmental Systems Research Institute (Esri) **MS:** Married **SPN:** Laura Dangermond **ED:** Honorary Doctor of Science, University of Minnesota (2008); Master's Degree in Landscape Architecture, Harvard Graduate School of Design (1969); MArch in Urban Planning, University of Minnesota; Bachelor's Degree in Landscape Architecture and Environmental Science, California State Polytechnic University, Pomona, CA **C:** President, Co-founder, Environmental Systems Research Institute (ESRI), Redlands, CA (1969-Present) **CR:** Advisory Committee, NASA; Advisory Committee, United States Environmental Protection Agency; Advisory Committee, National Academy of Sciences; Advisory Committee, NCGIA **CIV:** Signatory, The Giving Pledge **AW:** Named One of the Forbes 400: Wealthiest Americans (2019); Named to the Billionaires' List, Forbes Magazine (2019); Named One of the Richest in Tech, Forbes Magazine (2017); Named One of the Richest Persons in America's 50 Largest Cities, Forbes Magazine (2016); Audubon Medal, National Audubon Society (2015); Fellow, University Consortium for Geographic Information Science (UCGIS) (2012); Patron's Medal, Royal Geographical Society (2010); Co-recipient, Alexander Graham Bell Medal, National Geographic Society (2010); Named One of the Forbes 400: Richest Americans, Forbes (2009); Carl Mannerfelt Gold Medal, International Cartographic Association (2007); Cullum Geographical Medal, American Geographical Society (1999); Anderson Medal, Association of American Geographers (AAG) (1998); John Wesley Powell Award, U.S. Geological Survey (1996); Horwood Distinguished Service Award, Urban and Regional Information Systems Association (URISA) (1988); EduCause Medal; Named Officier, Orde van Oranje Nassau; Recipient, Numerous Awards **MEM:** Eurasian Academy Society; Numerous Organizations

DANGERMOND, LAURA, T: Co-founder **I:** Environmental Services **CN:** Environmental Systems Research Institute (Esri) **MS:** Married

SPN: Jack Dangermond **C:** Co-founder, Environmental Systems Research Institute (Esri) (1969-Present) **CIV:** Signatory, The Giving Pledge

DANIELIAN, ARSEN, SHAREHOLDER, DIRECTOR, OFFICER, T: Attorney at Law **I:** Law and Legal Services **CN:** Baker, Olson, LeCroy & Danielian **MS:** Married **SPN:** Hasmik Danielian, EdD **CH:** Alfred Danielian, M.D., FACC, FACS ; Nyree Kolanjian, Esq. **ED:** LL.D., Honorary Degree, Armenian State Pedagogical University (2010); JD, University of La Verne (1984); MA in Political Science, University of La Verne, California(1982); LL.B., National University of Iran (1978) **C:** Attorney, Partner, Halstead, Baker & Olson (1993-1995) **CR:** Chairman of the General Assembly (World Congress), Catholicosate of the Holy See of Cilicia, Antelias, Lebanon (2002-2009); Chairman, Executive Council of the Western Prelacy of the Armenian Apostolic Church of America (2000-2002); Member, Central Executive Council of the Holy See of Cilicia (1996-2000); Vice-Chairman, Executive Council of the Western Prelacy of the Armenian Apostolic Church of America (1992-1996); Member, Governing Board of Adventist Health, Glendale, CA; Former Chairman, Board of Directors, Healthcare Foundation of the Glendale Adventist Medical Center; Former Chairman, Board of Trustees, Armenian Society of Los Angeles; Former Chairman, Ambassadors of Faith of the Western Diocese of the Armenian Church of North America; Former Member, Diocesan Council of the Western Diocese of the Armenian Church **CW:** Author, Numerous Political, Legal, and Literary Articles, English, Armenian, and Persian Publications; Public Speaker, Lecturer, Keynote Speaker, Master of Ceremonies at Numerous Civic, Community, and Academic Events as well as Graduation Ceremonies **AW:** Certificate of Commendation, Los Angeles County Board of Supervisors for Dedicated Service to the Affairs of L.A. County (2019); Erwin J. Remboldt Founder's Award, Glendale Adventist Medical Center for Outstanding Philanthropy (2014); St. Nerses Shnorhali Medal of Honor and Pontifical Encyclical, Supreme Patriarch and Catholicos of All Armenians (2014) **MEM:** Board of Directors, be.group Foundation (Formerly SCPH) (2008-2014); Civic Advisory Board of Davidian Mariamian Educational Foundation (2007-2012); Chairman, National Representative Assemblies of the Western Prelacy (1999, 200, 2003-2004); Central Committee of the Armenian Cultural Foundation Western United States (1997-2000); Board of Directors, Armenian Educational Foundation (1992-1996); Secretary, Board of Directors, United Armenian Fund (1992-1996); Arroyo-Verdugo Sub-Region Advisory Council, Southern California Association of Governments (1993-1994); Executive Committee of the Board of Trustees of the American Armenian International College of the University of La Verne (1990-1991); Chairman of the Education Council of the Schools of the Western Prelacy of the Armenian Apostolic Church of America (1987-1991); Secretary, Board of Trustees, Holy Martyrs Armenian Apostolic Church and Ferrahian School of Encino (1982-1983); Chairman of the Executive Board, Garikian Scholarship Fund of the Western Prelacy (1981-2000); Member/Vice President of the Board of Directors of the Glendale Symphony Orchestra Association; Member of the Board of Directors of the Glendale Rotary Club; State Bar of California, International Law Section; Los Angeles County Bar Association, Immigration Law Section; American Immigration Lawyers Association **BAR:** California; Supreme Court of the United States **AS:** Mr. Danielian attributes his success to being close to people and earning their trust. **B/I:** Mr. Danielian became involved in his profession because he always wanted to be a lawyer. He would have preferred to become a diplomat. But since he was born in Iran and is a Christian Armenian, there wasn't many opportunities for him in diplomacy. When he was young he acted as an associate of a prominent international lawyer Dr. Y.D. Papazian, O.B.E. in Iran; Their law firm was the legal counsel to 14 foreign embassies in Iran. After immigrating to the United States, he continued his legal education and, after admission to the California Bar in 1985, he continued to practice law in Los Angeles, California.

DANIELS, JEFF, T: Actor **I:** Media & Entertainment **DOB:** 02/19/1955 **PB:** Clarke County **SC:** GA/USA **PT:** Robert Lee Daniels; Marjorie J. (Ferguson) Daniels **MS:** Married **SPN:** Kathleen Treado (07/13/1979) **CH:** Ben; Lucas; Nellie **ED:** Honorary DFA, University of Michigan (2009); Coursework, Central Michigan University **C:** Founder, Purple Rose Theatre Co., Chelsea, MI (1991-Present); Executive Director, Purple Rose Theatre Co.; Apprentice, Circle Repertory Co., New York, NY **CW:** Actor, "The Catcher Was A Spy" (2018); Actor, "The Looming Tower" (2018); Actor, "Godless" (2017); Actor, "The Divergent Series: Allegiant - Part 1" (2016); Actor, "Steve Jobs" (2015); Actor, "The Martian" (2015); Actor, "The Newsroom" (2012-2014); Actor, "Dumb and Dumber To" (2014); Actor, "Looper" (2012); Actor, "Howl" (2010); Actor, "State of Play" (2009); Actor, "Paper Man" (2009); Actor, "Away We Go" (2009); Actor, "God of Carnage" (2009); Actor, "Space Chimps" (2008); Actor, "Traitor" (2008); Actor, "Turn of the Century" (2008); Actor, "Short-Changed Review, Blackbird" (2007); Actor, "The Lookout" (2007); Actor, "RV" (2006); Actor, "Infamous" (2006); Actor, "Because of Winn-Dixie" (2005); Actor, "The Squid and the Whale" (2005); Actor, "Good Night, and Good Luck" (2005); Actor, "Imaginary Heroes" (2004); Actor, "The Goodbye Girl" (2004); Actor, "The Five People You Meet in Heaven" (2004); Actor, "Gods and Generals" (2003); Actor, "I Witness" (2003); Across the Way" (2002); Actor, Director, Writer, "Super Sucker" (2002); Actor, "Blood Work" (2002); Actor, "The Hours" (2002); Actor, Director, Writer, "Escanaba in da Moonlight" (2001); Actor, "Chasing Sleep" (2000); Actor, "The Crossing" (2000); Actor, "Cheaters" (2000); Actor, "My Favorite Martian" (1999); Actor, "All the Rage" (1999); Actor, "Pleasantville" (1998); Actor, "Trial and Error" (1997); Actor, "Fly Away Home" (1996); Actor, "2 Days in the Valley" (1996); Actor, "101 Dalmatians" (1996); Actor, "Redwood Curtain" (1995); Escanaba in da Moonlight" (1995); Thy Kingdom's Coming" (1994); Actor, "Speed" (1994); Actor, "Dumb and Dumber" (1994); The Vast Difference" (1993); Actor, "Gettysburg" (1993); Actor, "Redwood Curtain" (1993); Actor, "Disaster in Time" (1992); The Tropical Pickle" (1992); Actor, "The Butcher's Wife" (1992); Playwright, "Shoeman" (1991); Actor, "Arachnophobia" (1990); Actor, "Welcome Home, Roxy Carmichael" (1990); Actor, "Love Hurts" (1990); Actor, "Grand Tour" (1989); Actor, "Checking Out" (1989); Actor, "No Place Like Home" (1989); Actor, "The House on Carroll Street" (1988); Actor, "Sweet Hearts Dance" (1988);); Actor, "The Caine Mutiny Court Marshall" (1988); Actor, "Radio Days" (1987); Actor, "Heartburn" (1986); Actor, "Something Wild" (1986); Actor, "Marie" (1985); Actor, "The Purple Rose of Cairo" (1985); Actor, "The Golden Age" (1984); Actor, "Three Sisters" (1982-1983); Actor, "Terms of Endearment" (1983); Actor, "An Invasion of Privacy" (1983); Actor, "Johnny Got His Gun" (1982); Actor, "The Fifth of July" (1978, 1979, 1980-1981); Actor, "Ragtime" (1981); Actor, "A Rumor of War" (1980); Actor, "Lulu" (1978); Actor, "Slugger" (1978); Actor, "My Life" (1977); Actor, "Brontosaurus" (1977); Actor, "Feedlot" (1977); Actor, "The Farm" (1976); Singer, "Grandfather's Hat, Jeff Daniels Live and Unplugged" **AW:** Outstanding Lead Actor in a Drama Series, Emmy Awards (2013); Emmy Award, Outstanding Supporting Actor in a Limited Series or Movie; Obie Award

DANIELS, LEE, T: Producer, Director **I:** Media & Entertainment **DOB:** 12/24/1959 **PB:** New York **SC:** NY/USA **CW:** Writer, "Good People" (2020); Writer, "Empire" (2016-2019); Co-creator, "Star" (2016); Co-Creator, "Empire" (2015); Producer, "Lee Daniels' The Butler" (2013); Producer, "The Paperboy" (2012); Producer, "Precious" (2009); Producer, "Tennessee" (2008); Producer, "Shadowboxer" (2005); Producer, "The Woodsman" (2004); Actor, "Agnes und Seine Bruder" (2004); Producer, "Monster's Ball" (2001); Actor, "A Little Off Mark" (1986)

DANNELS, MARK J., T: Sheriff **I:** Law and Legal Services **CN:** Cochise County Sheriffs Office **ED:** MA in Criminal Justice Management, Aspen University, Denver, CO (2011); BA in Criminal Justice Administration, Columbia Southern University, Orange Beach, AL **CT:** Certified Public Manager, Arizona State University **C:** Sheriff, Cochise County Sheriff's Department, AZ (1986-Present); Officer, Bisbee County Sheriff's Department, AZ (1984-1986) **CR:** Teacher, Organizational Leadership & Team Building, Cochise College; Teacher, Wayland Baptist University **CIV:** Advisory Council, Department of Homeland Security; Chairman, National Sheriff's Association for Border Security; Past President, Arizona Sheriff's Association; President, Just Kids Inc.; President, CASA; Coach, High School Basketball; Past President, San Pedro Kiwanis; Past President, San Pedro Boys & Girls Club **MIL:** United States Army **AW:** Good Conduct Medal, United States Army; Medal of Valor. United States Army; Distinguished Service Award, United States Army; Deputy of the Year, United States Army; Western Sheriff of the Year, United States Army; National Police Hall of Fame, United States Army **MEM:** Arizona Sheriff's Association; National Sheriff Association **AS:** Sheriff Dannels attributes his success to having the trust of his community, as well as the men and women that serve the mission of the Sheriff's Department. He surrounds himself with bright, passionate workers. Sheriff Dannels' motto is "Don't be position driven because that is temporary. Be people-driven because they last a lifetime." **B/I:** Sheriff Dannels grew up in a rural farm community in northern Illinois. It was always a childhood dream of his to have a career in law enforcement. He remembers the local Sheriff would come to his house, as he had a positive relationship with Sheriff Dannels' family and the surrounding community. Sheriff Dannels always admired that connection. After high school, he joined the military. He was stationed at Fort Huachuca in Arizona before being discharged in 1984. Following his honorable discharge, Sheriff Dannels was hired by the Bisbee Police Department, where he worked until 1986. He was then hired by the Sheriff's Department of Cochise, where he remains today. **THT:** Sheriff Dannels acknowledges that his position is an elected position. His main focus is the quality of life within his communities. He breaks that down into three priorities, education, prevention, and enforcement. He makes it a priority to build trust and gain the respect of his community, ensuring that every citizen feels safe. Sheriff Dannels was the first Sheriff in the history of the country to be appointed to the Department of Homeland Security's advisory council.

DANTZIC, CYNTHIA MARIS, T: Senior Professor Emerita, Artist **I:** Education/Educational Services **CN:** Long Island University **DOB:** 01/04/1933 **PB:** New York **SC:** NY/USA **PT:** Howard Arthur Gross;

Sylvia Hazel (Wiener) Gross **MS:** Widowed **SPN:** Jerry Dantzic (06/15/1958) **CH:** Grayson "Gray" Ross Dantzic **ED:** MFA, Pratt Institute (1963); BFA, Yale University (1955); Coursework, Bard College (1950-1952); Coursework, Brooklyn Museum Art School, Brooklyn, NY (1947-1950) **C:** Senior Professor Emerita, Long Island University (2019-Present); Professor, Long Island University, Brooklyn, NY (1975-Present); Faculty, Long Island University, Brooklyn, NY (1964-Present); Senior Professor, Long Island University (2009-2019); Adjunct Professor of Art, The Cooper Union (1999-2002); Adjunct Associate Professor of Art, The Cooper Union (1992-1999); Chair, Art Department, Long Island University, Brooklyn, NY (1980-1986); Instructor of Art, Bronx Community College, CUNY, Bronx, NY (1963-1964); Coordinator of Art Progressive, Instructor, North Shore Community Arts Center, Roslyn, NY (1962-1964); Head, Art Department, Bentley School, New York, NY (1958-1962); Teacher of Art, The Baldwin School, Bryn Mawr, PA (1955-1958) **CR:** Lecturer, Presenter in Field; Exhibiting Artist; Author **CIV:** Trustee, Park Slope Civic Council (1991-2015) **CW:** Group Show Exhibit, The National Arts Club (2005, 2008, 2016, 2017, 2019); Solo Exhibit, Resnick Gallery, Long Island University, Brooklyn, NY (1983, 1989, 1995, 2000, 2017); Author, Chapter in "Robert Engman: Structural Sculpture" (2017); Author, "100 New York Calligraphers" (2015); Author, Illustrator, "Alphabet City: Signs of New York" (2010); Author, Illustrator, "100 New York Photographers" (2009); Group Show Exhibit, Spring St. Gallery, New York, NY (2005-2008); Group Show Exhibit, Blue Mountain Gallery, New York, NY (1984-1985, 1994-1998, 2001-2002, 2004-2008); Author, Illustrator, "100 New York Painters" (2006); Solo Exhibit, Crosby Studio Gallery, New York, NY (2005); Author, Illustrator, "Antique Pocket Mirrors: Pictorial & Advertising Miniatures" (2002); Author, Illustrator, "Drawing Dimensions: A Comprehensive Introduction" (1999); Solo Exhibit, St. John's University Gallery (1995); Author, Illustrator, "Design Dimensions: An Introduction to the Visual Surface" (1990); Group Show Exhibit, Hillwood Gallery, Greenvale, NY (1985); Commissioned Artist, Edition of Photo Collages, Brooklyn Arts and Culture Association (1983); Author, Illustrator, "Sounds of Silents" (1976); Author, Illustrator, "Stop Dropping BreAdcrumBs on my YaCht" (1974); Solo Exhibit, East Hampton Gallery, New York, NY (1965-1966); Represented in Permanent Collections, Brooklyn Museum, NY, Rose Art Museum, MA, Bard College, NY, Adirondack Museum, NY; Contributor, Articles, Professional Journals **AW:** Long Island University Faculty Research Grantee (1985-Present); 50-Year Faculty Award, Long Island University (2018); 40-Year Faculty Medal, Long Island University (2007); Trustees Lifetime Award for Scholarly Achievement in Art and Art Education, Long Island University (1999); Trustees Award, Single Work (1990); Newton Teaching Excellence Award (1988); Mellon Grantee (1984) **MEM:** Photography and Imaging, American Photography Archives Group (2016-Present); Vice President, Society of Scribes (2015-Present); The National Arts Club (2010-Present); Board of Governors, Society of Scribes (2003-Present); Executive Committee, Long Island University Faculty Federation: LIUFF (1975-Present); Board Member, New York Society for General Semantics (2010-2015); American Association of University Professors; International Society of Copier Artists; College Art Association of America, Inc. **MH:** Albert Nelson Marquis Lifetime Achievement Award; Marquis Who's Who Top Professional **AS:** Ms. Greciano attributes her success to professional parents who expected her to succeed, as well as effort, enthusiasm, and quite a bit of good luck. **B/I:** Ms. Greciano

became involved in her profession because from her earliest days, she knew she was going to be an artist. At Yale, Josef Albers asked her to accept a teaching position with one of his Black Mountain students in Bryn Mawr, Pennsylvania. Later, after receiving an MFA at Pratt in 1963, she joined the faculty at Long Island University, and has been there ever since. **AV:** Playing piano; Traveling ; Collecting Americana, tribal, and folk art **PA:** Democrat **THT:** Ms. Greciano is very proud of her son, Grayson, who put together a photo presentation of his father's photographs of Billie Holiday for the Smithsonian Institution Traveling Exhibition Service(SITES). These photographs will be sent around the country for four years. She assisted in the editing process.

DARST, DAVID EARL, BTH, BS, MED, MBA, T: Finance Educator, Pastor **I:** Religious **DOB:** 09/26/1946 **PB:** Lancaster **SC:** OH/USA **PT:** Darrell Clellan Darst; Thelma Marie Darst **MS:** Married **SPN:** Pauline Mae (Bertram) Darst (11/27/1976) **CH:** Sara Jane (Darst) Rowland **ED:** MBA, Bowling Green State University, Bowling Green, OH (1991); MEd, Bowling Green State University, Bowling Green, OH (1990); BS, Accounting, Franklin University, Columbus, OH (1975); BTh, Apostolic Bible Institute, St. Paul, MN (1969) **CT:** Ordained Minister, United Pentecostal Church, Weldon Spring, MO (1972-Present); Certified Fraud Examiner, Association of Certified Fraud Examiners (2006-2012) **C:** Instructor, New Life Christian Center Campus, Purpose Institute, Lancaster, OH (2019, 2016-2017); Accounting Professor, Central Ohio Technical College, Newark, OH (1994-2012); Instructor, Anchor Church Campus, Purpose Institute, Zanesville, OH (2015); Adjunct Instructor, Ohio State University at Newark, Newark, OH (2001-2008); Accounting Instructor, Zane State College, Zanesville, OH (1992-1994); Graduate Teaching Assistant, Business Education and Accounting Departments, Bowling Green State University, Bowling Green, OH (1989-1991); Accounting Instructor, Detroit Lakes Technical College, Detroit Lakes, MN (1989); Accounting Instructor, Wooster Business College, Wooster, OH (1978-1979) **CR:** Controller, Snappy Air Distribution Products, Detroit Lakes, MN (1984-1987); Cost Control Manager, Woodside Fireplaces (1979-1984); Cost Accountant, Mansfield Products, Mansfield, OH (1978-1979); President, Faculty Council, Central Ohio Technical College; Vice President of Faculty Council, Central Ohio Technical College; President Ex-Officio, Faculty Council, Central Ohio Technical College **CIV:** New Life Christian Center, Lancaster, OH (2013-Present); Chairman, Ohio District United Pentecostal Church Audit Committee (2001-Present); Ohio District United Pentecostal Church Audit Committee (1991-Present); Minister, United Pentecostal Church (1969-Present); Central Ohio Woodturners, Columbus, OH (2017-2018); Association of Certified Fraud Examiners (2006-2012); Pastor, Kirkersville Apostolic Church, Kirkersville, OH (2002-2012); Pastor, Gibonburg United Pentecostal Church, Gibsonburg, OH (1989-1991); North Dakota United Pentecostal Church District Board (1988-1989); Pastor, Changing Lives Tabernacle, West Fargo, ND (1987-1989); Ohio District United Pentecostal Church Home Missions Boar (1981-1984); Pastor, United Pentecostal Church, West Salem, OH (1978-1984); Pastor's Assistant, United Pentecostal Church, Circleville, OH (1973-1976); Evangelist, United Pentecostal Church International (1969-1973); Testified as a Special Witness, Licking County Ohio Court Case **CW:** Author, Contributor, Numerous Short Articles, Sermonettes, Pastor of the New Life Christian Church, Lancaster, OH; Writer, Numerous Scripts, Upward Thoughts Radio Program, Sponsored by New Life Christian Church, Lancaster, OH;

Clarinet Player, Orchestra, Kirkersville Apostolic Church **AW:** Listee, Who's Who in America (2010); Numerous Commendations for Academic Leadership and Theological Leadership; Special Recognition, United Pentecostal Church International, Weldon Spring, MO; Letter of Recognition and Commendation for Excellence in Leadership as Chairman of the Central Ohio Technical College Faculty Council, Donna Alvarado, Chairperson of the Central Ohio Technical College Trustee Board, Newark, OH; Letter of Recognition and Commendation for Excellence in Leadership as Chairman of the Central Ohio Technical College Faculty Council, Dr. Rafael Cortada, Dean-Director of Central Ohio Technical College-Ohio State University, Newark, OH; Listee, Who's Who Among America's Teachers **MEM:** New Life Christian Center, Lancaster, OH (2013-Present); Ohio District Audit Committee, United Pentecostal Church International (1991-Present); Central Ohio Woodturners, Columbus, OH (2017-2018); Association of Certified Fraud Examiners (2006-2012); Institute of Management Accountants **MH:** Albert Nelson Marquis Lifetime Achievement Award; Marquis Who's Who Top Professional; Distinguished Humanitarian **AS:** First of all, Mr. Darst attributes his success to the Lord Jesus Christ and to the principles instilled in him by his parents. Hard work, determination, perseverance, and the drive to be the best he could be were all very important. He never gave up and always faced the challenges of success and moving forward with grit and gumption. **B/I:** Mr. Darst became involved in his profession because of his initial quest to become a pastor. His family was Apostolic, and he was raised in an Apostolic church. At an early age, he felt that the Lord was calling him to minister and to make a difference in people's lives through His ministry. As a result, Mr. Darst felt compelled by the Lord to do with his life. He went to the Apostolic Bible Institute in St. Paul Minnesota for theological training a few years after he graduated from high school. He graduated in 1969 and subsequently was granted a ministerial license by the United Pentecostal Church. He was ordained in 1972. After evangelizing for four years, he accepted a position as an assistant to the pastor in a small town in Ohio. It was always Mr. Darst's ultimate goal to pastor a small church, and he knew that most pastors of small churches are bi-vocational in order to support their families. While serving as a pastor's assistant, he enrolled in the accounting program at Franklin University. After graduating from Franklin University, he ultimately accepted an accounting position in addition to serving as the pastor's assistant. **AV:** Reading; Crocheting; Woodturning; Traveling **RE:** United Pentecostal Church **THT:** Mr. Darst believes life is broader than our vocation and our career. As professionals, our lives should not be defined just by our position but by our character, compassion, honesty, integrity, principles, values and our desire and willingness to help other people along life's pathway. Selfless service is important if one is to be successful in life. We must never forget our obligation to our families, our children, and those individuals who have supported us and contributed to our success both as professionals and as individuals. Professionals must never sacrifice their relationship with their wives and children on the altar of career advancement and success in our professions.

DAS, SUMIT, T: Product Engineer **I:** Engineering **CN:** TE Connectivity **SC:** India **PT:** Amid Das; Nivedita Das **ED:** MS, Michigan Technological University **C:** Product Engineer, TE Connectivity (2018) **AS:** Mr. Das attributes his success to the traits he possesses: sincerity, honesty and hard work. Those traits have always been with him. **B/I:**

Mr. Das entered his profession because he had a childhood passion for the automotive field and his father and mother motivated him to pursue that passion and receive the education to move forward. **AV:** Playing music; Listening to music

DASH, ANIL, T: Chief Executive Officer **I:** Information Technology and Services **CN:** Glitch Inc. **SC:** PA/USA **MS:** Married **SPN:** Alaina Browne **CH:** One Son **C:** Chief Executive Officer, Glitch (2016-Present); Co-founder, Managing Director, Activate (2010-2016); Co-founder, Chief Executive Officer, Makerbase (2015-2016); Co-founder, Chief Executive Officer, ThinkUp (2012-2016); Contributing Editor, Wired Magazine (2012); Director, Expert Labs, American Association for the Advancement of Science (2009-2012); Vice President, Evangelism, Six Apart Ltd. (2003-2009); New Media Development, Village Voice Media (2001-2003) **CR:** Member, Board of Directors, Lower Eastside Girls Club of New York (2015-Present); Member, Board of Directors, Data & Society Research Institute (2013-Present); Board Director, Stack Overflow, Stack Exchange Inc. (2011-Present); Speaker in the Field **CW:** Featured, "Media Matters," PBS (2003)

DASILVA, RODRIGO, T: Managing Partner, Restaurateur **I:** Food & Restaurant Services **CN:** RHS Hospitality Group **DOB:** 05/24/1979 **SC:** Brazil **PT:** Vincente DaSilva; Ana Maria DaSilva **ED:** Marketing Degree, Earned in Brazil **C:** Managing Partner, Co-founder, RHS Hospitality Group (2016-Present); Multi-unit General Manager, OTG Management (2014-2016); Multi-unit General Manager, Partner, Burger Bound-Handcrafted Organic Burgers (2011-2014); General Manager, Operations Manager, Rio Rodizio Churrascaria/Newark and Union Locations, NJ (2006-2011); Manager, AGM, 22 West-New American Cuisine (2004-2006); Floor Captain, Manager, Alfama Fine Portuguese Cuisine (1999-2004) **AS:** Mr. DaSilva attributes his success to a lot of hard work, and the perseverance of trying to get better everyday. **B/I:** Mr. DaSilva became involved in his profession because he always worked in customer service, always dealt with people, and it was something he enjoyed doing. **THT:** Mr. DaSilva is a dedicated restaurant and hospitality professional who has worked over 20 years in the industry. A seasoned multi-unit operations restaurateur, he is well-rounded in many facets of the hospitality industry. Working with many hospitality projects, Mr. DaSilva is a proven leader adept at working established high profile, high energy and high grossing concepts, as well as start-ups. For Mr. DaSilva, the most rewarding aspect of his profession was seeing all the accomplishments the professionals that started in his organization are having today. Mr. DaSilva has observed many changes in his field, including that everything is more computerized and his fear that human interaction will become less and less. He has managed restaurants in hotels and some lounges, mostly in the Newark, NJ area.

DATCHER, JEWELL A., T: Mathematics Teacher (Retired) **I:** Education/Educational Services **DOB:** 08/21/1948 **PB:** Detroit **SC:** MI/USA **PT:** Mack A. Junior; Julia Maria (Oliver) McCartha **MS:** Married **SPN:** William Jerome Datcher (9/7/1968) **CH:** Antonia Latrec **ED:** Postgraduate Coursework, Word of Faith International Christian Center, School of Ministry (1995-1997); MEd in Instructional Technology, Wayne State University (1995); BA in Business Administration, Marygrove College, Detroit, MI (1992); BRE, William Tyndale College, Cum Laude, Farmington Hills, MI (1984) **CT:** Ordained (2003); Certified Teacher, Elementary K-5, Math 6-8 Self Contained **C:** Teacher, Detroit Public School (2008-2016); Worked for Orthodontist (1997-2008);

Project Coordinator, Benefit Delivery Services (1994-1997); Team Leader, Instructional Developer, Blue Cross-Blue Shield of Michigan, Detroit, MI (1991-1994); Interim Supervisor, Team Leader, Blue Cross-Blue Shield of Michigan, Detroit, MI (1992-1993); Lead Performance Analyst, Blue Cross-Blue Shield of Michigan, Detroit, MI (1990-1991); Technology Writer, Blue Cross-Blue Shield of Michigan, Detroit, MI (1989-1990); Director, Christian Education, Detroit Institute for Biblical Studies (1988-1989); Supervisor, Training and Quality, Blue Cross-Blue Shield of Michigan, Detroit, MI (1987-1989); Senior Trainer, Blue Cross-Blue Shield of Michigan, Detroit, MI (1985-1987); Customer Service Representative II, Blue Cross-Blue Shield of Michigan, Detroit, MI (1966-1985) **CR:** Representative, Missions Tour to Ecuador, South America, William Tyndale College (1980); Consultant, Delegate, Afro-American Mennonite Association, Detroit, MI (1979) **CIV:** Member, TMBC Pastor's Chorus; Staff Member, Salvation Temple Church (Non-denominational) **AW:** Marygrove Scholar, Marygrove College (1985-1992); Grosse Pointe Women's Auxiliary Scholar, William Tyndale College (1983) **MEM:** American Society for Training and Development; National Association for the Advancement of Colored People; National Management Association; Marygrove College Alumni Association; William Tyndale College Alumni Association **B/I:** Ms. Datcher became involved in her profession because she felt called in the ministry to go out and help in the community. She got the biblical training she needed and moved on from there. She was now a teacher and a pray director at the Salvation Temple Church, in Hazel Park Michigan.

DATTA, SUBHENDU KUMAR, DR., T: Mechanical Engineer, Educator **I:** Education/Educational Services **DOB:** 01/15/1936 **PB:** Howrah **SC:** India **PT:** Srish Chandra; Prabhabati Datta **ED:** PhD, Jadavpur University (1962); MSc, Calcutta University (1956); BSc, Presidency College, with Honors, Kolkata, India (1954) **C:** Professor Emeritus, University of Colorado (2007-Present); Assistant Professor to Professor, University of Colorado, Boulder (1968-2007); Assistant Professor, University of Manitoba, Winnipeg, Canada (1967-1968); Assistant Professor, Indian Institute of Technology, Kanpur (1965-1967); Postdoctoral Fellow, Rensselaer Polytechnic Institute, Troy, NY (1963-1964); Lecturer, Mathematics Research Center, Madison, WI (1962-1963) **CR:** Consultant, National Institute Standards and Technology, Boulder, CO (1985-2004); Visiting Assistant Professor, University of Colorado, Boulder (1964-1965) **CW:** Contributor, Articles, Professional Journals; Co-author, "Elastic Waves in Composite Media and Structures" **AW:** Grantee, Department of Energy (1995-2003); Grantee, Office of Naval Research (1985-1992); Grantee, National Science Foundation (1970-1988); Fulbright Award (1986, 1962) **MEM:** Board Director, American Academy of Mechanics (1995-1998); Fellow, American Society of Mechanical Engineers; Fellow, American Academy of Mechanics **MH:** Albert Nelson Marquis Lifetime Achievement Award

DAVENPORT, G. WILLIAM, T: U.S. Administrative Law Judge (Retired) **I:** Law and Legal Services **CN:** U.S. Government **DOB:** 07/26/1949 **PB:** Birmingham **SC:** AL/USA **PT:** George Martin Davenport; Marjorie Salma (Lee) Davenport **MS:** Married **SPN:** Virginia Carolyn Davis Davenport (12/23/2017) **CH:** William Matthew; Samantha Christine; Andrew Stephen **ED:** JD, Duke University (1977); PhD in Political Science, International Law, Political Philosophy, International Relations, Duke University (1976); MA in Political Science, Duke University

(1974); BA in History, Philosophy, Political Science, Birmingham Southern College, Magna Cum Laude (1972) **C:** Retired, United States Administrative Law Judge, Social Security Administration, Savannah, GA (1995-2015); Retired, United States Administrative Law Judge, Social Security Administration, Middlesboro KY (1994-1995); Senior Trial Attorney, United States Equal Employment Opportunity Commission (EEOC), Birmingham AL (1979-1994); Associate, Dawson & Thomson, Birmingham AL (1977-1979) **CW:** Author, "Controlling the Multinational Corporations" (1976); Author, Various Law Review Articles, Professional Journals **AW:** Fellow, Sigma Xi (1976); Best PhD Dissertation Award (1976); Faculty Fellow, Duke University (1972-1976) **MEM:** American Bar Association; ATLA; Phi Beta Kappa; Omicron Delta Kappa; MENSA **BAR:** Georgia (2017); United States Courts of Appeals for the 11th Circuit (1981); United States Courts of Appeals for the 5th Circuit (1978); United States District Court for the Northern District of Alabama (1977); United States District Court for the Middle District of Alabama (1977); United States District Court for the Southern District of Alabama (1977); Alabama (1977) **MH:** Albert Nelson Marquis Lifetime Achievement Award **AS:** Plato defined justice as giving each man what he truly deserves. In the law, it is Judge Davenport's job to help bring out the truth. He works hard and uses fair means to prove each case. He does his best to be fair; as he gained experience, victories have come his way more frequently. **B/I:** As a young man, Judge Davenport wanted a public service career. He had a passion for strategic thinking and thought of being a career military officer, but later considered careers in both the law and academics. The more he pursued either of those professions, the more he realized he wanted to do both, which is how he got to where he is today. **AV:** Eclectic reading; Practicing martial arts; Swimming **PA:** Independent **RE:** Christian, Methodist Denomination **THT:** Judge Davenport always does his best. He is never afraid to fail. He believes in the end, history judges us all, as does God.

DAVID, LARRY, T: Television Scriptwriter, Producer, Actor **I:** Media & Entertainment **DOB:** 07/02/1947 **PB:** Brooklyn **SC:** NY/USA **PT:** Morty David; Rose David **MS:** Married **SPN:** Ashley Underwood (2020); Laurie Lennard (03/31/1993, Divorced 2007) **CH:** Cazzie; Romy **ED:** BA in History, University of Maryland, College Park, MD **CW:** Executive Producer, Writer, Actor, "Curb Your Enthusiasm" (2000-Present); Actor, Writer, Producer, "Saturday Night Live" (2015-2017); Actor, Writer, Producer, "May & Marty" (2016); Actor, Writer, Producer, "The League" (2015); Actor, Writer, "A Fish in the Dark" (2015); Actor, Writer, Producer, "Triptank" (2014); Actor, Writer, Producer, "Clear History" (2013); Executive Producer, Actor, "The Three Stooges" (2012); Actor, "The Paul Reiser Show" (2011); Executive Producer, Actor, "Whatever Works" (2009); Actor, "Entourage" (2004); Executive Producer, Co-creator, "Seinfeld" (1990-1998); Writer, Director, "Sour Grapes" (1998); Executive Producer, Actor, "New York Stories" (1989); Creator, Writer: Norman's Corner" (1989); Executive Producer, Co-creator, "The Seinfeld Chronicles" (1989); Executive Producer, Actor, "Radio Days" (1987); Staff Writer, "Saturday Night Live" (1984-1985); Executive Producer, Actor, "Can She Bake a Cherry Pie?" (1983); Staff Writer, "Fridays" (1980-1982) **AW:** Award for Best Comedy Series, AFI (2001); Emmy Award for Outstanding Comedy Series, Television Academy (1993); Emmy Award for Outstanding Writing in a Comedy Series, Television Academy (1993)

DAVIDS, SHARICE LYNETTE, T: U.S. Representative from Kansas **I:** Government Administration/Government Relations/Government Services **CN:** U.S. House of Representatives **DOB:** 05/22/1980 **PB:** Frankfurt **SC:** West Germany **PT:** Crystal Herriage **ED:** Doctor of Jurisprudence, Cornell Law School (2010); Bachelor of Arts in Business Administration, University of Missouri-Kansas City (2007); Coursework, University of Kansas; University of Johnson County Community College; Coursework, Haskell Indian Nations University **C:** Member, U.S. House of Representatives from Kansas' Third Congressional District (2019-Present); Professional Mixed Martial Artist (2013-Present); White House Fellow, Department of Transportation (2016) **AW:** Named, One of the Pride50, Queerty (2019) **PA:** Democrat

DAVIDSON, THOMAS M., T: Corporate Financial Executive **I:** Financial Services **DOB:** 12/14/1937 **PB:** New York **SC:** NY/USA **PT:** Alfred Edward Davidson; Claire Helen (Dreyfus) Davidson **MS:** Married **SPN:** Ruth Elizabeth Bovenkerk (12/08/1962) **CH:** Douglas Edward; Anne Elizabeth **ED:** MBA, Columbia University (1961); BA, Vanderbilt University (1959) **C:** Managing Director, Ash Creek Capital Advisors, LLC (2001-Present); President, Chief Executive Officer, International Technologies, Inc., Greenwich, CT (1993-2008); President, Chief Executive Officer, Medical Information International (1995-1998); Board of Directors, Arrow Electronics, Inc., Greenwich, CT (1981-1994); Board of Directors, Global TeleSystems Group (1990-1993); President, Chief Executive Officer, Global TeleSystems Group (1989-1993); Executive Vice President, Arrow Electronics, Inc., Greenwich, CT (1987-1989); Executive Vice President, Chief Financial Officer, Arrow Electronics, Inc., New York, NY (1981-1987); Senior Vice President of Finance, Chief Financial Officer, Director, Texas Gas Transmission Corp., Owensboro, KY (1977-1981); Vice President, Treasurer, White Motor Corp., Eastlake, OH (1976-1977); President, Chief Executive Officer, White Motor Credit Corp., Cleveland, OH (1975-1977); Senior Vice President, Chief Operating Officer, White Motor Credit Corp., Cleveland, OH (1973-1975); Director of Credit Operations, White Motor Corp., Eastlake, OH (1972-1973); Manager, Ford Motor Co., Dearborn, MI (1963-1972); Board of Directors, White Motor Credit Corp., Cleveland, OH **CR:** Member, AMG Capital Advisors, LLC (2011-Present); Managing Director, Southporter Management Group (2002-Present); Director, Digital Attractions Inc. (2008-2009); Sequas Corp. (2005-2007); Co-Founder, Senior Vice President, Vytek Wireless, Inc. (2000-2001); Board of Directors, Chair, Chief Executive Officer, XXI Century Hotel Network Ltd. (1998-2000); Board of Directors, Baltic Communications, Ltd., Russia; Board of Directors, SOVAM Teleport Russia, Sovintel, Russia **MIL:** U.S. Army Reserve (1959-1964) **CW:** Contributor, Articles, Professional Journals **MEM:** Manager of Tennis Team, New York Athletic Club **MH:** Albert Nelson Marquis Lifetime Achievement Award **B/I:** Mr. Davidson became involved in his profession because throughout his life, businesses have faced problems in communication and he is a problem solver. He has always been a problem solver in each of the positions he's held. In addition, Mr. Davidson sees himself as a team player. **AV:** Playing tennis; Swimming; Running; Gardening

DAVIDSON, WARREN EARL, T: U.S. Representative from Ohio **I:** Government Administration/Government Relations/Government Services **CN:** U.S. House of Representatives **DOB:** 03/01/1970 **PB:** Troy **SC:** OH/USA **ED:** Master of Business Administration, University of Notre Dame Mendoza College of Business (2000); Bachelor of Arts, United States Military Academy (1995) **C:** Member, U.S. Representative from Ohio's Eighth Congressional District (2016-Present); Member, Committee on Financial Services **PA:** Republican

DAVIS, ANTHONY JR., T: Professional Basketball Player **I:** Athletics **DOB:** 03/11/1993 **PB:** Chicago **SC:** IL/USA **PT:** Anthony Davis; Erainer Davis **ED:** Coursework, University of Kentucky, Lexington, KY (2011-2012) **C:** Professional Basketball Player, Forward, Center, Los Angeles Lakers, NBA (2019-2020); Professional Basketball Player, Forward, Center, New Orleans Pelicans, NBA (2012-2019) **CR:** U.S. National Team, Summer Olympic Games, London, England, United Kingdom (2012) **AW:** Named NBA All-Star Game MVP (2017); Named to All-NBA First Team (2015, 2017); Named to NBA All-Defensive Second Team (2015, 2017); Named NBA Blocks Leader (2014, 2015); Named to NBA All-Rookie First Team (2013); Named a Unanimous First Team All-American, The Associated Press, U.S. Basketball Writers Association, The Sporting News, National Association of Basketball Coaches (2012); Named NCAA Final Four Most Outstanding Player (2012); Named College Basketball Player of the Year, The Associated Press (2012); Named College Basketball Player of the Year, The Sporting News (2012); Named Defensive Player of the Year, National Association of Basketball Coaches (2012); Named National Freshman of the Year, U.S. Basketball Writers Association (2012); Named Southeastern Conference Player of the Year (2012); Southeastern Conference Defensive Player of Year (2012); Named Southeastern Conference Freshman of the Year (2012); Gold Medal, Men's Basketball, Summer Olympic Games (2012); Pete Newell Big Man Award, National Association of Basketball Coaches (2012); Oscar Robertson Trophy, U.S. Basketball Writers Association (2012); John R. Wooden award, Los Angeles Athletic Club (2012); Adolph F. Rupp Trophy, Commonwealth Athletic Club of Kentucky (2012); Naismith Trophy, Atlanta Tipoff Club (2012); NCAA Champion (2012)

DAVIS, DANIEL, "DANNY" K., T: U.S. Representative **I:** Government Administration/Government Relations/Government Services **DOB:** 09/06/1941 **PB:** Parkdale **SC:** AR/USA **MS:** Married **SPN:** Vera Davis (1974) **CH:** Jonathan; Stacey **ED:** PhD, Union Institute (1977); MA, Chicago State University (1968); BA, Arkansas AM & N College (Now University of Arkansas at Pine Bluff) (1961) **C:** U.S. Representative, Illinois' Seventh Congressional District, United States Congress (1997-Present); Member, Committee on Ways and Means, United States Congress; Member, Committee on Education and Workforce, United States Congress; Member, Subcommittee of Census, United States Congress; Member, Committee on Government Reform and Oversight, United States Congress; Member, Committee on Small Business, United States Congress **CIV:** Commissioner, Cook County, IL (1990-1996); Co-Chairman, Clinton/Gore/Moseley-Braun Illinois Campaigns (1992); Candidate, Chicago Mayor (1991); Chicago Alderman (1979-1990); Founder, President, The Westside Association for Community Action; President, National Association of Community Health Centers, Inc.; Board of Directors, National Housing Partnership **AW:** Power 150, Ebony Magazine (2008); One of the Most Influential Black Americans (2006) **MEM:** Alpha Phi Alpha Fraternity, Inc. **PA:** Democrat

DAVIS, ERNESTINE BADY, T: PMA Director, Nurse Educator, Administrator, Professor Emerita of Nursing (Retired) **I:** Education/Educational Services **CN:** University of North Alabama **DOB:** 04/08/1943 **PB:** Atlanta **SC:** GA/USA **PT:** Rev. Henry Benjamin; Martha (Shropshire) Bady **MS:** Widow **SPN:** Luther Davis Jr. (08/14/1965, Deceased) **CH:** Luther Davis III; Dr. Ella Michelle Temple **ED:** Doctor of Education, University of Alabama, Tuscaloosa, AL (1979); Master of Science in Nursing, Medical College of Georgia, Augusta, GA (1973); Bachelor of Science in Nursing, Tuskegee University, Tuskegee, AL (1965) **C:** Professor Emerita of Nursing, University of North Alabama, Florence, AL (2018-Present); Assistant Professor, University of Alabama Weekend College, Tuscaloosa, AL (1977-1980); Instructor, Tuskegee University, Alabama (1971-1977); Nurse, Various Hospitals, Arizona, Virginia, California, and Japan (1965-1971); Professor of Nursing, University of North Alabama, Florence, AL; Assistant Professor, Capstone College of Nursing, University of Alabama, Tuscaloosa, AL **CR:** Assistant to President of Minority Affairs, Cultural Diversity Consultant, Alabama Early Intervention **CIV:** Volunteer, Local Church; Mentoring Students **CW:** Author, "Essential Strategies to Success" (2017); Author, "Enhancing Academic Success of Underrepresented Students," International Journal of Nursing and Clinical Practice (2016); Co-Author, "A Brief Overview: How to Use Qualitative Research When Identifying Health Care in Disadvantaged Families"; Textbook Reviewer, Lippincott and Wilkins Textbooks; Textbook Reviewer, Byrne Guide for Inclusionary Cultural Content; Textbook Reviewer, The Science for Nursing Research and Path-Physiology and Conceptual Approach; Published, JOJ Nursing & Health Care Advising and Caring **AW:** Lillian Harvey Award, Alabama State Nurses Association (2000); Shoals Community Outstanding Service Award, University of North Alabama; President Award, University of North Alabama; Award of Excellence in Recognition of Exemplary Dedication to PMA Students, University of North Alabama; Diversity Award, University of North Alabama; Leadership Award, Omicron Delta; Inspiration Award, University of North Alabama; Leroy Finch Education Award, National Association for the Advancement of Colored People; Named, Outstanding Young Women of America; Named, Zeta Woman of Year, Zeta Phi Beta Society; Notable American Women Award; Tri-County Branch, National Association for the Advancement of Colored People; $1.3 Million Nursing Workforce Diversity Grantee, Health Resources and Services Administration **MEM:** American Cancer Society; Board Director, Ala Gerontological Society; Alabama Ethics/Human Rights Committee; Sigma Theta Tau Nursing Society; Delta Sigma Theta; Phi Kappa Phi **MH:** Albert Nelson Marquis Lifetime Achievement Award **AS:** Dr. Davis attributes her success to her deep and abiding Christian faith. **B/I:** Dr. Davis became involved in her profession because of her upbringing. As one of eight children, her parents worked very hard and instilled within their kids the value of a college education. Long fascinated with nursing, she resolved to aim her career aspirations accordingly. **AV:** Reading; Camping **RE:** African Methodist Episcopal Church

DAVIS, JACQUETTA, "JACQUE" ANDERSON, T: English Language Educator **I:** Education/Educational Services **DOB:** 01/16/1958 **PB:** Philadelphia **SC:** PA/USA **PT:** Jacob Jenkins; Mary Geneva Anderson Brown **MS:** Married **SPN:** Eddie Davis (01/15/1990) **CH:** Mary Wehma; Decontee Johanna **ED:** Coursework, Studying to Become Herbalist (2019-Present); MEd, The College of New Jersey (1985); Bachelor in Elementary Education, The College of New Jersey (1981); Bachelor in Bible, Philadelphia College of the Bible (Now Cairn University) (1979) **CT:** Certified Master Gardener and Master Food Preserver, NJ (2016-2019); Certified Community and School Garden Educator, NJ (2016-2019); Certified Beginner Farmer, NJ

(2016-2019); Elementary Education Teacher, NJ; English as a Second Language Teacher, NJ; Basic Skills Teacher, NJ **C:** Retired (2006); Curriculum Writer, English as a Second Language, East Windsor Regional School District, Hightstown, NJ (1981-2006); Missionary and Evangelist, Various Churches, PA and NJ (1975-1990); Foreign Missionary to Fiji Islands, United Missionary Fellowship, Inc., Sacramento, CA (1978) **CR:** New Jersey Teachers of English to Speakers of Other Languages (Now New Jersey Teachers of English to Speakers of Other Languages/New Jersey Bilingual Educators) (1986, 1994, 1995); Central Jersey Network of Black Women for Education (Now Central Jersey Network of Black Women, Inc.) (1993, 1994); Workshop Presenter, National Teachers English to Speakers of Other Languages Conference, Miami, FL and Chicago, IL (1985, 1986) **CIV:** Member, Faith International Baptist Church, Kissimmee, FL (2019-Present); Board Member, The Educational Voices of Change (2016-Present); Presenter, Food Preservation and Gardening, Rutgers, The State University of New Jersey (2016-2019); NJ Bilingual Spanish Voting Board Worker (2008-2019); Member, Faith Baptist Church, Hamilton, NJ (1991-2019); Sunday School Teacher, Various Churches, Mercer County, NJ (1991-2010); Guest Speaker to Women and Children, Various Churches, PA and NJ (1978-2006) **CW:** Co-author, English as Second Language Curriculum Management Program, "English as a Second Language Management Program K-12" (1986) **AW:** Action Grantee, Software and Material for Schoolwide Reading Program in English and Spanish, East Windsor Regional School District (1995); Kappa Delta Pi Honorary Mention for Distinguished Educator Award, Trenton State College Chapter (1991) **MEM:** NJREA (New Jersey Education Association) (2006-Present); New Jersey Education Association (1981-2019); New Jersey Teachers of English to Speakers of Other Languages/New Jersey Bilingual Educators (1981-2006) **MH:** Who's Who of Professional Women (2020); Albert Nelson Marquis Lifetime Achievement Award (2019) **AS:** Mrs. Davis attributes her success to being raised by a strong, independent Black matriarch in a close-knit supportive conservative Christian family. She also credits being led by God to marry Mr. Eddie B. Davis and duplicate that in a family of their own! **B/I:** The mother of Mrs. Davis always knew she was to be a teacher. But, she was only able to attend one year of her college scholarship because her father became blind and she had to return home to work and take care of the family. Growing up, her mother always took the family to pick their fresh fruits and vegetables on the farms, but, she eventually went blind at the end of her life. She taught and inspired everyone around her, even though she never was able to fulfill her dream of having an official teaching career. Mrs. Davis' stepfather had a landscaping business and as the family grew, he started a cleaning service. She and her siblings helped out as he taught them all he knew. However, he eventually closed them both down to move the growing family into their first home in another state. Likewise, he was never able to return to entrepreneurship. Mrs. Davis' father was a brick mason/construction worker by trade, but an avid gardener at home. She would help him, whether at his home or when doing odd jobs for family, neighbors and friends. And, lastly, since her parents never quit got to fulfill all that they wanted to do, she purposed in her heart to take all that they had taught her, reared with a strong religious upbringing that, first of all, taught her to impact folks on spiritual matters, then inspire others to get as much education as they possibly can but mostly to pay it forward before you die! **AV:** Bible study and reading; Writing; Poetry; Visiting hospital and nursing home patients; Assisting

homeowners and schools with gardening setup and maintenance; Working on, and some day publishing, the family memoir; Herbalist-in-training **PA:** Independent **RE:** Protestant **THT:** Mrs. Davis says, "My reflections on my life Scripture verse: John 14:6KJV: "Jesus saith unto him, I am the way, the truth, and the life: no man cometh unto the Father, but by me." "Jesus said, "I am the way", so, without Him there is no going." "Jesus said, "I am the truth", so, without Him there is no knowing." "Jesus said, "I am the life", so, without Him there is no living."

DAVIS, LECOUNT R. SR., CHAIRMAN EMERITUS, T: CFP(R) **I:** Financial Services **CN:** Association of African American Financial Advisors **DOB:** 08/18/1937 **PB:** Washington **SC:** DC/USA **PT:** Henry Davis; Daisy Davis **MS:** Married **SPN:** Jewel **CH:** Three Children **ED:** Master's Degree in Accounting, Southeastern University, Washington, DC (1960); Bachelor's Degree, Southeastern University, Washington, DC **CT:** Certification in Financial Planning, College for Financial Planning, Denver, CO (1978); Certified Planner, Board of Standards **C:** Independent Financial Planner (1978-2020); Chair Emeritus, Association of African American Financial Advisors **CR:** Adjunct Professor, Accounting, Howard University; Lecturer, Financial Management, Howard University School of Continuing Education; Host, Financial Television Program, Common Cents, Station WHMM **CIV:** Founder, Chairman, Emeritus Board Member, Association for African American Financial Advisors (AAAA); Chair, Family Financial Literacy Ministry, Mount Calvary Baptist Church **CW:** Author, "One Step Back, Two Steps Forward - The Dance of My Ultimate Plan" (2020); Author, "Finance and the African American Family" **AW:** Eagle Award, Society for Education and Professional Development (2018); Inaugural Award, Lifetime Achievement Award, Investment News (2018); Lifetime Achievement Award, Financial Planning Association (2008); Trail Blazer Award, Association for African American Financial Advisors (2006); Listee, Nation's Best Certified Financial Planners, Money Magazine (1987); 2000 Service Award, Alpha Kappa Alpha Sorority **MEM:** President, DC Chapter, International Association for Financial Planning; Association for African American Financial Advisors (AAAA) **MH:** Marquis Who's Who Top Professional **AS:** Mr. Davis attributes his success to the woman who introduced him to financial planning, Alexandra Armstrong. He met her at a symposium where he was the only person of color; she invited him in and asked him to join several committees. He is endlessly grateful for her faith in his skills. **B/I:** Mr. Davis was inspired to work in finance after meeting the financial guru of his neighborhood. Later in life, he worked for this man, and it was in this role that Mr. Davis found his love for the field. He wanted to take a holistic approach to how society handles money. He believes that the more society knows about the benefits of financial planning and how they can help handle financial and social problems that could negatively impact our communities' growth and prosperity, the better off society will be. **AV:** Appreciating sports and music; Attending church **RE:** Baptist **THT:** Mr. Davis believes God has a plan for every individual.

DAVIS, M. DENISE, T: Reading Consultant, Tutor **I:** Education/Educational Services **DOB:** 10/10/1948 **PB:** Washington **SC:** DC/USA **PT:** Joseph Davis; Maebelle Virginia (Renn) Davis **MS:** Single **ED:** MEd in Reading Instruction, University of Virginia (1997); MEd in Interdisciplinarity, Frostburg State University (1986); BS in Social Sciences, Frostburg State University (1972); Student, Business

Administration and Engineering, Southern Maryland Community College **CT:** Certified Reading Teacher; Psychosocial Rehabilitation Counselor, Virginia; Registered Sanitarian, Maryland **C:** Psychosocial Rehabilitation Counselor, Rappahannock Area Community Services, Fredericksburg, VA (2006-2011); Teacher, English and Reading, King George Public Schools, Virginia (2003-2004); Classroom Aide, Reading Tutor, After-school Tutor, Rockingham County, VA (2001-2003); Employment Counselor, Department of Rehabilitative Services, Harrisonburg, VA (2000-2001); Assistant Librarian, Rockingham Community Library (1999-2000); Instructor, Danville Reading Center, Danville, VA (1998-1999); Chief Executive Officer, President, Instructor, The Learning Station Inc., Danville, VA (1996-1998); Psychosocial Rehabilitation Counselor, Danville-Pittsylvania Community Services (1990-1998); Sanitarian, Calvert County, Anne Arundel County, MD (1980-1989); Laboratory Technician, Engineer Assistant, Washington Suburban Sanitary Committee, Hyattsville, MD (1973-1980) **CR:** Instructor, English as a Second Language, Harrisonburg, VA (2000-2002) **CIV:** Leader, Arts and Crafts, Exercise, Bay Ageing Senior Center, Colonial Beach, VA (2012-2018); District Representative, Virginia Conference Methodist Singles Ministry, Richmond, VA (1995-2002); Member, Danville Literature Council (1994-1997); Program Chair, Trinity Singles, Danville, VA (1991); President, 4-H, Prince Frederick, MD (1987-1989); 4th Youth Leader, Cooperative Extension Service, Prince Frederick, MD (1981-1989); Big Brothers./Big Sisters, Prince Frederick, MD (1983-1984); President, Stage Manager, Tidewater Theatre, Prince Frederick, MD (1981-1983); Member, Advisory Board, Arts Council of Calvert County, Prince Frederick, MD (1980-1983); Rails-to-Trails Conservancy **AW:** Nominee, Employee of the Month **MEM:** International Reading Association (1995-2000); Dan River Trail Association (1993-1998); National Camping Association (1983-1991); Association for Curriculum and Instruction **MH:** Albert Nelson Marquis Lifetime Achievement Award; Marquis Who's Who Top Professional **B/I:** Ms. Davis became involved in her profession because, although she wanted to be a math teacher while in high school, when she got to college, she realized she could do the math problems but could not do the theorems; she then took an Introduction to Sociology class and thought it was interesting, so she switched to social studies. When she got out of college, she started looking for a job and found one in the Washington Suburban Sanitary Commission. It was more of an office position but a position in the wastewater laboratory became available and she applied for it and she got it. After four or five years, she decided to try the engineering assistant position. Her brother-in-law was working as a health inspector, and Ms. Davis decided she would try and apply for a position as the sanitarian in Calvert County, which she got. She then found a position in Danville, Virginia, with the community services board, worked with the psychosocial program, and was in charge of the kitchen. She then became responsible for the clerical unit. She left the position and moved to Harrisburg, Virginia, and worked in the Rockingham Community Library as an assistant Librarian. Ms. Davis then started working for the Department of Rehabilitative Services as an employment counselor for a year and a half. In the midst of these positions, she finished her certificate for reading teacher requirement and subsequently served as a classroom aide and tutor for Rockingham School District. Ms. Davis then moved on to being a teacher of English and reading at King George Public Schools in Virginia. She then went back to Fredericksburg, Virginia, where she started working as a psychosocial rehabilitation counselor at

Rappahannock Area Community Services up until her retirement in 2011. **AV:** Reading; Home decorating; Gardening; Hiking **PA:** Independent **RE:** Messianic Jewish, Seventh-day Adventist Church

DAVIS, RICHARD J., T: Lawyer, Government Official (Retired) **I:** Law and Legal Services **DOB:** 03/27/1946 **PB:** New York **SC:** NY/USA **PT:** Herbert H.; Sylvia (Ginesin) Davis **MS:** Married **SPN:** Nancy R. Davis **CH:** Ann S. Davis **ED:** Doctor of Jurisprudence, Columbia Law School, Magna Cum Laude (1969); Bachelor of Arts in History, University of Rochester, with Honors (1966) **C:** Law Offices of Richard J. Davis (2012-Present); Partner, Weil, Gotshal & Manges LLP (1981-2011); Assistant Secretary Treasurer for Enforcement and Operations, U.S. Department of Treasury, Washington, DC (1977-1981); Associate, Weil, Gotshal & Manges LLP, New York, NY (1976-1977); Assistant Special Prosecutor, Watergate Special Prosecution Force, Washington, DC (1973-1975); Member, Criminal Division, Assistant Chief, Appellate Attorney Corruption Unit, U.S. Attorney's Office for the Southern District of New York (1970-1973); Law Clerk to Judge Jack B. Weinstein, U.S. District Court for the Eastern District of New York (1969-1970) **CIV:** Member, Board of Trustees, Goucher College (2015-Present); Member, New York City Campaign Finance Board (2009-Present); Member, Board of Directors, Boys & Girls Harbor Inc. (1992-2011); Chair, Randall Island Sports Foundation (1995-2010); Chairperson, Pier Park & Playground Association (1999-2005); Chair, Mayor's Commission Combat Police Corruption (1996-2002); Member, Mayor's Task Force on Police-Community Relations (1997); Member, Citizens Task Force on the Use & Security of Central Park (1987-1991) **CW:** Contributor, Articles to Professional Journals, Chapters to Books **AW:** Servant of Justice Award, Legal Aid Society (2018); Public Service Award, New York Law Journal (2016); Examiner, Caesars Bankruptcy (2015-2016); Champion for Children's Award, Randall's Island Sports Foundation (2010); Whitney North Seymour award, Federal Bar Council (2000); Ari Halberstam Award, Jewish Children's Museum (2000); Curtis J. Berger Award, The Bridge Inc. (1999); Law Society Award, Lawyers for the Public Interest **MEM:** Chairperson, Board of Directors, Legal Aid Society (2010-Present); Board of Directors, Citizens Union (1998-2009); Chairperson, Board of Directors, Citizens Union (2004-2008); Foundation Chairperson, Citizens Union (2004-2008); Chairperson, Criminal Justice Council, New York City Bar Association (2000-2003); American Bar Association **BAR:** District of Columbia (1974); New York (1970); U.S. Court of Appeals for the District of Columbia Circuit; Supreme Court of the United States; United States District Court for the Southern District of New York **MH:** Albert Nelson Marquis Lifetime Achievement Award; Marquis Who's Who Top Professional **B/I:** Mr. Davis first became involved in his profession after having dabbled in real estate law and tax law. After clerking for Judge Jack B. Weinstein, however, he became more interested in criminal cases.

DAVIS, RODNEY LEE, T: U.S. Representative **I:** Government Administration/Government Relations/Government Services **DOB:** 01/05/1970 **PB:** Des Moines **SC:** IA/USA **MS:** Married **SPN:** Shannon Davis (1995) **CH:** Griffin; Toryn; Clark **ED:** BA in Political Science, Millikin University (1992) **C:** U.S. Representative, Illinois' 13th Congressional District, United States Congress, Washington, DC (2013-Present); U.S. House Committee on Transportation and Infrastructure (2013-Present); U.S. House Committee on Agriculture (2013-Present); Campaign Manager, John Shumkus' Congressional Campaign (1998); Staff Member to Represen-

tative John Shimkus, U.S. House of Representatives (1997-2012); Staff Member to Secretary of State George Ryan, State of Illinois, Springfield, IL (1992-1996) **CIV:** Member, Board of Education, St. Mary's Church; Volunteer Athletic Director, St. Mary's Church; Coach, Taylorville Junior Football; Member, Taylorville Optimist Club; Board of Directors, Christian County Senior Center **PA:** Republican **RE:** Roman Catholic

DAVIS, RUSS ERIK, PHD, T: Oceanographer; Educator **I:** Sciences **DOB:** 03/08/1941 **PB:** San Francisco **SC:** CA/USA **PT:** Henry Fairfax Davis; Enid L. (Kuchel) Davis Wood **MS:** Married **SPN:** Geraldine F. Caron (08/25/2012); Linda D. Welzig (11/06/1995); Sandra Powell (06/21/1963, Divorced 1972) **CH:** Erik Russ **ED:** PhD in Chemical Engineering, Stanford University (1967); MS in Chemical Engineering, Stanford University (1967); BS in Chemical Engineering, University of California Berkeley (1963) **C:** Research Oceanographer, Scripps Institution of Oceanography, La Jolla, CA (2000-2019); Professor of Oceanography, Scripps Institution of Oceanography, La Jolla, CA (1969-2000); Chairman, Ocean Research Division, Scripps Institution of Oceanography, La Jolla, CA (1979-1983); Assistant Research Geophysicist, Scripps Institution of Oceanography, La Jolla, CA (1967-1969) **CW:** Contributor, More Than 110 Articles to Professional Journals **AW:** Maurice Ewing Medal, American Geophysical Union (2015); Henry Stommel Medal, American Meteorological Society (2000); A.G. Huntsman Award (1997); Named, David Packard Distinguished Lecturer; Prince Albert I Gold Medal, International Association for the Physical Sciences of the Oceans (IAPSO) **MEM:** Fellow, American Geophysical Union; Fellow, American Meteorology Society; American Academy of Arts and Science; National Academy of Sciences **MH:** Albert Nelson Marquis Lifetime Achievement Award; Marquis Who's Who Top Professional **AS:** Dr. Davis attributes his success to good luck and a lot of friends. **B/I:** Dr. Davis entered his profession because it was fun. All of his degrees are in chemical engineering, but he only did oceanography. While he was in graduate school, there was a program that he participated in that allowed students to go to Woods Hole Oceanographic Institution and he had so much fun. Dr. Davis had an advisor with uncommon understanding and grace. His dissertation was on internal waves. He pursued oceanography ever since. In addition, what made him take the leap and go into being an oceanographer was blind luck because he didn't do it. He started out as a chemical engineer and the last year of his bachelor degree, one of his professors took them to a chemical plant in Richmond, California and it looked like an oil distillery. So, he looked at it and said, "Wait a minute, do I want to spend my life making good ugly things that work well and make stinky stuff?" and he said, "No, I am going to go for something else that doesn't make much money." So, he thought about going into things that had something to do with natural sciences to get away from the machines that were ugly, but worked. In grad school there was a program to go to Woods Hall Oceanographic Institution, Cape Cod, where students go in the summer and establish oceanography; he jumped at the opportunity because he was accepted and would be able to work with Stuart Turner, one of the most amazing oceanographers ever. Stuart Turner also ended up being Dr. Davis's advisor for that summer's work. They would do experiments like make waves in the ocean, things that they could see and test out, which matched Dr. Davis's approach to life, like why things did what they did in the ocean. He did his thesis on that and it kind of made him go in the direction of being an ocean-

ographer after that. Furthermore, his mentor, Dr. Cox, thought of "an acoustic Doppler current profiler" after the Doppler shift, which proved that motion can change the tone of something. The simplest example are trains that had a whistle and the sound changes when it comes toward you and goes away. Dr. Davis and his graduate students made this invention happen. It was with a big team, but it was something that he helped create with Dr. Cox. **AV:** Flying (Had His Own Planes) ; Kayaking; Gardening; Sailing **THT:** Another invention created after ARGO is now called an "underwater glider." The invention is more clouded than his and most people would say Dr. Davis invented it but he had little association with it. It is one of the things out of the floats except it has wings on it and instead of going straight up and down it goes like a model airplane, but the wings allow it to go sideways and the operator can instruct it where to go. There are fewer of them than there are the floats and the fact that they go means that people have places they want them to go, so they go up and down fairly rapidly to go somewhere so they don't last as long. But, they do many more dives than the floats.

DAVIS, SUSAN CAROL, T: U.S. Representative from California **I:** Government Administration/Government Relations/Government Services **DOB:** 04/13/1944 **PB:** Cambridge **SC:** MA/USA **PT:** George R. Alpert; Dorothy M. (Wexler) Alpert **MS:** Married **SPN:** Steven Davis **CH:** Jeffrey; Benjamin **ED:** MA in Social Work, University of North Carolina (1968); BA in Sociology, University of California Berkeley (1965) **C:** Member, U.S. Representative from California's 53rd Congressional District, United States Congress (2003-2019); Member, U.S. Representative from California's 49th Congressional District, United States Congress (2001-2003); Member, District 76, California State Assembly (1994-2000); Executive Director, Aaron Price Fellowship Progressive, San Diego, CA (1990-1994); Development Associate, KPBS-TV, San Diego, CA (1979-1983); Development Associate, KPBS-FM, San Diego, CA (1977) **CR:** President, Board of Education, San Diego Unified School District (1983-1992); Executive Board Member, New Democrat Coalition; Member, National Conference for Christians and Jews (NCCJ); San Diego Consortium and Private Industry Council; Vice President, Democratic Leadership Council **CIV:** Youth Volunteer, United Way; Volunteer, June Burnett Institute for Children, Youth and Families, San Diego, CA **MEM:** President, San Diego League of Women Voters (1977) **PA:** Democrat **RE:** Jewish

DAVIS, VIOLA, T: Actress **I:** Media & Entertainment **DOB:** 08/11/1965 **PB:** Saint Matthews **SC:** SC/USA **PT:** Dan Davis; Mary Davis **MS:** Married **SPN:** Julius Tennon (06/23/2003) **CH:** Genesis (Adopted); Two Stepchildren **ED:** Coursework, Juilliard School; Coursework, Rhode Island College **C:** Actress (1992-Present) **CW:** Actress, "How to Get Away with Murder" (2014-Present); Appearance, Executive Producer, "Giving Voice" (2020); Actress, "Troop Zero" (2019); Actress, "Widows" (2018); Actress, "Suicide Squad" (2016); Actress, "Fences" (2016); Actress, Executive Producer, "Custody" (2016); Actress, Executive Producer, "Lila & Eve" (2015); Actress, "Blackhat" (2015); Actress, "The Disappearance of Eleanor Rigby: Them" (2014); Actress, "Get on Up" (2014); Actress, "Beautiful Creatures" (2013); Actress, "Prisoners" (2013); Actress, "The Disappearance of Eleanor Rigby: Him" (2013); Actress, "The Disappearance of Eleanor Rigby: Her" (2013); Actress, "Ender's Game" (2013); Actress, "Sofia the First" (2013); Actress, "Won't Back Down" (2012); Actress, "The Help" (2011); Actress, "Extremely Loud and Incredibly

Close" (2011); Actress, "Knight and Day" (2010); Actress, "Eat Pray Love" (2010); Actress, "It's Kind of a Funny Story" (2010); Actress, "Fences" (2010); Actress, "United States of Tara" (2009); Actress, "Madea Goes to Jail" (2009); Actress, "State of Play" (2009); Actress, "The Andromeda Strain" (2008); Actress, "Law & Order: Special Victims Unit" (2003-2008); Actress, "Nights in Rodanthe" (2008); Actress, "Doubt" (2008); Actress, "Fort Pit" (2007); Actress, "Jesse Stone: Sea Change" (2007); Actress, "Traveler" (2007); Actress, "Disturbia" (2007); Actress, "Jesse Stone: Night Passage" (2006); Actress, "Jesse Stone: Death in Paradise" (2006); Actress, "Life Is Not a Fairytale: The Fantasia Barrino Story" (2006); Actress, "The Architect" (2006); Actress, "World Trade Center" (2006); Actress, "Stone Cold" (2005); Actress, "Syriana" (2005); Actress, "Get Rich or Die Tryin'" (2005); Actress, "Century City" (2004); Actress, "Far from Heaven" (2002); Actress, "Antwone Fisher" (2002); Actress, "Solaris" (2002); Actress, "Father Lefty" (2002); Actress, "The Shrink Is In" (2001); Actress, "Kate & Leopold" (2001); Actress, "King Hedley II" (2001); Actress, "Amy & Isabelle" (2001); Actress, "City of Angels" (2000); Actress, "Traffic" (2000); Actress, "The Pentagon Wars" (1998); Actress, "Grace & Glorie" (1998); Actress, "Out of Sight" (1998); Actress, "The Substance of Fire" (1996); Actress, "Seven Guitars" (1996) **AW:** Named One of the 100 Most Influential People in the World, TIME Magazine (2012, 2017); Academy Award for Best Supporting Actress, Academy of Motion Picture Arts and Sciences (2016); Golden Globe Award for Best Supporting Actress, Hollywood Foreign Press Association (2016); Outstanding Performance by a Female Actor in a Drama Series, Screen Actors Guild Awards, SAG-AFTRA (2015, 2016); Outstanding Actress in a Drama Series, NAACP Image Awards (2015); Favorite Actress in a New TV Series, People's Choice Awards (2015); Outstanding Lead Actress in a Drama Series, Emmy Awards, Television Academy (2015); Outstanding Actress in a Motion Picture, NAACP Image Awards (2013); Lead Actress award, African American Film Critics Association (2012); Best Actress, Critics' Choice Movie Awards (2012); Outstanding Performance by a Female Actor in a Leading Role, Screen Actors Guild, SAG-AFTRA (2012); Tony Award for Best Performance by a Leading Actress in a Play (2010); Recipient, Virtuoso Award, Santa Barbara International Film Festival (2009); Best Breakthrough Performance - Female, National Board of Review (2008); Tony Award for Best Performance by a Leading Actress in a Play (2001)

DAVIS III, EGBERT LAWRENCE, T: Retired Partner **I:** Law and Legal Services **CN:** Womble Bond Dickinson **DOB:** 12/30/1937 **PB:** Winston-Salem **SC:** NC/USA **PT:** Egbert Lawrence Davis Junior; Eleanor Layfield Davis **MS:** Married **SPN:** Alexandra Holderness (08/25/1962) **CH:** Alexandra Davis Hipps; Egbert L. Davis IV; Lucinda Davis; Pamela Davis **ED:** MBA, George Washington University (1966); LLB, Duke University (1963); AB, Princeton University (1960) **C:** Retired, Of Counsel, Womble, Carlyle, Sandridge & Rice, Raleigh, NC (1997-2015); Partner, Womble, Carlyle, Sandridge & Rice, Raleigh, NC (1982-1997); Partner, Womble, Carlyle, Sandridge & Rice, Winston-Salem, NC (1970-1982); Associate, Womble, Carlyle, Sandridge & Rice, Winston-Salem, NC (1965-1970) **CR:** Discussion Group Leader, Bible Study Fellowship (1983-1990); Secretary, Wachovia Realty Investments, Winston-Salem, NC (1979-1982); Co-Chair, Young Life Winston-Salem **CIV:** Board of Directors, North Carolina Foundation for Economic Education (1996-2006); Board of Directors, Center for Citizenship, Enterprise, and Government (2003-2005); Co-Chairman, Raleigh Wake Leadership Foundation (2002-2004);

Board of Directors, Haven House Services Inc. (1983-1998); Executive Committee, Eastern Center for Regional Development (1996-1997); State Council, North Carolina Prison Fellowship (1994-1997); Chairman, North Carolina Family Business Forum (1993-1994); Chairman, North Carolina Democratic Party (1989-1991); Chairman, Board of Trustees, North Carolina Baptist Hospital, Winston-Salem, NC (1981-1982); Co-Chair, Winston-Salem Young Life Committee (1980-1981); Chairman, Northwest Environmental Preservation Committee, Inc., Winston-Salem, NC (1980); Senator, North Carolina Senate (1974-1978); Representative, North Carolina House Of Representatives (1970-1974); North Carolina Courts Committee (1972-1974); Deacon, Elder, Sunday School Teacher, Stephen Minister, White Memorial Presbyterian Church **MIL:** Captain, U.S. Army (1963-1965) **CW:** Author, "The Life & Times of Jim Henry Shore" (2020); Editorial Board, Duke University Law Journal (1963) **AW:** Inductee, Order of the Long Leaf Pine (2019); Inductee, U.S. Jaycees (1973); Freedom Guard Award, North Carolina Jaycees (1973); Young Man of the Year, Winston-Salem Jaycees (1972); Citizen of the Year, Winston-Salem Mayor's Committee on Employment of the Handicapped (1971) **MEM:** Board of Directors, George A. Coburn Foundation Inc. (1998-2014); Board of Directors, Duke University Law School Alumni Association (2006-2012); Board of Directors, Coastal Conservation Association (1997-2006); President, Raleigh Rotary Club (1986-1987); Board of Governors, North Carolina Bar Association (1979-1982) **BAR:** North Carolina (1963) **AS:** Mr. Davis attributes his success to the help of the good Lord, as well as his family and friends. **B/I:** Mr. Davis became involved in his work as a direct result of the range of opportunities that were presented to him. **AV:** Researching history; Writing; Biking; Swimming; Spending time with family **RE:** Christian **THT:** Mr. Davis looks at life as a gift that enables one to give to others.

DAWSON, PETER J., MD, T: Pathologist, Educator **I:** Medicine & Health Care **DOB:** 02/17/1928 **PB:** Wolverhampton **SC:** United Kingdom **PT:** Sydney Dawson; Bertha (Richards) Dawson **MS:** Widower **SPN:** Elizabeth Ann Coombs (03/01/1982, Deceased 2019); Nancy Sexton Taylor (04/10/1953, Divorced 1969) **CH:** Christopher (Deceased); Susan; Deborah; Phobie; Alan; Patrick **ED:** MD, Cambridge University (1960); MA, Cambridge University (1953); MB, BChir, Cambridge University (1952); BA, Cambridge University (1949) **CT:** Diplomate, American Board of Pathology **C:** Professor Emeritus, University of South Florida (1999-Present); Chief, Pathology and Laboratory Services, James Haley VA Hospital, Tampa, FL (1994-1999); Professor, Pathology and Laboratory Medicine, University of South Florida, Tampa, FL (1989-1999); Professor, Pathology, Director of Laboratory Surgical Pathology, University of Chicago (1977-1989); Professor, Pathology, University of Oregon, Portland, OR (1967-1976); Associate Professor, University of Oregon, Portland, OR (1964-1967); Lecturer, University of Newcastle Upon Tyne, England (1962-1964); Visiting Assistant Professor, University of California, San Francisco, CA (1960-1962); Resident, Royal Postgraduate Medical School (1959-1960); Resident, Royal Postgraduate Medical School (1954-1955); Demonstrator in Pathology, St. George's Hospital, Medical School of London (1953-1954); Intern, Victoria Hospital For Children (1953); Intern, Royal Berkshire Hospital, Reading, England (1952-1953) **MIL:** Captain, Royal Army Medical Corps (1955-1958) **CW:** Author, "Dorothy in a Man's World: An biography of Dorothy Reed Mendenhall" (2016); Contributor, Over 100 Articles, Professional Journals **MEM:** Vice President, President, Chicago Pathology Society

(1984-1988); Fellow, Royal College of Pathologists; International Academy of Pathology; American Association of Cancer Research; Arthur Purdy Stout Society of Surgical Pathologists **MH:** Albert Nelson Marquis Lifetime Achievement Award **B/I:** Dr. Dawson grew up in wartime Britain. His choice of a profession was fortuitous. In England, there was an exam called the School Leaving Certificate, which he took at the age of 16. After getting the results, Dr. Dawson's father made an appointment to see the headmaster of the school and he began studying chemistry. This led him to pursue medicine later in life. **AV:** Sailing **RE:** Episcopalian

DAY, DONALD, "DONNY" GENE JR., T: Owner, President, Chief Executive Officer **I:** Health, Wellness and Fitness **CN:** Peak Zone Fitness **DOB:** 07/27/1989 **SC:** United States **PT:** Donald Day Sr.; Marilyn Day **MS:** Married **SPN:** Lyndi Day **CH:** Aden Letch; Lawson Letch; George Anagnostics **ED:** Collin College, Plano, TX **CT:** National Academy of Sports Medicine; American Fitness Training of Athletics; American Council on Exercise; Pilates; Personal Training Fundamentals; Corrective Exercise Specialist; Walking & Running Certification; General Nutrition; Sports Specific Nutrition; The Fundamentals of Fitness, Bally Total Fitness **C:** Owner, President, Chief Executive Officer, Peak Zone Fitness (2013-Present); Area Fitness Manager, Just Fitness 4U, Dallas, Plano, Mesquite, Carollton, Hurst, and Addison, TX (2011-Present); Training General Manager, LA Fitness, Hollywood, California (2009-2010); Fitness Director, Manager, Bally Total Fitness, Plano, Mesquite, Richardson, and Carollton, TX (2007-2009) **CR:** Mentor to more than 100 Fitness Managers, 1000 Personal Trainers, and More Than 40,000 Clients **AW:** MINDBODY Visionary Award (2019); "People Love Us on Yelp" Award (2016, 2017, 2018); Awarded "Best Trainers" in Dallas, Best Business; Voted "Best Place to Workout in Lake Highlands"; Next Door Favorites, Nextdoor **AS:** Mr. Day attributes his success to being extremely ambitious and his hard work at a young age. **B/I:** Mr. Day became involved in his profession because he grew up wanting to be a trainer. He grew up training his friends in school, and it was something that was a passion of his. To him it was a natural progression, because he was already having success working out and training others. Mr. Day began his career selling gym memberships in 2007, and worked his way up to a personal trainer. He eventually became known as a fitness manager, and a regional manager of fitness clubs. He eventually worked his way up to a president position, running a $20 million fitness company, and added seven additional gyms. He eventually opened his own business, which he has been for the past six years.

DAYANANDA, MYSORE A., PHD, T: Professor Emeritus of Materials Engineering **I:** Education/Educational Services **CN:** Purdue University **DOB:** 07/01/1934 **PB:** Mysore City **SC:** India **PT:** Tekhalli Srinivasarao Ananthamurthy; Kapila Ananthamurthy **MS:** Married **SPN:** Prema Kumari Rao (07/05/1972) **CH:** Ila **ED:** PhD, Purdue University (1965); MS, Purdue University (1961); DSc, Indian Institute of Science, Bengaluru, India (1957); Honorary BSc, Mysore University (1955) **C:** Professor Emeritus, School of Materials Engineering, Purdue University (2017-Present); Associate Head, School of Materials Engineering, Purdue University (2005-2007); Interim Head, School of Materials Engineering, Purdue University (1999); Professor, Purdue University (1975-2017); Associate Professor, Purdue University (1970-1975); Assistant Professor of Materials Engineering, Purdue University (1966-1970); Postdoctoral Research Associate, Purdue University (1965-1966); Senior Research

Assistant, Indian Institute of Science, Bengaluru, India (1957-1958) **CR:** Visiting Professor, Indian Institute of Science, Bengaluru, India (1992); Visiting Professor, University of Münster, Germany (1980) **CW:** Editor, Four Books; Contributor, 120 Articles, Professional Journals; Contributor, "Acta Materialia"; Contributor, "Scripta Materialia"; Contributor, "Philosophical Magazine"; Contributor, "Metallurgical & Materials Transactions"; Contributor, "Transactions of the Materials Society"; Contributor, "Materials Science and Engineering"; Contributor, "Journal of Nuclear Materials"; Contributor, "Journal of Phase Equilibria & Diffusion" **AW:** Recipient, Albert Easton White Distinguished Teacher Award, ASM International (2017); Recipient, Visiting Lectureship, ASM International (2015); Recipient, Engineering Faculty Engagement/Service Excellence Award, Purdue University (2003); Recipient, Best Teacher Award, Purdue University School of Materials Engineering (1982, 1990) **MEM:** Fellow, American Society for Metals; American Institute of Mining; American Association for the Advancement of Science; Microbeam Analysis Society; American Society for Engineering Education; Sigma Xi **MH:** Albert Nelson Marquis Lifetime Achievement Award **B/I:** Dr. Dayananda's story goes back to when he came to this country in 1958. As a student, he wanted to study engineering at Purdue University, so he earned a master's degree and PhD and decided to work in the industry. He was stopped by Purdue University and asked to continue his academic career as a professor. Dr. Dayananda was promoted up through the university. His favorite thing was getting involved with is research, how atoms interact as they move in solids.

DAYHOFF, NANCY, EDD, RN, T: Managing Partner **I:** Medicine & Health Care **CN:** Clinical Solutions, LLC **ED:** EdD, Indiana University (1985); MSN in Education, Indiana University (1960); BSN, Indiana University Bloomington **C:** Senior Consultant, Clinical Solutions, LLC (2019-Present); Associate Professor Emeritus, School of Nursing, Indiana University (2001-Present); Chief Executive Officer, Managing Partner, Clinical Solutions, LLC (2000-Present)

DAY-LEWIS, DANIEL, T: Actor **I:** Media & Entertainment **DOB:** 04/29/1957 **SC:** London/England **PT:** Cecil Day-Lewis; Jill (Balcon) Day-Lewis **MS:** Married **SPN:** Rebecca Miller (11/11/1996) **CH:** Gabriel-Kane; Ronan Cal; Cashel Blake **ED:** Honorary LittD, University of Bristol (2010); Coursework, Bedales and Bristol Old Vic Theatre School **CW:** Actor, "Phantom Thread" (2017); Actor, "Lincoln" (2012); Actor, "Nine" (2009); Actor, "There Will Be Blood" (2007); Actor, "The Ballad of Jack and Rose" (2005); Actor, "Gangs of New York" (2003); Actor, "The Boxer" (1997); Actor, "The Crucible" (1996); Actor, "The Age of Innocence" (1993); Actor, "In the Name of the Father" (1993); Actor, "The Last of the Mohicans" (1992); Actor, "Eversmile, New Jersey" (1989); Actor, "Hamlet" (1989); Actor, "My Left Foot" (1989); Actor, "The Unbearable Lightness of Being" (1988); Actor, "Stars and Bars" (1988); Actor, "A Room with a View" (1986); Actor, "My Beautiful Laundrette" (1986); Actor, "Nanou" (1986); Actor, "The Insurance Man" (1986); Actor, "My Brother Jonathan" (1985); Actor, "The Bounty" (1984); Actor, "Ghandi" (1982); Actor, "How Many Miles to Babylon?" (1982); Actor, "Frost in May" (1982); Actor, "Artemis 81" (1981); Actor, "Sunday Bloody Sunday" (1971); Actor, "Class Enemy"; Actor, "Funny Peculiar"; Actor, "Look Back in Anger"; Actor, "Dracula"; Actor, "Another Country"; Actor, "Futurists"; Actor, "Romeo"; Actor, "Thisbe"; Actor, "R.S.C." **AW:** Knight Commander, Most Excellent Order

of the British Empire (KBE), Her Majesty Queen Elizabeth II (2014); British Academy of Film and TV Arts (2013); Golden Globe Award, Hollywood Foreign Press Association (2013); Outstanding Performance by a Male Actor in a Leading Role, Screen Actors Guild (2013); Academy Award for Best Actor (2013); Listee, 100 Most Influential People in the World, Time Magazine (2013); Best Actor, Critics Choice Awards (2012); Critics Choice Award, Broadcast Film Critics Association (2008); Golden Globe Award, Hollywood Foreign Press Association (2008); Outstanding Performance by a Male Actor in a Leading Role, Screen Actors Guild (2008); Best Leading Actor, British Academy Film and TV Arts (2008); Academy Award for Best Actor in a Leading Role (2008); Best Actor, New York Film Critics Circle (2007); Best Actor in Leading Role, British Academy Film and TV Arts (2003); Academy Award for Best Actor, 1989, British Academy Film and TV Arts (1990); Best Actor, New York Film Critics Circle; Best Actor, Boston Society of Film Critics; Best Actor, National Society of Film Critics; Best Performance by an Actor in a Motion Picture-Drama

DE BLASIO, BILL, "BILL", T: Mayor of New York City **I:** Government Administration/Government Relations/Government Services **DOB:** 05/08/1961 **PB:** New York **SC:** NY/USA **PT:** Warren Wilhelm; Maria (de Blasio) Wilhelm **MS:** Married **SPN:** Chirlane McCray (1994) **CH:** Dante; Chiara **ED:** Master of Arts in International and Public Affairs, Columbia University (1987); Bachelor of Arts, New York University (1984) **C:** Mayor, New York, NY (2014-Present); Candidate, Democratic Nominee, 2020 Presidential Election (2019); Public Advocate, New York, NY (2010-2013); City Councilman, District 39, New York City Council (2001-2009); Campaign Manager, Hillary Clinton's Senatorial Campaign (2000); Regional Director, U.S. Department of Housing and Urban Development, New York, NY (1996-1999); Campaign Manager, U.S. Representative Charles Rangel, United States Congress (1994); Political Organizer, Quixote Center, MD (1987); With, Urban Fellows Program, New York City Department of Juvenile Justice (1984); Aide to Deputy Mayor Bill Lynch, New York, NY **CR:** Chairperson, General Welfare Committee, New York City Council **CIV:** Volunteer Coordinator, David Dinkins' Mayoral Campaign (1989); Member, Community School Board 15, New York, NY **PA:** Democrat

DE CASAL, CAROLE A., T: Education Educator **I:** Education/Educational Services **DOB:** 10/05/1948 **PB:** Nyack **SC:** NY/USA **ED:** Master of Business Administration, Novus University, California (2007); Doctor of Education, University of Utah, Salt Lake City, UT (1980); Master of Education, University of Utah, Salt Lake City, UT (1978); Bachelor of Science, University of Utah, Salt Lake City, Utah (1971) **CT:** Teaching Certifications, 9-12 Spanish, K-12 English, K-12 Bilingual/ESL Education, K-12 Special Education, K-12 Reading, Elementary Ed, Secondary Ed, K-12 Language Arts, K-12 International TESOL/TEFL/TESL, K-12; Administrator Certifications, Community College, K-12 Superintendent, K-12 Supervisor, K-12 Principal, K-12 Teacher and Principal Evaluation; K-12 Principal Evaluation; K-12 Instructional Leadership; Administrative Hearing Officer; Mediator; Paralegal; Federal and State Tax Accountant; International Tour Manager; International Tour Guide **C:** Professor of Leadership in Law Labor Relations and Policy for Executive Leaders, Tennessee State University, Nashville, TN (2008-Present); Department Head, Educational Leadership, Tennessee State University, Nashville, TN (2008-2012); Associate Dean, Internal Operations, Director of International Programs,

Director of Accreditation, Director of Teacher Education, and Professor of Leadership at University of Colorado, Colorado Springs (2006-2008); Assistant Dean, Strategic Planning and Accreditation, Director of Teacher Education and Professor of Leadership at University of Southern Mississippi (2004-2006); Department Head for Educational Leadership, Winthrop University, Rock Hill, SC (2004-2006) **CR:** State Director, Civil Rights, State Director of Special Population Programs, and State Monitor for Molly Hootch Consent Decree Compliance at Alaska Department of Education; Executive Director, Disability Association, Austin, TX; Disability Specialist, Law Firm in Austin, TX **CIV:** City Councilor; Contributor, Rotary International; Volunteer, Education Supplies and Constructing in Bolivia, Honduras, Mexico and the Bahamian Islands; Assistant, Translator, Study Abroad Program, Tennessee State University **CW:** Co-Author, National/State Sample Refereed Publication, "A Service Learning Project to Imbue Strategic Thinking in a University Graduate Level Strategic Management Course," Tennessee Journal of Servicing & Community Engagement (2018); Co-Author, International Sample Refereed Publication, "Differentiating Cognitive Essential Competencies from Behavioral Essential Competencies in Nursing Preparation Programs: Implementations for Curriculum Revision," International Journal of Scientific Research (2017); Co-Author, National/State Sample Refereed Publication, "Service-Learning or Community Service? That is the Question!" Serve InDEED: Tennessee Journal of Service-Learning and Civic Engagement (2017); Co-Author, National/State Sample Refereed Publication, "Assessment Policies for Non-English Speaking Students: Incongruencies in the Current Policies," Education Law Association 52nd Annual Conference, Conference Proceedings (2006); Author, Book Chapter, "Employment Discrimination in Under Title VII," Contemporary Issues in Higher Education Law (2005); Author, Book Chapter, "Enhancing Educational Opportunities for Diverse Student Populations," Texas School Administration and Organization (2002); Author, Book Chapter, "Student Diversity in the New Millennium," Texas School Administration and Organization" (2000); Author, Book Chapter, "Meeting Diverse Students' Educational Needs," Texas School Administration and Organization (1995); Author, Book Chapter, "Meeting the Needs of Special Populations," Texas School Administration and Organization (1992); Contributor, Articles to Professional Journals, to Monographs; Contributor, Book Chapters; Frequent National and International Speaker, Author, and Consultant **AW:** Woman of Distinction in Education (2016); National Professional Woman of the Year in Higher Education, National Association of Professional Women (2012); Distinguished Educator Award, State of Tennessee Department of Education (2001); Blue Ribbon Committee Award, University of Memphis (2001); Service Award, Education Law Association (1997-2000); Women Excelling in Leadership, Texas Council of Women School Executives (1990); Teaching Excellence Award Finalist, University of Texas at Austin (1989); World Who's Who of Women (1987); Who's Who in the west (1981-1985); Meritorious Service Award, Phi Delta Kappa Community College Honor Fraternity (1981); Service Award, Phi Theta Kappa, Omega Upsilon Chapter (1980-1981); Excellent Educator Award for Tennessee; Oxford University International Women in Leadership Invited Speaker; UCEA Jack Culbertson Outstanding Professor National Award **MEM:** International Congress for School Effectiveness and Improvement; Education Law Association; Council for Exceptional Children;National Association of Vocational Special Needs; State Supervisors of Special Needs;

Texas Council of Women School Executives; Texas Professors of Educational Administration; Tennessee Teachers of English as a Second Language; American Association of School Administrators **MH:** Albert Nelson Marquis Lifetime Achievement Award; Marquis Who's Who Top Professional **AS:** Dr. de Casal, a second-generation American and a first-generation college attendee and graduate, attributes her success to pure grit and determination taught to her by her immigrant grandparents' stories of coming to America, as well as their trials and many tribulations as non-English speaking persons in a strange land. **B/I:** Dr. de Casal became involved in her profession because she had wanted to become a teacher by the fourth grade. She went to college as an education major and never looked back. In addition, she chose her profession in education because she is a voracious reader. **AV:** Traveling; Cultural anthropology; Reading leadership biographies; Gemology **PA:** Depends on the times **RE:** Methodist

DE CRUZ-SÁENZ, MICHÈLE S., PHD, T: Language Educator, Researcher **I:** Education/Educational Services **DOB:** 01/05/1949 **PB:** Mount Vernon **SC:** NY/USA **PT:** Sebastian Joseph Schiavone; Rosa Antonia (Greco) Schiavone **MS:** Divorced **SPN:** Gonzalo Francisco Cruz-Sáenz (06/05/1971, Divorced 11/1991) **CH:** Sebastian Francis; Gonzalo Edward Cruz-Schiavone **ED:** PhD, University of Pennsylvania (1976); MA, University of Pennsylvania (1974); Teaching Fellow, University of Pennsylvania, Philadelphia, PA (1972-1974); Teaching Fellow, Ohio University, Athens, Ohio (1971-1972); AB, Connecticut College (1971) **CT:** Certified Secondary Teacher, States of Connecticut and New York, and Commonwealth of Pennsylvania **C:** Adjunct Professor, Delaware County Community College (2014-Present); Chair, Foreign Language Department, Wallingford-Swarthmore School District (1999-2012); Teacher, Wallingford-Swarthmore School District, PA (1982-2012); Assistant Professor, The George Washington University, Washington, DC (1978-1982); Assistant Professor, Beaver College (Now Arcadia University), Glenside, PA (1976-1978); Lecturer, Swarthmore College, PA (1974-1976); Lecturer, University of Pennsylvania, Philadelphia, PA (1973-1975); Instructor, Haverford College, PA (1974-1975) **CR:** Consultant A.P. Program, ETS (1985-Present); Revised Teachers Guide for A.P. Language Course, ETS (1992); Member, Committee, Middle States Evaluation (1987, 1989) **CW:** Author, "Traditional Spanish Ballads of Aragon" (1995); Author, "Manuscript of the Biblioteca Escorial III-K-4" (1993); Author, "Resource Guide: Medieval Ballads of Hispania" (1990); Author, "El Romancero Tradicional de Costa Rica" (1986); Author, "The Life of St. Mary of Egypt" (1979) **AW:** Grantee, Ministry of Culture of Spain (1994, 1995); Award for Excellence in Teaching, Business Week (Now Bloomberg Businessweek) (1990); Grantee, National Endowment for the Humanities (1990); Grantee, Ludwig Vogelstein Foundation (1985); Grantee, American Philosophical Society (1975, 1979, 1983) **MEM:** Treasurer, The American Association of Teachers of Spanish and Portuguese (1998-Present); President, The American Association of Teachers of Spanish and Portuguese, Delaware Valley Chapter (1991-1997); Modern Language Association of America; Northeast Modern Language Association; The American Association of Teachers of Spanish and Portuguese; Asociación Internacional de Hispanistas; The Medieval Academy of America **MH:** Albert Nelson Marquis Lifetime Achievement Award **B/I:** Dr. Cruz-Sáenz was the first to be a teacher in her family, however, her mother and father were teachers in their own right. **AV:** Opera and classical music; Mystery and suspense novels; Soccer **PA:** Independent **RE:** Roman Catholic

DE JAGER, NIKKIE, "NIKKIETUTORIALS", T: Makeup Artist, Beauty Vlogger **I:** Internet **CN:** Nikkie Tutorials **DOB:** 03/02/1994 **PB:** Wageningen **SC:** Netherlands **ED:** Coursework, B Academy, Amsterdam, The Netherlands **C:** Makeup Artist, Nikkie Tutorials, YouTube (2008-Present) **CR:** Global Beauty Adviser, Marc Jacobs Beauty (2019-Present); Makeup Artist, Colourfool Agency (2011-2014); Collaborator, Ofra; Collaborator, Maybelline; Promoter, Haus Labs **CW:** Appearance, "The Ellen DeGeneres Show" (2020); Host, "Eurovision Song Contest," Rotterdam, The Netherlands (2020); Guest Judge, "Glow Up" (2019); Competitor, Wie is de Mol? (2019); Participant, "The Big Escape" (2017); Head Makeup Artist, "I Can Make You a Supermodel" (2014) **AW:** Top Ten Beauty Influencers, Forbes Magazine (2017); YouTube Guru Award, Ninth Annual Shorty Awards (2017); Teen Choice Award, Choice Web Star: Fashion/Beauty (2017)

DE LA RENTA, OSCAR, T: Fashion Designer **I:** Apparel & Fashion **DOB:** 07/22/1936 **PB:** Santa Domingo **SC:** Dominican Republic **PT:** Oscar Avelino de la Renta; Carmen Maria Antonia (Fiallo) de la Renta **MS:** Married **SPN:** Annette Engelhard (12/26/1989); Francoise de Langlade (1967, Deceased 1983) **CH:** Moises (Adopted) **ED:** Honorary Doctorate, Hamilton College, NY (2013); Coursework, Royal Academy of Fine Arts of San Fernando, Madrid, Spain **C:** Designer, Oscar de la Renta, Ltd. (1966-2014); Designer, Tortuga Bay Hotel (2006); Designer, Pierre Balmain, Paris, France (1993-2002); Chairman, Board of Directors, Chief Designer, Oscar de la Renta, Ltd. (1974-2014); Designer, Oscar de la Renta for Jane Derby (1965-1966); Designer, Custom Clothing, Elizabeth Arden, Inc., New York, NY (1963-1965); Couture Assistant, Lanvin, Paris, France **CR:** Launched, Fragrance, Intrusion (2002); Launched, Fragrance for Men, Pou Lui, Oscar for Men (1995); Launched, Signature Fragrance, Oscar (1977) **CIV:** Board of Directors, La Casa del Nino Orphanage & School, Santo Domingo, The Metropolitan Opera, NY, Carnegie Hall, WNET, New Yorkers for Children, Americas Society (Now Americas Society/Council of the Americas), Queen Sofia Spanish Institute, NY; Ambassador-at-large, Dominican Republic **AW:** Carnegie Hall Medal of Excellence (2014); Founder's Award, CFDA (2013); Superstar Award, Night of Stars (2009); Womenswear Designer of the Year Award, CFDA (2000, 2007); Named Grand Marshall, New York Hispanic Day Parade (2000); Decorated Gold Medal of Bellas Artes, King of Spain (2000); Lifetime Achievement Award, Hispanic Heritage Society (1996); Living Legend Award, American Society of Perfumers (1995); Perennial Success Award, The Fragrance Foundation (1991); Lifetime Achievement Award, CFDA (1990); Named to American Fashion Critics' Hall of Fame (1973); Named to the International Best-Dressed List Hall of Fame (1973); Golden Tiberius Award (1968); Neiman Marcus Award (1968); Coty Award (1967, 1968); La Gran Cruz Award, Order al Mérito de Juan Pablo Duarte; Award, Order of Cristóbal Colón, Dominican Republic **MEM:** President, CFDA (1973-1976, 1986-1988)

DE NIRO, ROBERT ANTHONY, T: Actor **I:** Media & Entertainment **DOB:** 08/17/1943 **PB:** New York **SC:** NY/USA **PT:** Robert De Niro Sr.; Virginia (Admiral) De Niro **MS:** Separated **SPN:** Grace Hightower (06/17/1997, Separated 2018); Diahnne Abbott (12/28/1976, Divorced 1988) **CH:** Raphael Eugene; Drina (Stepchild); Elliot; Helen Grace; Aaron Kendric DeNiro; Julian Henry De Niro **ED:** Coursework, Stella Adler Studio of Acting; Coursework, Lee Strasberg's Actors Studio (Now The Lee Strasberg Theatre & Film Institute); Coursework, HB Studio **C:** Owner, Locanda Verde, New York, NY (2009-Present); Owner, Ago, Los Angeles, CA (2008-Present); Co-founder, Tribeca Film Festival (2002-Present); Co-owner, Rubicon, San Francisco, CA (1994-Present); Co-owner, Nobu, New York, NY (1994-Present); Co-owner, Tribeca Grill (1990-Present); Co-founder, Tribeca Productions, Tribeca Enterprises LLC (1988-Present); Owner, Ago, New York, NY; Co-owner, Greenwich Hotel **CW:** Actor, "The Comeback Trail" (2020); Actor, "Father of the Bride, Part 3(ish)" (2020); Actor, "The War with Grandpa" (2020); Producer, "Artemis Fowl" (2020); Actor, Producer, "The Irishman" (2019); Actor, "Joker" (2019); Actor, "The Comedian" (2016); Actor, "Hands of Stone" (2016); Actor, "Dirty Grandpa" (2016); Actor, Executive Producer, "The Wizard of Lies" (2016); Executive Producer, "For Justice" (2015); Actor, "Joy" (2015); Actor, "Heist" (2015); Actor, "The Intern" (2015); Actor, "The Bag Man" (2014); Actor, "American Hustle" (2013); Actor, "Grudge Match" (2013); Actor, "Motel" (2013); Actor, "Last Vegas" (2013); Actor, "The Family" (2013); Actor, "Killing Season" (2013); Actor, "The Big Wedding" (2013); Actor, "Silver Linings Playbook" (2012); Actor, "Freelancers" (2012); Actor, "Being Flynn" (2012); Actor, "Red Lights" (2012); Actor, "New Year's Eve" (2011); Actor, "Limitless" (2011); Actor, "Killer Elite" (2011); Actor, "Little Fockers" (2010); Actor, "Stone" (2010); Actor, "Machete" (2010); Appearance, "I Knew It Was You: Rediscovering John Cazale" (2010); Actor, "Everybody's Fine" (2009); Actor, "What Just Happened?" (2008); Actor, "Righteous Kill" (2008); Actor, "Stardust" (2007); Voice Actor, "Arthur and the Invisibles" (2006); Actor, Director, "The Good Shepherd" (2006); Producer, "Rent" (2005); Actor, "Hide and Seek" (2005); Voice Actor, "Shark Tale" (2004); Actor, Producer, "Meet the Fockers" (2004); Actor, "Godsend" (2004); Producer, "Stage Beauty" (2004); Actor, "City by the Sea" (2002); Actor, "Analyze That" (2002); Actor, "Showtime" (2002); Producer, "About a Boy" (2002); Actor, "The Score" (2001); Actor, Executive Producer, "Meet the Parents" (2000); Executive Producer, "Holiday Heart" (2000); Executive Producer, "Navy Driver" (2000); Executive Producer, "Conjugating Niki, (2000); Actor, "Flawless" (1999); Actor, "Analyze This" (1999); Producer, "Entropy" (1999); Actor, "15 Minutes" (1999); Actor, Producer, "The Adventures of Rocky and Bullwinkle" (1999); Narrator, "Lenny Bruce: Swear to Tell the Truth" (1998); Actor, "Great Expectations" (1998); Actor, "Copland" (1997); Actor, Producer, "Wag the Dog" (1997); Actor, "Sleepers" (1996); Actor, "Marvin's Room" (1996); Executive Producer, "Faithful" (1996); Actor, "The Fan" (1996); Actor, "Heat" (1995); Actor, "Casino" (1995); Actor, "Mary Shelley's Frankenstein" (1994); Actor, "This Boy's Life" (1993); Actor, Director, "A Bronx Tale" (1993); Actor, "Mad Dog and Glory" (1993); Executive Producer, "Tribeca" (1993); Co-producer, "Thunderheart" (1992); Actor, "Night and the City" (1992); Actor, "Mistress" (1992); Actor, "Guilty by Suspicion" (1991); Actor, "Cape Fear" (1991); Actor, "Backdraft" (1991); Actor, "Awakenings" (1991); Actor, "Goodfellas" (1990); Actor, "Stanley & Iris" (1990); Actor, "Jacknife" (1989); Actor, Executive Producer, "We're No Angels" (1989); Actor, "Midnight Run" (1988); Narrator, "Dear America: Letters Home from Vietnam" (1987); Actor, "The Untouchables" (1987); Actor, "Angel Heart" (1987); Actor, "The Mission" (1985); Actor, "Brazil" (1984); Actor, "Falling in Love" (1984); Actor, "Once Upon a Time in America" (1984); Actor, "The King of Comedy" (1982); Actor, "Strange Show" (1982);

Actor, "True Confessions" (1981); Actor, "Raging Bull" (1980); Actor, "The Deer Hunter" (1978); Actor, "New York, New York" (1977); Actor, "Taxi Driver" (1976); Actor, "Nineteen Hundred" (1976); Actor, "The Last Tycoon" (1976); Actor, "The Godfather, Part II" (1974); Actor, "Mean Streets" (1973); Actor, "Bang the Drum Slowly" (1973); Actor, "The Gang That Couldn't Shoot Straight" (1971); Actor, "Born to Win" (1971); Actor, "Jennifer on My Mind" (1971); Actor, "Bloody Mama" (1970); Actor, "Hi, Mom!" (1970); Actor, "The Wedding Party" (1969); Actor, Numerous Films **AW:** Lifetime Achievement Award, SAG-AFTRA (2020); Critics' Choice Award, Best Movie Cast (2020); Presidential Medal of Freedom, The White House (2016); Cecil B. DeMille Award, Hollywood Foreign Press Association (2011); Honoree, Kennedy Center Honors, John F. Kennedy Center for the Performing Arts (2009); Named Greatest Living Movie Star, Empire Magazine (2004); Golden Lion Honorary Award, Venice Film Festival (1993); D.W. Griffith Award for Best Actor (1990); Academy Award for Best Actor, Academy of Motion Picture Arts and Sciences (1981); Golden Globe Award, Best Actor in a Motion Picture - Drama, Hollywood Foreign Press Association (1981); Hasty Pudding Award, Hasty Pudding Institute of 1770, Harvard University (1979); Academy Award for Best Supporting Actor, Academy of Motion Picture Arts and Sciences (1975); Recipient, Numerous Awards

DE SANTO, JOSEPH ROBERT, T: Engineering Educator **I:** Education/Educational Services **DOB:** 11/04/1940 **PB:** Pittston **SC:** PA/USA **PT:** Joseph De Santo; Rose De Santo **MS:** Married **SPN:** Barbara F. De Santo (08/22/1964) **CH:** Ron; Gary **ED:** Coursework in Physics, New York University (1963-1966); MS in Physics, Fordham University (1963); BS in Physics, University of Scranton (1961) **C:** Retired (2017); Chairman, Department of Engineering Technology, Luzerne County Community College (1993-2017); Professor of Engineering Technology, Luzerne County Community College (1983-2017); Associate Professor of Engineering Technology, Professor of Engineering Technology, Luzerne County Community College (1974-1982); Assistant Professor of Engineering Technology, Luzerne County Community College (1969-1973); Engineer, General Precision Laboratories (1966-1969) **MEM:** IEEE; American Physical Society **MH:** Albert Nelson Marquis Lifetime Achievement Award **B/I:** Mr. De Santo became involved in his profession because he majored in physics in college, which prepared him for his first professional role with General Precision Laboratories. Over the years, he was afforded many grants that allowed him the opportunity to pursue basic research and development into the use of magnetic resonance to detect the movement of metal carried by enemy troops over long distances from the electromagnetic source of radiation during the Vietnam War. In 1969, he was given the opportunity to be transferred to one of two locations within General Precision Laboratories or become a teacher at a nearby school. He chose to stay close to home and served with Luzerne County Community College for nearly 50 years.

DE SHIELDS, ANDRÉ, T: Actor, Singer, Choreographer **I:** Media & Entertainment **DOB:** 01/12/1946 **PB:** Baltimore **SC:** MD/USA **PT:** John De Shields; Mary Gunther **ED:** Honorary DFA, University of Wisconsin-Madison (2007); MA, New York University Gallatin School of Individualized Study (1991); BA in English Literature, University of Wisconsin-Madison (1970); Coursework, Wilmington College **CR:** Adjunct Professor, New York University Gallatin School of Individualized Study **CW:** Actor, "Hadestown" (2019-Present); Actor, "John Mulaney & the Sack Lunch Bunch" (2019); Actor, "Gotta Dance" (2015-2016); Actor, "The Fortress of Solitude" (2012, 2014); Actor, "The Jungle Book" (2013); Actor, "Impressionism" (2009); Actor, "Black Nativity" (2007); Actor, "Prymate" (2004); Actor, "The Full Monty" (2000); Actor, "Play On!" (1997); Actor, "Extreme Measures" (1996); Actor, "Another World" (1995-1996); Writer, Director, "Saint Tous" (1991); Actor, "Prinson" (1988); Actor, "Revival" (1988); Actor, "Ain't Misbehavin'" (1978, 1988); Actor, "Stardust" (1987); Actor, "Cotton Club Gala" (1985); Director, "The Adventures of Rhubarb: The Rock and Roll Rabbit" (1985); Actor, "I Dream of Jeannie - 15 Years Later" (1985); Writer, Director, Composer, Choreographer, "André De Shields' Haarlem Nocturne" (1984); Writer, Director, "Judith and the Cohen Sisters in Midnight in Manhattan" (1983); Actor, "Alice in Wonderland" (1983); Actor, "Stardust: The Mitchell Parrish Musical" (1981); Actor, "The Wiz" (1975, 1978); Actor, "Thoughts" (1974); Actor, "Rachael Lily Rosenbloom (And Don't You Ever Forget It)" (1973); Actor, "Warp" (1973); Actor, "Sacred Guard" (1973); Actor, "The Me Nobody Knows" (1970); Actor, "Hair" (1969); Actor, "Gulliver's Trilogy"; Actor, "Dancing on Moonlight"; Actor, "Death of a Salesman"; Actor, "Avenue X"; Actor, "Waiting For Godot"; Actor, "The Man Who Came to Dinner"; Actor, "Death of a Salesman"; Actor, "Dusyanta: A Tale of Kalidasa"; Actor, "The Gospel According to James"; Actor, "Camino Real"; Actor, "Cosby"; Actor, "Sex and the City"; Actor, "Great Performances"; Actor, "Lipstick Jungle"; Actor, "Law & Order"; Actor, "Law & Order: Special Victims Unit" **AW:** Grammy Award, Best Musical Theater Album, The Recording Academy (2020); Drama Desk Award, Outstanding Featured Actor in a Musical (2019); Tony Award, Best Featured Actor in a Musical (2019); Outer Critics Circle Award, Outstanding Featured Actor in a Musical (2001, 2019); Bistro Award, Bob Harrington Lifetime Achievement Award (2018); Special Achievement AUDELCO Award, Audience Development Committee, Inc. (2014); Grantee, Fox Foundation Fellowship for Distinguished Achievement (2013); Jeff Award, Outstanding Achievement in the category of Actor in a Supporting Role – Musical (2013); Living Legend Award, National Black Theatre Festival (2009); AUDELCO Recognition Award, Outstanding Performance in a Musical, Audience Development Committee, Inc. (2009); Obie Award for Sustained Excellence of Performance (2007); AUDELCO Recognition Award, Outstanding Performance by a Lead Actor in a Play, Audience Development Committee, Inc. (2004); AUDELCO Recognition Award, Excellence in Black Theatre, Audience Development Committee, Inc. (1992); AUDELCO Recognition Award, Outstanding Choreography of a Musical, Audience Development Committee, Inc. (1984); AUDELCO Recognition Award, Outstanding Direction of a Musical, Audience Development Committee, Inc. (1984); Primetime Emmy Award, Outstanding Individual Performance in a Variety or Music Program, Television Academy (1982)

DE SILVA, DEEMATHIE, PHD, T: University Administrator, Educator **I:** Education/Educational Services **DOB:** 04/27/1939 **PB:** Galle **SC:** Sri Lanka **PT:** Peter Dantanarayana; Wilhelmina (Silva) Dantanarayana **MS:** Married **SPN:** Dharma de Silva (04/11/1962) **CH:** Harshini (Deceased); Mahinda; Duminda; Lathika **ED:** PhD, Columbia Pacific University (1988); MA, Stanford University (1964); Graduate Coursework, Government Teachers College, Colombo, Sri Lanka **CT:** Certified Teacher, State of Kansas **C:** President, Transcultural Marketing Communications, Wichita, KS (1995-Present); Co-Principal Investigator, Ronald D. McNair Post Baccalaureate Achievement Program (1995-1999); Director, Grant Writer, Student Support Services, Wichita State University (1985-1997); UB-Math Science Regional Center (1992-1995); Instructor, Anthropology, Wichita State University (1982-1983); Research Associate, College of Business, Wichita State University (1979-1981); Lecturer, Biology, Wichita State University (1980); Testing Coordinator, Women's Equity Program, Wichita State University (1977-1978) **CR:** Consultant Trainer, TRIO Directors Nationwide, Western Kentucky University (1994-1997); Director, Operation Success, Wichita State University (1985-1997); Member, Kansas Delegation to Washington, DC (1984-1997); Presenter, Change Management Seminars, Numerous Distinguished Institutions (1983-1997); Chair, Upward Bound Math-Science Advisory Council (1992-1995); Trainer, Impact of Culture on Productivity, Beech Top Managers (1994); Chair, Session on International, Kansas White House Conference on Small Business (1994); Chair, Session on Kansas Governor's Economic Development Conference (1990); Chair, Ten State Professional Development Conference (1984); Assistant Professor, Director, Grant Writer, SSS Trio Program; Executive Trainer, Team Building, Headstart Educators; Presenter, Participant, Numerous Conferences and Symposia; Diversity Trainer, Numerous International Organizations **CIV:** World Trade Council, Wichita, KS (1989-2015); Executive Board of Directors, Global Learning Center, Wichita, KS (1991) **CW:** Writer, "Cultural and Diversity," Student Affairs Bi-Monthly Newsletter, Division of Student Affairs, Wichita State University (1992-1993); Co-Author, "A Tutor Handbook for TRIO Programs" (1987); Contributor, Numerous Articles, Professional Journals **AW:** Trio Legacy Award, Wichita State University (2019); World Peace Through Trade Award, Kansas World Trade Center, Wichita, KS (2004); Brotherhood Sisterhood Award, National Conference Community and Justice, Wichita, KS (2001); Listee, 200 Notable American Women (1990); Grantee, National Science Council Sri Lanka (1977); Fellow, American Association of University Women (1975-1976); Fellow, National Science Foundation (1964); Scholar, Fulbright Foundation (1963-1964); Kansas International Special Recognition, Kansas World Trade Center, Wichita, KS **MEM:** Society for Intercultural Education, Training, and Research (1984-Present); Director, Southeast Region, Independent Scholars Of Asia (1985-1995); Missouri-Kansas-Nebraska Association; International Society for Intercultural Education and Research; Executive Board of Directors, Archivist, Mid-America Association Educational Opportunity Program Personnel; Executive Member, World Trade Council, Wichita, KS; Sri Lanka Association for Advancement of Science **MH:** Albert Nelson Marquis Lifetime Achievement Award; Marquis Who's Who Top Professional; Distinguished Humanitarian **B/I:** Dr. de Silva became involved in her profession because her father, a Fulbright recipient and professor of physics, often traveled around the world. She admired the respect he received, and she knew she wanted to be just like him. Under the positive influence of her father, Dr. de Silva decided to pursue academia, which led her to become a university professor, administrator, and educator. **RE:** Buddhist

DEAN, MADELEINE CUNNANE, T: U.S. Representative from Pennsylvania **I:** Government Administration/Government Relations/Government Services **DOB:** 06/06/1959 **PB:** Glenside **SC:** PA/USA **PT:** Bob Dean; Mary Dean **MS:** Married **SPN:** Patrick Cunnane **CH:** Three Sons **ED:** JD, Widener University Delaware Law School; BA, La Salle University, Magna Cum Laude; Coursework, Fels Institute of Government, University of Pennsylvania **C:** Member, U.S. House of Representatives from Pennsylvania's Fourth Congressional District (2019-Present); Member, 153rd District, Pennsylvania House of Representatives (2012-2018); Assistant Professor of English, La Salle University; In-house Counsel, Bicycle Business; Founder, Small Law Practice, Glenside, PA; Executive Director, Philadelphia Trial Lawyers Association **CW:** Contributor, The Philadelphia Inquirer, Philadelphia Daily News, The Patriot News and Other Publications **PA:** Democrat

DEAR, RONALD BRUCE, T: Social Work Educator (Retired) **I:** Education/Educational Services **DOB:** 09/23/1933 **PB:** Philadelphia **SC:** PA/USA **PT:** John David Dear; Margaret (McDade) Dear **CH:** Bruce W. Dear **ED:** PhD in Social Work, Columbia University (1972); MSW, University of Pittsburgh (1957); Honors Certificate, The University of Aberdeen, Scotland, United Kingdom (1955); BA in Psychology, Bucknell University (1955) **CT:** Certified Social Worker, States of New York and Washington; National Academy of Certified Social Workers **C:** Professor Emeritus, University of Washington (2001-Present); Professor, University of Washington, Seattle, WA (1970-2001); Residence Director, Horizon House, Inc., Philadelphia, PA (1961-1964); Chief Social Worker, Mental Hygiene Consultation Service, Aberdeen Proving Grounds, MD (1958-1960) **CR:** President, University of Washington Retirement Association (2007-2008); Invitational Address, "What Every Social Worker Should Know About Political Action," Fourth Annual Policy Conference on Politics, Social Policy, and Social Change, Charleston, SC (2001); Master Teacher, Council on Social Work Education (1991, 1993, 1994, 1997); Presidential Search Committee, University of Washington (1996-1997); Visiting Professor, University of Trondheim (Now Norwegian University of Science and Technology), Trondheim, Norway (1996); UW Faculty President, University of Washington (1993-1995); University Faculty Legislative Representative, Olympia, WA (1983-1985, 1988-1991); Visiting Professor, University of Bergen, Norway (1984); Selected Positions, Various Committees Including University Budget Committee and Senate Committee on Planning and Budgeting, University of Washington **CIV:** Advisory Committee, Washington State Economic Services (1996-2004); Appearance, Centennial Program, Columbia University School of Social Work (1998); Co-founder, National Organization, Influencing State Policy, U.S. Schools of Social Work (1997); Human Services Policy Center (1996); Governor Appointed Member, Income Assistance Advisory Committee (1987-1993); Member, Advisory Committee for Washington State Department of Social and Health Services (1980-1983) **MIL:** Acting Chief, Chief Social Worker, Neuropsychiatric Clinic, M.A.S.H. Unit, 7th Infantry Division, Korea (1960-1961); First Lieutenant, Neuropsychiatric Clinic, M.A.S.H. Unit, 7th Infantry Division, Korea (1959-1961); Chief Social Worker, Mental Hygiene Consultation Service, Aberdeen Proving Grounds, MD (1958-1960); Second Lieutenant, Neuropsychiatric Clinic, M.A.S.H. Unit, 7th Infantry Division, Korea (1957-1959) **CW:** Author, "Conan Doyle, Sherlock Holmes and the Strand Magazine: A Few More Words on the Sacred Writings," BCW Journal, Summer (2006); Author, "Social Welfare Policy: Trends and Issues, Sixth Edition" (2001); Author, "Should MSW Curricula Be Extended to Three Years? Yes!" Journal of Social Work Education (1999); Contributor, Editorial Review Board Member, "The Dictionary of Social Work," Four Editions (1987-1999); Contributor, Policy Text, "Becoming an Effective Policy Advocate..." (1999); Contributor, "Social Welfare Policy," "Encyclopedia of Social Work, 19th Edition" (1995, 1997); Author, "Welfare Reform in the Post-Industrial

Era" (1990); Author "What's Right with Welfare? The Other Face of AFDC"(1989); Co-author with R. Patti of "Legislative Advocacy" in "Encyclopedia of Social Work, 18th Edition" (1987); Author "No More Poverty in America? A Critique of Martin Anderson's Theory of Welfare" (1982); Co-author with R. Patti, "Legislative Advocacy: Seven Effective Tactics" (1981); Author, "Social Welfare: A Critical Aspect of Population Policy" (1978); Co-author with R. Patti, "Legislative Advocacy: One Path to Social Change"(1975); Author "The Current Crisis in Social Welfare" (1974); Co-author with Douglas, Textbook, "Poverty in Perspective: A Critical Analysis of the Social Welfare Problem" (1973); Contributor, Amicus Curiae Brief, Shapiro v. Thompson (1969); Contributor, Articles to Professional Journals **AW:** Named Social Worker of the Year, State of Washington (1981) **MEM:** Charter Member, National Association of Social Workers (1955); National Academy of Certified Social Workers **MH:** Albert Nelson Marquis Lifetime Achievement Award; Marquis Who's Who Top Professional **B/I:** Dr. Dear had been accepted by the University of Aberdeen, Scotland to study honors psychology from September 1954 to June 1955. This was a time before students commonly traveled abroad to study. It took extraordinary effort to convince Bucknell to allow him to travel abroad for his senior year and to grant him a nonresident senior credit for it. Aberdeen had an exceptionally well recognized and talented faculty in their Department of Psychology. For example, they were among the first in the world to start experiments using LSD; also, they were leaders in behavioral psychology, as opposed to Freudian based treatment psychology that was almost universally used and taught in the USA. That was the context of Dr. Dear beginning his career in psychology, and later, in social work. At the end of his studies in Aberdeen, he talked with his professor/advisor, Dr. Rex Knight, Chair of Psychology, and President of the British Psychological Association. He thought Dr. Dear worked well with people, had creative ideas, and believed that he should pursue some sort of people/idea profession. Dr. Dear returned for his final summer at Bucknell when the possibility of studying for a master's degree in social work at nearby University of Pittsburgh was brought to his attention; classes started the following month, September 1955. He applied, was accepted and for financing, was awarded a stipend from the Pennsylvania Department of Welfare. To his new courses at Pitt, he introduced some of the ideas and concepts he had learned in Scotland, often deeply at odds with those in his current classes. He came to realize then, and increasingly in years to come, that to really assist people, in addition to direct and personal interventions of psychotherapy, be they Freudian or behavioral, we may need additional levels and types of intervention. Perhaps more political? He became more keenly interested in legislative policy and its influence on direct practice. **AV:** Solo overland travel in over 50 countries, some remote and rarely visited, often on foot; Photography

DEBERTIN, JAY D., T: Chief Executive Officer and President **I:** Agriculture **CN:** CHS Inc. **ED:** MBA, University of Wisconsin, Madison (1984); Bachelor's Degree in Economics, University of North Dakota, Grand Forks (1982) **C:** Chief Executive Officer, President, CHS Inc. (2017-Present); Executive Vice President and Chief Operating Officer, Energy & Foods, CHS, Inc. (2011-Present); Executive Vice President and Chief Operating Officer, Processing, CHS, Inc., Inver Grove Heights, MN (2005-2010); Senior Vice President of Energy Operations, CHS, Inc., St. Paul, MN (2001); Vice President of Crude Oil Supply, CHS, Inc., Denver, CO (1998-2001); With,

Petroleum Division, CHS, Inc. (1984) **CR:** Board of Directors, USA BioEnergy (2006-Present); Board of Directors, Ventura Foods, LLC; Board of Director, Horizon Milling; Board of Directors, National Cooperative Refinery Association

DEBEVOISE, CHARLES HENRY, T: Shareholder, Lawyer **I:** Law and Legal Services **CN:** Davis, Malm & D'Agostine PC **DOB:** 05/17/1958 **PB:** Providence **SC:** RI/USA **PT:** Charles Conklin DeBevoise; Dolores Annette (Anderson) DeBevoise Brunt **MS:** Married **SPN:** Janet Shensa **CH:** Robert Raymond; Edward Raymond; Henry Morton **ED:** JD, American University, Washington, DC (1983); BA in Political Science, Providence College, Providence, RI, Cum Laude (1980) **C:** Shareholder, Davis, Malm & D'Agostine, Professional Corporation, Boston, MA (2004-Present); Partner, Bowditch & Dewey, Framingham, MA (1999-2004); Partner, Edwards & Angell, Providence, RI, Boston, MA (1992-1995); Associate, Edwards & Angell, Providence, RI (1987-1992); Law Clerk, Supreme Court of Rhode Island, Providence, RI (1983-1984) **CIV:** Boston Committee on Foreign Relations (2015); Senior Warden, St. Dunstan's Episcopal Church, Dover, MA (2000-2003); Boston Minuteman Council, Boy Scouts of America, Boston, MA (2001-2002); Board of Directors, Narragansett Council, Boy Scouts of America, Providence, RI (1987-1995) **AW:** AV Preeminent Rating, Martindale-Hubbell; Silver Beaver Award, Boy Scouts of America **MEM:** Board of Governors, Dedham Country and Polo Club (2006-2009); Rhode Island Bar Association; Massachusetts Bar Association; Bar Association of the District of Columbia (BADC); Boston Bar Association; Chicago Bar Association; Dedham Country and Polo Club; Eagle Scout, Boy Scouts of America; Pi Sigma Alpha; The University Club of New York; The University Club, Providence, RI **BAR:** Washington, DC (1985); U.S. District Court for the District of Rhode Island (1984); Massachusetts (1984); Rhode Island (1983) **MH:** Albert Nelson Marquis Lifetime Achievement Award **AV:** Reading; Playing tennis; Playing golf; Gardening **PA:** Republican **RE:** Episcopalian

DEFAZIO, PETER ANTHONY, T: U.S. Representative **I:** Government Administration/Government Relations/Government Services **DOB:** 05/27/1947 **PB:** Needham **SC:** MA/USA **MS:** Married **SPN:** Myrnie L. Daut **ED:** MS in Public Administration and Gerontology, University of Oregon, Eugene, OR (1977); BA in Economics and Political Science, Tufts University, Medford, MA (1969) **C:** Ranking Member, The House Committee on Transportation and Infrastructure (2014-Present); Ranking Member, Natural Resources Committee, U.S. House of Representatives (2013-Present); U.S. Representative, Oregon's Fourth Congressional District, United States Congress (1987-Present); Chairman, Lane County Board of Commissioners (1985-1986); Commissioner, Lane County Board of Commissioners, Eugene, OR (1983-1986); Director, Constituent Services, U.S. House of Representatives (1980-1982); Legislative Assistant, Washington Office, U.S. House of Representatives (1978-1980); Senior Issues Specialist, District Field Office of Congressman Jim Weaver, U.S. House of Representatives, OR (1977-1978) **CIV:** Board of Directors, Eugene-Springfield Metropolitan Partnership, Inc. **MIL:** Air Force Reserve (1967-1971) **AW:** Rail Leadership Award, American Passenger Rail Coalition (2006); Human Lifetime Achievement Award, The Humane Society of the United States (2002); Congressional Award, Military Production Network (1995); DC Distinguished Alumnus Award, Alumni Association, University of Oregon (1994)

MEM: National Association of Counties; Association of Oregon Counties **PA:** Democrat **RE:** Roman Catholic

DEFRANCO, JASON, T: President **I:** Medicine & Health Care **CN:** Team Solution Dental Lab **CT:** Certified Dental Technician, National Board of Certification (2006-Present) **C:** President, Team Solutions Dental Lab (2013-Present); Executive Director of Operations, National Dentex Corporation (2006-2013); Vice President, Prodontic Laboratories (1995-2005); Computer Communications Expert, U.S. Air Force (1989-1993) **CIV:** Partner, Wounded Warriors; Partner, St. Jude's; Partner, Give Back a Smile; Partner, Dental Lifeline Network; Pro Bono Casework **AW:** Award, National Dentex (2013); Most Improved Laboratory, National Dentex (2012); Laboratory of the Year (2012); Air Force Achievement Medal, USAF (1991); Air Force Outstanding Unit Award (1991); Southwest Asia Service Medal (1990); Fastest Growing Laboratory, Lab Management Today Magazine; Below-the-Zone Promotion, U.S. Air Force; Joint Meritorious Unit Award, JTF Proven Force; Michael Perri Creative Writing Award **MEM:** Florida Dental Laboratory Association **AS:** Mr. DeFranco attributes his success to his commitment to integrity and hard work. **B/I:** Mr. DeFranco became involved in his profession due to the influence of his father, who owned a dental lab.

DEGETTE, DIANA LOUISE, T: U.S. Representative, Lawyer **I:** Government Administration/Government Relations/Government Services **DOB:** 07/29/1957 **PB:** Tachikawa **SC:** Japan **PT:** Richard Louis DeGette; Patricia Anne (Rose) DeGette **MS:** Married **SPN:** Lino Sigismondo Lipinsky (09/15/1984) **CH:** Raphaela Anne; Francesca Louise **ED:** JD, New York University School of Law (1982); BA in Political Science, Colorado College, Magna Cum Laude (1979) **C:** U.S. Representative, Colorado's First Congressional District, United States Congress (1996-Present); Assistant Minority Leader, Colorado House of Representatives (1995-1996); Of Counsel, McDermott & Hansen, Denver, CO (1993-1996); Member, Colorado House of Representatives (1992-1996); Sole Practice, Denver, CO (1986-1993); Associate, Coghill Group, PC, Denver, CO (1984-1986); Deputy State Public Defender, Office of the Colorado State Public Defender, Denver, CO (1982-1984); Member, Committee on Education and the Workforce; Member, Committee on Armed Services; Vice-chair, Committee on Energy and Commerce; Chief Deputy Whip, First Congressional District, United States Congress **CR:** Chair, Denver Democratic Party (1986); Lead-Whip, State Children's Health Insurance Progressive; Co-Chair, Congressional Diabetes Caucus; Co-Chair, Congressional Bipartisan Pro-Choice Caucus; Member, Mayor's Management Review Commission on Social Services; Member, Denver Women's Commission on Resolutions **CIV:** Board of Directors, New York University School of Law (1986-1992); Board of Directors, Planned Parenthood of the Rocky Mountains **CW:** Author, "Sex, Science, and Stem Cells: Inside the Right Wing Assault on Reason," The Lyons Press (2008); Editor, Trial Talk Magazine (1989-1992) **AW:** Vanderbilt Medal (1982); Root-Tilden Scholar, New York University School of Law (1979) **MEM:** Board of Governors, Colorado Bar Association (1989-1991); Board of Directors, Executive Committee, Colorado Trial Lawyers Association (1986-1992); Denver Bar Association; Colorado Women's Bar Association; Pi Gamma Mu Honor Society; The Phi Beta Kappa Society **BAR:** Supreme Court of the United States (1989); United States Court of Appeals for the 10th Circuit (1984); United States

District Court District of Colorado (1982); Colorado Bar Association (1982) **AV:** Reading; Backpacking; Gardening **PA:** Democrat

DEITRICK, GEORGE A., MD, T: Physician, Surgeon **I:** Medicine & Health Care **DOB:** 04/17/1946 **PB:** Ashland **SC:** PA/USA **PT:** George Albert Deitrick; Sabina Mary (Cortellini) Deitrick **MS:** Married **SPN:** Tara Lynne Gleason (11/28/1981) **CH:** Taryn Christine **ED:** MD, Temple University, Philadelphia, PA (1976); BA, Gettysburg College (1970) **CT:** Certification in Surgery, American Board of Physical Medicine and Rehabilitation (1993, 2003, 2013); Certification in Spinal Cord Injury Medicine, American Board of Physical Medicine and Rehabilitation (2003); American Board of Surgery (1983); National Board of Medical Examiners (1981) **C:** Attending Surgeon, Spinal Cord Injury Physician, James J. Peters Veterans Affairs Medical Center, Bronx, NY (2000-Present); Principal, Interlink Healthcare Consulting, Garden City, NY (1997-2000); Vice President, Medical Affairs, Curative Health Services, Curative Techs., East Setauket, NY (1991-1997); Attending Surgeon, Assistant Professor of Surgery, School of Medicine, Pennsylvania Hospital, University of Pennsylvania, Philadelphia, PA (1981-1991); Intern, Resident in Surgery, Pennsylvania Hospital, University of Pennsylvania, Philadelphia, PA (1976-1981) **CR:** Consultant, Gerson Lehrman Group, New York, NY (2002-Present); Associate Professor, Surgery, Mount Sinai School of Medicine (2000-Present); Integrated Medical Services, Highwood, IL (2000-Present); Editorial Board, European Journal of Wound Management (2009); Editor, European Journals of Wound & Burn Management **CW:** Contributing Editor, Advances in Wound Care (2001-Present); Contributor, Articles, Professional Journals **AW:** Teaching Award, Pennsylvania Hospital Residents (1986) **MEM:** Fellow, American College of Surgeons; Life Member, Alpha Kappa Kappa; Life Member, Sigma Alpha Epsilon **MH:** Albert Nelson Marquis Lifetime Achievement Award **B/I:** Dr. Deitrick became involved in his profession because his father and grandfather were surgeons; they inspired him. His grandfather was first licensed to practice surgery and medicine in the commonwealth of Pennsylvania in 1910. His influence continues to influence Dr. Deitrick today. **AV:** Golfing; Rose gardening; Cooking

DEJOY, JIM, T: Teacher/Athletic Director **I:** Education/Educational Services **CN:** Sycamore Junior High School **DOB:** 02/12/1966 **PB:** Cleveland **SC:** OH/USA **PT:** James M. DeJoy; Carol (Fox) DeJoy **MS:** Married **SPN:** Jill Cierley (06/08/1991) **CH:** Two Daughters **ED:** Postgraduate Coursework, Xavier University, Cincinnati, OH (1993); BA in Physical Education, Ohio University (1989) **C:** Athletic Director, Sycamore Junior High School (2015-Present); Teacher, Physical Education, Junior High School, Sycamore Schools, Cincinnati, OH (1991-2015); Teacher, Physical Education, Elementary School, Sycamore Schools, Cincinnati, OH (1989-1991) **CIV:** Counselor, Raquette Lake Camps (1986, 1988); The Sandwich Project **AW:** Educator of the Year Award, Blue Ash Montgomery Rotary Club (2016) **MEM:** Member Alliance for Health; Ohio Alliance for Health; The Ohio Health and Physical Education Recreation and Dance Association for Ohio State and National; National Athletic Directors Association **MH:** Marquis Who's Who Top Professional **AS:** Mr. DeJoy likes to work with children. He believes his success is a direct result of his passion for teaching, mentoring, and learning with his students. **B/I:** Mr. Dejoy's mother was a teacher; she inspired him to pursue the field. He also had many other family members who were in the education industry. By the time he gradu-

ated high school, he knew he wanted to become a teacher. **AV:** Exercising; Playing sports **RE:** Roman Catholic **THT:** Mr. Dejoy treats others the way he would like to be treated.

DEL CONTE, LAVADA CATHERINE, M.SPL. EDUCATION, T: Special Education Educator **I:** Education/Educational Services **DOB:** 06/08/1955 **PB:** Montour Falls **SC:** NY/USA **PT:** Leon Clarence May; Dorothy Louise May **MS:** Married **SPN:** Richard Del Conte (04/08/1995); Douglas Kelsey (08/02/1973) **CH:** Henry Lee Kelsey; Bryon Douglas Kelsey **ED:** MEd in Special Education, George Mason University, Fairfax, VA (2000); MPA in Geriatrics, SUNY Brockport (1986); BSW, SUNY Brockport (1983); AA in Human Services, Genesee Community College, Batavia, NY (1981) **CT:** Renewal of Special Education Educator License (2019-2029) **C:** Special Education Educator (2011); Learning Disabilities/Special Education Teacher, Fairfax County Public Schools, Annandale, VA (1998-2006);Case Manager, Jewish Social Services, Rockville, MD (1995-1997); Case Manager, State of Maryland/Great Oaks MR Center (1994-1995); Case Manager, Brice Warren Corporation, Washington, DC (1992-1994); Case Manager, We Care, Incorporated, Washington, DC (1991-1992) **CR:** Member, Attendance Advisory Committee Annandale High School (2003-2004); Lead Teacher, Remediation Program (1999-2002); Historian, Phi Delta Kappa/George Mason University, (1998-2000); Court-Appointed Specialist, Fairfax County, Fairfax, VA (1991-1993) **AW:** Women of Distinction (2018) **MH:** Albert Nelson Marquis Lifetime Achievement Award; Marquis Who's Who Top Professional **B/I:** Ms. Del Conte became involved in her profession because she began as a case manager working with people with developmental disabilities. As a child growing up, she came from a poor area in the country, and she was bussed into a city school. Because of her background, being from the country, people did not expect much from her. Back in those times, they did not diagnose learning disabilities, so she struggled and was not expected to graduate high school. She was the first in six generations in her family to complete her education. Ms. Del Conte had the desire to help kids that were like herself and give them the proper care and education services they required. **AV:** Hiking; Reading; Working out; Poetry; Learning new things, Keeping his mind active through classes at local community college **PA:** Democrat

DEL ROSARIO, NESTOR, MD, T: Physician **I:** Medicine & Health Care **CN:** Del Rosario Medical Clinic **CH:** Two Children **ED:** Fellowship, Pulmonary and Critical Care, University of California Irvine (1994); Residency, University of California Los Angeles (1990); MD, Eastern Virginia Medical School, VA (1987); MS in Medicine, University of California at Irvine Medical Center (1994) **C:** Founder, Del Rosario Medical Clinic, Hawaii (1998-Present); Internist, Pulmonary Critical Care Specialist, Various Hawaii Hospitals (1997-1998); With, City of Hope (1994-1997) **AW:** Named Teacher of the Year **MEM:** American Medical Association; Past President, Philippine Medical Association of Hawaii (PMAH); Critical Care Chest Society **AS:** Dr. Del Rosario attributes his success to his heart, the passion for helping and the love he has for the work. **B/I:** Dr. Del Rosario always was an outstanding student in school. Initially, he had aspirations to become a priest or lawyer, but his grandmother, (who he was raised by), chose his brother to be the doctor of the family. His brother did not follow through with their desire for him and made his mother cry. Seeing his mother cry, he told her that he would do anything to make her happy. She asked would he become a doctor? He began to feel he did have the mind for it, and so he followed through. He currently has no regrets at all for the decision that he made. While doing medical missions in the Philippines, he saw how poor the people were and felt like they needed help. He then decided to enroll in medical school in the Philippines, before eventually transferring to East Virginia University in the United States.

DEL TORO, GUILLERMO, T: Film Director **I:** Media & Entertainment **DOB:** 10/09/1964 **PB:** Guadalajara **SC:** Jalisco/Mexico **MS:** Married **SPN:** Lorenza Newton (1986) **CH:** Mariana; Marisa **ED:** Coursework, University of Guadalajara **C:** Film Teacher, Mexico; Founder, The Tequila Gang, Mexico; Founder, Necropia, Mexico; Make-Up Supervisor **CR:** Judge, Mentor, NHK Awards (2000); Jury Member, Independent Film Project's Spirit Awards (1999, 2000) **CW:** Director, The Shape of Water" (2017); Writer, Director, Producer, "Crimson Peak" (2015); Producer, "The Thin Yellow Line" (2015); Writer, "The Hobbit: The Battle of the Five Armies" (2014); Writer, Director, "Pacific Rim" (2013); Executive Producer, "Mama" (2013); Writer, "The Hobbit: The Desolation of Smaug" (2013); Writer, "The Hobbit: An Unexpected Journey" (2012); Executive Producer, "Rise of the Guardians" (2012); Executive Producer, "Kung Fu Panda 2" (2011); Executive Producer, "Puss in Boots" (2011); Co-Author, "The Night Eternal" (2011); Writer, Producer, "Don't Be Afraid of the Dark" (2010); Producer, "Julia's Eyes" (2010); Executive Producer, "Splice" (2009); Producer, "Rage" (2009); Writer, Director, "Hellboy II: The Golden Army" (2008); Producer, "Rudo y Cursi" (2008); Executive Producer, "The Orphanage" (2007); Writer, Director, Producer, Pan's Labyrinth" (2006); Executive Producer, "Chronicles" (2004); Writer, Director, "Hellboy" (2004); Executive Producer, "I Murder Seriously" (2002); Director, Blade II" (2002); Writer, Director, Executive Producer, "The Devil's Backbone" (2001); Writer, Director, "Mimic" (1997); Writer, Director, "Cronos" (1993); Executive Producer, "Dona Herlinda and Her Son" (1985); Producer, "Hora Marcada" **AW:** Golden Globe for Best Director (2018); Best Picture, National Society of Film Critics (2007); BAFTA Award for Best Film Not in the England Language (2007); Listee, 50 Smartest People in Hollywood, Entertainment Weekly (2007); Academy Award for Best Director

DELANEY, JOHN KEVIN, T: Former U.S. Representative **I:** Government Administration/Government Relations/Government Services **DOB:** 04/16/1963 **PB:** Wood-Ridge **SC:** NJ/USA **PT:** Jack Delaney; Elaine (Rowe) Delaney **MS:** Married **SPN:** April McClain (1990) **CH:** Four children **ED:** JD, Georgetown Law (1988); BA, Columbia University (1985) **C:** Candidate, Democratic Nominee, 2020 Presidential Election (2017-2020); U.S. Representative, Maryland's Sixth Congressional District, United States Congress, Washington, DC (2013-2019); Member, Joint Economic Committee (2013-2019); Member, U.S. House Financial Services Committee (2013-2019); Co-Founder, Executive Chairman, CapitalSource, Chevy Chase, MD (2000-2012); Co-Founder, HealthCare Financial Partners, Inc. (1993-1999); Associate, Shaw Pittman, Potts, & Troubridge (Now Pillsbury Winthrop Shaw Pittman LLP) (1988-1993) **CR:** Founder, Blueprint Maryland (2011-Present) **CIV:** Board of Directors, National Symphony Orchestra; Board of Directors, Georgetown University; Board of Directors, ICRW; Chairman, St. Patrick's Episcopal Day School **AW:** Entrepreneur of the Year Award, Ernst & Young (Now EY) (2004) **PA:** Democrat **RE:** Catholic

DELAURO, ROSA LUISA, T: U.S. Representative from Connecticut **I:** Government Administration/Government Relations/Government Services **DOB:** 03/02/1943 **PB:** New Haven **SC:** CT/USA **PT:** Theodore J. DeLauro; Luisa (Canestri) DeLauro **MS:** Married **SPN:** Stanley Greenberg **CH:** Anna; Kathryn; Jonathan **ED:** MA in International Politics, Columbia University (1966); BA in History and Political Science, Marymount College, Cum Laude (1964); Master's Degree, Queen Mary University of London School of Economics **C:** Co-chair, U.S. House Committee on Democratic Steering (2003-Present); Member, U.S. House Committee on Policy (2003-Present); Member, U.S. House of Representatives from Connecticut's Third Congressional District, United States Congress (1991-Present); Executive Director, EMILY's List (1989-1990); Executive Director, Countdown '87 (1987-1988); Chief of Staff to Senator Christopher Dodd, U.S. Senate, Washington, DC (1981-1987); Campaign Manager to Senator Christopher Dodd, U.S. Senate (1979); Executive Assistant, Development Administrator, City of New Haven, CT (1977-1978); Campaign Manager, City of New Haven, CT (1977); Executive Assistant to Mayor Frank Logue, City of New Haven, CT (1976-1977); Assistant Director, Director, National Urban Fellows (1972-1975); Administrative Assistant, National Urban Fellows (1969-1972); Training Associate, Community Progress Inc., New Haven, CT (1967-1969); Committee on Appropriations **CR:** Regional Director, Dukakis for President Campaign (1988); State Director, Mondale-Ferraro Presidential Campaign, NJ (1986); City Coordinator, Carter-Mondale Presidential Campaign, New Haven, CT (1977-1979); Instructor, International Relations, Albertus Magnus College, New Haven, CT (1967-1968) **CIV:** Anti-Crime Youth Council (1993-Present); Founder, Rosa's Readers (1999); Founder, Kick Butts Connecticut; Organizer, Connecticut Jobs Fair **AW:** Bartels Fellow, University of New Haven; Corneilius Driscoll Award, New Haven St. Patrick's Day Committee **MEM:** Honorary Board Member, National Organization of Italian American Women (NOIAW); Leader, Catholic Democrats **PA:** Democrat **RE:** Roman Catholic

DELBENE, SUZAN KAY, T: U.S. Representative from Washington **I:** Government Administration/Government Relations/Government Services **DOB:** 02/17/1962 **PB:** Selma **SC:** AL/USA **PT:** Barry Oliver; Beth Oliver **MS:** Married **SPN:** Kurt DelBene (1997) **CH:** Zach; Becca **ED:** MBA, University of Washington Foster School of Business (1990); BS in Biology, Reed College (1983) **C:** Member, U.S. House of Representatives from Washington's First Congressional District, United States Congress, Washington, DC (2013-Present); Member, U.S. House Judiciary Committee (2013-Present); Member, U.S. House Committee on Agriculture (2013-Present); Director of Revenue, State of Washington, Olympia, WA (2010-2012); Management Consultant, Strategic Advisor, Global Partnerships (2008-2009); Corporate Vice President, Mobile Communications Business, Microsoft Corp. (2004-2007); Chief Executive Officer, Nimble Technology (2000-2003); Vice President, Drugstore.com (1998-2000); Director of Marketing and Business Development, Interactive Media Group, Microsoft Corp., Redmond, WA (1989-1998) **PA:** Democrat

DELCOLLE, MICHAEL, T: Owner **I:** Food & Restaurant Services **CN:** Del's Bar & Grill **DOB:** 07/29/1971 **PB:** Glen Cove **SC:** NY/USA **PT:** Frank DelColle; Phyllis Minicozzi DelColle **MS:** Married **ED:** Bachelor's in Business Management, State University of New York at Old Westbury; Associate in Business Administration, Nassau Community College **CT:** Class A Firefighter **C:** Owner, Del's Bar & Grill; With, Town of Oyster Bay; With, Prism Visual Software, Inc.; With, TelCom Corporation, NetTel USA, Inc., Fibernet Corp. AT&T and MCI (Now Verizon); Salesman, Clothes **CIV:** Firefighter, Oyster Bay Fire Department (24 Years) **AW:** 20-Year Service Award, Oyster Bay Fire Department; Brooke Jackman Award, Brooke Jackman Foundation **MEM:** Oyster Bay Fire Department; Oyster Bay-East Norwich Chamber of Commerce, Oyster Bay, NY; Oyster Bay Italian American Club, Oyster Bay, NY; Race Director, Brooke Jackman Foundation **B/I:** Mr. DelColle became involved in his profession because his dad opened the business in 1975 and ran the bar for 20 years and Mr. DelColle took it over for another two years. He moved onto a different livelihood after the bar closed, which was selling clothes imported from India with a friend. First, they started out in a basement and then moved the business to a 3,000 square-foot warehouse in New York City. After that, Mr. DelColle worked for TelCom, NetTel, Fibernet, AT&T and MCI. Route accounting software was his next endeavor at Prism Visual Software where he worked full-time for a year and part time for 13 years. He finally settled at being a garbage man for the Town of Oyster Bay for 14 years, while also working part-time for Prism. Mr. DelColle has also been an active fireman for the Oyster Bay Fire Department for 24 years. In 2007, he bought the building that his dad owned and hired a chef with 15 years of experience, who was also a garbage man, and his business has been very successful since.

DELGADO, ANTONIO RAMON, T: U.S. Representative from New York **I:** Government Administration/Government Relations/Government Services **DOB:** 01/28/1977 **PB:** Schenectady **SC:** NY/USA **PT:** Tony Delgado; Thelma P. Hill **MS:** Married **SPN:** Lacey Schwartz (2011) **CH:** Maxwell; Coltrane **ED:** JD, Harvard Law School (2005); Coursework, The Queens College, University of Oxford (2001); BA, Colgate University (1999) **C:** Member, U.S. House of Representatives from New York's 19th District (2019-Present); With, Akin Gump Strauss Hauer & Feld LLP **CW:** Rap Artist, AD the Voice, Album (2007) **PA:** Democratic

DELGADO, MANUEL EDUARDO, T: Architect, Urban Designer, Educator **I:** Education/Educational Services **CN:** Wentworth Institute of Technology **DOB:** 08/28/1949 **PB:** Caracas **SC:** Venezuela **PT:** Manuel Delgado; Gladys Arteaga Delgado **MS:** Married **SPN:** Lisette Ávila **CH:** Patricia Delgado; Oriana Silva (Grandchild); Camila Silva (Grandchild) **ED:** MS in Urban Studies and Planning, Massachusetts Institute of Technology (MIT) (2001); BArch, Universidad Central de Venezuela (1988); MA in Museography, Escuela Nacional de Conservación, Restauración, y Museografía, Churubusco, Mexico (1974) **CT:** Colegio de Arquitectos de Venezuela #1123; Colegio de Ingenieros de Venezuela #14.323 **CIV:** Board of Directors, Fenway Community Development Corporation (2007-2014); Urban Planning Committee (2002-2007); Academic Faculty Council, Elected Member, Facultad de Arquitectura y Urbanismo, Central University of Venezuela (1992-1996); Founder, Board Member, Fundación Instituto de Arquitectura Urbana (1978-1981) **CW:** Co-Author, "Urbanismo Ecológico en America Latina", Mohsen Mostafabi, Harvard University (2019); Project Manager, Urban Designer, Chief Architect, San Agustín District Master Plan, Boulevard and Public Buildings, Centro Simón Bolívar C.A., Caracas, Beltrán Alfaro (1984-1987); Architect, Benedictine Abbey of San José, Güigüe, Edo. Carabobo, Venezuela (1983-1984) **AW:** First Prize, International Design Competition, Parque Verde Metropolitano (2012); Honorable Mention, Macagua Company Airport, IX Bienal de Arquitectura, Santiago, Chile, EDELCA (1995); Research

Honorable Mention, VIII Bienal de Arquitectura de Caracas (1987) **AS:** Mr. Delgado doesn't consider what he does as a success, nor does he consider himself successful. He will always continue working. In architecture, each project is an opportunity for success. **B/I:** Mr. Delgado started teaching as a part-time professor in the Universidad Central de Venezuela when he was very young. Teaching is the path to learning, in his opinion. He became involved in his profession by sharing his experience in Mexico, where he learned from the students and connected with people in different places.

DELL, MICHAEL SAUL, T: Chairman, Chief Executive Officer, Founder **I:** Technology **CN:** Dell **DOB:** 02/23/1965 **PB:** Houston **SC:** TX/USA **PT:** Alexander Dell; Lorraine Charlotte (Langfan) Dell **MS:** Married **SPN:** Susan Lynn Lieberman (10/23/1989) **CH:** Alexa; Zachary; Juliette; Kira **ED:** Honorary Doctorate in Economic Science, University of Limerick (2002); Coursework, The University of Texas at Austin (1984) **C:** Chairman, Chief Executive Officer, Dell, Round Rock, TX (2007-Present); Chairman, Dell, Round Rock, TX (2004-2007); Chairman, Chief Executive Officer, Dell, Round Rock, TX (1984-2004); Founder, Dell Computer Corp. (Formerly PC's Ltd.), Austin, TX (1984) **CR:** Board of Directors, Startup America Partnership, LLC (2011-Present); Investor, ValleyCrest (Now BrightView Holdings, Inc.) (2006-Present); Founder, MSD Capital, L.P., New York, NY (1998-Present); Board of Directors, Dell (1984-Present); Board Member, Catalyst **CIV:** Governing Board, Indian School of Business, Hyderabad, India (2003-Present); Co-Founder, Michael & Susan Dell Foundation, Austin, TX (1999-Present); Advisory Board, Tsinghua University School of Economics and Management, Beijing, China; Global Advocate for Entrepreneurship, United Nations Foundation **CW:** Co-Author, "Direct from Dell: Strategies that Revolutionized an Industry" (1999) **AW:** One of the World's Richest People, Forbes Magazine (2007-Present); The Richest People in America, The Forbes 400 (2005-Present); Billionaires List, Forbes Magazine (2019); Named One of the World's Richest People, Business Insider (2019); Named One of the Top 50 Best CEOs of Large Companies, Comparably (2018); One of the Most Powerful People, Forbes Magazine (2018); One of the Richest in Tech, Forbes Magazine (2017); One of the Richest Persons in America's 50 Largest Cities, Forbes Magazine (2016); Bower Award for Business Leadership, Franklin Institute (2013); One of the 50 Who Matter Now, CNNMoney.com Business 2.0 (2006); One of the Top 10 Most Powerful People in Business, Fortune Magazine (2003, 2004); Chief Executive of the Year, Chief Executive Magazine (2001); Customer Satisfaction Award, JD Power (1991, 1993); CEO of the Year, Financial World Magazine (1993); Entrepreneur of the Year, Inc. Magazine (1990) **MEM:** Fellow, American Association for the Advancement of Science; Honorary Member, Foundation Board, World Economic Forum; Executive Committee, International Business Council; Technology CEO Council; The Business Council; Business Roundtable **PA:** Republican **RE:** Jewish

DELONG, BONNIE, T: Owner, Principal **I:** Education/Educational Services **CN:** Bonnie DeLong Designs **DOB:** 01/31/1954 **PB:** Bellingham **SC:** WA/USA **PT:** Orville Edward Brooks; Elizabeth Brooks **MS:** Married **SPN:** Charles Paul DeLong (07/24/1976) **CH:** Jennifer DeLong; Nicole Sunwall; Robert DeLong **ED:** Degree in Residential Design, Art Institute of Seattle, with Honors (2011); BA in Education, Washington State University (1976) **CT:** Certificate, American Society of Interior Designers; Certificate, Interior Design Continuing Edu-

cation Council **C:** Interior Designer, BDL Designs, Bonnie DeLong Designs (2011-Present); Elementary Principal, Heritage Christian School, Bothell, WA (2000-2004); Kindergarten Teacher, Heritage Christian School, Bothell, WA (1990-2000); Pre-School Teacher, Heritage Christian School, Bothell, WA (1988-1990); First Grade Teacher, Clark County Christian School, Vancouver, WA (1976-1977) **CR:** Gymnastics Coach, Junior High School (1977-1978) **CIV:** Administrator of Ministry Team, First Baptist Church, Bothell, WA (2000); Leader of Group, Bothell High Fellowship Group (1997-2000); Youth Leader, Junior and Senior High School Elim Baptist, Seattle, WA (1977-1980) **CW:** Designer, "Cinderella" Christmas Tree, Everett Providence Gala Evening **AW:** AIS graduated with Honors **MEM:** American Society of Interior Designers **MH:** Albert Nelson Marquis Lifetime Achievement Award; Marquis Who's Who Top Professional **AS:** Ms. DeLong attributes her success to her supportive husband. He always encouraged her to go after her desires and dreams. She additionally credits her supportive father for loving and encouraging her. **B/I:** Ms. DeLong entered her profession because she had a first grade teacher that taught her to read and made her feel good about herself. After that experience, she was inspired to become a teacher. She had been at the school as a parent and then as a teacher for a long time. The school had a need for a principle and they asked her. When they asked her to be a principal, Ms. DeLong completed her accreditation quickly in order to accept the position. Becoming a principle choose her, she didn't choose it she loved teaching. **AV:** Gardening; Reading; Walking; Skiing; Decorating **THT:** Be kind and generous to all. Go after your dreams. Don't give up.

DEMCHAK, WILLIAM STANTON, T: Chairman, President, Chief Executive Officer **I:** Business Management/Business Services **CN:** The PNC Financial Services Group Inc. **ED:** BS, Allegheny College (1984); MBA in Accounting, University of Michigan **C:** Chairman, PNC Financial Services Group, Inc. (2014-Present); President, Chief Executive Officer, PNC Financial Services Group, Inc., Pittsburgh, PA (2013-Present); President, PNC Financial Services Group, Inc., Pittsburgh, PA (2012-2013); Senior Vice Chairman, PNC Financial Services Group, Inc., Pittsburgh, PA (2009-2012); Head of Corporate and Institutional Banking, PNC Financial Services Group, Inc., Pittsburgh, PA (2005-2009); Vice Chairman, Chief Financial Officer, PNC Financial Services Group, Inc., Pittsburgh, PA (2002-2009); Global Head, Structured Finance & Credit Portfolio, J.P. Morgan Chase & Co. (1997-2002) **CR:** Board of Directors, PNC Financial Services Group, Inc. (2013-Present); Board of Directors, "Black Rock, Inc." (2003-Present) **CIV:** Board of Directors, Blue Mountain Credit Alternatives Ltd; Board of Directors, YMCA of Pittsburgh; Board Member, Extra Mile Education Foundation; Board Member, Greater Pittsburgh Council, Boy Scouts of America **MEM:** Financial Services Roundtable

DEMINGS, VALDEZ, "VAL" VENITA, T: U.S. Representative from Florida **I:** Government Administration/Government Relations/Government Services **DOB:** 03/12/1957 **PB:** Jacksonville **SC:** FL/USA **PT:** James Butler; Elouise Butler **MS:** Married **SPN:** Jerry Demings (1988) **CH:** Three Children **ED:** MPA, Webster University (1996); BS, Florida State University (1979) **C:** Member, U.S. House of Representatives from Florida's 10th Congressional District (2017-Present); Police Chief, Orlando Police Department (2007-2011); Commander of Special Operations (2003-2006); With, Police Office, Orlando Police Department (1983-2007); Member,

Committee on Homeland Security; Member, Committee on Oversight and Government Reform; Social Worker, Jacksonville, FL **PA:** Democrat

DEMONIC, BETTY, T: Music Educator, Retired **I:** Education/Educational Services **SC:** WV/USA **PT:** Oscar Lee Gray; Alice Elizabeth Parker **MS:** Married **SPN:** James R. DeMonic (8/3/1984) **CH:** Holly Metz **ED:** MusM in Education, West Virginia University, Morgantown, WV (1973); BS in Music Education, Concord College (1971) **CT:** Certification in Music, Elementary Education **C:** Teacher, Vocal Music, Musical Theater, Franklin HS, Somerset, NJ (1984-2015); Teacher, Voice, Musical Theater, American Academy of Dramatic Arts, New York, NY (2009-2013); Teacher, Vocal Production, American Academy of Dramatic Arts, New York City, NY (1988-1995); Teacher, Vocal Music, Drama, John Dickinson High School, Wilmington, DE (1975-1983); Teacher, Vocal Music, Sabraton Junior High School, Morgantown, WV (1974-1975); Teacher, Vocal Music, Morgantown Junior High School (1972-1974) **CR:** Director, Madrigal Singers Franklin High School **CW:** Director, Numerous Musical Theater Productions; Director, Costumes, Numerous Productions **AW:** Franklin Township Teacher of the Year, Marconel Foundation (2012-2013); New Jersey Governor's Award for Excellence in Teaching (1992, 2004); Distinguished Educator Award, Princeton University (1997) **MEM:** National Education Association; American Choral Directors Association; Music Educators National Convention; New Jersey Educators Association **MH:** Albert Nelson Marquis Lifetime Achievement Award **AS:** Ms. DeMonic attributes her success to her love for vocal performance. She loves to teach the practice to whoever she can, which is why she became a teacher. Her students were always eager to learn; it made everything all the more enjoyable. **B/I:** Ms. DeMonic became involved in her profession because it was always the only career she wanted to pursue. She liked performing as well; her big moment was working on "Madame Butterfly." She studied voice with former opera singers Francis Yend and James Benner. They taught dialect classes, inspiring Ms. DeMonic to sing in all languages. **AV:** Designing fashion and costumes **RE:** Episcopalian

DEMPSEY, MARY LU, T: Director of Health Insurance Benefits Administration **I:** Insurance **CN:** Commonwealth of Kentucky **DOB:** 03/29/1940 **PB:** Hopkinsville **SC:** KY/USA **PT:** Frank McIntosh; Lucille (Morgan) Miller **MS:** Married **SPN:** Rodney Parrish Dempsey (04/10/1965) **CH:** Frank Leslie; Thomas Parrish **ED:** BA in Journalism, University of Kentucky (1961); Coursework, Sophia Newcomb College (1957-1958) **CT:** First Certified, State and Local Government Benefits Administrators, State and Local Government Benefits Association **C:** Retired (2003); Director, Health Insurance Benefits Administration, Department of Personnel, Commonwealth of Kentucky (1986-1996); Director of Personnel, City of Hopkinsville (1982-1986); Staff Assistant, Pennyrile Area Development District, Hopkinsville, KY (1981); Operator, Sound System, Kentucky General Assembly, Frankfort, KY (1978-1980); Women's Editor, Kentucky New Era, Hopkinsville, KY (1972-1975); Information Specialist, Office Governor, Commonwealth Kentucky, Frankfort, KY (1964-1965); Women's Writer, Fort Lauderdale News (1962-1964); Reporter, Evansville Press (1961-1962) **CR:** Vice President of Marketing, National Health Care Services, Louisville, KY (1996-2003) **CIV:** President, La Jardinere Garden Club, Frankfort, KY (1980); President, Grace Episcopal Church Women, Hopkinsville, KY (1970); Publicity Chair, Democratic Women of Kentucky, Frankfort, KY (1965-1967) **CW:** Creator,

"KENTUCKY KARE"; Initiator, Accredited Program, State and Local Government Healthcare Administrators, SALGBA; Assistant Editor, Woman's Page, Fort Lauderdale Sun; Editor, Woman's Page, Hopkinsville, KY **AW:** Community Appreciation Award, City of Hopkinsville (1968); Best Women's Page, Kentucky Press Association **MEM:** Board of Directors, President, State and Local Government Benefits Association (1989-1992); Chartered, Board of Directors, President, Kentucky Intergovernmental Personnel Association (1984-1985) **MH:** Albert Nelson Marquis Lifetime Achievement Award **B/I:** Ms. Dempsey was inspired to pursue healthcare during her time as a personnel director for the City of Hopkinsville. She was successful, which later provided her with a foundation on which to become the president of the State and Local Government Benefits Administrators (SALGBA) of the United States. **AV:** Gardening; Traveling; Reading **PA:** Democrat **RE:** Disciple of Christ

DENCH, JUDI, T: Actress **I:** Media & Entertainment **DOB:** 12/09/1934 **PB:** York **SC:** England/United Kingdom **PT:** Reginald Arthur Dench; Eleanora Olave (Jones) Dench **SPN:** Michael Williams (02/05/1971, Deceased 01/11/ 2001) **CH:** Tara Cressida Frances **ED:** Honorary ArtsD, University of Winchester (2019); Honorary ArtsD, Harvard University (2017); Honorary Doctor of the University, University of Stirling (2013); Honorary LittD, Nottingham Trent University (2010); Honorary LittD, University of St. Andrews (2008); Honorary LittD, Trinity College (2003); Honorary LittD, University of Leeds (2002); Honorary LittD, University of Durham (2001); Honorary LittD, Queen Margaret University (2000); Honorary LittD, University of Oxford (2000); Honorary LittD, York University (1983); Honorary LittD, Warwick University (1978); Coursework, Central School Speech Training (Now Royal Central School of Speech and Drama) **CW:** Actress, "Artemis Fowl" (2020); Actress, "Cats" (2019); Actress, "All Is True" (2018); Actress, "Red Joan" (2018); Actress, "Nothing Like a Dame" (2018); Actress, "Tulip Fever" (2017); Actress, "Victoria & Abdul" (2017); Actress, "Murder on the Orient Express" (2017); Actress, "Miss Peregrine's Home for Peculiar Children" (2016); Voice Actress, "Schadenfreude" (2016); Actress, "Roald Dahl's Esio Trot" (2015); Actress, "The Vote" (2015); Actress, "The Second Best Exotic Marigold Hotel" (2015); Actress, "The Vote" (2015); Actress, "The Winter's Tale" (2015); Actress, "Philomena" (2013); Actress, "National Theatre Live: 50 Years on Stage" (2013); Actress, "Peter and Alice" (2013); Actress, "Run for Your Wife" (2012); Actress, "Stars in Shorts" (2012); Actress, "Skyfall" (2012); Actress, "Pirates of the Caribbean: On Stranger Tides" (2011); Actress, "Jane Eyre" (2011); Actress, "J. Edgar" (2011); Actress, "My Week with Marilyn" (2011); Actress, "The Best Exotic Marigold Hotel" (2011); Author, "And Furthermore" (2011); Actress, "A Midsummer Night's Dream" (2010); Actress, "Madame de Sade" (2009); Actress, "Nine" (2009); Actress, "Quantum of Solace" (2008); Actress, "Cranford" (2007); Actress, "Hay Fever" (2006); Actress, "The Merry Wives of Windsor" (2006); Voice Actress, "Doogal" (2006); Actress, "Casino Royale" (2006); Actress, "Notes on a Scandal" (2006); Actress, "Pride & Prejudice" (2005); Actress, "Mrs. Henderson Presents" (2005); Actress, "The Chronicles of Riddick" (2004); Actress, "Ladies in Lavender" (2004); Voice Actress, "Home on the Range" (2004); Actress, "All's Well That Ends Well, London and Stratford-upon-Avon" (2003-2004); Actress, "Iris" (2002); Actress, "The Shipping News" (2002); Actress, "The Importance of Being Ernest" (2002); Actress, "Die Another Day" (2002); Actress, "The Breath of Life" (2002); Actress, "The Royal Family"

(2001); Actress, "The Last of the Blond Bombshells" (2000); Actress, "Chocolat" (2000); Actress, "Tea With Mussolini" (1999); Actress, "The World Is Not Enough" (1999); Actress, "Amy's View," NY (1999); Actress, "Shakespeare in Love" (1998); Actress, "Filumena," London, United Kingdom (1997, 1998); Actress, "Tomorrow Never Dies" (1997); Actress, "GoldenEye" (1995); Actress, "A Little Night Music" (1995); Actress, "Jack & Sarah" (1994); Actress, "The Seagull," Aldwych, United Kingdom (1994); Actress, "The Gift of the Gorgon," Aldwych, United Kingdom (1992-1993); Actress, "The Sea, Coriolanus," Aldwych, United Kingdom (1992); Actress, "The Cherry Orchard," Aldwych, United Kingdom (1989, 1990); Actress, "Henry V" (1989); Actress, "A Handful of Dust" (1988); Actress, "Mr. and Mrs. Edgehill" (1988); Actress, "Mr. and Mrs. Nobody," Aldwych, United Kingdom (1988); Actress, "Wetherby" (1985); Actress, "Juno and the Paycock," Aldwych, United Kingdom (1981); Actress, "Cymbeline," Royal Shakespeare Company, Stratford, United Kingdom (1979); Actress, "The Way of the World," Royal Shakespeare Company, London, United Kingdom (1977-1978); Actress, "King Lear," Royal Shakespeare Company, Stratford, United Kingdom (1976-1977); Actress, "The Good Companions," London, United Kingdom (1974-1975); Actress, "The Gay Lord Quex," London, United Kingdom (1975); Actress, "The Wolf," Oxford and London, United Kingdom (1974); Actress, "London Assurance," London, United Kingdom (1973); Actress, "Twelfth Night," Royal Shakespeare Company, Stratford, United Kingdom (1972); Actress, "The Duchess of Malfi," Royal Shakespeare Company, Stratford, United Kingdom (1971); Actress, "London Assurance," United Kingdom (1970); Actress, "A Winter's Tale," United Kingdom (1969); Actress, "Sally Bowles in Cabaret," London, United Kingdom (1968); Actress, "The Promise," Oxford and London, United Kingdom (1966-1967); Actress, "Talking to a Stranger" (1966); Actress, "He Who Rides a Tiger" (1965); Actress, "A Study in Terror" (1965); Actress, "Four in the Morning" (1965); Actress, "Romeo and Jeanette," Oxford (1964); Actress, "A Penny for a Song," Royal Shakespeare Company, Stratford, United Kingdom (1961-1962); Actress, "Romeo and Juliet," The Old Vic (1959-1961); Actress, "Romeo and Juliet," (Paladino d'Argentino), Venice Festival (1961); Actress, "Twelfth Night," The Old Vic (1957-1958); Actress, "Hamlet," The Old Vic; Actress, "Midsummer Night's Dream," The Old Vic; Actress, "The Importance of Being Earnest," The Old Vic; Actress, "As You Like It," The Old Vic; Actress, "The Cherry Orchard," Royal Shakespeare Company, Stratford, United Kingdom; Actress, "Measure for Measure," Royal Shakespeare Company, Stratford, United Kingdom; Actress, "Midsummer Night's Dream," Royal Shakespeare Company, Stratford, United Kingdom; Actress, "The Alchemist," Oxford Playhouse; Actress, "The Three Sisters," Oxford Playhouse; Actress, "Twelfth Night, Royal Shakespeare Company, London, United Kingdom; Actress, "The Merchant of Venice, Royal Shakespeare Company, Stratford, United Kingdom; Actress, "Much Ado About Nothing," Royal Shakespeare Company, Stratford, United Kingdom; Actress, "The Comedy of Errors," Royal Shakespeare Company, Stratford, United Kingdom; Actress, "Macbeth," Royal Shakespeare Company, Stratford, United Kingdom; Actress, "Pillars of the Community," Royal Shakespeare Company, London, United Kingdom; Actress, "A Kind of Alaska," Aldwych, United Kingdom; Actress, "The Importance of Being Earnest," Aldwych, United Kingdom; Actress, "Pack of Lies," Aldwych, United Kingdom; Actress, "Antony and Cleopatra," Aldwych, United Kingdom ; Actress, "Gertrude in Hamlet," Aldwych, United Kingdom;

Actress, "The Blough and the Stars," Aldwych, United Kingdom; Director, "Much Ado About Nothing"; Director, "Look Back in Anger"; Director, "The Boys from Syracuse"; Director, "Romeo and Juliet"; Actress, "Major Barbara"; Actress, "Jackanory"; Actress, "Neighbours"; Actress, "Marching Song"; Actress, "Days to Come"; Actress, "The Comedy of Errors"; Actress, "Macbeth"; Actress, "Village Wooing"; Actress, "Love in a Cold Climate"; Actress, "A Fine Romance"; Actress, "The Cherry Orchard"; Actress, "Going Gently"; Actress, "Saigon"; Actress, "Ghosts"; Actress, "Make and Break"; Actress, "Behaving Badly"; Actress, "Can You Hear Me Thinking"; Actress, "Torch"; Actress, "Absolute Hell"; Actress, "As Time Goes By"; Actress, "A Midsummer Night's Dream"; Actress, "The Third Secret"; Actress, "Dead Cert"; Actress, "A Room with a View"; Actress, "84 Charing Cross Road"; Actress, "Mrs. Brown" **AW:** Praemium Imperiale (2011); Lucy Cavendish College Fellow, Cambridge, England (2005); Named to Order of the Companions of Honour (2005); Olivier Award Lifetime Achievement (2004); Evening Standard Theater Award (2004); BAFTA Fellow (2001); Walpole Medal, New York (2000); Benjamin Franklin Medal, Royal Society of the Arts (The RSA), London, United Kingdom (2000); Golden Globe Award for Best Supporting Actress, Hollywood Foreign Press Association (2000); Tony Award for Best Performance by a Leading Role in a Play (1999); Academy Award for Best Supporting Actress for Shakespeare in Love, Academy of Motion Picture Arts and Sciences (1999); UK Entertainment Personality of Year, Variety (1999); Academy Award for Best Supporting Actress, Academy of Motion Picture Arts and Sciences (1998); Critics Circle Drama Award (1997); British Academy Film and TV Arts Scotland Award (1997); Critics Circle Film Award (1997); Golden Globe Award for Best Actress, Hollywood Foreign Press Association (1997); Rothermore Award for Lifetime Achievement (1997); Oliver Award for Best Actress in a Musical (1996); Olivier Award for Best Actress (1996); BAFTA Award for Best Actress in a Supporting Role (1989); BAFTA Award for Best Actress (1968); BAFTA Award for Most Promising Newcomer (1965); ACE Award; BAFTA Award for Best Actress; Standard Best Actress Award; Plays and Players Awards for Best Actress; SWET Best Actress Awards; Evening Standard Drama Award for Best Actress; Variety Club Award for Actress of the Year; Laurence Olivier Theatre Award; Evening Standard Drama Award; Drama Magazine Award; Critics Circle Award for Outstanding Service to the Arts; Tony Award for Best Actress; Named Dame, Commander, Order of the British Empire **MEM:** Honorary Member, American Academy of Arts & Sciences **RE:** Religious Society of Friends

DENEGALL, JOHN P. JR., T: Construction Executive **I:** Architecture & Construction **CN:** Nico Asphalt Paving Inc. **DOB:** 03/21/1959 **PB:** Tarrytown **SC:** NY/USA **PT:** John P. Denegall Sr.; Edna D. (Kirkaldy) Denegall **MS:** Divorced **SPN:** Johnnie Lou Jarrett (02/27/1982, Divorced) **CH:** John P. Denegall III; Revisa Taylor Denegall **ED:** Coursework, Westchester Community College, Vahalla, NY (1977-1980); Diploma in Mechanical Engineering and Design, Thomas A. Edison Career and Technical Education High School, Jamaica, NY (1977) **CT:** Notary Public, State of New York (2001) **C:** Vice President, Nico Asphalt Paving Inc., Brooklyn, NY (1999-Present); Risk Manager, City Wide Asphalt Paving Co. Inc., Brooklyn, NY (1996-1999); Senior Insurance Claims Representative, Crum & Forster Commercial Insurance, New York, NY (1985-1996); Insurance Claims Adjuster, Liberty Mutual Insurance, New York, NY (1981-1985); Manager, Radio Shack, Yorktown Heights, NY (1980-1981);

Manager, Elmsford Raceway Inc., NY (1976-1980) **CR:** Founder, Moran Bay Equities (2008-Present); Board of Directors, Harlemads.com (2004); Founding Partner, Family-Tree Investments (1999); President, Eva's Laundry Inc., Bronx, NY (1989-1994); Denegall Properties, Inc., Jamaica, NY (1986-1989); Arbitrator, Insurance Arbitration Forum, New York, NY (1986) **CIV:** President, Briarwood Community Association **MH:** Albert Nelson Marquis Lifetime Achievement Award; Marquis Who's Who Top Professional **B/I:** Mr. Denegall became involved in his profession due to his interest in automotive engineering, particularly in regards to race cars. He worked in numerous different professions, and eventually learned more about business and entrepreneurship. **AV:** Bicycling; Auto racing; Basketball **PA:** Republican **RE:** Presbyterian

DENMARK-WESNER, FLORENCE HARRIET, DHL, PHD, T: Distinguished Research Professor **I:** Education/Educational Services **CN:** Pace University **DOB:** 01/28/1931 **PB:** Philadelphia **SC:** PA/USA **PT:** Morris Levin; Minnerva (Sharkis) Levin **MS:** Married **SPN:** Robert W. Wesner; Stanley J. Denmark (06/07/1953, Divorced 1973) **CH:** Valerie; Pamela (Deceased); Richard **ED:** DHL, Allegheny College (1998); PsyD, Illinois School of Professional Psychology, Argosy University (1995); DHL, Cedar Crest College (1988); DHL, Massachusetts School of Professional Psychology (Now William James College) (1985); PhD, University of Pennsylvania (1958); AM, University of Pennsylvania (1954); AB, University of Pennsylvania (1952) **C:** Adjunct Professor, City University of New York (1990-Present); Robert Scott Pace, Distinguished Research Professor, Psychology, Pace University, New York, NY (1988-Present); Chairman, Psychology Department, Pace University, New York, NY (1988-Present); Professor, Psychology, City University of New York (1984-1990); Professor, City University of New York (1964-1990); Instructor, City University of New York (1964-1990); Affiliate, Doctoral Faculty of Psychology, City University of New York (1967-1987); Lecturer in Psychology, City University of New York (1959-1966) **CR:** Organizer, Lecturer, International Counsel of Psychologists (2017); Fellow, New York Academy of Sciences (1966); Fellow, American Psychological Association **CW:** Co-Editor, "Psychology of Women," Third Edition (2017); Co-Editor, "Engendering Psychology" (2000); Co-Editor, "Females and Autonomy: A Life-Span Perspective" (1999); Co-Editor, "Violence and the Prevention of Violence" (1995); Editor, "Psychology: The Leading Edge Into the Unknown" (1980); Co-Editor, "Women: Dependent or Independent Variable?" (1975); Editor, "Who Discriminates Against Women?" (1974); Co-Editor, "Hand Book of the Psychology of Women, Third Edition"; Contributor, Chapters, Books; Contributor, Articles, Professional Journals **AW:** Recognition for Mentoring and Co-Founding, Association for Women in Psychology (2019); Distinguished Contributions to International Psychology Award, American Psychological Association (1999); Inter-American Award, Inter-American Society of Psychology, Inc. (1997); Distinguished Contributions to International Psychology Award, American Psychological Association (1996); Distinguished Career Award, The Association for Women in Psychology (1996); Margaret Floy Washburn Award, New York State Psychological Association (1996); Allen V. Williams Jr. Memorial Award, New York State Psychological Association (1994); Distinguished Contributions to Psychology in Public Interest, American Psychological Association (1993); Centennial Award, American Psychological Association (1992); Carolyn Wood Sherif Award, New York State Psychological Association (1992); Wilhelm Wundt Award, New York State Psychological Asso-

ciation (1988); Outstanding Women in Science Award, The Association for Women in Psychology (1980); Kurt Lewin Award, New York State Psychological Association (1978); Mellon Scholarship, St. Olaf College (1977); Grantee, Center for Human Relations, University of Pennsylvania; Recipient, Grant, U.S. Office of Education (Now U.S. Department of Education); Grantee, Research Foundation for the State University of New York; Grantee, New York Community Trust; Grantee, National Science Foundation; Grantee, Ford Foundation; Grantee, National Endowment for the Humanities; Grantee, National Institute of Mental Health; Grantee Muskowini Fund; Grantee, Pace University **MEM:** Psychology Advisory Committee, New York Academy of Sciences (1971-Present); President, Division 52, American Psychological Association (1999); Committee on Accreditation, American Psychological Association (1998); President, Academy Division, New York State Psychological Association (1990-1991); Board of Directors, Eastern Psychological Association (1988-1991); President, Division of Social Psychology, New York State Psychological Association (1989-1990); President, International Council of Psychologists (1989-1990); Vice President, The New York Academy of Sciences (1984-1987); President, Eastern Psychological Association (1986); Executive Board Member, The President's Council (1983-1984); President, American Psychological Association (1980); National President, Psi Chi, the International Honor Society in Psychology (1978-1980); American Psychological Society; Interamerican Society of Psychology; Vice President, International Organization for the Study of Group Tensions; Secretary, President's Council; International Council of Psychologists; Association for Women in Psychology; Society for the Advancement of Social Psychology; Council of Graduate Departments of Psychology; Otto Klineberg Intercultural and International Relations Awards Committee, Society for Psychological the Study of Social Issues; Century Association; Chemists' Club **MH:** Albert Nelson Marquis Lifetime Achievement Award; Marquis Who's Who Top Professional; Marquis Who's Who Humanitarian Award **AV:** Opera; Ballet; Theater; Travel; Sports **THT:** Dr. Denmark-Wesner has a book that was released in 2018 called "Women in Leadership," which she co-edited with Michele Paludi, PhD.

DENNEHY, BRIAN MANION, T: Actor **I:** Media & Entertainment **YOP:** 2020 **DOB:** 07/09/1938 **PB:** Bridgeport **SC:** CT/USA **PT:** Edward Dennehy; Hannah (Mannion) Dennehy **MS:** Married **SPN:** Jennifer Arnott (1988); Judith Scheff (1959, Divorced 1974) **CH:** Five Children **ED:** BA in History, Columbia University (1965) **MIL:** United States Marines (1958-1963) **CW:** Actor, "Son of the South" (2020); Actor, "3 Days with Dad" (2019); Actor, "Master Maggie" (2019); Actor, "Driveways" (2019); Actor, "The Song of Sway Lake" (2018); Actor, "Tag" (2018); Actor, "The Seagull" (2018); Actor, "A Very Merry Toy Store" (2017); Actor, "Hap and Leonard" (2017); Actor, "The Blacklist" (2016-2019); Actor, "The Ultimate Legacy" (2016); Actor, "Public Morals" (2015); Actor, "Knight of Cups" (2015); Actor, "Cocked" (2015); Actor, "Love Letters" (1993, 2014); Actor, "The Big C" (2013); Actor, "The Challenger Disaster" (2013); Voice Actor, "Kinect Fun Labs: Kinect Rush – A Disney Pixar Adventures: Snapshot" (2012); Actor, "The Good Wife" (2012); Actor, "Twelfth Knight" (2012); Actor, "The Big Year" (2011); Actor, "The Big Year" (2011); Actor, "Alleged" (2010); Actor, "The Next Three Days" (2010); Actor, "Rizzoli & Isles" (2010); Actor, "Meet Monica Velour" (2010); Actor, "Every Day" (2010); Actor, "Nolan Knows Best" (2010); Actor, "Carrie Underwood: Temporary Home" (2010); Actor, "Bunker Hill" (2009); Actor, "Rules of Engagement"

(2009); Actor, "Righteous Kill" (2008); Actor, "Cat City" (2008); Actor, "30 Rock" (2008); Actor, "War Eagle, Arkansas" (2007); Actor, "Welcome to Paradise" (2007); Actor, "Masters of Science Fiction" (2007); Actor, "Ratatouille" (2007); Actor, "Marco Polo" (2007); Actor, "Law & Order: Special Victims Unit" (2007); Actor, "The Ultimate Gift" (2006); Actor, "Everyone's Hero" (2006); Actor, "The 4400" (2006); Actor, "10th & Wolf" (2006); Actor, "Our Fathers" (2005); Actor, "The West Wing" (2005); Actor, "The Exonerated" (2005); Actor, "Assault on Precinct 13" (2005); Actor, "Category 6: Day of Destruction" (2004); Actor, "She Hates Me" (2004); Actor, "Behind the Camera: The Unauthorized Story of 'Three's Company'" (2003); Actor, "Just Shoot Me" (1998-2003); Actor, "The Roman Spring of Mrs. Stone" (2003); Actor, "The Agency" (2003); Actor, "The Crooked E: The Unshredded Truth About Enron" (2003); Actor, "Great Performances" (1981-2002); Actor, "A Season on the Brink" (2002); Actor, "Stolen Summer" (2002); Executive Producer, Actor, "Three Blind Mice" (2001); Actor, "Summer Catch" (2001); Director, Actor, "Night Visions" (2001); Co-executive Producer, Actor, "The Fighting Fitzgeralds" (2001); Executive Producer, Actor, "Warden of Red Rock" (2001); Actor, "Dish Dogs" (2000); Actor, "Fail Safe" (2000); Actor, "American Experience" (2000); Executive Producer, Actor, "Death of a Salesman" (2000); Actor, "Silicon Towers" (1999); Actor, "Sirens" (1999); Actor, "Out of the Cold" (1999); Actor, "Too Rich: The Secret Life of Doris Duke" (1999); Actor, "Net-Force" (1999); Actor, "Voyage of Terror" (1998); Actor, "Thanks of a Grateful Nation" (1998); Director, Executive Producer, Actor, "Indefensible: The Truth About Edward Brannigan" (1997); Actor, "Nostromo" (1996-1997); Director, Writer, Co-Executive Producer, Actor, "Jack Reed: Death and Vengeance" (1996); Actor, "Romeo + Juliet" (1996); Actor, "Undue Influence" (1996); Actor, "Dead Man's Walk" (1996); Actor, "A Season in Purgatory" (1996); Director, Writer, Actor, "Jack Reed: A Killer Among Us" (1996); Director, Writer, Executive Producer, Actor, "Shadow of a Doubt" (1995); Director, Writer, Co-executive Producer, Actor, "Jack Reed: One of Our Own" (1995); Actor, "The Stars Fell on Henrietta" (1995); Actor, "Tommy Boy" (1995); Actor, "Screen Two" (1994); Director, Writer, Co-executive Producer, Actor, "Jack Reed: A Search for Justice" (1994); Actor, "Leave of Absence" (1994); Actor, "Birdland" (1994); Actor, "Murder in the Heartland" (1993); Co-Executive Producer, Actor, "Jack Reed: Badge of Honor" (1993); Actor, "Final Appeal" (1993); Actor, "Prophet of Evil: The Ervil LeBaron Story" (1993); Actor, "Foreign Affairs" (1993); Actor, "Deadly Matrimony" (1992); Actor, "Teamster Boss: The Jackie Presser Story" (1992); Actor, "The Great Diamond Robbery" (1992); Actor, "Gladiator" (1992); Actor, "The Burden of Proof" (1992); Actor, "To Catch a Killer" (1992); Actor, "F/X2" (1991); Actor, "In Broad Daylight" (1991); Actor, "Presumed Innocent" (1990); Actor, "Rising Son" (1990); Actor, "A Killing in a Small Town" (1990); Actor, "The Last of the Finest" (1990); Actor, "Pride and Extreme Prejudice" (1989); Actor, "Perfect Witness" (1989); Actor, "Seven Minutes" (1989); Actor, "Indio" (1989); Actor, "Day One" (1989); Actor, "Cocoon: The Return" 1988); Actor, "Miles from Home" (1988); Actor, "The Lion of Africa" (1988); Actor, "Return to Snowy River" (1988); Actor, "A Father's Revenge" (1988); Actor, "Miami Vice" (1987); Actor, "Best Seller" (1987); Actor, "The Belly of an Architect" (1987); Actor, "Faerie Tale Theatre" (1987); Actor, "Legal Eagles" (1986); Actor, "The Check in the Mail" (1986); Actor, "Acceptable Risks" (1986); Actor, "F/X" (1986); Actor, "Evergreen" (1985); Actor, "The Last Place on Earth" (1985); Actor, "Tall Tales & Legends" (1985); Actor, "Twice in a

Lifetime" (1985); Actor, "Silverado" (1985); Actor, "Cocoon" (1985); Actor, "The Ferret" (1984); Actor, "The River Rat" (1984); Actor, "Hunter" (1984); Actor, "Pigs vs. Freaks" (1984); Actor, "Finders Keepers" (1984); Actor, "Cagney & Lacey" (1984); Actor, "Gorky Park" (1983); Actor, "Never Cry Wolf" (1983); Actor, "Blood Feud" (1983); Actor, "I Take These Men" (1982); Actor, "Star of the Family" (1982); Actor, "First Blood" (1982); Actor, "Split Image" (1982); Actor, "BBC2 Playhouse" (1982); Actor, "Darkroom" (1981); Actor, "Dynasty" (1981); Actor, "Skokie" (1981); Actor, "Fly Away Home" (1981); Actor, "Knots Landing" (1980); Actor, "A Rumor of War" (1980); Actor, "The Seduction of Miss Leona" (1980); Actor, "Little Miss Marker" (1980); Actor, "Big Shamus, Little Shamus" (1979); Actor, "10" (1979); Actor, "Butch and Sundance: The Early Days" (1979); Actor, "Dummy" (1979); Actor, "The Jericho Mile" (1979); Actor, "Silent Victory: The Kitty O'Neil Story" (1979); Actor, "A Real American Hero" (1978); Actor, "Pearl" (1978); Actor, "Foul Play" (1978); Actor, "Dallas" (1978); Actor, "F.I.S.T." (1978); Actor, "A Death in Canaan" (1978); Actor, "Ruby and Oswald" (1978); Actor, "The Tony Randall Show" (1978); Actor, "Ants!" (1977); Actor, "Semi-Tough" (1977); Actor, "Looking for Mr. Goodbar" (1977); Actor, "Lou Grant" (1977); Actor, "The Fitzpatricks" (1977); Actor, "Lucan" (1977); Actor, "Bumpers" (1977); Actor, "Handle with Care" (1977); Actor, "M*A*S*H" (1977); Actor, "Police Woman" (1977); Actor, "Lannigan's Rabbi" (1977); Actor, "Johnny, We Hardly Knew Ye" (1977); Actor, "Serpico" (1977); Actor, "Kojak" (1977) **AW:** Inductee, American Theater Hall of Fame (2010); Tony Award for Best Actor in a Play (1999, 2003); Screen Actors Guild Award for Outstanding Performance by a Male Actor in a Miniseries or Television Movie, SAG-AFTRA (2001); Award for Outstanding Producer, of Long-Form Television, Producers Guild of America (2001); Golden Globe Award for Best Actor - Miniseries or Television Film (2001); Drama Desk Award for Outstanding Actor in a Play (1999); CableAce Award for Best Actor in a Miniseries or a Movie (1994)

DENTON, ROBERT, "PETE" WILLIAM, T: Chief Executive Officer **I:** Business Management/Business Services **CN:** Related Enterprises of R.W. Denton Co. **DOB:** 05/27/1944 **PB:** Wilmington **SC:** DE/USA **PT:** William R. Denton; Margaret L. (Mitchell) Denton **MS:** Married **SPN:** Donna Hughes Denton (12/20/1978) **CH:** Dyanna C. Brown; Rhett W. Denton; Whitney E. Denton **ED:** Postgraduate Coursework, Harvard University (1985); EdD, University of South Carolina (1980); Postgraduate Coursework, University of Kentucky (1975); Master's Degree in Accountancy, University of South Carolina (1973); MBA, University of South Carolina (1967); BBA, University of South Carolina (1966) **CT:** Licensed Real Estate Broker in Charge, South Carolina and North Carolina; Licensed General Insurance Agency, South Carolina and North Carolina; Licensed as Master Mariner, United States Coast Guard; United States Private Instrument Rated Pilot **C:** President, Dominion Sovereign Financial Service (1996-Present); Residential Real Estate (1996-Present); President, Alpine of South Carolina, Commercial Real Estate (1996-Present); President, Better Enterprises, Car Care Centers (1996-Present); Chief Executive Officer, R.W. Denton Co. (1994-Present); Emeritus Treasurer, Vice President, University of South Carolina (1996); Special Assistant to the President, University of South Carolina, Columbia (1994-1996); University of South Carolina, Columbia, SC (1966-1996); Treasurer, Executive Vice President, Business and Finance, University of South Carolina, Columbia, SC (1988-1994); Senior Vice President, Business and Finance, University of South Carolina, Colum-

bia (1983-1988); System Vice President, Fiscal Affairs, University of South Carolina, Columbia, SC (1981-1983); Vice President, Finance, University of South Carolina, Columbia, SC (1977-1981); Assistant Vice President, Finance, University of South Carolina, Columbia, SC (1976-1977); Instructor, Assistant Budget Director, Budget Director, Director of Accounting Staff Training, University of South Carolina, Columbia (1967-1976) **CR:** Expert Advisor, Board of Directors, Southern Association of Colleges and Universities; Criteria and Review Committee, Southern Association of Colleges and Universities; Visiting Accreditation Committees, Southern Association of Colleges and Universities; Chairman, Board of Directors, Faculty House of Carolina; Chairman, Board of Directors, University of South Carolina Auxiliary Services Foundation; Board of Directors, National Association of College and University Business Officers; Chair, Professional Development Committee, National Association of College and University Business Officers; Board of Directors, President, Executive Committee, Program Committee, Audit Committee, News Letter Editor, Southern Association of College and University Business Officers; Board Member, Southeastern Manufacturing Tech Center; Board of Directors, South Carolina Student Loan Corporation; Car Care Trade Associations **CIV:** Chairman, Board of Directors, Better Business Bureau, Inc.; Executive Committee, Commissioned, Admiral of Texas Navy; Commissioned, Kentucky Colonel; Order of The Palmetto for the State of South Carolina **CW:** Author, "The Shopping Mall on Campus: A Guide for Planning, Implementing, and Administering" (1993); Co-Author, "Current Issues in College and University Human Resources" (1993); Author, "A Study Guide for Use with Financial Accounting: A Basic Approach" (1980); Contributor, Articles, Professional Journals **AW:** Order of the Palmetto, State of South Carolina **MEM:** South Carolina Associates; University of South Carolina Alumni Association; Ducks Unlimited; The Palmetto Club; Beta Alpha Psi; Beta Gamma Sigma; Phi Delta Kappa Omicron Delta Epsilon; Omicron Delta Kappa; Kappa Sigma **BAR:** Admitted to Practice as Expert, Business Financial and Accounting, State of South Carolina Courts **MH:** Albert Nelson Marquis Lifetime Achievement Award **AS:** Dr. Denton attributes his success to having a wonderful upbringing and being given opportunities. He grew up in a small town and was raised with an appreciation for hard work and strong ethics. His father was a businessman, and his mom provided strict lessons in social skills and proper behavior. He was inspired by unselfish acts by many mentors, both known and unknown. **B/I:** Dr. Denton became involved in his work as a result of those who mentored him. His strong work ethic and drive to make the world a better place was a consistent motivator. **AV:** Sailing; Flying as an instrument-related pilot in command; Traveling; Practicing horticulture; Sportfishing **PA:** Republican **RE:** Christian

DEPP, JOHNNY, T: Actor **I:** Media & Entertainment **DOB:** 06/09/1963 **PB:** Owensboro **SC:** KY/USA **PT:** John Depp; Betty Sue (Palmer) Wells **MS:** Divorced **SPN:** Amber Heard (02/03/2015, Divorced 05/2016); Lori Anne Allison (12/20/1983, Divorced 1985) **CH:** Lily-Rose Melody; Jack Christo **CIV:** Honorary Member, Comanche Nation, OK **CW:** Actor, "Minamata" (2020); Actor, "Waiting for the Barbarians" (2019); Actor, "City of Lies" (2018); Actor, "The Professor" (2018); Actor, "London Fields" (2018); Actor, "Sherlock Gnomes" (2018); Actor, "Fantastic Beasts: The Crimes of Grindelwald" (2018); Actor, "Richard Says Goodbye" (2018); Actor, "Labyrinth" (2018); Actor, "Pirates of the Caribbean: Dead Men Tell No Tales" (2017); Actor, "Murder on the Orient Express" (2017);

Actor, "Donald Trump's The Art of the Deal: The Movie" (2016); Actor, "Yoga Hosers" (2016); Actor, "Alice Through the Looking Glass" (2016); Actor, "Fantastic Beasts and Where to Find Them" (2016); Actor, Producer, "Mortdecai" (2015); Actor, "Black Mass" (2015); Actor, "London Fields" (2015); Actor, "Transcendence" (2014); Actor, "Tusk" (2014); Actor, "Into the Woods" (2014); Actor, Executive Producer, "The Lone Ranger" (2013); Actor, "For No Good Reason" (2012); Actor, Producer, "Dark Shadows" (2012); Voice Actor, "Rango" (2011); Actor, "Pirates of the Caribbean: On Stranger Tides" (2011); Actor, "The Rum Diary" (2011); Actor, "Life's Too Short" (2011); Actor, "Alice in Wonderland" (2010); Actor, "The Tourist" (2010); Actor, "Public Enemies" (2009); Actor, "Spongebob Squarepants" (2009); Actor, "This American Life" (2008); Actor, "Pirates of the Caribbean: At World's End" (2007); Actor, "Sweeney Todd: The Demon Barber of Fleet Street" (2007); Narrator, "Deep Sea 3D" (2006); Actor, "Pirates of the Caribbean: Dead Man's Chest" (2006); Voice Actor, "Kingdom Hearts II" (2005); Actor, "Charlie and the Chocolate Factory" (2005); Voice Actor, "Corpse Bride" (2005); Voice Actor, "King of the Hill" (2004); Actor, "Secret Window" (2004); Actor, "Ils se Marièrent et Eurent Beaucoup D'Enfants" (2004); Actor, "Finding Neverland" (2004); Actor, "The Libertine" (2004); Actor, "Pirates of the Caribbean: The Curse of the Black Pearl" (2003); Actor, "Once Upon a Time in Mexico" (2003); Actor, "Blow" (2001); Actor, "From Hell" (2001); Actor, "The Man Who Cried" (2000); Actor, "Chocolat" (2000); Actor, "The Fast Show" (2000); Actor, "The Vicar of Dibley" (1999); Actor, "The Source" (1999); Actor, "The Ninth Gate" (1999); Actor, "Just to Be Together" (1999); Actor, "The Astronaut's Wife" (1999); Actor, "Sleepy Hollow" (1999); Actor, "The Source" (1999); Actor, "The Vicar of Dibley" (1999); Actor, "The Astronaut's Wife" (1998); Actor, "L.A. Without a Map" (1998); Actor, "Fear and Loathing in Las Vegas" (1998); Actor, "Donnie Brasco" (1997); Writer, Director, Actor, "The Brave" (1997); Actor, "Nick of Time" (1996); Actor, "Arizona Dreamer, Don Juan DeMarco" (1995); Actor, "Dead Man" (1995); Actor, "Ed Wood" (1994); Actor, "Benny & Joon" (1993); Actor, "What's Eating Gilbert Grape" (1993); Actor, "American Dreamers" (1992); Actor, "Freddy's Dead: The Final Nightmare" (1991); Actor, "Cry-Baby" (1990); Actor, "Edward Scissorhands" (1990); Actor, "21 Jump Street" (1987-1990); Actor, "Hotel" (1987); Actor, "Platoon" (1986); Actor, Producer, "Slow Burn" (1986); Actor, "Lady Blue" (1985); Actor, "Private Resort" (1985); Guitar, Rock City Angels (1985); Actor, "A Nightmare on Elm Street" (1984); Guitarist, The Flame; Guitarist, the Kids **AW:** Named Favorite Animated Voice, People's Choice Awards (2012); MTV Generation Award, MTV Movie Awards (2012); Recipient, People's Choice Awards (2010, 2011, 2012); Recipient, Nickelodeon Kids' Choice Awards (2008); Named Best Comedic Performance, MTV Movie Awards (2008); Named Best Villain, MTV Movie Awards (2008); Golden Globe for Best Performance by an Actor in a Motion Picture - Musical or Comedy, Hollywood Foreign Press Association (2008); Named Choice Movie Villain, Teen Choice Awards (2008); Named One of the 100 Most Powerful Celebrities, Forbes.com (2007, 2008); Named Favorite Male Movie Star (2006, 2008); Named One of the 50 Smartest People in Hollywood, Entertainment Weekly (2007); Named One of the Top 25 Entertainers of the Year (2007); Named Favorite Male Star, Favorite Male Action Star & On-screen Matchup (Keira Knightly) (2007); Named Best Performance, MTV Movie Awards (2007); Named Choice Movie Actor: Action Adventure, Teen Choice Awards (2007); Named Choice Movie Actor: Comedy, Teen Choice Awards (2006); Named Choice Movie Actor: Drama/Action

Adventure, Teen Choice Awards (2006); Named One of the 50 Most Powerful People in Hollywood, "Premiere" (2004, 2005, 2006); Named 100 Most Influential People, TIME Magazine (2005); Screen Actors Guild Award for Best Actor, SAG-AFTRA (2004)

DERN, LAURA ELIZABETH, T: Actress, Director, Producer **I:** Media & Entertainment **DOB:** 02/10/1967 **PB:** Los Angeles **SC:** CA/USA **PT:** Bruce Dern; Diane Ladd **MS:** Divorced **SPN:** Ben Harper (2005, Divorced 2013) **CH:** Ellery Walker; Jaya; Charles (Stepson); Harris (Stepdaughter) **ED:** Coursework, Lee Strasberg Institute; Coursework, Royal Academy of Dramatic Art, London, England, United Kingdom **C:** Actress (1973-Present); Director; Producer **CIV:** Activist, Down Syndrome Awareness, Women's Rights, Immigrants' Rights, Gender Pay Parity, Combating Gun Violence and Climate Change **CW:** Producer, "The Way I See It" (2020); Narrator, "Crazy, Not Insane" (2020); Actress, "Little Women" (2019); Actress, "Marriage Story" (2019); Actress, "Cold Pursuit" (2019); Actress, "The Tale" (2018); Actress, "JT LeRoy" (2018); Actress, "Big Little Lies" (2017); Actress, "The Last Man on Earth" (2017); Actress, "Unbreakable Kimmy Schmidt" (2017); Actress, "Twin Peaks" (2017); Actress, "Wilson" (2017); Actress, "The Good Time Girls" (2017); Actress, "Downsizing" (2017); Actress, "Star Wars: The Last Jedi" (2017); Actress, "Wilson" (2016); Actress, "The Founder" (2016); Actress, "Certain Women" (2016); Actress, "The Mindy Project" (2015); Actress, "F is for Family" (2015); Actress, "Bravetown" (2015); Actress, "The Fault in Our Stars" (2014); Actress, "When the Game Stands Tall" (2014); Actress, "Wild" (2014); Actress, "99 Homes" (2014); Actress, "Kroll Show" (2014); Actress, "Drunk History" (2014); Director, "Call Me Crazy: A Five Film" (2013); Actress, Executive Producer, Writer, "Enlightened" (2011-2013); Actress, "The Master" (2012); Actress, "Little Fockers" (2010); Actress, "Everything Must Go" (2010); Actress, "Tenderness" (2009); Actress, "Recount" (2008); Actress, "Year of the Dog" (2007); Actress, "Lonely Hearts" (2006); Actress, Co-producer, "Inland Empire" (2006); Actress, "Happy Endings" (2005); Actress, "The Prize Winner of Defiance, Ohio" (2005); Actress, "We Don't Live Here Anymore" (2004); Voice Actress, "King of the Hill" (2003); Actress, "Damaged Care" (2002); Guest Appearances, "The West Wing" (2002); Co-producer, "Damaged Care" (2002); Actress, "Daddy and Them" (2001); Actress, "Jurassic Park III" (2001); Actress, "Novocaine" (2001); Actress, "I Am Sam" (2001); Actress, "October Sky" (1999); Actress, "The Baby Dance" (1998); Guest Appearances, "Ellen" (1997); Actress, "Citizen Ruth" (1996); Actress, "Bastard Out of Carolina" (1996); Actress, "Ruby Ridge" (1996); Guest Appearances, "Frasier" (1995); Executive Producer, "Down Came a Blackbird (1995); Director, "The Gift" (1994); Actress, "Jurassic Park" (1993); Actress, "Fallen Angels (Murder, Obliquely)" (1993); Actress, "A Perfect World" (1993); Guest Appearances, "Fallen Angels" (1993); Actress, "Afterburn" (1992); Actress, "Rambling Rose" (1991); Actress, "Wild at Heart" (1990); Actress, "Fat Man & Little Boy" (1989); Actress, "Haunted Summer" (1988); Actress, Theater, "The Palace of Amateurs," NY (1988); Actress, "Blue Velvet" (1986); Actress, "Mask" (1985); Actress, "Smooth Talk" (1985); Actress, "Teachers" (1984); Actress, "The Three Wishes of Billy Grier" (1984); Actress, "Happy Endings" (1983); Actress, "Ladies and Gentlemen, the Fabulous Stains" (1982); Guest Appearances, "Shannon" (1981); Actress, "Foxes" (1980); Actress, "Alice Doesn't Live Here Anymore" (1974); Actress, "White Lightning" (1973); Actress, Theater, "Brooklyn Laundry," Los Ange-

les, CA; Stage Appearances, Plays **AW:** Golden Globe Award for Best Supporting Actress in a Motion Picture, Hollywood Foreign Press Association (2020); Screen Actors Guild Award for Best Female Actor in a Supporting Role, SAG-AFTRA (2020); Award for Best Supporting Actress, AARP's Movies for Grownup Awards (2020); Award for Best Supporting Actress, National Society of Film Critics (2020); Award for Best Supporting Actress, North Dakota Film Critics Association (2020); Award for Best Supporting Actress, Hawaii Film Critics Society (2020); Co-recipient with Florence Pugh for "Little Women," Award for Best Supporting Actress, Denver Film Critics Society (2020); Robert Altman Award, Film Independent Spirit Awards (2020); Award for Best Supporting Actress, Dallas–Fort Worth Film Critics Association (2019); Named Best Supporting Actress, Indiewire Critics' Poll (2019); Award for Best Supporting Actress, Phoenix Film Critics Society (2019); Award for Best Supporting Actress, Southeastern Film Critics Association (2019); Award for Best Supporting Actress, Toronto Film Critics Association (2019); Award for Best Supporting Actress, Vancouver Film Critics Circle (2019); Award for Best Supporting Actress, Detroit Film Critics Society (2019); Award for Best Supporting Actress, Florida Film Critics Society (2019); Award for Best Supporting Actress, Atlanta Film Critics Circle (2019); Award for Best Supporting Actress, Boston Society of Film Critics (2019); Golden Globe Award for Best Supporting Actress in a Series, Miniseries or Motion Picture Made for Television, Hollywood Foreign Press Association (2018); Award for Best Miniseries/TV Movie Actress, Gold Derby Television Awards (2018); Emmy Award for Outstanding Supporting Actress in a Limited Series or Television Movie, Television Academy (2017); Award for Best Miniseries/TV Movie Supporting Actress, Gold Derby Television Awards (2017); Golden Globe Award for Best Actress in a Television Series – Musical or Comedy, Hollywood Foreign Press (2012); Inductee, Hollywood Walk of Fame (2010); Golden Globe Award for Best Supporting Actress in a Series, Miniseries or Motion Picture Made for Television, Hollywood Foreign Press Association (2009); Golden Globe Award for Best Performance by an Actress in a Supporting Role in a Series, Mini-Series or Motion Picture Made for Television, Hollywood Foreign Press Association (2009); Special Distinction Award (Shared with David Lynch), Film Independent Spirit Awards (2007); Award for Best Supporting Actress, Boston Society of Film Critics (2004); Independent Vision Award, Sundance Film Festival (1999); Award, Best Actress, Montreal World Film Festival (1996); Golden Globe Award for Best Actress in a Miniseries or Motion Picture – Television, Hollywood Foreign Press Association (1993); Award, Best Actress, Montreal World Film Festival (1991); New Generation Award, Los Angeles Film Critics Association (1985); Named Miss Golden Globe, Hollywood Foreign Press Association (1982)

DESALVA, CHRISTOPHER, T: Attorney, Consultant, Entrepreneur **I:** Law and Legal Services **CN:** The Law Offices of Christopher Joseph DeSalva **DOB:** 06/16/1950 **PB:** Milwaukee **SC:** WI/USA **PT:** Salvatore Joseph DeSalva; Elaine Mae DeSalva **MS:** Married **SPN:** Erika Marie De Salva (05/24/1975) **CH:** Jessica Anne; One Son **ED:** PhD, California State Christian University (2012); Postgraduate Coursework, California Coast University (1994); MBA, California Coast University (1993); JD, American College of Law, Summa Cum Laude (1987); BA in Political Science, St. Vincent College (1972) **C:** Attorney, Consultant, Entrepreneur, Private Practice, Indio, CA (1994-Present); Founder, Owner, C.J. DeSalva & Associates Investment and

Marketing Services of La Quinta (now C.J. De Salva & Associates) La Quinta, CA (1979-Present); Temp Court Judge, Riverside County Superior Court (2006-2009); Private Practice, San Diego, CA (1996-1998); Private Practice, La Quinta, CA (1994-1998) **CR:** Real Estate Broker, DeSalva Realty California (1980-Present); Life and Disability Insurance Agent, C.J. DeSalva Insurance Agency (1978-Present); Adjunct Faculty, Property Law, American College of Law, Brea, CA (1989-1990, 1992-1995); Chief Executive Officer, President, The Kings Vault Gallery, Inc. (1985); Tax Consultant, Preparer, Christopher DeSalva Tax Consultants; Consultant, Christopher DeSalva Business and Management Consultants; Lecturer, Property Law, American College of Law **MIL:** First Lieutenant, U.S. Marine Corps (1974-1977) **CW:** Author, "NAFTA, The Hidden Agenda" (1995) **AW:** Ronald Reagan Medal (2004); International Law Legal Professional Gold Medal, Cambridge University (2004); American Jurisprudence Scholarship Award, American College of Law **MEM:** American Bar Association; Association of Trial Lawyers; Vietnam Era Veterans; Veterans of Latin America; National Society of Public Accountants; California Bar Association **BAR:** U.S. Supreme Court (2000); U.S. District Court for the Central District of California (1995); U.S. District Court for the Southern District of California (1995); U.S. Court of Federal Claims (1995); U.S. Tax Court (1995); California (1994) **MH:** Albert Nelson Marquis Lifetime Achievement Award **B/I:** When Mr. DeSalva was a teenager, he was arrested for something he did not do. It took a while, but he was eventually cleared of this crime. This is what inspired him to pursue law. Likewise, he was always good at arguing his point of view. This only further inspired him to pursue a career in the field. **AV:** Playing music; Playing sports, Writing songs

DESANTIS, RONALD, "RON" DION, T: Governor of Florida **I:** Government Administration/ Government Relations/Government Services **DOB:** 09/14/1978 **PB:** Jacksonville **SC:** FL/USA **PT:** Ronald DeSantis; Karen (Rogers) DeSantis **MS:** Married **SPN:** Casey Black (2010) **CH:** One daughter; One son **ED:** Diploma, Naval Justice School (2005); JD, Harvard Law School (2005); BA in History, Yale University (2001) **C:** Governor, State of Florida (2019-Present); Member, United States House Committee on Oversight and Reform (2013-Present); Member, United States House Judiciary Committee (2013-Present); Member, United States House Foreign Affairs Committee (2013-Present); Member, Florida's Sixth Congressional District, United States Congress, Washington, DC (2013-2018); Prosecutor, United States Attorney's Office, Middle District of Florida, The United States Department of Justice (2008-2010); Legal Adviser to Commander SEAL Team, Special Operations Task Force-West, Fallujah, Iraq (2007); Military Prosecutor, Joint Task Force-Guantanamo Commander, Cuba **CR:** Instructor of United States Military Law, Florida Coastal School of Law **MIL:** Lieutenant, United States Navy Judge Advocate General's Corps, U.S. Navy Reserve (2010-Present); Served, U.S. Navy (2004-2010) **CW:** Author, "Dreams from Our Founding Fathers: First Principles in the Age of Obama" (2011); Contributor, National Review, The Washington Times, The American Spectator, Human Events, and American Thinker **AW:** Decorated Iraq Campaign Medal; Bronze Star; Navy and Marine Corps Commendation Medal; Global War on Terrorism Service Medal **MEM:** VFW; The American Legion **PA:** Republican **RE:** Roman Catholic

DESAULNIER, MARK JAMES, T: U.S. Representative from California **I:** Government Administration/ Government Relations/Government Services **CN:**

U.S. House of Representatives **DOB:** 03/31/1952 **PB:** Lowell **SC:** MA/USA **CH:** Two Children **ED:** Bachelor of Arts in History, College of the Holy Cross **C:** U.S. Representative from California's 11th Congressional District (2015-Present); Member, District Seven, California State Senate (2009-Present); Chair, Committee on Growth Management, California State Assembly (2007-2008); Member, District 11, California State Assembly (2006-2008); Former Mayor, Concord, CA (1993); Council Member, Concord, CA (1991-1993); Member, Committee on Elections, Reapportionment and Constitutional Amendments; Member, Committee for Transportation and Housing, California State Senate; Member, Committee on Budget and Fiscal Review, California State Senate; Chair, Committee on Labor and Industrial Relations, California State Senate **CR:** Co-Chair, World Fuel Cell Conference, Lucerne, Switzerland (2002); Speaker, Japanese Automotive Research Institute, Tokyo, Japan **AW:** Fellow, Leadership Program, Harvard Kennedy School, John F. Kennedy School of Government and Symposium on Affordable Housing (2003) **MEM:** Metropolitan Transportation Commission; California Air Resources Board; Bay Area Air Quality Management District; Association of Bay Area Governments; Future Fund; Board Supervisor, Children & Families Commission; Board Supervisor, Contra Costa County; Afterschool Alliance **PA:** Democrat

DESJARLAIS, SCOTT EUGENE, MD, T: U.S. Representative from Tennessee; Physician **I:** Government Administration/Government Relations/Government Services **DOB:** 02/21/1964 **PB:** Des Moines **SC:** IA/USA **PT:** Joe DesJarlais; Sylvia DesJarlais **MS:** Married **SPN:** Amy DesJarlais (2002); Susan DesJarlais (Divorced 1998) **CH:** Tyler; Ryan; Maggie **ED:** MD, University of South Dakota Sanford School of Medicine (1991); BS in Chemistry and Psychology, University of South Dakota (1987) **C:** Member, U.S. House of Representatives from Tennessee's Fourth Congressional District, United States Congress, Washington, DC (2011-Present); Member, U.S. House Committee on Oversight and Government Reform, Washington, DC (2011-Present); Member, Committee on Foreign Affairs (2011-Present); Member, U.S. House Committee on Education and the Workforce, Washington, DC (2011-Present); Member, U.S. House Committee on Agriculture, Washington, DC (2011-Present); Physician, General Practitioner, Grand View Medical Center, Jasper, TN (1993-Present) **PA:** Republican **RE:** Episcopalian

DESTEFANO, JOHNNY, T: Director, Office of Presidential Personnel **I:** Government Administration/Government Relations/Government Services **ED:** Bachelor of Arts, St. Louis University, Missouri (2001) **C:** Counselor to the President (2018-2019); Director, Office of Presidential Personnel (2017-2018); Senior Advisor, John Boehner (2011-2013); Political Director, Congressman John Boehner (2007-2011); Deputy Executive Director, National Republican Congressional Committee, Washington, DC (2007); Campaign Manager, Deborah Pryce's Congressional Campaign, Ohio (2006); Coalitions Director, U.S. House of Representatives Conference (2001-2006) **AW:** The Fabulous 50, Roll Call (2009)

DETILLION, LINDA KAY, T: Geriatrics Rehab Nurse **I:** Medicine & Health Care **DOB:** 03/03/1947 **PB:** Bucyrus **SC:** OH/USA **PT:** Gordon Lee; Darlene Marie (Knieriemen) Clady (biological); Mary Katherine Fligor Clady **MS:** Widowed **SPN:** Gary Lee Detillion (07/09/1966, Deceased 11/03/2001) **CH:** Brian Russell; Kenneth Roy; Lisa (Daughter-in-Law) **ED:** Associate Degree in Nursing, Northcen-

tral Technical College, Wausau, WI, with Honors (1990) **CT:** Licensed Practical Nurse, Northcentral Technical College, Wausau, WI (1985) **C:** Private Care Legal Nurse, Consultant (1992-Semi-Retired); Supervisor, Heartland of Bucyrus, Bucyrus, OH (1991-1992); With, Crestline Hospital (1991); Pool Nurse, Mansfield Personnel Pool, Ohio (1986-1990); Charge Nurse, Oakwood Manor, Bucyrus, OH (1985-1986) **CIV:** Fundraiser Volunteer, Women of the Moose **MEM:** Secretary-Treasurer, Organization of Associate Degree Nurses; National Association for Practical Nurse Education and Service, Inc. (NAPNES); The Veterans of Foreign Wars (Formerly The Veterans of Foreign Wars of the US) **MH:** Albert Nelson Marquis Lifetime Achievement Award; Marquis Who's Who Top Professional **B/I:** Ms. Detillion became involved in her profession because when she was 6 years old, she had to have her tonsils taken out and was impacted by the nurse who helped her through the process. The nurse was so kind to her and she was fascinated by all that those in the profession did. After that experience, she knew she wanted to be a nurse.

DEUTCH, THEODORE, "TED" ELIOT, T: U.S. Representative from Florida, Chair of the House Ethics Committee **I:** Government Administration/Government Relations/Government Services **CN:** U.S. House of Representatives **DOB:** 5/7/1966 **PB:** Bethlehem **SC:** PA/USA **PT:** Bernard Deutch; Jean (Mindlin) Deutch **MS:** Married **SPN:** Jill (Weinstock) Deutch (1992) **CH:** Gabrielle; Serena; Cole **ED:** Doctor of Jurisprudence, University of Michigan Law School (1990); Bachelor of Arts, University of Michigan (1988) **C:** Chair, House Ethics Committee (2019-Present); Member, U.S. House of Representatives from Florida's 22nd Congressional District, United States Congress, Washington, DC (2017-Present); Ranking Member, House Ethics Committee (2017-2019); Member, U.S. House of Representatives from Florida's 21st Congressional District, United States Congress, Washington, DC (2013-2017); Member, U.S. House of Representatives from Florida's 19th Congressional District, United States Congress, Washington, DC (2010-2013); Member, District 30, Florida State Senate, Tallahassee, FL (2006-2010); Attorney **CW:** Editor-in-Chief, Consider Magazine **AW:** James and Marjorie Baer Leadership Award, Jewish Federation of South Palm Beach County; Harry S. Truman Scholarship **MEM:** American Bar Association; Florida Bar Association; Century Village Democratic Club; Lake Worth West Democratic Club; Greater Boynton Beach Democratic Club; United South County Democratic Club; Deerfield Beach Democratic Club; League of Women Voters; Women's Foundation of Florida; National Safety Council; University of Michigan Alumni Association; The Jewish Federations of North America; Jewish Federation of South Palm Beach County; Voter's Coalition; Forum Club; National Conference of State Legislatures **PA:** Democrat **RE:** Jewish

DEUTCH, ZOEY FRANCIS, T: Actress **I:** Media & Entertainment **DOB:** 11/10/1994 **PB:** Los Angeles **SC:** CA/USA **PT:** Howard Deutch; Lea Thompson **MS:** Single **ED:** Coursework, Los Angeles County High School for the Arts; Coursework, Young Actors Space; Coursework, Oakwood School; Coursework, Los Angeles County Museum of Art **CIV:** Participant, Women's March (2017-2018); Planned Parenthood; Performer, Alzheimer's Association, "What a Pair!" Org; Corazón de Vida; Embrace Ambition Campaign, Tory Burch Foundation; Celebrity Ambassador, Seventh Annual Shop for Success, Dress or Success; Time's Up **CW:** Actress, "The Politician" (2019-Present); Actress, "Zombieland: Double Tap" (2019); Producer, Actress, "Buffaloed" (2019); Actress, "The Profes-

sor" (2018); Actress, "Set It Up" (2018); Co-Producer, Actress, "The Year of Spectacular Men" (2017); Actress, "Flower" (2017); Actress, "The Disaster Artist" (2017); Actress, "Rebel in the Rye" (2017); Appearance, Music Video, "Perfect" (2017); Actress, "Before I Fall" (2017); Actress, "Why Him?" (2016); Actress, "Good Kids" (2016); Actress, "Vincent N Roxxy" (2016); Actress, "Everybody Wants Some!!" (2016); Actress, Short Film, "Of Dogs and Men" (2016); Actress, "Vampire Academy" (2014); Appearance, Music Video, "Opium" (2014); Guest Appearance, "Under the Gunn" (2014); Guest Appearance, "Swiched at Birth" (2013); Actress, "Beautiful Creatures" (2013); Actress, "The Amazing Spider-Man" (2012); Actress, "Ringer" (2011-2012); Actress, "Mayor Cupcake" (2011); Actress, "Hallelujah" (2011); Guest Appearance, "Criminal Minds: Suspect Behavior" (2011); Guest Appearance, "NCIS" (2011); Actress, "The Suite Life on Deck" (2010-2011); Actress, "Most Dangerous Game" **AW:** Next Generation of Hollywood Award, Hollywood Critics Association (2020); Ischia Actress of the Year, Ischia Global Film and Music Festival (2019); Rising Star Award, SCAD Savannah Film Festival (2017); Diff Shining Star Award, Dallas International Film Festival (2017); MAXMARA Face of the Future, Women in Film Crystal + Lucy Awards (2017); Chandon Rising Star, Napa Valley Film Festival (2016) **RE:** Jewish

DEVGAN, ONKAR DAVE N., PHD, T: Technologist, Consultant **I:** Technology **DOB:** 10/11/1941 **PB:** Lahore **SC:** Panjab/India **PT:** Thakar Dass Devgan; Sohag Wati Sharma Devgan **MS:** Married **SPN:** Veena Devgan (07/20/1969) **CH:** Sanjay; Pooja **ED:** MBA, Temple University (1975); Postdoctoral Fellow, National Institutes of Health (1967-1970); PhD, Vikram University (1966); MS, Vikram University (1963); BS, Panjab University (1960); Coursework, The Wharton School, University of Pennsylvania **C:** Technology and Management Consultant, Devgan Associates, Sunnyvale, CA (1991-Present); Director, Technology and Operations, Polylithics Inc., Santa Clara, CA (1989-1990); Director, Microelectronics, Northrop Corporation, Los Angeles, CA (1986-1988); Engineering Manager, Fairchild Semiconductor, Palo Alto, CA (1983-1984, 1988); Program Manager, Varian Associates, Palo Alto, CA (1984-1986); Manager, Material Development, Senior Engineer, Texas Institute for Surgery, Dallas, TX (1978-1983); Consultant, Visiting Professor, The University of Texas at Dallas (1976-1978); Scientist, C-E Glass, Pennsauken, NJ (1973-1976); Instructor, Research Associate, University of Pennsylvania, Philadelphia, PA (1970-1973); Co-Founder, President, Paragon System Technician **CR:** Member, Semi Automation Committee, Mount View, CA (1984-1986); Co-Chairman, Semi GaAs Committee, Mount View, CA (1984-1985); Adviser, Semi Equipment Uptime Committee, Mount View, CA; Chair, Session on Process Control and Monitoring, International Semiconductor Manufacturing Science Symposium, San Francisco, CA **CW:** Author, "Democracy When the Head is High and The Mind is Free"; Author, "Pure Science Based: Integrated System/System Integrated Universal"; Contributor, Articles, Technology and Business Journals **AW:** Council of Science and Industrial Research Senior Fellow, Indian Associates of Science at Calcutta (1966-1967); PhD Fellow, Government of India (1963-1966) **MEM:** IEEE; American Chemical Society; Food Technology **MH:** Albert Nelson Marquis Lifetime Achievement Award **B/I:** Dr. Devgan became involved in his profession because he was supposed to be a doctor; his family consisted of advisers to the King and lived in a ranch-style house. His brothers went to work and his father stayed with his dad. His eldest uncle, who was strong-minded, came up with a contract for the government, which he submitted. It was 10 times less than the others guy's contract, and they gave it to him. **AV:** Working; Exercising

DEVITO, DANNY, T: Actor **I:** Media & Entertainment **DOB:** 11/17/1944 **PB:** Asbury Park **SC:** NJ/USA **PT:** Daniel DeVito; Julia (Moccello) DeVito **MS:** Married **SPN:** Rhea Perlman (January 28, 1982) **CH:** Lucie Chet; Gracie Fan; Jacob Danie **ED:** Graduate, American Academy of Dramatic Arts (1966) **C:** Owner, DeVito South Beach, Miami, FL (2007-Present); Co-Founder, Jersey Films (1992) **CW:** Actor, "It's Always Sunny in Philadelphia" (2006-Present); Executive Producer, "Reno 911" (2003-Present); Actor, "Dumbo" (2019); Actor, "Smallfoot" (2018); Actor, "Animal Crackers" (2017); Actor, "Jim & Andy: The Great Beyond" (2017); Actor, "Wiener-Dog" (2016); Actor, "Curmudgeons" (2016); Actor, "Deadbeat" (2015); Actor, "All the Wilderness" (2014); Producer, Director, "St. Sebastian" (2013); Voice Actor, "Dr. Seuss' The Lorax" (2012); Actor, "Hotel Noir" (2012); Actor, "Girl Walks Into a Bar" (2011); Actor, "When in Rome" (2010); Actor, "House Broken" (2009); Actor, "Just Add Water" (2008); Actor, "The Good Night" (2007); Actor, "Nobel Son" (2007); Producer, "Freedom Writers" (2007); Actor, Executive Producer, "Reno 911!: Miami" (2007); Actor, Producer, "Relative Strangers" (2006); Executive Producer, "Bye Bye Benjamin" (2006); Actor, "The OH in Ohio" (2006); Actor, "Even Money" (2006); Actor, "Deck the Halls" (2006); Actor, Producer, "Be Cool" (2005); Actor, "Marilyn Hotchkiss' Ballroom Dancing Charm School" (2005); Executive Producer, "Garden State" (2004); Producer, "Along Came Polly" (2004); Executive Producer, "Karen Sisco" (2003-2004); Actor, "Family of the Year" (2004); Voice Actor, "Father of the Pride" (2004); Voice Actor, "Catching Kringle" (2004); Actor, "Friends" (2004); Actor, "Christmas in Love" (2004); Actor, "Marx Brothers" (2003); Actor, Director, "Duplex" (2003); Producer, "Camp" (2003); Actor, "Anything Else" (2003); Actor, "Big Fish (voice)" (2003); Actor, "Ed" (2002); Actor, "Austin Powers in Goldmember" (2002); Executive Producer, "The American Embassy" (2002); Actor, Director, "Death to Smoochy" (2002); Executive Producer, "Kate Brasher" (2001); Executive Producer, "UC: Undercover" (2001); Producer, "The Caveman's Valentine" (2001); Actor, "What's the Worst That Could Happen" (2001); Actor, "Heist" (2001); Actor, Producer, "How High" (2001); Actor, Executive Producer, "Drowning Mona" (2000); Producer, "Erin Brokovich" (2000); Actor, "Screwed" (2000); Actor, "The Virgin Suicides" (1999); Actor, "The Big Kahuna" (1999); Actor, Producer, "Man on the Moon" (1999); Actor, Producer, "Living Out Loud" (1998); Producer, "Out of Sight" (1998); Producer, "Gattaca" (1997); Actor, "The Rainmaker" (1997); Actor, "Actor, "Pearl" (1997); Voice Actor, "Hercules" (1997); Actor, Director, Producer, "Matilda" (1996); Actor, "Mars Attacks!" (1996); Producer, "Sunset Park" (1996); Producer, "Feeling Minnesota" (1996); Actor, Producer, "Get Shorty" (1995); Co-Executive Producer, "Pulp Fiction" (1994); Producer, "Reality Bites" (1994); Co-Producer, "8 Seconds" (1994); Actor, "Renaissance Man" (1994); Actor, "Junior" (1994); Voice Actor, "Last Action Hero" (1993); Voice Actor, "Look Who's Talking Now" (1993); Actor, "Jack the Bear" (1993); Actor, Director, Producer, Hoffa" (1992); Voice Actor, "The Simpsons" (1989, 1991, 1992); Actor, "Batman Returns" (1992); Actor, "Other People's Money" (1991); Actor, Director, "The War of the Roses" (1989); Actor, "Twins" (1988); Actor, Director, "Throw Momma From the Train" (1987); Actor, "Tin Men" (1987); Actor, "Amazing Stories" (1986); Actor, "Wise Guys" (1986); Voice Actor, "My Little Pony" (1986); Actor, "Ruthless People"

(1986); Actor, "Head Office" (1985); Actor, "Jewel of the Nile" (1985); Actor, Director, All the Kids Do It" (1984); Actor, Director, The Ratings Game" (1984); Actor, "Romancing the Stone" (1984); Actor, "Johnny Dangerously" (1984); Actor, "Terms of Endearment" (1983); Actor, "Taxi" (1978-1983); Actor, "Going Ape!" (1981); Actor, Director, Valentine" (1979); Actor, "Swap Meet" (1979); Actor, "Hot Dogs for Gaugin, Goin' South" (1978); Actor, Director, The World's Greatest Lover" (1977); Actor, "Starsky and Hutch" (1977); Actor, "Police Woman" (1977); Actor, "The Money" (1976); Actor, Director, Selling of Vince D'Angelo" (1976); Actor, "One Flew Over the Cuckoo's Nest" (1975); Actor, "The Many Wives of Windsor," New York Shakespeare Festival (1974); Actor, "Where Do We Go From Here?" (1974); Actor, "Hurry Up, or I'll Be 30" (1973); Actor, "A Phantasmagoria Historia of D. Johann Fauster Magister, Ph.D, M.D., D.D., D.L., etc." (1973); Actor, "Scalawag" (1972); Actor, "DuBarry Was a Lady" (1972); Actor, "The Shrinking Bride" (1971); Actor, "One Flew Over the Cuckoo's Nest" (1971); Actor, "Lady Liberty" (1971); Actor, "Dreams of Glass" (1970); Actor, "The Man With a Flower in His Mouth," Sheridan Square Playhouse (1969) **AW:** Star, Hollywood Walk of Fame (2011); Inductee, New Jersey Hall of Fame (2010); Crystal Globe Prize for Contribution to Cinema, Karlovy Vary Film Festival (2007); Emmy Award for Outstanding Supporting Actor in a Comedy or Variety or Music Series (1981); Golden Globe Award for Best TV Actor in a Supporting Role (1980)

DEVOS, ELISABETH, "BETSY" DEE, T: United States Secretary of Education **I:** Education/Educational Services **DOB:** 01/08/1958 **PB:** Holland **SC:** MI/USA **PT:** Edgar Dale Prince; Elsa D. (Zwiep) Prince **MS:** Married **SPN:** Richard M. DeVos Jr. (1979) **CH:** Four Children **ED:** BSc in Business Administration, Calvin College (Now Calvin University) (1979) **C:** United States Secretary of Education, United States Department of Education, Washington, DC (2017-Present); Member, National Republican Committee (1996-Present); Chairman, Kent County (Michigan) Republican Finance Committee, MI (1985-1988, 1996-Present); Chairman, Michigan State Republican Party (2003-2017); Chairman, Michigan State Republican Party (1996-2000); Republican National Committeewoman, State of Michigan (1992-1997); Co-chairman, Kent County Republic Finance Committee, MI (1983-1984) **CR:** Market Research Analyst, Amway Corporation (1979-1981); President, The Windquest Group **CIV:** Board of Directors, Ada Christian School, MI (1992-Present); Board of Directors, Blodgett Memorial Medical Center, Spectrum Health (1986-Present); Member, Republican Congressional Leadership Council **MEM:** The Economic Club of Grand Rapids **AV:** Travel; Boating; Skiing

DEWINE, RICHARD, "MIKE" MICHAEL, T: Governor of Ohio **I:** Government Administration/Government Relations/Government Services **DOB:** 01/05/1947 **PB:** Springfield **SC:** OH/USA **PT:** Richard DeWine; Jean DeWine **MS:** Married **SPN:** Frances Struewing (06/03/1967) **CH:** Patrick; Jill; Rebecca; John; Brian; Alice; Mark; Anna **ED:** JD, Ohio Northern University Pettit College of Law (1972); BS in Education, Miami University, Oxford, Ohio (1969) **C:** Governor, State of Ohio (2019-Present); Attorney General, State of Ohio, Columbus, Ohio (2011-2019); Instructor, Center for Political Sciences, Cedarville University (2007-2010); United States Senator, State of Ohio, Washington, DC (1995-2007); Lieutenant Governor, State of Ohio, Columbus, Ohio (1991-1994); Member, Ohio's Seventh Congressional District, United States Congress, Washington, DC (1983-1990); Member, Ohio

State Senate, Columbus, Ohio (1981-1982); Prosecuting Attorney, Greene County, Xenia, Ohio (1977-1981); Assistant Prosecuting Attorney, Greene County, Xenia, Ohio (1973-1975) **CIV:** Member, National Commission on Drug-Free Schools **AW:** Champion Award, Campaign for Tobacco-Free Kids (2005); Congressional Recognition Award, International Association of Fire Fighters (2001); Excellence in Public Service Award, American Academy of Pediatrics (1997); Watchdog of the Treasury Award, National Taxpayers Union (NTU); Spirit Enterprise Award, United States Chamber of Commerce; National Security Leadership Award, American Security Council; MADD Award; Guardian Small Business Award, National Federation of Independent Business; Golden Eagle Award, Council of National Defense; Donald E. Santarelli Public Policy Award, National Organization for Victim Assistance; Nathan Davis Award, American Medical Association **BAR:** Supreme Court of the Unites States (1977); State of Ohio (1972) **PA:** Republican **RE:** Roman Catholic

DEWITT, WILLIAM O. JR., T: Managing Partner **I:** Athletics **DOB:** 08/31/1941 **PB:** St. Louis **SC:** MO/USA **PT:** William O. DeWitt; Margaret H. DeWitt **MS:** Married **SPN:** Katharine Cramer **CH:** Katie; Bill; Andrew; Margot **ED:** Master of Business Administration, Harvard School Business, Cambridge, Massachusetts (1965); Bachelor of Arts in Economics, Yale University, New Haven, CT (1963) **C:** Managing Partner and Chairperson, St. Louis Cardinals (1996-Present); Co-founder and President, Reynolds, DeWitt & Co. (1979-Present); With, Gradison & Co., Cincinnati (1974-1979) **CR:** Member, Foreign Intelligence Advisory Board, Washington, DC (2001-Present); Chairman, Board of Directors, Gateway Group Inc.; Board of Directors, U.S. Playing Card Co.; Board of Directors, Williams Inc.; Board of Directors, Sena Weller Rohel; Co-chairman, Restaurant Management Inc. **CIV:** Cabinet Member, Multiple Sclerosis Society; Cabinet Member, United Way Cincinnati; Cabinet Member, Cincinnati Fine Arts Fund; Member, Development Board, Yale University; President, Republican Finance Committee, Hamilton County, Ohio; President, William O. & Margaret H. DeWitt Foundation; President, Fund for Independent Schools, Cincinnati; Board of Directors, Salvation Army; Board of Directors, Taft Museum; Board of Directors, Cincinnati Art Museum; Board of Directors, Semple Foundation

DIAMOND, HARRIS, T: Chairman, Chief Executive Officer **I:** Advertising & Marketing **CN:** McCann Worldgroup **DOB:** 02/05/1953 **PB:** New York **SC:** NY/USA **MS:** Married **SPN:** Amy Simon (03/26/1956) **ED:** JD, Brooklyn Law School (1983); MBA, Fairleigh Dickinson University (1978); BA, Drew University (1975) **C:** Chairman, Chief Executive Officer, McMann Worldgroup (2012-Present); Chairman, Chief Executive Officer, Constituency Management Group (CMG) (Now IPG DXTRA) (2004-2012); Chief Executive Officer, Weber Shandwick, Inc., New York, NY (2001-2012); Chairman, True North Diversified Companies (1999-2001); Director, Bozell Jacobs Kenyon & Eckert (Now Bozell) (1996-2001); Chairman, Chief Executive Officer, BSMG Worldwide (Now Weber Shandwick, Inc.,) (1996-2001); Chief Operating Officer, Robinson, Lerer, Sawyer & Miller (Now Weber Shandwick, Inc.) (1993-1995); Partner, Chairman, Management Committee, Sawyer Miller Group (Now Weber Shandwick, Inc.), New York, NY (1986-1993); Confidential Assistant to District Attorney, Office of Kings County District Attorney Elizabeth Holtzman, Brooklyn, NY (1982-1985); Various Management Positions, Prudential Insurance Co. (Prudential Financial, Inc.), Newark, NJ (1975-1980)

CR: Political Analyst, Network and Local Television; Speaker, Crisis Communications, Industry and Company Forums; Board of Directors, Caremark (Now CVS Caremark) **CIV:** Board Member, New York City Center (2014-Present); Board of Directors, Ad Council (2013-Present); Chairman, Ronald McDonald House, NY (2006-Present); Board of Visitors, Drew University, Madison, NJ (1991-Present); New York City Community Board (1980-1983) **AW:** Named Agency of the Year, Clio Award (2019); Named A-List Executive of the Year, Advertising Age (2015); PRSA Foundation Paladin Award (2014); Named PR Agency Executive of Decade, The Holmes Report (2010); Named One of the 100 Most Influential PR People in the 20th Century, PRWeek **MEM:** Board of Directors, Rolling Hills Country Club, Wilton, CT **BAR:** State of New York (1984)

DIAMOND, JARED MASON, T: Writer, Ecologist, Biologist **I:** Writing and Editing **DOB:** 09/10/1937 **PB:** Boston **SC:** MA/USA **PT:** Lewis K. Diamond; Flora (Kaplan) Diamond **MS:** Married **SPN:** Marie Cohen **CH:** Max; Joshua **ED:** Honorary PhD, Westfield State University (2009); Honorary DLitt, Sejong University, Korea (1995); PhD in Physiology and Biophysics, University of Cambridge, England (1961); BA in Biochemical Sciences, Harvard University (1958); Honorary PhD, Katholieke Universiteit Leuven, Belgium **C:** Writer (1992-Present); Professor of Physiology, David Geffen School of Medicine, UCLA (1968-Present); Associate Professor of Physiology, David Geffen School of Medicine, UCLA (1966-1968); Associate in Biophysics, Harvard Medical School (1965-1966); Junior Fellow, Society Fellows, Harvard University (1962-1965); Professor of Geography, UCLA **CR:** Board of Directors, World Wildlife Fund (1993-Present); Contributing Editor, Discover Magazine (1984-Present); Research Associate of Ornithology, LA County Museum of Natural History (1985-Present); American Museum of Natural History (1973-Present) **CW:** Author, "The Third Chimpanzee for Young People: The Evolution and Future of the Human Animal" (2015); Author, "The World Until Yesterday: What Can We Learn from Traditional Societies?" (2012); Co-Editor, with James A. Robinson, "Natural Experiments of History" (2010); Author, "Collapse: How Societies Choose to Fail or Succeed" (2005); Co-Author, "The Birds of Northern Melanesia: Speciation, Ecology, and Biogeography" (2001); Author, "Why is Sex Fun? The Evolution of Human Sexuality" (1997); Author, "Guns, Germs, and Steel: The Fates of Human Societies" (1997); Author, "The Third Chimpanzee: The Evolution and Future of the Human Animal" (1991); Co-Author, "Birds of New Guinea" (1986); Co-Editor, with T.J. Case, "Community Ecology" (1986); Co-Editor, with M.L. Cody, "Ecology and Evolution of Communities" (1975); Author, "The Avifauna of the Eastern Highlands of New Guinea" (1972); Contributor, Book Chapters; Member, Editorial Board, "Skeptic Magazine" **AW:** Humanist of the Year, American Humanist Association (2016); Co-Recipient, Wolf Foundation Prize for Agriculture (2013); Dickson Prize in Science (2006); Lewis Thomas Prize for Writing about Science (2002); Tyler Prize for Environmental Achievement (2001); Lannan Literary Award for Nonfiction (1999); National Medal of Science (1999); Pulitzer Prize (1998); Cosmos Prize, Japan (1998); Rhone-Poulenc Science Book Prize (1998); Aventis Prize for Science Books (1998); Elliott Coues Award, American Ornithologists' Union (1998); International Cosmos Prize (1998); Phi Beta Kappa in Science Book Prize (1997); Skeptics Society Randi Award (1994); Zoological Society of San Diego Conservation Medal (1993); Rhone-Poulenc Prize for Science Books (1992); Archie Carr Medal (1989);

MacArthur Foundation Fellowship (1985); Franklin L. Burr Medal, National Geographic Society (1979); Nathaniel Bowditch Prize (1976); Distinguished Achievement Award, American Gastroenterology Association (1975); Los Angeles Times Book Prize **MEM:** Fellow, American Academy of Arts and Sciences; National Academy of Sciences; Institute of Medicine; American Philosophical Society

DIAMOND, LISA, T: Chief Executive Officer **I:** Biotechnology **CN:** Pinpoint Science Inc. **PB:** San Francisco **SC:** CA/USA **PT:** Bernard Lee Diamond; Ann Landy Diamond **CH:** Erica Katya Diamond **ED:** Visiting Scholar in Biological Sciences, Stanford University, Palo Alto, CA (2004); Coursework in Programming and Computer Graphics, University of Illinois, Chicago, IL (1978); Coursework in Mathematics and Dramatic Arts, University of California Berkeley (1969) **C:** Chief Executive Officer, Pinpoint Science Inc. (2014-Present); Principal Systems & Software Architect, Global Viral, San Francisco, CA (2015-2017); Consultant, International Livestock Research Institute, Kenya, Nairobi (2014); Systems Architect, Developer, Stanford Genome Technology Center, Palo Alto, CA (2004-2013); Co-founder, Developer, Pathogenica, Cambridge, MA (2010-2011); Co-founder, Chief Technology Officer, Coyote Group, San Francisco, CA (2005-2006); Visiting Scholar, Stanford University, Biological Sciences, Palo Alto, CA (2003-2004); Vice-President of Engineering, Black Pearl, San Francisco, CA (2001-2002); Vice President, Reuters/Tibco Finance Technology, Palo Alto, CA (1999-2001); Vice-President, Architecture and Strategy, Merrill Lynch (1994-1999); Senior Systems Engineer, Fusion Systems Group (1992-1994); Senior Systems Engineer, Dubner Computer, Grass Valley Group, Tektronix, New Jersey (1984-1991); Programmer, New York Times, New York, NY (1983); Programmer, Atari/Warner Communications, New York, NY (1980-1982); Programmer, New York Telephone, New York, NY (1979-1980); Programmer, Datalogics, Chicago, IL (1977-1978) **CR:** Current Support NIH RADx (2020); Past Support, Templeton Foundation, Boundaries of Life Initiative (2015-2017); NHGRI Center Grant, Stanford Genome Technology Center (2004-2013); Teacher, Graduate Seminars, Stanford University **CW:** Contributor, Articles, Professional Journals; Developer, Novel Software, Metagenomic Analysis of Vaginal Microbiome; Co-Inventor, Nanosensor Chip, Rapid Molecular Diagnostic Technologies **AS:** Ms. Diamond attributes her success to the scientific inspiration and the intellectual generosity of the various mentors she has had over the years. She has benefited greatly from the rich research environment of the Bay Area, which nurtures innovation and collaboration to harness novel technology to address global health challenges. **B/I:** Ms. Diamond became involved in her field due to the influence of a longtime family friend, who was a biochemist. Inspired, she began working in research laboratories at Stanford and Berkeley at the age of 13. For the last 20 years, Diamond has focused on developing breakthrough technologies to tackle pandemic disease and other global health challenges.

DIAMOND, NEIL, T: Singer **I:** Media & Entertainment **DOB:** 12/24/1941 **PB:** Brooklyn **SC:** NY/USA **PT:** Akeeba Diamond; Rose (Rapaport) Diamond **MS:** Married **SPN:** Katie McNeil (04/21/2012); Marcia Murphey (12/05/1969, Divorced 1995); Jaye Posner (1963, Divorced 1969) **CH:** Marjorie; Elyn; Jesse; Micah **ED:** Coursework, New York University **CW:** Singer, "50th Anniversary Collection" (2017); Singer, "Acoustic Christmas" (2016); Singer, "Melody Road" (2014); Singer, "The Classic Christmas Album" (2013); Singer, "The Very Best

of Neil Diamond" (2011); Singer, "Dreams" (2010); Singer, "Hot August Night/NYC" (2009); Singer, "A Cherry Cherry Christmas" (2009); Singer, "Home Before Dark" (2008); Singer, "Gold" (2005); Singer, "12 Songs" (2005); Singer, "Play Me" (2002); Singer, "Three Cord Opera" (2001); Singer, "The Essential" (2001); Singer, "Best of Neil Diamond" (1999); Singer, "Best of The Movie Album" (1999); Singer, "As Time Goes By-Movie Album" (1998); Singer, "Neil Diamond: Under a Tennessee Moon" (1996); Singer, "His 12 Greatest Hits" (1996); Singer, "Live in America" (1994); Performer, "Neil Diamond's Christmas Special" (1993); Singer, "Neil Diamond The Greatest Hits: 1966-1992" (1992); Singer, "The Christmas Album" (1992); Singer, "Neil Diamond Glory Road 1968-1972" (1992); Singer, "Lovescape" (1991); Singer, "The Best Years of Our Lives" (1989); Singer, "Neil Diamond: Greatest Hits Live" (1988); Singer, "Hot August Night II" (1987); Singer, "Headed For the Future" (1986); Singer, "Primitive" (1984); Singer, "Live Diamond" (1982); Singer, "Heart Light" (1982); Singer, "Song Sung Blue" (1982); Singer, "Best Of" (1981); Singer, "Solitary" (1981); Singer, "Love Songs" (1981); Singer, "On the Way to the Sky" (1981); Composer, Actor, "The Jazz Singer" (1980); Singer, "September Morn" (1980); Singer, "Jazz Singer" (1980); Singer, "Neil Diamonds" (1979); Singer, "You Don't Bring Me Flowers" (1978); Singer, "20 Golden Greats" (1978); Composer, "Every Which Way but Loose" (1978); Singer, "Live at the Greek" (1977); Singer, "I'm Glad You're Here With Me Tonight" (1977); Singer, "Beautiful Noise" (1976); Singer, "And the Singer Sings His Song" (1976); Singer, "Diamonds" (1975); Singer, "Focus On" (1975); Singer, "Greatest Hits" (1974); Singer, "Serenade" (1974); Singer, "Gold 1" (1974); Singer, "Gold 2" (1974); Composer, "Jonathan Livingston Seagull); Singer, "Rainbow" (1973); Singer, "Jonathan Livingston Seagull" (1973); Singer, "Hot August Nights" (1972); Singer, "Moods" (1972); Singer, "Stones" (1971); Singer, "Do It!" (1971); Singer, "Gold" (1970); Singer, "Tap Root Manuscript" (1970); Singer, "Shilo" (1970); Singer, "Touching You, Touching Me" (1969); Singer, "Brother Love's Travelling Salvation Show" (1969); Singer, "Neil Diamond's Greatest Hits" (1968); Singer, "Velvet Gloves and Spit" (1968); Singer, "Just for You" (1967); Singer, "The Feel of Neil Diamond" (1966) **AW:** Star, Hollywood Walk of Fame (2012); Inductee, Rock and Roll Hall of Fame (2011); Kennedy Center Honors, John F. Kennedy Center for the Performing Arts, Washington, DC (2011); MusiCares Person of Year, National Academy Recording Arts and Sciences (2009); Golden Globe Award for Best Original Score (1974); Grammy Award for Best Score Soundtrack (1973); Guest Artist, Various Network Television Shows

DIAMONDSTONE, FRED ALAN, T: Lawyer **I:** Law and Legal Services **DOB:** 03/08/1952 **PB:** Redwood City **SC:** CA/USA **PT:** Albert Harold Diamondstone; Judith Mildred (Uslander) Diamondstone **MS:** Married **SPN:** Mary Elizabeth Monschein (11/21/1981) **CH:** David **ED:** JD, University of Washington (1976); Intern, Congressman Robert Leggett of California, Washington, DC (1974); AB, University of California Berkeley, with Distinction (1973) **C:** Attorney, Sole Practice (1995-Present); Associate, Groshong, Lehet & Thornton, Seattle, WA (1993-1995); Attorney, Sole Practice, Seattle, WA (1977-1993); Clerk, Smith, Kaplan & Withey, Seattle, WA (1975); Teaching Assistant, University of Washington School of Law, Seattle, WA (1974-1975) **CR:** Arbitrator, King County Superior Court (1987-Present); Cooperating Attorney, ACLU of Washington (1980-Present); Mediator, CR 39.1 Panel, United States District Court for the Western District of Washington (1997-2003, 2008-2011); Mediator, Settlement Now! (1992-1998); Seminar

Co-chair, "Government Accountability," Washington State Trial Lawyers Association (WSTLA) (1997); Seminar Chair, "Legal Issues Facing Non-profits," Washington State Trial Lawyers Association (WSTLA) (1994-1995); Seminar Co-chair, "The Use and Abuse of Rule 11 CLE," National Lawyers Guild (1991); Faculty, Northwest Regional Program, National Institute of Trial Advocacy (1991); Seminar Chair, "Taking the Government to Court CLE," National Lawyers Guild (1983); Co-chair, "Police Misconduct CLE," National Lawyers Guild (1979); Speaker in Field **CIV:** Committee Chair, Homeless to Renter Program, Temple Beth Am (2014-Present); CLE Co-chair, "A Look at Police and People of Color-Racial Progress or a Deepening Racial Divide?," Washington State Bar Association (2017); CLE Co-chair, "Police Misconduct-From Ferguson to Pasco," WSAJ (2015); Social Action Committee, Temple Beth Am (1996-2013); Advisory Board, Families and Friends of Missing Persons & Violent Crime Victims (Now Victim Support Services) (2004-2009); Board of Directors, Temple Beth Am (2001-2005); Captain, Neighborhood Block Watch (1993-2002); Board Member, Coalition for a Jewish Voice (1999-2001); Chair, Social Action Committee, Temple Beth Am (1999-2000); Board of Directors, ACLU of Washington, Seattle, WA (1982-1986); Delegate, ACLU National Biennial Conference (1985); Board of Directors, Youth Advocates, Inc., Seattle, WA (1977-1981) **CW:** Author, "Police Misconduct: Qualified Immunity Cases Emphasize Need for Thorough Analysis," Trial News (2018); Contributor, "WSAJ Civil Right Deskbook" (2011); Author, "Rethinking the Empty Chair Problem/Opportunity," Trial News (2000); Author, "Civil Rights: A Look at the Supreme Court's 1999 Term," Trial News (1999); Author, "Civil Rights Redux, Dancing Angels in America," Trial News (1997); Author, "Civil Rights–A Retrospective," Trial News (1996); Author, "Drug Sentencing Law Reform?," Washington State Bar News (1993); Author, "Police Dogs--Bark or Bite? Time for a Muzzle?," Trial News (1992) **AW:** Named Super Lawyer, Washington Law & Politics (2000); President's Award, Washington State Bar Association (1999); Public Justice Award, Washington State Trial Lawyers Association (WSTLA) (1997); AV Preeminent Rating, Martindale-Hubbell **MEM:** Executive Committee, Civil Rights Law Section, Washington State Bar Association (2017-Present); Chair, Civil Rights Section, Washington State Association for Justice (2011-2012); Court Rules Committee, Washington State Bar Association (2004-2007); Alternative Dispute Resolution Standing Committee, Washington State Bar Association (1999-2001); Chair, Court Rules Committee, Washington State Bar Association (1998-1999); Court Rules Committee, Washington State Bar Association (1996-1999); Chair, Civil Rights Section, Washington State Trial Lawyers Association (WSTLA) (1996-1998); Legislative Steering Committee, Washington State Trial Lawyers Association (WSTLA) (1993-1998); Alternative Dispute Resolution Task Force, Washington State Bar Association (1996-1997); Civil Rights Committee, Washington State Bar Association (1993-1996); Chair, Corrections Committee, Washington State Bar Association (1991-1992); Corrections Committee, Washington State Bar Association (1989-1992); Delay Reduction Task Force, Joint Bench/Bar Task Force (1987-1989); President, Seattle Chapter, National Lawyers Guild (1987-1988); Court Congestion Committee, King County Bar Association (1986-1988); Chair, Task Force on Lawyer Specialization, Young Lawyers Section, King County Bar Association (1985); Minority Representation in the Law Committee, Young Lawyers Section, King County Bar Association (1982-1984); American Civil Liberties Union (ACLU) **BAR:** United States District Court for the Eastern District of Washing-

ton (1980); United States Court of Appeals for the Ninth Circuit (1979); State of Washington (1976); United States District Court for the Western District of Washington (1976) **MH:** Albert Nelson Marquis Lifetime Achievement Award; Marquis Who's Who Top Professional; Marquis Who's Who Humanitarian Award **B/I:** Mr. Diamondstone was a child of the 1960s and he was always interested in doing social justice work. **AV:** Swimming; Hiking; Skiing; Biking **RE:** Jewish

DIAZ, DALILA, T: Principal **I:** Religious **CN:** Tamiami United Methodist Church **PB:** Cuba **SC:** Cuba **MS:** Married **SPN:** Camilo Torres **CH:** Emmanuel Torres; David Torres; Constanza Torres **ED:** Coursework in Architecture, Univesidad Central de Costa Rica (2008-2009); CEAC, Internal Design, Chile (2000-2002); Coursework, Construction Drawing, José Martí Polytechnic Institute of Construction, Cuba (1985-1988); Coursework, Primary and Secondary Studies, Cuba (1975-1985) **CT:** Fluent in Spanish; 2nd English Level Certified, Miami Dade College **C:** Daycare Director, Private School Principal, Tamiami United Methodist Church Daycare, Elementary, and Middle School (2012-Present); Teacher, Edward Childcare, Kendall, FL (2011-2012); Design, Logistics, Marketing, Toy Products (2009-2011); Professor, Internal Design, Boston University (2004-2009); Designer, Salesperson, Azkent Furniture Store, San Jose, Costa Rica (2002-2003); Design, Budget, Drawing, Road Sewers, Road Sanitation, Chile (1997-2002); Design, Drawing, Several Hotel Projects, Havana Cuba Architecture and Engineering Company (1988-2002) **MEM:** NICE **AS:** Ms. Diaz attributes her success to God's blessings, as well as helping immigrant families. **B/I:** Ms. Diaz came to the United States from Cuba with her family. At the time, her uncle was a pastor and worked at Tamiami, a church that also had a school, which was in need of a teacher. After acquiring the necessary certifications in 2011, she began teaching adults. In 2012, she earned the position of director at the school. **RE:** Christian

DIAZ QUINONES, JUAN J., MD, T: Chief of the General OB/GYN Division, Vice Chair of Quality and Safety **I:** Medicine & Health Care **CN:** Temple University Hospital **ED:** Executive MBA, Fox School of Business, Temple University, Philadelphia, PA (2017); MD, Instituto Tecnológico de Santo Domingo, Dominican Republic (2002) **CT:** Licensure, Pennsylvania (2009-Present); Board Certification, American Board of Obstetrics and Gynecology (2011) **C:** Associate Clinical Professor, Lewis Katz School of Medicine, Temple University, Philadelphia, PA (2018-Present); Assistant Professor, Lewis Katz School of Medicine, Temple University, Philadelphia, PA (2012-2018); Clinical Assistant Professor, Lewis Katz School of Medicine, Temple University, Philadelphia, PA (2009-2012); Intern, Resident, Temple University Hospital, Philadelphia, PA (2009) **CR:** Vice Chair of Quality and Safety, Department of Obstetrics and Gynecology, Temple University Hospital (2019-Present); Director, Family Planning Clinic (2017-Present); Board of Directors, Society of Ibero Latin American Medical Professionals, Philadelphia, PA (2016-Present); Chief, Division of General Obstetrics and Gynecology, Temple University Hospital (2014-Present); Chief, General OB/GYN Division (2014-Present); Clinical and Residency Adviser for Medical Students (2014-Present); Attending Physician, Temple University Hospital (2009-Present); Physician, Outpatient Services, General OB/GYN, Greater Philadelphia Health Action (2009-2012) **CIV:** Member, Abstract/Video Grading Committee for AAGL Global Congress (2015-2018); Liaison Committee for Medical Edu-

cation: Re-Accreditation of the School of Medicine (2015-2016); Translator, Medical History Collector, Heart Care International (2002-2004) **CW:** Author, Contributor, Numerous Peer-Reviewed Articles (2014-2019); Co-Presenter, 24th Annual Meeting, Mid-Atlantic Gynecologic Oncology Society, Hot Springs, VA (2009); Co-Presenter, "Outcome of Stage II and III Cervical Cancer: Importance of Optimal Therapy," 23rd Annual Meeting, Mid-Atlantic Gynecologic Oncology Society, Washington, DC (2008); Author, Contributor, Numerous Abstracts **AW:** Excellence in Teaching Award, Association of Professors of Gynecology and Obstetrics, Temple University Hospital (2013); Member of the Year, Temple University Hospital (2013) **MEM:** Society of Academic Specialist in General Obstetrics and Gynecology (2019-Present); Society of Ibero Latin American Medical Professionals; Obstetrical Society of Philadelphia; Fellow, American Congress of Obstetrics and Gynecology; Fellow, College of Physicians of Philadelphia; Fellow, American College of Surgeons **AS:** Dr. Diaz Quinones attributes his success to being very dedicated and persistent, as well as his inclusivity. He has recently completed Safe Zone training to learn about LGBTQ identities, gender and sexuality, and examine prejudice, assumptions and privilege. He welcomes patients from the LGBTQ community in his practice. **B/I:** Dr. Diaz Quinones became involved in his profession because his grandfather was a doctor and they were very close. His grandfather served as a great inspiration throughout his early life.

DIAZ-BALART, MARIO RAFEL CABALLERO, T: U.S. Representative from Florida **I:** Government Administration/Government Relations/Government Services **DOB:** 09/25/1961 **PB:** Fort Lauderdale **SC:** FL/USA **PT:** Rafael Diaz-Balart; Hilda Caballero Brunet **MS:** Married **SPN:** Tia Diaz-Balart **CH:** Cristian Rafael **ED:** Coursework, University of South Florida **C:** Member, U.S. House of Representatives from Florida's 25th Congressional District, United States Congress (2003-2011, 2013-Present); Member, U.S. House of Representatives from Florida's 21st Congressional District, United States Congress (2011-2013); Member, District 112, Florida House of Representatives, Tallahassee, FL (2001-2002); Member, District 37, Florida State Senate, Tallahassee, FL (1993-2000); Member, District 115, Florida House of Representatives, Tallahassee, FL (1989-1992); Administrative Assistant to Mayor Xavier Suarez, City of Miami, FL (1985-1988); President, Gordon Sloan Diaz-Balart, Boca Raton, Miami, FL **AW:** Named Legislator of the Year, Florida Optometric Association (2000); Award, Florida Association of Realtors (Florida Realtors) (2000); Top Pillar Award, Florida International University (2000); Lifetime Legislative Achievement Award, Florida Association of Community Colleges (Now Association of Florida Colleges) (2000); Legislator of Distinction Award, MADD (2000); Golden Shovel Award, Miami River Marine Group (2000); Claude Pepper Memorial Award, United HomeCare Services (2000); Top Forty Award, Florida Chamber of Commerce (1996, 2000); Named Conservationist of the Year, Biscayne Bay Foundation (1999); Named Senator of the Year, Florida Association of Life Underwriters (Now NAIFA-Florida) (1998); Distinguished Leadership Award, National Alliance on Mental Illness (NAMI) (1997); Award, Florida Police Benevolent Association (PBA) (1996); Government Recognition Award, American Association of Poison Control Centers (AAPCC) (1996); Legislator of Courage Award, Labor Council for Latin American Advancement (LCLAA) (1996); Furtherance of Justice Award, Florida Municipal Attorneys Association (1994); Leadership Award, Florida Association of State Troopers (1993, 1996); Public Service Award, Spanish American League

Against Discrimination (S.A.L.A.D.) (1992) **MEM:** Spanish American League Against Discrimination (S.A.L.A.D.); National Association of Latino Elected and Appointed Officials (NALEO); Westchester Lions Club **AV:** Reading; Biking; Diving **PA:** Republican **RE:** Roman Catholic

DICAPRIO, LEONARDO WILHELM, T: Actor; Activist **I:** Media & Entertainment **DOB:** 11/11/1974 **PB:** Hollywood **SC:** CA/USA **PT:** George DiCaprio; Irmelin (Indenbirken) DiCaprio **CIV:** Founder, The Leonardo DiCaprio Charitable Foundation (1998-Present) **CW:** Narrator, "Ice on Fire" (2019); Actor, "Once Upon a Time in Hollywood" (2019); Actor, "Omniverse" (2018); Appearance, "Before the Flood" (2016); Producer, "Delirium" (2016); Actor, "The Revenant" (2015); Appearance, "Saturday Night Live" (2014); Executive Producer, "Cowspiracy: The Sustainability Secret" (2014); Actor, "The Great Gatsby" (2013); Producer, "Out of the Furnace" (2013); Producer, "Runner, Runner" (2013); Actor, "The Wolf of Wall Street" (2013); Actor, "Django Unchained" (2012); Producer, "Red Riding Hood" (2011); Executive Producer, "The Ides of March" (2011); Actor, "J. Edgar" (2011); Actor, "Shutter Island" (2010); Actor, "Inception" (2010); Producer, "Orphan" (2009); Actor, "Greensburg" (2008); Actor, "Body of Lies" (2008); Actor, "Revolutionary Road" (2008); Writer, Narrator, "The 11th Hour" (2007); Actor, "The Departed" (2006); Actor, "Blood Diamond" (2006); Actor, Producer, "The Aviator" (2004); Executive Producer, "The Assassination of Richard Nixon" (2004); Actor, "Gangs of New York" (2002); Actor, "Catch Me If You Can" (2002); Actor, "Don's Plum" (2001); Actor, "The Beach" (2000); Actor, "The Man in the Iron Mask" (1998); Actor, "Celebrity" (1998); Actor, "Titanic" (1997); Actor, "Romeo and Juliet" (1996); Actor, "Marvin's Room" (1996); Actor, "The Quick and the Dead" (1995); Actor, "The Basketball Diaries" (1995); Actor, "Total Eclipse" (1995); Actor, "This Boy's Life" (1993); Actor, "What's Eating Gilbert Grape?" (1993); Actor, "Growing Pains" (1991-1992); Actor, "Critters III" (1991); Actor, "Parenthood" (1990); Actor, "Santa Barbara" (1990); Actor, Producer, Numerous Television Shows, Documentaries, Films **AW:** Golden Globe Award for Best Performance by an Actor in a Motion Picture - Drama, Hollywood Foreign Press Association (2005, 2016); Critics' Choice Award for Best Actor (2016); Screen Actors Guild Award for Outstanding Performance by a Male Actor in a Leading Role, SAG-AFTRA (2016); BAFTA Award for Best Actor (2016); Academy Award for Best Actor, Academy of Motion Picture Arts & Sciences (2016); Golden Globe Award for Best Performance by an Actor in a Motion Picture - Comedy or Musical, Hollywood Foreign Press Association (2014); Critics' Choice Award for Best Actor in a Comedy (2014); Messenger of Peace, United Nations (2014); Favorite Dramatic Movie Actor, People's Choice Awards (2014); Spotlight Award for Career Collaboration with Martin Scorsese, National Board of Review (2013); Award for Best Supporting Actor, National Board of Review (2012); Teen Choice Award for Choice Movie Actor: Horror/Thriller (2010); International Green Award, Cinema for Peace (2009); Listee, 100 Most Powerful Celebrities, Forbes.com (2008); Listee, Most Influential People in the World, Time Magazine (2007); Listee, 50 Most Powerful People in Hollywood, Premiere Magazine (2003-2006); Commander, Order of Arts and Letters, France (2005); Platinum Award, Santa Barbara International Film Festival (2005); Green Cross Millennium Award for Entertainment Industry Environmental Leadership, Global Green USA (2003); Recipient, Numerous Awards

DICKELMAN, THOMAS S., T: Founder, Senior Minister **I:** Religious **CN:** The Community Church of Lake Forest & Lake Bluff **DOB:** 02/26/1956 **PB:** Geneva **SC:** IL/USA **PT:** C.O. Dickelman Jr.; Lois Dickelman **MS:** Married **SPN:** Jean **CH:** Tommy; Kate; Annie **ED:** Intern, Fourth Presbyterian Church, Chicago, IL; Doctor of Ministry in Organizational Revitalization and Marketing, McCormick Theological Seminary (1991); MDiv, McCormick Theological Seminary (1983); BS in Sociology, The University of Utah (1978) **CT:** Ordained Presbyterian Minister, PC(USA)Certified Windsurfing Instructor (SSS & BIG) **C:** Founder, Senior Minister, The Community Church of Lake Forest & Lake Bluff (1999-Present); Assistant Minister, Second Presbyterian Church - Indianapolis; Minister, Union Church of Lake Bluff **CR:** Founder, Windblessed Weddings; Founder, The Center for Innovative Ministry **CIV:** President, Rotary Club of Lake Forest-Lake Bluff, Rotary International; Board, CROYA; Board, Dickinson Hall, The City of Lake Forest; Board, Lake Forest Cable Commission; Steering Committee, Lake Bluff Middle School; Board, McCormick Theological Seminary; Founder, KidsUganda **CW:** Creator and Host, "A Spirited Take" **MEM:** Presbytery of Chicago **AS:** Dr. Dickelman attributes his success to his commitment to never give up, and his loving and supportive family and friends. He has also been blessed with an inordinate number of supportive and caring members and coaches throughout his life. **B/I:** Dr. Dickelman became involved in his profession with support from two ministers, Dr. William Enright and Dr. Charles Alcorn. His father passed away while he was a freshman in high school, and he was informally adopted by these two men, who had a major influence on his life and career path. **AV:** Founder, Member, Dancing Bohemian Ukulele Team **RE:** Non-denominational Christian **THT:** Dr. Dickelman believes, "Angels can fly because they take life lightly." - G.K. Chesterton. Dr. Dickleman also follows the words, "Life is not a problem to be solved but a reality to be experienced." - Soren Kierkegaard

DICKERSON, GARY E., T: President, Chief Executive Officer **I:** Engineering **CN:** Applied Materials, Inc. **ED:** MBA, University of Missouri-Kansas City, MO; BS in Engineering Management, Missouri University of Science and Technology, Rolla, MO **C:** Chief Executive Officer, Applied Materials, Inc. (2013-Present); President, Applied Materials, Inc. (2012-Present); Chief Executive Officer, Varian Semiconductor Equipment Associates Inc. (Now Applied Materials, Inc.) (2004-2012); President, KLA-Tencor Corp. (Now KLA Corporation), San Jose, CA (2002-2004); Chief Operating Officer, KLA-Tencor Corp. (Now KLA Corporation), San Jose, CA (1999-2004); Various Roles, KLA-Tencor Corp. (Now KLA Corporation), San Jose, CA (1986-1999); Head, Photo Engineering Section, AT&T Technologies; With, Delco Electronics Division, General Motors **CR:** Member, Board of Directors, Applied Materials, Inc. (2013-Present)

DICKERSON, MATTIE FRY, T: Church of the Lord Jesus Christ, Academy of Jesus Christ **I:** Religious **CN:** Administrator

DICKEY, NANCY WILSON, T: Professor, Physician **I:** Medicine & Health Care **DOB:** 09/10/1950 **PB:** Watertown **SC:** SD/USA **PT:** Edward Wilson; Mary Wilson **MS:** Married **SPN:** Franklin Wells (Champ) Dickey **CH:** Danielle; Wilson; Elizabeth **ED:** MD, University of Texas Health Science Center at Houston, Houston, TX (1976); BA, Stephen F. Austin State University, Nacogdoches, TX (1972) **CT:** Diplomate, American Board of Family Practice; Fellow, American Academy of Family Physicians **C:** Executive Director, A&M Rural and Community Health Institute, College Station, TX (2013-Present); President Emeritus, Texas A&M University Health Science Center (2012-Present); Physician, Texas A&M Health Science Center, College Station, TX (2002-Present); Professor, Family Medicine, Texas A&M College of Medicine (1996-Present); President, Texas A&M Health Science Center, College Station, TX (2002-2012); Vice-Chancellor, Health Affairs, Texas A&M University System, College Station, TX (2002-2012) **CR:** Honorary Staff, Polly Ryon Memorial Hospital, Richmond, TX; Courtesy Staff, College Station Medical Center, College Station, TX; Courtesy Staff, CHI St. Joseph Health Regional Hospital, Bryan TX; Medical Director, Free Clinic, Bryan, TX **CIV:** Sponsor, United Methodist Youth Fellowship (1991-1995); Coach, Youth Soccer (1986-1988); Board of Directors, Hastings Center, Office of Early Childhood Development; American Heart Association; Christ United Methodist Church, College Station, TX **CW:** Founding Editor, Journal of Patient Safety; Reviewer, Journal of American Medical Association; Editorial Advisory Board, Patient Care; Editorial Advisory Board, Medical World News; Medical Ethics Adviser, Archives of Family Medicine; Editor, Swanson's Family Medicine Review **AW:** The Secretary of Defense Medal for Outstanding Public Service (2019); John G Walsh Award for Lifetime Contributions to Family Medicine (2019); Elected, Texas' Women's Hall of Fame (2010); Elected, Institute of Medicine (2007); Citation of Merit, Texas Society of Pathologists (1995); Alpha Omega Alpha, University of Texas Houston (1979); Outstanding Young Alumnus, Stephen F. Austin State University, Nacogdoches, TX; Distinguished Alumni Award, University of Texas Medical School **MEM:** Rotary Club of College Station (2001-Present); President, American Medical Association (1998); Chair, Board of Trustees, American Medical Association (1995-1997); Board of Trustees, American Medical Association (1989-1997); Vice-Chair, American Medical Association (1994-1995); Secretary-Treasurer, American Medical Association (1993-1994); Institute of Medicine; Texas Academy of Family Physicians; Texas Medical Association; Alpha Omega Alpha; Academy of Medicine, Engineering, and Science of Texas **MH:** Albert Nelson Marquis Lifetime Achievement Award; Marquis Who's Who Top Professional **AS:** Dr. Dickey attributes her success to her supportive parents, who encouraged her to tackle any goal with hard work and determination. Likewise, she credits her husband, who generously met her half-way on every path she took. **B/I:** Dr. Dickey became involved with her profession because she has always liked people and was interested in science. Throughout high school and college, she worked as a nurses aide in hospitals. She enjoyed watching health professionals conquer the various challenges of medicine; this is what inspired her to join the field. She tells her students that it is a lifelong learning position. Dr. Dickey enjoys all that she can do with just one degree. She had a private practice for 20 years and worked as an administrator for 15 years. Additionally, she has been in academics and has worked in rural health care for the past five years. **AV:** Reading; Skiing; Golfing; Traveling; Spending time with grandchildren

DIDION, JOAN, T: Writer **I:** Writing and Editing **DOB:** 12/05/1934 **PB:** Sacramento **SC:** CA/USA **PT:** Frank Reese Didion; Eduene Jerrett Didion **SPN:** John Gregory Dunne (01/30/1964, Deceased 12/30/2003) **CH:** Quintana Roo (Deceased) **ED:** Honorary LittD, Yale University (2011); Honorary LittD, Harvard University (2009); BA in English, University of California Berkeley (1956) **C:** Associate Feature Editor, "Vogue" (1956-1963); Contributor, New York Review of Books; Former Columnist, "Esquire"; Former Columnist, "Life"; Former Columnist, "Saturday Evening Post" **CR:** Speaker in Field **CW:** Author, "Blue Nights" (2011); Playwright, "The Year of Magical Thinking" (2007); Author, "We Tell Ourselves Stories in Order to Live: Collected Nonfiction" (2006); Author, "The Year of Magical Thinking" (2005); Author, "Where I Was From" (2003); Author, "Fixed Ideas: America Since 9.11" (2003); Author, "Political Fictions" (2001); Screenwriter, "Up Close and Personal" (1996); Author, "The Last Thing He Wanted" (1996); Author, "After Henry" (1992); Screenwriter, "Hills Like White Elephants" (1991); Author, "Miami" (1987); Author, "Democracy" (1984); Author, "Salvador" (1983); Screenwriter, "True Confessions" (1981); Author, "The White Album" (1979); Author, "A Book of Common Prayer" (1977); Screenwriter, "A Star Is Born" (1976); Screenwriter, "Play It As It Lays" (1972); Co-author (with John Gregory Dunne), "The Panic in Needle Park" (1971); Author, "Play It As It Lays" (1970); Author, "Slouching Towards Bethlehem" (1968); Author, "Run, River" (1963) **AW:** National Humanities Medal (2013); Medal for Distinguished Contribution to American Letters, National Book Foundation (2007); Evelyn F. Burkey Award for Contributions Bringing Honor and Dignity to Writers Everywhere, Writers Guild of America (2007); Hubert Howe Bancroft Award (2006); Golden Plate Award (2006); Inductee, The Academy of Achievement (2006); Gold Medal in Belle Lettres and Criticism, American Academy of Arts and Letters (2005); National Book Award (2005); George Polk Award (2001); Columbia Journalism Award (1999); Edward MacDowell Medal (1996); Morton Dauwen Zabel Prize, American Academy of Arts and Letters (1978); First Prize, Prix de Paris, Vogue (1956) **MEM:** American Academy of Arts and Letters; Council on Foreign Relations; American Academy of Arts and Sciences

DIENES, TIMOTHY, "TIM" PAUL, T: Mathematician, Educator **I:** Education/Educational Services **DOB:** 04/18/1960 **PB:** Cleveland **SC:** OH/USA **PT:** William; Ruth Marilyn Dienes **MS:** Single **ED:** MS in Applied Statistics, University North Carolina, Charlotte (1992); BA in Math., University North Carolina, Chapel Hill (1982) **C:** Instructor, Mathematics, Central Piedmont Community College, Charlotte, NC (2003-Present); Instructor, Mathematics, Cabarrus College of Health Sciences (2004-2005); Instructor, Mathematics, Carolinas College Health Sciences, Charlotte, NC (2003-2010); Document control, Bechtel Corp., Charlotte, NC (2000-2002); Teacher, Mathematics, Resurrection Christian School, Charlotte, NC (1997-1999); Rate auditor, United Parcel Service, Charlotte, NC (1993-1997); Production control, Absorba, Inc., Hendersonville, NC (1983-1989) **CW:** Author, "Waters Run Deep"; Author, "Song of Silent Reliance" **AW:** National Merit Scholar, Bendix Corp., (1978-1982) **MEM:** America Mensa; ManKind Project **MH:** Albert Nelson Marquis Lifetime Achievement Award **AS:** Mr. Dienes attributes his success to faith, foundation and work ethic of his parents. He also acknowledges his perseverance through bouts of depression, and a deep sense that there is much more to be made manifest. **B/I:** Mr. Dienes became involved with his profession because it seemed like the most natural thing to do. A high "academic comfort score" on the Strong-Campbell Interest Inventory at a key juncture with a career counselor was pivotal. **AV:** Contradance; Writing **PA:** Independent **RE:** Lutheran **THT:** Viewed on the whole, it has a wicked acceleration to it, which by the time we realize it, half our lives are past. That said, our timeless souls may daydream much as they did in our earliest years, knowing that there is a permanence which is ours. Sooner or

later we realize that it is not so desirable to keep our options open, but to make some kind of long-term commitment, the timing of which, varies widely among us. Lord deliver us from pernicious perfectionism and comparisons, and give us the courage to live out our lives as our conscience dictates. John 14:6, 2 Tim 1:7.

DIESEL, VIN, T: Actor **I:** Media & Entertainment **DOB:** 07/28/1967 **PB:** New York **SC:** NY/USA **PT:** Delora Vincent **CH:** Hania Riley; Vincent Sinclair; Pauline **ED:** Coursework, Hunter College **CW:** Actor, "Bloodshot" (2020); Voice Actor, "Fast and Furious Spy Racers" (2019); Voice Actor, "Avengers: Infinity War" (2018); Voice Actor, "Ralph Breaks the Internet" (2018); Actor, "The Fate of the Furious" (2017); Actor, "Guardians of the Galaxy Vol. 2" (2017); Actor, "Avengers Infinity War" (2017); Actor, "xXx Return of Xander Cage" (2017); Actor, "Furious 7, Billy Lynns Long Halftime Walk" (2016); Actor, "The Last Witch Hunter" (2015); Actor, "Furious 7" (2015); Voice Actor, "Guardians of the Galaxy" (2014); Executive Producer, "Life Is a Dream" (2014); Actor, Producer, "Fast & Furious 6" (2013); Actor, "Riddick" (2013); Producer, "A War Hero" (2012); Actor, "Fast Five" (2011); Actor, "Fast & Furious" (2009); Actor, "Babylon A.D." (2008); Executive Producer, "Hitman" (2007); Actor, "Find Me Guilty" (2006); Actor, "The Fast and the Furious: Tokyo Drift" (2006); Actor, "Be Cool" (2005); Actor, "The Pacifier" (2005); Actor, Producer, "The Chronicles of Riddick" (2004); Actor, "A Man Apart" (2003); Actor, Executive Producer, "XXX" (2002); Actor, "The Fast and the Furious" (2001); Actor, "Knockaround Guys" (2001); Actor, "Boiler Room" (2000); Actor, "Pitch Black" (2000); Actor, "Into Pitch Black" (2000); Voice Actor, "The Iron Giant" (1999); Actor, "Saving Private Ryan" (1998); Actor, "Strays" (1997); Actor, Director, Producer, Writer, "Multi-facial" (1994)

DILGEN, REGINA, PHD, T: Professor, Chairperson **I:** Education/Educational Services **CN:** Palm Beach State College **PB:** Brooklyn **SC:** NY/USA **PT:** **SPN:** William Tignor **CH:** Mia Tignor; Francesca Tignor **ED:** Doctor of Philosophy, Comparative Studies, Florida Atlantic University (2011); Master of Arts in Library and information Science, University of South Florida (1990); Master of Arts in English, Florida Atlantic University (1985) **CT:** Certificate in Women's Studies, Florida Atlantic University (2006); Certificate in Community College Education, University of Central Florida (2003) **C:** Professor, Department Chairperson of English, Palm Beach State College, Lake Worth, FL

DILLABOUGH, DENILLE LYNNE, T: Women's Health and Critical Care Nurse **I:** Medicine & Health Care **DOB:** 08/19/1948 **PB:** Watertown **SC:** NY/USA **PT:** Orra Glenford Mitchell; Beverly Jean (Viau) Mitchell **MS:** Married **SPN:** Richard Dillabough **CH:** Shannon Orra Dillabough; Darcy Lynne Dillabough **ED:** AS in Nursing, Regents College (Now Excelsior College), Albany, NY (1994); Coursework Towards BSN, Jacksonville University; Diploma, Massena School of Practical Nursing (1971) **C:** Director of Infection Control/Perinatal Services (2001); Nurse, Memorial Hospital (1972); Nurse, Medical Surgical Unit (1971); Nurse , Newborn Nursery ICU and Emergency Room, Massena Memorial Hospital, St. Lawrence Health System, NY; Nursing Supervisor, Massena Memorial Hospital, St. Lawrence Health System, NY; Director of Infection Control/Central Sterile Supply; House Supervision **CR:** Initiated Bioterrorism Surveillance, Particularly in Emergency Room; Reports to New York State Department of Health (NYSDOH) **CIV:** Member, Calvary Baptist Church **MEM:** New York State Nurses Association; Association for Pro-

fessionals Infectious Control (APIC); Local County Infection Control Group **MH:** Albert Nelson Marquis Lifetime Achievement Award; Marquis Who's Who Top Professional **B/I:** Mrs. Dillabough always wanted to be a nurse from the time she was little; her mother was a nurse. She was not able to attend nursing school, however the State of New York had a Man Power Program on practical nursing and she was a part of that program. It was called Massena School of Practical Nursing and she trained there for 10 months. It was the best educational program and it helped her to be a nurse. **AV:** Reading; Knitting; College courses (Bible); Piano **PA:** Republican **RE:** Baptist **THT:** Mrs. Dillabough says, "9/11 changed my life in Infection Control; I initiated bioterrorism surveillance, particularly in the ER." She gave frequent reports to the NYSDOH. Drug resistant organisms and c-difficile were on the rise and required monitoring and patient placement. She required safety devices to protect all care providers, personal protective equipment, apparel and hand care hygiene which was a huge but necessary undertaking.

DILLER, BARRY CHARLES, T: Chairman, Senior Executive **I:** Business Management/Business Services **CN:** IAC/InterActiveCorp, Expedia **DOB:** 02/02/1942 **PB:** San Francisco **SC:** CA/USA **PT:** Michael Diller; Reva (Addison) Diller **MS:** Married **SPN:** Diane von Furstenberg (2/2/2001) **ED:** Coursework, UCLA (1959-1961) **C:** Chairman, Senior Executive, IAC/InterActiveCorp, New York, NY (2010-Present); Chairman, Expedia Group (2005-Present); Chairman, Live Nation Entertainment, Live Nation Worldwide, Inc. (2010); Chairman, Ticketmaster Entertainment, Inc. (2008-2010); Chairman, Chief Executive Officer, IAC/InterActiveCorp, New York, NY (1995-2010); Co-Chief Executive Officer, Vivendi Universal (2002-2003); Chairman, Chief Executive Officer, Home Shopping Network, Inc. (Now HSN, Inc.) (1996-1998); Chairman, Chief Executive Officer, Silver King Communications, Inc. (1995-1998); Chairman, Chief Executive Officer, QVC Network, Inc. (Now QVC, Inc.) (1992-1994); Chairman, Chief Executive Officer, Fox, Inc. (1984-1992); Chairman, Chief Executive Officer, Twentieth Century Fox Film Corp. (20th Century Studios), TCF Holdings, Los Angeles, CA (1984-1985); President, Gulf + Western Entertainment and Communications Group (Simon & Schuster, Inc., Madison Square Garden Company, SEGA) (1983-1984); Chairman, Paramount Pictures Corporation (1974-1984); Vice President, Primetime Television, ABC (1973-1974); Vice President, Feature Films and Movies of the Week, ABC (1971-1973); Vice President, Feature Films and Program Development, ABC (1969-1971); Executive Assistant to Vice President of Programming and Director of Feature Films, ABC (1968-1969); Assistant to Vice President in Charge of TV Programming, ABC (1966-1968); William Morris Agency, Endeavor Operating Company, LLC (1961-1966); Vice President of Development, ABC (1965) **CR:** Board of Directors, The Coca-Cola Company (2002-Present); Board of Directors, The Washington Post (2000-Present); Board of Directors, Hotels.com; Board of Directors, Brightcove, Inc.; Board of Directors, Interactive Network Inc.; Board of Directors, Seagram Co., Ltd. **CIV:** Executive Board of Medical Sciences, UCLA; Dean's Council, Tisch School of the Arts, New York University; Board of Trustees, New York University; Board of Councilors, School of Cinematic Arts, University of Southern California; Board of Directors, Conservation International; Board of Directors, The New York Public Library; Board of Directors, Museum, TV & Radio (Now The Paley Center for Media); Co-Founder, Diller-von Furstenberg Family Foundation **AW:** The Richest People in

America, The Forbes 400 (2006-Present); 50 Who Matter Now, CNNMoney.com Business 2.0 (2006-2007) **PA:** Democrat

DILLER, ELIZABETH E., T: Partner, Architect **I:** Architecture & Construction **CN:** Diller Scofidio + Renfro **SC:** Poland **MS:** Married **SPN:** Ricardo Scofiño **ED:** Bachelor of Architecture, The Irwin S. Chanin School of Architecture, Cooper Union (1979) **C:** Partner, Architect, Artist, Diller Scofidio + Renfro, New York, NY (1979) **CR:** Professor of Architecture, Princeton University, NJ (1990-Present) **CW:** Co-publisher with Ricardo Scofidio, "Blur: The Making of Nothing," Abrams (2002); Architect, Media Pavillion for Swiss EXPO (2002); Artist, Slow House, "At the End of the Century: One Hundred Years of Architecture," Museum of Contemporary Art (1998); Artist, "The American Lawn: Surface of Everyday Life," Canadian Centre for Architecture, Montreal, Canada (1998); Artist, "Public Faces/Private Places," Pusan International Arts Festival, Korea (1998); Artist, "His/Her Bathroom," Thomas Healy Gallery, NY (1998); Artist, "Dress Code," Landesmuseum, Linz, Austria (1998); Artist, "EJM1: Man Walking at Ordinary Speed" and "EJM2: Inertia" (1998); Multi-media Work for Stage, Collaboration with Builders Association; Artist, "Jet Lag" (1998); Artist, "Master/ Slave," Fondation Cartier pour L'Art Contemporain, Paris, France, InterClone Hotel, Ataturk Airport for Istanbul Biennial (1997); Artist, "Pelts," Thaddeus Ropac Gallery, Paris, France (1997); Interactive Video Installation, Biennial Nagoya, Japan, (1997); Artist, Electronic Project, "Subtopia," Interstate Commerce Commission Gallery, Tokyo, Japan (1997); Artist, "Non-Place," San Francisco Museum of Modern Art (1997); Artist, Video Installation, Pageant, Johannesburg Biennial & Rotterdam Film Festival (1997); Permanent Installation, "X,Y," Kobe, Japan (1997); Co-publisher with Ricardo Scofidio, "Flesh: Architectural Probes," Princeton Architectural Press (1995); Artist, "Desiring Eye, I'dentity and Difference," Triennale, Milan, Italy (1994); Co-publisher with Ricardo Scofidio, "Back to the Front: Tourisms of War, FRAC Basse-Normandie" (1994); Artist, Apparatus Drawing, Museum of Modern Art, NY (1993); Artist, Apparatus Drawing, New Museum (1993); Artist, Apparatus Drawing, Dysfunction, Center d'Art Contemporian de Castres, France (1993); Designer, Museum of Contemporary Art, Chicago, IL (1992); Permanent Collection, Installation, "The Desiring Eye: Reviewing the Slow House," Gallery MA, Tokyo, Japan (1992); Architect, Works Include Institute of Contemporary Art, Boston, MA, Seagrams, NY, Museum of Art & Technology, NY, Blur Building; Designer, Viewing Platform for Ground Zero, NY, Brasserie Restaurant, NY, Slither, Gifu, Japan, Loophole; Permanent Collections, Travelogues, International Arrivals Terminal 4, JFK Airport, NY; Touring Exhibition, Dance Collaborations with Lyon Ballet Opera, France and Charleroi Danses, Belgium; Artist, Web Project, "Refresh," Dia Art Foundation; Public Art Commission, Permanent Video Marques, "Jump Cuts," United Artists Cineplex, San Jose, CA; Collaborative Dance Work, Charleroi Danses, "Moving Target"; Collaborative Theater Work, Dumb Type and Hotel Pro Forma, "Business Class," Copenhagen Cultural Capital; Interactive Video Installation, "Indigestion," Barbican Art Gallery, London, England; Interactive Video Installation, Walter Phillips Gallery, Banff, Canada; Installations Commissioned by Museum of Modern Art, Whitney Museum, New Museum of Contemporary Art, Walker Art Center, MN, Cartier Foundation, Palais des Beauz-Arts Brussels, and Gallery Ma Tokyo; Permanent Collections, Museum of Modern Art, Museum of Modern Art San Francisco, Fonds National d'Art Contempo-rain, Several Fonds Regional d'Art Contemporain, France, Musee de la Mode, Paris, France and Many Private Collections; Several Other Projects **AW:** Listee, AD100, Architectural Digest (2019); Named, One of the 100 Most Influential, Time Magazine (2018); Named, One of the World's Most Influential People, Time Magazine (2009); Named, One of the 100 Most Influential Women in New York City Business, Crain's New York Business (2007); Brunner Prize in Architecture, American Academy of Arts and Letters (2003); MacArthur Foundation Award (1999); Graham Foundation Fellowship (1998-1999); Chrysler Award for Innovation in Design (1988-1989); Chicago Institute for Architecture and Urbanism Fellowship; Progressive Architecture Design Award; James Beard Foundation Award for Best New Restaurant Design; Obie Award for Creative Achievement; MacDermott Award for Creative Achievement, Massachusetts Institute of Technology **MEM:** Fellow, American Academy of Arts & Sciences

DILLMAN, KRISTIN MMUS, T: Elementary School Educator (Retired), Musician, College Educator, Accompanist, Private Teacher **I:** Education/ Educational Services **DOB:** 11/07/1953 **PB:** Fort Dodge **SC:** IA/USA **PT:** Winford Lee; Helen Caroline (Brown) Egli **MS:** Married **SPN:** David D. Dillman (04/13/1990); Kirk Michael Wicker (01/01/1982, Deceased 1982) **CH:** Alek Joseph; Andrew Dillman **ED:** MM, University of South Dakota, Vermillion, SD (1983); BM in Music Education, Morningside College, Sioux City, IA (1976); AA, Iowa Central Community College (1974) **CT:** Certified Teacher, State of Iowa **C:** Double Bass Instructor, Morningside College, Sioux City, IA (2016-2018); Church Musician (1994-2018); Private Bass and Piano Teacher (1985-2018); Double Bassist, Sioux City Symphony (1974-2014); Teacher, Instrumental Music, Sioux City Community Schools, Iowa (1977-2010); Western Iowa Tech (2008-2009); Teacher, Instrumental Music, Garrigan Affiliated Schools, Algona, IA (1976-1977) **AW:** National Daily Point of Light Award (2006); Teacher of the Year, Sioux City Community Schools (1988-1989) **MEM:** National Education Association; Iowa Education Association; Zeta Sigma; Mu Phi Epsilon **MH:** Albert Nelson Marquis Lifetime Achievement Award; Marquis Who's Who Top Professional **AS:** Being a lifelong learner, Ms. Dillman attributes her success to her love of music and the many mentors, teachers, and fellow colleagues who have helped her throughout her career. **B/I:** Ms. Dillman became involved in her profession because she was involved in music from a young age; it quickly became an important part of her life. She began piano lessons at age nine and was encouraged by her extended musical family and teachers to further pursue her talents. In the years since honing her talents, she has taught elementary through college-level students in both orchestra and band. **AV:** Golfing; Walking; Gardening; Volunteering **PA:** Independent **RE:** Lutheran

DILLMAN, RICHARD HOWARD, PHD, T: English Language Educator, Professor Emeritus of English and American Literature **I:** Education/Educational Services **CN:** St. Cloud State University **DOB:** 12/16/1942 **PB:** Washington **SC:** DC/USA **PT:** Richard Howard Dillman; Anna (Zeilik) Dillman **MS:** Married **SPN:** Diane Marie Barabas (06/18/1966) **CH:** Christopher Sean; Meredith Anne **ED:** PhD in English, University of Oregon (1978); Doctor of Arts in English, University of Oregon (1976); MA in English, University of Oregon (1975); MA in English, Southern Connecticut State University (1972); BA in Economics, University of Connecticut (1965) **C:** Professor Emeritus of English and American Literature, St. Cloud State University, MN (2016-Present); Full Professor of English, St. Cloud State University, MN (1987-2016); Faculty, St. Cloud State University, MN (1978-2016); Chairman, Department of English, St. Cloud State University, MN (1989-1995, 2012-2013); Director of Composition, St. Cloud State University, MN (2008-2011); Graduate Teaching Fellow/Postdoctoral Fellow, University of Oregon, Eugene, OR (1974-1977, 1977-1978); Teacher of English, Cheshire High School, Cheshire, CT (1969-1972); Teacher of English, Kolbe High School, Bridgeport, CT (1966-1969) **CR:** Visiting Professor of English, Consultant, Western Washington University, Bellingham, WA (1984-1985); Assistant Director of Composition, University of Oregon, Eugene, OR (1974-1976) **CIV:** Executive Board Member, Cinosam Lakes Association (2005-2018); Committee Secretary, St. Cloud School District, Board of Education (1983-1984) **CW:** Grant Review, Research Council of Canada (2006); Manuscript Review, Canadian Literature (2005); Author, Editor, "The Major Essays of Henry David Thoreau" (2000); Author, "Essays on Henry David Thoreau, Rhetoric, Style and Audience" (1993); Author, Editor, "The Essays of Henry David Thoreau" (1992); Editor, Compiler, "Thoreau's Comments on the Art of Writing" (1987); Editor, "The Minnesota English Journal" (1985-1989); Co-Director, St. Cloud Area Writing Project (1985-1987); Editorial Board, "Rhetoric Society Quarterly" (1983-1989); Assistant Editor, "Rhetoric Society Quarterly" (1980-1983); Author, "Thoreau's Psychological Rhetoric," University of Oregon (1978); Author, Numerous Articles, Professional Journals **AW:** 35-Year Service Award, St. Cloud State University (2013); Sabbatical Awards, St. Cloud State University (1988-1989, 1998-1999, 2010); Grantee, Minnesota State University System (1987, 1989, 1992); Outstanding Contribution Award, St. Cloud State University (1990); Grantee, Canada Embassy Studies (1989); Distinguished Teacher Award, St. Cloud State University (1988); Grantee, National Endowment of the Humanities (1984); 20-Year Service Award, St. Cloud State University **MEM:** The Thoreau Society; Former Member, Minnesota Council of Teachers of English; Former Member, College of English Association; Former Member, Society for Study of Midwestern Literature; Former Member, Midwest American Studies Association; MLA Associated Departments of English; Former Member, Rhetoric Society of America; Former Member, Association of Literary Scholars and Critics **MH:** Albert Nelson Marquis Lifetime Achievement Award **AS:** Dr. Dillman attributes his success to hard work, dedication, setting reasonable goals, and striving to meet them. **B/I:** Dr. Dillman became involved in his profession because he originally wanted to be a lawyer but then changed his mind. When he graduated from the University of Connecticut, the Vietnam War was raging, which limited his career options. He obtained a position teaching English at an inner-city high school with a minor in English and received a three-year draft deferment for that. He was required to raise his English minor to a major and take several education courses to become a certified teacher. He had never studied English in much depth, except for his minor. He was intrigued by the field and wanted to learn as much as possible about it. Dr. Dillman went from the inner-city high school to a public high school, and while there, he completed a master's degree in medieval British literature and the history of the English language. He was interested in blending linguistics, literature, and rhetoric with all the components of a well-developed English department. He became fascinated with these three related areas of English. He was able to combine these related areas throughout his six years of graduate study at the University of Oregon. While there, he was encouraged to teach a wide range of English courses in literature, rhetoric/writing, and methods of teaching composition as part of his fellowship. As a graduate student, he was also asked to serve as assistant director of composition for the entire university, which gave him valuable administrative experience. **AV:** Reading; Book collecting; Practicing photography; Biking; Kayaking; Writing **RE:** Christian

DIMAS, MARILYN J., T: Health Products Executive **I:** Medicine & Health Care **DOB:** 01/24/1944 **PB:** Portland **SC:** OR/USA **PT:** John Davidson Dow; Gladys Victoria (Lewis) Thompson **MS:** Married **SPN:** John F. Bass; George Dimas (Divorced 1981) **CH:** Ron Farr; Kimberly Farr **ED:** MPA, New York University (1978); MSN, University of Oregon (1970); BS, University of Oregon (1967) **C:** President, Healthcare Quality Improvement Resources, Inc., New York, NY (1988-2009); Associate Executive Director, Woodhall Hospital, Brooklyn, NY (1986-1990); President, Marilyn Dimas & Associates, New York, NY (1978-1988); Executive Director, Boley Manor, St. Petersburg, FL (1984-1986); Executive Director, Richmond Fellowship of New York, New York, NY (1978-1984); Assistant Director, American Lung Association, New York, NY (1974-1976); Deputy Director, National Council on Alcoholism, New York, NY (1973-1974); Director, Psychiatric Crisis Unit Medical School, University of Oregon, Portland, OR (1970-1973) **CR:** National Health Council, New York, NY (1975-1976); Consultant, American Lung Association, New York, NY (1974); Director, Western Institute of Drug Problems Summer School, Portland, OR (1970-1972) **CW:** Author, "Standards for Voluntary Health Organizations" (1976); Author, "Standards for State Alcoholism Associations" (1971) **AW:** Named One of the Outstanding Young Women of America (1980); Gold Plaque, NIAAA (1974) **MEM:** American Hospital Association; National Association for Healthcare Quality; New York State Quality Assurance Professionals **MH:** Albert Nelson Marquis Lifetime Achievement Award **B/I:** Ms. Dimas became involved in her profession because she was a student nurse within the medical school at the University of Oregon. She was selected to head up a team to prepare the University of Oregon's medical center for their first joint commission accreditation. That was her first experience as a student nurse and from there, she became the director of the crisis unit and her mother, Gladys Victoria (Lewis) Thompson, was the director of a geriatric hospital in the Bronx. Her mother had lost their accreditation at the hospital and called her, asking if she could come out and help them get their accreditation because she knew she had done that for the medical center. The first consulting job she did was from her mother's hospital in New York. That was how she got involved as a student nurse. **AV:** Swimming; Horseback riding; Jogging; Cooking

DIMON, JAMIE, T: Chairman, Chief Executive Officer, and President **I:** Financial Services **CN:** JPMorgan Chase & Co. **DOB:** 03/13/1956 **PB:** New York **SC:** NY/USA **PT:** Theodore Dimon; Themis Dimon **MS:** Married **SPN:** Judith Kent (05/21/1983) **CH:** Julia; Laura; Kara Leigh **ED:** MBA, Harvard Business School (1982); BA in Psychology and Economics, Tufts University (1978) **C:** Chairman Emeritus, JPMorgan Chase Bank, N.A. (2013-Present); Chairman, President, Chief Executive Officer, JPMorgan Chase & Co., New York, NY (2006-Present); Chairman, JPMorgan Chase Bank, N.A. (2006-2013); President, Chief Executive Officer, JPMorgan Chase & Co., New York, NY (2005-2006); President, Chief Operating Officer, JPMorgan Chase & Co., New York, NY (2004-2005); Chairman,

Chief Executive Officer, Bank One Corporation, Chicago, IL (2000-2004); President, Citigroup, Inc. (1998-2000); Chairman, Co-Chief Executive Officer, Salomon Smith Barney Holdings Inc. (1998-2000); President, Chief Operating Officer, The Travelers Group Inc. (1993-1998); Chief Financial Officer, The Travelers Group, Inc. (1988-1995); President, Primerica Corporation, New York, NY (1990-1993); Executive Vice President, Chief Financial Officer, Primerica Corporation, New York, NY (1989-1990); Senior Vice President, Chief Financial Officer, Commercial Credit Company, Baltimore (1986-1988); Vice President, Assistant to President, American Express Co., New York, NY (1982-1985) **CR:** Chairman The Clearing House Payments Co. (2007-Present); Board of Directors, The Federal Reserve Bank of New York (2007-Present); Board of Directors, JPMorgan Chase & Co. (2000-Present); Board of Directors, Yum! Brands, Inc. (1997-2004); Board of Directors, The Financial Services Roundtable; Board of Directors, Catalyst Inc. **CIV:** Board of Directors, United Negro College Fund; Board of Directors, National Center on Addiction and Substance Abuse; Member, Council on Foreign Relations; Board of Directors, Mount Sinai Medical Center & Health Systems; Board of Directors, Economic Club of Chicago; Board of Directors, Chicago Council on Global Affairs; Board of Directors, Partnership for New York City; Member, Trustees Committee, Chicago Community Trust; Civic Committee, Commercial Club of Chicago; Trustee, New York University Medical Center; Trustee, University of Chicago **AW:** The World's Most Powerful People, "Forbes" (2009-2014); 50 Most Influential People in Global Finance, "Bloomberg Markets" (2011-2013); Executive of the Year, University of Rochester Simon Graduate School of Business (2012); 100 Most Influential People in the World, "TIME" (2006, 2008, 2009, 2011); Business People of the Year, "Fortune" (2010); Banker of the Year, "American Banker" (2009); The Top 25 Market Movers, "US News & World Report" (2009); The Global Elite, "Newsweek" (2008); The 25 Leaders Reshaping New York, "Crain's New York" (2008); The 25 Most Powerful People in Business (2007); Golden Plate Award, Academy Achievement (2006) **PA:** Democrat

DINGELL, DEBORAH, "DEBBIE" ANN, T: U.S. Representative, Lobbyist (Retired) **I:** Government Administration/Government Relations/Government Services **DOB:** 11/23/1953 **PB:** Detroit **SC:** MI/USA **MS:** Widowed **SPN:** John Dingell (1981, Deceased 2019) **CH:** Four children **ED:** Master's Degree in Liberal Studies, Georgetown University (1998) **C:** U.S. Representative, Michigan's 12th Congressional District (2015-Present); Lobbyist, General Motors (1977); Member, House Committee on Energy and Commerce; Former Executive Director, Global Community Relations and Government Relations, General Motors **CIV:** Board of Governors, Wayne State University, Detroit, MI (2006); Co-Founder, The Children's Inn at NIH, Bethesda, MD; Vice Chairman, General Motors Foundation; Member, Executive Committee, Barbara Ann Karmanos Cancer Institute; Co-Chair, Breast Cancer Committee, Barbara Ann Karmanos Cancer Institute; Co-Chair, Government Relations Committee, Barbara Ann Karmanos Cancer Institute; Vice Chair, Barbara Ann Karmanos Cancer Institute; Member, Democratic National Committee; Founding Chair, NWHN **AW:** One of the 100 Most Powerful Women in DC, Washingtonian Magazine (2009)

DINKLAGE, PETER, T: Actor **I:** Media & Entertainment **DOB:** 06/11/1969 **PB:** Morristown **SC:** NJ/USA **PT:** John Dinklage; Diane Dinklange **MS:** Married **SPN:** Erica Schmidt (4/16/2005) **CH:** Zelig **ED:** BA in Drama, Bennington College, Vermont

(1991); Attended, Welsh School Music & Drama, Cardiff, Wales; Attended, Royal Academy Dramatic Arts, London **CW:** Actor, "I Care a Lot" (2020); Actor, "Between Two Ferns: The Movie" (2019); Voice Actor, "The Angry Birds Movie 2" (2019); Actor, "Game of Thrones" (2011-2019); Actor, "I Think We're Alone Now" (2018); Actor, "Avengers Infinity War" (2018); Actor, "My Dinner with Herve" (2018); Actor, "Rememory" (2017); Actor, "Three Billboards Outside Ebbing, Missouri" (2017); Actor, "Three Christs" (2017); Actor, "The David S Pumpkins Animated Halloween Special" (2017); Actor, "The Boss" (2016); Voice Actor, "Angry Birds" (2016); Actor, "Taxi" (2015); Actor, "Pixels" (2015); Actor, "Low Down" (2014); Actor, "X-Men: Days of Future Past" (2014); Actor, "The Angriest Man in Brooklyn" (2014); Actor, "A Case of You" (2013); Host, "Saturday Night Live" (2013); Host, "Sesame Street" (2013); Actor, Executive Producer, "Knights of Badassdom" (2013); Voice Actor, "Ice Age: Continental Drift" (2012); Actor, "A Little Bit of Heaven" (2011); Actor, "I Love You Too" (2010); Actor, Producer, "Pete Smalls Is Dead" (2010); Actor, "The Last Rites of Ransom Pride" (2010); Actor, "Saint John of Las Vegas" (2009); Actor, "The Chronicles of Narnia: Prince Caspian" (2008); Actor, "Death at a Funeral" (2007); Actor, "Ascension Day" (2007); Actor, "Underdog" (2007); Actor, "Threshold" (2005-2006); Actor, "Nip/Tuck" (2006); Actor, "Ultra" (2006); Actor, "The Limbo Room" (2006); Actor, "Find Me Guilty" (2006); Actor, "Little Fugitive" (2006); Actor, "Penelope" (2006); Actor, "Testing Bob" (2005); Actor, "The Baxter" (2005); Actor, "Escape Artists" (2005); Actor, "Lassie" (2005); Actor, "Fortunes" (2005); Actor, "89 Seconds at Alcázar" (2004); Actor, "Jail Bait" (2004); Actor, "Surviving Eden" (2004); Actor, "I'm with Her" (2004); Actor, "The Station Agent" (2003); Actor, "Tiotoes" (2003); Actor, "Elf" (2003); Actor, "13 Moons" (2002); Actor, "Just a Kiss" (2002); Actor, "Never Again" (2001); Actor, "Human Nature" (2001); Actor, "Pigeonholed" (1999); Actor, "Safe Men" (1998); Actor, "Bullet" (1996); Actor, "Living in Oblivion" (1995) **AW:** Emmy Award for Outstanding Supporting Actor in a Drama Series (2011, 2015, 2018); Golden Globe Award for Best Performance by an Actor in a Supporting Role in a Series, Mini-Series or Motion Picture Made for TV (2012)

DION, CELINE MARIE CLAUDETTE, T: Singer **I:** Media & Entertainment **DOB:** 03/30/1970 **PB:** Charlemagne **SC:** QC/Canada **PT:** Adhémar-Charles Dion; Thèrése (Tanguay) Dion **MS:** Widowed **SPN:** René Angélil (12/17/1994, Deceased 2016) **CH:** René-Charles; Eddy; Nelson **ED:** Honorary MusD, University of Laval, Quebec City, Quebec, Canada (2008) **CR:** Launched, Gender Neutral Clothing Line, Celinununu (2018-Present); Owner, Feeling Productions Inc. (2016-Present); Celine Dion Parfums, Coty, Inc. (2003-Present); Founder, Nickels Restaurant (1990-1997); Co-founder, Le Mirage Golf Club; Co-Founder, Schwartz's Restaurant; Co-Owner, Pure, Caesar's Palace **CIV:** Goodwill Ambassador, United Nations (2010-Present); Supporter, Cystic Fibrosis Canada (1982-Present); Participant, World Children's Day (2003); Supporter, T.J. Martell Foundation, Diana Princess of Wales Memorial Fund, Numerous Health and Educational Organizations **CW:** Singer, "Courage" (2019); Performer, "Celine," Residency, The Colosseum, Caesars Palace, Las Vegas, NV (2011-2019); Singer, "Encore un Soir" (2016); Appearance, "Muppets Most Wanted" (2014); Singer, "Loved Me Back to Life" (2013); Appearance, "Sur la Post due Marsupilami" (2012); Singer, "Sans Attendre" (2012); Appearance, "Celine: Through the Eyes of the World" (2010); Appearance, "Céline sur les Plaines" (2008); Singer, "Taking Chances" (2007);

Singer, "Ihre Schönsten Weihnachstlieder" (2007); Singer, "En Amour" (2007); Singer, "D'Elles" (2007); Performer, "A New Day...," Residency, The Colosseum, Caesars Palace, Las Vegas, NV (2003-2007); Singer, "D'Amour Francaise" (2006); Singer, "Du Soleil au Coeur" (2006); Singer, "On Ne Change Pas" (2005); Singer, "A New Day" (2004); Singer, "Miracle" (2004); Singer, "1 Fille & 4 Types" (2003); Singer, "One Heart" (2003); Singer, "A New Day Has Come" (2002); Singer, "Classique: A Love Collection" (2001); Singer, "The French Album" (2001); Singer, "All the Way" (1999); Singer, "These are Special Times" (1998); Singer, "S'il Suffisait d'Aimer" (1998); Singer, "My Heart Will Go On," Original Motion Picture Soundtrack, "Titanic" (1997); Singer, "Let's Talk About Love" (1997); Singer, "C'est Pour Vivre" (1997); Singer, "Falling into You" (1997); Singer, "The Collection" (1982-1988, 1997); Singer, "Live à Paris" (1996); Singer, "Des Mots Qui Sonnent" (1995); Singer, "Beauty and the Beast," Peabo Bryson's "Through the Fire" (1994); Singer, "Dion Chante Plamondon" (1994); Singer, "Premieres Anees" (1994); Singer, "When I Fall in Love," Original Motion Picture Soundtrack, "Sleepless in Seattle" (1993); Singer, "Colour of My Love" (1993); Singer, "Celine Dion" (1992); Singer, "Beauty and the Beast," Original Motion Picture Soundtrack, "Beauty and the Beast" (1991); Singer, "Unison" (1990); Singer, Original Motion Picture Soundtrack, "Real Love" (1979); Appearance, "Touched by an Angel"; Appearance, "The Nanny"; Appearance, "All My Children"; Appearance, "La Fureur de Celine"; Appearance, "Des Fleurs sur la Neige"; Appearance, "Quest for Camelot"; Appearance, "Hell's Kitchen"; Performer, Numerous Worldwide Tours **AW:** Icon Award, Billboard Music Awards (2016); Companion, Order of Canada, Governor General of Canada (2013); Named, 100 Most Powerful Celebrities, Forbes Magazine (2008); Légion d'Honneur, France (2008); Best-selling Canadian Artist, World Music Awards (2008); Legend Award (2007); Chopard Diamond Award, Best-selling Female Artist of All Time (2004); Star, Hollywood Walk of Fame (2004); Star, Canada's Walk of Fame (1999); Grammy Award, Record of the Year, Recording Academy (1999); Grammy Award, Best Female Pop Vocal, Recording Academy (1999); Billboard Music Award for Best Soundtrack Single (1998); Billboard Music Award for Best Album (1998); Grammy Award, Album of Year, Recording Academy (1997); Grammy Award, Best Pop Album, Recording Academy (1997); Grammy Award, Best Pop Performance by a Duo or Group with Vocal, Recording Academy (1992); Grammy Award, Best-selling Single, Recording Academy (1992); Academy Award, Best Song, Academy of Motion Picture Arts and Sciences (1992); Album of the Year (1990); Numerous Awards

DIRKS, LEE EDWARD, T: Newspaper Executive (Retired) **I:** Writing and Editing **DOB:** 08/04/1935 **PB:** Indianapolis **SC:** IN/USA **PT:** Raymond Louis Dirks; Virginia Belle (Wagner) Dirks **MS:** Married **SPN:** Donna Mary Bradley; Judith Ann Putman (12/28/2001, Deceased 11/01/2012); Barbara Dee Nutt (06/16/1956, Divorced 01/1985) **CH:** Stephen Merle Dirks; Deborah Virginia Dirks; David Louis Dirks **ED:** MA, The Fletcher School, Tufts University (1957); BA, DePauw University (1956) **C:** Chairman, Dirks, Van Essen & April (1980-2008); Vice President, General Manager, Detroit Free Press (1977-1980); Assistant to President, Detroit Free Press (1976-1977); Securities Analyst, CSM Advisors, LLC (1975-1976); Delafield Clinic-Children's Wisconsin (1971-1975); Dirks Brothers (1969-1971); News Editor, National Observer (1966-1968); Reporter, National Observer (1962-1965); Reporter, Boston Globe (1957); Copy Editor, Wall Street Journal (1954-1956) **CIV:** Honorary Trustee,

Georgia O'Keeffe Museum (2012-Present); President, Georgia O'Keeffe Museum (2000-2004, 2011-2012); Board of Directors, Santa Fe Opera (1998-2004); Board of Directors, National Ghost Ranch Foundation (1973-1997) **MIL:** Special Agent, Office of Special Investigations, U.S. Air Force (1957-1961) **CW:** Publisher, Dirks Newspaper Newsletter (1970-1976); Author, "Religion in Action" (1965) **AW:** Religion Writer of Year, Religious Newswriters Association (1964) **MEM:** The Phi Beta Kappa Society; Lambda Chi Fraternity; The Club at Las Campanas; The Loxahatchee Club; Japanese Art Society of America **B/I:** **RE:** Episcopalian

DISNEY, BENJAMIN O., T: Small Business Owner **I:** Business Management/Business Services **CN:** Xentropa Services **MS:** Married **CH:** One Daughter **CT:** Certified Handyman Professional, ACHP **C:** Owner, Xentropa Services (2006-Present) **CIV:** Nonprofit Community Outreach **MEM:** Association of Certified Handyman Professionals **AS:** Mr. Disney attributes his success to his parents and his incredible drive to do something with purpose. **B/I:** Mr. Disney never completed college, although he always loved to learn. He then decided to take a trip across the country; it ended up lasting four years. During that time, while traveling, Mr. Disney would stop at various places to work. Luckily, he met great people who noticed his intelligence and would teach him new skills. Each place he worked, he acquired a new skill, and it led him to new places where he learned new skills. Mr. Disney was inspired to keep learning because of his family. It got him to where he is today. **THT:** Mr. Disney's motto is, "It's a beautiful day, regardless of the day." The name Xentropa, which he named his company after, means "skillful and artful solutions to problems." Mr. Disney tries to apply that to his life every day.

DISPENZIERE, PATRICIA, T: Professional Artist **I:** Fine Art **CN:** Pat Dispenziere **ED:** BFA, The Ohio State University (1995); BA in Art Education, The Ohio State University **CW:** Published in "Splash 7," "Watercolor Magic," "Artistic Touch 5," and "The Artist's Magazine" **MEM:** Signature Member, National Watercolor Society; Watercolor West; San Diego Watercolor Society, California Watercolor Association, Louisiana Watercolor Society, Rocky Mountain Watercolor Society; Watercolor Art Society - Houston, Texas and Philadelphia Water Color Society; Texas Watercolor Society; Western Federation of Watercolor Societies; Western Colorado Watercolor Society, Juried Member, Los Angeles Printmaking Society; Juried Member, Women Painters West **B/I:** When Ms. Dispenziere moved to California there were many workshops. They had an art center in Palace Verdes. She got very involved and started selling her work. She was young and she did many art shows.

DITKOWSKY, KENNETH K., T: Lawyer **I:** Law and Legal Services **DOB:** 07/12/1936 **PB:** Chicago **SC:** IL/USA **PT:** Samuel J. Ditkowsky; Lillian (Plavnik) Ditkowsky **MS:** Married **SPN:** Judith Goodman (09/09/1959) **CH:** Naomi; Deborah; R. Benjamin **ED:** JD, Loyola University, Chicago, IL; BS, University of Chicago **C:** Retired (2013); Partner, Ditkowsky & Contorer, Chicago, IL (1961-2013) **CIV:** Juvenile Protection League **CW:** Mark of the Title Act; Condominium Declaration **MEM:** Illinois Bar Association **BAR:** U.S. Supreme Court (1975); U.S. Tax Court (1973); U.S. Court Appeals for the 7th Circuit (1973); U.S. District Court for the Northern District of Illinois (1962); Illinois (1961) **MH:** Albert Nelson Marquis Lifetime Achievement Award **B/I:** Mr. Ditkowsky got involved in the law after work-

ing with a real estate entrepreneur. They covered a case that got bad results, which suggested one of them attend law school. Mr. Ditkowsky did so.

DIVITTORIO, JENN, T: Independent Consultant **I:** Cosmetics **CN:** Rodan & Fields **ED:** BA in English and Spanish, The Pennsylvania State University, Centre County, PA (1996) **C:** Independent Consultant, Rodan & Fields (2011-Present) **AW:** Featured as Success Story for Funding Endowment and Fellowship in Parents' Names for Brain Repair Research at The Pennsylvania State University, Kiplinger Magazine **B/I:** Ms. DiVittorio became involved in her profession because she had been in pharmaceutical sales for 10 years. Prior to that she was at Novartis for eight years and she ended up getting laid off one Thanksgiving. The following January, she happened to be watching the "Today Show" and a beauty editor from L'Oreal magazine was on that day. They spoke about their products and some of what they sold and because she was a product enthusiast, she started to research it and realized there was a business opportunity behind it. She was looking for a way to make money and be independent and also for something that would give her more flexibility than traditional sales jobs. Therefore she decided to start her own business. In addition, it was her dad who was always in sales and was an inspiration.

DIXON, JO-ANN C., T: Management Consultant **I:** Business Management/Business Services **DOB:** 08/05/1942 **PB:** Orange **SC:** NJ/USA **PT:** Rocco Louis Conte; Antoinette (DeRosa) Conte **MS:** Married **SPN:** Michael Eugene Dixon (07/26/1964) **CH:** Christopher Michael; Peter Eugene **ED:** Pursuing MA, Drew University (1985-Present); BA, Thomas A. Edison College (Now Thomas State Edison University) (1978); AA, Thomas A. Edison College (Now Thomas State Edison University) (1976) **CT:** Certificate in Gestalt Psychotherapy, Montclair State College (Now Montclair State University) (1994) **C:** Chief Executive Officer, Principal, JCD Consulting, LLC (2013-Present); Chief Executive Officer, Principal, MatchPlay, Inc. (2008-2013); Acting Chief Executive Officer, Home Health Service and Staffing Association, NJ (2007-2008); Regional Director, American Management Associate (1996-2007); President, MatchPlay, Inc. (1989-1996); President, Principal Consultant, Q, Inc., Essex Fells, NJ (1980-1989); Director, Rapidata, Inc., Fairfield, NJ (1980-1981); Manager Corporate Training Department, Rapidata, Inc., Fairfield, NJ (1979-1980); Administrator, Corporate Training Department, Rapidata, Inc., Fairfield, NJ (1978-1979); Market Research Analyst, Harkness & Associates, Inc., San Francisco, CA (1976-1978); Owner, Organization Unlimited, Glen Ridge, NJ (1972-1978); Teacher, St. Raphael's School, Livingston, NJ (1963-1968) **CR:** Chairman, Board of Trustees, National Institute for Organizational and Management Research, Essex Fells, NJ (1987-Present); President, West Essex Community Health Services (1993-1995); Trustee, Mount St. Dominic Academy (1989-1995); Development Chair, West Essex Community Health Services (1988-1993); Board Director, Alumni Affairs/Development Officer, Seton Hall University School of Law, Newark, NJ (1984-1985); Director, Management of Development, Rutgers University Graduate School of Management (Now Rutgers Business School) (1983-1984); Director, Alumni Relations, New Jersey Institute of Technology, Newark, NJ (1981-1983); Speaker in the Field **CIV:** Strategic Planning Chair, New Jersey District of Kiwanis (Kiwanis International) (2017-Present); New Jersey District of Kiwanis (Kiwanis International) (2015-Present); NNJ Executive Women's Golf Association (Now LPGA Amateur Golf Association), Northern NJ (2002-Present); President,

LPGA Amateur Golf Association, Northern NJ (2017-2019); Public Relations Chair, New Jersey District of Kiwanis (Kiwanis International) (2013-2015); Secretary, Board of Directors, Garden State Woman's Education Foundation (2002-2008); President, Executive Women of New Jersey (2003-2004); President, National Executive Women's Golf Association (Now LPGA Amateur Golf Association) (2001-2004); President, Kiwanis Club of Caldwell-West Essex, NJ (1998-1999); Vice Chairman, Board, Passaic River Coalition, Basking Ridge, NJ (1983-1988); Chairman, Board, Passaic River Coalition, Basking Ridge, NJ (1976-1983); Member, President, Home and School Board, Glen Ridge, NJ (1978-1979); Member, New Jersey Governor's Task Force for Passaic River (1976-1978); Regional Coordinator, Passaic River Coalition, Basking Ridge, NJ (1971-1976); Chairman, Mayor's Committee on Environmental, Glen Ridge, NJ (1974-1975); Youth Protection Chair, New Jersey District of Kiwanis (Kiwanis International) AW: Named One of 50 Best Women in Business, NJBIZ Magazine (2010); Named Woman of Distinction, Girl Scouts of the United States of America (2004); Named Business Person/Committee Leader of the Year, West Essex Chamber of Commerce (2001); Charles T. Morgan Award for Excellence in Training and Development, ATD (1989); Named Dame of Malta, Order of St. John of Jerusalem (1986); National Trust for Historic Preservation Scholar (1977); Recipient, Citation, Borough of Glen Ridge; Professional Excellence Award, ATD MEM: Vice President, Kiwanis Club of Caldwell-West Essex (2009-Present); National Board Member, LPGA Amateur Golf Association (2008-Present); Carrington Swain Fellowship (2013); Strategic Planning Member, EWNJ (2006-2010); Sponsorship Chair, LPGA Amateur Golf Association (2006-2007); President, LPGA Amateur Golf Association (2004-2006); Leadership Chair, LPGA Amateur Golf Association (2004); President, EWNJ (2002-2004); Lieutenant Governor Division 12, Kiwanis Club of Caldwell-West Essex (2002-2003); Sectional Director, Metro Northeast Chapter, LPGA Amateur Golf Association (2001-2002); President-elect, EWNJ (1999-2002); Hixson Fellow (2001); Chair, Pediatrics Trauma Program, New Jersey District (1999-2001); Vice President, LPGA Amateur Golf Association (1999-2000); President, Kiwanis Club of Caldwell-West Essex (1998-1999); Strategic Planning Chair, EWNJ (1996-1999); President-elect, Kiwanis Club of Caldwell-West Essex (1997-1998); Founder, Committees Chair, LPGA Amateur Golf Association (1997-1998); Secretary, Kiwanis Club of Caldwell-West Essex (1996-1998); Vice President, Kiwanis Club of Caldwell-West Essex (1996-1997); Secretary, Board of Directors, Foundation of the New Jersey District of Kiwanis (1990-1993); Board of Trustees, Foundation of the New Jersey District of Kiwanis (1990-1992); Vice President, West Essex Chamber of Commerce (1990-1991); Board of Directors, West Essex Chamber of Commerce (1988-1989); Knights of Malta, Order of St. John of Jerusalem (1986); American Society for Training and Development (Now ATD); Vice President, Communications, ATD; League of Women Voters; Executive Women of New Jersey (Now EWNJ); West Essex Chamber of Commerce; Executive Women's Golf Association of Northern New Jersey (Now LPGA Amateur Golf Association); Founder, Glen Ridge Historical Society MH: Albert Nelson Marquis Lifetime Achievement Award B/I: Mrs. Dixon became involved in her profession because when she was 12 years old, her parents were building a house in Caldwell, NJ, and that meant relocating to a new school district as well. She was reading in the newspaper about a school for girls in Caldwell called the Mount St. Dominic Academy and she told her mom that it looked like a really good school which she would like to attend. Her mother told her if they had the money it would be possible and she told her to fill out the application. When she received the letter, she read she was accepted to the Mount St. Dominic Academy. She believed the one thing that inspired her more than anything else was watching her parents. Although they did not have a lot of money, they made a wonderful life for their children. The sisters at St. Dominic Academy were women who promoted women going after what they really wanted in life. When people ask her where she learned to become a leader, she always says Mount St. Dominic Academy in Caldwell. AV: Reading; Birdwatching; Golf; Writing PA: Independent RE: Roman Catholic

DJOKOVIC, NOVAK, T: Professional Tennis Player I: Athletics DOB: 05/22/1987 SC: Belgrade/Serbia PT: Srdjan Djokovic; Dijana Djokovic MS: Married SPN: Jelena Ristiç (7/10/2014) CH: Stefan C: Professional Tennis Player, ATP Tennis (2003-Present) CW: Author, "Serve to Win: The 14-Day Gluten-Free Plan for Physical and Mental Excellence" (2013) AW: ATP Player of the Year (2014-2015, 2017); ATP Player of the Year (2011-2012); Arthur Ashe Humanitarian Award (2012); Listee, 100 Most Influential People in the World, Time (2012); Order of Serbian National Defense in America (2011); Order of St. Sava, Patriarch Irinej of Serbia (2011); ATP Most Improved Player (2007); ATP Most Improved Player (2006) RE: Serbian Orthodox Christian

DOERR, JOHN, T: Venture Capitalist I: Fundraising CN: Kleiner Perkins DOB: 6/29/1951 PB: St. Louis SC: MO/USA MS: Married SPN: Ann Dowland CH: Two Children ED: Master of Business Administration, Harvard Business School (1976); Master of Science in Electrical Engineering, Rice University (1974); Bachelor of Science in Electrical Engineering, Rice University (1973) C: Advisory Board Member, Generation Investment Management Inc. (2007-Present); Founder, Chief Executive Officer, Silicon Compilers (1981-Present); Partner, Kleiner Perkins Caulfield & Byers, Menlo Park, CA (1980-Present); Member, USA Economic Recovery Advisory Board (2009-2017); Salesman, Intel Corp. (1974-1980) CR: Board of Directors, Zynga Inc. (2013-Present); Board of Directors, iControl Networks Inc. (2008-Present); Board of Directors, Amyris Biotechnologies Inc. (2006-Present); Board of Directors, Zazzle.com Inc. (2005-Present); Board of Directors, Google Inc. (1999-Present); Board of Directors, Netscape Communications Corp. (1994-Present); Board of Directors, Homestore.com (1998-Present); Member, President's Economic Recovery Advisory Board (2009-2011); Board of Directors, Amazon.com (1996-2010); Board of Directors, Move Inc. (1998-2008); Board of Directors, Intuit (1990-2007); Board of Directors, Sun Microsystems Inc. (1982-2006); Board of Directors, Palm Inc. (2003-2005); Board of Directors, Drugstore.com (1998-2004); Board of Directors, Handspring Inc. (1998-2003) AW: Listee, The Forbes 400: Richest Americans (2006-Present); Inductee, California Hall of Fame (2010); Fellow, American Academy of Arts and Sciences (2009); Listee, America's Best Leaders, US News & World Report (2009); Listee, The 50 Most Important People on the Web, PC World (2007); Named, Distinguished Alumnus, Rice University (1997) MEM: Fellow, American Academy Arts and Sciences

DOGGETT, LLOYD ALTON II, T: U.S. Representative from Texas I: Government Administration/ Government Relations/Government Services DOB: 10/06/1946 PB: Austin SC: TX/USA PT: Lloyd Alton Doggett; Alyce Paulin (Freydenfeldt) Doggett MS: Married SPN: Elizabeth "Libby" Belk (1969) CH: Lisa; Catherine ED: JD, The University of Texas School of Law, with Honors (1970); BBA, The University of Texas at Austin (1967) C: Member, U.S. House of Representatives from Texas' 35th Congressional District, United States Congress (2013-Present); Member, U.S. House of Representatives from Texas' 25th Congressional District, United States Congress (2005-2013); Member, U.S. House of Representatives from Texas' 10th Congressional District, United States Congress (1995-2005); Justice, Texas Supreme Court, Austin, Texas (1989-1994); Partner, Doggett & Jacks, Austin, Texas (1975-1988); Member, District 14, Texas State Senate (1973-1985) CR: Chair, Task Force on Judicial Ethics, Texas Supreme Court (1992-1994); Adjunct Professor, The University of Texas School of Law (1989-1994) CIV: Board of Directors, Consumers Union of US (1976-1981, 1986-1989) AW: Named Best Elected Official, Austin Chronicle (2010); Legislator Achievement Award, American Association of Retired Persons (AARP) (2008); Environmental Champion Award, Texas League of Conservation Voters (2006); Named Business Advocate of the Year, Texas Association of Mexican American Chamber of Commerce (TAMACC) (2006); Named an Outstanding Jurist in Texas, Mexico American Bar Association (1993); Named an Outstanding Jurist in Texas, Mexican American Bar Association (1993); James Madison Award, Freedom of Information Foundation of Texas (1990); First Amendment Award, National Society of Professional Journalists (1990); Named One of the Best Legislators, Texas Monthly Magazine (1979, 1981); Named an Outstanding State Senator, Common Cause (1980); Named One of the Five Outstanding Young Texans, Texas Jaycees (1977); Arthur B. DeWitty Award for Outstanding Achievement in Human Rights, Austin Chapter, NAACP MEM: President, Texas Consumer Association (1973) BAR: United States District Court for the Western District of Texas (1972); United States Court of Appeals for the Fifth Circuit (1972); State of Texas (1971) RE: Methodist

DOLCE, PHILIP C., T: Professor of History, Chair of the Suburban Studies Group, Social Sciences I: Education/Educational Services DOB: 11/29/1941 PB: New York SC: NY/USA PT: Joseph Philip Dolce; Emma Veronica (Gallo) Dolce MS: Married SPN: Patricia Francine (Pasciuto) Dolce (07/16/1963) CH: Susan Elizabeth; Michael Joseph ED: Doctor of Philosophy, Fordham University, Bronx, NY (1971); Master of Arts, Fordham University, Bronx, NY (1966); Bachelor of Arts, St. John's University, New York, NY (1963) CT: Management Development Certificate, Harvard University, Cambridge, MA (1990) C: Former Dean, Professor of History, Chair of the Suburban Studies Group, Social Sciences, Bergen Community College, Paramus, NJ (1972-Present); Assistant Professor, St. John's University, New York, NY (1966-1972); Teacher, St. Helena's High School, Bronx, NY (1963-1966) CR: Executive Director, Eastern Educational Consortium, Paramus, NJ (1978-1986); Bergen County Police Training Advisory Committee, Mahwah, NJ CW: Creator, Television and Radio Programs, Now Part of the Permanent Collections of the Paley Center for Media in New York City, The National Archives in Washington, DC, the FBI Academy Library in Virginia, the Schomburg Center for Black Cultures in New York City and the John F. Kennedy Library in Massachusetts (2000-2008); Moderator, TV Program, "The Black Middle Class" (2002); Coordinator, TV Documentary, "The Cubans of New Jersey" (1986); Producer, CBS TV Series, "Science and Society: A Humanistic View" (1980); Editor, "Suburbia: The America Dream and Dilemma" (1976); Co-Editor, "Power and the Presidency" (1976); Co-Editor, "Cities in Transition: From the Ancient World to Urban America"

(1974); Producer, Host, Weekly WPAT Radio Series; Creator, TV Series, "The American Suburbs and American Health Care"; Current Research and Publications Focused on the American Suburbs; Speaker, Member, Panel Presenter, On Such Topics as Suburbia, Immigration and Teaching, National Meetings of the League for Innovation, the Community College Futures Assembly, the Organization of American Historians, the National Council for Black Studies, the American Sociological Association, the Popular Culture Association, the Society for American City and Regional Planning History, the National Education Association and More **AW:** John and Suzanne Roueche Excellence Award, League of Innovation (2017); Excellence in the Art of Teaching Award, National Education Association (2002); John L. Blackburn Award, Exemplary Administrative Leadership from the American Association of University Administrators (2000); Radio Enterprise Award (1995); Radio Feature Award (1995); Radio Public Service Award, Society of Professional Journalists (1991); Administrative Innovation and Team Leadership Award, American Association of University Administrators (1990); CAPE Documentary TV Award, Cable TV Network, New Jersey (1987); Finalist, Award, International Film and TV Festival (1986); Immigration Fellow, New Jersey Department Higher Education, Trenton, NJ (1985-1986); International Global Finalist Award for Social Commitment in the Field of Health Care **MEM:** Columbia University Seminar on the City; Former Member, New Jersey Business and Labor State Advisory Committee, Trenton, NJ; Former Member, Bergen County Police Advisory Committee, Mahwah, NJ **MH:** Albert Nelson Marquis Lifetime Achievement Award; Marquis Who's Who Top Professional **B/I:** Dr. Dolce became involved in his profession because he always liked history. He was always interested in current events and building his local community.

DOLE, ELIZABETH ALEXANDER, T: Founder, Author, Former U.S. Senator **I:** Nonprofit & Philanthropy **CN:** The Elizabeth Dole Foundation **DOB:** 7/29/1936 **PB:** Salisbury **SC:** NC/USA **PT:** John Van Hanford; Mary Ella (Cathey) Hanford **MS:** Married **SPN:** Robert Joseph Dole (12/06/1975) **CH:** Robin **ED:** Doctor of Jurisprudence, Harvard Law School (1965); Master of Arts in Education and Government, Harvard University (1960); Postgraduate Coursework, Oxford University, England (1959); Bachelor of Arts in Political Science, Duke University, with Distinction (1958) **C:** U.S. Senator, State of North Carolina (2003-2009); Chair, National Republican Senatorial Committee (2005-2007); Secretary, U.S. Department of Labor (1989-1990); With, Robert Dole Presidential Campaign (1987-1988); Secretary, U.S. Department of Transportation (1983-1987); Assistant to President for Public Liaison, The White House (1981-1983); Director, Human Services Group, Office of Executive Branch Management, Office of President-elect (1980); Chairperson, Voters for Reagan-Bush (1980); Commissioner, Federal Trade Commission, Washington, DC (1973-1979); Deputy Assistant to President, The White House, Washington, DC (1971-1973); Associate Director of Legislative Affairs, Then Executive Director, President's Committee for Consumer Interests, Washington, DC (1968-1971); Private Law Practice, Washington, DC (1967-1968); Staff Assistant to Assistant Secretary for Education, U.S. Department of Health Education & Welfare, Washington, DC (1966-1967) **CR:** Nominating Committee, North Carolina Consumer Council (1972); Student Teacher, Melrose High School, Melrose, MA (1959-1960) **CIV:** Founder, Elizabeth Dole Foundation (2006-Present); Honorary Chair, Project RoundHouse (2001); President, The American National Red Cross (1991-1999); Council,

Harvard Law School Association (1992-1995); Visiting Committee, Harvard School of Public Health (1992-1995); Board of Overseers, Harvard University (1989-1995); Trustee, Duke University (1974-1988); Honorary Board Member, Wings of Hope **CW:** Author, "Hearts Touched with Fire: My 500 Most Inspirational Quotes" (2006); Co-author, with Bob Dole, Richard Norton Smith and Kerry Tymchuk, "Unlimited Partners: Our American Story" (1996) **AW:** Named to Society of World Changers, Indiana Wesleyan University (2014); Named, One of the Most Powerful Women in the World, Forbes Magazine (2005); S. Roger Horchow Award for Greatest Public Service by a Private Citizen (1999); Named, Third Most Admired Woman in America, Good Housekeeping (1996, 1998); Named, One of the 10 Most Fascinating People, Barbara Walter's Special, (1996); Named, One of the Most Inspiring Political Figures, MSNBC (1996); Christian Woman of the Year Award (1996); Raoul Wallenberg Award for Humanitarian Service (1995); Inductee, National Women's Hall of Fame (1995); Leadership Award, League of Women Voters (1994); Maxwell Finland Award, National Foundation for Infectious Diseases (1994); Lifetime Achievement Award for Breaking the Glass Ceiling, Women Executives in State Government (1993); North Carolinian of the Year Award, North Carolina Press Association (1993); Radcliffe Medal (1993); Selectee, Safety and Health Hall of Fame International (1993); North Carolina Award (1991); Distinguished Service Award, National Safety Council (1989); Humanitarian Award, National Commission Against Drunk Driving (1988); Voted One of the World's 10 Most Admired Women (1988); Distinguished Alumni Award, Duke University (1988); Named, One of America's 200 Young Leaders, TIME Magazine (1974); Arthur S. Flemming Award, U.S. Government (1972) **MEM:** The Phi Beta Kappa Society; Pi Lambda Theta; Pi Sigma Alpha **BAR:** District of Columbia Bar (1966) **PA:** Republican **RE:** Methodist

DOLE, ROBERT, "BOB" JOSEPH, T: Former U.S. Senator from Kansas; Special Counsel **I:** Government Administration/Government Relations/Government Services **CN:** Alston & Bird LLP **DOB:** 07/22/1923 **PB:** Russell **SC:** KS/USA **PT:** Doran Ray Dole; Bina (Talbott) Dole **MS:** Married **SPN:** Elizabeth Hanford (12/06/1975); Phyllis Holden (1948, Divorced 1972) **CH:** Robin **ED:** Honorary Doctorate, The University of Kansas (2012); Honorary LLD, Washburn University, Topeka, KS (1969); LLB, Washburn Municipal University (Now Washburn University), Topeka, KS (1952); AB, Washburn Municipal University (Now Washburn University), Topeka, KS (1952); Coursework, The University of Arizona (1948-1949); Coursework, The University of Kansas (1941-1943) **C:** Special Counsel, Alston & Bird LLP, Washington, DC (2003-Present); Of Counsel, Verner, Liipfert, Bernhard, McPherson & Hand (1997-2002); Senate Majority Leader (1985-1987, 1995-1996); Senate Minority Leader (1987-1995); Chairman, U.S. Senate Finance Committee (1981-1985); Chairman, Republican National Committee (1971-1973); U.S. Senator, State of Kansas (1969-1996); Member, U.S. House of Representatives from Kansas' First Congressional District, United States Congress, Washington, DC (1963-1969); Member, U.S. House of Representatives from Kansas' Sixth Congressional District, United States Congress, Washington, DC (1961-1963); Attorney, Sole Practice, Russell, KS (1953-1961); Member, Kansas House of Representatives (1951-1953) **CR:** Co-chair, President Commission on Care for America's Returning Wounded Warriors (2007-Present); Chairman, International Commission on Missing Persons in the Former Yugoslavia (1997-2001); Republican Candidate, U.S. Presidential Election

(1996); Member, Martin Luther King Jr. Federal Holiday Commission (1984); Member, National Commission on Social Security Reform (1983); Advisor, General Agreement on Tariffs and Trades, Ministerial Trade Conference (1982); Member, U.S. Delegate to the United Nations Food and Agricultural Organization (1965, 1968, 1974, 1975, 1977, 1979); Member, Commission on Security and Cooperation in Europe (1977); Republican Vice Presidential Candidate, U.S. Presidential Election (1976); Member, U.S. National Commission for UNESCO (1970, 1973); Member, U.S. Delegate to Study the Arab Refugee Problem (1967); Member, President's Delegate to Study the Food Crisis in India (1966) **CIV:** Chairman, National WWII Memorial (1997-2004); Chairman, Dole Foundation **MIL:** Honorary Colonel, United States Army, World War II (1942-1948) **CW:** Author, "One Soldier's Story: A Memoir" (2005); Co-author with George McGovern and Donald Messer, "Ending Hunger Now: A Challenge to Persons of Faith" (2005); Author, "Great Presidential Wits (...I Wish I Was in the Book): A Collection of Humorous Anecdotes and Quotations" (2001); Author, "Great Political Wit: Laughing (Almost) All the Way to the White House" (1998); Co-author with Elizabeth Dole, Richard Norton Smith and Kerry Tymchuk, Autobiography, "Unlimited Partners: Our American Story" (1996) **AW:** Congressional Medal of Freedom (2018); Named One of the 50 Top Lobbyists, Washingtonian Magazine (2007); Theodore Roosevelt Award, NCAA (1998); Presidential Medal of Freedom, The White House (1997); Horatio Alger Award, The Horatio Alger Association of Distinguished Americans, Inc. (1988); Decorated Bronze Star with Oak Cluster; Two Purple Hearts **MEM:** DAV; VFW; 4-H Fair Association; The American Legion; Kiwanis International; Elks; Shriners International; Masons; Kappa Sigma Fraternity **BAR:** State of Kansas (1952) **PA:** Republican **RE:** Methodist

DOLIM, HENRY P. JR., DOB: 03/27/1942 **PB:** Balboa **SC:** Panama **PT:** Henry Philip Dolim; Virginia Ridge Dolim **MS:** Widowed **SPN:** Charlene Joy Mundorf (12/17/1966, Deceased) **CH:** Scott; Anthony; David **ED:** MS in Systems Management, University of Southern California, Los Angeles, CA (1974); BS in Industrial Engineering, University of Southern California, Los Angeles, CA (1965) **CT:** Certification, Project Management Institute, Inc. (2006) **C:** Adjunct Professor, Industrial and Systems Engineering, University of Southern California (2006-2015); Systems Engineer, Northrop Grumman Corporation, Hawthorne and El Segundo, CA (1986-2006) **MIL:** Officer, United States Air Force (1966-1986) **AW:** Distinguished Flying Cross with Two Oak Leaf Clusters, United States Air Force; Air Medal with 15 Oak Leaf Clusters, United States Air Force **MEM:** Air Force Association; Military Officers Association of America **MH:** Albert Nelson Marquis Lifetime Achievement Award **B/I:** Mr. Dolim became involved in his profession with influence from his father, who served in the United States Air Force as a pilot during World War II. After the war, his father continued to fly airplanes and pursued aeronautical engineering. Mr. Dolim decided to follow in his footsteps. **AV:** Photography; Travel; Amateur radio **THT:** During his time in the United States Air Force, Mr. Dolim piloted the T-38A, AT-38B, F-5BEF and F-4CDE aircrafts.

DOMINGUEZ, MICHELLE, T: Executive Vice President of Compliance **I:** Media & Entertainment **CN:** Vision Media **DOB:** 06/19/1974 **CH:** Mary **ED:** Doctor of Jurisprudence, Northwestern California School of Law (2023) **C:** Executive Vice President of Compliance, Vision Media (2019-Present); Senior Director, Entertainment Services (2018-Present); Director, Process Management, Vision Media Management LLC (1998-Present) **CIV:** Will Rogers Program **MH:** Marquis Who's Who Top Professional **AS:** Ms. Dominguez attributes her success to her drive and determination. She strives to always do better. **B/I:** Ms. Dominguez became involved in her profession after graduating from high school. After working at one particular company for more than five years, a client offered her a job, which she eagerly accepted. **THT:** Always let the best idea win.

DOMINGUEZ-WEISS, THERESA, RN, T: President, Director **I:** Other **CN:** Power Places **DOB:** 08/16/1950 **PB:** Los Angeles **SC:** CA/USA **PT:** Richard Joseph Dominguez; Norma (Romero) Dominguez **MS:** Widowed **SPN:** F. T. Weiss, PhD (2008, Deceased) **CH:** Rebecca **ED:** Registered Nurse, Rio Hondo College, Whittier, CA (1975); Advanced Certificate, Family Nurse Practitioner Program, UC Davis School of Medicine **CT:** Registered Nurse **C:** President, Director, Power Places (2008-Present); Co-Owner, Vice President, Director, Power Places (1985-2008); Medical Consultant, Administrator, Headache Institute, Newport Beach, CA (1987-1989); Medical Consultant, Administrator, Health Management Center, Orange, CA (1984-1987); Junior Faculty Medicine, University of California, Irvine (1982-1984); Co-Director, Cardiac Rehabilitation Center, Whittier, CA (1978-1979); Critical Care Nurse, Beverly Hospital, Montebello, CA (1975-1978); Rehabilitation Nurse Pediatric and Spinal Cord, Rancho Los Amigos Hospital, Downey, CA (1969-1975) **CR:** Researcher, In-Field Instructor, Prenatal Care, Coastline Community College, Costa Mesa, CA (1985); Researcher, In-Field Instructor, Prenatal Care, Chope Hospital, San Mateo, CA (1982) **CW:** Author, "Transformational Journeys with Death & Dying" **MEM:** National Association for Female Executives; American Nurses Association; California Nurses Association; California Association for Nurse Practitioners; Laguna Art Museum **MH:** Albert Nelson Marquis Lifetime Achievement Award **B/I:** Ms. Weiss became involved in her profession because her grandparents escaped the Mexican revolution and settled in Southern California. Her family members were all successful immigrants, with her grandfather being one of the first Mexican-Americans to be involved in the movie industry. They came from a close-knit family and a loving environment. Her parents worked hard to send her and her siblings to private school to give them the best education. She felt secure growing up as a kid in that environment, which inspired her to follow her dreams. She believes it was she became a candy striper because of her father. Whenever she or her siblings got cuts or bruises, their father would clean them up and explain the process as he did so. She wanted to emulate him and that's how her career began, first as a candy striper then eventually an registered nurse.

DOMKE, GARY EDWARD, T: Securities Company Executive **I:** Business Management/Business Services **PB:** St. Louis **SC:** MO/USA **PT:** Charles Fred Domke; Eleanor (Webbers) Domke **MS:** Married **SPN:** Lee Krieger (05/06/1995); Yvonne Anderson; Constance Lowe **CH:** Yvette Lynn **ED:** Coursework, St. Louis University (1977-1980); Coursework, University of Missouri, St. Louis, MO (1971-1976) **CT:** Registered Principal; Registered Investment Advisor; Registered Options Principal; General Agent, Missouri Insurance, Life, Health & Variable Annuities **C:** Vice President, Huntleigh Securities, Inc., Clayton, MO (2004-Present); Vice President, Private and Corporate Accounts, Oppenheimer & Co., Inc., Clayton, MO (1996-Present); Registered Independent Associate, CFD Investments (2017); Chief Compliance Officer, Chairman of the Board,

Oakbridge Financial (2010); Vice President, Resident Manager, Stifel Nicolaus & Co. Inc. (1994-1996); Vice President, Prudential Securities, St. Louis, MO (1982-1994); Vice President, Tax Shelters, Mutual Funds, WZW Cornerstone, St. Louis, MO (1980-1982); Registered Representative, R. Rowland & Co., St. Louis, MO (1971-1980); Registered Representative, R. G. Mills And Co., St. Louis, MO (1969-1971) **CR:** Consultant, Various CPA and Law Firms **MIL:** First Lieutenant Captain, Company Commander, Ordinance Corps, U.S. Army (1965-1969) **MH:** Albert Nelson Marquis Lifetime Achievement Award **B/I:** When Mr. Domke got released from active duty in the United States Army, he had to find a job and ended up working for an executive search firm for a bit. He did a search for an information technology chief officer for an investment banking firm; unfortunately, though, they did not hire his candidate. He reached out to the president to discuss his confusion regarding their decision, and the president told him he hired a candidate who would take less money. This experience made it clear to Mr. Domke that he was working in the wrong industry. He then transitioned to where he is today. **AV:** Golfing; Skiing; Exploring computers; Woodworking; Practicing photography **RE:** Republican

DONALD, AARON, T: Professional Football Player **I:** Athletics **CN:** Los Angeles Rams **DOB:** 05/23/1991 **PB:** Pittsburgh **SC:** PA/USA **ED:** Degree in Communications, University of Pittsburgh (2020) **C:** Professional Football Player, Los Angeles Rams (2014-Present) **AW:** First-team All-Pro (2015–2019); Winner, Pro Bowl (2014–2019); AP NFL Defensive Player of the Year (2017-2018); NFL Defensive Rookie of the Year (2014); PFWA All-Rookie Team (2014); ACC Defensive Player of the Year (2013); Bronko Nagurski Trophy (2013); Chuck Bednarik Award (2013); Lombardi Award (2013); Outland Trophy (2013); Unanimous All-American (2013); First-team All-ACC (2013); First-team All-Big East (2012); Second-team All-Big East (2011); Invited, NFL 2010s All-Decade Team

DONALDSON, JOHN RILEY, T: Physics Educator **I:** Education/Educational Services **DOB:** 11/24/1925 **PB:** Dallas **SC:** TX/USA **PT:** John Riley Donaldson; Marguerette Hoover (Atkinson) Donaldson **MS:** Single **SPN:** Ruth Heise Reynolds (2007, Deceased 2017); Shirley Jean Brown (06/30/1951, Deceased 2006) **CH:** Nancy Gullett; Dorothy Chaffee; Jack Donaldson; Jane Hollingsworth **ED:** PhD, Yale University (1951); MS, Yale University (1949); MA, Rice University (1947); BS, Rice University (1945) **C:** Professor Emeritus, California State University, Fresno (1991-Present); Chairman, Department of Physics, California State University, Fresno (1983-1991); Professor, California State University, Fresno (1967-1991); Assistant Professor then Associate Professor, California State University, Fresno (1956-1967); Physicist, U.S. Army, Frederick, MD (1954-1956); Associate Professor, University of Arizona (1953-1954); Physicist, California Research and Development, Livermore, CA (1950-1953) **CR:** Visiting Professor, Swiss Federal Institutes of Technology, Zürich, Switzerland (1967-1968, 1982-1983) **CIV:** Choir Director, College Community Congregational Church, Fresno, CA (1956-1996); Elected Supervisor, Fresno County, CA (1973-1980); Moderator, College Community Congregational Church, Fresno, CA (1960-1961); Volleyball Player, National AAU All American (1951); National AAU Discus Champion (1945); Member, United Church of Christ **MIL:** Private to Specialist Third Class (SP3), U.S. Army (1954-1956) **AW:** Democratic Award **MEM:** American Association for the Advancement of Science; American Physical Society; American Association of Physics Teachers

MH: Albert Nelson Marquis Lifetime Achievement Award **AS:** Dr. Donaldson attributes his success to having several lucky breaks, a leaked IQ test in fifth grade, assignment to a high-IQ class in seventh grade, being a high school valedictorian, and arriving in the Army in Frederick, Maryland, just as the big Methodist church needed a choir director. Directing a church was a huge part of his life for 42 years; he loved it. **B/I:** Dr. Donaldson became involved in his profession because he had good algebra and chemistry teachers in high school who were inspiring. He had a physics teacher who would allow him to use the lab freely after school ended and in addition he had a biology teacher who was close to retirement and after his first exam would allow him to make up exams for her. In the seventh grade, he joined the arithmetic team and that helped a lot. He learned to speed his work which helped his entire career. His dad was an engineer and his best teacher in high school was a chemist so he started as a chemical engineer at Rice University and he did not like it, so he switched to physics after his junior year. got his degree in four years and took an extra year to finish the required physics courses. Harold A. Wilson was a very supportive teacher at Rice University at that time. **AV:** Singing; Conducting; Sports **PA:** Democrat **RE:** Atheist **THT:** Dr. Donaldson is still enjoying life at 94.

DONNELLY, KATAYOUN, T: Attorney **I:** Law and Legal Services **CN:** Azizpour Donnelly LLC **PB:** Tehran **SC:** Iran **CH:** One Son **ED:** Doctor of Jurisprudence, University of Denver, Sturm College of Law (2006); Coursework, The Hague Academy of International Law, The Netherlands (2001); Bachelor of Laws, with Honors, University of Tehran; Bachelor's Degree in Law, Tehran University **C:** Attorney, Owner, Azizpour Donnelly LLC (2012-Present); Associate, Baker & Hostetler LLP (2011-2012); Law Clerk for the Honorable Stephanie K. Seymour, United States Court of Appeals for the Tenth Circuit (2009-2010); Law Clerk for the Honorable Edward W. Nottingham, United States District Court for the District of Colorado (2008) **CIV:** Board of Directors, Board of Trustees, American Inns of Court (2016-Present); Board of Trustees, Colorado Supreme Court's Attorneys' Fund for Client Protection (2015-Present); Temple Bar Scholarship Selection Committee, American Inns of Court (2015-Present); Chief Justice's Commission on the Legal Profession (2012-Present); Judge William E. Doyle American Inn of Court (2007-Present); Board of Governors, Denver Bar Association Representative, Colorado Bar Association (2011-2013); Board of Directors, Colorado Lawyers Committee; Volunteer, Moot Court Competitions; Mentor, Colorado Attorney Mentoring Program, Colorado Supreme Court **AW:** Listee, Super Lawyers Rising Stars (2014-2017); Temple Bar Scholar (2010) **MEM:** Appellate CLE Faculty, Colorado Bar Association (2016-Present); Appellate Practice Subcommittee, Colorado Bar Association (2009-Present); Co-Chair, Pro Bono Subcommittee, Appellate Practice, American Bar Association **MH:** Marquis Who's Who Top Professional **AS:** Ms. Donnelly credits her success on the encouragement of her family, as well as her various colleagues. **B/I:** Ms. Donnelly became involved in her profession despite a lifelong interest in mathematics and physics, deciding instead to enter law school. She eventually developed a fascination in appeals, civil and criminal law. **AV:** Tennis; Skiing

DONNELLY, SCOTT CHRISTOPHER, T: Chairman, President, Chief Executive Officer **I:** Other **CN:** Textron Inc. **ED:** BEE, University of Colorado (1984) **C:** Chairman, President, Chief Executive Officer, Textron, Inc., Providence, RI (2010-Present); President, Chief Executive Officer, Textron, Inc., Providence, RI (2009-2010); President, Chief Operating Officer, Textron, Inc., Providence, RI (2009); Executive Vice President, Chief Operating Officer, Textron, Inc., Providence, RI (2008-2009); President, Chief Executive Officer, General Electric Aviation (2005-2008); Senior Vice President, Director, GE Global Research, Schenectady, NY (2000-2005); Vice President of Global Technology System, GE Medical Systems (1997-2000); General Manager, GE Industrial Systems Technology (1995-1997); With, GE Aerospace, Syracuse, NY (1989-1995) **CR:** Board of Directors, Textron Inc. (2009-Present) **CIV:** Board of Directors, United Way of Greater Cincinnati; Member, Visiting Committee on Advanced Technology, National Institute of Standards and Technology; Member, Engineering Advisory Committee, Center for Innovation in Minimally Invasive Therapy, Massachusetts General Hospital; Member, Engineering Advisory Committee, Cornell University; Member, Engineering Advisory Committee, University of Colorado; Trustee, Siena College

DONOHUE, JOYCE, PHD, T: Educator (Retired); Scientist; Chemical Risk Assessor **I:** Sciences **DOB:** 01/27/1940 **PB:** Holyoke **SC:** MA/USA **PT:** Richard Charles Morrissey; Anna Elizabeth (Joyce) Morrissey **MS:** Divorced **SPN:** John Thomas Donohue (01/27/1973) **CH:** Maura Joyce; John Thomas; Sean Richard; Eric Patrick **ED:** PhD in Biochemistry, The University of New Hampshire (1972); MS in Nutrition Research, University of Massachusetts (1964); BS in Education in Foods and Nutrition, Framingham State College (Now Framingham State University), Framingham, MA (1961) **CT:** Certified Secondary School Teacher in Science, Commonwealth of Massachusetts; RD (Registered Dietitian) **C:** Chemical Risk Assessor, Health Scientist, Office of Water, United States Environmental Protection Agency, Washington, DC (1996-Present); Adjunct Associate Professor, Northern Virginia Community College, Annandale, VA and Woodbridge, VA (1974-2008); Adjunct Professor of Nutrition, Virginia Polytechnic Institute and State University, Falls Church, VA (1979-1997); Manager, Toxicology, NSF International, Washington, DC (1994-1996); Program Manager, Toxicologist, Life Systems Incorporated, Arlington, VA (1990-1994); Service Manager, Toxicology, Washington Area, Law Environmental, Woodbridge, VA (1989-1990); Health Scientist, V.J. Ciccone & Associates, Woodbridge, VA (1981-1989); Associate Professor of Biochemistry, Framingham State College (Now Framingham State University) (1972-1973); Assistant Professor of Biochemistry and Nutrition, Framingham State College (Now Framingham State University) (1971-1972); Instructor of Chemistry and Nutrition, Framingham State College (Now Framingham State University) (1966-1968); Teacher of Chemistry and Biology, West Springfield High School, MA (1962-1966) **CIV:** Wetlands Board, Department of Public Works, Prince William County Government (1989-Present); Council of Environmental and Public Health Advisors, UL LLC (2006-2017); Solid Waste Management Citizens' Advisory Committee, Prince William County Government (1986-2000); School Lunch Advisory Committee, Prince William County Public Schools (1982-1985) **AW:** Silver Medal, United States Environmental Protection Agency (2018); Gold Medal, United States Environmental Protection Agency (2000, 2015, 2018); Joseph Seifter Award for Human Health Risk Assessment, United States Environmental Protection Agency (2010); Scientific and Technological Achievement Award, Health Effects Research and Human Health Risk Assessment, United States Environmental Protection Agency (2008); Alumni Achievement Award, Framingham State College

(Now Framingham State University) (1986) **MEM:** American Association for the Advancement of Science; Academy of Nutrition and Dietetics; Northern Virginia Academy of Nutrition and Dietetics; Board Member, Independent Association of Framingham State Alumni **MH:** Albert Nelson Marquis Lifetime Achievement Award **B/I:** Dr. Donohue became involved in her profession with inspiration from her high school chemistry teacher, and because of her longtime passion for cooking, which started in middle school. She was always curious about what would happen if she made subtle recipe changes, and applied this interest to the study of carbohydrates, fats and DNA in chemistry, food science and nutrition. **AV:** Collecting historic American clothing **PA:** Democrat **RE:** Roman Catholic

DOOCY, STEVE, T: Author, Television Personality **I:** Media & Entertainment **DOB:** 10/19/1956 **PB:** Algona **SC:** IA/USA **ED:** BS in Journalism, University of Kansas **C:** Host, "All American New Year" (2004); Co-Host, "Fox and Friends" (1998) **CW:** Tales from the Dad Side (2008); Author, "The Mr. and Mrs. Happy Handbook (2007)

DORN, ROOSEVELT F., JD, DD, T: Retired Superior Court Judge, Retired Mayor of the City of Inglewood **I:** Government Administration/Government Relations/Government Services **DOB:** 10/29/1935 **PB:** Checotah **SC:** OK/USA **PT:** William M. Dorn; Nettie (Brinkley) Dorn **MS:** Married **SPN:** Joyce Evelyn Glosson Dorn (1965) **CH:** Bryan Keith Dorn; Dr. Renee Felicia Dorn; Atty. Rochelle Francine Dorn-Hayes; Randy Dorn; Irvin Dorn **ED:** DD, Southern California School of Ministry (1998); Graduate Coursework, Earl Warren Legal Institute (1982); Graduate Coursework, California Judicial College, University of California Berkeley School of Law (1979); JD, Whittier College (1969) **C:** Mayor, City of Inglewood (1997-2010); Superior Court Judge, Los Angeles County and the State of California, Los Angeles, CA (1980-1997); Municipal Court Judge, Inglewood Judicial District (1979-1980); Assistant City Attorney, Los Angeles City Attorney's Office (1970-1979); Deputy Sheriff, Los Angeles County (1961-1969) **CIV:** Founder, Project Hope, Multi-Organization to Fight Truancy, Inglewood, CA (1983-Present); President, Board of Directors, 100 Black Men, Inc., Los Angeles, CA (1983-1993); RDM Scholarship Fund, Inglewood, CA (1983); Bible Teacher, Local Elder, First African Methodist Episcopal Methodist Church, Los Angeles, CA; Foundation for At Risk Youth; Past President and Vice President, National Conference of Black Mayors of America, Inc.; Past Member, U.S. Conference of Mayors, Inc.; Life Member, Past Vice President, Past President, Board of Directors, 100 Black Men of Los Angeles Inc.; Past Board of Directors, Young Black Scholars, 100 Black Men of Los Angeles, Inc.; Past Chairman of the Board, Los Angeles Community Sports and Arts Foundation for At Risk Youth; Life Member, National Association for the Advancement of Colored People (NAACP); Life Member, New Frontier Democratic Club; Founder, Life Member, Inglewood Democratic Club; Ordained Minister, First AME Church, Los Angeles, CA; Man-Child Mentoring Program for Male Youth at Risk, First AME Church **MIL:** U.S. Air Force (1954-1958) **CW:** Featured, Los Angeles Magazine; Featured, KNBC TV, Channel 4; Featured, KCET TV, Channel 28 **AW:** Certificate of Recognition, Paralyzed Veterans of America (2018); Certificate of Recognition, Veterans of Foreign Wars of the United States (2015); Certificate of Recognition, Inglewood Area Ministerial Association, Inc. for National Prayer Day (2012); Barack Obama Community Service Award, Fifth Episcopal District, African Methodist Episcopal Church, Ingle-

wood Area Ministers' Association (2012); Certificate of Recognition, Prayer Breakfast (2010); Neighborhood Watch Award, Heights at Ladera HOA (2009); Glory Award (2008); Healthy Kleen Award in Recognition of Efforts to Bring Fairness, Honesty, and Encouragement of Small and Large Businesses, City of Inglewood (2007); Project "Read For Hope" Award, Stephanie Starks HOPE Foundation (2006); Thank You for Your Leadership Dedication, Positive Image in Our Community, Heights at Ladera Neighborhood Watch (2005); Citizen of the Year Award, Phi Beta Beta Graduate Chapter, Omega Psi Phi Fraternity, Inc. (2004); Support of NAUW Programs Award, National Association of University Women's 64th Biennial National Convention (2003); Freedom and Justice Award, World Literacy Crusade International (2002); Frontline Soldier Award, A Gathering of Men (2001); Legacy Award, National Association for the Advancement of Colored People (1995); Distinguished Service Award, 33rd Degree Prince Hall, Masons (1995); Professional Service Award, People Who Care Center, Inc. (1990); Certificate of Special Congressional Recognition, Congressman Julian Dixon (1990); Certificate of Commendation, Mayor of Los Angeles (1990); Outstanding Service to Education and Welfare of Youth Award, Prairie View A&M University Alumni Association (1989); Special Service Award, Martin Luther King Committee, Inglewood, CA (1989); Christ's Caring Presence Award, Los Angeles Baptist Mission Society (1988); Special Volunteer Award, Young Black Scholars (1988); Public Service Award, Probation Department, City of Inglewood (1987); Meritorious Service Youth Award, Inglewood Teachers Association (1985); Outstanding Community Service Award, Harmony Missionary Baptist Church (1985); National Top Ladies of Distinction Humanitarian Award (1984); Letter of Commendation, President Bush and Gov. Deukmejian; Centinela District Good Scout Award, Los Angeles Area Boy Scouts of America; FAME First to Serve Award, First African Methodist Episcopal Church of Los Angeles, Rev. Dr. John J. Hunter; Letter of Commendation for Leadership in Inglewood, Congresswoman Maxine Waters; Certificate of Membership, Greater Los Angeles African American Chamber of Commerce; President's Heritage Hall of Honor Award, Baptist Minister's Conference of Los Angeles and Southern California; Political and Religious Hall of Fame Award, Black American Political Association of California (BAPAC); Amanda Guruge Lifetime Commitment Award, Violence Prevention Conference, Stop the Violence, Increase the Peace Foundation; Democrat of the Year, 51st Assembly District, Los Angeles County Democratic Party; Several Commendations; Certificate of Appreciation, New Anointing Deliverance Church, Los Angeles, CA; Certificate of Appreciation, Recognition of Outstanding Service, Educating Young Minds; Two Certificates of Acknowledgement, U.S. Department of Housing and Urban Development, HUD Secretary Alphonso Jackson; Partner in Education Award, Inglewood Unified School District; Spirit of the Community Award, Association for Better Living and Education (ABLE) International; Gov. Arnold Schwarzenegger Recognition, John M. Langston Bar Association; Award, Congress of Racial Equality; Yvonne Brathwaite Burke Master of Law Award, Recycling Black Dollars "11th Annual Honors Luncheon to Acknowledge Your Body of Work and Service to Our Community"; City of Inglewood Good Example/Moral Leadership Award, Concerned Businessmen Association of America; City of Los Angeles Political Partners for "Real Men Cook" Foundation Award, Mayor Antonio R. Villaraigosa; "Spirit Of Peace" Award, Stop the Violence, Increase the Peace; Inductee, Langston Bar Association of Los Angeles Hall of

Fame; Political Achievement Award, New Frontier Democratic Club; Outstanding Contributions Award, Little Belize Independence Day Streetfest; Commendation, Supervisor of the Second District Yvonne Brathwaite Burke, County of Los Angeles; History Pacemaker Award for Historical Contributions in Legal and Community Leadership, First Baptist of South Los Angeles; Man of Valor Civic Award, Los Angeles NAACP Youth Council; Award for Continued Dedication to Public Education and Support of Animo Inglewood High School, Animo Inglewood Student Body; Certificate of Appreciation, Employee Support of the Guard and Reserve; Named, 57 Most Intriguing Blacks in America, Ebony Magazine; Outstanding Leadership Award, Whittier College of Law; Angel Leadership Award, WISDYM, Inc.; WISDYM Tribute of Heartfelt Service Award, County of Los Angeles Board of Supervisors Yvonne Brathwaite Burke of the Second District; Award for Dedication in the Fight Against Domestic Violence, Agape Foundation Against Domestic Violence, Inc.; Economic Development Award, 100 Black Men of Los Angeles, Inc. and County of Los Angeles Supervisor Yvonne Brathwaite Burke of the Second District; Public Service Award, Inter-Denominational Ministerial Alliance; Recipient, Numerous Industry Awards **MEM:** American Bar Association; National Association for the Advancement of Colored People (NAACP); National Bar Association; Los Angeles County Bar Association; Los Angeles Trial Lawyers Association; California District Attorneys Association; California Judges Association; California Black Lawyers and Judges Association; Judges' Division, John M. Langston Bar Association; Board of Directors, Young Black Scholars; 33rd Degree Prince Hall, Masons; New Frontier Democratic Club; Inglewood Democratic Club; 100 Black Men of Los Angeles, Inc. **BAR:** State of California (1970) **MH:** Albert Nelson Marquis Lifetime Achievement Award **AS:** Mr. Dorn attributes his success to his faith in God, his wife, Joyce Evelyn Dorn, his parents, sisters, and brothers, and his children. **B/I:** Mr. Dorn became involved in his profession because of a superior court judge, Ralph A. Nutter, who was a Harvard graduate that inspired him while he was working as a bailiff. He offered him a letter of recommendation if he chose to attend law school. He later encouraged him to study in his chambers. Mr. Dorn studied hard, and he had a lot of respect for Judge Nutter. **AV:** Reading; Watching old movies and sports; Traveling; Fishing; Playing cards with friends **PA:** Democrat **RE:** African Methodist Episcopal **THT:** Mr. Dorn believes one gets out of life what one puts in. He encourages staying close to God, praying often, and understanding and learning from one's mistakes. Likewise, always be willing to forgive and help those in need, never carry a grudge, and pass on blessings.

DORNFELD, KAYLA MARIE, T: Teacher **I:** Education/Educational Services **CN:** Mapleton Elementary School **PT:** Deb Hoerth **MS:** Married **CH:** Two stepchildren **ED:** MEd in Elementary Education, University of North Dakota; BS in Early Childhood Education, University of North Dakota **C:** Teacher, Mapleton Elementary School (2015-Present); Teacher, West Fargo Public Schools (2013-2015); Teacher, East River Falls Minnesota Schools (2002-2013) **CR:** International Keynote Speaker; TedxTalk **CIV:** Volunteer, Lutheran Church; Volunteer, Ronald McDonald House **CW:** Two Published Books **AW:** Master Tech of the Year Award, ASE (2019); North Dakota Teacher of the Year (2019); Sioux Award Winner (2018); Internationally-Recognized Third-Grade Teacher **MEM:** National Education Association; North Dakota United **AS:** Ms. Dornfeld attributes her success to finding the right people to share and spend her time with. Her mom

was her number one mentor since she started teaching. Her mother taught kindergarten prior to her retiring. She taught with such care and love for kids. She really looked up to her not only as a mother but as a teacher. **B/I:** Ms. Dornfeld became involved in her profession because her parents were both teachers and inspired her to go into the profession herself.

DORSEY, JACK, T: Internet Company Executive, Software Architect **I:** Internet **DOB:** 11/19/1976 **PB:** St. Louis **SC:** MO/USA **PT:** Tim Dorsey; Marcia (Smith) Dorsey **ED:** Coursework, University of Missouri-Rolla (1995-1998); Coursework, University of California-Berkeley; Coursework, New York University **C:** Co-Founder, Chief Executive Officer, Square, Inc., San Francisco, CA (2009-Present); Chief Executive Officer, Twitter, Inc., San Francisco, CA (2015-Present); Executive Chairman, Twitter, Inc., San Francisco, CA (2011-Present); Non-Executive Chairman, Twitter, Inc., San Francisco, CA (2008-2011); Chief Executive Officer, Twitter, Inc., San Francisco, CA (2007-2008); Co-Founder, Twitter, Inc., San Francisco, CA (2007); Creator, Twitter.com, San Francisco, CA (2006); Co-Founder, Obvious Ventures (2006); With, Odeo (2006); Owner, Web-Based Dispatch Company, CA (2000); With, Dispatch Company, Manhattan, NY (1999-2000) **CR:** Member, Advisory Board, Ustream. tv (2009-Present); Board of Directors, The Walt Disney Company (2013-Present); Board of Directors, BUILD (2011-Present); Board of Directors, Square, Inc. (2009-Present); Board of Directors, Twitter, Inc. (2007-Present) **AW:** 40 Under 40, Fortune (2011-2014); Innovator of the Year Award, American Banker (2012); Innovator of the Year Award, The Wall Street Journal (2012); The 100 Most Influential People in the World, Time (2009); Technology's Best & Brightest Young Entrepreneurs, BusinessWeek; Inductee, TR35, MIT Technology Review

DORSEY, ROBERT FRANCIS, T: Managing Member, President **I:** Law and Legal Services **CN:** Dorsey Associates LLC **DOB:** 01/02/1947 **PB:** Worcester **SC:** MA/USA **PT:** Jeremiah Edmund Dorsey; Mary Theresa (Zelesky) Dorsey **MS:** Married **SPN:** Lynne McGrail; Edna M. Dorsey **CH:** Christopher; Robyn **ED:** MBA, Babson College, Wellesley, MA (1974); BSBA, Nichols College, Dudley, MA (1973) **C:** Managing Member, President, Dorsey Associates LLC, New Bern, NC (2008-Present); President, Chief Executive Officer, Wilson-Epes Printing Company, Inc., Washington, DC (1993-2016); President, Chief Executive Officer, Cling Surface Company, Orchard Park, NY (1991-1993); Senior Vice President, Finance, The Metholatum Company, Buffalo, NY (1985-1991); Corporate Controller, Champion Products, Rochester, NY (1982-1985); Corporate Credit Manager, Champion Products, Rochester, NY (1979-1980); Corporate Credit Manager, Lee-Norse Company, Pittsburgh, PA (1978-1979); General Credit Manager, Ingersoll-Rand Equipment Corporation (1974-1978); Management Trainee, Ford Motor Credit Corporation, Southboro, MA (1973-1974) **CIV:** Board of Trustees, Nichols College, Dudley, MA (2008-2012); Administrator, Robert F. Dorsey Charitable Foundation; Buffalo Club; New Bern Golf & Country Club; Dunes Club of Atlantic Beach **MIL:** Active Duty, Active Reserve, Staff Sergeant, E-6, U.S. Marine Corps (1968-1976) **AW:** Listee, Outstanding Young Men in America (1979); Fellow Award, National Institute of Credit, New York, NY (1978) **MEM:** Life Member, Financial Executives International; Life Member, American Legion **B/I:** Mr. Dorsey became involved in his profession because of the Soldiers and Sailors Act, which meant that his older brother was drafted into the

military out of law school. He had an automobile accident in 1967 and missed a semester of school, and, since the act had not been revised, his hometown, which consisted of 23 colleges and universities, had no able-bodied "cannon fodder." His uncle drafted him and Mr. Dorsey spent a year in school, trying to fight the draft, but gave in eventually and enlisted in the Marine Corps. After finishing his undergraduate coursework, he pursued graduate school. **AV:** Traveling; Reading; Riding collectible motorcycles **PA:** Independent **RE:** Roman Catholic

DORSEY, SHERRELL, T: Publisher **I:** Writing and Editing **CN:** The Plug **ED:** Master's Degree in Data Journalism, Graduate School of Journalism, Columbia University (2018); Coursework, Growing the Minority Business Executive Program, Tuck School of Business, Dartmouth College (2018); Bachelor of Science in International Trade and Marketing, Fashion Institute of Technology **C:** Publisher, The Plug (2016-Present); Senior Consultant, Build the Good (2016-Present); Correspondent, Fast Company, Essence, Next City, Black Enterprise, Others (2010-Present); Consultant, Marketing and Community Engagement, Tresata (2018-2019); Sales Analyst, Google Fiber Account, MarketSource Inc. (2016-2017); Marketing Manager, Uber (2014-2015); Communications Manager, Sustain Charlotte (2014); Public Policy Fellow, Office of the Mayor, Bridget, The ZOOM Foundation (2013-2014) **CR:** Reality Tech Fellow, Schusterman Foundation, Israel (2018); Zoom Fellowship (2013) **CIV:** Board President, INTech Camp for Girls (2019-Present); Co-Chair of Talent, Governor's Entrepreneurship Council, State of North Carolina (2019-Present); Pitch Advisory Board, SXSW (2018-Present); Selection Advisory Council, GreenLight Fund (2018-Present); Founding Board Member, Great Oaks Charter School NYC (2014) **CW:** Author, "A Growing Group of Black Angel Investors Is Making Up for the Funding Biases in Venture Capital," Fast Company; Author, "Portland Fund Fuels Minority and Women Entrepreneurs," Next City; Author, "Steve Case's Quest to Make Innovation Regionally and Racially Inclusive," Fast Company; Contributor, "The Rise of Black-Owned Co-Working Spaces," VICE/Motherboard **AW:** Named, Interesting Women of Tech to Follow, CNET (2018); Anne O'Hare McCormick Memorial Scholarship, Columbia University (2017); HIVE Global Leader (2015); Recognizing Rockstars Award, Campaign for Safe Cosmetics (2013)

DORTCH, CLARENCE III, ESQ., T: Lawyer **I:** Law and Legal Services **DOB:** 05/16/1962 **PB:** Talladega **SC:** AL/USA **PT:** Clarence Dortch Jr.; Peggy (White) Dortch **MS:** Married **SPN:** Floretta James Dortch **CH:** Clarence Dortch IV; Thayer Johnetta Dortch **ED:** JD, Temple University (1986); BA, Talladega College (1983) **C:** Private Practice Talladega County, AL (2000-Present); Private Practice, Birmingham, AL (1989-2000); Law Clerk, Alabama Supreme Court, Birmingham, AL (1988-1989); Associate, Oscar W. Adams III Law Offices, Birmingham, AL (1987-1988); Law Clerk, Schoel, Ogle, & Benton, Birmingham, AL (1986-1987); Law Clerk, Reid & Thomas, Attorneys, Anniston, AL (1986); Law Clerk, Love, Love & Love, Talladega, AL (1985-1986) **MEM:** Alabama Lawyers Association; Talladega County Bar Association; National Bar Association; Magic City Bar Association; Association of American Trial Lawyers; International Platform Association; Alpha Phi Alpha; Phi Alpha Theta; Prince Hall Mason 33rd Degree **BAR:** United States District Court for the Southern District of Alabama (2012); United States District Court (2012); United States Eleventh Circuit Court of Appeals (2004); Alabama (1987); United District Court for the

Northern District of Alabama (1987) **MH:** Albert Nelson Marquis Lifetime Achievement Award **AS:** Mr. Dortch attributes his success to not only his faith in God but also the support and encouragement of his family, friends, and colleagues. **B/I:** Dortch grew up in a small town in Alabama. Throughout his youth, he witnessed numerous injustices, all of which compelled him to take action to correct the law. Naturally, the best way for him to do so was to pursue a career in law. **PA:** Democrat **RE:** Methodist **THT:** The foundations of Mr. Dortch's life are God, family, and the law. He prioritized his life in that order.

DOUB, JOSEPH PEYTON, CEP, PWS, T: Senior Environmental Scientist **I:** Government Administration/Government Relations/Government Services **CN:** United States Nuclear Regulatory Commission **DOB:** 06/09/1960 **PB:** Baltimore **SC:** MD/USA **PT:** William Doub; Mary Graham (Boggs) Doub **MS:** Single, Never Married **ED:** MS in Plant Physiology, University of California Davis (1984); BS in Plant Sciences, Cornell University (1982); Coursework, Various Training Courses **CT:** NRC Contracting Officers Representative (2017); Duke NEPA Certificate, Duke Environmental Leadership Program (2014); Environmental Technical Reviewer Qualification, United States Nuclear Regulatory Commission (2009); Contracting Officer Technical Representative, United States Nuclear Regulatory Commission (2008); Maryland Forest Conservation Act Qualified Professional, Maryland Department of Natural Resources (2004); Certified Environmental Professional, Academy of Board Certified Environmental Professionals (1996); Professional Wetland Scientist, Society of Wetland Scientists and Professional Certification Program (1995); Wetland Delineator, United States Army Corps of Engineers (1993) **C:** Senior Environmental Scientist, Terrestrial Ecologist, United States Nuclear Regulatory Commission (2008-Present); Senior Environmental Scientist, Tetra Tech NUS, Inc. (1989-2008); Consultant in Vegetation Management, Baltimore Gas and Electric Company (1987-1988) **CR:** Environmental Representative, Working Group on Advanced Microreactors (2018-Present); Subject Matter Expert on Ecology and Land Use for Generic EIS for Advanced Reactors (2020-2022); Technical Reviewer, Early Site Permit Application for Small Modular Reactor, Tennessee Valley Authority Clinch River Site, Oak Ridge, TN (2017-Present); Terrestrial Ecologist, Update to Environmental Standard Review Plans (2014-Present); Land Use Technical Reviewer, Combined License and Early Site Permit Applications for New Reactors (2008-Present); Ecologist, Revision 3 to Regulatory Guide 4.2 "Preparation of Environmental Reports for Nuclear Power Stations" (2014-2018); Expert Witness in Terrestrial Ecology and Land Use, Combined License Mandatory Hearings (2015-2017); Technical Lead, Development of Regulatory Guide 4.24 "Aquatic Environmental Studies for Nuclear Power Stations" (2014-2017); Assistant Instructor, NEPA for the Uninitiated, NRC Professional Development Center (2016); Terrestrial Ecology Technical Reviewer, Combined License Applications for New Reactors (2008-2016); Expert Witness in Terrestrial Ecology, Combined License Contested Hearings for Levy Units 1 and 2 and Fermi Unit 3 (2012-2014); Technical Lead, Revision 2 to Regulatory Guide 4.11, Terrestrial Environmental Studies for Nuclear Power Stations (2008-2013); Instructor, NRC Wetlands Orientation Session, Pacific Northwest National Laboratory (PNNL) (2008); Wetlands Permitting Task Leader, Environmental Services for Proposed Exelon Nuclear Texas Project, Exelon Nuclear, Inc., Matagorda and Victoria Counties, Texas (2007-2008); Terrestrial Ecology Task Leader, Environmental Report for Proposed UniStar Nuclear Calvert Cliffs Units 3 and 4, Lusby, MD (2006-2008); Task Manager, Monitoring of Wetland Mitigation Projects on Naval District Washington, West Area, Dahlgren Site, J.M. Waller Associates (Now Versar, Inc.), Dahlgren, VA (2003-2008); Task Leader, Phase I Environmental Baseline Survey/Environmental Condition of Property Survey for GM-38 Tract, Bethpage, NY (2007); Project Manager, Forest Stand Delineation and Forest Conservation Plan for Fort George G. Meade Uncontrolled Waste Site, Anne Arundel County, MD (2007); Task Leader, Community Environmental Response Facilitation Act (CERFA) Reports for BRAC PMO Northeast Closing Bases, Various Locations, United States Navy BRAC Project Management Office Northeast, Philadelphia, PA (2006-2007); Task Leader, Ecological Risk Assessment for Aberdeen Proving Ground Open Burn and Open Detonation Units, United States Army Corps of Engineers, Mobile District, Aberdeen, MD (2005-2007); Task Manager, Wetland Delineation of Raven Rock Mountain Complex, United States Army, Adams County, PA (2006); Task Manager, Ecological Communities Survey and Terrestrial Mammal Survey, Engineer Proving Ground, United States Army Garrison, Baltimore District, United States Army Corps of Engineers, Fort Belvoir, VA (2006); Expert Witness, Endangered Species Issues Related to Turkey, Point Units 6 & 7 Mandatory Hearing; Presenter, NRC Knowledge Management Seminars, Office of New Reactors, Department of Site Safety and Environmental Analysis, Environmental Technical Support Branch; Several Others **CIV:** Lector, St. Paul's Episcopal Church, Sharpsburg, MD **CW:** Author, "The Endangered Species Act: History, Implementation, Successes, and Controversies," CRC Press Taylor & Francis (2012); Author, "Preparing NEPA Environmental Assessments: A User's Guide to Best Professional Practices," CRC Press Taylor & Francis (2012); Author, "Wetland Mitigation and Monitoring on Hazardous Waste Remediation Sites, United States Environmental Protection Agency (USEPA)/ US Army Corps of Engineers (USACE)," Conference on Design and Construction Issues at Hazardous Waste Sites, Philadelphia, PA (2007); Author, "A Systematic Tool for Determining the Need for Specialized Expertise in NEPA," Environmental Practice (2003); Author, "Case Studies Demonstrating a Systematic Process for Integrating the National Environmental Policy Act with Regulatory Agency Consultation," Environmental Practice (2003); Author, "Improving Biological Resources Impact Assessment," Proceedings of the 22nd Annual Conference of the National Association of Environmental Professionals (1997); Author, "Nationwide Wetland Delineation: Identifying Wetland Boundaries Anywhere in the United States," Wetland Journal (1995); Author, "Wetlands Protection and Permitting for Industrial Development in Virginia," Proceedings of Environment of Virginia (1994); Author, "Delineation of Playa Features in the Western Great Basin," Wetland Journal; Contributor, Articles, Professional Journals **AW:** Performance Awards for Work Performed in Fiscal Years (2011-2019) **MEM:** Elected Member-at-large, Board of Directors, National Association of Environmental Professionals (2019-Present); Certification Review Board, Academy of Board Certified Environmental Professionals (ABCEP) (2017-Present); Open and Collaborative Work Environment Working Group, NRC Office of New Reactors (2017-Present); Board of Trustees, Academy of Board Certified Environmental Professionals (ABCEP) (2011-2017); Certification Review Board, Academy of Board Certified Environmental Professionals (2000-2011); American Nuclear Society **AS:** Mr. Doub attributes his success to the Lord and to his father, a great role model for him. He also credits his mother, Mary Graham, and his brother, Albert. **B/I:** Mr. Doub was interested in environmental science, particularly botany and wetlands. In addition, it was an evolving interest. He actually started out in college by majoring in agriculture. He always liked the outdoors, and when he saw that there was an opportunity to work in the environment, he thought it was a good place for a career. The coursework and training were highly overlapping. **AV:** Writing; Birding; Crossword puzzles **RE:** Episcopalian **THT:** Mr. Doub's motto is, "Be of strong faith, pray often, work hard, dream intensely, keep learning, enjoy nature, take vacations, give to charity, and don't sweat the small stuff."

DOUGHERTY, JAMES D., T: Lawyer **I:** Law and Legal Services **DOB:** 12/29/1936 **PB:** Baldwin **SC:** NY/USA **PT:** Thomas Francis Dougherty; Jean May (Young) Dougherty **MS:** Married **SPN:** Nancy Harrington Decker (12/29/1971) **ED:** Graduate, Advanced Management Program, Harvard Business School (1983); LLB, Columbia University (1963); BA, Dartmouth College (1958) **C:** President, Supermarkets General Corporation (1987-1989); Executive Vice President, Supermarkets General Corporation (1983-1987); Senior Vice President, Supermarkets General Corporation (1981-1983); Vice President, Supermarkets General Corporation 1975-1981); Former Secretary, General Counsel, Supermarkets General Corporation (1972); Associate General Counsel, Supermarkets General Corporation (1971-1972); Associate, Shea & Gould (1969-1971); Associate, Hughes Hubbard & Reed (1963-1969) **CR:** Board of Advisers, Arkwright Boston Insurance Company (1983-1989); President, Director, 132 East 19th Street, Inc. (1964-1978); Lecturer, Practicing Law Institute (1970-1974) **CIV:** President, Gramercy Neighborhood Associates Inc. (1990-Present); Chairman, Nature Conservancy (1990-Present); Trustee, Nature Conservancy (1982-Present) **MIL:** Junior Grade Lieutenant, U.S. Navy (1958-1960) **MEM:** Supervisor, Town of Shelter Island (2008-2017); Special Committee on Electronic Transfer Funds, Association of the Bar of the City of New York (1976-1979); American Bar Association **BAR:** New York State Bar Association (1963) **MH:** Albert Nelson Marquis Lifetime Achievement Award; Marquis Who's Who Top Professional **B/I:** Mr. Dougherty became involved in his profession because his dad, Thomas Francis, became a lawyer during the depression. He became a very successful lawyer in suburban Long Island. **PA:** Democrat

DOUGLAS, ALEXANDER, T: Chief Executive Officer **I:** Retail/Sales **CN:** Staples Inc. **ED:** Degree, University of Virginia **C:** Chief Executive Officer, Staples Inc. (2018-Present); Senior Vice President, Coca Cola Company (2013-2018); President, Chief Operating Officer, North America Group, The Coca-Cola Company (2006-2010); Global Chief Commercial Officer, Coca Cola Company (2003-2006)

DOUGLAS, MICHAEL KIRK, T: Actor **I:** Media & Entertainment **DOB:** 09/25/1944 **PB:** New Brunswick **SC:** NJ/USA **PT:** Kirk Douglas; Diana Douglas **MS:** Married **SPN:** Catherine Zeta-Jones (11/18/2000); Diandra Morrell Luker (03/20/1977, Divorced 2000) **CH:** Cameron Morrell; Dylan Michael; Carys Zeta **ED:** Honorary LittD, The University of St. Andrews, Scotland, United Kingdom (2006); BA, University of California Santa Barbara (1967) **CW:** Appearance, "Avengers: Endgame" (2019); Actor, "Ant-Man and the Wasp" (2018); Actor, "Unlocked" (2017); Actor, "Flatliners" (2017); Producer, "We Have Always Lived in the Castle" (2017); Actor, "Ant-Man" (2015); Actor, Producer, "Beyond the Reach" (2014); Actor, "And So

It Goes" (2014); Actor, "Behind the Candelabra" (2013); Actor, "Last Vegas" (2013); Actor, "Haywire" (2011); Actor, "Wall Street: Money Never Sleeps" (2010); Actor, "Ghosts of Girlfriends Past" (2009); Actor, "Solitary Man" (2009); Actor, "Beyond a Reasonable Doubt" (2009); Actor, "King of California" (2007); Actor, "You, Me and Dupree" (2006); Actor, Practice, "The Sentinel" (2006); Producer, "Godspeed, Lawrence Mann" (2004); Actor, Producer, "It Runs in the Family" (2003); Actor, Producer, "The In-Laws" (2003); Actor, Producer, "One Night at McCool's" (2001); Actor, "Don't Say a Word" (2001); Actor, "Wonder Boys" (1999); Actor, "Still Life" (1999); Actor, "Traffic" (1999); Actor, "A Perfect Murder" (1998); Actor, "The Game" (1997); Producer, "The Rainmaker" (1997); Actor, Producer, "The Ghost and the Darkness" (1996); Actor, "A Song for David" (1996); Actor, "The American President" (1995); Actor, "Disclosure" (1994); Producer, "Made in America" (1993); Actor, "Falling Down" (1993); Actor, "Shining Through" (1992); Actor, "Basic Instinct" (1992); Producer, "Flatliners" (1990); Actor, "Black Rain" (1989); Actor, "The War of the Roses" (1989); Actor, "Wall Street" (1987); Actor, "Fatal Attraction" (1987); Actor, "A Chorus Line" (1985); Actor, Producer, "Jewel of the Nile" (1985); Actor, Producer, "Romancing the Stone" (1984); Actor, "The Star Chamber" (1983); Actor, "It's My Turn" (1981); Actor, Producer, "The China Syndrome" (1979); Actor, "Running" (1979); Actor, "Coma" (1978); Actor, "Streets of San Francisco" (1972-1976); Producer, "One Flew Over the Cuckoo's Nest" (1975); Actor, "Napoleon and Samantha" (1972); Actor, "Summertree" (1971); Actor, "Adam at 6 A.M." (1970); Actor, "Hail Hero" (1969); Actor, "Cast a Giant Shadow" (1966) **AW:** Genesis Award, Genesis Prize Foundation (2015); Golden Globe Award for Best Performance by an Actor in a Mini-Series or Motion Picture Made for TV, Hollywood Foreign Press Association (2014); Screen Actors Guild Award for Outstanding Performance by a Male Actor in a TV Movie or Miniseries, SAG-AFTRA (2014); Emmy Award for Outstanding Lead Actor in a Miniseries or Movie, Television Academy (2013); Named to New Jersey Hall of Fame (2012); David O. Selznick Achievement Award, Producers Guild of America (2009); Award, American Film Institute (2009); Lifetime Achievement Award, Savannah Film Festival (2007); Career Achievement Award, National Board of Review (2007); Cecil B. DeMille Award, Hollywood Foreign Press Association (2004); Academy Award for Best Actor in a Leading Role, Academy of Motion Picture Arts and Sciences (1987); Golden Globe Award for Best Performance by an Actor in a Motion Picture - Drama, Hollywood Foreign Press Association (1987); BAFTA Award for Best Film (1977); Academy Award for Best Picture, Academy of Motion Picture Arts and Sciences (1975); Golden Globe Award for Best Motion Picture - Drama, Hollywood Foreign Press Association (1975); National Board of Review Award for Best Actor

DOUGLASS, H. ROBERT DDES, FAIA, T: Architect, Health Care Consultant, Educator, Artist **I:** Architecture & Construction **DOB:** 03/27/1937 **PB:** McCook **SC:** NE/USA **PT:** Harry William Douglass; Irma Ruth Douglass **MS:** Married **SPN:** Darlene Thompson **CH:** William; Stephanie; Jennifer **ED:** DDes, Harvard University (1994); MDes, Harvard Graduate School of Design (1992); Graduate Coursework, Owner-President Management Program, Harvard University Business School (1985); MArch, American Hospital Association-American Institute of Architects Fellow, University of Minnesota (1966); BArch, University of Nebraska (1963) **CT:** Fellow, American Institute of Architects; Emeritus Architect, Texas; Certified Healthcare Architect, Academy of Architecture for Health, Ameri-

can Institute of Architects; Certified Healthcare Executive, American College of Healthcare Executives **C:** Owner, Douglass Planning and Architecture (1996-2006); Architect, Watkins Carter Hamilton, Houston, TX (1995-1996); Private Practice, Houston, TX (1994-1995); Teaching Fellow, Harvard University, Cambridge, MA (1991-1994); Private Practice, Cambridge, MA (1991-1994); Partner-in-charge, Douglass Group of Deloitte & Touche, Houston, TX (1988-1991); Chairman, Chief Executive Officer, Robert Douglass Associates Inc., Hospital Consultants, Houston, TX (1973-1988); Vice President, Director of Architecture, CE Maguire Inc., Boston, MA (1971-1973); Vice President, Health Facilities Division, Caudill Rowlett Scott, Houston, TX (1968-1971); Associate, Design Team Leader, Leo A. Daly Co., Omaha, NE (1964-1968) **CR:** Visiting Professor, Holder, Thomas A. Bullock Chair in Leadership and Innovation, College of Architecture, Texas A&M University (2001-2002); Practice Curriculum Committee, Harvard Graduate School of Design (1993-1995); Lecturer, Healthcare Planning, University of Houston, University of Colorado, University of Missouri (1980-1991); Associate Professor, Director, Graduate Programs, Healthcare Planning and Design, Rice University School of Architecture, University of Texas School of Public Health, Houston, TX (1973-1976) **CIV:** Robert Douglass Associates Scholarship in Health Care Administration, University of Minnesota (1983-Present); Professional Advisory Council, University of Nebraska College of Architecture (1983-2018); Douglass Fellowship in Architecture for Health, University of Nebraska College of Architecture (2006); Founding Fellow, Academy of Architecture for Health (1996); Endowed, Douglass Professorship in Architecture (1991) **CW:** Artist (2006-Present); Author, "Managing the Health Facility Development Process," Association of University Programs in Health Administration (1988); Contributor, "Facilities Planning and Construction," The AUPHA Manual of Health Services Management, An Aspen Publication (1992); Guest Editor, "Medical Facilities" Issue, Progressive Architect Magazine (1992); Editorial Board, Journal, Health Administration Education (1980-1991); Guest Editor, "Hospitals" Issue, Progressive Architecture Magazine (1972); Contributor, Articles, Professional Journals **AW:** Professional Advisory Committee, University of Nebraska College of Architecture (1983-2018); Harvard Business School Alumni Board (2016); University Master Award, University of Nebraska (2006); Distinguished Alumnus Award, University of Nebraska College of Architecture (1998); Elected Fellow, American Institute of Architects (1986); Honoree, INC Magazine "INC 500" (1983-1985); Progressive Architecture Honor Award, H. Lee Moffitt Cancer Hospital and Research Center, University of South Florida (1985); Presidential Silver Medal, National Endowment for the Arts for Boston's Charles River Project (1984) **MEM:** Founding Member, American Academy Healthcare Architects (1998); National Committee on Architecture for Health, American Institute of Architects (1984-1996); Chairman, Houston AIA Fellowship Committee (1991-1992); Fellow, American Institute of Architects (1986); Board of Directors, American Association of Hospital Planning (1975-1980); American College of Healthcare Executives, Society of Hospital Planners; Fellow, American Association of Healthcare Consultants **MH:** Albert Nelson Marquis Lifetime Achievement Award; Marquis Who's Who Top Professional **AS:** Mr. Douglass attributes his success to his foundation, values, and work ethic. He loves solving problems artistically. Likewise, he has benefited tremendously from his courageous and visionary clients. He additionally credits his wife, Darlene, who became his partner in both work and

his personal life. Mr. Douglass also was inspired by his key mentors who coached, encouraged, and motivated him to succeed. **B/I:** Mr. Douglass was influenced by his father's dream of becoming an engineer and working in construction. This, combined with a love of art and design, made architecture a natural choice. **AV:** Painting; Practicing journalism **PA:** Democrat **RE:** Unitarian **THT:** Mr. Douglass believes in working hard, playing fair, and giving back.

DOVALE, FERN LOUISE, T: Civil Engineer **I:** Engineering **DOB:** 05/11/1956 **PB:** Fort Leavenworth **SC:** KS/USA **PT:** Riel Stanton Crandall; Beatrice Marie (Mayor) Crandall **SPN:** Antonio Joseph DoVale Jr. (10/17/1981) **CH:** Antonio Joseph DoVale III; Jennifer Louise DoVale; Elizabeth Rose DoVale **ED:** MSCE, Columbia University (1982); BSCE, Massachusetts Institute of Technology (1978) **CT:** Registered Professional Engineer, New Jersey **C:** Retired Civil Engineer (1993); Engineering Manager, Integrated Engineering Software, Inc., Englewood Cliffs, NJ (1992-1993); Engineering Manager, NPS Technologies Group, Inc., Elmwood Park, NJ (1989-1992); Project Manager, NPS Technologies Group, Inc., Secaucus, NJ (1988-1989); Project Engineer, Nuclear Power Services, Inc., Secaucus, NJ (1986-1988); Lead Engineer, Nuclear Power Services, Inc., Secaucus, NJ (1985-1986); Senior Engineer, Nuclear Power Services, Inc., Secaucus, NJ (1983-1985); Engineer, Nuclear Power Services, Inc., Secaucus, NJ (1980-1983); Associate Engineer, M.W. Kellogg Co., Hackensack, NJ (1978-1980) **CIV:** Girl Scout Leader (2000-2013) **CW:** Author, Editor, Computer Manuals **AW:** Joseph Wenick Award, Alumni, Massachusetts Institute of Technology (1992) **MEM:** President, Club of Northern New Jersey, MIT Alumni Association (1985-1986, 1994-1995); Board of Directors, Club of Northern New Jersey, MIT Alumni Association (1979-1995); Program Vice President, Club of Northern New Jersey, MIT Alumni Association (1984-1985, 1992-1994); Executive Committee, Northern New Jersey Section, American Nuclear Society (1986-1989, 1991-1994); Membership Vice President, Club of Northern New Jersey, MIT Alumni Association (1982-1984, 1989-1992); American Nuclear Society; American Society of Civil Engineers; American Society of Mechanical Engineers; National Society of Professional Engineers; Educational Council, Massachusetts Institute of Technology Society of Women Engineers; Girl Scouts of the United States of America **MH:** Albert Nelson Marquis Lifetime Achievement Award **AV:** Playing crochet; Teaching archery and canoeing for the Girl Scouts **RE:** Catholic

DOWDEN, CARROLL VINCENT, T: Publishing Company Executive **I:** Media & Entertainment **DOB:** 04/09/1933 **PB:** Louisville **SC:** KY/USA **PT:** Charles Merrill Dowden; Regina Celestine (Popham) Dowden **MS:** Married **SPN:** Eleanor Therese Dion (11/23/1956) **CH:** Mark Vincent; Laura Anne; Amy Alexandra; Beth Regina **ED:** MS in Journalism, Columbia University (1960); BA, University of Notre Dame (1955) **C:** Founder, Chairman, Wainscot Media, Park Ridge, NJ (2006-Present); Founder, President, Dowden Health Media, Montvale, NJ (1988-2005); Chairman, American Business Media LLC (1997-1998); Chairman, Washington Legal Committee, American Business Press (1979-1985, 1992-1995); Group Vice President, Cahners Publishing Company, New York, NY (1986-1988); Vice President, International Thomson Organization (1985-1986); President, International Thomson Business Press (1984-1985); Vice President, BPA Worldwide (1984-1985); Director, BPA Worldwide (1981-1985); President, Medical Economics, MJH Life Sciences (1977-1984); Various Positions, Medical Economics, MJH Life Sciences, Oradell, NJ (1963-1984); President, Next Publishing Company, New York, NY (1979-1981); Executive Vice President, Medical Economics, MJH Life Sciences (1976-1977); Publisher, Medical Economics Magazine, MJH Life Sciences (1973-1977); General Manager, Drug Topics Magazine, MJH Life Sciences (1972-1973); Assistant Financial Editor, The Courier-Journal, Louisville, KY (1957-1963); Associate Editor, Indiana University News Bureau, Bloomington, IN (1956-1957); Assistant Financial Editor, The Louisville Times (1955-1956) **CIV:** Zoning Board of Adjustment, Saddle River, NJ (2003-2018); Trustee, Hackensack Meridian Pascack Valley Medical Center (1976-1983); Vice President of the Board, Hackensack Meridian Pascack Valley Medical Center (1978-1980) **MIL:** Captain, U.S. Army (1956, 1961-1962) **AW:** Inductee, Medical Advertising Hall of Fame (2014); Pulitzer Travelling Fellowship, Columbia University (1960-1961) **MEM:** Society of Professional Journalists; Hackensack Golf Club, Oradell, NJ; The Union League Club, New York, NY; Philadelphia Country Club, Gladwyne, PA; PGA National Resort & Spa, Palm Beach Gardens, FL **MH:** Albert Nelson Marquis Lifetime Achievement Award

DOWNEY, ROBERT JR., T: Actor **I:** Media & Entertainment **DOB:** 04/04/1965 **PB:** New York **SC:** NY/USA **PT:** Robert Downey Sr.; Elsie Ford **MS:** Married **SPN:** Susan Levin (08/27/2005); Deborah Falconer (05/29/1992-04/26/2004) **CH:** Indio; Exton Elias; Avri Roel **C:** Co-Founder, Team Downey (2010) **CW:** Actor, "Dolittle (Also Referred to as "The Voyage of Dr Dolittle")" (2019); Actor, "Avengers: Endgame" (2019); Actor, "Avengers: Infinity War" (2018); Actor, "All Star Weekend" (2018); Actor, "Spider Man Homecoming" (2017); Actor, "Captain America: Civil War" (2016); Actor, "The Nice Guys" (2016); Actor, "Avengers: Age of Ultron" (2015); Executive Producer, "Playing It Forward: Imagine Dragons" (2015); Actor, "Chef" (2014); Actor, Executive Producer "The Judge" (2014); Actor, "Iron Man 3" (2013); Actor, "The Avengers" (2012); Actor, "Sherlock Holmes: A Game of Shadows" (2011); Actor, "Iron Man 2" (2010); Actor, "Due Date" (2010); Actor, "The Soloist" (2009); Actor, "Sherlock Holmes" (2009); Actor, "Iron Man" (2008); Actor, "Tropic Thunder" (2008); Actor, "Zodiac" (2007); Actor, "Lucky You" (2007); Actor, "Charlie Bartlett" (2007); Actor, Co-producer, "A Guide to Recognizing Your Saints" (2006); Actor, "The Shaggy Dog" (2006); Actor, "A Scanner Darkly" (2006); Actor, "Fur: An Imaginary Portrait of Diane Arbus" (2006); Voice Actor, "Family Guy" (2005); Actor, "Game 6" (2005); Actor, "Kiss, Kiss, Bang, Bang" (2005); Actor, "Good Night and Good Luck" (2005); Actor, "Eros" (2004); Singer, "The Futurist" (2004)); Actor, "The Singing Detective" (2003); Actor, "Whatever We Do" (2003); Actor, "Gothika" (2003); Actor, "Lethargy" (2002); Actor, "Ally McBeal (2000-2002); Actor, "Wonder Boys" (2000); Actor, "Auto Motives" (2000); Actor, "In Dreams" (1999); Actor, "Friends & Lovers" (1999); Actor, "Bowfinger" (1999); Actor, "Black and White" (1999); Actor, "The Gingerbread Man" (1998); Actor, "US Marshals" (1998); Actor, "One Night Stand" (1997); Actor, "Hugo Pool" (1997); Actor, "Two Girls and a Guy" (1997); Actor, "Danger Zone" (1996); Actor, "Richard III" (1995); Actor, "Home for the Holidays" (1995); Actor, "Mr. Willowby's Christmas Tree" (1995); Actor, "Natural Born Killers" (1994); Actor, "Only You" (1994); Actor, "Restoration" (1994); Actor, "Hail Caesar" (1994); Actor, "Heart and Souls" (1993); Actor, Writer, "The Last Party" (1993); Actor, "Short Cuts" (1993); Actor, "Chaplin" (1992); Actor, "Too Much Sun" (1991); Actor, "Soapdish" (1991); Actor, "That's Adequate" (1990); Actor, "Air America" (1990);

Actor, "True Believer" (1989); Actor, "Chances Are" (1989); Actor, "Johnny Be Good" (1988); Actor, "Rented Lips" (1988); Actor, "Nineteen Sixty-Nine" (1988); Actor, "Less Than Zero" (1987); Actor, "The Pick-Up Artist" (1987); Actor, "America" (1986); Actor, "Saturday Night Live" (1985-1986); Actor, "Back to School" (1986); Actor, "Deadwait" (1985); Actor, "Mussolini: The Untold Story" (1985); Actor, "To Live and Die in LA" (1985); Actor, "Tuff Turf" (1985); Actor, "Weird Science" (1985); Actor, "Firstborn" (1984); Actor, "Fraternity" (1984); Actor, "American Passion" (1983); Actor, "Alms for the Middle Class" (1983); Actor, "Baby It's You" (1983); Actor, "Up the Academy" (1980); Actor, "Greaser's Palace" (1972); Actor, "Pound" (1970) **AW:** Favorite Dramatic Movie Actor, People's Choice Awards (2015); Generation Award, MTV Movie Awards (2015); Favorite Movie Actor (2013, 2015); Favorite Action Movie Star (2014); Number One, Forbes' List of Hollywood's Highest-Paid Actors (2013); American Cinematheque Award (2011); Best Performance by an Actor in a Motion Picture-Comedy or Musical, Golden Globe Award, Hollywood Foreign Press Association (2010); Listed, "The 10 People Who Mattered," Newsweek (2008); Listed, "The 100 Most Influential People in the World," TIME USA, LLC (2008)

DOYLE, MICHAEL, "MIKE" F. JR., T: U.S. Representative from Pennsylvania **I:** Government Administration/Government Relations/Government Services **DOB:** 08/05/1953 **PB:** Swissvale **SC:** PA/USA **PT:** Michael Doyle; Rosemarie (Fusco) Doyle **MS:** Married **SPN:** Susan Erlandson **CH:** Four Children **ED:** BS in Community Development, The Pennsylvania State University (1975) **C:** Member, U.S. House of Representatives from Pennsylvania's 14th Congressional District, United States Congress (2003-Present); Member, U.S. House of Representatives from Pennsylvania's 18th Congressional District, United States Congress (1995-2003); Co-Founder, Agent, Eastgate Insurance Agency, Pittsburgh, PA (1983-1994); Chief of Staff to Senator Frank Pecora, Harrisburg, PA (1979-1994); Executive Director, Turtle Creek Valley Citizens Union, PA (1977-1979); Committee on Energy and Commerce **CR:** Swissvale Borough Council (1977-1981) **MEM:** National Democratic Club; Italian Sons & Daughters of America; Ancient Order of Hibernians; Lions Clubs International **AV:** Golfing; Italian cooking; Playing piano **PA:** Democrat **RE:** Roman Catholic

DOYLE, WENDELL E., T: Band Director (Retired), Educator (Retired) **I:** Education/Educational Services **DOB:** 07/08/1940 **PB:** Higbee **SC:** MO/USA **PT:** Travis E. Doyle; Hattie Erma (Webb) Doyle **SPN:** Julia Ann Vail (06/23/1963) **CH:** Dora Michelle; Michael E.; Melissa Kae **ED:** MEd in Music, University of Missouri (1967); BS in Education, Northeast Missouri State University (1962) **CT:** Certified Lifetime Teacher, Missouri **C:** Retired (1992); Band Director, Platte County R-3 School District, Platte City, MO (1972-1992); Band Director, Brookfield R-III School District, Brookfield, MO (1968-1972); Band Director, Braymer C-4 School District, Braymer, MO (1962-1968) **CR:** Exchange Teacher, Platte County R-3 School District, Warwickshire, England (1984) **CIV:** President, Barry Heights Homes Association (1986-1987); Minister of Music, Northgate Baptist Church, Kansas City, MO (1972-1985); Minister of Music, Park Baptist Church, Brookfield, MO (1968-1972) **AW:** Inductee, Hall of Fame, Missouri Bandmasters Association (1997); Outstanding Band Director Award, Lambda Chapter, Phi Beta Mu (1993) **MEM:** President, Clay/Platte Area Retired School Employees Association (2006-Present); President, Phi Beta Mu (1990-1991); President, Greater Kansas City Dis-

trict, Missouri State Teachers Association (1978); Music Educators National Conference; Missouri Music Educators Association; Secretary, Missouri Bandmasters Association; Missouri Bandmasters Association; Phi Beta Mu **MH:** Albert Nelson Marquis Lifetime Achievement Award **B/I:** Mr. Doyle became involved in his profession because he had been interested in music his whole life. He started playing the piano when he was 5 years old and always wanted to teach. It was the summer before he entered college when he decided to pursue music as a career. **AV:** Fishing; Reading; Traveling **PA:** Democrat

DRAVILLAS, SPELEOS G., T: Vice President of Global Sales **I:** Telecommunications **CN:** Percipia **ED:** Crain's ExecEdge, Executive Leadership Training for Mid-level to Senior Managers, Lake Forest Graduate School of Management (2017); Bachelor of Science in Biology and Political Science, Loyola University, IL **C:** Vice-President, Chicago Chapter, Hospitality Financial & Technology Professionals (2018-Present); Vice President, Global Sales, Percipia, Chicago, IL (2017-Present); Director of International Sales, Mitel (2006-2017); Chief Business Development Officer, BTI Communications (1993-2006) **CIV:** Little League Boys Baseball Head Coach, Welles Park Parents Association (2015-Present); Chairman, Food Fest, Annunciation Greek Orthodox Cathedral (2006-2015); Parish Council President, Parish Treasurer **AW:** President's Club Award, Mitel **MEM:** Vice President, Hospitality Financial & Technology Professionals; Hospitality Tech Next Generation **B/I:** Mr. Dravillas began his career in unified communications. He subsequently specialized in verticals and, eventually, hospitality. In this capacity, he utilized future technology to better service guests and provide additional lines of revenue.

DREYER, WILLIAM MD, T: Professor of Pediatrics **I:** Education/Educational Services **CN:** Baylor College of Medicine **CH:** One Son **ED:** Fellowship, Baylor College of Medicine (1988); Residency, University of California San Francisco (1984); Internship, Children's Hospital At Vanderbilt University (1982); MD, University of Florida College of Medicine (1981); BS in Biology, Furman University (1977) **CT:** National Board of Medical Examiners; American Board of Pediatrics **C:** Professor, Pediatrics-Cardiology, Baylor College of Medicine **MEM:** American Academy of Pediatrics; American College of Cardiology; American Heart Association; Council on Basic Science, American Heart Association; Council on Cardiovascular Disease in the Young, American Heart Association; Harris County Medical Association; Texas Medical Society; Society for Pediatric Research; Houston Cardiology Society; Texas Pediatric Society; International Society for Heart & Lung Transplantation **MH:** Albert Nelson Marquis Lifetime Achievement Award

DREYFUSS, RICHARD, T: Actor **I:** Media & Entertainment **DOB:** 10/29/1947 **PB:** New York **SC:** NY/USA **PT:** Norman Dreyfuss; Geraldine (Robbins) Dreyfuss **MS:** Married **SPN:** Svetlana Erokhin (03/16/2006); Janelle Lacey (05/30/1999, Divorced 2005); Jeramie Rain (03/20/1983, Divorced 08/1995) **CH:** Emily; Benjamin; Harry **ED:** Coursework, San Fernando Valley State College (Now California State University, Northridge) **CIV:** Alternate Military Duty Service, LA County General Hospital (Now LAC+USC Medical Center) (1969-1971); Participant, Civil Rights Marches; Lobbyist for Amnesty Bills **CW:** Actor, "Astronaut" (2019); Actor, "Daughter of the Wolf" (2019); Actor, "Polar" (2019); Actor, "The Last Laugh" (2019); Actor, "Bayou Caviar" (2018); Actor, "Book Club" (2018); Actor, Producer, "Shots Fired" (2017); Actor,

"Madoff" (2016); Actor, "Zipper" (2015); Actor, Producer, "Your Family or Mine" (2015); Actor, "Very Good Girls" (2013); Actor, "Paranoia" (2013); Actor, "Squatters" (2013); Actor, "Cas & Dylan" (2013); Actor, "Coma" (2012); Actor, Producer, "Parenthood" (2011); Actor, "The Big Valley" (2011); Actor, Producer, "Weeds" (2010); Actor, "Piranha 3D" (2010); Actor, "Red" (2010); Executive Producer, "The Lightkeepers" (2009); Actor, "My Life in Ruins" (2008); Actor, "W." (2008); Actor, "Prophesy and Honor" (2007); Actor, "Poseidon" (2006); Actor, "Coast to Coast" (2004); Actor, "The Producers" (2004); Actor, "Sly Fox" (2004); Actor, "Silver City" (2004); Actor, Producer, "Copshop" (2004); Actor, Producer, "The Education of Max Bickford" (2001-2002); Actor, "Who Is Cletis Tout?" (2001); Actor, "The Day Reagan Was Shot" (2001); Voice Actor, "Rudolph the Red-Nosed Reindeer and the Island of Misfit Toys" (2001); Actor, "The Crew" (2000); Actor, "The Old Man Who Read Love Stories" (2000); Actor, "Fail Safe" (2000); Actor, "Lansky" (1999); Actor, "Krippendorf's Tribe" (1998); Actor, "A Fine and Private Place" (1998); Actor, "Night Falls on Manhattan" (1997); Voice Actor, "The Call of the Wild: Dog of the Yukon" (1997); Actor, Producer, "Oliver Twist" (1997); Actor, "Mad Dog Time" (1996); Voice Actor, "James and the Giant Peach" (1996); Actor, "Mr. Holland's Opus" (1995); Actor, "The Last Word" (1995); Co-author, "The Two Georges" (1995); Director, Writer, "Present Tense, Past Perfect" (1995); Actor, "The American President" (1995); Executive Producer, "Quiz Show" (1994); Actor, "Silent Fall" (1994); Actor, "Lost in Yonkers" (1993); Actor, "Another Stakeout" (1993); Actor, "Death and the Maiden" (1992); Actor, Producer, "Once Around" (1991); Actor, Producer, "Prisoner of Honor" (1991); Host, "The Class of the 20th Century" (1991); Actor, "What About Bob?" (1991); Actor, "Rosencrantz and Guildenstern Are Dead" (1991); Actor, "Postcards from the Edge 1990); Actor, "Let It Ride" (1989); Actor, "Always" (1989); Actor, "Moon Over Parador" (1988); Actor, "Tin Men" (1987); Actor, "Stakeout" (1987); Actor, "Nuts" (1987); Actor, "Down and Out in Beverly Hills" (1986); Actor, "Stand By Me" (1986); Actor, "The Buddy System" (1984); Actor, "Total Abandon" (1983); Actor, "Whose Life Is It Anyway?" (1981); Actor, "The Competition" (1980); Actor, "Othello" (1979); Actor, Producer, "The Big Fix" (1978); Actor, "Julius Caesar" (1978); Actor, "The Big Fix" (1978); Actor, "Close Encounters of the Third Kind" (1977); Actor, "The Goodbye Girl" (1977); Actor, "Victory at Entebbe" (1976); Actor, "Jaws" (1975); Actor, "Inserts" (1975); Actor, "The Apprenticeship of Duddy Kravitz" (1974); Actor, "The Second Coming of Suzanne" (1974); Actor, "American Graffiti" (1973); Actor, "Catch-22" (1973); Actor, "Dillinger" (1973); Actor, Producer, "The Mod Squad" (1973); Actor, Producer, "Gunsmoke" (1973); Actor, Producer, "A Touch of Grace" (1973); Actor, Producer, "The New Dick Van Dyke Show" (1973); Actor, "Two for the Money" (1972); Actor, "Shadow of a Gunman" (1972); Actor, "Untold Damage" (1971); Actor, Producer, "The Young Lawyers" (1971); Actor, Producer, "The Bold Ones: The New Doctors" (1970); Actor, Producer, "Room 222" (1970); Actor, Producer, "The Ghost & Mrs. Muir" (1969); Actor, Producer, "The New People" (1969); Actor, "Hello Down There" (1969); Actor, Producer, "Judd for the Defense" (1968); Actor, Producer, "Felony Squad" (1968); Actor, "The Young Runaways" (1968); Actor, Producer, "The Big Valley" (1967); Actor, Producer, "Occasional Wife" (1967); Actor, Producer, "That Girl" (1967); Actor, Producer, "Hey, Landlord" (1967); Actor, Producer, "Please Don't Eat the Daisies" (1967); Actor, Producer, "The Second Hundred Years" (1967); Actor, "Valley of the Dolls" (1967); Actor, "The Graduate" (1967); Actor, Producer, "Gidget"

(1966); Actor, Producer, "Bewitched" (1966); Actor, Producer, "Ben Casey" (1965); Actor, Producer, "Karen" (1964) **MEM:** American Federation of Television and Radio Artists (Now SAG-AFTRA); ACLU; Actors' Equity Association; Screen Actors Guild (Now SAG-AFTRA)

DRUMMOND, ANDRE JAMAL, T: Professional Basketball Player **I:** Athletics **CN:** Cleveland Cavaliers **DOB:** 08/10/1993 **PB:** Mount Vernon **SC:** NY/USA **ED:** Diploma, St. Thomas More School, Oakdale, CT (2011) **C:** Professional Basketball Player, Cleveland Cavaliers (2020-Present); Professional Basketball Player, Detroit Pistons (2012-2020) **AW:** Two-Time NBA All-Star (2016, 2018); All-NBA Third Team (2016); Gold Medal, FIBA World Cup, Spain (2014); NBA All-Rookie Second Team (2013); Gold Medal, FIBA World U17 Championship, Hamburg, Germany (2010); Gold Medal, FIBA Americas U16 Championship, Argentina (2009)

DRYFOOSE, GEORGIA, T: Retired Elementary School Educator **I:** Education/Educational Services **DOB:** 08/24/1942 **PB:** Cincinnati **SC:** OH/USA **PT:** Robert Arthur Reif; Edith Telitha (Clark) Reif **MS:** Widowed **SPN:** Earl Daniel Dryfoose Jr. (3/26/1970, Deceased 12/2016) **ED:** MS in Education, Indiana University (1980); BS in Education, University of Cincinnati (1964) **C:** Retired, Brown County School Corp., Nashville, IN (1997); Kindergarten Teacher, Brown County School Corp., Nashville, IN (1976-1997); Reading Aide, Brown County School Corp., Nashville, IN (1975-1976); Second-Grade Teacher, Brown County School Corp., Nashville, IN (1970-1975); Kindergarten Teacher, Oak Hills School District (1969-1970); Kindergarten Teacher, Cincinnati Public Schools (1964-1969) **CR:** Curriculum Committee, Brown County School Corp. (1986-1997); Curriculum Revision Committee Cincinnati Public Schools (1966-1969); Head Teacher, Operation Head Start (1965-1966) **CIV:** Brown County Historical Society (1998-Present); Young Republican Club, Cincinnati, OH (1964-1969); Secretary, House Chairman, Mariemont Players, Inc., Cincinnati OH (1964-1969); Founding Member, Brown County Community Theatre **AW:** Teacher of the Year Award, American Academy of Pediatrics, Cincinnati, OH (1964-1965); Grover Brown Award, National Indiana Historical Society **MEM:** Vice President, President, Xi Chapter, Delta Zeta (1961-1963); Indiana Retired Teachers Association; National Muzzle Loading Rifle Association; Phi Delta Kappa **MH:** Albert Nelson Marquis Lifetime Achievement Award **B/I:** Passionate about learning, Ms. Dryfoose knew she wanted to pursue a career in education from a young age. As a child, she often played school with her friends, always playing the role of the teacher, which provided her with semi-practical experience in the field. In high school, her biology teacher encouraged her to pursue medicine, but she knew she wanted to be an educator. **AV:** Reading; Learning Indian lore; Traveling

DRYMAN, AMY, DSC, T: Manager **I:** Research **PT:** Irving A. Dryman; Sylvia Dryman **ED:** DSc, School of Hygiene and Public Health (Now Bloomberg School of Public Health), Johns Hopkins University, Baltimore, MD (1987); BA, Yale University, New Haven, CT (1981) **C:** Manager, Pfizer, Inc., New York, NY (2001-2004); Assistant Director, Pfizer, Inc. (1999-2001); Project Leader, Pfizer, Inc. (1993-1999); Consultant, Pfizer, Inc. (1993); Research Scientist, Research Associate, Bloomberg School of Public Health, Johns Hopkins University, Baltimore, MD (1987-1988) **CIV:** Donor, Charities Relevant to Professional and Personal Concerns **CW:** Contributor, Research Papers, Professional Journals **MEM:** American Medical Writers Associa-

tion; International Society for Medical Publication Professionals **MH:** Albert Nelson Marquis Lifetime Achievement Award; Marquis Who's Who Top Professional **B/I:** As a researcher in public health, Dr. Dryman sought to contribute to an improved understanding of risk factors for mental health problems. **AV:** Reading the news

DUBOSE, JAMES DAULTON, DMD, T: Dentist **I:** Medicine & Health Care **DOB:** 07/14/1938 **PB:** Turbeville **SC:** SC/USA **PT:** Robert Alvin DuBose; Olive (Dennis) DuBose **MS:** Married **SPN:** Kathy Elizabeth Johnson (03/14/1974) **CH:** Olive Elizabeth; Dixie Daulton **ED:** DMD, University of Louisville (1965); BS, University of South Carolina (1961) **C:** Dentistry Practice, Manning, SC (1972-2002); Dentistry Practice, Aiken, SC (1970-1972); Dentistry Practice, Bishopville, SC (1965-1970) **CR:** Staff Member, Clarendon Memorial Hospital (Now McLeod Health Clarendon), Manning, SC; President, DMD Enterprises; Owner, Bluff Plantation, Colleton County, SC; Vice President, R.A. DuBose, Incorporated; President, Best Western Inn, Three D. Inc., Santee, SC; Board Member, SMG Pharmaceuticals; President, Four Seasons Inn, NC **CIV:** Trustee, Clarendon Hall School (1985-2000); Chairman, Heart Fund, Lee County, SC (1966); Trustee, Deacon, Summerton Baptist Church **MEM:** American Dental Association; American Society of Dentistry for Children; Augusta Dental Society; Pee Dee District Society, Columbia, SC; Sertoma; Lions International; Delta Sigma Delta - An International Dental Fraternity **MH:** Albert Nelson Marquis Lifetime Achievement Award; Marquis Who's Who Top Professional **B/I:** Dr. DuBose earned his Bachelor's from the University of South Carolina, but he hadn't quite come to grips yet on what he wanted to do for a living. A roommate of his said, "Why don't you apply to dentistry?" So he did, sending a dollar and his transcript to the University of Louisville. They accepted him on probation within a week, and this surprising turn of events led to a lifelong career. **AV:** Ranching; Water resources **PA:** Republican **RE:** Baptist

DUBOVSKY, STEVEN L. MD, T: Professor, Chair **I:** Education/Educational Services **CN:** University at Buffalo **ED:** Residency in Psychiatry, University of Colorado Medical Center (1973); Fellowship, Teaching Fellow (Chief Resident) in Psychiatry, University of Colorado (1973); Internship, Mixed Medical, Vancouver General Hospital (1970); MD, Medicine, New York University School of Medicine (1969); AB, New York University, Magna Cum Laude (1965) **CT:** Diplomat, American Board of Psychiatry and Neurology; EMT-B; Peace Officer; Firefighter **C:** Professor and Chair, Psychiatry, Jacobs School of Medicine and Biomedical Sciences, University at Buffalo, The State University of New York (2004-Present); Adjoint Professor, Psychiatry and Medicine, University of Colorado School of Medicine (2004-Present); Visiting Professor, Department of Psychiatry, Cornell University (2009); Visiting Professor, University of Massachusetts, Worcester, MA (2008); Visiting Professor, University of New Mexico, Albuquerque, NM (2007); Advisory Board, Biovail (2005-2007); Consultant, Invesco (2001-2004); Vice-Chair for Academic and Clinical Affairs, University of Colorado School of Medicine (2000-2004); Consultant, Community Care Inc, Denver (1998-2004); Consultant in Psychobiology, Boulder Community Hospital (1990-2004) **CIV:** Interior Firefighter, New York; Reserve Deputy Sheriff, Erie County, NY **CW:** Clinical Guide, Psychotropic Medication (2005); Concise Guide, Mood Disorders (2002); Mind, Body Conceptions (1995); Concise Guide, Psychiatry (1994); "Clinical Psychiatry In Primary Care" (1985); Editor, Psychiatric Decision Making (1984); Pyschotherapeutics

In Primary Care (1981); Author, 200 Peer-Reviewed Articles, Book Chapters **AW:** SUNY Chancellor's Award for Faculty Service (2020); Exceptional Scholar, University at Buffalo, The State University of New York (2011); Award for Outstanding Contributions to Medical Student Education (2009); Dean's Award, University at Buffalo, The State University of New York (2007); Nancy D. Smith Memorial Award (2005); Community Service Award, Crisis Services, Buffalo, NY (2005); Outstanding Achievement Award, Colorado Psychiatric Society (2004); 21st Gold Medal Award for Distinction and Excellence (1991); Ninth Eleanor Steele Award for Inspirational Teaching and Supervision (1990) **MEM:** Distinguished Life Fellow, American Psychiatric Association; Fellow, American College of Psychiatric; Group of Advancement Psychiatry; Western NY Psychiatric Society; Phi Beta Kappa; Eggertsville Hose Company; Erie County Sheriffs Office **AS:** Dr. Dubovsky attributes his success to stubbornness. **B/I:** Dr. Dubovsky became involved in his profession because he came from a family of doctors and he knew a lot about medicine; he always liked it. He liked psychiatry because it integrated medical issues with mental health. **THT:** Dr. Dubovsky believes in standing fast.

DUCEY, DOUGLAS, "DOUG" ANTHONY, T: Governor of Arizona **I:** Government Administration/ Government Relations/Government Services **DOB:** 04/09/1964 **PB:** Toledo **SC:** OH/USA **MS:** Married **SPN:** Angela Ducey **CH:** Jack; Joe; Sam **ED:** BS in Finance, Arizona State University (1986) **C:** Governor, State of Arizona (2015-Present); State Treasurer, State of Arizona (2011-2015); Chief Executive Officer, Cold Stone Creamery; With, Proctor & Gamble; With, Hensley & Co. (Now Hensley Beverage Company) **CR:** Former President, Greater Phoenix Economic Club; Former President, Arizona Chapter, Young Entrepreneur's Organization; Member, State Land Election; Board Surveyor, General Chairman, State Loan Commission; Member, Arizona State Board of Investment **AW:** Tom and Madena Stewart Lifetime Compassion Award, Arizona Chapter, Make-A-Wish Foundation of America (2012); Father of the Year, Father's Day Council, American Diabetes Association (2009); Entrepreneurial Fellow, Eller College of Management, University of Arizona (2006); Inductee, W.P. Carey Alumni Hall of Fame, W. P. Carey School of Business, Arizona State University (2004); Golden Chain Award, Multi-Unit Foodservice Operators; Spirit of Philanthropy Award, Association of Fundraising Professionals **PA:** Republican

DUCKWORTH, LADDA, "TAMMY" TAMMY, T: U.S. Senator from Illinois **I:** Government Administration/Government Relations/Government Services **DOB:** 03/12/1968 **SC:** Bangkok/Thailand **PT:** Franklin Duckworth; Lamai (Sompornpairin) Duckworth **MS:** Married **SPN:** Bryan Bowlsbey (1994) **CH:** Abigail O'Kalani; Maile **ED:** PhD in Human Services, Capella University (2015); BA in Political Science, University of Hawai'i (1989); PhD Coursework, Northern Illinois University; MA in International Affairs, Elliott School of International Affairs, The George Washington University **C:** U.S. Senator, State of Illinois (2017-Present); Member, U.S. House Armed Services Committee (2013-Present); Officer, Illinois National Guard (1996-Present); Member, U.S. House Select Committee on the Events Surrounding the 2012 Terrorist Attack in Benghazi (2014-2016); Member, U.S. House of Representatives from Illinois' Eighth Congressional District, United States Congress, Washington, DC (2013-2017); Member, U.S. House Oversight & Government Reform Committee (2013-2015); Assistant Secretary for Public & Intergovernmental Affairs, U.S. Department of Veterans Affairs, Washington,

DC (2009-2011); Director, Illinois Department of Veterans Affairs, Springfield, IL (2006-2009); Manager, Club and District Administration Department, Asia-Pacific Region, Rotary International (2002-2004) **CR:** Coordinator, Center for Nursing Research, Northern Illinois University (1999-2001) **MIL:** Lieutenant Colonel, Illinois National Guard (1992-2014); Officer, United States Army Reserve (1992); Battle Captain, Assistant Operations Officer, Iraq; Commander, B/1-106th Aviation, Chicago Midway Airport; Logistics Officer, 106th Aviation Battalion, Peoria, IL **CW:** Contributor, Articles, Professional Journals **AW:** Veterans Leadership Award, Iraq & Afghanistan Veterans of America (2007); Decorated Senior Army Aviator Badge; Combat Action Badge; Army Reserve Components Achievement Medal with Four Oak Leaf Clusters; Meritorious Service Medal; Army Commendation Medal with Oak Leaf Cluster; Air Medal; Purple Heart; National Defense Service Medal; Army Service Ribbon; Dame Grand Cross, First Class, Order of the Crown of Thailand **PA:** Democrat

DUDZINSKI, DIANE MARIE, PHD, T: Biology Educator **I:** Sciences **DOB:** 07/23/1946 **PB:** Erie **SC:** PA/USA **PT:** Maxim John Dudzinski; Sophie (Wisniewski) Dudzinski **MS:** Single **ED:** American Society of Science and Engineers Educators Fellowship, NASA Ames Research Center, Stanford University (1982-1984); PhD, Fordham University (1974); MS, Fordham University (1970); BS, Villa Maria College (Now Gannon University) (1968) **CT:** Certified Power Boat Pilot; Secondary School Teacher, States of Pennsylvania and New York **C:** Professor of Biology, Washington State Community College (1991-2012); Professor of Biology, Mercyhurst University (1986-1991); Professor of Biology, College of Santa Fe (1981-1986); Chairperson, Department of Science and Mathematics, College of Santa Fe (1982-1985); Associate Professor of Biology, College of Santa Fe (1978-1981); Assistant Professor of Biology, Manhattan College (1975-1978); Instructor, Manhattan College (1973-1975); Teaching Fellow, Fordham University (1972-1974); Instructor, Pace University (1972-1973); Laboratory Assistant, Fordham University (1969-1972); Instructor, Ladycliff College (1970-1971); Villa Maria College (1964-1968) **CR:** Controls for Environmental Pollution, Santa Fe, NM (1979-1981); Environmental Consultant (1979-1980) **CW:** Contributor, Articles, Professional Journals **AW:** Distinguished Alumni Award, Villa Maria College (1986); Fellowship, NASA (1982-1984); Grant, National Institutes of Health (1980-1981); Grant, National Science Foundation (1976-1980); Fellowship, U.S. Fish & Wildlife Service (1977); Named First Woman Participant, US-USSR Joint Oceanographic Expedition to Bering Sea **MEM:** Board of Directors, Heritage Society, Gannon University (2018); Zonta Club of Mid-Ohio Valley (1995-2013); Board of Directors, New Mexico Network for Women in Science and Engineering (1985-1987); Treasurer, (1981-1982, 1985-1986); Student Chapter Moderator, Manhattan College, American Institute of Biological Science (1975-1978); Audiovisual Director, International Congress, The American Society of Parasitologists (1977); American Association for the Advancement of Science; The American Society for Microbiology; Pennsylvania Academy of Science; TriBeta; Sigma Xi, The Scientific Research Honor Society **MH:** Albert Nelson Marquis Lifetime Achievement Award; Marquis Who's Who Top Professional **AS:** Dr. Dudzinski attributes her success to her work ethic, support from family and friends and desire to be a lifelong learner. **B/I:** Dr. Dudzinski became involved in her profession because of her high school teachers. **AV:** Snorkeling; Swimming; Gardening; Antiquing;

Traveling **PA:** Democrat **RE:** Roman Catholic **THT:** Dr. Dudzinski states, "Always do the best that you can do, be kind to others and be willing to learn."

DUERIG, G.F., "JILL", T: Interim Executive Director **I:** Government Administration/Government Relations/Government Services **DOB:** 03/08/1953 **PB:** Milwaukee **SC:** WI/USA **PT:** William R. Frey; Germaine M. (Reback) Frey **MS:** Married **SPN:** Thomas W. Duerig **CH:** Kristin; Lara; Thomas J **ED:** Doctor of Jurisprudence, Santa Clara University, Santa Clara, CA (2000); Master of Science in Chemical Engineering, University of Pittsburgh, Pittsburgh, PA (1978); Bachelor of Science in Fundamental Science, Lehigh University, Bethlehem, PA (1974) **CT:** Registered Civil Engineer, California; Certified Operator, Grades T5/D4, California **C:** Interim Executive Director, Department of Consumer Affairs, Sacramento, CA, May (2018-Present); General Manager, Zone 7 Water Agency, Livermore, California (2005-2018); General Manager, Chief Engineer, Scotts Valley Water District, California (2003-2005); Attorney, Wendel, Rosen, Black & Dean LLP, Oakland (2000-2003); Law Clerk Environmental Protection, Alameda County District Attorney's Office, Oakland, California, (1998-2000); Production Manager, Alameda County Water District, Fremont, California (1992-1998); Division Engineer, Alameda County Water District, Fremont, CA (1989-1992); Associate Engineer, Alameda County Water District, Fremont, CA (1988-1989); Assistant Engineer, Alameda County Water District, Fremont, CA (1986-1988); Director, Water Quality, Western Pennsylvania Water Co., Pittsburgh, PA (1979-1980); Water Quality Supervisor, Western Pennsylvania Water Co., Pittsburgh, PA (1977-1979); Chemist, Western Pennsylvania Water Co., Pittsburgh, PA (1975-1977) **CR:** Board of Directors, State and Federal Contractors Water Agency (2008-2018); Board of Directors, Association of California Water Agencies (2014-2017); CUWA Board (2007-2018); Co-Chair, Watereuse-Potable Reuse Subcommittee, American Water Works Association (1992-1994); Member, Hazardous Waste Technical Advisory Committee, Alameda County, CA (1990-1992) **MEM:** President-Elect, Livermore Valley Rotary Club (2005); Rotary (2003); California Bar Association **BAR:** California **MH:** Albert Nelson Marquis Lifetime Achievement Award **B/I:** Ms. Duerig became involved in her profession because she was incredibly interested in water science, particularly as it pertains to marine life. She drew inspiration from her mentor, Dr. Jack Pearce, who served as her teacher at the Sandy Hook Marine Laboratory.

DUFFIELD, DAVID A., T: Co-Chief Executive Officer **DOB:** 09/21/1940 **PB:** Shaker Heights **SC:** OH/USA **MS:** Married **SPN:** Cheryl Duffield **CH:** Nine Children **ED:** MBA, Cornell University (1964); BS in Electrical Engineering, Cornell University (1962) **C:** Co-founder, Workday, Incline Village, NV (2005-Present); Founder, Chairman, PeopleSoft Inc., Pleasanton, CA (1987-2004); Chief Executive Officer, PeopleSoft Inc., Pleasanton, CA (2004); Chief Executive Officer, PeopleSoft Inc., Pleasanton, CA (1987-1999); President, PeopleSoft Inc., Pleasanton, CA (1987-1999); Founder, Chairman, Integral Systems Inc., Walnut Creek, CA (1972-1987); Co-founder, Information Associates; Marketing Representative, System Engineer, IBM (1964-1969) **CR:** Co-founder Maddie's Fund, Alameda, California (1999-Present) **CIV:** Maddie's Fund (1994) **AW:** Forbes 400: Richest Americans (2006-Present)

DUFFY, SEAN PATRICK, T: Senior Counsel; Former U.S. Representative from Wisconsin **I:** Government Administration/Government Relations/Government Services **CN:** BGR Group **DOB:** 10/3/1971 **PB:** Hayward **SC:** WI/USA **PT:** Thomas Walter Duffy; Carol Ann (Yackel) Duffy **MS:** Married **SPN:** Rachel Campos (04/04/1999) **CH:** Nine Children **ED:** JD, William Mitchell College of Law, St. Paul, MN (1999); BA in Marketing, St. Mary's University, San Antonio, Texas (1994) **C:** Senior Counsel, BGR Group, Washington, DC (2019-Present); Member, U.S. House of Representatives from Wisconsin's Seventh Congressional District, United States Congress (2011-2019); Member, U.S. House Financial Services Committee (2011-2019); District Attorney, Ashland County, WI (2002-2010) **CW:** Color Commentator, "Great Outdoor Games," ESPN (2003); Cast Member, "Real World/Road Rules Challenge: Battle of the Seasons," MTV (2002); Cast Member, "Road Rules: All Stars," MTV (1998); Cast Member, Reality Series, "The Real World: Boston," MTV (1997) **AW:** Named One of the Politics 40 Under 40, TIME Magazine (2010) **PA:** Republican **RE:** Roman Catholic

DUGAN, ROBERT M., T: President **I:** Business Management/Business Services **CN:** Thor Guard **DOB:** 02/01/1953 **PB:** Albany **SC:** NY/USA **PT:** Walter James Dugan; Grace (Kennedy) Dugan **MS:** Married **SPN:** Susan Diane Seligman (05/31/2018); Nancy Ann Larsen (07/27/1977, Divorced 1984) **ED:** BA, College of the Holy Cross (1975); Coursework, La Salle Institute, Troy, NY (1971) **C:** President, Thor Guard, Inc. (2000-Present); Owner, Thor Guard, Inc., Sunrise, FL (1991-Present); Owner, Loomis Golf (2003-2012); Owner, G. Loomis (1988-1992); Consultant, Thor Guard, Inc. (1988-1991); Owner, Mind Power Golf (1988-1990); Executive Search Consultant, Dugan Associates (1984-1989); Executive Search Consultant, Mitchell/Wolfson Associates, Bannockburn, IL (1982-1984); Executive Search Consultant, Howe/Corey Consulting Group, Barrington, IL (1980-1982); Territory Sales Manager, Cerro Metals Division, Marmen Group, Oak Brook, IL (1976-1980); Golfer, PGA Tours (1975-1977) **CR:** Board of Directors, Thor Guard **CIV:** Board of Directors, Loomis Golf (2005); Board of Directors, Northern Amateur Golf Championship (1988-1992); Board of Directors, Dewar's Profile, Chicago, IL **CW:** Creator, "Mind, Power, Golf: Subliminal Golf Improvement Audio Tapes" **MEM:** American Compensation Association; United States Power Squadrons; Lightning Protection Institute; Boat Owners Association of The United States; Florida State Golf Association; United States Golf Association **MH:** Albert Nelson Marquis Lifetime Achievement Award; Marquis Who's Who Top Professional **AS:** Mr. Dugan attributes his success to hard work, flexibility with fellow work associates, setting high goals and professional and personal standards, and having a supportive and loving wife. **B/I:** Mr. Dugan became involved in his profession by playing golf professionally. After becoming a PGA professional, he worked for a company that sponsored him and his career grew from there. He was later recruited by another company to become an executive search consultant, where he specialized in retained searches for insurance actuaries. That experience led him to eventually opening his own firm. **AV:** Boating; Fishing; Skiing; Golfing; Playing piano; Listening to music **RE:** Roman Catholic

DUNAWAY, FAYE, T: Actress **I:** Media & Entertainment **DOB:** 12/14/1941 **PB:** Bascom **SC:** FL/USA **PT:** John Dunaway; Grace Dunaway **MS:** Divorced **SPN:** Terrence O'Neill (1983, Divorced 03/1987); Peter Wolf (08/07/1974, Divorced 1979) **CH:** Liam Walker **ED:** Diploma in Theater, Boston University (1962); Coursework, Florida State University; Coursework, University of Florida **CW:** Actress, "The Bye Bye Man" (2017); Actress, "The

Case for Christ" (2017); Actress, "Inconceivable" (2017); Co-executive Producer, "Faye Dunaway: Live from the TCM Classic Film Festival" (2017); Co-executive Producer, "Documentary Now!" (2016); Actress, "Master Class" (2014); Co-executive Producer, "A Family Thanksgiving" (2010); Actress, "The Magic Stone" (2009); Actress, "The Seduction of Dr. Fugazzi" (2009); Actress, "The Bait" (2009); Actress, "21 and Wake-Up" (2009); Co-executive Producer, "Midnight Bayou" (2009); Actress, "Dr. Fugazzi" (2008); Actress, "La Rabbia" (2008); Co-executive Producer, "Pandemic" (2007); Actress, "The Gene Generation" (2007); Actress, "Cougar Club" (2007); Actress, "Say it in Russian" (2007); Actress, "Flick" (2007); Actress, "Rain" (2006); Actress, "Love Hollywood Style" (2005); Actress, "Blind Horizon" (2004); Actress, "The Last Goodbye" (2004); Actress, "El Padrino" (2004); Actress, "Jennifer's Shadow" (2004); Actress, "Ghosts Never Sleep" (2004); Co-executive Producer, "Anonymous Rex" (2004); Co-executive Producer, "Back When We Were Grownups" (2004); Actress, "Alias" (2002, 2003); Actress, "Changing Hearts" (2002); Actress, "The Rules of Attraction" (2002); Actress, "Soul Food" (2002); Actress, "Mid-Century" (2002); Actress, "The Calling" (2002); Co-executive Producer, "The Biographer" (2002); Actor, Director, Producer, "The Yellow Bird" (2001); Actress, "Touched by an Angel" (2001); Co-executive Producer, "Running Mates" (2000); Actress, "The Yards" (2000); Actress, "Stanley's Gig" (2000); Actress, "Love Lies Bleeding" (1999); Actress, "The Messenger: The Story of Joan of Arc" (1999); Actress, "The Thomas Crown Affair" (1999); Actress, "Fanny Hill" (1998); Co-executive Producer, "Gia" (1998); Co-executive Producer, Actress, "A Will of Their Own" (1998); Co-executive Producer, "Rebecca" (1997); Co-executive Producer, Actress, "Twilight of the Golds" (1997); Actress, "Drunks" (1997); Co-executive Producer, "The People Next Door" (1996); Actress, "En Brazos de la Mujer Madura" (1996); Actress, "The Chamber" (1996); Actress, "Albino Alligator" (1996); Actress, "Dunston Checks In" (1996); Actress, "Don Juan DeMarco" (1995); Co-executive Producer, "A Family Divided" (1995); Actress, "Road to Avonlea" (1995); Author, "Looking for Gatsby: My Life" (1995); Co-executive Producer, "Columbo: It's All in the Game" (1995); Co-executive Producer, "Mother Love" (1995); Actress, "Even Cowgirls Get the Blues" (1994); Actress, "Arizona Dream" (1993); Actress, "The Temp" (1993); Actress, "It Had to Be You" (1993); Actress, "Double Edge" (1992); Actress, "Arrowtooth Waltz" (1991); Actress, "The Handmaid's Tale" (1990); Actress, "Three Weeks in Jerusalem" (1990); Actress, "Scorchers" (1990); Co-executive Producer, "Silhouette" (1990); Co-executive Producer, "Cold Sassy Tree" (1989); Actress, "The Gamble" (1989); Actress, "On a Moonlit Night" (1989); Actress, "Wait Until Spring, Bandini" (1989); Actress, "Burning Secret" (1988); Actress, "La Partita" (1988); Actress, "Midnight Crossing" (1988); Actress, "Barfly" (1987); Actress, "Casanova" (1987); Actress, "Beverly Hills Madame" (1986); Actress, "Raspberry Ripple" (1986); Actress, "Christopher Columbus" (1985); Actress, "13 at Dinner" (1985); Actress, "TV Miniseries: Ellis Island" (1984); Actress, "Ordeal by Innocence" (1984); Actress, "Supergirl" (1984); Actress, "The Wicked Lady" (1982); Actress, "Curse of the Aching Heart" (1982); Actress, "The Country Girl" (1982); Actress, "Evita Peron" (1981); Actress, "Mommie Dearest" (1981); Actress, "The First Deadly Sin" (1980); Actress, "The Champ" (1979); Actress, "The Eyes of Laura Mars" (1978); Actress, "Network" (1976); Actress, "The Voyage of the Damned" (1976); Actress, "The Disappearance of Aimee" (1976); Actress, "The Four Musketeers"

(1975); Actress, "Three Days of the Condor" (1975); Actress, "Chinatown" (1974); Actress, "After the Fall" (1974); Actress, "The Towering Inferno" (1974); Actress, "Oklahoma Crude" (1973); Actress, "The Three Musketeers" (1973); Actress, "The Woman I Love" (1972); Actress, "Doc" (1971); Actress, "La Maison Sous les Arbres" (1971); Actress, "Hogan's Goat" (1971); Actress, "Little Big Man" (1970); Actress, "The Puzzle of a Downfall Child" (1970); Actress, "A Place for Lovers" (1969); Actress, "The Arrangement" (1969); Actress, "The Extraordinary Seaman" (1969); Actress, "The Thomas Crown Affair" (1968); Actress, "The Happening" (1967); Actress, "Bonnie and Clyde" (1967); Actress, "Hurry Sundown" (1967); Actress, "The Trials of O'Brien" (1966); Actress, "Seaway" (1965) **AW:** Special Tribute Award, Almería International Film Festival (2007); Golden Alexander Award, Thessaloniki Film Festival (2001); Career Achievement Award, Chicago International Film Festival (2001); Golden Globe Awards for Best Supporting Actress – Series, Miniseries or Motion Picture Made for Television, Hollywood Foreign Press Association (1985, 1999); Lifetime Achievement Award, ShoWest (Now CinemaCon, National Association of Theatre Owners (NATO)) (1995); Emmy Award for Guest Actress in Drama, Television Academy (1994); Academy Award for Best Actress, Academy of Motion Picture Arts and Sciences (1977); Golden Globe Award for Best Actress in a Motion Picture - Drama, Hollywood Foreign Press Association (1977); Most Promising Newcomer Award, British Film Academy (1968); Recipient, Numerous Awards

DUNCAN, DANIEL W., T: Labor Union Adminstrator **I:** Infrastructure **DOB:** 02/21/1956 **PB:** Cleveland **SC:** OH/USA **PT:** James Ward Duncan; Patricia (Madison) Duncan **MS:** Married **SPN:** Karen Fernand (06/26/1983) **ED:** Bachelor of Arts, University of Tennessee at Chattanooga (1978) **C:** Executive Secretary-Treasurer, American Federation of Labor and Congress of Industrial Organizations, Maritime Trades Department (2011-Present); Executive Director, American Federation of Labor and Congress of Industrial Organizations, Maritime Trades Department, Washington, DC (2000-2011); Communications Director, Seafarers International Union, Camp Springs, MD (1996-2000); Managing Editor, Seafarers International Union, Camp Springs, MD (1993-1996); Assistant Editor, Seafarers International Union, Camp Springs, MD (1991-1993); Associate Editor, Seafarers International Union, Camp Springs, MD (1989-1991); Field Political Reporter, Seafarers International Union, Jacksonville, FL (1987-1989); Director, SASC/Senior AIDES, Fort Lauderdale, FL (1983-1986); Assistant to Administrator, Family Health Centers, Hollywood, FL (1981-1983); Reporter, Hollywood Sun-Tattler, Florida (1981); Sports Editor, Photographer, Herald-Chronicle, Winchester, TN (1980-1981); Claims Adjuster, Progressive Insurance, Santa Clara, CA (1979) **CR:** Chairman, Organizer, South Florida Title V Directors, Fort Lauderdale, FL (1985-1986) **CIV:** Member, Fairfax Hospital Bone Marrow Transplant Survivors, Virginia (1994-Present); Delegate, Northern Virginia Central Labor Council (1992-Present); Member, Fairfax County Democratic Committee, Virginia (1992-2017); President, Northern Virginia Labor Federation (2007-2016); 11th Congressional District Democrats and Virginia State Democrats Central Committee (1998-2007); Delegate, Democratic National Convention (1988, 2000, 2004); District Chairman, Duval Democratic Committee (1988-1989); COPE Director, North Florida Central Labor Council (1987-1989); With, Duval County Young Democrats (1987-1988); Executive Director, Florida Young Democrats, Tallahassee (1987-1988); President, Broward County Young Democrats, Fort

Lauderdale, FL (1985-1987); Editor, Broward Democratic Committee, Fort Lauderdale (1984-1987); President, The University of Tennessee at Chattanooga Democrats (1975-1977) **CW:** Treasurer, District of Columbia Area Browns Backers (1999-2002); Editor, District of Columbia Area Browns Backers (1989-1993) **AW:** John Sturdivant Award, 11th Congressional District Democrats (2013); Washington-Baltimore News Guild Herbert Block Award (2008); Lion of the Year (1985); Named, Young Democrat of the Year, Broward County Young Democrats (1984) **MEM:** Executive Committee, Community Services Agency of Washington (2002-Present); Lions (1980-Present); President, Alexandria Lincolnia Chapter, Lions (1993-1994, 2002-2006); Board of Governors, Washington Propeller Club (2001-2006); Vice President, Northern Virginia APRI (1996-2000); Chaplain, North Florida Coalition Black Trade Unionists (1989); Sergeant-at-Arms, North Florida Community Services Union Counselor Association (1989); Second Vice President, Fort Lauderdale Downtown Chapter, Lions (1986-1987); Secretary, Miramar Chapter, Lions (1983-1986); Editor, District 12, Lions (1980-1981) **MH:** Albert Nelson Marquis Lifetime Achievement Award; Marquis Who's Who Top Professional **B/I:** Mr. Duncan first became involved in his profession after receiving a union membership card in 1973 while working at a grocery store chain in Tennessee. Likewise, he was inspired by his parents, who encouraged him to help others. **AV:** Photography; Collecting presidential campaign buttons; Lionel trains **RE:** Methodist

DUNCAN, JEFFREY DARREN, T: U.S. Representatives from South Carolina **I:** Government Administration/Government Relations/Government Services **CN:** U.S. House of Representatives **DOB:** 01/07/1966 **PB:** Greenville **SC:** SC/USA **PT:** John T. Duncan; Dianne M. Duncan **MS:** Married **SPN:** Melody Ann Hodges (12/03/1988) **CH:** Graham; John Philip; Parker **ED:** Bachelor of Arts, Clemson University (1988); Diploma, South Carolina Bankers School **CT:** Accredited Auctioneer; Real Estate Designation; Certified, Auctioneers Institute Designation **C:** Member, U.S. House of Representatives from South Carolina's Third Congressional District, United States Congress, Washington, DC (2011-Present); Member, U.S. House Committee on Natural Resources, Washington, DC (2011-Present); Member, U.S. House Homeland Security Committee, Washington, DC (2011-Present); Member, U.S. House Committee on Foreign Affairs, Washington, DC (2011-Present); Chairperson, South Carolina House Committee on Agriculture, Natural Resources and Environmental Affairs (2007-2011); Member, District 15, South Carolina House of Representatives (2002-2010); Member, Republican Study Committee; President, Corporate Auctioneer, J. Duncan Associates, Clinton, SC **CR:** Member, Clinton Board of Zoning Appeals (1995-1999) **CIV:** Board of Directors, Laurens County Chamber of Commerce (2002-2007); Board of Directors, Piedmont Wilderness Institute, Clinton, SC (2001-2006); Board of Directors, South Carolina Waterfowl Association (1997-2002); Board of Directors, Clinton Uptown Development Association (1993-1997) **AW:** Award, South Carolina Wildlife Federation (2007); Guardian of Small Business Award, National Federation of Independent Business (2006); Palmetto Leadership Award, South Carolina Policy Council (2003); Named, Legislator of the Year, South Carolina Recreation & Parks Association **PA:** Republican **RE:** Baptist

DUNCAN, TIM, T: Professional Basketball Player **I:** Athletics **DOB:** 04/25/1976 **PB:** Christiansted **SC:** VI/USA **PT:** William Duncan; Ione Duncan **MS:** Married **SPN:** Amy Sherrill (07/2001-11/2013)

CH: Sydney; Draven **ED:** BA in Psychology, Wake Forest University (1997) **C:** Center, Forward, San Antonio Spurs (1997-2016) **CR:** Member, U.S. Olympic Men's Basketball Team, Athens (2004) **CIV:** Founder, Executive Vice President, Tim Duncan Foundation **AW:** Teammate of the Year, NBA (2015); Western Conference All-Star Game, NBA (1998, 2000-2011, 2013); All-NBA First Team (1998-2005, 2007, 2013); All-Defensive First Team, NBA (1999-2003, 2005, 2007-2008); Shooting Stars Champion, NBA (2008); MVP, NBA Finals (1999, 2003, 2005); Sportsman of Year, Sports Illustrated (2003); MVP, NBA (2002, 2003); NBA Player of Year, The Sporting News (2002, 2003); Co-MVP, NBA All-Star Game (2000); Rookie of the Year, NBA (1998); NCAA Men's Basketball Player of Year, Associated Press (1997); John R. Wooden Award (1997); Naismith Player of the Year Award (1997)

DUNGY, TONY, T: NFL Coach **I:** Athletics **DOB:** 10/06/1955 **PB:** Jackson **SC:** MI/USA **PT:** Wilbur Dungy; Cleomane Dungy **MS:** Married **SPN:** Lauren Harris **CH:** Tiara; Jade; Eric; Jordan; Justin; James (Deceased) **ED:** BA in Business Administration, University of Minnesota (1977) **C:** Analyst, Football Night in America, NBC Sports (2009-Present); Head Coach, Indianapolis Colts (2002-2009); Head Coach, Tampa Bay Buccaneers, Florida (1996-2001); Defensive Coordinator, Minnesota Vikings (1992-1995); Defensive Backs Coach, Kansas City Chiefs (1989-1991); Defensive Coordinator, Pittsburgh Steelers (1984-1988); Defensive Back Coach, Pittsburgh Steelers (1982-1983); Defensive Assistant, Pittsburgh Steelers (1981-1983); Defensive Backs Coach, University Minnesota (1980); Professional Football Player, New York Giants (1980); Professional Football Player, San Francisco 49ers (1979); Professional Football Player, Pittsburgh Steelers (1977-1978) **CIV:** Active, American Diabetes Association; Active, United Way Central Indiana; Active, Indiana Black Expo; Active, Black Coaches Association National Convention; Active, Basket of Hope; Active, All Pro Dad; Active, Boys & Girls Clubs; Active, Big Brothers Big Sisters; Active, Athletes in Action; Founder, Mentors for Life, Tampa Bay; Active, Prison Crusade Ministry; Active, Fellowship Christian Athletes **CW:** Author, "You Can Be a Friend" (2011); Co-author, "Uncommon" (2009); Author, "Quiet Strength: The Principles, Practices, & Priorities of a Winning Life" (2007) **AW:** Pro Football Hall of Fame (2016); Indianapolis Colts Ring of Honor (2010); Indiana Hall of Fame (2008); Named Best Coach-Manager, ESPY Awards (2007); World's Most Influential People, "TIME" (2007); Amos Alonzo Coaching Award (2007); Fatherhood Award, National Fatherhood Initiative (2002); NFL 2000s All-Decade Team, Super Bowl Champion, XIII, XLI; Bestseller, Publisher's Weekly; Bestseller, "New York Times"

DUNLEAVY, MICHAEL, "MIKE" JAMES, T: Governor of Alaska **I:** Government Administration/Government Relations/Government Services **DOB:** 05/05/1961 **PB:** Scranton **SC:** PA/USA **MS:** Married **SPN:** Rose Newlin **CH:** Maggie; Catherine; Ceil **ED:** Bachelor of Arts in History, Misericordia University (1983); Master's Degree in Education, University of Alaska Fairbanks **CT:** Certified Teacher **C:** Governor, State of Alaska (2018-Present); Member, Alaska Senate E District (2015-2018); Member, Alaska Senate D District (2013-2015) **CR:** Teacher, Principal and Superintendent, Northwest Alaska; Member, Matanuska-Susitna Borough Board; Past President, Matanuska-Susitna Borough Board **AV:** Outdoor capacities; Hunting; Fishing; Snowmachining; Camping **PA:** Republican

DUNN, MICHAEL L., T: Lawyer **I:** Law and Legal Services **CN:** Michael L Dunn, Attorney at Law **PT:** Aubrey Dunn; Teresa Dunn **MS:** Married **ED:** Coursework in Nutrition, Erie Community College (1996); Coursework in Microbiology, Niagara County Community College (1996); Coursework in Anatomy and Physiology, Niagara County Community College (1995); Coursework in Immersion German, Dartmouth College (1989); Coursework in Immersion German, Goethe-Institut, Germany (1989); Coursework in Electronics, National Technical School, (1980); JD, University of Houston (1968); BA in Chemistry, Indiana University (1962) **CT:** Genetic Engineering Seminar Certificate (1985); Certified Rescue Diver **C:** Attorney, Michael L Dunn, Attorney at Law (1972-Present) **MIL:** Honorable Discharge, United States Marine Corps (1968) **MEM:** Life Member, The American Legion **BAR:** New York; New Jersey; North Carolina; Admission to U.S. Patent Bar **AS:** Mr. Dunn attributes his success to his true love of education. He never stopped, it's something he likes to do. He would like to learn anything, from languages, technology, etc. **B/I:** When Mr. Dunn was 12 years old, he thought he might want to be a patent lawyer. He changed his mind a few times but after he received his technical degree, he decided he wanted to do law and technology. **AV:** Scuba diver; Chess

DUNN, NEAL PATRICK, T: U.S. Representative from Florida **I:** Government Administration/Government Relations/Government Services **CN:** U.S. House of Representatives **DOB:** 02/16/1953 **PB:** New Haven **SC:** CT/USA **MS:** Married **SPN:** Leah Dunn **CH:** Three Sons **ED:** Medical Internship, Walter Reed Army Medical Center; Doctor of Medicine, George Washington University School of Medicine & Health Sciences; Bachelor of Science, Washington and Lee University **C:** Member, U.S. House of Representatives from Florida's Second Congressional District (2017-Present); Member, Committee on Agriculture; Member, Committee on Science, Space and Technology; Member, Committee on Veterans' Affairs; Member, Republican Study Committee **CR:** Co-founder, Panama City Urological Center; Co-founder, Panama City Surgery Center; Founding Chairperson, Summit Bank **MIL:** Advanced through Grades to Major, United States Army

DUPERREAULT, BRIAN, T: Chief Executive Officer, President **I:** Insurance **CN:** American International Group, Inc. **DOB:** 05/08/1947 **PB:** Hamilton **SC:** Bermuda **ED:** BS, St. Joseph's University, Philadelphia (1969) **C:** President, Chief Executive Officer, American International Group, Inc. (2017-Present); President, Chief Executive Officer, Marsh & McLennan Companies, Inc., New York, NY (2008-2012); Chairman, ACE Ltd. (1994-2007); Chief Executive Officer, ACE Ltd. (1994-2004); President, ACE Ltd. (1994-1999); Chairman, Chief Executive Officer, American International Underwriters, American International Group, Inc.; Executive Vice President, Foreign General Insurance, American International Group, Inc. **CR:** Board of Directors, Tyco International Ltd. (2004-Present); Chairman, Board of Directors, ACE Ltd. (1994-2007); Board of Directors, Bank N.T. Butterfield & Sons Ltd. **CIV:** Member, Board of Trustees, St. Joseph's University; Board of Directors, Insurance Information Institute, Center on Philanthropy, New York, NY

DURANT, KEVIN WAYNE, T: Professional Basketball Player **I:** Athletics **CN:** Brooklyn Nets **DOB:** 09/29/1988 **PB:** Washington, DC **SC:** DC/USA **PT:** Wayne Pratt; Wanda (Durant) Pratt **ED:** Coursework, The University of Texas at Austin (2006-2007) **C:** Professional Basketball Player, Brooklyn Nets, NBA (2019-Present); Forward-guard, Golden

State Warriors, NBA (2016-2019); Forward-guard, Oklahoma City Thunder, NBA (2008-2016); Forward-guard, Seattle SuperSonics, NBA (2007-2008) **CR:** Member, U.S. National Team, Summer Olympic Games, London, England, United Kingdom (2012); Member, FIBA World Championships, Turkey (2010) **AW:** Named to All-NBA Second Team (2016, 2017, 2019); Named NBA All-star (2010-2019); NBA Champion (2017, 2018); Named NBA Finals MVP (2017, 2018); All-NBA First Team (2010-2014, 2018); NBA Most Valuable Player (2014); Named NBA Scoring Champion (2010-2012, 2014); Named to Western Conference All-Star Team, NBA (2010-2013); Named to First Team All-NBA, NBA (2010-2013); Gold Medal for Men's Basketball, Summer Olympic Games (2012); Named NBA All-star Game MVP (2012); Gold Medal, FIBA World Championship (2010); Named First Team All-Rookie (2008); Named NBA Rookie of Year, The Associated Press (2008); Named National Player of the Year (2007); Named First Team NCAA All-American (2007); Named College Basketball Player of Year, The Sporting News (2007); Named Division 1 Player of Year, National Association of Basketball Coaches (2007); John R. Wooden Award (2007); Naismith College Player of the Year Award, Atlanta Tipoff Club (2007); Adolph Rupp Trophy (2007); Oscar Robertson Trophy, US Basketball Writers Association (2007); Named Jordan All-American Classic Game MVP (2006); Named McDonald's All-American Game Co-MVP (2006); Named to McDonald's All-American Team (2006)

DURBIN, RICHARD, "DICK" JOSEPH, T: U.S. Senator from Illinois **I:** Government Administration/Government Relations/Government Services **DOB:** 11/21/1944 **PB:** East St. Louis **SC:** IL/USA **PT:** William Durbin; Ann Durbin **MS:** Married **SPN:** Loretta Schaefer (06/24/1967) **CH:** Christine Ann (Deceased); Paul; Jennifer **ED:** JD, Georgetown University Law Center, Washington, DC (1969); BS in Economics, Georgetown University, Washington, DC (1966) **C:** Senate Minority Whip (2015-Present); Assistant Minority Leader (Minority Whip) (2015-Present); Chairman, U.S. Senate Defense Appropriations Subcommittee (2013-Present); U.S. Senator, State of Illinois (1997-Present); Senate Majority Whip (2007-2015); Assistant Majority Leader (Majority Whip) (2007-2015); Assistant Minority Leader (Minority Whip) (2005-2007); Member, U.S. House of Representatives from Illinois' 20th District, United States Congress (1983-1997); Partner, Durbin & Lestikow, Springfield, IL (1979-1982); Staff Minority Leader, Illinois State Senate (1972-1977); Parliamentarian, Illinois State Senate (1969-1977); Chief Legal Counsel to Lieutenant Governor Paul Simon, State of Illinois (1969-1972) **CR:** Associate Professor, Medical Humanities, Southern Illinois University (1978-Present); Co-chairman, Democratic Platform Committee (2000) **CIV:** Advisor, American Council of Young Political Leaders (1981); Candidate for Illinois Lieutenant Governor (1978); Staff, Office of Illinois Department of Business and Economic Development, Washington, DC and CT; Board of Directors, Springfield Youth Soccer; Board of Directors, Springfield Old Capitol Art Fair; Board of Directors, United Way of Springfield (Now United Way of Central Illinois); Board of Directors, Catholic Charities **AW:** Public Service Award, American Chemical Society (2005); Leadership Award, National Organization on Fetal Alcohol Syndrome (2005); Ground Water Protector Award, National Ground Water Association (2005); Excellence in Immunization Award, National Partnership for Immunization (NPI) (2001); Friend of Agriculture Award, Illinois Farm Bureau, Illinois Agricultural Association (2000); Lifetime Achievement Award, American Lung Association **MEM:** NAACP; Trial Lawyers Association; Sangamon County Bar Association; Illinois State Bar Association **BAR:** State of Illinois (1969) **PA:** Democrat **RE:** Roman Catholic

DURFEE, WAYNE KING, PHD, T: Aquaculture Educator, Researcher, Professor **I:** Education/Educational Services **CN:** The University of Rhode Island **DOB:** 10/01/1924 **PB:** North Scituate **SC:** RI/USA **PT:** Alvin William Durfee; Mildred Amey (King) Durfee **MS:** Widowed **SPN:** Bernice Claire Anderson (06/23/1951, Deceased 12/11/2019) **CH:** Bonita R.; William K. **ED:** PhD, Rutgers, The State University of New Jersey (1963); Poultry Physiology Research Fellow for P.D. Sturkie; MS in Poultry Science, The University of Rhode Island, Kingston, RI (1953); BS in Poultry Science, The University of Rhode Island, Kingston, RI (1950) **C:** Professor Emeritus, The University of Rhode Island (1989-Present); Professor, Fisheries, Aquaculture and Pathology, The University of Rhode Island (1978-1989); Research Project Manager, Rhode Island Agricultural Experiment Station, Kingston, RI (1976-1983); Associate Professor, The University of Rhode Island (1964-1978); Ombudsman, The University of Rhode Island (1974-1976); Assistant Professor, The University of Rhode Island (1957-1964); Instructor, The University of Rhode Island (1951-1957) **MIL:** Torpedoman 2/C, USS Ira Jeffery (DE - 63), United States Navy Reserve, World War II (1943-1945) **CW:** Contributor, 21 Articles, Professional Journals **MEM:** American Association of University Professors; Rhode Island Aquaculture Association; National Shellfisheries Association; World Mariculture Society; AF and AM Masons Lodge; Sigma Xi, The Scientific Research Honor Society **MH:** Albert Nelson Marquis Lifetime Achievement Award **AS:** Dr. Durfee attributes his success to many factors. He credits, "being able to acquire what you need, live comfortable, avoid debt at all cost, enjoy your good health and pay for continued good health; the knowledge to know what you're doing in life so that you can maintain a healthy lifestyle, helping others when you can." **B/I:** Dr. Durfee went to the University of Rhode Island, and Professor William H. Wiley was head of the poultry department. He was a personable man and Dr. Durfee enjoyed his lectures, his manner of speaking and also his delivery. He developed an association with him, and Professor Wiley urged him to go on and do graduate work. Dr. Durfee always enjoyed chicken growing up as child. His father was a highway engineer after World War I and he gave Dr. Durfee very strong work ethics. **AV:** Woodworking; Gardening **RE:** Protestant

DURNIN, TIMOTHY, DC, T: Chiropractic Physician **I:** Medicine & Health Care **CN:** Lansing Chiropractic Clinic and Wellness Medical Centers **MS:** Married **SPN:** Heather **CH:** Gabriella **ED:** BASc in Molecular Genetics, Eastern Illinois University (1996); BS, Doctor of Chiropractic, National University of Health Sciences (1991); BS in Aerospace, Aeronautical and Astronautical Engineering, Western Michigan University (1984) **C:** Clinic Director, Wellness Medical, S.C., Lansing, IL (1991-Present); Chief Clinician, Lansing Chiropractic Clinic & Wellness Medical Center (1991-Present); Co-Admitting Orthopedics, Olympia Fields Osteopathic Medical Center (1991-1999); Resident, Sacred Heart Hospital (1991) **MEM:** American Association of Spinal Physicians; American Chiropractic Association; Illinois Chiropractic Association (Now Illinois Chiropractic Society); Aircraft Owners and Pilots Association; Experimental Aircraft Association (EAA); Professional Association of Diving Instructors (PADI) **AS:** Mr. Durnin attributes his success to having bad influences growing up and doing the opposite of the negative things he was a witness to. He advises others, "Live every day like it's your last..." **B/I:** Mr. Durnin became involved in his profession because his father was a pioneer in the chiropractic field. His father's office was in the front of his childhood home, so he was exposed to the profession his entire life. At first, he was in pursuit of his degree in zoology but different opportunities and circumstances arose leading him back to follow in his father's footsteps. At one point, he wanted to be a fighter pilot, but was told that he was too tall. **THT:** Mr. Durnin describes his wife Heather as "indispensable..." and feels that he could not have done any better in finding a wife. When he nearly lost his leg and life in a 4-wheeling accident, Mrs. Durnin quit her job as an accountant and nursed him back to health.

DUTHIE, TRACEE, T: Attorney **I:** Law and Legal Services **CN:** Van Law Firm **PB:** Spokane **SC:** WA/USA **PT:** Ruth Dashiell-Duthie **MS:** Married **SPN:** Michael McNeely **ED:** JD, UIC John Marshall Law School, Chicago, IL (2003); BS in Human Resources Management, University of Nevada, Las Vegas, NV (2000) **C:** Attorney, Van Law Firm, Las Vegas, NV (2018-Present); Partner, Resnick & Louis, P.C., Las Vegas, NV (2017-2018); Trail Consulting, Local Firms, Las Vegas Area, NV (2014-2017); Of Counsel, Patti Sgro Lewis & Roger, Las Vegas, NV (2013-2014); Of Counsel, Gazda & Tadayon Injury Law Firm, Las Vegas, NV (2012-2013); Associate Attorney, Cooksey, Toolen, Gage, Duffy & Woog (2007-2012); Attorney, Bremer Whyte Brown & O'Meara, LLP (2004-2006); Attorney, Selman Breitman LLP (2004); Paralegal/Law Clerk, Ashby & Ranalli, LLP (2003-2004) **CIV:** Contributor, Various Charities **AW:** Named One of the 10 Best Attorneys in Client Satisfaction (2019); Named One of the 10 Best Attorneys in Nevada, American Institute of Personal Injury Attorneys (2019) **BAR:** State of Nevada **AS:** Mrs. Duthie attributes her success to hard work, great education and massive amounts of dedication to the practice. Also Mrs. Duthie's mother is a CPA and the first in her family to go to college. Her mother, Ruth, made education a priority in her family. **B/I:** Mrs. Duthie recalls watching the show, "Matlock," at only 4 years old, and deciding then and there that she would be a lawyer growing up. She knew from a very young age she would succeed with that skill set. She spent her youth studying the law and spending time around advocates, judges and attorneys to become better prepared for the ethical practice of law. **AV:** Travel **THT:** Mrs. Duthie's motto is "Veritas Vincit - truth prevails."

DUTKOWSKY, ROBERT M., T: Chief Executive Officer (Retired) **I:** Technology **CN:** Tech Data Corporation **DOB:** 01/02/1955 **ED:** BS in Industrial Engineering and Labor Relations, Cornell University (1977) **C:** Chief Executive Officer, Board of Directors, Tech Data Corporation, Clearwater, FL (2006-2018); Chairman, President, Chief Executive Officer, Egenera Inc., Marlboro, MA (2004-2006); Chairman, President, Chief Executive Officer, J.D. Edwards & Company, Inc. (2002-2004); President, Assembly Test Division, Teradyne Inc. (2001-2002); Chairman, President, Chief Executive Officer, GenRad Inc. (2000-2002); President, Data General, EMC Corp. (1999); Executive Vice President, Marketing and Channels, EMC Corp. (1997-1999); Various Senior Management Positions, IBM (1977-1997) **CR:** Board of Directors, McAfee Inc. (2001-2007); Sepaton Inc. **AW:** Ellis Island Medal of Honor (2000)

DUVALL, ROBERT, T: Actor **I:** Media & Entertainment **DOB:** 01/05/1931 **PB:** San Diego **SC:** CA/USA **PT:** William Howard Duvall **MS:** Married **SPN:** Luciana Pedraza (10/06/2004); Sharon Brophy (05/01/1991, Divorced 1996); Gail Youngs

(08/1982, Divorced 1986); Barbara Benjamin (1964, Divorced 1975) **ED:** Diploma, Principia College, IL; Coursework, Neighborhood Playhouse, New York, NY **MIL:** With, United States Army (1953-1954) **CW:** Director, Writer, "Widows" (2018); Director, Writer, "In Dubious Battle" (2016); Director, Writer, "Wild Horses" (2015); Actor, Director, Writer, "The Judge" (2014); Actor, Producer, Writer, "A Night in Old Mexico" (2013); Actor, Executive Producer, "Hemingway & Gellhorn" (2012); Actor, "Jayne Mansfield's Car" (2012); Actor, "One Shot" (2012); Actor, "Jack Reacher" (2012); Actor, "Seven Days in Utopia" (2011); Actor, "The Road" (2009); Actor, "Get Low" (2009); Actor, Producer, "Crazy Heart" (2009); Actor, "Four Christmases" (2008); Actor, "Lucky You" (2007); Actor, "We Own the Night" (2007); Actor, Executive Producer, "Broken Trail" (2006); Actor, "Kicking & Screaming" (2005); Actor, "Thank You for Smoking" (2005); Actor, "Gods and Generals" (2003); Actor, "Open Range" (2003); Actor, "Secondhand Lions" (2003); Actor, Director, Producer, Writer, "Assassination Tango" (2002); Actor, "John Q" (2002); Actor, "Gone in Sixty Seconds" (2000); Actor, "A Shot at Glory" (2000); Actor, "The Sixth Day" (2000); Actor, "A Civil Action" (1999); Actor, "Deep Impact" (1998); Actor, "Gingerbread Man" (1997); Actor, Director, Producer, Writer, "The Apostle" (1997); Actor, "Sling Blade" (1996); Actor, "Phenomenon" (1996); Actor, "A Family Thing" (1996); Actor, "The Man Who Captured Eichmann" (1996); Actor, "The Stars Fell on Henrietta" (1995); Actor, "The Scarlet Letter" (1995); Actor, "The Paper" (1994); Actor, "Falling Down" (1993); Actor, "Geronimo" (1993); Actor, "Wrestling Ernest Hemingway" (1993); Actor, "Newsies" (1992); Actor, "Stalin" (1992); Actor, "Rambling Rose" (1991); Actor, "Convicts" (1990); Actor, "Roots in a Parched Ground," (1990); Actor, "The Handmaid's Tale" (1990); Actor, "A Show of Force" (1990); Actor, "Days of Thunder" (1990); Actor, "Lonesome Dove" (1989); Actor, "Colors" (1988); Actor, "Hotel Colonial" (1987); Actor, "Belizaire the Cajun" (1986); Actor, "The Lightship" (1986); Actor, "Let's Get Harry" (1986); Actor, "The Stone Boy" (1984); Actor, "The Natural" (1984); Director, Writer, "Angelo My Love" (1983); Actor, "The Terry Fox Story" (1983); Actor, "Tender Mercies" (1983); Actor, "True Confessions" (1981); Actor, "The Pursuit of D.B. Cooper" (1981); Actor, "The Great Santini" (1980); Actor, "Ike: The War Years" (1980); Actor, "Ike" (1979); Actor, "Apocalypse Now" (1979); Actor, "The Betsy" (1978); Actor, "The Eagle Has Landed" (1977); Actor, "The Greatest" (1977); Actor, "American Buffalo" (1977); Director, "We're Not the Jet Set" (1977); Actor, "Network" (1976); Actor, "The Seven Per Cent Solution" (1976); Actor, "Breakout" (1975); Actor, "The Killer Elite" (1975); Actor, "The Outfit" (1974); Actor, "The Conversation" (1974); Actor, "The Godfather Part II" (1974); Actor, "Lady Ice" (1973); Actor, "Badge 373" (1973); Actor, "The Godfather" (1972); Actor, "Tomorrow" (1972); Actor, "The Great Northfield Minnesota Raid" (1972); Actor, "Joe Kidd" (1972); Actor, "THX-1138" (1971); Actor, "Lawman" (1971); Actor, "M*A*S*H" (1970); Actor, "The Revolutionary" (1970); Actor, "True Grit" (1969); Actor, "The Rain People" (1969); Actor, "Countdown" (1968); Actor, "The Detective" (1968); Actor, "Bullitt" (1968); Actor, "Wait Until Dark" (1966); Actor, "Fame Is the Name of the Game" (1966); Actor, "The Chase" (1965); Actor, "A View from the Bridge" (1965); Actor, "Captain Newman, M.D." (1964); Actor, "To Kill a Mockingbird" (1963) **AW:** Lifetime Achievement Award, San Francisco International Film Festival (2010); Primetime Emmy for Outstanding Lead Actor in a Miniseries or a Movie & Outstanding Miniseries, Television Academy (2007); Primetime Emmy for Outstanding Miniseries, Television Academy

(2007); National Medal of Arts, National Endowment for the Arts (2005); Recipient, Star, Hollywood Walk of Fame (2003); Golden Globe Award for Best Performance by an Actor in a Mini-Series or Motion Picture Made for TV, Hollywood Foreign Press Association (1993); Golden Globe Award for Best Performance by an Actor in a Mini-Series or Motion Picture Made for TV, Hollywood Foreign Press Association (1990); Academy Award for Best Actor, Academy of Motion Picture Arts and Sciences (1984); Golden Globe Award for Best Performance by an Actor in a Motion Picture - Drama, Hollywood Foreign Press Association (1984); BAFTA Award for Best Supporting Actor (1980); New York Film Critics Award for Best Supporting Actor (1972); Obie Award; National Association of Theatre Owners Award; Decorated National Defense Service Medal

DUVERNAY, AVA MARIE, T: Film Director, Producer **I:** Media & Entertainment **DOB:** 8/24/1972 **PB:** Long Beach **SC:** CA/USA **PT:** Joseph Marcel DuVernay III; Darlene (Sexton) DuVernay; Murray Maye (Stepfather) **ED:** Diploma, Saint Joseph High School, Lakewood, CA (1990); Bachelor of Arts in English Literature and African American Studies, University of California Los Angeles **C:** Founder, The DuVernay Agency (1999); Junior Publicist, 20th Century Fox, Savoy Pictures, Others; Intern, CBS News **CR:** Launched, Urban Beauty Collective (2003) **CW:** Director, Writer, Executive Producer, "Cherish the Day" (2020); Director, Writer, Executive Producer, "When They See Us" (2019); Executive Producer, "The Red Line" (2019); Director, "A Wrinkle in Time" (2018); Director, Writer, Producer, "Family Feud" (2017); Director, Writer, Producer, "Queen Sugar" (2016); Director, Writer, Producer, "August 28: A Day in the Life of People" (2016); Director, Writer, Producer, "13th" (2016); Director, Executive Producer, "For Justice" (2015); Director, "Chapter 1, Chapter 2, Chapter 3" (2015); Director, Writer, Producer, "Selma" (2014); Director, Writer, Producer, "The Door" (2013); Director, Writer, "Venus Vs" (2013); Director, Producer, "Say Yes" (2013); Director, "HelloBeautiful Interludes Live: John Legend" (2013); Director, "Scandal" (2013); Director, Writer, Producer, "Middle of Nowhere" (2012); Director, Writer, "TV One Night Only: Live From the Essence Music Festival" (2010); Director, Producer, "My Mic Sounds Nice" (2010); Director, Writer, Producer, "I Will Follow" (2010); Director, Writer, Producer, "Essence Presents: Faith Through the Storm" (2010); Director, Writer, Producer, "This is the Life: How the West Was One" (2008); Director, "Producer, "Compton in C Minor" (2007); Director, Producer, "Saturday Night Live" (2006) **AW:** Television Showman of the Year Award (2020); Named, Time 100 Most Influential (2017); Primetime Emmy for Outstanding Documentary, (2016); Primetime Emmy for Outstanding Writing for Nonfiction Programming **MEM:** Honorary Member, Alpha Kappa Alpha

DWYER, ANN ELIZABETH, T: Editor **I:** Writing and Editing **CN:** Crain's Chicago Business **ED:** Coursework, University of Illinois at Urbana-Champaign **C:** Editor, Crain's Chicago Business (2019-Present); Copy Editor, Chicago Tribune Media Group, Tribune Publishing (1994-1995); Copy Editor, Danville Commercial-News, Commercial-News.com (1993-1994); Staff Writer, Wolfram Research Inc. (1990-1993); Reporter, Joliet Herald-News, The Herald-News (1989-1990); Editor, Reporter, Illini Media Company (1986-1989)

DWYER, LAURAINE THERESA RN, MS, T: Ambulatory Care Administrator, Rehabilitation Nurse **I:** Medicine & Health Care **DOB:** 02/29/1948 **PB:** Detroit **SC:** MI/USA **PT:** Thomas Z. Dwyer; Mary

Alice (Parker) Dwyer **MS:** Single **ED:** MS in Nursing, Arizona State University (1976); BSN, Arizona State University (1970) **CT:** Certified Rehabilitation Nurse (CRRN) (1980); Certificate, Adult Nurse Practitioner, California State University, Long Beach (1979) **C:** Retired (2006); Director, Ambulatory Care Services, VA Medical Center, San Diego, CA (1997-2006); Associate Chief, Nursing Service, Ambulatory Care, VA Medical Center, San Diego, CA (1991-1997); Associate Chief, Nursing Service, Spinal Cord Injury (SCI) Unit/Ambulatory Care/Extended Care, VA Medical Center, San Diego, CA (1987-1991); Clinical Services Director, Outpatient Department, VA Medical Center, San Diego, CA (1986-1987); Clinical Nurse Specialist, SCI, VA Medical Center, San Diego, CA (1985-1986); Spinal Cord Injury Nurse Practitioner, VA Medical Center, Phoenix, AZ (1980-1985); Rehabilitation Clinical Nurse Specialist, Carl T. Hayden VA Medical Center, Phoenix, AZ (1977-1985); Staff & Charge Nurse, Neurology & Rehabilitation Unit, Carl T. Hayden VA Medical Center, Phoenix, AZ (1976-1977);Staff and Charge Nurse, SCI Unit, Banner Good Samaritan Hospital, Phoenix, AZ (1970-1975) **CR:** Chair, Planning Committee, VA National Telephone Care Conference (1998); Chair, Logistics Committee, 17th Annual Veterans Wheelchair Games (1996-1997); Task Force, Future Directions in Ambulatory Care, VA Central Office (1993); Planning for SCI Clinics in non-SCI VA Medical Centers, VACO (1983); Member, ARN Delegation to the People's Republic of China (1981) **CIV:** Spokane County WA Juvenile/Family Court (2018-Present); Chair, Logistics Committee, 17th Annual National Veterans Wheelchair Games (1996-1997); Court-Appointed Special Advocate (CASA) **CW:** Author, "Who Leads Tomorrow?" in Advance for Nurses (2008); Abstract Editor, SCI Nursing (1994-1996); Member, Editorial Board, REHAB Management (1991-1994); Author, "Triage & Advice: A Model for Managing Non-Emergent Patients in VA Medical Center", Innovations in Ambulatory Care Nursing (1993); Author, "For the Health of It," Paralyzed Veteran of America (PVA) publication (1986-1987); Co-Editor, SCI Nursing (1982-1986); Producer, Video, "Spinal Cord Injuries & the Road to Recovery" (1986); Author, "Bowel & Bladder Care" in Nursing Spinal Cord Injuries (1985); Author, Book Review, in Rehabilitation Nursing, journal of the Assn. of Rehabilitation Nursing (1983); Producer, Video, "Range of Motion Exercises for Home Care Patients" (1975) **AW:** Disabled American Veterans Service Award, San Diego Chapter, DAV (1995); Distinguished Service Award, American Association of SCI Nurses (1994); Nominee, GEICO National Public Service Award (1985); Certificate of Appreciation, PVA National Headquarters (1983); Service Award, San Diego Chapter, Paralyzed Veterans of America (PVA) (1982); Nurse of the Year, Arizona Nurses Association (1982); Barrier Buster Award, PVA Arizona Chapter (1981) **MEM:** Association of California Nurse Leaders (2002-2006); National Association of VA Ambulatory Care Managers (1997-2006); Chair, VA Special Interest Group, American Academy of Ambulatory Care Nursing (1991-2006); Sigma Theta Tau, Gamma Gamma Chapter, San Diego University, (1985-2006); Founding Member, American Association of SCI Nurses (1982-2000); Association of Rehabilitation Nurses (1974-2000); Organization of Nurse Executives - California (1991-1998); Secretary, San Diego Chapter, National Association of VA Ambulatory Care Managers (1994-1996); Abstract Editor, American Association of SCI Nurses (1994-1996); Editorial Board, SCI Nursing, journal of American Association of SCI Nurses (1982-1996); Editorial Board, SCI Nursing, Journal of American Association of SCI Nurses (1982-1996); Board of Directors, American Association of SCI Nurses (1991-1994);

Treasurer, San Diego Chapter, Association of Rehabilitation Nurses (1990-1994); Chair, Editorial Board, American Association of SCI Nurses (1988-1994); Society of Ambulatory Care Professionals of the American Hospital Association (1991-1993); Chair, Program Committee, 13th Annual Education Conference, Association of Rehabilitation Nurses, Anaheim, CA (1986-1987); Co-Editor, SCI Nursing, American Association of SCI Nurses (1982-1986); Distinguished Service Award Committee, Association of Rehabilitation Nurses (1984-1985); Arizona Nurses Association (1979-1985); Sigma Theta Tau, Beta Mu Chapter, Arizona State University, (1977-1985); Chair, Paper/Poster Committee, 8th Annual Education Conference, Association of Rehabilitation Nurses, Denver, CO (1981-1982); Treasurer, District 18, Arizona Nurses Association (1979-1980); Founding President, Arizona Chapter, Association of Rehabilitation Nurses (1978-1980) **MH:** Marquis Who's Who Top Professional (2020); Albert Nelson Marquis Lifetime Achievement Award **AS:** Ms. Dwyer attributes her success to having a deep affinity for helping others achieve their goals, which led her to work with patients who found themselves paralyzed after traumatic events or the result of neurological illness. A childhood friend was injured in a car crash while they were in college; he was admitted to the SCI Unit in a Phoenix hospital, where she worked as a nursing assistant one summer. At first, she had no intention of making this specialty a career, but caring for him that summer and helping him become independent and return to college while using a wheelchair was very fulfilling. She also discovered she was good at it. She wanted to learn more and work to improve such care processes. Her career was now set. **B/I:** Ms. Dwyer became involved in her profession because she is the oldest of six children. When she was 9 years old, she was admitted to a pediatric unit at a local Phoenix hospital for a severe respiratory illness. She was placed in a crib in a four-bed infant/toddler room because the unit had no other beds available. She was not happy about the crib and expressed her objections to a nurse, who then found a regular hospital bed that was moved into the room she shared with much younger patients, making her feel more comfortable and less "like a baby." This nurse inspired her because she listened to her patient and paid attention to her needs. Ms. Dwyer knew at that very young age that she wanted to be like that nurse and help others who were ill to get better and teach them how to live healthy lives. **RE:** Roman Catholic **THT:** Ms. Dwyer said, "We only get one life, so it's important to make the most of it by sharing knowledge, love of your profession, leadership and care for others. Helping and modeling leadership for those nursing leaders who came after me was my goal as a health care and nursing leader. I think I succeeded!"

DWYER, MAUREEN E., T: Of Counsel **I:** Law and Legal Services **CN:** Goulston & Storrs PC **SPN:** Mark Hennigh **CH:** Jason; Jonathan **ED:** JD, Columbus School of Law, Catholic University of America (1978); BA, Smith College (1973) **C:** Of Counsel, Goulston & Storrs PC (2010-Present); Managing Partner, Pillsbury Winthrop Shaw Pittman LLP (2005-Present); Partner, Real Estate Group, Pillsbury Winthrop Shaw Pittman LLP (2000-Present); Shareholder, Wilkes Artis (1978-2000) **CIV:** Former Chairman, Eugene and Agnes E. Meyer Foundation; Former Chairman, Advisory Board, The Salvation Army **AW:** One of 100 Most Powerful Women in Washington, Washingtonian Magazine (2001) **MEM:** President, Commercial Real Estate Women (1989-1991); Federal City Council, DC Chamber of Commerce; Urban Land Institute; Greater Washington Board of Trade; District of Columbia Build-

ing Industry Association **BAR:** United States Court of Appeals District of Columbia Circuit (1979); Supreme Court of the United States **MH:** Albert Nelson Marquis Lifetime Achievement Award; Marquis Who's Who Top Professional **B/I:** Ms. Dwyer became involved in her profession because her father encouraged her to go into law. While Ms. Dwyer was in law school, she was a paralegal for a firm in New York that did contract litigation and she thought that was something she wanted to pursue. However, her son was born between her second and third year of law school, so her priorities changed. She wanted to pursue a type of law that was more local in order to have regular hours.

DYSINGER, WILLIAM MD, MPH, T: Emeritus Professor and Emeritus Associate Dean **I:** Education/Educational Services **DOB:** 05/24/1927 **PB:** Burns **SC:** TN/USA **PT:** Paul Clair Dysinger; Mary Edith (Martin) Dysinger **MS:** Married **SPN:** Yvonne Mae (Minchin) Dysinger (05/11/1958) **CH:** Edwin; Wayne; John; Janelle **ED:** MPH., Harvard University (1962); MD, Loma Linda University (1955); BA, Southern Adventist University (1951) **CT:** Diplomate, National Board of Medical Examiners; American Board of Preventive Medicine **C:** Associate Dean Emeritus, School of Public Health, Loma Linda University (2004-Present); Clinical Professor Emeritus, Preventive Medicine, Loma Linda University (2004-Present); Chairman of the Board, Development Services International, Williamsport, TN (1992-2014);Director, Preventive Medical Residency, School of Medicine, Loma Linda University (1983-1988); Associate Dean for Academic Affairs, Loma Linda University (1971-1979); Assistant Dean for Academic Affairs and International Health, School of Public Health, Loma Linda University (1969-1971); Assistant to Dean, Chairman, Department of Tropical Health, School of Public Health, Loma Linda University (1967-1969); Administrative Assistant, Division of Public Health, Loma Linda University (1964-1967); Director, Field Station, Western Tanganyika, Loma Linda University (1962-1964); Research Associate, Department of Preventive Medicine, Loma Linda University (1960-1962); Physician, Medical Advisor, American Embassy, Phnompenh, Cambodia (1958-1960); Senior Assistant Surgeon, U.S. Public Health Service (1958-1960); Intern, Washington, DC (1955-1956); Emeritus Professor And Emeritus Associate Dean **CR:** Local Director, CHIP, (2007-Present); Country Director, ADRA, Yemen (1998-1999); Senior Health Advisor, Adventist Development and Relief Agency (1988-1992); Chief, Preventive Medicine, Pettis Memorial VA Hospital, Loma Linda, CA (1984-1988); Medical Consultant, Department of Vocational Rehabilitation, Riverside, CA (1964-1988); Teacher, Consultant, South America and the Caribbean (1981-1983); Medical Director, Village Health Program, Punjab, Pakistan (1980-1981); Mother and Child Health Consultant, Ministry of Health, Tanzania (1978-1980) **CW:** Contributor, Articles, Medical Publications; Author, "Heavens Lifestyle Today"; Author, "Health to the People" **AW:** Rural Health Practitioner of the Year, Rural Health Association of Tennessee (2012); Distinguished Service Award, Loma Linda University (2000); Distinguished Service Award, Southern Adventist University (1999); Fellow, World Health Organization (1969) **MEM:** President, Adventist International Medical Society (1983-1984); National President, Delta Omega (1977-1978); Fellow Royal Society Tropical Medicine and Hygiene; American Public Health Association; American College Preventive Medicine; President, International Health Society; member American Medical Association; Global Health Council **MH:** Albert Nelson Marquis Lifetime Achievement Award; Marquis Who's Who Top Professional **B/I:** Dr. Dysinger's mother

studied nursing but never completed her studies. His father strongly encouraged his education. Dr. Dysinger was also influenced by his aunt and uncle, who were missionaries throughout South America. They were highly involved with medical missionary work. They would organize events and speeches about their adventures. Since they only had daughters, his aunt and uncle would incorporate the young Dr. Dysinger in their programs. He found himself genuinely interested in the work and committed himself at that young age to become a medical missionary in South America. To be specific, he had ambitions to go to Peru, but did not make it to Peru until well into his retirement. **AV:** Collecting stamps; Traveling; Taking photography **RE:** Adventist

EARHARDT, AINSLEY HAYDEN, T: News Correspondent **I:** Media & Entertainment **DOB:** 09/20/1977 **MS:** Married **SPN:** Kevin Wayne McKinney (04/09/2005) **ED:** BA in Mass Communications, University of South Carolina **C:** Host, Fox and Friends (2016-Present); Correspondent, FOX News Channel, New York, NY (2007-Present); Weekday News Anchor, KENS-TV, San Antonio (2004-2007); News Correspondent, WLTX-TV, Columbia, SC (2000-2004) **AW:** Listee, Most Beautiful Women on Planet Earth, MoFoPolitics.com (2011); Young Alumni Award, University of South Carolina (2007); Outstanding Young Alumna, University South Carolina School Journalism & Mass Communications (2007); Best Personality of the Year, Columbia Metropolitan Magazine (2004)

EASTERBROOK, STEVE, T: Chief Executive Officer and President **I:** Food & Restaurant Services **CN:** McDonald's Corporation **PB:** Watford **SC:** Hertfordshire/England **ED:** Coursework, Durham University **C:** President, Chief Executive Officer, McDonald's Corporation (2015-Present); Chief Brand Officer, McDonald's (2013-2015); Chief Executive Officer, PizzaExpress Ltd. and Wagamama Ltd. (2011-2013); Senior Executive Vice President, Chief Global Office, McDonald's Corp. (2013-2015); Corporate Executive Vice President, Chief Brand Officer then President, McDonald's Europe, McDonald's Corporation (2010-2011); Senior Vice President, Division President, Northern Europe, McDonald's Corporation (2007-2010); President, Chief Executive Officer, McDonald's UK division, McDonald's Corporation (2006-2007); Deputy Managing Director, McDonald's UK, McDonald's Corp. (2005-2006); Regional Vice President, UK's Southern Region, McDonald's Corporation (2001-2005); Various Positions in Finance, Operations and Supply Chain, including Financial Reporting Manager, McDonald's Corp. (1993-2001); Accountant, Price Waterhouse Cooper

EASTWOOD, CLINT, T: Actor, Director **I:** Media & Entertainment **DOB:** 05/31/1930 **PB:** San Francisco **SC:** CA/USA **PT:** Clinton Eastwood; Margaret Ruth Eastwood **MS:** Divorced **SPN:** Dina Ruiz (03/31/1996, Divorced 12/2014); Maggie Johnson (12/19/1953, Divorced 05/14/1984) **CH:** Kyle; Alison; Kimber; Francesca; Ruth; Scott; Kathryn; Morgan **ED:** Honorary DFA, Wesleyan University (2000); Coursework, Los Angeles City College **CR:** Owner, Malpaso Records Co.; Mission Ranch Resort (Now Mission Ranch Hotel and Restaurant), Carmel, CA; Tehama Golf Club, Carmel, CA; Co-founder, Partner, Tehama Inc.; Co-owner, Pebble Beach Company **CIV:** National Spokesman, Take Pride in America (2005-Present); California State Parks Commissioner, Carmel, CA (2002-Present); Mayor, City of Carmel, CA (1986-1988); Member, National Council of Arts (1972-1978); Board Member, Monterey Jazz Festival; Chairman, Monterey Peninsula Foundation; Honorary Board of Governors, Entertainment Industry Foundation; Vice-chair, California State Parks and Recreation Commission **CW:** Director, Producer, "Richard Jewell" (2019); Actor, Director, Producer, "The Mule" (2018); Producer, "The 15:17 to Paris" (2018); Producer, "A Star is Born" (2018); Director, Executive Producer, "Indian Horse" (2017); Director, Producer, "Sully" (2016); Director, Producer, "Jersey Boys" (2014); Director, Producer, "American Sniper" (2014); Actor, Producer, "Trouble with the Curve" (2012); Director, Producer, "J. Edgar" (2011); Director, Producer, "Hereafter" (2010); Director, Producer, "Invictus" (2009); Director, Producer, "Changeling" (2008); Actor, Producer, "The Exchange" (2008); Actor, Director, "Gran Torino" (2008); Director, Producer, "Flags of Our Fathers" (2006); Director, Producer, "Letter from Iwo Jima" (2006); Actor, Director, Producer, "Million Dollar Baby" (2004); Director, Producer, "Mystic River" (2003); Director, "The Blues-(Piano Blues Episode)" (2003); Actor, Director, Producer, "Blood Work" (2002); Actor, Director, Producer, "Space Cowboys" (2000); Actor, Director, Producer, "True Crime" (1999); Actor, Director, Producer, "Absolute Power" (1997); Director, Producer, "Midnight in the Garden of Good and Evil" (1997); Actor, Director, Producer, "The Bridges of Madison County" (1995); Producer, "The Stars Fell on Henrietta" (1995); Actor, "In the Line of Fire" (1993); Actor, Director, Producer, "A Perfect World" (1993); Actor, Director, Producer, "Unforgiven" (1992); Actor, Director, Producer, "White Hunter Black Heart" (1990); Actor, Director, "The Rookie" (1990); Executive Producer, "Thelonious Monk-Straight, No Chaser" (1989); Actor, "Pink Cadillac" (1989); Director, Producer, "Bird" (1988); Actor, "The Dead Pool" (1988); Director, "Amazing Stories (Vanessa in the Garden Episode)" (1985); Actor, Director, Producer, "Heartbreak Ridge" (1986); Actor, Director, Producer, "Pale Rider" (1985); Actor, Producer, "Tightrope" (1984); Actor, "City Heat" (1984); Actor, Director, Producer, "Sudden Impact" (1983); Actor, Director, Producer, "Firefox" (1982); Actor, Director, Producer, "Honkeytonk Man" (1982); Singer, "Rowdy, For You, For Me, For Evermore, Cowboy in a Three Piece Suit" (1981); Singer, "Unknown Girl" (1981); Actor, Director, "Bronco Billy" (1980); Actor, "Any Which Way You Can" (1980); Actor, "Escape from Alcatraz" (1979); Actor, "Every Which Way But Loose" (1978); Actor, Director, "The Gauntlet" (1977); Actor, Director, "The Outlaw Josey Wales" (1976); Actor, "The Enforcer" (1976); Actor, Director, "The Eiger Sanction" (1975); Actor, "Thunderbolt and Lightfoot" (1974); Actor, "Magnum Force" (1973); Actor, Director, "High Plains Drifter" (1973); Director, "Breezy" (1973); Actor, "Joe Kidd" (1972); Actor, "The Beguiled" (1971); Actor, "Dirty Harry" (1971); Actor, Director, "Play Misty for Me" (1971); Actor, "Two Mules for Sister Sara" (1970); Actor, "Kelly's Heroes" (1970); Actor, "Paint Your Wagon" (1969); Actor, "Hang 'Em High" (1968); Actor, "Coogan's Bluff" (1968); Actor, "Where Eagles Dare" (1968); Actor, "The Witches" (1967); Actor, "Rawhide" (1959-1966); Actor, "The Good, the Bad and the Ugly" (1966); Actor, "For a Few Dollars More" (1965); Actor, "A Fistful of Dollars" (1964); Singer, "Rawhide's Clint Eastwood Sings Cowboy Favorites" (1962); Actor, "Ambush at Cimarron Pass" (1958); Actor, "Lafayette Escadrille" (1958); Actor, "Escapade in Japan" (1957); Actor, "Never Say Goodbye" (1956); Actor, "The First Travelling Saleslady" (1956); Actor, "Star in the Dust" (1956); Actor, "Away All Boats" (1956); Actor, "Revenge of the Creature" (1955); Actor, "Francis in the Navy" (1955); Actor, "Lady Godiva" (1955); Actor, "Tarantula" (1955) **AW:** National Board of Review Award for Best Director (2009, 2014); James Smithson Bicentennial Medal, Smithsonian Institution (2012); Career Achievement Award, Palm Springs International Film Society (2009); Modern Master Award, Santa Barbara Film Festival (2009); Golden Palm Award, Cannes Film Festival (2009); Named Legion d'Honneur Commander, Government of France (2009); National Medal of Arts Award, National Endowment for the Arts (2009); National Board of Review Award for Best Actor (2008); Special Prize, Festival de Cannes (2008); Jack Valenti Humanitarian Award, Motion Picture Association of America (Now Motion Picture Association, Inc.) (2007); Named to Legion d'Honneur Order, Government of France (2007); Milestone Award, Producers Guild of America (2006); Lifetime Achievement Award, Directors Guild of America (DGA) (2006); Stanley Kubrick Britannia Award for Excellence in Film, BAFTA/LA (2006); Golden Boot award, Motion Picture & Television Fund (2006); Inductee, California Hall of Fame, California Museum (2006); Named One of the 100 Most Influential People, TIME Magazine (2005); Golden Globe Award for Best Director, Hollywood Foreign Press Association (2005); Director's Guild Award for Best Feature, DGA (2005); Academy Award for Best Director and Best Picture, Academy of Motion Picture Arts and Sciences (1992, 2005); Hank Award, Henry Mancini Institute (2003); Lifetime Achievement Award, Screen Actors Guild Awards, SAG-AFTRA (2003); Honoree, Kennedy Center Honors, John F. Kennedy Center for the Performing Arts (2000); Lifetime Career Achievement Award, New York National Board of Review (2000); Life Achievement Award, Film Society at Lincoln Center (1996); Award, American Film Institute (1996); Irving G. Thalberg Memorial Award, Academy of Motion Picture Arts and Sciences (1995); Golden Globe Award for Best Director, Hollywood Foreign Press Association (1993); Cecil B. DeMille Award, Hollywood Foreign Press Association (1988); Henrietta Award for World Film Favorite, Hollywood Foreign Press Association (1971) **MEM:** Fellow, American Academy Arts & Sciences

EBERHART, ROBERT N., PHD, T: Professor of Research **I:** Education/Educational Services **CN:** Stanford University **MS:** Married **CH:** Three Children **ED:** PhD in Management Science and Engineering, Stanford University, CA (2013); MA in Economics, University of Michigan (1986); BA in Finance, Michigan State University (1981) **CT:** Private Pilot, Federal Aviation Administration (1976) **C:** Visiting Scholar, Stanford University (2019-Present); Editorial Board, Organization Science (2016-Present); Assistant Professor, Organization Theory & Entrepreneurship, Santa Clara University (2013-Present); STVP Fellow, Project Leader, Stanford Technology Ventures Program, Stanford University (2013-2016); Visiting Scholar, Stanford University (2007-2011); Entrepreneur in Residence, Actium Ventures (2007-2010); CEO, WineInStyle (1999-2007); President, Plantronics Japan (1999); Director, QA, Plantronics (1996-1999); Manager, Applied Materials (1993-1996) **CIV:** Vice-Chairman, United States-Japan Joint Commission on Innovation Entrepreneurship, United States Department of State; Academic Board Member, Green Bay Packers Town Development Program; Board of Directors, Dynetics Corporation; Advisory Board, Japan Innovation Network; Board of Directors, Japan Society Of Northern California; American Chamber of Commerce, Japan **CW:** Contributor, Articles, Professional Journals; Speaker, Invited Presentations **AW:** University Research Grant, Santa Clara University (2019); Best Paper Award, Western Academy of Management (2018); Best Published Theory Paper Award, The Academy of Management (2018); Dean's Outstanding Scholar Award, Santa Clara University (2017); WAMMY Best Paper Award, Western Academy of Management (2016); Outstanding Dissertation Award, The Academy of Management (2014); Best Student Paper Award, Fondation du France, Japon de l'Hess (2012); Best Paper Proceedings Award, Academy of Management (2012) **MEM:** Academy of Management; International Society for New Institutional Economics; Society for the Advancement of Socio-Economics; Institute for Operations Research and Management Sciences **AS:** Dr. Eberhart attributes his success to hard work and realizing that nothing comes easily. **B/I:** Dr. Eberhart has always been a curious person. He wanted to understand the world more, which inspired him to pursue his work. By age 50, he decided he wanted to find a career in which he could be his own boss.

EBERLE, ANNE, T: Artist **I:** Fine Art **DOB:** 03/21/1932 **PB:** St. Louis **SC:** MO/USA **PT:** Chandler Fay Rinehart; Elizabeth Sarah (Milbank) Rinehart **MS:** Widow **SPN:** Robert Todd Eberle **CH:** Sarah Butler **ED:** Coursework, Louisiana Tech University (1978-1986); Coursework, Kansas City Art Institute (1954-1956); MA in Painting, Northeast Louisiana University (1975); BS in Applied Design with Distinction, Purdue University, West Lafayette, IN (1954) **C:** Freelance Artist, Monroe, LA (1975-Present); Instructor, Northeast Louisiana University (1982); Instructor, Masur Museum of Art, Monroe, LA (1980-1986); Graduate Assistant, Northeast Louisiana University (1973-1975); Instructor, People's Art Center, St. Louis, MO (1956-1958); Staff Artist, Hallmark, Inc., Kansas City, MO (1954-1956) **CR:** Instructor, Watercolor Media **CIV:** President, Education Chairman, Trustee, Twin City Art Foundation, Monroe, LA (1974-Present); Mayor's Committee for Visual Arts, Monroe, LA (1979-1982) **CW:** Two-Person Exhibit, Schepis Museum (2008); Irving Art Association, Texas and Neighbors (1996); Group Show, Watercolor Energies (1990); Group Show, Art Options, Inc. Chagrin Falls, OH (1990); Group Show, Creative Influences (1990); Group Show, Masur Museum of Art, Monroe, LA (1990); One-Woman Show, Snyder Museum (1988); One-Woman Show, The Peck House (1989); One-Woman Show, The Biederharn Foundation (1991); One-Woman Show, Water Works Wafer Gallery (1991); Group Show, Rountree Gallery (1983); Group Show, Barucci Gallery (1989); Jury Exhibit, American Watercolor Society (1985) **AW:** Exhibit Award, Kentucky Aqueous (1984, 1991, 1984, 1985, 1997); Exhibit Award, Louisiana National (1983, 1984, 1994); Oklahoma National Award (1983, 1985, 1988, 1994); First-Place Award, New England Fine Arts Institute (1993); Exhibit Award, Mid Southern Watercolor (1981, 1987, 1989) **MEM:** Local President, Chi Omega (1970-1971); Secretary, Monroe Art Association (1968-1970); Association for Women in Communications; Associate, American Watercolor Society; Louisiana Watercolor Society; Mid-South Watercolorists; Secretary, Kentucky Watercolor Society; Phi Kappa Phi **MH:** Albert Nelson Marquis Lifetime Achievement Award **B/I:** Ms. Eberle feels that she did not choose her profession, but that her profession chose her. She had a talent for art since she was in grade school, and her career has evolved ever since then. **RE:** Episcopalian

EBOZUE, BENSON O., CPA, CGMA, T: Financial Analyst, Certified Public Accountant (CPA), Chartered Global Management Accountant (CGMA) **I:** Financial Services **DOB:** 11/14/1960 **PB:** Onitsha **SC:** Anambra/Nigera **PT:** Benjamen A. Ebouzue; Regina A. Abanafo **MS:** Married **SPN:** Uche Ebouzue (06/13/2016) **CH:** Benson Onyeka Junior; Jessie Mezue Nna **ED:** Certificate, University of Texas, Arlington (1992); BBA, Dallas Baptist University (1991); Diploma in Accounting, School of Accountancy & Management, Aba, Imo, Nigeria (1982) **CT:** Certified Public Accountant, Texas; Certified Administrative Accountant, United Kingdom C: Owner, Benson O. Ebozue CPA, Cedar Hill, TX (2001-Present); Senior Accountant, Federal Management System, Inc., Washington (2000-2010); Accounting Analyst, Sunbelt National Mortgage, Dallas, TX (1992-1997); Manager, Owner, Diamond Shamrock (BCE Mart), Dallas, TX (1998-1999); President, Chief Financial Officer, Home Health Care Response, Dallas, TX (1997-1998); Default Auditor, FTB Mortgage Services, Dallas, TX (1992-1997); Loan Auditor, Mortgage Bankers Consultant, Dallas, TX (1991-1992); Accounts Payable Assistant, CompUsa, Dallas, TX (1989); Accounts Payable Assistant, Makai Brothers, Orlando, FL (1984-1988); Senior Accounting Assistant, Ekwenibe & Sons Trading Co., Onitsha (1982-1984); Tutor, School of Commerce, Onitsha (1980-1981) CR: Staff Auditor, Logan & Associates, CPA, Cedar Hill, TX (1999-Present) CIV: Tutor, Dallas Independent School District (1991-1992); Volunteer, Boys Brigade, Onitsha (1971-1976) MEM: American Institute of Certified Public Accountants; Texas Society of CPAs MH: Albert Nelson Marquis Lifetime Achievement Award B/I: Mr. Ebozue has a love for numbers and that love for numbers and to work with numbers led him to be a Certified Public Accountant. He would read the accountant books around him. He took the opportunity from the resources around him. Teaching became interesting to him, he first did not like it but after mentoring the children he found it to be beneficial to the students. AV: Soccer; Ping pong/table tennis

ECKSTEIN, PETER C., T: Labor Union Economist (Retired) I: Other DOB: 11/14/1936 PB: Chicago SC: IL/USA PT: Charles Nathan Eckstein; Virginia (Bosch) Eckstein MS: Divorced SPN: Janet Neary (06/10/1958, Divorced 1979) CH: Anne Elizabeth ED: PhD in Economics, Harvard University (1971); AM in Sociology, Harvard University (1960); BA in Economics, University of Michigan (1958) C: Retired Labor Union Economist (1999); Research Director, Michigan AFL-CIO (1982-1983, 1986-1999); Executive Director, Governor's Commission on Jobs and Economic Development, Lansing, MI (1983-1986); Research Associate, United Auto Workers International Union (Now UAW), Detroit, MI (1975-1982); Associate Professor of Economics, Western Michigan University, Kalamazoo, MI (1971-1975); Assistant Professor of Economics, University of Michigan, Ann Arbor, MI (1967-1971); Editor, The Student, International Magazine (1961-1964) CR: Board of Directors, Michigan's Children (1994-2012); Member, Michigan Governor's Council of Economic Advisors (2003-2010); Michigan Prospect (2000-2009); Michigan Partners for Education Task Force, Lansing, MI (1987-1992); Board of Economists, Detroit Free Press (1980-1990); Michigan School Finance Commission (1987); Member, Governor's Advisory Commission on Financial Institutes, Lansing, MI (1976-1977) CIV: Board of Directors, Michigan Technical Council, Statewide (1992-1995); Board of Directors, South Central Division, Michigan Technical Council (1986-1995); Board of Directors, Midwest Technical Development Institute, Minneapolis, MN (1986-1988) CW: Co-author, "Basic Economic Concepts," Chinese Edition (1984); Co-author, "Basic Economic Concepts," Spanish Edition (1979); Co-author, "Basic Economic Concepts, Second Edition" (1977); Co-author, "Basic Economic Concepts" (1974); Editor, The Michigan Daily (1957-1958) MEM: Former Member, Economic History Association; Society for History of Technology (SHOT); Michigan Democratic Party; The Tiara Club; The Henry Ford Museum MH: Albert Nelson Marquis Lifetime Achievement Award PA: Democrat THT: Dr. Eckstein has one daughter, Anne Elizabeth, who is married to Deron Brod. While at the AFL-CIO, he researched on public policy issues, testified before the legislature on public policy issues, wrote speeches and represented the AFL-CIO on various study committees and commissions.

EDGERTON, CYNTHIA, T: Veterinary Corps Officer I: Veterinary Care CN: U.S. Army Veterinary Corps ED: DVM, University of Minnesota (2018); BS in Biology and Military Science, Saint Michael's College C: Captain, U.S. Army Veterinary Corps (2018-Present) CIV: Volunteer, Vaccination Clinics; Volunteer, Spay and Neuter Clinics, Costa Rica, Thailand; Volunteer, Homeless Shelter, Colorado Springs, CO AW: Physical Fitness Award, U.S. Army AS: Dr. Edgerton grew up in Vail, Colorado, with a strong family who encouraged her to work hard in school. They gave her the support she needed to earn good grades, as did some of her teachers. B/I: Dr. Edgerton always had a love for animals. Her grandfather had been in the military, so she grew up hearing all of his stories about traveling through Korea and Germany, which greatly influenced her. When she found out that the Army needed veterinarians, she knew she had found her calling. The combination of working with animals, being in the military, and traveling was exactly what she had been looking for.

EDWARDS, BRUCE GEORGE, MD, T: Ophthalmologist, Captain, U.S. Navy (Retired) I: Military & Defense Services CN: United States Navy, Medical Corps DOB: 05/06/1942 PB: Idaho Springs SC: CO/USA PT: Bruce Norwood; Evelyn Alice (Kohut) Edwards MS: Single ED: Doctor of Medicine, University of Colorado, Denver, CO (1968); Bachelor of Arts, University of Colorado (1964) CT: Diplomate, American Academy Ophthalmology C: Retired (1997); Ophthalmology Department Head, U.S. Navy, Medical Corps, Camp Pendleton Naval Hospital (1985-1997); Director, Surgical Services, U.S. Navy, Medical Corps, Camp Pendleton Naval Hospital (1990-1992); Physician Advisor for Quality Assurance, U.S. Navy, Medical Corps, Camp Pendleton Naval Hospital (1985-1986); Ophthalmologist, Chief of Medical Staff, U.S. Naval Hospital, Naples, Italy (1983-1985); Member, Ophthalmology Staff, U.S. Navy, Medical Corps, Camp Pendleton Naval Hospital (1976-1983); Resident in Ophthalmology, U.S. Naval Hospital, Oakland, California (1973-1976); Resident in Ophthalmology, University of California San Francisco (1973-1976); General Medical Officer, U.S. Naval Dispensary, Treasure Island, San Francisco, CA (1972-1973); General Medical Officer, U.S. Naval Hospital, Taipei, Taiwan (1970-1972); Medical Officer, U.S. Navy, USS Long Beach (1969-1970); Intern, U.S. Naval Hospital, San Diego, CA (1968-1969) CR: Volunteer, International Eye Foundation, Harar, Ethiopia (1975) MIL: Advanced through Grades to Captain, Medical Corps, U.S. Navy (1980); Commissioned Ensign, Medical Corps, U.S. Navy (1964) AW: Colorado DeMolay of the Year, Order of DeMolay (1961); U.S. Naval Achievement Medal; Viet Nam Service Medal; U.S. Presidential Certificate of Appreciation for Service in the Armed Forces of the United States MEM: Colorado State Secretary, Order of DeMolay (1961-1962); Fellow, American Academy of Ophthalmology; American Medical Association; California Medical Association; California Association of Ophthalmologists; American Society of Contemporary Ophthalmologists; Association of U.S. Military Surgeons; American Legion; Pan American Association of Ophthalmology MH: Albert Nelson Marquis Lifetime Achievement Award AV: Piano; Camping; Hiking; Bicycling; Travel PA: Republican RE: Methodist

EDWARDS, BRUCE L., T: Investment Company Representative I: Financial Services DOB: 10/10/1948 PB: Decatur SC: IL/USA PT: Roy W. Edwards; Lila L. (Severe) Edwards MS: Married SPN: Lynn V. Edwards (05/16/1982) ED: MBA, University of Denver (1977); BS in Mechanical Engineering, Bradley University (1970) CT: Licensed Professional Engineer C: Investments Representative, LPL Financial CIV: Past President, Rotary International; Past Member, Lake City - Columbia County Chamber of commerce AW: Named Five-star Investment Advisor MEM: Rotary International MH: Albert Nelson Marquis Lifetime Achievement Award AS: Mr. Edwards attributes his success to hard work and great communication skills. B/I: Mr. Edwards was a project manager of finance in the engineering field; that's why he became an investment advisor. AV: Travel; Golf; Fishing RE: Christian THT: Mr. Edwards loves his family. He has been working for 54 years.

EDWARDS, JOHN BEL, T: Governor of Louisiana I: Government Administration/Government Relations/Government Services DOB: 09/16/1966 PB: Amite SC: LA/USA PT: Frank M. Edwards Jr.; Dora Jean (Miller) Edwards MS: Married SPN: Donna Hutto CH: Sarah Edwards; Samantha Edwards; John Miller Edwards ED: JD, Louisiana State University Paul M. Herbert Law Center (1999); BS in Engineering, United States Military Academy (1988); Diploma, Airborne School (1986) C: Governor, State of Louisiana (2015-Present); Minority Leader, Louisiana House of Representatives (2012-2015); Member, District 72, Louisiana House of Representatives (2008-2015); Chair, Special Committee on Military and Veterans Affairs Committee, Louisiana House of Representatives; Member, Civil Law and Procedure Committee, Louisiana House of Representatives; Member, Education Committee, Louisiana House of Representatives; Member, Judiciary Committee, Louisiana House of Representatives; Member, House Committee on Homeland Security, Louisiana House of Representatives; Member, Joint Committee on Homeland Security, Louisiana House of Representatives; Attorney PA: Democrat RE: Roman Catholic

EDWARDS, JOHN CARVER, PHD, T: Archivist I: Library Management/Library Services DOB: 12/8/1939 PB: Charleston SC: SC/USA PT: John Pelham Edwards; Elizabeth Carver Edwards MS: Married SPN: Judith Task Edwards CH: Leigh Edwards Davis; John Spann Edwards; Liam Morgan Quinlan; Kelly Harris Quinlan ED: PhD, University of Georgia (1975); MA, University of Georgia (1966); BA, Wofford College, With Honors (1964) C: Emeritus (Retired), University of Georgia, Athens, GA (2000-Present); Special Projects Archivist, University of Georgia, Athens, GA (1993-2000); Official Archivist, Ecological Society of America (1983-2000); Professional Archivist (1977-2000); Archivist, University of Georgia, Athens, GA (1977-1993); Records Officer, University of Georgia, Athens, GA (1972-1977); Head, Manuscripts Division, Georgia Department of Archives and History, Atlanta, GA (1970-1972) CR: Library Journal Book Reviewer (1996-Present); Program Co-Director, Exhibit Preparer and Conference Organizer, "And Deliver Them From Evil: A Commemoration Of Americas Role In The Global War Against Fascism, 1941-1945" (1994); Program Co-Director, Exhibit Preparer and Conference Organizer, "All Blood Runs Red: The Life Of Gene Bullard, Americas First Black Fighter Pilot, Columbus Georgia Native, WWI" (1989); Program Co-Director, Exhibit Preparer and Conference Organizer, "A Memorial Day Salute To Denmark Groover: Georgia's Black Sheep Squadron 214/WWII" (1987); Program Co-Director, Exhibit Preparer and Conference

Organizer, Archives and Records Management/ Viable Partnership, University Of Georgia Bicentennial Observance (1985) **CIV:** Active, Various Political Campaigns, Cleveland, GA (2002-Present) **CW:** Author, "And Orvilles Aviators: Outstanding Alumni Of The Wright Flying School, 1910-1916" (2009); Author, "Flying For Orville: Howard Rineharts Life Of Adventure" (2004); Author, "Airmen Without Portfolio: U.S. Mercenaries In Civil War Spain" (1997); Author, "Berlin Calling: American Broadcasters In Service To The Third Reich" (1991); Author, "Patriots In Pinstripe: Men Of The National Security League" (1982); Contributor, Five Essays, Encyclopedia of World War I; Radio Guest, "Berlin Calling," National Public Radio; Radio Guest, "Flyers of Fortune," National Public Radio; Author, 32 Academic Articles, 25 Professional Publications; Author, Biography on Thomas Etholen Selfridge **AW:** Honorable Mention Award (1999); Best Documentary Award, Society of Professional Journalists, Public Radio News Directors, Inc., and Georgia Association of Broadcasters (1994); Commendation, Library Journal **MEM:** League of WWI Aviation Historians; Charter Member, Academy of Certified Archivists; Society of American Archivists; Associate Member, Delta Tau Kappa; Associate Member, Pi Gamma Mu; Associate Member, Phi Alpha Theta; Associate Member, Phi Kappa Phi **MH:** Albert Nelson Marquis Lifetime Achievement Award (2018) **AV:** Military modeling; Reading; Walking; Baseball; Fishing **PA:** Independent **RE:** Episcopalian

EFFRON, MARC, T: Founder **I:** Medicine & Health Care **CN:** Legacy Healing Center **MS:** Married **SPN:** Massiel **CH:** Mavin; Max **C:** Founder, Legacy Healing Center **CIV:** Coaching his son's athletics teams; Treatment Owners Retreat; United Way **MEM:** National Association of Addiction Treatment Providers **MH:** Marquis Who's Who Top Professional **AS:** Mr. Effron attributes his success to his employees and not watering down the vision of why he opens Legacy Healing Center in the first place. **B/I:** Mr. Effron became involved in his profession because he spent 20 years in the financial industry. He was the vice president of a major investment company. He ran divisions/teams and was a keynote speaker for half that career. He has been clean himself for over a decade. He realized there wasn't a facility that if any of his kids became addicted that he would feel comfortable sending them to. He knew what he was capable of at sobriety and professional standpoint. He felt It in his heart and realized there's a big void in behavioral health he started to realize after doing research and learning the laws and meeting people in his community he realized there isn't really anyone like him in Florida he was committed to making a company that foster the idea that they were ladies and gentlemen caring for ladies and gentlemen and every other treatment center and there's over 14,585 programs in the country its still not enough to treat the epidemic, but Mr. Effron knew the one thing that he had control over and he had the team of leadership standpoint and the medical staff, critical staff and everybody that had the experience that he didn't he had a leadership quality, he knew that he could carry the vision that they can impact families and their love ones far better than his personal experience back in 2006 to 2008 when he finally stayed sober, he did it because there's was just not a good place for his kids so it felt personal and at that time there was so many that to leave a career that he was good at, he made good money, it was cushy at home, everyone was happy because dad was always around but in a short period of time they turned into a behavioral health provider not just in Florida they're out of state now he has 161 employees they're the sole

provider for mental health training for American Airlines and work extremely close with United Way as well. **AV:** Playing golf; Coaching football, soccer, and baseball; Being active in his community; Skiing; Reading **THT:** Mr. Effron's mottos are "The past is not equal to the future"; it' is important "to be stronger than any excuse he can give himself"; "Fear is not real, it is just in the mind"; and "All things through God, who strengthens me."

EGGERT, JAMES E., T: Educator, Writer **I:** Education/Educational Services **DOB:** 02/03/1943 **PB:** Chicago **SC:** IL/USA **PT:** Robert John Eggert; Alice Elizabeth Bauer Eggert **MS:** Married **SPN:** Patricia Ellen Stock (05/08/1971) **CH:** Anthony Robert; Leslie Louise **ED:** MA in Economics, Michigan State University (1968); BA in Economics, Lawrence University (1967) **C:** Professor Emeritus, University of Wisconsin-Stout, Menomonie, WI (2001-Present); Faculty, Economics, University of Wisconsin-Stout, Menomonie, WI (1968-2001) **CR:** Staff, Visiting Faculty, Northern Arizona University, Flagstaff, AZ (1978) **CIV:** Plan Commission Town of Colfax, Wisconsin (2003-2015); Adviser, GreenSense Environment Club (1991-2002); Volunteer, Peace Corps, Kenya, East Africa (1964-1966) **CW:** Author, "Meadowlark Economics: Exploring Values for a Sustainable Future, Revised" (2015); Author, "Greenspan's Anguish Thoreau as Economic Prophet and Other Selected Essays" (2013); Author, "Meadowlark Economics: Collected Essays on Ecology, Community and Spirituality" (2009); Author, "The Wonder of the Tao: A Meditation on Spirituality and Ecological Balance" (2004); Author, "What is Economics?" (1997); Author, "Song of the Meadowlark: Exploring Values for a Sustainable Future" (1998); Author, "A Cosmic Journey" (1995); Author, "What Is Economics?" (1993); Author, "Invitation to Economics: Macroeconomics and Microeconomics" (1991); Author, "Milton Friedman, Thoreau & Grandfather Pine: Essays and Poetry" (1986); Author, "Invitation to Economics: A Friendly Guide Through the Thickets of the Dismal Science" (1984); Author, "Low-Cost Earth Shelters" (1982); Author, "Investigating Microeconomics" (1979); Contributor, Articles, Professional Journals **AW:** Teacher of the Year, University of Wisconsin-Stout (1987); Outstanding Faculty, Ethnic Services (1984-1985) **MEM:** Sierra Club; Thoreau Society; Wisconsin Conservation Voters **AS:** Mr. Eggert attributes his success to his passion for learning. **B/I:** Mr. Eggert became involved in his profession because he wanted to help his students build lifelong learning techniques. **AV:** Taking photographs; Listening to music; Playing tennis; Studying astronomy and field botany; Practicing Tai Chi; Reading books on evolution and religion

EICHBERG, STEVEN J., T: Attorney at Law **I:** Law and Legal Services **CN:** The Law Offices of Steven J. Eichberg **MS:** Married **SPN:** Linda Albarici **CH:** Lindsay **ED:** JD, Southwestern Law School (1974); BA, California State University, Los Angeles (1971) **C:** Owner, Attorney, The Law Offices of Steven J. Eichberg (1977-Present); Senior Partner, Goldfarb, Sermon Agrobac & Eichberg, Attorney, Mediator, Co-Founder, Southern California Mediation Partners, LLC (2009-2012);Attorney, FASTFRAME Expert Picture Framing (1987-2011); Owner, LA Research Associates (1971-1974) **CIV:** Youngest Director, Member, Anti-Defamation League, HIV/ AIDS Village, Lily in the Valley, Pella, South Africa (2004-2011); Director, Biggest Fundraiser for Lily in the Valley, Lovefest (2004-2011) **AW:** Honoree, Top 1% of Lawyers in the United States, Lawyers of Distinction (2017-2019); Top Lawyer, American Law Society (2018); Lifetime Achievement Award, Cornerstone Ministry (2011); Award for Directing, Lovefest (2011); Honoree, Top 1% of Lawyers,

National Association of Distinguished Council **B/I:** Mr. Eichberg became involved in his profession because he was a leader in the Jewish community and always involved in politics. The assassination of Robert F. Kennedy in 1968 is what got him into law. **THT:** Mr. Eichberg's treats his clients how he would want to be treated himself. He has lived his life by the motto, "A closed mouth is never fed," meaning he will not stop until he does not have a chance of getting rejected. He does whatever he can to obtain things for his clients.

EICHELBERGER, IKE, T: Broker, Owner **I:** Real Estate **CN:** Builder Realty Group LLC **MS:** Married **SPN:** Lucille **CH:** Miller; Bydal; Kim; Phyllis; Patrice; Trent (Stepchild); Sparkle (Stepchild) **ED:** BA in United States History and Sociology, Westfield State University (1974) **C:** Broker, Owner, Builders Realty Group, LLC (2001-Present);Ramp Supervisor, Customer Service Supervisor, Customer Service Representative, United Airlines (1967-2002) **CIV:** Broker, Professional Opinions **AW:** Five Star Professional, 5280 Magazine **MEM:** Colorado Association of Realtors; National Association of Realtors **MH:** Marquis Who's Who Top Professional **AS:** Mr. Eichelberger attributes his success to being driven. **B/I:** Mr. Eichelberger previously worked for United Airlines. While working there, he decided to start working in real estate because he figured he could sell homes to the individuals he worked with at United Airlines. **AV:** Golfing

EICHENWALD, DEREK, T: Chief Executive Officer **I:** Financial Services **CN:** Triumph Capital Management **DOB:** 06/09/1980 **PB:** Framingham **SC:** MA/USA **ED:** BBA in Finance and Real Estate, Colorado State University (2002) **CT:** Certificate in Retirement and Estate Planning, Accounting and Finance, Wharton School of the University of Pennsylvania (2006); Licensure, Series 7, 66, 24; Licensure, Disability, Health, and Long Term Care Insurance **C:** Chief Executive Officer, Senior Investment Executive, Triumph Capital Management (2016-Present); Chief Executive Officer, JP Turner & Company (2009-2015); Senior Portfolio Manager, Financial Advisor, Raymond James (2008-2009); Vice President, AXA Advisors (2003-2008) **CIV:** Volunteer, Jewish Charities; Volunteer, Denver Chamber of Commerce **AW:** Top Ranked Investment Manager and Financial Planner, Denver Business Journal (2015-2020); Five-Star Awarded Wealth Manager (2014-2020) **MEM:** Financial Planning Association **MH:** Marquis Who's Who Top Professional **B/I:** From a young age, Mr. Eichenwald was interested in financial planning and estate management. He was introduced to the field from his local newspaper's section on finance, and the interest stayed with him throughout his entire life. **AV:** Skiing **RE:** Jewish **THT:** Mr. Eichenwald believes in the motto, "Work until you can't work anymore."

EIGUREN, ROY L., JD, T: Managing Partner **I:** Law and Legal Services **CN:** Eiguren Ellis **MS:** Married **CH:** Two Children **ED:** Executive Management Program, Public Policy Analysis, Dartmouth College (1983); JD, University of Idaho College of Law (1977); Bachelor's Degree in Political Science and Government, University of Idaho (1974) **C:** Co-Owner, Intelligent Office (2014-Present); Teacher, College Law, University of Idaho (2014-Present); Founder, Managing Partner, Eiguren Ellis Public Policy (2010-Present); Director, Idaho Independent Bank (2001-Present); Special Assistant to the Chief Executive Officer, Bonneville Power Administration (1981-1984); Deputy Attorney General, Division Chief for Administrative and Legislative Affairs, Idaho Attorney General (1979-1981); Deputy Prosecuting Attorney, Ada County,

ID (1977-1978) **CIV:** Advisory Board, School of Public Service, Boise State University (2017-Present); Chairman, Board of Directors, American Red Cross of Greater Idaho (2017-Present); Chairman, Advisory Board of Directors, Tolsma USA (2016-Present); Board of Directors, Idaho Independent Bank (1995-Present); Chairman of the Board, Boise Metro Chamber of Commerce (2000); Chairman, Capitol Commission of the State of Idaho (1999-2005); Capitol Camping Chairman for the Idaho State Museum **AW:** Lifetime Achievement Award, Idaho Business Review (2018); Listee, Lawyers of Distinction for Excellence in Governmental Relations and Public Policy Law; Listee, Best Lawyers for Public Policy **MEM:** American Red Cross **AS:** Mr. Eiguren attributes his success to education and hard work. **B/I:** Mr. Eiguren's interest in law started in high school. He had a family friend who was a lawyer, which inspired his interest in the field. **AV:** Hiking; Reading; Traveling

EIN, DANIEL MD, T: Director **I:** Education/Educational Services **CN:** George Washington University **DOB:** 11/26/1938 **PB:** Liege **SC:** Belgium **PT:** Max Motel Ein; Sabine (Toeman) Ein **MS:** Married **SPN:** Marina Wallach (04/10/1988); Marion Hess (06/25/1961, Divorced 1978) **CH:** Mark David; Jon Spencer; Jacqueline A. Deal (Stepdaughter); Arthur (Tory) Newmyer (Stepson) **ED:** MD, Albert Einstein College of Medicine, Yeshiva University, with Honors (1965); Intern, Bronx Municipal Hospital (1964-1965); AB, Columbia University, New York, NY (1959) **CT:** American Board of Internal Medicine; Diplomate, American Board of Allergy and Immunology **C:** Director, Division of Allergy, George Washington University (2005-2020); Private Practice (1971-2005); Senior Investigator, National Cancer Institute (1969-1971); Assistant Instructor, Harvard Medical School (1968-1969); Residency, Massachusetts General Hospital (1968-1969); Clinical Associate, National Cancer Institution (1967-1968); Staff Associate, National Cancer Institution (1965-1968); Fellowship, National Cancer Institute **CR:** Director, Division Allergy (2005-Present); Clinical Professor, Medicine, George Washington University, Washington, DC (1984-Present); Founder, President, Capital Physicians Network (1994-1999) **CIV:** Sharon Pratt Kelly Mayoral Transition Team; DC State Health Planning Agency; Food and Drug Administration (FDA) Advisory Committee, Allergen Immunotherapy **MIL:** U.S. Public Health Service **CW:** Contributor, Articles, Professional Journals, Newspapers **AW:** Best Doctors, Castle-Connolly (2020, 2018, 2016, 2014, 2012, 2009); Best Doctors in America (2006-2020, 2002, 2000, 1997-1998); Distinguished Fellow Award, American College of Allergy, Asthma and Immunology (2013); Distinguished Fellow (2012); Distinguished Service Award, American College of Allergy, Asthma and Immunology (2010); Distinguished Service Award, Medical Society of the District of Columbia (2008); Part-Time Physician Award, Medical House Officers, George Washington University School of Medicine (1974); Top Doctor to Date, U.S. News & World Report; Who's Who in America; Who's Who in the World **MEM:** Board of Directors, American College of Allergy (2000-2009); President, American College of Allergy (2007); President, Joint Council of Allergy (1998-2000); American Medical Association Delegate, American Academy of Allergy (1994); President, Medical Society of the District of Columbia (1991); President, Greater Washington Allergy Society (1979); Washington Academy of Medicine; Alpha Omega Alpha; Cosmos Club; Jacobi Society of Washington; Academy of Medicine, Washington, DC **MH:** Albert Nelson Marquis Lifetime Achievement Award; Marquis Who's Who Top Professional **AS:** Dr. Ein attributes his success to good genes

and hard work. **B/I:** Dr. Ein became involved in his profession because he has loved biology since high school. He was always curious and interested in the field. His father was a big influence on his choice of career as well. Having been a Holocaust survivor, he frequently pointed out to Dr. Ein frequently that medicine was the only profession that could be easily translated and practiced anywhere. **AV:** Traveling; Photography; Museums; History **RE:** Jewish

EINHORN, DAVID A., T: Lawyer **I:** Law and Legal Services **DOB:** 12/11/1961 **PB:** Brooklyn **SC:** NY/USA **PT:** Harold Einhorn; Jane Ellen (Wiener) Einhorn **MS:** Married **SPN:** LeAnne **CH:** Felicia; Diana **ED:** JD, Columbia University (1986);BA in Computer Science, Columbia University, Magna Cum Laude (1983) **C:** Partner, Scarinci Hollenbeck (2017-Present); Partner, Baker & Hostetler LLP (2008-2017); Partner, Anderson Kill & Olick, PC, New York, NY (1989-2008);Associate, Kaye, Scholer, Fierman, Hays & Handler, New York, NY (1986-1989) **CR:** Arbitrator National Arbitration Forum (2002-Present) **CIV:** Board of Trustees, Chemists Club **MIL:** Lt. Col., Judge Advocate General's Corps (JAG Corps), Army Division, New York Guard (1987-2016) **CW:** Editor in Chief, Intellectual Property Laws in Cyberspace (Updated Annually); Co-Author, Two-Volume Treatise, Patent Licensing Transactions; Contributor, Articles, Professional Journals **AW:** Encore Business Volunteer of Year Award, Arts and Business Council (2004); Long and Faithful Service Award, New York Society of Military Naval Officers (1998); National Prize, Nathan Burkan Copyright Essay Competition (1985); Harlan Fiske Stone Scholar, Columbia University (1985); New York State Defense of Liberty Medal for World Trade Center service; Off Off Broadway Review Award for Producing Ionesco Festival **MEM:** Vice President, Chemists Club (2014-Present); Representative to ICANN, Intellectual Property Owners Association (2013-Present); Vice President, Board of Directors, Tasters Guild (1997-Present); Chairman, Board of Directors, Producing Director, Treasurer, Untitled Theater Company 61, Limited (1994-Present); President, 36 Sutton South Corporate (2014-2016); Chairman, Committee, Online Copyright Issues, American Bar Association (2004-2005); Chairman, Committee, Online Trademark Issues, American Bar Association (2002-2007); Chairman, Broadcasting, Sound Recordings, and Performing, Artists Committee, American Bar Association (2000-2002); Software Copyright Subcommunications, American Bar Association (1995-1996); Software Licensing Subcommunications, American Bar Association (1991-1995); Chairman, Software Patent Subcommittee, American Bar Association (1988-1991); Lecturer, Licensing Executives Society; Computer Law Section, DC Bar Association; International Trademark Association; Former Chairman, Copyright Committee, New York Intellectual Property Law Association; American Intellectual Property Law Association **BAR:** New York; Washington DC **MH:** Albert Nelson Marquis Lifetime Achievement Award **B/I:** Mr. Einhorn became involved in his profession because his father, Harold, was also an attorney who graduated from Columbia University, so he was naturally inspired by his good experiences and influence. **AV:** Tennis; Wine tasting; Theater **RE:** Jewish

EINISMAN, MYRON, "MIKE" SACHAR, I: Nonprofit & Philanthropy **DOB:** 03/13/1940 **PB:** Chicago **SC:** IL/USA **PT:** William; Ada Joyce (Brenner) E **MS:** Married **SPN:** Margaret Movius Boland (09/26/1977) **ED:** Doctor of Jurisprudence, University of Louisville (1966); Master of Business Administration, University of Chicago (1963);

Bachelor of Arts in Liberal Arts, University of Chicago College (1962) **C:** President of Publishing, OMG/Philanthropy Publication, Chicago, IL (1994-2004); Vice President of Marketing, OMG/Publications, Chicago, IL (1982-1994); Chief Consultant, I.D.C. Corporation, Chicago, IL (1976-1982); Director, Development and Public Relations, United Charities of Chicago (1973-1976); Consultant, Charles R. Feldstein & Co., Chicago, IL (1971-1973); Development Officer, University of Chicago (1967-1971); Attorney, National Labor Relations Board, Los Angeles, CA (1966-1967) **CR:** Head, Michael Einisman, IDC Corporation (2004-Present); Founding Chairperson, Student and Alumni Theatre Committee, University of Chicago (1992-1996) **CIV:** Co-chairperson, College Reunion, University of Chicago College (1992); Consultant, Advisor, Recovery Inc. (1986-1987); Consultant, Charitable Groups in Health, Education and Arts (1967-1986); Student Editor, Chairperson, University of Louisville Law School Brandeis Lecture Series (1963-1965); Officer, Friends of Union League Library; Co-writer, Class Column Class of 1962, University of Chicago Alumni Magazine **CW:** Author, Syndicated Articles on Charitable Finance Planning (1990-Present); Publisher, Project Editor, Audiotapes, "Masterpieces of Legal Fiction" (1997); Co-publisher, Reprints of Artist Drawings used in Original Sherlock Holmes Magazine Stories (1988) **AW:** Outstanding Alumni Service Award, University of Chicago Theatre Alumni, Chicago, IL (1994) **MEM:** Quadrangle Club, University of Chicago (2004-Present); Member, Union League Club of Chicago (1998-2008); Club of Chicago Library; Phoenix Society, University of Chicago **MH:** Albert Nelson Marquis Lifetime Achievement Award; Marquis Who's Who Top Professional **AS:** Mr. Einisman attributes his success to his conceptualization of success, which is not based in financial asset accumulation or public recognition. **B/I:** Mr. Einisman became involved in his profession after helping with fundraising efforts since high school, such as a donation towards finding a cure for polio. **AV:** Collector of autographed mystery books **PA:** Democrat

EISENBERG, HOWARD M., T: R.K. Thompson Professor **I:** Education/Educational Services **CN:** University of Maryland School of Medicine and Medical Systems **DOB:** 05/04/1939 **PB:** New York **SC:** NY/USA **PT:** Monroe L. Eisenberg; Regina (Fish) Eisenberg **MS:** Married **SPN:** Doris Zografos **CH:** Nancy M. Hoy; John A. **ED:** Clinical Fellow in Surgery, Harvard Medical School, Harvard University (1969-1970); Fellow in Neurology, National Hospital for Nervous Disease, London England (1967-1968); Resident, Neurology Surgery, Children's Hospital Medical Center and Peter Bent Brigham Hospital (1966-1970); Fellow in Surgery, Cornell University (1965-1966); Intern, Resident, Assistant Surgeon, General Surgery, New York Hospital (1964-1966); MD, Downstate Medical Center, State University of New York (1964); BA, Syracuse University (1960) **CT:** Diplomate, American Board of Neurological Surgery; Licensure, Maryland; Licensure, Texas; Licensure, Massachusetts; Licensure, New York **C:** R.K. Thompson Professor, Department of Neurosurgery, University of Maryland School of Medicine and Medical Systems (2019-Present); R.K. Thompson Professor and Chairman, Department of Neurosurgery, University of Maryland School of Medicine and Medical Systems (2000-2019); Professor, Chair, Department of Neurosurgery, University of Maryland School of Medicine and Medical Systems (1996-2000); Director, Program in Trauma, R. Adams Cowley Shock Trauma Center, University of Maryland School of Medicine and Medical Systems (1995-1997); Director, Medical Services and Program in Trauma, R. Adams Cowley Shock

Trauma Center, University of Maryland School of Medicine and Medical Systems (1993-1997); Professor, Head, Division of Neurological Surgery, University of Maryland School of Medicine and Medical Systems (1992-1996); Professor of Surgery (Neurosurgery) and Pediatrics, University of Texas Medical Branch (1981-1992); Chief of Neurological Surgery, University of Texas Medical Branch (1980-1992); Associate Professor of Surgery (Neurosurgery) and Pediatrics, University of Texas Medical Branch (1977-1981); Assistant Professor of Surgery (Neurosurgery) and Pediatrics, Attending Neurosurgeon and Head of Pediatric Neurosurgery, University of Texas Medical Branch (1975-1977); Consultant, Neurosurgery, Boston Hospital for Women, Robert Breck Brigham Hospital, Veteran's Administration Hospital, Pondville Hospital, Massachusetts Hospital School (1973-1975); Instructor of Surgery (Neurosurgery), Harvard Medical School, Junior Associate, Neurosurgery, Peter Bent Brigham and Children's Hospital Medical Center (1972-1975) **CR:** Consultant, Brainlab, Munich, Germany (2015-Present); Consultant, InSightec, Israel (2015-Present); Neurotrauma Consultant, National Football League (2013-Present); Consultant, Focused Ultrasound Surgery Foundation (2009-Present); Snodgras Visiting Professor, University of Texas Medical Branch (2011); 2nd Alumni Visiting Professor, Department of Neurosurgery, Brigham and Women's Hospital, Harvard University (2010); Matson Visiting Professor, Harvard University (2003); Marshall Visiting Professor, University of Toronto (2002); Wagner Visiting Professor, Medical College of New Jersey (2002); Principal Investigator, Co-Investigator, Numerous Grant Support Work **CIV:** Member, Developer Board, Houston Grand Opera (1989-1992); Chair, National Institutes of Health, Study Section, Neurology; Member, Science Advisory Committee, Moody Foundation **MIL:** Chief, Department of Neurosurgery, Naval Hospital (1971-1972); Lieutenant Commander U.S. Navy Reserve (1970-1972) **CW:** Author, Co-Author, Numerous Articles in Peer-Reviewed Journals (1970-Present); Member, Editorial Advisory Board, World Surgery (2009-2015); Member, Editorial Advisory Board, Journal of Neurosurgery (1999-2015); Co-Chairman, Editorial Board, Journal of Neurosurgery (1997-1999); Co-Author, "Catastrophic Brain Injury" (1995); Co-Author, "Frontal Lobe Function and Dysfunction" (1991); Co-Author, "Neurosurgery Clinics of North America: Management of Head Injury" (1991); Speaker, Presenter, Panelist, Numerous Presentations and Invited Talks (1990-2019); Member, Editorial Board, Critical Reviews in Neurosurgery (1990-1997); Member, Editorial Board, Journal of Neurosurgery (1989-1999); Co-Author, "Mild Head Injury" (1989); Member, Editorial Board, Journal of Neurotrauma, Mary Ann Liebert, Inc. (1988-1995); Co-Author, "Neurobehavioral Recovery from Head Injury" (1988); Consulting Editor, Brain Injury and Recovery (Serial), The Guilford Press (1985-1995); Member, Editorial Board, Brain Injury, college Hill Press, San Diego, Taylor & Francis Ltd., London (International) (1985-1990); Member, Editorial Board, Journal of Central Nervous System Trauma, Mary Ann Liebert, Inc. (1984-1988); Co-Author, "The Cerebral Microvasculature: Investigation of the Blood-Brain Barrier" (1980); Author, Co-Author, Book Chapters; Co-Author, Numerous Instructional Materials **AW:** Distinguished Service Award, Society of Neurological Surgeons (2008); William Fields Caveness Award, National Head Injury Foundation, Inc. (1994); Lecture and Trauma Award, American Association of Neurological Surgeons/Congress of Neurological Surgeons, Trauma, Joint Section on Trauma (1991); Wakeman Award, Duke University (1990); Honored Guest, Japanese Society of Neurotraumatology (1990)

Recipient Wakeman award, 1990; William Caverness award National Head Injury Foundation, 1994; numerous grants in field **MEM:** Appeals Panel Neurosurgery, Accreditation Council for Graduate Medical Education (2004-Present); Vice Chair, Residency Review Committee for Neurosurgery, Accreditation Council for Graduate Medical Education (2001-2002); Residency Review Committee for Neurosurgery, Accreditation Council for Graduate Medical Education (1996-2002); Chairman, Board of Directors, American Board of Neurological Surgeons (1995-1996); Secretary-Treasurer, American Board of Neurological Surgeons (1992-1995); Ex-Officio Member, Residency Review Committee for Neurosurgery, American Board of Neurological Surgeons (1990-1996); Representative, American Board of Medical Specialties, American Board of Neurological Surgeons (1990-1996); Chairman, Neurology Study Section A, National Institutes of Health Review Groups (1987-1991); Neurology Study Section A, National Institutes of Health Review Groups (1983-1987); Society of Neurological Surgeons; American Academy of Neurological Surgery; American Association of Neurological Surgeons/Congress of Neurological Surgeons; American College of Surgeons; American Association for the Advancement of Science; American Association of Neurological Surgeons; Section on Tumors, Section on Trauma, Section on Pediatric Neurosurgery, Section on Basic Science, American Association of Neurological Surgeons; American Board of Neurological Surgery; American College of Surgeons; American Epilepsy Society; American Medical Association; Founding Member, American Society for Pediatric Neurosurgery; American Surgical Association; Baltimore City Medical Society; Congress of Neurological Surgeons; Epilepsy Foundation of America; Galveston County Medical Society; International Society for Pediatric Neurosurgery; Maryland Neurosurgical Society; Massachusetts Medical Society; Medical and Chirurgical Faculty of Maryland; New England Neurosurgical Society; New York Academy of Sciences; North American Skull Base Society; Research Society of Neurological Surgeons; Rocky Mountain Neurosurgical Society; Sigma Xi, the Scientific Research Society; Society for Neuroscience; Society of Neurological Surgeons; Southern Neurosurgical Society; Texas Neurosurgical Association; Halsted Society; Vice President, Academy of Neurosurgery **BAR: MH:** Marquis Who's Who Top Professional **B/I:** Dr. Eisenberg became involved in his profession because he was interested in neuroscience and decided to become a doctor. However, there were no doctors in the family, so he did not follow in the footsteps of anybody. **AV:** New York Yacht Club

EISENBERG, LEE, T: Film and Television Producer, Writer **I:** Media & Entertainment **DOB:** 04/05/1977 **PB:** Needham **SC:** MA/USA **ED:** Graduate, Connecticut College (1999) **C:** Co-Founder, Quantity Entertainment **CW:** Co-Screenwriter, "Good Boys" (2019); Co-Screenwriter, "Bad Teacher" (2009); Co-Screenwriter, "Year One" (2009); Writer, "The Office"; Co-Executive Producer, "Trophy Wife"; Co-Executive Producer, "Bad Teacher"; Co-Writer, Co-Executive Producer, "Hello Ladies"; Co-Writer, "Pulling"

EK, DANIEL, T: Entrepreneur, Technologist **I:** Technology **CN:** Spotify **DOB:** 02/21/1983 **PB:** Stockholm **SC:** Sweden **MS:** Married **SPN:** Sofia Levander (2016) **CH:** Two Children **ED:** Coursework, KTH Royal Institute of Technology, Sweden **C:** Co-founder, Chief Executive Officer, Spotify, London, England (2006-Present); Founder, Advertigo; Chief Executive Officer, Torrent; Chief Technology Officer, Stardoll; Chief Technology Officer,

Jajja Communications **AW:** Named to the Power 100, Billboard (2019); Named One of the 100 Most Influential People in the World, TIME Magazine (2012, 2017); Named One of the 40 Under 40, Fortune Magazine (2011-2013)

ELBA, IDRIS, T: Actor, Singer **I:** Media & Entertainment **DOB:** 09/06/1972 **PB:** London **SC:** England **PT:** Winston Elba; Eve Elba **MS:** Married **SPN:** Sabrina Dhowre (2019); Sonya Nicole Hamlin (2006); Hanne "Kim" Nørgaard (1999-2003) **CH:** Isan; Winston **CW:** Actor, Producer, "A Hundred Streets" (2016); Voice Actor, "Zootopia" (2016); Voice Actor, "The Jungle Book" (2016); Actor, "Bastille Day" (2016); Voice Actor, "Finding Dory" (2016); Actor, "Star Trek Beyond" (2016); Actor, Producer, "Beasts of No Nation" (2015); Executive Producer, "Mandela, My Dad and Me" (2015); Actor, "The Gunman" (2015); Actor, "Avengers: Age of Ultron" (2015); Actor, Executive Producer, "Luther" (2010-2015); Actor, "Second Coming" (2014); Actor, "No Good Deed" (2014); Actor, "Pacific Rim" (2013); Actor, "Mandela: Long Walk to Freedom" (2013); Actor, "Thor: The Dark World" (2013); Actor, "Prometheus" (2012); Actor, "They Die by Dawn" (2012); Executive Producer, "Idris Elba's How Clubbing Changed the World" (2012); Executive Producer, "Demons Never Die" (2011); Actor, "Ghost Rider: Spirit of Vengeance" (2011); Actor, "Thor" (2011); Actor, Executive Producer, "Legacy" (2010); Actor, "The Losers" (2010); Actor, "The Big C" (2010); Actor, "Takers" (2010); Singer, "High Class Problems Vol. 1" (2010); Singer, "Kings Among Kings" (2009); Actor, "The Unborn" (2009); Actor, "Obsessed" (2009); Actor, "The Office" (2009); Actor, "Prom Night" (2008); Actor, "Rockn-Rolla" (2008); Actor, "The Human Contract" (2008); Actor, "Daddy's Little Girls" (2007); Actor, "The Reaping" (2007); Actor, "28 Weeks Later" (2007); Actor, "American Gangster" (2007); Actor, "This Christmas" (2007); Actor, "All in the Game" (2006); Singer, "Big Man" (2006); Actor, "The Gospel" (2005); Actor, "Sometimes in April" (2005); Actor, "World of Trouble" (2005); Actor, "The Wire" (2002-2004); Actor, "One Love" (2003); Actor, "CSI: Miami" (2003); Actor, "London's Burning" (2001); Actor, "Buffalo Soldiers" (2001); Actor, "Sorted" (2000); Actor, "Dangerfield" (1999); Actor, "Ultraviolet" (1998); Actor, "Insiders" (1997); Actor, "Silent Witness" (1997); Actor, "Ruth Rendell Mysteries" (1996); Actor, "The Governor" (1996); Actor, "Absolutely Fabulous" (1995) **AW:** Screen Actors Guild Award for Outstanding Performance by a Male Actor in a Supporting Role (2016); Critics' Choice Award for Best Actor in a Movie Made for TV or Limited Series (2016); Screen Actors Guild Award for Outstanding Performance by a Male Actor in a TV Movie or Mini-Series (2016); National Association for the Advancement of Colored People Image Award for Outstanding Actor in a TV Movie, Mini-Series or Dramatic Special (2011, 2014); Golden Globe Award for Best Performance by an Actor in a Mini-Series or Motion Picture Made for TV (2012); Best Actor, BET Awards (2010, 2011)

ELGAZZAR, ANDREW J., T: Chief Executive Officer **I:** Law and Legal Services **CN:** QUiVX **DOB:** 03/04/1978 **MS:** Married **SPN:** Carrie Elgazzar **CH:** Kylie; Summer **ED:** AA in Technology, Heald College (1999) **C:** Co-Founder, Chief Executive Officer, Quivx.com (2008-Present); Vice President, Information Services, Publicly Traded International Staffing Company; Director, Operations, Firetalk, San Francisco, CA **CIV:** Warren W. Eukel Teacher Trust; Church Elder **AS:** Mr. Elgazzar attributes his success to his hard work and dedication. **B/I:** From a young age, Mr. Elgazzar was especially interested in information technology, and he was drawn to the opportunities of what was, at the time, an up-and-coming industry. As it became more demanding, though, Mr. Elgazzar began feeling the effects of burnout. His entrepreneurial spirit took over, and he decided to start his own company with his cousin. His risk has paid off exponentially. **PA:** Republican **RE:** Christian **THT:** Mr. Elgazzar's motto emphasizes that there is always a way to succeed.

ELIZONDO, ROY J. III, T: Managing Attorney **I:** Law and Legal Services **CN:** The Elizondo Law Firm **CH:** One Child **ED:** JD in Trial Advocacy Law, South Texas College of Law, Houston, TX (2002); BA, Yale University, New Haven, CT (1998) **CT:** Southern District of the United States (2003-Present); State Bar of Texas (2002-Present) **C:** Partner, Green & Barton, Houston, TX (2016-Present); Managing Member, The Elizondo Law Firm, PLLC, Houston, TX (2007-Present); Senior Trial Attorney, Law Offices of Thomas J. Henry, Houston, TX (2015-2016); Associate Attorney, Griffith & Garza, LLP, McAllen, TX (2005-2007); Associate Attorney, Watson, Kowis & Rossick, PC, Houston, TX (2003-2005); Associate Attorney, The Ahn Law Firm, PC, Houston, TX (2002-2003); Briefing Law Clerk, O'Quinn Laminack & Pirtle, PC, Houston, TX (2000-2002) **AW:** Listee, SuperLawyers, Texas Monthly; Texas Rising Star Award **MEM:** Texas Wears Association; Texas Young Lawyers Association; Houston Bar Association **MH:** Marquis Who's Who Top Professional **AS:** Mr. Elizondo attributes his success to his mindset to "out-work" the other side, solve problems creatively, and think outside of the box for ways to explain to the jury. He also strives to empathize with his clients for a successful outcome. He doesn't prepare any case to settle. Every case, from day one, is prepared as if he is walking in a courtroom to convince 12 strangers to grant his client money. Mr. Elizondo always likes to make sure he is improving daily and that his skills are always sharp. **B/I:** Mr. Elizondo became involved in his profession because, in high school, as captain of the debate team, he discovered that he enjoyed being on a stage. He originally wanted to become a trial lawyer. He was influenced by a man named John O'Quinn, from whom he received a clerkship, which introduced him to civil trial law.

ELKINS, LEE HAND, T: Deputy Public Defender **I:** Law and Legal Services **CN:** Office of Public Defender **MS:** Married **SPN:** Jane Fosbender **CH:** Harry **ED:** JD, Boston University School of Law, Boston, MA (1976); BA in Liberal Arts, St. John's College, Annapolis, MD (1973) **CT:** Permanency Planning Certification, National College of Juvenile and Family Law, Child Abuse and Neglect Institute, Reno, NV; Drug Court Management Certification, Family Drug Court Planning Initiative, National Drug Court Institute **C:** Deputy Public Defender, Washoe County, NV (2012-Present); Family Court Judge, State of New York (1995-2012); Adjunct Clinical Professor, Judicial Clinic, Brooklyn Law School (2002-2005); Judge, Criminal Court of the City of New York (1995) **CR:** Law Clerk, Supreme Court of the State of New York; Special Assistant, Attorney General, Office of the Special Prosecutor; Staff Attorney, Criminal Defense Division, Legal Aid Society of New York; Legal Intern, Office of General Counsel, Massachusetts Department of Mental Health; Panelist in Field; Intensive Judicial Training, Therapeutic Jurisprudence; Panelist, Open Adoption, Bar Association of the City of New York; Panelist, Legal Representation for Parents, Family Court; Panelist, Domestic Violence and Child Protection, Fordham University; Panelist, Conference on Achieving Justice for Parents Involved in the Child Welfare System, Fordham University; Panelist, Adoption and Safe Families Act, New York State Judicial Institute; Panelist, Ethics in the Interdisci-

plinary Representation of Parents in Child Welfare Cases, Fordham University; Speaker, Roundtable, Proposed Permanency Legislation, Albany, NY; Panelist, Domestic Violence, New York State Judicial Institute; Panelist, Crisis in the Family Court, New School of Social Research; Moderator, Panel, Effects of the Internet of Adolescent Development; Panelist, Effective Representation of Parents Counsel; Designated Speaker, Nevada Legislature, Washoe County Public Defender **CIV:** Chair, Advisory Committee, Juvenile Justice, Chief Judge of Family Court (2010-2012); Coach, 78th Precinct Youth Council Little League (2005-2011); Assistant Theatrical Director, Reno Youth Opera; Volunteer, C.H.I.P.S. Homeless Shelter Monitor; Consultant, Permanent Judicial Commission, Justice for Children; Advisory Office, Family Court Advisory and Rules Committee **CW:** Author, "Two Volume Treatise on the Law of Domestic Violence in New York" (1998); Author, "New York Law of Domestic Violence," Thomson West (1998); Author, "Assault and Related Offenses," New York Criminal Practice, Matthew Bender; Author, Assault and Related Offenses," New York Criminal Practice, Matthew Bender; Author, "Competence to Stand Trial," Criminal Trial Techniques, Matthew Bender; Author, "The Good Faith Defense," Proving Criminal Defenses, Matthew Bender; Co-Author, "The value of court employed social workers to Family Court Judges overseeing agency efforts toward permanency for children in foster care," Fordham University; Author, "Office of Court Administration online manual for delinquency judges"; Author, "Comparing interpretation and application of ASFA time frames across jurisdictions"; Author, 20 Decisions, New York Miscellaneous Reports; Featured Law Day Speaker, Kings County Family Court; Speaker, Address, New York City Council Committee on General Welfare **AW:** Highest Grade in Mental Health and the Law, Public Defender Clinic; New York State Foster/Adoptive Parent Association Award, Outstanding Services and Dedication to Foster/Adoptive Families **MEM:** School Justice Partnership Task Force (2011-2012); Family Court Advisory and Rules Committee (2001-2012); National Criminal Defense College; Past Member, Criminal Justice Operations and Budget Committee, Legal Problems of the Mentally Ill; Past Chair, Family Court Subcommittee, New York State Bar **BAR:** New York; Nevada; Massachusetts (Inactive); New Mexico (Inactive) **AS:** Mr. Elkins attributes his success to reading a lot. **B/I:** Mr. Elkins became involved in his profession because of the civil rights movement in the 1960s.

ELKINS, THOMAS ARTHUR, T: Chief Scientist **I:** Sciences **DOB:** 01/25/1965 **PB:** San Pedro **SC:** CA/USA **PT:** Thomas O. Elkins; Carolyn M. (Bench) Elkins **MS:** Divorced **ED:** MS in Data Science, Southern Methodist University (2017); BS in Computer Science, California State University (1988); BA in Physics, California State University (1988) **C:** Chief Scientist, Mercury Solutions, Inc. (2001-Present); Owner, Spectrum Solutions, Palmdale, CA (1997-2003); Computer Engineer, 413th Flight Test Squadron, Edwards Air Force Base, CA (1993-1997); Rocket Propulsion Analyst, Air Force Phillips Laboratory, Edwards Air Force Base, CA (1988-1993); Teaching Assistant, California State University, Dominguez Hills, CA (1986-1987, 1988); Computer Scientist, Air Force Astronautics Laboratory, Edwards Air Force Base, CA (1987-1988) **MIL:** With, United States Navy (1983-1985) **CW:** Contributor, Articles to Professional Journals **AW:** Professional Performance Award, United States Air Force (1988, 1992-1997); Philip Johnson Scholar, California State University (1987) **MEM:** Mensa International Limited **MH:** Albert Nelson Marquis Lifetime Achievement Award **B/I:** Mr. Elkins got

into his profession because he always liked solving problems. Some people got excited when they built something but for him struggling with something or seeing a problem or a question, he would say to himself, "that's interesting" and think about it. He would get an emotional high with solving problems, which was something he just loved to do. When he was in the Navy, he injured himself and so that ended his Naval career and astronaut training. He went to civilian college to obtain his degree and one of his professors had submitted him for a scholarship, which he won. At the award ceremony, a guy approached the table with his family and himself and introduced himself as the director of the Air Force rocket propulsion lab and he offered him a job right then and there. So that was how he ended up there.

ELLEN-ELLIS, JENNIFER, T: Owner **I:** Business Management/Business Services **CN:** Olde Towne Toys **MS:** Married **CH:** Emily; Connor **ED:** BA in Speech Communications, University of Georgia (1989) **C:** Owner, Olde Towne Toys (2002-Present) **CR:** Residential Real Estate Mogul **CIV:** Habitat for Humanity **MEM:** American Specialty Toy Retailers Association **AS:** Mrs. Ellen-Ellis attributes her success to her customer service skills and having a consistent quality selection for her customers. **B/I:** Mrs. Ellen-Ellis went with her then 4-year-old to a toy store in Pennsylvania and thought St. Augustine should have a similar store. So, she opened her own.

ELLINGSEN, MARK, T: Professor of Church History **I:** Religious **CN:** Interdenominational Theological Center **DOB:** 06/18/1949 **PB:** Brooklyn **SC:** NY/USA **PT:** Emil Ellingsen; Edna (Nilssen) Ellingsen **MS:** Married **SPN:** Betsey Shaw Ellingsen **CH:** Patrick John Ellingsen; Elizabeth Ann Santos; Peter Ellingsen **ED:** PhD, Yale University (1980); MA, Yale University (1975-1976); MPhil, Yale University (1975-1976); MDiv, Yale Divinity School, Magna Cum Laude (1974); BA, Gettysburg College, Magna Cum Laude (1971) **CT:** Ordained to Ministry, Evangelical Lutheran Church of America **C:** Professor, Interdenominational Theological Center, Atlanta, GA (1993-Present); Pastor, St. John's Lutheran Church, Asheboro, NC (1990-1993); Pastor, Haven Lutheran Church, Salisbury, NC (1988-1990); Associate Professor, Institute for Ecumenical Research, Strasbourg, France (1982-1988); Professor, Luther-Northwestern Seminary, St. Paul, MN (1979-1982); Vice Pastor, Central Pocono Lutheran Parish, Scotrun, PA (1977-1978); Vice Pastor, St. Luke's Lutheran Church, Hellertown, PA (1975-1977) **CR:** Guest, KPFP Houston (2018); Guest, AIB TV, Atlanta, GA (2017); Guest, AIB TV, "How Ancient African Christianity Shaped American Religious and Political Life" (2013); Guest, AIB TV, Atlanta (2012); Guest, AIB TV, Atlanta (2011); Guest, KUCI, Los Angeles, CA (2009); Guest, WMUZ, Detroit, MI (2009); Guest, FM 107.1, St. Paul, MN (2007); Guest, CNN TV (2007); Guest, WVHU (2007); Guest, 99FM New Orleans (2007); Guest, WNRR Augusta (2007); Guest, WIBA Madison (2007); Guest, KGMW Seattle (2007); Guest, WDRC Hartford (2007); Guest, KGMW Seattle, WA (2003); Guest, KFFB San Francisco (2003); Part-Time Instructor, Randolph C.C., Asheboro, NC (1992-1993); Guest, KXL NPC, Portland, OR (1989); Guest, WCBM Baltimore (1989); Guest, WILY, Centralia (1989); Guest, KUOM Minneapolis (1989); Guest, WMFR, Highpoint (1989); Guest, WWCM Detroit, "Religion in the 80s" (1989); Presenter in Field; 21-Time Guest, Numerous Radio and Television Shows **CIV:** Faith Study Task Force (1997-Present); Christ Lutheran Church, Marietta, GA (1994-Present); Volunteer Chaplain, Atlanta Detention Center (1998-2007); Consultant, Ecumenical Affairs Committee, Southeastern Synod

Evangelical Lutheran Church of America (1995-1998); Recruiter, Participant, March of Dimes Walkathon, Asheboro, NC (1992-1993); Participant, Crop Walk for Hunger, Salisbury, NC (1989-1990); Big Brother, Big Brothers Big Sisters (1978-1979) **CW:** Author, "Ever Hear of Feuerbach?" (2020); Author, "Theological Formation" (2020); Author, "A Rebellious Faith" (2018); Author, "Martin Luther's Legacy" (2017); Author, "African Christian Mothers and Fathers" (2015); Author, "Lectionary Preaching Workbook, Cycle A" (2013); Author, "Lectionary Preaching Workbook, Cycle C" (2012); Author, "Lectionary Preaching Workbook, Cycle B" (2011); Author, "Sin Bravely" (2009); Author, "Making Black Ecumenism Happen" (2008); Author, "Jesus Vision of a Fun Free Life, Not Driven By Purpose" (2007); Author, "When Did Jesus Become Republican?" (2007); Author, "The Richness of Augustine" (2005); Author, "Blessed Are the Cynical" (2003); Author, "A Word That Sets Free" (2000); Author, "Reclaiming Our Roots, Vols.1-2" (1999); Author, "A Common Sense Theology" (1995); Author, "The Cutting Edge: How Churches Speak on Social Issues" (1993); Author, "Preparation and Manifestation" (1992); Author, "The Integrity of Bible Narrative" (1990); Author, "The Evangelical Movement" (1988); Author, "Doctrine and Word" (1983); Contributor, Over 600 Articles, Professional Journals; Contributor, Newspapers; Author, 23 Books **AW:** Grantee, Institute for the Study of American Evangelicals Grant for work on "The Changing Terrain of American Protestant Missions" (2009-2011); Coca Cola/ITC Faculty Award of Excellence (2008-2009); Listee, 2000 Outstanding Scholars of the 21st Century (2003,2004); Reader's Choice Award, Christianity Today (1992); Aid Association of Lutherans Fellowship for Lutheran Seminary Professor (1981) **MEM:** American Academy of Religion; Sixteenth Century Studies Conference; Phi Beta Kappa **MH:** Albert Nelson Marquis Lifetime Achievement Award **AS:** Dr. Ellingsen attributes his success to the grace of God, the powerful nurturing of his parents, and the guidance of educated professors. Likewise, he credits his wife, Betsey, who is endlessly supportive. **B/I:** Being an immigrant, Dr. Ellingsen was raised biculturally in a religiously conservative but socially liberal family. Although he was initially interested in civil rights legal studies, he fell in love with philosophy and theology along the way. **AV:** Researching theology; Staying updated on current events and politics; Playing guitar; Traveling; Playing sports **PA:** Democrat **RE:** Lutheran Christian **THT:** In Dr. Ellingsen's opinion, life is a happy, surprising adventure, filled with wonderful opportunities to serve and interact with others. Life is about joyfully rebelling against injustice and meaninglessness alongside healthy doses of giving thanks, he says.

ELLIOTT, ANNE, T: Gifted and Talented Education Educator (Retired) **I:** Education/Educational Services **DOB:** 04/16/1947 **PB:** Hickory **SC:** NC/USA **PT:** Robert William; Reba Blanton (Whisnant) Elliott **MS:** Married **SPN:** George Thomas Pitner (1/1/1980, Divorced 1999); Allen Eugene Caldwell (6/9/1968, Divorced 1978) **CH:** Catherine Anne Elliott Mims (Kenneth Derrick Mims Jr.) **ED:** Master of Arts, Lenoir-Rhyne University (1990); Bachelor of Arts, University of North Carolina, Greensboro, NC (1968) **CT:** Certified Teacher Elementary Gifted and Talented **C:** Retired (2000); Teacher, Newton-Conover City Schools, North Carolina (1970-2000); Teacher, Raleigh Public Schools, North Carolina (1968-1969) **CR:** Consultant, North Carolina Geographical Alliance (1988-1998) **CIV:** Volunteer, Catawba Science Center **AW:** Frances Moody Volunteer of the Year, Hickory Landmarks Society (2004); Named, Technical Volunteer of the Year, Hickory Community Theatre (2002, 2003); Out-

standing Elementary Mathematics Teacher Award, North Carolina Council of Teachers of Mathematics (1991); Distinguished Teaching Achievement Award, National Council for Geographical Education (1990); Excellence in Geography Teaching Regional Award, Rand McNally (1990) **MEM:** Local Secretary, North Carolina Association of Educators (1970); Association for Supervision and Curriculum Development; North Carolina Association for the Gifted and Talented; North Carolina Council of Social Studies; North Carolina Science Teachers Association; Gamma Rho Chapter, Gamma Eta Chapter, Alpha Delta Kappa; Hickory Community Theatre Guild; Hickory Landmark Society; Hickory Museum of Art; John Hoyle Chapter, Daughters of the American Revolution **MH:** Albert Nelson Marquis Lifetime Achievement Award; Marquis Who's Who Humanitarian Award **AS:** Ms. Elliott attributes her success to the influence of her parents and upbringing. **B/I:** Ms. Elliott was inspired to become an educator due to the influence of her family, which has a history in the profession. **AV:** Walking; Reading; Knitting; Painting; Gardening **RE:** Baptist

ELLIOTT, MISSY, T: Musician **I:** Media & Entertainment **DOB:** 07/01/1971 **PB:** Portsmith **SC:** VA/USA **CW:** Guest, "Star" (2017); Guest, "Taraji P. Henson's White Hot Holidays" (2016); Voice Actress, "American Dad!" (2016); Guest, "The Voice" (2015); Guest, "What Chilli Wants" (2010); Guest, "Party Monsters Cabo" (2009); Musician, "Block Party" (2009); Guest, "Ego Trip's Miss Rap Supreme" (2008); Guest, "My Super Sweet 16" (2008); Guest, "America's Best Dance Crew" (2008); Musician, "We Run This" (2006); Musician, "Just for Kicks" (2005); Musician, "The Cookbook" (2005); Host, "The Road to Stardom with Missy Elliott" (2005); Musician, "Lose Control" (2005); Musician, "Fade to Black" (2004); Musician, "Shark Tale" (2004); Musician, "Ultrasounds: Hip Hop Dollars" (2003); Musician, "Honey" (2003); Guest, "Eve" (2003); Guest, "Punk'd" (2003); Musician, "This Is Not A Test!" (2003); Musician, "Under Construction" (2002); Musician, "Work It" (2002); Musician, "Scream aka Itchin" (2002); Musician, "Miss E...So Addictive" (2001); Musician, "Get Ur Freak On" (2001); Musician, "One Minute Man" (2001); Musician, "Pootie Tang" (2001); Musician, "Da Real World" (1999); Musician, "Hot Boyz" (1999); Guest, "The Wayans Bros." (1998); Musician, "Supa Dupa Fly" (1997); Musician, "The Rain (Supa Dupa Fly)" (1997); Guest, "All That" (1997); Guest, "Family Matters" (1997) **AW:** Best Female Hip-Hop Artist Award, BET Awards (2006, 2008); MTV Video Music Award for Video Special Effects (2006); Grammy Award for Best Short Form Music Video (2006); Best Dance Video and Best Hip Hop Video, MTV Video Music Awards (2005); Favorite Female Hi-Hop Artist Award, American Music Awards (2003, 2005); Grammy Award for Best Female Rap Solo Performance (2004); Grammy Award for Best Female Rap Solo Performance (2003); Soul Train Music Award for Best R&B/Soul or Rap Music Video (2003); 50 Greatest Hip-Hop Artists, VH1 (2003); Best Song and Best Music Video, Soul Train Lady of Soul Awards (2003); Video of the Year and Best Hip Hop Video, MTV Video Music Awards (2003); Best Single, Rolling Stone (2002); Soul Train Lady of Soul Award for Best R&B/Soul or Rap Music Video (2002); Best Female Hip-Hop Artist, BET (2002); Best Female Artist, Best R&B Artist, Rolling Stone (2002); Soul Train Lady of Soul Award for Best R&B/Soul or Rap Music Video (2001, 2002); Grammy Award for Best Rap Solo (2002); Best Single of Year, Rolling Stone (2001); Top Hot R&B/Hip Hop Single and Top Hot Rap Single, Billboard Year-End Charts (2000, 2001); Top Hot Rap Artist and Top Hot Female Rap

Artist (2000); Best Rap Artist of the Year, Rolling Stone (1997); Best Video of the Year, Rolling Stone (1997); Best Clip and Best New Artist, Billboard Video Music Awards (1997)

ELLIS, ANNE ELIZABETH, T: Fundraiser **I:** Nonprofit & Philanthropy **DOB:** 08/21/1945 **PB:** Orngestad **SC:** Aruba **PT:** Thomas Albert Wolfe; Anne Elizabeth (Belis) Wolfe **MS:** Married **SPN:** Earl Edward Ellis (02/14/1970) **CH:** Sunni Elizabeth **ED:** BS, Louisiana State University (1967) **C:** Volunteer Work (1988-Present); Executive Director, Nassau County Museum of Fine Art Association, Roslyn, NY (1985-1988); Assistant Buyer, J.C. Penney, Inc., Dallas, TX (1970-1973); Fashion Distributor, J. C. Penney Company, Inc., Arlington, TX (1969-1970); Buyer, I.H. Rubensteins., Baton Rouge, LA (1967-1968); Textile Researcher, Louisiana State University, Baton Rouge, LA (1965-1967); Fashion Coordinator, Baton Rouge, LA (1962-1967) **CR:** Speaker, C.W. Post University, Greenvale, NY (1988-Present); Consultant in Field **CIV:** Foundation Board, Sand Hills Community College, Pine Hurst, NC (2014-Present); Trustee, Long Island University (1998-2007); Chairman, Advisory Board, Long Island Chapter, Save the Children (1995-2001); Member, Executive Board, Executive Vice President, Trustee, WLIW, Long Island Public TV (1990-2001); Chairman, Board of Directors, WLIW, Long Island Public TV (1997-1999); Executive Board, Dowling College, Oakdale, NY (1997-1998); Trustee, Dowling College, Oakdale, NY (1993-1998); Advisory Board, Westbury Gardens (1993-1997); Board of Directors, Benefit Co-chairman, Nassau County Family Association Services, Hempstead, NY (1988-1996); Board of Directors, Committee Chairman, Congregational Church, Manhasset, NY (1975-1996); Trustee Community Foundation of Oyster Bay (1991-1994); Benefit Vice-chairman, Glen Cove/North Shore Community Hospital (1989-1993); Executive Vice President, Board of Directors, Committee Chairman, Junior League International Benefit Gala Chairman, Committee Chairman, Grenville Baker Boys & Girls Club, Locust Valley, NY (1983-1991); President, Board, Vice-chairman, Community Outreach, Benefit Gala Chairman, Tilles Performing Art Center, Long Island University, Greenvale, NY (1985) **CW:** Chairman, Editor, Cookbook, Specialties of the House (1981-1983) **AW:** Women of Achievement Award, Junior League Long Island (2000); Distinguished Service Medal, Long Island State Parks Foundation (1999); Outstanding Community Volunteer Award, Junior League of Long Island (1991-1992); Distinguished Leadership Award, Long Island, NY (1991); Juliette Low Award, Nassau County Girl Scouts, Long Island, NY (1991); Outstanding Volunteer Services and Commitment Award, County of Nassau (1989); Volunteer of Year Award, Junior League Long Island (1984, 1985) **MEM:** President, P.E.O. (1985-1987); Alumna President, Kappa Kappa Gamma (1971-1972); The Creek Inc.; Meadowbrook Club Inc.; Lost Tree Club; Forest Creek Club; Brights Creek Club **MH:** Albert Nelson Marquis Lifetime Achievement Award **B/I:** Mrs. Anne Ellis's was inspired by the work her family did in the community, they believed in giving back. Mrs. Ellis was a buyer for JCPenney and and for distribution, she had 80 stores. She bought by district Junior Dresses and she bought for approximately 15 hundred stores at the time. It was the first use of the computerized system and that was the beginning of Retail Stores using a computerized system. She started in distribution and worked her way up to the buying office. **AV:** Golf; Gardening; Needlepoint **PA:** Republican **RE:** Congregationalist

ELLIS, GEORGE FITZALLEN, REAR ADMIRAL U.S. NAVY (RETIRED), T: Two Star Admiral (Retired); Corporate Vice President (Retired) **I:** Oil & Energy **CN:** Energy Services Company **DOB:** 05/04/1923 **PB:** Salisbury **SC:** NC/USA **PT:** George F. Ellis; Lena (Ramsay) Ellis **MS:** Married **SPN:** Dr. Carol Andrews Ellis; Rachel Trexler (Deceased) **CH:** Susan Snider; George F. Ellis III (Deceased) **ED:** MS, Rensselaer Polytechnic Institute, Troy, NY (1957); BS, U.S. Naval Academy (1944); Coursework, Armed Forces Staff College **C:** Retired Corporate Vice President (1988); Vice President, Government Operations, McDermott International, Inc., and Babcock & Wilcox Enterprises, Inc., Washington, DC (1979-1988); Director, Government Relations, Babcock & Wilcox Enterprises, Inc., Washington, DC (1978-1979); Director, International Business, Babcock & Wilcox Enterprises, Inc., Lynchburg, VA (1976-1978) **CR:** Board of Directors, John Hanson Savings Bank, MD (1989-1990); Board of Trustees, American University, Washington, DC (1982-1991) **CIV:** Trustee, Church of the Covenant, Arlington, VA (1981-1982) **MIL:** Retired Two Star Admiral, United States Navy (1976); Commander, United States Navy, South Atlantic Force (1975-1976); Staff Supreme, United States Navy, Allied Command Europe (1974-1975); President, U.S. Naval Academy Class of 1945 (1945); Senior Military Officer, Staff, U.S. Ambassador to NATO, United States Navy, Brussels, Belgium; Submarine Service, United States Navy, Pacific World War II, Advanced through Grades to Rear Admiral, United States Navy **AW:** Decorated Legion Merit with Four Clusters; Meritorious Service Medal with Two Clusters; Navy Commendation Medal; Joint Service Commendation Medal; Vietnam Service Medal; Republic of Vietnam Campaign Medal; Numerous World War II Campaign and Service Medals **MEM:** The Army and Navy Club, Washington, DC; Vero Beach Yacht Club; Annapolis Yacht Club; Naval Academy Club; Annapolis Metropolitan Club; Army Navy Country Club; International Club **MH:** Albert Nelson Marquis Lifetime Achievement Award **B/I:** Mr. Ellis became involved in his profession because his father was in the Navy in World War I and his two uncles were admirals in World War II. The brothers of his mother and father were both graduates of the Naval Academy, along with his brother, who was also a graduate of the Naval Academy and he went into the Air Force. His first cousin was a graduate of the Naval Academy and is now a retired captain of the Navy. **PA:** Republican **RE:** Christian **THT:** Mr. Ellis spent 32 years of service in the United States Navy.

ELLIS, TRAYVON, T: Recording Artist, Producer, Songwriter **I:** Media & Entertainment **CN:** Billion Dollar Bangaz LLC **ED:** BA in Media Productions, American Intercontinental University (2008) **C:** Driver, Uber (2015-Present); Inventory Stocker, Victoria's Secret (2011-Present); Producer, Artist, Billion Dollar Bangaz, LLC (2011-Present); Information Technology Technician Lead, GDH Consulting (2011-Present); Chief Executive Officer, Billion Dollar Bangaz, LLC (2005-Present); Computer Specialist, Best Buy (2007-2008) **CIV:** Volunteer, Homeless Organizations **MEM:** ASCAP; The Recording Academy **AS:** Mr. Ellis attributes his success to God, his mother and his life experiences. **B/I:** Mr. Ellis became involved in his profession after going to school for media productions. **THT:** Mr. Ellis states, "hope stands for 'holding on to positive energy.'"

ELLISON, JULIAN JR., T: Economist (Retired) **I:** Financial Services **DOB:** 12/16/1942 **PB:** Albany **SC:** GA/USA **PT:** Julian Ellison; Johnnie Ruth (White) Ellison **MS:** Married **SPN:** Nirleeta (Young) (Bing) Ellison; Patricia E. Bynoe (January 31,

1970, Divorced 1974); Barbara A. Britton, (September 1974, Divorced 1976); Chirleeta **CH:** Akissi M.; Kiani; Kofi; Afouqe; Teloria; LeTia; Alvin III **ED:** Doctorate of Ministry, New York Theological Seminary, (2014); Master of Ministry, New York Theological Seminary (2012); PhD, Economics, Columbia University (1974); MA, Columbia University (1972); AB, Lincoln University, PA (1967) **CT:** Certificate of Ministry, NY Theological Seminary (2003) **C:** Retired (2004); Economist, U.S. Treasury Department (1991-2004); President, Director, Mid-Atlantic Economic Research Corp., Washington, DC (1976-1990); Visiting Assistant Professor, Research Associate, Susquehanna University, Selinsgrove, PA (1983-1985); Director, Economic Development Programs, National Rural Center, Washington, DC (1977-1979); Assistant Professor, Hunter College, City University of New York, New York, NY (1977); Instructor, College of New Rochelle, Bronx, NY (1977); Economist, Senior Economist, Black Economic Research Center, New York, NY (1972-1976); Instructor, Economics and Afro-American Studies, Brooklyn College, City University of New York (1970-1972); Economic Planner, Brownsville Community Council, Brooklyn, NY (1969-1971); Economist, New York City Community Development Administration (1968); Intern, U.S. Department Defense, Washington, DC (1967) **CR:** Committee on Small Business (1972-1977); Consultant, Subcommittee on Africa U.S. House of Representatives, Washington, DC (1972-1973); Board of Directors Emeka Enterprises, New York, NY; Board of Directors, West Africa Timber Imports Inc., Wilmington, DE **CIV:** Dar-29-Salaam, Tanzania President Committee for Cooperative Development, Washington, DC (1979-1982); Candidate, U.S. Congress (1979-1980); Member, TransAfrica, Washington, DC (1979); Associate Secretary General, 6th Pan-African Congress, Washington, DC (1973-1974) **MIL:** U.S. Army (1960-1966); Sergeant, U.S. Army (1960-1963) **CW:** Editor, "The Economic Theory of Transfer Pricing," (2002); Editor, "American Economic Review" (1991); Author, "Abram L. Harris, Junior, Economist: A Biography," (1990); Editor, "Celestial Mechanics and the Location Theory of William H. Dean Junior, 1930-1952"; Contributor, Articles, Professional Journals **AW:** Rockefeller Brothers Fund, (1977-1979); Opportunity Funding Corp., Washington, DC (1975-1976); Chicago Economic Development Corp., (1975-1976); Presbyterian Economic Development Corp., New York, NY (1975-1976); Grantee, Ford Foundation, New York, NY (1972); Fellow, Southern Fellowships Fund, Atlanta, GA (1968-1970); Fellow, Woodrow Wilson Foundation, Princeton, NJ (1967-1968) **MEM:** National Economic Association (Director, 1969-1973); African Heritage Studies Association; Association for Study of African American Life and History; American Finance Association; Association for Evolutionary Economics; Association for Social Economics; American Economic Association **MH:** Albert Nelson Marquis Lifetime Achievement Award **B/I:** Mr. Ellison became involved in his career because his family was very poor and he wanted to study something that could help them move from that position. When he retired from economics field in 2004, he decided to pursue a career in ministry. **AV:** Playing Chess; Bao; Listening to Jazz **PA:** Democrat **RE:** Baptist

ELLISON, KEITH MAURICE, T: Attorney General from Minnesota **I:** Government Administration/Government Relations/Government Services **DOB:** 08/04/1963 **PB:** Detroit **SC:** MI/USA **PT:** Leonard Ellison; Clida (Martinez) Ellison **MS:** Divorced **SPN:** Kim Ellison (1987, Divorced 2012) **CH:** Amirah; Jeremiah; Elijah; Isaiah **ED:** JD, University of Minnesota Law School (1990); BA in Economics, Wayne State University, Detroit, MI (1987) **C:**

Attorney General, State of Minnesota (2019-Present); Member, U.S. House of Representatives from Minnesota's Fifth Congressional District, United States Congress, Washington, DC (2007-2019); Deputy Chair, Democratic National Committee (2017-2018); District 58B, Minnesota House of Representatives, Minneapolis, MN (2003-2007); Attorney, Hassan & Reed Ltd. (1998-2007); Executive Director, Legal Rights Center (1993-1998); Associate, Linquist & Vennum (Now Ballard Spahr LLP) (1990-1993); Committee on Financial Services, United States Congress; Committee on Foreign Affairs, United States Congress; Judiciary Committee, United States Congress **CW:** Author, "My Country 'Tis of Thee" (2014) **AW:** Distinguished Service Award, Sierra Club (2011); Listee, Utne Reader (2011); Trailblazer Award, American-Arab Anti-Discrimination Committee (2007) **PA:** Democrat **RE:** Muslim

ELLISON, LARRY, T: Entrepreneur **I:** Business Management/Business Services **DOB:** 08/17/1944 **PB:** New York **SC:** NY/USA **MS:** Married **SPN:** Melanie Craft (December 18, 2003-2010); Barbara Boothe (1983-1986); Nancy Wheeler (1976-1977); Ada Quinn (1967-1974) **CH:** David; Megan **ED:** Coursework, University of Chicago (1965-1966); Coursework, University of Illinois Urbana-Champaign (1963-1965) **C:** Executive Chairman, Chief Technology Officer, Oracle Corp., Redwood, CA (2014-Present); Chief Executive Officer, Oracle Corp., Redwood, CA (1977-2014); Chairman, Oracle Corp., Redwood, CA (1995-2004);President, Oracle Corp., Redwood, CA (1978-1996); Chairman, Oracle Corp., Redwood, CA (1990-1992);Co-founder (with Bob Miner & Ed Oates), Oracle Corp., Redwood, CA (1977); President Systems Division, Omex Corp. (1972-1977); With, Amdahl, Inc., Santa Clara, CA (1967-1971); Systems Architect, Amdahl, Inc., Santa Clara, CA **CR:** Board of Directors, Oracle Corp. (1977-Present); Board of Directors, Apple Computer, Inc. (1997-2002); Trustee, US Council International Business **AW:** The Forbes 400: Richest Americans (2006-Present); The World's Richest People, "Forbes" (1999-Present); Forbes Fifth Wealthiest in the United States, Eighth Wealthiest in the World (2018); World's Most Powerful People, "Forbes" (2013); The Business People of the Year, "Fortune" (2010); The 50 Who Matter Now, CNNMoney.com Business 2.0 (2006); Named Bio-IT Champion, Bio-ITWorld (2002); Industry Achievement Award (1997); Distinguished Information Sciences Award, Association Information Technology Professionals (1996); Leadership Award for Global Integration (1994); Entrepreneur of the Year, Harvard Business School (1990) **AV:** Yachting; Tennis; Guitar **RE:** Jewish

ELVIN-LEWIS, MEMORY PATIENCE FREDRIKA, PHD, DSC HONORIS CAUSA, T: Microbiology Educator, Researcher, Ethnobotanist **I:** Education/Educational Services **DOB:** 05/20/1933 **PB:** Vancouver **SC:** British Columbia/Canada **PT:** Richard James Elvin; May Winnifred (Foster) Elvin **MS:** Married **SPN:** Walter Hepworth Lewis (02/02/1957) **CH:** Memoria Florence Richenda May Lewis; Walter Hepworth, Jr. **ED:** Doctor of Science, Honoris Causa, University of British Columbia (2012); Doctor of Science, Honoris Causa, Andrews University, Michigan (2003); PhD in Medical Microbiology, University of Leeds, School of Medicine, Leeds, England (1966); MSc in Virology and Epidemiology, Baylor University, School of Medicine, Houston, TX (1960); MSc in Medical Microbiology, University of Pennsylvania, School of Medicine, Philadelphia, PA (1955); BA in Bacteriology and Genetics, University of British Columbia, Vancouver, Canada (1952) **CT:** Professional Diploma, American Society of Medical Technologists (1954);

Professional Diploma, Canadian Society of Laboratory Technologists (1953) **C:** Faculty Scholar, Institute for Public Health (2015-Present); Professor Emeritus, Washington University (2018); Professor of Biomedicine in Microbiology and Ethnobotany, Washington University (1991-2018); Adjunct Professor of Biology, Washington University, School Arts and Science, St. Louis, MO (1967-2018); Assistant, Associate, Professor of Microbiology, Washington University School of Dental Medicine (1967-1991); Assistant Professor, Washington University School of Botany (1966-1967); Lecturer, Washington University School of Botany (1965) **CR:** Affiliated Faculty, Graduate Program in Organizational Dynamics, University of Pennsylvania (2018-Present); Clinical Professor Emeritus, Drexel University (2017-Present); Faculty Scholar, Institute for Public Health, Washington University in St. Louis, Missouri (2015-Present); Vice President, International Society of Herbal Medicine, India (2003-Present); Strategy Contributor, Wharton Blog Network (2013-Present); Director, Robert Wooler Company (1983-Present); Professor Emeritus, Institute for Public Health, Washington University in St. Louis, Missouri (2018); Professor of Biomedicine in Microbiology and Ethnobotany, Washington University in St. Louis, Missouri (1991-2018); Adjunct Professor of Biology, School of Arts and Science, Washington University in St. Louis, Missouri (1967-2018); Alan Lesniewicz Memorial Lecturer, The University of Illinois at Chicago College of Pharmacy, National Institutes of Health Center for Botanical Dietary Supplements Research (2014, 2017); Lecturer, Graduate Program in Organizational Dynamics, University of Pennsylvania (1997-1999); Convention Coordinator, Society for Economic Botany, St. Louis MO (1997); Counselor, Society for Economic Botany (1993-1996); Senior Consultant, Wharton Center for Applied Research (1987-1992); Assistant, Associate, Professor of Microbiology, School of Dental Medicine, Washington University in St. Louis, Missouri (1967-1991); Consultant, Neem Toothpaste (1983); Consultant, World Health Organization (1982-1983); President, International Association of Dental Research (1982-1983); Senior Field Associate, American Center for the Quality of Work Life (1979-1982); Faculty Fellow, Productivity Research, United States Office of Personnel Management (1979-1981); Consultant, Calcutta Chemical Company (1975); Consultant, Colgate-Palmolive Research Center (1974); President, Microbiology Section, American Association of Dental Schools (1973-1974); Speaker, 58 Invited Lectures **CW:** Advisory Board, "Scholara Journals: Pharmacy and Pharmacology Journal" (2015-Present); Reviewer, African Journal of Plant Science (2012-Present); Reviewer, International Journal of Molecular Sciences (2012-Present); Advisory Board, "Herbalgram" (2012-Present); Reviewer, Journal of Pharmacy and Pharmacology, African Journal of Traditional, Complementary and Alternative Medicines (2011-Present); Advisory Board, International Journal of Green Pharmacy (2010-Present); Advisory Board, "A Quarterly Bulletin of International Institute of Herbal Medicine," International Institute of Hotel Management (2010-Present); Advisory Board, African Journal of Traditional, Complementary and Alternative Medicines (2004-Present); Reviewer, Journal of Ethnopharmacology (2003-Present); Contributor, "An Ethnobotanist's Circuitous Route to the Amazon," The American Society of Pharmacognosy Newsletter (2018); Reviewer, ScienceDomain.org (2012); Senior Editor, Journal of Biological and Chemical Research, India (1989); Editorial Board, Indian Journal of Dental Research (1989); Editorial Board, Journal of Preventive Dentistry (1980); Contributor, 11 Selected Publications in Field; Contributor,

30 Papers and Presentations; Contributor, Six Editorials, Professional Publications; Author, Eight Book Reviews **AW:** Listee, Significant Canadian Scientists, 150th Anniversary of Canada, Canada 150: Discovery Way Exhibit, Ontario Science Centre, Toronto, Ontario, Canada (2019); Alumni Award of Distinction, University of British Columbia (2012); Dr. E.K. Janaki Ammal Gold Medal, Society of Ethnobotanists, India (2008); MBA-Level Distinguished Teaching Awards (2001, 2004-2008); Distinguished Economic Botanist, Society of Economic Botany (2006) **MEM:** Vice President, International Society of Herbal Medicine, India (2003-Present); Mexican Academy of Traditional Medicine, XV Internacional Congreso de Medicina Tradicional y Alternatives Terapéuticas, Mexico City, Mexico (2001); Convention Coordinator, Society for Economic Botany, St. Louis MO (1997); Lifetime Member, International Association of Dental Research (1996); Counselor, Society for Economic Botany (1993-1996); Fellow, International Society of Herbal Medicine (India) (1995); Fellow, Linnean Society (1995); Life Member, Asian Federation of Clinical Pharmacognosists (1989); Honorary Life Member, International Society of Herbal Medicine (1989); President, International Association of Dental Research (1982-1983); President, Microbiology Section, American Association of Dental Schools (1973-1974) **MH:** Albert Nelson Marquis Lifetime Achievement Award **B/I:** Ms. Elvin-Lewis became involved in her profession because she adored science. She got into academia because it was her husband's career. He then encouraged Ms. Elvin-Lewis to venture out on her own after she acquired a degree. **AV:** Gourmet cooking; Collecting antiques

ELWOOD-AKERS, VIRGINIA, T: (Retired) Librarian, Writer, Archivist, Researcher **I:** Library Management/Library Services **DOB:** 11/09/1938 **SC:** LA/USA **PT:** George Henry Elwood; Eileen Edythe Elwood **MS:** Widow **SPN:** Roy Stanley Akers (04/12/1980, Deceased 2003) **ED:** MA in Mass Communications, California State University, Northridge, Los Angeles, CA (1981); MLS, University of Oregon (1972); BA, University of California Los Angeles (1964); Associate's Degree, Santa Monica City College, Santa Monica, CA (1961) **C:** Librarian, Archivist, California State University, Northridge, Los Angeles, CA (1972-2001); Writer, University of California Los Angeles (1971-1972); Editor, University of California Los Angeles (1970-1971) **CW:** Author, "Caroline Severance" (2010); Author, "Women War Correspondents in the Vietnam War" (1988); Contributor, Articles, Professional Journals; Researcher, "California Women Win the Vote"; Researcher, "Inez Milholland" **AW:** Medal of Honor, Veteran Feminist of America, Women & Media (2013); Grantee, California State University Foundation; Grantee, California State University Library **MEM:** Western Association of Women Historians; Women Writing the West **MH:** Albert Nelson Marquis Lifetime Achievement Award **AS:** Ms. Elwood-Akers loves her work, which is the key to success in her opinion. She has always had good luck as well, which has worked in her favor. **B/I:** Ms. Elwood-Akers was 36 when she became a librarian. Her prior experience writing and editing at the University of California Los Angeles worked positively in her favor. **THT:** Ms. Elwood-Akers believes in being positive and kind.

EMANUEL, RAHM ISRAEL, T: Former Mayor of Chicago; Former White House Chief of Staff **I:** Government Administration/Government Relations/Government Services **DOB:** 11/29/1959 **PB:** Chicago **SC:** IL/USA **PT:** Benjamin M. Emanuel; Marsha (Smulevitz) Emanuel **MS:** Married **SPN:** Amy Merritt (Rule) (06/05/1994) **CH:** Zacharias;

Ilana; Leah **ED:** Honorary Doctorate in Public Service, The George Washington University (2009); MA in Speech and Communications, Northwestern University (1985); BA in Liberal Arts, Sarah Lawrence College, Bronxville, NY (1981) **C:** Contributor, "ABC News," ABC (2019-Present); Senior Counselor, Centerview Partners Holdings LP (2019-Present); Mayor, City of Chicago, IL (2011-2019); Chief of Staff to the President, The White House, Washington, DC (2009-2010); Chairman, U.S. House Democratic Caucus (2006-2009); Member, U.S. House of Representatives from Illinois' Fifth Congressional District, U.S. Congress, Washington, DC (2003-2009); Managing Director, Dresdner Kleinwort Wasserstein, Chicago, IL (1999-2002); Director of Special Projects, Senior Adviser for Policy and Strategy, The White House, Washington, DC (1995-1998); Assistant to the President, Director of Political Affairs, Deputy Director of Communications, The White House, Washington, DC (1993-1995); National Finance Director, Clinton/Gore Campaign (1991-1992); Senior Adviser, Chief Fundraiser, Mayoral Campaign of Richard M. Daley (1988-1989); National Campaign Director, Democratic Congressional Campaign Committee (DCCC) (1987-1988); Senior Adviser, Chief Fundraiser, Representative Paul Simon's Campaign for U.S. Senate (1984); Member, Illinois Public Action Council (1981-1983); Finance Director, David L. Robinson Campaign for U.S. Congress (1980) **CR:** Board of Directors, Freddie Mac (Federal Home Loan Mortgage Corporation) (2000-2001); Vice Chairman, Chicago Illinois Housing Authority (1998); Co-Director, Presidential Inaugural Committee (1993) **CIV:** Member, Anshe Sholom B'nai Israel Congregation, Chicago, IL **CW:** Author, "Chicago 2011 Transition Plan" (2011); Co-Author (With Bruce Reed), "The Plan: Big Ideas for America" (2006) **AW:** Named One of the 100 Agents of Change, Rolling Stone Magazine (2009); Named One of the 50 Most Powerful People in DC, GQ Magazine (2007, 2009); Named One of the Global Elite, Newsweek Magazine (2008); Great Laker Award, Healing Our Waters-Great Lakes Coalition (2007); Alumni Achievement Citation, Sarah Lawrence College (2001) **AV:** Cycling; Triathlons **PA:** Democrat **RE:** Jewish

EMBLIDGE, ROBERT WILLIAM, PHD, T: Principal Scientist **I:** Sciences **DOB:** 09/11/1960 **PB:** Syracuse **SC:** NY/USA **PT:** William Robert, Jr.; Dorothy Mae (Hill) Emblidge **MS:** Married **SPN:** Lisa Anne Sabatini (09/04/1988) **CH:** Two foster children **ED:** PhD in Physical Organic Chemistry, Northwestern University (1992); MS, University of Rochester (1984); BS, Ohio Wesleyan University (1982) **C:** Principal Scientist, AdvanSix (2016-Present); Lead Scientist, Engineer, Honeywell International Inc. (2009-2016); Senior Process Chemist, Sunoco (1999-2009); Associate Research Specialist, Dow (1992-1997); Associate Biochemist, Carter-Wallace, Inc. (1986-1988) **CW:** Contributor, Articles, The Journal of Organic Chemistry; Contributor, Articles, Journal of the American Chemical Society; Contributor, Articles, Journal of Physical Organic Chemistry **AW:** PPG Fellow, Northwestern University (1989); Sherman Clarke Fellowship, University of Rochester (1982-1983); R.E. Hall Fellowship, Ohio Wesleyan University (1981-1982); NSF-URP Summer Fellowship, Ohio Wesleyan University (1981) **MEM:** American Association for the Advancement of Science; The New York Academy of Sciences; American Chemical Society; The Phi Beta Kappa Society; Sigma Xi, The Scientific Research Society; Phi Lambda Upsilon **MH:** Albert Nelson Marquis Lifetime Achievement Award **B/I:** Dr. Emblidge became involved in his profession because of his infatuation with science and technology. **PA:** Democrat **RE:** Presbyterian

EMERY, RITA, "EM", T: Physical Education Educator **I:** Education/Educational Services **DOB:** 09/21/1939 **PB:** Berkley **SC:** CA/USA **PT:** Byron Elden Emery; Charlotte Antoinette (Siwinski) Emery **ED:** MA, Washington State University (1977); BA, Chico State College (Now California State University, Chico) (1963); AA, Contra Costa College (1960) **CT:** Certified Teacher, State of California **C:** With, Senior Coalition Center (2019); Physical Education Instructor, Vallejo City Unified School District (2000-2007); Teacher, Vallejo City Unified School District (1996); Director of Junior Programming, ClubSport of Pleasanton, CA (1995); Elementary Physical Education Specialist, Coach, Vacaville Unified School District, CA (1990-1995); Instructor of Physical Education, Campbell Union School District, CA (1989-1990); Instructor of Physical Education, Coach, Athletic Director, St. Leonard School, Fremont, CA (1985-1989); Coach, Women's Softball, Oregon State University, Corvallis, OR (1977-1980); Coach, Women's Volleyball, Contra Costa College, San Pablo, CA (1977); Instructor of Physical Education, Coach, Department Chair, Lower Lake High School, CA (1967-1976); Instructor of Physical Education, Coach, Churchill County High School, Fallon, NV (1963-1965); Teacher and Mentor, After School Program, Vacaville School District (Now Vacaville Unified School District) **CR:** With, Suisun Wildlife Center (2015-Present); Girls Basketball Coach, Will C. Wood High School, Vacaville, CA (1993-1995); Teen Youth Coordinator, Fremont Leisure Services (1988-1993); Instructor of Youth Sports, Fremont Leisure Services (1988-1990); Coach Coordinator of Recreation, Holy Spirit Church, Fremont, CA (1980-1985); Intramural Director, Contra Costa College (1957-1960) **CIV:** Volunteer, Hall of Health/Kids Safe Program, Berkeley, CA (1990); Speaker, Alameda County Chapter, American Heart Association, Inc. (1983-1990); Volunteer Coach, Officer, Official Fremont Centerville Little League (1983-1986) **CW:** Author, Children Book (2020); Co-author, "Melange: Musings on Life from a Writer's Pen" (2018) **AW:** Award, Senior Coalition of Solano County (2018); Named Teacher of the Year, Ulatis Elementary School, Vacaville, CA (1992); Named Volunteer of Year, American Heart Association, Inc. (1986, 1988); Named Coach of the Year (Softball), Oregon State University (1979, 1980); Graduate Student Honors, The Honor Society of Phi Kappa Phi, Washington State University (1977); Named Female Athlete of the Year, Contra Costa College (1960) **MEM:** Advisory Committee for Development of Athletic Training Council, Alliance for Health, AccentCare; California Association of Health; Physical Education, Recreation and Dance **MH:** Albert Nelson Marquis Lifetime Achievement Award; Marquis Who's Who Top Professional **B/I:** Ms. Emery started her career as an instructor of physical education. She worked as a playground director and a coach during the summers. She always wanted to be a surgeon, because she always liked operating on things when she was younger, however, the more she became involved with physical education, the more she enjoyed it and that is how she became a physical education teacher. When she was growing up, they only had sport days within the school. As she got older, she did AAU basketball and other sports. When she attended Contra Costa College, there was a gentleman there who looked after her and he made her the intramural director at the college. She has taught physical education from third grade all the way to college. **AV:** Bicycling; Walking; Cacti gardening; Traveling; Watching men and women basketball; Working with seniors **THT:** For more information on Ms. Emery's book, please visit: http://www.goodreads.com/book/show/42600412-melange

EMMER, THOMAS, "TOM" EARL JR., T: U.S. Representative from Minnesota **I:** Government Administration/Government Relations/Government Services **CN:** U.S. House of Representatives **DOB:** 03/03/1961 **PB:** South Bend **SC:** IN/USA **MS:** Married **SPN:** Jacqueline Emmer (1993) **CH:** Tripp; Jack; Bobby; Katie; Joey; Billy; Johnny **ED:** Doctor of Jurisprudence, William Mitchell College of Law (1988); Bachelor of Arts in History, University of Alaska Fairbanks (1984) **C:** Member, U.S. House of Representatives from Minnesota's Sixth Congressional District, United States Congress, Washington, DC (2014-Present); Managing Partner, Emmer Law Firm (2005-Present); Member, District 19B, Minnesota House of Representatives (2005-2011); Member, Health Policy and Finance Committee, Minnesota House of Representatives (2005-2006); Councilman, City of Delano, MN (2003-2004); Councilman, City of Independence, MN (1995-2002); Member, Committee on Financial Services; Member, Republican Study Committee **PA:** Republican **RE:** Roman Catholic

EMMETT, JAMES ROBERT, T: Attorney (Retired) **I:** Oil & Energy **DOB:** 01/24/1940 **PB:** Gary **SC:** IN/USA **YOP:** 2018 **PT:** Robert Gerald Emmett; Jeannette Lois (Pinkerton) Emmett **MS:** Married **SPN:** Marian Carol Yanney (01/28/1967) **CH:** Jennifer Kathleen Emmett Demmon; Robert (Robb) Yanney Emmett **ED:** JD, Indiana University (1966); BCE, Purdue University (1963) **C:** Retired (2000); Senior Tax Attorney, Amoco Corporation (1986-2000); State Tax Attorney, Amoco Corporation (1974-1986); Property Tax Representative, Amoco Corporation (1972-1974); Real Estate Attorney, Amoco Corporation (1970-1972); Design Engineer, Snyder & Associates 1968-1970) **BAR:** Supreme Court of the United States (1993); United States Court of International Trade (1993); Indiana State Bar Association (1967); United States District Court Southern District of Indiana (1967) **MH:** Albert Nelson Marquis Lifetime Achievement Award **AV:** Golfing; Playing guitar and drums; Riding horses; Reading

EMMICH, CLIFF, T: Actor of Film, Television, and Stage **I:** Media & Entertainment **DOB:** 12/13/1936 **PB:** Cincinnati **SC:** OH/USA **PT:** Clifford Joseph Emmich; Winifred Lucile (Hahn) Emmich **ED:** Graduate, High School, Pasadena, CA **CT:** Screen Actors Guild-American Federation of Television and Radio Artists (SAG-AFTRA); Academy of Motion Picture Arts and Sciences; National Academy of Television Arts & Sciences **C:** Actor, Film, Television, and Stage (59 Years) **MIL:** Airman 2nd Class, Photographer, U.S. Air Force (1956-1960) **CW:** Actor, "Murder, She Wrote" (1995); Actor, "Baywatch" (1995); Actor, "Columbo" (1994); Actor, "Adam-12" (1990); Actor, "Dragnet" (1990); Actor, "A Different World" (1990); Actor, "Andrew Dice Clay Special," HBO; Actor, "Simon & Simon"; Actor, "It's Garry Shandling's Show"; Actor, "Hunter'"; Actor, "Private Eye"; Actor, "Charlie's Angels"; Actor, "Happy Days"; Actor, "The Odd Couple"; Actor, "Night Court"; Actor, "Ironside"; Actor, "Fantasy Island"; Actor, "Police Woman"; Actor, "Police Story"; Actor, Numerous Films, including "Return to Horror High," "Hellhole," "All the Marbles," "Halloween II," "Telefon," "Out of Control," "Jackson County Jail," "Aloha Bobby and Rose," "Payday," "Thunderbolt and Lightfoot," and Others; Actor, Numerous TV Movies and Miniseries, Including "Gus Brown and Midnight Brewster," Dempsey," "Wheels," "The Freedom Riders," "Mallory," "Little House on the Prairie," and Others; Actor, Numerous Other TV Shows; Actor, More Than 50 Commercials; Actor, More Than 50 Professional Stage Productions **MEM:** Academy of Motion Picture Arts and Sciences; Academy of Television Arts & Sciences; Pasadena Playhouse Alumni and Associates **MH:**

Albert Nelson Marquis Lifetime Achievement Award **AS:** Mr. Emmich attributes his success to being discovered by the casting director of the Dorothy Chandler Pavilion at the Pink Garter Theater in Jackson Hole, Wyoming, in the summer of 1968. The casting director was responsible for his casting in "Captain Brassbound's Conversion" and made it possible to gain his Actors Equity card. Additionally, he attributes it to director Hal Ashby, who cast him in "Gaily Gaily," a film he also co-produced. That casting made it possible to gain his Screen Actors Guild card. Both cards were needed to work in the Industry. **B/I:** Mr. Emmich became involved in his profession because his father, Clifford Joseph, was one of the pioneers of the exotic car market, whose clients were from the motion picture industry, including people like Gary Cooper. **AV:** Photography; Auto racing; Horses; Western lore **PA:** Conservative **RE:** Baptist **THT:** As a single man, the support that Mr. Emmich received from his parents and three sisters meant a lot to him. He is also moved by all the appreciation of his work from critics, fans, directors, producers, and other actors, which has brought great joy to his life. He has found it rewarding to see life through the eyes of the hundreds of characters he has had the chance to portray. He has been lucky to follow his dream and cherish his memories.

EMMONS, DIANE NEAL, EDM, CAS, T: Career Development Consultant **I:** Consulting **DOB:** 09/09/1932 **PB:** Detroit **SC:** MI/USA **PT:** Kirke Albert Neal; Dorothy Becker Neal **MS:** Widowed **SPN:** Curtis Prout (12/07/1985, Deceased 12/02/2001) **CH:** Elizabeth Brooks Emmons; Catherine Davies Emmons; Robert Wales Emmons III; Anne Neal Emmons Barton; Chiinga Louise Musonda (Foster Daughter) **ED:** EdM, Harvard University (1978); BA, Smith College (1955) **CT:** Certificate of Advanced Study in Marital and Family Therapies, Boston University; Certificate of Advanced Study in Employee Assistance Programs (CAS), Boston University **C:** Career Development Consultant, Manchester, MA (1982-Present); Assistant Director, Office of Career Services, Harvard University, Cambridge, MA (1980-1983); Assistant to the Dean of Academy Programs, Harvard Medical School, Boston, MA (1979-1980); Teacher, Brookwood School, Manchester, MA (1973-1977) **CR:** Director, Manchester Community Center (2005-Present); President, College Luncheon Series (2002-Present); President, Board of Directors, Directions: Greater Boston Counseling Services (1978-1982) **CIV:** Class Fund Agent, Smith College, Northampton, MA (1980-Present); Board of Directors, Family Homes, Incorporation, Manchester, MA (1975-Present); Board of Directors, KALOS (2005-2011); President, General Assembly (1980); Board of Directors, YMCA of Greater Boston (1963-1978); Board of Directors, Boston Children's Services (1972-1973); Board of Directors, Secretary, The Church Home Society, Boston, MA (1963-1973); Community Preservation Committee, Manchester by the Sea; Board of Directors, Manchester Community Center; Elected Measurer of Wooden Bark, Town of Manchester, MA **AW:** Service Award, YMCA of Greater Boston (1980-1982) **MEM:** American Society for Training & Development (Now ATD); The Vincent Club, Boston, MA; American Mental Health Counselors Association; Harvard Club of the North Shore **MH:** Albert Nelson Marquis Lifetime Achievement Award **AS:** Ms. Emmons attributes her success to God, her father, her education, her friends, and good luck. Her father was her hero; she was very close to him. **B/I:** Ms. Emmons has been interested in pursuing her profession for as long as she can remember. **AV:** Feeding seagulls **PA:** Semi-Democrat **RE:** Episcopalian **THT:** Ms. Emmons was a single parent; she balanced working alongside raising her four children on a singular income from 1977 to 1985.

ENEYO, UGWEM I., T: Chief Executive Officer **I:** Business Management/Business Services **CN:** Solstice Energy **ED:** MS, PhD in Civil and Environmental Engineering, Stanford University (2014-2019); BS in Civil and Environmental Engineering, University of Illinois (2013) **C:** Co-Founder, Chief Executive Officer, Solstice Energy Solutions (2016-Present); Environmental, Regulatory and Socioeconomic Adviser, ExxonMobil (2013-2014)

ENGEL, ELIOT LANCE, T: U.S. Representative from New York **I:** Government Administration/Government Relations/Government Services **DOB:** 02/18/1947 **PB:** New York **SC:** NY/USA **PT:** Philip Engel; Sylvia (Bleend) Engel **MS:** Married **SPN:** Patricia Ennis Engel **CH:** Three Children **ED:** JD, New York Law School (1987); MS in Guidance and Counseling, Herbert H. Lehman College, The City University of New York (1973); BA in History, Hunter-Lehman College, The City University of New York (1969) **C:** Chair, House Foreign Affairs Committee (2019-Present); Member, U.S. House of Representatives from New York's 16th Congressional District, United States Congress (2013-Present); Ranking Minority Member, House Committee on Foreign Affairs (2013-Present); Member, U.S. House of Representatives from New York's 17th Congressional District (1993-2013); U.S. House of Representatives from New York's 19th Congressional District (1989-1993); Member, District 81, New York State Assembly (1977-1988); Guidance Counselor, New York Public Schools (1973-1975); Teacher, Department Chairman, New York Board of Education (1969-1976); Counselor, Advisor, New York Urban Corps (1968) **CIV:** District Leader (1976); President, New Democratic Club Co-op City (1975-1976); Judicial Delegate, New York Supreme Court Convention, First Judicial District (1975-1976); Vice President, Bronx Committee for Democratic Voters (1975-1976); Delegate, Bronx Committee for Democratic Voters (1971-1976); Founder, New Democratic Club Co-op City (1975); President, Independent Democrats of Co-op City (1974-1975); Member, Executive Council, New York State New Democratic Coalition (1973-1975); Vice President, Independent Democrats of Co-op City (1972-1973); Delegate, Member, Steering Committee, Youth Caucus, Democratic National Convention (1972); Committeeman, Bronx County Democratic Committee, NY (1972); Vice President, Park-East Independent Democratic Club, NY (1970-1971) **CW:** Columnist, Co-op City News (1972) **AW:** Named Honorary Citizen of Pec, Kosovo (2011); Named Friend of the Farm Bureau, American Farm Bureau Federation and New York Farm Bureau (2008); Named Distinguished Community Health Superhero, National Association of Community Health Centers, Inc. (2008); National Association of Public Hospitals Safety Net Award (2007); AIDS Institute National HIV/AIDS Care and Treatment Award (2007); Legislator of the Year, Children are Precious (1990); Man of the Year Award, FDR Independent Democratic Club (1976); Notable Americans Award, Historic Preservation of America; Humanitarian Award, United Field of Representatives and Staff Union; Distinguished Service Award, National Council of Negro Women, Inc. **MEM:** Board of Directors, Americans for Democratic Action, NY (1974); United Fund Teachers (UFT) (Now United Federation of Teachers); Zionist Organization of America; The Knights of Pythias **PA:** Democrat **RE:** Jewish

ENGELBERT, CATHY, T: Chief Executive Officer **I:** Financial Services **ED:** Bachelor of Science in Accounting, Lehigh University (1986) **C:** Chief Executive Officer, Deloitte (2015-Present); Partner, Deloitte (1986-Present); Chairperson, Chief Executive Officer, Deloitte & Touche (2014-2015)

ENGELHARDT, HERMANN PHD, T: Faculty Emeritus **I:** Education/Educational Services **CN:** California Institute of Technology **DOB:** 10/20/1936 **PB:** Augsburg **SC:** Germany **PT:** Johannes Engelhardt; Frieda (Dörwald) Engelhardt **MS:** Widowed **SPN:** Luise Köhler Engelhardt (09/09/1963, Deceased 2010) **CH:** Michael; Katharina **ED:** Habilitation, University of Münster (1986); Doctor Rerum Naturalium, Technische Universität, Munich, Germany (1964) **C:** Faculty Emeritus, California Institute of Technology, Pasadena, CA (2009-Present); Senior Research Associate, California Institute of Technology, Pasadena, CA (1988-2009); Professor, Eidgenössische Technische Hochschule, Zurich, Switzerland (1987-1988); Lecturer, University of Münster (1986-1988); Senior Research Associate, University of Münster (1982-1986); Professor, University of Munich, Germany (1980-1981); Senior Research Fellow, California Institute of Technology, Pasadena, CA (1976-1980); Associate Professor, University del Valle, Cali, Colombia (1974-1976); Scientist, National Research Council, Ottawa, Canada (1969-1970); Lecturer, Polytechnic School, Munich, Germany (1961-1962); Adjunct Faculty, Department of Appalachian Laboratories, University of Maryland **CR:** Consultant, Jet Propulsion Laboratory, NASA, Pasadena, CA (2000-2010) **CIV:** Deacon, Word and Service, Evangelical Lutheran Church in America (2014-Present) **CW:** Author, Editor, "Physics of Ice" (1969); Contributor, Over 90 Articles, Professional Journals **MEM:** International Glaciological Society; American Geophysical Union; American Polar Society **MH:** Albert Nelson Marquis Lifetime Achievement Award **B/I:** Dr. Engelhardt had excellent physics teachers during his time as a student. One of his teachers was Nobel Laureate, Werner Heisenberg. Just listening to Mr. Heisenberg's lectures convinced Dr. Engelhardt to pursue physics. **AV:** Skiing; Playing trumpet and piano **RE:** Lutheran

ENGELHARDT, MARK DOUGLAS, T: Professor of Education, Statistics and Research Methods **I:** Education/Educational Services **DOB:** 11/05/1952 **PB:** Cape Girardeau **SC:** MO/USA **PT:** W. Gene; Delba Aletha (Hartle) E. **MS:** Married **SPN:** Gelina Lee Ann Bridges (07/27/1975) **CH:** Douglas Lee; Diana Lee Ann; Dana Lee **ED:** Doctor of Philosophy, St. Louis University, with Distinction (1990); Education Specialist, St. Louis University, with Distinction (1989); Master of Education, Southeast Missouri State University (1981); Bachelor of Science in Engineering, Southeast Missouri State University, Summa Cum Laude (1974) **CT:** Missouri Certification, Secondary School Social Studies Teacher; Missouri Certification, Middle School Social Studies; Missouri Certification, Secondary Principal; Missouri Certification, Early Childhood; Missouri Certification, Early Childhood Special Education; Missouri Certification, Superintendent **C:** Professor of Education, Statistics & Research Methodology, Missouri Baptist University (1999-Present); Education Site Coordinator, MBU Troy/Wentzville Regional Learning Center (1999-2016); Chapter Member, Liaison for Eastern Missouri, Phi Delta Kappa International (2004-2009); Assistant Superintendent, Special Services School of the Osage (1998-1999); Elementary Principal, Director of Federal Programs, Special Education and Transportation, Woodland R-IV School District (1995-1998); High School Principal, Athletic Director, Woodland R-IV School District (1992-1995); Middle School Principal, Maplewood Richmond Heights School District (1986-1992); Adjunct Professor of Psychology, Saint Louis University (1979-1986); High School Social Studies Teacher, Coach, Hazelwood School District (1974-1986) **CR:** Educational Consultant, Nine K-12 Schools in the Middle East (2010-2013) **CIV:** Lay Leader, Wentzville United Methodist (2012-Present); Councilor, Wentzville United Methodist Church (2012-Present); Member and Past Chair of Photography Committee (2007-Present); St. Louis Alumni Board Member, Southeast Missouri State University (1999-Present); Past Board of Trustees Member, Lake Saint Louis Sailing and Paddling Club (1999-Present); Wentzville United Methodist Church Men (1999-Present); Certified Lay Speaker, United Methodist Church (1992-Present); East Central Administrators Association (1999-2018); Career and Technical Education Committee, Wentzville School District (2010-2017); Habitat for Humanity (2008-2016); PTA, Wentzville School District (1999-2015); Technology Committee, Lincoln Co. RIII School District (2008-2012); Member of Legislative Committee, St. Louis Symphony Volunteers Association (2007-2011); A+ Committee, Wentzville School District (2004-2010); St. Louis Worlds Fair Association (2003-2010); Board Member, St. Louis Symphony Volunteer Association (2009); Past Vice President, Lake Saint Louis Artist Association (1999-2008); Council Member, Boy Scouts of America Troop 24 (1995-1998); Board of Advisors, KRCU 90.9 FM (1995-1998); Past President, Kiwanis Club (1986-1992) **CW:** Author of Peer Reviewed Publications, Including for the Journal for Missouri Counselors and Others (2014); Author, Professional Development Folio Guide for Teachers and Library Media Specialists (1999) **AW:** Elected, Kappa Delta Pi; Elected, Phi Alpha Theta; Elected, Pi Lambda Theta; Elected, Phi Delta Kappa; International Service Key, Phi Delta Kappa; Outstanding Young Men in America **MEM:** Kappa Delta Pi President; Phi Alpha Theta Parliamentarian; Phi Delta Kappa President; Delegate, Research Representative, Historian, Vice President Programs, Chapter Member Liaison, Eastern Missouri Association of Supervision and Curriculum Development; Committee Chairperson, Greater Saint Louis Association of Supervision and Curriculum Development; President, Missouri State Teachers Association; Hazelwood CTA; President, Board of Directors, Greater Saint Louis Missouri State Teachers Association; Member, National Council of Teachers of Mathematics; Member, National Science Teachers Association; Fellow, St. Louis and Missouri Principal Academy **MH:** Albert Nelson Marquis Lifetime Achievement Award **AS:** Dr. Engelhardt attributes his success on the influence of his family, as well as his spouse, teachers, colleagues and friends. Likewise, he credits his love for learning. **B/I:** Dr. Engelhardt became involved in his profession because it was a calling that he felt from as long as he could remember. **AV:** Saxophone and clarinet playing; Boating; Camping; Ballroom dancing; Golf **PA:** Independent **RE:** United Methodist

ENGLE, ROBERT FRY III, T: Economist, Finance Educator **I:** Financial Services **DOB:** 11/10/1942 **PB:** Syracuse **SC:** NY/USA **MS:** Married **SPN:** Marianne Eger (08/10/1969) **CH:** Jordan; Lindsey **ED:** Doctorate (Honorary), HEC International Business School, Paris (2005); Doctor (Honorary), University of Southern Switzerland (2003); PhD in Economics, Cornell University, Ithaca, NY (1969); MS in Physics, Cornell University, Ithaca, NY (1966); BS in Physics, Williams College, with Honors, Williamstown, MA (1964) **C:** Professor Emeritus and Research Professor, University of California, San Diego (2003-Present); Michael Armellino Professor Management of Financial Services, Stern School of Business, New York University (2000-Present); Emeritus Professor and Distinguished Research Professor, University of California, San Diego (2003-Present); Professor of Economics, University of California, San Diego (1977-2003); Chair, Department of Economics, University of California, San Diego (1990-1994); Associate Professor, University of California, San Diego (1975-1977); Associate Professor, Massachusetts Institute of Technology, Cambridge (1974-1975); Assistant Professor, Massachusetts Institute of Technology, Cambridge, Massachusetts (1969-1974) **CR:** Research Associate, National Bureau of Economic Research (1987-Present) **CW:** Member, Editorial Board, "Real Estate Economics" (2004-Present); Associate Editor, "Journal of Applied Econometrics" (1988-Present); Associate Editor, "Journal of Regional Science (1978-Present); Associate Editor "Journal of Forecasting" (1985-Present); Editor, "Cointegration, Causality, and Forecasting: A Festschrift in Honour of Clive W. J. Granger: A Festschrift in Honour of Clive W. J. Granger" (1999); Co-Editor, "Journal of Applied Econometrics" (1985-1989); Contributor, Articles, Professional Journals **AW:** Recipient Nobel Prize in Economics (2003); Excellence in Teaching Award, MIT Graduate Economics Association (1974-1975) **MEM:** Council Member, Econometric Society (1994); Fellow, Institute for Quantitative Research in Finance; American Financial Association; American Statistical Association; American Academy of Arts & Sciences; Society of Financial Econometrics; Founding Member, American Economic Association; National Academy of Sciences

ENTIN, PETER, T: Former Vice President of Theatre Operations **I:** Media & Entertainment **CN:** Shubert Organization **C:** Former Vice President of Theatre Operations, Shubert Organization (1974-2017) **AW:** Tony Honor For Excellence In Theatre (2019)

ENZI, MICHAEL, "MIKE" BRADLEY, T: U.S. Senator from Wyoming **I:** Government Administration/Government Relations/Government Services **DOB:** 02/01/1944 **PB:** Bremerton **SC:** WA/USA **PT:** Elmer Jacob Enzi; Dorothy (Bradley) Enzi **MS:** Married **SPN:** Diana (Buckley) Enzi (06/07/1969) **CH:** Amy; Emily; Brad **ED:** MBA, Daniel College of Business, University of Denver (1968); BBA, George Washington University (1966) **C:** Chairmen, Senate Budget Committee (2015-Present); U.S. Senator, State of Wyoming (1997-Present); Chairman, U.S. Senate Committee on Health, Education, Labor and Pensions (2005-2007); Accounting Manager, Dunbar Well Service, Inc., Gillette, WY (1985-1997); Commissioner, Western Interstate Commission for Higher Education, Wyoming State Senate (1995-1996); Member, Wyoming State Senate, Cheynne, WY (1991-1996); President, NZ Shoes, Inc., Sheridan, WY (1983-1996); President, NZ Shoes, Inc., Gillette, WY (1969-1995); Member, Wyoming House of Representatives, Cheynne, WY (1986-1991); Mayor, City of Gillette, WY (1975-1982) **CR:** Member, Education Commission of the States (1989-1993) **CIV:** Board of Directors, Black Hills Corporation (1992-1996); President, Wyoming Association of Municipalities, Cheyenne, WY (1980-1982); Chairman, Board of Directors, First Wyoming Bank, Gillette, WY (1978-1988); Eagle Scout, Boy Scouts of America; Coach, Youth Soccer; Elder, Teacher, Sunday School, Presbyterian Church **MIL:** With, United States Air Force (1967-1973) **AW:** Named Policy Maker of the Year, Association for Career & Technical Education (ACTE) (2005); Named Legislator of the Year, BIO (2005); TechNet Founders Circle Award (2005); Leadership Award, National Organization on Fetal Alcohol Syndrome (2005); Congressional Leadership Award, Food Industry Association (2005); Award, ASCP (2004); Small

Investor Empowerment Award, Nareit (2002); W. Stuart Symington Award, Air Force Association (2001) **MEM:** President, Wyoming Jaycees (1973-1974); State Master Councilor, Wyoming Order of DeMolay (1963-1964); Lions Clubs International; Wyoming Jaycees; Shriners International; Masons; Wyoming Order of DeMolay; Scottish Rite; Sigma Chi Fraternity; Alpha Kappa Psi Fraternity **AV:** Fishing; Bicycling; Soccer; Hunting; Reading **PA:** Republican **RE:** Presbyterian

EPSTEIN, THEO NATHAN, T: Professional Sports Team Executive **I:** Athletics **DOB:** 12/29/1973 **PB:** New York **SC:** NY/USA **PT:** Leslie Epstein; Ilene Epstein **MS:** Married **SPN:** Marie Whitney (01/01/2007) **CH:** Jack **ED:** JD, University of San Diego (1998); BA in American Studies, Yale University (1995) **C:** President of Baseball Operations, Chicago Cubs (2011-Present); Executive Vice President, General Manager, Boston Red Sox (2006-2011); General Manager, Boston Red Sox (2002-2005); Director of Baseball Operations, San Diego Padres (2000-2002); Baseball Operations Assistant, San Diego Padres (1998-2000); Summer Intern, Media Relations, San Diego Padres (1992-1998) **AW:** 100 Most Influential People, "TIME" (2017); Sporting News Executive of the Year (2016); Esurance MLB Award for Best Executive (2016); Recipient, Executive of the Decade, The Sporting News (2009); Major League Baseball Executive of Year, Baseball America (2008); Carl Maddox Sport Management Award, US Sports Academy (2007)

ERGEN, CHARLES W., T: Chairman **I:** Telecommunications **DOB:** 03/01/1953 **PB:** Oak Ridge **SC:** TN/USA **MS:** Married **SPN:** Cantey Ergen **CH:** Five Children **ED:** MBA, Wake Forest University (1976); BS in Business & Accounting, University of Tennessee, Knoxville (1974) **C:** Chairman, Dish Network Corporation (2017-Present); President, Chief Executive Officer, Dish Network Corporation, Englewood, CO (2015-Present); Chairman, Dish Network Corporation, Englewood, CO (2011-Present); Chairman, EchoStar Corporation, Inverness, CO (2009-Present); Chairman, Chief Executive Officer, Dish Network Corporation (2015-2017); Founder, Chairman, President, Chief Executive Officer, Dish Network Corporation, Englewood, CO (1980-2011); Chairman, President, Chief Executive Officer, EchoStar Corporation, Inverness, CO (2007-2009); Financial Analyst, Frito-Lay (1976-1980); Professional Blackjack Player, Las Vegas, NV **CR:** Board of Directors, EchoStar Corporation (Now Dish Network Corporation) (1980-Present) **AW:** The World's Richest People (2000-Present); The Forbes 400: Richest Americans (1999-Present); Inductee, Consumer Electronics Hall of Fame (2012); Top 10 CEOs, "Forbes" (2007); CEO of the Year, Frost & Sullivan (2001); Business Person of the Year, Rocky Mountain News (1996, 2001); Space Industry Business Man of Year, Aviation Week Magazine (2000); Rocky Mountain Region Master Entrepreneur of the Year, "INC." (1991); Star Award, Home Satellite TV Association (1988) **MEM:** Co-Founder, Satellite Broadcasting Communications Association **AV:** Mountain climbing; Poker; Basketball

ERICKSON, JEANNE, RPH, T: Pharmacist; Real Estate Company Officer **I:** Pharmaceuticals **DOB:** 11/17/1921 **PB:** Warroad **SC:** MN/USA **PT:** Edward James Holland; Henrietta (Berglund) Holland **MS:** Widowed **SPN:** Martin A. Erickson II (06/21/1941, Deceased 2005) **CH:** Martin A. Erickson III; Marilyn J.; Kirk E. **ED:** BS in Pharmacy, University of Minnesota (1946); Coursework, Macalester College (1939-1940) **CT:** Registered Pharmacist, State of Minnesota (1947) **C:** Vice President, Retail Sales-rental Property, Warroad Heritage Inc. (1975-Present); Pharmacy Consultant, Member, Infection

Control Committee, Warroad Care Center (1979-2009); Pharmacist-in-charge, Heritage Pharmacy, Warroad, MN (1975); Manager, Rembrandt Pharmacy, Edina, MN (1971-1975); Member, Advisory Committee, Minnesota Board of Pharmacy (1973); Staff Pharmacist, Olson Brothers Pharmacy, Edina, MN (1966-1971); Pharmacist-in-charge, Holland Pharmacy, Warroad, MN (1946-1956); Analyst, Minnesota Board of Pharmacy, Minneapolis, MN (1943-1946) **CIV:** Crusade Chairman, Erie County Unit American Cancer Society, Inc., Hamburg, NY (1965); Director, Religious Education, Hamburg Schools Release Time Education, NY (1963-1966); Vice President, PTA, Wanaka, NY (1962); Leader, Girls Scouts of the United States of America, NY; Leader, Girls Scouts of the United States of the United States, MN; Sunday School Teacher, Christ Presbyterian Church **AW:** Warroad High School Award for Outstanding Achievement (2004); Appreciation Award, Warroad Care Center (1985); Named to Hall of Fame, Rembrandt Corp. (1972) **MEM:** Delegate, Minnesota Pharmacists Association (Now MPhA) (1972-1974); Minnesota Alumni; American Legion Auxiliary; Society of Hospital Pharmacists; National Association of Retail Pharmacists; American Pharmacists Association; Order of the Eastern Star **MH:** Albert Nelson Marquis Lifetime Achievement Award **B/I:** Mrs. Erickson's father, Edward James, was a pharmacist; he was born in Canada, his uncle was a former mayor of the city Winnipeg, and every year they have Easter and they would go up to Fort Gary. There, they would have the Easter brunch and visit his memorial. She spent a lot of time in the pharmacy with her father; it was something that she wanted to do because of her dad. **AV:** Swimming; Music; Flying; Boating; Socializing **PA:** Republican **RE:** Protestant

ERICKSON, SUSAN PHILLIANS, T: Secondary School Educator **I:** Education/Educational Services **DOB:** 07/31/1947 **PB:** Uniontown **SC:** PA/US **PT:** John William Phillians; Louise (Grannell) Phillians **MS:** Married **SPN:** Philip Milton Erickson (07/01/1972) **CH:** Spencer P. Erickson Philip **ED:** Coursework, Fredonia, State University of New York (1974-1992); Coursework, West Virginia University (1970-1971); BA, Thiel College (1969) **CT:** Lifetime Certification, Teacher, State of New York (1969) **C:** Retired, Jamestown Board of Education, Jamestown Public Schools, NY (2002); Teacher, Jamestown Board of Education, Jamestown Public Schools, NY (1969-2002) **CR:** Consultant, Jamestown Public Schools, NY (2003-2004); Coordinator, Lessing-Gymnasium, Frankfurt, Germany (1993-1998); Coordinator, German-American Partnership Program, Jamestown Public Schools and Maximilian-Kolbe-Gymnasium (1978-1992) **MEM:** District Liaison Committee, Jamestown Teachers Association (1976-1979); American Association Teachers German; American Association of Teachers of French (AATF); New York Association of Foreign Language Teachers (NYSAFLT); National Education Association, NY; New York State Retired Teachers Association (NYSTRS); Jamestown Teachers Association; Association of Certified Swimming Officials of New York State, Jamestown Area Chapter, NY; National Society Daughters of the American Revolution (NSDAR); Norden Women's Club; PTA; Delta Epsilon Phi **MH:** Albert Nelson Marquis Lifetime Achievement Award **AV:** Gardening; Sewing; Knitting; Travel; Reading **PA:** Republican **RE:** Methodist

ERICSON, DAVID PAUL, PHD, T: Philosophy of Education Educator **I:** Education/Educational Services **DOB:** 10/29/1949 **PB:** Kansas City **SC:** MO/USA **PT:** Paul Jacob Ericson; Jane Marie (Miller) Ericson **MS:** Married **SPN:** Rieko O. Ericson

(08/22/1999); Bonnie Lynn Ohrlund (05/28/1971, Divorced) **CH:** Kristin Elisabeth; Marisa Jane **ED:** PhD, Syracuse University (1976); Postgraduate Coursework, University of London (1974-1975); MA in Philosophy, Syracuse University (1973); BA, St. Olaf College, Cum Laude (1971); Coursework, Cambridge, England, United Kingdom (1970) **C:** Partner, Consultant Group (2019-Present); Professor Emeritus, Chair, Department of Educational Foundations, University of Hawai'i at Manoa College of Education, Honolulu, Hawaii (1992-2019); Associate Professor, University of California Los Angeles (1986-1992); Assistant Professor, University of California Los Angeles (1979-1986); Assistant Professor, Virginia Polytechnic Institute and State University, Blacksburg, VA (1977-1979) **CR:** Consultant, Nichinoken Institute, Yokahama, Japan (1989-Present); Partner, Mid-Pacific International Higher Education Consulting (2008-2019); Researcher, Pacific Rim Center, University of California Los Angeles (1989-1995) **CIV:** Faculty Athletic Representative, NCAA, Office of the Chancellor, University of Hawai'i at Manoa (2014-2019); Acting Associate Dean for Research and Graduate Education, College of Education; Shared Faculty Senate, University of Hawai'i at Manoa **CW:** Co-author, "Predicting the Behavior of the Education System" (1980, 1997); Editor-in-chief, "Studies in Philosophy and Education" (1989-1994) **AW:** Fulbright Scholar (2008-2013); Pacific Rim Center, University of California Los Angeles (1989); Grantee, Spencer Foundation (1981-1986) **MEM:** Fellow, The Philosophy of Education Society; American Educational Research Association; Comparative and International Education Society **MH:** Albert Nelson Marquis Lifetime Achievement Award **B/I:** Dr. Ericson was in college as an undergraduate. He was a philosophy major and he spent a year at the University of Cambridge in England. He had various tutors and he really enjoyed that year of studies; it led him not only into philosophy, but also philosophy of education as an endeavor. By taking a course in philosophy of education, he saw that this was an area of philosophy that was relatively undeveloped, and it was an opportunity for Dr. Ericson to make a solid contribution. **AV:** Fly-fishing; Sailing; Golf; Investing **PA:** Independent

ERIVO, CYNTHIA ONYEDINMANASU CHINASA-OKWU, T: Actress **I:** Media & Entertainment **DOB:** 01/08/1987 **SC:** Stockwell/England **ED:** Coursework, Royal Academy of Dramatic Art; BA in Music Psychology, University of East London; Diplomate, La Retraite Roman Catholic Girl's School **CW:** Actress, "The Outsider" (2020); Contestant, "American Idol" (2019); Recording Artist, "Anthem: Homunculus" (2019); Actress, "Harriet" (2019); Actress, "Broad City" (2017-2019); Actress, "Bad Times at the El Royale" (2018); Actress, "Widows, Belle" (2018); Voice Actress, "The Boss Baby: Back in Business" (2018); Actress, "The Tunnel" (2016); Actress, "Mr. Selfridge" (2016); Recording Artist, "The Color Purple" (2016); Actress, "The Last Five Years" (2016); Actress, "Chewing Gum" (2015); Actress, "The Color Purple" (2013); Actress, "Lift" (2013); Actress, "Sister Act" (2011-2012); Actress, "The Umbrellas of Cherbourg" (2011) **AW:** Best Actress in a Musical, Tony Awards (2016); Breakthrough Award, Palm Springs Film Festival; Drama Desk Award for Outstanding Actress in a Musical; Best Musical Theatre Album, Grammy Award; Daytime Emmy Award, Outstanding Musical Performance in a Daytime Program

ERLICHMAN, STANTON ROY, PHD, CEDS-S, CAP, FIAEDP, T: Industrial Consultant, Psychotherapist **I:** Medicine & Health Care **DOB:** 03/24/1939 **PB:** Detroit **SC:** MI/USA **PT:** William Isaiah Erlichman; Lydia (Bloom) Erlichman **MS:** Married **SPN:** Gail

Fried Erlichman **CH:** Karen Erlichman; Daniel East; William Mann; Terri Starr Lipkin (Stepchild); Ronald Starr (Stepchild) **ED:** PhD, Union Institute, Ohio (1977); MA, Goddard College, Vermont (1975); BA, Franklin and Marshall College, Pennsylvania (1961); Postgraduate Coursework, Eastern Pennsylvania Psychiatric Institute; graduate, Philadelphia School of Psychoanalysis. Philadelphia, Pennsylvania; Training, Family Institute of Philadelphia, Philadelphia, PA **CT:** Licensed Marriage and Family Therapist; Certified Eating Disorders Specialist, International Association of Eating Disorders Professionals, Approved Eating Disorders Supervisor and Certified Addictions Professional, State of Florida **C:** Partner, Erlichman Associates, Bala Cynwyd, PA (1972-Present); Partner, G.T. Manufacturing Corporation, San Juan, Puerto Rico (1972-Present); President, Richards Manufacturing Company, Philadelphia, PA (1962-1973). **CR:** Co-Director, ERE Associates, South Miami, FL (1980); Instructor, Addictions Training Institute, Florida School Addiction Studies, Miami, FL; Board of Directors, Vice President, Compugen Corporation, Malvern, PA; Member of Field Faculty, Goddard College; Past President and Member Board of Directors, International Association of Eating Disorders Professionals; Frequent Presenter and Trainer at Lectures and Conferences throughout the United States and Abroad; Specialist in Psychodynamic Psychotherapy and Family Therapy **CW:** Author, Professional Article; Associate Editor, Perspectives **CIV:** Member, Lower Merion Township Recycling Committee, Pennsylvania (1969-1972); Psychotherapy Training Institute, Miami, FL **AW:** Recipient, Lifetime Achievement Award, International Association of Eating Disorders Professionals (2016); Recipient Spirit Award, Sierra Tucson; Fellow, International Association of Eating Disorders Professionals; Phi Beta Kappa. **MEM:** Fellow, American Orthopsychiatric Association; Diplomate, American Board of Medical Psychotherapists; Florida Alcohol and Drug Abuse Association; International Association of Eating Disorders Professionals; American Counseling Association; American Orthopsychiatric Association; National Psychological Association for Psychoanalysis; Clinical Member, American Association for Marriage and Family Therapy; National association for the Advancement of Psychoanalysis; Zeta Beta Tau Fraternity ; Phi Beta Kappa. **MH:** Albert Nelson Marquis Lifetime Achievement Award **B/I:** Dr. Erlichman initially started his career in business but was discontented, although successful. His wish was to work with people clinically, as a psychotherapist and as an educator to other professionals. Dr. Erlichman wanted comprehensive clinical education in psychotherapy and advanced training in psychoanalysis and family therapy. The educational path he pursued addressed and fulfilled his goals.

ERNST, JONI KAY, T: U.S. Senator from Iowa **I:** Government Administration/Government Relations/Government Services **DOB:** 07/01/1970 **PB:** Red Oak **SC:** IA/USA **PT:** Richard Ernst; Marilyn Ernst **MS:** Divorced **SPN:** Gail Ernst (1992, Divorced 2019) **CH:** Three Children **ED:** MPA, Columbus College (Now Columbus State University) (1995); BA in Psychology, Iowa State University (1992) **C:** U.S. Senator, State of Iowa (2015-Present); Vice Chair, Senate Republican Conference (2019-Present); Member, U.S. Senate Small Business and Entrepreneurship Committee (2015-Present); Member, U.S. Senate Armed Services Committee (2015-Present); Member, U.S. Senate Homeland Security and Governmental Affairs Committee (2015-Present); Member, U.S. Senate Committee on Agricultural Nutrition and Forestry (2015-Present); Member, 12th District,

Iowa State Senate (2011-2014); Member, District 48, Iowa State Senate (2011-2014); Auditor, Montgomery County, Iowa (2004-2010); Emergency Coordinator, Montgomery County, Iowa (2001-2003); Job Training Partnership Act Coordinator, Midlands Technical College (1997-1999); Human Resources Applicant Tester, Blue Cross Blue Shield Association (1996-1997); Saleswoman, Parisian Shoes (1993-1995) **CR:** Montgomery County Chair, Romney for President (2011-2012); Co-chair, Montgomery County Republican Party (2006-2012) **CIV:** Sunday School and Confirmation Teacher, Mamrelund Lutheran Church of Stanton (2004-Present); Coordinator, Santa Lucia Festival of Lights Coronation Ceremony (2011-2013); National Guard Voting Assistance Officer (2009-2012); Volunteer Crisis Counselor, ACCESS Women's Shelter (1991-1992) **MIL:** Company Commander, 1168th Transportation Company, United States Army Reserve, Iraq War (2003-2004); Advanced through Grades, Lieutenant Colonel, Iowa National Guard (1993-2015); Commanding Officer, 185th Combat Sustainment Support Battalion, Iowa Army National Guard, Camp Dodge **MEM:** Lifetime Member, Montgomery County Republican Women; Lifetime Member, Veterans of Foreign Wars Post 2265; Lifetime Member, Montgomery County Veterans Memorial Court of Honor; Lifetime Member, Altrusa International; Lifetime Member, PEO, Chapter HB; Lifetime Member, National Rifle Association of America; Montgomery County Farm Bureau **PA:** Republican **RE:** Christian

ERSEK, HIKMET, T: President, Chief Executive Officer **I:** Financial Services **CN:** Western Union **PB:** Istanbul **SC:** Turkey **MS:** Married **SPN:** Dr. Nayantara Ghosh-Ersek **CH:** One son **ED:** MS in Economics, Vienna University of Economics and Business; Coursework in Economics and Business Administration, Vienna University of Economics and Business **C:** President, Chief Executive Officer, Director, Western Union (2010-Present); Chief Operating Officer, Western Union (2010); Executive Vice President, Managing Director for Europe, Middle East, Africa and Asia Pacific Region, Western Union (2008-2009); Executive Vice President, Managing Director of Europe, Middle East, Africa and South Asia, Western Union (2006-2008); Senior Vice President of Europe, Middle East, Africa and South Asia, Western Union (2004-2006); Senior Vice President of Europe, Middle East and Africa, Western Union (2002-2004); Regional Vice President for Central And Eastern Europe, Western Union (2001-2002); Regional Vice President for South Europe, Western Union (1999-2001); General Electric Capital (1996); Europay/Mastercard, Austria (1986-1996); National Executive, General Electric Capital, Austria; National Executive, General Electric Capital, Slovenia **CR:** Former Member, Board of Directors, Fexco Financial Services; Chairman, Western Union **AV:** Playing basketball

ERTZ, JULIE BETH, T: Professional Soccer Player **I:** Athletics **CN:** Chicago Red Stars **DOB:** 4/6/1992 **PB:** Mesa **SC:** AZ/USA **PT:** David Johnston; Kristi Johnston **MS:** Married **SPN:** Zach Ertz (3/26/2017) **ED:** Diploma, Dobson High School (2010); Coursework, Santa Clara University **C:** Professional Soccer Player, Chicago Red Stars (2014-Present); Soccer Player, Santa Clara Broncos (2010-2013); Soccer Player, Sereno Soccer Club (2004-2010); Soccer Player, Arizona Arsenal Soccer Club (2000-2004); Soccer Player, AYSO Region 503 **CR:** Professional Soccer Player, U.S. National Team (2013-Present); Professional Soccer Player, FIFA Women's World Cup, France (2019); Professional Soccer Player, FIFA Women's World Cup, Canada (2015) **AW:** SheBelieves Cup Winner (2016, 2018, 2020); CONCACAF Women's Olympic Qualifying Tournament

Winner (2016, 2020); Gold Medal, FIFA Women's World Cup, France (2019); IFFHS Women's World Team Award (2019); USWNT Player of the Year (2017, 2019); CONCACAF Women's Championship Golden Ball (2018); Tournament of Nations Winner (2018); NWSL Second XI (2016-2018); CONCACAF Women's Championship (2014, 2018); Gold Medal, FIFA Women's World Cup, Canada (2015); Algarve Cup Winner (2015); NWSL Best XI (2015); FIFA FIFPro World XI (2015); NWSL Rookie of the Year (2014); College Sports Madness WCC Player of the Year (2013); WCC Player of the Year (2013); U.S. Soccer Young Female Athlete of the Year (2012); FIFA U20 Women's World Cup (2012); CONCACAF U20 Women's Championship (2012); Top Drawer Soccer Team of the Year (2012); Preseason All-WCC (2011); WCC Freshman of the Year (2010) **RE:** Christian

ERVIN, SPENCER, T: Lawyer **I:** Law and Legal Services **DOB:** 11/25/1932 **PB:** Bala **SC:** PA/USA **PT:** Spencer Ervin; Miriam Williams Roberts Ervin **MS:** Married **SPN:** Florence Wetherill Schroeder **CH:** Margaret; Mary; Miriam; Helen **ED:** JD, Harvard Law School (1959); BA, Harvard College (1954) **C:** Private Practice (1998-2018); Counsel, Largay Law Offices, P.A. (1996-1997); Partner, Hepburn, Willcox, Hamilton & Putnam (1992-1996); Partner, Bennett Bricklin & Saltzburg LLC (1972-1992); Partner, Ringe, Tate & Ervin (1964-1972); Associate, Ringe & Dewey (1962-1964); Staff Counsel, Philco Corporation (1959-1962) **CR:** Board of Directors, MDI Biological Laboratory (2000-2017) **CIV:** Board of Directors, Officer, The Neighborhood Club of Bala Cynwyd (1969-1989) **MIL:** Commissioned Lieutenant, U.S. Naval Reserve (1954-1956) **MEM:** American Bar Association; Pennsylvania Bar Association; Philadelphia Bar Association; Maine State Bar Association; Findlay/Hancock County Bar Association **BAR:** Maine State Bar Association (1995); Supreme Court of the United States (1963); Pennsylvania Bar Association (1960) **MH:** Albert Nelson Marquis Lifetime Achievement Award; Marquis Who's Who Top Professional **B/I:** Mr. Ervin became involved in his profession because he was inspired by his father, who was a lawyer. While on active duty, he applied to law school and has never looked back. **PA:** Democrat **RE:** Episcopalian

ERVING, JULIUS, T: NBA Player (Retired) **I:** Athletics **DOB:** 02/22/1950 **PB:** East Meadow **SC:** NY/USA **PT:** Julius Erving; Callie Lindsey **MS:** Married **SPN:** Turquoise Erving (1972) **CH:** Cheo; Julius III; Jazmin; Cory; Alexandra Stevenson **ED:** Graduate, University of Massachusetts (1986); Honorary Doctorate, University of Massachusetts (1983); Honorary Doctorate, Temple University (1983) **C:** President, The Erving Group (1997-Present); Co-Owner, Coca-Cola Bottling Co., Philadelphia, PA (1987-2007); Executive Vice President, Orlando Magic (1997-2003); Vice President, RDV Sports, Orlando, FL (1997-2003); In-Studio Analyst, NBC Sports (1993-1997); Forward, Guard, Philadelphia 76ers (1976-1987); Forward, Guard, New York Nets, American Basketball Association (1973-1976); Forward, Guard, Virginia Squires, American Basketball Association (1971-1973); President, JDREGI **CR:** Former Member, Board of Directors, Fusion Telecommunications (2003-Present); Former Member, Board of Directors, Meridian Bancorp; Former Member, Board of Directors, Converse Shoe Co.; Former Member, Board of Directors, Darden Restaurants, Inc.; Former Member, Board of Directors, The Sports Authority; Former Member, Board of Directors, LCI; Former Member, Board of Directors, Saks Inc. **CIV:** Trustee, NBA International, Basketball Hall of Fame; Board of Directors, New York State Sports Commission **CW:** Actor, "The Fish That Saved Pittsburgh" (1979) **AW:** Inductee,

Nassau County Sports Hall of Fame (2004); NBA 50th Anniversary All-Time Team (1996); 40 Most Important Athletes of All Time (1994); Naismith Memorial Basketball Hall of Fame (1993); NBA Eastern Conference All-Star Team (1977-1987); Sportsman of Year, David Zinkoff Memorial Foundation (1986); Man of the Year, American Express (1985); Sports Award, Big Brothers Inc., New York, NY (1985); Appreciation Award, Lupus Foundation of America (1985); Whitney M. Young Award, Urban League (1984); Father Flanagan Award, Boys Town Nebraska (1984); Biddy Basketball Award (1984); Walter Kennedy Citizenship Award (1983); Jackie Robinson Award, "Ebony" (1983); NBA All-Star Game MVP (1977, 1983); First Team All-NBA (1978, 1980-1983); Certificate of Appreciation, Easter Seals (1982); Best Friend Award, Police Athletic League of Philadelphia (1982); MVP, NBA (1981); Inductee, Hall of Fame, University of Massachusetts (1980); NBA 35th Anniversary All-Time Team (1980); Liberty Bell Award, Philadelphia Mayor Frank Rizzo (1978); First Team All-ABA (1973-1976); American Basketball Association MVP (1974-1976); American Basketball Association Playoffs MVP (1974, 1976); First Team American Basketball Association All-Def. (1976); American Basketball Association Eastern Conference All-Star Team (1972-1976); Rookie of Year, American Basketball Association (1972)

ERXLEBEN, JORG, T: Chief Executive Officer, President, Owner **I:** Business Management/Business Services **CN:** Jotatech LLC **DOB:** 12/11/1963 **MS:** Married **SPN:** Teresa (1999) **CH:** Two Sons **ED:** MS in Chemistry, University of Hamburg (1989); BS in Chemistry, Technical Commercial School of Hamburg, Germany (1982) **C:** Chief Executive Officer, Jotatech LLC (2019-Present); R&D Manager, VIPI Produtos Odontologicos, Brazil (1999-Present); Quality Manager, TDV Dental Limited, Brazil (1998); Section Development Leader, VOCO GmbH, Germany (1992-1997); Group Development Leader, Heraeus Kulzer GmbH, Germany (1989-1991) **CR:** Consulting, Health and Beauty Industry **CIV:** Director, Editorial Board, Full Science and Dentistry **CW:** Contributor, Articles, Professional Journals **MEM:** Rotary International **AS:** Mr. Erxleben's philosophy is to "work, work, and work." He also likes to teach others how to find their own success. **B/I:** When Mr. Erxleben graduated from college, he was hired by a dental material manufacturing company in Germany. From there, he worked his way up into the R & D department, continuing to grow. Mr. Erxleben later worked as a consultant in Brazil and made connections with other dental material producing companies. After the new management of his company came in, they made him give up consulting for other companies. He was not fond of the idea and, so, he decided to begin his own company.

ESCOBAR, VERONICA, T: U.S. Representative from Texas **I:** Government Administration/Government Relations/Government Services **DOB:** 09/15/1969 **PB:** El Paso **SC:** TX/USA **MS:** Married **SPN:** Michael Pleters **CH:** Two Children **ED:** MA, New York University; BA, The University of Texas at El Paso **C:** Member, U.S. House of Representatives from Texas' 16th Congressional District (2019-Present); County Judge, El Paso County (2011-2017); County Commissioner, El Paso County (2006-2011) **CR:** Instructor, English and Chicano Literature, The University of Texas at El Paso and El Paso Community College **PA:** Democratic

ESHOO, ANNA A., T: U.S. Representative from California **I:** Government Administration/Government Relations/Government Services **DOB:** 12/13/1942 **PB:** New Britain **SC:** CT/USA **PT:** Fred

Georges; Alice Alexandre Georges **MS:** Divorced **SPN:** George Eshoo (Divorced) **CH:** Karen Elizabeth; Paul Frederick **ED:** AA in English, Canada College, With Honors (1975) **C:** Member, U.S. House of Representatives from California's 18th Congressional District, United States Congress (2013-Present); Member, U.S. House of Representatives from California's 14th Congressional District, United States Congress (1993-2013); San Mateo County Board of Supervisors (1982-1992); President, San Mateo County Board of Supervisors (1986); Chair, San Mateo Democratic Party (1978-1982); Arcata National Corporation (1966-1970); Alcoa Corporation (1963-1966); Committee on Agriculture; Committee on Natural Resources **CR:** Democratic National Committee (1981-1992); National Committee Presidential Nominations (1981); Chief-of-Staff to Speaker Leo McCarthy, California State Assembly (1981) **CIV:** Chair, Board of Directors, San Mateo County General Hospital (1984-1992); Co-Founder, San Mateo County Women's Hall of Fame **AW:** Listee, One of the 10 Most Powerful Women of Silicon Valley, San Jose Mercury News (2011) **MEM:** League of Women Voters; League of Conservation Voters; Democratic Activists for Women Now; Junior League Palo Alto-Mid Peninsula **PA:** Democrat **RE:** Roman Catholic

ESLINGER, KENNETH NELSON, T: Social Sciences Educator **I:** Education/Educational Services **CN:** John Carroll University **DOB:** 03/02/1944 **PB:** Hennepin **SC:** MN/USA **PT:** Kenneth N.; Pearl May E. **MS:** Married **SPN:** Denise Marie Juba (07/22/1979) **ED:** PhD, The Ohio State University, Columbus, Ohio (1971); MA, The Ohio State University, Columbus, Ohio (1968); BA, Indiana State University, Terre Haute, IN (1963) **C:** Associate Professor of Sociology, John Carroll University (1985-Present); Chair, Department of Sociology, John Carroll University (1997-2005); Acting Chair, Department of Sociology, John Carroll University (1995-1996); Assistant Professor of Sociology, John Carroll University, University Heights, Ohio (1980-1985); Assistant Professor of Sociology, Cleveland State University (1973-1980); Assistant Professor of Sociology, The Ohio State University, Lima Campus, Ohio (1972-1973) **CIV:** Member, Democratic National Committee (1993-2003); Advisory Committee, Congressman, Cleveland, Ohio (1983-1984); Organizer, Higher Education Field, Gubernatorial Campaign, Cleveland, Ohio (1982) **CW:** Contributor, Four Publications, International Encyclopedia in Social Sciences (2008); Contributor, Articles, Professional Journals **MEM:** Vice President, North Central Sociological Association (1997-1999); American Sociological Association; The Society for the Study of Social Problems (SSSP); National Council on Family Relations (NCFR) **MH:** Albert Nelson Marquis Lifetime Achievement Award; Marquis Who's Who Top Professional **B/I:** Dr. Eslinger became involved in his profession because he was interested in history, social change, and why societies are organized and how they change. He was also interested in how social institutions influence social behavior and had an interest in sociology from an undergraduate background in history. Dr. Eslinger was a history major as an undergraduate and decided he was interested in patterns of social change and studied the history of uniqueness of specific societies. He was concerned about social institutions and how the organizations of society is an entity into itself. He felt that sociology could do that better than history could. **AV:** Bass fishing; Fly fishing

ESPAILLAT, ADRIANO DE JESUS, T: U.S. Representative from New York **I:** Government Administration/Government Relations/Government

Services **DOB:** 09/27/1954 **PB:** Santiago **SC:** Dominican Republic **PT:** Ulises Espaillat; Melba Rodriguez Espaillat **MS:** Married **SPN:** Martha Madera (1980) **CH:** Adriano Ulises Jr.; Natalia **ED:** BS in Political Science, Queens College, CUNY (1978) **C:** Member, U.S. House of Representatives from New York's 13th Congressional District (2017-Present); Member, District 31, New York State Senate (2011-2016); Member, District 72, New York State Assembly (1997-2010); Director, Project Right Start (1994-1996); Director, Washington Heights Victim Services Community Office (1992-1994); Manhattan Court Services Coordinator, New York City Criminal Justice Agency (1980-1988); Member, Committee on Education and the Workforce; Member, Committee on Foreign Affairs; Member, Committee on Small Business **CR:** Member, Governor's Dominican American Advisory Board, NY (1991-1993); Member, Executive Board, Community Planning Board 12 (1986-1991); Past President, 34th Precinct Community Council **CIV:** Mediator, Washington Heights Inwood Coalition Mediation Program, NY; Board of Directors, Dominican American National Roundtable **PA:** Democrat

ESPER, MARK THOMAS, PHD, T: United States Secretary of Defense; Former United States Secretary of the Army **I:** Government Administration/Government Relations/Government Services **DOB:** 04/26/1954 **PB:** Uniontown **SC:** PA/USA **PT:** Thomas Joseph Esper; Pauline "Polly" (Reagan) Esper **MS:** Married **SPN:** Leah Lacy (1989) **CH:** Three Children **ED:** PhD in Public Policy, The George Washington University (2008); MPA, Harvard Kennedy School, John F. Kennedy School of Government (1995); BS in Engineering, Unites States Military Academy (1986) **C:** United States Secretary of Defense, Washington, DC (2019-Present); Acting United States Secretary of Defense, Washington, DC (2019); United States Secretary of the Army, Washington, DC (2017-2019); Vice President, Government Relations, Raytheon Company (2010); Executive Vice President, Global Intellectual Property Center (2008-2010); Vice President for Europe and Eurasia, U.S. Chamber of Commerce (2008-2010); National Policy Director, U.S. Senator Fred Thompson's Presidential Campaign (2007-2008); Executive Vice President, Aerospace Industries Association (2006-2007); Director for National Security Affairs, U.S. Senate (2004-2006); Deputy Assistant Secretary of Defense, Negotiations Policy, Washington, DC (2002-2004); Policy Director, House Armed Services Committee (2001-2002); Senior Professional Staffer, Senate Committee on Foreign Relations and Senate Governmental Affairs Committee, U.S. Senate, Washington, DC (1998-2002); Senior Policy Advisor, Legislative Director for U.S. Senator Chuck Hagel **CIV:** Chief of Staff, The Heritage Foundation (1996-1998) **MIL:** Advanced through Grades to Lieutenant Colonel, United States Army (1986-2007); United States Army Reserve; Virginia Army National Guard; Infantry Officer, 101st Airborne Division, United States Army **AW:** Listee, Top Corporate Lobbyists, The Hill (2015, 2016); Combat Infantryman Badge; Legion of Merit; Bronze Star; Department of Defense Medal for Distinguished Public Service

ESPOSITO, PHILIP ANTHONY, T: Retired Professional Hockey Player **I:** Athletics **DOB:** 02/20/1942 **PB:** Sault St. Marie **SC:** ON/Canada **PT:** Patrick J. Esposito; Frances S. (Dipietro) Esposito **MS:** Married **SPN:** Donna Esposito (08/07/1976) **CH:** Laurie; Carrie **ED:** Coursework, Public Schools, Sault Ste. Marie, Ontario, Canada **C:** President, General Manager, Alternate Governor, Tampa Bay Lightning, Tampa, FL (1992-1997); Head Coach, New York Rangers, New York, NY (1986, 1987, 1989); Vice President, General Manager, New York Rangers,

New York, NY (1986-1989); TV Commentator, New York Rangers, New York, NY (1981-1986); Player, New York Rangers, New York, NY (1975-1981); Player, Boston Bruins (1967-1975); Player, Chicago Black Hawks (1963-1967) **CW:** Co-Author, "Winning Hockey for Beginners" (1976); Co-Author, "Hockey is My Life" (1972); Co-Author, "We Can Teach You How to Play Hockey" (1972) **AW:** Art Ross Trophy for Leading Scorer (1969, 1971-1974); Player of the Year, Sporting News E Division (1971-1973); Hart Memorial Trophy for Most Valuable Player, NHL (1969); Inductee, Hall of Fame **MEM:** Order of Canada

ESSIN, EMMETT M., PHD, T: Professor Emeritus **I:** Education/Educational Services **CN:** East Tennessee State University **MS:** Married **SPN:** Sally (Goodman) Essin **CH:** Elizabeth Christin Essin; Emmett Matthew Essin **ED:** Doctor of Philosophy, Texas Christian University, Fort Worth, TX (1968); Master of Arts, Texas Christian University, Fort Worth, TX (1965); Bachelor of Arts, Austin College, Sherman, TX (1964); Coursework, Abilene Christian University, Abilene, TX (1961) **CT:** Certified, National Track Official, USA Track & Field **C:** Professor Emeritus, Department of History, East Tennessee State University, Johnson City, TN (2014-Present); Professor, East Tennessee State University, Johnson City, TN (1975-2017); Distinguished Professor, East Tennessee State University, Johnson City, TN (1976); Associate Professor, East Tennessee State University, Johnson City, TN (1970-1975); Assistant Professor, East Tennessee State University, Johnson City, TN (1967-1970); University Fellow, Texas Christian University, Fort Worth, TX (1966-1967); Teaching Assistant, Texas Christian University, Fort Worth, TX (1965-1966) **CR:** Director, Division of Developmental Studies, East Tennessee State University, Johnson City, TN (1986-2003); Interim Director, Division of Developmental Studies, East Tennessee State University, Johnson City, TN (1985-1986) **CIV:** Board of Directors, Southwest Social Sciences Association (1999-Present); Director of Workshops and Special Events, Southwest Social Sciences Association (1995-2008); Chairperson, Finance Committee, Southwest Social Sciences Association (1998-2001); Member, Johnson City Park and Recreation Board (1983-1998); Chairperson, Johnson City Park and Recreation Board (1987-1991); Vice Chairperson, Johnson City Park and Recreation Board (1985-1987); Board of Directors, Appalachian Consortium (1980-1987); Chairperson, Board of Directors, Appalachian Consortium (1984-1986); Chairperson, Western Historical Association Membership Committee (1983-1986); Vice Chairperson, Board of Directors, Appalachian Consortium (1981-1984) **CW:** Author, "Shavetails and Bell Sharps: The History of the United States Army Mule," The University of Nebraska Press (1997); Contributor, Chapter, "United States Calvary Mounts," Western Horse Tails (1993); Contributor, Chapter, "The Ox-Bow Route," American Pioneer Trails, Caxton Press (1985); Contributor, Chapter, "Frontier Women," Working Papers from the Regional Economics History Center (1983); Contributor, Chapter, "The Southern Cheyenne," Forked Tongues and Broken Indian Treaties, Caxton Press (1976); Editor, "Appalachia: Family Traditions in Transition" (1975); Contributor, Chapter, "Political Parties: Their Values and Functions," Contemporary America: Issues and Problems (1968); Contributor, Numerous Articles to Professional Journals; Contributor, Numerous Chapters to Books; Author, Dissertation, "The Calvary and the Horse"; Contributor, Numerous Book Reviews to Journals **AW:** Distinguished Service Award, Southwest Social Science Association (2009); Distinguished Service Award, Phi Alpha Theta (2008); Named, Committee Chairman of the Year, Metro

Kiwanis Club (1990-1991); Distinguished Faculty Award for the College of Arts and Sciences, East Tennessee State University (1976); Inductee, Johnson City Wall of Fame **MEM:** Long Range Planning Committee, Phi Alpha Theta (1998-2003); Metro Kiwanis Club (1977-2003); Lieutenant-Governor, Division 7 Kentucky-Tennessee District, Kiwanis (2000-2001); National Advisor, Phi Alpha Theta (1995-1999); National Counselor, Phi Alpha Theta (1993-1995); President, Metro Kiwanis Club (1966); Western History Association; Southwest Social Science **AS:** Dr. Essin attributes his success as a professor to the influence of his doctoral professor, Dr. Donnell Lee Worcester. **B/I:** Dr. Essin became involved in his profession because, as a child, he learned much about books and reading from his father. That is how he got started with history. Likewise, he enjoyed the influence of his high school history teacher, Ms. Jean Blooke, who made the subject come alive.

ESTEFAN, GLORIA MARIA MILAGROSA, T: Singer **I:** Media & Entertainment **DOB:** 09/01/1957 **PB:** Havana **SC:** Cuba **PT:** Jose Fajardo; Gloria (Garcia) Fajardo **MS:** Married **SPN:** Emilio Estefan Jr. (09/02/1978) **CH:** Nayib Emil; Emily Maria **ED:** Honorary Doctor of Music, Berklee College of Music (2007); Honorary Doctor of Law, Barry University (2002); Honorary Doctor of Music, University of Miami, Florida (1993); Bachelor of Arts in Psychology, Minor in French, University of Miami, Florida (1979) **C:** Co-owner, Miami Dolphins, NFL (2009-Present); Co-owner, Costa d'Este, Vero Beach, FL (2008-Present); Co-owner, Bongos Cuban Cafe, Miami, FL (2000-Present); Co-owner, Bongos Cuban Cafe, Orlando, FL (1997-Present); Co-owner, Bongos Cuban Cafe, Puerto Vallarta and Mexico City, Mexico and Hollywood, FL; Vice President, Estefan Enterprises, Inc.; Co-owner, The Cardozo, Miami, FL; Co-owner, Cabana Beach Resort, Vero Beach, FL; Co-owner, Cafe Cardozo; Co-owner, Larios on the Beach **CR:** Board of Directors, Univision Communications Inc. (2007-Present); Speaker, TEDx Via della Conciliazione (2013); Board of Trustees, University of Miami; English/Spanish/French Translator, Customs Department, Miami International Airport **CIV:** Founder, The Gloria Estefan Foundation (1997-Present) **CW:** Singer, "Brazil305" (2020); Actress, "One Day at a Time" (2019); Host, Kennedy Center Honors (2018); Appearance, "Q85: A Musical Celebration for Quincy Jones" (2018); Actress, "A Change of Heart" (2017); Appearance, "Jane the Virgin" (2016); Writer, "On Your Feet!," Marquis Theatre, New York, NY (2015); Appearance, "Glee" (2012, 2015); Singer, "The Standards" (2013); Appearance, "The Next: Fame is at Your Doorstep" (2012); Appearance, "The X Factor" (2011); Singer, "Miss Little Havana" (2011); Featured, Documentary, "Recording: The History of Recorded Music" (2010); Appearance, "The Marriage Ref" (2010); Voice Actress, "G-Force" (2009); Appearance, "Kathy Griffin: My Life on the D-List" (2009); Appearance, "Marley & Me" (2008); Co-author, "Estefan Kitchen" (2008); Guest Mentor, "American Idol" (2008); Appearance, Documentary, "Your Mommy Kills Animals" (2007); Singer, "90 Millas" (2007); Featured, "Your Mommy Kills Animals" (2007); Featured, Documentary, "90 Millas Documentary" (2007); Author, "Noelle's Treasure Tale" (2006); Appearance, "The Chris Isaak Show" (2006); Author, "The Magically Mysterious Adventures of Noelle the Bulldog" (2005); Appearance, "A Capitol Fourth" (2005); Singer, "Unwrapped: Remixes" (2004); Singer, "Unwrapped" (2003); Featured, Documentary, "Famous: The Making of Unwrapped" (2003); Narrator, Short Film, "Little Angelita" (2000); Appearance, "Frasier" (2000); Singer, "Alma Caribbean -

Caribbean Soul" (2000); Actress, TV Film, "For Love or Country: The Arturo Sandoval Story" (2000); Actress, "Music of the Heart" (1999); Appearance, "Blue's Clues" (1998); Singer, "Party Time!" (1998); Singer, "Bailando!" (1998); Singer, "Gloria!" (1998); Appearance, "Elmopalooza" (1998); Singer, "Destiny" (1996); Singer, "Abriendo Puertas" (1995); Singer, "Hold Me, Thrill Me, Kiss Me" (1994); Singer, "Christmas Through Your Eyes" (1993); Singer, "Mi Tierra" (1993); Singer, "Twelve Inch Mixes" (1993); Appearance, "The Hypnotic World of Paul McKenna" (1993); Singer, "Into the Light" (1991); Appearance, "Postcard From... with Clive James" (1989); Singer, "Cuts Both Ways" (1989); Singer, with Miami Sound Machine, "Let It Loose/Anything for You" (1987); Actress, "Club Med" (1986); Singer, with Miami Sound Machine, "Primitive Love" (1985); Singer, with Miami Sound Machine, "Eyes of Innocence" (1984); Singer with Miami Sound Machine, "A Toda Maquina" (1984); Singer with Miami Sound Machine, "Rio" (1982); Singer with Miami Sound Machine, "Otra Vez" (1981); Singer with Miami Sound Machine, "MSM" (1980); Singer, with Miami Sound Machine, "Imported" (1979); Singer, with Miami Sound Machine, "Miami Sound Machine" (1978); Singer, with Miami Sound Machine, "Live Again/Renacer" (1977); Singer, Musician, Solo Songs and Several Compilation Albums; Appearances, Television Shows **AW:** Gershwin Prize for Popular Song, Library of Congress (2019); Honoree, Kennedy Center Honors, John F. Kennedy Center for the Performing Arts (2018); Co-recipient, Presidential Medal of Freedom, The White House (2015); Co-recipient, Caribbean American Mover and Shakers Lifetime Achievement Award (2014); Spirit of Hope Award, Billboard Latin Music Awards (2011); Named to All Time Top Adult Contemporary Artists, Billboard Top 50 Adult Contemporary Artist Ever (2011); Two Awards for Billboard Top 100 Adult Contemporary Songs Ever (2011); Co-recipient, Las Vegas Walk of Stars Award (2010); Award for Icon of the Year, BMI Awards (2009); Latin Grammy Awards for Best Tropical Latin Song, Best Traditional Tropical Album, Person of the Year, The Latin Recording Academy (2008); Dial Radio Award (2008); Awards for Tropical Airplay Track of the Year, Tropical Album of the Year, Billboard Latin Music Awards (2008); St. Jude Hospital for Children Humanitarian Award (2008); Named, One of the All-time Top Artists, Five All-time Top Latin Songs, Billboard Hot 100 50th Anniversary (2008); Award for Tropical Airplay Track of the Year, Billboard Latin Music Awards (2005); Named, One of the Top Pop Artists of the Past 25 Years (2004); Award for Latin Pop Airplay Track of the Year, Billboard Latin Music Awards (2004); Magic 106 Exceptional Woman of the Year Award (2004); Buoniconti Fund Humanitarian Award (2003); Medallion of Excellence, Congressional Hispanic Caucus Institute (2002); Grammy Award for Best Traditional Tropical Latin Album, The Recording Academy (2001); Award for Best Tropical/Salsa Album, Billboard Latin Music Awards (2001); Latin Grammy Award for Best Music Video, The Latin Recording Academy (2000); Award of Merit, American Music Awards (2000); Award for Favorite Song from a Movie, Blockbuster Awards (2000); Harry Chapin Memorial Humanitarian Award (2000); Award for Best Latin Singer, Amigo Music Awards (2000); Hall of Fame Award, International Women's Forum (2000); Awards for Outstanding Music Video, Outstanding Host in a Variety/Music/Comedy Special or Series, Ricardo Montalban Lifetime Achievement Award, ALMA Awards (1999); Award for Best Latin Dance Club Play Track of the Year, Billboard Latin Music Awards (1999); Named, One of the 100 Greatest Women in Rock and Roll, VH1 (1999); Award for Best Latin Female Artist, Amigo Music Awards (1998); Award for Best Female Latin Artist, American Music Awards (1997); Prestigious President's Award, BMI Awards (1997); Inductee, Songwriters Hall of Fame (1997); Grammy Awards for Best Tropical Latin Album, The Recording Academy (1994, 1996); Award for Music Video of the Year, Billboard Music Awards (1995); Awards for Top Tropical/Salsa Latin Artist, Top Tropical/Salsa Latin Album, Billboard Year-end Charts (1995); Award for Bestselling Latin Performer, World Music Awards (1994); Named, Person of the Year, MusiCares (1994); Award for Tropical/Salsa Song of the Year, Billboard Latin Music Awards (1994); Awards for Top Latin 50 Album Artist, Top Latin 50 Album, Top Tropical/Salsa Latin Artist, Top Tropical/Salsa Latin Album, Billboard Year-end Charts (1994); Ellis Island Medal of Honor (1993); Hispanic Heritage Award (1993); Spirit of Hope Award (1993); Humanitarian of the Year Award, National Music Foundation (1993); Recipient, Star, Hollywood Walk of Fame (1993); Excellence Award, Premios lo Nuestro a la Musica Latina (1992); Award for Songwriter of the Year, BMI Awards (1991); International Viewer's Choice Award - MTV Internacional, MTV Video Music Awards (1990); Award for Favorite Pop/Rock Band/Duo/Group, American Music Awards (1989); Award for Songwriter of the Year, American Billboard Music Awards (1989); Named Female Vocalist of the Year, Performance Magazine (1988); First Prize, Annual Tokyo Music Fair (1986); Awards for Top Adult Contemporary Single, Top New Pop Artist, Top Pop Singles Artist, Billboard Music Awards (1986); Numerous Awards **MEM:** Honorary Member, Sigma Alpha Iota International Music Fraternity, Sigma Chi Chapter, University of Miami (2017) **RE:** Catholic

ESTES, KENNETH WILLIAM, PHD, LT. COL. USMC (RET.), T: Military Officer; History Professor; Defense Consultant **I:** Education/Educational Services **DOB:** 08/25/1947 **PB:** Seattle **SC:** WA/USA **PT:** Victor Guy Estes; Lois Bernice Horth Estes **MS:** Married **SPN:** Genevieve Perrin (09/24/2002) **CH:** Caroline; Gwendolyn; Hugo; Ivan **ED:** PhD, University of Maryland (1984); MA, Duke University (1974); BSc, United States Naval Academy (1969) **CT:** Certified, Marine Corps Command and Staff College (1985) **C:** Professor of History (1993-Present); Retired, Defense Consultant, United States Marine Corps (2000-2008); Professor of History, The College for International Studies, Madrid, Spain (1995-1997); Historical Writer, United States Marine Corps Historical Center, Washington, DC (1992-1993); Visiting Assistant Professor, Duke University (1981-1984); Marine Officer Instructor, Duke University (1981-1983); Instructor of History, United States Naval Academy (1974-1978) **CR:** Senior Research Fellow, Marine Corps University, Quantico, VA (2006-2008); Contract Historian, First Armored Division, United States Army, Wiesbaden, Germany (2005); Research Fellow, Emirates Center for Strategic Studies and Research (2002); Consultant, United States Marine Corps Combat Development Command (1996-2001); Consultant, Computing Technologies, Inc., Falls Church, VA (1996-2001); Writer and Publisher, Self-employed **MIL:** Retired, Lieutenant Colonel, United States Marine Corps (1993); Lieutenant Colonel, United States Marine Corps (1969-1993); Head, International Affairs Branch, Office of Defense Cooperation, Madrid, Spain (1991-1992); United States Marine Corps Liaison Officer, Bilateral Affairs Officer, Office of Defense Cooperation, Madrid, Spain (1989-1991); Head, Amphibious Requirements Section, Operations Division, Headquarters, United States Marine Corps (1988-1989); Assistant Operations Officer (G-3), III Marine Amphibious Force, Japan (1985-1986); Head, Marine Air-Ground Task Force Concepts Section, Operations Division, Headquarters, United States Marine Corps (1986-1988); Operations Officer (S-3), Second Tank Battalion, United States Marine Corps (1980-1981); Company Commander, H&S Company, Second Tank Battalion, United States Marine Corps (1979-1980); Company Commander, C Company, Second Tank Battalion, United States Marine Corps (1978-1979); Logistics Officer (S-4), Second Tank Battalion, United States Marine Corps (1978); Company Commander, B Company, Third Motor Transport Battalion, United States Marine Corps (1973); Operations Officer (S-3), Third Motor Transport Battalion, United States Marine Corps (1972-1973); Tank Company Executive Officer, Battalion Assistant Operations Officer, Second Tank Battalion, United States Marine Corps (1971-1972); Tank Platoon Commander, Second Tank Battalion, United States Marine Corps (1970-1971) **CW:** Author, "German Heavy Fighting Vehicles of the Second World War: From Tiger to E-100," Fonthill Media (2018); Author, "M50 Ontos and M56 Scorpion 1956-70: US Tank Destroyers of the Vietnam War," Osprey Publishers, London, United Kingdom (2016); Author, "A European Anabasis: Western European Volunteers in the German Army and Waffen-SS, 1940-1945, Revised," Helion & Co. (2015); Author, "Super-heavy Tanks of World War II," Osprey Publishers, London, United Kingdom (2014); Author, "M103 Heavy Tank 1950-1974," Osprey Publishers, London, United Kingdom (2013); Author, "Into the Breach at Pusan: The 1st Provisional Marine Brigade in the Korean War," University of Oklahoma Press, Norman, Ohio (2012); Author, "U.S. Marines in Iraq. Vol. II 2004-2005: Into the Fray," History Division, U.S. Marine Corps, Washington, DC, Print (2011); Author, "U.S. Marines in Iraq. Vol. II 2004-2005: Into the Fray," History Division, U.S. Marine Corps, Washington, DC Online Text Only (2009); Compiler, Editor, "Guidebook for Marines,19th Edition," Marine Corps Association, Quantico, VA (2009); Editor, "The Marine Officer's Guide, Seventh Edition," USNI Press, Annapolis, MD (2008); Editor, "Handbook for Marine NCOs, Fifth Edition" USNI Press, Annapolis, MD (2008); Author, "US Army Soldier: Baghdad, 2003-2004," Osprey Publishers, London, United Kingdom (2007); Author, "US Marine Corps Tank Crewman 1941-45," Osprey Publishers, Pacific London, United Kingdom (2005); Editor, Co-author with Daniel Kowalsky, "The Spanish Civil War [History in Dispute, Volume 18]," St. James Press, Detroit, MI (2004); Co-author with Robert M. Neiman, "Tanks on the Beach: a Marine Tanker in the Pacific War," Texas A&M University Press, College Station, Texas (2003); Author, "A European Anabasis: Western European Volunteers in the German Army and Waffen-SS, 1940-1945," Columbia University Press (EPIC), NY (2003); Author, "Marines Under Armor: The Marine Corps and the Armored Fighting Vehicle, 1916-2000," USNI Press, Annapolis, MD (2000); Editor, "Handbook for Marine NCOs, Revised Edition" USNI Press, Annapolis, MD (2000); Editor, "The Marine Officer's Guide, Revised Edition," USNI Press, Annapolis, MD (2000); Editor, "The Marine Officer's Guide, Sixth Edition," USNI Press, Annapolis, MD (1995); Editor, "Handbook for Marine NCOs, Fourth Edition" USNI Press, Annapolis, MD (1995); Editor, "Handbook for Marine NCOs, Third Edition" USNI Press, Annapolis, MD (1988); Editor, "The Marine Officer's Guide, Fifth Edition," USNI Press, Annapolis, MD (1985); Author, 16 Books; Contributor, Articles **AW:** Gutenberg e-Prize, American Historical Association (2001); Third Place Award as Outstanding Navy ROTC Instructor, American Defense Preparedness Association (Now National Defense Industrial Association) (1983); European Academy Fellowship, Federal Republic of Germany (1982);

Decorated, Cruz de Merito (Naval) con Distinctivo Blanco Kingdom of Spain; Decorated, Defense Meritorious Service Medal; Decorated, Meritorious Service Medal **MEM:** United States Naval Institute; Society for Military History; United States Commission on Military History; American Historical Association **B/I:** Born in Seattle, WA, Dr. Estes was inspired to enter his profession because Seattle was still very much a Navy town in the 1950s and television reflected much of the country's militarism from the Cold War. There were series such as "West Point," "Men of Annapolis" and "Navy Log." The Navy's documentary series, "Victory at Sea," occupied prime time Sunday evenings. His father noticed this and one Navy Day took the family down to the Piers 90-91 of the Naval Supply Depot where the usual squadron of ships was conducting port call and holding open house to the public. Dr. Estes was amazed to see one of the largest aircraft carriers tied up at Pier 91 USS Midway. The tour was excellent, but he was enthralled by riding the aircraft elevators up and down and viewing the large number of aircraft still on board for the visit. This event set the hook in Dr. Estes and he thereafter read books, collected photos, built models and learned to carve 1:600 scale waterline ship models in wood of his favorite vessels as the model kits were too limited in their offerings. He visited ships and shipyards, writing to ships coming to port for special tours, such as the USS Seadragon, after becoming the third submarine to surface at the North Pole in 1962. One did not tour nuclear subs normally in those days. Dr. Estes applied for the NROTC and the Naval Academy in 1964, and received appointments to both, entering the United States Naval Academy in June 1965. In addition, he went to the Naval Academy to be a submariner and naval architect and came out a historian and a Marine. He thinks that this is one of the values of the American education because he was able to start out doing one thing and ended up doing another without being shoehorned into one particular direction. **THT:** Dr. Estes was satisfied with his sustained excellent performance as an officer, a scholar and a consultant.

ESTES, RONALD GENE, T: U.S. Representative from Kansas **I:** Government Administration/Government Relations/Government Services **DOB:** 07/19/1956 **PB:** Topeka **SC:** KS/USA **PT:** Billy Dale Estes; Mary Lou (Hendrickson) Estes **MS:** Married **SPN:** Susan Oliver Estes **CH:** Three Children **ED:** MBA, Tennessee Tech University College of Business (1983); BS in Civil Engineering, Tennessee Tech University (1978) **CT:** Certified, American Production and Inventory Control Society (Now APICS) **C:** Member, U.S. House of Representatives from Kansas' Fourth Congressional District (2017-Present); State Treasurer, State of Kansas (2011-2017); Treasurer, Sedgwick County, KS (2004-2010); Team Manager, Procter & Gamble, Jackson, TN (1979-1981); Member, Committee on Education and the Workforce; Member, Committee on Homeland Security; Member, Republican Study Committee; Management Information Consultant, Andersen Consultant, Nashville, TN; With, Koch Industries, Inc.; With, Bombardier Learjet **AW:** Named One of the Outstanding Young Men of America (1985) **MEM:** Chairman, Sectional 70, Alpha Phi Omega (1983-1985); Board of Directors, Tennessee Tech Alumni Association, Tennessee Tech University (1979-1981); American Production and Inventory Control Society (Now APICS); Tennessee Tech Alumni Association, Tennessee Tech University ; Alpha Phi Omega; Omicron Delta Kappa; The Honor Society of Phi Kappa Phi; Beta Gamma Sigma **AV:** Athletics **PA:** Republican **RE:** Methodist

ESTEVEZ, ELIA F., PHD, T: Mathematics Educator **I:** Education/Educational Services **DOB:** 02/02/1961 **PB:** Rio de Janeiro **SC:** Brazil **PT:** Benito Fernandez; Maria Tereza (Vidal) Fernandez **MS:** Married **SPN:** Jose Estevez (06/03/1984) **CH:** Adriana; Gabriel; Alexis **ED:** PhD in Mathematics Education, Columbia University (2005); MS, Columbia University (2002); MA, Hofstra University (1991); BS, Hofstra University (1988) **CT:** Certified Secondary Math Teacher with Bilingual Extension **C:** Math Teacher, Grades 7-12, Hempstead High School, NY (1992-Present); Math Teacher, Grades 7-12, Long Beach Public Schools, NY (1989-1991) **CR:** Summer Mathematics Teacher (1991-1993); Researcher, Hofstra University, Hempstead, NY (1991) **CW:** Compiled Questions from Regents and Translated to Spanish; E-Math, Took Algebra Translated in Spanish; Translated Curriculum to Spanish; Lesson Plan for Geometry Translated to Spanish **MH:** Albert Nelson Marquis Lifetime Achievement Award **B/I:** Dr. Estevez is the oldest of five children and when she was a child, her job was to help her siblings with their homework. When she came to the United States to study, her easiest subject was mathematics. She originally wanted to be an engineer, however English was difficult, so he pursued her education in teaching mathematics. **AV:** Travel; Writing; Reading; Dance

ETELAMAKI, SUSAN LOUISE SHELDRICK, BFA, T: Production Potter/Owner **I:** Fine Art **CN:** South Hill Pottery **DOB:** 03/25/1955 **PB:** Landstuhl **SC:** Germany **PT:** William Leroy Sheldrick, USAF Lieutenant Colonel (Ret.); Eileen May Courtois Sheldrick **MS:** Married **SPN:** Gordon Gene Etelamaki (06/11/1983) **CH:** Heather Sue Etelamaki; Heidi Tess Willard **ED:** BFA, University of Nebraska (1977); Diploma, (1973) **CT:** Teaching Certificate, Kansas (1986); Teaching Certificate, Nebraska (1977); **C:** Production Potter/Owner, South Hill Pottery; Fine Arts Teacher, Nebraska, K-12, NE (7 Years); Fine Arts Teacher, 3rd and 4th Grade Classroom Teacher in Axtell, Kansas (5 Years) **CIV:** Board Member, Chamber of Commerce **AW:** First Place, Blue Ribbon, Landscape Painting, Marshall County Fair, KS (2014); First Place, State DAR Poster Contest for "9/11" Celebration (2002); Honorable Mention, Paternayan Yarn Contest (1978); First Place, South Central Division Winner, Chapter Report, "400th Anniversary Mayflower Voyage and Settling of Plymouth Colony," DAR, **MEM:** Past Member, National Art Teachers Association; Daughters of the American Revolution (Now National Society Daughters of the American Revolution (NSDAR)) (32 Years); The Marysville Retailers Organization **AS:** Mrs. Etelamaki feels that one of the things that has helped her the most was getting into Girl Scouts. The scouting program was exciting, challenging, educational, and rewarding, all at the same time. She gained confidence in her abilities every time she tackled new tasks in the badge requirements and completed them successfully. She learned to work as a team in activities the troop did. She learned to work with people which helps her in her business. Mrs. Etelamaki's school teachers in junior high encouraged her to be the best she could be, reach for the stars and always face a challenge with confidence. Her parents have always been very supportive through her life and encouraged her in every undertaking. **B/I:** In junior high school, Mrs. Etelamaki had an interest in art and it turned into working in the arts in her junior and high school years. When she completed high school she attended the University of Nebraska, did their fine art programs and received her Bachelor's in Fine Arts. She started teaching fine arts at a rural school in North East Nebraska and taught there for seven years before she met her husband. He taught math and geometry in a

nearby school. They married and moved to Kansas where he got a teaching job in math and as there was no opening for her to teach art, she found an empty building that was available and turned that into her pottery studio. Kids would come to the studio for lessons and in 2015, she found another building in downtown Kansas. After its renovation she worked part-time there, eventually moving to full-time in 2018. She got into her profession because when she entered the University of Nebraska, she took classes in pottery and ceramic and she loved it from the first moment she was in the class. She was fascinated by it especially when she started using the potters wheel and when her pieces were fired she really thought hard on how she would glaze them. She loved to hear the "Ooh and Aah" responses from the people who surveyed her work. She got her own potter's wheel; she connected with a potter and would attend his weekend art shows. **AV:** Baking; Quilting; Painting (artwork); Crocheting; Knitting; Sewing; Most all kinds of crafts; Singing in the church choir; Helping with community service projects **RE:** Episcopalian **THT:** Mrs. Etelamaki hopes she has have been an inspiration to her daughters in their lives and showed them that they can do anything they put their minds to. She is so proud of all they have accomplished and the people they have become.

EVANS, DAVID LYNN, T: Founder, Chief Executive Officer **I:** Nonprofit & Philanthropy **CN:** Center for Global Reasoning **DOB:** 06/26/1941 **PB:** Red Oak **SC:** IA/USA **PT:** John Louis Evans; Margaret Alice (Young) Evans **MS:** Maried **SPN:** Mary Susan Ricke **CH:** John Louis Evans; Mary Lynn Evans; Sarah Leigh Evans; Michael Ricke Evans **ED:** MBA, University of Pennsylvania (1966); BS, Iowa State University (1964) **C:** Founder, Chief Executive Officer, Center for Global Reasoning (2015-Present); Director of Finance, Deere & Company (1966-1992); Vice President, General Manager, John Deere Information Systems; Executive Vice President, Chief Financial Officer, Rocky Mountain Internet; Vice President, Chief Financial Officer, Peak Internet; President, Chief Executive Officer, Evanwood Corporation; Manager, Chief Executive Officer, Rose Creek Ridge, LLC; Manager, Chief Executive Officer, Evans Bros., LLC **CR:** Board Member, Audit Committee Chair, Pearl Mutual Funds; Board Member, Audit Committee Chair, Data Transmission Network Corporation; Board Member, John Deere Receivables, Inc.; Board Member, John Deere Receivables, LLC **CIV:** Board Member, Various World Affairs Associations (1967-Present); Board Member, World Federalist Association (1970-1980); Founding Member, World Denver; Board Member, Colorado Foothills World Affairs Council; Chief Executive Officer, Writer, Blog, Center for Global Reasoning **CW:** Creator, Corporate Financial Simulation Model; Speaker, Seminars, Harvard Business School **MEM:** World Denver; Colorado Foothills World Affairs Association **MH:** Albert Nelson Marquis Lifetime Achievement Award; Marquis Who's Who Top Professional **AS:** Mr. Evans attributes his success to education, drive, and willingness to accept constructive criticism and luck. He feels that luck is of the utmost importance. **B/I:** Mr. Evans began his business career in high school when he created a spray painting business, which focused on painting farm buildings and homes. With income from his business, he began investing in the stock market at age 16. After college, which he paid for through his spray painting operation, he was recruited by the Deere & Company. After retiring, he was hired by Deere as a consultant to work in China. He also did consulting work in India. During his experiences abroad, he came to the idea of creating the non-profit, the Center for Global Reasoning. **AV:** Skiing; Practicing foreign affairs; Traveling **PA:** Independent **RE:** Presbyterian **THT:** Mr. Evans' thoughts on life center around the objectives of the Center for Global Reasoning. The Center for Global Reasoning focuses research on the greatest issues facing civilization. These include managing global warming, governing the planet when China becomes the dominant country, and reducing intolerance of all kinds.

EVANS, DWIGHT E., T: U.S. Representative from Pennsylvania **I:** Government Administration/Government Relations/Government Services **CN:** U.S. House of Representatives **DOB:** 05/16/1954 **PB:** Philadelphia **SC:** PA/USA **PT:** Henry Evans; Jean E. Odoms **ED:** Diploma, La Salle University (1975); Diploma, Community College of Philadelphia (1973) **C:** Member, U.S. House of Representatives from Pennsylvania's Second Congressional District (2016-Present); Chairperson, Democratic Appropriations Committee (1991-Present); Member, District 203, Pennsylvania House of Representatives (1981-2016); Member, Northwest Political Coalition and Pennsylvania Council of Neighborhoods; Member, City-wide Political Alliance; Vice Chairperson, Democratic County Executive Committee, PA; Former Elementary School Teacher; Former Counselor, Urban League Pennsylvania **CR:** Board of Directors, Pennsylvania Black Alliance for Educational Options; Board of Directors, National Black Alliance for Educational Options **CIV:** Board of Directors, American Diabetes Association; Board of Directors, Fox Chase Cancer Center, Temple University Health System Inc.; Board of Directors, Public School Employees' Retirement System; Board of Directors, Pennsylvania Convention Center and Visitors' Bureau; Board of Directors, The American National Red Cross, Pennsylvania **AW:** Distinguished Gentleman Award, African American Heritage Celebrations (1993); Outstanding Achievement Award, Pennsylvania Legal Service (1979, 1993); Service Award, Pennsylvania Child Care Association **AV:** Reading; Patron of the arts; Sports **PA:** Democrat **RE:** Baptist

EVANS, HAROLD RAY, I: Education/Educational Services **CN:** Musician, Educator **DOB:** 04/25/1926 **PB:** Altadena **SC:** CA/USA **PT:** William Edward; Vera (Stillings) E. **MS:** Married **SPN:** Donna Carsbeta (2017) **CH:** Diane (Deceased) **ED:** Student, Pasadena City College, 1942-48;Studied, Dick Shanahan Les Brown's Drummer, John Jacob CBS Studio staff, 1950 Percussionist **C:** Freelance Instructor of Percussion, San Diego, CA (1981-1990); Leader, Percussionist, Ray Evans Combo, Los Angeles, CA (1965-1981); Freelance Percussionist, Various Bands, Los Angeles, CA (1949-1965); Entertainer, Band Leader, Various Shows, Los Angeles, CA (1944) **CR:** With, Rumbleseat Rascals (1999, 2007); Performer and Teacher, Various Concerts, San Diego, CA (1990-1996, 1999); With, Walt Disney Studio Musicians John Lucas, Blues Blowers (1949-1965); With, Carl Hoffman's Orchestra **MIL:** 25th Division Band, 24th Regional Band Philippines-Japan Occupation, (1945-1947); Sergeant, U.S. Army (1944-1946); Swing Band **MEM:** Museum of Making Music (1998-2019); Lifetime Member, American Federation of Musicians; San Diego North County **MH:** Albert Nelson Marquis Lifetime Achievement Award **B/I:** Mr. Evans became involved in his profession due to a childhood interest in musical instruments, as well as the inspiration of his teacher, Mr. Stafford. **AV:** Photography; Music; Concerts **PA:** Democrat **RE:** Christian

EVANS, HARRY L. MD, T: Pathologist **I:** Medicine & Health Care **DOB:** 06/11/1948 **PB:** Mobile **SC:** AL/USA **PT:** Aurelius A. Evans; Anne (Hatha-

way) Evans **MS:** Divorced **SPN:** Cheryl J. Winfrey (06/06/1970, Divorced 1990) **CH:** Thomas H.; Sarah S. **ED:** MD, University of Florida (1974); BS, Stetson University (1970) **CT:** Diplomate, American Board of Pathology **C:** Clinical Professor, The University of Texas MD Anderson Cancer Center (2010-Present); Professor, The University of Texas MD Anderson Cancer Center (1990-2010); Associate Professor, The University of Texas MD Anderson Cancer Center (1982-1990); Assistant Professor, Pathology, The University of Texas MD Anderson Cancer Center (1978-1982); Fellow in Dermatopathology, Mayo Clinic, Rochester, MN (1977-1978); Fellow in Pathology, The University of Texas MD Anderson Cancer Center (1975-1977); Resident in Pathology, Vanderbilt University Medical Center, Nashville, TN (1974-1975) **CW:** Contributor, Articles, Medical Journals **AW:** Houston Pathology Society Award **MH:** Albert Nelson Marquis Lifetime Achievement Award **AV:** Mountain climbing; Appreciating music; Finishing crossword puzzles

EVERETT, PAUL, T: President, Owner **I:** Business Management/Business Services **CN:** Sabir General Services **PT:** Jimmy Brooks Sr.; Hester Liza Johnson **ED:** AS, Trinity Valley Community College, Athens, TX (1994) **C:** Chief Executive Officer, President, Owner, Sabir General Services (2008-Present) **CIV:** Volunteer, Fathers Flannigans Boys Home; Volunteer, St. Josephs Indian School; Kids Wish Network **AS:** Mr. Everett attributes his success to quality service. Word of mouth can go very far in a business. **B/I:** From a young age Mr. Everett watched his father and was infatuated with seeing him in a suit and with a briefcase. He wanted that for himself one day. **THT:** If we don't know, then we know who does.

EVERS, ANTHONY, "TONY" STEVEN, T: Governor of Wisconsin **I:** Government Administration/Government Relations/Government Services **DOB:** 11/05/1951 **PB:** Plymouth **SC:** WI/USA **MS:** Married **SPN:** Kathy Evers **CH:** Three Children **ED:** PhD, University of Wisconsin-Madison (1986); MA, University of Wisconsin-Madison (1976); BA, University of Wisconsin-Madison (1973) **C:** Governor, State of Wisconsin (2019-Present); State Superintendent of Public Instruction, Wisconsin Department of Public Instruction (2009-2019); Deputy State Superintendent, Wisconsin Department of Public Instruction, Madison, WI (2001-2009); Chief Administrative Officer, Cooperative Educational Service Agency 6 (CESA 6), Oshkosh, WI (1992-2000); Superintendent, Verona Area School District and School District of Oakfield; Teacher, Tomah, WI **MEM:** President, Deputy State Superintendent Leadership Commission, Council of Chief State School Officers (CCSSO); Council of Chief State School Officers (CCSSO) **PA:** Democrat

EVERT, CHRIS, T: Former Professional Tennis Player **I:** Athletics **DOB:** 12/21/1954 **PB:** Fort Lauderdale **SC:** FL/USA **PT:** James Evert; Colette Evert **MS:** Married **SPN:** Greg Norman (2008); Andy Mill (07/30/1988, Divorced 2006); John Lloyd (04/17/1979, Divorced 1987) **CH:** Alexander James; Nicholas Joseph; Colton Jack **C:** Owner, Evert Enterprises/IMG, Boca Raton, FL (1989-Present); Olympics Commentator, CBS Sports (1992); Professional Tennis Player (1972-1989) **CR:** Host and Organizer, Chris Evert Pro-Celebrity Tennis Classic (1989, 1990, 1992, 1993, 1994, 1995, 1996, 1997, 1998, 1999); Commentator, NBC Sports Tennis Events; Corporate Spokesperson and Representative; Special Advisor to U.S. National Tennis Team, USTA; Board of Directors, International Tennis Hall of Fame (ITHF); Trustee, Women's Sports Foundation **CIV:** Founder, Chris Evert Charities, Inc.; Healthy Start **AW:** Named to Tennis Channel

Top 100 of All Time, Special Merit from the International Tennis Hall of Fame (2013); Inductee, International Tennis Hall of Fame (ITHF) (1995); Inductee, Madison Square Garden Walk of Fame (1993); Providencia Award, Palm Beach County Convention and Visitors Bureau (1991); Flo Hyman Award, Women's Sports Foundation (1990); Named One of the Top 10 Romantic People of 1989, Korbel (1989); Winner, European Women's Open, Geneva (1987); Winner, Eckerd Open (1987); Player Service Award, Women's Tennis Association (1981, 1986, 1987); Winner, Virginia Slims (1972, 1973, 1975, 1977, 1987); Winner, French Open Singles (1974, 1975, 1979, 1980, 1983, 1985, 1986); Named Greatest Woman Athlete of the Last 25 Years, Women's Sports Foundation (1985); Winner, Australian Open (1982, 1984); Winner, U.S. Open (1975, 1976, 1977, 1978, 1980, 1982); Winner, Wimbledon Singles (1974, 1976, 1981); Named Female Athlete of Year, The Associated Press (1974, 1975, 1977, 1980); Sportmanship Award, Women's Tennis Association (1979); Winner, Doubles (1976); Named Athlete of the Year, Sports Illustrated (1976); Top Women's Singles Player Award, U.S. Lawn Tennis Association (1974); LeBair Sportsmanship Trophy (1971); Winner, U.S. Junior Championship (1970, 1971); Winner, Numerous Tournaments **MEM:** U.S. Lawn Tennis Association; National Honor Society; Board of Directors, Florida Sports Foundation; President, Women's Tennis Association; Executive Committee, Women's Tennis Association

EYBERG, SHEILA MAXINE, PHD, T: Psychology Educator **I:** Medicine & Health Care **CN:** PCIT International **DOB:** 12/31/1944 **PB:** Omaha **SC:** NE/USA **PT:** Clarence George Eyberg; Geraldine Elizabeth (Gilbert) Eyberg **MS:** Divorced **SPN:** John Richard Graham-Pole (11/10/1985) **CH:** George; Katherine **ED:** PhD in Clinical Psychology, University of Oregon, Eugene, OR (1972); MA in Psychology, University of Oregon, Eugene, OR (1970); BA in Psychology, University of Nebraska Omaha (1967) **CT:** Diplomate in Clinical Child and Adolescent Psychology, American Board of Clinical Child and Adolescent Psychology (2003); Diplomate in Clinical Psychology, American Board of Professional Psychology (1996); Licensed Psychologist, Florida State Board of Psychological Examiners (1985); National Register of Health Service Providers (Now National Register of Health Service Psychologists) (1978); Licensed Psychologist, Oregon State Board of Psychologist Examiners (1974); Master Trainer, Parent-Child Interaction Therapy International (PCIT International) **C:** Distinguished Professor Emerita, University of Florida, Gainesville, FL (2011-Present); Distinguished Professor, University of Florida, Gainesville, FL (2005-2011); Affiliate Professor in Psychology, University of Florida, Gainesville, FL (1988-2011); Affiliate Professor in Pediatrics, University of Florida, Gainesville, FL (1987-2011); Associated Chair for Research, Department of Clinical and Health Psychology, University of Florida (2003-2007); University of Florida Foundation Research Professor (2003-2006); Professor of Clinical and Health Psychology, University of Florida, Gainesville, FL (1985-2005); Visiting Associate Professor of Clinical Psychology, University of Florida, Gainesville, FL (1984-1985); Associate Professor, Medical Psychology, Oregon Health & Science University, Portland, OR (1981-1985); Assistant Professor, Medical Psychology, Oregon Health & Science University, Portland, OR (1974-1981) **CR:** Professor, Introduction to Research in Psychology, University of Florida (1989-Present); Professor, Advanced Parent-Child Interaction Therapy, University of Florida (2008-2011); Professor, Parent-Child Interaction Therapy: Theory, Research, and Practice, University of Florida (2000-2011); Professor, Doctoral Research, University of Florida (1986-2011); Professor, Independent Research, University of Florida (1986-2011); Professor, Child Practicum, University of Florida (1985-2011); Professor, Lifespan Psychopathology, University of Florida (2010); Professor, Child Psychotherapy: Theory, Research, and Practice, University of Florida (1992-2000); Teacher, Advanced Child Psychotherapy, Department of Clinical & Health Psychology, University of Florida (1985-1991); Professor, Seminar in Pediatric Psychology, University of Florida (1988-1990); Professor, Psychological Assessment of Children, University of Florida (1986); Professor, Medical Psychology, Oregon Health & Science University School of Medicine (1982-1985); Professor, Child Health, Oregon Health & Science University School of Medicine (1973-1985); Professor, Developmental Psychology, Oregon Health & Science University School of Nursing **CIV:** Parent-Child Interaction Therapy International (PCIT International) **CW:** Editorial Board, Journal of Pediatric Psychology (1977-Present); Editorial Board, Child & Family Behavior Therapy (2000-2015); Editorial Board, Journal of Clinical Child and Adolescent Psychology (2010-2013); Editorial Board, Clinical Child Psychology and Psychiatry (1995-2013); Editorial Board, Vulnerable Children and Youth Studies (2005-2011); Editorial Board, Clinical Child and Family Psychology Review (1997-2010); Editorial Board, Journal of Consulting and Clinical Psychology (2003-2008); Editorial Board, Journal of Clinical Child and Adolescent Psychology (1982-2007); Editorial Board, Clinical Psychology: Science and Practice (1994-2005); Editorial Board, Behavior Therapy (1998-2000); Current Literature Contributor, Ambulatory Child Health (1997-1998); Associate Editor, Behavior Therapy (1995-1998); Associate Editor, Journal of Clinical Child Psychology (1992-1996); Editorial Advisory Board, Handbook of Pediatric Psychology (1988); Reviewer, Journal of Consulting and Clinical Psychology; Reviewer, Journal of Abnormal Child Psychology; Reviewer, Journal of Clinical Child and Adolescent Psychology; Reviewer, Psychological Assessment; Developer, Parent-Child Interaction Therapy; Founder, Parent-Child Interaction Therapy International; Author, Parent-Child Interaction Therapy Manual for Research and Training; Author, Dyadic Parent-Child Interaction Coding System; Author, Eyberg Child Behavior Inventory; Author, Sutter-Eyberg School Behavior Inventory; Author, Therapy Attitude Inventory; Author, Revised Edition of the School Observation Coding System; Contributor, Numerous Articles to Professional Journals **AW:** William N. Friedrich Memorial Lecture Award, Mayo Clinic (2011); Trailblazer Award, Association for Behavioral and Cognitive Therapies (ABCT) (2009); Nicholas Hobbs Award, Society for Child and Family Policy and Practice (2008); Distinguished Career Award, Society for Clinical Child and Adolescent Psychology (2008); Lee Salk Award for Distinguished Service to Pediatric Psychology (2002); Distinguished Contributions to Education and Training Award, American Psychological Association (2007); Regent's Scholar, University of Nebraska Omaha (1964-1967); Research Award, Atlantic Coast Social Behavioral and Economic Sciences Alliance (AC-SBE); Diplomate in Clinical Psychology; Grant Recipient, National Institute of Mental Health and Others25306 **MEM:** President, Parent-Child Interaction Therapy International (PCIT International) (2009); President, Society for Child and Family Policy and Practice (2001); President, Southeastern Psychological Association (2000); President, Society of Pediatric Psychology (1987); President, Society of Clinical Child and Adolescent Psychology (1987); Executive Committee, Society of Clinical Psychology; Fellow, American Psycho-

logical Association (1984); Portland Athletic Club; Heritage Club; Alpha Lambda Delta; The Honor Society of Phi Kappa Phi **MH:** Albert Nelson Marquis Lifetime Achievement Award; Who's Who in American Colleges and Universities; Marquis Who's Who in the West; Marquis Who's Who of American Women; Who's Who in the Biobehavioral Sciences; Marquis Who's Who in the South and Southwest; Marquis Who's Who of Emerging Leaders in America; Marquis Who's Who Among Human Service Professionals; Marquis Who's Who in American Education; Who's Who in Science and Engineering; Marquis Who's Who in Medicine and Healthcare **AS:** Dr. Eyberg attributes his success to unconditional positive regard from his parents. **B/I:** Dr. Eyberg became involved in his profession by being a "counselor" to his friends when growing up; it was personally rewarding. **AV:** Tennis; Skiing; Swimming; Running; Photography; Leisure travel **PA:** Democrat **RE:** Religious Science

EYO, IKEMESIT, "KEM" A., T: Senior Associate Attorney **I:** Law and Legal Services **CN:** Waggoner Hastings LLC **ED:** JD, Georgia State University College of Law (2006); MPA, Georgia State University (2006); MHA, Tulane University (1998); BS in Mathematical Science, Clemson University (1995) **C:** Associate Attorney, Waggoner Hastings LLC (2015-Present); Associate Attorney, Warner, Bates, McGinnis & Portnoy, PC (Now Warner Bates) (2013-2014); Solo Practitioner, The Law Office of Kem Eyo, LLC (2007-2013); Legal Department Manager, Community Management Associates, Inc. (CMA) (2005-2006); Program Specialist, Georgia Department of Community Health (2000-2004) **CIV:** Pro Bono Work, Atlanta Bar Association **AW:** Named, Excellence in Family and Divorce, Lawyers of Distinction (2017-2019); 10 Best Client Satisfaction Award, American Institute of Family Law Attorneys (2016-2019); Named One of the Top 30 National Academy of Family Law Attorneys (2016-2019); Named to 2018 Lawyers of Distinction (2018); Named Top Lawyer, The Global Directory of Who's Who (2016); Named One of the Top 10 Under 40, National Academy of Family Law Attorneys (2015) **MEM:** State Bar of Georgia; Family Law Section, Atlanta Bar Association; Family Law Section, Cobb County Bar Association; Family Law Section, Georgia Association of Black Woman Attorneys (GABWA); Georgia Association for Women Lawyers (GAWL) **BAR:** United States District Court for the Northern District of Georgia (2008); Court of Appeals of Georgia (2006); Georgia Supreme Court (2006); Georgia (2006) **AS:** Ms. Eyo attributes her success to drive. She is a first-generation American; both her parents came to this country for education. Her father passed away when she was 10, and her mother had to take care of three kids, while a full-time student working on her PhD and working full-time. Somehow, she did it; both her sisters are doctors. Her mother taught her through example how to keep working and striving to excel and achieve. **B/I:** When Ms. Eyo was in college, she had a couple of male friends who were treated poorly by the legal system and she felt that it was the fact that they were males. She didn't like that; she felt there should be less of a focus on the gender of a parent and more of a focus on the quality of a parent. She thought that the better way of trying to make a difference in how that works was to be part of the ones making a decision in how it worked. **THT:** Ms. Eyo lives by the motto, "Reach for the moon, that way if you fail, you will be among the stars."

EYSTER, JOHN W., T: Adjunct Professor **I:** Education/Educational Services **DOB:** 10/12/1940 **PB:** Lake Geneva **SC:** OH/USA **PT:** Walter C.; Bessie Eva (Adlard) E. **MS:** Married **SPN:** Marilyn M.

Philpott (06/04/1965) **CH:** Beth Kari; Mark Erik **ED:** Master of Arts, in Educational Administration, University of Wisconsin-Madison (1979); Master of Arts in Teaching and History, University of Wisconsin, Whitewater, WI (1971); Master of Divinity in Theology, Wesley Theological Seminary (1966); Bachelor of Arts in International Relations, American University (1962) **CT:** Minister, United Church of Christ (1984); Elder, United Church of Christ (1966); Ordained Deacon, United Church of Christ (1963) **C:** Lecturer, University of Wisconsin, Waukesha, WI (2006-2011); Legislator Liaison, School District of Janesville, Wisconsin (2000-2008); Lecturer, University of Wisconsin, College Systems, Rock County Campus, Wisconsin (2003-2006); Chairman, Social Studies Department, Parker High School, Janesville, WI (1986-2000); Social Studies Teacher, Parker High School, Janesville, WI (1971-2000); Pastor, Hebron United Methodist Church, Fort Atkinson, WI (1968-1971) **CR:** Teacher, Wisconsin Virtual School (2005-2010); Consultant, Advanced Placement, Government and Politics, Midwest Region College Board, Evanston, IL (1976-2006); Democracy Education Curriculum Committee, Wisconsin Department of Public Instruction (2000-2005); Reader, Advanced Placement Government and Politics Exam Educational Testing Services (1987-2004); Developer, Educational Program, Washington Seminar, Civics Education Task Force (1998-2000); Tentmaker, Pastor, Emerald Grove Church, United Church of Christ (1973-1995); Speaker in Field; Lecturer In Field **CIV:** Advisory Council, Wisconsin Advanced Placement **CW:** Co-author, "Roads to Learning" (1977); Co-author, Curriculum Book, "Profiles of Promise #7 - Integrated Social Studies" (1972) **AW:** Featured, Profile, Salute to American Teachers, Disney Channel (1993); Fellow, Kohl Educational Foundation (1991); Outstanding Social Studies Program, Wisconsin Council for Social Studies (1990); Outstanding Teacher, Beloit College (1988); Named, Outstanding U.S. History Teacher, National Society of Daughters of Colonial Wars (1981); Valley Forge Teacher's Medal, Freedoms Foundation (1978) **MEM:** Wisconsin Alliance for Excellent Schools; Sons of Norway **MH:** Albert Nelson Marquis Lifetime Achievement Award **AV:** Running; Cross country skiing; Reading; Writing **PA:** United Church of Christ **RE:** Christian

FACEY, LA-TOYA, T: Franchise Owner, Entrepreneur, Instructional Facilitator, Author **I:** Business Management/Business Services **CN:** Bodytek Pembroke Pines LLC **DOB:** 05/20/1983 **PB:** Brooklyn **SC:** NY/USA **MS:** Married **SPN:** David Walker (6/13/2020) **CH:** Two Daughters **ED:** EdD in Educational Leadership and Administration, University of Phoenix (2020); Master's Degree in Elementary Education, Florida Memorial University (2008); Bachelor's Degree in Elementary Education and Reading, Florida Memorial University (2005) **CT:** Certification in Educational Leadership, State of Florida **C:** Franchise Owner, Entrepreneur, Instructional Facilitator, Bodytek Pembroke Pines LLC (2019-Present); Professional Development Specialist, School Board of Broward County (2018-Present); Master Coach, Office of Talent Development, School Board of Broward County (2015-Present); Instructional Facilitator, Student Services, School Board of Broward County (2015); Literacy Coach, Walker Elementary School, School Board of Broward County (2011-2015); Educator, Fairway Elementary School, School Board of Broward County (2005-2011) **CR:** Owner, Facey's Foster Home (2010-Present); Author **CIV:** Mentor, Coach, Cambell Foster Home **CW:** Author, "Brielle-Elaine Tries to Fit In!" (2011) **MEM:** Alpha Kappa Alpha **MH:** Marquis Who's Who Top Professional **AS:** Ms. Facey attributes her success to her mother; she was a single mother, working multiple jobs to ensure both Ms. Facey and her sister had everything they needed. Education was always at the forefront. Ms. Facey had to go to school and do well, as it was her mother's highest expectation. Without her encouragement, she wouldn't be where she is today. **B/I:** Ms. Facey wanted to make a difference in the school system. She has always been motivated to help students struggling with academics

FAIRBANK, RICHARD D., T: Chief Executive Officer, Chairperson **I:** Financial Services **CN:** Capital One Financial Corporation **DOB:** 09/19/1950 **ED:** Master of Business Administration, Stanford University (1981); Bachelor of Arts in Economics, Stanford University (1972) **C:** Chairperson, Chief Executive Officer, Founder, Capital One Bank USA NA (2008-Present); Chairperson, President, Chief Executive Officer, Capital One Financial Corporation, McLean, VA (2003-Present); Chairperson, US Region, MasterCard, Inc. (2002-2004); Chairperson, Chief Executive Officer, Capital One Financial Corp., McLean, VA (1994-2003); Consultant, Strategic Planning Associates (1981-1987) **CR:** Board of Directors, MasterCard International Global Board (2004-Present); Board of Directors, MasterCard US Region (1995-2004) **AW:** Business Leader of the Year, "Washingtonian"; Best Chief Executive Officer, "Institutional Investor"

FAKHOURY, RAMI, T: Managing Director **I:** Law and Legal Services **CN:** Fakhoury Global Immigration **MS:** Married **SPN:** Carmen Saleh Fakhoury **CH:** Three Children **ED:** JD in International Law, Michigan State University College of Law, East Lansing, MI, Cum Laude (1993); BS in Finance and Business Economics, Wayne State University, Detroit, MI (1989) **C:** Founder, Managing Director, Fakhoury Global Immigration, USA PC (1997-Present) **CIV:** Co-Founder, Board Member, Global Detroit; Board of Directors, Informal Legal Counsel, FBI Citizens Academy; Save the Children; Sarah's House; Wounded Veterans; Alke-Bulan Village; Abel Ogundokun Odeleye Foundation **CW:** Author, Immigration Law Book, "The PERM Book, 3rd Edition" (2018); Editor, "The Consular Posts Book" (2015-2016); Author, "The Immigration Practitioner's Guide to U.S. Export Control Regulations" (2011); Editor, "USCIS Immigration Procedures and U.S. State Department Consular Processes" (2009); Organizer, Informational Sessions and Webinars for Businesses, Universities, and Other Stakeholders Worldwide; Presenter, American Immigration Lawyers Association (AILA); Contributor, Hundreds of Policy Articles, Professional and Trade Group Presentations and White Papers **AW:** Thought Leader, Who's Who Legal - Corporate Immigration (2019-2020); Top Lawyers in Metro Detroit, dBusiness Magazine (2011-2014, 2017-2020); SuperLawyers (2014-2020); Martindale Hubbell AV Preeminent Attorney (2014-2020); Most Honored Professionals - Top 1%, American Registry (2019); dBusiness, Top Attorney in Michigan (2019); Leading Lawyer and Equity Member, Alliance of Business Immigration Lawyers (2018); dBusiness Top Lawyer Hall of Fame (2017); Global Detroit Champion Award, Global Detroit (2016) **MEM:** International Law Section, State Bar of Michigan; Immigration Law Committee, International Business Association; Centre of International Legal Studies, Salzburg, Austria; Alliance of Business Immigration Lawyers; American Immigration Lawyers Association; Economic Club of Detroit; Detroit Chamber of Commerce; Global Detroit **BAR:** State Bar of Michigan (1994); U.S. District Court for the Eastern District of Michigan (1994) **MH:** Who's Who International for Corporate Immigration **AS:** Mr. Fakhoury attributes his success to

believing that "if you focus on what you are passionate about, it creates a wonderful momentum and it is not just a career...it is a lifelong commitment." He also enjoys directing his business and in helping people in numerous ways. His passionate dedication to his clients and his commitment to his staff is what keeps him and his firm going. **B/I:** Mr. Fakhoury became involved in his profession because he is an immigrant himself. He was born in Jordan and relocated to the United States when he was two months old. He grew up in various immigrant communities. Mr. Fakhoury feels that the United States is the one country where peoples' aspirations have the greatest chance of success. In his view, helping America to seek and retain the best and brightest people in the world is an act of true patriotism. He also feels it is a win-win because "skilled and enterprising individuals can make better lives for themselves here in the U.S., and the nation enjoys the economic benefits of their talent and ambition." Immigrants, Mr. Fakhoury says, "contribute considerably to keeping America on the cutting edge - in my home state of Michigan, immigrants create more new businesses than U.S. citizens. We are the greatest melting pot in the world and it has made us a much more resilient country and society." **AV:** Travel; Squash; Hiking; Reading; Concerts **THT:** The greatest good you can do for yourself is to serve the needs of others. There is nothing so satisfying as knowing that you have helped other people to realize their dreams.

FALCK, FRANCIS, MD, PHD, MS, T: Eye Surgeon **I:** Medicine & Health Care **CN:** Falck Eye Center, LLC **DOB:** 02/13/1951 **SC:** RI/USA **MS:** Married **CH:** Two Children **ED:** Fellowship in Anterior Segment Eye Surgery & Glaucoma, University of Michigan (1992); Residency in Ophthalmology, University of Rochester (1991); MD, University of Connecticut (1986); PhD in Public Health, University of Michigan (1982); MPH in Public Health, University of Michigan (1982) **C:** Ophthalmologist, Falck Eye Centers LLC (1991-Present); Chief Executive Officer, Falck Medical Incorporated, Mystic, CT **CIV:** Founder, Community Glaucoma Screening Program, Hartford, CT (1999-Present) **AW:** Man of the Year in Medicine, World Forum, Cambridge University (2010) **MEM:** American Academy of Ophthalmology; Connecticut Society of Eye Physicians and Surgeons **AS:** Dr. Falck attributes his success to perseverance. He believes that is what it takes to overcome any obstacle in one's way. He says, "There will always be something that will test your commitment, but it is important to persevere." **B/I:** Dr. Falck believes that vision is the most precious sense in the world. Sight keeps individuals connected to the world so that society can continue to appreciate the beauty around it. When choosing a profession, he knew that he wanted to do something worthwhile, which drew him to ophthalmology.

FALDO, NICK, T: Professional Golfer **I:** Athletics **DOB:** 07/18/1957 **PB:** Hertfordshire **SC:** England **MS:** Married **SPN:** Valerie Faldo **CH:** Natalie; Matthew; Georgia; Emma **C:** Professional Golfer, PGA (1976-Present); Captain, European Ryder Cup Team (2008); Member, World Cup Team (1977, 1991, 1998); Member, European Ryder Cup Team (1977, 1979, 1981, 1983, 1985, 1987, 1989, 1991, 1993, 1995, 1997); Member, Dunhill Cup Team (1985, 1986, 1987, 1988, 1991, 1993); Member, Four Tours Championship Team (1990); Member, Kirin Cup Team (1987); Member, Nissan Cup Team (1986); Member, Hennessy Cognac Cup Team (1978, 1980, 1982, 1984) **AW:** Payne Stewart Award (2014); Knight Bachelor (2009); Winner,

UBS Cup (2001, 2002, 2003); Member of the British Empire (1998); Winner, Nissan Open (1997); Elected, World Golf Hall of Fame (1997); Winner, Masters Tournament (1989, 1990, 1996); Winner, Doral/Ryder Open (1995); Winner, Alfred Dunhill Open (1994); Winner, Johnnie Walker Classic (1990, 1993); Winner, Carroll's Irish Open (1991, 1992, 1993); Leading Money Winner, European Tour (1983, 1992); Winner, Scandinavian Masters (1992); Winner, GA European Open (1992); Winner, Toyota World Matchplay (1992); Winner, British Open (1987, 1990, 1992); PGA Player of the Year (1990); Suntory World Match Play (1989, 1990); Winner, Open de France (1983, 1988, 1989); Winner, Volvo PGA Championship (1989); Winner, Dunhill British Masters (1989); BBC Sports Personality of the Year (1989); Winner, Volvo Masters (1988); Winner, Spanish Open (1987); Winner, Car Care Plan International (1983, 1984); Winner, Sza Pines Heritage Classic (1984); Winner, Martini International (1983); Winner, Lawrence Batley International (1983); Winner, Ebel European Masters Swiss Open (1983); Winner, Haig Whiskey TPC (1982); Winner, British PGA Championship (1978, 1980, 1981); Winner, ICL Tournament (1979); Winner, Skol Laeger Individual (1977); European Rookie of the Year (1977); Winner, British Youths Amateur Championship (1975); Winner, English Amateur Championship (1975)

FALK, JAMES ROBERT, PHD, T: President **DOB:** 05/31/1952 **PB:** New York **SC:** NY/USA **PT:** Arthur E. Falk; Ruth A. Falk **MS:** Married **SPN:** Karen V. Falk **CH:** Kathleen Anne; Kevin James **ED:** PhD, Fordham University (1980); MA, Fordham University (1976); BS, Fordham University (1974) **C:** President and Principal Consultant, Comstat Research Corporation (2015-Present); Senior Systems Analyst, Davis Polk & Wardwell LLP (1989-2015); Vice President, Lopez & Associates, Inc. (1987-1989); Research Analyst, Mocatta Corporation (1986-1987); Instructor of Computer Programming, Concentric Associates (1984-1985); Research Psychologist, Cornell University Medical College, New York Hospital (Now NewYork-Presbyterian Hospital), White Plains, NY (1980-1983); Adjunct Instructor of Psychology, Mercy College (1975-1983); Research Psychologist, Gould Inc., Simulation Systems Division, NY (1979-1980); Research Assistant in Psychology, New York State Psychiatric Institute and Columbia Presbyterian Hospital (Now NewYork-Presbyterian Hospital) (1977); Research Assistant in Psychology, Fordham University (1975-1977); Electronics Consultant, Psychological Research, New York University Medical Center, NYU Langone Health (1972-1974); Adjunct Instructor of Psychology, Marymount College (Now Marymount University); Adjunct Instructor of Psychology, Fordham University **CIV:** Knights of Columbus **CW:** Contributor, Articles to Professional Journals **AW:** Fordham University Loyola Fellow **MEM:** American Psychological Association; American Association for the Advancement of Science; The New York Academy Sciences; Sigma Xi, The Scientific Research Honor Society; American Computer Machinery Organization (Now ACM, Inc.) **MH:** Albert Nelson Marquis Lifetime Achievement Award; Marquis Who's Who Top Professional **B/I:** Dr. James Falk received his Doctorate in Psychology. He started out as an Experimental Psychologist, performing human factors engineering for an aerospace company and that gave him an opportunity to move on to clinical research at Cornell University Medical College. Shortly from there, he went into consulting, performing data analysis and statistical work on research projects. He became an instructor at AT&T Technicians, teaching them how to program. Ultimately, he stayed in computers. He went back into being a research psychologist for Lopez and Associates, an organizational and psychology company. His main world there was developing computer software for psychological assessments. From there, he went to Davis Polk as a Senior Systems Analyst, which was all computer work, writing software to do various things. He retired around 2015 and then reactivated his own project, Comstat, a consulting firm performing data analysis and computer programming. **AV:** Sailing; Traveling

FALK, THOMAS J., T: Executive Chairman **I:** Manufacturing **CN:** Kimberly-Clark Corporation **PB:** Waterloo **SC:** IA/USA **MS:** Married **SPN:** Karen Falk **CH:** One Child **ED:** MS in Management, Stanford University (1988); Bachelor in Accounting, University of Wisconsin (1980) **C:** Executive Chairman, Kimberly-Clark Corporation, Texas (2003-Present); Chief Executive Officer, Kimberly-Clark Corporation, Texas (2002-2019); Board of Directors, Kimberly-Clark Corporation, Texas (1999-Present); Chief Operating Officer, Kimberly-Clark Corporation (1999-2002); President, Kimberly-Clark Corporation (1999-2003); Group President, Global Tissue, Pulp and Paper, Kimberly-Clark Corporation (1998-1999); Group President, North America Consumer Products, Kimberly-Clark Corporation (1995); Group President Infant and Child Care, Kimberly-Clark Corporation (1993); Senior Vice President Analysis and Administration, Kimberly-Clark Corporation (1991); Vice President of Operations Analysis and Control, Kimberly-Clark Corporation (1990); Operations Manager of Infant Care, Diaper Plant, Kimberly-Clark Corporation, Beech Island, SC (1989); Director of Corporate Strategic Analysis, Kimberly-Clark Corporation (1987); Senior Financial Analyst, Kimberly-Clark Corporation (1986); Senior Auditor, Kimberly-Clark Corp. (1984); With, Internal Audit Staff, Kimberly-Clark Corporation, Neenah, WI (1983); With, Alexander Grant & Co. **CR:** Board of Directors, Centex Corporation (2003-Present); Grocery Manufacturers America, Inc.; Dallas Regional Advisory Board, JP Morgan Chase; Member, Board of Directors, Catalyst, University of Wisconsin Foundation; Centex Corporation **CIV:** Board of Governors, Boys & Girls Clubs of America; Board of Directors, University of Wisconsin Foundation **AW:** Sloan Fellow, Stanford University Graduate School of Business (1988)

FALLON, JIMMY, T: Talk Show Host, Actor **I:** Media & Entertainment **DOB:** 09/19/1974 **PB:** New York **SC:** NY/USA **PT:** James W. Fallon; Gloria (Feeley) Fallon **MS:** Married **SPN:** Nancy Juvonen (12/22/2007) **CH:** Winnie Rose; Frances Cole **ED:** Bachelor of Arts in Communications, The College of Saint Rose, Albany, NY (2009) **C:** Television Personality (1998-Present) **CW:** Host, The Tonight Show Starring Jimmy Fallon (2014-Present); Host, 74th Golden Globe Awards (2017); Actor, "May & Marty" (2016); Actor, "Popstar: Never Stop Never Stopping" (2016); Actor, "Get Hard" (2015); Actor, "Ted 2" (2015); Actor, "Jurassic World" (2015); Actor, "Jem and the Holograms" (2015); Actor, "Lip Sync Battle" (2015); Actor, "Louie" (2015); Actor, "The Spoils Before Dying" (2015); Actor, "The Jim Gaffigan Show" (2015); Author, "Your Baby's First Word Will Be DADA" (2015); Host, "Late Night with Jimmy Fallon" (2009-2014); Host, "Saturday Night Live" (2013); Executive Producer, Writer, Creator, "Guys With Kids" (2012-2013); Performer, "Blow Your Pants Off" (2012); Voice Actor, "Rise of the Guardians" (2012); Author, "Thank You Notes 2" (2012); Actor, "30 Rock" (2009-2012); Actor, "Bucky Larson: Born to Be a Star" (2011); Author, "Thank You Notes" (2011); Host, 62nd Primetime Emmy Awards (2010); Voice Actor, "Arthur 3: The War of the Two Worlds" (2010); Actor, "Whip It" (2009); Voice Actor, "Arthur and the Revenge of Malt-

azard" (2009); Actor, "Gossip Girl" (2009); Voice Actor, "Family Guy" (2009); Actor, "The Year of Getting to Know Us" (2008); Voice Actor, "Doogal" (2006); Voice Actor, "Arthur and the Invisibles" (2006); Actor, "Factory Girl" (2006); Actor, "Fever Pitch" (2005); Author, "Snowball Fight" (2005); Host, MTV Movie Awards (2005); Actor, "Taxi" (2004); Actor, "Saturday Night Live" (1998-2004); Performer, "The Bathroom Wall" (2003); Actor, "Anything Else" (2003); Actor, "The Entrepreneurs" (2003); Host, MTV Video Music Awards (2002); Co-host, MTV Movie Awards (2001); Actor, "Band of Brothers" (2001); Actor, "Almost Famous" (2000); Co-author, with Gloria Fallon, "I Hate This Place: The Pessimist's Guide to Life" (1999); Actor, "Spin City" (1998) **AW:** People's Choice Award for Favorite Late Night Talk Show Host (2013-2017); Favorite Late Night Talk Show Host, People's Choice Awards (2016); Favorite Late Night Talk Show Host, People's Choice Awards (2012, 2013, 2015); Primetime Emmy for Outstanding Creative Achievement in Interactive Media (2010, 2015); Named Entertainer of Year, Entertainment Weekly (2014); Primetime Emmy for Outstanding Interactive Program (2014); Outstanding Guest Actor in a Comedy Series, Emmy Awards (2014); 100 Most Influential People in the World, "TIME" (2013); Best Comedy Album, Grammy Awards (2013); Grammy for Best Comedy Album (2013); Webby Person of the Year, International Academy of Digital Arts & Sciences (2009); The 50 Most Beautiful People, "People" (2002)

FAMA, EUGENE FRANCIS, T: Economics Professor **I:** Education/Educational Services **DOB:** 02/14/1939 **PB:** Boston **SC:** MA/USA **MS:** Married **ED:** Honorary DSc, Tufts University (2002); Honorary DSc, Tufts University, Medford, MA (2002); Honorary DSc, Catholic University of Leuven, Belgium (1995); Honorary LLD, De Paul University, Chicago, IL (1989); Honorary LLD, University of Rochester (1987); PhD, The University of Chicago (1964); MBA, The University of Chicago (1963); BA in Romance Languages, Tufts University, Medford, MA, Magna Cum Laude (1960) **C:** Robert R. McCormick Distinguished Service Professor of Finance, The University of Chicago Booth School of Business (1993-Present); Theodore O. Yntema Distinguished Service Professor of Finance, The University of Chicago Booth School of Business (1984-1993); Theodore O. Yntema Professor of Finance, The University of Chicago Booth School of Business (1973-1984); Professor, The University of Chicago Booth School of Business (1968-1973); Associate Professor, The University of Chicago Booth School of Business (1966-1968); Assistant Professor of Finance, The University of Chicago Booth School of Business (1963-1965) **CR:** Board of Directors, Dimensional Fund Advisors (1982-Present); Director of Research, Dimensional Fund Advisors (1982-Present); Member, Investment Strategy Committee, Dimensional Fund Advisors (1982-Present); Visiting Professor, UCLA Anderson Graduate School of Management (1982-1995); Visiting Professor, Catholic University of Leuven & European Institute for Advanced Studies in Management, Belgium (1975-1976) **CW:** Advising Editor, Journal of Financial Economics (1974-Present); Associate Editor, Journal of Monetary Economics (1984-1996); Associate Editor, Journal of Finance"(1971-1973, 1977-1980); Associate Editor, "American Economic Review" (1975-1977); Author, "Foundations of Finance" (1976); Co-author with M. Miller, "The Theory of Finance" (1972); Contributor, Articles, Various Professional Journals **AW:** Co-recipient, Nobel Memorial Prize in Economic Sciences (Sveriges Riksbank Prize), Royal Swedish Academy of Sciences (2013); Graham and Dodd Best Perspective Award, Financial Analysts Journal

(2012); Onassis Prize in Finance (2009); Morgan Stanley American Financial Association Award for Excellence in Finance (2007); Fred Arditti Innovation Award, Chicago Mercantile Exchange (CME Group Inc.) (2007); Nicholas Molodovsky Award, Chartered Financial Analyst Institute (CFA Institute) (2006); Deutsche Bank Prize in Financial Economics (2005); Inductee, Malden Catholic High School Athletic Hall of Fame (1992); Named Chaire Francqui (1982) **MEM:** Fellow, American Finance Association; American Academy of Arts & Sciences; The Econometric Society; American Economic Association; Beta Gamma Sigma

FANNING, THOMAS ANDREW, T: Chairman, President, and Chief Executive Officer **I:** Oil & Energy **CN:** Southern Company **DOB:** 03/12/1957 **PB:** Morristown **SC:** NJ/USA **PT:** James E. Fanning; Marjorie (Van Morstein) Fanning **MS:** Married **SPN:** Beverly Booher (03/14/1987) **CH:** Matthew Ryan; Bradley Stephen **ED:** MS in Finance, Georgia Institute of Technology, Atlanta, GA (1980); BS in Industrial Management, Georgia Institute of Technology, Atlanta, GA (1979) **C:** Chairman, President, Chief Executive Officer, Southern Company (2010-Present); President, Southern Company (2010); Executive Vice President, Chief Operating Officer, Southern Company (2008-2010); Executive Vice President, Chief Financial Officer, Treasurer, Southern Company (2003-2008); President, Chief E Gulf Power, Southern Company (2002-2003); Executive Vice President, Chief Financial Officer, Georgia Power, Southern Company (1999-2002); Vice President, Chief Financial Officer, Mississippi Power, Southern Company; Director Corporate Finance, Southern Company Services, Atlanta, GA (1988); Supervisor, Southern Company Services, Atlanta, GA (1988); Senior Vice President Strategy, Southern Company; Treasurer, Southern Electrical International, Atlanta (1986); With, Southern Company Services, Atlanta, GA (1983-1986); Financial Analyst, Southern Company, Atlanta, GA (1980) **CR:** Chairman, Board of Directors, Federal Reserve Bank (2015-Present); Board of Directors, Southern Company (2010-Present); Member, Board of Directors, Vulcan Materials **AW:** National Merit Scholar Advisory Board, Georgia Institute of Technology (2003-Present); Georgia Federal Management Scholar (1979) **MEM:** Phi Eta Sigma National Honor Society, Inc.

FARBER, JOHN PHD, T: Chairman of the Board **I:** Engineering **CN:** iCC Industries Inc. **DOB:** 08/23/1925 **PB:** Timisoara **SC:** Romania **PT:** Eugene; Magda (Reiter) F. **MS:** Married **SPN:** Maya Kleyman (06/28/1953) **CH:** Sandra; Deborah; Michael; Claudia **ED:** Doctor of Philosophy in Chemistry, Polytechnic Institute of Brooklyn, New York (1956); Master of Science, University of Cluj, Timisoara, Romania (1948) **C:** Chairman, Frutarom Limited (1996-Present); Founder, Chairman, International Chemical Company Industries Incorporated (1953-Present); Consultant, Asahi Chemical Industry Company, Limited, Tokyo, Japan (1953-1956); Research Chemist, Sun Chemical Company (1951-1952); Chairman, Dover Chemical Corporation, Ohio; President, Dover Chemical Corporation, Ohio; Chairman, Primex Plastics Corporation, New Jersey; Consultant, Chemische Fabrik Kalk GmbH, Koln, Kalk, Germany; Consultant, Foster Grant Company, Incorporated, Leominster, Massachusetts; Consultant, Verneba A.G. Neuallschwill, Basel, Switzerland; Consultant, Society des Peintures et Vernis Bouvet, Tournus, France **CR:** Chairman, Board of Directors, Frutarom Limited **AW:** Lifetime Achievement Award, the Society of Plastics Engineers (2018) **MEM:** American Chemical Society; Society of the Plastics Industry; Society of Plastics Engineers; National Petroleum Refiners

Association; Chemical Manufacturers Association **MH:** Albert Nelson Marquis Lifetime Achievement Award; Marquis Who's Who Top Professional **B/I:** Dr. Farber became involved in his profession after traveling to America to study at the Polytechnic Institute of Brooklyn. While he was in school, he worked as a chemist in a paint company. He created paint and sold it under his own label. He is known for working in plastics and established a plastics company called Primex Plastics.

FARBER, MAYA M., T: Artist **I:** Fine Art **DOB:** 01/24/1936 **PB:** Timi?o-ara **SC:** Romania **MS:** Married **SPN:** John Farber **CH:** Sandra; Deborah; Michael; Claudia **ED:** BA, Hunter College, New York, NY; Coursework, Pratt Institute, Hans Hofmann School of Fine Arts; Coursework, Art Students League With Reginald Marsh and Will Barnett **C:** Director, Frutarom Industries Ltd. (1996-Present); Director, Electrochemical Industries Ltd. (1952); Director, ICC Industries, Inc., New York, NY **AW:** Artist Over 60, The Artist Magazine (2012) **MEM:** Signature Member, National Collage Society **MH:** Marquis Who's Who Top Professional **B/I:** Ms. Farber lived for some years in Managua, Nicaragua, and the vivid tropical colors inspired many of her works.

FARBER, ROBERT, "ROB" J., T: Senior Research Scientist **I:** Sciences **CN:** Atmospheric Clarity **DOB:** 05/02/1946 **PB:** Oak Ridge **SC:** TN/USA **PT:** Milton Farber; Constance (Baldwin) Farber **MS:** Married **SPN:** Anna Lee Farber (10/2/1976) **CH:** Devon Lance; Shannon Nicole **ED:** PhD in Environmental Engineering, University of Washington (1975); MS in Atmospheric Sciences, University of Washington (1972); BS in Chemistry, Yale University (1968) **C:** Senior Research Scientist, Southern California Edison, Rosemead, CA (1976-2013) **CIV:** Captain, U.S. Air Force (1968-1981) **MIL:** Air Force Officer; National Guard and Reserve Weather Forecaster **CW:** Contributor, Articles, Professional Journals **AW:** Delivery and Applications Award, EPRI Environmental Division (1998) **MEM:** Secretary, Technical Committee, Air and Waste Management Association (1980-Present); American Meteorological Society **MH:** Albert Nelson Marquis Lifetime Achievement Award **AS:** Dr. Farber attributes his success to his ideal family upbringing. His parents emphasized academics and a well-rounded lifestyle. From an early age, he was exposed to sports and fine arts. He started playing the piano at the age of 5, which he still does today. Likewise, his mother was an avid gardener, and Dr. Farber continues to garden today. **B/I:** From an early age, Dr. Farber enjoyed the outdoors. His family consisted of entirely outdoorsy individuals, so he was always able to care for nature. This is what inspired him to become an air quality and management research scientist. **AV:** Gardening; Playing tennis; Practicing classical piano; Hiking; Skiing; Backpacking; Sailing; Biking; Swimming; Water-skiing, Golfing; Appreciating opera, ballet, and symphonies **PA:** Democrat **RE:** Christian Scientist **THT:** Dr. Faber believes in finding one's passions in life and going after them.

FARES, AHMAD AL, T: Founder and Chief Executive Officer **I:** Telecommunications **CN:** Celitech Inc. **DOB:** 05/26/1982 **PB:** Baalbeck **SC:** Lebanon **MS:** Married **SPN:** Hiba Edgheim **CH:** Celine **ED:** Executive Education, Strategic Financial Analysis, Harvard Business School (2013); MBA in General Management, INSEAD (2008); BE in Electrical Engineering and Physics, American University of Beirut, with Distinction (2004); Baccalaureate in Mathematics, National Protestant College, with Distinction (2000) **CT:** Cloud Computing Practitioner **C:** Member, Forbes Technology Council (2018-Pres-

ent); Founder, Chief Executive Officer, Celitech Inc. (2017-Present); Chief Financial Officer, General Manager, Keystone Group & Acsys Technologies (2010-2017); Senior Consultant (Associate), Roland Berger Strategy Consultants (2009-2010); Engineering & BD Manager, Pertrofac (2004-2008) **CR:** Inventor, Seven U.S. and International Utility Patents **CIV:** Judge, Hult Prize Foundation (2017); Mentor, The Mowgli Foundation (2015-2016) **AW:** Overall Wireless Broadband Solution of the Year, Mobile Breakthrough Awards (2019); Best Tech Startup, The Tech Tribune (2018); US Green Card holder under "Extraordinary Ability" category (2017); INSEAD Diversity Scholarship (2008); "Best Paper in Electrical Engineering," Third FEA Student Conference, American University of Beirut (2004); Speaker, Sixth International Symposium on Communications and Information Technologies, ISCIT, Japan (2004) **MEM:** Forbes Technology Council; INSEAD Alumni Association; Institute of Electrical and Electronics Engineers (IEEE) **MH:** Marquis Who's Who Top Executive for 2020 **AS:** Mr. Fares attributes his success to the notion that "ease is a greater threat to progress than hardship." **B/I:** Mr. Fares became involved in his profession because he saw a real need for more accessible and affordable wireless internet, starting within global travel. In 2000, when he graduated college, he was fascinated by the new world being created by the internet and the dot-com boom. Mr. Fares wanted to pursue electrical engineering to be part of shaping internet technologies and making them deeper enabler to human life, from access to information and opportunity to better travel. **AV:** Skiing; Playing soccer; Traveling **THT:** For more information on Mr. Fares and his work, see:https://www.linkedin.com/in/ahmadfares; https://www.forbes.com/sites/forbestechcouncil/2019/08/30/will-esim-change-the-way-you-travel-internationally/#7249813047ac; https://ieeexplore.ieee.org/document/1413828

FARMER, ANTHONY DREW, T: Director **I:** Health, Wellness and Fitness **CN:** Bay Area Enterprises **DOB:** 12/17/1985 **PB:** Coos Bay **SC:** OR/USA **MS:** Married **SPN:** Jillian **ED:** BS in Sociology, Portland State University (2012) **CT:** Individual Placements and Supports Supervisor, Rockville Institute (2017) **C:** Director, Bay Area Enterprises (2018-Present); Employment Specialist, Mental Health Association, North Bend, OR (2016-2018); Executive Assistant, Chuck Bracelin Transportation, Inc., Coos Bay, OR (2013-2016); Personnel Specialist, U.S. Navy, San Diego, CA (2005-2009) **CIV:** Board of Directors, League of Oregon Cities (2018-Present); City Councilor, Coos Bay, OR (2016-Present); Board Member, League of Oregon Cities Board; Board Member, Local Library **AW:** Volunteer Service Award, Armed Services YMCA **AS:** The greatest driver for Mr. Farmer's success is seeing a need or an objective and then seeing that it has not been fully addressed yet, which goes back to his family and his upbringing. There is a long history of veterans in his family, and the mission-driven perspective is a trait they all share. **B/I:** The field of mental health has always been interesting to Mr. Farmer. After he finished his undergraduate studies, he moved back to his hometown. It was a small and rural town, so it was difficult to find work at times. After finding initial work as a trucker, he moved into other fields. Each venture has been a continuation of his interests in mental health. Mr. Farmer has always had a desire to help others.

FARNSWORTH, BROOKE, JD, T: Lawyer **I:** Law and Legal Services **CN:** Farnsworth & vonBerg, LLP **DOB:** 03/16/1945 **PB:** Grand Rapids **SC:** MI/USA **PT:** George Llelwyn Farnsworth; Gladys Fern (Kennedy) Farnsworth **MS:** Married **SPN:** Connie

D. Hedblom (06/15/1996) **CH:** Leslie Erin; T Brooke **ED:** JD, Indiana University Robert H. McKinney School of Law, Indianapolis, IN (1971); BS in Business, Indiana University, Indianapolis, IN (1967) **C:** Principal, Farnsworth & vonBerg, LLP, Houston, Texas (1990-Present); Principal, Farnsworth & Associates, PC, Houston, Texas (1978-1990); Counsel, Damson Oil Corp., Houston, Texas (1974-1978); Associate, Butler, Binion, Rice, Cook & Knapp, Houston, Texas (1971-1974); Administrative Assistant to Treasurer of State of Indiana, Indianapolis, IN (1968-1971) **CIV:** Law Advisor Board Member, Energy Institute **CW:** Contributor, Articles on Law to Professional Journals **AW:** AV Preeminent Rating, Martindale-Hubbell **MEM:** Fellow, Texas Bar Foundation, Houston Bar Association; College of the State Bar of Texas; American Bar Association (ABA); State Bar of Texas; Champions Golf Club; The Olympic Club **BAR:** United States Court of Appeals for the Tenth Circuit (2003); United States District Court for the Northern District of Texas (1994); United States District Court for the Western District of Texas (1998); United States Court of Appeals for the Eleventh Circuit (1982); Supreme Court of the United States (1978); United States Court of Appeals for the District of Columbia Circuit (1977); United States Court of Appeals for the Fifth Circuit (1977); United States Tax Court (1972); United States District Court for the Southern District of Texas (1972); Texas (1971) **MH:** Albert Nelson Marquis Lifetime Achievement **AS:** Mr. Farnsworth attributes his success to a caring attitude toward his clients and their issues as well as, in litigation, remembering the three rules: preparation, preparation and preparation. **B/I:** Mr. Farnsworth's decision to become involved in his profession of law came from reading a book while in college called "Clarence Darrow for the Defense" by Irving Stone. **AV:** Golf **PA:** Republican **RE:** Protestant

FARR, DAVID NELSON, T: Chairman and Chief Executive Officer **I:** Oil & Energy **CN:** Emerson Electric Company **MS:** Married **CH:** Two Children **ED:** MBA, Owen Graduate School of Management, Vanderbilt University (1981); BS in Chemistry, Wake Forest University (1977) **C:** Chairman, Chief Executive Officer, Emerson Electric Company (2010-Present); Chairman, President, Chief Executive Officer, Emerson Electric Company (2005-2010); Chairman, Chief Executive Officer, Emerson Electric Company (2004-2005); Chief Executive Officer, Emerson Electric Company (2000-2004); From Staff Member to Chief Executive Officer, Emerson Electric Co., St. Louis (1981-2000) **CR:** Board directors IBM Corp. (2012-Present); DPH Holdings Corporation (2002-2009); Member, The Business Council, Washington, DC; The Delphi Corporation; United Way of Greater St. Louis **CIV:** Member, Civic Progress; Board of Directors, Greater St. Louis Area Council, Boy Scouts of America; Board of Directors, Municipal Theatre Association of St. Louis

FARRELL, MARK MACAULAY, T: Bank Executive (Retired) **I:** Financial Services **PB:** Troy **SC:** NY/USA **PT:** John J. Farrell; Mary-Elizabeth (O'Brien) Farrell **MS:** Married **SPN:** Cathleen (Purnell) Farrell **CH:** Elizabeth L. Farrell; Helen G. Farrell **ED:** MBA, Columbia University (1987); Intern, Citibank (Citigroup, Inc.), New York, NY (1986); PhD, University of North Carolina at Chapel Hill (1982); MA, Tufts University (1975); AB, Hamilton College (1974); Postgraduate Coursework, University of Goettingen, Germany (1981); Postgraduate Coursework, University of Tuebingen, Germany (1974-1975) **CT:** Series 7 and 63 Securities Licenses **C:** Senior Vice President, National Director of Government and Institutional Banking, Washington Federal (Now WaFd Bank, Formerly Wedbush Bank), Portland,

OR (2011-2017); Vice President, Senior Relationship Manager, KeyBank, Portland, OR (1997-2011); Vice President, Bank of America (Bank of America Corporation, Formerly Security Pacific Bank), Portland, OR (1990-1997); Assistant Treasurer, Bank of New York (Now The Bank of New York Mellon Corporation, Formerly Irving Trust Company), New York and White Plains, NY (1987-1989); Assistant Professor, East Carolina University, Greenville, NC (1983-1985); Assistant Professor, Bowdoin College, Brunswick, Maine (1982-1983); Graduate Teaching Fellow, University of North Carolina at Chapel Hill (1976-1982) **CR:** Invited speaker and participant, Washington Federal Leadership Conference, 2014, 2016; Corporate banking executive participant Security Pacific Bank Management Exchange, 1991 **CIV:** President, Hamilton College Alumni Council, Oregon Region (2010-2016); Volunteer Coach, Willamette United Soccer Club, West Linn, OR (2002-2006); Guest Speaker, Graduation, University of Portland Pamplin School of Business (1999); Corporate Fundraiser, Oregon Independent College Foundation, Portland, OR (1998); United Way, Portland, OR (1992, 1994); United Way, Westchester County, New York, NY (1989); United Way, New York, NY (1988) **CW:** Contributor, Articles to Professional Journals; Frequent Speaker at Professional Conferences **AW:** National Business Development Leadership Awards, KeyBank (2000-2004); Kent James Brown Fellow, (1981) **MEM:** Special Districts Association of Oregon (1998-2017); Oregon Association of School Business Officials (OASBO) (1998-2017); Oregon Association of County Treasurers and Finance Officers (1998-2017); Member, Committee Participant, Oregon Government Finance Officers Association (1995-2017); Council of Development Finance Agencies (2006) **MH:** Albert Nelson Marquis Lifetime Achievement Award

FARRELL, NAOMI, RN, MS, BS, T: Editor, Journalist, Medical Writer, Nurse Researcher, Poet, Artist **I:** Writing and Editing **DOB:** 04/21/1941 **PB:** Glasgow **SC:** Scotland **PT:** Rev. Louis; Minnie (Przestrzeleniec) F **ED:** Master of Science, Social Science and International Affairs, Long Island University (1979); United Nations Studies Certificate, Long Island University (1978); Bachelor of Science in Nursing, Hunter College (1973); Associate of Applied Science, City University of New York, with Honors (1970) **CT:** Certificate, Medical-Surgical Specialist (1991); Registered Nurse **C:** Features Writer, Jerusalem Post (1995-Present); Mideast Correspondence, United Nations Observer and International Report (1993-Present); United Nations Correspondent, The New Middle East Magazine (1994-1995); Associate Editor, Al Hoda, New Lebanese American Journal, New York, NY (1979-1995); Nurse, Researcher, Cornell Medical Center, New York, NY (1977-1980); Administrator, Health Insurance Plan, New York, NY (1964-1965); TV Performer, Canada (1959-1963); United Nations Correspondent, Freelance Writer, Technion University Report, Israel; United Nations Correspondent, Freelance Writer, Al Ahram Weekly, Egypt; United Nations Correspondent, Freelance Writer, Globe And Mail Of Canada **CR:** Consultant, International Medical Tourism (1985); Dancer, Model, Actress (1957-1966) **CIV:** International Advisory Board, Symphony for United Nations (1986) **CW:** Author, Numerous Articles and Poems for Newspapers and Magazines and Books **AW:** Research Paper on World Hunger Accepted by United Nations Research and Training Library, Used in Presidential Commission on World Hunger, Washington, DC (1979) **MEM:** Vice President, Society Writers of the United Nations (1985-1986); Associate Editor, United Nations Correspondents Association (1985); Citation for Position Paper,

United Nations Association (1978); Foreign Press Association; Society of International Development; New York Academy of Sciences; American Nurses Association; Voices Israel, English Poets Society **MH:** Albert Nelson Marquis Lifetime Achievement Award **B/I:** Ms. Farrell became involved in her profession because her father, Reverend Louis Farrell, served as a great inspiration to her. He used to write poetry, so it was the background of her father that spurred her to love knowledge and remain curious.

FARROW, RONAN, T: Television Personality, Former Federal Agency Administrator **I:** Media & Entertainment **DOB:** 12/19/1987 **PB:** New York **SC:** NY/USA **PT:** Woody Allen; Mia Farrow **ED:** Honorary Doctor, Dominican University, California (2012); JD, Yale Law School, New Haven, CT (2009); BA, Bard College, Annandale-on-Hudson, NY (2004) **C:** Host, Ronan Farrow Daily, MSNBC (2014-2015); Special Advisor, to the Secretary for Global Youth Issues, United States State Department (2011-2012); Special Advisor, Humanitarian and NGO Affairs in the Office of the Special Representative for Afghanistan and Pakistan, United States State Department, Washington, DC (2009-2011); Spokesperson for Youth, UNICEF; Legal Counsel, United States House of Foreign Affairs Committee, Washington, DC; Summer Associate, Davis Polk & Wardell, New York, NY **CR:** Representative, United to End Genocide (Formerly Genocide Intervention Network) **CW:** Author, "To Catch and Kill" (2019); Guest Actor, TV Series, Unbreakable Kimmy Schmidt (2019); Author, "War on Peace: The End of Diplomacy and the Decline of American Influence" (2018); Voice-over Actor, The Wind Rises (2013); Voice-over Actor, From Up on Poppy Hill (2011); Contributor, Articles, Various Publications including the LA Times, International Herald Tribune and Wall St Journal **AW:** Named, 40 Under 40, Connecticut Magazine (2019); Named, Time Magazine's 100 Most Influential (2018); Point Courage Award, Point Foundation (2018); Recipient, Excellence in Exploration and Journalism, Reach the World (2014); Named, Man of the Year of His Birth, Esquire Magazine (2013); Rhode Scholar, Oxford University (2012); Named one of The 30 Under 30 in Law & Policy, Forbes Magazine (2011); Named Up-and-Coming Politician of Year, Harper's Bazaar (2011); Named, New Activist of Year, New York Magazine (2009); McCall-Pierpaoli Humanitarian Award, Refugee's International (2008) **PA:** Democrat

FARRUGIA, GIANRICO, MD, T: Gastroenterologist, Researcher **I:** Research **CN:** Mayo Clinic **DOB:** 12/24/1963 **PB:** Balzan **SC:** Malta **PT:** Paul Farrugia; Maria Farrugia **MS:** Married **SPN:** Geraldine Farrugia **CH:** Luca; Stefan **ED:** MD, University of Malta (1987) **CT:** Certified in Gastroenterology (1993); Certified in Internal Medicine (1991) **C:** Professor, College of Medicine and Science, Mayo Clinic (2004-Present); Associate Director, Rochester Research Committee, Mayo Clinic, Rochester, MN (2006); Chair of Research In Gastroenterology and Hepatology, Mayo Clinic, Rochester, MN (2004-2005); From Assistant To Associate Professor, College of Medicine and Science, Mayo Clinic (1994-2004); Senior Associate Consultant, Mayo Foundation for Medical Education and Research, Rochester, MN (1994-1997) **CR:** Consultant and Lecturer in Field; Faculty Director, Center for Gastrointestinal Endoscopy Research and Development **CIV:** Advisory Board Member, Vanderbilt Digestive Disease Research Center (2001-Present) **CW:** Editorial Board, American Journal of Physiology, Gastrointestinal and Liver Physiology (2003-Present); Associate Editor, Neurogastroenterology and Motility (2001-Present); Contributor, Chapters,

Books; Contributor, Articles, Professional Journals **AW:** Grantee, Solvay (2005); Grantee, Novartis (2004); Grantee, National Institutes Of Health (1997, 2000-2002, 2004); Research Group Young Investigator Award, American Gastroenterological Association (2003); Janseen Award (2000); Award, American Federation Research (1996); Young Investigator Award, American Gastroenterological Association (1992); Decorated Knight, Sovereign Military Hospitaller Order of Saint John of Jerusalem, of Rhodes and of Malta **MEM:** American College of Physicians; American Medical Association; American Society of Clinical Investigation; American Motility Society; American Gastroenterological Association; American Physiological Society; American Federation of Research; American Society for Gastroenterological Endoscopy; American College of Gastroenterology; International Motility Society; Minnesota Medical Association; Zumbro Valley Medical Association **AV:** Sailing; Playing soccer

FARWELL, DOROTHY, "DOTTY", T: Educator (Retired) **I:** Education/Educational Services **DOB:** 03/21/1936 **PB:** Grand Forks **SC:** ND/USA **PT:** Philip William West; Tenney Constance (Johnson) West **MS:** Married **SPN:** Robert William Farwell (06/30/1984); Gerald Alpha Freeman (08/18/1956, Divorced 1965) **CH:** Jeffrey West Freeman **ED:** MEd, Louisiana State University, Baton Rouge, LA (1973); BS in Education, Louisiana State University, Baton Rouge, LA (1958) **CT:** Licensed, Louisiana, Certified Clinical Competence; Supervisor of Student Teaching; Assessment Teacher; Child Search Coordinator; Parish or City School Supervisor/Director of Special Education; Special School Principal **C:** Speech and Language Pathologist, St. Tammany Parish School Board, Covington, LA (1986-1989); Assistant Coordinator, Pupil Appraisal, East Baton Rouge Parish School Board, Baton Rouge, LA (1984-1986); Compliance Consultant, Pupil Appraisal, East Baton Rouge Parish School Board, Baton Rouge, LA (1982-1984); Supervisor, Student Teachers, Louisiana State University, Baton Rouge, LA (1967-1982); Speech and Language Pathologist, East Baton Rouge Parish School Board, Baton Rouge, LA (1966-1982); Assistant Dean, Women, Louisiana State University, Baton Rouge, LA (1961-1966); Speech and Language Pathologist, St. Helena Parish School Board, Greensburg, LA (1959-1961) **CR:** Substitute Teacher, Hancock County School District and Pass Christian Public School District, Mississippi (2002-2017); Speech and Language Pathologist, St. Tammany Schools, Covington, LA (1986-1989); Assistant to Coordinator, Pupil Appraisal Services (1984-1986); Compliance Consultant, Pupil Appraisal (1982-1984); Compliance Consultant, Pupil Appraisal (1982-1984); Supervisor, Student Teachers, Louisiana State University, Baton Rouge, LA (1967-1982); Speech and Language Pathologist, East Baton Rouge Parish Schools, Baton Rouge, LA (1966-1982); Assistant to Dean of Women, Louisiana State University, Baton Rouge, LA (1961-1966); President, Alumnae Chapter, Baton Rouge Mortar Board (1960-1962); Speech and Language Pathologist, St. Helena Parish Schools, Greensburg, LA (1959-1961); Recruitment Consultant, Numerous Universities **CIV:** Secretary, Timber Creek Condominium Association, Mandeville, LA (1990); President, Timber Creek Condominium Association, Mandeville, LA (1987); Vice President, Timber Creek Condominium Association, Mandeville, LA (1986); President, Lakeside Villa Condominium Association, Diamondhead, MS (1980-1982); Secretary, Lakeside Villa Condominium Association, Diamondhead, MS (1978-1979) **AW:** Loyalty Award (2016); Greek Excellence Award, Louisiana State University (2015); Delta Gamma Fraternity Cable Award (1980); Honorary Graduate Fellowship Honoree (1979) **MEM:** American Speech-Language-Hearing Association; Mortar Board; Foundation Board of Trustees; North Shore Alumnae Association **B/I:** Ms. Farwell became involved in her profession because she always wanted to be a teacher but did not want to work in the classroom, which is why she went into speech pathology. She was led into the field because of her high school speech teacher, Oren Teague. **AV:** Traveling; Reading; Needlecrafting; Cooking **PA:** Republican **RE:** Presbyterian **THT:** Ms. Farwell's father, Philip W. West, was previously featured in a Who's Who publication, as was her husband, Robert W. Farwell.

FARWELL, ROBERT WILLIAM, PHD, T: Physicist **I:** Sciences **DOB:** 05/11/1927 **PB:** Providence **SC:** RI/USA **PT:** Robert Reo Farwell; Marie Harriett (Reilly) Farwell **MS:** Married **SPN:** Dorothy Anne West (06/30/1984); Charlotte Charmaine Stricker (03/31/1956, Divorced 1981) **CH:** William Reo; Bradley Alan **ED:** Doctor of Philosophy, Pennsylvania State University (1960); Master of Science, Pennsylvania State University (1955); Bachelor of Science, Yale University **C:** Physicist, U.S. Naval Research Laboratory, Stennis Space Center, MS (1983-1994); Associate Professor, Applied Research Laboratory, Pennsylvania State University, State College (1963-1983); Assistant Professor, Ordnance Research Laboratory, Pennsylvania State University, State College (1960-1963); Graduate Assistant, Physics Department, Pennsylvania State University, University Park (1958-1960); Research Assistant, Research Associate, Ordnance Research Laboratory, Pennsylvania State University, State College (1951-1958) **CR:** Substitute Teacher, Hancok School District (2002-Present) **CIV:** Chairman, Zoning Hearing Board, College Township, State College (1974-1978) **MIL:** U.S. Navy (1945-1946) **CW:** Contributor, Articles to Professional Journals **MEM:** Administrative Council, Institute of Electrical and Electronics Engineers (1988-Present); Acoustical Society of America (1989-Present); Chairman, Technician Committee on Underwater Acoustics, Institute of Electrical and Electronics Engineers (1988-Present); Technician Committee on Underwater Acoustics, Acoustical Society of America (1970-1973) **MH:** Albert Nelson Marquis Lifetime Achievement Award **AV:** Running; Investments; Reading; Traveling **PA:** Republican **RE:** Protestant

FASSBENDER, MICHAEL, T: Actor **I:** Media & Entertainment **DOB:** 04/02/1977 **SC:** Heidelberg/Germany **PT:** Josef Fassbender; Adele Fassbender **C:** Owner, Peanut Productions **CW:** Actor, "X-Men: Dark Phoenix" (2019); Actor, "Song to Song" (2017); Actor, "Alien: Covenant" (2017); Actor, "The Snowman" (2017); Actor, Producer, "Assassin's Creed" (2016); Actor, "X-Men: Apocalypse" (2016); Actor, "Weightless" (2016); Actor, "Trespass Against Us" (2016); Actor, "The Light Between Oceans" (2016); Actor, "Macbeth" (2015); Actor, "Steve Jobs" (2015); Actor, Executive Producer, "Slow West" (2015); Actor, "Frank" (2014); Actor, "X Men: Days of Future Past" (2014); Actor, "12 Years a Slave" (2013); Actor, "The Counselor" (2013); Actor, "Haywire" (2012); Actor, "Prometheus" (2012); Actor, "Jane Eyre" (2011); Actor, "X-Men: First Class" (2011); Actor, "A Dangerous Method" (2011); Actor, "Shame" (2011); Actor, "Centurion" (2010); Actor, "Jonah Hex" (2010); Voice Actor, "Fable III" (2010); Actor, "Blood Creek" (2009); Actor, "Fish Tank" (2009); Actor, "Inglourious Basterds" (2009); Actor, "Hunger" (2008); Actor, "The Devil's Whore" (2008); Actor, "Eden Lake" (2008); Actor, "Wedding Belles" (2007); Actor, "Angel" (2007); Actor, "300" (2006); Actor, "Trial & Retribution" (2006); Actor,

"Agatha Christie's Poirot" (2006); Actor, "William and Mary" (2005); Actor, "Murphy's Law" (2005); Actor, "Our Hidden Lives" (2005); Actor, "Hex" (2004-2005); Actor, "Gunpowder, Treason & Plot" (2004); Actor, "A Most Mysterious Murder: The Case of Charles Bravo" (2004); Actor, "A Bear Named Winnie" (2004); Actor, "Sherlock Holmes and the Case of the Silk Stocking" (2004); Actor, "Carla" (2003); Actor, "NCS Manhunt" (2002); Actor, "Holby City" (2002); Actor, "Band of Brothers" (2001); Actor, "Hearts and Bones" (2001) **AW:** Spotlight Award, National Board of Review (2011)

FAULKNER, JUDITH, "JUDY" R., T: Co-Founder, Chief Executive Officer **I:** Technology **CN:** Epic Systems **DOB:** 08/01/1943 **PT:** Louis Greenfield; Del Greenfield **MS:** Married **SPN:** Gordon Faulkner, MD **CH:** Three Children **ED:** BS in Mathematics, Dickinson College (1965); Diploma, Moorestown Friends School (1961); MS in Computer Science, University of Wisconsin-Madison **C:** Chief Executive Officer, Epic Systems Corporation, Verona, WI (1979-Present); Co-Founder, Human Services Computing, Inc. (Now Epic Systems Corporation) (1979-Present); Health Care Software Developer; Instructor, Computer Science, University of Wisconsin-Madison **AW:** Named, Forbes 400: Richest Americans (2012-Present); Named, Top 50 Health Care Technology CEOs, Healthcare Technology Report (2019); Named, America's Top 50 Women in Tech, Forbes Magazine (2018); Named, 100 Most Powerful Women, Forbes Magazine (2014); Named, 100 Most Influential People in Healthcare, Modern Healthcare Magazine (2011); Alice Paul Merit Award, Moorestown Friends School (2011); Named, Most Powerful Woman in Healthcare, Forbes Magazine

FAULKNER, WILLIAM, T: Partner **I:** Law and Legal Services **CN:** McManis Faulkner **SC:** CA/USA **ED:** JD, UC Hastings College of the Law (1978); BA, Stanford University (1973) **C:** Partner, McManis Faulkner **CIV:** Officer, Board of Trustees, San Jose Museum of Art **CW:** Author, "Avoiding Avoidance: Keeping Payments After Client Bankruptcy," Daily Journal; Author, "Rent Overpayment: Return to Sender?," California Real Estate Journal **AW:** Named, Top 100, Northern California Super Lawyers (2016-2020); Northern California Super Lawyers (2004, 2006-2020); Listed, Corporate Counsel Edition, Northern California Super Lawyers; Senior Fellow, Litigation Counsel of America; Fellow, American Bar Foundation; Best Lawyers in America in Commercial Litigation, Real Estate Litigation, and Trusts & Estates Litigation **MEM:** Santa Clara County Bar Association; Santa Clara County Trial Lawyers Association; Trustee, Officer, San Jose Museum of Art; Former Managing Attorney, Legal Counseling Office, Associated Students of Stanford University; Former Trustee, Los Altos Educational Foundation **BAR:** State Bar of California; U.S. District Court for the Northern, Central, Southern and Eastern Districts of California; U.S. Court of Appeals for the Ninth and Federal Circuits **AS:** Mr. Faulkner attributes his success to hard work and teamwork. **B/I:** Mr. Faulkner became involved in his profession because he saw it as a way he could help people; they do a lot of civil right cases and pro bono work. **AV:** Rugby **THT:** Mr. Faulkner's motto is "Excellence, integrity and kindness."He regularly represents one of Silicon Valley's premier companies in Federal and State Court litigation; obtained an arbitration award of more than $15 million to recover debt owed to clients in a real estate partnership; subsequently secured a series of arbitration orders that allowed the clients to buy out their partners on favorable terms; obtained a defense judgment, including an award of all attorney's fees, in defending a real

estate fraud claim against client by wealthy individuals seeking more than $25,000,000 in damages; and successfully recovered a substantial portion of sums paid through early settlement on behalf of a major telecommunications client that was overcharged under the terms of a commercial lease.

FAUST, DREW GILPIN, T: Former President, Professor of History **I:** Education/Educational Services **CN:** Harvard University **DOB:** 09/18/1947 **PB:** New York **SC:** NY/USA **PT:** McGhee Tyson Gilpin; Catharine (Mellick) Gilpin **MS:** Married **SPN:** Charles E. Rosenberg (06/07/1980); Stephen Faust (12/28/1968, Divorced 1976) **CH:** Jessica; Leah (Stepchild) **ED:** Honorary LLD, Princeton University (2010); Honorary Doctor, Peking University (2008); Honorary Doctor, University of Pennsylvania (2008); Honorary Doctor of Humanities, Yale University (2008); Honorary LHD, Bowdoin College (2007); PhD, University of Pennsylvania (1975); MA, University of Pennsylvania (1971); BA, Bryn Mawr College, Magna Cum Laude (1968) **C:** Lincoln Professor of History, Harvard University, Cambridge, MA (2001-Present); President, Harvard University, Cambridge, MA (2007-2018); Dean, Radcliffe Institute for Advanced Study, Harvard University, Cambridge, MA (2001-2007); Annenberg Professor of History, University of Pennsylvania, Philadelphia, PA (1989-2000); Stanley I. Sheerr Professor of History, University of Pennsylvania, Philadelphia, PA (1988-1989); Professor, University of Pennsylvania, Philadelphia, PA (1984-1989); Associate Professor, University of Pennsylvania, Philadelphia, PA (1980-1984); Assistant Professor in American Civilization, University of Pennsylvania, Philadelphia, PA (1976-1980) **CR:** Board of Directors, Staples, Inc. (2012-Present) **CIV:** Trustee, The Andrew W. Mellon Foundation (2002-2007) **CW:** Editorial Board, Journal of American History (1991-Present); Author, "This Republic of Suffering: Death and the American Civil War" (2008); Author, "Mothers of Invention: Women of the Slaveholding South in the American Civil War" (1996); Author, "Southern Stories: Slaveholders in Peace and War" (1992); Editorial Board, Pennsylvania Magazine of History and Biography (1986-1989); Author, "The Creation of Confederate Nationalism: Ideology and Identity in the Civil War South" (1988); Editorial Board, Journal of Southern History (1981-1986); Author, "James Henry Hammond and the Old South: A Design for Mastery" (1982) ; Author, "A Sacred Circle: The Dilemma of the Intellectual in the Old South" (1977); Editorial Board, Contributor, Articles, Professional Journals **AW:** Named One of "100 Most Powerful Women," Forbes (2007-2009, 2011-2014); Bancraft Prize, Columbia University (2009); Named One of "100 Most Influential People in the World," TIME Magazine (2007); Elizabeth Hall Fellow, Concord Academy (2003); Fellow, Massachusetts Historical Society (2002); Francis Parkman Prize, Society of American Historians (1997); Avery O. Craven Prize, Organization of American Historians (1996); Article Prize, Berkshire Conference of Women Historians (1991); Award, John Simon Guggenheim Memorial Foundation (1987); Award, American Council of Learned Societies (1986); Award, Stanford University Humanities Center (1983-1984); Charles Sydney Award (1983); Jules and Frances Landry Award (1982) **MEM:** Council Member, American Historical Association (1992-Present); Membership Committee, Southern Association for Women Historians (1988-Present); Council Member, Organization of American Historians (1999-2002); President, Southern Historical Association (1999-2000); President, Southern Association for Women Historians (1998-1999); Chair, Avery Craven Prize Committee, Organization of American Historians (1991, 1997); Chair, Nominating Committee, Southern Historical Association (1993); Vice President, Professional Division, American Historical Association (1992); Board Member, Historical Society of Pennsylvania (1988-1991); Executive Council, Southern Historical Association (1987-1990); Council Member, American Studies Association (1988-1990); Chair, Progressive Committee, Organization of American Historians (1987); The American Philosophical Society; American Academy Arts & Sciences

FAUST, MARJORIE JARETTA, T: Nursing Administrator (Retired) **I:** Medicine & Health Care **DOB:** 04/29/1937 **PB:** Dilliner **SC:** PA/USA **PT:** Sanford Griffin; Virginia Pearle (Hart) Griffin **MS:** Widow **SPN:** James R. Faust (09/13/1958) **CH:** Cynthia Ann; James Christian (Deceased); Frederick Allan **ED:** BSN, West Virginia University (1981); Diploma, Washington School of Nursing (1958) **CT:** Certificate in Nursing Administration, University of Minnesota (1989); RN, States of Pennsylvania, West Virginia, New Mexico **C:** Retired, Chief Nursing Officer, Carlsbad Medical Center (2000-2003); Vice President, Patient Care Services, Eastern New Mexico Medical Center, Roswell, NM (1992-1998); Director of Nursing, Eastern New Mexico Medical Center, Roswell, NM (1991-1992); Staff Nurse, Director of Nursing, Clinical System, West Virginia University Hospital, Morgantown, WV (1961-1991); Instructor, Kings Daughter Hospital School of Nursing, Martinsburg, WV (1960-1961); General Staff Nurse, St. Vincent Pallott Hospital, Morgantown, WV (1958-1960) **CR:** Advisory Board, Chavez County Ambulance, Roswell, NM (1986-Present); Board of Directors, St. Francis Clinic, Carlsbad, NM; Researcher, Southern Regional Board Research Project, School of Nursing, University of Texas MD Anderson Cancer Center; Founder, West Virginia Ostomy Association **CIV:** Board of Directors, Chavez County United Way, Roswell, NM (1996-1998); Southeastern Green Community Health Clinic, Greensboro, PA (1987-1990) **CW:** Contributor, Articles, Professional Journals **AW:** Inductee, Hall of Fame, AARP (2017) **MEM:** State of New Mexico Executive Council (2011-2018); Representative, New Mexico Organization of Nurse Executives (1997-1998); Scholarship Reviewer, American Organization of Nurse Executives (1995); N.M.O.N.E.; Sigma Theta Tau; President, AARP Chapter #651 **MH:** Albert Nelson Marquis Lifetime Achievement Award **B/I:** Ms. Faust enrolled in nursing school after graduating from high school. While she did not anticipate pursuing the career, she was excited to see where it would take her. After completing her entrance exams, she excelled in her classes. Though her nursing career was an accident, Ms. Faust has never sought professional success elsewhere. **AV:** Dancing; Listening to music; Traveling; Gambling

FAUST, WALTER LUCK, PHD, T: Physicist (Retired) **I:** Sciences **CN:** U.S. Naval Research Laboratory **DOB:** 02/13/1934 **PB:** Benton **SC:** AR/USA **PT:** Walter Hendrix Faust; Laura Louise (Tynes) Faust **MS:** Married **SPN:** Dorothy C. Faust; Alice Anna Toth (06/15/1957, Deceased 08/1991) **CH:** Laurel Anne; Walter Louis; Kathleen Susan Faust Lee **ED:** PhD in Physics, Columbia University (1961); AB, Columbia College (1956) **C:** Senior Scientist, U.S. Naval Research Laboratory, Washington, DC (1975-Present); Branch Head, U.S. Naval Research Laboratory, Washington, DC (1972-1975); From Associate Professor to Professor, University of Southern California, Los Angeles, CA (1967-1972); Member of Staff, Bell Telephone Laboratory, Murray Hill, NJ (1961-1967) **CW:** Contributor, Articles to Professional Journals **AW:** Fellow, American Physical Society **MEM:** Fellow, American Phys-

ical Society **MH:** Albert Nelson Marquis Lifetime Achievement Award **B/I:** Dr. Faust became involved in his profession because he was a second year student at Columbia University and had won a scholarship in high school. The superintendent of his high school, Jeff Matthews, had a practice for finding scholarships and he was the one to get him that scholarship. In Columbia, he was approached by Leon Letterman and Allan Fax, who both suggested he should do physics and that influenced him to change to physics. **PA:** Democrat

FAUSTINO, REY, T: Chief Executive Officer, Founder **I:** Nonprofit & Philanthropy **CN:** One Degree Inc. **ED:** Master of Science in Social and Urban Policy, Kennedy School of Government, Harvard University (2012); Bachelor of Science in Business Entrepreneurship, University of Southern California (2003) **CT:** Y Combinator, W14 **C:** Chief Executive Officer, Founder, One Degree Inc. (2011-Present); Education Pioneers Graduate School Fellow, Highland Street Foundation (2011); Youth Facilitator, Rap Director, College Summit (2007-2011); Site Director, BUILD (2008-2010); Incubator Manager, BUILD (2005-2008); English Teacher, Hachiouji School, Tokyo, Japan (2003-2004); Co-Executive Director, Troy Camp (2001-2003) **CR:** Residential Student Leader, University of Southern California (2000-Present) **CIV:** Board of Directors, St. Anthony Foundation (2018-Present); Editor, Harvard LGBTQ Policy Journal; With, Education Professional Interest Council; With, LGBTQ Caucus; With, APA Caucus; With, Harvard University **AW:** Harvard Emerging Global Leader Award, Harvard University (2017) **MEM:** Skull and Dagger Honor Society (2003-Present); Mortar Board (2002-Present)

FEDERER, ROGER, T: Professional Tennis Player **I:** Athletics **DOB:** 08/08/1981 **PB:** Basel **SC:** Switzerland **PT:** Robert Federer; Lynette Federer **MS:** Married **SPN:** Mirka Vavrinec (4/11/2009) **CH:** Charlene Riva; Myla Rose; Leo; Lenny **C:** Founder, RF-RogerFederer Fragrance Line (2003-Present); Professional Tennis Player, Association of Tennis Professionals (1998) **CR:** Swiss National Team, Davis Cup (1999-Present); Swiss National Team, Summer Olympic Games, London, England (2012); Swiss National Team, Summer Olympic Games, Beijing, China (2008); Swiss National Team, Summer Olympic Games, Athens, Greece (2004); Swiss National Team, Summer Olympic Games, Sydney, NSW, Australia (2000) **CIV:** Goodwill Ambassador, UNICEF (2006-Present) **AW:** ATP Sportsmanship Award (2004-2009, 2011-2017); ATP Fan Favorite (2003, 2008-2017); Arthur Ashe Humanitarian Award (2013); Silver Medal in Men's Singles, Summer Olympic Games (2012); ATP Player of the Year (2006-2007, 2009); Gold Medal in Men's Doubles (2008); Named, 100 Most Powerful Celebrities, Forbes.com (2008); Named, Most Influential People in World of Sports, Business Week (2007); Named, World's Most Influential People, "TIME" (2007); International Tennis Federation World Champion (2004-2007); Arthur Ashe Humanitarian of the Year Award, ATP (2006); Sportsman of the Year, Laureus World Sports Awards (2006); Academy Outstanding Athlete of the Year, U.S. Sports Academy (2005-2006); Ambassador for Tennis, International Tennis Writers Association (2004-2006); Player of the Year (2004-2006); ATPtennis. com Fans' Favorite (2004-2006); Stefan Edberg Sportsmanship Award (2004, 2006); BBC Sports Overseas Personality of the Year (2004, 2006); ATP Player of the Year (2004, 2006); Swiss of the Year (2003) **AV:** Golf; Soccer; Skiing; Music; Video games; Playing cards

FEDEROFF, HOWARD J., T: Dean **I:** Education/Educational Services **DOB:** 03/24/1953 **PB:** Chicago **SC:** IL/USA **PT:** Harry Federer; Esther (Rosen) Federer **MS:** Married **SPN:** Wendy P. Solovay (10/16/1983) **CH:** Allison; Monica **ED:** MD, Albert Einstein College of Medicine (1983); PhD, Albert Einstein College of Medicine (1979); BA, Earlham College (1974) **CT:** Diplomate in Internal Medicine and in Endocrinology and Metabolism, American Board of Internal Medicine **C:** Dean, University of California (2015-Present); Professor, University Rochester School Medicine and Dentistry (1995-Present); Associate Professor, Albert Einstein College Medicine, Bronx, NY (1993-1995); Assistant Professor, Albert Einstein College Medicine, Bronx, NY (1988-1993); Clinical and Research Fellow, Massachusetts General Hospital, Boston, MA (1985-1988); Intern, Resident, Massachusetts General Hospital, Boston, MA (1983-1985) **CR:** Consultant, Astra Arcus Pharmaceuticals (1995); Science Advisory Board, Alexion Pharmaceuticals, New Haven, CT (1994-1995) **CW:** Contributor, Numerous Papers and Articles, Professional Journals

FEENEY, CHARLES, "CHUCK" FRANCIS, T: Founder **I:** Nonprofit & Philanthropy **CN:** The Atlantic Philanthropies **DOB:** 4/23/1931 **PB:** Elizabeth **SC:** NJ/USA **MS:** Married **SPN:** Helga Feeney; Danielle J. Feeney (Divorced) **CH:** Juliette M. Feeney-Timsit; Caroleen A.; Diane V.; Leslie D. Feeney-Baily; Patrick A. **ED:** Honorary Doctor of Law (2012); Diploma, St. Mary of the Assumption High School (1949); Graduate, School of Hotel Administration, Cornell University **C:** Founder, The Atlantic Philanthropies (1982-Present) **CIV:** Participant, The Giving Pledge (2011-Present); Donor, St. Mary of the Assumption High School; Donor, New York City Tech Campus of Cornell University; Donor, University of Limerick; Donor, Dublin City University **MIL:** Radio Operator, U.S. Air Force **CW:** Author, "The Billionaire Who Wasn't: How Chuck Feeney Made and Gave Away a Fortune Without Anyone Knowing" (2007); Featured, Documentary, "Secret Billionaire: The Chuck Feeney Story" **AW:** Honorary Queensland Great (2019); UCSF Medal (2012); Presidential Distinguished Service Award (2012); Cornell Icon of Industry Award (2010) **MEM:** Alpha Sigma Phi; Sphinx Head Society

FEINSTEIN, DIANNE EMIEL BERMAN, T: U.S. Senator **I:** Government Administration/Government Relations/Government Services **DOB:** 06/22/1933 **PB:** San Francisco **SC:** CA/USA **PT:** Leon Goldman; Betty (Rosenburg) Goldman **MS:** Married **SPN:** Richard C. Blum (01/20/1980); Bertram Feinstein (11/11/1962, Deceased 1978) **CH:** Katherine Anne **ED:** Honorary LHD, University of San Francisco (1988); Honorary JD, Mills College (1985); Honorary JD, Antioch University (1983); Honorary Doctor in Public Service, University of Santa Clara (1981); Honorary Doctor in Public Administration, University of Manila (1981); Honorary LLB, Golden Gate University (1977); BA in History, Stanford University (1955) **C:** U.S. Senator from California (1992-Present); Ranking Member, Senate Judiciary Committee (2017); Vice Chair, Senate Intelligence Committee (2015-2017); Chair, U.S. Senate Narcotics Caucus (2009-2015); Chair, U.S. Senate Select Committee on Intelligence (2009-2015); Chair, Joint Committee on Printing (2009-2013); Chair, U.S. Senate Rules & Administration Committee (2007-2009); Chair, Joint Committee on the Library (2007); Mayor, City of San Francisco (1978-1988); President, San Francisco Board Supervisors, San Francisco, CA (1970-1971, 1974-1975, 1978); Member, Mayor's Committee on Crime, Chairman, Advisory Committee, Adult Detention (1967-1969); With, California Women's Board of Terms and Parole (1960-1966); Fellow, Coro Foundation, San Francisco, CA (1955-1956) **CR:** Democratic Nominee, Governor of California (1990); Member, Executive Committee, U.S. Conference of Mayors (1983-1988); Member, National Committee on U.S.-China Relations **CIV:** Member, San Francisco Bay Area Conservation & Development Commission (1973-1978) **AW:** One of the Most Powerful Women, Forbes Magazine (2005); Outstanding Member of the U.S. Senate Award, National Narcotic Officers' Association Coalition (2005); Funding Hero, Breast Cancer Research Foundation (2004); Leadership Award, AltaMed Health Services Corporation (2004); Pat Brown Legacy Award (2004); Lifetime of Idealism Award, City Year (2004); Legislator of the Year Award, California School Resource Officers' Association (2004); National Distinguished Advocacy Award, American Cancer Society, Inc. (2004); Women of Achievement Award, Century City Chamber of Commerce (2004); Friend of Watershed Award, Association of Water Agencies of Ventura County (2004); Public Service Award, American Society of Hematology (2003); Torch of Liberty Award, Anti-Defamation League (2002); Dr. Nathan Davis Award, American Medical Association (2002); Woodrow Wilson Award, Woodrow Wilson International Center for Scholars (2001); Winning Spirit Award, Women's Information Network Against Breast Cancer (2000); One of the Top 50 Members of Congress, Congressional Quarterly (2000); Recognition Award, Susan G. Komen Breast Cancer Foundation (2000); Congressional Award, National Association of Police Organizations (1999); Celebration of Courage Award, Handgun Control, Inc. (1999); Congressional Champion Award, Coalition for Cancer Research (1999); Abraham Lincoln Award, Illinois Council Against Handgun Violence (1998); Paul E. Tsongas Award, Lymphoma Research Association of America (1997); Congressional Excellence Award, MADD (1997); Donald Santarelli Award, National Organization for Victims Assistance (1996); Awareness Achievement Award, Board of Sponsors, Breast Cancer Awareness (1995); Person of the Year, The National Guard Association of California (1995); Lifetime Achievement Award, National AIDS Foundation (1993); President's Medal, University of California San Francisco (1988); Coro Leadership Award (1988); Distinguished Civilian Award, United States Navy (1987); Number One Mayor, All-Pro City Management Team, City and State Magazine (1987); Commander's Award, U.S. Army (1986); Brotherhood/Sisterhood Award, National Conference of Christians and Jews (1986); French Legion of Honor (1984); Scopus Award, American Friends of the Hebrew University (1981); Coro Foundation Award (1979); Woman of Achievement Award, Business and Professional Women's Clubs of San Francisco (1970); Distinguished Woman Award, San Francisco Examiner (1970) **MEM:** President, Japan Society of Northern California; Trilateral Commission; Inter-American Dialogue; National Committee on U.S.-China Relations **PA:** Democrat **RE:** Jewish

FEINZAIG, LESLIE, T: Chief Executive Officer; Founder **I:** Business Management/Business Services **CN:** Female Founders Alliance **ED:** MBA, Harvard Business School (2007); Bsc in Industrial Relations, London School of Economics (2001) **C:** Chief Executive Officer, Founder, Female Founders Alliance (2017-Present); Judge, Mentor, Social Venture Partners Seattle (2017-Present); Mentor, Techstars (2015-Present); Owner, Venture Kits LLC (2016-2019); Organizer, Seattle Startup Week (2017-2018); Vice President, Digital Experience, Julep Beauty (2014-2015); Vice President, Product Management, Julep Beauty (2014); Director, Product Management and Marketing, Big Fish

(2013-2014); Senior Product Manager, Kinect for Windows, Microsoft (2012-2013); Senior Product Planner, Online Services Division, Microsoft (2008-2012); Senior Associate, Innosight (2007-2008); Summer Associate, McKinsey & Company (2006) **CIV:** Board Member, Washington Technology Industry Association (WTIA) (2019-Present) **CW:** Contributor, Articles to Professional Journals **AW:** Named One of the 100 Most Powerful Women, Forbes Centroamerica (2018); Named One of the 40 Under 40, Puget Sound Business Journal (2018); Gold Star Award, Microsoft (2011); Excellence in Product Management Award, Microsoft (2010); People's Choice Award, Microsoft (2010)

FELIX, ALLYSON MICHELLE, T: Track and Field Athlete **I:** Athletics **DOB:** 11/18/1985 **PB:** Los Angeles **SC:** CA/USA **PT:** Paul Felix; Marlean Felix **MS:** Married **SPN:** Kenneth Ferguson **CH:** Camryn **ED:** Bachelor's Degree in Elementary Education, University of Southern California **C:** Professional Sprinter (2003-Present) **CR:** U.S. National Team, Summer Olympic Games, Rio de Janeiro, Brazil (2016); U.S. National Team, Summer Olympic Games, London, England (2012); U.S. National Team, IAAF World Championships, Daegu, Republic Of Korea (2011); U.S. National Team, IAAF World Indoor Championships, Doha, Qatar (2010); U.S. National Team, IAAF World Championships, Berlin, Germany (2009); U.S. National Team, IAAF World Athletics Final, Thessaloniki, Greece (2007, 2009); U.S. National Team, Summer Olympic Games, Beijing, China (2008); U.S. National Team, IAAF World Championships, Osaka, Japan (2007); U.S. National Team, IAAF World Athletics Final, Stuttgart, Germany (2006); U.S. National Team, IAAF World Athletics Final, Monte Carlo, Monaco (2005); U.S. National Team, IAAF World Championships, Helsinki, Finland (2005); U.S. National Team, Summer Olympic Games, Athens, Greece (2004); U.S. National Team, IAAF World Championships, Paris Saint-Denis, France (2003) **CIV:** SportsUnited Sports Envoy, U.S. Department of State (2014) **AW:** Gold Medal, Mixed Relay, 4x400 M Relay, World Championships, Doha, Qatar (2019); Gold Medal, 4x400 M Relay, 4x100 M Relay, World Championships, London, England (2017); Bronze Medal, 400 M, World Championships, London, England (2017); Gold Medal, 4x400 M Relay, 4x100 M Relay, Olympic Games, Rio de Janeiro, Brazil (2016); Silver Medal, 400 M, Olympic Games, Rio de Janeiro, Brazil (2016); Gold Medal, 400 M, World Championships, Beijing, China (2015); Silver Medal, 4x400 M Relay, 4x100 M Relay, World Championships, Beijing, China (2015); Silver Medal, 4x100 M Relay, World Relay Championships, Nassau, Bahamas (2015); Gold Medal, 4x400 M Relay, 4x100 M Relay, 200 M, Olympic Games, London, England (2012); Gold Medal, 4x400 M Relay, 4x100 M Relay, World Championships, Daegu, Republic of Korea (2011); Silver Medal, 400 M, World Championships, Daegu, Republic of Korea (2011); Bronze Medal, 200 M, World Championships, Daegu, Republic of Korea (2011); Gold Medal, 4x400 M Relay, World Indoor Championships, Doha, Qatar (2010); Gold Medal, 4x400 M Relay, 200 M, World Championships, Berlin, Germany (2009); Gold Medal, 4x400 M Relay, Olympic Games, Beijing, China (2008); Silver Medal, 200 M, Olympic Games, Beijing, China (2008); Gold Medal, 4x400 M Relay, 4x100 M Relay, 200 M, World Championships, Osaka, Japan (2007); Gold Medal, 200 M, World Championships, Helsinki, Finland (2005); Silver Medal, 200 M, Olympic Games, Athens, Greece (2004); Gold Medal in 4x100 M Relay, Bronze Medal in 200 M, Pan American Games, Santo Domingo, Dominican Republic (2003); Gold Medal, Medley Relay and 100 M, World Youth Championships, Debrecen, Hungary (2001)

FELSENTHAL, STEVEN ALTUS, T: Lawyer **I:** Law and Legal Services **PT:** Jerome Felsenthal; Eve Felsenthal **MS:** Married **SPN:** Carol Judith Felsenthal **CH:** Rebecca; Julia; Daniel **ED:** JD, Harvard University (1974); AB, University of Illinois (1971) **C:** Senior Partner, Sugar Felsenthal Grais & Helsinger LLP, Chicago, IL (2011-Present); Senior Partner, Sugar & Felsenthal LLP (Now Sugar Felsenthal Grais & Helsinger LLP) (2008-2011); Senior Partner, Sugar, Friedberg & Felsenthal (Now Sugar Felsenthal Grais & Helsinger LLP), Chicago, IL (1984-2008); Partner, Levenfeld, Eisenberg, Janger, Glassberg & Lippitz, Chicago, IL (1980-1984); Partner, Levenfeld & Kanter, Chicago, IL (1978-1980); Associate, Levenfeld, Kanter, Baskes & Lippitz, Chicago, IL (1974-1978) **MEM:** American Bar Association (ABA); Illinois State Bar Association; The Chicago Bar Association; Chicago Council of Lawyers; Chicago Estate Planning Council, National Association of Estate Planners & Councils; Harvard Law Society of Illinois; Standard Club; Harvard Club of Chicago; Harvard Club of New York City; The Economic Club Chicago; The Phi Beta Kappa Society **BAR:** Michigan (2014); United States Court of Appeals for the Seventh Circuit (1981); United States Court of Federal Claims (1975); United States Tax Court (1975); Illinois (1974); United States District Court for the Northern District of Illinois (1974); **MH:** Albert Nelson Marquis Lifetime Achievement Award

FENG, PAUL, PT: Chih-Chung Feng; Pao-Ru Hu Feng **MS:** Married **SPN:** Marie R. Feng; Mary S. Feng (Deceased) **CH:** Joseph; Dorothy (Hamamura); Alphonso **ED:** MBA, The University of Chicago (1991); JD, DePaul University (1986); PhD, Washington University in St. Louis (1954); Graduate Fellow, National Beijing University (1947-1948); BS, Fu Jen Catholic University (1947) **CT:** CPA, University of Illinois Board of Examiners (1996) **C:** Private Law Practice, IL (1986-Present); Of Counsel, Lamet Kanwit and Davis, Brezina and Ehrlich (1990-2000); Professor, Marquette University, Milwaukee, WI (1987-1988); Associate Professor, Marquette University (1966-1970); National Research Council Professor and Dean, National Tsinghua University, Hsinchu, Taiwan (1973-1974); Fulbright Lecturer, National Taiwan University (1965); Science Advisor, IIT Research Institute (1962-1966); Manager, IIT Research Institute (1955-1966); Adjunct Associate Professor, Illinois Institute of Technology (1964-1966); Technical Director, Manu-Mine Research and Development Co., Reading, PA (1953-1955); Teacher, Wen-Hua High School, Beijing, China (1945-1947) **CR:** President, North Suburban Bar Association, Skokie, IL (1996-1997); Senior Advisor, National Research Council, Taiwan (1973-1974); Consultant, Chung-Shan Institute of Technology, Taoyuan, Taiwan (1973-1974); Apollo Program-NASA, Washington, DC (1968); United States Army Natick Laboratories, Natick, MA (1966-1974); Technical Advisor, United States Delegation to Second UN Conference on Peaceful Uses of Atomic Energy, Geneva (1958) **CIV:** Director, Neighborhood Assistance Foundation (1992-1996); Chinese Advisory Committee, Cultural Relations in America, Washington, DC (1960-1964); Member, Committee for Chinese Refugee Relief (1962) **CW:** Contributor, Articles, Professional Journals; Contributor, Chapters in Books; Author, "Dividend Reinvestment Handbook" **AW:** Research Grantee, United States Air Force, United States Atomic Energy Commission (1955-1974); Achievement Award, National Youth Commission, Taiwan (1971) **MEM:** Career Consultant, American Chemical Society (1992-1996); President, Marquette Chapter, Sigma Xi, The Scientific Research Honor Society (1973-1974); Phoenix Society, American Chemical Society; Overture Society; Life Member, Elliott

Society; Sigma Xi, The Scientific Research Honor Society **BAR:** United States Tax Court (1994); United States Patent Bar (1989); United States Court of Appeals for the Seventh District (1986); United States District Court for the Northern District of Illinois (1986); Federal Trial Bar (1986); Illinois (1986) **MH:** Albert Nelson Marquis Lifetime Achievement Award; Marquis Who's Who Top Professional **B/I:** Dr. Feng became involved in his profession because he started with his studies in China doing scientific education. When he got to the United States, he continued studying and was offered different opportunities as well. **AV:** Travel (Life status, American Airlines Platinum); Classical music; Languages **PA:** Independent **RE:** Roman Catholic

FENNER, WILLIAM, "BILL", T: Associate Manager **I:** Consumer Goods and Services **CN:** The Kraft Heinz Company **DOB:** 06/28/1981 **PB:** New Haven **SC:** CT/USA **PT:** Ellen Fenner **CH:** Lily; Claire **ED:** MBA, The College of Saint Rose, Albany, NY (2007); BA in History, Siena College (2003) **C:** Associate Manager, In-store Sales, The Kraft Heinz Company (2018-Present); Customer Development Manager, Sales, Marketing, Technology, Advantage Solutions (2017-2018); National Account Manager, Russell Stover Candies (Now Russell Stover Chocolates, LLC) (2010-2017); Division Manager, Russell Stover Candies (Now Russell Stover Chocolates, LLC), New England (2008-2010); Sales Representative, Russell Stover Candies (Now Russell Stover Chocolates, LLC), Albany, NY (2006-2008); Part-time Store Manager, Kirkland's, Albany, NY (2006); Assistant Project Manager, Certified Reports Inc., Kinderhook, NY (2005-2006) **CIV:** Volunteer, Soup Kitchens **CW:** Author, Publication (2015) **AW:** The Griffin Report of the Northeast, Shelby Publication (2015); Listee, The Griffin Report's Top 40 Grocery Industry Rising Leaders 40 Under 40, Special Report Feature **MEM:** Phi Alpha Theta National History Honor Society **MH:** Marquis Who's Who Top Professional **AS:** Mr. Fenner has always had a great work ethic. He has always worked smartly, as well as put in the necessary time and effort. He always had goals that he strives for. **B/I:** Back in 2006, before Mr. Fenner started working with Russell Stover, he was working in a retail store, part-time, in Albany, New York. He knew that he needed retail experience because he wanted to at some point be able to apply for a job with a well-known and respected company in order to achieve his long term career objectives. He worked hard to become the best salesperson he could before he applied for a job at Russell Stover. His experience helped him interview well, and he told the hiring manager that he was looking for a long-term commitment. He was offered the job, worked very hard, and within two years was promoted to a division manager position. **RE:** Roman Catholic

FENTY, ROBYN RIHANNA, T: Singer **I:** Media & Entertainment **DOB:** 02/20/1988 **PB:** Saint Michael **SC:** Barbados **PT:** Ronald Fenty; Monica (Braithwaite) Fenty **CR:** Launched, Lingerie, Savage X Fenty (2018-Present); Founder, Fenty Beauty, LVMH (2017-Present); Co-Owner, Tidal (2015-Present); Model, Spokesperson, Covergirl (2007-Present); Launched, Fragrance, Nude (2014); Launched, Fragrance, Rebelle (2012); Launched, Fragrance, Reb'l Fleur (2011) **CIV:** Founder, Clara Lionel Foundation (2012-Present); Founder, Believe Foundation (2006-Present); Named, Cartier Love Charity Bracelet Ambassador; Performer, Benefit Concerts **CW:** Actress, "Guava Island" (2019); Actress, "Ocean's 8" (2018); Actress, "Valerian and the City of a Thousand Planets" (2017); Singer, "ANTI" (2016); Voice Actress, "Home" (2015); Actress, "Annie" (2014); Singer

with Eminem, "Monster" (2013); Singer, "Unapologetic" (2012); Actress, "Battleship" (2012); Singer, "Diamonds" (2012); Singer, "Talk That Talk" (2011); Singer, Featuring Calvin Harris, "We Found Love" (2011); Singer, with Eminem, "Love the Way You Lie" (2011); Singer, "Only Girl (in the World)" (2010); Singer, "Loud" (2010); Singer, "Rated R" (2009); Singer, with Jay-Z and Kanye West, "Run This Town" (2009); Singer, with T.I., "Live Your Life" (2008); Singer, Featuring Jay-Z, "Umbrella" (2007); Singer, "Shut Up and Drive" (2007); Singer, "Don't Stop the Music" (2007); Singer, "Good Girl Gone Bad" (2007); Singer, "A Girl Like Me" (2006); Actress, "Bring It On: All or Nothing" (2006); Singer, "Music of the Sun" (2005); Singer, Solo and Collaborations; Actress, Appearances, Television Shows, Films **AW:** President's Award, NAACP Image Awards (2020); Awards for Favorite Soul/R&B Female Artist, American Music Awards (2007, 2008, 2010, 2013, 2015, 2018); Fan-Voted Billboard Chart Achievement Award, Billboard Music Awards (2016); Michael Jackson Video Vanguard Award, MTV Video Music Awards (2016); Grammy Award for Best Rap/Sung Collaboration, The Recording Academy (2015); Grammy Award for Best Urban Contemporary Album, The Recording Academy (2014); One of the 100 Most Powerful Women in Entertainment, The Hollywood Reporter (2014); Award for Favorite R&B Artist, People's Choice Awards (2012, 2013); Icon Award, American Music Awards (2013); Award for Best Short Form Music Video, MTV Video Music Awards (2013); Awards for Top R&B Artist, Top Radio Songs Artist, Top R&B Album, Top R&B Song, Billboard Music Awards (2013); Awards for Favorite Soul/R&B Album, American Music Awards (2011, 2012); One of the 100 Most Influential People in the World, Time Magazine (2012); Award for Top Streaming Artist, Billboard Music Awards (2012); Award for Video of the Year, MTV Video Music Awards (2012); Choice Breakout in a Film, Teen Choice Awards (2012); Grammy Award for Best Dance Recording, The Recording Academy (2011); Award for Top Rap Song, Billboard Music Awards (2011); Female R&B Artist Award, BET Awards (2011); Sexiest Woman Alive, Esquire (2011); Award for Top Female Artist, Billboard Music Awards (2011); Viewer's Choice Award, BET Awards (2009, 2010); Award for Favorite Pop Artist, Favorite Song, People's Choice Awards (2010); Award for Top Dance Club Artist, Billboard Music Awards (2010); Grammy Awards for Best Rap/Sung Collaboration, Best Rap Song, The Recording Academy (2010); Award for Best Hip-Hop Song of the Year, Soul Train Music Awards (2010); One of the Women of the Year, Glamour Magazine (2009); Award for Top Digital Song Artist of the Decade, Billboard Music Awards (2009); Award for Best Hip-Hop Collaboration, BET Hip-Hop Awards (2009); Award for Favorite Music Collaboration, People's Choice Awards (2009); Award for Female Artist of the Year, Billboard Music Awards (2006, 2008); Grammy Award for Best Rap/Sung Collaboration, The Recording Academy (2008); Award for Best R&B/Urban Dance Track, International Dance Music Awards (2008); Award for Favorite Pop/Rock Female Artist, American Music Awards (2008); Choice R&B Artist Award, Teen Choice Awards (2006, 2007); Awards for Monster Single of the Year, Video of the Year, MTV Video Music Awards (2007); Award for Favorite R&B Song, People's Choice Awards (2007); One of the Top 25 Entertainers of the Year, Entertainment Weekly (2007); Awards for Entertainer of the Year, Best Female Pop Artist, Best Female R&B Artist, World Music Awards (2007); Female Breakout Artist Award (2006); Numerous Awards Including 33 Barbados Music Awards

FERENCZ, ROBERT M., PHD, T: Division Leader **I:** Research **CN:** Lawrence Livermore National Laboratory **DOB:** 03/28/1957 **PB:** Cleveland **SC:** OH/USA **PT:** Bruce J. Ferencz; Catherine R. Wheeler Ferencz **MS:** Married **CH:** Stephen **ED:** PhD in Mechanical Engineering, Stanford University (1989); MSME, Stanford University (1984); MSCE, Case Western Reserve University (1981); BSCE, Case Western Reserve University (1980) **C:** Division Leader in Computational Engineering, Lawrence Livermore National Laboratory (2015-Present); Group Leader of Methods Development, Lawrence Livermore National Laboratory (2002-2015); Project Leader, Lawrence Livermore National Laboratory (1998-2002); Vice President of Research and Development, Centric Engineering Systems, Inc. (1996-1998); Director of Software Development, Centric Engineering Systems, Inc. (1994-1996); Manager of Quality Assurance, Centric Engineering Systems, Inc. (1990-1993); Engineer, Code Developer, Lawrence Livermore National Laboratory (1984-1989); Engineer, Analyst, Lawrence Livermore National Laboratory (1980-1983) **CR:** Member, Standard Subcommittee on Verification and Validation in Computational Solid Mechanics, The American Society of Mechanical Engineers **CW:** Co-Author, Book Chapter, "The Finite Element Method" (1987); Contributor, Textbook Chapter **MEM:** The Tau Beta Pi Association, Inc.; Sigma Xi, The Scientific Research Society; The American Society of Mechanical Engineers; American Society of Civil Engineers; American Academy of Mechanics **MH:** Albert Nelson Marquis Lifetime Achievement Award **B/I:** Dr. Ferencz became involved in his profession because like many engineers he was always curious as to how things worked. His father was also an engineer and he would hold the flash light while he took many things apart. **AV:** Performing arts; Studying history; Hiking; Gardening **RE:** Unitarian Universalist

FERGUS, GARY S, JD, T: Lawyer **I:** Law and Legal Services **CN:** Fergus **DOB:** 04/20/1954 **PB:** Racine **SC:** WI/USA **PT:** Russell Malcolm Fergus; Phyl Rose (Muratore) Fergus **MS:** Married **SPN:** Isabelle Sabina Beekman (9/28/1985) **CH:** Mary Marckwald Beekman Fergus; Kirkpatrick Russell Beekman Fergus **ED:** LLM, New York University (1981); JD, University of Wisconsin (1979); AB, Stanford University (1976) **C:** Founder, Law Office, Fergus, San Francisco, CA (2002-Present); Senior Partner, E-commerce Anti-trust Group, Brobeck, Phleger & Harrison, San Francisco, CA (2000-2001); Managing Partner, Products Liability, Insurance Coverage, Brobeck, Phleger & Harrison, San Francisco, CA (1996-2000); Partner, Brobeck, Phleger & Harrison, San Francisco, CA (1986-2001); Associate, Brobeck, Phleger & Harrison, San Francisco, CA (1980-1986) **CIV:** Federal Committee, Golden Gate National Park **AW:** AV Rating, Martindale-Hubbell **MEM:** American Bar Association **BAR:** California State Bar (1980); Wisconsin Bar (1979) **MH:** Albert Nelson Marquis Lifetime Achievement Award; Marquis Who's Who Top Professional

FERGUSON, ANDERSON, "DREW" DREW IV, T: U.S. Representative from Georgia **I:** Government Administration/Government Relations/Government Services **CN:** U.S. House of Representatives **DOB:** 11/15/1966 **PB:** Langdale **SC:** AL/USA **MS:** Married **SPN:** Elizabeth Ferguson **CH:** Four Children **ED:** Doctor of Dental Medicine, Medical College of Georgia, Augusta University (1992); Diploma, University of Georgia (1988) **C:** Member, U.S. House of Representatives from Georgia's Third Congressional District (2017-Present); Mayor, West Point, GA (2008-2016); Dentist, Family Dental Practice, GA (1998-2016); Member, West Point Board of Alderman (1997-1999);

Member, Committee on Budget; Member, Committee on Education and the Workforce; Member, Committee on Transportation and Infrastructure

FERGUSON, JIM T., T: Vice President Operations **I:** Manufacturing **CN:** Gold Eagle **MS:** Married **ED:** BA in Business, Management, Marketing, and Related Support Services, Penn Foster (1995) **CT:** Six Sigma Black Belt **C:** Vice President, Operations, Gold Eagle Company (2018-Present); Senior Director of Operations, Amcor Rigid Packaging (2004-2018); Plant Manager, Consolidated Container Company, LLC (2002-2003); Vice President, General Manager, The Plastics Group Inc (1999-2002); Director of Operations, Mattel, Inc (1995-1999) **MIL:** U.S. Army (1978-1981) **AW:** LSSBB **AS:** He attributes his success to his family. **B/I:** Mr. Ferguson was a military veteran. His father was in the plastic business, He is the Vice President of Operations and he followed in his footsteps. **THT:** When you have to make priorities in life, take care of God, family and the organization first.Alot of times, we focus on work and we forget about what allows us to be able to work. Motto: Do better today than what we did yesterday.

FERGUSON, ROBERT WATSON, T: Attorney General of Washington **I:** Government Administration/Government Relations/Government Services **DOB:** 02/23/1965 **PB:** Seattle **SC:** WA/USA **PT:** Murray Ferguson; Betty Ferguson **MS:** Married **SPN:** Colleen Ferguson **CH:** Jack; Katie **ED:** JD, New York University School of Law (1995); BA in Political Science, University of Washington **C:** Attorney General, State of Washington (2013-Present); With, King County Council (2003-2012); Litigator, Preston, Gates & Ellis, Seattle, WA; Chief Clerk to Judge Myron Bright, United States Court of Appeals for the Eighth Circuit; Law Clerk for Chief Judge William Fremming Nielsen, United States District Court Eastern District of Washington, Spokane, WA **CIV:** Volunteer, Jesuit Volunteer Corps Northwest **AW:** One of the 100 Most Influential People, TIME Magazine (2017) **PA:** Democrat

FERGUSON, ROGER WALTER JR., T: Chief Executive Officer and President **I:** Financial Services **CN:** Teachers Insurance and Annuity Association of America (TIAA) **DOB:** 10/28/1951 **PB:** Washington **SC:** DC/USA **MS:** Married **SPN:** Annette LaPorte Nazareth (05/03/1986) **CH:** Two Children **ED:** PhD in Economics, Harvard University (1981); JD, Harvard University, Cum Laude (1979); BA in Economics, Harvard University, Magna Cum Laude (1973); PhD (Honorary), Webster University; PhD (Honorary), Lincoln College **C:** President, Chief Executive Officer, Teachers Insurance & Annuity Foundation College Retirement Equities Fund (TIAA-CREF), New York, NY (2008-Present); Group Financial Market Strategist, Swiss Reinsurance Company, Zurich, Switzerland (2006-2008); Member, Executive Board, Swiss Reinsurance Company, Zurich, Switzerland (2006-2008); Chairman, Swiss Re American Holdings Corp., Armonk, NY (2006-2008); Vice Chairman, Federal Reserve Systems, Washington, DC (1999-2006); Member, Board of Governors, Federal Reserve Systems, Washington, DC (1997-2006); Associate to Partner, McKinsey & Co., Inc., New York, NY (1984-1997); Attorney, Davis Polk & Wardwell, New York, NY (1981-1984) **CR:** Member, President's Economic Recovery Advisory Board (2009-Present); Chairman, Financial Stability Forum (2003-Present); Chairman, Committee on the Global Financial System (2003-Present); Group Ten Working Party on Financial Sector Consolidation (1999-2001); Joint Year (2000); Council (1998-2000) **CIV:** Board of Overseers, Harvard University (2003-Present); Past Treasurer, Friends of Education; Board of

Trustees, Carnegie Endowment for International Peace; Board of Trustees, Institute for Advanced Study (2004); Trustees' Committee, Museum of Modern Art, New York, NY **AW:** Honorary Fellow, University of Cambridge Pembroke College (1973-1974, 2004-Present); 25 Leaders Reshaping New York, "Crain's New York" (2008); Distinguished Service Award, Bond Market Association **MEM:** Council on Foreign Relations **BAR:** New York State Bar Association (1983) **PA:** Democrat

FERREIRA, STACEY, T: Chief Executive Officer **I:** Business Management/Business Services **ED:** Coursework, Xavier College Preparatory (2011); BA in Creativity and Innovation, New York University (2011) **C:** Board of Directors, Watermark (2017-Present); Chief Executive Officer, Co-Founder, Forge (2015-Present); Technology Advisory Board Member, Xavier College (2014-Present) **CW:** Author, "2 Billion Under 20" (2015)

FERRELL, WILL, T: Actor **I:** Media & Entertainment **DOB:** 07/16/1967 **PB:** Irvine **SC:** CA/USA **PT:** Lee Ferrell; Kay Ferrell **MS:** Married **SPN:** Viveca Paulin (08/12/2000) **CH:** Magnus; Mattias; Axel **ED:** BA in Sports Information, University of Southern California (1989) **C:** Comedian, Actor (1997-Present); Comedian, The Groundlings **CW:** Actor, "Downhill" (2020); Actor, "Between Two Ferns: The Movie" (2019); Actor, "Zeroville" (2019); Actor, "Life in Front of a Studio Audience: Norman Lear's 'All in the Family' and 'The Jeffersons'" (2019); Actor, "Drunk Parents" (2019); Actor, "The Lego Movie 2: The Second Part" (2019); Actor, "Drunk History" (2015-2019); Actor, "The 2019 Rose Parade Hosted by Cord & Tish" (2019); Actor, "Holmes and Watson" (2018); Actor, "I Love You, America" (2018); Actor, "Zeroville" (2018); Producer, "LA to Vegas" (2018); Producer, "Succession" (2018); Actor, "Daddy's Home" (2017); Actor, "The House" (2017); Executive Producer, "No Activity" (2017); Actor, "Daddy's Home 2" (2017); Producer, "The Boss" (2016); Actor, "Zeroville" (2016); Actor, "Zoolander 2" (2016); Actor, Producer, "Get Hard" (2015); Actor, Producer, "Daddy's Home" (2015); Actor, Executive Producer, "A Deadly Adoption" (2015); Executive Producer, "Drunk History" (2013-2015); Executive Producer, "Mission Control" (2014); Actor, Producer, "Welcome to Me" (2014); Actor, "The Spoils of Babylon" (2014); Voice Actor, "The Lego Movie" (2014); Executive Producer, "Assistance" (2013); Actor, Producer, Writer, "Anchorman 2: The Legend Continues" (2013); Actor, Executive Producer, "Eastbound & Down" (2009-2012); Actor, Producer, "Tim and Eric's Billion Dollar Movie" (2012); Actor, Producer, "Casa de mi Padre" (2012); Actor, Producer, "The Campaign" (2012); Producer, "Bachelorette" (2012); Actor, "The Office" (2011); Actor, "Papanatos" (2011); Actor, "Funny or Die Presents" (2010-2011); Actor, "Everything Must Go" (2011); Actor, "The Other Guys" (2010); Voice Actor, "Megamind" (2010); Actor, "The Merrick & Rosso Show" (2009); Actor, "You're Welcome America: A Final Night With George W. Bush" (2009); Voice Actor, "SpongeBob SquarePants" (2009); Actor, "Land of the Lost" (2009); Actor, Writer, Executive Producer, "Step Brothers" (2008); Actor, "Semi-Pro" (2008); Actor, "Blades of Glory" (2007); Executive Producer, "Hot Rod" (2007); Actor, Producer, Writer, "Talladega Nights: The Ballad of Ricky Bobby" (2006); Actor, "Stranger Than Fiction" (2006); Voice Actor, "Curious George" (2006); Actor, "The Wendell Baker Story" (2005); Actor, "Kicking & Screaming" (2005); Actor, "Bewitched" (2005); Actor, "Wedding Crashers" (2005); Actor, "The Producers" (2005); Actor, "Winter Passing" (2005); Voice Actor, "Family Guy" (2001" (2005);

Actor, "Melinda and Melinda" (2004); Actor, Writer, "Anchorman: The Legend of Ron Burgundy" (2004); Actor, "Old School" (2003); Actor, "Elf" (2003); Actor, "Saturday Night Live" (1995-2002); Actor, "Jay and Silent Bob Strike Back" (2001); Actor, "Zoolander" (2001); Actor, "Strangers with Candy" (2000); Actor, "Drowning Mona" (2000); Actor, "The Ladies Man" (2000); Actor, "The Suburbans" (1999); Actor, "Austin Powers: The Spy Who Shagged Me" (1999); Actor, "Dick" (1999); Actor, "Superstar" (1999); Voice Actor, "King of the Hill" (1999); Actor, "The Thin Pink Line" (1998); Actor, Writer, "A Night at the Roxbury" (1998); Voice Actor, "Cow and Chicken" (1997); Actor, "Austin Powers-International Man of Mystery" (1997); Actor, "Men Seeking Women" (1997); Actor, "Bucket of Blood" (1995); Actor, "Grace Under Fire" (1995); Actor, "Living Single" (1995) **AW:** Honoree, Hollywood Walk of Fame (2015); Comedian of the Year, British GQ Men of the Year (2015); Mark Twain Prize for American Humor, John F. Kennedy Center for the Performing Arts (2011); 100 Agents of Change, "Rolling Stone" (2009); The 50 Smartest People in Hollywood, "Entertainment Weekly" (2007); The Top 25 Entertainers of the Year (2007); The 50 Most Powerful People in Hollywood, "Premiere" (2005-2006); Numerous Primetime Emmy Awards

FERRIOLA, JOHN J., T: Chairman and Chief Executive Officer **I:** Engineering **CN:** Nucor Corporation **ED:** Bachelor's Degree in Electrical Engineering, Maritime State University of New York **C:** Chairman, Nucor Corporation, Charlotte, NC (2014-Present); Chief Executive Officer, Nucor Corporation, Charlotte, NC (2013-Present); President, Nucor Corporation (2011-Present); President, Chief Operating Officer, Nucor Corporation, Charlotte, NC (2011-2013); Chief Operating Officer, Steelmaking Operations, Nucor Corporation, Charlotte, NC (2007-2011); Executive Vice President, Nucor Corporation, Charlotte, NC (2002-2007); Vice President, Nucor Corporation, Charlotte, NC (1996-2001); General Manager, Nucor Steel, Crawfordsville, IN (1998-2001); General Manager, Nucor Steel, Norfolk, NE (1995-1998); General Manager, Vulcraft, Grapeland, TX (1995); Manager, Maintenance and Engineering, Nucor Steel, Jewett, TX (1992-1995) **CR:** Chairman World Steel Association (2016-Present); Chairman, American Iron and Steel Institute

FERRY, KRISTINA, T: Community Services Director **I:** Medicine & Health Care **CN:** The Mayflower Retirement Community **ED:** Bachelor of Arts in Health, Health Care Administration and Management, Winter Park, FL (2019); Associate of Arts, Valencia College, Orlando, FL **C:** Community Services Assistant, The Mayflower Retirement Community (2019-Present); Intern, Florida Hospital, Orlando, FL (2018-Present); Employee Training and Human Resources, Winter Park, FL (2003-Present); Activities Director, The Mayflower Retirement Community, Winter Park, FL (2015-2018) **CIV:** Fundraising Coordinator, Alzheimer's Association (2017); Court Watch, Chicago Metropolitan Battered Women's Network (2011); Volunteer, Shedd Aquarium (2011) **AW:** Academic Excellence, Rollins College (2019); President's List **MEM:** American Medical Informatics Association; Voice of Women Club **AS:** Ms. Ferry attributes her success to her background. Her mother was very headstrong and a fierce role model, having spent much of her time at work in order to provide for three children. Ms. Ferry found herself alone a lot of the time and was forced to mature very early. **B/I:** Ms. Ferry became involved in her profession after being presented with an opportunity in her eventual career field, which she accepted. Though she never saw herself in such a vocation, she eventually became passionate for it.

FETTER, TREVOR, T: Chairman (Retired) **I:** Financial Services **CN:** The Hartford Financial Services Group **DOB:** 01/16/1960 **PB:** San Diego **SC:** CA/USA **MS:** Married **CH:** Two Children **ED:** MBA, Harvard University (1986); BS in Economics, Stanford University (1982) **C:** Lead Independent Director, The Hartford Financial Services Group (2007-Present); Chairman, TH Medical (2015-2017); President, Chief Executive Officer, TH Medical, Dallas, TX (2003-2015); President, Acting Chief Executive Officer, TH Medical, Dallas, TX (2003); President, TH Medical, Dallas, TX (2002-2003); Chairman, Chief Executive Officer, Broad Lane, Inc., San Francisco (2000-2002); Executive Vice President, Chief Financial Officer, TH Medical, Dallas, TX (1996-2000); Executive Vice President, TH Medical, Dallas, TX (1995-1996); Senior Vice President, MGM/UA Communications Co. (1988); Executive Vice President, Chief Financial Officer, MGM; With, Investment Banking Division, Merrill Lynch Capital Markets **CR:** Board of Trustees, Healthcare Leadership Council; Member, Board, The Hartford Financial Services Group **CIV:** Chairman, Board of Directors, Catalina Island Conservancy; Trustee, Santa Barbara Zoo

FETTERMAN, LISA, T: Chief Executive Officer **I:** Business Management/Business Services **ED:** BA in Journalism, Metropolitan Studies and American Studies, New York University (2006-2010) **C:** Founder and Chief Executive Officer, Nomiku (2012-Present); Chief Executive Officer, Lower East Kitchen (2010-2012); Editor, "SMITH" (2008-2011) **AW:** Listee, 30 Under 30, Zagat; Listee, 30 Under 30, "Inc"

FEUER, STEVEN Z., ESQ., T: Lawyer **I:** Law and Legal Services **DOB:** 03/06/1959 **PB:** Los Angeles **SC:** CA/USA **PT:** Marvin J. Feuer; Brenda C. (Chalin) Feuer **MS:** Married **SPN:** Gail M. Graben (07/8/1984) **CH:** Michael Ian **ED:** JD, Golden Gate University (1984); BA in Political Science, Binghamton University State University of New York (1981) **CT:** New York State Bar Association (1985); United States District Court Northern District of New York (1985) **C:** Private Practice, Oneonta, NY (1987-Present); Associate, The Joyce & Holbrook Law Firm (1985-1987); Legal Assistant, Law Office Philip J. Devine, Oneonta, New York (1984-1985); Legal Assistant, Bushnell, Caplan, Fielding & Rudy (1983-1984) **CR:** General Counsel, Rental Company One, Inc. (2000) **CIV:** Chairman, Temple Beth-El Cemetery (2000-Present); President, Men's Club, Temple Beth El, Oneonta, NY (1986-Present); Path Director, Oneonta Rotary Fund (2006-2010); Otsego County Democratic Committee Member (2002-2006); President, Temple Beth El, Oneonta, NY (1991-1994); Vice President, Temple Beth El, Oneonta, NY (1988-1990); Coach, Little League Baseball Team; Traveling Soccer Coach; Scout Master, Boy Scouts **MEM:** Director, Oneonta Chapter, Rotary International (2006-2009); President, Seagul County Bar Association (2007-2008); New York State Bar Association; Otsego County Bar Association; Pi Sigma Alpha **MH:** Albert Nelson Marquis Lifetime Achievement Award **B/I:** Mr. Feuer became involved in his profession because when he was very young he knew that he wanted to be a lawyer. **AV:** Golfing; Doing archery **RE:** Jewish

FEULNER, EDWIN JOHN, PHD, T: Think Tank Executive (Retired) **I:** Research **CN:** The Heritage Foundation **DOB:** 08/12/1941 **PB:** Chicago **SC:** IL/USA **PT:** Edwin John Feulner Sr.; Helen Joan (Franzen) Feulner **MS:** Married **SPN:** Linda Claire Leventhal (03/08/1969) **CH:** Edwin John III; Emily V. Lown **ED:** Honorary LHD, Thomas More College, Manchester, NH (2005); Honorary Doctorate in Public Service, Hillsdale College, MI (2004); Honorary LLD, St. Norbert College, De Pere, WI (2002); Honorary LLD, Pepperdine University, Malibu, CA (2000); Honorary DLitt, Grove City College, PA (1994); Honorary LLD, Gonzaga University, Spokane, WA (1992); Honorary LLD, Bellevue College (Now Bellevue University), Nebraska (1987); Honorary Doctorate in Social Sciences, Hanyang University, Seoul, Republic of Korea (1982); Honorary Degree, Universidad Francisco Marroquin, Guatemala City, Guatemala (1982); Honorary LHD, Nichols College, Dudley, MA (1981); PhD, University of Edinburgh, Scotland (1981); MBA, University of Pennsylvania, Philadelphia, PA (1964); BS, Regis University, Denver, CO (1963) **C:** Founder, The Heritage Foundation (2013-Present); President, The Heritage Foundation, Washington, DC (2017-2018); Chairman, Asian Studies Center, The Heritage Foundation (2013-2018); Chung Ju-Yung Fellow, The Heritage Foundation (2013-2018); President, The Heritage Foundation, Washington, DC (1977-2013); Counselor to Vice Presidential Candidate Jack Kemp (1996); Chairman, Institute for European Defense & Strategic Studies (1977-1996); Executive Director, U.S. House Republican Study Committee (1974-1977); Administrative Assistant to Republican Philip M. Crane, U.S. House of Representatives (1970-1974); Campaign Manager, Crane for Congress Committee (1972); Confidential Assistant to Secretary Melvin Laird, U.S. Department of Defense (1969-1970); Research Analyst, U.S. House of Republican Conference (1968-1969); Public Affairs Fellow, Hoover Institution (1966-1968); Fellow, Center for Strategic and International Studies (1965-1966); Richard Weaver Fellow, London School of Economics (1965) **CR:** Advisory Board, Public Diplomacy Collaborative, John F. Kennedy School of Government, Harvard Kennedy School (2009-Present); Distinguished Visiting Professor, Hanyang University, Seoul, Republic of Korea (2001-Present); Member, Gingrich/Mitchell Task Force on United Nations Reform (2005-2008); Congressional Policy Advisory Board (1997-2001); Member, International Financial Institute Advisory Committee (1999-2000); Member, National Advisory Board, Center for Education and Research in Free Enterprise, Texas A&M University (1995-1996); Vice Chairman, National Committee on Economic Growth and Tax Reform (1995-1996); Member, Advisory Committee on American Political Channel (1994-1996); U.S. Advisory Committee on Public Diplomacy (1982-1994); Member, U.S. Committee on Improving Effectiveness of the United Nations (1989-1993); Chairman, U.S. Information Agency (1982-1991); Distinguished Fellow, Mobilization Concepts, Development Center, National Defense University (1983-1989); White House Consultant on Domestic Policy (1987); Member, Carlucci Commission on Foreign Assistance (1983); Public Delegate, United Nations Second Special Session on Disarmament (1982); Member of President's Commission, White House Fellows (1980-1981); Member, Executive Committee, Presidential Transition (1979-1980); U.S. Delegate, IMF/World Bank (1974-1976) **CIV:** Life Trustee, Regis University (2013-Present); Member, Executive Council, America's Future Foundation (1998-Present); Trustee, Sarah Scaife Foundation (1988-Present); Vice Chairman, Board of Directors, Roe Foundation (1983-Present); Vice Chairman of Board, Intercollegiate Studies Institute (1979-Present); Vice Chairman of Board, Aequus Institute (1989-2015); Trustee, Regis University (2005-2013); Trustee, National Chamber Foundation (1998-2011); Chairman, Intercollegiate Studies Institute (2003-2006); Member, Multimedia Supercorridor International Advisory Council, Malaysia (2001-2005); Secretary, Korea-U.S. Exchange Council (2001-2004); Member, Board of Visitors, George Mason University (1996-2004); Trustee, Acton Institute (1995-2002); Trustee, International Republican Institute (1995-2001); Member, Executive Committee, Council on National Policy (1993-2001); Trustee, Regis University (1991-2001); Trustee, Sequoia National Bank (1987-1999); Trustee, St. James School (1990-1998); Chairman, Intercollegiate Studies Institute (1989-1993); Trustee, American Council on Germany, NY (1982-1992); Trustee, Lehrman Institute (1981-1990); Chairman, Citizens for American Education Foundation (1985-1989); Trustee, Institute for Research on Economics Taxation (1980-1987); Vice Chairman, Trustee, Manhattan Institute Policy Studies (1977-1986); Trustee, Foundation Francisco Marroquin; Member, Council of Advisers, Bryce Harlow Foundation **CW:** Author, "The American Spirit" (2012); Author, "Getting America Right" (2006); Author, "Public Policy Review" (1977-2001); Author, "Leadership for America" (2000); Author, "Intellectual Pilgrims" (1999); Author, "The March of Freedom" (1998); Author, "Conservatives Stalk the House" (1983); Author, "Looking Back" (1981); Author, "Congress and the New International Economic Order" (1976); Contributor, Articles, Professional Journals and Newspapers; Contributor, Chapters to Books **AW:** Presidential Gold Medal, Czech Republic (2014); Ronald Reagan Lifetime Achievement Award, Council of National Policy (2013); Bradley Prize (2012); Named, One of the Most Influential United States Conservatives, The Daily Telegraph (2010); Charles Hoeflich Lifetime Achievement Award, Intercollegiate Studies Institute (2009); Named, One of the Seven Most Powerful Conservatives, Forbes Magazine (2009); Named, One of the 50 Most Powerful People in Washington, D.C., GQ Magazine (2007); Truman-Reagan Medal of Freedom (2006); Walter Judd Freedom Award, Fund for American Studies (2004); Thomas Jefferson Servant Leadership Award, Council of National Policy (1996); Named, Man of the Year, The Wharton School, University of Pennsylvania (1993); Director's Service Award, U.S. Information Agency (1992); Superior Public Service Award, U.S. Department of the Navy (1987); Named, Free Enterprise Man of the Year, Texas A&M University (1985); Distinguished Alumni Award, Regis University (1985); American Eagle Award, Invest-in-American National Council (1983); Washington Award, Freedom Foundation (1979-1980); Decorated, Presidential Recognition Medal; Decorated, Order of Diplomatic Service Merit; Decorated, Merit-Gwanghwa Medal, Republic of Korea; Decorated, Order of Brilliant Star with Grand Cordon, Republic of China **MEM:** President, The Philadelphia Society (2013-2014); Treasurer, Mont Pelerin Society (2000-2014); Senior Vice President, Treasurer, Mont Pelerin Society (1998-2000); President, Treasurer, Mont Pelerin Society (1996-1998); Treasurer, Mont Pelerin Society (1979-1996); Chairman, International Committee of the G.K. Chesterton Society (1989-1992); President, The Philadelphia Society (1982-1983); Treasurer, The Philadelphia Society (1964-1979); The Union League Club, New York, NY; Metropolitan Club; Reform Club, London, England; Bohemian Club, San Francisco, CA; Knights of Malta; Knights of the Holy Sepulchre; Alpha Kappa Psi; American Economics Association; Instituts d'études politiques **MH:** Albert Nelson Marquis Lifetime Achievement Award; Marquis Who's Who Top Professional **AV:** Model railroading **PA:** Republican **RE:** Roman Catholic

FEY, TINA, T: Actress, Comedian **I:** Media & Entertainment **DOB:** 05/18/1970 **PB:** Upper Darby **SC:** PA/USA **PT:** Donald Fey; Jeanne (Xenakes) Fey **MS:** Married **SPN:** Jeff Richmond (06/03/2001) **CH:** Alice Zenobia; Penelope Athena **ED:** BA in Drama, University of Virginia (1992) **C:** Performer, Second City Comedy Troupe, Chicago, IL **CW:** Actress, "Modern Love" (2019); Actress, "Wine Country" (2019); Guest, "Great News" (2017); Guest, "Maya & Marty" (2016); Guest, "Difficult People" (2016); Guest, "The Kicker" (2016); Actress, "Whiskey Tango Foxtrot" (2016); Actress, Producer, "Whiskey Tango Foxtrot" (2016); Co-Host, "The 72nd Golden Globe Awards" (2015); Co-Host, "Family Fortune" (2015); Guest, "Unbreakable Kimmy Schmidt" (2015); Guest, "Inside Amy Schumer" (2015); Guest, "Saturday Night Live" (2015); Actress, "Monkey Kingdom" (2015); Actress, "Sisters" (2015); Actress, Producer, "Sisters" (2015); Narrator, "Monkey Kingdom" (2015); Actress, "Family Fortune" (2015); Co-Host, "The 71st Golden Globe Awards" (2014); Executive Producer, "Cabot College" (2014); Actress, "Muppets Most Wanted" (2014); Actress, "This Is Where I Leave You" (2014); Actress, "Admission" (2013); Actress, "Anchorman 2: The Legend Continues" (2013); Co-host, "The 70th Golden Globe Awards" (2013); Actress, Writer and Co-Producer, "30 Rock" (2006-2013); Author, "Bossypants" (2011); Actress, "Date Night" (2010); Voice Actress, "Megamind" (2010); Actress, "The Invention of Lying" (2009); Actress, "Baby Mama" (2008); Guest, "Saturday Night Live: Presidential Bash" (2008); Voice Actress, "Aqua Teen Hunger Force Colon Movie (2007); Actress, "Saturday Night Live" (2000-2006); Writer, "Saturday Night Live" (1997-2006); Actress, "Man of the Year" (2006); Actress, "Beer League" (2006); Actress, Writer, "Mean Girls" (2004); Writer, "The Colin Quinn Show" (2002); Writer, "NBC 75th Anniversary Special" (2002); Guest, "The Real World/Road Rules Extreme Challenge" (2001); Guest, "Upright Citizens Brigade" (1999); Writer, "Saturday Night Live: 25th Anniversary" (1999) **AW:** Listee, The 100 Most Powerful Women in Entertainment, The Hollywood Reporter (2008-2014); Emmy Award for Outstanding Writing for a Comedy Series (2013); Screen Actors Guild Award for Outstanding Performance by a Female Actor in a Comedy Series (2008, 2010, 2013); Mark Twain Prize for American Humor, John F. Kennedy Center for the Performing Arts (2010); Teen Choice Award for Choice Movie Actress: Comedy (2010); Danny Thomas Producer of the Year Award in Episodic TV - Comedy, Producers Guild of America (2009-2010); Golden Globe Award for Best TV Series - Musical Or Comedy, Hollywood Foreign Press Association (2009); Listee, The 100 Agents of Change, Rolling Stone Magazine (2009); Funny Female Star, People's Choice Awards (2009); Writers Guild of America Award for Best Comedy Series (20Emmy Award for Outstanding Guest Actress in a Comedy Series, Academy TV Arts & Sciences (2009); Golden Globe Award for Best Performance by an Actress in a TV Series - Musical or Comedy, Hollywood Foreign Press Association (2008, 2009); Listee, The 100 Most Influential People in the World, Time Magazine (2007, 2009); Emmy Award for Outstanding Comedy Series, Academy of TV Arts & Sciences (2007, 2008); Producers Guild of America Award for Best Episodic TV-Comedy (2008); Emmy Award for Outstanding Lead Actress in a Comedy Series, Academy TV Arts & Sciences (2008); Listee, 10 People Who Mattered, Newsweek (2008); Listee, 25 Leaders Reshaping New York, Crain's New York Magazine (2008); Listee, The Ten Most Fascinating People of 2008, Barbara Walters Special (2008); Listee, The 100 Most Powerful Celebrities, Forbes.com (2008); Listee, The 50 Most Powerful Women in New York City, New York Post (2007, 2008);

Entertainer of the Year, Associated Press (2008); Listee, The Top 25 Entertainers of Year, Entertainment Weekly (2007); Entertainer of the Year, Entertainment Weekly (2001)

FIELD, ROBERT BUNTEN, T: Lawyer **I:** Law and Legal Services **DOB:** 02/08/1943 **PB:** San Francisco **SC:** CA/USA **PT:** Robert Bunten Field; Jean (Pierce) Field **MS:** Married **SPN:** Elizabeth C. Hoopes Field (10/02/1971) **CH:** Robert Bunten III; Charles S.; Victoria E. **ED:** JD, Boston University (1970); AB, Dartmouth College (1964) **C:** Sole Practitioner, Robert B. Field, Jr., PLLC (2011-2015); Founding Member and Partner, Colliander, Field, & Brown, P.A., Portsmouth, NH (1999); Partner, Sheehan, Phinney, Bass & Green P.A. (Now Sheehan Phinney), Manchester and Portsmouth, NH (1980-1999); Partner, Hamblett & Kerrigan P.A., Nashua, NH (1970-1980) **CR:** Board of Directors, Pease Development Authority, New England Trade Adjustment Assistance Corp. (Now New England Trade Adjustment Assistance Center), Boston, MA; Board, Gundalow Company, Portsmouth, NH **CIV:** Trustee, Cuttyhunk Historical Society (1994-1997); Cuttyhunk Yacht Club, Commodore (1984-1986); Past Trustee and Chairman, Children's Museum Portsmouth, RiverWoods Group; Exeter **MIL:** USS Longbeach (CGN9), Anchored at Da Nang Harbor, Vietnam (1968-1969); New Hampshire Lieutenant, Junior Grade, United States Naval Reserve (1964-1968) **MEM:** Board of Governors, Nashua Country Club (1978-1980); New Hampshire Bar Association; Rockingham County Bar Association; Warwick Club; Member, Board of Governors, Treasurer, Cuttyhunk Yacht Club; Nashua Country Club; Abenaqui Country Club; Rye Beach Club, The Beach Club; Rotary International **BAR:** New Hampshire (1970) **MH:** Albert Nelson Marquis Lifetime Achievement Award **B/I:** Mr. Field became involved in his profession because his grandfather was an attorney in Portland, Maine, so he was inspired by him. He believed in justice and was an honest, upright person and was inspired to help other people. **AV:** Travel **PA:** Republican **RE:** Congregationalist

FIGWER, J. JACEK, T: Acoustics Consultant (Retired) **I:** Media & Entertainment **CN:** Jacek Figwer Associates Inc **DOB:** 03/16/1928 **PB:** Mielec **SC:** Poland **PT:** Jozef M. Figwer; Zofia (Haladej) Figwer **MS:** Widowed **SPN:** Magda L. Rzadkowska (09/15/1955, Deceased) **CH:** Kai J.; Ulla T. **ED:** Doctor of Philosophy in Applied Acoustics, Research Institute of Film and Photo, Moscow, Russia (1958); Master of Science in Electrical Engineering, Silesian University of Technology, Gliwice, Poland (1951) **C:** Retired (Present); Acoustics Consultant, Principal Consultant, Jacek Figwer Associates, Inc., Concord, MA (1978); Supervisor, Consultant, Bolt Beranek and Newman, Cambridge, MA (1962-1978); Engineer of Research and Development, Deutsche Grammophon GmbH, Hannover, Germany (1960-1962); Engineer of Research and Development, Motion Picture Industry, Warsaw, Poland (1951-1960) **MEM:** Fellow, Acoustical Society of America; Audio Engineering Society **MH:** Albert Nelson Marquis Lifetime Achievement Award; Marquis Who's Who Top Professional **AS:** Mr. Figwer attributes his success to his mentor, Tadeusz Zagajewski, a professor of electronics at the Silesian University of Technology in Gliwice, Poland, because he taught him to seek in-depth solutions to problems, rather than superficial answers. **B/I:** Mr. Figwer became involved in his profession due to a longstanding interest in electrical engineering, particularly regarding radio receivers and sound equipment. After securing employment in the film industry, he was involved in the introduction of magnetic recording to replace optical sound tracks. **AV:** Glider pilot;

Private pilot aircraft; Single engine land **THT:** Mr. Figwer believes that the most important aspect of successful work as a consultant is to establish a close and supportive cooperation with other professionals working on the project. The most rewarding aspect of his profession is following the history of his completed projects and seeing that they are being used successfully.

FILYAW, LISTON NATHANIEL, T: Director of Student Activities (Retired) **I:** Education/Educational Services **DOB:** 10/31/1949 **PB:** New Haven **SC:** CT/USA **PT:** Macceo Nathaniel Filyaw; Katheryn Dorothy Filyaw **ED:** MS in Elementary Education, Eastern Connecticut State University (1976); MA in Rehabilitation Counseling, University of Connecticut (1978); BA in Sociology, University of Connecticut (1972); AA in Liberal Arts, South Central Community College, New Haven, CT (1970) **C:** Contract Work, Various Organizations, CT (2003-2020); Director of Student Activities, Manchester Community College (2002-2003); Director of Minority Student Programs, Manchester Community College (1993-2002); Counselor, Center for Academic Programs, University of Connecticut, Storrs, CT (1986-1993); Assistant Director, H. Fred Simons African American Cultural Center (AACC), University of Connecticut, Storrs, CT (1983-1986); Coordinator, Programs, Employment, Hartford Housing Authority (Now The Housing Authority of the City of Hartford), CT (1979-1981) **CR:** Private Consultant, Various Organizations, CT (1981-1983) **CIV:** Co-founder, Vice President, Journey Writers, Inc.; Chartered Member, Co-founder, Former President, Vital Elements of the Arts, Inc.; Former Board Member, American School for the Deaf; Former Board Member, Queen Ann Nzinga Center for Cultural, Education and Social Change (QANC); Former President, African Americans in Higher Education **CW:** Author, Several Plays; Actor; Director; Singer **AW:** Community Service Award, Greater Hartford Interdenominational Ministerial Alliance (2017); Leadership in Service, The Connecticut Department of Higher Education (1999); Mildred Mitchell Arts and Culture Service Award, The Connecticut Senate (1997); Official Citation, City of New Haven (1994) **MEM:** Former Member, New England Association Educational Opportunity Program Personnel; Former Member, Connecticut Council Black Students and Professionals; Former Member, Connecticut Association of Educational Opportunity Programs; Former Member, University of Connecticut Professional Employees Association, American Federation of Teachers, AFL-CIO; Former Member, Connecticut State Federation of Teachers; Former Member, American Federation of Teachers, American Federation of Teachers, AFL-CIO; Former Member, Union Representative, AFL-CIO; Former Member, Charter Member, Co-chair, Black Employees Association **MH:** Albert Nelson Marquis Lifetime Achievement Award **AS:** Ms. Filyaw has always worked hard to achieve her goals. Once she set her mind on a particular task, she never stopped until it was completed. That persistence included her educational pursuits, as well as her artistic endeavors. **B/I:** Ms. Filyaw has always enjoyed being in a learning environment, both as a student and as an employee at institutions of higher education. Working with students has been her greatest reward and fulfillment, as she watched them grow, eventually graduate, and secure profession careers. **AV:** Playwriting; Drama; Music **PA:** Democrat **THT:** Ms. Filyaw says, "It is my belief that we enter life to fulfill many purposes. I also believe that life is precious and we are all connected in one way or another. We each have the capacity to make contributions that can enhance the lives of others, society and the world. This can be accomplished by valuing each person's individuality, in addition to respecting differences, and appreciating what each one has to offer. First, we must be aware of our own thought patterns and work to address areas in our lives we would like to change. It is also important to continue to enhance our personal growth through self-reflection and other means and methods that works for each person. Being aware of our own thought processes helps us to become more open to accepting other's joys, challenges and concerns. Finally, we must be open to change. With each generation comes new ways of thinking, processing, new methods of learning, scientific discoveries and technological advancements. We must therefore be prepared for it."

FINCHER, HUGH MCCOMMON, T: Foreign Language Educator **I:** Education/Educational Services **DOB:** 11/29/1945 **PB:** Gaffney **SC:** SC/USA **PT:** Hugh McCommon Fincher, Jr. (Deceased 1989); Flora Neva (Bonner) Fincher (Deceased 1983) **ED:** PhD in Humanities, Florida State University, Tallahassee, FL (1979); MA in Classics, University of North Carolina, Chapel Hill, NC (1969); AB in Classics, University of North Carolina, Chapel Hill, NC, with Honors (1967) **CT:** Licensed Teacher, South Carolina (1982); Licensed Teacher, North Carolina (1982) **C:** Teacher of Spanish, The Village School, Gaffney, SC (2009-2010); Teacher of Spanish, Union County Schools, Union, SC (2007-2009); Teacher, Cherokee County Schools, Gaffney, SC (1984-2007); Teacher of Latin, French, Spanish, and German, Cherokee County Schools, Gaffney, SC (1984-2007); Adjunct Professor, Latin, Converse College, Spartanburg, SC (1988-1992); Adjunct Professor, French, Limestone College, Gaffney, SC (1985-1987); Teacher, Trinity School, Rutherfordton, NC (1982-1984); Teacher, Headmaster, Gaffney Day School, Gaffney, SC (1975-1982); Instructor, English, University of Alabama, Huntsville, AL (1973-1975); Assistant Professor, Classics, Birmingham-Southern College, Birmingham, AL (1969-1970) **CR:** Developer, English as Second Language Program (1993-1996); Developer, Teacher, French, FLES Program, Cherokee County Schools, Gaffney, SC (1990-1993); Member, State Committees, Department of Education, South Carolina (1988-1995) **CIV:** Volunteer Translator, Hispanic Community **CW:** Editor, "Caesar's Bellum Helveticum" (Copyrighted, Not Published) **MEM:** National Education Association; Carolina Teachers English to Speakers Other Languages; Classical Association Midwest and South; South Atlantic Modern Language Association; American Association of Teachers of French; American Association of Teachers of German **MH:** Albert Nelson Marquis Lifetime Achievement Award **B/I:** Dr. Fincher became involved in his profession because he enjoyed Latin and Greek and wanted to work with people. He has always loved teaching, and was inspired to become a teacher because of the interaction he had with several of his teachers, especially his high school Latin teacher. He admired her a great deal. **AV:** Languages; Linguistics; Genealogy **RE:** Presbyterian

FINE, JASON E., T: Editor **I:** Writing and Editing **CN:** Rolling Stone **ED:** Master in History and Journalism, University of California Berkeley; BA in History and Journalism, University of California Berkeley **C:** Editor, Rolling Stone (2018-Present); Managing Editor, Rolling Stone (2015-Present); Editorial Director, Men's Journal (2015-2017); Editor-at-large, Rolling Stone (1997-2015)

FINE, JEFFREY SCOTT, MD, T: Vice Chairman of Rusk Rehabilitation **I:** Medicine & Health Care **CN:** NYU Grossman School of Medicine **ED:** Residency, Mount Sinai School of Medicine, Rehab Medicine

(1997); MD, New York Medical College (1993); MD, New York Medical College; MD, George Washington University **CT:** American Board of PM&R (ABPMR) (2016); American Board of PM&R (ABPMR) (2004); American Board of PM&R (ABPMR) (2003) **C:** Clinical Assistant Professor, Department of Psychiatry; Associate Professor, Department of Rehabilitation Medicine; Clinical Associate Professor, Ronald O. Perelman Department of Emergency Medicine; Clinical Associate Professor, Department of Pediatrics; Chief, Physical Medicine and Rehabilitation Service, NYU Langone Hospital-Brooklyn; Vice-Chair, Network Development, NYU Langone Hospital-Brooklyn, Rusk Rehabilitation **CR:** Vice Chairman of Rusk Rehabilitation, NYU Grossman School of Medicine **MH:** Marquis Who's Who Top Professional **B/I:** Dr. Fine became involved in his profession because it was one of the things for him to do at the time, to do with his life, as he had experience working with his father in his office. His father was a surgeon.

FINE, JEREMY S. MD, T: Physician **I:** Medicine & Health Care **CN:** Jeremy Fine MD, Inc. **DOB:** 09/06/1974 **PB:** Johanessburg **SC:** South Africa **MS:** Married **CH:** Four Children **ED:** Resident, Internal Medicine, Cedars Sinai Medical Center, Los Angeles, CA (2002-2004); Residency, Cedar Sinai Medical Center (2001-2004); Coursework, Tel Aviv University Sackler School of Medicine (1997-2001); BA in Biology, University of California, Yeshiva University, Los Angeles, CA and New York, NY (1997) **CT:** Board Certified, Internal Medicine, State of California **C:** Physician, Jeremy Fine MD Incorporated (2005- Present); Clinical Instructor of Medicine, David Geffen School of Medicine at UCLA, (2004-2006); Clinical Instructor of Medicine, University of Southern California Keck School of Medicine (2003-2005) **CIV:** Issie Shapiro, Center for Developmentally Disabled Children **AW:** Named Top Doctor, Los Angeles, LA Magazine; Named Most Compassionate Doctor; Named One of Hollywood's Favorite Doctors **AS:** Dr. Fine attributes his success to a love of hard work and enjoying what he does. He also always tries to better himself each day. **B/I:** Dr. Fine has always had a love of science and social interactions. He also had a desire to help others and their families improve their lives.

FINK, LAURENCE DOUGLAS, T: Chief Executive Officer **I:** Financial Services **CN:** BlackRock **ED:** Master of Business Administration, Real Estate, University of California Los Angeles (1976); Bachelor of Arts in Political Science, University of California Los Angeles (1974) **C:** Chairperson, Chief Executive Officer, BlackRock (1988-Present); Managing Director, First Boston Corporation (1976-1988)

FINK, RAYMOND, PHD, T: Medical Educator **I:** Medicine & Health Care **DOB:** 04/21/1927 **PB:** New York **SC:** NY/USA **PT:** William; Yetta (Rales) F. **MS:** Married **SPN:** Louise Berenson (01/27/1983); Ruth Ursula Gebhard (5/28/1961, Divorced 1982) **CH:** William D.; David S. **ED:** Doctor of Philosophy, Cornell University (1956); Master of Arts, University Denver (1949); Bachelor of Business Administration, City College of New York (1947) **C:** Director of Research, Mid-Hudson Family Health Institute, New Paltz, NY (1999-2001); Director, Health Services Research, New York Medical College, Valhalla, NY (1990-2000); Professor of Community and Preventive Medicine, New York Medical College, Valhalla, NY (1978-2000); Director, Health Policy Management, New York Medical College, Valhalla, NY (1982-1990); Vice President, Research and Statistics, Health Insurance Plan Greater New York, New York, NY (1962-1978); Associate Director, Drinking Practices Study, California State Department

Public Health, Berkeley, CA (1960-1962); Research Associate, Bureau Social Science Research, Washington, DC (1957-1960); Survey Statistician, U.S. Bureau Census, Suitland, MD (1949-1950, 1956); Research Associate, Human Resources Research, George Washington University, Washington, DC (1952-1953); Statistician, Opinion Research Center, University of Denver (1949) **CR:** Advisor to President, Hofstra University Public Health Program (2011-2018); Epidemiologic and Services Review Committee, National Institute of Mental Health (1980-1985); Chairperson, Task Force on HMOs, National Institute of Mental Health, Rockville, MD (1971-1972); Chairperson, Social Science Advisor Committee, Executive Committee, Planned Parenthood Federation of America, New York, NY (1966-1971); Mental Health Advisory Committee, United Auto Workers (1967-1970) **CIV:** Trustee, Health Services Improvement Fund, New York, NY (1986-2000); Active, United Hospital Fund, New York **MIL:** Sergeant, U.S. Army, Office of the Secretary of Defense (1950-1952) **CW:** Contributor, Articles to Professional Journals **AW:** Grantee, Robert Wood Johnson Foundation (1990-1994); Grantee, Social Science Research Council (1982-1983); Grantee, National Cancer Institute (1972-1978); Grantee, National Institute of Mental Health (1968-1972); Distinguished Service Award; Grantee, New York Association of Public Opinion Research **MEM:** President, Herman Biggs Society (1994-1998, 2006-2010); Chairperson, Medical and Health Research Association (1975-2002); Co-Editor, American Association of Public Opinion Research (1968-1969); Councilor at Large, New York Association of Public Opinion Research; Association for Health Services Research; American Public Health Association **MH:** Marquis Lifetime Achievement Award **AS:** Dr. Fink attributes his success on the educational opportunities provided to him by New York City, the state and by the GI Bill. **RE:** Jewish

FINKENAUER, ABBY LEA, T: U.S. Representative from Iowa **I:** Government Administration/Government Relations/Government Services **DOB:** 12/27/1988 **PB:** Dubuque **SC:** IA/USA **ED:** BA in Public Relations, Drake University **C:** Member, U.S. House of Representatives from Iowa's First Congressional District (2019-Present); Member, 99th District, Iowa House of Representatives (2015-Present); Page, Pat Murphy, Democratic Speaker of the House, Iowa (2007); Page, Representative Jim Nussle (2006); Legislative Aide, Iowa Democratic State Representative Todd Taylor; Communications Specialist, Community Foundation of Greater Dubuque **PA:** Democrat

FINNEGAN, JOHN VIANNEY, CIC, T: Adjunct Professor of Risk Management **I:** Education/Educational Services **DOB:** 11/26/1951 **PB:** Buffalo **SC:** NY/USA **PT:** Francis Thomas Finnegan; Catherine Virginia Finnegan **MS:** Married **SPN:** Nancy A. Finnegan **CH:** Shannon; Amy Catherine Little; Jacob (Grandson); Isaac (Grandson); Benjamin (Grandson); Anna (Granddaughter) **ED:** BA, University of Maine, Orono, ME (1975); AA, University of Maine, Augusta, ME (1973); Degree in Liberal Studies, University of Maine, Augusta, ME (1972) **CT:** Certification, Society of Certified Insurance Counselors, Texas (1987) **C:** President, Macomber Farr & Whitten, Augusta, ME (1975-2014); Director of Treatment, Kennebec County Correctional Facility, Augusta, ME (1972-1975) **CR:** Assistant Professor of Risk Management, University of Maine (2004-Present); Adjunct Professor, University of Maine (2004-Present); Chairman, City Of Augusta Health and Welfare Appeals Board, Member, Outstanding Alumni, University of Maine (2008); Chairman, Board of Visitors, University of Maine (2006-2007); Past President, Maine Independent

Insurance Agents, Augusta, ME (1993-1994); Chairman, Augusta Parking District (1981) **CIV:** Chairman, Whatever Family Festival, Augusta, ME (1998-2008); Director, Augusta Board Trade (1997-2008); President, University of Maine Foundation (2000-2007); Director, Global Review Universal Healthcare, University of Maine **CW:** Director, Organist, Christmas Chorale; Songwriter, Professional Keyboardist, Musician; Author, Historical Novel, Pending Publication **AW:** Boy Scouts of America Citizenship Award (2014); Businessperson of the Year, Chamber of Commerce (2013); Distinguished Service Award, University of Maine (2006); Chairman Award, American Association of Managing General Agents (1989) **MEM:** Director Emeritus, Kennebec Valley Chamber of Commerce (1997-2008); Chairman, Board Member, Kennebec Valley Chamber of Commerce (2000-2001); Kennebec Valley Chamber of Commerce **B/I:** Mr. Finnegan became involved in his profession because he had a dual major in English and Criminal Justice in college. When he got out of college, he was the director of a prison treatment program. Being young and idealistic, he wanted to save people from crime but realized it was not as easy as he thought. He gained a lot of experience from that, but ended up unemployed and in need of a job. He came from a financial family as his father was a banker and retired as the vice president of a large bank. However, his twin brother was the one who followed in the banking footsteps and one day he saw an ad for insurance and felt it might be interesting as he had some experience in sales. He decided to try it and ended up in an independent insurance agency, which was family-owned. He was hired as the secretary with no experience and came in at the lowest level and learned everything about insurance. They sent him to Boston to some commercial insurance schools and he really got interested in it. Eventually, after 40 years, the boss made him president over his two sons. **AV:** Music; Writing **PA:** independent **RE:** Roman Catholic

FINNEY, KATHRYN REBECCA, T: 1) Founder, Chief Executive Officer 2) Founder, Chief Executive Officer **I:** Business Management/Business Services **CN:** 1) DigitalUndivided 2) Budget Fashionista **PB:** Milwaukee **SC:** WI/USA **MS:** Married **SPN:** Tobias Wright **ED:** Honorary Doctorate, Mount Holyoke College (2017); MS in International Epidemiology, Yale University; BA in Political Science and Women's Studies, Rutgers, the State University of New Jersey **C:** Founder, Chief Executive Officer, DigitalUndivided (2012-Present); Author, Random House/Ballantine Books (2006-Present); Executive Producer, #ReWriteTheCode Documentary (2015-2016); Adviser, All Star Code (2014-2016); Adviser, MentorMe, Inc. (2013-2016); Editor-at-Large, BlogHer (2012-2014); Founder, Chief Executive Officer, The Budget Fashionista (2004-2014); Founder, Chief Executive Officer, Simply Good Productions (2003-2011) **CR:** Board of Directors, Public Radio International (2017-Present); Global Fellow, Echoing Green (2016-Present); Fellow, French-American Foundation (2017); Fellow, Eisenhower Fellowships (2015-2017) **CIV:** National Advisory Council on Innovation and Entrepreneurship (2016); Women Entrepreneurs and Investors Advisory Council, SUNY Levin Institute (2013-2014) **CW:** Author, "How to Be a Budget Fashionista: The Ultimate Guide to Looking Fabulous for Less" (2006) **AW:** One of the 100 Most Powerful Women in Business, Entrepreneur Magazine (2019); Young Leader, French-American Foundation (2017); One of the 50 Most Powerful Mothers, Working Mother (2017); Woke 100 List, Essence Magazine (2017); Grace Hopper Celebration ABIE Award, Anita Borg Institute (2016); Woman to Watch, Entrepreneur Magazine (2016); One of the Women to Watch, Marie Claire (2015); Game Changer Award, Spelman College (2015); One of the 100 List of Top Innovators, UPSTART Business Journal (2015); Most Influential New York Business Woman, New York Business Journal (2015); One of the Grio 100 (2014); One of the Ebony Power 100, Ebony Magazine (2013); White House Champion of Change (2013); SXSW Black Innovators Award, SXSW/Blacks in Technology (2013); One of the Top 10 Women in Money, AOL (2012); One of the 40 Stars Under 40, Black Enterprise Magazine (2012)

FINNEY, ROBERT, "DR. BOB" G. PHD, PHD, T: Professor Emeritus **I:** Education/Educational Services **DOB:** 03/31/1935 **PB:** Newark **SC:** NJ/USA **PT:** Gerald Joseph Finney; Helen Marguerite (Kaufhold) Finney **MS:** Married **SPN:** Scarlett Vanessa Davis (5/19/1985); Barbara Jayne Carr (11/19/1960, Divorced 1/1982) **CH:** Torin; Tara; Tal; Tanya; Treg; Tasha **ED:** PhD, The Ohio State University (1971); MA, The Ohio State University (1957); AB, Marietta College (1956) **C:** Professor Emeritus; Chair, Senior Citizen Advisory Commission, Long Beach, CA (2016-Present); Distinguished Professor, Department of Film & Electronic Arts, California State University Long Beach (1993-2015); Professor, Chairman, Department of Radio-TV-film, California State University Long Beach (1977-1993); Professor, James Madison University, Harrisonburg, VA (1973-1977); Associate Professor, Memphis State University (1971-1973); Associate Professor, Dean, School of Communication, Shaw University, Raleigh, NC (1968-1971); Teaching Associate, The Ohio State University, Columbus, OH (1966-1968); Instructor, University of Cincinnati (1964-1966); Personnel Director, Radio Corp. of America (1961-1964) **CR:** Professional Musician, Band Leader, Scarlett and the Dr. Bob Finney Jazz Group (2003-Present); Research Director, Great Escapes Travel TV Show (1985); Adjunct Senior Lecturer, School of Journalism, University of Southern California (1979-1989); Director, Museum of Broadcast Communications, Board of Directors, Broadcast Education Association (1978-1986); Consultant in Field; Board of Directors, Station KOCE-TV, Huntington Beach, CA, Station KLON-FM, Long Beach, CA **CIV:** Scoutmaster, Los Alamitos California Council, Boy Scouts of America (1981-1986) **MIL:** Retired, Captain (0-6), United States Navy (1957-1988) **CW:** Editor, Feedback Magazine (1976-1982); Producer, Radio Show, "Encounter: Public Policy" (1974-1977); Producer, TV Program, "Town Hall" (1973-1977); Producer, TV Program, "Face to Face" (1973-1977) **AW:** Honored as California State University Outstanding Professor (1993); Grantee, Virginia Council on Humanities (1973-1977); Grantee, U.S. Office of Education (1967-1971) **MEM:** Board of Directors, 30 Year Committee, Broadcast Education Association (1986); Academy of TV Arts and Sciences; Association of Communication Administrators; Life Member, Naval Reserve Association; American Federation of Musicians; Life Member, National Eagle Scout Association; Broadcaster Foundation **MH:** Albert Nelson Marquis Lifetime Achievement Award **AS:** Dr. Finney attributes his success to hardwork. **B/I:** Dr. Finney became involved in his profession because when he graduated from getting his master's degree in 1957, he was tired of school so he enrolled in the U.S. Navy. When he left the U.S. Navy, he worked for RCA for several years and it was around the last three years there that he had an epiphany and decided he wanted to be a teacher. He gave up a big promotion and salary to go back to school to get his doctorate. **PA:** Democrat **RE:** Roman Catholic

FINUCANE, ANNE, T: Vice Chair **I:** Financial Services **CN:** Bank of America **DOB:** 07/12/1952 **PB:** Boston **SC:** MA/USA **PT:** William Finucane; Mary Finucane **MS:** Married **SPN:** Mike Barnicle **CH:** Four children; Three stepchildren **ED:** BA, University of New Hampshire, Durham, NH **C:** Vice Chair, Bank of America (2015-Present); Global Chief Strategy and Marketing Officer, Bank of America (2005-2015); Chief Marketing Officer, Fleet Bank (1995-2004); Executive Vice President, Hill Holliday (1980-1994); Office of Cultural Affairs, City of Boston, Massachusetts (1975-1977) **CIV:** Board of Directors, CVS Caremark (2011-Present); Board of Directors, Brigham and Women's Hospital; Board of Directors, Carnegie Hall; Board of Directors, JFK Library Foundation; Board of Directors, National September 11 Memorial and Museum; Board of Directors, American Ireland Fund; Board of Directors, International Center for Journalists; Board of Directors, Boston Public Library Foundation; Board of Directors, Museum of Fine Arts, Boston; Board of Directors, John F. Kennedy Presidential Library; Board of Directors, Partners HealthCare; Board of Trustees, Special Olympics; Council on Foreign Relations; President, Massachusetts Women's Forum **AW:** Advertising Woman of the Year, Advertising Women of New York (2013); New York Women in Communications Matrix Award (2013); Inaugural International Women's Media Foundation Leadership Award; 25 Most Powerful Women in Banking, American Banker Magazine

FIORAVANTI, SHIRLEY J.S., T: Retired Language Educator **I:** Education/Educational Services **DOB:** 08/04/1930 **PB:** Oneida **SC:** NY/USA **PT:** L. Raymond Serviss; Irma May (Sager) Serviss **MS:** Widowed **SPN:** Joseph A. Fioravanti (9/3/1983, Deceased 2009) **CH:** Christopher (Deceased); Donna (Deceased); Steven; Susan; Michael **ED:** MA, Syracuse University (1957); BA, University at Albany, State University of New York (1952); Postgraduate Coursework, Syracuse University **CT:** Licensed Teacher, New York (1952) **C:** Retired (1990); Associate Professor, Spanish, State University of New York College at Oneonta (1961-1990); Spanish Teacher, Shaker High School, North Colonie, NY (1958-1961); Spanish Teacher, North Rose Central School (1952-1958) **CIV:** Advisory Board, Center of Continuing Adult Learning, Oneonta, NY (2002-Present); Teacher, Center of Continuing Adult Learning, Oneonta, NY (1994-Present); Vice President, National Federation of Republican Women (2000); President, AUW **MEM:** Former Member, League of Women Voters; Garden Club; Historian, Eastern Star **MH:** Albert Nelson Marquis Lifetime Achievement Award **B/I:** In sixth grade, Mrs. Fioravanti decided that she wanted to work with the United Nations. She was influenced by the many popular Spanish singers around her, as well as her experience in her local church. **AV:** Reading; Traveling **PA:** Republican **RE:** Presbyterian

FIRE, ANDREW ZACHARY, T: Biologist, Pathology Professor **I:** Education/Educational Services **DOB:** 04/27/1959 **PB:** Palo Alto **SC:** CA/USA **ED:** PhD in Biology, Massachusetts Institute of Technology (1983); BA in Mathematics, University of California, Berkeley (1978) **C:** Professor, Department of Pathology and Genetics, Stanford University School of Medicine, California (2003-Present); Staff Member, Department of Embryology, Carnegie Institution of Washington, Baltimore, MD (1986-2003); Postdoctoral Fellow, Medical Research Council Laboratory Molecular Biology, Cambridge, England (1983-1986) **CR:** Adjunct Professor of Biology, Johns Hopkins University, Baltimore, MD (1989-2003); Member, Board of Science Counselors National Center of Biotechnology, National Institutes of Health **CW:** Contributor, Articles, Professional Journals **AW:** Paul Ehrlich & Ludwig Darmstaedter Prize, Germany (2006); Nobel Prize in Physiology/Medicine (2006); Massry Prize (2005);

Lewis S. Rosenstiel Award, Brandeis University (2005); Gairdner Foundation International Award (2005); Dr. H.P. Heinken Prize in Biochemistry and Biophysics, Netherlands Academy Arts & Sciences (2004); Wiley Prize, Rockefeller University (2003); Award in Molecular Biology, National Academy of Sciences (2003); Meyenburg Prize, Germany (2002); Genetics Society of America Medal (2002); Maryland Distinguished Young Scientist Award (1997) **MEM:** Fellow, American Academy of Arts & Sciences; National Academy of Sciences; Institute of Medicine

FIRTH, COLIN ANDREW, T: Actor **I:** Media & Entertainment **DOB:** 09/10/1960 **PB:** Grayshott **SC:** England **PT:** David Norman Lewis Firth; Shirley Jean (Rolles) Firth **MS:** Married **SPN:** Livia Giuggioli (06/21/1997) **CH:** Will; Luca; Mateo **ED:** Coursework, Barton Peveril College **CW:** Actor, "1917" (2019); Actor, "The Command" (2018); Actor, "The Happy Prince" (2018); Actor, "The Mercy" (2018); Actor, "Mamma Mia! Here We go Again" (2018); Actor, "Mary Poppins Returns" (2018); Actor, "Red Nose Day Actually" (2017); Actor, "Kingsman: The Golden Circle" (2017); Actor, "Genius" (2016); Actor, "Deep Water" (2016); Actor, "Bridget Jones's Baby" (2016); Producer, "Loving" (2016); Producer, "Amá" (2015); Producer, "Eye in the Sky" (2015); Actor, "Magic in the Moonlight" (2014); Actor, "Before I Go to Sleep" (2014); Actor, "Kingsman: The Secret Service" (2014); Actor, "The Railway Man" (2013); Actor, "Devil's Knot" (2013); Actor, "Arthur Newman" (2012); Actor, "Gambit" (2012); Actor, "Tinker Tailor Soldier Spy" (2011); Executive Producer, "The People Speak UK" (2010); Actor, "The King's Speech" (2010); Actor, "Main Street" (2010); Actor, "A Single Man" (2009); Actor, "Mamma Mia!" (2008); Actor, "Easy Virtue" (2008); Actor, "The Last Legion" (2007); Executive Producer, "In Prison My Whole Life" (2007); Actor, "And When Did You Last See Your Father?" (2007); Actor, "Then She Found Me" (2007); Actor, "Where the Truth Lies" (2005); Actor, "Nanny McPhee" (2005); Actor, "Bridget Jones: The Edge of Reason" (2004); Actor, "What a Girls Wants" (2003); Actor, "Girl with the Pearl Earrings" (2003); Actor, "Love Actually" (2003); Actor, "Hope Springs" (2003); Actor, "The Importance of Being Earnest" (2002); Actor, "Bridget Jones's Diary" (2001); Actor, "Conspiracy" (2001); Actor, "Relative Values" (2000); Actor, "Three Days of Rain" (1999); Actor, "My Life So Far" (1999); Actor, "The Secret Laughter of Women" (1999); Actor, "Blackadder Back & Forth" (1999); Actor, "Shakespeare in Love" (1998); Actor, "Nostromo" (1997); Actor, "Fever Pitch" (1997); Actor, "A Thousand Acres" (1997); Actor, "The English Patient" (1996); Actor, "Circle of Friends" (1995); Actor, "Pride and Prejudice" (1995); Actor, "The Widowing of Mrs. Holroyd" (1995); Actor, "Master of the Moor" (1994); Actor, "The Deep Blue Sea" (1994); Actor, "Playmaker" (1994); Actor, "Chatsky" (1993); Actor, "Hostages" (1993); Actor, "The Hour of the Pig" (1993); Actor, "Femme Fatale" (1991); Actor, "The Caretaker" (1991); Actor, "Out of the Blue" (1991); Actor, "Wings of Fame" (1990); Actor, "Tumbledown" (1989); Actor, "Valmont" (1989); Actor, "Apartment Zero" (1988); Actor, "A Month in the Country" (1987); Actor, "Desire Under the Elms" (1987); Actor, "Tales from the Hollywood Hills: Pat Hobby Teamed with Genius" (1987); Actor, "The Secret Garden" (1987); Actor, "Lost Empires" (1986); Actor, "The Lonely Road" (1985); Actor, "Dutch Girls" (1985); Actor, "Nineteen Nineteen" (1985); Actor, "Camille" (1984); Actor, "Another Country" (1983); Actor, "Another Country" (1981) **AW:** 100 Most Influential People in the World, TIME (2011); Best Performance by an Actor in a Motion Picture-Drama, Golden Globe Awards (2011); Outstanding Performance by a Male Actor in a Leading Role, Screen Actors Guild (2011); Outstanding Performance by a Cast in a Motion Picture, Screen Actors Guild (2011); Best Actor in a Leading Role, Academy Awards (2011); Best Actor, Critics' Choice Movie Awards (2011); Best Leading Actor, British Academy of Film and Television Arts (2010); Best Actor, New York Film Critics Circle (2010); Best Dressed Actor Award, "Elle" (2010) **MEM:** Royal Shakespeare Company

FISCHER, DEBRA, "DEB" LYNELLE, T: U.S. Senator **I:** Government Administration/Government Relations/Government Services **DOB:** 03/01/1951 **PB:** Lincoln **SC:** NE/USA **PT:** Gerold Carl Strobel; Florence M. (Bock) Strobel **MS:** Married **SPN:** Bruce Fischer (02/05/1972) **CH:** Adam Carl; Morgan Thomas; Luke Christopher **ED:** BS in Education, University of Nebraska-Lincoln (1988) **C:** U.S. Senator, State of Nebraska (2013-Present); Member, U.S. Senate Small Business and Entrepreneurship Committee (2013-Present); Member, U.S. Senate Committee on Indian Affairs (2013-Present); Member, U.S. Senate Environment and Public Works Committee (2013-Present); Member, U.S. Senate Committee on Commerce, Science and Transportation (2013-Present); Member, U.S. Senate Armed Services Committee (2013-Present); Rancher, Sunny Slope Ranch (1972-Present); Member, District 43, Nebraska State Legislature (2005-2013) **CR:** Commissioner, Nebraska Coordinating Commission for Postsecondary Education (2000) **CIV:** Member, Valentine Rural High School Board of Education (1990-2004) **MEM:** P.E.O. Sisterhood; Society for Range Management; Sandhills Cattle Association **PA:** Republican **RE:** Presbyterian

FISH, DANIEL, T: Theater Director **I:** Media & Entertainment **ED:** Bachelor of Science in Performance Studies, Northwestern University **C:** Assistant Director, Shakespeare Theatre Company (1989-1993) **CR:** Instructor, Yale School of Drama, Princeton University, University of California San Diego, The New School, Bard College; Visiting Artist, American Academy in Rome **CW:** Director, "Oklahoma!" (2019) **AW:** Nominee, Outstanding Director of a Musical, Drama Desk Awards and Outer Critics Circle (2019); Nominee, Best Direction of a Musical, Tony Awards (2019)

FISH, JAMES C. JR., T: President of Waste Management **I:** Facility Management **CN:** Waste Management, Inc. **ED:** Bachelor's Degree in Accounting, Arizona State University; MBA in Finance, The University of Chicago **CT:** CPA **C:** President and Chief Executive Officer, Waste Management, Inc. (2017-Present); Executive Vice President and Chief Financial Officer, Waste Management, Inc. (2012-2016); Senior Vice President, Eastern Group, Waste Management, Inc. (2011-2012); Director of Financial Planning and Analysis, Waste Management, Inc. (2001-2003)

FISHBURNE, LAURENCE, T: Actor **I:** Media & Entertainment **DOB:** 07/30/1961 **PB:** Augusta **SC:** GA/USA **PT:** Laurence John Fishburne Jr.; Hattie Bell Crawford Fishburne **MS:** Divorced **SPN:** Gina Torres (09/20/2002, Divorced 2018); Hajna O. Moss (07/01/1985, Divorced 1990) **CH:** Langston Issa; Montana Isis; Delilah **ED:** Honorary HHD, Howard University (2009) **CW:** Actor, Producer, "Black-ish" (2014-Present); Actor, "Where'd You Go Bernadette" (2018); Actor, "Ant Man and the Wasp" (2018); Actor, "Madiba" (2017); Actor, "Last Flag Flying" (2017); Actor, "Roots" (2016); Actor, "Batman v Superman: Dawn of Justice" (2016); Actor, "Passengers" (2016); Actor, "Roots" (2016); Actor, "John Wick: Chapter Two" (2016); Actor, "The Muppets" (2015); Actor, "Standoff" (2015); Actor, "Ride Along" (2014); Actor, "The Signal" (2014); Actor, "Rudderless" (2014); Actor, "Hannibal" (2013-2014); Actor, "The Colony" (2013); Actor, "Man of Steel" (2013); Actor, "Khumba" (2013); Actor, "Contagion" (2011); Actor, "Have a Little Faith" (2011); Actor, "Thurgood" (2011); Actor, "CSI: Crime Scene Investigation" (2008-2011); Actor, "Predators" (2010); Actor, Executive Producer, "Black Water Transit" (2009); Actor, "Armored" (2009); Actor, "Twenty-One" (2008); Actor, "Thurgood" (2008); Voice Actor, "TMNT" (2007); Voice Actor, "Fantastic 4: Rise of the Silver Surfer" (2007); Actor, "The Death and Life of Bobby Z" (2007); Actor, Producer, "Five Fingers" (2006); Actor, Producer, "Akeelah and the Bee" (2006); Actor, "Mission Impossible III" (2006); Actor, "Fences" (2006); Actor, "Bobby" (2006); Actor, "Assault on Precinct 13" (2005); Actor, "Biker Boyz" (2003); Actor, "The Matrix Reloaded" (2003); Actor, "Mystic River" (2003); Actor, "The Matrix Revolutions" (2003); Voice Actor, "Osmosis Jones" (2001); Actor, Director, Producer, Writer, "Once in the Life" (2000); Actor, "The Matrix" (1999); Actor, Executive Producer, "Always Outnumbered" (1998); Actor, "Miss Ever's Boys" (1997); Actor, Executive Producer, "Hoodlum" (1997); Actor, "Before Your Eyes" (1996); Actor, "Event Horizon" (1997); Actor, "Fled" (1996); Actor, "Bad Company" (1995); Actor, "Just Cause" (1995); Actor, "Othello" (1995); Actor, "Higher Learning" (1995); Actor, "The Tuskegee Airmen" (1995); Actor, "What's Love Got to Do With It" (1993); Actor, "Tribeca" (1993); Actor, "Searching For Bobby Fischer" (1993); Actor, "Two Trains Running" (1992); Actor, "Deep Cover" (1992); Actor, "Cadence" (1991); Actor, "Class Action" (1991); Actor, "Boyz N the Hood" (1991); Actor, "King of New York" (1990); Actor, "Decoration Day" (1990); Actor, "The Equalizer" (1989); Actor, "School Daze" (1988); Actor, "Red Heat" (1988); Actor, "Loose Ends" (1988); Actor, "Urban Blight" (1988); Actor, "Gardens of Stone" (1987); Actor, "The Father Clements Story" (1987); Actor, "Pee-wee's Playhouse" (1986" (1987); Actor, "Cherry 2000" (1987); Actor, "Spenser: For Hire" (1987); Actor, "A Nightmare on Elm Street 3: Dream Warriors" (1987); Actor, "Band of the Hand" (1986); Actor, "Quicksilver" (1986); Actor, "Miami Vice" (1986); Actor, "The Color Purple" (1985); Actor, "The Cotton Club" (1984); Actor, "Short Eyes" (1984); Actor, "I Take These Men" (1983); Actor, "For Us the Living: The Medgar Evers Story" (1983); Actor, "Rumble Fish" (1983); Actor, "Death Wish II" (1982); Actor, "Strike Force" (1982); Actor, "M*A*S*H" (1982); Actor, "Trapper John, M.D." (1981); Actor, "Hill Street Blues" (1981); Actor, "The Six O'Clock Follies" (1980); Actor, "A Rumor of War" (1980); Actor, "Willie and Phil" (1980); Actor, "Apocalypse Now" (1979); Actor, "Fast Break" (1979); Actor, "Eden" (1976); Actor, "Cornbread, Earl and Me" (1975); Actor, "Section D" (1975); Actor, "If You Give a Dance, You Gotta Pay the Band" (1972) **AW:** Image Award for Outstanding Actor in a TV Movie, Mini-Series or Dramatic Special, NAACP (2015); Image Award for Outstanding Supporting Actor in a Comedy Series, NAACP (2015); Drama Desk Award for Outstanding Solo Performance (2008); Artist of the Year Award, Harvard University (2007); Image Award for Outstanding Lead Actor in a TV Movie or Mini-Series, NAACP (1998); Image Award for Outstanding Supporting Actor in a Motion Picture, NAACP (1996); Image Award for Outstanding Actor in a TV Movie or Mini-Series, NAACP (1996); Tony Award for Best Featured Actor" (1992)

FISHER, DORIS F., T: Co-Founder **I:** Apparel & Fashion **CN:** The Gap, Inc. **PT:** B. Joseph Feigenbaum; Dorothy Bamberger **MS:** Widowed **SPN:** Donald G. Fisher (Deceased) **CH:** Robert J.; William S.; John J. **C:** Board Director, Gap, Inc.

(1969-Present); Merchandiser, Gap, Inc. (1969-2003); Co-Founder, Gap, Inc. (1969) **CIV:** Trustee, Stanford University **AW:** Named, Forbes 400: Richest Americans (2009); Named, Top 200 Collectors, ARTnews (2004-2008); Named, Most Powerful Women, Forbes Magazine (2005)

FISHER, ROBERT J. PHD, T: Marketing and Corporate Executive **I:** Advertising & Marketing **CN:** Bobs Solution Co. Inc. **DOB:** 04/29/1940 **PB:** Belleforte **SC:** PA/USA **PT:** Donald J. Fisher; Gladys C. (Bish) Fisher **MS:** Married **SPN:** Judy C. Lucas (06/06/1944) **CH:** Timothy D.; Daniel R.; Ruth S.Fisher; Marten Langdon; Foster **ED:** MS, State University of New York at Brockport (1975); Degree, Moody Bible Institute (1965); BS, Pennsylvania State University (1962); PhD, University of London **CT:** Certified Financial Planner (1972); Ordained, Baptist Church (1965) **C:** Corporate Counselor (2017-Present); Medicare and Senior Benefits Counselor (2011-Present); New York State Director, CEF (2003-2018); Chief Executive Officer, National Team Concepts (2000-2006); President, Open Door Bible Institute (2001-2004); Divisional Director, KareMore International, Inc. (1999-2001); President, Founder, National Team Concepts, Inc., Churchville, NY (1996-1999); Area Marketing Manager, National Telephone and Communications Inc., Rochester, NY (1994-1996); Vice President, Monitrend Investment Management Inc., Rochester, NY (1988-1994); President, Rochester Fund Distributor, Inc. (1982-1988); Financial Planner, F, H, and Z, Rochester, NY (1979-1982); Assistant Pastor, Grace Baptist Church (1978-1981); President, Rochester Fund Distributor (1975-1979); Private Money Manager, Investment Advisor, Faithful Stewards, Inc., Rochester, NY (1975-1979); Regional Sales Manager, Baptist Life Associates, Buffalo, NY (1970-1975); Stock Broker, Mayflower Securities, Rochester, NY (1967-1970); Assistant Department Head, Eastman Kodak Co., Rochester, NY (1965-1967); Assistant Pastor, Ministry By Berean Bible Fellowship (1965) **CR:** Conductor, National Seminars; Board of Directors, Officer, Monitrend Investment Management, Inc., Nashville, TN **CV:** New York State Board of Directors, Child Evangelism Fellowship (1994-2002); Board of Officers, Board of Directors, New York Family Research Foundation (1984-1994); Assistant Pastor, Grace Baptist Church (1978-1981) **MIL:** Air Force Reserves **CW:** Author, "Instrument Flight Curriculum" (1975); Author, "FARs Made Easy" (1975); Author, "Commercial Flight Curriculum" (1974); Author, 'Private Pilot Flight Curriculum" (1973) **AW:** American Medal of Honor (1979); Outstanding Teacher of the Year (1970); 2nd Runner Up, National Championship of Wrestling (1963); Salesman of the Year, West Penn Power Co.(1961); Outstanding Wrestler of the Year (1958) **MEM:** Board of Directors, Genuine Technologies (2004-Present); Charman, Board of Directors, CEF of New York (1997-2004); Board of New Yorkers for Constitutional Freedom (1979-1997); Board of Directors, International Association of Financial Planners (1984-1986); President, Monroe County Bee Keepers Association (1979-1983); Aircraft and Pilots Association **MH:** Albert Nelson Marquis Lifetime Achievement Award; Marquis Who's Who Top Professional **AS:** Dr. Fisher attributes his success to his excellent listening skills. He is steadfast and persistent. Likewise, he credits his deep faith in Jesus Christ. **B/I:** Dr. Fisher got involved in his work to help and serve others. **AV:** Fishing; Hunting; Golfing; Flying; Boating **PA:** Republican **RE:** Baptist

FISHER-DALLY, PATRICIA A., T: President, Owner **I:** Insurance **CN:** Sunrise Title Services, Inc. **DOB:** 07/22/1957 **SC:** NJ/USA **PT:** Dewey; Betty Engel **MS:** Married **SPN:** Gerard **CH:** Dana; Archie

ED: High School **CT:** Licensed Title Officer of New Jersey and Pennsylvania; Notary Public of New Jersey and Pennsylvania **C:** President, Partner, Sunrise Title Services (2006-Present);Partner, Majestic Title Agency (1998-2006) **AW:** Outstanding Player Award, Softball; Numerous Honors, Longest Drive for Women in Golf Outings **MEM:** BNI Networking Group; Former Member and Officer, Soroptimists of Hackettstown **MH:** Albert Nelson Marquis Lifetime Achievement Award; Marquis Who's Who Top Professional **AS:** Ms. Fisher-Dally attributes her success to a positive attitude and having good people surrounding her. **B/I:** Ms. Fisher-Dally became involvement in her profession because it was a natural progression. Right out of high school, she started working with a land surveyor and worked with him for about nine years. He moved his office location, then she worked for an attorney's office doing the real estate in the office. She and a girlfriend thought "Why are we doing all the work and the attorney is getting all the money?", which is when they started the first title agency, Majestic Title. Her husband had passed away during that time period, and her partner at the time wanted to take the business in a direction she was not comfortable with and so she walked out the door and started her own company. **AV:** Playing golf; Playing softball; Glamping

FISHMAN, LAWRENCE MARTIN, MD, FACP, T: Professor Emeritus of Medicine **I:** Education/Educational Services **CN:** University of Miami Miller School of Medicine **DOB:** 12/20/1933 **PB:** Brooklyn **SC:** NY/USA **PT:** Matthew Fishman; Ruth Janet (Frank) Fishman **MS:** Married **SPN:** Suzanne Marian **CH:** Matthew Edward; Charles Neal; Betsy Rachel; Andrew Klein **ED:** Intern, Peter Bent Brigham Hospital (Now Brigham and Women's Hospital), Boston, MA (1960-1961); MD, Harvard University (1960); AB, Harvard College, Magna Cum Laude (1955) **CT:** Diplomate, National Board of Medical Examiners; American Board Internal Medicine, Sub-specialty in Endocrinology and Metabolism **C:** Professor Emeritus of Medicine, University of Miami Miller School of Medicine (2008-Present); Professor, University of Miami Miller School of Medicine (1975-2008); Associate Professor, University of Miami Miller School of Medicine (1972-1975); Assistant Professor of Medicine, University of Miami Miller School of Medicine (1967-1972); Fellow in Diabetes and Endocrinology, Vanderbilt School of Medicine, Nashville, TN (1965-1967); Clinical Associate in Endocrinology, National Cancer Institute, National Institutes of Health, Bethesda, MD (1962-1965); Assistant Resident in Medicine, Peter Bent Brigham Hospital (Now Brigham and Women's Hospital), Boston, MA (1961-1962) **CR:** Research Subject Advisory Program, University of Miami Miller School of Medicine General Clinical Research Center (Now Don Soffer Clinical Research Center) (2004-2006); Associate Chief of Staff for Research, VA Medical Center, Miami, FL (1975-2003); Chief, Endocrinology and Metabolism Section, VA Medical Center, Miami, FL (1967-1999) **CW:** Contributor, Chapters to Books, Articles to Professional Journals **MEM:** Fellow, American College of Physicians; American Federation Clinical Research; Endocrine Society; The Southern Society for Clinical Investigation; The Phi Beta Kappa Society; Sigma Xi, The Scientific Research Honor Society; Alpha Omega Alpha Honor Medical Society **B/I:** Dr. Fishman's father was a general practitioner and he remembers spending time with him and seeing how invested he was at taking care of his patients. He really admired that and it was his inspiration to pursue a career in medicine as well. He jokes that he

wouldn't tell people that he had his mind made up to become a physician, just to seem like he was keeping his options open.

FITCH, WILLIAM C., T: Professional Basketball Coach (Retired) **I:** Athletics **DOB:** 05/19/1934 **PB:** Cedar Rapids **SC:** IA/USA **ED:** Coursework, Coe College **C:** Coach, L.A. Clippers (1994-1998); Coach, New Jersey Nets (1989-1992); Coach, Houston Rockets (1983-1988); Coach, Boston Celtics (1979-1983); Coach, Cleveland Cavaliers (1970-1979); Basketball Coach, University of Minnesota, Minneapolis, MN (1968-1970); Basketball Coach, Bowling Green State University (1967-1968); Basketball Coach, University of North Dakota, Grand Forks, ND (1962-1967); Basketball Coach, Coe College, Cedar Rapids. IA (1958-1962) **AW:** Chuck Daly Lifetime Achievement Award (2012-2013); Coach, NBA Championship Team (1981); NBA Coach of the Year (1976, 1980); Top 10 Coaches in NBA History

FITHIAN, PETER STALKER, T: Retail Executive **I:** Retail/Sales **DOB:** 07/07/1928 **PB:** Bridgeport **SC:** CT/USA **PT:** Roswell Curtis Fithian; Ada Allerton (Stalker) Fithian **MS:** Married **SPN:** Roberta Bernice Wong (1970); Jean Simons (06/1950, Divorced 02/1958) **CH:** Peter Junior; Marsha Jean **ED:** BS in Hotel Administration, Cornell University (1951) **C:** President, Greeters of Hawaii (1957-Present); Assistant Manager, Kaiser's Hawaiian Village (1956-1957); Manager, Kona Inn (1955-1956); Manager, Augusta National G.C. (1955); Assistant Treadway Inns (1954) **CR:** Participant, Small Company Management Program, Harvard University (1980) **CIV:** Board of Directors, The Billfish Foundation (1986-1994); Founder, Chairman, Hawaiian International Billfish Association (1976-1994); Pacific Ocean Research Association (1976-1994); Trustee, International Gamefish Association (1985-1992); National Coalition Marine Consultant (1987-1992); Aloha Festivals (1980-1982); Member, Western and Central Pacific Fisheries Commission (1976-1980); Chairman, Hawaii Visitors & Convention Bureau (1969-1971) **MIL:** Junior Grade Lieutenant, U.S. Navy (1951-1954) **MEM:** Chairman, Hawaii Chapter, Cornell Hotel Society (1980-1985); American Society of Travel Advisors; Society for Incentive Travel Excellence; Pacific Asia Travel Association; Waialae Country Club; Lifetime Member, Balboa Angling Club **BAR: MH:** Albert Nelson Marquis Lifetime Achievement Award **B/I:** Mr. Fithian became involved in his profession because of his interest in hotel administration. **AV:** Fishing; Golfing; Walking

FITTERLING, JIM RAY, T: Chief Executive Officer **I:** Manufacturing **CN:** Dow Chemical Company **SC:** MO/USA **C:** Chief Executive Officer, Dow Chemical Company (2018-Present); Chief Operating Officer, Dow Chemical Company (2015-Present); Vice President, Polyethylene, Dow Chemical Company (2005-Present); Chief Executive Officer, The OPTIMAL Group (2002-Present); Chief Operating Officer, President, Dow Chemical Company (2016-2018); President, Basic Plastics, Dow Chemical Company (2007-2009)

FITTIPALDI, EMERSON, T: Semi-Retired Racing Driver **I:** Automotive **DOB:** 12/12/1946 **PB:** Sao Paulo **SC:** Brazil **PT:** Wilson Fittipaldi; Juze Fittipaldi **MS:** Married **SPN:** Teresa Fittipaldi (1983) **CH:** Tatiana; Juliana; Jayson **ED:** Coursework, Jim Russell School of Motor Racing **C:** Winner, Marlboro Challenge (1992); Winner, Indianapolis 500 (1989); Race Car Designer, Car Dealership Owner, Brazil (1982-1984); Winner, Formula One

World Title (1972); Formula One Racer, Europe (1970); Founder, Fittipaldi Motoring Accessories **AW:** Inductee, Motorsport Hall of Fame (2001)

FITZGERALD, OSCAR P. IV, PHD, T: Adjunct Professor **I:** Museums & Institutions **DOB:** 05/17/1943 **PB:** Charleston **SC:** WV/USA **PT:** Oscar P. Fitzgerald III; Anne Gordon (Stevenson) Fitzgerald **MS:** Married **SPN:** Toby Lee Feldman (06/25/1965) **CH:** Michael Collins; Molly Louise **ED:** PhD, Georgetown University (1971); MA, Georgetown University (1968); BA, Vanderbilt University, Cum Laude (1965) **C:** Director, National Museum of the U.S. Navy (1985-1994); Associate Director, National Museum of the U.S. Navy (1979-1985); Historian, Naval Heritage Center (1966-1979) **CR:** Adjunct Professor, Smithsonian, George Washington University (2017-Present); Decorative Arts Consultant (1995-Present); Visiting Professor, Marymount University (1976, 2005, 2018); Adjunct Professor, Smithsonian, George Mason University (2011-2017); Adjunct Professor, Smithsonian, Corcoran Master's Program in the History of the Decorative Arts (2006-2011); Adjunct Professor, Smithsonian, Parson's Master's Program in the History of the Decorative Arts (1999-2006); Lecturer, Cruise Ships **CIV:** Vice Chairman of the Board, Alexandria Library (2007-Present); Board of Trustees, Monteagle Sunday School Assembly (2000-2006); Board Member, Chair, Alexandria Board of Architectural Review (1991-2003); Board Member, Historic Alexandria Foundation (1988-1991); First Chairman, Historic Alexandria Resources Commission (1982-1986); Chairman, Friends of the Carlyle House; Former Chairman, Architectural Review Committee, Monteagle Sunday School Assembly; Member, Alexandria Archaeological Commission; Trainer, Literacy Council of Northern Virginia **CW:** Author, "American Furniture: 1650 to the Present" (2018); Author, "New Masters of the Wooden Box: Expanding the Boundaries of Box Making" (2009); Author, "Studio Furniture of the Renwick Gallery: Smithsonian American Art Museum" (2007); Author, "Four Centuries of American Furniture" (1995); Author, "The Green Family of Cabinetmakers: An Alexandria Institution, 1817-1887" (1986); Co-Author, "United States Navy and the Vietnam Conflict. From Military Assistance to Combat, 1959-1965" (1986); Author, "Three Centuries of American Furniture" (1982) **AW:** Alexandria Beautification Award (2004); Walter Mess Northern Virginia Regional Park Authority Award (2000); Achievement Award, Alexandria Association (1982); James Renwick Research Fellowship **MEM:** Alexandria Library; The Alexandria Association; Friends of Carlyle House; Friends of Dumbarton House **MH:** Albert Nelson Marquis Lifetime Achievement Award **AS:** Mr. Fitzgerald attributes his success to his family's great advice. **B/I:** Mr. Fitzgerald became involved in his profession because of his interest in history. **AV:** Gardening; Woodworking; Playing handball; Restoring an 1840s log cabin **PA:** Republican **RE:** Episcopalian

FITZPATRICK, BRIAN KEVIN, T: U.S. Representative from Pennsylvania **I:** Government Administration/Government Relations/Government Services **CN:** U.S. House of Representatives **DOB:** 12/17/1973 **PB:** Levittown **SC:** PA/USA **ED:** Doctor of Jurisprudence, Dickinson Law, The Pennsylvania State University (2001); Master of Business Administration, The Pennsylvania State University Smeal College of Business (2001); Bachelor of Science in Business Administration, La Salle University (1996) **C:** Member, U.S. House of Representatives from Pennsylvania's Eighth Congressional District (2017-Present); National Supervisor, Bureau's Public Corruption Unit (2002-2016); Judicial Clerk, Eastern District of Pennsylvania

(2001-2002); Member, Committee on Foreign Affairs; Member, Committee on Homeland Security; Member, Committee on Small Business

FITZSIMMONS, KIMBERLY, T: President **I:** Financial Services **CN:** JP Morgan Chase **DOB:** 09/18/1965 **MS:** Divorced **CH:** 2 Children **ED:** Bachelor of Arts in Business Administration, University of Mississippi, School of Business Administration (1987) **C:** President, Global Merchant Services, JP Morgan Chase & Company (2019-Present); U.S. President, Chase Commerce Solutions, JP Morgan Chase & Company (2014-2019); Strategic Advisor, Cynergy Data (2014-2014); Chief Executive Officer, Cynergy Data (2012-2013); Executive Vice President, Merchant Services & Community Banks, First Data Corporation (2004-2012); Senior Vice President, Concord EFS (2003-2004); Principal, Founder, H & F Services, DBA EFS Card Services (1996-2003); Senior Vice President, Concord EFS (1988-1996) **CR:** Past President, Electronic Transaction Association; Past President, WNet **CIV:** Board of Directors, Healthy Kids Foundation; With, Peer Power **AW:** Listed, Top 100 Global Sales Leaders in 2020; Listed, One of the Industry's Most Influential Women in Payments; Lifetime Achievement Award, Midwest Acquirers Association **MEM:** WNet **AS:** Ms. Fitzsimmons attributes her success to her large drive for success and her disdain for losing. She has a very competitive nature. Likewise, she credits her propensity for honesty and moral integrity. **B/I:** Ms. Fitzsimmons got a job opportunity and continued to expand on it until she received a leadership role. She loves client facing teams, growing and building teams, and capitalizing on different opportunities that were presented to her at the time.

FIX WOLF, BERNICE, T: Vice Mayor, Educator **I:** Government Administration/Government Relations/Government Services **PB:** Cincinnati **SC:** OH/USA **PT:** Arthur Howard Fix; Lillian (Kursban) Fix **MS:** Widowed **SPN:** Raymond Bernard Wolf (1948, Deceased) **CH:** Randall Kevin Wolf, MD; Bradley Rex Wolf, MD; Leslie Rae Dye, MD **ED:** Bachelor of Education, University of Cincinnati (1950); Bachelor of Arts, University of Cincinnati (1949) **CT:** Certified Tree Farmer, State of Indiana; Pest Control License **C:** Vice Mayor, Coffeyville, KS (1989-1993); Teacher, Dearborn County High School, Indiana (1962-1965); Teacher, Walnut Hills High School, Cincinnati, OH (1950-1952); Teacher, Whitewater Township, IN **CIV:** Volunteer, Polo Club **CW:** Unofficial Publicist, Cincinnati Polo Club **MEM:** American Association of University Women; National League of Cities; Kansas Municipal League; Southeast Kansas Cities Coalition; Coffeyville Country Club; Parents as Teachers; Rotary International; Indian Hill Welcomers Club; Cincinnati Polo Club; National Rifle Association of America **MH:** Albert Nelson Marquis Lifetime Achievement Award **AV:** Painting; Swimming; Golf; Tennis; Bridge; Horseback riding; Travel; Forestry

FLAHERTY, TIMOTHY T., I: Medicine & Health Care **PB:** Fond du Lac **SC:** WI/USA **MS:** Married **SPN:** Joan Flaherty **CH:** Four Children **ED:** Residency in Radiology, University of Wisconsin, Madison (1963-1966); Fellowship, University of Wisconsin, Madison (1964-1965); Internship, St. Mary's Hospital (1959-1960); MD, Marquette University (1959); Honorary Doctoral Degree, Medical College of Wisconsin **CT:** Diplomate, American Board of Radiology **C:** Private Practice (1968-2003) **CR:** Board of Trustees, Department of Radiology, Theda Clark Regional Medical Center (1980-1995); Trustee, Novus Health Group (1988-1994); Secretary, Board of Directors, National Patient Safety Foundation; Founding Director, Physicians Insur-

ance Company; Executive Committee, Underwriting Committee, Investment Committee, Governor's Task Force on Health Reform; Founding Director, SMS Services, Inc.; Board of Directors, Bank One of Appleton; Clinical Professor, Department of Radiology, University of Wisconsin **MIL:** Major General, U.S. Air Force **AW:** First-Time Lifetime Achievement Award Winner, Wisconsin Radiology Society (2006) **MEM:** Chair, Finance Committee, American Medical Association (1996-1997); Counselor, Radiological Society of North America (1991-1997); Director, Commission on Office Laboratory Assessment (1996); Executive Committee, American Medical Association (1995); Fellow, American College of Radiology; American Pacific; Vice Chair, Board of Directors, Wisconsin Medical Society; Former President, Wisconsin Radiological Society; Society of Medical Consultants to the Armed Forces; Aerospace Medical Association; Association of Military Surgeons; Society of Air Force Flight Surgeons **MH:** Albert Nelson Marquis Lifetime Achievement Award **B/I:** Dr. Flaherty became involved in his profession because he has always wanted to be a doctor. His cousin was a family practitioner and that also gave him the inspiration to practice medicine.

FLAKE, JEFFRY LANE, T: Former U.S. Senator from Arizona **I:** Government Administration/Government Relations/Government Services **DOB:** 12/31/1962 **PB:** Snowflake **SC:** AZ/USA **PT:** Dean Maeser Flake; Nerita (Hock) Flake **MS:** Married **SPN:** Cheryl (Bae) Flake (1985) **CH:** Five Children **ED:** MA in Political Science, Brigham Young University (1987); BA in International Relations, Brigham Young University (1986) **C:** Contributor, "CBS News," "CBS This Morning" and "CBS Evening News," CBS (2019-Present); U.S. Senator, State of Arizona (2013-2019); Member, U.S. Senate Special Committee on Aging (2013-2019); Member, U.S. Senate Judiciary Committee (2013-2019); Member, U.S. Senate Committee on Energy and Natural Resources (2013-2019); Member, U.S. Senate Committee on Foreign Relations (2013-2019); Member, U.S. House of Representatives from Arizona's Sixth Congressional Congress, U.S. Congress, Washington, DC (2003-2013); Member, U.S. House of Representatives from Arizona's First Congressional Congress, U.S. Congress, Washington, DC (2001-2003); Executive Director, Goldwater Institute, AZ (1992-1999); Lobbyist, Rossing Uranium (1990-1992); Executive Director, Foundation for Democracy, Namibia (1989-1990) **CIV:** Missionary, Church of Jesus Christ of Latter-day Saints, South Africa **CW:** Appearance, Television Special, "Rival Survival" (2014); Appearance, Documentary, "How Democracy Works Now: Twelve Stories" (2010) **AW:** Named One of the 10 Best Members of Congress, Esquire Magazine (2008) **PA:** Republican **RE:** Church of Jesus Christ of Latter-day Saints

FLAM, BERNARD VINCENT, T: Secondary School Educator (Retired), Actor, Author, Painter, Radio Personality **I:** Education/Educational Services **DOB:** 06/06/1945 **PB:** Bronx **SC:** NY/USA **PT:** Abraham Flam; Anna (Aptowitzeer) Flam **MS:** Married **SPN:** Lydia Esther Nieves (06/07/1969, Divorced 1989) **CH:** Rachel; Elliot **ED:** Bachelor of Science in Psychology, City College of New York (1969) **CT:** Registered Junior High School Mathematics Teacher, New York City **C:** Teacher, Mathematics, Intermediate School 192, Bronx, NY (1975-2002); Teacher, Mathematics, Intermediate School 52, Bronx, NY (1969-1975); Radio Personality, WKQW Nanuet (1972-1974); Actuarial Clerk, National Health & Welfare, New York, NY (1968-1969) **CIV:** Member, 801 Bronx River Rd. Coop Board (2001-2008); President, Stratford Ave. Block Association, Bronx, NY (1969-1971); Secretary, Sound-view-Throgs Neck Community Mental Health Center, Bronx, NY (1970) **CW:** Author, Two Books; Actor, "Law and Order"; Actor, "Third Watch"; Actor, "Kiss Me Again"; Actor, "Sarbanes-Oxley" **AW:** Recognized as Inspirational Teacher, Fordham Preparatory School (1995) **MEM:** Chapter Chairman, Intermediate School 192, United Federation Teachers (1992-1994); American Federation of Teachers; International Society of Photographers **MH:** Albert Nelson Marquis Lifetime Achievement Award **B/I:** Mr. Flam became involved in his profession during the Vietnam War draft, during which time he was about to graduate college and received a deferment for entering the profession of teaching. **AV:** Running; Opera; Music; Supporting homeless shelters in New York City, Yonkers, New York and Gallup, New Mexico; Providing support to students **PA:** Independent **RE:** Jewish

FLATTAU, EDWARD BA, T: Environmental Columnist **I:** Writing and Editing **CN:** Global Horizons Syndicate **DOB:** 05/18/1937 **PB:** New York **SC:** NY/USA **SPN:** Pamela **CH:** Jeremy; Victoria **ED:** Postgraduate Coursework, Columbia Law School (1958-1960); BA, Brown University (1958) **C:** President Columnist, Self Syndicated Columnist, Global Horizons Syndicate, Washington, DC (1972-Present); Environmental Columnist, Los Angeles Times Syndicate (1972-1977); Assistant Director of Information, European Community (1971-1972); Legislative Assistant, Representative Benjamin Rosenthal, Washington, DC (1969-1971); Congressional Correspondent, United Press International, Washington, DC (1967-1969); Political Correspondent, United Press International, Albany, NY (1962-1966); Environmental Columnist **CW:** Author, "From Green to Mean" (2016); Author, "Green Morality" (2010); Author, "Peering Through the Bushes" (2004); Author, "Evolution of a Columnist" (2003); Author, "Tracking the Charlatans" (1998); Contributor, Articles, Magazines **AW:** Top Columnist, Washingtonian Magazine (2011); Global Media Award, Population Institute (1986); Lorax Award, Global Tomorrow Coalition (1985); Distinguished Journalism Citation, Scripps Howard Foundation (1978) **MEM:** Society of Environmental Journalists **MH:** Albert Nelson Marquis Lifetime Achievement Award **B/I:** Mr. Flattau became involved in his profession after growing up in the shadow of the American Museum of Natural History in New York City. The museum inspired and stimulated his interest in environmental issues. **AV:** Playing tennis; Golfing; Researching Civil War history

FLEISCHMANN, CHARLES, "CHUCK" JOSEPH, T: U.S. Representative from Tennessee; Lawyer **I:** Government Administration/Government Relations/Government Services **DOB:** 10/11/1962 **PB:** New York **SC:** NY/USA **PT:** Max Fleischmann; Rose Marie Fleischmann **MS:** Married **SPN:** Brenda M. Fleischmann (1986) **CH:** Charles; James; Jeffrey **ED:** JD, The University of Tennessee College of Law, Knoxville, TN (1986); BA in Political Science, University of Illinois at Urbana-Champaign, Magna Cum Laude (1983) **C:** Member, U.S. House of Representatives from Tennessee's Third Congressional District, United States Congress, Washington, DC (2011-Present); Member, U.S. House Committee on Small Business, Washington, DC (2011-Present); Member, Committee on Appropriations, Washington, DC (2011-Present); Member, U.S. House Committee on Science, Space and Technology, Washington, DC (2011-Present); Member, U.S. House Committee on Natural Resources, Washington, DC (2011-Present); Founder, Partner, Fleischmann & Fleischmann, Chattanooga, TN (1987) **CR:** Past Chairman, Chattanooga Lawyers Pro Bono Committee **CIV:** Board of Directors, FACES:

The National Craniofacial Association; Board of Directors, Cherokee Area Council, Boy Scouts of America, Chattanooga, TN **CW:** Radio Talk Show Host, "Chuck Fleischmann Show," Chattanooga, TN **MEM:** Past President, Chattanooga Bar Association; The Phi Beta Kappa Society **PA:** Republican **RE:** Roman Catholic

FLEISCHMANN, ROGER JUSTICE, T: Lawyer (Retired) **I:** Law and Legal Services **CN:** Fleischmann & Fleischmann **DOB:** 09/23/1934 **PB:** Buffalo **SC:** NY/USA **PT:** Edwin Fleischmann; Clover Fleischmann **MS:** Married **SPN:** Martha Ann Stennis (06/27/1959) **CH:** Roger Justice Fleischmann Jr.; Susan (Fleischmann) Brazeal **ED:** LLB, Harvard University (1959); BA, Harvard University, Magna Cum Laude (1956) **C:** Partner, Fleischmann & Fleischmann, San Francisco, CA (1979-1998); Partner, Private Practice, Graham & James, San Francisco, CA (1968-1969); Associate, Bledsoe, Smith, Carthcart, Johnson & Phelps, San Francisco, CA (1960-1962); Represented, Toshiba Ltd., Marubeni Corporation, Komatsu Ltd., Varilux Corporation and Bank of Tokyo, Ltd. and Their Subsidiaries, Other Related Companies, Other Clients, Worldwide; Helped Set Up the "Madrigal" Gold, Copper and Zinc Mine, and Negotiated Supply Contracts for Its Owners, Peru **CR:** Lecturer, Golden Gate University School of Law (1973); Counsel, California "Buy American" Act Declared Unconstitutional, Bethlehem Steel Corporation vs. Board of Commissioners, Department of Water & Power, City of Los Angeles, CA (1969) **CIV:** Commissioner, Asian Art Museum (1986-1992); Member, Mayor's Task Force on Foreign Investment, San Francisco, CA (1985-1986) **MIL:** With, U.S. Army (1959-1964) **CW:** Co-Author, "Countertrade: International Trade Without Cash" (1983); Author, Undergraduate Thesis, "The United States and into China" (1945-1954) **MEM:** Board of Directors, Japan Society (1976-1999); President, Japan Society (1979-1980); California State Bar Association; San Francisco Bar Association; Japan Society **BAR:** Supreme Court of the United States (1967); California (1960); U.S. District Court for the Northern District of California (1960) **MH:** Albert Nelson Marquis Lifetime Achievement Award **B/I:** Mr. Fleischmann became involved in his profession because he was born in Buffalo, where his uncles operated one of the biggest law firms. His grandfather, Simon Fleischmann, was a lawyer in the Buffalo area as well. **AV:** Playing golf; Playing tennis; Traveling; Hiking

FLEISS, JENNIFER, T: Co-Founder **I:** Luxury Goods & Jewelry **CN:** Rent the Runway **PB:** New York **SC:** NY/USA **ED:** MBA, Harvard Business School (2009); BA, Yale University, Cum Laude (2005) **C:** Co-Founder, Head of Business Development, Board Director, Rent the Runway **CR:** Asset Management Group, Lehman Brothers; Strategic Planning Group, Morgan Stanley **AW:** Forbes Disruptors (2013); 40 Under 40, Fortune; Most Powerful Women Entrepreneurs, Fortune; 30 Under 30, Inc.; Most Influential Women in Technology, Fast Company; Finalist, Entrepreneur of the Year, New York Area Region, EY; Most Influential People in New York Fashion, Fashionista.com

FLEMING, MARCELLA, T: Journalist (Retired) **I:** Writing and Editing **PB:** Paoli **SC:** IN/USA **PT:** Kenneth Fleming; Neva Fleming **MS:** Married **SPN:** Brian D. Smith **ED:** AB in Journalism and English, Indiana University (1978) **CT:** Certification in Teaching **C:** Writer, The Indianapolis Star (1995-2004); Education Reporter, The Indianapolis News (1992-1995); National Editor, Indianapolis CEO, Columbus CEO Magazines (1991-1992); Freelance Writer, Indianapolis Monthly Magazine (1989-1991); City Editor, Marion Chronicle-Tribune (1990-1991); Editor, Pub-

lications, Children's Museum Indianapolis (1988-1990); City Reporter, Feature Writer, Copy Editor, Sunday Editor, Fort Wayne Journal-Gazette (1983-1988); Reporter, Marion Chronicle-Tribune (1980-1983); Reporter, Wabash Plain Dealer (1978-1980) **CR:** Judge, Thomas R. Keating Writing Competition (1990); Judge, Numerous Reporting and Writing Contests, Society of Professional Journalists; Judge, Numerous Reporting and Writing Contests, Associated Press Managing Editors Association **AW:** Best Columnist, Indiana Society Of Professional Journalists (2000); Feature Writing, Hoosier State Press Association (1999); Deadline Reporting, Associated Press Managing Editors Association (1998); Deadline News, Society of Professional Journalists (1998); Deadline Reporting, Hoosier State Press Association (1997); Deadline News, Society of Professional Journalists (1996); Feature Writing, Associated Press Managing Editors Association (1995); Hoosier State Press Association's Top Award, Indiana's Blue Ribbon Daily Newspaper, The Indianapolis News (1995); Breaking News Story, Distinguished Achievement, Educational Press Association Of America (1994); Best Newsletter, Best Feature Story, Best News Story Awards, Editor's Forum (1990); Best Annual Report Award, International Association of Business Communicators (1990); Award of Excellence, National Down Syndrome Congress (1988); The National Education Contest, Benjamin Fine Award (1986); Community Service Award, Hoosier State Press Association (1985); Best News Series, United Press International (1985); Best News Story on Deadline, Hoosier State Press Association (1985); Best News Story on Deadline, Associated Press Managing Editors Association (1985); Best News Story on Deadline, Hoosier State Press Association (1984); Best Feature Series, Hoosier State Press Association (1979); Co-Recipient, The National Benjamin Fine Award (1986); Publications Editor Award, The Children's Museum Of Indianapolis **MEM:** Former Member, Educational Press Association (1994) **AV:** Researching genealogy and U.S. political history; Playing music

FLEMING, PEGGY GALE, T: Former Olympic Figure Skater **I:** Athletics **DOB:** 07/27/1948 **PB:** San Jose **SC:** CA/USA **PT:** Albert Eugene Fleming; Doris Elizabeth (Deal) Fleming **MS:** Married **SPN:** Greg Jenkins (06/13/1970) **CH:** Andy; Todd **ED:** Coursework, Colorado College (1966) **C:** Figure Skater (1958-1968) **CR:** Skating Commentator, "Wide World of Sports," ABC; Actress, Commercials, Concord Watch **CIV:** National Chairman, Easterseals; Trustee, Women's Sports Foundation **CW:** Actress, "Blades of Glory" (2007); Performer, Ice Capades (1968); Performer, Ice Follies; Performer, Television Specials; Guest, "Fantasy Island" **AW:** Lombardi Award of Excellence (2003); Inductee, Colorado Hall of Fame (1969); Named Woman of the Year, Reader's Digest (1969); Gold Medal, Winter Olympics (1968); Named Female Athlete of the Year, The Associated Press (1968); First Place, U.S. Championships (1964-1968); First Place, World Championships (1966-1968); First Place, North American Championships (1967); Sports Award, ABC-TV (1967) **MEM:** U.S. Figure Skating Association Clubs; Broadmoor Figure Skating, Colorado Springs, CO

FLETCHER, ELIZABETH, "LIZZIE" ANN, T: U.S. Representative from Texas; Lawyer **I:** Government Administration/Government Relations/Government Services **DOB:** 02/13/1975 **PB:** Houston **SC:** TX/USA **MS:** Married **SPN:** Scott Fletcher **ED:** JD, William & Mary Law School, VA (2006); BA, Kenyon College, Ohio **C:** Member, U.S. House of Representatives from Texas' Seventh Congressional District (2019-Present); Member, House Committee on

1912 • Esteemed Listees

Who's Who in America

Transportation and Infrastructure (2019-Present); Member, House Committee on Science, Space and Technology (2019-Present); Partner, Ahmad, Zavitsanos, Anaipakos, Alavi & Mensing P.C. (2015-2018); With, Vinson & Elkins LLP **CW:** Editor-in-chief, William & Mary Law Review **AW:** Gambrell Professionalism Award, William & Mary Law School (2006) **MEM:** The Phi Beta Kappa Society **PA:** Democrat

FLETCHER, JOHN DEXTER, PHD, I: Government Administration/Government Relations/Government Services **CN:** Institute for Defense Analyses **DOB:** 12/09/1940 **PB:** Providence **SC:** RI/USA **PT:** John Dexter Fletcher; Agnes Belle (McClelland) Fletcher **MS:** Married **SPN:** Sheila Ann Gates (6/17/1968) **CH:** Scott; Jeffrey; Brian, Paul **ED:** PhD in Educational Psychology, Stanford University (1973); MS in Computer Science, Stanford University (1973); BA in English, The University of Arizona, with Honors (1965) **C:** Research Staff Member, Institute for Defense Analyses (1986-Present); Assistant Director, Science & Technology Division, Institute for Defense Analyses (1991-1995); Adjunct Professor of Information Systems and Systems Engineering, George Mason University (1986-1994); Research Psychologist, U.S. Army Research Institute for the Behavioral and Social Sciences (1985-1986); Associate Professor of Computer Science and Educational Psychology, University of Oregon (1983-1985); Director, WICAT Education Institute (1981-1983); Research Psychologist, U.S. Army Research Institute for the Behavioral and Social Sciences (1980-1981); Program Manager, Defense Advanced Research Projects Agency (1978-1980); Manager, Functional Tests, Xerox Corporation (1977-1978); Supervisory Personnel Research Psychologist, Personnel Research & Development Center, U.S. Navy (1974-1977); Research Associate, Stanford University (1969-1973); Assistant Professor of Psychology & Computer Science, The University of Illinois at Chicago **CR:** Consultant, Bell Labs; Consultant, Brigham Young University; Consultant, Computer Curriculum Corporation; Consultant, Cubic Corporation; Consultant, Data General; Consultant, Department of Defense; Consultant, U.S. Air Force; Consultant, U.S. Army; Consultant, U.S. Navy; Consultant, International Development and Evaluation Association; Consultant, Educational Testing Service; Consultant, Essex Corporation; Consultant, Fairfax County Public Schools; Consultant, Honeywell International Inc.; Consultant, Indian Affiliates Inc.; Consultant, Institute for Defense Analyses; Consultant, International Policy and Planning Research Corporation; Consultant, Job Corps, Department of Labor; Consultant, McGraw-Hill Education; Consultant, Minnesota Educational Computing Consortium, The Learning Company; Consultant, Northwest Regional Educational Laboratory (Now Education Northwest); Consultant, Pan American World Airways; Consultant, SAIC; Consultant, Smithsonian Institute **CW:** Educational Psychology"; Reviewer, "Review of Educational Research"; Reviewer, "Artificial Intelligence Journal" (1993-Present); Associate Editor, "Information and Decision Technologies" (1989-1994); Reviewer, "Computer Surveys"; Reviewer, "Human Factors"; Reviewer, "Journal of Abnormal Psychology"; Reviewer, "Journal of Computer-Base Institutional Systems"; Reviewer, Journal of Designer, Computer-assisted Instruction Programs; Developer, Computer-assisted Instruction Programs; Contributor, Articles, Professional Journals **AW:** Service Award, ACM, Inc. (1984-1986); James Baird Scholarship, The University of Arizona (1964-1965) **MEM:** Fellow, American Psychological Association; Fellow, American Association for the Advancement of Science; Fellow, IEEE; Amer-

ican Educational Research Association; American Psychological Society; ACM, Inc.; Association for the Development of Computer-Based Institutional Systems; Human Factors and Ergonomics Society; Society for Applied Learning Technology; The Honor Society of Phi Kappa Phi **MH:** Albert Nelson Marquis Lifetime Achievement Award

FLETCHER, LOUISE, T: Actress **I:** Media & Entertainment **DOB:** 7/22/1934 **PB:** Birmingham **SC:** AL/USA **PT:** Robert Capers Fletcher; Estelle (Caldwell) Fletcher **SPN:** Jerry Bick (1959-1978) **CH:** John Dashiell; Andrew Wilson **ED:** Honorary Doctor of Humane Letters, Western Maryland College (1986); Honorary Doctor of Humane Letters, Gallaudet University (1982); Bachelor of Arts, University of North Carolina (1957); Acting Student, Jeff Corey **CIV:** Board of Directors, Deafness Research Foundation (1980-Present) **CW:** Actress, "Girlboss" (2017); Actress, "A Perfect Man" (2013); Actress, "Shameless" (2011-2012); Actress, "Of Two Minds" (2012); Actress, "Private Practice" (2010-2011); Actress, "Cassadaga" (2011); Actress, "The Genesis Code" (2010); Actress, "Heroes" (2009); Actress, "The Last Sin Eater" (2007); Actress, "Fat Rose and Squeaky" (2006); Actress, "A Dad for Christmas" (2006); Actress, "Dancing in Twilight" (2005); Actress, "Aurora Borealis" (2005); Actress, "7ᵗʰ Heaven" (2005); Actress, "Clipping Adam" (2004); Actress, "Joan of Arcadia" (2004); Actress, "Finding Home" (2003); Actress, "A Time to Remember" (2003); Actress, "Manna from Heaven" (2002); Actress, "Touched by a Killer" (2001); Actress, "After Image" (2001); Actress, "Very Mean Men" (2000); Actress, "Silver Man" (2000); Actress, "Seeing in the Dark" (2000); Actress, "Big Eden" (2000); Actress, "Star Trek: Deep Space Nine" (1993-1999); Actress, "The Devil's Arithmetic" (1999); Actress, "Time Served" (1999); Actress, "A Map of the World" (1999); Actress, "More Dogs than Bones" (1999); Actress, "Cruel Inventions" (1999); Actress, "Time Served" (1999); Actress, "Love Kills" (1998); Actress, "The Practice" (1998); Actress, "Brimstone" (1998); Actress, "Twisted Path" (1997); Actress, "Breastmen" (1997); Actress, "Married to a Stranger" (1997); Actress, "Profiler" (1997); Actress, "Heartless" (1997); Actress, "Picket Fences" (1996); Actress, "Stepford Husbands" (1996); Actress, "The Girl Gets Moe" (1996); Actress, "Heartless" (1996); Actress, "Virtuosity" (1995); Actress, "Mulholland Falls" (1995); Actress, "2 Days in the Valley" (1995); Actress, "Edie & Pen" (1995); Actress, "High School High" (1995); Actress, "VR5" (1994, 1995); Actress, "The Haunting of Cliff House, Dream On" (1994); Actress, "Someone Else's Child" (1994); Actress, "Return to Two Moon Junction" (1993); Actress, "Tollbooth" (1993); Actress, "Civil Wars" (1993); Actress, "The Fire Next Time" (1992); Actress, "Tales from the Crypt" (1991); Actress, "In a Child's Name" (1991); Actress, "Boys of Twilight" (1991); Actress, "The Player" (1991); Actress, "Blind Vision" (1990); Actress, "The Hitchhiker" (1990); Actress, "Best of the Best" (1989); Actress, "Shadowzone" (1989); Actress, "Final Notice" (1989); Actress, "The Karen Carpenter Story" (1988); Actress, "Nightmare on the 13ᵗʰ Floor" (1988); Actress, "The Twilight Zone" (1988); Actress, "Blue Steel" (1988); Actress, "Flowers in the Attic" (1987); Actress, "Two Moon Junction" (1987); Actress, "Hoover" (1986); Actress, "Nobody's Fool" (1986); Actress, "Invaders from Mars" (1985); Actress, "The Boy Who Could Fly" (1985); Actress, "Maverick" (1959); Actress, "Second Serve" (1985); Actress, "A Summer to Remember" (1984); Actress, "Island" (1984); Actress, "Firestarter" (1983); Actress, "Overnight Sensation" (1983); Actress, "Strange Invaders" (1982); Actress, "Once Upon a Time in America" (1982); Actress, "Brainstorm" (1981); Actress,

"Strange Behavior" (1980); Actress, "The Lucky Star" (1979); Actress, "Natural Enemies" (1979); Actress, "The Lady in Red" (1979); Actress, "The Magician" (1978); Actress, "Alfred Hitchcock, Thou Shalt Not Commit Adultery" (1978); Actress, "The Cheap Detective" (1977); Actress, "Exorcist II: The Heretic" (1976); Actress, "One Flew Over the Cuckoo's Nest" (1975); Actress, "Russian Roulette" (1974); Actress, "Thieves Like Us" (1973); Actress, "The Millionaire" (1960); Actress, "Wagon Train" (1959-1960); Actress, "Lawman" (1959); Actress, "Playhouse 90" (1958) **MEM:** Advisory Board, National Institute of Deafness and Other Communicable Disorders

FLOOD, VERONICA H., MD, T: Associate Professor, Pediatric Hematology **I:** Education/Educational Services **CN:** Medical College of Wisconsin **MS:** Married **SPN:** Dave Olson **CH:** Matthew; Eric; Caitlin **ED:** MD, Tufts University School of Medicine (1999); BS in Biological Anthropology, Harvard University (1995); Internship, Residency, Phoenix Children's Hospital **C:** Associate Professor, Medical College of Wisconsin (2006-Present); Instructor, Oregon Health & Science University, Portland, OR (2005-2006); Fellow, Oregon Health & Science University, Portland, OR (2002-2005) **AW:** Outstanding Medical Student Teacher (2017); Eberhard F. Mammen Young Investigator Award (2013) **MEM:** American Society of Hematology; International Society on Thrombosis and Hemostasis; National Hemophilia Foundation; Hemostasis and Thrombosis Research Society **AS:** Dr. Flood attributes her success to her passion for her work and her great mentors for helping her along the way. **B/I:** Dr. Flood became involved in her profession because ever since she was a child, she was intrigued by medicine. She recalls a book she came across called "Dr. Spock's Baby and Child Care." Her parents had a copy and she would sit down and read chapters of it. She became interested in hematology when she began her pediatric residency. She had the opportunity to work with a fantastic pediatric hematology physician. Within three days of her rotation with him, it was clear to her that was what she wanted to do. She began writing fellowship applications and it was hematology the rest of the way. That was the benefit of having great mentors and one of the reasons she is so committed to mentoring. **AV:** Reading **THT:** Dr. Flood advised medical students to "be persistent because there are a lot of times where you face challenges and it will be easy to give up, but people who have the persistence and are willing to try something, fail and get back up will be the ones who succeed in the long run. Also pick what you love and enjoy because you must be happy with the work you do, or else it will be extremely difficult, and detrimental to not only your patients but yourself as well..."

FLORA, JAIRUS D. JR., T: Statistician **I:** Research **CN:** KWA, Inc. **DOB:** 03/27/1944 **PB:** Northfield **SC:** MN/USA **PT:** Jairus Dale Flora; Betty Ruth (Garvin) Flora **MS:** Married **SPN:** Sharyl Ann Hughes (08/18/1967) **CH:** Edward Hughes Flora **ED:** PhD, Florida State University (1971); MS, Florida State University (1968); Postgraduate Coursework, Karlsruhe Institute of Technology (1965-1966); BS, Midland Lutheran College (Now Midland University), Magna Cum Laude (1965) **C:** Statistical Consultant, KWA Inc. (1999-Present); Principal Statistician, KWA Inc. (1999); Clinical Professor of Biostatistics, School of Medicine, University of Missouri-Kansas City (1984-2008); Senior Advisor for Statistics, MRI Global (1991-1999); Principal Statistician, MRI Global (1984-1990); President, Council of Principal Scientists, MRI Global (1986); Professor of Biostatistics, School of Public Health,

University of Michigan (1981-1984); Research Scientist, Transportation Research Institute, University of Michigan (1981-1984); Associate Professor of Biostatistics, School of Public Health, University of Michigan (1976-1981); Associate Research Scientist, Highway Safety Research Institute, University of Michigan (1976-1981); Assistant Professor, Highway Safety Research Institute, University of Michigan (1973-1976); Assistant Research Scientist, Highway Safety Research Institute, University of Michigan (1973-1976); Assistant Professor of Biostatistics, School of Public Health, University of Michigan (1971-1973) **CR:** Statistics Consultant, The National Burn Information Exchange (1971-1976) **CIV:** Administration Board, Valley View UMC (1989-1992); Volunteer Leader, Boy Scouts of America **CW:** Editorial Collaborator, "Annals of Thoracic Surgery" (1979-1990); Editorial Collaborator, "Mathematical Biosciences" (1979-1990); Editorial Collaborator, "Biometrics, Accident Analysis and Prevention" (1979-1990); Contributor, Articles, Professional Journals; Patentee, Fieldwork **AW:** Patent Award (1993); Directors Award (1987); CPS Enterprise Award (1985); Research Grantee, National Highway Traffic Safety Administration (1974-1981); Trainee, National Institutes of Health (1969-1971); Trainee, National Aeronautics and Space Administration (1966-1969); German Academy Exchange Service Fellowship (1965-1966); Diamond Donor, Kansas Masonic Foundation C-Club; Platinum Donor, Kansas Masonic Foundation C-Club **MEM:** Past Area Deputy Grand Master Masons (2005-2006); Past Deputy Grand Master, Local Area, Masons (2003-2005); Vice President, Kansas City Chapter, Sigma Xi, The Scientific Research Honor Society (1994-1996); President, Kansas City Chapter, Sigma Xi, The Scientific Research Honor Society (1990-1991); American Statistical Association; 33rd Degree Scottish Rite; Knight Commander Court of Honor, York Rite; Masonic Societas Rosiercruciana in Civitatibus Foederatus; Blue Key Honor Society; Past Master, Masons **AS:** Dr. Flora attributes his success to his ability to communicate with people in a wide variety of disciplines and understand their work. He can then assist them in applying logic and statistics to their data to identify the most significant findings. Likewise, he can write well on both the scientific and more general levels to communicate research findings to other scientists and the general public. **B/I:** Dr. Flora was always interested in math and science. As a statistician, he had the opportunity to work with leading scientists and engineers in several different areas of science and apply statistics to help analyze the data in many fields. These have ranged from physics and chemistry to biology and medicine to environmental sciences. **AV:** Painting; Reading; Woodworking **PA:** Republican **RE:** Methodist **THT:** Dr. Flora's motto is, "It's not the destination so much as the journey; enjoy the ride." He says if one always aims to do things halfway reasonable, one won't miss the mark by very much.

FLORA, ROBERT M., PHD, T: Biochemist (Retired) **I:** Sciences **DOB:** 10/01/1938 **PB:** Richmond **SC:** VA/USA **PT:** Jacob Parker Flora; Ora Mae (Flora) Flora **MS:** Widowed **SPN:** Evelyn Gayle Long (1965, Deceased 2019) **CH:** Jonathan; Susan **ED:** PhD, Virginia Polytechnic Institute and State University (1965); BA, Bridgewater College, VA, Cum Laude (1960) **C:** Vice President, Research and Development,, Biotechnology Group, Pharmacia Inc., Piscataway, NJ (1983-1991); Senior Consultant Scientist, Millipore Corp., Bedford, MA (1979-1983); Director, Research Product Development, Worthington Biochemical Corporation, Freehold, NJ (1974-1979); Research Scientist, Worthington Biochemical Corporation, Freehold,

NJ (1968-1974); Assistant Professor of Chemistry, American University, Washington, DC (1966-1968); Research Associate, Vanderbilt University School of Medicine, Nashville, TN (1964-1966) **MEM:** Former Member, American Association for the Advancement of Science; American Chemical Society; Former Member, Industrial Biotechnology Association (Now Biotechnology Innovation Organization (BIO)); Sigma Xi, The Scientific Research Honor Society; The Honor Society of Phi Kappa Phi; Phi Lambda Upsilon **MH:** Albert Nelson Marquis Lifetime Achievement Award; Marquis Who's Who Top Professional **AS:** Dr. Flora attributes his success to his education and good problem solving skills. **B/I:** Dr. Flora became involved in his profession because majoring in general science as an undergraduate, the understanding of life processes became an appealing interest.

FLORENCE, ALFRED WILLIAM, T: Multidiscipline Systems Engineer (Retired) **I:** Engineering **CN:** The MITRE Corporation **DOB:** 04/15/1939 **PB:** Las Vegas **SC:** NM/USA **PT:** Alfonso Frank Florence; Cora Margret (Paiz) Florence **MS:** Married **SPN:** Harumi Uchida Florence **CH:** Bryan Florence; Daniel Florence **ED:** Master's Degree Coursework in Computer Science, UCLA, University of Southern California; BS in Mathematics, Physics and Art, The University of New Mexico; Postgraduate Coursework **CT:** Lean Six Sigma Black Belt, Harrington Management Systems; Certified in Capability Maturity Model Integration, Carnegie Mellon University **C:** Shell Oil Company; Hughes Aircraft Company; Software Engineer, Technical Lead, TRW; Technical Manager, Martin Marietta; Senior Manager, SAIC; The MITRE Corporation **CIV:** Spanish Colonial Arts Society **MIL:** U.S. Army **AW:** Accommodation, The MITRE Corporation; Technical Certificates and Commendations, Department of Homeland Security; Art Ribbons **MEM:** Hyperloop Advanced Research Partnership **MH:** Albert Nelson Marquis Lifetime Achievement Award **AS:** Mr. Florence attributes his success to his open mind and willingness to find the answers to necessary questions. **B/I:** Mr. Florence became involved in his profession because of his studies. He chose to pursue mathematics, physics and art. **AV:** Volunteering **PA:** Democrat

FLORES, WILLIAM, "BILL" HOSE SR., T: U.S. Representative from Texas; Former Oil Industry Executive **I:** Government Administration/Government Relations/Government Services **DOB:** 02/25/1954 **PB:** Cheyenne **SC:** WY/USA **PT:** Joe Pete Flores; Ruth Ann Theresa (Kennedy) Flores **MS:** Married **SPN:** Gina Lynn (Bass) Flores (06/17/1978) **CH:** William Hose Jr.; John Patrick **ED:** MBA, Houston Baptist University (1985); BBA in Accounting, Texas A&M University, Cum Laude (1976) **CT:** CPA, State of Texas (1978) **C:** Member, U.S. House of Representatives from Texas' 17th Congressional District, Unites States Congress, Washington, DC (2011-Present); Member, U.S. House Committee on Natural Resources, Washington, DC (2011-Present); Member, U.S. House Budget Committee, Washington, DC (2011-Present); Chairman, Republican Study Committee (2015-2017); Co-founder, President, Chief Executive Officer, Phoenix Exploration Co. LP, Houston, Texas (2006-2009); Senior Vice President, Chief Financial Officer, Gryphon Exploration Co., Houston, Texas (2001-2005); Senior vice President, Chief Financial Officer, Transenergy USA, Houston, Texas (1999); Corporate Senior Vice President, Chief Financial Officer, Western Atlas Inc., Houston, Texas (1997-1998); Executive Vice President, Director of Marine Drilling, Chief Financial Officer, Marine Drilling Cos., Inc., Sugar Land, Texas (1991-1997); Vice President of Finance, Keyes Offshore Cos., Sugar Land, Texas

(1980-1990); Controller, ABC, Houston, Texas (1978-1980); Senior Accountant, Peat, Marwick & Mitchell Co. (Now KPMG International Cooperative), Houston, Texas (1976-1978); Staff Accountant, Peat, Marwick & Mitchell Co. (Now KPMG International Cooperative), Amarillo, Texas (1976); Member, Committee on Energy and Commerce, United States Congress **CIV:** Board of Trustees, Houston Baptist University; Commissioner, Texas Real Estate Commission; Board of Directors, Alley Theatre, Houston, Texas; Board of Directors, Past President, The Association of Former Students of Texas A&M University; Member, Central Baptist Church **AW:** Distinguished Alumnus Award, Houston Baptist University (2013); Named to the Hall of Honor, Texas A&M University Corps of Cadets (2012); Boss of the Plains Award, National Ranching Heritage Center, Texas Tech University (2011); Distinguished Alumnus Award, Texas A&M University (2010); Outstanding Alumnus Award, Mays Business School, Texas A&M University (2004); Numerous Congressional Service Awards **AV:** Skiing; Flying **PA:** Republican **RE:** Methodist

FLOYD, GEORGE PERRY JR., I: Other **DOB:** 10/14/1973 **PB:** Fayette **SC:** NC/USA **CH:** Five Children **ED:** Coursework, Texas A&M University; Coursework, South Florida Community College **C:** Security Guard, Minnesota (2020); Truck Driver, Minnesota (2014); Bouncer, Conga Latin Bistro, Minnesota (2014); Automotive Customizer, Houston, TX **CIV:** With, Local Ministry, Resurrection Houston, Houston, Texas (2014); Mentor and Defacto Community Leader **CW:** Featured, Anti-Gun Violence Video (2017); Rap Artist, Screwed Up Click (1994) **AV:** Basketball **THT:** His death sparked protests and demonstrations held in all 50 states and globally against police brutality and lack of accountability, justice for his death, and furthering the Black Lives Matter movement (2020); Numerous colleges established a memorial scholarship in his honor, including North Central University, Alabama State University, Oakwood University, Missouri State University, Southeast Missouri State University, The Ohio University, SUNY Buffalo State, Cooper Mountain College (2020); Numerous murals created in his memory (2020); June 9th named George Perry Floyd Jr. Day, Harris County, TX (2020)

FLOYD, KIMBERLY, "KIM" HAYES, T: Lawyer **I:** Law and Legal Services **CN:** Joe D. Floyd, PA, Law Firm **DOB:** 01/10/1958 **PB:** Greensboro **SC:** NC/USA **PT:** Joe Don Floyd; Bonita Jean (Hayes) Floyd **MS:** Single **ED:** Doctor of Jurisprudence, Campbell University, Buies Creek, NC (1983); Postgraduate Coursework, London School of Economics, London, England (1982); Bachelor of Science, Campbell University, Buies Creek, NC (1980) **C:** Joe D. Floyd, PA, Law Firm, High Point, NC (1985-Present) **CR:** Presidential Advisory Board, Campbell University, Buies Creek, NC (2002-Present) **CIV:** Board Member, Salvation Army of High Point (2019-Present); Junior League of High Point (1990-Present); President, High Point Bar Association (2016-2017); Delegate, Republican National Convention (1996); Speaker, Green Street Baptist Church Women's Conference (1995); Public Speaker, Child Watch Committee in Cooperation with Guilford County Department of Social Services (1992-1994); Secretary, Treasurer, Guilford County Bar Association (1992-1993) **AW:** Distinguished Alumna Award, Campbell University, Buies Creek, NC (1997); Named, One of the Outstanding Young Women of America (1988, 1991) **MEM:** North Carolina State Bar; High Point Bar Association; High Point Judicial District Bar; North Carolina Association of Women Attorneys; North Carolina Advocates For Justice; North

Carolina Bar Association **BAR:** United States District Court for the Eastern District of North Carolina (1994); Supreme Court of the United States (1991); United States District Court for the Middle District of North Carolina (1986); State of North Carolina (1985) **MH:** Albert Nelson Marquis Lifetime Achievement Award; Marquis Who's Who Top Professional; Life Member of the National Registry of Who's Who; Who's Who in American Law **AS:** Ms. Floyd attributes her success to her Christian upbringing, as well as her parents, who encouraged her to be the best person she possibly can. She tries her best to treat people fairly, just as she would want to be treated. **B/I:** Ms. Floyd became involved in her profession because she wanted to follow in her father's footsteps. Since she was in the second grade, her father took her to court with him. Her mother was also very instrumental in encouraging her to pursue her dreams. Ms. Floyd's favorite memory was when she sat with a female judge and wrote down whether she thought the person on trial was guilty or innocent. Her great uncle was also a federal judge. It was very endearing to her to see how they treated people fairly. Ms. Floyd's father has been a highly respected attorney, and her great uncle was also a very respectable judge, and she was fortunate to have had their influence in her life. **PA:** Republican **RE:** Baptist

FLOYD, RAYMOND, T: Professional Golfer **I:** Athletics **CN:** Professional Golfers' Association of America (PGA of America) **DOB:** 09/04/1942 **PB:** Fort Bragg **SC:** NC/USA **PT:** Loren B. Floyd; Edith (Brown) Floyd **MS:** Married **SPN:** Maria **CH:** Raymond Loran; Robert Loran; Christina Loran **ED:** Coursework, University of North Carolina (1960) **C:** Professional Golfer, Senior Professional Golfers' Association of America (PGA of America) (1992-Present); Professional Golfer, PGA of America (1961-1992) **CR:** Assistant Captain, United States Team, Ryder Cup (2008); Member, US Team, Ryder Cup (1969, 1975, 1977, 1981, 1983, 1985, 1991, 1993); Captain, US Team, Ryder Cup (1989) **AW:** Winner, Wendy's Champion Tour Skins (2006); Runner-up, The Boeing Championship (2006); Three Top Ten Finishes in Nine Starts (2006); Winning U.S. Team, UBS Cup (2004); Winner, 2000 Ford Senior Players Championship; Winner, Ford Senior Players Championship (2000); Winner, Senior Tour Championship (1994); Winner, Northville Long Island Classic Senior PGA (1993); Winner, Doral Ryder Open (1992); Winner, GTE North Classic (1992); Winner, World Golf Hall of Fame (1989); Winner, Vardon Trophy (1983); Winner, Byron Nelson (1983); Rookie of the Year, Golf Magazine (1963, 1977); Player of the Year (1976)

FODY, EDWARD P., T: Pathologist, Laboratory Director **I:** Sciences **DOB:** 06/11/1947 **PB:** Baltimore **SC:** MD/USA **PT:** Edward Paul Fody; Frances Dorothy (Schultz) Fody **MS:** Married **SPN:** Nancy June Keipe (07/19/1974) **ED:** MD, Vanderbilt University (1975); Residency in Pathology, Vanderbilt University Hospital, Nashville, TN (1975-1978); MS, University of Wisconsin (1971); BS, Duke University (1969) **CT:** Diplomate, American Board of Pathology **C:** Pathologist, Holland Hospital (2013-Present); Chief of Pathology, Western Michigan Pathology Associates, Holland Hospital (2004-2013); Chief Pathologist, Erlanger Health System, Chattanooga, TN (1997-2004); Chief Pathologist, Bethesda Hospital, Cincinnati, OH (1987-1996); Associate Professor of Pathology, University of Arkansas for Medical Sciences (1981-1987); Chief, Laboratory, Veterans Affairs Hospital, Little Rock, AR (1981-1987); Assistant Professor of Pathology, McGovern Medical School, UT Health (1980-1981); Fellow in Chemistry, McGovern Medical School, UT Health (1979-1980) **CW:** Editor, Author, "Clinical Chemistry" (1984) **MEM:** Fellow, College of American Pathologists; American Society for Clinical Pathologists; American Medical Association; American Association for Clinical Chemistry; American Society for Microbiology; Michigan State Medical Society; Ottawa County Medical Society **MH:** Albert Nelson Marquis Lifetime Achievement Award; Marquis Who's Who Top Professional **B/I:** Dr. Fody became involved in his profession because of his lifelong interest in science and desire to study cancer. While at the University of Wisconsin, he studied the impact of chemical compounds on cancer therapy, and he continued that work when he became a physician. **AV:** Boating; Taking photographs **PA:** Republican **RE:** Lutheran

FOGARTY, JAMES VINCENT, EDD, T: Chief Executive Officer, Special Education Administrator, Educator **I:** Education/Educational Services **CN:** A+ Schools **DOB:** 12/12/1945 **PB:** New York **SC:** NY/USA **PT:** James Vincent Fogarty; Dorothy (Hummender) Fogarty **MS:** Married **SPN:** Susan Mitsos (2011-Present) **CH:** Ann Denise; Brian James; Andrea; Shannon **ED:** CAS in Administration, Hofstra University (1974); MS in Special Education, Adelphi University (1971); BS in Biology, State University of New York, Stony Brook (1967); Ed.D., Nova Southeastern University **CT:** School District Administrator, New York State (SDA) **C:** Chief Executive Officer, Galway Consultants Inc. (2002-Present); Associate Director Phi Delta Kappa (2001-2002); Executive Director, Board of Cooperative Education Services, 2nd Supervisory District, Patchogue, NY (1997-2000); Executive Director, Division of Special Education & Occupation Technical Education & Adult Education, Board of Cooperative Education Services, 2nd Supervisory District, Patchogue, NY (1996-2000); Director, Special Education, Board of Cooperative Education Services, 2nd Supervisory District, Patchogue, NY (1983-1996); Deputy Assistant Director, Board of Cooperative Education Services, 2nd Supervisory District, Patchogue, NY (1977-1983); Assistant Center Administrator, Board of Cooperative Education Services, 2nd Supervisory District, Patchogue, NY (1974-1977); Teacher, Town of Oyster Bay, NY (1970-1974); Teacher, Curriculum and Intellectually Disabled, Board of Cooperative Education Services, Rosemary Kennedy Center, Nassau County, NY (1967-1974) **CR:** Adjunct Professor, Hofstra University, Hempstead, NY (1986-Present); Adjunct Professor, Dowling College, Oakdale, NY (1988-1995); Consultant, New York City Board Education (1981); Adjunct Faculty, Long Island University, Greenvale, NY (1980) **CIV:** President, Chapters 72 and 653, Council Exceptional Children (1968-Present) National Christina Foundation (1985-2000); Suffolk County Handicapped Advisory Board, Hauppauge, NY (1985-2000) **CW:** Author, Articles on Education **AW:** County Service Award, St. Charles Hospital, (1997); Educator of Year, Columbia University (1989); Stephen Apter Leadership Award; New York State Educators Emotionally Disturbed (1989, 2002); Recipient, Service Award, Association for Children with Down Syndrome (1981); Research Scholar, Grantee, National Science Foundation (1967) **MEM:** Phi Delta Kappa **MH:** Albert Nelson Marquis Lifetime Achievement Award; Marquis Who's Who Top Professional; Marquis Who's Who Humanitarian Award **B/I:** Mr. Fogarty became involved with his profession after studying at Long Island University and later accepting a position as a teachers aide. During that time, he worked with children who were mentally handicapped. He enjoyed the position so much, that he made the decision to get all his degrees in education. **AV:** Fishing, Whitewater rafting; Gardening; Traveling **PA:** Independent **RE:** Catholic

FOLES, NICHOLAS EDWARD, T: Professional Football Player **I:** Athletics **CN:** Chicago Bears **DOB:** 01/20/1989 **PB:** Austin **SC:** TX/USA **PT:** Larry Foles; Melissa Foles **MS:** Married **SPN:** Tori Moore (2014) **CH:** Lily James **ED:** Master of Divinity Candidate, Liberty University; Coursework, University of Arizona; Diploma, Westlake High School **C:** Professional Football Player, Chicago Bears (2020-Present); Professional Football Player, Jacksonville Jaguars (2019); Professional Football Player, Philadelphia Eagles (2017-2018); Professional Football Player, Kansas City Chiefs (2016); Professional Football Player, St. Louis Rams (2015); Professional Football Player, Philadelphia Eagles (2012-2014) **CW:** Author, "Believe It: My Journey of Success, Failure, and Overcoming the Odds" (2018) **AW:** Super Bowl Champion (2017); Super Bowl MVP (2017); Pro Bowl Champion (2013) **RE:** Christian

FOLEY, HARRIET E., T: School Librarian (Retired) **I:** Library Management/Library Services **DOB:** 08/11/1935 **PB:** Franklin **SC:** OH/USA **PT:** Milo A. Fealy; Nora Lucile (Babb) Fealy **MS:** Married **SPN:** Thomas R. Foley (11/22/1969) **ED:** Postgraduate, Kent State University (1965); Master of Science in Library Science, University of Kentucky (1961); Bachelor of Arts in Education, College of Mount St. Joseph, Cincinnati (1957) **CT:** Certified Teacher of Elementary Education Ohio; Certification in Library Science **C:** School Librarian, Carlisle Schools, Ohio (1961-1982); Teacher of Secondary French, Carlisle Schools, Ohio (1961-1963); Elementary Teacher, Carlisle Schools, Ohio (1957-1961) **CIV:** Secretary, Conover Health Center (2017-Present); Trustee, Conover Health Center (2016); Trustee, Secretary, Carlisle Federal Credit Union (1962-2008); Various Committees, Otterbein-lebanon Retirement Community Committee (1990-1998); Bicentennial Committee, Franklin (1996) **CW:** Editor, "The History of Franklin on the Great Miami Valley" (1982, 2004); Co-author, "Foleys from County Clare, Ireland" (1994); Co-author, "History of St. Mary Parish: 1867-1967"; Editor, "Carlisle, the Jersey Settlement in Ohio: 1800-1980"; Editor, "Carlisle, the Jersey Settlement in Ohio: 1800-1990"; Co-author, "150 Year History of St. Mary Church: 1868-2018" **AW:** Named, Citizen of the Year of Franklin (2007); Inductee, Franklin High School Hall of Fame (2003) **MEM:** Treasurer, Warren County Genealogical Society (1982, 1994-Present); Local Chapter Treasurer, Daughters of the American Revolution (1988-Present); Treasurer, Franklin Area Historical Society (1999-2018); Editor, Newsletter, Franklin Area Historical Society (1986-2015); Editor, Heir Lines, Warren County Genealogical Society (1982-2015); President, Warren County Genealogical Society (1991); Secretary, Treasurer, Ohio Association of School Libraries (1970-1975); American Library Association; Ohio Educational Library Media Association; Lifetime Member, Ohio Retired Teachers Association; Ohio Genealogical Society; Plantagenet Society; Magna Carta Dames; First Families of Ohio; First Families of Belmont County, Ohio; First Families of Clark County, Ohio; Early Settlers of Warren County, Ohio; Civil War Families of Warren County, Ohio **B/I:** Ms. Foley became involved in her profession because father dad was an elementary school principal and her mother was a Latin, French and English teacher, all of which inspired her to follow their example. **AV:** Genealogy; Local history **PA:** Republican **RE:** Roman Catholic

FONDA, JANE, T: Actress **I:** Media & Entertainment **DOB:** 12/21/1937 **PB:** New York **SC:** NY/USA **PT:** Henry Fonda; Frances (Seymour) Fonda **SPN:** Ted Turner (1991, Divorced 2001); Tom Hayden (01/20/1973, Divorced 1990); Roger Vadim (08/14/1965, Divorced 01/16/1973) **CH:** Vanessa; Troy Garity; Mary **ED:** Coursework, Vassar College **CW:** Voice Actress, "Elena of Avalor" (2017-Present); Actress, "Grace and Frankie" (2015-Present); Actress, "The Newsroom" (2012-Present); Actress, "Book Club" (2018); Actress, "Our Souls at Night" (2017); Voice Actress, "Elena and the Secret of Avalor" (2016); Actress, "Youth" (2015); Actress, "Fathers and Daughters" (2015); Voice Actress, "The Simpsons" (2014); Actress, "Better Living Through Chemistry" (2014); Actress, "This Is Where I Leave You" (2014); Actress, "Lee Daniels' The Butler" (2013); Actress, "All Together" (2011); Actress, "Peace, Love & Misunderstanding" (2011); Host, "Jane Fonda's Prime Time: Trim, Tone & Flex" (2011); Author, "Prime Time: Love, Health, Sex, Fitness, Friendship, Spirit-Making the Most of Your Life" (2011); Host, "Jane Fonda's Prime Time: Firm & Burn" (2011); Host, "Jane Fonda: Prime Time Walkout" (2010); Host, "Jane Fonda: Prime Time Fit & Strong" (2010); Actress, "33 Variations" (2009); Actress, "Georgia Rule" (2007); Author, "My Life So Far" (2005); Actress, "Monster-in-Law" (2005); Actress, "A Century of Women" (1994); Actress, "Stanley and Iris" (1990); Author, "Jane Fonda's New Pregnancy Workout & Total Birth Program" (1989); Actress, "Old Gringo" (1988); Actress, "Retour" (1987); Actress, "Leonard Part 6" (1987); Author, "Jane Fonda's New Workout & Weight-Loss Program" (1986); Actress, "The Morning After" (1986); Actress, "Agnes of God" (1985); Author, "Women Coming of Age" (1984); Actress, "The Dollmaker" (1984); Host, "Jane Fonda's Workout" (1982); Actress, "Lily: Sold Out" (1981); Author, "Jane Fonda's Workout Book" (1981); Actress, "Rollover" (1981); Actress, "On Golden Pond" (1981); Actress, "Nine to Five" (1980); Actress, "The China Syndrome" (1979); Actress, "Electric Horseman" (1979); Actress, "California Suite" (1978); Actress, "Comes a Horseman" (1978); Actress, "Coming Home" (1978); Actress, "Julia" (1977); Actress, "The Blue Bird" (1976); Actress, "Steelyard Blues" (1973); Actress, "A Doll's House" (1973); Actress, "All's Well" (1972); Actress, "Klute" (1970); Actress, "Spirits of the Dead" (1969); Actress, "They Shoot Horses, Don't They?" (1969); Actress, "Barbarella" (1968); Actress, "The Game Is Over" (1967); Actress, "Hurry Sundown" (1967); Actress, "Barefoot in the Park" (1967); Actress, "The Chase" (1966); Actress, "Any Wednesday" (1966); Actress, "Cat Ballou" (1965); Actress, "La Ronde" (1964); Actress, "Sunday in New York" (1963); Actress, "In the Cool of the Day" (1963); Actress, "The Love Cage" (1963); Actress, "Strange Interlude" (1963); Actress, "A Walk on the Wild Side" (1962); Actress, "The Chapman Resort" (1962); Actress, "Period of Adjustment" (1962); Actress, "The Fun Couple" (1962); Actress, "A String of Beads" (1961); Actress, "There Was a Little Girl" (1960); Actress, "Tall Story" (1960) **AW:** Lifetime Achievement Award, New York Women's Agenda (2009); Inductee, California Hall of Fame (2008); Women in Hollywood Tribute Award, ELLE (2008); Career Achievement Award, National Board of Review (2005); People's Choice Award for Favorite Motion Picture Actress (1980-1983); Golden Apple Prize for Female Star of the Year, Hollywood Women's Press Club (1977); Golden Globe Award for Most Promising Newcomer, Hollywood Foreign Press Association (1962)

FONTAINE, DANI, T: Owner/Product Developer **I:** Cosmetics **CN:** Nature's Root Spa **MS:** Single **CH:** One Son **ED:** High School Diploma **C:** Co-owner, HGH Seed Inc. (2017-Present); Owner/Product Developer, Natures Root Labs (2015-Present); Co-owner, Nature's Root Spa (2014-Present); Co-owner, Colorado Hemp Project (2013-Present);Owner, Nature's Root (2008-Present) **CIV:** Building a House and Donating it to Someone in Jamaica **AW:** Named Cannabis Woman of the year, Cannabis Business Awards (2018); Best Hemp Product Award, Cannabis Business Awards (2016-2018); Named Best Innovative Product (2016) **MEM:** HGH Seed, Inc.; Local Farms; Nature's Root; Natures Root Labs, Hemp International Association **AS:** Ms. Fontaine attributes her success to her plants and her son. **B/I:** Ms. Fontaine went to college for a few month until she realized it wasn't for her; she wanted to be an entrepreneur. There are many of entrepreneurs in her family. She has been involved in cannabis since she was 12 as a caregiver. **THT:** Nature's Roots was originally created of her first hemp farm. She had no buys but needed to find some kind of income stream to show that her first hemp crop was successful. She used the lab to make a body care product line, which then turned into something more educational, which developed into her spa. Her motto is, "Its a mission not a competition. Do things with intention, do things but set boundaries and always look for the greater cause."

FONTANA, SANTINO ANTHONY, T: Actor **I:** Media & Entertainment **DOB:** 03/21/1982 **PB:** Stockton **SC:** CA/USA **PT:** Ernest John Fontana; Sharon Marie (Simarro) Fontana **MS:** Married **SPN:** Jessica Hershberg (2015) **CH:** Grace **ED:** BFA, Guthrie Theater Actor Training Program, University of Minnesota (2004); Diploma, Richland High School (2000); Coursework in Theatre Arts, Interlochen Arts Camp, Interlochen Center for the Arts; Coursework in Arts, Academy of Children's Theatre **CW:** Actor, "Impossible Monsters" (2019); Guest Appearance, "Fosse/Verdon" (2019); Voice Actor, "Frozen II" (2019); Actor, "Tootsie," Cadillac Palace Theatre and Marquis Theatre (2018-2019); Actor, "Off the Menu" (2018); Actor, Short Film, "Papercop" (2018); Actor, "The Vanishing Princess" (2018); Actor, "Hello, Dolly!," Shubert Theatre, The Shubert Organization, Inc.(2018) Actor, "Mozart in the Jungle" (2014-2018); Actor, "Shades of Blues" (2016-2017); Guest Appearance, "BrainDead" (2016); Actor, "1776" and "Kurt Vonnegut's God Bless You, Mr. Rosewater," Encores! New York City Center (2016); Actor, "Crazy Ex-Girlfriend" (2015-2016); Musician, "Keep Christmas with You" (2015); Voice Actor, Short Film, "Frozen Fever" (2015); Actor, "Sisters" (2015); Actor, "Act One," Vivian Beaumont Theatre, Lincoln Center Theater (2014); Actor, "Jack Ryan: Shadow Recruit" (2014); Guest Artist, "A Summer Celebration of Song" (2014); Actor, "Fade to White" (2014); Actor, "Submissions Only" (2011-2014); Actor, "Cinderella," The Broadway Theatre, The Shubert Organization, Inc. (2013); Actor, Short Film, "Marion Knapp Doesn't Smile" (2013); Voice Actor, "Frozen" (2013); Actor, "Nancy, Please" (2012); Guest Appearance, "A Gifted Man" (2012); Guest Appearance, "Royal Pains" (2012); Guest Appearance, "Made in Jersey" (2012); Actor, Short Film, "Newsworthy" (2011); Actor, "The Importance of Being Earnest," American Airlines Theatre, Roundabout Theatre Company (2011); Guest Appearance, "Nurse Jackie" (2011); Actor, "Sons of the Prophet," Laura Pels Theatre, Roundabout Theatre Company (2011); Guest Appearance, "The Good Wife" (2010); Actor, "A View from the Bridge," Cort Theatre, The Shubert Organization, Inc. (2010); Actor, "Brighton Beach Memoirs" and "Broadway Bound," Nederlander Theatre, Nederlander Organization, Inc. (2009); Actor, "Sunday in the Park with George," Roundabout Theatre Company (2008); Actor, "Billy Elliot the Musical," Imperial Theatre, The Shubert Organization, Inc. (2008); Actor, "Noel Coward's Hay Fever," Old Globe Theatre, The Old Globe (2007); Actor, "Hamlet," Guthrie Theater, University of Minnesota (2006); Actor, "The Fantasticks" (2006); Co-writer, Actor, "Perfect Harmony," Studio Tisch, New York University (2005); Actor, "Six Degrees of Separation," Guthrie Theater, University of Minnesota (2003); Actor, "A Christmas Carol," Guthrie Theater, University of Minnesota; Actor, "La Traviata," Washington East Opera; Actor, "Death of a Salesman," Guthrie Theater, University of Minnesota, and Gaiety Theatre; Actor, "As You Like It," Guthrie Theater, University of Minnesota; Actor, "Once in a Lifetime," "9/11 Project," "On the Verge," "Loves Labour's Lost," Chautauqua Theater Company, Chautauqua Institution **AW:** Best Thriller/Suspense Audiobook, "The Institute," Audie Awards (2020); Outstanding Actor in a Musical, "Tootsie," Outer Critics Circle Awards (2019); Outstanding Actor in a Musical, "Tootsie," Drama Desk Awards (2019); Best Actor in a Musical, "Tootsie," Tony Awards (2019); Best Actor, "Papercop," Williamsburg Independent Film Festival (2018); Best Actor in a Touring Production, "Tootsie," BroadwayWorld Chicago Awards (2018); Best Vocal Ensemble in a Feature Film, "Frozen," Behind the Voice Actors Award: People's Choice and Feature Film (2014); Co-recipient, Favorite Onstage Pair, "Cinderella," Broadway.com Audience Awards (2013); Outstanding Lead Actor, "Sons of the Prophet," Lucille Lortel Awards (2012); Performance Award, "Sons of the Prophet," Obie Awards (2012); Most Promising Male Performer, "The Importance of Being Earnest," Clarence Derwent Awards (2011); Outstanding Featured Actor in a Play, "Brighton Beach Memoirs," Drama Desk Awards (2010)

FORD, HARRISON, T: Actor **I:** Media & Entertainment **DOB:** 7/13/1942 **PB:** Chicago **SC:** IL/USA **PT:** Christopher Ford; Dorothy Nidelman Ford **MS:** Married **SPN:** Calista Flockhart (2010); Melissa Mathison (March 14, 1983-January 6, 2004); Mary Marquardt (June 18, 1964-October 3, 1979) **CH:** Willard; Benjamin **ED:** Completed Coursework, Ripon College **CIV:** Board of Directors, Archaeological Institute of America, Boston (2008-Present); Honorary Board Member, Wings of Hope; Board of Directors, Conservation International **CW:** Actor, "The Call of the Wild" (2020); Actor, "Star Wars: The Rise of Skywalker" (2019); Voice Actor, "The Secret Life of Pets 2" (2019); Actor, "Toxic Puzzle- Hunt for the Hidden Killer" (2017); Actor, "Blade Runner 2049" (2017); Actor, "The Age of Adaline" (2015); Actor, "Star Wars: The Force Awakens" (2015); Actor, "The Expendables 3" (2014); Actor, "42" (2013); Actor, "Paranoia" (2013); Actor, "Ender's Game" (2013); Actor, "Anchorman 2: The Legend Continues" (2013); Actor, "Cowboys & Aliens" (2011); Actor, "Morning Glory" (2010); Actor, Executive Producer, "Actor, "Extraordinary Measures" (2010); Actor, "Crossing Over" (2009); Actor, "Indiana Jones and the Kingdom of the Crystal Skull" (2008); Actor, "Firewall" (2006); Actor, "Hollywood Homicide" (2003); Actor, Executive Producer, "K-19: The Widowmaker" (2002); Actor, "What Lies Beneath" (2000); Actor, "Random Hearts" (1999); Actor, "Six Days Seven Nights" (1998); Actor, "Air Force One" (1997); Actor, "Devil's Own" (1996); Actor, "Sabrina" (1995); Actor, "A Hundred and One Nights" (1995); Actor, "Clear and Present Danger" (1994); Actor, "The Fugitive" (1993); Actor, "The Young Indiana Jones Chronicles" (1993); Actor, "Patriot Games" (1992); Actor, "Regarding Henry" (1991); Actor, "Presumed Innocent" (1990); Actor, "Indiana Jones and the Last Crusade" (1989); Actor, "Frantic" (1988); Actor, "Working Girl" (1988); Actor, "Mosquito Coast"

(1986); Actor, "Witness" (1985); Actor, "Indiana Jones and the Temple of Doom" (1984); Actor, "Return of the Jedi" (1983); Actor, "Blade Runner" (1982); Actor, "Raiders of the Lost Ark" (1981); Actor, "The Empire Strikes Back" (1980); Actor, "Hanover Street" (1979); Actor, "More American Graffiti" (1979); Actor, "The Frisco Kid" (1979); Actor, "Apocalypse Now" (1979); Actor, "Force 10 From Navarone" (1978); Actor, "Star Wars" (1977); Actor, "Heroes" (1977); Actor, "The Possessed" (1977); Actor, "James A. Michener's Dynasty" (1976); Actor, "Judgement: The Court-Martial of Lieutenant William Calley" (1975); Actor, "Kung-Fu" (1974); Actor, "Petrocelli" (1974); Actor, "The Conversation" (1974); Actor, "Gunsmoke" (1972-1973); Actor, "American Graffiti" (1973); Actor, "Dan August" (1971); Actor, "The Intruders" (1970); Actor, "Getting Straight" (1970); Actor, "Zabriske Point" (1970); Actor, "My Friend Tony" (1969); Actor, "F.B.I." (1969); Actor, "Love, American Style" (1969); Actor, "The Mod Squad" (1968); Actor, "The Men From Shiloh" (1967); Actor, "Ironside" (1967); Actor, "Luv" (1967); Actor, "The Long Ride Home" (1967); Actor, "Dead Heat on a Merry-Go-Round" (1966) **AW:** Board of Governors Award, American Society of Cinematographers (2012); Jules Verne Spirit of Nature Award (2006); Lifetime Achievement Award, American Film Institute (2000) **PA:** Democrat

FORD, TOM, T: Fashion Designer **I:** Apparel & Fashion **DOB:** 08/27/1962 **PB:** Austin **SC:** TX/USA **PT:** Tom Ford; Shirley Burton **MS:** Married **SPN:** Richard Buckley **CH:** Alexander John Buckley Ford **ED:** BFA in Architectural Design, Parsons School of Design, New York, NY (1986); Coursework, New York University **C:** Founder, President, Chief Executive Officer, Tom Ford Co. (2005-Present); Creative Director Yves Saint Laurent Rive Gauche, YSL Beauté Line, Gucci (2000-2004); Creative Director, Gucci (1994-2004); Design Director, Gucci (1992-1994); Chief Women's Ready-to-Wear Designer, Gucci (1990-1992); Design Director, Perry Ellis Women's American Division (1988-1990); Senior Designer, Cathy Hardwick (1986-1988); Intern, Chloé, Paris **CR:** Tom Ford for Estee Lauder (2005-Present) **CW:** Director, Writer, Producer, "Nocturnal Animals" (2015); Director, Writer, Producer, "A Single Man" (2009) **AW:** Satellite Auteur Award (2016); Menswear Designer of Year, Council Fashion Designers America (2008, 2015); Geoffrey Beene Lifetime Achievement Award, Council Fashion Designers of America (2014); 100 Most Influential People in the World, "TIME" (2011); Maverick, "Details" (2007); Accessory Designer of Year (2002); Designer of Year for Yves Saint Laurent Rive Gauche, VH1/Vogue Fashion Awards (2002); Womenswear Designer of Year (2001); Designer of Year, "GQ" (2001); Best Fashion Designer "TIME" (2001); Best Designer of Year, Fashion Editor's Club Japan (2001); Superstar Award, Fashion Group International Night Stars (2000); International Man of the Year, British GQ (2000); Commitment to Life Award, AIDS Project, LA (1999); Womenswear Designer of the Year (1996, 1999); Style Icon Award, Elle Style Awards (1999); International Designer of the Year (1996); Menswear Designer of the Year (1996); Future's Best New Designer (1995)

FORDE, PATRICIA, "PAT" ANN, T: Executive Director **I:** Medicine & Health Care **CN:** LHC DBA Life Care at Home **DOB:** 04/20/1953 **PB:** Providence **SC:** RI/USA **PT:** William T. Forde; Lena E. (Fera) Forde **MS:** Single **ED:** MBA, Providence College (1985); MSN, University of Maryland (1977); BA in Psychology, University of Rhode Island (1975); BSN, University of Rhode Island (1975) **CT:** Certified OASIS Field Specialist (CFOS) **C:** Director of Nursing, Executive Director, LHC Group DBA Life Care at Home, Cranston, RI (2014-Present); Director of Clinical Services, Pinnacle Home Care, Warwick, RI (2011-2014); Primary Field Nurse, Case Manager, Home Care Advantage, LLC, Cranston, RI (2009-2010, 2010-2011); Director, Clinical Services, Assisted Daily Living, Inc., Warwick, RI (2010); Admission Nurse, Case Manager, Amedisys Home Care (2008-2009); Quality Assurance Coordinator, TLC Home Care (Now Amedisys Home Care) (2005-2008); Case Manager, Home Care, TLC Home Care (Now Amedisys Home Care), Providence, RI (2003-2005); Director of Hospice/Administrative Services, Hospice of Nursing Placement/Nursing Placement, Inc., Pawtucket, RI (2000-2003); Vice President, Clinical Services, VNS Home Health Services, Narragansett, RI (1996-2000); Interim Chief Executive Officer, VNS Home Health Services, Narragansett, RI (1998); Director, Manager, Case Management/Medical Management, First Allmerica Financial Life Insurance Company, Worcester, MA (1995-1996); Consultant, Boston & West Casualty Claims, Woodville, MA (1991-1996); Professional Nurse, Per Diem/Home Care/Private Duty/Hospital, Nursing Placement, Inc., Pawtucket, RI (1980-1996); Administrator, Senior Nurse Consultant, Claims Medical Management, Metropolitan Property & Casualty Insurance Company, MetLife Services and Solutions, LLC, Warwick, RI (1988-1995); Manager, Claims Medical Management, Metropolitan Property & Casualty Insurance Company, MetLife Services and Solutions, LLC, Warwick, RI (1985-1988); Consultant, Clinical Specialist, Rhode Island Hospital, Providence, RI (1979-1985); Clinical Liaison, Boston University, Boston, MA (1980-1982); Manager, Oncology/Endocrinology Unit, Roger Williams Hospital (Roger WIlliams Medical Center), Providence, RI (1979); Manager, Med/Surg and ICU/CCU, Good Samaritan Hospital, MedStar Health, Baltimore, MD (1977-1979); Per Diem Professional Nurse, Charge Nurse, Mercy Hospital (Mercy Medical Center), Baltimore, MD (1976-1977) **CR:** Consultant, Boston and West Casualty Claims, Woodville, MA (1990); Guest Lecturer, Various Healthcare Seminars and Insurance Events **CIV:** Member, Professional Education Committee, American Cancer Society, Inc. (1980-1985); CPR Instructor, American Heart Association, Inc. (1977-2003) **CW:** Reviewer, Editor, Programmed Technical Insurance Claims Training Textbooks for Professional Publishing Firm; Author, Article for Insurance Industry Magazine Regarding the Development of New Cost Containment Unit **AW:** Listee, Worldwide Leaders in Healthcare (2018); Named Top Registered Nurse, International Nurses Association **MEM:** Sigma Theta Tau International Honor Society of Nursing; American Organization for Nursing Leadership, American Hospital Association **MH:** Albert Nelson Marquis Lifetime Achievement Award; Marquis Who's Who Top Professional; Marquis Who's Who Humanitarian Award **AS:** Ms. Forde reports that she has always been blessed with the support and encouragement of her family. She attributes that support to starting her on her path to choosing and pursuing her chosen vocation in nursing and healthcare. Once she set her goals, she cites the importance of her never losing sight of them and of pursuing them with determination and a strong work ethic learned from her parents. It is also important, she notes, to build a solid foundation by being open to change and to opportunities to learn new skills along with learning from your mistakes. Having a sense of humor and a willingness to laugh and enjoy life's adventures is extremely important to keeping your life in balance, and having friends to share these adventures is important as well. She notes that her sense of humor and the ability to laugh at herself has helped her through some tough spots through the years. **B/I:** Ms. Forde became involved in her profession because when she was young, she knew she wanted to be a nurse and her grandmother and parents encouraged her. As time moved on, she went into nursing, did some CNA work, and when she was at the University of Rhode Island, she became fascinated by psychology. She then pursued her degree in psychology, along with nursing. Ms. Forde went on to the University of Maryland to receive her master's degree. Shortly after receiving her master's degree, she was contacted to do teaching and taught for Towson University as a guest lecturer. When she returned back to Rhode Island, she was a master's-prepared nurse and a clinical specialist, with her field being oncology and medical-surgical nursing. Following her return to Rhode Island, she taught for Boston University and also Rhode Island College. **AV:** Dog obedience training and competing; Traveling; Reading fiction and mystery; Arts and crafts; Theater; Singing in community chorus; Playing piano **PA:** Independent **RE:** Catholic **THT:** Ms. Forde believes it is important to enjoy the people, places and experiences we have to the fullest. She talks about how wonderful it is to share her time with friends and her large extended family, but also with her pets, who she feels add so much quality to her life. She has a list of places that she wants to travel to and to explore and learn about the culture and people. She believes that if people focused their energy more on their likenesses than on their differences, they would be able to appreciate each other's uniqueness and qualities. She believes that life is what you make it, so make it good.

FORGIONE, DANA A., PHD, T: Endowed Chair of the Jessie Francis Neal Foundation & Clifton W. Coonrod Endowment, and Professor of Accounting **I:** Education/Educational Services **CN:** Texas A&M University Corpus Christi **ED:** Doctor of Philosophy in Accounting, University of Massachusetts Amherst (1987); Master of Science in Accounting, University of Massachusetts Amherst (1980); Master of Business Administration in Accounting, University of Massachusetts Amherst (1977); Bachelor of Business Administration in Accounting and Information Systems, University of Massachusetts Amherst (1975) **CT:** Certified in Church Ministries, Heritage Baptist Institute, Springfield, MA (1983); Certified in Christian Leadership, Heritage Baptist Institute, with High Honors, Springfield, MA (1979); Certified Fraud Examiner; Certified Management Accountant, Certified Public Accountant, States of Florida, Texas and Maryland **C:** Endowed Chair of the Jessie Francis Neal Foundation & Clifton W. Coonrod Endowment, and Professor of Accounting in the College of Business at Texas A&M University Corpus Christi (2020-Present); Graduate Faculty, Translational Science Doctorate Program, Graduate School of Biomedical Sciences, University of Texas (2015-Present); Adjunct Professor, Department of Cardiothoracic Surgery, School of Medicine, University of Texas (2011-Present); Adjunct Professor, Department of Pediatrics, School of Medicine, University of Texas (2008-Present); Adjunct Professor, School of Public Health, University of Texas (2007-Present); Professor of Accounting, Department of Accounting, The University of Texas at San Antonio (2006-2020); Janey S. Briscoe Endowed Chair in Business Health, College Business, University of Texas at San Antonio (2006-2016); Professor, Director, Center for Accounting, Auditing and Tax Studies, School Accounting, Florida International University, Miami, FL (2006); Director, Professor, School of Accounting, Florida International University, Miami, FL (2001-2005); Affiliate Professor, University of Maryland, Baltimore (2000-2001); Professor, University of Baltimore

(2000-2001); Affiliate Associate Professor, School of Pharmacy, University of Maryland, Baltimore (1996-2000); Advisor of MBA Specialization in Healthcare Management, University of Baltimore (1993-2001); Associate Professor, Merrick School of Business, University of Baltimore (1993-2000); Director of Professional MBA Program, Merrick School of Business, University of Baltimore (1993-2000); Assistant Professor, College Business Administration, Graduate School of Business, Texas A&M University, College Station, TX (1987-1993); Assistant Professor, School of Business, Western New England College, Springfield, MA (1983-1987); Assistant Professor, C.W. Post Center School of Professional Accountancy, Long Island University, Greenvale, NY (1981-1983) **CR:** Technological University of Berlin and Belgian Health Care Knowledge Center (2014); Federal Health Insurance Review Agency, Republic of Korea (2012); Principal, Global Anti-Fraud Consultant Inc., Baltimore, MD (1998-2001); Consultant, United States Department of Veterans Affairs (1997); Consultant in Field **CIV:** Litigation Support, Expert Testimony, Consultant, Texas Attorney General (1992-1993) **CW:** Member, Editorial Board, Journal on Governmental and Nonprofit Accounting (2015-Present); Editorial Board, Journal of Forensic and Investigative Accounting (2011-Present); Associate Editor, Financial Accountability and Management (1998-Present); Member, Editorial Board, Financial Accountability and Management (1994-Present); Member, Editorial Board, Public Budgeting, Accounting and Finance Management (1994-Present); Co-Author, "Costly Reflections in a Midas Mirror, Third Edition" (2012); Senior Editor, Managing Editor, "Research in Healthcare Finance Management" (2000-2009); Member, Editorial Board, Journal on Health Care Finance (1996-2009); Member, Editorial Board, Research in Government and Nonprofit Accounting (1996-2009); Reviewer, Governmental and Nonprofit Accounting (1992-2009); Member, Editorial Board, Issues in Accounting Education (1998-2007); Senior Editor, "Research in Healthcare Finance Management" (1994-2000); Co-Author, "Costly Reflections in a Midas Mirror, Second Edition" (1999); Chairman, Editorial Review Board, "The White Paper" (1996-1999); Reviewer, Issues in Accounting Education (1997-1998); Co-Author, "Laser Logos Inc., Second Edition" (1997); Member, Editorial Board, Journal on Economics and Finance (1992-1995); Co-Author, "Costly Reflections in a Midas Mirror" (1994); Co-Author, "Pet Polygon Manufacturing Company Management Accounting Case, Third Edition," Laser Logos Inc. (1994); Columnist, Journal on Health Care Finance; Reviewer, International Journal on Public Administration (1993); Member, Editorial Board, Today's CPA (1992-1993); Co-Author, "Pet Polygon Manufacturing Company Management Accounting Case" (1992); Contributor, More than 158 Articles to Professional Journals; Reviewer, Government Accountants Journal **AW:** Enduring Lifetime Achievement Award, Government and Non-Profit Section, American Accounting Association (2017); Outstanding Research Paper Award, Government and Non-Profit Section, American Accounting Association (2008); Research Fellowship, Center for Accounting, Audit and Tax Research, Florida International University (2005-2006); Honorary Diploma, National University of San Marcos, Peru (2004); Honorary Professor, Ricardo Palma University, Peru (2004); Best Faculty Award, Florida International University Accounting Associate (2004); Black and Decker Research Award, Merrick School Business, University of Baltimore (1999); Division Award, International Association Management (1998); International Regional Publication Award, International Association Management (1996);

Named, Top 10 List, Merrick School of Business (1995); Black and Decker Research Award, Merrick School Business, University of Baltimore (1995); Curriculum Funds Development Award, Merrick School of Business (1994); Outstanding Faculty Member Award, Beta Alpha Psi (1992); Incentive Grant for Teaching, Center for Teaching Excellence, Texas A&M University (1992); Symposium Fellow, Office for Government Accounting Research and Education, University of Illinois at Chicago (1984); Honorary Mention Manuscript Award, Massachusetts Society of CPAs (1976); Chancellor's Citation for Undergraduate Instructors, University of Massachusetts (1973); Manuscript Award, National Association of Accountants **MEM:** Regent Emeritus, Association of Certified Fraud Examiners (2001-Present); Member of National Council, American Accounting Association (2011-2014); Director, International Society for Research in Healthcare Finance Management (1994-2011); Member of National Council, American Accounting Association (2005-2006); President, Government and Nonprofit Section, American Accounting Association (2005-2006); Secretary, Treasurer, Government and Nonprofit Section, American Accounting Association (2003-2004); Member of Executive Committee, Mid-Atlantic Region, American Accounting Association (1994-2001); Board of Regents, Association of Certified Fraud Examiners (1999-2000); Chairman, Healthcare Management Division, International Association Management (1997-1998); Senior Editor of Journal, International Association Management (1996-1998); President, Mid-Atlantic Region, American Accounting Association (1996-1997); Member of National Council, American Accounting Association (1996-1997); Chairman, Board of Directors, Morningside Ministries Senior Living; International Associate, Institute Public Sector on Accounting Research, University of Edinburgh; Founder, International Society for Research in Healthcare Finance Management **MH:** Albert Nelson Marquis Lifetime Achievement Award **AS:** Mr. Forgione attributes his success to a great deal of hard work, and his adherence to Christianity **B/I:** Mr. Forgione initially became involved in his profession after studying accounting while in business school. Upon graduating, he secured his first accounting job as a junior accountant at a hospital. Following this, he attended school again and subsequently began teaching. **AV:** Computers; Biblical chronology; Woodworking **RE:** Baptist

FORMAN, CHARLES, T: Attorney **I:** Law and Legal Services **CN:** Forman Holt **ED:** JD, Seton Hall University School of Law, Newark, NJ (1976); BS in Industrial Engineering, New Jersey Institute of Technology, Newark, NJ (1972) **C:** Member, U.S. Bankruptcy Court for the District of New Jersey Registry of Mediators (2016-Present); Member, Private Panel of Trustees, District of New Jersey (1982-Present); Managing Member, Forman Holt (2017-2019); Officer, LeClairRyan, PC (2016-2017); Managing Member, Forman Holt & Eliades LLC (Now Forman Holt) (1997-2016); Member, Private Panel of Trustees, District of Delaware (2010-2015); Senior Member, Forman Stern P.C. (1995-1997); Sole Proprietor, Charles M. Forman & Associates (1988-1995); Managing Member, Rodino Forman & D'Uva LLC (Now Forman Holt) (1979-1988); General Counsel, Clinton Bogert Association, Consulting Engineers (1977-1979); Special Assistant to Commissioner, New Jersey Department of Environmental Protection (1976-1977) **CR:** Frequent Lecturer, Bankruptcy and Commercial Law Matters, New Jersey State Bar Association, American Bankruptcy Institute, and Turnaround Management Association **CW:** Contributor, Pub-

lished Various Articles on Topics Involving Chapter 7 and Chapter 11 Practice and Trustee Issues, Substantial Abuse, Non-Dischargeability Issues, and Ethical, Criminal, and Fraud Issues **AW:** Lifetime Achievement Award, New Jersey Law Journal (2016); U.S. Department of Justice Director's Award for Outstanding Achievement, U.S. Department of Justice (2002); Pi Delta Epsilon National Medal of Merit Award (1971) **MEM:** Advisory Committee, Mid-Atlantic Region, American Bankruptcy Institute (2015-2020); President, New Jersey Bankruptcy Lawyers Foundation (NJBLF); President, New Jersey Institute of Technology Alumni Association; President, Independent Alumni of NJIT; Master, New Jersey Bankruptcy Inn of Court; President, Federal Bar Association of New Jersey (Now Association of the Federal Bar of New Jersey); New Jersey State Bar Association; New York State Bar Association; District of Columbia Bar Association (Now The Bar Association of DC); American Bar Association (ABA); Turnaround Management Association; Commercial Law League of America; New York Institute of Credit (NYIC); Mensa International Limited **BAR:** State of New Jersey; State of New York; United States District Court for the District of Columbia; United States District Court for the District of New Jersey; United States District Court for the Southern District of New York; United States Court of International Trade; United States Court of Appeals for the Third Circuit; Supreme Court of the United States **AS:** Mr. Forman attributes his success to being the best that he can be and being kind to others. **B/I:** Mr. Forman became involved in his profession because he went to school for engineering before law school. He faced some childhood experiences that made him independent. He realized while he was in engineering school that the likelihood of having control over his future would be a challenge. Many engineers work for someone else. He noted that "If you pick the wrong company to work for, after a couple of years, you need to reinvent yourself." Mr. Forman wanted to be his own boss and serve others. **THT:** Mr. Forman's motto is, "Do onto others that you would like done to you."

FORSLEFF, LOUISE STEWART PETERSON, T: Psychologist, Educator **I:** Education/Educational Services **DOB:** 10/07/1933 **PB:** Portland **SC:** ME/USA **PT:** Roland Peterson; Gertrude Peterson **MS:** Widowed **SPN:** Elmer Andrew Forsleff (12/24/1965, Deceased 06/04/1993) **CH:** Mary Anne; John Clark **ED:** PhD, Michigan State University (1967); MA, Western Michigan University (1962); AB, Lake Erie College (1959) **CT:** Licensed Psychologist, State of Michigan; Certification, Council for the National Register of Health Service Providers in Psychology; Certified Practitioner, Jin Shin Jyuesu **C:** Professor Emerita, Western Michigan University (1998-Present); Professor, School of Community Health Services, Western Michigan University (1990-1998); Associate Vice President, Student Services, Western Michigan University (1985-1990); Director, University Counseling Center, Western Michigan University (1968-1985); Counselor, University Counseling Center, Western Michigan University (1962-1968); Testing, Research, Kalamazoo Public Schools (1962) **CR:** Consultant in Field (1998-2000); Teacher, Holistic Medicine; Advisor to the Board, West Michigan of Holistic Medicine, American Holistic Centers (1995-1996); Coordinator, Professional Exchange Clearing House (1977-1979) **CIV:** Board of Directors, West Main Hill Neighborhood Association (1993-1997); Board of Directors, Homestead, Incorporated (1990-1997); Loaned Executive, United Way (1988) **CW:** Presenter, Elder Housing, Environmental Design Research Association of Sweden, Ontario (1994); Contributor, Editor, "An Outline of Sexology" (1993) **AW:**

Grantee, Faculty Research Grant, Western Michigan University (1992) **MEM:** Delegate, Threads to the Future Conference New Zealand, Institute of Noetic Sciences (1996); Board of Directors, President, International Association Counseling Services (1976-1985); Society of Human Ecology; National Register of Health Service Providers in Psychology **B/I:** Dr. Forsleff was influenced by the headmistress of the preparatory school she went to in Maine, who said it was important to have guidance as she went through the educational experience. That stuck with Ms. Forsleff throughout her career. She strives to always implement that philosophy in her work. **AV:** Gardening; Traveling; Practicing environmental design; Practicing alternative health methods **RE:** Society of Friends

FORSYTH, ERIC BOYLAND, T: Electrical Engineer **I:** Engineering **DOB:** 04/16/1932 **PB:** Bolton **SC:** England **PT:** Frank; Elizabeth (Scrivens) **MS:** Widowed **SPN:** Edith Millicent Meyer **CH:** Colin; Brenda **ED:** MASc, University of Toronto (1960); BSc, Manchester University (1953) **CT:** Registered Professional Engineer, Ontario **C:** Retired (1990); Chairman, Accelerator Development Department, Brookhaven National Laboratory (1986-1990); Senior Engineer, Brookhaven National Laboratory (1977-1986); Engineer, Brookhaven National Laboratory (1965-1977); Associate Engineer, Brookhaven National Laboratory (1962-1965); Assistant Engineer, Brookhaven National Laboratory (1960-1962); Research Engineer, Applied Industrial Technologies (1957-1959); Research Engineer, AVRO Aircraft (1955-1957) **CR:** Panel on Superconductivity, National Academy of Sciences (1987-1988); Invited Lecturer, The Institute of Electrical Engineers of Japan (1985) **MIL:** Flying Officer, Royal Air Force (1950-1957); Fighter Pilot, 613 Squadron **CW:** Author, "An Inexplicable Attraction: My Fifty Years of Ocean Sailing (2016); Patentee in Field; Author, 120 Articles, Two Book Chapters **AW:** Herman Halperin Electric Transmission and Distribution Award, IEEE (2007); Blue Water Medal, Cruising Club of American (2000) **MEM:** Invited Lecturer, Fellow, IEEE (1983); Bentley Drivers Club Limited **MH:** Albert Nelson Marquis Lifetime Achievement Award **B/I:** Mr. Forsyth became involved in his profession because as a child he played with surplus electronic equipment which had been left behind by the recent war in England. **AV:** Appreciating antique cars; Cruising

FORTE, DOMENIC J., PHD, T: Associate Professor **I:** Education/Educational Services **CN:** University of Florida **PB:** Staten Island **SC:** NY/USA **ED:** PhD in Electrical Engineering, University of Maryland (2013); MSEE, University of Maryland (2010); BSEE, Manhattan College, Summa Cum Laude (2006) **C:** Associate Professor, University of Florida (2019-Present); FICS Research Security and Assurance (SCAN) Lab Director, University of Florida (2016-Present); Assistant Professor, University of Florida (2015-2019); Assistant Professor, University of Connecticut (2013-2015); Research Assistant, University of Maryland (2009-2013); Teaching Assistant, University of Maryland (2006-2010); Co-Op Student Intern, National Institutes of Health (2007-2009); REU Student, Maryland Engineering Research Internship Teams, College Park, MD (2005) **CR:** Co-Instructor, University of Florida (2016); Guest Lecturer, University of Connecticut (2014); Co-Instructor, University of Maryland (2013); Northrop Grumman Fellowship (2012-2013); Mentor, Teaching Assistant, Training and Development, University of Maryland (2010-2012); Advisor, Undergraduate, Graduate, and Postdoctoral Students; Speaker in Field **CW:** Associate Editor, ACM Journal on Emerging Technologies in Computing (2019-present); Associate Editor,

Springer Journal of Hardware and System Security (2016-Present); Guest Editor, "Hardware Reverse Engineering and Obfuscation," Springer Journal of Hardware and System Security (2018); Reviewer, ACM Transactions on Design Automation of Electronic Systems, IEEE Journal of Solid-State Circuits, Transactions on Biomedical Engineering, IEEE Transactions on Embedded Computing Systems, IEEE Transactions on Industrial Electronics (2018); Reviewer, ACM Transactions on Privacy and Security, IEEE Transactions on Dependable and Secure Computing, Image and Vision Computing (2017); Co-Author, "Security Opportunities in Nano Devices and Emerging Technologies," CRC Press (2017); Co-Author, "Hardware Protection through Obfuscation," Springer (2017); Reviewer, IEEE Transactions on Computer-Aided Design of Integrated Circuits (2016-2018); Reviewer, IEEE Transactions on VLSI Systems (2013-2018); Reviewer, IEEE Transactions on Computers (2015-2017); Reviewer, IEEE Transactions on Circuits and Systems I, IEEE Transactions on Information Forensics and Security (2014-2017); Reviewer, IEEE Transactions on Embedded Computing Systems, Journal of Electronic Testing: Theory and Applications (2016); Guest Editor, "Supply Chain Security for Cyber-Infrastructure," IEEE (2016); Reviewer, ACM Transactions on Design Automation of Electronic Systems (2014-2016); Reviewer, ACM Journal on Emerging Technologies in Computing Systems, IEEE Access, IEEE Journal on Emerging and Selected Topics in Circuits and Systems, IEEE Transactions on Emerging Topics in Computing, IEEE Transactions on Multi-Scale Computing Systems, IEEE Transactions on Nanotechnology (2015); Co-Author, "Counterfeit Integrated Circuits: Detection and Avoidance," Springer (2015); Reviewer, IEEE Communications Letters, IEEE Design & Test, IEEE Transactions on Circuits and Systems II, IEEE Transactions on Computer-Aided Design of Integrated Circuits, IET Computers & Digital Techniques (2014); Reviewer, IEEE Transactions on Emerging Topics in Computing (2013); Contributor, 12 Chapters, Books; Contributor, 54 Peer-Reviewed Articles, Professional Journals; Contributor, 89 Peer-Reviewed Conference/Workshop Publications; Author, 25 Non-Refereed Conference Papers; Patentee, Eight Patents in Field **AW:** Presidential Early Career Award for Scientists and Engineers (2019); Pramod R. Khargonekar Award (2018-2019); ACM TODAES Best Paper Award (2018); Provost's Excellence Award for Assistant Professors, University of Florida (2017-2018); NSF Faculty Early Career Development Award (2017); Outstanding Paper Award, International Symposium for Testing and Failure Analysis (2017); Best Student Paper Award, International Joint Conference on Biometrics (2017); Hardware Category, ACM Computing Reviews Notable Computing Books and Articles (2016); Young Investigator Award, Army Research Office (2016); IBest Paper Award, EEE International Symposium on Hardware Oriented Security and Trust (2016); Best Paper Nomination, IEEE International Symposium on Hardware Oriented Security and Trust (2016); Schloss Dagstuhl NSF Support Grant for Junior Researchers (2016); Best Paper Award, IEEE International Symposium on Hardware Oriented Security and Trust (2015); Jacob K. Goldhaber Travel Award, University of Maryland (2013); Best Paper Nomination, Design Automation Conference (2012); Best Student Paper Award, NASA/ESA Conference on Adaptive Hardware and Systems (2011); George Corcoran Outstanding Teaching Award, University of Maryland (2008); Distinguished Teaching Assistant Award, University of Maryland (2007-2008); Co-Recipient, Medal for Electrical Engineering, Manhattan College (2006); Next in Merit, Draddy Medal for General Excel-

lence in Engineering, Manhattan College (2006); Society of Military Engineers Scholarship (2005); Manhattan College Presidential Scholarship (2002); New York State Academic Excellence Scholarship (2002) **MEM:** Scribe, TAME Hardware Vulnerability Database Working Group (2018-Present); IEEE P1735 Working Group (2018-Present); Program Chair, International Symposium on Hardware-Oriented Security and Trust (2019); Publicity Chair, IEEE Computer Society Annual Symposium on VLSI (2019); EEL 4242 Power Electronics 1 ABET Course Committee, University of Florida (2017-2019); EEE 4404 Mixed Signal IC Testing I ABET Course Committee, University of Florida (2016-2019); EEE 4310 Digital Integrated Circuits ABET Course Committee, University of Florida (2015-2019); Vice Program Chair, International Symposium on Hardware-Oriented Security and Trust (2018); Reverse Engineering Track Chair, International Symposium for Testing and Failure Analysis (2018); Publicity Chair, Workshop on Attacks and Solutions in Hardware Security (2018); Proposal Panelist/Reviewer, National Science Foundation Critical Infrastructure Resilience Institute (2018); Faculty Search Committee, University of Florida (2017-2018); Publicity Chair, IEEE Asian Hardware-Oriented Security and Trust Symposium (2016-2018); Graduate Recruiting & Admissions Committee, University of Florida (2015-2018); Program Co-Chair, International Verification and Security Workshop (2017); Tutorial Chair, International Symposium on Hardware-Oriented Security and Trust (2017); Poster Chair, FICS Research Annual Conference on Cybersecurity (2017); Proposal Panelist/Reviewer, American Association for the Advancement of Science Army Research Office (2017); EEL 3111 Circuits 1 ABET Course Committee, University of Florida (2015-2017); Reverse Engineering Track Chair, International Symposium for Testing and Failure Analysis (2016); Proposal Panelist/Reviewer, National Science Foundation (2016); Publicity Chair, International Symposium on Hardware-Oriented Security and Trust (2015-2016); Department Judge, First Annual Graduate Poster Competition, University of Connecticut (2015); Course and Curriculum Committee, University of Connecticut (2014-2015); Hardware Security Challenge Co-Chair, CSI Cybersecurity, Education & Diversity Challenge Week (2014); Senior Member, Institute of Electrical and Electronics Engineers (IEEE); Program Committees, Several Symposia in Field **AS:** Dr. Forte attributes his success to hard work. He additionally credits good mentorship and support from his family, senior faculty, and his advisor. **B/I:** Dr. Forte was always a gifted student; he liked the university environment. As an undergraduate student, he had the opportunity to participate in research for the undergraduate program at the University of Maryland one summer, which exposed him to the life of a graduate student. Later, when he went to graduate school, he was not always sure he would pursue a career in academia. As he gained more experience in teaching and research, both aspects of academic life grew on him. He received multiple accolades in teaching and research, which only further drew him to this career. He finds his profession to be rewarding because it allows him to inspire and train students, perform cutting-edge research in any direction he chooses, make an impact on an emerging field, and become globally recognized for his work. **PA:** Independent

FORTENBERRY, JEFFREY LANE, T: U.S. Representative **I:** Government Administration/Government Relations/Government Services **DOB:** 12/27/1960 **PB:** Baton Rouge **SC:** LA/USA **MS:** Married **SPN:** Celeste Gregory **CH:** Five Children **ED:** ThM, Franciscan University of Steubenville, Ohio

(1996); Master's Degree in Public Policy, Georgetown University, Washington, DC (1986); BA in Economics, Louisiana State University (1982) **C:** U.S. Representative, Nebraska's First Congressional District, United States Congress (2005-Present); Sales Representative, Sandhills Publishing (Now Sandhills Global) (1998-2005); At-Large Member, City Council, Lincoln, NE (1997-2001); Public Relations Foundation Activities Director, Sandhills Publishing (Now Sandhills Global), Lincoln, NE (1995-1998); Assistant Director, Downtown Development District, Baton Rouge, LA (1989-1992); Research Associate Economist, Gulf South Research Institute, New Iberia, LA (1987-1989); Member, Economic Analysis Team, U.S. Senate Subcommittee for Intergovernmental Relations (1986); Member, Committee on Agriculture; Member, Committee on Foreign Affairs; Member, Republican Study Committee; Member, Committee on Small Business **PA:** Republican **RE:** Roman Catholic

FOSS, ERIC J., T: Chairman, President, Chief Executive Officer **I:** Other **CN:** Aramark **DOB:** 03/13/1958 **ED:** BS in Marketing, Ball State University (1980) **C:** Chairman, Aramark (2015-Present); President, Chief Executive Officer, Aramark (2012-Present); Chief Executive Officer, PepsiCo (2010-2011); Chairman, Chief Executive Officer, Pepsi Bottling Group, Inc. (2008-2010); President, Chief Executive Officer, Pepsi Bottling Group, Inc. (2006-2008); Chief Operating Officer, Pepsi Bottling Group, Inc. (2005-2006); President, North American Section, Pepsi Bottling Group, Inc. (2001-2005); Executive Vice President, General Manager for North America, Pepsi Bottling Group, Inc. (2000-2001); Senior Vice President of U.S. Sales and Field Marketing, Pepsi Bottling Group, Inc. (1999-2000); General Manager for Central Europe, PepsiCo (1996-1999); General Manager for North America's Great West Business Unit, PepsiCo (1994-1996); Vice President of Retail Strategy for North America, PepsiCo (1990-1994); Various Sales, Marketing and Management Positions, PepsiCo (1982-1990) **CR:** Member, Industry Affairs Council, Grocery Manufacturers Association; Board of Directors, United Dominion Realty Trust

FOSTER, GEORGE, "BILL" WILLIAM, T: U.S. Representative from Illinois; Physicist **I:** Government Administration/Government Relations/Government Services **DOB:** 10/07/1955 **PB:** Madison **SC:** WI/USA **PT:** George William Foster; Jeanette Raymond Foster **MS:** Married **SPN:** Aesook Byob (11/2008); Ann Christine Oswall (03/31/1983, Divorced 10/1996) **CH:** George Billy; Christine **ED:** PhD, Harvard University (1983); BA in Physics, University of Wisconsin-Madison (1976) **C:** Member, U.S. House of Representatives from Illinois' 11th Congressional District, United States Congress (2013-Present); Member, U.S. House Financial Services Committee (2008-2011, 2013-Present); Member, U.S. House of Representatives from Illinois' 14th Congressional District, United States Congress, Washington, DC (2008-2011); Research Physicist, Fermi National Accelerator Laboratory, Batavia, IL (1984-2006); Founder, Chief Executive Officer, Electronic Theatre Controls, Inc., Middleton, WI (1976-1979); Member, Committee on Science, Space and Technology **CR:** Board of Directors, Electronic Theatre Controls, Inc., Middleton, IL **CIV:** Board of Directors, Batavia Foundation for Educational Excellence (1996-2001) **AW:** Particle Accelerator Science and Technology Award, IEEE NPSS (1999); Fermilab Technology Award for Digital Multiplier Integrated Circuit (1999); Federal Energy and Water Management Award, U.S. Department of Energy (1998); Rossi Prize for Astrophysics, American Astronomical Society (1989) **MEM:** Fellow, American Physical Society **PA:** Democrat

FOSTER, NORMAN, T: Architect **I:** Architecture & Construction **DOB:** 06/01/1935 **PB:** Reddish **SC:** England/United Kingdom **PT:** Robert Foster; Lilian (Smith) Foster **MS:** Married **SPN:** Elena Ochoa **ED:** Honorary DSc, University of Dundee (2008); Honorary DSc, London Institute (2001); Honorary DSc, Negev, Israel (2001); Honorary DSc, London, United Kingdom (1996); Honorary DSc, Oxford, United Kingdom (1996); Honorary DSc, Eindhoven, Netherlands (1996); Honorary DSc, Kent Institute of Art & Design (1994); Honorary DSc, Manchester, United Kingdom (1992); Honorary DSc, Humberside, United Kingdom (1992); Honorary DSc, Valencia College (1992); Honorary DSc, Royal College of Art (1991); Honorary DSc, Bath, United Kingdom (1986); Honorary LittD, East Anglia, United Kingdom (1980); MArch, Yale University (1962); Diploma in Architecture, Manchester University (1961) **C:** President, Norman Foster Foundation (2017-Present); Principal, Foster + Partners, London, United Kingdom (1967-Present); Consultant Architect, University of East Anglia (1978-1987) **CR:** Visiting Professor, Harvard University Graduate School of Design (2000); Visiting Professor, Bartlett School of Architecture (1998-1999); Collaborator with Buckminster Fuller (1968-1983); With, London Polytechnic (Now University of Westminster); With, Bath Academy of Arts; With, Royal College of Art (1981); Vice President, Architectural Association Council (1974); External Examiner, Royal Institute of British Architects (1971-1973); Architectural Association Council (1969-1971); Teacher, University of Pennsylvania; With, Architectural Association, London, United Kingdom **CW:** Architect, Comcast Center, Comcast Corporation's Global Headquarters (2014); Architect, Deutsche Bank Place, Sydney, Australia (2002–2006); Architect, Dresden Hauptbahnhof Reconstruction, Dresden, Germany (2006); Architect, Hearst Tower, New York, NY (2006); Contributor, Articles, Architectural and Technical Publications (2005); Architect, Supreme Court Building, Singapore (2005); Architect, Western Årsta Bridge, Stockholm, Sweden (2005); Architect, 40 Luxury Apartments, St. Moritz, Switzerland (2005); Architect, National Police Memorial, The Mall, London, United Kingdom (2005); Architect, The Philological Library at the Free University of Berlin, Germany (2005); Architect, Tower 2, World Trade Center Site (2005); Architect, The Millau Viaduct, France (2004); Architect, Medical Research Center, Stanford University (2000); Architect, National Botanic Gardens of Wales (2000); Architect, Citibank Headquarters, London, United Kingdom (2000); Architect, Millennium Bridge, London, United Kingdom (2000); Architect, British Museum, Great Court, London, United Kingdom (2000); Architect, Reichstag New German Parliament (1999); Architect, Hong Kong International Airport (1998); Architect, Congress Centre, Valencia, Spain (1998); Architect, Microelectronic Centre, Duisburg, Germany (1998); Architect, American Air Museum (IWM), Duxford, United Kingdom (1997); Architect, Commerzbank Headquarters, Frankfurt, Germany (1997); Architect, Bilbao Metro Systems (1995); Architect, University of Cambridge Faculty Law (1995); Architect, Joslyn Art Museum Addition, Omaha, NE (1994); Architect, Carré d'Art Arts Centre, Nîmes (1993); Architect, Library, Cranfield University (1993); Architect, Lycee School, Fréjus, France (1993); Architect, Barcelona Telecommunications Tower (1992); Architect, King's Cross Master Plan, London, United Kingdom (1991); Architect, Third London Airport Terminal Zone at Stansted (1991); Architect, Century Tower, Tokyo, Japan (1991); Architect, Sackler Galleries, Royal Academy of Arts, London, United Kingdom (1991); Architect, Stockley Park B3 (1989); Architect, Hong Kong and Shanghai Banking Corp. Headquarters (1986); Architect, Centre for Renault Car Co., United Kingdom (1983); Featured Artist, The Museum of Modern Art, New York, NY (1979); Architect, Sainsbury Centre for Visual Arts, Norwich, United Kingdom (1977); Architect, Head Office, Willis, Faber and Dumas, Ipswich, United Kingdom (1975); Architect, Pilot Head Office, IBM, Hampshire, United Kingdom (1971); Featured Artist, Various Galleries in Barcelona, Madrid, Valencia and Bilbao, Spain, London, Glasgow, Norwich, and Manchester, United Kingdom, Copenhagen, Denmark, Paris, Nîmes and Bordeaux, France, Parma, Florence, Venice and Milan, Italy, Berlin, Frankfurt and Munich, Germany, Tokyo, Japan, Zurich, Switzerland, Hong Kong, Antwerp, Belgium, Helsinki, Finland; Architect, Leslie L. Dan Pharmacy Building, University of Toronto; Featured Artist, Permanent Collection, The Museum of Modern Art, New York, NY **AW:** Prince of Asturias Award (2009); German Order Pour le Mérite for Sciences and Arts (2002); Auguste Perret Prize (2002); Praemium Imperiale Award for Architecture (2002); Fifth South Bank Show Award (2001); Visual Arts Award (2000); Pritzker Architecture Prize, The Hyatt Foundation (1999); Structural Steel Award (1972, 1978, 1980, 1984, 1986, 1992, 1999); Benedictus Award (1993, 1999); Named Life Peer (1999); Silver Medal, Chartered Society of Designers (1997); Prince Philip Designers Prize (1997); Order of Merit (1997); Named Man of the Year, MIPIM (1996); Queens Export Achievement Award (1995); Named to Order of North Rhine-Westphalia (1995); Interiors USA Award (1988, 1992, 1993, 1994); Gold Medal, AIA (1994); Winner, Competition in Berlin (1993); Premio Alcantara Award (1993); Industrial Architecture Award, Financial Times (1967, 1970, 1971, 1974, 1981, 1984, 1993); Arnold W. Brunner Memorial Prize (1992); Gold Medal, French Academy of Architecture (Académie d'Architecture) (1991); Mies van der Rohe Pavilion Award (1991); Knighthood (1990); Trustees Medal, RIBA (1990); Chicago Arts Award (1990); Berlin Art Grand Prize (1989); R.S. Reynolds International Memorial Award (1976, 1979, 1986); Royal Gold Medal for Architecture (1983); IBM Fellow, Aspen Design Conference (1980); Ambrose Congreve Award (1980); Named Officer of the Order of Arts and Letters Ministry of Culture, France; R.S.A. Business and Industry Awards; International Design Awards; Finniston Award; RIBA Awards; Concrete Society Awards **MEM:** Fellow, AIA; Honorary Member, Royal Incorporation of Architects in Scotland; Honorary Member, Royal Academy of Engineering; Honorary Member, The Institution of Structural Engineers; Foreign Honorary Member, American Association for the Advancement of Science; Associate, C.S.D., Royal Academy; The RSA; Association of Academie Royale de Belgique; Foreign Member, Royal Academy of Fine Arts Sweden; European Academy of Sciences and Arts; Honorary Member, Bund Deutscher Architeken; Royal Designer for Industry, International Academy of Architecture

FOSTER, TIM, T: Fastpitch Director **I:** Athletics **CN:** Indiana USSSA **PT:** Ralph Foster **MS:** Married **SPN:** Jennifer **CH:** Chris; Macie; Raegyn **CT:** Certification in Sports Management, University of Indianapolis (1994) **C:** Fastpitch Director, Indiana USSSA; Founder, UTrippin Sports Academy **CIV:** Fundraiser, Autism Awareness; Fundraiser, Military Veterans **AW:** National Director of the Year Award **MEM:** Columbus Chamber of Commerce; Regional Director, Fastpitch Board **B/I:** Mr. Foster always loved sports. He played baseball and basketball, going on to work in the parks and recreation department, where he met the woman in charge of a softball association. He eventually got involved in this organization, as he wanted to work with female athletes and give them the recognition they deserve. He is currently working on keeping the United States Women's Fastpitch team enrolled in the Olympics. **THT:** Mr. Foster's lives every day as if it is his last. He believes in the saying, "It's not the day you were born or the day that you die on your tombstone that matters. What matters is that dash in the middle." He is straightforward, fair, and honest.

FOSTER-RANDLE, ELLEN EUGENIA DR., EDD, MA, BA, T: Opera and Classical Singer; Educator **I:** Media & Entertainment **DOB:** 10/02/1948 **PB:** New Haven **SC:** CT/USA **PT:** Rev. Dr. Richard A.G. Foster; Thelma Lousie (Brooks) Foster **MS:** Married **SPN:** Rev. Dr. John Willis Randle (12/24/1983); Ira James William (1968, Divorced 1972) **ED:** Psychotherapy Intern of Senior Peer Counseling Program, City of Fremont, CA (1999-2000); EdD in International Multicultural Education, University of San Francisco (1998); MA in Marriage and Family Therapy, University of San Francisco (1994); MA in Counseling and Psychology, University of San Francisco (1990); Coursework with Patricia Goehl, Munich, Germany (1979); Coursework with Madam Eleanor Steber, Graz, Austria (1979); MA in Music, Lone Mountain College (1978); Coursework, University of California Berkeley (1977); BA in World History, Lone Mountain College (1976); Coursework with Tito Gobbi, Florence, Italy (1974); Coursework, Graduate School of Fine Arts (Florence School of Fine Arts), Florence, Italy (1974); Coursework with Boris Goldovsky (1970); Coursework, Sonoma State College (Now Sonoma State University) (1970) **C:** Director, Reflection (2006-2011); Private Practice, with Dr. Harmesh Kumar, Director of Residential Services, Therapeutic Residential Care Service, Inc., Concord, CA (2004-2006); Family Consultant, Positive Options Family Services, Sacramento, CA (2002-2004); Family Facilitator, EMQ Family and Children Services (Now Uplift Family Services), Sacramento, CA (2002); Psychotherapist, Marriage Family Therapist Intern, Portia Bell Human Behavioral Health and Training Center (The Hume Center), Concord, CA (2000-2001); Instructor of African American Culture and Humanities, Mission College, Santa Clara, CA (1997-2000); Instructor, Peralta Community College District, Oakland, CA (1998); Assistant Artistic Director, Opera Piccola, Oakland, CA (1990-1992) **CR:** Adjunct Professor, University of Phoenix, Northern CA (2001-Present); Adjunct Professor, University of Phoenix (1999-2000); Instructor, Las Positas College, Livermore, CA (1999-2000); Instructor of East Bay Center for the Performing Arts, Richmond, CA (1986); Instructor, Chapman College (Now Chapman University) (1986); Lecturer in Field **CIV:** Art Commissioner, City of Richmond, CA; Volunteer, Church; Appointed Member, California Annual Conference, African Methodist Episcopal Zion Church (AME Zion Church) **CW:** Assistant Artistic Director, Opera Piccola, Oakland, CA (1990-Present); Lecturer, Guangxi University, China (2014); Invited Speaker, Presentation on Stress and Coping Skills, African American Studies, Association of Hispanic Latino Studies and Association Conference, Mexico (2001); Music Director, "Natural Man," Berkeley, CA (1986); Singer, Opera Production, "The Magic Flute," Oakland, CA (1984); Singer, Opera Production, "Madame Butterfly," Oakland, CA (1982-1983); Singer, Opera Production, "La Traviata," Oakland, CA (1981-1982); Singer, Opera Production, "Aida," Oakland, CA (1981-1982); Singer, Opera Production, "Porgy and Bess," Oakland, CA (1980-1981); Actor, "SABAR, Life is a Dance," International Independent Films Festival, Canada and Africa; Performer, Television Specials, Religious Concerts and Musicals; Singer, Cassette, "Holiday Festivals" **AW:** Award, Book Contract for Historical Section of Dissertation, "The History of the African American (Negro) Spirituals (1600-1885)," The Edwin Mellen International Scholarly Publisher of Advanced Research (2011); Black American Achievement Award **MEM:** Former President, Doctoral and Graduate Student Council, University of San Francisco (1996-1997); Former Member, Music Teachers National Association; Lifetime Member, Local #5; International Black Writers and Artists Inc.; National Council of Negro Women, Inc.; Former Member, National Association of Negro Musicians, Inc.; Former Member, California Arts Federation; Former Member, The California-Nebraskan Organization, Inc.; Former Member, San Francisco Chapter, California Association of Marriage and Family Therapists; Former Member, San Francisco Commonwealth Club (Now The Commonwealth Club of California), San Francisco, CA; International Black Poets **MH:** Albert Nelson Marquis Lifetime Achievement Award **AS:** Dr. Foster-Randle's parents were her role models. Dr. John Lewis, PhD, was her music teacher at McClymonds High School in Oakland, CA. Another inspiration was the late Maestro Marco Sorisio, from Oakland, CA. **B/I:** Dr. Foster-Randle entered her profession because she was inspired by her father, who was an African American preacher, & politician. The late Rev. Dr. Richard A.G. Foster was in the African Methodist Episcopal Zion Church. In July 1952, Rev. Dr. Foster moved the family out to Oakland. Dr. Foster-Randle was just 3 1/2 years old at the time. The church to which her father was assigned had a former pastor who was a magnificent choir director and vocal music teacher. The choir at the church also recorded on vinyl 33 records and traveled across the country performing. Her father became the custodian of these records, so at the age of 4, Dr. Foster-Randle started listening to the choir members perform, both live at church and at home, on her record player. She remembers saying, "Lord, I want to sing like that, but a little bit different... like nobody else." Kids have magical imaginations, so she never believed that her dream would come true. But as a pastor's child singing in the choirs and the public school system, her desire to perform began to grow. It wasn't until she was 15 years old singing a solo at church in a Christmas evening program, that people at church began to cry as she performed "O Holy Night." She went home and told her sister, Ricarda, what happened at church. She asked for me to sing "O Holy Night" to her and she did. Ricarda convinced her mother and her Godmother to pay for her to take classical voice lessons. This is when her voice started to show; it changed and there was a difference, since the female voice matures gradually every five years or so. Dr. Foster-Randle's voice type would still be growing into the age of 40 plus years. Dr. Foster-Randle voice was labeled a German Soprano. When she auditioned at Lone Mountain College in San Francisco, her forte was singing the works of Verdi and Puccini. Her instructors believed that her voice would not fully mature until she was in her forties. She earned a scholarship, kept progressing musically, and eventually met her instructors' expectations in full. In Germany, she was labeled and placed into the category of a German Soprano. Her voice is a gift from the Lord. It has opened doors to advance her education at every level into her doctoral program; she wrote her dissertation about racism in European classical music. African American classical singers, male and female, must have a benefactor to pave the way for their careers in the European classical music industry, which is a racist industry.

Dr. Foster-Randle says, "We just can't win auditions like white performers. We must have a benefactor who help with the money to open music festivals' and opera houses' doors around the world. This has been documented since the 1820s with the young classical pianist, Blind Tom, who was an African American enslaved in the 1850s with Elizabeth Taylor Green, an African American/Native American enslaved person. Both artists, their owners were their benefactors. They performed all over the United States and in Europe. Their owners paid for their enslaved artists to perform in European classical concerts halls in the US and in Europe." **AV:** Cooking **PA:** Democrat **RE:** Methodist Episcopal **THT:** Dr. Foster-Randle says, "As an artist, plus an African American woman, I must stay grounded in my faith and in my relationship with the Lord Jesus Christ, who is the creator of my singing voice. Voice teachers teach vocal technique, they cannot make a voice. I have a Bell Canto technique of singing which was developed in the 10th century in Italy. It takes 10 years to learn how to breathe correctly. In the United States, colleges and universities do not teach this vocal technique. It takes too long just to learn how to master the breathing technique. I started to take voice lessons at the age of 15 years old. I only have had two voice teachers in my lifetime to teach me this vocal technique. The almighty U.S. dollar is not a value one should place on yourself to being successful. I learned this from my parents."

FOTOVICH, URSULA ANN, T: Nun; Archivist and Local Historian **I:** Religious **CN:** Congregation of St. Joseph **DOB:** 02/21/1952 **PB:** Kansas City **SC:** KS/USA **PT:** Stephen Vida Fotovich; Helen Barbara Fotovich **ED:** MS in Educational Administration, University of Dayton (1986); BS in Education, Emporia State University (1974); AA, Kansas City Kansas Community College (1972) **CT:** Certified Teacher, State of Kansas **C:** Archivist/Local Historian, Congregation of St. Joseph, Wichita, KS (2012-Present); Nun, Sisters of St. Joseph, Wichita, KS (1974-Present); Diocesan Director of Missions, Catholic Diocese of Wichita, KS (2000-2012); Elementary Teacher, St. Cecilia Catholic School, Haysville, KS (1998-1999); Elementary Teacher, St. Anne Catholic School, Wichita, KS (1996-1998); Congressional Secretary, Sisters of St. Joseph, Wichita, KS (1993-1996); Elementary Principal, St. Mary Catholic School, Newton, KS (1990-1992); Elementary Principal, Holy Savior Catholic School, Wichita, KS (1984-1990); Elementary Teacher, Holy Name Catholic School, Coffeyville, KS (1981-1984); Elementary Teacher, Parsons Catholic School, Parsons, KS (1977-1981); Level 1 Teacher of Special Education, Holy Family Center, Wichita, KS (1974-1975) **CIV:** Volunteer, Lord's Diner, Wichita, KS **MEM:** The United States Catholic Mission Association, Inc. **B/I:** Sister Fotovich became involved in the teaching profession because she liked to help people and she liked being around children. As far as the religious community, God knew where he wanted her to be and he used many different avenues to guide her to the Sisters of St. Joseph. **AV:** Playing brac (stringed instrument); Quilting; Embroidery; Crafts

FOWLER, VIVIAN DELORES, T: Insurance Company Executive **I:** Insurance **DOB:** 09/26/1946 **PB:** Knoxville **SC:** TN/USA **PT:** Rance James Pierce Compton; Margaret Willadene (Crowe) Compton **MS:** Married **SPN:** James Hubert Fowler (05/12/1979) **CH:** James Hubert Fowler Jr. **ED:** Coursework, The University of Tennessee, Knoxville **CT:** Certified Insurance Counselor, Society of Certified Insurance Counselors (1987); Certified Professional Insurance Woman, National Association of Insurance Women (1975); Chartered

Property and Casualty Underwriter **C:** Retired, Fireman's Fund/Alliance (2013); Commercial Senior Professional, Fireman's Fund Insurance Co., Alpharetta, GA (2006-2013); Senior Commercial Underwriting Professional (2006-2013); Regional Assistant Manager, Small Business Unit Commercial Lines, The Travelers Insurance Co. (The Travelers Indemnity Company), Atlanta, GA (1993-2005); Regional Underwriting Manager, Select Accounts Marketing, Travelers/Aetna Insurance Co. (Name Changed to St. Paul Travelers), Atlanta, GA (1996); Account Manager, The Travelers Insurance Co. (The Travelers Indemnity Company), Nashville, TN (1990-1993); Senior Account Analyst, The Travelers Insurance Co. (The Travelers Indemnity Company), Nashville, TN (1989-1990); Commercial Account Analyst, The Travelers Insurance Co. (The Travelers Indemnity Company), Nashville, TN (1986-1989); Commercial marketing assistant, The Travelers Insurance Co. (The Travelers Indemnity Company), Knoxville, TN (1984-1986); Administrative Staff, The Travelers Insurance Co. (The Travelers Indemnity Company), Knoxville, TN (1984); Clerk, The Travelers Insurance Co. (The Travelers Indemnity Company), Knoxville, TN (1967-1984) **CIV:** Yarn Tales-Knit Ministry (2013); Friends of the Library (2013); Spiritual Growth Officer, Regional Atlanta-Roswell United Methodist Women (2010); District Education and Interpretation Officer, Atlanta-Roswell United Methodist Women (2009); Knot for Profit (2008); Tiny Stitches, Alpharetta GA (2000); Active Member, Arthritis Foundation (1991); Charter Member, Saint Thomas Hospital Foundation Society, Saint Thomas Health (1990); Lay Witness Speaker, United Methodist Church, Knoxville TN (1979-1982) **MEM:** Christian Insurance Professionals of Atlanta (2010); Insurance Professionals of Atlanta (1998); National Association of Female Executives (NAFE); Society of Chartered Property and Casualty Underwriter; Society of Certified Insurance Counselors; National Association of Insurance Women; The International Platform Association **MH:** Albert Nelson Marquis Lifetime Achievement Award **B/I:** Mrs. Fowler studied more in management and marketing when she got her first job with Travelers Insurance, which was not her first choice in careers, however, she started working as a personal line underwriter. Shortly after, she learned more about the position, and she realized she enjoyed what she was doing. All the things she learned in school seemed to fit the position. When she went into commercial insurance, she learned so much about how to run a business. **AV:** Knitting for charity; Reading; Taking classes on books of the Bible by online study; Teaching Bible study (28-week course); Composing the study guides

FOX, MICHAEL ANDREW J., T: Actor **I:** Media & Entertainment **DOB:** 06/09/1961 **PB:** Edmonton **SC:** AB/CAN **PT:** William Fox; Phyllis (Piper) Fox **MS:** Married **SPN:** Tracy Pollan (07/16/1988) **CH:** Sam Michael; Aquinnah Kathleen; Schuyler Frances; Esme Annabelle **ED:** Honorary LLD, Justice Institute of British Columbia (2012); Honorary MD, Karolinska Institute (2010); GED (1995) **CR:** Founder, The Michael J. Fox Foundation for Parkinson's Research (2000-Present); Founder, Lottery Hill Entertainment (1996-2003) **CW:** Actor, "The Good Fight" (2020); Voice Actor, "Corner Gas Animated" (2019); Voice Actor, "A.R.C.H.I.E. 2" (2018); Actor, "Designated Survivor" (2018); Appearance, "Oscars" (2017); Appearance, "Nightcap" (2016); Voice Actor, "A.R.C.H.I.E." (2016); Appearance, "Jimmy Kimmel Live" (2015); Appearance, "Mr. Calzaghe" (2015); Appearance, "Back in Time" (2015); Appearance, "Being Canadian" (2015); Appearance, "Annie" (2014); Actor, Executive Producer, "The Michael J. Fox Show" (2013-2014); Appear-

ance, "Drew: The Man Behind the Poster" (2013); Actor, "Curb Your Enthusiasm" (2011); Actor, "The Good Wife" (2010-2013); Author, "A Funny Thing Happened on the Way to the Future" (2010); Author, "Always Looking Up: The Adventures of an Incurable Optimist" (2009); Actor, "The Magic 7" (2009); Actor, "Rescue Me" (2009); Voice Actor, "Stuart Little 3: Call of the Wild" (2006); Actor, "Boston Legal" (2006); Actor, "Scrubs" (2004); Actor, "Interstate 60" (2002); Voice Actor, "Stuart Little 2" (2002); Executive Producer, "Otherwise Engaged" (2002); Voice Actor, "Atlantis: The Lost Empire" (2001); Author, "Lucky Man: A Memoir" (2001); Executive Producer, "Anna Says" (1999); Voice Actor, "Stuart Little" (1999); Actor, "I Am Your Child" (1997); Actor, "Spin City" (1996-2000); Voice Actor, "Homeward Bound II: Lost in San Francisco" (1996); Actor, "Mars Attacks!" (1996); Actor, "The Frighteners" (1996); Actor, "Cold Blooded" (1995); Actor, "Blue in the Face" (1995); Actor, "The American President" (1995); Actor, "Greedy" (1994); Actor, "Life With Mikey" (1993); Actor, "For Love or Money" (1993); Actor, "Where the Rivers Flow North" (1993); Voice Actor, "Homeward Bound: The Incredible Journey" (1993); Actor, "The Hard Way" (1991); Actor, "Tales from the Crypt" (1991); Actor, "Back to the Future, Part III" (1990); Actor, "Casualties of War" (1989); Actor, "Back to the Future, Part II" (1989); Actor, "Bright Lights, Big City" (1988); Actor, "The Secret of My Success" (1987); Actor, "Light of Day" (1986); Actor, "Back to the Future" (1985); Actor, "Teen Wolf" (1985); Actor, "Poison Ivy" (1985); Actor, "High School USA" (1985); Actor, "Night Court" (1984); Actor, "The Love Boat" (1983); Actor, "Family Ties" (1982-1989); Actor, "Class of '84" (1981); Actor, "Trapper John, M.D." (1981); Actor, "Midnight Madness" (1980); Actor, "Family" (1980); Actor, "Palmerstown USA" (1980); Actor, "Letters from Frank" (1979); Actor, "Lou Grant" (1979); Actor, "Leo and Me" (1976) **AW:** Golden Apple Award, Casting Society of America (2013); Lifetime Achievement International, Golden Camera Award (2011); Officer of the Order of Canada (2010); Grammy Award, Best Spoken Word Album, The Recording Academy (2010); Emmy Award, Outstanding Guest Actor in a Drama Series, Academy of Television Arts & Sciences (2009); One of America's Best Leaders, U.S. News & World Report (2007); One of the 100 Most Influential People in the World, TIME Magazine (2007); Golden Plate Award, Academy of Achievement (2005); Star, Hollywood Walk of Fame (2002); Golden Globe Award, Best Actor in Comedy Series, Hollywood Foreign Press Association (1989, 1998, 1999, 2000); SAG Award for Outstanding Performance by a Male Actor in a Comedy Series, SAG-AFTRA (1999, 2000); Emmy Award, Best Actor in Comedy Series, Academy of Television Arts & Sciences (2000); Honoree, Family Television Awards (2000); Star, Canada's Walk of Fame (2000); Emmy Award, Outstanding Lead Actor in a Comedy Series, Academy of Television Arts & Sciences (1986, 1987, 1988); Numerous Awards

FOXX, JAMIE, T: Actor, Comedian **I:** Media & Entertainment **CN:** Foxxhole Productions Inc. **DOB:** 12/13/1967 **PB:** Terrell **SC:** TX/USA **PT:** Shahid Abdulah (Darrell Bishop); Louise Annette Dixon **CH:** Corinne Bishop; Anelise **ED:** Coursework, U.S. International University (Now Alliant International University), San Diego, CA (1986-1988); Coursework, Classical Piano, The Juilliard School **C:** Owner, Foxxhole Productions, Inc. **CW:** Host, Executive Producer, "Beat Shazam" (2017-Present); Host, "The Foxxhole," Sirius XM Radio (2008-Present); Actor, "Just Mercy" (2019); Actor, "Live in Front of a Studio Audience: Norman Lear's All in the Family and The Jeffersons" (2019); Actor, "Robin Hood" (2018); Actor, "All Star Week-

end" (2018); Actor, "Sleepless" (2017); Actor, "Baby Driver" (2017); Actor, "White Famous" (2017); Actor, "Jackie Robinson" (2016); Singer, "Hollywood: A Story of a Dozen Roses" (2015); Voice Actor, "Rio 2" (2014); Actor, "The Amazing Spider-Man 2" (2014); Actor, "Horrible Bosses 2" (2014); Actor, "Annie" (2014); Actor, "A Million Ways to Die in the West" (2014); Actor, "White House Down" (2013); Actor, "David Blaine, Real or Magic" (2013); Actor, "Django Unchained" (2012); Voice Actor, "Rio" (2011); Actor, "Horrible Bosses" (2011); Actor, "When I Was 17" (2011); Director, "Night Tales" (2011); Executive Producer, "In the Flow with Affion Crockett" (2011); Singer, "Best Night of My Life" (2010); Actor, "Valentine's Day" (2010); Actor, "Due Date" (2010); Actor, "The Soloist" (2009); Actor, "Law Abiding Citizen" (2009); Executive Producer, Writer, "From G's to Gents" (2008-2009); Singer, with T-Pain, "Blame It" (2008); Singer, "Intuition" (2008); Actor, "The Kingdom" (2007); Actor, "Miami Vice" (2006); Actor, "Dreamgirls" (2006); Actor, "Stealth" (2005); Actor, "Jarhead" (2005); Singer, with Kanye West, "Gold Digger" (2005); Singer, "Unpredictable" (2005); Actor, "Redemption: The Stan Tookie Williams Story" (2004); Actor, "Breakin' All the Rules" (2004); Actor, "Collateral" (2004); Actor, "Ray" (2004); Actor, "Shade" (2003); Comedian, Executive Producer, Writer, "Jamie Foxx: I Might Need Security" (2002); Actor, "Date from Hell" (2001); Actor, "Ali" (2001); Actor, "Bait" (2000); Actor, "Held Up" (1999); Actor, "Any Given Sunday" (1999); Actor, "The Players Club" (1998); Actor, "Booty Call" (1997); Actor, "The Truth About Cats and Dogs" (1996); Voice Actor, "C-Bear and Jamal" (1996); Actor, Director, Producer, Writer, "The Jamie Foxx Show" (1996); Singer, "Peep This" (1994); Actor, "The Great White Hype" (1996); Actor, "Toys" (1992); Actor, "In Living Color" (1991-1994) **AW:** Entertainer of the Year, NAACP Image Awards (2013); Grammy Award for Best R&B Performance by a Duo or Group with Vocals, The Recording Academy (2010); Outstanding Male Artist, NAACP Image Awards (2006, 2009); Star, Hollywood Walk of Fame (2007); Best Album, Soul Train Awards (2007); Best Duet, Video of the Year, BET Awards (2006); Favorite Male Artist, Soul/Rhythm & Blues, American Music Awards (2006); Golden Globe Award for Best Actor in a Musical or Comedy, Hollywood Foreign Press Association (2005); Outstanding Performance by a Male Actor in Leading Role, Screen Actors Guild Awards (2005); Academy Award for Best Actor in a Leading Role, Academy of Motion Picture Arts and Sciences (2005); One of the 10 Most Fascinating People, Barbara Walters Special (2005); One of the 100 Most Influential People in the World, TIME Magazine (2005); Best Actor, National Board of Review of Motion Pictures (2004); Best Actor, Boston Film Critics Awards (2004); Outstanding Supporting Actor in a Motion Picture, NAACP Image Awards (2002); Outstanding Lead Actor in a Comedy Series, NAACP Image Awards (1997)

FOYT, ANTHONY, "A.J." JOSEPH JR., T: Auto Racing Crew Chief, Professional Auto Racer (Retired) **I:** Business Management/Business Services **CN:** A.J. Foyt Enterprises **DOB:** 01/16/1935 **PB:** Houston **SC:** TX/USA **PT:** Anthony Foyt, Sr.; Emma Evelyn (Monk) Foyt **MS:** Married **SPN:** Lucy Zarr (1955) **CH:** A.J. Foyt III; Jerry; Terry Lynn **ED:** Coursework, Public Schools **C:** Auto Racer (1953-1982); Owner, Conseco/A.J. Foyt Enterprises Corporation (Now A.J. Foyt Enterprises) **CR:** Professional Horse Breeder and Trainer; Member, Houston Board of Directors, Riverway Bank, Houston, TX; Board Member, SCI Corporation, Houston, TX **AW:** Inductee, International Motorsports Hall of Fame (2000); Inductee, National Sprint Car

Hall of Fame (1990); Inductee, Motorsports Hall of Fame of America (1989); Inductee, National Midget Auto Racing Hall of Fame (1988); One of NASCARS 50 Greatest Drivers (1998); Outstanding American Driver of the Year (1967); Racing Driver of the Year, Auto Racing Fraternity of Greater New York (1963)

FRALINGER, JACK BRUCE, MD, T: Surgeon **I:** Medicine & Health Care **CN:** Gallup Indian Medical Center (GIMC) **DOB:** 12/07/1967 **PB:** Baltimore **SC:** MD/USA **PT:** Jack Martin Fralinger; Audrey Ann Fralinger **MS:** Married **SPN:** Ona Lynn **CH:** Bethany; Emma; Dandro; Jackson **ED:** Resident in Surgery, Waterbury Surgical Residency, CT (2001-2006); Resident in Surgery, Swedish Medical Center, Swedish Health Sciences, Seattle, WA (1996-1999); MD, University of Minnesota (1996); BA in History, University of Nevada (1992); BS in Zoology, University of Nevada (1990) **CT:** Board Certified in General Surgery **C:** Trauma Director, Gallup Indian Medical Center (GIMC) Level 3 Trauma Center (2010-Present); Surgeon, Gallup Indian Medical Center (GIMC), NM (2006-Present); Physician, NorthEast Washington Medical Group, Colville, WA (2001); Physician, Indian Health Service, Neah Bay, WA (2001) **CR:** Trauma Director, Gallup Indian Medical Center (2010-Present) **CIV:** Instructor, "Stop the Bleed," American College of Surgeons (2018-Present) **MEM:** American College of Surgeons; Association of American Indian Physicians **AV:** Travel; Cooking; Hiking; Hunting

FRANCAVILLA, BARBARA JEAN, I: Other **DOB:** 11/18/1955 **PB:** Montclair **SC:** NJ/USA **PT:** John Joseph Francavilla; Angela (Rapa) Francavilla **ED:** MA, Montclair State University (1995) **CT:** Licensed Professional Counselor; Licensed Clinical and Drug Counselor **C:** Owner, Equality 4 Children (2019-Present); Counselor, School District (2000-2019); Director of Youth and Community Services, Saint Barnabas Medical Center (1995-2000); Prevention Specialist, Institute for Prevention and Recovery, RWJ Barnabas Health (1995-2000); Mental Health Counselor, Community Substance Abuse Program, Saint Clare's Health (1992) **CIV:** Former Board Member, Livingston Municipal Alliance Committee (1995-2000) **AW:** Who's Who of American Women; Who's Who Registry of Executives and Professionals **MEM:** American Counseling Association; New Jersey Counseling Association; The Honor Society of Phi Kappa Phi; Alpha Kappa Delta International Honor Society; CHADD; Understood For All Inc. **MH:** Albert Nelson Marquis Lifetime Achievement Award **B/I:** Ms. Francavilla became involved in her profession because of personal experiences in her adolescent years. Having an understanding of people's struggles and difficulties, as well as being an empathetic listener made her realize she had the skills to be a counselor.

FRANCHITTI, DARIO MARINO, T: Sports Commentator, Race Car Driver (Retired) **I:** Athletics **DOB:** 05/19/1973 **PB:** Edinburgh **SC:** Scotland **MS:** Married **SPN:** Eleanor Robb (2014-Present); Ashley Judd (2001-2013) **CH:** Valentina; Sofia **C:** Commentator, Formula E (2014-2018); Race Car Driver, NASCAR, Ganassi Racing (2008-2013); Race Car Driver, IndyCar Series, Andretti Green (2003-2007) **AW:** First Place, Indy 500, Indianapolis Motor Speedway (2007, 2010, 2012); Named IndyCar Series Champion, Indy Racing League (2007); Jerry Titus Award, American Automobile Racing Writers & Broadcasters Association (2008); Second Place, ABC Supply Company A.J. Foyt 225, Milwaukee Mile (2005, 2007); First Place, Peak Antifreeze Indy 300, Chicagoland Speedway (2007); Second Place, Honda 200, Mid-Ohio Sports Car Course (2007); First Place, Iowa Corn Indy 250, Iowa Speedway (2007); First Place, SunTrust Indy Challenge, Richmond International Raceway (2007); Second Place, Firestone Indy 200, Nashville Speedway (2007); Second Place, Kansas Lottery Indy 300, Kansas Speedway (2007); Second Place, Indy Grand Prix Sonoma, Infineon Raceway (2006); First Place, Toyota Indy 400, California Speedway (2005); First Place, Firestone Indy 200 (2005); Second Place, SunTrust Indy Challenge (2005); First Place, Honda Indy 225, Pikes Peak International Raceway (2004); First Place, Menards A.J. Foyt 225 (2004) **AV:** Reading; Playing video games; Skiing

FRANCIS, ELIZABETH, "BETH ANN" ANN, BHPP, BHT, T: Recovery Support Specialist **I:** Medicine & Health Care **CN:** Connections Health Solutions **DOB:** 11/22/1981 **PB:** Willingboro **SC:** NJ/USA **PT:** Robert Afflerback; Elizabeth Afflerback **MS:** Married **SPN:** James **CH:** Emma **ED:** Diploma in Cosmetology, Burlington County Institute of Technology (2000); Diploma, High School **CT:** Certified, Recovery Support Specialist (2016)Currently working on certification as a Doula, and a certification from Arizona western college as a Community healthcare worker **C:** Recovery Support Specialist, Connections Health Solutions (2014-Present); Unit Coordinator, Crisis Response Network, Southern AZ (2012-2015); Medical Records Specialist, Audit Clerk, Providence Corporation, Tucson, AZ (2008-2012); Front Desk Receptionist, Animal Birth Control, Tucson, AZ (2008); Accounting Clerk, Front Desk Receptionist, BrakeMax Corporation, Tucson, AZ (2007); Multiple Dealership Titles, Clerk, Classic Chevrolet, Moorestown, NJ (2002-2007) **CIV:** Co-founder, Support Group for Peers; Volunteer, Suicide Walk; Volunteer, Various Community Events **AW:** Ben's Bells Award for Work in the Community (2009); Edward J. Bloustein Distinguished Scholar (2000) **MEM:** Life Member, International Association of Peer Supporters, Inc.; National Honor Society; Council Member, Order of the White Rabbit **MH:** Marquis Who's Who Top Professional **AS:** Mrs. Francis attributes her success to the wonderful team with whom she works. She feels they are all doing their work because they want to help people, inspire hope and instill motivation and courage to keep trying no matter what happens. To her mom and dad, for instilling in her independence and a strong work ethic. To her husband, for supporting her and believing in her. To Tyler Logan, her friend and manager for believing she had what it took to do this work and bringing her out of her shell. **B/I:** Mrs. Francis was unaware that her profession even was one for a long time. However, when she found out about it, she knew she had finally found a way to help people. Mrs. Francis was hired at the crisis response center in 2012, and got her first exposure to this profession. Mrs. Francis is a suicide survivor, suffering the loss of her husband in 2011. After dealing with that, and a long time dealing with anxiety and depression issues herself, she wanted to give back and help others to find their reasons for living and learning to cope. **AV:** Gardening; Reading; Classic car shows with club; Musical entertainment; Community service; Cooking **PA:** Republican **RE:** Catholic **THT:** Mrs. Francis says, "Life is nothing more than a giant roller coaster ride, it has ups and downs. It's what you do with the downs that gives you strength to go up and do it again."

FRANCO, JAMES EDWARD, T: Actor, Teacher, Writer **I:** Media & Entertainment **DOB:** 4/19/1978 **PB:** Palo Alto **SC:** CA/USA **PT:** Douglas Eugene Franco; Betsy Lou (Verne) Franco **ED:** Master of Fine Arts, Columbia University School of the Arts (2010); Bachelor of Arts in English, University of California Los Angeles (2008) **C:** Teacher, Film and English Departments, New York University; Teacher, Film and English Departments, California Institute of the Arts; Teacher, Film and English Departments, University of California Los Angeles; Teacher, Film and English Departments, University of Southern California **CR:** Co-founder, Co-owner, Rabbit Bandini Productions **CW:** Actor, "The Long Home" (2018); Actor, "Artic Justice Thunder Squad" (2018); Actor, "Kin" (2018); Actor, "Pretenders" (2018); Actor, "The Ballad of Buster Scruggs" (2018); Actor, "The Institute" (2017); Actor, "The Disaster Artist" (2017); Actor, "Alien Covenant" (2017); Actor, "Don't Come Back From the Moon" (2017); Actor, "The Vault" (2017); Actor, "This is Your Death" (2017); Actor, "The Heyday of the Insensitive Bastards" (2017); Actor, "Actors Anonymous" (2017); Actor, "Kill the Czar" (2017); Actor, "High School Lover" (2017); Actor, "The Deuce" (2017); Actor, "Angie Tribeca" (2016); Actor, "11.22.63" (2016); Actor, "Mother May I Sleep with Danger?" (2016); Actor, "The Labyrinth" (2016); Actor, "Goat" (2016); Actor, "Sausage Party" (2016); Actor, "Burn Country" (2016); Actor, "King Cobra" (2016); Voice Actor, "The Labyrinth" (2016); Actor, Director, Writer, Producer, "Black Dog, Red Dog" (2016); Actor, "The Caged Pillows" (2016); Actor, "In Dubious Battle" (2016); Actor, "Why Him?" (2016); Actor, Director, "Zeroville" (2016); Actor, "The Little Prince" (2015); Actor, Producer, "I am Michael" (2015); Actor, Producer, "The Adderall Diaries" (2015); Writer, Director, "Bukowski" (2015); Actor, "Memoria" (2015); Actor, "Queen of the Desert" (2015); Actor, "Every Thing Will Be Fine" (2015); Actor, "Wild Horses" (2015); Voice Actor, "The Little Prince" (2015); Actor, "Richard Peter Johnson" (2015); Actor, "The Night Before" (2015); Actor, "Deadbeat" (2015); Actor, Executive Producer, "Don Quixote: The Ingenious Gentleman of La Mancha" (2015); Actor, Executive Producer, "Memoria" (2015); Actor, Executive Producer, "Yosemite" (2015); Appearance, "SNL" (2014); Writer, Producer, "Holy Land" (2014); Actor, "Good People" (2014); Actor, "The Interview" (2014); Actor, "True Story" (2014); Actor, "Naked and Afraid" (2014); Author, "A California Childhood" (2013); Actor, Director, Writer, Producer, "Child of God" (2013); Actor, Director, Producer, "Interior.Leather.Bar." (2013); Author, "Actors Anonymous" (2013); Appearance, "Comedy Central Roast of James Franco" (2013); Actor, "The Mindy Project" (2013); Actor, "Spring Breakers" (2013); Actor, "Lovelace" (2013); Actor, "Oz the Great and Powerful" (2013); Actor, "This is the End" (2013); Actor, "Palo Alto" (2013); Actor, "Third Person" (2013); Actor, "Homefront" (2013); Actor, "Hollywood Heights" (2012); Author, "Strongest of the Litter" (2012); Actor, "The Stare" (2012); Actor, "About Cherry" (2012); Actor, "The Iceman" (2012); Actor, "The Letter" (2012); Actor, "Maladies" (2012); Actor, "Tar" (2012); Actor, "General Hospital" (2009-2012); Actor, Director, Writer, "Sal" (2011); Actor, "Your Highness" (2011); Actor, "Rise of the Planet of the Apes" (2011); Actor, Director, Writer, Producer, "The Broken Tower" (2011); Author, "Palo Alto: Stories" (2010); Actor, "Date Night" (2010); Actor, "Eat Pray Love" (2010); Actor, "127 Hours" (2010); Actor, "Pineapple Express" (2008); Actor, "Nights in Rodanthe" (2008); Actor, "Milk" (2008); Actor, "Good Times Max" (2007); Actor, "An American Crime" (2007); Actor, "Finishing the Game" (2007); Actor, "Camille" (2007); Actor, "Spider-Man 3" (2007); Actor, "In the Valley of Elah" (2007); Actor, Director, Writer, "Good Time Max" (2007); Actor, "Tristan & Isolde" (2006); Actor, "Annapolis" (2006); Actor, "The Wicker Man" (2006); Actor, "Flyboys" (2006); Actor, "The Great Raid" (2005); Actor, "Fool's Gold" (2005); Actor, "Spider-Man 2" (2004); Director, Executive Producer, Writer, "The Ape" (2004); Actor, "Mean People Suck" (2003); Actor, "The Car Kid" (2003);

Actor, "Spider-Man" (2002); Actor, "Deuces Wild" (2002); Actor, "City by the Sea" (2002); Actor, "Sonny" (2002); Actor, "Some Body" (2001); Actor, "James Dean" (2001); Actor, "Blind Spot" (2001); Actor, "Whatever It Takes" (2000); Actor, "At Any Cost" (2000); Actor, "If Tomorrow Comes" (2000); Actor, "Freaks and Geeks" (1999-2000); Actor, "To Serve and Protect" (1999); Actor, "Profiler" (1999); Actor, "Never Been Kissed" (1999); Actor, "Pacific Blue" (1997) **AW:** Golden Globe Award for Best Actor in a Motion Picture Musical or Comedy (2018); Named, Man of the Year, Hasty Pudding Theatrical Society (2009); Golden Globe Award for Best Actor in a Miniseries or Television Film, Hollywood Foreign Press Association (2002)

FRANCONA, TERRY, "TITO" JON, T: Professional Baseball Manager, Professional Baseball Player (Retired) **I:** Athletics **CN:** Cleveland Indians **DOB:** 04/22/1959 **PB:** Aberdeen **SC:** SD/USA **PT:** Tito Francona; Roberta Jackson **MS:** Divorced **SPN:** Jacque Lang (01/09/1982-2011) **CH:** Nick; Alyssa; Leah; Jamie **ED:** Coursework, University of Arizona **C:** Manager, Cleveland Indians (2012-Present); Baseball Analyst, "Sunday Night Baseball," ESPN (2011-2012); Manager, Boston Red Sox (2004-2011); Bench Coach, Oakland A's (2003); Bench Coach, Texas Rangers (2002); Special Assistant of Baseball Operations, Cleveland Indians (2001); Manager, Philadelphia Phillies (1997-2000); Third Base Coach, Detroit Tigers (1996); Manager, Dominican Winter League (1995); Manager, Birmingham AA (1993-1995); Manager, Chicago Single-A South Bend (1992); Hitting Instructor, Gulf Coast Rookie League, Chicago White Sox Organization, Sarasota, FL (1991); First Baseman, Outfielder, Milwaukee Brewers (1989-1990); First Baseman, Outfielder, Cleveland Indians (1988); First Baseman, Outfielder, Cincinnati Reds (1987); First Baseman, Outfielder, Chicago Cubs (1986); First Baseman, Outfielder, Montreal Expos (1981-1985) **CW:** Author, "Francona: The Red Sox Years" (2013) **AW:** American League Manager of the Year, Major League Baseball (2013, 2016); Top Managerial Prospect in Minors, Baseball America (1994); Minor League Manager of the Year (1993); Southern League Manager of the Year (1993); Golden Spikes Award, USA Baseball (1980) **AV:** Golfing

FRANGIPANE, ASHLEY, "HALSEY" NICOLETTE, T: Singer **I:** Media & Entertainment **DOB:** 09/29/1994 **PB:** Edison **SC:** NJ/USA **PT:** Chris Frangipane; Nicole Frangipane **MS:** Single **ED:** Diploma, Warren Hills Regional High School, Washington, NJ (2012); Coursework, Rhode Island School of Design **CIV:** Participant, March for Our Lives, Washington, DC (2018); Speaker, Women's March (2018); Donor, Planned Parenthood (2017); Participant, "I'm Listening," Entercom (2017) **CW:** Featured Musician, "Be Kind" (2020); Musician, "Experiment on Me" (2020); Featured Musician, "The Other Girl" (2020); Guest Appearance, "Scooby-Doo and Guess Who?" (2020); Musician, "Manic" (2020); Appearance, Web Series, "Road to Manic" (2019-2020); Appearances, "Saturday Night Live" (2018-2020); Musician, "Nightmare" (2019); Featured Musician, "¿" (2019); Featured Musician, "Boy with Luv" (2019); Featured Musician, "11 Minutes" (2019); Contributing Musician, "Earth" (2019); Featured Musician, "Die for Me" (2019); Performer, Victoria's Secret Fashion Show (2018); Cameo, "A Star is Born" (2018); Guest Advisor, Performer, "The Voice" (2018); Celebrity Guest, "The Doctors" (2018); Guest Judge, "RuPaul's Drag Race" (2018); Voice Actress, "Teen Titans Go! To the Movies" (2018); Featured Musician, "Love is Madness" (2018); Featured Musician, "Eastside" (2018); Featured Musician, "Him & I" (2017); Guest Appearance, "American Dad!" (2017); Musician,

"Hopeless Fountain Kingdom" (2017); Featured Musician, "Damage" (2017); Musician, "Not Afraid Anymore" (2017); Featured Musician, "Closer" (2016); Featured Musician, "Tokyo Narita (Freestyle)" (2016); Musician, "Complementary Colors" (2016); Featured Musician, "Hands" (2016); Guest Appearance, "Roadies" (2016); Featured Musician, "Free Love" (2016); Musician, "Badlands" (2015); Musician, "Spotify Sessions" (2015); Musician, "Room 93: 1 Mic 1 Take" (2015); Musician, "Room 93: The Remixes" (2015); Featured Musician, "The Feeling" (2015); Musician, "Room 93" (2014); Co-Director, Five Music Videos **AW:** Rising Star Award, Global Awards (2019); Fangirls Award, iHeartRadio Music Awards (2019); Two Winning Songs, "Bad at Love" and "Him & I," iHeartRadio Titanium Awards (2019); Most Viewed YouTube Music Video in 24 Hours by a K-Pop Group, Most Viewed YouTube Music Video in 24 Hours, Most Viewed YouTube Video in 24 Hours, "Boy with Luv," Guinness World Records (2019); Hal David Starlight Award, Songwriters Hall of Fame (2019); Choice Summer Female Artist, Choice Collaboration, "Boy with Luv," Teen Choice Awards (2019); Best K-Pop, "Boy with Luv," MTV Video Music Awards (2019); Favorite Pop/Rock Song, "Without Me," American Music Awards (2019); Outstanding Music Artist, GLAAD Media Awards (2018); Dance Song of the Year, "Closer," iHeartRadio Music Awards (2017); Top Hot 100 Song, Top Collaboration and Top Dance/ Electronic Song, "Closer," Billboard Music Awards (2017); Best Video, "Closer," MTV Italian Music Awards (2017); Best International Video, "Closer," Myx Music Awards (2017); Rising Star, Billboard Women in Music (2016)

FRANK, JOACHIM, PHD, T: Structural Biologist; Professor; Biophysicist **I:** Education/Educational Services **CN:** Columbia University **DOB:** 09/12/1940 **PB:** Siegen **SC:** Germany **MS:** Married **SPN:** Carol Saginaw (1983) **CH:** Ze; Mariel **ED:** PhD in Biophysics, Technical University of Munich (1970); MS in Physics, University of Munich; BS in Physics, University of Freiburg **C:** Professor, Biochemistry and Molecular Biophysics, Columbia University (2008-Present); Distinguished Scientist, Structural Biology, Wadsworth Center, Albany, NY; Director, Laboratory of Computational Biology and Macromolecular Imaging, Wadsworth Center, Albany, NY **CR:** Investigator, Howard Hughes Medical Institute (1998-Present); Research Professor, Cell Biology, NYU Grossman School of Medicine; Adjunct Professor, Biochemistry and Molecular Biophysics, Columbia University, NY; Professor, Biology, State University of New York, Albany **CW:** Author, Five Books; Contributor, 200 Articles to Scientific Journals **AW:** Nobel Prize in Chemistry (2017); Wiley Prize in Biomedical Sciences (2017); Benjamin Franklin Medal in Life Science (2014); National Academy of Sciences (2006); Fellow, American Academy of Arts & Sciences (2006); Humboldt Research Award (1994); Elizabeth Roberts Cole Award, Biophysical Society (1993) **MEM:** Fellow, American Academy of Arts & Sciences; Fellow, Biophysical Society; Fellow, American Association for the Advancement of Science; National Academy of Sciences

FRANK, JOHN L., T: Commissioner, Lawyer (Retired); Educator (Retired) **I:** Law and Legal Services **DOB:** 03/13/1952 **PB:** Eau Claire **SC:** WI/ USA **PT:** George LeRoy Frank; Frances Elaine (Torgerson) Frank **MS:** Single **ED:** JD, University of Wisconsin - Madison, Cum Laude (1977); BS, University of Wisconsin - Eau Claire, Summa Cum Laude (1974) **C:** Chair, West Central Wisconsin Regional Planning Commission, WI (2018-Present); Member, Executive Committee, West Central Wisconsin Regional Planning Commission, WI (2011-Present);

Commissioner, West Central Wisconsin Regional Planning Commission, Eau Claire, WI (1998-Present); Vice Chair, West Central Wisconsin Regional Planning Commission, WI (2016-2018); Instructor, Chippewa Valley Technical College (1989-1993, 1997-2016); Chair, Department of Behavioral Science and Civic Effectiveness, Chippewa Valley Technical College (2013-2015); Chair, Department of Liberal Arts Program, Chippewa Valley Technical College (2009-2013); Chair, Department of Behavioral Science and Civic Effectiveness, Chippewa Valley Technical College (2003-2008); Private Law Practice (1990-1993, 1997-2005); Director, Paralegal Program, Chippewa Valley Technical College (1992-1993, 1997-2001, 2003-2004); Deputy Chief Counsel, House Committee on Agriculture, Washington, DC (1995-1997); Counsel, Congressman Steve Gunderson, Washington, DC (1993-1997); Deputy Minority Counsel, House Committee on Agriculture, Washington, DC (1993-1995); Counsel, Minority Consultant, House Subcommittee on Livestock, Washington, WI (1993-1995); Staff Coordinator, 92 Group, Washington, DC (1987-1989); Chief of Staff, Counsel, Congressman Steve Gunderson, Washington, DC (1985-1989); Legislative Director, Counsel, Congressman Steve Gunderson, Washington, DC (1981-1985); Associate, Garvey, Anderson, Kelly & Ryberg, Eau Claire, WI (1977-1981); Instructor of Law, University of Wisconsin - Madison (1976-1977) **CR:** Political Analyst, Commentator, WEAU-TV, Eau Claire, WI (1998-Present); Visiting Professor Lakeland College (Now Lakeland University) (1999-2001, 2015-2016); With, University of Wisconsin - Stout (2006-2014); With, University of Wisconsin - Eau Claire (2002-2003); Member, Bush-Cheney Transition Advisory Committee (2001) **AW:** Lifetime Achievement Award (2017); Award of Excellence (2012); Fuerstenberg Outstanding Teacher Award, Chippewa Valley Technical College (2011); President's Award (2009); Named Teacher of the Year (2006); Named Wisconsin Teacher of the Year (2006); Hambrecht Award, Wisconsin Association for Career & Technical Education (ACTE) (2005); Region III Award of Merit, Association for Career & Technical Education (ACTE) (2003); Distinguished Achievement Award, University of Wisconsin-Eau Claire Alumni Association (2001); Durance Award, Phi Gamma Delta (1978) **MEM:** Government Affairs Committee, Eau Claire Area Chamber of Commerce (2016-Present); Vice President, The Presto Foundation (2000-Present); Board of Directors, The Presto Foundation (2000-Present); Good Government Council, Eau Claire Area Chamber of Commerce (2000-Present); Board of Directors, Chippewa Valley Museum Foundation (2012-2018); Board of Directors, Wisconsin Association for Career & Technical Education (ACTE) (2010-2013); President, Wisconsin Association for Career & Technical Education (ACTE) (2010-2012); Legislative Committee Chair, Wisconsin Association for Career & Technical Education (ACTE) (2010-2011); Re-organization Committee, Association for Career & Technical Education (ACTE) (2005-2007); Board of Directors, Wisconsin Association for Career & Technical Education (ACTE) (2000-2004); Legislative Committee, Association for Career & Technical Education (ACTE) (2003-2007); Nominations Committee Chair, Wisconsin Association for Career & Technical Education (ACTE) (2004-2005); Paralegal Task Force, Wisconsin Bar Association (1998-2005); Conference Committee Chair, Wisconsin Association for Career & Technical Education (ACTE) (2003-2004); Board of Directors, Wisconsin Association for Career & Technical Education (ACTE) (2000-2004); President, Wisconsin Association for Career & Technical Education (ACTE) (2002-2003); Strategic Planning Committee Chair, Wisconsin Association for Career & Technical Education (ACTE) (2001-2002); Legislative Committee Chair, Wisconsin Association for Career & Technical Education (ACTE) (2000-2001); Board of Directors, The Presto Foundation (1992-1993); Vice President, The Presto Foundation (1992-1993); University of Wisconsin Alumni Association; Phi Gamma Delta; The International Legal Honor Society of Phi Delta Phi; The Honor Society of Phi Kappa Phi; Phi Eta Sigma National Honor Society, Inc.; Omnicron Delta Kappa; Omicron Delta Epsilon, The International Economics Honor Society **BAR:** Supreme Court of the United States (1982); Wisconsin (1977); United States District Court for the Western District of Wisconsin (1977) **MH:** Albert Nelson Marquis Lifetime Achievement Award **B/I:** Mr. Frank became involved in his profession because he always had an interest in politics and the law since he was in grade school. His interest came about from watching the news on television.

FRANK, ROBERT ALLEN, T: Media Consultant **I:** Media & Entertainment **DOB:** 09/26/1932 **PB:** Albany **SC:** NY/USA **PT:** Edward Frank; Marian (Kostelanetz) Frank **MS:** Married **SPN:** Cynthia Tull (8/1984) **CH:** David; Chelsea; Alison **ED:** MBA, Amos Tuck School of Business Administration, Dartmouth College (1958); BA, Colby College (1954) **C:** Chief Strategist, Noetic Partners (2011-2012); Private Consultant (2003-2004); Vice Chairman, Media Planning Group USA, New York, NY (2001-2002); President, CEO, SFM Media LLC, New York, NY (1998-2000); President Media Service Division, SFM Media Corp., New York, NY (1981-1997); Executive Vice President, Co-founder, SFM Media Corp., New York, NY (1969-1997); Account Executive, Radio Network Sales, CBS, Inc., New York, NY (1962-1969); TV Sales Service Account Executive, CBS, Inc., New York, NY (1961); Corporate Auditor, CBS, Inc., New York, NY (1959-1960); Cost Control Administrator, ABC-TV, New York, NY (1958-1959) **CIV:** Board of Directors, Library Programs, Judge Rotenberg Education Center (2006-2011); Board of Directors, Judge Rotenberg Education Center (2004-2009); Vice Chairman, National Child Labor Committee (1994-1996); Trustee, National Child Labor Committee (1984-1996); Du Pont for President (1988); Inner Circle, Republican National Senatorial Committee (1985-1988); Trustee, Myasthenia Gravis Foundation (1984-1993); Citizens Republican President Committee (1984-1988); Leadership Council, President's Club (1984-1988); Reagan for President (1980); Bush for President (1980); Ford for President (1976); Radio and TV Consultant, National Kidney Fund (1974); Richard Nixon for President (1972); Robert Kennedy for Senator (1964); Leadership Council, Republican National Committee; Leadership Council, National Republican Congressional Committee **MIL:** Captain, U.S. Air Force (1954-1956) **AW:** Lifetime Achievement Award, Media Week (2001) **MEM:** Board of Directors, President, Amos Tuck Alumni Association New York (1976-1979); Pi Gamma Mu; International Radio and Television Society **MH:** Albert Nelson Marquis Lifetime Achievement Award **B/I:** Mr. Frank began his career at the Tuck School, where he got the opportunity to work at ABC. This was an exciting opportunity; he started in their training program in the cost control department. He then went to CBS to work in the corporate auditing department and eventually moved to television and radio network sales.

FRANK, STUART M., PHD, T: Founding Director **I:** Museums & Institutions **CN:** Scrimshaw Forensics Laboratory **DOB:** 06/14/1948 **PB:** New York **SC:** NY/USA **PT:** Robert M.; Pearl K. Frank **MS:** Married **SPN:** Marry Malloy **ED:** Doctor of Philosophy,

Brown University (1985); Master of Arts, Brown University (1981); Degrees, Frank C. Munson Institute of American Maritime Studies (1972, 1973); Master of Arts in Religion, Yale University (1972); Bachelor of Arts, Wesleyan University (1970) **CT:** Fellow, Massachusetts Historical Society; Research Fellow, Nantucket Historical Association; Laureate, Old Time Country Music Association Hall of Fame **C:** Senior Curator, New Bedford Whaling Museum (2001-2016); Executive Director, Kendall Whaling Museum, Sharon, MA (1981-2001); Faculty Member, Massachusetts Bay Maritime Studies Consortium (1985-1987); Visiting Professor, Sea Education Association (1980-1985); Lecturer of Literature, Williams College Program Maritime Studies, Mystic, CT (1979-1981); Teaching Fellow, Brown University (1979-1981); Research Associate, Mystic Seaport Museum (1972-1979); Scholar in Residence, Virginia Museum of Fine Arts (1977-1978); Artist-in-Residence, Virginia Museum (1976-1977); Lecturer of Humanities, University of New Haven (1971-1972); Instructor of Philosophy, University of Bridgeport, CT (1971-1972) **CR:** PhD Review Committee on Maritime History, University of Leiden, The Netherlands (2006-2008); Editorial Board: The American Neptune (1983-2003); Confederate Naval Historical Society (1988-2000); Kendall Whaling Museum Newsletter (1981-2001); Secretary of the Interior's Advisory Committee on Maritime Resources (1998-1999); International Journal Maritime History (1988-1995); Founder and Director, Scrimshaw Forensics® Laboratory (1989); Munson Institute of American Maritime Studies (1977-1987); Emmanuel College Graduate School (1983-1984); Lesley College Graduate School (1982); Brown University (1980-1981); Executive Board and Program Committee Chair, International Congress of Maritime Museums; Adjunct Faculty, Wesleyan University (1968-1970); Advisory Committee, Massachusetts Board of Underwater Archaeological Resources; Collection Consultant, Australian National Maritime Museum; Collection Consultant, Cape Cod Maritime Museum; Collection Consultant, Mystic Seaport Museum; Collection Consultant, Nantucket Historical Association; Collection Consultant, New Bedford Whaling National Historical Park; Collection Consultant, San Francisco Maritime National Historical Park; Collection Consultant, Taiji Whale Museum, Japan; Collection Consultant, Whale Museum, Lahaina, Maui, HI **CW:** Author, "Scrimshaw on Nantucket: The Collection of the Nantucket Historical Association" (2019); Author, "Dutch and Flemish Old Master Paintings in the New Bedford Whaling Museum" (2018); Author, "Classic Whaling Prints" (2016); Author, "Scrimshaw and Provenance" (2013); Author, "Ingenious Contrivances, Curiously Carved: Scrimshaw in the New Bedford Whaling Museum" (2012); Author, "The New Book of Pirate Songs" (2012); Author, "Jolly Sailors Bold: Ballads and Songs of the American Sailor" (2011); Composer, Recording, "Classic Sea Music" (2004); Composer, Recording, with Mary Malloy, "Pirate Songs" (2001); Author, "The Book of Pirate Songs" (1998); Author, "More Scrimshaw Artists" (1998); Composer, Recording, with Mary Malloy, "Sailor's Songs and Ballads" (1991); Author, "Dictionary of Scrimshaw Artists" (1991); Composer, Recording, with Mary Malloy and Jeff Warner, "Traditional Sailors' Songs and Chanteys" (1988); Author, "Herman Melville's Picture Gallery" (1986); Composer, Recording, "Songs of Sea and Shore" (1980); Composer, Recording, "Songs of the Sea: San Francisco Sea Music Festival" (1979); Composer, Recording, with Stuart Gillespie and Ellen Cohn, "Sea Shanties and Forecastle Songs at Mystic Seaport" (1978); Contributor, 75 Scholarly and Popular Journal Articles and 10 Monographs on Maritime Art, History, Literature

and Song **AW:** John Gardner Maritime Research Award, Mystic Seaport (2017); Inductee, Old Time Country Music Hall of Fame, National Traditional Country Music Association (2014); Bookmakers of Boston Book Award (2013); Best Book of 2012, New England Prize (2012); John Lyman Book Award, North American Society for Oceanic History (1991); National Maritime Alliance Award for Excellence (1990); Graphic Design Citation, Philip Brady, Using Type Right, Cincinnati (1988); John Lyman Book Award, North American Society for Oceanic History (1987); Elected, Most Innovative Teacher, University of Bridgeport (1972); Yale University Fellowship (1971); Griffin Prize, Wesleyan University (1970); Underwood Prize, Wesleyan University (1970) **MEM:** Boston Museum on Fine Arts; Buffalo Bill Historical Center; Friends of the Brown University Library, John Carter Brown Library, and Wesleyan University Library; Friends of the Netherlands Scheepvaartmuseum, Amsterdam; International Congress of Maritime Museums; Massachusetts Historical Society; Nantucket Historical Association; National Music Museum, Vermillion, South Dakota; New Bedford Port Society; New Bedford Whaling Museum; Worcester Art Museum; Ticknor Society **AS:** Dr. Frank attributes his success to his conscientious self-application over long periods of time, as well as his penchant for collaborating with colleagues and fellow travelers. **B/I:** Dr. Frank became involved in his profession by default. He studied philosophy and theology in graduate school, whereupon he was awarded with a summer position as a musician at Mystic Seaport Museum. Following this accomplishment, he returned to graduate school and worked at both Mystic Seaport and as a teacher at Brown University. When he took over the Kendall Whaling Museum in 1981, it already possessed the largest and finest scrimshaw collection in the world. He began to perform a great deal of research on the subject, which laid the groundwork for future achievements. **AV:** Early music; Antiquarian books; Antiquarian sheet music **PA:** Independent

FRANKEL, BETHENNY R., T: Entrepreneur **I:** Business Management/Business Services **DOB:** 11/04/1970 **PB:** New York **SC:** NY/USA **PT:** Robert Frankel; Bonnie Parisella Frankel **MS:** Divorced **SPN:** Jason Hoppy (03/28/2010, Divorced 07/2016); Peter Sussman (10/07/1996, Divorced 1997) **CH:** Bryn Casey **ED:** Coursework, Boston University; Coursework, New York University; Coursework, Natural Gourmet Institute for Health and Culinary Arts **C:** Founder, Skinnygirl Brand (2009); Founder, BethennyBakes **CR:** Spokesperson, Pepperidge Farm Baked Naturals and Deli Flats; Founder, Skinnygirl Margarita **CIV:** Model, PETA (2009); Founder, BStrong **CW:** Guest Appearance, "Shark Tank" (2017-2019); Actress, "The Real Housewives of New York City" (2008-2010, 2015-2019); Guest Appearance, "Bar Rescue" (2018); Guest Appearance, "The Real Housewives of Beverly Hills" (2016, 2018); Actress, "Bethenny & Fredrik" (2017); Guest Appearance, "Million Dollar Listing New York" (2017); Author, "I Suck at Relationships So You Don't Have To: 10 Rules for Not Screwing Up Your Happily Ever After" (2016); Guest Judge, "Beat Bobby Flay" (2016); Guest Appearance, "The Ellen DeGeneres Show" (2010-2015); Author, "Skinnygirl Cocktails: 100 Fabulous and Flirty Cocktail Recipes and Party Foods for Any Occasion, Without the Guilt" (2014); Author, "Cookie Meets Peanut" (2014); Author, "Skinnygirl Solutions: Simple Ideas, Extraordinary Results" (2014); Host, "Bethenny" (2013-2014); Guest Appearance, "The Neighbors" (2013); Author, "Skinnydipping: A Novel" (2012); Actress, "Bethenny Ever After" (2010-2012); Guest Appearance, "Chelsea Lately" (2010-2012); Author, "A Place of Yes: 10 Rules for Getting Everything You Want Out of Life" (2011); Contestant, "Skating with the Stars" (2010); Author, "Body by Bethenny: Body-Sculpting Workouts to Unleash Your SkinnyGirl" (2010); Author, "The Skinnygirl Dish: Easy Recipes for Your Naturally Thin Life" (2009); Guest Appearance, "Z Rock" (2009); Author, "Naturally Thin: Unleash Your SkinnyGirl and Free Yourself from a Lifetime of Dieting" (2009); Contestant, "The Apprentice: Martha Stewart" (2005); Actress, "Wish Me Luck" (1995); Actress, "Wish Me Luck" (1994); Actress, "Soiree Sans Hors D'oeuvres" (1993) **AW:** 100 Most Powerful Women in Entertainment, Hollywood Reporter (2011)

FRANKEL, LOIS JANE, T: U.S. Representative from Florida **I:** Government Administration/Government Relations/Government Services **DOB:** 05/16/1948 **PB:** New York **SC:** NY/USA **CH:** Benjamin **ED:** JD, Georgetown University Law Center (1973); BA, Boston University, Magna Cum Laude (1970) **C:** Member, U.S. House Committee on Transportation and Infrastructure (2013-Present; Member, U.S. House Committee on Foreign Affairs (2013-Present); Mayor, City of West Palm Beach, FL (2003-2011); Minority Leader, Florida House of Representatives (2000-2002); Member, District 85, Florida House of Representatives (1995-2003); Member, District 83, Florida House of Representatives, Tallahassee, FL (1987-1993); Partner, Searcy Denney, Scarola, Barnhart & Shipley (1978-1994); Assistant Public Defender, West Palm Beach, FL (1974-1978); Law Clerk to Honorable David Norman, DC Superior Court, Washington, DC (1973-1974) **CR:** Chair, AIDS Task Force (1986-1990) **CIV:** Founder, Domestic Assault Shelter; Director, Jewish Family and Children's Services, Palm Beach County, FL; Board of Directors, American Cancer Society, Inc., Palm Beach County, FL **AW:** Rookie of the Year Award, American Cancer Society, Inc. (1994); Award, American Heart Association, Inc. (1992); Political Courage Award, American Lung Association (1992); Leadership Award, Executive Women of the Palm Beaches Foundation, Inc. (1991); Commissioner's Award for Prevention of Child Abuse and Neglect, U.S. Department of Health and Human Services (1991); Award, Child Care Connection, Inc. (1990); Annual Legislator Award, Children's Forum, Inc., FL (1990); First Legislative Award, Florida Nursing Students Association (1990); Outstanding Legislator Award, Florida Federation of Business and Professional Women's Clubs, Inc. (BPW/FL) (1990); Outstanding Legislator Award, Academy of Florida Trial Lawyers (Now Florida Justice Association) (1990); Named Citizen of the Year, National Association of Social Workers (1989); Named Child Advocate of the Year (1989); Award, Children's Home Society of America (1989); Florida Brotherhood Award (1989); Weizmann Institute of Science Award (1989); Brotherhood Award, The Arc of Florida, Inc. (1989); Allen Morris Most Promising Freshman Award (1988); Up and Comers Government Award, South Florida Business Journal-Price Waterhouse (PwC) (1988); Nelson Poynter Civil Liberties Award (1988); Named Freshman Friend of Education, FTP-NEA (1987); Freshman Award, Academy of Florida Trial Lawyers (Now Florida Justice Association) (1987) **MEM:** Past President, Palm Beach County Chapter, Florida Association for Women Lawyers, Inc.; National Organization for Women; League of Women Voters; Florida Bar Association; Academy of Florida Trial Lawyers (Now Florida Justice Association); Florida Association for Women Lawyers, Inc.; Palm Beach County Bar Association; Jewish Federation of Palm Beach County; Executive Women of the Palm Beaches Foundation, Inc.; The Economic Council of Palm Beach County; Gold Coast Business and Professional Women's Group; American Cancer Society, Inc.; Jewish Family and Children's Services **AV:** Sports; Music **PA:** Democrat **RE:** Jewish

FRANKLIN, KIRK DEWAYNE, T: Singer **I:** Media & Entertainment **DOB:** 01/26/1970 **PB:** Fort Worth **SC:** TX/USA **MS:** Married **SPN:** Tammy Collins (1/20/1996) **CH:** Kerrion; Carrington; Kennedy; Caziah **ED:** Coursework, Oscar Dean Wyatt High School **C:** Choir Leader, Kirk Franklin & The Family (1992-Present); Choir Leader, God's Property; Choir Leader, Kirk Franklin's Nu Nation **CW:** Musician, "Ling Live Love" (2019); Musician, "Losing My Religion" (2015); Musician, "Hello Fear" (2011); Musician, "The Fight of My Life" (2007); Musician, "Hero" (2005); Musician, "The Rebirth of Kirk Franklin" (2002); Musician, "Kirk Franklin Presents 1NC" (2000); Musician, "The Nu Nation Project" (1998); Musician, "God's Property from Kirk Franklin's Nu Nation" (1997); Musician, "Whatcha Lookin' 4" (1996); Musician, "Kirk Franklin & the Family Christmas" (1995); Musician, "Kirk Franklin & The Family" (1993) **AW:** Best Gospel/Inspirational Award, Soul Train Awards (2019); Contemporary Gospel Recorded Song of the Year, "Love Theory," Dove Awards (2019); Best Gospel Performance/Song, "Never Alone," Grammy Awards (2019); Gospel Artist of the Year, Dove Awards (2019); Contemporary Gospel/Urban Recorded Song of the Year, "My World Needs You," Dove Awards (2017); Best Gospel Album, "Losing My Religion," Grammy Awards (2017); Best Gospel Performance/Song, "God Provides," Grammy Awards (2017); Contemporary Gospel/Urban Album of the Year, Dove Awards (2016); Gospel Artist of the Year, Dove Awards (2016); Best Gospel Performance/Song, "Wanna Be Happy?," Grammy Awards (2016); Traditional Gospel Recorded Song of the Year, "Take Me to the King," Dove Awards (2014); Song of the Year, "Take Me to the King," Stellar Awards (2014); Contemporary Gospel Recorded Song of the Year, "I Smile," Dove Awards (2012); Song of the Year, CD of the Year, "I Smile," Stellar Awards (2012); Contemporary Gospel Album of the Year, "Hello Fear," Dove Awards (2012); Best Gospel Album, Best Gospel Song, "Hello Fear," Grammy Awards (2012); Producer of the Year, Contemporary CD of the Year, "Hello Fear," Dove Awards (2012); Urban Album of the Year, "The Fight of My Life," Dove Awards (2009); Best Gospel Act, Urban Music Awards (2009); Best Contemporary R&B Gospel Album, "The Fight of My Life," Grammy Awards (2009); Best Gospel Song, "Help Me Believe," Grammy Awards (2009); Urban/ Inspirational Single / Performance of the Year, "Declaration: (This is It)," Stellar Awards (2008); Urban Recorded Song of the Year, "Imagine Me," Dove Awards (2007); Best Contemporary R&B Gospel Album, "Hero," Grammy Awards (2007); CD of the Year, "Hero," Stellar Awards (2007); Best Gospel Song, "Imagine Me," Grammy Awards (2007); Urban Gospel Album of the Year, "Hero," Dove Awards (2006); Favorite Contemporary Inspirational Artist, American Music Awards (2006); Urban Song of the Year, "Looking for You," Dove Awards (2006); Contemporary Gospel Album of the Year, "The Rebirth of Kirk Franklin," Dove Awards (2003); Artist of the Year, Producer of the Year, CD of the Year, "The Rebirth of Kirk Franklin," Stellar Awards (2003); Song of the Year, Music Video of the Year, "Hosanna," Stellar Awards (2003); Urban Recorded Song of the Year, "Thank You," Dove Awards (2002); Urban/Inspirational Performance of the Year, Rap/Hip Hop Gospel CD of the Year, "Kingdom Come," Stellar Awards (2002); Urban Gospel Album of the Year, "Kirk Franklin Present 1NC," Dove Awards (2001); Urban Song of the Year, "Revolution," Dove Awards (2000); Artist of the Year, Song of the Year and Music Video of the Year for "Lean on Me," Producer of the Year, CD of the Year, Contemporary CD of the Year, Contemporary Choir of the Year and Rap Hip-Hop Gospel CD of the Year for "The Nu Nation Project," Stellar Awards (2000); Urban/Inspirational Performance of the Year, "Thank You," Stellar Awards (2000); Best Contemporary Soul Gospel Album, "The Nu Nation Project," Grammy Awards (1999); Urban Album of the Year, "God's Property," Dove Awards (1998); Urban Song of the Year, "Stomp," Dove Awards (1998); Best Gospel Choir or Chorus Album, "God's Property," Grammy Awards (1998); Best Contemporary Soul Gospel Album, "Whatcha Lookin' 4," Grammy Awards (1997); Contemporary Gospel Album of the Year, "Whatcha Lookin' 4," Dove Awards (1996); Traditional Gospel Album of the Year, "Kirk Franklin and the Family," Dove Awards (1993); Traditional Gospel Song of the Year, "Why We Sang," Dove Awards (1993)

FRANKS, DONALD, LLC, T: Owner **I:** Business Management/Business Services **CN:** New Focus Consulting LLC **MS:** Married **SPN:** Eva (32 years) **CH:** Three Children **ED:** MS in Business Management, Human Resources, Excelsior College, Albany, NY (2016); BS in Business Administration & Management, Minor in Information Systems, Excelsior College, Albany, NY (2013) **C:** Owner, New Focus Consulting LLC; Former Training Liaison, Northrop Grumman, VA (2018-Present); Counselor, Zeiders LLC, VA (2016-2018); Comcast (2014-2018); General Dynamics (2011-2014); L3 Communications (2010-2011) **MIL:** With, United States Military (1984-2010) **AS:** Mr. Franks attributes his success to his parents. Their example of knowing the difference between what is morally right and wrong has exemplified how to handle various situations to Mr. Franks. He believes in showing leadership by example. **B/I:** Since childhood, Mr. Franks always wanted to make life better. He learned that if one is not part of the solution, they are part of the problem. He uses his life experiences to help inspire others and show them that they can step up and make a difference. **THT:** Mr. Franks wants to work on, "developing people to not only look up for help but to look into themselves and others to become better than they were yesterday."

FRANZESE, CHRIS J., PHARMD, T: Principal & Clinical Leader **I:** Pharmaceuticals **CN:** Matchstick LLC **ED:** PharmD, Fairleigh Dickinson University (2018); MHS, Fairleigh Dickinson University (2018); BS in Biology, Loyola University (2012); Coursework, Monash University, Melbourne, Australia (2010) **CT:** Advanced Cardiac Life Support; Basic Life Support for Healthcare Providers; Pediatric Advanced Life Support; Registered Pharmacist, State of New Jersey; Six Sigma Green Belt Certified; Pharmacy-Based Immunization Delivery; Pharmacist & Patient-Centered Diabetes Care; Delivering Medication Therapy Management Services **C:** PGY1 Pharmacy Resident, Atlantic Health System (2019-Present); Principal & Clinical leader, Matchstick LLC (2018-Present); Advanced Pharmacy Practice Extern, Project Informatics, Atlantic Health System (2018); Advanced Pharmacy Practice Extern: Operational Informatics, Atlantic Health System (2018); Lead Clinical Analyst, Matchstick LLC (2015-2018); Advanced Pharmacy Practice Extern, Community Pharmacy, Walgreens (2017); Advanced Pharmacy Practice Extern, Institutional Pharmacy, Capital Health (2017); Advanced Pharmacy Practice Extern, Acute Care/Neurointensive Care, Capital Health (2017); Advanced Pharmacy Practice Extern, Transitions of Care, Capital Health (2017); Clinical Analyst, Matchstick LLC (2014-2015); Clinical Research

Associate, LifeBridge Health (2012-2014) **MEM:** Rho Chi Society; Industry Pharmacists Organization (IPhO); American Society of Health-System Pharmacists (ASHP); American Pharmacists Association (APhA); New Jersey Pharmacists Association (NJPhA) **AS:** Dr. Franzese attributes his success to being open to learning and tenacious. He always strives to be better at his craft. **B/I:** Dr. Franzese always had an interest in science. Unfortunately, his father passed at a young age due to a cerebral aneurysm. This event, in particular, inspired Dr. Franzese to pursue a medical path. His first exposure to research was when he volunteered at a lab in Baltimore, Maryland, where he saw patients streamline their therapies as a result of the diagnostics performed in his lab. He went to pharmacy school with the intent to apply science to impact patients on a global scale. Upon starting pharmacy school, Dr. Franzese was offered a unique opportunity at Matchstick (his current company) to place clinicians at the forefront of device development. He has since dedicated his career to this venture. **THT:** Dr. Franzese's motto is, "There is nothing too complicated for anyone to learn."

FRAZIER, ANTHANY V.E., T: Founder, President **I:** Consulting **CN:** AVEF Volunteer Management Consultants & Trainers, The STOPGAP Ministry **DOB:** 05/16/1951 **PB:** Chicago **SC:** IL/USA **PT:** Sidney Louis Frazier; Roxie Marie Frazier **MS:** Married **SPN:** Ruth Mary Fairfax Frazier (01/12/1970) **CH:** Annika Shielmara Frazier Muhammad; Darrius Rafi Frazier; Ajani Zameer Asad Osuntaka Frazier (Grandchild); Beatriz Ruth Bibiana C. Frazier-Iyah (Grandchild); Hamza Ibn Omar Frazier Muhammad (Grandchild); Nala Annabelle Graham Muhammad (Grandchild); Yahzariyah Eva C. Frazier-Iyah (Grandchild) **ED:** Completed and/or Directed More Than 200 Professional Business Development Programs sponsored by the Executive, Legislative, and Judicial Branches of the United States Government (1982-2017); Graduate Business Executive Fellow, Chicago Upward Bound (CUB) Program, Chicago Region V, Social Security Administration (SSA) (2005); Certificate of Completion, Addictions Studies, Harold Washington College, University of Illinois, Chicago Hospital and Health Sciences System, Department of Psychiatry, Division of Addictive Behaviors, Chicago, IL (2002); Certificate of Completion, Managing Technical Professionals and Organizations, Sloan School of Management, Massachusetts Institute of Technology, Cambridge, MA (1997); Certificate of Completion, Law Program for Community Developers and Social Workers, John Marshall Law School, Chicago, IL (1996); Certificate of Completion, Minority Business Executive Program, Amos Tuck School of Business Administration, Dartmouth College, Hanover, NH (1992); MA in Behavioral Sciences, Governors State University (GSU), University Park, IL (1992); Certificate of Completion, International Trade Executive Program, University of Illinois, Illinois World Trade Center, Chicago, Illinois (1991); Certificate of Completion, International Marketing Program, Kellstadt Center for Commerce, DePaul University, Chicago, IL (1991); Certificates of Completion, Graduate and Advanced Legislative Institutes for Staff Members of the United States Congress, Congressional Research Service (CRS), Library of Congress, Washington, D.C. and Richmond, Virginia (1990); BA in Behavioral Sciences, Chicago State University (CSU), Chicago, IL (1977) **CT:** Certified Access User & Cable Television Producer, Expert in Field Editing, In-Studio, NLE Edit, Portable Hand, PVOM, Chicago Access Network Television (CAN-TV), Chicago, IL; Emeritus, Social Media Content Developer, YouTube eMarketing Innovator & Brand Man-

agement Business Executive, Broadcast Journalist Emeritus, Social Security Administration (SSA), Chicago Access Network Television (CAN-TV), Chicago, IL; Authorized Homeland Security Presidential Directive 12 (HSPD–12) certified sponsor and issuer of the PIV smartcard credentials and trainer for registered Virtual Private Network (VPN) users, Social Security Administration (SSA); Professional Educator, Diversity Trainer, Expert in the Field of Aging; Illinois Driver's License, 15 Driver Safety Awards, Illinois Secretary of State **C:** Vice Chairman, Member, Illinois Council on Aging, Illinois Department on Aging (IDoA) (2000-Present); Founder & President, AVEF Volunteer Management Consultants and Trainers & The STOPGAP Ministry (1992-Present); Adjunct Community Professor, Motivational Speaker, and Guest Lecturer at the University of Oxford, England, UK, Roosevelt University, Oakton Community College, and Chicago Public Schools (CPS) (1982-Present); Public Broadcast Team Leader, Area VII Chicago Metro Speakers Bureau Cadre Leader/Member, Emeritus, Social Security Administration (1993-2017); Area VII Systems Coordinator (ASC), Chicago Metro, Provided SSA Employee Automation/Software Training and Performed Complex, Hardware System Support Services for the Busiest, Largest, and Most Culturally Diverse SSA Field Offices (FO) within the Chicago Metropolitan Area, Social Security Administration (SSA) (2007-2012); Federal Grants and Contracts Manager, Legislative/Staff Assistant, Administrator and Congressional Liaison for the Aging, Housing, Small Business, Economic Development Task Forces, and Print Media Outlets Coordinator/Op-ed Writer, The Honorable Congressman Charles Arthur Hayes (D-IL), U.S. House of Representatives, Washington DC, Chicago, IL, and the Former Vice-President of the United Food and Commercial Workers International Union (UFCW) (1981-1993); Legislative/Staff Assistant, Administrator and Congressional Liaison for the Aging, Economic Development, Housing, Community Development, Technology Transfer/Commercialization Task Forces, The Honorable U.S. Senator Alan John Dixon (D-IL), U.S. Senate, Washington, DC, Chicago, IL, and the Former Chairman of the U.S. Defense Base Realignment and Closure Commission (1982-1987) **CR:** Entertainer, Mental Health Wellness Counselor, Life Coach, Motivational Speaker, Community Organizer, Multi-Instrumentalist, Musician, Novelist, Spiritual Consultant, Social Media Content Developer & Brand Executive Manager, and Writer, A.V.E.F. Management Consultants and Trainers & The STOPGAP Ministry (1992 – Present); Cable TV Host and Public Television Broadcast Producer, Emeritus, Chicago Access Network Television (CAN-TV), SSA YouTube Videos, Social Security Administration (SSA) (2004-2017); International Diplomat, Presenter, Participant, 2nd Annual University of Oxford International Health & Homelessness Conference, England, UK (2006); Co–Author, Six-State Regional, SSA "Communications Strategic Plan, and Deputy Commissioner of Operation (DCO) Operating Plan," and served as a SSA regional public affairs expert for the Medicare Modernization Act (MMA) legislation, which created the Medicare Part D prescription drug coverage programs, Chicago Region V, Social Security Administration (SSA) (2006); Worked as a SSA Regional Public Affairs Spokesman During the Implementation of Executive Order (EO) 13123, and the Installation of the Mega-Million Dollar, 110-kilowatt, Rooftop Solar Photovoltaic (PV) System at Chicago's Harold Washington Social Security Center (HWSSC) (2006); Chairman Emeritus, Aging, Technology Transfer, Research And Development, Physically Disabled Subcommittee, The Minority Business Resource Advisory Com-

mittee (MBRAC), Creator and Designer, Unisex Clothing Attire and Commemorative Patches and Space Flight Emblems National Aeronautics & Space Administration (NASA) (1992-1996); Co-Chairman Emeritus, Economic Development Specialist, Economic Development Subcommittee (EDS), The Chicago Community Development Advisory Committee (CDAC) (1987-1993) **CIV:** Judge, Illinois Department on Aging (IDoA), Senior Illinoisans Hall of Fame (2010-2019); Aging Specialist, Guest Lecturer, Workshop Convener, Illinois Governors Annual Conference on Aging and Human Services (2002-2011); Guest Lecturer and Honoree Annual Principal For The Day Ceremonial Program, Chicago Board Of Education, Chicago Public Schools (2004-2010) **CW:** Composer, Presenter, Original Commemorative Resolution to Honor the Legacy of Joan Diane Adams-Alsberry, Former Member, Illinois Council on Aging (ICoA), Illinois Department on Aging (IDoA) (2019); Co-Author, Team Leader, Created First Online Virtualized, "ICoA Orientation Manual and Internet Resource Portal," Illinois Council on Aging (ICoA), Illinois Department on Aging (2018); Sponsor, Talent Coordinator, Convener of Free Inter-Generational Music Concerts, and Mental Health Wellness Forums, Social Security Administration (SSA) (1993-2017); Original Music Performer, Theatrical Stage Actor, Combined Federal Campaign (CFC) Celebratory Kickoff Events, Social Security Administration (SSA), The Office of Personnel Management (2007); Composer, Registered Original Music Composition, "Sista Rosa Louise Parks: Girlfriend Your Life Efforts Have Not Been In Vain" (1994); Designer, Constructor, Art Exhibition Display to Commemorate the Rich Historical Tradition of the African-American Involvement in the Chicago Labor Trade Unions Movement, Consulting with the American Federation of State, County and Municipal Employees (AFSCME), Chicago History Museum; Coalition of Black Trade Unionist (CBTU), DuSable Museum of African American History; Museum of Science and Industry (MSI); The Smithsonian Institution, and the United Food and Commercial Workers International Union (UCFW) (1987–1993); Contributor, "Tribute To Chicago Blues Patriarch Willie James Dixon and Chess Records" Published in the Congressional Record of the 102nd Congress, Second Session by The Honorable Congressman Charles Arthur Hayes (D-IL), U.S. House of Representatives (1992) **AW:** Alfred Nelson Marquis Lifetime Achievement Award, Marquis Who's Who (2020); 30-Year Certificate of Appreciation, "Distinguished Public Service and Loyalty to the United States Government," Social Security Administration (SSA), Baltimore, Maryland and Chicago, Illinois (2017); Certificate of Recognition for "Exceptional Contributions to Federal Service," Chicago Federal Executive Board, Social Security Administration (SSA), Chicago, Illinois (2014); Certificate of "Appreciation and Recognition," The Recording Academy, The Grammy Awards, Chicago, Illinois (2010); Letter of Appreciation, Parkside Academy, Chicago, Illinois (2010) **AV:** Designing exteriors and men's fashion clothing; Environmentalist; Fishing; Filmmaking; Gardening; Historian; Motivational speaking; Musical entertainment and composition; Team sports; Volunteering; Writing **PA:** Democrat **RE:** Baptist

FRAZIER, KENNETH CARELTON, T: Chairman, President, Chief Executive Officer **I:** Business Management/Business Services **CN:** Merck & Co., Inc. **DOB:** 12/17/1954 **PB:** Philadelphia **SC:** PA/USA **PT:** Otis Frazier **MS:** Married **SPN:** Andrea Frazier **CH:** Two Children **ED:** JD, Harvard Law School (1978); BA in Political Science, The Pennsylvania State University (1975) **C:** Chairman, President, Chief Executive Officer, Merck & Co., Inc. (Formerly

Schering-Plough Corp.), Whitehouse Station, NJ (2011-Present); President, Merck & Co., Inc. (Formerly Schering-Plough Corp.), Whitehouse Station, NJ (2010-Present); Executive Vice President, President, Global Human Health, Merck & Co., Inc. (Formerly Schering-Plough Corp.), Whitehouse Station, NJ (2007-2010); Executive Vice President, General Counsel, Merck & Co., Inc. (Formerly Schering-Plough Corp.), Whitehouse Station, NJ (2006-2007); Senior Vice President, General Counsel, Merck & Co., Inc. (Formerly Schering-Plough Corp.), Whitehouse Station, NJ (1999-2006); Vice President, Deputy General Counsel, Merck & Co., Inc. (Formerly Schering-Plough Corp.), Whitehouse Station, NJ (1999); Vice President of Public Affairs, Assistant General Counsel, Merck & Co., Inc. (Formerly Schering-Plough Corp.), Whitehouse Station, NJ (1997-1998); Vice President, Public Affairs, Merck & Co., Inc. (Formerly Schering-Plough Corp.), Whitehouse Station, NJ (1994-1996); Vice President, General Counsel, Secretary, Astra Merck (1992-1994); Partner, Department of Litigation, Drinker Biddle & Reath LLP (1978-1992) **CIV:** Board of Directors, Merck & Co., Inc. (2011-Present); Board of Directors, Exxon Mobil Corporation (2009-Present); CLO Roundtable-U.S.; Corporate Executive Board's General Counsel, Roundtable; Advisory Board, CorporateProBono. Org; Advisory Board, Rand Institute for Civil Justice; Advisory Board, Health Law and Policy Center, Seton Hall University; Advisory Board, Law and Economic Center, University of Pennsylvania; Chairman, Ethics Resource Center; Board of Directors, Legal Services of New Jersey; Board of Directors, Cornerstone Christian Academy; Board of Directors, The Pennsylvania State University **MEM:** American Bar Association; The American Law Institute; Pennsylvania Bar Association; Council on Foreign Relations; American Philosophical Society; The Business Council; American Academy of Arts & Sciences **BAR:** Supreme Court of the United States (2002); United States Court for the Eastern District of Pennsylvania (1978); Pennsylvania (1978)

FREDERICK, JAMES PAUL, T: Chemical Engineer **I:** Engineering **DOB:** 07/22/1943 **PB:** Billings **SC:** MT/USA **PT:** John William Frederick; Alice Murtle (Avery) Frederick **MS:** Married **SPN:** Beverly Ann Halliday Walker Grimmett (09/01/2001); Karen Ann Roth (08/03/1962, Divorced 03/01/2001) **CH:** Rand John Frederick; Johnathan Uriel Halliday; Ardith Jean Frederick Flight; Rodney Rydell Walker; Muriel Denise Walker Jones; Myia Charnett Walker (Deceased); Sharis Renee Walker; Carmen Elaine Grimmett Smith **ED:** BSChemE, Montana State University (1968) **CT:** Registered Professional Engineer, States of Wyoming, Colorado, Ohio, Montana and Texas **C:** Retired (2018); Self-Employed Technical Consultant (2007-2018); General Manager, Partner, Maumee Research & Engineering, Perrysburg, OH (2002-2007); General Manager, SGI International (1998-2002); Technical Manager, Zeigler Coal Company (1992-1998); Project Manager, Shell Mining Company (1977-1992); Chemical Engineer, Shell Oil Company (1968-1977) **CIV:** Antelope Valley Homeowners Association; AARP **CW:** Contributor, Articles, Professional Journals; Designer, Operator, ENCOAL Clean Coal Demonstration Partnership, U.S. Department of Energy; Patentee in Field **MEM:** Rocky Mountain Elk Foundation; Train Collectors Association; Lionel Collectors Club of America **MH:** Albert Nelson Marquis Lifetime Achievement Award **B/I:** Mr. Frederick became involved in his profession because of an English project he did in high school. He had to write a paper on what he wanted to be and due to his scientific prowess and innate curiosity, he wrote about wanting to be an engineer. **AV:** Playing handball; Collecting model trains; Listening to music; Hunting; Fishing

FREDERICKS, MARGARET, T: Physician, Surgeon **I:** Medicine & Health Care **MS:** Single **ED:** PhD, Johns Hopkins University; BSc with Honors, University WisconsinRoyal College of Surgery, EnglandRoyal College of Physicians, England **CW:** Contributor, Articles, Professional Journals **AW:** Best Dermatologist, Imperial Valley Press (2019); Top Dermatologists, Top Doctors Awards, (2019); Best Doctor Award, Indian Wells, CA (2018, 2019); University Scholar, McGill University; Sir Edmund Henry Botterel Prize for Best Woman Freshmen, Royal Victoria College, McGill University; Sigma Epsilon Sigma; Mortar Board, Phi Kappa Phi, University of Wisconsin-Madison; Deans Scholarship, Johns Hopkins University School of Medicine; Richard Ellis Prize in Pediatrics; Charles Oldham Prize in Ophthalmology; Deans Fellowship, Stanford University; Excellence Award in Cosmetic Surgery, American Academy of Cosmetic Surgery **MEM:** American Med Association; Johns Hopkins Medical and Surgical Association; American Academy of Cosmetic Surgery; American Association of Physician Specialists; Royal College of Surgeons; Royal College of Physicians **MH:** Who's Who in America (2007-2015, 2019)

FREE, KENNETH A., T: Athletic Conference Commissioner **I:** Athletics **DOB:** 06/08/1936 **PB:** Greensboro **SC:** NC/USA **PT:** Lee W. Free; Margaret (McMurray) Free **CH:** Delana (Deceased); Kenneth Jr.; Benjamin **ED:** BS, North Carolina A&T State University (1970) **C:** Commissioner, Mid-Eastern Athletic Conference MEAC, Greensboro, NC (1978-Present); Consultant, Parks and Recreation, North Carolina Department of Resources, Fayetteville, NC (1970-1978); Administrator, Recreation Center, Greensboro Parks and Recreation (1968-1969); Professional Baseball Player, Central Motor Lines, Greensboro, NC (1964-1967); Professional Baseball Player, New York Mets (1960-1964); Professional Baseball Player, Hickory Negro Baseball League (1960); Professional Baseball Player, Detroit Stars, Kansas City Negro Baseball League (1959) **CR:** NCAA Pro Sports Liason (1993); NCAA Executive Committee, Overland Park, KS (1992); NCAA Men's Basketball Committee, Overland Park, KS (1987-1992); Board of Directors, NCAA Honda Award, Overland Park, KS; NCAA Postgraduate Scholarship Committee, NASC **CIV:** Board of Directors, North Carolina Parks and Recreation Foundation; Guilford County AIDS Task Force Member; Citizens' Advisory Committee, Greensboro Bats; Greensboro Sports Commission; Greensboro Sports Council; Trustee, Planning Committee, Greensboro Coliseum; Member, Chancellor, Choir, United Methodist Church **MIL:** With, United States Army (1955-1958) **AW:** Named to National All-star Team, Negro Baseball League (1959); Named to CIAA Basketball and Football Officials Hall of Fame; Named to North Carolina A&T Sports Hall of Fame; Recipient, The Order of the Long Leaf Pine Society, NC; Recipient, Key to the City of Garner, NC **MEM:** Fellow, North Carolina Recreation & Parks Association; Collegiate Commissioners Association; National Basketball and Football Coaches Association; Executive Committee, National Association of Collegiate Directors of Athletics; University Commissioners Association; Masons; Kappa Alpha Psi Fraternity, Inc. **MH:** Albert Nelson Marquis Lifetime Achievement Award **B/I:** Growing up in what Mr. Free describes as "the hood" in Pennsylvania, then moving to North Carolina, there were so many people volunteering to help the youth, he felt compelled to do the same. His father instructed him to go back to college, because he had stopped to play professional baseball. His father told him in order to be in a position to help someone, he needed to be educated to do so. Following his father's advice, he went back to school and volunteered much of his time to coaching and mentoring the youth. The work he was doing brought him a great amount of joy. While working for the parks and recreation center, Mr. Free was eventually promoted to community center director. Eventually the state opened up a regional office to administer outdoor recreation funding for cities and towns. A job for commissioner of the Mid-Eastern Athletic Conference became available and he felt that he could help student athletes by creating programs for the conference that would encourage professional teams to look at their athletes. The first conference game he spearheaded was the Freedom Bowl. His first Freedom Bowl was a certified NCAA all-star game where seven of his athletes were recruited to try out in NFL camps. Four out of the seven made it to the NFL. One of the men that helped him organize the first game is currently the commissioner of the NFL, Roger Goodell. **AV:** Football; Basketball official (15 years)

FREEL, STEVEN, T: President, Chief Executive Officer **I:** Business Management/Business Services **CN:** Studsvik Scandpower **ED:** MBA in Business Strategy, University of Maryland, Robert H. Smith School of Business (2007); BS in Mechanical Engineering, Pennsylvania State University (1987) **CT:** SCRUM Master **C:** President, Chief Executive Officer, Studsvik Scandpower (2016-Present); President, Freelance Performance (2015-2016); Chief Operating Officer, GSE Systems (2012-2014); Chief Technology Officer, GSE Systems (2011-2014); Director, Business Development, GSE Systems (2006-2010); Director, Ontology Works (2004-2006); Manager, Solution Collaboration Center, Raytheon (2002-2005); Project Manager, SAIC (1996-1999); Engineering Manager, Product Manager, Developer, Systems Engineer, GSE Systems (1988-1996) **CIV:** Co-Owner, Area 405 (2002-Present); Volunteer, Station North Tool Library (2014) **MEM:** American Nuclear Society; ASME **AS:** Mr. Freel attributes his success to hard work, and thinking outside of the box. The ability to innovative. **B/I:** Mr. Freel was born an engineer. He started out in engineering at the university and came into software as he worked in engineering.

FREEMAN, MORGAN, T: Actor, Narrator **I:** Media & Entertainment **DOB:** 6/1/1937 **PB:** Memphis **SC:** TN/USA **PT:** Morgan Porterfield Freeman; Mayme Edna (Revere) Freeman **MS:** Divorced **SPN:** Myrna Colley-Lee (1984, Divorced 2010); Jeanette Adair Bradshaw (1967, Divorced 1979) **CH:** Alphonso; Saifoulaye; Deena; Morgana **ED:** Coursework, Los Angeles City College **MIL:** Automatic Tracking Radar Repairman to Airman First Class, United States Air Force (1955-1959) **CW:** Actor, "The Nutcracker and the Four Realms" (2018); Actor, "Going in Style" (2017); Actor, "Just Getting Started" (2017); Actor, "London Has Fallen" (2016); Actor, "Going in Style" (2016); Actor, "Now You See Me 2" (2016); Actor, "Ben-Hur" (2016); Actor, "Madam Secretary" (2014-2016); Actor, "Last Knights" (2015); Actor, "Ted 2" (2015); Actor, "Momentum" (2015); Executive Producer, "Through the Wormhole" (2010-2015); Narrator, "We the People" (2014); Voice Actor, "The Lego Movie" (2014); Actor, "Life Itself" (2014); Actor, "5 Flights Up" (2014); Actor, "Transcendence" (2014); Actor, "Lucy" (2014); Actor, "Dolphin Tale 2" (2014); Narrator, "Island of Lemurs: Madagascar" (2014); Actor, "Olympus Has Fallen" (2013); Actor, "Oblivion" (2013); Narrator, "JFK: A President Betrayed" (2013); Actor, "Now You See Me" (2013); Actor, "Last Vegas" (2013); Actor, "The Magic of Belle Isle" (2012); Actor, "The

Dark Knight Rises" (2012); Actor, "We the People" (2012); Narrator, "Born to Be Wild" (2011); Actor, "Dolphin Tale" (2011); Actor, "Red" (2010); Appearance, "Saturday Night Live" (2010); Actor, "Invictus" (2009); Actor, Producer, "The Maiden Heist" (2009); Actor, "The Country Girl" (2008); Actor, "Wanted" (2008); Actor, "The Dark Knight" (2008); Actor, "Smithsonian Channel's Sound Revolution" (2008); Actor, "Stephen Fry in America" (2008); Actor, "Gone Baby Gone" (2007); Actor, "The Bucket List" (2007); Actor, "Lucky Number Slevin" (2006); Actor, "10 Items or Less" (2006); Actor, "Unleashed" (2005); Voice Actor, "Batman Begins" (2005); Narrator, "War of the Worlds" (2005); Narrator, "March of the Penguins" (2005); Actor, "An Unfinished Life" (2005); Actor, "Edison" (2005); Voice Actor, "Slavery and the Making of America" (2005); Actor, "The Big Bounce" (2004); Actor, "Million Dollar Baby" (2004); Actor, "Dreamcatcher" (2003); Actor, "Bruce Almighty" (2003); Actor, "Levity" (2003); Actor, "High Crimes" (2002); Actor, "The Sum of All Fears" (2002); Actor, "Along Came a Spider" (2001); Actor, "Nurse Betty" (2000); Actor, Executive Producer, "Under Suspicion" (2000); Actor, "Water Damage" (1999); Actor, "Mutiny" (1999); Actor, "Mutiny" (1999); Actor, "Hard Rain" (1998); Actor, "Deep Impact" (1997); Actor, "Kiss the Girls" (1997); Actor, "Chain Reaction" (1996); Actor, "The Long Way Home" (1996); Actor, "Moll Flanders" (1996); Actor, "Outbreak" (1995); Actor, "Seven" (1995); Actor, "The Shawshank Redemption" (1994); Director, "Bopha!" (1993); Actor, "Unforgiven" (1992); Actor, "Robin Hood: Prince of Thieves" (1991); Actor, "The Bonfire of the Vanities" (1990); Actor, "Lean on Me" (1989); Actor, "Johnny Handsome" (1989); Actor, "Driving Miss Daisy" (1989); Actor, "Glory" (1989); Actor, "The Gospel at Colonus" (1988); Actor, "Clinton and Nadine" (1988); Actor, "Clean and Sober" (1988); Actor, "Street Smart" (1987); Actor, "Flight for Life," (1987); Actor, "Resting Place" (1986); Actor, "The Atlanta Child Murders" (1985); Actor, "Teachers" (1984); Actor, "Medea and the Doll" (1984); Actor, "Harry and Son" (1983); Actor, "Buck" (1983); Actor, "Othello," Dallas Shakespeare Festival (1982); Actor, "All's Well That Ends Well," Dallas Shakespeare Festival (1982); Actor, "The Marva Collins Story" (1981); Actor, "Mother Courage and Her Children" (1980); Actor, "Attica" (1980); Actor, "Brubaker" (1980); Actor, "Eyewitness" (1980); Actor, "Coriolanus," New York Shakespeare Festival (1979); Actor, "Hollow Image" (1979); Actor, "Julius," New York Shakespeare Festival (1979); Actor, "Mighty Gents" (1978); Actor, "White Pelicans" (1978); Actor, "Cockfight" (1977); Actor, "Sisyphus and the Blue-Eyed Cyclops" (1975); Actor, "The Electric Company" (1971-1977); Actor, "Black Visions" (1972); Actor, "Who Says I Can't Ride a Rainbow" (1971); Actor, "Purlie," American National Theatre and Academy Theatre, New York, NY (1970); Actor, "Jungle of Cities" (1969); Actor, "The Recruiting Officer" (1969); Actor, "Scuba-Duba" (1969); Actor, Debut, "Niggerlover" (1967); Actor, "Hello Dolly" (1967) AW: Named, Favorite Movie Icon, People's Choice Awards (2012); Cecil B. DeMille Award, Hollywood Foreign Press Association (2012); Life Achievement Award, American Film Institute (2011); Career Achievement Award, Palm Springs International Film Festival (2010); National Board of Review Award for Best Actor (2009); African-American Film Critics Association Award for Best Actor (2009); Kennedy Center Honors, John F. Kennedy Center for the Performing Arts (2008); Spencer Tracy Award, University of California Los Angeles (2006); Screen Actors Guild Award for Outstanding Performance by a Male Actor in Supporting Role (2005); Academy Award for Best Supporting Actor, Academy of Motion Picture Arts and Sciences (2005); Golden Globe Award for Best Performance by an Actor in a Motion Picture-Drama, Hollywood Foreign Press Association (1990); Obie Award (1988); Clarence Derwent Award (1978); Drama Desk Award (1978)

FREY, JOHN WARD, T: Landscape Architect (Retired) **I:** Architecture & Construction **PT:** Philip Rockel Frey; Sarah Helen (Dempwolf) Frey **SPN:** Wilma Emma Weggel (02/11/1961) **CH:** Holly Frances; Allison Margaret; Frederika Elizabeth; Marietta Isabel **ED:** Master's Degree in Landscape Architecture, Harvard University (1955); Bachelor of Arts in Mathematics, College of Wooster (1952) **C:** Partner, Mason and Frey, Landscape Architects (1963-2004); Associate, Designer, Sasaki Associates Inc. (1957-1962); Urban Designer, The Architects Collaborative (1955) **CR:** Registered Landscape Architect, New York, Connecticut, Massachusetts **CIV:** Member, Lexington Minuteman Commuter Bikeway Committee (1993-1995); Member, Massachusetts Recreational Trails Advisory Committee (1993); Member, Lexington Tree Committee (1990); Chairperson, Design Advisory Committee, Lexington, MA (1988); Member, Revere Beach Design Review Board (1976-1978); Member, Advisory Committee to Planning Board, Lexington Design (1973-1976) **MIL:** U.S. Army, 18th Engineer Brigade, Fort Leonard Wood, MO **CW:** Principal Architect, Southwest Corridor Park, Section III, Jamaica Plain, Boston, MA (1988); Principal Architect, Arlington Bicentennial Park, Massachusetts (1975); Principal Architect, Burlington High School, MA (1968-1974); Principal Architect, Murray Hill, Manchester (1973); Principal Architect, Sandoz Pharmaceutical, East Hanover, NJ (1964, 1973); Principal Architect, Wellesley College Science Center (1973); Principal Architect, State University College, Geneseo, NY (1963-1973); Principal Architect, State University Agricultural and Technical College, Farmingdale, New York (1963-1971); Principal Architect, Fulton Montgomery C.C., Johnstown, NY (1967-1970); Principal Architect, Polaroid Corp., Waltham, MA (1970); Principal Architect, Lexington Center Mall (1967) **AW:** Presidential Design Award, Federal Design Achievement Award, National Education Association (1988); Merit Award, American Society of Landscape Architects (1973); Award, Boston Society of Architects (1973); "A" Citation, Massachusetts Audubon Society (1968); Industrial Plant Beautification Award, Governors Conference on Natural Beauty (1967) **MEM:** Trustee, Boston Chapter, American Society of Landscape Architects (1980-1983); Member, Examining Board, Boston Society of Landscape Architects (1971-1975); Member, Public Service Committee, Boston Society of Landscape Architects (1963-1971); Treasurer, Boston Society of Landscape Architects (1966-1967); Program Committee, Boston Society of Landscape Architects (1966-1967); Member, Committee on Landscape Architectural Registration in Massachusetts, Boston Society of Landscape Architects (1966-1967); Charles River Watershed Association; Appalachian Mountain Club; Appalachian Trail Conference; The Nature Conservancy; Massachusetts Audubon Society; Rails to Trails Conservancy **MH:** Albert Nelson Marquis Lifetime Achievement Award **B/I:** Mr. Frey became involved in his profession out of a childhood love for gardening, which evolved into a passion for landscaping and architecture. **AV:** Gardening; Bicycling; Canoeing; Jogging **PA:** Democrat

FREY, SHERWOOD CHARLES JR., T: Professor Emeritus **I:** Education/Educational Services **CN:** University of Virginia **DOB:** 11/07/1942 **PB:** Washington **SC:** DC/USA **PT:** Sherwood Charles Frey; Mary (Mazy) Goss Frey **MS:** Married **SPN:** Jill Ann Wohlrabe (2017); Marietta Kirkup (10/11/1969, Deceased 2013) **CH:** Christopher Eldon; Matthew Joseph; Katie Marie; Elizabeth Jean **ED:** Doctor of Philosophy, Johns Hopkins University (1969); Master of Science in Engineering Science, University of California Berkeley (1965); Bachelor of Arts in Mathematics, University of California Berkeley (1964) **C:** Emeritus Ethyl Corporation Professor of Business Administration, Darden School, University of Virginia (2010-Present); Ethyl Corporation Professor of Business Administration, Darden School, University of Virginia (1979-2010); Visiting Professor, Ivey Business School, London, ON, Canada (1998-1999); Associate Professor of Business Administration, Harvard Business School (1970-1979); Consultant, Kappa Systems, Rosslyn, VA (1968-1970); Faculty, International Teachers Program, Versailles, France (1963-1986) **CR:** Sherwood C. Frey, Jr. & Associates, Charlottesville, VA (1979-2019) **CW:** Author, "Quantitative Business Analysis - Text and Cases"; Author, "Quantitative Business Analysis Casebook"; Author, "Quantitative Methods in Management"; Contributor, Management Science, Operations Research, Author, Over 100 Business Cases and Technical Notes **AW:** Inaugural Recipient, University Award for Faculty Mentoring (2007); Henry St. George Tucker Award (2005); BBSF Award (1993, 2001, 2003); All-University Teaching Award (2002); Elected, Faculty Class Marshall (1982, 1987, 1989, 2001); Friend of the Student Award (2000); Fred Morton Leadership Award (1998); University Day Honoree (1997); Outstanding Faculty Award (1995); Raven Society Award (1992) **MH:** Albert Nelson Marquis Lifetime Achievement Award **AS:** Prof. Frey attributes his success on hard work, insightful mentoring and supportive spouses. **B/I:** Prof. Frey became involved in his profession after having worked in consultation with the Pentagon for two years. He had taught as a graduate student and found it was not as rewarding as he had hoped. Following this revelation, he decided he needed to get back to his passion, which was teaching. **AV:** Hiking; Cooking; Woodworking

FRIDAY, ERIN, CPA, T: President, Chief Executive Officer **I:** Financial Services **CN:** Main Line Accounting LLC **DOB:** 01/07/1968 **PB:** Philadelphia **SC:** PA/USA **PT:** Robert James; Irene Anne (Halasz) Farley **MS:** Married **SPN:** John Eric Friday (4/13/1991) **CH:** Colin; Sean; Shannon **ED:** Master of Business Administration, Villanova University (1993); Bachelor of Science in Mathematics, Villanova University (1989); Bachelor of Arts in Liberal Arts, Villanova University (1989); Bachelor of Science in Accountancy, Villanova University (1989) **CT:** Certified Public Accountant, Pennsylvania (1993) **C:** President, Chief Executive Officer, Thousand Hills Accounting Ltd (2019-Present); President, Chief Executive Officer, Main Line Accounting LLC (2007-Present); Chief Financial Officer, LEAF Pharmaceuticals LLC, Gulph Mills, PA (2016-2018); Business Development Manager, Carlton Services LLC, Wayne, Pennsylvania, PA (2003-2007); Controller, ADVISORport, Plymouth Meeting, Pennsylvania (2003-2005); Controller, Kistler Tiffany Benefits Company, Wayne, PA (1993-2003); Financial Analyst, Milliman & Robertson, Radnor, PA (1991-1993); Auditor, Coopers & Lybrand, Philadelphia, PA (1989-1991) **CIV:** Volunteer, Shooting Touch Program, Kigali, Rwanda (2017-Present); Volunteer, Gashora Girls Academy of Science & Technology, Gashora, Rwanda (2017-Present); Board of Directors, Philadelphia Youth Basketball, Philadelphia, PA (2016-Present); Presenter, St. Philip Neri PreCana Program, Lafayette Hill, PA (2014-Present); Volunteer, Villanova Alumni Recruitment Network, Villanova, PA (2010-Present); Track and Field Official, U.S. Athletic Association, Philadelphia, PA (1980-Present); Home & School President, Epiphany of Our Lord School, Pennsylvania (2006-2012); Assistant Cubmaster, EOL Cub Pack 117, Plymouth Meeting, Pennsylvania (2006-2012); Basketball Coach, EOL Instructional Basketball League, Plymouth Meeting, Pennsylvania (2006-2012); Board of Directors, Kistler-Tiffany Foundation, Wayne, PA (1994-1996, 2002-2003); Volunteer, Laurel House, Norristown, PA (1988-1990); President's Advisory Council, Academy of Notre Dame, Villanova, PA **AW:** Faces of Philanthropy Award, Philadelphia Business Journal (2018); Featured Guest, Women to Watch Radio Program (2017); Growth Award, Baird Women's Lifestyle Conference (2017); Steinbrenner Family Heritage Award, Penn Relays (2007) **MEM:** American Institute of Certified Public Accountants; Pennsylvania Institute of CPAs; Phi Beta Kappa; Beta Gamma Sigma **AV:** Golf; Travel; Basketball; Education; Philanthropy **RE:** Roman Catholic

FRIEDHEIM, STEPHEN B., T: Educational Consultant **I:** Education/Educational Services **DOB:** 11/13/1934 **PB:** Joplin **SC:** MO/USA **PT:** Robert Wray Friedheim; Virginia Grace (Bailey) Friedheim **MS:** Married **SPN:** Jan V. Eisenhour (09/01/1984) **CH:** Neeneh Marie; Stephen Bailey II; Robert William **ED:** Honorary DAM, Central New England College, Worcester, MA (1984); Honorary DBA, Johnson and Wales University, Providence, RI (1978); BA, University of Arkansas (1952-1956) **CT:** Certified Association Executive **C:** Founder, Education Systems & Solutions, LLC (2001-Present); Vice President, Public Relations, College of American Services, Inc. (2001-2011); Principal, Education Solutions For Students LLC (1991-2001); President, ESS College of Business (Formerly Executive Secretarial School), Dallas, TX (1984-2001); Senior Vice President, Campbell Communications, Dallas, TX (1984-1990); Senior Vice President, King Education Services (1984-1989); President, Association of Independent Colleges and Schools, Washington, DC (1976-1984); Executive Vice President, American Society of Medical Technology, Houston, TX (1966-1976); Director of Public Relations, American Personnel and Guidance Association, Washington, DC (1961-1966); Newsman, Station KFSB (1957); Announcer, Station KBRS, Springdale, AR (1956-1957); Senior Vice President, Campbell Communications, Bethesda, MD **CR:** Consultant, College American (2002-Present); Consultant, Johnson & Wales University (2002-2006); Consultant, Vatterott Colleges (2003-2005); Consultant, KD Studio Actors Conservatory (2002-2005); Founder, Managing Director, EdVerify (1998-2000); Consultant, Paradigm Publishing (1999); Consultant, Masters Institute (1997); National Task Force on Image of the Secretary (1980-1997); President, American Education Alliance (1988-1990); Consultant, South-Western Publishing Co. (1984-1988); Consultant, Professional Sciences (1980-1982); Task Force, Transfer Credit, Council on Postsecondary Accreditation (1977-1978) **CIV:** Trinity River Arts Center (2002-2006); Vice-Chairman Workforce Leadership Texas (2000-2001); Chairman, Vice-Chairman, Board of Directors, Texas Discovery Gardens (1999-2001); Founding Member, Local County Workforce Development Board, Dallas, TX (1996-2001); Trustee, Dollars for Scholars (1982-1984); Board of Directors, St. Aidan's School, Alexandria, VA (1979-1982); Vestry, Man Ascension Church, Houston, TX (1973-1976); Narrator, Minnesota Symphony Orchestra (1972) **MIL:** U.S. Army (1957-1961) **CW:** Editor, Texas Times (1994-2004); Editor, The Lead Generation (1984-1990) **AW:** 1st Place Award, Washington Society of Association Executives (1990, 1991); Broadcasting Award, American Legion Auxiliary (1963); Freedoms Foundation Award (1960, 1962) **MEM:** Board of Directors, Career Colleges and

Schools of Texas (2000-2004); Board of Directors, National Association of Workforce Boards (2000-2001); Business Advisory Committee, National Alliance of Business (1994-2000); Board of Directors, Trustee, Career Training Foundation (1992-2000); Board of Directors, President, Metropolitan Association of Career Schools (1985-1999); Strategic Alliance Committee for Education, National Court Reporters Association (1994-1995); Board of Directors, Chairman, Career College Association (1991-1995); Board of Directors, President, Southwestern Association of Independent Colleges And Schools (1985-1992); Treasurer, Board of Directors, Chairman, Association Independent Colleges and Schools (1985-1991); Fellow, Australasian College of Bio-Medical Scientists; American Society of Association Executives; National Association for Trade and Technology Schools; Association of Independent Colleges And Schools; WorkForce Commission Creative Service, Washington Society of Association Executives; American Association of Higher Education; American Vocational Association; National Business Education Association; American Vocational Association; National Association of Executives; National Association of Concerned Veterans; Career College Association; Center for Workforce Preparation and Quality Education **MH:** Albert Nelson Marquis Lifetime Achievement Award; Marquis Who's Who Top Professional **B/I:** Mr. Friedheim began his career in radio, proceeding to fulfill a four-year tour in the United States Army. He then decided to pursue association management.

FRIEDMAN, ADENA TESTA, T: Chief Executive Officer **I:** Financial Services **CN:** Nasdaq, Inc. **PT:** Michael D. Testa; Adena W. Testa **MS:** Married **SPN:** Michael Friedman (08/21/1993) **CH:** Two Children **ED:** MBA, Owen Graduate School of Management, Vanderbilt University, Nashville, TN, With Honors (1993); BA in Political Science, Williams College, MA (1991) **C:** President, Chief Executive Officer, Nasdaq, Inc. (2017-Present); President, Chief Operating Officer, Nasdaq, Inc. (2015-2016); President of Global Corporate, Information and Technology Solutions, Nasdaq OMX Group, Inc. (2014-2015); Chief Financial Officer, Managing Director, The Carlyle Group, LLC, Washington, DC (2011-2014); Executive Vice President, Chief Financial Officer, Nasdaq OMX Group, Inc. (2009-2011); Executive Vice President of Corporate Strategy, Nasdaq OMX Group, Inc. (2003-2011); Executive Vice President of Global Data Products, Nasdaq OMX Group, Inc. (2000-2009); Vice President, OTC Bulletin Board, Mutual Fund Quotation Service And Nasdaqtrader.Com, Nasdaq OMX Group, Inc. (2000-2001); Director of Trading and Market Services, Nasdaq OMX Group, Inc. (1997-2000); Marketing Manager, Trading And Market Services, Nasdaq OMX Group, Inc. (1995-1997); Nasdaq OMX Group, Inc. (1993) **CR:** Board of Directors, Nasdaq Dubai Ltd. (2008-2010); OTC Bulletin Board and Mutual Fund Quotation Service (1997-2000) **AW:** 100 Most Powerful Women, Forbes Magazine (2014); Crain's 40 Under 40, Crain's New York Business (2005)

FRIEDMAN, IRWIN, T: Medical Educator **I:** Education/Educational Services **CN:** State University of New York at Buffalo **DOB:** 12/15/1929 **PB:** New York **SC:** NY/USA **PT:** Dave Friedman; Lillie (Shapiro) Friedman **ED:** Resident, Mary Imogene Bassett Hospital, University of Utah (1958-1960); Intern, Buffalo Hospital (1955-1960) **C:** Clinical Professor, Medicine, State University of New York at Buffalo (1961-Present) **MIL:** Captain, U.S. Army (1956-1958) **MEM:** American College of Physicians

FRIEDMAN, MONROE, PHD, T: Professor of Psychology **I:** Education/Educational Services **CN:** Eastern Michigan University **YOP:** 2020 **PT:** Isadore Friedman; Pearl Friedman **SPN:** Rita Joyce Shaffer (09/02/1956) **CH:** Ethan; Mark; Jordan **ED:** Coursework in Gerontology Research, University of Michigan (1988-1999); Postdoctorate Fellow, National Institute on Aging, University of Michigan (1988-1989); Coursework in Cultural Anthropology, University of California Berkeley (1987-1988); Coursework in Labor History, Wayne State University (1981); PhD in Psychology, University of Tennessee (1959); BS in Psychology, Brooklyn College (1956) **C:** Emeritus Professor of Psychology, Eastern Michigan University, Ypsilanti, MI (2005-Present); Professor, Eastern Michigan University, Ypsilanti, MI (1964-2005); Editorial Consultant, Prentice-Hall (1991-1992); Editorial Consultant, Greenwood Press (1991-1992); Director, Contemporary Issues Center, Eastern Michigan University, Ypsilanti, MI (1970-1979); Congressional Fellow, American Political Science Association (1966-1967); Human Factors Scientist, System Development Corporation, Santa Monica, CA (1959-1964); Fellow, Division of Population, Environment, and Conservation Psychology, Division of Consumer Psychology, American Psychological Association; Charter Fellow, Division of Study Peace, Conflict, and Violence, Division of Aesthetics, Creativity, and the Arts, American Psychological Association; Fellow, American Council on Consumer Interests **CR:** Presenter in Field, Board of Directors, FAME Santa Monica Redevelopment Corporation (2010); Insight Panel, New York Times (2006-Present); Co-Editor, Journal of American Culture (2011); Senior Peer Counselor, Center for Healthy Aging, Santa Monica, CA (2007-2008); Reviewer, Consumer Education Literacy Federal Reserve Board, Washington, DC (2004); Board of Directors, Consumer Interest Research Institute, Washington, DC (1984-2000); Consultant, ACLU Foundation, New York, NY (2001-2002); Visiting Professor, University of Leuven (1992-1993); Visiting Professor, Tilburg University, Netherlands (1982-1983); Consultant, Federal Trade Commission, Washington, DC (1976-1977); Consultant, Giant Food, Inc. (1974-1975); Board of Directors, United States General Accounting Office, Washington, DC (1973-1974); Board of Directors, National Science Foundation, Washington, DC (1973-1974); Board of Directors, Consumer Interests Foundation, Washington, DC (1972-1973); President's Committee on Consumer Interests, Washington, DC (1966); Speaker, Over 50 International Research Presentations **CIV:** Executive Council, Emeritus College, Santa Monica, CA (2005-2011); Secretary-Treasurer, Santa Monica Commission for the Senior Community (2008-2010); President, American Council on Consumer Interests (1989-1990) **CW:** Editorial Advisory Board, Journal of Consumer Affairs (2012-Present); Editorial Advisory Board, Journal of Personal Finance (2011-Present); Editorial Advisory Board, Journal of Popular Culture (2005-Present); Editorial Advisory Board, Journal of American Culture (2004-Present); Editorial Advisory Board, Journal of Consumer Policy (1976-Present); Editorial Advisory Board, Journal of Public Policy and Marketing (2006-2012); Editorial Board, Journal of Consumer Affairs (1998-2012); Co-Editor, Journal of American Culture (2011); Editor, Journal of American Culture (2007); Editorial Advisory Board, Journal of Interdisciplinary 20th Century Studies (2005); Author, "Consumer Boycotts" (1999); Editorial Board, Journal of Consumer Affairs (1984-1993); Author, "A Brand New Language" (1991); Editor, Journal of Social Issues (1991); Co-Editor, "Frontier of Research in the Consumer Interest" (1988); Editorial Advisory Board, Journal of Consumer Research (1982-1985); Editor, Journal of Consumer

Affairs (1980-1984); Editorial Advisory Board, Journal of Consumer Research (1973-1977); Contributor, Hundreds of Articles, Professional Journals **AW:** Outstanding Academic Title of the Year, Association for College and Research Libraries (2000); Distinguished Applied Consumer Economics Award, American Council on Consumer Interests (1997); Research Grantee, AARP Andrus Foundation (1992); Distinguished Applied Consumer Economics Award, American Council on Consumer Interests (1991); Research Grantee, AARP Andrus Foundation (1990); Distinguished Faculty Award, Michigan Board of Regents (1983); Research Grant, Michigan Council for Humanities (1975); Bronze Prize for Educational Films, International Film Festival, Berlin, Germany (1975) **MEM:** Chair, Fellows Selection Committee, Division of Adult Development and Aging and Division of Psychological Study Social Issues, American Psychological Association (2014-Present); Speakers Bureau, American Psychological Association (2009-Present); Media Referral Panel, American Psychological Association (2008-Present); Program Review Committee, Division of Media Psychology and Technology, American Psychological Association (2015); Consumer Reports Foundation, American Psychological Association (2015); Fellows Selection Committee, Division of Adult Development and Aging and Division of Psychological Study of Social Issues, American Psychological Association (2010-2014); Judge, Division 1 Graduate Student Awards Committee, American Psychological Association (2011-2013); Program Review Committee, American Council on Consumer Interests (2008); Program Review Committee, Division of Teaching Psychology and Division of International Psychology, American Psychological Association (2007-2009); United States Representative, Board of Trustees, Economic Psychology Division, International Association of Applied Psychology (1988-2005); Representative, Board of Trustees, International Association for Research in Economic Psychology (1982-2005); Scientific Committee, International Association for Research in Economic Psychology (2001-2002); Scientific Committee, International Association of Applied Psychology (1998); Chair, Research Agenda Committee, Foundation for Society of Consumer Affairs Profiles (1984-1987); Fellows Selection Committee, American Psychological Association (1977-1978); Trustee, Foundation for Society of Consumer Affairs **MH:** Albert Nelson Marquis Lifetime Achievement Award **AS:** Dr. Friedman believes a successful contributor to any field needs good ideas, passion, and perseverance, as well as a lot of luck and supportive friends. Likewise, supportive work environments are helpful. **B/I:** Dr. Friedman was always fascinated by human behavior in many areas, which is why he immersed himself in the field.

FRIEDMAN, RICHARD I., T: Public Defender (Retired) **I:** Law and Legal Services **DOB:** 10/02/1947 **PB:** Newark **SC:** NJ/USA **PT:** Irving R. Friedman; Esther Friedman **MS:** Married **SPN:** Harriet Bronfield (09/23/1982) **CH:** Rebecca; Natasha **ED:** JD, Rutgers, The State University of New Jersey (1980); MSW in Community Practice, University of Michigan (1971); BA in Political Science, Rutgers, The State University of New Jersey (1969) **CT:** Certified in Staff Training, Behavior Modification, School Social Worker, New Jersey **C:** Deputy Public Defender, Managing Attorney, New Jersey Office of the Public Defender, Newark, NJ (2018-Present); Assistant Deputy Public Defender, New Jersey Office of the Public Defender (2014-2018); Assistant Deputy Public Defender, New Jersey Office of the Public Defender, Newark, NJ (1996-1998); Special Counsel, New Jersey Office of the Public Defender, Newark, NJ (1995-1996); Attorney, Division for Mental Health and Guardianship Advocacy, New Jersey Office of the Public Defender, Newark, NJ (1994-1995); Assistant Deputy Public Advisor, New Jersey Department of the Public Advisor (1981-1994); Field Representative, Division of Mental Health Advocacy, New Jersey Department of the Public Advisor (1971-1981); Program Coordinator, North Essex Drug Abuse Council, Inc. (1973-1974); Social Worker, South Orange-Maplewood Board of Education (1972); Teacher, Secondary School, Newark, NJ (1971-1972); Researcher, community Action Program, United Auto Workers, Michigan (1970-1971); Researcher, Analyst Legal Services Bail Project, New Jersey Administrative Office of Courts (1970); Community Organizer, Northwest Interfaith Centers for Racial Justice, Detroit, MI (1969-1970); Caseworker, Essex County Welfare Board (1969) **CR:** Chair, Individual Rights, New Jersey Bar Association (2019-Present); Adjunct Professor, New York Law School (2002-Present); Member, Adjunct Professor, Rutgers University Law School, Newark, NJ (1994, 1997); Adjunct Professor, Seton Hall Law School (1996); Krol Coordinator (1992-1998); Consultant to Director, New Jersey Council of Churches (1973); Producer, Host, Station WFMU, East Orange, NJ (1971-1972); Researcher, New Jersey ACLU (1971-1972) **CIV:** Member, Blue Ribbon Committee Transfer, Essex County Hospital Center (1999); Member, State Wide Task Force for Outpatient Civil Commitment, New Jersey Federation YM-YWHA's Camps (1999); Board of Governors, New Jersey Federation YM-YWHA's Camps (1981-1997); Legal Advisor, SANE (1980-1985); Member, New Jersey State Committee, SANE (1972-1980); President, Orange Tenants Association (1976) **MEM:** Ethics Committee, Division of Government and Public Sector Lawyers, American Bar Association (1994-1996); American Association for Justice; New Jersey Bar Association; New York Bar Association; Essex County Bar Association **BAR:** United States Court of Appeals for the Third Circuit (1996); Supreme Court of the United States (1991); New York (1989); New Jersey (1980); United States District Court for the District of New Jersey (1980) **MH:** Albert Nelson Marquis Lifetime Achievement Award

FRIEDMAN, SONIA ANNE PRIMROSE, T: Theater Producer **I:** Media & Entertainment **CN:** Sonia Friedman Productions **PT:** Leonard Friedman; Clair Llewelyn (Sims) Friedman **ED:** Coursework, The Royal Central School of Speech and Drama **C:** Founder, Sonia Friedman Productions (2002-Present); Producer, Ambassador Theatre (1998-Present); Co-founder, Out of Joint (1993-Present); Various Roles Including Stage Manager, Education Manager, Head of Education and Producer of Mobile Productions and Theatre for Young People, National Theatre (1988-1993) **CW:** Producer, "Harry Potter and the Cursed Child," NY (2018-Present); Producer, "The Ferryman," Melbourne, Australia (2018); Producer, "The Jungle," Bernard B. Jacobs Theatre, NY (2018); Producer, "Consent," Playhouse Theatre and Harold Pinter Theatre (2018); Producer, "The Birthday Party," NY (2018); Producer, "Mean Girls," Harold Pinter Theatre (2018); Producer, "Travesties," NY (2018); Producer, "Farinelli and the King," Duke of York's Theatre (2017, 2018); Producer, "The Ferryman" (2017, 2018); Producer, "Who's Afraid of Virginia Woolf?" (2017); Producer, "1984," Harold Pinter Theatre (2017); Producer, "Ink," NY (2017-2018); Producer, "Harry Potter and the Cursed Child" (2016-2018); Producer, "Dreamgirls" (2016-2018); Producer, "The Book of Mormon" (2013-2018); Producer, "The Glass Menagerie" (2017); Producer, "Travesties" (2017); Producer, "Funny Girl," United Kingdom Tour (2017); Producer, "Our Ladies of Perpetual Succour," Royal Court Theatre (2017); Producer, "Hamlet," Gielgud Theatre (2017); Producer, "Sunny Afternoon," United Kingdom Tour (2016); Producer, "Nice Fish" (2016); Producer, "Funny Girl" (2016); Producer, "1984," United Kingdom and NY (2013, 2015-2016); Producer, "Bend It Like Beckham," NY (2015); Producer, "Hamlet" (2015); Producer, "Farinelli and the King" (2015); Producer, "A Christmas Carol," NY (2015); Producer, "King Charles III," United Kingdom and NY (2014, 2015); Producer, "Shakespeare in Love" (2014); Producer, "Electra," Frank McGuinness Translation (2014); Producer, "Sunny Afternoon" (2014); Producer, "The River" (2014); Producer, "The Nether" (2014); Producer, "Old Times" (2013); Producer, "Merrily We Roll Along" (2013); Producer, "Chimerica" (2013); Producer, "The Sunshine Boys" (2013); Producer, "Twelfth Night," Los Angeles, CA (2013); Producer, "Richard III," Los Angeles, CA (2013); Producer, "Mojo" (2013); Producer, "Ghosts" (2013); Producer, "A Chorus of Disapproval" (2012-2013); Producer, "Richard the Third" (2012-2013); Producer, "Twelfth Night (2012-2013); Producer, "Master Class" (2012); Producer, "Absent Friends" (2012); Producer, "Hay Fever" (2012); Producer, "Death of a Salesman" (2012); Producer, "Nice Work If You Can Get It" (2012-2013); Producer, "The Sunshine Boys" (2012); Producer, "La Cage Aux Folles," United Kingdom and United States (2010, 2011-2012); Producer, "Jerusalem," United Kingdom and United States (2010, 2011-2012); Producer, "The Children's Hour" (2011); Producer, "Clybourne Park" (2011); Producer, "Arcadia" (2011); Producer, "Jerusalem" (2011); Producer, "The Book of Mormon" (2011); Producer, "Much Ado About Nothing" (2011); Producer, "Betrayal" (2011); Producer, "Top Girls" (2011); Producer, "The Mountaintop," United States Tour (2011); Producer, "Private Lives" (2010); Producer, "The Prisoner of Second Avenue" (2010); Producer, "All My Sons" (2010); Producer, "A View from the Bridge" (2010); Producer, "Shirley Valentine and Educating Rita" (2010); Producer, "La Bete" (2010); Producer, "A Flea in Her Ear" (2010); Producer, "Boeing-Boeing," United Kingdom Tour (2009); Producer, "Dancing at Lughnasa" (2009); Producer, "A View from the Bridge" (2009); Producer, "A Little Night Music" (2009); Producer, "The Norman Conquests" (2009); Producer, "The Mountaintop" (2009); Producer, "Arcadia" (2009); Producer, "Othello" (2009); Producer, "Prick Up Your Ears" (2009); Producer, "After Miss Julie" (2009); Producer, "Legally Blonde" (2009); Producer, "A Little Night Music" (2009); Producer, "Boeing-Boeing," United States and Australia (2008); Producer, "That Face" (2008); Producer, "Under the Blue Sky" (2008); Producer, "The Seagull (2008); Producer, "No Man's Land" (2008); Producer, "La Cage Aux Folles" (2008); Producer, "Maria Friedman: Re-Arranged" (2008); Producer, "Donkeys' Years" (2006, 2007); Producer, "King of Hearts" (2007); Producer, "The Dumb Waiter" (2007); Producer, "Boeing-Boeing" (2007); Producer, "In Celebration (2007); Producer, "Rock 'n' Roll (2007); Producer, "Is He Dead?" (2007); Producer, "Hergé's Adventures of Tintin" (2007); Producer, "Dealer's Choice" (2007); Producer, "On the Third Day (2006; Producer, "Eh Joe" (2006); Producer, "Bent (2006); Producer, "Faith Healer (2006); Producer, "Love Song (2006); Producer, "Rock 'n' Roll" (2006); Producer, "By the Bog of Cats" (2005); Producer, "Whose Life is it Anyway" (2005); Producer, "The Home Place" (2005); Producer, "As You Like It" (2005); Producer, "Shoot the Crow" (2005); Producer, "Celebration" (2005); Producer, "Otherwise Engaged" (2005); Producer, "The Woman in White" (2005); Producer, "Calico" (2004); Producer, "Endgame" (2004); Producer, "Guantánamo" (2004); Producer, "The Woman in White" (2004); Producer, "Ragtime" (2003); Producer, "A Day in the Death of Joe Egg" (2003); Producer, "Sexual Perversity in Chicago" (2003) Producer, "Absolutely! (Perhaps)" (2003); Producer, "Hitchcock Blonde" (2003); Producer, "See You Next Tuesday" (2003); Producer, "Jumpers" (2003); Producer, "Benefactors" (2002); Producer, "Up for Grabs" (2002); Producer, "Afterplay" (2002); Producer, "What the Night Is For" (2002); Producer, "Macbeth" (2002); Producer, "A Day in the Death of Joe Egg" (2001); Producer, "Noises Off" (2000); Producer, "Speed the Plow" (2000); Producer, "Spoonface Steinberg" (1999); Producer, "The Steward of Christendom" (1997); Producer, "Three Sisters" (1997); Producer, "Blue Kettle/ Heart's Desire" (1997); Producer, "Shopping and Fucking" (1996); Producer, "The Libertine (1995); Producer, "The Queen and I (1994); Producer, "Tartuffe" (1991); Producer, "Accidental Death of an Anarchist" (1990) **AW:** Named One of the 100 Most Influential People, TIME Magazine (2018); Equity Services to the Theatre Award, WhatsOnStage Awards (2018); Named Producer of the Year, Stage Awards (2017); Named Officer, Order of the British Empire (2016)

FRITTS, STEPHEN J., MS, I: Education/Educational Services **CN:** Warren Hills Regional Board of Education **MS:** Married **SPN:** Shelley Stauffer **CH:** Courtney; Erin; Casey **ED:** MS in Health Education, East Stroudsburg University, PA (1988); BA in Health & Physical Education, Penn State University (1973); 12 Credits, Health, Certified Health Instructor in Physical Education, The Pennsylvania State University **CT:** Certified in Health, Health Physical Education, Ohio and New Jersey **C:** Health and Physical Education Teacher (Retired), Warren Hills Regional Board of Education (33 Years) **AW:** Inductee, Warren Hills Athletics Hall of Fame (2010); Warren Hills Special Recognition Award, Outstanding Contributions for the Athletic Program (2004); Middle School Teacher of the Year, Warren Hills Middle School (2000); Special Achievement Award, Star Gazette Local Newspaper (1991) **MEM:** Eagle Scout, Boy Scouts of America **AS:** Mr. Fritts attributes his success to refusing to ever give up on his goals or his dreams. **B/I:** Mr. Fritts became involved in his profession because he has played sports for all of his life. He began playing sports at the age of 5. His eighth grade teacher and his freshman football coach Mr. Bob Fluck is why he chose his career path. In addition, there were a lot of things that he worked hard on for example he used to stutter. He drove an oil truck in the winter and worked in the summer, he even worked for a tire warehouse. But, he worked hard at it all because he wanted to get a teaching job right away. So, he kept working at it until he got a job. **RE:** Lutheran

FRITZ, LANCE M., T: Chairman, President, Chief Executive Officer **I:** Other **CN:** Union Pacific Corporation **ED:** MBA, Northwestern University; Bachelor's Degree in Mechanical Engineering, Bucknell University **C:** President, Chairman, Chief Executive Officer, Union Pacific Corporation (2015-Present); Chief Operating Officer, Union Pacific Corporation (2014-2015); Executive Vice President of Operations, Union Pacific Corporation (2010-2014); Vice President of Operations, Union Pacific Corporation (2009-2010); Vice President of Labor Relations, Union Pacific Corporation (2008-2009); Regional Vice President, Southern Region, Union Pacific Corporation (2006-2008); Regional Vice President, Northern Region, Union Pacific Corporation (2005-2006); Vice President, General Manager of Energy, Union Pacific Corporation (2000-2005); General Manager, Fiskars Inc. (1997-2000); Business Analyst, Cooper Industries (1991-1994); Various Marketing and Operations Positions,

Cooper Industries; Various Operations and Manufacturing Management Positions, General Electric **CR:** Board of Directors, Union Pacific Corporation (2015-Present); Board of Directors, Association of American Railroads; Member, Business Roundtable, STRATCom Consultation Committee **CIV:** Board of Directors, Omaha Symphony; Board of Directors, United Way of the Midlands

FROILAND, KATHRYN, "KATHY" G., T: Oncology Clinical Educator **I:** Pharmaceuticals **CN:** GlaxoSmithKline Oncology **PT:** Phyllis June Froiland; Alfred Wilhelm Froiland **ED:** Master of Science in Nursing, University of Texas, Houston, TX (1994); Bachelor of Science in Nursing, St. Olaf College, Northfield, MN (1979) **CT:** Advanced Oncology Certified Nurse Specialist; Certified Wound, Ostomy and Continence Nurse **C:** Oncology Nurse Educator, Tesaro (2015-Present); Oncology Nurse Educator, Tesaro (2015-2019); Oncology Clinical Educator, Glaxo Smith Kline (2003-2015); Program Director, Wound Ostomy Continence Nurse Education Program, University of Texas MD Anderson Cancer Center, Houston, TX (2001-2003); Senior Wound Ostomy Continence Nurse, University of Texas MD Anderson Cancer Center, Houston, TX (1995-2001); Senior Nursing Instructor, University of Texas MD Anderson Cancer Center, Houston, TX (1991-1994); Hospice Nurse, Mayo Clinic Foundation, Rochester, MN (1989-1991); Assistant Head Nurse, Methodist Hospital, Minneapolis, MN (1988-1989); Assistant Head Nurse, Station Instructor, Charge Nurse, Staff Nurse, University of Minnesota Hospitals and Clinics, Minneapolis, MN (1979-1988) **CIV:** Volunteer, American Cancer Society, Houston, TX (1991-Present) **CW:** Author, Chapter on Pressure Ulcers and Wounds, "Textbook of Palliative Medicine and Supportive Care," Second Edition (2015) **AW:** Distinguished Alumna Award, University of Texas Health Science Center at Houston School of Nursing (2002); Named, Wound, Ostomy, and Continence Nurse of the Year, South Central Region of the Wound Ostomy Continence Nursing Society (2001); Excellence in Clinical Care Award, NurseWeek (2001); Mary Mazzaway Scholarship Award, Oncology Nursing Society; Excellence in Patient Care & Clinical Education Award; Inductee, MD Anderson Gynecologic Oncology Fellows Class of 2000 **MEM:** Houston Chapter Secretary, President-Elect, President, Board Director, Oncology Nursing Society (1995-2000); Wound Ostomy Continence Nursing Society; Sigma Theta Tau **MH:** Albert Nelson Marquis Lifetime Achievement Award; Marquis Who's Who Top Professional **AS:** Ms. Froiland attributes her success to her desire to be a continual learner, and her dedication in contributing to the betterment of others. **B/I:** Ms. Froiland became involved in her profession as a medical educator after joining the staff of the University of Minnesota. **PA:** Independent **RE:** Lutheran

FROMM, ERWIN FREDRICK, T: Insurance Company Executive (Retired) **I:** Insurance **DOB:** 10/24/1933 **PB:** Kalamazoo **SC:** MI/USA **PT:** Erwin Carl Fromm; Charlotte Elizabeth (Wilson) Fromm **ED:** Postgraduate Studies, Illinois State University (1970-1972);BA, Kalamazoo College (1959); Student, Flint Junior College (1952-1953); Student, University of Michigan (1951-1952) **CT:** Chartered Property and Casualty Underwriter, Chartered Life Underwriter; Certified Nursing Home Administrator **C:** Vice President, Metropolitan Property & Liability Insurance Company, Warwick, RI (1974-Present);Assistant Vice President, Metropolitan Property & Liability Insurance Company, Warwick, RI (1973-1974); Director, Underwriting and Policyholders Services, Metropolitan Property & Liability Insurance Company, Warwick,

RI (1973); Consultant, Metropolitan Property & Liability Insurance Company, Warwick, RI (1972-1973); Underwriter, State Farm Insurance (1959-1972) **CR:** President, Royal Monarch Consultant, Inc. (1990-Present); American Certified Long-Term Care Ombudsman (1998-2013); Nursing Home Executive, Royal Crest Health Care Center, In. (1990-1992); Senior Vice President, Royal Insurance Company, Charlotte, NC (1979-1990); Past Chairman, All Industry Insurance Committee for Arson Control; Chairman, National Council on Compensation Insurance; Past Chairman, Commercial Lines Committee Insurance Service Office; Past Member, Advisory Committee, Underwriting Program, Insurance Institute **CIV:** California Senior Legislature (2000-2014); Past Member, Advisory Council, Business School, University of Rhode Island; Past Member, Board of Directors, Charlotte Symphony; Member, North Carolina Insurance Education; Member, Advisory Council on Aging, Board of Directors, California Foundation on Aging; Past Member, Board of Directors, Compulsive Gambling Institute; Member, Advisory Council, RSVP-Riverside Company, California **MIL:** 1st Lt., U.S. Army **MEM:** Chartered Member, California Chapter, Property and Casualty Underwriter Association; Chartered Life Member, California Chapter, Underwriter Association; Masons; Shriners **MH:** Albert Nelson Marquis Lifetime Achievement Award **B/I:** Ms. Fromm became involved in her profession because it was simply an opportunity at the time he was looking for a job. The choice he made worked out for the best. Eventually he began to take the educational courses pertaining to his profession. **RE:** Lutheran

FROST, PATRICIA, T: Chairman Emeritus **I:** Museums & Institutions **CN:** Smithsonian Institution **MS:** Married **SPN:** Phillip Frost **C:** Chairman Emeritus, Smithsonian Institution

FROST, PHILLIP, T: Chief Executive Officer **I:** Business Management/Business Services **CN:** Okpo Health **MS:** Married **SPN:** Patricia Orr **ED:** MD, Albert Einstein College, Bronx, NY (1961); BA, University of Pennsylvania (1957) **C:** Chairman, Teva Pharmaceuticals Industries, Ltd. (2010-Present); Chairman, Chief Executive Officer, Opko Health, Inc. (2007-Present); Chairman, Ladenburg Thalmann Fin. Services, Inc. (2006-Present); Vice-Chairman, Teva Pharmaceuticals Industries, Ltd. (2006-2010); Executive Vice President, Chief Scientific Officer, Imclone Systems Inc., New York, NY (2006); Interim CEO, Imclone Systems Inc., New York, NY (2005-2006); Founder, Chairman, Chief Executive Officer, Ivax Corp., Miami, FL (1987-2006); President, Ivax Corp., Miami, FL (1991-1995); Chairman Department Of Dermatology, Mount Sinai Medical Center, Miami, FL (1972-1990); Chairman, Key Pharmacies, Miami, FL (1972-1986) **CR:** Board of Directors, Castle Brands Inc. (2008-Present); Chairman, Ladenburg Thalmann Financial Services (2006-Present); Vice Chairman, Teva (2005-2007); Board of Directors, Ladenburg Thalmann Financial Services (2001-2002); Board of Directors, Ideation Acquisition Corp.; Prolor Biotech Inc.; Kidville Inc.; Co-Vice-Chairman, Board of Governors, American Stock Exchange; Board of Directors, Cellular Technical Services; Continucare Corp.; Northrop Grumman Corp.; Chairman, IVAX Diagnostics, Inc. **CIV:** Trustee, Scripps Research Institute; Board of Regents, Smithsonian Institute; Trustee, Past Chairman, University of Miami **AW:** Listee, Forbes 400: Richest Americans (2006-Present)

FUDGE, BRENDA, T: Owner **I:** Food & Restaurant Services **CN:** Ray's Diner **DOB:** 10/04/1963 **PB:** Topeka **SC:** KS/USA **MS:** Married **SPN:** Jay

(2012) **CH:** Two Children **C:** Owner, Ray's Diner (2004-Present); Restaurant Worker; Owner, Bed and Breakfast **AW:** Award for Garbage Sandwich (2015); Most Pepsi Memorabilia, Pepsi Magazine **AS:** Ms. Fudge attributes her success to her caring attitude. She truly cares about the work she does and values her relationships with customers. **B/I:** Ms. Fudge dropped out of high school at age 16 to begin and pursue her career in the restaurant industry. 46 years later, she is the owner of a diner and was previously the owner of a local bed and breakfast before selling the establishment. **AV:** Spending time with family **THT:** Ms. Fudge has been involved in the restaurant business for 46 years.

FUDGE, MARCIA LOUISE, T: U.S. Representative from Ohio **I:** Government Administration/Government Relations/Government Services **DOB:** 10/29/1952 **PB:** Cleveland **SC:** OH/USA **ED:** JD, Cleveland-Marshall College of Law, Cleveland State University (1983); BS in Business Administration, The Ohio State University, Columbus, OH (1975) **C:** Member, U.S. House of Representatives from Ohio's 11th Congressional District, United States Congress (2009-Present); Mayor, City of Warrensville Heights, Ohio (2000-2008); Chief of Staff to Representative Stephanie Tubbs Jones, U.S. House of Representatives (1999-2001); Member, Committee on Agriculture; Member, Committee on Science, Space, and Technology; Staff, Personal Property Tax Department, Cuyahoga County Auditor's Office; Various Positions Including Director of Budget and Finance, Cuyahoga County Prosecutor's Office, Cleveland, Ohio **CR:** Chairperson, Congressional Black Caucus (2013-Present) **CIV:** Member, AIPAC Mission-Israel (2008); Visiting Referee, Acting Judge, Bedford Municipal Court, Cuyahoga County, Ohio; Active Member, Glenville Church of God **AW:** American Voice Award (2014); Named Municipal Leader of the Year, Northeast Ohio Municipal Leader Magazine (2007); Patricia Roberts Harris Medallion Award for Excellence in Government Service (2007); Russell T. Adrine Citizen of the Year Award (2005); Trailblazer of the Year Award, Norman S. Minor Bar Association (2005) **MEM:** Co-chair, National Social Action Commission, Delta Sigma Theta Sorority, Inc. (2000-2004); President, Delta Sigma Theta Sorority, Inc. (1996-2000) **PA:** Democrat **RE:** Baptist

FUJIOKA, JO ANN FUJIKO, PHD, T: President, Consultant **I:** Education/Educational Services **CN:** Fujioka Consultants **DOB:** 04/30/1939 **PB:** Bellflower **SC:** CA/USA **PT:** Richard Masayoshi; Lillian Chiyono (Ihara) Ota **MS:** Widowed **SPN:** Arthur Fujioka (02/19/1961) **CH:** Dana Kay Nami Fujioka **ED:** PhD, Colorado State University (1987); MSN, University of Colorado (1970); BSN, University of Colorado (1961) **CT:** Certified Administrator; Certified Superintendent; Certified Special Education Director; Certified School Nurse; Certified Vocational Education Administrator; Registered Nurse **C:** Retired (1996); Consultant, Fujioka Consultants (1995-Present); Area Manager for Special Education and Related Services, Building Administrator K-6, Jefferson County School District (1979-1995); Supervisor, School Nursing and School Health Program, Jefferson County School District (1976-1979); School Nurse, Jefferson County School District (1971-1976); Psychiatric Public Nurse Health, Denver General Hospital (1961-1971) **CR:** President, Denver Council Parent Teacher Student Association (2019-Present); Vice President, Advocates for Public Education Policy (2019-Present); Vice President, Diversity and Inclusion Chair, Colorado Parent Teacher Association (2016); Board of Directors, Colorado Parent Teacher Association (2015); Resolutions Chairperson, National Parent Teacher Association (2013); Board of Directors, National Parent Teacher Association (2008); Delegate to China, People to People International (2007); Delegation Leader to China, Phi Delta Kappa (2007); Board of Governors, Phi Delta Kappa (2006); Vice President, PDK International (2006); Colorado Mediation Project (1998); Colorado Association of Family and Children's Agencies (1997); Denver Children's Home (1996); Consultant, Central Kansas Board of Cooperative Educational Services (1992) **CIV:** Secretary House District 6, Colorado Democratic Party (2019-Present); Precinct Committee Person, Colorado Democratic Party (2007-Present); Representative, Colorado Coalition for Gun Violence Prevention, Colorado Parent Teacher Association (2018-Present); Captain-at-Large, Denver Democratic Party (2018-Present); Honorary Member, Board of Directors, Colorado Women's Hall of Fame (2002-2015); Chair, Bernie Sanders Delegation, Democratic National Convention (2016); Chair, Denver Democrats Education Study, Democratic National Convention (2016); Chairman, Board of Directors, Creative Exchange (1999-2001); Vice Chairman, Board of Directors, Creative Exchange (1997-1999); Alliance of Professional Consultants; League of Women Voters **CW:** Author, "School Health Team Model for Delivering Comprehensive School Health Programs," American Journal of School Health; Author, "A Continuum of Interventions for Sexual Behavior Problems in Elementary Schools," Colorado's Children **AW:** Scholarship, University of Colorado; Gabbard Institute Scholarship, PDK International; Who's Who in the World; Who's Who of American Women; Administrators Award, Institute for Special Education, Harvard University; Full Scholarship, University of Denver; Leadership Award, PDK International; Lifetime Service Key Award, Colorado Parent Teacher Association **MEM:** Colorado Board of Directors, National Parent Teacher Association (2009-Present); Colorado Diversity and Inclusivity Chair, National Parent Teacher Association (2009-Present); Board of Directors, UC Health Seniors Clinic (2000-Present); International Coordinator for Ethical Leadership Project, UC Health Seniors Clinic (2000-Present); Fall Conference Chair, UC Health Seniors Clinic (1993-2005); American Association of University Women; National Organization of Women; Jefferson County Administrators Association; American Society of Association Executives **MH:** Albert Nelson Marquis Lifetime Achievement Award **AS:** Dr. Fujioka attributes her success to her fairness, integrity and honesty. **B/I:** Dr. Fujioka became involved in her profession because from childhood she always wanted to be a nurse. She grew up at a time when women either became secretaries, nurses or teachers. Due to her interest in helping others, her first career was in nursing and then education. Her passion for education stemmed from her experience being interned in an American concentration camp as a young child because she was a Japanese American. Her family had to leave everything they had in California when an executive order was issued by the president notifying anyone with Japanese ancestry that they had three days to evacuate to a concentration camp. Throughout her life, her father always said that she had to get an education as "that is the one thing that can never be taken from you." Her mother died when she was seven because they could not find a doctor in Denver who would treat her uterine cancer because she was Japanese American. Her mother's needless death and her father's emphasis on the importance of an education led Dr. Fujioka to pursue her life's work. Over the years, her parents' passion for fairness and equity have instilled in Dr. Fujioka the need to become civically involved to fight for equity and justice for all. The oppression of people of color in education and justice are the focus of her endeavors to right the many wrongs in our society. Through all the strife and hardship endured by her father and the family, he always said to her that in spite of the many faults, America is still the best place in the world to live. These beliefs have been the driving force for her whole life and career. **AV:** Doing crossword and jigsaw puzzles; Crocheting; Practicing Tai Chi; Reading **PA:** Democrat **RE:** Buddhist

FUKUYAMA, FRANCIS, PHD, T: Political Scientist; Author; Director, Professor **I:** Education/Educational Services **CN:** Stanford University **DOB:** 10/27/1952 **PB:** Chicago **SC:** IL/USA **PT:** Yoshio Fukuyama; Toshiko Kawata Fukuyama **MS:** Married **SPN:** Laura Holmgren **CH:** Julia; David; John **ED:** Honorary Doctorate, Doane College, Crete, NE (2001); Honorary Doctorate, Connecticut College, New London, CT (1995); PhD in Soviet Foreign Policy, Harvard University (1981); Intern, U.S. Arms Control and Disarmament Agency (1976); BA in Classics, Cornell University (1974); Honorary Doctorate, Doshisha University, Japan **C:** Olivier Nomellini Senior Fellow, Freeman Spogli Institute for International Studies, Resident, Center for Democracy, Development and the Rule of Law, Stanford University, CA (2010-Present); Bernard Schwartz Professor of International Political Economy, Director of International Development Program, Johns Hopkins University School of Advanced International Studies (2001-2010); Omer L. and Nancy Hirst Professor of Public Policy, Director of International Commerce and Policy Program, George Mason University, VA (1996-2001); Senior Social Scientist, RAND Corporation, Santa Monica, CA (1995-1996); Consultant, RAND Corporation, Santa Monica, CA (1990-1994); Deputy Director, Policy Planning Staff, U.S. Department State, Washington, DC (1989-1990); Senior Staff Member, Political Science Department, RAND Corporation, Santa Monica, CA (1983-1989); Policy Planning Staff, U.S. Department of State, Washington, DC (1981-1982); Associate Social Scientist, RAND Corporation, Santa Monica, CA (1979-1981); Consultant, Pan Heuristics, Inc., Los Angeles, CA (1978-1979) **CR:** Co-Founder, The American Interest (2005-Present); Co-Director, Project on the Information and Biological Revolution, RAND/George Mason University (1996-1999); Director, New Sciences Project, Johns Hopkins University School of Advanced International Studies (1996-1999); Director, SAIS Telecommunications Project (1994-1996); Fellow, Foreign Policy Institute (1994-1996); Visiting Lecturer, Department of Political Science, University of California Los Angeles (1989); Advisory Board, FINCA International, Inter-American Dialogue, National Endowment for Democracy, National Interest, New American Foundation (1986) **CIV:** President's Council on Bioethics (2001-2005); U.S. Delegate, Egyptian-Israeli Talks on Palestinian Autonomy (1981-1982); Board of Trustees, RAND Corporation; Board of Governors, Pardee RAND Graduate School; Executive Board, Inter-American Dialogue; Board Member, Global Financial Integrity; Board of Counselors, Pyle Center of Northeast Asian Studies, National Bureau of Asian Research; Steering Committee, Scooter Libby Legal Defense Trust; Fellow, World Academy of Art & Science **CW:** Author, "Identity: The Demand for Dignity and the Politics of Resentment" (2018); Author, "Political Order and Political Decay: From the Industrial Revolution to the Present Day" (2014); Author, "The Origins of Political Order" (2011); Author, "Falling Behind: Explaining the Development Gap between Latin America and the United States" (2008); Author, "America at the Crossroads: Democracy, Power, and the Neoconservative Legacy" (2006); Author,

"State-Building: Governance and World Order in the 21st Century" (2004); Author, "Our Posthuman Future: Consequences of the Biotechnology Revolution" (2002); Author, "The Great Disruption: Human Nature and the Reconstitution of Social Order" (1999); Co-Editor, "Information and Biological Revolutions: Global Governance Challenges-Summary of a Study Group" (1999); Co-Author, "The Virtual Corporation and Army Organization" (1997); Author, "The End of Order" (1997); Author, "Trust: The Social Virtues and the Creation of Prosperity" (1995); Co-Author, "The US-Japan Security Relationship After the Cold War" (1993); Author, "The End of History and the Last Man" (1992); Author, "Gorbachev and the New Soviet Agenda in the Third World" (1989); Author, "Soviet Civil-Military Relations and the Power Projection Mission" (1987); Author, "Moscow's Post-Brezhnev Reassessment of the Third World" (1986); Editorial Board, Journal of Democracy; Chairman, Editorial Board, The American Interest; Contributor, Chapters, Books; Contributor, Articles, Professional Journals **AW:** Graduate Fellow, National Security Program, Center for International Affairs, Harvard University (1979); Graduate Fellow, Center for Science and International Affairs, Harvard University (1978-1979) **MEM:** Council for Civil Society; Board of Directors, National Endowment for Democracy; Global Business Network; Founding Member, Pacific Council on International Policy; American Political Science Association (APSA); Council on Foreign Relations **AV:** Photography

FULCHER, RUSSELL M., T: 1) U.S. Representative from Idaho 2) Real Estate Broker **I:** Government Administration/Government Relations/Government Services **CN:** 1) U.S. House of Representatives 2) Mark Bottles Real Estate **DOB:** 03/09/1962 **PB:** Boise **SC:** ID/USA **MS:** Divorced **SPN:** Kara Fulcher (Divorced 2018) **CH:** Three Children **ED:** Diploma, Micron Technology Inc. (1993); Master of Business Administration, Boise State University College of Business and Economics (1988); Bachelor of Business Administration, Boise State University (1984) **C:** Member, U.S. House of Representatives from Idaho's First Congressional District (2019-Present); Commercial Agent, Mark Bottles Real Estate (2006-Present); Majority Caucus Chairperson, Idaho State Senate (2008-2012, 2013-2014); Member, 22nd District, Idaho Senate (2012-2014); Member, District 21, Idaho State Senate (2005-2012); Vice President, Sales and Marketing, PRECO Electronics (1998-2006); Manager and Director, Sales and Marketing, Micron Technology Inc. (1983-1998) **CR:** Adjunct Instructor, International Business, Boise State University (2002-2003) **PA:** Republican

FULFORD, ELIZABETH, T: Director of Integrated Care Management **I:** Medicine & Health Care **CN:** Indiana University Health **CH:** One Son **ED:** MSN, MBA, Indiana Wesleyan University (2016); BS, University of Southern Indiana (2011) **C:** Program Director, Indiana University Health (2016-Present); Director, Integrated Care Management, Indiana University Health Care Alliance Services (2015-Present); Manager, Integrated Care Management, Indiana University Health (2016); RN, Case Manager Team Lead, Indiana University Methodist Hospital (2014-2016); RN, Case Manager, Indiana University Health (2013-2014); RN, Indiana University Health Bloomington Hospital (2012-2013) **CIV:** Volunteer, Nursing Assistant, Nineveh Hensley Jackson School Corporation; Habitat for Humanity **AS:** Ms. Fulford attributes her success to her drive. She has had great mentors and preceptors, all of whom have been a blessing to her. She fed off the information they gave her and always looked for the next challenge. **B/I:** Ms. Fulford became

involved in her profession because, ever since middle school, she knew she wanted to be a nurse. Throughout her entire academic journey, she participated in classes that would further her success in healthcare.

FULKS, ROBERT, T: Computer Company Executive **I:** Technology **CN:** Cadence Design Systems **DOB:** 04/08/1936 **PB:** Kansas City **SC:** MO/USA **PT:** Hilburne Grady; Dora Elouise (Johnson) Fulks **MS:** Married **SPN:** Nancy Sundra Fulks **CH:** Stephanie, Scott Grady, Sham, Raj, Kristen **ED:** Master of Science in Electrical Engineering, Massachusetts Institute of Technology (1959); Bachelor of Science in Electrical Engineering, Massachusetts Institute of Technology (1958) **C:** Vice President, Cadence Design Systems, Chelmsford, MA (1992-1996); Group Vice President, Product Division, Valid Logic Systems (1989-1991); Vice President, General Manager, PCB CAD Division, Valid Logic Systems (1987-1989); Vice President, Engineering, Telesis Systems Corp., Chelmsford, MA (1986-1987); General Manager, Advanced Technology Division, GenRad Inc., Phoenix, AZ (1980-1986); Founder, President, Omnicomp Inc., Phoenix, AZ (1975-1980); President, Micro Systems Inc. (1973-1975); Engineer, Chief Engineer, Vice President, Engineering and Product Marketing, GenRad Inc., Concord, MA (1959-1973) **CR:** Board Director, Office Tech. Ltd., Boston, MA; Board Director, Markwood Inc., Phoenix, AZ; Board Director, Custon Data Management Inc., Phoenix, AZ; Board Director, Texcon Corp., Phoenix, AZ; Board Director, Cirrus Sigma Ltd., Fareham, England **CW:** Contributor, Articles to Professional Journals; 10 Patents in the Field **MEM:** Institute of Electrical and Electronics Engineers; Association Computing Machinery; Board Director, Chairperson, Finance Committee, Concord Chamber of Commerce; Sigma Xi **MH:** Albert Nelson Marquis Lifetime Achievement Award; Marquis Who's Who Top Professional

FULMER, RUSSELL FRANCIS, T: Librarian (Retired) **I:** Library Management/Library Services **CN:** Georgia Highlands College **DOB:** 11/28/1946 **PB:** Birmingham **SC:** AL/USA **PT:** John A. Fulmer; Agnes E. (Parker) Fulmer **ED:** MLS, The University of Alabama at Birmingham, AL (1972); AB, Dickinson College (1968) **C:** Librarian, Georgia Highlands College (1994-2015); First Year Experience Teacher, Georgia Highlands College (1994-2015); Assistant Director of Library for Technical Services, Colorado School of Mines, Golden, CO (1983-1991); Coordinator of Technology Services, Jackson Hinds Library System (1974-1983); Cataloger, The University of Alabama, Tuscaloosa (1971-1974) **CR:** Consultant, Mississippi Library Association (1983); Database Quality Advisory Committee, Southwestern Library Network (1979-1981) **CIV:** Mission Committee, St. Christopher's Episcopal Church of the Ascension, Jackson, MS (1981-1983); Volunteer, Mississippi Region, Easterseals (1975-1976); Consultant in Computerized Library Systems (CARL); Board of Directors, CARL **CW:** Assistant Editor, "Mississippi Libraries" (1980-1981) **MEM:** Chairman, Technology Services and Automation Division, Colorado Association of Libraries (1987-1988); President, Library School Alumni Association (1972); American Library Association; Southeastern Library Association; Mississippi Library Association; Beta Phi Mu-The International Library and Information Studies Honor Society **MH:** Albert Nelson Marquis Lifetime Achievement Award; Marquis Who's Who Top Professional **B/I:** Mr. Fulmer didn't intend to be a librarian. He originally intended to do something with history, as he was a history major in college. He really liked doing research and books. His parents realized that he did really well with books, so

they arranged for him to talk to some people who were in libraries. He went to the medical library at the University of Alabama at Birmingham, Alabama, and talked to the librarians there. They said a brand new library school was just opening up, so he went and applied and got into the first class at the University of Alabama's School of Library Service. He managed to do that, and was one of the first two graduates. **RE:** Episcopalian

FULMER, SHIRLEY MINUS PERSON, T: Art Educator **I:** Education/Educational Services **DOB:** 04/30/1933 **PB:** Columbia **SC:** SC/USA **PT:** Richard Oliveros Person; Dorothy May (Minus) Person **MS:** Married **SPN:** Henry Lynn Fulmer (01/27/1956) **CH:** Richard Person Fulmer; Cynthia Lynn Fulmer Dettman; Paul Minus Fulmer **ED:** BA in Art and Education, University of South Carolina (1955) **CT:** Certified Teacher, State of South Carolina **C:** Private Practice Art Teacher, Greenville, SC (1959-Present); Art Teacher, Wardlaw Junior High School, Columbia, SC (1958-1959); Director, Christian Education, First Presbyterian Church, Columbia, SC (1956-1958); Receptionist, University of South Carolina, Columbia, SC (1955-1956) **CIV:** Member, Metropolitan Arts Council (MAC) (2005) **MEM:** President, Carolina-Piedmont Branch, National League of American Pen Women (NLAPW) (1994-1998, 2000-2002, 2004-Present); President, Hillcrest Garden Club (2003-2005); Vice President, Hillcrest Garden Club (2003); President, State of South Carolina, National League of American Pen Women (NLAPW) (1996-2012); National League of American Pen Women (NLAPW); Upcountry Plein Air Artists; Upstate Visual Arts, University of South Carolina; Hillcrest Garden Club; Kudzu Art Society; Greenville Council Garden Club; Life, Greenville Council Garden Club **B/I:** Mrs. Fulmer feels that she was born an artist. She has been drawing since she was young, and her grandmother was an artist as well, though she died before Mrs. Fulmer was born. **AV:** Art and crafts; Painting **PA:** Republican **RE:** Presbyterian

FULSON, LULA M., T: Educator **I:** Education/Educational Services **DOB:** 06/20/1938 **PB:** Chicago **SC:** IL/USA **PT:** Alice Mae Jones **SPN:** Larry E. Fulson (06/09/1957, Deceased 1994) **CH:** Darrell (Deceased 2009); Larry; Daphne; Zachary; Stephanie **ED:** MEd, National Louis University (1988); BA, National Louis University (1983) **C:** Retired (2005); Instructor, Coordinator, South Suburban College, South Holland, IL (1985-2005); Retention Counselor, South Suburban College, South Holland, IL (1984-1985) **CIV:** Corresponding Secretary, Windy City Travelers, Chicago, IL (1995-Present); Second Vice President, People's Party, Robbins, IL (1995-Present); Trustee, Treasurer, William Leonard Public Library, Robbins, IL (1995- Present); Secretary Theda Hambright Scholarship, South Holland, IL (1990-Present) **CW:** Co-Editor, Robbins Bulletin Newspaper (1995-Present); Author, "Memoirs of a Widow" (1996) **AW:** 2017 Outstanding Resident of the Year, Mayor Tyrone Ward, Village of Robbins (2017); Noteworthy Senior Award, Mayor, Village of Robbins (2014); Outstanding Citizen and Board Member, Chicago Youth Center/Robbins (1996); Named Outstanding County Chairwoman, Moms Association Inc., University of Illinois (1993-1994); Living Black History Award Harvey Public Library Youth Services (1988); Certificate of Appreciation, Public Service, Mayor, Village of Robbins **MEM:** Junior Director, Senior Director, Illinois Adult and Continuing Education Association (1984-1986); Citizens United for Progress **MH:** Albert Nelson Marquis Lifetime Achievement Award **B/I:** Ms. Fulson became involved in her profession because she has always been strong and independent. Upon losing both her mother and father, she had to make some decisions. At the age of 13, she traveled from Mississippi to Chicago on the train alone to live with her aunt. She has always wanted to help because her young life was difficult. She worked eight hours a night and went to high school. She had a friend, Austin Barnett, who tutored her with her math so she could have an opportunity to go to college. **AV:** Singing; Camping; Bowling; Sports; Reading **RE:** Member, Church of Christ

FUNDERBURK, ELEANOR JO, T: Terrain Vehicle Company Executive, Realtor **I:** Real Estate **DOB:** 03/31/1943 **PB:** Monroe **SC:** LA/USA **PT:** Hugh Franklin Calhoun: Clotea Elizabeth (Mayes) Calhoun **MS:** Married **SPN:** Shelby Dean Funderburk (12/29/1964); Robert Andrew Heacock (8/25/1961, Deceased 1963) **ED:** Graduate, Calhoun High School (1961) **CT:** Graduate, Real Estate Institute **C:** Realtor, Hogan Realty (1978-Present); Rural Carrier, USPS (1989-2012); Sales, One Million Plus Motor Homes (1986-1989); Secretary, Treasurer, Funderburk 3-Wheeler (1980-1986); Inventory Control Clerk, Secretary, Olinkraft, Inc. (1966-1978); Teller, Secretary, Ouachita Independent Bank (1964-1966); Secretary, Rivers Ford (1963-1964); Receptionist, Secretary, Dr. R.E. Harvey (1961-1963); Sales Clerk, S.H. Kress, Monroe, LA (1958-1961) **AW:** Eight Regional Titles, One Multiple State Title, One Tri-State Title, Twelve State Titles, National Championship, USTA **MEM:** USTA; Former Member, National Association of Realtors; Former Member, Louisiana Realtors; Former Member, Monroe Chamber of Commerce **AS:** Ms. Funderburk attributes her success to her mother, Clotea Elizabeth Mayes Calhoun. **B/I:** Ms. Funderburk became involved in her profession because she wanted to go into business with her husband. **AV:** Plants **PA:** Republican **RE:** Baptist

FURLONG, GEORGE, "SKIP" MORGAN, I: Aviation **PB:** Muskogee **SC:** OK/USA **PT:** George M. Furlong; Anna (Moore) Furlong **MS:** Married **SPN:** Ryland Hagood Blakey (06/05/1956) **CH:** Morgan; William **ED:** Student, U.S. Nuclear Power School (1972-1973); BS in Aeronautical Engineering, U.S. Naval Postgraduate School (1963); BS in Naval Science, U.S. Naval Academy (1956) **C:** Director of Development, Baptist Health Foundation, Pensacola, FL (1997-2001); Executive Vice President, National Naval Aviation Museum, Pensacola, FL (1986-1997); Deputy Chief of Naval Education and Training, Pensacola, FL (1983-1985); Commander, Fighter Airborne Early Warning Wing, U.S. Pacific Fleet, Naval Air Station, Miramar, San Diego, CA (1981-1983); F-14 Program Manager, Fleet Introduction of the F-14 Tomcat; Director, Air Warfare Systems Analysis Staff, Office of the Chief of Naval Operations; Chief of Staff, U.S. Sixth Fleet, Gaeta, Italy; Commander, F-4 Fighter Squadron, Vietnam; Air Commander, USS Enterprise, CVN-65; Commanding Officer, Fleet Oiler, USS Ponchatoula, AO-148, Peal Harbor, Hawaii; Commanding Officer, USS Independence, CV-62, Norfolk, VA **MIL:** Navy Fighter Pilot, More Than 4,500 Hours Flight Time, 930 Carrier Landings and 230 Combat Missions, Vietnam **MEM:** Naval Aviation Museum Foundation Board; AmSouth Bank Board; ACTS Retirement-Life Communities Board **MH:** Albert Nelson Marquis Lifetime Achievement Award **B/I:** Admiral Furlong became involved in his profession because because his first flight in an airplane was in the 1933-1934 time frame and the pilot was Wiley Post, who had recently circumnavigated the earth for the first time in the Winnie May, the aircraft that SKIP flew in. One thing led to another and before he knew it, he was flying airplanes.

FURPHY, DANIEL G., ABA, T: Legislator; Banker (Retired) **I:** Government Administration/Government Relations/Government Services **DOB:** 01/15/1951 **PB:** Laramie **SC:** WY/USA **PT:** Robert L. Furphy; Donna (Dixon) Furphy **MS:** Married **SPN:** Kandi A. Freese (08/20/1983) **CH:** Matthew; Evan Slafter **ED:** College for Financial Planning (1996); ABA, National Commercial Lending School (1984); MBA, University of Wyoming, Laramie, WY (1979); BS in Finance, University of Wyoming, Laramie, WY (1975) **C:** President, Chief Executive Officer, First National Bank of Wyoming, Laramie, WY (1991-2010); President, American National Bank (Now First National Bank of Wyoming), Laramie, WY (1986-1991); Senior Vice President, American National Bank (Now First National Bank of Wyoming), Laramie, WY (1983-1986); Executive Officer, United Bank, Steamboat Springs, CO (1982-1983); Assistant Vice President, Controller, First Interstate Bank, Laramie, WY (1977-1982); Auditor, First Interstate Bank, Laramie, WY (1976-1977); Management Intern, First Interstate Bank, Laramie, WY (1974-1976) **CR:** Wyoming House of Representatives (2017-Present); Laramie Chamber Business Alliance, Laramie, WY (2013-2016); President, Capital West Bankshares (2010-2013); Laramie City Council (1997-2001) Board of Directors, First National Bank, Steamboat Springs, CO, Professional Bank, Denver, CO **CIV:** Chairman, Board of Directors, Trustee, Ivinson Memorial Hospital, Laramie, WY (1988-Present); President, United Way of Albany County, Laramie, WY (1992-1994); Board of Directors, Invinson Memorial Foundation; Board of Directors, University of Wyoming American Heritage Center; Board of Directors, Wyoming Territorial Park; Board of Directors, American Heart Association; Board of Directors, Wyoming Council Economics Education **CW:** Speaker, Numerous Conferences and Universities **MEM:** Board of Directors, Wyoming Bankers Association (1990-Present); Lieutenant Governor, Rotary, Kiwanis (1990); President, Rotary, Kiwanis (1986-1987); President, Rocky Mountain Chapter, Bank Marketing Association (1986-1987); Laramie County Club; Laramie Athletic Club; Former President, Wyoming Bankers Association **MH:** Albert Nelson Marquis Lifetime Achievement Award **B/I:** Mr. Furphy became involved in his profession because he has always had an interest in finance and investing, so when he was given the opportunity to start as an intern that opportunity worked extremely well for him. He knew at that point that banking was the right career choice for him. His father was very hard working and that gave him the motivation to pursue his career He served on the hospital board and on the city council in Wyoming, so he decided to jump in and run for the state house and was fortunate to get elected and re-elected. **AV:** Skiing; Running; Weightlifting; Playing golf; Windsurfing **RE:** Christian

FUTTER, ELLEN VICTORIA, T: President; Music Administrator **I:** Museums & Institutions **CN:** American Museum of Natural History **DOB:** 09/21/1949 **PB:** New York **SC:** NY/USA **PT:** Victor Futter; Joan Babette (Feinberg) Futter **MS:** Married **SPN:** John Shutkin (1974) **CH:** Anne Victoria; Elizabeth Jane **ED:** Honorary Diploma, Williams College (2004); Honorary Diploma, Skidmore College (2003); Honorary DHL, Yale University (2000); Honorary DHL, The City College of New York (1996); Honorary DHL, Long Island City College (1995); Honorary DHL, Hofstra University (1994); Honorary LLD, Hamilton College (1985); Honorary LLD, Columbia University, New York, NY (1984); Honorary DHL, Amherst College; Honorary LLD, New York Law School; JD, Columbia Law School, New York, NY (1974); AB, Barnard College, Magna Cum Laude, New York, NY (1971); Coursework,

University of Wisconsin - Madison **C:** President, American Museum of Natural History, New York, NY (1993-Present); President, Barnard College (1981-1993); Acting President, Barnard College (1980-1981); Associate, Milbank, Tweed, Hadley & McCloy (Now Milbank LLP), New York, NY (1974-1980) **CIV:** Board of Directors, Consolidated Edison Company of New York, Inc. (1997-Present); Board of Directors, Viacom (Now ViacomCBS Inc.) (2006-2007); Board of Directors, American International Group, Inc. (AIG) (1999-2008); Board of Directors, Bristol-Myers Squibb Company (1999-2005); Board of Directors, JPMorgan Chase & Co. (1997-2013); Chair, Federal Reserve Bank of New York (1992-1993); Board of Directors, Federal Reserve Bank of New York (1988-1993); Board of Overseers, Memorial Sloan Kettering Cancer Center **AW:** Rachel Carson Award, National Audubon Society (2014); Named One of the 50 Most Powerful Women in New York, Crain's New York Business (2009, 2011); Mark Schubart Award in Education, Lincoln Center Institute for the Arts in Education (Now Lincoln Center Education) (2008); Lawrence A. Wien Prize for Social Responsibility, Columbia Law School (2008); Named One of the 100 Most Influential Women in New York City Business (2007); Woman of Achievement Award, Women in Development, New York (2006); Alexander Hamilton Award, Manhattan Institute for Policy Research, Inc. (2002) **MEM:** Fellow, American Academy of Arts & Sciences; ABA; Council on Foreign Relations; National Institute of Social Sciences; Association of the Bar of the City of New York; New York State Bar Association; The Economic Club of New York; Academy of American Poets; Century Club; Cosmopolitan Club; The Phi Beta Kappa Society **BAR:** New York (1975)

GABBARD, TULSI, T: U.S. Representative from Hawaii **I:** Government Administration/Government Relations/Government Services **DOB:** 04/12/1981 **PB:** Leloaloa **SC:** HI/USA **PT:** Gerald Mike Gabbard; Carol (Porter) Gabbard **MS:** Married **SPN:** Abraham Williams (2015); Eduardo Tamayo (2002, Divorced 06/05/2006) **ED:** BBA in International Business, Hawai'i Pacific University (2009); Diploma, Alabama Military Academy Accelerated Officer Candidate School (2007) **C:** Candidate, Democratic Nominee, Presidential 2020 Election (2019-Present); Member, U.S. House of Representatives from Hawaii's Second Congressional District, United States Congress, Washington, DC (2013-Present); Member, U.S. House Homeland Security Committee (2013-Present); Member, U.S. House Committee on Foreign Affairs (2013-Present); City Councilwoman, District Six, City of Honolulu, Hawaii (2011-2012); Legislative Aide to Senator Daniel K. Akaka, U.S. Senate (2006-2009); Member, District 42, Hawaii House of Representatives (2002-2004) **CR:** Vice-Chair, Democratic National Committee (2013-2016); Co-Founder, Stand Up for America (SUFA) (2011); Co-Founder, Health Hawaii Coalition (HHC) (2000) **MIL:** Major, Hawaii Army National Guard, United States Army (2003-Present) **AW:** Friend of the National Parks Award, National Parks Conservation Association (2015); Listee, 10 Most Powerful Women in DC, Elle Magazine (2014); John F. Kennedy New Frontier Award, Harvard Kennedy School, John F. Kennedy School of Government (2013); Decorated German Armed Forces Badge for Military Proficiency in Gold; Combat Medical Badge; Army Good Conduct Medal; Army Achievement Medal with Oak Leaf Cluster; Army Commendation Medal; Meritorious Service Medal, U.S. Army **MEM:** Life Member, Military Police Regimental Association (MPRA); Life Member, The National Guard Association of the United States **AV:** Surfing **PA:** Democrat **RE:** Hindu

GABELLI, MARIO JOSEPH, T: Chief Executive Officer **I:** Financial Services **CN:** GAMCO Investors, Inc. **DOB:** 06/19/1942 **PB:** The Bronx **SC:** NY/USA **MS:** Married **SPN:** Regina Gabelli **CH:** Four Children **ED:** Honorary PhD, Roger Williams University, RI; MBA, Columbia University (1967); Diploma, Fordham University, Summa Cum Laude (1965) **C:** Chairman, Chief Executive Officer, GAMCO Investors, Inc., NY (2007-Present); Vice Chairman, Lynch Corporation (2001-Present); Chairman, Chief Executive Officer, Chief Investment Officer, GAMCO Investors, Inc. (1999-Present); Chief Executive Officer, Director, Lynch Interactive Corporation (1999-Present); Founder, Gabelli Funds, LLC, GAMCO Investors, Inc. (1977-Present); Chairman, Lynch Interactive Corporation (1999-2002); Chief Executive Officer, Chairman, Lynch Corporation (1986-2001) **CR:** Board of Advisors, Health Point Capital Partners; Eastside Partner, Van Biema Value Fund LP (Now van Biema Value Partners, LLC); Caymus Governor, American Stock Exchange (Now NYSE American, Intercontinental Exchange, Inc.) **CIV:** Board of Directors, National Mentoring Partnership (Now MENTOR National); Board of Directors, National Italian American Foundation; Trustee, Winston Churchill Foundation; Lake Isle Association; Eastchester Zoning Board; Board of Governors, American Stock Exchange (Now NYSE American, Intercontinental Exchange, Inc.); Board of Trustees, Fordham Preparatory School; Board of Directors, Foundation for Italian Art and Culture; Board of Directors, American-Italian Cancer Foundation (Now AICF); Board of Trustees, Boston College; Chairman, Patron's Committee, Immaculate Conception School, Bronx, NY; Trustee, E.L. Wiegand Foundation, Reno, NV; Board of Directors, Bruce Museum; Board of Trustees, Roger Williams University; Board of Trustees, Fairfield University; Board of Overseers, Columbia University Business School **AW:** Discovery Award (2005); Public Service Award (2000); Ellis Island Medal of Honor for Business Leaders Award (1996); Columbus Citizens Foundation Award (1994); Cavaliere Award, Italian Legions of Merit

GABELLI, REGINA, T: Director of Institutional Marketing **I:** Advertising & Marketing **CN:** Gabelli Asset Management Company Investors **MS:** Married **SPN:** Mario Gabelli **C:** Director of Institutional Marketing, Gabelli Asset Management Company Investors **CIV:** Donor, Columbia University and Boston College (2017); Trustee, Boston College (2015); Donor, Fordham University (2010); Co-Founder, The Gabelli Foundation; Participant, The Giving Pledge

GABRIEL, RICHARD L., T: Supreme Court Justice **I:** Law and Legal Services **CN:** Colorado Supreme Court **DOB:** 03/03/1962 **PB:** Brooklyn **SC:** NY/USA **MS:** Married **SPN:** Jill Wichlens **CH:** Two daughters **ED:** JD, Carey School of Law, University of Pennsylvania (1987); BA in American Studies, Yale University, Cum Laude (1984) **C:** Supreme Court Justice, Colorado Supreme Court (2015-Present); Judge, Colorado Court of Appeals (2008-2015); Private Practice (1988-2008); Partner, Holme Roberts & Owen LLP (1994-2008); Associate, Holme Roberts & Owen LLP (1990-1994); Associate, Shea & Gould, New York, NY (1988-1990); Law Clerk, Honorary J. Frederick Motz, U.S. District Court District of Maryland, Baltimore (1987-1988) **CIV:** Vice Chair, Judicial Liaison Section, Colorado Bar Association (2016-Present); Chair, Our Courts (2015-Present); Fellow, American Bar Foundation (2013-Present); Professionalism Coordinating Council, Denver Bar Association, Colorado Bar Association (2009-Present); Minoru Yasui American Inn of Court (2009-Present); Chair, Content Committee, Our Courts (2009-Present); Judi-

cial Liaison Section, Colorado Bar Association (2008-Present); Executive Committee Member, Our Courts (2008-Present); Fellow, Colorado Bar Foundation (2003-Present); Director, Colorado Judicial Institute (1999-Present); Trumpeter, Colorado Wind Ensemble (1990-Present); Chief Justice's Commission on Professional Development (2011-2019); Board of Trustees, Denver Bar Association (2013-2016); Representative, Denver Bar Association (2010-2016); Chair, Professionalism Working Group, Chief Justice's Commission on Professional Development (2014-2015); Secretary, Judicial Liaison Section, Colorado Bar Association (2013-2015); President, Minoru Yasui American Inn of Court (2013-2014); Vice President, Denver Bar Association (2012-2013); Vice President, Minoru Yasui American Inn of Court (2012-2013); Federal Courts Committee, Our Courts (2007-2008); President, Colorado Wind Ensemble (1994-2008); Director, Colorado Wind Ensemble (1993-2008); Chair, Colorado Judicial Institute (2004-2006); Civil Litigator Column Editor, Colorado Lawyer (1996-2005); Vice Chair, Colorado Judicial Institute (2001-2002) **CW:** Author, Numerous Continuing Legal Education Papers (1990-Present); Co-Author, "Friending, Following, and Liking: Social Media and the Courts," 48 Colo. Law. 9 (July 2019); Co-Author, "Chapter on Rule 26," Colorado Civil Procedure Forms and Commentary (Debra Knapp ed. 1996, 2019); "Our Courts: A Model for Adult Education," 47 Colo. Law. 10 (July 2018); "One of the Greatest: Daniel S. Hoffman," 46 Colo. Law. 54 (July 2017); "Reflections on Colorado's State Appellate Courts," 45 Colo. Law. 81 (July 2016); "Six of the Greatest: James E. Bye," 44 Colo. Law. 41 (July 2015); Co-Author, "Caveat Advocatus: Some Traps for the Unwary in the Colorado Court of Appeals," 44 Colo. Law 51 (Jan. 2015); Co-Author, "The Mentoring Relationship: How to Make it Work and Why it Matters," 42 Colo. Law. 53 (Oct. 2013); "Professionalism in Today's Competitive Legal Market," 39 Colo. Law. 65 (June 2010); "Rule 606(b): Competency of Jurors as Witnesses," 25 Colo. Law 47 (Mar. 1996); Book Review, "Modern Evidence: Doctrine and Practice," 25 Colo. Law. 48 (Feb.1996); "Rule 615: Exclusion of Witnesses," 24 Colo. Law. 1299 (June 1995); "Rule 501: The Privilege of Self-Critical Analysis," 23 Colo. Law. 1291 (June 1994); "Rule 1006: Admissibility of Summary Evidence," 22 Colo. Law. 35 (Jan. 1993); "Rule 702: Admissibility of Expert Testimony Regarding Eyewitness Identification," 21 Colo. Law. 927 (May 1992); "The Strickland Standard for Claims of Ineffective Assistance of Counsel: Emasculating the Sixth Amendment in the Guise of Due Process," 134 U. Pa. L. Rev. 1259 (1986) **AW:** Pursuit of Justice Lifetime Achievement Award, Rocky Mountain Children's Law Center (2019); Award of Merit, Denver Bar Association (2014); Chambers' Leading Lawyers for Business (2007-2008); Colorado Super Lawyer (2007-08); Lawyer of the Year, Lawyers USA (2007); Intellectual Property Lawyer of the Year, Law Week Colorado (2007); Forty Under 40, Denver Business Journal (2002); Richard Marden Davis Award, Denver Bar Foundation (2002); Champion for Children, Rocky Mountain Children's Law Center (1997); Winner, Keedy Cup Moot Court Competition (1987) **MEM:** American Bar Association; Colorado Bar Association; Denver Bar Association; New York State Bar Association **BAR:** Colorado Bar Association (1990); New York State Bar Association (1987); Supreme Court of the United States

GADSBY, ROBIN EDWARD, T: Chemicals Executive **I:** Manufacturing **DOB:** 03/22/1939 **PB:** St Leonards-on-Sea **SC:** England **PT:** John Ernest Gadsby; Emily Louisa (Burt) Gadsby **MS:** Married **SPN:** Georgeann Portkalis (11/8/2014); Margaret

Alice Fuessel (12/29/1983, Divorced 2006); Olwyn Diane Bowen (08/05/1961, Divorced 1981) **CH:** Tricia Clare; Tracey Carolyn **ED:** Master of Business Administration, University of Chicago (1982); Master of Engineering, Cambridge University, England (1961); Master of Arts in Natural Sciences, Cambridge University, England (1960) **CT:** Chartered Financial Analyst **C:** President, Chemical and Polymers Group, ICI Americas Inc., Wilmington, DE (1990-1997); President, Polyurethanes Group Director, ICI Americas, Inc., Wilmington, DE (1986-1997); President, International Isocyantel Institute (1989); General Manager, Rubicon Chemicals Inc., Wilmington, DE (1984-1986); President, Katalco Corporation, Oak Brook, IL (1978-1983); Catalysts Research Group Manager, ICI PLC Agricultural Division, Billingham, England (1976-1977); Process Technical Manager, ICI PLC Agricultural Division, Billingham, England (1970-1976); Chemical Engineering Manager, ICI PLC Agricultural Division, Billingham, England (1967-1970); Plant Manager, ICI PLC Agricultural Division, Heysham, England (1965-1967); Corporate Planner, ICI Billingham Division, England (1962-1965); Chemical Engineer, ICI Billingham Division, England (1961-1962) **CR:** Chairman, Cempra Pharmaceutical (2006-2009); Board of Directors, Callard, Madden & Associates (1991-1998) **MEM:** President, International Isocynates Institute (1990-1991); UK Editorial Board, Institute of Chemical Engineers (1976-1977); American Institute of Chemical Engineers; American Chemical Society; Chartered Financial Analyst Institute; New York Academy of Sciences; Financial Analysts Society of Philadelphia; Lely Resort and Country Club, Florida; University of Chicago Chapter, Beta Gamma Sigma; Financial Analysts Society, Naples, FL; The Club at Pelican Bay, Naples, FL **MH:** Albert Nelson Marquis Lifetime Achievement Award **AS:** Mr. Gadsby attributes his success to the inspiration he has always drawn from science. **THT:** All skills and experiences combine to create the shape of life, so be attentive.

GAETZ, MATTHEW, "MATT" LOUIS, T: U.S. Representative from Florida; Lawyer **I:** Government Administration/Government Relations/Government Services **DOB:** 05/07/1982 **PB:** Hollywood **SC:** FL/USA **PT:** Don Gaetz; Victoria (Quertermous) Gaetz **ED:** JD, William & Mary Law School, Williamsburg, VA (2007); BS, Florida State University, Tallahassee, FL (2003) **C:** Member, U.S. House of Representatives from Florida's First Congressional District (2017-Present); Member, District Four, Florida House of Representatives, Tallahassee, FL (2010-2017); Attorney, Fort Walton Beach, FL **CR:** Member, Niceville Valparaiso Chamber of Commerce; Member, Navarre Beach Area Chamber of Commerce; Member, Greater Fort Walton Beach Chamber of Commerce; Member, Destin Area Chamber of Commerce **CIV:** Board Member, AMIkids, Emerald Coast, FL **MEM:** Okaloosa Bar Association **PA:** Republican **RE:** Baptist

GAHAN, DAVE, T: Singer **I:** Media & Entertainment **CN:** Depeche Mode **DOB:** 05/09/1962 **PB:** Epping **SC:** England **PT:** Len Callcott; Sylvia Callcott **MS:** Married **SPN:** Jennifer Sklias; Teresa Conroy (Divorced); Joanne Fox (Divorced) **CH:** Three Children **ED:** Student, Barstable School **C:** Lead Vocalist, Depeche Mode (1980-Present) **CW:** Musician, "Spirit" (2017); Musician, "Angels and Ghosts" (2015); Musician, "Delta Machine" (2013); Musician, "The Light the Dead See" (2012); Musician, "Sounds of the Universe" (2009); Musician, "Hourglass" (2007); Musician, "Playing the Angel" (2005); Musician, "Paper Monsters" (2003); Musician, "Exciter" (2001); Musician, "Ultra" (1997); Musician, "Songs of Faith and Devotion" (1993); Musician, "Violator" (1990); Musician, "Music for the Masses" (1987); Musician, "Black Celebration" (1986); Musician, "Some Great Reward" (1984); Musician, "Construction Time Again" (1983); Musician, "A Broken Frame" (1982); Musician, "Speak and Spell" (1981) **AW:** Inductee, Rock and Roll Hall of Fame (2020); Best International Group, Echo Awards (2010, 2014); Best International Video, "Tour of the Universe: Barcelona 20/21. 11.09," Porin (2011); Best Alternative Video, "Personal Jesus 2011," UK Music Video Awards (2011); Wood Pencil, "Wrong," D&AD Awards (2010); Best Narrative Video, Best Cinematography, "Wrong," Antville Music Video Awards (2009); Best Cinematography, "Wrong," Camerimage (2009); Pop Award, "Precious," BMI London Awards (2007); Best Dance Artist (Group), International Dance Music Awards (2006-2007); Best Group, MTV Europe Music Awards (2006); Best Group, Music Television Awards (2006); Popkomm Music DVD Award, "One Night in Paris," Popkomm Awards (2002); Innovation Award, Q Awards (2002); Best Artist Site Award, MidemNet Awards (2001); Best International Artist, Viva Comet Awards (2001); Best Album, "Ultra," Music Television Awards (1997); Best British Single, "Enjoy the Silence," Brit Awards (1991); Best Foreign Group, Rockbjornen (1990); Best Rock Group (Bronze), Bravo Otto Awards (1986-1987); Numerous Other Awards

GAIMAN, NEIL RICHARD, T: Novelist, Comics Writer, Screenwriter **I:** Writing and Editing **DOB:** 11/10/1960 **SC:** Portchester/England **PT:** David Bernard; Sheila Gaiman **MS:** Married **SPN:** Amanda Palmer (2011); Mary T. McGrath (1985, Divorced 2007) **CH:** Michael; Holly; Madeleine; Anthony **ED:** Coursework, Whitgift School, Croydon, England (1974-1977); Coursework, Ardingly College, England (1970-1974); Coursework, Fonthill School, East Grinstead, England **C:** Author, Short Fiction Novels, Comic Books, Graphic Novels, Nonfiction, Audio Theater, Films (1984-Present) **CIV:** Patron, Science Fiction Foundation; Patron, Open Rights Group;Supporter, Board Member, Comic Book Legal Defense Fund **CW:** Author, "Trigger Warning" (2015); Author, "The Ocean at the End of the Lane" (2013); Author, "Make Good Art Speech" (2013); Co-Editor, "Unnatural Creatures" (2013); Author, "Chu's Day" (2013); Author, "Fortunately the Milk" (2013); Author, "The Absolute Death (2009); Author, "Odd and the Frost Giants" (2008); Author, "The Graveyard Book" (2008); Author, "The Dangerous Alphabet" (2008); Author, "Interworld" (2007); Author, "M is for Magic" (2007); Executive Producer, Writer, "Beowulf" (2007); Producer, "Stardust" (2007); Author, "Fragile Things: Short Fictions and Wonders (2006); Author, "Anansi Boys" (2005); Author, "Mirrormask: A Really Useful Book" (2005); Co-Author, "The Alchemy of Mirror Mask" (2005); Writer, "MirrorMask" (2005); Author, "American Gods: The Monarch of the Glen" (2004); Author, "Melinda" (2004); Author, "The Wolves in the Walls" (2003); Writer, Director, "A Short Film About John Bolton" (2003); Author, "A Walking Tour of the Shambles" (2002); Author, "Adventures in the Dream Trade" (2002); Author, "Coraline" (2002); Author, "American Gods" (2001); Author, "Stardust" (1999); Writer, "Day of the Dead," "Babylon" (1998); Author, "Smoke & Mirrors" (1998); Writer, "Princess Mononoke" (1997); Author, "The Day I Swapped My Dad for Two Goldfish" (1997); Author, "Neverwhere" (1996); Writer, "Neverwhere" (1996); Author, "The Sandman" (1989-1996); Author, "Angels and Visitations: A Miscellany (1993); Author, "Now We Are Sick" (1991); Author, Novel, "Good Omens" (1990); Co-Author, "The Sandman: Book of Dreams"; Author, Numerous Works of Prose, Graphic Novels and Comics **AW:** May Hill Arbuthnot Honor Lecture Award, Association for Library Service to Children (ALSC), American Library Association (2020) Award, Literary Lights for Children, Boston Public Library (2010); Kurt Vonnegut Junior Award for Literature (2010); Galaxy Award for Most Popular Foreign Author, China (2009-2010); John Newbery Medal, American Library Association (2009); Comic-Con Icon Award (2007); Bob Clampett Humanitarian Award (2007); Mythopoeic Fantasy Award for Adult Literature (1999, 2006); Quill Book Award for Graphic Novels (2005); Angoulême International Comics Festival Prize (2004); Bram Stoker Award for Best Illustrated Narrative (2000, 2004); Hugo Award for Best Novella (2003); Nebula Award for Best Novella (2003); Locus Award for Best Young Adult Book (2003); Hugo Award for Best Novel (2002); Nebula Award for Best Novel (2002); Locus Award for Best Fantasy Novel (2002): Bram Stoker Award for Best Work for Young Readers (2001); Bram Stoker Award for Best Novel (2001); Sproing Award, Norway (1998); Nax Und Moritz Award for Best Foreign Writer (1998); HQ Award for Best Foreign Writer, Comic, Brazil (1994-1998); Lucca Award for Best Writer, Italy (1997); Yellow Kid Award (1995); Haxtur Award, Spain (1993-1995); Kemi Award for Best International Writer, Finland (1994); Squiddy Award for Best Writer (1990-1994); Defender of Liberty Award, Comic Book Legal Defense Fund (1993); Named Favorite Writer, Comics Buyer's Guide (1991-1993); World Fantasy Award (1991)

GALDA, DWIGHT WILLIAM, T: Principal **I:** Financial Services **CN:** Crescent Wealth Counsel **DOB:** 12/19/1942 **PB:** Brooklyn **SC:** NY/USA **PT:** Fred C.; Audrey D. **MS:** Married **SPN:** Suzanne Galda (05/20/2004) **CH:** Cynthia A. **ED:** MPA, MS, University of Texas (2002); MBA, Texas Christian University (2000); BA, Pennsylvania Military College (1964) **CT:** Chartered Financial Consultant, American Electric Power Company; Chartered Life Underwriter **C:** Principal, Crescent Wealth Counsel, Scottsdale, AZ (1997-Present); Regional Executive, USPA and IRA, Fort Worth, TX (1992-1996); District Executive, USPA and IRA, Fort Worth, TX (1986-1992); Representative, United Services Planning Association and Independent Research Agency, Fort Worth, TX (1983-1986) **CR:** Adjunct Economic and Management Professor, Flagler College (2015-2017); Adjunct Economic and Management Professor, Embry-Riddle Aeronautical University (2013-2017); Adjunct Economic and Management Professor, University of Advancing Technology (2009-2014); Adjunct Economic and Management Professor, Western International University (2003-2012) **MIL:** Lt. Col., U.S. Army (1964-1982); Army Attaché U.S. Embassy, Cambodia (1973-1975) **CW:** Creator, U.S. Army Opposing Force Program (1976); Contributor, Articles, Professional Journals **AW:** Pace Award, U.S. Department of Army (1976, 1977); Bronze Star with V and Two Oak Leaf Clusters; Legion of Merit; Meritorious Service Medal with Four Oak Leaf Clusters; Air Medal with V and Four Oak Leaf Clusters; Joint Services Commendation Medal; Army Commendation Medal; Purple Heart; Vietnamese Cross of Gallantry with Silver Star; Cambodian National Defense Service Medal with Gold Star; Presidential Unit Citation **MEM:** Fellow, CFA Institute; CFA Society Phoenix; Central Arizona Estate Planning Council **MH:** Albert Nelson Marquis Lifetime Achievement Award (1997-2020) **AS:** Mr. Galda attributes his success to energy, hard work, and creativity. **B/I:** Mr. Galda became involved in his profession because of his desire to make a difference in others' lives. **AV:** Running; Chamber music; Traveling **RE:** Episcopalian **THT:** Mr. Galda said, "You get what you give."

GALISON, PETER LOUIS, T: Scientist **I:** Education/Educational Services **CN:** Harvard University **DOB:** 05/17/1955 **PB:** New York **SC:** NY/USA **MS:** Married **SPN:** Caroline A. Jones (1987) **CH:** Two Children **ED:** Doctor of Philosophy in Physics and History Science, Harvard University (1983); Master of Philosophy in History and Philosophy Science, Cambridge University (1978); Bachelor of Arts, Master of Arts, in History Science, Harvard College, Summa Cum Laude (1977) **C:** Joseph Pellegrino University Professor, Harvard University (2006-Present); Mallinckrodt Professor of the History of Science and Physics, Harvard University (1994-2006); Harvard College Professor, Harvard University (2001); Chairperson, Department of the History of Science, Harvard University (1993-1997); Professor of Physics, Harvard University (1992); Professor of the History of Science, Harvard University (1992); Assistant Professor to Professor of Philosophy and Physics, Stanford University (1982-1992); Director, Collection of Historical Scientific Instruments, Harvard University **CR:** Fellow, John D. and Catherine T. Mac Arthur Foundation (1997-2002); Board of Directors, Center for Philosophy and History of Science, Boston University (1993-1996); Visitor, Institute of Advanced Study (1994-1995); Co-Chairperson, Program on the History of Science (1990-1992); Fellow, Center for the Advanced Study of Behavioral Science (1989-1990); Howard Foundation Fellow (1985); Visiting Assistant Professor, Department of History, Princeton University (1985); Visiting Professor, L'Ecole Normale Supérieure, Center for the Sociology of Innovation, L'Ecole Des Mines; Fellow, American Association for the Advancement of Science; Fellow, American Academy of Arts and Sciences; Fellow, American Physical Society **CW:** Producer, Co-Director, "Secrecy" (2008); Co-Author, "Objectivity" (2007); Author, "Einstein's Clock, Poincare's Maps: Empires of Time" (2003); Co-Editor, "Scientific Authorship" (2003); Co-Editor, "Atmospheric Flight in the Twentieth Century" (2000); Writer, Producer, "Films Ultimate Weapon: The H-Bomb Dilemma" (2000); Co-Author, "Picturing Science, Producing Art" (1998); Author, "Historian Mysteries of the Universe: A Science Odyssey" (1998); Author, "Image and Logic: A Material Culture of Microphysics" (1997); Co-Editor, "The Disunity of Science: Contexts, Boundaries and Power" (1996); Co-Editor, "Big Science: The Growth of Large-Scale Research" (1992); Author, "How Experiments End" (1987); Contributor, Articles, Professional Journals; Editorial Board, Critical Inquiry **AW:** Max Planck Prize, Max Planck Society and Alexander Von Humboldt Foundation (1999); Marta Sutton Weeks Faculty Scholar in Humanities (1989-1992); Presidential Young Investigator Award, National Science Foundation (1986-1991); Pfizer Prize for the Best Book in the History of Science **MEM:** Council, History of Science Society (1993-1995); International Society of the History of Science; Sigma Xi

GALKIN, ROBERT T., T: Company Executive **I:** Business Management/Business Services **DOB:** 09/18/1926 **PB:** Providence **SC:** RI/USA **PT:** Athur Sherman Galkin; Shirley (Mann) Galkin **MS:** Widow **SPN:** Wini Blacher (11/2/1952) **CH:** Ellen Lee Kenner; Jane S. Litner; Debra L. Krim **ED:** Postgraduate Coursework, Oxford University (1950); BA, Brown University (1949) **C:** President, Natco Home Fashions (1994-Present); President, Valley Hydro (1984-Present); President, New England Warehouse Co. (1984-Present); President, Valley Industries (1970-Present); President, Arctic Development (1965-Present); President, Norwood Development Corp. (1965-Present); President, Natco Products (1975-1994); President, NPC South (1985); Vice President, Natco Products (1960-

1975); Sales Manager, Natco Products Corp., West Warwick, RI (1949-1960) **CR:** Leader, Recycling Industry (1975-Present); Active, Development of Low Power Hydroelectric, Rhode Island **CIV:** U.S. Navy (1944-1945); City Council, Good Government Candidate, Cranston (1956); Advisory Board, Bryant College Institute of Family Enterprise **CW:** Writing; Collecting fine art and history **AW:** Rhode Island College Doctor of Humanities, Rhode Island Heritage Hall of Fame (2017); Newport Preservation Society Laurel Award (2013); Williams Award for Outstanding Contributions to Brown University **MEM:** Naval War College Association; Ledgemont Country Club; Goat Island Yacht Club; Brown Club; Rhode Island Commodores; President's Circle, Brown University; University Club; Newport Preservation Society; American Society **MH:** Albert Nelson Marquis Lifetime Achievement Award; Marquis Who's Who Top Professional **B/I:** Mr. Galkin's profession chose him; he did not choose his profession. He feels lucky to have found the many opportunities that eventually brought him his success.

GALLAGHER, DIANE, T: Nursing History and University Archivist **I:** Education/Educational Services **DOB:** 12/31/1936 **PB:** New York **SC:** NY/USA **PT:** Dwyer William; Leona (MacDonald) Shugrue **CH:** Maura; William; Katherine; Claire **ED:** Bachelor of Science in Organizational Behavior, Lesley College (1988); Coursework, Neighborhood Playhouse School of the Theatre (1957-1958); Associate of Arts in Theatre Arts, Colby Sawyer College (1957) **C:** Nursing History and University Archivist, Boston University (2000-Present); Director of Recruitment, U.S. Census Bureau, Boston, MA (1998-2000); Staff Representative, Peace Corps, Boston, MA (1993-1998); Volunteer, Peace Corps, Cape Verde, West Africa (1990-1992); Human Resources Consultant, Analog, Houghton-Mifflin, Boston, MA (1989-1990); Human Resources Representative, Fidelity Investments, Boston, MA (1985-1988); Human Resources Representative, Wang Laboratories, Lowell, MA (1983-1985); Placement Director, Katharine Gibbs School, Boston, MA (1979-1983); Partner, Bare Cove Art Gallery, Scituate, MA (1967-1982); TV Talk Show Host, WBZ TV, Boston, MA (1974-1977); Newspaper Columnist, South of Boston Mirror, Scituate, MA (1973-1976) **CR:** Career Counselor, Roxbury High School, Massachusetts (1981-1990); Member, Boston Council of International Visitors (1970-1980); Board Member, Greater Boston Rehabilitation Services, Cambridge, MA **CIV:** Active, Harvard Host Family Program (1970-Present); Board Member, Harvard Park Condo Association, Brookline, MA (1993-1996); Board Member, Marion Court College (1982-1988); Board Member, Massachusetts College Art (1972-1978); Commissioner, National Commission on the Observance of International Women's Year, Boston, MA (1976); Commissioner, Governor's Commission on the Status of Women, Boston, MA (1971-1976); Board Member, Advisor to President Colby, Sawyer College (1970-1976); Chairwoman, Child Care Task Force, Boston, MA (1974); Advisory Board of Directors, Cape Verde Coalition, Boston, MA **CW:** Author, "Lure of Service: My Peace Corps. Adventures at Middle Age" (2012) **AW:** Distinguished Alumni Award, Colby Sawyer College; Who's Who of American Women; Appointed by President Carter to the International Women's Year Commission; Appointed by Governor Dukakis to the Governor's Commission on the Status of Women; Appointed by Governor Sargent to the Governor's Commission on the Status of Women; U.S. Presidents' Volunteer Award; The Lillian Carter Award; Honorary Member, Sigma Theta Tau **MEM:** Returned Peace Corps Association **MH:** Albert Nelson Marquis Lifetime Achievement

Award; Marquis Who's Who Top Professional **B/I:** Ms. Gallagher first became involved in her profession in 1974, after she secured a position writing newspaper columns related to women. **AV:** Horse back riding; Swimming; Tennis; Writing non-fiction; Modern dance

GALLAGHER, MICHAEL, "MIKE" JOHN, PHD, T: U.S. Representative from Wisconsin **I:** Government Administration/Government Relations/Government Services **CN:** U.S. House of Representatives **DOB:** 3/3/1984 **PB:** Green Bay **SC:** WI/USA **ED:** Doctor of Philosophy in Government and International Relations, Georgetown University (2015); Master of Arts in Government, Georgetown University (2013); Master of Arts in Security Studies, Georgetown University (2012); Master of Science in Strategic Intelligence, National Intelligence University (2010); Bachelor of Arts, Woodrow Wilson School of Public and International Affairs, Princeton University (2006) **C:** Member, U.S. House of Representatives from Wisconsin's Eighth Congressional District (2017-Present); Foreign Policy Advisor, Committee on Foreign Relations (2015-Present); Member, Committee on Armed Services; Member, Committee on Homeland Security **MIL:** With, United States Marine Corps Reserves (2006-2013)

GALLAGHER, THOMAS C., T: Chairman **I:** Automotive **CN:** Genuine Parts Company **C:** Chairman, Genuine Parts Company (2017); Chairman, Chief Executive Officer, Genuine Parts Company (2012-2016); Chairman, President, Chief Executive Officer, Genuine Parts Company (2005-2012); President, Chief Executive Officer, Director, Genuine Parts Company (2004-2005); President, Chief Operating Officer, Director, Genuine Parts Company (1990-2004); Executive Vice President, Genuine Parts Company (1989-1990); With, SP Richards Company (1983); Joined, Genuine Parts Company (1963) **CR:** Board of Directors, STI Classic Funds, Oxford Industries

GALLEGO, RUBEN MARINELARENA, T: U.S. Representative from Arizona **I:** Government Administration/Government Relations/Government Services **DOB:** 11/20/1979 **PB:** Chicago **SC:** IL/USA **PT:** Elisa Gallego **MS:** Divorced **SPN:** Kate Widland Gallego (2010, Divorced 2017) **CH:** One Child **ED:** BA in International Relations, Harvard University **C:** Member, U.S. House of Representatives from Arizona's Seventh Congressional District (2015-Present); Member, District 16, Arizona House of Representatives (2011-2015); Member, Committee on Armed Services; Member, Committee on Natural Resources; Vice Chairman, Arizona Democratic Party; Chief of Staff, Councilman Michael Nowakowski, Phoenix, AZ; With, Riester, AZ; Director, Latino and New Media Operations, Strategies 360 **CR:** Board of Directors, Valley Citizens League; Board of Directors, Children's Museum **MIL:** Advanced through Grades, Corporal, United States Marine Corps Reserve (2000-2006) **CW:** Contributor, Articles, Phoenix Business Journal **AW:** Named Distinguished Freshman Lawmaker, The Arizona Republic (2011) **MEM:** Sigma Chi Fraternity **PA:** Democrat

GALLI, MIKE R., ESQ., T: Attorney **I:** Law and Legal Services **CN:** Office of the District Attorney for the County of Santa Clara **DOB:** 03/30/1958 **PB:** San Francisco **SC:** CA/USA **PT:** David Alfred Bonelli (Deceased); Ann Galli Atkinson (Deceased) **MS:** Single **ED:** JD, Santa Clara University School of Law, Santa Clara, CA (1983); BA in Political Science and Government, University of San Francisco, San Francisco, CA, Cum Laude (1980); AA in History, Foothill College, Los Altos, CA, with Honors (1978) **CT:**

POST Certified Level 1 Instructor (2011); Licensed (1983) **C:** Unit Member, Case Issuance Unit, Office of the District Attorney for the County of Santa Clara, San Jose, CA (2010-Present); Instructor, Robert Presley Institute of Criminal Investigation (2007-Present); Deputy District Attorney, Office of the District Attorney for the County of Santa Clara, San Jose, CA (1984-Present); Assistant Unit Leader, Felony Narcotics Unit, Office of the District Attorney for the County of Santa Clara, San Jose, CA (2009-2010); Assistant Supervisor, Felony Narcotics Unit, Office of the District Attorney for the County of Santa Clara, San Jose, CA (2008-2009); Unit Member, Restitution Services Unit, Office of the District Attorney for the County of Santa Clara, San Jose, CA (2007-2008); Unit Member, North County Division, Office of the District Attorney for the County of Santa Clara, San Jose, CA (2004-2007); Unit Member, San Martin Division, Office of the District Attorney for the County of Santa Clara, San Jose, CA (2003-2005); Unit Member, Motions, Writs and Appeals Unit, Office of the District Attorney for the County of Santa Clara, San Jose, CA (2001-2002); Unit Supervisor, Welfare Fraud Unit, Office of the District Attorney for the County of Santa Clara, San Jose, CA (1998-2001); Unit Member, Motions, Writs and Appeals Unit, Office of the District Attorney for the County of Santa Clara, San Jose, CA (1997-1998); Unit Member, Preliminary Examination Unit, Office of the District Attorney for the County of Santa Clara, San Jose, CA (1996-1997); Unit Member, Economic Crimes Felony Unit, Office of the District Attorney for the County of Santa Clara, San Jose, CA (1994-1996); Unit Supervisor, Asset Forfeiture Unit, Office of the District Attorney for the County of Santa Clara, San Jose, CA (1989-1994); Assistant Supervisor, Felony Narcotics Unit, Office of the District Attorney for the County of Santa Clara, San Jose, CA (1986-1989); Special Assistant, United States Attorney, Office of the District Attorney for the County of Santa Clara, San Jose, CA (1985-1986); Unit Member, Narcotics Unit, Office of the District Attorney for the County of Santa Clara, San Jose, CA (1985-1986); Unit Member, Juvenile Unit, Office of the District Attorney for the County of Santa Clara, San Jose, CA (1984-1985); Unit Member, Misdemeanor Driving Under the Influence Unit, Office of the District Attorney for the County of Santa Clara, San Jose, CA (1984) **CR:** Instructor, Robert Presley Institute of Criminal Investigation (ICI) (2007-Present); Technical Adviser and Instructor, California District Attorneys Association Search Warrant Law Seminar (2006-Present); Instructor on Informant, Search Warrant Law, and Search Warrant Drafting, San Jose Police Department Bureau of Investigation (1987-2014); Guest Lecturer, Stanford University Citizens Academy on Fourth Amendment Law (2012); Instructor, California District Attorneys Association High Technology Seminar (2008-2010); Instructor, Fourth Amendment Legal Updates, Los Gatos Police Department (1992-2001); Guest Lecturer, Numerous University and College Classes on Topics Related to Criminal Prosecution, Including Santa Clara University School of Law, Peninsula University Law School, Gavilan College, and West Valley College; Instructor, California Asset Forfeiture Law, California State Conference for the California Association for Property & Evidence (CAPE) and California Governor's Conference on Victims Services and Public Safety **CW:** Author, "Search Warrant Law & Practice Manual, Fifth Edition" (2019); Author, "Search Warrant Law & Practice Manual, Fourth Edition" (2016); Author, "California Electronic Communication Privacy Act" Police Technical (2016); Author, "Search Warrant Law & Practice Manual, Third Edition" (2014); Author, "Warrantless Searches" Police Technical (2014); Guest Lecturer, Stanford

University Citizen's Academy (2012); Author, "People v. Diaz: Right Result, but Wrong Rationale," California District Attorneys Association, Firewall (2012); Author, "Search Warrant Law & Practice Manual, Second Edition" (2012); Author, "Cell Phone Searches," California District Attorneys Association, Firewall (2009); Author, "Search Warrant Law & Practice Manual, First Edition," California District Attorneys Association (2009); Author, "Chapter II, Search and Seizure," California District Attorneys Association High Technology Crimes Manual (2008); Author, "Tracking Devices and the Fourth Amendment," California District Attorneys Association, Firewall (2008); Author, "Search Warrants," Santa Clara County Superior Court Judge's Duty Manual (2007); Author, "Chapter IV, Search Warrants, Second Edition," California District Attorneys Association, Hate Crimes Monograph, Prosecutor's Notebook (2006); Author, "Chapter IV, Search Warrants," California District Attorneys Association, Hate Crimes Monograph, Prosecutors Notebook (1999); Editor, "High-Technology Crime," KSK Publications (1995); Author, "Basic Search & Seizure & Search Warrants," Santa Clara County Superior Court Judge's Duty Manual (1994); Author, "Drafting Narcotics Search Warrants," California District Attorneys Association, Prosecutor's Brief (1988); Contributor of Numerous Articles **AW:** Named Prosecutor of the Year, California Narcotic Officers' Association, Region One (2016); Named Author of the Year, California District Attorneys Association (2009); Excellence Award, San Jose Police Department (1992); Named Santa Clara County Employee of the Month (1990); San Jose Police Department Narcotics Unit Commendation Letter (1989); San Jose Police Department Burglary Prevention Unit Commendation Letter (1989) **MEM:** High Tech Crime Committee, California District Attorneys Association (2007-Present); American Bar Association (ABA) (1985-Present); Public Fraud Committee, California District Attorneys Association (1998-2001); Asset Forfeiture Committee, California District Attorneys Association (1989-1994); California District Attorneys Association; Litigation Section, American Bar Association (ABA); Life Member, California Narcotics Officers' Association **BAR:** United States District Court for the Northern District of California (1983); California (1983) **AS:** Mr. Galli attributes his success to hard work. Following his parents' divorce, he was raised by his maternal grandparents (Robert G. & Anna C. Galli). They instilled a strong work ethic in him and believed strongly in education. **B/I:** Mr. Galli became involved in his profession because his father was shot in the head in the middle of a robbery in 1975. He fortunately survived it. There was a district attorney in San Francisco named Joe Freitas. They did not see this as a attempted murder, but as a robbery; the man who shot him went to jail for just two years and that bothered him a bit. Mr. Galli wanted to bring people like this to justice, so he became a prosecutor. **THT:** Mr. Galli's motto is, "The future doesn't belong to the timid," and John Wayne's observation that "Courage is being scared to death and saddling up anyway."

GALLUP, EMILY BRADFORD, T: Information Systems Consultant **I:** Information Technology and Services **CN:** Self-employed **DOB:** 02/09/1941 **PB:** Newton **SC:** NJ/USA **PT:** Winslow S. Gallup; Esther (Hoagland) Gallup **MS:** Divorced **SPN:** Rick Fayen (02/17/1973, Divorced 1982) **ED:** Master of Public Administration in Information Science, American University; BS in Mathematics and Physics, University of Maryland **C:** Office Administrator, Neighborhood Association of the Back Bay (NABB) (2012-2016); IT Consultant, (1964-2012); General Manager, EOS International, Boston, MA (1996-

2003); Director, Library Products, IME Group Ltd., Dedham, MA (1992-1996); Director, Information Systems, University of Pennsylvania, Philadelphia, PA (1984-1992); Assistant Director, Libraries, University of Pennsylvania, Philadelphia, PA (1984-1992); Director, Library Automation, Dartmouth College (1979-1984); Programmer, Analyst, Norris Cotton Cancer Center-Dartmouth College, Hanover, NH (1977-1979); Reference Librarian, Fiske Free Library, Claremont, NH (1976-1977); Consultant, U.S. Government (1972-1976); Senior Engineer, Creare, Inc., Hanover, NH (1973-1974); Senior Systems Analyst, Computer Sciences Corp., Falls Church, VA (1968-1973); Operations Research Analyst, Food and Drug Administration, Washington DC (1968); Technology Document Analyst, Naval Ship Research and Development, Carderock, MD (1965-1968); With, Documentation, Inc., Bethesda, MD (1963-1965) **CR:** Adjunct Professor, Drexel University (1989-Present); Lecturer, U.S. Information Agency AMPART, Europe (1987) **CIV:** Neighborhood Association of the Back Bay (NABB) **CW:** Co-author with F.W. Lancaster, "Information Retrieval"; Contributor, Numerous Articles, Various Scholarly and Professional Publications as Emily Gallup Fayen **AW:** Award, Best Information Science Book (1974) **MEM:** ARL/ILL Task Force, Indonesia National Academy of Sciences (1993-Present); Chairman, Special Interest Group on Technology Information Society, American Society of Information Science (1982-1983, 1989-1990); National Research Council Task Force, Indonesia National Academy of Sciences (1986-1987); Users Online Interaction, American Society of Information Science (1983-1984); American Library Association; Association Computing Machinery **MH:** Albert Nelson Marquis Lifetime Achievement Award **AS:** Ms. Gallup attributes her success to having a feeling of accomplishment. It could be all kinds of things as important as getting the bulletin out on time to making sure that all the abstracts got there properly. Doing a creditable, quality job is very important. **B/I:** She's not sure, her father was an electrical engineer and her mom was a fine arts major and Ms. Gallup has got some wonderful things from both of them. She's sure the technology part came from her father, she always found it fascinating. She always wanted not to serve technology, but to have it serve us–that was the fascination: to make all the new stuff work for us. **AV:** Sports car, owns a 1958 Porsche 356 Cabriolet

GANGAS, LILIBETH, T: Chief Technology Community Officer **I:** Business Management/Business Services **CN:** Kapor Center **ED:** MBA, Strategy and Finance, Leonard N. Stern School of Business, New York University (2013); BSEE, University of Southern California **CT:** Product Management, General Assembly **C:** Chief Technology Community Officer, Kapor Center (2016-Present); Tech for Good Fellow, New America CA (2018-2019); Associate Principal, Open Innovation, Accenture (2016); Lead Associate, Open Innovation and Crowdsourcing Services, Booz Allen Hamilton (2016); Associate, Open Innovation and Crowdsourcing Services, Booz Allen Hamilton (2013-2015); Entrepreneurial Institute Programs MBA Intern, New York University (2013); Business Development and Ops Fellow, NYU Stern Social Impact Fellowship, InVenture (Now Tala) (2012); Pre-MBA Consulting Track, MBA JumpStart (2011); Los Angeles Volunteer Captain, StartingBloc (2010-2011); Senior Multi Disciplined Engineer, Raytheon (2008-2011); Pre-MBA Global Immersion Consultant, MBA Diversity (2010); Multi Disciplined Engineer, Raytheon (2004-2008) **CR:** Board Member, Unity Council (2020-Present); Lecturer, Mills College, Oakland, CA (2019-Present); Board Member, One Degree,

Inc. (2017-Present) **CIV:** Advisory Board Member, AI4ALL (2017-Present); Oakland Organizer, Startup Weekend (2016-Present); Mentor, East Bay College Fund (2017-2019); Advisory Council Member, DreamWakers (2017-2018); Diversity and Inclusion Digest, Startup Digest (2017-2018); Business Mentor, Stanford Latino Entrepreneurship Initiative, Stanford University Graduate School of Business (2016-2017); Social Impact Edition, Startup Weekend (2015); Small Business Administration Startup in a Day Judge, U.S. Small Business Administration (2015); Panelist, Data Innovation, Council of Women and Girls, The White House (2015); Panelist, Mentoring Kickoff, Women Who Code (2015); Innovation Panelist, Central Intelligence Agency (2015); Social Venture Business Plan Competition Mentor, George Washington University (2014); Womens Edition Co-Organizer, Global Startup Battle DC Pitch Coach Organizer, Startup Weekend (2014); Boston Fellow, StartingBloc (2010) **AW:** Named, Most Influential Women in Business, San Francisco Business Times (2019); Named, 40 Under 40: Tech Diversity – Silicon Valley, theREGISTRY Bay Area and Digital Diversity Network (2016); Culture Catalyst, Innovation and Inclusion Awards, Digital Diversity Network (2016); Center for Engineering Diversity Student Leader Award, University of Southern California (2004); Scholarship, Leonard N. Stern School of Business, New York University **MEM:** Net Impact (2011-Present); USC Student Vice President, Society of Women Engineers (2003-2004); USC Student Vice President, Corporate Relations, Society of Hispanic Professional Engineers (2002-2004); Consortium for Graduate Study in Management, MBA JumpStart Diversity Forum, Vice President of Corporate Relations of the Management Consulting Association, Vice President of Treks of the Entertainment, Media and Technology Association, Student Consultant of Charter Cities, Ashoka Youth Venture, Leonard N. Stern School of Business, New York University

GARAMENDI, JOHN RAYMOND, T: U.S. Representative from California **I:** Government Administration/Government Relations/Government Services **DOB:** 01/24/1945 **PB:** Camp Blanding **SC:** FL/USA **PT:** Raymond V. Garamendi; Mary Jane (McSorley) Garamendi **MS:** Married **SPN:** Patricia Wilkinson **CH:** Six Children **ED:** MBA, Harvard Business School (1974); BA in Business, University of California Berkeley (1966) **C:** Member, U.S. House of Representatives from California's Third Congressional District, United States Congress, Washington, DC (2013-Present); Member, Committee on Agriculture (2013-Present); Member, Committee on Natural Resources (2013-Present); Member, Republican Study Committee (2013-Present); Member, U.S. House of Representatives from California's 10th Congressional District, United States Congress, Washington, DC (2009-2013); Lieutenant Governor, State of California (2007-2009); Insurance Commissioner, State of California (1991-1995, 2003-2007); Partner, The Yucaipa Companies (1998); Deputy Secretary, U.S. Department of the Interior (1995-1998); Member, District One, California State Senate (1977-1991); Member, District Seven, California State Assembly (1975-1977); Rancher, Sacramento County, CA **CIV:** Member, Ocean Protection Council (2007-2009); Member, California Emergency Council (2007-2009); Chair, California State Lands Commission (2007-2009); Chair, California Commission on Economic Growth (2007-2009); Trustee, California State University (2007-2009); Regent, University of California Santa Barbara (2007-2009); Chairman, University of California Merced Foundation (UC Merced Foundation) (1999-2009); Board Member, International Fund for Animal Welfare (IFAW) (1998-2009);

Member, Advisory Board, University of California Santa Barbara Bren School of Environmental Science & Management (1998-2009); Board Member, Operation Respect (1998-2002); Board Member, National Heritage Institute (1998-2002); Member, National Park Foundation (1998-2001); Member, National Association of Service and Conservation Corps (Now The Corps Network) (1998-2001); Volunteer, Peace Corps (1966-1968) **AW:** Glenn Seaborg Award, University of California (2009) **PA:** Democrat **RE:** Christian

GARCETTI, ERIC MICHAEL, T: Mayor of Los Angeles **I:** Government Administration/Government Relations/Government Services **DOB:** 02/04/1971 **PB:** Los Angeles **SC:** CA/USA **PT:** Gil Garcetti; Sukey (Roth) Garcetti **MS:** Married **SPN:** Amy Elaine Wakeland (01/04/2009) **CH:** Maya Juanita (Adopted) **ED:** MA in International Relations, Columbia University, NY; BA in International Relations, Columbia University, NY; Coursework, London School of Economics; Coursework, University of Oxford **C:** Mayor, City of Los Angeles, CA (2013-Present); President, Los Angeles City Council (2006-2012); Councilman, District 13, Los Angeles City Council (2001-2013); Assistant Professor of Diplomacy and World Affairs, Occidental College, Los Angeles, CA; Instructor of International Affairs, University of Southern California **CR:** Board of Directors, Roth Family Foundation; Board of Directors, International Criminal Court Alliance; Founding Board Member, Pobladores Fund, Liberty Hill Foundation **CIV:** Board of Directors, California Committee, Human Rights Watch; Board of Directors, Parents International Ethiopia; Board of Directors, Democratic Leadership for the 21st Century; Board of Directors, LA County Young Democrats **MIL:** Lieutenant, United States Navy Reserve Information Dominance Corps (2005-2013) **AW:** Person of the Year, NAACP (2014); Grantee, Young Leaders Fellow, French-American Foundation (2006); Asia 21 Fellow, Asia Society (2006); One of the 25 Angelenos Who Stand Out for Potential to Shape Lives in LA, LA Business Journal (2004); LA's Favorite Elected Official, LA Alternative Press (2003); Olson Award, Human Rights Watch (2002); Next Generation Leadership Fellow, The Rockefeller Foundation (1998); John F. Kennedy New Frontier Award; Green Cross Millennium Award, President Mikhail Gorbachev; Tiger Award, Valley Industry & Commerce Association; Rhodes Scholar **AV:** Taking photographs; Playing piano and jazz piano **PA:** Democrat

GARCIA, JESÚS, "CHUY" G., T: U.S. Representative from Illinois **I:** Government Administration/Government Relations/Government Services **DOB:** 4/12/1956 **PB:** Durango **SC:** Mexico **MS:** Married **SPN:** Evelyn Garcia (1980) **CH:** Three Children **ED:** Bachelor of Arts, University of Illinois at Chicago (1980) **C:** Member, U.S. House of Representatives from Illinois' Fourth Congressional District (2019-Present); Member, Seventh District, Cook County Board of Commissioners, (2011-Present); Member, First District, Illinois State Senate (1993-1999); Alderman, City of Chicago, IL (1986-1992); Deputy Commissioner, Department of Water (1984-1986); Assistant Director, Little Village Neighborhood Housing Service (1980-1984); Paralegal, Legal Assistance Foundation (1977-1980) **CR:** Chairperson, Aviation Committee; Member, Committee on Budget and Government Operations; Member, Committee on Education; Member, Finance Committee

GARCIA, JORGE, T: Head Band Director **I:** Education/Educational Services **CN:** United ISD - Trautmann Middle School **MS:** Married **CH:** Four Children **ED:** MA in Music, Texas A&M University, Kingsville, Texas (2000); BA in Music Education, Texas A&M University, Kingsville, Texas (1998) **C:** Head Band Director, United ISD - Trautmann Middle School (2005-Present); Teacher, United High School (2004-2005) **CR:** Teacher, Bigger Classes **CIV:** Volunteer, Feeding Veterans; Volunteer, Ronald McDonald House Charities (RMHC) **AW:** Nominated, Golden Apple Award (2013); Nominated, Teacher of the Year; Nominated, Teacher of the Month **MEM:** Texas Music Educators Association (TMEA); Texas Music Adjudicators Association (TXMAA) **MH:** Marquis Who's Who Top Professional **B/I:** Growing up, Mr. Garcia was surrounded by the school environment. His mom worked as a library aide at the local elementary school. He saw how she interacted with the kids. When he was in high school, he saw how passionate his band director was. He helped him out by being a section leader and enjoyed it. Senior year, Mr. Garcia was given a scholarship and decided to do what he loves, so he went into music education. He is passionate about teaching middle school children because he has the ability to mold them and set the foundation for when they move on to high school. **AV:** Family time; Working on his cars (3); Traveling; Plays with a community musical group called "USD Wind Symphony" **THT:** Mr. Garcia's motto is, "In order to be the best you can, never stop improving."

GARCIA, JOSE ZEBEDEO, T: Political Science Educator (Retired) **I:** Education/Educational Services **DOB:** 01/02/1945 **PB:** Saint Helena **SC:** CA/USA **PT:** Jose Zebedeo; Marjorie Louise (Lathrop) Garcia **MS:** Married **SPN:** Olivia Nevarez (04/23/1984); Barbara Hiller (04/1973, Divorced 12/1976) **CH:** Monica Luisa; Cristina **ED:** PhD, The University of New Mexico (1974); MA, Tufts University (1968); BA, Occidental College (1966) **C:** Retired (2014); Secretary of Higher Education, State of New Mexico (2010-2014); Assistant to Associate Professor, New Mexico State University, Las Cruces, NM (1975-2010); Assistant Professor, California State University, Chico, CA (1972-1975) **CR:** Speaker, U.S. Department of State, Various Latin American Countries (1984-Present); Consultant, Various Political Campaigns (1979-Present); Distinguished Visiting Professor, United States Army School of the Americas, Fort Benning, GA (1989-1991); Observer, Paraguayan Elections, Asuncion, Paraguay (1989); Chairman, New Mexico 529 Education Plan **CIV:** Director, Center for Latin American Studies, New Mexico State University (1991); Party Chairman, Democratic Party of Dona Ana County, Las Cruces, NM (1979-1983) **CW:** Author, "Governing New Mexico"; Contributor, Articles to Professional Journals **AW:** Fulbright Fellow, Ecuador (1966-1967); Teacher of the Year Award, United States Army School of the Americas **MEM:** Latin American Studies Association; American Political Science Association (APSA); Rocky Mountain Latin American Studies Council **MH:** Albert Nelson Marquis Lifetime Achievement Award; Marquis Who's Who Top Professional **AV:** Running; Reading; Photography

GARCIA, SYLVIA RODRIGUEZ, T: U.S. Representative from Texas; Chief Judge **I:** Government Administration/Government Relations/Government Services **DOB:** 09/06/1950 **PB:** San Diego **SC:** TX/USA **PT:** Rick Luis Garcia; Antonia (Rodriguez) Garcia **ED:** JD, Texas Southern University Thurgood Marshall School of Law (1978); BS, Texas Woman's University (1972) **C:** Member, U.S. House of Representatives from Texas' 29th Congressional District (2019-Present); Member, Sixth District, Texas Senate (2013-Present); Chief Judge, Municipal Court, City of Houston, TX (1987-Present); Harris County Commissioners Court (2002-2010);

Hearings Examiner, Equal Employment Opportunity Commission, Houston, TX (1985-1986); Sole Practice, Houston, TX (1985); Partner, Hubacker and Garcia, Houston, TX (1984-1985); General Manager, Counsel, ASI Universal Corp., Houston, TX (1981-1984); Vice-chairman, Appraisal Review Board, Houston, TX (1982-1983); Attorney, Gulf Coast Legal Foundation, Houston, TX (1978-1981); Law Clerk, City of Houston, TX (1978) **MEM:** Judicare Committee, Houston Bar Association (1985); Council, Women in Law Section, State Bar of Texas (1981-1982); Legislation Public Interest Committee, State Bar of Texas (1980-1981); Legal Services to Indigent Committee, State Bar of Texas (1979-1981); BA; State Bar of Texas; Houston Bar Association; Mexican-American Bar Association **BAR:** United States Court of Appeals for the Fifth Circuit (1981); United States District Court for the Southern District of Texas (1979); State of Texas (1978)

GARDNER, CHRISTOPHER, "CHRIS" PAUL, T: Chief Executive Officer **I:** Business Management/Business Services **CN:** Happyness **DOB:** 02/09/1954 **PB:** Milwaukee **SC:** WI/USA **PT:** Thomas Turner; Bettye Jean Gardner; Freddie Triplett (Stepfather) **MS:** Divorced **SPN:** Sherry Dyson (06/18/1977, Divorced 1986) **CH:** Christopher Jarrett Jr.; Jacintha **C:** Founder, Chief Executive Officer, Gardner Rich & Co. (Now Christopher Gardner International Holding Co.) (1987-2006); Bear Stearns & Co. (1983-1987); Intern, Dean Witter Firm (1981-1982); Research Assistant, University of California San Francisco; Medical Equipment Salesman; Motivational Speaker **CIV:** Board Director, National Fatherhood Initiative; Board Director, National Educated Foundation; Volunteer, Donor, Cara Progressive, Chicago, IL; Volunteer, Donor, Glide Memorial United Methodist Church, San Francisco, CA **MIL:** U.S. Navy (1970-1974) **CW:** Co-Author, "Start Where You Are: Life Lessons in Getting from Where You Are to Where You Want to Be" (2009); Co-Author, "The Pursuit of Happyness" (2006); Associate Producer, "The Pursuit of Happyness" (2006); Featured, "Evening News with Dan Rather," "20/20," "Oprah," "Today Show," "The View," "Entertainment Tonight," CNN, CNBC, Fox News Channel, Profiles in People, USA Today, Associated Press, The New York Times, Fortune, Jet, Reader's Digest, Trader Monthly, Chicago Tribune, San Francisco Chronicle, New York Post and Milwaukee Journal Sentinel **AW:** Best Biography or Autobiography, NAACP Image Awards (2007); Friends of Africa Award, Continental Africa Chamber of Commerce (2006); Award, Peace Over Violence (2006); Humanitarian Awards-Spirit Award, Los Angeles Commission on Assaults Against Women (2006); Named, New York Times and Washington Post Bestseller Lists (2006); Father of the Year, National Fatherhood Initiative (2002)

GARDNER, CORY SCOTT, T: U.S. Senator from Colorado **I:** Government Administration/Government Relations/Government Services **CN:** U.S. Senate **DOB:** 08/22/1974 **PB:** Yuma **SC:** CO/USA **PT:** John W. Gardner; Cindy L. (Pagel) Gardner **MS:** Married **SPN:** Jaime Gardner **CH:** Thatcher; Caitlyn; Alyson **ED:** Doctor of Jurisprudence, University of Colorado Law School (2001); Bachelor of Arts in Political Science, Colorado State University, Summa Cum Laude (1997) **C:** U.S. Senator, State of Colorado, Washington, DC (2015-Present); Member, Committee on Commerce, Science, and Transportation (2015-Present); Member, Committee on Energy and Natural Resources (2015-Present); Member, Committee on Foreign Relations (2015-Present); Member, Committee on Small Business and Entrepreneurship (2015-Present); Chairperson, National Republican Senatorial Committee (2017-2019); Member, U.S. House of Representatives from Colorado's Fourth Congressional District, United States Congress, Washington, DC (2011-2015); Member, U.S. House Committee on Energy and Commerce, Washington, DC (2011-2015); Minority Whip, Colorado House of Representatives, Denver, CO (2007-2011); Member, District 63, Colorado House of Representatives, Denver, CO (2005-2011); Farm Equipment Dealer (1997-1998, 2005-2011); Legislative Director to Senator Wayne Allard, U.S. Senate, Washington, DC (2002-2005); Communications Director to Senator Wayne Allard, U.S. Senate, Washington, DC (2001-2002) **PA:** Republican **RE:** Lutheran

GARDNER, SONIA ESTHER, T: Hedge Fund Manager **I:** Financial Services **CN:** Avenue Capital Group **DOB:** 02/16/1962 **PB:** Marrakech **SC:** Morocco **CH:** One Child **ED:** JD, Benjamin N. Cardozo School of Law (1986); Bachelor of Philosophy, Clark University, with Honors (1983) **C:** Co-founder, President, Managing Partner, Avenue Capital Group (1995-Present); Senior Portfolio Manager, Debt Brokerage Firm (1990-1995); Co-founder, Amroc Investments (1989-1990); Senior Attorney, Bankruptcy and Corporate Reorganization Department, Cowen and Company (Now Cowen Inc.) **CIV:** Board Member, 100 Women in Hedge Funds; Former Board Member, Her Justice; Board Member, Mount Sinai Medical Center **CW:** Featured, "The Alpha Masters: Unlocking the Genius of the World's Top Hedge Funds" (2012) **AW:** Women's Entrepreneurship Day Pioneer Award, United Nations (2017); Named One of the 25 Most Powerful Women on Wall Street, Business Insider (2013); Named One of the Top 50 Women in Hedge Funds, The Hedge Fund Journal (2010-2011); Industry Leadership Award, 100 Women in Hedge Funds (2008) **MEM:** Chair, Global Association Board Leadership, 100 Women in Hedge Funds (2015); Executive Committee, Former Board of Directors, Managed Funds Association

GARLAND, GREGORY CYRIL, T: Chairman, Chief Executive Officer **I:** Utilities **CN:** Phillips 66 Company **ED:** BSChemE, Texas A&M University (1980) **C:** Chairman, Chief Executive Officer, Phillips 66 Company (2012-Present); Senior Vice President of Exploration and Production Americas, ConocoPhillips, Houston, TX (2010-2012); President, Chief Executive Officer, Chevron Phillips Chemical Company LLC., The Woodlands, TX (2008-2010); Senior Vice President of Planning and Specialty Products, Chevron Phillips Chemical Company LLC. (2001-2008); Senior Vice President of Planning and Strategic Transactions, Chevron Phillips Chemical Company LLC. (2000-2001); General Manager for Qatar/Middle East, Chevron Phillips Chemical Company LLC. (1997-2000); General Manager of Natural Gas Liquids, Chevron Phillips Chemical Company LLC. (1995-1997); Manager of Planning and Development, Chevron Phillips Chemical Company LLC. (1994-1995); Manager, K-Resin Business Unit, Chevron Phillips Chemical Company LLC. (1992-1994); Manager, Olefins Business Unit, Chevron Phillips Chemical Company LLC. (1989-1992); Business Development Director, Chevron Phillips Chemical Company LLC. (1988-1989); Business Service Manager for Advanced Materials, Chevron Phillips Chemical Company LLC. (1986-1988); Sales Engineer for Plastics Resins, Chevron Phillips Chemical Company LLC. (1982-1986); Project Engineer, Plastics Technology Center, Chevron Phillips Chemical Company LLC., Bartlesville, OK (1980-1982) **CR:** Board of Directors, Amgen, Inc. (2013-Present); Board of Directors, Phillips 66 Company (2012-Present) **CIV:** Member, Chemical Engineering Industrial Advisory Board, Texas A&M University; Board of Directors, Executive Committee; American Chem-

istry Council; Board of Directors, Junior Achievement of Southwest Texas **MEM:** Board of Directors, Executive Committee, National Petrochemicals & Refiners Association

GARLAND, MERRICK BRIAN, T: Chief Judge **I:** Government Administration/Government Relations/Government Services **CN:** United States Court of Appeals District of Columbia Circuit **DOB:** 11/13/1952 **PB:** Chicago **SC:** IL/USA **PT:** Cyril Garland; Shirley Garland **MS:** Married **SPN:** Lynn Rosenman (09/19/1987) **CH:** Two daughters **ED:** JD, Harvard Law School, Magna Cum Laude (1977); BA, Harvard University, Summa Cum Laude (1974) **C:** Chief Judge, United States Court of Appeals for the District of Columbia, Washington, DC (2013-Present); Judge, United States Court of Appeals for the District of Columbia, Washington, DC (1997-2013); Principal Associate Deputy Attorney General, The United States Department of Justice, Washington, DC (1994-1997); Deputy Assistant Attorney General, Criminal Division, The United States Department of Justice, Washington, DC (1993-1994); Partner, Arnold & Porter Kaye LLP (Now Arnold & Porter Kaye Scholar LLP), Washington, DC (1992-1993); Assistant U.S. Attorney, The United States Department of Justice, Washington, DC (1989-1992); Associate Independent Counsel, The United States Department of Justice, Washington, DC (1987-1988); Partner, Arnold & Porter LLP (Now Arnold & Porter Kaye Scholar LLP), Washington, DC (1985-1989); Associate, Arnold & Porter LLP (Now Arnold & Porter Kaye Scholar LLP), Washington, DC (1981-1985); Special Assistant to Attorney General, The United States Department of Justice, Washington, DC (1979-1981); Law Clerk to Justice William J. Brennan Jr., Supreme Court of the United States, Washington, DC (1978-1979); Law Clerk to Honorable Henry J. Friendly, United States Court of Appeals for the Second Circuit, NY (1977-1978) **CR:** Member, Committee on Judicial Security, U.S. Judicial Conference (2008-Present); Member, Committee on Judicial Branch (2001-2005); Lecturer, Harvard Law School (1985-1986) **CIV:** President, Harvard University (2009-2010); Member, Board of Overseers, Harvard University (2003-2010) **CW:** Author, "Antitrust and State Action," Yale Law Journal (1987); Author, "Antitrust and Federalism," Yale Law Journal (1987); Author, "Deregulation and Judicial Review," Harvard Law Review (1985) **MEM:** The American Law Institute; The Phi Beta Kappa Society **BAR:** The United States Court of Appeals for the Tenth Circuit (1996); Supreme Court of the United States (1983); United States Court of Appeals for the Fourth Circuit (1980); United States Court of Appeals, District of Columbia Circuit (1980); United States Court of Appeals for the Ninth Circuit (1980); United States District Court District of Columbia (1980); The District of Columbia Bar (1979)

GARMS, DAVID JOHN, PHD, T: Manager, Foreign Service Officer **I:** Government Administration/Government Relations/Government Services **DOB:** 10/19/1942 **PB:** Worthington **SC:** MN/USA **PT:** Leonard John Garms; Gladys Anna Hinkeldey **MS:** Married **SPN:** Barbara F. Carter-Garms **CH:** Doria Jean; Diantha Barnwell **ED:** PhD, La Salle University, New Orleans, LA (2005); MPA, University of the Philippines, Manila (1978); BA in Sociology and Social Work, Gustavus Adolphus College, St. Peter, MN (1964) **C:** Manager, Shenandoah Cedar (2009-Present); Retired, Foreign Service Officer, U.S. Agency for International Development (1997); Consultant, Emergency Relief Programs, U.S. Agency for International Development (1997); Alternate Permanent Representative, U.S. Mission to the United Nations, Rome, NY (1993-1997); Chief Office of Program, U.S. Agency for International

Development (USAID), Colombo, Sri Lanka (1988-1993); Officer-in-charge, Sri Lanka/Nepal/Maldives Affairs, U.S. Agency for International Development (USAID), Washington, DC (1985-1988); Program Officer, U.S. Agency for International Development (USAID), Lilongue, Malawi (1981-1985); Program Officer, U.S. Agency for International Development (USAID), Lilongue, Malawi (1981-1985); Officer-in-charge of India Affairs, U.S. Agency for International Development (USAID), Washington, DC (1978-1981); Assistant Program Officer, U.S. Agency for International Development (USAID), Manila, Philippines (1976-1978); Education Officer, U.S. Agency for International Development (USAID), Dhaka, Bangladesh (1972-1976); Program Analyst, Development Planning for Africa Bureau, U.S. Agency for International Development (USAID), Washington, DC (1971-1972); Rehabilitation Officer, U.S. Agency for International Development (USAID), Saigon, Vietnam (1967-1971) **CR:** Chairman, Sri Lanka Rehabilitation Task Force, Washington, DC (1987-1988); Member, Peace Corps-Agency for International Development Task Force, Washington, DC (1986-1988); Secretary, U.S.-India Joint Commission, Washington, DC (1978-1980) **CIV:** Volunteer, Peace Corps, India (1964-1966) **CW:** Author, "With the Dragon's Children, Second Edition" (2015) **AW:** Superior Honor Award, U.S. Agency for International Development (USAID) **MEM:** President, Sri Lanka-America Society (1990-1991); American Foreign Service Association; Sri Lanka-America Society **MH:** Albert Nelson Marquis Lifetime Achievement Award; Marquis Who's Who Humanitarian Award **AS:** Dr. Garms attributes his success to inspiration from Bill Ruser and Tom Riley, and his paternal grandparents, John and Rosa Garms. **B/I:** Dr. Garms became involved in his profession because he wanted to do something in the humanitarian area. **AV:** Nature exploration; Writing **RE:** Lutheran **THT:** Dr. Garms' book can be purchased through http://www.davidgarms.com

GARNETT, KEVIN MAURICE, T: Former Professional Basketball Player **I:** Athletics **DOB:** 05/19/1976 **PB:** Mauldin **SC:** SC/USA **PT:** O'Lewis McCullough; Shirley Irby Garnett **MS:** Divorced **SPN:** Brandi Padilla (07/2004, Divorced 2019) **CH:** Kapri; Kavalli **C:** Consultant, Los Angeles Clippers, NBA (2017); Consultant, Milwaukee Bucks, NBA (2016-2017); Broadcaster, "Inside the NBA," TNT (2016); Host, "Area 21," "Inside the NBA," TNT (2016); Forward, Minnesota Timberwolves, NBA (1995-2007, 2015-2016); Forward, Boston Celtics, NBA (2007-2013); Forward, Brooklyn Nets, NBA (2013-2015) **CR:** Member, U.S. Olympic Men's Basketball Team, Sydney, Australia (2000); Owner, Official Block Family, Inc. **CW:** Actor, "Uncut Gems" (2019) **AW:** Named to Eastern Conference All-star Team, NBA (2008-2011, 2013); Named to NBA All-defensive First Team (2000-2005, 2008, 2011); Named to All-NBA First Team (2000, 2003-2004, 2008); NBA Championship, Boston Celtics (2008); Named Defensive Player of Year, NBA (2008); Named One of the 100 Most Powerful Celebrities, Forbes.com (2008); Named to Western Conference All-Star Team, NBA (1997, 1998, 2000-2007); J. Walter Kennedy Citizenship Award (2006); Named NBA Player of the Year, The Sporting News (2004); Named NBA Most Valuable Player (2004); Espy Award, Best NBA Player, ESPN (2004); Named NBA All-star Game Most Valuable Player (2003); Gold Medal, Sydney Olympic Games (2000); Named One of the Most Influential People of the Next Decade, Newsweek (1997) **AV:** Yoga; Music

GAROPPOLO, JAMES, "JIMMY" RICHARD, T: Professional Football Player **I:** Athletics **CN:** San Francisco 49ers **DOB:** 11/2/1991 **PB:** Arlington Heights **SC:** IL/USA **PT:** Tony Garoppolo Sr.; Denise

(Malec) Garoppolo **ED:** Coursework, Eastern Illinois University (2010-2013); Diploma, Rolling Meadows High School, IL (2010) **C:** Quarterback, San Francisco 49ers (2017-Present); Professional Football Player, New England Patriots (2014-2017) **AW:** Two-time Super Bowl Champion (2014, 2017); Walter Payton Award (2013); OVC Offensive Player of the Year (2013); First-team All-OVC (2013); Two-Time OVC Champion (2012-2013); Second-team All-OVC (2012)

GARRETT, GEOFFREY, PHD, T: Dean **I:** Education/Educational Services **CN:** University of Southern California Marshall School of Business **ED:** PhD, Duke University (1990); MA, Duke University (1984); BA, Australian National University (1980) **C:** Dean, University of Southern California Marshall School of Business (2020-Present); Dean, Reliance Professor, Management and Private Enterprise, The Wharton School, The University of Pennsylvania, Philadelphia, PA (2014-2020); Dean, Professor of Business, University of New South Wales Business School, Sydney, Australia (2013-2014); Dean, The University of Sydney Business School (2012-2013); Founding Chief Executive Officer, Professor, Political Science, U.S. Studies Centre (2008-2012); Senior Fellow, Pacific Council on International Policy, Sydney, Australia (2008-2009); President, Pacific Council on International Policy, Sydney, Australia (2005-2008); Professor, International Relations, Business Administration, Communications and Law, University of Southern California (2001-2005); Dean, University of California Los Angeles International Institute (2001-2005); Director, Ronald W. Burkle Center on International Relations, University of California Los Angeles (2001-2005); Vice Provost, International Studies, Professor, Political Sciences, University of California Los Angeles (2001-2005); Founding Director, Leitner Program in International Political Economy, Yale University (1999-2001); Director, Program in Ethics, Politics and Economics, Yale University (1999-2001); Professor, Political Science, Yale University, New Haven, CT (1997-2001); Founding Co-Director, European Studies Council, Yale University (1998-2000); Associate Professor, Multinational Management, The Wharton School, The University of Pennsylvania (1995-1997); Assistant Professor to Full Professor, Stanford University (1988-1997); Fellow in Politics, University College, University of Oxford (1986-1988) **CR:** Board of Directors, The Asia Foundation (2012-Present); Board of Directors, The Asia Foundation, Australia (2010-Present); Member, Editorial Board, European Political Science Review (2007-Present); Member, Editorial Board, Review of International Organizations (2004-Present); Board of Directors, CEMS (2011-2013); Board of Directors, Capital Markets Cooperative Research Centre (2011-2013); Board of Directors, U.S. Studies Centre (2008-2013); Member, Editorial Board, World Politics (2004-2010); Member, Editorial Board, Global Policy (2008); Board of Directors, Pacific Council on International Policy (2005-2008); Member, Editorial Board, Comparative Political Studies (1996-2005); Member, Editorial Board, Political Research Quarterly (1996-2005); Member, Editorial Board, International Organization (1997-2003); Visiting Fellow, Juan March Institute (1998); Member, Editorial Board, Political Behavior (1989-1995); National Fellow, Stanford University Hoover Institution (1993-1994); Visiting Professor, Stanford Graduate School of Business (1993-1994); Visiting Fellow, Wissenschaftszentrum, Berlin, Germany (1990-1993); Visiting Fellow, Public Policy Program, Australian National University (1992); Fellow, Center for Advanced Study in the Behavioral Sciences (1991-1992); Board of Advisers, Indian School of Business; Board of Advisers, Tsinghua

University School of Economics and Management **CW:** Co-Editor (with James Alt, Simone Chambers, Margaret Levi and Paula McClain), "The Encyclopedia of Political Science" (2010); Co-Editor (with Frank Dobbin and Beth Simmons), "The Global Diffusion of Markets and Democracy" (2008); Author, "Partisan Politics in the Global Economy" (1998) **AW:** Named One of the Top 50 Most Influential People in Education, The Australian (2012); Fulbright Scholar (1981-1986) **MEM:** Fellow, Academy of the Social Sciences in Australia Inc.; Council on Foreign Relations

GARTEN, INA, T: Cookbook Author; Television Show Host **I:** Food & Restaurant Services **DOB:** 02/02/1948 **PB:** Brooklyn **SC:** NY/USA **PT:** Charles H. Rosenberg; Florence (Rich) Rosenberg **MS:** Married **SPN:** Jeffrey Garten (12/22/1968) **ED:** MBA, The George Washington University; Coursework, Syracuse University **C:** Co-founder, Barefoot Contessa Pantry (2006-Present); Specialty Food Store Owner, Manager, Chef, Barefoot Contessa, Southampton, NY (1978-1985, 1985-1996, 2004); Budget Analyst, Office Management and Budget, The White House (1972-1978) **CIV:** Member, Design Review Board, East Hampton, NY **CW:** Columnist, "Entertaining," O, The Oprah Magazine (2003-Present); Host, "Barefoot Contessa: Back to Basics," Food Network (2002-Present); Columnist, "Entertaining is Fun!," Martha Stewart Living Magazine (1999-Present); Author, "Cook Like a Pro" (2018); Author, "Cooking for Jeffrey" (2016); Author, "Barefoot Contessa: Make It Ahead" (2014); Author, "Barefoot Contessa Foolproof: Recipes You Can Trust" (2012); Appearance, "30 Rock" (2010-2011); Actor, "Barefoot Contessa: How Easy is That?" (2010); Columnist, "Ask the Barefoot Contessa," House Beautiful Magazine (2006-2010); Actor, "Barefoot Contessa: Back to Basics" (2008); Author, "Barefoot Contessa at Home" (2006); Author, "Barefoot in Paris" (2004); Author, "Barefoot Contessa Family Style" (2002); Author, "Barefoot Contessa Parties!" (2001); Author, "Barefoot Contessa Cookbook" (1999) **AW:** Daytime Emmy Award for Best Culinary Host, The National Academy of Television Arts & Sciences (2009) **RE:** Jewish

GARUTTI, RANDY, T: Chief Executive Officer **I:** Food & Restaurant Services **CN:** Shake Shack **PB:** Hackensack **SC:** NJ/USA **ED:** BS, School of Hotel Administration, Cornell University (Cornell SHA) (1997) **C:** Director of Operations, Union Square Hospitality Group, New York, NY; General Manager, Union Square Cafe, New York, NY; General Manager, Tabla Restaurant, New York, NY; From Assistant General Manager to General Manager, Canlis Restaurant, Seattle, WA; Assistant General Manager, Chart House, Lahaina, Maui, HI; Manager, Chart House, Aspen, CO **CIV:** Board of Directors, Columbus Avenue Business Improvement District **AW:** Named, Nation's Restaurant News Annual Power List, NRN (2017); Named, 40 Under 40, Crain's New York Business (2006)

GARVIN, CHARLES DAVID, PHD, T: Professor Emeritus; Consultant; Therapist **I:** Education/Educational Services **CN:** University of Michigan **DOB:** 06/11/1929 **PB:** Chicago **SC:** IL/USA **PT:** Hyman Garvin; Etta (Raphaelson) Garvin **MS:** Married **SPN:** Janet Louise Tuft (01/27/1957) **CH:** David; Amy; Tony **ED:** PhD, The University of Chicago (1968); AM, The University of Chicago (1951) **CT:** Certified Social Worker **C:** Professor Emeritus, University of Michigan (2002-Present); Professor, University of Michigan, Ann Arbor, MI (1965-2002); Research Associate, The University of Chicago (1964-1965); Social Worker, Jewish Community Centers (JCC Chicago), Chicago, IL (1956-1964); Social Worker, Henry Booth House,

Chicago, IL (1948-1956) **CR:** Chairman, Committee for the Advancement of Social Work with Groups, New York, NY (1982-1986) **CIV:** Active, Model Cities Policy Board, Ann Arbor, MI (1970-1973); Board Member, Jewish Family Service, Ann Arbor, MI **MIL:** Served to Corporal, United States Army (1952-1954) **CW:** Co-author with Ortega, "Socially Just Practice in Groups: A Social Work Perspective" (2019); Co-author with Tolman, & Macgowan, "Group Works Research" (2016); Co-editor with Gutierrez & Galinsky, "It," and "Book of Social Work with Groups, Second Edition" (2016); Co-author with R. Fisch, "Social Work and Social Justice" (2016); Author, "Contemporary Group Work, Third Edition" (1997); Author, "Social Work in Contemporary Society" (1992); Author, "Interpersonal Practice in Social Work" (1985); Author, "The Work Incentive Experience" (1974); Author, Over 50 Articles **AW:** Lifetime Achievement Award, Council of Social Work Education (2012); Grantee, U.S. Health Service, National Institute of Mental Health (1986-1989); Fellow, U.S. Department of State, Pakistan (1973-1974); Grantee, U.S. Department of Labor (1969-1973) **MEM:** Fellow, American Orthopsychiatry Association, American Psychological Association; National Association of Social Workers; American Sociological Association; Council on Social Work Education; International Association for Social Work with Groups **MH:** Albert Nelson Marquis Lifetime Achievement Award; Marquis Who's Who Top Professional **B/I:** At age 19, Dr. Garvin went as a volunteer to a settlement house called Henry Booths House in Chicago, Illinois in 1948. He saw the impact of poverty and poor housing while volunteering. He eventually became a paid employee and went back to the settlement house to work after the Military. Working at the settlement house inspired Dr. Garvin to become a social worker because of his experience and wanting to help people in poverty. **AV:** Yoga **RE:** Jewish **THT:** Dr. Garvin's wife is also a social worker and they have been married for 62 years. Two of Dr. Garvin's children followed in his footsteps; his son, Dave, is the vice president of Catholic Social Services in Warsaw County and his daughter, Amy, is the manager of Adoptions for Children's Home Aid Society in West Palm Beach, Florida. For more information on Dr. Garvin's work, please see: http://www.iaswg.org/ and http://www.fsannarbor.org/

GARY, WILLIE, "THE GIANT KILLER" E., T: Partner **I:** Law and Legal Services **CN:** Gary, Williams, Parenti, Watson & Gary, PLLC **DOB:** 07/12/1947 **PB:** Eastman **SC:** GA/USA **PT:** Turner Gary; Mary Ella (McNarr) Gary **MS:** Married **SPN:** Gloria R. Gary (08/25/1978) **CH:** Kenneth; Sekou; Ali; Kobie **ED:** JD, North Carolina Central University (1974); BA in Business Administration, Shaw University (1971) **C:** Partner, Gary, Williams, Parenti, Finney, Lewis, McManus, Watson, & Sperando, P.L. (Now Gary, Williams, Parenti, Watson & Gary, P.L.L.C.), Stuart, FL (1976-Present); Private Practice, Martin County, FL (1975-1976) **CR:** Founder, MTBC Network **CIV:** Founder, The Gary Foundation; Chairman, Building Fund, Evergreen Baptist Church of Indiantown; Member, Adult Choir; Past President, Young Men's Progressive Association of Martin County; Chairman, Board of Trustees, Shaw University; Member, NAACP; Member, Urban League; Member, Civitan International; Member, Florida Guardsmen, Inc.; Member, United Way of Martin County; Member, Council, Martin Memorial Hospital Foundation; Contributor to Various Charities **CW:** Featured, "60 Minutes," "The Oprah Winfrey Show," "World News Tonight with Peter Jennings" **AW:** Named to the Power 150, Ebony Magazine (2008); Named One of the 100 Most Influential Black Americans, Ebony Magazine (2002, 2006); Named One of America's Top Black Lawyers, Black Enterprise Magazine

(2003); Horatio Alger Award, Horatio Alger Society (1999); Golden Trumpet Award, Turner Broadcasting Co. (1997); Learned Hand Award, American Jewish Committee (1996); Named Role Model of the Year, Bethune-Cookman College (Now Bethune-Cookman University) (1989); Named One of Two College Alumni of the Year, United Negro College Fund (1989); Named Lawyer of the Year, National Bar Association **MEM:** American Bar Association; Martin County Bar Association; St. Lucie County Bar Association, Inc.; Past Member, Board of Governors, Florida Bar Association; Past President, Florida Chapter, National Bar Association; Florida Bar Association; National Bar Association; Florida Academy Trial Lawyers (Now Florida Justice Association); American Trial Lawyers Association (Now American Association for Justice); Million Dollar Verdict Club, LLC; Phi Alpha Delta Law Fraternity, International **BAR:** U.S. District Court for the Middle District of Florida; U.S. District Court for the Southern District of Florida; State of Florida

GASE, MARY ELLEN, T: Music Teacher (Retired) **I:** Education/Educational Services **DOB:** 09/17/1937 **PB:** Saginaw **SC:** MI/USA **PT:** Louis A. Gase; Blanche A. (Pelkey) Gase **MS:** Single **ED:** Master's Degree in Humanities, California State University, Dominguez Hills, Carson, CA (1981); MA, California State University, Dominguez Hills, Carson, CA (1978); BS in Music Education, Saint Mary-of-the-Woods College (1959) **CT:** Registered Music Educator, National Association for Music Education (1990); Certified Teacher, K-12, State of Michigan **C:** Music Teacher, Saginaw Arts & Sciences Academy (1981-1999); Music Teacher, Saginaw ISD (1959-1981); Music Teacher, Summer School, Saginaw Schools **CR:** Certified Registered National Music Teacher, National Association for Music Education (1990) **CIV:** Junior League of the Great Lakes Bay Region (1962-Present) **CW:** Editor, "Keys to Success, Piano Books Volumes I-VIII" (1992-1999); Contributor, Articles on Music **AW:** Excellence in Teaching Award, Saginaw Community Foundation (1996); Excellence in Teaching Award, Michigan Department of Education (1993); Fellowship Grant, Henry and Leigh Bienen School of Music, Northwestern University (1984); National Guitar Curriculum Award (1980-1981) **MEM:** Immaculate Heart of Mary Parish (2002-2020); St. Stephen Church (1959-2002); Various Teacher Organizations (1959-1999) **MH:** Albert Nelson Marquis Lifetime Achievement Award **AS:** Ms. Gase attributes her success to her parents and to S. Laurette Bellamy, her piano teacher, who inspired her during her freshman and sophomore years of college. **B/I:** Ms. Gase became involved in her profession because of her parents, Louis A. Gase and Blanche A. Pelkey Gase. Her mother was a violinist and her dad was a singer and played the banjo. **AV:** Traveling in Europe and Asia; Taking photographs; Attending concerts; Writing poetry; Playing piano and guitar; Attending opera, ballet and symphony orchestra concerts; Taking continued education classes **PA:** Republican **RE:** Roman Catholic

GASICH, WELKO ELTON, T: Retired Aerospace Defense Executive, Management Consultant **I:** Aviation **DOB:** 03/28/1922 **PB:** Cupertino **SC:** CA/USA **PT:** Elija J. Gasich; Catherine (Paviso) Gasich **MS:** Married **SPN:** Patricia Ann (Gudgel) Gasich **CH:** Mark David Gasich **ED:** Sloan Executive Fellow, Stanford University (1967); Aeronautical Engineer, California Institute of Technology (1948); MS in Mechanical Engineering, Stanford University (1947); AB in Mechanical Engineering, Stanford University, Cum Laude (1943) **CT:** Certificate in Finance and Economics, Stanford Uni-

versity (1967) **C:** Aerospace Consultant, Encino, CA (1988-2000); Retired, Northrop Corp., Los Angeles, CA (1988); Executive Vice President, Programs, Northrop Corp., Los Angeles, CA (1985-1988); Senior Vice President, Advanced Projects, Northrop Corp., Los Angeles, CA (1979-1985); Corporate Vice President, Executive Aircraft Group, Northrop Corp., Los Angeles, CA (1976-1979); Corporate Vice President, General Manager, Aircraft Division, Northrop Corp., Los Angeles, CA (1971-1976); Corporate Vice President, General Manager, Northrop Ventura Division, Northrop Corp., Los Angeles (1967-1971); Vice President, Assistant General Manager, Technology, Northrop Corp., Los Angeles, CA (1961-1966); Director, Advanced Systems, Northrop Corp., Los Angeles, CA (1956-1961); Chief, Preliminary Design Aircraft Division, Northrop Corp., Los Angeles, CA (1953-1956); Chief, Aero Design, Rand Corp. (1951-1953); Supervisor, Aeroelastics, Douglas Aircraft Co. (1947-1951); Aerodynamicist, Douglas Aircraft Co. (1943-1944) **CIV:** Chairman, Advisory Council, Stanford School of Engineering (1981-1983); Chairman, United Way (1964); Chairman, Scout-O-Rama, L.A. Council, Boy Scouts of America (1964); Chairman, Explorer Scout, Executive Committee, Boy Scouts of America (1963-1964); Past Member, Advisory Council, Stanford Graduate School of Business **MIL:** Navy Reserve (1946-1954); Lieutenant, U.S. Navy (1944-1946) **CW:** Author, "40 Years of Ferrari V-12 Engines," SAE (1990) **MEM:** President, Stanford Graduate School of Business Alumni Association (1971); Fellow, American Institute of Aeronautics and Astronautics; Fellow, Society of Automotive Engineers; National Academy of Engineering (NAE); Navy League; Bel Air Country Club; Conquistadores del Cielo Club **MH:** Albert Nelson Marquis Lifetime Achievement Award **AV:** Reading; Stamp collecting; Formula race cars **PA:** Republican **RE:** Protestant

GASOL, MARC, T: Professional Basketball Player **I:** Athletics **CN:** Los Angeles Lakers **DOB:** 01/29/1985 **PB:** Barcelona **SC:** Spain **ED:** Diploma, Lausanne Collegiate School, Memphis, TN **C:** Center, Los Angeles Lakers (2020-Present); Center, Toronto Raptors (2019-2020); Center, Memphis Grizzlies (2008-2019); Center, Girona (2006-2008); Center, Barcelona Team (2003-2006) **AW:** Gold Medal, World Cup, China (2019); NBA Champion (2019); Bronze Medal, EuroBasket, Turkey (2017); Three-Time NBA All-Star (2012, 2015, 2017); All-NBA First Team (2015); Euroscar Player of the Year (2014); All-NBA Second Team (2013); NBA Defensive Player of the Year (2013); Bronze Medal, Euro-Basket, Slovenia (2013); NBA All-Defensive Second Team (2013); Silver Medal, Olympic Games, London, England (2012); Gold Medal, EuroBasket, Lithuania (2011); NBA All-Rookie Second Team (2009); Gold Medal, EuroBasket, Poland (2009); All-Spanish League Team (2008); Spanish League MVP (2008); Silver Medal, Olympic Games, Beijing, China (2008); Silver Medal, EuroBasket, Spain (2007); Gold Medal, World Cup, Japan (2006); Spanish League Champion (2004)

GATES, BILL HENRY III, T: Entrepreneur; Software Company Executive; Philanthropist **I:** Technology **CN:** Bill & Melinda Gates Foundation **DOB:** 10/28/1955 **PB:** Seattle **SC:** WA/USA **PT:** William Henry Gates Sr.; Mary (Maxwell) Gates **MS:** Married **SPN:** Melinda (French) Gates (01/01/1994) **CH:** Jennifer Katherine; Rory John; Phoebe Adele **ED:** Honorary LLD, Harvard University (2007); Coursework, Harvard University **C:** Technology Advisor, Microsoft, Redmond, WA (2014-Present); Non-executive Chairman, Microsoft, Redmond, WA (2008-2014); Chairman of the Board, Microsoft, Redmond, WA (1981-2008); Chief Software

Architect, Microsoft, Redmond, WA (2000-2006); Chief Executive Officer, Microsoft, Redmond, WA (1981-2000); Executive Vice President, Development Activities, Microsoft, Redmond, WA (1982-1983); President, Microsoft, Redmond, WA (1977-1982); General Partner, Microsoft, Redmond, WA (1975-1977); Co-founder, Microsoft, Albuquerque, NM (1975); Co-founder, Traf-O-Data Co., Seattle, WA (1972-1973) **CR:** Board of Directors, Berkshire Hathaway Inc. (2004-Present); Board of Directors, Microsoft (1981-Present); Speaker, Consumer Electronics Show (2006, 2008); Board of Directors, ICOS Corporation (1990-2005); Founder, Corbis (1989); Chairman, Chief Executive Officer, Cascade Investment LLC, Kirkland, WA **CIV:** Co-Founder, The Giving Pledge (2009-Present); Co-founder, Co-chair, Trustee, Bill & Melinda Gates Foundation (2000-Present); Co-founder, Gates Learning Foundation (Formerly Gates Library Foundation) (1997-2000); Founder, Chairman, William H. Gates Foundation (1994-2000) **CW:** Author, "Business at the Speed of Thought" (1999); Co-author with Nathan Myhrvold and Peter Rinearson, "The Road Ahead" (1995) **AW:** Named One of the Forbes 400: Richest Americans (1986-Present); Named One of the World's Richest People, Business Insider (2019); Presidential Medal of Freedom, The White House (2016); Named One of the World's Most Powerful People, Forbes Magazine (2009-2014); Co-recipient with Melinda Gates, Lasker-Bloomberg Public Service Award, Albert & Mary Lasker Foundation (2013); Bower Award for Business Leadership, Franklin Institute (2010); Silver Buffalo Award, Boy Scouts of America (2010); Indira Gandhi Prize for Peace, Disarmament and Development for Work with Gates Foundation (2009); Named One of the 100 Agents of Change, Rolling Stone Magazine (2009); Named to the Global Elite, Newsweek Magazine (2008); Einstein Award, Hebrew University (2008); Named Honorary Trustee, Peking University (2007); Named One of the 25 Most Powerful People in Business, Fortune Magazine (2007); Named Innovator of the Year, Consumer Electronics Association (2006); James C. Morgan Global Humanitarian Award (2006); Named One of the 50 Who Matter Now, CNNMoney.Com Business 2.0 (2006); Named One of the 100 Most Influential People in the World (2004, 2005, 2006); Named One of the Three Persons of the Year (2005); Named Knight Commander of British Empire (KBE), Her Majesty Queen Elizabeth II (2005); Named One of the Top 200 Collectors, ARTnews Magazine (2004); Named One of the Top 100 Most Influential People in Media, The Guardian (2001); Named One of the Top 50 Cyber Elite, TIME Magazine (1998); Named One of the World's Richest People, Forbes Magazine (1996); Named CEO of the Year, Chief Executive Magazine (1994); National Technology Medal, U.S. Department of Commerce (1992); Howard Vollum Award, Reed College, Portland, OR (1984) **AV:** Art; Reading; Golfing; Bridging; Playing Tennis

GATES, MELINDA ANN, T: Charitable Foundation Administrator **I:** Nonprofit & Philanthropy **CN:** Bill and Melinda Gates Foundation **DOB:** 08/15/1964 **PB:** Dallas **SC:** TX/USA **PT:** Raymond Joseph French; Elaine Agnes (Amerland) French **MS:** Married **SPN:** Bill Gates (01/01/1994) **CH:** Three Children **ED:** Honorary LHD, Duke University (2013); Honorary Doctorate, University of Cambridge (2009); MBA, Duke University Fuqua School of Business (1987); BS in Computer Science & Economics, Duke University (1986) **C:** Co-Chair, Trustee, Bill & Melinda Gates Foundation, Seattle, WA (2000-Present); General Manager, Information Products, Microsoft Corp., Redmond, WA (1987-1996) **CR:** Board of Directors, The Washington Post Co. (2004-2010); Board of Directors, Drugstore.com (1999-2006) **CIV:** Trustee, Duke

University (1996-2003); Co-Chair, Washington State Governor's Commission on Early Learning **AW:** Legion of Honour (2017); Otto Hahn Peace Medal (2016); Presidential Medal Of Freedom (2016); Padma Bhushan (2015); Named, 100 Most Powerful Women, Forbes Magazine (2005-2014); Dame Commander Of The Order Of The British Empire (2013); Co-Recipient, Lasker-Bloomberg Public Service Award, Albert & Mary Lasker Foundation (2013); Named, Global Elite, Newsweek Magazine (2008); Named, 50 Women To Watch, Wall Street Journal (2006, 2008); Named, World's 100 Most Influential People, TIME Magazine (2006); Named, Three Persons Of Year (2005); Named, Time 100 Most Influential **MEM:** Bilderberg Group **AV:** Running **RE:** Roman Catholic

GAVAN, WILLIAM HUTCHESON, T: Military Officer **I:** Military & Defense Services **DOB:** 07/28/1938 **PB:** Fort Sill **SC:** Oklahoma/USA **PT:** Paul Amos Gavan; Anne De Armond Gavan **MS:** Married **SPN:** Kathryn Rush **CH:** James; Annie; Retired Captain William H. Gavan Junior; Colonel Sean E. Gavan **ED:** MEd, North Carolina State College (1972); BS, West Point Military Academy (1962); Valley Forge Military Academy **C:** Assistant Division Command Support, 9th division, Fort Lewis, WA (1990-1992) Deputy Commander of Combat development activity Combined arms training Center Fort Levenworth, KS (1989-1990); Chief of staff, garrison Commander, U.S. Army Training Center, Fort Dix, NJ (1987-1989); Regiment Commander 29th infantry regiment, Fort Benning, GA (1985-1987); Chief of staff 3d infantry division, Wurtzburg, Federal Republic Germany (1983-1984); Chief of force mod. division, Pentagon, Washington DC (1980-1983); Branch chief inspections division, Pentagon, Washington DC (1979); Battalion Commander 8th infantry division (1977-1978); Officer Brigade XO, 2d Brigade 8th infantry division, Baumholder, Federal Republic Germany (1975-1976); Major, U.S. Military Academy, Fort Belvoir, VA (1974); Director military NGASSTC, U.S. Military Academy, Fort Belvoir, VA (1969-1972); Battalion advisor, U.S. Army, Vietnam (1967-1969); Aide de camp to commanding general Fred Weyand , U.S. Army, Vietnam (1966-1967); Company Commander 25th infantry division, U.S. Army, Vietnam (1965-1966); Advanced through grades to colonel, U.S. Army; Commissioned Second Lieutenant, U.S. Army (1962) **CR:** General Manager, West Virginia Turnpike (1992-1999) **AW:** Decorated Bronze Star with Two V Clusters; Silver Star; Four Purple Hearts; Three Legions of Merit; **MH:** Albert Nelson Marquis Lifetime Achievement Award **AV:** Hunting; Fishing; Golfing **RE:** Episcopalian

GAVIN, DONALD GLENN, T: Lawyer, Educator, Arbitrator, Public Speaker **I:** Law and Legal Services **DOB:** 10/12/1942 **PB:** Newark **SC:** NJ/USA **PT:** Louis Brooks Gavin; Elizabeth (Nievert) Gavin **MS:** Married **SPN:** Irene Dunn (11/25/1965) **CH:** Andrew Scott Gavin; Mitchell Bryant Gavin **ED:** LLM, George Washington University (1972); JD, University of Pennsylvania (1967); BS in Economics, Wharton School of Business, University of Pennsylvania (1964) **C:** Arbitrator, Mediator, Akerman, Sentefitt, Wickwire (2017-Present); Shareholder, Akerman, Senterfitt, Wickwire, Gavin (2006-2017); Founding Partner, Wickwire, Gavin Professional Corporation, Washington, LA, and Vienna, VA (1974-2006); Associate to Partner, Lewis, Mitchell & Moore, Washington, LA, and Vienna, VA (1972-1974); Law Clerk, Courts of Common Pleas, Philadelphia, PA (1967-1968) **CR:** Lecturer, Federal Publications Inc.; Lecturer, Nationwide for Hank Kaiser; Lecturer, Nationally and Internationally **CIV:** Past President, National Board, American Ceramic Circle; Construction

Committee at Temple; Washington Performing Arts **MIL:** Captain, Judge Advocate General's Corps, U.S. Army (1968-1972) **CW:** Contributor, Articles, Professional Journals **AW:** Outstanding Service Award, U.S. Court of Federal Claims **MEM:** Fellow, Numerous Positions, American Bar Foundation; Fellow, International Academy of Construction Lawyers; American Bar Foundation; American College Construction Lawyers; U.S. Council for International Business; International Bar Association; International Construction Project Committee, Chicago, Buenos Aires, Tokyo, Singapore, Madrid; Pennsylvania Bar Association; Virginia Bar Association; U.S. Court of Federal Claims Committee; Federal Bar Association **BAR:** Virginia (1973); D.C. (1972); Pennsylvania (1967) **MH:** Albert Nelson Marquis Lifetime Achievement Award; Marquis Who's Who Top Professional; Marquis Who's Who Humanitarian Award **B/I:** Mr. Gavin became involved in his profession because his dad was a lawyer and there was not much discussion on what he was going to do; it was destined that he was attending law school. He was in the military for four years and went to work for Judge Advocate General's Corps (JAG Corps) because when he came back to duty in 1968, it was the height of the Vietnam War. He went down to the Pentagon. Already commissioned to ROTC, he found out that he would be diffusing bombs and went to work for the JAGS office to be safer. For a while, they had him teaching at the Corps of Engineers headquarters, which he really enjoyed. One night, a neighbor was getting ready to leave and suggested that Mr. Gavin take his job, which was a contracting officers advisor position at headquarters and he volunteered. He was already in the midst of getting his master's degree when he started doing contracts; he just hooked it with a government contracts group. When he got out, he applied to many law firms and the offers he received were all with government contract firms. He went to work for Roy Mitchell of Lewis, Mitchell & Moore in 1972 and worked his way to partner in two years. In the later years, Mr. Gavin became the founding partner of Wickwire, Gavin. He then became an arbitrator as he became a shareholder with Akerman, Senterfitt, Wickwire, Gavin. Mr. Gavin also became interested in international arbitration through a friend, Jim Meyers, who led him to the International Bar Association. Mr. Gavin has arbitrated for the International Chamber of Commerce, headquarters out of Paris. There were many other countries involved. Mr. Gavin went out and made himself available to other groups.

GAVRITY, JOHN D., T: Retired Insurance Company Executive **I:** Insurance **DOB:** 10/26/1940 **PB:** Staten Island **SC:** NY/USA **YOP:** 2018 **PT:** John S. Gavrity; Eleanor R. (Decker) Gavrity **MS:** Married **SPN:** Camille Appello (04/16/1998) **CH:** John; Joseph **ED:** BS, Wagner College (1963) **C:** Retired (1998); Executive Vice President, Chief Actuary, USLife Corporation, New York, NY (1997-1998); Actuary, Executive Vice President, Financial Actuary, USLife Corporation, New York, NY (1975-1997); Staff, Associate Actuary, USLife Corporation, New York, NY (1963-1974) **MEM:** Fellow, Society of Actuaries; American Academy of Actuaries **MH:** Albert Nelson Marquis Lifetime Achievement Award **PA:** Republican **RE:** Roman Catholic

GAW, JERRY LEWIS, PHD, T: Historian, Minister **I:** Religious **DOB:** 03/12/1952 **PB:** Gainesboro **SC:** TN/USA **PT:** Lewis Ambrose Gaw; Sylvia Gerlene (Hix) Gaw **MS:** Married **SPN:** Vicki Renee (Clayton) Gaw **CH:** David Clayton Gaw **ED:** PhD, Mississippi State University, Starkville, MS (1990); MA, Northwestern State University, Natchitoches, LA (1983); BA, David Lipscomb College (Now Lipscomb

University), Nashville, TN, Magna Cum Laude (1974) **C:** Minister, Church of Christ at Cheap Hill, Chapmansboro, TN (1998-Present); Full Professor, History, Lipscomb University, Nashville, TN (2002-2020); Associate Professor, History, Lipscomb University, Nashville, TN (1996-2001); Assistant Professor, History, Lipscomb University, Nashville, TN (1991-1996); Instructor, History, Lipscomb University, Nashville, TN (1981-1982, 1984-1990); Graduate Teaching Assistant, Mississippi State University, Starkville, MS (1982-1984); Associate Minister, Huntington Park Church of Christ, Shreveport, LA (1980-1981); Graduate Teaching Assistant, Northwestern State University, Natchitoches, LA (1979-1980); Minister, Cotton Valley Louisiana Church of Christ (1978-1980); Teacher, Shreve Christian School, Shreveport, LA (1978-1979); Minister, Church of Christ at Fort Walton Beach, Fort Walton Beach, FL (1976-1978); Teacher, Escambia Christian School, Pensacola, FL (1974-1976) **CR:** Chair, Membership Committee, European History Section, Southern Historical Association (2010-2012); Visiting Assistant Professor, Summer History Courses, Vanderbilt University, Nashville, TN (1991, 1993); Editorial Advisory Board, World Civilization, Collegiate Press, Alta Loma, CA (1989-1990) **CIV:** Introducer, Southern Festival of Books, Nashville, TN; Panelist, Community Access Television Series, Nashville, TN; Judge, Metro Social Science Fair, Nashville, TN; Interviewee, The Tennessean, Nashville, TN; Guest Speaker, Tennessee Military Collectors Association, Nashville, TN; Guest Speaker, World War II 50th Anniversary, Legislative Plaza, Nashville, TN; Guest Speaker, Senior Neighbor Outreach, Donelson, TN **CW:** Author, "A Time to Heal: The Diffusion of Listerism in Victorian Britain, Transactions of the American Philosophical Society" (1999); Author, "Joseph Lister, 1827-1912," Research Guide to European Historical Biography (1993); Author, "Edward Jenner, 1749-1823," Research Guide to European Historical Biography (1993); Author, "'Refuge in a Hostile White World': The Negro Church in North Louisiana during Reconstruction," North Louisiana Journal (1980); Reviewer, Six Books; Reviewer, Three Articles; Reviewer, Two Papers; Lecturer, Four Sessions of Lifelong Learning Program; Presenter, Six Papers, Various Professional Conferences; Author, "David Lloyd George: The Politics of Religious Conviction" **AW:** Nominee, John Frederick Lewis Award, American Philosophical Society's Best Book (1999); David Laine Memorial Award, Lipscomb University (1994); Second Place Essay Winner, Overdyke Student Award for North Louisiana History (1980); Grantee, The National Society of The Colonial Dames in the State of Tennessee (1974) **MEM:** Lifetime Member, Chapter President, Phi Alpha Theta (1974-1984); European History Section, Southern Historical Association **AS:** Professor Gaw attributes whatever success he has achieved in life to Jehovah God and his son, Jesus Christ, as well as the Holy Spirit. He was blessed with hardworking, devoted parents but now has a loving wife and son who continue to support him. Great professors and amazing colleagues have also encouraged him in his accomplishments. The church's leaders, as well as members, have always kept him motivated to preach the plain and simple truth in love. **B/I:** Professor Gaw started out to be a full-time minister but decided he would need another vocation. He always loved history. He was inspired by his history teachers alongside the popular television programs depicting the wonders of the past. He has combined his work as a historian with the ministry for a non-consecutive total of 32 years now. The roles have worked well together. **AV:** Traveling **PA:** Nonpartisan **RE:** Church of Christ **THT:** Professor Gaw knows life is a blessing from the Creator. All live, move, and have their being in Him (Acts 17:28). Each breath and heartbeat are due to him. Everyone should glorify him in thought, word, and deed.

GAYAM, VIJAY, MD, T: Attending Physician/Chief Hospitalist, Assistant Program Director; Clinical Assistant Professor of Medicine, Adjunct Professor of Medicine **I:** Medicine & Health Care **CN:** Interfaith Medical Center **PT:** Udhakar Gayam; Reddy Gayam **MS:** Married **ED:** MD, Internal Medicine Resident, Interfaith Medical Center, Brooklyn, NY (2012-2015); Bachelor of Medicine, Bachelor of Surgery (MB, BChir), Osmania Medical College, Hyderabad, India (2008); Intern, Osmania Medical College, Hyderabad, India (2007-2008) **CT:** Advance Cardiac Life Support for Healthcare Provider (2018-Present); Basic Life Support for Healthcare Provider (2018-Present); Certified, American Heart Association, Inc. (2018); Diplomat, American Board of Internal Medicine (2015); Certificate, Education Commission for Foreign Medical Graduates (2011); Medical License, State of New York **C:** Assistant Program Director, Interfaith Medical Center (2017-Present); Chief Hospitalist, Interfaith Medical Center (2016- Present); Teaching Attending Physician, Research Head and Quality Control Director, Department of Medicine, Interfaith Medical Center (2015-Present); Medical Director, Department of Psychiatry, Interfaith Medical Center (2017); PGY4 Chief Resident, Interfaith Medical Center (2015-2016); PGY3 Chief Resident, Interfaith Medical Center (2014-2015) **CR:** Adjunct Professor of Medicine, American University of Antigua (2015-Present); Clinical Assistant Professor, State University of New York (2015-Present); Clinical Observership, Departments of Medicine and Gastroenterology, University of Pennsylvania, Philadelphia, PA (2011); Clinical Externship, Department of Medicine, Swedish Covenant Hospital (Now Swedish Hospital), Chicago, IL (2011); Clinical Externship, Department of Emergency Medicine, East Texas Medical Center (2010-2011) **CIV:** Volunteer, New York Department of Health Medical Reserve Corps (2018); Pulse Polio Immunization Program, India (2003-2007); Research Associate, Division of Gastroenterology, Department of Medicine, New York University Langone Health, New York University School of Medicine; Graduate Medical Education Committee, Pharmacy and Therapeutics Committee, Cardiac Arrest Committee, Quality Assurance Committee, Risk Management Committee, Interfaith Medical Center; Health Camp in Rural Villages, Hyderabad, India; Volunteer, Urgent Care, Comprehensive Care and Health Education for Underserved Communities, Hyderabad, India **CW:** Editor, Nova Science Publishers, Intech Open Publishers, Gastroenterology & Hepatology International Journal (2019-Present); Reviewer, American Journal of Medicine, Annals of Internal Medicine, Journal of Internal Medicine, Therapeutic Advances in Gastroenterology, CUREUS, Quantitative Imaging in Medicine and Surgery (2019-Present); Editorial Board Member, Gastroenterology Online Journal, Trends in Case Reports (2019-Present); Editorial Board Member, Gastroenterology Research, Journal of Investigative Medicine High Impact Case Reports, Journal of Community Hospital Internal Medicine Perspectives, SCIREA Journal of Clinical Medicine, SCIREA Journal of Medicine, Journal of Clinical and Experimental Gastroenterology (2018-Present); Reviewer, Gut and Liver, Medical Science Monitor, American Federation for Medical Research, Journal of Community Hospital Internal Medicine Perspectives, Pan African Medical Journal, PLOS ONE, Gastroenterology Research, SAGE Open Medical Case Reports (2018-Present); Contributor, 52 Peer-reviewed Articles, Eight Book Chapters, Three Oral Presentations, 19 Poster Presentations **AW:** Outstanding Clinician in General Medicine, Venus International Foundation (2018-2019); Equity in Prevention and Treatment Award, New York Department of Health Viral Hepatitis Research Symposium (2018); Presidential Poster Award, American College of Gastroenterology (2018); Charles Cherubin Award, Interfaith Medical Center (2016-2017); PGY4 Chief Resident Award, Interfaith Medical Center (2015-2016); PGY3 Chief Resident Award, Outstanding PGY3 of the Year Award, Interfaith Medical Center (2014-2015); Best PGY2 and PGY3 Resident of the Month, Interfaith Medical Center (2014); Outstanding PGY2 Award of the Year, Interfaith Medical Center (2013-2014); Best PGY1 Resident of the Month, Interfaith Medical Center (2012); Grantee in Field **MEM:** Councilor, Eastern Section, American Federation for Medical Research (2018-Present); American College of Physicians; American College of Gastroenterology; American Association for the Study of Liver Diseases; Indian Medical Association; Andhra Pradesh Medical Council, India **AS:** Dr. Gayam attributes his success to his passion and hard work. He had the desire to come to the U.S. and follow his dream to become a doctor. **B/I:** Dr. Gayam is from India. He is the only one in his family that is highly educated. His parents always supported him. **THT:** Dr. Gayam follows the teachings in "Think and Grow Rich" by Napoleon Hill.

GEBBIA, JOE JR., T: Chief Product Officer **I:** Leisure, Travel & Tourism **CN:** Airbnb, Inc. **DOB:** 08/21/1981 **PB:** Atlanta **SC:** GA/USA **PT:** Joe Gebbia Sr.; Eileen Gabbia **ED:** BFA in Graphic and Industrial Design, Rhode Island School of Design (2005); Coursework in Business, Brown University and Massachusetts Institute of Technology **C:** Co-Founder, Neighborhood (2017-Present); Co-Founder, Chief Product Officer, Airbnb, Inc. (2008-Present) **CIV:** Participant, The Giving Pledge (2016-Present); Donor, Rhode Island School of Design (2014); Board of Trustees, Rhode Island School of Design **AW:** 40 Under 40, Fortune Magazine (2013)

GEHRY, FRANK OWEN, T: Architect **I:** Architecture & Construction **CN:** Gehry Partners, LLP **DOB:** 02/28/1929 **PB:** Toronto **SC:** Canada **PT:** Irving Goldberg; Sadie Thelma (Caplan) Goldberg **MS:** Married **SPN:** Panamanian Berta Isabel Aguilera (1975); Anita Snyder (1952, Divorced 1966) **CH:** Leslie; Brina; Alejandro; Samuel **ED:** Honorary Doctorate, University of Oxford (2017); Honorary Doctorate, University of Technology Sydney (2015); Honorary Doctorate, Juilliard School (2014); Honorary Doctorate, Princeton University (2013); Honorary Doctorate, University of Edinburgh (2000); Honorary Doctorate, Harvard University (2000); Honorary Doctorate, Yale University (2000); Honorary Doctorate, University of Southern California (2000); Honorary LLD, University of Toronto (1998); Honorary Doctorate, Southern California Institute of Architecture (1997); Honorary Doctorate, California College of Arts and Crafts (Now California College of the Arts); Honorary Doctorate, Whittier College (1995); Honorary HHD, Occidental College (1993); Honorary DEng, Technical University of Nova Scotia (1989); Honorary Doctorate of Visual Arts, California Institute of Arts (1987); Honorary DFA, Otis Art Institute at Parsons School of Design (1989); Honorary DFA, Rhode Island School of Design (1987); Postgraduate Coursework, Harvard University (1956-1957); BArch, University of Southern California (1954) **CT:** Registered Professional Architect, State of California **C:** Principal, Gehry Partners, LLP (Formerly Frank O. Gehry & Associates and Gehry & Krueger, Inc.), Santa Monica, CA (1962-Present); Planning, Design and Project Director, Victor Gruen Associates (Now Gruen Associates), Los Angeles, CA (1958-1961); Project Designer, Planner, Pereira & Luckman, Los Angeles, CA (1957-1958); Designer, Victor Gruen Associates (Now Gruen Associates), Los Angeles, CA (1953-1954) **CR:** Charlotte Davenport Professorship in Architecture, Yale University (1982, 1985, 1987-1989, 1999); Visiting Professor, UCLA (1998); Visiting Scholar, Swiss Federal Institute of Technology, Zürich, Switzerland (1996-1997); Eliot Noyes Chair, Harvard University (1984); William Bishop Chair, Yale University (1979); Distinguished Professor, Architecture, Columbia University, NY **CIV:** Trustee, Hereditary Disease Foundation, Santa Monica, CA (1970-Present) **CW:** Architect, Biomuseo, Panama City, Panama (2014); Architect, Louis Vuitton Foundation, Paris, France (2014); Architect, New World Center, Miami Beach, FL (2011); Architect, Opus Hong Kong (2011); Architect, Cleveland Clinic Lou Ruvo Center for Brain Health, Las Vegas, NV (2010); Architect, Peter B. Lewis Library, Princeton University, NJ (2008); Architect, IAC/Interactive Corp. East Coast Headquarters, New York, NY (2007); Architect, Marqués de Riscal Winery, Elciego, Spain (2006); Architect, MARTa, Headford, Germany (2005); Architect, IAC/InterActive Corp. West Coast Headquarters, Los Angeles, CA (2005); Architect, Pritzker Pavilion, Millennium Park, Chicago, IL (2004); Architect, Peter B. Lewis Weatherhead School of Management, Case Western Reserve University, Cleveland, Ohio (2003); Architect, Ray and Maria Stata Center for Computer, Information, and Intelligence Sciences (Building 32), Massachusetts Institute of Technology, Cambridge, MA (2003); Architect, Walt Disney Concert Hall, Los Angeles, CA (2002); Architect, Bard College Center for the Performing Arts (Now Fisher Center), Annandale-on-Hudson, NY (2001); Architect, DG Bank Headquarters, Berlin, Germany (2000); Architect, Experience Music Project, Seattle, WA (2000); Architect, Vontz Center for Molecular Studies, University of Cincinnati, Ohio (1999); Architect, Der Neue Zolihof, Dusseldorf, Germany (1999); Architect, Guggenheim Museum, Bilbao, Spain (1997); Architect, Nationale-Nederlanden Building, Prague, Czech Republic (1996); Architect, Team Disneyland Administration Building, Anaheim, CA (1995); Architect, Dancing House, Prague, Czech Republic (1995); Architect, EMR Communication and Technology Center, Bad Oeynhausen, Germany (1995); Architect, Vitra International Headquarters, Basel, Switzerland (1994); Architect, American Center, Paris, France (1994); Architect, Walt Disney Concert Hall, Los Angeles, CA (1993); Architect, Frederick R. Weisman Art Museum, Minneapolis, MN (1993); Designer, Golden Fish Sculpture, Olympic Village, Barcelona, Spain (1992); Architect, Advanced Technology Laboratories Building, University of Iowa, Iowa City, Iowa (1992); Architect, University of Toledo Center for Visual Arts, Toledo, Ohio (1992); Architect, Chiat/Day Headquarters (Now TBWA/Chiat/Day), Venice, CA (1991); Architect, Vitra International Manufacturing Facility and Design Museum, Weil am Rhein, Germany (1989); Architect, Engineering Research Laboratory and Engineering Center, UCI Donald Bren School of Information & Computer Sciences, Irvine, CA (1986-1988); Architect, Frances Howard Goldwyn - Hollywood Regional Library, Hollywood, CA (1986); Architect, Aerospace Museum of California (1984); Architect, Temporary Contemporary Museum (Now The Geffen Contemporary at MOCA) (1983); Architect, Loyola Law School, Los Angeles, CA (1978-1992); Architect, Numerous Buildings, Exhibition Designs; Featured, Major Architectural Publications Including Newsweek, TIME Magazine, Forbes, The Economist, Vanity Fair, Art in America, The Wall Street Journal, The New York Times, Los Angeles Times, Washington

Post, Le Monde, L'Express, El Correo and Frankfurter Allgemeine **AW:** Canada's Walk of Fame (2019); Neutral Medal (2018); Presidential Medal of Freedom, The White House (2016); Harvard Arts Medal (2016); J. Paul Getty Medal (2015); Prince of Asturias Award (2014); Golden Lion for Lifetime Achievement, La Biennale di Venezia, Fondazione di Venezia (2008); Lifetime Achievement Award, Americans for the Arts (2000); Gold Medal, The American Institute of Architects (1999); Lotus Medal of Merit, Lotos Club (1999); Gold Medal, Royal Architectural Institute of Canada (1998); Friedrich Kiesler Prize, Friedrich Kiesler Foundation (1998); National Medal of Arts, National Endowment of the Arts (1998); Chancellor, City of Bilbao, Spain (1998); Honorary Consul (1997); Dorothy and Lilian Gish Award (1994); Praemium Imperiale Award, Japan Art Association (1992); Wolf Prize in Art, Wolf Foundation (1992); Pritzker Architecture Prize, The Hyatt Foundation (1989); Arnold W. Brunner Memorial Prize in Architecture, American Academy of Arts and Letters (1983) **MEM:** Honorary Academician, Royal Academy of Arts (1998); Academician, National Academy of Design (1994); Trustee, American Academy of Rome (1989); Fellow, The American Institute of Architects; Fellow, American Association for the Advancement of Science; Fellow, American Academy of Arts and Letters

GEIGER, MARK J., T: Attorney **I:** Law and Legal Services **CN:** Mark J. Geiger, Attorney at Law **PB:** Milwaukee **SC:** WI/USA **PT:** Shirley Geiger; Joseph Geiger **MS:** Married **SPN:** Pam **ED:** JD, Willamette University College of Law, Salem, OR (1983); BA in English, Carroll College (Now Carroll University), Waukesha, WI (1979) **C:** Lawyer, Mark J. Geiger, Attorney at Law (1984-Present) **CIV:** Golden Bond Rescue of Oregon; American Humane; American Society for the Prevention of Cruelty to Animals **CW:** Author, "The Trinity Effect"; Author, Six Screenplays **AW:** Named to Top 100 Trial Lawyers of America; Recipient, Top DUII Award **MEM:** Oregon Criminal Defense Lawyers Association (OCDLA); Marion County Association of Defenders; Oregon State Bar; Marion County Bar Association (MCBA) **BAR:** Oregon; United States Federal Court **AS:** Mr. Geiger attributes his success to his creativity. **B/I:** Mr. Geiger became involved in his profession because of his motivation to help the "underdogs." **AV:** Loves football (especially The Green Bay Packers), the Milwaukee Bucks and golf; Playing trumpet; Animals, especially dogs; Hiking with wife in Lake Tahoe and central Oregon **THT:** Mr. Geiger has been an attorney since 1984. He has successfully defended people charged with murder, and has won several post-conviction cases involving innocent individuals convicted of murder. Mr. Geiger has won appellate cases in which innocent people's convictions have been overturned. He works very hard to achieve a just result for his clients, but is always realistic about what he can and cannot do. Mr. Geiger is a published author; he discovered his aptitude for creative writing while he was a law student. His guiding principles encourage striving for the best and prioritizing honesty. Mr. Geiger used to play trumpet when he was in high school and college, and recently has started playing again. He loves animals, especially dogs. He always has two dogs, usually Golden Retrievers and German Shepherds. He and his wife, Pam, love to hike, often in Lake Tahoe and central Oregon.

GELB, PETER, T: Performing Company Executive **I:** Media & Entertainment **CN:** Metropolitan Opera Association **PT:** Arthur Gelb; Barbara Gelb **MS:** Married **SPN:** Keri Lynn Wilson **CH:** Two Children **ED:** Honorary Doctorate, Manhattan School

of Music (2019); Honorary Doctorates, Hamilton College, William E. Macaulay Honors College of City University of New York **C:** General Manager, Metropolitan Opera (2006-Present); General Manager Designate, Metropolitan Opera, New York, NY (2005-2006); President, Sony Classical (1995-2004); Head, American Division, Sony Classical (1993-1995); Founder, President, CAMI Video, Division of Columbia Artists Management (1982-1993); Assistant, Press Office, Boston Symphony Orchestra (1978-1981); Manager, Vladimir Horowitz **CW:** Executive Producer, "Dvořák in Prague: a Celebration" (1993); Executive Producer, "New Year's Eve Concert 1992: Richard Strauss Gala" (1992); Executive Producer, "The Metropolitan Opera Gala" (1991) **AW:** Gold Medal, National Institute of Social Science (2019); Sanford Prize, Yale School of Music (2013); Chevalier de la Légion d'honneur, French President (2013); Diplomacy Award, Foreign Policy Association (2012); Tribeca Disruptive Innovation Award (2011); Officier dans l'Ordre des Arts et des Lettres (2010); Named, 25 Leaders Reshaping New York, Crain's New York Magazine (2008); Named, 100 Most Influential People In The World, TIME Magazine (2008); Decorated Officier Dans l'Ordre Des Arts Et Des Lettres, France; Six Emmy Awards; Peabody Awards

GENADER, ANN MARIE, T: Educator, Journalist, Church Musician **I:** Education/Educational Services **DOB:** 05/28/1932 **PB:** West Milford **SC:** NJ/USA **PT:** Arthur Genader; Verina Agnes (Mathews) Genader **MS:** Domestic Partner **SPN:** Jack Brooks **ED:** MA, William Paterson College (1969); BS, Jersey City State College (1954) **CT:** Teaching Certification, New Jersey **C:** Organist, Church of Good Shepherd (2013-Present); Organist, Episcopal Church of Incarnation, West Milford, NJ (1977-1992); Organist, Our Lady Queen of Peace Catholic Church, West Milford, NJ (1960-1984); Organist, St. Joseph's Catholic Church, West Milford, NJ (1947-1967); Retired, Educator, Journalist; Church Musician **CR:** Teacher, West Milford Board of Education (1963-1997); Oakland Board of Education (1959-1963); Pompton Lakes Board of Education (1954-1959); Reporter, West Milford Messenger Newspaper; Freelance Writer, Multiple Newspapers and Magazines **AW:** Passaic County Teacher of Year (1991); West Milford Top Teacher of the Year (1990-1991) **MH:** Albert Nelson Marquis Lifetime Achievement Award **B/I:** Ms. Genader started playing the organ when she was 12 years old, teaching herself slowly but surely. She often played for services in the church. Ms. Genader's mother, Verina Agnes Genader, was an organist and teacher. She was Ms. Genader's teacher for four years. She additionally helped her mother in her classroom, becoming acquainted with the role of a teacher. She had always wanted to become a writer. She is happy to have pursued all of her early interests. **AV:** Practicing art and music; Reading; Painting

GENNETTE, JEFFREY, T: Chairman, Chief Executive Officer **I:** Retail/Sales **CN:** Macy's Inc. **ED:** BA in English & Art History, Stanford University, California (1983) **C:** Chairman, Macy's Inc (2018-Present); Chief Executive Officer, Macy's Inc (2017-Present); President, Macy's Inc. (2014-2017); Chief Merchandising Officer, Macy's, Inc. (formerly Federated Department Stores Inc.) (2009-2014); Chairman, Chief Executive Officer, Macy's West, Macy's, Inc. (formerly Federated Department Stores Inc.) (2008-2009); Chairman, Macy's Northwest, Macy's, Inc. (formerly Federated Department Stores Inc.), Seattle, WA (2005-2008); Executive Vice President, Director, Stores, Macy's Central, Macy's, Inc. (formerly Federated Department Stores Inc.), Atlanta, GA (2004-2005); Senior Vice President, General Merchandise Manager, Macy's West, Macy's, Inc.

(formerly Federated Department Stores Inc.) (2001-2004); Regional Vice President, Broadway Stores, Carter Hawley Hale Stores Inc.;Vice President, Manager, Emporium/Weinstocks stores, Carter Hawley Hale Stores Inc. (1994); Vice President, Store Manager, Macy's, Inc. (formerly Federated Department Stores Inc.), Minneapolis, MN (1993-1994); Store Manager, Macy's, Inc. (formerly Federated Department Stores Inc.), Santa Rosa, CA (1990-1993); Store Manager, Food and Agriculture Organization Schwarz Union Square, San Francisco, CA (1989-1990); Various Positions in Stores & Merchandise, Macy's, Inc. (Formerly Federated Department Stores Inc.) (1983-1989); Joined Macy's West Division, Macy's, Inc. (formerly Federated Department Stores Inc.), San Francisco, CA (1983) **CR:** Board of Directors, Macy's Inc. (2006-Present)

GEORGE, DANIEL, T: President **I:** Apparel & Fashion **CN:** Daniel George Custom Suits **ED:** Bachelor of Science, University of Central Florida (1990) **C:** Founder, Owner, Daniel George Custom Suits (2012-Present) **CIV:** Donator, Suited for Success **B/I:** Mr. George became involved in his profession despite lacking any formal training in fashion - instead, it was a lifelong passion. Drawing influence from his parents, who were very stylish people, he won multiple accolades for his impeccable dress sense, and this is what drew him toward the industry.

GEORGE, PAUL CLIFTON ANTHONY, T: Professional Basketball Player **I:** Athletics **CN:** Los Angeles Clippers **DOB:** 05/02/1990 **PB:** Palmdale **SC:** CA/USA **PT:** Paul George; Paulette George **ED:** Coursework, California State University, Fresno (2008-2010) **C:** Small Forward, Los Angeles Clippers (2019-Present); Small Forward, Oklahoma City Thunder (2017-2019); Small Forward, Indiana Pacers (2010-2017) **AW:** All-NBA First Team (2019); Two-Time NBA All-Defensive First Team (2014, 2019); Six-Time NBA All-Star (2013-2014, 2016–2019); Four-Time All-NBA Third Team (2013-2014, 2016, 2018); Gold Medal, Olympic Games, Rio de Janeiro, Brazil (2016); Two-Time NBA All-Defensive Second Team (2013, 2016); NBA Most Improved Player (2013); NBA All-Rookie Second Team (2011); Second-Team All-WAC (2010)

GEORGE, WILLIAM KYLE, T: Partner **I:** Law and Legal Services **CN:** Hartiens & Faulk **MS:** Married **CH:** One Child **ED:** MBA in Business Admistration, University of Louisiana at Lafayette (2008); MA in Accounting, University of Louisiana at Lafayette (2008) **C:** Partner, Hartiens & Faulk; Staff, Darnell, Sykes & Frederick **CIV:** President-Elect, Arcadian Chapter, Louisiana Certified Public Accountants **MEM:** Society of Louisiana Certified Public Accountants **AS:** Mr. George feels that gratitude and hard work are never wasted. Loyalty, as well, has kept his safe for many years. He additionally never followed only the money; instead, Mr. George prioritizes his clients. He feels the three primary factors behind his success are his gratitude, loyalty, and work ethic. **B/I:** Mr. George's father ran a successful small business. Despite his retail success, he always wished he was better at accounting. Because of this, accounting called to Mr. George. He decided to pursue the industry because it offered him the ability to work as much as he wanted.

GERARD, REDMOND, "RED", T: Snowboarder **I:** Athletics **DOB:** 06/29/2000 **PB:** Rocky River **SC:** OH/USA **AW:** First Overall, Toyota Grand Prix, Mammoth, CA (2019); First Place, Slopestyle, Burton U.S. Open (2019); Gold Medal, Slopestyle, Winter Olympics Gold Medal (2018); First Place,

Aspen Toyota Grand Prix (2018); Second Place, Mammoth Toyota Grand Prix (2018); First Place, Mammoth Toyota Grand Prix (2017); First Overall, Slopestyle, FIS Snowboard World Cup

GERE, RICHARD TIFFANY, T: Actor **I:** Media & Entertainment **DOB:** 08/31/1949 **PB:** Philadelphia **SC:** PA/USA **PT:** Homer Gere; Doris Ann (Tiffany) Gere **MS:** Married **SPN:** Alejandra Silva (04/2018); Carey Lowell (11/09/2002, Divorced 10/2016); Cindy Crawford (12/12/1991, Divorced 12/1995) **CH:** Homer James Jigme; Alexander Gere **ED:** Coursework, University of Massachusetts Amherst **CIV:** Co-founder, Tibet House US (THUS); Creator, The Gere Foundation; Chairman, Board of Directors, International Campaign for Tibet **CW:** Actor, "MotherFatherSon" (2019); Actor, "The Dinner" (2017); Actor, "Three Christs" (2017); Actor, "Norman: The Moderate Rise and Tragic Fall of a New York Fixer" (2016); Actor, "The Second Best Exotic Marigold Hotel" (2015); Actor, "The Benefactor" (2015); Actor, Producer, "Time Out of Mind" (2014); Actor, "Movie 43" (2013); Voice Actor, "Henry & Me" (2013); Actor, "Arbitrage" (2012); Actor, "The Double" (2011); Actor, "Brooklyn's Finest" (2009); Actor, "Amelia" (2009); Actor, Producer, "Hachiko: A Dog's Story" (2009); Actor, "Nights in Rodanthe" (2008); Actor, "The Hoax" (2007); Actor, "The Hunting Party" (2007); Actor, "I'm Not There" (2007); Actor, "Bee Season" (2005); Actor, "Shall We Dance?" (2004); Actor, "The Mothman Prophecies" (2002); Actor, "Unfaithful" (2002); Actor, "Chicago" (2002); Actor, "Autumn in New York" (2000); Actor, "Dr. T and the Women" (2000); Actor, "Runaway Bride" (1999); Actor, "An Alan Smithee Film: Burn Hollywood Burn" (1998); Author, "Pilgrim Photo Collection" (1998); Actor, "Red Corner" (1997); Actor, "The Jackal" (1997); Actor, "Primal Fear" (1996); Actor, "First Knight" (1995); Actor, "Intersection" (1994); Actor, Executive Producer, "Mr. Jones" (1993); Actor, Executive Producer, "Sommersby" (1993); Actor, "And the Band Played On" (1993); Actor, Executive Producer, "Final Analysis" (1992); Actor, "Rhapsody in August" (1991); Actor, "Internal Affairs" (1990); Actor, "Pretty Woman" (1990); Actor, "Miles from Home" (1988); Actor, "Power" (1986); Actor, "No Mercy" (1986); Actor, "King David" (1985); Actor, "The Cotton Club" (1984); Actor, "Breathless" (1983); Actor, "Beyond the Limit" (1983); Actor, "An Officer and a Gentleman" (1982); Actor, "American Gigolo" (1980); Actor, "Yanks" (1979); Actor, "Days of Heaven" (1978); Actor, "Blood Brothers" (1978); Actor, "Looking for Mr. Goodbar" (1977); Actor, "Baby Blue Marine" (1976); Actor, "Report to the Commissioner" (1975); Actor, "Strike Force" (1975); Actor, "Kojak" (1973); Actor, "Taming of the Shrew," "Midsummer Night's Dream," "Habeas Corpus," "Bent," "Grease"; Actor, "Killer's Head," "Richard Farina: Long Time Coming and Long Time Gone," "Back Bog Beast Bait"; Actor, "Great God Brown," "Camino Real," "Rosencrantz," and "Guildenstern Are Dead," Provincetown Playhouse; Actor, Composer, "Volpone," Seattle Repertory Theatre; Musician, Trumpet, Piano, Guitar and Bass, Composer, Music, Various Musical Groups; Actor, Appearances, Television Shows, Films **AW:** Medal of Gratitude, Albanian President Bamir Topi (2012); George Eastman Award for Distinguished Contribution to the Art of Film, George Eastman Museum (2012); Joel Siegel Humanitarian Award, Critics Choice Awards (2009); Independent Spirit Robert Altman Award (2008); Marian Anderson Award, City of Philadelphia, PA (2007); SAG Award for Outstanding Performance by a Cast in a Motion Picture, SAG-AFTRA (2003); Golden Globe Award for Best Actor – Motion Picture Musical or Comedy, Hollywood Foreign Press Association (2003); Award for Best Cast, Broadcast Film Crit-

ics Association (2003); Freedom of Expression Award, National Board of Review (1997); David di Donatello Award for Best Foreign Actor (1979)

GERKE, HEATHER D., T: Owner **I:** Health, Wellness and Fitness **CN:** True REST Float Spa **DOB:** 08/02/1973 **PB:** Wooster **SC:** OH/USA **PT:** Stephen Ferrell; Sharon Ferrell **MS:** Married **SPN:** Patrick Gerke **CH:** Three Children **C:** Owner, True REST Float Spa, Powell, Ohio (2014-Present); Director of Advertising and Marketing, The Robb Report (2002-2005) **AW:** Named Top Sales, Mind Body (2018); Named Best of Groupon (2017, 2018); Ranked Five Stars, Google Rating; Ranked A Grade, Better Business Bureau **MH:** Marquis Who's Who Top Professional **AS:** Mrs. Gerke attributes her success to her competitive and driven nature. Also just knowing that she started something; she always wants a successful outcome. Her hard work and dedication, not to mention the fulfillment in seeing the reward for people has been a driving factor behind her desire to keep going. **B/I:** In 2013, Mrs. Gerke received a text message from her husband saying "We're going to open a float spa..." and she responded "What the heck is that?" He heard about it as a form of therapy for veterans. Her husband, also being a veteran, became very intrigued by the idea and passed his interest along to Mrs. Gerke. Her husband is a former United States Marine, who battled with PTSD and so they decided to take a drive to Chicago from Ohio because it was the closest float spa at the time. He loved his experience. Mrs. Gerke already had prior executive experience in advertising and marketing and so she began to put her skills into play and follow through with opening the spa. **AV:** Hiking; Traveling; Camping; Reading **THT:** Mrs. Gerke says, "If you work, hard things pay off...I think that, just having goals is so important... Keeping your finger on the pulse, staying in tune with your community and business as well as running it to the best of your abilities is key..."

GERKEN, HEATHER KRISTIN, T: Dean; Professor **I:** Education/Educational Services **CN:** Yale Law School **DOB:** 02/19/1969 **PB:** Bolton **SC:** MA/USA **MS:** Married **SPN:** David Simon **ED:** JD, University of Michigan, Summa Cum Laude (1994); AB, Princeton University, Summa Cum Laude (1991) **C:** Dean, Yale Law School, New Haven, CT (2017-Present); Sol & Lillian Goldman Professor of Law, Yale Law School (2017-Present); Co-founder, Adviser, San Francisco Affirmative Litigation Project, Yale Law School (2006-Present); J. Skelly Wright Professor of Law, Yale Law School (2008-2017); Professor, Yale Law School (2006-2008); Visiting Professor of Law, Yale Law School (2005-2006); Professor, Harvard Law School, Cambridge, MA (2005-2006); Eugene P. Beard Faculty Fellow, Harvard University Center for Ethics and the Profession (Now Edmond J. Safra Center for Ethics) (2003-2004); Assistant Professor of Law, Harvard Law School (2000-2005); Associate, Jenner & Block LLP (1996-2000); Law Clerk for Justice David H. Souter, Supreme Court of the United States, Washington, DC (1995-1996); Law Clerk for Honorable Stephen Reinhardt, United States Court of Appeals for the Ninth Circuit, Los Angeles, CA (1994-1995) **CR:** Senior Adviser, Obama for America (2008); Member, Academic Steering Committee; Chair, Democratic Governance Working Group; Academic Advisor, The Tobin Project; Board of Supervisors, Roosevelt Institute; Board of Supervisors, Center on Law and Redistricting **CIV:** Trustee, Princeton University; Trustee, Campaign Legal Center; Trustee, Yale Law Journal **CW:** Author, "The Democracy Index: Why Our Election System is Failing and How to Fix It" (2009); Editor-in-chief, Michigan Law Review; Contributor, Articles to Professional Journals **AW:**

Yale Law Women Faculty Teaching Award, Yale Law School (2009); Sachs-Freund Award for Teaching Excellence, Harvard Law School (2003) **MEM:** Fellow, American Academy of Arts & Sciences (2017); ABA; Redistricting Task Force, ABA; American Law Institute; Order of the Coif **BAR:** District of Columbia (1998); Maryland (1997)

GERMANOTTA, STEFANI (LADY GAGA) JOANNE ANGELINA, T: Singer, Songwriter; Actress **I:** Media & Entertainment **DOB:** 03/28/1986 **PB:** Yonkers **SC:** NY/USA **PT:** Joseph Germanotta; Cynthia (Bissett) Germanotta **ED:** Coursework, New York University Tisch School of the Arts, New York, NY **C:** Creative Director, Polaroid (2010-2014); Former Songwriter, Interscope Records **CIV:** Co-founder, Born This Way Foundation (2012-Present) **CW:** Actress, "A Star Is Born" (2018); Singer, "Joanne" (2016); Actress, "American Horror Story" (2015-2016); Singer with Tony Bennett, "Cheek to Cheek" (2014); Actress, "Sin City: A Dame to Kill For" (2014); Singer, "ARTPOP" (2013); Actress, "Machete Kills" (2013); Actress, "Men in Black 3" (2012); Singer, Song, "Born This Way" (2011); Performer, Television Special, "Lady Gaga Presents The Monster Ball Tour at Madison Square Garden" (2011); Singer, Song, "Born This Way" (2011); Host, "A Very Gaga Thanksgiving" (2011); Singer, Song, "Alejandro" (2010); Singer Featuring Beyoncé, "Telephone" (2010); Appearance, "Gossip Girl" (2009); Singer, Song, "Bad Romance" (2009); Singer, "The Cherrytree Sessions" (2009); Singer, "The Fame Monster" (2009); Singer, Song, "Poker Face" (2008); Singer, Song, "Just Dance" (2008); Singer, "The Fame" (2008) **AW:** Grammy Award for Best Pop Duo/Group Performance, Recording Academy (2018); Golden Globe for Best Performance by an Actress in a Leading Role in a Series, Limited Series or Motion Picture Made for TV, Hollywood Foreign Press Association (2016); Grammy Award for Best Traditional Pop Vocal Album, Recording Academy (2015); Named Most Powerful Popstar, Guinness World Records (2015); Named One of the 100 Most Powerful Women, Forbes Magazine (2010-2014); Named One of the 100 Most Powerful Women in Entertainment, Hollywood Reporter (2011, 2013); Named Top Dance Album, Billboard Music Awards (2012); Named Favorite Album of Year, People's Choice Awards (2012); Named Top Dance Artist, Billboard Music Awards (2011, 2012); Named Top Pop Artist, Billboard Music Awards (2011); Grammy Awards for Best Female Pop Vocal Performance, Best Pop Vocal Album, Best Short Form Music Video, Recording Academy (2011); Named Top Electronic/Dance Album, Billboard Music Awards (2011); Named Best Pop Dance Track, International Dance Music Awards (2011); Fashion Icon award, Council Fashion Designers America (CFDA) (2011); Randy Shilts Visibility Award, Servicemembers Legal Defense Network (SLDN) (2011); Awards for Best Video with a Message, Best Female Video, MTV Video Awards (2011); Named Best Album of the Year, Best New Artist, Best Pop/Rock Artist, Best Song of the Year, World Music Awards (2010); Named Best International Album, Brit Music Awards (2010); Named Crossover Artist of Year, Latin Billboard Music Awards (2010); Awards for Best Collaboration, Best Female Video, Best Pop Video, Best Dance Music Video, Video of the Year, MTV Video Music Awards (2010); Grammy Awards for Best Dance Recording, Best Electronic or Dance Album, Recording Academy (2010); Named Video of Year, BET Awards (2010); Named Favorite Pop/Rock Female Artist, American Music Awards (2010); Named Favorite Pop Artist, Favorite Breakout Music Artist, People's Choice Awards (2010); Named One of the 100 Most Influential People in the World, TIME Magazine (2010); Best Dressed of the Year Award, Vogue Magazine

(2010); GLAAD Media Award for Outstanding Music Artist (2010); Teen Choice Award for Choice Music: Female Artist (2010); International Breakthrough Act Award, Brit Music Awards (2010); International Female Solo Artist Award (2010); Named Best Pop Dance Track, Breakthrough Solo Artist, International Dance Music Awards (2009); Named Best New Artist, MTV Video Music Awards (2009); Named to Barbara Walters' 10 Most Fascinating People of Year (2009)

GERSH, BERNARD J., MB, CHB, D.PHIL, T: Professor of Medicine **I:** Medicine & Health Care **CN:** Mayo Clinic **DOB:** 10/02/1941 **PB:** Johannesburg **SC:** South Africa **PT:** Maurice Gersh; Revee Gersh **SPN:** Ann Gersh (10/28/1977); Alison D. Brunette (1967, Divorced 1973) **CH:** Brunette; Jonathan; Amanda; Kate and Sarah (Twins); One Stepchild **ED:** DPhil, Oxford University, England (1970); MBChB, University of Cape Town, South Africa (1965); PhD. University of Coimbra, Portugal, Cum Laude **C:** Professor of Medicine, Mayo Clinic College of Medicine and Science, Rochester, MN (1985-1993, 1993-1998, 1998- Present); Consultant, Mayo Clinic, Rochester, MN (1978-1993, 1998); Chief, Division of Cardiology, Georgetown University Medical Center, Washington, DC (1993-1998); W. Proctor Harvey Teaching Professor, Georgetown University Medical Center, Washington, DC (1993-1998); Professor of Medicine, Georgetown University Medical Center, Washington DC **CR:** Senior Specialist, Senior Lecturer, Groote Schuur Hospital, University of Cape Town (1973-1978) **CIV:** Past Chairman, Council on Clinical Cardiology, American Heart Association (1995-1998) **CW:** Editor, Author, 148 Book Chapters; Contributor, More Than 1,180 Articles, Professional Journals **AW:** Gold Medal, European Society of Cardiology 2017; Distinguished Scientist Award, American Heart Association (2016); James B. Herrick Award, American Heart Association (2012); Silver Medal, European Society of Cardiology (2011); Distinguished Service Award, American College of Cardiology (2007); Distinguished Service Award, American College of Cardiology (2004); Rhodes Scholar (1965); Distinguished Achievement Award, Council on Clinical Cardiology; Distinguished Achievement Award, American Heart Association **MEM:** Trustee, American College of Cardiology (1995-2000); Fellow, Royal College of Physicians; Association of University Cardiologists; American Clinical and Climatological Association; Cosmos Club; Western Province Cricket Club; Marylebone Cricket Club **MH:** Albert Nelson Marquis Lifetime Achievement Award; Marquis Who's Who Top Professional **B/I:** Dr. Gersh became involved in his profession because in his last year of school, he had an illness and was hospitalized for three months and recovered. That event stimulated his interest in becoming a doctor.

GERTH, DONALD, "DON" R., T: University President, Educator (Retired) **I:** Education/Educational Services **DOB:** 12/04/1928 **PB:** Chicago **SC:** IL/USA **PT:** George C. Gerth; Madeleine (Canavan) Gerth **MS:** Married **SPN:** Beverly J. Hollman Gerth (10/15/1955) **CH:** Annette Schofield; Deborah Houghan **ED:** Doctor of Philosophy, University of Chicago (1963); Master of Arts, University of Chicago (1951); Bachelor of Arts, University of Chicago (1947) **C:** President, Professor Emeritus, California State University (2003-Present); President, Professor of Public Policy and Administration, California State University, Sacramento, CA (1984-2003); President, Professor of Political Science, California State University, Dominguez Hills, CA (1976-1984); Chairperson, Commission on Extended Education, California State University (1977-1982); Vice President of Academy Affairs,

California State University (1970-1976); Professor of Political Science, California State University (1964-1976); Coordinator, Institute for Local Government and Public Service (1968-1970); Associate Vice President of Academy Affairs, Director of International Programs, California State University (1969-1970); Co-Director, Danforth Foundation Research Project (1968-1969); Dean of Students, California State University, Chico (1964-1968); Associate Dean of Institutional Relations and Student Affairs, California State University (1963-1964); Associate Dean of Students, Admissions and Records, Member, Department of Political Science, San Francisco State University, San Francisco, CA (1958-1963); Admissions Counselor, University of Chicago (1956-1958); Assistant to President, Shimer College (1951); Field Representative, Southeast Asia, World University Service (1950) **CR:** Chairperson, American Council for the U.N. University (2004-2009); Member, American Council for the U.N. University (1998-2009); Vice Chairperson, U.N. Universal Council (2002-2004); Board of Governors, U.N. Universal Council (1998-2004); Chairperson, World Trade Center, North California (1996-2003); Past Chair, Accrediting Commission for Senior Colleges and Universities of Western College Association, California State University (1974-2003); Chairperson, Admissions Council, California State University (1974-2003); President, Association University (1996-1999); Chairperson, California State University Institute (1997-1998); Member, World Trade Center, North California (1996); Board of Directors, Ombudsman Foundation, Los Angeles, CA (1968-1971); With, Claremont Graduate School and University Center (1965-1969); Lecturer, University of the Philippines (1953-1954) **CIV:** Member, Committee on Governmental Relations, American Council on Education (1992-2002); Chairperson, South Bay Hospital Foundation (1995-1996); Executive Committee, Sacramento Area United Way (1991-1996); Chairperson-Elect, Sacramento Area United Way (1994-1995); Vice Chairperson, Sacramento Area United Way (1992-1994); Board of Directors, Committee Chairperson, Sacramento Area United Way (1991-1992); Member, Cultural Commission, Los Angeles, CA (1981-1984); Member, Varsity Scouting Council (1980-1984); Chairperson, United Way Campaign, California State University (1981-1982); Board of Directors, South Bay Hospital Foundation (1979-1982); Advisory Committee, Justice Programs, Butte College (1970-1976); Member, Personnel Commission, Chico Unified School District (1969-1976); Chairperson, Personnel Commission, Chico Unified School District (1971-1974) **MIL:** Served to Rank of Captain, U.S. Air Force (1952-1956) **CW:** Author, "The People's University: A History of the California State University" (2009); Contributing Editor, Papers on the Ombudsman in Higher Education (1979); Author, Editor, "An Invisible Giant" (1971); Contributing Editor, Education for the Public Service (1970); Co-author, "The Learning Society" (1969) **MEM:** Vice Chairperson, United Nations University Council (2001-2004); Board of Governors, United Nations University Council (1998-2004); President, International Association of University Presidents (1996-1999); Chairperson, Board of Directors, California State University Institute (1997-1998); Board of Directors, American Association of State Colleges and Universities (1990-1992); Chairperson, Association of Public Administration Educators (1973-1974); Advisory Committee, United Nations Educational, Scientific and Cultural Organization; American Political Science Association; American Society for Public Administration; Society for College and University Planning; Western Governmental Research Association; World Affairs Council of Northern California;

Western Political Science Association **MH:** Albert Nelson Marquis Lifetime Achievement Award **AV:** Reading **PA:** Democrat **RE:** Episcopalian

GERVAIS, RICKY DENE, T: Actor; Comedian **I:** Media & Entertainment **DOB:** 06/25/1961 **PB:** Reading **SC:** Berkshire/United Kingdom **PT:** Lawrence Raymond "Gerry" Gervais; Eva Sophia (House) Gervais **MS:** Partner **SPN:** Jane Fallon (1982) **ED:** BA in Philosophy, University College of London **C:** Host, "Ricky Gervais is Deadly Sirius," Sirius XM (2017-Present); Member, David Brent and the Foregone Conclusion (2013); Contributor, "Mary Anne Hobb's Radio 1 Show"; Disc Jockey, XFM Radio Station, London, England, United Kingdom; Assistant Events Manager, University of London Union; Manager, Suede; Seona Dancing **CW:** Actor, Writer, Director, Executive Producer, "After Life" (2019-Present); Host, Golden Globe Awards (2011, 2012, 2016, 2020); Performer, "Ricky Gervais: Humanity" (2018); Author, "Blazing Samurai" (2017); Author, "Special Correspondents" (2016); Author, "David Brent: Life on the Road" (2016); Actor, "Galavant" (2015); Actor, "BoJack Horseman" (2015); Voice Actor, "The Little Prince" (2015); Actor, "Muppets Most Wanted" (2014); Actor, "Night at the Museum: Secret of the Tomb" (2014); Actor, Writer, Executive Producer, Director, "Derek" (2012-2014); Actor, Writer, Director, Executive Producer, "Life's Too Short" (2011-2013); Voice Actor, "Escape from Planet Earth" (2013); Executive Producer, "The Making of Derek" (2013); Writer, Producer, "The Office," U.S. Version (2005-2013); Actor, Writer, Executive Producer, "The Ricky Gervais Show" (2010-2012); Voice Actor, "Spy Kids: All the Time in the World in 4D" (2011); Writer, Voice Actor, "The Simpsons" (2006, 2011); Director, Co-writer, "Cemetery Junction" (2010); Performer, "Out of England 2: The Stand-Up Special" (2010); Actor, Director Co-writer, "The Invention of Lying" (2009); Actor, "Night at the Museum: Battle of the Smithsonian" (2009); Performer, "Out of England: The Stand-Up Special" (2008); Actor, "Ghost Town" (2008); Author, "Flanimals: The Day of the Bletching" (2007); Author, "Flanimals: A Complete Natural History" (2007); Actor, "Stardust" (2007); Actor, Writer, Director, "Extras" (2005-2007); Author, "More Flanimals" (2006); Actor, "For Your Consideration" (2006); Actor, "Night at the Museum" (2006); Author, "Flanimals of the Deep" (2006); Author, "Flanimals" (2005); Voice Actor, "Valiant" (2005); Performer, "Comic Relief 2003: The Big Hair Do" (2003); Voice Actor, "Legend of the Lost Tribe" (2002); Actor, Writer, Director, "The Office," U.K. Version (2001-2003); Writer, "The Sketch Show" (2001); Actor, "Dog Eat Dog" (2001); Actor, "Meet Ricky Gervais" (2000); Writer, "Bruiser" (2000); Host, Writer, "Meet Ricky Gervais" (2000); Actor, "The 11 O'Clock Show" (1998); Performer, Stand-up Comedy Specials; Actor, Writer, Producer, Television Shows; Author, Books **AW:** Listee, 100 Most Influential People in the World, Time Magazine (2010); Golden Globe Award for Best TV Series - Musical or Comedy, Hollywood Foreign Press Association (2008); Primetime Emmy Award for Outstanding Lead Actor in a Comedy Series, Academy of Television Arts & Science (2007); Award for Best Television: Comedy Series, Writers Guild of America (2007); BAFTA Award for Best Comedy Performance, Best Situation Comedy Award (2002, 2003, 2004, 2006); Primetime Emmy Award for Outstanding Comedy Series, Academy of Television Arts & Sciences (2006); Co-Recipient, Rave Award for Podcast, Wired Magazine (2006); London's Funniest Man, Time Out Magazine (2004); Ranked Number Three, British Culture's Top 50 Movers and Shakers, BBC 3 (2004); Golden Globe Award for Best Actor in a

TV Series - Musical or Comedy, Hollywood Foreign Press Association (2004); O.K. Comedy Award (2003); Numerous Awards

GERWIG, GRETA CELESTE, T: Actress, Director **I:** Media & Entertainment **DOB:** 08/04/1983 **PB:** Sacramento **SC:** CA/USA **PT:** Gordon Gerwig; Christine (Sauer) Gerwig **MS:** Life Partner **SPN:** Noah Baumbach (2011) **CH:** Harold **ED:** Diploma, St. Francis High School (2002); Degree in English and Philosophy, Barnard College **CW:** Actress, "Three Sisters," New York Theatre Workshop (2020); Director, Writer, "Little Women" (2019); Voice Actress, "Isle of Dogs" (2018); Voice Actress, "The Meyerowitz Stories" (2017); Guest Appearance, "Saturday Night Live" (2017); Director, Writer, "Lady Bird" (2017); Actress, "Wiener-Dog" (2016); Actress, "Jackie" (2016); Guest Appearance, "The Mindy Project" (2016); Actress, "20th Century Women" (2016); Co-writer, Co-producer, Actress, "Mistress America" (2015); Guest Appearance, "Portlandia" (2015); Actress, "Maggie's Plan" (2015); Voice Actress, "China, IL" (2011-2015); Actress, "How I Met Your Dad" (2014); Actress, "Eden" (2014); Actress, "The Village Bike," MCC Theater (2014); Actress, "The Humbling" (2014); Actress, "Lola Versus" (2012); Actress, "The Corrections" (2012); Actress, "To Rome with Love" (2012); Co-writer, Actress, "Frances Ha" (2012); Actress, "No Strings Attached" (2011); Actress, "Damsels in Distress" (2011); Actress, "Arthur" (2011); Actress, "Greenberg" (2010); Actress, "Art House" (2010); Co-writer, Actress, "Northern Comfort" (2010); Actress, "The Dish and the Spoon" (2010); Actress, "You Won't Miss Me" (2009); Actress, "The House of the Devil" (2009); Actress, "Baghead" (2008); Actress, "Yeast" (2008); Co-director, Co-writer, Co-producer, Actress, "Nights and Weekends" (2008); Actress, Short Film, "Quick Feet, Soft Hands" (2008); Actress, "I Thought You Finally Completely Lost It" (2008); Co-writer, Actress, "Hannah Takes the Stairs" (2007); Actress, "LOL" (2006) **AW:** Named Best Picture, "Little Women," Boston Society of Film Critics (2019); Named Best Adapted Screenplay, "Little Women," Critics' Choice Movie Awards (2019); Named Best Adapted Screenplay, "Little Women," Florida Film Critics Circle (2019); Golden Globe Award for Best Motion Picture – Musical or Comedy, "Lady Bird," Hollywood Foreign Press Association (2018); Named One of the 100 Most Influential, TIME Magazine (2018); Auteur Award, "Lady Bird," Satellite Awards (2018); Rare Pearl Award, "Lady Bird," Denver International Film Festival (2017); MVFF Award, "Lady Bird," Mill Valley Film Festival (2017); Named Best Director, "Lady Bird," National Board of Review (2017); New Generation Award, Los Angeles Film Critics Association (2017); Named Best Director, Best Screenplay, "Lady Bird," Houston Film Critics Society (2017); Named Best Screenplay, "Lady Bird," Independent Spirit Awards (2017); Named Best Actress, "Damsels in Distress," Dublin International Film Festival (2012) **RE:** Unitarian Universalist

GEWITZ, MICHAEL H., T: William Russell McCurdy Physician-in-Chief **I:** Medicine & Health Care **CN:** Maria Fareri Children's Hospital at WMCHealth **PT:** Ruth And Henry Gewitz **MS:** Married **SPN:** Judith **CH:** Emily, Andrew **ED:** MD, Drexel University, College of Medicine (aka Hahnemann University) (1974); BA, Yale University (1970) **CT:** MD; Fellow, American Academy of Pediatrics, Fellow, American College of Cardiology; Fellow, American Heart Association **C:** Physician-in-Chief, Maria Fareri Children's Hospital, Valhalla, NY (2004-Present); Chief, Pediatric Cardiology, Maria Fareri Children's Hospital, Valhalla, NY (2004-Present); Professor, Vice Chair, Department of Pediatrics, New York Medical College, Valhalla, NY (1992-Present); Chief, Pediatric Cardiology, New York Medical College (1983-Present); Executive Director, Maria Fareri Children's Hospital, Valhalla, NY (2004-2008); Director, Department of Pediatrics, Chief, Pediatric Cardiology, Westchester Medical Center, Valhalla, NY (1991-2004); President, Medical Staff, Westchester Medical Center (1998-2002); Assistant Professor of Pediatrics, Perelman School of Medicine, University of Pennsylvania, Philadelphia, PA (1979-1983); Director, Noninvasive Cardiology, Children's Hospital of Philadelphia (1979-1983); Fellow, Yale New Haven Hospital (1977-1979); Registrar, The Hospital for Sick Children (Now Great Ormond Street Hospital) (1976-1977); Resident, Children's Hospital of Philadelphia (1975-1976); Intern, Children's Hospital of Philadelphia (1974-1975) **CR:** Chairman, Council on Cardiovascular Disease in the Young, American Heart Association (2010-12) Science Advisory Committee and Manuscript Oversight Committee, American Heart Association (2010-2012); Organizing Committee and Scientific Committee, Third, Fourth, and Fifth International Scientific Meetings, Kawasaki Disease **CIV:** Cor Vitae Society; Consultant, American Heart Association; Gift of Life International; Board of Directors, American Heart Association; Founders Affiliate, American Heart Association **CW:** Section Editor, "Cardiovascular Reviews" (2004-Present); Associate Editor, "Heart Diseases" (1999-2004); Editor, "Primary Pediatric Cardiology" (1995); Author, Co-Author, More Than 130 Scientific Publications and Communications **AW:** Edith Macey Award for Community Service, Westchester Children's Association (2018); Ellis Island Award (2014); Outstanding Service Award, Council on Cardiovascular Disease in the Young, American Heart Association (2010); Paul Harris Fellow, Rotary International (1998); Physician of the Year, Westchester Medical Center (1995); Young Investigator Award, American Academy of Pediatrics (1983) **MEM:** Executive Committee, Cardiovascular Disease in Young, American Heart Association (1999-2014); Chairman, American Heart Association (2010-2012); Numerous Positions, American Heart Association; Fellow, American Academy of Pediatrics; American College of Cardiology; New York Academy of Medicine; American College of Physician Executives; Pediatric Academic Societies **B/I:** Dr. Gewitz became involved in his profession because his father became ill before high school, so he became interested in medicine around that time. **AV:** Black and white photography **THT:** Dr. Gewitz's mentors are Richard Weinerman and William Raskind. His motto is, "Never give up."

GIACCHINO, MICHAEL, T: Musician, Composer **I:** Fine Art **DOB:** 10/10/1967 **PB:** Riverside Township **SC:** NJ/USA **ED:** BFA in Film Production, School of Visual Arts, New York, NY (1990); Diploma, Holy Cross High School, Delran Township, NJ (1986); Postgraduate Coursework in Composition, The Juilliard School **C:** Assistant Producer, Disney Interactive; Feature Film Publicity Department, Disney Studios, Burbank, CA; Intern, Universal Pictures **CW:** Composer, "Extinct" (2020); Composer, "An American Pickle" (2020); Composer, "Jojo Rabbit" (2019); Composer, "Spider-Man: Far From Home" (2019); Composer, "Bad Times at the El Royale" (2018); Composer, "Jurassic World: Fallen Kingdom" (2018); Composer, "Incredibles 2" (2018); Composer, Video Game, "Lego The Incredibles" (2018); Composer, "Coco" (2017); Composer, "War for the Planet of the Apes" (2017); Composer, "Spider-Man: Homecoming" (2017); Composer, "The Book of Henry" (2017); Composer, "Rogue One: A Star Wars Story" (2016); Composer, "Doctor Strange" (2016); Composer, "Star Trek Beyond" (2016); Composer, "Zootopia" (2016); Composer, "Inside Out" (2015); Composer, "Jurassic World" (2015); Composer, "Tomorrowland" (2015); Composer, "Jupiter Ascending" (2015); Composer, "This is Where I Leave You" (2014); Composer, "Dawn of the Planet of the Apes" (2014); Composer, "Star Trek Into Darkness" (2013); Composer, "John Carter" (2012); Composer, "Mission: Impossible-Ghost Protocol" (2011); Composer, "50/50" (2011); Composer, "Monte Carlo" (2011); Composer, "Super 8" (2011); Composer, "Cars 2" (2011); Composer, "Let Me In" (2010); Composer, "Lost" (2004-2010); Composer, Documentary, "Earth Days" (2009); Composer, "Land of the Lost" (2009); Composer, "Up" (2009); Composer, "Star Trek" (2009); Composer, Video Game, "Up" (2009); Conductor, 81st Academy Awards (2009); Producer, Video Game, "Fracture" (2008); Composer, Video Game, "Lost: Via Domus" (2008); Composer, Video Game, "Turning Point: Fall of Liberty" (2008); Composer, "Speed Racer" (2008); Composer, "Cloverfield" (2008); Co-Composer, "Fringe" (2008); Composer, "Ratatouille" (2007); Composer, Video Game, "Medal of Honor: Heroes 2" (2007); Composer, Video Game, "Medal of Honor: Airborne" (2007); Composer, Video Game, "Medal of Honor: Vanguard" (2007); Composer, "Six Degrees" (2006-2007); Co-Composer, Video Game, "Black" (2006); Composer, "Mission: Impossible III" (2006); Composer, "Looking for Comedy in the Muslim World" (2006); Composer, "Alias" (2001-2006); Composer, "The Family Stone" (2005); Composer, TV Movie, "The Muppets' Wizard of Oz" (2005); Composer, "Sky High" (2005); Composer, Video Game, "The Incredibles: Rise of the Underminer" (2005); Composer, Video Game, "Mercenaries: Playground of Destruction" (2005); Composer, Video Game, "The Incredibles" (2004); Composer, Video Game, "Alias" (2004); Composer, Video Game, "Call of Duty: Finest Hour" (2004); Composer, Video Game, "Call of Duty: United Offensive" (2004); Composer, "The Incredibles" (2004); Composer, "Sin" (2003); Composer, Video Game, "Secret Weapons Over Normandy" (2003); Composer, Video Game, "Call of Duty" (2003); Composer, Video Game, "Medal of Honor: Frontline" (2002); Composer, Video Game, "Medal of Honor: Allied Assault" (2002); Composer, "The Trouble with Lou" (2001); Composer, Video Game, "Medal of Honor: Underground" (2000); Composer, Video Game, "Muppet Monster Adventure" (2000); Composer, Video Game, "Medal of Honor" (1999); Composer, Video Game, "Warpath: Jurassic Park" (1999); Composer, Video Game, "T'ai Fu: Wrath of the Tiger" (1999); Composer, "My Brother the Pig" (1999); Composer, Video Game, "Small Soldiers" (1998); Composer, Video Game, "Chaos Island" (1997); Composer, Video Game, "The Lost World: Jurassic Park" (1997); Composer, "Legal Deceit" (1997); Composer, Video Game, "Maui Mallard in Cold Shadow" (1995); Composer, Video Game, "Gargoyles" (1995); Composer, Video Game, "Mickey Mania: The Timeless Adventures of Mickey Mouse" (1994); Composer, "The Batman"; Composer, "Jurassic World: Dominion"; Composer, Numerous Short Films, Holiday Specials, Television Pilots and Theme Park Attractions **AW:** Music in a Feature Production, "Incredibles 2," Annie Awards (2019); Music in a Feature Production, "Coco," Annie Awards (2018); Music in a Feature Production, "Inside Out," Annie Awards (2016); Composer of the Year, World Soundtrack Academy Awards (2015); Best Music, "Super 8," Saturn Awards (2012); Best Original Score, "Up," Academy Awards (2010); Best Score Soundtrack Album for Motion Picture, Television or Other Visual Media, Best Instrumental Composition, "Up," Grammy Awards (2010); Best Original Music, "Up," British Academy Film Awards (2010); Best Original Score-Motion Picture, "Up," Golden

Globe Awards (2010); Best Score, "Up," Broadcast Film Critics Association Awards (2010); Music in a Feature Production, "Ratatouille," Annie Awards (2008); Best Score Soundtrack Album for Motion Picture, Television or Other Visual Media, "Ratatouille," Grammy Awards (2008); Composer of the Year, StreamingSoundtracks.com Awards (2007); Best Score for a Short Film, "Lifted," Film & TV Music Awards (2007); Music in a Feature Production, "The Incredibles," Annie Awards (2005); Outstanding Music Composition for a Series (Dramatic Underscore), "Lost," Primetime Emmy Awards (2005); Excellence in Audio, "Call of Duty," Game Developers Choice Awards (2004); Score of the Year, "The Incredibles," Composer of the Year, IFMCA Awards (2004); Original Music Composition, "Medal of Honor: Frontline," Interactive Achievement Awards (2003); Excellence in Audio, "Medal of Honor: Allied Assault," Game Developers Choice Awards (2003); Original Music Composition, "Medal of Honor: Underground," Interactive Achievement Awards (2001)

GIANFORTE, GREGORY, "GREG" RICHARD, T: U.S. Representative, Former Information Technology Executive **I:** Government Administration/Government Relations/Government Services **DOB:** 04/17/1961 **PB:** San Diego **SC:** CA/USA **PT:** Frank Richard Gianforte; Dale (Douglass) Gianforte **MS:** Married **SPN:** Susan Gianforte (1988) **CH:** Four children **ED:** Honorary PhD in Computer Science, Montana State University (2007); BEE, Stevens Institute of Technology (1983); MS in Computer Science, Stevens Institute of Technology **C:** U.S. Representative, Montana's At-Large Congressional District (2017-Present); Member, Natural Resources Committee, U.S. House of Representatives (2017-Present); Member, House Committee on Oversight and Reform (2017-Present); Founder, RightNow Technologies, Inc. (1995-Present); Founder, President, Brightwork Development Corp. (Now McAfee Associates) (1986-1994); Chairman, President and Chief Executive Officer, RightNow Technologies, Inc. (Now Oracle); Vice President, North America Sales, McAfee Associates, Inc.; Managing Director, Bozeman Technology Incubator Inc.; With, AT&T Bell Laboratories **CIV:** Founder, Gianforte Family Foundation (2004-Present); Founder, Bootstrap Montana; Board, Friedman Foundation for Educational Choice (Now EdChoice) **CW:** Publisher, "Eight to Great: Eight Steps to Delivering an Exceptional Customer Experience" (2008); Author, "Bootstrapping Your Business: Start and Grow a Successful Company with Almost No Money" **AW:** Inductee, Hall of Fame, CRM (2007); Entrepreneur of the Year, EY (2003); Stevens Honor Award, Stevens Institute of Technology (2003)

GIANNET, DINA, T: Executive Director, Activity Consultant **I:** Consulting **DOB:** 05/10/1937 **PB:** Jersey City **SC:** NJ/USA **MS:** Married **CH:** Three Children **ED:** Doctor of Ministry, Covington Theological Seminary; Diploma in German Language, Darmstadt University; Studiengemeinschaft Werner Kamprath, Germany; Diploma in Proficiency in English, Greek-American Cultural Institute, Athens, Greece **CT:** Certified Activity Consultant, National Certification Council for Activity Professionals (1993); Certified, OneStroke Painting **C:** Executive Director, Giannet Consulting Services, Inc. **CR:** Teacher, Foreign Language and English Education (1970-Present); Teacher, One-Stroke Painting **CW:** Author, "Words to Live By: Inspiring Quotes that Will Touch Your Heart"; Author, "Between the Raindrops" **AW:** Editor's Choice Award, National Library of Poetry **MEM:** Toast Masters International **AV:** Painting; Spending time with family; Writing; Writing poetry; Public speaking; Teaching; Playing piano, accordion,

guitar, ukulele, recorder, and flute; Advocating for the elderly; Protecting animals and nature **RE:** Greek Orthodox Christian **THT:** Dr. Giannet has been an activity professional serving the elderly in assisted living and long-term care facilities for 35 years. In this capacity, she has enhanced the quality of life of the elderly psychologically, physically and spiritually, and provided training to professionals who serve this population. Additionally, as the executive director of Giannet Consulting Services, Inc., an organizational and healthcare training corporation focused on training a variety of professionals in the long-term/assisted living industry, and as a Certified Activity Consultant from the National Certification Council for Activity Professionals since 1993, she has been offering the Modular Education Program for Activity Professionals, the required course all activity professionals must complete to obtain certification, for two decades.

GIBBS, BETTY CALDWELL, T: Educational Administrator **I:** Education/Educational Services **DOB:** 09/03/1932 **PB:** Griffin **SC:** GA/USA **PT:** William Thomas Caldwell; Winnie Cleo (Kennedy) Caldwell **MS:** Married **SPN:** Billy Dan Gibbs (05/23/1952) **ED:** EdD, Nova University, Fort Lauderdale, FL (1987); MEd, Mercer University (1976); BS in Elementary Education, Tift College, Forsyth, GA (1967) **CT:** Commercial Certification, Tift College, Forsyth, GA (1950); Certified Life Elementary Teacher, Administrator, Supervisor, Georgia **C:** Assistant Superintendent, Special Instruction, Henry County Board of Education, Mcdonough, GA (1991); Director, Special Education, Henry County Board Education, Mcdonough, GA; Teacher, Special Education, Henry County Board Education, Mcdonough, GA **AW:** Outstanding Young Educator-Community Award; Teacher of the Year Award **MEM:** President, Alpha Iota Chapter, Delta Kappa Gamma; Phi Delta Kappa **MH:** Albert Nelson Marquis Lifetime Achievement Award **B/I:** Growing up, every time Ms. Gibbs would get together to play with her friends, she insisted they would play school and she would be the teacher. She knew from a young age that she wanted to pursue a career in education. **AV:** Traveling; Reading; Participating in church activities **THT:** Mrs. Gibbs considers herself to be truly blessed for good health. She feels lucky to have had the opportunity to do what she loves and succeed in life.

GIBBS, JAMIE, "TERWILLIGER", T: Principal Designer **I:** Architecture & Construction **CN:** Jamie Gibbs Associates **PT:** Irvin Lee; Glenna Lillian (Reid) G. **MS:** Married **SPN:** Hipoleto Argiz **CH:** Jaron Argiz **ED:** Master of Arts in Historic Preservation, Columbia University (1981); Bachelor of Science and Arts, Master of Science and Arts, Purdue University (1977); Bachelor of Science in Landscape Architecture and Horticulture, Purdue University **CT:** Certified Landscape Architect; Registered Interior Designer **C:** Owner, Principal Designer, Jamie Gibbs Associates (1979-Present); Director, Bronx Frontier Development Corporation, New York (1979-1981); Principal Designer, Stoeppelwerth and Associates, Indianapolis, IN (1978-1979); Director of Design, State of Indiana, Division of State Parks, Indianapolis, IN (1977-1978) **CR:** Adjunct Professor, Parsons School of Design (1988-2017); Consultant, Tapestria Division of Hunter Douglas (2001-2002) **CIV:** Board of Directors, Indianapolis Opera Company (2012-Present); With, The Fund for Park Avenue, New York, NY (2008-Present); With, The Horticultural Society Newfields, the Indianapolis Museum of Art (2012-2019); With, Hudson River Park Alliance (1998-2010); With, CityLore, New York (1992-2010); With, Coalition to Save City and Suburban Homes, New

York, NY (1995-2001); With, New York Council on Alcoholism (1997-2000); Chairman Associates Committee, Federation of Protestant Welfare Agencies Inc., New York, NY (1987-2000); With, Grosvenor Neighborhood House, New York, NY (1990-1997); Advisory Board, New York Foundation for Senior Citizens, New York, NY (1988-1997); With, Counseling in Schools Inc., New York, NY (1982-1992) **CW:** Designer, Selection of Trims and Fabrics, The Jamie Gibbs Vintage Collection (2002); Editorial Board, Window Fashions (1994-2002); Editorial Board, Fine Furniture International (1995-1998); Author, "All About Roses" (1990); Author, "Landscape It Yourself" (1988); Contributor, Articles to Popular Magazines, Professional Journals; Designer, Residential Buildings and Resorts in New York, Connecticut, New Jersey, Pennsylvania, Indianapolis, Puerto Rico, St. Maarten, Moscow, Rio de Janeiro, Jamaica, Hilton Head, North Carolina **AW:** Fellow, Walter Blackburn Foundation (2019); Best of Danville Award in Interior Design (2013, 2019); Fashion Arts Society of Distinguished Talent (2018); Design Scholar, Columbia University (1980); Various Certificates of Appreciation **MEM:** American Society of Landscape Designers; American Society of Interior Designers; Association of Professional Landscape Designers; Allied Board of Trade; International Furniture and Design Association **MH:** Albert Nelson Marquis Lifetime Achievement Award **AS:** Mr. Gibbs attributes his success to the enjoyment he derives from working with people and creating beautiful living environments, with an emphasis on history, sustainability and quality. **B/I:** Mr. Gibbs became involved in his profession because it was a professional area where he had not only an interest, but a talent. **AV:** Collecting 18th and 19th century high style furniture and decorative objects **PA:** Democrat **RE:** Episcopalian

GIBBS, JOE JACKSON, T: Professional Sports Team Executive; Former Professional Football Coach **I:** Athletics **CN:** Joe Gibbs Racing **DOB:** 11/25/1940 **PB:** Mocksville **SC:** NC/USA **PT:** Jackson Ceufud Gibbs; Winnie Era (Blalock) Gibbs **MS:** Married **SPN:** Pat Gibbs (1966) **CH:** Coy; J.D. (Deceased) **ED:** MS, San Diego State University (1966); BS, San Diego State University (1964); Coursework, Cerritos Junior College (Now Cerritos College) **C:** Founder, JGRMX (2008-Present); Founder, Owner, Joe Gibbs Racing (1991-Present); Special Adviser to Owner, Washington Redskins, National Football League (NFL) (2008-2012); Head Coach, Team President, Washington Redskins, National Football League (NFL) (2004-2007); Head Coach, Washington Redskins, National Football League (NFL) (1981-1992); Offensive Coordinator, San Diego Chargers, National Football League (NFL) (1979-1980); Offensive Coordinator, Tampa Bay Buccaneers, National Football League (NFL) (1978); Running Backs Coach, St. Louis Cardinals, National Football League (NFL) (1973-1977); Running Backs Coach, University of Arkansas, National Football League (NFL) (1971-1972); Offensive Line Coach, University of Southern California (1969-1970); Offensive Line Coach, Florida State University (1967-1968); Offensive Line Coach, San Diego State University (1964-1966) **CR:** Sports Commentator, NBC (1993-1998) **CW:** Author, "Game Plan for Life" (2009); Co-Author (with Ken Abraham), "Racing to Win: Establish Your Game Plan for Success" (2003); Co-Author (with Jerry B. Jenkins), "Joe Gibes: Fourth and One" (1992) **AW:** Named to NASCAR Hall of Fame (2020); Winner, NASCAR Championships (2000, 2002, 2005, 2015); Named One of the Most Influential People in the World of Sports, Business Week (Now Bloomberg Businessweek) (2007); Named to Pro Football Hall of Fame (1996); Winner, Washington Redskins,

Super Bowl (1983, 1988, 1992); Winner, Sporting News COY, (1982-1983, 1991); Named NFL Coach of the Year, Sporting News (1982, 1983, 1991); Named Coach of the Year, The Associated Press (1982, 1983); Winner, Sporting News Cup (1982-1983); Named Coach of the Year, United Press International (1982); Named to Redskins' Ring of Fame; Five-time NASCAR Cup Series Champion

GIBBS, ROBERT, "BOB" BRIAN, T: U.S. Representative **I:** Government Administration/Government Relations/Government Services **DOB:** 06/14/1954 **PB:** Peru **SC:** IN/USA **MS:** Married **SPN:** Jody Cox (1977) **CH:** Adam; Amy; Andrew **ED:** BA, Agricultural Technical Institute, The Ohio State University (1974) **C:** U.S. Representative, Ohio's Seventh Congressional District, United States Congress, Washington, DC (2013-Present); Member, U.S. House Committee on Transportation and Infrastructure (2011-Present); Member, U.S. House Committee on Agriculture (2011-Present); U.S. Representative, Ohio's 18th Congressional District, United States Congress, Washington, DC (2011-2013); Member, District 22, Ohio State Senate (2009-2010); Owner, Gibbs Enterprises LLC (2004-2009); Member, District 97, Ohio House of Representatives (2003-2008); Co-Founder, Owner, Hidden Hollow Farms LLC, Holmes County, Ohio (1978-2004) **AW:** Guardian of Small Business Award, National Federation of Independent Business (2004); Watchdog Treasury Award, United Conservatives of Ohio (2004); Legislator of the Year Award, Ohio Restaurant Association; All-American Award, National Pork Producers Council **MEM:** Board of Trustees, Ohio Farm Bureau Federation (1985-Present); Former President, Ohio Farm Bureau Federation; National Federation of Independent Business; The Ashland Area Chamber of Commerce; Wadsworth Area Chamber of Commerce; Holmes County Chamber of Commerce; Ohio Farm Bureau Federation **PA:** Republican **RE:** United Methodist

GIBSON, BOB, T: Former Professional Baseball Player **I:** Athletics **DOB:** 11/09/1935 **PB:** Omaha **SC:** NE/USA **PT:** Pack Gibson; Victoria Gibson **MS:** Married **SPN:** Wendy Nelson (1979); Charline Johnson (Divorced) **CH:** Chris; Annette; Renee **ED:** Coursework, Creighton University **C:** Special Advisor, St. Louis Cardinals, MLB (1995); Special Advisor to American League President Gene Budig, MLB (1998); Color Commentator, ESPN (1990); Broadcaster, KMOX Sports Division, St. Louis, MO (1985-1989); Coach, Atlanta Braves, MLB (1982-1984); Coach, New York Mets, MLB (1981-1982); Pitcher, St. Louis Cardinals, MLB (1959-1975) **CW:** Co-author with Reggie Jackson and Lonnie Wheeler, "Sixty Feet, Six Inches: A Hall of Fame Pitcher and a Hall of Fame Hitter Talk About How the Game is Played" (2009); Co-author with Lonnie Wheeler, "Stranger to the Game: The Autobiography of Bob Gibson" (1996) **AW:** Inductee, St. Louis Cardinals Hall of Fame Museum (2014); Named to All-century Team, MLB (1999); Inductee, National Baseball Hall of Fame and Museum (1981); Golden Glove Award (1965-1973); Named to National League All-star Team (1962, 1965-1970, 1972); Cy Young Award, National League (1968, 1970); Named MVP, National League (1968); Named World Series Most Valuable Player (1964, 1967); Winner, St. Louis Cardinals, World Series Championship (1964, 1967)

GIBSON, KEVIN, T: Professor of Medicine, Clinical, and Translational Science **I:** Education/Educational Services **CN:** University of Pittsburgh School of Medicine/UPMC **MS:** Married **SPN:** Virginea (2017) **CH:** One Son **ED:** MD, Rutgers New Jersey Medical School, (now Robert Wood Johnson Medical School) (1980); Bachelor's in Zoology, Drew University, Madison, NJ (1976) **CT:** Board-Certified in Internal Medicine, Pulmonary Medicine, Critical Care Medicine **C:** Medical Director, The Simmons Center for Interstitial Lung Disease at UPMC (2002-Present); Professor of Medicine, Clinical, and Translational Science, University of Pittsburgh School of Medicine (2012-Present); Associate, Assistant Professor, University of Pittsburgh School of Medicine (1984-2012) **CR:** Internship in Internal Medicine, Emory University Affiliated Hospitals, Atlanta, GA; Residency in Internal Medicine, Emory University Affiliated Hospitals, Atlanta, GA; Fellowship in Pulmonary Medicine and Critical Care, University of Pittsburgh **CIV:** Board Member, Kinsley Association; Board Member, Institutional Review Boards (IRB) **CW:** Author, 30 Abstracts and Articles **AW:** Listee, Best Doctors in Pittsburgh (2011-Present); Listee, Best Doctors in America (2007-Present) **MEM:** American Thoracic Society **AS:** Dr. Gibson attributes his success to the support of his family and friends. Likewise, he credits his work ethic and passion for helping others. **B/I:** Dr. Gibson always wanted to be a physician. He excels in both research and patient care, and he runs a center for scar and lung disease. His interests in research and academic medicine developed a little bit later.

GIBSON, MEL COLMCILLE GERARD, T: Actor, Film Director, Producer **I:** Media & Entertainment **DOB:** 1/3/1956 **PB:** Peekskill **SC:** NY/USA **PT:** Hutton Peter Gibson; Anne Patricia (Reilly) Gibson **MS:** Divorced **SPN:** Robyn Denise Moore (1980, Divorced 2011) **CH:** Hannah; Edward; Christian; William; Louis; Milo; Thomas; Lars; Lucia **ED:** Honorary Doctor of Humane Letters, Loyola Marymount University (2003); Diploma, National Institute of Dramatic Art, Sydney, Australia (1977) **C:** Co-founder, Icon Productions (1989-Present) **CW:** Actor, "Force of Nature" (2020); Actor, Producer, "The Professor and the Madman" (2019); Actor, "Dragged Across Concrete" (2018); Actor, "Daddy's Home" (2018); Actor, "The Bombing" (2018); Actor, "Daddy's Home 2" (2017); Actor, "Bloody Father" (2016); Director, "Hacksaw Ridge" (2016); Actor, "The Expendables 3" (2014); Producer, "Stonehearst Asylum" (2014); Actor, "Machete Kills" (2013); Screenwriter, Actor, Producer, "Get the Gringo" (2012); Actor, "The Beaver" (2011); Actor, "Edge of Darkness" (2010); Executive Producer, "Carrier" (2008); Appearance, "Who Killed the Electric Car?" (2006); Screenwriter, Director, Producer, "Apocalypto" (2006); Executive Producer, "Leonard Cohen: I'm Your Man" (2005); Actor, Director, Producer, Complete Savages (2004-2005); Producer, Clubhouse (2004-2005); Actor, Producer, Paparazzi (2004); Screenwriter, Director, Producer, "The Passion of the Christ" (2004); Producer, "Family Curse" (2003); Actor, Producer, "The Singing Detective" (2003); Actor, "We Were Soldiers" (2002); Actor, "Signs" (2002); Producer, "Invincible" (2001); Producer, "The Three Stooges" (2000); Actor, "What Women Want" (2000); Actor, "The Patriot" (2000); Voice Actor, "Chicken Run" (2000); Actor, "The Million Dollar Hotel" (2000); Voice Actor, "The Simpsons" (1999); Actor, "Payback" (1999); Actor, "Lethal Weapon 4" (1998); Actor, "Father's Day" (1997); Actor, "Conspiracy Theory" (1997); Actor, "FairyTale: A True Story" (1997); Actor, "Ransom" (1996); Actor, Director, Producer, "Braveheart" (1995); Appearance, "Casper" (1995); Voice Actor, "Pocahontas" (1995); Narrator, World of Discovery (1995); Actor, "Maverick" (1994); Actor, Director, "The Man Without a Face" (1993); Actor, "Love Letters" (1993); Actor, Producer, "Forever Young" (1992); Actor, "Lethal Weapon 3" (1992); Actor, "Hamlet" (1990); Actor, "Air America" (1990); Actor, "Bird on a Wire" (1990); Actor, "Lethal Weapon 2" (1989); Host, "Saturday Night Live" (1989); Actor, "Tequila Sunrise" (1988); Actor, "Lethal Weapon" (1987); Actor, "Mad Max Beyond Thunderdome" (1985); Actor, "Mrs. Soffel" (1984); Actor, "The River" (1984); Actor, "The Bounty" (1984); Actor, "Cop Shop" (1977-1984); Actor, "The Sullivans" (1976-1983); Actor, "The Year of Living Dangerously" (1982); Actor, "Attack Force Z" (1982); Actor, "Death of a Salesman" (1982); Actor, "Mad Max II: The Road Warrior" (1981); Actor, "Gallipoli" (1981); Actor, "Punishment" (1981); Actor, "No Names, No Pack Frill" (1981); Actor, "The Chain Reaction" (1980); Actor, "Mad Max" (1979); Actor, "The Hero" (1979); Actor, "Tim" (1979); Actor, "On Our Selection" (1979); Actor, "Waiting for Godot" (1979); Actor, "Romeo and Juliet" (1979); Actor, "I Never Promised You a Rose Garden" (1977); Actor, "Summer City" (1977); Actor, Appearances, Plays, Television Shows, Films; Director, Producer, Films **AW:** Award for Producer of the Year, Hollywood Film Awards (2004, 2016); Named, One of the 50 Most Powerful People in Hollywood, Premiere Magazine (2003-2006); Innovator of the Year Award, The Hollywood Reporter (2004); Named, World's Most Powerful Celebrity, Forbes Magazine (2004); Awards for Favorite Motion Picture Actor, People's Choice Awards (2001, 2003, 2004); Global Achievement Award, Australian Film Institute (2002); Award for Favorite Motion Picture Star in a Comedy, People's Choice Awards (2001); Award for Favorite Motion Picture Actor, People's Choice Awards (2001); Named, Man of the Year, Hasty Pudding Theatricals (1997); Named Honorary Officer, Order of Australia (1997); Awards for Favorite Motion Picture Actor, People Choice Awards (1991, 1997); Academy Awards for Best Director, Best Picture, Academy of Motion Picture Arts & Sciences (1996); Golden Globe Award for Best Director, Hollywood Foreign Press Association (1996); Special Achievement in Filmmaking Award, National Board of Review (1995); Critics' Choice Award for Best Director (1995); Named, Sexiest Man Alive, People Magazine (1985)

GIDDENS, ANGELA, T: Teacher (Retired), Caretaker **I:** Education/Educational Services **CN:** SPUR Enterprise Schools **ED:** Bachelor's Degree, Harding University (1987) **C:** Substitute Teacher, SPUR Enterprise Schools **CIV:** Former President, PTO (Parent Teacher Organization) **AS:** Ms. Giddens attributes her success to living through and getting over obstacles, leaving them behind and being able to move forward. **B/I:** Ms. Giddens became involved in her profession because since she was in third grade, she knew she wanted to be a teacher and this aspiration carried throughout her upbringing. She also wanted to work in a children's home, which she did right after graduating college. Ms. Giddens was able to be there every day to get her children up in the morning and put them to bed at night.

GIELE, JANET ZOLLINGER, T: Sociologist, Educator **I:** Education/Educational Services **CN:** Brandeis University **DOB:** 08/23/1934 **PB:** Wadsworth **SC:** OH/USA **PT:** Albert Zollinger; Ellen Esther Nestor **MS:** Married **SPN:** David Lester Giele (08/24/1957) **CH:** Elizabeth Ellen; Benjamin Zollinger **ED:** PhD, Harvard University (1961); MA, Harvard University, Cambridge, MA (1958); BA, Earlham College, Richmond, IN (1956) **C:** Professor Emerita, Brandeis University (2004-Present); Professor, Sociology, Social Policy Women's Studies, Heller School for Social Policy and Management, Brandeis University (1989-2004); Acting Dean, Heller School, Brandeis University (1993-1994); Associate Professor, Heller School Brandeis University, Waltham, MA (1976-1989); Ford Faculty Fellow, Harvard University (1974-1975); Fellow, Bunting Inst Radcliffe College, Cambridge, MA

(1970-1974); Instructor to Assistant Professor, Wellesley College (1962-1970) **CR:** Consultant, National Institute on Aging (1982-1984); Consultant, Research on Women's Changing Life Patterns from Lilly Endowment (1981-1983); Consultant, Research Grants on Family Policy, National Science Foundation (1974); Principal Consultant, Task Force on Rights and Responsibilities of Women, Ford Foundation (1972-1974) **CIV:** Wellesley Town Meeting (2007-Present); Warden, Vestry Member, St. Andrew's Episcopal Church (1986-1989) **CW:** Co-editor, "The Craft of Life Course Research, Japanese Edition" (2013); Author, "Family Policy and the American Safety Net" (2012); Co-editor, "The Craft of Life Course Research" (2009); Co-editor, "Changing Life Patterns in Western Industrial Societies" (2004); Co-author, "Women's Equality in the Workplace" (2003); Co-editor, "Methods of Life Course Research: Qualitative and Quantitative Approaches, Japanese Edition" (2003); Co-editor, "Methods of Life Course Research: Qualitative and Quantitative Approaches" (1998); Author, "Two Paths to Women's Equality: Temperance, Suffrage, and the Origins of American Feminism" (1995); Co-editor, "Women's Work and Women's Lives: The Continuing Struggle Worldwide (1992); Editor, "Women in the Middle Years: Current Knowledge and Directions for Research and Policy" (1982); Author, "Women and the Future: Changing Sex Roles in Modern America" (1978); Co-editor, "Women: Roles and Status in Eight Countries" (1977); Contributor, Chapters, Books; Contributor, Scientific Papers, Articles, Professional Journals **AW:** Distinguished Life Course Award, Pepperdine University (2013); Mentoring Award, Heller School, Brandeis University (2004); Graduate Society Award, Radcliffe Alumnae Association (2000); Fellowship, Radcliffe Institute , Harvard University (1999-2000); Fellow, Rockefeller Foundation, Bellagio Center (1993); German Marshall Fund Fellowship (1992-1993); Outstanding Alumni Award, Earlham College (1990); Fellowship for Study of Gender, Rockefeller Foundation (1987-1988); Ford Foundation Faculty Fellow (1975-1976) **MEM:** St. Andrew's Wellesley; Wellesley Club; Wellesley Neighbors; League of Women Voters **MH:** Albert Nelson Marquis Lifetime Achievement Award **AS:** Dr. Giele attributes her success to the support for her education from her parents, husband, and teachers. Scholarships and fellowships that recognized her work and potential. Her family were independent minded and thoughtful and encouraged hard work and achievement. **B/I:** She was always an outstanding student and was recognized as having potential for being a teacher and a scholar. But being a woman in the time she came of age presented a potential conflict between being a homeworker or a career woman. So her response was to study the issue. How had the first women's movement developed; who were the leaders and how were there lives different from the majority. These questions were at the heart of her dissertation. She then went on to do research on the different life patterns of contemporary women and the different life experiences that led to different outcomes. Various research grants allowed her to survey several thousand college women of different generations as well as conduct qualitative interviews of 50 college educated women, both African American and Caucasian, some of whom were homemakers with children and others had children but were also in the work force. Questions about their lives and upbringings revealed different themes in the two groups. **AV:** Gardening; Cooking; Knitting; Choral singing **PA:** Democrat **RE:** Episcopalian

GIER, KARAN, PHD, T: Psychologist (Retired) **I:** Education/Educational Services **CN:** University of Alaska **DOB:** 12/07/1947 **PB:** Sedalia **SC:** MO/USA **PT:** Ioda Clyde Hancock; Lorna (Campbell) Hancock **MS:** Married **SPN:** Thomas Robert Gier (09/28/1968) **ED:** Doctor of Philosophy, Pacific Western University (1989); Master of Education in Guidance and Counseling, University of Alaska (1981); Master of Arts in Counseling Psychology, Western Colorado University (1981); Master of Education, Webster University (1974); Bachelor of Arts, University of Missouri, Kansas City, MO (1971) **CT:** National Certified Counselor **C:** Director, OMNI Counseling Services, Anchorage, AK (1984-2005); Professor, University of Alaska Anchorage, Anchorage, AK (1982-2005); Professor, Chapman College, Anchorage, AK (1988-1993); Counselor, U.S. Air Force, Anchorage, AK (1985-1986); Counselor, University of Alaska Anchorage, Anchorage, AK (1982-1983); College Preparatory Instructor, Alaska Native Foundation, Anchorage, AK (1982); Program Coordinator, Education, Western Regional Resource Center, Anchorage School District, Anchorage, AK (1980-1981); Instructor, Counselor, Bethel Regional High School, Bethel, AK (1975-1980); Consultant, ArtsTech, Kansas City, MO (1973-1975); Instructor, Diocese of Kansas City–St. Joseph (1969-1973) **CIV:** Center for Environmental Education, Beta Sigma Phi, Bethel, AK (1976-1981) **CW:** Co-Editor, "The Tutor Training Handbook" (1996); Co-Author, "Helping Others Learn: A Guide to Peer Tutoring" (1985); Co-Author, "Coping with College" (1984); Co-Author, "A Student's Guide to College Success" (1983); Contributing Author, "Developmental Yup'ik Language Program" (1981); Contributor, Articles, Professional Journals **AW:** Robert Griffin Award for Long and Outstanding Service, College Reading & Learning Association (1998); Special Recognition Award, College Reading & Learning Association (1994-1995); Outstanding Adjunct Faculty, University of Alaska, Anchorage, AK (1992-1993); Certificate of Appreciation, College Reading & Learning Association (1986-1993); Meritorious Service Award, University of Alaska Anchorage (1984-1988); Notable Achievement Award, U.S. Air Force (1986); Third Place, Color Photo Award, Yukon-Kuskokwim State Fair (1978) **MEM:** Newsletter Editor, Peer Tutor, Special Interest Group, College Reading & Learning Association (1988-1995); President-Elect, Alaska Counseling Association (1989-1990); American Counseling Association; National Rehabilitation Counseling Association; The National Rehabilitation Association; Alaska Chapter, National Career Development Association; Board Director, Alaska State Chapter, College Reading & Learning Association; Coordinator, International Tutor Training Program, College Reading & Learning Association; Wolf Song of Alaska; The Humane Society of the United States; Wolf Haven International **MH:** Albert Nelson Marquis Lifetime Achievement Award; Marquis Who's Who Top Professional **B/I:** Dr. Gier became involved in her profession when she developed a desire to teach history during her time as an undergraduate. She pursued every opportunity available to her, and eventually relocated to Alaska. **AV:** Traveling; Wolf preservation; Photography; Music; Acting

GIESE, HERBERT ADOLPH, T: Pediatrician **I:** Medicine & Health Care **DOB:** 12/22/1937 **PB:** Alexandria **SC:** VA/USA **PT:** Herbert Adolph; Vohnda Avonelle (Pilgrim) Giese **MS:** Married **SPN:** Carol Jean Dauenhauer (08/10/1959) **CH:** Paul Thomas (Deceased); Vohnda Maria; Rosanne Celeste; Scott Damian; Mark Michael; Brent Edward **ED:** Master of Public Health, Tulane University (1970); Doctor of Medicine, Louisiana State University (1963); Bachelor of Science, Loyola University of South, New Orleans, LA (1960) **CT:** Past Diplomate, American Board Pediatrics **C:** Pediatrician, Washington Pediatric Medical Association, Redlands, CA (1979-2016); Associate Director of Pediatrics, San Bernardino County Medical Center, California (1975-1979); Pediatrician, Beaver Medical Clinic, Redlands, CA (1973-1975); Director of Pediatric Education, St. Jude Children's Hospital, Memphis, TN (1972-1973); Pediatrician, Holzer Medical Clinic, Gallipolis, OH (1970-1972); Pediatrician, 3535th U.S. Air Force Hospital, Mather Air Force Base, California (1966-1968); Resident in Pediatrics, Wilford Hall U.S. Air Force Hospital, San Antonio, TX (1964-1966); Intern, Keesler U.S. Air Force Hospital, Biloxi, MS (1963-1964) **CR:** Medical Director, Children in Crisis Center, San Bernardino, CA (1988-Present); Board of Directors, Coalition for Prevention of Abuse to Women and Children, San Bernardino, CA (1977-1984); U.S. Public Health Service Trainee in Pediatric Infectious Diseases, Tulane University (1968-1970); Consultant in Infectious Diseases **CIV:** Juvenile Justice and Delinquency Prevention Commission, San Bernardino, CA (1988-Present); Children's Network, San Bernardino, CA (1988-Present); Board of Directors, Bethlehem House Battered Women's Shelter, San Bernardino, CA (1988); Member, Child Abuse and Neglect Prevention and Intervention Commission, San Bernardino, CA (1984-1986); Treasurer, Seniors in Retirement, Redding, CA **MIL:** Major, U.S. Air Force (1963-1968) **CW:** Author, "Sexual Abuse in a Premenarchal Child?", Southwestern Medical Society (1991); Co-author, "Comparison of Three Agents Used in Surgical Scrubs," Ohio Medical Journal (1972) **AW:** Gingerbread House Award, Child Advocates of Nevada County (2000); Outstanding Efficiency Report, Wilford Hall Ambulatory Surgical Center (1996); Martha Lou Berke Award, for Child Abuse Training Task Force, San Bernardino, CA (1991); Volunteer of the Year, National Volunteer Center of Riverside, CA (1983); Outstanding Service for the Protection of Children, San Bernardino County (1982); San Bernardino Community Mental Health Award, San Bernardino County Board of Supervisors (1978); Outstanding Service In Leadership, Redlands YMCA (1976); Recognition for Teen Pregnancy Task Force Regional Access Project, Board of Supervisors, Riverside, CA **MEM:** Fellow, American Academy of Pediatrics; American Society for Microbiology; International Society for the Prevention of Child Abuse and Neglect; American Professional Society on the Abuse of Children; Hinterlands Pediatric Society; Undersea and Hyperbaric Medical Society **MH:** Albert Nelson Marquis Lifetime Achievement Award **B/I:** Dr. Giese became involved in his profession because of his mother, who was one of the first nurse anesthetists in Shreveport, Louisiana. **AV:** Scuba diving; Underwater photography **PA:** Democrat **RE:** Catholic

GILBERT, DAN, T: Co-Founder **I:** Financial Services **CN:** Quicken Loans **DOB:** 11/17/1962 **PB:** Detroit **SC:** MI/USA **MS:** Married **SPN:** Jennifer Gilbert **CH:** Five Children **ED:** JD, Wayne State University Law School; Bachelor's Degree, Michigan State University; Diploma, Southfield-Lathrup High School **CT:** Real Estate Agent's License **C:** Co-Founder, Chief Executive Officer, Quicken Loans (2000-Present); Co-Founder, Rock Financial (1985-2000) **CR:** Owner, Cleveland Gladiators (2012-Present); Owner, Canton Charge (2011-Present); Owner, Cleveland Monsters (2007-Present); Majority Owner, Cleveland Cavaliers (2005-2018); Chairman, Quicken Loans, Inc.; Founding Partner, Rockbridge Growth Equity LLC; Investor in Field; Co-Founder, StockX; Casino Operator **CIV:** The Giving Pledge (2012-Present); Donor, Breslin Center, Michigan State University (2016); Donor,

Wayne State University Law School (2016); Donor, Chris Christie Presidential Campaign (2015); Launched, Bizdom (2007); Founder, Two Neurofibromatosis Research Clinics, Children's National Medical Center, Washington, DC, Dana Children's Hospital at Sourasky Medical Center, Tel Aviv, Israel; Board Member, Children's Tumor Foundation, Cleveland Clinic, Children's Hospital Foundation; Vice Chairman, M-1 RAIL **AW:** Named, Fortune 100 Best Companies to Work for (2005–2017); NBA Champion (2016); Best Team ESPY Award (2016); Calder Cup Champion (2016); 16-Time Winner, JD Power Highest Customer Satisfaction Award **MEM:** 100 Thieves **BAR:** State of Michigan

GILBY, STEVE W., PHD, T: Metallurgical Engineering Researcher **I:** Engineering **DOB:** 09/22/1939 **PB:** Dayton **SC:** OH/USA **PT:** Ray Gilby; Marjorie Gilby **MS:** Married **SPN:** Betty **CH:** Joan; Karen; David **ED:** PhD in Material Science and Engineering, The Ohio State University, Columbus, OH (1966); BS in Metallurgical Engineering, University of Cincinnati, Cincinnati, OH (1962) **C:** Professor, Office of Professional Practice, University of Cincinnati (2002-2015); Consulting, Nucor Steel and Mitta Steel (2003-2009); Adjunct Associate Assistant to the President, Armco Research and Technician, Middletown, OH (1997-2000); Vice President, Research and Technology, Armco Research and Technician, Pittsburgh, PA (1992-1997); Director, Process Research, Armco Steel Company (Now AK Steel Holding) (1987-1992); Manager, Steelmaking and Casting Research, Armco Steel Company (Now AK Steel Holding) (1975-1987); Senior Engineer and Senior Staff Engineer, Youngstown Steel Company (1966-1975) **CR:** Advisory Board, Controlled Rolling Corp (2002-2007); Member, External Advisory Commission, Materials Science and Engineering Department, Ohio State University, Columbus, OH (1985-1995) **AW:** William Eisenmann Award for Chapter Leadership, ASM (American Society for Metals) (2012); Ohio State Alumni Distinguished Mershon Award for Service (1985); Ohio State Distinguished Engineering Alumni (1983) **MEM:** American Iron and Steel Association; ASM International (American Society for Metals) **MH:** Albert Nelson Marquis Lifetime Achievement Award **B/I:** Dr. Gilby became involved in his profession because when he was 12, his Boy Scout Troop toured the Armco Steel Company facility, where he eventually became employed at. He recalls being fascinated by the complexity and size of a modern steel plant. From that experience alone, Dr. Gilby began and continued the path to become a metallurgical engineering researcher. **AV:** Golfing

GILL, GEORGE W., PHD, T: Anthropologist (Retired); Distinguished Professor Emeritus **I:** Education/Educational Services **CN:** University of Wyoming - Laramie **DOB:** 06/28/1941 **PB:** Sterling **SC:** KS/USA **PT:** George Laurance Gill; Florence Louise (Jones) Gill **MS:** Married **SPN:** Denise Ann Gill **CH:** George Scott Gill; John Ashton Gill; Jennifer Florence Gill; Bryce Thomas Gill **ED:** PhD in Anthropology, The University of Kansas (1971); MPhil in Anthropology, The University of Kansas (1970); BA in Zoology, The University of Kansas, with Honors (1963) **CT:** Diplomate, The American Board of Forensic Anthropology (1978) **C:** Professor Emeritus of Anthropology, University of Wyoming, Laramie, WY (2006-Present); Member, Faculty, University of Wyoming, Laramie, WY (1971-Present); Distinguished Emeritus Professor, University of Wyoming College of Arts and Sciences (2007); Professor of Anthropology, University of Wyoming, Laramie, WY (1985-2006); Chairman, Department of Anthropology, University of Wyoming, Laramie, WY (1993-1996); Director, Anthropology Museum, University of Wyoming, Laramie,

WY (1979-1987) **CR:** Forensic Anthropologist, Law Enforcement Agencies (1972-Present); Science Leader, Easter Island Anthropological Expedition (1981); Chairman, Rapa Nui Rendezvous: International Conference Easter Island Research, University of Wyoming (1993) **CIV:** Paul Harris Fellow, Rotary Club of Laramie **MIL:** Captain, United States Army (1963-1967) **CW:** Co-editor with Vincent H. Stefan and George W. Gill, Main Author, "Skeletal Biology of the Ancient Rapanui (Eastern Islanders)," Cambridge University Press (2016); Co-editor with Rick L. Weathermon, "Skeletal Biology & Bioarchaeology of the Northwestern Plains" (2008); Co-editor with S. Rhine, "Skeletal Attribution of Race" (1990); Author, Articles, Monographs **AW:** Outstanding Former Faculty Award, University of Wyoming College of Arts and Sciences (2015); Co-grantee, Museum Inventory and Curation, BLM, Bureau of Reclamation, Wyoming Department of Transportation, Fish and Wildlife Services (1994-1999); Grantee, Kon-Tiki Museum, Oslo, Norway (1987, 1989, 1994, 1996); Grantee, World Monuments Fund (1989); John P. Ellbogen Meritorious Classroom Teaching Award (1983); Research Grantee, University of Wyoming (1972, 1978, 1982); Grantee, National Geographic Society (1980); Grantee, Center for Field Research (1980); Fellow, National Defense Education Act (1970); Grantee, National Science Foundation (1963, 1970) **MEM:** Chairman, American Academy of Forensic Sciences (1987-1988); Secretary, Physical Anthropology Section, American Academy of Forensic Sciences (1985-1987); Fellow, American Academy of Forensic Sciences; The American Board of Forensic Anthropology; Wyoming Archaeological Society; Plains Anthropological Society; American Association of Physical Anthropologists **MH:** Albert Nelson Marquis Lifetime Achievement Award **B/I:** Dr. Gill became involved in his profession because he watched with fascination the balancing of the different kinds of work of his undergraduate professor of biological anthropology, Dr. Bass. **AV:** Creator & active breeder of Wyoming Mountain Dog **PA:** Republican **RE:** Secular

GILL, GERALD LAWSON, MA, T: Professor Emeritus **I:** Education/Educational Services **CN:** James Madison University **DOB:** 11/13/1947 **PB:** Montgomery **SC:** AL/USA **PT:** George Ernest Gill; Marjorie (Hackett) Gill **MS:** Married **SPN:** Andrea Konst (10/07/2016); Nancy Argroves (03/05/1977, Divorced 1982) **ED:** Postgraduate Coursework in Business Administration, James Madison University, Harrisonburg, VA (1978-1979); MA in Library Science, University of Wisconsin-Madison, Madison, WI (1973); AB in History, Philosophy, and Religion, University of Georgia, Athens, GA (1971) **CT:** Certified Professional Librarian, Virginia **C:** Professor Emeritus, James Madison University, Harrisonburg, VA (2010-Present); Head of Reference and Government Documents, James Madison University, Harrisonburg, VA (2003-2010); Professor, James Madison University, Harrisonburg, VA (2002-2010); Government Documents Librarian, James Madison University, Harrisonburg, VA (1998-2003); Associate Professor, James Madison University, Harrisonburg, VA (1990-2002); Business Reference Librarian, James Madison University, Harrisonburg, VA (1987-1999); Assistant Professor, James Madison University, Harrisonburg, VA (1980-1990); Reference Librarian, James Madison University, Harrisonburg, VA (1976-1987); Instructor, James Madison University, Harrisonburg, VA (1974-1980); Cataloger, James Madison University, Harrisonburg, VA (1974-1976) **CR:** Faculty, Senate, James Madison University (1996-1998); University Council, James Madison University (1996-1998); Chair, Curriculum and Instruction Committee, James Madison University (1978-1979); Faculty,

Senate, James Madison University (1975-1979); Secretary, Curriculum and Instruction Committee, James Madison University (1976-1978); Lecturer and Speaker, National and Regional Groups; Consultant in Field **CIV:** Member, Democratic National Committee (2016-Present); Board Member, Minor Hill Manorhomes Homeowners Association (2006-2016); President, Minor Hill Manorhomes Home Owners Association (2004-2005); Member, Library Advisory Committee, State Council for Higher Education in Virginia (1986-1987); Virtual Virginia Coordinator, Management Business Committee **CW:** Member, Editorial Board, James Madison Journal (1977-1980); Reviewer, American Reference Books Annual; Contributor, Articles to Professional Journals **AW:** Gale Research Award for Excellence in Business Librarianship, American Library Association (1991) **MEM:** Phi Beta Delta Honor Society for International Scholars (2007-Present); Chairman, Business Reference Services Committee, American Library Association (1984-1986); Secretary, Law and Political Science Section, American Library Association (1982-1985); Chairman, Business Reference Services Discussion Group (1986-1987); Chairman, Business Reference, Academy Libraries Committee (1988-1991); Council, Virginia Library Association (1986-1987); President, Virginia Chapter, Special Libraries Association (1986-1987); Treasurer, Virginia Chapter, Special Librarians Association (1983-1985); Parliamentarian, Virginia Library Association (1981); Parliamentarian, Virginia Library Association (1979) **MH:** Albert Nelson Marquis Lifetime Achievement Award **AS:** Mr. Gill attributes his success in many ways, to being at the right place at the right time, but beyond that loving the work that he did. Librarianship was the perfect choice and he enjoyed the contributions he was able to make. **B/I:** Mr. Gill became involved in his profession because when he was a freshman at the University of Georgia, he went to the career counseling center and was tested; he ranked high in the fields of journalism and mathematics, but was most qualified to become a librarian. He then did his research to be part of the program. **AV:** Art collecting; Writing **PA:** Democrat **RE:** Roman Catholic **THT:** With others, Mr. Gill tries to understand what makes them tick: why they do the things they do and why they make certain choices.

GILL, VINCE, T: Singer, Songwriter **I:** Media & Entertainment **DOB:** 04/12/1957 **PB:** Norman **SC:** OK/USA **PT:** J. Stanley Gill; Jerene Gill **MS:** Married **SPN:** Amy Grant (03/2000); Janis Oliver (1980, Divorced 1997) **CH:** Jenny; Corrina **ED:** Diploma, Northwest Classen High School, Oklahoma City, OK **C:** Solo Artist (1984-Present); Member, The Time Jumpers (2010); Member, Cherry Bombs (1981); Member, Pure Prairie League (1979-1981); Member, Sundance; Member, Boone Creek; Member, The Blue Grass Alliance **CW:** Singer, "Okie" (2019); Performer, Eagles Tour (2017); Singer, "Down to My Last Bad Habit" (2016); Singer, "Bakersfield" (2013); Singer, "Guitar Slinger" (2011); Singer, "These Days" (2006); Singer, "Next Big Thing" (2003); Singer, "Christmas" (2003); Singer, "Let's Make Sure We Kiss Goodbye" (2000); Singer, "The Key" (1998); Singer, "High Lonesome Sound" (1996); Singer, "Souvenirs" (1995); Singer, "When Love Finds You" (1994); Singer, "Vince Gill and Friends" (1994); Singer, "Let There Be Peace on Earth" (1993); Singer, "I Never Knew Lonely" (1992); Singer, "I Still Believe in You" (1992); Singer, "Pocket Full of Gold" (1991); Singer with Dire Straits, "On Every Street" (1991); Singer, "The Best of Vince Gill" (1989); Singer, "When I Call Your Name" (1989); Singer, "The Way Back Home" (1987); Singer, "The Things That Matter" (1985); Singer, "Turn Me Loose" (1984); Performer, Duets with

Reba McEntre, Emmylou Harris, Patty Loveless, Ricky Skaggs, Kelly Clarkson; Appearances, Television Shows **AW:** CMA Humanitarian Award, CMA Country Music Association Inc. (2017); Grammy for Best American Roots Song, Recording Academy (2017); BMI Icon Award (2014); Irving Waugh Award of Excellence, CMA Country Music Association Inc. (2014); Recipient, Star, Hollywood Walk of Fame (2012); Grammy Awards for Best Country Instrumental Performance, Recording Academy (1998, 2001, 2009); Grammy Awards for Best Male Country Performance, Recording Academy (1990, 1992, 1994-1998, 2003, 2007); CMA Award for Vocal Event of the Year, CMA Country Music Association Inc. (1996, 2007); Named to Country Music Hall of Fame (2007); Grammy Award for Best Country Album, Recording Academy (2007); Academy of Country Music Home Depot Humanitarian Award (2006); Named to Nashville Songwriters Hall of Fame (2005); Grammy Award for Best Country Gospel Album, Recording Academy (2005); Orville H. Gibson Lifetime Achievement Award (1997); Recipient, Christian Country Music Association Awards (1996); Recipient, BMI Awards (1987, 1991-1993, 1995, 1996); Recipient, TNN/Music City News Awards (1991-1994, 1996); Recipient, Nashville Music Awards (1994-1996); CMA Awards for Song of the Year, CMA Country Music Association Inc. (1992, 1993, 1996); Grammy Awards for Best Country Collaboration with Vocals, Recording Academy (1991, 1996); Grammy Awards for Best Country Song, Recording Academy (1992, 1995); CMA Award for Male Vocalist of the Year, CMA Country Music Association Inc. (1991-1995); Outstanding Nashvillian of Year Award, Kiwanis (1994); Tennessean of the Year Award (1994); Award for Country Single of the Year, American Music Awards (1994); CMA Award for Entertainer of the Year, CMA Country Music Association Inc. (1993, 1994); Recipient, Music City News Songwriters Awards (1990-1994); Minnie Pearl Award (1993); Harmony Award (1993); CMA Award for Album of the Year, CMA Country Music Association Inc. (1993); Award for Country Single of the Year, Academy of Country Music Awards (1984, 1992, 1993); Instrumentalist of the Year Award, The Nashville Network/Music City News (1991); CMA Award for Single of the Year, CMA Country Music Association Inc. (1990); Numerous Awards

GILLIBRAND, KIRSTEN ELIZABETH, T: U.S. Senator from New York **I:** Government Administration/Government Relations/Government Services **DOB:** 12/09/1966 **PB:** Albany **SC:** NY/USA **PT:** Douglas Paul Rutnick; Polly Edwina (Noonan) Rutnick **MS:** Married **SPN:** John Gillibrand (2001) **CH:** Theodore; Henry; Nelson **ED:** JD, UCLA School of Law (1991); AB in Asian Studies, Dartmouth College, Hanover, NH, Magna Cum Laude (1988) **C:** U.S. Senator, State of New York, Washington, DC (2009-Present); Candidate, Democratic Nominee, 2020 Presidential Election (2019); Member, U.S. House of Representatives from New York's 20th Congressional District, United States Congress, Washington, DC (2007-2009); Partner, Commercial Litigation Practice, Boies Schiller Flexner LLP, Albany, NY (2001-2007); Special Counsel to Secretary, U.S. Department of Housing and Urban Development, Washington, DC (2000-2001); Associate, Davis, Polk & Wardwell LLP (1993-2000); Law Clerk to Honorable Roger J. Miner, United States Court of Appeals for the Second Circuit (1992-1993); Associate, Davis Polk & Wardwell LLP (1991-1992) **CIV:** Member, Advisory Board, Brennan Center for Justice at NYU Law; Board Member, Commission Greenway Heritage Conservancy, Hudson River Valley; Board Member, Eleanor Roosevelt Legacy Committee; Chairman, Women's Leadership Forum Network **CW:** Author, "Off the Sidelines: Raise Your

Voice, Change the World" (2014) **AW:** Named One of the 100 Most Influential People in the World, TIME Magazine (2014); Named One of the 50 Most Powerful Women in New York, Crain's New York Business (2009, 2011); American Jurisprudence Book Award **MEM:** Chairman, Committee on Government Ethics, The Association of the Bar of the City of New York (1998-1999, 2000-Present); ABA; New York Women's Bar Association; Blue Dog Coalition; The Association of the Bar of the City of New York **BAR:** The District of Columbia (1993); State of New York (1992); United States District Court for the Southern District of New York; United States District Court for the Eastern District of New York **PA:** Democrat **RE:** Roman Catholic

GILMAN, SHELDON G., T: Lawyer **I:** Law and Legal Services **DOB:** 07/20/1943 **PB:** Cleveland **SC:** OH/USA **PT:** Sol J. Gilman; Adella M. Gilman **MS:** Married **SPN:** Nancy **CH:** Stephen; Scott **ED:** JD in Business Organizations and Tax Law, Case Western Reserve University, Cleveland, OH (1967); BBA in Business Finance and Accounting, Ohio University, Athens, OH (1965) **C:** Retired (2017); Lynch, Cox, Gilman & Goodman, P.S.C. (1987-2017); Partner, Barnett Alagia (1982-1986); Associate, Partner, Handmaker, Weber and Myer (1972-1982) **CR:** Adjunct Faculty of Employee Benefits, Brandeis Law School, University of Louisville (1994); General Counsel, Louisville Association of Life Underwriters (1977-1978, 1990); Adjunct Professor, School of Law, University of Louisville **CIV:** Chair, Louisville Jewish Community's Life & Legacy Program (2017-Present); Board of Directors, Law Alumni Association, Case Western Reserve University (2017-Present); Board of Directors, Jewish Community Federation of Louisville (2000-2009); Committee on Congregational Standards (1996-2000); Board of Directors, United Synagogue of Conservative Judaism, New York, NY (1992-2000); Regional President, Ohio Valley Region, United Synagogue of Conservative Judaism (1992-1996); President, Congregation Adath Jeshurun, Louisville, KY (1986-1988); Vice President, Secretary, Louisville Orchestra (1984-1986); Chairman, Louisville Minority Business Resource Center, Louisville Chamber of Commerce (1975-1980); Member, Vietnam Veterans of America **MIL:** Captain, U.S. Army Reserve (1968-1972); Judge Advocate General's Corps, U.S. Army; United States Army Missile Command, Redstone Arsenal, Huntsville, AL; Office of The Judge Advocate General, Department of the Army, Washington, DC; Secretary of the Army Designee to Conscientious Objector Review Board, Washington, DC; Counsel, The Office of the Secretary Defense, Washington, DC **CW:** Author, "Kentucky Estate Planning, Fifth Edition" (2014); Contributor, Chapters, Books; Contributor, Articles, Professional Journals; Contributor, Estate Planning for UK/CLE-Guides; Speaker, Numerous Conferences and Presentations **AW:** Wilson Wyatt Award for Excellence in Philanthropic Advising, Community Foundation of Louisville; 25-Year Award of Preeminent "AV" Rated Lawyer, Martindale-Hubbell; Who's Who in American Law; Who's Who in America; Who's Who in the World **MEM:** Ethics "Hotline," Kentucky Bar Association (1990-2011, 2013-Present); Ethics Committee, Kentucky Bar Association (1982-1986, 1990-2011, 2013-Present); Professional Responsibility Committee, American College of Trust and Estate Counsel (2002-2006); Employee Benefits Committee, American College of Trust and Estate Counsel (1999-2002); General Counsel, Louisville Association of Life Underwriters (1977-1978, 1990-2000); Model Rules Committee, Kentucky Bar Association (1988); President, Louisville Employee Benefits Council (1980); Section of Real Property, Probate and Trust Law, American Bar Association;

Fellow, American Bar Foundation **BAR:** The Florida Bar; Indiana State Bar Association; Kentucky Bar Association; Ohio State Bar Association; Tennessee Bar Association; The District of Columbia Bar; United States Court of Appeals for the Armed Forces; United States Tax Court; Supreme Court of the United States; United States District Court Western District of Kentucky **MH:** Albert Nelson Marquis Lifetime Achievement Award **B/I:** Mr. Gilman became involved in his profession because of President John F. Kennedy. In his inaugural speech, President Kennedy said, "ask not what your country can do for you, ask what you can do for your country." Mr. Gilman responded by joining the Army ROTC and serving as an Army officer. While in college, Mr. Gilman's major area of concentration was finance and accounting, and one of his classes was in tax accounting law, which he found to be fascinating. He increased his semester course work so he could graduate from Ohio University in January 1965, and, thereby, start law school in February 1965. From his days in college, Mr. Gilman developed an interest in the law and then always wanted to be in the private practice. Over many years he had opportunities to leave the private practice but rejected all of them. **AV:** Listening to music; Running on the treadmill; Swimming; Reading a lot; Enjoying exercise six days a week **PA:** Democrat **RE:** Jewish

GINGRICH, NEWT LEROY, T: U.S. Representative, Writer **I:** Government Administration/Government Relations/Government Services **DOB:** 06/17/1943 **PB:** Harrisburg **SC:** PA/USA **PT:** Newton Searles McPherson; Robert Bruce Gingrich (Stepfather); Kathleen (Daugherty McPherson) Gingrich **MS:** Married **SPN:** Callista Bisek (08/18/2000); Marianne Ginther (08/08/1981, Divorced 2000); Jacqueline May Battley (06/19/1962, Divorced 02/1981) **CH:** Linda Kathleen; Jacqueline Sue **ED:** PhD in European History, Tulane University, New Orleans, LA (1971); MA, Tulane University, New Orleans, LA (1968); BA, Emory University, Atlanta, GA (1965) **C:** Founder, Center for Health Transformation (2003-Present); Panelist, "Crossfire," Cable News Network (2013-2014); Founder, Committee for New American Leadership, Washington, DC (2000); Political Analyst, Fox News Channel (1999-2011); Chairman, The Gingrich Group (1999-2011); Speaker of House, Georgia's Sixth District, United States Congress, Washington, DC (1995-1999); U.S. Representative, Georgia's Sixth Congressional District, United States Congress, Washington, DC (1979-1999); Assistant Professor of History, West Georgia College, Carrollton, GA (1970-1978) **CR:** Distinguished Visiting Fellow, Hoover Institution, Stanford University (1999-Present); Senior Fellow, American Enterprise Institute (1999-Present); Candidate for Republican Nomination, U.S. Presidential Election (2012); Adjunct Professor, Reinhardt College, Waleska, GA (1994-1995); Co-Founder, Conservative Opportunity Society; Speaker, Chairman Emeritus, GOPAC **CW:** Author, "Trump vs China: America's Greatest Challenge" (2019); Author, "Trump's America: The Truth about Our Nation's Great Comeback" (2018); Author, "Understanding Trump" (2017); Author, "Treason: A Novel" (2016); Co-Author, "Duplicity: A Novel" (2015); Author, "Breakout: Pioneers of the Future, Prison Guards of the Past and the Epic Battle that Will Decide America's Fate" (2013); Co-Author, Nonfiction, "Rediscovering God in America" (2012); Author, "$2.50 a Gallon: Why Obama is Wrong and Cheap Gas is Possible" (2012); Author, "Victory at Yorktown: A Novel" (2012); Author, "The Battle of the Crater: A Novel" (2011); Author, "A Nation Like No Other: Why American Exceptionalism Matters" (2011); Author, "To Try Men's Souls: A Novel of George Washington and the Fight for American Freedom" (2010); Author, "To Save America: Stopping Obama's Secular-Socialist Machine" (2010); Author, "Valley Forge: George Washington and the Crucible of Victory" (2010); Executive Producer, Documentary, "America at Risk" (2010); Executive Producer, Documentary, "Nine Days that Changed the World" (2010); Executive Producer, Documentary, "Rediscovering God in America II: Our Heritage" (2009); Co-Author, "Real Change: From the World that Fails to the World that Works" (2008); Author, "Drill Here, Drill Now, Pay Less: A Handbook for Slashing Gas Prices and Solving Our Energy Crisis" (2008); Author, "Days of Infamy" (2008); Author, "Pearl Harbor: A Novel of December 8th" (2007); Author, "Rediscovering God in America: Reflections on the Role of Faith in Our Nation's History and Future" (2006); Author, "Never Call Retreat: Lee and Grant: The Final Victory" (2005); Author, "Winning the Future: A 21st Century Contract with America" (2005); Author, "Gettysburg: A Novel of the Civil War" (2003); Author, "Grant Comes East: A Novel of the Civil War" (2003); Author, "Lessons Learned the Hard Way: A Personal Report" (1998); Author, Nonfiction, "To Renew America" (1995); Co-Author, "Nineteen Forty-Five" (1995); Co-Author, "Window of Opportunity: A Blueprint for the Future" (1984) **AW:** One of the 50 Highest-Earning Political Figures, Newsweek (2010); Carl E. Sander Political Leadership Scholar, University of Georgia School of Law (2009); One of the 25 Most Influential Republicans, Newsmax Magazine (2008); Award, National Minority Health Month Foundation (2005); Health Quality Award, National Committee for Quality Assurance (2005); Scientific Pioneer Award, The Science Coalition (2001); Legislative Conservationist of the Year, Georgia Wildlife Foundation (1998); Georgia Citizen of the Year, March of Dimes (1995); Man of the Year, Time Magazine (1995) **MEM:** American Association for the Advancement of Science; Georgia Conservancy; Kiwanis International **PA:** Republican **RE:** Roman Catholic

GINSBERG, BENJAMIN, PHD, T: Political Science Educator **I:** Education/Educational Services **DOB:** 04/01/1947 **PB:** Pocking **SC:** Germany **PT:** Herman; Anna (Wolfstein) G. **MS:** Married **SPN:** Sandra Joy Brewer (12/15/1968) **CH:** Cynthia; Alexander **ED:** Doctor of Philosophy in Political Science, University of Chicago (1973); Master of Arts in Political Science, University of Chicago (1970); Bachelor of Arts in Political Science, University of Chicago (1968) **C:** Director, Master of Arts in Government Program, Johns Hopkins University, Baltimore, MD (1993-Present); David Bernstein Professor of Political Science, Chairperson, Center for Government Studies, Johns Hopkins University, Baltimore, MD (1992-Present); Director, Washington Program, Cornell University, Ithaca, NY (1988-1991); Director, Institute of Public Affairs, Cornell University, Ithaca, NY (1987-1991); Professor, Cornell University, Ithaca, NY (1983-1991); Director, Survey Research Facility, Cornell University, Ithaca, NY (1985-1986); Associate Professor, Cornell University, Ithaca, NY (1978-1983); Assistant Professor of Government, Cornell University, Ithaca, NY (1972-1978) **CR:** William Weber Lecturer, Kalamazoo College (2005); Exxon Foundation Lecturer, University Chicago (1992); Taft Memorial Lecturer, University of Cincinnati (1992); Consultant, New York Times, New York, NY (1984-1985) **CW:** Author, "Congress, The First Branch" (2019); Author, "Analytics Policy and Governance" (2017); Author, "What Washington Gets Wrong" (2016); Author, "Presidential Government" (2015); Author, "The Worth of War" (2014); Author, "The Value of Violence" (2013); Author, "How the Jews Defeated Hitler" (2013); Author, "The Fall of the Faculty" (2011);

Author, "Political Science as Public Philosophy" (2010); Author, "Moses of South Carolina" (2010); Author, "Understanding the U.S. Constitution" (2008); Author, "The American Lie" (2007); Author, "Presidential Power: Unchecked and Unbalanced" (2007); Author, "Making Government Manageable" (2003); Author, "Downsizing Democracy" (2002); Author, "We the People" (1997); Author, "Embattled Democracy" (1995); Author, "Democrats Return to Power" (1994); Author, "The Fatal Embrace" (1993); Author, "American Government: Readings and Cases" (1992); Author, "Politics by Other Means" (1990); Author, "Freedom and Power in American Government" (1989); Author, "The Captive Public" (1986); Author, "Do Elections Matter?" (1985); Author, "The Consequences of Consent" (1982); Author, "Poliscide" (1976) **AW:** George E Owen Award for Outstanding Teaching, Johns Hopkins University (2016); Deans Award for Excellence in Research, John Hopkins University (2014); Fellow, National Academy Public Administration (2010); George Owen Award for Outstanding Teaching and Service (2000); Oraculum Award for Excellence in Teaching (1993); Grantee, Kellogg Foundation (1987); Jonathan Meigs Grantee, Cornell University (1985); Grantee, U.S. Department of Justice (1984); National Institute of Mental Health Fellow, University of Chicago (1968-1972); Trustees' Scholar, University of Chicago (1964-1968) **MEM:** President, National Capital Area, American Political Science Association (2002) **MH:** Albert Nelson Marquis Lifetime Achievement Award **B/I:** Mr. Ginsberg became involved in his profession due to the inspiration of Hans J. Maurgenthau, a famous professor of international relations. **RE:** Jewish

GIRMA, HABEN, T: American Disability Rights Advocate **I:** Social Work **DOB:** 07/29/1988 **PB:** Oakland **SC:** CA/USA **ED:** JD, Harvard Law School, Cambridge, MA (2013); BA, Lewis & Clark College, Portland, OR (2010) **C:** Attorney, Skadden Fellow, Disability Rights Advocates (DRA), Berkeley, CA (2015-2016) **CR:** Speaker, Apple Worldwide Developers Conference (2016); Speaker, TEDxBaltimore (2014) **CIV:** Volunteer, buildOn **CW:** Author, "Haben: The Deafblind Woman Who Conquered Harvard Law" (2019); Contributing Author, The Washington Post (2018) **AW:** Listee, Top 30 Thinkers Under 30, Pacific Standard (2016); Listee, Forbes 30 Under 30, Law & Policy (2016); Champion of Change, Obama Administration (2013) **MEM:** Board Member, Helen Keller Services for the Blind (2015) **AV:** Surfing; Rock climbing; Kayaking; Cycling; Dancing

GIULIANI, RUDOLPH, "RUDY" WILLIAM LOUIS, T: Lawyer, Mayor of New York City (Retired) **I:** Law and Legal Services **DOB:** 05/28/1944 **PB:** Brooklyn **SC:** NY/USA **PT:** Harold Angelo Giuliani; Helen (D'Avanzo) Giuliani **MS:** Divorced **SPN:** Judith Nathan (05/24/2003, Separated 2018); Donna Hanover (04/15/1984, Divorced 07/10/2002); Regina Peruggi (10/26/1968, Annulled 1982) **CH:** Andrew; Caroline **ED:** Honorary LLD, Earle Mack School of Law (Now Thomas R. Kline School of Law), Drexel University (2008); Honorary Doctorate in Public Administration, The Citadel (2007); Honorary Diploma, Middlebury College (2005); Honorary Diploma, Loyola College (2005); JD, School of Law, New York University, Magna Cum Laude (1968); BA, Manhattan College (1965) **C:** Attorney to President Donald Trump (2018-Present); Senior Adviser to Executive Chairman, Greenberg Traurig, LLP (2016-Present); Chairman, Chief Executive Officer, Giuliani Partners LLC, New York, NY (2002-Present); Informal Cybersecurity Adviser to Donald Trump (2017); Partner, Bracewell & Giuliani LLP (Now Bracewell LLP), New

York, NY (2005-2016); Chairman, Chief Executive Officer, Giuliani Capital Advisors LLC (Acquired by Macquarie Group), New York, NY (2004-2007); Mayor, New York, NY (1994-2001); Attorney, Anderson Kill Olick & Oshinsky PC (Now Anderson Kill P.C.), New York, NY (1990-1993); Attorney, White & Case LLP, New York, NY (1989-1990); U.S. Attorney, United States District Court Southern District of New York, The U.S. Department of Justice, New York, NY (1983-1989); Associate Attorney General, The U.S. Department of Justice, Washington, D.C (1981-1983); Attorney, Patterson Belknap Webb & Tyler LLP, New York, NY (1977-1981); Associate Deputy Attorney General, The U.S. Department of Justice, Washington, DC (1975-1977); Executive Assistant U.S. Attorney, Chief Narcotics Section and Chief Special Prosecutions Section, The U.S. Department of Justice, Washington, DC (1973-1975); Assistant U.S. Attorney, United States District Court Southern District of New York, The U.S. Department of Justice, New York, NY (1970-1973); Law Clerk to Honorable Lloyd Francis McMahon, United States District Court Southern District of New York, New York, NY (1968-1970); Chair, Cybersecurity and Crisis-Management Practice **CR:** Member, Iraq Study Group (2006); Speaker, Republican National Convention, New York, NY (2004); Republican Candidate, Mayor, New York, NY (1989, 1993, 1997) **CW:** Appearance, Film, "Anger Management" (2003); Co-Author, with Ken Kurson, "Leadership" (2002) **AW:** One of the 50 Highest-Earning Political Figures, Newsweek (2010); Special Achievement Award for Public Service, National Italian-American Foundation (2007); Margaret Thatcher Medal of Freedom (2007); Margaret Thatcher Medal of Freedom, Atlantic Bridge (2007); Golden Plate Award, Academy of Achievement (2003); Ronald Reagan Freedom Award (2002); Fiorella LaGuardia Public Service Award for Valor and Leadership in the Time of Global Crisis, Episcopal Diocese of New York (2002); Knight Commander of the British Empire, Her Majesty Queen Elizabeth II (2002); Consultant of the Year, Consultant Magazine (2002); Person of the Year, TIME Magazine (2001); Order of the Merit of Savoy (2001); Gold Medal Award, The Hundred Year Association of New York (1998) **PA:** Republican **RE:** Roman Catholic

GLASER, MICHAEL, "MIKE" LANCE, JD, T: Communications Law, Business Litigator **I:** Law and Legal Services **CN:** Law Offices of Michael L. Glaser, LLC **DOB:** 06/09/1939 **PB:** Washington, DC **SC:** USA **PT:** Theodore Allen Glaser; Margaret Esther (Bielaski) Glaser **MS:** Widowed **SPN:** Catherine Mary Connor (12/08/1941, Deceased 05/16/2015) **CH:** Michael Lance; Casey Lynn; Shannon Michele; Timothy Edwin; Regan Marie **ED:** JD, George Washington University, with Honors (1965); BA in Economics, George Washington University (1961) **C:** Attorney, Law Offices of Michael L. Glaser, LLC (2009-Present); Partner, Holme, Roberts & Owen, LLP (1990-1992); Partner, Gardner, Carton & Douglas, LLP, Washington, DC and Denver, CO (1981-1990); Partner, Glaser, Fletcher & Johnson, PC, Washington, DC (1971-1981); Partner, Bilger & Glaser, Washington, DC (1968-1970); Associate, Smith & Pepper, Washington, DC (1966-1968); Law Clerk, Associate Judge Frank Meyers, District of Columbia Court of Appeals, Washington, DC (1965-1966) **CR:** Member, Atomic Safety and Licensing Board, U.S. Nuclear Regulatory Commission, Atomic Energy Commission, Washington, DC (1972-1982) **AW:** Named Best Lawyer in America (2013-Present); AV Rating (5.0 out of 5), Martindale-Hubbell (1977-Present) **MEM:** American Bar Association (ABA); Federal Communications Bar Association; Colorado Bar Association; Denver Bar Association; The District of Columbia

Bar **BAR:** Supreme Court of the United States; District of Columbia Court of Appeals; Maryland Court of Appeals; Supreme Court of Colorado **MH:** Marquis Lifetime Achievement Award **B/I:** Mr. Glaser became involved in his profession because when he was in high school, he always thought he wanted to be a lawyer, and graduated from law school with honors (cum laude). He got into law because he wanted to help people. **RE:** Roman Catholic

GLASSMAN, JEFFREY L., T: Chairman **I:** Financial Services **CN:** Covington Capital Management **MS:** Married **SPN:** Cecelia **CH:** Four Children **ED:** JD, Loyola Law School, Loyola Marymount University, Magna Cum Laude; BA in Political Science, UCLA **C:** Chairman, Covington Capital Management (2018-Present); Chief Executive Officer, Covington Capital Management (2007-Present); Managing Director, Bingham Legg Advisers LLC; Principal, Riordan & McKinzie **CIV:** Vice Chair, Board of Directors, Los Angeles Jewish Home; Board of Directors, Mark Hughes Foundation; Board of Directors, Skirball Cultural Center; Board of Directors, Los Angeles Sports and Entertainment Commission; Vice Chair, Board of Directors, ArtCenter College of Design; Board of Trustees, California Science Center; Former Board of Directors, International Foundation for Electoral Systems (IFES) **AS:** Mr. Glassman attributes his success to being trustworthy and having good judgement. **B/I:** Mr. Glassman became involved in his profession because he wasn't sure what direction he wanted to go in, but he had two friends that attended law school a year before he did, so he applied. He ended up graduating second in his class at law school, where he discovered it was something he was good at. He was a trust and estates lawyer for his entire law career. When his law firm merged with a large national firm that had a money management firm, he was asked to open the Los Angeles office of the money management firm, which he did in 2002. When the money management firm was sold to Wilmington Trust, Mr. Glassman and a partner bought the LA office and merged it to Covington Capital Management.

GLAUBER, ROY JAY, PHD, T: Theoretical Physicist, Professor **I:** Sciences **CN:** Harvard University **DOB:** 09/01/1925 **PB:** New York **SC:** NY/USA **PT:** Emanuel B. Glauber; Felicia (Fox) Glauber **MS:** Divorced **SPN:** Cynthia Marshall Rich (1960, Divorced 1975) **CH:** Jeffrey M.; Valerie M. **ED:** Honorary Doctorate, Friedrich-Alexander University, Germany (2006); Honorary Doctor of Science, The University of Arizona, Tucson, AZ (2006); Honorary Doctorate, University of Essen, Germany (1997); Doctor of Philosophy in Physics, Harvard University (1949); Master of Arts, Harvard University (1947); Bachelor of Science in Physics, Harvard University, Summa Cum Laude (1946) **C:** Mallinckrodt Professor of Physics, Harvard University, Cambridge, MA (1976-2018); Professor, Harvard University (1962-1976); Associate Professor, Harvard University (1956-1962); Assistant Professor, Harvard University (1953-1956); Lecturer, Harvard University (1952-1953); Lecturer, California Institute of Technology, Pasadena, CA (1951-1952); Research Fellow, Swiss Federal Polytechnic Institute, Zürich, Switzerland (1950); Member, Institute for Advanced Study, Princeton, NJ (1949-1951); Staff, Theoretical Physics Division, Los Alamos Laboratory, NM (1944-1946) **CR:** Board of Directors, Center for Arms Control and Non-proliferation (2006-2018); Adjunct Professor of Physics, The University of Arizona, Tucson, AZ (1988-2018); Advisory Board, Program for Science and Technology for International Security, Massachusetts Institute of Technology (1983-

2018); Honorary Professor, Zhejiang University, Hangzhou, China (2007); Honorary Professor, Xian Jiaotong University, China (2007); Honorary Professor, Tongji University, Shanghai, China (2007); Trustee, Ivy Fund (1961-1992, 1995-2004); Director, Mackenzie Funds Inc. (1993-2004); Racah Lecturer, Hebrew University, Jerusalem, Israel (1988); Touschek Lecturer, Frascati Laboratory, Italy (1988); Freese Lecturer, Rensselaer Polytechnic Institute (1986); Visiting Staff, European Organization of Nuclear Research, Geneva, Switzerland (1983); Visiting Professor, College of France, Paris, France (1983); Visiting Professor, NORDITA, Copenhagen, Denmark (1974); Lorentz Professor, University of Leiden, The Netherlands (1974); Guest Professor, European Organization of Nuclear Research, Geneva, Switzerland (1972-1973); Visiting Lecturer, City University of New York (1970); Director, Enrico Fermi International School of Physics, Varenna, Italy (1967); Visiting Lecturer, University of Leningrad, USSR (1964); Visiting Lecturer, Ecole d'Été de Physical, Théorique, Les Houches, France (1954, 1964); Visiting Lecturer, University of California Berkeley (1955, 1957, 1963); Visiting Lecturer, University of Colorado Boulder (1958, 1961); Visiting Lecturer, Brandeis University, Waltham, MA (1961); Visiting Lecturer, University of Washington, Seattle, WA (1960); Consultant, Clinton Anderson Laboratory and Los Alamos National Laboratory, NM **CW:** Author, "Quantum Theory of Optical Coherence" (2007); Editor, "Quantum Optics" (1989-1995); Member, Editorial Board, Nuclear Physics B. (1972-1993); Member, Editorial Board, Journal of Mathematical Physics (1961-1963); Contributor, Articles to Professional Journals **AW:** Willis E. Lamb Prize (2006); Co-recipient, Nobel Prize in Physics (2005); Dannie N. Heineman Prize in Mathematical Physics, American Physical Society (1996); Heineman Prize (1996); A. von Humbolt Research Award (1989); Max Born Award, The Optical Society (1985); A.A. Michelson Medal, Franklin Institute (1985); Fellow, John Simon Guggenheim Foundation (1966-1967, 1972-1973); Named, Fulbright Lecturer (1954); Fellow, Frank B. Jewett Bell Laboratories (1950-1951); Fellow, Atomic Energy Commission (1949-1950); Fellow, National Research Council (1946-1949) **MEM:** Fellow, Royal Society (1997); Fellow, American Academy of Arts and Sciences; Fellow, American Physical Society; Fellow, The Optical Society; Honorary Fellow, Royal Society of New Zealand; National Academy of Sciences; Foreign Member, Royal Society of London; Advisory Board, National Center of Arms Control Non-Proliferation; Phi Beta Kappa; Sigma Xi

GLAVINE, TOM MICHAEL, T: Former Professional Baseball Player **I:** Athletics **DOB:** 05/25/1966 **PB:** Concord **SC:** MA/USA **PT:** Fred Glavine; Millie Glavine **MS:** Married **SPN:** Christine Glavine (1998); Carri Dobbins (11/07/1992, Divorced 1997) **CH:** Kienan Patrick; Peyton; Mason; Jonathan (Stepson); Amber **ED:** Diploma, Billerica Memorial High School, with Honors, MA (1984) **C:** Special Assistant to Atlanta Braves' President (2010); Pitcher, Atlanta Braves, MLB (1987-2002, 2008-2009); Pitcher, New York Mets, MLB (2002-2007); Guest Analyst, SportSouth and Fox Sports South **CR:** Former Atlanta Braves' Team Representative (1991); National League Player's Representative, Major League Baseball Players Association (MLBPA) **CIV:** Released, Charity Wine, Cabernet Glavington, CURE Childhood Cancer (2008); Spokesman, Operation Backpack, Volunteers of America (2005); Host, Georgia Transplant Foundation Annual Spring Training; Honorable Chairman, Georgia Council on Child Abuse, Inc.; Volunteer, National Sports Committee and Leukemia Society of America, Inc. (Now The Leukemia & Lymphoma

Society) **AW:** Inductee, National Baseball Hall of Fame (2014); Inductee, Braves Hall of Fame (2010); Good Guy Award, Baseball Writers' Association of America, New York Chapter (2007); Named to National League All-star Team (1991-1993, 1996-1998, 2000, 2002, 2004, 2006); Bart Giamatti Award for Community Service, Baseball Assistance Team (2006); Joan Payson Award for Humanitarian Service, Baseball Writers' Association of America, New York Chapter (2004); Good Guy Award, New Jersey Sports Writers Association (2004); Named National League Pitcher of the Year, Sporting News (1991, 2000); Silver Slugger Award (1991, 1995-1996, 1998); National League Cy Young Award (1991, 1998); Named World Series Most Valuable Player (1995); Winner, Atlanta Braves, World Series Championship (1995); Babe Ruth Award (1995)

GLEASON, WALLACE A. JR., MD, T: Medical Educator and Researcher **I:** Medicine & Health Care **CN:** McGovern Medical School **DOB:** 07/26/1944 **PB:** Fargo **SC:** ND/USA **PT:** Wallace Anselm Gleason; Elizabeth Madeline (Powers) Gleason **MS:** Widower **SPN:** Mary Jo-Ann Hofer (11/25/1972, Deceased) **CH:** Michael Andrew Gleason; Dennis Patrick Gleason **ED:** Residency in Pediatrics, St. Louis Children's Hospital (1970-1972); MD, University of Minnesota (1969); BS, University of Minnesota (1967); Coursework, Creighton University (1962-1965) **CT:** Diplomate, The American Board of Pediatrics; Pediatric Gastroenterology, The American Board of Pediatrics **C:** Associate Dean, Admissions and Student Affairs, The University of Texas Health Science Center at Houston (1998-Present); Professor, Pediatric Gastroenterology, Hepatology and Nutrition, The University of Texas Health Science Center at Houston (1996-Present); Associate Professor, Pediatric Gastroenterology, The University of Texas Health Science Center at Houston (1984-1996); Associate Professor, University of Texas Health Science Center at San Antonio (1982-1984); Assistant Professor, University of Texas Health Science Center at San Antonio (1977-1982); Assistant Professor, School of Medicine, Saint Louis University (1975-1977); Instructor, Pediatrics, School of Medicine, Saint Louis University (1974-1975); Instructor, Pediatrics, School of Medicine, Washington University in St. Louis, St. Louis, MO (1973-1974); Assistant, Pediatrics, School of Medicine, Washington University in St. Louis, St. Louis, MO (1969-1973); Intern, Pediatrics, St. Louis Children's Hospital (1969-1970) **CW:** Contributor, Articles, Professional Journals **MEM:** Fellow, American Academy of Pediatrics; American Gastroenterological Association; NASPGHAN; The Southern Society for Pediatrics Research; Society for Pediatric Research; Houston Pediatric Society; Houston Gastroenterology Society **MH:** Albert Nelson Marquis Lifetime Achievement Award; Marquis Who's Who Top Professional **B/I:** Dr. Gleason became involved in his profession as a result of inspiration from his father, who was a physician, and his interest in science. He sought a career that would make a difference in people's lives. Dr. Gleason especially enjoyed his medical school experience in pediatrics and ultimately remained in the field. **RE:** Roman Catholic

GLICK, RICHARD STEPHEN, MD, T: Physician, Rheumatologist **I:** Medicine & Health Care **CN:** Richard S. Glick, MD **DOB:** 05/18/1947 **PB:** Pittsburgh **SC:** PA/USA **PT:** William Glick; Ruthe (Scher) Glick **MS:** Married **SPN:** Joan Marie Skaf (11/02/1986) **CH:** William Spencer; Michael Andrew **ED:** Fellow, Albany Medical College Hospital (1978-1979); Fellow, Hospital of the University of Pennsylvania (1977-1978); Resident, University of Michigan Hospital, Ann Arbor, MI (1974-1977); Intern, University of Michigan Hospital, Ann

Arbor, MI (1973-1974); MD, Perelman School of Medicine, University of Pennsylvania (1973); BA, University of Pennsylvania, Cum Laude (1969) **CT:** Diplomate, American Board of Internal Medicine; Subspecialty, Rheumatology Board **C:** Practice, Medicine Specializing in Rheumatology and Internal Medicine, Fort Lauderdale, FL (1979-Present); Medical Staff, Holy Cross Hospital, Fort Lauderdale, FL; Medical Staff, Broward Health Imperial Point, Fort Lauderdale, FL; Medical Staff, Broward Health Medical Center, Fort Lauderdale, FL **CR:** Chief, Division of Rheumatology, Holy Cross Hospital, Fort Lauderdale, FL (2005-2006, 2011-2014) **CW:** Contributor, Professional Journals **AW:** Honoree, "Top Doctors," Fort Lauderdale Illustrated Magazine (2020); Honoree, "Top Doctors," Publications in Broward and Palm Beach Counties rated by Castle Connolly (2007-2019) **MEM:** Alpha Omega Alpha Honor Medical Society, University of Pennsylvania School of Medicine (1972); Phi Beta Kappa, University of Pennsylvania (1968); American College of Rheumatology; Florida Society of Rheumatology **MH:** Who's Who in America (2006-Present); Who's Who in Medicine and Healthcare; Who's Who in Science and Engineering; Who's Who in the World **AS:** Dr. Glick attributes his success to the love and support of his family. **B/I:** Dr. Glick became involved in his profession because in his hometown of Mount Pleasant, Pennsylvania, his cousin was a general practice physician and his own family doctor when he was a boy. His dedication and the respect he earned caring for his patients inspired his younger self to follow in his footsteps. He was also most fortunate to have trained both in residency and fellowship under several renowned rheumatologist mentors at the University of Michigan and the University of Pennsylvania, including Dr. William D. Robinson, Dr. William N. Kelley, Dr. Joseph Lee Hollander, and Dr. H. Ralph Schumacher.

GLIMCHER, SABRINA P. R., T: Chief Commercial Counsel **I:** Law and Legal Services **CN:** Global Jet Capital, Inc. **DOB:** 07/11/1985 **MS:** Married **SPN:** Daniel Glimcher **CH:** Karen; Mila **ED:** JD, Case Western Reserve University School of Law (2010); BA in Political Science, The Ohio State University (2003-2007) **C:** Senior Counsel, Global Jet Capital (2016-Present); Chief Commercial Counsel, Global Jet Capital (2019); Associate General Counsel, Global Jet Capital (2019); Staff Attorney, Waypoint Leasing Limited (2014-2015); Associate Attorney, Jones Day (2010-2014) **AS:** Ms. Glimcher attributes her success to taking ownership of the work that she produces, regardless of its quality. She doesn't make the same mistake twice. **B/I:** Ms.Glimcher came from a family that traveled frequently. When she was 9, she took a trip to Tel Aviv on the third-largest aircraft ever made. In 1993, the Hungarian airport did not have traditional gates. Being a 9-year-old next to the airliner, she remembered looking back at it and asking her dad how such a heavy machine could fly. Together, they got into reading about flights and physics, which inspired Ms. Glimcher's fascination with the aviation industry. Eventually, she broached the legal side of the field, finding the perfect place for her to succeed.

GLOR, JEFFREY, "JEFF" TODD, T: News Correspondent **I:** Media & Entertainment **CN:** CBS News **DOB:** 07/12/1975 **PB:** Buffalo **SC:** NY/USA **MS:** Married **SPN:** Nicole Glab (2003) **CH:** Two Children **ED:** BA in Journalism and Economics, Syracuse University, Magna Cum Laude, NY (1997) **C:** Co-host, "CBS This Morning: Saturday" (2019-Present); Special Correspondent, CBS News (2019-Present); Anchor, CBS Evening News (2017-2019); Correspondent, "60 Minutes Sports" (2015-2016); Anchor, Sunday Edition, CBS Evening News, CBS News (2012-2016);

News Anchor, "The Early Show," CBS News (2011-2012); Special Correspondent, "CBS This Morning," CBS News (2011); Anchor, Saturday Edition, CBS Evening News, National Correspondent, CBS News (2009-2010); National Correspondent, "The Early Show," CBS News, New York, NY (2007-2010); News Anchor, Weekday Reporter, WHDH-TV, Boston, MA (2003-2007); Co-anchor, Reporter, Evening News, WSTM-TV (2000-2003); Morning News Anchor, WSTM-TV (1997-2000); News Writer, WSTM-TV, Syracuse, NY (1997) **CW:** Creator, Producer, Blog; Author **AW:** Named Best Male News Anchor, Syracuse New Times; Henry J. Wolff Prize, Syracuse University

GLOVER, DONALD, T: Actor, Writer, Director **I:** Media & Entertainment **DOB:** 09/25/1983 **PB:** Edwards Airforce Base **SC:** CA/USA **CW:** Actor, "The Lion King" (2019); Actor, "Solo: A Star Wars Story" (2018); Actor, "Spider-Man: Homecoming" (2017); Recording Artist, "Awaken, My Love" (2016); Actor, "Atlanta" (2016); Actor, "The Martian" (2015); Actor, "The Lazarus Effect" (2015); Actor, "Magic Mike XXL" (2015); Actor, "Ultimate Spider-Man" (2015); Actor, "China, Il" (2015); Actor, "Alexander and the Terrible, Horrible, No Good, Very Bad Day" (2014); Actor, "Chicken and Futility" (2014); Recording Artist, "Because the Internet" (2013); Actor, "The To Do List" (2013); Actor, "Clapping for the Wrong Reasons" (2013); Actor, "Sesame Street" (2013); Actor, "Girls" (2013); Actor, "Adventure Time" (2013); Actor, "Donald Glover Weirdo" (2012); Recording Artist, "Camp" (2011); Actor, "Regular Show" (2011); Actor, "The Muppets" (2011); Actor, "Robot Chicken" (2010); Actor, "Comedy Central Presents Donald Glover" (2010); Actor, "Mystery Team" (2009); Actor, "Community" (2009); Actor, "Human Giant" (2007); Actor, "30 Rock" (2006) **AW:** Grammy for Record of the Year, Song of the Year, and Best Rap/Song Performance, "This Is America" (2018)

GLUSKI, ANDRÉS R., T: Director, President, Chief Executive Officer **I:** Utilities **CN:** AES Corporation **ED:** Doctor of Philosophy in Economics, University of Virginia; Master of Arts, University of Virginia; Bachelor of Arts, Wake Forest University **C:** Director, President, Chief Executive Officer, AES Corporation, Arlington, VA (2011-Present); Executive Vice President, Chief Operating Officer, AES Corporation, Arlington, VA (2007-2011); Executive Vice President, Regional President, Latin America, AES Corporation, Arlington, VA (2006-2007); Senior Vice President, Caribbean & Central America, AES Corporation, Arlington, VA (2003-2006); Manager, Venezuela and Chile, AES Corporation, Arlington, VA (1997-2003); Executive Vice President of Corporate Banking, Banco de Venezuela; Executive Vice President of Finance, CANTV, Venezuela **CR:** Board Member, U.S.-Brazil Chief Executive Officer Forum; Board Member, U.S.-India Chief Executive Officer Forum; Board Member, AES Corporation, Waste Management and AES Gener; Chairperson, Council of the Americas; Director, Edison Electric Institute **MEM:** Phi Beta Kappa

GODARD, JEAN-LUC, T: Film Director **I:** Media & Entertainment **DOB:** 12/03/1930 **PB:** Paris **SC:** France **PT:** Paul Godard; Odile (Monod) Godard **MS:** Divorced **SPN:** Anne Wiasemsky (07/22/1967, Divorced 1979); Anna Karina (03/03/1961, Divorced 1967) **ED:** Coursework, Lycée Buffon, Paris, France **C:** Journalist, Film Critic, Cahiers du Cinema (1951); Co-founder, Gazette du Cinema (1950) **CR:** Telephone Switchboard Operator, Construction Worker, Plaz Fleuri **CW:** Artist, "Le Studio d'Orphee," Fondazione Prada, Milan, Italy (2019); Director, "Image et Parole" (2018); Director, "Goodbye to Language" (2014); Director, "Bridges of Sara-

jevo" (2014); Director, "Film Socialisme" (2010); Director, "Vrai Faux Passeport" (2006); Director, "Reportage Amateur Maquette Expo" (2006); Director, "Notre Musique" (2004); Director, "In Praise of Love" (2001); Director, "The Old Place" (2000); Director, "For Ever Mozart" (1996); Director, "JLG by JLG" (1995); Director, "Helas Pour Moi" (1993); Director, "Momentous Events: Russia in the 90s" (1993); Director, "Contre L'Oubli" (1992); Director, "Allemagne Neuf Zero" (1991); Director, "Nouvelle Vasue" (1989); Director, Writer, Actor, Executive Producer, "King Lear" (1988); Author, "Godard on Godard: Critical Writings by Jean-Luc Godard" (1986); Director, Writer, "Hail Mary" (1985); Director, Co-writer, "Detective" (1985); Director, Actor, "First Name: Carmen" (1984); Director, Co-writer, Editor, "Passion" (1982); Director, Co-writer, "Sauve Qui Peut" (1980); Director, Co-writer, Editor, Producer, "Every Man for Himself" (1980); Director, "Bugsy" (1979); Co-director, Writer, Narrator, "Ici et Ailleurs" (1976); Director, Co-writer, Appearance, "Numero Deux" (1975); Co-director, Co-writer, "Tout va Bien" (1972); Co-director, Co-writer, Editor, "Vladmir et Rosa" (1971); Director, "Lotte in Italia" (1970); Co-director, Writer, "British Sounds" (1969); Director, "One American Movie: 1 A.M." (1969); Co-director, Co-writer, Editor, "Le Vent D'Est" (1969); Director, "One Plus One" (1968); Director, "Un Film Comme les Autres" (1968); Director, Writer, "Week-end" (1967); Director, Writer, "La Chinoise" (1967); Director, "Sympathy for the Devil" (1967); Director, "Lion du Vietnam" (1967); Director, "Le Plus Vieux Metier du Monde" (1967); Director, "Vangelo '70" (1967); Director, "Made in U.S.A." (1966); Director, "Masculine-Feminine" (1966); Director, Writer, "Alphaville: Une Etrange Aventure de Lemmy Caution" (1965); Director, Writer, "Pierrot le Fou" (1965); Director, Writer, Narrator, "Une Femme Mariée" (1964); Director, Writer, Narrator, "Band of Outsiders" (1964); Director, "Les Plus Belles Escroqueries du Monde" (1963); Director, Writer, Actor, "The Little Soldier" (1963); Director, Writer, "The Carabiniers" (1963); Director, Writer, Voice Actor, "Vivre et sa Vie" (1962); Director, Writer, "Une Femme est une Femme" (1961); Co-director with Jean Vigo, "Le Sept Peches Captiaux" (1961); Director, "A Bout de Souffle" (1959); Director, Writer, Editor, Voice Actor, "Charlotte et Son Jules" (1958); Director, "Tous les Garçons S'Appelent Patrick" (1957); Director, "Une Femme Coquette" (1955); Director, Producer, Writer, "Opération Béton" (1954); Director, Writer, Numerous Films and Documentaries **AW:** Honorary Academy Awards, Academy of Motion Pictures Arts & Sciences (2011); Special Prize, Festival of Venice (1962); Prix Pasinetti (1962) **MEM:** Superior Council of the French Language

GODLESKI, JOHN J., MD, T: Professor of Pathology Emeritus **I:** Medicine & Health Care **CN:** Harvard Medical School **DOB:** 07/24/1943 **PB:** Nanticoke **SC:** PA/USA **PT:** John Godleski; Sophie Godleski **MS:** Married **SPN:** Mary Lou Moss Godleski (06/14/1969) **CH:** Teresa Louise Sheedy; Daniel Peter; David (Son-in-Law) **ED:** MD, University of Pittsburgh, Pittsburgh, PA (1969); BS, King's College, Wilkes-Barre, PA (1965); Internship, Pathology, Residency in Pathology, Massachusetts General Hospital, Boston, MA; Fellowship in Pulmonary Research, Harvard School of Public Health, Boston, MA **CT:** Board Certification, Pathological Anatomy, American Board of Pathology (1975) **C:** Professor Emeritus, Pathology, Harvard Medical School, Boston, MA (2018-Present); Professor, Pathology, Harvard Medical School, Harvard University, Boston, MA (2015-2017); Associate Professor, Harvard Medical School, Harvard University, Boston, MA (1984-2015); Professor of Pathology, Brigham and Women's Hospital; Leader of Pulmonary Pathology Unit, Brigham and Women's Hospital (1978-2015); Assistant Professor of Pathology, Medical College of Pennsylvania, Philadelphia, PA (1973-1978); Commissioned Officer, United States Public Health Service, U.S. Environmental Protection Agency Research, Research Triangle Park, North Carolina **CR:** Consultant, John J. Godleski, MD PLLC; Associate Director, Harvard EPA Clean Air Research Center; Leader of Inhaled Particles Research Core, National Institute of Environmental Health Sciences Center, Harvard T.H. Chan School of Public Health; Head of Electron Microscopy Laboratory, National Institute of Environmental Health Sciences Center, Harvard T.H. Chan School of Public Health; Collaborative Research Programs, Scientists in Poland, Germany and Japan; Participant, International Pleural Mesothelioma Program, Brigham and Women's Hospital **CIV:** Coordinator/Director, Harvard School of Public Health-University of Sao Paulo Medical Student Research Training Program (2006-2016); Krakowiak Polish Dancers of Boston, Member of Board of Directors (1984-1988); Publicity Chair, Polish Festival Week in Boston (1987); Weston-Rombas international Exchange Program Committee (1988-1994) Treasurer (1991-1993); Member of Graduation Committee, CCBEU Language School Sao Bernardo, Brazil **MIL:** Surgeon, U.S. Public Health Service, North Carolina (1971-1973) **CW:** Contributor, More than 170 Peer-Reviewed Articles, Professional Journals **AW:** Outstanding Alumni Professional Achievement Award, King's College, Wilkes-Barre, PA (2019); Research Grants, National Institutes of Health (1979-2017); Cub Scout Hero Award, Quincy, MA (2016); Honorary Lifetime Fellowship, Polish Society of Pathologists, Warsaw, Poland (1989); Father of the Year, Town of Weston, MA (1981); Golden Apple Award for Outstanding Teaching, Medical College of Pennsylvania (1978) **MEM:** American Thoracic Society; Pulmonary Pathology Society; Microscopy Society of America; American Society for Investigative Pathology; New England Society of Pathologist; International Academy of Pathology; Secretary, Treasurer, Academy of Biological Sciences; Aquinas Society; Co-Chair, Annual Heart Panel Program, American Heart Association; French Club **MH:** Albert Nelson Marquis Lifetime Achievement Award; Marquis Who's Who Top Professional **AS:** Dr. Godleski attributes his success to his ability to identify the perfect wife in Mary Lou, to whom he has been married since 1969. In addition, he attributes it to his ability to choose great trainees, employees, and collaborators, which has been the basis of his professional success. **B/I:** Dr. Godleski became involved in his profession because in college, he was trying to decided whether he should go to medical school or earn a PhD in biological research. He met a pathologist who convinced him that pathology was both an interesting career and a great way to pursue research. It turned out to be the exact right field for Dr. Godleski. **RE:** Roman Catholic **THT:** Dr. Godleski's research focuses on the pulmonary and systemic responses to inhaled ambient air particles. His studies use cardiac and pulmonary mechanical measurements as well as cell and molecular biological approaches with inhalation exposure of experimental animal models to concentrated ambient air particles or ambient source particles. The overall hypothesis being tested in his laboratory is: Ambient urban air particles are complex mixtures with intrinsic toxicity; particulate exposure results in stimulation of lung receptors, release of reactive oxygen species, and induction of pro-inflammatory mediators that lead to local and systemic effects especially on the cardiovascular system, which ultimately account for epidemiologic associations between adverse health effects and particulate air pollution. Other

work in Dr. Godleski's laboratory uses analytical electron microscopy to quantify and identify environmental, therapeutic, diagnostic, and personal use product materials in human tissues.

GOETZ, JIM, T: Venture Capitalist **I:** Financial Services **CN:** Sequoia Capital **MS:** Married **SPN:** Alicia Goetz **ED:** MSEE in Computer Systems and Networking, Stanford University (1990); BS in Electrical and Computer Engineering, University of Cincinnati (1988) **C:** Partner, Sequoia Capital (2004-Present); Partner, Accel Partners (2000-2004); Co-Founder, Vital Signs (1996-1999); Vice President of Network Management, SynOptics Communications (1989-1996) **CIV:** Board of Directors, Dashlane (2019-Present); Board of Directors, Intel Corporation (2019-Present); Board of Directors, Observable (2018-Present); Board of Directors, Carbon 3D (2013-Present); Board of Directors, Chartboost (2013-Present); Board of Directors, Pocket Gems (2010-Present); Board of Directors, Metaswitch Networks (2008-Present); Board of Directors, Palo Alto Networks (2005-Present); Board of Directors, GitHub (2015-2019); Board of Directors, Drawbridge, Inc. (2011-2019); Board of Directors, Barracuda Networks (CUDA) (2005-2018); Board of Directors, Appirio (2008-2017); Board of Directors, Nimble Storage (NMBL) (2007-2016); Board of Directors, Ruckus Wireles (RKUS) (2012-2015); Board of Directors, WhatsApp Inc. (2011-2015); Board of Directors, Jive Software (2007-2015); Board of Directors, eMeter Corporation (2009-2012); Board of Directors, Clearwell Systems (2006-2011); Board of Directors, AdMob (2005-2010)

GOFF, GREGORY J., T: Executive Vice Chairperson (Retired) **I:** Oil & Energy **CN:** Marathon Petroleum Corporation **ED:** Master of Business Administration, University of Utah (1981); Bachelor of Science, University of Utah (1978) **C:** Retired (2019); Executive Vice Chairperson, Marathon Petroleum Corporation (2018-2019); President, Chief Executive Officer, Andeavor (2017-2018); President, Chief Executive Officer, Tesoro Corp. (2010-2017); Senior Vice President, Commercial, ConocoPhillips (2008-2010); President, Strategy, Integration and Specialty Business, Refining, Marketing and Transportation, ConocoPhillips (2006-2008); President, Continental United States and Latin America Exploration and Production Business, ConocoPhillips (2004-2006); President, Europe and Asia Pacific Downstream Activities, ConocoPhillips (2002-2004); Chairperson, Managing Director, Conoco Ltd., England (2000); Managing Director, Chief Executive Officer, Conoco JET Nordic, Conoco Inc. (1998-2000); Joined, Conoco Inc. (1981) **CR:** Board of Directors, ChevronPhillips Chemical Co.,; Board of Directors, PolyOne Corporation; Board of Directors, American Fuel and Petrochemical Manufacturers **CIV:** Downstream Committee, American Petroleum Institute; National Advisory Board, University of Utah Business School

GOGGINS, DAVID, T: Athlete **I:** Athletics **DOB:** 02/17/1975 **PB:** Buffalo **SC:** NY/USA **C:** Motivational Speaker; Professional and Collegiate Athlete **CR:** Athlete, Ultramarathons Including Badwater-135, San Diego One Day and Las Vegas Marathon **CIV:** Fundraising Athlete, Special Operations Warrior Foundation **MIL:** SEAL Team Five, U.S. Navy; U.S. Air Force **CW:** Author, "Can't Hurt Me: Master Your Mind and Defy the Odds" (2018) **AW:** Hero of Running, Runner's World (2008); Third Place, Badwater-135 (2007); Second Place, Ultraman World Championships Triathlon, Hawaii (2006)

GOHMERT, LOUIE BULLER JR., T: U.S. Representative, Judge (Retired) **I:** Government Administration/Government Relations/Government Services **DOB:** 08/18/1953 **PB:** Pittsburg **SC:** TX/USA **PT:** Louis Buller Gohmert; Erma Sue (Brooks) Gohmert **MS:** Married **SPN:** Kathryn Ann (Bledsoe) Gohmert (06/24/1978) **CH:** Kathryn Blair; Caroline Sue; Sarah Louise **ED:** JD, School of Law, Baylor University, Waco, TX (1977); BA in History, Texas A&M University (1975); Coursework, School for International Training, Putney, VT **C:** U.S. Representative, Texas' First Congressional District, United States Congress (2005-Present); Judge, 12th Court of Appeals (2002-2003); Judge, Smith County District Court, Tyler, TX (1992-2002); Private Practice Attorney, Tyler, TX (1986-1992); Partner, Freeman, Smithson & Gohmert, Tyler, TX (1986); Associate, Potter Guinn Law Firm, Tyler, TX (1982-1986); Assistant District Attorney, 76th Judicial District, Mount Pleasant, Texas (1978); Member, Committee on the Judiciary; Member, Committee on Natural Resources; Member, Republican Study Committee **CIV:** Deacon, Green Acres Baptist Church, Tyler, TX **MIL:** Captain, Judge Advocate General Corps, U.S. Army, Fort Benning, GA (1978-1982) **MEM:** Treasurer, Smith County Bar Association (1989); President, Texas Agricultural and Mechanical Alumni Association (Now The Association of Former Students of Texas A&M University), Smith County Chapter, Texas (1988); State Bar of Texas; Rotary International **BAR:** Supreme Court of the United States (1986); United States Court of Appeals for the Fifth Circuit (1986); United States District Court Eastern District of Texas (1978); United States District Court Southern District of Texas (1978); State Bar of Texas (1978) **AV:** Watching sports; Writing **PA:** Republican **RE:** Baptist

GOLD, ALLAN PHILIP, NCSP, T: District Psychologist **I:** Education/Educational Services **CN:** Reed Union School District **DOB:** 08/09/1946 **PB:** San Francisco **SC:** CA/USA **PT:** Benjamin Gold; Dorothy Gold **MS:** Married **SPN:** Alan Ferrara **ED:** PhD in Educational Psychology, University of California Berkeley (1978); BA in Psychology, University of California Berkeley (1973); MA in Statistics, University of California Berkeley (1969); BA in Mathematics, University of California Berkeley, Summa Cum Laude (1967) **CT:** Nationally Certified School Psychologist **C:** District Psychologist, Reed Union School District (1976-Present); Adjunct Professor, University of California Berkeley (1980-1987) **CIV:** Volunteer; President, Local Synagogue; Chairman of the Board, "Being Adept" **MIL:** U.S. Army Reserves **AW:** Outstanding School Psychologist Awards, California Association of School Psychologists (1991, 2017); Rotary Club Award (2014); First Educator Award for Outstanding Educators, Reed School District (1994) **MEM:** California Association of School Psychologists; National Association of School Psychologists **MH:** Marquis Who's Who Top Professional **AS:** Dr. Gold has extremely varied roles in his job as a school psychologist. In addition to assessing children with disabilities, he does a lot of individual and group counseling. He also runs groups for children who have parents that are divorced or ill, as well as children who have special-needs siblings. Dr. Gold additionally helps children develop social skills by consulting with parents, teachers, and administrators to assist the kids academically, socially, and emotionally. He attributes his success to humanizing the provision of mental health. He runs weekly math clubs to challenge students, all of which stem from his own love of math and his education in that field. He likes to show kids that he can be funny and human. Most importantly, he wants to demonstrate that seeking mental health support should not be stigmatizing. **B/I:** Dr. Gold was always interested in teaching and education. His father was a high school math and science teacher. While Dr. Gold was in graduate school, he joined the U.S. Army reserves, becoming part of a medical unit. That is where he was introduced to psychology. He then decided to return to school, earn a bachelor's degree in psychology, and then applied to the psychology program at the University of California Berkeley. There, he earned a PhD in educational psychology. **AV:** Stamp collecting; Painting **PA:** Democrat **RE:** Jewish **THT:** Dr. Gold always tries to do good for others. He feels fulfilled in his life as a result of his career, which has helped him to solve problems, demonstrate empathy and compassion, and make a difference in the world through mental health.

GOLDBERG, SUSAN, T: Editor-in-Chief **I:** Writing and Editing **CN:** National Geographic Magazine **SC:** MI/USA **MS:** Married **SPN:** Geoffrey Etnire; Gary Blonston (Deceased 1999) **CH:** Colin **ED:** BA in Journalism, Michigan State University, East Lansing, MI **C:** Editor-in-Chief, National Geographic Magazine, New York (2014-Present); Executive Editor, Bloomberg News, San Francisco, CA (2010-2014); Editor, The Plain Dealer, Cleveland, Ohio (2007-2010); Executive Editor, San Jose Mercury News (2003-2007); Vice President, San Jose Mercury News (2001-2007); Managing Editor, San Jose Mercury News (1999-2003); Deputy Managing Editor, USA Today (1989-1999); Assistant City Editor, San Jose Mercury News (1987-1989); Acting City Editor, San Jose Mercury News; Assistant City Editor, Detroit Free Press; Reporter, Seattle Post-Intelligencer **CR:** Board of Directors, Accrediting Council on Education in Journalism and Mass Communications (ACEJMC); Chair, Managing Editors Leadership and Management Committee, The Associated Press **CIV:** Board Member, American Cancer Society, Inc, Silicon Valley Chapter, California (2003-Present); Member, Board of Visitors, Northwestern University Medill School of Journalism; Member, Board of Directors, The City Club; Member, Board of Directors, Business Volunteers Unlimited; Board Member, National Museum for Women in the Arts; Board Member, Reporters Committee for Freedom of the Press; Member, Board of Directors, American Society of News Editors **CW:** Author, "Talking Toilets with Matt Damon," National Geographic (2017) **AW:** Named One of the Most Powerful Women, Washingtonian Magazine (2017) **MEM:** Rotary Club of San Jose

GOLDBERG, WHOOPI, T: Actress; Comedian **I:** Media & Entertainment **DOB:** 11/13/1955 **PB:** Manhattan **SC:** NY/USA **PT:** Robert James Johnson Jr.; Emma (Harris) Johnson **MS:** Divorced **SPN:** Lyle Trachtenberg (10/01/1994, Divorced 1995); David Claessen (09/01/1986, Divorced 1988); Alvin Martin (1973, Divorced 1979) **CH:** Alexandrea Martin **ED:** Studied with Uta Hagen, HB Studio, NY **C:** Member, Blake Street Hawkeyes, Berkeley, CA (1980-1984); Member, San Diego Repertory Theatre (1975-1980) **CW:** Co-host, "The View" (2007-Present); Actress, "The Stand" (2020); Appearance, "Rupaul's Drag Race" (2020); Voice Actress, "Scooby-Doo and Guess Who?" (2019); Voice Actress, "Summer Camp Island" (2019); Actress, "The List" (2018); Actress, "9/11" (2017); Actress, "King of the Dance Hall" (2016); Actress, "Black Dog, Red Dog" (2015); Voice Actress, "Savva. Heart of the Warrior" (2015); Actress, "Delores & Jermaine" (2015); Actress, "Teenage Mutant Ninja Turtles" (2014); Actress, "Top Five" (2014); Actress, "Big Stone Gap" (2014); Actress, Executive Producer, "A Day Late and a Dollar Short" (2014); Actress, "Once Upon a Time in Wonderland" (2013-2014); Actress, "Sensitive Men" (2013); Actress, "Glee" (2012-2014); Author, "Whoopi Goldberg: Inside the Whoopi Cushion" (2012); Actress, "A Little Bit of Heaven" (2011); Executive Producer, "Wow, I Never Knew That!" (2011); Executive Producer, "Moms Mabley: I Got Somethin' to Tell You" (2011); Co-author, "Sugar Plum Ballerinas #5: CATastrophe" (2011); Producer, Broadway, "Sister Act" (2011); Actress, "For Colored Girls" (2010); Voice Actress, "Toy Story 3" (2010); Voice Actress, "The Little Engine That Could" (2010); Author, "Is It Just Me?, Or Is It Nuts Out There?" (2010); Co-author, "Sugar Plum Ballerinas # 3: Perfectly Prima" (2010); Co-author, "Sugar Plum Ballerinas #4: Terrible Terrel" (2010); Actress, "Madea Goes to Jail" (2009); Actress, "The Cleaner" (2009); Co-author, "Sugar Plum Ballerinas # 2: Toeshoe Trouble" (2009); Voice Actress, "Snow Buddies" (2008); Actress, "A Muppets Christmas: Letter to Santa" (2008); Actress, "Xanadu" (2008); Appearance, "Entourage" (2008); Actress, "Life on Mars" (2008); Co-author, "Sugar Plum Ballerinas # 1: Plum Fantastic" (2008); Actress, "If I Had Known I Was Genius" (2007); Actress, "Doogal" (2006); Actress, "Everyone's Hero" (2006); Actress, "Everybody Hates Chris" (2006); Author, "Whoopi's Big Book of Manners" (2006); Host, "Wake-up with Whoopi," 103.5 KTU-FM (2006); Actress, "Racing Stripes" (2005); Actress, "Jiminy Glick in La La Wood" (2004); Actress, "Littleburg" (2004); Voice Actress, "Pinocchio 3000" (2004); Actress, "Blizzard" (2003); Actress, Producer, "Good Fences" (2003); Actress, Executive Producer, "Whoopi" (2003); Actress, Producer, "Ma Rainey's Black Bottom" (2003); Actress, "Star Trek: Nemesis" (2002); Actress, "Funny Girl" (2002); Actress, "Liberty's Kids" (2002); Voice Actress, "Madeline: My Fair Madeline" (2002); Actress, "It's a Very Muppet Christmas Movie" (2002); Actress, "Kingdom Come" (2001); Actress, "Monkeybone" (2001); Actress, Executive Producer, "Call Me Claus" (2001); Actress, "What Makes a Family" (2001); Actress, "Rat Race" (2001); Narrator, "Golden Dreams" (2001); Executive Producer, "Ruby's Bucket of Blood" (2001); Actress, "More Dogs Than Bones" (2000); Executive Producer, "Strong Medicine" (2000); Voice Actress, "A Second Chance at Life" (2000); Actress, "Deep End of the Ocean" (1999); Actress, "Jackie's Back!" (1999); Producer, "Oh What a Time It Was" (1999); Co-producer, "The Mao Game" (1999); Actress, "Jackie's Back!" (1999); Actress, "The Magical Land of the Leprechauns" (1999); Actress, "Alice in Wonderland" (1999); Actress, "Girl, Interrupted" (1999); Actress, "Foxbusters" (1999); Producer, "Hollywood Squares" (1998-2002); Actress, "How Stella Got Her Groove Back" (1998); Voice Actress, "The Rugrats Movie" (1998); Actress, "A Knight in Camelot" (1998); Actress, "Alegria" (1998); Actress, "A Funny Thing Happened on the Way to the Forum" (1996-1998); Voice Actress, "A Christmas Carol" (1997); Actress, "In the Gloaming" (1997); Voice Actress, "Mother Goose: A Rappin' and Rhymin' Special" (1997); Actress, "Happily Ever After: Fairy Tales for Every Child" (1997); Author, "Whoopi Goldberg Book" (1997); Actress, "Cinderella" (1997); Actress, "Bogus" (1996); Actress, "The Ghost of Mississippi" (1996); Actress, "Eddie" (1996); Actress," Tales from the Crypt Presents: Bordello of Blood" (1996); Actress, "The Associate" (1996); Actress, "Boys on the Side" (1995); Actress, "Moonlight and Valentino" (1995); Actress, "Theodore Rex" (1995); Actress, "The Little Rascals" (1994); Actress, "Corrina, Corrina" (1994); Actress, "Star Trek: Generations" (1994); Voice Actress, "The Lion King" (1994); Voice Actress, "The Pagemaster" (1994); Actress, "Naked in New York" (1993); Voice Actress, "Yuletide in the 'hood" (1993); Actress, "Made in America" (1993); Actress, "National Lampoon's Loaded Weapon 1" (1993); Actress, "Sister Act 2: Back in the Habit" (1993); Host, "The Whoopi Goldberg Show" (1992-1993); Author, "Alice" (1992); Actress, "The Player" (1992); Actress, "Sister Act" (1992); Actress, "House Party 2" (1992); Actress, "Sarafina!" (1992); Actress, "Defenders of Dynatron City" (1992); Actress, "Soapdish" (1991); Actress, "Blackbird Fly" (1991); Actress, "The Long Walk Home" (1990); Actress, "Ghost" (1990); Appearance, "Circus of the Stars #15" (1990); Featured, "Tales from the Whoop: Hot Rod Brown, Class Clown" (1990); Voice Actress, "Captain Planet and the Planeteers" (1990); Actress, "Baghdad Cafe" (1990); Actress, "Homer and Eddie" (1989); Actress, "Beverly Hills Brats" (1989); Actress, "My Past is My Own" (1989); Actress, "Kiss Shot" (1989); Actress, "Comicitis" (1989); Actress, "Star Trek: The Next Generation" (1988-1994); Actress, "Living on the Edge of Chaos" (1988); Actress, "Clara's Heart" (1988); Actress, "The Telephone" (1987); Actress, "Fatal Beauty" (1987); Actress, "Jumpin' Jack Flash" (1986); Director, Writer, Performer, "Comic Relief" (1986); Actress, "Burglar" (1986); Actress, "The Color Purple" (1985); Actress, Writer, "Whoopi Goldberg on Broadway" (1984-1985); Actress, "Citizen" (1982); Producer, Broadway, "Thoroughly Modern Millie"; Actress, Producer, Theater, Television Shows, Films **AW:** Emmy Award for Outstanding Talk Show Host, Academy of Television Arts & Sciences (2009); Named One of the World's Most Influential People, TIME Magazine (2009); Tony Award for Best Musical (2002); Emmy Award for Outstanding Special Class Special, Academy of Television Arts & Sciences (2002); Mark Twain Prize for American Humor, John F. Kennedy Center for the Performing Arts (2001); Recipient, Star, Hollywood Walk of Fame (2001); Academy Award for Best Supporting Actress, Academy of Motion Picture Arts and Sciences (1991); Golden Globe for Best Supporting Actress in a Motion Picture, Hollywood Foreign Press Association (1991); Named Entertainer of the Year, NAACP (1990); Humanitarian of the Year Award, Starlight Foundation (1989); California Theatre Award for Outstanding Achievement (1988); Hans Christian Andersen Award for Outstanding Achievement by a Dyslexic (1987); Golden Globe for Best Actress in a Motion Picture Drama, Hollywood Foreign Press Association (1986); Grammy Award for Best Comedy Recording, The Recording Academy (1985); Numerous Awards **MEM:** National Rifle Association of America

GOLDEN, JARED FORREST, T: U.S. Representative from Maine **I:** Government Administration/Government Relations/Government Services **CN:** U.S. House of Representatives **DOB:** 7/25/1982 **PB:** Lewiston **SC:** ME/USA **MS:** Married **SPN:** Isobel (Moiles) Golden **ED:** Bachelor of Arts, Bates College; Coursework, University of Maine at Farmington **C:** Member, U.S. House of Representatives from Maine's Second Congressional District (2019-Present); Member, 60th District, Maine House of Representatives (2014-Present) **MIL:** With, United States Marine Corps (2002-2006) **PA:** Democrat

GOLDENBERG, JEAN, T: Speech Language Pathologist **I:** Education/Educational Services **DOB:** 03/29/1950 **PB:** Buffalo **SC:** NY/USA **PT:** Samuel Deitsch; Freda (Gandel) Deitsch **MS:** Widowed **SPN:** Herbert Goldenberg (09/02/1974, Deceased 07/2015) **CH:** Yehuda; Yerucham; Peretz; Bracha; Chaim; Zvi; Nachman; Menachem; Chaya Raizel; Asher; Binyamin; Yaakov **ED:** MA, Queens College (1974); BA, Queens College (1972); Teaching Certificate, Rika Breuer Teachers College (1971) **CT:** Certified Teacher, State of Florida **C:** Contract Services, Orange Tree Staffing: Contract Services Communications Consultants (2018-Present); Speech Language Pathologist, Contract Services, North Miami, FL (1992-Present); Speech Language Pathologist, Dade County Schools, North Miami, FL (1989-2016); Speech Clinic Supervisor, Nova University, Broward, FL (1987-1989); Speech Pathologist, Joy Felton Contract Services, North Miami Beach, FL (1986-1987); Speech Pathologist, New York City Schools, Queens, NY (1980-1986); Speech Pathologist, Willowbrook State School, Staten Island, Queens, NY (1974-1978); Various Positions in Private Schools, New York, NY (1972-1974) **CR:** Consultant, Various Elementary and Secondary Schools, Miami, FL; New York, NY, Adjunct Lecturer, New York Institute of Technology - Long Island Campus (1974-1978); Leader, Workshops on Low-Functioning Children, New York; Sewing Instructor, "You Can Make It" **CW:** Contributor, Journal of Childhood Communication Disorders (1981); Co-Author (Under Tova Goldenberg Nickname), with Donna J. Thal, "Programming Diversity of Response: A Method for Teaching Flexibility of Language Use"; Contributor, Advanced Newsletter for Speech Pathologists; Contributor, Standardized Speech Tests **MEM:** American Speech and Hearing Association; Florida Speech and Hearing Association **MH:** Albert Nelson Marquis Lifetime Achievement Award **AS:** Mrs Goldenberg grew up with learning disabilities. She became the object of jokes regarding her response mess ups during her school years. At that time she vowed to obtain a master's degree and higher to prove to everyone that she was not the dummy that people pretended she was. **B/I:** Ms. Goldenberg entered her profession because she had a Hebrew teacher who had a deaf child and he inspired some of the students to work with the deaf. She went to Queens College to look at different departments, and went to the speech department and saw them working with the kids and she decided then that she would go into speech. **AV:** Copy editing; Sewing; Knitting; Homemaking; Instructing sewing

GOLDENBERG, MYRNA GALLANT, PHD, T: Holocaust Educator, Professor Emerita of English Language and Literature **I:** Education/Educational Services **DOB:** 03/08/1937 **PB:** Brooklyn **SC:** NY/USA **PT:** Harry (Deceased) Gallant; Fay (Solomon) Gallant **MS:** Married **SPN:** Neal Goldenberg **CH:** Elizabeth; David Brian; Eve Lisa **ED:** PhD, University of Maryland (1987); MA, University of Arkansas (1961); BS, The City College of New York, Cum Laude (1957) **C:** Professor Emerita, English Department, Montgomery College, Rockville, MD (2004-Present); Professor, English Department, Montgomery College (1971-2004); Founder and Director, The Paul Peck Humanities Institute, Montgomery College, Rockville, MD (1997-2003); Coordinator, Women's and Gender Studies Program, Montgomery College, Rockville, MD (1990-1994); Coordinator, General Education Program, Montgomery College, Rockville, MD (1981-1990); Chair, English Department, Montgomery College, Rockville, MD (1979-1981) **CR:** Project Director, Curriculum Mainstreaming and Teaching Initiative, Ford Foundation (1993-1994); Chairman, Arts and Humanities Council of Montgomery County (1984-1991); Project Co-director, Towson State University/Community College Advisory Committee on Curriculum Integration, Fund for the Improvement of Postsecondary Education, U.S. Department of Education (1988-1990); Chairman, Title IX Advisory Committee, Montgomery County Public Schools (1985-1989); Lecturer, Johns Hopkins University Krieger School of Arts & Sciences; Lecturer, Holocaust and Genocide Studies, Women's Studies, Jewish Women's Studies, English Honors Program, University of Maryland **CIV:** Jewish Historical Society of Greater Washington, DC (1997-Present); Maryland Humanities Council (1997-2003); Board of Directors, Jewish Community Council (1997-2002); Arts and Humanities Council (2000-2002);

Volunteer Librarian, Synagogue; Former Docent, United States Holocaust Memorial Museum **CW:** Contributing Editor, "Before All Memory is Lost: Women's Voices from the Holocaust" (2016); Contributor, "Anguished Hope: Holocaust Scholars Confront the Palestinian-Israeli Conflict" (2008); Contributing Editor, "Testimony, Tensions, and Tikkun: Teaching the Holocaust in Colleges and Universities" (2007); Contributing Editor, "Experience and Expression: Women, the Nazis, and the Holocaust" (2003); Editor, "Community College Humanities Review" (1990-2002); Contributing Editor, "Belles Lettres" (1989-1998); Contributor, "Memoirs of Auschwitz Survivors: The Burden of Gender," "Women in the Holocaust" (1998); Contributor, Preface, "The Beautiful Days of My Youth: My Six Months in Auschwitz and Plaszow" (1997); Contributor, "Lessons Learned from Gentle Heroism: Women's Holocaust Narratives," "The Annals of the American Academy of Political and Social Science," Volume 548 (1996); Contributing Editor, "Testimony, Narrative, and Nightmare: The Experiences of Jewish Women in the Holocaust," "Active Voices: Women in Jewish Culture" (1995); Contributor, "Writing Everybody In" (1994); Contributor, "Different Horrors/Same Hell: Gender and the Holocaust," "Thinking the Unthinkable: Human Meanings of the Holocaust" (1991); Co-editor, "Community College Guide to Curriculum Change" (1990); Contributor, "Common and Uncommon Concerns: The Complex Role of Community College Department Chair," "Enhancing Departmental Leadership: The Role of the Chairperson" (1990); Dissertation, Annie Nathan Meyer, University of Maryland (1987); Contributor, Articles, Professional Journals **AW:** IPPY Award, "Before All Memory is Lost: Women's Voices from the Holocaust" (2018); Canadian Jewish Literary Award, "Before All Memory is Lost: Women's Voices from the Holocaust" (2017); Finalist, National Jewish Book Award, "Before All Memory is Lost: Women's Voices from the Holocaust," Jewish Book Council (2017); Brilliant Diamond Award, Montgomery College (2006); Ida E. King Distinguished Visiting Scholar, Sara & Sam Schoffer Holocaust Resource Center, Richard Stockton College (Now Stockton University), NJ (2005-2006); Comcast Excellence in the Humanities Award (2002); William H. Meardy Faculty Member Award, ACCT (1996); Teaching Award, MD-AHEAD, Association on Higher Education and Disability (1991); Outstanding Faculty Award, Montgomery College (1990); Distinguished Humanities Educator Award, Community College Humanities Association (1989); Lowenstein Wiener Fellowship, The Jacob Rader Marcus Center of the American Jewish Archives (1983); ACE Fellow, American Council on Education (1981-1982) **MEM:** Board of Directors, Jewish Historical Society of Greater Washington, DC (1997-2002); Cosmos Club, Washington, DC (2001-Present); Secretary, Jewish Community Council ; Secretary, National Women's Studies Association; Association for Jewish Studies; NCTE; The Honor Society of Phi Kappa Phi **MH:** Albert Nelson Marquis Lifetime Achievement Award **AS:** Dr. Goldenberg attributes her success to an active curiosity about many subjects, including literature, history, visual arts, religion, and political/cultural trends and influences. She also credits devotion to truth and love of learning. **B/I:** Dr. Goldenberg became involved in her profession by following her heart and her head. Following a traumatizing trip to Vienna, Austria, and a visit to a concentration camp and its gas chamber, Dr. Goldenberg began immersing herself in Holocaust scholarship, reading everything she possibly could. Her ambition to learn became a matter of personal urgency, as she started to make connections with her own history; her mother's family was murdered by Nazis. She

could sense that something was missing in her field, and decided to devote her career to activism through academia. Dr. Goldenberg has never stopped educating herself on global racism. **AV:** Walking; Traveling; Writing; Reading; Knitting **PA:** Democrat **RE:** Jewish **THT:** Dr. Goldenberg tried to follow her father's maxims, "Leave this world better than you found it." She also follows Hillel's sayings, "What is hateful to you do not do to your fellow [sic]" and "If I am not for myself, who is for me? And when I am only for myself, what am I?"

GOLDFARB, STANLEY, MD, T: Professor of Medicine **I:** Education/Educational Services **CN:** University of Pennsylvania **DOB:** 12/18/1943 **PB:** New York **SC:** NY/USA **PT:** Robert Melvin; Mary Ann (Siegel) G. **MS:** Married **SPN:** Rayna Lynne Block (8/30/1970) **CH:** Rachael; Michael **ED:** Master of Science, University of Pennsylvania (1986); Doctor of Medicine, University of Rochester (1969); Bachelor of Arts, Princeton University (1965) **C:** Professor of Medicine, University of Pennsylvania, Philadelphia, PA (1988-1994); Associate Professor, University of Pennsylvania, Philadelphia, PA (1984-1988); Assistant Professor, University of Pennsylvania, Philadelphia, PA (1974-1984); Resident, Hospital, University of Pennsylvania, Philadelphia, PA (1970-1973); Intern, Hospital, University of Pennsylvania, Philadelphia, PA (1969-1970) **CR:** Member, Nephrology Board, American Board of Internal Medicine, Philadelphia, PA (1988-Present); Editor, Journal of the American Society of Nephrology (2007-2013); Chairperson, University of Pennsylvania, Philadelphia, PA (2004-2007) **CIV:** Board of Directors, National Kidney Foundation of Pennsylvania, Philadelphia, PA (1988-1990); Board of Directors, Board of Regents, American College of Physicians; Board Member, Measey Foundation **CW:** Editor, Hormones, Autocoids and Kidney (1991) **MEM:** President, The College of Physicians of Philadelphia (2006-2010); American Society of Clinical Investigation **MH:** Albert Nelson Marquis Lifetime Achievement Award **B/I:** Mr. Goldfarb became involved in his profession because he was mainly interested in doing research, which he performed at the University of Pennsylvania for many years. **AV:** Golf

GOLDGRABEN, GERALD ROBERT, T: Company Executive **I:** Consulting **DOB:** 08/11/1940 **PB:** New York **SC:** NY/USA **PT:** Henry Lawrence Goldgraben; Shirley (Altman) Goldgraben **MS:** Divorced **SPN:** Renee Glattstein (06/16/1966, Divorced 1986) **CH:** Felice Michelle; Haley Lynn **ED:** MBA, Marymount University, Arlington, VA (1985); Master in Chemical Engineering, New York University (1965); BA, Hunter College, NY (1961) **C:** President, New Carrolton Metro Gas 'N Go, Inc., (DBA Purse Strings 'N Things) (1997-2013); President, New Carrolton Metro Gas 'N Go, Inc., MD (1988-1997); Regional Executive Director, United Synagogue of Conservative Judaism (USCJ) (1996-1997); Manager, Center of Operations, United Synagogue of Conservative Judaism (USCJ) (1991-1993); Group Leader, United Synagogue of Conservative Judaism (USCJ) (1979-1991); Technical Staff, United Synagogue of Conservative Judaism (USCJ) (1976-1978); Senior Engineer/Project Manager, NUS Corp., Rockville, MD (1974-1976); President, North American Scientific Co., Dobbs Ferry, NY (1971-1974); President, Genic Construction Corp., Dobbs Ferry, NY (1971-1974); President, Ambient Systems, Inc., Dobbs Ferry, NY (1971-1974); Manager, Field Operations, New York City Department of Air Resources (1966-1971); Research/Development Chemist, Technicon Corp., Ardsley, NY (1964-1966); Clinical Chemist, Montefiore Hospital (Montefiore Medical Center), New York, NY (1962-1963); Clinical Chemist, Bronx-Lebanon Hospital, New York, NY (1961-1962); With,

The Mitre Corp., McLean, VA **CR:** President, Chief Executive Officer, VERTICAST Concrete Systems Corp. (1991-Present); Lecturer (1966-1975); Board of Directors, Wave Hill Environmental Institute, New York, NY (1967-1970) **CIV:** Founder, First Vice President, Mills Farm Potomac Hunt Civic Association, Gaithersburg, MD (1987-1989); President, Westleigh Citizen's Association, Gaithersburg, MD (1981-1982); Member, Solid Waste Advisory Committee, Montgomery County, MD (1976-1980); Chairman, Environmental Quality Control Commission, Town of Greenburgh, NY (1971-1974) **CW:** Co-author, "Organic Chemicals Manufacturing Hazards" (1981); Co-author, Contributor, Two Books; Author/Co-author, More Than 40 Papers; Lecturer, High Schools, Colleges, and Professional Society Courses; Patentee in Field, U.S. and International **MEM:** American Institute of Chemical Engineers; American Society for Testing and Materials (ASTM); American Chemical Society; Delta Epsilon Sigma **MH:** Albert Nelson Marquis Lifetime Achievement Award **B/I:** Mr. Goldgraben became involved in his profession as a result of a progressive series of positions. He started out as a clinical biochemist working for two hospitals. He completed a Master's in Chemical Engineering and was hired by the company that had developed the new, automated blood analysis device with which he developed an expertise in his hospital work. He was tasked with developing it for commercial/industrial applications, one of which was air pollution monitoring. He was later offered a job by the city of New York and was given a federal grant to design and implement an automated environment air pollution monitoring system. As head of Field Operations at the New York City Department of Air Pollution Control, he took control of the federal grant and designed and implemented the first computerized, automated, and telemetered air pollution monitoring system in the world in New York City. That was how he ended up in the environmental field. **AV:** Amateur radio; Tennis; Travel; Coin collecting/numismatics **PA:** Democrat **RE:** Jewish **THT:** Mr. Goldgraben's motto is, "Do not be afraid to be imaginative."

GOLDMAN, EMANUEL, PHD, T: Professor **I:** Education/Educational Services **CN:** Rutgers New Jersey Medical School **DOB:** 02/19/1945 **PB:** New York **SC:** NY/USA **PT:** Yehuda Goldman; Anne (Slochower) Goldman **MS:** Married **SPN:** Naomi Weinshenker, MD (08/30/1998); Jill Katherine Brannis (03/14/1986, Divorced 1992); M. Joan Wendy Millner (05/29/1966, Divorced 1975) **CH:** Theodore Joel Goldman; Lila Amy Goldman **ED:** PhD in Biochemistry, Massachusetts Institute of Technology (1972); BA, Brandeis University (1966); Diploma, Bronx High School of Science, with Honors (1962) **C:** Professor of Microbiology, New Jersey Medical School, Newark, NJ (1993-Present); Associate Professor of Microbiology, New Jersey Medical School, Newark, NJ (1983-1993); Assistant Professor of Microbiology, New Jersey Medical School, Newark, NJ (1979-1983); Assistant Research Microbiologist, University of California Irvine, CA (1977-1979); Associate of Medical Microbiology, University of California Irvine, CA (1975-1977); Research Fellow in Pathology, Harvard Medical School, Boston, MA (1973-1975); Fellow in Viral Oncology, Public Health Research Institute, New York, NY (1972-1973) **CR:** Editorial Board, Applied Environmental Microbiology (2011-Present); Editorial Board, Protein Expression and Purification (1996-Present); Genetic Mechanisms in Cancer, Peer Review Committee, American Cancer Society (1998-2002); Coordinator, New York Area Research Club, Columbia University (1982-1985); Consultant, Pathology, Harvard Medical School (1976) **CIV:** Outside Reviewer, Appointments,

Promotions (1999-2002); Performed Piano, Charity Events, Faculty Organization Parties, New Jersey Medical School (1981-2009); Active, American Civil Liberties Union (ACLU); Sierra Club; National Organization of Women; American Vegan Society **CW:** Co-author, "Gene Expression: Lessons from Bacteria with Comparisons to Eukaryotes" (2018); Co-author, "Phage Identification of Bacteria," Practical Handbook of Microbiology, Third Edition (2015); Co-author, "Introduction to Bacteriophages," Practical Handbook of Microbiology, Third Edition (2015); Co-author, "Survey of Selected Clinical, Commercial, and Research-model Eubacterial Species," Practical Handbook of Microbiology, Third Edition (2015); Co-author, "tRNA and the Human Genome," Encyclopedia of Life Sciences (2011); Co-author, "Introduction to Bacteriophages" Practical Handbook of Microbiology, Second Edition (2009); Author, "Translation Control by RNA," Encyclopedia of Life Sciences (2008); Co-author, "Fluorescence Enhancement on Silver Nanostructures: Studies of Components of Ribosomal Translation in Vitro," Single Molecule Spectroscopy and Imaging (2008); Author, "Translation Control by Proteins," Encyclopedia of Life Sciences (2007); Author, "Transfer RNA," Encyclopedia of Life Sciences (2008); Co-author, "Expression of Non-open Reading Frames Isolated from Phage Display Due to Translation Reinitiation," FASEB (2003); Co-author, "Genetic Analysis of the Basis of Translation in the -1 Frame of an Unusual Non-ORF Sequence Isolated from Phage Display," Gene Expression (2002); Co-author, "Reversal of Inhibition by the T7 Concatemer Junction Sequence on Expression from a Downstream T7 Promoter," Gene Expression (2001); Co-author, "Absence of Effect of Varying Thr-Leu Codon Pairs on Protein Synthesis in a T7 System," Biochemistry (2001); Author, "Stop Bugging Me," Viva! (2001); Co-author, "Efficiencies of Translation in Three Reading Frames of Unusual Non-ORF Sequences Isolated from Phage Display," FASEB (2000); Co-author, "The T7 Concatemer Junction Sequence Interferes with Expression from a Downstream T7 Promoter in Vivo," (1999); Co-author, "Modified Nucleosides in the First Positions of the Anticodons of tRNA 4Leu and tRNA 5Leu," Escherichia Coli B (1999); Co-author, "Messenger RNA Release from Ribosomes During 5'-translational Blockage by Consecutive Low-usage Arginine but not Leucine Codons," Eschericha Coli (1998); Co-author, "Use of SDS-polyacrylamide Gel Electrophoresis to Resolve mRNA and its Protein Product in One Gel," FASEB (1997); Co-author, "Lack of Correlation Between Agglutinability, the Surface Distribution of Con-A and Postconfluence Inhibition of Cell Division in Ten Cell Lines," Cell (1996); Co-author, "Evidence that Uncharged tRNA Can Inhibit a Programmed Translational Frameshift Escherichia Coli," Escherichia Coli (1995); Co-author, "Role of Carboxy-terminal Region in Proofreading Function of Methionyl-tRNA Synthetase," Escherichia Coli (1994); Author, "Clustering of Low Usage Codons and Ribosome Movement," Journal of Theoretical Biology (1994); Co-author," Methionine-mediated Lethality in Yeast Cells at Elevated Temperature," Journal of Bacteriology (1993); Author, "Effects of Consecutive AGG Codons on Translation in E. coli Demonstrated with a Versatile Codon Test System," Journal of Bacteriology (1993); Author, "Synthesis of Homocysteine Thiolactone by MethionyltRNA Synthetase in Cultured Mammalian Cells," FEBS Letters (1993); Co-author, "Effects of Consecutive AGG Codons on Translation in E. coli Demonstrated with a Versatile Codon Test System," Journal of Bacteriology (1993); Author, "Excerpted in Electrophoresis: Theory, Techniques and Biochemical and Clinical Applications," University Press (1981); Author, "Use of Protein Synthesis

in Vitro to Study Codon Recognition by Escherichia coli tRNA Leu Isoaccepting Species," Transver RNA: Biological Aspects (1980); Co-author, "Analysis of Host Range of Nontransforming Polyoma Virus Mutants," Virology (1975); Co-author, "Competition Between Bacteriophage f2 RNA and Bacteriophage T4 Messenger RNA," Biochemical and Biophysical Research Communications (1975); Co-author, "Indirect Complementation of a Non-transforming Mutant of Polyoma Virus," Cold Spring Harbor Symposium of Quantitative Biology (1974); Co-author,"T4 Phage and T4 Ghosts Inhibit f2 Phage Replication by Different Mechanisms," Journal of Molecular Biology (1973); Co-author, "Specificity of Protein Synthesis by Bacterial Ribosomes and Initiation Factors: Absence of Change After Phage T4 Infection," Journal of Molecular Biology (1972); Co-author, "Inhibition of Replication of Ribonucleic Acid Bacteriophage f2 by Superinfection with Bacteriophage T4," Journal of Virology (1971) **AW:** Celebration of Scholarship Award, Rutgers University Libraries, Rutgers, The State University of New Jersey (2017); Certificate of Outstanding Contribution in Reviewing (2015); Basic Sciences Faculty of the Year, Faculty Organization, New Jersey Medical School (2000); Faculty Extramural Support Incentive Award, New Jersey Medical School (1987); Kani Medal, National Cancer Center (National Cancer Center Research Institute), Tokyo, Japan (1986); Research Career Development Award, National Cancer Institute, National Institutes of Health (1983-1988); Faculty Exceptional Merit Awards, University of Medicine and Dentistry of New Jersey (1980, 1982); Lievre Senior Fellow, California Division, American Cancer Society, Inc. (1977-1979); Damon Runyon Fellow (1973-1975); Chemistry Department Prize, Brandeis University (1966) **MEM:** Officer, Program Coordinator, Molecular Biology Club (1985-Present); President, American Association of University Professors (AAUP), University of Medicine and Dentistry (1997-1999); Coordinator, Boston Area Tumor Virus Journal Club, Harvard Medical School (1974-1975); American Society for Biochemistry and Molecular Biology; The American Society for Microbiology; American Society for Microbiology, NJ; North America Vegetarian Society **MH:** Albert Nelson Marquis Lifetime Achievement Award; Marquis Who's Who Top Professional **AV:** Vegetarian nutrition; Cinema; Classical music **PA:** Democrat **RE:** Jewish

GOLDMAN, LEE, MD, T: Dean; Cardiologist; Professor **I:** Education/Educational Services **CN:** Columbia University Irving Medical Center **DOB:** 01/06/1948 **PB:** Philadelphia **SC:** PA/USA **PT:** Marvin Goldman; Kathryn (Schwartz) Goldman **MS:** Married **SPN:** Jill Steinhardt (03/21/1971) **CH:** Jeff; Daniel; Robyn Sue **ED:** Fellow in Cardiology, Yale New Haven Hospital, Yale New Haven Health (1976-1978); Resident in Medicine, Massachusetts General Hospital, Boston, MA (1975-1976); Resident in Medicine, University of California San Francisco (1974-1975); Intern, University of California San Francisco (1973-1974); MPH, Yale University (1973); MD, Yale University (1973); BA, Yale University (1969) **CT:** Diplomate, American Board of Internal Medicine; Diplomate, American Board of Cardiovascular Disease **C:** Harold and Margaret Hatch Professor, Executive Vice President, Health and Biomedical Sciences, Dean, Faculties of Health Sciences and Medicine, Columbia University Vagelos College of Physicians and Surgeons, New York, NY (2006-2020); Chair, Department of Medicine, University of California San Francisco (1995-2006); Professor, Harvard Medical School (1989-1995); Associate Professor, Harvard Medical School (1983-1989); Assistant Professor of Medicine, Harvard Medical School (1978-1983); Chief Executive, Columbia University Irving Medical Center; Professor, Associate Dean, University of California San Francisco **CR:** Member, Institute of Medicine (1995-Present); President, Association of Professor of Medicine (APM), Alliance for Academic Internal Medicine (2002); Board of Directors, Association of Professor of Medicine (APM), Alliance for Academic Internal Medicine (1998-2000); Board of Directors, UCSF Stanford Health Care (1997-2000); Member, Association of Professor Medicine (APM), Alliance for Academic Internal Medicine (1995-2006); Member, Operating Committee, Partners Healthcare Inc. (Now Mass General Brigham Incorporated) (1993-1995) **CIV:** Board of Directors, American Board of Internal Medicine (1996-Present); President, Board of Directors, Temple Shir Tikva, Wayland, MA (1986-1988) **CW:** Editor-in-chief, American Journal of Medicine (1997-2005); Associate Editor, New England Journal of Medicine (1989-1995); Author, "Too Much of a Good Thing"; Lead Editor, Goldman-Cecil Medicine; Contributor, Numerous Articles to Professional Journals **AW:** Robert Williams Award (2009); Henry J. Kaiser Family Foundation Scholar (1982-1987); John Phillips Award, American College of Physicians **MEM:** Fellow, Former President, Association of American Physicians; Fellow, American College of Cardiology; Fellow, American Association for the Advancement of Science; National Academy of Medicine; National Academy of Sciences

GOLDSMITH, PETER S., T: Chairperson **I:** Information Technology and Services **CN:** LISTnet **PB:** Bronx **SC:** NY/USA **PT:** Alfons Goldsmith; Lotte Goldsmith **MS:** Married **SPN:** Joyce Goldsmith **CH:** Matthew Goldsmith **ED:** Honorary Doctorate, Briarcliffe College (2001); Master of Business Administration, St. John's University, with Honors (1978); Bachelor of Business Administration, City College of New York (1964) **CT:** Eagle Scout **C:** Co-Manager, Digital Ballpark (2016-Present); Chairperson, Long Island Software & Technology Network (LISTnet) (1995-Present); President, LISTnet (1995-2016); Director of Operations, Grumman Data Systems (1975-1995); Director of A&R Operations, CBS Records (1967-1975); Adjunct Professor, Hofstra University **CR:** Board Member, United Way; Board Member, Urban League; Board Member, Touro Law School; Board Member, Stony Brook University College of Engineering **CIV:** Huntington Chamber of Commerce; Hauppauge Chamber Difference Maker **MIL:** U.S. Army Reserve (1964-1970) **AW:** Who's Who in the East (1985-1986); Who's Who in Finance and Industry (1981-1982); Have a Heart, American Heart Association; Friends of Justice, Touro Law School; Rough Riders, Boy Scouts of America; Eagle Scout, Boy Scouts of America; Listee, Kings of Long Island, Star Network; Power List, Long Island Press; Long Island Top Leaders, Long Island Business News; Tech Hall of Fame, Stony Brook University **MEM:** Beta Gamma Sigma; Alpha Phi Omega **AS:** Mr. Goldsmith attributes his success to realizing that it's not how many ideas one has, it's how many one makes happen. **B/I:** Mr. Goldsmith became involved in his profession out of a desire to help technology companies and startups grow on Long Island. **RE:** Jewish

GOLDSTEIN, KEITH S., MD, MPH, FAAFP, DABPM, T: Occupational Medicine Program Director; Consultant **I:** Medicine & Health Care **CN:** CareATC, Inc.; RB Health Partners, Inc. **DOB:** 07/04/1955 **PB:** Bronx **SC:** NY/USA **PT:** Stanley Irving Goldstein; Horty (Silverstein) Goldstein **MS:** Married **SPN:** Staci Marta Willner **CH:** Keiren Jack; Hali **ED:** Postgraduate Coursework Towards MPH, Medical College of Wisconsin (1991); Residency in Family Practice, Niagara Falls Memorial Medical Center, Niagara Falls, NY; Residency in General Surgery, Brookdale University Hospital Medical Center, Brooklyn, NY; MD, Ross University School of Medicine, with Honors (1982); BS in Biology, Tulane University, with Honors (1976) **CT:** MRO (Medical Review Officer) Certification (2012); Certified PALS (Pediatric Advanced Life Support) (2012); Certified, Radiation Medical, U.S. Department of Energy (2012); Designated Physician, U.S. Department of Energy (2012); ACLS (Advanced Cardiac Life Support) Experienced Instructor Certification (2012); CPR/AED (Basic Cardiac Life Support) Instructor (2012); Security Clearance, U.S. Department of Energy (1994-2012); Certified Human Resources Specialist (2007); Certified, BAT (Breath Alcohol Technician) (2004); Designated, Pre-Hospital Physician, PA Department of Health (2000); Certified, Base Station Emergency Medical Command (MC-3), Commonwealth of Pennsylvania (1994); Certified ATLS (Advanced Trauma Life Support) (1993); Team Physician Certification (1991); Board Certification in Occupational Medicine; Diplomate, American Board of Preventive Medicine **C:** Chief Medical Consultant, RB Health Partners, Inc., Tampa, FL (2015-Present); Occupational Medicine Clinic Director, CareATC, Inc., Tampa, FL (2012-Present); Attending Physician, Department of Family Practice, Scranton State General Hospital, PA (1988-Present); Global Occupational Medical Program Director, Bettis Atomic Power Laboratory, Naval Nuclear Laboratory, Pittsburgh, PA (1994-2012); Private Family Practice, Scranton, PA (1987-1989); Medical Director, Wellness Program, Towanda Memorial Hospital (Now Guthrie Towanda Memorial Hospital), The Guthrie Clinic, PA (1992-1994); Attending Physician, Department of Emergency Medicine, Towanda Memorial Hospital (Now Guthrie Towanda Memorial Hospital), The Guthrie Clinic, PA (1988-1994); Attending Physician, Department of Emergency Medicine, Scranton State General Hospital, PA (1987-1989) **CR:** With, Wyalusing Ambulance (1991-1994); With, Canton Ambulance (1991-1994); Medical Director, Tri-Township EMS (1990-1994); With, Scranton Plasma Center (1988-1994); With, Bradford County Fall Run (1991); With, Endless Mountains (Bradford County) Triathlon, Bradford County, PA (1990-1991); Team Physician Assistant, All Bradford County Pennsylvania School Teams (1988-1994); Assistant, Sports Medicine Clinic, Towanda Memorial Hospital (Now Guthrie Towanda Memorial Hospital), The Guthrie Clinic, PA (1988-1994); Visiting Professor of Anatomy, Niagara County Community College School of Nursing, Sanborn, NY (1985); Lecturer in Field **CIV:** Police Entry Team Physician Participant, Smithton Borough, PA (1994-2012) **CW:** Member, Editorial Board, Journal of Contemporary Surgery (1987-Present); Co-investigator, Use of Ca-DTPA and Zn-DTPA as a Chelating Agent for Treatment of Internal Contamination by Transuranic Elements, Oak Ridge Institute for Science Education, Idaho (1994-2012); Presenter, "Chemical Hazards" Lecture, American College of Osteopathic Emergency Physicians Conference, Las Vegas, NV (1996); Surgery Opinion Panel, Journal of Contemporary Surgery (1987-1996); Author, Bimonthly Article, "Patient Medical Information Series," Wyalusing Ambulance Newsletter, Wyalusing, PA; Medical Software Review Committee, "Computers in Emergency Medicine," American College of Emergency Physicians Section; Contributor, Articles to Professional Publications **AW:** Physician Recognition Award, American Medical Association (1991, 1993, 1995, 1997, 2011); Fellow, American Academy of Family Physicians **MEM:** Florida Medical Association; Florida Association of Occupational Physicians; Florida Academy of Family Physicians; American Board of Sports Medicine, American Board of Family Medicine, Inc.; American College of Occupational and Environmental Medicine (ACOEM); American College of Preventive Medicine; American Medical Association; American Association of Physician Specialists - Emergency Medicine, American Medical Association of Sports Medicine Physicians; American Academy of Family Physicians; American College of Sports Medicine (ACSM); American College of Emergency Physicians; Pennsylvania Medical Society, American Association of Trauma Specialists; National Association of Emergency Medical Technicians; B'nai B'rith International **AS:** Dr. Goldstein attributes his success to encouragement from his parents, his amazing wife, Staci, his amazing children, Keiren and Hali, and best friend, Salvatore Galante, MD. Their invaluable support and advice have helped him to navigate life and his career goals. He will always be grateful to them. **AV:** Private pilot; Amateur radio: KG1MD; Scuba diving; Computer programming; Poetry; 3D Printing; Innovator; Inventor **PA:** Conservative Republican **RE:** Jewish

GOLDSTEIN, RONALD E., DDS, T: Dentist, Author, Educator, Consultant, Lecturer **I:** Medicine & Health Care **DOB:** 11/01/1933 **PB:** Atlanta **SC:** GA/USA **PT:** Irving Goldstein; Helen (Mendel) Goldstein **MS:** Married **SPN:** Judy **CH:** Cary; Cathy; Ken; Rick **ED:** DDS, School of Dentistry, Emory University (1953-1957); University of Michigan (1951-1953); Oglethorpe University (1953); Georgia State University (1952) **C:** Adjunct Professor of Comprehensive Dentistry, The University of Texas Health Science Center at Houston (2011-Present); Clinical Professor of Restorative Sciences, Dental College of Georgia, Augusta University (1993-Present); Adjunct Clinical Professor of Prosthodontics, Henry M. Goldman School Dental Medicine, Boston University (1990-Present); Visiting Professor in Oral and Maxillofacial Imaging and Continuing Education, School of Dentistry, University of Southern California (1993-2011); Special Lecturer in Esthetic Dentistry (1980-1993); Adjunct Professor of Restorative Dentistry, The University of Texas at San Antonio (1983-1985); Clinical Professor, Department of Oral Rehabilitation, School of Dentistry, Medical College of Georgia (1983-1993); Special Lecturer in Periodontology, School of Dentistry, Emory University (1972-1979); Private Practice Dentist, Goldstein, Garber, & Salama **CR:** Founder, Tomorrow's Smile (2008-Present); Consultant, PM Magazine (1979-1982); Producer, More Than 70 Television Programs on Dental Health (1979-1982); Volunteer-in-Charge of Cosmetic Dentistry, Ben Massell Dental Clinic (1967-1980) **CIV:** Evander Holyfield Foundation (2003-Present); Jewish Family and Children's Services (1969-Present); Center for Dental Information (1995-1996); Scientific Adviser, Princeton Dental Resource Center (1991-1995); Trustee, Achim Gate City Lodge (1970); Board of Advisers, Anti-Defamation League (1970); Board of Directors, Family Counseling Service Society (1963-1969); Board of Directors, Atlanta USO-JWB (1966-1968); Board of Directors, Metropolitan Atlanta Community Chest (1964-1968); Board of Directors, Metropolitan Atlanta Mental Health Association (1964-1967); President, Atlanta Health Council (1964-1966); Former Chairman, Governor's Committee on Employment of the Emotionally Restored (1961-1963, 1964-1966); Vice President, Georgia Association for Mental Health (1964); Creator, National Program in Mental Health and Retardation, U.S. Junior Chamber of Commerce (1963); Founder, Atlanta Health Council (1962); Board of Directors, Achim Gate City Lodge, B'nai B'rith International (1961-1962) **MIL:** Captain, Army Dispensary, The Pentagon (1957-1959); Dentist, U.S. Army Dental Corps (1957-1959) **CW:** Editorial Advisory Board, Inside Dentistry Magazine (2005-Present); Editorial Advisory Board, New Beauty Magazine (2005-Present); Co-Author, "Ronald E. Goldstein's Esthetics in Dentistry Volume II, Third Edition" (2018); Author," Change Your Smile, Fourth Edition" (2009); Co-Editor-in-Chief, Journal of Esthetic Dentistry (1993-2000); Author, "Change Your Smile, Third Edition" (1997); Co-Author, "Complete Dental Bleaching" (1995); Co-Author, "Porcelain and Composite Inlays and Onlays (1994); Co-Author, "Porcelain Laminate Veneers" (1988); Co-Author, "Bleaching Teeth" (1987); Author, "Change Your Smile" (1984); Contributing Editor, "The Wonderful World of Modern Dentistry" (1972); Editorial Board Member, Current Opinion in Dentistry (1972); Author, More Than 700 Courses and Lectures, 400 Professional Journal Articles, 375 Consumer Magazine Articles; Featured, More Than 100 Professional Videos, 245 Consumer Television, Radio and Internet Interviews **AW:** Top Four Lecturers in Esthetic Dentistry, Dentist Magazine (1989-Present); EB Clark Award for Exceptional Leadership and Outstanding Contributions in Research, Education and the Application of Color Science and Art in the Dental Profession (2015); Lifetime Achievement Award, Georgia Academy of Cosmetic Dentistry (2013); Distinguished Alumni Award, Dental Alumni Association, Emory University (2001); Fellow, International College of Dentists (1997); Achievement Medal, Alpha Omega International Dental Fraternity (1997); Featured Practice, Dentistry Today (1991, 1994); Fellow, American College of Dentists (1992); Charles L. Pincus Award for Contribution to Esthetic Dentistry, American Academy of Esthetic Dentistry (1992); John Muir Medical Film Festival Award (1982); Outstanding Contribution to Cosmetic Dentistry Award, American Academy of Cosmetic Dentistry (1992); Citizen of the Week, Station WPLO (1963); Outstanding Young Man of the Year Award, Atlanta Junior Chamber of Commerce (1962); Winner, First Annual Writing Award, American College of Dentists (1957) **MEM:** Society for Color and Appearance in Dentistry (2008-Present); Honorary Member, The Venezuelan Academy of Esthetic Dentistry (2004-Present); Honorary Member, Japanese Academy of Esthetic Dentistry (1997-Present); Lifetime Member, American Academy of Fixed Prosthodontics (1986-Present); American Association for Dental Research (1985-Present); International Association for Dental Research (1985-Present); Fellow, American Academy of Esthetic Dentistry (1978-Present); Northern District Dental Society, American Dental Association (1959-Present); American Dental Association (1958-Present); Georgia Dental Association (1953-Present); Former President, Fifth District Dental Society **MH:** Albert Nelson Marquis Lifetime Achievement Award **B/I:** Dr. Goldstein became involved in his profession because his father was a dentist. Dr. Goldstein was a journalist and his father suggested he pursue dentistry as well because the industry needed good writers. **AV:** Taking photographs; Painting; Writing; Traveling **PA:** Republican **RE:** Jewish

GOMEZ, JIMMY, T: U.S. Representative from California **I:** Government Administration/Government Relations/Government Services **DOB:** 11/25/1974 **PB:** Fullerton **SC:** CA/USA **MS:** Married **SPN:** Mary Hodge **ED:** Master's in Public Policy, Harvard Kennedy School John F. Kennedy School of Government; BA in Political Science, University of California Los Angeles; Coursework, Riverside Community College **C:** Member, U.S. House of Representatives from California's 34th Congressional District (2017-Present); Member, Committee on Oversight and Government Reform (2017-Present); Member, Committee on Natural Resources (2017-Present); Member, Committee on Ways and Means (2017-Present); Member, District 51, California State Assembly (2012-2017); Majority Whip, State Assembly (2013-2014) **CR:** Member, Congressional Hispanic Caucus; Member, Congressional Asian Pacific American Caucus (CAPAC); Member, Congressional Progressive Caucus (CPC); Vice-chair, Future Forum

GOMEZ, SELENA MARIE, T: Actress; Singer **I:** Media & Entertainment **DOB:** 07/22/1992 **PB:** Grand Prairie **SC:** TX/USA **PT:** Ricardo Joel Gomez; Amanda Dawn "Mandy" (Cornett) Teefey **C:** Founder, Lead Singer, Selena Gomez & the Scene (2008) **CIV:** Goodwill Ambassador, UNICEF (2009-Present); Disney's Friends for Change (2009-2012); Ambassador, DoSomething.org; Ambassador, Ryan Seacrest Foundation; Spokesperson, State Farm Insurance **CW:** Singer, "Rare" (2020); Actress, "The Voyage of Doctor Dolittle" (2019); Voice Actress, "Hotel Transylvania 3" (2018); Actress, "A Rainy Day in New York" (2018); Actress, "Puppy!" (2017); Actress, "In Dubious Battle" (2016); Appearance, "Inside Amy Schumer" (2016); Host, "Saturday Night Live" (2016); Actress, "The Revised Fundamentals of Caregiving" (2016); Actress, "Neighbors 2: Sorority Rising" (2016); Actress, "In Dubious Battle" (2016); Singer, "Revival" (2015); Actress, "The Big Short" (2015); Voice Actress, "Hotel Transylvania 2" (2015); Appearance, "The Voice" (2015); Actress, "Rudderless" (2014); Actress, "Behaving Badly" (2014); Appearance, "We Day" (2014); Singer, "Stars Dance" (2013); Actress, "Getaway" (2013); Actress, Executive Producer, "The Wizards Return: Alex versus Alex" (2013); Actress, "Spring Breakers" (2012); Voice Actress, "Hotel Transylvania" (2012); Actress, "Aftershock" (2012); Actress, "Wizards of Waverly Place," (2007-2012); Actress, "Monte Carlo" (2011); Singer, Selena Gomez & the Scene, "When the Sun Goes Down" (2011); Singer, Selena Gomez & the Scene, "A Year Without Rain" (2010); Actress, "Ramona and Beezus" (2010); Singer, Selena Gomez & the Scene, "Kiss & Tell" (2009); Actress, "Princess Protection Program" (2009); Actress, "Wizards of Waverly Place: The Movie" (2009); Actress, "Another Cinderella Story" (2008); Voice Actress, "Horton Hears a Who!" (2008); Actress, "Hannah Montana" (2007-2008); Actress, "The Suite Life of Zack & Cody" (2006); Actress, "Spy Kids 3-D: Game Over" (2003); Actress, "Barney & Friends" (2002-2003) **AW:** Woman of the Year, Billboard Music Award (2017); Favorite Animated Movie Voice, People's Choice Awards (2016); Best Pop Video, MTV Video Music Awards (2013); Choice Music Group, Selena Gomez & the Scene, Teen Choice Awards (2012); Favorite TV Actress, Nickelodeon Kids' Choice Awards (2009, 2010, 2011); Recipient, Numerous Awards

GÓMEZ, LAURA I., T: Founder, Former Chief Executive Officer **I:** Business Management/Business Services **CN:** Atipica **ED:** Coursework, University of California Berkeley; Coursework, Education Abroad Program in Brazil in Economics, History, and Portuguese, Pontifícia Universidade Católica do Rio de Janeiro/PUC-Rio; MA, University of California San Diego **CT:** Post Baccalaureate in Counseling and Psychology Professions, Health Advocacy, University of California Berkeley Extension (2020) **C:** Chief Executive Officer, Founder, Atipica (2014-2020); Internalization, Localization and International Product, Jawbone (2013-2014); Head of Localization, Twitter (2009-2012); Head of Twitter en Español, Twitter (2009-2012); Ad Operations, Asia Pacific and Latin America, YouTube (2007-2008); International Campaign Management, AKQA (2006-2007) **CR:** Health Educator **CIV:** Volunteer Crisis Counselor, Crisis Text Line (2020-Present); Board of Advisors, Flexability (2019-Present);

Women of Color Council, Anita Borg Institute for Women and Technology (2017-Present); Diversity Council, Code.org (2017-Present); Founding Advisor, Project Include (2016-Present); Board Member, Operation Code (2015-2017); Board Member, Digital NEST Inc. (2015-2016); Speaker, International Women's Day, Google (2014) **CW:** Author, "Portrait of the Dream" (2013) **AW:** Hispanics in Philanthropy Award (2015); Kennedy Laureate, John F. Kennedy University (2014); Listee, Women Techmakers, Google (2014); Listee, 50 Most Powerful Women, Forbes México (2013); Listee, Most Influential Women in the Bay Area, Division of American City Business Journals, The Business Journals (2013); Listee, 40 Under 40, Silicon Valley Latino (2013); Listee, Top 100, HITEC (2012); Person of the Year, Social Pioneer, GQ México (2012); Listee, TechWomen, State Department of the United States (2012) **AV:** Traveling; Reading; Cooking

GONZALEZ, ANTHONY E., T: U.S. Representative from Ohio; Former Professional Football Player **I:** Government Administration/Government Relations/Government Services **DOB:** 09/18/1984 **PB:** Cleveland **SC:** OH/USA **MS:** Married **SPN:** Elizabeth Gonzalez **CH:** One Son **ED:** MBA, Stanford Graduate School of Business; BA, The Ohio State University **C:** Member, U.S. House of Representatives from Ohio's 16th Congressional District (2019-Present); Wide Receiver, New England Patriots, NFL (2012); Wide Receiver, Indianapolis Colts, NFL (2007-2011) **PA:** Republican

GONZALEZ, ERIKA G., MD, T: Chief Executive Officer, Physician **I:** Medicine & Health Care **CN:** South Texas Allergy and Asthma Medical Professionals **PT:** Heriderto; Laura **MS:** Married **SPN:** Joel Reyes **CH:** Lucas; Evan **ED:** Doctor of Medicine, The University of Texas Medical Branch at Galveston (2002); Bachelor of Science in Biology, St. Mary's University, San Antonio, TX (1998) **CT:** Board Certified, American Board of Allergy and Immunology; Board Certified, American Board of Pediatrics **C:** Chief Executive Officer, President, Physician, South Texas Allergy and Asthma Medical Professionals (2014-Present); Chief of Allergy, Immunology & Rheumatology, Children's Hospital of San Antonio (2014-2017); Staff Allergist, United States Air Force (2002-2011); Fellowship, Allergy and Immunology, Wilford Hall Medical Center, San Antonio, TX; Internship, Residency in Pediatrics, Keesler Air Force Base, Biloxi, MS **CR:** Associate Professor, Baylor College of Medicine (2014-2017) **CIV:** With, Latino Victory; Chairperson, San Antonio Hispanic Chamber of Commerce **AW:** Air Force Meritorious Service Award (2006, 2011); Air Force Longevity Award with Clover Leafs (2004, 2010); Air Force Commanders Award (2008); Air Force Commendation Medal (2006); St. Mary's University Distinguished Alumni; San Antonio Women's Leadership Award **MEM:** American Academy of Allergy Asthma and Immunology; American College of Allergy Asthma and Immunology **AS:** Dr. Gonzalez attributes her success on the wonderful support system she enjoyed through her colleagues and family. **B/I:** Dr. Gonzalez became involved in her profession due to a lifelong interest in medicine. After undertaking her pediatric residency, she fell in love with the specialty. She likens it to investigative work, as much of the discipline involves determining what people are reacting to. **AV:** Traveling; Reading; Spending time with family

GONZALEZ, RICHARD A., T: Chief Executive Officer, Chairman **I:** Pharmaceuticals **CN:** AbbVie Inc. **DOB:** 01/21/1954 **ED:** BS in Biochemistry, University of Houston (1976); MS in Biochemistry, University of Miami **C:** Chief Executive Officer,

Chairman, AbbVie Inc. (2013-Present); Executive Vice President, Pharmaceutical Products Group, Abbott Labs (Now AbbVie Inc.) (2010-Present); President Abbot Ventures, Inc., Abbott Labs (Now AbbVie Inc.) (2009-2013); President, Chief Operating Officer, Abbott Labs (Now AbbVie Inc.) (2006-2007); President, Chief Operating Officer of Medical Products, Abbott Labs (Now AbbVie Inc.) (2001-2006); Senior Vice President for Hospital Products, Abbott Labs (Now AbbVie Inc.) (1998-2001); Vice President, Health Systems Division, Abbott Labs (Now AbbVie Inc.) (1995-1998); Divisional Vice President, General Manager, Abbott Labs (Now AbbVie Inc.) (1992-1995); Numerous Positions in Diagnostics Division, Abbott Labs (Now AbbVie Inc.) (1977-1992); Research Biochemist, Miller School of Medicine University of Miami **CR:** Board of Directors, Abbott Labs (Now AbbVie Inc.) (2001-2007) **CIV:** Board of Directors, Shedd Aquarium; Board of Directors, Lyric Opera of Chicago **AW:** One of 50 Most Important Hispanics in Technology and Business, Hispanic Engineer & Information Technology (2005)

GONZALEZ, SARAH, T: Chief Operating Officer **I:** Financial Services **CN:** First Guaranty Mortgage Corporation **DOB:** 11/16/1978 **PB:** Willingboro **SC:** NJ **PT:** Johnny O. Bushnell; Luann Bushnell **MS:** Married **SPN:** Saul Gonzalez **CH:** Alani; Sofia; Sebastian **ED:** Coursework, Purdue Global University (2020); Coursework in Business, Collin College (2004) **CT:** Direct Endorsement **C:** Chief Operation Officer, First Guaranty Mortgage Corporation (2018-Present); Senior Vice President, Strategic Business Operations, Stearns Lending (2017-2018); Senior Vice President, Correspondent Operations, Stearns Lending (2015-2017); Vice President, Change Management, Stearns Lending (2014-2015); Vice President, Correspondent Operations, Nationstar Montage (2013-2014); Vice President, Correspondent Operations, Citi (2011-2013); AVP Manufacturing Quality Assurance, Bank of America (2010-2011); DE Mortgage Underwriter, Bank of America (2009-2010); Production Specialist III: Manufactured Quality Assurance, Bank of America (2007-2009); AVP Production, Countrywide Financial (2004-2007) **CR:** Member, Board of Directors, ALICE Executive Women's Summit; Advisory Board Member, NEXT Mortgage Events **AW:** Top 100 in Real Estate (2020); Women of Influence, HousingWire (2019); Keystone Finalist, Culture, Five Star Institute (2019); 75 Elite Women, Mortgage Professionals of America (2017); 2017 Elite Women (2017); 2016 Insider Award (2016); Industry MVP, HousingWire (2016) **MEM:** Mortgage Bankers Association; National Association of Professional Women; Women for Women International **AS:** Ms. Gonzalez attributes her success to having two parents that were in the military. She was raised to set goals, obtain goals, have a routine and be accountable for her actions. She has also enjoyed the influence of many great people in her adult life, many of whom have given her a chance when others would not. **B/I:** Ms. Gonzalez became involved in her profession because her first mortgage job was answering calls at a mobile home lot. A fellow employee was on maternity leave and she was asked to fill in, after which she excelled in the position. **RE:** Christian

GONZALEZ, VICENTE JR., T: U.S. Representative from Texas, Lawyer **I:** Government Administration/Government Relations/Government Services **CN:** U.S. House of Representatives **DOB:** 09/04/1967 **PB:** Corpus Christi **SC:** TX/USA **MS:** Married **SPN:** Lorena (Saenz) Gonzalez **ED:** Doctor of Jurisprudence, Texas A&M University School of Law (1996); Bachelor of Science in Aviation Business Administration, Embry-Riddle Aeronautical University (1992); Associate's Degree in Banking and Finance, Del Mar College **C:** Member, U.S. House of Representatives from Texas' 15th Congressional District (2017-Present); Member, Committee on Financial Services (2017-Present); Founder, Lawyer, V. Gonzalez & Associates PC (1997-Present) **BAR:** Texas; New York

GONZÁLEZ, FRANCY, T: Director **I:** Media & Entertainment **CN:** Univision Network **DOB:** 06/10/1965 **SC:** Havana/Cuba **CIV:** Children's Defense Fund **CW:** Director, "¡Despierta América!" (1997-Present); Host, "Premio lo Nuestro a la música Latina" (2006-2011); Host, "Premios juventud" (2005, 2008-2010); Director, "Nuestra Belleza Latina" (2009); Host, "Latin Grammy Celebra José José" (2008); Director, "Lente loco" (1990) **AW:** Outstanding Morning Program in Spanish, "¡Despierta América!," Daytime Emmy Awards (2019) **AV:** Meditating; Practicing yoga and sports; Spending quality time with family

GONZÁLEZ COLÓN, JENNIFFER AYDIN, T: Resident Commissioner of Puerto Rico **I:** Government Administration/Government Relations/Government Services **DOB:** 08/05/1976 **PB:** San Juan **SC:** Puerto Rico **ED:** LLM, Inter American University of Puerto Rico School of Law, San Juan, Puerto Rico; JD, Inter American University of Puerto Rico School of Law, San Juan, Puerto Rico; BA, University of Puerto Rico, Rio Piedras, Puerto Rico **C:** Resident Commissioner of Puerto Rico (2017-Present); Chair, Puerto Rico Republican Party (2015-Present); Minority Leader, Puerto Rico House of Representatives (2013-2017); Member, At-large District, Puerto Rico House of Representatives (2005-2017); Speaker, Puerto Rico House of Representatives (2009-2013); Member, Fourth District, Puerto Rico House of Representatives (2002-2005); Chair, House Government Affairs Committee, Puerto Rico House of Representatives; Ranking Member, Budget Committee, Puerto Rico House of Representatives; Member, Committee on San Juan Development, Puerto Rico House of Representatives; Member, Committee on Women's Affairs, Puerto Rico House of Representatives; Member, Committee on Internal Affairs, Puerto Rico House of Representatives; Member, Joint Commission for the Revision of the Civil Code of Puerto Rico **CR:** Chair, San Juan New Progressive Party Youth Organization **PA:** New Progressive

GOOD, KENNETH R., PHD, T: Anthropology Educator **I:** Education/Educational Services **CN:** New Jersey City University **DOB:** 09/04/1942 **PB:** Philadelphia **SC:** PA/USA **PT:** Thomas William Good; Virginia (Candelori) Good **MS:** Married **SPN:** Yarima Good (6/17/1986) **CH:** David; Vanessa; Daniel **ED:** PhD, University of Florida (1989); MA, Pennsylvania State University (1973); BA, Pennsylvania State University (1968); BA, Pennsylvania State University (1965) **C:** Associate Professor, Anthropology, Jersey City State College (1990-Present); Adjunct Assistant Research Scientist, University of Florida, Gainesville, FL (1989-1990); Adjunct Assistant Research Scientist, University of Florida, Gainesville, FL (1982); Visiting Research Fellow, Max-Planck Institute, Munich, Germany (1978-1981); Research Assistant, Pennsylvania State University (1974-1977); Anthropology Instructor, Central University of Venezuela (1971-1972); Field Assistant, Archaeological Excavation, Tula, Hidalgo, Mexico, University of Missouri (1970); Research Assistant, Pennsylvania State University (1969-1970) **CR:** Presenter in Field **CW:** Co-Author, "Into the Heart" (1991); Television Appearance, National Geographic Explorer Series; Contributor, Articles, Professional Journals **AW:** Fulbright Fellowship, Bolivia **MEM:** Phi Kappa Phi **MH:** Albert Nelson Marquis Lifetime Achievement Award **B/I:** Dr. Good's interest in anthropology solidified when he learned about the Yanomami. He wrote a dissertation on the tribe, who practiced warfare and were considered to be extremely fierce. The dissertation examined the reasons for the hostility they displayed between villages; he concluded that the main ecological factor may have been related to their diet.

GOOD, LYNN JONES, T: Chairman, President, and Chief Executive Officer **I:** Oil & Energy **CN:** Duke Energy Corporation **DOB:** 04/18/1959 **ED:** BS in Systems Analysis & Accounting, Miami University, Oxford, OH (1981) **CT:** Certified Public Accountant (CPA) **C:** Chairman, President, Chief Executive Officer, Duke Energy Corporation (2016-Present); Vice Chair, President, Chief Executive Officer, Duke Energy Corporation, Charlotte, NC (2013-2016); President, Chief Executive Officer, Duke Energy Corporation, Charlotte, NC (2013); Group Executive, Chief Financial Officer, Duke Energy Corporation, Charlotte, NC (2009-2013); Group Executive, President, Commercial Business, Duke Energy Corporation, Charlotte, NC (2007-2009); Senior Vice President, Treasurer, Duke Energy Corporation, Charlotte, NC (2006-2007); Executive Vice President, Chief Financial Officer, Cinergy (2005-2006); Vice President, Finance, Controller, Cinergy (2005); Vice President, Controller, Cinergy (2003-2005); Vice President, Finance Project Strategy, Cinergy (2003); Partner, Deloitte & Touche LLC, Cincinnati, OH (2002-2003); Partner, Arthur Andersen (1992-2002); Numerous Positions, Arthur Andersen (1981-2002) **CR:** Board of Directors, Duke Energy Corporation (2013- Present); Board of Directors, Hubbell Inc. (2009-Present) **CIV:** Board Member, Bechtler Museum of Modern Art, Charlotte, NC **AW:** Named One of "The 50 Most Powerful Women in Business," Fortune Magazine (2013-2015)

GOODE, SHARON S., BS, MHA, RNC, T: Certified RN, Master of Science and Hospital Administration **I:** Health, Wellness and Fitness **CN:** Presence McAuley Manor (Ascension Senior Living) **DOB:** 01/29/1940 **PB:** Pana **SC:** IL/USA **PT:** Joseph Spinner; Mary (Broux) Spinner **MS:** Widowed **SPN:** Paul B. Goode **CH:** Steve Heitmeier; Michael Goode; Patrick Goode **ED:** Diploma, St. John's Hospital School of Nursing (St. John's College of Nursing), Springfield, IL (1962); Master in Hospital Administration, University of St. Francis, Joliet, IL; BS, University of St. Francis, Joliet, IL **CT:** Certified Gerontological Nurse; Illinois Rehabilitation Nursing Certification, St. Francis Hospital (OSF St. Francis Medical Center), OSF Healthcare System), Peoria, IL **C:** Director of Nursing, Presence McAuley Manor (Ascension Senior Living), Aurora, IL; In-service Coordinator, Presence McAuley Manor (Ascension Senior Living), Aurora, IL; Coordinator of Nursing, Bethesda Lutheran Home (Bethesda Lutheran Communities), Aurora, IL; Assistant Director of Nursing, Au Sable Valley Home, Fairview, MI **MEM:** Past President, Chapter Founder, Beta Sigma Phi **MH:** Albert Nelson Marquis Lifetime Achievement Award; Marquis Who's Who Top Professional **B/I:** Mrs. Goode entered her profession because her cousin, Geradine, was a nurse. When Mrs. Goode was 10 years old, she knew she was going to be a nurse because she admired her cousin so much. She never looked back; she kept moving forward from one achievement to another. **AV:** Spending time with cat; Spending time with family; Church **PA:** Democrat **RE:** Catholic

GOODEN, LANCE CARTER, T: U.S. Representative from Texas **I:** Government Administration/Government Relations/Government Services

DOB: 12/01/1982 **PB:** Terrell **SC:** TX/USA **PT:** Tom Ed Gooden **MS:** Married **SPN:** Alexa Calligas (2016) **CH:** Liam **ED:** BBA in Finance, The University of Texas at Austin; BA in Government, The University of Texas at Austin **C:** Member, U.S. House of Representatives from Texas' Fifth Congressional District (2019-Present); Member, District Four, Texas House of Representatives (2011-2015, 2017-Present); Legislative Aide to Betty Brown **CIV:** Member, Rockwall and Brin Church of Christ, Terrell, TX **PA:** Republican

GOODING, CUBA MARK JR., T: Actor **I:** Media & Entertainment **DOB:** 01/02/1968 **PB:** Bronx **SC:** NY/USA **PT:** Cuba Gooding Sr.; Shirley (Sullivan) Gooding **MS:** Married **SPN:** Sara Kapfer (03/13/1994) **CH:** Spencer; Mason; Piper **CW:** Actor, "Bayou Caviar" (2018); Actor, "Chicago" (2018); Actor, "American Crime Story: The People v. O.J. Simpson" (2016); Actor, "American Horror Story: Roanoke" (2016); Actor, "Empire" (2015); Actor, "Forever" (2015); Actor, "Big Time in Hollywood, FL" (2015); Actor, "The Book of Negroes" (2015); Actor, "Selma" (2014); Actor, Executive Producer, "Freedom" (2014); Actor, "Deception" (2013); Actor, "Something Whispered" (2013); Actor, "Summoned" (2013); Actor, "The Butler" (2013); Actor, "Guilty" (2013); Actor, "The Trip to Bountiful" (2013); Actor, "Machete Kills" (2013); Actor, "Red Tails" (2012); Actor, "One in the Chamber" (2012); Actor, "Firelight" (2012); Actor, "The Hit List" (2011); Actor, "Sacrifice" (2011); Actor, "The Devil's Tomb" (2009); Actor, "Lies & Illusions" (2009); Actor, "Hardwired" (2009); Actor, "Wrong Turn at Tahoe" (2009); Actor, "Gifted Hands: The Ben Carson Story" (2009); Actor, "Hero Wanted" (2008); Actor, "Linewatch" (2008); Actor, Producer, "Harold" (2008); Actor, "Norbit" (2007); Actor, "What Love Is" (2007); Actor, "Daddy Day Camp" (2007); Actor, "American Gangster" (2007); Actor, "End Game" (2006); Actor, "Lightfield's Home Videos" (2005); Actor, "Shadowboxer" (2005); Actor, "Dirty" (2005); Voice Actor, "Home on the Range" (2004); Actor, "Psychic" (2003); Actor, "The Fighting Temptations" (2003); Actor, "Radio" (2003); Actor, "Boat Trip" (2002); Actor, "Pearl Harbor" (2001); Actor, "Rat Race" (2001); Actor, "In the Shadows" (2001); Actor, "Men of Honor" (2000); Actor, "Instinct" (1999); Actor, "What Dreams May Come" (1998); Actor, "As Good As It Gets" (1997); Actor, Producer, "A Murder of Crows" (1999); Actor, "Jerry Maguire" (1996); Actor, "The Audition" (1996); Actor, "Losing Isaiah" (1995); Actor, "Outbreak" (1995); Actor, "The Tuskegee Airmen" (1995); Actor, "Lightning Jack" (1994); Actor, "Judgement Night" (1993); Actor, "Daybreak" (1993); Actor, "Gladiator" (1992); Actor, "A Few Good Men" (1992); Actor, "Hitz" (1992); Actor, "Murder with Motive: The Edmund Perry Story" (1992); Actor, "Boyz N the Hood" (1991); Actor, "Kill or Be Killed" (1990); Actor, "MacGyver" (1989-1991); Actor, "Sing" (1989); Actor, "Coming to America" (1988); Actor, "Hill Street Blues" (1986-1987) **AW:** Award for Outstanding Actor in a TV Movie, Mini-Series or Dramatic Special, NAACP Image Awards (2013); Award for Outstanding Actor in a Motion Picture, NAACP Image Awards (2003); Blockbuster Entertainment Award for Favorite Supporting Actor – Comedy/Romance (1996, 1998); Academy Award for Best Supporting Actor, Academy of Motion Picture Arts and Sciences (1996); SAG Award for Outstanding Performance by a Male Actor in a Supporting Role, SAG-AFTRA (1996); American Comedy Award for Funniest Supporting Actor in a Motion Picture (1996); Award for Best Supporting Actor, Broadcast Film Critics Association (1996); Award for Best Supporting Actor, Chicago Film Critics Association (1996); Satellite Award for Best Supporting Actor - Motion Picture (1996)

GOODLIN, NICK, T: President **I:** Advertising & Marketing **CN:** Design Thumbprint **ED:** Bachelor of Arts in Supply Chain Management, Michael F. Price College of Business, University of Oklahoma (2004) **C:** President, Design Thumbprint (2016-Present); International Account Executive (2010-2015); Trade Direct Account Executive (2006-2010); Senior Account Executive, UPS Supply Chain Solutions (2006); Director of Supply Chain Management, Primatech Medical Systems (2004-2006) **CIV:** Oklahoma City Chamber of Commerce; Edmond Chamber of Commerce; Volunteer, City Rescue Mission **AW:** Expertise Award, Best Digital Marketing Company in Oklahoma City (2017, 2018) **AS:** Mr. Goodlin attributes his success toward his company's focus on keeping client risk low and manageable. Trust is a cornerstone of his business model.

GOODMAN, JOHN STEPHEN, T: Actor **I:** Media & Entertainment **DOB:** 06/20/1952 **PB:** Affton **SC:** MO/USA **PT:** Leslie Francis Goodman; Virginia Roos (Loosmoore) Goodman **MS:** Married **SPN:** Annabeth Hartzog (10/27/1989) **CH:** Molly Evangeline **ED:** BFA in Theater, Southwest Missouri State University (Now Missouri State University) (1975); Coursework, St. Louis Community College, Meramec **CW:** Actor, "The Righteous Gemstones" (2019-Present); Actor, "The Conners" (2018-Present); Actor, "The Freak Brothers" (2020); Narrator, "Birds of a Different Game: The 80s Cardinals" (2020); Actor, "Captive State" (2019); Actor, "Roseanne" (1988-1996, 2018); Actor, "Bunyan and Babe" (2017); Actor, "Kong Skull Island" (2017); Actor, "Atomic Blonde" (2017); Actor, "Once Upon a Time in Venice" (2017); Actor, "Transformers the Last Knight" (2017); Actor, "Valerian and the City of a Thousand Planets" (2017); Actor, "10 Cloverfield Lane" (2016); Voice Actor, "Ratchet and Clank" (2016); Actor, "Going West" (2016); Actor, "The Coldest City" (2016); Actor, "Patriots Day" (2016); Actor, "Trumbo" (2015); Actor, "Love the Coopers" (2015); Actor, "Spring Break '83" (2014); Actor, "The Monuments Men" (2014); Voice Actor, "Transformers: Age of Extinction" (2014); Actor, "The Gambler" (2014); Actor, "Alpha House" (2013-2014); Actor, "Dancing on the Edge" (2013); Actor, "The Hangover Part III" (2013); Actor, "The Internship" (2013); Voice Actor, "Monsters University" (2013); Actor, "Inside Llewyn Davis" (2013); Actor, "Downwardly Mobile" (2012); Voice Actor, "SpongeBob SquarePants: It's a SpongeBob Christmas!" (2012); Actor, "Alpha House" (2012); Actor, "Flight" (2012); Voice Actor, "ParaNorman" (2012); Actor, "Argo" (2012); Actor, "Trouble with the Curve" (2012); Actor, "Community" (2011-2012); Voice Actor, "Happy Feet Two" (2011); Actor, "Red State" (2011); Actor, "The Artist" (2011); Actor, "Extremely Loud and Incredibly Close" (2011); Actor, "Damages" (2011); Actor, "Treme" (2010-2011); Actor, "You Don't Know Jack" (2010); Actor, "Drunkboat" (2010); Actor, "Confessions of a Shopaholic" (2009); Actor, "Alabama Moon" (2009); Actor, "Waiting for Godot" (2009); Actor, "Pope Joan" (2009); Voice Actor, "The Princess and the Frog" (2009); Actor, "Speed Racer" (2008); Actor, "Gigantic" (2008); Actor, "In the Electric Mist" (2008); Actor, "Drunkboat" (2007); Actor, "Death Sentence" (2007); Actor, "Evan Almighty" (2007); Voice Actor, "Bee Movie" (2007); Voice Actor, "King of the Hill" (2007); Voice Actor, "The Emperor's New School" (2007); Voice Actor, "The Year Without a Santa Claus" (2006); Actor, "The Odd Job Jack" (2006); Actor, "Studio 60 on the Sunset Strip" (2006); Voice Actor, "Cars" (2006); Actor, "Cat on a Hot Tin Roof" (2005); Actor, "Marilyn Hotchkiss Ballroom Dancing & Charm School" (2005); Actor, "Center of the Universe" (2004-2005); Voice Actor, "Father of the Pride" (2004-2005); Actor, "Home of Phobia" (2004); Voice Actor, "Clifford's Really Big Movie" (2004); Actor, "Beyond the Sea" (2004); Actor, "The West Wing" (2003-2004); Actor, "Masked and Anonymous" (2003); Voice Actor, "The Jungle Book 2" (2003); Actor, "Freedom: A History of Us" (2003); Actor, "Dirty Deeds" (2002); Actor, "Storytelling" (2001); Actor, "Happy Birthday" (2001); Voice Actor, "Monsters, Inc." (2001); Actor, "On the Edge" (2001); Actor, "Ed" (2001); Actor, "Coyote Ugly" (2000); Actor, "O Brother, Where Art Thou?" (2000); Actor, "What Planet Are You From?" (2000); Actor, "Hitting the Wall" (2000); Actor, "The Adventures of Rocky & Bullwinkle" (2000); Actor, "My First Mister" (2000); Actor, "One Night at McCool's" (2000); Voice Actor, "The Emperor's New Groove" (2000); Actor, "Normal, Ohio" (2000); Actor, "Pigs Next Door" (2000); Actor, "Now and Again" (1999-2000); Voice Actor, "The Simpsons" (1999); Voice Actor, "Futurama" (1999); Actor, "The Jack Bull" (1999); Actor, "The Runner" (1999); Actor, "Bringing Out the Dead" (1999); Voice Actor, "Rudolph the Red Nosed Reindeer: The Movie" (1998); Voice Actor, "The Real Macaw" (1998); Actor, "Dirty Work" (1998); Actor, "Blues Brothers 2000" (1998); Actor, "The Big Lebowski" (1998); Actor, "Soul Man" (1997-1998); Actor, "The Borrowers" (1997); Actor, "Combat" (1997); Actor, "Fallen" (1997); Actor, "Mother Night" (1996); Actor, "Pie in the Sky" (1996); Actor, Producer, "Kingfish: A Story of Huey P. Long" (1995); Actor, "A Streetcar Named Desire" (1995); Actor, "The Flinstones" (1994); Actor, "The Hudsucker Proxy" (1994); Voice Actor, "We're Back! A Dinosaur's Story" (1993); Actor, "Born Yesterday" (1993); Actor, "Matinee" (1993); Actor, "Grace Under Fire" (1993); Voice Actor, "Frosty Returns" (1992); Actor, "The Babe" (1992); Actor, "Barton Fink" (1991); Actor, "Grand" (1990); Actor, "King Ralph" (1990); Actor, "Arachnophobia" (1990); Actor, "Stella" (1990); Actor, "Always" (1989); Actor, "Sea of Love" (1989); Actor, "Punchline" (1988); Actor, "Everybody's All-American" (1988); Actor, "The Wrong Guys" (1988); Actor, "Murder Ordained" (1987); Actor, "The Equalizer" (1987); Actor, "Moonlighting" (1987); Actor, "Raising Arizona" (1987); Actor, "Burglar" (1987); Actor, "The Big Easy" (1987); Actor, "True Stories" (1986); Actor, "Big River" (1985); Actor, "Sweet Dreams" (1985); Actor, "Maria's Lovers" (1985); Actor, "C.H.U.D." (1984); Actor, "The Face of Rage" (1983); Actor, "Heart of Steel" (1983); Actor, "Chiefs" (1983); Actor, "Revenge of the Nerds" (1984); Actor, "Eddie Macon's Run" (1983); Actor, "The Survivors" (1983); Actor, "Loose Ends" (1979); Actor, "Jailbait Babysitter" (1977); Performer, Dinner and Children's Theater Productions, Off-Broadway and Broadway Plays **AW:** Disney Legend Award (2013); SAG Award, Outstanding Performance by a Cast in a Motion Picture, SAG-AFTRA (2013); Spotlight Award, National Board of Review (2012); Emmy Award, Outstanding Guest Actor in a Drama Series, Academy of Television Arts & Sciences (2007); Golden Globe Award, Best Performance by an Actor in a TV Series - Comedy/Musical, Hollywood Foreign Press Association (1993); American Comedy Awards, Funniest Male Performer in a TV Series (Leading Role) Network, Cable or Syndication (1989, 1990); Numerous Awards

GOODMAN, SHIRA D., T: Chief Executive Officer (Retired) **I:** Other **CN:** Staples, Inc. **PB:** Chicago **SC:** IL/USA **ED:** JD, Harvard Law School; BA, Princeton University, New Jersey; MS in Strategy and Marketing, MIT Sloan School of Management **C:** Executive Vice President, Human Resources, Staples, Inc., Framingham, MA (2009-Present); Chief Executive Officer, Staples Inc. (2016-2018); Executive Vice President of Marketing, Staples, Inc., Framingham, MA (2001-2009); Senior Vice President, Staples

Direct, Staples, Inc., Framingham, MA (1992); Numerous Management Positions, Bain & Co., Inc. (1986-1992); Senior Vice President of Business Delivery, Staples, Inc., Framingham, MA **CR:** Board of Directors, CarMax Business Services, LLC (2007-Present); Board of Directors, Stride Rite Corporation (2002-2007) **RE:** Jewish

GOODNIGHT, JAMES HOWARD, T: Co-founder, Chief Executive Officer; Information Technology Executive **I:** Business Management/Business Services **CN:** SAS Institute Inc. **DOB:** 01/06/1943 **PB:** Salisbury **SC:** NC/USA **PT:** Albert Goodnight; Dorothy Patterson **MS:** Married **SPN:** Ann Goodnight **CH:** Three Children **ED:** PhD in Statistics, North Carolina State University; MA in Statistics, North Carolina State University (1968); Bachelor in Applied Mathematics, North Carolina State University (1972-1976) **C:** President, Chief Executive Officer, Co-founder, Chairman, SAS Institute Inc., Cary, NC (1976-Present); Faculty, North Carolina State University (1972-1976) **CR:** Adjunct Professor, North Carolina State University (1976-Present); Co-owner, Prestonwood Country Club and The Umstead Hotel and Spa **CIV:** Co-founder, Cary Academy, Cary, NC (1996); Active Participant, Business Roundtable and Business Council; Started, SAS in School; Speaker, Participant, World Economic Forum **AW:** Named One of the World's Richest People, Forbes Magazine (2001-Present); Named One of the Forbes 400: Richest Americans, Forbes Magazine (1999-Present); "CEO Great Place to Work for All Leadership" Award, Great Place to Work (2020); Named One of the Richest in Tech, Forbes Magazine (2017); Named One of America's 25 Most Fascinating Entrepreneurs, Inc. Magazine (2004); Named One of the 20th Century's Great American Business Leaders, Harvard Business School (2004) **MEM:** Fellow, American Statistical Association; Tau Kappa Epsilon, Beta Beta Chapter

GOODYEAR, NANCY L., EDD, T: Biology Educator **I:** Education/Educational Services **DOB:** 10/13/1945 **PB:** Silver City **SC:** NM/USA **PT:** Howard R. Goodyear; Audrey Willela (Lee) Goodyear **ED:** EdD in Science Education, Auburn University, Auburn, AL (1976); MS in Bacteriology, University of Wisconsin-Madison, Madison, WI (1967); BA in Biology, MacMurray College, Jacksonville, IL (1967) **C:** Adjunct Professor, Medical Microbiology, North Georgia College & State University (University of North Georgia), Dahlonega, GA (2011); Biology Adjunct, Assistant Professor, Biology, San Joaquin Delta College, Stockton, CA (2003-2011); Adjunct Professor, Biology, Solano Community College, Fairfield, CA (2006-2008); Adjunct Professor, Biology, Napa Valley College, Napa, CA (2003-2004); Adjunct Professor, Biology, Cosumnes River College, Sacramento, CA (2003); Adjunct Professor, Biology, Tallahassee Community College, Tallahassee, FL (1992-2002); Professor, Biology, Bainbridge State College, Bainbridge, GA (1976-2001); Secondary Science Teacher, Pine Bluff School District, AR (1971-1976); Secondary Teacher, Foreign Mission Board, Southern Baptist Convention, Richmond, VA (1969-1971); Secondary Science Education Teaching Assistant, Auburn University, Auburn, AL; Microbiology Research Assistant, Food Research Institute, University of Wisconsin–Madison, Madison, WI; Biology Research Assistant, MacMurray College, Jacksonville, IL **CR:** Director, Junior Master Gardener Program, Lumpkin County Elementary School, Dahlonega, GA (2017-2018); Faculty Member of e-Core Curriculum, Writer of Environmental Science Course, University System of Georgia (2000) **CIV:** Volunteer, St. Marks Wildlife Refuge Association **CW:** Contributor, "Reaction Time to a Fixed and Pseudo-Random Auditory Stimulus," Laboratory Manual for Physiology, Volume 1 (2005); Contributor, "The Use of a Regional Science Fair to Generate an Organic Collaboration," Journal of College Science Teaching (1990); Author, "My Lizard Friend" (1989); Contributor, Numerous Articles to Professional Journals; Author, Poetry **AW:** Named, Distinguished Professor of the Year, Bainbridge State College Association of Educators (2000); Appreciation for Hosting the First Regional Association for Biology Laboratory Education Workshop (1996); Certificate of Appreciation for Helping with The Decatur Co. Science Fair, GA (1996); Recipient, Mini-Grant to Enhance Computer Technology Skills, Bainbridge State College (1996); Recipient, Faculty Enrichment Grant, Bainbridge State College (1992, 1994, 1996); Meritorious Faculty Award, Bainbridge State College (1992); Faculty Enrichment Grant, Bainbridge State College (1984, 1986, 1988, 1991); Grantee, Georgia Endowment for the Humanities (1984); Named, Outstanding Young Women of America (1978); Original Poetry Award, Bahamian Art and Drama Festival (1971) **MEM:** Dahlonega Woman's Club (2011-2017);Membership Chairman, Delta Kappa Gamma (DKGSI) (1997-2002); Chairman, Nominations Committee and Lab Initiative Grants, Association for Biology Laboratory Education (2000-2001); Member-at-large, Association for Biology Laboratory Education (1998-2001); Association for Biology Laboratory Education (1983-2001); Chairman, Regional Meetings, Association for Biology Laboratory Education (1999-2000); Treasurer, Delta Kappa Gamma (DKGSI) (1983-1996); Program Chairman, Delta Kappa Gamma (DKGSI) (1984-1986) **MH:** Albert Nelson Marquis Lifetime Achievement Award; Marquis Who's Who Top Professional; Marquis Who's Who Humanitarian Award **B/I:** Dr. Goodyear became involved in her profession because of her inspirational high school biology teacher, Ms. Formby. Dr. Goodyear became a biology teacher because of her mentor. Her older brother encouraged her when they were outside playing to pick up snakes and other reptiles. Thus she learned not to fear but to respect and enjoy local animals. Dr. Goodyear grew up loving the outdoors and nature. **AV:** Reading; Gardening; Traveling; Large cross-stitching; Watching birds

GOOLD, RUPERT, CBE, T: Theatre Director **I:** Media & Entertainment **DOB:** 02/18/1972 **PB:** Highgate **SC:** England **MS:** Married **SPN:** Kate Fleetwood (2001) **CH:** Raphael; Constance **ED:** Degree in English Literature, Trinity College, Cambridge University (1994); Coursework in Performance Studies, New York University, Fulbright Scholar **C:** Associate Director, Royal Shakespeare Company (2010-Present); Artistic Director, Headlong Theatre Co., London, England (2005-2013); Artistic Director, Derngate Theatre, Northampton, England (2002-2005); Artistic Director, Royal Theatre, Northampton, England (2002-2005); Associate Artist, Salisbury Playhouse (1996-1997); Trainee Director, Donmar Warehouse (1995-1996) **CW:** Director, "Judy" (2019); Director, "Shipwreck" (2019); Director, "Ink" (2017, 2019); Director, "Albion" (2017); Director, "King Charles III" (2014, 2017); Director, "Richard III" (2016); Director, "True Story" (2015); Director, "Medea" (2015); Director, "Made in Dagenham" (2014); Director, "The Merchant of Venice" (2011, 2014); Director, "American Psycho: A New Musical Thriller" (2013); Director, "The Effect" (2012); Director, "Richard II" (2012); Director, "Decade" (2011); Director, "Earthquakes in London" (2010); Director, "Macbeth" (2007, 2010); Director, "Romeo and Juliet" (1998, 2010); Director, "ENRON" (2009); Director, "Oliver!" (2009); Director, "King Lear" (2008); Director, "No Man's Land" (2008); Director, Writer, "Six Characters in Search of an Author" (2008); Director, "The Last Days of Judas Iscariot" (2008); Director, "Rough Crossings" (2007); Director, "The Glass Menagerie" (2007); Director, "Faustus" (2006); Director, "Restoration" (2006); Director, "The Tempest" (2006); Director, "Speaking Like Magpies" (2005); Director, "Hamlet" (2005); Writer, "Faustus" (2004); Director, "Insignificance" (2004); Director, "Summer Lightning" (1998, 2004); Director, "Othello" (2003); Director, "Sunday Father" (2003); Director, "Waiting for Godot: The Weir" (2003); Director, "Betrayal" (2002); Director, "Arcadia" (2002); Director, "The Wind in the Willows" (2001); Director, "Scaramouche Jones" (2001); Director, "Privates on Parade" (2001); Director, "Gone to LA" (2000); Director, "Broken Glass" (1999); Director, "The Colonel Bird" (1999); Director, "Habeas Corpus" (1999); Director, "Dancing at Lughnasa" (1998); Director, Writer, "The End of the Affair" (1997); Director, "Travels with My Aunt" (1997) **AW:** Commander of the Order of the British Empire (2017)

GOPEZ, EVELYN V., MD, T: Professor of Pathology **I:** Education/Educational Services **CN:** The University of Utah **SC:** Philippines **MS:** Married **CH:** Three Children **ED:** Graduate, Executive Leadership in Academic Medicine (ELAM) Program, University of Utah School of Medicine, Salt Lake City, Utah (2013); Fellow in Surgical Pathology, University of Pennsylvania, Philadelphia, PA (1995-1996); Fellow in Cytopathology, University of Pennsylvania, Philadelphia, PA (1994-1995); Chief Resident, Berkshire Medical Center, Berkshire Health Systems, Pittsfield, MA (1993-1994); Resident in Anatomic and Clinical Pathology, Berkshire Medical Center, Berkshire Health Systems, Pittsfield, MA (1990-1994); Intern in Psychiatry, Harvard Medical School, Boston, MA (1989-1990); Resident in Anatomic Pathology, University of Santo Tomas, Espana, Manila, Philippines (1980-1982); MD, University of Santo Tomas, Manila, Philippines (1979); BS, University of Santo Tomas, Espana, Manila, Philippines (1975) **CT:** Licensed Physician, Utah (1999-Present); Board Certification, Cytopathology, The American Board of Pathology (1997-Present); Board Certification, Anatomic and Clinical, The American Board of Pathology (1996-Present); Licensed Physician, Education Commission for Foreign Medical Graduates (1981-Present) **C:** Professor, Department of Pathology, University of Utah School of Medicine, Salt Lake City, Utah (2010-Present); Associate Dean, Office of Inclusion and Outreach, University of Utah School of Medicine, Salt Lake City, Utah (2012-2019); Professor of Pathology, University of Utah, Salt Lake City, Utah (2003-2019); Associate Vice President, Inclusion, Health Sciences, University of Utah, Salt Lake City, Utah (2012-2014); Assistant Dean, University of Utah School of Medicine, Salt Lake City, Utah (2010-2012); Associate Professor, Department of Pathology, University of Utah School of Medicine, Salt Lake City, Utah (2003-2010); Associate Professor, University of Utah, Salt Lake City, Utah (2002-2007); Assistant Professor, Department of Pathology, University of Utah School of Medicine, Salt Lake City, Utah (1997-2003); Assistant Professor, University of Utah, Salt Lake City, Utah (1997-2002); Director of Cytology, Veteran's Administration Medical Center, Salt Lake City, Utah (1998-2001) **CR:** Laboratory Director, Midvale Family Health Clinic, Midvale, Utah (2013-Present); Founder, Faculty Adviser, Health Sciences Multicultural Student Association (2013-Present); Founder, Faculty Adviser, Resident Interdisciplinary Council (2013-Present); Faculty Adviser, Asian Pacific Association of Medical Students, University of Utah School of Medicine, Salt Lake City, UT (2009-Present); Program Director, Pathology Residency Training, University of Utah School of Medicine, Salt Lake City, Utah (2005-2012); Director, Cytology Laboratory, University of Utah School of Medicine, Salt Lake City, Utah (2009-2011); Medical Director, School of Cytotechnology, University of Utah, Salt Lake City, Utah (2004-2010); Assistant Medical Director, Cytology Laboratory (2004-2010); Course Director, Mini-fellowship Program in Anatomic and Clinical Pathology (1998-2004) **CW:** Author, Contributor, Numerous Peer-reviewed Journal Articles (1992-2017); Contributor, Numerous Non Peer-reviewed Journal Articles (2010-2011) **AW:** Award, American Health Council (2019); NIH Scholar, National Institutes of Health (2015); Health Care Heroes Award (2015); Advisor Service Award, Latino Medical Student Association (LMSA) (2013-2014); Certificate of Appreciation, Latino Medical Student Association (LMSA) (2011-2012); Certificate of Excellence, Latino Medical Students Association (LMSA) (2010-2011) **MEM:** Association of American Medical Colleges (AAMC); American Society of Clinical Pathology; College of American Pathologists **AS:** Dr. Gopez attributes her success to her persistence and the interest that she has in her work. She is also very eager to share her knowledge with others. Dr. Gopez says, "If you like what you're doing, you'll be great at it, and everything else will fall into place." **B/I:** Dr. Gopez became involved in her profession due to "the amount of time you get for your work as a pathologist." Additionally, pathology was something of interest to her. When she applied for an associate dean position, she had to let go of 50% of her practice. She sat down with her staff and asked "How could we get children more involved in wanting to go to medical school?" The idea arose that they should receive a hands-on experience. **AV:** Reading; Drinking tea **THT:** Dr. Gopez is passionate about health disparity and educating our future physicians about health and how its management could differ from one culture to another.

GORDER, JOE, T: Chief Executive Officer, President **I:** Oil & Energy **CN:** Valero Energy Corporation **ED:** MBA, Our Lady of the Lake University (1992); BBA, University of Missouri, St. Louis (1979) **C:** President, Chief Executive Officer, Valero Energy Corp. (2014-Present); President, Chief Operating Officer, Valero Energy Corp., (2012-2014); Executive Vice President, Marketing & Supply, Chief Commercial Officer, Valero Energy Corp., (2011-2012); Executive Vice President, Marketing & Supply, Valero Energy Corp., (2005-2011); Senior Vice President, Corporate Development, Valero Energy Corp., San Antonio, TX (2003-2005); Vice President, Business Development, Ultramar Diamond Shamrock; Director of Sales, Diamond Shamrock; Assistant Treasurer, Diamond Shamrock; Director Information Systems, Diamond Shamrock

GORDON, JEFF MICHAEL, T: Professional Stock Car Racer (Retired), Sportscaster, Sports Team Executive **I:** Athletics **CN:** Fox Sports **DOB:** 08/04/1971 **PB:** Vallejo **SC:** CA/USA **PT:** William Grinnell Gordon; Carol Ann (Houston) Bickford **MS:** Married **SPN:** Ingrid Vandebosch (11/07/2006); Brooke Sealy (11/26/1994, Divorced 06/2003) **CH:** Ella Sofia; Leo Benjamin **C:** Announcer, Fox NASCAR (2015-Present); Global Business Adviser, Axalta (2015-Present); Retired Professional Stock Car Driver (2015); Professional Stock Car Driver, NASCAR, Hendrick Motorsports (1993-2015) **CIV:** Founder, Jeff Gordon Children's Foundation (1999-Present) **AW:** Bristol Motor Speedway Legends Plaza (2016); The Order of the Long Leaf Pine Society (2016); Denise McCluggage Award (2016); Nation Motorsports Press Association Spirit Award (2015); Bill France Award of Excellence (2015); Chevrolet Lifetime Achievement Award (2015); First Place, Ford EcoBoost 400, Homestead-Miami Speedway (2012); Heisman Humanitarian Award (2012); First Place, Pennsylvania 400, Pocono Raceway (2012); First Place, Subway Fresh Fit 500, Phoenix International Raceway (2007, 2011); First Place, Pocono 500 (2007, 2011); First Place, Labor Day Classic 500, Atlanta Motor Speedway (2011); First Place, Samsung 500, Texas Motor Speedway (2009); One of the 100 Most Powerful Celebrities, Forbes.com (2008); First Place, Aaron's 499 (2004, 2005, 2007); First Place, Dodge Avenger 500, Darlington Raceway (2007); First Place, UAW-Ford 500, Talladega Superspeedway (2007); First Place, Bank of America 500, Lowe's Motor Speedway (2007); One of the Most Influential People in the World of Sports, Business Week (Now Bloomberg Businessweek) (2007); First Place, Dodge/Save Mart 350, Infineon Raceway (2004, 2006); First Place, USG Sheetrock 400, Chicagoland Speedway (2006); First Place, Subway 500 (2003, 2005); First Place, Daytona 500, Daytona International Speedway (1997, 1999, 2005); First Place, Advanced Auto Parts 500, Martinsville Speedway (2005); First Place, Brickyard 400, Indianapolis Motor Speedway (1994, 1998, 2001, 2004); First Place, Pepsi 400 (1995, 1998, 2004); First Place, Auto Club 500, California Speedway (2004); First Place, Bass Pro Shops MBNA 500 (2003); First Place, Virginia 500 (2003); First Place, Protection One 400, Kansas Speedway (2001, 2002); First Place, Mountain Dew Southern 500 (1995-1997, 2002); First Place, Sharpie 500, Bristol Motor Speedway (2002); Driver of the Year, NASCAR (1995, 1997, 1998, 2001); Winston Cup Series Champion (1995, 1997, 1998, 2001); First Place, UAW-Daimler Chrysler 400, Las Vegas Motor Speedway (2001); First Place, Kmart 400, Michigan International Speedway (2001); First Place, Global Crossing, Glen Watkins Glen International Raceway (2001); First Place, MBNA Platinum 400, Dover International Speedway (2001); First Place, DieHard 500 (1996, 2000); First Place, Chevrolet Monte Carlo 400, Richmond International Raceway (2000); First Place, Save Mart/Kragen 350 (1998-2000); First Place, California 500 (1997, 1999); First Place, Frontier at the Glen (1999); First Place, NAPA AutoCare 500 (1999); First Place, Cracker Barrel 500 (1999); First Place, UAW-GM Quality 500 (1999); First Place, Coca-Cola 600 (1994, 1997, 1998); First Place, Bud at the Glen (1997, 1998); First Place, CMT 300, New Hampshire International Speedway (1997, 1998); First Place, Pepsi 400 (1998); First Place, Pennsylvania 500 (1998); First Place, Pepsi Southern 500 (1998); First Place, NAPA 500 (1998); First Place, Air Corps Delco 400, North Carolina Speedway (1998); First Place, GM Goodwrench Service Plus 400 (1998); First Place, Goodwrench Service 400 (1997); First Place, Goody's Headache Powder 500 (1997); First Place, Pocono 500 (1997); First Place, MBNA 500 (1995, 1996); First Place, Tyson Holly Farms 400, North Wilkesboro Speedway (1996); First Place, Hanes 500 (1996); First Place, UAW-GM Teamwork 500 (1996); First Place, Pontiac Excitement 400 (1996); First Place, TranSouth Financial 400 (1996); First Place, Miller 500 (1996); First Place, Food City 500 (1995-1998); First Place, Slick 50 300 (1995); First Place, Goodwrench 500 (1995); First Place, Purolator 500 (1995); McDonald's All-Star Team (1994, 1995); Rookie of the Year (1993); Numerous Awards

GORDON, MARK, T: Governor of Wyoming **I:** Government Administration/Government Relations/Government Services **DOB:** 03/14/1957 **PB:** New York **SC:** NY/USA **MS:** Married **SPN:** Jennie Muir Young (2000); Sarah Hildreth Gilmore (03/07/1981, Deceased 1993) **CH:** Anne; Aaron; Bea; Spencer **ED:** Bachelor of Arts, Middlebury College (1979) **C:** Governor, State of Wyoming (2019-Present); Treasurer, State of Wyoming (2012-2019) **CR:** Owner, Merlin Ranch, East Buffalo and Johnson County, WY **AW:** Excellence in Rangeland Stewardship Award, Society for Range Management, Wyoming Section (2009) **PA:** Republican

GORDON, ROY G., PHD, T: Chemistry Professor **I:** Education/Educational Services **CN:** Harvard University **DOB:** 01/11/1940 **PB:** Akron **SC:** OH/USA **PT:** Nathan Gold Gordon; Frances (Teitel) Gordon **MS:** Married **SPN:** Myra Sheila Miller (12/24/1961) **CH:** Emily Francine; Steven Eric **ED:** Doctor of Philosophy in Chemical Physics, Harvard University (1964); Master of Arts in Physics, Harvard University (1962); Bachelor of Arts, Harvard University, Summa Cum Laude (1961) **C:** Professor of Chemistry and Chemical Biology, Harvard University (1969-Present); Assistant Professor of Chemistry and Chemical Biology, Harvard University (1964-1966) **CIV:** Exhibitor on Energy Conserving Windows, Boston Museum of Science and the Corning Museum **AW:** Eni Award, The Boston Museum of Science (2019); Esselen Award, American Chemical Society (1996); Research and Development Award (1991); Baekeland Award, American Chemical Society (1979); American Chemical Society Award in Pure Chemistry (1972); Achievement Award for Atomic Layer Deposition, American Vacuum Society; Research Partnership Award for Energy Efficiency and Renewable Energy, U.S. Department of Energy; Israel Einstein Fellowship; Sloan Foundation Fellowship; Faraday Society Bourke Award; R & D 100 Award **MEM:** Fellow, American Physical Society; American Chemical Society; Faraday Society; Union of Concerned Scientists; National Academy of Sciences; American Academy Arts and Sciences; Phi Beta Kappa; Sigma Xi; National Academy of Sciences; American Academy of Arts and Sciences; European Academy of Arts Sciences and Humanities **MH:** Albert Nelson Marquis Lifetime Achievement Award **B/I:** Dr. Gordan has been interested in chemistry since he was a young boy, having built his own laboratory in his basement. He was able to enter the field because he had friends who were chemists or pharmacists. **AV:** Playing the violin; Swimming; Hiking

GORDON, SHARON ANN, T: Mathematics Educator (Retired) **I:** Education/Educational Services **CN:** Sparta High School **DOB:** 08/08/1945 **PB:** Newton **SC:** NJ/USA **PT:** Kenneth William Gordon; Hazel Emma (Pascoe) Gordon **ED:** MEd, Montclair State University (1970); BA in Mathematics, Chemistry, History, Drew University (1967); Coursework, Centenary College (Now Centenary University) (1963-1964) **CT:** Certified Secondary School Mathematics Teacher, Grades 7-12, The State Board of Examiners, State of New Jersey (1969) **C:** Retired (2011); Preschool Teacher Aide, Circle of Friends Preschool, Sparta Township, NJ (2000-2011); Mathematics Teacher, Sparta High School (1968-2000) **CIV:** Choir Member, Sparta United Methodist Church (1956-Present) **AW:** Creative Writing Award, Centenary University (1963) **MEM:** National Education Association; Sussex County Retired Educators Association; New Jersey Education Association; Jack Russell Terrier Club of America; Phi Theta Kappa Honor Society **MH:** Albert Nelson Marquis Lifetime Achievement Award; Marquis Who's Who Top Professional **AV:** Writing poetry; Baking; Cooking; Counted cross stitch; Reading **RE:** Methodist

GORDON-LEVITT, JOSEPH LEONARD, T: Actor **I:** Media & Entertainment **DOB:** 02/17/1981 **PB:** Los Angeles **SC:** CA/USA **PT:** Dennis Levitt; Jane Gordon **MS:** Married **SPN:** Tasha McCauley (12/20/2014) **CH:** Two Sons **ED:** Coursework, Columbia University; Diploma, Van Nuys High School (1999) **C:** Co-founder, hitRECord (2005-Present) **CW:** Actor, "Knives Out" (2019); Host, "Sesame Street's 50th Anniversary Celebration" (2019); Actor, "7500" (2019); Actor, "Endgame" (2018); Voice Actor, "Star Wars: The Last Jedi" (2017); Actor, "Snowden" (2016); Actor, "The Walk" (2015); Actor, "The Night Before" (2015); Actor, "Sin City: A Dame to Kill For" (2014); Voice Actor, "The Wind Rises" (2013); Actor, Director, Writer, "Don Jon" (2013); Actor, Executive Producer, "Looper" (2012); Actor, "The Dark Knight Rises" (2012); Actor, "Premium Rush" (2012); Actor, "Lincoln" (2012); Actor, "50/50" (2011); Actor, "Inception" (2010); Actor, "Hesher" (2010); Director, Producer, Writer, Composer, "Sparks" (2009); Actor, "Big Breaks" (2009); Actor, "Women in Trouble" (2009); Actor, "500 Days of Summer" (2009); Actor, "G.I. Joe: The Rise of Cobra" (2009); Actor, "Stop-Loss" (2008); Actor, "Miracle at St. Anna" (2008); Actor, "Uncertainty" (2008); Actor, "Killshot" (2008); Actor, "The Lookout" (2007); Actor, "Brick" (2005); Actor, "Havoc" (2005); Actor, "Shadowboxer" (2005); Actor, "Mysterious Skin" (2004); Actor, "Latter Days" (2003); Voice Actor, "Treasure Planet" (2002); Actor, "Manic" (2001); Actor, "Picking Up the Pieces" (2000); Actor, "Forever Lulu" (2000); Actor, "10 Things I Hate About You" (1999); Actor, "Sweet Jane" (1998); Actor, "3rd Rock from the Sun" (1996-2001); Actor, "The Juror" (1996); Actor, "The Great Elephant Escape" (1995); Actor, "Holy Matrimony" (1994); Actor, "The Road Killers" (1994); Actor, "Angels in the Outfield" (1994); Actor, "Roseanne" (1993-1995); Actor, "Partners" (1993); Actor, "Gregory K" (1993); Actor, "The Powers That Be" (1992-1993); Actor, "A River Runs Through It" (1992); Actor, "Dark Shadows" (1991); Actor, "Changes" (1991); Actor, "Hi Honey - I'm Dead" (1991); Actor, "Plymouth" (1991); Actor, "Stranger on My Land" (1988); Actor, "Settle the Score" (1988); Actor, Television Shows, Films; Musician **AW:** Emmy Award for Outstanding Creative Achievement in Interactive Media – Social TV Experience, Academy of Television Arts & Sciences (2014); Award for Best Young Actor Under 10 in a Motion Picture, Young Artist Awards (1992)

GORDY, BERRY III, T: Recording Industry Executive; Film Producer; Entrepreneur **I:** Media & Entertainment **DOB:** 11/28/1929 **PB:** Detroit **SC:** MI/USA **MS:** Divorced **SPN:** Grace Eaton (07/17/1990, Divorced 1993); Raynoma Mayberry Liles (1960, Divorced 1964); Thelma Coleman (1953, Divorced 1959) **CH:** Berry IV; Hazel Joy; Terry James; Kerry A.; Sherry R.; Kennedy William; Stefan Kendal; Rhonda Suzanne Ross-Kendrick **ED:** Honorary PhD in Music, Eastern Michigan University (1971) **C:** Chairman, Board of Directors, West Grand Media (1998-Present); Founder, Jobete Music Co., Inc. (1997-Present); Founder, Motown Record Corporation (1961-Present); Executive Producer, Motion Pictures **CW:** Writer, "Motown: The Musical" (2013-2015); Writer, "Lennon" (2005); Author, "To Be Loved: The Music, the Magic, the Memories of Motown" (1994); Executive Producer, "Berry Gordy's the Last Dragon" (1984); Executive Producer, "Bingo Long Traveling All-Stars and Motor Kings" (1975); Director, "Mahogany" (1975); Executive Producer, "Lady Sings the Blues" (1972); Writer, "Money - That's What I Want"; Producer, Writer, Composer and Lyricist **AW:** National Medal of Arts (2016); Pioneer Award, Songwriters Hall of Fame (2013); Named to Michigan Rock and Roll Legends Hall of Fame (2009); Candle Award for Lifetime Achievement in Arts and Entertainment, Morehouse College (2005); Wall St. Project Millennium Award, RainbowPUSH Coalition (2000); A.G. Gaston Lifetime Achievement Award, Black Enterprise/Bank of America Corporation (2001); Legend Award, RainbowPUSH Coalition (2001); Legend Award, Black Entertainment and Sports Lawyers Association (1998); Lifetime Achievement Award, NABOB (1998); American Legend Award, American Society of Composers Pop Music Awards (1998); Junior Achievement Award, National Business Hall of Fame (1998); Recipient, Star, Hollywood Walk of Fame (1996); Generation Award, Congressional Black Caucus Foundation (1993); Lifetime Achievement Award, Black Business Association (1993); Abe Olman Publisher Award, Songwriters Hall of Fame (1993); 20th Century Award, Black Radio Exclusive (1993); Trustees Award, National Academy of Recording Arts and Sciences (1991); Named to Rock and Roll Hall of Fame (1988); Gordon Grand Fellow, Yale University (1985); Named to Minority Hall of Fame, Clark Atlanta University School of Business Administration (1981); Whitney M. Young Junior Award, Los Angeles Urban League (1980); Named One of the Leading Entrepreneurs of the Nation, Babson College (1978); Second Annual American Music Award for Outstanding Contribution to Music Industry (1975); Golden Mike, NATRA (1969); Martin Luther King Jr. Leadership Award (1969); Business Achievement Award, Interracial Council for Business Opportunity (1967) **MEM:** NAACP; ASCAP; BMI; DGA

GORE, ALBERT, "AL" ARNOLD JR., T: 45th Vice President of the U.S.; Environmental Activist **I:** Environmental Services **DOB:** 03/31/1948 **PB:** Washington **SC:** DC/USA **PT:** Albert Gore Sr.; Pauline (LaFon) Gore **MS:** Married **SPN:** Mary Elizabeth "Tipper" Aitcheson (05/19/1970, Separated 06/01/2010) **CH:** Karenna; Kristin; Sarah; Albert III **ED:** Honorary Doctorate, University of Melbourne (2017); Honorary Doctorate, Hamilton College (2011); Honorary Doctorate, Tilburg University (2010); Honorary LLD in Ecology and Evolutionary Biology, University of Tennessee Knoxville, TN (2010); Honorary LHD in Ecology and Evolutionary Biology, University of Tennessee Knoxville, TN (2010); Honorary Doctorate, Concordia University (2007); Honorary Doctorate, Aalborg University (2007); Coursework, Vanderbilt University Law School (1974); AB, Harvard University, Cum Laude (1969); Coursework, Vanderbilt University Divinity School, Nashville, TN; **C:** Partner, Head Climate Change Solutions Group, Kleiner Perkins Caufield & Byers (Now Kleiner Perkins), Menlo Park, CA (2007-Present); Co-founder, Chairman, Generation Investment Management LLP, London, England (2004-Present); Co-founder, Chairman, Current TV, San Francisco, CA (2005-2013); Democratic Candidate, Presidential Election (2000); Vice President of the United States, Washington, DC (1993-2001); U.S. Senator, State of Tennessee (1985-1993); Member, U.S. House of Representatives from Tennessee's Sixth Congressional District, United States Congress, Washington, DC (1983-1985); Member, U.S. House of Representatives from Tennessee's Fourth Congressional District, United States Congress, Washington, DC (1977-1983); Homebuilder and Land Developer, Tanglewood Home Builders Co. (1971-1976); Investigative Reporter, Editorial Writer, The Tennessean (1971-1976) **CR:** Chairman, Alliance for Climate Protection, Climate Reality Project (2006-Present); Board of Directors, World Resources Institute (2005-Present); Board of Directors, Apple Inc. (Formerly Apple Computer Inc.) (2003-Present); Visiting Professor, University of California Los Angeles (2001-Present); Senior Advisor, Google, Inc. (2001-Present); Visiting Professor, Middle Tennessee State University (2001); Visiting Professor, Fisk University (2001); Visiting Professor, Columbia Journalism School (2001) **MIL:** With, United States Army (1969-1971) **CW:** Author, "The Future: Six Drivers of Global Change" (2013); Author, "Our Choice: A Plan to Solve the Climate Crisis" (2009); Author, Children's Book, "An Inconvenient Truth: The Crisis of Global Warming" (2007); Author, "The Assault on Reason: How the Politics of Fear, Secrecy, and Blind Faith Subvert Wise Decision Making, Degrade Our Democracy, and Put Our Country and Our World in Peril" (2007); Author, "An Inconvenient Truth: The Planetary Emergency of Global Warming and What We Can Do About It" (2006); Host, Co-producer, Documentary, "An Inconvenient Truth" (2006); Co-author with Tipper Gore, "Joined at the Heart: The Transformation of the American Family" (2002); Co-author with Joseph Kaufman, "The World According to Al Gore: An A-to-Z Compilation of His Opinions, Positions, and Public Statements" (2000); Author, "Let the Glory Out: My South and It's Politics" (2000); Author, "Earth in the Balance: Ecology and the Human Spirit" (1992) **AW:** Named One of the 50 Highest-earning Political Figures, Newsweek (2010); Grammy Award for Best Spoken Word Album for Audio Book, The Recording Academy (2009); Named One of the 100 Agents of Change, Rolling Stone Magazine (2009); James C. Morgan Global Humanitarian Award, Tech Museum (Now The Tech Interactive) (2009); Dan David Prize, Dan David Foundation (2008); Named One of the World's Most Influential People, TIME Magazine (2006, 2007); Nobel Peace Prize, Norweigan Nobel Committee (2007); Quill Book Award for Current Events (2006, 2007); Principe de Asturias Prize, Fundación Príncipe de Asturias (2007); Founders Award, International Academy of Television Arts & Sciences (2007); Named Policy Leader of the Year, Scientific American Magazine (2006); World Technology Award for Policy, The World Technology Network (2006); Special Award for "An Inconvenient Truth," Humanitas Prize Board (2006); Webby Lifetime Achievement Award, International Academy of Digital Arts and Sciences (IADAS) (2005) **MEM:** Fellow, American Academy of Arts & Sciences; American Farm Bureau Federation; Tennessee Jaycees; The American Legion; VFW **PA:** Democrat **RE:** Baptist

GORELIK, ALEXANDER V., PHD, T: Associate Professor of Mass Communication **I:** Education/ Educational Services **CN:** Benedict College **DOB:** 01/03/1969 **PB:** Kharkiv **SC:** Ukraine **PT:** Irina Gorelik; Valeriy Gorelik **MS:** Married **SPN:** Alina Likholatnikova **ED:** PhD in Media Economics, University of South Carolina (2002) **C:** Associate Professor of Mass Communication, Benedict College, Columbia, SC (2010-Present); Assistant Professor of Mass Communication, Benedict College, Columbia, SC (2009-2010); Program Coordinator, Mass Communication, Benedict College, Columbia, SC (2009-2010); Research Consultant, Market Probe Canada, Toronto, Canada (2006-2009); Senior Research Analyst, Market Probe Canada, Toronto, Canada (2006-2009); Consultant, Competitor Research and Intelligence, Sigma-KC, Sigma-Audit, Kharkiv, Ukraine (2005-2007); Research Associate, Transaction Network Services, Canadian Facts, Toronto, Canada (2002-2006) **CR:** President, South Carolina Media Educators Association (2013-2015); Association for Education in Journalism and Mass Communication; Broadcast Education Association; National Communication Association **CW:** Co-Presenter, "When Big Data Eclipses God," Bureau of Economic Analysis (2018); Conference, Las Vegas, NV (2018); Co-Presenter, "Crises, Organizations and Communication Practices: Conceptualizing the Initial Haiti earthquake response among Christian relief organizations," South Carolina Media Educators Association Conference, Columbia, SC (2015); Presenter, "Mass Self-Communication, eSelf and The Public Sphere: a framework of interdisciplinary discourse," Convergence and Society Conference, Las Vegas, NV (2013); Presenter, "Public Administration: Challenges of the 21st Century," Proceedings of the 13th International Congress, Kharkov, Ukraine (2013); Co-Presenter, "Information-Seeking Behavior of HBCU College Students: an exploratory case study," South Carolina Media Educators Association Conference, Columbia, SC (2012) Co-Presenter, "Toward cogent understanding of communication practices: initial Haiti earthquake response among Christian relief organizations," National Communication Association, Religious Communication Association Conference, San Francisco, CA (2010); Co-Presenter, "Convergent Newsrooms: Ukrainian Visions 2009," Convergence and Society Conference, Reno, NV (2009); Presenter, "Knowledge as a Source of Competitiveness in a Transforming Industry: Two Comparative Case Studies of Ukrainian Shipbuilding Companies," American Society for Competitiveness Conference, Alexandria, VA (2002); Presenter, "The Public Sphere and eSelf: toward a theoretical framework of networked democracy" **MEM:** President, South Carolina Media Educators Association (2013-2015); Vice President, South Carolina Media Educators Association (2011); Broadcast Education Association; National Communication Association; Association for Education in Journalism and Mass Communication **AS:** Mr. Gorelik attributes his success to his dedication to his student's improvement. He believes that in a changing world, one has to be a "learner." He feels it's important to keep an open mind, and always be available to take in new information. Mr. Gorelik feels he learns most when he is in situations with people who know more than he does. **B/I:** Mr. Gorelik became involved in his profession while he was studying literature in Ukraine. He helped found the first non-government television station in Ukraine, and founded a small public relations firm there. At the television station, Mr. Gorelik met representatives from the World Bank, who encouraged him to study public relations. Mr. Gorelik went on to earn his master's degree in public relations and a PhD in media economics from the University of North Carolina. Mr. Gorelik's interest in knowledge management grew as he earned his degrees. **THT:** Mr. Gorelik is a researcher and educator with more than a decade of combined experience in consulting, research, and management in organizational communication. He has worked as a consultant and published in the United States, Ukraine, and Canada. As a research manager, he sees his professional role at the intersection of data providers, data scientists and decision makers. His management roles focus on strategic clients in small business, banking, insurance, and local government sectors. He built inter-disciplinary and inter-departmental partnerships to complete national market and organizational studies. Mr. Gorelik currently directs an academic program at Benedict College, a historically black institution that serves under-privileged populations and adult learners. His former students work as journalists, content creators, radio DJs, researchers, business executives, and marketers.

GORMAN, JAMES P., T: Chairman, President, Chief Executive Officer **I:** Other **CN:** Morgan Stanley **DOB:** 07/14/1958 **PB:** Melbourne, Victoria **SC:** Australia **ED:** MBA, Columbia University (1987); LLB, University of Melbourne (1982); Bachelor's Degree, University of Melbourne **C:** Chairman, President, Chief Executive Officer, Morgan Stanley, New York, NY (2012-Present); Chairman, Morgan Stanley Smith Barney LLC (2009-Present); President, Chief Executive Officer, Morgan Stanley, New York, NY (2010-2011); Co-President, Co-Head, Strategic Planning, Morgan Stanley, New York, NY (2007-2009); President, Chief Operating Officer, Global Wealth Management Group, Morgan Stanley, New York, NY (2005-2008); Executive Vice President, Acquisitions, Strategy and Research, Merrill Lynch & Co., Inc. (2005); President, Global Private Client, Merrill Lynch & Co., Inc. (2002-2005);Head, USPC Client Relationship Group, Merrill Lynch & Co., Inc. (2001-2002);Executive Vice President, Chief Marketing Officer, Merrill Lynch & Co., Inc. (1999-2001); Senior Partner, McKinsey & Co., New York, NY (1997-1999); Member, Partner Election Committee, McKinsey & Co. (1997-1999); Chairman, New York Personnel Operating Committee, McKinsey & Co. (1996-1999); Co-Head, Personal Financial Services Practice, North America, McKinsey & Co. (1992-1996); Partner, McKinsey & Co. (1992-1997); Attorney, Phillips Fox & Masel, Melbourne, Australia (1982-1985) **CR:** Board of Directors, Morgan Stanley (2010-Present); Board of Directors, MSCI Inc. (2007-2009); Chairman, Security Industry & Financial Markets Association (2006) **CIV:** Trustee, Columbia Business School; Chairman, Board of Directors, Graham-Windham **AW:** Named One of the 50 Most Influential People in Global Finance, Bloomberg Markets (2011, 2014)

GORSKY, ALEX, T: Chairman and Chief Executive Officer **I:** Consumer Goods and Services **CN:** Johnson & Johnson **DOB:** 05/24/1960 **MS:** Married **SPN:** Pat Gorsky **CH:** Nicholas **ED:** MBA, The Wharton School, The University of Pennsylvania (1996); BS, U.S. Military Academy, West Point, NY (1982); Honorary Doctorate, Thomas Jefferson University **C:** Chairman, Chief Executive Officer, Johnson & Johnson, Johnson & Johnson Services, Inc. (2012-Present); Vice Chairman, Executive Committee, Johnson & Johnson, Johnson & Johnson Services, Inc. (2011-2012); Worldwide Chairman, Medical Devices & Diagnostics Group (MD&D), Executive Committee, Johnson & Johnson, Johnson & Johnson Services, Inc. (2009-2011); Chief Executive Officer, Head, Pharma North America, Novartis Pharmaceuticals Corp., Novartis AG (2005-2008); Chief Operating Officer, Head, General Medicines, Novartis Pharmaceuticals Corp., Novartis AG (2004-2005); Group Chairman, Europe, the Middle East & Africa, Johnson & Johnson, London, England, United Kingdom (2003-2004); President, Janssen Pharmaceutica, Inc., Janssen Global Services, LLC (2001-2003); Various Positions Including Sales Representative, Sales & Marketing Divisions, Janssen Pharmaceutica, Inc., Janssen Global Services, LLC (1988-2001) **CR:** Board of Directors, Johnson & Johnson, Johnson & Johnson Services, Inc. (2012-Present); Board of Directors, IBM; Board of Directors, Congressional Medal of Honor Society; Board of Directors, National Academy Foundation **CIV:** Board of Directors, Doylestown Hospital (Now Doylestown Health) **AW:** Named, Top 50 Healthcare Technology CEOs, The Healthcare Technology Report (2019); Honorable Mentor, Healthcare Businesswomen's Association (2009); Named, 100 Most Inspiring Leaders, PharmaVOICE; Joseph Wharton Award for Leadership; Named Humanitarian of the Year Award, CADCA **MEM:** Philadelphia College of Pharmacy (Now University of the Sciences); National Alliance on Aging; National Alliance on Mental Illness (NAMI); The Business Council; Business Roundtable **AV:** Running

GORSUCH, NEIL MCGILL, T: Associate Justice **I:** Law and Legal Services **CN:** Supreme Court of the United States **DOB:** 08/29/1967 **PB:** Denver **SC:** CO/USA **PT:** David Ronald Gorsuch; Anne (McGill Burford) Gorsuch **MS:** Married **SPN:** Marie Louise (Burleston) Gorsuch (06/22/1996) **CH:** Belinda Loveday; Emma Louise **ED:** Doctor of Jurisprudence, Harvard Law School, Cum Laude, Cambridge, MA (1991); Bachelor of Arts, Columbia University, with Honors (1988); Doctor of Philosophy, University of Oxford, England **C:** Associate Justice, Supreme Court of the United States, Washington, DC (2017-Present); Adjunct Professor, University of Colorado Law School (2007-2017); Judge, United States Court of Appeals for the 10th Circuit, Denver, CO (2006-2017); Principal Deputy Associate Attorney General, Acting Associate Attorney General, U.S. Department of Justice, Washington, DC (2005-2006); Partner, Kellogg, Hansen, Todd, Figel & Frederick PLLC, Washington, DC (1998-2005); Associate, Kellogg, Hansen, Todd, Figel & Frederick, PLLC, Washington, DC (1995-1997); Law Clerk to Justice Byron R. White and Justice Anthony M. Kennedy, Supreme Court of the United States, Washington, DC (1993-1994); Law Clerk to Honorable David B. Sentelle, United States Court of Appeals for the District of Columbia Circuit (1991-1992) **CR:** Board of Directors, Executive Committee, Judicial Conference of the United States Committee on Rules of Practice and Procedure (2010-Present); Board of Directors, Federal Judges Association (2009-Present) **CIV:** Honorary Chairperson, National Constitution Center (2019-Present) **CW:** Contributor, Articles to Professional Journals **AW:** Joseph Stevens Public Service Award, Harry S. Truman Foundation (2007); Edmund J. Randolph Award for Outstanding Service, U.S. Department of Justice (2006); Marshall Scholar (1992-1995); Harry S. Truman Scholar (1987-1990) **MEM:** American Bar Association; American Association for Justice; Republican National Lawyers Association; New York State Bar Association; Colorado Bar Association; The Bar Association of DC; The Phi Beta Kappa Society **BAR:** The District of Columbia (1997); State of Colorado (1994); State of New York (1992)

GOSAR, PAUL ANTHONY, DDS, T: U.S. Representative from Arizona; Dentist **I:** Government Administration/Government Relations/Government Services **DOB:** 11/27/1958 **PB:** Rock Springs **SC:** WY/USA **PT:** Antone John Gosar; Bernadette M. (Erramouspe) Gosar **MS:** Married **SPN:** Maude Gosar **CH:** Three Children **ED:** DDS, School of Dentistry, Creighton University (1985); BS, Creighton University (1981) **C:** Member, U.S. House of Representatives from Arizona's Fourth Congressional District, U.S. Congress, Washington, DC (2013-Present); Member, U.S. House Committee on Natural Resources (2011-Present); Member, U.S. House Committee on Oversight and Government Reform Committee (2011-Present); Member, U.S. House of Representatives from Arizona's First Congressional District, United States Congress, Washington, DC (2011-2013); Private Dental Practice, Flagstaff, AZ **AW:** Dentist of the Year, Arizona Dental Association; Inductee, Hall of Fame, Arizona Dental Association **MEM:** Past Vice Chairman, Council on Government Affairs, American Dental Association; Past President, Arizona Dental Association; Northern Arizona Dental Society **PA:** Republican **RE:** Roman Catholic

GOSLING, RYAN THOMAS, T: Actor **I:** Media & Entertainment **DOB:** 11/12/1980 **PB:** London **SC:** ON/Canada **PT:** Thomas Ray Gosling; Donna Gosling **MS:** Partner **SPN:** Eva Mendes **CH:** Esmeralda Amada; Amada Lee **CR:** Co-Owner, Tagine, Beverly Hills, CA (2004-Present) **CIV:** Volunteer, Clean-up Effort, Hurricane Katrina; Supporter, PETA, Invisible Children, Generation Progress, and Enough Project **CW:** Actor, "First Man" (2018); Actor, "Song to Song" (2017); Actor, "Blade Runner 2049" (2017); Solo Artist, Artist with Emma Stone, "City of Stars," "La La Land: Original Motion Picture Soundtrack" (2016); Artist, with Emma Stone, "A Lovely Night," "La La Land: Original Motion

Picture Soundtrack" (2016); Actor, "Weightless" (2016); Actor, "The Nice Guys" (2016); Actor, "La La Land" (2016); Guest Host, "Saturday Night Live" (2015-2017); Actor, "The Big Short" (2015); Producer, Director, Writer, "Lost River" (2014); Executive Producer, "White Shadow" (2013); Actor, Executive Producer, "Only God Forgives" (2013); Actor, "Gangster Squad" (2013); Actor, "The Place Beyond the Pines" (2012); Actor, "Crazy, Stupid, Love" (2011); Actor, "Drive" (2011); Artist, "You Always Hurt the One You Love," "Blue Valentine: Original Motion Picture Soundtrack" (2011); Actor, "The Ides of March" (2011); Producer, "ReGeneration" (2010); Actor, Executive Producer, "Blue Valentine" (2010); Musician, with Dead Man's Bones, "Dead Man's Bones" (2009); Actor, "All Good Things" (2010); Actor, "Fracture" (2007); Actor, "Lars and the Real Girl" (2007); Actor, "Half Nelson" (2006); Actor, "Stay" (2005); Actor, "I'm Still Here" (2005); Actor, "The Notebook" (2004); Actor, "The United States of Leland" (2003); Actor, "Murder by Numbers" (2002); Actor, "The Slaughter Rule" (2002); Actor, "The Believer" (2001); Actor, "Remember the Titans" (2000); Actor, "The Unbelievables" (1999); Actor, "Hercules: The Legendary Journeys" (1999); Actor, "Young Hercules" (1998-1999); Actor, "Nothing Too Good for a Cowboy" (1998); Actor, "Breaker High" (1997-1998); Actor, "Ready or Not" (1996); Actor, "Flash Forward" (1996); Actor, "The Adventures of Shirley Holmes" (1996); Actor, "Goosebumps" (1996); Actor, "Road to Avonlea" (1996); Actor, "Kung Fu: The Legend Continues" (1996); Actor, "PSI Factor: Chronicles of the Paranormal" (1996); Actor, "Frankenstein and Me" (1996); Appearance, "Are You Afraid of the Dark?" (1995); Actor, "The Mickey Mouse Club" (1993-1994) **AW:** Golden Globe Award for Best Actor in a Motion Picture - Musical or Comedy, Hollywood Foreign Press Association (2017); Award for Best Cast, National Board of Review (2015); Satellite Award for Best Actor in a Motion Picture - Drama (2011); Satellite Award for Best Actor in a Motion Picture - Comedy or Drama (2007); Award for Best Breakthrough Performance - Male, National Board of Review (2006); Independent Spirit Award for Best Male Lead (2006)

GOSSARD, STONE CARPENTER, T: Musician **I:** Media & Entertainment **DOB:** 07/20/1966 **PB:** Seattle **SC:** WA/USA **PT:** David W. Gossard Jr.; Mary Carolyn Carpenter **MS:** Married **SPN:** Vivian Wang; Liz Weber (Divorced) **CH:** Vivian Sparks **C:** Solo Artist (2001-Present); Co-Founder, Loosegroove Records (1994-2000); Guitarist, Pearl Jam (1991-2001); Member, Temple of the Dog (1990-1991); Member, Mother Love Bone (1988-1990); Member, Green River (1985-1988) **CW:** Solo Artist, "Moonlander" (2013); Musician, with Pearl Jam, "Lightning Bolt" (2013); Musician, with Pearl Jam, "Backspacer" (2009); Musician, with Mother Love Bone, "The Road Mix: Music from the Television Series One Tree Hill, Volume 3" (2007); Musician, with Pearl Jam, "Pearl Jam" (2006); Musician, with Green River, "Sleepless in Seattle: The Birth of Grunge" (2006); Musician, with Pearl Jam, "Riot Act" (2002); Solo Artist, "Bayleaf" (2001); Musician, with Mother Love Bone, "Alternative Moments" (2001); Musician, with Green River, "Wild and Wooly: The Northwest Rock Collection" (2000); Musician, with Pearl Jam, "Binaural" (2000); Musician, with Pearl Jam, "Yield" (1998); Musician, with Mother Love Bone, "Proud to Be Loud" (1997); Musician, with Green River, "Hype!: The Motion Picture Soundtrack" (1996); Musician, with Pearl Jam, "No Code" (1996); Musician, with Mother Love Bone, "Alterno-Daze: Natural 90s Selection" (1995); Musician, with Pearl Jam, "Vitalogy" (1994); Musician, with Pearl Jam, "Vs." (1993); Musician, with Mother Love Bone, "Thrash and Burn: The Metal Alterna-

tive" (1993); Musician, with Mother Love Bone, "The Best of Grunge Rock" (1993); Musician, with Mother Love Bone, "Mother Love Bone" (1992); Musician, with Green River, "Afternoon Delight: Love Song from Sub Pop" (1992); Musician, with Pearl Jam, "Ten" (1991); Musician, with Pearl Jam, "Alive" (1991); Musician, with Temple of the Dog, "Temple of the Dog" (1991); Musician, with Green River, "Endangered Species" (1990); Musician, with Mother Love Bone, "Apple" (1990); Musician, with Green River, "Dry as a Bone" (1990); Musician, with Green River, "This House is Not a Motel" (1989); Musician, with Green River, "Sub Pop Rock City" (1989); Musician, with Green River, "Another Pyrrhic Victory: The Only Compilation of Dead Seattle God Bands" (1989); Musician, with Mother Love Bone, "Shine" (1989); Musician, with Green River, "Sub Pop 200" (1988); Musician, with Green River, "Rehab Doll" (1988); Musician, with Green River, "Dry as a Bone" (1987); Musician, with Green River, "Come on Down" (1985); Musician, Numerous Collaborations **AW:** Inductee, Rock and Roll Hall of Fame (2017); Grammy Award for Best Recording Package, The Recording Academy (2015); One of the Top 20 New Guitar Gods, Rolling Stone Magazine (2007); Award for Favorite Alternative Artist, American Music Awards (1999); Grammy Award for Best Hard Rock Performance, The Recording Academy (1996); Awards for Favorite Alternative Artist, Favorite Heavy Metal/Hard Rock Artist, American Music Awards (1996); Awards for Favorite Pop/Rock New Artist, Favorite New Heavy Metal/Hard Rock Artist, American Music Awards (1993); Awards for Video of Year, Best Group Video, Best Metal/Hard Rock Video, Best Direction, MTV Music Video Awards (1993)

GOTO, LORI, T: Realtor **I:** Real Estate **CN:** Realty Austin **PB:** Honolulu **SC:** HI/USA **CT:** ABR; CLHMS; CNE; CRS; E-pro; GREEN **C:** Realtor, Realty Austin, Austin, TX (2006-Present) **CIV:** President, Asian Real Estate Association of America; Volunteer, Habitat for Humanity; Volunteer, Foundation Communities; Volunteer, Rebuilding Together; Fundraiser, Cottey College; Fundraiser, Austin Children's Shelter **AW:** 5-Star Professional, Platinum Top 50 (2012-Present); Community Service Award, Wells Fargo; Community Service Award **MEM:** Austin Board of Realtors; National Association of Realtors; Texas Realtors; Asian Real Estate Association of America **AS:** Ms. Goto began her real estate career with Keller Williams Real Estate. They have a great training program and she started with a big team, working with a large number of leads. In her first year, she sold 24 houses. Ms. Goto says, "You can have whatever you want if you give people what they want first." **B/I:** Ms. Goto always wanted to have her own business, and she thought that real estate would be more flexible on hours. Initially, she was trying to purchase a franchise business for the gym, Curves. She looked for a place to start the business and began the process but was eventually denied. Her next decision was to go into real estate, try it for a year, and see how it goes. Many years later, Ms. Goto has found a lot of success in real estate. **THT:** Ms. Goto makes her relationship with her clients deeper than a transaction. She enjoys fulfilling their desires and likes to keep in touch with them, even after the transaction is done.

GOTTESMAN, NOAM, T: Co-Founder **I:** Business Management/Business Services **CN:** GLG Partners **DOB:** 05/24/1961 **SC:** Israel **PT:** Dov Gottesman **MS:** Married **SPN:** Bianca Dueñas (2015); Geraldine Gottesman (Divorced) **CH:** Five Children **ED:** BA, Columbia University, New York, NY **C:** Non-Executive Chairman, GLG Partners LP (2012-Present); Co-Founder, Managing Director

of U.S. Equities, Senior Fund Manager, GLG Partners LP, New York, NY (2000-Present); Chairman, Board of Directors, GLG Partners LP (2007-2012); Co-Chief Executive Officer, GLG Partners LP (2005-2012); Chief Executive Officer, GLG Partners LP (2000-2005); Co-Founder, GLG Partners Division, Lehman Brothers International (1995-2000); Fund Manager, Goldman Sachs Private Client Services (1985-1995) **CR:** Co-Owner, MonsterDaata, Inc. **CIV:** Dia Art Council; Tate Modern Gallery Council **AW:** Listee, Forbes Richest Americans (2008, 2012); Listee, Top 200 Collectors, ARTnews Magazine (2006-2012) **AV:** Collecting contemporary art

GOTTHEIMER, JOSH, T: U.S. Representative from New Jersey **I:** Government Administration/ Government Relations/Government Services **CN:** U.S. House of Representatives **DOB:** 3/8/1975 **PB:** Livingston **SC:** NJ/USA **MS:** Married **SPN:** Marla Tusk (2006) **CH:** Two Children **ED:** Doctor of Jurisprudence, Harvard Law School (2004); Bachelor of Arts, University of Pennsylvania (1997); Coursework, Pembroke College, University of Oxford **C:** Member, U.S. House of Representative from New Jersey's Fifth Congressional District (2017-Present); Member, Committee on Financial Services (2017-Present); General Manager for Advertising and Strategy, Microsoft (2012-2015); Senior Counselor, Chairperson of the Federal Communications Commission (2010-2012); Special Assistant/ Speechwriter for Hilary Clinton (1998-2001); With, Burson-Marsteller; With, Ford Motor Company **CW:** Author, "Power in Words: The Stories Behind Barack Obama's Speech's from the State House to the White House" (2011); Author, "Ripple of Hope: Great American Civil Rights Speeches" (2003) **AW:** Thouron Fellow, University of Oxford **PA:** Democrat

GOTTLIEB, DANIEL S., T: Attorney **I:** Law and Legal Services **CN:** Hillis Clark Martin & Peterson P.S. **DOB:** 09/19/1954 **PB:** Los Angeles **SC:** CA/USA **PT:** Seymour Gottlieb (Deceased 2015); Blanche Joyce (Kaufman) Gottlieb (Deceased 2000) **MS:** Married **SPN:** Marilynn Jeanne Payne (07/21/1985) **CH:** Gwendolyn Z.; Rebecca Lucinda **ED:** JD, Harvard University (1980); BA, Columbia University, Summa Cum Laude (1976) **C:** Principal/Attorney, Hillis Clark Martin & Peterson P.S., Seattle, WA (2013-Present); Member, Gottlieb, Fisher & Andrews, PLLC, Seattle, WA (1997-2013); Principal, Graham & James LLP/Riddell Williams P.S., Seattle, WA (1996-1997); Partner, Riddell, Williams, Bullitt & Walkinshaw, Seattle, WA (1986-1995); Associate, Riddell, Williams, Bullitt & Walkinshaw, Seattle, WA (1980-1986) **CR:** Chairman, Washington State Access to Justice Board (2008-2010); Member, Washington State Access to Justice Board (2004-2010); Coordinator, Southeast Legal Clinic, Seattle, WA (1984-1986) **CIV:** President, Kitsap Regional Library (KRL) (2014-2015, 2020-Present); Member, Board of Trustees, Kitsap Regional Library (KRL) (2012-Present); Member, Seattle Fremont Advisory Committee (1987-1988) **CW:** Co-author, "Tax-Exempt Bond Financing and Long Term Financing," Chapter 22, Washington Health Law Manual, Third Edition (2019) **AW:** Helen M. Geisness Award, King County Bar Association (2001); Achievement Award, Economic Development Council of Seattle & King County (1990) **MEM:** President, King County Bar Association (1997-1998); First Vice President, King County Bar Association (1996-1997); Second Vice President, King County Bar Association (1995-1996); Vice President, Secretary, Shir Hayam (1993-1995); Treasurer, King County Bar Association (1993-1995); Chairman, King County Bar Association (1989-1990); Board of Directors, Young Lawyers Division, King County Bar Association (1987-1990); Vice-chairman,

King County Bar Association (1988-1989); Treasurer, King County Bar Association (1987-1988); Chairman, Legal Information and Referral Clinics Committee, King County Bar Association (1986-1987); American Bar Association (ABA) (1980); Washington State Bar Association (1980); National Association Bond Lawyers; King County Bar Association; Washington State Association Municipal Attorneys (WSAMA); Washington State Society of Healthcare Attorneys (WSSHA); Chavurat Shir Hayam **BAR:** Oregon (2004); United States District Court for the Western District of Washington (1980); Washington (1980) **MH:** Albert Nelson Marquis Lifetime Achievement Award **B/I:** Mr. Gottlieb became involved in his profession because at first he did not want to go into law, as he wanted to be an Egyptologist. He went to grad school for three weeks but then got an ulcer and decided to do something different. Both of his parents were lawyers and they encouraged him to go to law school, which ended up working out very well. **AV:** Tuba; Hiking; Bicycling **RE:** Jewish **THT:** Mr. Gottlieb has played in a band as a tuba player for 40 years.

GOWER, PATRICIA E., PHD, T: Professor Emeritus (Retired) **I:** Education/Educational Services **DOB:** 11/28/1950 **PB:** Carrizo Springs **SC:** TX/USA **PT:** Daniel W. Gower; Gail A. Gower **MS:** Married **SPN:** Thomas May (10/10/1998) **CH:** Jennifer Ross; Melissa Lamkin; Travis Lamkin (Deceased) **ED:** PhD in American History, Texas Agricultural and Mechanical University (1996); MA, Angelo State University (1990); BA, University of Texas at El Paso (1972) **C:** Professor Emeritus (2017-Present); Professor, Chair, Department of History, University of the Incarnate Word, San Antonio, TX (1995-2017); Graduate Assistant, Texas A&M University (1993-1995) **CW:** Co-Author, "'Well, Bless Your Heart!': Rhetoric and Power in Dallas Women During the Progressive Era," East Texas Historical Association Journal (2014); Co-Author, "Chapter Study Questions for History 2" (2013); Author, "Contrasts in Neglect: Progressive Municipal Reform in Progressive-Era Dallas and San Antonio," Seeking Civil Rights: Texans and the Quest for Social Justice, Texas A&M Press (2009); Co-Author, "Blacks in San Angelo: Relations Between Fort Concho and the City, 1875-1889," Slavery to Integration: Black Americans in West Texas, State House Press (2008); Co-Author, "Unintended Consequences: The San Antonio Pecan Shellers Strike of 1938," Journal of South Texas (2004); Author, "The Price of Exclusion: Dallas Municipal Policy and Its Impact on African Americans," East Texas Historical Association Journal (2001); Author, "Seeking Consensus: Experiments in Dallas Municipal Policy," Legacies: Journal of the Dallas Historical Society (2000); Author, "Dissertation: Dallas in the Progressive Era, 1898-1920" (1996); Author, "Blacks in San Angelo: Relations Between Forts Concho and the City, 1875-1889," West Texas Historical Association Year Book (1990); Author, "The Black Troops of Fort Concho," El Companario (1990); Author, "Fort Concho: The Lost Years, 1889-1939," Fort Concho Report (1988); Contributor, Numerous Presentations, Refereed Papers; Reviewer, Numerous Books, Textbooks **AW:** Title V Grant (2009); Humanities Texas Grant (2006); Faculty Development Funds Award (2002-2003); Outstanding Advisor, History Club (1999); McDonald's Award for Excellence in Teaching for Graduate Teaching Assistants, Texas A&M University (1995) **MEM:** CHASS Internal Committee on Rank and Tenure (2015-2016); CHASS Internal Committee for Rank and Tenure Review (2014-2015); Program Review for Department History (2013-2014); University-Wide Education Committee (2013); Subcommittee on Writing Assessment Tool (2013); Focus Faculty Group (2009-2013); First Faculty Group (2008-2013); IDS Advisory Committee (1999-2013); Advisory Board for Education, University of the Incarnate Word (1996-2013); World History Association of Texas (2009); CORE Advisory Council (2007); Search Committee for H-E-B School of Business (2006); Goal 5 Committee for International Initiatives (2006); 2 Search Committees for H-E-B School of Business (2004); Faculty Affairs Committee (2003-2004); Rank and Tenure Committee (2001-2003); Faculty Senate (2001); Faculty Development Funds Committee (1998-2000); Committee for the ExCet Examination and the Interdisciplinary Studies Program, Education Department (1998-2000); Earth Day Committee (1999) **MH:** Albert Nelson Marquis Lifetime Achievement Award **B/I:** Dr. Gower became involved in her profession because she was surrounded by history while growing up. She got her degree in 1972 but was not sure what she was going to do with it. She and her mother opened a ceramic store in 1983, where she taught ceramic classes, building off her experience teaching as a graduate student. Professor Gower earned a PhD in 1996. **AV:** Arts and crafts; Needle felting; Cross stitching; Practicing ceramics

GRACE, DANIEL H., T: Secretary-Treasurer **I:** Business Management/Business Services **CN:** Teamsters Local 830 **ED:** AS in Automotive Diesel Technology, Lincoln Technical School **C:** Secretary-Treasurer, Business Manager, Teamsters Local Union 830 (2001-Present); Transport Driver, Pepsi Bottling Group (1976-1995) **CIV:** Volunteer, Aid for Friends; Commissioner, Delaware River Joint Toll Bridge Commission; Board Member, Bucks County Prison; Board of Directors, Self-Help **AW:** Pioneer Award, National Association for the Advancement of Colored People (2019) **MEM:** Irish Society **AS:** Mr. Grace attributes his success to being honest with the members of his team and doing his best on a daily basis. **B/I:** Mr. Grace's family was involved in the Teamsters when he was a child. He always admired what they did, looked up to them, and aspired to do it himself when he became of age.

GRAF, STEFFI, T: Former Professional Tennis Player **I:** Athletics **DOB:** 06/14/1969 **PB:** Mannheim, Baden-Württemberg **SC:** Germany **PT:** Peter Graf; Heidi Graf **MS:** Married **SPN:** Andre Agassi (10/22/2001) **CH:** Jaden Gil; Jaz Elle **C:** Designer, Steffi Graf Handbags (2002-Present); Founder, Steffi Graf Marketing (1996); Professional Tennis Player, WTA Tour, Inc. (1982-1999) **CIV:** Founder, Children for Tomorrow (1998-Present); Ambassador, World Wildlife Fund; Numerous Benefit Exhibition Matches **AW:** Named to German Sports Hall of Fame (2008); Named to International Tennis Hall of Fame (2004); Named to Tennis Hall of Fame (2004); Winner, French Open (1993, 1995, 1996, 1999); Named German Sportsperson of the Year (1986-1989, 1999); Olympic Medal of Honor, IOC (1999); Female Athlete of the Decade, Espy Awards (1999); Named Greatest Female Tennis Player of the 20th Century, The Associated Press (1999); Winner, U.S. Open (1989, 1993, 1995, 1996); Winner, Wimbledon (1989, 1991, 1992, 1993, 1995, 1996); International Tennis Federation World Champion (1987-1990, 1993, 1995-1996); Winner, Australian Open (1989, 1990, 1994); Named WTA Player of Year, WTA Tour, Inc. (1987-1990, 1993-1996); Winner, Golden Grand Slam (Australian Open, French Open, Wimbledon, U.S. Open, Olympics) (1988); Winner, Berlin Open (1988); Olympic Gold Medal (1988); Winner, Numerous Professional Women's Tennis Tournaments

GRAFFIUS, BRENDA L., RN, T: Manager **I:** Medicine & Health Care **DOB:** 06/13/1961 **PB:** Fairmont **SC:** WV/USA **PT:** Donald E. Graffius; Helen M. (Prahl) Graffius **MS:** Married **SPN:** Charles Barna **ED:** MS in Information Systems Technology, The George Washington University, Magna Cum Laude (2000); BSN, West Virginia University, Magna Cum Laude (1984); AS, Fairmont State College (Now Fairmont State University), with Honors (1981) **C:** Manager, KPMG Healthcare and Government Solutions (Now KPMG LLP), Greenville, SC; Clinical Systems Manager, Suburban Hospital, The Johns Hopkins University, Bethesda, MD; Operating Room Clinical Nurse, The George Washington University Hospital, WA; Medical Staff Nurse, Fairmont General Hospital (Now Fairmont Medical Center), WVU Medicine **CIV:** Habitat for Humanity International; United Way Hands on Greenville; Special Olympics **AW:** Award for Opening a Prisma Carolina Hospital, Prisma Health (2005) **MEM:** Association Operating Room Nurses; Sigma Theta Tau International Honor Society of Nursing **MH:** Albert Nelson Marquis Lifetime Achievement Award **B/I:** Mrs. Graffius has always wanted to take care of other people, even when she was a small child. She watched her mother take care her parents and her father's parents and her mother encouraged her to be a nurse. About 15 years into her career, she decided to do something else in the healthcare field, so she leaned towards the information technology side of healthcare and that is when she went back to school to receive her master's degree in information technology. **AV:** Golf; Beach; Biking; Travel

GRAHAM, ASHLEY, T: Model **I:** Apparel & Fashion **DOB:** 10/30/1987 **PB:** Lincoln **SC:** NE/USA **MS:** Married **SPN:** Justin Ervin (2010) **CH:** Isaac **ED:** Diploma, Lincoln Southwest High School (2005) **C:** Model, Ford Models (2003-Present); Designer, Lingerie for Addition Elle (2013); Model, Wilhelmina Models (2001-2003) **CW:** Host, Executive Producer, "American Beauty Star" (2019); Author, "A New Model: What Confidence, Beauty, and Power Really Look Like" (2017); Backstage Host, Miss Universe (2016-2018); Backstage Host, Miss USA (2016-2017); Judge, "America's Next Top Model" (2016); Model, Numerous Magazines Including Harper's Bazaar and Sports Illustrated's Annual Swimsuit Issue; Appearances, Numerous Television Shows, Music Videos **AW:** Named, One of the 100 Most Influential People, TIME Magazine (2017)

GRAHAM, AUBREY, "DRAKE" DRAKE, T: Singer, Rapper; Actor **I:** Media & Entertainment **DOB:** 10/24/1986 **PB:** Toronto, Ontario **SC:** Canada **PT:** Dennis Graham; Sandra "Sandi" Graham **CH:** Adonis **ED:** Diploma (2012); Coursework, Vaughan Road Academy; Coursework, Forest Hill Collegiate Institute **C:** Co-founder, Virginia Black Whiskey (2016-Present); Spokesperson, Apple Music (2015-Present); Co-founder, OVO Sound, Warner Records Inc. (2012-Present) **CIV:** Global Ambassador, Toronto Raptors, NBA (2013-Present) **CW:** Artist, "Toosie Slide" (2020); Artist Featuring Giveon, "Chicago Freestyle" (2020); Executive Producer, "Euphoria" (2019); Executive Producer, "Top Boy" (2019); Appearance, "Remember Me, Toronto" (2019); Artist, "Scorpion" (2018); Artist, "Scary Hours" (2018); Appearance, Executive Producer, "The Carter Effect" (2017); Artist, "More Life" (2017); Host, Performer, "Saturday Night Live" (2014, 2016); Artist, "Views" (2016); Artist, "If You're Reading This It's Too Late" (2015); Appearance, "Think Like a Man" (2014); Actor, "Anchorman 2: The Legend Continues" (2013); Artist, "Nothing Was the Same" (2013); Artist, "Hold On, We're Going Home" (2013); Voice Actor, "Ice Age: Continental Drift" (2012); Artist, "Take Care" (2011); Performer, "Saturday Night Live" (2011); Artist Featuring Lil Wayne, "HYFR" (2011); Artist, "Thank Me Later" (2010); Artist, "Best I Ever

Had" (2009); Artist, "So Far Gone" (2009); Actor, "Degrassi: The Nest Generation" (2001-2009); Artist, "Comeback Season" (2007); Artist, "Room for Improvement" (2006); Artist, Numerous Singles, Albums; Actor, Television Shows and Films **AW:** Brit Award for International Male Solo Artist (2019); Grammy Awards for Best Rap Song, Best Song, The Recording Academy (2017, 2019); Award for Video of the Year, BET Awards (2018); Award for Top Rap Artist, Billboard Music Awards (2016); Awards for Favorite Rap/Hip-Hop Artist, Favorite Rap/Hip-Hop Album, Favorite Rap/Hip-Hop Song, Favorite Soul/R&B Song, American Music Awards (2016); IFPI Global Recording Artist (2016); Award for Best Hip-Hop Video, MTV Video Music Awards (2012, 2014); Grammy Award for Best Rap Album, The Recording Academy (2013); Named Best Male Hip-Hop Artist, BET Awards (2012); Hal David Starlight Award, Songwriters Hall of Fame (2011); Award for Rap Recording of the Year, Juno Awards (2010); Award for Top Rap Song, Billboard Music Awards (2009); Award for Top New Hip-Hop Artist/R&B Artist, Billboard Music Awards (2009); Numerous Awards

GRAHAM, CLARA ANNE, T: Accountant, Operational Analyst **I:** Financial Services **DOB:** 10/26/1943 **PB:** Dover **SC:** DE/USA **PT:** John Harper; Anne Elizabeth (Thompson) Jones **MS:** Married **SPN:** Robert Myles Elliott (06/15); Richard Terrell Graham (08/13/1964, Divorced 1978) **CH:** Richard Cary; Jocylyn Anne **ED:** AA in Accounting, Business Administration. Goldey-Beacom College, with Honors (1963) **C:** Internal Auditor, Community Health Care, Inc., Naples, FL (1990-Present); Accountant, Office Manager Supervisor, HCMF Corporation, Blacksburg, VA (1984-1990); Comptroller, Bonomo's Incorporated, Blacksburg, VA (1977-1984); Accountant, Office Manager, Estaa Hess Associate, Richlands, VA (1976-1977) **CIV:** Vice President, League of Women's Voters of Collier County; President, League of Women Voters of Lee County Florida; Treasurer, League of Women's Voters, State of Florida; Chair, State of Florida for Climate Change Task Force; League of Women Voters of the United States; Florida Climate Change Task Force; International Host, Student Program, Virginia Tech University; Vice President, Blacksburg in the Eighties; Candidate, Blacksburg Town Council; Co-chair, Blacksburg Cancer Crusade; President, Blacksburg Newcomers; Stakeholder, Southwest Environmental Impact Study, US Army Corps of Engineers **AW:** Distinguished Alumni Award, Goldey-Beacom College **MEM:** Vice President, League of Women Voters, Collier County, FL (1991-Present); President, League of Women Voters, Montgomery County, VA (1980-1982, 1984-1986); National Association for Female Executives (NAFE); League of Women Voters; National Association of Accountants; Association of Healthcare Internal Auditors (AHIA); Virginia Tech University Club (Now University Club at Virginia Tech); President, Blacksburg Junior Women's Club **MH:** Albert Nelson Marquis Lifetime Achievement Award

GRAHAM, FRANKLIN III, T: President, Chief Executive Officer, Missionary **I:** Religious **CN:** Billy Graham Evangelistic Association **DOB:** 07/14/1952 **PB:** Asheville **SC:** NC/USA **PT:** Billy Graham; Ruth Bell Graham **MS:** Married **SPN:** Jane Austin Cunningham (1974) **CH:** William Franklin Iv; Roy; Edward; Jane Austin **ED:** Bachelor of Arts, Appalachian State University, Boone, NC (1978); Honorary Doctorate, Liberty University; Honorary Doctorate, National University; Honorary Doctorate, Lees-McRae College; Honorary Doctorate, LeTourneau University; Honorary Doctorate, Toccoa Falls College; Honorary Doctorate, Whitworth University **C:** President, Billy Graham Evangelistic Associ-

ation (2001-Present); Chief Executive Officer, Billy Graham Evangelistic Association (2000-Present); First Vice Chairperson, Billy Graham Evangelistic Association (1995-Present); Evangelist, Billy Graham Evangelistic Association (1989-Present); President, Chief Executive Officer, Samaritan's Purse (1979-Present); Board Member, Samaritan's Purse (1978) **CR:** Board of Directors, Harvest Christian Fellowship **CW:** Author, "The Sower" (2012); Author, "A Wing and a Prayer" (2005); Co-author, with R. Rhoads, "All for Jesus: A Devotional" (2003); Author, "Kids Praying for Kids" (2003); Author, "It's Who You Know: The One Relationship that Makes All the Difference" (2002); Author, "The Name" (2002); Author, "Living Beyond the Limits" (1998); Author, "Miracle in a Shoebox" (1995); Author, "Rebel with a Cause" (1995); Author, "Bob Pierce: This One Thing I Do" (1983) **AW:** Named, Daniel of the Year, World Magazine (2002); Named, Tar Heel of the Year, The News & Observer, Charlotte, NC (1992); William Booth Award, Salvation Army **PA:** Republican **RE:** Evangelist

GRAHAM, LINDSEY OLIN, T: U.S. Senator from South Carolina **I:** Government Administration/ Government Relations/Government Services **DOB:** 07/09/1955 **PB:** Central **SC:** SC/USA **PT:** Florence James Graham; Millie Graham **ED:** Honorary Doctor in Public Administration, The Citadel, Charleston, SC; Honorary Doctor in Public Service, Presbyterian College, Clinton, SC; Honorary HHD, Francis Marion University, Florence, SC; Honorary LHD, Allen University, Columbia, SC; Honorary LHD, College of Charleston, SC; Honorary LHD, Winthrop University, Rock Hill, SC; Honorary LLD, Coker College (Now Coker University), Hartsville, SC; Honorary LLD, Erskine College, Due West, SC; Honorary LLD, South Carolina State University, Orangeburg, SC; Honorary LLD, Southern Wesleyan University, Central, SC; Honorary LLD, University of South Carolina; JD, University of South Carolina School of Law (1981); MPA, University of South Carolina (1978); BS in Psychology, University of South Carolina (1977) **C:** Chairman, Senate Judiciary Committee (2019-Present); Member, U.S. Senate Committee on Homeland Security and Governmental Affairs (2009-Present); Member, U.S. Senate Select Committee on Aging (2007-Present); Member, U.S. Senate Committee on Veterans' Affairs (2007-Present); Member, U.S. Senate Budget Committee (2004-Present); U.S. Senator, State of South Carolina (2003-Present); Member, U.S. Senate Armed Services Committee (2002-Present); Member, U.S. Senate Judiciary Committee (2002-Present); Member, U.S. Senate Select Committee on Intelligence (2007-2009); Member, U.S. Senate Committee on Agriculture, Nutrition and Forestry (2007-2009); Member, U.S. Senate Committee on Health, Labor, Education and Pensions (2002-2004); Member, U.S. House Armed Services Committee (1999-2002); Member, U.S. House Judiciary Committee (1997-2002); Member, U.S. House Committee on Education and Workforce (1995-2002); Member, U.S. House of Representatives from South Carolina's Third Congressional District, United States Congress (1995-2001); Member, U.S. House Committee on International Relations (1995-1998); Member, South Carolina House of Representatives (1992-1995); City Attorney, Central, SC (1990-1994); Attorney, Private Practice (1988-1994); Assistant County Attorney, County of Oconee, SC (1988-1992); Circuit Trial Counsel, United States Air Force in Europe (1984-1988); Area Defense Counsel, Shaw Air Force Base (Shaw AFB) (1982-1984) **CR:** Candidate, 2016 Republican Party Presidential Nomination (2016) **CIV:** Member, Anderson Area Chamber of Commerce; Board of Directors, Rosa Clark Free Medical Clinic (Now Rosa Clark Clinic),

Seneca, SC; Member, Corinth Baptist Church **MIL:** With, United States Air Force Reserve (1995-2015); With, Air National Guard (1989-1995); With, United States Air Force (1982-1988) **AW:** Minuteman of the Year Award, Reserve Officers Association of the United States (Now Reserve Organization of America) (2004); Decorated Meritorious Service Medal **MEM:** Retired Officers Association of the United States (Now Reserve Organization of America); Fundraising Chairman, American Cancer Society, Inc., Oconee County Chapter; Seneca Sertoma, Inc.; The American Legion Post 120; Walhalla Rotary Club **PA:** Republican **RE:** Baptist

GRAMMER, KELSEY, T: Actor **I:** Media & Entertainment **DOB:** 02/21/1955 **PB:** Saint Thomas **SC:** U.S. Virgin Islands **PT:** Frank Allen Grammer Jr.; Sally (Cranmer) Grammer **MS:** Married **SPN:** Kayte Walsh (02/25/2011); Camille Donatacci (08/02/1997, Divorced 2011); Leigh-Anne Csuhany (09/11/1992, Divorced 1993); Doreen Alderman (05/30/1982, Divorced 1990) **CH:** Auden James Ellis; Kelsey Gabriel Elias; Jude Gordon; Faith Evangeline Elisa; Mason Olivia; Kandace Greer; Spencer **ED:** Coursework, The Juilliard School, New York, NY **C:** Founder, Grammnet Productions **CW:** Actor, "Money Plane" (2020); Actor, "Carol's Second Act" (2020); Actor, "The Boy Friend" (2020); Actor, "Proven Innocent" (2019); Voice Actor, "You're Not a Monster" (2019); Actor, "Man of La Mancha" (2019); Actor, "Grand Isle" (2019); Narrator, "Arrow" (2018-2019); Actor, "Like Father" (2018); Actor, "Guardians of the Galaxy" (2018); Voice Actor, "Bunyan and Babe" (2017); Actor, "Modern Family" (2017); Actor, "Neighbors 2: Sorority Rising" (2016); Voice Actor, "Storks" (2016); Actor, "Nest" (2016); Actor, "The Last Tycoon" (2016); Voice Actor, "Trollhunters" (2016); Actor, "Finding Neverland" (2015-2016); Actor, "Baby, Baby, Baby" (2015); Actor, "Killing Jesus" (2015); Featured, "Best of Enemies" (2015); Actor, Narrator, "Killing Jesus" (2015); Actor, "Think Like a Man Too" (2014); Actor, "Partners" (2014); Actor, "Reach Me" (2014); Actor, "Transformers: Age of Extinction" (2014); Actor, "The Expendables 3" (2014); Actor, "Breaking the Bank" (2014); Actor, "Who Do You Think You Are?" (2014); Actor, "Partners" (2014); Voice Actor, "Legends of Oz: Dorothy's Return" (2013); Executive Producer, "The Game" (2006-2013); Actor, "Boss" (2011-2012); Executive Producer, "Medium" (2005-2011); Actor, "Boss" (2011); Actor, "I Don't Know How She Does It" (2011); Actor, "La Cage aux Folles" (2010); Actor, "The Troop" (2010); Actor, "30 Rock" (2010); Actor, "Middle Men" (2010); Actor, "Crazy on the Outside" (2010); Actor, "Hank" (2009-2010); Voice Actor, "The Simpsons" (1990-2010); Actor, "Fame" (2009); Actor, "Swing Vote" (2008); Actor, "Back to You" (2007-2008); Actor, "Back to You" (2007); Actor, "X-Men: The Last Stand" (2006); Actor, "Even Money" (2006); Executive Producer, "Kelsey Grammer Presents: The Sketch Show" (2005); Actor, "Frasier" (1993-2004); Executive Producer, "Gary the Rate" (2003); Executive Producer, "In-Laws" (2002); Actor, "15 Minutes" (2001); Actor, "The Sports Pages" (2001); Actor, "Macbeth" (1981, 2000); Voice Actor, "Toy Story 2" (1999); Actor, "15 Minutes" (1999); Actor, "New Jersey Turnpikes" (1999); Actor, "Standing on Fishes" (1999); Voice Actor, "Bartok the Magnificent" (1999); Actor, "Animal Farm" (1999); Actor, "The Hand Behind the Mouse: The Ub Iwerks Story" (1999); Actor, "The Pentagon Wars" (1998); Actor, "The Real Howard Spitz" (1998); Voice Actor, "Anastasia" (1997); Executive Producer, "Fired Up" (1997); Actor, "London Suite" (1996); Actor, "Down Periscope" (1996); Author, "So Far" (1995); Actor, "The Innocent" (1994); Actor, "Cheers" (1984-1993); Actor, "Beyond Suspicion" (1993);

Actor, "Dance 'til Dawn" (1988); Actor, "Crossings" (1986); Actor, "George Washington" (1984); Actor, "Kennedy" (1983); Actor, "Sunday in the Park with George" (1983); Actor, "Plenty" (1982); Actor, "Othello" (1981); Actor, "Kate and Allie," "Wings," "Tracy Ullman Show"; Actor, "A Month in the Country" and "Quartermaine's Terms"; Actor, Plays, Television Shows and Films **AW:** Emmy Award for Outstanding Performer in an Animated Program, Academy of Television Arts & Sciences (2017); Tony Award (as Producer) for Best Revival of a Musical (2016); Golden Globe Award for Best Performance by an Actor in a TV Series - Drama, Hollywood Foreign Press Association (2012); Emmy Award for Outstanding Voice-Over Performance, Academy of Television Arts & Sciences (2006); Emmy Award for Outstanding Lead Actor in a Comedy Series, Academy of Television Arts & Sciences (2004); People's Choice Award for Favorite Male Television Performer (2002); Star, Hollywood Walk of Fame (2001); Golden Globe Award for Best Actor in TV Series, Hollywood Foreign Press Association (1996, 2000); Screen Actors Guild Award for Outstanding Performance by an Ensemble in a Comedy Series, SAG-AFTRA (2000); Emmy Award for Best Lead Actor in a Comedy Series, Academy of Television Arts & Sciences (1994, 1995, 1998); People's Choice Award for Favorite Male in a New Television Series (1994); Numerous Awards

GRANGER, NORVELL, "KAY" KAY, T: U.S. Representative from Texas **CN:** U.S. House of Representatives **DOB:** 01/18/1943 **PB:** Greenville **SC:** TX/USA **CH:** Three Children **ED:** Bachelor of Science, Texas Wesleyan University, Magna Cum Laude (1965); Honorary Doctor in Public Service, Tennessee Wesleyan College; Honorary Doctor of Humane Letters, Texas Wesleyan University **C:** Member, U.S. House of Representatives from Texas' 12th Congressional District, United States Congress (1997-Present); Vice Chair, House of Representatives Conference, United States Congress from Texas' 12th Congressional District (2007-2009); Mayor, Fort Worth, TX (1991-1995); City Councilwoman, Fort Worth, TX (1989-1991); Member, Private Industry Council, Fort Worth, TX (1988-1989); Member, Zoning Committee, Fort Worth, TX (1981-1989); Principal, Owner, Kay Granger & Associates; Principal, Owner, G&R Insurance Agency, Fort Worth, TX; Teacher, English and Journalism; Member, Committee on Appropriations **CIV:** Board of Visitors, United States Air Force Academy; Board of Trustees, Southwestern University, Georgetown, Texas; Member, United Methodist Church **CW:** Author, "What's Right About America?" (2006) **AW:** Brotherhood/Sisterhood Citation, The Multicultural Alliance, Fort Worth/Tarrant County Region (2006); National Association of Manufacturers Award (2006); Community Health Defender Award, National Association of Community Health Centers Inc. (2006); Inductee, Texas Women's Hall of Fame (1999); Named Distinguished Alumnus, Eastern Hills High School (1993); Inductee, Fort Worth Business Hall of Fame **MEM:** Board of Directors, East Fort Worth Business and Professional Association; Meadowbrook Business and Professional Women's Association; East Fort Worth Business and Professional Association; Sister Cities International; APA; East Area Council, Fort Worth Chamber of Commerce **PA:** Republican **RE:** Methodist

GRANNIS, WAYNE E., T: Judge **I:** Law and Legal Services **CN:** Cobb County Juvenile Court **MS:** Married **CH:** Two Children **ED:** JD, Georgia State University (2003); BA in Criminal Justice, Georgia State University (1989) **C:** Judge, Cobb County Government (2018-Present); Senior Assistant District Attorney, Cobb County Government (2017-Pres-

ent); Deputy District Attorney, Fulton County Government (2012-2017); Senior Assistant District Attorney, Fulton County Government (2007-2012); Child Advocate Attorney, Fulton County Government (2005-2007); Staff Attorney, Fulton County Government (2003-2005); Juvenile Probation Officer, Fulton County Government (1994-2003) **CIV:** Developed and Presented Program, LEAPS (Legal Education for Parents and Students Program), Local Schools; Volunteer, Boys to Men to Mentor Youth Program; Created, Specialty Court for Gang Prevention, RISING (Rebuild, Invest, Support, Integrate, Navigate, Graduate) **AW:** National Recognition for Being Distinguished for Gang Prevention **MEM:** Cobb County Bar Association; Georgia Bar Association; American Bar Association (ABA); The Phi Beta Kappa Society **BAR:** State Bar of Georgia **B/I:** From an early age, Judge Grannis had an interest in the law and became a parole officer upon graduating college. He became disenchanted with the system and took on a position as a juvenile probation officer to address the problems in criminogenic behavior at its inception. He was mentored by Juvenile Court Judge Sanford Jones, who brought him on as a staff attorney upon his graduation from law school. Judge Jones inspired Judge Grannis to become a patient and compassionate advocate for children and their families. **AV:** Reading; Playing golf; Hiking; Spending time with his family **THT:** Judge Grannis aims to be a kind, compassionate, and loving husband and father. He'd like to remain healthy and to continue learning and improving himself. He'd also like to remain aware of the developments in the field of child welfare law and to be a patient, compassionate, fair and attentive judge. Judge Grannis' motto is the Golden Rule, "Do unto others as you would have them do unto you."

GRANT, ELISABETH FRANZ, T: Elementary School Educator (Retired) **I:** Education/Educational Services **DOB:** 06/30/1931 **PB:** Hempstead Gardens **SC:** NY/USA **PT:** Carl Joseph Franz; Margaretha Laubner Franz **MS:** Widowed **SPN:** Robert Myron Grant (05/29/1954, Deceased 08/1990) **CH:** Sharon Clark; Cheryl Beach **ED:** BS in Education, SUNY Geneseo (1953) **CT:** Certified School Teacher, State of New York (1953) **C:** Kindergarten Teacher, York Central School District (1968-1993); First Grade Teacher, York Central School District (1960-1968); Kindergarten Teacher, Perry Elementary School (1955-1959); Fourth Grade Teacher, Perry Elementary School (1954-1955); Kindergarten Teacher, Plainedge School (1953-1954) **CR:** Moderator, Judge, Brainstormers (1995-1999) **CIV:** Member, Committee Advisory Panel, Arkema Plant, Piffard, NY (1999-Present); Public and Program Chairperson, York-Leicester Field Days (1995-Present); The Rochester Chorus (1993-2017); Song of the Lakes Sweet Adelines Chorus (1977-1992) **CW:** Author, Industry Publications; Author, Twelve Musical Plays for Children **AW:** Senior Citizen Of The Year (2008); Member, Rochester Chorus (2006); Contributions as Assistant Director, Genesee Valley Chorus (1990); Two-Time Winner, Sweet Adeline of the Year (1983) **MEM:** Genesee Valley Council of the Arts; National Warplane Museum; Livingston County RTA; Rochester Ski Club **MH:** Albert Nelson Marquis Lifetime Achievement Award **B/I:** Ms. Grant became involved in her profession because she has always enjoyed it. **AV:** Skiing; Golfing; Hiking; Gardening **RE:** Episcopalian

GRANTS, VALDIS, T: Engineering Manager **I:** Engineering **DOB:** 03/05/1942 **PB:** Liepaja **SC:** Latvia **PT:** Karlis Voldemars Grants; Meta Mudite (Grinvalds) Grants **MS:** Married **SPN:** Yvette Marie (Guhl) **CH:** Kristine Marie; Carl Raymond

(Deceased) **ED:** MS in Electrical Engineering, University of Michigan (1967); BS in Engineering Mathematics, University of Michigan (1965); BS in Science Engineering, University of Michigan (1964) **C:** Manager, Product Safety, Rockwell Automation, Mayfield Heights, OH (1995-2008); Engineer Manager, Allen-Bradley Co., Highland Heights, OH (1977-1995); Engineering Supervisor, Allen-Bradley Co., Highland Heights, OH (1976-1977); Senior Design Engineer, Allen-Bradley Co., Highland Heights, OH (1971-1976); Senior Design Engineer, Information Instruction, Inc., Ann Arbor, MI (1970-1971); Research Engineer, University of Michigan, Ann Arbor, MI (1965-1970) **CW:** Patentee in Field **MEM:** IEEE; American Society for Quality; Tau Beta Pi; Eta Kappa Nu; Phi Kappa Phi **MH:** Albert Nelson Marquis Lifetime Achievement Award **B/I:** Mr. Grants became involved in his profession because his dad was an engineer. When he came to this country at the age of 7, he did not know what he wanted to do. He really wanted to be an astronomer but his dad talked him out of it. He told him he would not be able to make a living out of that and engineering was the way to go. **AV:** Astronomy; Photography; Personal computers; Jogging; Reading

GRASSLEY, CHARLES, "CHUCK" ERNEST, T: U.S. Senator from Iowa **I:** Government Administration/Government Relations/Government Services **DOB:** 09/17/1933 **PB:** New Hartford **SC:** IA/USA **PT:** Louis Arthur Grassley; Ruth (Corwin) Grassley **MS:** Married **SPN:** Barbara Ann Speicher (1954) **CH:** Lee; Wendy; Robin; Michele; Jay **ED:** Postgraduate Coursework, The University of Iowa (1957-1958); MA in Political Science, University of Northern Iowa (1956); BA, University of Northern Iowa (1955) **C:** President, Pro Tempore, U.S. Senate (2019-Present); Chairman, U.S. Senate Committee on Finance (2003-2007, 2019-Present); Chairman, U.S. Senate Judiciary Committee (2015-Present); U.S. Senator from Iowa (1981-Present); Chairman, U.S. Senate Narcotics Caucus (2015-2019); Chairman, Congressional Joint Committee on Taxation (2005-2006); Chairman, U.S. Senate Special Committee on Aging (1997-2001); Member, U.S. House of Representatives from Iowa's Third District, United States Congress, Washington, DC (1975-1981); Iowa House of Representatives (1959-1975); Assembly Line Worker (1961-1971); Instructor, Political Science, Charles City College (1967-1968); Instructor, Political Science, Drake University (1962); Member, Sheet Metal Shearer (1959-1961); Farmer **AW:** Health Policy Hero Award, National Research Center for Women & Families (2009); National Energy Leadership Award, National Biodiesel Board (2003); Named Legislator of the Year, Biotechnology Industry Organization (2003); National Leadership Award, National Citizens' Coalition for Nursing Home Reform (2002); Patients' Champions Award, American Chiropractic Association (2001); Excellence in Public Service Award, American Academy of Pediatrics (2001); Bipartisan Hero Award, National Association of Pediatric Nurse Practitioners (2001); American Financial Leadership Award, Financial Services Roundtable (2001); Ester Peterson Senior Advocate Award, United Seniors Health Cooperative (2000); Excellence in Health Service Award, National Association of Community Health Centers (1998); Congressional Award, Community Anti-Drug Coalitions of America (1997) **MEM:** American Farm Bureau Federation; State Historical Society of Iowa; Cedar Falls Historical Society, Black Hawk County, Iowa; Masons; Pi Gamma Mu Honor Society; Kappa Delta Pi, International Honor Society in Education; Alpha Gamma Rho **PA:** Republican **RE:** Baptist

GRAUER, PETER, T: Chairman of the Board **I:** Financial Services **CN:** Bloomberg LP **PB:** Philadelphia **SC:** PA/USA **PT:** Frederick M. Grauer; Frances (Thacher) Graeur **MS:** Married **SPN:** Laura McCord **CH:** Three Children **ED:** Bachelor of Arts, University of North Carolina (1968) **C:** Chairperson, Bloomberg LP (2001-Present); Managing Director, Senior Partner, CSFB Private Equity (2002); Managing Director, Credit Suisse First Boston (2000-2002); Managing Director, Donaldson, Lufkin & Jenrette (1992-2000); Co-Chairperson, Founder, Grauer & Wheat Merchant Banking Partners (1989-1992); Founder, President, Treasurer, Chairperson, DLJ Merchant Banking Partners **CR:** Board of Directors, Glencore Xstrata Plc (2013-Present); Lead Independent Director, Davita Inc. (2003-Present); Board of Directors, Decisionone Holdings Corp. (1997-Present); Board of Directors, Davita Inc. (1994-Present); Board of Directors, Formica Corp. (1998-2001); Board of Directors, Bloomberg LP (1986) **CIV:** Chairperson Emeritus, Board of Directors, Big Apple Circus; President, Board of Trustees, Inner City Scholarship Fund, New York, NY; Trustee, Pomfret School **AW:** Peterson Business Award, Greenwich Library (2010); Papal Order of Merit

GRAVELY, WILLIAM, "WILL" BERNARD, T: Professor Emeritus **I:** Education/Educational Services **CN:** University of Denver **DOB:** 08/19/1939 **PB:** Pickens **SC:** SC/USA **PT:** W. Marvin Gravely; Artie L. (Hughes) Gravely **MS:** Married **SPN:** Mary Liles (03/14/1992) **CH:** Julie G. McAllister **ED:** Honorary Degree in the Humanities, Wofford College (2020); PhD, Duke University (1969); BD, Drew University, Magna Cum Laude (1964); BA in History, Wofford College, Magna Cum Laude (1961) **CT:** Licensed Preacher, Ordained Deacon and Elder, United Methodist Church (1958-1975) **C:** Professor Emeritus, University of Denver (2001-Present); Professor of Religious Studies, University of Denver (1987-2001); Director, Joint PhD Program with Iliff School of Theology and University Denver (1990-1993); Associate Professor, Department of Religion, University of Denver (1972-1987); Director of American Studies Undergraduate Program, University of Denver (1972-1975); Assistant Professor, Department of Religion, University of Denver (1968-1972) **CR:** Book Tour, SC, NC, and CO (2019); Organization of American Historians (2009); International Rebecca West Society (2007); Clemson and Furman Universities Conference on South Carolina Upstate (2007); American Society of Church History, Emory University Conference on Racial Violence (2003); Citadel Conference on Civil Rights Movement in South Carolina (2003); Parliament of the World's Religions, Cape Town, South Africa (1999); Core Curriculum Director, University of Denver (1990-1993); Furman University Symposium on Lynching of Willie Earle (1990); Institutional Representative, University of Denver on Rocky Mountain United Methodist Conference Board Higher Education (1988-1990); Director of National Endowment for the Humanities Curriculum Grant, University of Denver (1985-1988); Chair, Board, Campus Ministry, Rocky Mountain Conference (1971-1975); Presenter of Research, National and Regional, American Academy of Religion **CIV:** Precinct Committee Chairperson, Arapahoe County Democrats (2004-2019); Active Member, United Methodist Campus Ministries, Duke University and University of Denver (1964-2000); PTA University Park Elementary (1974-1981) **CW:** Author, "They Stole Him Out of Jail – Willie Earle, South Carolina's Last Lynching Victim" (2019); Author, "Race, Truth and Reconciliation in the US: Reflections on Desmond Tutu's Proposal," Journal of Religion Society (2001); Author, "You Must Not Kneel Here" [Richard Allen], Christian History (Christianity Today) (1999); Author, "Reliving SC's Last Lynching: Tessie Earle Robinson," SC Review (1997); Contributor, "Dialectic of Double-Consciousness in Black American Freedom Celebrations, 1808-63," Journal of Negro History (1982); Author, "Gilbert Haven, Methodist Abolitionist" (1973); Author, Articles, Reprints and Reviews on Abolitionism, African-American Religious History and Lynching to Professional Journals; Contributor, 11 Anthologies, Six Dictionaries and Five Encyclopedias **AW:** Research Editor for African American Religion Documents Collections, Lilly Foundation, Lilly Endowment, Inc. (1987-1993); Research Grant for "Memory and Violence" on the Willie Earle Lynching, Harry Frank Guggenheim Foundation (1988-1990); University Teachers Fellowship, National Endowment for the Humanities (1988-1989); Research Grant, American Council of Learned Societies (1981-1982); Ethnic Minorities Fellowship, National Endowment for the Humanities (1974-1975); Jesse Lee Prize, General Commission on Archives and History, United Methodist Church (1970); The Phi Beta Kappa Society (1961) **MEM:** American Academy of Religion (1968-2001); Co-chair, African American Religious History Group, American Academy of Religion (1985-1987); American Society of Church History; Society for Values in Higher Education; Organization American of Historians; Association for the Study of African American Life and History (ASALH) **MH:** Albert Nelson Marquis Lifetime Achievement Award **AS:** Though without access to college, both of Dr. Gravely's parents were valedictorians in their high school classes and were an intellectually curious couple. Small town Pickens, SC had networks of persons who mentored and supported the next generation. Dr. Gravely also had such in Lewis P. Jones at Wofford, H. Gordon Harland at Drew, H. Shelton Smith at Duke and James A. Kirk in Denver. Without classroom teaching experience during graduate school, he learned to teach introductory courses in American religious history and historiography, works of Walker Percy, "In the Steps of Thoreau," religion and sexuality and social justice movements. His engagement in interdisciplinary humanities collaborative team teaching occurred in the University of Denver's American Studies Program (1970-1981), NEH Core curriculum courses (1975-1980, 1985-1993) and the doctoral program of Religion and Social Change. **B/I:** Dr. Gravely went to theological school to become a pastor. Some faculty at Drew encouraged him to study to be a college professor. He ended up at Duke in 1964 and became a research assistant for a mentor there. The project he was conducting was related to the work Dr. Gravely was doing for his PhD dissertation which later became a book. Their work revolved around religion and social change dealing with race issues. He was then hired in the summer of 1967 by the Methodist board of education to work in Atlanta with the African American seminaries moving library materials from one facility to another. All of it documented African American religious history. Dr. Gravely spent the next 25 years in libraries and archives to identify further sources in Black American religious history and to bring such to mainstream scholarly focus. Dr. Gravely considers himself fortunate enough to become immersed in such studies despite being a blue-eyed, white, southern male. He learned the importance of passing over in other people's traditions and learning what you could from them. Dr. Gravely also recalls an African American woman named Ms. Beatrice Holiday, who would take care of him growing up. He had affectionate feelings for her and she taught him how to learn from, respect and treat others the way they want to be treated. **AV:** Staying alert to public issues; Genealogy; Walking dogs; Television and book mysteries; Sports on television **PA:** Democrat (1960-Present) **RE:** Episcopalian (1995-Present); Methodist **THT:** Surviving in a pandemic has taught Dr. Gravely how creative and generous people can be against the lure of the sovereign individual who lives in an ego bubble. It illustrates Reinhold Niebuhr's observation about how a value, of every individual, can house a defect that ironically promotes a detrimental outcome. He remains amazed at how corporate institutionalized evil can take ever new forms so that all struggles for justice must continually be renewed. Those who carry those banners illustrate a religious orientation taken from Jesus' appeal in Matthew 25 to attend to the needy, the hungry, the imprisoned, the stranger. Dr. Gravely's motto dating from 1961 comes from Niebuhr: "We must study the past not only because it shows us how finite we are, what creatures of our determinations, but we must also study the past to free ourselves for the future." Learning to trust intuition and synchronicity has given him delightful pleasures. Dr. Gravely is a birthright Methodist named after a local minister; his uncle, Horace Edward Gravely Sr., perished in the North Atlantic in February 1943 as an Army chaplain aboard the USS Henry Mallory. He is now Episcopalian.

GRAVES, GARRET NEAL, T: U.S. Representative from Louisiana **I:** Government Administration/ Government Relations/Government Services **CN:** U.S. House of Representatives **DOB:** 1/31/1972 **PB:** Baton Rouge **SC:** LA/USA **PT:** John Graves; Cynthia (Sliman) Graves **MS:** Married **SPN:** Carissa Vanderleest **CH:** Three Children **ED:** Coursework, American University, Washington, DC (1996); Coursework, Louisiana Tech University (1993-1995); Coursework, The University of Alabama, Tuscaloo, AL (1990-1991) **C:** Member, U.S. House of Representatives from Louisiana's Sixth Congressional District (2015-Present); Manager, Louisiana Coastal Protection and Restoration Authority (2008-2014); Legislative Aide, U.S. Senator David Vitter, Committee on Commerce, Science and Transportation (2005-2008); Member, Committee on Natural Resources; Member, Committee on Transportation; Member, Republican Study Committee; Aide, U.S. Representative Billy Tauzin; With, U.S. Senator John Breaux; Chief Legislative Aide, U.S. Senate Committee on Environment and Public Works **PA:** Republican

GRAVES, JOHN, "TOM" THOMAS JR., T: U.S. Representative from Georgia **I:** Government Administration/Government Relations/Government Services **DOB:** 02/03/1970 **PB:** St. Petersburg **SC:** FL/USA **MS:** Married **SPN:** Julie Howard (1996) **CH:** JoAnn; John; Janey **ED:** BBA in Finance, University of Georgia; Diploma, Coverdale Leadership Institute **C:** Member, U.S. House of Representatives from Georgia's 14th Congressional District, U.S. Congress (2013-2019); Member, U.S. House of Representatives from Georgia's Ninth Congressional District, U.S. Congress, Washington, DC (2010-2013); Member, District 12, Georgia House of Representatives (2005-2010); Member, District 10, Georgia House of Representatives (2003-2005); Member, Committee on Agriculture; Member, Committee on Education and the Workforce **CIV:** Active Member, Belmont Baptist Church, Calhoun, GA **AW:** Award, Ninth District Republican Party (2009); Award, American Legislative Exchange Council (2009); Named Legislator of the Year, Georgia Retail Association; Legislative Entrepreneur of the Year Award, FreedomWorks Foundation; Guardian of Small Business Award, National Federation of Independent Business **MEM:** American Legislative Exchange Council **PA:** Republican **RE:** Baptist

GRAVES, JOHN WILLIAM, T: Edgar and Margurite Henley Professor of American History **I:** Education/Educational Services **DOB:** 06/25/1942 **PB:** Little Rock **SC:** AK/USA **PT:** William A. Graves; Mabel (Morehart) Graves **ED:** Doctor of Philosophy in History, University of Virginia (1978); Master of Arts in History, University of Arkansas (1967); Bachelor of Arts in History, University Arkansas (1964); Diploma, Lions Township High School, La Grange, IL, Western Springs, IL (1960) **C:** Edgar and Margurite Henley Professor of American History, Henderson State University, Arkadelphia, AK (1985-Present); Chairman, Department of Social Science, Henderson State University, Arkadelphia, AK (2003-2015); College Assistance Migrant Program, Freshman Studies Coordinator, Basic Skills Specialist, Lecturer, St. Edward's University, Austin, TX (1979-1985); Instructor of History, Texas State University, San Marcos, TX (1972-1977); Research Assistant, University Virginia, Charlottesville, VA (1971-1972); Instructor of History, University of Louisiana at LaFayette (1966-1968); Graduate Teaching Assistant, University of Arkansas (1965-1966) **CR:** Representative, Department of Social Science Faculty Senate (2002-2003); Representative, School Liberal Arts Faculty Senate (1987-1988) **CIV:** Advisory Board Department, Arkansas Heritage Mosaic Templars Building Preservation Society (1993-Present); Board of Directors, Society for Preservation of Mosaic Templars of America; Builder, Hillcrest Residents Association, Little Rock, AK; Black History Commission, State of Arkansas **CW:** Author, "Town and Country: Race Relations in an Urban-Rural Context, Arkansas, 1865-1905" (1990); Contributor, Articles to Professional Journals **AW:** Distinguished Research Award, Henderson State University (2001-2002); Distinguished Service Award, Henderson State University (1999-2000); Commendation Award, American Association for the Study of State and Local History (1993); Arkansiana Award, Arkansas Library Association (1991); Philip Francis DuPont Fellowship, University of Virginia (1969-1971); Stonewall Jackson Memorial Fellowship, Arkansas History Commission (1965); Award of Commendation, American Association for the Study of State and Local History **MEM:** President of Chapter, American Association of University Professors (1999-2001); President, Arkansas Historical Association (1992-1996); Vice President, Arkansas Historical Association (1987-1992); President, Audubon Society, Bastrop County, Texas (1985); Graduate School Representative, University of Arkansas (1965-1966); President, Tau Kappa Epsilon (1964); Southern Historical Association; Arkansas Secretary of State, Arkansas History Council; Defenders of Wildlife; Arkansas Nature Conservancy; National Trust for Historical Preservation; Historic Preservation Alliance of Arkansas; Quapaw Quarter Association; Student Senator, University of Arkansas; Phi Alpha Theta, History Honor Society **MH:** Albert Nelson Marquis Lifetime Achievement Award

GRAVES, SAMUEL BRUCE JR., T: U.S. Representative from Missouri **I:** Government Administration/Government Relations/Government Services **DOB:** 11/07/1963 **PB:** Tarkio **SC:** MO/USA **PT:** Samuel Bruce Graves; Janice A. (Hord) Graves **MS:** Divorced **SPN:** Lesley Hickok (1986, Divorced 2012) **CH:** Three Children **ED:** BS in Agronomy, University of Missouri, Columbia, MO (1986) **C:** Ranking Member, House Transportation Committee (2019-Present); Member, U.S. House of Representatives from Missouri's Sixth Congressional District, United States Congress (2001-Present); Chairman, U.S. House Committee on Small Business (2011-2015); Member, District 12, Missouri State Senate (1995-2000); Member, District Four, Missouri House of Representatives (1993-1995) **AW:** Voice of Missouri Business Award, Associated Industries (1999); Missouri Physical Therapy Association Award (1997); Named Outstanding Young Farmer in U.S., Missouri Junior Chamber of Commerce (1996); Tarkio, Missouri Community Betterment Award (1995); Named Outstanding Young Farmer in the U.S., American Farm Bureau Federation (1991); Named Outstanding Young Farmer in Missouri, Missouri Farm Bureau (1990) **MEM:** American Farm Bureau Federation; Rotary International **PA:** Republican **RE:** Southern Baptist

GRAVINO, STACY, T: Town Clerk **I:** Government Administration/Government Relations/Government Services **CN:** Town of East Haven **DOB:** 04/16/1969 **PB:** New Haven **SC:** CT/USA **PT:** Frank Gravino; Beverly Gravino **ED:** BS in Biology, Albertus Magnus College (1991) **C:** Town Clerk, Town of East Haven, CT (2009-Present) **AW:** Paul Harris Award, Rotary International **MEM:** Rotary Club; East Haven Chamber of Commerce **AS:** Ms. Gravino attributes her success to having a good work ethic, having a drive, and the example her parents set. Her parents always made sure they treated people as they wanted to be treated and always helped others. She also enjoys working with the public and is passionate about the work she does. **B/I:** Ms. Gravino had been working in a laboratory setting for about 17 years before deciding that she needed a career change. The former town clerk was retiring, and Ms. Gravino was approached to put her name in as a candidate to run for town clerk. At first, she wasn't sure because she knew nothing about the job, but after some thought, she knew that she did want a career change, so she gave it a try. After finding out more about the position and the work the position entails, she realized how similar it was to her background in biology, especially in the aspect of analytics of various town statistics and filing of reports. **AV:** Reading; Relaxing; Spending time with her dog **THT:** Ms. Gravino lives by the motto, "She believed she could, so she did."

GRAY, GLENDA ELISABETH, MBBCH, T: President, Chief Executive Officer, Physician **I:** Medicine & Health Care **CN:** South African Medical Research Council **DOB:** 12/14/1962 **PB:** Boksburg **SC:** South Africa **MS:** Married **SPN:** Jacobus Kloppers **CH:** Three Children **ED:** Honorary Doctor of Law, Rhodes University (2019); Bachelor of Medicine, Bachelor of Surgery, Colleges of Medicine of South Africa; Diploma, University of the Witwatersrand **C:** President, Chief Executive Officer, South African Medical Research Council; Research Professor of Paediatrics, University of the Witwatersrand; Executive Director, Pediatric HIV Research Unit, Chris Hani Baragwanath Hospital; Co-founder, Perinatal HIV Clinic **CR:** Co-principal Investigator, HIV Vaccine Trails Network; Member, Vaccine and Infectious Disease Division, Fred Hutchinson Cancer Research Center **CW:** Contributor, Articles to Professional Journals **AW:** Named, One of Africa's 50 Most Influential People, Forbes Africa (2020); Named, One of the 100 Most Influential People, TIME Magazine (2017); Outstanding African Scientist Award, European and Developing Countries Clinical Trials Partnership (2013); Silver Award, Order of Mapungubwe (2010); Mandela Award for Health and Human Rights (2002); International Fogarty Fellowship (1999); Rated "A" Scientist, National Research Foundation; Named, One of the Icons of the Century, Longevity Magazine's Millennium Collectors Issue **MEM:** African Academy of Sciences (2015); Academy of Science of South Africa; Foreign Associate, National Academy of Medicine; Fellow, American Academy of Microbiology

GRAYSON, JULIA, T: Chief Executive Officer **I:** Business Management/Business Services **CN:** Grayson De Vere **CH:** Seven Children **ED:** Degree in Interior Architecture & Design, Inchbald School of Design, United Kingdom (2015); Degree in Interior Design, New York School of Interior Design (2010); BS in Business/Economics, Vanderbilt University, Nashville, TN (1982) **C:** Owner, Principal Design, Grayson De Vere, Greenwich, CT, East Hampton, NY (1998-Present); Retired, Investment Banker (1992) **CIV:** Board Member, American Red Cross **MEM:** Affiliate, American Society of Interior Designers **AS:** Ms. Grayson attributes her success to her love and passion for her work. She has great spacial awareness and loves to work with people. **B/I:** Ms. Grayson always wanted to be an Architect. Even as a child she was always interested in design and architecture. Her mother did not approve and told her she would be an investment banker, which she eventually became. She retired as an investment banker in 1992 while living in London. The first house that she owned was an estate outside of London, previously owned by John Lennon. While renovating the house she used it as an opportunity to study drafting and become more engaged in the process. She used it as her first design project and everyone loved the work that she did. People eventually began to spread the word, and would ask her to do projects for them before she decided to start her own interior design company in 1998.

GRBAC, NICHOLAS A., T: Broadcast Engineer **I:** Media & Entertainment **DOB:** 01/26/1957 **PB:** Cincinnati **SC:** OH/USA **PT:** Nick A. Grbac; Carol Myrtle (Thomson) Grbac **ED:** BA in Broadcast Communications Arts, San Francisco State University, Cum Laude (1979) **CT:** Society of Broadcast Engineers; Certified Broadcast Technician; Certified Television Operator **C:** Engineering Technician, Master Control Crew Chief, Station KRON-TV, San Francisco, CA (1984-Present); Videotape Engineer, Station KTLA-TV/Golden West Video Tape, Hollywood, CA (1983-1984); Vacation Relief Engineer, Station KRON-TV, San Francisco, CA (1983); Technical Director, Station KNTV, San Jose, CA (1982-1983); Master Control Engineer, Station KNTV, San Jose, CA (1981-1982); Air Operations Engineer, Station KGSC-TV, KICU-TV, San Jose, CA (1979-1981) **CW:** Publisher, Society of Broadcast Engineers (2015); Compiled, "Technical Orientation Manual" (1986); Co-Author, "Television Operations: A Handbook of Technical Operations for TV Broadcast, On Air, Cable, Mobile, and Internet" **MEM:** Broadcast Engineering and Operations Professionals; Film & TV Tech Professionals **MH:** Albert Nelson Marquis Lifetime Achievement Award; Marquis Who's Who Top Professional **B/I:** Mr. Grbac attended Jesuit College Preparatory High School, where he learned about standards and morals. As a child, he was always interested in how things worked versus how they appeared. Luckily, Mr. Grbac's high school had a small television department and he was able to take a class on how television media worked. Initially, he was going to study music in college, but he ultimately discovered a passion for television. Mr. Grbac then decided to attend a well-known college, San Francisco State University, and he majored in broadcasting programming. He then received a bachelor's degree in broadcasting communication of arts in 1979. **AV:** Spending time with dogs and animals; Listening to music; Collecting television nostalgia; Researching San Francisco history **PA:** Democrat **RE:** Roman Catholic

GRECIANO, SANDRA, T: Voice Educator **I:** Education/Educational Services **PB:** Malden **SC:** MA/USA **PT:** Fletcher Nichols Eames; Doris G. Rich **MS:** Widowed **SPN:** Anton D. Greciano

(12/21/1976, Deceased 09/11/2004); Alfons Faeh (Divorced) **CH:** Thomas J. Faeh **ED:** Coursework, Manhattan School of Music (1964); BFA in Opera Theater, Boston University (1960) **CT:** Certified, National Association of Teachers of Singing, Inc.; Certified, American Guild of Variety Artists; Certified, Actors' Equity Association **C:** Voice Coordinator, Point Park University, Pittsburgh, PA; Teaching Artist, Point Park University, Pittsburgh, PA; Performer, Equity Theater, New York, NY **CR:** Instructor, Juventis Institute, Zurich, Switzerland; Founder, Vocalist, Peterswood Trio, Pittsburgh, PA **AW:** Scholarship, Manhattan School of Music (1964); Scholarship, Boston University (1960) **MEM:** Chairman, Opera Workshop, Tuesday Musical Club (1983-1991); Producer, Opera Workshop, Tuesday Musical Club (1983-1991); President, Tuesday Musical Club (1987-1988); Pittsburgh Concert Society; National Association of Teachers of Singing; Tuesday Musical Club **MH:** Albert Nelson Marquis Lifetime Achievement Award; Marquis Who's Who Top Professional **B/I:** Ms. Greciano became involved in her profession because she wanted to sing. She studied piano first, but her friend told her about voice lessons. She found a voice teacher that would come to town once a week. He was a bel canto style teacher, which means he taught in the old style; the old style emphasized phrasing, expression, and vibrato. The teacher helped her to get a scholarship to the New England Conservatory of Music.

GREEN, ALEXANDER, "AL" N., T: U.S. Representative from Texas **I:** Government Administration/Government Relations/Government Services **DOB:** 09/01/1947 **PB:** New Orleans **SC:** LA/USA **ED:** JD, Texas Southern University Thurgood Marshall School of Law (1974); BA, Tuskegee Institute of Technology (Now Tuskagee University), AL; Coursework, Florida Agricultural and Mechanical University **C:** Member, U.S. House of Representatives from Texas' Ninth Congressional District, United States Congress (2005-Present); Justice of the Peace, Harris County, Texas (1977-2004); Founder, Managing Partner, Green, Wilson, Dewberry & Fitch, Houston, TX (1974) **CIV:** Past President, Houston Branch, NAACP **AW:** Named One of the 100 Most Influential Black Americans, Ebony Magazine (2006); Named to the Power 150 (2008); Mickey Leland Humanitarian Award, NAACP (2006); Citation for Service, American Federation of Teachers (1983); Outstanding Leadership Award, Black Heritage Society (1981); Distinguished Service Award, Houston Citizens Chamber of Commerce (1978) **MEM:** Alpha Phi International **PA:** Democrat **RE:** Baptist

GREEN, CEELO, T: Singer, Songwriter, Record Producer **I:** Media & Entertainment **DOB:** 5/30/1975 **PB:** Atlanta **SC:** GA/USA **PT:** Sheila J. Tyler-Callaway **MS:** Divorced **SPN:** Christina Johnson (2000, Divorced 2005) **CH:** Kingston; Sierra (Stepdaughter); Kalah (Stepdaughter) **C:** Solo Artist, Member, Gnarls Barkley (2006-Present); Member, Goodie Mob (1991-1998) **CW:** Contestant, "The Masked Singer," United Kingdom Version (2020); Contestant, "Lip Sync Battle" (2016); Singer with Goodie Mob, "Heart Blanche" (2015); Reality TV Personality, "CeeLo Green's The Good Life" (2014); Singer, "Cee-Lo's Magic Moment" (2012); Voice Actor, "Hotel Transylvania" (2012); Singer, "Cee-Lo Green...Is Everybody's Brother" (2012); Vocal Coach, Judge, "The Voice" (2011-2013); Singer with Melanie Fiona, "Fool for You" (2011); Singer, "The Lady Killer" (2011); Singer, "Forget You!" (2010); Singer with Gnarls Barkley, "The Odd Couple" (2008); Singer, "Run" (2008); Singer with Gnarls Barkley, "St. Elsewhere" (2006); Singer, "Crazy" (2006); Singer, "Smiley Faces" (2006); Singer,

"Art of Noise: The Best of Cee-Lo" (2006); Singer, "Closet Freak: The Best of Cee-Lo Green the Soul Machine" (2006); Singer "Cee-Lo Green...Is the Soul Machine" (2004); Singer, "Cee-Lo Green & His Perfect Imperfections" (2002); Singer with Goodie Mob, "World Party" (1999); Singer with Goodie Mob, "Still Standing" (1998); Singer with Goodie Mob, "Soul Food" (1995); Appearances, Television Shows **AW:** Grammy Awards for Best R&B Song, Best Traditional R&B Vocal Performance, The Recording Academy (2012); Grammy Award for Best Urban/Alternative Performance, The Recording Academy (2011); Named Best International Male, BRIT Awards (2011); Awards for Best Art Direction, Best Choreography, MTV Video Music Awards (2008); Grammy Award for Best Urban/Alternative Performance, The Recording Academy (2007); Grammy Award for Best Alternative Music Album, The Recording Academy (2007); Award for Best Editing, MTV Video Music Awards (2007); Award (with Gnarls Barkley) for Best Group, BET Awards (2007); Ranked Number One, Top 50 Songs of the Decade, Rolling Stone Magazine (2000–2009); Numerous Awards

GREEN, JOHN MICHAEL, T: Author; Vlogger **I:** Writing and Editing **DOB:** 08/24/1977 **PB:** Indianapolis **SC:** IN/USA **PT:** Michael Green; Sydney Green **MS:** Married **SPN:** Sarah Urist (05/21/2006) **CH:** Two Children **ED:** BA in English and Religious Studies, Kenyon College (2000) **C:** Co-Creator, VidCon (2010-Present); Vlogger, Numerous Videos, YouTube (2007-Present); Production Editor, NPR; Former Contributor, "All Things Considered," NPR; Former Contributor, WBEZ Public Radio; Book Critic, The New York Times Book Review; Publishing Assistant, Production Editor, Booklist; Student Chaplain, Nationwide Children's Hospital, Columbus, OH **CIV:** Co-Founder, Life's Library Book Club (2018-Present); Co-Creator, Project for Awesome, YouTube (2007-Present) **CW:** Host, "The Anthropocene Reviewed" (2018-Present); Co-Host, "Dear Hank & John" (2015-Present); Co-Creator, "Crash Course" (2012-Present); Co-Creator, Video Blogs, "Brotherhood 2.0," "Vlogbrothers," YouTube (2007-Present); Host, "Mental Floss," YouTube (2013-2018); Author, "Turtles All the Way Down" (2017); Author, "The Fault in Our Stars" (2012); Author, "Double on Call and Other Short Stories" (2012); Author, "Reasons" (2011); Author, "Will Grayson, Will Grayson" (2010); Author, "Freek the Geak" (2009); Author, "Let it Snow: Three Holiday Romances" (2008); Author, "The Great American Morp" (2007); Author, "The Approximate Cost of Loving Caroline" (2006); Author, "An Abundance of Katherines" (2006); Author, "Looking for Alaska" (2005); Vlogger, Videos, YouTube; Producer, Podcasts, Numerous Videos and Films **AW:** Visionary Award, MTVU Fandom Awards (2014); Los Angeles Times Book Prize, Innovator Award (2013); Children's Choice Book Award (2013); Indiana Authors Award (2012); Corine Literature Prize (2010); Edgar Allan Poe Award (2009); Michael L. Printz Award, American Library Association (2006); Listee, Top 10 Best Books for Teens (2005)

GREEN, KIRSTEN, T: Venture Capitalist **I:** Financial Services **CN:** Forerunner Ventures **PB:** San Francisco **SC:** CA/USA **ED:** Bachelor of Arts in Business Economics, University of California Los Angeles (1993) **CT:** CPA; CFA **C:** General Partner/Founder, Forerunner Ventures (2010-Present); Advisor, TSG Consumer Partners (2009-2010); Equity Research Analyst, Bank of America (1998-2002); Associate, Donaldson, Lufkin & Jenrette (1996-1997); Senior Accountant, CPA, Deloitte and Touche (1993-1996) **CR:** Angel Investor and Independent Consultant (2003-2009) **CIV:** Board of Directors, Curated (2019-Present); Board of

Directors, Modern Fertility (2019-Present); Board of Directors, The Yes (2018-Present); Board of Directors, Faire (2018-Present); Board of Directors, Prose (2017-Present); Board of Directors, Ritual (2015-Present); Board of Directors, INTURN (2014-Present); Board of Directors, ReSci (2013-Present); Board of Directors, Glossier Inc. (2013-Present); Board of Directors, Bonobos (2012-2017); Board of Directors, Dollar Shave Club (2012-2016) **AW:** Named, Time 100 (2017)

GREEN, MARK EDWARD, MD, T: U.S. Representative from Tennessee; Physician **I:** Government Administration/Government Relations/Government Services **DOB:** 11/08/1964 **PB:** Jacksonville **SC:** FL/USA **MS:** Married **SPN:** Camie Green **CH:** Two Children **ED:** Honorary HHD, Williamson College, Franklin, TN (2015); MD, Wright State University; MA, University of Southern California; BS in Quantitative Business Management, United States Military Academy at West Point (1986) **C:** Member, U.S. House of Representatives from Tennessee's Seventh Congressional District (2019-Present); Member, 22nd District, Tennessee Senate (2012-Present); Founder, Chief Executive Officer, Align MD **CR:** Board Member, American Physician Partners, LLC; Board Member, Align MD; Board Member, Rural Physician Partners **CIV:** Member, Advisory Board, Latinos for Tennessee (2015-Present); Board Member, Middle Tennessee Council, Boy Scouts of America **MIL:** Advanced through Grades to Major, United States Army (1986-2006) **CW:** Author, "A Night With Saddam" (2011) **AW:** Bronze Star; Meritorious Service Medal; Army Commendation Medal; Army Achievement Medal; Two Air Medals with Valor; Combat Medical Badge; Air Assault Badge; Flight Surgeon Badge; Ranger Tab; Senior Parachutist Badge **PA:** Republican

GREENBERG, ARLINE, T: Artist **I:** Fine Art **PB:** New York **SC:** NY/USA **PT:** Yetta (Teller) Skolnick **MS:** Married **SPN:** Sidney Greenberg **ED:** AS, Parsons School for Design, The New School, New York, NY; Coursework, Pratt Institute, New York, NY; Postgraduate Coursework, New York University; BA in Art and Design, Hunter College; Coursework in Fabrics, Beading and Draping, Fashion Institute of Technology **CT:** Six-month Coursework on Technical Information on Fabric, The City College of New York **C:** Fashion Director, Burlington Klopman Fabrics, New York, NY (1988-1992); Vice President, Reliable Textile Co., New York, NY; Independent Practice Consultant, Firm in Jewelry and Design **CR:** Cohn-Hall-Marx Division, United Merchants & Manufacturers, Inc. (1959-1972); Cohama Division, United Merchants & Manufacturers, Inc.; Guest Lecturer, Hunter College **CIV:** Preservation Society; The Metropolitan Museum of Art; Smithsonian Institution; Metropolitan Opera Guild; Citizens Union; Frick Museum (The Frick Collection) **CW:** Contributor, Articles, Newspapers **AW:** Medal in Fine Arts; Scholar, New York University; Named, Yearly Forecaster of Color, Color Association of the US **MEM:** Metropolitan Chapter, Victorian Society in America; Color Association of the US **MH:** Albert Nelson Marquis Lifetime Achievement Award **B/I:** Mrs. Greenberg became involved in her profession because she got her start in public school. Although her mother, Yetta Skolnick, wanted her to be a teacher, she is a very free spirit and decided to go into art and design. She received a Bachelor's from Hunter College and from there did her postgraduate work at New York University. She also attended Parsons School of Design and Pratt Institute. At some point, she started an independent practice consultant firm in jewelry and design and worked her way up to Fashion Director of Burlington Klopman Fabrics in New York City. **AV:** Travel; Art; Architecture; Opera; Attending Julliard classes; Drawing the figure for about 30 years

GREENBERG, DONNA, T: Associate Professor of Psychiatry **I:** Education/Educational Services **CN:** Harvard Medical School **ED:** MD, University of Rochester School of Medicine & Dentistry (1975); BA in Psychology, Cornell University (1971); Residency, Boston Medical Center; Residency, Massachusetts General Hospital **CT:** Internal Medicine; Psychiatry **C:** Associate Professor of Psychiatry, Harvard Medical School (1999-Present) **AW:** Various Teaching Awards **MEM:** Academy of Consultation-Liaison Psychiatry; The American Psychiatric Association College of Physicians; The Association of Medicine and Psychiatry; American Society of Psychosocial Oncology (Now American Psychosocial Oncology Society (APOS)) **AS:** Dr. Greenberg attributes her success to good teachers. **B/I:** Dr. Greenberg is trained as an internist and psychiatrist. Bringing the knowledge of psychiatry to the care of medical patients has been her mission.

GREENBERG, LILLIAN, T: Elementary School Educator (Retired) **I:** Education/Educational Services **DOB:** 05/09/1924 **PB:** Philadelphia **SC:** PA/USA **PT:** Solomon Simons; Florence (Bloom) Simons **MS:** Married **SPN:** William Greenberg (06/20/1948) **CH:** Janet Ellen; Michael Robert **ED:** MA in Teaching, William Paterson College, Wayne, NJ (1967); BA, Hunter College, New York, NY (1945) **C:** Elementary Teacher, Upper Saddle River Board of Education **CIV:** Chair of Fundraising and Hospitality, Friends of the New Milford Public Library (1980-2006) **AW:** New Jersey Governor's Award for Outstanding Teaching (1987) **MEM:** Bergen County Retired Education Association; New Jersey Education Association; National Education Association; Kappa Delta Pi **MH:** Albert Nelson Marquis Lifetime Achievement Award

GREENE, BRIAN, T: President, Chief Executive Officer **I:** Financial Services **CN:** Houston Food Bank **ED:** Master of Arts in Economics, University of Tennessee-Knoxville **C:** President, Chief Executive Officer, Houston Food Bank (2005-Present); Executive Director, Second Harvest Food Bank of Greater New Orleans and Acadiana (1993-2005); Executive Director, Second Harvest Food Bank of East Tennessee (1988-1993)

GREENE, CHRISTINE ELIZABETH, T: Artist **I:** Fine Art **CN:** Caricatures by Chris Greene **DOB:** 03/29/1945 **PB:** Chelm **SC:** Poland **PT:** Stanley Lipert; Irene (Gering) Lipert **MS:** Married **SPN:** Stephen M. Greene (1974) **CH:** Valerie I. **ED:** Coursework, Art Students League of New York (1976); Bachelor of Fine Arts, Moore College of Art and Design (1968); Diploma, Newark School of Fine and Industrial Arts (1965) **C:** Owner, Caricatures by Chris Greene (1983-Present); Party Caricaturist, Syosset, NY (1981-Present); Textile Designer, Schwartz & Liebman Textiles, New York, NY (1970-1977); Textile Designer, Jos H. Lowenstein & Sons, New York, NY (1969-1970) **CR:** Contributor, Metropolitan Museum of Art, New York, NY (1989-Present); Contributor, Smithsonian Institution, Washington, DC (1982-Present); Contributor, Public TV, Channel 13, WLIW21 **CIV:** Saint Edward the Confessor Church, Syosset, NY **CW:** Illustrator, "The Story of Us" (2020); Group Show, AARP Artists 50+ Exhibit at Islip Art Museum, Islip NY (2019); Solo Show, b. j. spoke gallery, "Figurations" (2019); Group Show, "Art of the Figure," Gallery North, Setauket, NY (2012); Illustrator, "French Fries for Siblings: The Forgotten Children of Autism" (2009); Artist, Various Figurative Paintings **AW:** Honorable Mention, "A Quotidian Life - Finding Beauty

in the Ordinary," Art League of Long Island, Dix Hills, NY (2017); Charles Merendino Memorial Award, Suburban Art League (2017); Certificate of Excellence, Holbein Inc., Independent Art Society (2016); Award of Merit, Suburban Art League (2016); Award of Excellence, Emily and Ira L. Waxberg Memorial Award, Suburban Art League (2015); Award of Excellence, Suburban Art League (2013); Award of Excellence, Huntington Township Art League (1983); Award of Excellence, Channel 21 Art Show (1982); Art Award, Grumbacker Art Supplies (1981) **MEM:** Independent Art Society, Plainview, NY; Suburban Art League, Syosset, NY; National League of American Pen Women; B.J. Spoke Gallery, Huntington, NY **MH:** Albert Nelson Marquis Lifetime Achievement Award; Marquis Who's Who Top Professional **AS:** Ms. Greene attributes her success to her belief in God, one's self, hard work and perseverance. **B/I:** From a young age, Ms. Greene knew that she wanted to be an artist, so she pursued it all her life. She has been a textile designer, portrait artist, fine artist and caricature artist for parties and events. **AV:** Gardening; Painting **PA:** Republican **RE:** Roman Catholic

GREENE, CYNTHIA, T: Of Counsel **I:** Law and Legal Services **CN:** Young, Berman, Karpf & Karpf, P.A. **MS:** Single **ED:** JD, University of Miami School of Law (1979); BA, University of Miami, Cum Laude (1975) **C:** Of Counsel, Young, Berman, Karpf & Karpf, P.A. **BAR:** Marital and Family Law, Board of Legal Specialization and Education, The Florida Bar; Licensed to Practice, Supreme Court of the United States; American Academy of Matrimonial Lawyers **MH:** Marquis Who's Who Top Professional **AS:** Ms. Greene believes if you want to be successful you need to put in the work and the effort. **B/I:** Ms. Greene had a journalism degree and wanted to be able to write. She heard if you had a law degree you are able to write things, such as briefs. She thought that it was a good idea.

Greengard, Paul, T: Neuroscientist, Educator **I:** Sciences **DOB:** 12/11/1925 **PB:** New York **SC:** NY/USA **ED:** Doctor of Philosophy in Biophysics, Johns Hopkins University, Baltimore, MD (1953); Bachelor of Arts in Mathematics and Physics, Hamilton College, Clinton, NY (1948) **C:** Director, Fisher Center for Alzheimer's Disease Research, Rockefeller University, New York, NY (1995-Present); Vincent Astor Professor, Laboratory of Molecular & Cellular Neuroscience, Rockefeller University, New York, NY (1983-Present); Professor of Pharmacology and Psychiatry, Yale University School of Medicine, New Haven, CT (1968-1983); Director of Biochemistry, Geigy Research Laboratories, Ardsley, NY (1959-1967); Visiting Scientist, National Heart Institute, National Institutes of Health (1958-1959); Fellow, National Institute of Neurological Diseases & Blindness, National Institutes of Health, Bethesda, MD (1956-1958); Paraplegia Foundation Fellow, National Institute of Medical Research, England (1955-1956); March of Dimes Fellow, Molteno Institute, Cambridge University, England (1954-1955); National Science Foundation Fellow in Neurochemistry, Institute of Psychiatry, University London (1953-1954) **CR:** Andrew D. White Professor at Large, Cornell University, Ithaca, NY (1981); Visiting Associate Professor of Pharmacology, Albert Einstein College of Medicine, New York, NY (1961-1970); Visiting Professor, Vanderbilt University, Nashville, TN (1967-1968); Board of Scientific Governors, Scripps Research Institute, La Jolla, CA **CIV:** Co-founder, Pearl Meister Greengard Prize, Annual Award for Women Scientists; Board of Directors, Michael Stern Parkinson's Research Foundation **AW:** Nobel Prize in Physiology and Medicine, The Nobel Foundation (2000); Senior Scholar Award, Ellison Medical Foundation (1999);

Award for Medical Research, Metropolitan Life Foundation (1998); Mayor's Award for Excellence in Science and Technology, New York, NY (1998); Award for Pioneering Achievements in Health, Charles A. Dana Foundation (1997); Thudichum Medal, Biochemical Society (1996); Lieber Prize, National Alliance for Research on Schizophrenia and Depression (1996); Gerard Prize, Society of Neuroscience (1994); Karl Spencer Lashley Prize, American Philosophical Society (1993); Goodman & Gilman Award in Receptor Pharmacology (1992); Bristol-Myers Award for Distinguished Achievement in Neuroscience Research (1989); 3M Life Sciences Award, Federation of American Societies for Experimental Biology (1987); Award in Biology & Medical Sciences, New York Academy of Sciences (1980); Ciba-Geigy Drew Award (1979); Dickson Prize & Medal in Medicine, University of Pittsburgh (1977) **MEM:** National Academy of Sciences, National Alliance for Research on Schizophrenia and Depression; Society of Neuroscience; American Association for the Advancement of Science; American Neurological Association

GREENHOUSE, LINDA JOYCE, T: Knight Distinguished Journalist-in-residence, Joseph M. Goldstein Lecturer in Law **I:** Education/Educational Services **CN:** Yale Law School **DOB:** 01/09/1947 **PB:** New York **SC:** NY/USA **PT:** Herman Robert Greenhouse; Dorothy Eleanor (Greenlick) Greenhouse **MS:** Married **SPN:** Eugene R. Fidell (01/01/1981) **CH:** Hannah Margalit **ED:** Honorary LLD, The Pennsylvania State University (2011); Honorary LLD, University of Hartford (2009); Honorary LLD, Roger Williams University (2008); Honorary LLD, Skidmore College (2007); Honorary LLD, Georgetown University (2004); Honorary LLD, University of Miami (2004); Honorary LLD, City University of New York (1997); Honorary LLD, Northeastern University (1997); Honorary LLD, Colgate University (1993); Honorary DHL, Binghamton University (2006); Honorary DHL, Brown University (1991); LLM, Yale University (1978); BA, Radcliffe College (1968) **C:** Knight Distinguished Journalist-in-residence, Joseph Goldstein Lecturer in Law, Yale Law School (2009-2015); Supreme Court Correspondent, The New York Times, Washington, DC (1988-2008); Congressional Correspondent, The New York Times, Washington, DC (1986-1988); Supreme Court Correspondent, The New York Times, Washington, DC (1978-1985); State Political Reporter, The New York Times, New York, NY (1974-1977); Metropolitan Reporter, The New York Times, New York, NY (1970-1974); Assistant to James Reston, The New York Times, New York, NY (1968-1969) **CR:** Fellow, American Academy of Arts and Sciences **CIV:** Board of Overseers, Harvard University (2009-2015); Schlesinger Library Council, Radcliffe Institute for Advanced Study, Harvard University (2003-2009); Advisory Committee, Schlesinger Library on the History of Women in America, Radcliffe Institute for Advanced Study, Harvard University (1995-2002); Board of Directors, Yale Law School Fund, New Haven, CT (1984-1991) **CW:** Co-author, "The U.S. Supreme Court: A Very Short Introduction" (2012); Co-author, "Before Roe V. Wade: Voices That Shaped the Abortion Debate Before the Supreme Court's Ruling" (2010); Author, "Becoming Justice Blackmun: Harry Blackmun's Supreme Court Journey" (2005) **AW:** Constitution Project Annual Award (2008); Matrix Award, New York Women in Communications, Inc. (2008); Award of Merit, Yale Law School Association (2007); Medal, Radcliffe Institute for Advanced Study, Harvard University (2006); Medal of Distinction, Barnard College (2006); William Green Award for Professional Excellence, University of Richmond School of Law (2005); Anvil of Freedom Award, Estlow International Center for Journalism and New Media, University of Denver (2005); John Chancellor Award for Excellence in Journalism (2004); President's Special Award, New York Women's Bar Association (2004); Goldsmith Career Award, John F. Kennedy School of Government, Harvard University (2004); Golden Pen Award, Legal Writing Institute (2002); Henry J. Friendly Medal, American Law Institute (2002); Carey McWilliams Award, American Political Science Association (2002); Pulitzer Prize in Journalism for Beat Reporting (1998) **MEM:** Vice President, The American Philosophical Society (2013-Present); Board of Directors, The American Philosophical Society (2009-Present); Senate, The Phi Beta Kappa Society (2009-Present); Council, American Academy of Arts & Sciences (2004-Present); Council, The American Philosophical Society (2009-2013); Visiting Scholar, The Phi Beta Kappa Society (2004-2006); Vice President, Women's Forum of Washington, DC (Now International Women's Forum) (2003-2005); Honorary Member, American Law Institute; Executive Committee, Yale Law Association (1993-1997); Board of Directors, Harvard Club of Washington (1989-1992) **MH:** Albert Nelson Marquis Lifetime Achievement Award

GREENSTEIN, SCOTT, T: President, Chief Content Officer **I:** Technology **CN:** Sirius XM Radio Inc. **ED:** JD, George Washington University; BA, Tulane University **C:** President, Chief Content Officer for Entertainment and Sports, Sirius XM Radio Inc., New York, NY (2004-Present); Chairman, USA Films, New York, NY (1999-2004); Co-President, October Films (1997-1999); Senior Vice President, Motion Pictures, Music, New Media and Publishing, Miramax Films, New York, NY (1993-1997); Vice President, Law Department, Viacom International, Inc., New York, NY (1992-1993); Attorney, Viacom Entertainment, New York, NY (1989-1992); Attorney, Loeb & Loeb, LLP, Los Angeles, CA (1987-1989); Attorney, Cahill Gordon & Reindel LLP, New York, NY (1984-1987) **AW:** Power 100, Billboard (2019); First Knight, Royal Order of the Polar Star, King of Sweden (2009); Honoree, LIFEbeat (2006)

GREGG, ROSALIE, T: Social Service Agency Administrator **I:** Social Work **DOB:** 09/17/1920 **PB:** Hayden **SC:** NM/USA **PT:** John Patterson Mann; Lona Estella (Butler) Mann **SPN:** Robert Nolen Gregg (12/16/1945) **CH:** Sherry Lynn Gregg Harris; Marsha Jill Gregg Eder; Robbie Zane Gregg Weaver; Dana Rene Gregg Brooks **ED:** Coursework, Decatur Baptist Junior College (1942) **C:** Adoption Investigator, Wise County (1982-1990); Administrative Assistant, Wise County Council on Alcoholism, Decatur, TX (1976-1984); Secretary, Decatur Chamber of Commerce (1968-1975); Insurance Clerk, Allied Insurance Agency, Decatur, TX (1965-1968); Secretary, Government of Wise County (1957-1965); Secretary, Texas Department Public Welfare (1945-1957); Secretary, Office Price Administration (1940-1944) **CR:** Chairman, Wise County Historical Commission (1964-2014); Treasurer, Wise County Historical Society Inc., Wise County Historical Commission; Executive Director, Wise County Heritage Museum **CIV:** Executive Director, Wise County Historical Society (1970-Present); Secretary, Annual Meetings, Lost Battalion and U.S. Ship Houston CA30 (1954-2015); Chairman, Wise County Historical Commission (1964-2014); Chairman, Family Living Department; Pioneer, District Women's Clubs; Secretary-Treasurer, Wise County Little Theater Guild; Pleasant Grove Cemetery Association **CW:** Editor, "History of Wise County, A Link with the Past, Vol. 1" (1975); Editor, "Do You Know About Wise County" (1965); Contributor, Monthly Historical Newsletter **AW:** Decatur Woman of the Year (1987); Woman of the Year, Decatur Chamber of Commerce (1986); DAR

Preservationist of the Year **MEM:** Military Order of Purple Heart; DAV Auxiliary; Texas Historical Foundation; Texan Museum; Secretary-Treasurer, American Legion Auxiliary; Past President, Decatur Woman's Club; Treasurer, AARP **MH:** Albert Nelson Marquis Lifetime Achievement Award **B/I:** Ms. Gregg got involved in her field after completing her college education. When she got an opportunity to work for the government of Wise Country as a secretary, she took it. In the years since then, her career has progressed naturally. **PA:** Democrat **RE:** Methodist

GREGORY, DOROTHY ALICE L., T: Critical Care Nurse **I:** Medicine & Health Care **DOB:** 02/13/1946 **PT:** Willie Heyward Love; Millie Mae (Robertson) Love **MS:** Married **SPN:** Thomas C. Gregory (09/18/1969) **CH:** John Clyburn Gregory **ED:** AS in Nursing, University of South Carolina (1967); Coursework, Columbia College, SC (1965) **CT:** Certified Critical Care Registered Nurse; Certified Advanced Cardiac Life Support Instructor; Certified Basic Life Support Instructor **C:** Nursing Educator, Administrative Assistant to Chief Nursing Officer, Springs Memorial Hospital, Lancaster, SC (1998-2003); Home Care Giver to Mother (1996-1997); Critical Care Nurse Manager of Intensive Care Unit, Medical Surgical Nurse Manager, Acting Chief Nursing Officer, Springs Memorial Hospital, Lancaster, SC (1996); Critical Care Nurse Manager of Intensive Care Unit, Medical Surgical Nurse Manager, Springs Memorial Hospital, Lancaster, SC (1995); Acting Director of Nursing, Elliott White Springs Hospital, Lancaster, SC (1994); Critical Care Nurse Manager of Intensive Care Unit and Emergency Room, Elliott White Springs Hospital, Lancaster, SC (1992-1994); Head Nurse of Intensive Care Unit, Elliott White Springs Hospital, Lancaster, SC (1972-1992); Staff Nurse of Intensive Care Unit, Elliott White Springs Hospital, Lancaster, SC (1967-1972) **CR:** Poster Presenter, National Teaching Institute for Critical Care, Atlanta, GA (1994) **CW:** Developer, Critical Care Nurse Skills Assessment Plan and Practice Lab, Springs Memorial Hospital, Lancaster, SC (1994) **MEM:** American Association of Critical-Care Nurses **MH:** Albert Nelson Marquis Lifetime Achievement Award **B/I:** Mrs. Gregory went into nursing because she played nurse with her dolls as a little girl; she would pretend to stick needles in their arms as a nurse would. As a child, Mrs. Gregory's oldest brother contracted polio at 14 months. He would go on to have multiple surgeries until he was 15-years-old. She would watch her brother go through this and would go to the hospital to see him. Mrs. Gregory wanted to give back to the profession that helped her brother regain the use of his legs. Many of her family members have gone into the medical field. **AV:** Cooking; Entertaining; Flower arranging; Interior decorating; Making cards **RE:** Southern Baptist

GREGORY, JACKIE S., FNP, T: Family Nurse Practitioner **CN:** Texas Tech University Health Sciences Center (TTUHSC) **DOB:** 11/26/1946 **PB:** Amarillo **SC:** Texas/USA **PT:** Albert Ray Horner; Rosa Inez (Bryson) Horner **MS:** Divorced **CH:** Larry; Paula; Justin **ED:** MSN, West Texas A&M University (1997); BSN, West Texas A&M University (1989) **CT:** RN-APN, State of Texas; Certified Family Nurse Practitioner **C:** PCP, Texas Tech University Health Science Center (TTUHSC) Correctional Health (2014-Present); PCP, The University of Texas Medical Branch at Galveston Correctional Medical (2001-2013); HIV Coordinator, Dallas County Inmate Health Services (1999-2001); Charge Nurse Practitioner, Case Manager, Community Neighborhood Clinic (1998-1999); Charge Nurse, Case Manager, Coalition of Health Services Inc. (1997-1998); Charge Nurse, Case Manager, South Plains Health

Provider, Amarillo, Texas (1996-1997); Administrator, Angel Home Health Inc., Malakoff, Texas (1995-1996); Administrator, Associates Home Health Inc., Jacksonville, Texas (1994-1995); Staff Nurse, Vascular ICU, Baylor University Medical Center, Dallas, Texas (1991-1993) **CR:** Part-time Primary Care, Special Health Resources, East Texas (2002-2004); Cameron Clinical Instructor, Cameron University, Lawton, OK (1990-1993) **CIV:** VA Hospital, Dallas, Texas (1989-1991); Volunteer, Hospice Program, Visiting Nurse Association of America (VNAA) (1989-1990) **CW:** Contributor, Articles to Professional Journals **AW:** U.S. Public Health Service Scholar (1988-1989) **MEM:** Sigma Theta Tau International Honor Society of Nursing **MH:** Albert Nelson Marquis Lifetime Achievement Award **B/I:** Mrs. Gregory has always been scientifically oriented; she had the opportunity to help people and combine science with it, and that appealed to her. She liked people so it was the perfect opportunity to mix science and her love for people to become something that came naturally to her. **THT:** Mrs. Gregory's motto is, "Do the best you can at whatever you are doing. Always be honest."

GREGORY, ROGER LEE, T: Chief Judge **I:** Law and Legal Services **CN:** United States Court of Appeals for the Fourth Circuit **DOB:** 07/17/1953 **PB:** Philadelphia **SC:** PA/USA **PT:** George Lee Gregory; Fannie Mae (Washington) Gregory **MS:** Married **SPN:** Carla Eugenia (Lewis) (09/06/1980) **CH:** Adriene Leigh; Rachel Leigh **ED:** JD, University of Michigan Law School (1978); BA, Virginia State University, Summa Cum Laude (1975) **C:** Chief Judge, United States Court of Appeals for the Fourth Circuit, Richmond, VA (2016-Present); Judge, United States Court of Appeals for the Fourth Circuit, Richmond, VA (2001-2016); Managing Partner, Chairman, Litigation Secretary, Wilder & Gregory (Now Harrell & Chambliss LLP), Richmond, VA (1982-2001); Associate Attorney, Hunton & Williams (Hunton Andrew Kurth), Richmond, VA (1980-1982); Associate Attorney, Butzel, Long, Gust, Klein & Van Zile (Now Butzel Long), Detroit, MI (1978-1980) **CR:** Board of Visitors, Virginia Commonwealth University, Richmond, VA (1985-Present); Adjunct Professor, Virginia State University (1981-1985) **CIV:** Board of Directors, YMCA of Greater Richmond, Richmond, VA (1989-Present); Board of Directors, Industrial Development Authority, Richmond, VA (1984-Present) **MEM:** Board of Directors, Metro Richmond Chamber of Commerce (1989-Present); Executive Committee, Central Virginia Legal Aid Society, Inc.; President, ODBA; Board of Directors, The Bar Association of the City of Richmond; Alpha Kappa Mu Honor Society; Alpha Mu Gamma; Omega Psi Phi Fraternity, Inc.; Sigma Pi Phi Fraternity **BAR:** United States Court of Appeals for the Fourth Circuit (1980); Commonwealth of Virginia (1980); State of Michigan (1978); United States Court of Appeals for the Sixth Circuit (1978) **RE:** Baptist

GREIDER, CAROLYN, "CAROL" WIDNEY, PHD, T: Professor, Molecular Biologist **I:** Education/Educational Services **CN:** Johns Hopkins University School of Medicine **DOB:** 04/15/1961 **PB:** San Diego **SC:** CA/USA **MS:** Divorced **SPN:** Nathaniel C. Comfort (1992, Divorced) **CH:** Two Children **ED:** PhD in Molecular Biology, University of California Berkeley (1987); BA in Biology, University of California Santa Barbara (1983) **C:** Daniel Nathans Professor and Director, Department of Molecular Biology and Genetics, Johns Hopkins University School of Medicine, Baltimore, MD (2003-Present); Professor of Oncology, Johns Hopkins University School of Medicine, Baltimore, MD (2001-Present); Interim Director, Department of Molecular Biology and Genetics, Johns Hopkins University

School of Medicine, Baltimore, MD (2002-2003); Professor, Johns Hopkins University School of Medicine, Baltimore, MD (1999-2003); Associate Professor, Department of Molecular Biology and Genetics, Johns Hopkins University School of Medicine, Baltimore, MD (1997-1999); Investigator, Cold Spring Harbor Laboratory, NY (1994-1997); Associate Staff investigator, Cold Spring Harbor Laboratory, NY (1992-1994); Assistant Investigator, Cold Spring Harbor Laboratory, NY (1990-1992); Fellow, Cold Spring Harbor Laboratory, NY (1988-1990) **CR:** Consultant, Amgen, Inc. (1998-2002); Member, National Bioethics Advisory Commission (1996-2001); Organizer, Gordon Research Conference of Nucleic Acids, Providence, RI (1998); Visiting Lecturer, State University of New York, Stony Brook, NY (1991-1997); Member, Scientific Advisory Board, Geron Corporation (1992-1996) **CW:** Member, Editorial Board, Molecular Cancer Research (2003-Present); Member, Editorial Board, Cancer Cell (2001-Present); Contributor, Numerous Articles and Reviews, Professional Journals; Contributor, Chapters, Books **AW:** Nobel Prize in Physiology/Medicine (2009); Louisa Gross Horwitz Prize, Columbia University (2007); Albert Lasker Award for Basic Medical Research (2006); Wiley Prize in Biomedical Sciences (2006); Lila Gruber Cancer Research Award (2006); Richard Lounsbery Award, National Academy of Sciences (2003); Lewis S. Rosenstiel Award, Brandeis University (1999); Passano Foundation Award (1999); Gairdner Foundation International Award (1998); Senior Scholar Award, Ellison Medical Foundation (1998); Gertrude Elion Cancer Research Award, American Society for Biochemistry and Molecular Biology (1997); Schering-Plough Scientific Achievement Award, American Society for Biochemistry and Molecular Biology (1997); Glenn Foundation Award, American Society of Cell Biology (1995); Pew Biomedical Sciences Scholar (1990-1994); Regents Scholar, University of California (1981) **MEM:** Council Member, American Society of Cell Biology (1998-2001); Fellow, American Association for the Advancement of Science; Fellow, American Academy of Microbiology; Fellow, American Academy of Arts & Sciences; National Academy of Sciences; Institute of Medicine; American Society for Biochemistry and Molecular Biology; American Society for Microbiology; American Association for Cancer Research; American Society for Cell Biology; The Phi Beta Kappa Society

GRETZKY, WAYNE DOUGLAS, T: Former Professional Hockey Player; Former Professional Hockey Coach **I:** Athletics **DOB:** 01/26/1961 **PB:** Brantford **SC:** Ontario/Canada **PT:** Walter Gretzky; Phyllis Leone (Hockin) Gretzky **MS:** Married **SPN:** Janet Jones (07/16/1988) **CH:** Paulina; Ty Robert; Trevor Douglas; Tristan Wayne; Emma Marie **C:** Partner, Vice Chairman, Oilers Entertainment Group (2016-Present); Special Adviser, Team Canada, Olympic Games, Vancouver, Canada (2010); Head Coach, Phoenix Coyotes, NHL (2005-2009); Director of Hockey Operations, Alternate Governor, Phoenix Coyotes, NHL (2001-2009); Managing Partner, Phoenix Coyotes, NHL (2000-2009); Investor, Los Arcos Sports LLC/Phoenix Coyotes, NHL (1999-2009); Executive Director, Team Canada, Olympic Games, Torino, Italy (2006); Executive Director, Team Canada, World Cup of Hockey (2004); Executive Director, Team Canada, Olympic Games, Salt Lake City, Utah (2002); Center, New York Rangers, NHL (1996-1999); Center, St. Louis Blues, NHL (1996); Center, Los Angeles Kings, NHL (1988-1996); Center, Edmonton Oilers, NHL (1979-1988); Center, Indianapolis Racers, World Hockey Association (1978); Center, Sault Ste. Marie Greyhounds (1977-1978); Center, Peterborough Petes, Junior Ontario Hockey Association (1977-1978)

AW: Named Legend of the Game, World Hockey Association Hall of Fame (2010); Named One of the Most Influential People in the World of Sports, Business Week (Now Bloomberg Businessweek) (2008); Named One of the Top 60, Hockey News Book (2007); Named to Centennial All-Star Team, International Ice Hockey Federation (2004); Named to Ontario Sports Hall of Fame (2004); World Cup of Hockey Champion (2004); Named All-star Game MVP (1983, 1989, 1999); Named to Hockey Hall of Fame (1999); Named to NHL All-Star Team (1980-1994, 1997-1999); Art Ross Memorial Trophy, NHL (1981-1987, 1989-1990, 1990-1991, 1993-1994); Lady Byng Memorial Trophy (1979-1980, 1990-1991, 1991-1992, 1993-1994); Lester Patrick Trophy (1993-1994); Winner, Edmonton Oilers, Stanley Cup (1984, 1985, 1987, 1988); Conn Smythe Trophy (1985, 1988); Emery Edge Award (1983-1984, 1984-1985, 1986-1987); Named Dodge Performer of the Year (1984-1985, 1986-1987); Lester B. Pearson Award (1982, 1984-1985, 1986-1987); Named Canadian Athlete of the Year (1985); Named Sportsman of the Year, Sports Illustrated (1982); Named NHL Player of the Year, Sporting News (1981-1987); Named Man of the Year (1981); Hart Memorial Trophy (1974-1980); Named Rookie of the Year, World Hockey Association (1978-1979); Lemms Family Award (1977-1978); William Hanley Trophy (1977-1978)

GRIFFIN, BLAKE AUSTIN, T: Professional Basketball Player **I:** Athletics **CN:** Detroit Pistons **DOB:** 03/16/1989 **PB:** Oklahoma City **SC:** OK/ USA **PT:** Tommy Griffin; Gail Griffin **MS:** Single **CH:** One Son; One Daughter **ED:** Coursework in Pre-Health and Exercise Science, University of Oklahoma, Norman, OK (2007-2009); Diploma, Oklahoma Christian School, Edmond, OK **C:** Forward, Detroit Pistons (2018-Present); Forward, Los Angeles Clippers (2009-2018) **CR:** Endorser, Panini America (2011); Production Intern, "Funny or Die," Los Angeles, CA (2011); Spokesman, Kia Motors, Subway, Vizio, GameFly **CIV:** Donor, Little Caesars Arena (2020); Founder, Dunking for Dollars; Fundraiser, Team Blake, Stand Up to Cancer **CW:** Actor, "The Female Brain" (2018) **AW:** Two-Time All-NBA Third Team (2015, 2019); Six-Time NBA All-Star (2011-2015, 2019); Three-Time All-NBA Second Team (2012-2014); NBA Rookie of the Year (2011); NBA All-Rookie First Team (2011); NBA Slam Dunk Contest Champion (2011); National College Player of the Year (2009); Consensus First-Team All-American (2009); Big 12 Player of the Year (2009); McDonald's All-American (2007); Third-Team Parade All-American (2007) **RE:** Christian

GRIFFITH, HOWARD, "MORGAN" MORGAN, T: U.S. Representative, Lawyer **I:** Government Administration/Government Relations/Government Services **DOB:** 03/15/1958 **PB:** Philadelphia **SC:** PA/ USA **PT:** A. Hundley Griffith; Charlotte Virginia (Burford) Griffith **MS:** Married **SPN:** Hilary Davis **CH:** Davis; Starke; Abby (Stepchild) **ED:** JD, School of Law, Washington and Lee University, Lexington, VA (1983); BA, Emory & Henry College, VA, with Honors (1980) **C:** U.S. Representative, Virginia's Ninth Congressional District, United States Congress, Washington, DC (2011-Present); Member, U.S. House Committee on Energy and Commerce, Washington, DC (2011-Present); Partner, Head, Roanoke/Salem Office, Albo & Oblon LLP (2007-Present); Majority Leader, Virginia House of Delegates (2000-2010); Member, District Eight, Virginia House of Delegates (1994-2010); Partner, Griffith & Varney, Salem, VA (1987-1989); Private Practice, Salem, VA (1984-1987, 1989-2007); Associate, Lutins & Shapiro, Roanoke, VA (1983-1984) **CIV:** Board of Directors, Stonegate Swim Club, Salem, VA (1991-Present); Chairman, Salem Republican

Party (1986-1988, 1991-1994); Board of Directors, Legal Aid Society of Roanoke Valley (1991-1992); Adviser, Sponsor, Legal Explorers Post, Boy Scouts of America, Salem, VA (1988-1989); District Chairman, Boy Scouts of America (1988-1991); Chairman, Catawba District, Boy Scouts of America (1984-1986); Board of Visitors, Emory & Henry College; Member, Blue Ridge Mountains Council, Boy Scouts of America; Member, State Central Committee, Republican Party of Virginia; Member, St. Paul's Episcopalian Church, Salem, VA; Board of Trustees, Jamestown-Yorktown Foundation; Former Member, Board of Directors, Easterseals, VA **AW:** Silver Beaver Award, Boy Scouts of America (1994) **MEM:** President, Salem/Roanoke County Bar Association (1995-1996); Board of Directors, Lions International (1988-1990); Virginia Bar Association **BAR:** United States District Court District of Virginia (1985); The Virginia Bar Association (1983) **AV:** Swimming; Studying ornithology and ichthyology **PA:** Republican **RE:** Episcopalian

GRIFFITH, TRICIA, T: Chief Executive Officer **I:** Insurance **CN:** Progressive Corporation **ED:** Bachelor of Science, Illinois State University **C:** Chief Executive Officer, Progressive Corporation (2015-Present); Personal Lines Chief Operating Officer, Progressive Corporation (2014-2016); Claim Group President, Progressive (2008-2014); Chief Human Resources Officer, Progressive (2002-2008) **AW:** Fortune 100 Most Powerful Women (2016)

GRIFFITH JOYNER, FLORENCE DELOREZ, T: Professional Track and Field Athlete (Retired) **I:** Athletics **DOB:** 12/21/1959 **PB:** Los Angeles **SC:** CA/USA **PT:** Robert Griffith; Florence Griffith **MS:** Married **SPN:** Al Joyner (1984) **CH:** Mary Ruth Joyner **ED:** Honorary PhD, American University, Washington, DC (1994); BA in Psychology, UCLA (1983); Coursework, California State University, Northridge **C:** Co-Owner, NUCO Nails, Camarillo, CA (1994-1998) **CIV:** Co-Chairperson, President Council on Physical Fitness and Sports (1993-1998); Founder, The Florence Griffith Joyner Youth Foundation **CW:** Designer, Line of Sportswear, Uniforms, Indiana Pacers, NBA; Actress, "The Chaser"; Actress, "Santa Barbara"; Guest Appearance, "227"; Guest Appearances, Numerous Talk Shows; Host, Commentator, Various Sports Events **AW:** Award for Outstanding Contribution to the Field of Athletics, Harvard Foundation (1989); Sports Award for Extraordinary Accomplishments in Athletics, Essence Magazine (1989); Golden Camera Award, German Advertising Industry (1989); James E. Sullivan Memorial Award for Most Outstanding Athlete in America (1989); Sports Woman of the Year, U.S. Olympic Committee (1988); Three-Time Winner, Gold Medal, 100 Meters, 200 Meters, 4 x 100 Meters, Summer Olympic Games, Seoul, South Korea (1988); Two-Time Recipient, Silver Medal, 200 Meters and 4 x 400 Meters, Summer Olympic Games, Seoul, South Korea (1988); International Jesse Owens Award for Most Outstanding Amateur Athlete (1988); Most Outstanding Physique of the 1980s, International Federation of Bodybuilders (1988); Jesse Owens Outstanding Track and Field Athlete, TAC (1988); Sports Personality of the Year, Tass News Agency (1988); Athlete of the Year, Track and Field (1988); Gold Medal, 4 x 100 Meter Relay, World Championships (1987); Silver Medal, 200 Meters, World Championships (1987); Silver Medal, 200 Meters, Olympic Games, Los Angeles, CA (1984); Collegiate Champion, 200 Meters, NCAA (1983); Collegiate Champion, 400 Meters, NCAA (1981)

GRIJALVA, RAÚL MANUEL, T: U.S. Representative from Arizona **I:** Government Administration/Government Relations/Government Services **DOB:** 02/19/1948 **PB:** Tucson **SC:** AZ/USA **MS:** Married **SPN:** Ramona F. Grijalva **CH:** Adelita; Raquel; Marisa **ED:** BA in Sociology, University of Arizona (1988) **C:** Member, U.S. House of Representatives from Arizona's Third Congressional District, U.S. Congress (2013-Present); Ranking Member, Committee on Natural Resources (2013-Present); Ranking Member, U.S. House Committee on Natural Resources (2007-Present); Member, U.S. House of Representatives from Arizona's Seventh Congressional District, U.S. Congress (2003-2013); Member, Pima County Board of Supervisors (1989-2003); Chairman, Pima County Board of Supervisors (2000-2002); Assistant Dean, Hispanic Student Affairs, University of Arizona (1987); Director, El Pueblo Neighborhood Center (1975-1986); Board Member, Tucson Unified School District (1974-1986) **AW:** Inductee, Sunnyside High School Alumni Hall of Fame (2004) **PA:** Democrat **RE:** Roman Catholic

GRIMSLEY, JAMES EDWARD, T: Newspaper Editor, Syndicated Columnist **I:** Writing and Editing **DOB:** 05/25/1927 **PB:** Buchanan County **SC:** VA/USA **PT:** James Lowry Grimsley; Almeda (Thomas) Grimsley **MS:** Married **SPN:** Ann Neblett (3/3/1951) **CH:** Martha Grimsley Blumenthal; James Edward Junior (Deceased); Anna Grimsley Ashworth; Six Grandchildren; Two Great-Grandchildren **ED:** BA in Government, College William and Mary (1951) **C:** Chairman, Editorial Board, Richmond Times-Dispatch (1992-1995); Editor, Editorial Page, Richmond Times-Dispatch (1970-1992); Reporter, Columnist, Richmond Times-Dispatch (1953-1970); Director, Press Relations, College William and Mary, Williamsburg, VA (1952-1953); Reporter, United Press International, Richmond, VA (1951-1952) **CR:** Member, Pulitzer Prize Nominating Jury, New York, NY (1985) **CIV:** Member, Board of Visitors, College of William and Mary (1990-Present); Rector of College (1999-2001) **MIL:** U.S. Navy (1945-1946) **CW:** Author, "First Let's Kill All The Humorlists" (1997); Author, "Coming Through Awry" (1967) **AW:** Awards for Editorials, U.S. Industrial Council Education Foundation (1977); Award for Editorials, Freedoms Foundation, Valley Forge, PA (1976); Awards for Editorials and Columns, Virginia Press Association **MEM:** National Conference of Editorial Writers; Society of Professional Journalists; Sigma Delta Chi; American Society of Newspaper Editors **MH:** Albert Nelson Marquis Lifetime Achievement **AV:** Golf; Bridge **PA:** Independent **RE:** Presbyterian

GRISCHKOWSKY, DANIEL RICHARD, PHD, T: Professor Emeritus **I:** Education/Educational Services **CN:** Oklahoma State University **DOB:** 04/17/1940 **PB:** St. Helens **SC:** OR/USA **PT:** Oscar Edward Grischkowsky; Christine Hazel (Olsen) Grischkowsky **MS:** Married **SPN:** Frieda Rosa Bachmann **CH:** Timothy; Stephanie; Daniela **ED:** Postdoctoral Studies, Columbia University, New York, NY (1968-1969); PhD in Physics, Columbia University (1968); AM in Physics, Columbia University (1965); BS, Oregon State University (1962) **C:** Professor Emeritus, School of Electrical and Computer Engineering, Oklahoma State University, Stillwater, OK (2001-Present); Regents Professor, Bellmon Chair, Optoelectronics, School of Electrical and Computer Engineering, Oklahoma State University, Stillwater, OK (1993-2001); Manager, Ultra-Fast Science With Lasers Group, IBM Watson Research Center, Yorktown Heights, NY (1983-1993); Manager, Atomic Physics With Lasers Group, IBM Watson Research Center, Yorktown Heights, NY (1979-1983); Science Adviser to Director of Research Division, IBM, Yorktown Heights, NY (1978); Research Staff, IBM Watson Research Center, Yorktown Heights, NY (1969-1977) **CR:** Chairman, International Council on Quantum Electronics (1989-1993); American Physical Society/Optical Society of America/IEEE Joint Council on Quantum Electronics (1989-1993); Fellow, IEEE (1992); Fellow, OSA (1988); Fellow, American Physical Society (1982) **CW:** Contributor, Articles, Professional Journals; Patents in Field **AW:** Kenneth J. Button Prize (2012); Honorary Professor, Tianjin University, China (2008); William F. Meggers Award, Optical Society of America (2003); R. W. Wood Prize (1989); Boris Pregel Award, New York Academy of Sciences (1985) **MEM:** Chairman, Laser Science Topical Group, American Physical Society (1993-1994); Optical Society of America **MH:** Albert Nelson Marquis Lifetime Achievement Award; Marquis Who's Who Top Professional **B/I:** Dr. Grischkowsky became involved in his profession because he has been this way since he was a child; he just always wanted to know where things came from in nature and had a determination to follow his North Star. He wanted to understand the universe he was in. He is a born problem-solver and has a tremendous focus on things. **RE:** Christian

GRISHAM, MICHELLE LYNN, T: Governor of New Mexico **I:** Government Administration/Government Relations/Government Services **DOB:** 10/24/1959 **PB:** Los Alamos **SC:** NM/USA **PT:** Buddy Lujan; Sonja Lujan **MS:** Widowed **SPN:** Gregory Grisham (Deceased 2004) **CH:** Taylor; Erin **ED:** JD, The University of New Mexico School of Law (1987); BA, The University of New Mexico (1981) **C:** Governor, State of New Mexico (2019-Present); Co-owner, Delta Consulting Group (2008-Present); Member, United States House Committee on Oversight & Government Reform (2013-2019); Member, United States House Budget Committee (2013-2019); Member, United States House Agricultural Committee (2013-2019); Member, New Mexico's First Congressional District, United States Congress, Washington, DC (2013-2019); Commissioner, Bernalillo County, NM (2011-2012); Secretary, New Mexico Department of Health, Santa Fe, NM (2004-2007); Director, New Mexico Area Agency on Aging (1992-2004); Director, Lawyer Referral for the Elderly Progressive, State Bar of New Mexico **PA:** Democrat **RE:** Roman Catholic

GRISHAM, STEPHANIE, T: White House Press Secretary; White House Communications Director **I:** Government Administration/Government Relations/Government Services **DOB:** 07/23/1976 **MS:** Divorced **SPN:** Dan Marries (Divorced) **CH:** Two Children **C:** White House Press Secretary, White House Communications Director, Washington, DC (2019-Present); Deputy Press Secretary, Washington, DC (2017-2019); Press Aide, Donald Trump's Presidential Campaign (2016); Press Coordinator, Pope Francis' Visit to Philadelphia, PA (2015); Mitt Romney's Presidential Campaign (2012); Spokeswoman, AAA Arizona (2007); Spokeswoman, Arizona House of Representative Republican Caucus; Spokeswoman, Attorney General Tom Horne

GRONKOWSKI, ROB JAMES, T: Professional Football Player **I:** Athletics **CN:** Tampa Bay Buccaneers **DOB:** 05/14/1989 **PB:** Amherst **SC:** NY/USA **PT:** Gordon Gronkowski; Diane Gronkowski **MS:** Life Partner **SPN:** Camille Kostek (2015) **ED:** Coursework in Pre-Business, University of Arizona, Tucson, AZ; Diploma, Woodland Hills High School, Pittsburgh, PA **C:** Tight End, Tampa Bay Buccaneers (2020-Present); Tight End, New England Patriots (2010-2018) **CR:** Cameo, André the Giant Memorial Battle Royal, WrestleMania 33 (2017); Launched, Gronk Beverage, Coca-Cola (2016); Launched, Gronk's Hot Sauce, PLB Sports (2015); Launched, Gronk Flakes, PLB Sports (2012); Endorser, Nike, Dunkin Donuts, Visa, T-Mobile, Tide, Lyft, JetBlue, Zynga, Cheerios, Oberto, SixStar Pro, Bodyarmor SuperDrink, DraftKings, Kids Footlockers, "Mobile Strike," "Halo," Others **CIV:** Donor, Boston Medical Center, St. Joseph's Regional Medical Center (2019-2020); Founder, Gronk Nation Youth Foundation; Participant, One Mission Buzz Off for Kids; Supporter, Make-A-Wish Foundation, Patriots Foundation **CW:** Actor, "Boss Level" (2020); Executive Producer, "Game On!" (2020); Appearance, Music Video, "I'll Wait" (2020); Host, WrestleMania 36 (2020); Cameo, "Deported" (2020); Guest Appearance, "WWE Backstage" (2019); Executive Producer, "Shark Week's 50 Best Bites" (2018); Executive Producer, "Unsportsmanlike Comedy with Rob Gronkowski" (2018); Executive Producer, "MVP" (2017); Appearance, Music Video, "Swish Swish" (2017); Cameo, "American Violence" (2017); Appearance, Music Video, "On My Mind" (2017); Cameo, "The Clapper" (2017); Guest Appearance, "Seven Bucks Digital Studios" (2017); Actor, "You Can't Have It" (2017); Actor, TV Film, "The Lit Party" (2017); Guest Appearance, "Family Guy" (2017); Guest Appearance, "Entourage" (2015); Featured, "A Gronking to Remember" (2014); Numerous Others **AW:** Winner, WWE 24/7 Championship (2020); Wish Hero Award, Make-A-Wish Foundation MA/RI (2019); Merit Award, United Service Organizations (2019); Three-Time Super Bowl Champion (2014, 2017-2018); Five-Time Pro Bowl (2011-2012, 2014-2015, 2017); Four-Time First-Team All-Pro (2011, 2014-2015, 2017); Ron Burton Community Service Award, New England Patriots (2016); NFL Comeback Player of the Year (2014); First-Team All-Pac-10 (2008); Third-Team All-American (2008); NFL 100th Anniversary All-Time Team; NFL 2010s All-Decade Team **AV:** Wrestling

GROSS, CHARLES MERIDITH, T: Broadcast Executive **I:** Media & Entertainment **DOB:** 07/31/1952 **PB:** Norfolk **SC:** VA/USA **PT:** Harold W. Gross; Mary E. Greenlee Gross **MS:** Widowed **ED:** Coursework, University of North Carolina (1970-1973) **C:** Travel Manager, Guide and Host, AAA Connecticut Motor Club (1995-2015); Manager of Operations, Station 960 WELI-AM, iHeartMedia, Inc., New Haven, CT (1982-1995); Vice President of Programming, Insilco Broadcasting (1983-1985); Manager of Operations, Station 920 KYST-AM, Houston, Texas (1981-1982); Manager of Operations, Station KSET-AM and FM, El Paso, Texas (1977-1980) **CIV:** President, Foxwood Crossing Home Owner's Association (1991-1994); Chairman, New Haven 4th of July Committee, CT (1984-1987); Board of Directors, American Cancer Society, Inc., New Haven, CT (1983-1985); Member, Volunteer Action Center **AW:** Award, American Liver Foundation (1993); 10 Year Service Award, Connecticut Girl Scouts of the United States of America (1992); Community Service Award, Volunteer Action Center (1990); Hamden Probus Club Service Award (1990); Panasonic National Science Achievement Award (1970) **MH:** Albert Nelson Marquis Lifetime Achievement Award **B/I:** At the age 10, Mr. Gross knew he wanted to be a broadcaster. When he was a child, he received a hobby called "101 Projects You Can Make with Parts," and the one thing he could make was a wireless microphone that had a broadcasting range of 100 feet. When Mr. Gross was a small boy, he ran an antenna up a tree and he was able to record music and fake commercials; he was able to create his first pirate radio station. As he got older, he became involved in other aspects of broadcasting, so when he received the scholarship from the National Society of Professional Engineers, he was thinking of being a civil engineer, not an electrical engineer. The engineering club started a campus radio station at USC Charlotte; they had plenty of engineers but no one knew what to put on the radio so he became in charge of programming. Due to health related problems, his education was pushed back for a moment and he felt he was missing out on the job market, so he decided to be a broadcaster. He wanted to attend the Carolina School of Broadcasting but it was too expensive. Mr. Gross drove out to the countryside to a day-time radio station and accepted a position as a broadcaster. **AV:** Travel; Music; Fantasy baseball; Reading

GROSS, DAVID JONATHAN, PHD, T: Physicist; Professor **I:** Education/Educational Services **CN:** University of California, Santa Barbara **DOB:** 02/19/1941 **PB:** Washington **SC:** DC/USA **PT:** Bertram M. Gross; Nora (Faine) Gross **MS:** Married **SPN:** Jacquelyn Savani (08/12/2001); Shulamith Toaff (03/30/1962, Divorced) **CH:** Ariela; Elisheva; Miranda Savani (Stepdaughter) **ED:** Honorary Doctorate, University of Chinese Academy of Sciences (2016); Doctor Philosophiae Honoris Causa, Universidad Nacional de Tucumán, Argentina (2016); Honorary Doctorate, University Libre de Bruxelles (2010); Honorary Doctorate, University of Cambodia (2010); Honorary Doctorate, Hong Kong University of Science and Technology (2008); Honorary Doctorate, University of Cambridge, England, United Kingdom (2008); Honorary Doctorate, De La Salle University, Manila, Philippines (2008); Honorary Doctorate, The Ohio State University (2007); Honorary Doctorate, Sao Paulo University, Brazil (2006); Honorary Doctorate, Hebrew University, Jerusalem, Israel (2001); Honorary Doctorate, University of Montpellier (2000); PhD, University of California, Berkeley (1966); BSc, Hebrew University, Jerusalem, Israel (1962) **C:** Professor of Physics, University of California, Santa Barbara (1997-Present); Jones Professor of Physics Emeritus, Princeton University (1997-Present); Gluck Professor, Theoretical Physics, University of California, Santa Barbara (2001-2002); Frederick W. Gluck Chair of Theoretical Physics, Director, Kavli Institute for Theoretical Physics, University of California, Santa Barbara (1997-2012); Jones Professor of Physics, Princeton University (1995-1997); Eugene Higgens Professor of Physics, Princeton University (1986-1995); Professor, Princeton University (1973-1986); Associate Professor, Princeton University (1971-1973); Assistant Professor of Physics, Princeton University (1969-1971); Junior Fellow, Harvard Society of Fellows, Harvard University (1966-1969) **CR:** Member, Solvay Science Committee of Physics (2006-Present); Member, Franqui Prize Committee (2012); Chair, XXV Solvay Conference of Physics (2011); Solvay Centenary Chair, Solvay Institute, Brussels, Belgium (2011); Solvay Professor, University of Brussels (2008); Rothschild Professor, University of Cambridge (2007); Member, XXIII Solvay Conference of Physics (2005); Chair, Evaluation Committee, Scuola Internazionale Superiore di Studi Avanzati, Italy (1994); Visiting Professor, European Organization of Nuclear Research, Geneva, Switzerland (1993); Visiting Professor, Lawrence Radiation Laboratory, Berkeley, CA (1992); Visiting Professor, Ecole Normale Superioure, Paris, France (1988-1989); Visiting Professor, Hebrew University, Jerusalem, Israel (1984); Visiting Professor, Paris, France (1983); Visiting Professor, Geneva, Switzerland (1968-1969); Member, International Advisory Committee, Indian Center for Theoretical Studies, Bangalore, India; Invited Lecturer, Several Universities **CIV:** Director, Jerusalem Winter School (1999-Present) **CW:** Associate Editor, Nuclear Physics (1972-Present) **AW:** Medal of Honor, Joint Institute for Nuclear Research, Dubna, Russia (2016); Richard E. Prange Prize, University of Maryland (2013); San Carlos Boromero Award, University of San Carlos, Philippines (2008); Nobel Prize in Physics (2004); Co-recipient, High Energy and Particle Physics Prize, European Physical Society (2003); Golden Plate Award, Academy of Achievement (2005); Grande Médaille, French Academy of Sciences (2004); Oscar Klein Medal, Stockholm University (2000); Harvey Prize, Technion-Israel Institute of Technology (2000); Dirac Medal, International Center for Theoretical Physics (1988); MacArthur Prize Fellow (1987); J. J. Sakurai Prize, American Physical Society (1986); Alfred P. Sloan Fellow (1970-1974); Named Honorary Professor, Several Universities **MEM:** Member, Institute for Quantum Studies, Chapman University, CA (2011-Present); Foreign Member, Chinese Academy of Sciences (2011-Present); Chair, International Advisory Committee, International Institute of Physics (2009-Present); Academie Internationale de Philosophie des Sciences (2009-Present); American Philosophical Society (2007-Present); The Academy of Sciences for the Developing World (Now The World Academy of Science) (2007-Present); European Academy of Sciences (2004-Present); Fellow, American Association for the Advancement of Science; Fellow, American Physical Society; Fellow, American Academy of Arts and Sciences; National Academy of Sciences; Tata Institute of Fundamental Research

GROSS, MARK, T: Chief Executive Officer (Retired) **I:** Food & Restaurant Services **CN:** Super-Valu, Inc. **ED:** JD, Carey Law School, University of Pennsylvania, Cum Laude (1990); BA in History, Dartmouth College (1985) **C:** President, Chief Executive Officer, SupeValu, Inc. (2016-Present); Owner, Surry Investment Advisors LLC (2006-2016); Co-President, C&S Wholesale Grocers, Inc. (1997-2006); Attorney, Skadden, Arps, Slate, Meagher & Flom (1990-1997) **CW:** Editor, Journal of International Business Law **MEM:** Phi Delta Alpha

GROSSER, MORTON, T: President **I:** Consulting **CN:** MG Consulting **DOB:** 12/25/1931 **PB:** Philadelphia **SC:** PA/USA **PT:** Albert J. Grosser; Esther (Mendel) Grosser **MS:** Widowed **SPN:** Janet Dolores Zachs (06/28/1953, Deceased 08/30/2004) **CH:** Adam **ED:** National Institutes of Health Postdoctoral Fellow, UCLA Medical Center; PhD in History of Science/Astrophysics, Stanford University (1961); MS in Fiber Mechanics, Massachusetts Institute of Technology (1954); BS in Mechanical Engineering, Massachusetts Institute of Technology (1953) **CT:** Registered Securities Representative; Financial Principal **C:** President, Management and Technology Consultant, MG Consulting, Palo Alto and Menlo Park, CA (1967-1983, 1987-Present); Faculty, Venture Capital Institute, Emory University (2017-2020); General Partner, Managing Director, L.H. Alton & Co., San Francisco, CA (1984-1987); Director of Publications, Boeing Scientific Research Laboratories, Boeing, Seattle, WA (1964-1966); Head of Design, Clevite Transistor Products, Development Division, Waltham, MA (1956-1957); Engineering Designer, Raytheon Corp., Waltham, MA (1955-1956); Research Associate, Massachusetts Institute of Technology, Cambridge, MA (1954-1955) **CR:** Entrotech Life Sciences (2014-2018); Control Point Medical (2014-2017); Microfabrica Corp. (2002-2008); Chroma Group (1997-2006); Lazer-Tron Corporation (1994-2000); Redem Corporation (1988-1991); Director, I-Flow Corporation (1985-1987); Scientific Advisory Boards, Sunshine Medical Instruments, Inc., Therox Corporation, Percutaneous Systems, Inc., Venture Capital Co-investor with CompassTechnology Partners, Institutional Venture Partners, Kleiner Perkins Caulfield & Byers, Life Science Angels; Distinguished Corporate Lecturer, Apple Computer, Boeing Corporation, E.I. Dupont de Nemours & Co., Electronic Arts, Google, Inc., LSI Logic, and Tektronix Inc. **CW:** Consulting Editor, "100 Inventions That Shaped World History" (1993); Author, "The Fabulous Fifty" (1990); Author, "On Gossamer Wings" (1982); Author, "Gossamer Odyssey: The Triumph of Human-Powered Flight" (1981); Author, "Diesel: The Man and the Engine" (1978); Author, "The Snake Horn" (1973); Author, "The Hobby Shop" (1967); Author, "The Discovery of Neptune" (1962); Editor, Boeing Scientific Research Laboratories Review; Contributor, Papers to Peer-reviewed Professional Journals; Contributor, Fiction, Nonfiction, and Poetry to Literary Magazines Including The Atlantic, Harper's, and The New Yorker; Inventor, Holder, 17 U.S. Patents, Licensed and Pending **AW:** Commonwealth Club Medal for Literary Excellence (1991); Stegner Creative Writing Fellowship (1963-1964); National Institutes of Health Postdoctoral Fellowship (1961-1962); Ford Foundation Fellowship (1960); Stanford Teaching Fellowship (1959-1960); Coats & Clark Graduate Fellowship, Massachusetts Institute of Technology (1954); Fellow, Society of Mechanical Engineers (Now The American Society of Mechanical Engineers); Associate Fellow, American Institute of Aeronautics and Astronautics **MEM:** Associate Fellow, American Institute of Aeronautics and Astronautics; Fellow, The American Society of Mechanical Engineers; Authors Guild **B/I:** When Mr. Grosser was a child, he loved writing and was also talented at math and science. He had a high school creative writing teacher who encouraged him to write, a professor at MIT who mentored him in science and engineering, and a professor at Stanford who mentored him in history. He continued writing throughout his science and engineering education at MIT and Stanford University, and incorporated it into his professional career as a technologist, inventor, and Venture Capital investor and consultant. **AV:** Aviation; Fitness; Modelbuilding; Photography **THT:** Dr. Grosser's motto is, "Why not?"

GROSSMAN, ROBERT IVIN, MD, T: Chief Executive Officer; Dean; Neuroradiologist **I:** Medicine & Health Care **CN:** NYU Langone Health; New York University School of Medicine **DOB:** 09/28/1947 **PB:** New York **SC:** NY/USA **ED:** Honorary Doctorate, University of Bordeaux, France (2010); Fellow in Neuroradiology, Massachusetts General Hospital, Boston, MA (1979-1981); Resident in Radiology, University of Pennsylvania Perelman School of Medicine, Philadelphia, PA (1976-1979); Resident in Neurosurgery, University of Pennsylvania School of Medicine, Philadelphia, PA (1974-1976); Intern, Beth Israel Hospital, Boston, MA (1973-1974); MD, University of Pennsylvania Perelman School of Medicine, Philadelphia, PA (1973); BS, Tulane University (1969) **CT:** Certification in Neuroradiology and Radiology **C:** Chief Executive Officer, NYU Langone Health (2007-Present); Saul J. Farber Dean, New York University School of Medicine (2007-Present); Louis Marx Professor of Radiology, Chairman, Department of Radiology, Professor of Neurosurgery, Neurology, Physiology and Neuroscience, New York University School of Medicine (2001-Present); Chairman, Diagnostics Radiology Study Section, University of Pennsylvania Medical Center (1997-2000); Chief of Neuroradiology, University of Pennsylvania Medical Center (1987); Professor of Radiology, Neurosurgery and Neurology, University of Pennsylvania Perelman School of Medicine (1987); Associate Professor, University of Pennsylvania Perelman School of Medicine (1984-1987); Assistant Professor, Radiology, University of Pennsylvania Perelman School of Medicine (1981-1984) **CR:** National Advisory Council for Biomedical Imaging and Bioengineering, National Institutes of Health (2003-2007); Chairman, National Advisory Council for Biomedical Imaging and Bioengineering, National Institutes of Health (1997-2000); Diagnostic Radiology Study Section, National Institutes of Health (1995-2000) **CW:** Associate Editor, Magnetic Resonance Medicine (1991-Present); Author, "Magnetic Resonance Techniques in Clinical Trials in Multiple Sclerosis" (1999); Author, "Neuroradiology: The Requisites" (1994); Contributor, Articles, Medical Journals **AW:** Lifetime Achievement Award of the Emeritus Class, Tulane University (2019); Listee, 50 Most Influential Healthcare Leaders Who Changed the State of Healthcare in America, Time Magazine (2018); "Living Landmark," New York Landmarks Conservancy (2013); Gold Medal, ISMRM (2010); Named Distinguished Graduate, University of Pennsylvania Perelman School of Medicine (2010); Award for Outstanding Contributions in Research, American Society of Neuroradiology Education and Research Foundation (Now The Foundation of the American Society of Neuroradiology) (2004); Javits Neuroscience Investigator Award, National Institutes of Health (1999) **MEM:** President-Elect, American Society of Neuroradiology (2005-2006); Former Vice President, American Society of Neuroradiology; Fellow, International Society of Magnetic Resonance in Medicine (ISMRM); Fellow, American College of Radiology; American Society of Neuroradiology; Alpha Omega Alpha Honor Medical Society

GROSSMANN, IGNACIO E., T: Professor of Chemical Engineering **I:** Education/Educational Services **CN:** Carnegie Mellon University **PB:** Mexico City **SC:** Mexico **PT:** Donat Grossmann; Marie-Louise (Epper) Grossmann **MS:** Married **SPN:** Blanca Espinal Zabalza (11/26/1977) **CH:** Claudia, PhD; Andrew; Thomas **ED:** PhD in Chemical Engineering, Imperial College London, London, England, United Kingdom (1977); Honorary Diploma, Imperial College London, London, England, United Kingdom (1975); MSc in Chemical Engineering, Imperial College London (1975); BSc in Chemical Engineering, Ibero-American University (1974) **C:** Rudolph and Florence Dean Professor of Chemical Engineering, Carnegie Mellon University, Pittsburgh, PA (1990-Present); Director, Center for Advanced Process Decision-Making, Carnegie Mellon University, Pittsburgh, PA (2004-2016); Head, Department of Chemical Engineering, Carnegie Mellon University, Pittsburgh, PA (1994-2002); Professor, Carnegie Mellon University, Pittsburgh, PA (1986-1990); Associate Professor, Carnegie Mellon University, Pittsburgh, PA (1983-1986); Assistant Professor, Chemical Engineering, Carnegie Mellon University, Pittsburgh, PA (1979-1983); Research and Development Engineer, Instituto Mexicano del Petroleo, Mexico City, Mexico (1978); Professor of Chemical Engineering **CR:** Member, Advisory Board, Singapore University of Technology and Design (2013-Present); Member, Advisory Board, Rutgers, The State University of New Jersey (2010-Present); Academic Trustee, Computer Aids for Chemical Engineering (CACHE) Committee (1983-Present); Chair, Chemical Engineering Section, National Academy of Engineering (2018-2019); Vice Chair, Chemical Engineering Section, National Academy of Engineering (2017-2018); Member, Advisory Board, Cornell University (2008-2013); Member, Advisory Board, Princeton University (2006-2013); Member, Advisory Board, Purdue University (2005-2011); Member, Advisory Board, The Pennsylvania State University (2005-2010); Board Director, American Institute of Chemical Engineers (AIChE) (2007-2009); Chair, Pan American Institute Study on Emerging Trends in Process Systems Engineering, Mar del Plata, Argentina (2008); Chair, Chemical Engineering Section, National Academy of Engineering (2007-2008); Vice-Chair, Chemical Engineering Section, National Academy of Engineering (2006-2007); Member, Chemical Engineering Section, Peer Committee, National Academy of Engineering (NAE) (2004-2006); Chair, Pan American Institute Study on Process Systems Engineering, Iguazu Falls, Argentina (2005); Chair, Chemical Engineering Chairs Session, Annual Meeting Council of Chemical Research, Chair of Fourth International Conference on Foundations of Computer-Aided Process Operations (FOCAPO2003), Coral Springs, FL (2003); Chair, International Committee, Member, Awards Committee, American Institute of Chemical Engineers (AIChE) (1999-2002); University Professor, Carnegie Mellon University (2001); Member, Steering Committee, Challenges for the Chemical Sciences in the 21st Century, National Research Council (1999-2002); Member, Governing Board, Council for Chemical Research, American Institute of Chemical Engineers (1998-2001); Co-chairman, CEPAC Workshop on Process Systems Engineering, Santa Fe, Argentina (1999); Co-chairman, "Pan-American Conference for Collaboration in Chemical Engineering", Rio de Janeiro, Brazil (1998); Vice Co-chairman, Third International Conference "Foundations of Computer Aided Process Design," Snowmass (1989); Chairman, National Program Committee of AIChE: Area 10c - Computers in Management and Information Processing (1987-1988); Vice-Chairman, National Program Committee of AIChE: Area 10c - Computers in Management and Information Processing (1985-1986); Served on National Program Committee of AIChE: Area 10c - Computers in Management and Information Processing (1980-1984) **CW:** Member, Editorial Advisory Board, Computers and Chemical Engineering, Journal of Global Optimization, Optimization and Engineering, Latin American Applied Research, Optimization Letters, Sustainable Production and Consumption, Computers and Operations Research, Theoretical Foundations of Chemical Engineering (2016-Present); Author, More Than 700 Publications, Professional Journals **AW:** Founders Award for Outstanding Contributions to the Field of Chemical Engineering, American Institute of Chemical Engineers (AIChE) (2019); Top Cited Scientist in Computer Science and Electronics: 53 Worldwide, 38 National, 115 H-Index (2019); Award for Long-term Achievements in Computer Aided Process Engineering, Working Party on CAPE, European Federation of Chemical Engineering (2017); ETH Zurich Chemical Engineering Medal (2017); Tsinghua Forum Award of Chemical Engineering, Tsinghua University, Beijing, China (2016); Constantin Caratheodory Prize, International Society of Global Optimization (2015); Named One of the Most Influential Scientific Minds, Thompson Reuters (2015); Chemical Engineering Division's Lectureship Award, ASEE, Seattle, WA (2015); Sargent Medal, Institution of Chemical Engineers, London, England, United Kingdom (2015); PROSE Award for Chapter in the Book, "Distillation: Fundamentals and Principles" (2015); Award, Best Technical Paper (2014); Named Ashland Padma Vibhushan Professor C.N.R. Rao Medal and CHEMCON Distinguished Speaker Award, Indian Institute of Chemical Engineers, Mumbai (2013); Distinguished Professor of Engineering Award, Carnegie Mellon University (2014); Luis Federico Leloir Award for International Cooperation, Buenos Aires, Argentina (2012); Research Excellence in Sustainable Engineering Award, American Institute of Chemical Engineers (AIChE) (2011); Warren Lewis Award for Excellence in Education, American Institute of Chemical Engineers (AIChE) (2009); Named One of the "100 Engineers of the Modern Era," American Institute of Chemical Engineers (AIChE) (2008); Outstanding Contributed Paper Award, FOCAPO Meeting (2008); INFORMS Computing Society Prize (2003); Named One of the Top 15 Most Cited Author in Computer Science, ISI (2002); Steven J. Fenves Award for Systems Research, CIT, Carnegie Mellon University (2000); Award, Best Technical Paper, Computers & Chemical Engineering (2000); Technical Achievement Award in Academic Research, HENAAC (2000); Gambrinus Award, Technical University of Dortmund (1999); William H. Walker Award for Excellence in Contributions to Chemical Engineering Literature, American Institute of Chemical Engineers (AIChE) (1997); Award, Best Technical Paper, Computers and Chemical Engineering (1988); Presidential Young Investigator Award, National Science Foundation (1984); Medal, Best Student of Mexico, National Council on Science and Technology (CONACYT) (1974); Citation for Leadership in Mixed Integer Nonlinear Programming (MINLP) Model Formulation and Solution for Process Design and Operation; Recipient, Numerous Distinguished Lectureships, Numerous Recognitions and Accolades **MEM:** American Institute of Chemical Engineers; Institute for Operations Research and Management Science (INFORMS); Institution of Chemical Engineers (IChemE); Mathematical Optimization Society; American Chemical Society; American Society Engineering Education (ASEE); National Academy of Engineering; Mexican Academy of Sciences; Mexican Academy of Engineering **MH:** Albert Nelson Marquis Lifetime Achievement Award; Marquis Who's Who Top Professional **AS:** Dr. Grossmann attributes his success to the impact of his teachers and colleagues who promoted passion for education and research, and by setting very high standards. They most notably include Ing. Alejandro Puron de la Borbolla at Universidad Iberoamericana, Mexico City, Prof. Roger Sargent, his PhD advisor at Imperial College, London, and Prof. Arthur Westerberg and Prof. Egon Balas at Carnegie Mellon University. **B/I:** Dr. Grossmann became involved in his profession because he always liked mathematics, and it became a matter of combining mathematics and science and applying it to practice. **AV:** Classical music; History of mathematics **RE:** Roman Catholic **THT:** Dr. Grossman's motto is, "It always pays to dream."

GROTH, EDWARD JOHN III, T: Professor **I:** Education/Educational Services **CN:** Princeton University **DOB:** 05/13/1946 **PB:** St. Louis **SC:** MO/USA **PT:** Edward J. Groth, Jr. (Deceased 2003); Marion Catherine (Winkel) Groth (Deceased 1991) **MS:** Widowed **SPN:** Jane Ellen Stevenson (06/15/1968, Deceased 2015) **CH:** Jeffrey Todd; Amy Carina **ED:** PhD in Physics, Princeton University (1971); BS in Physics, California Institute of Technology (1968) **C:** Professor Emeritus, Princeton University (2015-Present); Professor, Princeton University (1986-2015); Associate Professor, Princeton University (1978-1986); Assistant Professor, Princeton University (1972-1978); Instructor, Department of Physics, Princeton University (1971-1972) **CR:** Consultant, Cornell Technical Services LLC (2015-Present); Associate Chair, Department of Physics, Princeton University (2004-2008); Consultant, American Cash Exchange (2001-2016); Deputy Principal Investigator, Wide Field and Planetary Camera (1990-1995); Data and Operations Team Leader, Hubble Space Telescope, NASA (1977-1995); Consultant, Princeton Telecommunications (1986-1991); Consultant, HP, Corvallis, OR (1982-1983); Consultant, TRW, Redondo Beach, CA (1981-1982) **CIV:** Hopewell Valley Arts Council; Sourland Conservancy **AW:** Medal for Excep-

Council on Education (2015); Americanism Award, Anti-Defamation League (2014); Honorary Fellow, London School of Economics (2013); Woman of Spirit Award, The National Multiple Sclerosis Society (2012); Named Distinguished Daughter of Pennsylvania (2010); Centennial Medal, Harvard University (2003); Senior Scholar Award (1999-2003); President's Distinguished Teaching Award (2000); Fellowship, University of Hong Kong (1998-1999); Bertram Mott Award, American Association of University Professors, Rider College (Now Rider University) (1998); Grant, The Spencer Foundation (1995-1998); Award, Gustavus Myers Center for the Study of Bigotry and Human Rights in North America (1997); Ralph J. Bunche Award, American Political Science Association (APSA) (1997); Book Award, North America Society for Social Philosophy (1996-1997); Fellowship, American Council of Learned Societies (1978-1979); Fellowship, National Endowment for the Humanities (1977); Numerous Awards **MEM:** Executive Committee, Association for Practical and Professional Ethics (1990-Present); President, American Society for Political and Legal Philosophy (2001-2004); Fellow, American Academy of Arts & Sciences; National Academy of Education; The American Academy of Political and Social Science; The Phi Beta Kappa Society

GUTWILER, SHARON, T: School System Administrator **I:** Education/Educational Services **DOB:** 06/13/1942 **PT:** Elmer L.; Lola (Thimmes) Bixler **MS:** Married **SPN:** Patrick J. Gutwiler (07/02/1960) **CH:** Michael; Linda Gutwiler Coppess; Janet; Kathy Gutwiler Kelley; Brian **ED:** Diploma, Stanwood High School (1960) **C:** Secretary, Jack's Feed and Grain, Inc. (1987-Present); Member, Lincoln Board of Education (1986-1992); Secretary, Rockwell International (1963-1965) **CIV:** Stanwood Union Church (1960-Present); Member, Core Committee, Stanwood Sesquicentennial (1992-1994); Member, Hootn-Tootn Days Committee (1992, 1993); Secretary, United Taxpayers of Iowa (1988-1990) **AW:** The Community Impact Award, North Cedar Community School District (2019); Honorary Chapter Farmer, Future Farmers of America, Lincoln, NE (1982); Alumni Community Impact Award **MEM:** Treasurer, Stanwood Lions Club (1990-Present) **MH:** Albert Nelson Marquis Lifetime Achievement Award **AV:** Spending time with grandchildren; Sewing; Boating; Bowling; Camping **PA:** Republican

GUY, GEORGE, "BUDDY", T: Guitarist **I:** Media & Entertainment **DOB:** 07/30/1936 **PB:** Lettsworth **SC:** LA/USA **PT:** Sam Guy; Isabel Guy **MS:** Divorced **SPN:** Jennifer Guy (1975, Divorced 2002); Joan Guy (1959, Divorced) **CH:** Charlotte; Carlise; Colleen; George; Gregory; Geoffrey; Rashawnna; Michael **C:** Professional Guitar Player, Chicago, IL (1957-Present); Owner, Buddy Guy Legends, Chicago, IL; Touring Musician in Field **CIV:** Former Member, Nominating Committee, Rock and Roll Hall of Fame **CW:** Musician, "The Blues Is Alive and Well" (2018); Musician, "Born to Play Guitar" (2015); Musician, "Rhythm & Blues" (2013); Musician, "Living Proof" (2010); Musician, "Skin Deep" (2008); Contributing Musician, "He's My Blues Brother" (2006); Musician, "Bring 'Em In" (2005); Musician, "Blues Singer" (2003); Musician, "Sweet Tea" (2001); Musician, "Heavy Love" (1998); Musician, "Slippin' In" (1994); Contributing Musician, "All Star Chicago Blues Session" (1994); Contributing Musician, "Better Off with the Blues" (1993); Musician, "Feels Like Rain" (1993); Musician, "Damn Right, I've Got the Blues" (1991); Contributing Musician, "Bad Luck Boy" (1983); Contributing Musician, "The Red Hot Blues of Phil Guy" (1982); Musician, "DJ Play My Blues" (1982); Contributing Musician,

"Buddy & Phil" (1981); Contributing Musician, "Going Back" (1981); Musician, "Breaking Out" (1980); Musician, "The Blues Giant" (1979); Contributing Musician, "Pleading the Blues" (1979); Contributing Musician, "Play the Blues" (1972); Musician, "Hold That Plane!" (1972); Contributing Musician, "Southside Reunion" (1971); Contributing Musician, "Southside Blues Jam" (1970); Contributing Musician, "Buddy and the Juniors" (1970); Contributing Musician, "Coming at You" (1968); Musician, "A Man and the Blues" (1968); Musician, "I Left My Blues in San Francisco" (1967); Contributing Musician, "It's My Life, Baby!" (1966); Contributing Musician, "Chicago/The Blues/Today!, Vol. 1" (1966); Contributing Musician, "Hoodoo Man Blues" (1965) **AW:** Traditional Blues Album, "The Blues is Alive and Well," Grammy Awards (2019); Inductee, Austin City Limits Hall of Fame (2019); Blues Album, "Born to Play Guitar," Grammy Awards (2016); Lifetime Achievement Award, Grammy Awards (2015); Lifetime Achievement Award, National Academy of Recording Arts and Sciences (2015); Inductee, Musicians Hall of Fame and Museum (2014); Kennedy Center Honors (2012); Contemporary Blues Album, "Living Proof," Grammy Awards (2011); Inductee, Louisiana Music Hall of Fame (2008); Inductee, Rock and Roll Hall of Fame (2005); Traditional Blues Album, "Blues Singer," Grammy Awards (2004); National Medal of Arts (2003); Rock Instrumental Performance, "SRV Shuttle," Grammy Awards (1997); Contemporary Blues Album, "Slippin' In," Grammy Awards (1996); Inductee, Guitar Center's Hollywood Rockwalk (1996); Contemporary Blues Album, "Feels Like Rain," Grammy Awards (1994); Century Award, Billboard Magazine (1993); Contemporary Blues Album, "Damn Right, I've Got the Blues," Grammy Awards (1992); 23-Time Recipient, W.C. Handy Awards; Greatest Living Electric Blues Guitarist

GWYNN, REGINA, T: Co-Founder, Chief Executive Officer **I:** Business Management/Business Services **CN:** TresseNoire **ED:** MBA in Marketing, Entrepreneurship and Strategy, Northwestern University Kellogg School of Management (2009); BS in Marketing, Rutgers, the State University of New Jersey (2001); Coursework in Fashion Buying and Merchandising, Fashion Institute of Technology (1997) **C:** Co-Founder, Black Women Talk Tech (2017-Present); Co-Founder, Chief Executive Officer, TresseNoire (2014-Present); Senior Advisor, Culture Shift Labs (2013-2017); With, Marketing, The Apparel Group (2011-2015); Consultant, Monitor Group (2010-2011); Marketing Manager, Macy's Merchandising Group, Inc. (2005-2007); Associate Marketing Manager, Menswear and Kids Brands, Macy's Merchandising Group, Inc. (2003-2005); Product Assistant, Dress Accessories, Macy's Merchandising Group, Inc. (2001-2003) **CIV:** Vice-Chair, Rising Tide Capital (2010-2012)

GYLLENHAAL, JAKE BENJAMIN, T: Actor **I:** Media & Entertainment **DOB:** 12/19/1980 **PB:** Los Angeles **SC:** CA/USA **PT:** Stephen Gyllenhaal; Naomi (Achs) Foner Gyllenhaal **ED:** Coursework, Columbia University **CW:** Appearance, "Saturday Night Live" (2020); Actor, "John Mulaney & the Sack Lunch Bunch" (2019); Actor, "Spider-Man: Far from Home" (2019); Actor, "Velvet Buzzsaw" (2019); Actor, "Sea Wall/A Life" (2019); Actor, "The Sisters Brothers" (2018); Actor, "Wildlife" (2018); Actor, "Stronger" (2017); Actor, "Okja" (2017); Actor, "Lief" (2017); Actor, "Sunday in the Park with George" (2016-2017); Actor, "Nocturnal Animals" (2016); Appearance, "Inside Amy Schumer" (2016); Actor, "Demolition" (2015); Actor, "Everest" (2015); Actor, "Southpaw" (2015); Actor, "Accidental Love" (2015); Actor, "Little Shop of Horrors" (2015); Actor,. "Constellations" (2014-2015); Actor,

Producer, "Nightcrawler" (2014); Actor, "Nailed" (2014); Actor, "Enemy" (2013); Actor, "Prisoners" (2013); Actor, "If There is I Haven't Found It Yet" (2012); Actor, Executive Producer, "End of Watch" (2012); Actor, "Source Code" (2011); Actor, "Love and Other Drugs" (2010); Actor, "Prince of Persia: The Sands of Time" (2010); Actor, "Brothers" (2009); Actor, "Rendition" (2007); Actor, "Zodiac" (2007); Actor, "Proof" (2005); Actor, "Jarhead" (2005); Actor, "Brokeback Mountain" (2005); Actor, "The Day After Tomorrow" (2004); Actor, "The Good Girl" (2002); Actor, "Moonlight Mile" (2002); Actor, "This is Our Youth" (2002); Actor, "Highway" (2002); Actor, "Lovely and Amazing" (2001); Actor, "Bubble Boy" (2001); Actor, "Donnie Darko" (2001); Actor, "October Sky" (1999); Actor, "Homegrown" (1998); Actor, "A Dangerous Woman" (1993); Actor, "Josh and S.A.M." (1993); Actor, "City Slickers" (1991); Appearance, Television Shows, Theater, Music Videos, Films **AW:** Listee, 50 Most Powerful People in Hollywood, Premiere Magazine (2006); BAFTA Award for Best Actor in a Supporting Role (2006); Award for Best Performance, Best Kiss MTV Movie Awards (2006); Listee, 50 Most Beautiful People, People Magazine (2006); Award for Best Supporting Actor, National Board of Review (2005); London Evening Standard Theatre Award for Outstanding Newcomer (2002); Recipient, Numerous Awards **AV:** Woodworking; Cooking

HAALAND, DEBRA, "DEB" ANNE, T: U.S. Representative from New Mexico **I:** Government Administration/Government Relations/Government Services **DOB:** 12/02/1960 **PB:** Winslow **SC:** AZ/USA **PT:** J.D. "Dutch" Haaland; Mary Toya Haaland **CH:** One Daughter **ED:** JD in Indian Law, The University of New Mexico, Albuquerque, NM (2006); BA in English, The University of New Mexico, Albuquerque, NM (1994) **C:** Member, U.S. House of Representatives from New Mexico First Congressional District (2019-Present); Chair, New Mexico Democratic Party (2015-2017); Tribal Administrator, San Felipe Pueblo, NM (2013-2015); Owner, Pueblo Salsa **MIL:** Honorary Commander, Kirtland Air Force Base (2016-Present) **AV:** Marathon running; Gourmet cooking **PA:** Democrat **RE:** Catholic

HAAS, THOMAS AVERILL HOGAN, "T. HOGAN" HOGAN MR., T: Chief Executive Officer, Executive Director **I:** Fine Art **CN:** Huntington Symphony Orchestra (HSO) **DOB:** 09/30/1955 **PB:** Greenfield **SC:** OH/USA **PT:** Franklyn Haas; Dolores Haas **MS:** Independent **CH:** Mr. Haas highly respects his sister, Kathy Haas McGinnis, whom he considers the smartest and most talented person he knows. **ED:** MBA, University of Maryland, Baltimore (1992);BSBA, Berea College, Berea, KY (1980); Ironton High School (1973) **C:** Chief Executive Officer, Executive Director, Huntington Symphony Orchestra (2007-Present) **CIV:** The City Club of Huntington (2007); Rotary Club of Huntington (2006) **AW:** Person of the Year Award (2018) **AS:** Mr. Haas attributes his success to staying current, saying "If your brain and attitude is current thus your life will be fresh...one cannot demand respect, it is very simply earned. No one is entitled to any factor; earn respect and your entitlements will grow." **B/I:** Mr. Haas became involved in his profession because his teacher, Janet Bromley, was a huge inspiration to him. They met at the beginning of his career. She has since passed, but he still talks to her son to this day. **AV:** Training and handling Great Danes; Dogs; Health and fitness **PA:** Republican/Independent **RE:** Catholic **THT:** Mr. Haas advises others to "look forward to reach[ing] your goal and beware of the gossip and the people connected."

HABER, MICHAEL, T: Attorney **I:** Law and Legal Services **CN:** Law Offices of Michael S. Haber **MS:** Married **CH:** Two children **ED:** JD, School of Law, Saint John's University (1986); BS, University of Bridgeport (1979) **C:** Attorney, Law Offices of Michael S. Haber, New York, NY (1991-Present) **CIV:** Volunteer, Arbitrator; Pro Bono Legal Services, Animal Rights **CW:** "CPLR Art. 9: Statute is to be Applied Liberally to Permit Class Certification of Plaintiff Shareholders with Substantially Similar Claims in Actions Against Corporate Directors," St. John's Law Review (1985) **MEM:** New York State Bar Association **BAR:** New York State Bar Association (1986); Connecticut Bar Association (1986) **MH:** Marquis Who's Who Top Professional **AS:** Mr. Haber attributes his success to the fact that he listens and that he actually cares about positive results. Also he cannot stand to lose. **B/I:** Mr. Haber became involved in his profession because he felt that litigation was the way to advance society.

HABERMAN, MAGGIE LINDSY, T: White House Correspondent **I:** Writing and Editing **CN:** The New York Times Company **DOB:** 10/30/1973 **PB:** New York **SC:** NY/USA **PT:** Clyde Haberman; Nancy (Spies) Haberman **MS:** Married **SPN:** Dareh Ardashes Gregorian (2003) **CH:** Three Children **ED:** BA, Sarah Lawrence College (1995) **C:** White House Correspondent, The New York Times (2015-Present); Political Analyst, Cable News Network (CNN) (2014); Senior Reporter, Politico (2010-2014); Reporter, New York Post (1996-1999, 2008-2010); Reporter, New York Daily News **AW:** Co-Recipient, Pulitzer Prize for National Reporting (2018); Aldo Beckman Memorial Award, White House Correspondents' Association (WHCA) (2018); Front Page Award for Journalist of the Year, The Newswomen's Club of New York (2018)

HACKETT, JAMES PATRICK, T: Chief Executive Officer, President **I:** Automotive **CN:** Ford Motor Company **DOB:** 04/22/1955 **PB:** Columbus **SC:** OH/USA **ED:** Bachelor in General Studies, University of Michigan (1977) **C:** President, Chief Executive Officer, Ford Motor Company (2017-Present); Chairman, Ford Smart Mobility (2016-2017); Chief Executive Officer, Steelcase, Inc., Grand Rapids, MI (2013-2014); President, Chief Executive Officer, Steelcase, Inc., Grand Rapids, MI (1994-2013); Executive Vice President, Chief Operating Officer for North America, Steelcase, Inc., Grand Rapids, MI (1994); Executive Vice President, Steelcase Ventures, Steelcase, Inc., Grand Rapids, MI (1994); President, Turnstone Subsidiary, Steelcase, Inc., Grand Rapids, MI (1993-1994); Senior Vice President of Sales and Marketing, Steelcase, Inc., Grand Rapids, MI (1990-1993); Director of National Accounts, Steelcase, Inc., Grand Rapids, MI (1986-1990); Regional Manager, Steelcase, Inc., Houston, TX (1984-1986); Management Positions, Steelcase, Inc., Grand Rapids, MI (1981-1984);Various Sales and Management Positions, The Proctor & Gamble Co., (1977-1981) **CR:** Trustee, University of Michigan (2013-Present); Board of Directors, Ford Motor Company (2013-Present); Fifth Third Bancorp (2001-Present); Northwestern Mutual Life (2000-Present)

HACKMAN, GENE ALLEN, T: Actor **I:** Media & Entertainment **DOB:** 1/30/1930 **PB:** San Bernardino **SC:** CA/USA **PT:** Eugene Ezra Hackman; Anna Lyda Elizabeth (Gray) Hackman **MS:** Married **SPN:** Betsy Arakawa (12/1991); Faye Maltese (01/01/1956, Divorced 1986) **CH:** Christopher Allen; Elizabeth Jean; Leslie Anne **ED:** Studied, Pasadena Playhouse (1956); Coursework in Journalism and Television Production, University of Illinois **MIL:** Radio Operator, United States Marines (1948-1951) **CW:** Narrator, "We, the Marines" (2017); Narrator, "The Unknown Flag Raiser of Iwo Jima" (2016); Author, "Pursuit" (2014); Author, "Payback at Morning Peak" (2011); Co-author, "Escape from Andersonville: A Novel of the Civil War" (2008); Co-author, "Justice for None: A Novel" (2004); Actor, "Runaway Jury" (2003); Actor, "The Mexican" (2001); Actor, "Heartbreakers" (2001); Actor, "Heist" (2001); Actor, "The Royal Tenenbaums" (2001); Actor, "Behind Enemy Lines" (2001); Co-author with Daniel F. Lenihan, "Wake of the Perdido Star: A Novel" (2000); Actor, "The Replacements" (2000); Actor, Executive Producer, "Under Suspicion" (1999); Actor, "Enemy of the State" (1998); Voice Actor, "Antz" (1998); Actor, "Twilight" (1998); Actor, "The Magic Hour" (1997); Actor, "Absolute Power" (1997); Actor, "Extreme Measures" (1996); Actor, "The Chamber" (1996); Actor, "The Birdcage" (1996); Actor, "The Quick and the Dead" (1995); Actor, "Crimson Tide" (1995); Actor, "Get Shorty" (1995); Actor, "Wyatt Earp" (1994); Actor, "The Firm" (1993); Actor, "Geronimo: An American Legend" (1993); Actor, "Unforgiven" (1992); Actor, "Company Business" (1991); Actor, "Loose Cannons" (1990); Actor, "Narrow Margin" (1990); Actor, "The Package" (1989); Actor, "Postcards from the Edge" (1989); Actor, "Class Action" (1989); Actor, "Another Woman" (1988); Actor, "Bat*21" (1988); Actor, "Split Decisions" (1988); Actor, "Mississippi Burning" (1988); Actor, "Full Moon in Blue Water" (1988); Actor, "Superman IV: The Quest for Peace" (1987); Actor, "No Way Out" (1987); Actor, "Power" (1986); Actor, "Target" (1985); Actor, "Twice in a Lifetime" (1985); Actor, "Misunderstood" (1984); Actor, "Eureka" (1984); Voice Actor, "Two of a Kind" (1983); Actor, "Under Fire" (1983); Actor, "Uncommon Valor" (1983); Actor, "All Night Long" (1981); Actor, ""Reds" (1981); Actor, "Superman II" (1980); Actor, "Superman" (1978); Actor, "A Bridge Too Far" (1977); Actor, "The Domino Principle" (1977); Actor, "March or Die" (1977); Actor, "The French Connection II" (1975); Actor, "Bite the Bullet" (1975); Actor, "Night Moves" (1975); Actor, "Lucky Lady" (1975); Actor, "The Conversation" (1974); Actor, "Zandy's Bride" (1974); Actor, "Young Frankenstein" (1974); Actor, "Scarecrow" (1973); Actor, "Prime Cut" (1972); Acotr, "The Poseidon Adventure" (1972); Actor, "Doctor's Wives" (1971); Actor, "The Hunting Party" (1971); Actor, "The French Connection" (1971); Actor, "Cisco Pike" (1971); Actor, "Marooned" (1970); Actor, "Riot" (1969); Actor, "The Gypsy Moths" (1969); Actor, "Downhill Racer" (1969); Actor, "I Never Sang for My Father" (1969); Actor, "The Split" (1968); Actor, "Shadow on the Land" (1968); Actor, "My Father and My Mother" (1968); Appearance, "I Spy" (1968); Appearance, "The Iron Horse" (1967); Actor, "First to Fight" (1967); Actor, "A Covenant with Death" (1967); Actor, "Bonnie and Clyde" (1967); Actor, "First to Fight" (1967); Appearance, "The F.B.I." (1967); Appearance, "The Invaders" (1967); Appearance, "The Trials of O'Brien" (1966); Actor, "Hawaii" (1966); Actor, "Lilith" (1964); Appearances, "The Defenders" (1961, 1963); Appearance, "Look Up and Live" (1963); Appearance, "Naked City" (1963); Appearance, "The DuPont Show of the Week" (1963); Appearance, "East Side/West Side" (1963); Actor, "Ride with Terror" (1963); Appearances, "The United States Steel Hour" (1959, 1960, 1962); Actor, "Mad Dog Coll" (1961); Actor, Theater Plays, Television Shows and Films **AW:** Cecil B. DeMille Award, Golden Globe Awards, Hollywood Foreign Press Association (2003); Award for Best Actor, Chicago Film Critics Association (2002); Award for Best Actor, National Society of Film Critics (1988, 2002); Award for Best Actor, American Film Institute (2002); Golden Globe Award for Best Actor - Motion Picture Musical or Comedy, Hollywood Foreign Press Association (2001); Academy Award for Best Supporting Actor, Academy of Motion Picture Arts & Sciences (1993); Award for Best Actor, New York Film Critics Association (1971, 1992); Golden Globe Award for Best Supporting Actor - Motion Picture, Hollywood Foreign Press Association (1992); Award for Best Actor, Los Angeles Film Critics Association (1992); Award for Best Actor, Boston Film Critics Association (1992); Award for Best Actor, National Society of Film Critics Awards (1992); Award for Best Actor, National Board of Review (1971, 1974, 1988); Named Star of the Year, National Association of Theatre Owners (1974); Cannes Film Festival Award (1973); British Academy Award (1972); Academy Award for Best Actor, Academy of Motion Picture Arts & Sciences (1971); Golden Globe Award for Best Actor - Motion Picture Drama, Hollywood Foreign Press Association (1971); Numerous Awards

HACKMAN, JUDITH, T: University Administrator, Researcher **I:** Education/Educational Services **PT:** John Burrel; Elva Hannah (Smith) Dozier **MS:** Widow **SPN:** J. Richard Hackman (Deceased) **CH:** Julia Beth Hackman Proffitt; Laura Dianne Hackman Codeanne **ED:** Doctor of Philosophy, University of Michigan, 1983; Graduate School Special Student, Yale University, 1979-1980;Master of Science, Southern Connecticut State University, 1970;Bachelor of Arts, University of Illinois, 1963;Coursework, MacMurray College, 1959-1962 **C:** Provost, The Graduate Institute (2016-Present); Director, Teaching Fellow Program, Yale Graduate School (1999-2015); Associate Dean, Yale College (1998-2015); Director, Corporate and Foundation Relations, Yale University (1996-1998); Associate Dean, Yale College (1987-1995); Director, Institutional Research, Yale University (1982-1987); Associate Director, Institutional Research, Yale University (1979-1982); Special Projects, Yale University (1974-1979); Director, Criteria Study, Yale University (1971-1973); Researcher, Yale University, New Haven (1966-1971); Teacher, Oakwood High School, Fithian, IL (1963-1966) **CR:** Guest Lecturer, Numerous Universities; Consultant, Education Research Associates **CIV:** Board Member, Neighborhood Music School (2012-Present); Trustee, Macmurray College (2003-Present); Vice Chair, United Way of Greater New Haven (2006-2015); Board Member, United Way of Greater New Haven (2004-2014); With, WYBC-FM Radio (1991-1996); Member, Greater New Haven Community Loan Fund (1988-1996); President, Greater New Haven Community Loan Fund (1993-1995); Member, Town Democratic Committee, Bethany (1984-1989); Moderator, Church Council, Battell Church of Christ in Yale, New Haven, CT (1985-1986); Board of Directors, Information and Counseling Service for Women, New Haven, CT (1972-1977, 1979-1980); Board of Directors, New Careers for Women, New Haven, CT (1974-1980); Board of Directors, Bethany Community Schools, Connecticut (1978-1979) **CW:** Contributor, 17 Articles to Professional Journals; Contributor, 2 Book Chapters **AW:** Volunteer of the Year, United Way of Greater New Haven (2006); Yale and New Haven Elm Ivy Award (2004); Best Dissertation Award, University of Michigan (1984); Outstanding Alumnus Award, Southern Connecticut State University (1983) **MEM:** Board Director, Association for the Study of Higher Education (1988-Present); Accreditation Liaison Officer for Yale, New England Association of Schools and Colleges (1983-1988, 2008-2015); Editorial Board, Society of College and University Planning (1986-1994); Past President, Chairman, Nominating Committee, Association for the Study of Higher Education (1991-1992); President, Association for the Study of Higher Education (1990-1991); President-Elect, Association for the Study of Higher Education (1989-1990); College Advisory Board, Washington Office, New England Association of Schools and Colleges (1987-1989); Publications Board, Association for Institutional Research (1987-1989); Nominating Committee, Association for Institutional Research (1986-1987); Chairman, Nominating Committee, North East Association for Institutional Research (1986-1987); Program Chairman, Association for the Study of Higher Education (1987); Forum Panel Committee, Association for Institutional Research (1985-1986); President, North East Association for Institutional Research (1985-1986); Program Chairman, North East Association for Institutional Research (1984-1985); Program Vice Chairman, Association for the Study of Higher Education (1984-1985) **MH:** Albert Nelson Marquis Lifetime Achievement Award; Marquis Who's Who Top Professional **AV:** Baritone horn **RE:** United Church of Christ

HACKWELL, GLENN A., PHD, T: Professor Emeritus of Zoology, Consultant **I:** Education/Educational Services **DOB:** 01/20/1931 **PB:** Manti **SC:** UT/USA **PT:** Alfred Henry Hackwell; Delma (Sudweeks) Hackwell **MS:** Widower **SPN:** Dorothy Alice Rasmussen (09/06/1955, Deceased 2019) **CH:** Burke Henry; Melissa **ED:** PhD, Oregon State University (1967); MS, Brigham Young University (1958); BS, Brigham Young University (1957) **CT:** Registered Professional Entomologist **C:** Professor Emeritus, California State University Stanislaus, Turlock, CA (2000-Present); Professor, California State University Stanislaus, Turlock, CA (1972-2000); Assistant Professor, Associate Professor, California State University Stanislaus, Turlock, CA (1961-1972) **CR:** Consultant, Campbell Soup Co., Modesto, CA (1983-1985); Consultant, United Nations Food and Agricultural Organization, Islamabad, Pakistan (1981-1982); Consultant, Fenimore Chemical Co., Los Angeles, CA (1973-1979); Consultant, Gallo Wine Co., Modesto Co., Los Angeles, CA (1968-1970) **CIV:** Trustee, Turlock Mosquito Abatement Project (1983-Present); Board of Directors, Turlock School Board (1975-1981) **MIL:** United States Air Force (1948-1952) **CW:** Contributor, Articles, Professional Journals **MEM:** International Society of Hymenopterists **MH:** Albert Nelson Marquis Lifetime Achievement Award **B/I:** When Dr. Hackwell was young, he would go hiking often. One time, he and his friends found some very large wasps, and Dr. Hackwell was fascinated. He quickly took a liking to hymenopterans; this interest stayed with Dr. Hackwell for the rest of his career. **AV:** Hiking; Insect collecting; Traveling; Reading **PA:** Democrat **RE:** Church of Latter-Day Saints

HADDISH, TIFFANY, T: Actress; Comedian **I:** Media & Entertainment **DOB:** 12/03/1979 **PB:** Los Angeles **SC:** CA/USA **PT:** Tsihaye Reda Haddish; Leola Haddish **ED:** Coursework, Santa Monica College **C:** Comedian, Various Comedy Shows; Customer Service Representative, Air New Zealand and Alaska Airlines, Los Angeles International Airport **CW:** Voice Actress, "Tuca & Bertie" (2019-Present); Actress, "Bad Trip" (2020); Actress, "Like a Boss" (2020); Appearance, "Between Two Ferns: The Movie" (2019); Actress, "The Kitchen" (2019); Voice Actress, "The Angry Birds Movie 2" (2019); Host, "Kids Say the Darndest Things" (2019); Voice Actress, "Crank Yankers" (2019); Voice Actress, "The Lego Movie Sequel" (2019); Voice Actress, "The Secret Life of Pets 2" (2019); Actress, "Night School" (2018); Actress, "The List" (2018); Actress, "Drunk History" (2018); Appearance, "The Last O.G." (2018); Actress, "Uncle Drew" (2018); Actress, "Mad Families" (2017); Featured, "Tiffany Haddish: She Ready! From the Hood to Hollywood" (2017); Host, "Saturday Night Live" (2017); Author,

"The Last Black Unicorn" (2017); Actress, "Girls Trip" (2017); Actress, "Boosters" (2017); Actress, "Kean" (2016); Actress, "Legends of Chamberlain Heights" (2016); Actress, "If Loving You is Wrong" (2015); Actress, "The Carmichael Show" (2015); Actress, "All Between Us" (2015); Actress, "4Play" (2014); Actress, "Patterns of Attraction" (2014); Actress, "Wishes" (2014); Actress, "New Girl" (2014); Actress, "Trip Tank" (2014); Actress, "School Dance" (2014); Actress, "Real Husbands of Hollywood" (2013-2014); Actress, "Christmas Wedding" (2013); Actress, "What My Husband Doesn't Know" (2012); Actress, "Driving by Braille" (2011); Actress, "Wax On, F*ck Off" (2010); Actress, "Janky Promoters" (2009); Actress, "In the Motherhood" (2009); Actress, "Secret Girlfriend" (2009); Actress, "Meet the Spartans" (2008); Actress, "Racing for Time" (2008); Appearance, "Nick Cannon Presents: Short Circuitz" (2007); Actress, "Just Jordan" (2007); Appearance, "Bill Bellamy's Who's Got Jokes?" (2006); Actress, "My Name is Earl" (2006); Actress, "It's Always Sunny in Philadelphia" (2006); Actress, "The Underground" (2006); Actress, "The Urban Demographic" (2005); Actress, "That's So Raven" (2005); Actress, Appearances, Music Videos, Television Shows, Films **AW:** Listee, 100 Most Influential People, Time Magazine (2018); BET Award for Best Actress (2018); Black Reel Awards for Best Supporting Actress and Outstanding Breakthrough Performance (Female) (2018); Emmy Award for Outstanding Guest Actress in a Comedy Series, Academy of Television Arts & Sciences (2018)

HAFKENSCHIEL, JOSEPH HENRY, T: President (Retired) **I:** Medicine & Health Care **DOB:** 06/06/1946 **PT:** Joseph Henry Hafkenschiel; Lucinde Buchanan (Thomas) Hafkenschiel **MS:** Married **SPN:** Cynthia Rusth Easton (09/28/1972) **CH:** Erin; Alexander **ED:** Master of Business Administration, University of California Berkeley (1970); Bachelor of Arts, Swarthmore College (1968) **CT:** Certified Association Executive (1991) **C:** President, California Association for Health Services at Home, Sacramento, CA (1986-2012); Executive Director, California Health Facilities Commission, Sacramento, CA (1980-1985); Chief, Office of Planning and Program Analysis, California Department of Health Services, Sacramento, CA (1978-1980); Senior Health Planning Analyst, California Department of Health, Sacramento, CA (1975-1978); Economist, Communications Workers, Washington, DC (1972-1975); Research Analyst, U.S. Department of Labor, Washington, DC (1971-1972) **CR:** Chairperson of the Board, California Society of Association Executives (2001-2002); Governing Council, American Public Health Association (1988-1990); American Society of Association Executives; National Association for Home Care **CIV:** Health Insurance Counseling and Advocacy; Sacramento Children's Home **CW:** Co-Principal Investigator, Uniform Home Health Database and Patient Classification Project, CAHSAH Foundation (1994-1998) **AW:** Lois C. Lillick Award for Outstanding Contributions to Home Care, California Association for Health Services at Home (2012) **MEM:** American Society of Association Executives; California Society of Association Executives; Park Terrace Club **MH:** Albert Nelson Marquis Lifetime Achievement Award **B/I:** Mr. Hafkenschiel became involved in his profession after serving in the U.S. government as a health and safety worker for several decades. Likewise, he served in the Communications Workers of America, which was the labor union that represented Bell Systems employees. Following this period, he became the president of the California Health Association at Home. **AV:** Reading; Gardening; Cooking **PA:** Independent **RE:** Society of Friends

HAFNER, JOSEPH A. JR., T: Food Products Executive **I:** Food & Restaurant Services **DOB:** 10/09/1944 **PB:** San Bernadino **SC:** CA/USA **PT:** Joseph Albert Hafner; Mary Florence (McGowan) Hafner **MS:** Married **SPN:** Merrill Hafner **CH:** John Michael; Daniel Stephen; Caroline Elizabeth **ED:** MBA, Amos Tuck School Business Administration, With High Distinction (1967); AB, Dartmouth College, Cum Laude (1966) **CT:** Certified Professional Accountant (CPA) **C:** Chairman, Riviana Foods Inc. (2005-Present); Director, Riviana Foods Inc., Houston, TX (1985-Present); President, Chief Executive Officer, Riviana Foods Inc., Houston, TX (1984-2005); President, Chief Operating Officer, Riviana Foods Inc., Houston, TX (1981-1984); Vice President, Riviana Foods Inc., Houston, TX (1977-1981); Treasurer, Vice President of Finance, Riviana International, Inc., Houston, TX (1973-1977); Controller, C/A Division, Riviana International, Inc., Guatemala City, Guatemala (1972-1973); Senior Consultant, Arthur Andersen & Co., Houston, TX (1969-1971); Intern, Cornell University-Ford Foundation, Lima, Peru (1967-1969) **AW:** CPA Gold Medal, Arkansas State Board of Public Accountancy (1969) **MEM:** American Institute of Certified Public Accountants; Council on Foreign Relations **MH:** Albert Nelson Marquis Lifetime Achievement Award **B/I:** As an undergraduate, Mr. Hafner got the opportunity to travel to Peru. This experience showed him the many wonders of the food industry, as he worked for the largest beer company in the city. His career progressed naturally in the future.

HAGAN, MICHAEL P., MD, T: Physician **I:** Medicine & Health Care **CN:** The McGuire Veterans Hospital **MS:** Married **SPN:** Silvia **CH:** Seven Children **ED:** MD, Baylor College of Medicine, Houston, TX (1989); PhD in DNA Damage, University of Illinois; MS in Nuclear Engineering, University of Illinois; BS in Engineering, United States Military Academy, West Point, NY **C:** National Director of Radiology and Oncology, McGuire VA Medical Center; Private Practice, Virginia Commonwealth University; Residency, Massachusetts General Hospital/Harvard University; Internship in Internal Medicine, Baylor Medical College **CIV:** Senior Executive Service, United States Government (2009) **MIL:** United States Military **AW:** Fellowship in Physics, Department of Energy (1974); Fellow, Atomic Energy in Physics (1970) **MEM:** American Society of Radiation Oncology; European Society for Radiation Oncology; Radiation Research Society; American Society for Biology; American Medical Association; Phi Kappa Phi **AS:** Dr. Hagan attributes his success to his passion for the job, as well as the mindset that causes him to refuse to go home until his work is done. **B/I:** Dr. Hagan always had an interest in science. He began his career as a physicist, studying the effects of ionizing radiation in living systems. That is what began his interest in working with DNA damage repair. Dr. Hagan completed his thesis in part at the Argonne National Laboratory in Illinois, studying proton and neutron therapy for patients. When he began working with patients, he knew immediately that was what he wanted to do. When he went to medical school, his mission was to apply the radiation biology that he previously studied in the treatment of patients.

HAGEDORN, JAMES, "JIM" LEE, T: U.S. Representative from Minnesota **I:** Government Administration/Government Relations/Government Services **CN:** U.S. House of Representatives **DOB:** 08/04/1962 **PB:** Blue Earth **SC:** MN/USA **PT:** Tom Hagedorn; Kathleen Hagedorn **MS:** Married **SPN:** Jennifer Carnahan **ED:** Bachelor of Arts in Government and Politics, George Mason University (1993) **C:** Member, U.S. House of Representatives from Minnesota's First Congressional District (2019-Present); Director, Legislative and Public Affairs, Financial Management Service, United States Department of the Treasury (1991-1998); Legislative Assistant, Minnesota Congressman Arlan Stangeland **CIV:** Member, St. Paul Lutheran Church, Blue Earth, MN **PA:** Republican **RE:** Lutheran

HAGLER, TZVI Y., ESQ., T: Partner **I:** Law and Legal Services **CN:** Law Office of Tzvi Y. Hagler **MS:** Married **CH:** Four Children **ED:** JD, Hofstra University (2008) **C:** Partner and Founder, Law Office of Tzvi Y. Hagler (2011-Present) **MEM:** Nassau County Bar Association; New York State County Bar Association **BAR:** Nassau County Bar Association; New York **MH:** Marquis Who's Who Top Professional; Marquis Who's Who Humanitarian Award **AS:** Mr. Hagler attributes his success to his ability to listen to and understand what his clients want from him. He always works hard to successfully represent them. **B/I:** Mr. Hagler became involved in his profession because he liked working with people to solve problems.

HAGLUND, ELAINE J., PHD, T: Emerita Professor **I:** Education/Educational Services **CN:** California State University, Long Beach **DOB:** 04/01/1937 **MS:** Single **ED:** Doctorate in International Education; Master's Degree in International Education **C:** Professor Emerita, California State University, Long Beach (2009-Present); Professor, California State University, Long Beach (1971-2009) **CR:** Founder, Endowment for the Global Studies Institute, California State University, Long Beach; Coordinator, Global Studies Institute, Mission "To Make International Integral to What It Means to be Educated"; Instructor, Institutions Across the World, including Ecuador, Turkey, Mexico, South Korea, Kazakhstan, Nepal, Vietnam, Northern Cyprus, Morocco, and Peking Graduate School in China, Among Others; Former Teacher, Overseas Schools in Germany and Japan **AW:** Award for Distinguished Teaching; Numerous Awards Representing her Academic Leadership in the Fields of Higher Education and International Education; Three Fulbright Fellowships, Africa **MEM:** Orange County Peace Corps Association; Comparative and International Education Society; National Association for Multicultural Association; Fulbright **MH:** Marquis Who's Who Top Professional **PA:** Democrat **RE:** Christian **THT:** Dr. Haglund has a competition internationalizing her student's coursework, which makes it possible for two African history courses to be part of the curriculum.

HAHN, RICHARD WAYNE, T: Retired Hospital Administrator **I:** Medicine & Health Care **DOB:** 06/12/1942 **PB:** Phillipsburg **SC:** NJ/USA **PT:** Albert L. Hahn; Irene S. (Nagy) Hahn **MS:** Married **SPN:** Gregory; Anne Lenora Waugh (04/12/1969) **CH:** Gregory; Susan **ED:** MHA, University of Minnesota (1970); BS, Trinity University, San Antonio, TX (1964) **C:** Retired Hospital Administrator, Dunn Memorial Hospital (1997); Executive Director, Dunn Memorial Hospital (1978-1997); Administrator, Syosset Hospital, Syosset, NY (1976-1978); Assistant Administrator, Montana Deaconess Hospital (1973-1976); Assistant Administrator, United Hospitals, Newark, NJ (1969-1973) **CR:** U.S. Air Force Reserve, Chanute Air Force Base (1987-1992); Air National Guard (1978-1986); New York Air National Guard (1976-1978); Clinic Administrator, Montana Air National Guard (1973-1976) **CIV:** Elder, First Presbyterian Church (1984-Present) **MIL:** Lieutenant Colonel, U.S. Air Force Reserve (1973-1992); U.S. Army (1967-1968) **AW:** Decorated Bronze Star, U.S. Army **MEM:** Life Fellow, American College of Hospital Administrators; Rotary **MH:** Albert

Nelson Marquis Lifetime Achievement Award; Marquis Who's Who Top Professional; Distinguished Humanitarian **B/I:** Mr. Hahn became involved in his profession because, when he was in Vietnam, he was a platoon commander for a civil affairs platoon. In that position, he developed an interest in civil affairs for Vietnamese people, especially in providing medical services. He then learned about a career in hospital administration, which was when he applied to graduate school. Mr. Hahn was selected to go to the University of Minnesota, where he would partake in the program for hospital administration. He was the first individual to attend college in his family. **AV:** Hunting; Fishing; Outdoor activities; Listening to music **PA:** Republican **RE:** Presbyterian

HALABE, UDAYA, T: Civil Engineering Educator, Researcher **I:** Education/Educational Services **PT:** Gangadhar Bhatta; Shailaja Bhatta Halabe **MS:** Married **SPN:** Anjali Marathe **CH:** Esha Bhatta H.; Shivali Bhatta H. **ED:** PhD in Civil Engineering, Massachusetts Institute of Technology (1990); MS in Management, Massachusetts Institute of Technology (1990); MS in Civil Engineering, Massachusetts Institute of Technology (1988); Master in Technology, Civil Engineering, Indian Institute of Technology, Kanpur, India (1985); BE in Civil Engineering, University of Roorkee, India (1984) **CT:** Registered Professional Engineer, West Virginia **C:** Professor, West Virginia University, Morgantown (2001-Present); Associate Professor, West Virginia University, Morgantown (1996-2001); Assistant Professor, West Virginia University, Morgantown (1990-1996) **CW:** Contributor, Numerous Articles, Professional Journals and Conference Proceedings; Contributor, Over 125 Journal and Conference Papers; Contributor, Over 50 Research Reports **AW:** Statler College Outstanding Advisor Award (2016, 2017); WVASCE Outstanding Civil Engineering Educator of the Year Award (2016); National James M. Robbins Excellence Teaching Award (2012) **MEM:** Fellow, American Society of Civil Engineers; Fellow, Structural Engineering Institute; Fellow, American Society of Nondestructive Testing; American Concrete Institute; Chi Epsilon; Tau Beta Pi **MH:** Albert Nelson Marquis Lifetime Achievement Award; Marquis Who's Who Top Professional **AS:** He attributes his success to continuous hard work. **B/I:** He had interest in civil engineering from early childhood. **AV:** Walking; Reading; Tennis; Swimming **PA:** Independent **RE:** Hindu **THT:** Everyone should maintain high level of honesty and professional integrity, and contribute to the well-being of the society.

HALASI-KUN, ADAM T., LTC, USAR (RET.), T: Manager **I:** Utilities **DOB:** 11/29/1943 **PB:** Budapest **SC:** Hungary **PT:** Tibor Halasi-Kun; Eva (Metzger) Halasi-Kun **MS:** Widowed **SPN:** Karen M. Cherubin (10/17/1970, Deceased) **CH:** Karen Mary (Cherubin) Halasi-Kun (Deceased) **ED:** Coursework, Command and General Staff College (1978); MBA, St. John's University (1975); Coursework, Civil Affairs Advanced Course (1973); Coursework, Defense Civil Preparedness Staff College Course (1973); BS, New York University (1966) **CT:** Certified Compensation Professional (CCP), American Compensation Association (1985) **C:** Manager, Customer Services/Employee Benefits, Con Edison (Consolidated Edison Company of New York, Inc.) (1990-2003); Manager, Performance Improvement and Organization Development, Con Edison (Consolidated Edison Company of New York, Inc.), New York, NY (1980-1990); Organization Development Consultant, Con Edison (Consolidated Edison Company of New York, Inc.), New York, NY (1976-1980); Manager, Director, Food Services, Saga Admin Corporation, Menlo

Park, CA (1968-1971) **CIV:** Chairman, New Milford Conservation Commission; Chairman, Sexton for Upper Merryall Cemetery Association **MIL:** With, United States Army Reserve (1969-1994); With, Civil Affairs/Special Operations Assignments, United States Army (1966-1968); Second Lieutenant, Lieutenant Colonel, Assigned to Supply, Finance, and Infantry Units, United States Army **CW:** Author, "Upper Merryall Cemetery: A Brief History" (2017); Author, "Karen Halasi-Kun, A Life Partner: Her Story" (2017) **AW:** Army Meritorious Service Medal (1994); Army Commendation Medal with Oak Leaf (1993) **MEM:** Former Member, American Compensation Association (Now WorldatWork); Civil Affairs Association; Reserve Officers Association (Now Reserve Organization of America; American Society for Training and Development (Now ATD); Organization Development Network; Appalachian Trail Council, Appalachian Trail Conservancy; Appalachian Mountain Club; President, Weantinoge Heritage Land Trust **MH:** Albert Nelson Marquis Lifetime Achievement Award; Marquis Who's Who Top Professional **B/I:** Mr. Halasi-Kun became involved in his profession because when he graduated from New York University, it was during the height of the Vietnam War. Everyone was being drafted, so he decided to enlist instead of being drafted. New York University had a Reserve Officer Training Corps (ROTC) program, which he joined and therefore joined the Army as a second lieutenant rather than a private. He was eventually sent to Vietnam, but before he went there, they sent him to an open mass management program, which is how to run military clubs and feeding operations. When he went to Vietnam, he was initially a supply officer, then a finance audit officer for non-appropriate funds. For a while, he was in an infantry company, where he was the commanding officer or the executive officer, depending on how they were structured. From that, he came back home. In 1968, he got a job in Virginia with a company in Chicago, Illinois, and then Menlo Park, California, running hospitality-type businesses. He stayed in both organizations for 28 years. Upon completing active duty, separating military members were required to serve additional time in the reserves, both active and inactive. Mr. Halasi-Kun took advantage of this opportunity to join a civil affairs unit that provided ample temporary for active duty assignments. He was able to have a dual career track. As a condition, Con Edison stated that voluntary absences could not exceed six months and was to be unpaid while the Army would not accept employment conflicts as an excuse for non-attendance. Upon completing active duty, Mr. Halasi-Kun elected to stay in the Army and joined an active reserve unit. With the support of Con Edison, he was able to pursue dual career tracks. **AV:** Traveling; Photography; Woodsman/outdoors; Golfing **PA:** Republican **RE:** Roman Catholic

HALE, LEE L., JD, T: Lawyer **I:** Law and Legal Services **CN:** Lee Hale Attorney-at-Law **DOB:** 10/17/1948 **PB:** Atlanta **SC:** GA/USA **PT:** Jack Lee Hale (Deceased 08/22/1994); Margaret Louise (Deano) Hale (Deceased 01/25/2020) **MS:** Married **SPN:** Margareth D. Hale (11/24/2001) **CH:** Lee Louis Jr. (JD); Lauren Alyce; John Robert **ED:** JD, Duke University (1973); BA, Spring Hill College, Summa Cum Laude (1970); Coursework, McGill Institute (1966) **CT:** Archdiocese of Mobile, Toolen Institute for Parish Services, Ecclesial Lay Ministry (1992) **C:** Lawyer, Solo Practitioner (1992-Present); Special Judge, Probate Court (2017-2018); Partner, Hale, Hughes & Teague, Mobile, AL (1984-1992); Special Assistant, Attorney General for Security Fraud Prosecutions (1981-1984); Deputy Attorney General, State of Alabama (1979-1980); Assistant

District Attorney, Mobile County, AL (1974-1979); Associate, Hamilton & Butler, Mobile, AL (1973-1974) **CR:** Strategist, Graddick for Chief Justice, State of Alabama (2012); Strategist, Windom for Governor (2002); Strategist, Lt. Governor Windom, Opposition to the Alabama Lottery Constitutional Amendment (1999); Strategist, Windom for Lt. Governor (1998); Strategist, Windom for State Senate (1989-1994); Lecturer, Continuing Legal Education, Alabama State Bar (1980-1983); Lecturer, Alabama Judicial College (1979); Campaign Manager, Graddick for Attorney General (1978); Adjunct Professor, Law, Alabama Judicial College (1975-1978); Professor in Criminal Justice, Troy State University, Bay Minette, AL (1975-1978); Campaign Manager, Graddick for District Attorney (1974) **CIV:** Criminal Code Committee, Alabama Law Institute (2005-2018); Criminal Warrants and Indictments Committee, Alabama Law Institute (2007-2008); Election Law Committee, Alabama Law Institute (2003-2005); Strategist and Adviser, Campaign for Lieutenant Governor Steve Windom (1998); Chairman, Parish Council, St. Ignatius Catholic Church (1992-1995); Strategist and Adviser, Campaign for Senate for Steve Windom (1989, 1990, 1994); Drug Law Review Committee, Alabama Law Institute (1980); Form Indictment Committee, Alabama Law Institute (1979-1980) **CW:** Draftsman, Chief Representative, Attorney General's Amendments to the Criminal Code (1979); Catholic Churches in Mobile, "Addiction: Openness to the Fullness of God's Love and Grace"; Speaker, Instructor, Numerous Catholic Churches in Mobile County, Toolen Institute for Parish Services **AW:** Named Alabamians Attorney of the Year, Legal Services of Alabama Private Attorney Program, Fighting for Equal Justice for Low Income (2011); Named Outstanding Young Man, American US Jaycees (1977, 1980) **MEM:** Vice Chairman, Program Committee, Mobile Bar Association (1983-1984); Alabama State Bar **BAR:** United States Court of Appeals for the Eleventh Circuit (1982); United States District Court for the Middle District of Alabama (1982); Supreme Court of the United States (1977); United States District Court of Alabama (1973); State of Alabama (1973) **MH:** Albert Nelson Marquis Lifetime Achievement Award; Marquis Who's Who Top Professional **AS:** Mr. Hale attributes his success to always seeking the truth. He works with his clients as hard as he possibly can to reveal the details of the truth in each case. He never seeks an agenda driven outcome, but he encourages his client to work with him as they join to seek the truth. After they have done all they can to develop the facts of the case, the time comes to set out the truth of the case. He asks the Spirit to send to him and his client his words that are far better than any words he could use to describe the true facts of the case. Once the truth of the case is developed, he then develops the law that applies to this unique case. Mr. Hales reads all of the statutes and then the cases that relate to the facts of the case. He attempts to absorb the entire body of the case law and determine where the appellate courts are going with this body of law as it applies to the facts of the case, now and in the years to come when the case will reach the appellate courts in the future. At times, a case will present facts which will permit him to develop further the law in a way that also benefits his client. Then, he can take this case wherever the case needs to go: settlement, trial and at times, appeals in which the law is developed in the case as never before, a case of first impression. He has been gifted with six cases of first impression in his state's appellate courts. He has totally enjoyed the practice of law. He looks forward to each new day in the law. So, he is not doing a job. He is having fun when he practices law

as he helps others who need his help as they work together to do justice. **B/I:** Mr. Hale was the oldest of six children who wanted to be a lawyer since he was 12 years old. His father, Jack Lee Hale, was a businessman who formed a company called Forestry Equipment in 1949 in Pritchard, Alabama. Lee Hale's father was a strong source of encouragement to his children. He wanted he and his brother to become professionals so they would not have to work as hard as he had worked (Obviously, Jack Hale had never heard that the law is a jealous mistress). Jack Hale encouraged his son to become a lawyer. When Mr. Hale was ready for college, he applied for scholarships. Mr. Hale took an exam sponsored by Spring Hill College which, if you were in the top 10, would award a scholarship. Mr. Hale received one. Mr. Hale wanted to attend Tulane College in New Orleans, Louisiana, because that is where his mother was from, but he attended Spring Hill College, as requested by his father. When he arrived at Spring Hill College, he found that he loved the honors programs in which he was enrolled full-time. In the first two years, the program consisted of an integrated study program with courses in literature, philosophy, theology, history and art history, following the same time period which began in ancient Sumer and extended through the classical, then medieval, renaissance, reformation period, baroque and ended just before World War I. The program required reading almost a thousand pages a week. In the last two years, Spring Hill encouraged Mr. Hale to take courses with a heavy emphasis on writing. In effect, Spring Hill College taught what every lawyer needs to know: how to read in many different thought processes and how to write in an organized form with clarity and precision. Mr. Hale graduated from Spring Hill College with his bachelor's degree in History, summa cum laude, in 1970. After he received an academic scholarship from Duke University School of Law, he graduated with his Juris Doctorate in 1973. Duke Law trained well in the tools a lawyer needs to apply to his profession, the ability to analyze complex matters and then to synthesize huge amounts of data. **AV:** Golf; Swimming; Improving the Tiff Turf grass in his yard; Enjoying Duke basketball and Coach K.; Enjoying Alabama football and Coach Saban **PA:** Conservative **RE:** Catholic **THT:** Mr. Hales says, "The Good Lord has provided each of us with so many gifts. These gifts are usually revealed to us when we use these gifts for the benefit of others. When we exercise our gifts well, we are filled with the joy which comes from using well our gifts. As a lawyer who represents citizens, I have found that I need to encourage my clients to help me find the truth of the case, a far more complex and arduous task than most believe. To set out the truth in a case is hard work. After the client, witnesses, documents, and the processes of the law help us to set out the truth, my goal then is to develop fully the law and then to apply the law to the truth that we have developed. At times, I have had to set out to the client that the law will not provide a remedy for him. However, when the law does provide a remedy for the facts of the case, the law almost always fulfills that promise. The client is overjoyed when that result occurs and I am blessed to share in his joy. The practice of law in this regard means that I am not doing a job whose primary purpose is to generate fees. The primary purpose of my profession is to fulfill my calling and to provide for the client the justice that the law mandates. As long as my health permits me to sustain this practice, I will continue to help my clients who trust me with the most important activity of their lives as we work together on the case. True fulfillment, true joy." Mr. Hale enjoys Duke basketball with Coach K. and Alabama football with Coach Saban;

these two are great coaches who inspire him to bring to his profession in a small way what they have brought to their professions in ways he could never have imagined.

HALEY, NIKKI RANDHAWA, T: United States Ambassador (Retired) **I:** Government Administration/Government Relations/Government Services **CN:** United Nations **DOB:** 01/20/1972 **PB:** Bamberg **SC:** SC/USA **PT:** Ajit Singh Randhawa; Raj Kaur Randhawa **MS:** Married **SPN:** Michael Haley (09/06/1996) **CH:** Rena; Nalin **ED:** Bachelor of Science in Accounting, Clemson University (1994) **C:** Ambassador to the United Nations, Washington, DC (2017-2018); Governor, State of South Carolina, Columbia, SC (2011-2017); Majority Whip, South Carolina House of Representatives, Columbia, SC (2006-2010); Member, District 87, South Carolina House of Representatives, Columbia, SC (2004-2010); Chief Financial Officer, Exotica International Inc. (1996-2004); Accounting Supervisor, FCR Inc. (1994-1996) **CR:** Board of Directors, Lexington County Sheriff's Foundation (2004-2006); Board of Directors, Lexington Medical Center Foundation (2004) **CIV:** Board Member, Mount Horeb United Methodist Church **CW:** Author, Memoir, "Can't is Not an Option: My American Story" (2012) **AW:** Named, One of the Politics 40 Under 40, TIME Magazine (2010); Named, One of the 50 Politicos to Watch, Politico (2010) **MEM:** National Rifle Association of America; West Metro Republican Women; Rotary Club of Lexington **PA:** Republican **RE:** Methodist

HALL, ANNA CHRISTENE, T: Government Official (Retired) **I:** Government Administration/Government Relations/Government Services **CN:** United States Department of Labor **DOB:** 12/18/1946 **PB:** Tyler **SC:** TX/USA **PT:** Willie B. Hall; Mary Christine Hall **MS:** Single **ED:** BA in Political Science, Southern Methodist University (1969) **CT:** Certified Grant Officer; Certified Contract Officer; Specialized Training (e.g. Public Speaking); Management Training (258 Hours); Contract Courses (120 Hours) **C:** Retired (2002); Subject Matter Expert, DTI & Associates, Dallas, Texas (2004-2007); Director, Office of Adult Services, Employment & Training Administration (ETA), United States Department of Labor, Dallas, Texas (2000-2002); Office Director, United States Department of Labor, Dallas, Texas (1988-2001); Executive Assistant, United States Department of Labor, Washington, DC (1987-1988); Division Chief, United States Department of Labor, Washington, DC (1984-1987); Program Analyst, United States Department of Labor, Washington, DC (1980-1984); Federal Representative, United States Department of Labor, Dallas, Texas (1970-1980); Clerk Stenographer, Employment & Training Administration (ETA), United States Department of Labor, Dallas, Texas (1970) **CR:** Part-time Consultant, DTI Associates (2004-2007) **AW:** Distinguished Career Service Award (2002); Outstanding Leadership Award, DFW Federal Executive Boards (Now Dallas-Fort Worth FEB) (2000); Secretary's Exceptional Achievement Awards (1997-2002); Meritorious Achievement Award (1986) **MEM:** Partnership for Employment and Training; National Honor Society **AS:** Ms. Hall attributes her success to her faith in God, parental leadership, and dedicated hard work. **B/I:** While attending high school, Ms. Hall took shorthand and typing like most girls in schools. She worked for four summers and two Christmas vacations for two different federal agencies – the Federal National Mortgage Association (FNMA) and the Defense Contractor Administration Services Region (DCASR). During her first two summers, she worked for FNMA and took dictation from seven different men and transcribed their letters. She also typed deeds of trust. The last two summers, she worked for DCASR and typed contracts related to the Vietnam War. She also prepared daily reports for the agency's commander. **AV:** Reading; Theater; Playing piano **PA:** Democrat **RE:** Presbyterian

HALL, BARRY G., T: Evolutionary Biologist **I:** Education/Educational Services **DOB:** 07/17/1942 **PB:** New York **SC:** NY/USA **SPN:** Susan M. (Werlein) (05/02/1964) **CH:** Steven; Scott; Rebecca Hathaway **ED:** PhD in Genetics, University of Washington, Seattle (1971); BS in Genetics, University of Wisconsin, Madison (1968) **C:** Adjunct Professor, Center of Genomic Science, Allegheny-Singer Research Institute, Pittsburgh, PA (2009-Present); Director, Bellingham Research Institute, Portland, OR (2004-Present); Professor Emeritus, University of Rochester, New York (2003-Present); Professor, University of Rochester, New York (1989-2003); Full Professor, University of Connecticut, Storrs (1985-1989); Associate Professor, University of Connecticut, Storrs (1980-1985); Assistant Professor, University of Connecticut, Storrs (1977-1980); Assistant Professor, Memorial University Newfoundland and Medical School, St. John's, Newfoundland, Canada (1974-1977) **CR:** Editor-in-Chief, "Molecular Biology and Evolution" (1993-1998); Profeseur Invité Université Paris-Sud, Orsay, France (1993); Protocols Editor, "Molecular Biology and Evolution" (2018); Editorial Board, Journal of Bacteriology; Editorial Board, Journal of Molecular Evolution; Editorial Board, Genetica; Editorial Board, Molecular Biology and Evolution; Co-founder, Gordon Conference on Microbial Population Biology; Organizer, 10 Scientific Conferences; Invited Speaker, 153 Universities and Scientific Meetings **CW:** Author, "Phylogenetic Trees Made Easy" (Five Editions); Author, Over 140 Peer Reviewed Scientific Research Articles; Author, Six Significant Computer Programs, Bioinformatics Analysis **AW:** Grantee, National Institutes of Health (2000-2004, 1992-1996, 1986-1992, 1978-1986); Grantee, American Cancer Society (1996-1998); Grantee, National Science Foundation (1989-1993); Fulbright Senior Scholar (1984); National Institutes of Health Research and Career Development Awardee (1980) **MEM:** Society for Molecular Biology and Evolution **MH:** Albert Nelson Marquis Lifetime Achievement Award **AS:** Professor Hall attributes his success to his PhD training in the University of Washing Genetics Department under Dr. J. Gallant, Dr. H. Roman, and Dr. L. Sandler. **B/I:** Professor Hall was inspired by a man named Dr. James Crow, who was a professor and member of the National Academy of Scientist and one of the founders of field population biology and one of the best teachers he had ever met. He was working as a glassware washer at a Laboratory next door to Crow's and he decided to try to take genetics because he liked biology. Professor Hall at the time was looking at the prospects of being a lawyer, however once he took Dr. Crow's course, he changed his direction. **AV:** Playing jazz trumpet

HALL, CAROLYN S., T: Retired Special Education Educator **I:** Education/Educational Services **DOB:** 08/14/1947 **PB:** Zanesville **SC:** OH/USA **PT:** Harold Wesley Monroe; Florence Marjorie (Grier) Monroe **MS:** Married **SPN:** Kenneth Harold Hall (01/06/1968) **CH:** Adrian Monroe Hall; Melinda Elizabeth Hall Yerian **ED:** BEd, Ohio University (1987) **CT:** Certification in Secondary Education in Social Studies; Certification in Secondary Education in Biological Science **C:** Retired, Multihandicap Teacher, Morgan Local School District, Mcconnelsville, OH (1991-2008); Multihandicap Teacher, Perry County MR/DD, New Lexington, OH (1988-1991); Multihandicap Teacher, Mary Ham-

mond MR/DD, Mcconnelsville, OH (1987-1988) **CR:** Coach, Morgan Special Olympics, McConnelsville, OH (1988-Present); Advisor, Handicapped 4-H, McConnelsville, OH (1991-2003) **CIV:** Behavior Board; Board of Developmental Disabilities **MEM:** Parent-Teacher Association; Daughters of the American Revolution **MH:** Albert Nelson Marquis Lifetime Achievement Award **AS:** Ms. Hall attributes her success to a promise she made to her father. Because of this promise, she graduated from college. **B/I:** Ms. Hall started her teaching career in elementary education, slowly transitioning to secondary education. She eventually started substitute teaching as well, which is what introduced her to special education. She found she enjoyed working with special-ed students, proceeding to naturally progress in her career. **AV:** Reading; Crafting **PA:** Republican **RE:** Methodist

HALL, ELLA TAYLOR, PHD, T: Clinical School Psychologist **I:** Education/Educational Services **DOB:** 11/30/1948 **PB:** Macon **SC:** MS/USA **PT:** Essex; Mamie (Roland) Taylor **CH:** Banyikaai Monique (Deceased); Motiqua Shante **ED:** PhD, George Peabody College (1978); MA, Fisk University (1973); BA, Fisk University (1971) **CT:** Licensed Psychologist; Certified in School Psychology **C:** School Psychologist, Abbott Union Free School District (1985-2011); Clinical Consultant, Abbott House, Irvington, NY (1982-1985); Clinical Psychologist, Wiltwyck Residential Treatment Center, Ossining, NY (1979-1981); Associate Psychologist, Bronx Psychiatric Center (1979); Mental Health Specialist, Behavioral Science Division, Meharry Medical College, Nashville, TN (1976-1977) **CIV:** Lay Reader, Acolyte Episcopal Church Member, Committee on Special Education, Kids Program Africa; Consultant Psychologist, Youth Theater Interactions, Inc.; Volunteer Knitter, Seamen's Church Institute **CW:** Art Exhibition, Mixed Media (2017-2019); Author, Poem, "To Behold These Precious Moments" (2015); Author, Poem, "Farewell to a Friendship" (2015); Author, Poem, "Seeking Meaning Everyday" (2013); Author, Poem, "If a Sidewalk Could Talk" (2013); Author, Poem, "The Overseen" (2012); Author, Poem, "Can You Ever Imagine" (2011); Author, Poem, "How Will Your Words Lie on the Heart of a Child (2010); Author, Poem, "What Do Of This Moment?" (2009); Author, "Blood Silence" (2000); Author, "Secret Garden" (2000); Author, "Young Wilted Flower" (2000); Author, "Ordinary" (1996); Author, "These Times" (1995); Author, "Mama Sis" (1995); Author, "Down My Three Rows" (1995); Author, "Maple Tree at Dawn" (1995); Author, "Double Twister, Somebody, Clinging Tears" (1994) **AW:** Grant, National Institute of Mental Health; Crusade Fellowship; Salutatorian, B. F. Liddel High School **MEM:** President Elect, Abbott School Teachers Association (2008); Schomburg Center for Research in Black Culture; New York State Psychological Association; New York Botanical Society; Wildlife Conservation Society; Delta Sigma Theta **B/I:** Dr. Hall became involved in her profession because she was fascinated by what psychology entailed and how people functioned. **AV:** Taking photographs

HALL, GEOFFREY, T: Adjunct Professor **I:** Education/Educational Services **CN:** Northampton Community College **DOB:** 12/04/1946 **PB:** Easton **SC:** PA/USA **MS:** Divorced **ED:** Coursework, Northampton Community College (2018); Coursework, Princeton University, Princeton, NJ (2015); Coursework, Cedar Crest College, Allentown, PA (2014); Docent, Lehigh Valley Zoo (2011); Coursework, Lafayette College, Easton, PA (2000); Coursework, Penn State University, Allentown, PA (1983); Master of Arts, Marshall University, Huntington, WV (1975); Bachelor of Science, Presbyterian College, Clin-

ton, SC (1973); Coursework, University of Graz, Austria (1972) **CT:** Certificate, LAN Administrator, Northampton Community College, Bethlehem, PA (1998) **C:** Adjunct Instructor, DeSales University (2001-Present); Adjunct Instructor, Warren County Community College, Washington, NJ (2001-Present); Adjunct Instructor, Northampton Community College, Bethlehem, PA (2001-Present); MBA Coordinator, DeSales University Graduate Program (2001-2003); Senior Compensation Specialist, Guardian Insurance Company, Bethlehem, PA (1997-2001); Systems and Training Consultant (1997-2001); Part-time Teacher, Massachusetts (1997-2001); Customer Services Manager, Programming Resources Co., Hartford, CT (1992-1994); Automation Systems and Training Manager, Cigna Insurance Corporation, Quincy, MA (1983-1992); Underwriter, Marketer, Inland Mutual Insurance Co., Huntington, WV (1979-1983); Senior Planning Analyst, Cigna Corporation, Philadelphia, PA; Training Specialist, Cigna Corporation, Philadelphia, PA; Underwriting Services Supervisor, Allentown, PA; Salesman, Jefferson-Pilot Life; Salesman, Metropolitan Life Insurance Company **CR:** Instructor, Northampton Co. Prison (2012-2018); Teacher, Northampton Community College (2004-2018); Teacher, DeSales University (2001-2004); Teacher, Marshall University, Huntington, WV (1980-1982); Teacher, Ohio University, Athens, OH (1980-1982); Teacher, Huntington College of Business (1980-1982) **CIV:** Volunteer, Northampton County Jail, Easton, PA **MIL:** Staff Sergeant, U.S. Air Force (1966-1970) **CW:** Senior Thesis, "Self-Concept of the Incarcerated," South Carolina Journal of Law **AW:** Air Force Commendation Citation, U.S. Air Force (1970); Outstanding Unit Citation, U.S. Air Force (1970); Appreciation Award for Working With Inmates at Local Jail **MEM:** Alpha Kappa Delta; National Association for the Advancement of Colored People **MH:** Marquis Who's Who Top Professional **AS:** Mr. Hall attributes his success to his constant hard work. **B/I:** Mr. Hall became involved in his profession because, while he worked in the insurance industry for almost 30 years, he wanted to make a change. He worked for Cigna Corporation in Boston, Massachusetts, but the office was closed due to cuts. He decided to enter teaching out of passion, not for monetary gain. **AV:** Violin; Banjo **PA:** Independent **RE:** Protestant

HALL, KEITH D., PHD, T: Former Director **I:** Government Administration/Government Relations/Government Services **CN:** Congressional Budget Office **ED:** PhD in Economics, Purdue University; MS in Economics, Purdue University; BA in Economics, University of Virginia **C:** Director, Congressional Budget Office (2015-2019); Commissioner, U.S. Bureau of Labor Statistics, U.S. Department of Labor (2008-2012); Chief Economist, Council of Economic Advisers, Executive Office of President; Chief Economist, Economics and Statistics Administration, U.S. Department of Commerce; Senior International Economist, Research Division, U.S. International Trade Commission; Chief, Division of Applied Economics, U.S. International Trade Commission

HALL, KENDRA, RN, BSN, M, MSN, T: Nursing Administrator, Educator, Research Nurse **I:** Medicine & Health Care **DOB:** 06/26/1945 **PB:** LA **SC:** CA/USA **PT:** Kenneth Eugene; Loretta Gene (Hurlburt) Hall **MS:** Married **SPN:** Jeffrey E. Prag (09/17/2000) **CH:** Madelyn Chand; Rosie Steinbrenner **ED:** Bachelor of Science in Nursing, California State University, Sacramento, CA (1982); Associate of Science, Sacramento City College, with Highest Honors (1980); Bachelor of Arts in Psychology, University of California Davis (1970); Postgraduate, California State University, Sacramento **C:** Chart

Center Coordinator, Case Manager, Hospice of San Joaquin, Stockton, CA (1999-Present); Research Associate, Crossroads Program, Consolidated Science Inc., Stockton, CA (1998-1999); Neurology Nurse Clinician, Research Nurse, VA Northern California Health Care System, Sacramento, CA (1991-1998); Research And Pain Care Nurse, Department Anesthesia, University California Davis Medical Center, Sacramento, CA (1988-1991); Instructor of Medicine, Surgery and Nursing, Sacramento City College (1988); Assistant Director Nurses, Sutter Healthcare Systems, Sacramento, CA (1987); Clinical Nurse, Neurosurgical ICE, University California Davis Medical Center, Sacramento, CA (1981-1986) **CR:** Lecturer of Neurology, Sacramento Community Critical Care Course **CW:** Contributor, Articles to Professional Kournals **MEM:** Stockton Chapter, American Association of University; American Nurses Association; California Nurses Association; American Association of Neuroscience Nurses; Northern California Nursing Research Network; Central Valley Birding Consortium; Assistance League; Sierra Club; Audubon; Sigma Theta Tau; Phi Kappa Phi **MH:** Albert Nelson Marquis Lifetime Achievement Award **B/I:** Ms. Hall became involved in the profession of nursing due to her longstanding passion for psychology and biology, which synergized well with her field.

HALL, ROBERT B., T: Program Manager **I:** Other **CN:** Raytheon Technologies Corporation **DOB:** 01/15/1945 **PB:** Dayton **SC:** OH/USA **PT:** Earl Brent Hall; Mary Louise (Meehan) Hall **MS:** Married **SPN:** A. Jane Graber (05/23/1964) **CH:** Thomas; Robert; Michael; Kathleen; Stephen **ED:** MS, Vanderbilt University (1981); AA, BS, University of Maryland (1980); AS, Miami Dade College (1977) **CT:** Certified Engineering Specialist, Resource Manager, National Security Agency; PGI Certified Display Operator, PGI, Inc. **C:** Program Manager, Raytheon Technologies Corporation (1982-Present); Senior Configuration Management Analyst, Ford Aerospace (1978-1982); Systems Engineer, Tech Plan, Inc. (1977-1978); Cryptologic Technician, United States Navy (1964-1977) **CIV:** Executive Board Member, Nittany Mountain District, Juniata Valley Council, Boy Scouts of America (1992-Present); Council Training Chairman, Nittany Mountain District, Juniata Valley Council, Boy Scouts of America (1991-Present); District Training Chairman, Nittany Mountain District, Juniata Valley Council, Boy Scouts of America (1985-1991) **MIL:** United States Navy (1964-1977) **AW:** Silver Beaver Award, Juniata Valley Council Boy Scouts America (1988); Award, Boy Scouts of America (1986); District Award of Merit, Nittany Mountain District **MEM:** Pennsylvania Apple Microcomputer Users' Group (1986-1988); Nittany Valley Chapter, ATD **MH:** Albert Nelson Marquis Lifetime Achievement Award **AV:** Camping; Watching fireworks; Reading

HALLAL, DIANA, T: Founder, Chief Executive Officer **I:** Financial Services **CN:** DH Financing **MS:** Single **CH:** Sarah; Ryan **ED:** BA in French Literature, St. Joseph University; Degree in Business Administration, Saddleback College **C:** Founder, Chief Executive Officer, DH Financing (2017-Present); Senior Vice President, Business Development, TMC Financing (2015-2017); Director, Senior Business Development Officer, Union Bank (2011-2015); Senior Vice President, Senior Relationship Manager, Vice President, Commercial Loan Officer, Wachovia, A Wells Fargo Company (2007-2011); Vice President, Business Development, Bank of America (1993-2007) **CIV:** Vice President, San Diego Advisory Council; Contributor, Habitat for Humanity; Blood Bank; Contributor, The Cancer Society **MEM:** CREW (Commercial Real Estate for Women); AIR (Association Industrial Real Estate);

SIOR (Society of Industrial & Office Realtors) **B/I:** Ms. Hallal became involved in her profession by accident, not knowing where she wanted to be. Initially, she was a part-time teller at the Bank of America while she was going to school. She has always been driven and she has always been someone that wanted to do more; she enjoys people. She loved the interaction with people and helping, as she is a natural giver. Slowly, Ms. Hallal found herself naturally selling. When she discovered the business aspect of banking, that took her to another level. She comes from a family of business owners. She watched her father start his business. Failing is not an option for Ms. Hallal, it is instead an experience to get to something better. She stumbled into banking as a young female going to school, though she always knew she was an entrepreneur at heart. It took her some time to get where she is now because she was very cautious as to when to start her own business because she was a single mom raising two children. However, she has found much success.Ms. Hallal began working as a part-time teller while she was attending school. Like most young people, her career goals were not yet fully formed, but the job was a good fit with her class schedule. She soon found that finance suited her. She was good with numbers, she enjoyed the discipline that banking required and she especially liked the daily interactions with customers from all walks of life. The bank afforded a boots-on-the-ground perspective on the integral role that banking and finance plays in the lives of individuals and businesses. When she realized that a career in finance would give her the opportunity to make a real difference in people's lives, she was hooked. **AV:** Outdoor activities; Working out; Healthy habits; Playing golf **THT:** Ms. Hallal believes one should always do the right thing. Ms. Hallal, Founder & Chief Executive Officer of DH Financing, based in Beverly Hills, California, is a 20-year veteran in the banking and financial service industry specializing in financing commercial buildings. Her passion for real estate and helping businesses grow is what led her to start DH Financing. She has worked for top banks such as Bank of America, Wells Fargo and Union Bank and has achieved and exceeded annual goals on a regular basis. Diana has built a solid foundation of lenders – working with over 100 of them nationally. She is responsible for the company's day to day operations in addition to new business development. Diana Hallal embodies integrity, vigor, and proficiency in every detail of her financial services. She is well-respected in her field. Diana is active in her community and is involved with several nonprofit organizations and associations including CREW (Commercial Real Estate for Women), AIR (Association Industrial Real Estate), SIOR (Society of Industrial & Office Realtors). Ms. Hallal graduated from St. Joseph University with a degree in French literature, and from Saddleback College with a degree in Business Administration. Her varied skills and experiences have molded her into who she is today – a finance expert with a track record of success.

HALLENGREN, HOWARD E., T: President and Chairman **I:** Real Estate **CN:** Falcon Real Estate Investment Management Ltd. **DOB:** 09/08/1930 **PB:** Chicago **SC:** IL/USA **PT:** Charles Hallengren; Julia Hallengren **MS:** Single **ED:** MBA, The University of Chicago Booth School of Business (1958); AB in English Literature, Princeton University, Cum Laude (1952) **C:** President and Chairman, Falcon Real Estate Investment Management, Ltd. (1991-Present); Co-founder with Jack Miller, Falcon Real Estate Investment Management, Ltd. (1991); Chief Investment Officer, International Private Banking, Chase Manhattan Bank (1982-1991);

Chief Investment Officer, The First National Bank of Chicago (1970-1977) **CIV:** Volunteer, Supporter, Oriental Institute of the University of Chicago; Volunteer, Supporter, Music Theater Works, Wilmette, IL **CW:** Author, "Reminiscences of an Accidental Embezzler" (2016) **AW:** Award, Support, Oriental Institute of the University of Chicago (2019) **MH:** Albert Nelson Marquis Lifetime Achievement Award; Marquis Who's Who Top Professional **AS:** Mr. Hallengren attributes his success to hard work and determination. **B/I:** Mr. Hallengren became involved in his profession because he had a general interest in the stock market and investments. When he graduated from Princeton University, the First National Bank of Chicago offered him a job in the investment division and he thought that it would be very interesting. Mr. Hallengren was always interested in the stock market. He got involved in this profession because he was the Chief Investment Officer at the First National Bank of Chicago and then Chase hired him to be the Chief Investment Officer. He had been at First National Bank of Chicago for 30 years in the investment area before he went to Chase. **AV:** Writing and developing pure fiction

HALLER, KAREN S., BS IN EDUCATION, T: Writer **I:** Writing and Editing **DOB:** 04/25/1935 **PB:** St. Louis **SC:** MO/USA **PT:** Frank Michael Kratoville; Frieda Catherine (Hartmann) Kratoville **MS:** Married **SPN:** Albert John Haller **CH:** Christopher Karl; Debra Lynn; Angela Haller (Daughter-in-Law) **ED:** BS in Education, University of Missouri (1956) **C:** Hearing Testing Technician, Special School District, St. Louis County (1975-1976); Elementary School Teacher, Ladue School District (1956-1960) **CR:** Teacher (2002-Present); Volunteer, Interpreter, Sophie M. Sachs Butterfly House (1998-2002); Earthwatch Volunteer, Bees and Orchids of Brazil Project (1998) **CIV:** Advisor, Co-Ed Explorer Post, Boy Scouts of America (1976-1980); Junior Girl Scouts Troop (1970-1971); Assistant Leader, Leader, Brownie Troop, Girl Scouts of America (1969-1970); Bus Tour Guide, Chairman, St. Louis Visiting Center (1966-1970); Member of Mortar Board, University of Missouri, Columbia, MO (1955) **CW:** Author, Photographer, "Walking with Wildflowers" (1994); Contributing Photographer, "Wildflowers of North America" (1987); Contributing Photographer, "Wildflowers of Arkansas" (1984); Contributing Photographer, "Sensitive Plants of St. Francis National Forests" (1984) **AW:** Award for 20 Years of Outstanding Service, Missouri Botanical Garden Program (2018); Erna R. Eisendrath Education Award, Missouri Native Plant Society (1994); Dorr Scholarship, National Audubon Society (1989); Annual Scholarship to the Wisconsin Audubon Camp, National Audubon Society (1958) **MEM:** Board of Directors, Missouri Parks Association (2000-Present); Board of Directors, Missouri Parks Association (2000-2008); President, Missouri Native Plant Society (1991-1993); Awards Chairman, National Audubon Society (1990); Program Chairman, National Audubon Society (1987-1990); Conservation Chairman, Webster Groves Nature Study Society (1983-1986); President, Webster Groves Nature Study Society (1978-1980); President, Jaycee Wives (1963-1964); Vice President, President, Treasurer, Secretary, Naiads; Board of Directors, Missouri Parks Association; Vice President, President, Naiads Swim Club; Sierra Club **MH:** Albert Nelson Marquis Lifetime Achievement Award; Marquis Who's Who Top Professional **B/I:** When Mrs. Haller was growing up, generally women could only be teachers, nurses, or, like her mother, work in a bank. Mrs. Haller had an interest in teaching, so that is the career path she chose. She was always interested in the outdoors, so she joined various outdoor clubs knowing that they would be interesting to her. The Butterfly House was a local club she joined that she is still a part of today. Mrs. Haller is also a member of a botany group with the Webster Grove Nature Society, they go on weekly trips and occasionally they go on one-week trips where they would go to another part of the state to study plants, insects, snakes, or whatever would appear as they were out there. There was a point in time when she decided that she had to have pictures of all the things that she was seeing, thus, she became interested in photography. **AV:** Hiking; Canoeing; Camping; Traveling; Synchronized swimming

HALLERMANN, GISELA ELISABETH, MBA, T: Insurance Agent (Retired) **I:** Insurance **DOB:** 10/12/1936 **PB:** Herne **SC:** Germany **PT:** Ferdinand Bleckmann; Emilie Anna (Loecker) Bleckmann **MS:** Married **SPN:** Franz-Josef Hallermann (02/20/1965); Alfred Schmidt (04/12/1961, Deceased 1962) **CH:** Henning Hallermann; Detlef Hallermann; Petra Hallermann; Sven Hallermann **ED:** MBA, Texas A&M University-Corpus Christi, Corpus Christi, TX (1984); Teaching Degree, Pedagogische Academie, Dortmund, Germany (1961) **C:** Account Executive, W.L. Dinn Co Inc., Subsidiary of Hilb Rogal and Hamilton Corpus Christi (1989-1999); Account Executive Insurance Agent, Swantner and Gordon, Corpus Christi, TX (1984-1989); Fundraiser, Corpus Christi Symphony (1980); Vice President, Rekortan Sports Corporation, Seattle, WA (1979-1984); Fundraiser, Incarnate World Academy, Corpus Christi, TX (1973-1980) **AV:** Theater; Bridge; Travel; Aerobic exercise; Art history **PA:** Republican **RE:** Roman Catholic

HALLIN, DAVID ANTHONY, T: Pilot (Retired) **I:** Aviation **DOB:** 11/02/1945 **PB:** Ancon **SC:** Panama Canal Zone **PT:** Henry Emerson Hallin Sr.; Theodora (Moses) Hallin **MS:** Married **SPN:** Pamela J. (Williams) Hallin **ED:** Designated Naval Aviator, Naval Air Training Command, Pensacola, FL (1969); BSBA, University of Arkansas, Fayetteville, AR (1968) **C:** MD-11/MD-10 Captain (2000-2005); Pilot, Flight Instructor, Check Airman, Assistant Chief Pilot, Federal Express Corporation (Now FedEx), Memphis, TN (1973-2005); DC-10 Flight Manager/Assistant Chief Pilot, Federal Express Corporation (Now FedEx), Memphis, TN (1989-1999); Instructor, B-727 (1978-1984); Line Captain, Fan Jet Falcon (1975-1978); First Officer, DA-20 Falcon Fan Jet, Federal Express Corporation (Now FedEx) (1973-1975) **CIV:** Board of Directors, Humphreys Center Owners Association (2010-Present); Poll Worker, Shelby County Election Commission, 2020 Elections, Shelby County Government, TN (2020); Kimbrough Green Condominiums Homeowners Association, Germantown, TN (1983-1984); President, Woodshire Townhouse Homeowners Association, Germantown, TN (1978-1979); Board Member, President, Ashley Gardens Homeowners' Association; Board of Directors, Beethoven Club of Memphis; Lindenwood Christian Church **MIL:** Retired Colonel, United States Marine Corps Reserve (1992); Officer-in-charge, 4th MAW Detachment, United States Marine Corps Reserve, NAS Memphis, TN (1992); With, 4th MAW Detachment, United States Marine Corps Reserve, NAS Memphis, TN (1989-1992); Commanding Officer, VMA-124, United States Marine Corps, NAS Memphis, TN (1986-1987); Served, VMA-124, United States Marine Corps Reserve, NAS Memphis, TN (1972-1987); Naval Air Command, NAS Meridian, MS with VT-9 and 19, United States Marine Corps Reserve (1971-1972); Forward Air Controller, VMO-2 Operating OV-10 Bronco Aircraft, United States Marine Corps Reserve, Vietnam (1970-1971); Naval Aviator, United States Marine Corps Reserve (1969);

Commissioned Second Lieutenant, United States Marine Corps Reserve (1968) **CW:** Contributor, "B727 Operations Manual," Federal Express (FedEx) (1983) **AW:** 15 Air Medals, United States Marine Corps; Navy Commendation Medal with Combat "V," United States Marine Corps; Vietnam Service Medal, United States Marine Corps; 13 Bravo Zulu Awards, United States Marine Corps; Other Letters of Commendation, United States Marine Corps **MEM:** Military Officer Association of America (MOAA); Marine Corp Aviation Association (MCAA); Beethoven Club of Memphis; Memphis Symphony League, Memphis Symphony Orchestra; FedEx Retiree Club; Gray Falcons Pilot Associations; Association of Naval Aviation (ANA); OV-10 Bronco Associations; Arkansas Alumni Association **AS:** Mr. Hallin attributes his success to scrupulous honesty, conscientious effort, and hard work. **B/I:** The Vietnam War required young men to choose how to serve. Mr. Hallin chose and was selected to become a Marine Corps Officer and Naval Aviator, a career in which he would have remained had it not been for a reduction in force [RIF] in 1972. He moved immediately to the Marine Corps Reserve. He discovered that civilian companies would not hire an aviator for other occupations, as they feared such employees would leave when the airlines began hiring. By coincidence, Mr. Hallin learned that the Federal Express Corporation was training and hiring pilots in Little Rock, Arkansas. Mr. Hallin paid for his training with the assistance of the GI Bill and was hired as the 864th employee of what became FedEx. **AV:** Travel; Light exercise; Singing in church choir; Attending reunions **PA:** Independent **RE:** Christian **THT:** Mr. Hallin says, "As a business management student at the University of Arkansas, I learned under the auspices of Dr. Robert D. Hay that a business will succeed if it satisfies the needs and wants of customers, employees, suppliers and others. At Federal Express, I found that same, or similar, philosophy in the mantra "People, Service, Profit," promulgated by Frederick W. Smith, founder and, now, Chairman of the Board. The term "servant leader," I believe, is a key to the success of leaders in any environment whether it be in business, military, community, church or family. Service to others is our most important mission in life."

HAM, KAY, T: Adjunct Faculty **I:** Education/Educational Services **CN:** University of Oklahoma **CH:** One Daughter **ED:** Diploma, University of Oklahoma **C:** Adjunct Faculty, University of Oklahoma (2003-2009); Director of Health and Safety Services, The American National Red Cross **CR:** Teacher, Online Classes, Conflict Resolution, Organizational Development; Teacher, First Aide, Swimming, The American National Red Cross **CW:** Co-Author, Chapter, "The Handbook of Human Resource Management in Government" **AW:** Rufus Hall Outstanding Professor Award **MEM:** Chair, City of Norman Human Rights Commission; Mediator, Cleveland County Court System; Chair, Staff Parish Relations Committee **MH:** Marquis Who's Who Top Professional **AS:** Ms. Ham attributes her success to her passion for her work. She enjoys creating programs, working with students, and making connections. **B/I:** Ms. Ham's mother was a teacher and many of her relatives were teachers, so that prompted her to choose the profession. She really enjoys it. **AV:** Swimming; Bicycling; Bird-watching

HAMADY, THEODORE M., T: Marketing Company Executive (Retired) **I:** Advertising & Marketing **DOB:** 08/11/1937 **PB:** Flint **SC:** MI/USA **PT:** Robert Michael Hamady; Millie (Salha) Hamady **MS:** Married **SPN:** Saniya Al-Faquih Hamady (07/30/1960) **CH:** Michael Geoffrey; Peter Winston; Linda Claire

ED: MBA, The George Washington University (1978); BBA, University of Michigan, With High Distinction (1975); BA, University of Michigan (1960) **C:** President, T.M. Hamady, Inc. (1984-2005); Executive Vice President, Director, Boles World Trade Corp., Washington, DC (1979-1984); Vice President, Director, Boles World Trade Corp., Washington, DC (1974-1979); Chairman, Hamady Brothers, Inc., Flint, MI (1969-1974); Vice President, Hamady Brothers, Inc., Flint, MI (1964-1968) **CIV:** Rotary Club, Washington, DC (1986-Present); Board of Trustees, Board of Directors, The Valley School (1973-1975); Vice President, Leadership Flint (1973-1975); Flint Institute of Music (1973-1974) **AW:** Writing and Research Award, National Air and Space Museum, Smithsonian Institution; Outstanding Article in Air Power History, Air Force Historical Foundation; International Service Award, Rotary International **MEM:** American Marketing Association; American Management Association; Masons; University Club, Rotary Club, Washington, DC; Bethesda-Chevy Chase Chapter, Izaak Walton League of America; Aero Club of Washington; Company of Military Historians; Commemorative Air Force **MH:** Albert Nelson Marquis Lifetime Achievement Award **AV:** Studying aviation military history; Publishing aviation history; Flying

HAMILL, PETE, T: Journalist **I:** Writing and Editing **DOB:** 06/24/1935 **PB:** Brooklyn **SC:** NY/USA **PT:** Billy Hamill; Anne Devlin **MS:** Married **SPN:** Fukiko Aoki (1987); Ramona Negron (1962-1970) **ED:** Honorary LittD, St. John's University (2010); Honorary Doctorate, Pratt Institute (1980); Coursework, Mexico City College (1956-1957); Honorary Diploma, Regis High School, New York, NY; Coursework, School of Visual Arts **C:** Columnist, The New York Post (1965); Feature Writer, The New York Herald Tribune (1964); Correspondent, Saturday Evening Post (1963-1964); Reporter, The New York Post (1960-1963); Art Director, The Atlantis (1958); Editor, The Post; Editor-in-Chief, The Daily News **MIL:** U.S. Navy (1952) **CW:** Appearance, Documentary, "Breslin and Hamill: Deadline Artists" (2019); Author, "Tabloid City" (2011); Author, "North River" (2007); Author, "Downtown: My Manhattan" (2004); Author, "Forever" (2003); Author, "Diego Rivera" (1999); Author, "Why Sinatra Matters" (1999); Author, "News is a Verb" (1998); Author, "Snow in August" (1998); Author, "Piecework" (1996); Author, "A Drinking Life: A Memoir" (1995); Author, "Tokyo Sketches: Short Stories" (1992); Author, "Loving Women" (1989); Author, "The Guns of Heaven" (1984); Author, "The Invisible City: Short Stories" (1980); Author, "The Deadly Piece" (1979); Author, "Flesh and Blood" (1977); Author, "Dirty Laundry" (1978); Author, "The Gift" (1973); Author, "Irrational Ravings" (1971); Author, "A Killing for Christ" (1968) **AW:** George Polk Career Award (2014); Louis Auchincloss Prize, Museum of the City of New York (2010); Ernie Pyle Lifetime Achievement Award, National Society of Newspaper Columnists (2005); Grammy Award (1975); Distinguished Writer in Residence, Arthur L. Carter Journalism Institute **RE:** Catholic

HAMILTON, ARLAN, T: Founder, Managing Partner **I:** Media & Entertainment **CN:** Backstage Capital **ED:** Coursework in Investments, Stanford Continuing Studies (2015); Diploma, Lake Highlands High School (1999) **C:** Founder, Managing Partner, Backstage Capital (2015-Present); Tour Manager, Janine and the Mixtape (2015-Present); Production Coordinator, Toni Braxton (2014); Tour Manager's Assistant, Jason Derulo (2014); Production Coordinator, Chromeo (2014); Talent Wrangler, Pharrell Williams (2014); Tour Director, Nico Turner (2013); Tour Director, UK/Europe, Amanda Palmer (2013); Production Coordinator, CeeLo Green (2012-2013);

Production Coordinator, Kirk Franklin/King's Men Live Nation Tour (2012); Blogger, Arlan Was Here Productions (2006-2012); Production Assistant, Director's Assistant, Various Programs (2009-2011); Tour Manager/Booking Agent, Terra Naomi (2002-2009); Tour Manager/Booking Agent, Goldenboy (2002-2004) **CW:** Founder, Publisher, Editor, INTERLUDE Magazine (2002-2008)

HAMILTON, JACKIE STEWART, MS PSYCHOLOGY, T: Executive Director **I:** Health, Wellness and Fitness **CN:** Hamilton House Child Safety Center **PB:** Booneville **SC:** AR/USA **PT:** Chester Austin Stewart; Verna Moore Stewart **MS:** Married **SPN:** Gary (01/2013) **CH:** Shawn; Shea **ED:** MS in Psychology, University of Arkansas; BS in Psychology, University of Arkansas **C:** Founder, Executive Director, Hamilton House Child Safety Center, Fort Smith, AR (2011-Present); Owner, Learning Consultants, AR **AW:** "Buddy A Coach" Award, Mid-America District Exchange Clubs (2018); Award, Outstanding Commitment in the Prevention of Child Abuse **MEM:** Board Member, Child Advocacy Support Association (CASA); Noon Exchange Club; National Exchange Student Counselor **AS:** Mrs. Hamilton attributes her success to her choices to always do the right thing. **B/I:** Mrs. Hamilton credits her grandmother, May Stewart, for the reason behind why she became involved in her career path. She believes the lessons she taught her growing up had a great impact on her life choices. She would always say "Jackie, you always do the right thing...and sometimes the right thing causes undesirable results but you still must do the right thing..." **THT:** Mrs. Hamilton was the first person in the state of Arkansas to write a criminal disposition sentence for a sex offender.

HAMILTON, MARGARET, T: Garden Designer **I:** Business Management/Business Services **DOB:** 12/31/1940 **PB:** Luray **SC:** VA/USA **PT:** James Raymond; Margaret (Stewart) Mims **MS:** Widowed **SPN:** William Thornley Hamilton (12/22/1959, Deceased 2009) **CH:** Jenny S. Keck; Ann C. Swanson (Deceased, 1995); Amy R. Hamilton (Deceased, 2016) **ED:** BA, Otterbein College (1973) **C:** Owner, Gardens By Design, Denver, CO (1989-2009); Executive Director, Action for Children, Columbus, OH (1979-1983); Program Director, Action for Children, Columbus, OH (1977-1979); Director of Services, Community Coordinated Child Care, Columbus, OH (1974-1977); Teacher, North Broadway Children's Center, Columbus, OH (1973-1974) **CR:** Community Volunteer, Board of Directors, Massanutten Regional Library System (2015-Present); Consultant, Denver, CO (1989-2010) **MEM:** President, State Conference Chair, National Association Education of Young Children (1978-1982); American Association of University Women; Denver Art Museum; Denver Natural History Museum; The Philadelphia Gallery; The Virginia Museum of Fine Arts; The National Museum of Women in the Arts; The Barnes Foundation **MH:** Albert Nelson Marquis Lifetime Achievement Award **B/I:** Ms. Hamilton became involved in gardening because her mother and grandmother were gardeners, so it came naturally to her. She initially wanted to work in child care but she quickly found she was more inclined to work with gardens. For the first few months of her time as a gardener, she often helped clients for free. However, after gaining confidence, she began charging people for her time. In the years since making this decision, she has found a multitude of professional success. **AV:** Gardening; Drawing; Painting with watercolors; Reading; Making collages **RE:** Episcopalian

HAMILTON, MATT, T: Reporter **I:** Media & Entertainment **CN:** The Los Angeles Times **ED:** MJ, University of Southern California (2012-2014); Bachelor's Degree, Boston College (2009) **C:** Metro Reporter, The Los Angeles Times (2014-Present); Stringer, The New York Times (2013-2014); Reporting Intern, The Los Angeles Times (2013); Editor, Al-Faridah for Specialized Publications (2010-2011); Trip Leader, Alford Lake Camp (2009) **AW:** Pulitzer Prize for Investigative Reporting (2019) **MEM:** Phi Beta Kappa

HAMILTON, SUSAN BOYD, T: Assistant Professor **I:** Education/Educational Services **CN:** Tarrant County College **DOB:** 07/21/1957 **SC:** USA **PT:** Bill Boyd; Sarah Boyd **MS:** Married **SPN:** Bruce Hamilton **ED:** MSN in Nursing Education, Child Health Nursing, The University of Texas at Arlington (1990); BSN in Registered Nursing/Registered Nurse, Baylor University, Cum Laude (1979) **CT:** Registered Nurse; CPR Instruction, American Heart Association, Inc.; Pediatric Advanced Life Support (PALS) Certified **C:** Assistant Professor of Nursing, Tarrant County College (2013-Present) **CR:** Coordinator, Exito Juntos **CIV:** Volunteer, Broadway Baptist Church; American Heart Association, Inc.; Mentor, Fourth Grade Hispanic Student, Academy 4; Hispanic Wellness Coalition; Girl Scouts of the United States of America; Short-term Missions to Venezuela **CW:** Author, Video, "Intramuscular & Subcutaneous Injections"; Author, "Kindness Matters"; Author, Poster Presentation, "SOAR" **AW:** Chancellor's Award Nominee for Student Success, Tarrant County College; Named to Great 100 Nurses of Dallas-Fort Worth; Named Best Clinical Instructor, The University of Texas at Arlington **MEM:** American Nurses Association; Texas Nurses Association; Baylor Alumni Association; National League for Nursing **AS:** Mrs. Hamilton attributes her success to her compassion and enthusiasm. **B/I:** Mrs. Hamilton wanted to be a nurse since junior high school. Her mother was training to become a nurse but quit because she married her father. She loves people and she loves science, and nursing is a way she can use both. **RE:** Baptist **THT:** My personal goal is to make a positive difference in other people's lives. Mrs. Hamilton has a rescue English Cocker Spaniel named Autumn.

HAMLIN, JEFFERSON DAVIS, T: Retired Information Technology Executive **I:** Technology **DOB:** 03/21/1932 **PB:** Danville **SC:** VA/USA **PT:** James Turner Hamlin; Nell (Davis) Hamlin **MS:** Married **SPN:** Winborne Leigh Hamlin (07/27/1959) **CH:** Jefferson; John; Frank **ED:** BEE, University of Virginia (1959); BA, University of Virginia (1954) **C:** Retired, Senior Vice President, Chief Financial Officer, Electronic Data Systems Group, Dallas, TX (1986-1994); Board of Directors, Electronic Data Systems Group, Dallas, TX (1986-1994); Vice President, Electronic Data Systems Corp., Dallas, TX (1969-1986); Branch Manager, Electronic Data Systems Corp., Atlanta, GA (1966-1969); Corporate Staff Systems Engineer, IBM, White Plains, NY (1965-1966); Manager, Systems Engineer, IBM, Lancaster, SC (1964-1965); Systems Engineer, IBM, Lancaster, SC (1960-1963); Applied Science Representative, IBM, Lancaster, SC (1959-1960) **CIV:** Board of Directors, Dallas Symphony Opera Association (1986-Present); United Way, Dallas, TX (1989); Council of Arts and Sciences, University of Virginia (1986); Vestry Member, St. Michael and All Angels Church, Dallas, TX (1975-1978) **MIL:** Active Duty, U.S. Navy (1954-1956) **MEM:** Eta Kappa Nu **MH:** Albert Nelson Marquis Lifetime Achievement Award; Marquis Who's Who Top Professional **B/I:** During his time in the ROTC at the University of Virginia, Mr. Hamlin became involved in electronic equipment management. Though at the time, he knew nothing about electronics, he quickly found an interest in the field. Once he completed his active duty, he returned to the University of Virginia and earned a degree in electronic engineering. **RE:** Episcopalian

HAMM, JON DANIEL, T: Actor **I:** Media & Entertainment **DOB:** 03/10/1971 **PB:** St. Louis **SC:** MO/USA **PT:** Daniel Hamm; Deborah (Garner) Hamm **ED:** BA in English, University of Missouri, St. Louis, MO (1993); Coursework, University of Texas **CW:** Appearance, "Curb Your Enthusiasm" (2020); Actor, "Medical Police" (2020); Actor, "Unbreakable Kimmy Schmidt" (2015-2020); Voice Actor, "Good Omens" (2019); Actor, "Richard Jewell" (2019); Actor, "The Jesus Rolls" (2019); Actor, "Lucy in the Sky" (2019); Actor, "The Report" (2019); Actor, "Bad Times at the El Royale" (2018); Actor, "Beirut" (2018); Actor, "Nostalgia" (2018); Actor, "Tag" (2018); Actor, "SpongBob SquarePants" (2017); Actor, "Tour De Pharmacy" (2017); Actor, "Big Mouth" (2017); Actor, "Travel Man" (2017); Actor, "Majorie Prime" (2017); Actor, "Baby Driver" (2017); Actor, "Aardvark" (2017); Actor, "Wander Over Yonder" (2016); Actor, "Angie Tribeca" (2016); Narrator, "All or Nothing" (2016); Actor, "The Last Man on Earth" (2016); Actor, "Absolutely Fabulous: The Movie" (2016); Actor, "Marjorie Prime" (2016); Actor, "Aardvark" (2016); Actor, "Keeping Up with the Joneses" (2016); Actor, "Wet Hot American Summer: First Day of Camp" (2015); Actor, "TripTank" (2015); Appearance, "Toast of London" (2015); Actor, "7 Days in Hell" (2015); Voice Actor, "Minions" (2015); Actor, Producer, "Mad Men" (2007-2015); Actor, "Million Dollar Arm" (2014); Actor, "Parks and Recreation" (2014-2015); Voice Actor, "The Congress" (2013); Actor, "Clear History" (2013); Actor, Executive Producer, "A Young Doctor's Notebook" (2012-2013); Actor, "Friends with Kids" (2012); Actor, "The Increasingly Poor Decisions of Todd Margaret" (2012); Actor, "Bridesmaids" (2011); Voice Actor, "Shrek Forever After" (2010); Voice Actor, "The Simpsons" (2010); Actor, "The Town" (2010); Host, "Saturday Night Live" (2008, 2010); Actor, "The Day the Earth Stood Still" (2008); Actor, "The Ten" (2007); Actor, "What About Brian" (2006-2007); Actor, "The Unit" (2006-2007); Actor, "Ira and Abby" (2006); Actor, "Charmed" (2005); Actor, "CSI: Miami" (2005); Actor, "Point Pleasant" (2005); Actor, "The Division" (2002-2004); Actor, "We Were Soldiers" (2002); Actor, "Gilmore Girls" (2002); Actor, "Early Bird Special" (2001); Actor, "Kissing Jessica Stein" (2001); Actor, "Providence" (2000-2001); Actor, "Space Cowboys" (2000); Actor, "The Hughleys" (2000); Actor, "The Trouble with Normal" (2000); Actor, "The Trouble with Normal" (2000); Actor, "Ally McBeal" (1997); Appearance, "The Big Date" (1996); Actor, Television Shows and Films; Actor, Commercials Including Mercedes-Benz and H&R Block **AW:** Golden Globe Award for Best Performance by an Actor in a TV Series - Drama, Hollywood Foreign Press Association (2008, 2016); Emmy Award for Outstanding Leading Actor in a Drama Series, Academy of Television Arts & Sciences (2015); Television Critics Association Award for Individual Achievement in Drama (2011, 2015); Critics Choice Award for Best Actor (2011); National Board of Review Award for Best Ensemble Cast (2010); International Man Award, GQ Magazine (2010); SAG Award for Outstanding Performance by an Ensemble in a Drama Series, SAG-AFTRA (2009, 2010); Named Sexiest Man Alive, People Magazine (2008); Named One of the Entertainers of the Year, People Magazine (2008); Named Sexiest Man Living, Salon.com (2007); Satellite Award for Best Performance by an Ensemble Cast - Television (2007)

HAMMERGREN, JOHN HARVEY, T: Chairman, Chief Executive Officer **I:** Business Management/Business Services **CN:** McKesson Corporation **DOB:** 02/20/1959 **PB:** St. Paul **SC:** MN/USA **ED:** MBA, Xavier University (1987); BBA, University of Minnesota (1981) **C:** Chairman, Chief Executive Officer, McKesson Corporation (2002-Present); President, McKesson Corporation (2001-2018); Co-President, Co-Chief Executive Officer, McKesson Corporation (1999-2001); Chief Executive Officer of Supply Chain Management, McKesson Corporation (1997-1999); Group President, McKesson Health Systems (1997-1999); Executive Vice President, President, Chief Executive Officer, Supply Management Business, McKesson HBOC, Inc. (1996-1999); President, Medical/Surgical Division, Kendall Healthcare Products Co., Mansfield, MA (1991-1996); With, Baxter Healthcare Corp./American Hospital Corp. & Lyphomed Inc. (1981-1991) **CR:** Board of Directors, McKesson Corporation (1999-Present); Board of Directors, HP (2005-2013); Chairman, Healthcare Leadership Council (2008-2009); The Business Roundtable; The Business Council **CW:** Co-Author, with Phil Harkins, "Skin in the Game: How Putting Yourself First Today Will Revolutionize Healthcare Tomorrow" (2008) **AW:** Warren Bennis Award for Leadership (2004); Cap Gemini Ernst & Young Leadership Award for Global Integration (2004)

HANDLER, BETH ANN, EDD, T: Language and Learning Disabilities Specialist **I:** Education/Educational Services **DOB:** 06/09/1946 **PB:** Jersey City **SC:** NJ/USA **PT:** Harry Handler; Theresa (Kaplan) Handler **CH:** Lauren Handler **ED:** EdD, Columbia University (1993); EdM, Columbia University (1979); MA, New York University (1970); BS, Boston University (1968) **CT:** Certified Reading Teacher, Teacher of Classes for the Emotionally Handicapped, Teacher of Nursery, Kindergarten and Elementary Grades, State of New York; Certified Reading Teacher, Teacher of Classes for the Emotionally Handicapped, Teacher of Common Branches, New York, NY **C:** Language and Learning Specialist, Private Practice, New York, NY (1973-Present); Learning Specialist, Trinity School, New York, NY (1985-1994); Instructor, Teachers College, Columbia University, New York, NY (1982-1984); Project Associate, Reading Specialist, New York Board of Education, New York, NY (1977-1979); Classroom Teacher, New York Board of Education, New York, NY (1975-1977); Teacher, Reading and Language, New York Board of Education Facility, New York State Psychiatric Institute, NewYork-Presbyterian Hospital, New York, NY (1969-1975); Program Coordinator, Program for the Education of Autistic Adolescents **CR:** Member, NGO Committee on Mental Health, United Nations, New York, NY (1997-Present); Implemented, Further Developed Volunteer Tutoring Program (1996-2000); Designed, Developed and Executed Reading Program, The Gift of Literacy, The Jewish Community Center of the Upper West Side (Now Marlene Meyerson JCC Manhattan), NY (1990-1992) **CIV:** Member, New York City Task Force for Education, New York, NY (1993) **CW:** Creator, Programs for Autistic Students, New York State Psychiatric Institute (1969-1975); Co-coordinator, Training Video, "New Diagnostic Procedures and Remedial Techniques for Educating Autistic Children" (1973); Collaborator, Training Video, "Behavioral Changes in a Schizophrenic Child During Treatment" (1972) **AW:** Full Scholarship to Study Advanced Methods of Preverbal Therapy, St. Luke's Hospital (Now Mount Sinai Morningside), New York, NY (1979-1980); Full Scholarship for Graduate Training at New York University, New York, NY (1969-1970); Named to Kappa Delta Pi, International Honor Society in Education, Teachers College, Columbia University **MEM:** President, Council for Educational Diagnostic Services, NY (1994-1995); Association for Supervision and Curriculum Development (ASCD); International Dyslexia Society (International Dyslexia Association); Council for Exceptional Children (CEC); Council for Educational Diagnostic Services, NY; International Reading Association (Now International Literacy Association); The Orton Dyslexia Society (Now International Dyslexia Association) **MH:** Albert Nelson Marquis Lifetime Achievement Award (2019); Who's Who Award in Education (1996-1997) **AS:** Dr. Handler was extremely fortunate to work at the New York State Psychiatric Institute early in her career where the principal of the school in which she taught, Dr. Pearl Berkowitz, allowed her the time to be mentored by three outstanding professionals each of her nine years there. Among them were Drs. Kim Puig-Antich, Howard Hunt, Donald Dunton, Martha Denckla, Lauretta Bender, and Sam Anderson. Dr. Jeannette Jansky and Mrs. Katrina de Hirsch, at the Babies Hospital, Columbia Presbyterian Hospital, taught her the essentials for responding to individual needs and developing programs for individuals who learn differently. Years later, she spent a summer studying with the Neo Piagetians at the University of Geneva. Sher attended a year of seminars with Dr. Shoshana Mafdali-Goldman studying early language development and pathology at the Learning-Disabilities Unit at St. Luke's Hospital, New York and trained in the Orton-Gillingham method at the Churchill School, New York. Dr. Handler learned the University of Kansas Reading, Writing and Vocabulary Strategies from Mrs. Anita Friede and studied the Sound Reading Solutions Program from its developer, Bruce Howlett. She attended the Concepts Phonics Program taught by Phyllis Fischer. She was then fortunate to learn many additional programs that facilitate mastery of reading, writing, math, spelling, study, and reasoning skills and later able to choose aspects of programs that would work best with each student of hers. **B/I:** Dr. Handler was inspired to go into her profession when she was at Boston University. She was student teaching off campus and encountered four learning-disabled students; she was fascinated by them and wanted to figure out how to best teach them. **AV:** Reading; Knitting; Travel; The arts **THT:** Dr. Handler believes in being a compassionate listener and tuning into the needs of individuals is essential.

HANEY, BRIAN, T: Counsel **I:** Law and Legal Services **CN:** Sweder & Ross LLP **ED:** JD, Suffolk University Law School (2004); BA, University of Vermont (2000) **C:** Counsel, Sweder & Ross LLP, Boston, MA (2013-Present); Associate, Cooley Manion Jones LLP, Boston, MA (2005-2012); Law Clerk to Justices, Massachusetts Superior Court, Boston, MA (2004-2005) **CIV:** American Ireland Fund; Boys & Girls Clubs of Boston; TENacity **CW:** Contributing Author, "Alcohol, Good Service, and Entertainment Licensing" (2017); Author, "Contrasting the Prosecution of Witness Tampering Under 18 U.S.C."; Contributor, Publications **AW:** "Super Lawyer," SuperLawyers (2015-Present); "Rising Star," SuperLawyers (2011-2014) **AS:** Mr. Haney attributes his success to two things. He has never been afraid of hard work and has been fortunate to have wonderful mentors, who taught him how to be a better lawyer. He has said, "You can never be professional enough, and your hard work is the only thing that you can control..." **B/I:** Mr. Haney became involved in his profession because his father and grandmother were attorneys. His grandmother graduated from law school in 1937 and his father graduated in 1981. When Mr. Haney was a child, he went to work with his father, and "nipped at his heels." He knew from a very early age that law would be the perfect profession for him. **THT:** Mr. Haney said, "A recognition of what I have accomplished and a recognition that I am capable and likely to accomplish a great deal more in the future..."

HANKS, TOM JEFFREY, T: Actor **I:** Media & Entertainment **DOB:** 07/09/1956 **PB:** Concord **SC:** CA/USA **PT:** Amos Mefford Hanks; Janet Marilyn (Frager) Hanks **MS:** Married **SPN:** Rita Wilson (04/30/1988); Samantha Lewes (01/24/1978, Divorced 03/19/1987) **CH:** Colin; Elizabeth; Chester Marlon; Truman Theodore **ED:** Coursework, California State University, Sacramento; Coursework in Theater, Chabot College, Hayway, CA **CW:** Actor, Screenwriter, "Greyhound" (2020); Appearance, "Borat Subsequent Moviefilm" (2020); Actor, "A Beautiful Day in the Neighborhood" (2019); Voice Actor, "Toy Story 4" (2019); Appearance, Executive Producer, "The Movies" (2019); Producer, "Mamma Mia! Here We Go Again" (2018); Appearance, "Last Week Tonight with John Oliver" (2014, 2017); Author, "Uncommon Type" (2017); Actor, "The Circle" (2017); Actor, "Mark Felt: The Man Who Brought Down the White House" (2017); Actor, "The Post" (2017); Executive Producer, "The Nineties" (2017); Voice Actor, "The David S. Pumpkins Animated Halloween Special" (2017); Actor, "Inferno" (2016); Executive Producer, "The Eighties" (2016); Actor, "Maya and Marty" (2016); Producer, "My Big Fat Greek Wedding 2" (2016); Actor, Producer, "A Hologram for the King" (2016); Actor, "Sully" (2016); Actor, Executive Producer, "Ithaca" (2015); Actor, "Bridge of Spies" (2015); Executive Producer, "The Seventies" (2015); Executive Producer, "The Sixties" (2014); Executive Producer, "Olive Kitteridge" (2014); Appearance, "The Greatest Event in Television History" (2014); Voice Actor, "Toy Story That Time Forgot" (2014); Actor, "Killing Lincoln" (2013); Voice Actor, "Toy Story of Terror" (2013); Actor, "The Assassination of President Kennedy" (2013); Actor, "Captain Phillips" (2013); Producer, "Parkland" (2013); Actor, "Killing Lincoln" (2013); Actor, "Lucky Guy" (2013); Actor, "Saving Mr. Banks" (2013); Executive Producer, "Game Change" (2012); Actor, "Cloud Atlas" (2012); Actor, "Extremely Loud and Incredibly Close" (2011); Executive Producer, "The 3 Minute Talk Show" (2011); Actor, "30 Rock" (2011); Executive Producer, "He Has Seen War" (2011); Actor, Producer, Director, "Larry Crowne" (2011); Executive Producer, "Big Love" (2006-2011); Actor, "The Pacific" (2010); Voice Actor, "Toy Story 3" (2010); Executive Producer, "My Life in Ruins" (2009); Actor, "Angels & Demons" (2009); Executive Producer, "Where the Wild Things Are" (2009); Producer, "Beyond All Boundaries" (2009); Actor, "The Great Buck Howard" (2008); Actor, "John Adams" (2008); Voice Actor, "The Simpsons Movie" (2007); Actor, "Charlie Wilson's War" (2007); Actor, "Neil Young: Heart of Gold" (2006); Actor, "The Ant Bully" (2006); Actor, "The Da Vinci Code" (2006); Voice Actor, "Cars" (2006); Actor, "Connie and Carla" (2004); Actor, "The Terminal" (2004); Actor, "The Ladykillers" (2004); Appearance, "Elvis Has Left the Building" (2004); Voice Actor, "The Polar Express" (2004); Actor, "Road to Perdition" (2002); Actor, "Catch Me if You Can" (2002); Producer, "My Big Fat Greek Wedding" (2002); Executive Producer, "We Stand Alone Together" (2001); Appearance, Director, Writer, Producer, "Band of Brothers" (2001); Actor, "Cast Away" (2000); Voice Actor, "Toy Story 2" (1999); Actor, "The Green Mile" (1999); Actor, "Saving Private Ryan" (1998); Actor, "You've Got Mail" (1998); Producer, Director, Writer, "From the Earth to the Moon" (1998); Actor, "I Am Your Child" (1997); Actor, Writer, Director, "That Thing You Do!" (1996); Actor, "Apollo 13"

(1995); Voice Actor, "Toy Story" (1995); Actor, "Forrest Gump" (1994); Actor, "Sleepless in Seattle" (1993); Actor, "Philadelphia" (1993); Actor, "Radio Flyer" (1992); Actor, "A League of Their Own" (1992); Actor, "Joe Versus the Volcano" (1990); Actor, "The Bonfire of the Vanities" (1990); Actor, "Turner and Hooch" (1989); Actor, "The 'Burbs" (1989); Actor, "Punchline" (1988); Actor, "Big" (1988); Actor, "Dragnet" (1987); Actor, "The Money Pit" (1986); Actor, "Nothing in Common" (1986); Actor, "Every Time We Say Goodbye" (1986); Actor, "Volunteers" (1985); Actor, "The Man with One Red Shoe" (1985); Actor, "Splash" (1984); Actor, "Bachelor Party" (1984); Actor, "Mazes and Monsters" (1982); Actor, "Bosom Buddies" (1980-1982); Actor, "He Knows You're Alone" (1980); Actor, Producer, Television, Documentaries and Film **AW:** Cecil B. DeMille Award, Golden Globe Awards, Hollywood Foreign Press Association (2020); Named Honorary Citizen of Greece (2019); Presidential Medal of Freedom, The White House (2016); Named to French Legion of Honor (2016); Emmy Awards for Outstanding Limited Series, Academy of Television Arts & Sciences (1998, 2002, 2008, 2010, 2015); Honoree, Kennedy Center Honors, John F. Kennedy Center for the Performing Arts, Washington, DC (2014); David L. Wolper Producer of the Year Award in Long-form TV, Producers Guild America (2009, 2013); Emmy Award for Outstanding Television Movie, Academy of Television Arts & Sciences (2012); Norman Lear Achievement Award in Television, Producers Guild of America (2011); Named One of the World's Most Influential People, TIME Magazine (2009); Honoree, Film Society of Lincoln Center (2009); Named One of the 100 Most Powerful Celebrities, Forbes.com (2007); Named Honorary Member, United States Army Ranger Hall of Fame (2006); Douglas S. Morrow Public Outreach Award (2006); Named One of the 50 Most Powerful People in Hollywood, Premiere Magazine (2004-2006); Britannia Award for Excellence in Film, BAFTA Los Angeles (2004); Emmy Award for Outstanding Directing for a Limited Series, Television Movie or Special, Academy of Television Arts & Sciences (2002); Named Actor of the Year, Hollywood Film Festival (2002); AFI Life Achievement Award, American Film Institute (2002); Golden Globe Award for Best Actor in a Motion Picture - Drama, Hollywood Foreign Press Association (1994, 1995, 2001); New York Film Critics Circle Award for Best Actor (2000); Distinguished Public Service Award, United States Navy (1999); Screen Actors Guild Award for Outstanding Performance by an Ensemble Cast in a Motion Picture, SAG-AFTRA (1996); American Comedy Awards for Funniest Actor in a Motion Picture (1989, 1995); Named Man of the Year, Hasty Pudding Theatrical Society (1995); Screen Actors Guild Award for Outstanding Performance by a Male Actor in a Leading Role in a Motion Picture, SAG-AFTRA (1995); Academy Award for Best Actor, Academy of Motion Picture Arts and Sciences (1993, 1994); Award for Best Actor, National Board of Review (1994); Louella O. Parsons Award, Hollywood Women's Press Club (1994); American Comedy Award for Funniest Supporting Actor in a Motion Picture (1993); Recipient, Star, Hollywood Walk of Fame (1992); Golden Globe Award for Best Actor in a Motion Picture - Musical or Comedy, Hollywood Foreign Press Association (1989); Golden Apple Award, Hollywood Women's Press Club (1988); Numerous Awards **MEM:** Vice President, Academy of Motion Picture Arts and Sciences (2007-2009, 2009-Present); American Federation of TV and Radio Artists (Now SAG-AFTRA); Screen Actors Guild (Now SAG-AFTRA); International Thespian Society, Educational Theatre Association; Academy of Motion Picture Arts and Sciences; Actors' Equity Association **AV:** Collector of typewriters

HANNA-ATTISHA, MONA, MD, T: 1) Physician, Pediatric Residency Director, 2) Assistant Professor 3) Public Health Advocate **I:** Medicine & Health Care **CN:** 1) Hurley Medical Center 2) Michigan State University **DOB:** 11/24/1976 **PB:** Sheffield **SC:** United Kingdom **MS:** Married **SPN:** Elliott Attisha **CH:** Two daughters **ED:** Chief Residency, Residency, Wayne State University/Children's Hospital of Michigan; MD, College of Human Medicine, Michigan State University; MPH in Health Management and Policy, School of Public Health, University of Michigan; BS, School for Environment and Sustainability, University of Michigan **C:** Physician, Hurley Medical Center; Pediatric Residency Director, Associate Professor, Department of Pediatrics and Human Development, Michigan State University **CIV:** Honorary Co-Chair, March of Science (2017-Present); Appointed Member, Flint Water Interagency Coordinating Committee, Michigan Child Lead Poisoning Elimination Board and Michigan Public Health Commission (2016) **AW:** Vilcek-Gold Award for Humanism in Healthcare, Vilcek Foundation and the Arnold P. Gold Foundation (2019); Inductee, Michigan Women's Hall of Fame (2018); Heinz Award, Heinz Family Foundation (2017); One of the 100 Most Influential People, Time Magazine (2016); Politico 50 (2016); One of 10 Outstanding Young Americans (2016); Ridenhour Prize for Truth-Telling (2016); Got Science? Champion, Union of Concerned Scientists (2016); James C. Goodale Freedom of Expression Award, PEN American Center; Rose Nader Award for Arab American Activism, American-Arab Anti-Discrimination Committee; Champion of Justice, Arab Community Center for Economic and Social Services

HANNER, PAT, T: Artist, Retired Nurse **I:** Fine Art **DOB:** 07/19/1940 **PB:** Ontario **SC:** CA/USA **PT:** Joseph William Hanner; Dorothy Candy Hanner **ED:** BA in Public Administration, California Polytechnic State University, Pomona, CA (1982); ADN, Chaffey College, Alta Loma, CA (1978) **CT:** RN, Florida, California **C:** Owner, Pat Hanner Art Gallery, Ontario, CA (1964-2011); Director, Psychiatric Nursing Education, Lanterman Development Center, Pomona, CA (1964-2003); Board of Directors, Pacific Federal Credit Union, Pomona, CA **CR:** Board of Directors, Here We Grow Child Care Center, Pomona, CA **CIV:** Donor, Faith Community Home Church; Donor, American Cancer Society; Donor, American Red Cross; Donor, Feed the Children; Donor, Father Flannigan's Boys Town; Donor, Joyce Myers Ministry; Donor, Life Outreach International; Donor, Parkinson's Resource Center, Palm Springs, CA **CW:** Author, "Continuous Quality Improvement, New American Governor" (2009); Author, "A Miracle in the Making" (1993); Author, "Ontario City Sewer System" (1980) **AW:** Employee of the Year, Lanterman Development Center (2003); Employee of the Month, Lanterman Development Center (2003) **MEM:** American Red Cross **MH:** Albert Nelson Marquis Lifetime Achievement Award **AV:** Art; Gardening; Aerobics; Swimming

HANNITY, SEAN PATRICK, T: Political Commentator; Author **I:** Media & Entertainment **CN:** Fox News; iHeartMeadia, Inc. **DOB:** 12/30/1961 **PB:** New York **SC:** NY/USA **PT:** Hugh Hannity; Lillian (Flynn) Hannity **MS:** Divorced **SPN:** Jill Rhodes (01/09/1993, Divorced 2019) **CH:** Patrick; Merri **ED:** Honorary PhD, Southeastern University (2006); Honorary Diploma, Liberty University (2005); Coursework, Adelphi University; Coursework, New York University **C:** Host, "Hannity," FOX News Channel (2009-Present); Host, "The Sean Hannity Show," iHeartMedia, Inc. (2007-Present); Host, "The Sean Hannity Show," ABC Radio Network, New York, NY (2001-Present); Host, "Hannity's America," FOX News Channel (2007-2009); Co-Host, "Hannity & Colmes," FOX News Channel, New York, NY (1996-2009); Afternoon Drive Host, 77 WABC Radio, New York, NY (1998-2001); Late Night Host, 77 WABC Radio, New York, NY (1997-1998); Substitute Host, 77 WABC Radio, New York, NY (1996); Staff, Station WGST, Atlanta, GA (1992-1996); Staff, Station WVNN, Huntsville, AL (1990-1992) **CIV:** Host, Benefit Shows, Freedom Concerts (2003-2010) **CW:** Author, "Live Free or Die" (2020); Executive Producer, "Let There Be Light" (2017); Author, "Conservative Victory: Defeating Obama's Radical Agenda" (2010); Author, "Deliver Us From Evil: Defeating Terrorism, Despotism, and Liberalism" (2004); Author, "Let Freedom Ring: Winning the War of Liberty Over Liberalism" (2002) **AW:** Inductee, National Radio Hall of Fame (2017); Listee, 50 Highest-Earning Political Figures, Newsweek (2010); Listee, 100 Most Important Talk Show Hosts, Talkers Magazine (2009); Marconi Award for Network Syndicated Personality of the Year, National Association of Broadcasters (2007); National Talk Show Host of the Year Award, Radio & Records Magazine (2003, 2004); Marconi Award for Talk Show Host of the Year, National Association of Broadcasters (2003); Freedom of Speech Award, Talkers Magazine (2003); Listee, Top 100 Talk Hosts in America, Talkers Magazine (2003) **PA:** Republican **RE:** Roman Catholic

HANSEN, LARS PETER, PHD, T: Professor; Economist **I:** Education/Educational Services **CN:** The University of Chicago **DOB:** 10/26/1952 **PB:** Urbana **SC:** IL/USA **PT:** Roger Gaurth Hansen; Anna Lou (Rees) Hansen **MS:** Married **SPN:** Grace Renjuei Tsiang (08/25/1984) **ED:** PhD in Economics, University of Minnesota (1978); BS in Mathematics and Political Science, Utah State University (1974) **C:** David Rockefeller Distinguished Service Professor, Economics, Statistics and the College, The University of Chicago (2010-Present); Founding Director, Becker Friedman Institute for Research in Economics, The University of Chicago (2009-Present); Homer J. Livingston Professor, Economics, The University of Chicago (1990-2010); Chairman, Department of Economics, The University of Chicago (1998-2002); Director, Graduate Studies, The University of Chicago (1988-1994); Professor, The University of Chicago (1984-1990); Associate Professor, The University of Chicago (1982-1984); Associate Professor, Carnegie-Mellon University, Pittsburgh, PA (1980-1981); Assistant Professor, Economics, Carnegie-Mellon University, Pittsburgh, PA (1978-1980) **CR:** Visiting Professor, Keio University School of Business and Commerce (2009); Nemmers Visiting Professor, Department of Economics, Northwestern University (2007); Visiting Research Professor, The University of Chicago Booth School of Business (2003-2005); Visiting Research Professor, Stanford Graduate School of Business (1989-1990); Visiting Associate Professor, Harvard University, Cambridge, MA (1986); Visiting Associate Professor, Massachusetts Institute of Technology, Boston, MA (1983); Visiting Associate Professor, Economics, The University of Chicago (1981-1982); Board of Governors, Stevanovich Center for Financial Mathematics, The University of Chicago **CW:** Co-editor, Econometrica (1986-Present); Contributor, Articles to Professional Journals **AW:** Nobel Memorial Prize in Economic Sciences (Sveriges Riksbank Prize), Royal Swedish Academy of Sciences (2013); BBVA Foundation Frontiers of Knowledge Award in Economics, Finance and Management (2011); Award, CME Group-MSRI in Quantitative Applications (2008); Erwin Plein Nemmers Prize in Economics (2006); Co-recipient, Frisch Medal (1984); Sloan Fellow (1982) **MEM:** President, The Econometric Society (2007); Fellow, The Econometric Society;

The American Finance Association (AFA); National Academy of Sciences; American Association for the Advancement of Science **AV:** Skiing

HARBAUGH, EDITH, T: Chief Executive Officer **I:** Other **CN:** LaunchDarkly **ED:** BS in Engineering, Harvey Mudd College; Degree in Economics, Pomona College **C:** Mentor, HMC INQ (2017-Present); Chief Executive Officer, Co-Founder, Launch-Darkly (2014-Present); Contributing Writer, Readwrite (2015-Present); Co-Host, To Be Continuous, DevOp.Com (2015-Present); Startup Mentor, Alchemist Accelerator (2015-Present)

HARBAUGH, JIM JOSEPH, T: College Football Coach; Former Professional Football Coach; Former Professional Football Player **I:** Athletics **CN:** University of Michigan Wolverines **DOB:** 12/23/1963 **PB:** Toledo **SC:** OH/USA **PT:** Jack Avon Harbaugh; Jacqueline M. (Cipiti) Harbaugh **MS:** Married **SPN:** Sarah Feuerborn Harbaugh (01/05/2008); Miah (Burke) Harbaugh (1996, Divorced 2006) **CH:** Jay; James Jr.; Grace; Addison: Katherine; Jack; John **ED:** BA in Communications, University of Michigan (1987) **C:** Head Football Coach, University of Michigan Wolverines, Ann Arbor, MI (2014-Present); Head Football Coach, San Francisco 49ers, NFL (2011-2014); Head Football Coach, Bradford M. Freeman Director of Football, Stanford University Cardinals (2006-2011); Head Football Coach, University of San Diego Toreros (2004-2006); Offensive Assistant, Oakland Raiders, NFL (2002-2003); Quarterback, Carolina Panthers, NFL (2001); Quarterback, San Diego Chargers, NFL (1999-2000); Quarterback, Baltimore Ravens, NFL (1998-1999); Volunteer Assistant Coach, Western Kentucky University Athletics, Bowling Green, KY (1994-2001); Quarterback, Indianapolis Colts, NFL (1994-1998); Quarterback, Chicago Bears, NFL (1987-1993) **CR:** Co-owner, Founding Partner, Panther Racing (1997-Present) **CIV:** With, Legal Services Corporation **CW:** Appearance, "Arli$$" (1977); Appearance, "Saved By the Bell: The New Class" (1996) **AW:** Named NFL Coach of the Year, NFC Champions (2012); Named NFL Coach of the Year, The Associated Press (2011); Woody Hayes Coach of the Year Award (2010); Named Pioneer League Champion (2005, 2006); Named to Indianapolis Colts' Ring of Honor (2005); Named to Pro Bowl Team, American Football Conference (1995); Named NFL Co-comeback Player of the Year, The Associated Press (1995); Named AFC Player of Year, United Press International (1995); Named NFL All-Pro (1995); Named Big 10 MVP (1986)

HARDEN, JAMES EDWARD JR., T: Professional Basketball Player **I:** Athletics **CN:** Houston Rockets **DOB:** 08/26/1989 **PB:** Los Angeles **SC:** CA/USA **PT:** James Harden Sr.; Monja Willis **MS:** Single **ED:** Coursework, Arizona State University, Tempe, AZ (2007-2009); Diploma, Artesia High School, Lakewood, CA **C:** Professional Basketball Player, Guard, Houston Rockets, NBA (2012-Present); Professional Basketball Player, Guard, Oklahoma City Thunder, NBA (2009-2012) **CR:** U.S. National Team, Summer Olympic Games, London, England, United Kingdom (2012) **AW:** Eight-time NBA All-Star (2013–2020); Five-time All-NBA First Team (2014-2015, 2017–2019); Named NBA Most Valuable Player (2018); Gold Medal, World Cup, Spain (2014); Named to All-NBA Third Team (2013); Gold Medal, Olympic Games, London, England, United Kingdom (2012); Named NBA Sixth Man of the Year (2012); Named to NBA All-Rookie Second Team (2010); Named to Consensus First-Team All-American (2009); Named Pac-10 Player of the Year (2009); Two-time First-team All-Pac-10 (2008-2009); Named to Second-team Parade All-American (2007)

HARDER, JOSHUA, "JOSH" KECK, T: U.S. Representative **I:** Government Administration/Government Relations/Government Services **DOB:** 08/01/1986 **PB:** Turlock **SC:** CA/USA **MS:** Married **SPN:** Pamela (Sud) Harder (2018) **ED:** MBA, Harvard Business School; MPP, Harvard University; BA in Political Science and Economics, Stanford University **C:** U.S. Representative, California's 10th Congressional District (2019-Present); Professor of Business, Modesto Junior College (2017-Present); Vice President, Bessemer Venture Partners, San Francisco, CA (2016-2017); With, Bessemer Venture Partners, NY (2014-2016) **PA:** Democrat

HARDISH, PATRICK, T: Librarian, Composer **I:** Media & Entertainment **DOB:** 04/06/1944 **PB:** Perth Amboy **SC:** NJ/USA **PT:** Stanley John Hardish; Mildred Elaine (Dafcik) Hardish **ED:** MS, Pratt Institute (1981); Postgraduate Coursework, Columbia University (1978-1981); BA, Queens College (1977); Coursework, The Julliard School (1969-1972) **C:** Music Library, New York Public Library, New York, NY (1984-Present); Library Assistant, Columbia University, New York, NY (1978-1984) **CR:** Editorial Board, The New Music Connoisseur (1985-Present); Interviewer, Music Scholarship, Russian Journal for Academic Studies (2016); Guest Composer, WNYC-FM Radio (1983, 1986); WKCR-FM (1979-1986); Consultant, Jewish Theological Seminary, New York, NY (1985); Composer-In-Residence, National Association for the Regional Ballet's Craft on Choreography Conference (1981) **CW:** Composer, "Two Poems," Composers Concordance Records (2011); Piano and Percussion Duet, Capstone Records (2001); Composer, "Solo for Pete," Composers Cordornance Records (2000); Sonorities VI, Calabrese Music (1998); Composer, "Sonorous" (1996); Composer, "Ave Maria" (1991); Composer, "Sonorities IV" (1990); Composer, "Suite for Wendy" (1989); Composer, "Sonorities III" (1986); Composer, "Sonorities III" (1986); Composer, "Tremotrill" (1981); Lecturer, New York University; Lecturer, Governs School of the Gifted (1981); Composer, "Accordioclusterville," Finnadar Records (1978); Composer, "Intensities II" (1978); Commission, Jamaica Symphony; Commission, North-South Consonance; Commission, Composers Guild of New Jersey **AW:** Grantee, Meet the Composer (1978, 1983, 1992, 1997); Sweet Briar Fellow, Virginia Center for the Creative Arts (1981-1982, 1985-1986, 1988) **MEM:** Dickens Fellowship of New York (2015-Present); Co-Director, Composers Concordance (1983-Present); Co-Founder, Co-Director, Composers Concordance (1983-2015); Vice Chairman, Music Library Association (1983-1985); American Federation of Musicians (1965-1984); American Music Center; New Jersey Guild of Composers; Broadcast Music Inc. **MH:** Albert Nelson Marquis Lifetime Achievement Award; Marquis Who's Who Top Professional **AV:** Attending concerts, movies, and plays; Reading; Walking

HARMENING, JEFFREY L., T: Chairman, Chief Executive Officer **I:** Retail/Sales **CN:** General Mills Inc. **ED:** MBA, Harvard University (1994); Bachelor's Degree, DePauw University, Greencastle, IN (1989) **C:** Chairman, General Mills Inc. (2018-Present); Chief Executive Officer, General Mills Inc. (2017-Present); President, Chief Operating Officer, General Mills Inc. (2016-2017); Executive Vice President, Chief Operating Officer of the U.S. Retail Segment, General Mills Inc. (2014-2016); Chief Executive Officer, Cereal Partners Worldwide, General Mills Inc. (2012-2014); Senior Vice President, General Mills Inc. (2011-2012); President, Big G Division, General Mills, Inc. (2007-2011); Vice President of Marketing, Cereal Partners Worldwide, General Mills, Inc., Lausanne, Switzerland (2003-2007); Marketing Director, Big G New Enterprises

and Food Service New Business, General Mills Inc. (2000-2003); With, General Mills Inc. (1994); Various Marketing Positions, Betty Crocker, Yoplait USA and Big G Cereals Divisions, General Mills Inc.

HARMON, MARK, T: Actor **I:** Media & Entertainment **DOB:** 09/02/1951 **PB:** Burbank **SC:** CA/USA **PT:** Tom Harmon; Elyse Knox **MS:** Married **SPN:** Pam Dawber (03/21/1987) **CH:** Sean; Ty Christian **ED:** BA in Communications, University of California Los Angeles, Cum Laude (1974); Associate Degree, Pierce College, Los Angeles, CA **CR:** Founder, Wings Productions (2014-Present); Merchandising Director **CW:** Actor, Executive Producer, "NCIS" (2008-Present); Actor, "NCIS: New Orleans" (2014-2018); Voice Actor, "Family Guy" (2012); Actor, "Certain Prey" (2011); Actor, "Certain Prey" (2011); Actor, "Justice League: Crisis on Two Earths" (2010); Actor, "Weather Girl" (2009); Actor, "Chasing Liberty" (2004); Appearance, "Retrosexual" (2004); Actor, "NCIS" (2003-2008); Actor, "JAG" (2003); Actor, "Freaky Friday" (2003); Actor, "The West Wing" (2002); Actor, "Local Boys" (2002); Actor, "The Legend of Tarzan" (2001); Actor, "Crossfire Trail" (2001); Actor, "And Never Let Her Go" (2001); Actor, "For All Time" (2000); Actor, "I'll Remember April" (2000); Actor, "The Amati Girls" (2000); Actor, "Chicago Hope" (1996-2000); Actor, "Fear and Loathing in Las Vegas" (1998); Actor, "The First to Go" (1997); Actor, "Casualties" (1997); Actor, "Strangers" (1996); Actor, "Charlie Grace" (1995-1996); Actor, "Original Sins" (1995); Actor, "The Last Supper" (1995); Actor, "Magic in the Water" (1995); Actor, "Wyatt Earp" (1994); Actor, "Reasonable Doubts" (1991-1993); Actor, "Cold Heaven" (1992); Actor, "Till There Was You" (1991); Actor, "Dillinger" (1991); Actor, "Long Road Home" (1991); Actor, "Fourth Story" (1991); Actor, "Shadow of a Doubt" (1991); Actor, "Sweet Bird of Youth" (1989); Actor, "Worth Winning" (1989); Actor, "Stealing Home" (1988); Actor, "The Presidio" (1988); Actor, "Summer School" (1987); Actor, "After the Promise" (1987); Actor, "Let's Get Harry" (1987); Actor, "Prince of Bel Air" (1986); Actor, "Deliberate Stranger" (1986); Actor, "St. Elsewhere" (1983-1986); Actor, "Intimate Agony" (1983); Actor, "Flamingo Road" (1981-1982); Actor, "Goliath Awaits" (1981); Actor, "The Dream Merchants" (1980); Actor, "240-Robert" (1979-1980); Actor, "Beyond the Poseidon Adventure" (1979); Actor, "Centennial" (1978-1979); Actor, "Getting Married" (1978); Actor, "Sam" (1978); Actor, "Little Mo" (1978); Actor, "Comes a Horseman" (1978); Actor, "Eleanor and Franklin: The White House Years" (1977); Actor, "Adam-12" (1975) **AW:** People's Choice Award for Favorite Crime Drama TV Actor (2016); Prism Award for Male Performance in a Drama Series (2013); Inductee, Inaugural Class, Pierce College of Athletic Hall of Fame (2010); Named Sexiest Man Alive, People Magazine (1986); National Football Foundation Award for All-around Excellence (1974)

HARMON, MARY L., CPA, ESQ, T: Managing Director, Tax Counsel, Head of Tax Planning (Retired) **I:** Financial Services **CN:** Goldman Sachs & Co. LLC **DOB:** 09/04/1953 **PB:** Paragould **SC:** AR/USA **PT:** Mayor Bill J. Harmon; Marvelle Harmon **MS:** Single **CH:** Luke L. Harmon **ED:** LLM in Taxation, New York University (NYU) School of Law (1984); JD, University of Arkansas at Little Rock, with High Honors (1983); BSBA in Accounting, Walton College, University of Arkansas (1976) **CT:** Certified Public Accountant (1976-1983) **C:** Managing Director, Tax Counsel, Head of Tax Planning and Advisory, Goldman Sachs & Co. LLC (1999-2020); Managing Director, Tax Counsel, Bankers Trust Company (1994-1999); Special Counsel, IRS Chief Counsel (1990-1993); Associate,

Clearly, Gottlieb, Steen & Hamilton (1986-1990); Acting Assistant Professor of Law, New York University (NYU) School of Law (1984-1986); Senior Field Auditor, Arkansas State Office of Legislative Audit (1976-1983); Partner, Hogan & Hartson (Now Hogan & Lovells) **CW:** Co-Author, "Tax Issues Raised by Financial Products: Shorts Against the Box, Collars, and Equity Derivatives," Journal of Civil Rights and Economic Development (1998); Author, "Civil Procedure–Quasi-in-Rem Jurisdiction–Attachment of Insurers Obligation to Nonresident Defendant (Seider Rule) Unconstitutional," University of Arkansas at Little Rock Law Review (1981); Panelist, "Practical Considerations in Dealing with the Tax Shelter Disclosure and List Maintenance Regulations," American Bar Association **AW:** Lifetime Achievement Award, University of Arkansas (2018); Chief Counsel Award for Service as Special Counsel, Chief Counsel, IRS (1993); American Jurisprudence Awards in Property Law, Conflicts of Law, and Legal Profession; Top Papers Awarded in Corporate Tax and Consolidated Tax Returns; Best Brief, Moot Court Competition; Law Journal Writing Award; Recipient, Numerous Law Journal Scholarships **MEM:** American Bar Association; Federal Bar Association; Sam M. Walton College of Business Dean's Advisory Board; Charter Member, Board of the Garrison Financial Institution; National Institute of Social Sciences; Active Supporter, New York Stem Cell Foundation; New York State Bar Association; DC Bar Association **BAR:** New York; District of Columbia; Arkansas **MH:** Albert Nelson Marquis Lifetime Achievement Award; Marquis Who's Who Top Professional **AS:** Ms. Harmon attributes her success to the network of successful tax lawyers, accountants, and friends that she has gained throughout her career. She gives most credit for her network building to the New York University tax program, which has a long-standing history of maintaining an active relationship among the students and professors. This was her network inspiration to maintain and continue to grow her personal network. She credits her work on several IRS guidance projects alongside her ability to bring a working group together to create regulations that provide workable rules and reflect the underlying congressional policy. **B/I:** Ms. Harmon became involved in her profession because she became a certified public accountant and obtained a position with the State of Arkansas Legislative Audit, which audited county and city governments. Auditing the county governments provided Ms. Harmon a bird's eye view of the courts and legal system in action. She had not focused on her preferred area of law, but a professor suggested that she combine her accounting background with her legal knowledge by obtaining an LLM in tax. Following up on that idea, she chose to attend the New York University School of Law, which is the most well-respected program in the country. After three and a half years at Cleary, she took the Special Counsel position at the IRS, subsequently leaving to become a partner at Hogan & Hartson (now Hogan & Lovells) and finally moved to the financial industry. Her role during this journey was that of a tax lawyer, which is where most of her post-education success and honors were earned. **PA:** Democrat **RE:** Christian

HARNER, STEPHEN GLEN, MD, T: Otolaryngologist (Retired) **I:** Medicine & Health Care **DOB:** 08/21/1940 **PB:** Winston-Salem **SC:** NC/USA **PT:** Casper Glendon Harner; Bessie Wanda (Carmichael) Harner **MS:** Married **SPN:** Carla June Kelly **CH:** Kelly Ann Patterson; Jeffrey Glenn Harner **ED:** Resident in Otolaryngology, Fitzsimons Army Hospital, Denver, CO (1968-1970); Resident in Surgery, Reynolds Army Hospital, Fort Sill, OK

(1966-1967); Intern, Brooke Army Hospital, San Antonio, TX (1965-1966); MD, University of Missouri (1965); AB, Washington University at St. Louis (1962) **CT:** Certified, Board of Otolaryngology (1971) **C:** Staff Otolaryngologist, Mayo Clinic, Rochester, MN (1973-2003); Resigned, U.S. Army (1973); Assistant Chief, Otolaryngology, Letterman Army Hospital, San Francisco, CA (1970-1973) **CR:** Professor, Otolaryngology Mayo Medical School (1994-Present) **CIV:** Member, Governor's Council on Developmental Disability (1993-1996); Board of Directors, Hiawatha Homes, Rochester, NY (1980-1994); President, Hiawatha Homes, Rochester, NY (1990-1992); Vice President, Hiawatha Homes, Rochester, NY (1989); Secretary, Hiawatha Homes, Rochester, NY (1986-1987); Volunteer, Channel One; Volunteer, Rochester Public Library **MIL:** Advanced through grades to Major, U.S. Army; Commissioned 2nd Lieutenant, U.S. Army (1964) **CW:** Contributor, Articles, Professional Journals **AW:** Named Teacher of Year, Mayo Fellow's Association (1979, 1984, 1986, 2003); Best Doctors in America (2001, 2002) **MEM:** Fellow, American College of Surgeons; Fellow, American Academy of Otolaryngology; Fellow, American Otologic Rhinologic & Laryngologic Association; Fellow, American Otologic Society; American Medical Association; Minnesota Medical Association; Zumbro Valley Medical Association; Society of University Otolaryngologists; American Neurotology Society; Medical Advisory Board, Acoustic Neuroma Association **MH:** Albert Nelson Marquis Lifetime Achievement Award; Marquis Who's Who Top Professional **B/I:** Dr. Harner's father was a physician. He decided at age 6 that being a physician was what he wanted to do too, and he became very focused on doing so. When he was in medical school, he was exposed to ENT by a professor and received training in the field which is where his career in otolaryngology began. In addition, he didn't go into what his father had done in terms of specialty and so on, but his father set an example that Dr. Harner wanted to follow. **AV:** Photography; Travel; Boating; Walking; Golf; Family; Genealogy **PA:** Independent

HAROON, NASREEN, T: Artist **I:** Fine Art **CN:** Nasreen Haroon Collections **DOB:** 12/10/1952 **PB:** Karachi **SC:** Pakistan **PT:** Ahmad; Amina (Dada) Adaya **MS:** Married **SPN:** Haroon Haji Husein (04/29/1972) **CH:** Omar; Sana **ED:** BA in Psychology, Philosophy and History, St. Joseph's College, Karachi, Pakistan (1972) **CR:** Design Consultant, Shangri-La Hotel, Santa Monica, CA (1983-1994); Speaker on Cultural, Ethnic, Religious Diversity (1991); Co-chair, Muslim Jewish Dialogue; Teacher, Master Classes in Art, Dubai, Abu Dhabi and Sharjah, United Arab Emirates; Lecturer, Ecole de Beaux Arts, Algiers **CIV:** Santa Monica Bay Interfaith Council, CA (1994-Present); Board of Directors, Islamic Center of Southern California (1999-2002); Vice President, Pakistan Arts Council, Pacific Asia Museum, Pasadena, CA (1997-1999); Development in Literacy, Pakistan Arts Council, Pacific Asia Museum, Los Angeles, CA (1996-1997); Pakistan Arts Council, Pacific Asia Museum, Pasadena, CA (1994-1996); President, Women's Association (1991); Co-chairman, Muslim Jewish Dialogue; Board of Directors, Cornerstone Theater Productions Co. (Cornerstone Theater Company) **CW:** Artist, Oil Paintings, Numerous Exhibitions (1992-Present); Featured, Premier Issue of Zarposh Magazine (1997); Regular Appearances, Adelphia Cable Television Program, "God Squad"; Paintings Selected for Art in Embassies Program, Displayed at U.S. Embassy, Pakistan, Senegal, United Arab Emirates, Algeria and Nigeria, Saudi Arabia; Cultural Envoy to State Department, United Arab Emirates and Algeria; Artist, Painted Mural, Battered Women's Shelter,

Algiers, Algeria **AW:** Award for Planning Youth Day, Westside Interfaith Council (1998); Trailblazer Award, NewGround: A Muslim-Jewish Partnership for Change **MH:** Albert Nelson Marquis Lifetime Achievement Award; Marquis Who's Who Top Professional; Marquis Who's Who Humanitarian Award **AS:** Mrs. Haroon attributes her success to wanting to change one person's mind in her class or wherever she is speaking, and to being able to teach others to be more accepting of other people. Mrs. Haroon wants to help others in anyway that she can without having expectations of something in return. **B/I:** Mrs. Haroon became involved in her profession because she always had interest in it. She went to Catholic convent school where a nun was giving after school oil painting classes, so she joined. Her father also encouraged her because the nun made him promise that she would stick with it. **AV:** Reading; Gardening; Jewelry Design; Photography; Travel **PA:** Democrat **RE:** Muslim **THT:** In 2008, Mrs. Haroon traveled on behalf of Art in Embassies to Algiers, Algeria. During the visit, Mrs. Haroon participated in children's art workshops and she coordinated the painting of a mural at a local NGO for battered women and children. Mrs. Haroon also held master classes at the Academy of Fine Arts, several presentations to the Museum of Fine Arts and the U.S. Embassy, and a roundtable discussion at a local art gallery. Her trip was publicized by several radio interviews and two TV interviews where she discussed her art and the Art in Embassies program. The events reached out to children, students, academics, cultural leaders, media, and the community at large. She truly served as a cultural ambassador and, at times, she was able to interject her background, her life as a Muslim American and her work on the interfaith council in Los Angeles. Mrs. Haroon also participated in televised events while in Algeria. On the "Bonjour Algerie" show, which is similar to "Good Morning America," she was on the show for over half an hour, which is a noteworthy occasion for the embassy. It was an opportunity to showcase the program, to reach out to the Algerian public, and to show the diversity of the U.S. society.

HARPER, BRYCE ARON MAX, T: Professional Baseball Player **I:** Athletics **CN:** Philadelphia Phillies **DOB:** 10/16/1992 **PB:** Las Vegas **SC:** NV/USA **PT:** Ron Harper; Sheri Harper **MS:** Married **SPN:** Kayla Varner (12/2016) **CH:** One Son **ED:** Coursework, College of Southern Nevada, North Las Vegas, NV (2009-2010) **C:** Right Fielder, Philadelphia Phillies, MLB (2019-Present); Outfielder, Washington Nationals, MLB (2010-2018); Catcher, College of Southern Nevada Coyotes (2009-2010) **AW:** Named All-star (2015-2018); Named National League MVP (2015); Hank Aaron Award, National League (2015); Named National League Home Run Leader (2015); Named to National League All-star Team, MLB (2012, 2013); Named National League Rookie of Year, Baseball Writers' Association of America (2012); Golden Spikes Award, USA Baseball (2010) **RE:** Latter-day Saints

HARPER, JACOB, T: Co-owner **I:** Food & Restaurant Services **CN:** Inner Circle Vodka Bar **ED:** Coursework, Oklahoma State University (2007) **C:** Co-owner, Inner Circle Vodka Bar, OK (2015-Present) **MEM:** Tulsa Young Professionals Organization **AS:** Mr. Harper attributes his success to the amount of time he spent in research before diving into the business. They spent a great amount of time creating a brand tailor-made for the particular demographic they wanted to reach. They were meticulous of each detail going into their business, down to the location. **B/I:** Mr. Harper began working in the restaurant business part-time as a student at Oklahoma State University. He had a passion for it and fell in love with the industry. It wasn't something he initially thought that he would be doing as a career but now he would not change it for the world. He loves the daily interaction between his staff and customers. The restaurant and bar community is very strong if you work well with other owners in the community. **THT:** For more information on the Inner Circle Vodka Bar, please visit: http://www.tulsaworld.com/lifestyles/food-and-cooking/behind-the-bar-inner-circle-vodka-bar-opens-downtown/article_b77ca6ef-6be0-508a-a2ea-c5e5e92eb179.html

HARRELSON, WOODY TRACY, T: Actor **I:** Media & Entertainment **DOB:** 07/23/1961 **PB:** Midland **SC:** TX/USA **PT:** Charles Voyde Harrelson; Diane Lou (Oswald) Harrelson **MS:** Married **SPN:** Laura Louie (12/28/2008); Nancy Simon (06/29/1985, Divorced 1986) **CH:** Deni Montana; Zoe Giordano; Makani Ravello **ED:** Honorary DHL, Hanover College, Hanover, IN (2014); BA in Theater Arts and English, Hanover College, Hanover, IN (1983) **CW:** Actor, "Live in Front of a Studio Audience" (2019); Actor, "Midway" (2019); Actor, "The Highwaymen" (2019); Actor, "Zombieland: Double Tap" (2019); Host, "Saturday Night Live" (2014, 2019); Actor, "Solo: A Star Wars Story" (2018); Actor, "Venom" (2018); Actor, "Shock and Awe" (2017); Actor, "Lost in London" (2017); Actor, "The Glass Castle" (2017); Actor, "Three Billboards Outside Ebbing Missouri" (2017); Actor, "The Edge of Seventeen" (2016); Actor, "LBJ" (2016); Actor, "The Duel" (2016); Actor, "Now You See Me 2" (2016); Actor, "Triple 9" (2016); Actor, "Wilson" (2016); Actor, "By Way of Helena" (2015); Actor, "The Hunger Games: Mockingjay - Part 2" (2015); Actor, "The Hunger Games; Mockingjay - Part 1" (2014); Actor, Executive Producer, "True Detective" (2014); Actor, "Now You See Me" (2013); Voice Actor, "Free Birds" (2013); Actor, "Out of the Furnace" (2013); Actor, "The Hunger Games: Catching Fire" (2013); Actor, "Game Change" (2012); Actor, "The Hunger Games" (2012); Actor, "Seven Psychopaths" (2012); Actor, "Friends with Benefits" (2011); Actor, "Rampart" (2011); Actor, "Defendor" (2009); Actor, "The Messenger" (2009); Actor, "Zombieland" (2009); Actor, "Semi-Pro" (2008); Actor, "Sleepwalking" (2008); Actor, "Transsiberian" (2008); Actor, "Seven Pounds" (2008); Actor, "Management" (2008); Actor, "The Walker" (2007); Actor, "No Country for Old Men" (2007); Actor, "The Grand" (2007); Actor, "Battle in Seattle" (2007); Actor, "A Prairie Home Companion" (2006); Voice Actor, "Free Jimmy" (2006); Actor, "A Scanner Darkly" (2006); Actor, "North Country" (2005); Actor, "The Prize Winner of Defiance, Ohio" (2005); Actor, "She Hate Me" (2004); Actor, "After the Sunset" (2004); Actor, "Anger Management" (2003); Actor, "Scorched" (2002); Actor, "Will & Grace" (2001); Actor, "American Saint" (2000); Actor, "EDtv" (1999); Actor, "Austin Powers: The Spy Who Shagged Me" (1999); Voice Actor, "Grass" (1999); Actor, "Play It to the Bone" (1999); Actor, "The Thin Red Line" (1998); Actor, "The Hi-Lo Country" (1998); Actor, "Wag the Dog" (1997); Actor, "The Sunchaser" (1996); Actor, "The People vs. Larry Flynt" (1996); Actor, "Kingpin" (1996); Actor, "The Cowboy Way" (1994); Actor, "I'll Do Anything" (1994); Actor, "Natural Born Killers" (1994); Actor, Director, Playwright, "Two on Two, Furthest from the Sun" (1993); Actor, "Indecent Proposal" (1993); Actor, "Cheers" (1985-1993); Actor, "White Men Can't Jump" (1992); Actor, "Doc Hollywood" (1991); Actor, "Ted and Venus" (1991); Actor, "L.A. Story" (1991); Host, "Comedy Club All-star IV" (1990); Actor, "Cool Blue" (1990); Actor, "Mother Goose Rock 'n' Rhyme" (1990); Actor, "Killer Instinct" (1988); Actor, "The Boys Next Door" (1987-1988); Actor, "Bay Coven" (1987);

Actor, "Eye of the Demon" (1987); Actor, "Wildcats" (1986); Understudy, Broadway Production, "Biloxi Blues" (1985-1986); Actor, "The Zoo Story"; Actor, Plays, Broadway, Off-Broadway, New York, and London's West End, United Kingdom **AW:** SAG Award for Outstanding Performance by a Cast in a Motion Picture, SAG-AFTRA (2008, 2018); Named PETA's Sexiest Vegetarian (2012); Award for Best Lead Actor, African American Film Critics Association (2011); Award for Best Supporting Actor, National Board of Review (2009); Emmy Award for Outstanding Supporting Actor in a Comedy Series, Academy of Television Arts & Sciences (1989); Numerous Awards

HARRIETT, JUDY A., T: Medical Equipment Company Executive (Retired) **I:** Medicine & Health Care **DOB:** 07/22/1960 **PB:** Walterboro **SC:** SC/USA **PT:** Billy Lee Harriett; Loretta (Rahn) Harriett **ED:** BS in Agricultural Business/Economics, Clemson University (1982) **C:** Retired (2018); With, Epiphany Healthcare (2013-2018); Vice President, Sales and Operations, Edisto Wood Preserving Company (2006-2012); Cardiology Sales Specialist, Alaris Medical Systems (Now BD), Redmond, WA (2001-2006); Regional Training Coordinator, Alaris Medical Systems (Now BD), San Diego, CA (1993-2000); Regional Training Coordinator, Imed Corp., San Diego, CA (1992-1993); Accountant Executive, Alaris Medical Systems (Now BD), San Diego, CA (1987-2001); Surgical Stapling Representative, Ethicon, Inc., Johnson & Johnson Corporation, Medical Device Business Services, Inc., Somerville, NJ (1985-1987); Sales Representative III, Monsanto Corp., Atlanta, GA (1982-1985) **CR:** Member, President Club (1993); Member, President, Advisory Panel (1991, 1992) **CIV:** Women's Center Benefit, Knoxville, TN (1990); Committee Member, Multiple Sclerosis Fundraising Benefit, Knoxville, TN (1988, 1989) **CW:** Author, "Time and Territory Management" (1984) **MEM:** National Association of Female Executives (NAFE); Life Member, President's Club **MH:** Albert Nelson Marquis Lifetime Achievement Award **B/I:** Ms. Harriett became involved in her profession because she grew up on a large farm and her father, Bille Lee, owned a business called Harriett farm supplies. During her high school and college years she dealt one on one with the farmers while she ran the store and loved working with the people. She learned everything she knew from her dad. **AV:** Golf; Reading; Skiing; Water-skiing; Travel **RE:** Republican

HARRINGTON, PÁDRAIG PETER, T: Professional Golfer **I:** Athletics **DOB:** 08/31/1971 **PB:** Dublin **SC:** Ireland **PT:** Patrick Harrington; Breda Harrington **MS:** Married **SPN:** Caroline Harrington (1997) **CH:** Patrick; Ciarán **CT:** Association of Chartered Certified Accountants **C:** Professional Golfer (1995) **CR:** Member, Great Britain and Ireland Team; Member, Team Europe; Member, Irish Team **AW:** Winner, Portugal Masters (2016); Winner, Honda Classic (2005, 2015); Winner, Grand Slam of Golf (2012); Winner, Ryder Cup (1999, 2002, 2004, 2006, 2008, 2010); Irish Golf Writers Professional of the Year Award (2008); Named RTÉ Sports Person of the Year (2008); Named European Tour Golfer of the Year (2007, 2008); Named Player of the Year, Association of Golf Writers (2007, 2008); Winner, British Open (2007, 2008); Winner, PGA Championship (2008); Named Player of the Year, Golf Writers Association of America (GWAA) (2008); Named European Tour Shot of the Year (2008); Named PGA Tour Player of the Year, PGA Tour Player of the Year (2008); Texaco Ireland Sportstar Golf Award (1996, 1999, 2001, 2002, 2004-2008); Winner, Irish Open (2007); Named to Order of Merit, PGA European Tour (2006); Winner, Dunlop Phoenix (2006); Winner, Seve Trophy (2000, 2002,

2003, 2005); Winner, Irish PGA Championship (1998, 2004, 2005); World Cup of Golf (1996-2005); Winner, Barclays Classic (2005); Winner, Omega Hong Kong Open (2004); Winner, Linde German Masters (2004); Winner, BMW Asian Open (2003); Winner, Deutsche Bank-SAP Open TPC of Europe (2003); Winner, Target World Challenge Presented by Williams (2002); Winner, Dunhill Links Championship (2002); Winner, Volvo Masters Andalucia (2001); Winner, Brazil Sao Paulo 500 Years Open (2000); Winner, BBVA Open Turespaña Masters Comunidad de Madrid (2000); Winner, Dunhill Cup (1996-2000); Winner, Peugeot Spanish Open (1996); Winner, Numerous Golf Events Including PGA European Tour and PGA Tour

HARRIS, ANDY, MD, T: U.S. Representative from Maryland **I:** Government Administration/Government Relations/Government Services **DOB:** 01/25/1957 **PB:** Brooklyn **SC:** NY/USA **PT:** Zoltán Harris; Irene Harris **MS:** Widowed **SPN:** Sylvia Harris (Deceased 08/28/2014) **CH:** Joseph; Rebecca; Irene; Jessica; Daniel **ED:** Master of Health Science in Health Policy and Management, Johns Hopkins University (1995); Intern, Resident, Johns Hopkins Hospital (1980-1984); MD, Johns Hopkins University (1980); BS in Human Biology, Johns Hopkins University (1977) **C:** Member, U.S. House of Representatives from Maryland's First Congressional District, Washington, DC (2011-Present); Member, U.S. House Committee on Transportation and Infrastructure (2011-Present); Member, U.S. House Committee on Space, Science and Technology (2011-Present); Member, U.S. House Committee on Natural Resources (2011-Present); Minority Whip, Maryland State Senate (2003-2010); Member, District Seven, Maryland State Senate (2002-2010); Member District Nine, Maryland State Senate (1998-2003); Member, Committee on Education, Health and Environmental Affairs; Member, Republican Study Committee; Associate Professor, Department of Anesthesiology and Critical Care Medicine, Johns Hopkins University School of Medicine; Chief Obstetric of Anesthesiology, Johns Hopkins Hospital **CIV:** Member, Board of Directors, Maryland Leadership Council (1995-Present); Vice President, St. Joseph's School, Home-School Association (HSA)(1992-1994); Member, Board of Directors, Sherwood Community Association (1987-1993); President, Thornleigh Improvement Association (1984-1986) **MIL:** Commander, United States Naval Reserve, Iraq (1988-2010); Commander, Johns Hopkins Naval Reserve Medical Unit (1989-1992) **MEM:** President, Maryland-DC Society of Anesthesiologists (2005-Present); Executive Committee, Maryland-DC Society of Anesthesiologists (1996-Present); Board of Directors, American Society for Obstetric Anesthesia & Perinatology (SOAP) (1996-Present); Maryland-DC Society of Anesthesiologists; American Society for Obstetric Anesthesia & Perinatology (SOAP) **PA:** Republican **RE:** Roman Catholic

HARRIS, ED ALLEN, T: Actor **I:** Media & Entertainment **DOB:** 11/28/1950 **PB:** Englewood **SC:** NJ/USA **PT:** Bob L. Harris; Margaret (Sholl) Harris **MS:** Married **SPN:** Amy Madigan (11/21/1983) **CH:** Lily Dolores **ED:** BFA, California Institute of the Arts, Valencia, CA (1975); Coursework, The University of Oklahoma, Norman, OK (1972-1973); Coursework, Columbia University (1969-1971) **CIV:** Trustee, California Institute of the Arts, Valencia, CA (1985-Present) **CW:** Actor, "Westworld" (2016-Present); Actor, "Resistance" (2020); Actor, "The Last Full Measure" (2019); Actor, "To Kill a Mockingbird" (2019-2020); Actor, "A Crooked Somebody" (2017); Actor, "Mother!" (2017); Actor, "Kodachrome" (2017); Actor, "Geostorm"

(2017); Actor, "In Dubious Battle" (2016); Actor, "Rules Don't Apply" (2016); Actor, "The Adderall Diaries" (2015); Actor, "Frontera" (2014); Actor, "Cymbeline" (2014); Actor, "Run All Night" (2014); Voice Actor, "Planes: Fire & Rescue" (2014); Actor, "Sweetwater" (2013); Actor, "Phantom" (2013); Actor, "Snowpiercer" (2013); Actor, "Pain & Gain" (2013); Voice Actor, "Gravity" (2013); Actor, "Game Change" (2012); Actor, "The Face of Love" (2013); Actor, "Man on a Ledge" (2012); Actor, "Salvation Boulevard" (2011); Actor, "That's What I Am" (2011); Actor, "The Way Back" (2010); Actor, "Once Fallen" (2010); Actor, "Virginia" (2010); Actor, "Touching Home" (2008); Actor, Director, Producer, Writer, "Appaloosa" (2008); Actor, "Cleaner" (2007); Actor, "Gone Baby Gone" (2007); Actor, "National Treasure: Book of Secrets" (2007); Actor, "The Armenian Genocide" (2006); Actor, "Wrecks" (2006); Actor, "Empire Falls" (2005); Actor, "Winter Passing" (2005); Actor, "A History of Violence" (2005); Actor, "Masked and Anonymous" (2003); Actor, "The Human Stain" (2003); Actor, "Radio" (2003); Actor, "Just a Dream" (2002); Actor, "The Hours" (2002); Actor, "Enemy at the Gates" (2001); Actor, "Buffalo Soldiers" (2001); Actor, "A Beautiful Mind" (2001); Actor, "Waking the Dead" (2000); Actor, Director, Producer, "Pollock" (2000); Actor, "The Prime Gig" (2000); Actor, "The Third Miracle" (1999); Actor, "Stepmom" (1998); Actor, "The Truman Show" (1998); Actor, "Absolute Power" (1997); Actor, Executive Producer, "Riders of the Purple Sage" (1996); Actor, "The Rock" (1996); Actor, "Taking Sides" (1996); Actor, "Simpatico" (1994, 1995); Actor, "Apollo 13" (1995); Actor, "Frasier" (1995); Actor, "Just Cause" (1995); Actor, "Eye for an Eye" (1995); Actor, "Nixon" (1995); Actor, "The Stand" (1994); Actor, "China Moon" (1994); Actor, "Milk Money" (1994); Actor, "Needful Things" (1993); Actor, "The Firm" (1993); Actor, "Glengarry Glen Ross" (1992); Actor, "Running Mates" (1992); Actor, "Paris Trout" (1991); Actor, "State of Grace" (1990); Actor, "The Abyss" (1989); Actor, "Bobby Gould in Hell" (1989); Actor, "Jacknife" (1989); Actor, "To Kill a Priest" (1988); Actor, "Walker" (1987); Actor, "The Last Innocent Man" (1987); Actor, "Precious Sons" (1986); Actor, "Pirates of Penzance," New York Shakespeare Festival, NY (1986); Actor, "Glass Menagerie," Long Wharf, New Haven, CT (1986); Actor, "Sweet Dreams" (1985); Actor, "Code Name: Emerald" (1985); Actor, "Scar" (1985); Actor, Repertory Plays, "Servant of Two Masters," Ohio and "Claptrap," Cambridge, MA (1985); Actor, "A Flash of Green" (1984); Actor, "Alamo Bay" (1984); Actor, "Fool for Love" (1983); Actor, "Places in the Heart" (1983); Actor, "The Right Stuff" (1982); Actor, "Swing Shift" (1982); Actor, "Under Fire" (1982); Actor, "Cassie and Co." (1982); Actor, "Lou Grant" (1979, 1980, 1981); Actor, "CHiPs" (1981); Actor, "Hart to Hart" (1981); Actor, "Creepshow" (1981); Actor, "Prairie Avenue" (1981); Actor, "Knightriders" (1980); Actor, "The Aliens Are Coming" (1980); Actor, "Dream On" (1980); Actor, "The Seekers" (1979); Actor, "Barnaby Jones" (1979); Actor, "The Rockford Files" (1978); Actor, "Coma" (1978); Actor, "Borderline" (1978); Actor, "The Amazing Howard Hughes" (1977); Actor, Plays, "A Streetcar Named Desire," "Sweet Bird of Youth," "Julius Caesar," "Hamlet," "Camelot," "Are You Lookin?," "Time of Your Life," "Learned Ladies," "Kingdom of Earth," "Grapes of Wrath," "Present Laughter," "Balaam," and "Killers' Head"; Actor, Theater, Television, Film **AW:** Recipient, Star, Hollywood Walk of Fame (2015); Golden Globe Award for Best Performance by an Actor in a Supporting Role in a Series, Miniseries or Motion Picture Made for TV, Hollywood Foreign Press Association (2013); National Society Film Critics Award for Best Supporting Actor (2006); Golden Globe Award for Best Performance by an Actor in a Supporting Role in a Motion Picture, Hollywood Foreign Press Association (1999); Screen Actors Guild Award for Outstanding Performance by a Cast, SAG-AFTRA (1996); Theatre World Award (1986); San Francisco Critics Award (1985); Obie Award (1983); Los Angeles Drama Critics Circle Award (1981); Numerous Awards **MEM:** SAG-AFTRA; Actors' Equity Association

HARRIS, JETTA BALLARD, MA, T: School Counselor (Retired) **I:** Education/Educational Services **DOB:** 11/25/2019 **PB:** Opelousas **SC:** LA/USA **PT:** Albert Louis Ballard; Lauvinia Agnes Ballard **MS:** Married **SPN:** Andrew Harris, Jr. (12/23/1967, Deceased 2019) **CH:** Stanley O.; Byron A. **ED:** Postgraduate Coursework, Indiana University (1964); MA in School Counseling, University of Colorado (1959); BA in Elementary Education, Xavier University (1954) **CT:** Certified in Elementary Education **C:** Retired (1995); School Counselor, DC State Board of Education, Washington, DC (1968-1995); Teacher, School Counselor, St. Landry Parish School Board, Opelousas, LA (1954-1968) **CR:** Restructuring Team Member, Mamie D. Lee School, Washington, DC (1996-1999); Teaching Consultant, School Counselor, Slowe Elementary School, Washington, DC (1996); Sponsor, Student Council Sponsor, 4-H Club **CIV:** Board of Directors, SJCS, Washington, DC (1999-Present); NAACP; Volunteer, District of Columbia Retired Educators Association **AW:** Best Administrator Award; Award for Excellence with the Student Council; Service Award, Local Church **MEM:** AAUW; American Counseling Association; District of Columbia Counseling Association; Washington Teachers Union; Greater Washington Urban League; Alumni Association, Xavier University; Alumni Association, University of Colorado; Louisiana Retired Teachers Association; Deaconess, Union Baptist Church, Brooklyn, NY **MH:** Albert Nelson Marquis Lifetime Achievement Award; Marquis Who's Who Humanitarian Award **B/I:** Ms. Harris became involved in her profession because her parents stressed the importance of education for her and her 13 siblings. Although she originally wanted to be a nurse, she followed in the footsteps of many of her family members and became an educator. **AV:** Sewing; Solving puzzles; Gardening; Reading; Crocheting; Cooking **PA:** Democrat **RE:** Baptist

HARRIS, MARK, T: Former U.S. Representative from North Carolina **I:** Government Administration/Government Relations/Government Services **DOB:** 04/26/1966 **PB:** Winston-Salem **SC:** NC/USA **MS:** Married **SPN:** Beth Harris **CH:** Three Children **ED:** Doctor of Ministry, Southeastern Baptist Theological Seminary; MDiv, Southeastern Baptist Theological Seminary; BA, Appalachian State University **C:** Member, U.S. House of Representatives from North Carolina's Ninth District (2019) **CIV:** Senior Pastor, First Baptist Church, Charlotte, NC (2017); Senior Pastor, Curtis Baptist Church, Augusta, GA (2000-2005); Lead Pastor, Trinity Baptist Church, Mooresville, NC; President, Baptist State Convention of North Carolina **PA:** Republican **RE:** Baptist

HARRIS, NEIL PATRICK, T: Actor **I:** Media & Entertainment **DOB:** 06/15/1973 **PB:** Albuquerque **SC:** NM/USA **PT:** Ronald Gene Harris; Sheila Gail (Scott) Harris **MS:** Married **SPN:** David Burtka (09/06/2014) **CH:** Gideon Scott; Harper Grace **CIV:** President, Board of Directors, Hollywood's Magic Castle; Supporter, Various Charities Including Elton John AIDS Foundation, Alex's Lemonade Stand Foundation, and Feeding America **CW:** Guest Judge, "Chopped" (2020); Actor, "Home Movie: The Princess Bride" (2020); Voice Actor, "Ghostwriter" (2019); Author, "The Magic Misfits: The Second Story" (2019); Host, Executive Producer, "Genius Junior" (2018); Author, "The Magic Misfits" (2017); Actor, Producer, "A Series of Unfortunate Events" (2017); Actor, "Mystery Science 3000" (2017); Appearance, "At Home with Amy Sedaris" (2017); Actor, "Downsizing" (2017); Host, "Best Time Ever with Neil Patrick Harris" (2015); Actor, "American Horror Story" (2015); Actor, "Ant & Dec's Saturday Night Takeaway" (2015); Author, "Neil Patrick Harris: Choose Your Own Autobiography" (2014); Actor, "Hedwig and the Angry Itch" (2014); Actor, "A Million Ways to Die in the West" (2014); Actor, "Gone Girl" (2014); Actor, "How I Met Your Mother" (2005-2014); Voice Actor, "The Smurfs 2" (2013); Voice Actor, "Cloudy with a Chance of Meatballs 2" (2013); Host, 65th Primetime Emmy Awards (2013); Director, "Nothing to Hide" (2013); Host, Annual Tony Awards (2009, 2011, 2012); Actor, "Neil's Puppet Dreams" (2012); Actor, "American Reunion" (2012); Actor, "Beastly" (2011); Actor, "Company" (2011); Voice Actor, "The Smurfs" (2011); Actor, "A Very Harold & Kumar 3D Christmas" (2011); Actor, "The Muppets" (2011); Actor, "The Best and the Brightest" (2010); Voice Actor, "The Penguins of Madagascar" (2009-2010); Voice Actor, "Robot Chicken" (2009); Host, 61st Primetime Emmy Awards (2009); Voice Actor, "Yes, Virginia" (2009); Voice Actor, "Cloudy with a Chance of Meatballs" (2009); Actor, "Glee" (2009); Actor, "Sesame Street" (2008); Host, World Magic Awards (2008); Actor, "Dr. Horrible's Sing-Along Blog" (2008); Actor, "Prop 8: The Musical" (2008); Voice Actor, "Justice League: The New Frontier" (2008); Actor, "Harold & Kumar Escape from Guantanamo Bay" (2008); Voice Actor, "Family Guy" (2007-2009); Actor, "Me, Eloise" (2006); Actor, "All My Sons" (2006); Actor, "Numb3rs" (2005); Actor, "The Christmas Blessing" (2005); Voice Actor, "The Golden Blaze" (2005); Actor, "Jack & Bobby" (2005); Actor, "Law & Order: Criminal Intent" (2004); Actor, "Assassins" (2004); Actor, "Harold and Kumar Go to White Castle" (2004); Actor, "Boomtown" (2003); Voice Actor, "Spider-Man" (2003); Voice Actor, "Spider-Man: The Animated Series" (2002); Voice Actor, "Justice League" (2002); Actor, "Undercover Brother" (2002); Actor, "Mesmerist" (2002); Actor, "Proof" (2002); Actor, "Touched by an Angel" (2002); Actor, "The Wedding Dress" (2001); Actor, "Sweeney Todd: The Demon Barber of Fleet Street in Concert" (2001); Voice Actor, "Static Shock" (2001); Actor, "Son of the Beach" (2001); Actor, "Ed" (2001); Actor, "The Mesmerist" (2001); Actor, "Will & Grace" (2000); Actor, "The Next Best Thing" (2000); Actor, "Stark Raving Mad" (1999); Actor, "Joan of Arc" (1999); Actor, "Sweeney Todd: The Demon Barber of Fleet Street" (1999); Actor, "Cabaret" (1998); Actor, "Romeo and Juliet" (1998); Actor, "The Christmas Wish" (1998); Actor, "The Proposition" (1998); Actor, "Rent" (1997-1998); Actor, "Homicide: Life on the Streets" (1997); Actor, "Starship Troopers" (1997); Actor, "The Outer Limits" (1996); Actor, "Animal Room" (1995); Actor, "Not Our Son" (1995); Actor, "Legacy of Sin: The William Coit Story" (1995); Actor, "My Antonia" (1995); Actor, "Snowbound: The Jim and Jennifer Stolpa Story" (1994); Actor, "The Man in the Attic" (1994); Actor, "Quantum Leap" (1993); Actor, "Sudden Fury: A Family Torn Apart" (1993); Actor, "Murder, She Wrote" (1993); Actor, "Roseanne" (1992); Voice Actor, "Capitol Critters" (1992); Actor, "Doogie Howser, M.D." (1989-1992); Actor, "Blossom" (1991); Actor, "A Stranger in the Family" (1991); Actor, "Fiddler on the Roof" (1991); Voice Actor, "Captain Planet and the Planeteers" (1990); Actor, "B.L. Stryker" (1989); Actor, "Home Fires Burning" (1989); Actor, "Cold Sassy Tree" (1989); Actor, "Clara's Heart" (1988); Actor, "The Purple People Eater" (1988); Actor, "Too Good to be True" (1988); Host, Numerous Award Shows

AW: Peabody Award for Entertainment, Children's & Youth Programming (2018); Drama Desk Award for Outstanding Actor in a Musical (2014); Tony Award for Best Leading Actor in a Musical (2014); Named Hasty Pudding Man of the Year (2014); Named One of Barbara Walters' 10 Most Fascinating People (2014); Named Favorite TV Comedy Actor, People's Choice Awards (2011, 2012); Emmy Award for Outstanding Guest Actor in a Comedy Series, Academy of Television Arts & Sciences (2010); Emmy Award for Outstanding Special Class Program, Academy of Television Arts & Sciences (2010); Named One of the 100 Most Influential People in the World, TIME Magazine (2010); Tannen's Magic Louis Award (2006); Young Artists Award for Best Young Actor in Series (1989, 1990, 1991, 1992); People's Choice Award for Favorite Male Performer in a New TV Series (1990); Numerous Awards AV: Magic

HARRIS, ROSEMARY ANN, T: Actress I: Media & Entertainment DOB: 09/19/1927 PB: Ashby-de-la-Zouch SC: England PT: Stafford Berkely Harris; Enid Maude Frances (Campion) Harris MS: Widowed SPN: John Ehie (1967, Deceased 2018); Ellis Rabb (1959, Divorced 1967) CH: Jennifer Ehie ED: Coursework, Royal Academy of Dramatic Art (1951-1952) CW: Actress, "My Fair Lady," Vivian Beaumont Theatre (2018-2019); Actress, "The von Trapp Family: A Life of Music" (2015); Actress, TV Film, "The Money" (2014); Actress, "Indian Ink," Laura Pels Theatre (2014); Actress, "This Means War" (2012); Actress, "The Road to Mecca," American Airlines Theatre (2012); Guest Appearance, "Law & Order: Special Victims Unit" (2010); Voice Actress, "Radio Free Albemuth" (2010); Actress, "The Royal Family," Samuel J. Friedman Theatre (2009); Actress, Short Film, "The Monday Before Thanksgiving" (2008); Actress, "Is Anybody There?" (2008); Actress, "Oscar and the Lady in Pink," Old Globe Theatre and Florence Gould Hall (2007-2008); Actress, "Before the Devil Knows You're Dead" (2007); Actress, "Spider-Man 3" (2007); Actress, "The Other Side," Manhattan Theatre Club (2005); Actress, TV Film, "Belonging" (2004); Actress, "Being Julia" (2004); Actress, "Spider-Man 2" (2004); Actress, "Spider-Man" (2002); Actress, "All Over," Gramercy Theatre (2002); Actress, "Blow Dry" (2001); Actress, "The Gift" (2000); Actress, "Sunshine" (1999); Actress, "Waiting in the Wings," Walter Kerr Theatre and Eugene O'Neill Theatre (1999); Actress, "My Life So Far" (1999); Voice Actress, Video Game, "Dark Side of the Moon" (1998); Actress, "Hamlet" (1996); Actress, TV Film, "Death of a Salesman" (1996); Actress, TV Film, "The Little Riders" (1996); Actress, "A Delicate Balance," Plymouth Theatre (1996); Actress, "An Inspector Calls," Royale Theatre (1994-1995); Guest Appearance, "Under the Hammer" (1994); Actress, "Summer Day's Dream," Lyric Theatre (1994); Actress, "Tom & Viv" (1994); Actress, "Lost in Yonkers," Richard Rogers Theatre and Royal Strand Theatre (1991-1993); Guest Appearance, TV Miniseries, "The Camomile Lawn" (1992); Actress, "The Bridge" (1992); Actress, "The Delinquents" (1989); Actress, "Crossing Delancey" (1988); Actress, "Hay Fever," Music Box Theatre (1985-1986); Actress, "Pack of Lies," Royale Theatre (1985); Actress, "The Ploughman's Lunch" (1983); Actress, "Heartbreak House," Circle in the Square Theatre and Theatre Royal (1983); Actress, TV Film, "To the Lighthouse" (1983); Actress, TV Miniseries, "The Chisholms" (1979-1980); Actress, TV Miniseries, "Holocaust" (1978); Actress, "The Boys From Brazil" (1978); Actress, TV Film, "The Royal Family" (1977); Actress, "The Three Sisters," "The New York Idea," Brooklyn Academy of Music (1977); Actress, "The Royal Family," Brooklyn Academy of Music and Helen Hayes Theatre (1975-

1976); Actress, TV Miniseries, "Notorious Woman" (1974); Actress, "A Street Car Named Desire," "The Merchant of Venice," Vivian Beaumont Theatre (1973); Actress, "Old Times," Billy Rose Theatre (1971-1972); Actress, "A Flea in Her Ear" (1968); Actress, TV Film, "Uncle Vanya" (1967); Actress, "War and Peace," "You Can't Take It With You," "The Wild Duck," Lyceum Theatre (1967); Actress, "The School for Scandal," Lyceum Theatre (1966-1967); Actress, TV Film, "Blithe Spirit" (1966); Actress, "We, Comrades Three," "Right You Are If You Think You Are," Lyceum Theatre (1966); Actress, "The Lion in Winter," Ambassador Theatre (1966); Actress, "Herakles," Lyceum Theatre (1965); Actress, "War and Peace," "Man and Superman," "Judith," Phoenix Theatre (1965); Guest Appearance, "Profiles in Courage" (1964); Actress, "Uncle Vanya" (1963); Actress, "Hamlet," Old Vic Theatre (1963); Actress, "Uncle Vanya," Chichester Festival Theatre (1963); Actress, "The Tumbler," Helen Hayes Theatre (1960); Guest Appearance, "Encounter" (1959); Guest Appearance, "DuPont Show of the Month" (1958); Guest Appearance, "Folio" (1958); Actress, TV Film, "Dial M for Murder" (1958); Guest Appearance, "Omnibus" (1958); Guest Appearance, "Suspicion" (1958); Actress, "The Disenchanted," Coronet Theatre (1958); Actress, "Interlock," "The Glass Eye," ANTA Playhouse (1957-1958); Actress, TV Film, "Twelfth Night" (1957); Actress, "The Shiralee" (1957); Actress, "Troilus and Cressida," Winter Garden Theatre (1956); Actress, TV Film, "Othello" (1955); Actress, "The Crucible," Bristol Old Vic (1954); Actress, "Beau Brummell" (1954); Actress, "The Seven Year Itch," Aldwych Theatre (1953-1954); Guest Appearance, "Studio One in Hollywood" (1952); Actress, "The Climate of Eden," Martin Beck Theatre (1952); Actress, TV Film, "A Cradle of Willow" (1952) AW: Lifetime Achievement in the Theatre, Tony Awards (2019); Golden Globe Award for Best Ensemble Cast, "Before the Devil Knows You're Dead," Hollywood Foreign Press Association (2007); Best Supporting Actress, "Tom & Viv," National Board of Review (1994); Actress in a Play, "Pack of Lies," Drama Desk Awards (1985); Golden Globe Award for Best Actress in a Television Series - Drama, "Holocaust," Hollywood Foreign Press Association (1978); Primetime Emmy Award for Best Lead Actress in a Limited Series, "Notorious Woman," Television Academy (1976); Actress in a Play, "The Royal Family," Drama Desk Awards (1976); Best Performance, "The Merchant of Venice," "A Streetcar Named Desire," Drama Desk Awards (1973); Best Performance, "Old Times," Drama Desk Awards (1972); Best Actress in a Play, "The Lion in Winter," Tony Awards (1966); Distinguished Performance by an Actress, "Judith," "Man and Superman," "War and Peace," Obie Awards (1965); Distinguished Performance by an Actress, "The Tavern," "The School for Scandal," "The Seagull," Obie Awards (1962)

HARRISON, LONNIE E., MD, T: Chief Executive Officer I: Medicine & Health Care CN: Harrison Heart, Vein & Vascular Center MS: Married SPN: Renee CH: Five Children ED: Doctor of Medicine, University of Arkansas for Medical Sciences College of Medicine (1988); Coursework in Analytical Chemistry, University of Arkansas; Bachelor of Arts in Theology, Central Bible College, Springfield, MO CT: Certified, Vascular Intervention C: Interventional Cardiologist, Saline Memorial Hospital (2016-Present); Founder, Chief Executive Officer, Harrison Heart, Vein & Vascular Center (2015-Present); Physician, Arkansas Heart Hospital; Co-Founder, Co-Director, Arkansas Heart Hospital Cardiac and Vascular Stem Cell Program CR: Medical Director, Arkansas Amputation Prevention Center (2015-Present) CIV: Arkansas

Amputation Prevention Foundation (2015-Present); Child Sponsor, Compassionate international Program; Volunteer, Local Church CW: Contributor, Multiple Research Papers in Major Medical Journals; Lecturer, National and International Conferences AW: Analytical Chemist of the Year, University of Arkansas System MEM: American College of Phlebology; International Society for Endovascular Specialists; Society for Vascular Medicine; International Society for Stem Cell Research AS: Dr. Harrison attributes his success to a dedication towards hard work and a desire for excellence. B/I: Dr. Harrison became involved in his profession after his father fell sick of a heart attack. After he received a coronary stent and bypass surgery, Dr. Harrison drew inspiration from the procedure and resolved to become a doctor himself.

HARRISON-INGRAM (MCCLAFFERTY), MONICA R., T: President I: Media & Entertainment CN: LA Film Locations DOB: 09/18/1964 PB: Panama City SC: Panama PT: Robert Edwin Harrison Melendez; Mireya de Rosario Ingram Jaen MS: Married SPN: James Thomas McClafferty CH: M. Connor McClafferty; John W. McClafferty (Jack); Mark H. McClafferty ED: BS in Economics, Minor in Spanish, University of Delaware (1986) CT: Women's Business Enterprise National Council; Women-Owned Small Business Association C: President, LA Film Locations (2003-Present); Asset Manager, The Boyt Company, Los Angeles, CA (1990-2015); C. Thomas Ruppert & Associates (1987-1990); Associate in Marketing, Equitec Properties, Los Angeles, CA (1987-1988) CIV: Assistance League; Single Mothers Outreach AW: Latino Business Awards (2016) MEM: Board Member, Santa Clarita Valley Chamber of Commerce; Location Managers Guild International; Latino Business Association AS: Ms. Harrison-Ingram McClafferty attributes her success to her grit and determination. B/I: Ms. Harrison-McClafferty became involved in her profession because of her ambition to fill an important gap in the film business. She recalls the need for a high-quality location service, and realized this field could be a good segway from commercial asset management into the entertainment industry. AV: Doing yoga; Traveling; Going to the beach PA: Independent RE: Roman Catholic THT: Ms. Harrison-Ingram McClafferty believes, "Love fiercely, because this all ends."

HARRY, DEBORAH ANN, T: Singer I: Media & Entertainment CN: Blondie DOB: 07/01/1945 PB: Miami SC: FL/USA PT: Richard Harry (Adoptive Father); Catherine (Peters) Harry (Adoptive Mother) MS: Single ED: AA, Centenary College, Hackettstown, NJ (1965); Diploma, Hawthorne High School (1963) C: Singer, Blondie (1974-1982, 1997-Present); Singer, The Stilettoes (1974); Singer, The Wind in the Willows (1968); Singer, Angel and the Snake CR: Secretary, BBC Radio; Waitress, Max's Kansas City; Go-Go Dancer, Union City, NJ; Playboy Bunny CW: Author, "Face It" (2019); Featured Musician, "#Liftmeup" (2019); Appearance, Documentary, "Bad Reputation" (2018); Musician, "Pollinator" (2017); Musician, "Ghosts of Download† (Blondie 4(0) Ever)" (2014); Cameo, "River of Fundament" (2014); Appearance, Short Film, "Believe the Magic" (2012); Cameo, Short Film, "Pipe Dreams" (2011); Contributor, "Debbie Harry and Blondie: Picture This" (2011); Musician, "Essential" (2011); Musician, "Panic of Girls" (2011); Cameo, Short Film, "The Mystery of Claywoman" (2009); Actress, "Elegy" (2008); Cameo, "Anamorph" (2007); Musician, "Necessary Evil" (2007); Featured Musician, "New York, New York" (2006); Actress, "Full Grown Men" (2006); Cameo, Short Film, "Honey Trap" (2005); Actress,

Short Film, "Patch" (2005); Actress, Short Film, "I Remember You Now..." (2005); Cameo, "My Life Without Me" (2003); Musician, "The Curse of Blondie" (2003); Actress, "A Good Night to Die" (2003); Actress, "The Tulse Luper Suitcases Part 1: The Moab Story" (2003); Actress, "Deuces Wild" (2002); Voice Actress, Video Game, "Grand Theft Auto: Vice City" (2002); Cameo, "Spun" (2002); Actress, "All I Want" (2002); Actress, "The Fluffer" (2001); Actress, "Red Lipstick" (2000); Featured Musician, "Command and Obey (Remix)" (1999); Musician, "No Exit" (1999); Actress, "Zoo" (1999); Cameo, "Joe's Day" (1998); Actress, "Cop Land" (1997); Actress, "Six Ways to Sunday" (1997); Featured Musician, "Command and Obey" (1997); Actress, TV Film, "L.A. Johns" (1997); Musician, "Denis" (1996); Actress, "Drop Dead Rock" (1996); Actress, "Heavy" (1995); Cameo, Short Film, "Sandman" (1995); Narrator, Short Film, "Rakthavira" (1994); Actress, "Dead Beat" (1994); Voice Actress, Video Game, "Double Switch" (1993); Actress, TV Film, "Body Bags" (1993); Musician, "Debravation" (1993); Musician, "Blonde and Beyond" (1993); Voice Actress, Short Film, "The Real Story of O Christmas Tree" (1991); Actress, "Tales from the Darkside: The Movie" (1990); Actress, TV Film, "Mother Goose Rock 'n' Rhyme" (1990); Cameo, "New York Stories" (1989); Musician, "Def, Dumb & Blonde" (1989); Musician, "Once More Into the Bleach" (1988); Actress, "Satisfaction" (1988); Actress, "Hairspray" (1988); Actress, "Forever, Lulu" (1987); Musician, "Rockbird" (1986); Actress, "Terror in the Aisles" (1984); Actress, "Videodrome" (1983); Voice Actress, "Rock & Rule" (1983); Cameo, "Wild Style" (1983); Musician, "The Hunter" (1982); Co-Author, "Making Tracks: The Rise of Blondie" (1982); Actress, "Downtown 81" (1981); Musician, "KooKoo" (1981); Actress, "Union City" (1980); Cameo, "Roadie" (1980); Musician, "Autoamerican" (1980); Musician, "Eat to the Beat" (1979); Actress, "The Foreigner" (1978); Musician, "Parallel Lines" (1978); Musician, "Plastic Letters" (1978); Actress, "Unmade Beds" (1976); Musician, "Blondie" (1976); Cameo, "Deadly Hero" (1975); Guest Appearances, Numerous TV Shows; Contributing Musician, Numerous Soundtracks AW: NME Award for Best Music Book (2020); Honorary Award for Outstanding Contribution to Music, Association of Independent Musicians Awards (2019); Style Icon, Elle Style Awards (2017); Inductee, "Heart of Glass," Grammy Hall of Fame (2016); Q Inspiration Award, Q Music Awards (1998, 2016); NME Godlike Genius Award (2014); Clio Honorary Award (2014); Inductee, Rock and Roll Hall of Fame (2006); Best Selling Single, "Heart of Glass," Juno Awards (1980); NME Award for Best Female Singer (1978); NME Award for Pin-up of the Year (1978)

HART, KEVIN DARNELL, T: Actor, Comedian **I:** Media & Entertainment **DOB:** 07/06/1979 **PB:** Philadelphia **SC:** PA/USA **PT:** Henry Hart; Nancy Hart **MS:** Married **SPN:** Eniko Parrish (08/13/2016); Torrei Hart (05/22/2003, Divorced 2011) **CH:** Kenzo; Heaven Leigh; Hendrix **ED:** Coursework, Community College of Philadelphia **CW:** Host, "Kevin Hart's Laugh Out Loud" (2019-Present); Comedian, Stand-Up Comedy Tour, "Kevin Hart: Don't F**k This Up" (2019-Present); Host, "Kevin Hart: What the Fit" (2018-Present); Comedian, Stand-Up Comedy Tour, "Kevin Hart: Irresponsible" (2019); Author, "I Can't Make This Up: Life Lessons" (2017); Comedian, Stand-Up Comedy Tour, "Kevin Hart: What Now?" (2016); Actor, "Ride Along 2" (2016); Actor, "Central Intelligence" (2016); Voice Actor, "The Secret Life of Pets" (2016); Actor, "The Wedding Ringer" (2015); Actor, "Get Hard" (2015); Actor, "Ride Along" (2014); Actor, "About Last Night" (2014); Actor, "Think Like a Man Too"

(2014); Actor, Writer, Executive Producer, "Keep It Together" (2014); Actor, "Top Five" (2014); Actor, Executive Producer, "Real Husbands of Hollywood" (2013-2015); Comedian, Stand-Up Comedy Tour, "Let Me Explain" (2013); Actor, "This is the End" (2013); Actor, "Grudge Match" (2013); Host, "MTV Video Music Awards" (2012); Actor, "Exit Strategy" (2012); Actor, "Think Like a Man" (2012); Actor, "The Five-Year Engagement" (2012); Actor, "Modern Family" (2011-2012); Actor, "Little in Common" (2011); Actor, "Let Go" (2011); Actor, "35 and Ticking" (2011); Comedian, Stand-Up Comedy Tour, "Laugh at My Pain" (2011); Comedian, Stand-Up Comedy Tour, "Seriously Funny" (2010); Actor, "Something Like a Business" (2010); Actor, "Death at a Funeral" (2010); Actor, "Little Fockers" (2010); Comedian, Stand-Up Comedy Tour, "I'm a Grown Little Man" (2009); Actor, "Party Down" (2009); Actor, "Not Easily Broken" (2009); Actor, "Fool's Gold" (2008); Actor, "Drillbit Taylor" (2008); Actor, "Superhero Movie" (2008); Actor, "Meet Dave" (2008); Actor, "Extreme Movie" (2008); Actor, "The Weekend" (2007); Actor, "Love, Inc." (2006); Actor, "Scary Movie 4" (2006); Actor, "The Last Stand" (2006); Actor, "Dante" (2005); Actor, "The 40-Year-Old Virgin" (2005); Actor, "In the Mix" (2005); Actor, "Barbershop" (2005); Actor, "The Big House" (2004); Actor, "Along Came Polly" (2004); Actor, "Soul Plane" (2004); Actor, "Death of a Dynasty" (2003); Actor, "Scary Movie 3" (2003); Actor, "Paper Soldiers" (2002); Actor, "Class of '06" (2002); Actor, "North Hollywood" (2001) **AW:** People Choice Award for the Comedy Act of 2018 (2018); Favorite Comedic TV Actor, People's Choice Awards (2017); Comedic Genius Award, MTV Movie Awards (2015); Entertainer of the Year for Outstanding Actor in a Comedy Series, NAACP Image Awards (2014); Outstanding Comedy Series, NAACP Image Awards (2014); BET Award for Best Actor (2012); Numerous Awards

HART, OLIVER D'ARCY, PHD, T: Lewis P. and Linda L. Geyser University Professor **I:** Education/Educational Services **CN:** Harvard University **DOB:** 10/09/1948 **PB:** London **SC:** United Kingdom **PT:** Philip D'Arcy Hart; Ruth D'Arcy (Meyer) Hart **MS:** Married **SPN:** Rita B. Goldberg (06/09/1974) **CH:** Daniel S.; Benjamin P. **ED:** Honorary PhD, Warwick University (2012); Honorary PhD, London Business School (2011); Honorary PhD, University of Paris-Dauphine (2009); Honorary PhD, Copenhagen Business School (2009); Honorary PhD, University of Basel, Switzerland (1994); Honorary PhD, Free University Brussels (1992); PhD, Princeton University (1974); MA, Warwick University, England (1972); BA, University of Cambridge (1969) **C:** Lewis P. and Linda L. Geyser University Professor, Harvard University (2020-Present); Andrew E. Furer Professor of Economics, Harvard University, Cambridge, MA (1997-2020); Professor of Economics, Harvard University, Cambridge, MA (1993-1997); Professor of Economics, Massachusetts Institute of Technology, Cambridge, MA (1984-1993); Professor of Economics, London School of Economics (1981-1985); Lecturer of Economics, University of Cambridge (1975-1981); Lecturer of Economics, University of Essex (1974-1975) **CR:** Centennial Visiting Professor, London School of Economics (1997-Present); Marvin Bower Fellow, Harvard Business School, Boston, MA (1988-1989) **CW:** Author, "Firms, Contracts, and Financial Structure" (1995); Editor, Review of Economic Studies (1979-1983); Contributor, Articles, Professional Journals **AW:** Co-Recipient, Nobel Prize in Economics (2016); Guggenheim Fellow (1987-1988) **MEM:** Council, Econometric Society (1983-Present); President, American Law and Economics Association (2006-2007); Vice President, American Economic Association (2006); Fellow,

Econometric Society; Fellow, American Academy of Arts & Sciences; Fellow, Correspondent, British Academy; American Law and Economics Association; American Economic Association; National Academy of Sciences **AV:** Listening to music

HARTZLER, VICKY JO, T: U.S. Representative from Missouri **I:** Government Administration/Government Relations/Government Services **DOB:** 10/13/1960 **PB:** Archy **SC:** MO/USA **MS:** Married **SPN:** Lowell Hartzler **CH:** Tiffany **ED:** MS in Education, State University of Central Missouri (1992);BS in Education, University of Missouri, Columbia, MO (1983) **C:** Member, U.S. House of Representatives from Missouri's Fourth Congressional District, United States Congress, Washington, DC (2011-Present); Member, U.S. House Armed Services Committee, Washington, DC (2011-Present); Member, U.S. House Committee on Agriculture, Washington, DC (2011-Present); Chairperson, Missouri Women's Council (2005-2007); Missouri House of Representatives, Jefferson City, MO (1995-2001) **CR:** Co-Owner, Hartzler Equipment Co. **CIV:** Former President, Cass County Farm Bureau **CW:** Author, "Running God's Way: Step by Step to a Successful Political Campaign" (2008) **PA:** Republican **RE:** Mennonite

HARVIN, WESLEY REID, T: Lawyer **I:** Law and Legal Services **CN:** Harvin & Harvin, LLP **DOB:** 01/04/1944 **PB:** Thomasville **SC:** GA/USA **PT:** Henry Ellis Harvin; Bertha Mae Harvin **MS:** Married **SPN:** Kay Kerce (08/09/1964) **CH:** Wesley Reid II **ED:** JD, Stetson University (1976); BA in Psychology, University of South Florida (1971) **C:** Lawyer, Harvin & Harvin LLP (1978-Present); Private Practice, Stuart, FL (1976) **CR:** Past Legal Counsel, St. Lucie County Code Enforcement Board; Past General Counsel, Thomas J. White Development Corporation **CIV:** Chairman, Planned Giving; Board of Directors, American Heart Association Martin County; Board of Directors, Treasure Coast Wildlife Hospital; Past Member, Board of Directors, First United Methodist Church Preschool; Past President, Martin County Band Boosters, Inc.; Past Assistant Scoutmaster, Boy Scouts of America; Founder, Annual Fundraiser Dinner **MIL:** Florida Army National Guard **AW:** AV Rating, Martindale Hubbell **MEM:** American Bar Association; Association of Trial Lawyers of America; Florida Bar Association; Martin County Bar Association; American Arbitration Association; President, Real Property Council of Martin County **BAR:** U.S. Supreme Court (1980); Florida Trial Bar (1977); U.S. District Court for the Southern District of Florida (1977); U.S. Court Appeals for the 11th Circuit (1977); Florida (1976) **MH:** Albert Nelson Marquis Lifetime Achievement Award **AV:** Exercising; Biking; Scuba diving; Fishing

HARYONO, IGNATIUS, PHD, DD, T: Retired Writer, Deacon **I:** Religious **SC:** Indonesia **PT:** Henricus Harjono Martodirjo; Anastasia Kusmaria Soemodirjo **MS:** Married **SPN:** Wijakti Karlina Harlim (12/24/1943) **ED:** DD, Roosevelt University (1981); PhD, Roosevelt University (1980) **C:** Assistant to Chaplain, Catholic Church (1990-2012); Assistant to Bishop, Diocese of Bandung (1978-1980); Assistant to Provincial, Order of the Holy Cross of Bandung (1975-1979); Professor, Parahyangan Catholic University (1972-1978); University Professor, Parahyangan Catholic University (1972-1979); Philosophy Docent, Pajajaran State University (1968-1973) **CR:** Religious Consultant (2000-Present); Postal Worker, Burbank Post Office, Burbank, CA (1989-1990); Director, USA Today, Glendale, CA (1985-1990) **CIV:** Director, Religious Education, Indonesian Catholic Community of Archdiocese, Los Angeles, CA (1994-2000); Director, Leader,

Bible Readers Club (1995); Lumen Christi Indonesian Catholic Bible Study **MIL:** Lieutenant Colonel, Titular Chaplaincy, Indonesian Army (1972-1979) **CW:** Author, "Was Mary Also Redeemed" (1989); Author, Poems, National Library of Poetry; Contributor, Articles, Religious Publications; Author, "Compendium" **AW:** Award, KKIA Inc. (2001); Indonesian Catholic Community Award (2001); Moderator Award, Cathedral Youth Organization (1978-1979); Presidential Award, W. Java Catholic Youth Organization (1973, 1979) **MEM:** Master, President, Owner, Iggy LLC (2000-2001) **MH:** Albert Nelson Marquis Lifetime Achievement Award **AV:** Traveling **PA:** Populist **RE:** Roman Catholic

HASHIMOTO, TOM TSUYOSHI, T: Engineer **I:** Engineering **DOB:** 07/28/2020 **PB:** Okayama-Shi **SC:** Japan **PT:** Taro Hashimoto; Yoshiko (Urata) Hahsimoto **MS:** Married **SPN:** Yoshiko Hashimoto (07/07/1970) **CH:** Dr. Clifton Hashimoto; Mark T. Hashimoto; Dr. Emily Y. Hashimoto Miotbo **ED:** BS in Engineering, University of Portland (1968); Coursework, Multnomah Junior College, Portland, OR (1963); Pre-Engineering Degree **C:** Owner, Hashimoto & Associates, Conroe, Texas (1993-2003); Engineering Manager, Dreco, Inc., Rosenberg, Texas (1991-1993); Vice President of Engineering and R&D, Branham Industries, Inc., Conroe, Texas (1978-1991); Project Engineer, Victoria Machine Works (1977-1978); Chief Structural Engineer, Skytop Brewster, Victoria, Texas (1974-1977); Design Engineer, Lee C. Moore Corporation (Now Lee C. Moore, A Woolslayer Company), Tulsa, OK (1966-1974) **CW:** Inventor, Five U.S. Patents; 49 Times Trip to Overseas as Engineering Assignments; Patentee in Field **AW:** Award for 25 Year Membership, American Welding Society **MEM:** The American Society of Mechanical Engineers; American Welding Society **MH:** Albert Nelson Marquis Lifetime Achievement Award **AS:** Mr. Hashimoto attributes his success to the oil crisis in 1974. They needed more oil rigs to drill, so he worked heard. There was a rig problem at the middle of the North Sea near the Atlantic Ocean so he went twice in 1971. There was only one drilling operating in the sea. The most oil drilling rigs are American made throughout the world. Mr. Hashimoto would like to visit others in the world. **B/I:** Mr. Hashimoto became involved in his profession because it was simple for him. He went all over the world and by the time he started the company, he opened there producing oil by using the derrick. One of the derricks drilled over five miles deep and set a world record. He also designed a portion of the derrick. **AV:** Hunting; Fishing; Travel **THT:** Mr. Hashimoto grew up in postwar Japan. Food was very scarce, organized crime was rampant and street gangs were the norm in this time of desperation. With money having little value, Japan was in state of depression. He struggled with high school, frequently flirting with trouble. He was unable to avoid fights and had at least one bad beating. This was the norm for young Japanese men. These things combined incensed in him to find a way out. As a "shot in dark," he wrote to Multnormah Junior College to apply for admission. Amazingly, he was accepted and with a quick trip to the consulate, he was cleared to leave the country! Mr. Hashimoto took a leap of faith by leaving his home in Japan, and boarding a ship across the Pacific Ocean. After a 21-day journey, he arrived in San Francisco, with nothing more than the $100 for the trip from his parents. He finally made his way to Oregon. Working his way through school was fraught with hardship. He had no money, spoke almost no English, and made many meals of the free crackers and ketchup from the cafeteria. If he failed, he faced being deported or even being drafted into the Vietnam war. This was a huge motivator for

Mr. Hashimoto to earn not only a pre-engineering degree, but also a Bachelor of Science and Engineering degree from the University of Portland. Upon completion of junior year, he traveled to Tulsa, Oklahoma, where he worked the summer as an intern. Happily, at the end of summer employment, Mr. Jenkins, VP of Engineering, urged him to return for full time employment upon completion of the degree. His next hurdle was his visa stated that upon graduation, he'd be required to return to Japan. Fortunately, his dedication and exceptional performance at the university had endeared him to the dean of engineering, who, conveniently, was a retired Navy Rear Admiral. When Dean Dr. Killian learned of his predicament, he immediately sent a letter to the State Department of Labor, stating the need for Mr. Hashimoto's extraordinary expertise in the American Industry. When graduation day finally arrived, and he was awarded his diploma on stage, he felt that this could only be described as a miracle. Mr. Hashimoto was so excited that he left the day after graduation and drove 2,029 miles straight without eating and sleeping to return to his work in Tulsa, OK. He received his first paycheck for the amount of $700 as a poor, skinny, half-starved recent college graduate. Eleven short years later, his mother strongly requested that it was time for him to return home to choose a wife! His mother had selected five lovely ladies for him to "interview," but after meeting Yoshiko, he knew that he need not look any further. Born in Japan, to Taro and Yoshiko Urata, he has been happily married to Yoshiko Hashimoto for 50 years. They are the proud grandparents of four wonderful grandchildren, whose parents are happy, well-educated, and enjoy successful professional careers. He and his wife are happily living in the scenic Cascade Mountains near the Pacific Ocean, where they enjoy the beautiful sunsets on the horizon. It is Mr. Hashimoto's wish to "have ashes spread across the Pacific Ocean to be able to eternally experience the bright sunrise shining on my mother's country."

HASLAG, JOSEPH, T: Professor and Kenneth Lay Chair in Economics **I:** Education/Educational Services **CN:** University of Missouri, Columbia **PT:** Harry G. Haslag; Marjorie L. (Bolten) Haslag **MS:** Married **SPN:** Sara M. Engler (05/21/1983) **CH:** Elizabeth; Stephen; Peter **ED:** PhD in Economics, Southern Methodist University (1987); MA, University of Missouri (1984); BS, University of Missouri (1982) **C:** Professor, Kenneth Lay Chair in Economics, University of Missouri, Columbia (2008-Present); Executive Director, Economic Policy Analysis and Research Center, University of Missouri, Columbia (2002-Present); Columnist, Columbia Business Times (2010-2014); Chief Economist, Show-Me Institute (2010-2008); Professor, University of Missouri, Columbia (2006-2008); Associate Professor of Economics, University of Missouri, Columbia (2000-2006); Visiting Scholar, Federal Reserve Bank of Kansas City (2001-2003); Visiting Scholar, Federal Reserve Bank of Atlanta (2000); Senior Economist, Policy Advisor, Federal Reserve Bank of Dallas (1995-2000); Visiting Professor, Southern Methodist University (1989-1998); Senior Economist, Federal Reserve Bank of Dallas (1990-1995); Economist, Federal Reserve Bank of Dallas (1988-1990); Economist, Research and Public Affairs Department, Federal Reserve Bank of St. Louis, MO (1987-1988); Adjunct Assistant Professor of Finance, University of Missouri, St. Louis, MO (1987-1988); Instructor, Department of Economics, Southern Methodist University (1986-1987); Instructor, Department of Economics, The University of Texas at Arlington (1986-1987) **CR:** Chief Executive Officer, Missouri Economic Consulting, LLC (2017-Present); Visiting Professor,

Michigan State University (2000); Visiting Scholar, Erasmus University Rotterdam, Netherlands (1991) **CW:** Author, "Modeling Monetary Economies, Fourth Edition" (2017); Author, "Modeling Monetary Economies, Third Edition" (2011); Author, "Macroeconomic Activity and Income Inequality in the US" (1989); Contributor, Articles to Professional Journals **MEM:** The Econometric Society; American Economic Association **MH:** Albert Nelson Marquis Lifetime Achievement Award **RE:** Christian

HASPEL, GINA CHERI, T: Director **I:** Government Administration/Government Relations/Government Services **CN:** Central Intelligence Agency **DOB:** 10/01/1956 **PB:** Ashland **SC:** KY/USA **MS:** Divorced **SPN:** Jeff Haspel (1976, 1985) **ED:** BA in Languages and Journalism, University of Louisville (1978); Coursework, University of Kentucky **CT:** Paralegal Certificate, Northeastern University (1982) **C:** Director, Central Intelligence Agency (2018-Present); Deputy Director, Central Intelligence Agency (2017-2018); Acting Director, National Clandestine Service, Central Intelligence Agency (2013); Deputy Group Chief, Counterterrorism Center, Central Intelligence Agency (2001-2003); Station Chief, Central Intelligence Agency, Europe (1990-2001); Several Undercover Overseas Positions Including Station Chief, Central Intelligence Agency, Ethiopia, Central Eurasia and Turkey (1987-1989); Reports Officer, Central Intelligence Agency (1985); Paralegal (1982-1985); Civilian Library Coordinator, Fort Devens, MA (1980-1981) **AW:** Donovan Award; Presidential Rank Award; Intelligence Medal of Merit; George H. W. Bush Award for Excellence in Counterterrorism

HASSAN, MARGARET, "MAGGIE" C., T: U.S Senator **I:** Government Administration/Government Relations/Government Services **DOB:** 02/28/1958 **PB:** Boston **SC:** MA/USA **PT:** Robert Coldwell Wood; Margaret (Byers) Wood **MS:** Married **SPN:** Thomas Edward Hassan (02/27/1988) **CH:** Benjamin Byers; Margaret McReynolds **ED:** JD, Northeastern University School of Law (1985); BA, Brown University (1980) **C:** U.S. Senator, State of New Hampshire (2017-Present); Governor, State of New Hampshire, Concord, NH (2013-2017); Majority Leader, New Hampshire State Senate (2008-2010); President Pro Tempore, New Hampshire State Senate (2006); Member, District 23, New Hampshire State Senate (2004-2006); Attorney, Sullivan, Weinstein & McQuay (1996-1999); Attorney, Assistant General Counsel, Brigham & Women's Hospital, Partners Healthcare (1993-1996); Attorney, Palmer & Dodge (1985-1992); Information Officer, Massachusetts Department of Social Services (1980-1982) **MEM:** New Hampshire Bar Association; Board Member, Disabilities Rights Center; American Bar Association **PA:** Democrat **RE:** Protestant

HASSETT, KEVIN ALLEN, T: Chairman (Retired) **I:** Financial Services **CN:** Council of Economic Advisers **DOB:** 03/20/1962 **PB:** Greenfield **SC:** MA/USA **MS:** Married **SPN:** Kristie Hassett **CH:** Two children **ED:** PhD in Economics, University of Pennsylvania; MA, University of Pennsylvania; BA in Economics, Swarthmore College **C:** Chairman, Council of Economic Advisors (2017-2019); Economic Adviser, Mitt Romney Campaign for President (2012); Economic Adviser, John McCain Campaign for President (2008); Economic Adviser, George W. Bush Campaign for President (2004); Director of Economic Policy Studies, AEI (2003); Resident Scholar, AEI (1997); Economist, Division of Research and Statistics, Federal Reserve Board of Governors (1992-1997); Associate Professor of Economics, Columbia Business School (1993-1994); Assistant Professor of Economics, Columbia Business School (1989-1993) **CW:** Author, Weekly Column, Bloomberg (2005-Present); Author, "Spending, Taxes and Certainty: A Road Map to 4%" (2012); Co-Editor, "Toward Fundamental Tax Reform" (2005); Author, "Bubbleology: The New Science of Stock Market Winners and Loser" (2002); Author, "Inequality and Tax Policy" (2001); Author, "Transition Costs of Fundamental Tax Reform" (2001); Co-Author, "Dow 36,000: The New Strategy for Profiting from the Coming Rise in the Stock Market" (1999); Author, "Tax Policy and Investment" (1999); Author, Monthly Column, National Review **PA:** Republican

HASSLER, DONALD, T: Language Educator **I:** Education/Educational Services **DOB:** 01/03/1937 **PB:** Akron **SC:** OH/USA **PT:** Donald Mackey Hassler; Frances Elizabeth (Parsons) Hassler **MS:** Married **SPN:** Sue Smith (09/13/1977); Diana Cain (10/08/1960, Deceased 1976) **CH:** Donald; David; Shelly **ED:** PhD, Columbia University (1967); MA, Columbia University (1960); BA, Williams College (1959) **C:** Emeritus Professor (2014-Present); Professor, Kent State University (1977-2014); Chair, Faculty Senate (2010-2012); Chair, Northeast Ohio Master of Fine Arts Hiring Committee, Kent State University (2007-2010); Chairman, Undergraduate Studies, Kent State University (1987-1991); Director, Kent State University (1973-1983); Acting Dean, Honors and Experimental College, Kent State University (1979-1981); Associate Professor, Kent State University (1971-1976); Assistant Professor, Kent State University (1967-1971); Instructor, English, Kent State University (1965-1967); Instructor, University of Montreal (1961-1965) **CR:** Arts And Sciences Advisory Council (2015-Present); Editorial Board, International Affairs (2011-Present); Chair, Chair Review Committee (2007-Present); Selection Committee, Northeast Ohio Master of Fine Arts Faculty (2005-Present); Secretary, Faculty Senate (1996-Present); Interim Chair, Department of English (2011-2012); Faculty Senate, Representative, Ohio Faculty Council (2009-2010); Coordinator, Major Program (1991-1994); Director, Wick Poetry Competition (1987-1991); Coordinator, Writing Certificate Program (1986-1991) **CIV:** President, Chair, Kent State Faculty Senate (2010-Present); Trustee, Covington Historical Society (2005-Present); Kent State University Press Board (2004-Present); Ohio Faculty Council (2009-Present); University Priorities and Budget Advisory Council (1998-Present); Elder, Secretary, Kent State Faculty Senate (1996-Present); Chancellors Faculty Advisory Committee (1996-Present); Elected Representative, Ohio Faculty Council (2013-2014); Speaker, Smithsonian Yesterdays Tomorrows Exhibit (2003); Co-Chairman, Kent American Revolution Bicentennial Commission (1974-1977); Deacon, Presbyterian Church (1971-1974) **CW:** Co-Editor, Editor, Executive Editor Friends of Arthur Machen (2008-Present); Editorial Board, "Paradoxa" (1994-Present); Author, Poems and Essays, Academic Questions (2015-2020); Author, Published Poems, Cornfield Review (2019); Author, Poems and Essays, New York Review of Science Fiction (2013-2019); Author, Reviews, Extrapolation (2013-2019); "High Latitudes" (2017); Co-Editor, "On The Origin of Exhibits" (2015); "Creative Non-Fiction in Great Lakes Book Projects" (2013); Author, Springer Springer eBook (2012); Author, "Emanations" (2011); Co-Editor, "New Boundaries in Political Science Fiction" (2008); Co-Editor, Political Science Fiction (1997); Co-Editor, "Letters of Arthur Machen and Montgomery Evans, 1923-1947" (1993); Author, "Isaac Asimov" (1991); Advisory Editorial Board, "Hellas" (1988); Managing Editor, Journal Extrapolation (1986-1987); Author, "Death and the Serpent" (1985); Author, "Patterns of the Fantastic II" (1984); Author, "Patterns of the

Fantastic" (1983); Author, "Hal Clement" (1982); Author, "Comic Tones in Science Fiction" (1982); Author, "Asimovs Golden Age: The Ordering of an Art" (1977); Author, "Erasmus Darwin" (1974); Author, "The Comedian as the Letter D: Erasmus Darwins Comic Materialism" (1973) **AW:** OFMC Gold Cup Chair of the Year (2012); Thomas D. Clareson Award, Science Fiction Research Association (2001); Finalist, Distinguished Scholar Award, Kent State University (1999); J. Lloyd Eaton Award, Eaton Library Collection, University of California Riverside (1993) **MEM:** Treasurer, President, Science Fiction Research Association (1983-1986, 2005-Present); President, Covington Historical Society (2015-2019); President, Phi Beta Kappa (1983-1984); Board of Directors, Kiwanis (1974-1976) **MH:** Albert Nelson Marquis Lifetime Achievement Award

HASTINGS, ALCEE LAMAR, T: U.S. Representative from Florida **I:** Government Administration/Government Relations/Government Services **CN:** U.S. House of Representatives **DOB:** 09/05/1936 **PB:** Altomonte Springs **SC:** FL/USA **PT:** Julius C. Hastings; Mildred L. Hastings **MS:** Married **CH:** Chelsea; Alcee Jr.; Leigh **ED:** Doctor of Jurisprudence, Florida A&M University College of Law (1963); Bachelor of Science in Zoology and Botany, Fisk University, Nashville, TN (1958); Coursework, Howard University School of Law **C:** Member, U.S. House of Representatives from Florida's 20th Congressional District, United States Congress (2013-Present); Member, U.S. House of Representatives from Florida's 23rd Congressional District, United States Congress (1993-2013); Private Practice Attorney (1989-1992); Judge, United States District Court for the Southern District of Florida (1979-1989); Judge, Circuit Court, Broward County, FL (1977-1979); Private Practice Attorney, Fort Lauderdale, FL (1966-1977); Associate, Allen & Hastings, Fort Lauderdale, FL (1963-1966); Member, Committee on Rule; Member, Commission on Security; Member, Cooperation in Europe **CR:** Lecturer, Consultant, Peace Corps Volunteers, Avon Park, FL (1966) **CIV:** Trustee, Bethune-Cookman University; Trustee, Broward College; Board of Directors, Broward County Council of Human Relations; Board of Directors, Florida Voters League Inc.; Board of Directors, Broward County Sickle Cell Anemia Foundation; Board of Directors, Child Advocacy Inc.; Board of Directors, Urban League of Broward County **CW:** Host, TV Series, "Pride," Station WPLG Columnist, West Side Gazette **AW:** Listee, Power 150 (2008); Named, One of the 100 Most Influential Black Americans, Ebony Magazine (2006); Chairman's Award, National Bar Association (1981); Glades Festival of Afro Arts Award, Zeta Phi Beta Sorority Inc. (1981); Named, Man of the Year, Committee of Italian American Affairs (1979); Named, Citizen of the Year, Zeta Phi Beta Sorority Inc. (1978); Sam Delevoe Human Rights Award, Community Relations Board, Broward County (1978); Humanitarian Award, Broward Young Democrats (1978) **MEM:** National Organization for Women; National Association for the Advancement of Colored People; Miami-Dade Chamber of Commerce; American Civil Liberties Union; The Family Christian Association of America Inc.; Kappa Alpha Psi **BAR:** State of Florida (1963) **PA:** Democrat

HASTINGS, WILMONT, "REED" REED JR., T: Chief Executive Officer **I:** Business Management/Business Services **CN:** Netflix **DOB:** 10/08/1960 **PB:** Boston **SC:** MA/USA **PT:** Wilmont Reed Hastings; Joan Amory (Loomis) Hastings **MS:** Married **SPN:** Patricia Ann Quillin **CH:** Two Children **ED:** MS in Computer Science, Stanford University, CA (1988); BA in Mathematics, Bowdoin College, Brunswick, Maine (1983) **C:** Co-founder, President, Chief Exec-

utive Officer, Netflix, Los Gatos, CA (1997-Present); Chief Executive Officer, Technology Network (1997-1999); Founder, Chief Executive Officer, Pure Atria Software (1991-1997); Software Engineer, Network Equipment Technologies (1990-1991); Software Engineer, Coherent Thought (1989-1990); Member, Technical Staff, Schlumberger Palo Alto Research (1988-1989); Lisp Instructor Assistant, Symbolics (1986) **CR:** Board of Directors, Facebook (2011-2019); Board Member, Dreambox (2010-2018); Board of Directors, Microsoft (2007-2012); Chairman, Netflix (1997, 1998) **CIV:** Board Member, Pahara Institute (2011-Present); Board Member, KIPP Foundation (2007-Present); Board Member, Hispanic Foundation of Silicon Valley (2014-2019); Board Member, California Charter Schools Association (2008-2016); President, California State Board of Education (2000-2004); Math Teacher, Peace Corp, Swaziland (1983-1985); Founding Member, EdVoice.net; Founding Member, Pacific Collegiate School; Founding Member, Aspire Public Schools; Founding Member, NewSchools.org **AW:** Named One of the Top 50 Best CEOs of Large Companies, Comparably (2018); Named One of the 100 Most Influential People in the World, Time Magazine (2005, 2011); Named Business Person of the Year, Fortune Magazine (2010); Named One of the 30 Most Respected CEOs, Barron's (2010); Named One of the 100 Agents of Change, Rolling Stone Magazine (2009); Named a Maverick, Details Magazine (2007); Named to the Video Business Hall of Fame (2007)

HATAJACK, FRANK JOSEPH, T: Respiratory Therapist **I:** Medicine & Health Care **DOB:** 07/01/1945 **PB:** Port Jefferson **SC:** NY/USA **PT:** Frank Joseph; Helen Lucy (Giaraputo) Hatajack **MS:** Divorced **SPN:** Susan Nelia Gray (02/18/1979, Divorced 11/1990) **ED:** AS in Biomedical Equipment Technology, Delgado Community College (1993); AS in Respiratory Care, Delgado Community College (1990); Diploma, Institute of Electronic Technology (1983); Diploma, Divers Institute of Technology (1972); BS in Geological Engineering, Michigan Technological University (1968) **CT:** Registered Respiratory Therapist, Registered Pulmonary Function Technologist, The National Board for Respiratory Care; Certification for the Biomedical Equipment Technician, International Certification Commission; Certified Electronic Technician, International Society of Certified Electronics Technicians; Neonatal Designation **C:** Retired (2010); Respiratory Therapist, LifeCare Hospitals, New Orleans, LA (1999-2010); Clinical Director, MedForce International (1989-1994); Supervisor, Diver, Welder, Taylor Diving (1973-1987); Assistant Junior Geologists, Consolidated Mining Corporation (1966); Respiratory Therapist, Charity Hospital, New Orleans, LA **CR:** Owner, Biomed Enterprises, Ltd. (1989-1996) **MIL:** U.S. Navy, Vietnam (1968-1972) **AW:** Respiratory Care Award for Academy Excellence, Delgado Community College (1990); Award, Best Research Paper, "Decompression Sickness," State of Louisiana, Louisiana Society for Respiratory Care (1989); Seymore Weiss Grantee, Delgado Community College (1988, 1989); Certificate, U.S. Merchant Marine (1983); Bell Diver Certification (1978); Boomer of the Month, Attack Squadron VA-165 (1972); National Defense Service Medal, U.S. Navy; Vietnam Service Medal, Two Stars, U.S. Navy; Republic of Vietnam Campaign Medal with Device, U.S. Navy; Good Conduct Medal, U.S. Navy; Seventh Fleet Citation, U.S. Navy **MEM:** American Association for Respiratory Care; The National Board for Respiratory Care; Mineralogical Society of America; Sigma Rho Fraternity **MH:** Albert Nelson Marquis Lifetime Achievement Award; Marquis Who's Who Top Professional **B/I:** Mr. Hatajack became involved in his profession because when he graduated from high school he was a right guard for the county and his coach sent a letter for him to get into college. After graduation, he enlisted in the service for four years and served as a shooter on the flight deck of the U.S.S. Constellation. Upon leaving the service, he channeled his expertise in deep sea diving into his career. For years, he worked as a deep sea diving welder before finally returning to school to become a respiratory therapist. **AV:** Studying mineralogy and radio astronomy; Exercising **RE:** Christian

HATHAWAY, ANNE JACQUELINE, T: Actress **I:** Media & Entertainment **DOB:** 11/12/1982 **PB:** Brooklyn **SC:** NY/USA **PT:** Gerard Hathaway; Kate (McCauley) Hathaway **MS:** Married **SPN:** Adam Shulman (09/29/2012) **CH:** Jonathan Rosebanks Shulman; Jack Shulman **ED:** Diploma, New York University Gallatin School of Individualized Study (2005); Coursework in English and Political Science, Vassar College; Coursework, American Academy of Dramatic Arts (1993) **CR:** Spokeswoman, Lancôme (2008) **CIV:** Board Member, Lollipop Theatre Network; Supporter, Freedom to Marry, Nike Foundation, The Girl Effect Program, World Bank, Creative Coalition, St. Jude Children's Research Hospital and Human Rights Campaign; UN Women Goodwill Ambassador **CW:** Actress, "The Last Thing He Wanted" (2020); Actress, "Sesame Street: Elmo's Playdate" (2020); Actress, "The Hustle" (2019); Actress, "Modern Love" (2019); Actress, "Dark Waters" (2019); Actress, "Serenity" (2019); Actress, "Ocean's 8" (2018); Actress, "Nasty Women" (2018); Actress, Producer, "The Children's Monologues" (2017); Appearance, "Documentary Now!" (2016); Actress, "Alice Through the Looking Glass" (2016); Actress, "Colossal" (2016); Actress, "The Intern" (2015); Actress, Producer, "Grounded" (2015); Appearance, "Hit Record on TV" (2015); Appearance, "Lip Sync Battle" (2015); Actress, "Interstellar" (2014); Actress, Producer, "Song One" (2014); Voice Actress, "Rio 2" (2014); Actress, "Don Peyote" (2014); Actress, "Don Jon's Addiction" (2013); Actress, "Les Misérables" (2012); Actress, "The Dark Knight Rises" (2012); Actress, "One Day" (2011); Voice Actress, "Rio" (2011); Co-host, 83rd Academy Awards (2011); Actress, "Alice in Wonderland" (2010); Actress, "Valentine's Day" (2010); Actress, "Family Guy" (2010); Voice Actress, "The Simpsons" (2009-2010); Actress, "Twelfth Night" (2009); Actress, "Bride Wars" (2009); Actress, "Passengers" (2008); Actress, "Rachel Getting Married" (2008); Guest Host, "Saturday Night Live" (2008); Actress, "Get Smart" (2008); Actress, "Becoming Jane" (2007); Actress, "Elmo's Christmas Countdown" (2007); Actress, "The Devil Wears Prada" (2006); Actress, "Brokeback Mountain" (2005); Actress, "Havoc" (2005); Voice Actress, "Hoodwinked" (2005); Actress, "Ella Enchanted" (2004); Actress, "The Princess Diaries 2: Royal Engagement" (2004); Voice Actress, "The Cat Returns" (2002); Actress, "Nicholas Nickleby" (2002); Actress, "The Princess Diaries" (2001); Actress, "The Other Side of Heaven" (2001); Actress, "Get Real" (1999-2000) **AW:** Recipient, Star, Hollywood Walk of Fame (2019); Named One of the Highest Paid Actresses, Forbes (2015); Critics Choice Award for Best Supporting Actress (2013); Golden Globe Award for Best Performance by an Actress in a Supporting Role in a Motion Picture, Hollywood Foreign Press Association (2013); SAG Award for Outstanding Performance by a Female Actor in a Supporting Role, SAG-AFTRA (2013); BAFTA Award for Best Supporting Actress (2013); Academy Award for Best Supporting Actress, Academy of Motion Picture Arts & Sciences (2013); Named Woman of the Year, Hasty Pudding Theatrical Society (2010); Choice Movie Actress: Comedy, Teen Choice Awards (2009); Named One of the Celebrity 100, Forbes (2009); National Board Review Award for Best Actress (2008); Critics Choice Award for Best Actress (2009); Women in Hollywood Tribute Award, Elle Magazine (2008); Numerous Awards

HATTON, MARY ELLEN, PHD, T: School Psychologist (Retired) **I:** Health, Wellness and Fitness **CN:** Sylvania Schools **DOB:** 09/26/1947 **PB:** Rochester **SC:** IN/USA **PT:** Robert Crosby Pletcher; Mildred Gail (Moore) Pletcher **MS:** Married **SPN:** Jerry Paul Hatton (12/28/1968) **CH:** Ethan Andrew; Joanna Lynn Gardner **ED:** PhD, Indiana University (1990); Intern, School Psychologist, Perrysburg Schools, Ohio (1988); MS in Education, Indiana University (1987); BA, North Central College (1969) **CT:** School Psychologist, States of Ohio and Michigan **C:** School Psychologist, Jackson County Intermediate School District, Jackson, MI (1995-2012); School Psychologist, Sylvania Schools, Ohio (1988-1995) **CR:** Researcher in Field; Adjunct Professor, Spring Arbor University **CIV:** Social Committee, Condo Board; Leader, Meditations, Local Church; Bible Study, Local Church; Quilt Group, Local Church **AW:** Recognition of Service Award (1990, 1991, 1992); Rose Award for Outstanding Work with Children **MEM:** Advisory Board, Learning Disabilities Association (LDA) (1992-1993); National Association of School Psychologists; Ohio School Psychologists Association (OSPA); Phi Lambda Theta **MH:** Albert Nelson Marquis Lifetime Achievement Award **B/I:** Dr. Hatton became involved in school psychology because it combined both her long-standing interest in psychology, as well as her love for teaching. A psychology course she took in high school with a fantastic teacher inspired her to pursue her career path. **AV:** Sewing; Painting; Needlecrafts

HAUCK, RACHEL, T: Scenic Designer **I:** Architecture & Construction **MS:** Life Partner **SPN:** Lisa Peterson **C:** Resident Scenic Designer, Eugene O'Neill Theater Center (2005-2014); Company Member, Actors' Gang (1993-2001); Art Direction Intern, Academy of Television Arts and Sciences (1990); Scenic Designer, Rachel Hauck Design; Usual Suspect, New York Theatre Workshop **CR:** NEA/TCG Design Fellow (1998-2000); Instructor, Brown University; Instructor, New York University/Playwrights Horizons; Instructor, Vassar College; Instructor, California Institute for the Arts **CIV:** Trustee, Eastern Region Executive Board, United Scenic Artists **CW:** Scenic Designer, "Perry Street" (2020); Scenic Designer, "The Wrong Man" (2019); Exhibited, "The Poor Itch," Prague Quadrennial, The Public Lab (2012); Exhibited, "House of Bernarda Alba," Prague Quadrennial, Mark Taper Forum (2004); Scenic Designer, "Hadestown"; Scenic Designer, "What the Constitution Means to Me"; Scenic Designer, "Latin History for Morons" **AW:** Tony Award for Best Scenic Design in a Musical, "Hadestown" (2019); Obie Award for Sustained Excellence in Scenic Design, American Theatre Wing (2016); Lilly Award for Excellence in Scenic Design (2011); Princess Grace Award for Theater (1998); Faberge Award (1998)

HAUGHT, WILLIAM DIXON, T: Partner **I:** Law and Legal Services **CN:** Haught & Wade, LLP **DOB:** 06/12/1939 **PB:** Kansas City **SC:** KS/USA **PT:** Walter Dixon Haught; Florence Louise (Rhoads) Haught **MS:** Married **SPN:** Julia Jane Headstream (07/22/1967) **CH:** Stephanie Jane Wade **ED:** LLM, Georgetown University (1968); LLB, University of Kansas (1964); BS, University of Kansas (1961) **C:** Partner, Haught & Wade (1996-Present); Private Practice, Little Rock, AR (1991-1995); Partner, Wright, Lindsey & Jennings, Little Rock, AR (1970-1991); Associate, Stanley, Schroeder, Weeks, Thomas & Lysaught, Kansas City, KS (1968-1970) **MIL:** Captain, U.S. Army Reserve, Korea (1964-1968) **CW:** Co-Author, "Arkansas Probate System, Seventh Edition" (2005); Author, "Probate and Estate Administration: The Law in Arkansas (1983); Co-Author, "Arkansas Probate System" (1977) **MEM:** American Bar Association; Regent, Editor Studies Program, State Chair, The American College of Trust and Estate Counsel; The International Academy Estate and Trust Law; The American Law Institute; Chairman, Probate Law Section, Arkansas Bar Association; Chairman, Economics of Law Practice Committee, Arkansas Bar Association; Chairman, Agricultural Law Committee, Arkansas Bar Association; Chairman, Juris Law Reform Committee, Arkansas Bar Association; Central Arkansas Estate Council; Pulaski County Bar Association; Country Club of Little Rock; Rotary International **BAR:** Arkansas Bar Association (1971); Kansas Bar Association (1964) **MH:** Albert Nelson Marquis Lifetime Achievement Award **B/I:** Mr. Haught became involved in his profession because in college he had teachers that inspired him and fostered his interest in law. He spoke to people and other attorneys and decided that law was what he wanted to do and had been doing it for a long time. **AV:** Enjoying art; Listening to music; Writing **RE:** Presbyterian

HAWKE, ETHAN GREEN, T: Actor **I:** Media & Entertainment **DOB:** 11/06/1970 **PB:** Austin **SC:** TX/USA **PT:** James Hawke; Leslie (Green) Hawke **MS:** Married **SPN:** Ryan Shawhughes (06/18/2008); Uma Thurman (05/01/1998, Divorced 07/20/2004) **CH:** Maya Ray Thurman-Hawke; Levon; Clementine Jane; Indiana **ED:** Coursework, Carnegie Mellon University (1988-1989) **C:** Co-Founder, Artistic Director, Malaparte Theatre Co., New York, NY (1992-2000) **CIV:** Board of Trustees, New York Public Library (2016-Present); Co-Founder, Young Lions Fiction Award (2001); Former Co-Chair, Young Lions Committee, New York Public Library; Supporter, Doe Fund **CW:** Actor, "Tesla" (2020); Actor, "The Good Lord Bird" (2020); Actor, "The Truth" (2019); Actor, "The Purge" (2019); Actor, Producer, "Adopt a Highway" (2019); Actor, "The Kid" (2019); Actor, "Stockholm" (2018); Actor, "Juliet, Naked" (2018); Actor, "Blaze" (2018); Actor, "Valerian and the City of a Thousand Planets" (2017); Actor, "First Reformed" (2017); Actor, "24 Hours to Live" (2017); Actor, "Maudie" (2016); Actor, "In a Valley of Violence" (2016); Actor, "The Magnificent Seven" (2016); Author, "Indeh: A Story of the Apache Wars" (2016); Actor, "10,000 Saints" (2015); Actor, "Sinister 2" (2015); Actor, "The Phenom" (2015); Actor, "Maggie's Plan" (2015); Actor, "Born to Be Blue" (2015); Actor, "Regression" (2015); Author, "Rules for a Knight" (2015); Actor, "Boyhood" (2014); Actor, "Predestination" (2014); Actor, "Cymbeline" (2014); Actor, "Good Kill" (2014); Director, Featured, "Seymour: An Introduction" (2014); Actor, Writer, "Before Midnight" (2013); Actor, Director, "Clive" (2013); Actor, "Macbeth" (2013); Actor, "Vigilandia" (2013); Actor, "The Purge" (2013); Actor, "Getaway" (2013); Actor, "Sinister" (2012); Actor, Producer, "Exit Strategy" (2012); Actor, "Ivanov" (2012); Actor, "The Woman in the Fifth" (2011); Actor, "Blood from a Stone" (2010-2011); Director, "A Lie of the Ming" (2010); Actor, "Daybreakers" (2009); Actor, "Brooklyn's Finest" (2009); Author, "The Last Outlaw Poet," Rolling Stone Magazine (2009); Actor, "The Cherry Orchard" (2009); Actor, "The Winter's Tale" (2009); Actor, "Life in New York" (2009); Actor, "What Doesn't Kill You" (2008); Actor, "Before the Devil Knows You're Dead" (2007); Actor, Writer, Director, "The Hottest State" (2007); Actor, "The Coast of Utopia (Part 3: Salvage)" (2007); Director, "Things

We Want" (2007); Actor, "The Coast of Utopia (Part 1: Voyage)" (2006); Actor, "The Coast of Utopia (Part 2: Shipwreck)" (2006); Actor, "Assault on Precinct 13" (2005); Actor, "Hurlyburly" (2005); Actor, Writer, "Before Sunset" (2004); Actor, "Taking Lives" (2004); Actor, "Sophistry" (2003-2004); Actor, "Henry IV" (2003-2004); Writer, Director, Actor, "Alias" (2003); Author, "Ash Wednesday" (2002); Voice Actor, "Waking Life" (2001); Actor, "Tape" (2001); Actor, "Training Day" (2001); Actor, "The Jimmy Show" (2001); Director, "Chelsea Walls" (2001); Actor, "Tell Me" (2000); Actor, "Hamlet" (2000); Actor, "Joe the King" (1999); Actor, "Snow Falling on Cedars" (1999); Actor, "Great Expectations" (1998); Actor, "The Newton Boys" (1998); Actor, "The Velocity of Gary" (1998); Actor, "Gattaca" (1997); Author, "The Hottest State" (1996); Actor, "Before Sunrise" (1995); Actor, "Search & Destroy" (1995); Director, "Straight to One" (1994); Actor, "Floundering" (1994); Actor, "Reality Bites" (1994); Actor, "White Fang II" (1994); Actor, "Quiz Show" (1994); Actor, "Alive" (1993); Actor, "Rich in Love" (1993); Actor, "A Midnight Clear" (1992); Actor, "Waterland" (1992); Actor, "A Joke" (1992); Actor, "The Seagull" (1992); Actor, "Casanova" (1991); Actor, "White Fang" (1991); Actor, "Mystery Date" (1991); Actor, "Dead Poet's Society" (1989); Actor, "Dad" (1989); Actor, "Lion's Den" (1988); Actor, "Explorers" (1985); Actor, Television Shows, Theater, Film **AW:** Chicago Film Critics Association Award for Best Actor (2017); Detroit Film Critics Society Award for Best Actor (2017); Gotham Independent Film Award for Best Actor (2017); Independent Spirit Award for Best Male Lead (2017); London Film Critics' Circle Award for Actor of the Year (2017); Los Angeles Film Critics Association Award for Best Actor (2017); National Society of Film Critics Award for Best Actor (2017); New York Film Critics Circle Award for Best Actor (2017); Louis XIII Genius Award, Critics' Choice Awards (2014); Boston Society of Film Critics Award for Best Cast (2014); Los Angeles Film Critics Association Award for Best Screenplay (2013); National Society of Film Critics Award for Best Screenplay (2013); Hollywood Film Award for Screenwriter of the Year (2013); Library Lion, New York Public Library (2010); Boston Society of Film Critics Award for Best Cast (2007); Gotham Independent Film Award for Best Ensemble Cast (2007); Satellite Award for Best Cast – Motion Picture (2007); Inductee, Texas Film Hall of Fame (2004); Recipient, Numerous Awards

HAWKINS, CARL G., T: President **I:** Law and Legal Services **CN:** Law Offices of Carl G. Hawkins, P.A. **PB:** Athens **SC:** Greece **MS:** Married **ED:** Intern, Michael Huyghue & Associates (2017); Legal Intern, Arcadier and Associates, PA- The Melbourne Legal Team (2014-2017); JD, Florida Coastal School of Law (2017); BA in Criminology, University of South Florida (2013) **CT:** Business Certificate, FCSL (2016) **C:** Corporate Counsel, Overwatch Partners, Inc. (2018-Present); President, Managing Attorney, Law Offices of Carl G. Hawkins (2017-Present); Founder, Carls Logistic Services (2013-2017); Manager, Epic Weapons (2006-2014) **CIV:** Certified Legal Intern, Public Defenders Office, 4th Judicial Circuit (2016); Volunteer, Coordinator, Judicial Campaign, 18th Judicial Circuit of Florida (2014) **AW:** CALI Book Award, Intellectual Property (2016); Silver Medalist, Syrtaki of Boca Dance Group, Hellenic Dance Festival (2009); Gold Medalist, Grecian Odyssey Dancers, Hellenic Dance Festival (2008); Bronze Medalist, Grecian Odyssey Dancers, Hellenic Dance Festival (2007); Southeast Region Orator Finalist, National Oratorical Contest **MEM:** Consultant, Greek American Association of Brevard; Florida Coastal School of Law Sports Law Society; American Bar Associ-

ation; Florida Bar Association **BAR:** Florida Bar **AS:** He attributes his success to wonderful parenting. His parents raised him with good ethics, good morals, good values, they were tough on him but at the same time showed him that they loved him, and his wonderful wife. **B/I:** Mr. Hawkins was inspired to become involved in his profession because of his mother. It was something that she had wanted to do but got pregnant at a young age. She was a wonderful mother, but getting pregnant cut her dream short. She always voiced that to him, he told her to come to law school with her, but she is involved in non profit work. Partially following in his mothers footsteps he wanted her to see that if she couldn't do it her son could. He is big on "use what god gave you", he is very spiritual, and he believes if god gives you a talent you explore that talent to you fullest potential. Growing up he was always arguing with his mom, and he noticed over time it was a good trait to have as a lawyer. While he learned to calm that down on the personal side, on the business side he is very good for advocating for his clients because it comes natural to him. He is also interested in getting involved with mediation, he has a talent for getting everyone involved.

HAWKINS, ELINOR DIXON, T: Librarian (Retired) **I:** Library Management/Library Services **DOB:** 09/25/1927 **PB:** Masontown **SC:** WV/USA **PT:** Thomas Fitchie; Susan (Reed) Dixon **MS:** Married **SPN:** Carroll Woodard Hawkins (06/24/1951) **CH:** John Carroll Hawkins **ED:** BS in Library Science, University of North Carolina (1950); AB, Fairmont State College (1949) **C:** Director, Craven-Pamlico-Carteret Regional Library, New Bern, NC (1962-1992); Librarian, Craven-Pamlico Library Service, New Bern, NC (1958-1962); Head, Circulation Department, Greensboro Public Library (1951-1956); Librarian, Enoch Pratt Free Library, Baltimore, MD (1950-1951) **CR:** Board of Directors, Triangle Bank of New Bern (1963); Storyteller, Children's Television Program, "Telestory Time" (1952-1958); Host, Children's Television Show, "Do You Know"; Board of Trustees, New Bern-Craven County Public Library **CIV:** Tryon Palace Commission (1974-Present); New Bern Historical Society (1973-Present); Advisory Board, Salvation Army **AW:** Order of Long Leaf Pine Award, Governor Bev Perdue (2012); William Booth Award, Salvation Army; Lifetime Membership Award, Salvation Army **MEM:** President, Pilot Club (1957-1958); Vice President, Pilot Club (1962-1963); Arc of the United States; Emeritus Member, Tryon Palace Commission; American Association of University Women; The English Speaking Union; Friends of the Cove City Cravens County Public Library; Friends of New Bern; Craven County Public Library; Church Club; Red Hat Society; Girl Scouts of America **MH:** Albert Nelson Marquis Lifetime Achievement Award **B/I:** Ms. Hawkins became involved in her profession because when she was in the sixth grade, a librarian asked her if she would like to help her after school. She enjoyed doing it and loved it so much that the librarian recommended her for helping the librarian in junior high. She helped there for three years; when Ms. Hawkins went to high school, the librarian there also sought out her assistance. She has technically been a librarian since sixth grade. **AV:** Collecting "The Nightmare Before Christmas" books **RE:** Baptist

HAWLEY, JOSHUA DAVID, T: U.S. Senator from Missouri **I:** Government Administration/Government Relations/Government Services **CN:** U.S. Senate **DOB:** 12/31/1979 **PB:** Springdale **SC:** AK/USA **MS:** Married **SPN:** Erin Morrow **ED:** Doctor of Jurisprudence, Yale Law School; Bachelor of Arts, Stanford University **C:** Senator, State of Missouri

(2019-Present); Associate Professor, University of Missouri Law School (2011-Present); Appellate Litigator, Hogan Lovells, Washington, DC (2008-Present); Attorney General, State of Missouri (2017-2019); Faculty Member, Blackstone Legal Fellowship (2013) **CW:** Author, "Theodore Roosevelt: Preacher of Righteousness" **PA:** Republican

HAYES, GREGORY JAMES, T: Chairman, President, Chief Executive Officer **I:** Technology **CN:** United Technologies Corporation **DOB:** 11/19/1960 **ED:** BS in Economics, Purdue University (1982) **CT:** Certified Public Accountant (CPA) **C:** Chairman, United Technologies Corporation (2016-Present); President, Chief Executive Officer, United Technologies Corporation, Hartford, CT (2014-Present); Senior Vice President, Chief Financial Officer, United Technologies Corporation, Hartford, CT (2008-2014); Vice President, Accounting & Investor Relations, United Technologies Corporation, Hartford, CT (2006-2008); Vice President, Accounting & Controls, United Technologies Corporation, Hartford, CT (2004-2006); Vice President, Controller, United Technologies Corporation, Hartford, CT (2003-2004); Financial Management Positions, Aerospace, Sundstrand Corporation (1989-1999); Accountant, Arthur Andersen **CR:** Board of Directors, Nucor Corporation (2014-Present); United Technologies Corporation (2014-Present)

HAYES, JAHANA, T: U.S. Representative from Connecticut **I:** Government Administration/Government Relations/Government Services **CN:** U.S. House of Representatives **DOB:** 03/08/1973 **PB:** Waterbury **SC:** CT/USA **MS:** Married **CH:** Four Children **ED:** Sixth-Year Certificate, University of Bridgeport (2014); Master of Arts in Curriculum and Instruction, University of Saint Joseph (2012); Bachelor of Arts, Southern Connecticut State University; Associate's, Naugatuck Valley Community College **C:** Member, U.S. House of Representatives from Connecticut's Fifth District (2019-Present); Teacher, Government and History, John F. Kennedy High School, Waterbury, CT; With, Southbury Training School, Connecticut; Member, Committee on Agriculture; Member, Committee on Education and Labor; Member, Congressional Black Caucus **CR:** Chair, SOAR Review Board, John F. Kennedy High School, Waterbury, CT; Co-adviser, HOPE, John F. Kennedy High School, Waterbury, CT **AW:** Named, Connecticut's Teacher of the Year (2016); Waterbury School District Educator of the Year (2015); John F. Kennedy Teacher of the Year (2015) **PA:** Democrat

HAYES, NICHELLE M., MPA, MLS, T: Leader **I:** Library Management/Library Services **CN:** Center for Black Literature & Culture Indianapolis Public Library **PT:** Sylvia Cleveland Hayes; Ronzo L. Hayes **MS:** Married **SPN:** Robert B. Davis **CH:** Alea Hayes-Davis; Shai Hayes-Davis **ED:** MLS, Indiana University (2011); MPA in Public Personnel Management, Valdosta State University (1998); BS in Human Resources, Valdosta State University (1995) **C:** Invited Guest Speaker, School of Education, Indiana University (2018-Present); Leader, Center for Black Literature & Culture, Indianapolis Public Library (2016-Present); Business Librarian, Indianapolis Public Library (2015-Present); Blogger, The Ties That Blind (2014-Present); Chief Executive Officer, Hayes Consulting (1998-Present); Library Media Specialist, K-5 School, IN (2008-2013); Consultant, National Council on Educating Black Children (2006-2007); Human Resources Recruiter, Indianapolis Power & Light (2002-2005); Human Resources Director, IRL (2001-2003) **CIV:** Board Member, YWCA Central Indiana; Former President, International African American Genealogy Group; President, Indiana Black Librarians Network; Board Member, Greater Indianapolis NAACP; Executive Board Member, Black Caucus of the American Library Association **AW:** Public & Community Service Award, Center for Leadership Development **B/I:** Ms. Hayes became involved in her profession because of her thirst for knowledge and her love of literature.

HAYES, SEAN PATRICK, T: Actor; Comedian **I:** Media & Entertainment **DOB:** 06/26/1970 **PB:** Chicago **SC:** IL/USA **PT:** Ronald Hayes; Mary Hayes **MS:** Married **SPN:** Scott Icenogle (2014) **ED:** Honorary Doctor of Philosophy, Illinois State University (2013); Coursework, Illinois State University **C:** Music Director, Pheasant Run Theatre, St. Charles, IL; Comedian, Second City Improvisational Comedy Group; Stand-up Comedian, Comedy Clubs, Los Angeles, CA and Chicago, IL **CR:** Co-founder, Production Company, Hazy Mills **CW:** Actor, "Lazy Susan" (2020); Actor, "Will & Grace" (1998-2006, 2017-2020); Actor, "Live in Front of a Studio Audience" (2019); Voice Actor, "Tangled: The Series" (2017); Voice Actor, "The Emoji Movie" (2017); Executive Producer, "Grimm" (2011-2017); Actor, "Hairspray Live" (2016); Actor, "Maya & Marty" (2016); Actor, "Crowded" (2016); Executive Producer, "The Soul Man" (2012-2016); Appearance, Executive Producer, "Hot in Cleveland" (2010-2015); Actor, "How Murray Saved Christmas" (2014); Actor, "The Comeback" (2014); Actor, "The Millers" (2014); Voice Actor, "How Murray Saved Christmas" (2014); Actor, Executive Producer, "Sean Saves the World" (2013-2014); Voice Actor, "Monsters University" (2013); Voice Actor, "Monsters University" (2013); Actor, "Smash" (2013); Actor, "Up All Night" (2012); Actor, "Portlandia" (2012); Actor, "Hit and Run" (2012); Actor, "The Three Stooges" (2012); Actor, "Promises, Promises" (2010); Voice Actor, "Cats & Dogs: The Revenge of Kitty Galore" (2010); Voice Actor, "Igor" (2008); Producer, "Man Stroke Woman" (2008); Actor, "Soul Men" (2008); Actor, "The Bucket List" (2007); Executive Producer, "What News?" (2007); Actor, "30 Rock" (2007); Executive Producer, "Stephen's Life" (2005); Executive Producer, "Situation: Comedy" (2005); Actor, "Win a Date with Tad Hamilton!" (2004); Actor, "Pieces of April" (2003); Actor, "The Cat in the Hat" (2003); Actor, "Martin and Lewis" (2002); Actor, "Cats & Dogs" (2001); Actor, "Scrubs" (2001); Voice Actor, "Buzz Lightyear of Star Command: The Adventure Begins" (2000); Actor, "Sin City Spectacular" (1999); Actor, "Billy's Hollywood Kiss" (1998); Actor, "Silk Stalkings" (1996); Actor, "A & P" (1996); Actor, Theater, Television, Films **AW:** SAG Award for Outstanding Performance by a Male Actor in a Comedy Series, Screen Actors Guild - American Federation of Television and Radio Artists (2002, 2003, 2006); SAG Award for Outstanding Performance by an Ensemble in a Comedy Series, Screen Actors Guild - American Federation of Television and Radio Artists (2001); Emmy Award for Outstanding Supporting Actor in a Comedy, Academy of Television Arts & Sciences (2000)

HAYES, WILLIAM J. III, T: Retired **I:** Writing and Editing **CN:** IGA, Inc. **PB:** Delafield **SC:** WI/USA **MS:** Divorced **CH:** Patrick **ED:** Coursework, Information Officers School; Coursework, Cold Weather Training School; Coursework, Nuclear, Biological, Chemical Warfare School; Coursework, Mess Officers School; Diploma, The Basic School, Quantico, VA; BA in Advertising/Journalism, Marquette University **C:** Retired (2004); Editor/Publisher, International Magazine, IGA (1992-2004); Senior Sales Person, Grocery Marketing Magazine, Chicago, IL (1990-1992); Director of National Accounts, Stroh Brewing Company (1982-1990); Director of National Accounts, Schlitz Brewing Company (1980-1982);

Regional Manager, Schlitz Brewing Company, CA (1968-1980); District Manager, Schlitz Brewing Company, Milwaukee, WI (1968-1980) **CIV:** Board of Directors, NROTC Alumni and Friends Association, Marquette University; United Fund **MIL:** Officer, United States Marine Corps (1963-1967); Information Services Officer, HNS Company (1965-1966); Executive Officer, Headquarters and Service Company, Camp Lejeune, NC (1964-1965); Platoon Commander, Camp Lejeune, NC (1963-1964) **MEM:** The American Legion; Board of Directors, Food Market Institute (FMI); Board of Associate Directors, National Association of Convenience Stories (NACS); National Liquor Store Association **AS:** Mr. Hayes was the oldest of seven children in his family, so he was always the first to try anything. He was eager to learn. He was very committed and dedicated to his craft. His education was definitely a big factor in his success. They were very competitive environments. **B/I:** Mr. Hayes always received the best grades in reading and writing. He went to Marquette High School which is prep school for the university. They were given the Cooter Preference Test during junior year. His marks in reading and writing were at the top of the chart. He was also great at art. He had to choose between art or writing. He realized that an art degree would not translate in the bulk in main professions, where journalism fit in different professions. He was also a director of national retail sales for Schlitz Brewing Company from 1980 until 1990.

HAYNES, MARION E., MBA, T: Oil Company Executive (Retired) **I:** Oil & Energy **DOB:** 02/01/1935 **PB:** Avoca **SC:** AR/USA **PT:** Arthur Monroe Haynes; Mary Grace (Snyder) Haynes **MS:** Married **SPN:** Janice Elaine Beebe (09/15/1973); Janice Georgene Lohman (08/01/1965, Deceased 2015); Shirley Ann York (06/06/1954, Deceased 1964) **CH:** Curtis Jerome; Sharman Lynn; Sara Marie **ED:** MBA, New York University (1970); BS, Arizona State University (1956); AA, Phoenix College (1954) **C:** Manager, Pensioner Relations, Shell Oil Company, Houston, TX (1985-1991); Management Development Specialist, Shell Oil Company, New York, NY, Houston, TX (1968-1985); Industrial Relations Specialist, Shell Oil Company, Los Angeles, CA (1967-1968); Division Employee Relations Manager, Shell Oil Company, Ventura, CA (1965-1967); Division Employee Relations Manager, Shell Oil Company, Bakersfield, CA (1960-1965); Employee Relations Generalist, Shell Oil Company, Los Angeles, CA (1956-1960) **CR:** Adjunct Lecturer, Houston Baptist University (1980-1989); Adjunct Lecturer, University of Houston (1975-1980) **CIV:** Board of Directors, International Society for Retirement Planning (1988-1996); President, International Society for Retirement Planning (1991-1993); Board of Directors Sheltering Arms, Houston, TX (1987-1991); Board of Directors, Meyerland Homeowners Association (Now Meyerland Community Homeowners Association), Houston, TX (1989) **CW:** Co-Author, "Comfort Zones" (2005); Author, "Prime Life Guide to Personal Success" (1996); Editor, "The Best of Retirement Planning" (1995); Author, "From Work to Retirement" (1993); Author, "Project Management" (1989); Author, "Effective Meeting Skills" (1988); Author, "Personal Time Management" (1987); Author, "Practical Time Management" (1985); Author, "Managing Performance" (1984); Author, "Stepping up to Supervisor" (1983); Contributor, Articles, Professional Journals **MEM:** Beta Gamma Sigma **MH:** Albert Nelson Marquis Lifetime Achievement Award **AS:** Mr. Haynes attributes his success to dedication to quality performance, hard work, and the support of colleagues and co-workers. **B/I:** Mr. Haynes became involved in his profession because he was born into a large family that was not well-off economically. His

encouragement to get an education came from his high school counselor and the minister at his church. That was his first step in recognizing that regardless of where he came from that educational opportunity existed and he should pursue it. A bachelors degree was the ticket to get an interview with a major organization. Mr. Haynes started college as a chemistry major and was good in science and math and was going to pursue those fields as a career. But it did not allow for sufficient work outside of school to pay the way so he transferred to the business school and chose that as a major. Mr. Haynes was recruited by Shell and spent his career there. **AV:** Family history research; Traveling **PA:** Republican **RE:** Methodist **THT:** Mr. Haynes said, "We have a unique calling to help others along their life's journey and in the process find fulfillment as we travel our own journey. My unique calling was adult education as presented through writing and classroom instruction."

HAYNES, ROBERT V., T: Professor Emeritus; Historian **I:** Education/Educational Services **CN:** Western Kentucky University **DOB:** 11/28/1929 **PB:** Nashville **SC:** TN/USA **PT:** Robert Raymond Haynes; Gladys Haynes **MS:** Widowed **SPN:** Martha Farr (12/25/1952, Deceased) **CH:** Catherine Anne; Carolyn Alice; Charles Allen **ED:** PhD in Philosophy, Rice University, Houston, Texas (1959); MA, Vanderbilt University George Peabody College, Nashville, TN (1953); BA, Millsaps College, Jackson, MS (1952) **C:** Professor Emeritus, Western Kentucky University, Bowling Green, KY (2010); Professor, Western Kentucky University (1984-2010); Vice President of Academic Affairs, Western Kentucky University (1984-1996); Deputy Provost, University Houston, Central Campus, Texas (1981-1984); Associate Provost, University of Houston, Central Campus (1980-1981); Director of Libraries, University of Houston, Central Campus (1978-1980); Interim Director of Libraries, University of Houston (1976-1978); Acting Director, Afro-American Studies, University of Houston (1969-1971); Professor of History, University of Houston (1967-1984); Associate Professor, University of Houston (1962-1967); Assistant Professor, University of Houston (1959-1962); Instructor, University of Houston (1956-1959) **CR:** Board of Editors, Journal of Mississippi History (1965-2010); Member, Advisory Planning Committee, Texas Conference on Library and Information Services (1978-1979); Director, Institute of Cultural Understanding (1971); Visiting Professor, Black Studies Consultant, The University of Alabama (1970) **CIV:** Past Member, Houston United Campus Christian Life Committee (1973-1981); Treasurer, Houston Committee on the Humanities (1978-1979); Past Chairman, Church and Society Committee, Synod of Texas, Presbyterian Church U.S.A. (Now PC (USA)) (1970-1973); Past Member, United Campus Ministry of Greater Houston **MIL:** Served, United States Air Force (1950-1951) **CW:** Editor, "In the Beginning: An Early History of the Presbyterian Church of Bowling Green, Kentucky" (2018); Author, "Bellewood: A Preshy Teriew Haven for Homeless Children" (2012); Author, "The Mississippi Territory and the Southwest Frontier (1795-1817)" (2010); Editor, The Houston Review (1981-1984); Author, "A Night of Violence: The Houston Riot of 1917" (1976); Author, "The Natchez District and the American Revolution" (1976); Contributor, Articles to Professional Journals **AW:** Natchez Literature Award (Now Richard Wright Literary Excellence Award), Natchez Literary and Cinema Celebration (NLCC) (2015); McLemore Prize, Mississippi Historical Society (2010); National Endowment for the Humanities Fellow (1973); Danforth Associate Fellow (1969); Carnegie Fellow, Carnegie Corporation of New York (1952-1953)

MEM: American Historical Association; Organization of American Historians; Southern Historical Association; Mississippi Historical Society; Omohundro Institute of Early American History and Culture; Past Chapter President, Texas Association of College Teachers; Past President, The Honor Society of Phi Kappa Phi **MH:** Albert Nelson Marquis Lifetime Achievement Award; Marquis Who's Who Top Professional **B/I:** Dr. Hayes always loved history. As a matter of fact, he is writing his own autobiography right now. When Dr. Hayes was growing up, he was somewhat lonely, so his parents gave him a book that had pictures of all of the presidents. He was probably 4 or 5 years old and he memorized all the presidents. **PA:** Democrat **RE:** Presbyterian

HAYNIE, FRED HOLLIS, T: Naval Officer, Materials Engineer (Retired) **I:** Engineering **DOB:** 02/08/1932 **PB:** Anniston **SC:** AL/USA **PT:** Fred Hollis Haynie; Mattie Lou (Gannaway) Haynie **MS:** Married **SPN:** Jean (Davis) Haynie (06/15/1955) **CH:** Christie Shook; Joy Ayscue; Steve Haynie; Ginny Ferrell **ED:** MS in Metallurgical Engineering, Ohio State University (1967); MS, Auburn University (1959); BS in Chemical Engineering, Auburn University (1954); Coursework, Georgia Technical University; Coursework, University of Pennsylvania; Coursework, University of Southern California **C:** Consultant in Atmospheric Corrosion, Research Triangle Park, NC (1991-Present); Branch Section, Chief of Environmental Engineering, Environmental Protection Agency, Research Triangle Park, NC (1969-1990); Senior Research Chemical Engineer, Battelle Columbus Laboratories (1964-1969); Engineer, Branch Chief, Naval Air Materials Center, Philadelphia, PA (1960-1964); Branch Chief, Naval Air Materials Laboratory, Philadelphia, PA (1960-1964); Commissioned Ensign, United States Navy (1954) **CIV:** Habitat for Humanity **MIL:** Advanced Through Grades to Captain, United States Navy; United States Naval Reserve **CW:** Contributor, Chapters, Books; Contributor, Articles, Professional Journals **AW:** Sam Tour Award, ASTM International **MH:** Albert Nelson Marquis Lifetime Achievement Award **B/I:** When Mr. Haynie enrolled at Auburn University, the Korean war had begun. In order for him to stay in college at the time, he had to undergo military training. During his military training, he decided the Navy would be a good fit for him. Mr. Haynie received his degree in the Navy and also became a commissioned officer. After his time serving, Mr. Haynie continued his career in the reserves but also continued his education to achieve two master's degrees. **AV:** Analyzing data; Working in yard; Exercising **RE:** Baptist

HAYS, MARILYN PATRICIA, JD, T: Lawyer, Real Estate Executive **I:** Law and Legal Services **DOB:** 09/19/1935 **PB:** Yarrow **SC:** MO/USA **PT:** John Dewey; Ruth McKim Hayes **MS:** Married **SPN:** Harold Clifton Ledbetter (12/13/1953, Divorced 1972) **CH:** Latricia Lyn; Lisa Ledbetter Janyes; David Clifton; Laura Lizanne; Harold Clifton Jr. **ED:** JD, Washburn University (1987); MA, University of Missouri (1983); BS, Missouri State University (1958) **CT:** Certified Broker University of Florida (1976); Licensed Real Estate Broker, Missouri, Kansas, Florida **C:** President of M P Hays Co., Ormond Beach, FL (1994-Present); President of M P Hays Co., Bucyrus, KS (1982-1994); President of M P Hays Co., Olathe, KS (1978-1982); Real Estate Broker, Kellogg Century 21, Daytona Beach, FL (1976-1978); Real Estate Sales Staff, Goldman's Associates, Daytona Beach, FL (1975-1976); Fashion Model (1950-1963); Instructor, Missouri Public Schools (1954-1961); Fashion Coordinator, Ashells and Regina's, Kirksville, MO (1951-1954)

CIV: Junior League of Daytona Beach, FL; Ormond Beach Historical Trust; Adviser, Ormond Beach Hospital Guild; President, Florida Osteopathic Medical Association Auxiliary; Teacher, CCD Holy Rosary Catholic Church, Bucyrus, KS; Parish Council, St Brendan Catholic Church, Ormond Beach, FL; Major Chairman, Association of Junior Leagues, Daytona Beach; Tillandsia Garden Club, Flower Federation garden Club, Incorporated; Member of the Angels, Hillside Cemetery **CW:** Contributor, Articles, Professional Journals **AW:** Outstanding Sales Achievement award, Kellogg Century 21 (1977); Most Successful Graduate Award, Class of 1952 High School 25th Reunion, Kirksville, MO **MEM:** American Association of University Women; American Bar Association; American Quarter Horse Association; Florida Association Women Lawyers; Volusia Flagler Association Women Lawyers; Volusia County Bar Association; Women's Legal Foru; Kansas Bar Association; The Florida Bar; Phi Delta Phi; Alpha Sigma Alpha **BAR:** Kansas; Florida; U.S. Supreme Court **MH:** Albert Nelson Marquis Lifetime Achievement Award **B/I:** Ms. Hays became involved in her profession because she was an instructor to help put her husband through medical school; she then retired from teaching for a while to have children and adopt a child. She went back to work in 1975, although she was not interested in teaching. At that point in her life, she wanted to have more flexible hours, and that is when she got her real estate and real estate brokers license in the 1970s and went to Kansas City, Missouri in the late 1970s to get her master's degree. She was invited to go to law school, which her friends encouraged her to do. She went and became a lawyer. **AV:** Photography; Horseback riding; Antiques; Duplicate bridge **PA:** Republican **THT:** Ms. Hays was the youngest certified teacher in Missouri Public Schools at the age of 18.

HAYWOOD, BETTY, "BJ" JEAN, MD, T: Anesthesiologist **I:** Medicine & Health Care **DOB:** 06/01/1942 **PB:** Boston **SC:** MA/USA **PT:** General Oliver Garfield Haywood Jr.; Helen Elizabeth (Salisbury) Haywood **MS:** Divorced **SPN:** Lynn Brandt Moon (08/29/1969, Divorced 08/1986) **CH:** Kaylin; Kristan; Kelly; Kasy R. **ED:** Graduate Coursework, Air War College, Air University (1997); MBA, Oklahoma City University (1993); Resident in Anesthesiology, The University of Arizona, Tucson, AZ (1972-1974); Resident in Pediatrics, The University of Arizona, Tucson, AZ (1971-1972); MD, University of Colorado (1968); BSc, Tufts University (1964) **CT:** Lean Six Sigma Black Belt (2017) **C:** Instructor, Department of Anesthesia, The University of Oklahoma Health Science Center, Oklahoma City, OK (1999-Present); Staff Anesthesiologist, St. Anthony Hospital, SSM Health, Oklahoma City, OK (1982-2000); Staff Anesthesiologist, South Community Hospital, Oklahoma City, OK (1977-2000); Chief of Anesthesia, Moore Municipal Hospital (1990-1994); Staff Anesthesiologist, Moore Municipal Hospital, (1981-1994); Director, Anesthesia Department, Pima County Hospital, Tucson, AZ (1975-1976) **CR:** Chief, Ethics Committee, Southwest Medical Center (1996) **CIV:** Medical Committee, Planned Parenthood, Oklahoma (1992-1994); Board of Directors, Treasurer, North America South Devon Association, Lynnville, IA (1978-1986) **MIL:** Colonel, United States Air Force Reserve (1968-2007); Colonel, Active Duty, United States Air Force, Operation Enduring Freedom, Wilford Hall Medical Center, Lackland AFB, Texas (2001-2002) **MEM:** U.S. Representative, South Devon World Association (1985, 1988); Treasurer, Chi Omega (1963-1964); American Society of Anesthesiologists (ASA); Representative, Tufts University Alumni Association **MH:** Albert Nelson Marquis Lifetime Achievement

Award **B/I:** Dr. Haywood became involved in her profession during her time in the United States Air Force. The Air Force had a good medical program, and Dr. Haywood was intrigued. She wanted to combine her interest in doing research with her intent on serving the country. As she grew in her career, Dr. Haywood switched to working in a clinical practice. **AV:** Skiing; Sailing **PA:** Republican **RE:** Presbyterian

HAYWOOD, KATHLEEN, "KATHIE" MARIE PHD, T: Professor Emerita **I:** Education/Educational Services **DOB:** 01/03/1950 **PB:** Saint Louis **SC:** MO/USA **PT:** Eugene W. Haywood; Mildred Soric Haywood **ED:** PhD in Physical Education, University of Illinois (1976); MA in Physical Education, Washington University (1973); BA in Psychology, Washington University (1972) **CT:** Certification in Teaching, K-12, Physical Education and Health;Certification in Archery Instruction, National Archery Association **C:** Retired, Professor, Associate Dean, University of Missouri (1976-2018) **CW:** Co-Author, "Advanced Analysis of Motor Development" (2012); Co-Author, "Life Span Motor Development"; Co-Author, "Archery: Steps to Success" **AW:** Mabel Lee Award, American Alliance of Health, Physical Education, Recreation, and Dance (1984); Central District Scholar Award **MEM:** President, North American Society of Psychology of Sports and Physical Activity (1999-2000); Fellow, National Academy of Kinesiology **MH:** Albert Nelson Marquis Lifetime Achievement Award; Marquis Who's Who Top Professional **AS:** Dr. Haywood attributes her success to being task-oriented. She does not let anything get in the way of her finishing a task. **B/I:** Dr. Haywood went into her profession because she wanted to teach and she wanted to influence the curriculum. **AV:** Playing tennis; Dog training; Traveling **RE:** Catholic

HAZARD, JOHN W. JR., T: Secondary School Educator (Retired) **I:** Education/Educational Services **CN:** Cranbrook Schools **DOB:** 06/04/1945 **PB:** Zanesville **SC:** OH/USA **ED:** Postgraduate Coursework, Wayne State University (1973-1978); Postgraduate Coursework, The University of Virginia (1971-1972); MA, Ohio University (1968); BA, Denison University (1967) **C:** Retired (2005); English Teacher, Cranbrook Schools, Bloomfield Hills, MI (1972-2005); English Instructor, The University of Memphis (1968-1971) **CR:** Community Service Developer and Coordinator, Cranbrook Schools (1987-Present) **CW:** Contributor, Poetry, Numerous Magazines **MEM:** Academy of American Poets **MH:** Albert Nelson Marquis Lifetime Achievement Award **B/I:** Mr. Hazard became involved in his profession because of his love of literature. **AV:** Playing guitar; Writing

HAZELIP, LINDA ANN, T: Musician **I:** Education/Educational Services **DOB:** 10/20/1952 **PB:** El Campo **SC:** TX/USA **PT:** Al Gareth Braswell; Annabelle (Black) Braswell **MS:** Divorced **SPN:** Richard Chris Hazelip (07/28/1972, Divorced 1984) **ED:** Diploma in Computer Programming and Data Processing, Massey Business College (1972) **CT:** Certified Teacher, Progressive Series, Intermediate-Level Piano, St. Louis Conservatory of Music (1971) **C:** Community Partnerships Administration, Harris County Department of Education, Head Start (2018-Present); Teacher, Voice, Organ, Piano (2000-Present); Business Owner, Organist, Choirmaster, Pianist, Vocalist, Sacred Occasions and Select Secular Special Occasions, Southeast and Houston, TX (1986-Present); Senior Administrative Assistant, The University of Texas MD Anderson Cancer Center (2016-2018); Secretary, Administrator, Management Assistant, Halliburton, Houston, TX (1991-1996); Executive Secretary, InterFirst

Bank, Post Oak, Houston, TX (1986); Director, Executive Secretary, Exponent Trading Co., Houston, TX (1983-1986); Secretary, St. Andrew's United Methodist Church, Houston, TX (1975-1979); Teacher, Basic Music and Piano (1971-1979); Bookkeeper, Millar Instruments, Houston, TX (1973-1974) **CR:** Organist for Traditional Worship, Southminster Presbyterian Church, Missouri City. TX (2017-Present); Choir Director, Covenant United Methodist Church, Houston, TX (1985-1986); Choir Director, Vocalist, Reid Memorial United Methodist Church, Houston, TX (1985); Organist, Choir Director, Vocalist, Parker Memorial United Methodist Church, Houston, TX (1984-1985); Organist, Vocalist, St. Stephen's United Methodist Church, Houston, TX (1983-1985); Organist, Vocalist, Music Director, St. John's United Methodist Church, Baytown, TX (1980-1984); Organist, Vocalist, Old River Terrace UMC, Channelview, TX (1978-1980); Organist, Vocalist, Pianist, Children's Music Director, Faith United Methodist Church, Houston, TX (1972-1977) **CIV:** First United Methodist Church, Houston, TX (1986-Present); Vocalist, Pianist, Open Door Mission, Houston, TX (1997-2014) **AW:** Woman of the Year, Skyscraper Chapter, ABWA Management LLC (1993-1994) **MEM:** Mu Alpha Theta; National Honor Society; American Guild of Organists; ABWA Management LLC; Choristers Guild **MH:** Albert Nelson Marquis Lifetime Achievement Award **AS:** Ms. Hazelip attributes her success to her Lord and Savior, as well as to her many wonderful mentors and supportive friends. **B/I:** Ms. Hazelip became involved in her profession because of her talent for and enjoyment of providing administrative support to executives and upper-level management in the business sector. Just as well, she is driven by her desire to use her God-given musical talents. **AV:** Taking Holy Land study tours **PA:** Republican **RE:** Methodist **THT:** Ms. Hazelip believes it is only by God's grace that she lives a normal life developing and using the talents given to her. Born with a dislocated hip, a team of doctors from around the world was selected her to try to help. She learned to walk three times before the age of five. At the age of 3, Jesus came to her in a dream and told her that she could walk. With childlike faith, she did walk while continuing her rehabilitation; it was a miracle in medical history. Ms. Hazelip's continual prayer is for her life to be a living testimony of what is possible with God if one believes.

HAZEN, SAMUEL N., T: Chief Executive Officer **I:** Medicine & Health Care **CN:** HCA Healthcare **DOB:** 07/30/1960 **MS:** Married **SPN:** Glenna Hazen **CH:** Luke; John **ED:** MBA, University of Nevada, Las Vegas (1988); Bachelor in Finance, University of Kentucky (1982) **C:** President, Chief Executive Officer, Chief Operating Officer, HCA Healthcare, Inc. (2019-Present); Various Positions, HCA, Inc. (Now HCA Healthcare, Inc.) (1983-Present); President, Chief Operating Officer, HCA Healthcare, Inc. (2017-2019); President, Chief Operating Officer, HCA Holdings Inc. (Now HCA Healthcare, Inc.) (2016-2017); Chief Operating Officer, HCA Holdings Inc. (Now HCA Healthcare, Inc.) (2015-2016); President, Operations, HCA Holdings Inc. (Now HCA Healthcare, Inc.) (2011-2015); President, Western Group, HCA, Inc. (Now HCA Healthcare, Inc.), TN (2001-2011); Chief Financial Officer, Western Group, HCA, Inc. (Now HCA Healthcare, Inc.) (1995-2001); Chief Financial Officer, North Texas Division, HCA, Inc. (Now HCA Healthcare, Inc.) (1994); Various Positions Including Financial Management Training Program, Humana (1983)

HEALY, PATRICIA COLLEEN, T: Social Worker, Retired **I:** Social Work **DOB:** 08/24/1935 **PB:** Denver **SC:** CO/USA **PT:** Cecil John Schulte; Gracia Maude (Walker) Schulte **MS:** Divorced **SPN:** John Patrick Healy III (8/3/1957, Divorced 1972) **CH:** Sean Patrick **ED:** Postgraduate Coursework, University of Kansas (1998); Postgraduate Coursework, Emporia University (1990); Postgraduate Coursework, Wichita State University (1974, 1975, 1989); MSW, University of Kansas (1983); BA, Sacred Heart College, Wichita, KS (1957) **CT:** Licensed Specialist Clinical Social Worker, Kansas **C:** Social Worker, Wichita, KS (2000); Social Worker, VA Medical Center, Wichita, KS (1983-2000); Veterans Benefits Counselor, VARO, Wichita, KS (1973-1983); Ward Clerk, Typist, VA Regional Office, VA Medical Center, Wichita, KS (1970-1973); Self-Employed Typist, Wichita, KS (1966-1970); Clerk, Typist, VA Regional Office, Wichita, KS (1963-1966); Clerk Typist, Air Force, Mcconnell AFB (1962-1963); Clerk Typist, Department of the Army, Fort Leavenworth, KS (1958-1960); Clerk Typist, National Sales, Inc., Wichita, KS (1954-1958); Proofreader, Wichita Publishing Company (1953); Board of Directors, Indiana Living Center of South Central Kansas **CIV:** Clinical Social Work Association (2003-Present); Community Services Advisory Board, Older Adult Alliance (2014-2015); Community Services Advisory Board, Visioneering Wichita (2008-2013); Board of Directors, Indiana Living Center, South Central Kansas (1990-1996); Former Member, Central Plains AAA Council on Aging; Board of Directors, Sedgwick County Department of Aging **CW:** Author, Filmstrip; Author, Columns; Author, Book Revisions; Author, Numerous Stories and Poems **MEM:** Academy of American Poets (2018-Present) **MH:** Albert Nelson Marquis Lifetime Achievement Award **B/I:** Ms. Healy initially began her career as a typist. However, after getting a divorce and dealing with the struggles of being a single parent, she decided to go back to school in pursuit of a degree in social work. She was inspired by her father's service as a religion teacher to the Black community during the height of segregation. He was a wonderful influence on Ms. Healy. She figured social work would be the perfect fit for her giving attitude. **AV:** Writing; Reading; Practicing photography; Listening to music; Knitting; Sewing **RE:** Cathedral of the Immaculate Conception, Tyler, TX

HEATH, MARK, T: Member **I:** Law and Legal Services **CN:** Spilman Thomas & Battle, PLLC **DOB:** 03/18/1961 **PB:** Smyrna **SC:** TN/USA **PT:** David William; Reba Mae Heath **MS:** Married **CH:** Two Daughters **ED:** JD, University of Kentucky College of Law (1986);BA in Journalism and History, Western Kentucky University, Cum Laude (1983) **C:** Member, Spilman Thomas & Battle, PLLC (2003-Present);Member, Heenan, Althen & Roles, LLP (1989-2002) **CR:** Co-Chair, OSHA & MSHA; Treasurer, Trustee, Ann. Institutes Energy & Mineral Law Foundation **CIV:** Board Member, Past Chair, Administrative Council, Elizabeth Memorial United Methodist Church **MIL:** Captain, Assistant Staff, Judge Advocate General's Corps, U.S. Army (1987-1990) **CW:** Contributor, Articles, Professional Journals **AW:** LEL Leadership Development Class, American Bar Association Labor and Employment Section (2016); Listed, Who's Who in America (2004); Recognized in Chambers USA: America's Leading Lawyers for Business for Labor & Employment; Nominated by his Peers for Inclusion in The Best Lawyers in America in the area of Energy Law; Decorated Army Commendation Medal, Fort McPherson, Georgia, Commandant's List, Judge Advocate General's Corps, U.S. Army **MEM:** Employee Co-Chair, Pro Bono and Community Outreach, Labor and Employment Section, American Bar Association; Occupational Safety and Health Law Committee, Section of Labor and Employment Law, Section of Litigation, American Bra Association; Chambers USA; Energy & Mineral Law Foundation; Kentucky Coal Association; Safety Committee, West Virginia Coal Association; Tug Valley Mining Institute; Kentucky Bar Association **BAR:** West Virginia State Bar; Kentucky State Bar; West Virginia Supreme Court of Appeals; Supreme Court of Kentucky; United States Supreme Court; U.S. District Courts for the Northern and Southern Districts of West Virginia; U.S. District Court for the Eastern District of Kentucky; U.S. Courts of Appeals for the Fourth and Sixth Circuits **MH:** Marquis Who's Who Top Professional **AS:** Mr. Heath attributes his success to providing good service to clients and, earlier in his career, working with some good lawyers to learn the area of the practice. **B/I:** Mr. Heath became involved in his profession because he always wanted to be an attorney. He knew since he was a child he wanted to pursue law. Although he did major in journalism in college. he went right to law school after undergraduate studies. **AV:** Traveling; History

HEATH, ROBERT, "BOB" THORNTON, PHD, T: Professor Emeritus **I:** Education/Educational Services **CN:** Kent State University **DOB:** 03/12/1942 **PB:** Chicago **SC:** IL/USA **PT:** Arthur Edwin Heath; Marian (Dillenbeck) Heath **MS:** Married **SPN:** Elizabeth Leigh Buchanan (07/26/1980); Linda Wilbert (08/06/1965, Divorced 06/1975) **CH:** David Edward; Tara Lyn **ED:** Postdoctoral Fellow, University of Georgia, Athens, GA (1975-1976); Postdoctoral Fellow, California Institute of Technology, Pasadena, CA (1968-1970); PhD, University of Southern California (1968); BS, University of Michigan (1963) **C:** Professor Emeritus, Kent State University, Ohio (2008-Present); Director, Water Resources Research Institute, Kent State University, Ohio (1993-2008); Professor, Department of Biological Sciences, Kent State University, Ohio (1970-2008); Resident Fellow, Great Lakes Environmental Research Laboratory, Ann Arbor, MI (1991-1992) **CR:** Member, Advisory Council, Ohio Coastal Resources (1997-Present); Consultant, Sea World Ohio, Solon, Ohio (1980-1981); Member, Advisory Council, Ohio Environmental Protection Agency; Source Water Advisory Group-Lake Erie; USEPA Science Advisory Board Committee: Lake Erie Phosphorus Review Panel **CIV:** Board of Directors, Cleveland Water Alliance (2008-Present); Board of Directors, Chair, Advisory Counsel, Old Woman Creek-National Estuarine Research Reserve, Huron, Ohio (1984-Present); Board of Presidents, Planned Parenthood of Summit, Portage, and Medina Counties, Ohio (2004-2006); Board of Directors, Planned Parenthood of Summit, Portage, and Medina Counties, Ohio (1996-2006); Executive Committee, Ohio Sea Grant (1991) **CW:** Contributor, Articles to Professional Journals; Contributor, Chapters to Books; Presenter in Field **AW:** Research Grantee, National Oceanographic and Atmospheric Administration (NOAA) (1986-2010); Ohio Lake Erie Award, Ohio Lake Erie Commission (2008); Anderson Everett Award, International Association for Great Lakes Research (2005, 2008); Research Grantee, United States Army Corps of Engineers (1982-1986) **MEM:** President, International Association for Great Lakes Research (2009-2010); President, The Ohio Academy of Science (2003-2004); Vice President, Ecology, The Ohio Academy of Science (1989-1991); Fellow, Cooperative Institute for Limnology and Ecosystem Research; American Association for the Advancement of Science; American Society of Limnology and Oceanography; Former Member, Ecological Society of America; Former Member, The American Society for Microbiology; Former Member, The Ohio Academy of Science; International Association for Great Lakes Research **MH:** Albert Nelson Marquis Lifetime Achievement Award **B/I:** Dr. Heath's father was a scientist, and he was his chief inspiration. From the time he was very young, his father was a lecturer at the Museum of Science and Industry in Chicago, IL, so he grew up in that museum. **AV:** Bonsai **PA:** Democrat **RE:** Presbyterian

HECK, DENNY LYNN, T: U.S. Representative **I:** Government Administration/Government Relations/Government Services **DOB:** 07/19/1952 **PB:** Vancouver **SC:** WA/USA **MS:** Married **SPN:** Paula Fruci (1976) **CH:** Bob; Trey **ED:** Coursework, Portland State University (1974-1975); BA, The Evergreen State College (1973) **C:** U.S. Representative, Washington's 10th Congressional District, United States Congress, Washington, DC (2013-2019); U.S. House Committee on Financial Services (2013-Present); Chief Executive Officer, TVW Television Network (1993-2003); Chief of Staff, Governor Booth Gardner, State of Washington (1990-1993); Minority Leader, Washington House of Representatives (1977-1985); Member, District 17, Washington House of Representatives (1976-1986); Member, House Permanent Select Committee on Intelligence; Co-Founder, Intrepid Learning Solutions **CR:** Board Director, Intrepid Learning Solutions (1999-2012) **CIV:** Board Member, Washington State History Museum; Trustee, The Evergreen State College; Member, Steering Committee, Washington Learns Commission **CW:** Author, Play, "Our Times" (2008); Author, "The Enemy You Know" (2002); Author, "Challenges and Opportunities: The Transformation of Washington's Schools" (1987) **PA:** Democrat

HECKMAN, JAMES JOSEPH, PHD, T: Professor; Economist **I:** Education/Educational Services **CN:** The University of Chicago **DOB:** 04/19/1944 **PB:** Chicago **SC:** IL/USA **PT:** John Jacob Heckman; Bernice Irene (Medley) Heckman **MS:** Married **SPN:** Lynne Pettler-Heckman (1979) **CH:** Jonathan Jacob; Alma Rachel **ED:** Honorary Doctorate, Pontifical University, Chile (2009); Honorary Doctorate, University of Montreal (2004); Honorary LHD, Bard College (2004); Honorary Doctorate, Mexico State Autonomous University (2003); Honorary Doctorate, University of Chile (2002); Honorary LLD, Colorado College (2001); PhD in Economics, Princeton University, NJ (1971); MA in Economics, Princeton University, NJ (1968); BA in Mathematics, Colorado College, Summa Cum Laude (1965) **C:** Director, Economics Research Center, The University of Chicago (1997-Present); Henry Schultz Distinguished Service Professor, Economics, The University of Chicago (1995-Present); Director, Center Program Evaluation, Harris School of Public Policy, The University of Chicago (1991-Present); Henry Schultz Professor, Economics, The University of Chicago (1985-1995); Professor, Economics, The University of Chicago (1976-1985); Associate Professor, Economics, The University of Chicago (1973-1976); Lecturer, Then Associate Professor, Columbia University (1970-1974); Aerospace Systems Engineer, Martin Marietta Corporation (1968) **CR:** Alfred Cowles Distinguished Visiting Professor, Yale University (2008-Present); Professor, Science and Society, University College Dublin (2006-Present); Senior Research Fellow, American Bar Foundation (1991-Present); Senior Research Associate, National Bureau of Economics Research (1977-1985, 1987-Present); Distinguished Chair, Microeconometrics, University College London (2004-2008); A. Whitney Griswold Professor, Economics, Yale University (1988-1990); Irving Fisher Professor, Economics, Yale University (1984); Research Associate, National Bureau of Economics Research (1970-1977) **CW:** Editorial Board, Journal of Applied Econometrics (2007-Present); Author, Editor, "Global Perspectives on the Rule of Law" (2010); Author, Editor, "Law and Employment: Lessons from Latin America and the Caribbean" (2004); Author, Editor, "Inequality in America: What Role for Human Capital Policy?" (2003); Author, Editor, "Longitudinal Analysis of Labor Market Data" (1985); Co-Author, Editor, "Handbook of Econometrics," Numerous Editions; Contributor, Articles to Professional Journals **AW:** Dan David Prize for Combating Poverty, Tel Aviv University (2016); Frisch Medal, The Econometric Society (2014); Spirit of Erikson Award (2014); Distinguished Contribution to Public Policy for Children Award, Society Research in Child Development (2009); Theodore W. Schultz Award, American Agricultural Economics Association Foundation (2007); Sun Yefang Economic Science Award (2007); Dennis J. Aigner Award for Applied Econometrics, Journal of Econometrics (2005, 2007); Ulysses Medal, University College Dublin (2006); Jacob Mincer Award for Lifetime Achievement, Society of Labor Economists (SOLE) (2005); Medal of Excellence, Center of Excellence for Children's Well-Being, Montreal University (2004); Statistician of the Year, American Statistical Association (2002); Nobel Prize in Economics (2000); Louis T. Benezet Distinguished Alumnus Award, Colorado College (1985); John Bates Clark Medal, American Economic Association (1983) **MEM:** Fellow, American Association for the Advancement of Science; Fellow, The Econometric Society; Fellow, American Academy of Arts. & Sciences; Fellow, Society of Labor Economists (SOLE); Fellow, Chicago Chapter, American Statistical Association; Fellow, International Statistical Institute; National Academy of Sciences; American Economic Association; American Philosophical Society; National Academy of Education; Life Member, Irish Economic Association; The Phi Beta Kappa Society

HECKMANN, RICHARD ANDERSON, T: Zoology Educator **I:** Education/Educational Services **DOB:** 12/07/1931 **PB:** Salt Lake City **SC:** UT/USA **MS:** Married **SPN:** Karen **CH:** Lisa; Nancy; Amy; Adam; Camille **ED:** Postgraduate Coursework, University of Utah (1985-1986); Postgraduate Coursework, Imperial College, England (1976); PhD in Zoology, Montana State University (1970); Postgraduate Coursework, University of California Berkeley (1963-1966); Postgraduate Coursework, University of Washington (1963); Postgraduate Coursework, University of Hawaii (1960-1961); Postgraduate Coursework, University of Pacific (1959); Postgraduate Coursework, University of California Davis (1958-1960); MS in Zoology, Utah State University (1958); BS in Zoology, Utah State University (1954) **C:** Professor Emeritus, Brigham Young University, Provo, UT (2002-Present); Assistant Professor, California State University Fresno (1970-1972); Teaching Assistant, Montana State University (1968-1970); Instructor, Contra Costa College (1962-1967); Teaching Assistant, University of California (1959-1961); Research Assistant, University of California (1958-1959); Teaching Assistant, Utah State University (1957) **CR:** Fulbright Professor, Egypt (2001); Alumni Professor, Brigham Young University (1995-1997); Visiting Professor, University of Ain Shams, University of Cairo, Egypt (1996); Visiting Professor, National Academy of Sciences, USSR, Poland (1989); Consultant, NARL Nielsen, Maxwell & Wangsgaard Engineers, Noorlander Corp. (1979, 1980); Consultant, BLM Deep Creek Mountains and Big Creek Impact Studies, Vaughn Hansen Associates (1978); Consultant, Diking Utah Lake Proposal Team (1976); Consultant, Westinghouse Electric Corp. (1974, 1975, 1976); Consultant, Central Utah Project (1974); Lecturer, California State University Fresno (1970); Consultant, Niagara Chemical Co. (1964, 1965, 1967); Consultant, U.S. Forest Service (1962); Director, Research Team to Guatemala **MIL:** First Lieu-tenant, United States Army (1954-1959); Honorable Discharge, Germany and Utah National Guard **CW:** Author, "Healing and Bacteriocidal Properties of Selected Herbal Extracts" (1988); Co-author, "Atlas of Animal Parasites" (1974); Editorial Board, California Fish and Game Magazine (1974); Editorial Board, Journal on Wildlife Diseases (1974); Author, "Laboratory Manual for Biology Part I and II" (1966); Patentee in Field; Contributor, Numerous Professional Journals; Contributor, Reviews, Dissertations for Pakistan **AW:** Silver Beaver Award, Boy Scouts of America (1989); Honored by Farmer to Farmer Program, USAID (1988, 1989); Grantee, Nevada Division of Wildlife Resources (1986, 1987, 1988-1989); Grantee, Binational Agricultural Research Development Fund (1986, 1987, 1988, 1989); Grantee, Brigham Young University (1987-1989); Grantee, Schering Corp. (1984); Grantee, Utah Power and Light (1979); Grantee, Naval Arctic Research Laboratory, University of Alaska (1979); Grantee, Arizona Fuels Corp. (1977, 1978, 1979); Grantee, Utah Division of Wildlife Resources (1975, 1978, 1979); Grantee, Westinghouse Corp. (1976); Faculty Research Awards (1972, 1973, 1974, 1975); Grantee, National Science Foundation (1971, 1972, 1975); Fellow, National Science Foundation (1963, 1966); Pauley Research Fellow (1960, 1961); Carl Raymond Grey Scholar (1950) **MEM:** American Institute of Fishery Research Biologist; Society of Protozoologist; Society of Parasitologists; Fish Health Section, Fish Culture Section, Public Committee, Chairman, Professional Standards Committee, Member, Endangered Species Committee, American Fisheries Society; World Malocologist's Society; Utah Public Health Association; SEM and EDAX Electron Microscopy **MH:** Albert Nelson Marquis Lifetime Achievement Award **B/I:** Dr. Heckmann admired the research of a professor at Utah State Dr. Deim Hammond, he was world renown for his work. After Dr. Heckmann got out of the service he asked if he would sponsor him and he said yes. **AV:** Hiking; Fishing **PA:** Republican **RE:** LDS

HEDRICK, STEVEN B., T: Chairman, Chief Executive Officer **I:** Business Management/Business Services **CN:** MATRIC, Inc. **SC:** WV/USA **MS:** Married **SPN:** Lana **CH:** Eli; Grant **ED:** Coursework in Three-Week EMBA Program, University of Notre Dame (2004); BS in Chemical Engineering, United States Military Academy at West Point (1989-1993) **C:** Chairman, Chief Executive Officer, Appalachia Development Group, LLC (2018-Present); Chairman, Chief Executive Officer, MATRIC, Inc., LLC (2013-Present); Vice President, Head, Institute Industrial Park, Bayer CropScience (2010-2013); Head, Director, Bayer Material Science, HSEQ-OS (2001-2010) **CIV:** Board Chairman, Charleston Area Alliance Board; Board Vice President, Advantage Valley; Board Member, Discover Real West Virginia Foundation; Board Member, West Virginia Chamber of Commerce; Board Member, West Virginia Manufacturers Association; Board Member, Clay Center for the Arts and Sciences of West Virginia **MIL:** Captain, U.S. Army (1993-1999) **AW:** Inter-Regional Government Tucker Award (2019); West Virginia Executive Magazine Sharp Shooter **MEM:** American Institute of Chemical Engineers (AIChE); Business Round Table of West Virginia **AS:** Mr. Hedrick was notoriously dissatisfied with the status quo growing up. He was stubborn, and nothing was ever good enough for him. Seeking an opportunity to improve life around him, he knew he had no choice but to be successful. **B/I:** Mr. Hedrick wanted to serve the United States, which inspired him to enlist in the United States Army. He was inspired by his father and uncles, all of whom excelled in the U.S. Air Force. However, he always had an interest in chemical engineering as well.

Thanks to his high school teacher, Shirley Kelley, and Billy Smith, his anatomy and physiology instructor, Mr. Hedrick decided to pursue the field.

HEEGER, ALAN JAY, PHD, T: Physicist, Professor Emeritus **I:** Education/Educational Services **CN:** UC Santa Barbara **DOB:** 01/22/1936 **PB:** Sioux City **SC:** IA/USA **PT:** Peter J. Heeger; Alice (Minkin) Heeger **MS:** Married **SPN:** Ruthann Chudacoff (08/11/1957) **CH:** Peter S.; David J. **ED:** Honorary DSc, University of Alicante, Spain (2006); Honorary DSc, Trinity College, The University of Dublin (2005); Honorary DSc, University of Nebraska (1999); Honorary PhD, Abo Akademie University, Finland (1998); Honorary Doctorate in Technology, Linköping University, Sweden (1996); Honorary DSc, University of Mons, Belgium (1993); PhD in Physics, University of California Berkeley (1961); BA, University of Nebraska, with High Distinction (1957); Honorary DSc, Bar Ilan University, Israel; Honorary Doctorate, Japan Advanced Institute of Science & Technology; Honorary DSc, Southern China University of Technology **C:** Professor Emeritus, UC Santa Barbara (2000-Present); Director, Institute for Polymers and Organic Solids, UC Santa Barbara (1983-2000); Professor of Physics, UC Santa Barbara (1982-2000); Acting Vice Provost of Research, University of Pennsylvania (1981-1982); Director, Research, Laboratory Structure of Matter, University of Pennsylvania (1974-1981); Professor of Physics, University of Pennsylvania (1966-1982); Associate Professor, University of Pennsylvania (1964-1966); Assistant Professor, University of Pennsylvania (1962-1964) **CR:** Co-Founder, Vice-Chairman, CytomX Therapeutics, Inc. (2006-Present); Co-Founder, Chairman, CBritu, Inc., Santa Barbara, CA (2005-Present); Co-Founder, Chief Scientist, Konarka Technologies, Inc., Lowell, MA (2001-Present); Founder, President, UNIAX Corporation, Santa Barbara, CA (1990-1994); Morris Loeb Lecturer, Harvard University (1973) **CW:** Author, "Never Lose Your Nerve" (2014); Editor-in-Chief, Synthetic Metals Journal (1983-2000); Contributor, Scientific Articles to Professional Journals **AW:** Italgas Prize, Eni Inc., Italy (2007); Co-Recipient, Nobel Prize in Chemistry (2000); President Medal, University of Pennsylvania (2000); Balzan Prize, Balzan Foundation, Italy/Switzerland (1995); John Scott Medal, City of Philadelphia, PA (1989); Buckley Prize for Solid State Physics, American Physics Society (1983); Alfred P. Sloan Fellowship **MEM:** Fellow, American Physics Society; National Academy of Engineering; National Academy of Sciences; Foreign Member, Korean Academy of Sciences **AV:** Skiing

HEES, BERNARDO VIEIRA, T: Chief Executive Officer **I:** Food & Restaurant Services **CN:** Kraft Heinz Company **ED:** MBA, University of Warwick, England; BA in Economics, Pontifícia Universidade Católica, Rio de Janeiro **C:** Chief Executive Officer, The Kraft Heinz Company (formally known as H.J. Heinz Co.), Pittsburgh, PA (2013-Present); Partner, 3G Capital Partners Ltd. (2010-Present); Chief Executive Officer, Burger King Holdings, Inc., Miami, FL (2010-2013); Chief Executive Officer, America Latina Logistica (2005-2010); Director, Superintendent, America Latina Logistica (2004); Operational Planning Manager, Chief Financial Officer, Commercial Officer, America Latina Logistica (2004); Chief Operating Officer, America Latina Logistica (2003); Vice President, Marketing, America Latina Logistica (2002-2003); Logistics Analyst, America Latina Logistica (1998-2000); With, Banco Marka (1995-1996); With, Shell Brazil; With, Banco Marka Nacional de Desenvolvimento Econômico e Social

CR: Board of Directors, Burger King Holdings, Inc. (2010-2013); Board of Directors, America Latina Logistica (2005-2010)

HEGDAL, RUTH MARGARET, T: Accountant, Retired CPA **I:** Financial Services **DOB:** 07/30/1931 **PB:** Seattle **SC:** WA/USA **PT:** Floyd Owen Payne; Ruth Margaret (Stevens) Payne **MS:** Married **SPN:** John R. Hegdal **CH:** Ian; Steven; Suzanne; Patricia; David **ED:** MBA, University of Alaska (1970); BA, University of Alaska (1969) **CT:** Certified Public Accountant, Washington **C:** Director, Small Business Management Program, Wenatchee Valley College (1987-Present); Private Practice Accounting, Oroville, WA (1974-1987); Assistant Professor, University of Alaska (1970-1974); Bookkeeper, Seattle First National Bank, Okanogan, WA (1974); Bookkeeper, Citizen's National Bank, Los Angeles, CA (1949) **CR:** CPA Private Practice, Weston, OR (2001-2017); Instructor, Wenatchee Valley College North Campus (1985-1999) **MEM:** Washington State Society CPA's **MH:** Albert Nelson Marquis Lifetime Achievement Award **B/I:** Ms. Hegdal, the daughter of an accountant, started out as a book keeper at age 16 although she did not actually attend college until she was in her mid-30's. She eventually ran the books for two stores, one of which required her to travel 13 hours away from home by bus for three days a week. Encouraged by her husband, she began school and was encouraged by faculty to begin to teach and so she pursued her masters and her CPA certificate so that she could achieve that. **AV:** Horse breeding; House and costume designing; Acting; Singing

HEGE, LINDA, T: Nurse (Retired) **I:** Medicine & Health Care **DOB:** 09/01/1945 **PB:** Lexington **SC:** NC/USA **PT:** Olin Grady; Kate Vivian (Walser) Hege **ED:** Bachelor of Science in Nursing, Lenoir Rhyne College (1967) **CT:** Medical Surgeon; ED; Certified Diabetes Educator **C:** Clinical Instructor, Forsyth Technical Community College, Winston-Salem, NC (1991-2011); Member, North Carolina Task Force National Disaster Medical Systems (1989-2011); Member, Special Operations Response Team Nurse (1988-2011); Patient Educator, CI Salem Family Practice (1994-2000); Associate Director, Forsyth Memorial Hospital, Winston-Salem, NC (1982-1994); Instructor, Forsyth County Heart Association, Winston-Salem, NC (1983); Lecturer, North Carolina Licensed Practical Nurse Association, Durham, NC (1982); Clinical Specialist, Forsyth Memorial Hospital, Winston-Salem, NC (1980-1982); Nursing Educational Instructor, Forsyth Memorial Hospital, Winston-Salem, NC (1980); Lecturer, Mitchell College, Statesville, NC (1979-1980); Assistant Head Nurse, Forsyth Memorial Hospital, Winston-Salem, NC (1975-1980); Staff Nurse, Forsyth Memorial Hospital, Winston-Salem, NC (1974-1975); Lecturer, Forsyth Technical Community College, Winston-Salem, NC (1970-1975); Assistant Head Nurse, Forsyth Memorial Hospital, Winston-Salem, NC (1969-1973); Staff Nurse, Forsyth Memorial Hospital, Winston-Salem, NC (1967-1969) **CIV:** Volunteer, Head Nurse, Shalom Project Clinic Remarkable 45 (2011-Present); Board Member, Triad Dream Center (2011-Present) **AW:** National Disaster Medical System Award; Volunteer of the Year, Shalom Project **MEM:** Representative, North Carolina Task Force on National Disaster Medical System, District III North Carolina Nurses Association (1990-Present); Chairman, Advisory Committee, Person-to-Person Program, United Way of Forsyth County (1989-Present); Loan Executive, United Way of Forsyth County (1988-Present); Chairman, Special Projects, District III North Carolina Nurses Association (1984-1989); American Nurses Association **MH:** Albert Nelson Marquis Lifetime Achievement Award **AS:**

Ms. Hege attributes her success to the support she received from her physicians and co-workers. **B/I:** Ms. Hege became involved with the profession of nursing due to a childhood aspiration to enter the field. **AV:** Reading; Swimming; Candlewicking **RE:** Methodist

HEGE, MIKE, MRE, T: Realtor **I:** Real Estate **CN:** Pridemore Properties **ED:** MA in Real Estate, REALTOR® University (2015); BBA, Gardner-Webb University (2006); AS in Registered Nursing, Central Piedmont Community College (2004) **CT:** Accredited Buyer's Representative (ABR®); Graduate, REALTOR® Institute (GRI), National Association of REALTORS®; GREEN Designation, National Association of REALTORS®; Certified Relocation Professional (CRP®), Worldwide ERC®; Military Relocation Professional (MRP); Residential Construction Certified™ (RCC) **C:** Owner, Real Estate Broker, Pridemore Properties Real Estate (2005-Present); Nursing, Carolinas Medical Center (Now Atrium Health) (1999-2004) **CIV:** Fundraiser Volunteer, Honor Home Program, Homes For Our Troops (2019-Present); Chair, Charlotte Regional Realtor® Association (2009-Present) **AW:** Five Star Real Estate Agent Award, Five Star Professional (2018, 2019); Vane Mingle Rookie of the Yea Award, Charlotte Regional Realtor® Association (2005); Dave Ramsey Endorsed Local Provider, Lampo Licensing, LLC **MEM:** Residential Real Estate Council; Knights of Columbus **AS:** Mr. Hege attributes his success to his determination to never stop learning; he values being adaptable and coachable in his profession. He also prioritizes being a reliable source for his clients when representing them in order to maximize their returns. Mr. Hege's business success relies on referrals, so the firm's reputation is of utmost importance to him. His approach to work and life is to move, ethically, one step at a time. **B/I:** Mr. Hege became involved in his profession over a long period of time. He began his career as a nurse, working nights in the emergency room. As he reflected on his father, who spent 40 years in a career he did not enjoy, he decided that working for the sake of supporting his family was not enough for him. Soon after he welcomed his first child, he was presented a real estate opportunity from which he never looked back. It was the perfect fit he'd been waiting for. Mr. Hege expresses gratitude to Scott Pridemore, his mentor and business partner to this day, for shepherding his real estate journey.

HEIDEN, ERIC ARTHUR, MD, T: Former Olympic Speed Skater; Former Professional Cyclist; Orthopedic Surgeon **I:** Athletics **DOB:** 06/14/1958 **PB:** Madison **SC:** WI/USA **MS:** Married **SPN:** Karen Drews (1995) **CH:** Zoe **ED:** Resident in Orthopedics, University of California, Davis (1996); MD, Stanford Medicine (1991); BS, Stanford University (1984); Coursework, University of Wisconsin - Madison **C:** Team Physician, U.S. Olympic Speed Skating Team (2002, 2006, 2010, 2014); With, Sports Clinic, Birmingham, AL (1997); Professional Speed Skater, Winter Olympics, Lake Placid, NY (1980); Professional Speed Skater, Winter Olympics (1976); Founding Member, 7-Eleven Cycling Team; Founder, Heiden Orthopaedics, Utah; Founder, The Orthopedic Specialty Hospital, Intermountain Healthcare, Murray, Utah; Team Physician, Sacramento Kings, NBA and Sacramento Monarchs, WNBA; Orthopedic Surgeon, Sacramento, CA **CW:** Co-author with Massimo Testa, MD, "Faster, Better, Stronger" (2008) **AW:** Named One of the 50 Greatest Athletes of the 20th Century (1999); Named to United States Bicycling Hall of Fame (1999); Named to Wisconsin Athletic Hall of Fame (1990); Winner, U.S. Professional Cycling Championship (1985); Named to U.S. Olympic Hall of Fame (1983);

Five-time Gold Medalist, Olympics (1980); James E. Sullivan Award, Amateur Athletic Union (1980); Named Athlete of the Year, United Press International (1980); Oscar Mathisen Award (1977-1980)

HEIDUCK, DONALD, "DONNIE" FRED, T: Law Enforcement Officer, Ranger **I:** Government Administration/Government Relations/Government Services **DOB:** 09/27/1956 **PB:** Cheyenne **SC:** WY/USA **PT:** Howard Fred Heiduck; Lillian Marie Stansbury Heiduck **MS:** Married **SPN:** Heather Dawn Heiduck **CH:** Ashley Victoria Wolf; Thomas Andrew Wolf; Sean Ryan O'Connor **ED:** BS in Administration of Justice, University of Wyoming (1992); AA in Criminal Justice, Laramie County Community College (1990); AA in History, Laramie County Community College (1985); AA in Anthropology, Laramie County Community College (1978) **CT:** Certified Deputy Coroner (1996-Present); Peace Officer's Standards and Training Certified Practitioner Lecturer (1996-Present); Qualified Witness, U.S. Federal Court **C:** Law Enforcement Ranger, Wyoming Parks (2019-Present); Adjunct Instructor, Laramie County Community College (2001-Present); Deputy Coroner, Laramie County Coroner's Office (1996-Present); Sheriff's Department, Laramie County (1993-2019); Reserve Deputy Sheriff, Laramie County (1987-1993); Adjunct Instructor, Chadron State College; Guest Lecturer, Wyoming Law Enforcement Academy; Security Officer, Teller Supervisor, Bookkeeping Supervisor, Equity Bank; Patrolman, Cheyenne Police Department; Police Dispatcher, Cheyenne Police Department **CR:** Co-Team Captain, National SWAT Competition (2008-2009); Operation Falcon, Operation Jessica, Operation No Joke, United States Marshal's Task Force; Warrant and Sex Offender Verification Task Force, U.S. Marshals Service **CIV:** Special Olympics; The Salvation Army; Empty Stocking Fund, Wyoming Tribune Eagle; Stamp Out Hunger Food Drive, USPS; Jail-in-Bail, March of Dimes; Blood Drive, Guns-n-Hoses; Judge, We the People **AW:** Lifesaving Award, Law Enforcement Officer of the Year, VFW Department of Wyoming (2019); Nominee, 100 Years of Eagle Scouts Publication (2012); Nominee, Community Service Award, Laramie County Community College Foundation (2010); Nominee, Outstanding Board Member, Laramie County Community College (2004, 2009); Employee Community Hero Award, Laramie County (2008); Nominee, Outstanding Young Men of American (1982, 1986); National Honor Society (1974-1975); E-Club in Basketball, Football and Track (1972-1975); Intramural Champion (1972-1975); Nominee, Civilian Youth Seminar (1974); Eagle Scout Award, Boy Scouts of America (1972); Community Service Award; Meritorious Service Commendation, Sheriff's Department, Laramie County; Lifesaving Commendation, Sheriff's Department, Laramie County; Community Service Commendation, Cheyenne Police Department; Honor Camper Award **MEM:** Vice President, The Arc of Laramie County; Treasurer, Vice President, Crime Stoppers Silent Witness of Laramie County; Vice President, President, Needs Inc.; Secretary, Local Chapter, The Salvation Army; ILEETA; Youth Alternatives Scholarship Selection Committee; Board Member, Historical Committee, Scholarship Committee, Wyoming Peace Officers Association; Chaplain, Treasurer, Wyoming Fraternal Order of Police; Vice President, Scholarship Committee, Laramie County Peace Officers Association; Board of Directors, Finance Committee, Development Committee, Laramie County Community College Foundation; Vice President, President, Rocky Mountain Division, International Association for Identification; Vice Chairman, Credit Union Compliance and Security Adviser, Cheyenne-Laramie County Employees Federal Credit Union; Presi-

dent, Laramie County Youth Development and Drug Education Board; American Criminal Justice Association; President, Scholarship Chairman, DUI Victim's Impact Panel; Law Enforcement Torch Run Committee, Special Olympics; Junior Leadership Board, Laramie County; Southeast Wyoming Search and Rescue Team **BAR:** Unauthorized Practice of Law Committee (2019-present); Proctor, Wyoming State Bar Exam (2018-Present) **AS:** Mr. Heiduck attributes his success to his parents, his wife and the opportunities he has been afforded throughout his life. **B/I:** Mr. Heiduck became involved in his profession because he wanted to follow in his father's footsteps. **RE:** Christian

HEILE, JOHN DAVID, T: Stockbroker **I:** Financial Services **DOB:** 04/16/1955 **PB:** Quebec City **SC:** QC/Canada **PT:** James E. Heile; Elaine (Ibold) Heile **ED:** BA in History, University of Cincinnati (1982) **C:** Retired Stockbroker, Ross, Sinclaire & Associates, LLC, Cincinnati, Ohio (1987-Present); Investment Broker, Legg Mason Investor Services, LLC, Cincinnati, Ohio (1983-1987); Owner, Manager, Trinities, Mobile, AL (1975-1980) **CR:** Board of Directors, Murdock Inc., Cincinnati, Ohio; Board of Directors, Caters of Tampa, Inc., FL; Board of Directors, Associated Outdoor Clubs, Inc. **CIV:** Fundraiser Explorers, Boy Scouts of America; Member, Ohio Republican Party **CW:** Contributor, Articles to Cincinnati Business Courier **MH:** Albert Nelson Marquis Lifetime Achievement Award **B/I:** Mr. Heile was fascinated with the stock market even in college. In 1974, the market was at a big low and he remembers seeing Mobil Oil asking if it was really a 9% yield, and there was talk about nationalizing the oil companies. People said that it might not be around. Mr. Heile thought he would take 9% any day, and that is where his interest started. In addition, the stock market was attractive to him and he was fascinated with it because he was buying gasoline when he was a teenager. He thinks it was Mobil. He called somebody up, someone older than him, a mentor, and Mr. Heile said, "Can I invest in Mobil?" and their reply was, "Yeah". Way back then, it had about a 7% yield, and they also said that "oil companies could be nationalized," however, Mr. Heile thought it would be great that he could get 7% on the dollar. So, that is how the fascination began. Also, the ability to buy into American industry and make a profit was fabulous. So, he thought, 'you can dig a ditch all day long or you could press a button and make the same amount of money. If you are smart, you would press the button instead of getting the shovel.' He chose to press the button. **AV:** Boating; Snow skiing; Trap shooting; Softball; Shooting skeet; Softball; Ice hockey **RE:** Roman Catholic

HEILICSER, BERNARD JAY, T: Emergency Physician **I:** Medicine & Health Care **DOB:** 01/19/1947 **PB:** New York **SC:** NY/USA **PT:** Murray; Esther (Dubrow) Heilicser **MS:** Married **SPN:** Marcia Cherry (06/02/1976) **CH:** Micah; Seth; Jacob **ED:** Doctor of Osteopathic Medicine, Des Moines University, Des Moines, IA (1976); Master of Science, Hahnemann University Hospital, Drexel University, Philadelphia, PA (1971); Bachelor of Arts, State University of New York at Binghamton, Binghamton, NY (1968) **CT:** Diplomate, American Board of Emergency Medicine **C:** Medical Director, EMS, South Cook County, Harvey, IL (1984-Present); Emergency Physician, Ingalls Hospital, Harvey, IL (1983-Present); Emergency Physician, Michael Reese Medical Center, Chicago, IL (1989-1991); Emergency Physician, St. Margaret Hospital, Hammond, IN (1979-1983); Assistant Professor of Emergency Medicine, Chicago College of Osteopathic Medicine, Midwestern University, Downers Grove, IL (1979); Staff Physician, Virginia Polytech-

nic Institute and State University, Blacksburg, VA (1977-1978); Instructor of Anatomy and Physiology, Hahnemann University Hospital, Drexel University, Philadelphia, PA (1971-1973) **CR:** Adjunct Assistant Professor, Neiswanger Institute for Bioethics and Healthcare Leadership, Stritch School of Medicine, Loyola University Chicago, Chicago, IL (2017-Present); Adjunct Assistant Professor, International Medical Corps' Emergency Response Team (2013-Present); Deputy Medical Director, Deputy Commander, Illinois Medical Emergency Response Team (2008-Present); Medical Adviser, Combined Agency Response Team (1999-Present); Member, Executive Council, Illinois Medical Emergency Response Team (1999-Present); Member, Ethics Committee, American College of Osteopathic Emergency Physicians (1997-Present); Chairperson, Disaster Committee, Region VII EMS, Emergency Medical Services (1997-Present); Chairperson, Ethics Committee, Ingalls Memorial Hospital, Harvey, IL (1994-Present); Faculty, Trauma Nurse Specialist, St. James Hospital, Chicago Heights, IL (1980-Present); Chairperson, Region VII EMS Advisory Council (2001-2004); Member, Adjunct Faculty, College of Health and Human Services, Governors State University, Chicago, IL (1999-2001); Member, Faculty, Chicago College of Osteopathic Medicine (1987-1999); Consultant, National Board of Osteopathic Medical Examiners, Harvey, IL (1994-1995); Fellow, MacLean Center for Clinical Medical Ethics, University of Chicago, Chicago, IL (1993-1994); Nurse Practitioner Preceptor, Purdue University Northwest, Hammond, IN (1981-1990) **CIV:** Lead Physician, Manager, Medical Team, Illinois Urban Search and Rescue Task Force (2004-Present); Volunteer Fireman, Flossmoor Fire Department, Flossmoor, IL (1985-Present); Volunteer, Matteson Fire Department, Matteson, IL (1980-1990) **CW:** Author, Featured Newspaper Articles, Local Papers, The Chicago Tribune; Columnist, Column, Emergency Medicine Magazine; Contributor, Articles to Professional Journals; Contributor, Numerous Chapters in Books **AW:** Distinguished Fellow, American College of Osteopathic Emergency Physicians (ACOEP) (2014-Present); Robert D. Aranosian Award for Excellence in EMS, American College of Osteopathic Emergency Physicians (2008); Behind the Scenes Award, Emergency Nurses Association (2009); Emergency Nursing Award, Illinois Nurses Association (2001); Special Recognition Award, Metropolitan Chicago Healthcare Council (1992) **MEM:** Fellow, American College of Emergency Physicians; American College of Osteopathic Emergency Physicians; American Osteopathic Association; National Association of EMS Physicians; National Association of Emergency Medical Technicians; Sigma Sigma Phi **AS:** Dr. Heilicser attributes her success to his spiritual beliefs and the love and support of his family. **B/I:** Dr. Heilicser became involved in his profession because he saw a lot of medical issues in his family growing up and wanted to dedicate himself to helping those who are sick. He found himself attracted to emergency medicine due to the excitement of it and the challenge of never knowing what is coming next. **AV:** Running; Basketball **RE:** Jewish **THT:** Follow your beliefs and strive to do what is right for humanity

HEILMANN, FLEMMING, T: Director **I:** Manufacturing **CN:** Whitlock Packaging Corporation **DOB:** 04/26/1936 **SC:** Malaysia **PT:** Poul Bent Heilmann; Hedvig Buchwald (Moller) Heilmann **MS:** Married **SPN:** Judith Lucy Tucker (09/15/1973) **CH:** Christian; Nicholas; Claire; Per; Niels **ED:** MA, University of Cambridge, England, United Kingdom (1957) **C:** Director, Board of Directors, Whitlock Packaging Corporation, OK (1998-2004); New York Representative, Danes Worldwide (1996-2001);

Chairman, Chief Executive Officer, Brockway Standard, Inc., Atlanta, GA (1989-1995); Director, President, Chief Executive Officer, American Can Canada, Inc. (Now Onex Packaging Inc.), Rexdale, Canada (1984-1989); Executive Vice President, Chief Administrative Officer, Continental Group, Inc., Stamford, CT (1981-1984); President, Continental Diversified Industries, Inc., Stamford, CT (1980-1981); President, Continental Group Europe, Brussels, Belgium (1978-1980); Vice President, Continental Can Company, Stamford, CT (1977-1978); Trustee, National Development and Management Foundation, South Africa (1970-1975); Managing Director, Chief Executive Officer, Metal Box South Africa Ltd., Johannesburg, South Africa (1970-1977); Director, Legal and General Insurance Company of South Africa (1972-1976) **CR:** Member, Advisory Council, University of Toronto Business School (Now University of Toronto Rotman School of Management) (1985-1992); Board of Directors, O'Shaughnessy Funds, Inc., Porter Chadburn PLC, Porter Chadburn, Inc. **CIV:** Chairman, Advisory Board, Danish American Cultural Exchange (2017-Present); Chairman, Advisory Board, Jacob A. Riis Museum, Ribe, Denmark (2016-Present); Chairman Emeritus, Jacob A. Riis Settlement, Inc., New York, NY (2012-Present); Trustee, The American-Scandinavian Foundation (1998-Present); Board of Directors, Jacob Riis Settlement, Inc. (1996-Present); Co-chair, Jacob Riis Exhibition Project 2014, Museum of the City of New York (2011-2017); Chairman, Board of Directors, Jacob Riis Settlement, Inc. (2006-2012); Exchange Program, Ribe Cathedral School, Denmark (2006); Member, Council, Cornell University (1996-2000, 2002-2006); Trustee, Paul Smith's College, St. Regis, NY (1999-2005); Danish American Coordinating Council of Greater New York (1991-2003); Board of Directors, Cambridge in America (1996-2002); Director, American Friends of Cambridge University (Now Cambridge in America) (1996-2001); President, Danish American Society (1996-2001); Attache Paralympic Games, Danish Sport Organization for Disabled, Atlanta, GA (1995-2001); Director, Danish American Society (1991-2001); Sponsor, Danish Documentary "Flash of a Dream" (1998); Speaker, Annual July Fourth Rebild Festival, Denmark (1997); Trustee, The American-Scandinavian Foundation (1996); Endowed Annual Scholarship, University of Copenhagen (1996); U.S. Representative, National Olympic Committee, Denmark (1993-1996); Second Term President, Danish Society, Johannesburg, South Africa (1973-1976); President, Danish Society, Johannesburg, South Africa (1965-1967); Established, Jacob Riis Settlement Youth; Volunteer, Danish American Community **CW:** Author, "The Unacceptable Face," Telemachus Press (2019); Author, "Odyssey Uncharted – A World War II Childhood Adventure and Education Wrapped in Mid-20th Century History," Telemachus Press (2017) **AW:** Elevated to Knight of the Order of Dannebrog First Rank (2013); Ellis Island Medal of Honor (2001); Named Knight, Order of Dannebrog (1998); Wilkins Fellowship, University of Cambridge Downing College (1999) **MEM:** Board of Directors, Danish-American Society (1990-2003); President, Danish-American Society (1996-2001); Director, Danish-American Chamber of Commerce (1995-2001) **MH:** Albert Nelson Marquis Lifetime Achievement Award; Marquis Who's Who Top Professional **B/I:** Mr. Heilmann was trained and educated as a lawyer and interested in being a barrister, but his parents had financial hardships because of WWII. He was responsible for his own finances at age of 14. Apprenticeship as a barrister cost too much money, so he had to work and went into industry. **PA:** Independent

HEIMBURGER, IRVIN LEROY, MD, T: Surgeon (Retired) **I:** Medicine & Health Care **CN:** Evansville Surgical Associates **DOB:** 09/28/1931 **PB:** Tsinan **SC:** China **PT:** LeRoy Francis Heimburger; Margaret Coleman (Smith) Heimburger **MS:** Married **SPN:** Marcia Jean Enlow (06/30/1963) **CH:** Angela R.; Jeffrey L.; Christian I. Heimburger; Jenny E. Heimburger Henneberger **ED:** Thoracic Fellowship, Leeds University Hospital (1963-1964); Residency in Surgery, Indiana University Health (1958-1963); Internship, Vanderbilt University Hospital (1957-1958); MD, Vanderbilt University (1957); BA, Drury University (1953) **CT:** Diplomate, American Board of Surgery; Diplomate, American Board of Thoracic Surgery **C:** Medical Staff, Deaconess Health System (1966-1998); Medical Staff, St. Mary Medical Center (1966-1998); Instructor, Clinical Associate Professor, Indiana University Hospital (1964-1980) **CR:** Registrar, Leeds General Infirmary (1963-1964) **CIV:** President, Vanderburgh County Medical Society (1977-1978) **CW:** Contributor, Archives of Surgery, Journal of Thoracic and Cardiovascular Surgery, Annals of Surgery, American Review of Respiratory Diseases, Journal of the Indiana State Medical Association **AW:** Champion of Champions, American Philatelic Society (2008) **MEM:** President, Indiana Chapter, American College of Surgeons (1977-1978); Central Surgical Association; International Society for Cardiovascular Disease Prevention; The Society of Thoracic Surgeons; Midwest Surgical Association; American Philatelic Society; Beta Iota Chapter, Kappa Alpha Order **MH:** Albert Nelson Marquis Lifetime Achievement Award; Marquis Who's Who Top Professional; Marquis Who's Who Humanitarian Award **AS:** Dr. Heimburger attributes his success to his faith and wonderful mentors. **B/I:** Dr. Heimburger became involved in his profession because he was inspired by his father and older brother both of whom were physicians. **PA:** Conservative **RE:** Christian

HEINRICH, MARTIN TREVOR, T: U.S. Senator **I:** Government Administration/Government Relations/Government Services **DOB:** 10/17/1971 **PB:** Fallon **SC:** NV/USA **PT:** Peter C. Heinrich; Shirley A. (Bybee) Heinrich **MS:** Married **SPN:** Julie Heinrich **CH:** Carter; Micah **ED:** BSc in Mechanical Engineering, University of Missouri (1995); Postgraduate Coursework, Community and Regional Planning Program, The University of New Mexico **C:** U.S. Senator, State of New Mexico (2013-Present); U.S. Senate Committee on Energy and Natural Resources (2013-Present); U.S. Senate Select Committee on Intelligence (2013-Present); U.S. Joint Economic Committee (2013-Present); U.S. Representative, New Mexico's First Congressional District, United States Congress (2009-2013); U.S. House Armed Services Committee (2009-2013); U.S. House Committee on Natural Resources (2009-2013); President, Albuquerque City Council (2006); Member, Albuquerque City Council (2003-2007); Natural Resources Trustee, State of New Mexico; With, U.S. Fish and Wildlife Service, AmeriCorps; With, Phillips Laboratories (Now Air Force Research Laboratory), Kirkland Air Force Base **CIV:** Founder, Public Affairs Consulting Firm (2002); Executive Director, Cottonwood Gulch Foundation (1996-2001); Board Member, Southeast Heights Neighborhood Association; Board Member, New Mexico Wilderness Alliance; Member, Open Space Advisory Board, City of Albuquerque **CW:** Appearance, Television Special, "Rival Survival" (2014) **PA:** Democrat **RE:** Lutheran

HEINSOHN, THOMAS, "TOM" WILLIAM, T: Professional Basketball Broadcaster; Former Professional Coach; Former Professional Player **I:** Athletics **DOB:** 08/26/1934 **PB:** Jersey City **SC:** NJ/USA **PT:** William B. Heinsohn; Bessie (Paul) Heinsohn **MS:** Married **SPN:** Diane Regenhard (09/02/1956) **CH:** Donna Marie; Paul T.; David **ED:** BSBA, Holy Cross College (1956) **CT:** Chartered Life Insurance Underwriter **C:** Commentator, CBS Sports, New York, NY (1980-Present); Coach, Boston Celtics, National Basketball Association (NBA) (1969-1978); Professional Basketball Player, Boston Celtics, National Basketball Association (NBA) (1956-1965); Life Insurance Underwriter, Boston, MA (1956) **AW:** Named (as Coach), to Naismith Memorial Basketball Hall of Fame (2015); Chuck Daly Lifetime Achievement Award, NBA Coaches Association (2009); Jack McMahon Award, National Basketball Coaches Association (1995); Named (as Player) to Naismith Memorial Basketball Hall of Fame (1986); Named NBA All-star Game Head Coach (1972-1974, 1976); Named NBA Coach of the Year (1973); Named NBA All-star (1957, 1961-1965); NBA Champion (1957, 1959-1965); Named to All-NBA Second Team (1963-1964); Named NBA Rookie of the Year (1957) **AV:** Painting; Playing golf

HELBERT, MICHAEL, T: Lawyer **I:** Law and Legal Services **DOB:** 12/30/1950 **PT:** Robert Lee Helbert; Carrollyn Jean (Stull) Helbert **MS:** Married **SPN:** Sandra Sue Ziegler Helbert (08/26/1978) **CH:** Michael; Ryan **ED:** Doctor of Jurisprudence, University of Kansas, Lawrence, KS (1975); Bachelor of Arts, University of Kansas, Lawrence, KS (1972) **C:** Private Practice, Helbert & Allemans, Emporia (1998-Present); Elected Member, Kansas Justice Initiative Commission (1997-Present); Principal, Emporia (1981-1997); Predecessor Firms, Emporia (1978-1981); Associate Law Firm, Atherton, Hurt & Sanderson, Emporia, KS (1975-1977); Intern, Douglas County Legal Aid, Lawrence (1974-1975); Partner, Helbert & Bell **CIV:** Chairman, Emporia Recreation Commission (2014-Present); Bench-Bar Committee (2007-Present); Member, School Board, United School District #253 (2007-2018); Treasurer, Lyon County Representative Central Committee (1986-1994); United Way Emporia (1978); Kansas University Endowment Association (1977-1981); Chairperson, Professional Division; Kansas Bar Association; Advisory Board; Paul Harris Fellow **CW:** Contributing Author, "Kansas Trial Lawyers Journal" (2007-2018) **AW:** Super Lawyers for Kansas of Missouri (2016-2020); Who's Who in the World (2011); Client Champion, Martindale-Hubbell; Top 100 National Trial Lawyers **MEM:** Fifth Judicial Nominating Committee, Lyon Chase County Bar Association (2000-Present); Board of Governors (1988-Present); President, Emporia Sunrise Rotary (2006-2007); President, Kansas Trial Lawyers Association (2000-2001); Vice President, Kansas Trial Lawyers Association (1997-1999); President, Lyon-Chase County Bar Association (1984); Director, Emporia Chamber of Commerce; Vice Chairperson, Emporia Chamber of Commerce; American Association for Justice **BAR:** U.S. Court of Appeals for the Tenth Circuit (1984); Supreme Court of the United States (1980); U.S. District Court for the District of Kansas (1975); Kansas (1975) **MH:** Albert Nelson Marquis Lifetime Achievement Award **B/I:** Mr. Helbert became involved in his profession due to the influence of his family, which always valued education. The first member of his family to graduate from college, he drew inspiration from legal dramas he had seen on television. **PA:** Republican **RE:** Presbyterian

HELIAS, VIRGINIE, T: Chief Sustainability Officer **I:** Cosmetics **CN:** Proctor & Gamble **ED:** MBA in Marketing, HEC Paris (1988) **C:** Non-executive Director, Chairman of the Sustainability Committee, Verallia (2019-Present); Chief Sustainability Officer, Proctor & Gamble (2016-Present); Global

Sustainability Director, Proctor & Gamble (2012-2016); Sustainability and Digital - Household Care, Proctor & Gamble (2011-2012); Marketing Director, Ariel Franchise, WE, Proctor & Gamble (2003-2011); Marketing Director, Feminine Care, WE, Proctor & Gamble (2001-2003); Marketing Director, Global Laundry - Developed Regions, Proctor & Gamble (1997-2001); Brand Management, Fabric Care, Baby Care and Hair Care, Proctor & Gamble (1988-1997) CIV: Advisory Steering Committee, Sustainable Brands (2020-Present); Advisory Board Member, APPAREAL (2019-Present); Co-Chair, Sustainable Lifestyle Working Group, World Business Council for Sustainable Development AV: Marathon running

HELLER, MARIELLE STILES, T: Actress, Director I: Media & Entertainment DOB: 10/01/1979 PB: Marin County SC: CA/USA PT: Steve Heller; Annie Heller MS: Married SPN: Jorma Taccone CH: Wylie Red Heller-Taccone ED: Diploma, Saint Joseph Notre Dame High School, Alameda, CA (1997); Coursework, University of California Los Angeles; Coursework, Royal Academy of Dramatic Art, London, England C: Actress, The Magic Theatre; Actress, The American Conservatory Theater; Actress, Berkeley Repertory Theatre; Actress, La Jolla Playhouse CR: Lynn Auerbach Screenwriting Fellowship; Maryland Film Festival Fellowship CW: Director, "A Beautiful Day in the Neighborhood" (2019); Director, "Can You Ever Forgive Me?" (2018); Director, "Casual" (2016); Actress, "Popstar: Never Stop Never Stopping" (2016); Actress, "Paper Anchor" (2016); Director, Writer, "The Diary of a Teenage Girl" (2015); Director, "Transparent" (2015); Actress, "A Walk Among the Tombstones" (2014); Actress, "MacGruber" (2010); Actress, "Single Dads" (2009); Actress, "All-For-Nots" (2008); Actress, "Awesometown" (2005); Actress, "The Liberation of Everyday Life" (2004); Actress, "Spin City" (2002); Actress, "White Power" (2001); Actress, "Peninsula"; Actress, "Much Ado About Nothing"; Actress, "King Lear"; Actress, "Hamlet"; Actress, "Continental Divide"

HELMS, BETTYANN S., T: Principal, Designer I: Architecture & Construction CN: Interiors by Betts; American Society of Interior Design (ASID) PB: Cleveland SC: OH/USA MS: Married SPN: Wade Farley Helms CH: Christina Stefanski; Ben Stefanski III; Ben Stefanski IV; Bridget Long; Luke Stefanski ED: BS in Interior Design, Case Western Reserve University (CRWU) (1964) CT: Certification, American Society of Interior Designers (ASID) C: Principal, Interiors by Betts (1969-Present); Past President, American Society of Interior Design (ASID) (2001-2002); Published Author, Numerous Articles, Professional Journals CR: Shaker Lakes Regional Nature Center (SLRNC): Past Chairman, House Committee; Intown Club of Cleveland; National Judge, General Electric; Nela Park Lighting Institute; Junior League of Cleveland; Past Chairman, Designer's Showhouse; American Cancer Society: Past Chairman, Designer's Showhouse; Designer, Multiple Showhouse Rooms; Designer, Theatres at Playhouse Square, Cleveland, OH; Designer, Row Houses on Prospect; Coordinator, Designer's Showhouse; Liaison, American Society of Interior Design (ASID); Liaison, American Cancer Society CIV: Junior League of Cleveland; Past Chair, Investment Club; Past Chair, VIP Cookbook; Hospitalier, Sovereign Order of St. John Knights (SOSJ): Past Commander, Vocational Guidance Services; Trustee Emeritus, Past Chairman, Annual Meetings and "Come for Lunch" Committees; Golden Age Centers of Cleveland; Cleveland Ballet; Past Board Member, Bratenahl Foundation AW: Presidential Citations for Distinguished Work; Citation, American Society of Interior Designers MEM:

Union Club of Cleveland; Shoreby Club; Sovereign Order of St. John (SOSJ); Junior League; American Society of Interior Designers AS: Ms. Helms attributes her success to finding creative solutions on time and remaining within budget. Likewise, she credits staying on top of her profession with continuing education. She was the first in her field to combine antiques with modern design. B/I: While planning to go to medical school, Ms. Helms took an elective course in interior architecture. She loved it and continued to study the field, graduating three years later. AV: Oil painting; Traveling; Playing pickleball; Practicing Sudoku; Investing; Gardening

HEMINGER, GARY R., T: Chief Executive Officer, Chairman I: Business Management/Business Services CN: Marathon Petroleum Corporation ED: MBA, University of Dayton (1982); Bachelor's Degree in Accounting, Tiffin University (1976) C: Chairman, Chief Executive Officer, Marathon Petroleum Corporation (2017-Present); Chairman, Chief Executive Officer, Mplx LP (2012-Present); President, Chairman, Chief Executive Officer, Marathon Petroleum Corporation (2011-2017); Executive Vice President Downstream, Marathon Oil Corporation (2005-2011); Executive Vice President, Marathon Oil Corporation (2001-2005); Executive Vice President of Supply Trans. & Marketing, Marathon Ashland Petroleum LLC (2001); Senior Vice President, Business Development, Marathon Ashland Petroleum LLC (1999-2001); Vice President, Business Development, Marathon Ashland Petroleum LLC (1998-1999); Manager, Business Development & Joint Interest, Marathon Oil Corp. (1996-1998); Vice President, West Division Speedway Superam., Marathon Oil Corp. (1991-1995); Management Positions, Marathon Oil Corp., Houston, TX (1976-1991) CR: Chairman, Downstream Committee, American Petroleum Institute; Oxford Institute of Energy Studies; Board of Directors, Fifth Third Bancorp. CIV: Chairman, Board of Trustees, Tiffin University

HEMSWORTH, CHRIS, T: Actor I: Media & Entertainment DOB: 08/11/1983 PB: Melbourne SC: Australia PT: Craig Hemsworth; Leonie (van Os) Hemsworth MS: Married SPN: Elsa Pataky (12/26/2010) CH: India Rose; Tristan; Sasha CW: Actor, Producer, "Extraction" (2020); Actor, "Avengers: Endgame" (2019); Actor, "Men in Black: International" (2019); Appearance, "Jay and Silent Bob Reboot" (2019); Actor, "Bad Times at the El Royale" (2018); Actor, "Avengers: Infinity War" (2018); Actor, "12 Strong" (2018); Actor, "Thor: Ragnarok" (2017); Actor, "Doctor Strange" (2016); Actor, "Ghostbusters" (2016); Actor, "The Huntsman: Winter's War" (2016); Actor, "In the Heart of the Sea" (2015); Actor, "Vacation" (2015); Actor, "Avengers: Age of Ultron" (2015); Host, "Saturday Night Live" (2015); Actor, "Blackhat" (2015); Actor, "Thor: The Dark World" (2013); Actor, "Rush" (2013); Actor, "Star Trek into Darkness" (2013); Actor, "Red Dawn" (2012); Actor, "Snow White and the Huntsman" (2012); Actor, "The Avengers" (2012); Actor, "The Cabin in the Woods" (2011); Actor, "Thor" (2011); Actor, "Ca$h" (2010); Actor, "Star Trek" (2009); Contestant, "Dancing with the Stars" (2006); Actor, "Home and Away" (2004-2007); Actor, "The Saddie Club" (2003); Actor, "Guinevere Jones" (2002); Actor, Television Shows, Films AW: Award for Favorite Movie Actor, Kids' Choice Awards (2017); Named Sexiest Man Alive, People Magazine (2014); Award for Favorite Action Movie Actor, People's Choice Awards (2013, 2016); Award for Best Fight, MTV Movie Awards (2013); Choice Summer Male Movie Star, Teen Choice Awards (2012)

HENDERSON, RICKEY HENLEY, T: Former Professional Baseball Player; Former Professional Baseball Coach I: Athletics DOB: 12/25/1958 PB: Chicago SC: IL/USA PT: John L. Henley; Bobbie Henley Henderson; Paul Henderson (Stepfather) MS: Married SPN: Pamela Palmer (1983) C: Special Instructor, Oakland Athletics, Major League Baseball (MLB) (2010); First Base Coach, New York Mets, Major League Baseball (MLB) (2007-2010); First Base Coach, New York Mets, Major League Baseball (MLB) (2007); Retired Professional Baseball Player, Major League Baseball (MLB) (2007); Special Instructor, New York Mets, Major League Baseball (MLB) (2006-2007); Outfielder, San Diego Surf Dawgs, Golden Baseball League (2005); Outfielder, Los Angeles Dodgers, Major League Baseball (MLB) (2003); Outfielder, Newark Bears, Atlantic League (2003); Outfielder, Boston Red Sox, Major League Baseball (MLB) (2002); Outfielder, San Diego Padres, Major League Baseball (MLB) (2001); Outfielder, Seattle Mariners, Major League Baseball (MLB) (2000); Outfielder, New York Mets, Major League Baseball (MLB) (1998-2000); Outfielder, Oakland Athletics, Major League Baseball (MLB) (1998); Outfielder, Anaheim Angels, Major League Baseball (MLB) (1997); Outfielder, San Diego Padres, Major League Baseball (MLB) (1995-1997); Outfielder, Oakland Athletics, Major League Baseball (MLB) (1993-1995); Outfielder, Toronto Blue Jays, Major League Baseball (MLB) (1993); Outfielder, Oakland Athletics, MLB (1989-1993); Outfielder, New York Yankees, Major League Baseball (MLB) (1984-1989); Outfielder, Oakland Athletics, Major League Baseball (MLB) (1979-1984); Draft Pick, Oakland Athletics, Major League Baseball (MLB) (1976) AW: Named to National Baseball Hall of Fame, Baseball Writers' Association of America (2009); Winner, Toronto Blue Jays, World Series Championship (1993); Named to American League All-star Team (1980, 1982-1988, 1990-1991); Named American League MVP (1990); Named to American League Silver Slugger Team, Sporting News (1981, 1985, 1990); Named American League Championship Series MVP (1989); Winner, Oakland Athletics, World Series Championship (1989); Golden Shoe Award, Sporting News (1983); Silver Shoe Award (1982); Golden Glove Award, American League (1981)

HENDRICKS, AILEEN ALANA, PHD, T: Theater Educator, Scholar, Director, Actress I: Fine Art CN: Louisiana Voices of Women Theatre Company DOB: 01/20/1940 PB: Bronx SC: NY/USA PT: Edwin Vincent Hendricks; Mary Frances (Taaffe) Hendricks MS: Married SPN: Donald Luke Couvillion; Robert William Wenck (01/03/1960, 04/21/1993) CH: August William II; Robert William, Jr. ED: PhD in Theater, Speech and English, Louisiana State University, Baton Rouge, LA (1988); MA in English and Theater, Texas A&M University, College Station, TX (1974); BA in English and Theater, Texas A&M University, College Station, TX (1971); Coursework, The University of Texas at Austin, Austin, TX (1966-1968) C: Tenured Professor, Department of Speech and Theater, Southern University, Baton Rouge, LA (2007-2013); Tenured Associate Professor, Departments of Visual and Performing Arts, Speech and Theater Section, and English, Southern University, Baton Rouge, LA (1999-2006); Assistant Professor, Departments of Visual and Performing Arts, Speech, Theater and English Sections, Southern University, Baton Rouge, LA (1995-1999); Instructor, Departments of Visual and Performing Arts, Speech and Theater Sections, Southern University, Baton Rouge, LA (1991-1995); Teacher of Drama and Speech, Sherwood and Glasgow Middle Schools, East Baton Rouge Parish School Board, Baton Rouge, LA (1990-1991); Assistant Professor, Communication and Theater Department, McNeese State University, Lake Charles, LA (1989-1990); Instructor, Speech Department, Nicholls State University, Thibodaux, LA (1988-1989); Teaching Assistant of Reading, Junior Division, Louisiana State University, Baton Rouge, LA (1987-1988); Theater Research and Teaching Assistant, Speech Department, Louisiana State University, Graduate Teaching Assistant, English Department, Louisiana State University, Baton Rouge, LA (1984-1986); Half-Time Instructor, English, Louisiana State University, Baton Rouge, LA (1983-1984); Three-Quarter-Time Instructor, Speech Department, Louisiana State University, Baton Rouge, LA (1981-1982); Graduate Assistant, Speech Department, Louisiana State University, Baton Rouge, LA (1978-1981); Consultant, Creative Dramatics, Conducting Workshops for Public School Teachers, Under a Grant from Texas Theater Council, Austin, TX (1976-1977) **CR:** Director of Premiere Players, Summer Theater Program for Teenagers, Department of English, Theater Arts Section, Texas A&M University (1974-1977); Half-Time Instructor, Theater Arts and English, Texas A&M University, College Station, TX (1974-1977); Graduate Assistant, Department of English, Texas A&M University, College Station, TX (1972-1974) **CIV:** YWCA (2003-2005,1995-Present); Women's Council of Greater Baton (1995-Present); Elected Vice President, Baton Rouge Council on Human Relations (2012); Social Justice Committee, Unitarian Church, Baton Rouge, LA (2009-2012); Facilitator, Governor's Capital Area Regional Conference for Louisiana's Women Leaders Statewide (2005); Active Participant, Secretary on the Board of Directors, Working Interfaith Network (2003-2005); Representative, Women's Council of Greater Baton Rouge, Community Action in Neighborhoods Developing Opportunities (2003); Steering Committee, Breakfast Committee, Women's Council of Greater Baton Rouge (2002); Facilitator, Baton Rouge 2000 Town Meeting, Centroplex, Baton Rouge, LA (2000); Create Baton Rouge Committee, Women's Council of Greater Baton Rouge (1998-1999); Harmony **CW:** Producer, One-Woman Show, "Haircrownicles" by Medina Perine, Red Shoes, Baton Rouge, LA (2018-2019); Performer, Readings of "Sirens" from "Ulysses" by James Joyce for the Irish Club of Baton Rouge at City Park Gallery of Baton Rouge (2018); Teaching, Acting Workshop for Women's Council of Greater Baton Rouge's Week-Long Celebration of Women (2018); Performer, Lynne in "Love, Loss, and What I Wore" by Nora and Delia Ephron, Produced by Red Magnolia Theater Company, Baton Rouge, LA (2018); Director, "Women on Fire" by Irene O'Garden, Theater Baton Rouge Studio (2018); Presenter, Session, "Using Women's Theater for Social Change," Justice Alliance Conference, Unitarian Church of Baton Rouge (2018); Costumer, "Blues for an Alabama Sky" by Pearl Cleage, Department of Theater, Frank Hayden Hall Theater, Southern University, Baton Rouge, LA (2012); Writer, Producer, Director, Play, "Seven Ages of Woman," Elizabeth Dent and LA VOW Theater Company, Woman's Club, Inc., Baton Rouge, LA (2009); Director, "The Story" by Tracy Scott Wilson, Department of Speech and Theater, Frank Hayden Hall Fine Arts Theater, Southern University, Baton Rouge, LA (2009); Director, "The Importance of Being Earnest" by Oscar Wilde, Department of Speech and Theater, Frank Hayden Hall Fine Arts Theater, Southern University, Baton Rouge, LA (2008); Writer, Reviser, Producer, Director, Performer, "Everywoman," Unitarian Church of Baton Rouge, LA (2007); Director, Presenter, Performer, "The Past-Reviving the Dead Ladies," Women Louisiana State Convention (2005); Writer, Reviser, Producer, Director, Performer, Two-Act Play, "Why Celebrate Women?" (2003); Director, "A Christmas Carol" by Charles Dickens, Beechwood Elementary School, Scotlandville, LA (2003); Writer, Two-Act Play, "Why Celebrate Women" (2002-2003); Co-Managing Editor, Blackstream (1997); Co-Author, Three-Act Play, "Cries That Bind Echoing in the Silence" **AW:** Silver Magnolia Award, Women's Council of Greater Baton Rouge (2014); Working Interfaith Network Service Award for 11 Years of Service as Secretary of the Board of Directors (2006); Most Distinguished Board Member Award, Working Interfaith Network (2006); Humanitarian Award (2006); Baton Rouge Council on Human Relations (2006); Women and Theatre Service Award for 20 Years of Membership and 10 Years of Service as a Treasurer (2004); Numerous Research Projects and Grants **MEM:** Founding Artistic Director, Board President, Louisiana Voices of Women Theater Company (2013); Board Member, Women's Council of Greater Baton Rouge (1994); The Society for Support of the Performing Arts; Board Member, American Association of University Women; WORTH; Irish Club of Baton Rouge; American Society for Theater Research; Black Theater Network; Southwest Teacher Association; Association of Theater in Higher Education; Black Theater Association; American Association of University Professors; American Association of University Women; American Society for Theatre Research; American Theatre and Drama Society; Association for Theatre in Higher Education; The Honor Society of Phi Kappa Phi; Irish American Cultural Institute **AS:** Dr. Hendricks attributes her success to God, her faith, women role models throughout history, the opportunities she has been afforded and her loving husband, Donald Luke Couvillion. **B/I:** Dr. Hendricks became involved in her profession because she loved theater. She never thought she would be a teacher since she wanted to be the world's greatest actress, but she discovered in college that she really loved to learn and was also a good teacher. **AV:** Reading poetry; Pursuing Irish-American studies; Traveling **PA:** Democrat **RE:** Roman Catholic **THT:** Dr. Hendricks states, "Believe in yourself and follow your dreams. Life is a physical, spiritual and intellectual journey that we have to be ready to adapt to and change according to the circumstances. Life is change and learning. When we cease to learn, we cease to live. Money and power are meant to be used for the good of everyone. Love is truly the greatest commandment."

HENDRICKS, DIANE MARIE, T: Co-Founder, Chairperson **I:** Business Management/Business Services **CN:** ABC Supply **SC:** WI/USA **MS:** Widowed **SPN:** Ken Hendricks (Deceased) **CH:** Seven Children **ED:** Diploma, Osseo-Fairchild High School (1965) **C:** Co-Founder, Chairperson, ABC Supply (1982-Present); Realtor (1975) **CIV:** Donor, WisconsinEye; Co-Chair, Rock County 5.0; Board Member, Stateline Boys and Girls Club, Beloit Memorial Hospital, Beloit Foundation, Forward Janesville, Kandu Industries, Blackhawk Bank, Hendricks Family Foundation; Board of Trustees, Beloit College **CW:** Producer, "Snowmen" (2010); Producer, "An American Carol" (2008); Producer, "The Stoning of Soraya M." (2008) **AW:** Listee, America's Richest Self-Made Women, Forbes (2018) **PA:** Republican

HENLEY, CHARLES E., T: Founding Dean **I:** Education/Educational Services **CN:** Sam Houston State University **MS:** Married **CH:** One Child **ED:** DO, Oklahoma State University College of Osteopathic Medicine, Tulsa, OK (1977); MPH in Epidemiology and Biostatistics, University of Hawaii Office of Public Health, Honolulu, Hawaii (1983); MS in Biochemistry, University of Oklahoma Health Sciences Center, Oklahoma City, OK (1974); BS in Chemistry, Northeastern State University, Tahlequah, OK (1971) **CT:** Licensed, Oklahoma State Board of Osteopathic Examiners (1997); Licensed, Texas State Board of Medical Examiners (1997); Licensed, Commonwealth of Virginia Department of Health Regulatory Boards (1980); Licensed, State of Indiana **C:** Founding Dean, Sam Houston State University College of Osteopathic Medicine, Huntsville, Texas (2016-Present); Founding Associate Dean for Clinical Affairs and Professor of Family Medicine, Marian University, Indianapolis, IN (2011-2016); Professor and Vice-Chair, Department of Family Medicine, The University of Oklahoma - Tulsa College of Medicine, School of Community Medicine, Tulsa, OK (2004-2011); Founders and Associates Endowed Chair for Clinical Research, The University of Oklahoma - Tulsa School of Community Medicine, Tulsa, OK (2004-2011); Professor and Chairman, Department of Family Medicine, Oklahoma State University College of Osteopathic Medicine, Tulsa, OK (1997-2004); Full Member, Group VI Biomedical Sciences Graduate Faculty, Oklahoma State University College of Osteopathic Medicine (2003-2007); Chairman, Department of Family and Community Medicine, U.S. DeWitt, Army Community Hospital (1990-1994); Director of Emergency Services, U.S. DeWitt, Army Community Hospital (1990-1994); Clinical Associate Professor, Department of Family Medicine, F. Edward Hebert School of Medicine, Uniformed Services University of the Health Sciences, Bethesda, MD (1990-1994); Clinical Assistant Professor, School of Public Health and Community Medicine, University of Washington School of Medicine, Seattle, WA (1989-1990); Clinical Assistant Professor, Department of Family Medicine, University of Washington School of Medicine, Seattle, WA (1986-1990); Program Director, Family Medicine Residency Program, Department of Family Medicine, Tripler Army Medical Center, Honolulu, Hawaii (1982-1985); Clinical Assistant Professor, Family and Community Medicine, John A. Burns School of Medicine, Honolulu, Hawaii (1981-1985); Faculty, Department of Family Medicine Residency Program, Tripler Army Medical Center, Honolulu, Hawaii (1980-1985) **CR:** Dean, Sam Houston State University, Huntsville, Texas (2016-Present); Inspector, Clinical Education, Commission on Osteopathic College Accreditation (COCA) (2012-Present); Associate Dean for Clinical Affairs, Marian University College of Osteopathic Medicine (2011-Present); Chairman, Research Committee, Uniformed Services Academy of Family Physicians Foundation (1992-Present); Member, AOA Bureau of Scientific Affairs and Public Health (2015-2016); Board Member, Indiana AHEC (2011-2016); Board Member, Indiana Rural Health Association (2013-2016); Board Member, COPTI (2012-2015); Board Chairman, Osteopathic Founders Foundation (2010-2011); Board Member, Osteopathic Founders Foundation (2006-2011); President, Tulsa Osteopathic Medical Society (2009-2010); Board Member, Tulsa Osteopathic Medical Society (2007-2009); Chairman, Clinical Department of Family Medicine, Tulsa Regional Medical Center (2002-2006); Member, Medical Executive Committee, Tulsa Regional Medical Center (2002-2006); President, Oklahoma State University College of Osteopathic Medicine Alumni Association (2004-2005); Chairman, Department of Family Medicine, Oklahoma State University College of Osteopathic Medicine (1997-2004); Chairman, Continuous Quality Assurance (CQI) Committee, Oklahoma State University Center for Health Sciences (2000-2002); Medical Director, CQI Oversight of Four Military PRIMUS Clinics in Northern Virginia (1990-1994); Member, Research Committee, American Academy of Family Physicians (1986-1990) **CIV:** Member,

Research Judges for Uniformed Services Academy of Family Physicians Research Competition (1985-Present); Past President, Osteopathic Founders Foundation; Volunteer, St. Vincent's De Paul Food Pantry; Board of Directors, Advisory Group, Indiana Area Health Education Centers Network (AHEC); Board of Directors, Indiana Rural Health Association **MIL:** Colonel, Medical Corps (MC) of the U.S. Army (1997); Commander, 41st Combat Support Hospital, Fort Sam Houston, San Antonio, TX (1995-1997); Chief of Clinical Policy, Consultants Division, U.S. Army Medical Command (MEDCOM), Office of the Surgeon General, San Antonio, TX (1994-1997); Chief Consultant to the Army Surgeon General, U.S. Army Medical Command (MEDCOM), Office of the Surgeon General, San Antonio, TX (1994-1997); U.S. Army Medical Corps (20 Years) **CW:** Author, Book Chapter, Gastroenteritis, "Taylor's Manual of Family Medicine" (2015); Co-author, Disease Prevention, "Essential Family Medicine" (2006); Author, Gastroenteritis, "Manual of Family Practice" (2000); Author, Insomnia, "The 10-Minute Diagnosis Manual" (2000); Author, Gastroenteritis, "Manual of Family Practice" (1996); Author, Editorial, "Military Family Practitioners Join the Ranks of the Journal of Family Practice" (1994); Member, Editorial Board, Journal of Family Practice (1991-1994); Author, Co-author, Numerous Refereed Journals (1988-2014); Author, Co-author, Numerous Non-Refereed Publications (1988-2013); Reviewer, Journal of Family Practice; Reviewer, Family Medicine; Reviewer, Annals of Family Medicine; Author, Diseases of the Rectum and Anus, "Taylor's Principles and Practices in Family Medicine"; Speaker, Numerous Invited Lectures and Presentations at State, Regional, and National Meetings **AW:** Named Physician of the Year, State of Indiana (2016); Dr. J.B. Kinsinger Award for Outstanding Service to the Profession, Indiana Osteopathic Association (2015); ACE Fellow (2007-2008); Teacher of the Year Award, Oklahoma State University College of Osteopathic Medicine (2004); Hammer Award, Presented by Vice President Al Gore (1994); "A" Designator Award for Academic Excellence; Named Educator of the Year, Oklahoma State University; Grantee, Research Grants and Contracts **MEM:** Indiana State Medical Association (2012-Present); Indiana Osteopathic Association (2011-Present); Indiana Academy of Family Physicians (2011-Present); Coastal Research Group (1999-Present); American College of Osteopathic Physicians (1985-Present); AOA (1977-Present); Tulsa Osteopathic Medical Society (2009-2011); Osteopathic Founders Foundation (2005-2011); American Public Health Association (2000-Present); Board of Directors, Uniformed Services Academy of Family Physicians (1991-1994); AAFP Delegate, American Cancer Society Workshop on Clinical Trials (1988); American Academy of Family Physicians (AAFP); American College of Osteopathic Family Practitioners; American Academy of Family Medicine; Uniform Services Academy of Family Physicians; Texas Academy of Family Physicians; Oklahoma Academy of Family Physicians; Oklahoma Osteopathic Association; Society of Teachers of Family Medicine (STFM); Dean's Advisory Group, University of Oklahoma College of Medicine **AS:** Dr. Henley attributes his success to his stubbornness. "If I only had one skill, its recognizing the skills and passions of others, and bringing them together to create value..." **B/I:** Dr. Henley became involved in his profession because when he was in college, he worked to pay his way through. He had a mentor that helped him get a NIH Fellowship, where he spent time taking courses at Georgetown University. That is where he was first introduced to the world of "higher level academia". The first thing he learned is, "its not where you go, it's what

you leave behind..." With that mindset, he made it his duty to always create value wherever he was. Working with patients seemed to be the place he felt he could make the biggest impact. **AV:** Artist; Voracious reader; Collecting books

HENNESY, GERALD C., T: Artist **I:** Fine Art **CN:** Studio of Hennesy **DOB:** 06/11/1921 **PB:** Washington, DC **SC:** USA **PT:** Gerald Craft Hennesy; Frances Lee (Moore) Hennesy **MS:** Widowed **SPN:** Elizabeth Ann Lovering (03/04/1950) **CH:** Kathleen; Paul; Brian; Shawn; Hugh; Craig **ED:** BS, University of Maryland, College Park, MD (1948); Student, The George Washington University, Washington, DC (1940); Student, Corcoran School of the Arts and Design, The George Washington University, Washington, DC (1939) **C:** Artist, Director, Studio of Hennesy, Clifton, VA (1972-Present); Assistant Director for Organization and Management, Atomic Energy Commission (1956-1972); Management Analyst, U.S. Air Force Headquarters, The Pentagon, Arlington, VA (1948-1952, 1953-1956) **MIL:** Naval Aviator, Korean War; Navy Fighter Pilot, U.S. Navy, World War II **CW:** Artist, One-Man Show, Marin-Price Galleries, Chevy Chase, MD (1995-1996, 1998, 2000, 2002, 2004, 2007, 2009, 2010, 2011, 2012, 2013, 2015); Artist, One-Man Show, Byrne Gallery, Middleburg, VA (2009, 2010, 2011, 2012, 2013); Artist, One-Man Show, Prince Royal Gallery, Alexandria, VA (1999, 2003, 2005); Artist, One-Man Show, Venable Neslage Galleries, Washington, DC (1993); Artist, One-Man Show, Tolley Galleries, Washington, DC (1983); Artist, Exhibition, Allied Artists of America, Inc., New York, NY (1974, 1975); Artist, One-Man Show, PLA Gallery, McLean, VA (1967); Artist, Exhibition, Corcoran Gallery of Art, Washington, DC (1957, 1959, 1967); Artist, Exhibition, Smithsonian Institute, Washington, DC (1962, 1964); Artist, Represented in Permanent Collections at U.S. House of Representatives, Governor's Mansion, American Legion National Headquarters, Daughters of the American Revolution National Headquarters Complex, and Federal Deposit Insurance Corporation (FDIC) **AW:** Decorated Air Medal With One Star **PA:** Republican **RE:** Catholic

HENRY, MARY KAY, T: President **I:** Other **CN:** Service Employees International Union **PB:** Wayne **SC:** MI/USA **MS:** Life Partner **SPN:** Paula Macchello **ED:** BA in Urban Studies and Labor Relations, Michigan State University (1979) **C:** International President, Service Employees International Union (2010-Present); International Executive Vice President, Service Employees International Union (2004-2010); Chief Health Care Strategist, International Executive Board, Service Employees International Union (1996); Service Employees International Union (1979); Medical Assistant, American Red Cross **CR:** Former Labor Adviser, Subcommittee on Catholic Health Care, United States Conference of Catholic Bishops **CIV:** Executive Board, Families USA **AW:** Washington's Top Lobbyists, The Hill (2010); Top 25 Women in Health Care, Modern Healthcare (2009) **RE:** Roman Catholic

HENSON, TARAJI PENDA, T: Actress **I:** Media & Entertainment **DOB:** 09/11/1970 **PB:** Washington **SC:** DC/USA **PT:** Boris Lawrence Henson; Bernice (Gordon) Henson **CH:** Marcell **ED:** Diploma, Howard University, Washington, DC (1995) **CR:** Launched, #MACTaraji Make-up Collection, MAC Cosmetics (2016) **CIV:** Co-spokesperson, Viva Glam Campaign, MAC Cosmetics HIV/AIDS Fund (2017); Supporter, PETA **CW:** Actress, "Coffee & Kareem" (2020); Actress, "What Men Want" (2019); Actress, "Proud Mary" (2018); Actress, "Arimony" (2018); Actress, "The Best of Enemies" (2018); Actress, "Wreck It Ralph 2" (2018); Appearance,

"Carpool Karaoke: The Series" (2017); Voice Actress, "The Simpsons" (2017); Actress, "Ice Age: The Great Eggscapade" (2016); Actress, "Term Life" (2016); Actress, "Hidden Figures" (2016); Actress, "Empire" (2015-2020); Narrator, "FIFA Women's World Cup Final" (2015); Actress, "SNL" (2015); Guest Co-host, "Live! with Kelly and Michael" (2015); Actress, "Season of Love" (2014); Actress, Executive Producer, "No Good Deed" (2014); Actress, "Think Like a Man Too" (2014); Actress, "From the Rough" (2013); Actress, "Think Like a Man" (2012); Actress, "Person of Interest" (2011-2015); Actress, "Taken from Me: The Tiffany Rubin Story" (2011); Actress, "The Good Doctor" (2011); Actress, "Larry Crowne" (2011); Actress, "Person of Interest" (2011); Voice Actress, "The Cleveland Show" (2010); Actress, "Date Night" (2010); Actress, "Once Fallen" (2010); Actress, "The Karate Kid" (2010); Actress, "Peep World" (2010); Actress, "Not Easily Broken" (2009); Actress, "I Can Do Bad All by Myself" (2009); Actress, "Hurricane Season" (2009); Actress, "The Family That Preys" (2008); Actress, "Eli Stone" (2008); Actress, "The Curious Case of Benjamin Button" (2008); Actress, "Boston Legal" (2007-2008); Actress, "Talk to Me" (2007); Actress, "Something New" (2006); Actress, "Smokin' Aces" (2006); Actress, "CSI: Crime Scene Investigation" (2006); Actress, "Half & Half" (2005); Actress, "House M.D." (2005); Actress, "All of Us" (2004); Actress, "Hustle & Flow" (2005); Actress, "Four Brothers" (2005); Actress, "Hair Show" (2004); Actress, "The Division" (2003-2004); Actress, "Holla" (2002); Actress, "All or Nothing" (2001); Actress, "Baby Boy" (2001); Actress, "Murder, She Wrote: The Last Free Man" (2001); Actress, "The Adventures of Rocky & Bullwinkle" (2000); Actress, "Strong Medicine" (2000); Actress, "Satan's School for Girls" (2000); Actress, "Pacific Blue" (1999); Actress, "Felicity" (1998-1999); Actress, "Streetwise" (1998); Actress, "ER" (1998); Actress, "Saved by the Bell: The New Class" (1998); Actress, "Smart Guy" (1997-1998); Actress, "Sister, Sister" (1997); Actress, Music Videos, Television Shows and Films **AW:** NAACP Image Awards for Outstanding Actress in a Drama Series (2016, 2017, 2018, 2019); BET Awards for Best Actress (2006, 2008, 2011, 2015, 2016, 2017); Award for Best Ensemble, African-American Film Critics Association (2017); SAG Award, Outstanding Performance by a Cast in a Motion Picture (2017); Golden Globe Award for Best Performance by an Actress in a TV Series - Drama, Hollywood Foreign Press Association (2016); NAACP Image Award for Outstanding Actress in a Motion Picture (2015); NAACP Image Award for Entertainer of the Year (2015); NAACP Image Award for Outstanding Supporting Actress in a Drama Series (2014); NAACP Image Award for Outstanding Supporting Actress in a Motion Picture (2009); Numerous Awards **RE:** Christian

HEO, JOONGHYEOK, "JOON", T: Assistant Professor **I:** Education/Educational Services **CN:** The University of Texas Permian Basin **PB:** Seoul **SC:** South Korea **MS:** Married **CH:** Two Children **ED:** PhD in Geology and Geophysics, Texas A&M University, College Station, Texas (2013); MSc in Earth and Environmental Sciences, Seoul National University, Seoul, South Korea (2006); BSc in Applied Geology, Chungnam National University, Daejeon, South Korea (2003) **CT:** Certificate, Applied Remote Sensing Training Program, National Aeronautics and Space Administration (2016); Certificate, College Teaching Program in STEM Education, University of Michigan, Ann Arbor, MI (2015); Certified Public School Teacher for Geosciences, Ministry of Education and Chungnam National University, South Korea (2003) **C:** Assistant Professor, Department of Geosciences, The

University of Texas Permian Basin, Odessa, Texas (2017-Present); Research Fellow, Energy Institute, University of Michigan, Ann Arbor, MI (2015-2017); Postdoctoral Researcher, Environment Research Division, Pohang University of Science and Technology (POSTECH), South Korea (2013-2015); Lecturer, Teaching Assistant, Department of Geology and Geophysics, Texas A&M University, College Station, Texas (2009-2012); Field Work Technician, College of Geosciences, Texas A&M University, College Station, Texas (2008-2009); Research Assistant, School of Earth and Environmental Sciences, Seoul National University, South Korea (2006-2008); Teaching Assistant, School of Earth and Environmental Sciences, Seoul National University, Seoul, South Korea (2006-2007); Teacher, Division of Geosciences, Dunsan Public School, Daejeon, South Korea (2003) **CW:** Co-author, Refereed Articles, Professional Journals; Contributor, Refereed Conference Proceedings and Presentations; Invited Speaker, Events and Presentations **AW:** Dow Postdoctoral Fellowship, Graham Sustainability Institute, University of Michigan (2015–2017); Travel Grant, Division of Postdoctoral Fellows, University of Michigan (2015); Distinguished Leader Award, Korean Student Association, Texas A&M University (2013); Graduate Research Assistantship, Texas A&M University (2010); Travel Grant, The Geological Society of America, Inc. Conference, Office of Graduate and Professional Studies, Texas A&M University (2010); Lechner Scholarship, Texas A&M University (2008); Academic Fellowship, Chungnam National University, South Korea (2000–2002) **AS:** Dr. Heo attributes his success to passionate hard work. He is proud to be held in high regard by his students, and enjoys collaborating with other researchers. **B/I:** Initially a public school teacher, Dr. Heo became involved in his profession when he commenced research for his doctoral dissertation. This immense project brought him to Texas and New Mexico, where he studied each state's water resource management system; Texas water resources are economically indispensable, while New Mexico's dry conditions and lack of surface water were scientifically interesting. Dr. Heo's research focused on the development of regional water resources and evaluated energy sources for each environment. **AV:** Tennis; Golf **THT:** Dr. Heo always makes himself available to his students, and encourages them to approach him with either personal or academic issues. He is an incredibly supportive educator.

HERBERT, GARY RICHARD, T: Governor of Utah **I:** Government Administration/Government Relations/Government Services **DOB:** 05/07/1947 **PB:** American Fork **SC:** UT/USA **PT:** Duane Barlow Herbert; Carol (Boley) Herbert **MS:** Married **SPN:** Jeanette Snelson **CH:** Nathan; Daniel; Bradley; Kimberli; Shannon; Heather **ED:** Coursework, Brigham Young University, Provo, UT **CT:** Licensed Real Estate Broker (1969) **C:** Governor, State of Utah (2009-Present); Chair, NGA (2015-2016); Lieutenant Governor, State of Utah (2005-2009); Commissioner, Utah County Commission, Salt Lake City, UT (1990-2004); President, Herbert & Associates, Orem, UT **CR:** President, Utah State Association of County Commissioners & Councils (2000); Chairman, Utah Advisory Council on Intergovernmental Relations; Chairman, Utah County Council of Governments, Mountainland Association of Governments **CIV:** Board of Directors, Provo-Orem Chamber of Commerce (Now Utah Valley Chamber of Commerce) **MIL:** Staff Sergeant, Utah National Guard **MEM:** President, Utah Association of Counties (2003); Vice President, Utah Association of Counties (2002); Chairman, Local Fiscal Affairs Committee, National Association of Realtors (1999); Past President, Utah Association

of Counties Insurance Mutual; Utah Association of Counties Insurance Mutual; Utah Association of Realtors; National Association of Realtors **AV:** Golfing; Playing tennis **PA:** Republican **RE:** Church of Jesus Christ of Latter-Day Saints

HERD, WHITNEY, T: Chief Executive Officer **I:** Business Management/Business Services **CN:** Bumble **DOB:** 07/01/1989 **PB:** Salt Lake City **SC:** UT/USA **PT:** Michael Wolfe; Kelly Wolfe **MS:** Married **SPN:** Michael Herd **CH:** One Son **ED:** Coursework in International Studies, Southern Methodist University; Coursework, Sorbonne University; Diploma, Judge Memorial Catholic High School **C:** Founder, Chief Executive Officer, Bumble (2014-Present); Vice President of Marketing, Tinder Inc. (2012-2014) **CR:** Investor, Chappy **AW:** Listee, Top 80 Richest Self-Made Women, Forbes (2019); Listee, Time Magazine Most Influential (2018) **MEM:** Kappa Kappa Gamma

HERN, KEVIN RAY, T: U.S. Representative from Oklahoma **I:** Government Administration/Government Relations/Government Services **DOB:** 12/04/1961 **PB:** Belton **SC:** MO/USA **MS:** Married **SPN:** Tammy Hern (1994) **CH:** Three Children **ED:** MBA, School of Business, University of Arkansas at Little Rock; BS, Arkansas Tech University (1986); Coursework in Astronautical Engineering, Georgia Institute of Technology **C:** Member, U.S. House of Representatives from Oklahoma's First Congressional District (2018-Present); McDonald's Franchisee (1997-Present); Aerospace Engineer, Rockwell **CIV:** Member, BattleCreek Church, OK **PA:** Republican

HERNANDEZ, FELIX, "KING FELIX" ABRAHAM, T: Professional Baseball Player **I:** Athletics **CN:** Atlanta Braves **DOB:** 04/08/1986 **PB:** Valencia **SC:** Venezuela **PT:** Felix Hernandez, Sr. **MS:** Married **CH:** One Son; One Daughter **C:** Pitcher, Atlanta Braves (2020); Pitcher, Seattle Mariners (2005-2019) **CR:** Member, Venezuelan National Team World Baseball Classic (2009, 2017) **AW:** Named to American League All-star Team, Major League Baseball (2009, 2011-2015); American League Cy Young Award, Baseball Writers Association of America (2010)

HERNANDEZ, MYRA, T: Owner **I:** Other **CN:** Hair It Is Salon **DOB:** 02/10/1973 **PB:** New York **SC:** NY/USA **CH:** Brianna Ruff; Kianna Aybar **ED:** Student, College **C:** Owner, Hair It Is Salon (2010-Present) **CIV:** Stylist, Free Cuts for Autism, First Sunday Every Month, Fox 35 **AW:** Superwoman Award "For a Different Salon Experience," Orlando Family Magazine (2019); Everyday Hero "For Autism Awareness and Autism Haircuts," Channel 13 (2018) **AS:** Ms. Hernandez attributes her success to her honesty with her clients. She is honest with them about their goals that can and cannot be achieved with their hair. That honesty evolves to trust, then friendship and eventually family. **B/I:** Ms. Hernandez became involved in her profession because she originally married a man in the U.S. military and by her third year of college at UMASS- Amherst, she dropped out, got married, and moved out of the country. She had a daughter who was born with autism and required special attention. After her divorce, she moved to Florida with her daughter. She wanted to spend time with her, but was unsure what she would do for herself as a career. Eventually she came upon being a hairdresser. Ten years later, the business is a success and her daughter works with her as well. In addition, she became involved as owner of her own salon because of her daughter, Brianna. She needed to create an environment that was safe for her after school. She did that for a safe haven for

her and now her daughter works alongside her. So, the dream came to pass because that was the whole plan: when she got to age 22, she would do so, and it has been a huge accomplishment.

HERNDON, JAMES RODNEY, T: Instructor (Retired) **I:** Education/Educational Services **CN:** Southern Illinois University Edwardsville **DOB:** 12/31/1949 **PB:** Cedar **SC:** MI/USA **PT:** Richard (1924-2007); Mary (1928-2017) **MS:** Married **SPN:** Jane Herndon (3/19/1971) **CH:** Matthew James; Jennifer Jane; **ED:** EDs in Educational Leadership, Southern Illinois University Edwardsville (1987); MS in Educational Administration, Southern Illinois University Edwardsville (1978); BS in Education, Southern Illinois University Edwardsville (1972) **C:** Instructor, Educational Leadership, Southern Illinois University Edwardsville (2005-2017); Professor, Mckendra University; Superintendent of Schools, High School Principal, Roxana School District (1994-2005); High School Principal, Roxana School District (1985-1994); Assistant High School Principal, Roxana School District (1978-1985); Teacher, Coach, Pleasant Hill School District (1974-1978); Classroom Teacher, Coach, Alton School District (1972-1974) **CIV:** Vice President, Community Teacher Federal Union; Served, United Methodist Village; Trustee, Chair, Church **CW:** Contributor, "Principal internships create exciting opportunities," Educational Leadership Magazine (2015); Contributor, School and Business Partnership, Illionic Community Magazine **AW:** SIUE Alumni Association Hall of Fame, SIUE Alumni Association (2019) **MEM:** President, South Western Illinois of School Supervision and Curriculum Development (1985-1988); Illinois Association of School Administrators; Former Member, Illinois Principal's Association; Former Member, Illinois Basketball Coaches Association; Illinois Retired Teachers Association; President, Madison County Retired Teachers Unit #2 **AS:** Mr. Herndon attributes his success to his mother and father. They were a positive driving force in his life. He thinks because of them, him and his siblings went into public service. **B/I:** Mr. Herndon is a third generation educator, both of his parents and his paternal grandfather were all teachers. His son is also a teacher. He was also very influenced by teachers and coaches he had a long the way during school. He wanted to have a similar impact on the next generation. **AV:** Family; Golfing; Reading **PA:** Democrat **RE:** United Methodist **THT:** A student's success is also a teachers success.

HERRERA, CAROLINA, T: Fashion Designer **I:** Apparel & Fashion **CN:** Carolina Herrera, Ltd. **DOB:** 01/08/1939 **PB:** Caracas **SC:** Venezuela **PT:** Guillermo Pacanins Acevedo; Maria Cristina Nino Passios **MS:** Married **SPN:** Reinaldo Herrera Guevara (1968); Guillermo Behrens Tello (1957, Divorced 1964) **CH:** Carolina Adriana; Patricia Cristina; Ana Luisa; Mercedes **C:** Founder, Head Designer, Carolina Herrera Ltd., New York, NY (1981-Present); Founder, Head Designer, CH Carolina Herrera Lifestyle Brand, Carolina Herrera Ltd. (2008); Founder, Head Designer, Herrera for Men, Herrera Studio and W by Carolina Herrera Clothing Lines, Carolina Herrera Ltd. (1992); Founder, Head Designer, Jewelry Collections, Carolina Herrera Ltd. (1990); Founder, Head Designer, Carolina Herrera Collection II Sportswear Line, Carolina Herrera Ltd. (1989); Founder, Head Designer, Fragrance Lines, Carolina Herrera Ltd. (1988); Founder, Head Designer, Couture Bridal Collection, Carolina Herrera Ltd. (1987); Publicist, Fashion House of Emilio Pucci, Caracas, Venezuela **CR:** Board of Directors, Mimi So (2004-Present) **CIV:** Board of Directors, Council of Fashion Designers of America (CFDA) (1999-Present) **AW:** Founder's Award, CFDA (2018);

Designer of Excellence Award, International Design Excellence Awards, Industrial Designers Society of America (2017); Designer of the Year, Style Awards (2012); Couture Council Award for Artistry of Fashion (2014); Geoffrey Beene Lifetime Achievement Award, CFDA (2008); Golden Plate Award, Academy of Achievement (2005); Glamour Award for the Fashion Force (2004); Womenswear Designer of the Year Award (2004); Spain's Gold Medal for Merit in Fine Arts, King Juan Carlos II (2002); Award for Special Distinction to Career in World of Design, International Fashion Center of New York (1995); Mary Ann Magnin Award (1994); Presidential Medal, Pratt Institute (1990); Latin America Designer Fashion Award (1987); Named to International Best-Dressed List, Vanity Fair Magazine (1971-1980)

HERRERA BEUTLER, JAIME LYNN, T: U.S. Representative from Washington **I:** Government Administration/Government Relations/Government Services **DOB:** 11/03/1978 **PB:** Glendale **SC:** CA/USA **PT:** Armando D. Herrera; Candice Marie (Rough) Herrera **MS:** Married **SPN:** Daniel Beutler (2008) **CH:** Abigail Rose; Ethan; Isana Mae **ED:** Intern, Office of Political Affairs, The White House; BA in Communications, University of Washington, Seattle, WA (2004); AA, Bellevue College (2003) **C:** Member, U.S. House of Representatives from Washington's Third Congressional District, United States Congress, Washington, DC (2011-Present); Member, U.S. House Committee on Transportation and Infrastructure, Washington, DC (2011-Present); Member, U.S. House Committee on Small Business, Washington, DC (2011-Present); Member, District 18, Washington House of Representatives (2007-2010); Senior Legislative Aide to Representative Cathy McMorris Rodgers, U.S. House of Representatives, Washington, DC (2005-2007); Assistant Minority Floor Leader, Washington House of Representatives; Member, Committee on Appropriations; Member, Republican Study Committee **CIV:** Volunteer, Ground Zero, 9/11, New York, NY (2001) **AW:** Named One of the Politics 40 Under 40, TIME Magazine (2010) **PA:** Republican **RE:** Christian

HERRIN, COLETTE M., T: Owner **I:** Other **CN:** Warranty Enterprises, LLC. **PB:** 12/30/1951 **MS:** Married **SPN:** Thomas **CH:** Kirk; Rebekah; Brian **ED:** AA in Computer Programming, South Puget Sound Community College (1984) **CT:** Certified Aflac Insurance Agent; Section 125 Specialist **C:** Owner, Bookkeeper, Consultant, Warranty Enterprises, LLC. (2008-Present); Avid Quilter (1994-Present); U.S. Army (1974-1977); Creative Consultant, Pfaff; Senior Systems Analyst; Programmer; Aflac Agent **CR:** Pastor (2014-Present) **MIL:** U.S. Army **CW:** Art Quilts **AW:** Employee of the Month, Washington State Department of Transportation (1992); Joint Service Commendation Medal for Meritorious Service (1977); Triple Crown Award for Sales, Aflac **AS:** Ms. Herrin attributes her success to her father. **B/I:** Ms. Herrin became involved in her profession because she tried accounting for a while and realized it wasn't for her. However, she did enjoy working with computers, so she pursued a career in the field. In addition, she wanted to become a pastor because of her Bible studies. **RE:** Christian **THT:** Ms. Herrin states, "The joy of the Lord is my strength."

HERRMAN, ERNIE, T: Chief Executive Officer **I:** Retail/Sales **CN:** TJX Companies Inc. **C:** Chief Executive Officer, TJX Companies Inc. (2016-Present); President, TJX Companies Inc. (2011-Present); Group President, TJX Companies Inc. (2008-2011); Senior Executive Vice President, TJX Companies Inc. (2007-2011); President, Marmaxx Group, TJX Companies Inc. (2007-2008); Executive Vice President, President, Marmaxx Group, TJX Companies Inc. (2005-2007); Executive Vice President, Chief Operating Officer, Marmaxx Group, TJX Companies Inc. (2004-2005); Executive Vice President, Merchandising, Marmaxx Group, TJX Companies Inc. (2001-2004); Senior Vice President, Merchandising, TJX Companies Inc. (1998-2001); Vice President, General Merchandise Manager, TJX Companies Inc. (1996-1998); Vice President, Senior Merchandise Manager, TJX Companies Inc. (1995-1996); Buyer, TJX Companies Inc., Framingham, MA (1989)

HERSHBERGER, TRUMAN VERNE, T: Retired Animal Nutritionist **I:** Veterinary Care **DOB:** 10/10/1927 **PB:** Walnut Creek **SC:** OH/USA **PT:** William James Hershberger; Minerva Hershberger **MS:** Married **SPN:** Diana Brueckner (02/14/2008); Dorothy Mae Steiner (08/28/1949, Deceased 9/21/2007) **CH:** Diana Hershberger **ED:** PhD, Ohio State University (1955); MS, Ohio State University (1951); BA, Goshen College (1949) **C:** Associate Professor of Animal Nutrition, The Pennsylvania State University, University Park, PA (1960-1991); Assistant Professor of Animal Nutrition, The Pennsylvania State University, University Park, PA (1955-1960); Instructor, Ohio Agricultural Experiment Station (1951-1955); Research Fellow, Ohio Agricultural Experiment Station (1950-1951) **CIV:** Board of Directors, United Campus Ministry, State College (1964-1992); Chairman, Board of Directors, International Friendship House, State College (1972-1974) **CW:** Editorial Board, Journal of Animal Science (1971-1975); Contributor, 46 Articles, Professional Journals **AW:** Postdoctoral Research Fellow, Ohio Agricultural Research & Development Center Library (OARDC) (1965-1966) **MEM:** Chairman, Numerous Committees, American Society Animal Science (1969-1970); Fellow, American Association for the Advancement of Science; American Scientific Affiliation; American Chemical Society; American Institute of Nutrition; New York Academy of Sciences; Nutrition Today Society; Council for Agricultural Science and Technology; Phi Lambda Upsilon; Sigma Xi **MH:** Albert Nelson Marquis Lifetime Achievement Award **B/I:** Dr. Hershberger originally wanted to pursue medical science; however, during his undergraduate studies, he realized animal nutrition would be a better field for him. **AV:** Playing table tennis; Running **PA:** Democrat **RE:** Mennonite

HERTZ, LAURA, T: Chief Executive Officer **I:** Business Management/Business Services **CN:** Gifts for Good **ED:** Coursework, Marshall School of Business, University of Southern California (2015-2017); BSBA, Haas School of Business, University of California Berkeley; Coursework, International Business, Finance, and Cantonese, University of Hong Kong; Diploma, Horace Greeley High School, Chappaqua, NY **CT:** Graduate Certificate in Impact Investing and Social Enterprise Management, Middlebury Institute of International Studies at Monterey (2015); Nonprofit Management and Leadership Certified, Nonprofit Leadership Alliance (2013); Global Reporting Initiative (GRI) Certified Training Course, G4 Reporting Guidelines; Social Impact Leadership Certified, Haas School of Business, University of California Berkeley **C:** Chief Executive Officer, Co-Founder, Gifts for Good (2017-Present); Creative Director, Cultural Outreach (2016-2017); Fellow in Impact Investing and Social Enterprise Management, Frontier Market Scouts (2015); Audit Senior Associate, Deloitte (2013-2015); International Sales Strategy Intern, Fair Trade USA (2013); Campus Ambassador, University of California Berkeley, Venture for America (2012-2013); Audit and Enterprise Risk Services Summer Associate, Deloitte (2012); Pacific Region Recruiter, AmeriCorps National Civilian Community Corps (NCCC) (2009-2011); Corps Member, Corps Ambassador Program Representative, AmeriCorps National Civilian Community Corps (NCCC) (2008-2009); Sales and Marketing Intern, Liquid Environmental Solutions (2008) **CIV:** Board of Directors, American Cancer Society (2019-Present); Gentefy (2016-Present); Bright Beverages (2015-Present); Share Practice (2016); Participant, AIDS/LifeCycle (2013); Susan Miller Dorsey High School Assistant Teacher and Tutor, Children Youth and Family Collaborative (2009); Construction Supervisor & Volunteer Coordinator, Habitat for Humanity of Lafayette (2009); Volunteer Coordinator & Mold Remediation Specialist, St. Bernard Project (2009); Wildfire Recovery Team, Volunteer San Diego (2008-2009); Director of Clothing Distribution Program, Sacramento Food Bank & Family Services (2008) **CW:** Co-Author, "2017 Best Real Estate Apps for Homebuyers Report: A Comprehensive Guide for Mortgage Lenders, Real Estate Professionals, and Homebuyers," Cultural Outreach (2016); Co-Author, "4 Tips on Capturing Real Estate Clients Through Pokémon Go," HousingWire (2016); Author, "Why Female Millennials Are Forever Changing How the Mortgage Industry Does Business," Mortgage Women Magazine (2016); Co-Author, "A Step-By-Step Guide to Section 342 Self Assessment," Mortgage Compliance Magazine **AW:** Listee, 30 Under 30 Social Entrepreneurs, Forbes (2019-Present); Marcia Israel Award, Top Graduate Student Enterprise, Lloyd Greif Center for Entrepreneurial Studies (2016); Frontier Market Scouts Scholar, Middlebury College (2015); Nominee, Women's Empowerment Day, Haas School of Business, University of California Berkeley (2013); Honor Roll, Haas School of Business, University of California Berkeley (2012); Dean's List, College of Natural Resources, University of California Berkeley (2010-2011); Bronze Congressional Service Award, Federal Corporation for National and Community Service (2009); Gold Presidential Volunteer Service Award, Federal Corporation for National and Community Service (2009) **MEM:** Los Angeles Chapter, Social Enterprise Alliance (2015-Present); Los Angeles Chapter, Young Women Social Entrepreneurs (2015-Present); Beta Gamma Sigma (2017); Alpha Phi International Fraternity (2009-2013)

HERZBERG-FREW, DOROTHY CREWS, T: Secondary School Educator (Retired) **I:** Education/Educational Services **CN:** West Contra Costa Unified School District **DOB:** 07/08/1935 **PB:** New York **SC:** NY/USA **PT:** Floyd Houston Crews; Julia (Lesser) Crews **MS:** Married **SPN:** Douglas Frew (01/2012); Hershel Zelig Herzberg (05/22/1962, Divorced 04/1988) **CH:** Samuel Floyd; Laura Jill; Daniel Crews **ED:** JD, San Francisco Law School (1976); MA, Stanford University, CA (1964); AB, Brown University, Providence, RI (1957) **CT:** San Francisco State Teaching Credentials, Secondary Life Credentials, Jr. College Life Credentials (1963) **C:** Retired (2005); Teacher, English as a Second Language, West Contra Costa Unified School District, Richmond, CA (1991-2005); Revenue Officer, IRS (1987-1989); Tax Preparer, H&R Block (1989); Registered Representative, Waddell and Reed, Inc. (1983-1984); Senior Administrator, Dean Witter Reynolds Co., San Francisco, CA (1980-1983); Investigator, Office of the District Attorney, San Francisco, CA (1978-1980); Legal Secretary, Various Law Firms, San Francisco, CA (1976-1978); Teacher, Secondary and University Levels, Peace Corps, Nigeria (1961-1963); Teacher, Mission Adult School, San Francisco, CA (1965-1966); Fresh Air Fund Summer 5354 Counselor; 57 Program Director; 61 Camp Director **CR:** Coordinator, Close-up Richmond and Kennedy High School (2001-2012);

Sponsor, Debate Team, Richmond High School (2001-2003) **CIV:** Board Member, United Nations Association East Bay (2012-2015); Board, North California Peace Corps (2015-2017); Board, ACLU Berkeley Chapter, CA (2008-2018); Board Director, Ujima (2012); Board Director, Greater Richmond Interfaith Programs (2004-2011); Chairperson, Social Justice Council, Unitarian Universalist Church of Berkeley (1997-2005); President, Miraloma Park Improvement Club, CA (1980-1981); Board of Directors, Miraloma Park Improvement Club, CA (1977-1985); Alternate Supervisor, San Francisco Mayor's Commission on Criminal Justice (1978); President, Council Cooperative Nursery Schools, San Francisco, CA (1969-1971); Member, Speakers Bureau (1967-1970); Board Director, League of Women Voters, San Francisco, CA (1965-1969); Volunteer, Peace Corps, Nigeria (1961-1963) **CW:** Author, "An Enduring Friendship"; Author, "Cameos," Through The Writer's Eye (2020); Author, Political Poetry, "Use Your Voice" (2018); Editor, Newsletters, Cooperative Nursery School Council (1969-1971); Author, "Me, Madam: Peace Peace Corps Letters from Nigeria" (1961-1963); Editor, "Miraloma Life" Newsletter (1976-1982); Editor, 17 Authors **AW:** Named, Woman of the Year, El Cenito by Assembly Resolution (2010-2011); Jefferson Award (2012); Schweitzer Award, Unitarian Universalist Church of Berkeley (2006); One of the First 400 Volunteers, Peace Corps, Nigeria (1961-1963) **MH:** Albert Nelson Marquis Lifetime Achievement Award **AV:** Swimming; Chorus **PA:** Democrat **RE:** Unitarian

HERZOG, JOHN ORLANDO, PHD, T: Mathematics Educator, University Administrator **I:** Education/Educational Services **DOB:** 04/06/1935 **PB:** Ulen **SC:** MN/USA **PT:** Herman Herzog; Olga (Renslow) Herzog **MS:** Married **SPN:** Colleen Strattford (Bone) Herzog (1991) **CH:** 12 Children Including Barbara; Michael; Jane; Kathleen; Daniel **ED:** PhD, University of Nebraska-Lincoln, Lincoln, NE (1963); MA, University of Nebraska-Lincoln, Lincoln, NE (1959); BA, Concordia College, Moorhead, MN (1957) **C:** Retired (1998); From Associate Professor to Professor of Mathematics, Pacific Lutheran University, Tacoma, WA (1967-1998); Chair, Department of Mathematics, Pacific Lutheran University, Tacoma, WA (1991-1992); Chairman, Department of Mathematics, Pacific Lutheran University, Tacoma, WA (1968-1974, 1983-1984); Chairman, Division of Science, Pacific Lutheran University, Tacoma, WA (1975-1981); Dean, Natural Sciences, Pacific Lutheran University, Tacoma, WA (1984-1990); From Assistant Professor to Associate Professor, Mathematics, Idaho State University, Pocatello, Idaho (1963-1967); Instructor, Mathematics, University of Nebraska-Lincoln, Lincoln, NE (1959-1961); Breakfast Cook, Yellowstone National Park (1953-1957) **CR:** Visiting Scholar, University of Canterbury, New Zealand (1991, 1993); Consultant, National Science Foundation, India (1967); Took 16 Students Backpacking to New Zealand **CIV:** Councilman, Trinity Lutheran Church, Tacoma, WA (1969-1971, 1982-1984) **AW:** Grantee, Department of Energy, Pacific Lutheran University, Tacoma, WA (1976-1985); Grantee, Pacific Lutheran University, Tacoma, WA (1968-1973); Grantee, National Science Foundation, Idaho State University, Pocatello, Idaho (1963-1967); National Science Foundation Fellow, University of Nebraska-Lincoln, NE (1961-1962) **MEM:** Chair, Mathematical Association of America (1989-1991); Treasurer, Mathematical Association of America (1976-1979); American Association of University Professors (AAUP); American Mathematical Society; National Council of Teachers of Mathematics; Washington State Mathematics Council **MH:** Albert Nelson Marquis Lifetime

Achievement Award; Marquis Who's Who Top Professional **B/I:** Dr. Herzog became involved in his profession because he has always had an interest in mathematics; he attended Concordia College in Minnesota and received his bachelor's degree in mathematics in 1957. Shortly after, he received his master's degree in mathematics from the University of Nebraska in 1959, and became an instructor at the same college. In 1963, he received his PhD from the University of Nebraska and became an assistant professor; he worked his way up to associate professor at Idaho State University. In 1984, he was named Dean of Natural Science at Pacific Lutheran University in Tacoma, WA, and then became chairman of the department of mathematics and the chairman of the division of science. In 1991, Dr. Herzog went to New Zealand on sabbatical leave and visited the University of Canterbury in Christchurch and met his wife, Colleen. They got married and promised that they would return every year and many years that they returned, they took a group of students to backpack through New Zealand. After his retirement, he continued to host students at his home in New Zealand. **AV:** Hiking; Gardening; Running; Beekeeping; Played baseball and basketball

HERZOG, WERNER, T: Screenwriter; Director **I:** Media & Entertainment **DOB:** 09/05/1942 **PB:** Munich **SC:** Germany **PT:** Dietrich Herzog; Elizabeth Stipetic **MS:** Married **SPN:** Lena Pisetski (1999); Christine Maria Ebenberger (1987, Divorced 1994); Martje Grohmann (1967, Divorced 1987) **CH:** Rudolph Amos Achmed; Simon; Hanna Mattes **ED:** Coursework, Duquesne University, Pittsburgh, PA; Coursework, University of Munich **CW:** Director, Writer, "Nomad: In the Footsteps of Bruce Chatwin" (2019); Actor, "The Mandalorian" (2019); Director, Writer, "Meeting Gorbachev" (2018); Producer, "A Gray State" (2017); Director, Producer, "Lo and Behold, Reveries of the Connected World" (2016); Producer, Writer, Director, Actor, "Salt and Fire" (2016); Director, Writer, "Into the Inferno" (2016); Director, Writer, "Queen of the Desert" (2015); Actor, "Parks and Recreation" (2015); Voice Actor, "Rick and Morty" (2015); Director, Writer, "The Look of Silence" (2014); Voice Actor, "Penguins of Madagascar" (2014); Voice Actor, "The Wind Rises" (2013); Actor, "Home from Home: Chronicle of a Vision" (2013); Director, Writer, "On Death Row" (2012-2013); Actor, "Jack Reacher" (2012); Executive Producer, "The Act of Killing" (2012); Artist, Exhibitions, Whitney Biennial, Whitney Museum of American Art (2012); Director, Writer, "Into the Abyss" (2011); Director, "Into the Abyss" (2011); Executive Producer, Writer, Co-director, "Happy People: A Year in the Taiga" (2011); Director, Writer, "Cave of Forgotten Dreams" (2010); Director, Co-writer, "Bad Lieutenant: Port of Call New Orleans" (2009); Director, Co-writer, "My Son, My Son, What Have Ye Done" (2009); Director, Writer, "Rescue Dawn" (2007); Director, Writer, "Encounters at the End of the World" (2007); Actor, "Mister Lonely" (2007); Actor, "The Grand" (2007); Director, Writer, "The Wild Blue Yonder" (2005); Director, Writer, "Grizzly Man" (2005); Director, Writer, "The White Diamond" (2004); Co-writer, Actor, "Incident at Loch Ness" (2004); Director, Writer, "Wheel of Time" (2003); Director, Writer, "Pilgrimage" (2001); Director, Writer, "Invincible" (2001); Director, Writer, "Wings of Hope" (2000); Actor, "Julien Donkey-Boy" (1999); Director, Writer, "My Best Fiend" (1999); Actor,"What Dreams May Come" (1998); Director, Writer, "Little Dieter Needs to Fly" (1997); Director, Writer, "Gesualdo: Death for Five Voices" (1995); Director, Writer, "The Transformation of the World into Music" (1994); Actor, "Tales from the Opera" (1994); Director, Writer, "Bells from

the Deep" (1993); Director, Writer, "Lessons of Darkness" (1992); Director, Writer, "Jag Mandir" (1991); Director, Co-writer, "Scream of Stone" (1991); Actor, "Hard to Be a God" (1990); Director, Writer, "Echoes from a Somber Empire" (1990); Actor, "Bride of the Orient" (1989); Director, Writer, "Wodaabe - Herdsmen of the Sun" (1989); Director, Writer, "Cobra Verde" (1987); Director, Writer, "The Dark Glow of the Mountains" (1984); Director, Writer, "Ballad of the Little Soldier" (1984); Director, Writer, "Where the Green Ants Dream" (1984); Actor, "Man of Flowers" (1983); Author, "Fitzcarraldo: The Original Story" (1983); Director, Writer, "Fitzcarraldo" (1982); Author, "Of Walking in Ice" (1981); Director, Writer, "God's Angry Man" (1980); Director, Writer, "Huie's Sermon" (1980); Writer, "Werner Herzog Eats His Shoe" (1980); Director, Writer, "Nosferatu the Vampyre" (1979); Director, Writer, "Woyzeck" (1979); Director, Writer, "Stroszek" (1977); Director, Co-writer, "Heart of Glass" (1976); Director, Writer, "How Much Wood Would a Woodchuck Chuck" (1976); Director, Writer, "The Enigma of Kaspar Hauser" (1974); Director, Writer, "The Great Ecstasy of Woodcarver Steiner" (1974); Director, Writer, "Aguirre, the Wrath of God" (1972); Director, Writer, "Handicapped Future" (1971); Producer, Writer, Director, "Land of Silence and Darkness" (1971); Director, Writer, "Fata Morgana" (1971); Director, Writer, "Even Dwarfs Started Small" (1970); Director, Writer, "The Flying Doctors of East Africa" (1969); Producer, Writer, Director, "Signs of Life" (1968); Director, Writer, Producer, Films, Documentaries and Operas; Author, Books **AW:** National Society Film Critics Award for Best Nonfiction Film (2011); Listee, 100 Most Influential People in the World, Time Magazine (2009); Film Society Directing Award, San Francisco International Film Festival (2006); Award for Outstanding Directorial Achievement in Documentary, DGA (2006); New York Film Critics Circle Award for Best Nonfiction Film (2005)

HERZOG, WHITEY, T: Professional Baseball Coach (Retired), Professional Baseball Player (Retired), Executive **I:** Athletics **DOB:** 11/09/1931 **PB:** New Athens **SC:** IL/USA **PT:** Edgar Herzog; Lietta Herzog **MS:** Married **SPN:** Mary Lou Herzog (1953) **CH:** Jim; Debbie **C:** Retired, MLB (1994); Senior Vice President, Director of Player Personnel, California Angels (Now Los Angeles Angels), MLB (1991-1994); Vice President, St. Louis Cardinals, MLB (1990); Manager, St. Louis Cardinals, MLB (1980-1990); Manager, Kansas City Royals, MLB (1975-1979); Coach, California Angels (Now Los Angeles Angels), MLB (1974-1975); Interim Manager, California Angels (Now Los Angeles Angels), MLB (1974); Manager, Texas Rangers, MLB (1973); Director of Player Development, New York Mets, MLB (1967-1972); Coach, New York Mets, MLB (1966); Coach, Kansas City Athletics, MLB (1965); Scout, Kansas City Athletics, MLB (1964); Infielder, Outfielder, Detroit Tigers, MLB (1963); Infielder, Outfielder, Baltimore Orioles, MLB (1961-1962); Infielder, Outfielder, Kansas City Athletics, MLB (1958-1960); Infielder, Outfielder, Washington Senators, MLB (1956-1958) **AW:** Inductee, St. Louis Cardinals Hall of Fame (2014); Inductee, National Baseball Hall of Fame (2009); National League Manager of the Year (1982, 1985, 1987); Winner, St. Louis Cardinals, World Series (1982); Man of the Year, Sporting News (1982); Executive of the Year, United Press International (1981-1982); American League Manager of the Year (1976); Inductee, Kansas City Royals Hall of Fame

HESS, STEVE, T: Chief Information Officer **I:** Medicine & Health Care **CN:** University of Colorado Health **ED:** BS in Computer Science, University of Delaware (1990) **C:** Chief Information Officer,

University of Colorado Health (2009-Present); Vice President, Chief Information Officer, Christiana Care Health System (2004-2009); Manager, Christiana Care Health System (1999-2003)

HEWSON, MARILLYN ADAMS, T: Chairman, President, Chief Executive Officer **I:** Military & Defense Services **CN:** Lockheed Martin Corporation **DOB:** 12/27/1953 **PB:** Junction City **SC:** KS/USA **ED:** MS in Economics, University of Alabama; BBA, University of Alabama **C:** President, Chief Executive Officer, Chairman, Lockheed Martin Corporation, Bethesda, MD (2013-Present); President, Chief Operating Officer, Lockheed Martin Corporation, Bethesda, MD (2012); Executive Vice President of Electronic Systems Business, Lockheed Martin Corporation, Bethesda, MD (2010-2012); President, Lockheed Martin Systems Integration, Lockheed Martin Corporation, Owego, NY (2008-2010); Executive Vice President for Global Sustainment, Aeronautics Division, Lockheed Martin Corporation, Fort Worth, TX (2007-2008); President, General Manager, Kelly Aviation Center, Lockheed Martin Corporation, San Antonio, TX (2006); General Manager of Logistics Services, Lockheed Martin Corporation (2006); Senior Vice President of Corporate Shared Services, Lockheed Martin Corporation (2001-2006); Vice President of Global Supply Chain Management, Lockheed Martin Corporation (2000-2001); Corporate Vice President of Internal Audits, Lockheed Martin Corporation, Bethesda, MD (1998-2000); Director of Consolidated Material Systems and Business Management, Aeronautics Material Management Center, Lockheed Martin Corporation, Fort Worth, TX (1995-1998); Director of Commercial Practices, Lockheed Martin Corporation (1995); Various positions, Director of Operations Control, Lockheed Martin Corporation (1993-1995); Senior Industrial Engineer Aeronautical Division, Lockheed Martin Corporation, Marietta, GA (1983);U.S. Bureau of Labor Statistics **CR:** Board of Directors, Lockheed Martin Corporation (2012-Present); E.I. DuPont de Nemours & Company (2007-Present); Chair, Board of Directors, Sandia Corporation (2010-2013); Carpenter Technology Corporation (2002-2006) **CIV:** Board of Visitors, Culverhouse College of Business, University of Alabama; Board of Trustees, Council of Trustees, Association of the United States Army **AW:** The 50 Most Powerful Women in Business, Fortune Magazine (2010-2015); One of The 100 Most Powerful Women, Forbes (2013-2014); Woman of the Year Award, United Service Organizations, Inc. (2012) **MEM:** The Economic Club of Washington D.C.

HEWSON, PAUL, "BONO" DAVID, T: Singer, Songwriter, Musician **I:** Media & Entertainment **DOB:** 05/10/1960 **PB:** Dublin **SC:** Ireland **PT:** Brendan Robert Hewson; Iris (Rankin) Hewson **MS:** Married **SPN:** Alison (Stewart) Hewson (08/21/1982) **CH:** Jordan; Memphis Eve; Elijah; John Abraham **ED:** Honorary LLD, University of Pennsylvania (2004); Honorary LLD, Trinity College, The University of Dublin (2003) **C:** Co-owner, Clarence Hotel, Dublin, Ireland (1992-Present); Singer, Songwriter, U2 (1978-Present); Member, Feedback (Later The Hype) **CR:** Managing Director, Co-founder, Elevation Partners, Menlo Park, CA (2004-Present) **CIV:** Board of Directors, Zipline (2019-Present); Founder, Spokesman, Board Director, Debt, Aids, Trade in Africa (DATA) (1999-Present); Launched, "Red" Campaign (2006); Performer, Benefit Concerts, Songs **CW:** Appearance, "Lost in London" (2017); Singer with U2, "Songs of Experience" (2017); Singer with U2, "Songs of Innocence" (2014); Appearance, "Arcade Fire in Here Comes the Night Time" (2013); Appearance, "Muscle Shoals" (2013); Composer, "Mandela: Long Walk to Freedom" (2013); Composer, "Ordinary Love" (2013);

Appearance, "B.B. King - The Life of Riley" (2012); Appearance, "The Resurrection of Victor Jara" (2012); Composer, Broadway, "Spider-Man: Turn Off the Dark" (2011); Appearance, "From the Sky Down" (2011); Appearance, "Anton Corbijn Inside Out" (2011); Appearance, "Bruno" (2009); Singer with U2, "No Line on the Horizon" (2009); Appearance, "U2 3D" (2008); Appearance, "Across the Universe" (2007); Appearance, "Rewind" (2007); Appearance, "American Idol" (2007); Co-author with U2 and Neil McCormick, "U2 by U2" (2006); Appearance, "Entourage" (2005); Singer with U2, "How to Dismantle an Atomic Bomb" (2004); Composer, "Gangs of New York" (2002); Singer with U2, "The Best of 1990-2000" (2002); Singer with U2, "Million Dollar Hotel" (2000); Singer with U2, "All That You Can't Leave Behind" (2000); Singer with U2, "Hasta la Vista Babe!: Live from Mexico City" (2000); Writer, Producer, Actor, "The Million Dollar Hotel" (2000); Appearance, "Entropy" (1999); Singer with U2, "The Best of 1980-1990" (1998); Singer with U2, "Pop" (1997); Composer, "Golden Eye" (1995); Composer, "In the Name of the Father" (1993); Appearance, "In Darkest Hollywood: Cinema & Apartheid" (1993); Singer with U2, "Zooropa" (1993); Singer with U2, "Achtung Baby" (1991); Featured, "U2: Rattle and Hum" (1988); Singer with U2, "Rattle and Hum" (1988); Singer with U2, "The Joshua Tree" (1987); Singer with U2, "Wide Awake in America" (1985); Singer with U2, "The Unforgettable Fire" (1984); Featured, "Under a Blood Red Sky: U2 Live at Red Rocks" (1984); Singer with U2, "War" (1983); Singer with U2, "Under a Blood Red Sky" (1983); Composer, "They Call it an Accident" (1982); Singer with U2, "October (1981); Singer with U2, "Boy" (1980); Singer, Songwriter, Composer, Songs and Albums **AW:** Named Man of the Year, Glamour Magazine (2016); Golden Globe Award for Best Original Song - Motion Picture, Hollywood Foreign Press Association (2014); Named (with U2) Top Touring Artist, Billboard Music Awards (2012); Named Person of the Year, TIME Magazine (2005, 2006, 2009); Named One of the 100 Agents of Change, Rolling Stone Magazine (2009); Man of Peace Prize, Paris, France (2008); Awards for Bestselling Irish Artist (with U2), World Music Awards (1993, 1998, 2007); Philadelphia Liberty Medal (2007); Named Honorary Knight Commander, Most Excellent Order of the British Empire, Queen Elizabeth II (2007); Liberty Medal for Humanitarian Work in Africa, National Constitution Center (2007); Board of Directors Special Tribute Award, Council of Fashion Designers of America (CFDA) (2007); Chairman's Award, NAACP Image Awards (2007); Grammy Awards for Best Rock Album, Album of the Year, Best Rock Group Performance, Song of the Year, Best Rock Song, The Recording Academy (2006); Named One of the 100 Most Influential People, TIME Magazine (2006); Neruda Award, Chile (2006); Award for World's Bestselling Rock Act, World Music Awards (2006); Named (with U2) to Rock and Roll Hall of Fame (2005); Portuguese Order of Liberty (2005); Ambassador of Conscience Award, Amnesty International (2005); Grammy Award for Best Rock Performance by a Duo or Group, The Recording Academy (2005); Named to UK Music Hall of Fame (2004); TED Prize, Technology, Entertainment and Design Conference (2004); Freedom Award, National Civil Rights Museum (2004); World Soundtrack Award for Best Original Song Written for a Film (2003); MusiCares Person of the Year (2003); Named the Most Powerful Artist in Music, Q Magazine (2002); Named One of VH1: 100 Sexiest Artists (2002); Grammy Awards for Album of the Year, Best Pop Performance, Best Rock Performance, Best Rock Album, The Recording Academy (2001); Grammy Award for Best Long Form Music Video, The Recording Academy (1995); Grammy

Award for Best Rock Group Vocal, The Recording Academy (1993); Grammy Awards for Best Album, Best Performance by a Group, The Recording Academy (1987); Numerous Awards

HIBBS, JOHN D., T: Computer Company Executive, Electrical Engineer, Small Business Owner **I:** Engineering **DOB:** 01/26/1948 **PB:** Del Norte **SC:** CO/USA **PT:** Alva Bernard Hibbs; Frances Ava (Cathcart) Hibbs **MS:** Married **SPN:** Ruthanne Johnson (02/28/1976) **ED:** Bachelor of Science in Electrical Engineering, University of Denver, Denver, CO (1970) **C:** Chairman, Board, Sport Sail Inc. (1996-1997); President, Owner, Hibbs Scientific Software, Boulder, CO (1986-1996); President, Owner, Computer Aided Lighting Analysis, Boulder, CO (1983-1986); Lighting Products Manager, Computer Sharing Services, Inc., Denver, CO (1979-1983); Lighting Engineer, Holophane Division Johns Manville, Denver, CO (1973-1979); Electrical Engineer, Merrick and Co., Denver, CO (1972-1973) **CR:** Co-Founder, Sport Sail Inc.; Investor in Apartment Buildings; Volunteer, Wood Furniture Projects for Colorado Music Festival in Boulder; Volunteer, Wood Furniture, 10th Mountain Huts **MIL:** U.S. Naval Reserve (1970-1972) **CW:** Author, Computer Aided Lighting Analysis **AW:** First Prize, San Luise Valley Science Fair (1963) **MEM:** Chairman, Computer Problem Set Committee, Computer Society of Institute of Electrical and Electronics Engineers (1991-1995); Chairman, Computer Committee, Illuminating Engineering Society of North America (1988-1991) **MH:** Albert Nelson Marquis Lifetime Achievement Award **AS:** Mr. Hibbs attributes his success to the influence of his family, as well as luck. **B/I:** Mr. Hibbs became involved in his profession because, from an early age, he had an inquisitive mind and enjoyed putting things together and taking them apart. He was infatuated with computers at an early age. **AV:** Woodworking; Bicycling; Sailing; Skiing; Painting **PA:** Democrat

HICE, JODY BROWNLOW, T: U.S. Representative **I:** Government Administration/Government Relations/Government Services **DOB:** 04/22/1960 **PB:** Atlanta **SC:** GA/USA **MS:** Married **SPN:** Dee Dee Hice (1983) **CH:** Two children **ED:** DMin, Luther Rice College & Seminary, Atlanta, GA; MDiv, Southwestern Baptist Theological Seminary, Fort Worth, TX; BA, Asbury University, Wilmore, KY **C:** U.S. Representative, Georgia's 10th Congressional District, United States Congress (2014-Present); Senior Pastor, The Summit Church, Loganville, GA (2011-2013); Senior Pastor, Bethlehem First Baptist Church (2005-2010); First Vice President, Georgia Baptist Convention (2004-2005); Professor of Preaching, Luther Rice College & Seminary; Member, Committee on Armed Services; Member, Committee on Natural Resources; Member, Committee on Oversight and Government Reform; Member, Republican Study Committee **CR:** Radio Show Host, "The Jody Hice Show" (Formerly "Let Freedom Ring") **MEM:** NRA; Georgia Carry; Georgia Gun Owners; Georgia Sports Shooting Association; Gun Owners of America **PA:** Republican

HICKENLOOPER, GEORGE L., T: Playwright, Educator **I:** Education/Educational Services **DOB:** 10/09/1935 **PB:** St. Louis **SC:** MO/USA **PT:** George Loening Hickenlooper; Helena White Hickenlooper **MS:** Married **SPN:** Jane Thatcher Hickenlooper (08/14/1982); Barbara Jo Wenger (07/14/1962, Divorced 06/15/1976) **CH:** George Hickenlooper III (Deceased) **ED:** Doctor of Fine Arts, Yale University, School of Drama, New Haven, CT (1967); Master of Arts in German, Washington University, St. Louis, MO (1960); Bachelor of Science in International Affairs, Georgetown University School Foreign Service, Washington, DC (1958)

C: Professor Emeritus, Lindenwood University, St. Charles, MO (2014-2019); Professor, Lindenwood University, St. Charles, MO (1992-2014); Adjunct Professor, St. Louis, MO (1982-1992); Freelance Writer, St. Louis, MO (1982-1992); Associate Professor, McKendree College, Lebanon, IL (1977-1982); Assistant Professor, Lincoln University, San Francisco, CA (1972-1976); Lecturer, San Jose State College, California (1970-1972); Artist-in-residence, Washington University, St. Louis, MO (1969-1970) **CR:** Board, Missouri Association Playwrights, St. Louis, MO (1978-Present) **CIV:** Teacher, Administrator, Voluntary Improvement Program Adult Education, St. Louis, MO (1965-1968) **CW:** Author, Play, "The Sleepwalker" (2010); Author, Play, "Sir Rogert Casement, Traitor" (2007); Author, Play, "All for his Own Good" (2000); Author, Play, "The Wave" (1989); Author, Play, "Nature's Gentleman" (1978) **AW:** Tony McAuley Award, for "Sir Roger Casement, Traitor," Oxford International Institute of Documentary and Conflict Transformation (2007); Buckham Alley Theater Playwright's Forum Award, for "All for his Own Good" (2000); Missouri Arts Council Award, for "Nature's Gentleman" (1978); Riverdale Contemporary Theater Award, for "Sir Roger Casement, Traitor" (1976) **MEM:** Dramatists Guild of America **MH:** Albert Nelson Marquis Lifetime Achievement Award **B/I:** Mr. Hickenlooper's parents encouraged him to be willing to make any sacrifice in order to pursue his education, and later on, his career. He enrolled in school at the Define Service School and then received the Attenhauer Fellowship to study at the University of Munich in Germany. During his time in Germany, Mr. Hickenlooper went to the theater and fell in love with the plays that he saw. **AV:** Traveling; Learning new languages **RE:** Roman Catholic

HICKEY, BENJAMIN M., T: Curator of Exhibitions **I:** Museums & Institutions **CN:** Paul and Lulu Hilliard University Art Museum **MS:** Married **CH:** Mac; Violet **ED:** Master of Arts in Art History, University of California Riverside, Riverside, CA (2008); Bachelor of Arts in History, Minor in Art History and Classics, Canisius College, Buffalo, NY (2004) **C:** Curator of Exhibitions, Paul and Lulu Hilliard University Art Museum, University of Louisiana at Lafayette, Lafayette, LA (2018-Present); Emily Cyr Bridges Endowed Professor of Art, Paul and Lulu Hilliard University Art Museum, University of Louisiana at Lafayette, Lafayette, LA (2018-Present); Trustee at Large, Association of Art Museum Curators (2015-Present); Co-Founder, Curator, Outside Gallery, Monroe, LA (2016-2018); Curator of Collections and Exhibitions, Masur Museum of Art, Monroe, LA (2010-2018); Member, Community Advisory Board, KEDM, Monroe, LA (2014-2017); Adjunct Professor, School of Design, Louisiana Tech University, Ruston, LA (2015-2016); Adjunct Professor, Art History, Canisius College, Buffalo, NY (2009-2010); Associate Preparator, Apprentice Cabinetmaker, Albright-Knox Art Gallery, Buffalo, NY (2008-2010); Assistant Preparator, Exhibitions Intern, Albright-Knox Art Gallery, Buffalo, NY (2004-2006) **CR:** Visiting Critic, University of Memphis (2017); Visiting Critic, University at Arkansas at Monticello (2017); Exhibitions Coordinator, Arts Council in Buffalo and Erie County, Buffalo, NY (2008-2010); Teaching Assistant, Department of the History of Art, University of California Riverside, Riverside, CA (2006-2008); Exhibitions Assistant, Registrar, Media Relations, College of Humanities, Arts, and Social Sciences, California Museum of Photography, Riverside, CA (2007) **CW:** Exhibition, "Malaika Favorite: The Alchemist," Paul and Lulu Hilliard University Art Museum (2020); Exhibition, "ROBERT C. TANNEN|BOX-CITY," Paul and Lulu Hilliard University Art Museum (2020); Exhibition, "Notes from the Schoolyard," Paul and Lulu Hilliard University Art Museum (2020); Author, Essay Describing John F. Simons Studio Practice, "Each Moment," 64 Parishes (2019); Exhibition Curator, "Paths and Loops: Automatic Drawings by John F. Simon, Jr," Paul and Lulu Hilliard University Art Museum (2019); Exhibition Curator, "Koto Ezawa: Two Views," Paul and Lulu Hilliard University Art Museum (2019); Exhibition Curator, "Gisela Colon: Pods," Paul and Lulu Hilliard University Art Museum (2019); Exhibition Curator, "Daniel Canogar: Echo," Paul and Lulu Hilliard University Art Museum (2019); Exhibition Curator, "Slavery, The Prison Industrial Complex: Photographs by Keith Calhoun and Chandra McCormick" (2019); Exhibition Curator, "Tripping Over Cypress: Recent Work by Cliff Tresner," Paul and Lulu Hilliard University Art Museum (2019); Exhibition Curator, "Land Displacement/Replacement," Paul and Lulu Hilliard University Art Museum (2019); Exhibition Curator, "Marina Zurkow: Mesocosm," Paul and Lulu Hilliard University Art Museum (2018); Exhibition Curator, "Shirin Neshat: Fervor," Paul and Lulu Hilliard University Art Museum (2018); Exhibition Curator, "Bill Viola: The Raft," Paul and Lulu Hilliard University Art Museum (2018); Exhibition Curator, "Ana Benaroya: Standing Before Evil," Masur Museum of Art (2018); Exhibition Curator, "Common Ground: Selina Atker & Anna Rowan," Masur Museum of Art (2018); Juror, 2017 International Louisiana Printmaking Exhibition, Moffett Gallery, F. Jay Taylor Visual Arts Center, School of Design, Louisiana Tech University (2017); Exhibition Curator, "Pat Phillips: Told You Not to Bring That Ball," Masur Museum of Art (2017); Exhibition Curator, "Social Vices," Outside Gallery, Alt-Ex Masur Museum Collaboriaton (2017); Exhibition Curator, "Marcus Journey: Missionary," Massur Museum of Art (2017); Exhibition Curator, "Caroline Youngblood: Becoming the Butterfly," Masur Museum of Art (2017); Exhibition Curator, "Escapism: Places & Spaces," Monroe Regional Airport, Alt-Ex Collaboration (2017); Exhibition Curator, "Lacey Stinson: Developing Thoughts on Small Worlds," Masur Museum of Art (2017); Exhibition Curator, "Will Work For Food," Outside Gallery, Alt-Ex Masur Collaboration (2017); Exhibition Curator, "It Made Angels Out of Everybody," Outside Gallery, Alt-Ex Masur Collaboration (2017); Exhibition Curator, "Moundbuilders: Ancient Architects of North America," University of Pennsylvania Museum of Archaeology and Anthropology (2017); Exhibition Curator, "Sequence of Events," Outside Gallery (2017); Exhibition Curator, "Children Are the Future," Outside Gallery (2017); Juror, 54th Juried Competition, Coordinated at the Masur Museum of Art (2017); Exhibition Curator, "Beili Liu: Artist in Residence," Masur Museum of Art (2016); Exhibition Curator, "Malik Perrilloux Is Just a Concept," Outside Gallery (2016); Exhibition Curator, "You Never Take Me Anywhere Nice," Outside Gallery (2016); Exhibition Curator, "Accalia and The Swamp Monster," Masur Museum of Art (2016); Group Exhibition, "Well Worn Truths," Masur Museum of Art (2015); Exhibition Curator, "Emily Caldwell, Naturally," Masur Museum of Art (2015); Permanent Collection, "Recent Acquisitions & Favorites," Masur Museum of Art (2015); Exhibition Curator, "Shared Earth: The Ancient Mounds Project," Masur Museum of Art (2014); Exhibition Curator, "Whispering Pines," Masur Museum of Art (2014); Exhibition Curator, "Elayne Goodmans Whispering Pines," Masur Museum of Art (2014); Exhibition Curator, "Not Again!?: Work by Greely Myatt," Masur Museum of Art (2014); Juror, 51st Annual Juried Competition, "Contemporary Art Museum St. Louis," Masur Museum of Art (2014); Exhibition Curator, "Narratives Near and Far: Selections from the Wells Fargo Corporate Collec-

tion," Masur Museum of Art (2013); Exhibition Curator, "Golden Anniversary: The Masur Celebrates Fifty Years," Masur Museum of Art (2013); Juror, 20th Annual Juried Competition, Kimball Art Museum, Coordinated at Maasur Museum of Art (2013); Exhibition Curator, "Improvisations in Time: Eugene J. Martin and the Masur Museum of Art" (2012); Exhibition Curator, "Non Sequitur: An Homage to Eugene J. Martin from the Permanent Collection," Masur Museum of Art (2012); Juror, 49th Annual Juried Competition, Phantom Galleries Los Angeles (PGLA), Coordinated at Masur Museum of Art (2012); Group Exhibition, "Outside In," Masur Museum of Art (2012); Exhibition Curator, "John James Audubon," Masur Museum of Art (2012); Exhibition Curator, "James Surls: Seeing & Believing," Masur Museum of Art (2011); Exhibition Curator, "Michal Manjarris Rate of Exchange," Masur Museum of Art (2011); Exhibition Curator, "River & Reverie: Paintings of the Mississippi River by Rolland Golden," Masur Museum of Art (2011); Exhibition Curator, "Oxbows: Acquiescence and Continuity, The Photography of Lee Estes," Masur Museum of Art (2010); Exhibition Curator, "Virginia Weiss Invitational," Arts Council & Erie County (2009); Exhibition Curator, "An Optical Experience," Canisius College/Albright-Knox Art Gallery (2004); Author, Contributor, Numerous Monograph Essays, Chapters, Articles; Speaker in the Field **MEM:** Association of Art Museum Curators (2012-Present); KEDM, NPR Affiliate, Monroe, LA (2010-2018); Art Advisory Panel, City of Monroe Transit Authority, Monroe, LA (2015-2017); Adviser, Louisiana Creative Communities Initiative, Downtown Arts Alliance, Monroe, LA (2013-2015) **AS:** Mr. Hickey attributes his success to his unconventional background. He started as a preparator at the Albright-Knox Art Gallery. He understands how exhibitions are put together and the importance of how scholarships are presented in an exhibition context. Because of that, he has always been in the position where he's the sole curator and can control the narrative within the museum. **B/I:** Mr. Hickey became involved in his profession because he couldn't understand why humans were driven to make artwork, whether it be outlines of psalms on cave walls or Tony Smith's "Die." People were always trying to make something that has cultural significance. It doesn't necessarily have a practical or functional significance. It is a compulsion that humans have; he finds that fascinating. He has realized that different artwork brings out different things in people. There is no one answer. **THT:** "Show up and embrace the grind."

HIDY, GEORGE M., D.ENG, T: Chemical Engineer, Engineering Executive **I:** Engineering **DOB:** 01/05/1935 **PB:** Kingman **SC:** AZ/USA **PT:** John William Hidy; Margaret (Coqueron) Hidy **MS:** Married **SPN:** Doris A. Wilson (09/28/1990); Dana Sexton Thomas (08/15/1958) **CH:** Anne; Adrienne; John; Larry; Tom; Diane **ED:** Doctorate of Engineering, Johns Hopkins University (1962); MSE, Princeton University (1958); BS, Columbia University, New York, NY (1957); AB, Columbia University, New York, NY (1956) **C:** Principal, Envair/Aerochem Associates, Placitas, NM (1995-Present); Interim Director, New Mexico State University Carlsbad Center for Environmental Monitoring/Research (2001-2002); Retired (1999); Principal, Envair Aerochem (1999); Alabama Industrial Professor, Environmental Engineering, University of Alabama, Birmingham, AL (1996-1999); Associate Director, College of Engineering, Center for Environmental Research, University of California Riverside (1994-1996); Vice President, Electric Power Research Institute, Palo Alto, CA (1987-1994); President, Desert Research Institute, Reno (1984-1987); Vice

President, Environmental Research & Technology, West Lake, CA (1976-1984); General Manager, Environmental Research and Technology, West Lake, CA (1974-1976); Associate Director, Rockwell International Science Center, Thousand Oaks, CA (1973-1974); Group Leader, Chemical Physics, Rockwell International Science Center, Thousand Oaks, CA (1969-1973); Assistant Director, Chemistry and Microphysics, National Center for Atmospheric Research, Boulder, CO (1967-1969) **CIV:** Chairman, El Pueblo Health Center (2004-2010); Board of Directors, El Pueblo Health Center (2003-2009); Commissioner, California Youth Soccer Association, Los Angeles, CA (1982-1984); El Pueblo Health Center **CW:** Author, "Aerosols: An Industrial and Environmental Science Paperback" (1984) **AW:** Sinclair Award, American Association of Aerosol Research (2009); Chambers Award, Air and Waste Management Association (2007) **MEM:** Fellow, American Association for the Advancement of Science; American Meteorological Society; American Chemical Society; American Geophysical Union; Air and Waste Management Association; American Association for Aerosol Research **MH:** Albert Nelson Marquis Lifetime Achievement Award **B/I:** Dr. Hidy became involved in his profession because his father, John William, was an electrical engineer and introduced him to the field. He urged him to pursue engineering because it was a growing field at the time.

HIEMSTRA, JOHN E., T: Reverend **I:** Religious **DOB:** 06/21/1928 **PB:** Oskaloosa **SC:** IA/USA **PT:** Frank Hiemstra; Gertrude H. (DeKock) Hiemstra **MS:** Married **SPN:** Norma Franklin Hiemstra (08/20/1948) **CH:** Carol; Ruth; Jean; Nancy **ED:** DD, Central University (1989); EdD, Rutgers, The State University of New Jersey (1978); MDiv, New Brunswick Theological Seminary (1955); BA, Central University (1952) **CT:** Ordained as Minister of Word **C:** Executive Secretary, The Regional Synod of New York, Tarrytown, NY (1979-Present); President, Reformed Church in America (1990-1991); Communication Director, United Ministries, New York, NY (1972-1979); Executive Minister, Reformed Church in America, New York, NY (1964-1972); Minister, Good Shepherd Church, Westland, MI (1959-1964); Minister, First Reformed Church, Waterloo, Iowa (1955-1959) **CR:** Member, New York City Church Council (Council of Churches of the City of New York) (1979-Present); Moderator, General Synod, Reformed Church in America (1991-1992); President, New York State Council of Churches, Syracuse, NY (1987-1989) **CIV:** Former Member, President, Hudson Area Housing Agency, Tarrytown, NY (1985-Present); Reform Church of Closter, NJ (1994-2005); Special Ministries to Japanese, Bronx, NY (1986) **AW:** Named Clergy of the Year, JFK Chapel, Our Lady of the Skies (2003); Named Man of the Year, Jaycees, Westland (1963) **MEM:** Association of Education; Aircraft Owners and Pilots Association; Classis of Rockland-Westchester; Rutgers Alumni Association; New Brunswick Theological Seminary Alumni Association **MH:** Albert Nelson Marquis Lifetime Achievement Award; Marquis Who's Who Humanitarian Award **B/I:** Dr. Hiemstra became involved in his profession because when he was about 7 years old, he looked at what his pastor, Reverend George Muyskens, was doing in Iowa and he decided he would like to model his life after him. From that time on, he was dedicated in serving through the church. **AV:** Pilot (had his own plane); Photography; Computer programming **PA:** Democrat **RE:** Reformed Church in America, Classic of Palisades

HIGGINS, BRIAN M., T: U.S. Representative from New York **I:** Government Administration/Government Relations/Government Services **DOB:** 10/06/1959 **PB:** Buffalo **SC:** NY/USA **PT:** Dan Higgins; Mary Higgins **MS:** Married **SPN:** Mary Jane Hannon **CH:** Maeve; John **ED:** MA in Public Policy and Administration, Harvard Kennedy School, John F. Kennedy School of Government (1996); MA in History, Buffalo State College, The State University of New York (1985); BS in Political Science, Buffalo State College, The State University of New York (1984) **C:** Member, U.S. House of Representatives from New York's 26th Congressional District, United States Congress (2013-Present); Member, U.S. House of Representatives from New York's 27th Congressional District, United States Congress (2005-2013); Member, District 145, New York State Assembly (1998-2004); Member, Buffalo Common Council (1987-1993); Lecturer, History and Economics, Buffalo State College, The State University of New York; Member, Committee on Foreign Affairs; Member, Committee on Homeland Security **AW:** Inaugural Western New York Harvard Graduate Fellowship (1995); Forty Under Forty Award, Business First Newspaper; Scholar, Judge John D. Hillary Scholarship Award **PA:** Democrat **RE:** Roman Catholic

HIGGINS, GLEN, "CLAY" CLAY, T: U.S. Representative from Louisiana **I:** Government Administration/Government Relations/Government Services **CN:** U.S. House of Representatives **DOB:** 08/24/1961 **PB:** New Orleans **SC:** LA/USA **MS:** Married **SPN:** Becca Higgins (2009); Kara Seymour (2003, Divorced 2007); Rosemary Rothkamm-Hambrice (1991, Divorced 1999); Eloisa Rovati (1983, Divorced 1991) **CH:** Four Children **ED:** Coursework, Louisiana State University (1979-1983, 1989-1990) **C:** Member, U.S. House of Representatives from Louisiana's Third Congressional District (2017-Present); Member, Committee on Homeland Security; Member, Committee on Science, Space, and Technology; Member, Committee on Veterans' Affairs **CIV:** City Marshal, Office of Marshal, City Court of Lafayette (2016-Present); Sheriff, St. Landry Parish (2008-2016); With, Port Barre Police Department (2007-2010); Reserve Officer, Opelousas, LA (2004-2008) **MIL:** With, United States Army (1979-1985) **AW:** Named, Kentucky Colonel (2016)

HIGGINSON, JERRY, "JAY" ALDEN, T: President, Chief Executive Officer **I:** Nonprofit & Philanthropy **DOB:** 07/21/1957 **PB:** Mount Vernon **SC:** IL/USA **PT:** Jerry Alden Higginson Sr.; Beverly Joyce (York) Higginson **MS:** Married **SPN:** Leah Jane Murray (06/11/1983) **CH:** Sara Elisabeth; Jon Patrick Alden **ED:** Master in Finance and Banking, Southern Methodist University (1988); Postgraduate Coursework, Southern Illinois University (1979); BA, Graceland College (Now Graceland University), Lamoni, Iowa (1979) **C:** Greater Randolph Area Services Program (2000-Present); Director of Development and Planned Giving, Jewish Family Service (1998-2000); Vice President, Norwest Bank, San Antonio, Texas (1997-1998); Vice President, City Manager, NationsBank of Texas, San Antonio, Texas (1982-1997); Trust Officer, MidAmerican Bank and Trust, Carbondale, IL (1980-1982); Trust Officer, Assistant Cashier, Salem National Bank, IL (1979-1980) **CR:** Instructor, American Institute Banking, San Antonio, Texas (1984-Present); Member, San Antonio Estate Planners Council, Texas (1982-Present); Member, Faculty, Palo Alto Community College (Palo Alto College) (1989-1990) **CIV:** Scoutmaster, Boy Scouts of America (2002-Present); Member, District Committee, Boy Scouts of America (2000-Present); Treasurer, Board of Directors, Las Casas Foundation (2000-Present); National Society of the Sons of the American Revolution (2000-Present); Musical Offerings (1997-Present); Member, Advisory Board, The Salvation Army USA (1994-Present); Treasurer, Mental Health Association of Texas (1992-Present); Chairman, Mental Health Association of Texas (1991-Present); President, National Society of the Sons of the American Revolution (2007-2008); Member, Board, Friends of San Antonio Public Library (1997-2001); Member, Regional Council, National Jewish Center for Immunology (Now National Jewish Center for Immunology and Respiratory Medicine) (1995-2000); Vice President, Board of Directors, Treasurer, Mental Health Association of Texas (1992-2005); Member, Board of Volunteers, Alamo Area Council, Boy Scouts of America (1990-2003); Planned Giving Council of San Antonio (PGCSA) (1993-2000); Treasurer, Planned Giving Council of San Antonio (PGCSA) (1993-2000); San Antonio Botanical Society (San Antonio Botanical Garden) (1992-2000); Board of Directors, Member, Development Board, Our Lady of Pillar (1992-2000); Board of Directors, Beautify San Antonio (1987-1998); Mission Road Developmental Center Chairman, Koehler Foundation (1991-1998); Board of Directors, San Antonio Junior Achievement (Junior Achievement of San Antonio) (1990); Board of Directors, Mental Health Association of Texas (1989-1990); President, Board of Trustees, San Antonio Area Foundation (1986-1990); President, Beautify San Antonio (1988-1989); President, Board of Directors, San Antonio Clean and Beautiful Committee (1987-1989); Past President, President, Keep San Antonio Beautiful Inc. (1986-1989); Treasurer, President, San Antonio Clean and Beautiful Committee (1986-1987); President, San Antonio Symphony Society (1985-1986); Member, Advisory Board, The Salvation Army USA, San Antonio, Texas; Board of Directors, Keep Texas Beautiful, Inc. **AW:** Various Service Awards **MEM:** Rotary Club of Randolph Metrocom (2000-Present); President, Knife and Fork Club San Antonio (1992-Present); Past President, Rotary Club of Randolph Metrocom (2009-2010); Board of Directors, San Antonio Botanical Garden (1992-2004); Board, The Witte Museum (1994-2000); Vice President, Knife and Fork Club San Antonio (1991-1992); Board of Directors, Knife and Fork Club San Antonio (1990-1991); National Society Fund Raising Executives (Now Association of Fundraising Professionals (AFP)); Symphony Society of San Antonio (Now San Antonio Symphony); San Antonio Baroque Music Society; San Antonio Conservation Society (Now The Conservation Society of San Antonio); San Antonio Botanical Society (Now San Antonio Botanical Garden); Knife and Fork Club San Antonio; The Witte Museum; San Antonio Genealogical and Historical Society; Alden Kindred of America; Mayflower Society of America (Now General Society of Mayflower Descendants) **MH:** Albert Nelson Marquis Lifetime Achievement Award **B/I:** Mr. Higginson began becoming involved with nonprofit organizations at the lowest level. He eventually worked his way up over the years to become a president of one. **AV:** Photography; Music; Travel **PA:** Republican **RE:** Protestant

HIGGS, GEOFFREY B., T: Doctor **I:** Medicine & Health Care **CN:** International Orthopaedic Surgery Consultants, LLC **ED:** Postdoctoral Fellowship in Sports Medicine, Harvard Medical School (1999); Residency in Orthopedic Surgery, Columbia University (1994); Postdoctoral Fellowship in Orthopedic Research, UC San Diego (1990); Internship in General Surgery, Columbia University (1989); MD, Columbia University (1988); BS in Systems Engineering, University of Virginia (1983) **CT:** Board Certified in Orthopedic Sports Medicine, American Board of Orthopedic Surgery (2007); Board Certified in Orthopedic Surgery, American Board of Orthopedic Surgery (1997) **C:** Founder, President, Excel Orthopedic Specialists (2018-Present); Head Team Physician, Dallas

Rattlers, Dallas Cowboys Star Center (2018-Present); Team Physician, Texas Legends (2018-Present); Head Team Physician, The University of Texas at Dallas (2018-Present); Head Team Physician, Texas Revolution (2018-Present); Head Team Physician, EXOS (2018-Present); Founder, Chief Executive Officer, International Orthopedic Surgery Consultants, LLC (2017-Present); Consultant, MedShape, Inc. (2010-Present); Chief Medical Officer, MedOne Texas (2018); Director of Orthopedic Surgery and Sports Medicine, Orthocare Institute (2017-2018); Orthopedic Surgeon, Sports Medicine Specialist, Advanced Orthopedics (2000-2016); Team Physician, Washington Redskins (2013-2015); Head Team Physician, Arena Football League (2002-2012); Team Physician, New England Revolution (1998-2000); Team Physician, New England Patriots (1998-2000); Team Physician, Harvard University (1998-2000); Team Physician, Boston Bruins (1998-2000); Consultant, Shoulder Fellowship, Royal Berkshire Hospital, England (1997); Stadium Physician, New York Rangers (1991-1994); Stadium Physician, New York Yankees (1991-1994); Stadium Physician, New York Knicks (1991-1994); Systems Engineer, The MITRE Corporation (1983-1984) **CR:** Clinical Assistant Professor of Orthopedic Surgery, Virginia Commonwealth University (2000-2017) **CIV:** Board of Directors, Fight for the Forgotten, The Justin Wren Foundation (2018-Present) **MIL:** Major, U.S. Army (1994-1998); Captain, First Lieutenant, Second Lieutenant (1984-1994); Assistant Chief of Orthopedic Surgery, 121st General Hospital, Seoul, South Korea, U.S. Army; Assistant Chief of Orthopedic Surgery, U.S. Army Hospital, Germany; Chief of Orthopedic Surgery, Combat Support Hospital, U.S. Army Hospital, Taszar, Hungary **CW:** Author, "Anterior Cruciate Ligament Fixation: Is Radial Force a Predictor of the Pullout Strength of Soft-Tissue Interference Devices?," The Knee (2012) **AW:** Oren Baab Award for Best Orthopedic Surgeon Resident, Columbia University **MEM:** American Academy of Orthopaedic Surgeons; American Orthopaedic Society for Sports Medicine; ISAKOS **AS:** Dr. Higgs attributes his success to his hard work and commitment to providing his patients with the best available care. **B/I:** Dr. Higgs became involved in his profession after suffering a sports-related injury. His surgeon inspired him to pursue a career in the field.

HIGHFILL-LAGO, APRIL, T: Library Director **I:** Library Management/Library Services **CN:** Prairie County Public Library System **MS:** Married **C:** Library Director, Prairie County Library (2016-Present); Manager, Prairie County Library; Clerk, Prairie County Library **AW:** Award for Excellence, Preservation through Rehabilitation, Board of Preserve Arkansas, Arkansas Preservation Awards Selection Committee **AS:** Mrs. Highfill-Lago attributes her success to hard work and dedication. She also credits being a go-getter, her drive and her caring ability. **AV:** Fishing; Camping; Gardening

HIGMAN, FRANCIS LEVI, T: Mathematics Educator **I:** Education/Educational Services **DOB:** 09/13/1932 **PB:** Carthage **SC:** NY/USA **PT:** Levi Christopher Higman; Anna May (Kelley) Higman **MS:** Widowed **SPN:** Barbara Joan Crowley (09/13/1958) **CH:** Sean Thomas; Kelley Ann; Meghan Ann; Kerry Lynn **ED:** Postgraduate Coursework, University of Minnesota (1968); MA in Mathematics, University at Buffalo (1963); MS in Education, Syracuse University (1957); BA, Niagara University (1954) **C:** Retired (1998); Professor of Mathematics, Niagara University (1982-1998); Associate Professor, Niagara University (1968-1982); Assistant Professor, Niagara University (1962-1968); Instructor, Niagara University (1956-1957) **CIV:** Treasurer,

Niagara County Chapter, American Cancer Society (1992-2012); Trustee, Niagara Catholic High School (1991-2012); President, Niagara University Lay Teachers Association (1978-1998); President, Niagara Catholic High School (1992-1993) **MIL:** First Lieutenant, U.S. Army Corps of Engineers (1954-1956) **MEM:** Mathematical Association of America **MH:** Albert Nelson Marquis Lifetime Achievement Award; Marquis Who's Who Top Professional **AS:** Mr. Higman attributes his success to being friendly with almost every faculty member on campus. **B/I:** Mr. Higman became involved in his profession because he originally wanted to teach high school mathematics but after receiving an offer to work at Niagara University, he never looked back. **AV:** Woodworking; Spending time with his grandchild **PA:** Democrat **RE:** Roman Catholic

HILL, FAITH, T: Singer **I:** Media & Entertainment **DOB:** 09/21/1967 **PB:** Ridgeland **SC:** MS/USA **PT:** Ted Perry; Edna Perry **MS:** Married **SPN:** Tim McGraw (10/06/1996); Daniel Hill (07/23/1988, Divorced 1994) **CH:** Gracie; Maggie; Audrey **ED:** Coursework, Hinds Community College, Raymond, MS **C:** With, Warner Brothers Records (1993-Present); Launched, Fragrance, True (2010); Launched, Fragrance, Faith Hill Parfums (2009) **CIV:** Founder, Faith Hill Family Literacy Project (1996-Present); Co-organizer, Nashville Rising Benefit Concert (2010) **CW:** Appearance, "The World's Best" (2019);Singer, "The Rest of Our Life" (2017); Appearance, "Pickler & Ben" (2017); Singer with Tim McGraw, "The Rest of Our Life" (2017); Singer, "Deep Tracks" (2016); Appearance, "The Voice" (2016); Appearance, "Dixieland" (2015); Singer, "Illusion" (2013); Performer, Soul2Soul, Las Vegas, NV (2012-2014); Appearance, "CMT Crossroads" (2011); Singer, "Joy to the World" (2008); Singer, "The Hits" (2007); Singer, "Fireflies" (2005); Singer, "Sunshine & Summertime" (2005); Singer, "Like We Never Loved at All" (2005); Actress, "The Stepford Wives" (2004); Singer, "Cry" (2002); Singer, "There You'll Be" (2001); Performer, Film Soundtrack, "Pearl Harbor" (2001); Performer, Film Soundtrack, "How the Grinch Stole Christmas" (2000); Singer, "Breathe" (1999); Singer, "Faith" (1998); Singer, "This Kiss" (1998); Singer, "Just to Hear You Say You Love Me" (1998); Singer, "Breathe" (1998); Singer with Tim McGraw, "Let's Make Love" (1998); Performer, Film Soundtrack, "Practical Magic" (1998); Singer, "It's Your Love" (1997); Actress, "Touched by an Angel" (1997); Singer, "Piece of My Heart" (1996); Singer, "It Matters to Me" (1995); Singer, "Take Me as I Am" (1993); Performer, Television Soundtrack, "King of the Hill" **AW:** Recipient, Star, Hollywood Walk of Fame (2019); Named Number One Adult Contemporary Artist of the Decade, Billboard (2009); Awards for Favorite Female Country Artist, American Music Awards (2001-2003, 2006); Grammy Award with Tim McGraw for Best Country Collaboration with Vocals, Recording Academy (2006); Grammy Award for Best Female Country Vocal Performance, Recording Academy (2003); Named Hottest Female Video of the Year, Country Music TV Flameworthy Video Music Awards (2003); Named Favorite Female Performer, People's Choice Awards (2001-2003); Award for Female Vocalist of the Year, Academy of Country Music Awards (1999, 2001); Award for Favorite Country Album, American Music Awards (2001); Named Top Selling Album, Canadian Country Music Association (Now Music Canada) (2001); Grammy Award for Best Country Album, Recording Academy (2001); Named One of the 30 Most Powerful Women in America, Ladies' Home Journal (2001); Named Female Vocalist of the Year, TNN/CTM Country Weekly Music Awards (2001); Grammy Awards for Best Country Vocal Performance, Best Country Album, Best Country Collaboration with

Vocals, Recording Academy (2001); Five Platinum Awards, Canadian Recording Industry Association (Now Music Canada) (2001); Award for Favorite Pop-Rock Female Artist, American Music Awards (2001); Named Female Country Artist of the Year, Country Weekly (2000); Named Hot 100 Singles Female Artist of the Year, Billboard (2000); Named Female Vocalist of the Year, TNN/Music City News (2000); Named Billboard Hot 100 Airplay Track of the Year (2000); Named Video of the Year, Single of the Year, Academy of Country Music (1999); Named Video of the Year, TNN/Music City News (1999); Named Vocal Event of the Year, Academy of Country Music (1999); Named Vocal Event of the Year, Song of the Year, Music City News (1999); Awards for Song of the Year, Single of the Year, Video of the Year, Vocal Event of the Year, Academy of Country Music Awards (1998); CMA Award for Video of the Year, CMA Country Music Association Inc. (1998); Named Female Star of Tomorrow (1995); Awards for Top Country Female Artist, Billboard (1994); Award for New Female Vocalist of Year, Academy of Country Music Awards (1993); Numerous Awards

HILL, JAMES, "FRENCH" FRENCH, T: U.S. Representative from Arkansas **I:** Government Administration/Government Relations/Government Services **DOB:** 12/05/1956 **PB:** Little Rock **SC:** AR/USA **MS:** Married **SPN:** Martha McKenzie (1988) **CH:** Two Children **ED:** BS in Economics, Vanderbilt University, Magna Cum Laude (1979) **C:** Member, U.S. House Financial Services Committee, Washington, DC (2015-Present); Member, Republican Study Committee (2015-Present); Member, U.S. House of Representatives from Arkansas' Second Congressional District, United States Congress, Washington, DC (2015-Present); Founder, Chairman, Chief Executive Officer, Delta Trust & Banking Corporation (Acquired by Simmons First National Corporation), Little Rock, AR (1999-Present); Executive Officer, First Commercial Corporation, Little Rock, AR (1993-1998); Special Assistant to President, Executive Secretary, Economic Policy Council, The White House (1991-1993); Deputy Assistant Secretary for Corporate Finance, U.S. Department of the Treasury, Washington, DC (1989-1993); Senior Economic Policy Official, U.S. Department of the Treasury (1989-1993); Director, Mason Best Company (1984-1989); Assistant to Senator John Tower, U.S. Senate Committee on Banking, Housing and Urban Affairs (1982-1984) **CR:** Chairman, Board Access Plans, Inc. (2009-Present); Board of Directors, HillAlliance HealthCard, Inc. (2009-Present); Board of Directors, Syair Designs LLC (2000-Present); Board of Directors, Research Solutions LLC (1999-Present); Board of Directors, Delta Trust & Banking Corporation (Acquired by Simmons First National Corporation) (1999-Present)Board of Directors, Access Plans USA Inc. (2003-2009); **AW:** Named One of the Most Powerful Men in Business, AY Magazine (2010); Henry Award, State of Arkansas (2007); Edwin Hanlon Award for Contributions to the City's Arts and Humanities (2002); Named Arkansas Museum Trustee of the Year (1999); Named to the 40 Under 40, Arkansas Business (1996); Named an Outstanding Young Arkansan, Arkansas Jaycees (1993); Distinguished Service Award, U.S. Department of the Treasury (1993) **MEM:** Phi Kappa Psi Fraternity **PA:** Republican

HILL, KATHERINE, "KATIE" LAUREN, T: Former U.S. Representaive from California **I:** Government Administration/Government Relations/Government Services **CN:** U.S. House of Representatives **DOB:** 08/25/1987 **PB:** Abilene **SC:** TX/USA **PT:** Mike Hill; Rachel Hill **MS:** Divorced **SPN:** Kenny Heslep (2010, Divorced 2019) **ED:** Master of Public Administration, California State University, Northridge;

Bachelor of Arts in English, California State University, Northridge **C:** Member, U.S. House of Representatives from California's 25th Congressional District, United States Congress, Washington, DC (2019); Executive Director, People Assisting the Homeless; Policy Advocate, People Assisting the Homeless **PA:** Democrat

HILL, LYDA, T: Chairman **I:** Business Management/Business Services **CN:** LH Capital, Inc. **DOB:** 09/17/1942 **PB:** Dallas **SC:** TX/USA **PT:** Albert Gatalyn Hill Sr.; Margaret (Hunt) Hill **ED:** BS in Mathematics, Hollins College (1964); Coursework, Stanford University (1960-1961) **C:** President, Hill Development CO., Dallas, TX (1985-Present); President, Seven Falls CO., Colorado Springs, CO (1985-Present); Chairman, Founder, Hill World Travel, Dallas, TX (1968-1986); President, Hill Development CO., Colorado Springs, CO **CR:** Chairman, LH Capital, Inc. **CIV:** President's Advisory Board, Private Sector Initiatives (1986-Present); Chairman, American Heart Association, Texas (1986-1987); Board of Directors, United Way, Dallas, TX (1983); President, Junior League of Dallas (1982-1983); Chairman, Crystal Charity Ball, Dallas, TX (1975); Board of Directors, Arts Magnet High School, Dallas, TX; Board of Directors, M.D. Anderson Hospital, Houston, TX; Board of Directors, American Heart Association; Board of Directors, Visiting Nurse Association; Board of Directors, Dallas Society of Crippled Children **AW:** President's Volunteer Action Award, National Federation of Republican Women (1986); Honorary Citizen, Fort Worth City Council (1985); Best American Award (1985) **MEM:** Kissing Camels Golf Club, Colorado Springs, CO; Garden Gods; Board of Directors, Dallas Chamber of Commerce; Charter 100; Committee 200; Young President Organization; Tower Club of Dallas; Dallas Country Club; Brook Hollow Club **AV:** Golf; Tennis; Skiing

HILL, MONTERO, "LIL NAS X" LAMAR, T: Rapper **I:** Media & Entertainment **DOB:** 04/09/1999 **PB:** Lithia Springs **SC:** GA/USA **PT:** Robert Stafford **MS:** Single **ED:** Coursework, University of West Georgia (2017-2018); Diploma, Lithia Springs High School (2017) **CW:** Musician, "7" (2019); Musician, "Banzup" (2019); Musician, "October 31st" (2018); Musician, "Nasarati" (2018) **AW:** Best Pop Duo/Group Performance, Best Music Video, "Old Town Road (Remix)," Grammy Awards (2020); Closet Door Bustdown Award, Queerty Awards (2020); Favorite Song - Rap/Hip-Hop, "Old Town Road (Remix)," American Music Awards (2019); Song of the Year, "Old Town Road," Apple Music Awards (2019); Single of the Year, Best Collab, Duo or Group, "Old Town Road (Remix)," BET Hip Hop Awards (2019); Musical Event of the Year, "Old Town Road (Remix)," Country Music Association Awards (2019); Song of the Year, Best Direction, "Old Town Road (Remix)," MTV Video Music Awards (2019); Winning Video, "Old Town Road (Remix)," MTV Video Play Awards (2019); Breakthrough Artist, Streamy Awards (2019); Choice Song: R&B/Hip-Hop, "Old Town Road (Remix)," Teen Choice Awards (2019)

HILLEGAS, WILLIAM J., PHD, T: Materials Scientist **I:** Sciences **DOB:** 08/31/1937 **PB:** Quakertown **SC:** PA/USA **MS:** Married **CH:** Five Children (One Deceased) **ED:** PhD, Northwestern University (1968); Graduate Coursework, Northwestern University, Evanston, IL (1963-1968); MS, Northwestern University (1967); BS, Drexel Institute of Technology (Now Drexel University) (1960); Student Engineer, Philco Corp., Lansdale, PA (1956-1960) **C:** Retired (2013); Vice President, Chief Technical Officer, Board of Directors, SoloHill Engineering, Inc., Ann Arbor, MI (1984-2013); Co-founder,

SoloHill Therapeutics, Inc., Pittsburgh, PA (1986); Co-founder, SoloHill Engineering Inc. (1984); Research Manager, KMS Fusion Inc., Ann Arbor, MI (1978-1984); Scientist, Xerox Corp., Rochester, NY (1968-1978); Engineer, Philco Corp., Lansdale, PA (1960-1963) **CIV:** County Committeeman, Democratic Committee, Monroe County, Rochester, NY (1971-1978) **CW:** Six Patents **AW:** SBIR Grants, National Cancer Institute and National Institute of Allergy and Infectious Diseases, National Institutes of Health, Washington, DC (1984-2000); Grantee, United States Navy, Washington, DC (1990); Grantee, Michigan State Research Fund, Lansing, MI (1988-1990); Grantee, American Iron and Steel Institute, Chicago, IL (1964-1968) **MEM:** American Association for the Advancement of Science; Past Member, The New York Academy of Science, American Institute of Chemical Engineers (AIChE), MRS and American Vacuum Society (Now AVS) **MH:** Albert Nelson Marquis Lifetime Achievement Award; Marquis Who's Who Top Professional **AV:** Travel

HILLENMEYER, HENRY, T: Restaurant Company Executive **I:** Food & Restaurant Services **DOB:** 11/13/1943 **PB:** Temple **SC:** TX/USA **PT:** Henry Reiling Hillenmeyer; Lucy Carolyn (Taylor) Hillenmeyer **MS:** Married **SPN:** Sallie Long Sigler (10/30/1976) **CH:** Henry Reiling; Edward Ferriday; Taylor Jennings; Morgan Andrew; Hunter Taverner **ED:** BA, Yale University (1965) **C:** President, Music City Flats, LLC (Now Lighthouse Property Management, Inc.) (2008-Present); Consultant, Compass Executives, LLC (2006-Present); Chairman, Chief Executive Officer, Director, Cooker Restaurant Corporation (1999-2004); Chairman, Chief Executive Officer, Director, Skillsearch Corporation, Nashville, TN (1995-1999); Chairman, President, Director, Southern Hospitality Corporation, Nashville, TN (1989-1994); President, Director, Southern Hospitality Corporation, Nashville, TN (1983-1989); Executive Vice President, Womco, Inc., Nashville, TN (1978-1982); President, Director, Ireland's Restaurants, Inc., Nashville, TN (1974-1978); Chairman, Director, CBM, Inc. (1972-1974); President, CBM, Inc. (1970-1972); Vice President, CBM, Inc., Cleveland, Ohio (1968-1970); Assistant Secretary, Kanawha Valley Bank (1967-1968); Trainee, Kanawha Valley Bank, Charleston, WV (1965-1967) **CIV:** Board of Directors, Junior Achievement, Nashville, TN (1985-Present); Board of Directors, Genetic Assays Inc. (2007); Chairman, Junior Achievement, Nashville, TN (1991-1992, 1997-1999); National Associate, Boys Clubs of America (Boys & Girls Clubs of America), New York, NY (1986-1990); Board of Directors, Special Olympics Tennessee, Nashville, TN (1986-1990); Trustee, Harding Academy, Nashville, TN (1985-1990) **MEM:** President, Yale Club of Middle Tennessee (1983-1988); World President Organization; Scroll and Key Society; Fence Club; Yale Club of Middle Tennessee **MH:** Albert Nelson Marquis Lifetime Achievement Award; Marquis Who's Who Top Professional **B/I:** Mr. Hillenmeyer became involved in his profession because he got into it by accident. When he graduated from Yale, he was first a banker and then he became the sixth founder of a computer company. The bank he worked for had an enormous trust department and he helped computerize the department, which was very complicated to do. There was no way they were going to be able to do that from scratch but he found a trust accounting system at the Bank of Southwestern, Houston, Texas, that dealt with all those issues. Ernst and Ernst were marketing that system but they were having difficulties getting other banks to successfully implement it but they were able to successfully implement it. What he did not know at the time was that the bank com-

puter system consultant at Ernst and Ernst was leaving them for another computer company. So they recruited him to join as one of the founders of that company. After advising the company that after six months they would run out of money, much to their denial, they did run out of funds. He was then offered the job of running the company at 26 years old and saved it. **PA:** Republican **RE:** Episcopalian

HILLESTAD, DONNA DAWN, T: Nurse (Retired) **I:** Medicine & Health Care **DOB:** 05/13/1938 **PB:** Merrill **SC:** WI/USA **PT:** Martin T. Dietrich; Edna (Frederick) Dietrich **MS:** Married **SPN:** John Curtis Hillestad (07/18/1959, Deceased 10/09/2012) **CH:** Dori Jean; David Jeffrey **ED:** Bachelor of Science in Nursing, Mankato University (1962) **CT:** Registered Nurse, Minnesota **C:** Charge Nurse, Supervisor, Lakeview Methodist Health Care Center, Fairmont, MN (1967-2000); Private Duty Public Health Nurse, Fairmont Clinic, Minnesota (1965-1967); Office Nurse, Fairmont Clinic, Minnesota (1963-1965) **CR:** Nurse Insurance Physical, Numerous Insurance Companies (1980-1997) **AW:** Numerous Awards, Bridge (2005-2018); Outstanding Achievement in Amateur Photography Award (2014); Gold Medal, Haines City Senior Olympics (1998); Three Silver Medals, Haines City Senior Olympics (1998); International Relations Award, American Association of University Women (1991); Multiple-Time Grand Champion, Martin County Fair; Numerous 1st Place Awards, Martin County Fair **MEM:** Chapter Secretary, Friendship Force, Southern Minnesota (1995-1997); Foundation Committee, Business and Professional Women (1990); Nominating Sunshine Committee, Business and Professional Women (1989-1990); Secretary, Business and Professional Women (1988-1989); Chairman, Hospitality, American Association of University Women (1987-1988); Public Relations Committee, American Association of University Women (1986-1987); Auditing Committee, Business and Professional Women (1986-1987); Chairman, International Relations, Business and Professional Women (1986); Bulletin Editor, American Association of University Women (1985-1986); Secretary, Business and Professional Women (1985-1986); Public Relations Committee (1984-1985); Historian, American Association of University Women (1982-1984); Emblem Chairman, Business and Professional Women (1982-1983); Cultural Interests Committee, American Association of University Women (1980-1981); Historian, Business and Professional Women (1976); Founder, Holiday Travel Club; Tourist Club; Community Club; Garden Club; Women's Club, Lake Wales **MH:** Albert Nelson Marquis Lifetime Achievement Award **AV:** Ham radio operator; World traveler; Crafts; Photography; Biking **RE:** Lutheran

HILSINGER WALLISER, KATHY ELLEN, T: President **I:** Real Estate **CN:** Acquirement LLC **DOB:** 11/02/1951 **PB:** St. Paul **SC:** MN/USA **PT:** Dolores Marie Tappe Hilsinger; Russell Jacob Hilsinger **SPN:** Gary Arnold Walliser (04/09/1972, Divorced 12/05/1988) **CH:** David N. Walliser; Deborah L. Walliser; Michelle A. Walliser; Michael J. Walliser **ED:** Doctoral Coursework in Biomedicine, Old Dominion University (2011-2013); Master of Science in Healthcare Administration, University of Maryland (2011); Bachelor of Science in Biological Sciences, East Carolina University (2006); Associate of Arts in Liberal Arts, Mission College, Santa Clara, CA (1993) **CT:** DOT Hazardous Materials Training for Regulated Medical Waste (2014); CME, New Trends in Blood Safety and Utilization, American Red Cross (2003); Certificate, Medical Response, Weapons of Mass Destruction, Signs and Symptoms, Greensboro Fire Department, HAZMAT (2003);

Certificate, International Humanitarian Law, American Red Cross (2002); Certificate International Services, American Red Cross (2002); Certificate, Tracing and Other International Services, American Red Cross (2002); Damage Assessment, American Red Cross (2001); Disaster Health Services, American Red Cross (2001); Disaster Welfare Inquiry Simulation, American Red Cross (2001); Family Services, Providing Emergency Assistance, American Red Cross (2001); Human Resources in Disaster, American Red Cross (2001); Introduction to Disaster Services, American Red Cross (2001); Disaster Preparedness Workshop, American Red Cross (2001); Conducting a Community Collaboration, American Red Cross (2001); Logistics Simulation, American Red Cross (2001); Logistics: An Overview, American Red Cross (2001); Mass Care: An Overview, American Red Cross (2001); Shelter Options, American Red Cross (2001); Shelter Simulation, American Red Cross (2001); Certificate, Medical Terminology, Dean-Vaughn Instruction (1991) **C:** President, Acquirement LLC (2017-Present); Moderator, Inventor Connection (2009-Present); Secretary of the Board, Compliance Officer and Project Specialist, HEAG Pain Management Center (2013-2016); Secretary of Institutional Review Board for Moses Cone Health System (2002-2004); Secretary of Institutional Review Board **CIV:** Founder, International Medical and Educational Fund (1993-Present); Donor, Freedom House, Greensboro, NC (2019); Volunteer, American Red Cross (1981-2006); Founder, Across the Sciences Award **CW:** Writer, Unlimited-Future (2011-Present); Author, I Come at Dusk, Poetry.com, (2006); Code-U Writer, Health Systems Magazine, Moses Cone Health System (2004) **AW:** Listee, Covington Whos Who (2014); National Deans List; Listee, 2,000 Most Notable American Women **MEM:** American Institute for Biological Sciences; Moderator, Inventor Connection Group, LinkedIn **AS:** Ms. Hilsinger Walliser credits her success on her ability to always try her hardest and learn all that she could. **B/I:** Ms. Hilsinger Walliser established Acquirement LLC in order to bring real estate projects to their highest level of use. **AV:** Inventor of energy bars **RE:** Christian

HILTON, LORRAINE ANN, MSED, T: Music Educator (Retired) **I:** Education/Educational Services **DOB:** 12/11/1946 **PB:** Plainfield **SC:** NJ/USA **PT:** Kenneth Edward Williams; Ruth Barbara Hatrick **MS:** Widowed **SPN:** Lawrence Raymond Hilton (06/26/2003, Deceased 2018); Richard Jon Robinson (06/28/1969, Divorced) **CH:** Lindsay Anne Williams; Kerry Eileen Cheney **ED:** MSEd, Trenton State College (1972); BA in Music Education, Montclair State College (1968) **CT:** Certified Supervisor, State of New Jersey (1972); K-12 Music Teacher, State of New Jersey (1968) **C:** Retired (2007); Instrumental Music Teacher, Franklin Township Board of Education (1968-2007) **CR:** Student Activities Bursar, Hillcrest School, Somerset, NJ (1996-2007); Student Council Advocate (1982-2007); Head Teacher, Conerly Road School, Somerset, NJ (1980-1982); Band Front Director, NJ (1968-1977); Assistant Band Director, NJ (1968-1978); Brass Ensemble Director, Franklin High School, Somerset, NJ (1973-1977); Concert Band Director, Franklin High School, Somerset, NJ (1973-1977) **CIV:** Trustee Emeritus, Company of Dance Arts, Red Bank, NJ (2001-Present); Treasurer, Rosary Alter Society, St. Elizabeth Ann Seton Church, Whiting, NJ (2017-2019); Vice-President, Rosary Alter Society, St. Elizabeth Ann Seton Church, Whiting, NJ (2019); Secretary, Board of Directors, Whiting, NJ (2012-2016); President, Board of Director, Whiting, NJ (2008-2012); Treasurer, Monmouth County Arts Council, Red Bank, NJ (1996-2003); Trustee, Company of Dance Arts, Red Bank, NJ (1990-2001);

Secretary, Company of Dance Arts, Red Bank, NJ (1997-1998); President, Company of Dance Arts, Red Bank, NJ (1992-1995) **AW:** Master Teachers Collaborative (2004); Fellow, National Endowment of the Humanities (1995) **MEM:** National Education Association; Music Educator's National Conference; Franklin Township Education Association; Somerset County Education Association; New Jersey Education Association; Beach Plum Quilters Guild **B/I:** Ms. Hilton became involved in her profession because she of a teacher she had as a child. Though she was younger than other children in the class, the teacher brought her forward, which made her feel included. She pursued a career in education in order to help children like her teacher had helped her. **AV:** Enjoying ballet, theater, visual arts and the symphony **PA:** Independent **RE:** Roman Catholic

HIMES, JAMES, "JIM" ANDREW, T: U.S. Representative from Connecticut; Former Nonprofit Organization Executive **I:** Government Administration/Government Relations/Government Services **DOB:** 07/05/1966 **SC:** Lima/Peru **PT:** James R. Himes; Judith A. Himes **MS:** Married **SPN:** Mary Scott (1994) **CH:** Emma; Linley **ED:** Honorary LHD, University of Bridgeport (2012); Master's Degree in Philosophy, University of Oxford, England (1990); BA, Harvard University (1988) **C:** National Finance Chairman, Democratic Congressional Campaign Committee (DCCC) (2013-Present); Member, U.S. House of Representatives from Connecticut's Fourth Congressional District, United States Congress (2009-Present); Vice President, Enterprise Community Partners, Inc. (Formerly Enterprise Foundation) (2007-2009); Head, Northeast Operations, Enterprise Community Partners, Inc. (Formerly Enterprise Foundation) (2004-2007); Joined, Enterprise Community Partners, Inc. (formerly Enterprise Foundation) (2003); Entry Level, Vice President, Goldman Sachs & Co. (1990-2002); Committee on Financial Services; Committee on Intelligence **CR:** Commissioner, Greenwich Housing Authority (2002); Chairman, Greenwich Democratic Town Committee; Board of Estimate & Taxation, Greenwich, CT **CIV:** Elder, First Presbyterian Church, Greenwich, CT; Board of Directors, Fairfield County Community Foundation; Advisory Board Member, Family Assets, Group, LLC, Bridgeport, CT; Former Chairman, Board of Directors, Aspira of Connecticut, Bridgeport, CT **AW:** Rhodes Scholar, St. Edmund Hall, University of Oxford, England **PA:** Democrat **RE:** Presbyterian

HINCH, ANDREW, "A.J." JAY, T: Former Manager **I:** Athletics **CN:** Houston Astros **DOB:** 05/13/1974 **PB:** Waverly **SC:** IA/USA **ED:** Diploma, Midwest City High School, Midwest City, OK (1992); Degree in Psychology, Stanford University **C:** Manager, Houston Astros (2015-2019); Manager, Arizona Diamondbacks (2009-2010); Professional Baseball Player, Philadelphia Phillies (2004); Professional Baseball Player, Detroit Tigers (2003); Professional Baseball Player, Kansas City Royals (2001-2002); Professional Baseball Player, Oakland Athletics (1998-2000) **CR:** Vice President of Professional Scouting, San Diego Padres (2010-2014) **AW:** World Series Champion (2017); Bronze Medal, U.S. Summer Olympics, Atlanta, GA (1996)

HINDS, ROBERT JAMES, T: Chemical Engineer **I:** Engineering **CN:** Chevron Research and Technology Company **DOB:** 09/29/1931 **PB:** Minot **SC:** ND/USA **PT:** Lonnie Robert Hinds; Mildred Louise Hinds **ED:** MS, Massachusetts Institute of Technology (1954); BS, Massachusetts Institute of Technology (1953) **CT:** Registered Professional Engineer, State of California **C:** Environmental Engineering Consultant, Chevron Research and Technology

Company, Richmond, CA (1998-Present); Senior Staff Engineer, Environmental Group, Chevron Research and Technology Company, Richmond, CA (1990-1997); Senior Staff Engineer, Engineering Technology Department, Chevron Corporation, Richmond, CA (1985-1989); Senior Environmental Engineer, Chevron Research Company, Richmond, CA (1975-1985); Manager, Computer and Systems Division, Chevron Research Company, Richmond, CA (1967-1974); Senior Engineering Associate, Chevron Research Company, Richmond, CA (1967); Group Supervisor, Chevron Research Company, Richmond, CA (1965); Research Engineer, Chevron Research Company, Richmond, CA (1962-1965); Chemical Engineer, E.I. duPont de Nemours & Company, Penns Grove, NJ, Antioch, CA, Louisville, KY (1956-1962) **CIV:** President, Knollwood Townhouses, Incorporated, San Rafael, CA (1977-1978) **MIL:** 1st Lt., U.S. Army (1954-1955) **CW:** Contributor, Articles, Professional Journals **MEM:** American Institute of Chemical Engineers; Aircraft Owners and Pilots Association; Commonwealth Club of California; Sigma Xi; Tau Beta Pi **MH:** Albert Nelson Marquis Lifetime Achievement Award **B/I:** Mr. Hinds became involved in his profession because he wanted to make a living. His specialty was design engineering. **AV:** Piloting

HINE, WILLIAM CLYDE, T: Dean Emeritus **I:** Education/Educational Services **CN:** Eastern Illinois University **DOB:** 01/02/1944 **PB:** Chicago **SC:** IL/USA **PT:** Maynard Hine; Harriett (Foulke) Hine **MS:** Married **SPN:** Betsy Nash (08/24/1968) **CH:** William; Charles **ED:** EdD, Indiana University, Bloomington (1973); MDiv, Christian Theological Seminary (1970); BS, Indiana University (1967) **C:** Dean, Eastern Illinois University (1986-2014); Associate Dean, University of Evansville (1980-1986); Chairperson, Indiana University East, Richmond (1973-1980); Graduate Assistant, Indiana University, Bloomington (1970-1973) **CR:** Consultant, Higher Education Institutions (1976-Present) **CW:** Contributor, Numerous Articles, Professional Journals **AW:** Outstanding Young Men America (1980) **MEM:** Chairperson, National Research Committee, Association for Continuing Higher Education (1984-Present); Publication Committee, Association for Continuing Higher Education (1982-Present); Region Chair, Board of Directors, Association for Continuing Higher Education (1988-1990); Board of Directors, American Association for Adult and Continuing Education (1987-1989); Vice President, American Association for Adult and Continuing Education (1987); Chairperson, Evaluation Committee, American Association for Adult and Continuing Education (1987); Chairperson, Adult Psychology, American Association for Adult and Continuing Education (1983-1985); Regional Planning Committee, Association for Continuing Higher Education (1981-1983); Committee for Private Higher Education, Association for Continuing Higher Education (1981-1982); American Association of Higher Education; Council for Advancement and Support of Education; American Association of Colleges for Teacher Education; American Society of Training and Development **MH:** Albert Nelson Marquis Lifetime Achievement Award **B/I:** Dr. Hine became involved in his profession because he was always interested in education. After finishing his seminary degree, he pursued graduate coursework and has excelled in higher education ever since. **AV:** Swimming; Golfing; Appreciating vintage automobiles **PA:** Republican **RE:** Christian

HINES, CURTIS LEE, EDD, T: Educational Consultant **I:** Education/Educational Services **DOB:** 04/03/1945 **PB:** Decatur **SC:** IL/USA **PT:** Sylvester Hines; Nobie (Hempstead) Hines **MS:** Married

SPN: Elinor Diane Ellis (07/25/1978) **CH:** Rayna Lynn; Shayla Ann; Kayla Karin; Curtis Lee Jr. **ED:** EdD in Educational Leadership, Nova Southeastern University (1996); EdS, University of Illinois, Urbana-Champaign, IL (1972); MEd in Counseling, Northeast Missouri State University (Now Truman State University) (1970); Bachelor's Degree in Physical Education, Northeast Missouri State University (Now Truman State University) (1969) **CT:** Certified Educational Counselor, School Administrator, State of Illinois **C:** Educational Consultant (Present); Director of Human Resources, North Chicago School District, North Chicago, IL (2001-2004); Assistant Superintendent, Hazel Crest School District (1999-2001); Principal, Lincoln Elementary School, Kenosha WI (1993-1999); Associate Principal, Bradford High School (1990-1993); Principal, Grant Elementary School, Rock Island, IL (1988-1990); Dean of Students, Evanston Township High School, IL (1974-1988); Part-time Instructor of Psychology, Sociology, Political Science, Health, Kankakee Community College (1972-1974); Counselor, Eastridge High School (1969-1974); Head Wrestling Coach, Eastridge High School (1969-1974); Part-time Counselor, Department of Public Aid, Kankakee, IL (1972); Driver's Education Teacher, Eastridge High School, Kankakee, IL (1969-1970) **CR:** Seminar, Teacher for Student Teachers, University of Wisconsin-Parkside, Kenosha, WI (2007-2008) **CIV:** African American Summit (1989); Program Activities Committee, Chicago Chapter, People United Save Humanity **CW:** Author, Doctoral Dissertation, "A Need for Change: Recruiting and Retaining a Multicultural Workforce in an Urban School District" **MEM:** Local School Commission Task Force, National Alliance of Black School Educators (NABSE) (1986-1988); Life Member, NAAC; Association for Supervision and Curriculum Development (ASCD); Kiwanis International; Omega Psi Phi Fraternity Inc.; Kappa Delta Pi, International Honor Society in Education **MH:** Albert Nelson Marquis Lifetime Achievement Award; Marquis Who's Who Top Professional **B/I:** Dr. Hines was inspired by educators he had, more specifically a wrestling coach that he had when he was in high school. **RE:** Christian

HINOJOSA, LYNARD, JD, LLB, T: Lawyer **I:** Law and Legal Services **DOB:** 05/03/1942 **PB:** Houston **SC:** TX/USA **PT:** Rudolph H. Hinojosa; Patricia Joy Hinojosa **MS:** Married **SPN:** Farahnaz H. Hinojosa (2/11/2006) **CH:** Chris; Kelly; Jeff **ED:** JD, University of California Los Angeles Law School (1967); BA, Yale University, New Haven, CT (1964) **C:** Partner, Hinojosa & Forer, Los Angeles, CA (2016-Present); Partner, Hinojosa & Wallet (1986-2016); Private Practice (1982-1986); Partner, Schibel & Hinojosa (1972-1982); Attorney, Los Angeles County Counsel (1967-1972) **CR:** Probate and Trust Executive Committee, California State Bar (1996-2002) **CW:** CEB Action Guide, "Handling a Probate" (2001, 2003, 2013, 2017); Co-Author, "Notification by Trustee: Two Views of the Requirements of New Probate Code §16061.7: The Sky is Not Falling", CA Trusts & Estates Quarterly (1998); Co-Author, "The Great Record Ripoff: Penal Sanctions and State Civil Remedies," University of West Los Angeles Law Review (1975); "The Publications: Ubiquitous Heirhunters," Probate Solutions; Editor, Co-Editor, "Action Guideline to Probate" **AW:** Listee, 100 Best Super California Lawyers (2019); Arthur K. Marshall Award, Los Angeles County Bar Association (2015); Listee, Super Lawyers **MEM:** Executive Committee, Los Angeles County Bar Association (1990-1996); Fellow, American College Trust and Estate Council; American Bar Association **BAR:** California State Bar **MH:** Albert Nelson Marquis Lifetime Achievement Award; Marquis Who's Who Top Professional **AS:** Mr. Hinojosa attributes his

success to his personality and his competitive nature. He additionally likes exchanging intellectual subjects with his peers. Likewise, he is aggressive, honest, and straightforward. **B/I:** Mr. Hinojoso decided to be a lawyer in order to support his family. He knew it was the right decision because he would be able to help others all the while making enough money for his family to be comfortable.

HIRONO, MAZIE KEIKO, T: U.S. Senator from Hawaii **I:** Government Administration/Government Relations/Government Services **DOB:** 11/3/1947 **PB:** Koori **SC:** Japan **PT:** Matabe Hirono; Laura Hirono **MS:** Married **SPN:** Leighton Kim Oshima (1987) **ED:** Doctor of Jurisprudence, Georgetown University Law Center (1978); Bachelor of Arts, University of Hawaii (1970) **C:** U.S. Senator, State of Hawaii (2013-Present); Member, U.S. Senate Committee on Veterans' Affairs (2013-Present); Member, U.S. Senate Judiciary Committee (2013-Present); Member, U.S. Senate Armed Services Committee (2013-Present); Member, U.S. House Ethics Committee (2011-2013); Member, U.S. House of Representatives from Hawaii's Second Congressional District, United States Congress (2007-2013); Lieutenant Governor, State of Hawaii (1994-2002); Member, District 22, Hawaii House of Representatives (1993-1994); Member, District 32, Hawaii House of Representatives (1985-1993); Member, Shim, Tam, Kirimitsu & Naito, Japan (1984-1988); Member, District 20, Hawaii House of Representatives (1983-1985); Member, District 12, Hawaii House of Representatives, Honolulu, Hawaii (1981-1983); Deputy Attorney General, State of Hawaii, Honolulu, Hawaii (1978-1980) **CR:** Board of Directors, National Asian Pacific American Bar Association; Chair, Hawaii Policy Group, National Commission on Teaching and America's Future (NCTAF); Member, Governor's Task Force on Science and Technology **CIV:** Board of Directors, Moiliili Community Center, Honolulu, Hawaii (1984-Present); Deputy Chair, Democratic National Committee (1997); Board of Directors, YMCA of Honolulu, Nu'uanu Branch (1982-2004) **MEM:** Bar of the Supreme Court of the United States; Hawaii Bar Association; The Phi Beta Kappa Society **PA:** Democrat **RE:** Buddhism

HITCHCOCK, KEN, T: Former Professional Hockey Coach **I:** Professional Training & Coaching **CN:** Edmonton Oilers **DOB:** 12/17/1951 **PB:** Edmonton **SC:** Alberta, Canada **ED:** Coursework, University of Alberta, Edmonton, Canada **C:** Head Coach, Edmonton Oilers, NHL (2018-2019); Head Coach, Dallas Stars, NHL (2017-2018); Head Coach, St. Louis Blues, NHL (2011-2017); Head Coach, Columbus Blue Jackets, NHL (2006-2010); Pro Scout, Philadelphia Flyers, NHL (2006); Head Coach, Philadelphia Flyers, NHL (2002-2006); Head Coach, Dallas Stars, NHL (1996-2002); Coach All-star Games, International Hockey League (IHL) (1993-1994, 1994-1995); Head Coach, Kalamazoo Wings (1993-1994); Assistant Coach, Philadelphia Flyers, NHL (1990-1993);Head Coach, Kamloops Blazers, Canadian League (CHL) (1984-1990) **CR:** Assistant Coach, Team Canada, Olympic Games, Sochi, Russia (2014); Assistant Coach, Team Canada, Olympic Games, Vancouver, Canada (2010); Head Coach, Team Canada, IIHF World Championships (2008) **AW:** Jack Adams Award, NHL (2012)

HITCHINS, KEITH ARNOLD, PHD, T: History Professor **I:** Education/Educational Services **CN:** University of Illinois at Urbana-Champaign **DOB:** 04/02/1931 **PB:** Schenectady **SC:** NY/US **PT:** Henry Arnold Hitchins; Lillian Mary Turrian **ED:** Honorary PhD, University of Bucharest, Bucharest, Romania

(2012); Honorary PhD, Constanta, Romania (2009); Honorary PhD, University of Iasi (Now Alexandru Ioan Cuza University), Iasi, Romania (2008); Honorary PhD, West University of Timisoara, Timisoara, Romania (2008); Honorary PhD, University of Medicine and Pharmacy of Targu Mures, Targu Mures, Romania (2005); Honorary PhD, "1 Decembrie 1918" University of Alba Iulia, Alba, Romania (2001); Honorary PhD, Lucian Blaga University of Sibiu, Sibiu, Romania (1993); Honorary PhD, Babes-Bolyai University, Cluj-Napoca, Romania (1991); PhD, Harvard University, Cambridge, MA (1964); AM, Harvard University, Cambridge, MA (1953); AB, Union College, Schenectady, NY (1952) **C:** Professor of East European History, University of Illinois at Urbana-Champaign, IL (1969-Present); Associate Professor, Professor of History, University of Illinois at Urbana-Champaign, IL (1967-Present); Assistant Professor of History, Rice University, Houston, Texas (1965-1967); Instructor, Assistant Professor of History, Wake Forest University, Winston-Salem, NC (1958-1965) **CR:** Lecturer, University of Bucharest (2015); Consultant, Joint Committee on Eastern Europe, American Council of Learned Societies and Social Science Research Council (1982-1989); Consultant, Council for International Exchange Scholars (CIEC) (1970-1979) **CW:** Author, "East or West: Romania 1919-2007" (2019); Author, "A Concise History of Romania" (2014); Author, "Ion I. C. Bratianu" (2011); Author, "The Identity of Romania" (2009); Editor, Journal of Kurdish Studies (1995-2008); Author, "Romanian-American Relations: Documents 1859-1901" (2001); Author, "A Nation Affirmed" (1999); Author, "A Nation Discovered" (1999); Author, "The Romanians, 1774-1866" (1996); Author, "Romania 1866-1947" (1994); Editor, Romanian Studies (1970-1986); Author, "The Idea of Nation: Romanians of Transylvania 1691-1849" (1985); Editor, Studies in East European Social History (1977-1981); Author, "Orthodoxy and Nationality" (1977); Author, "Romanian National Movement in Transylvania 1780-1849" (1969); Consultant, Caucasian Studies-Encyclopedia Iranica; Consultant, Kurdish Studies, Encyclopedia Iranica; Contributor, Articles, Kurdish History and Eastern European **AW:** National Order of Merit, Grand Officer, President of Romania (2016); National Order of Merit, President of Romania (2000) **MEM:** Honorary Member, Romanian Academy **MH:** Albert Nelson Marquis Lifetime Achievement Award; Marquis Who's Who Top Professional **B/I:** Dr. Hitchins' knowledge about the National Movements helped him get into Romanian studies and other peoples. His friends who lived in Paris told him to look into the Kurdish people. Dr. Hitchins read a lot of books about history. His two grandfathers talked to him about Europe and history. He was attracted to teach because it would enable him to develop his knowledge of history. **THT:** In graduate school and college, Dr. Hitchins developed an interest in Eastern Europe and also the Soviet Union. He thought he would maybe concentrate on Soviet and Russian history. In 1960, he was able to go to Romania to do research for his dissertation, and became acquainted with the people and the places. This stay in Romania is what convinced him to focus on Romania. Dr. Hitchins' advisor encouraged him to study Romania in graduate school. He can speak many languages which include Italian, Kurdish, Tajik, Romanian, Baltic, French, Spanish, and German.

HITT, DANNY, "DAN" LEON, T: Lawyer, Retired Executive, Vice President **I:** Manufacturing **CN:** 3M **DOB:** 12/13/1931 **PB:** Washington **SC:** DC/USA **PT:** Fred Raymond Hitt; Christie Nora (Crocker) Hitt **MS:** Married **SPN:** Marie Lavonne Prichett (10/02/1987) **CH:** Charles; Danny; Stacy; Ronald

ED: JD, University of Houston, Summa Cum Laude (1965); Coursework in Business Administration, University of Texas (1951); AS, University of Texas (1950) C: Federal Government Affairs Vice President, 3M, Washington, DC (1989-1992); Associate General Counsel, 3M, St. Paul, MN (1983-1989); Assistant General Counsel, 3M, St. Paul, MN (1979-1983); Associate Counsel, 3M, Brussels, Germany (1977-1978); Attorney, 3M, St. Paul, MN (1965-1977); Sales Correspondent, 3M, Dallas, TX (1954-1963) CR: Chairman, Vice-Chairman, Treasurer, Secretary, Minnesota State Bar International Law Section (1978-1989); Faculty, Bar Association Legal Seminars (1983-1988); Board of Directors, Sumitomo 3M, Japan; Hearing Examiner, Judge of Peer Court, Juvenile Justice Program, Seminole County, FL CIV: Bar Examinations Grader, Minnesota State Bar Association, St. Paul, MN (1967-1977); Member Committee, Secretary, Boy Scouts America, White Bear Lake, MN (1966-1970) MIL: Leading Journalist, Public Information Office, USS Franklin D. Roosevelt (CVA 42) (1957); Sports Publicity Director, USNTC Great Lakes (1956-1957); U.S. Navy (1955-1957) CW: Associate Editor, Author, Case Notes for Houston Law Review (1964-1965); Author, Articles, Newspapers (1956-1957); Columnist, Sports Editor, Great Lakes Bulletin (1955-1956) AW: Senior and Super Senior Golf Championships, Alaqua Country Club (1993-2001); Numerous Scholastic Awards, University of Houston College of Law (1963-1965); American Spirit Honor Medal, USNTC Great Lakes (1955) MEM: Vice President, Minnesota State Society, Washington DC (1990-1992); Chairman, International Law Section, Minnesota State Bar Association (1987-1989); International Business Law Section, American Bar Association (1979-1989); Tournament Players Club; White Bear Yacht Club; Alaqua Country Club; Legacy Country Club BAR: U.S. District Court of Minnesota (1967); Supreme Court, State of Minnesota (1966); American Bar Association; Minnesota State Bar Association MH: Albert Nelson Marquis Lifetime Achievement Award AS: Mr. Hitt attributes his success to hard work and his willingness to take a chance. Likewise, he is often in the right place at the right time. B/I: Mr. Hitt had a lifelong ambition to be a lawyer, starting in high school. However, there was a derailment of his plans and he had to make other decisions. Eleven years later, Mr. Hitt had found success in his personal life after marrying his wife and having children. He then took a leave of absence from his job at 3M and enrolled in the University of Houston Law school. He received a Juris Doctor 24 months later while working 48 hours per week as a night-time security guard. He graduated at the top of his class with Summa Cum Laude honors. AV: Golfing; Playing bridge; Hunting; Reading; Traveling; Spending time with family and his dog, Bogey PA: Independent RE: Presbyterian

HLAVAC, DANIEL C., T: Executive Director of Development I: Real Estate CN: Helm Equities CH: Three Children ED: Coursework, Academic Regents, Pearl River High School (1979); Coursework, Exploratory Architecture Program, Board of Cooperative Education Services (1979) CT: Architectural Drafting Certificate, Plaza School of Architectural Drafting (1981) C: Executive Director of Development, Helm Equities (2019-Present); Senior Project Executive, Chief Estimator, Kings Capital Construction (2017-2019); Senior Project Manager, Project Executive, Park Builders Group (2015-2017); Senior Project Manager, Account Executive, Lettire, New York (2013-2015); Project Manager, Flintlock Construction Services, New York (2012-2013); Director of Engineering and Field Operations, Quattro Construction Management, LLC, New York (2007-2013); Senior Project

Manager, Shaw's Super Markets, Creative Designs International CIV: Rockland County Planning Board; Chairman, Architectural Community Board of Review AW: Eponym, Dan Hlavac Day Award B/I: Mr. Hlavac's became involved in his profession because he wanted to follow in the footsteps of his father and grandfather.

HO, REGINALD C.S. MD, T: Medical Educator I: Medicine & Health Care DOB: 03/30/1932 PB: Hong Kong SC: China PT: Chow Ho; Elizabeth (Wong) Ho MS: Married SPN: Sharilyn Dang (11/14/1964) CH: Mark; Reginald; Gianna Masca; Timothy ED: MD, St. Louis University (1959); Coursework, St. Louis University (1954) CT: American Board of Internal Medicine (1963); Diplomate, National Board of Medical Examiners (1959) C: Retired, Associate Clinical Professor, Medicine, Jab School of Medicine (1977-2008); Physician, Department of Hematology and Oncology, Straub Clinic and Hospital, Honolulu, HI (1973-2008); Fellow in Hematology and Oncology, Barnes Hospital, Washington University (1962-1963); Resident in Internal Medicine, University of Cincinnati Hospitals (1960-1962); Rotating Intern, University of Cincinnati Hospitals (1959-1960); Private Practice CR: Adjunct Professor, Clinical Science Cancer Research Center of Hawaii (1989-Present); Principal Investigator, Hawaii Community Clinical Oncology Program, Honolulu, HI (1983-1986); Member, Various Committees CIV: Selected President, American Cancer Society (1992-1993); Board of Directors, Catholic Services for Families (1987-1991) CW: Contributor, Articles, Medical Journals MEM: Delegate, Director, Honorary Life Member, Executive Committee, American Cancer Society (1989-Present); Chair, Hawaii Cancer Commission, Hawaii Medical Association (1980-1990); American Medical Association; American College of Physicians; Alpha Omega Alpha MH: Albert Nelson Marquis Lifetime Achievement Award B/I: Dr. Ho decided to pursue hematology after starting college. He found it to be an attractive option in studying for his medical doctorate. He enjoys working with people and found the discipline conducive towards that desire. AV: Playing tennis; Reading RE: Roman Catholic

HOBERECHT, REYNOTTA JAHNKE, T: School System Administrator, Educator I: Education/Educational Services DOB: 03/26/1938 PB: Mattoon SC: WI/USA PT: Laurence Herman Jahnke; Magdalena Evelina (Waidelich) Jahnke MS: Widow SPN: Hal G. Hoberecht (09/19/1970, Deceased) CH: Marc ED: EdD, University of San Francisco (1998); MA, University of San Francisco (1978); BS, University of Wisconsin (1961) C: Administrative Assistant, Travis Unified Schools (1995-2003);Teacher, Travis Unified Schools (1971-1999) CR: Unidad de Paleontologia Expedition, Las Hoyas, Spain (1992) AW: Ecosystems Project Award, Travis School Board (1993) MEM: Treasurer, Secretary, California Teachers Association (1967-1968, 1994-1999) MH: Albert Nelson Marquis Lifetime Achievement Award B/I: Dr. Hoberecht remembers watching the rain soak into the soil when she was very young. While observing this, she began to notice strange objects embedded in the soil. Eventually, she was enlightened that these objects were flint, which was used by Native Americans for tools and arrows. From this moment on, she was interested in anthropology. AV: Playing with dog; Digging

HOBSON, MELLODY, T: Co-Chief Executive Officer I: Financial Services CN: Ariel Investments DOB: 04/03/1969 PB: Chicago SC: IL/USA PT: Dorothy Ashley MS: Married SPN: George Walton Lucas (06/22/2013) CH: Everest ED: BA, Princeton University Woodrow Wilson School of

International Relations (1991) C: President, Ariel Capital Management, Inc. (2000-Present); Senior Vice President, Director of Marketing, Ariel Capital Management, Inc. (1994-2000); Vice President of Marketing, Ariel Capital Management, Inc., Chicago (1991-1994); Chair, Board of Trustees, Ariel Investment Trust CR: Board of Directors, Groupon (2011-Present); Board of Directors, Starbucks Corp. (2005-Present); Board of Directors, Dreamworks Animation SKG, Inc. (2004-Present); Board of Directors, The Estée Lauder Companies Inc. (2003-Present); Spokesperson, Ariel/Schwab Black; Investor, Survey Columnist, Black Enterprise; Financial Correspondent, ABC's "Good Morning America" CIV: Chair, After School Matters (2012-Present); Board of Trustees, Princeton University; Board of Directors, Field Museum; Board of Directors, Chicago Public Library; Board of Directors, Chicago Public Education Fund; Board of Directors, Sundance Institute AW: Luminary Award, Girl Scouts Of Greater Chicago & Northwest Indiana (2010); Named, Top 25 Non-Bank Women In Finance, U.S. Banker (2009); Named, Power 150, Ebony Magazine (2008); Named, Woman To Watch, Fortune Magazine (2008); Named, 50 Women To Watch, Wall Street Journal (2008); Global Leader Of Tomorrow, World Economic Forum, Switzerland (2001); Named, 40 Under 40, Crain's Chicago Business (1999); Named, 30 Leaders Of The Future, Ebony Magazine MEM: Council on Foreign Relations

HOCHMAN, ROD, T: Chief Executive Officer I: Medicine & Health Care CN: Providence Health & Services ED: Fellow in Rheumatology, Dartmouth Medical School (1982-1984); Fellow in Internal Medicine, Harvard Medical School (1979-1982); MD, School of Medicine, Boston University (1979); BA, School of Medicine, Boston University (1979) C: Chief Executive Officer, President, Providence Health System (2016-Present); Chief Executive Officer, President, Providence Health & Services (2013-Present); Group President, Providence Health & Services (2012-2013); President, Chief Executive Officer, Swedish Medical Center (2007-2012); Executive Vice President, Sentara Healthcare (1998-2007)

HOCK, HANS HENRICH, T: Professor Emeritus I: Education/Educational Services CN: University of Illinois Urbana-Champaign DOB: 09/26/1938 PB: Moenchen-Gladbach SC: Germany PT: Helmut Hock; Helene (Gravenhorst) Hock MS: Married SPN: Zarina Manawwar (09/29/1973) CH: Heinrich Sharad ED: Honorary LittD, Deccan College, India (2018); PhD, Yale University (1971); MA, Northwestern University (1964) C: Professor Emeritus, University of Illinois Urbana-Champaign (2007-Present); Professor, University of Illinois Urbana-Champaign (1987-2007); Associate Professor, University of Illinois Urbana-Champaign (1975-1987); Assistant Professor, University of Illinois Urbana-Champaign (1971-1974); Linguistics Instructor, University of Illinois Urbana-Champaign (1967-1971); German Instructor, Tuskegee Institute, Alabama (1964) CR: Fulbright Lecturer, Jawaharlal Nehru University, New Delhi (1987); Visiting Lecturer, University of Pennsylvania, Philadelphia (1972) CW: Editor, "Veda and Vedic literature: Select papers from the panel on "Veda and Vedic Literature" at the 16th World Sanskrit Conference" (2016); Co-Editor, "The languages and linguistics of South Asia: A comprehensive guide" (2016); Editor, "Vedic studies: Language, culture, and philosophy" (2014); Co-Author, "Language, History, Language Change, and Language Relationship: An Introduction to Historical and Comparative Linguistics, 2nd Edition" (2009); Author, "An early Upanisadic Reader, with notes, glossary, and an appendix of related Vedic texts" (2007); Editor, "Historical, Indo-European, and Lexicographical Studies: A Festsschrift for Ladislav Zgusta" (1997); Co-Author, "Language, History, Language Change, and Language Relationship: An Introduction to Historical and Comparative Linguistics" (1996); Editor, "Studies in Sanskrit Syntax" (1991); Co-Editor, "Staefcraeft: Studies in Germanic Linguistics" (1991); Author, "Principles of Historical Linguistics, 2nd Edition" (1991); Editor, "Studies in Linguistic Sciences" (1988-1994); Author, "Principles of Historical Linguistics" (1986) **AW:** Travel Grantee (1980, 1982, 1989); Research and Travel Grantee, American Institute of Indian Studies (1980-1981); Research Grantee, American Philosophical Society (1974-1975) **MEM:** Invited Faculty, Linguistic Institute, The Ohio State University, Linguistic Society of America (1993); Executive Committee, Cosmopolitan Club (1972-1976); Lifetime Member, Linguistic Society of India; Society Linguistica Europaea; American Association for Applied Linguistics; American Oriental Society **MH:** Albert Nelson Marquis Lifetime Achievement Award; Marquis Who's Who Top Professional **B/I:** Dr. Hock became involved in his profession because he was a graduate student at Yale University during the civil rights movement. A number of Ivy League schools were sending student volunteers to help teach at traditionally Black colleges, and Dr. Hock volunteered because of his prior experience as an assistant at Northwestern University. He enjoyed his time in the position because anyone could succeed as long as there was a decent teaching curriculum; background didn't matter. His students were very happy to be succeeding.

HODES, BARTON LYLE, MD, T: Ophthalmologist, Educator **I:** Medicine & Health Care **DOB:** 08/21/1940 **PB:** Philadelphia **SC:** PA/USA **PT:** Philip J. Hodes, MD; Natalie Lansing Hodes **MS:** Married **SPN:** Stephanie Rudo Hodes **CH:** Tracy Hodes Sandler; Erica Robin Hodes **ED:** MD, Jefferson Medical College (1966); BA, University of Pennsylvania (1962) **CT:** Diplomate, American Board of Ophthalmology **C:** Retired (2017); Private Practice, Tucson, AZ (2000-2017); Professor of Ophthalmology, University of Arizona College of Medicine – Tucson, Tucson, AZ (1985-2000); Head, Ophthalmology, University of Arizona College of Medicine – Tucson, Tucson, AZ (1985-1989); Chairman, Integrated Department of Ophthalmology, Hershey Medical Center of Penn State University, Delaware (1980-1985); Associate Professor, Ophthalmology, Northwestern University Feinberg School of Medicine, Chicago, IL (1976-1979); Chief, Ophthalmology Clinics, Northwestern University Medical School, Chicago, IL (1976-1979); Program Director, Resident Training, Northwestern University Medical School, Chicago, IL (1974-1979); Practice, Ophthalmology, Chicago, IL (1970-1974); Chief Resident, Jefferson Medical College, Philadelphia, PA (1969-1970); Resident, Evanston Hospital (1967-1969); Intern, Evanston Hospital, Illinois (1966-1967) **CR:** Attending Physician, University of Arizona Medical Center (1986-2000); Chief of Ophthalmology, Tucson VA Medical Center, Tucson, AZ (1986-2000); Associate Examiner, American Board of Ophthalmology (1976-1996); Section Chief, Ophthalmology, Kino Community Hospital Tucson, AZ (1986-1992); Attending Physician, St. Joseph's Hospital, Tucson AZ (1986-1991); Professor of Surgery and Chief, Ophthalmology, Milton S. Hershey Medical Center, Pennsylvania State University (1980-1985); Representative of the American Academy of Ophthalmology to the Health Care Financing Administration (HCFA) and to the Prospective Payment System (PPS) of the American College of Surgeons **CIV:** Chairman, Safety Committee, Deerfield, IL (1972-1974) **MIL:** Lt.

Cmdr., U.S. Navy (1967-1974) **CW:** Editorial Board, Journal of Clinical Ultrasound (1974-1979); Consultant Editor, Archives of Ophthalmology; Author, 70 Articles, Refereed Medical Journals; Speaker, 27 Guest Lectureships; Presenter, 43 Formal Presentations, Regional and National Meetings **AW:** Certificate of Appreciation, 20 Years of Service as Associate Examiner, American Board of Ophthalmology (1996); Honor Award, American Academy Ophthalmology (1986) **MEM:** Executive Board, International Society Diagnosis with Ultrasound in Ophthalmology(1978-1980, 1986-Present); Vice President, International Society Diagnosis with Ultrasound in Ophthalmology (1982-1986); Secretary, International Society Diagnosis with Ultrasound in Ophthalmology (1981-1984); Fellow American College of Surgeons; American Academy Ophthalmology; American Association Ultrasound in Ophthalmology; World Federation Ultrasound in Medicine and Biology; Charter Member, International Association Ocular Surgeons; American Institute Ultrasound in Medicine; Arizona Ophthalmological Society **AS:** Dr. Hodes attributes his success to a combination of superb educational opportunities at all levels and having the support and encouragement of several mentors, who include, in no particular order, Dr. Thomas Duane, Dr. William Frayer, and Dr. David Shoch. **B/I:** Dr. Hodes became involved in his profession because his father was a physician and radiologist, which is why it was always his career goal to become a physician. He set his goal in medicine to become an ophthalmologist. He was influenced by the kindness and affection of his personal ophthalmologist, Irving H. Leopold, MD, whom he met when he was 8 years old.

HODGE, KATHLEEN, "KATHY" ANN, T: Reporting Analyst **I:** Information Technology and Services **CN:** Compulink Health Solutions **DOB:** 06/27/1954 **PB:** Rock Springs **SC:** WY/USA **PT:** Thomas Hodge; Frances (Whittaker) Hodge **MS:** Widow **SPN:** Judith Rosenfeld (Deceased 2003) **CH:** Bonnie Sioux Parker (Step-daughter); Vanessa (Grandchild); Danielle (Grandchild); Rick (Grandchild); Nolan (Grandchild); Michael (Grandchild); Johnny (Great-Grandchild); Ryan (Great-Grandchild); Justin (Great-Grandchild); Adrianna (Great-Grandchild); Elizabeth (Great-Grandchild) **ED:** Pursuing Bachelor's Degree in Business, Eastern Gateway Community College; Coursework in Philosophy, University of Utah; Coursework in Computer Programming, Orange Coast College; Coursework in Computer Programming, Antelope Valley College **CT:** Medical-Legal Disability Rating Certification (1990); Medical Assistant License; Certification in Phlebotomy **C:** Reporting Analyst, Compulink Health Solutions (2012-Present); Electronic Data Interchange (EDI) Supervisor, Compulink (2008-2012); Reporting Analyst and Medical Legal Analyst, Pepper Medical Management (Mesa Medical Group), Orange County, CA (2001-2002, 2005-2008); Programming, Technical and EDI Support, Santiago Data Systems, Newport Beach, CA (1995-2001); Network Administrator, Pacific West, Orange County, CA (1986-1993); Executive Director, Feminist Women's Health Center (FWHC), Orange County, CA (1981-1983); Human Resources Director, Feminist Women's Health Center (FWHC) (1979-1981); Staff, Feminist Women's Health Center (FWHC), Los Angeles, CA (1975-1979); Research Assistant, Researcher, University of Utah Medical Center (1972-1974) **CR:** Speaker in Field; Computer Programmer, Reporting Analyst, Santiago Data Systems **CIV:** Manager, Safe Harbor Sober Living Home, Desert Lighthouse Ministry, Lancaster, CA (2007); Incorporating Secretary, Area Family Planning, Orange County, CA (1980-1983); Coalition Against Police Abuse, Los Angeles, CA (1977-1979);

Union of Lesbians and Gay Men, Los Angeles, CA (1978); Educational Director, Young Socialist Alliance, Salt Lake City, UT (1972-1974) **CW:** Co-Author, "New View of a Woman's Body" (1978) **MEM:** National Women's Health Network; Southern Poverty Law Center; Amnesty International; Participant, Numerous Civic/Activist Organizations **MH:** Albert Nelson Marquis Lifetime Achievement Award **AS:** Ms. Hodge attributes her success to taking action to support her ideals all the while keeping her feet on the ground. As a young inventor, she was encouraged to dream of success by her high school teachers. **B/I:** During Ms. Hodge's time as a community clinic director, she became alarmed at the extreme complexity of medical billing in the insurance system in the United States. This is what motivated her to pursue a career in reporting analysis. She is now happy to see how hardware and software innovations have led society to a better place of overview. **AV:** Writing creatively; Exploring mathematics **PA:** Democrat **RE:** Lutheran **THT:** Ms. Hodge urges any young woman to understand the importance of advocating for their rights.

HODGE, RASHIDA A., T: Vice President **I:** Technology **CN:** IBM **ED:** MS in Industrial Engineering, North Carolina State University (2003); MBA, Fuqua School of Business, Duke University; BS in Industrial Engineering, North Carolina State University **C:** Vice President, Insurance Industry, IBM (2019-Present); Vice President, Watson AI Strategic Partnerships and Product Management, IBM (2017-2018); Director, Watson AI Worldwide Client Services Delivery, IBM (2014-2017); Chief of Staff to IBM Senior Vice President, IBM Watson Group, IBM (2013-2014); Strategy and Business Development Executive, Integrated Supply Chain, IBM (2012-2013); Europe Business Leader, Technical Support Services, IBM (2008-2011); Sales Operations Manager, IBM (2006-2008); Supply Chain Leadership Program, IBM (2004-2006); IBM Development and Research Program Manager, IBM (2003-2004) **CIV:** Board Member, Fuqua Minority Advisory Board, Duke University (2019-Present); Board Member, IBM Black Executive Council (2017-Present); Board Member, College of Engineering Foundation, North Carolina State University (2015-Present); Co-Founder, Get Right About Superior Performance **CW:** Four Patents in the Field **AW:** Distinguished Alumni Award, North Carolina State University (2019); Industrial Engineering Outstanding Alumni, North Carolina State University (2018); Presidential Award for Volunteer Services (2008) **MEM:** U.S. Virgin Islands Ambassador, U.S. Virgin Islands Department of Tourism (2019); Association for Operations Management; National Society of Black Engineers; Global Women of IBM Integrated Supply Chain; Bratislava Women in Action **AS:** Ms. Hodge attributes her success to her dedication, hard work, loyalty and networking. **B/I:** Ms. Hodge became involved in her profession due to her desire to work in the area of supply chain management. **AV:** Mentoring; Traveling; Swimming

HODGES, GEORGE A., T: Tooling, Facilites, & Production Supervisor (Retired) **I:** Automotive **CN:** General Motors **DOB:** 12/06/1950 **PB:** Morling **SC:** TX/USA **MS:** Married **CH:** Anthony Lynn; Brian Dean **ED:** MS in Manufacturing Management, Kettering University, Flint, MI (1995);BS in Business Management, Tarkio College, Tarkio, MO (1988) **C:** President, Self-Employed, Dallas/Fort Worth, TX (2015-Present); Mechanical Systems Consultant, Hodges Technologies, LLC (1998-2012); Facilities & Tooling Supervisor, General Motors (1994-2006); Tool & Die Maker, Facilities & Production Supervisor, General Motors Components Holdings, LLC (1990-2006); Tool & Die Maker, Model Maker Mechanical, Bendix K.C. Prime Contractor for Energy Commission (1969-1976) **AW:** MS in Manufacturing Management, Kettering University (1995); Tool and Die Maker Apprenticeship (1973); Graduate, Central High School, Kansas City, MO (1969) **MH:** Marquis Who's Who Top Professional **B/I:** Mr. Hodges became involved in his profession because he was seeking a job with a good income that would be able to provide his family with a middle class, or better, standard of life. When opportunities presented themselves, he definitely opted to go for them. In high school, he studied and explored electronics vocation. One of his assignments at the end of the year was to apply to the local electronics company to seek employment for vocational training. He was eventually hired and accepted employment upon his graduation, which essentially began his career in manufacturing.

HODGES, MAYME WEAVER, T: Retired Elementary Educator **I:** Education/Educational Services **DOB:** 12/14/1929 **PB:** Lakeland **SC:** FL/USA **PT:** Melvin Weaver; Alice (Haggins) Weaver **MS:** Married **SPN:** Thomas Hodges (07/05/1953) **CH:** Glenn T.; G. LaTanya Hodges Raffington **ED:** MEd, Stetson University (1981); BS in Education, Hampton University (1952) **C:** Elementary Teacher, Pinellas County Schools, Clearwater, FL (1955-1989); Elementary Teacher, Broward County Schools, Pompano, FL (1952-1954) **CR:** Board of Directors, Long Center, Clearwater; Nominating Commissioner, Board of City and County Commissioners **CIV:** Region IV Director (1996-1997); Board of Directors, Hunter Blood Center (1994-1997); Past Chairman, Neighborhood Affordable Housing Board (1994-1997); Executive Committee, Pinellas County Democratic Club (1987-1997); Nominating Commissioner, 6th Judicial Court (1993-1996); Interim City Commissioner, City of Clearwater (1992-1993) **AW:** Ms. Clearwater Award, Greater Clearwater Chamber of Commerce (1996); Liberty Bell Award, Clearwater Bar Association (1996); Community Service Award, Small Business Administration of Clearwater (1992) **MEM:** Region Director, President, District 6, (2012-2014); Co-President, President, North Pinellas Retired Educators (1994-2014); President, Vice President, Treasurer, Secretary, Alpha Kappa Alpha (1986-1988, 2010-2012); Volunteer Usher, Ruth Eckerd (1987-1988); North Pinella County Retired Educators **MH:** Albert Nelson Marquis Lifetime Achievement Award; Marquis Who's Who Top Professional **B/I:** Ms. Hodges got involved in her work because she was always interested in mathematics. **AV:** Playing bridge; Bowling; Playing tennis; Reading **PA:** Democrat **RE:** Methodist

HOEVEN, JOHN HENRY III, T: U.S. Senator from North Dakota **I:** Government Administration/Government Relations/Government Services **DOB:** 03/13/1957 **PB:** Bismarck **SC:** ND/USA **PT:** John Henry Hoeven Jr.; Patricia (Chapman) Hoeven **MS:** Married **SPN:** Mikey (Mical Laird) Hoeven **CH:** Marcela; Jack **ED:** MBA, Northwestern University Kellogg School of Management (1981); BA in History and Economics, Dartmouth College, Hanover, NH (1979) **C:** Chairman, U.S. Senate Committee on Indian Affairs (2017-Present); U.S. Senator, State of North Dakota, Washington, DC (2011-Present); Member, U.S. Senate Committee on Agriculture, Nutrition and Forestry, Washington, DC (2011-Present); Member, U.S. Senate Committee on Energy and Natural Resources, Washington, DC (2011-Present); Member, U.S. Senate Appropriations Committee, Washington, DC (2011-Present); Member, U.S. Senate Committee on Indian Affairs, Washington, DC (2011-2017); Governor, State of North Dakota, Bismarck, ND (2000-2010); President, Chief Executive Officer, Bank of North Dakota (BND) (1993-2000); Executive Vice President, First Western Bank, Minot, ND (1986-1993) **CR:** Chair, Committee on Health and Human Services; Chair, Committee on Natural Resources; Chair, National Governors Association; Chair, Midwestern Governors Association; Chair, Governors' Ethanol Coalition; Chair, Interstate Oil and Gas Compact Commission **CIV:** Trustee, Bismarck State College; Chair, Minot Area Development Corporation; Board of Directors, Harold Schafer Leadership Center; Board of Directors, Bismarck YMCA; Board of Directors, Economic Development Association of North Dakota (EDND); Board of Directors, North Dakota Small Business Investment Company (NDSBIC); Board of Directors, North Dakota Bankers Association; Board of Directors, First Western Bank & Trust **PA:** Republican **RE:** Roman Catholic

HOFFMAN, DUSTIN LEE, T: Actor **I:** Media & Entertainment **DOB:** 08/08/1937 **PB:** Los Angeles **SC:** CA/USA **PT:** Harry Hoffman; Lillian (Gold) Hoffman **MS:** Married **SPN:** Lisa Gottsegen (10/21/1980); Anne Byrne (05/04/1969, Divorced 10/06/1980) **CH:** Alexandra Lydia; Maxwell Geoffrey; Rebecca Lillian; Jacob Edward; Jenna; Karina (Adopted) **ED:** Studied with Barney Brown, Lonny Chapman & Lee Strasberg; Studied, Neighborhood Playhouse School of the Theatre, NY; Studied, Pasadena Playhouse; Coursework, Santa Monica College **CW:** Actor, "As Sick as They Made Us" (2020); Voice Actor, "The Curse of Molly McGee" (2020); Actor, "L'Uomo del Labrinto" (2019); Actor, "The Meyerowitz Stories" (2017); Voice Actor, "Kung Fu Panda 3" (2016); Actor, Producer, "Medici: Masters of Florence" (2016); Actor, Producer, "Roald Dahl's Esio Trot" (2015); Actor, "The Program" (2015); Actor, "Chef" (2014); Actor, "The Boychoir" (2014); Actor, "The Cobbler" (2014); Director, "Quartet" (2012); Actor, "Luck" (2011-2012); Voice Actor, "Kung Fu Panda 2" (2011); Actor, "Little Fockers" (2010); Voice Actor, "Kung Fu Panda" (2008); Voice Actor, "The Tale of Despereaux" (2008); Actor, "Last Chance Harvey" (2008); Actor, "Mr. Magorium's Wonder Emporium" (2007); Appearance, Music Video, 50 Cent Featuring Robin Thicke, "Follow My Lead" (2006); Actor, "Perfume: The Story of a Murderer" (2006); Actor, "Stranger Than Fiction" (2006); Voice Actor, "Racing Stripes" (2005); Actor, "The Lost City" (2005); Actor, "I Heart Huckabees" (2004); Actor, "Finding Neverland" (2004); Actor, "Meet the Fockers" (2004); Actor, "Lemony Snicket's A Series of Unfortunate Events" (2004); Actor, "Runaway Jury" (2003); Actor, "Confidence" (2003); Actor, "Moonlight Mile" (2002); Voice Actor, "Liberty's Kids" (2002); Voice Actor, "Tuesday" (2001); Producer, "A Walk on the Moon" (1999); Producer, "The Furies" (1999); Executive Producer, "The Devil's Arithmetic" (1999); Actor, "Messenger: The Story of Joan of Arc" (1999); Actor, "Sphere" (1998); Actor, "Wag the Dog" (1997); Actor, "Mad City" (1997); Actor, "Sleepers" (1996); Actor, "American Buffalo" (1996); Actor, "Outbreak" (1995); Actor, "Hero" (1992); Actor, "Hook" (1991); Actor, "Billy Bathgate" (1991); Actor, "A Wish for Wings That Work" (1991); Actor, "Dick Tracy" (1990); Actor, "Family Business" (1989); Actor, "The Merchant of Venice" (1989); Actor, "Rain Man" (1988); Actor, "Ishtar" (1987); Actor, "Death of a Salesman" (1985); Actor, "Death of a Salesman" (1984); Artist, "Death of a Salesman," Caedmon Records (1984); Actor, "Tootsie" (1982); Actor, "Agatha" (1979); Actor, "Kramer versus Kramer" (1979); Actor, Executive Producer, "Straight Time" (1978); Actor, "Straight Time" (1978); Actor, "All the President's Men" (1976); Actor, "Marathon Man" (1976); Actor, "Lenny" (1974); Actor, "Papillon" (1973); Actor, "Alfredo, Alfredo" (1972); Actor, "Who Is Harry Kellerman and Why Is He Saying Those Terrible Things About Me?" (1971); Actor, "Straw Dogs" (1971); Voice Actor, "The Point" (1971); Actor, "Little Big Man" (1970); Actor, "Madigan's Millions" (1969); Actor, "Sunday Father" (1969); Actor, "Midnight Cowboy" (1969); Actor, "John and Mary" (1969); Actor, "Jimmy Shine" (1968); Actor, "The Tiger Makes Out" (1967); Actor, "The Graduate" (1967); Actor, "The Star Wagon" (1967); Actor, "The Journey of the Fifth Horse" (1966); Actor, "Fragments" (1966); Actor, "Eh?" (1966); Actor, "Harry, Noon and Night" (1965); Actor, "Three Men on a Horse" (1964); Actor, Broadway Debut, "A Cook for Mr. General" (1961); Actor, "Endgame," "The Quare Fellow," "In the Jungle of Cities," "A Country Scandal," "The Dumbwaiter," "The Room," "Waiting for Godot," "Picnic on the Battlefield," "Dirty Hands," "The Cocktail Party," and All Theatre Company of Boston; Actor, Stage Debut, "Yes is for a Very Young Man," Sarah Lawrence College; Actor, Theater, Television Shows and Film **AW:** Lifetime Achievement Award, Gotham Awards (2017); Emmy Award for Best Performance by an Actor, Academy of Television Arts & Sciences (2015); Honoree, Kennedy Center Honors, John F. Kennedy Center for the Performing Arts, Washington, DC (2012); Honorary Commander, National Order of Arts and Letters, France (2009); Chairman's Award, Palm Springs International Film Society (2009); Honorary Cesar Medal, Cesar Awards (2009); Lifetime Achievement Award, American Film Institute (1999); Cecil B. DeMille Award, Golden Globes Awards, Hollywood Foreign Press Association (1996); Decorated Officer, National Order of Arts and Letters, France (1995); Academy Awards for Best Actor, Academy of Motion Picture Arts and Sciences (1979, 1988); Golden Globe Awards for Best Actor - Motion Picture Drama, Hollywood Foreign Press Association (1979, 1988); Emmy Award for Best Actor, Academy of Television Arts & Sciences (1986); Golden Globe Award for Best Actor - Miniseries or Television Film, Hollywood Foreign Press Association (1985); BAFTA Awards for Best Actor (1969, 1970, 1984); Drama Desk Awards (1967, 1984); Golden Globe Awards for Best Actor - Motion Picture Musical or Comedy, Hollywood Foreign Press Association (1982); Golden Globe Award for Most Promising Newcomer, Hollywood Foreign Press Association (1968); Verna Rice Award (1967); Theatre World Award (1967); Obie Award (1966); Numerous Awards **MEM:** Fellow, American Academy of Arts & Sciences

HOFFMAN, MICHAEL, T: Associate Professor of Medicine **I:** Medicine & Health Care **CN:** Bay Rheumatology **MS:** Married **CH:** Three Children **ED:** MD, State University of New York Downstate Medical Center College of Medicine (1965); BS, Brooklyn College **CT:** American Board of Internal Medicine **C:** Bay Rheumatology (1970-Present); Fellowship, Hospital for Special Surgery (1969-1970) **CR:** Acting Director of Rheumatology, Memorial Hospital (2000); Associate Professor, Rheumatology Department, Albert Einstein College of Medicine **AW:** Outstanding Physician Awards (2019-2020); Patients Choice Award (2010-2018); Compassionate Doctor Recognition (2010-2017); Various Teaching Awards, Albert Einstein College of Medicine **MEM:** American College of Rheumatology; Alpha Omega Alpha **MH:** Marquis Who's Who Top Professional **AS:** Dr. Hoffman attributes his success to his stubbornness in practice. He does what he wants to do, always helping his patients to the best of his ability. He is willing to do whatever it takes to help everyone that walks into his office. **B/I:** Dr. Hoffman went into rheumatology because it was the only specialty encompassing all of internal medicine. He decided to become a doctor because he was inspired by the people around him as he grew up, as they were the best physicians he ever met.

HOFSTADTER, DOUGLAS RICHARD, PHD, T: Professor, Author **I:** Education/Educational Services **CN:** Indiana University **DOB:** 02/15/1945 **PB:** New York **SC:** NY/USA **PT:** Robert Hofstadter; Nancy (Givan) Hofstadter **MS:** Married **SPN:** Baofen Lin (2012); Carol Ann Brush (1985, Deceased 1993) **CH:** Daniel Frederic; Monica Marie **ED:** PhD in Physics, University of Oregon (1975); MS, University of Oregon (1972); BS in Mathematics, Stanford University, with Distinction (1965) **C:** Distinguished Professor, Cognitive Science, Computer Science, Indiana University Bloomington (1988-Present); Walgreen Professor, Cognitive Science, University of Michigan, Ann Arbor, MI (1984-1988); Associate Professor, Indiana University Bloomington (1980-1984); Assistant Professor, Computer Science, Indiana University Bloomington (1977-1980) **CR:** Adjunct Professor, Psychology, Philosophy, History and Philosophy of Science, Comparative Literature, Director, Center for Research on Concepts and Cognition, Indiana University Bloomington **CW:** Co-author with Emmanuel Sander, "Surfaces and Essences: Analogy as the Fuel and Fire of Thinking" (2013); Author, "That Mad Ache" (2009); Author, "I am a Strange Loop" (2007); Author, "The Discovery of Dawn" (2007); Author, "Le Ton Beau de Marot" (1997); Author, "Rhapsody on a Theme by Clement Marot" (1996); Author, "Fluid Concepts and Creative Analogies" (1995); Author, "Eugene Onegin: A Novel Versification" (1991); Author, "Ambigrammi" (1987); Author, "Metamagical Themas" (1985); Columnist, Metamagical Themas, Scientific American (1981-1983); Co-Editor with Daniel C. Dennett, "The Mind's I" (1981); Author, "Godel, Escher, Bach: an Eternal Golden Braid" (1979); Author, Contributor, Papers, Books, Articles, Professional Journals **AW:** Los Angeles Times Book Prize for Science and Technology (2007); Fellow, John Simon Guggenheim Memorial Foundation (1980-1981); American Book Award (1980); Pulitzer Prize for General Nonfiction (1980) **MEM:** Cognitive Science Society; Association for the Advancement of Artificial Intelligence; ALTA

HOFSTETTER, JANE R., NWS, T: Artist, Educator, Author **I:** Fine Art **DOB:** 02/23/1936 **PB:** Oakland **SC:** CA/USA **PT:** Thomas O. Robinson; Fern (Worstell) Robinson **MS:** Married **SPN:** William R. Hofsetter (08/03/1958) **CH:** David; Glen **ED:** Coursework, Chouinard Art Institute, California Institute of the Arts, Los Angeles, CA; Coursework, San Francisco School of Design; Coursework, University of California Berkeley **CR:** Lecturer in Field **CW:** Author, "Seven Keys to Great Paintings" (2005); Represented in Permanent Collections, Triton Museum of Art, Santa Clara, CA; Represented in Permanent Collections, State of California Collection, Asilomar; Represented in Permanent Collections, San Ramon and Santa Clara City Halls; Represented in Permanent Collections, Kayser Hospital, CA; Represented in Permanent Collections, IBM Holdings and General Facilities, Gould Inc.; Represented in Permanent Collections, Northern California Savings and Loan; Represented in Permanent Collections, Systems Control Inc.; Represented in Permanent Collections, Zerox Corporation; Represented in Permanent Collections, Finance of America Companies; Judges Art Show; Painting Compositions, Best of Watercolor **AW:** International Award, National Watercolor Society (2017); Triton Museum of Art Award; Recipient, Numerous Other Award **MEM:** Signature Member, National Watercolor Society; Signature Member, Watercolor West Society; Signature Member, National Transparent Watercolor Society America (Now TWSA); Signature Member, Society of Western Artists; Signature Member, Watercolor Missouri (Now Missouri Watercolor Society); Georgia Watercolor Society; Texas Watercolor Society **MH:** Albert Nelson Marquis Lifetime Achievement Award; Marquis Who's Who Top Professional **B/I:** Since Mrs. Hofstetter was a child, she always painted. She won ascholarship to design school. She worked in Shenard and learned a lot about what pleases the eye. Her mother was a teacher and her father was a dental surgeon.

HOGAN, LAWRENCE, "LARRY" JOSEPH JR., T: Governor of Maryland **I:** Government Administration/Government Relations/Government Services **DOB:** 05/25/1956 **PB:** Washington, DC **SC:** DC/USA **PT:** Lawrence Joseph Hogan; Ilona (Modly) Hogan **MS:** Married **SPN:** Yumi (Kim) Hogan (2004) **CH:** Kim Velez (Stepchild); Jaymi Sterling (Stepchild); Julie Kim (Stepchild) **ED:** BA in Government and Political Science, Florida State University (1978) **C:** Governor, State of Maryland (2015-Present); Founder, President, Chief Executive Officer, The Hogan Companies, MD (1985-Present); Chair, National Governors Association (2019-2020); Vice Chair, National Governors Association (2018-2019); Governor-elect, State of Maryland (2014-2015); Cabinet Secretary to Governor Bob Ehrlich, State of Maryland, Annapolis, MD (2003-2007); Secretary, Appointments, State of Maryland (2003-2007) **CR:** Founder, Chairman, Change Maryland (2011-Present); Delegate to Republican National Convention (1976, 1980, 1984, 1988) **PA:** Republican

HOLCOMB, ERIC JOSEPH, T: Governor of Indiana **I:** Government Administration/Government Relations/Government Services **DOB:** 05/02/1968 **PB:** Indianpolis **SC:** IN/USA **MS:** Married **SPN:** Janet Holcomb **ED:** Honorary LLD, Anderson University (2019); BA, Hanover College (1990) **C:** Governor, State of Indiana (2017-Present); Lieutenant Governor, State of Indiana (2016-2017); Chief of Staff to Senator Dan Coats, United States Senate, Washington, DC (2013-2015); Chairman, Indiana Republican Party, Indianapolis, IN (2011-2013); Campaign Manager for Governor Mitch Daniels, IN (2008); Deputy Chief of Staff, Advisor for Governor Mitch Daniels, State of Indiana, Indianapolis, IN (2003-2011); With, Congressman John N. Hostettler (1997); With, Mayor Terry Mooney, City of Vincennes, IN **MIL:** Intelligence Officer, United States Navy **MEM:** Chapter President, Phi Gamma Delta **PA:** Republican

HOLDEN, MATTHEW, PHD, T: Political Scientist; Educator; Arbitrator; Energy Consultant **I:** Education/Educational Services **CN:** University of Illinois Springfield **DOB:** 09/12/1931 **PB:** Mound Bayou **SC:** MS/USA **PT:** Matthew Holden; Estelle (Welch) Holden **MS:** Widowed **SPN:** Dorothy Amanda Howard Holden (1932, Deceased 2016) **CH:** Paul C. Hendricks (Stepson); John Matthew Alexander Holden **ED:** Honorary LLD, Roosevelt University (2006); Honorary LHD, Virginia Theological Seminary (2000); Honorary LLD, Tuskegee University (1985); PhD, Northwestern University (1961); MA, Northwestern University (1956); BA, Roosevelt University (1952); Coursework, The University of Chicago (1946-1950) **C:** Wepner Distinguished Professor in Political Science, University of Illinois Springfield (2009-2015); Henry L. and Grace M. Doherty Professor, Government and Foreign Affairs, The University of Virginia, Charlottesville, VA (1981-2002); Commissioner, Federal Energy Regulatory Commission, Washington, DC (1977-1981); Professor, Political Science, University of Wisconsin-Madison (1969-1981); Commissioner, Public Service Commission of Wisconsin, Madison, WI (1975-1977); Member, U.S. Air Quality Advisory Board (1971-1974); Professor, Wayne State University, Detroit, MI (1967-1969); Member, Faculty, Wayne State University, Detroit, MI (1961-1963, 1966-1969); Associate Professor, Wayne State University, Detroit, MI (1966-1967); Assistant Professor, University of Pittsburgh (1963-1966) **CR:** Member, Panel on Commercial Arbitration, American Arbitration Association, New York City, NY (1982-Present); Director, Atlantic Energy, Inc. (AtlanticEnergy), NJ (1981-Present) **CIV:** Member, Standing Committee, The Episcopal Diocese of Virginia (1994-Present) **MIL:** With, Artillery, United States Army, Korea (1955-1957) **CW:** Editor, "Continuity & Disruption" (1996); Editor, National Political Science Review (1991-1995); Editor, "Varieties of Political Conservatism" (1974); Author, "The Divisible Republic" (1973); Editor, "What Answer, 204"; Current Research and Writing on Practice of Power in Executive Decision-making; Regulatory Policy and Performance; Author, "Divisible Republic in the 21st Century as Reassessment of World Compared to Forty Five Years Ago"; Contributor, Numerous Articles to Professional Journals **AW:** Award for Scholarship, Teaching and Service to the Profession, American Political Science Association (APSA) (1982) **MEM:** Executive Committee, National Association of Regulatory Commissioners (Now National Association of Regulatory Utility Commissioners) (1979-1981); Vice President, American Political Science Association (APSA) (1977); Vice President, Mid-America Regulatory Commissioners (1977); The Abraham Lincoln Association; National Academy of Public Administration; American Political Science Association (APSA); Mid-America Regulatory Commissioners; National Association of Regulatory Commissioners (Now National Association of Regulatory Utility Commissioners); Former Member, Board of Directors, Illinois State Historical Society; Mississippi Historical Society **MH:** Albert Nelson Marquis Lifetime Achievement Award; Marquis Who's Who Top Professional **B/I:** Dr. Holden became interested in politics when he was 7 years old, in a very small town. **AV:** Local history, especially Mississippi; Lincoln studies and connection to political science; History and politics of Department of Justice **PA:** Democrat **RE:** Episcopal **THT:** Dr. Holden's primary fields of interest are executive politics and public administration and public policy, and he continues to advocate a strong connection between the content of political science and the worlds of both private and public government.

HOLDEN, MATTHEW, T: President **I:** Utilities **CN:** 1st American Plumbing **CT:** Licensed Plumber, Dallas-Fort Worth Area, Texas (1996-2007) **C:** President, 1st American Plumbing (2018-Present); Vice President, SDL Plumbing Incorporated (2009-Present); Salesman, Southeast Region, Barco Pump, Texas (2007-2009) **AS:** Mr. Holden attributes his success to his training. He was trained by some of the best plumbers in the Dallas-Fort Worth Texas area. He received a wide variety of experiences from homes, hospitals, and repairs. He also attributes his success to his failures. **B/I:** Mr. Holden was pretty much caring and providing for himself by age 16. He was then recruited by a local plumbing company for work. Over his work experience, he developed a love for witnessing some homes he would work in go from "bad-shape to phenomenal". As his career progressed, he experienced and worked for companies whose values did not align with his standard of integrity. These experiences led Mr. Holden to open his own practice, and develop the slogan "Cheap isn't always good, and good isn't always cheap..."

HOLDING, GEORGE EDWARD BELL, T: U.S. Representative from North Carolina **I:** Government Administration/Government Relations/Government Services **CN:** U.S. House of Representatives **DOB:** 04/17/1968 **PB:** Raleigh **SC:** NC/USA **MS:** Married **SPN:** Lucy E. Herriott (1993) **CH:** Beatrice Elizabeth; Alice Margaret; Louisa Maggie; Royal **ED:** Doctor of Jurisprudence, Wake Forest Law (1996); Bachelor of Arts in Classical Studies, Wake Forest University, with Honors (1991) **C:** Member, U.S. House of Representatives from North Carolina's Second Congressional District, United States Congress, Washington, DC (2017-Present); Member, U.S. House Judiciary Committee (2013-Present); Member, U.S. House Committee on Foreign Affairs (2013-Present); Member, U.S. House of Representatives from North Carolina's 13ᵗʰ Congressional District, United States Congress, Washington, DC (2013-2017); United States Attorney, U.S. Department of Justice (2006-2011); First Assistant, United States Attorney for the Eastern District of North Carolina, U.S. Department of Justice (2002-2006); Attorney, Maupin Taylor, Raleigh, NC (2001-2002); Legislative Counsel to Senator Jesse Helms, U.S. Senate (1999-2001); Associate, Kilpatrick Stockton LLP, Raleigh, NC (1997-1998); Law Clerk to the Honorable Terrence Boyle, United States District Court for the Eastern District of North Carolina (1996-1997); Member, Committee on Ways and Means; Member, Republican Study Committee **PA:** Republican **RE:** Southern Baptist

HOLDITCH, KENNETH, PHD, T: Professor Emeritus **I:** Education/Educational Services **CN:** University of New Orleans **DOB:** 09/18/1933 **PB:** Ecru **SC:** MS/USA **PT:** Sidney Williamson Holditch; Dora Faye (Dickerson) Holditch **ED:** PhD in English, University of Mississippi (1961); MA in English, University of Mississippi (1957); Honorary BA, Southwestern at Memphis (Now Rhodes College) (1955) **C:** Research Professor Emeritus, University of New Orleans (1996-Present); Research Professor, University of New Orleans (1990-1996); Professor, University of New Orleans (1978-1990); Associate Professor, University of New Orleans (1969-1978); Assistant Professor, University of New Orleans (1964-1969); Instructor of American Literature, University of Mississippi, Oxford, MS (1957-1959) **CR:** Vice President, Tennessee Williams Festival, New Orleans, LA (1987-Present); Board of Directors, Tennessee Williams Festival, New Orleans, LA (1986-1997); Founder, Tennessee Williams Festival, New Orleans, LA, Clarksdale, MS, Columbus, MS **CIV:** Adviser, Clarksdale Tennessee Williams Festival (1992-Present); President, Friends of University of New Orleans Library (1990-1994); Tennessee Williams Walking Tour (30 years); Founder, Board of Directors, Pirate's Alley Faulkner Society **CW:** Founder, Publisher, The Tennessee Williams Journal (1989-Present); Contributor, "Dinner with Tennessee Williams" (2011); Co-Author, "Galatoire's: Biography of a Bistro" (2004); Co-Author, "Tennesee Williams and the South" (2002); Advisory Editor, South Central Journal (1990-1993); Editor, "In Old New Orleans" (1983); Author, Numerous Essays and Short Stories; Co-Editor, With Mel Gussow, Two Tennessee Williams Volumes, Library of America **AW:** Lifetime Achievement Award, Louisiana Endowment for the Humanities (2001); University Teacher of the Year, Liberal Arts, State of Louisiana (1980) **MEM:** Modern Language Association of America; South Central Modern Language Association **MH:** Albert Nelson Marquis Lifetime Achievement Award **B/I:** Dr. Holditch became involved in his profession because since he was in high school, he knew he wanted to pursue English as he was blessed with a wonderful English teacher, Florence Dogan, who introduced him to William Faulkner. In college, he had an English teacher who encouraged his interest in poetry, which he continued to read a great deal. He was born in a Ecru, Mississippi, which is the home of more authors than any other state and six miles away from where William Faulkner was born. His great-grandfather was the lieutenant under Faulkner's great-grandfather during the Civil War. Since he was born about 60 miles from where Tennessee Williams was born, he started reading him very early. He always wanted to move to New Orleans, so as soon as he could, he took a salary cut to go there to teach. Dr. Holditch has never regretted that move; it makes him very happy to be in a place that he loves. **AV:** Walking; Reading; Collecting glass; Going out to lunch; Giving 15 minute introductions on tours **THT:** Dr. Holditch attended junior high school with Elvis Presley, who was a year and a half younger and two grades behind him. Presley performed a couple times at an assembly and he and his friends laughed at him because they laughed at all the children younger than them. Then Presley performed at the Mississippi Alabama fair and dairy show and won second place in the talent contest. His cousin handed out the awards every year because he was president of the fair. After Elvis became famous, Dr. Holditch saw him come back to perform at the fair twice. He later met him in Memphis; he was very nice and charming, they talked about Tupelo, Mississippi.

HOLDREN, JOHN P., PHD, T: Educator, Physicist, Former Government Official **I:** Education/Educational Services **DOB:** 03/01/1944 **PB:** Sewickley **SC:** PA/USA **PT:** Raymond Andrew Holdren; Virginia June (Fuqua) Holdren **MS:** Married **SPN:** Cheryl E. Holdren (02/05/1966) **CH:** J. Craig Holdren; Jill Virginia Holdren **ED:** Honorary ScD, Rensselaer Polytechnic Institute (RPI) (2019); Honorary ScD, Green Mountain College (2016); Honorary ScD, University of the District of Columbia (2012); Honorary LLD, Sapienza Università di Roma (2010); Honorary DSc, Clark University (2003); Honorary DEng, Colorado School of Mines (1997); Honorary ScD, University of Puget Sound (1975); PhD, Stanford University, Palo Alto, CA (1970); MS, Massachusetts Institute of Technology (1966); BS, Massachusetts Institute of Technology (1965) **C:** Affiliated Professor, Harvard John A. Paulson School of Engineering and Applied Sciences, Harvard University (2018-Present); Professor, Environmental Science and Policy, Department of Earth and Planetary Sciences, Faculty of Arts and Sciences, Harvard University (2017-Present); Director, Office of Science and Technology Policy, Executive Office of the President of the United States, Washington, DC (2009-2017); Assistant to the President of the United States, Science and Technology, The White House, Washington, DC (2009-2017); Director, Woods Hole Research Center, Falmouth, MA (2005-2009); Director, Science, Technology, and Public Policy Program, Belfer Center for Science and International Affairs, Harvard Kennedy School, Harvard University, Cambridge, MA (1996-2009); Professor, Environmental Science and Public Policy, Department of Earth and Planetary Sciences, Faculty of Arts and Sciences, Harvard University, Cambridge, MA (1996-2009); Professor, Energy & Resources Group, University California, Berkeley (1978-1996); Chairman, Energy & Resources Group, University California, Berkeley (1983-1984); Associate Professor, Energy & Resources Group, University California, Berkeley (1975-1978); Assistant Professor, Energy & Resources Group, University California, Berkeley (1973-1975); Senior Research Fellow, California Institute of Technology, Pasadena, CA (1972-1973); Theoretical Physicist, Lawrence Livermore National Laboratory, Livermore, CA (1970-1973); Research Assistant, Institute for Plasma Research, Stanford University (1969-1970); Aerodynamic Engineer, Lockheed Missiles and Space Company, Sunnyvale, CA (1966-1967) **CR:** Co-Chair, President's Council of Advisors on Science and Technology, Office of Science and Technology Policy, The White House (2009-2017); Vice Chair, Board of Directors, Woods Hole Research Center (1994-2005); Distinguished Visiting Scholar, Woods Hole Research Center (1994-2005); President's Council of Advisors on Science and Technology, Office of Science and Technology Policy, The White House (1994-2001); Visiting Professor, Physics, Tor Vergata University of Rome (1997); Visiting Scholar, Woods Hole Research Center (1992-1994); Fusion Energy Sciences Advisory Committee, U.S. Department of Energy (1991-1994); Visiting Fellow, Defense and Arms Control Studies Program (Now MIT Security Studies Program), Massachusetts Institute of Technology (1988); Senior Investigator, Rocky Mountain Biological Laboratory, Crested Butte, CO (1974-1988); Visiting Fellow, Max-Planck-Gesellschaft, Starnberg, Germany (1987); Board of Editors, Bulletin of the Atomic Scientists, Chicago, IL (1984-1986); East-West Center, Honolulu, HI (1979-1980) **CIV:** Board of Directors, John D. and Catherine T. MacArthur Foundation (1991-2005); Chairman, Executive Committee, Pugwash Conferences on Science and World Affairs (1987-1997); Executive Committee, Pugwash Conferences on Science and World Affairs (1982-1997); Chairman, U.S. Pugwash Committee, Pugwash Conferences on Science and World Affairs, American Academy of Arts & Sciences, Cambridge, MA (1983-1995); Council, Smithsonian Institution (1988-1991) **CW:** Co-Author, "Confronting Climate Change: Avoiding the Unmanageable and Managing the Unavoidable" (2007); Co-Author, "Monitoring Nuclear Weapons and Nuclear-Explosive Materials: An Assessment of Methods and Capabilities" (2005); Co-Author, "Ending the Energy Stalemate: A Bipartisan Strategy to Meet America's Energy Challenges" (2004); Co-Author, "Controlling Nuclear Warheads and Materials: A Report Card and Action Plan" (2003); Co-Author, "Technical Issues Related to the Comprehensive Test Ban Treaty" (2002); Co-Editor, "Conversion of Military R&D" (1999); Co-Author, "Powerful Partnerships: The Federal Role in International Cooperation on Energy Innovation" (1999); Co-Author, "Federal Energy Research and Development for the Challenges of the Twenty-First Century" (1997); Co-Author, "The Future of U.S. Nuclear Weapons Policy" (1997); Co-Editor, "Earth and the Human Future" (1996); Co-Author, "Management and Disposition of Excess Weapons Plutonium" (1994); Co-Author, "Building Global Security through Cooperation" (1990); Co-Editor, "The Cassandra Conference: Resources and the Human Predicament" (1988); Co-Editor, "Strategic Defences and the Future of the Arms Race" (1987); Co-Author, "Strategic Defences and the Future of the Arms Race" (1987); Co-Author, "Energy in Transition 1985-2010" (1980); Co-Author, "Ecoscience: Population, Resources, Environment" (1977); Co-Author, "Human Ecology: Problems and Solutions" (1973); Co-Editor, "Man and the Ecosphere" (1971); Co-Author, "Energy: A Crisis in Power" (1971); Contributor, Articles, Professional Journals, Magazines, Blogs **AW:** Teresa and John Heinz Professor of Environmental Policy, Harvard Kennedy School, Harvard University (1996-2009, 2017-Present); Daniel Patrick Moynihan Prize, The American Academy of Political and Social Science (2019); Heinz Award, Public Policy (2001); Tyler Prize for Environmental Achievement (2000); Award for Excellence in Science and Environmental Policy, Kaul Foundation (1999); Leadership Award, Fusion Power Associates (1998); Class of 1935 Distinguished Professor of Energy, University California, Berkeley (1991-1996); Joseph A. Burton Forum Award, American Physical Society (1995); Volvo Environment Prize (1993); MacArthur Fellowship, John D. and Catherine T. MacArthur Foundation (1981-1986); FAS Public Service Award, Federation of American Scientists (1979) **MEM:** Board of Sponsors, Federation of American Scientists (1986-Present); Chairman, Board of Directors, American Association for the Advancement of Science (2007-2008); President, American Association for the Advancement of Science (2006-2007); Chairman, Committee on International Security and Arms Control, National Academy of Sciences (1993-2004); Committee on International Security and Arms Control, National Academy of Sciences (1992-2004); Vice Chairman, Committee on International Security Studies, American Academy of Arts & Sciences (1983-1997); Chairman, Federation of American Scientists (1984-1986); Vice Chairman, Federation of American Scientists (1981-1984); Council Member, Treasurer, Federation of American Scientists (1979-1980); Fellow, American Association for the Advancement of Science; National Academy of Sciences; National Academy of Engineering, National Academy of Sciences; The American Philosophical Society; American Academy of Arts & Sciences; The American Academy of Political and Social Science; American Physical Society; Federation of American Scientists; California Academy of Sciences **MH:** Albert Nelson Marquis Lifetime Achievement Award **B/I:** Reflecting on career impact, Professor Holdren gives credit to his elementary school teachers, as well as two influential books he read while in high school: "The Two Cultures" and "The Challenge of Man's Future." These works, written in the 1950s, inspired Professor Holdren to think seriously about a career bridging science, technology, and the humanities. His storied career owes largely to his drive to confront the challenges facing civilization. **AV:** Hiking; Fishing **PA:** Democrat **THT:** In 1995, Professor Holdren gave the acceptance lecture for the Nobel Peace Prize on behalf of the Pugwash Conferences on Sciences and World Affairs.

HOLICK, SALLY ANN, T: Biochemist, Researcher **I:** Sciences **DOB:** 12/11/1948 **PB:** Harrisburg **SC:** PA/USA **PT:** Paul Elwood Teats; Kathryn Mellie (Howard) Teats **MS:** Married **SPN:** Michael Francis Holick (05/28/1972) **CH:** Michael Todd Holick, J.D., M.B.A.; Emily Holick Nelson, M.D **ED:** Postdoctoral Fellow, Biochemistry, University of Wisconsin, Madison (1974-1975); PhD, University of Wisconsin (1974); BA, Bloomsburg University, Pennsylvania (1970) **C:** Chief Financial Officer, A&D Bioscience, Inc. (1988-2018); Research Scientist, Nutrition, Tufts University, Boston, MA (1985-1988); Research Scientist, Nutrition, Massachusetts Institute of Technology, Cambridge, MA (1982-1985); Instructor, Medicine, Massachusetts General Hospital and Harvard University Medical School, Boston, MA (1977-1982); Instructor, Chemistry, Boston University (1975-1977) **CIV:** Dartmouth College Women's Club of Boston; Middlebury College Friends of the Art Museum **CW:** Contributor, Articles, Professional Journals **AW:** National Institutes of Health Grant (1974-2008); Grantee-in-aid, Sigma Delta Epsilon (1981); Sigma Xi (1980) **MEM:** American Society of Biological Chemists; American Chemical Society; Sigma Delta Epsilon; Sigma Xi **AV:** Tennis; Gardening; Classical music **PA:** Independent **RE:** Lutheran

HOLIDAY, JRUE RANDALL, T: Professional Basketball Player **I:** Athletics **CN:** New Orleans Pelicans **DOB:** 06/12/1990 **PB:** Chatsworth **SC:** CA/USA **PT:** Shawn Holiday; Toya (DeCree) Holiday **MS:** Married **SPN:** Lauren Cheney (07/2013)

CH: Jrue Tyler **ED:** Coursework, University of California Los Angeles (2008-2009); Diploma, Campbell Hall School, Studio City, CA **C:** Professional Basketball Player, New Orleans Pelicans (2013-Present); Professional Basketball Player, Philadelphia 76ers (2009-2013) **AW:** NBA All-Star (2013); Gatorade National Player of the Year (2008); McDonald's All-American (2008); First-team Parade All-American (2008); California Mr. Basketball (2008); Third-team Parade All-American (2007) **RE:** Christian

HOLLAND, CINDY, T: Former Vice President of Content Acquisition **I:** Media & Entertainment **CN:** Netflix **ED:** Diploma, Stanford University **C:** Vice President of Content Acquisition, Original Series, Netflix (2002-2020); Vice President, Business Development, Kozmo (1999-2001); Head of Acquisitions, Mutual Film Company (1998-1999); Vice President of Development, Baltimore/Spring Creek Productions (1994-1998) **CR:** Board of Directors, Horizon Acquisition Corporation II (2020-Present) **AW:** Named One of the 100 Most Influential People, TIME Magazine (2018)

HOLLAND, WOODROW ALAN, T: Managing Member **I:** Law and Legal Services **CN:** Holland Law, PLLC **DOB:** 10/24/1947 **PB:** Houston **SC:** TX/USA **MS:** Married **SPN:** Frances **CH:** Four Children **ED:** JD, University of Texas (1974); BS in Civil Engineering, Southern Methodist University (1970) **C:** Managing Member, Holland Law, PLLC (1986-Present); Senior Vice President and General Counsel, Mariner Corporation (1982-1986); Secretary and General Counsel, Champion Realty Corporation (1978-1982) **CR:** Owner, Minas del Rio Sonora; Partner, Yorkshire Energy Corporation; Owner, Texas General Transportation, Texas City, TX; Partner, Solution Title Agency, Houston, TX; Club Flamingo, Houston, TX; Q Café, Houston, TX; Partner, Corsair Trading Company, Houston, TX; Partner, Galveston Houston Construction **CIV:** Board of Directors, Municipal Utility Districts; Boy Scouts of America **MIL:** U.S. Army Reserve (1970-1976) **MEM:** Board of Directors, Houston Young Lawyers Association (1974); State Bar of Texas; American Bar Association; Houston Bar Association **AS:** Mr. Holland attributes his success to his dedication to his businesses, as well as his ability to achieve at a high level. He also is proud of the way he has balanced his business interests with his family life. **THT:** Mr. Holland's motto is, "Treat others as you would like to be treated."

HOLLEIN, MAX, T: Director **I:** Fine Art **CN:** Metropolitan Museum of Art **DOB:** 07/07/1969 **SC:** Vienna/Austria **PT:** Hans Hollein; Helene Hollein **MS:** Married **SPN:** Nina Hollein **CH:** Three Children **ED:** MA in Art History, University of Vienna; MBA, Vienna University of Economics **C:** Director, Metropolitan Museum of Art (2018-Present); Director, Chief Executive Officer, Fine Arts Museums of San Francisco (2016-2018); Executive Assistant to the Director, Solomon R. Guggenheim Museum (1996-2000); Chief of Staff, Manager of European Relations, Solomon R. Guggenheim Museum (1998) **CR:** Director, Liebieghaus Skulpturensammlung; Städel Museum; Schirn Kunsthalle Frankfurt; Fundraiser, Traveling Exhibitions, Inauguration Activities, Guggenheim Bilbao **CIV:** Advisory Board, Deutsche Bank (2006-2012); International Advisory Board, State Hermitage Museum, St. Petersburg, Russia; Advisory Board, Hall Art Foundation; Advisory Board, Istanbul Modern; Jury Member, Nomura Art Award; International Advisory Board, University of Applied Arts Vienna; Advisory Board, University of Art and Design Offenbach am Main; Jury Member, Arts Sponsorship Award, Association of Arts and Culture of the German Economy **CW:** Author, "Julian Schnabel: Symbols of Actual

Life" (2019); Co-Author, "Odilon Redon: As in a Dream" (2007); Co-Editor, "Picasso and the Theater" (2007); Co-Editor, "Henri Matisse: Drawing with Scissors: Masterpieces from the Late Years" (2006); Co-Author, "Julian Schnabel: Malerei/Paintings 1978-2003" (2004); Freelancer, Business Section, Der Standard **AW:** Goethe Plaque, City of Frankfurt, Germany (2019); Goethe-Plakette des Landes Hessen (2016); Binding-Kulturpreis (2015); Austrian Cross of Honour for Science and Art (2010); Chevalier dans l'Ordre des Arts et des Lettres, French Minister of Culture (2009)

HOLLEMAN, JOHN, "SONNY" LINDSEY, T: Priest **I:** Religious **DOB:** 09/15/1940 **PB:** Mobile **SC:** AB/USA **PT:** Joseph Eugene; Audrey Gunn Holleman **MS:** Single **ED:** Licentiate of Sacred Theology, Gregorian University, Rome, Italy (1982); Bachelor of Letters in Theology, Christ Church College, Oxford, England (1974); Master of Arts in Philosophy, Tulane University (1971); Master of Divinity, General Theological Seminary, New York, NY (1968); Bachelor of Science in Mathematics, Tulane University (1962) **CT:** Ordained, Roman Catholic Church (1981); Ordained, Episcopal Church (1968) **C:** Catholic Priest (1981-Present); Retired Priest (2016); Production Manager, President, Hospitality TV Network, New Orleans, la (1995-2000); With, Various Parishes, Archdiocese of New Orleans (1988-1995); With, Immaculate Conception Church, Chicago Archdiocese (1986-1988); With, Various Parishes, Archdiocese of New Orleans (1982-1986); Teacher of Mathematics and Chemistry, Saint Ignatius College Preparatory, Chicago, IL (1978-1980); Episcopal Priest (1969-1978); With, Various Parishes, Episcopal Church, United States of America (1968-1978); With, Various Parishes, Archdiocese of Mobile **CR:** Missionary, Four Parishes in Alaska, Flying a Piper Warrior (2002-2005) **MIL:** Lieutenant, Junior Grade, U.S. Navy (1962-1964) **CW:** Author, Tract, "Why Confession?"; Author, Tract, "The Importance of Failure"; Author, Tract, "The Importance of Faith" **MEM:** Knights of Columbus **MH:** Albert Nelson Marquis Lifetime Achievement Award; Marquis Who's Who Humanitarian Award **AS:** Father Holleman credits his success on his adherence to his Christian faith. **B/I:** Father Holleman became a priest after having served in the U.S. Navy for several years, during which time he was stationed on the U.S.S. Putnam during the Cuban Missile Crisis. Following his discharge, he attended the General Theological Seminary in New York City and became a priest in Louisiana. **PA:** Republican **RE:** Roman Catholic

HOLLINGSWORTH, JOSEPH, "TREY" ALBERT III, T: U.S. Representative from Indiana **I:** Government Administration/Government Relations/Government Services **CN:** U.S. House of Representatives **DOB:** 09/12/1983 **PB:** Clinton **SC:** TN/USA **MS:** Married **SPN:** Kelly Francis (2014) **CH:** Joseph **ED:** Master in Public Policy, Georgetown University (2014); Bachelor of Science, The Wharton School, The University of Pennsylvania **C:** Member, U.S. House of Representatives from Indiana's Ninth Congressional District (2017-Present); Co-partner, Aluminum Remanufacturing Operation, Indiana (2008-Present); Member, Committee on Financial Services; Member, U.S. House Subcommittee on Investor Protection, Entrepreneurship, and Capital Markets; Member, U.S. House Financial Services Subcommittee on Diversity and Inclusion; Small Business Owner, Renovation and Rehabilitation of Industrial Sites **PA:** Republican

HOLLOWAY, ROBERT C., T: Musician, Composer (Retired) **I:** Media & Entertainment **PB:** Baltimore **SC:** MD/USA **PT:** George Albert Holloway; Edna Mildred (Smith) Holloway **MS:**

Widowed **SPN:** Leslee R. Seymour (06/04/1960) **CH:** Bruce; Collin; Christy; Heather; Deven; Duana **C:** Retired, President, Chelsea Music Service, Inc., New York, NY (1990-1992); Arranger, Orchestrator, Alvin Ailey Dance Co. (1952-1987) **CR:** Vice President, St. Croix Records **MIL:** U.S. Navy Reserves (1946-1954); U.S. Navy (1944-1946) **CW:** Arranger, Orchestrator, ABC-TV; Arranger, Orchestrator, CBS Radio; Arranger, Orchestrator, NBC Tonight Show; Arranger, Orchestrator, Radio City Music Hall; Arranger, Orchestrator, Children's TV Workshop, Sesame Street; Arranger, Orchestrator, U.S. Navy Band; Arranger, Orchestrator, Boston Pops Orchestra; Arranger, Orchestrator, PS Classics, San Antonio Symphony; Arranger, Orchestrator, Denver Symphony; Arranger, Orchestrator, Pacific Northwest Ballet; Orchestrator, "Internationale"; Orchestrator, "Piaf, Her Story, Her Songs," San Francisco Ballet; Orchestrator, "Odyssey"; Orchestrator, "Barnum"; Orchestrator, "Peter Pan"; Orchestrator, "Dancin'"; Orchestrator, "Sophisticated Ladies"; Orchestrator, "On Your Toes"; Orchestrator, "Jerome Robbins Broadway"; Vermont Jazz Ensemble; Jazz Experience; Composer, Prelude; Composer, Busybody; Composer, Southern Suite; Composer, Composer, Improvisations in Jazz; Composer, Celebration; Composer, Eastern Slope; Composer, Wildcat; Composer, Bone Fracture **MEM:** Jazz Network; American Society of Composers; American Society of Music Arrangers; American Federation of Musicians **MH:** Albert Nelson Marquis Lifetime Achievement Award **AS:** Mr. Holloway attributes his success to being very humble and working hard. **AV:** Boxing **RE:** Christian

HOLLOWAY, THOMAS M., PHD, T: Senior Vice President **I:** Financial Services **CN:** PNC Bank **DOB:** 07/25/1953 **SC:** MD/USA **PT:** McGlon T. Holloway; Ellen T. Holloway **CH:** Matthew Thomas; John Roger **ED:** Doctor of Philosophy in Decision Sciences, Walden University, Minneapolis, MN (2010); Master of Science in Economics, Texas Christian University, Fort Worth, TX (1976); Bachelor of Science in Economics, Texas Christian University, Fort Worth, TX, Summa Cum Laude (1975); Postgraduate Coursework, American University, Washington, DC **CT:** Competent Toastmaster **C:** Senior Vice President, Model Risk Management, PNC Bank, Pittsburgh, PA (2012-Present); Senior Director, Loss Forecasting, Risk Analysis, Credit Portfolio Management, Director, Model Management, Model Development, Director, Credit, Risk Assessment, Model Development Division, Freddie Mac, McLean, VA (1992-2012); Senior Economist, Mortgage Bankers Association, Washington, DC (1987-1992); Chief, Special Studies Branch, Bureau of Economic Analysis, U.S. Department of Commerce (1979-1987) **CR:** Part-Time Teacher, Macroeconomics, Microeconomics, Business, Texas Christian University, Texas Wesleyan University, University of Dallas; Part-Time Teacher, Money and Capital Markets, Mortgage Banker's Association School of Mortgage Banking **CIV:** Previous Member, Board of Governors, Credit Research Center, Georgetown University; Polling Monitor **CW:** Published, more than 50 Articles to Business and Professional Journals, such as Journal of Real Estate Finance and Economics, Journal of Money, Credit and Banking, Business Economics, Survey of Current Business, Mortgage Banking, International Journal of Forecasting, American Economist, Public Finance Quarterly; Nationwide Speaker in the Field **AW:** Freddie Mac Chairman's Discretionary Grant Award for Credit Scoring Work; Freddie Mac Premier Achievement Award for Loan Loss Reserves Work; Department of Commerce Recognition **MEM:** American Economics Association; Board of Governors, Georgetown University Credit Research Center; Competent Toastmaster, Designation by Toastmasters International; Mensa; Phi Beta Kappa **AS:** Mr. Holloway attributes his success to excellent mentors, training and long hours. He began his work at the National Bureau of Economic Analysis in the department of commerce, where he had the good fortune of working with Frank deLeeuw, the Chief Statistician of the Bureau. He and deLeeuw co-authored numerous articles on fiscal analysis. When Mr. Holloway moved to the Mortgage Bankers Association, he worked with Lyle Gramley, a former governor of the Federal Reserve Board, who mentored him in economical forecasting. Later, Mr. Holloway transitioned to Freddie Mac, where Henry Cassidy, who headed credit policy, and Mike Stamper, who was the Chief Risk Officer, provided guidance and support that enabled his future contributions in mortgage credit scoring. **B/I:** When he was an undergraduate, Mr. Holloway originally intended to pursue law. He had a broad interest in liberal arts and liked the analytics of law. However, he also always enjoyed quantifying things, and associated quantitative and analytic work. He was taking economics as part of the pre-law preparation and found that he was interested in that field more than legal service. **RE:** Methodist

HOLLUB, VICKI, T: President, Chief Executive Officer **I:** Oil & Energy **CN:** Occidental Petroleum Corporation **PB:** Birmingham **SC:** AL/USA **MS:** Married **ED:** Distinguished Engineering Fellow, College of Engineering, The University of Alabama (2016); Bachelor of Science in Mineral Engineering, The University of Alabama (1981) **C:** President, Chief Executive Officer, Occidental Petroleum Corporation (2016-Present); President, Worldwide, Occidental Oil and Gas Corporation (2015-Present); Chief Operating Officer, Occidental Petroleum Corporation (2015-2016); Senior Executive Vice President, Occidental Petroleum Corporation (2015); Executive Vice President, Occidental Petroleum Corporation (2014-2015); President, Americas, Occidental Oil & Gas Corporation (2014-2015); Vice President, Occidental Petroleum Corporation (2013-2014); Executive Vice President, U.S. Operations, Occidental Oil & Gas Corporation (2013-2014); Executive Vice President, California Operations, Occidental Petroleum Corporation (2012-2013) **CIV:** Board of Directors, Occidental Petroleum Corporation (2015-Present); U.S. Chair, U.S.-Colombia Business Council; Board Member, Khalifa University for Science and Technology; Board Member, American Petroleum Institute **MEM:** Society of Petroleum Engineers

HOLLY, RAMONA ANN, T: Elementary and Secondary Education Educator **I:** Education/Educational Services **DOB:** 02/11/1939 **PB:** Kissimmee **SC:** FL/USA **PT:** Horatio Abram Cobb; Lucindy (Hancock) Cobb **MS:** Widow **SPN:** Philip D. Anderson **CH:** Karl; Nick; Jamie **ED:** MA in American History and Education, Florida Atlantic University; BS in Geography, Florida Atlantic University; BA in Communications, Florida Atlantic University **CT:** Certified Elementary Teacher, Florida; Certification in Secondary School, Florida; Endorsed, Speakers of Other Languages (SOL); Certification in Special Education **C:** Teacher, Social Studies, English, Mathematics, Broward County Schools, Fort Lauderdale, FL (1987-1999); Teacher, Zion Lutheran School (1977-1987); Darkroom Technician, Lundy Technician Center, Pompano Beach, FL (1977-1986); Photographer, Photojournalist, Deerfield Beach Observer (1976-1982) **CIV:** Panel, Human Relations Board of Broward County (1976-1978); Board Member, Percy White Library, Deerfield Beach, FL; Singer, Various Local Church Choirs **AW:** Janet Rice Scholar, Florida Atlantic University (1975-1976) **MEM:** Deerfield Beach Historical Society; Garden Club of Sebring **MH:** Albert Nelson Marquis Lifetime Achievement Award; Marquis Who's Who Top Professional **B/I:** Mrs. Holly always knew she wanted to teach. She attributes her love for education to her mother, Lucindy Cobb, who was a Sunday school teacher but had aspirations of being a teacher herself. Mrs. Holly always had support from her father, Horatio Cobb, who was also a Sunday School teacher. He always stressed to her how vital education was in order to pursue her career. Mrs. Holly wanted to do the same for her students. **AV:** Traveling; Playing tennis; Gardening; Practicing needlecraft **PA:** Independent **RE:** Protestant

HOLM, GEORGE L., T: Chief Executive Officer and President **I:** Food & Restaurant Services **CN:** Performance Food Group Company **ED:** BS, Grand Canyon University **C:** President, Chief Executive Officer, Performance Food Group, Richmond, VA (2008-Present); President, Chief Executive Officer, Vistar Corporation, Centennial, CO (2002-2008); Chief Executive Officer, Roma Food Enterprises; Senior Management Positions, Alliant Foodservice Inc., US Foodservice Inc., Sysco Corporation

HOLMES, CECILE S., T: Associate Professor **I:** Education/Educational Services **CN:** School of Journalism and Mass Communications University of South Carolina **DOB:** 01/06/1955 **PB:** Columbia **SC:** SC/USA **PT:** James Gadsden Holmes; Anne Keene (Searson) Holmes **MS:** Widowed **SPN:** Jace Holloman **ED:** MA in Liberal Studies, UNC Greensboro (1994); Fellowship, University of North Carolina (1982); BA in Journalism, University of South Carolina, Magna Cum Laude (1977) **C:** Faculty, School of Journalism and Mass Communications, University of South Carolina (2000-Present); Religion Section Editor, Houston Chronicle (1989-2000); Religion Writer, Houston Chronicle (1987-1989); Religion Writer, Greensboro News and Record (1984-1987) **CR:** Faculty Member, Summer Journalism Workshop, Houston Chronicle (1988-1992); Co-Director, Minority Journalism Workshop, News and Record (1988) **CIV:** Mentor, Education for Ministry, Houston, TX (1989-Present); Adviser, Campaign for Homeless, United Way (1991); Ethics of Humane Care (1986); Moderator, NCCJ (1985); Hunger Commission Episcopal Diocese of North Carolina; South Carolina Christian Action Council **CW:** Author, "Witnesses to the Horror: North Carolinians Remember the Holocaust" (1988); Author, "Four Women, Three Faiths : Inspiring Spiritual Journeys"; Contributor, Articles, Professional Journals **AW:** Lifetime Achievement Award, Religion News Association (2016); Professor Newspaper Publishing Award, Association for Education in Journalism and Mass Communication (2005); Wilbur Award, Religion Communicators Council (1986); Public Service Award, North Carolina Press Association (1985); Community Journalism Award, North Carolina Agricultural and Technical State University (1984); Award, Piedmont Baptist Association (1984); Mark of Excellence Award, Society of Professional Journalists **MEM:** President, Religion News Association (1996-Present); First Vice President, Religion News Association (1994-1996); Second Vice President, Religion News Association (1992-1994); Treasurer, Religion News Association (1990-1992); Chapter President, Vice President, Society of Professional Journalists; Houston Press Club; Beta Sigma Phi; Kappa Tau Alpha; Omicron Delta Kappa **MH:** Marquis Who's Who Top Professional **AS:** Ms. Holmes attributes her success to her open-minded parents who exposed her to many religions at a young age. **AV:** Gardening; Taking photographs; Reading; Antiquing

HOLMES, RICHARD B., T: Chief Engineer **I:** Engineering **DOB:** 01/07/1959 **PB:** Milwaukee **SC:** WI/USA **PT:** Emerson Brooks Holmes; Nancy Anne Schaffter Holmes **MS:** Married **SPN:** Sandra Lynn Wong (06/27/1998) **ED:** MS, Stanford University (1983); BS, California Institute of Technology (1981) **C:** Chief Engineer, Nutronics, Inc., Longmont, CO (2019-Present); Chief Scientist, Boeing LTS (2010-2019); President, General Nutronics, Inc., Milpitas, CA (2001-2010); President, Nutronics, Inc., Cameron Park, CA (1998-2010); Senior Staff Scientist, Lockheed Martin Research Laboratories, Palo Alto, CA (1995-1998); Senior Member, Technical Staff, Rocketdyne Division Rockwell International, Canoga Park, CA (1990-1995); Principal Research Scientist, North East Research Associates, Woburn, MA (1988-1990); Senior Scientist, AVCO Everett Research Laboratory (1985-1988); Staff Scientist, Western Research, Arlington, VA (1983-1985); Senior System Analyst, Comptek Research, Vallejo, CA (1982-1983) **CR:** Consultant, North East Research Associates (1990) **CIV:** Wilderness Society, Washington, DC (1989); Northern California Scholarship Foundations, Oakland, CA (1977) **CW:** Contributor, Matched Asymptotic Expansions (1988); Contributor, Articles, Physical Review Letters; Contributor, Articles, Physical Reviews, Journal of the Optical Society of America; Contributor, Articles, IEEE Journal of Quantum Electronics; Author, "A Quantum Field Theory with Permutational Symmetry" **AW:** Presidential Medal of Merit (1992); Parsons Fellow, Massachusetts Institute of Technology (1990); Stanford Fellow, Stanford University (1982) **MEM:** Organizer, Senior Member, SPIE (1995-1999, 2011-2019); Fellow, The Optical Society; Fellow, Directed Energy Professional Society; American Physical Society; Topical Editor, Senior Member, Optical Society America

HOLMES NORTON, ELEANOR, T: Delegate to U.S. House of Representatives, Lawyer, Educator **I:** Government Administration/Government Relations/Government Services **DOB:** 06/13/1937 **PB:** Washington **SC:** DC/USA **PT:** Coleman Holmes; Vela (Lynch) Holmes **MS:** Widowed **SPN:** Edward Norton (Deceased 2014) **CH:** John Holmes; Katherine Felicia **ED:** LLB, Yale University (1964); MA in American Studies, Yale University (1963); BA, Antioch College (1960) **C:** Delegate to U.S. House of Representatives, District of Columbia's At-Large Congressional District (1990-Present); Professor of Law, Georgetown University, Washington, DC (1982-Present); Senior Fellow, Urban Institute, Washington, DC (1981-1982); Chairman, Equal Employment Opportunity Commission, Washington, DC (1977-1981); Chairman, New York City Commission on Human Rights (1970-1977); Executive Assistant to Mayor, City of New York, NY (1971-1974); Assistant Legal Director, American Civil Liberties Union (1965-1970); Law Clerk to Judge A. Leon Higgonbotham, Federal District Court (1964-1965); Member, Committee on Government Reform, United States Congress; Member, Committee on Transportation and Infrastructure, United States Congress **CIV:** Former Trustee, Rockefeller Foundation; Trustee, Numerous Public Service Boards; Board of Governors, The District of Columbia Bar; Board Member, Numerous Civil Rights and Other National Organizations **AW:** One of the 100 Most Powerful Women in DC, Washingtonian Magazine (2009); Power 150, Ebony Magazine (2008); One of the 100 Most Influential Black Americans, Ebony Magazine (2006); Citation of Merit for Outstanding Alumni, Yale Law School; Wilbur Cross Medal for Outstanding Alumni, Yale Graduate School of Arts and Sciences **BAR:** Supreme Court of the United States (1968); Pennsylvania Bar Association (1965) **PA:** Democrat

HOLST, SANFORD, T: Author, International Consultant **I:** Writing and Editing **DOB:** 11/04/1946 **PT:** William Walker Holst; Catherine (Loggie) Holst **CH:** Suzanne; Kristina **ED:** MBA, University of California, Los Angeles (UCLA) (1970); BS in Engineering, Massachusetts Institute of Technology (MIT) (1968) **C:** Author (1995-Present); Principal Consultant, Strategic Systems, Los Angeles, CA (1993-2003); Vice President, Computer Systems, Parsons Corporation, Pasadena, CA (1980-1993); Systems Analyst, Northwest Industries, Los Angeles, CA (1972-1980); Engineer, Advanced Design Group, Lockheed Aircraft Corporation, Los Angeles, CA (1968-1971) **CR:** Presenter, Academic Papers, Marquette University, Milwaukee, WI; Presenter, Academic Papers, Mary College, London, England; Presenter, Academic Papers, California State University, Long Beach, CA; Presenter, Academic Papers, Al Akhawayn University, Morocco; Presenter, Academic Papers, University of Ghent, Belgium **CIV:** Vice Chairman, Beverly Hills Bicentennial Committee (1976) **CW:** Author, "Origin of the Templars" (2017); Author, "Sworn in Secret" (2012); Author, "Phoenician Secrets" (2011); Author, "Phoenicians" (2005); Author, "Kombucha Phenemenon" (1995) **MEM:** Royal Historical Society (2008-Present); President, Alpha Mu Chapter, Phi Kappa Sigma (1967-1968) **AV:** Knights Templar; Freemasonry

HOLT, LESTER DON JR., T: News Correspondent; Anchor **I:** Media & Entertainment **CN:** NBC Universal **DOB:** 03/08/1959 **PB:** San Francisco **SC:** CA/USA **PT:** Lester Don Holt; June (DeRozario) Holt **MS:** Married **SPN:** Carol Hagen (05/08/1982) **CH:** Stefan; Cameron **ED:** Honorary Doctorate, Rutgers, The State University of New Jersey (2016); Honorary Doctorate, Pepperdine University (2012); Coursework in Government, California State University, Sacramento **C:** Anchor, "NBC Nightly News," NBC News (2015-Present); Anchor "Dateline NBC," NBC News, (2011-Present); Interim Anchor, "NBC Nightly News," NBC News (2015); Contributor, Weekend Anchor, "NBC Nightly News," NBC News (2007-2015); Co-Anchor, "Weekend Today," NBC News (2003-2015); Reporter, Correspondent, NBC News (2000-2003); Anchor, Evening News, WBBM-TV, Chicago, IL (1986-2000); Reporter, Weekend Anchor, WCBS-TV, New York, NY (1983-1986); Reporter, Weekend Anchor, KCBS-TV, Los Angeles, CA (1982-1983); Reporter, WCBS-TV, New York, NY (1981-1982) **CR:** Announcer, Westminster Kennel Club Dog Show, USA Network (2006-2008); Host, "Dateline on ID," Investigation Discovery Network **CW:** Appearance, "Fugitive"; Appearance, "Law & Order: Special Victims Unit"; Appearance, "30 Rock"; Appearance, Numerous Television Shows and Films **AW:** Walter Cronkite Award for Excellence in Journalism (2019); Alan B. DuMont Broadcaster of the Year, Montclair State University (2016); Journalist of the Year, National Association of Black Journalists (2016); Listee, 100 Most Influential People in the World, Time Magazine (2016); Inductee, California Hall of Fame (2015); Robert F. Kennedy Journalism Award (1990) **AV:** Playing upright and bass guitar

HOLTON, GREGORY ALLAN, PHD, T: Environmental Engineering Consultant **I:** Engineering **DOB:** 11/15/1948 **PB:** Jackson **SC:** MI/USA **PT:** Alvin LeRoy; Shirley Irene (Coy) Holton **MS:** Married **SPN:** Victoria M. Holton **CH:** Sue Ann Curtis; Gregory A. Holton, Jr. **ED:** PhD in Environmental Engineering, University of North Carolina (1981); MS in Environmental Engineering, University of North Carolina (1977); BS in Applied Science and Engineering, United States Military Academy West Point (1970) **CT:** Qualified Environmental Professional **C:** President, Holton Environmental Associates (1998-2017); Director of Air Services Group, Industrial Compliance (1993-1998); President, Chairman, Board of Directors, Holton & Dycus, Inc. (1989-1993); Office Manager, First Environment Inc. (1988-1989); Research Supervisor, JBF Associates (1985-1988); Research Associate, Maxima Corporation (1984-1985); Research Associate, Oak Ridge National Laboratory (1980-1984); Environmental Consultant (1977-1980); Environmental Engineer, Environmental engineer, United States Environmental Protection Agency (1976-1977) **CR:** Adjunct Professor, University of Alabama; Adjunct Professor, University of South Carolina; Adjunct Professor, University of Tennessee **CIV:** Consultant, Environmental Quality Advisory Board, Oak Ridge (1983) **MIL:** Lieutenant Colonel, Signal Corps, U.S. Army Reserve (1975-1978); Captain, Signal Corps, U.S. Army (1970-1975) **CW:** Editor, "Siting of Waste Management Facilities" (1988); Contributor, Articles, Professional Journals **AW:** Defense Meritorious Service Medal (1998); Small Business Innovation Research Grant, National Science Foundation (1985); Army Commendation Medal (1975) **MEM:** Chairman, Permitting and Siting Committee, Air & Waste Management Association (1984-1990) **MH:** Albert Nelson Marquis Lifetime Achievement Award **AS:** Dr. Holton attributes his success to graduating from West Point, which instilled in him a sense of determination and perseverance. **B/I:** Dr. Holton became involved in his profession because he has always enjoyed the outdoors and became concerned with the safety of the environment as he was growing up. **AV:** Fishing; Golfing; Skiing **PA:** Republican **RE:** Baptist

HOLUTIAK-HALLICK, STEPHEN P. JR., T: Army Officer (Retired), Businessman, Educator **I:** Business Management/Business Services **DOB:** 05/03/1945 **PB:** New York **SC:** NY/USA **PT:** Rev. Protopresbyter Stephen Holutiak-Hallick; Hope (Kukura) Hallick **MS:** Married **SPN:** Ann Marie Bazycki (07/29/1972) **CH:** Larissa Ann; Christine Michelle; Stephen Michael III **ED:** Diploma, St. Stephen's Course in Orthodox Theology, Antiochian House of Studies (2009); MBA in International Business, Mercer University (1992); Diploma, U.S. Army Command And General Staff College (1985); AS in Business Management, Community College of Allegheny County, Pennsylvania(1977); MA in Slavic Studies, University of Manitoba, Winnipeg, Canada (1969); BA in Liberal Arts/Russian Language/History, Penn State University (1967); Certificate in Russian Area Studies, Pennsylvania State University (1967) **C:** Owner, Director of Operations, TATO's Choice Vending Company, Duluth, GA (1995-2009); Management Consultant, Consortium Service Management Group, Ukraine (1995-2005); Management and Executive Consultant, George S. May Co. (1997); Manager of Expediting and Sub-contracts Administration (1984-1985), Administrator, Project Management Services, KHD Humboldt Wedag, New York-Montreal-Atlanta (1982-1984); Administrator and Expeditor of Projects, KHD Humboldt Wedag, New York-Montreal-Atlanta (1979-1982); Inspector and Expeditor, Robert W. Hunt Company, Pittsburgh, PA (1979-1982); Manager, Russian Translation Department, Translator, Interpreter, Purchasing Department Project Coordinator, Swindell-Dressler Engineering Co., Pittsburgh, PA (1972-1976) **CR:** Volunteer Instructor, Teacher of English as a Second Language, The Ukrainian National Association of America and the Prosvita Cultural Education Organization of Ukraine (1996-2003); Adjunct Instructor, American College, Atlanta (1997); Adjunct Instructor, Park College, Tinker Air Force Base, Oklahoma (1993-1995); Assistant Professor of Military Science, Clemson University, Clemson, SC

(1990-1992); Instructor of Ukrainian and Russian languages, Berlitz School of Languages, Pittsburgh, PA (1978-1979); Instructor of Russian language, Franklin Regional PTA Adult Continuing Education Program, Evening Division, Monroeville, PA (1974); Ukrainian Language Teacher, Grade 6, Ukrainian Language School "Ridna Shkola" Robert Morris Junior College (1973); Substitute Teacher, McKees Rocks School District, McKees Rocks, PA (1969-1970, 1971-1972); Russian Language Instructor, Harford Community College, BelAir, MD (1971) **CIV:** Member, Ukrainian Congress Committee, U.S. Observation and Inspection Team for SNAP Parliament Elections in Ukraine (2007); Initiator, Organizer, Chairman of Building Committee and benefactor of St. Andrew's Ukrainian Orthodox Church of Metropolitan Atlanta (1984 -2005); Member, Board of Regents, St. Sophia Ukrainian Orthodox Seminary (2000-2005); Member, Metropolitan's National Church Advisory Council, Ukrainian Orthodox Church of USA (1998-2001); Member and Escort for Friendship Force International: Ukraine-Atlanta (1997); Dumka Choir of NYC (1980-1982); Member, Board of Directors, Ukrainian Technological Society of Western Pennsylvania (1976); Chairman, 50ᵗʰ Anniversary Jubilee of Saint Vladimir's Ukrainian Orthodox Church, Pittsburgh, PA (1976); Western Pennsylvania Regional Choir of Ukrainian Orthodox League of USA (1968-1972); O. Koshetz Ukrainian National Choir, Winnipeg, Canada (1967-1969); Penn State University Chapel Choirs (1965-1967); President, Ukrainian Club at Penn State University (1965-1967); President, Eastern Orthodox Fellowship Penn State University (1965-1967); Member, Penn State ROTC Marching Band (1965-1967) **MIL:** Honorably Discharged at Rank of Lieutenant Colonel (1995); Inspector General, 95ᵗʰ Division (1992-1995); Staff Intelligence Officer, Forces Command Headquarters, U.S. Army (1985-1990); Inspector and Interpreter for On-Site Inspection Team for INF Treaty Verification and Inspections in USSR (1988); Chief, Intelligence Team 2, ODCSI, Forces Command Headquarters (1983-1985); Strategic Intelligence Officer, 432 Military Intelligence Detachment (Strategic) (1980-1983); Chief, Prisoner of War Interrogation Section, 394 Military Intelligence Detachment (SB) (1975-1980); Censorship Officer, 394 Military Intelligence Detachment (AFC) (1973-1975); Platoon Leader. 343 ASA Co. (1972); Executive Officer and Platoon Leader, 542 Military Intelligence Detachment, APG, Md. (1970-1971); Intelligence Analyst, Directorate of Intelligence Production, Fort Bragg, NC (1970); Military Schools (1967-1970) **CW:** Author, "J.B. Rudnyckyj and the Growth of Ukrainian Onomastics: Onomastic Bibliography 1935-1995" (1995); Author, "Dictionary of Ukrainian Surnames in the United States" (1994); Author, PhD and MA Theses on Orthodox Themes (1994); Author, "Slavistics at the Master's Level" (1994); Editorial Board, Rudnyckiana (1986-1992); Author, "Slavic Toponymic Atlas of the United States, Volume 1, Ukrainian" (1982); Author, "The Ukrainian Immigrants and Their Story in the United States" (1982); Author, "Eastern Orthodox Periodicals and Journals in the United States: 1948-1969" (1969); Contributor: Journals, Articles, Book Reviews, Anthologies; Author, More Than 70 Publications and Cited Acknowledgements of Research and Scholarship **AW:** Republican Presidential Honor Roll (2018-Present); Order of Merit, Republican National Committee (2013-Present); Certificate of Appreciation, Disabled American Veterans (1985-Present); Certificate of Appreciation, National Museum of the U.S. Army (2019); Order of the Orthodox Church of Ukraine (UOC): Ecclesiastical Jubilee Medal (2019); Certificate of Appreciation, National World War II Museum (2018); Commemorative Medallion, Statue of Liberty Museum in Recognition as Benefactor and Founder of Museum (2016); President George H.W. Bush Leadership Honor Roll (2013); Order of St. Michael (Medal 33), UApOC Ukraine (2011); 20ᵗʰ Anniversary Commemorative Medal (Medal No. 014), UAOC (2009); Ronald Reagan Award, Republican National Committee (2008); Certificate for Outstanding Service to the Nation and Army, Secretary of The US Army (2006); Order of St. Andrew (Medal 160), UAOC, Ukraine (2004); Cold War Recognition Certificate, US Secretary of Defense (2002); Three time recipient of US Army Meritorious Service Medal (1990, 1992, 1995); National Defense Service Medal (Service Star) (1970, 1991); U.S. Army Commendation Medals (1986, 1989); U.S. Armed Forces Reserve Medal (1970, 1989); U.S. Army Reserve Components Overseas Training Ribbon (1988); U.S. Army Achievement Medal (1983); U.S. Army Service Ribbon (1981); U.S. Army Reserve Components Achievement Medal (1977, 1981); Wasyl Swystun Prize of Ukrainian Studies, University of Manitoba (1967-1968); Senatorial Grantee to Penn State University, Pennsylvania State Senator Leonard B. Stacey (1963-1967); Danforth Leadership Award (1963); Honoree of Pittsburgh District Attorney, Edward C. Boyle at Pittsburgh Eagle Scout Recognition Dinner (1962); Eagle Scout, Boy Scouts of America (1960); Alpha Omega Orthodox Scouting Award (1960) **MEM:** The Heritage Foundation (2012-Present); American Legion, Post 251 (2005-Present); American Name Society (1969, 1984-Present); Friends of Harvard Ukrainian Research Institute (1980-Present); Friends of Ukrainian Free University (1975-Present); Reserve Officers Association of the United States (1974-Present); Georgia Historical Society (1987-2013); American Security Council: U.S. Congressional Advisory Board (1985-2006); Atlanta Committee on International Relations (1983-2006); Canadian Society for the Study of Names (1981-1997); Gwinnett County Historical Society (1985-1996); Military Intelligence Reserve Officers' Association of New York (1983-1995); 77ᵗʰ U.S. ARCOM Officers' Association (1977-1995); Project Management Institute (1985-1988); Ukrainian-American Professional and Businesspersons Association (1983-1988); Ukrainian Technological Society of Western Pennsylvania (1974-1979); Board of Directors, Ukrainian Technological Society of Western Pennsylvania (1976); Association of Teachers of Slavic and Eastern European Languages (1967, 1969); Founding Member, National Museum of the U.S. Army; Charter Member, National World War II Museum **MH:** Albert Nelson Marquis Lifetime Achievement Award (2019) **AS:** Mr. Holutiak-Hallick attributes his success to a desire to continue and contribute to his family motto and goal, which is "For God, for improving the fate and rights of Ukrainian people; and to create a free and independent Ukrainian Orthodox Church." **AV:** Reading; Traveling; Researching **RE:** Ukrainian Orthodox

HOLZENDORF, KING JR., T: City Councilman (Retired) **I:** Government Administration/Government Relations/Government Services **PB:** Jacksonville **SC:** FL/USA **MS:** Married **SPN:** Betty Smith **CH:** Kim Lockley; King III; Kevin; Kessler **ED:** Bachelor of Science, Edward Waters College, Jacksonville, FL **CT:** Certified Drug Counselor **C:** Member of Public Health and Safety Committee, City of Jacksonville, FL (1999-2003); Member Finance Committee, City of Jacksonville, FL (1999-2003); Chairman Recreation and Community Development Committee, City of Jacksonville, FL (1999-2003); City Councilman, City of Jacksonville, FL (1995-2003); Director, Task Program, River Region **CR:** Director, Court Service Unit, River Regional Human Service Inc.; Board of Directors, Florida Martin Luther King Junior Institute for Nonviolence **CIV:** Church **MIL:** Sergeant, First Class, Florida National Guard **MEM:** National Association for the Advancement of Colored People **MH:** Albert Nelson Marquis Lifetime Achievement Award **B/I:** Mr. Holzendorf became involved in his profession because he was going to school and needed employment. River Region offered him a job immediately as the director of the TASC program. Later, he was elected as the City Councilman for District 10, a position in which he served for eight years. **PA:** Democrat **RE:** African Methodist Episcopalian

HONEYWELL, LEIGH, T: Chief Executive Officer **I:** Business Management/Business Services **CN:** Tall Poppy **ED:** BS in Computer Science and Equity Studies, Innis College, University of Toronto (2011) **CT:** Psychological First Aid, Coursera Course Certificates (2016) **C:** Chief Executive Officer, Tall Poppy, San Francisco, CA (2018-Present); Technology Fellow, ACLU, San Francisco, CA (2017-2018); Security Response Manager, Slack, San Francisco, CA (2016-2017); Senior Staff Security Engineer, Slack, San Francisco, CA (2015-2016); Senior Platform Security Engineer, Heroku, San Francisco, CA (2014-2015); Security Program Manager II, Microsoft, Seattle, WA (2011-2014); Consultant, Independent, Toronto, ON, Canada (2006-2011); Malware Operations Engineer, Symantec (2008-2010); Technology Applications Specialist, Bell Canada (2005) **CR:** Venture Partner, Pioneer Fund, San Francisco, CA (2019-Present) **CIV:** Advisor, Open Technology Fund (2016-Present); Chief Security Officer, Double Union (2014-Present); Technical Advisor, Callisto Project, Sexual Health Innovations (2015-2017); Advisor, The Ada Initiative (2011-2015); Board Member, Seattle Attic Community Workshop (2013-2014); Co-Founder, HackLab.to (2008-2011) **CW:** Author, "Security for Snake People," Microsoft Bluehat (2016) **MEM:** Varsity Nordic Ski Team; Sexual Education and Peer Counseling Centre; Students' Administrative Council, Innis College; University of Toronto

HOOD, AMY ELIZABETH, T: Executive Vice President, Chief Financial Officer **I:** Technology **CN:** Microsoft **PB:** Nashville **SC:** TN/USA **MS:** Married **SPN:** Max Kleinman **ED:** BS in Economics, Duke University (1994); MBA, Harvard Business School **C:** Executive Vice President, Chief Financial Officer, Microsoft (2016-Present); CFO, Microsoft Corp. (2013-2016); CFO, Business Division, Microsoft Corp. (2010-2013); Microsoft Corp., Redmond, WA (2002); Investment Banking & Capital Markets Group, Goldman Sachs Group, Inc. (1994-2002); Chief of Staff, Server & Tools Division, Microsoft Corp. **AW:** Named, 100 Most Powerful Women, Forbes Magazine (2013-2014)

HOPKINS, ANTHONY, T: Actor **I:** Media & Entertainment **DOB:** 12/31/1937 **PB:** Port Talbot, South Wales **SC:** United Kingdom **PT:** Richard Arthur Hopkins; Muriel Annie (Yeates) Hopkins **MS:** Married **SPN:** Stella Arroyave (2003); Jennifer Ann Lynton (01/13/1973, Divorced 04/30/2002); Petronella Barker (09/1967, Divorced 1972) **CH:** Abigail **ED:** Honorary Fellow, St. David's College, Lampeter, Wales, United Kingdom (1992); Honorary LittD, University of Wales (1988); Coursework, Royal Academy of Dramatic Art, London, England, United Kingdom (1961-1963); Coursework, Royal Welsh College of Music & Drama, Cardiff, Wales, United Kingdom (1954-1956) **CIV:** Greenpeace; Patron, Rehabilitation for Addicted Prisoners Trust (Now The Forward Trust); President, Snowdonia Appeal, National Trust for Historic Preservation **CW:** Actor, "The Father" (2020); Actor, "The Two Popes" (2019); Actor, "King Lear" (2018);

Actor, "Transformers: The Last Knight" (2017); Actor, "Thor: Ragnarok" (2017); Actor, "Misconduct" (2016); Actor, "Collide" (2016); Actor, "Westworld" (2016); Actor, "The Dresser" (2015); Actor, "Kidnapping Freddy Heineken" (2015); Actor, "Blackway" (2015); Actor, "Noah" (2014); Actor, "Solace" (2014); Actor, "Red 2" (2013); Actor, "Thor: The Dark World" (2013); Actor, "Hitchcock" (2012); Actor, "Hannibal" (2012); Composer, "Composer" (2012); Actor, "The Rite" (2011); Actor, "Thor" (2011); Actor, "360" (2011); Composer, "And the Waltz Goes On" (2011); Actor, "The Wolfman" (2010); Actor, "You Will Meet a Tall Dark Stranger" (2010); Actor, "Fracture" (2007); Voice Actor, "Beowulf" (2007); Actor, Director, Writer, "Slipstream" (2007); Actor, "The City of Your Final Destination" (2007); Actor, "American Masters" (2007); Actor, Executive Producer, "Bobby" (2006); Actor, "All the King's Men" (2006); Actor, "Proof" (2005); Actor, "The World's Fastest Indian" (2005); Actor, "Alexander" (2004); Actor, "The Human Stain" (2003); Actor, "Freedom: A History of Us" (2003); Actor, "Bad Company" (2002); Actor, "Red Dragon" (2002); Voice Actor, "How the Grinch Stole Christmas" (2001); Actor, "Hannibal" (2001); Actor, "Hearts in Atlantis" (2001); Actor, "The Devil and Daniel Webster" (2001); Actor, "Mission Impossible II" (2000); Actor, "Instinct" (1999); Actor, "Titus" (1999); Actor, "The Mask of Zorro" (1998); Actor, "Meet Joe Black" (1998); Actor, "The Edge" (1997); Actor, "Amistad" (1997); Actor, "Surviving Picasso" (1996); Actor, "August" (1996); Actor, "Nixon" (1995); Author, "Anthony Hopkins' Snowdonia" (1995); Director, "August" (1994); Actor, "The Road to Welville" (1994); Actor, "Legends of the Fall" (1994); Actor, "Remains of the Day" (1993); Actor, "Shadowlands" (1993); Actor, "Selected Exits" (1993); Actor, "The Trial" (1993); Actor, "The Innocent" (1993); Actor, "Freejack" (1992); Actor, "Spotswood/The Efficiency Expert" (1992); Actor, "Howard's End" (1992); Actor, "Bram Stoker's Dracula" (1992); Actor, "Chaplin" (1992); Actor, "To Be The Best" (1992); Actor, "One Man's War" (1991); Actor, "Silence of the Lambs" (1991); Director, "Dylan Thomas: Return Journey" (1990); Actor, "A Chorus of Disapproval" (1989); Actor, "M. Butterfly," Shaftesbury Theatre, London, England, United Kingdom (1989); Actor, "Heartland" (1989); Actor, "Great Expectations" (1989); Actor, "The Tenth Man" (1988); Actor, "Across the Lake" (1988); Actor, "The Dawning" (1988); Actor, "Anthony & Cleopatra," National Theatre, London, England, United Kingdom (1987); Actor, "King Lear," National Theatre, London, England, United Kingdom (1986-1987); Actor, "84 Charing Cross Road" (1986); Actor, "Pravda," National Theatre, London, England, United Kingdom (1985-1986); Actor, "The Lonely Road," London, England, United Kingdom (1985); Actor, "The Good Father" (1985); Actor, "Mussolini and I" (1985); Actor, "Blunt" (1985); Actor, "A Married Man" (1984); Actor, "The Arch of Triumph" (1984); Actor, "Hollywood Wives" (1984); Actor, "Guilty Conscience" (1984); Actor, "The Bounty" (1984); Actor, "Strangers and Brothers" (1984); Actor, "Old Times," New York City, NY (1983); Actor, "The Hunchback of Notre Dame" (1982); Actor, "Othello" (1981); Actor, "Little Eyolf" (1981); Actor, "The Elephant Man" (1980); Actor, "The Bunker" (1980); Actor, "Peter and Paul" (1980); Actor, "A Change of Seasons" (1980); Actor, "The Tempest," Los Angeles, CA (1979); Actor, "Dark Victory" (1979); Actor, "Mayflower: The Pilgrim's Adventure" (1979); Actor, "International Velvet" (1978); Actor, "Magic" (1978); Actor, "Equus," Los Angeles, CA (1977); Actor, "A Bridge Too Far" (1977); Actor, "Audrey Rose" (1977); Actor, "The Lindbergh Kidnapping Case" (1976); Actor, "Victory at Entebbe" (1976); Actor, "Find Me" (1975); Actor, "A Childhood Friend" (1975); Actor, "Possessions" (1975); Actor, "All Creatures Great and Small" (1975); Actor, "Equus," New York City, NY (1974-1975); Actor, "The Girl from Petrovka" (1974); Actor, "Childhood" (1974); Actor, "Juggernaut" (1974); Actor, "A Doll's House" (1973); Actor, "Young Winston" (1972); Actor, "The Taming of the Shrew" (1972); Actor, "The Man Outside" (1972); Actor, "War and Peace" (1972); Actor, "Macbeth" (1972); Actor, "Vanya" (1971); Actor, "Hearts and Flowers" (1971); Actor, "Three Sisters" (1971); Actor, "The Peasant's Revolt" (1971); Actor, "Dickens" (1971); Actor, "Danton" (1971); Actor, "The Poet Game" (1971); Actor, "Decision to Burn" (1971); Actor, "War and Peace" (1971); Actor, "Cuculus Canorus" (1971); Actor, "Lloyd George" (1971); Actor, "Q.B. VII" (1971); Actor, "The Architect and the Emperor of Assyria" (1971); Actor, "When Eight Bells Toll" (1971); Actor, "A Woman Killed with Kindness" (1971); Actor, "Coriolanus" (1971); Appearance, "Department S" (1970); Actor, "Hamlet" (1969); Actor, "The Looking Glass War" (1969); Actor, "The Lion in Winter" (1968); Actor, "A Heritage and Its History" (1968); Actor, "Three Sisters" (1967); Actor, "Red, White and Zero" (1967); Actor, "The Dance of Death" (1967); Actor, "As You Like It" (1967); Actor, "A Flea in Her Ear" (1966); Actor, "Juno and the Paycock" (1966); Member, National Theatre Company (1966-1973); Actor, Stage Debut, "Julius Caesar," London, England, United Kingdom (1964); Actor, Director, Plays, Television Shows and Film; Composer, Music **AW:** Cecil B. DeMille Award, Golden Globe Awards, Hollywood Foreign Press Association (2006); Commander, Order of Arts and Letters, France (1996); One of the 100 Welsh Heroes (2004); Star, Hollywood Walk of Fame (2003); One of the Top 100 Movie Stars of All Time, Empire Magazine, United Kingdom (1997); Award for Best Actor, National Board of Review (1993); Award for Best Actor, National Society of Film Critics (1993); Knight's Bachelor, Order of the British Empire (1993); Academy Award for Best Actor, Academy of Motion Picture Arts & Sciences (1992); Award for Best Actor, Boston Film Critics Association (1992); Award for Best Actor, New York Film Critics Association (1992); BAFTA Award for Best Film Actor (1992); Decorated Commander, Order of British Empire (1987); Olivier Award (1985); Emmy Award for Outstanding Lead Actor in a Limited Series or a Special, Academy of Television Arts & Sciences (1980); Award for Best Actor, Los Angeles Drama Critics Circle Awards (1977); Emmy Award for Outstanding Lead Actor in a Drama or Comedy Special, Academy of Television Arts & Sciences (1976); Award for Best Actor, Drama Desk Awards (1975); Award for Best Actor, Outer Critics Circle (1975); Award for Best TV Actor, Society of Film and Television Arts (1972); Numerous Awards

HOPKINS, LINDA KAY, T: Intellectual Property Attorney (Retired) **I:** Law and Legal Services **DOB:** 11/03/1948 **PB:** St. Paul **SC:** MN/USA **PT:** Lyle E. Hopkins; Emily Griesman Hopkins **MS:** Married **SPN:** John Lindgren **ED:** Doctor of Jurisprudence, William Mitchell College of Law, St. Paul, MN (1998); Master of Arts, University of New Mexico, Albuquerque, NM (1987); Bachelor of Arts, University of Minnesota, Minneapolis, MN (1979); Master of Business Administration Certificate, University of St. Thomas, St. Paul, MN **CT:** Government Contracts; Certified Commercial Management (IACCM); Certified Information Systems Security Professional; Certified Commercial & Contract Professional (IACCM); Certified International Association Privacy Professionals (IAPP) **C:** Technology Attorney, Accenture LLP (2008-2013); Reporter, Upper Midwest Region, The Russian Magazine, San Diego, CA (1996-1998); Columnist, Tech Access Journal, Novate, CA (1995-1998); Chairperson, Working Group on Intellectual Property, Minnesota Government Information Access Council, St. Paul, MN (1995-1996); Contract Specialist, Department of Defense Contract Administration Office, Bloomington, IN (1989-1992); Contracting Officer, Veterans Medical Building, Bloomington, IN (1988-1989); Instructor, Special Education Director, Albuquerque Public Schools, Memorial Hospital (1987-1989); Hearing Assistant, Social Security Administration, Office of Appeals, Minneapolis, MN (1972-1980) **CR:** Consultant, United Nation, Agency for International Development on Behalf of the Government of Nepal; Speaker in the Field; Adjunct Professor, Graduate School, Public Administration, Hamline University, St. Paul, MN; Presenter, Workshops on Government Contracts Law; Moderator, National Information Infrastructure Advisory Council, Department of Commerce; Community Outreach Director, American Constitution Society, Minneapolis Office, MN; Policy Advisor and Legislative Drafter, Office of the President of the United States, National Economic Council; Small Business Administration, Department of Justice; Consultant and Trainer, IntelliWare, St. Paul, MN; Advisor, Patent Office of the Republic of Bulgaria **CIV:** Founder, TeamWomen, Minnesota, An Organization to Empower Women (2012-2017); Founder, Genetics, Law and Society Conference, Minneapolis, MN (1999); Community Director, Minnesota Chapter, American Constitution Society **CW:** Co-editor, "International Commercial and Contract Management, the Operational Guide"; Author, "Clementine Churchill, Linchpin of the British War Effort" (2020); Organizer, International Conference, "Genetics, Law and Society," St. Paul, MN (1999); Author, "Licensing Law Handbook, Federal Government Intellectual Property" (1994); Author, Newspaper Editorial, Minnesota Women's Press (1990) **AW:** Listed, Who's Who of Women Professionals (2019-2020); Listed, World's Who's Who of Women (2001); Listed, Who's Who in the Midwest (1998); Scholarship, National Contract Management Association (1984) **MEM:** Chairman, Government Intellectual Property Rights, Patents, and Technology Data, American Bar Association (1994-1995); American Bar Association; Minnesota Bar Association; Women's Bar Association of Minnesota; Christian Law Students of Minnesota; Biotechnology Association; National Contract Management Association; Toastmasters of Minnesota; Co-founder, Winston Churchill Legacy Book Club **BAR:** Minnesota **MH:** Albert Nelson Marquis Lifetime Achievement Award **AS:** Ms. Hopkins attributes her success to her need to learn and teach legal concepts and expand her intellectual horizons. **B/I:** Ms. Hopkins took an early interest in the profession of legal service. However, as a woman, she was always told that women in the law were not acceptable. Ms. Hopkins believed that women were equally capable of mastering the profession and that the laws as they stood were biased against the reality that women lived. It was important for her to be intellectually fulfilled and to be a mentor to other women who struggled to live without fear in the U.S. **AV:** Creative writing; Painting; Piano; Art study

HOPSON, SONYA, T: Chief Executive Officer, Founder **I:** Staffing and Recruiting **CN:** Hire Strategies **DOB:** 08/30/1975 **CH:** Bryanna; Braylen; Shaylah **ED:** Bachelor's Degree in Accounting and Financing; Master's Degree in Human Resources **C:** Chief Executive Officer, Founder, President, Hire Strategies (2013-Present) **CIV:** Volunteer, Boys and Girls Club; Volunteer, Habitat for Humanity; Volunteer, Local Domestic Violence Shelters **AW:** Top Minority-Owned Company (2019); Top Employment Agency (2013, 2015, 2017, 2018,

2019); Fast 50 Award, Fasting Growing Businesses (2017); Largest Staffing Company **MEM:** Women Presidents' Organization; NAWBO; The Alternative Board; Raleigh Chamber **MH:** Marquis Who's Who Top Professional **AS:** Ms. Hopson attributes her success to her tenancy, determination, and her desire to build a great future for her children. **B/I:** Ms. Hopson became involved in her profession because she was always interest in a sales position. She started with software sales, did that for about three years and really loved building relations with various clients. What she did not like was advocating for a company/software she was not passionate about. When she got into staffing, it felt more comfortable for her because she was selling herself as a resource. Ms. Hopson went to school for accounting and finance, and was convinced she wanted to be a stockbroker. She worked at her first job for about a year and discovered it was not something she wanted to do. After that position, she migrated into sales and quickly knew sales was the career for her. However, she was selling products so she found her way into staffing and loved it. She knew she could sell not necessarily products but her ability to help align clients with employees who are looking for jobs. That gave her a passion and a purpose. **AV:** Hiking; Weightlifting; Dancing **RE:** Christianity **THT:** Ms. Hopson does not compete with other people and other companies. She runs her own race and always strives to do the best she can to build a legacy she can be proud of and inspire others along with way.

HORN, KENDRA SUZANNE, T: U.S. Representative from Oklahoma; Lawyer **I:** Government Administration/Government Relations/Government Services **DOB:** 06/09/1976 **PB:** Chickasha **SC:** OK/USA **ED:** JD, Southern Methodist University Dedman School of Law; BA, The University of Tulsa; Coursework, International Space University, Strasberg, France **C:** Member, U.S. House of Representatives from Oklahoma's Fifth Congressional District (2019-Present); Lawyer, Founder, Solo Practice (2002-Present); Manager, Gubernatorial Campaign for Joe Dorman (2014); Press Secretary, United States Congressman Brad Carson (2004-2005); Manager of Communication and Media Relations, United States Congressman Brad Carson; With, Private Practice, Dallas, Texas **CIV:** Co-founder, Women Lead Oklahoma **AW:** Gold Award, Girls Scouts of the United States of America **PA:** Democrat **RE:** Episcopalian

HORN, WALLY EUGENE, T: Former Senator **I:** Government Administration/Government Relations/Government Services **CN:** The Iowa Legislature **DOB:** 11/28/1933 **PB:** Bloomfield **SC:** IA/USA **PT:** Lyle Horn; LaRetta Horn **MS:** Married **SPN:** Phyllis Peterson (1989) **CIV:** Member, Community Corrections Board; Member, Police and Fireman Retirement Board; Member, Kiwanis International; Associated General Contractors of America (AGC) **MIL:** With, United States Army (1953-1955) **CW:** Currently Working on Writing his Memoir **AW:** Defender of Freedom Award; Herbert Hoover Uncommon Public Service Award; Lifetime Achievement, Associated General Contractors of America (AGC); Inductee, Linn County Democratic Hall of Fame; Defender of Freedom, National Nursery Association; Award, The Iowa State Bar Association; Award, Associated General Contractors of America (AGC); Horticulture Award **MEM:** Executive Committee, National Conference of State Legislators, Executive Committee; Democratic Legislative Campaign Committee; The Council of State Governments; Midwest Legislative Executive Committee; Education Committee; Judiciary Committee **MH:** Marquis Who's Who Humanitarian Award **AS:** Mr. Horn attributes his success to always liking

to work with people. He added that young people kept him going. **B/I:** Mr. Horn became involved in his profession because he always wanted to coach and teach. After graduating, Mr. Horn was a high school coach. He coached football, tennis, track baseball, and golf. He went into government in order to better education, which was the thing that drove him to becoming a state senator. He wanted to support education at all levels. Mr. Horn was head of the teachers union in Cedar Rapids 46 years ago and education was what most people wanted. He had to draw the conclusion that he could do more as a state senator. At that point, he got into it and felt lucky that he won all of his elections. **AV:** Meeting people; Golfing; Traveling; Reading **PA:** Democrat **RE:** Christian Church **THT:** Mr. Horn tried to help everyone he was associated with. He cared about people and the government. He went into politics to better education. Upon retirement, Mr. Horn was the longest-serving legislator in the history of Iowa.

HORNBERGER, WALTER HENRY JR., T: Director of Quality Assurance (Retired) **I:** Other **DOB:** 12/13/1939 **PB:** Chicago **SC:** IL/USA **PT:** Walter Henry Hornberger; Elizabeth Wynne (Davies) Hornberger **MS:** Married **SPN:** Georgia Carol Bohmann (05/14/1966) **CH:** Donna Joyce; Carol Elizabeth, PhD (Deceased); Tamara Ann **ED:** Bachelor of Science in Metallurgical Engineering, Illinois Institute of Technology (1964); Coursework, Navy Pier, University of Illinois Urbana-Champaign; Diploma, Bowen High School, South Chicago, IL **CT:** Professional Engineer, State of Michigan (09/03/1974) **C:** Director of Quality Assurance, Weil McLain Division, United Dominion Industries Limited, Michigan City, IN (1993-2001); Quality Control Manager, Wells Vehicle Electronics, South Bend, IN (1987-1993); Quality Control Manager, Forged Products Division, National Standard Company, Buchanan, MI (1980-1987); Research Metallurgist, Plant Metallurgist, National Standard Company, Niles, MI (1967-1973, 1974-1980); Heat Treatment Manager, Plant Metallurgist, Rockwell International, Allegan, MI (1973-1974); Melt Shop Metallurgist, International Harvester-Wisconsin Steel, Chicago, IL (1964-1967); Blast Furnace Observer, South Works, U.S. Steel, Acme Steel (1962); Metallographic Technician, Acme Steel (1962); Laboratory Technician, Stainless-Steel Scrapyard (1961-1962); Laborer, International Harvester-Wisconsin Steel (1958-1961); Open Hearth Metallurgist, Wisconsin Steel **CR:** President, Board of Directors, NS Credit Union (1981-1989); Elected Member, Board of Directors, NS Credit Union (1980); Past Chairman, Notre Dame Chapter, ASM International, South Bend, IN (1978-1979) **AW:** Engineer of Year Award, National Society of Professional Engineers (1985) **MEM:** President, Blossomland Chapter, National Society of Professional Engineers (1984); President, Niles Optimist Club (1978); Masons; Shriners; Moose International; Board of Directors, Notre Dame Chapter, ASM International **MH:** Albert Nelson Marquis Lifetime Achievement Award **B/I:** Mr. Hornberger became involved in his profession because he grew up on the south side of Chicago in Illinois in an area surrounded by many steel mills. He remembers growing up and feeling that it would be a field full of lots of opportunity. He made a decision at around age 16 that he wanted to go into metallurgical engineering. Growing up, he didn't know who his grandfather was. He received a job at US Steel, Southworks. His father told him, while he was at work, to look around and he will find his grandfather's name in the building. It turned out that his grandfather, Herman Alexander Brassert, was the superintendent of the blast furnaces. He couldn't believe that he was walking in his grandfather's

footsteps. He continued to follow the family legacy and make choices to follow in his grandfather's footsteps. **AV:** Golfing; Studying family genealogy; Spending time with grandchildren; Traveling **THT:** Mr. Hornberger would like to acknowledge the success of his children, Donna Joyce, who completed a BS in computer science at Grand Valley State University; his daughter Carol Elizabeth, since passed away, who received a PhD in mechanical engineering at the University of Memphis and his daughter, Tamara Ann, who received a master's degree in civil engineering at the University of Memphis.

HOROWITZ, ROBERT B.G., T: Partner **I:** Law and Legal Services **CN:** Baker & Hostetler LLP **PB:** Mineola **SC:** NY/USA **PT:** Robert S. Horowitz; Audrey G. Schultz **MS:** Married **SPN:** Marie **CH:** 3 Sons **ED:** Doctor of Jurisprudence, University of Miami School of Law (1977); Bachelor of Arts, Ohio Wesleyan University (1974) **CIV:** President, Manhasset Bay Shipyard; President, Varsity Choral Society; Chair, Board of Trustees, Congregational Church of Manhasset **CW:** Author, Article Publishing on the Defend Trade Secrets Act, Federal Bar Council Quarterly (2016) **AW:** Listee, Legal Media Group, Guide to the World's Leading Trade Mark Law Practitioners (2002-Present); Listee in Intellectual Property and Trade Mark & Copyright, Chambers USA (2015-2020); Listee, WTR 1000 – The World's Leading Trademark Professionals (2012-2020); Listee, Who's Who Legal (2017-2020); Listee, New York Metro "Super Lawyer" (2010, 2012-2019); Best of the Best USA (2015-2019); AV Preeminent Rating, Martindale-Hubbell **MEM:** Federal Bar Council (2015-2019); Famous and Well Known Marks Team (2011-2019); Presenter on U.S. Perspectives for the Post Graphical Representation World for Non-Traditional Marks (2018); Trademark Dilution Issues Presenter (2012); Association Internationale pour la Protection de la Propriété Intellectuelle, Working Questions (2009-2011); Association of European Trade Mark Owners; International Trademark Association; Trademark Reporter Committee; Intellectual Property Law Committee **BAR:** United States District Court for the Northern District of New York (2002); United States Court of Appeals for the Second Circuit (1982); United States Court of Appeals for the Ninth Circuit (1982); United States District Court for the Eastern District of New York (1979); United States District Court for the Southern District of New York (1978); New York (1978) **MH:** Marquis Who's Who Top Professional **AS:** Mr. Horowitz attributes his success to hard work and luck. **B/I:** Mr. Horowitz became involved in his profession after clerking at a New York City law firm during his tenure at law school in Miami, Florida. **AV:** Boating and singing **PA:** Independent **RE:** Christian

HORSFORD, STEVEN ALEXANDER, T: U.S. Representative **I:** Government Administration/Government Relations/Government Services **DOB:** 04/29/1973 **PB:** Las Vegas **SC:** NV/USA **PT:** Gary Shelton; Pamela Horsford **MS:** Married **SPN:** Dr. Sonya Horsford **CH:** Benjamin; Bryson; Ella **ED:** BA, University of Nevada, Reno **C:** U.S. Representative, Nevada's Fourth Congressional District, U.S. House of Representatives (2013-2015, 2019-Present); Member, U.S. House Committee on Oversight and Government Reform (2013-Present); Member, U.S. House Committee on National Resources (2013-Present); Member, U.S. House Homeland Security Committee (2013-Present); Majority Floor Leader, Nevada State Senate (2009-2013); Member, District Four, Nevada State Senate, Clark County, NV (2005-2013); Chief Executive Officer, The Culinary Academy of Las Vegas (2001-2012); With, R&R Partners (1996) **CR:** Super Delegate, Democratic National Convention (2004); Member,

National Committee, Nevada State Democratic Party (2003); Aide, Governor Bob Miller's Re-Election Campaign (1994); Member, Board, Southern Nevada Workforce Investment **AW:** Distinguished Man of Southern Nevada, Dr. Martin Luther King Junior; One of the Top 40 Under 40, Business Las Vegas; Friend to Working Families Award **MEM:** NAACP; Latin Chamber of Commerce Nevada Inc.; Urban Chamber of Commerce; North Las Vegas Chamber of Commerce **PA:** Democrat

HOSCHEIT, CHARLES E., T: Park District Administrator **I:** Other **DOB:** 12/16/1935 **PB:** Peru **SC:** IL/USA **PT:** Charles M. Hoscheit **MS:** Married **SPN:** Nancy Sabotta Hoscheit (08/16/1958) **CH:** Laura; Becky; Charles **ED:** MS, University of Illinois (1974); BS, Illinois State University (1958) **C:** Executive Director, Fox Valley Park District, Aurora, IL (1977-1998); Executive Director, Lockport Township Park District (1965-1977); Teacher, Coach, Lockport West High School, Illinois (1962-1965) **CR:** Guest Teacher, University of Illinois; Guest Teacher, Moraine Valley Community College **CIV:** Chairman, United Way (1982); Member, Aurora Planning Commission (1982); Director, Will County Historic Preservation Council, Illinois (1974-1977); Chairman, Tomahawk Boy Scouts American Council (1972-1973) **CW:** Author, "Lockport Township Park & Recreation Plans" (1969) **AW:** FUPD Named Park Charles E. Hoscheit, Lockport TWP Parks District (1982); U.S. Gold Medal (1976, 1982) **MEM:** President, Finance Section, Illinois Park and Recreation Association (1981); President, Lockport, Lions Lodge (1977); President, South Suburban Parks and Recreation Association (1976); Midwest Institute of Park Executives; Illinois Association of Park Districts; National Recreation and Park Association; Toastmasters International; Elks Lodge; Moose Lodge **MH:** Albert Nelson Marquis Lifetime Achievement Award **B/I:** Mr. Hoscheit became involved in his profession because he was inspired by his high school coach at St. Bede Academy in Peru, Illinois. While Mr. Hoscheit was teaching, he worked summers in the Lockport Township Park District, and when the director passed away, he was asked to take over the park system. He taught and coached for seven years before he went into the park system. **AV:** Playing golf; Bowling **THT:** At the Lockport Township Park District, they were noted for extending the trail system in the early 1970s. At that time, they were the fastest-growing county in Illinois. Under Mr. Hoscheit's direction, the park system grew so fast they were dedicating a couple parks every month; they built numerous parks and golf courses.

HOULAHAN, CHRISTINA, "CHRISSY" MARIE, T: U.S. Representative from Pennsylvania **I:** Government Administration/Government Relations/Government Services **DOB:** 06/05/1967 **PB:** Naval Air Station Patuxent River **SC:** MD/USA **PT:** Andrew C.A. Jampoler **MS:** Married **SPN:** Bart Houlahan **CH:** Two Daughters **ED:** MS, Massachusetts Institute of Technology; BS, Stanford University **C:** Member, U.S. House of Representatives from Pennsylvania's Sixth Congressional District (2019-Present); Chief Operating Officer, AND1, The Basketball Marketing Company, Inc.; Chief Operating Officer, B-Lab **MIL:** Captain, United States Air Force **PA:** Democrat

HOUSTON, JUSTIN DONOVAN, T: Professional Football Player **I:** Athletics **CN:** Indianapolis Colts **DOB:** 01/21/1989 **PB:** Statesboro **SC:** GA/USA **ED:** Coursework, University of Georgia; Diploma, Statesboro High School **C:** Professional Football Player, Indianapolis Colts (2019-Present); Professional Football Player, Kansas City Chiefs (2011-2018) **AW:** Ed Block Courage Award (2016); Four-Time Pro Bowl (2012-2015); First-Team All-Pro (2014); Deacon Jones Award (2014); First-Team All-American (2010); First-Team All-SEC (2010)

HOWARD, DWIGHT DAVID II, T: Professional Basketball Player **I:** Athletics **CN:** Los Angeles Lakers **DOB:** 12/8/1985 **PB:** Atlanta **SC:** GA/USA **PT:** Dwight David Howard I; Sheryl Howard **MS:** Single **CH:** Five Children **ED:** Diploma, Southwest Atlanta Christian Academy, Atlanta, GA **C:** Professional Basketball Player, Los Angeles Lakers (2019-Present); Professional Basketball Player, Washington Wizards (2018-2019); Professional Basketball Player, Charlotte Hornets (2017-2018); Professional Basketball Player, Atlanta Hawks (2016-2017); Professional Basketball Player, Houston Rockets (2013-2016); Professional Basketball Player, Los Angeles Lakers (2012-2013); Professional Basketball Player, Orlando Magic (2004-2012) **CR:** Professional Basketball Player, Men's Senior National Basketball Team, U.S. Olympics, Beijing, China (2008); Professional Basketball Player, Men's Senior National Basketball Team, FIBA Americas Championship, Las Vegas, NV (2007); Professional Basketball Player, Men's Senior National Basketball Team, FIBA World Championship, Japan (2006) **CIV:** Co-Founder, Dwight D. Howard Foundation, Inc., College Park, GA (2004) **CW:** Featured, Documentary, "In the Moment" (2014); Guest Appearance, "Extreme Makeover: Home Edition" (2006) **AW:** Eight-Time NBA All-Star (2007–2014); Three-Time NBA Defensive Player of the Year (2009–2011); NBA Slam Dunk Contest Champion (2008); Gold Medal, Men's Senior National Basketball Team, U.S. Olympics, Beijing, China (2008); Gold Medal, Men's Senior National Basketball Team, FIBA Americas Championship, Las Vegas, NV (2007); Bronze Medal, Men's Senior National Basketball Team, FIBA World Championship, Japan (2006); Naismith Prep Player of the Year (2004); McDonald's All-American Game Co-MVP (2004); First-Team Parade All-American (2004); Mr. Georgia Basketball (2004) **RE:** Christian

HOWARD, GEORGE, "PETER" PRATT, T: Airport Economist **I:** Other **DOB:** 07/01/1930 **PB:** Altoona **SC:** PA/USA **PT:** George Charles Pratt; Margaret Elizabeth Pratt **MS:** Married **SPN:** Susan Waldron (11/11/1972); Carol Hamann (1957); Patchin Leo (1954) **CH:** Constance; Catherine; Virginia **ED:** MBA, New York University (1957); BA in Economics, University of Virginia (1951) **C:** Commissioner, Bradley International Airport (1996-1997); President, Airports Council International (1989-1996); President, North America Assistant Director of Aviation, Airports Council International (1965-1990); ADJ Professor of Airline Economics, The New School (1985-1986); Director of Marketing Research, Eastern Airlines LLC (1961-1964); Associate Director, Dun & Bradstreet, Inc. (1958-1961); Market Researcher, American Enka Company (1955-1957); Market Researcher, Ingersoll Rand (1951-1952) **CR:** Liaison, City-Wide Task Force on Tourism, Port Authority (1987-1988) **CIV:** President, Brooklyn Heights Association (1972-1974) **MIL:** First Lieutenant, U.S. Air Force (1952-1955) **CW:** Docent, Frick Collection, Wadsworth Atheneum Museum of Art (2003-2014); Docent, Guggenheim Museum (2003-2009); Editor, Contributing Author, "Airport Economic Planning," The MIT Press (1974); Docent, Outreach Program, The Yale University Art Gallery; Lecturer, Museo Tamayo **MEM:** Former Trustee, Deep River Historical Society; Board Member, Deep River Land Trust; Deep River Democratic Committee **MH:** Albert Nelson Marquis Lifetime Achievement Award **AV:** Traveling; Building a collection of 20th century Mexican photography

HOWARD, JEFFREY ROBERT, T: Chief Judge **I:** Government Administration/Government Relations/Government Services **CN:** U.S. Court of Appeals for the First Circuit **DOB:** 11/04/1955 **PB:** Claremont **SC:** NH/USA **MS:** Married **SPN:** Marie Howard **CH:** Two Children **ED:** JD, Georgetown University Law Center (1981); BA, Plymouth State University, Plymouth, NH (1978) **C:** Chief Judge, U.S. Court of Appeals for the First Circuit (2015-Present); Judge, U.S. Court of Appeals for the First Circuit (2002-2015); Private Practice, Jeffrey R. Howard, Esq. (2001-2002); Partner, Choate, Hall & Stewart LLP (1997-2001); Attorney General, State of New Hampshire (1993-1997); U.S. Attorney, District of New Hampshire, Concord, NH (1989-1992); Deputy Attorney General, State of New Hampshire (1988-1989); Attorney, Office of New Hampshire Attorney General (1981-1988) **CR:** Member, Attorney General Advisory Committee, Attorneys General Thornburgh and Barr **AW:** Named Citizen of the Year, Salisbury, NH (2000)

HOWARD, REDEMOUS A., T: Senior Passport Specialist **DOB:** 10/25/1947 **PB:** Petersburg **SC:** VA/USA **PT:** Redemous Howard; Jessie Lee (Cousins) Howard **MS:** Single **ED:** Bachelor of Social Work in Sociology, Virginia State University (1980) **C:** U.S. Department of State Bureau of Consular Affairs (1994-Present); U.S. Customs Service Import Specialist, U.S. Department of the Treasury (1991-1992); With, Defense Logistic Agency, Office of Telecommunications and Information Systems (1983-1991); Television Production Specialist, Nationwide Communications, Inc. WXEX-TV (Now WRIC-TV) (1972-1984); Television Film Technician, Petersburg Television Corp., WXEX-TV (Now WRIC-TV), Petersburg, VA (1966-1968) **CR:** U.S. Senatorial Club (1983-Present); Republican Presidential Task Force (1982-Present); Former Member, Commission Community Relations Affairs, Petersburg, VA; Former Member, Petersburg Junior Chamber of Commerce **CIV:** Founder, Neighborhood Tolerance Association, Petersburg, VA (1980) **MIL:** With, United States Air Force (1968-1972); With, ROTC, Virginia State University (1966-1967) **CW:** Owner-Operator, Independent Consultant, RAH47, Creative Services, Inc. (1980-1985) **AW:** Republican Presidential Medal of Merit (1984) **MH:** Albert Nelson Marquis Lifetime Achievement Award **B/I:** Mr. Howard became involved in his profession because his father worked in television and he would go and help him. While he was working in television he began thinking whether that was all he was ever going to do. Not liking that thought to become his reality, he left the television world to go to work for the government. He worked for the government since 1983, which included his military service. **AV:** Photography **PA:** Republican **RE:** Earth-based

HOWARD, TERRENCE DASHON, T: Actor **I:** Media & Entertainment **DOB:** 03/11/1969 **PB:** Chicago **SC:** IL/USA **PT:** Tyrone Howard; Anita (Hawkins) Williams **MS:** Divorced **SPN:** Mira Pak (2013, Divorced 2015); Michelle Ghent (01/20/2010, Divorced 2013); Lori McCommas (1989-2003, 2005-2008) **CH:** Hunter; Heaven; Aubrey; Qirin Love; Hero **ED:** Honorary LHD, South Carolina State University (2012); Coursework, Pratt Institute **CW:** Actor, "Empire" (2015-2020); Actor, "Gully" (2019); Actor, "Electric Dreams" (2017); Actor, "Cardboard Boxer" (2016); Actor, "Term Life" (2016); Actor, "Hada Madrina" (2016); Actor, "Wayward Pines" (2015-2016); Actor, "Sabotage" (2014); Actor, "St. Vincent" (2014); Actor, "Movie 43" (2013); Actor, "Dead Man Down" (2013); Actor, "House of Bodies" (2013); Actor, "The Butler" (2013); Actor, "Prisoners" (2013); Actor, "The Best Man Holiday" (2013); Actor, "Lullaby" (2013); Actor, "Hawaii Five-0" (2012); Actor,

"Red Tails" (2012); Actor, "On the Road" (2012); Actor, "The Company You Keep" (2012); Actor, "Little Murder" (2011); Actor, "Winnie" (2011); Actor, Co-executive Producer, "The Ledge" (2011); Actor, "Law & Order: LA" (2010-2011); Actor, "Fighting" (2009); Voice Actor, "The Princess and the Frog" (2009); Actor, "Cat on a Hot Tin Roof" (2008); Singer, "Shine Through It" (2008); Actor, "Iron Man" (2008); Actor, "Wifey" (2007); Actor, Executive Producer, "Pride" (2007); Actor, "The Brave One" (2007); Actor, "August Rush" (2007); Actor, "The Hunting Party" (2007); Actor, "Awake" (2007); Actor, "Idlewild" (2006); Actor, "Hustle & Flow" (2005); Actor, "Their Eyes Were Watching God" (2005); Actor, "The Salon" (2005); Actor, "Lackawanna Blues" (2005); Actor, "Four Brothers" (2005); Actor, "Animal" (2005); Actor, "Get Rich or Die Tryin'" (2005); Actor, "Ray" (2004); Actor, "Crash" (2004); Host, "Independent Lens" (2003-2007); Actor, "Biker Boyz" (2003); Actor, "Love Chronicles" (2003); Actor, "Street Time" (2003); Actor, "Hart's War" (2002); Actor, "Investigating Sex" (2001); Actor, "Angel Eyes" (2001); Actor, "Boycott" (2001); Actor, "Glitter" (2001); Actor, "Big Momma's House" (2000); Actor, "King of the World" (2000); Actor, Executive Producer, "Love Beat the Hell Outta Me" (2000); Actor, "Valerie Flake" (1999); Actor, "Best Laid Plans" (1999); Actor, "The Best Man" (1999); Actor, "Butter" (1998); Actor, "Mama Flora's Family" (1998); Actor, "Spark" (1998); Actor, "The Players Club" (1998); Actor, "Double Tap" (1997); Actor, "Sparks" (1996-1998); Actor, "Sunset Park" (1996); Actor, "Johns" (1996); Actor, "Mr. Holland's Opus" (1995); Actor, "Lotto Land" (1995); Actor, "The O.J. Simpson Story" (1995); Actor, "Shadow-Ops" (1995); Actor, "Dead Presidents" (1995); Actor, "Who's the Man?" (1993); Actor, "Tall Hopes" (1993); Actor, "The Jacksons: An American Dream" (1992) **AW:** NAACP Image Award for Outstanding Actor in a Drama Series (2016); NAACP Image Award for Outstanding Actor in a TV Movie, Mini-series or Dramatic Special (2006); SAG Award for Outstanding Performance by a Cast in a Motion Picture, SAG-AFTRA (2006); NAACP Image Award for Outstanding Supporting Actor in a Motion Picture (2006); National Board of Review Award for Breakthrough Performance Actor (2005); NAACP Image Award for Best Actor (2000); Numerous Awards **MEM:** Honorary Member, Phi Beta Sigma Fraternity, Inc.

HOWE, MARVINE HENRIETTA, T: Newspaper Reporter **I:** Writing and Editing **DOB:** 12/03/1928 **PB:** Shanghai **SC:** China **PT:** James Lewis Howe; Mary Scott (West) Howe **ED:** BLitt, Rutgers, The State University of New York (1950) **C:** Freelance Writer (1995-Present); Reporter, Metropolitan Staff, The New York Times, New York, NY (1984-1994); Bureau Chief, The New York Times, Athens (1984); Bureau Chief, The New York Times, Ankara (1980-1984); Bureau Chief, The New York Times, Beirut (1977-1980); Correspondent, The New York Times, Portugal and Angola (1975-1976); Bureau Chief, The New York Times, Rio de Janeiro, Brazil (1972-1975); Part-time Reporter, The New York Times, Algiers, Rabat, Lisbon (1957-1971); Part-time Reporter, Time-Life, Algiers, Rabat, Lisbon (1956-1965); Contributor, McGraw-Hill World News, Morocco (1958-1962); Contributor, British Broadcasting Corp., Rabat (1952-1955); News Broadcaster, Radio Maroc, Rabat, Morocco (1951-1955) **CR:** Lecturer, Rutgers University Journalism School (1991); Delegate, International Women's Media Conference, Washington DC (1986); Lecturer, University Center, Virginia (1959); Lecturer, Lycee, Fez, Morocco (1950-1951) **CW:** Author, "Al-Andalus Rediscovered - Iberia's New Muslims" (2012); Author, "Morocco: The Islamist Awakening and Other Challenges" (2005); Author, "Turkey Today: A Nation Divided Over Islam's Revival" (2000); Author, "The Prince and I or One Woman's Morocco" (1956); Author, Travel Articles; Contributor, Travel Guidebooks; Contributor, Articles, The Monitor, Scholastic, Middle East Journal, The Nation, New Republic, Africa Report, International Herald Tribune, World Policy Journal, Washington Report on Middle East Affairs **AW:** Adalaide Zagoren Fellow, Rutgers, The State University of New Jersey (1991); Poetry Award, Douglass College (1950) **MEM:** American Association of University Women; Silurians; Lisbon Foreign Press Association **MH:** Albert Nelson Marquis Lifetime Achievement Award **B/I:** Ms. Howe was born in Shanghai and she wanted to return to China. She was enrolled in the course in Asian studies in Columbia but then she got waylaid in Europe and happened to be there when colonialism started its fight to hang onto the colonies. She just happened to be in Europe at that time. She was 6 years old when she came to the United States, and she always wanted to go back and the only way she thought she could was as a journalist. **AV:** Theater; Classical music; Ballet; Travel **PA:** Democrat **RE:** Presbyterian

HOWELL, ROB STUART, T: Costume and Set Designer **I:** Media & Entertainment **SC:** England **C:** Designer, Royal National Theatre, Royal Court Theatre, Donmar Warehouse, Almeida Theatre, Royal Shakespeare Company; Resident Design Assistant, Royal Shakespeare Company **CW:** Designer, "The Ferryman" (2019); Designer, "Groundhog Day" (2015); Designer, "Le nozze di Figaro" (2014); Designer, "Matilda the Musical" (2013); Designer, "Ghost the Musical" (2012); Designer, "Private Lives" (2011); Designer, "The Norman Conquests: Living Together" (2009); Designer, "The Norman Conquests: Table Manners" (2009); Designer, "The Norman Conquests: Round and Round the Garden" (2009); Designer, "Boeing-Boeing" (2008); Designer, "Lord of the Rings" (2007); Designer, "The Graduate" (2002); Designer, "Betrayal" (2000); Designer, "True West" (2000); Designer, "Buried Child," "Chips with Everything," "Troilus and Cressida," "Battle Royal," "Howard Katz" **AW:** Best Costume Design of a Play, Best Scenic Design of a Play, "The Ferryman," Tony Awards (2019); Outstanding Set Design, "Matilda the Musical," Outer Critics Circle Awards and Drama Desk Awards (2013); Best Scenic Design of a Musical, "Matilda the Musical" (2013); Outstanding Set Design, "Ghost the Musical," Drama Desk Awards (2012)

HOXIE, CHAD, T: Vice President **I:** Insurance **CN:** Alliant Insurance Services, Inc. **MS:** Single **ED:** BA in History, San Diego State University (2003) **CT:** Strategic Decision and Risk Management, Stanford University (2008); Associate in Commercial Underwriting; Associate in Insurance Services; Associate in Risk Management for Public Entities; Associate in Risk Management; Chartered Property Casualty Underwriter **C:** Vice President, Alliant Insurance Services, Inc. (2014-Present); Analyst and Compliance Specialist, Preferred Employers Insurance Company (2013-2014); Production Underwriter, Preferred Employers Insurance Company (2009-2013); Claims Adjuster, State Compensation Insurance Fund (2007-2009); Auditor, State Compensation Insurance Fund (2005-2007) **AW:** Named to Hot 100, Insurance Business America (2019); Named One of the Agents of the Year, Insurance Journal (2018); Named One of the Rising Stars, Risk & Insurance Magazine (2018); Named Power Broker, Risk & Insurance Magazine (2018) **MEM:** California Restaurant Association; Honorary Member, Deputy Sheriff's Association **AS:** Mr. Hoxie attributes his success to a great deal of studying, listening and an unwavering desire to keep learning. **B/I:** Mr. Hoxie had a genuine interest in the industry. He was interested in the daily interactions between businesses and becoming a support system for those businesses. It seemed to be a very rewarding profession.

HOYE, VINCENT J., T: Correctional Education Administrator; Consultant **I:** Education/Educational Services **DOB:** 09/15/1933 **PB:** Boston **SC:** MA/USA **PT:** Vincent Joseph Hoye; Eleanor Z. (Walsh) Hoye **MS:** Married **SPN:** Sheila Maloney (08/20/1960) **CH:** Maura; Meeghan **ED:** Certificate of Advanced Graduate Studies in Occupational Education, University of Massachusetts Amherst (1991); Certificate of Advanced Graduate Studies in Education Administration, University of Massachusetts Boston (1983); MEd in Secondary Education, Boston State University (Now University of Massachusetts Boston (1981); AB in History and Government, Stonehill College, North Eaton, MA (1958) **CT:** Certified School Superintendent, Grades K-12; Principal; Teacher; Superintendent, Director of Regional Vocational-technical; Instructor, Commonwealth of Massachusetts **C:** Consultant, Correctional Education (1992-Present); Supervisor, Massachusetts Department of Corrections, Boston, MA (1991-1992); Retired (1992); Director, Massachusetts Department of Corrections, Boston, MA (1988); Vocational Coordinator, Education Division, Massachusetts Department of Corrections, Boston, MA (1985-1986); Instructor, Tri-County Regional Vocational Technical School District, MA (1979-1985); Consultant, New England Lobster Systems, Boston, MA (1973-1983); President, Hoye & Associates, Boston MA (1965-1973); Department Director, Massachusetts Department of Corrections, Boston, MA **CR:** Member, School Committee, Tri-County Regional Vocational Technical School District (1986-Present); Massachusetts Department of Education, Quincy, MA (1991); Member, Vocational Planning, Vocational Education Division, Virginia Department of Education, Richmond, VA (1989); Member, Standing Committee, Division of Occupational Education; Presenter, Conferences in Field **CIV:** Board of Directors, North Attleborough CD, MA (1980-1986); Trustee, North Attleborough Library (Now Richards Memorial Library) (1981-1985); Member, North Attleborough Democratic Town Committee **MIL:** With, United States Navy Air Force (1950-1955) **AW:** Silver Medal, Massachusetts Humane Society, Boston, MA (1947); Named Class President, Junior and Senior Year of College **MEM:** State Director, Correctional Education Association (1988); Chair, Energy Committee, Massachusetts Association School Committee (1987); American Association of School Administrators (Now AASA, The School Superintendents Association); American Correctional Association; Correctional Education Association; Massachusetts Association School Committee; American Vocational Association; Irish Cultural Association; Massachusetts Bureau of Pipefitters and Refrigeration Technicians; Pi Sigma Alpha; Pi Lambda Theta; Kappa Delta Pi, International Honor Society **MH:** Albert Nelson Marquis Lifetime Achievement Award; Marquis Who's Who Top Professional **B/I:** Mr. Hoye has always wanted to be able to make a contribution in education. **AV:** Walking; Hiking; Reading **PA:** Democrat **RE:** Roman Catholic **THT:** In the Navy, Mr. Hoye was an aviation petty officer and he mastered flying a blimp. He was also in charge over 700 teachers. Mr. Hoye was the emergency manager of his town and when he was 14 years old, he saved another young man from drowning.

HOYER, STENY HAMILTON, T: U.S. Representative from Maryland; House Majority Leader **I:** Government Administration/Government Relations/Government Services **DOB:** 07/14/1939 **PB:** New

York **SC:** NY/USA **PT:** Steen Theilgaard Hoyer; Jean (Baldwin Slade) Hoyer **MS:** Widowed **SPN:** Judith Elaine Pickett (06/17/1961, Deceased 02/1997) **CH:** Susan; Stefany; Anne **ED:** LLB, Georgetown University Law Center (1966); BS in Political Science, University of Maryland, College Park, MD, With High Honors (1963) **C:** House Majority Leader, United States Congress from Maryland's Fifth Congressional District (2007-2011, 2019-Present); Member, U.S. House of Representatives from Maryland's Fifth Congressional District, United States Congress, Washington, DC (1981-Present); Assistant Minority Leader (Minority Whip), United States Congress from Maryland's Fifth Congressional District (2003-2007, 2011-2019); Chairman, U.S. House Democratic Caucus (1989-1995); Vice-Chair, U.S. House Democratic Caucus (1989); Deputy Majority Leader (Deputy Majority Whip), United States Congress from Maryland's Fifth Congressional District (1987-1989); Private Law Practice (1981-1989); President, Maryland State Senate (1975-1979); Associate, Hoyer & Fannon, District Heights, MD (1969-1981); Member, Maryland State Senate (1966-1979); Associate, Haislip & Yewell, Marlow Heights, MD (1966-1969); Executive Assistant to Senator Daniel B. Brewster, U.S. Senate (1962-1966) **CIV:** Maryland Board of Higher Education (1979-1981); Baltimore Council on Foreign Relations; Board of Visitors, University of Maryland School of Public Affairs; Trustee, University of Maryland Alumni Association; Board of Trustees, St. Mary's College of Maryland; Board Member, International Foundation for Electoral Systems (IFES); Advisory Board Member, Center for the Study of Democracy **AW:** Nathan Davis Award for Outstanding Government Service, American Medical Association (2008); Leadership Award, National Organization on Fetal Alcohol Syndrome (NOFAS) (2005); Freedom Award, National Association of Secretaries of State (NASS) (2003); Excellence in Immunization Award, National Partnership for Immunization (NPI) (2001); Jack Niles Medal of Honor, Public Employees Roundtable (1999); Public Service Award, American Association of Public Health Dentistry (1997); Champion of Pediatric Research, Children's National Medical Center (Now Children's National Hospital) (1995); Excellence in Public Service Award, American Academy of Pediatrics (1991); Washingtonian of the Year, Washingtonian Magazine (1988); Outstanding Young Man, Maryland Jaycees (1975); State Official of the Year, Maryland Municipal League (1971) **MEM:** University of Maryland Alumni Association; Pi Sigma Alpha; Omicron Delta Kappa; Delta Theta Phi; Sigma Chi Fraternity **BAR:** State of Maryland (1966) **PA:** Democrat **RE:** Baptist

HROMATKO, WESLEY VINTON, D.MIN., T: Minister **I:** Religious **DOB:** 10/02/1947 **PB:** Slayton **SC:** MN/USA **PT:** Annel Jay Hromatko (Deceased 2007); Maybelle (Moffatt) Hromatko (Deceased 01/08/2011) **MS:** Widowed **SPN:** Marilyn Blitz-Stein (09/17/1978, Deceased 2015) **ED:** Doctor of Ministry, Meadville Lombard Theological School, Chicago, IL (1973); MA, Meadville Lombard Theological School, Chicago, IL (1971); BA, University of Minnesota, Cum Laude (1969) **CT:** Ordained to Ministry, Unitarian Universalist Association (1973) **C:** Tri State Unitarian Universalist Cluster, Speaker and Supply (1990-Present); Minister, First Congregational Parish Unitarian, Petersham, MA (1987-1990); Associate Minister, Church of Larger Fellowship, Boston, MA (1985-1990); Board of Directors, Chairman, Religious Education, Church of the Larger Fellowship, Boston, MA (1983-1986); Minister, All Souls All Souls Church, Braintree, MA (1982-1985); Minister, First Unitarian Church, Hobart, IN (1975-1982); Minister, Oaklandon Unitarian Universalist Church (1973-1975); Minister,

Abraham Lincoln Fellowship, Springfield, IL (1972-1973); Student Minister, Unity Temple, Oak Park, IL (1972-1973); Student Minister, Third Unitarian Church, Chicago, IL (1972-1973) **CR:** Owner, Century Farm, Brighton Corporation (2011-Present); Trustee, Chicago Area Unitarian Universalist Council (1976-1978); Member, Independent Unitarian-Universalist Legislature Conference (1973-1975); Chaplain Oaklandon Volunteer, Fire Department (1973-1974); Member, Independent Justice Project, Unitarian-Universalist Service Committee (1973-1974) **CIV:** Member, Petersham Arts Council (1987-1990); Member, Petersham Ecumenical Commission, Athol/Orange Food Bank (1988-1989); Member, North Braintree Civic Association (1984-1985); Member, Braintree Historical Society (1983-1985); Member, Protestant Social Services Bureau (1983-1985); Member, Prairie Group Program Committee, Save the Dunes Council (1973-1982); Board of Directors, Oaklandon Civic Association (1974-1975); Board of Directors, Eastern Lawrence Township Planning Commission (1974-1975); Member, Advisory Council, Religious Coalition for Abortion Rights (1974-1975); Member, Organization for Better Austin, Chicago, IL (1972); Member, Historical Society & Craft Center; Member, Hobart American Revolutionary Bicentennial Commission **CW:** Contributor, Articles "Hosea Ballou," "Unitarianism to 1961," New Encyclopedia of Unbelief (2007); Co-editor, "Appeal of the Irreligious" (1980); Contributor, Dictionary of Unitarian Universalist Biography; Contributor, "A Simple Faith"; Contributor, Various Denominational Publications **AW:** Entemann Ohanian Award (1975) **MEM:** Past Secretary, North Quabbin Interfaith Clergy Association (1988-1990); Secretary, Unitarian Universalist Ministers Association (1976, 1983-1985); Legal Panel, Northwest Independent Chapter, ACLU (1982-1983); Treasurer, Indianapolis, Americas United (1974-1975); Treasurer, Meadville Lombard Theological School Alumni Association (1973-1975); Unitarian Universalist Collegium; Unitarian Universalist Ministers Association; Prairie Star District Ministers Association; International Association Religious Freedom; Universalist Historical Society; Indianapolis Mental Health Association; Unitarian-Universalist Historical Society (Now Unitarian Universalist History and Heritage Society); Life Member, Meadville Lombard Theological School Alumni Association; Life Member, University of Minnesota Alumni Associations; Past Vice President, Hobart Ministerial Association; Former Board of Directors, Vice President, Unitarian-Universalist Advance **MH:** Albert Nelson Marquis Lifetime Achievement Award **AV:** Reading; Collecting stamps; Painting; Drawing; Buying and selling books **PA:** DFL (Democratic–Farmer–Labor Party-Minnesota) **RE:** Unitarian/Universalist

HUANG, SUEI-RONG, PHD, T: Chemistry Educator **I:** Education/Educational Services **DOB:** 01/01/1932 **PB:** Tainan **SC:** Taiwan **PT:** Shou Huang; Feng-ching (Wang) Huang **MS:** Married **SPN:** Lily P.T. Chen (01/30/1965) **CH:** Eric; Fritz; Jeffrey; Nina **ED:** PhD, Stevens Institute of Technology (1964); MS, New Mexico Highlands University (1960); BS, National Taiwan University (1954) **C:** Professor of Chemistry, Long Island University (1976-Present); Associate Professor, Long Island University (1970-1976); Assistant Professor of Chemistry, Long Island University (1964-1970) **CR:** Consultant, Seiken Industry (1972-Present) **CW:** Co-Author, "General Chemistry (1980); Co-Author, "Organic and Biochemistry" (1980) **MEM:** American Chemical Society; New York Academy of Sciences **MH:** Albert Nelson Marquis Lifetime Achievement Award **AV:** Playing tennis; Swimming

HUBBARD, LINCOLN B., T: Physicist **I:** Sciences **CN:** Rush University **DOB:** 09/08/1940 **PB:** Hawkesbury **SC:** ON/Canada **PT:** Carroll Chauncey Hubbard; Mary Lunn (Beals) Hubbard **MS:** Married **SPN:** Nancy Ann Krieger (04/03/1961) **CH:** Jill; Katrina **ED:** PhD, Massachusetts Institute of Technology (1967); BS in Physics, University of New Hampshire (1961) **CT:** Certified Health Physicist, American Board of Health Physics; Diplomate, American Board of Radiology **C:** Associate Professor of Medical Physics, Rush University (1986-Present); President, Hubbard, Zickgraf & Broadbent (1993-2018); Chief Physicist, Mount Sinai Hospital (1974-1975, 1979-2002); Partner, Griffith, Hubbard & Associate, Limited (1978-1993); Chief Physicist, Cook County Hospital (1975-1988); Assistant Professor of Physics, Furman University (1970-1974); Assistant Professor of Mathematics and Physics, Knoxville College (1968-1970); Postdoctoral Appointee, Argonne National Laboratory (1966-1968) **CW:** Co-Author, "Computers in Radiology" (1984); Co-Author, "Mathematics for Technologists" (1979) **AW:** Guest Examiner, American Board of Radiology **MEM:** Fellow, American College of Radiology; American Association of Physicists in Medicine **MH:** Albert Nelson Marquis Lifetime Achievement Award **B/I:** Dr. Hubbard became involved in his profession because of the academic opportunities that were available for physicists during the 1960s. With a degree from MIT, he found himself struggling to find a teaching job. Dr. Hubbard received a job at one of the top private schools in South Carolina at the time. Although the school was reputable, the salary simply was not enough to raise his family. Dr. Hubbard then decided to switch his focus to medical physics.

HUBBARD, STANLEY, "STUB", T: Broadcast Executive **I:** Media & Entertainment **CN:** Hubbard Broadcasting **PT:** Stanley E. Hubbard **MS:** Married **SPN:** Karen Hubbard **CH:** Kathryn Rominski; Stanley E.; Virginia Morris; Robert W.; Julia Hubbard Coyte **ED:** Bachelor's Degree, University of Minnesota **C:** Chairman, Chief Executive Officer, Hubbard Broadcasting (1983-Present); President, Hubbard Broadcasting (1967-1983); Hubbard Broadcasting (1951-1967) **CIV:** Donor, Our Principles PAC **AW:** Distinguished Service Award, National Association of Broadcasters (1995) **PA:** Republican

HUDLIN, REGINALD ALAN, T: Director **I:** Media & Entertainment **DOB:** 12/15/1961 **PB:** Centerville **SC:** IL/USA **PT:** Warrington W. Hudlin; Helen (Cason) Hudlin **MS:** Married **SPN:** Chrisette Suter (11/30/2002) **CH:** Two Children **ED:** BA, Harvard University, Cum Laude (1983) **C:** President of Entertainment, Chief Programming Executive, Black Entertainment TV (2005-Present); President, Hudlin Entertainment, New York, NY (1986-Present); Copywriter, Olgivy and Mather Advertising Agency, New York, NY (1986); Artist-in-Residence, Illinois State Arts Council (1984-1985) **CR:** Visiting Lecturer, Film, University of Wisconsin, Milwaukee, WI (1985-1986) **CIV:** Board Member, School of Theater, Film and Television, University of California Los Angeles **CW:** Director, "The Black Godfather" (2019); Director, Producer, "Marshall" (2017); Executive Producer, "Blazing Samurai" (2017); Executive Producer, "Blue & Green" (2017); Producer, "Burning Sands" (2017); Writer, "Black Panther: Doomwar" (2017); Author, "'Django Unchained' Producer on 'Selma' Oscar Snubs: Did Voters Have 'Racial Fatigue'?," The Hollywood Reporter (2015); Comic Adapter, "Django Unchained" (2014); President of Entertainment, BET's Comicview (2008-2013); Producer, "Django Unchained" (2012); Writer, "Black Panther: Power" (2010); Writer, "Captain America/Black Panther: Flags of Our Fathers" (2010); Writer, "Black Panther: The Deadliest of the Species" (2009); Network Executive, "Brothers to Brutha" (2008); Writer, "Black Panther: Little Green Men" (2008); Writer, "Black Panther: Black to the Future" (2008); Writer, "Black Panther: Back to Africa" (2008); Executive Producer, "The Boondocks" (2005-2008); Director, "Wifey" (2007); Writer, "Black Panther: Four the Hard Way" (2007); Writer, "Black Panther: Civil War" (2007); Writer, "Black Panther: The Bride" (2006); Writer, "Spider-Man: The Other" (2006); Executive in Charge of Co-Productions, "Somebodies" (2006); Writer, "Marvel Knights Spider-Man [Vol. 04], Wild Blue Yonder" (2005); Writer, "Black Panther: Who is the Black Panther" (2005); Director, Producer, "The Bernie Mac Show" (2002-2005); Writer, "Birth of a Nation: A Comic Novel" (2004); Director, "Serving Sara" (2002); Director, Actor, "The Ladies Man" (2000); Author, "If It's a Question of Money...," Los Angeles Times (2000); Producer, "Ride" (1998); Director, "The Great White Hype" (1996); Voice Actor, "Joe's Apartment" (1996); Executive Producer, Director, TV Film, "Cosmic Slop" (1994); Actor, "Posse" (1993); Executive Producer, Writer, Musician, "Bébé's Kids" (1992); Director, Actor, "Boomerang" (1992); Director, Writer, Actor, "House Party" (1990); Actor, "She's Gotta Have It" (1986); Director, Short Film, "The Kold Waves" (1986); Director, Short Film, "Reggie's World of Soul" (1985); Director, Writer, Short Film, "House Party" (1983); Various Roles, Numerous TV Specials; Guest Roles, Numerous TV Shows **AW:** Salute to Excellence Award, African-American Film Critics Association (2016); Icon Award, Comic Con (2015); Named, Top 10 Films, "Django Unchained," American Film Institute Awards (2012); Dramatic or Theatrical Special Award, "Cosmic Shop," CableACE (1995); Filmmakers Trophy, "House Party," Sundance Film Festival (1990); Black Independent Video and Film-maker's Awards, "House Party," Black American Cinema Society (1986) **MEM:** Co-Founder, Black Filmmakers Foundation (1978); Board of Governors, Academy of Motion Picture Arts and Sciences **AV:** Comic book collecting

HUDSON, JENNIFER KATE, T: Singer, Actress **I:** Media & Entertainment **DOB:** 09/12/1981 **PB:** Chicago **SC:** IL/USA **PT:** Samuel Simpson; Darnell Donnerson **CH:** David Daniel Otunga, Jr. **ED:** Coursework, Kennedy-King College; Coursework, Langston University **C:** With, Righteous Records (2002) **CR:** Spokesperson, Weight Watchers (2010-2014) **CIV:** Co-Founder, Julian D. King Foundation, Chicago, IL **CW:** Singer with Bono, Will.i.am and Yoshiki, "#SING4LIFE" (2020); Actress, "Cats" (2019); Actress, "All Rise" (2018); Coach, "The Voice" (2017-2019); Appearance, "Ant and Dec's Saturday Night Takeaway" (2017); Actress, "Sandy Wexler" (2017); Actress, "Sing" (2016); Actress, "Confirmation" (2016); Appearance, "Inside Amy Schumer" (2016); Actress, "Hairspray Live!" (2016); Actress, "The Color Purple" (2015); Actress, "Chi-Raq" (2015); Singer, "JHUD" (2014); Actress, "Lullaby" (2014); Actress, "Smash" (2013); Actress, "Call Me Crazy: A Five Film" (2013); Actress, "The Inevitable Defeat of Mister and Pete" (2013); Actress, "Black Nativity" (2013); Author, Memoir, "I Got This: How I Changed My Ways and Lost What Weighed Me Down" (2012); Actress, "The Three Stooges" (2012); Guest Judge, "The X Factor" (2011); Singer, "I Remember Me" (2011); Singer, "Star-Spangled Banner," Super Bowl XLIII (2009); Actress, "Fragments" (2009); Actress, "Sex and the City: The Movie" (2008); Actress, "The Secret Life of Bees" (2008); Singer, "Jennifer Hudson" (2008); Singer with Fantasia Barrino, "I'm His Only Woman" (2008); Actress, "Dreamgirls" (2006); Contestant, "American Idol" (2004) **AW:** Grammy Award for Best Musical Theater, The Recording Academy

(2017); Humanitarian Award, People's Choice Awards (2014); Outstanding Album, NAACP Image Awards (2009, 2012); Outstanding Music Video, NAACP Image Awards (2012); Grammy Award for Best R&B Album, The Recording Academy (2009); Outstanding Duo or Group, NAACP Image Awards (2009); Outstanding New Artist, NAACP Image Awards (2009); BAFTA Award for Best Actress in a Supporting Role (2007); Golden Globe Award for Best Performance by an Actress in a Supporting Role in a Motion Picture, Hollywood Foreign Press Association (2007); Critics Choice Award for Best Supporting Actress, Broadcast Film Critics Association (2007); SAG Award for Outstanding Performance by a Female Actor in a Supporting Role, SAG-AFTRA (2007); Academy Award for Best Supporting Actress, Academy of Motion Picture Arts & Sciences (2007); Outstanding Supporting Actress in a Motion Picture, NAACP Image Awards (2007); Best Actress, BET Awards (2007); Best New Artist, BET Awards (2007); Sammy Davis Junior Award for Entertainer of the Year, Soul Train Awards (2007); Award for Best Female Breakthrough Performance, National Board of Review (2006); Award for Best Supporting Actress, New York Film Critics Circle (2006); Award for Best Supporting Actress, African American Film Critics (2006); One of the 10 Actors to Watch, Variety (2006); ShoWest Female Star of Tomorrow Award, National Association of Theatre Owners (2006); Numerous Awards

HUDSON, RICHARD LANE JR., T: U.S. Representative **I:** Government Administration/Government Relations/Government Services **DOB:** 11/04/1971 **PB:** Franklin **SC:** VA/USA **MS:** Married **SPN:** Renee (Howell) Hudson (05/21/2010) **ED:** BA, UNC Charlotte (1996) **C:** U.S. Representative, North Carolina's Eighth Congressional District, United States Congress, Washington, DC (2013-Present); Member, Committee on Homeland Security, U.S. House of Representatives (2013-Present); Member, Education and Labor Committee, U.S. House of Representatives (2013-Present); House Agriculture Committee (2013-Present); Founder, Cabarrus Marketing Group, Concord, NC (2011-2012); Campaign Manager, Pat McCrory for Governor, NC (2008); Chief of Staff to Representative Mike Conaway, U.S. House of Representatives, Washington, DC (2009-2011); Chief of Staff to Representative John R. Carter, U.S. House of Representatives, Washington, DC (2006-2008); Chief of Staff to Representative Virginia Foxx, U.S. House of Representatives, Washington, DC (2005-2006); District Director to Representative Robin Hayes, U.S. House of Representatives, Washington, DC (2000-2005); Communications Director, North Carolina Republican Party (1997-1999); Customer Service, Carolina Power & Light Co. (1997); Deputy Campaign Manager, Steve Arnold for Lieutenant Governor, NC (1996); Field Director, Richard A. Vinroot for Governor, NC (1996); Member, Republican Study Committee **CIV:** Board of Trustees, Rowan-Cabarrus Community College (2001-2005); Chapter Secretary, Jaycees (2000-2004); Board of Governors, Alumni Association, UNC Charlotte (1999-2002) **AW:** Man of the Year, North Carolina Federation of Young Republicans (1999) **MEM:** President, Kappa Alpha Order, Alumni Chapter, The University of North Carolina at Charlotte (1998-Present); Magnolia Lodge No. 53, F.A.A.M.; The North Carolina State Society of Washington DC; The Texas State Society; RAMS; House Chief of Staff Associate; National Republican Club Capitol Hill; Order of Omega; Omicron Delta Kappa; Phi Eta Sigma National Honor Society, Inc. **AV:** Hunting **PA:** Republican **RE:** Methodist

HUFF, NORMAN NELSON, T: Computer Science Educator, International Lecturer, Engineer **I:** Education/Educational Services **PB:** San Diego **SC:** CA/USA **PT:** George Kleineburg Peabody Huff; Norma Nelson DeMetz **MS:** Married **SPN:** Sharon Kay Lockwood (9/30/1979) **ED:** Cultural Doctorate, World University, Benson, AZ (1987); Master of Business Administration, Golden Gate University, San Francisco, CA (1971); Associate of Arts, Victor Valley College (1971); Bachelor of Science in Mechanical Engineering, San Diego State University, San Diego, CA (1957) **CT:** Five Lifetime Teaching Credentials for California Community Colleges for Business Administration, Computer Science, and Mathematics Courses (1969-1988); Master's Teaching Program, Trade & Industry Certificate, University of California Los Angeles (1971); Masters Life Trade & Industry Certificate for Data Processing and Computer Science, University of California Los Angeles (1971); California Standard Designated Subjects Teaching Credential for Biology, Mathematics, and Chemistry (1968-1969) **C:** Substitute Teacher for Adult Education Classes, Regional Occupation Programs, Grammar/High School Classes, K-12 Grade Schools, Victorville, Apple Valley, Hesperia, San Bernardino, and Redlands, CA (1999-2003); U.S. Census Bureau, Apple Valley, CA (1999-2000); Treasurer, World University Roundtable for Intercultural Studies, Benson, AZ (1989-1993); Trustee, Instructor, Lecturer, World University Roundtable for Intercultural Studies, Benson, AZ (1989-1993); Founder, Consultant for Computer Center, Dr. Anthony O. Okafor, Enugu Anambra State, Nigeria (1990-1992); U.S. Census Bureau, Victorville, CA (1989-1990); Chair, Lecturer, Computer Science Department, Victor Valley Community College (1967-1988); Owner, High Desert Data Systems, Hesperia, CA (1972-1982); Adjunct Instructor for Computer Science and Quantitative Analysis Courses, Chapman College, Orange, CA, Golden Gate University, San Francisco, CA (1972-1976); Systems Programmer, California Mojave Water Agency, Victorville, CA (1972-1974); Systems Programmer for the Pfizer Inc. Cement Plant, Victorville, CA (1970-1972); U.S. Gypsum Co. Assistant Supervisor, U.S. Gypsum Mill Operation, Chemical Engineer, Quality Control Supervisor, Plaster City, CA (1957-1958); Team Member, ICBM Atlas Missile, Consolidated/Vultee Aircraft Co. (1954-1956); California Entomologist, San Diego, CA (1955); Rocket Engineering Team Member, Consolidated/Vultee Aircraft Co. (1953-1954); Research Chemist, Quality Control Inspector, Consolidated/Vultee Aircraft Co. (1953); Bergermeister Brewery Co., Oakland, CA (1952); Deep Sea Off Shore Drilling Crew Member, California Oil Company, Venice, LA (1950-1951); Shrimp Boat Fisherman, Pass Christian, MS (1949-1950) **CR:** Founding Member, American Air Museum in Britain Campaign, Washington (1993-Present); Trustee, Arizona (1991-Present); Treasurer, World University for Intercultural Studies, Benson, AZ (1991-Present); Instructor, Arizona (1990-Present); Chairman of Computer Science, Instructor, Victor Valley Community College, Victorville, CA (1967-1988); Deputy General, International Biographical Center (1987); Management Information System Consultant, Mojave Water Agency, California (1972-1974); Management Information System Consultant, Pfizer Inc. (1970-1972); Adjunct Professor, Chapman College, Orange, CA, Golden Gate University, San Francisco, CA; Lecturer, College Subjects; Trustee, World University Roundtable, Benson, AZ **CIV:** Donor, Lockheed Aircraft Company (1972); Vietnam Memorial Fund, Washington, DC; American Center for Law and Justice; Judicial Watch; Freedom Watch; Southeastern Legal Foundation; **MIL:** Combat Ready Jet Fighting Pilot, Senior Pilot Rating, 479th Field Maintenance Squadron, U.S. Air Force (1959-1967); U.S.

Air Force Primary Flight Training, Bainbridge, GA, Advance Jet Training, Big Springs, TX, U.S.; Captain, U.S. Air Force, Vietnam (1954-1967); Chief of Maintenance, 476th Tactical Fighter Squadron, U.S. Air Force, DaNang Airbase RV Vietnam, Republic of China, Taiwan (1965); General Aide, 82nd Airborne Divisions, U.S. Army (1964); Parachute Jump School, Fort Benning, GA, Combat Ready Jet Fighting Pilot, Senior Pilot Rating, U.S. Air Force (1961-1962); Advanced Tactical and Nuclear Training Program , Luke Air Force Base, Arizona, Advanced Fighter Weapons School, Las Vegas, NV (1959); VS-871, NAS, Las Alamitos, CA (1953-1954); Photographer, Radar Technician, Plane Captain U.S. Naval Air Reserve Weekend Warrior Program, New Orleans, LA (1950-1954); VF-871, Fashion 871, NAS, Oakland, CA (1951-1953); Plane Captain, NAS, New Orleans, LA (1950-1951); USS Antietam Aircraft Carrier, Pensacola, FL (1949-1950) **CW:** Author, Five Computer Science Texts, IBM (1972-1978); Author, "Design Engineering: Astrophysics, Designed an Intergalactic Space Ship using a Fusion Engine, Unlimited Specific Impulse" (1957) **AW:** Presidential Achievement Award (1982, 1986); Presidential Medal of Merit (1986); Presidential Medal of Merit (1983); Teacher of the Year, VVC (1967); Life Saver Award, Military Forces of Spain (1961); First Place Presenter, Intergalactic Space Ship, Annual Institute of Aeronautical Science Seminar, Los Angeles, CA (1957); Rifle Shooting Award, Expert, M1 Carbine, AFROTC, Davis Monthon AFB (1956); William Randolph Hearst Shooting Award (1951); Excellence in Academic Achievement in Chemistry/Physics, Gulf Coast Military Academy, Biloxi, MS (1951); Small Bore Shooting Award, Expert Marksman, First Place in U.S. Sixth Army Area, (1951); Armed Forces Expeditionary Medal With Bronze Service Star; Joint Services Commendation Medal; Air Force Longevity Service Award With Bronze Oak Leaf Cluster; Air Medal; Vietnamese Service Medal; National Defense Medal; 18 Other U.S. Army, Navy and Air Force Campaigns. **MEM:** Military Officers Association of America (2006-Present); Life Member, National Rifle Association (2000-Present); Division 74, California Teacher Retirement Program (1988-Present); Deputy Director, General International Biographical Center, Cambridge, England (1967-Present); LFIBA American Biological Institute, Raleigh, NC (1967-Present); Founding Member, American Air Museum, England (1991); Chair, Engineering Group, California Educational Computing Consortium (1968-1984); Treasurer, California Business Educational Association (1967-1973); Delta Xi Chapter, Sigma Chi, San Diego State University (1953-1957); President, Treasurer, Student Institute of Aeronautical Science Chapter, San Diego State University (1953-1957); Life Member, Veterans of Foreign Wars; American Legion **MH:** Albert Nelson Marquis Lifetime Achievement Award **B/I:** Mr. Huff was inspired to get involved in his profession due to random happenstance. After earning his honorable discharge from the U.S. Air Force, he was encouraged by a friend to obtain a computer science position at a nearby college. Following this period, he became a teacher. **AV:** Reading; Playing the electric organ, and five string banjo; Studying the cosmos, astronomy and medicine; Tutoring; Donating to animal groups, veterans and medical research; Holistic medicine **PA:** Republican **RE:** Catholic

HUFFINGTON, ARIANNA, T: Founder, Chief Executive Officer, Author **I:** Media & Entertainment **CN:** HuffPost News, Verizon Media, Thrive Global **DOB:** 07/15/1950 **PB:** Athens **SC:** Greece **PT:** Constantine Stassinopoulos; Helen Georgiadis **MS:** Divorced **SPN:** Michael Huffington (04/12/1986, Divorced 1997) **CH:** Christina; Isabella **ED:** MA in Economics, Girton College, University of Cambridge, England (1971) **C:** Syndicated Columnist, Tribune Media Services (1995-Present); Chair, President, Editor-in-Chief, Huffington Post Media Group (Now HuffPost News, Verizon Media), New York, NY (2011-2013); Co-founder, Editor-in-chief, Blogger, Huffington Post (Now HuffPost News, Verizon Media) (2005-2011) **CR:** Board Member, Committee to Protect Journalists; Board Member, The Center for Public Integrity; Board Member, PRISA; Board Member, El Pais **CIV:** Board of Trustees, Archer School for Girls; Board of Directors, A Place Called Home, Los Angeles, CA **CW:** Author, "The Sleep Revolution: Transforming Your Life, One Night at a Time" (2016); Author, "Thrive: The Third Metric to Redefining Success and Creating a Life of Well-Being, Wisdom, and Wonder" (2014); Author, "Third World America: How Our Politicians Are Abandoning the Middle Class and Betraying the American Dream" (2010); Author, "Right is Wrong: How the Lunatic Fringe Hijacked America, Shredded the Constitution, and Made Us All Less Safe" (2008); Author, "On Becoming Fearless:...in Love, Work, and Life" (2006); Author, "Fanatics and Fools: The Game Plan for Winning Back America" (2004); Author, "Pigs at the Trough: How Corporate Greed and Political Corruption are Undermining America" (2003); Author, "How to Overthrow the Government" (2000); Author, "Greetings From the Lincoln Bedroom" (1998); Author, "The Fourth Instinct" (1994); Author, "The Gods of Greece" (1993); Author, "Picasso: Creator and Destroyer" (1988); Author, "Maria Callas: The Woman Behind the Legend" (1981); Author, "After Reason" (1978); Author, "The Female Woman" (1974); Guest Appearances, "Larry King Live," "Oprah," "Nightline," "Inside Politics," "Charlie Rose," "Crossfire," "Hardball," "Good Morning America," "Today Show," "McLaughlin Group," and "the O'Reilly Factor"; Co-host, Nationally Syndicated Public Radio Progressive, "Left, Right & Center" **AW:** Named One of the 100 Most Powerful Women, Forbes Magazine (2010-2014); Pulitzer Prize for National Reporting (Website) (2012); Named One of the 100 Most Influential People in the World, Time Magazine (2006, 2011); Named One of the 50 Most Powerful Women in New York, Crain's New York Business (2011); Named One of the 50 Highest-Earning Political Figures, Newsweek (2010); Named One of the 100 Agents of Change, Rolling Stone Magazine (2009); Rave Renegade Award, WIRED Magazine (2007); Named One of the 50 Most Powerful Women in New York City, New York Post (2007); Named One of the 50 Who Matter Now, Business 2.0 (2007); Webby Award, International Academy of Digital Arts & Sciences (2006)

HUFFMAN, JARED WILLIAM, T: U.S. Representative **I:** Government Administration/Government Relations/Government Services **DOB:** 02/18/1964 **PB:** Independence **SC:** MO/USA **PT:** William Ward Huffman; Phyllis Jean Huffman **MS:** Married **SPN:** Susan E. Musgrove (05/13/1995) **CH:** Abby; Nathan **ED:** JD, School of Law, Boston College, Cum Laude (1990); BA in Political Science, University of California Santa Barbara, Magna Cum Laude (1986) **C:** Member, U.S. House Committee on Natural Resources (2013-Present);Member, U.S. House Budget Committee (2013-Present); U.S. Representative, California's Second Congressional District, Washington, DC (2013-Present); Member, District Six, California State Assembly (2006-2012); Partner, Boyd Huffman Williams & Urla, San Francisco, CA (1992-1996); Associate, McCutchen Doyle Brown & Enersen, San Francisco, CA (1990-1992); Senior Attorney, Natural Resources Defense Council; Partner, The Legal Solutions Group LLP, San Rafael, CA **CR:** Commissioner, Marin County Adult Criminal Justice Commission, San Rafael, CA (1996-Present); Board of Directors, Marin Municipal Water District, Corte Madera, CA **CW:** Contributing Editor, Legal Practice Guide (1995-1996) **AW:** Millennium Leadership Award, Marin Independent Journal and Marin Community Foundation (2000); Three-Time All-American, NCAA Volleyball, University of California Santa Barbara **MEM:** Rotary Club of San Rafael **BAR:** The State Bar of California (1990); United States District Court Northern District of California (1990) **AV:** Playing volleyball, golf, tennis and basketball; Fishing; Winemaking **PA:** Democrat

HUFFMAN, STEVE, "SPEZ", T: Chief Executive Officer **I:** Business Management/Business Services **CN:** Reddit **DOB:** 11/12/1983 **PB:** Warrenton **SC:** VA/USA **ED:** Diploma in Computer Science, University of Virginia (2005) **C:** Chief Executive Officer, Reddit (2015-Present); Owner, Founder, Reddit (2005-2006) **CIV:** Board of Advisers, Center for Technology and Society, Anti-Defamation League **AV:** Ballroom Dancer

HUG, JOYCE E., T: Founder, Director **I:** Religious **CN:** Sacred Waters **C:** Founder, Director, Sacred Waters (2000-Present) **AW:** Honoree, The Best Retreat Center in Mishawaka (2017) **AS:** Ms. Hug attributes her success to her passion for her work. She loves providing people with a place to experience their spiritual journeys, and she was happy to meet a need that was not being previously fulfilled in her community. **B/I:** Ms. Hug thought about starting her business for 20 years, but she never had the funds. She took the opportunity as soon as she was able.

HUGHES, LARRY NEAL, T: Civil and Environmental Engineer, Educator, Consulting Engineer **I:** Engineering **DOB:** 08/19/1941 **PB:** West Plains **SC:** MO/USA **PT:** Wilbur Emerson Hughes; Ruby Bernice (Johnson) Hughes **MS:** Married **SPN:** Carolyn Sue Mason Hughes (03/22/1968) **CH:** John Thomas; Amanda Christine **ED:** MS in Public Health Engineering, University of Hawaii (1967); BSCE, Bradley University (1964) **CT:** Board Certified in Water and Wastewater Engineering, American Academy of Environmental Engineers and Scientists; Certified Class 1 Sewage Treatment Works Operator, State of Illinois; Registered Professional Engineer, States of Florida and Illinois **C:** Retired (2008); Senior Project Manager, Maurer-Stutz, Inc. (2001-2008); Affiliated Instructor, Department of Civil Engineering, Bradley University (1992-2001); Director of Waste Treatment Facilities, Greater Peoria Sanitary District (1970-2001); Assistant District Chemist, Greater Peoria Sanitary District (1976-1970); Civil Engineer, Illinois Department of Transportation (1964-1965) **CR:** Scouting Coordinator, W. D. Boyce Council, Boy Scouts of America (1983-1990); Cubmaster, W. D. Boyce Council, Boy Scouts of America (1981-1983); Roundtable Commissioner Staff, W. D. Boyce Council, Boy Scouts of America (1981-1983); Assistant Cubmaster, W. D. Boyce Council, Boy Scouts of America (1980-1981); President, Jubilee District Explorer Scouts **CIV:** President, Association of Public Health Students, University of Hawaii (1965); Volunteer, Ground Observer Corps; Volunteer, Peoria Illinois Civil Defense; Chairman, Landfill Host Committee for East Peoria, Illinois City Council; Charity Accordion Performances, Illinois Nursing Homes, Retirement Homes, Senior Living Communities, Churches and Elementary Schools **CW:** Contributor, Articles, Professional Journals **AW:** Clarence Klassen Distinguished Service Award for Extraordinary Personnel Service in Water Pollution Control, Illinois Association of Water Pollution Control Operators (2018); Quarter Century Operators Club Award, Water Environment Federation (1992); William D. Hatfield Award, Water Environment Federation (1984, 1987); Operating Award, Central States Water Environment Association (1974); Eagle Scout; Order of the Arrow Brotherhood; Woodbadge Award; Scouters Training Award **MEM:** Commodore, Detweiller Yacht Club (1993-1994); Vice Commodore, Detweiller Yacht Club (1990-1993); Chairman, Water Quality Subcommittee, Illinois Association of Wastewater Agencies (1987-1990); President, Illinois Association of Water-Pollution Control Operators (1986-1987); Lifetime Member, Water Environment Federation; Fellow, American Society of Civil Engineers; Mayflower Descendants; Illinois Water Environment Association; American Academy of Environmental Engineers and Scientists; The Pi Kappa Alpha Fraternity; American Water Works Association **MH:** Albert Nelson Marquis Lifetime Achievement Award **AS:** Mr. Hughes attributes his success to his strong work ethic, honesty and the leadership opportunities he was afforded through the Boy Scouts of America. **B/I:** Mr. Hughes became involved in his profession because he had always wanted to know how things worked and would take things apart and put them back together again. **AV:** Boating; Traveling; Playing and teaching accordion; Modeling historic wooden ships **RE:** Elder, United Presbyterian Church of Peoria

HUIZENGA, WILLIAM, "BILL" PATRICK, T: U.S. Representative from Michigan **I:** Government Administration/Government Relations/Government Services **CN:** U.S. House of Representatives **DOB:** 01/31/1969 **PB:** Zeeland **SC:** MI/USA **MS:** Married **SPN:** Natalie Huizenga **CH:** Five Children **ED:** Bachelor of Arts, Calvin College (1991) **CT:** Real Estate License, State of Michigan **C:** Member, U.S. House of Representatives from Michigan's Second Congressional District, Washington, DC (2011-Present); Member, U.S. House Financial Services Committee, Washington, DC (2011-Present); Member, District 90, Michigan House of Representatives, MI (2003-2009); Director of Public Policy to Representative Pete Hoekstra, U.S. House of Representatives (1996-2002); Co-Chairman, Ottawa County Republican Party (2001); Board Director, Vanderbilt Public School Academy (1998-2001); Board Director, Holland Board of Realtors (1995-1996); Member, Republican Study Committee; Co-owner, Huizenga Gravel Company, Jenison, MI **CIV:** Member, Christian Reformed Church, Zeeland, MI **AW:** Named, Advisor of the Year, Alzheimer's Association, West Michigan Chapter (2000) **MEM:** National Federation of Independent Business **PA:** Republican

HULIN, FRANCES C., T: United States Attorney (Retired) **I:** Law and Legal Services **MS:** Married **SPN:** Charles **CH:** Andrew **ED:** JD, University of Illinois Urbana-Champaign (1971); BA, Northwestern University (1957) **C:** United States Attorney, U.S. Department of Justice (1993-2001); Prosecutor, U.S. Attorney's Office, Central District of Illinois (1978-1993); Assistant State Attorney, Macon County, IL (1977-1978); Assistant State Attorney, Champaign County, IL (1973-1976) **AW:** Distinguished Alumnae **BAR:** Illinois State Bar Association (1973) **MH:** Albert Nelson Marquis Lifetime Achievement Award **B/I:** Ms. Hulin became involved in her profession because of her experiences working in probation.

HULL, BOBBY MARVIN, T: Former Professional Hockey Player **I:** Athletics **DOB:** 01/03/1939 **PB:** Point Anne **SC:** Ontario/Canada **PT:** Robert Edward Hull; Lena (Cook) Hull **MS:** Married **SPN:** Deborah Lynn Wright (08/17/1984); Joanne McKay (1960, Divorced 1980) **CH:** Bobby Abbott; Blake Anthony; Brett Andrew; Bart Alexander; Michelle

C: Ambassador, Chicago Blackhawks, NHL (2007-Present); Left Wing, New York Ranger, NHL (1981); Left Wing, Hartford Whalers, NHL (1979-1980); Left Wing, Winnipeg Jets, NHL (1972-1979); Left Wing, Chicago Blackhawks, NHL (1957-1972) **CR:** Commissioner, World Hockey Association (2003-2004); Member, Team Canada, Canada Cup (1976); Commentator, Hockey Night, Canada; President, Bobby Hull Enterprises; Lecturer, United States and Canada **CW:** Author, "Hockey is My Game" (1967) **AW:** Named One of the 100 Greatest Hockey Players, The Hockey News (1998); Named to Hockey Hall of Fame (1983); Named Officer, Order of Canada (1978); Named Most Valuable Player, World Hockey Association (1973); Named to NHL First All-star Team (1960, 1962, 1964-1970, 1972); Named to NHL Second All-star Team (1963, 1971); Lester Patrick Trophy, NHL (1969); Art Ross Trophy (1960, 1962, 1966); Hart Memorial Trophy (1965, 1966); Lady Byng Memorial Trophy (1965); City of Hope Award (1965); Winner, Chicago Blackhawks, Stanely Cup (1961); Named to Canada Sports Hall of Fame; Named to Ontario Hall of Fame; Inaugural Inductee, World Hockey Association Hall of Fame; Named to Manitoba Sports Hall of Fame

HULL, CHRISTOPHER N., T: State Agency Biologist, Independent Researcher, Writer, Teacher, Conservationist **I:** Sciences **DOB:** 02/25/1953 **PB:** Flint **SC:** MI/USA **PT:** Darwin Hull; Rosemary Hull **ED:** Postgraduate Studies, Lansing Community College, Michigan (1984-1987, 1995); Postgraduate Studies, Michigan State University (1988-1990); MS in Natural Resources, University of Michigan, Ann Arbor, MI (1980); BS in Biology, University of Michigan, Flint, MI (1976) **CT:** Certified Instructor, Numerous Martial Arts; Numerous Others **C:** Water Quality Specialist; Aquatic Biologist; Michigan Department of Natural Resources; Michigan Department of Environmental Quality, Lansing, MI (1984-2010, Retired); Park Ranger, Parks Division, Michigan Department Natural Resources (1974-1983); Adult Education Instructor and Public School Teacher, Flint, Michigan Board of Education (1972-1983); Engineering Aide, Michigan Department of State Highways (1973); Deputy Dog Warden, Genesee Company, Michigan (1971-1972) **CR:** Contributor, USGS Breeding Bird Surveys (1985-2013); Principal Developer of Aquatic Life Protection Criteria, Michigan Water Quality Standards (1996-2010); Contributor, Michigan Frog and Toad Survey (1992-2001); Rotatory, Environmental Assistance Program (1999-2000); Contributor, USFWS and MDNR Kirtland's Warbler Census (1985-1997); Administrator, Statewide Toxins Monitoring Program, Annual Wastewater Report Program (1990-1996); District Biologist, (Conducted Biological Surveys, Permit Reviews, Chemical Evaluations, Fish Contaminant Monitoring, Remedial Action Plans, Grant Reviews) (1986-1990); MDNR/MDEQ Aquatic Biologist, Aquatic Toxicity Testing and Sampling (1984-1985); Conductor of numerous wildlife surveys, including National Audubon Society CBCs (1979); Author, Numerous Government Reports; Independent Instructor, Martial Arts and Self-Defense, Biology, Ecology, Natural History, Ornithology, Conservation, and Related Topics for Numerous Organizations (1973); Independent Researcher and Writer, in Ornithology (Especially Nesting Biology), Natural History, Wildlife, and Conservation Biology; Originator, Curator, Numerous Public and Private Partnership Projects in Wildlife and Endangered Species Conservation with Numerous Organizations, Agencies, and Private Entities; Leading Conservationist, American Chestnut; Licensed Wildlife Rehabilitator, Rescue and Rehabilitation of Domestic Animals and Wildlife **CIV:** Environmental Advocate; Orga-

nizer; Lobbyist **CW:** Contributing Author, "Michigan Breeding Bird Atlas II" (2011); Contributing Author, Regional Coordinator, Michigan Breeding Bird Atlas I (1991); Author, Quarterly Regional Natural History Journal, The Jack Pine Warbler (1987-1990); Author, Numerous Papers, Articles, and Educational Materials; Author, Numerous Books in Press **AW:** Volunteer of the Year, Fenner Nature Center, Lansing, MI (2007); Service Award for Independent Work with Michigan State Parks (1994); Earth Angel Award, Station WKAR-TV (1990); Outstanding Audubon Member Award, Michigan Audubon Society (1989); Commendation, MDNR Director, for Independent Work with the Nongame Wildlife Program (1987); Second Division Award, Flint Science Fair (1970) **MH:** Albert Nelson Marquis Lifetime Achievement Award **AS:** Mr. Hull attributes his success to the strong work ethic his parents and grandparents instilled in him throughout his life. **B/I:** Mr. Hull became involved in his profession because he recalls being "fascinated by nature in all of its forms..." since a child. As he grew older and it was time for him to pursue a career, he had a difficult time choosing between medicine and nature studies with his biology background.

HULL PYLE, JOAN, BSN, T: Director of Emergency Services (Retired) **I:** Medicine & Health Care **CN:** Orange County Government **DOB:** 05/25/1935 **PB:** Langdale **SC:** AL/USA **PT:** Raymond D. Hull; Velma (Solley) Hull **MS:** Married **SPN:** Jerry J. Pyle (08/06/1955) **CH:** Jerry J.; Daniel W.; Ellen Denise **ED:** BSN, The University of Alabama, Tuscaloosa, AL (1958) **CT:** Treatment of Burn Patients; Medical Coding **C:** President, Quality Trac, Orlando, FL (1994); Director of Emergency Medical Services, Orange County, Orlando, FL (1980-1994); Administrative Coordinator, Orlando Health Orlando Regional Medical Center, FL (1970-1980); Director of Nursing Service, Pineview Hospital, Hartselle, AL (1965-1970); Head Nurse, Huntsville Hospital, AL (1962-1965) **CIV:** Director, Christian Women Association (2005-2011); Member, Various Technology Advisory Councils, State of Florida **MEM:** Past President, Florida Association of Emergency Medical Providers; Executive Board, Florida Association of County Emergency Medical Services Directors; Central Florida Fire Chiefs Association (CFFCA); Organizer, Executive Board, Critical Incident Stress Debriefing, FL; Various National Committees, Federal Emergency Management Association (FEMA) **MH:** Albert Nelson Marquis Lifetime Achievement Award **B/I:** Mrs. Pyle became involved in her profession because when she was in the second grade, her brother got sick and they could not find nurses to take care of him. So her mother took turns in the hospital taking care of him and she thought in that moment that becoming a nurse was what she wanted to be. From that moment on, that was her desire, and although she took music classes, she was determined to be a nurse. **RE:** Protestant **THT:** Mrs. Pyle was instrumental in the passing of Florida's first DUI law, seat belt law, and child restrain laws.

HULLET, MICHAEL CRAIG, T: Artist, Designer, Art Researcher **I:** Fine Art **DOB:** 10/13/1953 **PB:** Fort Worth **SC:** TX/USA **PT:** Donna Hullet; Bob (O.W.) Hullet **MS:** Divorced **CH:** Gray Lawrence Hullet; Jack Vincent Hullet **ED:** Postgraduate Coursework, University of Utah (1987); Student, Light Metals Program, Rhode Island School of Design (1983-1984); BFA in Light Metals, University of Utah (1981); Pre-Architecture Coursework, University of Utah (1973-1975) **C:** Consultations and Prototype-Fabrication Services, Industrial Design LLC (2000-Present); Consultations, Provenance Researcher, Fine Art Research Consultants LLC (1999-Present); Independent Industrial Designer and Design Consultant, Salt Lake City, UT (1992-Present); Sculptor, Artist, Designer, Prototype Designer and Model Builder (1975-Present); Provenance Research, Fine Art Research Consultants LLC (2000-2015); 3-D Foundation Curriculum Committee, University of Utah (1994-1999); Art Collections Cataloguing Assistant, Utah and California (1993-1999); Educator, University of Utah (1980-1999); Adjunct Assistant Professor of Art, University of Art (1994-1998); Consultant, Assistant Collection Researcher, Private Art Collections (1992); Technical Consultant, Construction Industry (1992); Instructor, Department of Art, University of Utah (1988-1992); Art Director and Assistant Curator, Salt Lake Art Center, Salt Lake City, UT (1984-1985); Professional Studio Assistant, Numerous Regional and National Art Projects and Installations (1982-1984); Sculpture Studio Assistant, Salt Lake City, UT (1976-1984); Set Designer and Assistant, Bybee Studio, Salt Lake City, UT (1982); Art Director, "Expression Magazine," Contemporary Arts Journal, Salt Lake City, UT (1981-1982); Professional Photographic Studio Assistant, Salt Lake City, UT (1981) **CR:** Research Assistant, Private Art Collections, Los Angeles, CA (1993-2015); Co-Juror, Host, Unofficial Olympic Art Exhibit (2002); Metal Alloys Consultant for Light Speed Sports, Luge Sled Runners, Utah (2002); Invited Speaker, American Society of Interior Designers (ASID) National Conference, Collaborative Projects, Salt Lake City, UT (1996); Invited Juror, Department of Architecture, University of Utah, Salt Lake City, UT (1994); Invited Speaker, American Society of Interior Designers (ASID) National Conference, Industrial Design and Collaborative Projects, Salt Lake City, UT (1988); Lecturer, Design, Visual Arts Consultant; Lecturer, Numerous Lectures **CIV:** Salt Lake Arts Council, Gateway Project (2002); Host, Unofficial Olympic Art Exhibit (2002); Olympic Plan, Salt Lake Neighborhood Activist, District 3 (1995-1997); Guest Juror, Graduate School of Architecture (1996); Invited Juror and Presenter, Department of Architecture, University of Utah (1994); Mayor's Council, Invited Participant, The Role of Public Art Works Utah (1994); State Representative, Participant, Conference on Art in Public Places, Tucson, Arizona (1988); Active, Search and Rescue Groups; Former Participant, Mayor's Counsel **CW:** Featured Artist, Invitational Exhibit, Springville, UT (2001); Featured Artist, Interior Elements, Private Residence, Park City, UT (2000); Artist, Commission, Udvar Hazy School of Business (1994-1996); Artist, Commission, Utah State Tax Commission Headquarters (1994-1996); Artist, Commission, Utah One Center (Gallivan Center) (1993-1995); Featured Artist, Finalists Exhibit, Art in Public Places (1993); Artist, Commission. Utah State Capital, Data Processing (1992-1993); Artist, Private Collection, Hugh Evans, Washington, DC; Artist, Private Collection, Bruce Babbitt, Secretary of the Interior; Featured Artist, Faculty Show, Alvin Gittins Gallery, University of Utah (1992); Featured Artist, Faculty Show, Museum of Fine Arts, Salt Lake City, UT (1991); Featured Artist, 67th Spring Salon (1991); Featured Artist, Faculty Show, Alvin Gittins Gallery, University of Utah (1990); Artist, "ARTluminium", Alcan Aluminum, Montreal, Canada (1989); "Michael Hullet" Solo Exhibit, Gayle Weyher Gallery, Salt Lake City, UT (1988); Artist, "Michael Hullet" Solo Exhibit, MFA Graduate Show, Alvin Gittins Gallery, University of Utah (1987); Artist, "Michael Hullet" Solo Exhibit, Gayle Weyher Gallery, Salt Lake City, UT (1986); Artist, "20/20 Vision", Utah Arts Festival, Salt Lake City, UT (1986); Artist, 'Abstract and Non-Representational Art: A Utah Perspective', Salt Lake Art Center, Salt Lake City, UT (1985); Featured Artist, Group Exhibition, Gayle Weyher Gallery, Salt Lake City, UT

(1985); Artist, "Wearable Art," Salt Lake Art Center, Salt Lake City, UT (1985); "Utah '83", Salt Lake Art Center, Salt Lake City, UT (1983); Artist, "Kristi Krumbach & Michael Hullet", Salt Lake Art Center, Salt Lake City, UT (1982); Artist, "Utah Designer Craftsman Gallery, Group Exhibition", Brigham Young University Extension, Provo, UT (1980); Featured Artist, Group Show, Canyon Gallery, Alta, UT (1979) **AW:** Inductee, Utah's 100 Most Honored Artists (2002); Best of Show, Springville, Museum, Spring Salon, Springville, UT (2002); Nominee, James Beard 5th Annual Restaurant Design Awards, NYC, (1997); Finalist, Public Art Project Competition, Salt Lake City, UT (1992); Award of Merit, Sculpture, Springville Museum of Art (1991); Award of Merit, Graphic Design, American Museum Association (1988); Silver Award, Art Direction, Advertising Federation of Utah (1986); Award of Merit, Industrial Design, Utah Advertising Federation (1984); Intermountain Contractor, Design Award-Restaurant (1984); Award of Merit, Industrial Design, Los Angeles Art Directors Association (1984); Cash Stipend, Department of Light Metals, Rhode Island School of Design (1983); Achievement Award, University of Utah (1980); Merit Scholarship, University of Utah (1979); First Place Award, Art Department Exhibition, Alvin Gittins Gallery, University of Utah (1979); Merit Scholarship, University of Utah (1977-1978) **MEM:** Alta Club (2006-2011); Josie Johnston Memorial (2005); Southern Utah Wilderness Alliance (2001) **AS:** Mr. Hullet attributes his success to his mentors and their sacrifices; his friendships; marathons,; the meaning of one foot at a time; challenges; working at what he enjoyed; and seeking purpose in what he did as it exposed his path and responsibilities. He pursued an idea until he felt they worked or didn't. He didn't force outcomes, as he felt he lost an essential moment to be part of a process whose richness to teach himself, and also valued discovery. He noted that "failure has been a valued teacher, no less than successes." Exploring ideas has taught him patience, and to be relaxed with the unknown and more at ease with processes. He said, "Ideas are static and only a beginning" until he acts. He sees the struggle of a project to be difficult and a source of learning. **B/I:** Mr. Hullet became involved in his profession because, as a person exposed and taught to use one's hands to realize solutions presented by any number of problems and situations, he pursued his conviction to explore experiences that shaped many valued projects with highly successful outcomes. His earliest work was acutely influenced by an Asian philosophy bound to simplicity. Flight and its physical structures influenced his work. He earned a student's license and flew above New England's forests and coastlines.His pieces are partly inspired by shapes capable of flying, particularly with regard to tension and compression systems. Of equal beauty and curiosity were the antiquated structures that populated the agrarian environments he experienced in the Midwest, New England, and in Utah's deserts. He was inspired to appropriate elements from these worlds for use in his work and reassigned their original purposes as they spoke directly about relationships he found compelling. He strived to discover new ways of joining 'parts' together. He owes his desire to design and fabricate joints–largely in reaction to the industrial climate–to self-reliance and isolated cultures of limited resources. He observed how his immediate ancestors solved fundamentally basic and complex challenges. His personal experiences are undoubtedly reflected in his work. **AV:** Bicycling; Traveling; History; Archaeology; Personal and professional discovery through any medium **THT:** Mr. Hullet's art is about ideas; not precious, but about exploring possibilities

through processes which expose the potential of collective 'moments' and locating a balance in all criteria. He looks to his surroundings from contemporary technologies to nature as potential vocabularies to initiate the process of working. By nature, he is attentive to what his environment offers. His world is enriched by simple, dynamic artifacts from small, sensuous bone fragments having a patina pushed to exotic colors by the elements, to irresistible unknown objects that beg to be studied, used, or set on a shelf for investigation. As a sculptor and designer, he is basically an object maker, moving closer toward using symbols and the written word. While he did not serve in the military, he honored the contributions of those who did.

HULT, ALEX, T: Founder **I:** Food & Restaurant Services **CN:** Flights Restaurant Group **DOB:** 11/19/1984 **PB:** Falun **SC:** Sweden **ED:** Degree in Mathematics and Science, Sanda University (2004) **C:** Founder, Chief Executive Officer, Flights Restaurant Group (2017-Present);Restaurant Owner, Hult's Restaurant, Los Gatos, CA (2013-2017) **CIV:** President, Los Gatos Chamber of Commerce; Volunteer, American Cancer Society **AW:** Businessman of the Year, State of California (2017) **AS:** Mr. Hult attributes his success to his professional grit, hard work and positive mind set. **B/I:** Mr. Hult became involved in his profession while growing up in Sweden. He began playing hockey at a young age and ended up playing professionally for a number of years with the NHL team, the San Jose Sharks. Eventually, he was injured and was unable to play anymore so he followed in his mother's footsteps and pursued a career in hospitality.

HUME, RICHARD T., T: Chief Executive Officer **I:** Technology **CN:** Tech Data Corporation **ED:** BS in Accounting and Finance, The Pennsylvania State University (1982) **C:** Chief Executive Officer, Tech Data Corporation, Clearwater, FL (2018-Present); Executive Vice President, Chief Operating Officer, Tech Data Corporation (2016-2018); General Manager, International Business Machines (2008-2016); Chief Operating Officer, Global Technology Services, IBM (1984-2016) **CIV:** Board of Directors, Tech Data Corporation (2018-Present)

HUNGAR, JULIE YEARSLEY, T: Community College Administrator, Educator, Consultant **I:** Education/Educational Services **DOB:** 05/30/1931 **PB:** Bismark **SC:** ND/USA **PT:** Julian Clayton Yearsley; Gertrude (Bang) Yearsley **MS:** Widowed **SPN:** Gordan Earl Hungar (Deceased) **CH:** Ann Steel; Susan Hungar; Thomas Hungar; Paula Hungar **ED:** EdD, Educational Leadership, Seattle University (1982); MA in English Literature, University of Washington (1960); BA in English Literature, University of Washington (1954) **C:** Adjunct Lecturer, Seattle University (1982-1996); Vice Chancellor, Emerita, Seattle Community College (1984-1995); Division Chairman, Seattle Community College (1982-1984); Faculty Member, Seattle Community College (1980-1982); Development Coordinator, Seattle Community College (1978-1980); Faculty Member, Seattle Community College (1972-1977); Traffic, Promotion Director, KCTS-TV, Seattle, WA (1955-1957); News Editor, Traffic Manager, Station KBRC Radio, Mount Vernon, WA (1948-1951) **CR:** Strategic Planning Consultant (1996-2008); Consultant, Mills Consultant Associates, Seattle, WA (1982-1985) **CIV:** Seattle International District Rotary Club (1986-2014); Chairman (2010-2012); Elected Commissioner, Lake Forest Park Water District (2008-2012); President (2002-2004); Founding Board Member, Northwest International Bank, Seattle, WA (1998-2004); President (1993-1994); Vice President, Board of Directors, New Dimensions in Music, Seattle, WA (1968-1971); Founding Chairman, Citizens for Quality Integrated Education, Seattle, WA (1968-1969); Board of Directors, Allied Arts of Seattle (1965-1968); Board of Directors, Concert Chairman, Seattle Symphony Family Concerts (1963-1965) **CW:** Author, "The Wisdom Trail," with Janet Lieberman (2009); Author, "Life After 60? Yes!," with John Morford and Delight Willing (2005); Author, "Road to Equality," with Janet Lieberman (2001); Author, "Transforming Students' Lives," with Janet Lieberman (1998); Moderator, Producer, TV Series, "The Artist Among Us" (1965); Contributor, Chapters, Books; Contributor, Articles, Newspapers **MEM:** Treasurer, Washington C.C. Humanities Association (1984-1986); Washington Association C.C. Administrators; American Association for Women Community Colleges; National Council of Instructional Administrators; Phi Delta Kappa; Phi Beta Kappa **MH:** Albert Nelson Marquis Lifetime Achievement Award **AS:** She attributes her success to the late Janet Lieberman, who was a wonderful mentor and responsible for many women in community colleges achieving success.

HUNT, JOHNELLE TERRIA, T: Transportation Executive **I:** Logistics and Supply Chain **CN:** J.B. Hunt Transport Services **DOB:** 01/04/1932 **PB:** Heber Springs **SC:** AR/USA **MS:** Widowed **SPN:** Johnnie "J.B." Hunt (Deceased 2006) **CH:** Two Children **ED:** Coursework, University of Central Arkansas **C:** Co-Founder, J.B. Hunt Transport Services (1969-Present); Corporate Secretary, J.B. Hunt Transport Services (1969-2008); Credit Manager, J.B. Hunt Transport Services (1969-1986) **CR:** Advisory Council, Susan G. Komen Breast Cancer Foundation Ozark Affiliate; Advisory Board, Bernice Jones Eye Institute **AW:** Named, Forbes 400: Richest Americans (2009); Inductee, Arkansas Business Hall of Fame (2001); Worthen Professor Women of Distinction Award (1992) **MEM:** Washington County United Way; Founding Chairperson, Alexis de Tocqueville Society

HUNTER, DR. RICHARD C., "BUTCH", T: Professor Emeritus of Policy, Organization, and Leadership **I:** Education/Educational Services **CN:** University of Illinois at Urbana-Champaign **PB:** Omaha **SC:** NE/USA **PT:** Lloyd T. Hunter (Deceased); Lillian K. Hunter (Deceased) **MS:** Married **SPN:** Margo J. Hunter **CH:** Steve Jones; Kim Justin; Ricky Hunter; Dicky Clark; Wendell P. Clark; Emily M. Hunter **ED:** Honorary Doctor of Humane Letters, University of Richmond, Richmond, VA; Postdoctoral Coursework, Superintendents' Institute, Vanderbilt University, Nashville, TN; Postdoctoral Coursework, Advanced Studies Program, Vanderbilt University, Nashville, TN; Postdoctoral Coursework, Urban Superintendent's Seminar, University of Tennessee, Knoxville, TN; Postdoctoral Coursework, Superintendents' Work Conference, Columbia University, New York, NY; EdD in School Administration and Policy Planning, University of California Berkeley, Berkeley, CA; MA in Elementary School Administration, San Francisco State University, San Francisco, CA; BS in Elementary Education, University of Omaha (Now University of Nebraska Omaha), Omaha, NE **CT:** State Public School Superintendent of Schools Administrative Credentials, California, Maryland, Ohio, Virginia, Washington; State Public School Administrative Credentials, California, Maryland, Ohio, Virginia, Washington; State Public School Teaching Credentials, California (Life), Maryland, Ohio, Virginia, Washington; State Public Community College Teaching Credential, California (Life) **C:** Professor Emeritus of Educational Policy, Organization, and Leadership, University of Illinois at Urbana-Champaign, Champaign, IL; Professor of

Educational Administration, Educational Policy, Organization, and Leadership Department, University of Illinois at Urbana-Champaign, Champaign, IL; Professor of Educational Leadership, School of Education, University of North Carolina at Chapel Hill, Chapel Hill, NC; Department Head of the Educational Policy, Organization, and Leadership Department, University of Illinois at Urbana-Champaign, Champaign, IL; Program Chair of the Educational Leadership Program at the University of North Carolina at Chapel Hill, Chapel Hill, NC; Director of the Inter-institutional Doctoral Program in School Administration, University of North Carolina System and School of Education, University of North Carolina at Chapel Hill, both in Chapel Hill, NC; Superintendent, Baltimore City Public Schools, Baltimore, MD; Superintendent, Dayton Public Schools, Dayton, OH; Richmond City Public Schools, Richmond, VA; Public School District Assistant and Associate Superintendent, Seattle Public Schools, District #1, Seattle, WA; Public School District Assistant and Associate Superintendent, Richmond City Public Schools, Richmond, VA; Principal of Longfellow Intermediate/ University of California at Berkeley and Berkeley Unified School District, both in Berkeley, CA; Principal of Nystrom Elementary School and Compensatory Education Consultant, Richmond, Unified School District, Richmond, CA; Assistant Principal of Jefferson Elementary School, Berkeley Unified School District, Berkeley, CA; Assistant Project Coordinator of the Educational Park and Other School Desegregation Alternatives, Berkeley Unified School District, Berkeley, CA; Elementary and Secondary School Teacher, Franklin Elementary School, Berkeley Unified School District, Berkeley, CA; Elementary and Secondary School Teacher, Camp Drake Junior High School, Department of the United States Air Force Schools, Tokyo, Japan; Associate Director for Education at the United States Department of Defense Education Activity (DODEA), Arlington, VA; United States Full-time Regular Postal Clerk, Omaha, NE. **CR:** Fulbright Scholar, United States Department of State; Assigned Visiting Scholar, Bahrain Teachers College, University of Bahrain, Kingdom of Bahrain **CIV:** Baltimore College Bound Foundation, Baltimore, MD; Municipal Employees Credit Union, Baltimore, MD; Durham County Board of Education, Durham, NC; Dayton Art Institute, Dayton, OH; Dayton Science Museum, Dayton, OH; Central Virginia Educational Television Station, Richmond, VA; Richmond Renaissance Incorporated, Richmond, VA; Executive Committee of the Richmond Metropolitan Chamber of Commerce, Richmond, VA; Dominion National Bank Advisory Board, Richmond, VA; Public Library Board, Richmond, City of Richmond, VA; Mayor's Correct Census Count Committee, Richmond, VA; Mayor's Administrative Cabinet, Baltimore, MD; Served on Several State Committees Sppointed by two Governors of the Commonwealth of Virginia. **CW:** Editor, Hunter, Richard C., Brown, Frank, and Donahoo, Saran (2012); Editor, School Governance as part of a Book Series, Debating Issues in American Education: A Sage Reference Set, Thousand Oaks, CA; Brown, Frank, Hunter, Richard C., and Donahoo, Saran (2012); Series Editor, Five Book Series, Advances in Educational Administration, Volumes 6-10, Oxford, England, JAI-Elsevier Science (2007, 2006, 2006, 2004, 2003); Donahoo, Saran and Hunter, Richard C., (2007); Editor, No Child Left Behind and other Federal programs for urban school districts, Advances in Educational Administration, Volume 9, Tettegah, Sharon and Hunter, Richard C., (2006); Editor, Education and technology: Issues in applications, policy, and administration, Advances in Educational Administration, Volume 8, Alexander, Kern and Hunter, Richard C.,

(2004); Editor, Administering special education: In pursuit of dignity and autonomy, Advances in Educational Administration, Volume 7, Hunter, Richard C., and Brown, Frank (2003); Editor, Diversity in Public Education, as part of a Book Series, Debating Issues in American Education: A Sage Reference Set, Thousand Oaks, CA: Sage Publications; Hunter, Richard C., and Brown, Frank (1995); Editor, "Privatization in Public Education, Education and Urban Society, Corwin Press, Inc., Thousand Oaks, CA 27(2); Editor, Teaching leaders to lead teachers: Educational administration in the era of constant change, Advances in Educational Administration, Volume 10; Editor, Challenges of urban education and efficacy of school reform, Advances in School Administration, Volume 6; Member, Editorial Board, Journal of Education Finance, Sage Reference Set on Debating Issues in American Educational Administration, School Business Affairs, Education and Urban Society, Advances in Educational Administration, Series Editor for JAI-Elsevier Science, Urban Review, and High School Journal; Author, 28 Chapters, Books; Author, 49 Articals, Refereed Journals and Magazine; Author 4 Eric Documents, 24 Monographs, 57 National and International Conference Presentations; Consultant 25 Educational Organizations; Expert Witness, Several Federal District Court Public School Desegregation Cases **AW:** Fulbright Scholar, United States Department of State for service at Bahrain Teachers College, University of Bahrain, Kingdom of Bahrain; Outstanding Scholarship Award, Southern History Society; Outstanding Service to Education in America Award, National Institute for Education, Washington, D.C.; Outstanding Civilian Service Medal, United States Department of the Army, Washington, D.C.; Distinguished Library Service Award, American Association of School Librarians, Chicago, IL; Good Government Award, Richmond First Club, Richmond, VA; One of the 100 Best and Brightest School Executives in America, IBM Educational Service, Arlington, VA; Selected to the Minority Superintendent Training Program, Rockefeller Foundation, New York, NY; Appointed by Secretary William Cohen to the United States Senior Executive Service Program (SES) as the Associate Director for Educational Services for the Department of Defense Education Activity (DODEA); Appointed by the North Carolina State Department of Education as a Special Education Hearing Review Officer for the State of North Carolina; Selected by Berkeley Unified School District PTA to give testimony to the Select Committee on Equal Educational Opportunity of the United States Senate; Awarded the Honorary Doctor of Humane Letters Degree, University of Richmond, Richmond, VA; Outstanding Service Award, Dayton Human Relations Commission, Dayton, OH **MEM:** American Association of School Administrators (AASA); Illinois Association of School Administrators (IASA); American Education Research Association (AERA); National Alliance of Black School Educators (NABSE); National Association of Elementary School Principals (NAESP); International Association of School Business Officials (IASBO); American Association of School Personnel Administrators (AASPA); Phi Delta Kappa; The Horace Mann Society; Kappa Alpha Psi **MH:** Who's Who in America (2020) **AS:** Dr. Hunter attributes his success to hard work and being mentored by several caring and effective individuals. **B/I:** He became involved in his profession because of his teachers and other educators that were always highly regarded by him for their many contributions to young people. **AV:** International travel to many countries **PA:** Democrat **RE:** Protestant **THT:** Most people want to do good work and left to their devices will do so.

HUNTER, DUNCAN DUANE, T: U.S. Representative, Military Officer **I:** Government Administration/Government Relations/Government Services **DOB:** 12/07/1976 **PB:** San Diego **SC:** CA/USA **PT:** Duncan Lee Hunter; Lynne (Layh) Hunter **MS:** Married **SPN:** Margaret (Jankowski) Hunter **CH:** Duncan; Elizabeth; Sarah **ED:** Diploma, United States Marine Corps Officer Candidate School (2002); BBA, San Diego State University (2001) **C:** U.S. Representative, California's 50th Congressional District, United States Congress (2013-2019); U.S. Representative, California's 52nd Congressional District, United States Congress, Washington, DC (2009-2013); Member, Committee on Foreign Affairs; Member, U.S. House of Representatives Committee on Science, Space and Technology **MIL:** Active Duty, United States Marine Corps Reserve, Afghanistan (2007); Promoted to Captain, United States Marine Corps Reserve (2006); Lieutenant Battery A, First Battalion, 11th Marines, United States Marine Corps Reserve, Fallujah, Iraq (2004); Lieutenant, First Marine Division, United States Marine Corps Reserve, Iraq (2003); Lieutenant, United States Marine Corps Reserve (2002); Former Business Analyst, San Diego, CA **PA:** Republican **RE:** Baptist

HUPPERT, ISABELLE ANNE MADELEINE, T: Actress **I:** Media & Entertainment **DOB:** 03/16/1953 **PB:** Paris **SC:** France **PT:** Raymond Huppert; Annick (Beau) Huppert **MS:** Married **SPN:** Ronald Chammah (1982) **CH:** Lolita; Lorenzo; Angelo **ED:** Coursework, Conservatoire à Rayonnement Régional de Versailles (Conservatory of Versailles); Coursework, Conservatoire National Supérieur D'Art Dramatique; Coursework, Lycée de Saint-Cloud, Ecole Nationale des Langues Orientales Vivantes **CIV:** President, Jury, 62nd Cannes Film Festival (2009) **CW:** Actress, "The Glass Menagerie" (2020); Actress, "Mary Said What She Said" (2019); Actress, "The Mother" (2019); Actress, "Frankie" (2019); Actress, "White as Snow" (2019); Actress, "Golden Youth" (2019); Actress, "The Romanoffs" (2018); Actress, "Eva" (2018); Actress, "The Widow" (2018); Actress, "Une Jeunesse Doree" (2018); Actress, "Barrage" (2017); Actress, "Happy End" (2017); Featured, "I Love Isabelle Huppert" (2017); Actress, "Claire's Camera" (2017); Actress, "Reinventing Marvin" (2017); Actress, "Madame Hyde" (2017); Actress, "False Confessions" (2016); Actress, "Things to Come" (2016); Actress, "Elle" (2016); Actress, "Tout de Suite Maintenant" (2016); Appearance, "Closes Encounters with Vilmos Zsigmond" (2016); Actress, "Souvenir" (2016); Actress, "What Tears Us Apart" (2016); Actress, "Louder Than Bombs" (2015); Actress, "Valley of Love" (2015); Actress, "Macadam Stories" (2015); Actress, "Paris Follies" (2014); Appearance, "Dior and I" (2014); Actress, "Dead Man Down" (2013); Actress, "The Nun" (2013); Appearance, "Michael H - Profession: Director" (2013); Actress, "Tip Top" (2013); Actress, "Abuse of Weakness" (2013); Actress, "The Disappearance of Eleanor Rigby" (2013); Actress, "Captive" (2012); Actress, "Amour" (2012); Actress, "In Another Country" (2012); Actress, "Lines of Wellington" (2012); Actress, "Dormant Beauty" (2012); Actress, "My Little Princess" (2011); Actress, "My Worst Nightmare" (2011); Actress, "Copacabana" (2010); Actress, "Law & Order: Special Victims Unit" (2010); Actress, "Villa Amalia" (2009); Actress, "Home" (2008); Actress, "The Sea Wall" (2008); Actress, "Hidden Love" (2007); Actress, "Private Property" (2006); Actress, "Gabrielee" (2005); Actress, "Me and My Sister" (2004); Actress, "8 Women" (2002); Actress, "Ghost River" (2002); Actress, "Medee" (2001); Featured, "Isabelle Huppert, Une Vie Pour Jouer" (2001); Actress, "La Fausse Suivante" (2000); Actress, "Keep It Quiet" (1999); Actress, "The School of Flesh" (1998); Actress, "The Swindle" (1997); Voice Actress, "Gulliver's Travels" (1996); Actress, "Amateur" (1994); Actress, "La Séparation" (1994); Actress, "Malina" (1991); Actress, "Seobe" (1989); Actress, "Story of Women" (1988); Actress, "Entre Nous" (1983); Actress, "My Best Friend's Girl" (1983); Actress, "Godard's Passion" (1982); Actress, "Coup de Torchon" (1981); Actress, "Loulou" (1980); Actress, "Return to the Beloved" (1979); Actress, "The Lacemaker" (1977); Actress, "No Trifling with Love" (1977); Actress, "The Judge and the Assassin" (1976); Actress, "Serious as Pleasure" (1975); Actress, "The Common Man" (1975); Actress, "Rosebud" (1975); Actress, "The Big Delirium" (1975); Actress, "Successive Slidings of Pleasure" (1974); Actress, "Madame Baptiste" (1974); Actress, "Going Places" (1974); Actress, "Le Drakkar" (1973); Actress, "Faustine et le Bel Été" (1972); Actress, "The Bar at the Crossing" (1972); Actress, "César and Rosalie" (1972); Actress, "Le Prussien" (1971); Actress, Plays, Television Shows, Documentaries and Films **AW:** Honoree, Women in Motion Award, Cannes Film Festival (2017); Golden Globe for Best Picture, Hollywood Foreign Press Association (2017); Prix César for Best Actress (1978, 2017); Named Officier, Légion D'Honneur (2009); Stanislavsky Award (2008); Named Officier, Ordre National du Mérite (2005); Special Career Award, David di Donatello Awards (2003); Named Chevalier, Légion D'Honneur (1999); Named Chevalier, Ordre National du Mérite (1994); David di Donatello Award for Best Foreign Actress (1980); Gold Palm Award for Best Actress, Cannes Film Festival (1978); Prix D'Interpretation, Cannes Film Festival (1978); BAFTA for Most Promising Newcomer to Leading Film Roles (1978); Prix Susanne Bianchetti (1976); Prix Bistingo (1976); Numerous Awards

HURD, JON R., T: Nuclear Physicist **I:** Sciences **DOB:** 07/08/1945 **PB:** Columbus **SC:** OH/USA **PT:** Max Elden Hurd; Mildred Maxine (Baker) Hurd **MS:** Single **ED:** PhD, Florida State University (1979); MSc, Miami University, Ohio (1973); BSc, The Ohio State University (1968) **C:** Project Leader, Los Alamos National Laboratory (1989-Present); Member, Staff, Los Alamos National Laboratory (1984-Present); Research Associate, University of Virginia, Los Alamos, NM (1982-1984); Research Investigator, University of Pennsylvania, Philadelphia, PA (1979-1982) **MIL:** Vietnam Era Veteran; U.S. Army (1969-1971) **CW:** Contributor, Articles, Professional Journals **AW:** Award of Excellence for Significant Contribution to Nuclear Weapons Program Government of U.S. (1986); Army Commendation Medal **MEM:** Writing Committee, American National Standards Institute (1990-1994); American Association Physics Teachers; American Physical Society; Institute Nuclear Materials Management **MH:** Albert Nelson Marquis Lifetime Achievement Award **AS:** He attributes his success to his strong Christian faith, daily reading of the Holy Bible, and passionate love of mathematics and physics. **B/I:** He became a nuclear physicist because he knew that in high school, elementary and junior high school that he wanted to be a scientist. He always had an interest in science and loved to solve math problems. When he got to high school he knew he wanted to be a physicist and took physics at The Ohio State University. **AV:** Music (trumpet and piano); Chess; Bridge **PA:** Republican **RE:** Christian **THT:** The most important things in life are a strong faith, strong loving family with much laughter, good friends, and good health. With these, you can accomplish anything.

HURD, MARK VINCENT, T: Co-Chief Executive Officer **I:** Business Management/Business Services **CN:** Oracle Corporation **DOB:** 01/01/1957 **PB:** New York **SC:** NY/USA **MS:** Married **SPN:** Paula Kalupa **CH:** Kathryn; Kelly **ED:** BBA, Baylor University, Waco, TX (1979) **C:** Co-Chief Executive Officer, Oracle Corporation, Redwood City, CA (2014-Present); President, Oracle Corporation, Redwood City, CA (2010-2014); Chairman, President, Chief Executive Officer, Hewlett-Packard Co., Palo Alto, CA (2006-2010); President, Chief Executive Officer, Hewlett-Packard Co., Palo Alto, CA (2005-2006); President, Chief Executive Officer, NCR Corp., Dayton, OH (2003-2005); President, Chief Operating Officer, NCR Corporation, Dayton, OH (2002-2003); Co-President, NCR Corp., Dayton, OH (2001-2002); Chief Operating Officer, Teradata (2000-2002); Executive Vice President, NCR Corp. (2000-2001); Senior Vice President, Teradata Solutions Group (1998-2000) **CR:** Board of Directors, Oracle Corp. (2010-Present); News Corp. (2008-2010); Hewlett-Packard Co. (2005-2010) **CIV:** Board of Trustees, Dayton Area Chapter, American Red Cross; Board of Visitors, Fuqua School of Business, Duke University **CW:** Co-Author, "The Value Factor: How Global Leaders Use Information" (2004) **AW:** Listee, 25 Most Powerful People in Business, Fortune Magazine (2007); Listee, The 50 Who Matter Now, CNNMoney.com Business 2.0 (2006, 2007) **AV:** Playing tennis

HURD, WILLIAM, "WILL" BALLARD, T: U.S. Representative of Texas **I:** Government Administration/Government Relations/Government Services **DOB:** 08/19/1977 **PB:** San Antonio **SC:** TX/USA **PT:** Robert Hurd; Mary Alice Hurd **ED:** BS in Computer Science, Texas A&M University, College Station, TX (2000) **C:** Member, U.S. House of Representatives from Texas' 23rd Congressional District, United States Congress, Washington, DC (2015-Present); Senior Advisor, FusionX, LLC, San Antonio, Texas (2009-2014); Partner, Crumpton Group LLC, Arlington, VA (2009-2013); Case Officer, Central Intelligence Agency (2000-2009); Committee of Homeland Security, United States Congress; House Permanent Select Committee on Intelligence, United States Congress **CR:** Board Member, World Affairs Council, San Antonio, TX (2014-Present) **PA:** Republican **RE:** Christian

HURNY, BETH, T: Executive Director **I:** Other **CN:** Onondaga Council On Alcoholism Addictions Inc: Prevention Network **MS:** Married **SPN:** John Fricano **CH:** Amanda Salce; Anna Salce **ED:** MSW in Social Work, Syracuse University, New York (1997); BS in Human Services, Cornell University (1990) **C:** Executive Director, Onondaga Council On Alcoholism Addictions Inc: Prevention Network (2014-Present); Director of Youth & Parenting Services, Prevention Network, New York (2007-2014); Director of Evaluation Center, Helio Health (2005-2007); Clinical Supervisor, Family Counselor Services (1999-2005); Temporary Counselor, Family Counselor Services (1995-1999) **CIV:** Member, Community Services Board, Onondaga County; Member, Families Together, New York State; Board Member, Ophelia's Place **AS:** Ms. Hurny attributes her success to her belief in the grace of God. She has had great role models and support throughout her career. Additionally, her two daughters have been an incredible part of her success. Much of her professional success came in their lifetimes and she believes they are the reason. **B/I:** Ms. Hurny became involved in her profession because when she graduated from Cornell University with her degree in Human Services, she started working in the bookstore at Cornell. She was looking for any opportunity to dive in the human service field. She saw an ad for a substance abuse counselor job and decided to give it a shot. She was eventually hired even though she had no experience. She remained in the field ever since. Having battled with an eating disorder herself in the past and overcoming it, she felt that she could identify with the people who were afflicted with addiction. **AV:** Family time

HURT, WILLIAM MCCHORD, T: Actor **I:** Media & Entertainment **DOB:** 03/20/1950 **PB:** Washington, DC **SC:** DC/USA **PT:** Alfred McChord; Claire Isabel (McGill) Hurt; Henry Luce III (Stepfather) **MS:** Divorced **SPN:** Heidi Henderson (03/05/1989, Divorced 08/01/1993); Mary Beth Supinger (12/02/1971, Divorced 12/09/1982) **CH:** Sam; William Jr.; Alexander Devon; Jeanne **ED:** Honorary DFA, Tufts University (2005); Diploma, The Juilliard School (1976); BA in Drama, Tufts University (1972) **CT:** Private Pilot **C:** Joined, Circle Repertory Theatre, New York, NY (1977); Performer, Oregon Shakespeare Festival (1975) **CW:** Actor, "The Last Full Measure" (2019); Actor, "Avengers: Endgame" (2019); Actor, "Avengers: Infinity War" (2018); Actor, "The Miracle Season" (2018); Actor, "Condor" (2018); Actor, "The King's Daughter" (2017); Actor, "Race" (2016); Actor, "The Moon and the Sun" (2016); Actor, "Captain America: Civil War" (2016); Actor, "Beowulf: Return to the Shieldlands" (2016); Actor, "Trial" (2016); Actor, "Beowolf" (2016); Actor, "Goliath" (2016); Actor, "Humans" (2015); Actor, "Winter's Tale" (2014); Actor, "Days and Nights" (2014); Actor, "The Disappearance of Eleanor Rigby: Them" (2014); Actor, "The Host" (2013); Actor, "The Disappearance of Eleanor Rigby: Him" (2013); Actor, "The Disappearance of Eleanor Rigby: Her" (2013); Actor, "Bonnie and Clyde" (2013); Actor, "The Challenger Disaster" (2013); Actor, "Maddened by His Absence" (2012); Actor, "Shadows" (2011); Actor, "Late Bloomers" (2011); Actor, "Hellgate" (2011); Actor, "Too Big to Fail" (2011); Actor, "The River Why" (2010); Actor, "Robin Hood" (2010); Actor, "Damages" (2009); Actor, "End Game" (2009); Actor, "Yellow Hankerchief" (2008); Actor, "Vantage Point" (2008); Actor, "The Incredible Hulk" (2008); Actor, "Mr. Brooks" (2007); Actor, "Into the Wild" (2007); Actor, "Noise" (2007); Voice Actor, Co-producer, "The Legend of the Sasquatch" (2006); Actor, "Beautiful Ohio" (2006); Actor, "The Good Shepherd" (2006); Actor, "A History of Violence" (2005); Actor, "Hunt for Justice" (2005); Actor, "Neverwas" (2005); Actor, "Syriana" (2005); Actor, "Frankenstein" (2004); Actor, "The Blue Butterfly" (2004); Actor, "The Village" (2004); Actor, "The Tulse Luper Suitcases: The Moab Story" (2003); Actor, "Changing Lanes" (2002); Actor, "Nearest to Heaven" (2002); Actor, "Tuck Everlasting" (2002); Actor, "Master Spy: The Robert Hanssen Story" (2002); Actor, "Artificial Intelligence: AI" (2001); Actor, "The Contaminated Man" (2001); Actor, "Rare Birds" (2001); Actor, Riviere-des-Jeremie" (2001); Actor, "The Flamingo Rising" (2001); Actor, "Dune" (2000); Actor, "The Miracle Maker" (2000); Actor, "The Simian Line" (2000); Actor, "The Big Brass Ring" (1999); Actor, "Sunshine" (1999); Actor, "Do Not Disturb" (1999); Actor, "The 4th Floor" (1999); Actor, "Dark City" (1998); Actor, "Lost in Space" (1998); Actor, "One True Thing" (1998); Actor, "Loved" (1997); Actor, "Michael" (1996); Actor, "Jane Eyre" (1996); Actor, "A Couch in New York" (1996); Actor, "Smoke" (1995); Actor, "Trial by Jury" (1994); Actor, "Second Best" (1994); Actor, "Secrets Shared with a Stranger" (1994); Actor, "Mr. Wonderful" (1993); Actor, "The Plague" (1992); Actor, "The Doctor" (1991); Actor, "Until the End of the World" (1991); Actor, "Ivanov" (1991); Actor, "I Love You to Death" (1990); Voice Actor, "Marilyn Hotchkiss' Ballroom Dancing and Charm School" (1990); Actor, "Alice" (1990); Actor, "Beside Herself" (1989); Actor, "Love

Letters" (1989); Narrator, "The Polar Express" (1989); Actor, "The Accidental Tourist" (1988); Actor, "A Time of Destiny" (1988); Actor, "Broadcast News" (1987); Actor, "Children of a Lesser God" (1986); Actor, "Kiss of the Spider Woman" (1985); Actor, "Joan of Arc at the Stake" (1985); Actor, "Hurlyburly" (1984); Actor, "The Big Chill" (1983); Actor, "Gorky Park" (1983); Actor, "The Great Grandson of Jedediah Kohler" (1982); Actor, "Richard II" (1982); Actor, "A Midsummer Night's Dream" (1982); Actor, "Childe Byron" (1981); Actor, "The Diviners" (1981); Actor, "Eyewitness" (1981); Actor, "Body Heat" (1981); Actor, "All the Way Home" (1981); Actor, "Altered States" (1980); Actor, "Hamlet" (1979); Actor, "Mary Stuart" (1979); Actor, "Ulysses in Traction" (1978); Actor, "Verna: United Service Organizations Girl" (1978); Actor, "Lulu" (1978); Actor, "Fifth of July" (1978); Actor, "Henry V" (1977); Actor, "My Life" (1977); Actor, "The Best of Families" (1977) **AW:** New York Film Critics Circle Award for Best Supporting Actor (2005); Award for Best Supporting Actor, Austin Film Critics Association (2005); Award for Best Supporting Actor, Los Angeles Film Critics Association (2005); Award for Best Supporting Actor, North Texas Film Critics Association (2005); Award for Best Supporting Actor, Utah Film Critics Association (2005); First Spencer Tracy Award for Outstanding Screen Performances and Professional Achievement, University of California Los Angeles (1988); Golden Horse Award for Best Foreign Actor (1988); Academy Award for Best Actor, Academy of Motion Picture Arts and Sciences (1985); BAFTA Award for Best Actor (1985); Best Actor Award, Cannes Film Festival (1985); David di Donatello Award for Best Foreign Actor (1985); London Film Critics Circle Award for Actor of the Year (1985); Award for Best Actor, Los Angeles Film Critics Association (1985); Award for Best Actor, National Board of Review (1985)

HUSAIN, NADEEM, T: Medical Director **I:** Medicine & Health Care **CN:** South Mountain Cardiology **CH:** Three Children **ED:** Interventional Cardiology Fellowship, Henry Ford Hospital, Detroit, MI (2008-2009); Cardiology Fellowship, University of South Alabama (2005-2008); MD, Interventional Cardiology Residency, University of South Alabama (1997); Residency, University of South Alabama, Internal Medicine (1995-1997); Internship, University of South Alabama, Internal Medicine (1994-1995); Clinical Research, Children's Hospital, Islamabad, Pakistan (1993-1994); MBBS, Medicine, Surgery, Rawalpindi Medical College, India (1993) **CT:** Level II Certification, Cardiac CT (2008); Cardiology, Board Certified **C:** Medical Director, Owner, South Mountain Cardiology, Tempe, AZ (2012-Present); Interventional Cardiologist, Candler Cardiology, Candler, AZ (2010-2012); Interventional Cardiologist, Branson Heart Center, Branson, MO (2009); Assistant Professor, Medicine, University of South Alabama (2001-2005); Adjunct Assistant Professor, Physician Assistant Studies, University of South Alabama (1999-2005); Primary Care Physician, Family Health Clinic, Mobile County Health Department (1998-2001) **CIV:** Member, Phoenix Chapter, Islamic Circle of North America **CW:** Co-Author, "Pediatric Surgical Problems of the Head & Neck"; Presenter, Numerous Professional Presentations **AW:** Top Cardiologist, Top Doctor Award (2019); Inductee, Leading Physicians of the World (2015); America's Top Cardiologist (2012); Top Cardiologist, Top Doctor (2008); 1st Place, Annual American College of Cardiology, Alabama Chapter (1997); Best Resident Award, University of South Alabama; Young Trainee Award, Southern Societies (1996) **MEM:** American College of Cardiology **AS:** Dr. Husain attributes his success to hard work, lots of persistence, family support,

and luck. **B/I:** Dr. Husain became involved in his profession because he was drawn to cardiology as, to him, it was the most challenging field in the medical profession. **THT:** Dr. Husain lives his life by the motto of "Treat others the way you would like to be treated..."

HUSSAIN, FAISAL ROOMI, T: President, Chief Executive Officer **I:** Business Management/Business Services **CN:** Roomi Group Corporation **PT:** Hafiz Wajid Hussain; Sahira I. Hussain **MS:** Married **SPN:** Iram J. Hussain **CH:** Ibrahim; Iman; Hadi; Asiya; Hayah; Abdul Malik; Hamza; Hana **ED:** MBA in Finance, Harvard University, Cambridge, MA (2020); MBA, C.T. Bauer College of Business, University of Houston, Houston, TX (2009); BBA in Finance, C.T. Bauer College of Business, University of Houston, Houston, TX (2000) **C:** President, Roomi Group Corporation (2014-Present); Chief Executive Officer, Roomi Group Corporation (2011-Present); Vice President, Business Development, Roomi Group Corporation (2002-2008) **CIV:** Forever Foundation; Feeding the Homeless **AW:** Company Award, Top 100 Woodworkers in the World; Company Award for High-End Product and Project Delivery, Architectural Woodwork Institute **MEM:** Architectural Woodwork Institute (AWI); Associated General Contractors of America; American Institute of Architects (AIA) **MH:** Marquis Who's Who Top Professional **B/I:** Mr. Hussain became involved in his profession because he was born into commercial construction. He is a second-generation woodworker by trade with a layer of business acumen to help make decisions in engineering and building high-end woodwork. With the academics to become a doctor or lawyer, Mr. Hussain fell in love with the challenge and beauty of creating and producing tangible products from nothing. After that, he fell in love with the hardworking clients who demanded the best from him. The construction industry is similar to a video game, except it is based on one's own effort. He consistently pushes and "punishes" himself because, as he said, "We live once and I'd rather live to do my best daily. What better way than to enter a world where we have to build the impossible with nothing more than trust?"

HUTCHINSON, LAWRENCE, T: Veterinarian **I:** Medicine & Health Care **DOB:** 07/01/1937 **PB:** Bryn Mawr **SC:** PA/USA **PT:** Hamilton Hutchinson; Eva (Cohee) Hutchinson **MS:** Married **SPN:** Barbara Ann Bryson (08/16/1958) **CH:** Steven; Ben; Laura; Lee; Nathan **ED:** DVM, Cornell University (1962); BS, Pennsylvania State University (1959) **C:** Consultant Veterinarian, State College, PA (2002-Present); Retired (2002); Associate Professor to Professor, Pennsylvania State University, University Park, PA (1976-2002); Private Veterinarian Practice, Honey Brook, PA (1964-1976); Private Veterinarian Practice, Amsterdam, NY (1963-1964); Private Veterinarian Practice, Vergennes, VT (1962-1963) **AW:** Named Veterinarian of the Year, Pennsylvania Veterinary Medical Association (2002); Distinguished Service Award, Pennsylvania Veterinary Medical Association (2002); Distinguished Service Award, American Association of Bovine Practitioners (AABP) (1992); Named Veterinarian of the Year, American Association of Extension Veterinarians (1985) **MEM:** American Association of Bovine Practitioners (AABP) (2000); President, American Association of Bovine Practitioners (AABP) (1999); President, American Association of Extension Veterinarians (1985); President, Pennsylvania Veterinary Medical Association (1985); American Association of Extension Veterinarians; American Association of Bovine Practitioners (AABP);

Pennsylvania Veterinary Medical Association **MH:** Albert Nelson Marquis Lifetime Achievement Award

HUTCHINSON, PETER A., T: Artist **I:** Fine Art **DOB:** 03/04/1930 **SC:** London/England **PT:** Arthur William Woodhams Hutchinson; Linda Mary Woodhams (West) Hutchinson **MS:** Single **C:** Artist **CIV:** Artists Board Studio, Art Center, International Art Foundation, Firenze, Italy (2006-Present); Narrative Art, Galleria P420, Bologna, Italy (2011); Land Art, Ludwig Museum, Koblenz, Germany (2011); Active Fine Arts Work Center, Provincetown, MA (1988-1989, 1979-1985) **CW:** Galerie Blancpain, Geneva, Switzerland (2013); Galerie Bugdahn und Kaimer, Düsseldorf, Germany (2013, 2010, 2007, 2005, 1998); Ends of the Earth (2012); Dreamed Paradises, Arp Museum, Germany (2010); DNA Gallery, Provincetown, MA (1994-2009); Author, "Night Journals" (2008); Freight & Volume Gallery (2008); Museo Banco de Bogota, Columbia (2008); Musee Pompidou, Paris, France (2007); FRAC Limousin, Limoges, France (2006-2007); Author, "Thrown Rope" (2006); Frederieke Taylor Gallery, New York, NY (2005); Torch Gallery, Amsterdam, Netherlands (2005, 1998); Fondacion Joan Miro, Barcelona, Spain (2004); Galerie Blancpain/Stepczynski, Geneva, Switzerland (2004, 2001); Echigo-Tsumari Art, Triennial, Japan (2003); Lance Fung Gallery, New York, NY (2002); Galerie Lucien-Durand, Paris, France (1999); Galerie Helga De Alvear, Madrid, Spain (1998); Kunstverein, Ulm, Germany (1998); Biennale De France, Lyon, France (1998); Galerie Damasquine, Brussels (1997); James Mayor Gallery, London, England (1996); Author, "Dissolving Clouds" (1996); Oneman Show, "Holly Solomon Gallery" (1980-1990); Herter Gallery, Traveling Exhibition, University of Massachusetts (1989); Academy of Art, Berlin, Germany (1988); Venice Biennale, American Pavilion (1980); One-man Show, "John Gibson Gallery," New York, NY (1969-1980); Exhibited, Group Shows, Museum of Modern Art, New York, NY (1969); Journal "2012"; Contributor, Articles, Professional Journals; Contributor, Short Stories, Professional Journals **AW:** Grantee, Krasner-Pollack Foundation (1989); German Academic Exchange Service, Berlin, Germany (1988); Grantee, Adolph and Esther Gottlieb Foundation (1987); Fellow, National Education Association (1974); Fellow, Aspen Center for the Arts (1970-1971) **MH:** Albert Nelson Marquis Lifetime Achievement Award **B/I:** Mr. Hutchinson became involved in art while on vacation in New Orleans, Louisiana. After seeing a lot of beautiful art, he was inspired to enroll in art school and eventually finished at the top of his class. **AV:** Researching botany and history

HUTCHINSON, SCOTT W., T: Director of Tennis **I:** Athletics **CN:** Greater Atlanta Christian School **MS:** Married **SPN:** Kristy **CH:** Davis **ED:** BS in Marketing, Professional Tennis Management, Ferris State University (2003) **CT:** Elite Professional, United States Professional Tennis Association; High Performance/ITF Certified **C:** Director of Tennis, Greater Atlanta Chrisitan School (2017-Present); Head Tennis Professional, TPC Sugarloaf (2004-2016); Assistant Tennis Professional, The Shore and Country Club (2001-2003) **CIV:** Fundraiser, Wounded Warrior Project; Quarterly Volunteer, Hispanic Outreach; Volunteer, Local VA **MEM:** United States Professional Tennis Association; Georgia Professional Tennis Association; United States Tennis Association **AS:** Mr. Hutchinson attributes his success to his hard work and meeting people with similar viewpoints. He is a firm believer in what hard work can achieve. **B/I:** Mr. Hutchinson has a passion for coaching. When he got involved in tennis, his high school coach and

mentor planted the seed. He hopes to always be a coach, as he loves to see athletes find their way to success. **THT:** Mr. Hutchinson's motto is, "You dont get anywhere without hard work and putting the effort in. You have to be willing to go above and beyond if you want to succeed and progress."

HUTCHINSON, WILLIAM, "ASA" ASA II, T: Governor of Arkansas **I:** Government Administration/Government Relations/Government Services **DOB:** 12/3/1950 **PB:** Bentonville **SC:** AR/USA **PT:** John M. Hutchinson; Coral (Mount) Hutchinson **MS:** Married **SPN:** Susan Burrell **CH:** Asa III; Sarah; John; Seth **ED:** Doctor of Jurisprudence, University of Arkansas School of Law (1975); Bachelor of Science in Accounting, Bob Jones University (1972) **C:** Governor, State of Arkansas (2015-Present); Senior Partner, Asa Hutchinson Law Group PLC, Rogers, AR (2008-Present); Founding Partner, Chief Executive Officer, Hutchinson Group LLC, Washington, DC (2005-Present); Partner, Venable LLP, Washington, DC (2005-2006, 2007); Under Secretary for Border and Transportation Security, U.S. Department of Homeland Security, Washington, DC (2003-2005); Administrator, United States Drug Enforcement Administration, U.S. Department of Justice, Washington, DC (2001-2003); Member, Arkansas' Third Congressional District, United States Congress (1996-2001); Partner, Karr & Hutchinson, Fort Smith, AR (1986-1996); United States Attorney, Western District of Arkansas, U.S. Department of Justice (1982-1985); City Attorney, City of Bentonville, AR (1977-1978) **CR:** Board of Directors, The Constitution Project, SAFELINK Corporation (2005-Present); Delegate, White House Conference on Aging (1995); Chairperson, Arkansas State Republican Committee (1990-1995); Conductor, Democracy Workshops, Russia (1994); Fortress International Group Inc.; Pinkerton Government Services; Hexagon U.S. Federal **AW:** Named, One of the Ten Outstanding Young Leaders in Arkansas, Arkansas Jaycees (1986); Civic Star, Director General, Colombian National Police; Named, Orden al Merito Civil Libertador Simon Bolivar by President of Bolivia **MEM:** American Bar Association; National Association of Former United States Attorneys; Benton County Bar Association; Arkansas Bar Association **BAR:** United States Court of Appeals for the Fifth Circuit; United States Court of Appeals for the Eighth Circuit; Supreme Court of the United States; State of Arkansas **PA:** Republican **RE:** Baptist

HUTCHINSON, Y-VONNE, T: Founder, Chief Executive Officer **I:** Business Management/Business Services **CN:** ReadySet **MS:** Married **ED:** JD, Harvard Law School (2007); BFA, Carnegie Mellon University (2003) **C:** Founding Member, Project Include (2016-Present); Chief Executive Officer, ReadySet, Oakland, CA (2015-Present); Interim Chief Operating Officer, Senior Director of Law and Human Rights, La Isla Foundation, Leon, Nicaragua (2012-2015); Outreach Consultant, Broadway Impact (2010-2012); Rule of Law Fellow, International Rescue Committee, Thailand (2008-2009); Researcher, Magna Carta Institute (2008); Consultant, Management Systems International, Afghanistan (2007); Research Consultant, Altai Consulting, Afghanistan (2007); Legal Intern, U.S. Department of State (2006); Research Assistant, UN Institute for Disarmament Research (2005) **CIV:** Advisor, Tech Equity Collaborative (2016-Present); Judge, MIT Inclusive Innovation Challenge (2017-2020) **CW:** Author, "Avoiding the Snowball Effect How to Prevent the Collapse of the On-Demand Economy," Medium (2015); Author, "The Real Cost of Disruption," Medium (2015); Author, "Sickly Sweet: Human Rights Conditions for Sugarcane Workers in Nicaragua," La Isla Foundation (2014); Author,

"Anatomy of a Riot," La Isla Foundation (2013); Author, "Mesoamerican epidemic nephropathy. Report from the First International Research Workshop on MeN," SALTRA (2013); Author, "The Transference of Gender-based Norms in the Law Reform Process: A Reflection on my Work in Thailand," Querelles (2012); Author, "Miral: A Meandering, Uncomplicated Rendering of the Isreali/Palestinian Conflict," Rutgers Humanist (2011) **AW:** Legal Abstract of the Year, American Public Health Association Law Section (2013) **MEM:** International Human Rights and Policy Committees, American Public Health Association (2013-Present); Harvard Law School Institute for Global Law and Policy

HUTNER, MARTIN WOLFF, T: Interior Designer **I:** Fine Art **CN:** Martin Hutner Interiors **DOB:** 01/04/1938 **PB:** New York **SC:** NY/USA **PT:** Edward C. Hutner; Anne Hutner **MS:** Single **ED:** Master of Arts, Pratt Institute (1962); Bachelor of Arts, Queens College (1959) **C:** Founder, Owner, President, Martin Hutner Interiors, New York, NY (1969-Present); Chairman, Instructor, Fine Arts, Sands Point Academy, NY (1963-1969) **CR:** Lecturer and Author, Book Arts **CIV:** President, American Printing History Association (1988-Present); Trustee, Greenwich Village Society for Historical Preservation, New York, NY (1985-Present); Member, Landmarks Preservation Committee Planning Board 2, NY (1975-1996); President, West 9th Street Block Association, New York, NY (1982-1986); Trustee, Jefferson Market Garden **CW:** American Society of Interior Designers Article, The New York Times Company; Contributor, Numerous Publications on the Book Arts **AW:** NY State Senate Proclamation, Martin Hutner Appreciation Day (2017); The Golden Gingko Award, W9 St. BA (2017); Joseph A. Fielder Fellowship Award, NY Club of Printing Craftsmen (2003); 12 Year Board of Trustees Citation, Greenwich Village Society for Historical Preservation **MEM:** American Society of Interior Designers; The Grolier Club of New York; Metropolitan Museum of Art; The Morgan Library and Museum; Association of International Bibliophiles **MH:** Albert Nelson Marquis Lifetime Achievement Award **AS:** Mr. Hutner attributes his success to his interest in all forms of art. **B/I:** Mr. Hutner became involved in his profession because he was born into a family heavily involved in the arts, going all the way back to his maternal grandfather, including uncles and aunts. This includes the current generation. It was definitely not unusual for him to follow the same tradition. He was accepted into LaGuardia High School of the Arts, where his talent and enthusiasm led him to college, with a major in fine arts. He went to graduate school at the Pratt Institute and the Institute of Fine Arts in New York to pursue art history. After being accepted for membership in ASID, the New York Times published an illustrated article about his work, which increased his exposure exponentially. **AV:** Art and book collector

HUYSMAN, FREDERICK J., T: Newspaper Editor **I:** Writing and Editing **DOB:** 11/15/1946 **PB:** Pittsburgh **SC:** PA/USA **PT:** Robert Walter Huysman; Olive Margaret (Jadwin) Huysman **MS:** Married **SPN:** Janet Kritsky Huysman **CH:** Kristy Elizabeth (Huysman) Stoffman **ED:** BA in Journalism, The Ohio State University (1969) **C:** Retired (2012); With, Advertising, Giant Eagle, Inc. (2008-2012); Assistant Managing Editor/Sports, Pittsburgh Post-Gazette (1993-2007); Executive Sports Editor, Pittsburgh Post-Gazette (1987-1993); Assistant City Editor, Pittsburgh Post-Gazette (1982-1987); Reporter, Pittsburgh Post-Gazette (1976-1981);Reporter, The Valley Independent, Monessen, PA (1972-1976) **CR:** Member, Civil Justice Advisory Group, United States District Court for the Western District of Pennsylvania, Pittsburgh, PA (1991-1993) **CIV:** Board Member, Dapper Dan Charities (1987-2007) **MIL:** With, United States Army (1969-1971) **CW:** Author, "Greatest Moments in Penn Sate Football History" (1996); Author, "Greatest Moments in Steelers History" (1996); Author, "The Year the Panthers Roared" (1996) **AW:** Award for Best Investigative Reporting, Associated Press Sports Editors (1990); William A. Schnader Print Media Award, Pennsylvania Bar Association (1981) **MEM:** The Ohio State University Alumni Association; American Rose Society **MH:** Albert Nelson Marquis Lifetime Achievement Award **B/I:** Mr. Huysman has always been interested in writing and newspapers. He liked to read and would read the morning and the evening paper when he was young. He also liked to write because it is hard. He was interested in current events. It was an interesting field and he met a lot of interesting people over the years. **AV:** Golf; Roses; Freelance writing; Running; Enjoying the good life; Reading **PA:** Democrat **RE:** Episcopalian

HYDE-SMITH, CINDY, T: U.S. Senator **I:** Government Administration/Government Relations/Government Services **DOB:** 05/10/1959 **PB:** Brookhaven **SC:** MS/USA **PT:** Luther Hyde; Lorraine Hyde **MS:** Married **SPN:** Michael Smith **CH:** One child **ED:** BA, The University of Southern Mississippi; AA, Copiah-Lincoln Community College **C:** U.S. Senator, State of Mississippi (2018-Present); Commissioner, Mississippi Department of Agriculture and Commerce (2012-2018); Member, District 39, Mississippi State Senate (2000-2012); Congressional Affairs Consultant; Farmer **CR:** Member, Foundation Board, Copiah Lincoln Community College; Member, Mississippi National Guard Legislative Caucus **CIV:** Member, Macedonia Baptist Church **MEM:** Mississippi Cattlemen's Association; Mississippi Wildlife Federation; American Cancer Society, Inc.; NRA **PA:** Republican **RE:** Baptist

HYMAN, JENNIFER, T: Co-founder, Chief Executive Officer **I:** Business Management/Business Services **CN:** Rent the Runway **ED:** MBA, Harvard University, Cambridge, MA (2009); BA in Social Studies, Harvard University, Cambridge, MA (2002) **C:** Co-founder, Chief Executive Officer, Rent the Runway, New York, NY (2008-Present); Director of Business Development, IMG (2006-2007); Senior Manager, Sales, Wedding Channel (2005-2006); Senior Manager, Leisure Program Development, Starwood Hotels & Resorts Worldwide, Inc. (2002-2005) **CIV:** Member, Supervisory Board, Zalando SE (2020-Present); Board Member, Estee Lauder Companies Inc. (2018-Present) **AW:** Named One of the Most Creative People, Fast Company (2018); Named One of the CNBC Disruptor 50 (2015, 2018); Named to the Recode 100 (2017); Mid-Market Rising Star Award, CNBC (2015); Tribeca Film Festival Disruptive Innovation Award (2015); Named One of the 12 Most Disruptive Names in Business, Forbes Magazine (2013); Named One of the 11 People Who are Changing Business, Fortune Trailblazaers (2013); Named One of the 40 Under 40, Fortune Magazine (2012); Named One of the 40 Under 40, Crain's New York Business (2012); Named One of the Top 100 More Influential Women in Technology, Fast Company (2011)

HYTKEN, FRANKLIN HARRIS, T: Lawyer **I:** Law and Legal Services **DOB:** 12/25/1948 **PB:** Memphis **SC:** TN/USA **PT:** Mac E. Hytken; Florence B. Hytken **MS:** Divorced **SPN:** Louise Grace Parks (08/11/1979, Divorced 1999) **CH:** Rachel Lee Hytken **ED:** JD, Northwestern University, Evanston, IL (1972); BA, Northwestern University, Evanston, IL, Cum Laude (1969) **CT:** Certified in Civil Trial Law, Texas Board of Legal Specialization (1987-Present); Certified in Civil Trial Law, National Board of Trial Advocacy (1989-1999) **C:** President, Covesco Fund Management Co., Dallas, Texas (2005-Present); President, Franklin Harris Hytken, Professional Corporation, Dallas, Texas (1983-Present); President, Rhodus, Jones & Hytken, Professional Corporation, Dallas, Texas (1979-1983); Associate, Goins & Underkofler, Dallas, Texas (1977-1979) **CIV:** Chairman, Democratic Legislative District Executive Committee, Dallas, Texas (1984); Chairman, Ethics Committee, Dallas Bar Association **MIL:** Certified Military Judge, United States Department of the Navy (1976); Chief Prosecutor, Camp Foster (Camp Zukeran) (1975); Captain, Chief Defense Counsel, Third Marine Division (1974) **CW:** Author, "Pro-competitive Restraints of Trade" (1972) **AW:** Named Texas Businessman of the Year (2004-2005); Honorary State Chairman for Texas (2004); Named Boss of the Year, Dallas Association of Legal Secretaries (1983-1984) **MEM:** Secretary, Treasurer, North Dallas Bar Association (1985-1986); Chairman, North Dallas Chamber of Commerce (1984-1985); Chairman, Federal Practice Subcommittee, Texas Young Lawyers Association (TYLA) (1980); Founder, Society for Classical Reform Judaism (Now Roots of Reform Judaism); Fellow, Life Member, American Bar Foundation; Life Member, Texas Bar Foundation; Life Member, Dallas Bar Foundation; Dallas Chapter, American Jewish Committee; The American Legion; Business Executives for National Security; Vice President, Director, American Council for Judaism; John G. Tower Center Forum, Southern Methodist University; Dallas Committee on Foreign Relations (DCFR); College of the State Bar of Texas; B'nai B'rith International; North Dallas Chamber of Commerce; Dallas Bar Association **BAR:** Supreme Court of the United States (1978); Texas (1972); United States District Court for the Northern District of Texas; United States District Court for the Southern District of Texas; United States District Court for the Eastern District of Texas; United States District Court for the Western District of Texas; United States Court of Appeals for the Fifth Circuit; United States Court of Appeals for the Eleventh Circuit; United States Tax Court **MH:** Albert Nelson Marquis Lifetime Achievement Award **B/I:** Mr. Hytken became involved in his profession because he had always been interested in law and government. He also had friends of family who were accomplished attorneys. They were people he admired and achieved a lot in the field of law. He wanted to do the same. **AV:** Playing tennis; Golfing; Scuba diving

IACOCCA, LEE, T: Former Automobile Executive **I:** Automotive **DOB:** 10/15/1924 **PB:** Allentown **SC:** PA/USA **PT:** Nicola Iacocca; Antoinette (Perrotto) Iacocca **MS:** Divorced **SPN:** Darrien Earle (1991, Divorced); Peggy Johnson (04/17/1986, Annulled 1987); Mary McCleary (09/29/1956, Deceased 05/16/1983) **CH:** Kathryn Lisa Hentz; Lia Antoinette Nagy **ED:** ME, Princeton University (1946); BS, Lehigh University (1945) **C:** Founder, Olivio Premium Products (2000-2019); Founder, EV Global Motors (1999-2019); Principal, Iacocca Partners (1994-2019); Chairman, Chief Executive Officer, Chrysler Corporation, FCA US LLC, Highland Park, MI (1979-1993); President, Chief Operating Officer, Chrysler Corporation, FCA US LLC, Highland Park, MI (1978-1979); President, Ford Motor Company (1970-1978); With, Ford Motor Company, Dearborn, MI (1946-1978); Executive Vice President, Ford Motor Company (1967-1969); Vice President of Car and Truck Group, Ford Motor Company (1965-1969); General Manager, Ford Motor Company (1960-1965); Vehicle Market Manager, Ford Motor Company (1960); Car Marketing Manager, Ford Motor Company (1957-1960); Truck Market-ing Manager Division Office, Ford Motor Company (1956-1957); District Sales Manager, Ford Motor Company, Washington, DC (1946-1956); Vice President, Ford Motor Company; Successful Member of Field Sales Staff, Various Merchandising and Training Activities, Assistant Director of Sales Manager, Ford Motor Company, Philadelphia, PA; President, Lee Iacocca & Associates, Inc. **CIV:** Founder, The Iacocca Foundation (1984-2019); Chairman The Statue of Liberty-Ellis Island Foundation (1982) **CW:** Co-author with Catherine Whitney, "Where Have All the Leaders Gone?" (2007); Co-author with Sonny Kleinfeld, "Talking Straight" (1988); Actor, "Miami Vice" (1986); Co-author with William Novak, "Iacocca: An Autobiography" (1984) **AW:** S. Roger Horchow Award (1985); Named Portfolio 18th Greatest CEO of All Time; Wallace Memorial Fellow in Engineering, Princeton University **MEM:** NAE; The Tau Beta Pi Association, Inc.; Detroit Athletic Club

IBRAHIM, NUHAD KHALIL, T: Oncologist **I:** Medicine & Health Care **DOB:** 01/10/1954 **SC:** Lebanese Republic **MS:** Married **ED:** MB, ChB, Baghdad Medical College, Iraq (1980); BSc, American University of Beirut, Lebanon (1975) **CT:** Diplomate, American Board of Internal Medicine; Diplomate, Medical Oncology **C:** Professor of Medicine, Assistant Internist, University of Texas MD Anderson Cancer Center, Houston, TX (1995-Present); Fellow in Medical Oncology, University of Texas MD Anderson Cancer Center, Houston, TX (1991-1995); Resident in Internal Medicine, St. Luke's-Roosevelt Hospital, New York, NY (1990-1991); Resident in Internal Medicine, State University of New York Health Science Center, Brooklyn, NY (1988-1990); Attending Medical Oncologist, Lebanese Cancer Center, Byblos, Lebanon (1986-1987); Fellow, Clinical Hematology-Oncology, American University of Beirut Medical Center, Lebanon (1983-1986); Resident in General Surgery, American University of Beirut Medical Center, Lebanon (1981-1983); Surgical Internship, American University of Beirut Medical Center, Lebanon (1980-1981) **CW:** Contributor, Articles, Professional Journals **AW:** Travel Award, American Society of Clinical Oncology (1993); Research Grant Award, MD Anderson Cancer Center (1993) **MH:** Albert Nelson Marquis Lifetime Achievement Award **B/I:** Dr. Nuhad became involved in his profession because of his passion for taking care of his patients. Likewise, he was integral in developing the field and improving the standard of care by exploring new ways of managing patients.

ICAHN, CARL CELIAN, T: 1) Investment Company Executive, 2) Special Adviser to the President (Retired) **I:** Other **CN:** 1) Icahn Enterprises **DOB:** 02/16/1936 **PB:** New York **SC:** NY/USA **PT:** Michael Icahn; Bella (Schnall) Icahn **MS:** Married **SPN:** Gail Golden (1999); Liba Trejbal (1979, Divorced 1999) **CH:** Brett; Michelle Celia **ED:** PhB, Princeton University (1957); Coursework, New York University School of Medicine (Now NYU Grossman School of Medicine) **C:** Chairman, CVR Energy, Inc. (2012-Present); Chairman, Tropicana Entertainment Inc. (2010-Present); Chairman of the Board, XO Communications, LLC (2003-Present); Chairman, Board of Directors, American Railcar Industries, Inc. (1994-Present); Board Chairman, American Property Investors, Inc. (1990-Present); Founder, Icahn Capital, Inc. (1987-Present); Chairman, ACF Industries LLC, St. Charles, MO (1984-Present); Chairman, Board of Directors, Starfire Holding Corporation (1984-Present); Special Adviser, Regulatory Reform, President of the United States (2017); Chairman, Board of Directors, ImClone Systems Inc. (2006-2008); Chairman of the Board, GB Holdings (2000-2007); Chairman,

President, Icahn & Co., New York, NY (1968-2005); President, Stratosphere Corporation, Golden Entertainment (1998-2004); Board Chairman, Maupintour Holdings, LLC (1998-2002); Chairman, President, Chief Executive Officer, Trans World Airlines, Inc., New York, NY (1985-1993); Options Manager, Gruntal & Co. (1964-1968); Options Manager, Tessel, Patrick & Co. (Now Patrick & Co.), New York, NY (1963-1964); Apprentice Broker, Dreyfus Corporation (Now BNY Mellon Securities Corporation), New York, NY (1960-1963) **CR:** Non-Executive Chairman, Federal-Mogul Corporation, Tenneco Inc. (2008-Present); Board of Directors, Federal-Mogul Corporation, Tenneco Inc. (2007-Present); Board of Directors, WCI Communities, Inc. (2007-Present); Board of Directors, WestPoint International, Inc., Lenner Corporation (2005-Present); Board of Directors, Cadus Pharmaceutical Corporation (1993-2010); Board of Directors, Yahoo! Inc. (2008-2009); Founder, Foxfield Thoroughbreds (1985-2004) **CIV:** Founder, Carl C. Icahn Charter Schools, New York, NY; Founder, Icahn House, New York, NY **MIL:** Serviceman, U.S. Army (1960-1961) **AW:** Named, World's Richest People, Forbes Magazine (2007-Present); Named, Forbes 400: Richest Americans (2006-Present); Named, World's Richest People, Business Insider (2019); Named, 100 Most Influential People in the World, TIME Magazine (2014); Named, 50 Most Influential People in Global Finance, Bloomberg Markets (2013-2014); Named, Top 200 Collectors, ARTnews Magazine (2004); First Place, Breeders' Cup Juvenile Fillies (1990); Eclipse Award for Outstanding Two-Year-Old Filly (1990) **AV:** Collecting Old Master and impressionist art **RE:** Jewish

IDLE, JEFFREY, "JEFF" ROBERT, PHD, FRSC, FRSB, FBPHS, T: Director of Systems Pharmacology and Pharmcogenomic, Endowed Professor **I:** Research **CN:** Long Island University **DOB:** 09/17/1950 **PB:** Kendal **SC:** England **PT:** Robert William Idle; Margaret Joyce (Golightly) Idle **MS:** Single **CH:** Nadia Karim **ED:** PhD in Biochemistry, St. Mary's University (1976); BSc in Medicinal Chemistry, University of Hertfordshire, with First Class Honors (1973); BSc in Applied Chemistry, University of Hertfordshire (1972) **CT:** Chartered Scientist; Chartered Chemist; Chartered Biologist **C:** Endowed Professor, Director, Long Island University, Brooklyn, NY (2017-Present); Professor, University of Bern (2009-2017); Professor, Institute of Pharmacology, First Faculty of Medicine, Charles University, Prague, Czech Republic (2004-2009); Professor of Medicine and Molecular Biology, Norwegian University of Science and Technology (1995-2004); Chairman, Department of Pharmacological Sciences, University of Newcastle (1993-1995); Head, School of Clinical Medical Sciences, University of Newcastle (1992-1995); Professor, University of Newcastle, (1988-1995); Reader in Pharmacogenetics, University of London (1985-1988); Wellcome Trust Senior Lecturer, St. Mary's University (1983-1985); Lecturer in Biochemical Pharmacology, St. Mary's University (1976-1983); Lecturer in Biochemistry, St. Mary's University (1976); Research Chemist, Wander Ltd (1972); Technician, Geigy Ltd. (1971) **CR:** Consultant, Laboratory of Metabolism, National Cancer Institute, National Institutes of Health (2001-Present); Visiting Professor, University of Bern (2003-2009); Chief Executive, Genotypic Technology Pvt Ltd (1992-1995) **CW:** Founding Editor, Editor-in-Chief, Pharmacogenetics (1990-1998); Contributor, 350 Articles, Professional Journals **AW:** Research Grants **MEM:** Fellow, Royal Society of Chemistry; Fellow, Royal Society of Biology; Fellow, British Pharmacological Society; American Society for Biochemistry and Molecular Biology; American Chemical Society; Lifetime Member, Hungarian Society of Experimental and Clinical Pharmacology; American Society of Pharmacology and Experimental Therapeutics **AS:** Dr. Idle attributes his success to his hard work, excellent colleagues, serendipity and inspirational mentors. **B/I:** Dr. Idle became involved in his profession because of his lifelong interest in chemistry. He moved towards biology because his father passed away when he was very young. He therefore became interested in disease and the application of chemistry to medicine. **AV:** Listening to music; Studying languages, history and culture; Watching movies **THT:** Dr. Idle believes in personalized medicine because diagnosis and treatment aren't the same for everyone.

IFEDIORA, OKECHUKWU CHIGOZIE, T: Nephrologist; Educator **I:** Medicine & Health Care **DOB:** 03/01/1955 **PB:** Onitsha, Nigeria **SC:** Nigeria **PT:** Jeremiah Chukwudebe; Victoria Nonye (Menyua) Ifediora **MS:** Married **SPN:** Efeti Udaze Ifediora **CH:** Amala; Amaka; Chika; Kosi **ED:** Fellow in Nephrology, Lankenau Hospital (Lankenau Medical Center), Main Line Health, Philadelphia, PA (1990-1992); Resident, Harlem Hospital, New York, NY (1987-1990); Intern, General Hospital, Onitsha, Nigeria (1981-1982); Bachelor of Medicine and Bachelor of Surgery (MBChB), University of Ife (Now Obafemi Awolowo University), Nigeria (1981); BSc, University of Ife (Now Obafemi Awolowo University), Nigeria, with Honors (1978) **CT:** Diplomate, American Board of Internal Medicine; American Board of Nephrology **C:** Consultant, Vice President, Renal Associates, Monroe, LA (1997-Present); Consultant, Nephrology Consultant, Monroe, LA (1992-1997); Medical Officer, Apex Medical Center (Apex Orthopedic Hospital), Apex Specialists, Igbo-Ukwu, Nigeria (1982-1986) **CR:** Adjunct Assistant Clinical Professor, EA Conway Hospital (E.A. Conway Medical Center), Louisiana State University, Monroe, LA (1993-2003) **CIV:** Active participant in various civic, social, and religious activities in the community; Assisting with Healthcare, Medical Services Board, Nigeria, (2003-Present); Committees, Intensive Care Unit Project, Nigeria, (2018-Present); **CW:** Co-author with R.L. Benz, "Renal Papillary Necrosis in a Hemodialysis Patient," Clinical Nephrology (1993); Co-author with Brendan P. Teehan and Miles H. Sigler, "Solute Clearance in Veno-venous Hemodialysis," ASAIO Transactions (1992); Co-author with M.O. Sogbanmu, M.O. and A.E. Caxton-Martins, "Cytochemical Studies of Peripheral Blood Leukocytes in Pregnancy," African Journal of Medicine and Medical Sciences (1989) **AW:** Fellow, American College of Physicians (1996); AMA Physician Recognition Award, American Medical Association (1994); Nigerian National Merit Award for Academic Excellence (1975-1981); Nigerian Medical Association Prize, University of Ife (Now Obafemi Awolowo University), Nigeria **MEM:** Fellow American College of Physicians; American Medical Association; American Society Nephrology; International Society Nephrology; Ouachita Medical Society; National Kidney Foundation; Monroe Chambers of Commerce; Monroe Athletic Club **MH:** Marquis Lifetime Achievement Award **AS:** Dr. Ifediora attributes his success to family upbringing and support, as well as community expectations. These emphasized service to the community and humanity! **B/I:** Dr. Ifediora became involved in his profession because in Nigeria there were only a few professions that commanded respect. People and families were frightened, as success is measured by family and what society thinks about you, not what you think you are. People took pride in what you are, so the respected professions were in medicine, high military ranks, top religious positions, and a top attorney. Growing up, people wanted you to be at the top and Dr. Ifediora was the eldest of his brothers and cousins. Everyone thought he was bright and wanted him to be a physician. In Nigeria, when you step, you are representative of not only yourself, but your family and community. After graduating from medical school as a physician, he knew that had to be a good physician. In order to be at the top, he needed to acquire the best training and that is why he came to the United States. **AV:** Tennis; Golf; Photography; Swimming; Travel; Interests: Improving healthcare in Nigeria (his home state); **PA:** Independent **RE:** Christian **THT:** Dr. Ifediora's motto is, "Give a hand, whenever you can!"

IGE, DAVID YUTAKA, T: Governor of Hawaii **I:** Government Administration/Government Relations/Government Services **DOB:** 01/15/1957 **PB:** Pearl City **SC:** HI/USA **PT:** Tokio Ige; Tsurue Ige **MS:** Married **SPN:** Dawn Ige **CH:** Lauren; Amy; Matthew **ED:** MBA in Decision Sciences, University of Hawai'i at Manoa (1985); BS in Electrical Engineering, University of Hawai?i at Manoa (1979) **C:** Governor, State of Hawaii (2014-Present); Project Manager, Robert A. Ige & Associates Inc. (2003-Present); Member, District 16, Hawaii State Senate (2003-2014); Vice President of Engineering, Net Enterprise Inc. (2001-2002); Member, District 17, Hawaii State Senate (1995-2002); Project Manager, Pihana Pacific LLC (1999-2001); Senior Administrator, Gte-Hawaiian Telephone Co. (Now Hawaiian Telecom) (1981-1999); Member, District 43, Hawaii House of Representatives (1986-1993); Electronics Engineer and Analyst, Pacific Analysis Corporation; Board Director, Pacific Space Center; Vice Chairman, Media, Arts, Science and Technological Committee; Chairman, Intergovernmental Affairs Committee; Member, Commission to Commemorate the 90th Anniversary of Okinawan Immigration; Member, Task Force on Hawaiian Service; Member, Honolulu Finance Center Task Force; Former Chairman, Education Committee **AW:** Named One of University of Hawaii's Top 10 MBA Students, Hawaii Business Magazine (1986) **MEM:** IEEE; Newtown Estate Community Association; Pearl City Community Association; Vice President, Phi Delta Sigma Fraternity, Inc.; Treasurer, Phi Delta Sigma Fraternity, Inc. **PA:** Democrat

ILITCH, MARIAN, T: Co-Founder **I:** Business Management/Business Services **CN:** Little Caesar Enterprises Inc. **DOB:** 01/07/1933 **PB:** Dearborn **SC:** MI/USA **MS:** Widowed **SPN:** Michael Ilitch (1955, Deceased 2017) **CH:** Denise Ilitch-Lites; Ron; Mike Jr.; Lisa Ilitch-Murray; Atanas; Christopher; Carole **C:** Co-Founder, Vice-Chairman, Ilitch Holdings, Inc. (1999-Present); Co-Owner, Secretary-Treasurer, Hockeytown Cafe (1999-Present); Co-Owner, Secretary-Treasurer, Olympia Development LLC (1996-Present); Co-Owner, Secretary-Treasurer, The Second City (1993-Present); Co-Owner, Secretary-Treasurer, Little Foxes Fine Gifts (1992-Present); Co-Owner, Secretary-Treasurer, Detroit Tigers (1992-Present); Co-Owner, Secretary-Treasurer, Fox Theatre (1987-Present); Secretary-Treasurer, Olympia Arenas, Inc. (Olympia Entertainment Inc.) (1982-Present); Co-Owner, Secretary-Treasurer, Detroit Red Wings (1982-Present); Co-Owner, Secretary-Treasurer, Little Caesar International (1959-Present); Co-Owner, Secretary-Treasurer, Champion Foods; Co-Owner, Secretary-Treasurer, Uptown Entertainment; Co-Owner, Secretary-Treasurer, Blue Line Distributing **AW:** National Preservation Honor Award (1990); Pacesetter Award, Roundtable for Women in Foodservice (1988)

ILLIAN-MASQUELETTE, ALICE FONTAINE, T: Owner, Chief Executive Officer, Founder **I:** Medicine & Health Care **DOB:** 05/01/1954 **PB:** Poughkeepsie **SC:** NY/USA **PT:** Marc Francis Fountaine; Dorothy Mae Fountaine **MS:** Married **SPN:** David Simons Masquelette (05/03/2003); Mark Edward Illian (08/17/1974, Divorced) **CH:** Adam Edward (1979); Renee Fountaine (1985) **ED:** MSN in Nursing Administration, Texas Woman's University, Houston, TX (1990); BSN, Texas Woman's University, Houston, TX (1976) **CT:** RN Infusion (1990) **C:** Specialty Infusion Consultant, The Illian Consulting Group, Humble, TX (2015-Present): Nurse Manager, Alternate Branch Manager, Coram Healthcare, Houston, TX (2006-2015); Nursing Supervisor, Option Care, Houston, TX (2004-2006); Per Diem Infusion Nurse Clinician, Coram Healthcare, Houston, TX (2000-2004); President, Executive Director, National Association of Vascular Access Nurses, Draper, UT (1999-2000); Area Director of Nursing, Coram Healthcare, Denver, CO (1994-1999); National Director, Nursing HMSS, Inc., Houston, TX (1993-1994); Consultant, International Operations and Clinical Services, Curaflex Infusion Services, Houston, TX (1988-1993); Head Nurse, Clinical Coordinator, Adolescent Perinatal Program, University of Texas Medical School, Houston, TX (1986-1988); Head Nurse, Neonatal ICU, University Children's Hospital at Hermann, Houston, TX (1980-1985); Head Nurse, Newborn ICU, Jefferson Davis Hospital, Houston, TX; Charge Nurse, Women's Hospital at Texas; Staff Nurse, Women's Hospital at Texas **CR:** Contributing Author, Specialty Texts, Research Publications **CIV:** Fundraiser, American Heart Association; Fundraiser, Leukemia/Lymphoma Society; Local Church Music Ministry **AW:** Recipient, Numerous Awards in Field **MEM:** American Nurses Association; Texas Nurses Association; National Association of Vascular Access Networks; Infusion Nurse Society; Sigma Theta Tau; Omega Rho Alpha; National Association of Neonatal Nurses **MH:** Albert Nelson Marquis Lifetime Achievement Award **B/I:** Ms. Illian-Masquelette initially thought she wanted to be a physical therapist after graduating from high school. However, she quickly discovered it was not the field for her, which led her to discover nursing. In 1970, she began her journey to success as a nursing aide in her local emergency room. In the years that followed, Ms. Illian-Masquelette attended nursing school and got a degree, allowing her to exponentially further her career in the coming years. **AV:** Snow skiing; Running; Gardening **PA:** Independent **RE:** Episcopalian

IMAI, DOROTHY K., PHD, T: Psychotherapist (Retired) **I:** Health, Wellness and Fitness **PB:** Seattle **SC:** WA/USA **PT:** Kunizo Mayeno; Masaye (Kaita) Mayeno **MS:** Divorced **SPN:** William Brent Imai (Divorced) **CH:** W. Brent **ED:** PhD in Psychology, Summit University (1995); MA in Psychology, International College (1983); MA in Art Therapy, Goddard College (1978); BA in Human Services, University of California Los Angeles (1976) **C:** Retired (2013); Private Practice, Los Angeles, CA (1984-2013); Art Therapist, Wise Care Center, Santa Monica, CA (1990-1993); Instructor, Stress Management, Cardiac Therapy Group, YMCA of the USA, Los Angeles, CA (1985-1986); Art Therapist, ARTSreach Program, University of California Los Angeles (1980-1981); Program Director, Art Therapist, Founding Staff, Adult Day Center, Older Persons Information and Counseling Association, Los Angeles, CA (1979-1983); Art Therapist, The Jeffrey Foundation, Los Angeles, CA (1978-1980) **CR:** Art Therapy Exhibit, Rotunda Gallery, Los Angeles City Hall, CA (1992); Guest Speaker, Art Therapy Talks, Kodaira City, Tokyo, Japan (1991); Fellow, UCLA/USC Long-Term Care Gerontology Center (1983) **CIV:** Board of Directors, Westwood Center of the Arts, Los Angeles, CA (1976-1978); Representative,

United Way Welfare Planning Council, Los Angeles, CA (1967-1968); Officer, Mar Vista PTA, Los Angeles, CA (1965-1967); Chairman, Commission on Education, West Los Angeles United Methodist Church (1965-1966) **CW:** Exhibitor, Various Group Shows (1965-1974) **AW:** United Way Art Therapy Grantee (1990) **MEM:** Retired, UCLA Alumni Association (2013); Former Member, American Art Therapy Association; California Association of Marriage and Family Therapists; Cornerstone West Los Angeles, CA **MH:** Albert Nelson Marquis Lifetime Achievement Award **B/I:** Prior to entering her field, Dr. Imai got a divorce from her husband at the time. She wasn't sure what to do next, since she was a stay-at-home mom. Dr. Imai knew she needed to make a living, so she decided to attend the University of California Los Angeles with no specific career direction in mind. She had a love for learning and discovered her interest in psychology. **AV:** Traveling; Reading; Holistic health; Art; Music; Taizhi; Bible studies; Watching Lakers games **PA:** Independent **RE:** Christian

INFANTINO, GIANNI VICENZO, T: President; Sports Association Executive **I:** Athletics **CN:** FIFA **DOB:** 03/23/1970 **PB:** Brig **SC:** Switzerland **MS:** Married **SPN:** Leena Al Ashqar **CH:** Alessia; Sabrina; Shania Serena; Dhalia Nora **ED:** Coursework, University of Fribourg **C:** President, Federation of the International Football Association (FIFA) (2016-Present); General Secretary, Union European Football Associations (UEFA) (2009-2016); Deputy General Secretary and Director, Governance and Legal Affairs Division, Union European Football Associations (UEFA) (2007-2009); Interim Chief Executive Officer, Union European Football Associations (UEFA) (2007); Director, Legal Affairs and Club Licensing, Union European Football Associations (UEFA) (2004-2007); Joined, Union European Football Associations (UEFA), Nyon, Switzerland (2000); Secretary General, University of Neuchâtel International Centre for Sports Studies, Switzerland; Advisor to the Italian, Spanish and Swiss Football Leagues

INHOFE, JAMES, "JIM" MOUNTAIN, T: U.S. Senator **I:** Government Administration/Government Relations/Government Services **DOB:** 11/17/1934 **PB:** Des Moines **SC:** IA/USA **PT:** Perry Inhofe; Blanche Mountain Inhofe **MS:** Married **SPN:** Kay Kirkpatrick **CH:** James; Perry (Deceased); Molly; Katy **ED:** BA, The University of Tulsa (1973) **C:** Ranking Minority Member, U.S. Senate Committee on Environment and Public Works (2007-Present); U.S. Senator, State of Oklahoma (1994-Present); Chairman, Armed Services Committee (2018); Chairman, U.S. Senate Committee on Environment and Public Works (2015-2017); Chairman, U.S. Senate Committee on Environment and Public Works (2003-2007); U.S. Representative, Oklahoma's First Congressional District, United States Congress (1987-1994); Mayor, City of Tulsa, OK (1978-1984); Member, Oklahoma State Senate (1969-1977); Member, Oklahoma House of Representatives (1967-1969); President, Quaker Life Insurance Company **CIV:** Member, Tulsa Area Safety Council; Member, Tulsa Airport Authority **CW:** Author, "The Greatest Hoax: How the Global Warming Conspiracy Threatens Your Future" (2012) **AW:** National Guardian Award, Lincoln House, Heritage Foundation (2002); William S. Lee Award for Leadership, Nuclear Energy Institute (2001); Democracy Award, International Foundation for Electoral Systems (1996); Character and Leadership Award, United States Air Force Academy **MEM:** American Diabetes Association **PA:** Republican **RE:** Presbyterian

INSALACO-DE NIGRIS, ANNA MARIA THERESA, T: Middle School Educator **I:** Education/Educational Services **CN:** Longfellow Middle School **DOB:** 10/18/1947 **PB:** New York **SC:** NY/USA **PT:** Salvatore Insalaco; Rosaria (Colletti) Insalaco **MS:** Married **SPN:** Michael Peter De Nigris (07/12/1969) **CH:** Jenniffer Ann; Tamara Alicia **ED:** Postgraduate Coursework, The University of Virginia (2002); MA in English Linguistics, George Mason University (1988); BA in English and Languages, The City College of New York (1969) **CT:** Endorsement in Administration and Supervision, The University of Virginia (2002); Certified English Secondary Teacher, Virginia **C:** English Teacher, Longfellow Middle School (1994-1995); Teacher, Fairfax County Public Middle Schools (1990-2010); Teacher, English as a Second Language, Hammond Junior High School (Now Francis C. Hammond Middle School), Alexandria, VA (1988-1990); First Grade Teacher, Talent House Private Elementary School, Fairfax, VA (1987-1988); Teacher, Sunrise Acres Elementary School, Las Vegas, NV (1984-1985); English as a Second Language Specialist, Sunset Hills Elementary School, San Diego, CA (1980); Spanish and Core Subjects Teacher, St. John's, Rubidoux, CA (1969-1970) **CR:** Continuing Education, Board of Fairfax County (1998-Present); Steering Committee, Faculty of Advisory Committee, Reach for Tomorrow at Risk Youth (1995-Present); School-based Lead Mentor, Herndon Middle School, Fairfax County Public Schools (1998-2006); World English Speakers Team (2002-2005); Mentor and Teacher for New Teachers, Herndon Middle School, Fairfax County Public Schools (1999-2005); Coach, Krasnow Institute (2000-2004); Program Sponsor, Reach for Tomorrow at Risk Youth (1998-2004); Chair, WATESOL Secondary Interest Group (1999-2001); Co-Chair, WATESOL Secondary Interest Group (1998-1999); English as a Second Language Portfolio Assessment Committee, Virginia Department of Transportation (VDOT) (1993-1998); Human Relations Committee, Virginia Department of Transportation (VDOT) (1990-1996); Chairman for Multicultural Forum, Council for Applied R&D, George Mason University (1990-1994); School Adoption Committee, Virginia Department of Transportation (VDOT) (1991); School-based Member, Minority Achievement in Principals Cabinet, F.C. Hammond Junior High (Now Francis C. Hammond Middle School), Alexandria, VA (1989-1990); Teacher, Adult English as a Second Language, George Mason Junior/Senior High School, Falls Church, VA (1988-1989); Curriculum Advisory Committee for Social Studies with the County, George Mason University **CIV:** Summer Middle School Volunteer Assistant Principal, Longfellow Middle School (2002-2014); Leader, Girl Scouts of the United States of America (1980-1987); The American National Red Cross, Ohio and SC (1971-1973); Volunteer, Family Services, Wright-Patterson Air Force Base, Ohio (1971-1972); Scholarship Chair, Fairfax Education Association **CW:** Creator, Facilitator, World English Speakers Team Progress (2001-2006) **MEM:** Socio-political Concerns of Immigrant Rights Advocate, English as a Second Language Multicultural Convention (1995-Present); President, Italian American Caucus (2000-2004); Vice President, Italian American Caucus (1997-2000); Delegate, Virginia Education Association (1990-2008); Presenter, Facilitator, English as a Second Language Multicultural Convention (1989-2004); Delegate, Virginia Education Association; Delegate, National Education Association; School Representative, Scholarship Chairman, Fairfax Education Association; Virginia Association of Teachers of English (VATE); California Teachers of English as a Second Language; Washington Teachers of English as a Second Language; Teachers of English as a Second Language (TESOL

International Association); National Association of Bilingual Education **MH:** Albert Nelson Marquis Lifetime Achievement Award **AS:** Mrs. Insalaco-De Nigris attributes her success to her parents who always told her she could enter any profession she desired as long as she put her mind to it. Her tenacity and creativity have been an asset to achieve her goals. She is interested in helping others. **B/I:** Mrs. Insalaco-De Nigris wanted to go to a needs school because she was in tune with them, not a school where the students had what they needed. Ms. Insalaco-De Nigris never was a special education teacher, and she never took courses on special education. It just came naturally to her; she was told that by special education teachers in some of the schools where she taught. She always worked off the premise of "How would I want my own children treated?" **AV:** Writing; Reading; Politics; Helping others **RE:** Roman Catholic **THT:** Mrs. Insalaco-De Nigris speaks five languages. She learned Italian from her family, and she also lived in Germany.

INSERRA, BEN ANTHONY, T: Construction Management Company Executive, Consultant **I:** Architecture & Construction **DOB:** 04/05/1937 **PB:** Brooklyn **SC:** NY/USA **PT:** Rosario Inserra; Sylvia (Dovile) Inserra **MS:** Divorced **SPN:** Cecilia Avis Magann (09/26/1964, Divorced 1987) **CH:** Paul; Peter; Mark **ED:** MS, Massachusetts Institute of Technology (1958); BS, Massachusetts Institute of Technology (1957) **CT:** Registered Professional Engineer, New York **C:** Vice President, Director, Construction Management, Schumacher and Forelle, Inc., Great Neck, NY (1978-Present); Project Manager, March Construction Company, Inc., Merrick, NY (1962-1978); Project Administrator, Malan Construction Company, Inc., New York, NY (1960-1962) **CR:** Construction Consultant, Ben Inserra, Bellmore, NY (1991-Present) **CIV:** Volunteer, Cape Cares, Falmouth, MA (1991-Present) **MIL:** 1st Lt., U.S. Army Corps of Engineers (1958-1960) **MEM:** District Deputy, New York State Knights of Columbus (1979-1980); Grand Knight, Bellmore Knights of Columbus (1977-1978); Tau Beta Pi; Chi Epsilon; Sigma Xi **MH:** Albert Nelson Marquis Lifetime Achievement Award **AV:** Playing golf; Music; Playing tennis **PA:** Republican **RE:** Roman Catholic

INSLEE, JAY ROBERT, T: Governor of Washington **I:** Government Administration/Government Relations/Government Services **DOB:** 02/09/1951 **PB:** Seattle **SC:** WA/USA **PT:** Frank E. Inslee; Adele A. (Brown) Inslee **MS:** Married **SPN:** Trudi Anne Inslee (08/27/1972) **CH:** Jack; Connor; Joe **ED:** JD, Willamette University College of Law, Magna Cum Laude (1976); BA in Economics, University of Washington, Seattle, WA (1973); Coursework, Stanford University (1969-1970) **C:** Governor, State of Washington, Olympia, WA (2013-Present); Candidate, Democratic Nominee, 2020 Presidential Election (2019); Member, First Congressional District of Washington State, United States Congress (1999-2012); Regional Director, U.S. Department of Health & Human Services, Seattle, WA (1997-1998); Attorney, Gordon, Thomas, Honeywell, Malanca, Peterson & Daheim (Now Gordon Thomas Honeywell, LLP), Seattle, WA (1995-1996); Member, Fourth Congressional District of Washington State, United States Congress, Washington, DC (1993-1995); Member, District 14, Washington State House of Representatives (1988-1992); Attorney, Peters, Fowler & Inslee, Selah, WA (1976-1992) **CIV:** Charter Member, Hoopaholics, Seattle, WA (1988-Present); Board of Directors, Yakima, WA (1984-1988); Board of Directors, Selah, Washington

School Bond Committee (1980) **CW:** Co-Author, "Apollo's Fire: Igniting America's Clean Energy Economy" (2007) **PA:** Democrat **RE:** Protestant

IRESON, ROGER WILLIAM, ORDAINED MINISTER/GENERAL SECRETARY, T: General Secretary of Higher Education and Ministry **I:** Religious **CN:** The United Methodist Church **DOB:** 06/02/1939 **PB:** Saratoga **SC:** NY/USA **PT:** Orrin Francis Ireson; Elisabeth (Hempel) Ireson **MS:** Married **SPN:** Judith Ann Marsh (08/17/1963) **ED:** DLitt, Africa University, Zimbabwe (2013); Doctor Honoris Causa, Universidad del Centro Educativo Latinoamericano, Argentina (1999); Doctor Honoris Causa, Universidade Metodista de Piracicaba, Brazil (1998); DD, Huntingdon College (1998); Honorary DLitt, Dillard University (1994); Honorary DD, Willamette University (1992); Honorary DLitt, Florida Southern College (1989); Honorary DD, Iowa Wesleyan University (1988); PhD, Manchester University, England, United Kingdom (1974); MDiv, Garrett-Evangelical Theological Seminary (1966); BA, DePauw University (1962) **CT:** Ordained to Ministry, Elder, The United Methodist Church (1966) **C:** Professor of Philosophy and Religion, Martin Methodist College, TN (2001-2018); Professor of Philosophy and Religion, Green Mountain College, VT (2001-2009); General Secretary, Board of Higher Education and Ministry, The United Methodist Church, Nashville, TN (1988-2001); Senior Pastor, St. Timothy United Methodist Church, Detroit, MI (1979-1988); Pastor, St. Paul United Methodist Church, Bloomfield Hills, MI (1975-1979); Associate Pastor, Franklin Community Church, MI (1970-1975) **CR:** Founding President Emeritus, International Association of Methodist Schools, Colleges and Universities (IAMSCU), General Board of Higher Education and Ministry (2005); Trustee, Africa University, Zimbabwe and General Secretary-in-charge of the Development of the Institution (1988-2001); Board Member, Educational & Institutional Insurance Administrators, Inc. (1988-2000); Adjunct Professor of Philosophy and Theology, Vanderbilt University, Nashville, TN (1990-1993); Chairman, Board, Ecumenical Theological Center, MI (1980-1988); Lecturer on Humanities, Lawrence Technological University, Southfield, MI (1977-1987); Assistant Professor of Philosophy and Religion, Marygrove College, Detroit, MI; Member, Economic Club of Detroit (Detroit Economic Club) **CIV:** Trustee, American University, Washington, DC (1990-Present); World Methodist Council (1981-2001); Member, Community Affairs Forum, Detroit, MI (1980-1988); Meharry Medical College, Nashville, TN **CW:** Publication of a Festschrift, "Serving God with Heart and Mind: A Festschrift in Honor of Roger W. Ireson" (2001); Author, "Contrasting Values and Multicultural Society," Papers Presented at the International Conference at Charles University, Prague, Czech Republic (2001); Leading Delegation of Educators to Cuba and North Korea to Develop Programs of Educational Exchange for Students and Faculty (1999-2001); Author, "The Church in Education: Hope for a New Century," Paper Delivered at the Institute of Higher Education (1999); Contributor, Academy Publications; Author, "Education and Mission: A Global Vision," International Conference at University of Piracicaba, Brazil **AW:** Alumni Citation Award, DePauw University (1992); Alumni of the Year Award, Garrett-Evangelical Theological Seminary (1996); Alumni Citation Award, DePauw University (1992); Medallion, Methodist College (1989); Honored by Proclamation, Mayor of Detroit, MI (1989); University Studentship, Manchester University (1967-1969) **MEM:** American Academy of Religion; Society of Biblical Literature; The Oxford Institute of Methodist Theological Studies; Wesley Historical Society; World Meth-

odist Historical Society; Economic Club Detroit (Detroit Economic Club); Detroit Athletic Club **MH:** Albert Nelson Marquis Lifetime Achievement Award **B/I:** Dr. Ireson became involved in his profession because it was something he was always attracted to from his early studies at DePauw University where he majored in history and philosophy. He studied under great people and also spent a year at University of Cambridge in Manchester and met people all over the world who were of great inspiration. Later on, he became a great asset because he could call anywhere and get help with the projects they were promoting. **RE:** Christian - United Methodist

IRVING, DONALD J., T: University Dean **I:** Education/Educational Services **DOB:** 05/03/1933 **PB:** Arlington **SC:** MA/USA **SPN:** Jewel P. Irving **CH:** Kevin William; Todd Lawrence **ED:** EdD, Columbia University Teachers College (1963); MA, Columbia University Teachers College (1956); BA, Massachusetts College of Art (1955) **C:** Dean, Full Professor Faculty Fine Arts, University of Arizona, Tucson, AZ (1982-1990); Director, School Art Institute, Chicago, IL (1969-1982); Chairman, Art Department, Director, Peabody Museum of Art, George Peabody College of Teachers, Nashville, TN (1967-1969); Professor, Art, Dean, Moore College of Art, Philadelphia, PA (1963-1967); Instructor, Art, State University of New York at Oneonta (1960-1962); Teacher, Art, White Plains High School (1958-1960) **CR:** U.S. Delegate, Conference, National Society of Education Through Art, Prague, Czechoslovakia (1966); Consultant, Educational Television Series, "Art Now," WRCV-TV, Philadelphia, PA **CIV:** Merit Commission of Santa Cruz County (2012-Present); Volunteer, Civil Mediator, Sonoita Justice Court (2010-2019); Board of Directors, Arizonans for Cultural Development (1985-1990); President, Arizona Alliance for Arts in Education (1985-1987) **MIL:** U.S. Army (1957-1958) **CW:** Author, "Sculpture Material and Process" (1970); Contributor, Articles in Field, Professional Journals **MEM:** Director, Chairman, Indiana Arts Commission (1972-1982); Treasurer, Director, National Association Schools Art (1975-1977); Director, Federation of Illinois Colleges and Universities; National Art Education Association (1966-1968); Council, Manager, Eastern Arts Association (1964-1966); National Association of Land Grant Colleges and Universities; Director, National Council of Art Administrators; National Council of Arts in Education; International Society of Education Through Art; College Art Association; Phi Delta Kappa **MH:** Albert Nelson Marquis Lifetime Achievement Award **B/I:** Dr. Irving has always been interested in the visual arts. In elementary school, he was an artist. In high school, he played football and his coach was also his art teacher, which only further inspired his interests in the visual arts.

IRVING, KYRIE ANDREW, T: Professional Basketball Player **I:** Athletics **CN:** Brooklyn Nets **DOB:** 03/23/1992 **PB:** Melbourne **SC:** VIC/Australia **PT:** Drederick Irving; Elizabeth Irving (Deceased); Shetellia Irving (Stepmother) **MS:** Single **CH:** Azurie Elizabeth **ED:** Coursework, Duke University, Durham, NC (2010-2011); Student, St. Patrick High School Academy, Elizabeth, NJ; Student, Montclair Kimberley Academy, Montclair, NJ **C:** Professional Basketball Player, Brooklyn Nets (2019-Present); Professional Basketball Player, Boston Celtics (2017-2019); Professional Basketball Player, Cleveland Cavaliers (2011-2017) **CR:** Spokesman, Nike (2017-Present); Launched, PSD Underwear Collection (2015) **CIV:** Supporter, Standing Rock Indian Reservation **CW:** Actor, "Uncle Drew" (2018); Guest Appearance, "Family Guy" (2018); Guest Appearance, "We Bare Bears" (2016); Actor, Pepsi Max Advertisements (2012); Guest Appearance, "Kickin' It" (2012) **AW:** Six-Time NBA All-Star (2013-2015, 2017-2019); Best Team ESPY Award (2016); Gold Medal, Summer Olympics (2016); NBA Champion (2016); NBA All-Star Game MVP (2014); Gold Medal, FIBA Basketball World Cup (2014); USA Basketball Male Athlete of the Year (2014); FIBA Basketball World Cup MVP (2014); NBA Three-Point Contest Champion (2013); NBA Rookie of the Year (2012); Rising Stars Challenge MVP (2012); McDonald's All-American (2010); Nike Hoop Summit All-American (2010); Jordan Brand High School All-American (2010); First-Team Parade All-American (2010) **AV:** Reading; Singing; Dancing; Baritone saxophone

IRWIN, LINDY, PMA®-CPT, RN, T: Studio Owner **I:** Health, Wellness and Fitness **CN:** Authentic Pilates of Austin **PB:** St. Petersburg **SC:** FL/USA **MS:** Single **CH:** 1 Son **ED:** Bachelor of Science in Nursing, Registerd Nurse, Baylor University (2010); Bachelor of Fine Arts in Ballet, Texas Christian University (2000) **CT:** The Syllabus, MeJo Wiggin (2018); Advanced Teacher Training Bridge Program, The Pilates Center (2012); Master's Program, The Pilates Center, Amy Alpers & Rachel Segel Boulder, CO (2007); PilateSystem® Classical Comprehensive Program, Colleen Glenn, Dallas, TX (2002); Active Registered Nurse, TX; Pilates Method Alliance®-Certified, Pilates Teacher **C:** Pilates Studio Owner, Certified Pilates Instructor, Authentic Pilates of Austin (2018-Present); Pilates Instructor, Pilates Connection (2011-2013); Registered Nurse, Baylor Heart and Vascular Hospital (2011-2012); Pilates Instructor, Goodbody Wellness (2002-2007) **MEM:** Pilates Method Alliance **AS:** Ms. Irwin attributes her success to her compassion and willingness to listen to other people. **B/I:** Ms. Irwin was first exposed to pilates as a method for supplementary conditioning and rehab through ballet. She also entered the field of nursing in order to learn about different body systems. In this capacity, she learned about vascular surgery and pilates on her off days.

ISAACSON, WALTER, T: Professor of American History, Journalist, Historian **I:** Education/Educational Services **CN:** Tulane University **DOB:** 05/20/1952 **PB:** New Orleans **SC:** LA/USA **PT:** Irwin Isaacson; Betty Lee (Seff) Isaacson **MS:** Married **SPN:** Cathy Wright Isaacson **CH:** Betsy Isaacson **ED:** Diploma in History and Literature, Harvard University (1974); Diploma, Pembroke College, University of Oxford, First Class Honors **C:** Professor of History, Tulane University (2018); Advisory Partner, Perella Weinberg Partners (2018); President, The Aspen Institute (2003-2018); Chairman, Chief Executive Officer, Cable Network News (2001-2003); Editor, TIME Magazine (1996-2001); National Editor, Editor, Political Correspondent, New Media, TIME Magazine (1978-1996); With, New Orleans Times-Picayune; With, The Sunday Times, London, United Kingdom **CR:** Editor-at-Large, Senior Advisor, Arcadia Publishing (2019-Present) **CIV:** Co-chair, LaToya Cantrell Transition Team (2018); Member, New Orleans City Planning Commission (2016); Board Member, My Brother's Keeper Alliance (2015); Co-chair, New Orleans Tricentennial Commission (2014); Chairman, Broadcasting Board of Governors (2009-2012); Vice Chairperson, Louisiana Recovery Authority (2005); Chairperson, U.S.-Palestinian Partnership; Vice Chair, Partner for a New Beginning; Co-chair, U.S.-Vietnamese Dialogue on Agent Orange; Member, Innovation Advisory Board, U.S. Department of Defense; Chairperson Emeritus, Board, Teach for America; Board Member, United Airlines; Board Member, Tulane University; Board Member, The New Orleans Advocate/Times-Picayune; Board Member, New Schools New Orleans;

Board Member, Bloomberg Philanthropies; Board Member, Rockefeller Foundation; Board Member, Carnegie Institution for Science and the Society of American Historians **CW:** Co-host, "Amanpour & Company" (2018-Present); Host, "Trailblazers" (2017); Author, "Leonardo da Vinci" (2017); Author, "The Innovators: How a Group of Inventors, Hackers, Geniuses, and Geeks Created the Digital Revolution" (2014); Author, "Steve Jobs" (2011); Editor, "Profiles in Leadership: Historians on the Elusive Quality of Greatness" (2010); Author, "American Sketches" (2009); Author, "Einstein: His Life and Universe" (2007); Author, "Benjamin Franklin: An American Life" (2003); Author, "Kissinger: A Biography" (1992); Co-author, with Evan Thomas, "The Wise Men: Six Friends and the World They Made" (1986); Author, Books **AW:** Nichols-Chancellor's Medal, Vanderbilt University (2015); Jefferson Lecture, National Endowment for the Humanities (2014); Benjamin Franklin Medal, Royal Society of Arts (2013); Named, One of the Most Influential People in the World, TIME Magazine (2012); Gerald Loeb Award (2012); Rhodes Scholar **MEM:** Honorary Fellow, Pembroke College, University of Oxford; Fellow, Royal Society of Arts; American Academy of Arts & Sciences; American Philosophical Society

ISAKSON, JOHN, "JOHNNY" HARDY, T: U.S. Senator from Georgia (Retired) **I:** Government Administration/Government Relations/Government Services **DOB:** 12/28/1944 **PB:** Atlanta **SC:** GA/USA **PT:** Edwin Andrew Isakson; Julia (Baker) Isakson **MS:** Married **SPN:** Dianne (Davison) Isakson **CH:** John; Kevin; Julie **ED:** BBA, University of Georgia (1966) **C:** U.S. Senator, State of Georgia (2005-2019); Chairman, Senate Committee on Veterans' Affairs (2015-2019); Chairman, Senate Committee on Ethics (2015-2019); Vice Chairman, U.S. Senate Select Committee on Ethics (2009-2019); Member, U.S. House of Representatives from Georgia's Sixth Congressional District, United States Congress, Washington, DC (1999-2005); Member, Georgia State Senate (1994-1996); Republican Leader, Georgia House of Representatives (1983-1990); Member, Georgia House of Representatives (1976-1990) **CR:** Chairman, Georgia State Board of Education (1996-1999); Chief Executive Officer, Fairgreen Capital LP, Atlanta, GA (1996-1999); President, Northside Realty, Atlanta, GA (1979-1998) **CIV:** Sunday School Teacher, Mount Zion Methodist Church (1978-Present); Republican Primary Candidate for U.S. Senate (1996); Republican Candidate for Governor of Georgia (1990); Representative, Cobb County, GA; Advisory Board, Federal National Mortgage Association; Board of Trustees, Kennesaw State University; Board of Directors, The Georgia Club; Board of Directors, Metro Atlanta Chamber of Commerce; Board of Directors, Georgia Chamber of Commerce; Board of Directors, Riverside Bank, Salisbury Bank and Trust Company **MIL:** Staff Sergeant, SSG, Georgia Air National Guard (1967-1972); With, United States Air Force (1966-1967) **AW:** Blue Key Award, University of Georgia (1998); Best Legislator in America Award, Republican National Committee (1989); Tax Fighter Award, National Tax Limitation Committee; Hero of Taxpayers Award, Americans for Tax Reform; Guardian Small Business Award, National Federation of Independent Business; Distinguished Service Award, Georgia Municipal Association **MEM:** President, The Realty Alliance; Executive Committee, National Association of REALTORS; Sigma Alpha Epsilon Fraternity **PA:** Republican **RE:** Methodist

IVEY, KAY ELLEN, T: Governor of Alabama **I:** Government Administration/Government Relations/Government Services **DOB:** 10/15/1944 **PB:**

Camden **SC:** AL/USA **PT:** Boadman Nettles Ivey; Barbara Elizabeth Ivey **MS:** Divorced **ED:** BS, Auburn University (1967) **CT:** Certificate in Strategic Leadership for State Executives, Duke University (1989); Certificate in Marketing, University of Colorado (1975); Certificate in Banking, University of South Alabama **C:** Governor, State of Alabama (2017-Present); Lieutenant Governor, State of Alabama (2011-2017); Treasurer, State of Alabama (2003-2011); Director of Government Affairs, Alabama Commission on Higher Education (ACHE) (1985-1998); Executive Vice President, St. Margaret's Hospital Foundation (1982-1985); Reading Clerk, Alabama House of Representatives (1981-1982); Cabinet Officer, Office of the Governor, State of Alabama, Montgomery, AL (1979-1981); Assistant Vice President, Merchants National Bank, Mobile, AL (1970-1979); Teacher, Coach for Forensics, Rio Linda High School, CA (1968-1969) **CR:** Owner, Consultant, Ivey Enterprises, Montgomery, AL (1982-Present); Speaker in Field **CIV:** Secretary, Alabama Division, American Cancer Society, Inc. (1985-Present); Board of Directors, Alabama Girls State School (1983-1985); Member, Advisory Board, Raymond J. Harbert College of Business, Auburn University (1980-1983); Candidate, Alabama State Auditor (1982); Stetson Hoedown Rodeo Queen's Pageant, Montgomery, AL; Montgomery YMCA; Board of Trustees, Sheriff's Boys and Girls Ranches; Charter Trustee, Alabama Banking School **CW:** Editor, St. Margaret's Hospital Heart Tabloid (1983); Editor, Audio-Visual Presentation, "What Price Freedom" (1976) **AW:** Distinguished Citizen Award, Alpha Gamma Delta (1986); Award of Excellence for "What Price Freedom" (1976); Paul Harris Award, Montgomery Rotary Club **MEM:** State Chairman, National Society Daughters of the American Revolution (NSDAR) (1985-1986); Board of Directors, Public Relations Council of Alabama (1976-1982); Industrial Developers of Alabama; Young Men's Business League; Pub. Relations Council Alabama; National Society Daughters of the American Revolution (NSDAR); Past President, Alabama Young Bankers; Chairman, Education Committee, Alabama Bankers Association; Consultant, Alabama Bankers Association; Alabama Forestry Association; President, Alpha Gamma Delta; Director, Montgomery Rotary Club; Alabama Young Bankers; Alabama Bankers Association; Alpha Gamma Delta; Montgomery Rotary Club; Honorary Member, Homemakers of America; Future Farmers of America, National FFA Organization; Student Government Association **AV:** Horseback riding; Public speaking **PA:** Republican **RE:** Presbyterian

IZZO, THOMAS, T: College Basketball Coach **I:** Athletics **CN:** Michigan State University **DOB:** 01/30/1955 **PB:** Iron Mountain **SC:** MI/USA **MS:** Married **SPN:** Lupe Marinez (1992) **CH:** Raquel; Steven (Adopted) **ED:** Diploma, Northern Michigan University (1977); Honorary Diploma, Michigan State University; Honorary Diploma, Northern Michigan University **C:** Head Basketball Coach, Michigan State University Spartans, East Lansing, MI (1995-Present); Assistant Coach, Michigan State University Spartans, East Lansing, MI (1986-1995); Assistant Coach, Recruiting Coordinator, University of Tulsa Golden Hurricane (1986); Assistant Coach, Michigan State University Spartans, East Lansing, MI (1983-1986); Assistant Coach, Northern Michigan University Wildcats (1979-1983); Head Coach, Ishpeming High School, MI (1977-1979) **CR:** Head Coach, USA Pan American Games (2003); Assistant Coach, Goodwill Games (2001) **CIV:** Participant, Coach, Operation Hardwood (2005, 2006); Active Member, Coaches Vs. Cancer, American Cancer Society Inc.; Active Member, Catholic Social Services/St. Vincent Home for Children, Lansing, MI; Active Member, Sparrow Hospital, Sparrow Health System **AW:** Inductee, Naismith Memorial Basketball Hall of Fame (2016); Inductee, Basketball Coaches Association of Michigan (2016); Named, District V Coach of the Year, U.S. Basketball Coaches Association (2012); Dean Smith Award (2016); Named, Big 10 Conference Coach of the Year (2009, 2012); Named Division I Coach of the Year, National Association of Basketball Coaches (2001, 2012); Clair Bee Award (2005); Named, District XI Coach of the Year (1999, 2001); Winner, As Head Coach, Michigan State University Spartans, NCCA Men's Basketball National Championship (2000); Named, National Coach of the Year, Basketball News (1998); Named, National Coach of the Year, U.S. Basketball Writers' Association (1998); Named, National Coach of the Year, The Associated Press (1998); Inductee, Upper Peninsula Hall of Fame (1998); Henry Iba Award (1998); Named, Big 10 Coach of the Year (1998); Inductee, Northern Michigan University Hall of Fame (1990)

JACKLIN, KATHLEEN B., T: Archivist I: Education/Educational Services **DOB:** 11/17/1924 **PB:** Sayre **SC:** PA/USA **PT:** William Russell Jacklin; Hazel Marian (Kunzman) Jacklin **MS:** Single **ED:** MA, Cornell University (1958); AB, Elmira College (1950) **C:** Retired Archivist, Olin Library, Cornell University (1990); Archivist, Department of Manuscripts & University Archives, Olin Library, Cornell University, Ithaca, NY (1969-1990); Associate Curator and Archivist, Department of Manuscripts & University Archives, Olin Library, Cornell University, Ithaca, NY (1958-1969); Assistant Curator, Department of Manuscripts & University Archives, Olin Library, Cornell University, Ithaca, NY (1952-1958) **CW:** Editor, "Report of the Curator and Archivist" (1959, 1974); Author, Entries for Encyclopedias **MEM:** Former Member, Society of American Archivists (SAA); Former Member, American Historical Association; American Association of State and Local History (AASLH); International Council Archives; DeWitt Historical Society Tompkins County (Now The History Center in Tompkin County); Cornell Women's Club; Historic Ithaca **MH:** Albert Nelson Marquis Lifetime Achievement Award **AV:** Reading; Travel; Movies; Plays; Photography **PA:** Democrat **RE:** Methodist

JACKMAN, HUGH MICHAEL, T: Actor I: Media & Entertainment **DOB:** 10/12/1968 **PB:** Sydney **SC:** New South Wales/Australia **PT:** Christopher John Jackman; Grace McNeil (Greenwood) Jackman **MS:** Married **SPN:** Deborra-Lee Furness (04/11/1996) **CH:** Oscar Maximilian; Ava Eliot **ED:** Graduate Coursework, Western Australian Academy of Performing Arts (1994); BA in Journalism, University of Technology, Sydney, Australia (1991); Coursework, Actors' Centre, Sydney, Australia **C:** Owner, Laughing Man Coffee Company, New York, NY (2011-Present); Actor (1994-Present); Co-Founder, Seed Productions, Australia; Co-Founder, Seed Productions, Los Angeles, CA **CR:** Teacher, Physical Education, Uppingham School, England, United Kingdom **CIV:** Global Advisor, Global Poverty Project, Inc.; Fundraiser, Broadway Cares/Equity Fights AIDS **CW:** Actor, "Bad Education" (2019); Actor, "Missing Link" (2019); Actor, "The Man. The Music. The Show." (2019); Actor, "The Front Runner" (2018); Actor, "Logan" (2017); Actor, "The Greatest Showman" (2017); Actor "X-Men: Apocalypse" (2016); Actor, "Broadway 4D" (2016); Actor, "Eddie the Eagle" (2016); Actor, "Pan" (2015); Actor, "An Evening with Hugh Jackman" (2015); Actor, "Broadway to Oz" (2015); Actor, "Chappie" (2015); Actor, "The River" (2014-2015); Appearance, "WWE Raw" (2011, 2014); Host, Tony Awards (2003, 2004, 2005, 2014); Actor, "X-Men:

Days of Future Past" (2014); Appearance, "The Wolverine" (2013); Appearance, "Top Gear" (2013); Host, "Christmas in Washington" (2013); Actor, "Movie 43" (2013); Actor, "Prisoners" (2013); Actor, "Les Misérables" (2012); Voice Actor, "Rise of the Guardians" (2012); Actor, "Hugh Jackman: Back on Broadway" (2011-2012); Actor, "Snow Flower and the Secret Fan" (2011); Actor, "Butter" (2011); Host, "Saturday Night Live" (2011); Actor, "Real Steel" (2011); Appearance, "Sesame Street" (2010); Actor, "X-Men Origins: Wolverine" (2009); Host, 81st Academy Awards (2009); Actor, "A Steady Rain" (2009); Actor, "Uncle Jonny" (2008); Actor, "Australia" (2008); Actor, Producer, "Deception" (2008); Actor, "Viva Laughlin" (2007); Actor, "The Fountain" (2006); Actor, "X-Men: The Last Stand" (2006); Actor, "Scoop" (2006); Actor, "The Prestige" (2006); Voice Actor, "Flushed Away" (2006); Actor, "Happy Feet" (2006); Actor, "Van Helsing" (2004); Actor, "X2" (2003); Actor, "The Boy from Oz" (2003); Actor, "Standing Room Only" (2002); Actor, "Carousel" (2002); Actor, "Someone Like You" (2001); Actor, "Swordfish" (2001); Actor, "Kate & Leopold" (2001); Actor, "X-Men" (2000); Actor, "Oklahoma!" (1999); Actor, "Paperback Hero" (1999); Actor, "Erskineville Kings" (1999); Actor, "Hey Mr. Producer" (1998); Actor, "Halifax F.P.: Afraid of the Dark" (1998); Actor, "Beauty and the Beast" (1995); Actor, "Correlli" (1995); Actor, "Snowy River: The McGregor Saga" (1993); Actor, Performer, Plays, Musicals, Television Shows and Films **AW:** Grammy Award (as Producer) for Best Compilation Soundtrack for Visual Medial, The Recording Academy (2019); Golden Globe Award for Best Performance by an Actor in a Motion Picture-Comedy or Musical, Hollywood Foreign Press Association (2013); Star, Hollywood Walk of Fame (2012); Special Tony Award, Actors' Equity Association (2012); Favorite Action Star, People's Choice Awards (2010, 2012); Teen Choice Award for Choice Movie Actor: Action Adventure (2009); Sexiest Man Alive, People Magazine (2008); Emmy Award for Outstanding Individual Performance in a Variety or Musical Program, Academy of Motion Picture Arts and Sciences (2005); Tony Award for Best Actor in a Musical (2004); Drama Desk Award for Best Actor in a Musical (2004); Numerous Awards

JACKOBOICE, SANDRA KAY, T: Artist I: Fine Art **DOB:** 07/22/1936 **PB:** Detroit **SC:** MI/USA **PT:** Virgil Ellsworth; Lucille Elizabeth LeSeur **MS:** Widowed **SPN:** Edward James Jackoboice (01/11/1958) **CH:** Edward Michael Jackoboice; Timothy Jon Jackoboice **ED:** BA, Aquinas College, Grand Rapids, MI (1989) **C:** Owner, Color Plus Studio, Naples, FL (1983-Present); Art Program Director, the Franciscan Life Process Center in Lowell, Michigan (1990-1999); Wardrobe Consultant, Steketees, Grand Rapids, MI (1980-1982); Co-owner, Fashion Plate, Grand Rapids, MI (1975-1979) **CR:** Instructor, Pastel, Institute Ave. Maria University, Sub Pastel Class Students (2010); Frederik Meijer Gardens, Grand Rapids, MI (2006); Art League Fort Myers, FL (2003-2005); Art League, Marco Island, FL (2003-2006); Von Liebig Center Arts, Naples, FL (2001-2006) **CIV:** Board of Directors, United Arts Council of Collier County (2006-Present); Board of Directors, Arts Council of Greater Grand Rapids (1997-2000); Member, Grand Rapids Parking Commission (1993-1996); Member, Downtown Management Board, Grand Rapids, MI (1993-1996); Member, Junior League, Grand Rapids (1962-1996) **CW:** Solo Exhibitor, Sweet Art Gallery, The Englishman Gallery (2014); Exhibitor, Group Show, Philharmonic Center of Arts, Naples, FL (2008-2011); Featured in New Art Internet.- 2 Page Art (2008); Solo Exhibitor, Terryberry Gallery, Grand Rapids, MI (1997-2007);

Solo Exhibitor, Collier County Library, Naples, FL (2006); Solo Exhibitor, Betten Imports Gallery (2005-2006); Featured in Artists' Photo Reference Book, Pastel Artist International Magazine, Pastel Journal, The Ultimate Guide to Painting from Photographs (2005); Solo Exhibitor, Frederick Meijer Gardens (1998); Solo Exhibitor, FMB, Lowell (1993, 1995); Solo Exhibitor, City Hall, Bielsko-Biala, Poland (1995); Exhibitor, Group Shows, Botanical Images Exhibition, Lansing, MI, Ave Maria University, Florida, Artist Alliance Group Shows; Exhibitor, Permanent Collections, Aquinas College, Grand Rapids, MI, Ave Maria University, Florida, Florida State Capital, Tallahasee **AW:** Awards for Art Work **MEM:** Co-founder, Great Lakes Pastel Society; Signature Member, Pastel Society of America (2004-Present); Board of Directors, International Association of Pastel Societies (2003-Present); Publicity Chair, Membership Chair, International Association of Pastel Societies (2001-Present); Advisor, Board of Directors, Great Lakes Pastel Society (2001-Present); Vice President, International Association of Pastel Societies (2005-2007); President, Great Lakes Pastel Society (1997-2001); Naples Florida League Club; Grand Valley Artists; Artists Alliance; Life Member, Southwest Florida Pastel Society **MH:** Albert Nelson Marquis Lifetime Achievement Award **B/I:** Ms. Jackoboice became involved in her profession because her dad was a commercial artist for a while and she would play around with the things that he was using. He was always drawing or painting for commercial art magazines and her mother was not an artist but she could draw, however, she never pursued it as a career. She majored in art in high school and became very involved in pastels. **AV:** Travel; Art; Tennis; Golf **RE:** Republican

JACKSON, CHRIS, T: Publisher, Editor-in-Chief I: Writing and Editing **CN:** Random House **PB:** Harlem **SC:** NY/USA **ED:** Coursework, Columbia University; Diploma, Hunter College High School **C:** Head, One World, Random House (2016-Present); Executive Editor, Spiegel and Grau (2006-2016)

JACKSON, CURTIS, "50 CENT" JAMES III, T: Rap Artist; Actor; Entrepreneur I: Media & Entertainment **DOB:** 07/06/1976 **PB:** Queens **SC:** NY/USA **PT:** Curtis Jackson Jr.; Sabrina Jackson **CH:** Marquise; Sire **C:** Chief Executive Officer, Founder, SMS Audio; Founder, SK Energy; Chief Executive Officer, Founder, SMS Promotions; Owner, Sire Spirits **CIV:** Founder, G-Unity Foundation, Inc. **CW:** Executive Producer, "Power" (2014-Present); Actor, "For Life" (2020); Actor, "Escape Plan: The Extractors" (2019); Actor, "Den of Thieves" (2018); Actor, "Escape Plan 2: Hades" (2018); Actor, "The Pursuit" (2017); Appearance, "Popstar: Never Stop Never Stopping" (2016); Rap Artist, "Street King Immortal" (2015); Actor, "Southpaw" (2015); Actor, Producer, "The Frozen Ground" (2013); Actor, "Escape Plan" (2013); Actor, "Vengeance" (2013); Actor, Producer, "Freelancers" (2012); Actor, Producer, Writer, "All Things Fall Apart" (2011); Actor, Producer, "Setup" (2011); Actor, "Twelve" (2010); Actor, "Morning Glory" (2010); Actor, Executive Producer, "Caught in the Crossfire" (2010); Rap Artist, "Before I Self-Destruct" (2009); Author, "The 50th Law" (2009); Actor, "Righteous Kill" (2008); Rap Artist, "Curtis" (2007); Actor, "Get Rich or Die Tryin'" (2005); Author, Autobiography, "From Pieces to Weight: Once Upon a Time in Southside Queens" (2005); Rap Artist, "The Massacre" (2005); Rap Artist, "Get Rich or Die Tryin'" (2003); Rap Artist, "24 Shots" (2003); Rap Artist with G-Unit, "Beg for Mercy" (2003); Rap Artist, "In Da Club" (2003); Rap Artist, "Wanksta" (2002); Rap Artist, "Guess Who's Back?" (2002); Rap Artist,

"Power of the Dollar" (2000); Rap Artist, "How to Rob" (1999); Appearances, Television Shows, Video Games, Films **AW:** Grammy Award with Eminem and Dr. Dre for Best Rap Performance by a Duo or Group, The Recording Academy (2010); Named One of the 100 Most Powerful Celebrities, Forbes.com (2008); Award for Best Rap/Hip-Hop Artist, World Music Awards (2007); Awards for Best Male Pop Artist, Artist of the Year, Hip-Hop Artist of the Year, Rap Artist of the Year, Album of the Year, Hot 100 Artist of the Year, Top 200 Album of the Year, Billboard Music Awards (2005); Award for Favorite Rap Album, American Music Awards (2005); Award for Top R&B/Hip-Hop Song, Rap Song, Pop Songwriter of the Year, ASCAP (2004); Award for Best Group, BET Awards (2004); Awards for Best New Artist, Best Male Hip-Hop Artist, BET Awards (2003); Awards for Best Artist of the Year, Best New Artist, Best R&B Act, Best Hip-Hop Act, Best Pop Act, World Music Awards (2003); Numerous Awards

JACKSON, JESSE LOUIS, T: Civil Rights Activist; Clergyman **I:** Nonprofit & Philanthropy **CN:** RainbowPUSH **DOB:** 10/08/1941 **PB:** Greenville **SC:** SC/USA **PT:** Noah Louis Robinson; Charles Henry (Stepfather); Helen (Burns) Jackson **MS:** Married **SPN:** Jacqueline Lavinia Brown (12/31/1962) **CH:** Santita; Jesse Louis Jr.; Jonathan Luther; Yusef DuBois; Jacqueline Lavinia; Ashley **ED:** Honorary Doctorate, University of Edinburgh (2015); Honorary MDiv, Chicago Theological Seminary (2000); Honorary Doctorate, University of the District of Columbia; Honorary Doctorate, Georgetown University; Honorary Doctorate, Howard University; Honorary Doctorate, University of Rhode Island; Honorary Doctorate, Oral Roberts University; Honorary Doctorate, Oberlin University; Honorary Doctorate, Pepperdine University; Honorary Doctorate, North Carolina A&T State University; Coursework, Chicago Theological Seminary (1964-1966); BA in Sociology and Economics, N.C. A&T State University (1964); Coursework, University of Illinois (1959-1960) **CT:** Ordained to Ministry, Baptist Church (1968) **C:** Founder, The Wall St. Project (1997-Present); Founder, National President, Rainbow/Push Coalition, Inc. (Now RainbowPUSH), Chicago, IL (1996-Present); Special Envoy of the President and Secretary of State for the Promotion of Democracy in Africa, U.S. Department of State, Washington, DC (1997-2000); Shadow Senator, District of Columbia, United States Senate, Washington, DC (1991-1996); Founder, National President, National Rainbow Coalition Inc., Chicago, IL (1984-1996); Founder, PUSH-Excel and PUSH for Economic Justice (1977-1996); Founder, Executive Director, Operation PUSH (People United to Serve Humanity), Chicago, IL (1971-1996); Founder, Citizenship Education Fund (1984); National Director, Operation Breadbasket Project, Southern Christian Leadership Conference (1967-1971); Chicago Director, Operation Breadbasket Project, Southern Christian Leadership Conference, Chicago, IL (1966-1967) **CR:** Candidate, Democratic Nominee, United States Presidential Election (1983-1984, 1987-1988); Lecturer, Professor, High Schools and Colleges, United States and Europe **CIV:** Coalition for United Community Action (1969) **CW:** Appearance, Documentary, "The Nine Lives of Marion Barry" (2009); Host, "Both Sides with Jesse Jackson," CNN (1992-2000); Author, "It's About the Money: How You Can Get Out of Debt, Build Wealth, and Achieve Your Financial Dreams!" (1999); Co-Author (with Jesse L. Jackson Jr.), "Legal Lynching: Racism, Injustice, and the Death Penalty" (1996); Author, "Keep Hope Alive" (1989); Author, "Straight from the Heart" (1987) **AW:** Named to the Power 150, Ebony Magazine (2008); Honorary Fellowship, Edge Hill University

(2008); Named One of the Six New Leaders on the Rise, U.S. News World Report (2006); Named One of the 100 Most Influential Black Americans, Ebony Magazine (2006); Presidential Medal of Freedom, The White House (2000); Golden Doves for Peace, Italian Research Institute Archive Disarmo (1999); James Madison Award for Distinguished Public Service, American Whig-Cliosophic Society (1991); Spingarn Medal, NAACP (1989); Named Third Most Admired Man in America, Gallup Poll (1985); Jefferson Award for Greatest Public Service Benefiting the Disadvantaged (1979); Humanitarian Father of the Year Award, National Father's Day Committee (1971); Presidential Award, National Medical Association (1969)

JACKSON, MICHAEL J., T: Chairperson, Chief Executive Officer **I:** Automotive **CN:** AutoNation **C:** Chairperson, Chief Executive Officer, AutoNation Inc., Fort Lauderdale, FL (1999-Present); President, Chief Executive Officer, North America, Mercedes-Benz USA Inc.; Senior Marketing Executive, Mercedes-Benz USA Inc.; District Manager, Mercedes-Benz North America; Managing Partner, Euro Motorcars, Bethesda, MD; Technician, Mercedes-Benz Dealership, Cherry Hill, NJ **CR:** Chairperson, Board of Directors, Atlanta Federal Reserve Bank; Director, Fort Lauderdale Museum of Art **AW:** Listee, Fifty Visionary Dealers, Automotive News (2009); Inductee, Wayne Huizenga School of Business Entrepreneur Hall of Fame (2006); Jackson CEO of the Year, South Florida CEO Magazine (2006); Inductee, Automobile Hall of Fame (2003); Named, Automotive Industry Leader of Year (2003); All-Star Dealer Award, Sports Illustrated (1990); Two-time Member, Automotive Executives Dream Team, Automotive News; Four-time Listee, Marketing 100, Advertising Age

JACKSON, O'SHEA, "ICE CUBE", T: Rap Artist; Actor **I:** Media & Entertainment **DOB:** 06/15/1969 **PB:** Los Angeles **SC:** CA/USA **PT:** Hosea Jackson; Doris Jackson **MS:** Married **SPN:** Kim Woodruff (04/26/1992) **CH:** O'Shea Jr.; Darryl; Kereema; Shareef **ED:** Coursework, Phoenix Institute of Technology **C:** Solo Rap Artist (1990-Present); Founder, Lench Mob Records, Los Angeles, CA (1990-Present); Rapper, N.W.A. (1986-1989); Rapper, C.I.A. (1986) **CR:** Founder, CubeVision Production Company (1998-Present) **CW:** Actor, Producer, "The High Note" (2020); Actor, "Last Friday" (2018); Actor, "xXx: Return of Xander Cage" (2017); Actor, "Fist Fight" (2017); Actor, Producer, "Ride Along 2" (2016); Actor, Producer, "Barbershop: The Next Cut" (2016); Actor, "Straight Outta Compton" (2015); Executive Producer, "The Rebels" (2014); Actor, Producer, "Ride Along" (2014); Actor, "22 Jump Street" (2014); Actor, "The Book of Life" (2014); Rap Artist, "Everythang's Corrupt" (2014); Actor, "21 Jump Street" (2012); Actor, "Rampart" (2011); Executive Producer, "Are We There Yet?" (2010-2012); Actor, Executive Producer, "Lottery Ticket" (2010); Rap Artist, "I am the West" (2010); Actor, Producer, "The Janky Promoters" (2009); Rap Artist, "Raw Footage" (2008); Actor, "First Sunday" (2008); Actor, Producer, "The Longshots" (2008); Actor, Producer, "Are We Done Yet?" (2007); Executive Producer, "Black.White." (2006); Rap Artist, "Laugh Now, Cry Later" (2006); Actor, "xXx: State of the Union" (2005); Executive Producer, "Beauty Shop" (2005); Executive Producer, Television Show, "Barbershop" (2005); Actor, Producer, "Are We There Yet?" (2005); Actor, Executive Producer, "Barbershop 2: Back in Business" (2004); Actor, "Torque" (2004); Rap Artist (With Westside Connection), "Terrorist Threats" (2003); Actor, "Barbershop" (2002); Actor, Producer, "All About the Benjamins" (2002); Actor, Producer, "Friday After Next" (2002); Actor, "Ghosts of Mars" (2001);

Actor, Executive Producer, "Next Friday" (2000); Rap Artist, "War & Peace, Volume Two" (2000); Actor, "Three Kings" (1999); Actor, "I Got the Hook Up" (1998); Actor, Executive Producer, "The Players Club" (1998); Rap Artist, "War & Peace, Volume One" (1998); Actor, Executive Producer, "Dangerous Ground" (1997); Actor, "Anaconda" (1997); Rap Artist with Westside Connection, "Bow Down" (1996); Actor, Executive Producer, "Friday" (1995); Actor, "Higher Learning" (1995); Actor, Writer, "The Glass Shield" (1995); Rap Artist, "Lethal Injection" (1993); Actor, "Trespass" (1992); Rap Artist, The Predator" (1992); Actor, "Boyz n the Hood" (1991); Rap Artist, "Kill at Will" (1991); Rap Artist, "Death Certificate" (1991); Rap Artist, "Amerikkka's Most Wanted" (1990); Rap Artist (With N.W.A.), "Straight Outta Compton" (1989); Actor, Producer, Television Shows and Films **AW:** Star, Hollywood Walk of Fame (2017); Inductee (With N.W.A.), Rock and Roll Hall of Fame (2016); Award for Excellence in Entertainment, BET Awards (2014); Award for Outstanding Actor in a Comedy Series, NAACP Image Awards (2011); "I am Hip-Hop" Icon Award, BET Hip Hop Awards (2009); Quincy Jones Award, Soul Train Music Awards (2005); MECCA Movie Award for Acting Award (2002); Blockbuster Entertainment Award for Favorite Action Team (2000)

JACKSON, PHIL DOUGLAS, T: Former Professional Basketball Coach; Former Professional Basketball Player; Sports Team Executive **I:** Athletics **DOB:** 09/17/1945 **PB:** Deer Lodge **SC:** MT/USA **PT:** Charles Jackson; Elisabeth (Funk) Jackson **MS:** Divorced **SPN:** June Jackson (1974, Divorced 2001); Maxine Jackson (1967, Divorced 1972) **CH:** Ben; Chelsea; Charlie; Elizabeth; Brooke **ED:** Honorary LHD, University of North Dakota; BA in Religion, Psychology and Philosophy, University of North Dakota (1967) **C:** President, New York Knicks, NBA (2014-2017); Head Coach, Los Angeles Lakers, NBA (1999-2004, 2005-2011); Head Coach, Chicago Bulls, NBA (1989-1998); Assistant Coach, Chicago Bulls, NBA (1987-1989); Head Coach, Albany Patroons, Continental Basketball Association (1982-1987); Assistant Coach, New Jersey Nets, NBA (1980-1982); Forward, New Jersey Nets, NBA (1978-1980); Forward, New York Knicks, NBA (1967-1978) **CW:** Featured, "The Last Dance" (2020); Co-author with Hugh Delehanty, "Eleven Rings: The Soul of Success" (2013); Author, "Journey to the Ring: Behind the Scenes with the 2010 NBA Champion Lakers" (2010); Co-author with Michael Arkush, "The Last Season: A Team in Search of Its Soul" (2004); Co-author with Charley Rosen, "More Than a Game" (2002); Co-author with Hugh Delehanty, "Sacred Hoops: Spiritual Lessons of a Hardwood Warrior" (1996); Co-author with Charley Rosen, "Maverick" (1975); Co-author with George Kalinsky, "Take It All" (1970) **AW:** Winner (as Head Coach), Los Angeles Lakers, NBA Championship (2000-2002, 2009, 2010); Amos Stagg Coaching Award, Untied States Sports Academy (2002, 2010); Named NBA All-star Game Head Coach (1992, 1996, 2000, 2009); Named to Naismith Memorial Basketball Hall of Fame (2007); Named to Basketball Hall of Fame (2007); Winner (as Head Coach), Chicago Bulls, NBA Championship (1991-1993, 1996-1998); Named One of the NBA's 10 Greatest Coaches (1997); Named NBA Coach of the Year (1996); Theodore Roosevelt Rough Rider Award (1992); Winner, New York Knicks, NBA Championships (1970, 1973)

JACKSON, ROSA, MED, T: Elementary School Educator **I:** Education/Educational Services **DOB:** 12/08/1943 **PB:** Columbia **SC:** SC/USA **PT:** Alvin Oree, Jr.; Rosa Lee (Reese) Oree **MS:** Married **SPN:** Olin D. Jackson (06/14/1969) **CH:** Zandra Lalita; Delin Jawaski **ED:** MEd, South Carolina State University, Orangeburg, SC (1981); BA, Benedict College, Columbia, SC (1966) **CT:** Certified Teacher **C:** Second Grade Teacher, Richmond County Board of Education, Augusta, GA; Fifth Grade Teacher, Lancaster County Board of Education, Kershaw, SC; Second Grade Teacher, McDuffie County Board of Education, Thomson, GA; First Grade Teacher, Richmond County Board of Education, Augusta, GA **CR:** Leadership Team, Richmond County Schools **CIV:** Science Teacher in Residence; President, Reese Memorial Singers; Pulpit Aide; Senior Musical Choir; Nurses Guild; Chairperson, Kitchen Committee; Art Teacher, Vacation Bible School, Antioch Baptist Church; Volunteer Teacher, Richmond County School System, Augusta, GA **AW:** Service Recognition Award, Antioch Baptist Church; AARP Service Award **MEM:** Georgia Association of Educators; Research Center for Applied Education; National Education Association; National Science Teachers Association; Georgia Science Teachers Association; Georgia Staff Development Council; Association for Multicultural Science Education; Treasurer, Chapter 266, AARP **MH:** Albert Nelson Marquis Lifetime Achievement Award **B/I:** Ms. Jackson became involved in her profession because she knew she wanted to become a teacher from the time she was a child. **AV:** Flower decorating; Singing; Sewing; Cosmetology **THT:** Ms. Jackson attended the World Financial Group Conference with her son. She started singing at John W. Workhouse High School in 1971.

JACKSON, SAMUEL LEROY, T: Actor **I:** Media & Entertainment **DOB:** 12/21/1948 **PB:** Washington, DC **SC:** USA **PT:** Roy Henry Jackson; Elizabeth (Montgomery) Jackson **MS:** Married **SPN:** LaTanya Richardson (01/14/1980) **CH:** Zoe **ED:** BA in Drama, Moorehouse College, Atlanta, GA (1972) **CR:** Co-Founder, Just Us Theatre **CIV:** Launched Campaigns, One for the Boys and Alzheimer's Disease; Participant, Equal Rights Protests **CW:** Actor, "The Banker" (2020); Voice Actor, "Star Wars: The Clone Wars" (2020); Actor, "Staged" (2020); Voice Actor, "Star Wars: The Rise of Skywalker" (2019); Actor, "Son of Shaft" (2019); Actor, "Glass" (2019); Appearance, "Carpool Karaoke: The Series" (2019); Actor, "The Last Full Measure" (2019); Actor, "QTB: The First Eight" (2019); Actor, "Spider-Man: Far from Home" (2019); Voice Actor, "Incredibles 2" (2018); Actor, "Blazing Samurai" (2018); Actor, "Life Itself" (2018); Actor, "xXx:Return of Xander Cage" (2017); Actor, "Kong: Skull Island" (2017); Actor, "The Hitman's Bodyguard" (2017); Actor, "Unicorn Store" (2017); Actor, "Cell" (2016); Actor, "The Legend of Tarzan" (2016); Actor, "Miss Peregrine's Home for Peculiar Children" (2016); Actor, "Eating You Alive" (2016); Actor, "Kingsman: The Secret Service" (2015); Actor, "Barely Lethal" (2015); Actor, "Avengers: Age of Ultron" (2015); Actor, "Chi-Raq" (2015); Actor, "The Hateful Eight" (2015); Actor, "Reasonable Doubt" (2014); Actor, "RoboCop" (2014); Actor, "Black Dynamite" (2014); Actor, "Captain America: The Winter Soldier" (2014); Actor, "Kite" (2014); Actor, "Big Game" (2014); Actor, "Agents of Shield" (2013-2014); Actor, "Generations" (2013); Voice Actor, "Turbo" (2013); Actor, "Oldboy" (2013); Actor, "Curiosity" (2011, 2012); Host, Spike Video Game Awards (2012); Appearance, "The Colbert Report" (2012); Actor, "Meeting Evil" (2012); Actor, "The Avengers" (2012); Voice Actor, "Zambezia" (2012); Actor, "Django Unchained" (2012); Actor, Executive Producer, "The Samaritan" (2012); Actor, "The Mountaintop" (2011); Actor, "Captain America: The First Avenger" (2011); Actor, "Thor" (2011); Actor, "The Sunset Limited" (2011); Actor, "Prohibition" (2011); Actor, "Unthinkable" (2010); Actor, "Iron Man 2" (2010); Actor, "The Other Guys" (2010); Voice Actor, Producer, "Afro

Samurai: Resurrection" (2009); Voice Actor, "Astro Boy" (2009); Actor, "Mother and Child" (2009); Actor, "Jumper" (2008); Actor, "Star Wars: The Clone Wars" (2008); Actor, "Lakeview Terrance" (2008); Actor, "Soul Men" (2008); Actor, "The Spirit" (2008); Actor, Producer, "Cleaner" (2007); Actor, "Resurrecting the Champ" (2007); Actor, "1408" (2007); Actor, "Freedomland" (2006); Actor, "Snakes on a Plane" (2006); Actor, "Black Snake Moan" (2006); Actor, "Honor Deferred" (2006); Actor, "Home of the Brave" (2006); Voice Actor, "The Boondocks" (2005-2010); Actor, "xXx: State of the Union" (2005); Actor, "Star Wars: Episode III Revenge of the Sith" (2005); Actor, "The Man" (2005); Actor, "Coach Carter" (2005); Voice Actor, "The Incredibles" (2004); Actor, Kill Bill: Volume 2" (2004); Actor, "Twisted" (2004); Actor, "In My Country" (2004); Actor, "Basic" (2003); Actor, "S.W.A.T." (2003); Actor, "Changing Lanes" (2002); Actor, "Star Wars: Episode II - Attack of the Clones" (2002); Actor, "XXX" (2002); Actor, Executive Producer, "The Caveman's Valentine" (2001); Actor, Executive Producer, "Formula 51" (2001); Actor, "Unbreakable" (2000); Actor, "Shaft" (2000); Actor, "Deep Blue Sea" (1999); Actor, "Rules of Engagement" (1999); Actor, "Mefisto in Onyx" (1999); Actor, "Star Wars Episode I: The Phantom Menace" (1999); Actor, "Sphere" (1998); Actor, "Out of Sight" (1998); Actor, "The Negotiator" (1998); Actor, "Hard Eight" (1997); Actor, "Jackie Brown" (1997); Actor, "187" (1997); Actor, Producer, "Eve's Bayou" (1997); Actor, "The Great White Hype" (1996) Actor, "Trees Lounge" (1996); Actor, "The Search for One Eye Jimmy" (1996); Actor, "A Time to Kill" (1996); Actor, "The Long Kiss Goodnight" (1996); Actor, "Happily Ever After: Fairy Tales for Every Child" (1995-1999); Actor, "Losing Isiah" (1995); Actor, "Kiss of Death" (1995); Actor, "Fluke" (1995); Actor, "Die Hard with a Vengeance" (1995); Actor, "Hail Caesar" (1994); Actor, "Fresh" (1994); Actor, "The New Age" (1994); Actor, "Pulp Fiction" (1994); Actor, "Assault at West Point" (1994); Actor, "Against the Wall" (1994); Actor, "Simple Justice" (1993); Actor, "National Lampoon's Loaded Weapon 1" (1993); Actor, "Amos & Andrew" (1993); Actor, "Menace II Society" (1993); Actor, "Jurassic Park" (1993); Actor, "True Romance" (1993); Actor, "Juice" (1992); Actor, "White Sands" (1992); Actor, "Patriot Games" (1992); Actor, "Johnny Suede" (1992); Actor, "Jumpin' at the Boneyard" (1992); Actor, "Fathers and Sons" (1992); Actor, "Jungle Fever" (1991); Actor, "Strictly Business" (1991); Actor, "Dead and Alive: The Race for Gus Farace" (1991); Actor, "Common Ground" (1990); Actor, "A Shock to the System" (1990); Actor, "Def by Temptation" (1990); Actor, "Betsy's Wedding" (1990); Actor, "Mo' Better Blues" (1990); Actor, "The Exorcist III" (1990); Actor, "Goodfellas" (1990); Actor, "Return of Superfly" (1990); Voice Actor, "Mystery Train" (1989); Actor, "Do The Right Thing" (1989); Actor, "Sea of Love" (1989); Actor, "Coming to America" (1988); Actor, "School Daze" (1988); Appearance, "Eddie Murphy Raw" (1987); Actor, "Uncle Tom's Cabin" (1987); Actor, "Ragtime" (1981); Actor, "The Trial of the Moke" (1978); Actor, "Together for Days" (1972); Actor, Appearances, Plays, Television Shows, Films **AW:** Award for Outstanding Supporting Actor in a Motion Picture, NAACP Image Awards (2013); American Cinematheque Award (2008); Award for Outstanding Actor in a Motion Picture, NAACP Image Awards (2006); Recipient, Star, Hollywood Walk of Fame (2006); Dream Keeper Award, "I Have A Dream" Foundation (2005); BAFTA Award for Best Actor in a Supporting Role (1994); Numerous Awards

JACKSON LEE, SHEILA, T: U.S. Representative from Texas **I:** Government Administration/Government Relations/Government Services **DOB:**

01/12/1950 **PB:** Queens **SC:** NY/USA **PT:** Jason Cornelius Bennett; Erica Shelwyn Bennett **MS:** Married **SPN:** Elwyn C. Lee **CH:** Erica; Jason **ED:** JD, University of Virginia School of Law, Charlottesville, VA (1975); BA in Political Science, Yale University, New Haven, CT, With Honors (1972) **C:** Member, U.S. House of Representatives from Texas' 18th Congressional District, United States Congress (1995-Present); Councilwoman, Houston City Council (1990-1994); Associate Judge, City of Houston Municipal Court (1987-1989); Senior Attorney, United Energy Resources, Inc. (1980); Trial Attorney, Fulbright & Jaworski LLP (Now Norton Rose Fulbright US LLP) (1978-1980); Senior Counsel, Select Committee on Assassinations, United States Congress (1977-1978); Member, Committee on Homeland Security; Member, Committee on the Judiciary; Founder, Congressional Children's Caucus, Texas' 18th District, United States Congress **AW:** Listee, 100 Most Influential Black Americans, Ebony Magazine (2006); Listee, Power 150 (2008); Phillip Burton Immigration and Civil Rights Policy Award, Immigrant Legal Resource Center (2006); Top Women in Science Award, National Technical Association of Scientists and Engineers (1998) **MEM:** Texas Municipal Judges Association (Now TMCA); Justice Committee, State Bar Association **BAR:** State of Texas **PA:** Democrat

JACKSON-LOWMAN, HUBERTA, T: Professor **I:** Education/Educational Services **CN:** Florida Agricultural and Mechanical University **MS:** Married **CH:** Three Children **ED:** PhD, Clinical Psychology, University of Pittsburgh, Pennsylvania (1976); MA in Cinical-Experimental Psychology, Wichita State University, Kansas (1971); BA, Clinical-Experimental Psychology, Wichita State University, Kansas (1968) **C:** Full Professor, Florida Agricultural and Mechanical University (1996-Present); Chairperson, Psychology Department, Florida Agricultural and Mechanical University (2005-2013); Associate Professor, Department of Psychology, Florida Agricultural and Mechanical University (1996-2014); Co-Director, Institute for the Black Family, University of Pittsburgh, PA (1991-1995); Executive Director, Mayor's Commission on Families, Pittsburgh, PA (1987-1991) **CIV:** President, The Association of Black Psychologists, Incorporated (2015-Present); Implementer, Emotional Emancipation Circle, Train the Trainer Workshops & Group (2015); Senator, Famu Faculty Senate (2013-2016); Chair, African, Black Psychology Conference, Florida Agricultural and Mechanical University, Tallahassee, FL (2013); Co-Chair, African Black Psychology Conference, Florida Agricultural and Mechanical University Tallahassee, FL (2011); Co-Chair, African Black Psychology Conference, Florida Agricultural and Mechanical University Tallahassee, FL (2010); Faculty Research Associate, Juvenile Justice Institute, Florida Agricultural and Mechanical University (2009-2011); Area Coordinator, National Association of African American Studies (2008-2010); Project Director, Anago Fashion, African Religious Practices in Florida Conference, Office of Black Diasporan Culture, Florida Agricultural and Mechanical University (2008); Research Associatem FAMU Transportation Safety Research (2006-2009); Principal Investigator, Wisdombearers (2003-2006); Consultant, Regional Readiness Implementation Team (2001-2003); Tallahassee Community Healing Base **CW:** Speaker, "A Proposal for Addressing the Impact of Over Incarceration on Black Families & Communities," Colloquium on African American Health and Heath Policy, National Medical Association, Washington, DC (2019); Speaker, "Overcoming Engendered Racial Trauma in the Lives of Black Girls," 8th Annual Instilling Hope Conference, Tallahasee, FL (2019); Speaker, "The Historial, Political and Social Context of Trauma for Black Girls," Gwen's Girls, Pittsburgh, PA (2018-2019); Speaker, "Loving Black Girls Unconditionally through Culture, Consciousness and Commitment," Keynote Address, Equity Summit: The Village in Action to Advance Equity for Black Girls, Pittsburgh, PA (2018); Speaker, "Using Cultural Policy to Restore Ubuntu in Traumatized Black Communities," 7th Annual Instilling Hope Conference, Tallahassee, FL (2018); Speaker, Over 30 Professional Presentations **AW:** Travel Award, Florida Agricultural and Mechanical University (2015, 2013); Asa Hillard Scholar Travel Award, Elderhostel Inc. (2011); Awarded Certification, African Centered Psychologist, Diplomate & Fellow Status, Association of Black Psychologists (2009); Faculty Senate Travel Award (2009); Outstanding Scholarship Award for Reasearch, The Association of Black Psychologists (2008); Grantee, Florida Humanities Council (2008) **MEM:** Reviewer, Children and Youth Services (2018-Present); Reviewer, Journal of Black Psychology (2012-Present); National Association of African American Studies (2014-Present); Pan African Cultural Heritage Institute (2013-Present); North Florida Association of Black Psychologists (1996-Present); President, National Association of Black Psychologists (1992-Present); President-Elect, National Association of Black Psychologists (2015-2017); University Tenure & Promotion Committee (2014-2016); Association for the Study of African American Life and History (2013-2014); Elected Southern Regional Representative, The Association of Black Psychologists (2010-2014) **AS:** Dr. Lowman believes her success comes from her love, interest and commitment to her work. She is constantly learning and being stimulated by the progression of the field as well as growing with it. Success isn't what she chases, she simply is doing what she loves and expressing what defines her through her work. Success has become a bi-product. **B/I:** Dr. Lowman took a course in psychology in high school and became very interested. The idea of learning the science behind one's mind, especially her own, was intriguing to her. That was her inspiration and she never wavered from the path. **AV:** Travel; Spend more time with her grandchildren; Writing **THT:** She believes in the saying, "If you nourish an acorn, it will eventually become an oak tree. If you don't know the potential of an acorn, chances are it will not grow. Most people are like acorns. Some are aware of their potential and grow, and some are unaware and don't."

JACOBI, PETER P., T: Journalism Educator, Writer **I:** Writing and Editing **DOB:** 03/15/1930 **PB:** Berlin **SC:** Germany **PT:** Paul A. Jacobi; Liesbeth (Kron) Jacobi **MS:** Married **SPN:** Harriet Ackley (2008) **CH:** Keith Peter; John Wyn **ED:** MS in Journalism, Northwestern University (1953); BS in Journalism, Northwestern University (1952) **C:** Communications Consultant, Bloomington, IN (1985-Present); Retired (2017); Professor Emeritus, Indiana University Bloomington (1999-2017); Professor of Journalism, Indiana University Bloomington (1985-1999); Communications Consultant, Workshop Leader, New York, NY (1980-1984); Professor Journalism, Northwestern University, Evanston, IL (1969-1981); Journalism Faculty, Northwestern University, Evanston, IL (1955-1981); Associate Dean, Northwestern University, Evanston, IL (1966-1974); Associate Professor, Northwestern University, Evanston, IL (1966-1969); Assistant Professor, Northwestern University, Evanston, IL (1963-1966); Professional Lecturer, Northwestern University, Evanston, IL (1955-1963) **CR:** Music Critic, Columnist Bloomington Herald-Times (1985-Present); Columnist, Arts Indiana (1987-2001); Arts Correspondent, Christian Science Monitor (1956-1981);

Syndicated Commentator on Arts and Media, North American Radio Alliance (1978-1980); Arts Critic (1975-1977); Script Consultant, Goodman Theater, Chicago, IL (1973-1975); Music Columnist, Chicagoan Magazine (1973-1974); Theatre and Film Critic, Station WTTW, Chicago, IL (1964-1974); Theatre and Film Critic, Hollister Newspapers, Chicago, IL (1963-1970); Radio Commentator on Music and Opera (1958-1965); News Assignment Editor, Newscaster, NBC, Chicago, IL (1955-1961); News Editor, ABC, Chicago, IL (1951-1953) **MIL:** United States Army (1953-1955) **CW:** Co-Author, "From Budapest to Bloomington, Janos Starker and the Hungarian Cello Tradition" (1999); Author, "The Magazine Article: How to Think It, Plan It, Write It" (1991); Contributor, "Lyric Opera Companion" (1991); Co-Author, "Straight Talk about Videoconferencing" (1986); Author, "Writing with Style, The News Story and the Feature" (1982); Author, "The Messiah Book-The Life and Times of G.F. Handel's Greatest Hit" (1982); Editor, "Music Mag./Musical Courier," Chicago, IL (1961-1962); Editor, "Chicago Lyric Opera News" (1958-1961); Contributor, Articles, Professional Journals **AW:** Teaching Award, Indiana University; Teaching Award, Northwestern University; Award, Indiana Chapter, Society of Professional Journalists **MEM:** Chairman, Indiana Arts Commission (1990-1993); American Association of University Professors; National Academy of Television Arts and Sciences; Association of Education in Journalism; Society of Professional Journalists; Arts of the Midwest; Bloomington Community Arts Commission **MH:** Albert Nelson Marquis Lifetime Achievement Award; Marquis Who's Who Top Professional **B/I:** Mr. Jacobi grew up in Germany during World War II. His family was Jewish and knew they had to escape the country. Fortunately, they were able to move to the United States, where Mr. Jacobi quickly learned English. He grew to love the language, which drew him to begin working on his school's newspaper. This was how he discovered journalism and consequently decided to pursue a career in the field.

JACOBS, MARC, T: Fashion Designer **I:** Apparel & Fashion **DOB:** 04/09/1963 **PB:** New York **SC:** NY/USA **MS:** Married **SPN:** Charly Defrancesco (04/07/2019) **ED:** Coursework, Parsons School of Design, The New School, New York, NY **C:** Designer, Mark Jacobs, New York, NY (1988-Present); Launched, Marc by Marc Jacobs Line (2001-2015); Creative Director, Louis Vuitton, Paris, France (1997-2013); Head Designer, Perry Ellis, New York, NY (1989-1992); Debuted, Marc Jacobs Label (1986); Founder, Jacobs Duffy Designs Inc.; Designer, Ruben Thomas Inc. (Under Sketchbook Label), New York, NY; Stock Boy, Charivari, New York, NY **CR:** Creative Director, Diet Coke (2013); Co-Host, Metropolitan Museum of Art Costume Institute Gala (Now The Met Gala), New York, NY (2009) **CW:** Featured, "Scatter My Ashes at Bergdorf's" (2013); Actor, "Disconnect" (2012); Featured, "In Vogue: The Editor's Eye" (2012); Featured, "L'effet Mad Men" (2010); Featured, "The Red Carpet Issue" (2010); Featured, Documentary, "Marc Jacobs and Louis Vuitton" (2007) **AW:** MTV VMA Fashion Trailblazer Award (2019); Womenswear Designer of the Year Award, CFDA (1991, 1992, 1997, 2010, 2016); Geoffrey Beene Lifetime Achievement Award, Council of Fashion Designers of America (2011); Lifetime Achievement Award, CFDA (2011); Named One of the 100 Most Influential People in the World, TIME Magazine (2010); Named One of the 100 Agents of Change, Rolling Stone Magazine (2009); Named to Fragrance Foundation's Hall of Fame (2009); Designer of the Year Award, Accessories Council of Excellence (2007); Accessory Designer of the Year Award, CFDA (1998, 1999, 2003, 2005); Menswear Designer of

the Year Award, CFDA (2002); Perry Ellis Award for New Fashion Talent, CFDA (1987); Design Student of the Year Award, Parsons School of Design (1984); Chester Weinberg Gold Thimble Award (1984); Perry Ellis Gold Thimble Award, CFDA (1984) **PA:** Democrat

JACOBS, PATRICIA, "TRISH" LOUISE, CNA, T: Geriatrics Nurse Assistant **I:** Medicine & Health Care **DOB:** 02/27/1958 **PB:** Battle Creek **SC:** IA/USA **PT:** John Otto; Mary Ellen (Owens) Jacobs **MS:** Single **ED:** Nurse Aide Certificate, Western Iowa Tech Community College (1976) **CT:** Certified Nurse Assistant **C:** Nurse Assistant, Good Samaratin Home, Lennox, SD (1996-Present); With, Special Care Unit, Good Samaratin Center, Canton, SD (1996-2003); Nurse Assistant, Fellowship Village, Inwood, IA (1993-1996); Nurse Assistant, Julia's Valley Manor, Sioux City, IA (1991-1993); Nurse Assistant, Countryside Retirement Home, Sioux City IA (1989-1991); Nurse Assistant, Sunrise Manor, Sioux City, IA (1988-1989); Nurse Assistant, Hillhaven, West Des Moines, IA (1983-1986); Nurse Assistant, Beverly Enterprises, Las Vegas, NV (1979-1980); Nurse Assistant, Tommy Dale Development Center, Sioux City, IA (1977-1979); Nurse Assistant, Onawa, IA (1976-1979) **CR:** Nurse Assistant, Kimberly Nursing, West Des Moines, IA (1982-1983, 1986) **CW:** Author, "Together We Can" **B/I:** Ms. Jacobs became involved in her profession after attending an intake class in Las Vegas, during which she was pulled out and told that they required her on the floor, as she was already qualified. **AV:** Reading; Writing; Piano; Cross-stitch; Needlepoint **PA:** Republican **RE:** Christian

JACOBSZ ROSIER, RENE, "DUCKY" MARCEL, FOUNDER, T: President **I:** Logistics and Supply Chain **CN:** Transportation & Logistical Concepts/Periwinkles Powers Inc. **DOB:** 03/02/1971 **PB:** La Mirada **SC:** CA/USA **PT:** Donald Jacobsz Rosier **MS:** Married **SPN:** **CH:** Everett; Shelby **ED:** Bachelor's Degree in Electronic Engineering; Bachelor's Degree in Computer Science; Bachelor's Degree in Radiological Warfare **CT:** Certification in Chemical, Biological, Radiological Detection, and Ordinance Disposal **C:** Co-Owner, Periwinkles Powers Inc. (2019-Present); President, Transportation & Logistics Concepts (2014-2019); Calcon Command Freight Enterprises, Command Freight Systems, Pocino Foods **CR:** Founder, Logistical Consulting by Rene Jacobsz Rosier (2019-Present) **CIV:** Volunteer, Our Lady of Guadalupe; Sponsor, La Habra High School Women's Softball Team **MIL:** Active Duty, Reserves, U.S. Military (1992-1998) **AW:** 1st Place, National Geographic Amature Photographer **MEM:** Veterans Society; Veterans of Foreign Wars; Dutch Indonesian Society; Women's Rights **AS:** Mr. Jacobsz Rosier attributes his success to working hard and having the strength and courage to take risks. Though he has had troubles with his ex-wife, he has risen above their issues and remained successful. **B/I:** Mr. Jacobsz Rosier initially wanted to pursue engineering and computer science but changed his mind after getting involved with Pachino Foods. He then began working in transportation, which ended up being fun. It is an ever-changing industry. **AV:** Advocating for men's and women's rights **RE:** Buddist; Christian **THT:** Mr. Jacobsz Rosier believes in doing what one is passionate about, as well as having fun.

JAGGER, MICK PHILLIP, T: Singer **I:** Media & Entertainment **DOB:** 07/26/1943 **PB:** Dartford **SC:** Kent/United Kingdom **PT:** Basil Fanshawe "Joe" Jagger; Eva Ensley Mary (Scutts) Jagger **MS:** Divorced **SPN:** Bianca Perez Morena de Macias (05/12/1971, Divorced 11/1979) **CH:** Karis Hunt; Jade Sheena Jezebel; Elizabeth 'Lizzie' Scarlett;

James Leroy Augustin; Georgia May Ayeesha; Gabriel Luke Beauregard; Lucas Maurice Morad; Deveraux Octavian Basil **ED:** Coursework, London School of Economics (1962-1964) **C:** Lead Singer, The Rolling Stones (1962-Present); Lead Singer, SuperHeavy (2011); Member, Blues Incorporated **CW:** Actor, "The Burnt Orange Heresy" (2019); Singer, "Gotta Get a Grip/ England Lost" (2017); Producer, "Get On Up" (2014); Appearance, "Muscle Shoals" (2013); Singer (With The Rolling Stones), "GRRR!" (2012); Appearance, "Crossfire Hurricane" (2012); Featured, "The Rolling Stones: Charlie is My Darling" (2012); Singer (With SuperHeavy), "SuperHeavy" (2011); Singer (With SuperHeavy), "Miracles Worker" (2011); Co-Singer, "T.H.E." (2011); Performer, "Some Girls Live in Texas '78" (2011); Featured, "Stones in Exile" (2010); Singer, Performer, "Shine a Light" (2008); Producer, "The Women" (2008); Actor, "The Bank Job" (2008); Singer, "The Very Best of Mick Jagger" (2007); Performer, "The Biggest Bang" (2007); Actor, "The Knights of Prosperity" (2007); Singer (With The Rolling Stones), "A Bigger Bang" (2005); Singer (With The Rolling Stones), "Rarities 1971-2003" (2005); Singer, "Old Habits Die Hard" (2005); Singer (With The Rolling Stones), "Singles: 1965-1967" (2004); Singer (With The Rolling Stones), "Live Licks" (2004); Co-Singer, "Alfie" (2004); Actor, "Mayer of the Sunset Strip" (2003); Performer, "Four Flicks" (2003); Singer (With The Rolling Stones), "Forty Licks" (2002); Singer, "Goddess in the Doorway" (2001); Actor, "The Man from Elysian Fields" (2001); Producer, "Enigma" (2001); Featured, "Being Mick" (2001); Singer (With The Rolling Stones), "No Security" (1999); Singer (With The Rolling Stones), "Bridges to Babylon" (1997); Performer, "The Rolling Stones Bridges to Babylon Tour '97-98" (1997); Actor, "Bent" (1997); Singer (With The Rolling Stones), "The Rolling Stones Rock 'N' Roll Circus" (1996); Performer, "The Rolling Stones Rock 'N' Roll Circus" (1996); Singer (With The Rolling Stones), "Stripped" (1995); Performer, "Voodoo Lounge" (1995); Singer (With The Rolling Stones), "Voodoo Lounge" (1994); Singer (With The Rolling Stones), "Jump Back: The Best of the Rolling Stones" (1993); Singer, "Wandering Spirit" (1993); Actor, "Freejack" (1992); Performer, "Rolling Stones: Live at the Max" (1991); Singer (With The Rolling Stones), "Flashpoint" (1990); Singer (With The Rolling Stones), "Singles Collection: The London Years" (1989); Singer (With The Rolling Stones), "Steel Wheels" (1989); Featured, "25 X 5: The Continuing Adventures of the Rolling Stones" (1989); Singer, "Primitive Cool" (1987); Singer (With The Rolling Stones), "Dirty Work" (1986); Singer, "She's the Boss" (1985); Singer (With The Rolling Stones), "Rewind (1971-1984)" (1984); Singer (With The Rolling Stones), "Undercover" (1983); Performer, "Let's Spend the Night Together" (1983); Singer (With The Rolling Stones), "Still Life" (1982); Singer (With The Rolling Stones), "Sucking in the Seventies" (1981); Singer (With The Rolling Stones), "Tattoo You" (1981); Singer (With The Rolling Stones), Still Life American Concert (1981); Singer (With The Rolling Stones), "Emotional Rescue" (1980); Singer (With The Rolling Stones), "Some Girls" (1978); Singer (With The Rolling Stones), "Love You Live" (1977); Singer (With The Rolling Stones), "Black and Blue" (1976); Singer (With The Rolling Stones), "Metamorphosis" (1975); Singer (With The Rolling Stones), "Made in the Shade" (1975); Singer (With The Rolling Stones), "Rolled Gold+: The Very Best of the Rolling Stones" (1975); Singer (With The Rolling Stones), "It's Only Rock and Roll" (1974); Performer, "Ladies and Gentlemen: The Rolling Stones" (1974); Singer (With The Rolling Stones), "Goats Head Soup" (1973); Singer (With The Rolling Stones), "More Hot Rocks: Big Hits and Fazed Cookies" (1972); Singer, "Jamming with Edward" (1972); Singer (With The Rolling Stones), "Exile on Main Street" (1972); Singer (With The Rolling Stones), "Hot Rocks 1964-1971" (1971); Singer (With The Rolling Stones), "Sticky Fingers" (1971); Singer (With The Rolling Stones), "Get Yer Ya-Yas Out!: The Rolling Stones in Concert" (1970); Performer, "Gimme Shelter" (1970); Performer, "Sympathy for the Devil" (1970); Actor, "Ned Kelly" (1970); Actor, "Performance" (1969); Singer (With The Rolling Stones), "Let It Bleed" (1969); Singer (With The Rolling Stones), "Through the Past, Darkly (Big Hits Volume Two)" (1969); Singer (With The Rolling Stones), "Beggars Banquet" (1968); Singer (With The Rolling Stones), "Their Satanic Majesties Request" (1967); Singer (With The Rolling Stones), "Flowers" (1967); Singer (With The Rolling Stones), "Between the Buttons" (1967); Singer (With The Rolling Stones), "Got Live If You Want It!" (1966); Singer (With The Rolling Stones), "Aftermath" (1966); Singer (With The Rolling Stones), "Big Hits, High Tide, & Green Grass" (1966); Singer (With The Rolling Stones), "December's Children (And Everybody's)" (1965); Singer (With The Rolling Stones), "Out of Our Heads" (1965); Singer (With The Rolling Stones), "The Rolling Stones, Now!" (1965); Singer (With The Rolling Stones), "12 X 5" (1964); Singer (With The Rolling Stones), "England's Newest Hitmakers: The Rolling Stones" (1964) **AW:** Greatest Touring Band of All Time, World Music Awards (2006); Golden Globe Award for Best Original Song, Hollywood Foreign Press Association (2005); Inductee, UK Hall of Fame (2004); Honorary Knight Commander, Most Excellent Order of the British Empire, Her Majesty Queen Elizabeth II (2003); Grammy Award for Best Rock Album, The Recording Academy (1994); Inductee (With The Rolling Stones), Rock and Roll Hall of Fame (1989)

JAMALUDDIN, ABU SAEED, PHD, T: Advisor, Combustion & Heat Transfer Engineering (Retired) **I:** Oil & Energy **DOB:** 02/13/1949 **PB:** Dhaka **SC:** Bangladesh **PT:** A.K. Saifuddin; Raushanara Begum **MS:** Married **SPN:** Sufia Yasmeen **CH:** Nausheen Jamal; Sharmeen Jamal; Mehreen Jamal **ED:** PhD, The University of Newcastle, Australia (1985); MSc in Chemical Engineering, Bangladesh University of Engineering and Technology, Dhaka, Bangladesh (1980); BSc in Chemical Engineering, Bangladesh University of Engineering and Technology, Dhaka, Bangladesh (1972) **C:** Principal, Technical Consultant, Comprehensive Heater Support, LLC (2014-Present); Advisor, Combustion & Heat Transfer Engineering, Shell Global Solutions (2004-2014); Heat Transfer Specialist, Shell Deer Park Refining Company (1997-2004); Senior Research Engineer, Shell Development Company, Westhollow Technology Center, Houston, Texas (1990-1997); Senior Research Engineer, Babcock & Wilcox Company (Babcock & Wilcox Enterprises, Inc.), Alliance, Ohio (1988-1990); Postdoctoral Research Associate, Combustion Laboratory, Brigham Young University, Provo, Utah (1985-1988); Senior Engineer, Bangladesh Oil & Gas Corporation, Dhaka, Bangladesh (1978-1981); Cathodic Protection Engineer, Titas Gas Transmission and Distribution Company, Dhaka, Bangladesh (1975-1978); Graduate Research Scholar, Bangladesh University of Engineering and Technology, Dhaka, Bangladesh (1974-1975); Sales Engineer, Bangladesh Oxygen Company Ltd., Dhaka, Bangladesh (1972-1974) **CR:** Reviewer, Research Activities, Combustion Laboratories, Brigham Young University, The University of Utah and The Pennsylvania State University (1990-1993); Evaluator of Research Proposals, U.S. Department of Energy, Pittsburgh, PA (1989) **CIV:** Director, Participant, Musical and Cultural Programs, Indian and Bangladeshi Communities, Houston, Texas (1990-Present); Science Project Mentor, Judge, Alief Independent School District and Houston Science and Engineering Fair (1996-1997); Volunteer Scientist, Gulf Coast Texas Alliance for Minorities in Engineering (GCTAME), Houston, Texas (1995-1996) **CW:** Co-editor, Magazine, Bengali Language (1993); Author, Co-author, More Than 50 Publications in Peer-reviewed Journals and Conference Proceedings; Author, Co-author, More Than 100 Shell Reports, Internal Standards and Best Practice Documents; Reviewer, Technical and Scientific Papers for The American Society of Mechanical Engineers, American Institute of Aeronautics and Astronautics, Industrial Combustion, and Journal of the International Flame Research Foundation; Regular Contributor, Literary Magazine Published by the Bengali Community in Houston, Texas **AW:** Presidential Award of Excellence at Shell (1994, 2004); 12-time Recipient, Special Recognition Awards at Shell, Total of 12 Times/25 Years **MEM:** American Petroleum Institute (API); American Institute of Chemical Engineers; Combustion Institute; Sigma Xi, The Scientific Research Honor Society **MH:** Albert Nelson Marquis Lifetime Achievement Award; Marquis Who's Who Top Professional **B/I:** Dr. Jamaluddin became involved in his profession because part of it came from his parents. His parents wanted one of their kids to go into engineering and one in medicine, so he chose engineering, especially chemical engineering. When it came to a specialty, he liked combustion and heat transfer as his field and enjoyed the work he did. **AV:** Reading; Music; Traveling; Spending time with family

JAMBECK, JENNA, T: Professor **I:** Education/ Educational Services **CN:** University of Georgia **ED:** PhD in Environmental Engineering Sciences, University of Florida (2004); ME in Environmental Engineering Sciences, University of Florida (1998); BS in Environmental Engineering Sciences, University of Florida (1996) **CT:** EIT Credential **C:** Professor, College of Engineering, University of Georgia (2019-Present); Associate Professor, College of Engineering, University of Georgia (2015-2019); Assistant Professor, College of Engineering, University of Georgia (2009-2015); Research Assistant Professor of Environmental Engineering, University of New Hampshire (2005-2009); ORAU Post-Doc, U.S. Environmental Protection Agency (2004-2005); Graduate Research Assistant, University of Florida (2000-2004); Project Engineer, URS Corporation (1998-2000); Intern, Law Engineering and Environmental Services (1996) **CR:** National Geographic Fellow, Co-Lead Source to Sea Plastics Initiative, National Geographic (2018-Present); International Informational Speaker **CW:** Co-Author, "Plastic waste inputs from land into the ocean," Science/AAAS (2015); Co-Author, "Application of the Sustainable Neighborhoods for Happiness Index to Coastal Cities in the United States," Ocean and Coastal Management (2014); Co-Author, "Municipal Solid Waste Landfill Leachate Treatment and Electricity Production Using Microbial Fuel Cells," Applied Biochemistry and Biotechnology (2014); Co-Author, "The Sustainable Neighborhoods for Happiness Index: A Metric for Assessing a Community's Potential Influence on Residential Happiness," Ecological Indicators (2014); Co-Author, "Are Sustainable Cities 'Happy' Cities?: Associations Between Sustainable Development and Human Well-Being in Urban Areas of the United States," Environment, Development and Sustainability (2013); Co-Author, "Treatment of Landfill Leachate Using Microbial Fuel Cells: Alternative Anodes and Semi-Continuous Operation," Bioresource Technology (2013); Contributor, Science Publications **AW:** Creative Research

Medal, University of Georgia (2016) **MEM:** National Geographic Explorer, National Geographic Society (2018-Present)

JAMES, ASHLEY, T: Curator **I:** Fine Art **CN:** Guggenheim Museum **ED:** PhD Candidate in English Literature, African American Studies, Women's Gender and Sexuality Studies, Yale University; MA, Yale University; BA, Columbia University **C:** Curator, Guggenheim Museum (2019-Present); Assistant Curator of Contemporary Art, Brooklyn Museum **CR:** Mellon Curatorial Fellow in Drawing and Prints, Museum of Modern Art; Studio Museum, Harlem, NY; Yale University Art Gallery **CW:** Lead Curator, "Soul of a Nation: Art in the Age of Black Power," Brooklyn Museum; Organizer, "Eric N. Mack: Lemme Walk Across the Room"; Co-Curator, "John Edmonds: A Sidelong Glance"; Co-Organizer, "Odd Volumes: Book Art from the Allan Chasanoff Collection"; Contributor, Essays and Research for Books, Magazines and Catalogues

JAMES, LEBRON RAYMONE, T: Professional Basketball Player **I:** Athletics **DOB:** 12/30/1984 **PB:** Akron **SC:** OH/USA **PT:** Gloria James; McClelland Anthony **MS:** Married **SPN:** Savannah Brinson (9/14/2013) **CH:** LeBron Junior; Bryce Maximus; Zhuri Nova **C:** Forward, Los Angeles Lakers (2018-Present); Forward, Cleveland Cavaliers (2003-2010, 2014-2018); Forward, Miami Heat (2010-2014); Co-Founder, Partner, LRMR Innovative Marketing & Branding, Cleveland **CR:** Vice President, National Basketball Players Association (2015-Present); Member, U.S. National Team, Summer Olympic Games, London (2012); Member, U.S. National Team, Summer Olympic Games, Beijing (2008); Member, U.S. National Team, Summer Olympic Games, Athens, Greece (2004) **CIV:** Founder, Board of Directors, LeBron James Family Foundation (2004-Present) **CW:** Guest Appearance, "Entourage" (2009); Co-Author, "Shooting Stars" (2009); Cover Feature, Vogue (2008); Featured "More Than A Game" (2008); Co-Host, ESPY Awards Show (2007); Guest Host, Saturday Night Live (2007) **AW:** 100 Most Influential, Time (2017); All Star, NBA (2017); All-NBA 1st Team (2006, 2008-2014, 2017); MVP, NBA Finals (2012, 2013, 2016); All-Star Team, The Eastern Conference (2005-2016); MVP, NBA (2009-2010, 2012-2013); All-Defensive 1st Team, NBA (2009-2013); The Most Influential People in the World, Time Magazine (2005, 2013); Male Athlete of Year, Associated Press (2013); Sportsman of the Year, Sports Illustrated (2012); Gold Medal, Men's Basketball, Summer Olympic Games (2008, 2012); NBA Player of the Year, The Sporting News (2006, 2009); All-Star Game MVP, NBA (2006, 2008); Rookie of the Year, NBA (2004); National High School Player of the Year, USA Today (2003); One of the 10 Most Fascinating People, Barbara Walters Special (2010); The 40 Under 40, Fortune Magazine (2010); The 100 Agents of Change, Rolling Stone Magazine (2009); The Most Influential People in the World of Sports, Business Week (2007, 2008); The 100 Most Powerful Celebrities, Forbes.com (2008); The Power 150, Ebony Magazine (2008); Best Male Athlete Award, Black Entertainment TV (2006-2007); Bronze Medal, Men's Basketball (2004); All-Rookie First Team, NBA (2004)

JAMES, RAY ALLAN, T: Songwriter; Author; Singer; Insurance Adjuster **I:** Consulting **CN:** RJ Legal & Recreation Processing SVC **DOB:** 05/31/1958 **PB:** Wichita Falls **SC:** TX/USA **PT:** Ray Henry James; Betty Carol Jones; Jim Henry Jones (Stepfather) **MS:** Single **ED:** MA in Training and Development, Midwestern State University (2006); BS in Management Studies, Texas A&M Technology; Coursework, University of Maryland (1990);

AA in General Studies, University of Maryland (1987) **CT:** Licensed Adjuster, Property and Casualty, Texas Department of Insurance; Concealed Handgun Permit; Chartered Driver License; ESL **C:** Songwriter, Property Inspections, RJ Legal & Recreation Processing SVC (2004-Present); T-Square Logistics (2000-Present); Pinkerton Security and 9th Street Trailer Park Ct Security (1990-2014); Heavy Equipment Operator & Over-the-road Driver (1990-1999); FWISD Teacher(1988-1993); Union National Staff Insurance Sales Agent and United Insurance Sales Agent (1983-1985); Arlington Police Dispatch (1983); Halliburton Services Heavy Equipment Operator (1979-1982) **CR:** Over-the-road Truck Driver, Instructor (15 Years); Singer and Lyricist (15 Years); Communications Specialist (10 years); Administrative Technology (10 Years); Property Inspector (6 Years) **CIV:** MSU Graduate Senator; Scoutmaster, Boy Scouts of America, DeMolay **MIL:** Sergeant, United States Army Reserves; HHC, 59th Ord Bde (USAEUR), Colonel 158th Aviation Regiment, Grand Prairie, Texas; 425th MP Detachment, Fort Worth, Texas; 413th Civil Affairs, Lubbock, Texas; BNOC Fort Chaffee, AR; Basic Training & AIT Fort Jackson, SC 29207; 4159th Reserve School, Fort Worth, TX **CW:** Author, "A Sketch of My Life," "Legends from the Past," "Lovers Paradise Duet," "The Devils Run," "The Lamb of God," "The Land of the Believers," "The Test of Time is in God's Hands," "A Statue of You or Me," "Land of Opportunity," "Get a Life," "Turn Your Life Around," "He's My Brother, He Ain't Heavy," "Ambassadors of God," "The Land of the Believers," "A Pocket Full of Emotion," "I Got Friends in High Places," and "My True Love Forever"(1999-2020); Singer, Lyricist, Author, "The American Dream" (1993-2020); Author, "A Self-Help Approach to School Bus Issues and Emergency Procedures," (2006); Author, Singer, Composer and Lyricist, "The Blue Bonnet State," "Desert Storm," "No More Battlefield Cry," "The Chattanooga Dance," "A Touch of Mary Ann Hatfield," "God Bless America," "Ambassadors of God," "Santa's Coming to Town Tonight," "Let Me Tell You Now," "I've Said it Once, I'll Say it Again," and "Mrs. Right" **AW:** Named "The Ultimate Songwriter" (2019); Named Best Poet of the Year; Rated Top Singer for Garth Brooks, "We Shall Be Free" **MEM:** The Guild of International Songwriters & Composers; ASCAP; Nashville Songwriters Association International **MH:** Who's Who of Professional Songwriters & Services **AS:** Mr. James attributes his success to a well-rounded education and the many experiences he had while he was in the military. His leadership and writing ability are fully developed in country music with Nashville Stars & Demo Artists. **B/I:** In his early years, Mr. James always had a love for music. Music connected him with the people he really liked, including Kim, a young lady whom he sang with in junior high. He has written many songs, and additionally converted some, including, "He Ain't Heavy, He's My Brother." Mr. James also wrote a song recently for President Donald Trump, "God Bless America" and "Santa's Coming to Town Tonight." The intentions of these two songs were to tie in what is good about America and bring to light what is currently happening in Jerusalem. President Trump has listened to these songs and likes them. A lot of Mr. James songs are biographical and relevant to the times. He likes to write using his background in education, military and truck driving nationals and he felt he could say something that would help others.He likes to write using his background in education, military and truck driving nationals and he felt he could say something that would help others. **AV:** Nashville's Songwriters Association **PA:** Republican **RE:** Christian **THT:** Mr. James gives his knowledge and understanding of poli-

tics to enhance President Trump. He also reviews news media and puts quick decision-making skills on how best to help our country and other countries that are currently in need of advice. He has a contract for Pearl Records pending in reference to a collection of songs titled, "The American Dream." Some of Mr. James' songs can be found at the following links: https://soundcloud.com/ray-allan-james; https://soundcloud.com/ray-allan-james/james-ray-allan-the-test-of; https://soundcloud.com/ray-allan-james/james-ray-allan-mrsright-bootscoot-suggiemaster-1; https://soundcloud.com/ray-allan-james/james-ray-allan-the-land-of-1; https://soundcloud.com/ray-allan-james/james-ray-allan-rebuilding-faith-after-desert-storm; https://soundcloud.com/ray-allan-james/james-ray-allan-the-lamb-of; https://soundcloud.com/ray-allan-james/james-ray-allan-ambassadors-of; https://soundcloud.com/ray-allan-james/a-statue-of-you-or-me; https://soundcloud.com/ray-allan-james/james-ray-allan-mrsrightbootscoot-suggie-master; https://soundcloud.com/ray-allan-james/james-ray-allan-the-chattanooga-dance; https://soundcloud.com/ray-allan-james/james-ray-allan-a-touch-of-mary-ann-hatfield; https://soundcloud.com/ray-allan-james/james-ray-allan-desert-storm; https://soundcloud.com/ray-allan-james/james-ray-allan-the-blue-bonnet-state; https://soundcloud.com/ray-allan-james/i-got-friends-in-high-places; https://soundcloud.com/ray-allan-james/let-me-tell-you-now; https://soundcloud.com/ray-allan-james/james-ray-allan-the-land-of-the-believers; https://soundcloud.com/ray-allan-james/james-ray-allan-the-land-of-1; https://soundcloud.com/ray-allan-james/santa-coming-to-town-tonight-by-ray-allan-james; https://soundcloud.com/ray-allan-james/james-ray-allan-get-a-life; https://soundcloud.com/ray-allan-james/hes-my-brother-he-aint-heavy; https://soundcloud.com/ray-allan-james/james-ray-allan-santa-coming-to-town; https://soundcloud.com/ray-allan-james/no-more-battlefield-cry; https://soundcloud.com/ray-allan-james/james-ray-allan-lovers; https://soundcloud.com/ray-allan-james/my-true-love-forever; Singer and songwriter, Ray A. James, has also posted on YouTube, which can be seen at: https://youtu.be/da9Gcn1PbskA blog post from Mr. James can be read at: https://rayajames758304572.wordpress.com/2019/09/14/president-trump/. Additional information for Mr. James can be found at: https://educators-perform.webnode.com/#!

JAMSHIDI, MOHAMMAD, T: Electrical Engineer **I:** Engineering **DOB:** 05/10/1944 **PB:** Shiraz **SC:** Fars/Iran **PT:** Habib Jamshidi (Deceased); Kobra (Semsar) Jamshidi **MS:** Married **SPN:** Jila Salari (06/21/1974) **CH:** Ava; Nima H. **ED:** Honorary Doctor of Engineering, University of Waterloo, Canada (2004); Honorary Doctor of Engineering, Technical University of Crete, Greece (2004); Honorary Doctor of Science, Odlar Yourdu University, Baku, Azerbaijan (1998); PhD, University of Illinois (1971); MSEE, University of Illinois (1969); BSEE, Oregon State University (1967) **C:** Lutcher Brown Endowed Chair, Department of Electrical and Computer Engineering, The University of Texas at San Antonio, Texas (2006-Present); Regents Professor Emeritus and AT&T Professor Emeritus, The University of New Mexico (2003-2006); Director, Center for Autonomous Control Engineering, The University of New Mexico, Albuquerque, NM (1995-2006); AT&T Professor, The University of New Mexico, Albuquerque, NM (1991-2006); Professor, The University of New Mexico, Albuquerque, NM (1979-2006); Director of Research, CNRS-LAAS, Toulouse, France (1994-1995) **CR:** Vice Chair, IFAC Technical Committee on Large-Scale Systems (2010-Present); Visiting Professor of

System of Systems Engineering, Loughbrough University (2014-2017); Professor, Pahlavi University, Shiraz, Iran (1977-1979); IBM World Trade Fellow, Paris, France (1975-1977); Advisor, Department of Energy; Special Government Employee, Air Force Research Laboratory, NASA **CW:** Author, 74 Books in the Field; Contributor, Articles to Professional Journals; Patentee on Fuzzy Logic Video Printers, Cloud Computing **AW:** Named Advisor of Laboratory Excellence (2012-Present); Named Honorary Professor, Obuda University, Budapest, Hungary (2012-Present); Named Honorary Professor, University of Birmingham, United Kingdom (2011-Present); Named Honorary Chaired Professor, Deakin University, Deakin, Australia (2009-Present); IEEE-USA Career Award in Systems Engineering (2014); Invited Member of International Advisory Board of European Cyber-Physical Systems Network SOCIALCPS (2014); Career Contribution Award, IEEE-USA (2014); WAC Medal of Honor (2014); University of Texas at San Antonio College of Engineering Best Researcher Award (2014); Best Contribution Award, IEEE Systems Council (2013); Presidential Award for Advancing Globalization of Institution (2012); Best Paper Award, IEEE Systems Conference (2010); Best Paper Award, Kobe, Japan (2010); Distinguished Fellow, Cardiff University, Cardiff, Wales (2009-2010); Distinguished Visiting Research Fellow, Royal Academy of Engineering, United Kingdom (2009); Named Honorary Professor, Deakin University, Australia (2006-2008); IEEE SMC Society Distinguished Contribution Award (2006); Named Distinguished Alumni, Oregon State University (2006); IEEE Norbert Weiner Distinguished Research Award (2005); Fellow, The New York Academy of Sciences (2004); NASA Public Service Award (1999-2004); Named Honorary Chaired Professor, Deakin University, Deakin, Australia (2001); IEEE Control Systems Society Millennium Award (2000); Fellow ASME (1999); Fellow, American Association for the Advancement of Science (1998); Fellow, TWAS Developing World Academy of Sciences (1995); Winner, College of Engineering Outstanding Researcher of the Year, The University of New Mexico (1993); Fellow, IEEE (1989); IEEE Control Systems Society Distinguished Member Award (1985); Centennial Medal, IEEE (1984); Winner, General Electric College Bowl Scholarship, Oregon State University (1966-1967); Winner, Four-year Tuition Scholarship, Oregon State University (1963-1967); Named Eta Kappa Nu Electrical Engineering Outstanding Sophomore (1965); Named Honorary Chaired Professor, Nanjing Aeronautical University Nanjing, People's Republic of China; Named Honorary Chaired Professor, Xi'an University of Technology, Xi'an, People's Republic of China; Named Honorary Chaired Professor, East China Industrial Institute, Nanjing, People's Republic of China **MEM:** Committee on System of Systems Engineering, U.S. Department of Defense (2009-Present); Fellowship Review Board, US-Vietnam Education Foundation (2009-Present); US National Research Council Review Board, DOE and Ford Foundation (2001-2009); Russian Academy of Nonlinear Sciences (2000); Foreign Member, Hungarian Academy of Engineering (1999); Sigma Xi, The Scientific Research Honor Society (1980); Junior Honor Student, The Honor Society of Phi Kappa Phi (1966); IEEE - Eta Kappa Nu (1966); The Tau Beta Pi Association, Inc. (1966); Sigma Tau Engineering Honor Society (1966); Fellow, The World Academy of Science (TWAS); Hungarian Academy of Engineering; American Association for the Advancement of Science; Association of Mechanical Engineering; The New York Academy of Science; Fellow, IEEE; Fellow, The American Society of Mechanical Engineers (ASME); IFAC Group on Large-Scale Systems; Numerous IFAC and Other Conferences and Symposia Program Committees; NRC Committee on Manufacturing Engineer, National Academy of Science; Council, University of Texas Chancellor; Task Force on Aeronautical Engineering, National Academy of Engineering **MH:** Albert Nelson Marquis Lifetime Achievement Award **AS:** Dr. Jamshidi attributes his success to hard work and great time management. **B/I:** Dr. Jamshidi first arrived in America in 1963. He originally wanted to be a civil engineer. After spending a year at Oregon State University as a civil engineering major, he felt that it wasn't a real challenge to him. He then decided to change his focus to electrical engineering, which also associated heavily with the newly emerging computer industry at the time. It was a much more dynamic field for him. **AV:** Swimming; Travel; Stamp collection

JAN, CONCHITA TSENG, T: Music Educator **I:** Education/Educational Services **DOB:** 04/15/1941 **PB:** Hsin-Chu **SC:** Taiwan **MS:** Married **SPN:** Shan Jan **ED:** BA, Towson University (1982); The Royal Conservatory (1973); National Taiwan University of Arts (1968); Postgraduate Coursework, Towson University **C:** Private Piano Teacher, (1978-Present); Conductor, The Washington Chorus (1990-1998); Piano Accompanist, Tung-Hsin Choral Society, Potomac, MD (1982-1990) **CR:** Judge, Guild Audition, American College of Musicians (2001-Present); Judge, Maryland State Music Teachers Association (1982-Present) **MEM:** Vice President for Student Activities, Maryland State Music Teachers Association (2001-2005); Chair, Piano Solo Festival, Maryland State Music Teachers Association (2000-2005); Chair, Piano Concerto Competition, Maryland State Music Teachers Association (1996-2000); Chair, Piano Ensemble Festival, Maryland State Music Teachers Association (1983-1996) **MH:** Albert Nelson Marquis Lifetime Achievement Award **B/I:** Ms. Jan became involved in her profession because of her studies in Taiwan and at the Royal Conservatory in Spain. **AV:** Playing tennis; Gardening; Singing in choir **RE:** Catholic

JANAK, ROBERT, T: Foreign Language Educator **I:** Education/Educational Services **DOB:** 01/07/1945 **PB:** Schulenburg **SC:** TX/USA **PT:** Josef Peter; Edna Petrolina (Kubos) J. **ED:** Master of Arts in History, University of Kansas (1969); Fulbright Fellowship, Babes-Bolyai University, Cluj, Romania (1966); Bachelor of Arts in History, Lamar University, Beaumont, TX (1966) **CT:** Certified History and Spanish Teacher, Texas **C:** Creator of Czech Exhibit, Institute of Texan Cultures, San Antonio, TX (1999-2001); Spanish Teacher, West Brook High School, Beaumont, TX (1982-Present); Spanish Teacher, Hebert High School, Beaumont, TX (1970-1982) **CR:** Chairman, Foreign Language Department, West Brook High School, Beaumont, TX (1984-1990, 2003-2012); Co-chairman, Site-Based Decision Making Committee, Beaumont, TX (1992-1993); Teacher Leader, People to People Friendship Caravan, Soviet Union (1989); Chairman, Foreign Language Department, Hebert High School, Beaumont, TX (1972-1980) **CIV:** Campus Campaign Coordinator, United Way, Beaumont, TX (1987-2002, 2005-2007); Advisory Council, Czech Cultural Center, Houston, TX (1996); Leader of Student Group Masaryk University, Brno, Czechslovakia (1990); Delegate, Democratic Convention, Jefferson County, TX (1980, 1984, 1988, 1990) **CW:** Columnist, Cesky Hlas; Contributor, Articles to Professional Journals **AW:** Outstanding Teacher, West Brook High School (2005); Named, Honorary Citizen Town Council, Trojanovice, Czech Republic (1992); Texas Regional Teacher of the Year, Texas Education Agency (1992); Good Apple Award, Parent Teacher Association, Beaumont, TX (1989); Mirabeau B. Lamar Award, South Park Lodge 1320 A.F.&A.M, Beaumont, TX (1989); Outstanding Teacher, Beaumont A&M Club, Hebert High School (1976); Grantee, Kosciuszho Foundation, Jagiellonian University, Cracow, Poland (1969) **MEM:** Historian, Czech Heritage Society of Texas (1997-2016); Advisory Trustee, Czech Heritage Society of Texas (2008); Trustee, Czech Heritage Society of Texas (1988-2005); President, Czech Heritage Society of Texas (1982-1983, 1992-1993); Historian, Parent Teacher Association (1982-1985); Treasurer, Parent Teacher Association (1979-1981) **MH:** Albert Nelson Marquis Lifetime Achievement Award **AV:** Tombstone inscriptions; Genealogy; Local history **PA:** Democrat **RE:** Methodist

JANOS, JAMES, "JESSE VENTURA" GEORGE, T: Former Governor of Minnesota; Professional Wrestler (Retired) **I:** Government Administration/Government Relations/Government Services **DOB:** 07/15/1951 **PB:** Minneapolis **SC:** MN/USA **PT:** George William Janos; Bernice Martha (Lenz) Janos **MS:** Married **SPN:** Theresa Larson Masters (07/18/1975) **CH:** Tyrel; Jade **ED:** Coursework, North Hennepin Community College, Brooklyn Park, MN **C:** Visiting Fellow, John F. Kennedy School of Government, Harvard University (2004-Present); Host, "Jesse Ventura's America," MSNBC (2003); Governor, State of Minnesota, St. Paul, MN (1999-2003); Mayor, Brooklyn Park, MN (1991-1995); Commentator, World Championship Wrestling (1992-1994); Co-Host, "Saturday Night's Main Event" (1985-1990); Professional Wrestler, World Wrestling Federation (WWF) (Now WWE) (1973-1984); Bodyguard, Rolling Stones **CIV:** Member, Izaak Walton League of America; Volunteer, Football Coach, Champlin Park High School; Member, Advisory Board, Make-A-Wish Foundation of Minnesota **MIL:** Underwater Demolition Team 12, U.S. Navy (1969-1975) **CW:** Host, "Jesse Ventura Off the Grid" (2014-Present); Host, Television Series, "The World According to Jesse" (2017); Author, "Sh*t Politicians Say: The Funniest, Dumbest Most Outrageous Thing Ever Uttered by Our Leaders" (2016); Author, "Jesse Ventura's Marijuana Manifesto: How Lies, Corruption, and Propaganda Kept Cannabis Illegal" (2016); Voice Actor, "Teenage Mutant Ninja Turtles" (2014); Actor, "The Drunk" (2014); Co-Author, "They Killed Our President: 63 Reasons to Believe There Was a Conspiracy to Assassinate JFK" (2013); Co-Author, "DemoCRIPS and ReBLOODlicans: No More Gangs in Government" (2012); Author, "63 Documents the Government Doesn't Want You to Read" (2011); Himself, "Cubed" (2011); Co-Author, "American Conspiracies: Lies, Lies, and More Dirty Lies that the Government Tells Us" (2010); Actor, "Woodshop" (2010); Host, Producer, "Conspiracy Theory with Jesse Ventura" (2009-2012); Co-Author, "Don't Start the Revolution Without Me!" (2008); Actor, Film, "Borders" (2008); Voice Actor, "The Ringer" (2005); Actor, "Stuck on You" (2003); Co-Author, "Jesse Ventura Tells It Likes It Is: America's Most Outspoken Governor Speaks Out About Government" (2002); Co-Author, "Do I Stand Alone?: Going to the Mat Against Political Pawns and Media Jackals" (2000); Himself, "WWE Raw" (1999-2009); Actor, "20/20 Vision" (1999); Appearance, Documentary, "Beyond the Mat" (1999); Author, "The Wit and Wisdom of Jesse 'The Body–The Mind' Ventura" (1999); Author, "I Ain't Got Time to Bleed: Reworking the Body Politic from the Bottom Up" (1999); Actor, Television Series, "The Young and the Restless" (1999); Actor, "Batman and Robin" (1997); Actor, "The X-Files" (1996); Actor, "Arli$$" (1996); Host, Radio Program, KFAN 1130 and KSTP 1500 (1995-1998); Himself, "The History of SummerSlam" (1994); Himself, "Major League II" (1994); Actor, "Living and Working in Space: The Countdown Has Begun" (1993); Actor, "Demolition Man" (1993); Actor, "Renegade" (1992); Actor, "Zorro" (1991); Actor, "Ricochet" (1991); Actor, "Tagteam" (1991); Co-Host, Game Show, "The Grudge Match" (1991); Actor, "Hunter" (1990, 1985); Actor, "Abraxas, Guardian of the Universe" (1990); Actor, "No Holds Barred" (1989); Actor, "Thunderground" (1989); Co-Host, "Record Breakers" (1989); Actor, "The Running Man" (1987); Actor, "Predator" (1987) **AW:** Inductee, World Wrestling Entertainment (WWE) Hall of Fame (2004); Frank Gotch Award, International Wrestling Institute & Museum (2003); Ranked #239, Top 500 Singles Wrestlers During the "PWI Years," Pro Wrestling Illustrated (2003); Iron Mike Mazurki Award, Cauliflower Alley Club (1999); Best Color Commentator, Wrestling Observer Newsletter Awards (1987-1990); Wrestler of the Year, Ring Around The Northwest Newsletter (1976); Decorated Vietnam Service Medal; National Defense Service Medal; Ranked #67, Top 100 Tag Teams of the "PWI Years," Pro Wrestling Illustrated **MEM:** Screen Actors Guild (Now SAG-AFTRA); American Federation of Television and Radio Artists (Now SAG-AFTRA) **PA:** Independent

JARVIK, ROBERT KOFFLER, MD, T: Founder, President, Chief Executive Officer; Biomedical Research Scientist **I:** Medicine & Health Care **CN:** Jarvik Heart, Inc. **DOB:** 05/11/1946 **PB:** Midland **SC:** MI/USA **PT:** Norman Eugene Jarvik; Edythe (Koffler) Jarvik **MS:** Married **SPN:** Marilyn vos Savant (08/23/1987); Elaine Levin (1968, Divorced 1985) **CH:** Tyler; Kate **ED:** Honorary DSc, Hahnemann University (1985); Honorary DSc, Syracuse University (1983); MD, University of Utah School of Medicine (1976); MS in Medical Engineering, New York University (1971); BA, Syracuse University (1968) **C:** Founder, President, Chief Executive Officer, Jarvik Research Inc., New York, NY (Now Jarvik Heart, Inc.) (1988-Present); Assistant Research Professor of Surgery, The University of Utah, Salt Lake City, Utah (1979-1987); President, Symbion, Inc., Salt Lake City, Utah (1978-1987); Assistant Director of Experimental Laboratories, The University of Utah, Salt Lake City, Utah (1976-1982); Research Assistant, Division of Artificial Organs, The University of Utah, Salt Lake City, Utah (1971-1976) **CW:** Section Editor, International Journal of Artificial Organs (1979-1988) **AW:** Named Inventor of the Year, Intellectual Property Owners Association (1983); Golden Plate Award, American Academy of Achievement (1983); Gold Heart Award, Utah Heart Association (1983); John W. Hyatt Award, Society of Plastics Engineers (Now SPE-Inspiring Plastics Professionals) (1983)

JASWAL, TONY, T: Principal **I:** Oil & Energy **CN:** General Energy Corp **ED:** BE, University of Illinois **CT:** Certified Energy Manager (CEM) **C:** Principle, General Energy Corporation (2015-Present); Owner, Energy (2013-2015); Planning, Execution, and Closing of Energy Efficiency Projects, Bluestone Energy Services; Quality Check and Compliance, ComEd's Smart Ideas for Business program, Patrick Engineering, Inc.; Abbott Laboratories **CIV:** Volunteer, Weekly Food Drive **AW:** Named Entrepreneur of the Year, REA - Renewable Energy Association (2017) **MEM:** Green Energy Council **AS:** Mr. Jaswal will always strive for more because of the way he was raised; never settle, keep going and keep advancing. These are the values he was raised on and what has carried him thus far. **B/I:** Mr. Jaswal grew up with a single mother. She worked very hard, working two jobs to support and give him and his two siblings the opportunity to achieve their dreams and goals. That was very inspirational for him and the reason he became an entrepreneur and started his own company striv-

ing for even more. **AV:** Playing basketball; Spending time with family and friends hiking; provides community services to help the needy a couple of times a month **THT:** Mr. Jaswal's motto is, "Keep striving." Executive Vice President Mr. Jaswal is a mechanical engineering graduate and a certified energy manager (CEM). He is responsible for business development and assists in corporate matters and strategic planning. He has extensive industry experience while working with Bluestone Energy Services, Patrick Engineering, and Abbott Laboratories. For the last six years, he has developed many energy efficiency projects, including process cooling, refrigeration, indoor and outdoor lighting, chiller and boiler plant projects for industrial and commercial clients. Some of the major projects include Federal Mogul, Aurora Specialty Textile Group, Baker and Taylor, Metro-South Hospital, and Dr. Pepper. He is responsible of coordinating GEC effort to arrange funding of projects through funding from energy savings. Mr. Jaswal, while working with Bluestone Energy Services, was responsible for planning, execution, and closing of energy efficiency projects. At Patrick Engineering, he was responsible for quality check and compliance with ComEd's Smart Ideas for Business program. He is a BSME degree holder from the University of Illinois and a certified energy manager (CEM).

JATTAN-CUNNINGHAM, LYNETTE S., MD, FAAP, T: Pediatrician **I:** Medicine & Health Care **CN:** Conyers Pediatrics **DOB:** 10/07/1951 **PB:** Curepe **SC:** West Indies **PT:** David Gildharry Jattan (Deceased); Dolly Agnes Jattan **MS:** Married **SPN:** Ralph Cunningham **CH:** Katherine Cunningham **ED:** Residency in Pediatrics, Carolinas Medical Center (1993-1995); Diploma in Dermatology, University of London (1987); Intern, Port of Spain General Hospital (1983); MBBS, The University of the West Indies (1982); BS in Biochemistry, Minor in Pharmacology, Concordia University (1977) **C:** Conyers Pediatrics (1995-Present) **AW:** Numerous Reader's Choice Awards **MEM:** Fellow, American Academy of Pediatrics (1995) **MH:** Albert Nelson Marquis Lifetime Achievement Award; Marquis Who's Who Top Professional **AS:** Dr. Jattan-Cunningham attributes her success to having been afflicted with tetanus at a young age. She had to learn to walk again while recovering, which helped her appreciate great health care and led her on her current path. **B/I:** Dr. Jattan-Cunningham' became involved in her profession because she always tended to her siblings. That natural ability to nurture and care for others inspired her to pursue a career in medicine. **AV:** Playing tennis; Traveling; Spending time with family and friends; Going on medical missions **RE:** Christian

JAVOREK, RICHARD ALAN, T: History Educator (Retired), Lafayette Township Zoning Chairman, Consultant **I:** Education/Educational Services **DOB:** 11/16/1950 **PB:** Cleveland **SC:** OH/USA **PT:** Sylvester Richard Javorek; Elanor Javorek **MS:** Married **SPN:** Nancy Ruth Bublo Wagner Javorek (12/23/1978) **CH:** Maryann Rush; Carolyn Pen **ED:** Master's Degree in Curriculum and Instruction, Kent State University (1998); Bachelor's Degree in History, Baldwin Wallace College (1972) **CT:** Ordained Minister, Universal Life Church (2011) **C:** Social Studies Teacher, Brunswick City Schools (1974-2006) **CR:** Assistant District Commissioner, Venturing and Exploring, Chippewa District Great Trail Council, Boy Scouts of America (2012-Present); Project Citizen Evaluator, Ohio Center, Law-Related Education (2010-Present); Commissioner, Explore Boy Scouts America, Great Trail Council, Boy Scouts of America (2009-Present); Chair, Ohio Social Studies Resource Center

(2004-Present); Chair-Elect, Ohio Social Studies Resource Center (2004-Present); Planning Committee, Youth for Justice Program, Ohio Center for Law-Related Education (1996-Present); Youth Justice Trainer, Evaluator, People Evaluation Program, Ohio Center for Law-Related Education (2006-2012); Adjunct Professor, Bryant & Stratton College (2006-2009); Social Studies Curriculum Advisory Review Committee, Ohio Graduate Test Standards Setting Committee, Ohio Department of Education (2003-2005); Political Consultant, Local Politics **CIV:** Captain, Ohio History Connection (2007-Present) **CW:** Co-Host, "Touring Duffers" **AW:** Positive Image Award, North Eastern Ohio Education Association (1998); Golden Apple Achievement Award, Ashland (1990) **MEM:** Chairman, Lafayette Township Zoning Commission (2012-Present); Chair, Regional Coordinator's Council, Ohio Education Association (2005-2006); Liaison to Legislative Commission, Ohio Education Association (2004-2006); Resolutions Commission, Ohio Education Association (2003-2006); Ohio Representative, Resolutions Committee, National Education Association (2003-2006); Chair, Day Committee, North Eastern Ohio Education Association (2002-2006); Awards Committee, Ohio Education Association (2000-2006); Executive Committee, Ohio Education Association (2000-2006); Executive Committee, Unit Four, North Eastern Ohio Education Association (2000-2006); State Council Fund for Children and Public Education, Ohio Education Association (1992-2006); Representative, Educators Caucus, National Education Association (1998-2005); Chair, Internal Policy Action Committee, North Eastern Ohio Education Association (1990-1998); Chair, President Service Advisory Council, Ohio Education Association (1984-1998); Mid-Atlantic Regional Director, National Education Association **MH:** Albert Nelson Marquis Lifetime Achievement Award **AV:** Fishing; Golfing

JAYAPAL, PRAMILA, T: U.S. Representative **I:** Government Administration/Government Relations/Government Services **DOB:** 09/21/1965 **PB:** Chennai, Tamil Nadu **SC:** India **MS:** Married **SPN:** Steve Williamson **CH:** One child **ED:** MBA, Kellogg School of Management, Northwestern University (1990); BA, Georgetown University (1986) **C:** U.S. Representative, Washington's Seventh Congressional District (2017-Present); Member, 37th District, Washington Senate (2015-2016); Founder, Hate Free Zone (2001-2012); Member, Committee on Budget; Member, Committee on Judiciary; With, Sales and Marketing, Medical Company; Financial Analyst, PaineWebber **CW:** Author, "Pilgrimage: One Woman's Return to a Changing India" (2000) **PA:** Democrat

JEDLICKA, GERALD FRANK, T: Business/Accounting Educator **I:** Education/Educational Services **DOB:** 06/30/1941 **PB:** Kemp **SC:** TX/USA **PT:** Frank Jedlicka; Thelma (Wingo) Jedlicka **MS:** Married **SPN:** Judy Ann Jedlicka (06/01/1968) **CH:** Julie Thelane (Jedlicka) Nabors; Jerry Frank Jedlicka **ED:** MEd, East Texas State University (1967); BS, East Texas State University (1963); AS, Henderson County Junior College, Athens, TX (1961) **C:** Accounting Instructor, Trinity Valley Community College, Terrell, TX (1974-1999); Business Instructor, Blinn College, Brenham, TX (1967-1974); Business Instructor, Coach, Chapel Hill High School, Tyler, TX (1963-1967) **CR:** Sponsor, Phi Beta Lambda, Blinn College, Brenham, TX (1967-1974) **MEM:** Masons; Business Advisement Board (1988-1999) **MH:** Albert Nelson Marquis Lifetime Achievement Award **AS:** Mr. Jedlicka attributes his success to parental advisement. **AV:** Farming; Ranching **PA:** Democrat **RE:** Methodist **THT:** Mr. Jedlicka advised others: "Be honest and fair. Always work hard for what you want."

JEFFRIES, HAKEEM SEKOU, T: U.S. Representative from New York; Lawyer **I:** Government Administration/Government Relations/Government Services **DOB:** 08/04/1970 **PB:** Brooklyn **SC:** NY/USA **PT:** Marland Jeffries; Laneda Jeffries **MS:** Married **SPN:** Kennisandra (Arciniegas) Jeffries **CH:** Jeremiah; Joshua **ED:** JD, New York University School of Law, Magna Cum Laude (1997); MS in Public Policy, Georgetown University (1994); BA in Political Science, Binghamton University State Univerisity of New York (1992) **C:** Chair, Democratic Policy and Communications Committee (2017-Present); Member, U.S. House of Representatives from New York's Eighth Congressional District, Washington, DC (2013-Present); Member, U.S. House Judiciary Committee (2013-Present); Member, U.S. House Budget Committee (2013-Present); Member, District 57, New York State Assembly, Albany, NY (2007-2013); Litigation Counsel, CBS Corporation (2003-2006); Associate, Paul, Weiss, Rifkind, Wharton & Garrison, LLP (1999-2003); Law Clerk for the Honorable Harold Baer Jr., United States District Court for the Southern District of New York, NY (1998); Member, Committee on Education; Staff Member, Office of Mayor Sharon Pratt Kelly **CR:** Civil Rights, Civil Liberties Instructor, Crown Heights Youth Collective **CIV:** Member, Freedom Democrats, Brooklyn, NY; Member, 77th Precinct Community Council, NY **AW:** Named One of the 40 Under 40, Crain's New York Business (2006) **MEM:** President, Black Attorneys for Progress; Kappa Alpha Psi Fraternity, Inc. **PA:** Democrat **RE:** Baptist

JELINEK, WALTER CRAIG, T: Chief Executive Officer, President **I:** Retail/Sales **CN:** Costco Wholesale Corporation **DOB:** 08/08/1952 **SC:** CA/USA **ED:** BA, San Diego State University (1975) **C:** President, Chief Executive Officer, Costco Wholesale Corporation, Issaquah, WA (2012-Present); President, Chief Operating Officer, Costco Wholesale Corporation, Issaquah, WA (2010-2012); Executive Vice President, Chief Operating Officer, Merchandising, Costco Wholesale Corporation, Issaquah, WA (2004-2010); Executive Vice President, Chief Operating Officer, Northern Division, Costco Wholesale Corporation, Issaquah, WA (1995-2004); Senior Vice President of Operations, Northeastern Region, Costco Wholesale Corporation, Issaquah, WA (1992-1995); Vice President, Regional Operations Manager, Los Angeles Region, Costco Wholesale Corporation, Issaquah, WA (1986-1992); With, Costco Wholesale Corporation, Issaquah, WA (1984); With, Lucky Stores (1981-1984); Operations Manager, Los Angeles Division, FedMart (1969-1981); Various Positions, Gemco **CR:** Board of Directors, Costco Wholesale Corporation (2010-Present)

JENKINS, GAYE RANCK, BHS, MED, T: Adult Educator, Academic Specialist, Sociology Professor **I:** Education/Educational Services **DOB:** 12/27/1950 **PB:** Allenwood **SC:** PA/USA **PT:** Arthur Harry Ranck; Faith Newbury Ranck **MS:** Married **SPN:** Thomas Eugene Jenkins (09/14/1974) **CH:** Gregory West; Timothy Jenkins **ED:** Postgraduate Coursework, Pennsylvania State University, University Park (2001); MEd in Adult Education, Pennsylvania State University, University Park (2001); BHS, Pennsylvania College of Technology, Williamsport (1997); AAS, Pennsylvania College of Technology, Williamsport (1996) **C:** Academic Specialist, CSIU WATCH Project (2011-Present); Education Coordinator, Sullivan County Victim Services (2007-2008); Adjunct Graduate Faculty, Pennsylvania State Continuing Education, Univer-

sity Park (2004-2008); Adjunct Sociology Faculty, Pennsylvania College of Technology, Williamsport (2002-2019); Director, Women's Resource Center, Williamsport (1994-1996); Adult Recruiter, Hemlock Girl Scout Council, Montoursville, Pennsylvania (1993-1994); Volunteer Coordinator, Wise Options, YWCA, Williamsport, PA (1986-1992) **CR:** Liaison Between Academy, Community, Business Partners (2011-2019); Proposal Committee Member, Pennsylvania Adult Education Research Conference (2003); Intern, Adult Education Program, Pennsylvania State University (2001-2002); Practicum Teacher, World Campus, Pennsylvania State University (2000-2001); Presenter, Adult Education (1998-2008); Intern, Pennsylvania Coalition Against Domestic Violence, Harrisburg, PA (1997) **CIV:** Founding Member, Committee Community Directed Research and Education, Pennsylvania State University, University Park (1999-2005); Program Coordinator, 2nd Eastern Regional Adult Education Research Conference, University Park (2000); Board of Directors, Montgomery Area Historical Society **CW:** Editor, Newsletters, Pennsylvania State University Adult Education Program (1999-2001); Editor, Newsletters, Women's Resource Center Quarterly (1994-1996); Editor, Newsletters, Wise Options Quarterly (1991-1994); Contributor, Articles, Professional Journals **AW:** Pennsylvania State College Part-time Faculty, Excellence in Teaching Award, (2013); The Chancellor's List (2005-2006); Monk Professional Development Endowment, College of Education, Pennsylvania State University (2002); Volunteer of the Year, AIDS Resource Alliance (1994) **MEM:** Pennsylvania National Organization of Women; American Association of University Women; American Association Adult and Continuing Education; Pennsylvania Association Adult and Continuing Education; Pi Lambda Theta; Phi Delta Kappa **MH:** Albert Nelson Marquis Lifetime Achievement Award; Marquis Who's Who Top Professional; Marquis Who's Who Humanitarian Award **B/I:** Ms. Jenkins became involved in her profession because she was interested in women's issues and had worked in a variety of other areas. When she started working her motivation was because of a woman, Arlene Shaheen, who encouraged her due to the fact that she was helping a friend who was being abused. Arlene told her to come work for them so that was how it began. During that time she also considered going to college. **AV:** Card playing; Crossword puzzles; Reading; Listening to jazz and blues; Watching foreign films

JENKINS, JO ANN, T: Chief Executive Officer **I:** Business Management/Business Services **CN:** AARP **PB:** Mon Louis Island **SC:** AL/USA **ED:** BS in Political Science, Spring Hill College (1980); Graduate, Stanford Executive Program, Stanford Graduate School of Business; Honorary LHD, Spring Hill College; Honorary LHD, Washington College **C:** Chief Executive Officer, AARP (2014-Present); Chief Operating Officer, AARP (2013-2014); Senior Advisor, Chief of Staff, Chief Operating Officer, Library of Congress (1994-2010); Various Leadership Roles, U.S. Department of Housing and Urban Development, U.S. Department of Transportation, U.S. Department of Agriculture **CIV:** Board of Directors, AARP (2019-Present); President, AARP Foundation (2010-2013); Various Board/Advisory Positions, AARP Services, AARP Funds, Colonial Williamsburg Foundation, The Wall Street Journal CEO Council, Caring for Military Families; Board of Directors, National Symphony Orchestra, Kennedy Center; Board of Fellows, Stanford School of Medicine; U.S. Small Business Administration Council on Underserved Communities; Board of Directors, AVNET; Board for the Education, Gender, and Work System Initiative, World Economic Forum

Stewardship; Board of Governors, Health Systems Initiative, World Economic Forum **AW:** Baldrige Leadership Award (2019); Listee, World's 50 Greatest Leaders, Fortune (2019); Woman of Vision Award, WNET New York Public Media (2018); "Women Who Mean Business Award," Washington Business Journal (2018); Listee, Power and Influence Top 50, Nonprofit Times (2013-2016, 2018); Listee, Most Powerful Women in Business, Black Enterprise Magazine (2017); Actor's Fund Medal of Honor (2017); Presidential Award, International Association of Gerontology and Geriatrics (2017); Listee, Foreign Policy Global Thinker (2017); Listee, Power 100 – Washington's Most Influential People, Washington Life Magazine (2015-2017); Listee, Nonprofit Influencer of the Year (2015); Peace Corps Director's Award (2014); Malcolm Baldridge Fellow (2013)

JENNER, KENDALL NICOLE, T: Media Personality, Model **I:** Media & Entertainment **DOB:** 11/03/1995 **PB:** Los Angeles **SC:** CA/USA **PT:** Caitlyn Jenner; Kris Jenner **MS:** Single **ED:** High School Graduate (2014); Coursework, Sierra Canyon School **C:** Model, The Society Management, New York, NY; Model, Elite Model Management **CR:** Photographer (2016-Present); Model, Victoria's Secret Fashion Show (2015-2016); Launched, "Kendall + Kylie," Topshop (2015); Launched, Shoe and Handbag Line, Steve Madden's Madden Girl (2014); Launched, Jewelry Line, "Metal Haven by Kendall & Kylie," Pascal Mouawad's Glamhouse (2013); Launched, Clothing Line, "Kendall & Kylie Collection," PacSun (2013); Creative Director, "Gillette Venus Gets Ready with Kendall & Kylie Jenner" (2012); Launched, Nail Polish Line, Nicole by OPI (2011); Style Ambasador, Seventeen (2011) **CIV:** Fundraiser, Designers Against AIDS (2015); Participant, Kick'n It for Charity Celebrity Kickball Games, Glendale, CA (2014); Participant, Charity Bowling Game, Pinz, Studio City, CA (2014); Fundraiser, Children's Hospital Los Angeles (2013); Donor, Share Our Strength, No Kid Hungry and Greater Los Angeles Fisher House Foundation **CW:** "Keeping Up with the Kardashians" (2007-Present); Appearance, "I Think" (2019); Cameo, "Ocean's 8" (2018); Appearance, "Freaky Friday" (2018); Appearance, "Enchanté (Carine)" (2017); Guest Editor, Estée Edit (2016); Co-Author, "Time of the Twins" (2016); Appearance, "Where's the Love?" (2016); Appearance, "Taylor Swift: The 1989 World Tour Concert" (2015); Appearance, "I Am Cait" (2015); Co-Author, "Rebels: City of Indra" (2014); Guest Appearance, "Ridiculousness" (2014); Guest Appearance, "The High Fructose Adventures of Annoying Orange" (2014); Co-Host, Much Music Video Awards (2014); Appearance, Music Video, "Recognize" (2014); Guest Appearance, "America's Next Top Model" (2012); Guest Appearance, "Hawaii Five-0" (2012); Guest Appearance, "Khloé & Lamar" (2011); Guest Appearance, "Kourtney and Kim Take New York" (2011); Appearance, Music Video, "Blacklight" (2010); Guest Appearance, "Kourtney and Khloé Take Miami" (2009) **AW:** Icon of the Year, Revolve Awards (2018); Fashion Icon of the Decade, Daily Front Row Fashion Media Awards (2017); Choice Model, Teen Choice Awards (2017); Choice Model, Choice Female Hottie, Teen Choice Awards (2016); Social Media Star: Women (Readers' Choice), Models.com MDX Model of the Year Awards (2015); Internet Video: Viral Video, IADAS: The Lovie Awards (2015); Choice Model, Teen Choice Awards (2015); Breakout Star: Women (Readers' Choice), Models.com MDX Model of the Year Awards (2015); Choice TV Reality Star: Female, "Keeping Up with the Kardashians," Teen Choice Awards (2013)

JERVIS-WHITE, GWENDOLYN T., T: Mental Health Services Professional **I:** Health, Wellness and Fitness **CN:** Kaleida Health **DOB:** 07/15/1950 **PB:** New York **SC:** NY/USA **PT:** Nehemiah (Stepfather); Margaret Rose (Johnson) Campbell **MS:** Married **SPN:** Arnold White **ED:** MS, State University of New York (University at Buffalo), Buffalo, NY (1989); BS in Education, State University of New York (University at Buffalo), Buffalo, NY (1976) **C:** Retired 2013; Senior Counselor, Kaleida Health (2002-2013); Medical Social Worker, Kaleida Health (2001-2002); Mental Health Counselor, Kaleida Health (1987-2001); Coordinator Case Manager, Counselor, Geneva B. Scruggs Community Health Care Center, Buffalo, NY (1983-1987) **CR:** Clinical Liaison Women for Human Rights and Dignity, Buffalo, NY (1993-2001); Clinics Consultant, Conference Planner, Mental Health Association (1997) **CIV:** Consultant, Presenter, Strive for Women, Inc. (2002); Multicultural Diversity committee, Kalieda Health, Buffalo, NY (1995-1999) **AW:** Scholar, Neighborhood Youth Corp., Bronx, NY (1968) **MEM:** Historic Preservation, Hamlin Park Community Taxpayers Association; Parish Council for Catholic Diocese **MH:** Albert Nelson Marquis Lifetime Achievement Award **AS:** Mrs. Jervis-White attributes her success to her parents, who instilled a sense of civic duty and concern for the less fortunate within her. **B/I:** Mrs. Jervis-White initially planned on teaching English in high school but she felt unfulfilled in that area. At the time, she was going through a bad divorce and she was looking for a new, financially viable career option that could spark her interest. She went to interview for one such position; it was a part-time job, and the interviewer liked her personality, but did not think that she had the necessary mental health experience for the position. After telling her personal story to the interviewer, Mrs. Jervis-White asked how long it would take for her to accrue the needed experience, but she had impressed the interviewer so much that a position was created for her. She had always been interested in mental health; her grandmother was a victim of the mental health system in Georgia in the days where patients were simply locked up and put away. She resolved to work toward a better system. **AV:** Reading; Jazz; Travel; Mentoring **PA:** Democrat **RE:** Catholic

JETER, DEREK SANDERSON, T: Chief Executive Officer, Co-owner; Former Professional Baseball Player **I:** Athletics **CN:** Miami Marlins **DOB:** 06/26/1974 **PB:** Pequannock **SC:** NJ/USA **PT:** Sanderson Charles Jeter; Dorothy (Connors) Jeter **MS:** Married **SPN:** Hannah Davis (07/09/2016) **CH:** Bella; Story **ED:** Coursework, University of Michigan (1992) **C:** Chief Executive Officer, Co-owner, Miami Marlins, MLB (2017-Present); Founding Publisher, Jeter Publishing (2014-Present); Founder, The Players' Tribune (2014-Present); Shortstop, New York Yankees, MLB (1996-2014); Shortstop, New York Yankees, MLB (1995); Minor League Baseball Player (1992-1995) **CR:** Member, U.S. National Team, World Baseball Classic (2006, 2009) **CIV:** Founder, Turn 2 Foundation (1996-Present) **CW:** Co-author with Paul Mantell, "The Contract" (2014); Author, "Jeter Unfiltered" (2014); Appearance, "The Other Guys" (2010); Appearance, "Anger Management" (2003); Co-author with Jack Curry, "The Life You Imagine: Life Lessons for Achieving Your Dreams" (2001); Guest Host, "Saturday Night Live" (2001); Author, "Game Day: My Life On and Off the Field" (2001) **AW:** Named to New Jersey Hall of Fame (2015); Named to the American League All-star Team, MLB (1998-2002, 2004, 2006-2012, 2014); American League Silver Slugger Award (2006-2009, 2012); Named One of the 10 Most Fascinating People of 2011, Barbara Walters' Special (2011); American League Gold Glove Award (2004-2006, 2009, 2010); Roberto Clemente Award, MLB (2009); Named Sportsman of the Year, Sports Illustrated (2009); Hank Aaron Award (2006, 2009); World Series Champion, New York Yankees (1996, 1998-2000, 2009); Named One of the Most Influential People in the World of Sports, Business Week (Now Bloomberg Businessweek) (2007, 2008); Named to the Kalamazoo Central High School Athletic Hall of Fame (2003); Named All-star Game MVP, MLB (2000); Named World Series MVP (2000); Babe Ruth Award, Baseball Writers Association of America, New York Chapter (2000); Named American League Rookie of the Year, Baseball Writers Association of America (1996); Named Minor League Player of the Year, Baseball America (1994); Named Minor League Player of the Year, The Sporting News (1994); High School Player of the Year Award, Gatorade (1992); High School Player of the Year Award, American Baseball Coaches Association (1992); High School Player of the Year Award, USA Today (1992)

JEWELL, SARAH, "SALLY" MARGARET, T: Former U.S. Secretary of the Interior; Former Outdoor Apparel Company Executive **I:** Government Administration/Government Relations/Government Services **DOB:** 02/21/1956 **PB:** London **SC:** England/United Kingdom **PT:** Peter James Roffey; Anne (Murphy) Roffey **MS:** Marred **SPN:** Warren Jewell **CH:** Peter; Anne **ED:** BS in Mechanical Engineering, University of Washington (1978) **C:** Secretary, U.S. Department of Interior, Washington, DC (2013-2017); President, Chief Executive Officer, Recreational Equipment, Inc. (REI), Kent, WA (2005-2013); President, COO, Recreational Equipment, Inc. (REI), Kent, WA (2000-2005); President, Commercial Banking, Washington Mutual, Inc. (1996-2000); President, Chief Executive Officer, Westone Bancorp, Boise, ID (1992-1995); Executive Vice President, Security Pacific Bank, WA (1987-1992); Petroleum Engineer, Rainier Bank, Seattle, WA (1981-1987); Field Production Engineer, Mobil Oil Corporation, OK (1978-1981) **CR:** Board of Directors, Recreational Equipment, Inc. (REI) (1996-2013) **CIV:** Board of Regents, University of Washington (2002-2007, 2008-Present); Board Member, Mountains to Sound Greenway Trust (1991-Present); Board Member, Initiative for Global Development (IGD), IGD Leaders; Board Member, National Parks Conservation Association **AW:** Rachel Carson Award for Environmental Conservation, National Audubon Society (2009); Green Globe Environmental Catalyst Award (2008); Nonprofit Director of the Year Award, National Association of Corporate Directors (2008); Diamond Award for Distinguished Service, University of Washington College of Engineering (2007); Distinguished Leadership Award, University of Washington Foster School of Business (2006); Named CEO of the Year, Puget Sound Business Journal (2006) **AV:** Hiking; Camping **PA:** Democrat

JIMENEZ, HARLYN, LMT, NST, NMT, T: Founder, Chief Executive Officer **I:** Health, Wellness and Fitness **CN:** Six Degrees of Wellness **MS:** Married **CH:** Two Sons; Two Daughters **CT:** Massage Therapy License, High-Tech Institute, Orlando, FL (2003); NMT Certified **C:** Executive Creative Director, Six Degrees of Wellness, LLC (2019-Present); Executive Creative Director, Harlyn's Healing Touch, LLC (2017-Present); Executive Creative Director, Harlyn Touch Corporation (2012-Present); Executive Creative Director, Harlyn Jimenez, LLC (2015); Licensed Massage Therapist, Marriott (Marriott International, Inc.), Orlando, FL (2003-2008); Timeshare Sales, Westgate Resorts (2003-2004) **CR:** More than 40,000 Hours of Hands-on Massage Therapy Experience (2003-Present); Server, Bartender, Walt Disney World, Orlando, FL (1997-2010) **CIV:** Member, Rotary International **B/I:** Mr. Jimenez became involved in his profession because he was in a motorcycle accident and was told he may become an amputee; against the doctors' wishes, he went home and is now able to run a mile in eight minutes.

JINKERSON, MAXINE LOUISE, T: Facilitator for Gifted and Talented Education **I:** Education/Educational Services **DOB:** 08/10/1936 **PB:** Gary **SC:** IN/USA **PT:** Elias Daniel Spry; Vessey Jane (Ralph) Spry **MS:** Married **SPN:** Marvin Wayne Jinkerson (07/15/1985); Donald Howard Wintermute (08/11/1956, Divorced 1980) **CH:** Donine Marie Wintermute Schwartz; Mark Weston; Charles Martin; Bradford Wintermute **ED:** MA in Education, Southeast Missouri State University (1983); BA in Education, Harris Teachers College (Now Harris-Stowe State University) (1971); Coursework, University of Missouri (1964); Coursework, Northwest Missouri State University (1954-1956) **CT:** Certified Elementary Social Studies and Gifted Education Teacher, State of Missouri **C:** Organist, St. Andrews United Methodist Church (1977-Present); Gifted Education Teacher, Hillsboro R-3 School District (1983-1998); Fifth Grade Teacher, Hillsboro R-3 School District (1971-1983); Organist, Cedar Hill Presbyterian Church (1960-1963); Second Grade Teacher, Auxvasse Elementary School (1956-1959) **CR:** Coordinator, Autumn Acoustics Music Festival, Jefferson College, Hillsboro, MO (2002-2007); Coordinator, Jefferson County Conference for Gifted Children and Their Parents, Jefferson College, Hillsboro, MO (1988-1998) **CIV:** Member, National Society Daughters of the American Revolution (2002-Present) **MEM:** Missouri State Teachers Association; Gifted Association of Missouri; National Association for Gifted Children; P.E.O. Sisterhood; Jefferson County Square Dance Club **MH:** Albert Nelson Marquis Lifetime Achievement Award; Marquis Who's Who Top Professional **AS:** Ms. Jinkerson attributes her success to her focus on her students and her hard work. **B/I:** Ms. Jinkerson became involved in her profession because educational careers ran her family. **AV:** Playing the hammered dulcimer, organ and piano; Traveling' Studying genealogy; Writing **RE:** United Methodist

JITOMIRSKAYA, SVETLANA, T: Scientist **I:** Sciences **CN:** University of California, Irvine **DOB:** 06/04/1966 **PB:** Kharkov **SC:** Ukraine **MS:** Married **CH:** Three Children **ED:** PhD in Mathematics, Moscow State University (1991); BS, MS in Mathematics, Moscow State University, Summa Cum Laude (1987) **C:** Professor, Department Of Mathematics, University of California Irvine (2000-Present); Researcher, International Institute of Earthquake Prediction, Theory And Mathematics and Geophysics, Moscow, Russia (1990-Present); Associate Professor, University of California, Irvine (1997-2000); Assistant Professor, University of California, Irvine (1994-1997); Visiting Assistant Professor, California Institute of Technology (1996); Visiting Assistant Professor, University of California, Irvine (1992-1994); Lecturer, University of California, Irvine (1991-1992) **CR:** Research Professor, Mathematics and Sciences Research Institute (2003); Alfred P. Sloan Research Fellowship (1996-2000); Invited Professor, CPT, CNRS, Marseille, France (1998); Lecturer in Field **CW:** Contributor, Articles, Professional Journals; Reviewer in Field **AW:** Ruth Lyttle Satter Prize in Mathematics, American Mathematical Society (2005) **MEM:** Editorial Board Committee, American Mathematics Society (2002-2005)

JOBS, LAURENE, T: Educational Association Administrator; Philanthropist **I:** Education/Educational Services **CN:** Emerson Collective **DOB:** 11/06/1963 **PB:** West Milford **SC:** NJ/USA **MS:** Widowed **SPN:** Steve Paul Jobs (03/18/1991, Deceased 10/05/2011) **CH:** Reed Paul; Erin Sienna; Eve; Lisa Nicole Brennan-Jobs (Stepdaughter) **ED:** MBA, Stanford Graduate School of Business (1991); BA in Political Science, University of Pennsylvania School of Arts and Sciences (1985); BS in Economics, The Wharton School, The University of Pennsylvania (1985) **C:** Member, White House Council for Community Solutions (2010-Present); Founder, Chair, Emerson Collective (2004-Present); Co-founder, Board Chair, College Track (1997-Present); Co-founder, Terravera; Fixed-income Trading Strategist, Goldman Sachs; Fixed-income Trading Strategist, Merrill Lynch Asset Management **CR:** Chair, Board of Directors, XQ; Member, Chairman's Advisory Board, Council on Foreign Relations; Member, Board of Directors, Conservation International; Member, Board of Directors, Stand for Children; Member, Board of Directors, NewSchools Venture; Member, Board of Directors, Stanford Schools Corporation; Member, Board of Directors, New America Foundation; Member, Board of Directors, EdVoice; Member, Board of Directors, Global Fund for Women; Member, Board of Directors, Teach for America, Inc.; Member, Board of Directors, Achieva Credit Union; Member, Board of Directors, Udacity, Inc. **CIV:** Advisory Board, Stanford Graduate School of Business; Founding Member, Climate Leadership Council; Manager, Laurene Powell Jobs Trust **AW:** Named One of the World's Richest People, Business Insider (2019); Named One of the 100 Most Powerful Women, Forbes Magazine (2012-2014)

JOEL, BILLY MARTIN, T: Singer, Songwriter, Musician **I:** Media & Entertainment **DOB:** 05/09/1949 **PB:** Bronx **SC:** NY/USA **PT:** Howard "Helmut" Joel; Rosalind (Nyman) Joel **MS:** Married **SPN:** Alexis Roderick (07/04/2015); Katie Lee (10/02/2004, Divorced 2009); Christie Brinkley (03/23/1985, Divorced 08/26/1994); Elizabeth Weber Small (09/05/1973, Divorced 07/20/1982) **CH:** Remy Anne; Della Rose; Alexa Ray Joel **ED:** Honorary MusD, Stony Brook University, NY (2015); Honorary Doctorate in Musical Arts, Manhattan School of Music (2008); Honorary DFA, Syracuse University, NY (2006); Honorary MusD, Southampton College (Now Stony Brook University Graduate Center), NY (2000); Honorary LHD, Hofstra University, NY (1997); Honorary Doctorate, Berklee College of Music, MA (1993); Honorary LHD, Fairfield University, CT (1991) **C:** Performer, Franchise, Madison Square Garden (2014-Present); With, Universal Music Publishing Group (2012-Present); Solo Artist (1980-Present); Solo Artist, Bill Martin, Piano Bars, Los Angeles, CA (1973); Member, Attila (1969-1980); Member, The Hassles (1967-1969); Member, The Emeralds (1965-1967); Member, The Echoes (1965); Musician, Shrangri-Las (1964) **CR:** Co-founder, 20th Century Cycles, Oyster Bay, NY (2010-Present); Co-founder, Long Island Boat Company (1996-Present); **CIV:** Established, The Rosalind Joel Scholarship, City College of New York (1996); Singer, Benefit Concerts Including America: A Tribute to Heroes, 12-12-12: The Concert for Sandy Relief and Rise Up New York! **CW:** Songwriter, "Christmas in Fallujah" (2007); Singer, Musician, "12 Gardens Live" (2006); Author, "Goodnight My Angel: A Lullabye" (2005); Author, "New York State of Mind" (2005); Singer, Musician, "My Lives" (2005); Music Featured, Broadway Musical, "Movin' Out" (2002); Singer, Musician, "Fantasies & Delusions: Music for Solo Piano" (2001); Singer, Musician, "Essential Billy Joel" (2001); Singer, Musician, "2000 Years: Millennium Concert" (2000); Singer, Musician, "Billy Joel's Greatest Hits, Volume III" (1997); Singer, Musician, "River of Dreams" (1993); Singer, Musician, "Storm Front" (1989); Singer, Musician, "Kohuept: Live from the Soviet Union" (1987); Singer, Musician, "The Bridge" (1986); Singer, Musician, "Billy Joel's Greatest Hits, Volumes I and II" (1985); Singer, Musician, "An Innocent Man" (1983); Singer, Musician, "The Nylon Curtain" (1982); Singer, Musician, "Songs in the Attic" (1981); Singer, Musician, "Glass Houses" (1980); Singer, Musician, "52nd Street" (1978); Singer, Musician, "The Stranger" (1977); Singer, Musician, "Turnstiles" (1975); Singer, Musician, "Streetlife Serenade" (1974); Singer, Musician, "Piano Man" (1973); Singer, Musician, "Cold Spring Harbor" (1971); Singer with Attila, "Attila" (1970); Singer, "Hour of the Wolf" (1968); Singer with The Hassles, "The Hassles" (1967); Singer, Songwriter, Composer, Musician, Numerous Songs, Solo Albums and Collaborations; Appearances, Numerous Television Shows, Documentaries, Films **AW:** Gershwin Prize for Popular Song, Library of Congress (2014); Honoree, Kennedy Center Honors, John F. Kennedy Center for the Performing Arts, Washington, DC (2013); Named to Hit Parade Hall of Fame (2009); Named to Long Island Music Hall of Fame (2006); Recipient, Star, Hollywood Walk of Fame (2005); Named MusicCares Person of the Year (2002); Johnny Mercer Award, Songwriters Hall of Fame (2001); James Smithson Bicentennial Medal of Honor (2000); Named to Rock and Roll Hall of Fame (1999); Award of Merit, American Music Awards (1999); Founder's Award, ASCAP (1997); Billboard Century Music Award (1994); Named to Madison Square Garden Hall of Fame (1993); Named to Songwriters Hall of Fame (1992); Grammy Legend Award, The Recording Industry (1990); Humanitarian Award, Cathedral of St. John the Divine (1990); Grammy Award for Best Male Rock Vocal Performance, The Recording Academy (1980); Grammy Awards for Album of the Year, Best Male Pop Vocal Performance, The Recording Industry (1979); Numerous Awards

JOERGENSEN, JOHN, T: Senior Associate Dean **I:** Education/Educational Services **CN:** Rutgers, The State University of New Jersey **MS:** Married **CH:** Four Children **ED:** MS in Library Information Science, Drexel University (1997); JD, Temple University Law School (1992); MA in Philosophy, Fordham University (1985); BA in Philosophy, Fordham University (1983) **C:** Senior Associate Dean for Information Services, Rutgers, The State University of New Jersey (2016-Present); Associate Dean for Information Services, Rutgers Law School, Rutgers, The State University of New Jersey (2014-2016); Reference and Digital Services Librarian, Rutgers, The State University of New Jersey (1997-2012) **CIV:** Member, Free Access to Law Movement **MEM:** New Jersey State Bar Association **MH:** Marquis Who's Who Top Professional **THT:** Ms. Joergensen says, "Be willing to do the tedious things."

JOERGER, JAY HERMAN, T: Psychologist; Entrepreneur **I:** Health, Wellness and Fitness **DOB:** 10/23/1957 **PB:** Freeport **SC:** NY/USA **PT:** Herman Alexander Joerger; Ellen Rose (Becker) Joerger **MS:** Married **SPN:** Diana Marina Botero-Pareja **CH:** Nicholas Alexander; Richard Andrew **ED:** EdD, Columbia University (1987); MA, Colgate University (1981); BS, Union College (1980) **CT:** Registered in Texas and IME NYS WCB; Licensed Psychologist, Commonwealth of Pennsylvania and State of New York; Certified Medical Examiner; Registered Hypnotherapist; Certified Homeland Security; Board Certified in Forensic Medicine; Board Certified Forensic Examiner; Diplomate, Child Custody Evaluation; Evaluation and Testing; Psychology Assessment; Clinical Psychology; Substance Abuse Psychology **C:** Private Practice, Middletown, NY and PA (1991-Present); President, Mentors Resource and Development Corp. (1991-Present); Member, Group Practice, Center for Stress Reduction (1993-1997); Associate Psychologist, New York State, Wingdale, NY (1986-1996); Member, Group Practice, Carmel Psychological Associates (1993-1994); Vocational Rehabilitation Counselor, Community Workshop, Glens Falls, NY (1981-1983); Drug Abuse Counselor, Drug Abuse Council, Norwich, NY (1980-1981) **CR:** Admission and Hospital Privileges, Four Winds Hospital, Katonah, NY (1995-Present); Consultant, Four Winds Hospital, Katonah, NY (1988-Present); Board of Directors, Rapid Rabbit, Inc. (2004-2008); Adjunct Professor, Lehman College (1994-1997); Founding Coordinator, Alcoholism and Drug Abuse Counselor, Training Program, Lehman College (1996); Adjunct Assistant Professor, Iona College (1993-1995); Forensic Psychological Consultant and Expert Witness **CIV:** Physical Injury Specialist (2002-Present); Scout Master, Boy Scouts of America (2006-2015); Leader, Boy Scouts of America (2001-2006); Military Affiliate Radio Operator, Westchester Emergency Communications Association (WECA), Westchester County, NY (1983-1999); Board of Directors, Hudson Valley Labor Federation, Clintondale, NY (1987-1988); Merit Badge Counselor **MIL:** Amateur Radio Operator, United States Air Force **CW:** Co-author, Spirituality CD, "Letting Go of the Physical," (2018); Co-author, Book, CD, "Living Successfully: Relax and Enhance Your Life" (1996); Co-author, "The Physical, Psychological and Social Effects of Chemical Abuse - A Clinician's Workbook, Second Edition" (1995); Co-author, "Substance Abuse: Evaluation and Treatment Training Program" (1995); Co-author, "The Physical, Psychological and Social Effects of Chemical Abuse - A Clinician's Workbook" (1994); Author, "Living Successfully: A Self-Study Guide" (1993); Author, "A Participant Manual for Mentally Ill Chemical Abusers" (1989) **AW:** Excellence in Psychology Award, Medical Staff Organization, Harlem Valley Psychologists (1990) **MEM:** Liaison, Managed Care Task Force, New York State Psychological Association (NYSPA) (1994-1995); Secretary-treasurer, Addiction Division, New York State Psychological Association (NYSPA) (1993-1995); President, Industrial Organization Division, Westchester County Psychological Association (1992-1995); Life Member, American College of Forensic Examiners; New York State Psychological Association (NYSPA); Westchester County Psychological Association **MH:** Albert Nelson Marquis Lifetime Achievement Award; Marquis Who's Who Top Professional **B/I:** Dr. Jay Joerger came from an engineering background and he figured the most complex field that he would never be bored with, and would be perpetually interesting, is the human personality; you could not get more complex or convoluted than the human personality. So, he decided to pursue a career as a psychologist. He also is involved with chronic pain and injury. He went into psychology because he ran out of ways for people to fire him and liked doing things when he wanted on his own time. He wanted to be his own boss and private practice before managed care really afforded that opportunity. He liked solving problems and loved the complexity of it all. He liked helping people feel better and found it most rewarding. **AV:** Amateur radio

JOHLFS, CRAIG S., T: Certified Financial Planner **I:** Financial Services **CN:** Johlf's Financial Group **ED:** BA in Geographic Information Systems, Southern Illinois University, Carbondale, IL (2002) **CT:** AWMA, College for Financial Planning (2016); AAMS, College for Financial Planning (2016); Certified Financial Planner, Certified Financial Planner

Board of Standards, Inc. (2015); CMFC, College for Financial Planning (2008) **C:** President, Johlf's Financial Group (2007-Present); Financial Advisor, Waddell & Reed, Incorporated (2006-Present) **CIV:** Board Chair, Denver Children's Advocacy Center (2014-Present); Former Member, Denver Active 2030 Children's Foundation (2011-2016) **AW:** Presidents Council, Waddell & Reed (2019); Advisor Medalist-Platinum, Waddell & Reed (2016, 2017, 2018, 2019); Crest, Waddell & Reed (2016, 2017, 2018, 2019); Top Advisor Forum, Waddell & Reed; 40 Under 40, Denver Business Journal; Best in State Wealth Advisors, Forbes **MEM:** MDRT; Financial Planning Association of Colorado **AS:** Mr. Johlfs enjoys what he does. He also has a very consistent habit to be proactive and that is what he contributes to his success the most. His philosophy is to have fun, enjoy life and be happy. **B/I:** After college, Mr. Johlfs went to teach English in Japan for a year. He was having fun as a young guy, enjoying Tokyo. Shortly after, he caught "the travel bug" and began traveling constantly and ended up teaching English in South Korea. One day randomly, he got out of bed and decided he would become a financial advisor. He is not exactly sure how he arrived at the idea, though.

JOHN, DAYMOND GARFIELD, T: 1) Entrepreneur 2) Television Personality 3) Author, Motivational Speaker **I:** Other **CN:** 1) FUBU 2) Shark Tank **DOB:** 02/23/1969 **PB:** Brooklyn **SC:** NY/USA **C:** Founder, President, Chief Executive Officer, FUBU; Co-Founder, Chief Executive Officer, The Shark Group, New York, NY; Brand Ambassador, Shopify; Motivational Speaker **CR:** Co-Founder, Business Program, Daymond John's Success Formula (2015-Present) **CIV:** Board of Overseers, Volunteer, NFTE Events **CW:** Co-Host, "Shark Tank" (2009-Present); Co-Author, "Rise and Grind: Outperform, Outwork, and Outhustle Your Way to a More Successful and Rewarding Life" (2018); Co-Author, "The Power of Broke: How Empty Pockets, a Tight Budget, and a Hunger for Success Can Become Your Greatest Competitive Advantage" (2016); Co-Author, "The Brand Within" (2011); Co-Author, "Display of Power" (2011) **AW:** Marketer of the Year, Brandweek; Two-Time Winner, Entrepreneur of the Year Award, NAACP; Advertising Age Marketing 1000 Award for Outstanding Ad Campaign; Essence Award; 40 Under 40 Award, Crain's New York Business; New York Entrepreneur of the Year Award, EY; Asper Award for Excellence in Global Entrepreneurship, International Business School, Brandeis University; Most Influential Men, Details; Two-Time Winner, Congressional Achievement Award for Entrepreneurship

JOHN, ELTON HERCULES, T: Singer, Songwriter, Musician **I:** Media & Entertainment **DOB:** 3/25/1947 **PB:** Pinner **SC:** Middlesex/England **PT:** Stanley Dwight; Sheila Eileen (Harris) Dwight Farebrother **MS:** Married **SPN:** David Furnish (12/21/2014); Renate Blauel (02/14/1984, Divorced 02/20/1991) **CH:** Zachary Jackson Levon Furnish-John; Elijah Joseph Daniel Furnish-John **ED:** Honorary PhD, Royal Academy of Music, London, England, United Kingdom (2002); Coursework, Royal Academy of Music, London, England, United Kingdom (1959-1964) **C:** Solo Artist, Performer, Elton John Band (1969-Present); Staff Songwriter, DJM Records (1968); Member, Bluesology (1965-1967) **CIV:** Established, Elton John Aids Foundation (1992-Present); President, Watford Football Club (1990-Present); Chairman, Watford Football Club (1976-1990); Patron, Amnesty International; Patron, Scholarship Fund, Royal Academy of Music; Patron, The Globe Theatre; Patron, Terrence Higgins Trust; Patron, International AIDS Vaccine Initiative; Patron, Gus Dudgeon Founda-

tion **CW:** Author, "Me: Elton John Official Autobiography" (2019); Appearance, "Kingsman: The Golden Circle" (2017); Appearance, "Nashville" (2016); Artist, Musician, Composer, "Wonderful Crazy Night" (2016); Artist, Musician, Composer, "The Diving Board" (2013); Performer, Queen's Diamond Jubilee Concert, Outside Buckingham Palace, England, United Kingdom (2012); Co-artist with Pnau, Musician, Composer, "Good Morning to the Night" (2012); Performer, "The Million Dollar Piano," The Colosseum at Caesars Palace, Las Vegas, NV (2011-2018); Artist, Musician, Composer, "Gnomeo & Juliet" (2011); Performer, Piano Duet with Lady Gaga, 52nd Grammy Awards (2010); Co-artist with Leon Russel, Musician, Composer, "The Union" (2010); Featured, "Elton John: Me, Myself & I" (2007); Artist, Musician, Composer, "Rocket Man – Number Ones" (2007); Performer, Concert for Diana in Honor of Princess of Wales' 46th Birthday, Wembley Stadium, London, England, United Kingdom (2007); Artist, Musician, Composer, "The Captain & The Kid" (2006); Artist, Musician, Composer, "Lestat" (2006); Performer, Live 8 (2005); Artist, Musician, Composer, "Billy Elliot the Musical" (2005); Artist, Musician, Composer, "Peachtree Road" (2004); Performer, "The Red Piano Tour," The Colosseum at Caesars Palace, Las Vegas, NV (2003-2009); Actor, "The Country Bears" (2002); Artist, Musician, Composer, "Greatest Hits 1970-2002" (2002); Appearance, "Being Mick" (2001); Artist, Musician, Composer, "Songs from the West Coast" (2001); Artist, Musician, Composer, Narrator, "The Road to El Dorado" (2000); Artist, Musician, Composer, "Elton John One Night Only - The Greatest Hits" (2000); Artist, Musician, Composer, Broadway Musical, "Aida" (2000); Artist, Musician, Composer, "Elton John and Tim Rice's Aida" (1999); Artist, Musician, Composer, "The Muse" (1999); Artist, Musician, Composer, Broadway Musical, "The Lion King" (1998); Appearance, "Spice World" (1997); Artist, Musician, Composer, "The Big Picture" (1997); Performer, Funeral of Princess Diana, Westminster Abbey, England, United Kingdom (1997); Artist, Musician, Composer, "Love Songs" (1996); Artist, Musician, Composer, "Made in England" (1995); Artist, Musician, Composer, Soundtrack to Film, "The Lion King" (1994); Artist, Musician, Composer, "Duets" (1993); Performer, Freddie Mercury Tribute Concert (1992); Artist, Musician, Composer, "The One" (1992); Artist, Musician, Composer, "Greatest Hits 1976-1986" (1992); Artist, Musician, Composer, "To Be Continued" (1990); Artist, Musician, Composer, "Sleeping with the Past" (1989); Artist, Musician, Composer, "Reg Strikes Back" (1988); Artist, Musician, Composer, "Live in Australia with the Melbourne Symphony Orchestra" (1987); Artist, Musician, Composer, "Leather Jackets" (1986); Performer, Live Aid (1985); Artist, Musician, Composer, "Ice on Fire" (1985); Artist, Musician, Composer, "Breaking Hearts" (1984); Artist, Musician, Composer, "Too Low for Zero" (1983); Artist, Musician, Composer, "Jump Up!" (1982); Artist, Musician, Composer, "The Fox" (1981); Artist, Musician, Composer, "21 at 33" (1980); Artist, Musician, Composer, "Victim of Love" (1979); Artist, Musician, Composer, "A Single Man" (1978); Artist, Musician, Composer, "Greatest Hits Volume II" (1977); Artist, Musician, Composer, "Rock of the Westies" (1976); Artist, Musician, Composer, "Here and There" (1976); Artist, Musician, Composer, "Blue Moves" (1976); Artist, Musician, Composer, "Captain Fantastic and the Brown Dirt Cowboy" (1975); Actor, "Tommy" (1975); Artist, Musician, Composer, "Caribou" (1974); Artist, Musician, Composer, "Greatest Hits" (1974); Artist, Musician, Composer, "Don't Shoot Me I'm Only The Piano Player" (1973); Artist, Musician, Composer,

"Goodbye Yellow Brick Road" (1973); Artist, Musician, Composer, "Honky Chateau" (1972); Artist, Musician, Composer, "11.17.70" (1971); Artist, Musician, Composer, "Madman Across the Water" (1971); Artist, Musician, Composer, "Friends" (1971); Artist, Musician, Composer, "Elton John" (1970); Artist, Musician, Composer, "Tumbleweed Connection" (1970); Artist, Musician, Composer, "Empty Sky" (1969) **AW:** Academy Award for Best Original Song, Academy of Motion Picture Arts and Sciences (1995, 2020); Golden Globe Award for Best Original Song, Hollywood Foreign Press Association (2019); Grammy Award for Best Pop Collaboration with Vocals, The Recording Academy (2011); Tony Award (as Producer) for Best Play (2010); Named One of the 100 Most Influential People in the World, TIME Magazine (2010); PRS for Music Heritage Award (2010); New York Drama Critics' Circle Award for Best Musical (2009); Drama Desk Awards for Outstanding Musical, Outstanding Music (2009); Tony Award for Best Musical (2009); Named One of the Billboard Hot 100 Top All-Time Artists, Billboard Magazine (2008); Maori Award (2007); Named Disney Legend (2006); Honoree, Kennedy Center Honors, John F. Kennedy Center for the Performing Arts (2004); Grammy Legend Award, The Recording Academy (2001); Tony Award for Best Original Score (2001); Grammy Award for Best Musical Show Album, The Recording Academy (2001); Grammy Legend Award, The Recording Academy (1999); Decorated Knight Commander, Order of the British Empire, Queen Elizabeth II (CBE) (1998); Grammy Award for Best Male Pop Vocal Performance, The Recording Academy (1994, 1997); Named to Rock & Roll Hall of Fame (1994); Named to Songwriters Hall of Fame (1992); Grammy Award for Best Instrumental Composition, The Recording Academy (1991); Best British Male Artist Brit Award (1991); Grammy Award for Best Pop Performance by a Duo or Group, The Recording Academy (1987); Recipient, Star, Hollywood Walk of Fame (1975); 11 Ivor Novello Awards (1973-2000); Numerous Awards **MEM:** Fellow, The Ivors Academy

JOHNS, JASPER, T: Artist **I:** Fine Art **DOB:** 05/15/1932 **PB:** Augusta **SC:** GA/USA **PT:** Jasper Johns; Jean (Riley) Johns **ED:** Coursework, University of South Carolina (1947-1948) **CW:** Exhibition, National Gallery (2007); Exhibition, Kunstmuseum Basel, Switzerland (1979, 1990, 2007); Exhibition, Philadelphia Museum of Art (1999); Exhibition, Art Institute Chicago (1999); Exhibition, National Academy of Design, New York, NY (1996); Exhibition, Harvard Art Museums, Harvard University (1992); Exhibition, San Diego Museum Art (1992); Exhibition, Gagosian Gallery (1992); Exhibition, Palaus de Luppe, La Fondation Vincent Van Gogh, Arles, France (1992); Exhibition, Milwaukee Art Museum (1992); Exhibition, Galeria Weber Alexander Cobo, Madrid, Spain (1992); Exhibition, Saint Louis Art Museum (1991); Exhibition, Center for Fine Arts, Miami, FL (1991); Exhibition, Denver Art Museum (1991); Exhibition, Brooke Alexander Editions (Now Brooke Alexander, Inc.), New York, NY (1991); Exhibition, Cana Art Gallery, Seoul, South Korea (1991); Exhibition, Whitney Museum of American Art (1977, 1991); Exhibition, Walker Art Center, Minneapolis, MN (1990); Exhibition, The Museum of Fine Arts, Houston, TX (1990); Exhibition, Fine Arts Museum of San Francisco (1990); Exhibition, Montreal Museum of Fine Arts (1990); Exhibition, National Gallery of Art, Washington, DC (1990); Exhibition, Hayward Gallery, London, England (1990); Exhibition, Philadelphia Museum of Art (1988); Exhibition, The Museum of Contemporary Art, Los Angeles, CA (1987); Exhibition, Galerie Templon, Paris, France (1987); Exhibition, Wight

Art Gallery, University of California Los Angeles (1987); Exhibition, Kunsthalle (1986); Exhibition, The Museum of Modern Art (1986); Exhibition, St. Louis Art Museum (1985); Exhibition, Leo Castelli Gallery, New York, NY (1958, 1960, 1961, 1963, 1966, 1968, 1976, 1981, 1984); Exhibition, Des Moines Art Center (1983); Exhibition, Kunsthalle, Cologne, Germany (1978); Exhibition, Centre Pompidou, Paris, France (1978); Exhibition, Hayward Gallery, London, England, United Kingdom (1978); Exhibition, Seibu Museum, Tokyo, Japan (1978); Exhibition, San Francisco Museum of Modern Art (1978); Exhibition, Venice Biennale (1958, 1964, 1978); Exhibition, Arts Council of Great Britain (1974-1975); Exhibition, Minami Gallery, Tokyo, Japan (1965, 1975); Illustrator, "In Memory of My Feelings" (1967); Exhibition, National Collection of Fine Arts (Now Smithsonian American Art Museum) (1966); Exhibition, Pasadena Museum (1965); Exhibition, The Jewish Museum, New York, NY (1964); Exhibition, Whitechapel Gallery, London, England, United Kingdom (1964); Exhibition, Ileana Sonnabend, Paris, France (1963); Exhibition, Galerie Rive Droite, Paris, France (1959, 1961); Exhibition, Columbia Museum of Art (1960); Exhibition, Galleria D'Arte Del Naviglio, Milan, Italy (1959); Represented, Permanent Collections, Numerous Museums; Artist, Paintings, Sculptures, Prints, Permanent Collections and Exhibitions, Numerous Museums **AW:** Presidential Medal of Freedom, The White House (2010); National Medal of Arts, The White House (1990); Inductee, South Carolina Hall of Fame (1989); International Prize, Venice Biennale (1988); Wolf Prize for Painting, Wolf Foundation (1986); First Prize for Print, Biennale Ljubljana, Yugoslavia; Prize IX, Sao Paulo Biennale, Brazil; Skowhegan Medal for Painting, Skowhegan School of Painting & Sculpture; Skowhegan Medal for Graphics, Skowhegan School of Painting & Sculpture; Mayor's Award of Honor for Arts and Culture, City of New York; Gold Medal for Graphic Art, American Academy of Arts and Letters **MEM:** American Academy of Arts and Letters; Royal Academy of Arts; National Institute of Arts and Letters; American Academy of Arts & Sciences

JOHNSEN, EUGENE CARLYLE, RESEARCH & CONSULTING, T: Mathematician, Mathematical Social Scientist **I:** Research **CN:** University of California Santa Barbara **DOB:** 01/27/1932 **PB:** Minneapolis **SC:** MN/USA **PT:** Bernhardt Thorwald Johnsen; Esther Elvira (Eklund) Johnsen **MS:** Married **SPN:** Wanda Magee (05/10/2013); Marjorie Marie Wacklin (08/31/1957, Deceased 08/29/2011) **CH:** Emilka Furmanczyk (Stepdaughter) **ED:** PhD, The Ohio State University (1961); BChem, University of Minnesota (1954) **C:** Research and Consulting (1994-Present); Professor Emeritus, University of California Santa Barbara (1994-Present); Director of Summer Sessions, University of California Santa Barbara (1981-1994, 1994-1997); Professor, University of California Santa Barbara (1974-1994); Associate Professor, University of California Santa Barbara (1968-1974); Assistant Professor, University of California Santa Barbara (1964-1968); Lecturer in Mathematics, University of California Santa Barbara (1963-1964); NAS/NRC Research Associate, National Bureau of Standards, Washington DC (1962-1963) **CR:** Visiting Scholar in Sociology, Harvard University, Cambridge, MA (1984-1985); Visiting Lecturer in Mathematics, University of Michigan, Ann Arbor, MI (1968-1969); Instructor of Mathematics, The Ohio State University, Columbus, Ohio (1962); Mathematician, Sperry Rand, St. Paul, MN (1956-1957); Instructor of Chemistry and Mathematics, University of Minnesota (1956-1957); Organizer and Co-organizer, Mathematics Social Science Conferences; Reviewer, National Science Foundation **CIV:** L.A. Music Center Opera League (Now Opera League of Los Angeles) (1986-2009); Los Angeles County Museum of Art (Museum Associates) (1985-2008); Santa Barbara Region Chamber of Commerce, Business Advisory Committee, University of California Santa Barbara (1979-1984) **CW:** Co-author of book: "Social Influence Network Theory" (2011); Contributor, Articles in Professional Journals; Referee for Professional Journals; Editorial Board, Journal of Mathematical Sociology **AW:** Fulbright Travel Award Fellow, University of Tubingen (1969); Fellow, National Science Foundation (1959); Grantee, Department of Education, USAFOSR, National Science Foundation **MEM:** Board of Directors, Santa Barbara Chapter, The American-Scandinavian Foundation (2005-2008); President, Ivar Aasen Lodge, Sons of Norway (1999-2001, 2003-2006); Acting Chair to Chair, Mathematical Sociology Section, American Sociological Association; American Association for the Advancement of Science; American Mathematical Society; Mathematics Association of America; American Statistical Association; Society for Industrial and Applied Mathematics; International Network for Social Network Analysis; The Phi Beta Kappa Society; Sigma Xi, The Scientific Research Honor Society; Phi Lambda Upsilon; Pi Mu Epsilon; Alpha Chi Sigma; University of California Santa Barbara Faculty Club; Channel City Club **B/I:** When Dr. Johnsen went to the University of Minnesota, he was interested in chemistry, receiving a five-year BChem degree in the subject. After he graduated, he stayed in Minneapolis to take courses, such as philosophy of science. He was trying to decide what his career should be. He was unsure if chemistry was something he wanted to pursue further. He took mathematics courses at the suggestion of a friend, who gave him insight into the field. His friend was going to work in mathematics at Ohio State; this piqued his interest. **AV:** Music; Opera; Travel **THT:** Dr. Johnsen says, "As I look back in time, my thoughts on life are captured by the themes of affection, family, friends, music and science. I love the members of my family, am attracted to my friends, enjoy playing and listening to music, and am driven by curiosity with scientific problems. The loves of my life are my wives, Marjorie Johnsen and Wanda Johnsen, my stepdaughter Emilka, her husband, Pawel Furmanczyk, and their daughters, Aurelia and Lilliana. My deceased wife, Marjorie, played clarinet and I played the euphonium in the University of Minnesota band. Marjorie was also a lawyer, who received the Frank R. Crandall Pro Bono Community Service Award in Santa Barbara. My wife, Wanda, has continued studies in the paralegal program of UCSB Extension. She is also a registered nurse, who received the award of Traveller of the Year in 2010. My deceased brother, Julien Johnsen, served in the U.S. Army during World War II. I am proud of him for his military service. As my older brother, I truly looked up to him. Thus, my thoughts on life form an interconnected network of themes that bring harmony to my life.

JOHNSON, DAVID G., PHD, T: Chinese History Educator **I:** Education/Educational Services **DOB:** 07/15/1938 **PB:** Webster **SC:** SD/USA **PT:** George Andrew Johnson; Elizabeth Carolina (Herrlinger) Johnson **MS:** Married **SPN:** In Ja Rhee (06/06/1976) **CH:** Caroline **ED:** PhD, University of California Berkeley (1970); MA in Chinese History, University of California Berkeley (1964); AB in Modern European History, Harvard University, Cambridge, MA (1960) **C:** Professor of the Graduate School, Department of History, University of California Berkeley (2011-2014); Professor, Department of History, University of California Berkeley (1987-2011); Associate Professor, Department of History, University of California Berkeley (1983-1987); Research Associate, Department of East Asian Languages and Cultures, Columbia University, New York, NY (1981-1983); Senior Fellow, Society of Fellows in the Humanities, Columbia University, New York, NY (1979-1981); Assistant Professor, Department of East Asian Languages and Cultures, Columbia University, New York, NY (1970-1979) **CR:** Director, Chinese Popular Culture Project, University of California, Berkeley (1987-2011); Selection Committee, American Council of Learned Societies-Chiang Ching-Kuo Foundation Project (2004, 2005, 2006); America Council of Learned Societies-Social Science Research Council Joint Committee on Chinese Studies (1984-1989); Chairman, Grants Committee, Joint Committee on Chinese Studies (1986-1988); Editorial Board, Min-Su Ch'ü-i (Journal of Chinese Ritual, Theatre, and Folklore); Editorial Board, CHINOPERL Papers: Chinese Oral and Performing Literature **CW:** Author, "Spectacle and Sacrifice: The Ritual Foundations of Village Life in North China" (2009); Author, "'Confucian' Elements in the Great Temple Festivals of Southeastern Shansi in Late Im-perial Times" (1997); Author, "Mu-lien in Pao-chüan: The Performance Context and Religious Meaning of the Yu-ming pao-ch'uan" (1995); Editor, "Ritual and Scripture in Chinese Popular Religion," Five Studies (1995); Author, "Temple Festivals in Southeastern Shansi: The Sai of Nan-shê Village and Big West Gate" (1994); Co-Author, "Domesticated Deities and Auspicious Emblems: The Iconography of Everyday Life in Village China" (1992); Author, "Scripted Performances in Chinese Culture: An Approach to the Analysis of Popular Literature" (1990); Author, "Actions Speak Louder Than Words: The Cultural Significance of Chinese Ritual Opera" (1989); Editor, "Mu-lien Rescues His Mother" (1989); Author, "The City-God Cults of T'ang and Sung China" (1985); Author, "Communication, Class, and Consciousness in Late Imperial China" (1985); Co-Editor, "Popular Culture in Late Imperial China" (1985); Author, "Epic and History in Early China: The Case of Wu Tzu-hsü" (1981); Author, "The Wu Tzu-hsü Pien-wen and Its Sources" (1980); Author, "The Last Years of a Great Clan: the Li Family of Chao Chün in Late T'ang and Early Sung" (1977), Author, "The Medieval Chinese Oligarchy" (1977); Contributor, Articles, Professional Journals **AW:** Grantee, ACLS (1978, 1981, 1993); Grantee, National Endowment for the Humanities (1987-1991); Grantee, Rockefeller Foundation (1987-1991); Grantee, Committee on Scholarly Communications with the People's Republic of China (1984) **MEM:** Association for Asian Studies, China and Inner Asia Council (1988-1991) **MH:** Albert Nelson Marquis Lifetime Achievement Award **B/I:** Dr. Johnson studied modern European history as an undergraduate. Hoping to work in a less crowded field, he was fortunate to receive a fellowship upon graduation that allowed him to begin studying Chinese at the University of Hong Kong. After completing this fellowship, he knew he wanted to study Chinese history.

JOHNSON, DUSTIN, "DUSTY" M., T: U.S. Representative from South Dakota **I:** Government Administration/Government Relations/Government Services **DOB:** 09/30/1976 **PB:** Pierre **SC:** SD/USA **MS:** Married **SPN:** Jacquelyn Johnson **CH:** Three Children **ED:** MPA, The University of Kansas; BA, University of South Dakota **C:** Member, U.S. House of Representatives from South Dakota's At-large Congressional District (2019-Present); Chief of Staff, Governor of South Dakota (2011-2014); Member, South Dakota Public Utilities Commission (2005-2011); Senior Policy Advisor, Governor Mike Rounds (2003-2004) **CR:** Adjunct Professor, Dakota Wesleyan University **CIV:** State Advisor, South Dakota Teenage Republicans (2004-Present); Camp Leader, South Dakota Teenage Republicans, Black Hills, SD (2004-Present); Board of Directors, W.O. Farber Fund; Board of Directors, Abbott House; Board of Directors, South Dakota Attorney General's Open Government Task Force **MEM:** Phi Delta Theta Fraternity **PA:** Republican

JOHNSON, DWAYNE, "THE ROCK" DOUGLAS, T: 1) Founder 2) Actor, Former Professional Wrestler **I:** Media & Entertainment **CN:** 1) Seven Bucks Productions **DOB:** 05/02/1972 **PB:** Hayward **SC:** CA/USA **PT:** Rocky Johnson; Ata (Maivia) Johnson **MS:** Married **SPN:** Lauren Hashian (08/18/2019); Dany Garcia (1997, Divorced 2007) **CH:** Simone Alexandra; Jasmine; Tiana **ED:** Bachelor of General Studies in Criminology and Physiology, University of Miami (1995) **C:** Founder, Seven Bucks Productions (2012-Present); Professional Wrestler, World Wrestling Entertainment Inc. (1997-2013) **CW:** Host, Creator, Executive Producer, "The Titan Games" (2019-Present); Actor, Television Series, "Ballers" (2015-Present); Actor, Film, "Hobbs & Shaw" (2019); Actor, Film, "Shazam!" (2019); Actor, Film, "Rampage" (2018); Actor, Film, "Skyscraper" (2018); Appearance, Film, "Fighting with My Family" (2018); Host, Television Series, "Saturday Night Live" (2000, 2002, 2009, 2015, 2017); Voice Actor, Film, "Moana" (2017); Actor, Film, "The Fate of the Furious" (2017); Actor, Film, "Baywatch" (2017); Actor, Film, "Jumanji: Welcome to the Jungle" (2017); Guest Appearance, Executive Producer, Episode, "Lifeline" (2017); Actor, Film, "Central Intelligence" (2016); Actor, Film, "Furious 7" (2015); Actor, Film, "San Andreas" (2015); Wrestler, Television Series, "WWF Monday Night Raw" (1997-2015); Actor, Film, "Hercules" (2014); Guest Appearance, Creator, Executive Producer, Television Series, "Wake Up Call" (2014); Guest Appearance, Executive Producer, Television Series, "The Hero" (2013); Actor, Producer, Film, "Snitch" (2013); Actor, Film, "G.I. Joe: Retaliation" (2013); Actor, Film, "Empire State" (2013); Actor, Film, "Pain & Gain" (2013); Actor, Film, "Fast & Furious 6" (2013); Wrestler, Television Series, "WWE Smackdown!" (1999-2013); Actor, Film, "Journey 2: The Mysterious Island" (2012); Actor, Film, "Tooth Fairy" (2010); Actor, Film, "The Other Guys" (2010); Guest Appearance, Episode, Television Series, "Transformers Prime" (2010); Guest Appearance, Episode, Television Series, "Family Guy" (2010); Guest Appearance, Episode, Television Series, "Wizards of Waverly Place" (2009); Actor, Film, "Race to Witch Mountain" (2009); Voice Actor, Film, "Planet 51" (2009); Actor, Film, "Get Smart" (2008); Guest Appearance, Episode, Television Series, "Cory in the House" (2007); Guest Appearance, Episode, Television Series, "Hannah Montana" (2007); Actor, Film, "The Game Plan" (2007); Actor, Film, "Southland Tales" (2006); Actor, Film, "Gridiron Gang" (2006); Actor, Film, "Be Cool" (2005); Actor, Film, "Doom" (2005); Actor, Film, "Walking Tall" (2004); Wrestler, Television Series, "Sunday Night Heat" (1998-2004); Actor, Film, "The Rundown" (2003); Actor, Film, "The Scorpion King" (2002); Actor, Film, "The Mummy Returns" (2001); Actor, Episode, Television Series, "Star Trek: Voyager" (2000); Actor, Film, "Longshot" (2000); Actor, Film, "Beyond the Mat" (1999); Actor, Episode, Television Series, "That 70s Show" (1999); Guest Appearance, Television Series, "The Net" (1999); Wrestler, Television Series, "WWF Superstars of Wrestling" (1996) **AW:** Generation Award, MTV Movie & TV Awards (2019); Choice Comedy Movie Actor, Teen Choice Awards (2018); Favorite Movie Actor, Kids' Choice Awards (2018); Entertainer of the Year, NAACP Image Awards (2017); Favorite Premium Series Actor, People's Choice Awards (2017); Co-winner with Kevin Hart, Favorite BFFs, Kids' Choice Awards (2017); Choice Fantasy Movie Actor, Teen Choice Awards (2017); Star, Hollywood Walk of Fame (2017); Named, One of the 100 Most Influential People in the World, Time Magazine (2016, 2019); Named, Sexiest Man Alive, People Magazine (2016); Best Actor, Shorty Awards (2016); Favorite Premium Cable TV Actor, People's Choice Awards (2016); Mr. Olympia ICON Award (2016); Muscle & Fitness Man of the Century (2015); Favorite Male Butt Kicker, Kids Choice Awards (2013); CinemaCon Action Star of the Year (2012); Teen Choice Awards – Choice Movie Villain, Teen Choice Awards (2001); NCAAF National Championship with Miami Hurricanes (1991)

JOHNSON, EARVIN, "MAGIC" JR., T: Chairperson, Chief Executive Officer, Professional Basketball Player (Retired) **I:** Athletics **CN:** Magic Johnson Enterprises **DOB:** 08/14/1959 **PB:** Lansing **SC:** MI/USA **PT:** Earvin Johnson; Christine Johnson **SPN:** Earlitha "Cookie" Kelly (09/1991) **CH:** Andre Johnson; Earvin Johnson III; Elisa (Adopted) **ED:** Coursework, Michigan State University (1979) **C:** President, Los Angeles Lakers (2017-Present); Co-owner, Los Angeles Dodgers (2012-Present); Studio Analyst, NBA Countdown (2008-Present); Studio Analyst, ESPN, ABC Sports (2008-Present); Co-chairperson, Executive Steering Committee for Diversity, NASCAR (2004-Present); Chairperson, Magic Johnson Entertainment, Magic Johnson Productions & Magic Johnson Enterprises (1997-Present); Chairperson, Chief Executive Officer, Johnson Development Corp. (1993-Present); Owner, Los Angeles Sparks (2014); Vice President, Co-owner, Los Angeles Lakers (1994-2010); Studio Analyst, Turner Sports (2001-2008); Guard, Los Angeles Lakers (1996); Head Coach, Los Angeles Lakers (1994); Sportscaster, NBC-TV (1993-1994); Guard, Los Angeles Lakers (1979-1991) **CIV:** Founder, Magic Johnson Foundation (1991-Present) **CW:** Co-author, with Larry Bird and J. MacMullan, "When the Game Was Ours" (2009); Author, "32 Ways to Be a Champion in Business" (2008); Co-author, with William Novack, "My Life" (1992); Author, "What You Can Do to Avoid AIDS" (1992); Co-author, with Roy S. Johnson, "Magic's Touch" (1989); Author, Autobiography, "Magic" (1983) **AW:** Inductee, National Collegiate Basketball Hall of Fame (2009); AdColor Award (2008); Listee, Power 150, Ebony Magazine (2008); Named, One of the Most Influential People in the World of Sports, Business Week (2007, 2008); Named, One of the Most Influential Black Americans, Ebony Magazine (2006); Inductee, Naismith Memorial Basketball Hall of Fame (2002); Named, One of the 50 Greatest Players in NBA History (1996); J. Walter Kennedy Citizenship Award, NBA (1992); Gold Medal, Men's Basketball, Summer Olympic Games, Barcelona, Spain (1992); Inductee, Michigan State University Athletics Hall of Fame (1992); Named, NBA All-star Game MVP (1990, 1992); Named to the Western Conference All-star Team, NBA (1980, 1982-1992); Named to the First Team All-NBA (1983-1991); Named, NBA MVP (1987, 1989, 1990); Player of the Year, Sporting News (1987); Named, NBA Finals MVP (1980, 1982, 1987); All-around Contributions to Team Success Award, IBM (1984); Schick Pivotal Player Award (1984); Named, First Team All-Rookie (1980); Named, NCAA Final Four Most Outstanding Player (1979); Listee, First Team NCAA All-American, Associated Press (1979)

JOHNSON, EDDIE BERNICE, T: U.S. Representative **I:** Government Administration/Government Relations/Government Services **DOB:** 12/03/1935 **PB:** Waco **SC:** TX/USA **PT:** Lee Edward Johnson; Lillie Mae (White) Johnson **MS:** Married **SPN:** Lacy Kirk Johnson (07/05/1956, Divorced 10/1970) **CH:** Dawrence Kirk **ED:** Honorary LLD, Paul Quinn College (1993); Honorary LLD, Houston-Tillotson College (Now Houston-Tillotson University) (1993); Honorary LLD, Texas College (1989); Honorary LLD, Jarvis Christian College (1979); Honorary LLD, Bishop College (1979); MPA, Southern Methodist University, Dallas, TX (1976); BSN, Texas Christian University (1967); Diploma in Nursing, Saint Mary's College, University of Notre Dame, South Bend, IN (1955) **C:** Ranking Member, U.S. House of Representatives Committee on Science, Space and Technology (2010-Present); U.S. Representative, Texas' 30th Congressional District, United States Congress (1993-Present); Member, District 23, Texas State Senate (1987-1993); Vice President, Visiting Nurse Association of Texas (1981-1987); Executive Assistant to Administrator for Primary Health Care Policy, Department of Health, Education and Welfare, Washington, DC (1979-1981); Dallas Regional Director, Department of Health, Education and Welfare (1977-1979); Member, District 33, Texas House of Representatives (1973-1977); Chief Psychiatric Nurse, Veterans Administration Hospital, Dallas, TX (1956-1972) **CR:** Consultant, Division of Urban Affairs, Zales Corporation, Dallas, TX (1976-1977); Executive Assistant, Personnel Division, Neiman Marcus, Dallas, Texas (1972-1975); President, Eddie Bernice Johnson & Associates, Inc. **AW:** Power 150 (2008); One of the Most Influential Black Americans, Ebony Magazine (2006); Woman of the Year Award, 100 Black Men of America, Inc. (2001); Visionary Award, National Organization of Black Elected Legislative Women (2001); President's Award, National Conference of Black Mayors (2001); Heroes Award, NAACP (2000); Citizenship Award, National Conference for Christians & Jews (1985); 25th Anniversary Outstanding Achievement Award, National Black Caucus of State Legislators **MEM:** Alpha Kappa Alpha Sorority, Inc. **PA:** Democrat

JOHNSON, GERALD A., T: Health Facility Executive (Retired) **I:** Military & Defense Services **DOB:** 06/15/1941 **PB:** Rockford **SC:** IL/USA **PT:** LeRoy Gerald Johnson; Helen Winfred (Jensen) Johnson **MS:** Married **SPN:** Judy J. Johnson (1962) **CH:** David; Krista; Steven **ED:** MA, The George Washington University, Washington, DC (1971); BS, University of Illinois at Urbana-Champaign, Urbana, Champaign, IL (1964) **C:** President, Signum Primary Care, Durham, NC (1993-2000); Vice President of Development for Coastal Government Services, Coastal Healthcare Group, Durham, NC (1989-1993); Senior Health Services Administrator, United States Air Force (1979-1989); Health Services Administrator, United States Air Force (1964-1979) **CR:** Adjunct Assistant Professor, University of Alabama, Tuscaloosa, AL (1981) **CIV:** Commissioner, Scoutmaster, Boy Scouts of America; Past Lieutenant Governor, Kiwanis International; Past State President, Past Chapter President, Military Officers Association of America; Leader, Junior Chamber of Commerce; American Red Cross; Meals on Wheels; Military Officers Association of America; Representative of K-Kids Clubs, Kiwanis Districts, Project ELIMINATE, UNICEF; Kiwanis International Subcommittee, ELIMINATE Program **MIL:** Colonel, United States Air Force (1964-1989); Commissioned Officer, Medical Unit, United States Air Force, Athens, Greece; Temporary Hospital Administrator, United States Air Force, Bitburg, Germany; Hospital Administrator, United States Air Force, Madrid, Spain **CW:** Guest Speaker, Veterans Day Celebration, Milledgeville, GA (2019) **AW:** Recognition for Support of the Service Leadership Program, Kiwanis International (2012); Legion of Merit, U.S. Air Force (1989); Meritorious Service Medal, U.S. Air Force; Commendation Medal, U.S. Air Force **MEM:** Fellow, American College of Healthcare Executives **MH:** Albert Nelson Marquis Lifetime Achievement Award; Distinguished

Humanitarian **B/I:** Colonel Johnson became involved in his profession because he always had a quasi-interest in the military; for much of his life, he was in the Boy Scouts and took pride in unholding leadership roles. Colonel Johnson was more interested in leading the troops than working in skilled areas. While in high school, he joined the Junior ROTC and he rose to be a company commander, which was the second-highest rank in his school. Colonel Johnson then attended the University of Illinois, which had a requirement for two years of ROTC. He began with the United States Navy then transferred to the Air Force program, where he was able to apply his interest in hospital administration. **AV:** Traveling; Golfing

JOHNSON, HENRY, "HANK" CALVIN JR., T: U.S. Representative from Georgia, Lawyer **I:** Government Administration/Government Relations/ Government Services **CN:** U.S. House of Representatives **DOB:** 10/02/1954 **PB:** Washington **SC:** DC/ USA **MS:** Married **SPN:** Mereda Davis **CH:** Randi; Alex **ED:** Doctor of Jurisprudence, Texas Southern University Thurgood Marshall School of Law (1979); Bachelor of Arts, Clark University (1976) **C:** Member, U.S. House of Representatives from Georgia's Fourth Congressional District, United States Congress (2007-Present); Member, Committee on Armed Services; Member, Committee on the Judiciary; Partner, Johnson & Johnson Law Group LLC, Decatur, GA; Judge, State Court of Georgia; Judge, Magistrate Court, DeKalb County, GA **CR:** Chairperson, Budget Committee; Member, DeKalb County Board of Commissioners **AW:** Named to the Power 150, Ebony Magazine (2008) **MEM:** State Bar of Georgia, Georgia Lawyers Foundation; Georgia Association Criminal Defense Lawyers; DeKalb County Law Library, DeKalb County Superior Court **PA:** Democrat

JOHNSON, HOWARD A. JR., T: Corporate Executive, Operations Analyst, Financial Officer **I:** Financial Services **DOB:** 07/25/1952 **PB:** Indianapolis **SC:** IN/USA **PT:** Howard Arthur Johnson, Sr.; Joy (Nelson) Johnson **MS:** Married **SPN:** Teresa Thirsk (08/11/1979) **CH:** Jamie E. **ED:** MS in Software Engineering, University of Maryland, Cum Laude (2004); MA in International Studies and Management, University of Wyoming (1984); BA in Political Science and Operations Research Analysis, University of Kansas (1974) **CT:** Certification in ISO 9001 (2000, 2008); Certification in CMM Software Level 5; Certification in CMMI Systems Level 3 Series; Fagan Inspection Certified, Michael Fagan & Associates; Six Sigma Training, Green Belt, United Defense **C:** Co-Founder, CFO, Senior Consultant, Enterprise Architect and Engineer, Chief Security, SEER, Inc., Eden Prairie, MN (1992-Present); Senior Principal Systems Staff Engineer, Systems Engineering Manager, Honeywell, Inc. (1985-1992); Operations Research Analyst, Honeywell, Inc. (1985-1992); Operations Research Analyst, FMC Corp., Minneapolis, MN (1984-1985); Deputy to U.S. Director, Plans and Budgets, Royal Saudi Navy, Saudi Arabian Ministry Defense and Aviation, Riyadh (1981-1982); Operations Research Analyst, EG&G InterTech, Inc., Arlington, VA (1981-1984); Operations Research Analyst, Armament Systems, Inc., Fort Walton Beach, FL (1980-1981) **CR:** SEER, Inc. (2015-Present); United Healthcare Optum (2014-2015); BAE Systems (2012-2014, 2006-2010); Premier, Inc. (2010-2012); Medtronic (2004-2006); United Defense (1992-2004); Embassy Suites (1993); Consultant, U.S. Navy, Coronado, CA (1977-1978) **MIL:** Lieutenant, U.S. Navy (1974-1978) **AW:** Graduate Academic Scholar, University of Wyoming (1983-1984) **MEM:** American Association for the Advancement of Science; Institute of Electrical and Electronics Engineers (IEEE); Association

for Computing Machinery (ACM); HL7 Organization; Operations Research Society of America; Academy of International Business; Institute of Management Sciences; Foreign Policy Research Institute; Military Operations Research Society; Armed Forces Communications and Electronics Association; Washington Operations Research Management Science Council; Tau Kappa Epsilon **MH:** Albert Nelson Marquis Lifetime Achievement Award **B/I:** Mr. Johnson became involved in his profession because there were problems that needed to be solved in the field. He also felt there was an absence of skilled people to reach the needs of the field.

JOHNSON, JAMES, "MIKE" MICHAEL, T: U.S. Representative from Louisiana **I:** Government Administration/Government Relations/Government Services **CN:** U.S. House of Representatives **DOB:** 01/30/1972 **PB:** Shreveport **SC:** LA/ USA **PT:** James Patrick Johnson; Jeanne Johnson **MS:** Married **SPN:** Kelly Lary (1999) **CH:** Hannah; Abigail; Jack; Will **ED:** Doctor of Jurisprudence, Louisiana State University Paul M. Herbert Law Center (1998); Bachelor of Science in Business Administration, Louisiana State University (1995) **C:** Chairperson, Republican Study Committee (2019-Present); Member, U.S. House of Representatives from Louisiana's Fourth District (2017-Present); Member, District Eight, Louisiana House of Representatives (2015-2017); Trustee, Ethics and Religious Liberty Commission, Southern Baptist Convention (2004-2012); Member, Committee on the Judiciary; Member, Committee on Natural Resources; Constitutional Lawyer, Benton, Bossier Parish, LA **CW:** Appearances, "The O'Reilly Factor," "Fox & Friends," "Good Morning America," "The Today Show" and National Public Radio; Talk Show Host; Conservative Columnist **MEM:** Order of Omega; Kappa Sigma Fraternity **PA:** Republican

JOHNSON, JEFFREY MARK, T: Music Director **I:** Religious **CN:** Community Lutheran Church **DOB:** 03/24/1975 **PB:** Albuquerque **SC:** NM/USA **PT:** Steven Johnson; Linda Johnson **MS:** Married **SPN:** Elizabeth (2006) **CH:** Henry; Charles **ED:** MM in Choral Conducting, Azusa Pacific University, Azusa, CA (2003); BA in Music, California State University Northridge, Los Angeles, CA (2001); AA in Music and Liberal Arts, Los Angeles Pierce College, Los Angeles, CA (1997) **CT:** California Teaching Credential **C:** Music Director, Organist, Teacher, Community Lutheran Church, Escondido, CA (2015-Present); Worship Leader and Choir Director, Simi Covenant Church, Simi Valley, CA (2013-2015); Worship Director and Teacher, First Baptist Church, Salinas, CA (2008-2013); Director and Teacher, First Baptist Church, Woodland Hills, CA (1999-2008); Vocalist, Opera Santa Barbara (2004-2005); Music Music Director, First United Methodist Church, Van Nuys, CA (1996-1999) **CR:** Soloist, National FBI Annual Memorial Service; Manager, Local YMCA Musical Fundraiser; Honors Choir, Los Angeles Pierce College; Honors Choir, California State University Northridge; Pianist, Valley Center Symphony; Conductor, Community Players Theater **CIV:** Conductor, Valley Center Symphony (2016-Present) **CW:** Musician, "Jeffrey and Elizabeth's Wedding"; Musician, "Songs for the Soul"; Musician, "Hymns for the Heart" **AW:** Winner, Various Vocal Competitions **AS:** Mr. Johnson attributes his success to his Christian faith. **B/I:** Mr. Johnson became involved in his profession because he wanted to play piano and organ for as long as he could remember. His neighbor, Jason Robinowitz, who is currently a music producer for "The Math Club," inspired him. **AV:** Bike

riding with family; Exploring wild animal park; Camping; Listening to music; Watching movies **RE:** Christian

JOHNSON, JEFFRY LYNN, T: Projectionist **I:** Media & Entertainment **DOB:** 04/04/1961 **PB:** Sidney **SC:** OH/USA **PT:** Richard Wayne; Shirley Nellie (Rausch) J. **MS:** Married **SPN:** Andrea Johnson **CH:** Dylan Johnson **ED:** Student, Case Western Reserve University (1979-1982) **C:** Projectionist, Great Lakes Science Center, DOME Theater, (2016-Present); Projectionist, Sundance Film Festival, (2003-2006); Projectionist, Great Lakes Science Center OMNIMAX Theater (1997-2016); Projectionist, Centrum Theatre, Cleveland Heights, OH (1992-2000); Projectionist, Cedar Lee Theatre, Cleveland Heights, OH (1984-1992); Laboratory Technician Histocompatibility laboratory, Case Western Reserve University, University Hospitals of Cleveland, OH (1982-1997); Co-director, Case Western Reserve University Film Society, Cleveland, OH (1980-1983) **MEM:** Cleveland Motion Picture Projectionists; Video Technicians Union Local; Society Motion Picture and TV Engineers; British Kinematograph Sound and TV Society **MH:** Albert Nelson Marquis Lifetime Achievement Award **B/I:** Mr. Johnson became involved in his profession because of his father who took him to a movie called "2001: A Space Odyssey," when he was young. When he started working with the film society at Case Western he really enjoyed it, and this inspired him to continue.

JOHNSON, JIMMIE KENNETH, T: Professional Stock Car Racer **I:** Athletics **DOB:** 09/17/1975 **PB:** El Cajon **SC:** CA/USA **PT:** Gary Ernest Johnson; Catherine Ellen Johnson **MS:** Married **SPN:** Chandra Janway **CH:** Genevieve; Lydia **C:** Professional Race Car Driver, Hendrick Motorsports, NASCAR (2002-2020); Driver, Truck Series, Randy Moss Motorsports (2008) **CIV:** Co-founder, Jimmie Johnson Foundation (2006-Present); Spokesperson, Ban Bossy (2014) **CW:** Appearance, "24/7 Jimmie Johnson: Race to Daytona" (2010); Host, Weekly Radio Show, "Not What You Expected"; Spokesperson, Chevrolet Division, General Motors; Commentator, ESPN **AW:** Named NASCAR Driver of the Year (2006-2008, 2009-2010, 2013); NASCAR Nextel Cup Champion (2006-2010, 2013); First Place, Daytona 500, Daytona International Speedway (2006, 2013); First Place, Bojangles' Southern 500, Darlington Raceway (2012); First Place, FedEx 400, Dover International Speedway (2012); First Place, Tums Fast Relief 500, Martinsville Speedway (2012); First Place, AAA Texas 500, Texas Motor Speedway (2012); First Place, Crown Royal Curtiss Shaver 400, Indianapolis Motor Speedway (2012); Named One of the Most Influential Athletes, Forbes (2011-2012); First Place, Aaron's 499 Talladega Superspeedway (2011); First Place, Hollywood Casino 400, Kansas Speedway (2011); First Place, Shelby American, Las Vegas Motor Speedway (2010); First Place, AAA 400 (2010); First Place, Auto Club 500, California Speedway (2010); First Place, Lenox Industrial Tools 301, New Hampshire International Speedway (2010); First Place, Toyota/Save Mart 350, Infineon Raceway, Sonoma, CA (2010); First Place, Food City 500, Bristol Motor Speedway (2010); First Place, Bank of America 500, Lowes Motor Speedway (2009); Named Male Athlete of the Year, The Associated Press (2009); Named NASCAR Athlete of the Decade: 2000's, Sporting News (2009); First Place, Goody's Fast Pain Relief 500 (2009); First Place, Allstate 400, The Brickyard (2006, 2008, 2009); First Place, Pepsi 500 (2008, 2009); First Place, Dover 400 (2008, 2009); First Place, Checker O'Reilly Auto Parts 500 (2007-2009); First Place, Camping World RV 400 (2008); First Place, Subway Fresh Fit 500, Phoenix

International Raceway (2008); First Place, TUMS QuikPak 500 (2008); ESPY Award for Best Driver, ESPN (2008); First Place, Chevy Rock-n-Roll 400, Richmond International Raceway (2007, 2008); First Place, Crown Royal 400 (2007); First Place, Goody's Cool Orange 500 (2007); First Place, Subway 500 (2004, 2006, 2007); First Place, Dickies 500 (2007); First Place, UAW-DiamlerChrysler 400 (2006, 2007); First Place, Sharp AQUOS 500 (2007); First Place, Pep Boys Auto 500, Atlanta Motor Speedway, (2007); First Place, Kobalt Tools 500 (2007); First Place, MBNA RacePoints 400 (2005); First Place, United Auto Workers, DiamlerChrysler 400 (2005); First Place, United Auto Workers GM-Quality 500 (2004, 2005); First Place, Coca-Cola 600 (2003-2005); First Place, Mountain Dew Southern 500 (2004); First Place, Carolina Dodge Dealers 400 (2004); First Place, Pennsylvania 500, Pocono Raceway (2004); First Place, Pocono 500 (2004); First Place, Bass Pro Shops/MBNA 500 (2004); First Place, Sylvania 300 (2003); First Place, New England 300 (2003); First Place, NAPA Auto Parts 500 (2002); First Place, MBNA All-American Heroes 400 (2002); First Place, MBNA Platinum 400 (2002); Named Pat Schauer Memorial Rookie of the Year, American Speed Association (1998); Numerous Awards

JOHNSON, JIMMY WILLIAM, T: Sports Commentator; Former Football Coach **I:** Athletics **CN:** Fox Network **DOB:** 07/16/1943 **PB:** Port Arthur **SC:** TX/USA **MS:** Married **SPN:** Rhonda Rookmaaker (07/18/1999); Linda Kay Cooper (07/12/1963, Divorced 01/1990) **CH:** Two Sons **ED:** BA, University of Arkansas (1965) **C:** Co-Host, "Fox NFL Sunday," Fox Network (2002-Present); Head Coach, General Manager, Miami Dolphins, NFL (1996-1999); Sports Commentator, Football Analyst, Fox Network (1994-1995); Head Coach, Dallas Cowboys, NFL (1989-1994); Head Coach, University of Miami, Miami, FL (1983-1988); Head Coach, Oklahoma State University (1979-1983); Assistant Coach, University of Pittsburg (1977-1978); Assistant Coach, University of Arkansas (1973-1976); Assistant Coach, University of Oklahoma, Norman, OK (1970-1972); Assistant Coach, Iowa State University (1968-1968); Assistant Coach, Wichita State University (1967); Assistant Coach, Louisiana Tech University (1965) **CW:** Contestant, "Survivor: Nicaragua" (2010) **AW:** Inductee, Pro Football Hall of Fame (2020); Winner, Super Bowl XXVIII, NFL (1993); Winner, Super Bowl XXVII, NFL (1992); NFL Coach of the Year, Football Digest (1991); NFL Coach of the Year, College & Pro Football Newsweekly (1990); NFL Coach of the Year, United Press International (1990); NFL Coach of the Year, Associated Press (1990); Winner, NCAA Division I Championship (1987); Coach of the Year, Walter Camp Foundation (1986-1987); Seattle Gold Helmet Award (1986)

JOHNSON, JOHN HENRY, T: Film Director, Producer, Photographer; Educator **I:** Fine Art **DOB:** 10/31/1951 **PB:** Pueblo **SC:** CO/USA **PT:** William Admiral (Buddy) Johnson; Matilda Marie (Trabucco) Johnson **MS:** Married **SPN:** Nadine Sue (Milosavich) **CH:** Rebecca Sue (Becky); Thomas William **ED:** MFA, Cranbrook Academy of Art, Bloomfield Hills, MI (1977); Coursework with Ansel Adams, Brett Weston, Paul Caponigro and Others, Friends of Photography Workshop, Carmel, CA (1975); BFA, Rochester Institute of Technology, Rochester, NY, Summa Cum Laude, with Highest Honors (1975); AA, Colorado State University-Pueblo, CO, with Highest Honors (1973) **C:** President, Founder, Tamarack Productions, Inc., Pueblo, CO (1982-Present); With, Apple Inc. (2008-2017); Studio Cameraman, Director, Station KOAA-TV, Pueblo, CO (1997-2001); Custom Pho-

tographic Printer, Colorhouse Photographic Lab, Burbank, CA (1990-1993); Production Assistant, Metro-Goldwyn-Mayer (MGM), Canon City, CO (1983); Cinematographer, Production Assistant, Writer, Various Production Companies, CO (1979-1980); Photographer, Pueblo Chieftain and Star Journal (1975); Director, Cinematographer, Editor of Humanities Division Film Series, Colorado State University-Pueblo (1971-1972); Photographer, Colorado Highway Department (Now Colorado Department of Transportation), Eisenhower Tunnel, CO (1971); Studio Cameraman, Director, Station KOAA-TV, Pueblo, CO (1970) **CR:** Adjunct Professor of Filmmaking, Photography, Art Appreciation and Art History, Colorado State University-Pueblo (2009-Present); Adjunct Professor of Digital Photography and Mac Computers, Pikes Peak Community College, Colorado Springs, CO (2014-2015); Adjunct Professor of Art History, Red Rocks Community College (2009-2015); Adjunct Professor of Photography and Digital Photography, University of Colorado-Denver (2010); Adjunct Professor of Photography and Digital Photography, University of Colorado-Denver (2008); Adjunct Professor of Photography, Art Appreciation and Art History, Community College of Aurora (2004-2008); Adjunct Professor Filmmaking, Film Appreciation and Documentary Film, Colorado Film School (2004-2006); Adjunct Professor of Filmmaking, Photography, Art Appreciation and Art History, Colorado State University-Pueblo (2001-2004); Adjunct Professor of Photography, Filmmaking and Humanities, Pueblo Community College (1994-2002); Adjunct Professor of Filmmaking, Learning Tree University, Chatsworth, CA (1992-1993); Adjunct Professor of Filmmaking, Photography, Art Appreciation and Art History, Colorado State University-Pueblo (1980-1981); Adjunct Professor of Photography, Community College of Denver (1979); Instructor of Filmmaking, Photography and Design, Art Institute of Colorado, CO (1978-1979); Adjunct Professor of Filmmaking, Photography, Art Appreciation and Art History, Colorado State University-Pueblo (1978); Adjunct Professor of Photography, Arapahoe Community College, Littleton, CO (1978); Graduate Teaching Assistant of Photography, Cranbrook Academy of Art, Bloomfield Hills, MI (1977) **CW:** Author, Biographical Memoir, "Buddy Johnson - A Colorado Original" (2020); Artist, Exhibition, "Interpretations by Pueblo," Pueblo Community College San Juan Art Gallery (2018); Artist, Solo Exhibition, John Deaux Gallery, Pueblo, CO (2006, 2016); Artist, Exhibition, University of South Carolina-Sumter (2005); Artist, Exhibition, Texas Tech University, Lubbock, Texas (2004-2005); Artist, Exhibition, Washington Gallery of Photography, Bethesda, MD (2004); Artist, Exhibition, Rochester Institute of Technology Photography Centennial Celebration - 100 Years (2003); Photographer, "Photographic Materials & Processes, Second Edition" (2000); Photographer, "View Camera Technique, Eighth Edition" (1999); Photographer, "Visual Concepts for Photographers, Chinese Edition" (1998); Contributing Editor, "Focal Encyclopedia of Photography, Third Edition" (1993); Photographer, "View Camera Technique, Sixth Edition" (1993); Photographer, "Photographic Materials & Processes, Italian Edition" (1993); Director, Writer, Producer, Cinematographer, Editor, Invited Feature, International Science Fiction and Fantasy Film Festival, Rome, Italy (1990); Director, Writer, Producer, Cinematographer, Editor, "Curse of the Blue Lights" (1988); Photographer, "Orlin Helgoe-Shaman of the Prairie" (1986); Photographer, "View Camera Technique, Fifth Edition" (1986); Photographer, "Photographic Materials & Processes" (1986); Director, Writer, Producer, Cinematographer, Editor, "Zebulon Pike and The Blue

Mountain" (1984); Artist, Exhibition, Colorado Photography One, Colorado Springs Fine Arts Center at Colorado College (1982); Director, Cinematographer, Co-editor, "Damon Runyon's Pueblo" (1981); Photographer, "Visual Concepts for Photographers, First Edition" (1980); Artist, Exhibition, 17th Regional, Boulder, CO (1978); Artist, Exhibition, Chester County Art Association, West Chester, PA (1978); Artist, Exhibition, Michigan Photography, The Scarab Club Detroit (1976); Artist, Exhibition, Fourth All Colorado, Denver Art Museum (1976); Photographer, Southwest Fine Arts Biennial Exhibition, Museum of New Mexico (1976); Artist, Exhibition, Southwest Fine Arts Biennial, The Museum of New Mexico, Santa Fe, NM (1976); Artist, Solo Exhibition, Rochester Institute of Technology, Rochester, NY (1975); Artist, Solo Exhibition, Sangre de Cristo Art Center, Pueblo, CO (1975); Artist, Solo Exhibition, Pueblo Regional Library (1973) **AW:** Excellence in the Arts Award, Pueblo Arts Council (2006); Certificate of Commendation, American Association for State and Local History (AASLH), Nashville, TN (1986); CINE Golden Eagle Award, Council on International Nontheatrical Events, Washington, DC (1983, 1985); Grantee, National Endowment for the Humanities (1979); Grantee, Colorado Endowment for the Humanities (Now Colorado Humanities)(1979); Grantee, Colorado State University-Pueblo (1979); Grantee, Cranbrook Academy/Ford Foundation (1977); Grantee, Thatcher Foundation (1973-1977); Grantee, Professional Photographers of America (1974) **MH:** Albert Nelson Marquis Lifetime Achievement Award **AS:** Mr. Johnson attributes his success to not giving up; if there is something that you want, you keep working until you get it. **B/I:** Mr. Johnson entered his profession because his mother had worked in a photo lab. She was always involved with photography; when she married, she purchased a photo kit which she thought she would use, but never did. Decades later, one summer, Mr. Johnson and his friends were in the way and she told them to try out the kit and see if it still worked. He started printing pictures and never stopped. He always loved photography and art. That got him into photography and then to experimenting with filmmaking. Being around his father and growing up in a television studio, pointed Mr. Johnson in that direction. He made many short animated and experimental films starting in junior high. In high school, he made more ambitious films, including a 16-minute documentary "Concern 70", part of which was shown on local television. In college, his interests in photography and filmmaking took on a more professional nature, eventually leading to the creation of a production company and a number of award-winning films. Since he was 11, Mr. Johnson has split his time between photography and films, which eventually led him into teaching photography, film production, and art at all levels. **AV:** Photography; Music; Genealogy; Movies; History; Travel; Skiing **THT:** Mr. Johnson works on ideas that really interest him, in photography that would be pure, beautiful visual forms while his films have often dealt with local and regional history. For more information, please visit his website: http://www.johnhjohnson.net

JOHNSON, JOSEPH, "J.J.", T: Chef **I:** Food & Restaurant Services **CN:** Henry at Life Hotel **DOB:** 08/01/1984 **SC:** NY/USA **ED:** Bachelor's Degree in Culinary Arts/Chef Training, Culinary Institute of America (2007) **C:** Chef, Henry at Life Hotel, New York, NY (2018-Present); Executive Chef, The Cecil and Minton's Harlem, New York, NY (2013-2017); Executive Sous Chef, Morgan Stanley, New York, NY (2009-2013) **CR:** Chef/Co-Founder, InGrained Hospitality Concepts, New York, NY (2017-Present); Founder, Chef, FieldTrip **CW:** Co-Author,

"Between Harlem"; Co-Author, "Heaven" **AW:** Listee, Eater's Young Guns (2014); Listee, 30 Under 30, Zagat (2014); Listee, 30 Under 30 in Food and Wine Category, Forbes (2014); Winner, Rocco's Dinner Party, Bravo (2011); Best New Restaurant in America, Esquire

JOHNSON, JOSEPHINE POWELL, T: District Manager (Retired) **I:** Other **DOB:** 04/23/1941 **PB:** Goldsboro **SC:** NC/USA **PT:** William Howard Powell; Vennie Ann (Johnson) Powell **MS:** Widowed **SPN:** William Stephenson (12/24/1959, Deceased 02/1979); Amos James Johnson (08/15/1981) **CH:** Teresa Lynn (Deceased 2000); Amos James III; Edward; Brian Keith **ED:** Coursework, University of Mount Olive (1980-1983); Coursework, Fayetteville Technical Community College (1975-1979) **C:** Contract Worker, Carolina Power & Light Company (1995-1997); District Manager, Carolina Power & Light Company (1989-1995); Area Business Manager, Carolina Power & Light Company (1986-1987); Area Manager, Carolina Power & Light Company (1980-1986); Administrative Assistant to District Manager, Carolina Power & Light Company (1979-1980) **AW:** Woman of the Year, American Business Women's Association **MEM:** Vice President, Eastern North Carolina Chamber of Commerce (1980-Present); Chairman of the Board, Mt. Olive Family Medicine Center, Inc. (1997-2003); American Business Women's Association (1983-1995); Vice Chairman, Eastern North Carolina Chamber of Commerce (1992); Vice Chairman, North Carolina Board of Directors, Mt. Olive Family Medicine Center, Inc. (1984) **MH:** Albert Nelson Marquis Lifetime Achievement Award **AS:** Ms. Johnson attributes her success to the encouragement of her district managers, Herman Perry and Harry Oberbee. **B/I:** Ms. Johnson became involved in her profession because of her work in utilities at the start of her career. **PA:** Democrat

JOHNSON, JUDY DIANNE, T: Retired Elementary School Educator **I:** Education/Educational Services **DOB:** 10/01/1947 **PB:** Houston **SC:** TX/USA **PT:** Thomas Hunter Mitchell; Roxie Pauline (Swink) Mitchell **MS:** Married **SPN:** Dennis Carlton Johnson (06/04/1971) **CH:** Juli Lyn; Jill Nicole **ED:** BS in Elementary Education; MEd in Secondary Education **CT:** Certified Supervisor, Teacher, State of Texas **C:** Elementary Teacher, Katy Independent School District (1992-2006); Elementary Teacher, Humble Independent School District (1969-1992); Retired Elementary School Educator **CIV:** Cypress Assistance Ministries **MEM:** Texas Retired Teachers; National Wildlife Federation; Second Baptist Church; Bear Creek Book Club **MH:** Albert Nelson Marquis Lifetime Achievement Award; Marquis Who's Who Top Professional **AS:** Ms. Johnson attributes her success to her parents, who always encouraged her to do her best. **B/I:** Ms. Johnson knew from a young age that she wanted to be a teacher. There was no question that after she graduated she was going to get an education degree. She chose elementary education because she loves teaching smaller children. **AV:** Reading; Completing puzzles **PA:** Conservative **RE:** Baptist

JOHNSON, KEVIN, T: Chief Executive Officer, President **I:** Food & Restaurant Services **CN:** Starbucks Corporation **DOB:** 10/09/1960 **PB:** Bellevue **SC:** WA/USA **ED:** Bachelor of Arts in Business Administration, New Mexico State University **C:** President, Chief Executive Officer, Starbucks Corporation (2017-Present); President, Chief Operating Officer, Starbucks Corporation (2015-2017); Chief Executive Officer, Juniper Networks (2008-2013); President, Platform & Services (2007-2008); Co-President, Platform and Services (2005-2007)

JOHNSON, LAWRENCE TUFTS, T: Pilot (Retired) **I:** Aviation **PB:** Oakland **SC:** CA/USA **MS:** Married **ED:** Coursework in Electronic Engineering, Capital Technology Institute, Washington, DC; Diploma, Fork Union Military Academy (1964) **CT:** Certified, Burnside-Ott Aviation Training Center (1967); Commercial, Instrument; Graduate, Continental Airlines Pilot Certification Center; Engineer B-727, B-747; First Officer B727, DC-10; Captain B-737, 300, 500, 700, 800, 900; FAA Certification Courses; Certified, Flight Instructor **C:** Captain, Continental Airlines (1999-2002); First Officer, Continental Airlines (1995-1999); Flight Engineer, Continental Airlines (1988-1995); Captain, American Eagle (1986-1988); Pilot to Captain, Wings West Commuter Airlines, San Luis Obispo, CA (1980-1988); First Officer, American Eagle (1985-1986); Insurance Agency Manager (1983-1986); Owner, Aviation Insurance Business, Fresno Air Terminal, CA (1980-1985); Aviation Insurance Underwriter, Omni Aviation Managers, Inc. (1979-1983); Insurance Agency Manager, I. Berman Company, Aviation Insurance Broker (1976-1979); Chief Flight Instructor, Epps Aviation (1973-1976); Insurance Broker, Montgomery, AL (1972) **CR:** Auditor, Treasurer, Fresno County Democratic Committee; Chairman, Campaign Services Committee, Fresno County Democratic Party; Member, Fresno County Democratic Central Committee; Vice President, Internet Technology, California Democratic Council **MH:** Albert Nelson Marquis Lifetime Achievement Award **AS:** Mr. Johnson attributes his success to the desire to prove the many people who told him he would fail, wrong. **B/I:** In 1957, at age 11, Mr. Johnson's family was on a trip overseas in Cyprus. His father was on assignment with the Central Intelligence Agency (CIA). While there, a crew of pilots saw Mr. Johnson and asked would he like to see the inside of the cockpit of a military plane. He recalls, no less than 10 minutes leaving the cockpit, he knew exactly what he wanted to do with his life. **AV:** Computers; Aviation **PA:** Democrat

JOHNSON, MICHAEL DUANE, T: Professional Sprinter (Retired) **I:** Athletics **DOB:** 09/13/1967 **PB:** Dallas **SC:** TX/USA **MS:** Married **SPN:** Armine Shamiryan; Kerry D'Oyen (Divorced) **CH:** Sebastian **ED:** Coursework, Baylor University (1990) **C:** Founder, Michael Johnson Performance (2007-Present); Professional Sprinter (2000); Professional Sprinter (1986-2000) **CR:** Sports Commentator, BBC **CW:** Contestant, "Celebrity Apprentice" (2010); Contributor, Articles, Daily Telegraph, The Times **AW:** Inductee, National Track and Field Hall of Fame (2004); Gold Medalist, 400 Meters, 4 x 400 Meters, Summer Olympics, Sydney, Australia (2000); Gold Medal, 400 Meters, World Championship (1997); Named, Male Athlete of the Year, The Associated Press (1996); Gold Medal, 200 Meters and 400 Meters, Summer Olympics, Atlanta, GA (1996); Winner, 200 Meters, U.S. National Championships (1990-1992, 1995); Gold Medal, 200 Meters, Goodwill Games (1990, 1994); Named, Athlete of the Year, USA Track & Field (1993-1994); Winner, 400 Meters, World Athletic Championship (1993); Gold Medal, 4 x 100 Relay, Summer Olympics, Barcelona, Spain (1992); Winner, 200 Meters, World Athletic Championships (1991); Three-time Recipient, Jesse Owens Award

JOHNSON, RANDY, "THE BIG UNIT" DAVID, T: Former Professional Baseball Player **I:** Athletics **DOB:** 09/10/1963 **PB:** Walnut Creek **SC:** CA/ USA **PT:** Rollen Charles "Bud" Johnson; Carol Hannah Johnson **MS:** Married **SPN:** Lisa (1993) **CH:** Samantha; Tanner; Willow; Alexandria; Heather Renee Roszell **ED:** Coursework, University of Southern California **C:** Special Assistant to Team President, Arizona Diamondbacks (2015); Retired,

Major League Baseball (MLB) (2010); Pitcher, San Francisco Giants, Major League Baseball (MLB) (2008-2009); Pitcher, Arizona Diamondbacks, Major League Baseball (MLB), Phoenix, AZ (1999-2004, 2007-2008); Pitcher, New York Yankees, Major League Baseball (MLB) (2005-2006); Pitcher, Houston Astros, Major League Baseball (MLB) (1998); Pitcher, Seattle Mariners, Major League Baseball (MLB) (1990-1998); Pitcher, Montreal Expos, Major League Baseball (MLB), Canada (1988-1989) **AW:** Inductee, National Baseball Hall of Fame (2015); Recruited, National League All-Star Team (1999-2002, 2004); National League Babe Ruth Award (2001); World Series Championship, Arizona Diamondbacks, Major League Baseball (MLB) (2001); Sportsman of the Year, Sports Illustrated (2001); World Series Co-MVP, Major League Baseball (MLB) (2001); National League Outstanding Pitcher, Major League Baseball Players Association (2000); Warren Spahn Award, Oklahoma Sports Museum (1999-2002); National League Cy Young Award (1999-2002); Recruited, American League All-Star Team (1990, 1993-1995, 1997); American League Outstanding Pitcher, Major League Baseball Players Association (1995); Pitcher of the Year, The Sporting News (1995); American League Cy Young Award (1995); Inductee, Mariners Hall of Fame

JOHNSON, RICHARD DARRELL, T: Management Consultant **I:** Consulting **DOB:** 08/01/1935 **PB:** Columbus **SC:** OH/USA **PT:** Darrell Dean Johnson; Gretchen Price (Motz) Johnson **MS:** Married **SPN:** Ann Elizabeth Sektnan (04/09/1960, Deceased 2015) **CH:** Julie Ann Johnson; Jennifer Johnson Rehn; Douglas Richard Johnson **ED:** MBA, The Ohio State University (1962); Bachelor of Industrial Engineering, The Ohio State University (1958) **CT:** Certified Public Accountant, Illinois (1977); Certified Public Accountant, Ohio (1965); Professional Engineer, Ohio (1965); Certificate in Data Processing, Institute for Certification of Computer Professionals (1965) **C:** Consultant, Major Clients (1999-2001); Founder, Chairman, VIA International LLC, Offices in Chicago, London, New York, and Singapore (1992-1999); Founder, Change Management Service Line, Andersen Consulting (Now Accenture), Member, Global Management Team (1986-1991); Member, Chairman'Chief Executive Officer's Advisory Council, Arthur Andersen & Company (1976-1978); Managing Partner, Firm Services in Iran, Afghanistan, and Pakistan, Arthur Andersen & Company (1975-1977); Managing Partner, Cleveland Practice, Andersen Consulting (Now Accenture) (1971-1975); Partner, Arthur Andersen & Company (1970-1991); Numerous Management Responsibilities involving Audit, Tax, Consulting, and Professional Education, Andersen Consulting's Retail Industry Leader (1969-1975); Member, Information Technology Consulting Practice, Andersen Consulting (Now Accenture) (1962-1975) **CIV:** Member, Dean's Advisory Council, Fisher College of Business (2011-Present); Member, Chicago National Major Gifts Committee (1995-2015); Vice Chairman, The Ohio State University Alumni Association (2001-2004); Member, Board of Directors, The Ohio State University Alumni Association (1999-2004); Vice Chairman of the Board, Ravinia Festival, Chicago, IL (1999-2002); Member, Board of Trustees, Ravinia Festival, Chicago, IL (1988-2013); Member, Ruth Weimer Mount Leadership Initiative Stewardship Council (1997-2001); Director, United Way of Lake Forest-Lake Bluff (1981-2001); Member, President's Alumni Advisory Council, The Ohio State University (1996-1999); Chairman, Presidents Club Advisory Board, The Ohio State University (1996-1998); Member, Department of Industrial and Systems Engineering Alumni Advisory Council (1988-1992);

Member, College of Engineering Chicago Advisory Board (1988-1991); Member, Lake Forest District 67 Board of Education (1984-1990); Executive Vice President, Lake Forest Symphony Association Board of Trustees (1984-1989); Member, Lake Forest Symphony Association Board of Trustees (1979-1989); President, United Way of Lake Forest-Lake Bluff (1986-1988); Treasurer, United Way of Lake Forest-Lake Bluff (1984-1986); General Campaign Coordinator, Chicago, American Cancer Society (1983); President, Cleveland Chapter, Association for Systems Management (1973-1975); Member, Campaign Committees, Fisher College of Business **MIL:** Reserve Officer to the Rank of Captain, U.S. Air Force (1961-1967); Active Duty Officer to the Rank of First Lieutenant, U.S. Air Force (1958-1961) **CW:** Contributor, Articles, Professional Journals **AW:** Distinguished Service Award, The Ohio State University (2006); Significant Sig Award, Sigma Chi Fraternity (2002); Distinguished Alumni Award, Fisher College of Business, The Ohio State University (2002); Alumni Citizenship Award, The Ohio State University Alumni Association (1998); Gerlach Development Volunteer Award, The Ohio State University (1998); International Distinguished Service Award, Association for Systems Management (1976); Achievement Award, Association for Systems Management (1974); Merit Award, Association for Systems Management (1972) **MEM:** Sigma Chi Fraternity (1953-Present); Pelican Marsh Golf Club, Naples, FL (2002-2010); Pelican Isle Yacht Club, Naples, FL (1997-2010); Treasurer, Sloane Gardens Club of London, England (1993-1994); Vail Racquet Club, Colorado (1991-2003); Executives Club of Chicago (1990-2000); Sloane Gardens Club of London, England (1985-2018); Lake Forest Club (1977-1992); Lake Geneva Yacht Club, Wisconsin (1981-1990); Metropolitan Club of Chicago (1977-1993); Imperial Country Club, Tehran, Iran (1975-1977); Cleveland Athletic Club (1971-1977); Cleveland Yachting Club (1969-1978) **MH:** Albert Nelson Marquis Lifetime Achievement Award (2017); Marquis Who's Who Humanitarian Award (2017); Who's Who in Finance and Industry; Who's Who in America; Who's Who in the World **AV:** Skiing; Boating; Traveling; Golfing; Classical music **RE:** Presbyterian

JOHNSON, RICHARD N, PHD, T: President **I:** Machinery **CN:** Rockwind Venture Partners **DOB:** 01/04/1942 **PB:** Perry **SC:** IA/USA **PT:** Harding Richard Johnson; Dorothy Margret (Nelson) Johnson **MS:** Married **SPN:** Karen L. Friedman (05/18/1986); Lila Lee Herron (06/24/1978, Deceased 11/1984) **CH:** David; Rachel; Jana (Riley) **ED:** MBA, Roosevelt University, With Honors, Chicago, IL (1980); PhD in Engineering Mechanics, University of Wisconsin (1972); MS in Engineering Mechanics, Case Institute, Cleveland, OH (1968); BS in Applied Mathematics, University of Wisconsin (1964) **C:** President, Rockwind Venture Partner (2012-Present); Director, Engineering Outreach, Northern Illinois University (2004-2012); Research Department Manager, IIT Research Institute (1996-2004); Associate Director, Industrial Research Lab, Northwestern University, Evanston, IL (1991-1996); Department Manager, Packer Engineering, Naperville, IL (1989); Department Manager, Borg Warner Automotive Research, Des Plaines, IL (1981-1988); Department Manager, General American Research Division, GATX Corp, Niles, IL (1971-1981); Teaching Assistant, University of Wisconsin, Madison, WI (1970-1971); Project Manager, Lewis Research Division, NASA, Cleveland, OH (1964-1970) **CR:** Consultant, General Dynamics; Consultant, Psych Systems; Consultant, Axionix; Consultant, Legal Firms; Consultant to HomeCare Assistance Founder **CIV:** Renewable Energy and Manufacturing Rebuilding **CW:** Author, Several Chapters,

"Handbook of Manufacturing High Technology" (1986) **AW:** R&D 100 Award for Laser Assisted Cladding of Metals (2004); Research Grantee, NASA (1970); Lincoln Welding Award **MEM:** Society of Manufacturing Engineers; Institute of Industrial and Systems Engineers **MH:** Albert Nelson Marquis Lifetime Achievement Award **AS:** Dr. Johnson was raised in a very competitive family of Swedish immigrants with high aspirations for their children and a very supportive wife and family. He attributes his success to an enthusiasm for science and life-long learning. **B/I:** Dr. Johnson became involved in his profession because the space race inspired him to work at NASA. He then applied the knowledge he gained on metals during his time there to railroads and industrial machinery. Always dreamed of and acted on things that could be, not what existed. His enthusiasm for his ideas translated into being able to persuade R&D funding agencies to award him project funding. **AV:** Travel; Reading **THT:** Always question what is, and try to change and create what needs to be improved. Life is not a straight line; but offers many twists and turns, which if embraced can be exhilarating.

JOHNSON, RICHARD TURNER, T: Television Producer, Consultant **I:** Media & Entertainment **CN:** Community Arts Advocate **DOB:** 03/21/1933 **PB:** Seattle **SC:** WA/USA **PT:** B.E. Johnson; Marie (Turner) Johnson **MS:** Married **SPN:** Joyce Loraine McLeod (12/01/1957) **CH:** Richard (Rick) F. Johnson; Mark Robley Johnson **ED:** MA in Theater Arts, University of California, Los Angeles (1961); BA in Theater Arts, University of California, Los Angeles (1959) **C:** Assistant Program Director, Executive Producer, Station KHJ-TV Channel 9, Los Angeles, CA (1981-1990); Production Manager, Station KHJ-TV Channel 9, Los Angeles, CA (1972-1981); Producer, Director, Station KHJ-TV Channel 9, Los Angeles, CA (1967-1972); Television Stage Manager, Set Designer, Station KHJ-TV Channel 9, Los Angeles, CA (1962-1967) **CR:** Executive Director, Conejo Players Theater, Thousand Oaks, CA (1968-2010); Arts Commissioner, Thousand Oaks, CA (1986-1992) **CIV:** Chair, Board, California Museum of Art Thousand Oaks (2015-2019); Regional Art Museum Task Force, Vice Chair (2010-2014); Fundraising Chair (1991-1995); Cultural Center Planning Committee, Thousand Oaks (1985-1986); Civic Arts Plaza, Alliance For the Arts **MIL:** U.S. Naval Reserve (1954-1957) **CW:** Executive Producer, Television Program, "School Beat," KHJ-TV Channel 9, Los Angeles, CA (1986); Executive Producer, Television Program, "Taking "High" Out of High School," KHJ-TV Channel 9, Los Angeles, CA (1985); Executive Producer, Television Program, "Off-Hand," KHJ-TV Channel 9, Los Angeles, CA; Executive Producer, Television Program, "Teen Talk," KHJ-TV Channel 9, Los Angeles, CA; Director, Play, "Carousel," Conejo Players Theatre, Thousand Oaks, CA; Director, Play, "Kiss Me Kate," Conejo Players Theatre, Thousand Oaks, CA; Director, Play, "Peter Pan," Conejo Players Theatre, Thousand Oaks, CA; Director, Play, "Guys & Dolls," Conejo Players Theatre, Thousand Oaks, CA; Director, Play, "Tribute," Conejo Players Theatre, Thousand Oaks, CA; Director, Play, "Pipe Dream," Conejo Players Theatre, Thousand Oaks, CA; Director, Play, "How to Succeed in Business," Conejo Players Theatre, Thousand Oaks, CA; Director, Play, "Mikado," Conejo Players Theatre, Thousand Oaks, CA; Director, Play, "Champagne General," Conejo Players Theatre, Thousand Oaks, CA; Director, Play, "Amorous Flea," Conejo Players Theatre, Thousand Oaks, CA; Director, Play, "A Thousand Clowns," Conejo Players Theatre, Thousand Oaks, CA; Director, Play, "The Most Happy Fellow," Conejo Players Theatre, Thousand Oaks, CA; Director, Play, "Big

River," Conejo Players Theatre, Thousand Oaks, CA; Director, Play, "45 Seconds to Broadway," Conejo Players Theatre, Thousand Oaks, CA; Director, Play, "Bert & Eddie," Conejo Players Theatre, Thousand Oaks, CA; Director, Play, "Candide," Conejo Players Theatre, Thousand Oaks, CA **AW:** Arts Advocate Award, Conejo Players Theatre, Thousand Oaks, CA (2015); Twilight Award, Gold Coast Performing Arts (1995); Thousand Oaks Arts Commission Encore Award (1994); Los Angeles Emmy Award, "Teen Talk" (1983, 1989); Los Angeles Emmy Award, "Off-Hand" (1982, 1986, 1988); Los Angeles Emmy Award, "School Break" (1986); Los Angeles Emmy Award, "Taking "High" Out of High School" (1985) **MEM:** Alliance for the Arts; Academy of Television Arts & Sciences; Arts Council of the Conejo Valley; Conejo Players Theatre; UCLA Alumni Association **MH:** Albert Nelson Marquis Lifetime Achievement Award **AS:** Mr. Johnson attributes his success to the love and encouragement of his wife, Joyce. **B/I:** Mr. Johnson became involved in his profession because he has been interested in the arts since childhood; he began performing at a young age. During his time at Roosevelt High School, one of his teachers recommended that he audition for some of the school productions. He took that advice and found that he enjoyed the dramatic arts so much that, when moving from the University of Washington to UCLA in 1953, he changed his major from Art to Theater. He found that he enjoyed all types of art, including painting, drawing, and music. His mother, a teacher, saw his talent and encouraged him to pursue what he loved. As a career, Mr. Johnson discovered that he enjoyed all aspects of working in television, from designing graphics and sets to staging performers to directing cameras. He worked in television for many years and looked forward to going to work each day. **AV:** Painting; Carpentry; Swimming; Skiing

JOHNSON, RONALD, "RON" HAROLD, T: U.S. Senator **I:** Government Administration/Government Relations/Government Services **DOB:** 04/08/1955 **PB:** Mankato **SC:** MN/USA **PT:** Dale Robert Johnson; Jeanette Elizabeth (Thisius) Johnson **MS:** Married **SPN:** Jane Johnson (08/20/1977) **CH:** Carey; Jenna; Ben **ED:** BA in Business and Accounting, University of Minnesota (1977) **C:** Chairman, Committee on Homeland Security and Governmental Affairs, U.S. Senate (2015-Present); U.S. Senator, State of Wisconsin, Washington, DC (2011-Present); Member, Committee on Homeland Security and Governmental Reform, U.S. Senate, Washington, DC (2011-Present); Member, Special Committee on Aging, U.S. Senate, Washington, DC (2011-Present); Member, Appropriations Committee, U.S. Senate, Washington, DC (2011-Present); Member, Budget Committee, U.S. Senate, Washington, DC (2011-Present); Owner, President, Pacur, LLC (1997-Present); From Machine Operator and Accountant to General Manager, Pacur, LLC, Oshkosh, WI (1979-1997); Accountant, Jostens Inc., Minneapolis, WI (1977-1979) **CIV:** Active Member, Unified Catholic School Systems, Oshkosh, WI; Active Member, Oshkosh Chamber of Commerce; Member, Partners in Education Council **AW:** Stephen Mosling Commitment to Education Award, Oshkosh Chamber of Commerce (2009) **PA:** Republican **RE:** Lutheran

JOHNSON, WILLIAM, "BILL" LESLIE, T: U.S. Representative from Ohio **I:** Government Administration/Government Relations/Government Services **DOB:** 11/10/1954 **PB:** Roseboro **SC:** NC/USA **MS:** Married **SPN:** LeeAnn Johnson; Wanda Florence Porter (04/30/1975, Divorced) **CH:** Four Children **ED:** MA, Georgia Institute of Technology (1984); BA, Troy University, AL, Summa Cum

Laude (1979) **C:** Member, U.S. House of Representatives from Ohio's Sixth Congressional District, United States Congress, Washington, DC (2011-Present); Member, U.S. House Committee on Natural Resources, Washington, DC (2011-Present); Member, U.S. House Committee on Veterans' Affairs, Washington, DC (2011-Present); Member, U.S. House Committee on Foreign Affairs, Washington, DC (2011-Present); Chief Information Officer, Stoneridge Inc., Warren, Ohio (2006-2010); Co-Founder, J2 Business Solutions, Inc. (2003-2006); Co-founder, Johnson-Schley Management Group, Inc. (1990-2003); Member, Committee on Energy and Commerce; Member, Committee on Science, Space and Technology **MIL:** Lt. Col. (Retired), U.S. Air Force (1999); Director, Chief Information Officer Staff, U.S. Special Operations Command, U.S. Air Force (1973-1999) **AW:** Decorated National Defense Service Medal; Air Force Commendation Medal; Air Force Meritorious Service Medal; Named Distinguished Graduate, Air Force Reserve Officer Training Corps, Squadron Officer School and Air Command and Staff College **PA:** Republican **RE:** Protestant

JOHNSTONE, C. BRUCE, T: Investment Company Executive **I:** Business Management/Business Services **DOB:** 11/07/1940 **PB:** New York **SC:** NY/USA **PT:** Adam; Muriel S. (Smith) J **MS:** Married **SPN:** Helen Louise Lott (08/27/1963) **CH:** Brent Paul; Reed Evan **ED:** MBA, Harvard University (1966); AB, Harvard University, Cum Laude (1962) **CT:** Chartered Financial Analyst Certifications **C:** Senior Marketing Investment Strategist, Fidelity Investments (1992-Present); Managing Director, Fidelity Investments, Boston, MA (1983-Present); Chairman, Harvard Business School Fund (1998-2003); Chief Investment Officer, Managing Director, Fidelity International Ltd., (1990-1992); Executive Vice President, Chairman Investment Committee, Fidelity Management & Research Co., Boston, MA (1990); Board Directors, Fidelity Management & Research Co., Boston, MA (1989-1990);Senior Vice President, Fidelity Management & Research Co., Boston, MA (1984-1989); Senior Vice President, Fidelity Management Trust Co., Boston, MA (1982-1990); Portfolio Group Leader Income and Growth Funds, Fidelity Management & Research Co., Boston, MA (1981-1990); Vice President Portfolio Manager, Fidelity Equity Income Fund, Boston, MA (1972-1990) **CR:** Founding Member, Director, Needham Education Foundation **CIV:** Class Chair, Harvard University Business School (1966-Present), Class Secretary, (1986); Member, Committee on University Resources, Harvard University (1987) **MIL:** Lieutenant US Naval Reserve (1962-1968) **AW:** America's Best Income Investor, Money Magazine (1987) **MEM:** Member, Chartered Finance Analysts; Boston Security Analysts Society; Premiere Club; Wellesley Country Club; Harvard Varsity Club; Harvard Club Boston **MH:** Albert Nelson Marquis Lifetime Achievement Award **B/I:** Mr. Johnstone became involved in his profession because his father, Adam was a stock market enthusiast who invested for his family for many years. He was very successful at investing whatever he could save and put it in the stock market and it would become fruitful. He got him involved and convinced him by showing him the numbers which were good. That was what shaped his desire to get into the investment business.

JOLIE, ANGELINA, T: Actress **I:** Media & Entertainment **DOB:** 06/04/1975 **PB:** Los Angeles **SC:** CA/USA **PT:** Jon Voight; Marcheline Bertrand **MS:** Divorced **SPN:** Brad Pitt (08/23/2014, Divorced 2020); Billy Bob Thornton (03/05/2000, Divorced 05/27/2003); Jonny Lee Miller (03/03/1996, Divorced 02/03/1999) **CH:** Maddox Chivan

(Adopted); Pax Thien (Adopted); Zahara Marley (Adopted); Shiloh Nouvel; Knox Leon; Vivienne Marcheline **ED:** Coursework, New York University; Studied, Strasberg Theatre Institute, New York, NY **CR:** Former Professional Model, Los Angeles, CA, New York, NY and London, England **CIV:** Co-founder, Maddox Jolie-Pitt Foundation (MJP) (2006-Present); Goodwill Ambassador, UN High Commissioner for Refugees, Geneva, Switzerland (2001-Present) **CW:** Actress, "First They Killed My Father" (2017); Actress, "The Breadwinner" (2017); Voice Actress, "Kung Fu Panda 3" (2016); Actress, Producer, Director, Writer, "By the Sea" (2015); Actress, Executive Producer, "Maleficent" (2014); Producer, Director, "Unbroken" (2014); Director, "In the Land of Blood and Honey" (2011); Voice Actress, "Kung Fu Panda 2" (2011); Voice Actress, "Kung Fu Panda Holiday" (2010); Actress, "Salt" (2010); Actress, "The Tourist" (2010); Voice Actress, "Kung Fu Panda" (2008); Actress, "Wanted" (2008); Actress, "Changeling" (2008); Voice Actress, "Beowulf" (2007); Actress, "A Mighty Heart" (2007); Actress, "The Good Shepherd" (2006); Actress, "Mr. and Mrs. Smith" (2005); Actress, "Taking Lives" (2004); Voice Actress, "Shark Tale" (2004); Actress, "Sky Captain and the World of Tomorrow" (2004); Actress, "Alexander" (2004); Actress, "Lara Croft Tomb Raider: The Cradle of Life" (2003); Actress, "Beyond Borders" (2003); Actress, "Life or Something Like It" (2002); Actress, "Original Sin" (2001); Actress, "Dancing in the Dark" (2000); Actress, "Gone in Sixty Seconds" (2000); Actress, "Pushing Tin" (1999); Actress, "The Bone Collector" (1999); Actress, "Girl, Interrupted" (1999); Actress, "Hell's Kitchen" (1998); Actress, "Playing by Heart" (1998); Actress, "Gia" (1998); Actress, "George Wallace" (1997); Actress, "True Women" (1997); Actress, "Playing God" (1997); Actress, "Foxfire" (1996); Actress, "Mojave Moon" (1996); Actress, "Love Is All There Is" (1996); Actress, "Hackers" (1995); Actress, "Without Evidence" (1995); Actress, "Cyborg 2" (1993); Actress, "Angela & Viril" (1993); Actress, "Lookin' to Get Out" (1982); Appearances in Music Videos for Recording Artists Meat Loaf, Lenny Kravits, Antonello Venditti and The Lemonheads **AW:** Named, Honorary Dame Commander of the Most Excellent Order of the British Empire, Her Majesty Queen Elizabeth II (2014); Jean Hersholt Humanitarian Award, Academy of Motion Picture Arts & Sciences (2014); Named, One of the 100 Most Powerful Women, Forbes Magazine (2010-2014); Named, One of the 100 Most Powerful Women in Entertainment, The Hollywood Reporter (2008, 2014); Named One of Forbes' List of Hollywood's Highest-Paid Actresses (2013); Named, One of the 100 Most Powerful Celebrities (2007-2012); Nansen Refugee Award, United Nations (2011); Heart of Sarajevo Award (2011); Named, Favorite Female Action Star, People's Choice Awards (2009); Award for Best Actress, African American Film Critics Association (2008); Named, One of the 100 Most Influential People in the World, TIME Magazine (2006, 2008); Named, One of the 50 Smartest People in Hollywood, Entertainment Weekly (2007); Named, One of the Top 25 Entertainers of Year (2007); Named, One of Barbara Walters' 10 Most Fascinating People of Year (2006); Named, One of the 50 Most Powerful People in Hollywood, Premiere Magazine (2006); Global Humanitarian Award, United Nations Association of the USA (2005); Cambodian Citizenship for Conservation Work, King Norodom Sihamoni (2005); Academy Award for Best Supporting Actress, Academy of Motion Picture Arts & Sciences (2000); Golden Globe Award for Best Supporting Actress - Motion Picture, Hollywood Foreign Press Association (2000); SAG Award for Best Supporting Actress, Screen Actors Guild - American Federation of Tele-

vision and Radio Artists (2000); Broadcast Film Critics Award for Best Supporting Actress (2000); SAG Award for Best Actress, Screen Actors Guild - American Federation of Television and Radio Artists (1999); Golden Globe Award for Best Actress - Miniseries of Television Film, Hollywood Foreign Press Association (1999); Golden Globe Award for Best Supporting Actress, Hollywood Foreign Press Association (1998); National Board of Review Award for Best Breakthrough Performance (1998);

JOLY, HUBERT BERNARD, T: Former Chief Executive Officer, Executive Chairman **I:** Consumer Goods and Services **CN:** Best Buy **DOB:** 08/11/1959 **PB:** Nancy **SC:** France **PT:** Jean-Louis Joly; Denise (Grandjean) Joly **MS:** Married **SPN:** Nathalie Christine Motte (09/19/1981) **CH:** Stanislas; Agathe **ED:** MPA, Institute d'Etudes Politiques, Paris, France (1983); MBA, Ecole des Hautes Etudes Commercial, Jouy-en-Josas, France (1981) **C:** Chief Executive Officer, Best Buy, Richfield, MN (2012-2019); President, Chief Executive Officer, Carlson Companies, Inc., Minnetonka, MN (2008-2012); Executive Vice President, Monitoring US Assets, Deputy Chief Financial Officer, Vivendi Universal (2002-2004); Executive Vice President, Corporate Chief Information Officer, Vivendi Universal (2002); Senior Vice President, North American Integration, Vivendi Universal (2001-2002); Chief Executive Officer, Havas Interactive Inc. (1999-2000); Vice President, EDS Europe (1998-1999); President, EDS France, Paris, France (1996-1999); Chairman, EDS Progical (1996-1999); Co-leader, European Electronics Practice, McKinsey & Company, Paris, France (1994-1996); Principal, McKinsey & Company, Paris, France (1993-1996); Partner, McKinsey & Company (1982-1996); Principal, McKinsey & Company, New York, NY (1992-1993); Principal, McKinsey & Company, Paris, France (1990-1991); Manager, McKinsey & Company, Paris, France (1985-1989); Associate, McKinsey & Company, San Francisco, CA (1984-1985); Associate, McKinsey & Company, Paris, France (1983-1984); Assistant Chairman and Chief Executive Officer, Sacilor, Paris, France (1981-1982); Chief Executive Officer, Video Games Division, Vivendi Universal, Los Angeles, CA **CR:** Executive Chairman, Board of Directors, Best Buy (2012-Present); Board of Directors, Polo Ralph Lauren (2009-Present); Board of Directors, The Rezidor Hotel Group (Now Radisson Hotel Group) (2008-2012); Member, World European Forum, Global Leaders for Tomorrow (1996) **CIV:** Member, Advisory Board, U.S. Department of Commerce Travel & Tourism (2010-Present); Chairman, Board of Directors, CWT (2008-Present); Member, Board, Minneapolis Institute of Art (2008-Present); Member, Executive Committee, Minnesota Business Partnership (MNBP) (2008-Present); Member, Executive Committee, World Travel & Tourism Council (2008-Present); Board Member, American Chamber of Commerce in France (AmCham) (1998-Present) **CW:** Author, "Wake Up Europe!" (1999); Author, "Excellence in Electronics" (1993); Contributor, Articles to Professional Journals **AW:** Named One of the Top 50 Best CEOs of Large Companies, Comparably (2018) **MEM:** Centre d'Etude et de Prospective es Stratègique (CEPS)

JONAS, JEFF, T: Director, Chief Executive Officer **I:** Business Management/Business Services **CN:** Sage Therapeutics **ED:** MD, Harvard Medical School; BA, Amherst College **C:** Chief Executive Officer, Sage Therapeutics, Cambridge, MA (2003-Present); President, Regenerative Medicine Division, Shire PLC; Senior Vice President of Research and Development, Pharmaceuticals, Shire PLC; Executive Vice President, ISIS Pharmaceuticals; Chief Medical Officer and Executive Vice President, Forest Laboratories, Inc.; Upjohn Laboratories

CR: Resident in Psychiatry, Harvard University; Chief Resident in Psychopharmacology, McLean Hospital, Harvard Medical School CW: Publisher, Over 70 Scientific Papers and Chapters; Author, Over 100 Books, Scientific Articles and Abstracts AW: Innovation of the Year, Popular Science (2019) MEM: Board Member, Generation Bio and Karuna Therapeutics; Pharmaceutical Research and Manufacturers of America (PhRMA)

JONES, BARBARA EWER, T: Teacher, School Psychologist, Occupational Therapist, Disability Analyst I: Education/Educational Services CN: Monroe County Community School Corporation DOB: 01/28/1942 PB: Marion SC: IN/USA PT: J. Bertrand Ewer; Audrey May (Carter) Ewer MS: Married SPN: Jan Alden Fowler ED: Postgraduate Coursework, University of Indianapolis (1986-1993); MS, Indiana University–Purdue University Indianapolis (1978); Postgraduate Coursework, Butler University (1972-1980); MS, Indiana University (1970); BS, Indiana University (1965) CT: Training, Hadley School for the Blind (2011-2013); Permanent Teaching License (K-8); Special Education Endorsement, Emotional Handicapped, Learning Disability, Missouri Institute of Mental Health (MIMH); School Psychologist License; Occupational Therapy License, Training and Experience in Pediatrics, Stroke Rehab, Geriatrics, Alzheimer's Disease, Autism, Lower Cognitive, Children Born of Mothers of Drug Addiction; Teaching License, Social Studies C: Occupational Therapist, Teacher, Psychologist, Disability Analyst and Fellows, Inc. (2004-Present); Teacher of Blind, Hadley School for Blind, Butler University (2011-2013); Occupational Therapist, First Steps (1996-2013); Psychologist, Occupational Therapist, Master Level, Monroe County Community School Corporation, Bloomington, IN (1977-2004); Occupational Therapist, Skilled Care Unit, Independent Rehab Association, Evansville, IN (1996-1997); Evening Division Lecturer in Early Childhood Education, Butler University (1974-1981); Psychologist, Princeton University (1977); Director, Early Childhood Education, University of Indianapolis (1971-1975); Director of University Preschool, Holcolmb Estate, Butler University (1971-1975); Teacher of At-Risk First Graders, Decatur Township School System (Now MSD of Decatur Township), Indianapolis, IN (1967-1971); Contract Substitute Teacher, San Bernardino School Systems (Now San Bernardino City Unified School District), CA (1967); Teacher of First Grade, Marion School System, Marion, IN (1965-1967); Teacher, Marion School Systems (1965-1966); Consultation and In-service Trainer, Researcher, Monroe County Community School Corporation, Bloomington, IN (1990-Present); Retired, Occupational Therapist, First Steps Committee (2013); Lecturer, Evening Division, Butler University, Indianapolis, IN (1974-1981) CIV: Volunteer, Preschool Therapist, WellSpring (2015-Present); Volunteer, Horse Therapy, (2015-Present); Historian, Morgantown United Methodist Church, IN; Video Committee, Worship Committee, Altar Guild, Admission Committee, Missions Committee, Bell Choir, Morgantown United Methodist Church; Horse Therapy Volunteer, Agape; Camp Riley, Rlley Children's Foundation; WellSpring; Performer, Voices of Franklin, Franklin, IN CW: Contributor, Articles on Research on Children of Alcoholics, Professional Journals; Illustrator, "Little John", Series 1 and 2 AW: Awards in Photography, Sculpture, Watercolor Landscape Art, Fiber Art and Traditional Quilts (1978, 1986-1989) MEM: Indiana Occupational Therapy Association; American Occupational Therapy Association, Inc. MH: Albert Nelson Marquis Lifetime Achievement

Award; Marquis Who's Who Top Professional AS: Mrs. Jones attributes her success to her mentors standing behind her and encouraging her in her goals and skills. B/I: Mrs. Jones entered her profession when she started out as a teacher in her senior year at the University of Indiana; she was with a singing group called the Singing Hoosiers and she decided that she did not want to leave. Mrs. Jones put off her methods so she could not go due to her student teaching. One of the courses required her to complete work with a classroom at the lab school to perform and set up an assignment for the kids. Mrs. Jones taught them about white light. That experience within the call room and the white light experiment helped her to get accepted into student teaching at the lab school. She was one of the six out of 400 who were chosen to do the student teaching. Eventually, teaching was not enough. Mrs. Jones knew that she could do more. She went to Butler University for school psychology. She was close to three hours within the program, but they closed it, and she had to start over. Mrs. Jones eventually received her school psychology degree and received her license. AV: Sculpting; Painting; Quilting; Music; Acting; Working with children; Singing; Piano playing RE: Methodist THT: The most important aspect of Mrs. Jones' life right now is giving back. Four years ago, her house burned down; the whole area was on fire. A small community gave to Mrs. Jones and her family. Now, she feels, it is her turn. That is why Mrs. Jones volunteers. She enjoys giving her time to families and children and listening when stopped by a person that needs to talk. Mrs. Jones also volunteers for a group named WellSpring, an organization that works with homeless individuals. She volunteers as the preschool therapist and she works with children aged 3 to 7. She is additionally a volunteer for horse therapy at Agape, which helps build social emotional skills for children with behavioral issues.

JONES, CHARLES E., T: Chief Executive Officer I: Oil & Energy CN: FirstEnergy Corporation ED: BS, The University of Akron; Student, Reactor Technology Program, Massachusetts Institute of Technology C: Chief Executive Officer, President, Director, FirstEnergy Corporation (2015-Present); Executive Vice President, FirstEnergy Corporation (2014-2015); President of Utilities, FirstEnergy Corporation (2010-2013)

JONES, CHRISTOPHER ARLEN, EDD, T: Educator (Retired) I: Education/Educational Services DOB: 03/25/1943 PB: Detroit SC: MI/USA PT: Uyval Clinton Jones; Harriet Grace (Hostetter) Jones MS: Married SPN: Lynn Susan Klear (05/12/1967) CH: Sean C.; Stephanie L. ED: EdD, Boston University (1978); MS in Education, University of Pennsylvania (1969); BS, University of Michigan (1965) CT: Certified Teacher of Chemistry, Biology, Physics and German; Administration Certificate C: Assistant Professor, Bridgewater State University (2007-2015); Coach, Men's and Women's Swimming, Newton Schools (1976-2001); Teacher, Science, Newton Schools (1969-2001); Teacher, Science, Philadelphia Schools (1967-1969); Teacher, Science, United States Peace Corps, Amoud, Somalia (1965-1967) CR: Adjunct Professor, Brandeis University, Waltham, MA (1992-2015); Adjunct Professor, Boston College, Chestnuthill, MA (1981-1984) CIV: Boy Scout Master, Committee Troop 3, Westwood, MA (1990-1991) MEM: Pi Lambda Theta MH: Albert Nelson Marquis Lifetime Achievement Award B/I: Professor Jones graduated from the University of Michigan in 1965 and joined the Peace Corps that same year. He asked what kind of assignment was available and was told he could teach science in East Africa. Professor Jones

trained at Syracuse University and then went to Somalia. Ever since then, he has loved his work as a teacher. AV: Hiking; Canoeing; Skiing; Scuba diving; Researching cartography

JONES, CLARIS EUGENE JR., T: Botanist, Educator I: Education/Educational Services DOB: 12/15/1942 PB: Columbus SC: OH/USA PT: Claris Eugene Jones Senior; Clara Elizabeth (Elliott) Jones MS: Married SPN: Teresa Diane Wagner (06/26/1966) CH: Douglas Eugene; Philip Charles; Elizabeth Lynne Weise ED: PhD, Indiana University (1969); BS, Ohio University (1964) C: Professor Emeritus, School of Natural Science and Mathematics, California State University (1999-2010); Retired, Professor of Botany, California State University (1977-2010); Retired, Director, Faye Macfadden Herbarium, California State University (1969-2010); Chairman, Department of Biological Science, California State University (1989-2004); Director, Fullerton Arboretum, California State University (1970-1980); Associate Professor, California State University (1973-1977); Assistant Professor of Botany, California State University (1969-1973) CR: Founding Director, Designed Planting, Fullerton Arboretum CIV: Board of Director, Maui Kaanapali Villas (2001-Present) CW: Editor, "Handbook of Experimental Pollination Biology" (1983); Author, "A Dictionary of Botany" (1980); Contributor, Articles, Professional Journals AW: Distinguished Faculty Member, School of Natural Science and Mathematics, California State University, Fullerton, CA MEM: American Institute of Biological Science; American Association for the Advancement of Science; Botanical Society of America; International Association of Plant Taxonomy; American Society of Plant Taxonomists; Society of Study Evolution; Systematics Association; Ecological Society of America; California Botanical Society; Sigma Xi MH: Albert Nelson Marquis Lifetime Achievement Award; Marquis Who's Who Top Professional B/I: When Dr. Jones was in college, he majored in government and biology. Though he initially thought he wanted to be a lawyer, he changed his mind when he got further involved in the sciences. After taking a class on botany, he found he enjoyed it so much that he decided to pursue a career in the field. In later years, Dr. Jones earned a PhD in the field. RE: Methodist THT: He played football at Ohio University an won the Mid American conference championship in 1963 and he received his letter as a member of the University Football team.

JONES, DONALD KELLY, T: Head (Retired), Investment Promotion CN: Hong Kong Government DOB: 08/09/1944 PB: Fresno SC: CA/USA PT: Chester Jones; Helen Edith (Summers) Jones MS: Widowed SPN: Carolyn Wray Dolly (03/23/1979) ED: Master's in International Affairs, School of Advanced International Studies, Johns Hopkins University (1968); BA in History, Stanford University (1966) C: Deputy Commissioner, Senior Vice President, Chief Administrative Officer, Board of Directors, Empire State Development Corporation, New York, NY (1995); Senior Manager, Business Development, Nissho Iwai American Corporation, New York, NY (1986-1995); Director, International Trade, American Paper Institute, New York, NY (1984-1986); Senior Economist, General Motors Company, New York, NY (1975-1984); Assistant Professor, Davidson College (1973-1975); Head, Hong Kong Economic and Trade Office, New York CR: Member, U.S. Business and Industry Advisory Committee, Organisation for EconomicCo-operation and Development (OECD); President, Taxpayers Alliance of New York; Member, CATO Institute CIV: New York-Israel Economic Development Partnership (1999); Appointed Member, New York District Export Council (1996); Member,

Westchester County Budget Advisory Committee, White Plains, NY (1995); President, Taxpayers Alliance of New York, Hartsdale, NY (1994); Republican Party Candidate, New York State Assembly (1992) **CW:** Author, "Structure of American Government" (1975) **AW:** Outstanding Service Award, Cleveland World Trade Association (1993); Recognition of Service Award International Business Council, United Nations (1984) **MEM:** American Enterprise Institute; The Heritage Foundation; Cato Institute; Johns Hopkins University Alumni Association; Eastside Conservative Club (Eastside Republican Club) **MH:** Albert Nelson Marquis Lifetime Achievement Award **B/I:** Mr. Jones became involved in his profession because he is a specialist in the assessment and mitigation of political risks that investors face in overseas environments, with a particular interest in the Asian-Pacific region. **AV:** Classical music; Politics; Traveling **PA:** Republican

JONES, FRANKLIN, T: Chief Executive Officer/President/Owner **I:** Business Management/Business Services **CN:** First Consulting Group, LLC **DOB:** 12/30/1952 **MS:** Married **SPN:** Jacqueline Jones **CH:** Nicole; Nicole; Monique; Charise **ED:** MA, Embry Riddle Aeronautical University (1982); BASc, University of New Hampshire-Manchester (1982); BS, Embry Riddle Aeronautical University (1979) **CT:** Air Traffic Controller **C:** Owner, First Consulting Group, LLC (2000-Present); Regional Technical Manager, Dish Network (2000-2003); Regional Operations Manager (2000-2003) **CIV:** Minister, Freedom Christian Ministry **MIL:** U.S. Air Force **AW:** Five-Time Recipient, Meritorious Service Medals, U.S. Air Force; Two-Time Recipient, U.S. Air Force; Vietnam Service Medal, U.S. Air Force; Vietnam Cross of Gallantry, U.S. Air Force; Five-Time Recipient, Air Medal, U.S. Air Force; Space Com Senior Badge, U.S. Air Force; Air Traffic Control Badge, U.S. Air Force; Communications-Electronics Badge, U.S. Air Force; First Sergeant Diamond, U.S. Air Force **AS:** Mr. Jones attributes his success to his uncle and his cousin with whom he grew up; they were inspirational figures. He was raised in a difficult neighborhood but made it out, proceeding to join the military. **THT:** Mr. Jones' motto is, "Don't sweat the small stuff."

JONES, GORDON, "DOUG" DOUGLAS, T: U.S. Senator, Lawyer **I:** Government Administration/Government Relations/Government Services **DOB:** 05/04/1954 **PB:** Fairfield **SC:** AL/USA **PT:** Gordon Jones; Gloria Jones **MS:** Married **SPN:** Louise New Jones (12/12/1992) **CH:** Three children **ED:** JD, Cumberland School of Law, Samford University; BA, The University of Alabama **C:** U.S. Senator, State of Alabama (2018-Present); Member, Committee on Banking, Housing, and Urban Affairs (2018-Present); Member, Committee on Health, Education, Labor and Pensions (2018-Present); Member, Committee on Homeland Security and Governmental Affairs (2018-Present); Member, Special Committee on Aging (2018-Present); Founder, Jones & Hawley (2013-Present); General Special Master, Environmental Clean-up Case (2004); Lawyer, Private Practice (2001-2013); Attorney, Northern District of Alabama (1997-2001) **CR:** Advisory Board Member, Blackburn Institute, The University of Alabama **CIV:** Member, Canterbury United Methodist Church, Mountain Brook, AL **MEM:** Beta Theta Pi **PA:** Democrat **RE:** Methodist

JONES, HANNAH, T: Apparel Executive **I:** Apparel & Fashion **CN:** Nike Valiant Labs **ED:** Diploma, European Baccalaureate, European School of Brussels 1 (1996); BA in Art, Philosophy and French, University of Sussex (1990) **C:** Founder, President, Nike Valiant Labs, Nike, Portland, OR (2018-Present); Chief Sustainability Officer, Vice President of the Innovation Accelerator, Nike, Beaverton, OR (2014-2018); Vice President of Sustainable Business & Innovation, Nike, Beaverton, OR (2012-2014); Vice President of Corporate Responsibility & Labor Compliance, Nike, Beaverton, OR (2004-2012); Director of Corporate Responsibility, Europe, Middle East and Africa, Nike, Brussels, Belgium (1998-2004); Senior Consultant, FleishmanHillard for Microsoft, Paris, France, Dublin, Ireland, United Kingdom and Redmond, WA (1992-1995); European Manager, CSV Media, London, England, United Kingdom, and Brussels, Belgium (1992-1995); Reporter, BBC Radio One, BBC Radio Five & BBC World Service, London, England, United Kingdom (1990-1992) **CIV:** Founder, League of Badass Women (2015-Present); Co-founder, Co-chair, We Mean Business (2014-2017); Board Member, Purpose Climate Lab (Formerly Here Now) (2014-2017); Board Member, People Against Dirty (Method Soap and eCover) (2014-2017); Business Advisory Council, High Commissioner of the UNHCR (High Commission for Refugees) (2004-2009) **CW:** Co-author, "Nike Inc.'s Corporate Responsibility Report"; Co-author, "Sustainability Business Performance Report" **AW:** Top 500 Award in the Business of Fashion, Business of Fashion (2017); C.K. Prahalad Award for Global Business Sustainability Leadership, CEF (2013); Fast Company #8 Most Creative People Award (2010); Named Young Global Leader, World Economic Forum (2007)

JONES, JAMES EARL, T: Actor **I:** Media & Entertainment **DOB:** 01/17/1931 **PB:** Arkabutla **SC:** MS/USA **PT:** Robert Earl Jones; Ruth (Williams) Jones **MS:** Widowed **SPN:** Cecilia Hart (03/15/1982, Deceased 10/16/2016); Julienne Marie (1968, Divorced 1972) **CH:** Flynn Earl **ED:** Honorary ArtsD, Harvard University (2017); Honorary ArtsD, New York University (1994); Honorary LHD, Columbia College (1982); Honorary DFA, Yale University (1982); Honorary DFA, Princeton University (1980); Honorary LHD, University of Michigan (1970); Honorary Doctorate, Black American Cultural Festival (1969); Diploma, American Theatre Wing (1957); BA, University of Michigan (1955); Studied with Lee Strasburg, Tad Danielewski **MIL:** First Lieutenant, United States Army **CW:** Voice Actor, "The Lion King" (2019); Voice Actor, "Star Wars: The Rise of Skywalker" (2019); Actor, "Warning Shot" (2017); Actor, "Rogue One: A Star Wars Story" (2016); Actor, "The Angriest Man in Brooklyn" (2014); Actor, "Driving Miss Daisy" (2014); Actor, "Gimme Shelter" (2013); Actor, "Star Tours: The Adventures Continue" (2011); Actor, "Jack and the Beanstalk" (2010); Actor, "Quantum Quest: A Cassini Space Odyssey" (2009); Actor, "Welcome Home Roscoe Jenkins" (2008); Voice Actor, "Click" (2006); Actor, "Scary Movie 4" (2006); Actor, "Robots" (2005); Actor, "The Sandlot 2" (2005); Actor, "The Benchwarmers" (2005); Actor, "Finders Fee" (2001); Actor, "Our Friend Martin" (1999); Actor, "On the QT" (1999); Actor, "Undercover Angel" (1999); Actor, "The Annihilation of Fish" (1999); Voice Actor, "Fantasia 2000" (1999); Actor, "Primary Colors" (1998); Voice Actor, "The Lion King II" (1998); Actor, "Casper: A Spirited Beginning" (1997); Actor, "Gang Related" (1997); Actor, "A Family Thing" (1996); Actor, "Good Luck" (1996); Actor, "Jefferson in Paris" (1995); Actor, "Judge Dredd" (1995); Actor, "Naked Gun 33 1/3: The Final Insult" (1994); Actor, "Clean Slate" (1994); Voice Actor, "The Lion King" (1994); Actor, "Clear and Present Danger" (1994); Actor, "Dream Rider" (1993); Actor, "Sommersby" (1993); Actor, "The Sandlot" (1993); Actor, "The Excessive Force" (1993); Actor, "The Meteor Man" (1993); Actor, "Patriot Games" (1992); Actor, "Freddie as FRO7" (1992); Actor, "Sneakers" (1992); Actor, "Scorchers" (1991); Actor, "Convicts" (1990); Actor, "The Ambulance" (1990); Actor, "Grim Prairie Tales" (1990); Actor, "Three Fugitives" (1989); Actor, "Field of Dreams" (1989); Actor, "Best of the Best" (1989); Actor, "Coming to America" (1988); Actor, "Gardens of Stone" (1987); Actor, "My Little Girl" (1987); Actor, "Pinocchio and the Emperor of the Night" (1987); Actor, "Matewan" (1987); Actor, "Soul Man" (1986); Actor, "City Limits" (1985); Actor, "Return of the Jedi" (1983); Actor, "The Flights of Dragons" (1982); Actor, "Blood Tide" (1982); Actor, "Bushido Blade" (1981); Actor, "The Empire Strikes Back" (1980); Actor, "The Greatest" (1977); Actor, "Star Wars" (1977); Actor, "Exorcist II: The Heretic" (1977); Actor, "The Last Remake of Beau Geste" (1977); Actor, "The River Niger" (1976); Actor, "The Bingo Long Traveling All-Stars & Motor Kings" (1976); Actor, "Swashbuckler" (1976); Actor, "Deadly Hero" (1976); Actor, "Claudine" (1974); Actor, "Malcolm X" (1972); Actor, "The Man" (1972); Actor, "The End of the Road" (1970); Actor, "The Great White Hope" (1970); Actor, "King: A Filmed Record" (1970); Actor, "The Comedians" (1967); Actor, "The Comedians in Africa" (1967); Actor, "Dr.Strangelove" (1964); Spokesperson, Verizon (Formerly Bell Atlantic); Actor, Voice Actor, Numerous Films, Television Shows and Theatre Plays **AW:** Named Disney Legend (2019); Voice Icon Award, Society of Voice Arts and Sciences, Museum of Moving Image (2014); Marian Anderson Award (2012); Monte Cristo Award, Eugene O'Neill Theater Center (2011); Honorary Academy Award, Academy of Motion Picture Arts & Sciences (2011); Lifetime Achievement Award, SAG-AFTRA (2009); Special Award for Contributions to Theater, Drama Desk Awards (2008); Emmy Award for Outstanding Performance in a Children's Special, "Summer's End," Academy of Television Arts & Sciences (2000); John Houseman Award, The Acting Company (1995); Named Distinguished Artist, LA Music Center Club (1994); UCLA Medal (1993); National Medal of Arts for Outstanding Contribution to Cultural Life of Country (1992); Hall of Fame Image Award for Great Contribution to the Arts, NAACP (1992); National Medal of Arts (1992); Common Wealth Award for Distinguished Service in the Dramatic Arts, Bank of Delaware (1991); Emmy Award for Best Actor, Academy of Television Arts & Sciences (1991); Emmy Award for Best Supporting Actor, Academy of Television Arts & Sciences (1991); Jean Renoir Award, LA Film Teachers Association (1990); Emmy Award for Performance in Children's Programming, "Soldier Boys," CBS Schoolbreak Special, Academy of Television Arts & Sciences (1987-1988); First Recipient of Annie Glenn Award, National Association for Hearing and Speech Action (1987); Inductee, American Theater Hall of Fame (1985); Office of Black Ministries Toussaint Medallion (1982); Medal for Spoken Language, American Academy of Arts and Letters (1981); Grammy Award for Best Spoken Word, The Recording Academy (1977); Theatre World Award (1962); The Village Voice Off-Broadway Award (1962); Numerous Awards **MEM:** Presidential Appointee, National Council on the Arts (1970-1976); Presidential Appointment to Advisory Board, National Council on the Arts (1962); Board of Directors, Theatre Communications Group (1962); Fellow, American Academy of Arts & Sciences; National Council on the Arts; Actors' Equity Association; SAG-AFTRA; Theatre Communications Group

JONES, JERRAL, "JERRY" WAYNE, T: Professional Sports Team Owner **I:** Athletics **CN:** Dallas Cowboys **DOB:** 10/13/1942 **PB:** Los Angeles **SC:** CA/USA **PT:** J.W. "Pat" Jones; Arminta Pearl (Clark) Jones **MS:** Married **SPN:** Eugenia "Gene"

Jones **CH:** Stephen; Charlotte; Jerry Jr. **ED:** MBA, University of Arkansas (1970); Bachelor's Degree, University of Arkansas (1965); Diploma, North Little Rock High School (1960) **C:** Owner, President, General Manager, Dallas Cowboys (1989-Present); Executive Vice President, Modern Security Life, Springfield, MO (1965-1969); Founder, Jones Oil and Land Lease, Oklahoma **CR:** Business Ventures Committee, Special Committee on League Economics, Broadcast Committee, Management Council Executive Committee, Los Angeles Stadium Working Group, National Football League (NFL) **CIV:** National Advisory Board, Salvation Army (1998-Present); Co-Founder, Gene And Jerry Jones Family Center For Children (1998); Co-Founder, Gene And Jerry Jones Family Charities; The Rise School Of Dallas; The Family Place; Kent Waldrep Paralysis Foundation; Happy Hill Farm Academy/Home; Children's Medical Center Of Dallas; National Board, Boys And Girls Club Of America **CW:** Guest Appearance, "Entourage" (2010) **AW:** Named, Forbes 400: Richest Americans (2006-Present); Elected, Pro Football Hall Of Fame (2018); Named, 50 Most Influential People In Sports Business, Street & Smith's SportsBusiness Journal (2007-2009); Named, Most Influential People In The World Of Sports, Business Week (2007-2008); Hope Award, National Multiple Sclerosis Society (2005); Annette G. Strauss Humanitarian Award, Family Gateway Organization (2003); Children's Champion Award For Philanthropy, Dallas For Children Organization (2002); Chairman's Award, Boys And Girls Club Of America (2001); Evangeline Booth Award, Salvation Army (1999); Partner of the Year (1999) **MEM:** Salvation Army; William Booth Society **AV:** Hunting; Fishing; Playing tennis; Water-skiing; Skiing

JONES, JERRY FRANK, T: Attorney **I:** Law and Legal Services **CN:** Flaherty Jones Thompson PLLC **PB:** Hico **SC:** TX/USA **MS:** Married **SPN:** Madalyn **CH:** Three children **ED:** JD, The University of Texas at Austin (1971); BA, Williams College (1967); Mediation Training Coursework, Center for Public Policy Dispute Resolution, University of Texas **CT:** Board Certified in Estate Planning and Probate, State Bar of Texas; Bicycle Assembly and Maintenance, Barnett's Bicycle Institute **C:** Of Counsel, Brink Bennett Flaherty Golden (2017-Present); Of Counsel, Ikerd & Golden (1997-2017) **CR:** Supreme Court, Probate Forms Task Force, State Bar of Texas (2016); Pattern Jury Charges, Probate Subcommittee Chair, Family and Probate Law Volume (2009-2012); Family & Probate Co-Vice Chair, State Bar of Texas (2009-2012); Probate Code Committee, Section on Real Estate, Probate and Trust, State Bar of Texas (1989); Legislative Liaison, Real Estate, Probate and Trust Law Section, State Bar of Texas (1997-2003); Vice-Chairman, Committee on Planning and Administering Small Estates, American Bar Association (1988-1995); Co-Chair, Committee on Administration and Distribution of Estates and Trusts, American Bar Association (1996-1998); Chairman, Committee on Planning and Administering Small Estates and Trust of the Real Estate, Probate and Trust Law Section, American Bar Association (1995-1996); Real Estate, Probate, and Trust Law Section, State Bar of Texas; Bastrop County Bar Association; State Laws Committee, Fiduciary Litigation Committee, American College of Trust and Estate Counsel **CIV:** Planning Committee, Advanced Estate Planning and Probate Course (1990-2010); Board of Directors, Austin Alzheimer's Association; Combined Community Action Agency; City of Elgin Historical Review Board; Bastrop County Food Pantry **CW:** Conflicts of Laws, Article for Advanced Probate Texas (2015); Author, Numerous Articles, Professional Journals **AW:** The Best Lawyers in America (2006-

2018); Super Lawyer, Texas Monthly (2003-2017); Lawyer of the Year, Litigation-Trusts and Estates Austin, Best Lawyers (2015) **MEM:** The American College of Trust and Estate Counsel; American Bar Association; State Bar of Texas; Texas Academy of Probate Lawyers; Travis County Bar Association; Bastrop County Bar Association **BAR:** All Courts, State of Texas; United States District Court for the Western District of Texas; United States District Court for the Eastern District of Texas; United States Court of Appeals for the Fifth Circuit; United States Tax Court **AS:** Mr. Jones attributes his success to his parents, his brothers, his wife and his colleagues. He feels that he has been lucky in life. **B/I:** Mr. Jones became involved in his profession because he always wanted to be a lawyer. He chose the section of trust and estates because it is the crossroads of one generation to the next and a window to how people treat each other when they are sharing a family fortune. The field has math, logic, and psychology, which appeals to Mr. Jones. **AV:** Bicycling

JONES, K. C., T: Former Professional Basketball Coach; Former Professional Basketball Player **I:** Athletics **DOB:** 05/25/1932 **PB:** Taylor **SC:** TX/USA **ED:** Coursework, University of San Francisco **C:** Head Coach, New England Blizzard, ABL, Hartford, CT (1997-1998); Assistant Coach, Boston Celtics, National Basketball Association (NBA) (1977-1983, 1996-1997); Head Coach, Seattle SuperSonics, National Basketball Association (NBA) (1990-1992); Assistant Coach, Consultant Player Personnel Director, Seattle SuperSonics, National Basketball Association (NBA) (1989-1990); Vice President of Basketball Operations, Boston Celtics, National Basketball Association (NBA) (1988-1989); Coach, Boston Celtics, National Basketball Association (NBA) (1983-1988); Coach, Capital Bullets (Now Washington Wizards) (1973-1976); Coach, San Diego Conquistadores, ABL (1972-1973); Assistant Coach, Los Angeles Lakers, National Basketball Association (NBA) (1971-1972); Assistant Coach, Harvard University (1970-1971); Coach, Brandeis University, Waltham, MA (1967-1971); Point Guard, Boston Celtics, National Basketball Association (NBA) (1958-1967) **MIL:** United States Army (1956-1958) **AW:** Inductee, San Francisco Bay Area Sports Hall of Fame (1989); Inductee, Naismith Memorial Basketball Hall of Fame (1989); Winner (as Coach), NBA Championships (1984, 1986); NBA All-Star Game Head Coach (1975, 1984-1987); Winner, Boston Celtics, NBA Championship (1959-1966); NCAA Champion (1955, 1956); Gold Medal, USA Men's Basketball Team, Olympics (1956)

JONES, KENT, T: Director **I:** Media & Entertainment **CN:** New York Film Festival **C:** Director **CW:** Director, Writer, "Diane" (2018); Appearance, "Aware, Anywhere" (2017); Guest Appearance, "Cinéma, de notre temps" (2017); Appearance, "The Space in Between" (2017); Appearance, "Johnny Guitar: A Feminist Western?" (2016); Appearance, "Johnny Guitar: A Film Like No Other" (2016); Appearance, "Richard Linklater: Dream is Destiny" (2016); Director, Writer, "Hitchcock/Truffaut" (2015); Appearance, "Mr. X, a Vision of Leos Carax" (2014); Co-Writer, "Jimmy P." (2013); Appearance, "Martin Scorsese and Kent Jones on 'On the Waterfront'" (2013); Director, Writer, "A Letter to Elia" (2010); Moderator, "Redbelt: Q&A with David Mamet" (2008); Director, Writer, "Val Lewton: The Man in the Shadows" (2007); Guest Representative, "American Masters" (2005); Appearance, "French Beauty" (2005); Director, Writer, "Lady by the Sea: The Statue of Liberty" (2004); Creative Consultant, "The Blues" (2003); Writer, "My Voyage to Italy" (1999) **AW:** Named,

10 Directors to Watch, Variety (2019); Best Narrative Feature and Screenplay, Tribeca Film Festival (2018)

JONES, KIMBERLY, "LIL' KIM" DENISE, T: Rap Artist **I:** Media & Entertainment **DOB:** 07/11/1975 **PB:** Brooklyn **SC:** NY/USA **PT:** Linwood Jones; Ruby Mae Jones-Mitchell **CH:** Royal Reign **ED:** Diploma, Brooklyn College Academy **CW:** Appearance, "Girls Cruise" (2019); Appearance, "The Next Big Thing" (2019); Appearance, "Can't Stop Won't Stop: A Bad Boy Story" (2017); Performer, "Dancing with the Stars" (2009); Actress, "Superhero Movie" (2008); Appearance, "Life After Death: The Movie- Ten Years Later" (2007); Rap Artist, "The Naked Truth" (2005); Rap Artist, "The Meaning of Family" (2005); Voice Actress, "Lil' Pimp" (2005); Appearance, "There's a God on the Mic" (2005); Appearance, "Nora's Hair Salon" (2004); Appearance, "You Got Served" (2004); Actress, "Gang of Roses" (2003); Appearance, "American Dreams" (2003); Rap Artist, "La Bella Mafia" (2003); Actress, "Juwanna Mann" (2002); Composer, "Dr. Dolittle 2" (2001); Appearance, "Zoolander" (2001); Actress, "Moulin Rouge!" (2001); Appearance, "DAG" (2001); Appearance, "Moesha" (2001); Appearance, "Longshot" (2000); Rap Artist, "Notorious K.I.M." (2000); Appearance, "V.I.P." (1999); Actress, "She's All That" (1999); Actress, "Money Talks" (1997); Composer, "Booty Call" (1997); Composer, "Nothing to Lose" (1997); Composer, "High School High" (1996); Rap Artist, "Hard Core" (1996); Appearances, Television Shows, Films **AW:** "I Am Hip-Hop" Award, BET Hip-Hop Awards (2019); Power of Influence Award, City of New York (2018); New York City 12th Council District Arts and Music Award (2018); Hip-Hop Honoree, VH-1 (2016); Icon Award, WEEN Awards (2016); Named One of the 31 Female Rappers Who Changed Hip-Hop, Billboard Magazine (2014); Grammy Award for Best Collaboration with Vocals, The Recording Academy (2002); Numerous Awards

JONES, MILDRED PAULINE, T: Apparel Executive, Consultant **I:** Other **DOB:** 04/12/1936 **PB:** Kilgore **SC:** TX/USA **PT:** Paul Burleson Jones; Irma Nola (DeRamus) Doggett **MS:** Widowed **SPN:** Eugene Shirley Lacy (12/28/54) **CH:** Sheri Lynn (Deceased); Ivy Lance **ED:** Coursework, Hume Publishing (1985); Coursework, Commodore Discs (1984); Coursework, Hume Financial Education Service (1982-1983); Coursework, Harvard University (1961-1962) **C:** Executive Vice President, The Toggery (1971-Present); Style Show Producer, Director, Texas Liquor Convention (1980); Style Show Producer, Director, Civic Garden Club (1975); Co-Owner, The Toggery (1968); Co-Owner, The Toggery Shoe Salon (1963-1968); Executive Secretary to Personnel Manager, Notary Public, Home Savings (1959-1960); Bookkeeper, Randall & Hebbard General Insurance Agents (1955-1958); Legal Secretary, Neal & Girand, Hobbs, NM (1953-1954) **CR:** Fashion Marketing Teacher, Kilgore College **CIV:** Leader, Girl Scouts and Cub Scouts (1962-1969); Active, Various Benefit Style Shows, City Council Parent Teacher Association (1965-1967); Parent Teacher Association, Methodist Church (1963); Volunteer, Kilgore Restoration Association **CW:** Designed, Kilgore City Flag **AW:** Pauline's Pet, Stewart Weitzman (1986); City Merit Award (1982); Gold Belt, Alexis Kirk (1981); Promotion and Public Relations Award, Helene Sidel (1979); Yearbook Award, Parent Teacher Association of Texas (1966); National Republican Freedom Award **MEM:** Kilgore Area Chamber of Commerce, Texas Chamber of Commerce; Community Concert Association; National Association of Female Executives; Texas Retailers Association; Beta Sigma Phi **MH:** Albert Nelson Marquis Lifetime Achievement

Award **B/I:** Ms. Jones became involved in her profession because she wanted to go into business with her husband. **AV:** Reading; Gardening; Swimming **PA:** Republican **RE:** Methodist

JONES, RADHIKA, T: Editor-in-Chief **I:** Publishing **CN:** Vanity Fair **PB:** New York **SC:** NY/USA **PT:** Robert L. Jones; Marguerite Jones **MS:** Married **CH:** One Son **ED:** PhD in English and Comparative Literature, Columbia University, New York, NY; BA, Harvard University **C:** Editor-in-Chief, Vanity Fair (2017-Present); Executive Editor, Time Magazine (2011-2017); Assistant Managing Editor, Time Magazine (2009-2011); Arts Editor, Time Magazine (2008-2009); Managing Editor, Paris Review; Various Editorial Positions, Artforum; Various Editorial Positions, Grand St. Magazine; Various Editorial Positions, Moscow Times

JONES, TODD, T: Chief Executive Officer **I:** Food & Restaurant Services **CN:** Publix Super Markets Inc. **C:** Chief Executive Officer, Publix Super Markets Inc. (2016-Present); President, Publix Super Markets, Inc. (2007-Present); Senior Vice President, Product Business Development, Publix Super Markets, Inc., Lakeland, FL (2005-2007); Vice President, Jacksonville Division, Publix Super Markets, Inc. (2003-2005); Regional Director, Publix Super Markets, Inc. (1999-2003); District Manager, Publix Super Markets, Inc. (1997-1999); Store Manager, Publix Super Markets, Inc., Jacksonville, FL (1988-1997); Front Service Clerk to Various Store Level Positions, Publix Super Markets, Inc., New Smyrna Beach, FL (1980-1988)

JONES, TOMMY LEE, T: Actor **I:** Media & Entertainment **DOB:** 09/15/1946 **PB:** San Saba **SC:** TX/USA **PT:** Clyde L. Jones; Lucille Marie (Scott) Jones **MS:** Married **SPN:** Dawn Laurel (03/19/2001); Kimberlea Gayle Cloughley (05/30/1981, Divorced 03/1996); Kate Lardner (12/31/1971, Divorced 02/1978) **CH:** Austin Leonard; Victoria **ED:** Bachelor of Arts in English, Harvard University, Cum Laude (1969) **CW:** Actor, "Ad Astra" (2019); Actor, "Shock and Awe" (2017); Actor, "Just Getting Started" (2017); Actor, "Criminal" (2016); Actor, "Jason Bourne" (2016); Actor, "Mechanic: Resurrection" (2016); Actor, Director, Executive Producer, Writer "The Homesman" (2014); Actor, "The Family" (2013); Actor, "Men in Black III" (2012); Actor, "Hope Springs" (2012); Actor, "Lincoln" (2012); Actor, "Captain America: The First Avenger" (2011); Actor, Director, Executive Producer, "The Sunset Limited" (2011); Actor, "The Sunset Limited" (2011); Actor, "The Company Men" (2010); Actor, "In the Electric Mist" (2009); Actor, "In the Valley of Elah" (2007); Actor, "No Country for Old Men" (2007); Actor, "A Prairie Home Companion" (2006); Actor, "Man of the House" (2005); Actor, Director, Producer, "The Three Burials of Melquiades Estrada" (2005); Actor, "The Hunted" (2003); Actor, "The Missing" (2003); Actor, "Men in Black II" (2002); Actor, "Rules of Engagement" (2000); Actor, "Space Cowboys" (2000); Actor, "Double Jeopardy" (1999); Voice Actor, "Small Soldiers" (1998); Actor, "Men in Black" (1997); Actor, "Volcano" (1997); Actor, "U.S. Marshals" (1997); Actor, "Batman Forever" (1995); Actor, Director, Writer, "The Good Old Boys" (1995); Actor, "The Good Old Boys" (1995); Actor, "Blown Away" (1994); Actor, "The Client" (1994); Actor, "Natural Born Killers" (1994); Actor, "Blue Sky" (1994); Actor, "Cobb" (1994); Actor, "House of Cards" (1993); Actor, "Heaven and Earth" (1993); Actor, "The Fugitive" (1993); Actor, "Under Siege" (1992); Actor, "JFK" (1991); Actor, "Fire Birds" (1990); Actor, "Lonesome Dove" (1989); Actor, "The Package" (1989); Actor, "Stormy Monday" (1988); Actor, "Stranger on My Land" (1988); Actor, "April Morn-

ing" (1988); Actor, "Gotham" (1988); Actor, "The Big Town" (1987); Actor, "Broken Vows" (1987); Actor, "Yuri Nosenko, KGB" (1986); Actor, "Black Moon Rising" (1986); Actor, "The Park is Mine" (1985); Actor, "The River Rat" (1984); Actor, "Nate and Hayes" (1983); Actor, "The Rainmaker" (1982); Actor, "The Executioner's Song" (1982); Actor, "True West" (1981); Actor, "Back Roads" (1981); Actor, "Coal Mine's Daughter" (1980); Actor, "Eyes of Laura Mars" (1978); Actor, "The Betsy" (1978); Actor, "Rolling Thunder" (1977); Actor, "The Amazing Howard Hughes" (1977); Actor, "Smash-Up on Interstate 5" (1976); Actor, "Charlie's Angels" (1976); Actor, "Jackson County Jail" (1976); Actor, "Ulysses in Nighttown" (1974); Actor, "Blue Boys" (1972); Actor, "Eliza's Horoscope" (1972); Actor, "Life Study" (1972); Actor, "Four on a Garden" (1971); Actor, "Love Story" (1970); Actor, "A Patriot for Me" (1969); Actor, "Fortune and Men's Eyes" (1969) **AW:** SAG Award for Outstanding Performance by a Male Actor in a Supporting Role, Screen Actors Guild - American Federation of Television and Radio Artists (2013); SAG Award for Outstanding Performance by a Cast in a Motion Picture, Screen Actors Guild - American Federation of Television and Radio Artists (2008); Inductee, Texas Cowboy Hall of Fame (2009); Named, One of the Top 25 Entertainers of the Year, Entertainment Weekly (2007); Award for Best Acting by an Ensemble, National Board of Review (2007); Academy Award for Best Actor in a Supporting Role, Academy of Motion Picture Arts & Sciences (1994); Golden Globe Award for Best Performance by an Actor in a Supporting Role in a Motion Picture, Hollywood Foreign Press Association (1994); Star, Hollywood Walk of Fame (1994); Emmy Award for Outstanding Lead Actor in a Limited Series or Special, Academy of Television Arts & Sciences (1983); Numerous Awards

JORDAN, BOB, T: Partner **I:** Law and Legal Services **CN:** Jordan Law Firm PLLC **DOB:** 07/13/1950 **PB:** Lake City **SC:** FL/USA **PT:** James M. Jordan; Betty M. (Markham) Jordan **MS:** Married **SPN:** Linnie **CH:** Michael; Steven; Kathy; Jonathan; Christopher **ED:** MBA, Florida State University (1976); JD, Florida State University (1976); MS in Math and Computer Science, Purdue University (1972); BS in Math and Physics, University of Florida (1971) **C:** Partner, Grevior Jordan & Brannon (Now Jordan Law Firm PLLC), Lake City, FL (1994-Present); Partner, Grevior & Jordan, Fort Lauderdale, FL (1987-Present); Private practice, Fort Lauderdale, FL (1985-1987); Partner, Conrad, Scherer & James, Fort Lauderdale, FL (1976-1985) **CR:** Adjunct Professor, Nova Southeastern University Law School (1989-Present) **CIV:** Chairman, Columbia County Zoning Board; Florida Gateway College Real Estate Board; Board Member, YMCA; Board Member, Big Brother's; Pro Bono, Columbia County Humane Society **MEM:** American Bar Association (ABA); Association of Trial Lawyers of America (Now American Association for Justice); Academy of Florida Trial Lawyers (Now Florida Justice Association); Broward County Trial Lawyers Association; Defense Research Institute **BAR:** Supreme Court of the United States (1983); United States Court of Appeals for the Eleventh Circuit (1981); United States District Court for the Middle District of Florida (1977); Florida (1976); United States District Court for the Southern District of Florida (1976); United States Court of Appeals for the Fifth Circuit (1976) **MH:** Albert Nelson Marquis Lifetime Achievement Award **B/I:** Mr. Jordan had never thought to become a lawyer. He was influenced by a friend who was pursuing a career in law, and decided to give the law school entrance exam a chance. He did well on the exam and decided to continue the path to law school, just

to "try something different..." The more time he spent in law school, the more he began to love the field. Mr. Jordan began his career as a bankruptcy partner for a law firm. Over a couple of years, the law firm shrunk in size to about half of what it was when Mr. Jordan began. As the economy improved, bankruptcy work began to lessen and he began to be assigned personal injury work. Three or four years later, a lawyer who was the "premier medical malpractice defense lawyers" joined the firm. Mr. Jordan describes himself as "his gopher for a couple of years..." When he left the firm in 1985, everyone assumed that he would become a medical malpractice lawyer, and so people began sending him more and more cases in that area. It was not planned. Mr. Jordan says, "philosophically", he enjoys representing the injured people and their families better. He feels that it fit his personality better. **PA:** Democrat

JORDAN, JAMES, "JIM" DANIEL, T: U.S. Representative from Ohio **I:** Government Administration/Government Relations/Government Services **CN:** U.S. House of Representatives **DOB:** 02/17/1964 **PB:** Urbana **SC:** OH/USA **MS:** Married **SPN:** Polly Jordan **CH:** Rachel; Benjamin; Jessie; Isaac **ED:** Doctor of Jurisprudence, Capital University Law School, Columbus, OH (2001); Master of Arts in Education, Ohio State University, Columbus, OH (1991); Bachelor of Science in Economics, University of Wisconsin-Madison (1986) **C:** Member, U.S. House Select Committee on the Events Surrounding the 2012 Terrorist Attack in Benghazi (2014-Present); Member, U.S. House of Representatives from Ohio's Fourth District, United States Congress (2007-Present); Chairperson, Republican Study Committee (2011-2013); Member, District 12, Ohio State Senate (2001-2007); Member, District 85, Ohio House of Representatives, Columbus, Ohio (1995-2000); Assistant Wrestling Coach, Ohio State University Buckeyes, Columbus, Ohio; Member, Committee on the Judiciary; Member, Committee on Oversight and Government Reform **AW:** Named, National Legislator of the Year, Weyrich Award (2012); Leadership in Government Award, Ohio Roundtable/Freedom Forum (2001); Named, Pro-life Legislator of the Year, United Conservatives of Ohio (1998); Big Ten/NCAA Wrestling Champion (1985, 1986); Defender of Life Award, Ohio Right to Life Society **MEM:** Citizens Against Government Waste; Mad River Valley Young Republican Club **PA:** Republican **RE:** Evangelical

JORDAN, MICHAEL BAKARI, T: Actor **I:** Media & Entertainment **DOB:** 02/09/1987 **PB:** Santa Ana **SC:** CA/USA **PT:** Michael Jordan; Donna Jordan **MS:** Single **ED:** Graduate, Newark Arts High School, Newark, NJ **CR:** Former Model, Modell's Sporting Goods, Toys "R" Us **CW:** Producer, Actor, "Without Remorse" (2020); Producer, Actor, "Just Mercy" (2019); Executive Producer, Voice Actor, Web Series, "Gen:Lock" (2019); Executive Producer, Actor, "Raising Dion" (2019); Executive Producer, Actor, TV Film, "Fahrenheit 451" (2018); Actor, "Black Panther" (2018); Cameo, "Kin" (2018); Actor, "Creed II" (2018); Voice Actor, Video Game, "Creed: Rise to Glory" (2018); Appearance, Music Video, "Family Feud" (2017); Voice Actor, Video Game, "Wilson's Heart" (2017); Host, Video Game, "NBA 2K17" (2016); Guest Appearance, "Running Wild with Bear Grylls" (2015); Actor, "Fantastic Four" (2015); Actor, "Creed" (2015); Actor, "That Awkward Moment" (2014); Guest Appearance, "The Boondocks" (2014); Actor, "Fruitvale Station" (2013); Voice Actor, TV Movie, "Justice League: The Flashpoint Paradox" (2013); Actor, "Red Tails" (2012); Actor, "Chronicle" (2012); Guest Appearance, "House" (2012); Voice Actor, Video Game, "Gears of War 3" (2011); Actor, "Parenthood"

(2010-2011); Actor, "Friday Night Lights" (2009-2011); Guest Appearance, "Law & Order: Criminal Intent" (2010); Guest Appearance, "Lie to Me" (2010); Appearance, Music Video, "Did You Wrong" (2009); Guest Appearance, "Burn Notice" (2009); Actor, "Pastor Brown" (2009); Guest Appearance, "Bones" (2009); Actor, "The Assistants" (2009); Guest Appearance, "Cold Case" (2007); Actor, "Blackout" (2007); Guest Appearance, "CSI: Crime Scene Investigation" (2006); Guest Appearance, "Without a Trace" (2006); Actor, "All My Children" (2003-2006); Actor, "The Wire" (2002); Actor, "Hardball" (2001); Guest Appearance, "The Sopranos" (1999); Guest Appearance, "Cosby" (1999); Actor, "Black and White" (1999); Guest Appearance, "What If... ?" **AW:** Cinema Vanguard Award, "Black Panther," Santa Barbara International Film Festival (2019); Best Supporting Actor, "Black Panther," Online Film Critics Society (2019); Outstanding Performance by a Cast in a Motion Picture, "Black Panther," Screen Actors Guild Awards (2019); Best Villain, "Black Panther," MTV Movie & TV Awards (2018); Best Supporting Actor, "Black Panther," San Francisco Film Critics Circle (2018); Villain of the Year, "Black Panther," Seattle Film Critics Society (2018); Choice Villain, "Black Panther," Teen Choice Awards (2018); Breakout Performance, "Creed," African-American Film Critics Association (2015); Best Actor, "Creed," Boston Online Film Critics Association (2015); Outstanding Actor in a Motion Picture, "Creed," NAACP Image Awards (2015); Best Actor, "Creed," Black Reel Awards (2015); Best Actor, "Creed," National Society of Film Critics (2015); Hollywood Spotlight Award, "Fruitvale Station," Hollywood Film Awards (2013); Breakthrough Actor, "Fruitvale Station," Gotham Awards (2013); Breakthrough Actor, "Fruitvale Station," National Board of Review of Motion Pictures (2013); Breakthrough Award Performance, "Fruitvale Station," Satellite Awards (2013); Virtuoso Award, "Fruitvale Station," Santa Barbara International Film Festival (2013)

JORDAN, MICHAEL JEFFREY, T: Professional Sports Team Executive, Retired Professional Basketball Player **I:** Athletics **DOB:** 02/17/1963 **PB:** Brooklyn **SC:** NY/USA **PT:** James Jordan; Deloris Jordan **ED:** Student, University of North Carolina (1981-1984) **C:** Majority Owner, Chairman, Charlotte Hornets (Formerly Charlotte Bobcats) (2014-Present); Majority Owner, Chairman, Charlotte Bobcats (2010-2014); Minority Owner, Managing Member, Basketball Operations, Charlotte Bobcats (2006-2010); Retired Player, NBA (2003); Guard, Washington Wizards (2001-2003); President, Basketball Operations, Washington Wizards (1999-2000); Guard, Chicago Bulls (1995-1998); Minor League Baseball Player, Chicago White Sox AA Team (1994-1995); Guard, Chicago Bulls (1984-1993) **CR:** Founder MJ Basketball Holdings LLC, Jordan Brand Clothing (1997-Present); Owner, Michael Jordan's Restaurant (1993-Present) **CW:** Featured, Documentary Miniseries, "The Last Dance" (2020); Co-Author (with Tinker Hatfield), "Driven From Within" (2005); Actor, Film, "He Got Game" (1998); Actor, Film, "Space Jam" (1996); Author, "RareAir: Michael on Michael" (1993) **AW:** Presidential Medal of Freedom, The White House (2016); Inductee, Naismith Memorial Basketball Hall of Fame (2009); Named One of "The 100 Most Powerful Celebrities," Forbes.com (2008); "Most Influential People in the World of Sports," BusinessWeek Magazine (2007, 2008); Eastern Conference All-Star Team, NBA (1985-1993, 1996-1998, 2002-2003); Named NBA Finals MVP (1991,1993, 1996-1998); NBA All-Defensive Team (1988-1993, 1996-1998); NBA MVP (1988, 1991, 1992, 1996, 1998); All-NBA First Team (1987-1993, 1996-1998); NBA All-Star Game MVP (1988, 1996, 1998); Male

Athlete of the Year, Associate Press (1991, 1992, 1993); NBA Defense Player of the Year (1988); Slam Dunk Championship (1987, 1988); Seagram's NBA Player of the Year (1987); NBA Rookie of the Year (1985); Wooden Award (1984); Naismith Award (1984); First Team, All-American, Sporting News (1983-1984) **AV:** Playing golf

JORDAN, NOEL CHASE, T: President **I:** Leisure, Travel & Tourism **CN:** Naples Marine Group **DOB:** 08/17/1946 **PB:** Fargo **SC:** ND/USA **PT:** William Jordan; Alice Jordan **MS:** Married **SPN:** Carol **CH:** Todd; Tami; Katie; Christopher; Robert **ED:** MS in Industrial Engineering, North Dakota State University (1971); BS in Industrial Engineering, North Dakota State University (1971); MBA, Minnesota State University Moorhead **C:** Rear Admiral, Societe International De Geneve, Pour (2012-2020); Chief Executive Officer, President, Naples Marine Group (1995-2018); Chief Executive Officer, SkipperLiner Manufacturing; Numerous Positions, Trane Air Conditioning Company Worldwide; Partner, Numerous Organizations **CR:** Chief Executive Officer, American Marine, Sea Ray Dealer and Several Marinas; Owner, Several Cruise Boat Businesses **CIV:** President, Boy's Club; President, La Crosse Area Economic Development Authority; Numerous Boat Businesses; Sunday School Teacher, Congregational Church **MIL:** With, United States Army, Fort Ord, CA **CW:** Author, "New Product Release" (1971); Sports Editor, NDSU Spectrum **AW:** Two North Dakota State University Service Awards; Naples Profile of Distinction; Inductee, Wall of Fame and Margin of Excellence Boys Club **MEM:** BBCC **AS:** Mr. Jordan attributes his success to his great team and the hard work they put in. They paid a lot of attention to developing the staff as professionals. **AV:** Water skiing; Business development; Boating; Large boat design; Track; BB; CC **RE:** Congregational

JOSEPHS, BONNIE P., T: Lawyer **I:** Law and Legal Services **CN:** Law Office of Bonnie P. Josephs **DOB:** 10/11/1938 **PB:** Verona **SC:** NJ/USA **PT:** Paul Josephs; Helen (Joelson) Josephs **CH:** Melodie R. Winawer MD; Paul Josephs **ED:** JD, New York University (1966); BA, Smith College (1960) **C:** Principal, Law Office of Bonnie P. Josephs, New York, NY (1978-Present); Partner, Buttenwieser & Josephs, New York, NY (1976-1977); Partner, London, Buttenwieser, Bonem & Valente, New York, NY (1975); Associate, London, Buttenwieser & Chalif, New York, NY (1969-1974); Associate, Cravath, Swaine & Moore, LLP, New York, NY (1966-1969) **CW:** Contributor, Articles, Professional Journals; Author, "What Was She Thinking?" (2018); Co-author, "Political and Civil Rights" (1966); Co-author, "Child's Play" (1965); Editor, Grosset & Dunlap, New York, NY (1962-1963); Editor, Dell Publications (Now Penny Publications, LLC), New York, NY (1962); Editor, Hearst Magazines (Hearst Communications, Inc.), New York, NY (1961-1962); Editor, MacFadden Publications (Now MacFadden Communications Group), New York, NY (1960) **MEM:** Science and Law Committee, Association of the Bar of the City of New York (1989); Arbitration and Alternate Dispute Resolution Committee, Association of the Bar of the City of New York (1986-1989); Association for Trial Lawyers of America (Now American Association for Justice) **BAR:** New York (1966) **MH:** Albert Nelson Marquis Lifetime Achievement Award **B/I:** Ms. Josephs became involved in her profession after sitting in on the Education Committee at the United States Congress. Ms. Josephs was motivated by the women on the council, as well as her supportive parents. **AV:** Tennis; Science; Reading; Public gardening **PA:** Democrat **RE:** Jewish

JOYCE, DAVID PATRICK, T: U.S. Representative from Ohio, Lawyer **I:** Government Administration/Government Relations/Government Services **CN:** U.S. House of Representatives **DOB:** 03/17/1957 **PB:** Cleveland **SC:** OH/USA **MS:** Married **SPN:** Kelly Joyce (1990) **CH:** Trenton; Keighle; Bridey **ED:** Doctor of Jurisprudence, University of Dayton School of Law (1982); Bachelor of Science, University of Dayton (1979) **C:** Member, U.S. House of Representatives from Ohio's 14th District (2013-Present); Prosecutor, Geauga County, Ohio (1988-Present); Public Defender, Geauga County, Ohio (1985-1988); Public Defender, Cuyahoga Country, Ohio (1983-1984); Member, Committee on Appropriations

JOYCE, JOHN PATRICK, MD, T: U.S. Representative from Pennsylvania; Dermatologist **I:** Government Administration/Government Relations/Government Services **DOB:** 02/08/1957 **PB:** Altoona **SC:** PA/USA **MS:** Married **SPN:** Alice Joyce **ED:** Residency in Dermatology, Johns Hopkins Hospital; Internal Medicine Residency, Johns Hopkins Hospital; MD, Temple University Lewis Katz School of Medicine (1983); BS in Biology, University of Pennsylvania, University Park, PA, with Honors (1979) **C:** Member, U.S. House of Representatives from Pennsylvania's 13th Congressional District (2019-Present); Founder, Altoona Dermatology Associates; Chief Resident, Johns Hopkins Hospital **CR:** Clinical Instructor, Johns Hopkins Hospital **CIV:** Advisory Board, Altoona Campus, The Pennsylvania State University; Advisory Board, American Cancer Society, Inc.; Advisory Board, United Way; Advisory Board, Goodman Trust; Mentor, Eberly College of Science, The Pennsylvania State University; Volunteer, The Pennsylvania State University; Volunteer, St. Vincent de Paul Soup Kitchen; Lifelong Member, Cathedral of the Blessed Sacrament, Altoona, PA **MIL:** With, United States Navy, Portsmouth Naval Hospital, VA **AW:** Johns Hopkins Fellow, Baltimore, MD **MEM:** Fellow, American College of Physicians; Fellow, American Academy of Dermatology Association **PA:** Republican

JOYCE, THOMAS P. JR., T: Chief Executive Officer and President **I:** Technology **CN:** Danaher Corporation **C:** President, Chief Executive Officer, Member Board of Directors, Danaher Corporation (2014-Present); Executive Vice President, Danaher Corporation (2006-2014); Vice President, Group Executive, Danaher Corporation (2002-2006); President, Hach Company (Subsidiary of Danaher Corporation) (2001-2002); Joined, Danaher Corporation (1990); Various General Management Positions, Danaher Corporation

JOYCE-BRADY, MARTIN FRANCIS, T: Clinical Professor of Medicine **I:** Medicine & Health Care **CN:** The Pulmonary Center, Boston University School of Medicine **DOB:** 09/25/1953 **PB:** Wilmington **SC:** DE/USA **PT:** Robert Lawrence; Marjorie Theresa (Martin) Brady **MS:** Married **SPN:** Jean Marie Joyce Brady (09/17/1977) **CH:** Jessica; Erin; Emily **ED:** Doctor of Medicine, University of Maryland, Baltimore, MD (1979); Bachelor of Arts in Arts and Science, University of Delaware (1975) **C:** Clinical Professor of Medicine, Pulmonary Center, Boston University School of Medicine (1997-Present); Director, Pulmonary and Respiratory Therapy, Jewish Memorial Hospital and Radius Specialty Hospital, Boston, MA (1996-2014); Director, Ventilator Care Unit, Jewish Memorial Hospital and Radius Specialty Hospital, Boston, MA (1988-2014); Director, Pulmonary Function Laboratory, Boston City Hospital, Boston, MA (1987-1996); Assistant Professor of Medicine, Pulmonary Center, Boston University School Medicine, Boston, MA (1987-1996); Pulmonary Fellow, Pulmonary Center, Boston University School Medicine, Boston, MA (1982-1987); Chief Medical Resident, Boston City Hospital, Boston, MA (1982-1983); Medicine Resident, Boston City Hospital, Boston, MA (1980-1982); Medicine Intern, Boston City Hospital, Boston, MA (1979-1980) **CIV:** Past President, Pulmonary Society **CW:** Contributor, Articles to Professional Journals; Peer Reviewer, Articles to Professional Journals **AW:** Program Project Grantee On Lung Development, National Institutes Of Health (1991-1996, 1997-2002, 2002-2007); E.L. Trudeau Scholar, American Lung Association (1990-1992); H. Fletcher Brown Scholar, Bank of Delaware, Wilmington, DE (1975) **MEM:** Chair, Research Grant Committee, Massachusetts Thoracic Society (2003-Present); Fellow, American Theological Society (2019); American Physiological Society; American Association for the Advancement of Science; American Society of Cell Biology; Massachusetts Medical Society; American Thoracic Society **MH:** Albert Nelson Marquis Lifetime Achievement Award; Marquis Who's Who Top Professional **B/I:** Mr. Joyce-Brady became involved in his profession due to the example of his mother and aunt, who were nurses. **PA:** Democrat **RE:** Roman Catholic

JOYNER-KERSEE, JACKIE, T: Former Track and Field Athlete **I:** Athletics **DOB:** 03/03/1962 **PB:** East St. Louis **SC:** IL/USA **PT:** Alfred Joyner; Mary Joyner **MS:** Married **SPN:** Bob Kersee (01/11/1986) **ED:** Honorary DHL, Washington University in St. Louis (1999); Honorary DHL, Howard University (1999); Honorary DHL, Spelman College (1998); Honorary DHL, Fontbonne College (Now Fontbonne University), St. Louis, MO (1998); Honorary LLD, Iona College (1994); Honorary DHL, Harris-Stowe State College (Now Harris-Stowe State University) (1993); Honorary LLD, Washington University in St. Louis (1992); BA in History, University of California Los Angeles (1985) **C:** Retired (2001); Member, U.S. Track and Field Team, Summer Olympics (1984, 1988, 1992, 1996); Basketball Player, Richmond Rage, American Basketball League (1996) **CR:** President, Founder, JJK & Associates, Inc. **CIV:** Chairman Emeritus, St. Louis Sports Commission (2001-Present); Founder, JJK Youth Center Foundation (1997-Present); Founder, JJK Community Foundation (Now Jackie Joyner-Kersee Foundation) (1989-Present); Chairman, St. Louis Sports Commission (1996-2000); Founder, Jackie Joyner-Kersee Boys & Girls Club; Board of Directors, USA Track & Field **CW:** Author, "A Kind of Grace: The Autobiography of the World's Greatest Female Athlete" (1997); Co-author, "A Woman's Place is Everywhere" (1994) **AW:** Dick Enberg Award, College Sports Information Director of America (CoSIDA) (2011); Honoree, NCAA Silver Anniversary Awards (2010); Named to Order of Lincoln (2005); Named Laureate, The Lincoln Academy of Illinois (2005); Named to St. Louis Walk of Fame (2000); Jesse Owens Humanitarian Award (1999); Named Woman Athlete of the Century, Sports Illustrated (1999); Jack Kelly Fair Play Award (1997); Bronze Medal, Long Jump, Summer Olympics, Atlanta, GA (1996); Named Female Athlete of the Year, International Association of Athletics Federations (1994); Jackie Robinson "ROBIE" Award (1994); Jim Thorpe Award (1993); Winner, Heptathlon, World Championships, Stuttgart, Germany (1993); Gold Medal, Heptathlon, Summer Olympics, Barcelona, Spain (1992); Bronze Medal, Long Jump, Summer Olympics, Barcelona, Spain (1992); First Female Athlete of the Year Award, Sporting News (1988); Gold Medals, Heptathlon, Long Jump, Summer Olympics, Seoul, South Korea (1988); Winner, Hepthathlon, Goodwill Games, New York, NY (1998); American Black Achieve-

ment Award, Ebony Magazine (1987); Gold Medal, Long Jump, World Championships, Rome, Italy (1987); Winner, Mobil Indoor Grand Prix (1987); Winner, Long Jump, Pan American Games (1987); Named Female Athlete of the Year, The Associated Press (1987); Jesse Owens Award (1986, 1987); James E. Sullivan Award (1986); Named Athlete of the Year, Track & Field News (1986); Winner, Broderick Cup (1983, 1985); Silver Medal, Heptathlon, Summer Olympics, Los Angeles, CA (1984); Parenting Leader Award, Parenting Magazine; Humanitarian Award, Women Sports and Fitness; President's Award, National Conference of Black Mayors; Named St. Louis Ambassadors Sportswoman of the Year; Named Honorary Harlem Globetrotter; Named to National Boys and Girls Club Hall of Fame; Four-time Winner, National Junior Pentathlon Championships

JUDGE, AARON JAMES, T: Professional Baseball Player **I:** Athletics **CN:** New York Yankees **DOB:** 04/26/1992 **PB:** Linden **SC:** CA/USA **PT:** Wayne Judge (Adoptive Father); Patty Judge (Adoptive Mother) **MS:** Single **ED:** Coursework, California State University, Fresno; Diploma, Linden High School **C:** Professional Baseball Player, New York Yankees (2016-Present) **AW:** Wilson Defensive Player of the Year Award (2019); Two-Time All-Star (2017-2018); AL Rookie of the Year (2017); Silver Slugger Award (2017)

JULY, LISA, T: Vice President of Data Intelligence **I:** Information Technology and Services **CN:** J2E Technology LLC **PT:** Melvin; Mary July **MS:** Single **ED:** Bachelor of Science in Information Technology, Kaplan University (2014) **CT:** CM2-C (CM2 Comprehensive) Certification (2018); CompTIA Security + ce Certification, CompTIA (2018); l Configuration Management Assesor, Microsoft System Engineer **C:** Vice President of Data Intelligence, J2E Technology LLC (2015-Present); Contractor, TEKsystems (2013-2015); Business Analyst, Goodrich Aerostructures (2006-2013); Business Advisor, UGS (2000-2006); Engineer, Litton PRC (1999-2000); Training Specialist/Network Administrator, GRC International Inc. (1996-1999); Technical Support Representative, Dell (1995-1996); Workstation Analyst, TechForce Temporaries (1994-1995) **CIV:** Volunteer, San Diego Food Bank **MIL:** Data Systems Technican, U.S. Navy (1988-1994) **MEM:** Alpha Beta Kappa Honor Society; National Society of Collegiate Scholars (NSCS); National Management Association **AS:** Ms. July attributes her success to hard work and collaboration with the right people. **B/I:** Ms. July tested high for computer knowledge and those kind of skills, which led to her selecting the field of data management.

JUNE, CARL HOWARD, T: Immunologist **I:** Medicine & Health Care **DOB:** 07/13/1953 **ED:** Postdoctoral Training in Transplantation Biology, Fred Hutchinson Cancer Research Center, Seattle, WA (1983-1986); MD, Baylor College of Medicine, Houston, TX (1979); Graduate Training in Immunology and Malaria, World Health Organization, Geneva (1978-1979); BS in Biology, U.S. Naval Academy, Annapolis, MD (1971) **CT:** Certified in Medical Oncology, Diplomate, American Board of Internal Medicine **C:** Director, Translational Research Programs, Abramson Cancer Center, University of Pennsylvania, Philadelphia, PA (1999-Present); Professor, Pathology and Laboratory Medicine, University of Pennsylvania, Philadelphia, PA (1999-Present); Professor, Department of medicine, Department of Cell and Molecular Biology, Uniformed Services University, Bethesda, MD (1995-1999); Head, Department of Immunology, Founder, Immune Cell Biology Program, Naval

Health Research Center (NHRC), Maryland (1990-1995) **CR:** Investigator, Abramson Family Cancer Research Institute (1999-Present) **CW:** Contributor, Articles, Professional Journals **AW:** Listed, Time 2018 Most Influential (2018); Paul Ehrlich and Ludwig Darmstaedter Prize (2015); Taubman Prize for Excellence in Translational Medical Science (2014); Karl Landsteiner Memorial Award, AABB (2014); Hamdan Award for Medical Research Excellence (2014); Bristol-Myers Squibb Freedom to Discover Award (2005-2009); Federal Laboratory Award for Excellence in Technology Transfer (2005); William Osler Award, University of Pennsylvania School of Medicine (2002); Lifetime Achievement Award, Leukemia and Lymphoma Society of America (2002); Frank Brown Berry Prize in Federal Medicine (1997); Fellow, American College of Physicians (1991); Alpha Omega Alpha Medical Society (1978) **MEM:** Elected Member, American Academy of Arts and Sciences (2014); Elected Member, Institute of Medicine (2012); American Society of Clinical Oncology

JUSTICE, JAMES CONLEY II, T: Governor of West Virginia **I:** Government Administration/Government Relations/Government Services **DOB:** 04/27/1951 **PB:** Charleston **SC:** WV/USA **PT:** James Conley Justice; Edna Ruth (Perry) Justice **MS:** Married **SPN:** Cathy (Comer) Justice (1975) **CH:** Jay; Jill **ED:** MBA, Marshall University Brad E. Smith Schools of Business; BBA, Marshall University; Coursework, University of Tennessee, Knoxville, TN **C:** Governor, State of West Virginia (2017-Present); Businessman (1977-2017); Founder, Bluestone Farms (1977-2017); Developer, Stoney Brook Plantation, Monroe County, WV; Owner/Chief Executive Officer, The Greenbrier, Sulphur Springs, WV; Owner/Chief Executive Officer, Over 50 Businesses **CIV:** President, Beckley Little League (1992-Present); Supporter, Dream Tree for Kids Campaign; Donor, James C. Justice National Scout Camp, The Summit Bechtel Family National Scout Reserve; Donor, Marshall University; Donor, Cleveland Clinic

KACHURIN, ANATOLY, PHD, T: Director of Innovative Methods **I:** Biotechnology **CN:** VaxDesign Campus of Sanofi **DOB:** 02/20/1950 **PB:** Leningrad **SC:** Russia **PT:** Mark Kachurin; Rvekka Kachurin **MS:** Married **SPN:** Olga Kachurina **CH:** Alexander; Michael Kathchourine **ED:** PhD in Molecular and Radiation Biophysics, St. Petersburg Nuclear Physics Institute, Gatchina, Russia (1985) **C:** Director of Innovative Methods, VaxDesign Campus of Sanofi (Subdivision) (2000-Present); Petersburg Nuclear Physics Institute, USSR Academy of Sciences, Biophysics Department (20 Years); Postdoctoral Fellow, Oklahoma State University (Three Years); Private Company (Two Years) **AW:** Second Place in Science Award, North America Research and Development Hub, Sanofi (2015); Best Collaboration, DARPA Chemical and Biological Defense Science and Technology Conference (2009) **MEM:** Member, Central Florida Rifle and Pistol Club (Present) **AS:** Dr. Kachurin attributes his success to his capacity and working with brilliant people in Russia and the United States. Additionally, he found what he was doing very interesting. **B/I:** Dr. Kachurin became involved in his profession because in his early years, when he was a student, he followed his cousin, Alexey Kachurin, who was a biophysicist. That was why he entered the Polytechnic Institute in Leningrad, Russia, and became a certified biophysicist six years later. He got into the Department of Biophysics of Nuclear Physics Institute in 1973 and entered into a wonderful lab of biophysical spectroscopy. His teachers' names were Professor Symon Bresler and Dr. Victor Fomichev, and he was happy to stay in a lab throughout his whole career, which he has continued to do. **AV:** Traveling; Reading; Sailing; Spending time with his sons and grandsons; Shooting; Growing exotic plants **THT:** Since 2000, Dr. Kachurin has specialized in the development of molecular and biological assessments of immune response in close collaboration with his wife Olga, an experienced and gifted chemist. Throughout his career, he has obtained two Russian patents as well as 18 patents in the United States.

KADAMANI, ESTEBAN, T: Owner, Managing Director **I:** Other **CN:** Infinite Windows, LLC **DOB:** 06/02/1983 **SC:** Columbia **PT:** Hessam Kadamani **MS:** Married **SPN:** Karen **CH:** Victoria; Nicolas **ED:** Miami Dade College **C:** Official Member, YEC (2017-Present); Owner, Managing Director, Infinite Windows, LLC (2006-Present); Manager, Subway (2003) **CIV:** Volunteer, The Little Lighthouse Foundation (2014) **AW:** Best Entrepreneurial Companies in America, Entrepreneur Magazine (2019); DotCom Magazine Impact Company, Digital Journal (2019); Inc. 500, Inc Magazine (2018, 2019); Small Business of the Year, Doral Business Council (2015); Top 20 Under 40 Professionals, Brickell Magazine (2010) **AS:** Mr. Kadamani attributes his success to hard work. He thinks that its all about working hard and not giving up. There has been a lot of times where he could have closed doors but with his consistency and grit have been the main ingredient in staying successful. **B/I:** Mr. Kadamani became involved in his profession because he was inspired by his father, a real estate developer in Colombia. **AV:** Playing tennis

KAEPERNICK, COLIN RAND, T: Professional Football Player **I:** Athletics **DOB:** 11/03/1987 **PB:** Milwaukee **SC:** WI/USA **PT:** Rick Kaepernick (Adopted Father); Teresa Kaepernick (Adopted Mother); Heidi Russo (Mother) **ED:** Bachelor's Degree in Business Management, University of Nevada, Reno (2011) **C:** Free Agent, Professional Football Player (2016-Present); Quarterback, San Francisco 49ers, National Football League (NFL) (2011-2016) **CR:** Founder, Kaepernick Publishing **CIV:** Supporter, Mothers Against Police Brutality; Supporter, Numerous Charities in Oppressed Communities **AW:** Ambassador of Conscience Award, Amnesty International (2018); W.E.B. Du Bois Medal, Harvard University (2018); Citizen of the Year, GQ Magazine (2017); Muhammad Ali Legacy Award, Sports Illustrated (2017); Eason Monroe Courageous Advocate Award, American Civil Liberties Union (2017); Honoree, Puffin/Nation Prize for Creative Citizenship (2017); Listee, 100 Most Influential People, Time Magazine (2017); Offensive Player of the Year, Western Athletic Conference (2008, 2010); Most Valuable Player, Humanitarian Bowl (2008); Freshman of the Year (2007)

KAGAN, ELENA, T: Associate Justice; Professor **I:** Law and Legal Services **CN:** Supreme Court of the United States **DOB:** 04/28/1960 **PB:** New York **SC:** NY/USA **PT:** Robert Kagan; Gloria (Gittelman) Kagan **ED:** JD, Harvard Law School, Magna Cum Laude (1986); MPhil, Worchester College, University of Oxford, England (1983); BA in History, Princeton University, Summa Cum Laude (1981) **C:** Associate Justice, Supreme Court of the United States (2010-Present); Solicitor General, U.S. Department of Justice, Washington, DC (2009-2010); Charles Hamilton Houston Professor of Law, Dean, Harvard Law School, Cambridge, MA (2003-2009); Professor, Harvard Law School, Cambridge, MA (2001-2003); Visiting Professor of Law, Harvard Law School, Cambridge, MA (1999-2001); Deputy Assistant to President for Domestic Policy, Deputy Director, Domestic Policy Council, The White House, Washington, DC (1997-1999); Associ-

ate Counsel to President, The White House, Washington, DC (1995-1996); Professor, The University of Chicago Law School (1995); Assistant Professor, The University of Chicago Law School (1991-1995); Associate, Williams & Connolly LLP, Washington, DC (1989-1991); Law Clerk to Justice Thurgood Marshall, Supreme Court of the United States (1987-1988); Law Clerk to Honorable Abner Mikva, United States Court of Appeals for the District of Columbia Circuit (1986-1987) **CW:** Contributor, Articles, Professional Journals **AW:** Listee, 100 Most Influential People in the World, Time Magazine (2013); Listee, 100 Most Powerful Women, Forbes Magazine (2010); Listee, 10 Most Powerful Women in Washington, Fortune Magazine (2010); Listee, 100 Most Powerful Women in DC, Washingtonian Magazine (2009); Listee, Washington's Most Influential Women Lawyers, The National Law Journal (2010); Listee, 50 Most Influential Women Lawyers in America (2007); Teaching Excellence Award, The University of Chicago Law School (1993) **PA:** Democrat **RE:** Jewish

KAHN, GORDON JACQUES, T: Principal, Owner **I:** Architecture & Construction **CN:** Gordon Kahn, Professional Architect, PLLC **DOB:** 06/16/1057 **PB:** Manhattan **SC:** NY/USA **PT:** Roger Kahn; Joan R. Kahn **MS:** Married **SPN:** Ed Galloway **CH:** Carter; Joan; Harry **ED:** BA in Architecture, Columbia College (1980) **CT:** Licensed, States of New York, New Jersey, Vermont, New Hampshire, Connecticut, and Colorado **C:** Owner/Architecture, Gordon Kahn, Professional Architect, PLLC (1990-Present) **CIV:** Review Committee, Landmarks West; Pro Bono, Empire State Pride Agenda; Pro Bono, Harvey School **MEM:** American Institute of Architects (1991-Present) **B/I:** Mr. Kahn became involved in his profession because he had an interest in architecture from a young age. His parents built a house in a community that was laid out by Frank Lloyd Wright, it was known as Usonia, located in Pleasantville, New York. Having spent a lot of time there surrounded by people with a love and affection for Wright's work in general, Mr. Khan became inspired. In addition, Mr. Kahn became close with Aaron Resnick, who designed his childhood home. As a result of their friendship, Mr. Khan became even more interested in becoming an architect. He never wanted to do anything else with his life. **AV:** Going to the beach; Spending time with family; Boating; Gardening **THT:** Mr. Khan was inspired by Frank Lloyd Wright's projects for much of his life. Clients include Tina Fey, Bruce Willis, Andy Cohen and Penny Marshall.

KAHNEMAN, DANIEL, PHD, T: Professor Emeritus **I:** Education/Educational Services **CN:** Princeton University **DOB:** 03/05/1934 **PB:** Tel Aviv **SC:** Israel **PT:** Efrayim Kahneman; Rachel Kahneman **MS:** Widowed **SPN:** Anne Marie Treisman (1978, Deceased 2018) **CH:** Four Children **ED:** Honorary Doctorate, Erasmus University (2009); Honorary Doctorate, University of Rome (2007); Honorary Doctorate, University of Alberta (2006); Honorary Doctorate, University of Paris (2006); Honorary Doctorate, University of Milan (2005); Honorary Doctorate, University of Wurzburg (2004); Honorary Doctorate, University of East Anglia (2004); Honorary Doctorate, Harvard University (2004); Honorary Doctorate, University of British Columbia (2004); Honorary Doctorate, The New School, New York, NY (2003); Honorary Doctorate, Ben-Gurion University of the Negev (2003); Honorary Doctorate, University of Trento (2002); Honorary Doctor of Science, University of Pennsylvania (2001); Doctor of Philosophy in Psychology, University of California Berkeley (1961); Bachelor of Arts in Psychology and Mathematics, Hebrew University, Jerusalem, Israel (1954) **C:** Professor of

Public Affairs Emeritus, Senior Scholar, Princeton School of Public and International Affairs, Princeton University (2007-Present); Eugene Higgins Professor of Psychology Emeritus, Princeton University (2007-Present); Fellow, Center for Rationality, Hebrew University (2000-Present); Eugene Higgins Professor of Psychology, Professor of Public Affairs, Princeton University, NJ (1993-2007); Professor of Psychology, University of California Berkeley (1986-1994); Professor of Psychology, University of British Columbia, Canada (1978-1986); Professor, Hebrew University (1973-1978); Associate Professor, Hebrew University (1970-1973); Senior Lecturer, Hebrew University (1966-1970); Lecturer of Psychology, Hebrew University (1961-1966) **CR:** Visiting Scholar, Russell Sage Foundation (1991-1992); Associate Fellow, Canadian Institute of Advanced Research (1984-1986); Fellow, Center for Advanced Studies in the Behavioral Sciences, Stanford University, CA (1977-1978); Visiting Scientist, Applied Psychological Research Unit, University of Cambridge, England, United Kingdom (1968-1969); Lecturer of Psychology, Fellow, Center for Cognitive Studies, Harvard University (1966-1967); Visiting Scientist, Department of Psychology, University of Michigan (1965-1966) **MIL:** Second Lieutenant to Lieutenant, Israel Defense Forces (1954) **CW:** Author, "Thinking, Fast and Slow" (2011); Member, Editorial Board, Thinking and Reasoning; Member, Editorial Board, Environmental and Resource Economics; Contributor, Articles to Professional Journals **AW:** Named, the Seventh Most Influential Economist in the World, The Economist (2015); Presidential Medal of Freedom, The White House (2013); Named, One of the 50 Most Influential People in Global Finance, Bloomberg Markets (2011-2012); Named, One of the Top Global Thinkers, Foreign Policy (2011); Communication Award, National Academy of Sciences (2011); Talcott Parsons Prize, American Academy of Arts & Sciences (2011); Award for Outstanding Life Contributions to Psychology, American Psychological Association (2007); Frank P. Ramsey Medal, Decision Analysis Society (2006); Thomas Schelling Prize (2006); Career Achievement Award, Society for Medical Decision Making (2002); Grawemeyer Prize in Psychology, University of Louisville (2002); Nobel Prize in Economics, Royal Swedish Academy of Sciences (2002); Hilgard Award for Lifetime Contribution to General Psychology (1995); Warren Medal, Society of Experimental Psychologists (1995); Distinguished Scientific Contribution Award, Society for Consumer Psychology (1992); Distinguished Scientific Contribution Award, American Psychological Society (1982) **MEM:** President, Society for Judgement and Decision Making (1992-1993); Society of Experimental Psychologists (1992-1993); Fellow, The Econometric Society; Fellow, Canadian Psychological Association; Fellow, American Psychological Association; William James Fellow, American Psychological Society; American Academy of Arts & Sciences; National Academy of Sciences; Society for Judgment and Decision Making; Society of Economic Sciences; Psychonomic Society; Corresponding Member, British Academy

KAHRL, ROBERT, JD, LPCC, T: Lawyer **I:** Law and Legal Services **DOB:** 06/02/1946 **PB:** Mount Vernon **SC:** OH/USA **PT:** K. Allin Kahrl; Evelyn Sperry (Conley) Kahrl **MS:** Married **SPN:** La Vonne Rutherford Kahrl (07/12/1969) **CH:** Kurt Freeland; Eric Allin; Heidi Elizabeth **ED:** MACMHC, Ashland Theological Seminary (2013); MBA, Max M. Fisher College of Business, The Ohio State University (1975); JD, Moritz College of Law, The Ohio State University, Summa Cum Laude (1975); AB, Princeton University, Cum Laude (1968); Diploma, Naval Officer Candidate School, Newport RI **CT:**

Licensed Professional Clinical Counselor, State of Ohio (2019) **C:** Licensed Professional Counselor, Ohio (2013-Present); Distinguished Practitioner-in-Residence, School of Law, The University of Akron, Ohio (2010-Present); Partner, Jones, Day, Reavis & Pogue (Now Jones Day), Cleveland, OH (1985-2009); Practice Leader of Intellectual Property Practice Area, Jones Day (Formerly Jones, Day, Reavis & Pogue), Cleveland, OH (1991-2008); Associate, Jones, Day, Reavis & Pogue (Now Jones Day), Cleveland, OH (1976-1984); Law Clerk to Presiding Judge, United States Court of Appeals for the Sixth Circuit, Cleveland, OH (1975-1976) **CR:** Lecturer on Trademark Use, Forum on Franchising, Annual Meeting, American Bar Association (1998) **CIV:** Marriage Counselor, Christ Community Chapel **MIL:** Lt., U.S. Navy (1968-1972) **CW:** Author, "Patent Claim Construction, Second Edition" (2014); Co-Author, "Thesaurus of Claim Construction," Oxford University Press (2013); Author, "Patent Claim Construction," Aspen Law and Business (2001); Contributor, "Monograph Number Two," Antitrust Law Section, American Bar Association **MEM:** Member, Chairman Emeritus of Intellectual Property Section, Ohio State Bar Association; American Intellectual Property Law Association; Order of the Coif; American Association of Christian Counselors; Cleveland Intellectual Property Law Association **BAR:** Ohio (1975); Numerous Federal Courts **MH:** Albert Nelson Marquis Lifetime Achievement Award; Marquis Who's Who Top Professional **B/I:** Mr. Kahrl became involved in his profession because he decided to pursue his career after earning a higher score on the law board exam than on the business board exam. Hal Cooper, his mentor, encouraged him to work in intellectual property law. Mr. Kahrl also chose his job because he didn't want to be geographically limited in the way that many lawyers are. **AV:** High-performance automobiles; Playing piano; Exercising; Swimming; Playing golf **PA:** Republican **RE:** Protestant

KAINE, TIMOTHY, "TIM" MICHAEL, T: U.S. Senator from Virginia; Lawyer **I:** Government Administration/Government Relations/Government Services **DOB:** 02/26/1958 **PB:** St. Paul **SC:** MN/USA **PT:** Albert A. Kaine; Mary Kathleen (Burns) Kaine **MS:** Married **SPN:** Anne Bright Holton (11/24/1984) **CH:** Annella; Woody; Nat **ED:** JD, Harvard Law School, Cum Laude (1983); AB, University of Missouri, Summa Cum Laude (1979) **C:** U.S. Senator, Commonwealth of Virginia (2013-Present); Member, U.S. Senate Armed Services Committee (2013-Present); Member, U.S. Senate Committee on Foreign Relations (2013-Present); Member, U.S. Senate Budget Committee (2013-Present); Chairman, Democratic National Committee, Washington, DC (2009-2011); Governor, Commonwealth of Virginia (2006-2010); Lieutenant Governor, Commonwealth of Virginia (2002-2006); Mayor, City of Richmond, VA (1998-2001); Member, City Council, City of Richmond, VA (1994-1998); Private Law Practice, Richmond, VA (1984-2001); Law Clerk to the Honorable Robert Lanier Anderson III, United States Court of Appeals for the 11th Circuit (1983-1984) **CR:** Democratic Party Nominee for Vice President of the United States (2016); Chairman, Southern Governors Association (2008-2009); Professor of Law, University of Richmond School of Law **CIV:** Board of Directors, Historic Jackson Ward Association **CW:** Contributor, Articles, Professional Journals **AW:** Pro Bono Public Award, Richmond Bar Association (Now The Bar Association of the City of Richmond) (1995) **MEM:** ABA; The Virginia Bar Association; Richmond Bar Association (Now The Bar Association of the City of Richmond) **PA:** Democrat **RE:** Roman Catholic

KALING, MINDY, T: Actress; Writer, Television Producer **I:** Media & Entertainment **DOB:** 06/24/1979 **PB:** Cambridge **SC:** MA/USA **PT:** Avu Chokalingam; Swati Chokalingam **CH:** Katherine Swati **ED:** Honorary LHD, Dartmouth College, Hanover, NH (2018); BA in Playwriting, Dartmouth College (2001) **C:** Production Assistant, "Crossing Over with Jon Edward"; Intern, "Late Night with Conan O'Brien" **CR:** Minority-owner, Swansea City A.F.C., United Kingdom **CW:** Co-creator, Writer, Executive Producer, Actress, "Never Have I Ever" (2020-Present); Actress, "The Morning Show" (2019); Actress, Writer, Producer, "Late Night" (2019); Appearance, "Champions" (2018); Actress, "A Wrinkle in Time" (2018); Actress, "Ocean's 8" (2018); Appearance, "Animals" (2017); Appearance, "The Muppets" (2015); Author, "Why Not Me?" (2015); Voice Actress, "Inside Out' (2015); Actress, "The Night Before" (2015); Appearance, "Sesame Street" (2014); Actress, "This is the End" (2013); Actress, Executive Producer, Writer, "The Mindy Project" (2012-2017); Actress, "The Five-Year Engagement" (2012); Voice Actress, "Wreck-It Ralph" (2012); Actress, "No Strings Attached" (2011); Author, "Is Everyone Hanging Out Without Me? (And Other Concerns)" (2011); Voice Actress, "Despicable Me" (2010); Actress, "Unaccompanied Minors" (2006); Actress, "The 40 Year Old Virgin" (2005); Actress, Co-producer, "The Office" (2005-2012); Actress, "Curb Your Enthusiasm" (2005); Co-writer, Actress, "Matt & Ben" (2003); Featured, U.S. Comedy Arts Festival, Aspen, CO (2003); Appearances, Television Shows **AW:** Named One of the Women of the Year, Glamour Magazine (2014); Named One of the 100 Most Influential People in the World, TIME Magazine (2013); SAG Award for Outstanding Performance by an Ensemble in a Comedy Series, SAG-AFTRA (2007, 2008); Best Play Prize, New York International Fringe Festival (2003); Named One of the Top 10 Theatrical Events, TIME Magazine (2003)

KALLAKIS, ACHILLEAS M., I: Government Administration/Government Relations/Government Services **DOB:** 09/03/1968 **PB:** London **SC:** England **PT:** Michalis Kallakis; Erinoula (Angelinakis) Kallakis **MS:** Married **SPN:** Pamela Anne Stachowsky (1995) **CH:** Erinoula; Michalis; Aristotelis; Dionysios **ED:** BSc in Economics, London University, with Honors (1989) **CT:** Full Samaritans Training Course (2013); ICC Certification, Power Boat L II, Inland Waterways (2012) **C:** Ambassador of the Republic of San Marino to the Sultanate of Brunei (2007-Present); Pacific Risk Corp, London, England (2000-Present); Chief Executive Officer, Pacific Coffee Corp. (2000-Present); Hellenic Capital Management (2000-Present); Pacific Real Estate Corp. (2000-Present); Atlas Alliance Group (2000-Present); Development Board, National Portrait Gallery, London, England (2000-Present); British American Business, Inc. (2000-Present); Director, United States Chamber of Commerce, London (1997-Present); Bernouli Trust Corp., NY (1994-Present); South Pacific Advisory Board, Sydney (1994-Present); Chairman, Chief Executive Officer, Pacific Group of Companies, London, New York (1991-Present); Pacific Maritime, New York (1991-Present); Ocean Group, USA (1989-Present); Atlas E-Risk (2000-2001); Director, Global Transport, Delaware and New York (1981-1991); Chairman, Pacific Vending Group **CR:** Chief Advisor, Harvard Group (2018); Chief Advisor, Capital Real Estate (2018) **CIV:** ICCC Ambassador of Goodwill for the UK (2008-Present); Chief Advisor, Hermitage Syndicated Trust (1995-Present); Board Member, Prince Albert II Environmental Foundation, Monaco (2008); Committee, Youth Enterprise Initiative (1989-1992); Duke of Edinburgh Special Projects; Patron, English National Ballet **CW:** Author, "Transport Economics" (1996); Co-editor, "The Wonders of Italy" (1996); Author, "Maritime Registers of the World" (1994) **AW:** Icon Status, Winsdor Castle (2008); Bestowed Title of Chevalier, Order of Grimaldi, Monaco (2008); Gold Medal, Island of Mykonos, Greece (2007); Outstanding Emerging Leader Award, Office of Maritime Affairs (1997); Prime Minister's Award, South Pacific Action Forum (1996); President's Golden Honor Award, South Pacific Action, Foru (1995); Churchill Award for Excellence, Churchill Enterprise Foundation (1993) **MEM:** Fellow, Duke of Edinburgh International (2003-Present); Director, Friends of Florence (1997-Present); President, Youth Anglo-Hellenic Society of the United Kingdom (1986-1988); Royal Opera, London; Navy League; Fellow, Institute of Directors; Fellow, Institute of Transport and Tourism; Friends of Conservation; Queen's Club; Metropolitan Opera Guild, New York; Metropolitan Club, New York; National Trust, London; Society for the Protection of Ancient Buildings; Landmark Trust, London **MH:** Albert Nelson Marquis Lifetime Achievement Award **AV:** Travel; Italian studies; Backgammon; Fencing; Tennis; Antiques; Poker **RE:** Greek Orthodox

KALLAY, THOMAS, "TOM", T: Managing Attorney, 2nd Appellate District **I:** Government Administration/Government Relations/Government Services **CN:** California Court of Appeals **DOB:** 07/14/1937 **SC:** Budapest/Hungary **PT:** Nicholas Kallay; Piroska Kustar Kallay **MS:** Divorced **CH:** Maya Lewis; Tom C. Kallay **ED:** JD, University of California Los Angeles (1962); AB in Political Science, University of California Los Angeles (1958) **C:** Managing Attorney, 2nd Appellate District, California Court of Appeals (2011-Present); Senior Judicial Attorney, Second Appellate District, California Court of Appeals (2003-2011); Private Practice (1972-1976, 1988-2003); Executive Director, California Appellate Project of Los Angeles (1986-1988); Senior Research Attorney, California Court of Appeals (1970-1972); Deputy Attorney General, California Attorney General's Office (1967-1970) **CR:** Professor of Law, Southwestern University School of Law (1976-1986) **CIV:** Founding Executive Director, California Appellate Project of Los Angeles, California (1986-1988); Eagle Scout, Boy Scouts of America (1955) **MIL:** U.S. Navy (1963-1967); Lieutenant Commander, Judge Advocate General's Corps **CW:** Author, "A Conceptual Approach to California Summary Judgement" (2012); Book Reviewer, "Equity and the Constitution," 20 California Western Law Review 156 (1983); Book Reviewer, "Law Clerks and the Judicial Process," 28 UCLA Law Review 605 (1981); Author, "A Reappraisal of General and Limited Jurisdiction in California," 8 Pepperdine Law Review (1980); Author, "The Dismissal of Frivolous Appeals," California Courts of Appeal, 54 State Bar Journal 92 (1979); Author, "A Study in Rulemaking by Decision: California Court Adopt Federal Rule 54(b)," 13 Southwestern Law Review 7 **AW:** Fulbright Fellowship, University of Heidelberg, Germany (1959-1960); Inductee, Phi Beta Kappa, University of California Los Angeles (1958) **MEM:** California Academy of Appellate Lawyers (1984-Present); California State Bar; Los Angeles County Bar Association **BAR:** California (1963); U.S. District Court for the Central District of California (1963) **MH:** Marquis Who's Who Top Professional **AS:** Mr. Kallay attributes his success to never giving up; he always held faith in what a new day could bring. **B/I:** Mr. Kallay's father loved the law, which inspired him to follow in his footsteps. **AV:** Reading; Playing tennis and piano **RE:** Methodist

KALLEN, ELLIOT H., T: Chief Executive Officer, Financial Planner, Wealth Manager, Registered Principal **I:** Financial Services **CN:** Prosperity Financial Group, Inc. **DOB:** 03/05/1958 **PB:** Newark **SC:** NJ/USA **PT:** Fred Kallen; Lily Kallen **MS:** Married **SPN:** Tammy Carlson-Kallen **CH:** Cody; Alexa; Tyler; Lisa; Jake (Deceased) **ED:** BAS in Accounting and Economics, Minors in Business and Computer Science, Rutgers, The State University of New Jersey, Newark, NJ (1980) **C:** Chief Executive Officer, Financial Planner, Wealth Manager, Registered Principal, Owner, President, Financial Advisor, Partner, Prosperity Financial Group, Incorporated, San Ramon, CA (1993-Present); Financial Advisor, Registered Representative, Lincoln Financial Group (1993-2000) **CIV:** President, A Brighter Day Charity; Former President, Congregation B'nai Shalom; Former President, Boys & Girls Clubs of America **AW:** Named Best Boutique Independent Financial Planning Firm (2019); Named One of the Top Wealth Advisors in the Greater Bay Area, San Francisco Business Times (2011); Named to Top 100 Most Influential Advisors in the Country, 401k Wire Magazine (2010); Ronald Regan Gold Medal Award (2006); Congressional Order of Merit, United States Congress (2001-2006); Named Business Advisory Council Businessman of the Year, The Wall Street Journal (2003); Wealth Money Management Award **MEM:** Financial Planning Association **MH:** Named Business of the Year (2020) **AS:** Mr. Kallen attributes his success to lots of hard work and "sound decision making." He has been an entrepreneur his entire career and isn't afraid to make and take bold decisions to strive and become the industry leader. **B/I:** Mr. Kallen enjoys helping others. He enjoys helping them reach their financial and personal goals. He has been a leader in this industry for more than two decades and has spoken at industry and civic meetings to more than 10,000 people. **AV:** Hiking; Biking; Golf; Exercise at the gym **PA:** Independent **THT:** Mr. Kallen brings over 27 years of entrepreneurial business ownership experience to Prosperity's Financial Planning and advising practice. He is a keynote speaker on motivation and marketing in the independent financial advisor industry, utilizing his previous experience in international distribution to teach other investment professionals nationwide and in the San Francisco area. He is an Independent Financial Advisor and the founder of Prosperity Financial Group, Inc., a Registered Investment Advisory Firm. He holds Series 7, 24, 63, 65 and 66-licensed to offer securities. Since 1993, he has been licensed to offer insurance and annuities underwritten by a wide variety of the nation's insurers. Mr. Kallen's practice focuses on entrepreneurs, business owners, retirees, and millennials. He advises on retirement and estate planning, employee benefit planning, insurance and risk management and investment planning programs. He was awarded membership in International Who's Who of Professionals for 2000 and again in 2007. He holds Bachelor of Arts degrees in both accounting and economics from Rutgers University in New Jersey and serves on several boards of nonprofit and philanthropic organizations. Currently, Mr. Kallen is president of A Brighter Day, a 501©(3) charity he founded in memory of his youngest son. This charity unites stress and depression resources with teenagers throughout the Bay Area. He is actively involved with the Boys and Girls Clubs of the Diablo Valley. He has helped raise hundreds of thousands of dollars for this organization, which is on the front lines in providing athletic, social and cultural programming to the children of Diablo Valley. He formerly served as Board President. Mr. Kallen is also active with the Fallen Heroes Charity. He is also a former President of Congregation B'nai Shalom.

In 2003, he was recognized for his contribution to the Diablo Valley community, when he was named by the Business Advisory Council of the National Republican Congressional Committee as 2003 Businessman of the Year, which was featured in an article in The Wall Street Journal. In 2006, he received the Ronald Reagan Gold Medal Award. In 2011, he was named one of the Top 300 Advisors to the Defined Contribution 401K Industry. He is the proud father of two adult children, stepfather to two adult children and a grandfather. Mr. Kallen and his wife reside in Lafayette, CA.

KALTENEGGER, LISA, T: Astronomer **I:** Sciences **DOB:** 03/04/1977 **SC:** Austria **ED:** PhD in Astrophysics, University of Graz, Austria (2005); BS in Astrophysics, University of Graz, Austria (1999) **C:** Associate Professor of Astronomy, Cornell University (2014); Lecturer, University of Heidelberg (2011); Lecturer, Harvard University (2008); Emmy Noether Research Group Leader, Max Planck Institute for Astronomy, Heidelberg, Germany; Emmy Noether Research Group Leader, Harvard-Smithsonian Center for Astrophysics, Cambridge, MA **CR:** Founder, Director, Carl Sagan Institute, Cornell University **AW:** Science and Innovations, Christian Doppler Prize, Salzburg, Germany (2014); PI, Simon Origins of Life Initiative (2013); PI, Japanese Earth and Life Science Institute (2013); Heinz Maier-Leibnitz-Preis in Physics (2012); EC Role Model for the Women in Research & Science Campaign of the EU (2012); America's Young Innovator in Arts and Science, Smithsonian Magazine (2007); Paul Hertelendy Prize for Outstanding Young Scientist, Harvard Smithsonian Center for Astrophysics (2007); Named, Asteroid 7734 Kaltenegger

KAMILLI, ROBERT, "BOB" J., PHD, T: Scientist Emeritus **I:** Sciences **DOB:** 06/14/1947 **PB:** Philadelphia **SC:** PA/USA **PT:** Joseph George Kamilli; Marie Emma (Clauss) Kamilli **MS:** Married **SPN:** Diana Ferguson Chapman (6/28/1969) **CH:** Annie Chapman; Bobby Chapman **ED:** PhD in Geology, Harvard University (1976); AM in Geology, Harvard University (1971); BA in Geology, Rutgers, the State University of New Jersey, Summa Cum Laude (1969) **C:** Scientist Emeritus, U.S. Geological Survey (2014-Present); Research Geologist, U.S. Geological Survey (2007-2014); Scientist-in-Charge, U.S. Geological Survey (1996-2007); Project Chief, U.S. Geological Survey (2001-2006); Research Geologist, Project Chief, U.S. Geological Survey, Tucson, AZ (1989-1996); Mission Chief Geologist, U.S. Geological Survey, Saudi Arabian Mission (1987-1989); Geologist, U.S. Geological Survey, Saudi Arabian Mission, Jeddah, Saudi Arabia (1983-1987); Project Geologist, Climax Molybdenum Company, Golden, CO (1980-1983); Assistant Resident Geologist, Climax Molybdenum Company (1979-1980); Geologist, Climax Molybdenum Company, Empire, CO (1976-1979) **CR:** Adjunct Professor, Geosciences Department, University of Arizona, Tucson, AZ (1997-Present); Adjunct Professor, University of Colorado at Boulder (1981-1983) **CIV:** Board of Directors, Imago Dei Middle School, Tucson, AZ **CW:** Editor, "Geologic Highway Map of Arizona"; Contributor, Articles, Professional Journals **AW:** Henry Rutgers Scholar, Rutgers, the State University of New Jersey (1968-1969); Listed, Social Register **MEM:** Harvard Club Of Southern Arizona (2014-Present); Vice President, Arizona Geological Society (2004-Present); Counselor, Arizona Geological Society (2001-2003); Past President, Arizona Geological Society (2000); President, Arizona Geological Society (1999); Vice President, Arizona Geological Society (1995-1998); Fellow, Geological Society of America; Fellow, Society of Economic Geologists; Phi Beta Kappa; Sigma Xi **MH:** Albert Nelson Marquis Lifetime Achievement Award **B/I:**

When Dr. Kamilli was 5 years old, he sold quartz pebbles collected near his home in southern New Jersey. He would paint them bright colors and sell them to the neighbors. He also loved maps. From about the age of 8, he was the official navigator on family vacations. Fortunately, his parents did not object to his planning routes that passed near quarries and mine dumps. His father bought him his first rock hammer when he was 12. He did not know that maps had anything to do with rocks until he took a geology course at the Colorado School of Mines between his junior and senior years of high school, courtesy of the National Science Foundation. It was that geology course at the Colorado School of Mines that made him realize that he wanted to become a professional geologist. **AV:** Traveling; Swimming; Listening to music; Practicing photography; Singing; Playing the guitar and banjo **PA:** Democrat **RE:** Episcopalian

KANDARIAN, STEVEN A., T: Chairman, President, Chief Executive Officer **I:** Financial Services **CN:** MetLife Services and Solutions, LLC. **PB:** West Hartford **SC:** CT/USA **ED:** MBA, Harvard Business School (1980); JD, Georgetown University Law Center (1978); BA in Economics, Clark University (1974) **C:** Chairman, President, Chief Executive Officer, MetLife Services and Solutions, LLC. (2012-Present); President, Chief Executive Officer, MetLife Services and Solutions, LLC. (2011); Executive Vice President, Chief Investment Officer, MetLife Services and Solutions, LLC. (2005-2011); Executive Director, PBGC (2001-2004); President, Founder, Eagle Capital Holdings (1990-1993);Managing Director, Lee Capital Holdings, Boston, MA (1984-1990); With, State Street Bank; With, LCB Holdings, Inc.; Investment Banker, Rotan Mosle, Inc., Houston, TX; Founder, Managing Partner, Orion Energy Partners **CR:** Board of Directors, MetLife Services and Solutions, LLC. (2011-Present); Board of Trustees, Premier Global Fund, MassMutual; Board of Trustees, MassMutual Participation Investors

KANDEL, ERIC RICHARD, MD, T: Neuroscientist; Professor **I:** Education/Educational Services **CN:** Columbia University **DOB:** 11/07/1929 **PB:** Vienna **SC:** Austria **PT:** Herman Kandel; Charlotte (Zimels) Kandel **MS:** Married **SPN:** Denise Bystryn (1956) **CH:** Two Children **ED:** Honorary Doctorate, Norwegian University of Science and Technology (2011); Resident in Psychiatry, Harvard Medical School, Boston, MA (1960-1964); Intern, Montefiore Hospital (Montefiore Medical Center), New York, NY (1956-1957); MD, New York University Grossman School of Medicine (1956); BA, Harvard College (1952) **C:** Professor, Department of Biochemistry and Molecular Biophysics, Columbia University Irving Medical Center Vagelos College of Physicians & Surgeons, New York, NY (1992-Present); University Professor, Columbia University Irving Medical Center Vagelos College of Physicians & Surgeons (1983-Present); Professor, Department of Physiology and Psychiatry, Columbia University Irving Medical Center Vagelos College of Physicians & Surgeons (1974-Present); Founding Director, Center for Neurobiology and Behavior, Columbia University Irving Medical Center Vagelos College of Physicians & Surgeons (1974-1983); Associate Professor, Department of Physiology and Psychiatry, New York University Grossman School of Medicine (1965-1974); Staff Psychiatrist, Harvard Medical School, Boston, MA (1964-1965); Research Associate, Neurophysiology Laboratory, National Institutes of Health, Bethesda, MD (1957-1960) **CR:** Senior Investigator, Howard Hughes Medical Institute, Chevy Chase, MD (1984-Present) **CIV:** Member, Prize Committee, Kavli Prize in Neuroscience (2007-2010); Scientific Council, The Brain & Behavior Research Foundation **CW:** Author, Film, "In Search of Memory" (2008); Author, Book, "In Search of Memory: The Emergence of a New Science of Mind" (2007); Author, Autobiography, "In Search of Memory: The Emergence of a New Science of Mind" (2006); Author, "Psychiatry, Psychoanalysis, and the New Biology of Mind" (2005); Co-editor, "Principles of Neural Science" (2000); Author, "Essentials of Neural Science Value Pack" (1995); Co-author with James H. Schwartz and Thomas M. Jessell, "Essentials of Neural Science and Behavior" (1995); Editor, "Molecular Neurobiology in Neurology and Psychiatry" (1987); Co-editor, "Molecular Aspects of Neurobiology" (1986); Author, "Behavioral Biology of Aplysia: A Contribution to the Comparative Study of Opisthobranch Molluscs" (1979); Author, "A Cell Biological Approach to Learning" (1978); Author, "Cellular Biology of Neurons" (1977); Author, "Cellular Basis of Behavior: An Introduction to Behavioral Neurobiology" (1976); Contributor, Articles to Professional Journals **AW:** Grand Decoration of Honour in Silver with Star for Services to the Republic of Austria (2012); Viktor Frankl Award, Vienna, Austria (2008); Benjamin Franklin Medal for Distinguished Achievement in the Sciences (2006); Book Award for Science and Technology, Los Angeles Times (2006); Nobel Prize in Physiology/Medicine, The Nobel Foundation (2000); Heineken Prize (2000); Wolf Foundation Prize in Medicine, Israel (1999); Charles A. Dana Award for Pioneering Achievement in Health (1997); New York City Mayor's Award for Excellence in Science and Technology (1994); FO Schmitt Medal in Neuroscience (1993); Harvey Prize, Technion-Israel Institute of Technology (1993); Jean-Louis Signoret Neuropsychology Prize (1992); Warren Triennial Prize (1992); Award for Distinguished Achievement in Neuroscience Research, Bristol-Myers Squibb (1991); Award in Neuroscience, Robert J. & Claire Pasarow Foundation (1989); Distinguished Service Award, American Psychiatric Association (1989); National Medal of Science, The White House (1988); International Award, Gairdner Foundation (1987); Howard Crosby Warren Medal, Society of Experimental Psychologists (1984); Albert Lasker Award for Basic Medical Research, Albert And Mary Lasker Foundation (1983); Dickson Prize in Biology and Medicine, University of Pittsburgh (1982); Karl Spencer Lashley Prize in Neurobiology, The American Philosophical Society (1981); Solomon A. Berson Medical Alumni Achievement Award, New York University (1979); Lucy G. Moses Prize for Research in Basic Neurology (1977); Lester N. Hofheimer Prize for Research (1977); Henry L. Moses Award, Montefiore Hospital (Montefiore Medical Center) (1959) **MEM:** Honorary Fellow, The Royal Society of Edinburgh (2018); Foreign Member, The Royal Society (2013); President, Society for Neuroscience (1980-1981); Fellow, American Association for the Advancement of Science; National Academy of Sciences; Academy of Sciences, France; The American Philosophical Society; The New York Academy of Sciences; International Brain Research Organization (IBRO); Society for Neuroscience

KANE, DAVID LAWRENCE, T: Attorney **I:** Law and Legal Services **CN:** Kane Title, LLC; David L. Kane, P.C. **DOB:** 08/19/1969 **PB:** Corpus Christi **SC:** TX/USA **PT:** Jerry Kane; Glenda Kane **MS:** Married **SPN:** Marlo Kane **CH:** Sydney; Alexis; Josh **ED:** JD, Southern Methodist University, Texas, Cum Laude (1994); BBA in Business Administration-Marketing, University of Texas (1991) **C:** Escrow Officer, Kane Title, LLC, Texas (2013-Present); Attorney, David L. Kane, PC (2000-Present) **AW:** Named to Order of the Coif, Southern Methodist University (1994) **MEM:** State Bar of Texas; Texas Land Title Asso-

ciation (TLTA) **BAR:** United States District Court for the Southern District of Texas (1998); United States District Court for the Northern District of Texas (1997); Texas (1994) **AS:** Mr. Kane attributes his success to his empathy. He likes caring about people and he tries to be empathetic with clients so that he can be a better advocate for their position. If he cannot do so, he rarely would take the case. **B/I:** Growing up, everyone would tell Mr. Kane that he talked too much. They weren't wrong and he wanted to pursue a career where he could do something positive for people, aside from just talking about it. He decided his best use was as an attorney. Since then, he consistently strives to be a hero of some sort when advocating for others or when attempting to solve their problems. When people thank him for his work, it is the fulfilling feeling that fuels his daily efforts. **THT:** Mr. David Kane's grandfather, Sam Kane, was also included in Marquis Who's Who. Mr. Sam Kane was a Holocaust survivor, an American entrepreneur, and the best role model any grandson could ever hope to emulate. Mr. David Kane concludes with no better thought than to cite his grandfather Sam, who is always quoted as saying, "America is great!"

KANE, SARA WYN, T: Partner **I:** Law and Legal Services **CN:** Valli Kane & Vagnini LLP **DOB:** 08/01/1972 **PB:** Queens **SC:** NY/USA **PT:** Laura Grossman; Robert Grossman **ED:** Doctor of Jurisprudence, Hofstra University School of Law, with Distinction (1998); Bachelor of Fine Arts in Theatre, Boston University for the Arts, Cum Laude (1994) **C:** Co-founder, Partner, Valli Kane & Vagnini LLP (2005-Present) **CW:** Author, Article, "Have You Hit The Glass Ceiling?", Long Island Woman Magazine (2005); Proposal for a Model Employee Benefit Program, Benefits Quarterly (1998); Managing Editor, Hofstra Labor & Employment Law Journal **AW:** Selectee, Super Lawyers (2018, 2019, 2020); Legacy Award, National Association for the Advancement of Colored People (2017); Children, Families and the Law's Outstanding Women in the Law Award, Hofstra Law Center (2016); Long Island Business News Leadership in the Law Award, Hofstra Law Center (2016); Texas Lawyer's Award (2014); Listee, Top 100 Trial Lawyers, National Trial Lawyers **MEM:** National Association of Professional Women; Nassau County Bar Association; American Bar Associations; National Employment Lawyers Association; Legal Network for Gender Equity **BAR:** New York State Bar; United States District Court for the Southern District of New York; U.S. District Court for the Eastern District of New York; Supreme Court of the United States **MH:** Marquis Who's Who Top Professional **AS:** Ms. Kane attributes her success to working hard, as well as her compassion. **B/I:** Ms. Kane became involved in her profession due to the influence of her paternal grandfather, as well as her own mother. After receiving a fine arts degree in theater, she chose to leverage that training towards helping people in the field of legal service.

KANIA, ALAN J., I: Writing and Editing **DOB:** 11/30/1946 **PB:** Lawrence **SC:** MA/USA **PT:** Frank J.; Genievieve (Marcinonis) K. **MS:** Married **SPN:** Terry **ED:** Master of Public Affairs, University of Colorado, Denver, CO (1985); Bachelor of Science, Emerson College, Boston, MA (1971); Coursework, Boston University (1967-1969) **CR:** Conductor, Seminars, Conferences, American Hospital Association (1985, 1988); With, Grantsmanship Center Workshop (1984, 1985) **CIV:** Secretary of the Treasurer, Board of Directors, International Communications Forum of America (2003-2014); Board of Directors, Denver Press Club (1996-1997, 1997-1998, 2007-2008, 2008-2009); Board of Trustees, Board of Directors, Colorado's Ocean Journey

(1995-1996); President, Board of Directors, O. J. Goldrick Publishing Co. (1993-1996); Vice President, Secretary Board of Directors, Parker Fire District (1989-1994); Secretary, Board of Directors, Pension Fund, Parker Fire District (1989-1994); Secretary, Board of Directors, International Society for the Protection of Mustangs and Burros (1990-1992); Chairperson, Colorado Trail Master Plan Committee (1989-1991); Executive Secretary, Board of Directors, Colorado Trail Foundation (1987-1991); Member, Long-Range Planning Committee, Pinery Homeowners Association (1989); Member, Program Committee, Academy for Healthcare Marketing (1988-1989); Publicity Chairman, Board of Directors, Boulder County Horsemen's Association (1987); Strategic Planning Chairperson, Saint Anthony Foundation (1986-1987); Vice President, Board of Directors, Prospectors Point Condominium Association (1986-1987); Special Advisor, Western Colorado Historical Museum and Institute (1986); Member, Marketing Committee, Nonprofit Managers Association (1986); Executive Director, Chairman, Board of Directors, Center for Wild Horse and Burro Research (1983-1986); Newsletter Editor, Board of Directors, Sertoma Club Of Grand Junction (1975-1978); Board of Directors, Women's Resource Center, University of Colorado (1978); Public Relations Consultant, Catholic Services Association (1976); Member, Winterization Committee, Community Action Program (1976); Director Grand Junction Day Care Task Force (1976); Member, Editorial Director, Strategic Planning Committee, Colorado Mountain Club (1976); Member, State-wide CB Monitoring Program Committee, NADCO (1976); Board of Directors, Colorado National Monument Association (1976); Secretary, Board of Directors, Mesa County Historical Society (1976); Board of Directors, Women's Resource Center, Grand Junction, CO (1975); Executive Committee, Board of Directors, International Society for the Protection of Mustangs and Burros; President, Board of Directors, Friends of Castlewood Canyon **CW:** Author, "Bench and the Bar" (1991); Editor, Trail and Timberline Magazine (1984); Author, "John Otto of Colorado National Monument" (1984); Executive Editor, Health Care Strategic Management **AW:** First Prize, Colorado Society for Professional Journalists (1988, 1989); News Awards, Colorado Media, Agencies, Clients (1985, 1988); Journalism Awards for Excellence and Best in the Show, Society for Technical Communication (1983); Best TV Commercial Award (1983); Gold Leaf Awards, Best External Publication Award, Colorado Hospital Association, (1982, 1983); Best AV Presentation Award (1982, 1983) **MEM:** International Association of Business Communicators; Professional Photographers of America; British Kinematography; Sound and TV Society; Colorado Horseman's Council; Carriage Association of America; Denver Press Club; Colorado Mountain Club; Appalachian Mountain Club; Colorado Driving Society; Metro State College Society of Professional Journalists; Sigma Delta Chi **MH:** Albert Nelson Marquis Lifetime Achievement Award; Marquis Who's Who Top Professional

KANNAN, SANDRA JEAN, T: Elementary School Educator, Retired Teaching Assistant Principal **I:** Education/Educational Services **DOB:** 10/07/1943 **PB:** Lawrence **SC:** MA/USA **PT:** John Anthony Savinelli **MS:** Married **SPN:** William James Kannan (2/20/1970) **CH:** Cassandra Jean **ED:** MEd, Massachusetts University, Salem, MA (1996); BS, Suffolk University, Boston, MA (1967) **C:** Teaching Assistant Principal, Lawrence School Systems, Massachusetts (1970-2002); Teacher, Derry School District, New Hampshire (1967-1970) **CR:** Elementary Education Curriculum Committee, Addison Gallery, Phillips Academy, Andover, MA (1992-2002) **MEM:** Phi Kappa Phi **MH:** Albert Nelson Marquis Lifetime Achievement Award; Marquis Who's Who Top Professional; Marquis Who's Who Humanitarian Award **B/I:** Ms. Kannan's parents were immigrants and raised five children, and although her father had a limited education, he wanted his children to have more. Her mother was a reader and she it passed down to her children, and as a result, she loved reading and she has always been interested in history in every aspect of the world. She found that no other job allowed you to investigate things as much as teaching did. In addition, from a very young age, teaching was something that she has always wanted to do. **AV:** Painting; Gardening; Cooking; Reading; Travel; Dogs **PA:** Democrat **RE:** Roman Catholic

KANNANGARA, DON WALTER, MD, MSC, PHD, DTM&H, MRCP, T: Infectious Disease Consultant **I:** Medicine & Health Care **DOB:** 06/01/1942 **PB:** Bandaragama **SC:** Sri Lanka **PT:** Don Charles Kannangara; Donna Maggie (Edussuriya) Kannangara **MS:** Married **SPN:** Yoges Kanagaratnam (6/20/1968) **CH:** Nelum; Saman **ED:** PhD in Parasitology, University of London (1974); Diploma in Tropical Medicine, London School of Hygiene (1972); MSc in Parasitology, University of London (1971); MB BS, University of Ceylon, Sri Lanka (1966) **CT:** Diplomate, American Board of Internal Medicine; Diplomate, American Board of Infectious Disease; Diplomate, MRCP U.K. **C:** Assistant Professor, Medicine, Hahneman University, Philadelphia, PA (1981-Present); Assistant Professor, Medicine, Charles Drew Postgraduate School of Medicine (1979-1981); Lecturer in Parasitology, University of Ceylon, Sri Lanka (1968-1974) **CR:** Consultant, Infectious Diseases, St. Joseph Hospital, Girard Medical Center, Philadelphia, Easton Hospital, St. Luke's Hospital, Bethlehem, PA, Warren Hospital, Phillipsburg, PA **MIL:** Colonel Medical Corp, U.S. Army Reserve (Retired) **CW:** Contributor, Numerous Articles, Medical Journals; Contributor, Chapters, Books **AW:** Numerous Military Awards; Mark of Distinction, London University; Nominated Honoree, St. Luke's Hospital **MEM:** American Society of Microbiology; Infectious Disease Society of America; International Society of Infectious Diseases **MH:** Albert Nelson Marquis Lifetime Achievement Award; Marquis Who's Who Top Professional **B/I:** When Dr. Kannangaro studied in college and high school, people who excelled in grades went to medical school and people who received lower grades went into science or art. In addition, she chose her profession because of something that happened more than 50 years ago. Once she got involved in research she kept doing it. Furthermore, what attracted her was that in the beginning she was studying parasites and when she discovered two new species of parasites and the new life cycle so after that she stayed on that research and pathway. **AV:** Previously, ballroom dance; Gardening

KAO, MIN H., T: Co-Founder **I:** Technology **CN:** Garmin Ltd. **PB:** Zhushan **SC:** Taiwan **MS:** Married **SPN:** Fan Kao **CH:** Ken; Jen **ED:** PhD in Electrical Engineering, The University of Tennessee, Knoxville (1977); MS in Electrical Engineering, The University of Tennessee, Knoxville; BS, National Taiwan University **C:** Chairman, Garmin Corporation (Garmin Ltd.) (2007-Present); Chief Executive Officer, Garmin Corporation (Garmin Ltd.) (2007-2012); Co-Founder, Garmin Corporation (Garmin Ltd.) (1989); Systems Analyst, Teledyne Systems; With, Magnavox Advanced Products; With, AlliedSignal; Director, Garmin International, Inc.; Researcher, NASA and U.S. Army **AW:** Named One

of Forbes 400: Richest Americans (2006-Present); Named One of the 50 Who Matter Now, Business 2.0 (2007) **MEM:** National Academy of Engineering

KAPLAN, VIRGINIA, "GINI" LEE, T: Landscape Design & Plant Care **I:** Agriculture **CN:** Independent Contractor **DOB:** 06/07/1955 **PB:** Salem **SC:** OR/USA **MS:** Married **SPN:** Paul C. Kaplan **CH:** Aaron Lee; Sarah Elizabeth; Stephen Eli; Peter Benjamin **ED:** Coursework in Integrative Pest Management, Chemeketa Community College **CT:** Master Gardener **C:** Independent Contractor, Landscape Design & Plant Care **CW:** Author, Poems, "Hazy and Uncharted," "Boots Straps of the Heart," "Fabric of Our Flag," and "High Clouds" **AW:** Honorable Certificate of Academic Recognition, Chemeketa Community College **AS:** Mrs. Kaplan attributes her success to her high opinion of the living plants. When you go against what they need or if you harvest too many, then you have trouble. **B/I:** Mrs. Kaplan was outside a lot because she was a tomboy. Being with the plants was exciting and very calming. She knew she had a interest in horticulture when she graduated high school. **THT:** Mrs. Kaplan has been married to her husband, Paul, for 29 years. Her motto is, "Goodness, respect and decency is important."

KAPTUR, MARCIA, "MARCY" CAROLYN, T: U.S. Representative from Ohio **I:** Government Administration/Government Relations/Government Services **DOB:** 06/17/1946 **PB:** Toledo **SC:** OH/USA **PT:** Stephen Jacob Kaptur; Anastasia Delores (Rogowski) Kaptur **ED:** Honorary LLD, The University of Toledo (1993); MA in Urban Planning, University of Michigan, Ann Arbor, MI (1974); BA in History, University of Wisconsin-Madison (1968); Coursework, Massachusetts Institute of Technology; Coursework, The University of Manchester, England, United Kingdom **C:** Member, U.S. House of Representatives from Ohio's Ninth District (1983-Present); Assistant Director, Urban Affairs and Domestic, Executive Office of the President, The White House (1977-1979); Director of Planning, National Center of Urban Ethnic Affairs, Washington, DC (1975-1977); Urban Planner, Toledo-Lucas County Plan Commissions (1969-1975); Member, Committee on Appropriations **AW:** Ellis Island Medal of Honor (2002); Americanism Award, VFW (1999); Legislator of the Year Award, National Mental Health Association; Director's Award, Georgetown University Edmund A. Walsh School of Foreign Service **MEM:** A. Alfred Taubman College of Architecture and Urban Planning, University of Michigan Alumni Association; American Institute of Certified Planners (AICP); American Planning Association (APA); Polish American Historical Association; Democratic Women's Campaign Association; National Urban League; Fulton County Democratic Women's Club; Lucas County Democratic Business and Professional Women's Club **PA:** Democrat **RE:** Roman Catholic

KARDASHIAN WEST, KIM NOEL, T: Media Personality; Fashion Executive; Model **I:** Media & Entertainment **DOB:** 10/21/1980 **PB:** Los Angeles **SC:** CA/USA **PT:** Robert Kardashian; Kris Jenner; Bruce Jenner (Now Caitlyn Jenner) (Stepparent) **MS:** Married **SPN:** Kanye West (05/24/2014); Kris Humphries (08/20/2011, Divorced 06/03/2013); Damon Thomas (01/22/2000, Divorced 2004) **CH:** North; Chicago; Psalm; Saint **ED:** Diploma, Marymount High School **C:** Apprenticeship/Reading the Law (2019-Present); Clothing Co-designer, Kardashian Kollection (2011-Present); Clothing Co-designer, K-Dash by Kardashian (2010-Present); Contributing Beauty Editor, OK! Magazine (2009-Present); Co-creator, Retail Store, Kardashian Khaos, Las Vegas, NV (2011-2014); Co-de-

signer, Jewelry Line for Virgin Saints and Angels, Swag Designer Jewelry (2010); Co-owner, Clothing Store, DASH, Calabasas, CA, Miami, FL, New York, NY (2006-2017); Launched, Multiple Fragrances; Owner, Kimsaprincess, LLC; Fashion Stylist to the Stars; Closet Designer **CR:** Launched, Shape Wear Line, Kimono (Now Skims) (2019-Present); Creator, Designer, Mobile Game, "Kim Kardashian: Hollywood" (2014-Present); Co-founder, Chief Fashion Stylist, ShoeDazzle (2009-Present); Co-creator, Kardashian Glamour Tan (2010); Spokesmodel, PerfectSkin; Spokesperson, Skechers Shape-Ups **CW:** Appearance, "Keeping Up with the Kardashians" (2007-Present); Appearance, "Oceans 8" (2018); Appearance, "Dash Dolls" (2015); Appearance, "I am Cait" (2015); Appearance, "Kourtney & Khloe Take the Hamptons" (2014-2015); Appearance, "Celebrities Undercover" (2014); Featured, Cover, Paper Magazine (2014); Appearance, "Kourtney & Kim Take Miami" (2013); Actress, "Tyler Perry's Temptation" (2013); Voice Actress, "American Dad!" (2013); Appearance, "30 Rock" (2012); Actress, "Drop Dead Diva" (2012); Appearance, "Kourtney & Kim Take New York" (2011-2012); Co-author, "Dollhouse" (2011); Executive Producer, "SPINdustry" (2010); Co-author with Kourtney and Khloé Kardashian, "Kardashian Konfidential" (2010); Appearance, "90210" (2010); Appearance, "How I Met Your Mother" (2009); Actress, "CSI: NY" (2009); Featured, "Fit in Your Jeans by Friday" (2009); Featured, "Workout with Kim Kardashian" (2008); Actress, "Disaster Movie" (2008); Contestant, "Dancing with the Stars" (2008); Appearance, "Beyond the Break" (2006); Featured, Music Video, Fall Out Boy; Appearances, Television Shows, Music Videos **AW:** Named One of the 10 Most Fascinating People of 2013, Barbara Walters Special (2013); Named Favorite TV Celebrity Reality Star, People's Choice Awards (2012); Named One of the 10 Most Fascinating People of 2011, Barbara Walters Special (2011); Glamour Award for Entrepreneur of the Year (2011) **PA:** Democrat **RE:** Christian

KARP, DAVID, T: Founder; Internet Company Executive; Web Developer **I:** Technology **CN:** Tumblr **DOB:** 07/06/1986 **PB:** New York **SC:** NY/USA **PT:** Michael D. Karp; Barbara (Ackerman) Karp **C:** Founder, Chief Executive Officer, Tumblr Inc., New York, NY (2007-2017); Founder, Software Consulting Company, Davidville (2006-2007); Chief Technology Officer, UrbanBaby, Tokyo, Japan (2002-2006) **CR:** Adjunct Professor, New York University; Investor, Superpedestrian, Inc., Sherpaa, Inc., and Splash **CIV:** Board of Directors, Planned Parenthood Federation of America, Inc. **AW:** Named One of the 40 Under 40, Crain's New York Business (2011); Named One of the Top 35 Innovators in the World Under the Age of 35, MIT Technology Review (2010); Named the Best Young Tech Entrepreneur, Business Week (Now Bloomberg Businessweek) (2009)

KARPEL, CRAIG, T: Journalist, Editor **I:** Writing and Editing **PB:** Midland **SC:** TX/USA **MS:** Married **ED:** AB, Columbia University (1965) **C:** Contributing Editor, Harper's Magazine, New York, NY (1985-1992) **CW:** Author, "The 12-Step Guide for the Recovering Obama Voter" (2012); Author, "The Retirement Myth" (1995); Author, "The Rite of Exorcism" (1974); Contributor, Numerous Articles, Magazines and Newspapers, United States, South America, Europe, Africa and Asia

KATKO, JOHN MICHAEL, T: U.S. Representative, Lawyer **I:** Government Administration/Government Relations/Government Services **DOB:** 11/09/1962 **PB:** Syracuse **SC:** NY/USA **PT:** Andrew Katko; Mary Lou (O'Connor) Katko **MS:** Married

SPN: Robin Katko **CH:** Sean; Liam; Logan **ED:** JD, College of Law, Syracuse University, Cum Laude (1988); BA in Political Science, Niagara University, Cum Laude (1985) **C:** U.S. Representative, New York's 24th Congressional District, United States Congress, Washington, DC (2015-Present); Special Assistant United States Attorney, Eastern District of Virginia to Criminal Division, Narcotic and Dangerous Drug Section, The U.S. Department of Justice (1994-2014); Various Positions Including Supervisor, Narcotics Section, Narcotics Chief, Organized Crime Drug Enforcement Task Force Coordinator, Binghamton Office Supervisor, Team Leader and Grand Jury Coordinator **CIV:** Hockey Coach, Camillus Youth Hockey Association, NY **PA:** Republican **RE:** Roman Catholic

KATZ, JOEL, T: Information and Graphic Designer **I:** Graphic Design **CN:** Joel Katz Design **DOB:** 05/22/1943 **PB:** Hartford **SC:** CT/USA **PT:** Herman J. Katz; Gertrude B. Katz **MS:** Married **SPN:** Patricia Thompson (09/11/1983) **CH:** Benjamin T. Katz **ED:** MFA, Yale University; BFA, Yale University (1967); BA, Scholar of the House, Yale University, with Exceptional Distinction (1965) **C:** Principal, Joel Katz Design (1992-Present); Partner, Katz Wheeler Design, Philadelphia, PA (1979-1992); Senior Designer, Saul Bass, Herb Yager & Associates, Los Angeles, CA (1979); Principal, Joel Katz Design, Philadelphia, PA (1976-1979); Associate, Murphy Levy Wurman, Philadelphia, PA (1972-1976); Art Director, Investors Overseas Services SA, Geneva, Switzerland (1970-1971); **CR:** Adjunct Professor, University of the Arts, Philadelphia, PA (2009-2018); Lecturer, Philadelphia College of Art (1972-1983); Adjunct Professor of Graphic Design, Rhode Island School of Design, Providence, RI (1971); Instructor, Yale School of Art (1966) **CW:** Co-author, "And I Said No Lord" (2012); Co-author, "Designing Information" (2011); Co-author, "The Nature of Recreation" (1973); Co-author, "Aspen Visible" (1972); Associate Editor, Yale Alumni Publications, New Haven, CT (1967-1970); Exhibit, Group Shows, AIGA Communications Graphics, New York, NY, and AIGA Functional Graphics; Represented in Permanent Collections, The Museum of Modern Art, New York, NY, Cooper Hewitt Smithsonian Design Museum, The National Museum of Modern Art, Tokyo and The National Museum of Modern Art, Kyoto; Contributor, Articles to Professional Publications **AW:** Rome Prize, American Academy in Rome (2002-2003); Interior Designer's Choice Award, AIGA Mead Annual Report Show **MEM:** American Institute Graphic Arts (AIGA); Honorary Life Member, International Pediatric Nephrology Association (IPNA) **MH:** Albert Nelson Marquis Lifetime Achievement Award **AS:** Mr. Katz attributes his success to luck and hard work. **B/I:** Mr. Katz became involved in his profession because he was interested in graphic design when he was still in high school. Throughout undergraduate school and high school he designed various student publications, like the literary magazine. So from the middle of high school and onward, he knew that was what he wanted to do.

KATZ, JOEL ABRAHAM, T: Entertainment Attorney **I:** Law and Legal Services **CN:** Greenberg Traurig, LLP **DOB:** 05/27/1944 **PB:** Bronx **SC:** NY/USA **PT:** Harry Katz; Hilda (Weezenthal) Katz **MS:** Divorced **SPN:** Kane Swims (1994, Divorced 2015) **CH:** Leslie Helaine; Jeni Michelle **ED:** Honorary PhD, Kennesaw State University (2014); Honorary PhD, Hunter College, City University of New York (2008); JD, University of Tennessee, Knoxville (1969); BA in Economics, Hunter College, City University of New York (1966) **C:** Founding Partner, Katz, Smith & Cohen (1981-1998); Senior Partner, Galkin, Katz & Tye (1971-1981); Lawyer, Department of Housing and Urban Development (1969-1971); Law Professor, Georgia State University, (1969-1971); Law Clerk, Medium-sized Atlanta Law Firm (1969-1971); Founding Chairman, Global Entertainment and Media Practice, Greenberg Traurig, LLP; Founding Shareholder, Greenberg Traurig, LLP, Atlanta, GA; Co-managing Shareholder Emeritus, Greenberg Traurig, LLP; Member, Music Advisory Board, Hunter College, City University of New York **CR:** Board Member, Music Advisory Board, Hunter College, City University of New York (2011-Present); Special Counsel, Rock and Roll Hall of Fame (2006-Present); General Counsel, Recording Academy (2003-Present); General Counsel, Farm Aid; Member, Board of Directors, Farm Aid; Special Counsel, CMA Country Music Association, Inc; Former Vice Chairman, Gibson Foundation; Affiliate, Gibson Brands, Inc.; Former Vice Chairman, Baldwin; State Music Industry Representative, State of Georgia; Chairman, Entertainment Advisory Council, United Service Organizations; Presenter in Field **CIV:** Chairman, National Board of Directors, T.J. Martell Foundation (2017-Present); Board of Trustees, Clark Atlanta University (2017-Present); Board of Trustees, Berklee College of Music (2014-Present); Board Member, Initial Board of Directors, GRAMMY Museum (2008-Present); Board Member, National Board of Directors, T.J. Martell Foundation (2009-2017); Advisory Board of Directors, T.J. Martell Foundation (1995-2003); Advisory Board, Atlanta Committee for the Olympic Games (1991); Board Member, Berklee College of Music; Member, Board T.J. Martell Foundation, New York, NY; Board of Directors, Very Special Arts; Board of Directors, TouchTunes Music Corporation; Board of Directors, Kiz Toys Inc.; Board of Directors, Luxure Media Group; Board of Directors, MultiplyLive; Board of Directors, Charity Partners LLC; Board of Governors, Buckhead Club; Member, Board of Representatives, Sony/ATV Music Publishing; Director, Foundation Board, Recording Academy **AW:** Named Lawyer of the Year, Entertainment Law – Music, Atlanta, Best Lawyers in America (2014, 2020); Listed, Entertainment Law - Music, Best Lawyers in America (1989-2020); Listed, Entertainment Law - Motion Pictures and Television, Best Lawyers in America (1989-2020); Named to the Dealmakers Elite: New York, Variety (2017-2019); Named One of the Top Music Lawyers, Billboard (2017-2019); Named to the Power 100, Billboard (2012-2019); Listed, Intellectual Property, Chambers USA Guide (2008-2019); Listed, Georgia Super Lawyers (2004-2019); Named One of the Country Power Players, Billboard (2019); Named to the Power 100, Billboard (2019); Named One of Georgia's Most Influential Politically-Connected Attorneys, JAMES Magazine (2019); Named One of the Atlanta 500: Atlanta's Most Powerful Leaders, Atlanta Magazine (2019); Named One of Nashville Country Power Players, Billboard (2016-2018); Named Top Music Lawyer of the Year, Billboard (2017); Named One of the 100 Most Distinguished Alumnus, Centennial Alumnus 100th Anniversary Celebration, University of Tennessee, Knoxville (2017); Named to the Variety 500 (2017); Listed, Legal Impact Report: 50 Game-Changing Attorneys, Variety (2012-2013, 2017); Named to the Legal Elite, Georgia Trend Magazine (2009, 2011-2013, 2015-2017); Named One of the Top 100 Lawyers in Georgia (2008, 2012-2017); Named One of the Power Lawyers: Top 100 Most Influential Entertainment Lawyers in America, The Hollywood Reporter (2007-2017); Spirit of Life Award, City of Hope (2016); Honoree, King of Carnival, Seventh Annual Starfish Ball, NSORO Foundation (2016); Named One of Music's Most Powerful Attorneys, Billboard (2015); Named One of the Top 50 Nashville Players, Billboard (2015); Listed, Who's Who Legal: Sports & Entertainment (2015); Named One of the 100 Power Lawyers in Entertainment, The Hollywood Reporter (2007-2012); Spirit of Excellence Award, T.J. Martell Foundation (2007); "Outstanding Georgia Citizen," Secretary of State, The Mexican American Business Chamber (2007); Listed, Leading Lawyers in America, Lawdragon 500 (2005); Inductee, Hunter College Hall of Fame (2003); Spirit of Music Award, UJA Federation of New York and The Music for Youth Foundation (2003); Heroes Award, Atlanta Chapter of the Recording Academy (2002); Named One of the 100 Most Influential Georgians, Georgia Trend Magazine (2002); "University of Tennessee Founder's Day Medal" (1999); Inductee, Georgia Music Hall of Fame (1995); Listed, Super Lawyers; Ranked Number One Entertainment Attorney, Power 100, Billboard Magazine; AV Preeminent Rated, Martindale-Hubbell **MEM:** Fellow, Royal Society for Encouragement of Arts, Manufacturers and Commerce (RSA) (2005-Present); Chairman, Forum on the Entertainment and Sports Industries, ABA (1999-2001); Advisory Board Member, Atlanta Songwriters Association (1992); Past Vice President, Recording Academy; Past National Trustee, Recording Academy; National Chairman, Board of Trustees, Recording Academy, Atlanta Chapter; Chairman Emeritus, Recording Academy; Inaugural Advisory Board Member, Midem; Chairman, ABA; Atlanta Bar Association; Georgia Bar Association; Tennessee Bar Association; State Bar of Georgia **BAR:** State of Georgia (1971); U.S. Court of Appeals for the Eleventh Circuit (1971); U.S. District Court for the Eastern District of Tennessee (1970); State of Tennessee (1969) **MH:** Albert Nelson Marquis Lifetime Achievement Award (2017)

KATZMANN, ROBERT ALLEN, T: Chief Judge; Professor **I:** Law and Legal Services **CN:** United States Court of Appeals for the Second Circuit **DOB:** 08/22/1953 **PB:** New York **SC:** NY/USA **ED:** JD, Yale Law School (1980); PhD in Government, Harvard University (1978); MA in Government, Harvard University (1975); AB, Columbia University, Summa Cum Laude (1973) **C:** Chief Judge, United States Court of Appeals for the Second Circuit (2013-Present); Adjunct Professor of Law, New York University (2001-Present); Judge, United States Court of Appeals for the Second Circuit (1999-2013); William J. Walsh Professor of Government, Professor of Law, Georgetown University (1992-1999); President, The Governance Institute, Washington, DC (1986-1999); Fellow, The Brookings Institution, Washington, DC (1985-1999); Acting Director of Government Studies, The Brookings Institution, Washington, DC (1998); Adjunct Professor of Law, Public Policy, Georgetown University, Washington, DC (1984-1992); Research Associate, The Brookings Institution, Washington, DC (1981-1985); Law Clerk to Honorable Hugh H. Bownes, United States Court of Appeals for the First Circuit, Concord, NH (1980-1981) **CR:** Visiting Chair, Wayne Morse Professor of Law and Politics, University of Oregon (1992); Visiting Professor of Political Science, Washington Program, University of California Los Angeles (1990-1992); Consultant, Federal Courts Study Committee (1990) **CW:** Author, "When Legal Representation is Deficient: The Challenge of Immigration Cases for the Courts," 143 Daedalus (2014); Author, "Judging Statutes" (2014); Author, "Madison Lecture: Statutes" (2012); Author, "The Marden Lecture: The Legal Profession and the Unmet Needs of the Immigrant Poor," 21 Georgetown Journal of Legal Ethics 3 (2008); Co-Author, "Daniel Patrick Moynihan: The Intellectual in Public Life," Second Edition (2004); Co-Author, "Daniel Patrick Moynihan: The Intellectual in Public Life" (1998); Author, "Courts and Congress" (1997); Editor, "The Law Firm and the Public Good" (1995); Co-Editor, "Managing Appeals in Federal Courts" (1988); Editor, "Judges and Legislators" (1988); Author, "Institutional Disability: The Saga of Transportation Policy for the Disabled" (1986); Author, "Regulatory Bureaucracy: The Federal Trade Commission and Antitrust Policy" (1980); Article and Book Editor, Yale Law Journal (1979-1980); Contributor, Articles, Professional Journals **AW:** Vilcek Prize for Excellence in the Administration of Justice, Vilvek Foundation (2020); Charles Edward Merriam Award, American Political Science Association (2001) **MEM:** Chairman, Legislative Section, Association of American Law Schools (1999-2000); Board of Directors, American Judicature Society (1992-1998); Public Member, Administration Conference, ABA (1992-1995); Vice-Chair, Committee on Government Operations and Separation of Powers, American Bar Association (1991-1994); Fellow, American Academy of Arts & Sciences; Administrative Law Section, American Bar Association; Association of American Law Schools; American Political Science Association; American Judicature Society; The Phi Beta Kappa Society **BAR:** United States District Court for the District of Massachusetts (1984); The District of Columbia (1984); United States Court of Appeals for the First Circuit (1983); State of New York (1983); Massachusetts (1982)

KAUFMANN, CHARLES A., MD, T: Psychiatrist, Neuroscientist, Educator **I:** Medicine & Health Care **DOB:** 03/10/1951 **PB:** New York **SC:** NY/USA **PT:** Harold Joseph Kaufmann; Martha Marcia (Martel) Kaufmann **MS:** Widowed **SPN:** Joan Ruth Zoldessy (04/25/1980, Deceased 09/12/2018) **CH:** Sasha Zoldessy; Amelia Maude; Samuel Aslan **ED:** Residency in Psychiatry, Payne Whitney Psychiatric Clinic (1977-1981); Internship, New York Hospital (1977-1978); Internship, Department of Medicine, Memorial Sloan Kettering Cancer Center (1977); MD, Columbia University (1977); BS, Massachusetts Institute of Technology (1971) **CT:** Diplomate, American Board of Psychiatry and Neurology, Inc. (1982); Licensed Physician, State of New York **C:** Attending Psychiatrist, New York-Presbyterian Hospital (2008-2009); Associate Attending Psychiatrist, Presbyterian Church (1990-2008); Head, Molecular Neurobiology Laboratory, Department of Medical Genetics, New York State Psychiatric Institute (1988-2008); Psychiatrist II, New York State Psychiatric Institute (1986-2008); Science Director, Schizophrenia Research Unit, New York State Psychiatric Institute (1989-1999); Director, Diagnostic Center for Schizophrenia Linkage Studies, Columbia University (1989-1997); Assistant Attending Psychiatrist, Presbyterian Hospital (1986-1990); Guest Investigator, Neuropsychiatry Branch, National Institute of Mental Health (1986-1988); Postdoctoral Fellow, Molecular Neurobiology Laboratory, Center for Neurobiology and Behavior, Columbia University (1986-1988); Attending Psychiatrist, George Washington University Hospital (1982-1985); Attending Psychiatrist, St. Elizabeth's Hospital (1981-1985); Senior Staff Fellow, Adult Psychiatry Branch, National Institute of Mental Health (1981-1985); Ward Administrator, William A. White Division, St. Elizabeth's Hospital (1981-1982); Private Practice **CR:** Visiting Lecturer, Cornell University (1992-Present); Associate Professor, Columbia University (1990-Present); Epidemiology and Genetics Review Committee, National Institute of Mental Health (1992-1996); Residency Selection Committee, Department of Psychiatry, Columbia University (1994); Special Reviewer, Ontario Mental Health Foundation (1992); Assistant Professor of Clinical Psychiatry, Columbia University (1986-1990); Special Reviewer in Psychopathology, Clinical Biology Research Review

Committee, National Institute of Mental Health (1987); Examiner, American Board of Psychiatry and Neurology, Inc. (1985); Working Group on Mental Health Services to the Homeless (1985); Consultant, Sarah's House (1983-1985); Mental Health Task Force, Coalition for the Homeless (1982-1985); National Institute of Neurological Disorders and Stroke (1982-1985); Assistant Clinical Professor of Psychiatry and Behavioral Sciences, George Washington University (1982-1985); Visiting Associate Physician, Rockefeller University Hospital (1981); Instructor of Clinical Psychiatry, Cornell University (1980-1981); Guest Investigator, Laboratory of the Biology of Addictive Diseases (1979-1981); Research Assistant, Neal E. Miller Laboratory, The Rockefeller University (1977) **CW:** Author, "Schizophrenia: New Directions for Clinical Research and Treatment (1996); Co-Editor, "The American Psychiatric Press Review of Psychiatry, Volume 9" (1990); Contributor, Articles, Professional Journals **AW:** Grant, National Institute of Mental Health (1989-Present); Distinguished Investigator Award, NARSAD (Now The Brain & Behavior Research Foundation) (1997); Award, Scottish Rite Schizophrenia Research Program (1995-1997); Scientist Development Award, National Institute of Mental Health (1992-1997); Award, The G. Harold & Leila Y. Mathers Foundation (1994-1996); Physician Scientist Award, National Institute of Mental Health (1987-1992); Judith Silver Memorial Young Scientist Award, National Alliance on Mental Illness (1990); National Scholar, Massachusetts Institute of Technology (1967) **MEM:** Membership Committee, Society of Biological Psychiatry (1993; Distinguished Life Fellow, Falk Fellow, American Psychiatric Association (1979-1981); American Psychological Association; American Association for the Advancement of Science; NYAM; American Society of Clinical Psychopharmacology; American Society of Human Genetics, Incorporated; Association for Research in Nervous and Mental Disease; IBRO; New York Academy of Sciences; International Society of Psychiatric Genetics; Physicians for Social Responsibility; Society Neurosciences; The Phi Beta Kappa Society; Sigma Xi, The Scientific Research Society; Alpha Omega Alpha **MH:** Albert Nelson Marquis Lifetime Achievement Award **AS:** Dr. Kaufmann attributes his success to his intelligence and openness to new ideas. **B/I:** Dr. Kaufmann became involved in his profession because of the psychiatric care he received. **AV:** Hiking; Sea kayaking; Reading **RE:** Jewish

KAUFMANN, MICHAEL C., T: Chief Executive Officer **I:** Medicine & Health Care **CN:** Cardinal Health **ED:** Bachelor of Business Administration in Accounting and Management, Ohio Northern University (1985) **C:** Chief Executive Officer, Cardinal Health, Dublin, OH (2018-Present); Chief Financial Officer, Cardinal Health, Columbus, OH (2014-2017); Chief Executive Officer, Pharmaceutical Segment, Cardinal Health (2008-2014); Group President, Healthcare Supply Chain Services, Medical Segment, Cardinal Health, Columbus, OH (2007-2008) **CIV:** Executive Sponsor, Cardinal Health Women's Initiative Network, Cardinal Health; Board of Directors, MSC Industrial Direct Co. Inc.; Executive Board, Red Oak Sourcing; Trustee, Ohio Northern University; Former Member, Executive Committee, Healthcare Distribution Management Association; Former Member, Executive Committee, National Association of Chain Drug Stores

KAVASERRY, RAMAKRISHNAN, DPT CDN, T: Director, Physical Therapist **I:** Medicine & Health Care **CN:** RVA Physical Therapy **ED:** Doctorate Degree (2018); MS in Physical Therapy, Loma Linda University (2004); BS in Physical Therapy, Sri Ramachandra Institute of Higher Education and

Research (2002) **CT:** Board Certified in Physical Therapy; Board Certified in Myofascial Release; Certified Fitness Trainer; Direct Access, State of Virginia **C:** Director, Physical Therapist, RVA Physical Therapy (2015-Present); Physical Therapist, Welcome Home Care; Physical Therapist, Medical Services of America; Physical Therapist, Hilltop Manor **AW:** Listee, Virginia's Best (2015-Present); Top Doctor (2019) **MEM:** Virginia Physical Therapy Association; American Physical Therapy Association **AS:** Dr. Kavaserry attributes his success to his dedication; he is a very patience-orientated person. In his practice, his goal is never to have patients wait for him. He is happy to meet with them right away. **B/I:** Dr. Kavaserry wanted to be able to serve people in a simple way. He wanted to avoid all complications and surgeries, which inspired him to pursue physical therapy. This way, he can help his patients heal. Further, he used to have fluid accumulation in his brain, which required him to have a shunt. Unfortunately, one day, he had an infection and his doctors took the images of his brain, which showed his brain fluid levels were normal but his shunt was down in his chest. Consequently, the shunt was removed. This experience motivated Dr. Kavaserry to help others avoid the pain he went through.

KAWAMOTO, KENSAKU, T: Associate Chief Medical Information Officer **I:** Medicine & Health Care **CN:** The University of Utah **ED:** MS in Clinical Research, Duke University (2014); MD, Duke University School of Medicine (2008); PhD in Biomedical Engineering/Biomedical Informatics, Duke University (2006); BA in Biochemical Sciences, Harvard University (1999) **C:** Vice Chair of Clinical Informatics, Associate Professor, Department of Biomedical Informatics, The University of Utah (2018-Present); Co-Chair, Interoperability Standards Priorities Task Force, Office of the National Coordinator for Health Information Technology (2018-Present); Committee Member, Health IT Advisory Committee, Office of the National Coordinator for Health Information Technology (2017-Present); Associate Chief Medical Information Officer, The University of Utah (2013-Present); Assistant Professor, Department of Biomedical Informatics, The University of Utah (2011-2018); Assistant Professor, Duke University Health System (2006-2011) **CR:** Board Member, Health Level Seven International (2019-Present); Director, Knowledge Management and Mobilization, The University of Utah Hospitals and Clinics (2011-Present) **AW:** Top 25 Innovators, Modern Healthcare (2019)

KAZMIER, W. JAN, MD, PHD, T: President **I:** Medicine & Health Care **CN:** Regional Allergy, Asthma, and Immunology Center **DOB:** 05/27/1945 **PB:** Lódz **SC:** Poland **PT:** Jan Kazimierczak; Danuta Kazimierczak **MS:** Married **SPN:** Terica Michelle Kazmier **CH:** Peter; Magdalena; Lucas **ED:** Resident in Internal Medicine, Franklin Square Hospital Center, Baltimore, MD; Postdoctoral Fellow, Department of Allergy and Clinical Immunology, Johns Hopkins University, Baltimore, MD; MD, PhD, Medical University of Lodz, Lódz, Poland **CT:** Board Certified in Internal Medicine, Allergy, and Immunology **C:** Founder, President, Regional Allergy, Asthma, and Immunology Center, PC, Kingsport, TN (1989-Present) **CR:** Clinical Assistant Professor, College of Medicine, East Tennessee State University, Johnson City, TN; Research Fellow, Department of Pharmacology, University of Copenhagen, Denmark; Associate Professor, Polish Academy of Sciences, Lódz, Poland; Assistant, Pediatric Ear, Nose, and Throat, Medical University of Lodz, Lódz, Poland; Fellow, American Academy of Allergy, Asthma, and Immunology;

Research Consultant, National Science Foundation **CIV:** Friends in Need; CASA for Children **CW:** Contributor, 60 Research Papers **AW:** Innovation and Excellence Award, Corporate Livewire (2019) **MEM:** American Medical Association; Tennessee Medical Association **AS:** Dr. Kazmier attributes his success to curiosity, his love of medicine, and the need to help people. **B/I:** While studying medicine, Dr. Kazmier was introduced early on to research on the metabolism of histamine and allergic mediators. Since then, he continued research in this field, as well as academic teaching and clinical practice. **AV:** Travel; Photography **PA:** Independent **RE:** Undenominational

KEANE, MARGARET, T: Chief Executive Officer, President **I:** Financial Services **CN:** Synchrony Financial **ED:** Master of Business Administration, St. John's University, Queens, NY (1986); Bachelor of Arts in Government and Politics, St. John's University, Queens, NY (1981) **C:** President, Chief Executive Officer, U.S. Consumer Retail Finance, Synchrony Financial, Stamford, CT (2011-Present); President, Chief Executive Officer, Retail Consumer, Financial Unit, General Electric Capital (2004-2011); Senior Vice President, Operations for Consumer Finance, Americas, General Electric Capital (2002-2004); Chief Quality Officer, General Electric Capital, Stamford, CT (2000-2002); Retail Bank Operations Director, Citibank, New York, NY **AW:** Named, One of The 50 Most Powerful Women, Fortune Magazine (2015); Named, One of The 25 Most Powerful Women in Finance, American Banker (2011)

KEARFOTT, RALPH BAKER, PHD, T: Professor, Mathematician, Researcher, Educator; Computer Scientist **I:** Education/Educational Services **CN:** University of Louisiana **DOB:** 01/27/1954 **PB:** Salt Lake City **SC:** UT/USA **PT:** William E. Kearfott; Edith (Chamberlin) Kearfott **MS:** Married **SPN:** Ruth Constance Mentley (05/24/1976) **CH:** Frances Marie Kearfott **ED:** PhD in Mathematics, The University of Utah (1977); MA, The University of Utah (1974); BA, The University of Utah (1972) **C:** Professor Emeritus, University of Louisiana at Lafayette, Lafayette, LA (2019-Present); Professor, Mathematics, University of Southwestern Louisiana (Now University of Louisiana at Lafayette), Lafayette, LA (1977-2019); Senior Mathematician, ExxonMobil Research and Engineering, ExxonMobil Corporation, Clinton Township, NJ (1985-1986); Teaching Assistant, The University of Texas at Austin, Austin, Texas (1976-1977); Teaching Fellow, The University of Utah, Salt Lake City, Utah (1972-1976) **CR:** Chair, Microprocessor Standards Committee of the IEEE Computer Society, IEEE (2015); Computer Programmer, Center for Numerical Analysis, The University of Texas at Austin, Austin, Texas (1977) **CW:** Editor, "Reliable Computing" (1992-Present); Co-author, "Introduction to Interval Analysis" (2009); Author, "Rigorous Global Search: Continuous Problems" (1996); Contributor, Articles, Professional Journals; Contributor, Chapters, Books **AW:** Grantee, National Science Foundation (1992-1995) **MEM:** IEEE Computer Society, IEEE; American Mathematical Society; Society for Industrial and Applied Mathematics; Mathematical Programming Society; ACM, Inc. **MH:** Albert Nelson Marquis Lifetime Achievement Award **AS:** Dr. Kearfott attributes his success to work, perseverance and early encouragement from his family. **B/I:** Dr. Kearfott became involved in his profession because of his early interests in technology and mathematics, fostered by his family; his uncle was a mathematician, his grandfather was a biologist and his father came from a long line of civil engineers. One of Dr. Kearfott's sisters pursued nuclear engineering, and two other sisters became doctors of medicine.

AV: Competitive swimming; Participating in triathlons; Gardening; Beekeeping **THT:** Throughout his illustrious career, Dr. Kearfott has developed portable software libraries for nonlinear systems and for interval computations, and theory of preconditioning interval systems. He has supervised 13 PhD students, stewarded development of international standards for computer arithmetic, maintained the "Reliable Computing" journal, and advanced the state of the art in verified global optimization and interval computations.

KEARNS, MARTHA MARY, T: Professor, Humanities Educator, Author, Critic **I:** Education/Educational Services **DOB:** 03/23/1945 **PB:** Flint **SC:** MI/USA **PT:** Lewis Gamble Kearns; Mary Lucille (Williamson) Kearns **MS:** Single **ED:** Postgraduate Coursework in Education (1982); MS in Education, Antioch University (1977); BA, Arcadia University (1967) **C:** Adjunct Professor of Art, Moravian College (2003-Present); Lecturer in Art History, Lehigh University (2008-2010); Executive Director, Frankford Style (1992-2006); Professor, Department Chair, Department of Humanities, Antioch University (1988-1989); Artist-in-Residence, The Frankford Group Ministry (1986) **CR:** Curator, Contemporary African Art Meets Traditional, Payne Gallery (2019); Broadway Drama Critic, ICON (2008-2010); Connoisseur, New Art Examiner, Sculpture Magazine (1983-1999); Tyler School of Art, Temple University (1996); Lecturer, Goethe House (1987-1988); Book Critic, The Philadelphia Inquirer (1981-1985) **CIV:** Volunteer Guide, Rosenbach Museum of Library (2016-Present); Friends of UNIFAT (1994-Present); Outstanding Civic Leadership Award, Bridge-Pratt Business Association (1999); Outstanding Citizenship Award, Mayor Good, Philadelphia (1989) **CW:** Author, "Kaethe Kollwitz, Woman and Artist" (1976, 1977, 1991); Video Screenwriter, "Frankford Stories" (1988); Co-Arranger, "My Lifetime Listens to Yours (1982); Contributor, "Voice of Women" (1980) **AW:** Fulbright Fellow to The Netherlands, 1982; Humanities Fellow and Lecturer, Aston Magna Academy of Baroque Music and Art, 1977; WHYY Purchase Prize for video, Frankford Stories, 1988, First Prize, New Works of Merit Playwriting Contest, NYC, 2003; Pennsylvania Council on the Arts Playwriting Stipend Fellowship, 2002-2003, Antioch University Fellowship to the Vatican, Rome, 1986; Arts and Business Partnership Award to FrankfordStyle and Jack's Camera's given by the Arts and Business Council of Greater Philadelphia, 1999 **MEM:** St. Martin's (2016-Present); Dramatists Guild of America, Inc. (1982-Present); Cosmopolitan Club (1979-Present) **MH:** Albert Nelson Marquis Lifetime Achievement Award; Marquis Who's Who Top Professional **B/I:** Ms. Kearns became involved in her profession because of her parents and her long-standing desire to teach. **AV:** Gardening; Renovating and decorating her house; Teaching Sunday school; Reading **PA:** Democrat **RE:** Episcopalian

KEATING, CHRISTOPHER PATRICK, T: Capitol Bureau Chief, Reporter **I:** Media & Entertainment **DOB:** 09/02/1960 **PB:** New York **SC:** NY/USA **PT:** Francis A. Keating; Jeanne Gertrude (Scully) Keating **MS:** Married **SPN:** Margaret Grottola (06/30/1987) **ED:** MS, Columbia University (1984); BA, Fordham University (1982) **C:** Capitol Bureau Chief, Hartford Courant (1995-2000, 2002-Present); Reporter, Hartford Courant (1990-Present); Court Reporter (2001-2002); Reporter, Greenwich Time (1984-1990); Filer, Researcher, Newsweek, New York, NY (1981-1984) **AW:** Second Place, Video Storytelling (2016); Third Place, General Reporting (2015); Second Place, General Reporting (2012); First Place, Spot News Reporting 92011); Hon-

orable Mention, New England Associated Press Newspapers Editors Association (1990); Second Place for Business Reporting, Connecticut Chapter, Society of Professional Journalists (1990); First Place for Feature Writing, Connecticut Chapter, Society of Professional Journalists (1990); First Place for News In-Depth, Connecticut Chapter, Society of Professional Journalists (1987); Master Reporter Award, New England **MH:** Albert Nelson Marquis Lifetime Achievement Award

KEATING, WILLIAM, "BILL" RICHARD, T: U.S. Representative from Massachusetts; Former Prosecutor **I:** Government Administration/Government Relations/Government Services **DOB:** 09/06/1952 **PB:** Norwood **SC:** MA/USA **PT:** William B. Keating; Anna (Welch) Keating **MS:** Married **SPN:** Tevis Keating **CH:** Kristen; Patrick **ED:** JD, Suffolk University Law School (1985); MBA, Boston College (1982); BA, Boston College, Magna Cum Laude (1974) **C:** Member, U.S. House of Representatives from Massachusetts' Ninth Congressional District, United States Congress, Washington, DC (2013-Present); Member, U.S. House Homeland Security Committee (2013-Present); Member, U.S. House Committee on Foreign Affairs (2013-Present); Member, U.S. House Small Business Committee (2011-2013); Member, U.S. House of Representatives from Massachusetts' 10th Congressional District, United States Congress, Washington, DC (2011-2013); District Attorney, Canton, Norfolk County, MA (1999-2010); Member, Norfolk, Bristol and Plymouth District, Massachusetts State Senate, Boston, MA (1985-1998); Member, Eighth Norfolk District, Massachusetts House of Representatives (1979-1985); Member, 19th Norfolk District, Massachusetts House of Representatives, Boston, MA (1977-1979); Partner, Keating & Fishman **CR:** Former Chairman, Steering, Policy and Public Safety Committees, Massachusetts State Senate **AW:** Named Legislator of the Year, Massachusetts Bar Association (1992); Award, Mass Victim Witness Board (1989); Award, Massachusetts Police Association (1988); Award, Massachusetts Municipal Association (1980) **MEM:** LMV; Massachusetts Legislators Association; Massachusetts Bar Association; Knights of Columbus; Order Sons and Daughters of Italy in America; Jaycees **PA:** Democrat **RE:** Roman Catholic

KEATON, DIANE, T: Actress **I:** Media & Entertainment **DOB:** 01/05/1946 **PB:** Los Angeles **SC:** CA/USA **PT:** John "Jack" Newton Ignatius Hall; Jack and Dorothy Deanne (Keaton) Hall **CH:** Dexter (Adopted); Duke (Adopted) **ED:** Coursework, Neighborhood Playhouse, New York (1968); Coursework, Orange Coast College; Coursework, Santa Ana College **CW:** Actress, "Poms" (2019); Voice Actress, "Green Eggs and Ham" (2019); Actress, "Book Club" (2018); Actress, "Hampstead" (2017); Actress, "The Young Pope" (2016); Voice Actress, "Finding Dory" (2016); Actress, Executive Producer, "Love the Coopers" (2015); Actress, "And So It Goes" (2014); Author, "Let's Just Say It Wasn't Pretty" (2014); Actress, "5 Flights Up" (2014); Actress, "The Big Wedding" (2013); Actress, "Darling Companion" (2012); Author, "Then Again" (2011); Actress, "Tilda" (2011); Actress, "Morning Glory" (2010); Actress, "Mad Money" (2008); Actress, "Smother" (2007); Actress, "Mama's Boy" (2007); Actress, "Because I Said So" (2007); Actress, "The Family Stone" (2005); Actress, "Surrender, Dorothy" (2005); Actress, "Something's Gotta Give" (2003); Actress, "On Thin Ice" (2003); Actress, "Crossed Over" (2002); Actress, "Town and Country" (2001); Executive Producer, "Pasadena" (2001); Actress, "Plan B" (2001); Actress, "Sister Mary Explains It All" (2001); Actress, "Hanging Up" (2000); Actress, "The Other Sister" (1999); Actress, "The

Only Thrill" (1997); Executive Producer, "Northern Lights" (1997); Actress, "Marvin's Room" (1996); Actress, "First Wives Club" (1996); Actress, "Father of the Bride 2" (1995); Director, "Unstrung Heroes" (1995); Co-editor, "Mr. Salesman" (1994); Actress, "Amelia Earhart" (1994); Actress, "Manhattan Murder Mystery" (1993); Voice Actress, "Look Who's Talking Now" (1993); Actress, "Running Mates" (1992); Actress, "Father of the Bride" (1991); Director, "Wildflower" (1991); Actress, "The Lemon Sisters" (1990); Actress, "The Godfather, Part III" (1990); Actress, Producer, "The Lemon Sisters" (1990); Actress, "The Good Mother" (1988); Actress, "Radio Days" (1987); Director, Writer, "Heaven" (1987); Actress, "Baby Boom" (1987); Actress, "Crimes of the Heart" (1986); Actress, "Little Drummer Girl" (1984); Actress, "Mrs. Soffel" (1984); Co-Editor, "Still Life" (1983); Actress, "Shoot the Moon" (1982); Actress, "Reds" (1981); Author, "Reservations" (1980); Actress, "Manhattan" (1979); Actress, "Interiors" (1978); Actress, "Annie Hall" (1977); Actress, "Looking for Mr. Goodbar" (1977); Actress, "The Primary English Class" (1976); Actress, "Harry and Walter Go to New York" (1976); Actress, "Love and Death" (1975); Actress, "I Will, I Will...For Now" (1975); Actress, "The Godfather, Part II" (1974); Actress, "Sleeper" (1973); Actress, Film, "Play It Again Sam" (1972); Actress, "The Godfather" (1972); Actress, "Lovers and Other Strangers" (1970); Actress, Play, "Play It Again Sam" (1969); Actress, "Hair" (1968) **AW:** David di Donatello Award (2018); Lifetime Achievement Award, American Film Institute (2017); Trustees Award, International Center of Photography (2008); Golden Icon Award, Zurich Film Festival (2014); Honoree, Film Society of Lincoln Center (2007); Lifetime Achievement Award, Hollywood Film Awards (2005); Golden Globe Award for Best Actress in a Motion Picture-Musical or Comedy, Hollywood Foreign Press Association (1978, 2004); Best Actress, National Board of Review (2003); Elle Women in Hollywood Awards (1998); Woman of the Year, Hasty Pudding Theatricals Society (1991); Academy Award for Best Actress, Academy of Motion Picture Arts & Sciences (1978); BAFTA Award for Best Actress (1978); New York Film Critics Circle Award for Best Actress (1977); National Society Film Critics Award for Best Actress (1977); Numerous Awards **MEM:** Actors' Equity Association

KECK, TRISH HARRIS, T: Artist **I:** Fine Art **CN:** Corazon Gallery **MS:** Widowed **CH:** Lora Nova **ED:** Graduate Coursework, The University of New Mexico; Graduate Coursework, The University of Nevada; BFA, Eastern New Mexico University **C:** Artist, Denver, CO (1980-Present); Teacher, Bauder Fashion College, Arlington, Texas; Teacher, Public Schools, Las Vegas NV **AW:** Named Best of Show; Recipient, Several First Place, Second Place Award, Various Exhibits; Named Valedictorian, High School **MEM:** Trinidad Area Arts Association; Kappa Phi **MH:** Marquis Who's Who Top Professional **AS:** Mrs. Keck attributes her success to hard work and love of her art! **B/I:** Mrs. Keck grew up on a farm and was drawn to the arts. When she was younger, she had paper dolls and she would draw clothes on them. She believes art is something you are born with. She chose pottery as her forte because it kind of evolved. She took a couple of painting classes and painted for a while. It just felt like she needed her hands in the clay, mother Earth. **AV:** Dancing with her husband **THT:** Mrs. Keck is full of Native American spirit.

KEEHN, NEIL F., T: President, Chief Executive Officer **I:** Business Management/Business Services **CN:** The Engineer's Toolbox **DOB:** 10/24/1948 **PB:** Massillion **SC:** OH/USA **PT:** Russell Earl Keehn;

Mary (Danner) L. Keehn **MS:** Single **ED:** Postgraduate Coursework, Pardee Rand Graduate School (1977); Postgraduate Coursework, California Institute of Technology (1974); MS in Electrical Engineering, Arizona State University (1970); BS in Mathematics, Arizona State University (1970) **C:** President, Chief Executive Officer, The Engineer's Toolbox, Santa Monica, CA (2017-Present); President, Chief Executive Officer, The Knowledge Trust, Santa Monica, CA (1992-2006); Senior Systems Engineer, TRW, Inc., Redondo Beach, CA (1985-1992); Founder, President, Strategic Systems (1981-1990); Manager of Advanced Systems Concepts, SAIC, El Segundo, CA (1979-1980); Associate Program Manager, TRW, Inc., Redondo Beach, CA (1977-1979); Member, Technical Staff, Hughes Aircraft Company, El Segundo, CA (1974-1977); Consultant, Technical Staff, Technology Corporation, Santa Monica, CA (1972-1974); Associate Engineer, Martin-Marietta Corporation (1971-1972); Associate Engineer, Lockheed Electronics Company (1970-1971); Reliability Engineering Aide, General Electric Company (1968-1970) **CW:** Contributor, Articles to Professional Journals; Patentee in Digital Signal Processing; Contributor, Public Educational Materials **AW:** Several Awards for Organizing Two National Conferences on Aerospace Defense and Chairing the Aerospace Defense Systems Panel, IEEE **MEM:** The International Institute for Strategic Studies (1983-1993); American Institute of Aeronautics and Astronautics (1973-1993); U.S. Strategic Studies Institute (1973-1992); Chairman, Aerospace Defense System Panel, IEEE (1976-1979); Vice Chairman, Aerospace Defense System Panel, IEEE (1972-1976); IEEE **MH:** Albert Nelson Marquis Lifetime Achievement Award **B/I:** Mr. Keehn became involved in his profession because of his experiences in the MIT Science Reporter program in college. **AV:** Reading; Watching sports **PA:** Independent **RE:** Roman Catholic

KEEHNER, MICHAEL A.M., T: Owner and Managing Director **I:** Financial Services **CN:** Ore Hill Capital LLC **DOB:** 11/15/1943 **PB:** Cedar Rapids **SC:** IA/USA **PT:** Merl Keehner; Loraine Keehner **SPN:** Lee Ann Dunn **CH:** Brigham; Jonathon **ED:** MBA, Harvard Business School, Harvard University, Cambridge, MA, With High Distinction (1971); BS in Nuclear Physics, Massachusetts Institute of Technology (MIT), Cambridge, MA (1965) **C:** Adjunct Professor, Finance and Economics, Faculty Leader, Consultant, Sanford C. Bernstein & Co. Center for Leadership and Ethics, Columbia Business School, Columbia University (2005-Present); Owner and Managing Director, Ore Hill Capitol, LLC, New York, NY (1992-Present); Managing Partner, The Keehner Group, New York, NY (1994-2002); Executive Managing Director, Individual Investor Services, Kidder, Peabody & Co., New York, NY (1990-1994); Managing Director, Executive Committee, Board Member, Kidder Peabody International, New York, NY (1987-1994); President, Kidder Peabody International Corp., New York, NY (1989-1990); Investment Banking Manager, Corporate Finance Division, Kidder Peabody & Co., New York, NY (1971-1989); President, Chief Executive Officer, KP Exploration, Inc., New York, NY (1982-1988); Partner, Shareholder, Kidder Peabody & Co., New York, NY (1980); Engineering Manager, Radiological Engineer, General Dynamics Corporation, Quincy, MA (1965-1969) **CR:** Board of Directors, Oppenheimer Holdings, Inc. (2008-2017); Director, Inexco Oil Company, Lear Seigler Seating and Numerous Private Companies; Director, SO.P.AF.S.p.A., an Italian Merchant Bank, Beinto y Monjardin, a Spanish Investment Bank, and Euroclear Clearance System Public Limited Company; Guest Professor, Finance Department, University of New Mexico; Chairman, Kidder, Peabody Corporation; Adviser for Cor-

porate Leaders on a Range of Complex Strategic, Financial, and Business Issues; Investment, Credit, Strategic Planning and Commitment Committees, Kidder, Peabody & Co.; Management and Audit Committees, Kidder, Peabody Group, Inc.; Baker Scholar, Loeb Rhoades Fellow, Harvard Business School, Harvard University **CIV:** Adviser, Lecturer, Inspiring Capital (2013-Present); Private Tutor (2017); Associate, Brooklyn Museum; Past President, Heights Casino Athletic Club; Treasurer, Point O'Woods Association **MEM:** National Association of Corporate Directors (NACD) (2009-2016); Rembrandt Club; Long Island Wyandanch Club **MH:** Albert Nelson Marquis Lifetime Achievement Award; Marquis Who's Who Top Professional **B/I:** Mr. Keehner became involved in his profession because Harvard University inspired him to do so. **AV:** Sailing; Deep-sea diving; Early American history; Information technology

KEENE, LONNIE S., ESQ., I: Law and Legal Services **CN:** The Law Office of Lonnie S. Keene, Esq. **ED:** JD, New York University (1998); MPA, Harvard University (1984); BS, United States Military Academy West Point (1976) **C:** Attorney, The Law Office of Lonnie S. Keene, Esq. (2018-Present); Senior Ethics Officer, United Nations (2016-2017); Managing Director, Kroll (2013-2016); Court-Appointed Corporate Compliance Monitor, New York (2010-2013); Executive Vice President, Chief Compliance Officer, MoneyGram (2008-2010); Vice President, Associate General Counsel, Goldman Sachs (2002-2008); Associate, Wollmuth Maher & Deutsch LLP (2002); Associate, Milbank LLP (1999-2001); Associate, Linklaters (1998-1999); Policy Analyst, Office of Science & Technology Policy, The White House (1994-1995); Policy Planning Staff Member, U.S. Department of State (1990-1994); Assistant Army Attaché, U.S. Embassy, China (1988-1990); Assistant Professor, Instructor, United States Military Academy West Point (1984-1987) **MIL:** Lieutenant Colonel, U.S. Army (1976-1995) **AW:** Scholar, The Olmsted Foundation (1981-1983); Legion of Merit, U.S. Army; Meritorious Honor Award, U.S. Department of State **MEM:** Council on Foreign Relations; National Organization of Veterans' Advocates, Inc. **BAR:** New York State Bar Association; United States Court of Appeals for Veterans Claims **MH:** Albert Nelson Marquis Lifetime Achievement Award; Marquis Who's Who Top Professional **AV:** Golfing; Enjoying art; Traveling; Playing baseball

KEIDEL, ROBERT W., PHD, T: Management Consultant, Writer, Educator **I:** Consulting **CN:** Robert Keidel Associates **DOB:** 02/25/1943 **PB:** Philadelphia **SC:** PA/USA **PT:** Phillip Charles Keidel; Phyllis (Wooler) Keidel **MS:** Married **SPN:** Carole Anne Zneimer (09/28/1974) **CH:** Carly Margaret; Andrew Lewis (Deceased) **ED:** Doctor of Philosophy in Social System Sciences, Wharton School, University of Pennsylvania (1979); Master of Business Administration, Wharton School, University of Pennsylvania (1966); Bachelor of Arts, Williams College (1964) **C:** Principal, Robert Keidel Associates, Philadelphia, PA (1987-Present); Clinical Professor Emeritus, Management Department, Bennett S. LeBow College of Business, Drexel University, Philadelphia, PA (1999-2017); Assistant Professor, School of Business Administration, Temple University, Philadelphia, PA (1979-1983); Consultant, United States Office of Personnel Management, Washington, DC (1978-1979); Program Consultant, National Center for Productivity and Quality of Working Life, Washington, DC (1977-1978); Organization Consultant, Jamestown Area Labor Management Committee, New York (1975-1977); Management Research Analyst Management and Behavioral Science Center, Wharton School, University of Pennsylvania, Philadelphia,

PA (1974-1975); Corporate Project Manager, Walworth Company, Bala Cynwyd, PA (1972-1974); Management Analyst, Division of Science Management Corporation, Wofac Company, Moorestown, NJ (1970-1972) **CR:** Affiliated Faculty, Graduate Program in Organizational Dynamics, University of Pennsylvania (2018-Present); Strategy Contributor, Wharton Blog Network (2013-Present); Director, Robert Wooler Company, Dresher, PA (1983-Present); Clinical Professor, Drexel University, Philadelphia, PA (2010-2017); Visiting Associate Professor, Drexel University, Philadelphia, PA (1999-2010); Lecturer, Graduate Program in Organizational Dynamics, University of Pennsylvania, Philadelphia, PA (1997-1999); Senior Consultant, Wharton Center for Applied Research (1987-1992); Senior Fellow, Wharton Applied Research Center, University of Pennsylvania (1983-1987); Senior Field Associate, American Center for Quality of Working Life (1979-1982); Faculty Fellow of Productivity Research, United States Office of Personnel Management (1979-1981) **MIL:** Lieutenant, United States Navy (1966-1979) **CW:** Author, "The Geometry of Strategy" (2010); Author, "Say It with a Slogan," Wall Street Journal (1997); Author, "Seeing Organizational Patterns" (1995); Author, "Corporate Players" (1988); Author, "Game Plans" (1985); Author, "A New Game for Managers To Play," The New York Times (1985); Contributor, Numerous Articles to Professional Journals **AW:** Recipient, MBA-Level Distinguished Teaching Awards (2001, 2004-2008) **MH:** Albert Nelson Marquis Lifetime Achievement Award **AS:** Dr. Keidel attributes his success to his family and colleagues, and to a wide variety of professional experiences. **B/I:** Dr. Keidel decided to enter his profession because he wanted a mix of writing and teaching, as well as consulting. **AV:** Reading; Writing; Drawing; Golf **PA:** Independent

KEITH, TOBY, T: Singer, Songwriter **I:** Media & Entertainment **DOB:** 07/08/1961 **PB:** Clinton **SC:** OK/USA **PT:** Hubert K. Covel Jr.; Joan Covel **MS:** Married **SPN:** Tricia Lucus (03/24/1984) **CH:** Shelley Covel Rowland (Adopted); Krystal LaDawn Covel Sandubrae; Stelen Keith Covel **ED:** Honorary Doctorate, Villanova University, Villanova, PA **C:** Founder, Show Dog Nashville Records (2005-Present); Signed with, DreamWorks, Nashville, TN (1999); Signed with, Mercury Records, Nashville, TN (1984-1999); Defensive End, Oklahoma Outlaws, U.S. Football League (USFL); Defensive End, Oklahoma City Drillers, Minor League, Semipro Football Team; Member, Easy Money Band; From Derrick Hand to Operations Manager, Oil Fields **CW:** Singer, "35 MPH Town" (2015); Singer, "Drinks After Work" (2013); Singer, "Hope on the Rocks" (2012); Singer, "Clancy's Tavern" (2011); Singer, "Red Solo Cup" (2011); Singer, "Bullets in the Gun" (2010); Singer, "American Ride" (2009); Singer, "That Don't Make Me a Bad Guy" (2008); Writer, Producer, Actor, "Beer for My Horses" (2008); Singer, "Big Dog Daddy" (2007); Singer, "A Classic Christmas" (2007); Singer, "Love Me If You Can" (2007); Singer, "White Trash with Money" (2006); Actor, "Broken Bridges" (2006); Singer, "Honkytonk University" (2005); Singer, "As Good as I Once Was" (2005); Singer, "Greatest Hits 2" (2004); Singer, "20th Century Masters- The Millennium" (2003); Singer, "Whiskey Girl" (2003); Singer, "Shock 'n Y'all" (2003); Singer, "Unleashed" (2002); Singer, "Pull My Chain" (2001); Singer, "How Do You Like Me Now?" (2000); Singer, "How Do You Like Me Now?" (1999); Singer, "Greatest Hits, Volume One" (1998); Singer, "Dream Walkin'" (1997); Singer, "Blue Moon" (1996); Singer, "Boomtown" (1995); Singer, "Christmas to Christmas" (1995); Singer, "Toby Keith" (1993); Singer, "Should've Been a Cowboy" (1993); Appearances,

Television Shows **AW:** CMA Award for Music Video of the Year, CMA Country Music Association Inc. (2005, 2012); Award for Video of Year, Academy of Country Music Awards (2012); Tex Ritter Award, Academy of Country Music (2009); Awards for Favorite Male Country Artist, American Music Awards (2004, 2006); Named Country Artist of the Year, Billboard Music Awards (2005); Award for Hottest Video of the Year, Country Music Television, Inc. (2005); CMA Award for Country Album Artist of the Year, CMA Country Music Association Inc. (2005); Award for Best Country Album, American Music Awards (2004); Award for Album of the Year, Academy of Country Music Awards (2002, 2003); Named Entertainer of the Year (2002, 2003); Award for Top Male Vocalist, Academy of Country Music Awards (2000, 2003); Award for Favorite Country Album, American Music Awards (2003); Named Most Played Song of the 2000s, Billboard; Named Most Played Song of the Decade in the 90s, Billboard

KELLER, THOMAS A., T: Chef; Restaurateur; Author **I:** Food & Restaurant Services **DOB:** 10/14/1955 **PB:** Oceanside **SC:** CA/USA **MS:** Married **SPN:** Laura Cunningham **ED:** Honorary Degree of Culinary Arts, Johnson & Wales University (2003) **C:** Chef, Owner, Bouchon Bakery & Cafe, New York, NY (2011-Present); Chef, Owner, Ad Hoc, Yountville, CA (2006-Present); Chef, Owner, Per Se, New York, NY (2004-Present); Chef, Owner, Bouchon, Las Vegas, NV (2004-Present); Chef, Owner, Bouchon Bakery, Yountville, CA (1998-Present); Chef, Owner, The French Laundry, Yountville, CA (1994-Present); Chef, Owner, Bouchon Bar, Beverly Hills, CA (2009-2017); Chef, Owner, Bouchon Bakery, Beverly Hills, CA (2009-2017); Executive Chef, Checkers Hotel Kampinski, Los Angeles, CA (1991-1992); Consultant, John Clancey & Chez Louis Restaurants, NY (1990-1991); Chef, Owner, Rakel, NY (1986-1990); Chef de Cuisine, Restaurant Raphael, NY (1985-1986); Chef, Owner, Bouchon Bakery, Time Warner Center, NY; Executive Chef, Checkers Hotel, Los Angeles, CA; Guy Savoy and Taillevent, France; With, Restaurant, Palm Beach, FL **CR:** Board Trustee, Culinary Institute of America (2010); Advisory Board, California Milk (1997-1998); President, EVO, Inc. (1992); Consultant, "Spanglish"; Consultant, "Ratatouille"; Creator, Napa Valley Cabernet Modicum; Designer, White Porcelain Dinnerware by Raynaud, Hommage Point; Designer, Silver Hollow Ware by Christofle; Spokesperson, Hommage; President, Bocuse d'Or **CW:** Co-Author, "Bouchon Bakery" (2012); Author, "Ad Hoc at Home" (2009); Author, "Under Pressure: Cooking Sous Vide" (2008); Author, "Bouchon" (2004); Author, "The French Laundry Cookbook" (1999); Author, Introductions/Forwards, Several Other Cookbooks **AW:** Golden Plate Award, American Academy of Achievement (2014); Chevalier, French Legion of Honor (2011); America's Top Restaurant Award for Per Se, Zagat Survey (2008); Outstanding Restaurateur, James Beard Foundation (2007); Outstanding Restaurant Award, James Beard Foundation (2006); Illy Best New Restaurant Award (2005); Best Chef, Readers' Digest (2004); Best Wine Director, San Francisco Magazine (2002); America's Best Chef, Time Magazine (2001); Wedgewood Award, World Master in Culinary Arts (2001); Design Award, International Association of Culinary Professionals (1999); Versailles Cookbook Award (1999); Chef of the Year, Bon Appétit (1998); Best Chef, San Francisco Focus (1997); Outstanding Chef: America (1997); Robert Mondavi Culinary Award of Excellence (1997); Ivy Award, Restaurants & Institutions (1996); Named Best American Chef: California (1996); Listee, America's Best New Chefs, Food & Wine Magazine (1988); Cookbook of the Year; Julia Child First

Cookbook Award; Inductee, Culinary Hall of Fame **MEM:** Relais & Chateaux: Relais Gourmands, Traditions & Qualité

KELLEY, DAVID EDWARD, T: Executive Producer, Writer **I:** Media & Entertainment **DOB:** 04/04/1956 **PB:** Waterville **SC:** ME/USA **PT:** Jack Kelley; Ginny Kelley **MS:** Married **SPN:** Michelle Pfeiffer (11/13/1993) **CH:** John Henry; Claudia Rose (Adopted) **ED:** JD, Boston University (1983); BA, Princeton University (1979) **C:** Chief Executive Officer, David E. Kelley Productions, Inc., Los Angeles, CA **CW:** Creator, Writer, Executive Producer, "Goliath" (2016-Present); Creator, Writer, Executive Producer, "Big Little Lies" (2017-2019); Creator, Writer, Executive Producer, "Mr. Mercedes" (2017); Creator, Writer, Executive Producer, "The Crazy Ones" (2013-2014); Co-Creator, Writer, Executive Producer, "Monday Mornings" (2012-2013); Creator, Writer, Executive Producer, "Harry's Law" (2011-2012); Co-creator, Writer, Executive Producer, "Wonder Woman" (2011); Creator, Writer, Executive Producer, "Legally Mad" (2009-2010); Creator, Writer, Executive Producer, "Boston Legal" (2004-2009); Creator, Writer, Executive Producer, "Life on Mars" (2008); Creator, Writer, Executive Producer, "The Wedding Bells" (2006-2007); Creator, Writer, Executive Producer, "The Law Firm" (2005); Creator, Writer, Executive Producer, "The Brotherhood of Poland, New Hampshire" (2003-2004); Creator, Writer, Executive Producer, "The Practice" (1997-2004); Creator, Writer, Executive Producer, "Boston Public" (2000-2004); Creator, Writer, Executive Producer, "Girls Club" (2002); Creator, Writer, Executive Producer, "Ally McBeal" (1997-2002); Creator, Writer, Executive Producer, "Snoops" (1999-2000); Creator, Writer, Executive Producer, "Chicago Hope" (1994-2000); Writer, Producer, "Lake Placid" (1999); Creator, Writer, Executive Producer, "Picket Fences" (1992-1996); Creator, Writer, Executive Producer, "L.A. Law" (1986-1994); Writer, Story Editor, Executive Story Editor, Supervising Producer, Executive Producer, Television Shows and Films **AW:** Emmy Award for Outstanding Limited Series, Academy of Television Arts & Sciences (2017); Named to the Television Hall of Fame (2014); Peabody Awards (1998, 2002, 2005); Emmy Award for Outstanding Drama Series, Academy of Television Arts & Sciences (1998, 1999); Emmy Award for Outstanding Comedy Series, Academy of Television Arts & Sciences (1999); Emmy Award for Best TV Series - Musical or Comedy, Academy of Television Arts & Sciences (1997, 1998); Golden Globe Award for Best TV Drama, Hollywood Foreign Press Association (1998); Golden Globe Award for Best TV Series - Musical or Comedy, Hollywood Foreign Press Association (1997); Emmy Award for Outstanding Drama Series, Academy of Television Arts & Sciences (1989, 1990, 1993, 1994); Emmy Award for Outstanding Writing in a Drama Series, Academy of Television Arts & Sciences (1989, 1990); Numerous Awards

KELLMAN, BARNET, T: Professor, Robin Williams Endowed Chair in Comedy **I:** Education/Educational Services **CN:** University of Southern California School of Cinematic Arts **DOB:** 11/09/1947 **PB:** New York **SC:** NY/USA **PT:** Joseph A.G. Kellman; Verona D. (Kramer) Kellman **MS:** Married **SPN:** Nancy Mette (1982) **CH:** Katherine Mette; Eliza Mette; Michael Mette **ED:** PhD, Union Institute & University (1972); Postgraduate Coursework, Yale University (1970); BA, Colgate University, Magna Cum Laude (1969) **C:** Robin Williams Endowed Chair in Comedy, University of Southern California (2017-Present); Professor, School of Cinematic Arts, University of Southern California (2011-Present); Co-Founder, Director of Comedy, University of Southern California (2011-Present); Chair of Film and Television Production, School of Cinematic Arts, University of Southern California (2020); Director, New York Theatre (1971-1990) **CR:** Faculty, American Film Institute (2008-2011); Adjunct Faculty, Graduate Film Division, Columbia University (1984-1987); Teacher, Guest Director, UNCSA (1973-1980); Circle in the Square Acting School (1973-1977); Adjunct Faculty, City College of New York (1975-1976) **CW:** Director, "Murphy Brown" (2018) Director, "Out of the Mouths of Babes" (2016); Director, "The Middle" (2009-2011); Director, Producer, "Notes From The Underbelly" (2008-2010); Director, "Monk" (2008); Director, "My Boys" (2006); Director, "Four Kings" (2006); "Like Family" (2003); "Family Affair" (2003); "The George Lopez Show" (2002); Director, "Alias" (2002); "Mary and Rhoda" (2000); "Ally McBeal" (2000); "Once and Again" (2000); Director, "Defiled" (2000); "For Your Love" (1998); "Felicity" (1999); Director, "Slappy and the Stinkers" (1997); "Suddenly Susan" (1996); Director, "E.R." (1996); "Life with Roger" (1996); "Hope and Gloria" (1995); Co-Executive Producer, Director, "Bless This House" (1995); "If Not For You" (1995); Executive Producer, Director, "Something Wilder" (1994); Co-Executive Producer, Director, "Thunder Alley" (1994); Co-Executive Producer, Director, "The Second Half" (1993); Co-Executive Producer, Director, "Mad About You" (1992-1993); Co-Executive Producer, Director, "Good Advice" (1992-1993); Producer, Director, "Murphy Brown" (1989-1992); Director, "Straight Talk" (1992); Director, "The Loman Family Picnic" (1989); Director, "Designing Women" (1987); Director, "My Sister Sam" (1987); Director, "All is Forgiven" (1986); Director, "Key Exchange" (1985); Director, "Danny and the Deep Blue Sea" (1984); Director, "The Good Parts" (1982); Director, "Key Exchange" (1981); Director, "Breakfast with Les and Bess" (1982); Director, "Gemini," Showtime (1981); Associate Artistic Director, Williamstown Theatre Festival (1974-1975); Author, Contributor, Numerous Profiles, Interviews and Citations; Director, Six Seasons, Eugene O'Neill Theater Center **AW:** Emmy Award, Outstanding Direction of a Comedy Series, Murphy Brown (1992); Emmy Award, Outstanding Director in Comedy Series (1992); Emmy Award, Best Comedy, Murphy Brown (1991); Emmy Nomination, Outstanding Direction of a Comedy Series, Murphy Brown (1991); Director's Guild Award (1990); Emmy Nomination, Outstanding Direction of a Comedy Series, Murphy Brown (1990); Nomination, Directors Guild of America Award, Outstanding Direction of a Comedy Series, Murphy Brown (1990); Emmy Nomination, Producer, Best Comedy Murphy Brown (1990); Emmy Nomination, Outstanding Direction of a Comedy Series, Murphy Brown (1989); Viewers for Quality Television Award (1989); Directors Guild of America Award, Outstanding Direction of a Comedy, Murphy Brown (1989); Media Access Award (1989); Directors Guild of America Award Nomination, Outstanding Direction of a Comedy Series, Murphy Brown (1988); Emmy Nomination, Outstanding Direction of a Comedy Series, Murphy Brown (1988); Monitor Award, Best Director, Pepsi, To The Victors, Starring Martin Sheen (1985); Daytime Emmy Nomination, Best Direction, Another World (1981); Danforth Graduate Fellowship (1969 - 1975); Thomas J. Watson Fellowship (1969- 1971); Austen Colgate Scholar, The Phi Beta Kappa Society **MEM:** Stage Directors and Choreographers Society (1984-1986); Grant Auditor, Theatre Communications Group (1979); AEA; SAG-AFTRA; Directors Guild of America; Board of Directors, New Dramatists; Los Angeles Institute of the Humanities **MH:** Albert Nelson Marquis Lifetime Achieve-

ment Award **AS:** Mr. Kellman attributes his success to a passion for theater, an appreciation for comedy, doting parents, and numerous teachers that believed in him. **B/I:** Mr. Kellman became involved in his profession because of the media he consumed as a child and growing up just a short way from Broadway. **AV:** Playing tennis **RE:** Jewish **THT:** Mr. Kellman states, "Try to live in the moment even though it's hard."

KELLY, ALFRED F. JR., T: Chief Executive Officer **I:** Financial Services **CN:** Visa Inc. **ED:** MBA, Iona College (1981); BA in Liberal Arts, Iona College (1980) **C:** Chief Executive Officer, Visa Inc. (2016-Present); President, Head Global Consumer Group, American Express Company (2007-2010); Group President, U.S. Consumer & Small Business Service, American Express Company (2000-2007); President, Consumer Card Services Group, TRS, American Express Company (1998-2000); Executive Vice President, General Manager, Consumer Marketing, TRS, American Express Company (1998-2000); Executive Vice President, General Manager, Consumer Marketing, TRS, American Express Company (1997-1998); Head, Info Systems, The White House, Washington, DC (1985-1987); With, PepsiCo, Inc. (1981-1985); Adjunct Assistant Professor, Iona College, New Rochelle, NY (1980-1985); Executive Vice President, General Manager, U.S. Consumer Card Marketing, American Express Company **CR:** Board of Directors MetLife, Inc. (2009-Present); Board of Directors, Hershey Co. (2005-2007) **CIV:** Trustee, Iona College, New Rochelle, NY; Vice Chairman, Wall Street Charity Golf Classic; Board of Directors, Thomas and Agnes Carvel Foundation Children's Rehabilitation Center, St. Agnes Hospital; Board of Directors, Concern Worldwide USA; Board of Directors, Iona Preparatory School; Trustee, New York Presbyterian Hospital; Trustee, St. Joseph's Seminary & College **AW:** The Journal News Westchester Business Leader of the Year Award (2009) **MEM:** Council on Foreign Relations

KELLY, COLLEEN A., PHD, T: Secondary School Educator **I:** Education/Educational Services **DOB:** 02/04/1934 **PB:** Chicago **SC:** IL/USA **PT:** Patrick Bernard Kelly; Mabel Virginia (Smith) Kelly **MS:** Single **ED:** PhD, University of Connecticut (1983); MA, New York University (1974); MA, St. John's University, Jamaica, NY (1966); BA, Pace University (1955) **C:** Teacher, Fairfield High School, Fairfield, CT (1968-2006); Adjunct Professor, Central Connecticut State University, New Britain, CT (1987-1997); Chairman, Department of History, John F. Kennedy High School, Somers, NY (1961-1968); Teacher, Our Lady of Sorrows School, White Plains, NY (1960-1961); Teacher, St. John's School, Mahopac, NY (1958-1960); Instructor, Good Counsel College, White Plains, NY (1955-1958) **CR:** Commissioner, National Commission on Asia in the Schools (1999-Present); Consultant, McDougall, Littell & Company (1986-1987) **CW:** Author, Poetry Collection, "Dancing For Joy" (2018); Author, Poetry Collection, "Observations" (2018); Author, Poetry Collection, "I've Been Thinking" (2009); Author, Poetry Collection, "As I Was Saying" (2009); Editor, "Asia in Connecticut: A Catalogue of Asian Resources in Connecticut and Environments" (1996); Contributor, Writer Teachers Manual, "A World History, Links Across Time and Place" (1987); Editor, "A Catalogue of Asian Studies Resources in Connecticut" (1980); Co-Author, "Indian Summer" (1976, 1979); Co-Author, Filmstrip, "China's Communes" (1975) **AW:** Legacy Teacher Award, Fairfield High School, Fairfield, CT (2017); Pier Fellow, Yale University (1996-1997); Fulbright Grantee (1967, 1984); Grantee, University of Connecticut Research Foundation (1981);

International Scholar, Delta Kappa Gamma (1981); Named, Alumni of the Year, Pace University (1981) **MEM:** Delta Kappa Gamma Alpha Alpha Chapter (2018); Buchanan Prize Committee, Association for Asian Studies (2003-2005); Executive Committee, New England Conference, Association for Asian Studies; Comparative and International Education Society; Women of Distinction, Pace University **MH:** Albert Nelson Marquis Lifetime Achievement Award **B/I:** Dr. Kelly became involved in her profession because she intended to become a journalist but became "sidetracked." **AV:** Photography; Writing; Traveling; Art; Music **PA:** Democrat **RE:** Roman Catholic **THT:** Dr. Kelly is primarily writing poetry in her retirement. Her father, Patrick, was a defense attorney while her mother, Mabel, worked for an insurance company; both of them were great writers. Her sister, Patricia, was a principal of a junior high school in the Bronx, New York.

KELLY, GARY CLAYTON, T: Chairman, Chief Executive Officer **I:** Leisure, Travel & Tourism **CN:** Southwest Airlines Co. **DOB:** 03/12/1955 **PB:** San Antonio **SC:** TX/USA **PT:** Clayton Kelly; Carol G. Kelly **CH:** Caroline; Elizabeth **ED:** BBA in Accounting, University of Texas (1977) **CT:** Certified Public Accountant, State of Texas **C:** Chairman, Chief Executive Officer, Southwest Airlines Co., Dallas, TX (2008-Present); President, Southwest Airlines Co. (2008-2017); Chairman, Chief Executive Officer, Southwest Airlines Co., Dallas, TX (2008); Vice Chairman, Chief Executive Officer, Southwest Airlines Co., Dallas, TX (2004-2008); Executive Vice President, Chief Financial Officer, Southwest Airlines Co., Dallas, TX (2001-2004); Vice President of Finance, Chief Financial Officer, Southwest Airlines Co., Dallas, TX (1989-2001); Controller, Southwest Airlines Co., Dallas, TX (1986-1989); Controller, Systems Center Inc., Irving, TX; Audit Manager, Arthur Young & Co., Dallas, TX **CR:** Board of Directors, Jefferson-Pilot Corp. (2004-Present); Board of Directors, Air Transport Association America (2004-Present); Board of Directors, Southwest Airlines Co. (2004-Present) **CIV:** Member, Advisory Council, McCombs School of Business, The University of Texas at Austin **AW:** Tony Jannus Award for Distinguished Achievement in Commercial Air Transportation (2016); McLane Leadership in Business Award, Texas A&M University (2013); Inductee, The McCombs School Business Hall of Fame (2013); CEO of Year, Dallas Business Journal (2011); Distinguished Alumnus Award, The University of Texas at Austin (2010); One of The 25 Most Influential Executives, Business Travel News (2004) **AV:** Playing guitar

KELLY, GEORGE, "MIKE" JOSEPH JR., T: U.S. Representative from Pennsylvania **I:** Government Administration/Government Relations/Government Services **DOB:** 05/10/1948 **PB:** Pittsburgh **SC:** PA/USA **MS:** Married **SPN:** Victoria Kelly **CH:** George III; Brendan; Charlotte; Colin **ED:** BA, University of Notre Dame (1970) **C:** Member, U.S. House of Representatives from Pennsylvania's 16th Congressional District, United States Congress, Washington, DC (2019-Present); Member, U.S. House Committee on Oversight and Government Reform, Washington, DC (2011-Present); Member, U.S. House Committee on Foreign Affairs, Washington, DC (2011-Present); Member, U.S. House Committee on Education and the Workforce, Washington, DC (2011-Present); Owner, Mike Kelly Chevrolet Cadillac, Inc. (1995-Present); Member, U.S. House of Representatives from Pennsylvania's Third Congressional District, United States Congress, Washington, DC (2011-2019); Employee, Kelly Chevrolet-Cadillac, Inc., Butler, PA (1970-1995); Member, U.S. Committee on Ways and

Means **CR:** Former Member, Butler School Board of Education; Former Member, Butler City Council **AW:** Named to Butler County Sports Hall of Fame (1999) **PA:** Republican **RE:** Roman Catholic

KELLY, JOHN, "TRENT" TRENT, T: U.S. Representative from Mississippi **I:** Government Administration/Government Relations/Government Services **CN:** U.S. House of Representatives **DOB:** 03/01/1966 **PB:** Union **SC:** MS/USA **PT:** John Kelly; Barbara Kelly **MS:** Married **SPN:** Sheila Kelly **CH:** Three Children **ED:** Master of Arts, United States Army War College (2010); Doctor of Jurisprudence, University of Mississippi School of Law (1994); Bachelor of Business Administration, University of Mississippi; Associate's Degree, East Central Community College **C:** Member, U.S. House of Representatives from Mississippi's First Congressional District (2015-Present); District Attorney, Mississippi's First Judicial District (2012-2015); City Prosecutor, Tupelo, MS (1999-2011); Lawyer, Private Practice (1994-1999); Member, Committee on Agriculture; Member, Committee on Small Business; Member, Committee on House Armed Services Committee; Member, Republican Study Committee **MIL:** Brigadier General, Joint Force Headquarters, Mississippi Army National Guard (2018-Present); With, Mississippi Army National Guard (1985-Present) **MEM:** Phi Kappa Tau

KELLY, LAURA, T: Governor of Kansas **I:** Government Administration/Government Relations/Government Services **DOB:** 01/24/1950 **PB:** New York **SC:** NY/USA **MS:** Married **SPN:** Ted Daughety (1979) **CH:** Kathleen; Molly **ED:** MS in Therapeutic Recreation, Indiana University; BS in Psychology, Bradley University **C:** Governor, State of Kansas (2019-Present); Member, District 18, Kansas State Senate (2005-2019); Member, Joint Committee on Pensions, Investments and Benefits, Kansas State Senate; Member, Joint Committee on State Building Construction; Member, Public Health and Welfare Committee, Kansas State Senate; Member, Joint Committee on Health Policy Oversight, Kansas State Senate; Member, Joint Committee on Home and Community Based Services and KanCare Oversight, Kansas State Senate; Member, Judiciary Committee, Kansas State Senate; Member, Joint Committee on Legislative Budget, Kansas State Senate; Ranking Member, Ways and Means Committee, Kansas State Senate; Minority Whip, Kansas State Senate; Executive Director, Kansas Recreation and Park Association; Former Director of Recreation Therapy/Physical Education, National Jewish Hospital for Respiratory and Immune Diseases, National Jewish Health; Former ATM Use Instructor; Former Job Description Writer, Insurance Agency; Former Recreation Therapist, Rockland Children's Psychiatric Center **MEM:** Leadership Greater Topeka; Board Director, Sunflower State Games; North Topeka Business Alliance; Kansas Enrichment Network for Out-of-School Time **PA:** Democrat

KELLY, MEGYN MARIE, T: News Anchor; Journalist **I:** Media & Entertainment **DOB:** 11/18/1970 **PB:** Champaign **SC:** IL/USA **PT:** Edward Kelly; Linda Kelly **MS:** Married **SPN:** Douglas Brunt (03/01/2008); Daniel Kendall (2001, Divorced 2006) **CH:** Edward Yates; Yardley Evans; Thatcher Bray **ED:** Doctor of Jurisprudence, Albany Law School (1995); Bachelor of Arts in Political Science, Syracuse University, NY (1992) **C:** Host, "Megyn Kelly Today" (2018); Contributor, "Dateline NBC" (2018); Host, "Sunday Night with Megyn Kelly" (2017); Host, "The Kelly File," Fox News Channel (2013-2017); Host, "America Live," Fox News Channel (2010-2013); Host, "America's Newsroom," Fox News Channel (2007-2009); Contributor, "The O'Reilly Factor," Fox News Channel (2004-2010); General Assignment Reporter, Fox News Channel (2004-2007); General Assignment Reporter, WJLA-TV, Washington, DC (2004); Corporate Litigator, Jones Day, New York, NY, Chicago, IL, Washington, DC (1995-2004) **CW:** Author, "Settle for More" (2016) **AW:** Honoree, Variety's Power of Women (2016); Inductee, Bethlehem Central High School Hall of Fame (2015); Named, One of the 100 Most Influential People in the World, TIME Magazine (2014); Alumni Achievement Award, Albany Law School (2010); Award, Childhelp (2009) **RE:** Roman Catholic

KELLY, ROBIN LYNNE, T: U.S. Representative from Illinois **I:** Government Administration/Government Relations/Government Services **CN:** U.S. House of Representatives **DOB:** 04/30/1956 **PB:** New York **SC:** NY/USA **MS:** Married **SPN:** Nathaniel Horn (2003) **CH:** Kelly; Ryan **ED:** Doctor of Philosophy in Political Science, Northern Illinois University (2004); Master of Arts in Counseling, Bradley University (1982); Bachelor of Arts in Psychology, Bradley University (1977) **C:** Member, U.S. House of Representatives from Illinois' Second Congressional District, United States Congress, Washington, DC (2013-Present); Member, U.S. House Committee on Space, Science and Technology (2013-Present); Member, U.S. House Committee on Oversight and Government Reform (2013-Present); Chief Administrative Officer, Cook County, IL (2011-2013); Chief of Staff to Treasurer, State of Illinois, Springfield, IL (2007-2011); Member, District 38, Illinois House of Representatives (2002-2006); Director of Community Affairs, Village of Matteson, IL (1992-2006); Minority Student Services Director, Bradley University (1990-1992); Associate Director, The Youth Shelter (1987-1990); Director, Crisis Nursery, Crittenton Care and Counseling Center (1984-1987); Member, Committee on Foreign Affairs **CR:** Board Member, Hate Crimes Commission (2005-Present); Commissioner, Cook County Human Rights Commission (1998-Present) **CIV:** Trustee, Bradley University (2003-Present); Board Member, Bradley University Council (1998-Present); Board Member, Rich Township Food Pantry Board (1995-Present); Board Member, Illinois Theatre Center (1993-Present) **AW:** Inductee, Centurion Society, Bradley University (2009) **MEM:** Sigma Gamma Rho **PA:** Democrat

KELLY, THOMAS MICHAEL, T: Partner **I:** Law and Legal Services **CN:** Debevoise & Plimpton LLP **DOB:** 10/05/1958 **PB:** Atlanta **SC:** GA/USA **ED:** JD, Harvard University, Cum Laude (1983); AB, Columbia University, Cum Laude (1979) **C:** Partner, Debevoise & Plimpton, New York, NY (1993-Present); Associate, Debevoise & Plimpton, New York. NY (1984-1993); Law Clerk to Honorary Eugene Nickerson, U.S. District Court for the Eastern District of New York, Brooklyn, NY (1983-1984) **CR:** Member, Investment Committee, Social Science Research Council; Board of Directors, Royal Oak Foundation **CIV:** Chair, Insurance Law Committee, New York State Bar Association; Chair, Corporate Section of the Association of Life Insurance Counsel; Board of Directors, The Royal Oak Foundation **CW:** Co-Author, Article, "Federal Reserve Publishes Advance Notice of Proposed Rulemaking on Capital Requirements for Insurers," FC&S Legal (2016); Co-Author, Article, "Federal Reserve Proposes Enhanced Prudential Standards For Insurance SIFIs," FC&S Legal (2016); Author, Article, "Developments At The NAIC Spring Meeting," Parts 1–3, Law360 (2016); Author, Article, "Report On The NAIC 2015 Summer National Meeting," FC&S Legal (2015); Author, Article, "NAIC Begins To Develop A Group Capital Measure For U.S. Insurance Enterprises," FC&S Legal (2015); Author, Article, "NAIC 2015 Spring National Meeting," Insurance Coverage Law Report (2015); Author, Article, "IAIS Issues Consultation On Global Insurance Capital Standard," Canadian Insurance Regulation Reporter (2015); Author, Article, "Takeaways From The 21st Annual IAIS Conference," Law360 (2014); Author, Article, "Rector-Modified Recommendations to NAIC Task Force on Financing of XXX and AXXX Reserves," FC&S Legal (2014); Author, Article, "Citing Private Equity Concerns, New York Department of Financial Services Proposes Increased Scrutiny and Disclosure for Acquisitions of New York Domestic and Commercially Domiciled Insurers," FC&S Legal, and "Report on the NAIC 2014 Spring National Meeting," FC&S Legal's "Eye on the Experts" Blog (2014) **AW:** Leading Insurance Transnational and Regulatory Lawyer, Chambers USA (2018); Lawyer for Insurance: Non-Contentious, The Legal 500 US (2018); "Dealmaker of the Year," The American Lawyer (2002) **MEM:** Insurance Law Committee, Association of the Bar of the City of New York **BAR:** New York (1985) **PA:** Democrat

KEMBLE, BRIAN C., T: Director **I:** Business Management/Business Services **CN:** New Medical Management **DOB:** 10/16/1981 **PB:** Voorhees **SC:** NJ/USA **MS:** Married **SPN:** James Keenan **CH:** James; Jeannine; Jude Keenan **C:** Director of Operations, New Medical Management, Philadelphia, PA (2016-Present); Operations Manager, Joan Shepp, Philadelphia, PA (2010-2016); Office Manager, Accounting, Getaway Weekend Vacations, Inc., Cherry Hill, NJ (2008-2010); Operations Manager, Iron Butterfly, Inc., Mickleton, NJ (1998-2007); IT Telecom Consolidator, Cigna Insurance, Vorhees, NJ (2004-2005); Office Manager, Thrower Corp., Cherry Hill, NJ (2003-2004) **CIV:** Volunteer, Families of Fallen Police Officers **AS:** Mr. Kemble attributes his success to hard work. He has been able to dedicate most of his time to work, which has paid off with much success. **B/I:** Mr. Kemble became involved in his profession because he wanted to further his education. It initially started as a way to earn money; however, it eventually became more of an accomplishment to Mr. Kemble. The gratification he received from accomplishing tasks was what kept him motivated and on this career path.

KEMMERLING, LISA, T: Owner, Entrepreneur **I:** Apparel & Fashion **CN:** Clean Lines Fashion Consulting **MS:** Married **SPN:** T. Kemmerling **CH:** A. Kemmerling **ED:** BA in Business and Management, University of Phoenix (1994); Master's Coursework in Business Management, Suffolk University **C:** Chief Stylist, Clean Lines Fashion Consulting (2018-Present); Sales and Marketing Specialist, Hyperbaric Medical Services (2017-2018); District Director of Sales Development, Kindred Healthcare, LLC (2015-2016); Senior Clinical Sales Consultant, Medical Devices (2013-2015); Regional Sales Manager, Dynasplint Systems, Inc. (2013); Business Development Representative, Bioness Inc. (2012-2013); Senior Ortho Sales Consultant, Dynasplint Systems, Inc. (2011-2012); Sales Consultant, Dynasplint Systems, Inc. (2010-2011); Regional Coordinator, Muscular Dystrophy Association, Inc. (2008-2010); Senior Orthopedic Sales Consultant, Dynasplint Systems, Inc. (2004-2007); Regional Sales Manager, Dynasplint Systems, Inc. (1992-1997) **AW:** Named Top Sales Consultant; Ranked Number One Sales in Cash Receipts and in Net Revenue **MEM:** BNI Networking (Now BNI Global, LLC); Compass & Clock **AS:** Mrs. Kemmerling attributes her success to honesty and integrity for the people she has worked with! **B/I:** Mrs. Kemmerling has always had a passion for fashion. As a young adult, she wanted to be a fashion designer, instead went into medical sales. **THT:** Mrs. Kemmerling loves living her best life, by embracing the career she's chosen, which is fashion consulting. This has afforded her the opportunity to bring some level of happiness to the clients she serves. Never a day goes by, where she doesn't feel fulfilled to do what she loves.

KEMP, BRIAN PORTER, T: Governor of Georgia **I:** Government Administration/Government Relations/Government Services **DOB:** 11/02/1963 **PB:** Athens **SC:** GA/USA **MS:** Married **SPN:** Marty Argo **CH:** Jarrett; Lucy; Amy **ED:** BS in Agriculture, University of Georgia (1987) **C:** Governor, State of Georgia (2019-Present); Secretary of State, Atlanta, GA (2010-2018); Member, District 46, Georgia State Senate, Atlanta, GA (2002-2006); President, Kemp Development **CIV:** Former President, Athens Area Home Builders Association; Board of Directors, St. Mary's Health Care System, Athens, GA **PA:** Republican **RE:** Episcopalian

KENDALL, RICHARD PARKER, T: Principal Consultant **I:** Military & Defense Services **CN:** Department of Defense **DOB:** 07/13/1941 **PB:** Beaumont **SC:** TX/USA **PT:** James E.; Guinn H. Kendall **MS:** Married **SPN:** Linda E. Richards (03/25/1995) **CH:** John; Claire **ED:** MA in Mathematics, Rice University (1980); PhD in Mathematics, Rice University (1973); MA in Mathematics, University of Texas at Austin (1964); BA in Mathematics, University of Texas at Austin (1963) **C:** Software Engineering Consultant, DOD (Department of Defense), SEI/CMU Lorton, VA (2007-Present); Visiting Scientist, Software Engineering Institute, Pittsburgh, PA (2005-2007); Chief Information Officer, Los Alamos National Laboratory (2000-2003); Program Manager, Cyber Security, Los Alamos National Laboratory (1999-2000); Director, Testbed for Industry, Los Alamos National Laboratory, New Mexico (1995-1999); Chief Operating Officer, Western Atlas Software (1990-1992); Vice President, J. S. Nolen & Associates, Houston, TX (1982-1990); Senior Research Associate, Exxon Production Research Company, Houston, TX (1972-1982) **CR:** Visiting Professor of Mathematics, Wake Forest University (2013-2014); Advisor, Brown School of Engineering, Rice University (1980-1982); Adjunct Professor of Mathematics (1975-1980) **CIV:** Neighborhood Homeowners Association, Santa Fe, NM **CW:** Author, Contributor, Scientific Papers in Petroleum Engineering, Applied Mathematics and Software Engineering **AW:** Society of Petroleum Engineers (SPE) Distinguished Lecturer (1986-1987); U.S. Air Force Fellowship, Rice University (1965-1968) **MEM:** IEEE; Society Petroleum Engineers; Former Member, American Mathematical Society **MH:** Albert Nelson Marquis Lifetime Achievement Award; Marquis Who's Who Top Professional **AS:** Sometimes Dr. Kendall thinks it was shear dumb luck. He had wonderful teachers from junior high through graduate school–probably shear dumb-luck. He had the fervent backing of my parents–even when they thought that he had to be crazy. And the times were right– Sputnik, and computers launched his career. He was able to ride the wave of computers almost from the very beginning. **B/I:** Dr. Kendall knew at age 12 what he wanted to do for his career. In his first algebra class in junior high school, he was was overwhelmed by the idea that one simple formula described the area enclosed by any circle in the universe. The idea was so powerful that it set the direction of his career. **AV:** Opera; Ballet **RE:** Episcopalian **THT:** You have to engage and take chances.

KENDE, CHRISTOPHER BURGESS, JD, T: Lawyer, Educator **I:** Law and Legal Services **CN:** Cozen O'Connor **DOB:** 04/28/1948 **PB:** New York **SC:** NY/USA **PT:** Herbert Alexander Kende; Helga Henrietta (Wieselthier) Kende **MS:** Married **SPN:** Barbara Gonzales (05/22/1976) **ED:** JD, New York University (1973), MA, Brown University (1970); BA, Brown University (1970) **C:** Partner, Cozen O'Connor, New York, NY (1996-Present); Partner, Holtzmann, Wise & Shepard, New York, NY (1989-1996); Partner, Hill, Betts & Nash LLP, New York, NY (1982-1989); Associate, Hill, Betts & Nash LLP (1978-1982); Associate, Dewey Ballantine et al., New York, NY (1976-1978); Staff Attorney, Legal Aid Society, New York, NY (1973-1976) **CR:** Adjunct Professor of Maritime and Admiralty Law, Brooklyn Law School (2003-Present) **CW:** Contributor, Articles, Professional Journals **AW:** Manhattan Super Lawyer, Law & Politics (2006-2014); Silver Medal, French National Depository Bank (1984) **MEM:** President, Insurance Law Commission, Union Internationale des Avocats (2003-2006); Past Chairman, Committee on Admiralty and Maritime Law, New York County Lawyers Association (1998-1999); Tips Section, American Bar Association; Marine Ecology Committee, Committee on International Organizations and Standards, Maritime Law Association; French Maritime Law Association; India House; Edgartown Yacht Club; The University Club of New York; Travellers, Paris, France; Yacht Club de France; Order of the Coif; The Phi Beta Kappa Society **BAR:** The State Bar of California (1996); United States Court of Appeals for the Ninth Circuit (1996); The District of Columbia Bar (1988); United States Supreme Court (1978); United States Court of Appeals for the Second Circuit (1976); Massachusetts Bar Association (1975); State Bar of New York (1974); United States District Court for the Southern District of New York (1974); United States District Court for the Eastern District of New York (1974) **MH:** Albert Nelson Marquis Lifetime Achievement Award **AV:** Sailing; Motorcycling; Playing tennis; Having animal-assisted therapy; Gardening **PA:** Democrat **RE:** Presbyterian

KENNEDY, ANTHONY MCLEOD, T: Associate Justice (Retired) **I:** Law and Legal Services **CN:** Supreme Court of the United States **DOB:** 07/23/1936 **PB:** Sacramento **SC:** CA/USA **PT:** Arthur J. Kennedy; Gladys (McLeod) Kennedy **MS:** Married **SPN:** Mary Davis (06/29/1963) **CH:** Justin Anthony; Gregory Davis; Kristin Marie **ED:** Honorary JD, Santa Clara University (1988); Honorary JD, University of the Pacific (1988); LLB, Harvard University, Cum Laude (1961); Coursework, London School of Economics (1957-1958); BA in Political Science, Stanford University (1958) **C:** Associate Justice, Supreme Court of the United States, Washington, DC (1988-2018); Judge, United States Court of Appeals for the Ninth Circuit, Sacramento, CA (1975-1988); Adjunct Professor, Constitutional Law, McGeorge School of Law, University of the Pacific, California (1965-1988); Partner, Evans, Jackson & Kennedy (1967-1975); Private Practice, Sacramento, CA (1963-1967); Associate, Thelen, Martin, Johnson, & Bridges, San Francisco, CA (1961-1963) **CR:** Member, Federal Judicial Center (1987-1988); Chairman, Committee on Pacific Territories (1982-1988); Member, Committee on Pacific Territories (1979-1988); Member, Advisory Committee on Codes of Conduct (1979-1987); Member, Board of Student Advisers, Harvard Faculty, Harvard University (1960-1961) **MIL:** With, California Army National Guard (1961-1962) **AW:** One of the 100 Most Influential People in the World, TIME Magazine (2012); One of the 50 Most Powerful People in DC, GQ Magazine (2007); Golden Plate Award, Academy of Achievement (2005) **MEM:** Fellow, Honorary Member, American Bar Founda-

tion; Honorary Member, American College of Trial Lawyers; American Bar Association; Sacramento County Bar Association; The State Bar California; The Phi Beta Kappa Society **BAR:** United States Tax Court (1971); The State Bar of California (1962) **RE:** Roman Catholic

KENNEDY, JOHN NEELY, T: U.S. Senator from Louisiana **I:** Government Administration/Government Relations/Government Services **DOB:** 11/21/1951 **PB:** Centreville **SC:** MS/USA **MS:** Married **SPN:** Rebecca Stulb **CH:** Preston **ED:** BCL, Magdalen College, University of Oxford, First Class Honors (1979); JD, University of Virginia School of Law (1977); BA in Political Science, Philosophy & Economics, Vanderbilt University, Magna Cum Laude (1973) **C:** U.S. Senator, State of Louisiana (2017-Present); State Treasurer, State of Louisiana (2000-2017); Secretary, Department of Revenue (1996-1999); Special Counsel to Louisiana Governor (1988-1992); Attorney to Partner, Chaffe, McCall, Phillips, Toler and Sarpy, LLP, Baton Rouge, and New Orleans, LA **CR:** Adjunct Professor, Paul M. Hebert Law Center, Louisiana State University (2002-2016); Candidate, U.S. Senate, LA (2004); Board of Directors, Louisiana Workers' Compensation Corporation **CIV:** Founding Member, Volunteer Teacher, North Cross United Methodist Church; Board Director, Friends of the New Orleans Center for Creative Arts; Board Director, Council for a Better Louisiana **CW:** Author, "Louisiana State Constitutional Law," LSU Publications Institute (2012); Author, "The Dimension of Time in the Louisiana Products Liability Act," 42 Louisiana Bar Journal (1994); Author, "The Role of the Consumer Expectation Test Under Louisiana's Products Liability Doctrine," 69 Tulane Law Review 117 (1994); Author, "A Primer on the Louisiana Products Liability Act," 49 Louisiana Law Review 565 (1989); Author, "Assumption of the Risk, Comparative Fault and Strict Liability After Rozell," 47 Louisiana Law Review 791 (1987); Author, "The Federal Power Commission, Job Bias, and NAACP v. FPC," 10 Akron Law Review 556 (1977) **MEM:** South Regional Vice President, National Association of State Treasurers; The Phi Beta Kappa Society **PA:** Republican **RE:** Methodist

KENNEDY, JOSEPH, "JOE" PATRICK III, T: U.S. Representative from Massachusetts **I:** Government Administration/Government Relations/Government Services **DOB:** 10/04/1980 **PB:** Brighton **SC:** MA/USA **PT:** Joseph Patrick Kennedy II; Sheila Brewster (Rauch) Kennedy **MS:** Married **SPN:** Lauren Anne Birchfield (12/01/2012) **CH:** Eleanor; James Mattew **ED:** JD, Harvard Law School (2009); BS in Industrial Engineering, Stanford University (2003) **C:** Member, U.S. House of Representatives from Massachusetts' Fourth Congressional District, United States Congress, Washington, DC (2013-Present); Member, U.S. House Committee on Science, Space and Technology (2013-Present); Member, U.S. House Committee on Foreign Affairs (2013-Present); Assistant District Attorney, Middlesex County, MA (2011-2012); Prosecutor, Cape Cod and Islands, MA (2009-2011); Member, Committee on Energy and Commerce **CIV:** Volunteer, Peace Corps, Dominican Republic (2004-2006) **PA:** Democrat **RE:** Catholic

KENNEDY, KATHLEEN, T: President; Film Producer **I:** Media & Entertainment **CN:** Lucasfilm Ltd. **DOB:** 01/01/1954 **PB:** Berkeley **SC:** CA/USA **PT:** Donald R. Kennedy; Dione Marie (Dousseau) Kennedy **MS:** Married **SPN:** Frank Marshall (1987) **CH:** Two Children **ED:** BA in Telecommunications and Film, San Diego State University (1975) **C:** President, Lucasfilm Ltd., Walt Disney (2012-Present); Co-founder (with Frank Marshall), President,

Producer, Kennedy-Marshall Co. (1994-2012); Co-founder (with Steven Spielberg and Frank Marshall), President, Amblin Entertainment, Universal City, CA (1984-1992); Various Positions Including Camera Operator, Video Editor, Floor Director and News Production Coordinator, KCST, San Diego, CA **CR:** President, Producers Guild of America (2001-2006) **CIV:** Board Director, Michael J. Fox Foundation for Parkinson's Research **CW:** Producer, "The Mandalorian" (2019); Producer, "Star Wars: The Rise of Skywalker" (2019); Producer, "Solo: A Star Wars Story" (2018); Producer, "Star Wars: The Last Jedi" (2017); Executive Producer, "The BFG" (2016); Executive Producer, "The Girl on the Train" (2016); Producer, "Rogue One: A Star Wars Story" (2016); Producer, "Star Wars: Episode VII - The Force Awakens" (2015); Producer, "Lincoln" (2012); Co-producer with Steven Spielberg, "The Adventures of Tintin" (2011); Co-producer with Steven Spielberg, "War Horse" (2011); Executive Producer, "The Last Airbender" (2010); Executive Producer, "The Secret World of Arrietty" (2010); Executive Producer, "The Special Relationship" (2010); Producer, "Hereafter" (2010); Producer, "The Curious Case of Benjamin Button" (2008); Executive Producer, "Indiana Jones and the Kingdom of the Crystal Skull" (2008); Producer, "The Diving Bell and the Butterfly" (2007); Executive Producer, "Movies Rock" (2007); Producer, "War of the Worlds" (2005); Co-producer with Steven Spielberg, "Munich" (2005); Producer, "Seabiscuit" (2003); Producer, "The Young Black Stallion" (2003); Executive Producer, "Signs" (2002); Executive Producer, "The Sports Pages" (2001); Producer, "Artificial Intelligence: AI" (2001); Producer, "Jurassic Park III" (2001); Co-producer with Steven Spielberg, "The Six Sense" (1999); Producer, "Snow Falling on Cedars" (1999); Producer, "A Map of the World" (1999); Executive Producer, "Olympic Glory" (1999); Executive Producer, "Jurassic Park: The Lost World" (1997); Producer, "Twister" (1996); Co-producer with Clint Eastwood, "The Bridges of Madison County" (1995); Executive Producer, "Balto" (1995); Producer, "Congo" (1995); Producer, "The Indian in the Cupboard" (1995); Co-producer with Frank Marshall, "Milk Money" (1994); Co-producer with Frank Marshall, George R. Molen, David Kirschner, William Hanna, and Joseph Barbera, "The Flintstones" (1994); Co-producer with Robert Watts, "Alive" (1993); Executive Producer, "A Dangerous Woman" (1993); Co-producer with Steven Spielberg, "Schindler's List" (1993); Executive Producer, "Trail Mix-Up" (1993); Executive Producer, "A Far Off Place" (1993); Executive Producer, "We're Back! A Dinosaur's Story" (1993); Co-producer with Gerald R. Molen, "Jurassic Park" (1993); Co-producer with Peter Bogdanovich, "Noises Off" (1992); Co-producer with Frank Marshall and Gerald R. Molen, "Hook" (1991); Executive Producer, "Cape Fear" (1991); Co-producer with Frank Marshall and David Kirschner, "An American Tail: Fievel Goes West" (1991); Co-producer with Richard Vane, "Arachnophobia" (1990); Executive Producer, "Roller Coaster Rabbit" (1990); Executive Producer, "Gremlins 2: The New Batch" (1990); Executive Producer, "Back to the Future Part III" (1990); Executive Producer, "Joe Versus the Volcano" (1990); Producer, "Always" (1989); Executive Producer, "Dad" (1989); Executive Producer, "Back to the Future Part II" (1989); Co-producer with Frank Marshall and George Lucas, "Indiana Jones and the Last Crusade" (1989); Executive Producer, "TV Tummy Trouble" (1989); Co-producer with Steven Spielberg, "Who Framed Roger Rabbit" (1988); Co-producer with Frank Marshall, Steven Spielberg, and George Lucas, "The Land Before Time" (1988); Co-producer with Frank Marshall and Steven Spielberg, "Empire of the Sun" (1987); Co-producer with Frank Marshall, Steven Spielberg, Peter Guber, and Jon Peters, "Innerspace" (1987); Executive Producer, "*batteries not included" (1987); Co-producer with Frank Marshall and Art Levinson, "The Money Pit" (1986); Co-producer with Frank Marshall, Steven Spielberg, and David Kirschner, "An American Tail" (1986); Associate Producer, "Reform School Girls" (1986); Co-producer with Frank Marshall, "Fandango" (1985); Co-producer with Quincy Jones, Frank Marshall, and Steven Spielberg, "The Color Purple" (1985); Executive Producer, "The Goonies" (1985); Executive Producer, "Back to the Future" (1985); Executive Producer, "Young Sherlock Holmes" (1985); Associate Producer, "Indiana Jones and the Temple of Doom" (1984); Co-producer with Frank Marshall and Steven Spielberg, "Gremlins" (1984); Associate Producer, "Twilight Zone - The Movie" (1983); Producer, "E.T. The Extra-Terrestrial" (1982); Associate Producer, "Poltergeist" (1982); Producer, Television Shows, Films **AW:** Named One of the 50 Most Powerful Women in Busines, Fortune Magazine (2015); Named One of the 100 Most Powerful Women in Entertainment, The Hollywood Reporter (2006-2014); David O. Selznick Achievement Award in Theatrical Motion Pictures, Producers Guild of America (2008); Named One of the 50 Smartest People in Hollywood, Entertainment Weekly (2007); Academy Award for Best Picture, Academy of Motion Picture Arts and Sciences (1993)

KENNEDY, LESA DAWN, T: Vice Chairperson; Chief Executive Officer **I:** Business Management/Business Services **CN:** NASCAR; International Speedway Corporation **DOB:** 05/24/1961 **PT:** Bill France Jr.; Betty Jane France **MS:** Widowed **SPN:** Dr. Bruce Kennedy (Deceased 07/10/2007) **CH:** Ben **ED:** BA in Economics and Psychology, Duke University (1983) **C:** Chief Executive Officer, International Speedway Corporation (ISC) (2009-Present); President, International Speedway Corporation (ISC) (2003-2009); Executive Vice President, International Speedway Corporation (ISC) (1996-2003); Treasurer, International Speedway Corporation (ISC) (1989-1996); Secretary, International Speedway Corporation (ISC) (1987-1996); Board of Directors, International Speedway Corporation (ISC) (1984-1987); International Speedway Corporation (ISC) (1983) **CR:** Vice Chairperson, NASCAR **CW:** Listee, 30 Most Powerful Women in Sports, Adweek Magazine (2016); Most Powerful Woman in Sports, Forbes (2009); Most Influential Woman in Sports Business, Volusia Flagler Business Report (2006); Listee, 25 Most Influential People in NASCAR, Charlotte Observer (2001-2006); Most Influential Woman in Sports Business, Street & Smith's SportsBusiness Journal (2005); Listee, 10 Secret People Who Will Change The World, AutoWeek Magazine; Female Sports Executive of the Year, Street & Smith's SportsBusiness Journal

KENNEDY, THOMAS A., T: Chairperson, Chief Executive Officer **I:** Military & Defense Services **CN:** Raytheon Company **ED:** Doctorate Degree in Engineering, University of California Los Angeles; Master of Science, Air Force Institute; Bachelor of Science, Rutgers, The State University of New Jersey **C:** Chairperson, Forcepoint (2015-Present); Chief Executive Officer, Chairperson, Raytheon Company, 2014-Present); Chief Operating Officer, Raytheon Company (2013-2014); Vice President, Raytheon (2010-2013)

KENNEDY, TIMOTHY, "TIM" FRED, T: MMA Fighter **I:** Athletics **DOB:** 09/01/1979 **PB:** San Luis Obispo **SC:** CA/USA **ED:** Coursework, Dokan School of Martial Arts, Atascadero, CA (1996) **C:** MMA Fighter, Jackson Wink MMA Academy (2001-2003, 2006-2016); MMA Fighter, International Fight League (2007) **MIL:** U.S. Army Special Forces (2017); Special Forces Weapons Sergeant, Texas Army National Guard, U.S. Army (2009); Sniper, Sniper Instructor, Principal Combatives Instructor, Seventh Special Forces Group, Operational Detachments Alpha, U.S. Army (2007-2009); Basic Combat Training, Advanced Individual Training, Airborne School and Special Forces Qualification Course, U.S. Army (2004-2007) **AW:** Winner, Extreme Challenge Middleweight Tournament; Fight of the Night, Knockout of the Night, Ultimate Fighting Championship **RE:** Christian

KENNEY, JAMES, "JIM" FRANCIS, T: Mayor of the City of Philadelphia **I:** Government Administration/Government Relations/Government Services **DOB:** 08/08/1958 **PB:** Philadelphia **SC:** PA/USA **MS:** Divorced **SPN:** Maureen Kenney (Divorced 2018) **CH:** Brendan; Nora **ED:** BA in Political Science, La Salle University, Philadelphia, PA (1980) **C:** Mayor, City of Philadelphia, PA (2016-Present); Councilman-at-large, Philadelphia City Council, Philadelphia, PA (1992-2015); Chief of Staff to Senator Vincent J. Fumo, Pennsylvania State Senate, Harrisburg, PA (1984-1992); Administrative Assistant, Senator Vincent J. Fumo, Pennsylvania State Senate, Harrisburg, PA (1980-1984); Consultant, Vitetta Architects and Engineers; Adjunct Professor, University of Pennsylvania **CR:** Vice Chairman, Laws and Government Committee, Philadelphia City Council; Vice Chairman, Public Property and Public Works Committee, Philadelphia City Council; Vice Chairman, Rules Committee, Philadelphia City Council; Chairman, Environmental Committee; Chairman, Legislative Oversight Committee **CIV:** Delegate, Democratic National Convention (1980-1992); Member, Pennsylvania Democratic State Committee; Founding Member, Gallagher's St. Patrick's Day Observance; Board Member, Independence Blue Cross; Participant, Mummers Parade, Philadelphia, PA **MEM:** Columbus Civic Association, The Irish Society of Philadelphia; Jokers New Year's Association (Jokers NYA) **PA:** Democrat

KENT, JEANNE YVONNE, T: Artist, Poet **I:** Fine Art **DOB:** 02/06/1947 **PB:** Lawrence **SC:** MA/USA **PT:** Gerard George Galarneau; Cecile Fecteau Galarneau **MS:** Married **SPN:** Martin Joseph Kent (12/04/1971) **CH:** Sarah Hewett Fitzpatrick; Nicole Michelle Perez **ED:** BA in English and Creative Writing, University of Massachusetts (2003); BFA in Painting, Massachusetts College of Art, Boston, MA (1989); Coursework, Northeastern University, Boston, MA (1970-1973); Coursework, Lowell State College, Lowell, MA (1966-1968) **C:** Poetry Instructor, Kitty Dukakis Drug Rehabilitation for Women, Lemuel Shattuck Hospital, Jamaica Plain, MA (2009); Poetry Instructor, Roslindale Art Center, Roslindale, MA (2003); Art Instructor, Roslindale Art Center, Roslindale, MA (1996); Slide Lecturer, Weymouth North High School, East Weymouth, MA (1993, 1990); Instructor, Art, Leewards Arts and Crafts Store, Quincy, MA (1990); Private Art Instructor (1990's); Resident Assistant, Slide Lecturer, Elder Hostel, Massachusetts College of Art, Boston, MA (1988) **CR:** Invitational Poetry Readings: West Roxbury Public Library Intergenerational Poetry Contest, First Prize, (2012); West Roxbury Poetry Workshop 10th Anniversary Celebration, (2006); David Lang Studios, Ottonr Riccio's Poetry Workshop Invitational, (2004); University of Massachusetts, Boston, City Night Readings, (2003); Healey Library, University of Massachusetts, Boston, Hypergraphia Readings, (2003); Cambridge Public Library, John Holmes Prize Poem (2002); West Roxbury Intergenerational

Poetry Contest Reading, (1989); Other Readings: Barnes and Nobles, Express Cafe, Guilty Pleasures Coffee Shop, Java Joe's, The Wit's End Cafe, William Joiner Center **CW:** Group Show, The Jamaica Plain Open Studios (2016); Group Show, MassArt 25th Annual Benefit Art Auction (2013); Contributor, "Unlocking the Poem" (2009); One-Woman Show, Sweet Finnish Bakery, Jamaica Plain, MA (2005, 2006, 2007); Television Appearance, "It's All About Arts" Hosted by Glenn Williams, BNN-TV9, Boston, MA (1997, 2004, 2005); One-Woman Show, Olde Towne Realty, Roslindale, MA (2005); Group Show Exhibition, Women with Wild Roots, Cortland, NH (2005); Group Show Exhibition, It's All About Arts Gallery (2004); One-Woman Show, Lemuel Shadduck Hospital, Jamaica Plain, MA (2004); One-Woman Show, Emack & Bolio's, Roslindale, MA (2004); Author, Poems, "Watermark" (2003); Author, Poems, "Hypergraphia" (2003); Author, Poems, "Concrete Wolf" (2003); Group Show Exhibition, Massachusetts Coalition for the Homeless, Boston, MA (1999); Group Show Exhibition, Eliot School of Fine & Applied Arts, Jamaica Plain, MA (1998); Group Show Exhibition, Lowell St. Gallery, Cambridge Art Association (1998); One-Woman Show, Jamo's Restaurant, Roslindale, MA (1998); One-Woman Show, Jamaica Plain Branch of the Boston Public Library, Jamaica Plain, MA (1998); Group Show Exhibition, Boston City Hall, Boston, MA (1997); Group Show Exhibition, Greater Roslindale Art Association (1997); Group Show Exhibition, West Roxbury Public Library (1996-1997); Group Show Exhibition, Picture This Gallery, West Roxbury, MA (1996); One-Woman Show, Brookline Art Society, West Roxbury Branch of the Boston Public Library, West Roxbury, MA (1995); One-Woman Show, Public Library of Brookline, Brookline, MA (1995); Group Show Exhibition, Massachusetts College of Art and Design, Boston, MA (1995, 1988-1989); Group Show Exhibition, Arnold Arboretum of Harvard University, Jamaica Plain, MA (1992); Group Show Exhibition, Boston Visual Artist's Union (1990); Group Show Exhibition, Brookline Art Society, Brookline, MA (1989-1997); One-Woman Show, Rubin O'Barry's Coffee Shop, Jamaica Plain, MA (1989); Group Show Exhibition, Arts in the Parks, Boston, MA (1989); Poetry/Fiction/Non-Fiction Contributor, The Creatuve Impulse, Massachusetts College of Art (1987-1988); Poetry Contributor, Pegasus of Lowell State Teacher's College (1967) **AW:** Poetry, First Prize Award, West Roxbury Public Library Intergenerational Poetry Contest, West Roxbury, MA (2012); First Prize, Sonnet Contest (Adult Division) Heart of America Shakespeare Festival, Kansas City, MO (2011); Southwest Review, Morton Marr Poetry Prize Finalist (2010); Poetry Book Series Finalist, Concrete Wolf (2004, 2005); Honors in Creative Writing, English Department, University of Massachusetts, Boston (2001-2003); John Holmes Prize, New England Poetry Club (2002); Harold Taylor Prize, Academy of American Poets (2001); Juror's Choice Award, Image and Verse Show, Cambridge Art Association (1998); Honorable Mention for Poetry, Writers Digest Magazine (1998); Calendar Illustration Painting Award, First Annual Dedham Community Art Competition, Dedham Community House Gallery (1993); Fourth Place Painting Award, Dedham Arts and Crafts Fair, Massachusetts (1990); Inter-generational Poetry Honorable Mention Award, West Roxbury Branch of the Boston Public Library (1989) **MH:** Albert Nelson Marquis Lifetime Achievement Award; Marquis Who's Who Top Professional **AS:** Hard work, persistence, love of the arts, not being afraid of either failure or success and of course being at the right place at the right time. **B/I:** Ms. Kent became involved in her profession because she was inspired by her older brother Paul, an abstract expressionist painter who developed a mental illness. When he could no longer paint, he continued to encourage her saying she had talent. In high school she was voted "class poet." After an editor from the nearby Lawrence High School newspaper read one of her poems, she became a frequent contributor of humorous poems. From grammar school on, she noticed that she received more attention from teachers than she did at home, and so, she began to dream about being a teacher herself; she just wasn't sure which field to go into at the time. **AV:** Reading; Swimming; Diary-keeping; Gardening; Walking **RE:** Jehovah Witness

KERR, DONALD MACLEAN, PHD, T: Physicist, Federal Official **I:** Sciences **DOB:** 04/08/1939 **PB:** Philadelphia **SC:** PA/USA **PT:** Donald MacLean Kerr; Harriet (Fell) Kerr **MS:** Married **SPN:** Alison Richards Kyle (06/10/1961) **CH:** Margot; Kyle **ED:** PhD, Cornell University (1966); MS, Cornell University (1964); BEE, Cornell University (1963) **C:** Research Professor, Volgenau School of Engineering, George Mason University (2009-2012); Principal Deputy Director, Director of National Intelligence, National Reconnaissance Office (2007-2009); Director, National Reconnaissance Office (2005-2007); Deputy Director, Science and Technology, Central Intelligence Agency (2001-2009); Assistant Director, FBI (1997-2001); Executive Vice President, Board of Directors, Information Systems Laboratories, Inc. (1996-1997); Executive Vice President, Board of Directors, SAIC (1993-1996); President, Board of Directors, EG&G, Inc., Wellesley, MA (1989-1992); Executive Vice President, EG&G, Inc., Wellesley, MA (1988-1989); Senior Vice President, EG&G, Inc., Wellesley, MA (1985-1988); Director, Los Alamos National Laboratory (1979-1985); Deputy Assistant, Secretary, Energy Technology, U.S. Department of Energy (1979); Acting Assistant Secretary for Defense Programs, U.S. Department of Energy (1978); Deputy Assistant Secretary for Defense Programs, U.S. Department of Energy (1977-1979); Deputy Manager, Nevada Operations Office, U.S. Department of Energy, Las Vegas, NV (1976-1977); Alternate Energy Division Leader, Los Alamos National Laboratory (1975-1976); Staff, Los Alamos National Laboratory (1966-1976); Assistant Director, Los Alamos National Laboratory (1973-1975); Assistant Division Leader, Los Alamos National Laboratory (1972-1973); Group Leader, Los Alamos National Laboratory (1971-1972) **CR:** Chairman, The MITRE Corporation (2018-Present); Board of Directors, Orbis Operations, LLC (2012-Present); Board of Directors, Michael Baker International (2009-Present); Board of Directors, Resources for the Future, Washington (2009-2018); Board Member, Cornell University (1985); Defense Science Board (1993-1998); Joint Strategic Planning Staff, Science Advisory Group (1981-1991); Chairman, Committee on Research and Development, International Energy Agency (1979-1985); Board of Trustees, The MITRE Corporation; James Clerk Maxwell Fellow (1965-1966); Ford Foundation Fellow (1964-1965) **CIV:** Trustee, New England Aquarium (1989-1993) **AW:** Secretary of Defense Medal for Outstanding Public Service, U.S. Department of Defense (2009); National Intelligence Distinguished Service Medal (2009); Distinguished Intelligence Medal, Central Intelligence Agency (2005); Outstanding Services Award, U.S. Department of Energy (1979); National Merit Scholar, Cornell University (1963) **MEM:** San Diego Technology Council (1994-1997); Board of Directors, Atlantic Council (1991-1997); Corporate Draper Laboratory (1982-1997); Board of Directors, World Affairs Council, Boston (1988-1992); Board of Directors, National Association of Manufacturers (1986-1992); Advisory Committee of Naval Research (1982-1985); Advisory Board Member, Georgetown University Center of Strategic International Studies (1981-1987); Advisory Board, Geophysical Institute, University of Alaska Fairbanks (1980-1985); National Security Advisory Council, SRI International (1980-1989); Engineering Advisory Board, University of Nevada, Las Vegas (1976-1978); Science Advisory Panel, U.S. Army (1975-1978); Navajo Science Committee (1974-1977); Fellow, American Association for the Advancement of Science; American Physical Society; Southwestern Association of Indian Affairs; Sigma Xi, The Scientific Research Honor Society; The Tau Beta Pi Association, Inc.; Eta Kappa Nu, IEEE; American Geophysical Union **MH:** Albert Nelson Marquis Lifetime Achievement Award **B/I:** Dr. Kerr became involved in his profession because of his experiences at Los Alamos National Laboratory. While he was there, several faculty members helped him immensely. Paul Hartman, a member of the physics department, and Hans Bethe, the theoretical division leader at Los Alamos during World War II, both played a key role in Dr. Kerr's decision to pursue his career and move west.

KERR, VALERIE ANN, T: Public Health Nurse **I:** Medicine & Health Care **DOB:** 01/10/1940 **PB:** Alma **SC:** MI/USA **PT:** Floyd Arther Tomlin; Martha Ella (Wells) Tomlin **MS:** Widow **SPN:** Larry Lee Kerr (06/15/1961, Deceased 2011) **CH:** Kerry; Kristin; Karmen **ED:** BS, Central Michigan University (1983); Diploma, Saginaw General Hospital School Nursing (1961) **C:** Sunday School Teacher, First and Second Grade (2018-Present); Board Member, Alma Church of Nazarene (2010-2020); Public Health Nurse, Mid Michigan District Health Department, Stanton, MI (1989-2002); Supervisor, Michigan Masonic Home, Alma, MI (1986-1989); Instructor, Mid Michigan Community College, Harrison, MI (1982-1986); Clinical Nursing Instructor, Mid Michigan Community College, Harrison, MI (1978-1982); Migrant Program School Nurse, Montcalm Intermediate School District, Stanton, MI (1981); Nurse, Gratiot Community Hospital, Alma, MI (1961-1974) **CR:** Volunteer, Board Member, Office of Human Services, Pantry Thrift Store; Nursing Career included: Night Supervisor, Michigan Masonic Home, Pediatric Hospital Charge Nurse, Med/Surg Charge Nurse, LPN Student Instructor, Public Health Generalist Nurse (includes Epidemiology, Immunizations, HIV counseling/testing) **CIV:** Board Member, Saint Louis School Board (2019-Present); Chairperson, Board, Christian Life and Sunday School (1992-1995); Department Superintendent, Gratiot County Agricultural Society (1981-1983); Member, Michigan Farm Bureau, Gratiot Womens Organization (1978); Club Leader, Exchange Student Hostess, Michigan 4-H, Gratiot County, MI (1975-1977); Member, Alma Church Nazarene; St. Louis Friends of the Library; 4-H Leader **MEM:** Saginaw General Hospital School Nursing Alumni Association; Phi Kappa Phi (Former); Healthy Pine River Organization; Pine River Superfund Citizen Task Force; Gratiot County Historical and Genealogical Society **MH:** Albert Nelson Marquis Lifetime Achievement Award **AS:** She attributes her success to family and faith in God. **B/I:** Ms. Kerr became involved in her profession because she wanted to be a nurse as a child and helped her brother who had Down syndrome. This experience aided her in making the decision to become a professional nurse. **AV:** Perennial flower gardening; Watercolor painting **PA:** Independent **RE:** Church of the Nazarene

KERRY, JOHN FORBES, T: U.S. Secretary of State (Retired) **I:** Government Administration/Government Relations/Government Services **DOB:** 12/11/1943 **PB:** Denver **SC:** CO/USA **PT:** Richard John Kerry; Rosemary (Forbes) Kerry **MS:** Married **SPN:** Teresa Heinz (05/26/1995); Julia Stimson Thorne (05/23/1970, Divorced 07/25/1988) **CH:** Alexandra; Vanessa; Henry John IV (Stepchild); André (Stepchild); Christopher (Stepchild) **ED:** Honorary LLD, Boston College (2014); Honorary LLD, Kenyan College, Ohio (2006); Honorary Doctorate of Public Service, Northeastern University (2000); Honorary LLD, University of Massachusetts Boston (1988); JD, Boston College Law School (1976); BA in Political Science, Yale University (1966) **C:** Secretary, U.S. Department of State, Washington, DC (2013-2017); Chairman, U.S. Senate Committee on Foreign Relations (2009-2013); U.S. Senator, Commonwealth of Massachusetts (1985-2013); Member, Joint Select Committee on Deficit Reduction (2011); Senate Committee on Small Business and Entrepreneurship (2001-2003, 2007-2009); Democratic Nominee for President, U.S. Presidential Election (2004); Chairman, U.S. Chairman, Democratic Senatorial Campaign Committee (DSCC) (1987-1989); Lieutenant Governor, Commonwealth of Massachusetts, Boston, MA (1983-1985); Partner, Kerry & Sragow, Boston, MA (1979-1982); Assistant District Attorney, Middlesex County, MA (1976-1979); National Coordinator, Vietnam Veterans Against the War (VVAW) (1969-1971) **CIV:** Democratic Candidate for Congress, District Five, MA (1972); Board of Visitors, Walsh School of Foreign Service, Georgetown University **MIL:** Served to Lieutenant Junior Grade, United States Navy Reserve (1966-1969) **CW:** Author, "Every Day is Extra" (2018); Co-author with Teresa Heinz Kerry, "This Moment on Earth: Today's New Environmentalists and Their Vision for the Future" (2007); Author, "A Call to Service: My Vision for a Better America" (2003); Author, "The New War: The Web of Crime That Threatens America's Security" (1997); Author, "The New Soldier" (1971) **AW:** Named One of the 100 Most Influential People in the World, TIME Magazine (2014); Two Decorated Purple Hearts; Bronze Star with Oak Leaf Cluster; Silver Star **MEM:** Founder, Vietnam Veterans of America **BAR:** Commonwealth of Massachusetts (1976) **PA:** Democrat **RE:** Roman Catholic

KERSHAW, CLAYTON EDWARD, T: Professional Baseball Player **I:** Athletics **CN:** Los Angeles Dodgers **DOB:** 03/19/1988 **PB:** Dallas **SC:** TX/USA **PT:** Christopher George Kershaw; Marianne (Tombaugh) Kershaw **MS:** Married **SPN:** Ellen Melson (12/4/2010) **CH:** Cali Ann; Charley Clayton; Cooper Ellis **ED:** Student, Highland Park High School **C:** Pitcher, Los Angeles Dodgers (2008-Present) **CIV:** Volunteer, Arise Africa, Zambia (2011); Founder, Kershaw's Challenge **CW:** Co-Author, "Arise: Live Out Your Faith and Dreams on Whatever Field You Find Yourself" (2012) **AW:** Eight-Time All-Star (2011-2017, 2019); Four-Time Warren Spahn Award (2011, 2013-2014, 2017); Sporting News Player of the Year Award (2014); NL MVP (2014); Players Choice Awards for Player of the Year (2014); Baseball America Major League Player of the Year (2014); Marvin Miller Man of the Year Award (2014); Roy Campanella Award (2013-2014); Three-Time NL Cy Young Award (2011, 2013-2014); Sporting News Pitcher of the Year (2011, 2013-2014); Player's Choice Award for National League Outstanding Pitcher (2011, 2013-2014); Los Angeles Sports Council Sportsman of the Year (2011, 2014); Texas Professional Baseball Player of the Year Award (2009, 2011, 2014); Branch Rickey Award (2013); Roberto Clemente Award (2012); Triple Crown (2011); Rawlings Gold Glove Award (2011); Midwest League Prospect of the Year (2007); USA Today Baseball High School Player of the Year (2006); Gatorade National Player of the Year (2006); Eight-Time National League Player of the Week; Six-Time National League Pitcher of the Month **RE:** Methodist

KESSLER, MICHAEL WILLIAM, MD, T: Associate Professor **I:** Medicine & Health Care **CN:** MedStar Georgetown University Hospital **MS:** Married **CH:** Three Children **ED:** Fellowship, Department of Hand Surgery, Thomas Jefferson University Hospital at the Philadelphia Hand Center (2010-2011); Residency, Department of Orthopaedic Surgery, North Shore-Long Island Jewish Health System (Now Northwell Health) (2006-2010); Internship, Department of General Surgery, North Shore-Long Island Jewish Health System (Now Northwell Health) (2005-2006); MD, Albany Medical College, Albany, NY (2005); MPH, Mailman School of Public Health, Columbia University, New York, NY (2004); BS in Biomedical Science, Sophie Davis School of Biomedical Education, CUNY School of Medicine, City College of New York, New York, NY, Cum Laude (2002) **CT:** Certification, Subspecialty Board, Hand Surgery (2014, 2024); Board Certification, American Board of Orthopaedic Surgery (2013, 2023); Certification, AAMC Medical Education Research Certification (MERC) (2014); Course Completion, Orthopaedic Educators Course, American Academy of Orthopaedic Surgery (2012) **C:** Associate Professor of Orthopaedic Surgery, MedStar Georgetown University Hospital, Washington, DC (2011-Present); Chief, Division of Hand and Elbow Surgery, MedStar Georgetown University Hospital, Washington, DC (2011-Present); Residency Program Director, Department of Orthopaedic Surgery, MedStar Georgetown University Hospital, Washington, DC (2011-Present); Academic/Administrative Chief Resident, North Shore-Long Island Jewish Health System (Now Northwell Health), New Hyde Park, NY (2009-2010); Research Assistant, International Center for Health Outcomes and Innovation Research (InCHOIR), Columbia University, New York, NY (2003-2004) **CR:** Lecturer, Gross Anatomy (Limbs Module) (2018-Present); Special Reviewer, Graduate Medical Education Committee, Resident Dismissals, MedStar or Hospital Service (2015-Present); Faculty/Facilitator, Medical Education Journal Club (2014-Present); Member, Clinical Competency Committee, MedStar or Hospital Service (2014-Present); Chair, Program Evaluation Committee, MedStar or Hospital Service (2014-Present); Chair, Resident Admissions Committee (2012-Present); Preceptor, Ambulatory Care I & II (2011-Present); Member, Faculty, Orthopaedic Surgery, Medical School Clerkship (2011-Present); Fellow, Department of Hand Surgery, Thomas Jefferson University Hospital at the Philadelphia Hand Center, Philadelphia, PA (2010-2011); Resident, Department of Orthopaedic Surgery, Long Island Jewish Medical Center, Northwell Health, New Hyde Park, NY (2006-2010); Intern, Department of General Surgery, Long Island Jewish Medical Center, Northwell Health, New Hyde Park, NY (2005-2006) **CIV:** Co-Chair, Native American Health Service Committee, American Society for Surgery of the Hand (2018-Present); Question Writer, Self Assessment Committee, American Society for Surgery of the Hand (2016-Present); Hand Surgeon, Volunteer Faculty, Chinle Comprehensive Care Facility, Chinle, AZ (2016-Present); Question Writer, Maintenance of Certification Exam, Arthroscopy Association of North America (2015); Medical Mission to Uganda and Kenya, Africa (2003) **CW:** Lecturer, Invited Lectures (2016, 2019); Contributor, Numerous Original Papers, Refereed Journals (2005-2018); Contributor, Numerous Abstracts for Conference Papers and Posters (2009-2017); Reviewer, Yearbook of Hand and Upper Limb Surgery (2015, 2016); Co-Author, "Medical and Lateral Epicondylitis," Surgical Techniques of the Shoulder, Elbow, and Knee in Sports Medicine (2012); Presenter, Numerous Presentations (2009-2012); Co-Author, "Pathophysiology of Spinal Cord Injury," Spine Trauma and Critical Care (2007); Author, Editor, "Blueprints Orthopedics: A Pocket Guide" (2005) **AW:** Top Doctor, Washingtonian Magazine (2015-2019); Top 10 Poster "Patient Attitudes Towards Electronic Use in a Hospital-Based Orthopaedics Clinc: A Survey Study" (2017); Kenmore Award "for Excellence in Resident Education," Department of Orthopaedic Surgery, MedStar Georgetown University Hospital (2016); Top 10 Poster "Patient Attitudes Towards Orthopedic Surgeon Attire in a Hospital-Based Clinic: A Survey Study," American Orthopaedic Association (2016); Best Paper at Alumni Day, North Shore - Long Island Jewish Department of Orthopaedic Surgery (2010); Joseph H. Boyes Award, "Enhancement of tendon repair by blockade of matrix metalloproteinase," American Society for Surgery of the Hand (2009); Second Place, Residents and Fellows Night, "Augmentation of Zone II flexor tendon repair using GDF-5 in a rabbit model," New York Society for Surgery of the Hand (2009); Award for Excellence in Orthopaedic Research, Department of Orthopedics at Long Island Jewish Medical Center (2009) **MEM:** Associate Member, Georgetown University Medical Center Teaching Academy (2015-Present); American Orthopaedic Association (2018); American Society for Surgery of the Hand (2015); American Academy of Orthopaedic Surgery (2014); Washington D.C. Society for Surgery of the Hand (2011); Medical Society of the District of Columbia (2011); Council of Residency Directors, American Orthopaedic Association; Medical Society of the District of Columbia **AS:** Dr. Kessler attributes his success to being a perfectionist and not accepting mediocrity. **B/I:** Dr. Kessler became involved in his profession because he wants to be able to help others achieve success. **THT:** Dr. Kessler's motto is, "Do the best thing you can for the patient."

KETTLESON, DAVID NOEL, T: Retired Orthopaedic Surgeon, Timber Manager **I:** Medicine & Health Care **DOB:** 12/20/1938 **PB:** St. Paul **SC:** MN/USA **PT:** John Benton Kettleson Sr; Dorothy S. Kettleson **MS:** Married **SPN:** Karen Nordstrom Kettleson (08/25/1961) **CH:** EmKay; Daniel; Laura **ED:** Resident in Orthopaedic Surgery, University of Minnesota Hospital, Minneapolis, MN (1965-1969); Intern, St. Mary's Hospital, Duluth, MN (1964-1965); BS, MD, University of Minnesota (1964); BA, University of Minnesota (1960) **C:** Founder, Treasurer, Kettleson's Eagleview Farms, L.P. (2003-Present); Owner, Eagleview Farms, Crosslake, MN (1994-2003); Retired from Medical Practice (1994); President, Nebraska Spine Surgeons, Omaha, NE (1992-1994); Vice President, Secretary, Treasurer, Orthopaedic Surgery, Inc., Omaha, NE (1971-1992) **CR:** Chairman, Department of Orthopedics, Immanuel Medical Center, Omaha, NE (1978-1982) **MIL:** Served to Major, U.S. Air Force, Stationed at Tinker AFB, Oklahoma City and Offutt AFB, Omaha, NE (1969-1971) **AW:** Named, Minnesota Outstanding Tree Farmer of Year, American Forest Foundation (2001) **MEM:** Secretary, Nebraska Orthopaedic Society (1974-1985); Secretary, Mid Central States Orthopaedic Society (1974-1985); Fellow, North America Spine Society; American Medical Association; Scoliosis Research Society; American Tree Farm System **MH:** Albert Nelson Marquis Lifetime Achievement Award; Marquis Who's Who Top Professional **B/I:** Dr. Kettleson's mother was a nurse. He started in college majoring in forestry and wildlife management. His older brother went to school for Pre-Med, after the second year his brother started having health problems and had to drop out of school. At this time Dr. Kettleson changed his major to Pre-med. He did a four-year undergraduate program with chemistry, biology, and psychology majors.

KETTLEWELL, GAIL B., T: Global Development Education Professional **I:** Education/Educational Services **DOB:** 04/05/1939 **PB:** Dresden **SC:** OH/USA **PT:** Graydon Adams; Mildred K. (Cox) Biery **MS:** Widowed **SPN:** Charles G. Kettlewell (9/9/1960, Deceased 2016) **CH:** Christian; Abigail; Nathaniel **ED:** EdD, Virginia Polytechnic Institute and State University, Blacksburg, VA (1985); MA, Old Dominion University (1973); BA, Muskingum College (1961) **C:** Board of Directors, LEAD Foundation (2011-Present); Principal, International Center of Arts, Culture, and Education, George Mason University (2008-2012); Research Professor, Director of International Post Secondary Development, George Mason University (2006-2008); Director, Higher Education Program, George Mason University, Fairfax, VA (2002-2006); Provost, Northern Virginia Community College (1990-2002); Vice-Chancellor, Southern Arkansas University of Technology (1984-1990); Associate Professor, Tidewater Community College (1974-1983); Teacher, Portsmouth Public Schools (1962-1968, 1970-1972); Teacher, Fairfax County Public Schools, Alexandria, VA (1968-1970); Librarian, Knox County Library, Mount Vernon, OH (1961-1962) **CR:** Chairman, International Applied Arts and Sciences Institute (1999-2001) **CIV:** Gray Ghost Theater (2006-2009); New Chair Board, NCHS Alumni Endowed Scholarship Fund (2007); Prince William County Chapter, American Red Cross (1991-2005); Vice-Chairman, Managing Director, President, Prince William Habitat for Humanity (2001-2004); Prince William/I66 Partnership (1994-2002); Prince William/Manassas Convention and Visitors Bureau (2001); Manassas Center for the Arts (1994-1999); American Council Education Commission on Women (1994-1997); Manassas Tourism Council (1994-1996); Manassas Business Council (1994-1996); Manassas Museum Associates (1991-1994); Prince William Litter Control Council (1991); Arkansas Technology Committee, Little Rock, AR (1989-1990); Coordinator, Organizer, Ouachita-Calhoun Literacy Council, Camden, AR (1987-1989); Board of Directors, Arkansas Literacy Council, Little Rock, AR (1988) **CW:** Editorial Board, Workforce (1994); Co-Author, "Reading/Thinking/Writing" (1983); Author, "Guide for Peer Tutors" (1981); Co-Author, "An Approach to Language" (1978) **AW:** Fellow, Western Carolina University (1976); Fellow, Old Dominion University (1967); Community Service Award, Portsmouth, VA **MEM:** President, Federation Civic Clubs (1981-Present); Board of Directors, Vice President, President, Rotary (1992-2008); Board of Directors, Prince William/Greater Manassas Chamber of Commerce (1994-2002); Committee on Women, American Council Education (1994-1997); Phi Delta Kappa; Vice President, President, Delta Kappa Gamma (1980-1993); Senior President, Children American Revolution (1989-1990); North Central Association Schools and Colleges (1987-1990); President, Arkansas Association Development Education (1988-1989); Daughters of the American Revolution; National Association of Female Executives; American Association of University Women; American Society for Training and Development; PBD; Manassas Business Council; Virginia Association of Female Executives; Honorary Member, Phi Theta Kappa **AV:** Playing piano **RE:** Episcopalian

KEYS, ALICIA, T: Singer, Songwriter, Musician **I:** Government Administration/Government Relations/Government Services **DOB:** 01/25/1981 **PB:** Manhattan **SC:** NY/USA **PT:** Craig Cook; Teresa Augello **MS:** Married **SPN:** Kasseem Dean "Swizz Beatz" (07/31/2010) **CH:** Egypt Daoud Dean; Genesis Ali Dean **ED:** Coursework, Columbia University, New York, NY **C:** Global Creative Director, BlackBerry (2013) **CIV:** Co-founder, Global Ambassador, Keep a Child Alive; Performer, Numerous Benefit Concerts Including Live 8, America: A Tribute to Heroes, ReAct Now: Music & Relief, and Shelter from the Storm: A Concert for the Gulf Coast **CW:** Author, "More Myself: A Journey" (2020); Singer, "Alicia" (2020); Host, Grammy Awards (2019, 2020); Appearance, "Marriage Boot Camp" (2018); Judge, "The Voice" (2016, 2018); Performer, "Landmarks Live: Great Performances" (2017); Performer, "The Soundtrack of My Life" (2017); Performer, "Here in Times Square" (2016); Appearance, "The Gospel" (2016); Appearance, "CMT Crossroads" (2016); Singer, "Here" (2016); Singer, "Holy War" (2016); Singer, "Powerful" (2015); Singer, "Know Who You Are" (2015); Singer, "We Are Here" (2014); Actress, "The Ninth Wave" (2014); Author, "Blue Moon: From the Journals of MaMa Mae and LeeLee" (2014); Executive Producer, Composer, "The Inevitable Defeat of Mister and Pete" (2013); Executive Producer, "Firelight" (2012); Singer, Song and Album, "Girl on Fire" (2012); Singer, "Empire State of Mind (Part II) Broken Down" (2010); Singer, "Un-Thinkable (I'm Ready)" (2010); Singer, "The Element of Freedom" (2009); Singer with Jay Z, "Empire State of Mind" (2009); Actress, "The Secret Life of Bees" (2008); Singer, "Superwoman" (2008); Actress, "Smokin' Aces" (2007); Actress, "The Nanny Diaries" (2007); Singer, "No One" (2007); Singer, "As I Am" (2007); Singer, "Unbreakable" (2005); Singer, "Unplugged" (2005); Singer, "If I Ain't Got You" (2004); Singer, "Karma" (2004); Singer Featuring Tony! Toni! Toné!, "Diary" (2004); Singer with Usher, "My Boo" (2004); Author, "Tears for Water: Songbook of Poems and Lyrics" (2004); Actress, "American Dreams" (2003); Singer, "The Diary of Alicia Keys" (2003); Singer, "You Don't Know My Name" (2003); Singer, "Fallin" (2001); Singer, "Songs in A Minor" (2001); Performer, "Saturday Night Live" (2001); Actress, "Charmed" (2001); Appearance, "The Cosby Show" (1985); Singer, Songwriter, Musician, Collaborator, Solo Albums and Soundtracks; Host, Guest Host, Television Shows and Specials **AW:** Songwriter Icon Award, National Music Publishers Association (2018); Named One of the 100 Most Influential People in the World, TIME Magazine (2005, 2017); Award for Outstanding Song, NAACP Image Awards (2015); Recording Artists' Coalition Award, Recording Academy (2015); Grammy Award for Best R&B Album, Recording Academy (2014); Awards for Outstanding Female Artist, Outstanding Music Video, NAACP Image Awards (2013); Grammy Award for Best Rap Song, Best Rap/Sung Collaboration, Recording Academy (2011); Award for Outstanding Music Video, NAACP Image Awards (2011); Named One of the Top 20 Hot 100 Songwriters: 2000-2011, Billboard Magazine (2011); Named One of the 100 Greatest Artists of All Time, VH1 (2010); Awards for Artist of the Decade, Best Female R&B Artist, Best Collaboration, BET Awards (2010); Grammy Award for Best Female R&B Vocal Performance, Recording Academy (2009); Humanitarian Award, BET Awards (2009); Awards for Favorite R&B Song, Favorite R&B Song, People's Choice Awards (2009); Awards for Best R&B Female Artist, BET Awards (2005, 2008); Named Best Selling R&B Artist, World Music Awards (2002, 2004, 2008); Grammy Awards for Best Female R&B Vocal Performance, Best R&B Song, Recording Academy (2008); Named One of the 100 Most Powerful Celebrities, Forbes.com (2008); Named Best Album: Pop/Rock, Best Album: Soul/R&B, American Music Awards (2008); Awards for Outstanding Album, Outstanding Song, Outstanding Music Video, Outstanding Female Artist, NAACP Image Awards (2008); Awards for Outstanding Female Artist, Outstanding Song, Outstanding Music Video, NAACP Image Awards (2006); Awards for Best R&B Video, MTV Video Music Awards (2004, 2005); Grammy Award for Best R&B Album, Best Female R&B Performance, Best R&B Performance by a Duo or Group with Vocals, Best R&B Song, Recording Academy (2005); Named Songwriter of the Year, ASCAP (2005); Named Favorite Female Singer, People's Choice Awards (2005); Awards for Outstanding Music Video, Outstanding Song, NAACP Image Awards (2005); Hal David Starlight Award, Songwriters Hall of Fame (2005); Awards for Female R&B/Hip-Hop Artist of Year, Hot 100 Songwriter of the Year, Female Artist of the Year, R&B/Hip-Hop Single of the Year, R&B/Hip-Hop Airplay Single of the Year, R&B/Hip-Hop Albums Artist of the Year, R&B/Hip-Hop Singles Artist of the Year, Billboard Music Awards (2004); Awards for Favorite Female Soul/R&B Artist, American Music Awards (2004); Named One of the 50 Most Influential African-Americans, Ebony Magazine (2004); Grammy Awards for Best New Artist, Song of the Year, Best Female R&B Vocal Performance, Best R&B Song, Best R&B Album, Recording Academy (2002); Awards for Outstanding New Artist, Outstanding Female Artist, Outstanding Album, Outstanding Song, NAACP Image Awards (2002); Award for Best New Artist, BET Awards (2002); Awards for Favorite New Artist: Pop/Rock, Favorite New Artist: Soul/R&B, American Music Awards (2002); Award for Top R&B/Hip-Hop Album, Billboard R&B/Hip-Hop Awards (2002); Award for R&B/Soul Solo Artist Album of Year, Soul Train Lady of Soul Awards (2002); Awards for Female Artist of the Year, New R&B/Hip-Hop Artist of the Year, Billboard Music Awards (2001); Numerous Awards

KEYWELL, BRAD, T: Founder, Chief Executive Officer **I:** Technology **CN:** Uptake Technologies **DOB:** 10/27/1969 **PB:** Bloomfield Hills **SC:** MI/USA **ED:** JD, University of Michigan, Ann Arbor, MI (1993); BBA, University of Michigan, Ann Arbor, MI (1991); Coursework, London School of Economics (1990) **C:** Co-Founder, Director, Mediabank, LLC (2006-Present); Co-Founder, Director, Groupon, Inc. (2006-Present); Co-Founder, Director, Echo Global Logistics, Inc. (2005-Present); Co-Founder, Managing Director, Lightbank; Managing Partner, Meadow Lake Management, LLC; Equity Group Investments, LLC; Former President, HA-LO Industries; Co-Founder, Starbelly **CR:** Founder, Co-Curator, TEDxYouth/Midwest, TEDxMidwest, Chicago Ideas Week; Guest Lecturer, Medill School of Journalism and Kellogg Graduate School of Management, Northwestern University; Guest Lecturer, University of Michigan Business School; Adjunct Professor, Booth School of Business, University of Chicago **CIV:** Judge, University of Chicago Booth School New Venture Challenge; Special Advisor, Redmood Theatre Co., Chicago, IL; Founder, Digital Leadership Exchange; Founder, Connect to the Future Program, Chicago, IL; Appointed Member, Mayor's Chicago-China Friendship Initiative; Appointed Member, Mayor's Committee on Technology Infrastructure, Chicago, IL; Appointed Chairman, Illinois Innovation Council, Chicago, IL; Board of Directors, Warrior Productions; Board of Directors, Abraham Path Initiative; Advisory Committee, University of Chicago GSB Directors' College; Advisory Board of Directors, University of Michigan Law School College of Global Business; Board of Trustees, University of Michigan Hillel Foundation; Board of Trustees, University of Michigan Ross School of Business Zell Lurie Institute for Entrepreneurship; Board of Trustees, Imerman Angels; Board of Trustees, NorthShore University HealthSystem Foundation; Board of Trustees, Columbia College **CW:** Author, "Biz Dev 3.0: Changing Business as We Know It"; Co-Author, "Isabelle Speaks Up: A Story of Possibilities" **AW:** Ernst & Young World Entrepreneur of the Year (2019);

Conrad Hilton Distinguished Entrepreneur Award, Loyola Marymount University (2000); Named, Top 10 Collegiate Entrepreneurs, Association of Collegiate Entrepreneurs (1991); Named, Internet 100, Crain's Chicago Business **MEM:** Michigan Bar Association; State Bar of Illinois; Chairman, YPO Coaches Clinic, Young Presidents' Organization

KHAN, BADRUL, T: Information Technology Educator **I:** Technology **DOB:** 12/31/1958 **PB:** Chittagong **SC:** Bangladesh **PT:** Lokman Khan; Shabnom Khanam Sherwani **MS:** Married **SPN:** Komar Parveen Khan (05/04/1990) **CH:** Intisar Shewani; Inshat Sherwani **ED:** PhD, Indiana University (1994); BA, Indiana University (1988) **C:** Founder, Bookstoread.Com, Springfield, VA (1999-Present); Professor, Director, George Washington University, Washington, DC (1997-Present); Professor, Director, University of Texas (1994-1997); Evaluation Specialist, Independent Medical School, Indianapolis, IN (1994); Founder, Personal Website **CR:** Speaker, Web-Based Instruction; Speaker, E-Learning **CW:** Author, "E-Learning Strategies" (2002); Editor, "Web-Based Training" (2001); Editor, "Web-Based Instruction" (1997) **AW:** Inductee, Hall of Fame, United States Distance Learning Association (USDLA) (2014) **MEM:** Association for Educational Communications and Technology **MH:** Albert Nelson Marquis Lifetime Achievement Award **B/I:** Dr. Khan came to the United States in 1981 as an international student. He was studying chemistry as an undergraduate and always thought about sharing his knowledge with people in the world. He realized that coming from a small country, such as Bangladesh, he needed to have a focus on helping others. This was why he changed his major to instructional technology, as people could learn from using technology. From there, the invention of the internet provided Dr. Khan with various insights. He began using web technology to provide others with education. He then wrote an internet instruction book, which was a best seller in 1997. Today, 315 universities, including Harvard University, use the book as a reference guide and a textbook. **AV:** Cooking

KHAN, SHAHID, "SHAD", T: Chief Executive Officer, Manufacturing Executive, Professional Sports Team Executive **I:** Manufacturing **CN:** Flex-N-Gate Corporation **DOB:** 07/18/1950 **PB:** Lahore **SC:** Pakistan **MS:** Married **SPN:** Ann Carlson Khan (1977) **CH:** Shanna; Tony **ED:** Bachelor of Science in Mechanical Engineering, University of Illinois at Urbana-Champaign, IL (1971) **C:** Co-investor, All Elite Wrestling (2019-Present); Owner, Fulham FC, Barclays Premier League (2013-Present); Owner, Jacksonville Jaguars, NFL, Florida (2012-Present); Chief Executive Officer, President, Owner, Flex-N-Gate Corporation, Illinois (1980-Present); Founder, Auto Parts Designer and Manufacturer, Bumper Works (1978-1980); Product and Tooling Design Engineer, Flex-N-Gate Corporation, Illinois(1970-1978); Chairperson, Bio-Alternative LLC, Illinois; Chairperson, Smart Structures LLC, Illinois **CR:** Member, Daimler-Chrysler Minority Supplier Council **CIV:** Member, Business Advisory Council, University of Illinois Gies College Business; Member, Board of Visitors, University of Illinois Grainger College of Engineering; Board Member, NFL Foundation **AW:** Listee, Billionaires List, Forbes (2020); Named, One of the Forbes 400 (2019); Minority Business Leadership Award, National Minority Supplier Development Council (2007); Co-recipient, Alumni Award for Distinguished Service University of Illinois Grainger College of Engineering (2006); Distinguished Service Award, University of Illinois Alumni Association (2005); Mechanical and Industrial Engineering Dis-

tinguished Alumnus Award, University of Illinois at Urbana-Champaign (1999) **MEM:** World Presidents Organization

KHANNA, ROHIT, "RO", T: U.S. Representative from California; Lawyer **I:** Government Administration/Government Relations/Government Services **DOB:** 09/13/1976 **PB:** Philadelphia **SC:** PA/USA **MS:** Married **SPN:** Ritu Ahuja (2015) **CH:** Zara; Soren **ED:** JD, Yale Law School (2001); BA in Economics, The University of Chicago (1998) **C:** Member, U.S. House of Representatives from California's 17th Congressional District (2017-Present); Lawyer, Wilson Sonsini Goodrich & Rosati (2011-Present); Deputy Assistant Secretary, U.S. Department of Commerce (2009-2012); Member, Committee on Armed Services; Member, Committee on the Budget **CW:** Author, Novel, "Entrepreneurial Nation: Why Manufacturing is Key to America's Future" (2012)

KHOSROWSHAHI, DARA, T: Chief Executive Officer **I:** Business Management/Business Services **CN:** Uber **DOB:** 05/28/1959 **SC:** Tehran/Iran **PT:** Asghar "Gary" Khosrowshahi; Lili Khosrowshahi **MS:** Married **SPN:** Sydney Shapiro (12/12/2012) **CH:** Alex; Chloe; Hayes Epic; Hugo Gubrit **ED:** BSEE, Brown University (1991); Diploma, Hackley School, Tarrytown, NY (1987) **C:** Chief Executive Officer, Uber (2017-Present); Chief Executive Officer, Expedia, Inc., Bellevue, WA (2005-2017); Chief Financial Officer, IAC (1998-2005) **CIV:** Donor, Hillary Victory Fund, Sen. Patty Murray, Democratic National Committee, Sen. Mike Lee **MEM:** Sigma Chi

KICKLIGHTER, ALMA LOUISE, T: Communicable Diseases Specialist, Nurse, County Administrator **I:** Medicine & Health Care **DOB:** 01/12/1933 **PB:** Live Oak **SC:** FL/USA **PT:** Eugene Kicklighter; Mary Bell (Ashley) Young Kicklighter **MS:** Married **SPN:** Samuel Kicklighter **CH:** Carletta Ophelia; Harrell Alonzo; Samuel; June Renee **ED:** BSN, Florida Agricultural & Mechanical University (1958); Postgraduate Coursework, University of South Florida **C:** Owner, Operator, Ghettreal Community Services (2007-2016); Nursing Teacher, Pinellas County Schools (2000-2007); Public Health Nurse Supervisor, Florida Department of Health in Pinellas County (1964-2000); Nursing Program Specialist for Communicable Diseases, Florida Department of Health in Pinellas County (1990-1994); Supervisor of Epidemiology, Florida Department of Health in Pinellas County (1979-1994); Public Health Nurse, School Consultant, Florida Department of Health in Pinellas County (1959-1963); Charge Nurse, Medical, Surgical and Obstetrical Ward, Mercy Hospital (1958-1962); Teacher, Columbia County School District (1955) **CR:** Consultant **CIV:** HIV/AIDS Program, Florida Department of Health in Pinellas (2006-2016); Organizer, Open Door Bible Study (1980); Chair, Equal Employment Committee, HRS District Five; Former Second Vice President, St. Petersburg Citizens Council On Crime, Inc.; Former President, BRCHS PTSA **AW:** Plaque, Equal Employment Committee (1979); Woman of the Year, American Business Women's Association (1978-1979) **MEM:** American Nurses Association; Florida Nurses Association; Florida Public Health Association; Chi Eta Phi Sorority, Inc.; Delta Sigma Theta Sorority, Inc. **MH:** Albert Nelson Marquis Lifetime Achievement Award **B/I:** Ms. Kicklighter became involved in her profession because she was inspired by her grandmother, a midwife. **RE:** Democrat

KIDD, MICHEL, T: Environmental Health and Safety Specialist **I:** Environmental Services **CN:** BPI Coatings **ED:** Bachelor of Science in Natural

Sciences, Christian Brothers University, Memphis, TN (2014) **CT:** CPR/AED Certification, American Red Cross **C:** Environmental Health and Safety Specialist, AEROTEK/BPI Coatings, Olive Branch, MS (2018-Present); Microbiology Technician, APEX Life Sciences/Piramal Pharma Solutions, Lexington, KY (2018); Field Chemist, Tradebe Environmental, Nashville, TN (2015-2018); Wave Closure Clerk, Williams Sonoma, Olive Branch, MS (2014-2015) **CR:** Pharmacy Technician, Walgreens (2010-2014) **CIV:** Volunteers at Local Church **AS:** Ms. Kidd attributes her success to her son, who motivates her to do her best every day. **B/I:** Ms. Kidd became involved in her profession because she was working at a warehouse and decided she wanted to become a field chemist. She always had an interest in biological sciences and had a very inquisitive mind already, so the field was very interesting to her. **THT:** "Always strive to be better than yesterday."

KIEST, ALAN S., T: Senior Vice President, Co-Founder **I:** Financial Services **CN:** LTS Financial **DOB:** 05/14/1949 **PB:** Portland **SC:** OR/USA **PT:** Roger M. Kiest; Ellen Kiest **CH:** Jennifer S. **ED:** MPA, University of Washington (1979); BA in Political Science, University of Puget Sound (1970) **CT:** Associate Business Continuity Professional, Disaster Recovery Institute (2007); Certified Facilitator, The Pacific Institute (2006) **C:** Co-Founder, LTS Financial (2019-Present); Benefits Adviser, Aflac Incorporated (2015-2020); Regional Vice President, Freedom Equity Group (2018-2019); National Agency Manager, Virtual Financial Group (2016-2018); Community Services Office Administrator, Washington State Department of Social and Health Services (1982-2014); Service Delivery Coordinator, Washington State Department of Social and Health Services (1976-1982); Caseworker, Washington State Department of Social and Health Services (1972-1976); Welfare Eligibility Examiner, Washington State Department of Social and Health Services (1970-1972) **CR:** Chair, Budget Committee, Lake Forest Park (2006-2009); Member, City Council, Lake Forest Park (1990-2009); Vice Chair, Budget Committee, Lake Forest Park (1998-2005); Member, King County Human Services Roundtable (1995-2000); Chair, City Finance Committee, Lake Forest Park (1992-1997); Member, King County Managed Health Care Oversight Committee (1993-1995); Planning Commissioner, Lake Forest Park (1989) **CIV:** Regional State Judge, National History Day (2019-Present); Community Development Committee, United Way of King County (2003-2013); Member, Steering Committee, Reinvesting in Youth (2003-2006); Member, Executive Committee, United Way of King County (2001-2002); Member, Eastside Community Council, United Way of King County (1998-2002) **CW:** Co-Author, "Local WIN Program Managers as Constrained Entrepreneurs" (1981) **AW:** Three-Time Winner, Outstanding Employee, Regional Level, Washington State Department of Social and Health Services **MEM:** Community Emergency Response Team, Northshore Emergency Management Coalition (2015-Present); Suburban Cities Association (2000-2009) **MH:** Albert Nelson Marquis Lifetime Achievement Award **B/I:** Mr. Kiest became involved in his profession because of a series of fortunate opportunities within the state system. **AV:** Traveling; Listening to music

KILANOWSKI, DANA MARCOTTE, T: Historian, Writer, Filmmaker, Archaeologist **I:** Media & Entertainment **DOB:** 08/30/1946 **PB:** Grand Forks **SC:** ND/USA **PT:** Virgil Wallace Marcotte; Lucille Hogan (Weidel) Marcotte **MS:** Married **SPN:** Lt. Col. Samuel Joseph Kilanowski (08/30/1975) **CH:** Kristen Marcotte; Samantha Marcotte **ED:** BA, University of North Dakota, Grand Forks, ND (1975); Postgraduate Studies in History, Archaeology, Oral History Workshops and Short Courses, Oral History Association and Columbia University **C:** President, Dana Marcotte Kilanowski Productions, Palmdale, CA (1994-Present); Managing Partner, Kerosene Flats Entertainment LLC (2005-2010); Historian, Archaeologist, Computer Science Corporation, Edwards Air Force Base (1987-1994); Acting Director, Non-Academic Employment, University of North Dakota, Grand Forks, ND (1968-1971) **CR:** Oral Historian, The Society of Experimental Test Pilots (2005-Present); Guest Historian, The History Channel, New York, NY (1997) **CIV:** Vice-Chairman, Flight Test Historical Foundation, Lancaster, CA (2008-Present); Guest Lecturer, Antelope Valley Schools (1987-Present); Director, Flight Test Historical Foundation, Lancaster, CA (1991-2016); Parent-Teacher Association (PTA), Edwards Air Force Base (1986); President, Officers' Spouses Clubs, Edwards Air Force Base (1985-1986) **CW:** Chairwoman, Heroes & Legends, Aviation History Panels, L.A. County Air Shows (2017-Present); Executive Producer, "The Legends of Flight" (2004-Present); Oral Historian, Society of Experimental Test Pilots (SETP) (2018-2019); Guest Historian, Public Broadcasting Service (PBS) (2016); Guest Historian, "Space Men," Public Broadcasting Service (PBS) (2016); Contributor, Consultant, "Sonic Wind: The Story of John Paul Stapp and How a Renegade Doctor Became the Fastest Man on Earth" (2015); Co-Author, "Pancho Barnes and Tales From the Happy Bottom Riding Club" (2010); Producer, Historian, "The Legends of Flight" (2005); Featured, "Jackie Cochran" (2000); Contributor, Consultant, "Something New Under the Sun, Jets Come of Age," "Our American Century: A Century of Flight" (1999); Guest Historian, "Movies In Time," The History Channel (1998); Co-Author, Editor, "The Quest for Mach One: A First-Person Account of Breaking the Sound Barrier" (1997); Executive Co-Producer, "Mach One, The Times, The Team, The Sound Barrier," The History Channel (1997); Producer, "The Happy Bottom Riding Club" (1994); Co-Author, Co-Editor, "45th Anniversary Test Pilot School History Book," U.S. Air Force Test Pilots School, Edwards Air Force Base (1989); Co-Author, Co-Editor, "35th Anniversary Test Pilots School History Book," U.S. Air Force Test Pilots School, Edwards Air Force Base (1979); Interviewer, Over 160 Interviews, World's Leading Test Pilots and Astronauts; Contributor, Numerous Articles, Professional Journals **AW:** Best Book Award, "The Quest for Mach One," American Library Association (1998-1999); Key Research Historian Award, Department of Defense and Center Environmental Excellence (1997); Commendation, Jet Pioneers of America (1991); Commendation, Air Force Flight Test Center (1989) **MEM:** American Association of University Women; National Council of Public History; National Trust Historical Preservation; South West Oral History Association; Oral History Association; American Film Institute **MH:** Albert Nelson Marquis Lifetime Achievement Award **B/I:** Ms. Kilanowski became involved in her profession because of an aerospace historian from the Mercury, Gemini, and Apollo programs in the 1960s who truly inspired her. **AV:** Reading; Hiking; Swimming; Water-skiing **PA:** Independent **RE:** Christian

KILDEE, DANIEL, "DAN" TIMOTHY, T: U.S. Representative **I:** Government Administration/Government Relations/Government Services **DOB:** 08/11/1958 **PB:** Flint **SC:** MI/USA **MS:** Married **SPN:** Jennifer Kildee **CH:** Ryan; Katy; Kenneth **ED:** BS in Community Development Administration, Central Michigan University (2008) **C:** U.S. Representative, Michigan's Fifth District, United States Congress,

Washington, DC (2013-Present); Assistant Minority Whip, U.S. House of Representatives, Michigan's Fifth District, United States Congress (2013-Present); Member, U.S. House Committee on Financial Services (2013-Present); Founder, Chief Executive Officer, Genesee County Land Bank (2002-2009); Treasurer, Genesee County, MI (1997-2009); Commissioner, Genesee County, MI (1985-1997); Member, Flint Board of Education, MI (1977-1985); Youth Specialist, Whaley Children's Center (1976-1985); Member, Budget Committee; Member, Committee on Ways and Means **CR:** Co-Founder, President, Center for Community Progress (2009-2012) **PA:** Democrat

KILMEADE, BRIAN, T: Television and Radio Personality **I:** Media & Entertainment **CN:** Fox News **DOB:** 03/07/1964 **PB:** New York **SC:** NY/USA **MS:** Married **SPN:** Dawn (DeGaetano) Kilmeade **CH:** Brian; Kirstyn; Kaitlyn **ED:** BA, Long Island University Post, Brookville, NY (1986) **C:** Co-Host, "Fox & Friends," Fox News (2008-Present); Freelance Sports Anchor, WVIT, Hartford, CT (1997); Guest Co-Host, "The Five" (2012-2017); Host, "The Brian Kilmeade Show," Fox News Radio; Anchor, "Scoreboard Central"; Featured Reporter, Host, "Newsport Journal," Newsport TV; Sideline Reporter, MSG Network; Co-host, "The Jim Brown Shows," KLSD; Anchor, Host, KHSL-TV, Ontario, CA; Correspondent, Channel One News **CW:** Author, "Sam Houston and the Alamo Avengers: The Texas Victory That Changed American History" (2019); Author, "Andrew Jackson and the Miracle of New Orleans: The Battle That Shaped America's Destiny" (2017); Author, "Thomas Jefferson and the Tripoli Pirates: The Forgotten War That Changed American History" (2015); Author, "George Washington's Secret Six: The Spy Ring That Saved the American Revolution" (2013); Author, "It's How You Play the Game: The Powerful Sports Moments That Taught Lasting Values to America's Finest" (2007); Author, "The Games Do Count: America's Best and Brightest on the Power of Sports" (2004) **RE:** Roman Catholic

KILMER, DEREK CHRISTIAN, T: U.S. Representative from Washington **I:** Government Administration/Government Relations/Government Services **CN:** U.S. House of Representatives **DOB:** 01/01/1974 **PB:** Port Angeles **SC:** WA/USA **MS:** Married **SPN:** Jennifer Kilmer **CH:** Sophie; Tess **ED:** Doctor of Philosophy in Comparative Social Policy, Green Templeton College, University of Oxford (2003); Bachelor of Arts in Public Affairs, Princeton University Woodrow Wilson School Public and International Affairs (1996) **C:** Chair, New Democrat Coalition (2019-Present); Member, U.S. House of Representatives from Washington's Sixth Congressional District, Washington, DC (2013-Present); Member, U.S. House Armed Services Committee (2013-Present); Member, U.S. House Committee on Science, Space and Technology (2013-Present); Member, District 26, Washington State Senate (2007-2012); Member, District 26, Washington House of Representative (2005-2007); Management Consultant, McKinsey & Company; Vice President, Economic Development Board, Tacoma-Pierce Co.; Member, Committee on Appropriations **AW:** Named, Honorary Fire Chief, Washington Fire Chiefs; Legislator of the Year, Washington Council of Police & Sheriffs; Legislative Business Star Award, Enterprise Washington's Business Institute; Three-time Recipient, LEADER Award, Washington Economic Development Association; Marshall Scholarship, Department of Social Policy and Intervention, Green Templeton College, University of Oxford **PA:** Democrat **RE:** United Methodist Church

KIM, ANDREW, "ANDY" N., T: U.S. Representative from New Jersey **I:** Government Administration/Government Relations/Government Services **CN:** U.S. House of Representatives **DOB:** 7/12/1982 **PB:** Boston **SC:** MA/USA **MS:** Married **SPN:** Kammy Lai **ED:** Intern, United States Agency for International Development; Doctor of Philosophy, Magdalen College, University of Oxford; Master of Philosophy, Magdalen College, University of Oxford; Bachelor of Arts, Deep Springs College, The University of Chicago **C:** Member, U.S. House of Representatives from New Jersey's Third District (2019-Present); United States National Security Council Official, President Barack Obama **AW:** Rhodes Scholar; Harry S. Truman Scholarship, Magdalen College, University of Oxford **PA:** Democrat

KIM, DONGHWAN, T: Online Marketer **I:** Advertising & Marketing **CN:** stylemix77 **DOB:** 05/09/1985 **ED:** Master in International Business, Hult International Business School, Boston, MA (2015); BS in Accounting and Finance Management, Northeastern University, Boston, MA (2014); Foundation Degree in Art and Design, University of the Arts, London, England, United Kingdom (2007) **C:** Business Intelligence, Finance & Operations Senior Manager, Reebonz Korea, Seongdong-gu, Seoul, Korea (2013-Present); Actor, Director, Composer, Songwriter, Designer, Disc Jockey, Marketer, Merchandiser, Radiate Positive Vibes (2011-Present); Online Marketing Manager, Win Investment, Korea (2019); Online Marketing Manager, Solar Fintech, Korea (2018); Online Marketing Manager, The Zone Fund, Korea (2017); Operations, Project Manager, Groupon Korea, Gangnam-gu, Seoul, Korea (2011-2013); Consultant, Platform, Jung-gu, Seoul, Korea (2010-2011); Research Assistant, The Boston Consulting Group, Jung-gu, Seoul, Korea (2007-2008) **CIV:** Guardian Circle, UNICEF, United States (2013-Present); Combat Police, Daegu Metropolitan Police, Daegu, South Korea (2007-2009) **AS:** Mr. Kim attributes his success to hard work and a genuine love for the work that he does. It doesn't feel like work to him; he just does it. **B/I:** Mr. Kim initially attended art school to pursue his interests in art. He stayed up-to-date with current events by reading the news, but he often became depressed by what he read. After some time, he decided he wanted a career change. He chose his new career path by building off of the lessons that he learned in church. Mr. Kim knew it was his duty to be of service to others, but at first he wasn't sure how exactly he could do that. When he found marketing, he knew it was his way to help others and make a positive impact in their lives. Mr. Kim has studied many different religions and took their respective positive lessons and implemented them into his work life. His mission now is to strictly promote happiness and positivity through his work.

KIM, YJ, T: Master Instructor **I:** Athletics **CN:** Master Y.J. Kim's Martial Arts Center **DOB:** 12/20/1975 **PB:** Seoul **SC:** Republic of Korea **ED:** Bachelor of Sports Science, Dankook University, South Korea **CT:** Eighth Degree Black Belt in Taekwondo; Eighth Degree Black Belt in Chunkuhndo; Fifth Degree Black Belt in Kumdo (Sword Martial Arts); Fourth Degree Black Belt in Hapkido; First Degree Black Belt in Judo; Purple Belt in Brazilian Jiu-Jitsu; Certificate for Kensindo Master; Certificate of Sports Massage; Certificate of Sports Health; Certificate of Exercise Prescription Director; Certificate of Completion, Master Course for Poomsae, The Asian Taekwondo Union (Now World Taekwondo Asia); Certificate of Completion, Grandmaster Kim Soo, Founder of Chayon-Ryu; Certificate for High Level Leadership, Kukkiwon; Certified International Taekwondo Master

Instructor; Certified International Taekwondo Umpire; Certified USA National Taekwondo Referee; Instructor Certificate, World Chun Kuhn Taekwondo Federation; Master Instructor, Grandmaster H.K Lee Academy of Taekwondo, Herndon, VA; Ninth Degree Black Belt, Under Grandmaster H.K. Lee, Grandmaster H.K. Lee Academy of Taekwondo; Ninth Degree Black Belt, Under Grandmaster Eung Gil Choi, United States Taekwondo Martial Arts Academy, Leesburg, VA; 11th Degree Black Belt, World Chunkuhn Taekwondo Federation; Ninth Degree Black Belt, United States Taekwondo Association; Ninth Degree Black Belt, Home of International Taekwondo **C:** President, Washington DC Sports Association (2020-Present); President, DC Taekwondo Association, Washington, DC (2019-Present); President, Washington DC Ssireum Wrestling Association (2019-Present); Regional Manager, USA at WRTGM – Nonprofit Organization (2019-Present); Executive Director, Home of International Taekwondo (2017-Present); Director of Washington DC Taekwondo Team, Korean American Sports Festival (2017); Coach of Korea National Team, Umpire, Asia Taekwondo Championship (2011); Coach, Korea National Team, World Taekwondo Championship (2007); Master Instructor, Grandmaster H.K Lee Academy of Taekwondo, Herndon, VA; Master Instructor, United States Taekwondo Martial Arts Academy, Leesburg, VA; Former Technical Committee Chairman, Korea Taekwondo Association, USA **AW:** Silver Medalist in Ssireum Wrestling, Korean American Sports Festival (2019); Gold Medalist in Sparring, World Taekwondo Championship (2004); Presidential Physical Fitness Award, President Barack Obama; President's Volunteer Service Award, President Donald Trump; Certificate of Appreciation, Mayor Diane Gagner, Chatham- Kent, Ontario, Canada; Certificate of Commendation, Grandmaster Koang Woong Kim, United States Taekwondo Association; Certificate of Special Citation, Grandmaster Yoo Sun Lee, Home of International Taekwondo; Appreciation Award, Pan Am Taekwondo Union (PATU), World Taekwondo Pan America; Appreciation Award, Washington DC Sports Association; Appreciation Award, New York State Taekwondo Association; Appreciation Award, New Jersey State Taekwondo Association; Appreciation Award, Tournament Committee, Korea Taekwondo Association, USA; Award of Excellence, Korea Sports Association, USA; Certificate of Recognition, Greaten Korea Foundation; Appreciation Award, Ministry of Patriots and Veterans Affairs, Republic of Korea; Appreciation Award, U.S. Taekwondo and Martial Arts Grandmaster Federation; Certificate of Recognition, The Korean Women Veterans Association of Washington; Certificate of Appreciation, The Korean American Association of Greater New York; Letter of Commendation, Kukkiwon; Appreciation Award, Supreme Master Bok Man Kim, World Chunkuhn Taekwondo Federation

KIME, MILFORD, "MIL" BURTON PHD, T: Applied Physicist **I:** Sciences **DOB:** 10/31/1942 **PB:** Philadelphia **SC:** PA/USA **PT:** Roy Milford Kime; Sheila (Burton) Kime **MS:** Married **SPN:** Linda Joyce Almgren (07/29/1967) **CH:** Kristian Almgren Kime **ED:** MBA, Harvard University, Cambridge, MA (1972); PhD in Nuclear Science, Cornell University, Ithaca, NY (1971); BSEE, Princeton University, Princeton, NJ (1965) **CT:** Senior Reactor Operator, U.S. Army Environmental Command **C:** President, Kime Associates Investments (KAI Co) (1996-Present); Chairman, MicroContinuum, Inc., Cambridge, MA (1998-2000); Corporate Program Manager, Polaroid (1979-1995); Research Scientist, Simulation Physics Inc. (SPIRE) (1972-1978); Research Assistant, Atomic Energy Commission

(1966-1970) **CR:** Investor, Angel (1998-2008) **AW:** Winner, American Nuclear Society Graduate Paper Competition (1969) **MEM:** Life Member, Institute of Electrical and Electronics Engineers (IEEE); Life Member, American Physical Society (APS) **MH:** Albert Nelson Marquis Lifetime Achievement Award **AS:** Dr. Kime attributes his success to his extraordinary parents, family members, mentors, and friends. He additionally credits his exceptional educational background. **B/I:** Dr. Kime became involved in his field after reading an article in the Princeton Alumni Weekly journal that described Professor Lyman Spitzer's Matterhorn project for controlled nuclear fusion. He was immediately fascinated. **AV:** Practicing photography; Scouting; Skiing; Practicing marksmanship; Sprinting; Playing football; Mountain climbing; Offshore sailing

KIMMEL, JIMMY CHRISTIAN, T: Television Personality **I:** Media & Entertainment **DOB:** 11/13/1967 **PB:** Brooklyn **SC:** NY/USA **PT:** James John Kimmel; Joan (Iacono) Kimmel **MS:** Married **SPN:** Molly McNearney (07/13/2013); Gina Maddy (06/25/1998, Divorced 06/16/2002) **CH:** Katie; Kevin; Jane; William John **ED:** Honorary Doctorate, University of Nevada, Las Vegas (2013); Coursework, Arizona State University; Coursework, University of Nevada, Las Vegas **CR:** Co-Host, WRBQ-FM, Tampa, FL (1990-1991); Co-Host, "The Me and Him Show," KZOK-FM, Seattle, WA (1989-1990); Radio Host, KZZP-FM; Radio Personality, "Kevin and Bean," KRQQ, Tucson, AZ; Host, KCMJ, Palm Springs, CA; Writer, Promotions, Fox **CW:** Host, Writer, Executive Producer, "Jimmy Kimmel Live" (2003-Present); Host, "Who Wants to Be a Millionaire" (2020); Appearance, "Jeopardy! The Greatest of All Time" (2020); Co-Host, Executive Producer, "Revenge of the Nerds" (2020); Author, "The Serious Goose" (2019); Appearance, "Dads" (2019); Host, Academy Awards (2017, 2018); Appearance, "Curb Your Enthusiasm" (2017); Executive Producer, "Big Fan" (2017); Voice Actor, "The Boss Baby" (2017); Appearance, "Sandy Wexler" (2017); Appearance, "Brad's Status" (2017); Actor, "The Heyday of the Insensitive Bastards" (2017); Appearance, "The Grinder" (2016); Appearance, "The Real O'Neals" (2016); Appearance, "Trailer Park Boys" (2016); Appearance, "Pitch" (2016); Host, Primetime Emmy Awards (2012, 2016); Appearance, "Pitch Perfect 2" (2015); Appearance, "Ted 2" (2015); Actor, "Miss Famous" (2015); Appearance, "The Bachelor" (2015); Appearance, "Tim & Eric's Bedtime Stories" (2014); Appearance, "The Middle" (2014); Appearance, "Shark Tank" (2014); Appearance, "Brody Stevens: Enjoy It!" (2013); Voice Actor, "The Smurfs 2" (2013); Host, White House Correspondents' Dinner (2012); Appearance, "Hot in Cleveland" (2011); Executive Producer, "Sports Show with Norm Macdonald" (2011); Executive Producer, "Ace in the Hole" (2009); Executive Producer, "Alligator Boots" (2009); Executive Producer, "Big Night of Stars" (2008); Writer, Executive Producer, "The Andy Milonakis Show" (2005-2007); Host, Voice Actor, Writer, Executive Producer, "Crank Yankers" (2002-2007); Voice Actor, "Drawn Together" (2006); Voice Actor, "Robot Chicken" (2006); Actor, "Channel 101" (2006); Executive Producer, "The Adam Carolla Project" (2005); Appearance, "Entourage" (2004); Voice Actor, "Garfield" (2004); Co-Host, "Win Ben Stein's Money" (2001-2002); Actor, "Down to You" (2000); Voice Actor, "Road Trip" (2000); Host, Writer, "The Man Show" (1999-2003); Appearance, "Charmed" (1999); Numerous Appearances, Television Shows **AW:** Critics' Choice Television Award for Best Comedy Special (2020); Primetime Emmy Award for Outstanding Variety Special (Live), Academy of Television Arts & Sciences (2019); Critics' Choice Television Award for Best

Talk Show (2018); Award for Comedy, Writers Guild of America (2016); Star, Hollywood Walk of Fame (2013); Listee, 100 Most Influential People in the World, Time Magazine (2013); Variety's Power of Comedy Award (2013); Co-Recipient, Award for Best Comedy/Variety Series, Writers Guild of America (2012); Daytime Emmy Award for Outstanding Game Show Host, Academy of Television Arts & Sciences (1999) **RE:** Catholic

KIND, RONALD, "RON" JAMES, T: U.S. Representative from Wisconsin; Lawyer **I:** Government Administration/Government Relations/Government Services **DOB:** 03/16/1963 **PB:** La Crosse **SC:** WI/USA **PT:** Elroy Kind; Greta Kind **MS:** Married **SPN:** Tawni (Zappa) Kind **CH:** Johnny; Matthew **ED:** JD, University of Minnesota Law School (1990); MA, London School of Economics (1986); BA, Harvard University, with Honors (1985) **C:** Member, U.S. House of Representatives from Wisconsin's Third Congressional District, United States Congress (1997-Present); Chairman, New Democrat Coalition (2013-2017); Prosecutor, La Crosse County, WI (1992-1996); Associate, Quarles & Brady LLP, Milwaukee, WI (1990-1992); Member, Committee on Ways and Means **MEM:** New Democrat Network (NDN); La Crosse Optimists Club **PA:** Democrat **RE:** Lutheran

KING, ANGUS STANLEY JR., T: U.S. Senator **I:** Government Administration/Government Relations/Government Services **DOB:** 03/31/1944 **PB:** Alexandria **SC:** VA/USA **PT:** Angus Stanley King Sr.; Ellen Archer (Ticer) King **MS:** Married **SPN:** Mary J. Herman (1984) **CH:** Angus III; Duncan; James: Benjamin; Molly **ED:** Honorary LLD, Bowdoin College (2007); JD, School of Law, University of Virginia (1969); BA, Dartmouth College (1966) **C:** U.S. Senator from Maine (2013-Present); Member, U.S. Senate Select Committee on Intelligence (2013-Present); Member, U.S. Senate Committee on Rules and Administration (2013-Present); Member, U.S. Senate Budget Committee (2013-Present); Member, U.S. Senate Armed Services Committee (2013-Present); Distinguished Lecturer, Bowdoin College, Brunswick, Maine (2004-Present); Governor, State of Maine, Augusta, Maine (1995-2003); Partner, Smith, Lloyd & King, Brunswick (1975-1983); Chief Counsel to Senator William D. Hathaway, U.S. Senate Subcommittee on Alcoholism and Narcotics, Washington, DC (1972-1975); Staff Attorney, Pine Tree Legal Assistance, Showhegan, ME (1969-1972) **CR:** Founder, President, Northeast Energy Management Inc., Brunswick, ME (1989-1994); Vice President, General Counsel, Swift River Hafslund Company (1983) **CW:** Television Host, Co-Producer, "Maine Watch," Maine Public (1975-1993) **BAR:** Maine State Bar Association (1969) **PA:** Independent **RE:** Episcopalian

KING, BILLIE JEAN, T: Former Professional Tennis Player **I:** Athletics **DOB:** 11/22/1943 **PB:** Long Beach **SC:** CA/USA **PT:** Willard J. Moffitt; Betty (Jerman) Moffitt **MS:** Partner **SPN:** Ilana Kloss (1987); Larry King (09/17/1965, Divorced 1987) **ED:** Honorary PhD, University of Massachusetts (2000); Honorary PhD, University of Pennsylvania (1999); Honorary Doctorate, Trinity College (1998); Honorary PhD, California State University (1997); Coursework, California State University, Los Angeles, CA (1961-1964) **C:** Director, Official Spokesperson, World Team Tennis, Chicago, IL (1985-2017); Coach, Federal Cup, Women's Tennis Team (1995-1996, 1998-2003); Coach, USA Women's Tennis Team, Olympics (1996, 2000); Captain, Federal Cup, United States (1995); Member, World Team Tennis Recreational League (1985); Professional Tennis Player (1968-1984); Member, World Team Tennis Professional League (Now WTT, LLC)

(1981); President, World Team Tennis (WTT, LLC) (1973-1975, 1980-1981); Member, Tennis Challenge Series (1977, 1978); Sports Commentator, ABC-TV (1975-1978); Amateur Tennis Player (1958-1967); Commentator, Analyst, Wimbeldon and Other Tennis Events, HBO, New York, NY **CR:** Founding Member, Women's Sports Legends; Consultant, Virginia Slims World Championship Series; Tennis Teacher to Professionals **CIV:** Board of Directors, Philip Morris Incorporated (1999); Member, World Team Tennis Charities (1987); Founder, Women's Sports Foundation (1974); Member, President's Council for Fitness, Sports & Nutrition; Member, Planned Parenthood (Now Planned Parenthood Federation of America, Inc.), USPTA, Professional Tennis Registry, Chicago Area Women's Sports Association; Advisory Board, Arena Sports Award Nomination Committee, Jim Thorpe Pro Sports Award Nomination Committee; Sports Advisory Board, Vic Braden Neurology Research Institute, U..S Tennis Association Player Development Committee; Member, Board of Directors, Elton John AIDS Foundation, Challenger Center (Now Challenger Center for the Space Science Education, Inc.), S.A.F.E., National AIDS Fund, Altria Group, Inc., Women's Sports Foundation; Ambassador, Adventures in Movement; National Spokesperson, Literacy Volunteers of America (LVA) **CW:** Co-author with Cynthia Starr, "We Have Come a Long Way: The Story of Women's Tennis" (1988); Co-author with Frank Deford, "The Autobiography of Billie Jean King" (1982); Co-author with Greg Hoffman, "Tennis Love: A Parent's Guide to the Sport" (1978); Host, "The Lady Is a Champ" (1975); Co-author with Kim Chapin, "Billie Jean" (1974); Co-founder, Publisher, WomenSports Magazine (1974); Author, "Tennis to Win" (1970); Three-time Host, Colgate Women's Sports; TV Commentator, HBO-Sports Wimbeldon Coverage, HBO Sports; Co-founder, Publisher, Kingdom, Inc., San Mateo, CA **AW:** Named One of ESPNW'S Impact 25 (2014); Named to Southern California Tennis Hall of Fame (2011); Presidential Medal of Freedom, The White House (2009); Sunday Times Sports Women of the Year Lifetime Achievement Award (2007); Named to California Hall of Fame (2006); Phillipe Chatrier Award, International Tennis Federation (2003); Named to Court of Champions, U.S. Tennis Association (USTA) National Tennis Center (2003); Women & Sport World Trophy, International Olympic Committee (2002); Named Woman of the Year, Women in Sports & Events (2002); Radcliffe Medal, Radcliffe College (2002); National Association of Collegiate Women Athletic Administrators Award of Honor (2002); Capitol Award, GLAAD (2000); "Athletes Who Changed the Game Award, Sports Illustrated (1999); Named to Chicago LGBT Hall of Fame (1999); Arthur Ashe Award for Courage, ESPN (1999); Community Role Model Award, Los Angeles LGBT Center (1999); Elizabeth Blackwell Award for Courage, Hobart and William Smith Colleges (1998); Flo Hymnal Award, Women's Sports Foundation (1997); "Player Who Makes a Difference Award" (1997); Coach of the Year Award, U.S. Olympic Committee (1997); Honoree, National Women's Law Center (1997); Named One of the Top 40 Athletes (1994); Named Female Teaching Pro of the Decade (1994); Lifetime Achievement Award, March of Dimes (1994); Named One of the 100 Most Important Americans of the 20th Century, Life Magazine (1990); Named to National Women's Hall of Fame (1990); Named to International Tennis Hall of Fame (1987); WTA Honorable Membership Award, WTA Tour, Inc. (1986); Winner, Doubles, U.S. Open (1965, 1967, 1974, 1980); Winner, Doubles, Wimbledon (1961, 1962, 1965, 1967, 1968, 1970-1973, 1979); Winner, Federation Cup (1963-1967, 1976-1979); Winner, Wightman Cup (1961-1967, 1970, 1977, 1978); Named One of the 10 Most Powerful Women in America, Harper's Bazaar (1977); Named One of the 25 Most Influential Women in America, World Almanac (1977); Named Woman of the Year, TIME Magazine (1976); Winner, Singles, Wimbledon (1966-1968, 1972, 1973, 1975); Winner, Mixed Doubles, Wimbledon (1967, 1971, 1973, 1974); Winner, Singles, U.S. Open (1967, 1971, 1972, 1974); Winner, Mixed Doubles, U.S. Open (1967, 1971, 1973); Named Woman Athlete of the Year, The Associated Press (1967, 1973); Winner, Singles, French Open (1972); Named Top Woman Athlete of the Year (1972); Winner, Doubles, French Open (1972); Named Sportsperson of the Year (1972); Winner, Mixed Doubles, French Open (1967, 1970); Winner, Singles, Australian Open (1968); Winner, Mixed Doubles, Australian Open (1968); Named World Tennis Team All-star; Winner, Numerous Singles Champion Tournaments

KING, BRADLEY, T: Theatrical Lighting Designer **I:** Media & Entertainment **PB:** Baltimore **SC:** MD/USA **ED:** MFA in Design, Tisch School of the Arts, New York University; BFA in Theatrical Directing, Tisch School of the Arts, New York University; Diploma, Gilman School **CW:** Lighting Designer, "Lempicka" (2020); Lighting Designer, "Flying Over Sunset" (2020); Lighting Designer, "Endlings" (2020); Lighting Designer, "Moby Dick" (2019); Lighting Designer, "Little Shop of Horrors" (2019); Lighting Designer, "Alice by Heart" (2019); Lighting Designer, "Hadestown" (2016, 2018-2019); Lighting Designer, "Apologia" (2018); Lighting Designer, "Bernhardt/Hamlet" (2018); Lighting Designer, "The Last Match" (2017); Lighting Designer, "The Treasurer" (2017); Lighting Designer, "Burn All Night" (2017); Lighting Designer, "Natasha, Pierre and the Great Comet of 1812" (2013, 2016); Lighting Designer, "Preludes" (2015); Lighting Designer, "And I and Silence" (2014); Assistant Lighting Designer, "Mouth to Mouth" (2008); Assistant Lighting Designer, "The Black Eyed" (2007); Assistant Lighting Designer, "Richard II" (2006) **AW:** Outstanding Lighting Design (Play or Musical), "Hadestown," Outer Critics Circle Awards (2019); Outstanding Lighting Design for a Musical, "Hadestown," Drama Desk Awards (2019); Best Lighting Design in a Musical, "Hadestown," Tony Awards (2019); Outstanding Lighting Design, "Natasha, Pierre, & The Great Comet of 1812," Outer Critics Circle Awards (2017); Outstanding Lighting Design for a Musical, "Natasha, Pierre, & The Great Comet of 1812," Drama Desk Awards (2017); Best Lighting Design in a Musical, "Natasha, Pierre, & The Great Comet of 1812," Tony Awards (2017)

KING, CAROLE JOAN, T: Singer, Songwriter **I:** Media & Entertainment **DOB:** 02/09/1942 **PB:** Manhattan **SC:** NY/USA **PT:** Sidney N. Klein; Eugenia Klein **MS:** Divorced **SPN:** Rick Sorensen (1982, Divorced 1989); Rick Evers (1977, Deceased 1978); Charles Larkey (1970, Divorced 1976); Gerry Goffin (1959, Divorced 1968) **CH:** Louise; Sherry; Molly; Levi **ED:** Coursework, Queens College **C:** Solo Singer, Songwriter (1970-Present); Songwriter, Dimension Records; Songwriter; Secretary **CW:** Featured, "Beautiful: The Carole King Musical" (2014-2019); Appearance, "Gilmore Girls: A Year in the Life" (2016); Author, "A Natural Woman: A Memoir" (2012); Singer, "A Holiday Carole" (2011); Performer, "Live at the Troubadour" (2010); Singer, "Love Makes the World - Deluxe Edition" (2007); Performer, "Welcome to My Living Room" (2007); Singer, "The Living Room Tour" (2005); Appearance, "Gilmore Girls" (2002, 2005); Singer, "Love Makes the World" (2001); Singer, "Super Hits" (2000); Singer, "Pearls/Time Gone By" (1998); Singer, "The Carnegie Hall Concert" (1996); Performer, "In Concert" (1994); Singer, "A Natural Woman" (1994); Appearance, Broadway, "Blood Brothers" (1994); Singer, "Colour of Your Dreams" (1993); Appearance, "The Trials of Rosie O'Neill" (1991); Appearance, "Hider in the House" (1989); Appearance, "The Tracy Ullman Show" (1989); Appearance, Off-Broadway, "A Minor Incident" (1989); Singer, "City Streets" (1989); Appearance, "Russkies" (1987); Film Composer, Appearance, "Murphy's Romance" (1985); Film Composer, "The Care Bears Movie" (1985); Singer, "Speeding Time" (1983); Singer, "One to One" (1982); Singer, "Her Greatest Hits: Songs of Long Ago" (1978); Singer, "Really Rosie" (1975); Singer, "Thoroughbred" (1975); Singer, "Wrap Around Joy" (1974); Singer, "Fantasy" (1973); Singer, "Rhymes & Reasons" (1972); Singer, "Simple Things" (1972); Singer, "Pearls: Songs of Goffin and King" (1972); Singer, "Music" (1971); Singer, "Tapestry" (1971); Co-Writer, "It's Too Late" (1971); Film Composer, "Head" (1968); Co-Writer, Numerous Songs; Co-Writer, "Natural Woman"; Singer, Writer, Co-Writer, Various Artists and Solo, Numerous Songs **AW:** Honoree, Kennedy Center Honors, John F. Kennedy Center for the Performing Arts (2015); Golden Plate Award, American Academy of Achievement (2014); MusiCares Person of the Year, Grammy Awards, The Recording Academy (2014); Grammy Award for Best Musical Theater Album, The Recording Academy (2014); Lifetime Achievement Award, Grammy Awards, The Recording Academy (2013); Gershwin Prize for Popular Song, Library of Congress (2013); Recipient, Star, Hollywood Walk of Fame (2012); Named to Long Island Music Hall of Fame (2007); Grammy Trustees Award, The Recording Academy (2004); Johnny Mercer Award, Songwriters Hall of Fame (2002); Named to Rock and Roll Hall of Fame (1990); Co-Recipient, National Academy of Songwriters Lifetime Achievement Award (1988); Inductee, Songwriters Hall of Fame (1987); Grammy Awards for Album of the Year, Record of the Year, Song of the Year, Best Female Pop Vocal Performance, The Recording Academy (1972); Recipient, Numerous Awards **RE:** Jewish

KING, FRANCES, T: Education Educator (Retired) **I:** Education/Educational Services **DOB:** 11/14/1929 **PB:** Dallas **SC:** TX/USA **PT:** Grover W. Beckham; Clara (Blailock) Beckham **MS:** Married **SPN:** Erwin C. King, Jr. **CH:** Carol; Melody **ED:** Writer's Certificate, Children's Institute of Literature, Redding Ridge, CT (1987); BA, Austin College (1951) **CT:** Certified Teacher of the Mentally Impaired, Early Childhood and Learning Disabilities, State of Texas **C:** Subsidiary Teacher, Knox City-O'Brien District (1995-2005); Special Education and Adult Education Teacher, Knox City-O'Brien and Sweetwater District (1989-1995); Special Education Middle School Teacher, Knox City-O'Brien Consolidated Independent School District (1976-1978); Special Education Middle School Teacher, Knox City-O'Brien Consolidated Independent School District (1971-1976); Teacher, First Grade, Early Childhood/Special Education Teacher, Knox City Consolidated Independent School District (1961-1971); Teacher, Fourth Grade, O'Brien Consolidated Independent School District, Texas (1958-1962) **CR:** Spelling Coach, Knox City High School **CIV:** Program Chairman, Health Chairman, Local R.T.A (1999); Vice President, University of Mary Washington; Secretary for the Pink Lady, Hospital Auxiliary; Treasurer, Retired Teachers; Secretary, Harvest Day **CW:** Co-Author, Guide Program for Special Education **AW:** Named, Teacher of the Year, Special Education, Region IVX **MEM:** Local Health Chairman, Retired Teachers Association (2002); Local President, Association of Texas Professional Educators; Texas State Teachers Association **MH:** Albert Nelson Marquis

Lifetime Achievement Award **B/I:** Ms. King entered her profession because when she was four years old, she decided that teaching was something that she wanted to do. She lined all her dolls up and conducted school. When Ms. King was in the fifth grade, she taught second grade for a week because the teacher was sick; she was always a teacher. Ms. King had no way to go to college, yet she went and was able to go all four years and she returned as a teacher.

KING, GAYLE, T: Journalist **I:** Media & Entertainment **CN:** CBS News **PB:** Chevy Chase **SC:** MD/USA **MS:** Divorced **SPN:** William G. Bumpus (1982, Divorced 1993) **CH:** Two Children **ED:** BS, University of Maryland, College Park (1976) **C:** Co-Anchor, CBS This Morning (2012-Present); Co-Host, XM Satellite Radio's Oprah & Friends (2006-Present); Editor-at-Large, O at Home (2003-Present); Editor-at-Large, O, the Oprah Magazine (1999-Present); Host, "The Gayle King Show," OWN: Oprah Winfrey Network (2011); Host, XM Satellite Radio's "The Gayle King Show" (2006); Reporter, WFSB-TV, Hartford, CT (1981-1999); Host, "The Gayle King Show" (1997); Co-Host, "Cover to Cover" (1991); Reporter, Weekend Anchor, WDAF-TV, Kansas City, MO (1977-1980); Correspondent, "The Oprah Winfrey Show" **AW:** Named, 50 Most Powerful Women in New York City, New York Post (2007)

KING, HOWARD PICKETT, T: Circuit Court Judge, Of Counsel **I:** Law and Legal Services **CN:** Bryan Law Firm **DOB:** 04/13/1939 **PB:** Greenville **SC:** SC/USA **PT:** William George King; Maude (Pickett) King **MS:** Married **SPN:** Nancy Leslie Ariail (03/03/1962) **CH:** Nancy Leslie; Ariail Elizabeth **ED:** JD, University of South Carolina (1966); Postgraduate Coursework, The University of Tennessee (1964); BS in Business Administration, The Citadel (1961) **C:** Of Counsel, Bryan Law Firm (2020-Present); Retired (2006-2020); Resident Judge, Third Judicial Circuit (1996-2006); Partner, Bryan, Bahnmuller, King, Goldman & McElveen (Now Bryan Law Firm) (1969-1996); Associate, Bryan, Bahnmuller, King, Goldman & McElveen (Now Bryan Law Firm) (1966-1969) **CR:** Advisory Board Member, NationsBank (1986-Present) **CIV:** Trustee, Sumter County Library System (1980-1985) **MIL:** South Carolina National Guard (1963-1967); First Lieutenant, U.S. Army (1961-1963) **CW:** South Carolina Law Review **AW:** Order of the Palmetto (2006) **MEM:** President, South Carolina Bar (1990-1991); Fellow, Board of Directors, South Carolina Bar Foundation (1980-1982, 1989-1991); President-Elected, South Carolina Bar (1989-1990); Treasurer, South Carolina Bar (1988-1989); Secretary, South Carolina Bar (1987-1988); Chairman, House of Delegates South Carolina Bar (1980-1982); American Bar Association **BAR:** Supreme Court of the United States (1973); United States Court of Appeals for the Fourth Circuit (1970); South Carolina Bar (1966); United States District Court of South Carolina (1966) **MH:** Albert Nelson Marquis Lifetime Achievement Award **B/I:** Mr. King became involved in his profession because he was driven to help his fellow man. **RE:** Methodist

KING, PETER THOMAS, T: U.S. Representative, Lawyer **I:** Government Administration/Government Relations/Government Services **DOB:** 04/05/1944 **PB:** Manhattan **SC:** NY/USA **PT:** Peter E. King; Ethel M. (Gittins) King **MS:** Married **SPN:** Rosemary Wiedel (1967) **CH:** Sean; Erin **ED:** Honorary LLD, St. John's University (2013); JD, University of Notre Dame Law School (1968); BA in History, St. Francis College, Brooklyn, NY (1965) **C:** U.S. Representative, New York's Second Congressional District, United States Congress (2013-Present); Chairman, Committee on Homeland Secu-

rity, U.S. House of Representatives (2005-2007, 2011-2013); U.S. Representative, New York's Third Congressional District, United States Congress (1993-2013); Comptroller, Nassau County, NY (1981-1993); Town Council Member, Hempstead, NY (1977-1981); General Counsel, New York Off-Track Betting Corporation (1977); Executive Assistant to County Executive, Nassau County, NY (1974-1976); Deputy Attorney, Nassau County, NY (1972-1974); Private Law Practice (1968-1972); Member, Permanent Select Committee on Intelligence; Member, Committee on Financial Services **CW:** Author, "Vale of Tears" (2003); Author, "Deliver Us from Evil" (2002); Author, "Terrible Beauty" (1999) **AW:** Frederick Olmstead Award, Labor Enforcement Alliance (2003); Certificate of Achievement for Excellence in Financial Reporting, Government Finance Officers Association (1985-1991); Man of the Year, FBI Emerald Society; Patriot of the Year, Reserve Officers Association of the United States; Friend of Labor Award, Civil Service Employees Association; Guardian of Small Business Award, National Federation of Independent Business; Spirit of Enterprise Award, U.S. Chamber of Commerce; Interfaith Understanding Award, Jewish Chautauqua Society of the Wantagh Suburban Temple; Distinguished Service Award, Institute for Public Affairs of Orthodox Jewish Congregations of America; Huey Award, Veterans of Vietnam War; Certificate of Honor, Long Island Committee for Soviet Jewry; Certificate of Achievement, Catholic War Veterans & Auxiliary of the United States; Citizen of the Year, Knights of Columbus **MEM:** Honorary Member, Nassau County Firefighters Emerald Society; Catholic War Veterans and Auxiliary; Order Sons and Daughters of Italy in America; Veterans Corps 69th Regiment, Inc.; Life Member, AMVETS; The American Legion; Ancient Order of Hibernians; Knights of Columbus **BAR:** New York State Bar Association (1968) **PA:** Republican **RE:** Roman Catholic

KING, STEVEN, "STEVE" ARNOLD, T: U.S. Representative from Iowa **I:** Government Administration/Government Relations/Government Services **DOB:** 05/28/1949 **PB:** Storm Lake **SC:** IA/USA **PT:** Emmett A. King; Mildred Lila (Culler) King **MS:** Married **SPN:** Marilyn Kelly (1972) **CH:** Three Children **ED:** Coursework in Biology and Mathematics, Northwest Missouri State University (1967-1970) **C:** Member, U.S. House of Representatives from Iowa's Fourth Congressional District, United States Congress (2013-Present); Member, U.S. House of Representatives from Iowa's Fifth Congressional District, United States Congress, Washington, DC (2003-2013); Member, District Six, Iowa State Senate, Des Moines, Iowa (1997-2003); Founder, King Construction Company (1975-1996); Founder, Kiron Business Association; With, Iowa Land Improvement Contractors' Association; Member, Committee on Agriculture; Member, Committee on the Judiciary; Member, Committee on Small Business **CIV:** Member, St. Martin's Catholic Church; Board of Directors, Odebolt Community Housing **MEM:** Iowa Cattleman's Association; Land Improvement Contractors of America (LICA); U.S. Chamber of Commerce; Odebolt Iowa Chamber of Commerce; SAC County Farm Bureau; Alpha Kappa Lambda **PA:** Republican **RE:** Roman Catholic

KINGSLEY, BEN, T: Actor **I:** Media & Entertainment **DOB:** 12/31/1943 **PB:** Snainton **SC:** England **PT:** Rahimtulla Harji Bhanji; Anna Lyna Mary (Goodman) Bhanji **MS:** Married **SPN:** Daniela Lavender (2007); Alexandra Christmann (2003, Divorced 2005); Alison Sutcliffe (07/01/1978, Divorced 02/1992); Angela Morrant (1966, Divorced 1972) **CH:** Edmund; Ferdinand; Thomas; Jasmine **ED:** Honorary Master of Arts, University

of Salford; Diploma, Pendleton College, Salford, England **C:** Associate Artist, Royal Shakespeare Company, England, United Kingdom (1968) **CW:** Actor, "Perpetual Grace, LTD" (2019); Actor, "Spider in the Web" (2019); Actor, "The Red Sea Diving Resort" (2019); Actor, "Watership Down" (2018); Actor, "Intrigo: Death of an Author" (2018); Actor, "Night Hunter" (2018); Actor, "Operation Finale" (2018); Actor, "Backstabbing for Beginners" (2018); Actor, "Nomis" (2018); Actor, "The Ottoman Lieutenant" (2017); Actor, "War Machine" (2017); Actor, "An Ordinary Man" (2017); Actor, "Backstabbing for Beginners" (2017); Actor, "Security" (2017); Actor, "Watership" (2017); Voice Actor, "The Jungle Book" (2016); Actor, "Collide" (2016); Actor, "Tut" (2015); Voice Actor, "Knight of Cups" (2015); Actor, "Life" (2015); Actor, "Self/less" (2015); Actor, "The Walk" (2015); Actor, "Eliza Graves" (2014); Voice Actor, "The Boxtrolls" (2014); Actor, "Learning to Drive" (2014); Actor, "Robot Overlords" (2014); Actor, "Exodus: Gods and Kings" (2014); Actor, "Night at the Museum: Secret of the Tomb" (2014); Actor, "Garfunkel and Oates" (2014); Actor, "Iron Man 3" (2013); Actor, "A Birder's Guide to Everything" (2013); Actor, "Walking with the Enemy" (2013); Actor, "Ender's Game" (2013); Actor, "The Physician" (2013); Voice Actor, "Noah's Ark: The New Beginning" (2012); Actor, "The Dictator" (2012); Actor, "A Common Man" (2012); Actor, "Hugo" (2011); Actor, "Shutter Island" (2010); Actor, "Prince of Persia: The Sands of Time" (2010); Actor, "Shutter Island" (2010); Actor, "Prince of Persia: The Sands of Time" (2010); Actor, "Transsiberian" (2008); Actor, "War, Inc." (2008); Actor, "The Love Guru" (2008); Actor, "The Wackness" (2008); Actor, "Elegy" (2008); Actor, "Fifty Dead Men Walking" (2008); Actor, "You Kill Me" (2007); Actor, "The Last Legion" (2007); Actor, "The Inquiry" (2006); Actor, "Lucky Number Slevin" (2006); Actor, "The Sopranos" (2006); Actor, "A Sound of Thunder" (2005); Actor, "Mrs. Harris" (2005); Actor, "Mrs. Harris" (2005); Actor, "Oliver Twist" (2005); Actor, "BloodRayne" (2005); Actor, "Thunderbirds" (2004); Actor, "Suspect Zero," (2004); Actor, "House of Sand and Fog" (2003); Actor, "Tuck Everlasting" (2002); Voice Actor, "Artificial Intelligence: A.I." (2001); Actor, "The Triumph of Love" (2001); Actor, "Anne Frank: The Whole Story" (2001); Actor, "Sexy Beast" (2000); Actor, "Spooky House" (2000); Actor, "What Planet Are You From" (2000); Actor, "Rules of Engagement" (1999); Voice Actor, "A Force More Powerful" (1999); Actor, "The Confession" (1999); Actor, "Alice in Wonderland" (1999); Actor, "Crime and Punishment" (1998); Actor, "Parking Shots" (1998); Actor, "Crime and Punishment" (1998); Actor, "The Tale of Sweeney Todd" (1998); Actor, "The Assignment" (1997); Actor, "Photographing Fairies" (1997); Actor, "Weapons of Mass Distraction" (1997); Actor, "Moses" (1996); Actor, "Twelfth Night: Or What You Will" (1996); Actor, "Joseph" (1995); Actor, "Death and the Maiden" (1994); Actor, "Species" (1994); Actor, "Dave" (1993); Actor, "Innocent Moves" (1993); Actor, "Searching for Bobby Fisher" (1993); Actor, "Schindler's List" (1993); Voice Actor, "Freddie as F.R.O.7" (1992); Actor, "Sneakers" (1992); Actor, "Una Vita Scellerata" (1991); Actor, "L'Amore Necessario" (1991); Actor, "Bugsy" (1991); Actor, "The War That Never Ends" (1991); Actor, "Leini: The Train" (1990); Voice Actor, "Romeo-Juliet" (1990); Actor, "The Children" (1990); Actor, "O, Quinto Macacao" (1990); Actor, "Slipstream" (1989); Actor, "Pascali's Island" (1988); Actor, "Without a Clue" (1988); Actor, "Murderers Among Us: The Simon Weisenthal Story" (1988); Actor, "The Secret of the Sahara" (1987); Actor, "Silas Marner" (1987); Actor, "Maurice" (1987); Actor, "Testimony" (1987); Actor, "Stanley's Vision" (1986); Actor, "Oxbridge Blues" (1986);

Actor, "Othello" (1985-1986); Actor, "Harem" (1985); Actor, "Camille" (1984); Actor, "Turtle Diary" (1984); Actor, "Sleeps Six" (1984); Actor, "Betrayal" (1982); Actor, "Kean" (1982); Actor, "The Merry Wives of Windsor" (1982); Actor, "Edmund Kean" (1981-1983); Actor, "Gandhi" (1981); Actor, "Thank You Candidate" (1978); Actor, "Dickens of London" (1976); Actor, "Hamlet" (1975-1976); Actor, "The Brotherhood" (1975); Actor, "An Impeccable Elopement" (1975); Actor, "Remember Me" (1975); Actor, "Beata Beatrix" (1975); Actor, "The Artisan" (1975); Actor, "Antony and Cleopatra" (1974); Actor, "A Misfortune" (1973); Actor, "Barbara of the House of Grebe" (1973); Actor, "The Adventurer" (1973); Actor, "Wessex Tales" (1973): Actor, "Play for Today" (1973); Actor, "Fear is the Key" (1972); Actor, "Coronation Street" (1966-1967); Actor, "Orlando" (1966); Actor, "Skin Deep" (1966); Actor, "The Rhyme, But No Reason" (1966); Actor, Theater, Television Shows, Films **AW:** Fellowship Award, The Asian Awards (2013); Recipient, Star, Hollywood Walk of Fame (2010); Named, Knight Bachelor, New Year Honours, Queen Elizabeth II (2002); Screen Actors Guild Award for Outstanding Performance by a Male Actor in a Miniseries or Television Movie, Screen Actors Guild - American Federation of Television and Radio Artists (2001); Evening Standard Film Award for Best Actor, Academy of Motion Picture Arts and Sciences (1995); Distinguished Service Award (1989); Grammy Award for Best Spoken Word or Nonmusical Recording, The Recording Academy (1985); Padma Shri Award, Government of India (1984); Named Best Actor, Standard Film Awards, London, England (1983); Academy Award for Best Actor, Academy of Motion Picture Arts and Sciences (1982); BAFTA Award for Best Actor in a Leading Role (1982); Golden Globe Awards for Best Actor - Motion Picture Drama, New Star of the Year in a Motion Picture - Male, Hollywood Foreign Press Association (1982); Golden Camera Berlin Award; Numerous Awards **MEM:** Academy of Motion Picture Arts and Sciences; British Academy of Film and Television Arts

KINNE, FRANCES BARTLETT, PHD, T: Chancellor Emerita and Past President **I:** Education/Educational Services **CN:** Jacksonville University **DOB:** 05/23/1917 **PB:** Story City **SC:** IA/USA **PT:** Charles Morton Bartlett; Bertha (Olson) Bartlett **MS:** Widowed **SPN:** Colonel Harry L. Kinne, Jr. (Deceased); Colonel M. Wothington Bordley, Jr. (Deceased) **ED:** Honorary DHL, Jacksonville University (1995); Honorary DFA, Drake University, Des Moines, Iowa (1981); PhD in Music, English Literature, and Philosophy, Goethe University, Frankfurt, Federal Republic of Germany, Cum Laude (1957); Honorary LLD, Flagler College, St. Augustine, FL; Honorary DHL, Wagner College, NY; Honorary Diploma, Drake University, Des Moines, Iowa; Honorary Diploma, New York State University; Master of Music Education, Drake University, with Honors; Bachelor of Music Education, Drake University, with Honors; Two-Year Diploma, University of Northern Iowa, with Honors; Honorary LLD, Lenoir-Rhyne University **C:** Chancellor Emerita, Jacksonville University (1994-Present); Chancellor, Jacksonville University (1989-1994); President, Jacksonville University (1979-1989); Established Programs, College of Fine Arts, College of Business, College of Arts and Sciences, Dolphin Arts, Graduate Programs, Aviation Program, Executive MBA Program (1979-1989); Founder, Dean, College of Fine Arts, Jacksonville University (1961-1979); Professor of Humanities, Jacksonville University, Jacksonville, FL (1958-1961); Music Instructor, Iowa Public Schools, Des Moines, IA; Private Music Education Teacher in Piano, Story City, IA; Public School Music Teacher, Choral and Orchestra Conductor, Kelley Consolidated School, Kelley, IA; Supervisor, Choral, Instrumental Conductor and Church Choir Director, Boxholm Consolidated School, Boxholm, IA; Supervisor, Music, Des Moines Public Schools; World War II United States Army Hostess, Director of Service Club One, Camp Crowder, MO; World War II United States Army Hostess, Director of Three Clubs, Camp Crowder, MO; Recreation Director, Supervisor of Rehab Recreation, Veterans Administration, Wadsworth, KS; Lecturer, Music, English and Western Culture, Tsuda University, Kodaira, Tokyo; Creator, Volunteer Post-War Education of Japanese Students, Tokyo, Japan; Consultant, Music on Staff, U.S. Army General MacArthur's Headquarters, Tokyo, Japan; Assistant Piano Teacher **CR:** Board Member, Massachusetts Eye and Ear, Harvard University, Cambridge, MA; Board of Trustees, Massachusetts Eye and Ear, Harvard University, Cambridge, MA; Corporator, Schepens Eye Research Institute, Massachusetts Eye and Ear, Harvard University; Honorary Staff Member, Mayo Clinic, Jacksonville, FL; Contributor, Establishment of Mayo Clinic, Jacksonville, FL; Past Member, Advisory Council, National Society of Arts and Letters, Indiana Colleges and Universities; Past Member, Board of Trustees, Jacksonville University **CIV:** Trustee Emerita, Drake University (2009); Co-Champion, Dinner of Champions, Multiple Sclerosis (1993); Member Emerita, Past Member, Chairman, Advisory Board, Ronald McDonald House; Past Member, Board of Directors, Executive Committee, Eye Research Foundation; Board of Directors, Life Member, Jacksonville Symphony Association; Past Member, Advisory Council, Flagler College; Past Vice President, Community Development and Committee of 100, Jacksonville Chamber of Commerce; Past Member, Board of Governors, Jacksonville Chamber of Commerce; Trustee, Drake University; Advisory Board, Women's Eye Health Task Force, Harvard University; Past Member, National Advisory Council, OPTIC Foundation; Past Member, Jacksonville Symphony Women's Guild; Past Member, Jacksonville Coalition Against Pornography; Freedoms Foundation, Valley Forge, CA; Past Member, Vice President of Board, Eye Research Foundation; Past Member, Bert Thomas Scholarship Fund; Past Member, Civil Justice Reform Act Committee; Past Member, Doug Milne Foundation **CW:** Pianist, "Memories, Second Edition" (2012); Author, "Iowa Girl: The President Wears a Skirt, Second Edition" (2012); Pianist, "Memories" (2004); Co-Author, "Iowa Girl: The President Wears a Skirt, First Edition" (2000); Author, "A Comparative Study of British Traditional and American Indigenous Ballads" (1958); Author, Chapter, "How I Made the Sale that Did the Most for Me," Fifty Great Sales Stories, Mel Hickerson, NY; Author, "Band Training in the United States Army," Drake University; Author, "A Comparative Study of British Traditional and American Indigenous Ballads," Goethe University, Frankfurt, Germany; Featured, "Planning a Purposeful Life: Secrets of Longevity," The Wave Magazine, Kinne Century; Contributor, Numerous Articles, Professional Journals; Contributor, Chapters, Books **AW:** Guest Speaker Award, Rotary Club of Jacksonville, The Rotary Foundation (2017); Proclamation, Dr. Frances Bartlett Kinne Day, Awarded by Mayor Alvin Brown, City of Jacksonville, FL (2012); The Doctors Mayo Society, Mayo Clinic (2011); Named Woman of Vision, Girls, Inc. (2011); Named to Jacksonville University Sports Hall of Fame (2011); Distinguished Dolphin (2009); Leadership Character Inspiration Award, Turknett Leadership Group (2008); Award of Distinction, Mu Phi Epsilon (2008); Lifetime Achievement Award Honoree for Women's History (2008); Outstanding Philanthropist, National Philanthropy Day (2005); Outstanding Philanthropist Award (2005); Named Woman of Achievement, Ponte Vedra Women's Club (2005); Named Woman of the Year, American Biographical Institute (2005); Lifetime Achievement Award, Arthritis Foundation (2004); Psalm of Life, Rotary Club of Jacksonville (2001); Award, Women Business Owners of North Florida for Vital Contributions to Nation (1999); Outstanding Civic Leader Award, Civic Roundtable (1994); Heritage Society Charter Award, Drake University (1993); Mary L. Singleton Social Harmony Award (1993); Nominated as International Woman of the Year, World's Who's Who of Women (1992-1993); Hope Award, Multiple Sclerosis Society (1992); Cathedral Towers Appreciation Award (1989); Distinguished Educator Award, International Longshoreman's Association (1989); Appreciation for Outstanding Contributions, Museum of Science and History (1989); Woman of Achievement Award, First Coast Business and Professional Women's Club of Jacksonville (1987); Elaine Gordon Lifetime Achievement Award, Florida Federation of Business and Professional Women (1986); Inductee, Florida Women's Hall of Fame, Inducted by Florida Governor Bob Graham (1986); EVE Award in Education, Florida Publishing Company (1983); Memento of Appreciation, Men's Residence Hall Association and the Association of Women Students, Jacksonville University (1983); Nominee, Florida Women's Hall of Fame (1982); Top Management Award, Sales and Marketing Executives of Jacksonville (1981); Honoree Dinner, Outstanding Leadership and Loyal Service, St. Johns Dinner Club, Jacksonville, FL (1981); People of Vision Award, Prevent Blindness (1980); Recognition of Outstanding Service to Jacksonville University and the City of Jacksonville, The Women's Club of Jacksonville (1980); First EVE of the Decade Award, Florida Publishing Company (1970-1980) **MEM:** President, Downtown Rotary Club (2000); First Coast Chapter, National Philanthropy Day, November 19 (1997); Honorary Chairman, People of Vision (1996-1998); Honorary Chairman, Prevent Blindness (1992-1995); Life Member, TROA (1991); Life Member, American Military Retirement Association (1986); Past President, International Council of Fine Arts Deans (1974-1975); American Association of University Women (AAUW); PEO, Chapter CF; Advisory Council, National Society Arts and Letters; Southern Academy of Letters, Arts and Sciences; Past Chair, Independent Colleges and Universities of Florida (Two Years); Past Chairman, Region Seven, Executive Committee, Board of Governors, National Association of Schools of Music; Past President, Florida Music Education Association; Vice President, Florida Music Education Association; Life Member, Friday Musicale; Past Board of Governors, Association of American Colleges & Universities; Member, Executive Committee, Association of American Colleges & Universities; Past Board of Directors, Florida Music Education Association; Music Educators National Conference; Florida State Music Teachers Association; National Music Teachers Association; Honorary Member, Fine Arts Forum; Jacksonville Women's Network; Florida Women's Hall of Fame; Life Member, Delius Association of Florida; Honorary Member, Northeast Florida Chapter, Retired Officers Association; Honorary Member, Retired Officers Association, Mayport Chapter, Jacksonville Naval Air Station Chapter; River Club; Exchange Club; Past President, St. Johns Dinner Club; Board of Directors, Rotary Club of Jacksonville **MH:** Albert Nelson Marquis Lifetime Achievement Award **AV:** Public speaking **PA:** Republican **RE:** Christian

KINNEAR, JOHN KENYON JR., T: Architect **I:** Architecture & Construction **DOB:** 08/09/1948 **PB:** Brooklyn **SC:** NY/USA **PT:** John Kenyon Kinnear; Helen (Knowlton) Kinnear **MS:** Married **SPN:** Donna Manheim (11/27/1982); Alice Taylor (01/30/1971, Divorced 07/1982); Alicia Vargas Kinnear (10/10/2002) **ED:** BArch, Pratt Institute (1972) **CT:** Registered Architect, States of New York and Connecticut; Certification, National Council of Architectural Registration Boards **C:** Architect in Private Practice, New York, NY (2003-Present); Principal, Janko Rasic Architects, PLLC (1972-2003) **CR:** Chairman, Architectural Advisory Committee, Town of Ridgefield **CIV:** Board Member, The Eleanor Roosevelt Val-Kill Partnership; The American Scottish Foundation **CW:** British Memorial Garden; Hanover Square **AW:** Monsanto DOC National Design Award (1993) **MEM:** The American Institute of Architects; National Trust for Historic Preservation; The Nelson Society; The Society for Nautical Research; Vice President, The American Friends of the Georgian Group; Mashomack Preserve Club **MH:** Albert Nelson Marquis Lifetime Achievement Award; Marquis Who's Who Top Professional **B/I:** Mr. Kinnear became involved in his profession because of his lifelong interest in architecture and engineering. **AV:** Horseback riding; Modeling historic ship

KINNEY, JEFFREY, "JEFF" PATRICK, T: Author; Cartoonist **I:** Writing and Editing **DOB:** 02/19/1971 **PB:** Fort Washington **SC:** MD/USA **MS:** Married **SPN:** Julie Kinney (2003) **CH:** Will; Grant **ED:** BA, University of Maryland, College Park **C:** Co-owner, An Unlikely Story Bookstore & Cafe (2015-Present); Creator, Writer, Illustrator, Poptropica.com (2007-Present); Designer/Developer, Online Games, Boston, MA **CW:** Author, "Diary of a Wimpy Kid: The Deep End" (2020); Author, "Diary of a Wimpy Kid: Wrecking Ball" (2019); Author, "Diary of a Wimpy Kid: The Meltdown" (2018); Author, "Diary of a Wimpy Kid: The Getaway" (2017); Author, "Diary of a Wimpy Kid: Double Down" (2016); Author, "Diary of a Wimpy Kid: Old School" (2015); Author, "Diary of a Wimpy Kid: The Long Haul" (2014); Author, "Diary of a Wimpy Kid: Hard Luck" (2013); Author, "Diary of a Wimpy Kid: The Third Wheel" (2012); Author, "Diary of a Wimpy Kid: Cabin Fever" (2011); Author, "The Wimpy Kid Movie Diary" (2010); Author, "Diary of a Wimpy Kid: The Ugly Truth" (2010); Author, "Diary of a Wimpy Kid: The Last Straw" (2009); Author, "Diary of a Wimpy Kid: Dog Days" (2009); Author, "Diary of a Wimpy Kid Do-It-Yourself Book" (2008); Author, "Diary of a Wimpy Kid: Rodrick Rules" (2008); Author, "Diary of a Wimpy Kid" (2007); Executive Producer, "Diary of a Wimpy Kid" Series; Creator, "Igdoof," The Diamondback **AW:** Nickelodeon Kids Choice Award for Favorite Book (2010, 2011, 2012, 2014, 2015, 2016); Named One of the World's Most Influential People, TIME Magazine (2009)

KINS, GLORIA STARR, T: President of Public Relations Firm, Photojournalist, Writer, Editor **I:** Corporate Communications & Public Relations **DOB:** 02/23/1927 **PT:** Frank Starr; Claire Elias Starr **MS:** Divorced **CH:** Deborah Starr Kins Thomas; Victoria Starr Kins **ED:** Diploma, Gardner School, New York, NY **C:** International Society Editor, Washington International, U.N. Consular Corps (1995-Present); U.N. Correspondent, Station WQXR, New York, NY (1957-Present); Liaison to the United Nations, Oklahoma University, Irish Connections and Irish Examiner (Present); Senior Editor, Diplomatic World Bulletin (1990-1996); Publisher & Editor-in-Chief, Society and Diplomatic Review Accredited U.N. Publication, The Diplomatist Magazine, London, England (1970-1978); Founder, Society Editor, UN Correspondent, New York Voice, New York, NY (1960-1985); Society Editor of Curtis Publishing Encompassing Saturday Evening Post,

Holiday, Status Diplomat/Magazine, New York, NY (1968-1973); Deputy to Charles Van Rensselaer, Society Columnist, Cholly Knickerbocker Column, New York Journal-American, New York Post (1963-1970); Graduated to Managing Editor, Head, New York Office, Curtis Publishing Company (1970); Associate Producer, "Open Mind," NBC-TV, New York, NY (1960-1964); Associate Producer, "Sandy Lesberg Show," Station WOR, New York, NY (1960-1964); Society Editor, ITALAMERICAN Magazine, New York, NY (1957-1961); Associate Producer, Caspar Citron Show, WQXR; Chairperson, USA, Media Division, Observatory Cultural and Audio-visual Communication-Information Poverty Program; Managing Director, U.S., UBM Recording Co., Berlin, Germany; Managing Director, USA, Imphotismus, Berlin, Germany; Society Editor, Jewish Post; President, Kins Group Ltd, Publishing and International Public Relations Company; Government Liaison, Board of Directors, OCCAM Info Poverty World Conference **CR:** Board of Advisers, The Green Earth Enterprises, LLC; Vice-Chair, Center for Global Action for Sustainable Development (CGASD); Congress of Racial Equity Government Liaison and Protocol, I.C.C.C.; Vice Chairman, Earth Access; Committee Board of Directors, Harmonia Opera Company, Japan; Paul Robeson Foundation; New Jersey World Trade Council, New Jersey; Official Protocol & Cultural Partner, Saudi-American Healthcare Forum **CIV:** Founding Member, Manhattan Chapter, UNICEF (1978-Present); Board of Directors, UNICEF (1978-Present); Board of Directors, NGO, UN (1986); Executive Committee, U.S. Committee for Refugees, UN (1986); Board Member, International Affairs, The SNAP Student Foundation, Rochester, NY; Adviser, First Delegation of Tibet, U.N. **CW:** Editor, New Horizon Newspaper, London, England (1970); Society and Diplomatic Editor, Irish Connections, Irish Examiner; Contributing Editor, Eleph; Head, UN Operations, Station WOR **AW:** Official Protocol & Cultural Partner for the Saudi-American Healthcare Forum (2016); Named, Dame of the Sovereign Military Order of the Temple of Jerusalem (2002); Commander, Order of St. Stanislas (2002); Humanitarian Award, International Council for Caring Communities (2001); Certificate of Outstanding Public Service under the State of New York as Public Relations Adviser and New York State International Official Visitors Office under Nelson A. Rockefeller (1964); Honor, Dalai Lama for Volunteer Work on Tibetan Freedom (1963); National Honor of Merit, President Alfredo Stroesner of Paraguay (1959-1960) **MEM:** Lansdowne Club, London, England; Co-Founder, Islamic Council of Europe, London, England; Founder, Islamic Defense League, London, England; Acting Member, Islamic Heritage Society; National Committee on American Foreign Policy, Inc.; Cultural Exchange Committee, Nelson Rockefeller; Board Member, Pan American Society; Honorary Member, Afro-Asian Council; Acting Member, UN Delegations Women's Club; Head, North American Representative Office, Association de la Plume pour la Culture et le Development, Chad; Committee Member, The Hope Foundation USA and Kolkata, WIF, Advisory Committee of GLOCHA, Vienna, Austria; Former Member, La Confrérie de la Chaîne des Rôtisseurs **MH:** Albert Nelson Marquis Lifetime Achievement Award **AS:** Ms. Kins attributes her success to Governor Nelson Rockefeller and Osborne Elliot. **B/I:** Ms. Kins became involved in h profession because the principal at the Gardner School introduced her to the Herald Tribune International forums, the founding of the United Nations at Lake Success, and a U.N. spokesperson, Mr. Garcia, and ambassador, Mohsen Bader of Iran. **RE:** Catholic **THT:** Although hailing from a fashion empire, Ms. Kins took a different route into the world of diplomatic and international rela-

tions. Her father, Frank Starr, was one of the founders of Seventh Avenue in New York. He opened up business between India and China with the United States selling and producing textiles. Later on, her brother, Malcolm Charles Starr, took over the company, which later became synonymous with trendy glamour, where his pieces were a staple in every lady's closet.

KINSELLA, KATHLEEN E., T: Managing Director, Head Fixed Income, Money Market and Global Emerging Market Sales **I:** Business Management/Business Services **CN:** CIBC World Markets Inc. **SPN:** Connor Kinsella Stewart; Stewart Kinsella Stewart **ED:** BA in Economics and Sociology, Mount Holyoke College, South Hadley, MA (1986); College Exchange Program in Economics, Dartmouth College, Hanover, NH (1985); High School Diploma, Phillips Academy Andover, Andover, MA (1982) **CT:** Derivatives Certificate, New York University Stern School of Business (1995) **C:** Managing Director, Head of U.S. Fixed Income, Money Market and Global Emerging Markets Sales, CIBC World Markets Inc., New York, NY (2014-Present); Managing Director, Head, Americas EM Sales Team - FX, Rates & Credit, RBS Securities, Stamford, CT (2010-2014); Managing Director, Emerging Market Sales, Credit, IRD, Local Bonds, Citigroup, New York, NY (1998-2010); Vice President, Emerging Market Sales, Lehman Brothers, New York, NY (1996-1998); Vice President, Emerging Market Sales, Lehman Brothers, New York, NY (1987-1998); Vice President, Latam FI & Equity Derivative Trading & Structuring (1991-1995); Analyst, M&A - Financial Situations, New York, NY (1989-1991); Analyst, Corporate Finance, Natural Resources, London, England (1989-1991); Analyst, Management Training Program, Internal Consulting Group, JP Morgan, New York, NY (1987-1989) **CIV:** Board of Directors, EMpower; Board of Directors, Reach Within; Fundraiser, Various Charities **MEM:** Development Committee, Phillips Andover **AS:** Ms. Kinsella attributes her success to being straightforward, honest, and hardworking. **B/I:** Ms. Kinsella became involved in her profession because she was an economics major as an undergraduate. She had an interest in finance, and interviewed on campus and was given a job at JP Morgan. She had planned to go back to business school but she kept doing well, so she traveled up the ladder in multiple companies. Each job opportunity was sequential after the next.

KINZINGER, ADAM DANIEL, T: U.S. Representative **I:** Government Administration/Government Relations/Government Services **DOB:** 02/27/1978 **PB:** Kankakee **SC:** IL/USA **PT:** Rus Kinzinger; Betty Jo Kinzinger **ED:** BA, Illinois State University, Normal, IL (2000) **C:** U.S. Representative, Illinois' 16th Congressional District, United States Congress (2013-Present); Member, Committee on Energy and Commerce, U.S. House of Representatives, Washington, DC (2011-Present); Member, U.S. Representative, Illinois' 11th Congressional District, Washington, DC (2011-2013); Member, Committee on Foreign Affairs **CR:** Board Member, McLean County Government **MIL:** Captain, Pilot, U.S. Air Force (2005-Present); Lieutenant Colonel, U.S. Air Force (2003-Present); Second Lieutenant, U.S. Air Force (2003); With, Air Force Special Operations; With, Air Combat Command; With, Air Mobility Command; With, Wisconsin Air National Guard; With, U.S. Air Force **AW:** One of the Politics 40 Under 40, TIME Magazine (2010); Decorated Valley Forge Cross; Airman's Medal; Hero of the Year, Southeast Wisconsin Chapter, The American National Red Cross **MEM:** NRA; Illinois State Rifle Association **PA:** Republican **RE:** Christian

KIRBY, HARRY SCOTT, T: Priest in Charge **I:** Religious **CN:** The Episcopal Church **DOB:** 05/06/1938 **PB:** Richmond **SC:** VA/USA **PT:** William Alphus Kirby; Lucille Viola (Patterson) Kirby **MS:** Married **SPN:** Heather Patricia Roberts (06/22/1963) **CH:** Cheryl Christine; Robert Bruce **ED:** MDiv, The General Theological Seminary, New York, NY (1963); BA, University of Richmond, VA (1960) **CT:** Ordained Priest, Episcopal Church (1963) **C:** Priest in Charge, Grace Church, Rice Lake, WI (2005-2018); Dean, Christ Church Cathedral, Eau Claire, WI (1988-2005); Dean Emeritus, Christ Church Cathedral, Eau Claire, WI (2005-Present); Canon, Christ Church Cathedral, Salina, KS (1979-Present); Resident Director, Director of Development, St. Francis Academy (1979-1988); Rector, Church of St. John on the Mountain, Bernardsville, NJ (1973-1979); Rector, Church of St. John the Baptist, Dunkirk, NY (1966-1973); Curate, Church of the Advent, Kenmore, NY (1963-1966); Assistant to Rector, Cathedral Church of St. Luke and St. Paul, Charleston, SC (1963) **CR:** Vice President, House of Deputies, General Convention of the Episcopal Church, 77th General Convention (2012); Member, Title IV Committee (1997-2000); Development Consultant, St. Francis Academy, Salina, KS (1991-1994); Chairman, Long Range Planning, Diocese of Eau Claire (1989-1992); Member, Committee, Elect Presiding Bishop (1997-2000); Council of Advice, President, House of Deputies (1994-2000); Chair Committee, State of the Church (1994-1997); Dean, Chippewa Valley (1990-1996); President, Standing Committee, Chair, Liturgical Committee, Examining Chaplain, Diocese of Eau Claire; Executive Council, Visitation Committee for Council of Advice, Eau Claire Police Department Chaplain; Deputy, House of Deputies, General Convention of the Episcopal Church **CIV:** Chaplain, Seamen's Church Institute, Upper MI (Present); Board, Business Improvement District (1993-Present); Board of Directors, Episcopal Relief & Development (1985-1990); Member, The Episcopal Church in the USA **MIL:** Chaplain Captain, Civil Air Patrol **CW:** Contributor, Articles to Magazines **AW:** Distinguished Alumni Award, The General Theological Seminary (2015); Bishop's Service Award, Diocese of Western Kansas (1980); Longest Serving Ordained Deputy, House of Deputies, General Convention of the Episcopal Church **MEM:** Anglican Society **MH:** Albert Nelson Marquis Lifetime Achievement Award; Marquis Who's Who Top Professional **AS:** Rev. Kirby attributes his success to the example and witness of his parents, godparents, bishops, and pastors; their hard and dedicated service to the church set daily goals for his ministry. He also credits the excellent education and grounding that he received at the University of Richmond. The superior theological education and training at The General Theological Seminary and the support, and guidance of the dedicated dean and faculty set the framework for his daily work as a Christian priest. Each parish that he has served has also contributed to the ministry he has been privileged to maintain. His wife's love, support, and prayers sustained Rev. Kirby as they worked together in each parish and position to which he has been called to serve. **B/I:** Rev. Kirby always wanted to be a priest; he never knew a time in his life that he wanted to do anything else. His mother wanted him to be a dentist. Rev. Kirby disagreed. He then had an opportunity to attend the Naval Academy at Annapolis. He did not want to do that either. He went to seminary. Rev. Kirby's parents and his godparents were instrumental in his love for the church. **AV:** Music; Flying **RE:** Episcopalian

KIRKPATRICK, ANN LEILA, T: U.S. Representative **I:** Government Administration/Government Relations/Government Services **DOB:** 03/24/1950 **PB:** McNary **SC:** AZ/USA **PT:** Elliot Whittington Kirkpatrick; Nancy Jeanne (Cox) Kirkpatrick **MS:** Married **SPN:** Roger Curley **CH:** Whitney; Ashley **ED:** JD, James E. Rogers College of Law, The University of Arizona (1979); BA, The University of Arizona, Cum Laude (1972) **C:** U.S. Representative, Arizona's Second Congressional District, United States Congress (2019-Present); The House Committee on Transportation and Infrastructure (2013-Present); The House Committee on Veterans' Affairs (2013-Present); U.S. Representative, Arizona's First Congressional District, United States Congress (2009-2011, 2013-Present); U.S. Representative, Arizona's First Congressional District (2009-2011, 2013-2017); The House Committee on Veterans' Affairs (2009-2011, 2013-2017); Member, Committee on Small Business, U.S. House of Representatives (2009-2011); Member, Committee on Homeland Security, U.S. House of Representatives (2009-2011); Member, District Two, Arizona House of Representatives (2005-2007); Co-Founder, Kirkpatrick & Harris (1991); Associate, Mangum, Wall, Stoops & Warden, PLLC, Flagstaff, AZ (1985); Deputy Attorney, Pima County, Tucson, AZ (1982-1984); Private Practice, Secona, AZ (1981-1982); Deputy Attorney, Coconino County, Flagstaff, AZ (1980-1981) **CR:** Instructor of Business Law and Ethics, Coconino Community College (2004) **CIV:** Member, Civil Practice and Procedure Committee, Phoenix, AZ (1985-Present); Chairman of Funding, Board of Directors, IMPACT Victim-Witness Program, Flagstaff, AZ (1985-Present); Teacher, Sunday School, Flagstaff Federated Community Church, AZ (1985-Present); Consultant, Flagstaff Medical Center Foundation (1986-Present); Member, Mental Health Services Committee, Phoenix, AZ (1982-1984); Member, Mayor's Task Force, Tucson City Council (1982) **AW:** Outstanding Young Women in America (1985) **MEM:** American Bar Association; State Bar of Arizona; Coconino County Bar Association; American Academy of Hospital Attorneys (Now American Health Law Association); Arizona Hospital Association (Now Arizona Hospital and Healthcare Association) **BAR:** State Bar of Arizona (1979); United States District Court District of Arizona (1979) **AV:** Playing piano; Swimming; Skiing; Ice-skating **PA:** Democrat **RE:** Presbyterian

KIRSCH, DONALD, T: Financial Consultant **I:** Financial Services **DOB:** 10/09/1931 **PB:** New York **SC:** NY/USA **PT:** William Kirsch; Eva (Wasserman) Kirsch **MS:** Married **SPN:** Dorothy Ann Tejw (06/06/1959) **CH:** Mark Adam Kirsch; Dr.Karen Rebecca Hoffman; Jonathan Bradford **ED:** BS, New York University (1952) **CT:** Senior Securities Analyst, New York Society of Securities Analysts **C:** Chairman, Wall Street Group Inc., Los Angeles, CA (1963-Present); Chairman, President, The Wall Street Group Inc., New York, NY (1959-Present); President, Wall Street Consultant, New York, NY (1955-Present); Writer, Associated Press, New York, NY (1954-1955); Editorial Staffer, Wall Street Journal, New York, NY (1952-1953) **CR:** Founding Chairman, Talleres Graficos de Interamericanos, San Juan, Puerto Rico (1962-1980); Adjunct Associate Professor, New York University Graduate School of Arts and Science (1974-1979); Chairman, Eurofinancing Ltd. (1968); Board of Directors, Interstate National Dealers Services, Inc.; Board of Directors, Audiofidelity Enterprises Inc.; Board of Directors, Dialscan Systems, Medi-Mail, Inc.; Chairman, Strategic Planning Committee, MedNet Inc.; Board of Directors, Co-star Entertainment Inc.; Typesetting Products Inc. **CIV:** Treasurer, Board of Trustees, National Symphony Orchestra, John F. Kennedy Center for Performing Arts (1996-1998); Board of Managers, Episcopal Social Services, New York, NY; Trustee, Big Brothers; Trustee, Potter's Field; Trustee, Michael Moriarity's American Shakespeare School and Performance Art Center; Trustee, Corporate Headquarters Alcoholism Project **CW:** Author, "Financial and Economic Journalism: Analysis Interpretation and Reporting" (1978); Author, "Investor Relations for the Over-the-Counter or Newly Public Company"; Co-Author, "The Handbook of Investor Relations"; Contributor, Articles, Professional Journals **AW:** Librarian Association Award (1978); Inductee, New York Chapter, Journalism Honor Society (1976) **MEM:** Chairman, New York Metro Chapter, Young President's Organization (1976); Founding Member, American Associates Royal Academy Trust; Founding Member, Chief Executives Organization; Founding Member, Young President's Organization; Metropolitan President's Organization; Chief Executives Organization; New York Society Security Analysts; The Metropolitan Club of New York; Friar's Club; Economics Club of New York; Masons **AV:** Collecting art; Collecting first-edition books; Collecting glass; Traveling; Reading; Writing **PA:** Independent

KISSINGER, HENRY ALFRED, T: International Consulting Company Executive; Former U.S. Secretary of State **I:** Business Management/Business Services **CN:** Kissinger Associates Inc. **DOB:** 05/27/1923 **SC:** Fuerth/Germany **PT:** Louis Kissinger; Paula (Stern) Kissinger **MS:** Married **SPN:** Nancy Maginnes (03/30/1974); Ann Fleischer (02/06/1949, Divorced 1964) **CH:** Elizabeth; David **ED:** PhD, Harvard University (1954); MA, Harvard University (1952); AB in Political Science, Harvard University, Summa Cum Laude (1950) **C:** Founder, Chairman, Kissinger Associates, Inc., New York, NY (1982-Present); Chancellor, College of William & Mary (2001-2005); Secretary, U.S. Department of State, Washington, DC (1973-1977); Assistant to President for National Security Affairs, National Security Council, Washington, DC (1968-1975); Director, Defense Studies Program, Harvard University (1958-1969); Faculty Member, Department of Government and Center for International Affairs (Now Weatherhead Center for International Affairs), Harvard University (1954-1969); Executive Director, Harvard International Seminar (1951-1969); Associate Director, Center for International Affairs (Now Weatherhead Center for International Affairs), Harvard University (1957-1960) **CR:** Honorary Chair, Advisory Board, Bloomberg New Economy Forum (2018-Present); Honorary Counselor, Asia Society Policy Institute (2014-Present); Board Member, Theranos (2014-2017); Board of Directors, Freeport-McMoRan Copper & Gold Inc. (1995-2001); Board of Directors, American Express Company (1986-1996); President's Foreign Intelligence Advisory Board (1984-1990); Commission on the Integrated Long-term Strategy of the National Security Council and Defense Department (1986-1988); Chairman, National Bipartisan Commission on Central America (1983-1984); Consultant, U.S. Department of State (1965-1968); Consultant, RAND Corporation (1961-1968); Consultant, U.S. Arms Control and Disarmament Agency (1961-1968); Consultant, National Security Council (1961-1962); Weapons Systems Evaluation Group, U.S. Department of Defense (1959-1960); Director, Special Studies Project, Rockefeller Brothers Fund (1956-1958); Study Director, Nuclear Weapons and Foreign Policy, Council on Foreign Relations (1955-1956); Operations Coordinating Board (1955); Director, Psychological Strategy Board (1952); Operations Research Office (1950-1951) **CIV:** Board of Trustees, Institute of International Education, Inc. (1999-Present) **MIL:** Captain, Military Intelligence Reserve, United States Army (1946-1949); Counter Intelligence Corps, United States Army (1943-1946) **CW:** Author, "World

Order" (2014); Author, "On China" (2011); Author, "Crisis: The Anatomy of Two Major Foreign Policy Crises: Based on the Record of Henry Kissinger's Hitherto Secret Telephone Conversations" (2003); Author, "Vietnam: A Personal History of America's Involvement in and Extrication from the Vietnam War" (2002); Author, "Does America Need a Foreign Policy?: Toward a Diplomacy for the 21st Century" (2001); Author, "Years of Renewal" (1999); Co-author, "Kissinger Transcripts: The Top Secret Talks With Beijing and Moscow" (1999); Author, "Diplomacy" (1994); Author, "Observations: Selected Speeches and Essays 1982-1984" (1985); Author, "Years of Upheaval" (1982); Author, "For the Record: Selected Statements" (1981); Author, "White House Years" (1979); Author, "American Foreign Policy: Three Essays" (1969); Author, "The Troubled Partnership: A Re-Appraisal of the Atlantic Alliance" (1965); Editor, "Problems of National Strategy: A Book of Readings" (1965); Author, "The Necessity for Choice: Prospects of American Foreign Policy" (1961); Author, "Nuclear Weapons and Foreign Policy" (1957); Author, "A World Restored: Metternich, Castlereagh and the Problems of Peace, 1812-22" (1957); Contributor, Articles, Professional Journals **AW:** Henry A. Grunwald Award for Public Service, Lighthouse International (2013); Israel's President's Medal (2012); Theodore Roosevelt American Experience Award, Union League Club of New York (2009); Hopkins-Nanjing Award (2007); Woodrow Wilson Award for Public Service, Smithsonian Institution (2006); Honorary Knight Commander, Most Distinguished Order of St. Michael and St. George (1995); Medal of Liberty (1986); National Book Award, National Book Foundation (1980); Presidential Medal of Freedom, The White House (1977); Hope Award for International Understanding (1973); Dwight D. Eisenhower Distinguished Service Medal, Veterans of Foreign Wars (1973); Theodore Roosevelt Award, International Platform Association (1973); Distinguished Public Service Award, American Institute for Public Service (1973); Co-Recipient Nobel Peace Prize, Norwegian Nobel Committee (1973); Woodrow Wilson Prize for Best Book in Fields of Government, Politics and International Affairs (1958); Decorated Bronze Star **MEM:** American Academy Arts & Sciences; Council on Foreign Relations; American Political Science Association (APSA); Century Club; New York City Book Club; Metropolitan Club of the City of Washington; The Phi Beta Kappa Society **PA:** Republican **RE:** Jewish

KITCHENS, CLARENCE, "WES" WESLEY JR., T: Consultant **I:** Military & Defense Services **CN:** Wes Kitchens Consulting **DOB:** 11/08/1943 **PB:** Panama City **SC:** FL/USA **PT:** Clarence Wesley Kitchens, Sr; Voncile (Rudolph) Kitchens **MS:** Married **SPN:** Terry Lee Worsley (12/26/1966) **CH:** Kathy Lee; Mark Wesley **ED:** PhD, North Carolina State University (1970); MS, Virginia Polytechnic Institute and State University (1968); BS, Virginia Polytechnic Institute and State University (1966) **CT:** Registered Professional Engineer (Retired), Maryland; Charter Member, Army Acquisition Corps; Certified In Systems Planning, Research, Development, and Engineering, Level III; Original Classification Authority, Department of Defense Weapons Technologies **C:** Owner, Wes Kitchens Consulting (2017-Present); Manager, Wes Kitchens and Associates, LLC (2009-2017); Technical Fellow, Senior Advisor, Science Applications International Corp. (2004-2010); Vice President, Hicks and Associates, Inc., McLean, VA (2003-2004); Director, Chief Scientist, Department of Defense Weapon Systems Technology Information Analysis Center, Alexandria, VA (2000-2003); Principal Deputy for Technology, Army Materiel Command, Alexandria, VA (1998-2000); Director for Weapons Technolo-

gies, Office of Secretary of Defense, Washington, DC (1997-1998); Director, Army Benét Laboratories, Watervliet Arsenal, NY (1993-1996); Director, Army Research Laboratory Transition Office, Army Research Laboratory, Adelphi, MD (1992-1993); Chief, Terminal Ballistics Division, Army Ballistic Research Laboratory, Aberdeen Proving Ground, MD (1985-1992); Chief, Penetration Mechanics Branch, Army Ballistic Research Laboratory, Aberdeen Proving Ground, MD (1983-1985); Chief, Blast Dynamics Branch, Army Ballistic Research Laboratory, Aberdeen Proving Ground, MD (1980-1983); Leader, Fluid Dynamics Analysis Team, Army Ballistic Research Laboratory, Aberdeen Proving Ground, MD (1978-1980); Assistant to Director, Army Ballistic Research Laboratory, Aberdeen Proving Ground, MD (1977-1978); Research Aerospace Engineer, Army Ballistic Research Laboratory, Aberdeen Proving Ground, MD (1972-1977); Research and Development Coordinator, Army Ballistic Research Laboratory, Aberdeen Proving Ground, MD (1970-1972); Instructor, Engineering Mechanics, North Carolina State University, Raleigh, NC (1969-1970) **CR:** Department of Justice Expert Witness on Weapons Technologies (2012-2014); National Academies Panel on Armor and Armaments (2009-2012); American Institute of Aeronautics and Astronautics Weapons Systems Effectiveness Technical Committee (2006-2010); Science Applications International Corp. Engineering Science and Technology Council (2003-2010); National Academies Board on Army Science and Technology (2001-2007); (1998-2000); Co-Chair, United States Army/France Technology Working Group (1998-2000); Co-Chair, United States Army/United Kingdom Technology Working Group (1998-2000); Co-Chair, United States Army/Germany Technology Working Group (1998-2000); Army Performance Management Steering Committee (1999); Executive Secretary, White House Committee on National Security (1997-1998); U.S. National Leader, Conventional Weapons Technology Group, The Technology Cooperation Program (1997-1998); United States/Chile Defense Science and Technology Committee (1997-1998); Army Principal for Department of Defense Conventional Weapons Panel (1996); Co-Chair, United States Senior National Representatives Future Tank Main Armament Interoperability Working Group, U.S. Army (1993-1996); Chairman, Reliance Sub-Panel on Conventional Guns (1994-1995); U.S. National Leader, The Technical Cooperative Program Weapons Technology Technical Panel (1986-1992); U.S. National Leader, The Technical Cooperation Program Technical Panel on Terminal Effects (1985-1992); Chairman, Panel on Advanced Conventional Armament, DARPA Electrical Energy Gun Study (1988); Army Armor/Anti-Armor Net Assessment Team (1987); Armor/Anti-Armor Program Assessment Panel (1986); American Institute of Aeronautics and Astronautics Honors and Awards Committee (1985-1986); Armor Task Group, Defense Science Board Summer Study on Armor/Anti-Armor Competition (1985); Focus Officer for Kinetic Energy Penetrators, The Technical Cooperation Program (1983-1985) **CIV:** Director, Innisfree, Inc. (2007-Present) **MIL:** Captain, U.S. Army (1970-1972) **CW:** Contributor, Technical Articles, Professional Journals; Contributor, Chapters, Books **AW:** Presidential Exceptional Executive Rank Award (2000); U.S. Army Exceptional Civilian Service Award (1989, 2000); Honorary Order of Saint Barbara Award (1996); U.S. Army Superior Civilian Service Award (1996); Presidential Meritorious Executive Rank Award (1991); Firepower Award for Development, Picatinny Arsenal New Jersey Chapter of American Defense Preparedness Association (1990); U.S. Army Meritorious Civilian Service Award (1986); Ford Foundation Fellow-

ship (1968-1970); Inductee, Pi Mu Epsilon (1969); NASA Traineeship (1967-1969); Listee, Who's Who in American Colleges and Universities (1966); Inductee, Tau Beta Pi (1965); Inductee, Phi Kappa Phi (1965); Inductee, Omicron Delta Kappa (1965); Inductee, Kappa Theta Epsilon (1965); General Electric Scholarship for Undergraduate Studies (1962) **MEM:** Fellow, Associate, American Institute of Aeronautics and Astronautics; Fellow, Emeritus, U.S. Army Research Laboratory; Fellow, Emeritus, U.S. Army Laboratory Command; Fellow, Emeritus, Ballistic Research Laboratory; Technical Fellow, Emeritus, Science Applications International Corp.; Life-Member, Association of U.S. Army **MH:** Albert Nelson Marquis Lifetime Achievement Award **AS:** Dr. Kitchens attributes his success to his ability to work closely with others, effortlessly applying his knowledge and experience in a way that helps his team understand and solve difficult technical problems. He additionally can assess and improve research, technology, and development programs that are important to the United States' national security. **B/I:** Dr. Kitchens' interest in his career came from his knowledge and experience to help plan, conduct, and manage important science, technology, and engineering development activities. These included joint-service and international activities that contribute to national security. **AV:** Flyfishing; Fly tying; Upkeeping personal finances and investment management; Lifelong learning **PA:** Democrat **RE:** Methodist

KLARMAN, SETH ANDREW, T: Hedge Fund Manager **I:** Financial Services **CN:** Baupost Group **DOB:** 05/21/1957 **PB:** New York **SC:** NY/USA **MS:** Married **SPN:** Beth Schultz Klarman (1982) **ED:** MBA, Harvard Business School; BA in Economics, Cornell University, New York, NY **C:** Founder, President, The Baupost Group, Boston, MA (1983-Present) **CW:** Author, "Margin of Safety: Risk-Averse Value Investing Strategies for the Thoughtful Investor" (1991)

KLECKNER, KELLI, T: Office Manager **I:** Consumer Goods and Services **CN:** The Titus Company **C:** Officer Manager, The Titus Company (2016-Present); Commercial Business Insurance (1996-2016) **CIV:** Animal Rescue **AS:** Ms. Kleckner attributes her success to her honesty, hard work and dedication. **B/I:** Ms. Kleckner became involved her profession because she enjoys having relationships with people and helping them in any way that she can professionally and professionally. She started out as a receptionist and received her license and then was promoted to commercial business insurance. She saw her receptionist position as a blessing in disguise because she was able to grow and realize her capabilities. **AV:** Spending time with her cats **THT:** Ms. Kleckner believes that people should treat others how they'd like to be treated.

KLEGERMAN, MELVIN EARL, PHD, T: Biochemist, Biomedical Engineer **I:** Education/Educational Services **CN:** University of Texas Health Science Center at Houston (UTHealth) **DOB:** 08/30/1945 **PB:** Chicago **SC:** IL/US **PT:** Hyman Joseph Klegerman; Esther Elizabeth (Tartas) Klegerman **MS:** Married **SPN:** Maureen Goode, PhD (02/17/2014) **CH:** Robin Howard Allen; Joshua Sherwood Allen; Melanie Esther; Jessica Ann **ED:** PhD, Loyola University, Chicago, IL (1984); BA, University of Illinois at Chicago (1967) **C:** Professor, University of Texas, Houston, TX (2013-Present); President, Chief Executive Officer, EchoDynamics Inc. (2000-Present); Associate Professor, Medicine, Biochemistry and Biomedical Engineering, University of Texas, Houston, TX (2006-2013); President, Chief Executive Officer, Mid-Atlantic Biomedical Research Laboratory (1996-2002); Adjunct Assistant Professor, Pharmaceuticals, University of Illinois, Chicago, IL (1995-1998); Associate Director, Institute for Tuberculosis Research, University of Illinois at Chicago (1987-1996); Assistant Professor, Pharmaceuticals, University of Illinois, Chicago, IL (1988-1995); Research Associate, Rush-Presbyterian St. Luke's Medical Center, Chicago, IL (1986-1987); Research Investigator, Michael Reese Hospital and Medical Center, Chicago, IL (1980-1986); Research Associate, Evanston Hospital (1979); Research Associate, Loyola University Medical Center, Maywood, IL (1973-1978); Assistant Editor, Encyclopedia Britannica, Chicago, IL (1970-1973) **CR:** Founding Member, Zymo Pharmaceuticals, LLC (2012-Present) **CIV:** Volunteer, Brazos Bend State Park **CW:** Editor, "Pharmaceutical Biotechnology: Fundamentals and Essentials" (1992); Contributor, Articles, Journal of Laboratory and Clinical Medicine, Journal of Infectious Diseases, Cancer Letters, Journal of Controlled Release, Thrombosis Research, and Others **AW:** Grantee, National Institutes of Health (1981-Present); Grantee, Texas Ignition Fund (2009-2010); Grantee, Mallinkrodt Medical (1996-1997); Grantee, Organon Teknika Corporation (1988, 1993); Grantee, World Health Organization (1989) **MEM:** American Association for the Advancement of Science; American Society for Microbiology (ASM); American Association of Pharmaceutical Scientists (AAPS); American Heart Association; American Chemical Society **MH:** Albert Nelson Marquis Lifetime Achievement Award; Marquis Who's Who Top Professional **AS:** Dr. Klegerman attributes his success to his mentor, Hugh MacDonald, who was his PhD supervisor at Loyola University and allowed students to be self-motivated. **B/I:** Dr. Klegerman became involved in his profession because it all started with a Gilbert chemistry set his parents gave him when he was 8 years old. He knew he wanted to be a biochemist early on in life. In high school, his father was a chemistry hobbyist so they started their own home lab. **AV:** Reading; Drawing; Painting **PA:** Democrat **RE:** Buddhist

KLEID, WALLACE, T: Lawyer **I:** Law and Legal Services **DOB:** 06/25/1946 **PB:** Baltimore **SC:** MD/USA **PT:** Max E. Kleid; Bess (Hubberman) Kleid **MS:** Married **SPN:** Ina L. Sirkis **CH:** Kathy J. Kleid Tores; Micah Saul; Matthew Brett **ED:** JD, University of Maryland, Baltimore, MD (1971); BA, University of Maryland, Baltimore (1967) **CT:** Mediator, Circuit Courts of Baltimore City and Baltimore County **C:** SE Wallace Kleid Law LLC (2018-Present); Attorney, Hassan, Hassan, & Tuchman, Baltimore, MD (2001-2017); Attorney, Margolis, Prizker & Epstein, Towson, Annapolis, MD (1993-2001); Partner, Floam & Kleid, Baltimore, Towson, MD (1985-1993); Private Practice, Law, Baltimore, Towson, MD (1972-1985); Assistant States Attorney, States Attorney Baltimore County (1972-1977); Law Clerk, States Attorney Baltimore County, Maryland (1970-1972) **CR:** Attorney, Grievance Commission, Peer Review Panel (2001-Present); Co-Founder, MSAT-MD; Certified Mediator, Circuit Court, Baltimore County (1998-Present); Attorney, Grievance Commission (1982-2001); Consultant, Television Program, Women and the Law (1976-1977); Presenter, Testimony on Rape, Maryland General Assembly (1975); Rape Advisory Commission, Baltimore County (1974-1975); Presenter, Lecturer in Field **CIV:** Chair, American Friends of Magen David Adom, Greater Baltimore Region (2009-Present); University of Maryland Advocacy Network (1998-Present); Instructor, MSBA Professionalism Course for New Admittees (1995-Present); Watch Commander, Northwest Citizens Patrol (1990-Present); Executive Board, Israel Bonds of Maryland (1993-2007); Participant, Sar-El (2003);

Commentator, Workers Compensation Audiotape Series speaker, MWCEA Conference (2001, 2003); Treasurer, Summit Chase Home Owners Association (1996-1999); Troop Parents Committee (1993-1999); Board of Directors, Krieger-Schecter School (1990-1994); Den Leader, Boy Scouts of America (1988-1992); Citizens Democratic Club, Baltimore, MD (1972-1975); Board Director, Hadassah, Colonial Village Neighborhood Association, Baltimore (1969-1975); Prime Ministers Club, Development Corporation of Israel; Cheswolde Neighborhood Association, Baltimore; Maryland Institute of Continuing Professional Education of Lawyers **MIL:** Sgt., U.S. Army Reserve (1968-1974) **CW:** Contributor, Articles, Journals **AW:** Civilian Award, Baltimore County Police Department (1975) **MEM:** Negligence and Workers Compensation Committee, Baltimore County Bar Association (2004-Present); Alternate Dispute Resolution Committee, Baltimore County Bar Association (1999-Present); Workers Compensation Committee, Maryland Trial Lawyers Association (1998-Present); Negligence, Insurance and Workers Compensation Section Council, Maryland State Bar Association (1990-Present); Family Law Committee, Baltimore County Bar Association (1999-2009); Vice-Chair, Baltimore County Bar Association (2006-2007); Unfair Claims Practice Committee, Maryland Trial Lawyers Association (1998-2002, 2007); Teleconference Lecturer, Torts, Insurance Section, American Bar Association (2002); Contributing Editor, Women's Law Center's Family Law Manual, Volume Family Law Hotline (1995-1997); Board of Directors, Maryland Institute for Continuing Education Lawyers (1992-1996); Senior Vice Chair, Litigation Subcommittee, American Bar Association (1993-1994); Bench Bar Committee, Baltimore County Bar Association (1993-1994); Secretary, Maryland State Bar Association (1993-1994); Treasurer, Maryland State Bar Association (1991-1993); Vice Chairman, Baltimore County Bar Association (1988-1991); Entertainment Committee, Baltimore County Bar Association (1989-1990); Council, Maryland State Bar Association (1988-1990); Conference Planning Subcommittee, American Bar Association (1988-1989); Vice Chairman, General Practice Section, Liaison to National, State and Local Bar Leaders, American Bar Association (1987-1988); Chairman, Subcommittee, Associates Employment Agreements (1978-1988); Associates Employment Agreements, American Bar Association (1978-1988); Chairman, General Practice Section, Maryland State Bar Association (1985-1987); Consultant, Special Committee, Maryland State Bar Association (1985-1987); Chairman, Insurance Trust, Baltimore County Bar Association (1980-1987); Chairman Special Committee, Maryland State Bar Association (1984-1985); Lawyer Referral Committee, Baltimore County Bar Association (1976-1978); Association of Trial Lawyers of America; Federal Bar Association; Bench Bar Committee, Workers Compensation Committee, Alternate Dispute Resolution Committee, Baltimore City Bar Association; Maryland Criminal Defense Association; National Defense Attorneys Association; Maryland State Attorney's Association; Former Member, Maryland Association Justice; National District Attorneys Association; Washington, D.C. Bar Association; Zeta Beta Tau; American Friends of Magen David Adom **BAR:** States of Washington, DC (1982); United States Supreme Court (1975); U.S. Court of Appeals for the Fourth Circuit (1975); U.S. Court of Military Appeals (1973); Maryland (1972); U.S. District Court of Maryland (1972) **MH:** Albert Nelson Marquis Lifetime Achievement Award **B/I:** Mr. Kleid became involved in his profession because he could not master physics and chemistry, which thwarted his childhood dream of becoming an orthodontist. His parents owned a

bar, which had been handed down before prohibition from his grandparents. The state of Maryland had strived to build all the University of Maryland professional schools in Baltimore City. In order to build the surrounding campus, the state acquired the neighboring properties. Mr. Kleid's parent's bar was in that radius; the state wanted their property. At this time, Mr. Kleid had started law school. After being discharged from the United States Army mid-semester, he worked for a railroad, but he wanted to go back to law school. The state acquisition destroyed the bar's clientele, so the family received a pittance for the business. That aggravated Mr. Kleid. These events set him on the path to be a lawyer, as it also established his desire to give back through pro bono activities and bar association involvement. **AV:** Baltimore Orioles games; Concerts; Theater **PA:** Democrat **RE:** Jewish

KLEIN, BENJAMIN ENDSLEY, T: Theatre Director **I:** Media & Entertainment **CW:** Resident Director, "The Ferryman" (2018); Associate Director, "Carousel" (2018); Associate Director, "The Curious Incident of the Dog in the Night-Time" (2014); Associate Director, "Macbeth" (2013); Director, "Ann" (2013); Resident Director, "War Horse" (2011); Associate Director, "The Coast of Utopia (Part 3: Salvage)" (2007); Associate Director, "The Coast of Utopia (Part 2: Shipwreck)" (2006); Associate Director, "The Coast of Utopia (Part 1: Voyage)" (2006); Assistant Director, "Dirty Rotten Scoundrels" (2005)

KLEIN, CALVIN RICHARD, T: Fashion Designer **I:** Apparel & Fashion **DOB:** 11/19/1942 **PB:** Bronx **SC:** NY/USA **PT:** Leo Klein; Flore (Stern) Klein **MS:** Divorced **SPN:** Kelly Rector (09/1986, Divorced 04/2006); Jayne Centre (04/26/1964, Divorced 1974) **CH:** Marci **ED:** Honorary Doctorate, Fashion Institute of Technology, New York, NY (2003); Coursework, Fashion Institute of Technology, New York, NY **C:** Designer, Calvin Klein (PVH Corp.), New York, NY (2003-Present); Founder, President, Designer, Calvin Klein Ltd., New York, NY (1968-2003); Launched, Line of Coats and Dresses, Calvin Klein Ltd.; Expanded Line, Including Signature Jeans, Menswear, Womenswear, Lingerie, Home Furnishings, Eyewear, Swimwear and Various Perfumes for Men and Women, Calvin Klein Ltd.; Brands Include, Calvin Klein Watches and Jewelry, CK One Lifestyle, Calvin Klein Underwear, Calvin Klein Golf, The Khaki Collection, Calvin Klein Home, Calvin Klein Jeans, Calvin Klein Sport, Calvin Klein, CK Calvin Klein, and Calvin Klein Collection; Apprenticeship, Cloak and Suit Manufacturer, Dan Millstein **CW:** Narrator, "The Emperor's New Clothes: An All-Star Illustrated Retelling of the Classic Fairy Tale" (1998); Appearance, "30 Rock" **AW:** Lifetime Achievement Award, Council of Fashion Designers of America (CFDA) (2001); Named Womenswear/Menswear Designer of the Year, Council of Fashion Designers of America (CFDA) (1974, 1993); Named One of America's 25 Woolmark Award for Career Achievement (1987); Named Outstanding American Talent in Women's Fashion Design (1982, 1983, 1986); Named to International Best Dressed List (1983); Hall of Fame Award, Coty American Fashion Critics' Awards (1975); Named One of the Most Influential People, TIME Magazine **MEM:** Council of Fashion Designers of America (CFDA)

KLEIN, NAOMI, T: Journalist, Author **I:** Writing and Editing **CN:** The Nation Company LLC **DOB:** 05/08/1970 **PB:** Montreal **SC:** Canada **PT:** Michael Klein; Bonnie Sherr Klein **MS:** Married **SPN:** Avi Lewis **CH:** One Child **ED:** Honorary Doctorate, University of Amsterdam (2019); Honorary Doctorate,

Saint Thomas University (2011); Intern, The Globe & Mail, Toronto, Canada; Coursework, University of Toronto **C:** International Syndicated Columnist, Several Publications Including The Nation, The Nation Company LLC; Editor, This Magazine; Senior Correspondent, The Intercept; Puffin Writing Fellow, Type Media Center; Inaugural Gloria Steinem Endowed Chair, Media, Culture and Feminist Studies, Rutgers, the State University of New Jersey **CW:** Author, "On Fire: The (Burning) Case for a Green New Deal" (2019); Author, "The Battle for Paradise: Puerto Rico Takes on the Disaster Capitalists" (2018); Author, "No is Not Enough: Resisting Trump's Shock Politics and Winning the World We Need" (2017); Author, "This Changes Everything" (2015); Author, "This Changes Everything: Capitalism vs. The Climate" (2014); Appearance, "Catastroika" (2012); Author, "The Shock Doctrine," (2009); Author, "The Shock Doctrine: The Rise of Disaster Capitalism" (2007); Co-Director (with Avi Lewis), "The Take" (2004); Author, "Fences & Windows: Dispatches from the Front Lines of the Globalization Debate" (2002); Author, "No Logo: Taking Aim at the Brand Bullies" (2000); Syndicated Columnist, Toronto Star, The Nation, The New York Times, In These Times, Globe & Mail, This Magazine, The Guardian; Author, Chapters, Books; Author, Articles, Professional Journals **AW:** Sydney Peace Prize (2016); Named One of the Top 100 Nonfiction Books of All-time, The Guardian (2016); Hilary Weston Writers' Trust Prize for Nonfiction (2014); Named One of the 100 Notable Books of the Year, Book Review (2014); Named Book of the Year, The Observer (2014); Named to Readers' 10 Best Books of 2014, The Guardian (2014); Warwick Prize for Writing, England (2009); Named One of the 100 Agents of Change, Rolling Stone Magazine (2009); Named Critics' Pick of the Year, The New York Times (2007); Freda Kirchwey Fellow, Nation Institute (2005); Miliband Fellow, London School of Economics (2002); National Business Book Award, Canada (2001); Prix Médiations (2001); Named One of the Top 100 Nonfiction Books Published Since 1923, TIME Magazine (1999)

KLEINER, HEATHER SMITH, T: Academic Administrator (Retired) **I:** Education/Educational Services **DOB:** 03/31/1940 **PB:** New York **SC:** NY/USA **PT:** Henry Lee Smith Jr.; Marie (Ballou) Edwards **MS:** Married **SPN:** Scott Alter Kleiner (3/20/1961) **CH:** Greta (Deceased); Catherine **ED:** Postgraduate, University of Georgia (1974-1982); Master of Arts in Teaching in Education, Lynchburg College (1969); Bachelor of Arts in Sociology and Anthropology, Smith College (1961) **C:** Associate Director, Women's Studies Program, University of Georgia, Athens, GA (1990-2000); Assistant Director, Women's Studies Program, University of Georgia, Athens, GA (1988-1990); Academic Advisor, University of Georgia College Arts And Sciences, Athens, GA (1982-1988); Research Analyst, Edward Weiss Advertising, Chicago, IL (1963-1965) **CR:** Institute of Women Studies **CIV:** Board Director, Honorary Director, The Jeannette Rankin Women's Scholarship Fund, Athens, GA (1977-Present); Chairman, Partner Church Committee, Unitarian Universalist Fellowship of Athens (1992-2018); Trustee, Unitarian Universalist Fellowship of Athens, Georgia (2003-2006); Chairman, Capital Fund Drive, The Jeannette Rankin Women's Scholarship Fund, Athens, GA (1993-1996); Co-founder, First President, The Jeannette Rankin Women's Scholarship Fund, Athens, GA (1976-1977); Women and Girls in Georgia **AW:** Stewardship Award for Years of Service, Unitarian Universal Church, Sister Church, Romania (2016) **MEM:** League of Women Voters; American Association of University Women **MH:** Albert Nelson Marquis Lifetime Achievement Award **B/I:** Ms. Kleiner became involved in her profession following the start of the Civil Rights Movement in Lynchburg, Virginia. After working to integrate local schools, she joined the League of Women Voters and began to actively protest on behalf of women's rights. **AV:** Reading; Swimming **PA:** Democrat

KLEINSCHNITZ, BARBARA JOY, T: Oil Company Executive, Consultant **I:** Consulting **DOB:** 08/25/1944 **PB:** Granite Falls **SC:** MN/USA **PT:** Arthur William Green; Joy Ardys (Roe) Green **MS:** Divorced **SPN:** Charles Lewis Kleinschnitz (12/28/1963, Divorced) **CH:** Katheryn JoAnn Kleinschnitz Hartsock **ED:** BBA, University of Denver (1983); Coursework, Colorado Women's College **C:** Instructor, Institute of Business & Medical Careers, Inc. (1997-Present); Technical Writer, Management Tech. Inc. (1998-1999); Technical Writer, Computer Data Systems, Inc. (1993-1997); Training Specialist, Advanced-Data Concepts, Fort Collins, CO (1991-1993); Documentation Specialist, Q.C. Data, Inc. (1987-1991); Technical Consultant, Littleton, CO (1986-1987); Customer Support Manager, Energy Systems Tech., Inc., Englewood, CO (1983-1986); Technical Consultant, Tech. Log Analysis, Inc., Lakewood, CO (1982-1983); Supervisor, Log Processing, Scientific Software-Intercomp, Denver, CO (1976-1982); Leadman, Schlumberger Well Services, Denver, CO (1968-1976) **CR:** Energy Systems Technologies (1986-1993); Consultant, Tech. Log Analysis, Inc., Denver, CO (1983-1989) **CIV:** President, Denver Well Logging Society (1988-1989); Volunteer, Denver Police Reserve (1973-1975) **MEM:** Board of Directors, Vice President, Society of Professional Well Log Analysts (1989-1991); National Organization of Women; National Association of Female Executives; Association of Women Geoscientists; Denver Well Log Society **B/I:** Ms. Kleinschnitz became involved in her profession because, after she had her daughter, she decided she needed to return to work. She wanted a job that paid well and was on the cutting edge of technology, and the oil industry fit the bill. She was later hired at Schlumberger Well Services. In the years that followed, her career progressed naturally. **AV:** Playing racquetball; Swimming; Recording video cassettes; Exploring the internet; Traveling **PA:** Democrat **RE:** Roman Catholic

KLINE, KEVIN DELANEY, T: Actor **I:** Media & Entertainment **DOB:** 10/24/1947 **PB:** St. Louis **SC:** MO/USA **PT:** Robert Joseph Kline; Peggy (Kirk) Kline **MS:** Married **SPN:** Phoebe Cates (03/05/1989) **CH:** Owen; Greta **ED:** Diploma, Advanced Program, Drama Division, The Juilliard School, New York, NY (1972); BA in Speech and Theater, Indiana University Bloomington (1970) **C:** Founding Member, The Acting Company, New York, NY (1972-1976) **CR:** Artistic Associate, New York Shakespeare Festival (1993) **CIV:** Volunteer, Juvenile Diabetes Research Foundation **CW:** Actor, "Beauty and the Beast" (2017); Actor, "Dean" (2016); Actor, "Ricki and the Flash" (2015); Actor, "My Old Lady" (2014); Actor, "Last Vegas" (2013); Actor, "The Last of Robin Hood" (2013); Actor, "Darling Companion" (2012); Voice Actor, "Bob's Burgers" (2011-2014); Actor, "No Strings Attached" (2011); Actor, "The Conspirator" (2010); Actor, "Definitely, Maybe" (2008); Voice Actor, "The Tale of Despereaux" (2008); Actor, "Trade" (2007); Actor, "Cyrano de Bergerac" (2007); Actor, "King Lear" (2007); Actor, "Mother Courage" (2006); Actor, "A Prairie Home Companion" (2006); Actor, "As You Like It" (2006); Actor, "The Pink Panther" (2006); Actor, "De-lovely" (2004); Actor, "Henry IV, Parts I & II" (2003); Actor, "The Play What I Wrote" (2003); Actor, "The Emperor's Club" (2002); Actor, "Life as a House" (2001); Actor, "The Seagull" (2001); Actor, "The Anniversary Party" (2001); Voice Actor, "The Road to El Dorado" (2000); Actor, "Wild Wild West" (1999); Actor, "A Midsummer Night's Dream" (1999); Actor, "The Ice Storm" (1997); Actor, "In & Out" (1997); Actor, "Ivanov" (1997); Actor, "Fierce Creatures" (1997); Voice Actor, "The Hunchback of Notre Dame" (1996); Actor, "French Kiss" (1995); Actor, "Princess Caraboo" (1994); Voice Actor, "George Balanchine's The Nutcracker" (1993); Actor, "Measure for Measure" (1993); Actor, "Dave" (1993); Actor, "Chaplin" (1992); Actor, "Consenting Adults" (1991); Actor, "Grand Canyon" (1991); Actor, "Soap Dish" (1991); Actor, Director, "Hamlet" (1990); Actor, "I Love You to Death" (1989); Actor, "The January Man" (1989); Actor, "Much Ado About Nothing" (1988); Actor, "A Fish Called Wanda" (1988); Actor, "Cry Freedom" (1987); Actor, "Hamlet" (1986); Actor, "Violets are Blue" (1985); Actor, "Silverado" (1985); Actor, "Arms and the Man" (1985); Actor, "Henry V" (1984); Actor, "The Pirates of Penzance" (1983); Actor, "Richard III" (1983); Actor, "The Big Chill" (1983); Actor, "Sophie's Choice" (1982); Actor, "The Pirates of Penzance" (1980); Actor, "Loose Ends" (1979); Actor, "On the Twentieth Century" (1978) **AW:** Drama Desk Award for Best Actor (2004, 2017); Tony Award for Best Actor in a Play (2017); SAG Award for Outstanding Performance by a Male Actor in a TV Movie or Miniseries, SAG-AFTRA (2008); Lifetime Achievement Award, Lucille Lortel Awards (2007); Named Humanitarian of the Year, Juvenile Diabetes Research Foundation (2004); Academy Award for Best Supporting Actor, Academy of Motion Picture Arts & Sciences (1989); Obie Award (1980, 1986); Drama Desk Award for Outstanding Actor in a Musical (1981); Tony Award for Best Leading Actor in a Musical (1980); Tony Award for Best Performance by a Featured Actor in a Musical (1978); Drama Desk Award for Outstanding Featured Actor in a Musical (1978)

KLOBUCHAR, AMY JEAN, T: U.S. Senator from Minnesota **I:** Government Administration/Government Relations/Government Services **DOB:** 05/25/1960 **PB:** Plymouth **SC:** MN/USA **PT:** Jim Klobuchar; Rose Katherine (Heuberger) Klobuchar **MS:** Married **SPN:** John Bessler (1993) **CH:** Abigail Klobuchar Bessler **ED:** JD, The University of Chicago The Law School (1985); BA, Yale University (1982) **C:** Ranking Member, Senate Rules Committee (2017-Present); U.S. Senator, State of Minnesota (2007-Present); Candidate, Democratic Nomination, 2020 Presidential Election (2019-2020); Attorney, Hennepin County, MN (1999-2007); Partner, Gray Plant Mooty LLP (1993-1998); Associate Partner, Dorsey & Whitney LLP (1985-1993); Member, Minnesota Supreme Court Jury Task Force **CW:** Author, Autobiography, "The Senator Next Door: A Memoir from the Heartland" (2015); Author, "Uncovering the Dome" (1986) **AW:** Arabella Babb Mansfield Award, National Association of Women Lawyers (2017); Named the Mary Louise Smith Chair in Women and Politics, Carrie Chapman Catt Center, Iowa State University (2017); Goodwill Policy Award, Goodwill Industries (2016); Trumpeter Award, National Consumers League (2015); Congressional Justice Award, ABA (2015); Friends of Farm Bureau Award, American Farm Bureau Federation, Minnesota Branch (2014); Friend of CACFP, National Child and Adult Care Food Program (CACFP) Sponsors Association (2013); Leadership Award, Service Women's Action Network (SWAN) (2013); Legislator of the Year Award, Agricultural Retailers Association (2012); Sheldon Coleman Great Outdoors Award, American Recreation Coalition (2012); Named Best in Congress, Working Mother (2008); Achievement and Leadership Award, Ann Bancroft Foundation (2004); Named One of the 10 Attorneys of the Year, Minnesota Lawyer (2001); Leadership

Award, MADD (2001); Alumni of the Year Award, Wayzata High School (1999); Named One of the 40 Under 40, CityBusiness (1996); Named Super Lawyer, Minnesota Law & Politics **MEM:** President, Minnesota County Attorneys Association (2002-2003) **AV:** Cross Country Bicycling **PA:** Democrat

KLOSS, KARLIE ELIZABETH, T: Model **I:** Media & Entertainment **DOB:** 08/03/1992 **PB:** Chicago **SC:** IL/USA **PT:** Kurt Kloss; Tracy Kloss **MS:** Married **SPN:** Joshua Kushner (10/18/2018) **ED:** Coursework, New York University Gallatin School of Individualized Study (2015); Diploma, Webster Groves High School, Webster Groves, MO (2011) **C:** Model, IMG Models (2012-Present); Global Spokesmodel, Estee Lauder (2018); Model, Victoria Secret Angel (2011-2014); Model, NEXT Model Management (2008-2012); Spokesperson, Numerous Companies Including Jean Paul Gaultier, Nike, Donna Karan, Swarovski, and Chanel **CIV:** Founder, Kode with Klossy Camp (2015-Present) **CW:** Host, Executive Producer, "Project Runway" (2018-Present); Featured, Numerous Magazines **AW:** Listee, 100 Most Influential People, Time Magazine (2016)

KLOTMAN, MARY E., T: Dean **I:** Education/Educational Services **CN:** Duke University School of Medicine **MS:** Married **SPN:** Paul Klotman (11/28/1981) **CH:** Two Sons **ED:** Fellow in Infectious Diseases, Medicine, Duke University (1983-1985); Resident, Medicine, Duke University (1980-1983); MD, Duke University (1980) **C:** Dean, Duke University School of Medicine (2017-Present); Chair, Department of Medicine, Duke University School of Medicine (2010-2017); Professor, Medicine, Pathology, Molecular Genetics and Microbiology, Duke University School of Medicine; Irene and Dr. Arthur M. Fishberg Professor of Medicine, Chief of the Division of Infectious Diseases, Mount Sinai School of Medicine; Co-director, Global Health and Emerging Pathogens Institute, Mount Sinai School of Medicine (Now Icahn School of Medicine at Mount Sinai) **CW:** Editor, Annual Review of Medicine (2020-Present) **AW:** Duke University School of Medicine Distinguished Alumni Award (2015) **MEM:** National Academy of Medicine, National Academy of Sciences (2014)

KLUBER, COREY SCOTT, T: Professional Baseball Player **I:** Athletics **CN:** Texas Rangers **DOB:** 04/10/1986 **PB:** Birmingham **SC:** AL/USA **MS:** Married **SPN:** Amanda Kluber **CH:** Kendall; Kennedy; Camden **ED:** Coursework, Stetson University **C:** Pitcher, Texas Rangers, MLB (2019-Present); Pitcher, Cleveland Indians, MLB (2011-2019) **AW:** Lou Gehrig Memorial Award (2019); All-Star (2016, 2017); American League Cy Young Award (2014, 2017); American League Starting Pitcher of the Year, Sporting News (2016); Inductee, Atlantic Sun Conference Hall of Fame (2015); Inductee, Stetson Athletics Hall of Fame (2014); Inductee, Bob Feller Man of the Year (2014); Inductee, Atlantic Sun Conference Pitcher of the Year (2007) **AV:** Golfing

KLUM, HEIDI, T: Model **I:** Apparel & Fashion **DOB:** 06/01/1973 **PB:** Bergisch Gladbach **SC:** Germany **PT:** Günther Klum; Erna Klum **MS:** Married **SPN:** Tom Kaulitz (2019); Seal (05/10/2005, Divorced 2015); Ric Pipino (09/06/1997, Divorced 2002) **CH:** Leni; Henry Guenther; Johan Rily; Lou Sulola Samuel **C:** Launched, Womenswear Collection, New Balance, HKNB (2010-Present); Designer, Maternity Wear, Loved (2010-Present); Designer, Maternity Wear, Lavish (2010-Present); Co-Creator, Jewelry Collection, The Heidi Klum Collection, Mouawad (2007-Present); Designer, Makeup, Victoria's Secret, The Heidi Klum Collection (2007-2008); Model, Victoria's Secret Fashion Show (2001-2003); Designer, Birkenstocks; Launched,

Perfume Line, "Me"; Launched, Perfume Line, "Heidi Klum"; Spokesmodel, Victoria's Secret, Swatch, Peek & Cloppenburg, Otto, Nike, Katjes, Kathleen Madden, American Express, Amerige, Givenchy, Gerry Webber, Finesse, Bonne Bell; Cover Model, Cosmopolitan, Bride's, Glamour, Mademoiselle, Sports Illustrated, Elle **CIV:** Leader, Walk for Kids, Children's Hospital Los Angeles (2011); Elizabeth Glaser Pediatric AIDS Foundation; American Red Cross **CW:** Judge, "America's Got Talent: The Champions" (2019-Present); Host, Judge, "Germany's Next Topmodel" (2006-Present); Executive Producer, Appearance, "Making the Cut" (2020); Judge, "America's Got Talent" (2013-2018, 2020); Judge, "Queen of Drags" (2019); Voice Actress, "Arctic Dogs" (2019); Cameo, "Ocean's 8" (2018); Host, Judge, "Project Runway" (2004-2017); Voice Actress, "Littlest Pet Shop" (2012-2016); Guest Appearance, "Parks and Recreation" (2013); Cameo, "Hoodwinked Too! Hood vs. Evil" (2011); Host, "Seriously Funny Kids" (2011); Guest Appearance, "Desperate Housewives" (2010); Guest Appearance, "I Get That a Lot" (2009-2010); Host, "Perfect Stranger" (2007); Guest Appearance, "How I Met Your Mother" (2007); Cameo, "The Devil Wears Prada" (2006); Actress, "Ella Enchanted" (2004); Actress, "The Life and Death of Peter Sellers" (2004); Appearance, "Blue Collar Comedy Tour" (2003); Voice Actress, Video Game, "James Bond 007: Everything or Nothing" (2003); Guest Appearance, "CSI: Miami" (2003); Guest Appearance, "Malcolm in the Middle" (2002); Guest Appearance, "Yes, Dear" (2002); Actress, "Blow Dry" (2001); Guest Appearance, "Sex and the City" (2001); Cameo, "Zoolander" (2001); Actress, "Cursed" (2000); Cameo, "Spin City" (1999); Actress, "54" (1998) **AW:** Crystal Cross Award, American Red Cross (2014); Outstanding Host for a Reality or Reality-Competition Program, "Project Runway," Primetime Emmy Awards (2013)

KNIGHT, STEPHEN, "STEVE" THOMAS, T: U.S. Representative (Retired) **I:** Government Administration/Government Relations/Government Services **DOB:** 12/17/1966 **PB:** Edwards Air Force Base **SC:** CA/USA **MS:** Married **SPN:** Lily Knight **CH:** Christopher; Michael **ED:** AA, Antelope Valley College; Diploma, Palmdale High School **C:** U.S. Representative, California's 25th Congressional District, United States Congress, Washington, DC (2015-2019); Assistant Minority Leader, California State Assembly (2010-2012); Member, District 36, California State Assembly (2008-2015); Member, Palmdale City Council, CA (2005-2008); Member, Judiciary Committee, United States Congress; Member, Committee on Natural Resources, United States Congress; Member, Committee on Housing and Community Development, United States Congress; Member, Select Committee on Aerospace, California State Assembly; Member, Select Committee on Alcohol and Drug Abuse, California State Assembly; Vice Chair, Local Government Committee, California State Assembly; Officer, Community Resources Against Street Hoodlums (CRASH) Team, Los Angeles Police Department, CA **MIL:** With, United States Army Reserve (1987-1993); Tracked Vehicle Systems Mechanic, United States Army, Friedberg, Germany (1985-1987) **RE:** Roman Catholic

KNOSPE, WILLIAM H., MD, T: Medical Educator **I:** Medicine & Health Care **DOB:** 05/26/1929 **PB:** Oak Park **SC:** IL/USA **PT:** Herbert Henry Knospe; Dora Isabel (Spruce) Knospe **MS:** Married **SPN:** Adris M. (Nelson) Knospe (06/19/1954) **CH:** William A. Knospe; Elizabeth A. Knospe; David T. Knospe **ED:** MS in Radiation Biology, University of Rochester (1962); MD, University of Illinois (1954); BS, University of Illinois (1952); BA, University of

Illinois (1951) **CT:** Diplomate, American Board of Internal Medicine; Board on Hematology **C:** Emeritus, University of New Mexico, Albuquerque, NM (2002-Present); Professor Emeritus, Rush Medical College, Chicago, IL (1994-2002); Professor, Medicine, University of New Mexico, Albuquerque, NM (1994-2002); Professor, Medicine, Rush Medical College, Chicago, IL (1974-2002); Senior Attending Staff Physician, Presbyterian St. Luke's Hospital, Chicago, IL (1974-2002); Elodia Kehm Professor, Hematology, Rush Medical College, Chicago, IL (1986-1994); Director, Section Hematology, Rush-Presbyterian-St. Luke's Medical Center, Chicago, IL (1974-1993); Associate Professor, Medicine, Rush Medical College, Chicago, IL (1971-1974); Associate Attending Staff Physician, Presbyterian St. Luke's Hospital, Chicago, IL (1968-1974); Assistant Director, Hematology, Radiohematology Laboratory, Presbyterian St. Luke's Hospital, Chicago, IL (1967-1974); Associate Professor, University of Illinois (1969-1972); Assistant Professor of Medicine, University of Illinois (1967-1969); Assistant Attending Staff Physician, Presbyterian, St. Luke's Hospital, Chicago, IL (1967-1968); Assistant Chief, Hematology Service, Hematology Clinic, Walter Reed Army Institute of Research, Washington, DC (1964-1966); Investigator, Hematology, Assistant Chief, Department of Hematology, Walter Reed Army Institute Research (1964-1966); Fellow in Hematology, Walter Reed General Hospital, Washington, DC (1964-1965); Attending Physician, Medical Service, Walter Reed General Hospital, Washington, DC (1963-1964); Investigator, Radiation Biology, Walter Reed Army Institute Research, Washington, DC (1962-1964); Resident in Medicine, VA Research Hospital-Northwestern University Medical School, Chicago, IL (1956-1958); Resident in Medicine, Illinois Central Hospital, Chicago, IL (1955-1956) **CR:** Cancer Center, University of New Mexico (1992-1993); Visiting Professor, Medicine, University of Basel, Switzerland (1980-1981); Speaker, International Professional Conferences **CIV:** Trustee, Bishop Anderson House (1980-1994); Trustee, Illinois Chapter, Leukemia Society of America (1977-1988) **MIL:** Lieutenant Colonel, U.S. Army (1961-1966); Served to Captain, Medical Corps, U.S. Army Reserve (1958-1961) **CW:** Contributor, Numerous Articles, Professional Publications **MEM:** Fellow, American College of Physicians; American Federation of Clinical Research; American Medical Association; American Society of Hematology; American Society of Clinical Oncology; Central Society of Clinical Research; Chicago Medical Society; Institute of Medicine Chicago; International Society of Experimental Hematology; Radiation Research Society; Southeastern Cancer Study Group; Polycythemia Vera Study Group; Eastern Cooperative Oncology Group; Association of Hematology-Oncology Program Directors; Sigma Xi; Chicago Literary Club; Leukemia Foundation **MH:** Albert Nelson Marquis Lifetime Achievement Award; Marquis Who's Who Top Professional **B/I:** From the time that Dr. Knospe was 6 years old, he had a serious illness that required him to be under the care of doctors constantly. He eventually recovered, and his doctors became an inspiration to him. Because of their hard work, he was inspired to be a doctor. **PA:** Republican

KNOTT, STEPHEN F., PHD, T: Professor **I:** Education/Educational Services **CN:** United States Naval War College **DOB:** 06/14/1957 **PB:** Worcester **SC:** MA/USA **PT:** Frederick William Knott; Ruth Marie Knott **MS:** Married **SPN:** Maryanne **CH:** Maura **ED:** Honorary Doctor in Arts and Letters, Assumption University, Worcester, MA (2013); PhD in Political Science, Boston College, Boston, MA (1990); BA in Political Science, Assumption University,

Worcester, MA (1979) C: Professor, U.S. Naval War College, Newport, RI (2007-Present); Associate Professor, Miller Center of Public Affairs, University of Virginia, Charlottesville, VA (2001-2007); Associate Professor, United States Air Force Academy, Colorado Springs, CO (1996-2001); Assistant Professor, United States Air Force Academy, Colorado Springs, CO (1994-1996); Assistant Professor, Quinnipiac College (Now Quinnipiac University), Hamden, CT (1993-1994); Visiting Assistant Professor, Boston College, Chestnut Hill, MA (1993-1994); Visiting Assistant Professor, University of New Hampshire, Durham, (1991-1992) Executive Director, Friends of the Kennedy Library, Boston, MA (1985-1986); Supervisor, Visitor Services, John F. Kennedy Presidential Library and Museum, Boston (1984-1985) CW: Author, "The Lost Soul of the American Presidency: The Decline into Demagoguery and the Prospects for Renewal," The University Press of Kansas (2019); Author, "Washington and Hamilton: The Alliance That Forged America," Sourcebooks (2015); Author, "The Evolution of the Executive and Executive Power in the American Republic," Foreign Policy Research Institute E-Book (2014); Author, "Rush to Judgment: George W. Bush, the War on Terror, and His Critics," The University Press of Kansas (2012); Author, "At Reagan's Side: Insiders' Recollections from Sacramento to the White House," Rowman and Littlefield (2009); Author, "The Reagan Years," Facts on File, Inc. (2005); Author, "Alexander Hamilton and the Persistence of Myth," The University Press of Kansas (2002); Author, "Secret and Sanctioned: Covert Operations and the American Presidency," Oxford University Press (1996) AW: Outstanding Achievement Award, Assumption University Alumni Association (2009); Choice Award, "Secret and Sanctioned: Covert Operations and the American Presidency," American Association of College and Research Libraries, American Library Association; Doctoral Dissertation Award, Boston College MEM: American Political Science Association (APSA); Assumption University Alumni Association AS: Dr. Knott attributes his success to great parental mentors and influential teachers. B/I: Dr. Knott believes his parents' interest in history and politics played a major role in both his career path and aspirations. The types of books his parents read to him at a young age left a lasting impact on Dr. Knott; they formed his basic interests which eventually led to his career. AV: Reading; Writing and lecturing; Taking his dog for walks RE: Catholic

KNOWLES-CARTER, BEYONCÉ GISELLE, T: Singer; Actress **I:** Media & Entertainment **DOB:** 09/04/1981 **PB:** Houston **SC:** TX/USA **PT:** Matthew Knowles; Tina (Beyoncé) Knowles **MS:** Married **SPN:** Shawn Corey "Jay-Z" Carter (04/04/2008) **CH:** Blue Ivy; Rumi; Sir **C:** Solo Artist (2003-Present); Member, Destiny's Child (1997-2005) **CR:** Launched, Activewear, Ivy Park (2016-Present); Co-owner, Music Streaming Service, Tidal (2015-Present); Co-creator with Tina Knowles, Deréon by Beyoncé, C&A Clothing Stores (2010); Launched, Women's Fragrance, Beyoncé Heat (2010); Launched, Sasha Fierce for Deréon (2009); Launched, Women's Fragrance, Emporio Armani Diamonds (2007); Launched, Women's Fragrance, True Star Gold (2005); Launched, Fashion Line, House of Deréon (2005); Launched, Women's Fragrance, Tommy Hilfiger's True Star (2004); Spokesperson, L'Oreal, Pepsi, Nintendo, Vizio **CIV:** Ambassador, World Humanitarian Day (2012); Founder, Survivor Foundation (2005); With, Ban Bossy Campaign, LeanIn.org; Performer, Benefit Concerts **CW:** Performer, "Homecoming" (2019); Actress, "The Lion King" (2019); Singer, "Formation" (2016); Singer, "Hold Up" (2016); Singer, Song

and Album, "Lemonade" (2016); Singer, "Beyoncé" (2013); Singer, "7/11" (2014); Performer, Executive Producer, Director, "Life Is But a Dream" (2013); Voice Actress, "Epic" (2013); Singer Featuring Jay-Z, "Drunk in Love" (2013); Author, Article, "Eat, Play, Love," Essence Magazine (2011); Singer, "Love on Top" (2011); Singer, "4" (2011); Singer with Lady Gaga, "Telephone" (2010); Actress, "Obsessed" (2009); Singer, "Halo" (2009); Actress, "Cadillac Records" (2008); Singer, "Single Ladies (Put a Ring on It)" (2008); Singer, "I am...Sasha Fierce" (2008); Featured, Cover, Sports Illustrated Swimsuit Issue (2007); Actress, "The Pink Panther" (2006); Actress, "Dreamgirls" (2006); Singer, "Irreplaceable" (2006); Singer, "B'day" (2006); Singer with Destiny's Child, "#1's" (2005); Singer with Stevie Wonder, "So Amazing" (2005); Singer with Destiny's Child, "Destiny Fulfilled" (2004); Performer, "Live at Wembley" (2004); Singer with Luther Vandross, "The Closer I Get to You" (2004); Singer, "Dangerously in Love" (2003); Singer, "Dangerously in Love 2" (2003); Singer Featuring Jay-Z, "Crazy in Love" (2003); Actress, "The Fighting Temptations" (2003); Actress, "Austin Powers in Goldmember" (2002); Singer with Destiny's Child, "Survivor" (2001); Singer with Destiny's Child, "8 Days of Christmas" (2001); Singer with Destiny's Child, "Say My Name" (2000); Singer with Destiny's Child, "The Writing's on the Wall" (1999); Singer with Destiny's Child, "Destiny's Child" (1998); Performer, Singer, Solo and Collaborations **AW:** Named One of the 100 Women Who Defined the Last Century, TIME Magazine (2020); Awards for Video of the Year, Best Female Video, Best Direction, Best Cinematography, Best Editing, MTV Video Music Awards (2016); Fashion Icon Award, CFDA (2016); Named to BBC Radio 4's Woman's Hour Power List (2016); Award for Breakthrough Long Form Video, MTV Video Music Awards (2016); Award for Outstanding Female Artist, NAACP Image Awards (2009, 2015); Award for Best Editing, MTV Video Music Awards (2015); Grammy Awards for Best R&B Performance, Best R&B Song, Recording Academy (2015); Michael Jackson Video Vanguard Award, MTV Video Music Awards (2014); Award for Outstanding Female Artist, NAACP Image Awards (2014); Award for Favorite Soul/R&B Album, American Music Awards (2014); Named One of the 100 Most Influential People in the World, TIME Magazine (2013-2014); Named One of the 100 Most Powerful Women, Forbes Magazine (2010-2014); Awards for Favorite Female Soul/R&B Artist, American Music Awards (2009, 2011, 2012, 2014); Named One of the 100 Most Powerful Women in Entertainment, The Hollywood Reporter (2013); Grammy Award for Best Traditional R&B Performance, The Recording Academy (2013); Award for Best Female R&B Artist, BET Awards (2006, 2007, 2008, 2012); Writing Award, New York Association of Black Journalists (2012); Award for Top R&B Album, Billboard Music Awards (2012); Award for Video Director of the Year (with Alan Ferguson), BET Awards (2012); Named World's Most Beautiful Woman, People's Magazine (2012); Named One of the 100 Most Powerful Celebrities (2008-2012); Millennium Award, Billboard Music Awards (2011); Named Choice Music: R&B Artist, Teen Choice Awards (2010); Award for Best Collaboration, MTV Video Music Awards (2010); Grammy Awards for Best Female Pop Vocal Performance, Best Female R&B Vocal Performance, Best Contemporary R&B Album, Best R&B Song, Song of the Year, Recording Academy (2010); Named Choice Female Hottie, Teen Choice Awards (2009); Award for Album of the Year, Soul Train Music Awards (2009); Award for Best Female R&B/Soul Artist, Soul Train Music Awards (2009); Award for Video of the Year, BET Awards (2009); Awards for Best Choreography, Video of the Year, MTV Video Music Awards

(2009); Award for Song of the Year, Soul Train Music Awards (2009); Award for Best R&B Song, Teen Choice Awards (2009); Named One of the 50 Most Powerful Women in New York City, New York Post (2007, 2008); Award for Favorite Female Performer, People Choice Awards (2004, 2008); Award for Outstanding Contribution to the Arts, World Music Awards (2008); International Artist Award, American Music Awards (2007); Grammy Award for Best Contemporary R&B Album, Recording Academy (2007); Award for Video of the Year, BET Awards (2007); Award for Best Female R&B/Soul Single, Soul Train Music Awards (2007); Grammy Awards for Best R&B Performance by a Duo or Group with Vocals, Recording Academy (2002, 2004, 2006); Award for Female R&B/Hip-Hop Artist of the Year, Billboard Music Awards (2006); Award for Entertainer of the Year, NAACP Image Awards (2004); Award for Best International Female Solo Artist, BRIT Awards (2004); Named One of the 50 Most Influential African Americans, Ebony Magazine (2004); Award for Best Collaboration, BET Awards (2004); Grammy Awards for Best R&B Song, Best Rap/Sung Collaboration, Best Female R&B Vocal Performance, Best Contemporary R&B Album, Recording Academy (2004); Sammy Davis Junior Award for Entertainer of the Year, Soul Train Music Awards (2004); Award for Best Female R&B/Soul Album, Soul Train Music Awards (2004); Awards for Best Female Video, Best R&B Video, MTV Video Music Awards (2003); Grammy Awards for Best R&B Song, Best R&B Performance by a Duo or Group with Vocals, Recording Academy (2001); Numerous Awards

KNUTH, DONALD ERVIN, PHD, T: Computer Sciences Educator **I:** Education/Educational Services **CN:** Stanford University **DOB:** 01/10/1938 **PB:** Milwaukee **SC:** WI/USA **PT:** Ervin Henry Knuth; Louise Marie (Bohning) Knuth **MS:** Married **SPN:** Nancy Jill Carter (06/24/1961) **CH:** John Martin; Jennifer Sierra **ED:** DSc, University of Bordeaux (2007); Honorary DSc, National Academy of Sciences of the Republic of Armenia (2005-2006); Honorary DLitt, Concordia University, Wisconsin (2006); Honorary DSc, Eidgenössische Technische Hochschule Zürich (2005); Honorary DSc, Université de Montréal (2004); Honorary DSc, UAntwerpen (2003); Honorary DSc, Aristotle University of Thessaloniki (2003); Honorary DSc, Harvard University (2003); Honorary DSc, University of Oslo (2002); Honorary DSc, Athens University of Economics and Business (2001); Honorary DSc, University of Tübingen (2001); Honorary DSc, Williams College (2000); Honorary DLitt, University of Waterloo (2000); Honorary DSc, University of St Andrews (1998); Honorary DSc, Duke University (1998); Honorary DSc, Masarykova Univerzita (1996); Honorary DSc, Adelphi University (1993); Pochetnogo Doktora, St. Petersburg University (1992); Doctor Technology, KTH Royal Institute of Technology (1991); Honorary DSc, Concordia University (1991); Honorary DSc, Dartmouth College (1990); Honorary DSc, Grinnell College (1989); Honorary DSc, Valparaiso University (1988); Honorary DSc, Brown University (1988); Honorary DSc, University of Oxford (1988); Honorary DSc, Stony Brook University (1987); Honorary DSc, Université Paris-Sud (1986); Honorary DSc, University of Rochester (1986); Honorary DSc, University of Pennsylvania (1986); Honorary DSc, Muhlenberg College (1986); Honorary DSc, Lawrence University (1985); Honorary DSc, Luther College, Decorah, IA (1985); Honorary DSc, Case Western Reserve University (1980); PhD in Mathematics, California Institute of Technology (1963); MS, Case Institute of Technology (Now Case Western Reserve University) (1960); BS, Case Institute of Technology (Now Case Western Reserve University), Summa Cum

Laude (1960) **C:** Professor Emeritus, The Art of Computer Programming, Stanford University (1993-Present); Professor, Electrical Engineering, Stanford University (1977-Present); Professor, The Art of Computer Programming, Stanford University (1990-1992); Fletcher Jones Professor, Computer Science, Stanford University (1977-1989); Professor, Computer Science, Stanford University (1968-1977); Associate Professor, Mathematics, California Institute of Technology (1966-1968); Assistant Professor, Mathematics, California Institute of Technology (1963-1966) **CR:** Visiting Professor, Computer Science, University of Oxford (2002-2017); Guest Professor, Mathematics, University of Oslo (1972-1973); Staff Mathematician, Institute for Defense, Analysis-Communication Research Division (1968-1969); Consultant, Burroughs Corporation (Now Unisys), Pasadena, CA (1960-1968); Invited Lecturer in Field, University of Oxford **CW:** Member, Editorial Board, Transactions on Algorithms, Association for Computing Machinery (2004-Present); Member, Editorial Board, Theory of Computing (2004-Present); Member, Editorial Board, Journal of Graph Algorithms and Applications (1996-Present); Member, Editorial Board, Journal of Experimental Algorithmics (1996-Present); Member, Editorial Board, Electronic Journal of Combinators (1994-Present); Member, Editorial Board, The Mathematica Journal (1990-Present); Member, Editorial Board, Journal of Computer Science and Technology (1989-Present); Author, "The Art of Computer Programming" (1968-Present); Author, "Apocalyptica Illustrated" (2018); Author, "Fantasia Apocalyptica" (2018); Member, Editorial Board, Discrete and Computational Geometry (1986-2012); Member, Editorial Board, Journal of Computer and System Sciences (1969-2012); Member, Editorial Board, Random Structures & Algorithms (1990-2007); Member, Editorial Board, Software-Practice and Experience (1979-2007); Member, Editorial Board, Japan Journal of Industrial and Applied Mathematics (1997-2005); Member, Editorial Board, Journal of Algorithms (1979-2004); Member, Editorial Board, Applied Mathematics Letters (1987-2000); Author, "3:16 Bible Texts Illuminated" (1990); Author, "Concrete Mathematics" (1988); Member, Editorial Board, Combinatorica (1985-1998); Author, "Computers and Typesetting " (1986) **AW:** Honorary Fellow, Magdalen College, Oxford (2005-Present); Fellow, American Mathematical Society (2013); Faraday Medal, IET (2011); BBVA Foundation Frontiers of Knowledge Award (2010); Fellow, Society for Industrial and Applied Mathematics" (2009); Fellowship of the Royal Society (2003); Fellow, Computer History Museum (1998); Kyoto Prize, Inamori Foundation (1996); Harvey Prize, Israel Institute of Technology (1995); W. Wallace McDowell Award, IEEE (1995); John von Neumann Medal, IEEE (1995); Adelskold Medal, Swedish Academy of Science (1994); Fellow, Association for Computing Machinery (1994); Lester R. Ford Award, Mathematics Association of America (1993); Gold Medal Award, Case Alumni Association (1990); J.D. Warnier Prize (1989); Franklin Medal (1988); Steele Prize for Expository Writing, American Mathematics Society (1987); Steele Prize for Expository Writing, American Mathematics Society (1986); Recipient, Computer Science Education Award, Association for Computing Machinery (1986); Software Systems Award, Association for Computing Machinery (1986); Golden Plate Award, American Academy of Achievement (1985); W. Wallace McDowell Award, IEEE (1982); Computer Pioneer Award, IEEE (1982); Distinguished Fellow, British Computer Society (1980); Priestley Award, Dickinson College (1981); W. Wallace McDowell Award, IEEE (1980); National Medal of Science, President James Carter (1979); Distinguished Alumni Award, California Institute of Technology (1978); Lester R. Ford Award, Mathematics Association of America (1975); Alan M. Turing Award, Association for Computing Machinery (1974); Fellow, John Simon Guggenheim Memorial Foundation (1972-1973); Grace Murray Hopper Award, Association for Computing Machinery (1971); Fellow, National Science Foundation (1960); Fellow, Woodrow Wilson National Fellowship Foundation (1960) **MEM:** Honorary Member, London Mathematical Society (2015-Present); Foreign Member, Royal Society London (2003); Committee on Composition Technology, American Mathematics Society (1978-1981); Member, General Technology Achievement Awards Subcommittee, Association for Computing Machinery (1975-1979); National Lecturer, Association for Computing Machinery (1966-1967); Visiting Scientist, Association for Computing Machinery (1966-1967); Chairman, Subcommittee on ALGOL, Association for Computing Machinery (1963-1964); American Academy of Arts and Sciences; The Computer Museum; National Academy of Sciences; Honorary Member, Editorial Board, IEEE; Society Industrial and Applied Mathematics; Mathematics Association of America; Foreign Associate, Academy of Science, Paris; Foreign Associate, Academy of Science, Oslo; Foreign Associate, Academy of Science, Munich; Foreign Associate, Academy of Science, St. Petersburg; NAE; American Guild of Organists; American Philosophical Society; Foreign Member, Royal Society of London **MH:** Albert Nelson Marquis Lifetime Achievement Award **B/I:** Dr. Knuth became involved in his profession because he has wanted to be a teacher since first grade; he was most interested in teaching languages and then realized computer programming. **AV:** Playing pipe organ; Reading; Writing **RE:** Lutheran

KOBILKA, BRIAN KENT, MD, T: Professor; Molecular Biologist **I:** Sciences **CN:** Stanford University **DOB:** 05/30/1955 **PB:** Little Falls **SC:** MN/USA **PT:** Franklyn A. Kobilka; Betty L. (Faust) Kobilka **MS:** Married **SPN:** Tong Sun Thian **CH:** Jason; Megan **ED:** MD, Yale University School of Medicine, Cum Laude (1981); BS in Biology and Chemistry, University of Minnesota (1977) **C:** Co-founder, ConfometRX, Santa Clara, CA (2009-Present); Professor, Molecular and Cellular Physiology, Stanford University (1989-Present); Investigator, Howard Hughes Medical Institute (HHMI), Chevy Chase, MD (1987-2003); Assistant Professor of Medicine, Duke University; Research Fellow, Duke University; Internal Medical Research, Barnes-Jewish Hospital, St. Louis, MO **AW:** Co-recipient, Nobel Prize in Chemistry, Royal Swedish Academy of Sciences (2012); Award, National Academy of Sciences (2011); Javits Neuroscience Investigator, National Institute of Neurological Disorders and Stroke, National Institutes of Health (2004); John J. Abel Award in Pharmacology, American Society for Pharmacology and Experimental Therapeutics (ASPET) (1994) **MEM:** National Academy of Sciences **RE:** Roman Catholic

KOCH, CHARLES, T: Chemical Engineer **I:** Engineering **CN:** Koch Industries, Inc. **DOB:** 11/01/1935 **PB:** Wichita **SC:** KS/USA **PT:** Fred Chase Koch; Mary Clementine (Robinson) Koch **MS:** Married **SPN:** Elizabeth Koch (1972) **CH:** Chase; Elizabeth **ED:** Honorary DSc, George Mason University; Honorary JD, Babson College; Honorary PhD in Commerce, Washburn University; MSChemE, Massachusetts Institute of Technology (1959); MS in Mechanical Nuclear Engineering, Massachusetts Institute of Technology (1958); BS in General Engineering, Massachusetts Institute of Technology (1957) **C:** Chairman, Chief Executive Officer, Koch Industries, Inc., Wichita, KS (1967-Present); Chairman, Koch Engineering Co., Inc., Wichita, KS (1967-1978); President, Koch Industries, Inc., Wichita, KS (1966-1974); President, Koch Engineering Co., Inc., Wichita, KS (1963-1971); Vice President, Koch Engineering Co., Inc., Wichita, KS (1961-1963); Engineer, Arthur D. Little, Inc., Cambridge, MA (1959-1961) **CR:** Board of Directors, INTRUST Bank; Board of Directors, Mercatus Center at George Mason University **CIV:** Chairman, Institute of Humane Studies at George Mason University; Chairman, Claude R. Lambe Charitable Foundation; Chairman, Charles G. Koch Charitable Foundation **CW:** Author, "Good Profit: How Creating Value for Others Built One of the World's Most Successful Companies" (2015); Author, "The Science of Success: How Market-based Management Built the World's Largest Private Company" (2007); Author, "Market Based Management: The Science of Human Action Applied in the Organization" (2007) **AW:** Named, One of the Forbes 400: Richest Americans (2006-Present); Named, One of the World's Richest People, Forbes Magazine (1999-Present); Named, One of the World's Richest People, Business Insider (2019); Named, One of the 100 Most Influential People in the World, TIME Magazine (2011, 2014); Named, One of the World's Most Powerful People (2010-2014); Named, One of the 50 Most Influential People in Global Finance, Bloomberg Markets (2012); National Distinguished Service Award, Tax Foundation (2000); Director's Award for Global Vision in Energy, New York Mercantile Exchange (NYMEX) (1999); Leadership Award, NFTE; Adam Smith Award, American Legislative Exchange Council; Brotherhood/Sisterhood Award, National Conference of Christians and Jews (Now National Conference for Community and Justice (NCCJ); Distinguished Citizen Award, Boy Scouts of America; Free Enterprise Award, Council for National Policy (CNP); Spirit of Justice Award, Heritage Foundation; Spirit Excellence Award, Urban League of Kansas, Wichita, KS **MEM:** Flint Hills National Golf Club; The Mount Pelerin Society; The Vintage Club **PA:** Republican

KOCHARIAN, ARMEN N. DSC/PHD/PROF., T: Professor in Physics; Senior Research Scientist **I:** Sciences **CN:** California State University Los Angeles **DOB:** 01/03/1948 **PB:** Yerevan **SC:** Armenia **PT:** Norair M. Kocharian; Alisa V. Ter-Pogosian **MS:** Married **SPN:** Hasmik Agadjanian, PhD **CH:** Adrina Kocharian; David Kocharian; Vahan Kocharian **ED:** DSc in Physics & Mathematical Sciences, Supreme Attestation Board, Moscow (1991); PhD in Physics & Mathematical Sciences, P.N. Lebedevs' Physics Institute, Moscow, Russia (1977); Coursework, PhD Advisor Prof/Dr. D.I. Khomskii; M.S. & BA in Physics, M.V. Lomonosovs' Moscow State University, Summa Cum Laude (1972-1971) **CT:** Certificate of US Patent: Metal-containing nanoparticles & method of obtaining said nanoparticles, Solar Hydrogen Holdings, Inc. (2019) **C:** Director, Scientific Consultant, Nanomaterials and Nanoclusters Inc., Granada Hills, CA; Physics Professor, Department of Physics & Astronomy, CSU, Los Angeles, CA (2007-present); Faculty Professor, Physics & Planetary Sciences Department, Pierce College, Woodland Hills, CA (2001-Present); Faculty Professor, Santa Monica College (2007-Present); Visiting Research Professor, Physics Department, Tamkang University, Taiwan (1999); Visiting Research Professor, Laboratoire Leon Brilloin, Saclay, France (1999); Diploma Summa Cum Laude on Computer Systems and Programming from Computer Learning Center Inc. (1999); Adjunct Faculty, Department of Physics, CSU, Northridge (CSUN), Northridge, CA (1994-2006); Research Associate, Center for Computational Materials, Keck Laboratory, Northridge, CA (1996-1998); Visiting Professor, Trieste, Italy (1995-1996); Scholar in Residence, New York University (1995); Visiting Professor, Union College, Schenectady, NY (1993-1995); Senior Scientist, Department of Theoretical Physics, Yerevan Physics Institute, Yerevan, Armenia (1986-1993); Junior Researcher, Department of Theoretical Physics, Physics Institute, Moscow, Russia (1977-1985) **CIV:** Board of Directors, Analysis Research & Planning for Armenia (ARPA) in Science and Education (2013-Present) **CW:** Author, Book "Spin-dependent Transport in Magnetic Nanostructures" (2017); Author, Book Chapter, "Heterostructure Spin-Dependent Transport," "Dekker Encyclopedia of Nanoscience and Nanotechnology" (2017); Editorial Board Member, International Scholarly Research Network (ISRN) on Condensed Matter Physics (2012); Author, Book Chapter, "Spin and Charge Pairing Instabilities in Nanoclusters and Nanomaterials," "Scanning Probe Microscopy in Nanoscience and Nanotechnology" (2010); Peer-Reviewer, Numerous Journals; Author, Co-Author, Contributor and Corresponding Author, More than 150 Publications **AW:** Grantee, Centers of Research Excellence in Science and Technology (CREST) NSF-Grant on energy sustainability and saving (2020); Certificate of Inclusion for the Top 100 Academic Registry for Outstanding Achievement & Exemplary Leadership (2018); Two Years Seed Award Received from CSULA funded by the National Science Foundation (2015-2017); Partnerships for Research and Education in Materials (PREM) Grant from National Science Foundation (2016); Mini-Grant, Office of Research, Development at CSULA (2016); Certificate of Outstanding and Excellence in Reviewing Physics Letters A (2013, 2015); Certificate of Outstanding Contribution in Reviewing Material Letters (2015); Certificate of Outstanding Contribution in Reviewing Journal of Magnetism and Magnetic Materials (2015); CINT User Proposal Award at Los Alamos National Laboratory; Grantee, Sandia National Laboratories (2011-2015); Certification Associate Program, College of the Canyons (2009); Outstanding Instructor Award, Santa Monica Community College, Santa Monica, CA (2008); User Proposal Award at Center for Functional Nanomaterials, Brookhaven National Laboratory (2007-2015); NSF Chautauqua Short Courses for College Teachers Award, Eugene, OR (2004); Colloquium - For Lectures, by Lectures Appreciation Certificate for Contribution to the Success, California State Polytechnic University (2002, 2003, 2004); Strathmore's Who's Who Award (2003-2004); American Association of Physics Teachers (AAPT) Award (2002); Lucile Packard Foundation Grant, Lucile Packard Foundation for Participation in the Gordon Research Conference on Correlated Electron Systems in Colby College, Waterville, ME (2002); International Scientist of the Year, International Biographical Center of Cambridge, England (2001); American Association of Physics Teachers, (2001); Invitation Grant, Laboratoire Leon Brillouin, Saclay, France (1997); Fellowship Invitation, International Center for Theoretical Physics, Miramare-Trieste, Italy (1996); Honorary Scholar Diploma in Residence Award from New York University (1994) Personal Fellowship, Union College, Schenectady, NY (1993); Meyer Foundation Award, American Physical Society (1993) **MEM:** Foreign Member, Armenian National Academy of Sciences (2012); American Association of Physics Teachers (2001); Topical Group in Magnetism (1997); Material Research Society (1997); New York Academy Sciences (1996); American Physical Society (1993); Council on Physics of Rare-Earth Semiconductors, St. Petersburg, Russia (1983) **BAR: MH:** Who's Who in Science and Engineering (2000/2001) **AS:** Dr. Kocharian attributes his success to collaboration with colleagues and his former students in the US

and Armenia by conducting joint research on the problems in condensed matter & nanomaterials, theory of strong earthquakes, properties of chiral photonic crystal liquids, thermal properties of nuclear matter in discrete lattices, spin transport of electrons in magnetic nanostructures, entanglement properties and other fields. **B/I:** Dr. Kocharian became involved in his profession by following in his father's steps who was famous in Armenian Scientific Community and was the founder of the physics departments at Yerevan State University and the National Polytechnic University in Armenia. **AV:** Chess; Art; Drawing

KOCSIS, JOAN B., T: Elementary School Educator **I:** Education/Educational Services **DOB:** 02/06/1941 **PB:** Phillipsburg **SC:** NJ/USA **PT:** Frederick Bosco; Frances (Marina) Bosco **MS:** Married **SPN:** Gerald S. Kocsis Sr. (12/30/1961) **CH:** Gerald S. Jr.; Jacqueline Kocsis Morgan **ED:** MEd, University of North Carolina, Charlotte, NC (1987); BA in Elementary Education, Trenton State College (TCNJ, The College of New Jersey) (1962) **CT:** Certified Teacher, K-4; Certified, Early Childhood Education, Language Arts, K-12; Certified, Early Childhood Education, Social Studies 7-12; Certified Administration, Supervision and Curriculum, State of North Carolina **C:** Teacher, Grades 1-4, Union County Public Schools, Monroe, NC (1981-1988, 1989-Present); Teacher, First Grade, Charlotte-Mecklenburg Schools (1988-1989); Teacher, Kindergarten, Talented and Gifted, Hopewell Valley Regional Board of Education, Pennington, NJ (1976-1979); Teacher, K-3, Hamilton Township Board of Education, NJ (1962-1968) **CR:** Union County Council on Aging (2010); Teacher, Caregiver Classes **CIV:** Grand Advisory Committee, Union County Home and Community Care Block; Volunteer, Union County Council on Aging; Volunteer, Docent, Museum of the Waxhaws, Waxhaw, NC **CW:** Presenter, "Positively for Parents" (1992); Lecturer, "First Ladies, President and Various Historical Topics" **AW:** Presidential Award for Excellence in Teaching Science and Mathematics, National Science Foundation (1994) **MEM:** Treasurer, Union-Monroe Council, International Reading Association (Now International Literacy Association) (1993); National Education Association; National Science Teachers Association; NCSTA - North Carolina Science Teachers Association; Association of Presidential Awardees in Science Teaching (APAST) **MH:** Albert Nelson Marquis Lifetime Achievement Award **B/I:** Mrs. Kocsis always loved working with children. In high school, she was a member of future nurses and future teacher programs. Mrs. Kocsis decided on teaching because she was always drawn to children and she was concerned about getting sick **AV:** Reading; Collecting presidential artifacts; Antiquing; Shopping; Having fun **RE:** Roman Catholic

KOEHNKE, DONNA R., T: Secretary **I:** Government Administration/Government Relations/Government Services **DOB:** 04/25/1940 **PB:** Gorman **SC:** TX/USA **PT:** Herb Baker; Dema Baker **MS:** Married **SPN:** James Koehnke **CH:** Rodney Alan (Deceased, 8/9/1977); Cindy; Mark; Beth; Lynette; Brian **ED:** Associate of Applied Science, Northern Virginia Community College, Summa Cum Laude (1986) **C:** Secretary, United States International Trade Commission, Washington, DC (1993-2002); Secretary, Federal Communications Commission (1988-1993) **CIV:** Volunteer, Fauquier Health (2013-Present); Board Member, Cutting Edge Ministries (2012-Present); Election Officer (2001-2018); Board Member, Christian Clubs in Public Schools **AW:** Managing Award, Federal Communications Commission **MH:** Albert Nelson Marquis

Lifetime Achievement Award **AS:** Mrs. Koehnke attributes her success to her skills in management and her eagerness to finish her work. **B/I:** Mrs. Koehnke became involved in her profession after receiving a high score on the Civil Service exam. Much sought after, she was offered a position at the Federal Communications Commission. **AV:** Golf; Reading **PA:** Republican **RE:** Protestant

KOENIG, HAROLD PAUL, T: Management Consultant **I:** Consulting **CN:** H.P. Koenig Management Consultants **DOB:** 04/22/1926 **PB:** Mason City **SC:** IA/USA **PT:** Reuben Harold Koenig; Dorothea (Paule) Koenig **MS:** Married **SPN:** Barbara Anne Rucker (6/29/1974) **CH:** Kimberley Anne; Joseph Paul; Liberty Unique; Gerald Fred **ED:** MS, Illinois Institute of Technology (1956); BS, Iowa State University (1947); Coursework, Ohio Wesleyan University (1944-1945) **CT:** Ordained to Ministry, Baptist Church (1994); Registered Professional Engineer, States of Illinois, Minnesota, Indiana, Florida, Iowa **C:** Chairman, H.P. Koenig Management Consultant, Jupiter, Satellite Beach, Melbourne, FL (1990-Present); President, Chairman, Founder, Tele-Optics, Inc., West Palm Beach, FL (1986-1990); Chief Executive Officer, Tele-Optics, Inc., West Palm Beach, FL (1986-1990); Chief Operating Officer, Tel-Tech Devices, Inc., Fort Lauderdale, FL (1984-1986); Chairman, H.P. Koenig Management Consultant, Miami, FL (1980-1984); Director General, Canron Pipe & Hydraulics, Montreal, Quebec, Canada (1978-1980); Chief Executive Officer, Director General, Matisa, S.A., Lausanne, Switzerland (1977-1978); President, Chairman, Chief Executive Officer, Unionam., Inc., Windham Power Lifts, Elba, AL (1974-1976); President, Chairman, Chief Executive Officer, Founder, Ecological Science Corporation (1967-1973); Vice President, Dresser Industries, Inc., Dallas, TX (1964-1967); Engineer, Booz, Allen & Hamilton (1956-1964); Engineer Manager, Standard Oil Company, Whiting, IN (1953-1956); Chief Engineer, Grain Processing Corp., Muscatine, IA (1948-1950) **CR:** Certified Evangelical Explosion Lecturer, West Palm Beach, FL (1991-Present); Adviser, Citizens Democracy Corps, Ukraine (1998); Adviser, Citizens Democracy Corps, Russia (1996-1997); Supervising Counselor, Billy Grabam Crusade, Fort Lauderdale, FL (1985); Certified Trainer, Evangelical Explosion International, Fort Lauderdale, FL (1981-1984); Lecturer in Field **CIV:** Director, Grandparents Raising Grandchildren Brevard (2011-Present); Chaplain, Melbourne Florida International Airport (2002-Present); Founder, Chief Executive Officer, President, H.E.A.R.T. (1999-Present); Advisor for Drug Treatment, State of Florida (1998-Present); Citizens Democracy Corps, Ukraine (1998); Citizens Democracy Corps, Velikie Luki, Russia (1997); Citizens Democracy Corps, Khabarovsk, Sakhalin Island, Russia (1996); President Nixon's Committee on Environmental Quality (1969-1972); Witness on Environmental and Ecological Matters United States Congress, Washington, DC (1969-1971); Advisor, Founding Earth Day, United States Congress, President Richard Nixon (1970); Scoutmaster, Boy Scouts of America (1949-1950); Deacon, Baptist Church; Missionary to Kenya **MIL:** Seabees, Pacific Theater of Operations, U.S. Navy (1951-1953); Lieutenant Commander, U.S. Naval Reserve (1943-1946) **CW:** Author, "Winning Against Satan-Applying Military Principles to Spiritual Warfare" (1991); Contributor, Articles, Professional Journals **AW:** Ziegenhein Award, PREVENT of Brevard (2005); Meritorious Service Award, Government of Italy (1962); Eagle Scout Award With Bronze, Silver and Gold Palms, Boy Scouts of America (1942); Golden Owl Award, Phi Gamma Delta **MEM:** Phi Gamma Delta; Gideon **MH:** Albert Nelson Marquis Lifetime Achievement

Award **B/I:** Mr. Koenig got involved in his field due to a natural progression. **AV:** Playing tennis; Playing bridge; Playing chess **PA:** Republican

KOENIG, ROBERT AUGUST, PHD, T: Minister, Educator **I:** Financial Services **CN:** Internal Revenue Services **DOB:** 07/14/1933 **PB:** Red Wing **SC:** MN/USA **PT:** William C. Koenig; Florence E. (Tebbe) Koenig **MS:** Widowed **SPN:** Pauline Louise Olson-Koenig (Deceased 2/13/2018) **ED:** PhD, University of Minnesota (1973); MDiv, San Francisco Theological Seminary, Magna Cum Laude (1969); Postgraduate Coursework, Bennington College (1965); MA in Educational Administration, University of Minnesota (1965); BS, University of Wisconsin-Superior, Cum Laude (1955) **CT:** Ordained to Ministry, Presbyterian Church of the USA (1970) **C:** Stated Supply Pastor, Couderay and Radisson Presbyterian Churches, Wisconsin (1999-2009); Senior Pastor, First Presbyterian Church, South St. Paul, MN (1988-1998); Senior Pastor, Grove Presbyterian Church, Danville, PA (1985-1988); Pastor, First Presbyterian Church, Chippewa Falls, WI (1974-1985); Instructor, Inver Hills Community College, Inver Grove Heights, MN (1974); Coordinator of Commission and Personnel Services, Minnesota Higher Education Coordinating Board, St. Paul, MN (1972-1974); Assistant to Executive Director, Minnesota Higher Education Coordinator Board, St. Paul, MN (1972); Administrative Assistant to President, Lakewood State Community College, White Bear Lake, MN (1971-1972); Sawyer County Larger Parish, Wisconsin (1969-1974); Instructor of College Education, University of Minnesota (1969-1971); Teacher of General Music, Jordan Junior High School, Palo Alto, CA (1966-1969); Assistant to the Minister, St. John's Presbyterian Church, San Francisco, CA (1964-1965); Teacher of Instrumental Music and Humanities, Palo Alto Senior High School, California (1962-1965); Director of Instrumental Music, Chetek Public Schools, Wisconsin (1958-1962); Supervisor of Music, Florence High School, Wisconsin (1955-1956) **CR:** Established and Funded, Koenig Muilenburg History of Religion Seminar, San Francisco Theological Seminary (2010-Present); Established and Funded, Robert A. and Pauline L. Koenig Scholarship Fund, Chetek-Weyerhaeuser School District, Wisconsin (1998-Present); Member, Presbytery of Twin Cities Area (1988-Present); Led Chapel Services, Timber Hills Presbyterian Homes, Inver Grove Heights, MN (2010-2018); Member, South St. Paul Ministerial Association (1988-1998); President, South St. Paul Ministerial Association (1989-1990); President, Danville-Riverside Area Ministerial Association (1987-1988); Member of Christian Education Committee, Synod of the Trinity (1987-1988); Chairperson of Christian Education Committee, Presbytery of Northumberland (1987-1988); Member of Presbytery Council, Presbytery of Northumberland (1987-1988); Member of Committee on Ministry, Danville-Riverside Area Ministerial Association (1985-1988); Chairman, Presbytery of Northumberland (1982-1984); Synod Designation Pastor Plan Cabinet (1982-1984); Moderator, Presbytery of Northern Waters (1983); Chairman, Presbytery of Northern Waters (1981-1982); Member of Faculty, Communiversity (1977-1985); Member of Ministerial Relations Committee, Presbytery of Northern Waters (1977-1982); Member of International Coordinator Committee, Church Mission Synod Lakes and Prairies (1978-1979); Chairman, Third Annual Biblical Seminar (1977); Dean, Presbyterian Young Pastors Retreat (1977); Member of Faculty, University of Wisconsin Extension, Eau Claire, WI (1977); Adjunct Assistant Professor of Educational Administration, University of Minnesota, Minneapolis, MN (1976-1977); Member of Ministerial Relations Committee, Pres-

bytery of Chippewa (1974-1977); Member of Study Committee, Presbytery of Chippewa (1973-1974) **CIV:** Member, Veterans of Foreign Wars (1994-Present); President, College of Education and Human Development Alumni Society, University of Minnesota (2002-2004); Member of Executive Committee, College of Education and Human Development Alumni Society, University of Minnesota (2001-2005); Vice President, College of Education and Human Development Alumni Society, University of Minnesota (2001-2002); Board of Directors, College of Education and Human Development Alumni Society, University of Minnesota (1999-2005); President, Chippewa Valley Ecumenical Housing Association (1984-1985); Board of Directors of Development Foundation, North Central Career Development Center, Minneapolis, MN (1983-1985); Chairman of Finance Committee, North Central Career Development Center, Minneapolis, MN (1979-1984); Board of Directors, North Central Career Development Center, Minneapolis, MN (1978-1984) **MIL:** United States Army, Korea (1956-1958) **CW:** Contributor, Articles to Professional Journals **AW:** Nominee, One of the 100 Most Distinguished Alumni of University of Minnesota's College of Education and Human Development (2006); Recipient, Good Neighbor Award, WCCO (1974); Recipient, John Hay Fellowship, Bennington College **MEM:** Grand Chaplain, Wisconsin Chapter, Free & Accepted Masons (1977-1980, 1983-1985); Burton Society; College of Education, University of Minnesota; Heritage Society; University of Minnesota Elks; Free & Accepted Masons; Phi Delta Kappa; Veterans of Foreign Wars **MH:** Albert Nelson Marquis Lifetime Achievement Award; Marquis Who's Who Top Professional; Marquis Who's Who Humanitarian Award **B/I:** Dr. Koenig entered his profession because he felt a sense of calling, tested and found true.

KOENINGER, JIMMY G., PHD, T: Executive Director **I:** Medicine & Health Care **CN:** HOSA, Inc. **DOB:** 12/10/1942 **PB:** Duncan **SC:** OK/USA **PT:** Glen Koeninger; Dorthy Mae (Brooks) Koeninger **CH:** Jeffrey Glen; Jason Charles **ED:** PhD, Ohio State University (1973); MS, Oklahoma State University (1968); BS, Central State University, Edmond, OK (1965) **C:** Executive Director, HOSA, Inc. (1984-Present); President, Chief Executive Officer, Corporate Education Resources, Inc., Dallas/Fort Worth International Airport (1984-Present); Executive Vice President, Jobs for America's Graduates, Inc., Washington, DC (1984-2017); President, Leadership Development Institute, Fort Worth, TX (1976-1984); Associate Professor, College of Technology, University of Houston; Associate Professor, Oklahoma State University, Stillwater, OH; Assistant Professor, College of Business Administration, Oklahoma State University; Assistant Professor, Norris-Vincent College of Business, Angelo State University **CR:** Chief Executive Officer, TrainingMart.com (2011-Present) **CIV:** Vice Chair, Strategic Partnerships LLC (1995-Present) **CW:** Author training materials **MEM:** ASTD (American Society for Training & Development) (Now ATD) **MH:** Marquis Who's Who Top Professional **AS:** Dr. Koeninger attributes his success to being results-oriented. He said, "Whatever they do, they measure it and they are never satisfied." He is a lot older than most, and usually people have retired by his age. **B/I:** Dr. Koeninger became involved in his profession because he started as a professor, but felt that when working in a classroom setting, "you can only help those that enroll in your class." He believed that working with an association has a multiplier effect; he said, "You have the opportunity to work with many more." They influence those at a state level leadership, who then work with teachers below them, who then work with

students below them. They have an opportunity to work with 240,000 as opposed to a class room of 20 to 25 students. **AV:** Playing racquetball; Playing tennis; Playing golf; Fish breeding **PA:** Republican **RE:** Member, Christian Church (Disciples of Christ)

KOEPPE, PATSY PODUSKA, MD, T: Internist, Medical Educator **I:** Medicine & Health Care **DOB:** 11/18/1932 **PB:** Memphis **SC:** TN/USA **PT:** Ben F.; Lily Mae (Reid) Poduska **MS:** Married **SPN:** Douglas F. Koeppe Sr. (09/08/1967) **CH:** Douglas F. Jr. **ED:** Fellowship in Endocrinology and Metabolism, The University of Texas Medical Branch at Galveston (1963-1965); Residency in Internal Medicine, Lahey Health System, Inc. (1962-1963); Residency in Internal Medicine, Memphis VA Medical Center (1961-1962); Intern, Carilion Roanoke Memorial Hospital (1960-1961); MD, The University of Tennessee (1957); BA, Texas Woman's University (1954) **C:** Retired (1998); Professor, The University of Texas Medical Branch at Galveston (1994-1998); Graduate Faculty Member of Biomedical Sciences, The University of Texas Medical Branch at Galveston (1983-1998); Associate Professor, The University of Texas Medical Branch at Galveston (1987-1993); Acting Director, Division of Geriatrics, The University of Texas Medical Branch at Galveston (1991-1992); Assistant Professor of Internal Medicine, The University of Texas Medical Branch at Galveston (1969-1972, 1978-1987); Director, Weinberg Women's Health Center (1974-1977); Private Practice (1972-1973); Assistant Professor of Endocrinology, The University of Texas Medical Branch at Galveston (1969-1972); Instructor of Internal Medicine and Endocrinology, The University of Texas Medical Branch at Galveston (1965-1969) **CR:** Honorary Member, Medical Staff, The University of Texas Medical Branch at Galveston (1998) **MEM:** American Geriatrics Society; TMA; TMF Health Quality Institute; Galveston County Medical Society; Internal Medicine Alumni Society, The University of Texas Medical Branch at Galveston **MH:** Albert Nelson Marquis Lifetime Achievement Award; Marquis Who's Who Top Professional; Marquis Who's Who Humanitarian Award **AS:** Dr. Koeppe attributes her success to God and her supportive parents. **B/I:** Dr. Koeppe became involved in her profession of her lifelong desire to go into the medical field. **AV:** Reading; Studying the Bible **RE:** Presbyterian

KOHLHEPP, EDWARD JOHN SR., T: Founder, Chief Executive Officer **CN:** Kohlhepp Investment Advisors, Ltd. **DOB:** 08/11/1943 **PB:** Philadelphia **SC:** PA/USA **PT:** Edward H. Kohlhepp; Helen Kathleen (Egan) Kohlhepp **MS:** Married **SPN:** Elizabeth A. Bretschneider (06/21/1969) **CH:** Edward Joseph; Karen Ann; Mary Beth **ED:** MBA in Management, Temple University (1969); BS in Accounting, La Salle University (1967) **CT:** Certified Pension Consultant; Chartered Life Underwriter; Certified Financial Planner; Registered Principal NASD; Chartered Financial Consultant; Enrolled Actuary; Licensed FINRA Series 6, 7, 24, 63 and 65; Life, Health and Variable Annuity Licenses **C:** Founder, Chief Executive Officer, Kohlhepp Investment Advisors, Ltd. (1998-Present); President, Kohlhepp Investment Advisors, Ltd. (1998-2016); Representative, Cambridge Investment Research, Inc. (2004-2014); President, Manchester Financial Group (1994-1998); Principal, Manchester Benefits Group, Inc. (1994-1998); President, Van Buren & Kohlhepp, Ltd. (1987-1994); Private Practice (1980-1987); Assistant Professor to Senior Associate Professor, Bucks County Community College, Newtown, PA (1976-1986); Vice President, William L. Marshall Associates, Inc., Doylestown, PA (1979-1980); Consultant, Neil G. Kyde, Inc., Yardley, PA

(1975-1979); Secretary-treasurer, Lincoln Investment Planning, Inc., Jenkintown, PA (1972-1975); Instructor, Bucks County Community College, Newtown, PA (1969-1972) **CR:** Adjunct Faculty, Bucks County Community College (1999-2002) **CIV:** Karate Teacher, Children Ages 5-12 (2000-Present) **AW:** Named Man of the Year (2017) **MEM:** Financial Planning Association; American Academy of Actuaries; ASPPA; Bucks County Estate Planning Council, National Association of Estate Planners & Councils (NAEPC); Beta Gamma Sigma; Beta Alpha Psi **MH:** Albert Nelson Marquis Lifetime Achievement Award; Marquis Who's Who Top Professional **B/I:** Mr. Kohlhepp became involved in his profession after his interest evolved over a period of years. Upon leaving graduate school, he began teaching, but his father's business had some complex issues that he had to help deal with. When he started dealing with those issues and helping him out, he noticed there was an interest there. There was an interest in retirement plans, investments and insurance and that is how the evolution grew. **AV:** Saxophone; Golf; Shotokan karate; Long drives; Music

KOHNEN, MICHAEL PHILLIP, I: Business Management/Business Services **DOB:** 01/16/1942 **PB:** Eau Claire **SC:** WI/USA **PT:** Albert Rae Kohnen (Deceased); Virginia M. Green, Kohnen, Pehlke, (Deceased) **MS:** Divorced **CH:** Michael Phillip Kohnen II; Deloris Lydia Emily Kohnen; John Fitzgerald Kohnen; William Peter Kohnen; Nicole Lee Coker **ED:** Diploma Memorial High School, Eau Claire, WI; Coursework, Waldorf University, Forest City, IA; Associate Degree in Computer Sales Technology, Northwest Missouri State University, Maryville, MO (1974); Coursework, WI State University, Eau Claire, WI; Coursework, University of Wisconsin, Madison, WI; Coursework, United States Armed Forces Institute, Madison, WI **CT:** Licensed Wisconsin and Florida Insurance; RHU - Registered Professional Disability and Health Insurance Underwriter; President International Association of Health Insurance Underwriters; Licensed Real Estate Broker, Wisconsin **C:** Vice President, MPK Co. Clayton, WI (2010-Retired); Manufacturer of Inventions, Clayton Cars, Clayton Auto Body, Clayton Plastics, Wisconsin (1999); President, Kohnen Internacional S.A., San Jose, Costa Rica (1985); Master General Agent, Inter-State Assurance Co. (1982); Owner, President, Michael P. Kohnen, Rhu & Associates, Inc., Eau Claire, WI (1969; Insurance Agent, Eau Claire, WI (1967); President, Michael P. Kohnen, Rhu & Associates, Inc., Clayton, WI; Insurance Agent, Vero Beach, FL; WI Real Estate Broker; Networker **CR:** Sales Coordinator, National Safety Associates, Inc., Memphis, TN (1989); Real Estate Broker, Wisconsin (1973) **CIV:** Past PTA Treasurer; Senior Boy Scout Troop Leader, Randall School Eau Claire, WI; Junior Vice Commander, Disabled American Veterans Chapter 10, Clayton, WI **MIL:** Active Duty, Vietnam War, U.S. Air Force (1962-1966) **AW:** Administration Tech Briefs Grand Prize Winner (2010); Wisconsin Business Man of the Year (2010); American Spirit Honor Medal (1962); Voted Mr. Teenager, Eau Claire,WI (1959); Babe Ruth Baseball - pitcher 1957 WI State Babe Ruth Champions (1957); Freshman Varsity Hockey Letter Earner, Memorial High School - Eau Claire,WI (1957); Boy Scouts of America - Life Scout-leading the pledge of allegiance-Memorial Day Eau Claire, WI Band Schell (1955); Elected Student Council, Memorial High School, Eau Claire, WI; National Aeronautics & Space **MEM:** Wisconsin State President, National Association of Health Insurance Underwriters (1976-1977); Health Insurance Roundtable; Lifetime Member, Boy Scout Troop 89; Order of the Arrow; Life Scout, Eau Claire, WI **MH:** Albert

Nelson Marquis Lifetime Achievement Award **AS:** He attributes his success to attitude and the way he was raised. The people who were close to him were his mother Virginia Green Kohnen, Pehlke and his two aunts: Geraldine M. Green and Dorothy Green Lancor. They always lovingly furnished meals, bedding, clean/clothes, medical/dental care, haircuts, helped with his school work encouraging continuous learning, punctuality and always made sure he timely attended church. They were always there for him and couldn't do enough. **B/I:** To better understand and improve insurance and real estate for helping others. **AV:** Inland fishing with relatives and friends in Northern MN and Canada; Viewing pro and college football and college basketball; Current news; Time with relatives and friends **PA:** Republican **RE:** Lutheran **THT:** Practice the Golden Rule. Mr. Kohnen has also learned for whatever reason/s not to expect others to reciprocate in the same manner.

KOIRALA, NAVANEET, T: Principal **I:** Business Management/Business Services **CN:** Koirala & Associates LLC **DOB:** 05/27/1985 **PB:** Kathmandu **SC:** Nepal **PT:** Raghu Nath Koirala; Sujata Koirala **MS:** Married **SPN:** Puja Giri Koirala **CH:** Rayansh Koirala **ED:** BBA in Accounting, University of the District of Columbia, Summa Cum Laude (2010); AAS in Business Administration, Northern Virginia Community College (2007) **C:** Principal, Koirala & Associates (2019-Present); Revenue Accounting Supervisor, Citrix Systems, Inc., Fort Lauderdale, FL (2018-2019); Senior Revenue Accountant, Citrix Systems, Inc., Fort Lauderdale, FL (2016-2018); Senior Auditor, BDO USA LLP, Miami, FL (2015); Senior Assurance Associate, Ernst & Young LLP, Florida (2013-2014); Experienced Assurance Associate, PricewaterhouseCoopers LLP, Florida (2012-2013); Assurance Associate, Grant Thornton LLP, McLean, VA (2011); Intern Data Analyst, DC Government, Washington DC (2009-2010) **AW:** Leadership Award, Miami Chapter, National Association of Black Accountants, Inc. (2017); Good Citizenship Award for Participating in Junior Achievement, Grant Thornton LLP (2011); Thurgood Marshall College Fund Leadership Training Award (2010); Becker CPA Review Scholarship, National Association of Black Accountants, Inc. (2010); Johnson & Johnson Scholarship, National Association of Black Accountants, Inc. (2009); Bert Smith & Company Scholarship, National Association of Black Accountants, Inc. (2009); Peter Regis & Associate Scholarship, UDC School of Business (2009) **MEM:** Vice President, Miami Professional Chapter, National Association of Black Accountants, Inc. (2013-Present); Phi Eta Sigma National Honor Society (2009-Present); Member, American Institute of Certified Public Accountants (2009-Present); Financial Advisor, Safety NET (Nepal Earthquake Task Force), International Heath Initiatives (2015-2017); National Convention Committee, National Association of Black Accountants, Inc. (2016); SMS Director, Miami Professional Chapter, National Association of Black Accountants, Inc. (2012-2013) **AS:** Mr. Koirala attributes his success to his family, friends, and networking. **B/I:** Mr. Koirala became involved in his profession because of his passion for accounting and finance. Upon graduating with a Bachelor of Business Administration in accounting, he started working as an auditor. This gave him exposure to real-life experiences in various industries. Mr. Koirala's time as an auditor in some of the big 4's large global accounting firms and his career at Citrix Systems, Inc. helped him to become an entrepreneur and start his own corporate and personal financial consulting firm, Koirala & Associates LLC. **AV:** Traveling; Mentoring; Meditating **RE:** Hindu **THT:** Mr. Koirala is fluent in English, Nepali, and Hindi.

KOLKEY, DANIEL M., T: Former Judge, Lawyer **I:** Law and Legal Services **CN:** Gibson, Dunn & Crutcher LLP **DOB:** 04/21/1952 **PB:** Chicago **SC:** IL/USA **PT:** Eugene Louis Kolkey; Gilda Penelope (Cowan) Kolkey **MS:** Married **SPN:** Donna Christie Kolkey (05/15/1982) **CH:** Eugene; William; Christopher; Jonathan **ED:** JD, Harvard University, Cambridge, MA, Magna Cum Laude (1977); BA, Stanford University, Stanford, CA, with Distinction (1974) **C:** Partner, Gibson, Dunn & Crutcher LLP, San Francisco, CA (2003-2020); Associate Justice, California Court of Appeals for the Third Appellate District, Sacramento, CA (1998-2003); Counsel to Governor, Legal Affairs Secretary to California Governor Pete Wilson (1995-1998); Partner, Gibson, Dunn & Crutcher LLP, Los Angeles, CA (1985-1994); Associate, Gibson, Dunn & Crutcher LLP, Los Angeles, CA (1978-1984); Law Clerk, United States District Court Judge, New York, NY (1977-1978) **CR:** Vice President, California Supreme Court Historical Society (2018-Present); Director, Board of Directors, California Supreme Court Historical Society (2013-Present); Chair, California Reform Committee, Pacific Research Institute (PRI) (2013-Present); Chair, Rules Subcommittee, California Judicial Council Appellate Advisory Committee (2013-2019); Director, Board of Directors, Executive Committee, Central Pacific Region, Anti-Defamation League (2010-2016); Secretary, Executive Committee, Central Pacific Region, Anti-Defamation League (2011-2012); Adjunct Professor, University of the Pacific McGeorge School of Law (2001-2004); California State-Federal Judicial Council (2001-2003); Member, Blue Ribbon Commission on Jury Systems Improvement (1996); Chair, California Law Revision Commission (1994); Vice Chair, California Law Revision Commission (1993-1994); Arbitrator, Bi-national Panel for U.S.-Canada Free Trade Agreement (1990-1994) **CIV:** Member, Central Committee, California Republican Party (2017-Present); Member, Pacific Council on International Policy (1999-Present); California Delegate, Republican National Convention (1996); Member, Central Committee, California Republican Party (1995-1998); Member, Los Angeles Committee on Foreign Relations (1983-1995); Law and Justice Committee, Los Angeles Area Chamber of Commerce (1993-1994); Panel of Arbitrators, Arbitrator Large Complex Case Dispute Resolution Program, American Arbitration Association (1993-1994); Advisory Council, Executive Committee, Asia-Pacific Center for the Resolution of International Business Disputes (1991-1994); President, Los Angeles Center for International Commercial Arbitration (1990-1994); General Counsel, Citizens Research Foundation (1990-1994); Board of Directors, Los Angeles Center for International Commercial Arbitration (1986-1994); Alternate California Delegation, Republican National Convention (1992); Chairman, International Trade Legislative Subcommittee, International Commerce Steering Committee, Los Angeles Area Chamber of Commerce (1983-1991); Co-chairman, International Relations Section, Town Hall of California, Los Angeles, CA (1985-1990);Treasurer, Los Angeles Center for International Commercial Arbitration (1986-1988) **CW:** Co-editor, "Practitioner's Handbook on International Arbitration and Mediation" (2002); Contributor, Multiple Articles, Professional Journals, Newspapers **AW:** Named, Top 100 California Lawyers, San Francisco Daily Journal, Los Angeles Daily Journal (2004-2006, 2018, 2019); Clay Award, "Attorney of the Year," International Arbitration (2019); Clay Award, "Attorney of the Year," Sports Law (2017); Clay Award, "Attorney of the Year," Real Estate and Development (2015); Clay Award, "Attorney of the Year," Appellate Law (2006); Clay Award, "Attorney of the Year," Public Policy (2004); Master, Anthony M. Kennedy American Inn of Court (1996-1999); Inductee, The Phi Beta Kappa Society (1972); Clay Award, Multiple Years **MEM:** Vice President, California Supreme Court Historical Society (2018-Present); American Law Institute; Associate, Chartered Institute of Arbitrators, London, England, United Kingdom (1986-1994); Executive Committee, Friends of Wilton Park, Southern CA (1986-1994); Chairman, Executive Committee, Friends of Wilton Park, Southern CA (1986-1994) **BAR:** United States District Court of the Southern District of California (1994); United States District Court of Arizona (1992); Supreme Court of the United States (1983); United States District Court of the Northern District of California (1980); United States Court of Appeals for the Ninth Circuit (1979); United States District Court for the Central District of California (1979); United States District Court of the Eastern District of California (1978); California (1977) **MH:** Albert Nelson Marquis Lifetime Achievement Award **B/I:** Mr. Kolkey chose the law because of his interest in government. Since the sixth grade, he had decided that if he ever went into government, it would be important for him to be proficient in history, economics, and law. Accordingly, he majored in history at Stanford University, while also satisfying the requirements for an economics major, graduating with distinction and a straight-A average. He then went to Harvard Law School, where he graduated magna cum laude. **PA:** Republican

KOMARAVOLU, V.C. RAO, T: Engineering Educator **I:** Education/Educational Services **CN:** Michigan Technological University **DOB:** 08/03/1942 **PB:** Andhra Pradesh **SC:** India **MS:** Married **SPN:** Padma **CH:** Mala; Satya; Ravi **ED:** DAAD Fellowship, University of Stuttgart (1989); DAAD Fellowship, University of Karlsruhe (1981-1982); PhD in Mechanical Engineering, Indian Institute of Technology Madras (1980); MTech, Indian Institute Technology Madras (1968); Bachelor of Science in Mechanical Engineering, Sri Venkateswara University (1965) **CT:** Certified CAD/CAM Instructor, Ford and GM Motor Company **C:** Principal Lecturer, Michigan Technological University (2007-Present); Technical Consultant, Siemens, Bangalore, India (1999-2006); C3P Instructor, SDRC, Ford Motor Company (1998-1999); Lecturer, Michigan Technological University (1989-1999); Visiting Assistant Professor, Michigan Technological University (1989); Assistant Professor, Indian Institute of Technology Madras (1982-1989); Lecturer, Indian Institute of Technology Madras (1973-1981); Assistant Lecturer, Indian Institute of Technology Madras (1968-1973); Technical Teacher Trainee, Ministry of Education (1965-1968) **CR:** Acting Director, Innovation Center, Michigan Technological University (1995); Programmes and Publications Officer, Regional Centre for Energy, Heat and Mass Transfer (1978-1989); Part-Time Officer, Air Wing, National Cadet Crops, IIT, Madras, India (1975-1989); Faculty Advisor (1985-1988); Invited Lecturer, Indian Institute of Technology, Madras, India (1986); Director of Student Dormitory (Krishna) (1983-1986); Visiting Professor, XIV ICHMT Symposia, Dubrovnik, Yugoslavia (1982); Visiting Professor, University of Engineering and Technology, Lahore, Pakistan (1982); Participant, 17th International Seminar for Research and Education, University of Karlsruhe (1981-1982); Invited Lecturer, BHEL R&D, Hyderabad, India (1979-1980); Visiting Professor, University of Peradenia, Sri Lanka (1979); Invited Lecturer, Indian Institute of Technology, Madras, India (1978-1979); Invited Lecturer, Thiagarajar Polytechnic, Salem, Madras, India (1978); Visiting Professor, University of Stuttgart (1977); Investigator and Co-Investigator, Numerous Sponsored Research and Consultancy

Projects; Visiting Professor, Tribhuvan University, Kathmandu, Nepal; Advier to the Indian Student Association at MTU **MIL:** Air Wing NCC (National Cadet Corps) Flight Lieutenant **CW:** Reviewer, "Classical Thermodynamics," Prentice Hall (2008); Reviewer, "Fundamentals of Machine Elements," McGraw-Hill (1997-1998); Reviewer, "Engineering Heat Transfer," West Publishing (1995); Reviewer, Several Journal Papers and Published Books; Reviewer, ASME Journal of Mechanical Engineering; Contributor, 28 Articles, Professional Journals **AW:** DAAD Fellowship, German Academic Exchange Program **MEM:** MTU Coordinator, Partners for the Advancement of Collaborative Engineering Education (PACE); Advisor, India Students Organization (ISO); Life Member, Indian Society for Heat and Mass Transfer, India; American Society of Mechanical Engineers; Regional Centre for Energy, Heat and Mass Transfer **MH:** Albert Nelson Marquis Lifetime Achievement Award; Marquis Who's Who Top Professional **B/I:** Dr. Komaravolu became involved in his career because he always wanted to be a teacher. He was influenced by his father, who was a teacher as well. Once he began his career in engineering, he tried to get a job at a power plant, but received an opportunity to teach at an educational institution. He tied both influences together, received a PhD, and held his first teaching position in 1968 in India. **RE:** Hindu

KONKOL, RICHARD J., MD, PHD, T: Pediatric Neurologist **I:** Medicine & Health Care **DOB:** 01/05/1946 **PB:** Stevens Point **SC:** WI/USA **PT:** Leonard F. Konkol; Regina (Potoka) Konkol **MS:** Married **SPN:** Sherry Angel (05/12/2005); Elizabeth G. (Bendeich) Konkol (12/21/1974) **CH:** Jonathan R; Margaret E. **ED:** Doctor of Medicine, Georgetown University, Washington, DC, Cum Lade (1979); Doctor of Philosophy in Neuroanatomy and Neurochemistry, University of Iowa (1975); Bachelor of Arts in Biology, Natural Sciences, Philosophy and Theology, St. Mary's College (1968) **CT:** Diplomate, American Board of Psychiatry and Neurology, with Special Qualification in Child Neurology **C:** Chief of Pediatric Neurology, Senior Physician, Kaiser Permanente Northwest (1997-2015); Professor Emeritus of Neurology, Chief, Pediatric Neurology, Oregon Health Science University, Portland, OR (1992-2015); Associate Professor of Neurology, Chief of Pediatric Neurology, Medical College of Wisconsin, Milwaukee, WI (1987-1992); Assistant Professor of Neurology, Medical College of Wisconsin, Milwaukee, WI (1985-1987); Fellow in Epilepsy, Children's Hospital Medical Center, Harvard University, Boston, MA (1984-1985); Resident in Neurology, Children's Hospital Medical Center, Harvard University, Boston, MA (1981-1984); Resident in Pediatrics, Children's Hospital Medical Center, Harvard University, Boston, MA (1980-1981); Intern in Pediatrics, Children's Hospital Medical Center, Harvard University, Boston, MA (1979-1980); Postdoctoral Fellow, University of North Carolina at Chapel Hill (1974-1976); Consultant, Oregon Health Science University **CR:** Member, Advisory Board, Children with Hyperactivity Attention Disorder, Portland, OR (1994-1997) **CIV:** Member, Emergency Preparedness Group **CW:** Co-Author, "Prenatal Cocaine Exposure" (1996); Author, "Cocaine Baby"; Contributor, More Than 50 Articles to Professional Journals; Contributor, 12 Chapters in Textbooks **AW:** Peer Elected to Best Doctors in America (1995, 2001, 2007, 2009, 2011); Young Investigator Award, Child Neurology Society (1985); Putnam/Merritt Epilepsy Award, Park Davis (1984); Saul R. Korey American Academy of Neurology Award (1976) **MEM:** Former Member, American Epilepsy Society; Former Emeritus Member, Child Neurology Society; Former Member,

American Neurological Association; Professors of Child Neurology; American Academy of Neurology **MH:** International Who's Who of Professionals (1995); Who's Who in America (Science and Engineering) (1994); Albert Nelson Marquis Lifetime Achievement Award; Marquis Who's Who Top Professional **B/I:** Dr. Konkol became involved in his profession after he initially started in a religious direction as a Christian Brother for several years. Following this period, he taught high school and got interested in teaching. He served as a wrestling coach for several years, but knew that was not enough, so he proceeded to pursue his higher education with a doctorate in neuroanatomy and neurochemistry at the University of Iowa. **AV:** Hiking; Wine making; Fishing; Reading and working with public defender cases

KOOLHAAS, REMMENT LUCAS, T: Architect; Professor **I:** Education/Educational Services **CN:** Harvard University **DOB:** 11/17/1944 **PB:** Rotterdam **SC:** The Netherlands **PT:** Anton Koolhaas; Selinde Pietertje Roosenberg **MS:** Divorced **SPN:** Madelon Vriesendorp **CH:** Charlie; Tomas **ED:** Doctor Honoris Causa, Katholieke Universiteit Leuven (2007); Diploma, Architectural Association School, London, England, United Kingdom (1972) **C:** Co-founder, Volume Magazine (2005-Present); Professor, Practice of Architecture and Urban Design, Harvard University Graduate School of Design (1995-Present); Founder, Director, Office for Metropolitan Architecture, Rotterdam, The Netherlands (1978-Present); Founder, Office for Metropolitan Architecture, London, England, United Kingdom (1975-1978); Director, Office for Metropolitan Architecture, New York, NY; Former Journalist, Writer, Film Screenplays **CR:** Director, Project on the City, Harvard University (1995); Adjunct Professor, Architecture, Harvard University Graduate School of Design (1990-1995); Professor, Architecture, Rice University, Houston, Texas (1991-1992); Professor, Architecture, Technical University, Delft, The Netherlands (1988-1989); Architectural Associate, London, England, United Kingdom (1976) **CW:** Architect, Taipei Performing Arts Centre, Taipei, China (2012–Present); Architect, Marina Abramovic Community Centre Obod Cetinje – MACCOC, Cetinje (2012-Present); Architect, Bryghusprojektet, Danish Architecture Centre, Copenhagen, Denmark (2008–Present); Co-founder with Mark Wigley and Ole Bourman, Volume Magazine (2005-Present); Architect, The Factory, Manchester, England, United Kingdom (2019); Author, "Content" (2004); Architect, Garage Museum of Contemporary Art, Moscow, Russia (2014); Architect, De Rotterdam, Rotterdam, The Netherlands (2013); Author, "Project Japan: Metabolism Talks" (2011); Architect, 23 East 22nd Street, New York, NY (2010); Architect, New Court, St. Swithin's Lane, London, England, United Kingdom (2010); Architect, Riga Port City (2009); Architect, China Central TV Headquarters (2008); Author, "Serpentine Gallery: 24 Hour Interview Marathon" (2007); Co-author with Bernard Colenbrander and Michelle Provoost, "Dutchtown: A City Center Design by OMA" (2000); Co-author with Jacques Lucan, "OMA Rem Koolhaas Living, Vivre, Leben" (1999); Co-author with Bruce Mau, "S,M,L,XL" (1998); Architect, Maison at Bordeaux, France (1998); Architect, Educatorium Utrecht University, The Netherlands (1997); Author, "Rem Koolhaas Conversations with Students" (1996); Exhibition, The Museum of Modern Art (1988, 1994, 1995); Author, "Delirious New York: A Retroactive Manifesto for Manhattan" (1995); Architect, Lille Grand Palais, France (1994); Architect, Kunsthal, Rotterdam, The Netherlands (1992); Architect, Nexus Housing, Fukuoka, Japan (1991); Architect, Villa Dall'Ava, Paris, France (1991);

Exhibition, Stedelijk Museum, Amsterdam, The Netherlands (1990); Exhibition, Colegio de Arquitectos, Barcelona, Spain (1990); Exhibition, Musee des Beaux Arts, Lille, France (1990); Exhibition, Boymans Museum, Rotterdam, The Netherlands (1989); Exhibition, Institute of Francais d'Architecture, Paris, France (1989); Exhibition, Max Protech Gallery (1988); Exhibition, Architecture Museum, Basel, Switzerland (1988); Architect, Netherlands Dans Theater, The Hague (1987); Exhibition, Guggenheim Museum, New York, NY (1978); Architect, Netherlands Embassy, Berlin, Germany; Guest Editor, Wired Magazine **AW:** Johannes Vermeer Award (2013); Jencks Award, Royal Institute of British Architects (2012); Golden Lion of the Venice Biennale of Architecture for Lifetime Achievement (2010); Named One of the 100 Most Influential People, TIME Magazine (2008); Wired Rave Award in Architecture (2005); Named Legion d'Honneur (2001); Pritzker Architecture Prize, The Hyatt Foundation (2000); Named Best Building in Japan, Architectural Institute of Japan (1992); Prix d'Architecture, Le Moniteur, Paris, France (1991); Progressive Architecture Award (1974) **MEM:** Honorary Foreign Member, American Academy of Arts & Sciences

KOONTZ, DEAN RAY, T: Author **I:** Writing and Editing **DOB:** 07/09/1945 **PB:** Everett **SC:** PA/USA **PT:** Raymond Koontz; Florence (Logue) Koontz **MS:** Married **SPN:** Gerda Ann Cerra (1966) **ED:** Honorary LittD, Shippensburg University, PA (1989); BA in English, Shippensburg University, PA (1966) **C:** Freelance Writer, Orange, CA (1969-Present); Teacher, Mechanicsburg High School, PA (1967-1969); Teacher, Appalachian Poverty Progressive, Saxton, PA (1966-1967) **CW:** Author, "Devoted" (2020); Author, "The Crooked Staircase" (2018); Author, "The Silent Corner" (2017); Author, "The Whispering Room" (2017); Author, "Last Light" (2015); Author, "Ashley Bell" (2015); Author, "Ashley Bell" (2015); Author, "The City" (2014); Author, "Saint Odd" (2014); Author, "Odd Thomas: You are Destined to be Together Forever" (2014); Author, "Deeply Odd" (2013); Author, "Innocence" (2013); Author, "Odd Interlude #3" (2012); Author, "Odd Interlude #2" (2012); Author, "House of Odd," Graphic Novel (2012); Author, "Odd Interlude #1" (2012); Author, "Odd Apocalypse" (2012); Author, "Frankenstein: The Dead Town" (2011); Author, "The Moonlit Mind" (2011); Author, "77 Shadow Street" (2011); Author, "Nevermore" (2011); Author, "Dean Koontz's Nevermore" (2011); Author, "Frankenstein: Lost Souls" (2010); Author, "Odd is on Our Side," Graphic Novel (2010); Author, "Trixie & Jinx" (2010); Author, "Darkness Under the Sun" (2010); Author, "What the Night Knows" (2010); Author, "Fear Nothing, Volume One," Graphic Novel (2010); Author, "I Trixie, Who is Dog" (2009); Author, "Relentless" (2009); Author, "Frankenstein Book 3: Dead and Alive" (2009); Author, "Frankenstein: Prodigal Son," Graphic Novel (2009); Author, "Breathless" (2009); Author, "A Big Little Life" (2009); Author, "A Big Little Life: A Memoir of a Joyful Dog" (2009); Author, "Bliss to You: Trixie's Guide to a Happy Life" (2008); Author, "Bliss to You" (2008); Author, "Your Heart Belongs to Me" (2008); Author, "Odd Hours" (2008); Author, "In Odd We Trust" (2008); Author, "The Good Guy" (2007); Author, "The Darkest Evening of the Year" (2007); Author, "The Husband" (2006); Author, "Brother Odd" (2006); Author, "Velocity" (2005); Author, "Frankenstein Book 1: Prodigal Son" (2005); Author, "Christmas is Good!: Trixie Treats and Holiday Wisdom" (2005); Author, "Frankenstein Book 2: City of Night" (2005); Author, "Forever Odd" (2005); Author, "The Taking" (2004); Author, "Life Expectancy" (2004); Author, "Life is Good! Lessons in Joyful

Living" (2004); Author, "Robot Santa: The Further Adventures of Santa's Twin" (2004); Author, "Every Day's a Holiday: Amusing Rhymes for Happy Times" (2003); Author, "The Face" (2003); Author, "Odd Thomas" (2003); Author, "By the Light of the Moon" (2002); Author, "One Door Away from Heaven" (2001); Author, "The Paper Doorway: Funny Verse and Nothing Worse" (2001); Author, "From the Corner of His Eye" (2000); Author, "False Memory" (1999); Author, "Seize the Night" (1999); Author, "Fear Nothing" (1998); Author, "Demon Seed," Revised Version (1997); Author, "Sole Survivor" (1997); Author, "The Eyes of Darkness" (1996); Author, "Tick Tock" (1996); Author, "Santa's Twin" (1996); Author, "Intensity" (1996); Author, "Santa's Twin" (1996); Author, "Icebound" (1995); Author, "Strange Highways" (1995); Author, "Chase," Revised Version (1995); Author, "Winter Moon" (1994); Author, "Dark Rivers of the Heart" (1994); Author, "Dragon Tears" (1993); Author, "Mr. Murder" (1993); Author, "Hideaway" (1992); Author, "Cold Fire" (1991); Author, "The Bad Place" (1990); Author, "The Servants of Twilight" (1990); Author, "Shadow Fires" (1990); Author, "Midnight" (1989); Author, "Lightning" (1988); Author, "Oddkins: A Fable for All Ages" (1988); Author, "Twilight Eyes," Expanded Version (1987); Author, "Watchers" (1987); Author, "Strangers" (1986); Author, "Twilight Eyes" (1985): Author, as Richard Paige, "The Door to December" (1985); Author, "Twilight" (1984); Author, "Darkfall" (1984); Author, "Phantoms" (1983); Author, "The House of Thunder" (1982); Author, "The Eyes of Darkness" (1981); Author, "Whispers" (1980); Author, "The Voice of the Night" (1980); Author, "The Mask" (1981); Author, "How to Write Best-Selling Fiction" (1981); Author (as Owen West), "The Funhouse" (1980); Author (as Leigh Nichols), "The Key to Midnight," Revised (1979); Author, "The Vision" (1977); Author, "The Face of Fear" (1977); Author, "Night Chills" (1976); Author (as David Axton), "Prison of Ice" (1975); Author, "The Wall of Masks" (1975); Author, "Nightmare Journey" (1975); Author (as Aaron Wolfe), "Invasion" (1975); Author (as John Hill), "The Long Sleep" (1975); Author, "Dragonfly" (1975); Author (as Anthony North), "Strike Deep" (1974); Author, "After the Last Race" (1974); Author, "Surrounded" (1974); Author, "The Haunted Earth" (1973); Author, "Demon Seed" (1973); Author (as Brian Coffey), "Blood Risk" (1973); Author (as K. R. Dwyer), "Shattered" (1973); Author, "A Werewolf Among Us" (1973); Author, "Hanging On" (1973); Author, "Starblood" (1972): Author, "Chase" (1972); Author, "The Flesh in the Furnace" (1972); Author, "A Darkness in My Soul" (1972); Author, "Time Thieves" (1972); Author, "Writing Popular Fiction" (1972); Author, "Warlock!" (1972); Author, "Children of the Storm" (1972); Author, "Dance with the Devil" (1972); Author, "The Dark of Summer" (1972); Author (as Deanna Dwyer), "Demon Child" (1971); Author, "Legacy of Terror" (1971); Author, "The Crimson Witch" (1971); Author, "Anti-Man" (1970); Author, "Beastchild" (1970); Author, "Dark of the Woods" (1970); Author, "Soft Come the Dragons" (1970); Author (as Leonard Chris), "Hung" (1970); Author, "Hell's Gate" (1970); Author, "The Underground Lifestyles Handbook" (1970); Author, "The Pig Society" (1970); Author, "The Dark Symphony" (1969); Author. "The Fall of the Dream Machine" (1969); Author, "Fear That Man" (1969); Author, "Star Quest" (1968); Author, Numerous Short Stories, Books

KOPEL, ROBERT FRANK, T: Anesthesiologist **I:** Medicine & Health Care **CN:** Newport Harbor Anesthesia Consultants Medical Group Inc. **DOB:** 03/02/1954 **PB:** Detroit **SC:** MI/USA **PT:** Howard Frank Kopel; Sylvia Sara (Grushko) Kopel **MS:** Mar-

ried **SPN:** Ann Elizabeth Snyder (05/04/1986) **CH:** Eric Frank; Laura Ellen **ED:** Doctor of Medicine, Universidad Autonoma De Guadalajara, Mexico (1982); Bachelor of Arts, University of California Los Angeles (1978) **CT:** Anesthesiology Recertification, American Board of Anesthesiology (2009); Critical Care Medicine, American Board of Anesthesiology (1995); Anesthesiology, American Board of Anesthesiology (1995) **C:** Assistant Clinical Professor, Anesthesiology, University of California Los Angeles Medical Center (1991-Present); Staff Anesthesiologist, Hoag Memorial Hospital Presbyterian, Newport Beach, CA (1991-Present); President, Newport Harbor Anesthesia Consultants Medical Group Inc. (1998-2000, 2013-2016); Chairperson, Department of Anesthesiology (1998-2000); Anesthesiology Resident, University of California Los Angeles School of Medicine (1988-1991); Critical Care Physician, Greater Southeast Community Hospital, Washington, DC (1987-1988); Critical Care Medicine Fellow, University of Virginia School of Medicine, Charlottesville, VA (1986-1988); Critical Care Physician, Prince George's Hospital Center, Cheverly, MD (1986); Emergency Room Physician, Prince George's Hospital Center, Cheverly, MD (1985-1986); Chief Medical Resident, Prince George's Hospital Center, Cheverly, MD (1985-1986); Sexual Assault Physician, Prince George's Hospital Center, Cheverly, MD (1984-1986); Internal Medicine Resident, Prince George's Hospital Center, Cheverly, MD (1983-1986); Rotating Resident, Prince George's Hospital Center, Cheverly, MD (1982-1983); Paramedic, University of California Los Angeles Emergency Medicine Center (1974-1978) **CR:** President, Prince George's Hospital Housestaff Association (1984-1985) **CIV:** Pediatric Advanced Life Support Provider, American Heart Association (2016-Present); Advanced Cardiac Life Support Instructor, American Heart Association (1986-Present); Basic Cardiac Life Support Instructor, American Heart Association (1977-Present) **CW:** Contributor, Articles, Professional Journals; Invited Lecturer, Scientific Meetings **AW:** Hoag Hospital Outstanding Performance Improvement Award, Chairman of the Department of Anesthesiology (1998-1999); Chief Medical Resident (1985-1986); Best Junior Internal Medicine Resident (1983-1984) **MEM:** Trustee, Zeta Beta Tau (1977-Present); Fellow, American College of Physicians; Fellow, American College Chest Physicians; Fellow, American Society Anesthesiologists; California Society of Anesthesiologists; Society of Critical Care Medicine; Phi Delta Epsilon Medical Fraternity; Phi Alpha Theta History Honors Society **AS:** Dr. Kopel attributes his success on his tolerance and ability to empathize with others. He is thankful, grateful and resilient in the face of life's challenges. **B/I:** Dr. Kopel became involved in his profession because his paternal grandfather, who graduated from medical school in 1912, served as an early role model and inspired him to pursue the field. **AV:** Traveling; Hiking; Reading **PA:** Republican **RE:** Jewish

KOPROSKI, ALEXANDER R., KNIGHT OF MALTA, T: Real Estate Company Executive **I:** Real Estate **CN:** Al Koproski Realty **DOB:** 04/06/1934 **PB:** Stamford **SC:** CT/USA **PT:** Alexander J. Koproski; Gladys J. (Kryger) Koproski **MS:** Married **SPN:** Patricia A. Velliquette **CH:** Lisa; Susan; Gregory; Beth **ED:** BS in Marketing and Finance, Trine University, Angola, IN (1959); Coursework, University of Connecticut (1952-1954) **CT:** Licensed Real Estate Broker, States of New York and Connecticut **C:** Owner, Chief Executive Officer, Commercial and Industrial Broker, Al Koproski Realty, Stamford (1973-Present); Commercial and Industrial Broker, S.H. Silberman, Inc., Stamford (1960-1973) **CR:** Founder, American Center of Polish Culture Inc., Washington, DC (1990-2010);

Coastal Management Advisory Committee **CIV:** Trustee, Kosciuszko Foundation, New York, NY (2010-Present); Member, South End Revitalization Committee, Stamford, CT (1996-Present); Board Director, American Center Polish Culture, Incorporated, Washington DC (1990-2010); Board Director, Polish Slavic Information Center, Stamford, CT (1975-2010); 100th Anniversary Committee, Holy Name of Jesus Catholic Church, Stamford, CT (2002-2003); Grand Marshal, New York City Pulaski Parade, Stamford, CT (2000); Poles for Bush (2000); National Vice President, Polish National Youth Baseball Foundation (1997); Polish Studies Advisory Committee, Central Connecticut State University (1994); Co-Chairman, National Council, Kosciuszko Foundation; Trustee, Holy Name Jesus Christ of Church; Chairman, Kosciuszko New York, NY; Member Committee, Dedication of Pope John Paul II Statue, Stamford; Chairman, Founder, Little League, Dzialdowo, Poland; Treasurer, Fundraiser, American Center Polish Culture, Washington; Past Member, Stamford C.E.T.A. Manpower Program; Past Member, Mayor's South End Advisory Committee; Past Member, Polish American Affairs Council; Past Member, Resource Recovery Task Force; Past Member, Stamford Bicentennial Committee; Past Chairman, Stamford Pulaski Memorial Committee, Hartford; Past Chairman, Kosciuszko Park Memorial Committee; Past President, Holy Name Home and School Association; Past Chairman, Poles for Ford Committee; Lay Advisory Board, Holy Name of Jesus Catholic Church, Stamford; Past Chairman, 75th Annual Yearbook, Holy Name of Jesus Catholic Church, Stamford; Chairman, Board Director, American Center Polish Culture, Incorporated; Past Board Director, Polish American Central Committee Stamford; Past Board Director, Polish American Congress of Connecticut **MIL:** U.S. Army (1955-1957) **AW:** Chairman, Holy Name Church, Garden of Peace and Prayer (2009-2019); Honorary Award, Stamford Knights Of Columbus Council (2013); Medal, President of Poland (2012); Honorary Award, Polish Government (2012); Recipient, Award, Stamford Historical Society (2011); Honorary Award, Connecticut General Assembly Citation (2009); Official Citation Award, State Connecticut General Assembly (2009); Civic Achievement Award, Polish American Historical Association (2008); REAPS Award (2001); Urzad Kultury Fizcznej i Sportu Award, Government of Poland (2001); Polish Government Medal (2001); Excellence Award, Institute for Religious Education and Pastoral Studies, Sacred Heart University (2001); Ellis Island Medal of Honor (1998); Krzyzem Kawwalerskim Orderu Zaslugi Rzeczypospolitej Polskeij Medal, Government of Poland (1994); Layman of the Year, Stamford Kiwanis Club (1979); Citizen of Year, Polish American World, New York City (1978) **MEM:** Historian, President, Polish American Cultural Society (2002-President); Chairman, Kosciuszko Ball, New York City (2011); Board of Directors, Stamford Old Timers Athletic Association (2010); President, Stamford Old Timers Athletic Association (2007); Vice President, Stamford Old Timers Athletic Association (2005); President, Chief Executive Officer (1982); President, St. Davids Bluff Homeowners Association; Past President, Oceanview Beach and Tennis Club; Polish American Business and Professional Club; Exchange Club; National Fundraising Chairman, Washington Project, American Council Polish Cultural Club; American Association Military Order of Malta; Stamford Board Realtors; Honorary Member, Stamford Historical Society **MH:** Albert Nelson Marquis Lifetime Achievement Award **AS:** Mr. Koproski attributes his success to hard work. **B/I:** Mr. Koproski became involved in his profession because his father was a policeman who wanted him to be a doctor. He failed out of

three schools, and then went into the Army. He went to business school through the GI Bill. He worked in New York for three months as a commuter. An opportunity came up that his father had told him about, which is how he got into the real estate business. When he got out of college, he was one of the youngest men in the field and has since been in it for 60 years. He has been a commission man all of his life. A friend of his told him to go into insurance; he went to get his license and asked himself if he really wanted to go knocking on doors saying, "God forbid you pass away" or something like that, and this was NY Life, so he called the guy up and said, "This is not for me." However, he made a deal two weeks later and, as they say, the rest is history. **PA:** Republican **RE:** Roman Catholic

KORDESTANI, OMID R., T: Executive Chairman **I:** Internet **CN:** Twitter, Inc. **PB:** Tehran **SC:** Iran **MS:** Married **SPN:** Gisel Hissock (2011); Bita Daryabari (1991, Divorced 2009) **CH:** Four Children **ED:** MBA, Stanford Graduate School of Business (1991); BSEE, San Jose State University (1984) **C:** Executive Chairman, Twitter, Inc. (2015-Present); President, Global Sales Operations and Business Development, Chief Business Officer, Google, Inc., Mountain View, CA (2014-2015); Senior Advisor, Google, Inc. (2009-2014); Senior Vice President, Global Sales and Business Development, Google, Inc. (2006-2009); Senior Vice President, Worldwide Sales and Field Operations, Google, Inc., Mountain View, CA (1999-2006); Vice President, Business Development and Sales, Netscape (Now Verizon Media) (1995-1999); Director, Product Management, 3DO Co. (1993-1995); With, Business Development, GO Corp. (1991-1993); Product Marketing Manager, Hewlett Packard Company (Now Hewlett Packard Enterprise Development LP) (1984-1989) **CR:** Member, Board of Directors, Spotify AB (2014); Board of Directors, Vodafone Group Public Ltd. Co. (2013-2014) **AW:** Named One of the Forbes 400: Richest Americans (2006-Present); Named Persian Person of the Year, Persian Awards (2007); Named One of the 100 Most Influential People in the World, TIME Magazine (2006)

KOREN, EDWARD FRANZ JR., T: Chairperson Emeritus **I:** Law and Legal Services **CN:** Holland & Knight **DOB:** 08/06/1946 **PB:** Eustis **SC:** FL/USA **PT:** Edward Franz Koren Sr.; Frances (Boyd) Koren **MS:** Married **SPN:** Louise Poole (6/19/1970) **CH:** Daniel Edward; Susan Louise Hines **ED:** Doctor of Jurisprudence, Levin College of Law, University of Florida, with High Honors (1974); Bachelor of Science in Business Administration in Accounting, University of Florida (1971) **CT:** Florida Board Certified Wills, Trusts and Estates Lawyer; National Association of Estate Planners & Councils-Accredited Estate Planner **C:** Chair Emeritus, Holland & Knight (2016-Present); Chair, Private Wealth Services Department, Holland & Knight (2004-2016); Partner, Holland & Knight, Tampa, FL (1980-2016); Chairman, Trusts and Estates Department, Holland & Knight (1983-2004); Associate, Holland & Knight, Lakeland, FL (1975-1979); Instructor, University of Florida, Gainesville, FL (1974-1975) **CR:** Adjunct Professor, Graduate Estate Planning Progressive, University of Miami Law School (2000); Adjunct Professor, Graduate Tax Progressive, University of Florida, Gainesville, FL (1996); Speaker in Field **CIV:** Trustee, Treasurer, Community Foundation of Tampa Bay (2019) **MIL:** Captain, U.S. Army (1971-1972) **CW:** Author, "Estate and Personal Financial Planning, A Five-Volume Treatise," Thomson-West (1988-Present); Author, "Personal Planning Under the Tax Cuts and Jobs Act - Parts One and Two," Estate and Personal Financial Planning, Thomson-West (2018); Author, "Proposed Treasury

Regulations Would Severely Limit Valuation Discounts," Holland & Knight Alert (2016); Author, "U.S. Supreme Court Strikes Down State Laws Banning Same-Sex Marriage," Holland & Knight Alert (2015); Author, "Revenue Ruling Confirms that IRS Will Recognize Same-Sex Marriages, But Not Civil Unions or Registered Domestic Partnerships," Holland & Knight Alert (2013); Author, "United States v. Windsor: A New Direction in Planning for Same-Sex Couples," Holland & Knight Alert (2013); Author, "The American Taxpayer Relief Act of 2012: What It Means for You," Holland & Knight Alert (2013); Co-Author, "Principal & Income Act Updated," ActionLine (2013); Author, "Estate Planning in 2011 and 2012: Opening the Window of Opportunity," Daily Tax Report (2011); Author, "Important Estate, Gift and Generation-Skipping Provisions of the Tax Relief Act: Several December 31, 2010 Deadlines to Consider," Holland & Knight Alert (2010); Author, "Why is succession planning for family business so difficult?," Worth Magazine (2010); Author, "Formula Clauses: Hedging Value And Legislative Risks," Tax Notes (2010); Author, "Post-Mortem Access To Funds From Closely Held Business Interests," The Practical Tax Lawyer (2009); Author, "Select Task Force Issues Extensive Report on Transfer Tax Reform," Holland & Knight Newsletter (2005); Author, "Holland & Knight Announces Creation of Private Wealth Services Section," Holland & Knight Newsletter (2003); Author, "Estate and Elder Law Advisor" (2000); Author, "Estate and Personal Financial Planning" (2000); Author, "Florida Wills & Trusts" (1999) **AW:** Chambers High Net Worth Guide, Private Wealth Law, Eastern Region, Florida (2016-2019); Named, Florida Super Lawyers (2006-2019); Listed, Best Lawyers in America (1987-2019); Listed, Tax Estate Planning, Wealth Management: Eastern Region, Chambers USA – America's Leading Business Lawyers Guide (2007-2016); Listed, Private Client, Who's Who Legal 100 (2015); Trusts and Estates Lawyer of the Year, Tampa Litigation, Best Lawyers in America (2013); Holland & Knight's Chesterfield Smith Award (2012); Inductee, National Association of Estate Planners and Counsels Hall of Fame (2010); Distinguished Accredited Estate Planner, National Association of Estate Planners and Counsels (2010); Named, Top 100 Attorney, Worth Magazine (2009); Named, Top 100 Attorney, Worth Magazine (2005-2006); Gerald T. Hart Outstanding Tax Attorney, Florida Bar (2002-2003); Robert C. Scott Memorial Award, Real Property and Trust Law Section, Florida Bar (1991); Named, Florida Legal Elite, Florida Trend; A/V Preeminent Rating, Martindale-Hubbell **MEM:** Chairperson, Principal and Income Committee, Florida Bar (2000-Present); National Conference of Attorneys and Corporate Fiduciaries (1999-Present); Chairperson, Real Property, Probate and Trust Law Section, American Bar Association (2004-2005); Chairperson, Tax Section, Florida Bar (1990-1991); Chairperson, Real Property, Probate and Trust Law Section, Florida Bar (1988-1989); Chairperson, Real Property, Trust & Estate Law Section, American Bar Association; Past Chairperson, Regent, Estate and Gift Tax Committee, American College of Trust and Estate Counsel; Fellow, American College of Tax Counsel; Tampa Bay Leadership Counsel, Community Foundation; Fellow, American Bar Foundation; American Law Institute; Tampa Bay Estate Planning Council **BAR:** U.S. Court of Claims (1986); U.S. Tax Court (1985); U.S. Court of Appeals for the 11th Circuit (1981); Supreme Court of the United States (1980); United States District Court for the Middle District of Florida (1977); State of Florida (1975) **AS:** Mr. Koren attributes his success to his intense focus on his practice, strong leadership skills and ability to work with people. **B/I:** Mr. Koren became involved in his profession due to the influence of his father, who was a CPA. Despite initially dabbling in engineering, he decided to follow his father's example and become an accountant. However, he eventually pivoted toward legal service and estate planning. **PA:** Republican **RE:** Presbyterian

KORNBERG, ROGER DAVID, PHD, T: Professor in Medicine; Biochemist **I:** Sciences **CN:** Stanford University **DOB:** 04/24/1947 **PB:** St Louis **SC:** MO/USA **PT:** Arthur Kornberg; Sylvy Ruth (Levy) Kornberg **MS:** Married **SPN:** Yahli Deborah Lorch (09/18/1984) **CH:** Guy; Maya; Gil **ED:** PhD in Chemistry, Stanford University, CA (1972); BS in Chemistry, Harvard University, Cambridge, MA (1967) **C:** Winzer Professor of Structural Biology, Stanford University School of Medicine, Stanford Medicine (1978-Present); Chairman, Department of Structural Biology, Stanford University School of Medicine, Stanford Medicine (1984-1992); Assistant Professor, Biological Chemistry, Harvard Medical School (1976-1977); Member, Scientific Staff, MRC Laboratory of Molecular Biology, Cambridge, England, United Kingdom (1974-1975); Junior Fellow, MRC Laboratory of Molecular Biology (1973-1974); Postdoctoral Fellow, MRC Laboratory of Molecular Biology, Cambridge, England, United Kingdom (1972-1973) **CR:** Co-chairman, Skolkovo Science and Technical Council, Skolkovo Institute of Science and Technology (Skoltech) (2010-Present) **CW:** Contributor, Articles to Professional Journals **AW:** Louisa Gross Horwitz Prize, Columbia University (2006); Nobel Prize in Chemistry (2006); Dickson Prize in Medicine, University of Pittsburgh (2006); GM Cancer Research Award (2005); Massry Prize (2003); Pasarow Award in Cancer Research, Robert J. And Claire Pasarow Foundation (2003); Merck Award, American Society for Biochemistry and Molecular Biology (2002); Welch Foundation Award in Chemistry, The Welch Foundation (2001); Hoppe-Seyler Award, Society for Biochemistry and Molecular Biology, Germany (2001); Gairdner Foundation International Award (2000); Harvey Prize, Technion-Israel Institute of Technology (1997); CIBA-Drew Award (1990); Passano Award (1982); Eli Lilly Award in Biological Chemistry (1981) **MEM:** Foreign Member, The Royal Society; National Academy of Sciences; Foreign Associate, European Molecular Biology Organization (EMBO); American Academy of Arts & Sciences; Honorary Member, The Japanese Biochemistry Society

KOSHY, ELIZABETH, "LIZA" SHAILA, T: Actress, Television Host, Comedian, YouTuber **I:** Media & Entertainment **DOB:** 03/31/1996 **PB:** Houston **SC:** TX/USA **PT:** Jose Koshy; Jean Carol (Hertzler) Koshy **MS:** Single **ED:** Coursework, University of Houston, Houston, TX (2014-2015); Diploma, Lamar High School, Houston, TX (2014) **C:** YouTuber, YouTube (2016-Present); Co-Producer, "Liza on Demand," YouTube Premium (2018-Present); Comedian, Vine (2013-2017) **CIV:** Collaborator, The Giving Keys; Co-Chairperson, When We All Vote **CW:** Actress, Music Video, "Woke Up Late" (2019); Contestant, "To Tell the Truth" (2019); Host, TV Series, "Double Dare" (2018-2019); Host, "Total Request Live," MTV (2017-2019); Host, Golden Globe Awards (2017); Actress, "Escape the Night" (2017); Guest Appearance, "Ellen's Show Me More Show" (2017); Actress, "Freakish" (2016-2017); Actress, "Making a Scene with James Franco" (2016); Actress, "Jingle Ballin" (2016); Actress, "Boo! A Madea Halloween" (2016); Promoter, MTV Movie Awards (2016); Actress, "FML" (2016); Host, "Every Single Step" (2015-2016) **AW:** Listee, Forbes 30 Under 30 Hollywood & Entertainment List (2019); Listee, 25 Most Influential People on the Internet, Time Magazine (2019); Listee, 100 Next List, Time Magazine (2019); Nominee, Social

Star, People's Choice Awards (2019); Nominee, Favorite TV Host, Kids' Choice Awards (2019); Acting in a Comedy: Liza on Demand, Streamy Awards (2018); Comedy Series: Liza on Demand, Streamy Awards (2018); Nominee, Creator of the Year, Streamy Awards (2018); Choice YouTuber, Teen Choice Awards (2018); Choice Comedy Web Star, Teen Choice Awards (2018); Choice Female Web Star, Teen Choice Awards (2018); Nominee, Creator of the Decade, 10th Shorty Awards (2018); Favorite Funny YouTube Creator, Kids' Choice Awards (2018); Nominee, Editing, Streamy Awards (2017); Comedy, Streamy Awards (2017); Nominee, Creator of the Year, Streamy Awards (2017); Nominee, YouTuber of the Year, Shorty Awards (2017); Nominee, Choice YouTuber, Teen Choice Awards (2017); Nominee, Choice Comedy Web Star, Teen Choice Awards (2017); Choice Female Web Star (2017); Nominee, Favorite Social Media Star, People's Choice Award (2017); Listee, 15 Rising Crossover Stars, The Hollywood Reporter (2017); Listee, The Seven Female Comedians You Need to Know, Teen Vogue (2016); Breakout Creator, Streamy Awards (2016)

KOTB, HODA, T: News Correspondent; Television Personality **I:** Media & Entertainment **CN:** NBC **DOB:** 08/09/1964 **PB:** Norman **SC:** OK/USA **PT:** Abdel Kader Kotb; Sameha Kotb **MS:** Divorced **SPN:** Burzis Kanga (2005, Divorced 2008) **CH:** Haley Joy (Adopted); Hope Catherine (Adopted) **ED:** BA in Broadcast Journalism, Virginia Polytechnic Institute and State University (1986) **C:** Co-anchor with Savannah Guthrie, "Today," NBC (2018-Present); Correspondent, "Dateline NBC," New York, NY (1998-Present); Co-host with Kathie Lee, Fourth Hour Segment, "Today Show," NBC (2007-2019); Host, Syndicated Show, "Your Total Health," NBC (2004-2008); Anchor, Reporter, WWL-TV, New Orleans, LA (1992-1998); Weekend Anchor, Reporter, WINK-TV, Fort Myers, FL (1989-1991); Morning Anchor, General Assignment Reporter, WQAD-TV, Moline, IL (1988-1989); News Assistant, CBS News, Cairo, Egypt (1986); Anchor, WXVT-TV, Greenville, MS (1986) **CIV:** Board of Directors, Virginia Tech Alumni Association (2010-2012) **CW:** Author, "You are My Happy" (2019); Author, "I Really Needed This Today" (2019); Author, "Where We Belong: Journeys That Show Us the Way" (2016); Author, "Where They Belong: The Best Decisions People Almost Never Made" (2016); Author, "Ten Years Later: Six People Who Faced Adversity and Transformed Their Lives" (2013); Author, "Hoda: How I Survived War Zones, Bad Hair, Cancer and Kathie Lee" (2010) **AW:** Emmy Award for Outstanding Informative Talk Show, Academy of Television Arts & Sciences (2019); Webby Award (2015); Emmy Awards for Outstanding Morning Program, Academy of Television Arts & Sciences (2010, 2011, 2012); Gracie Award, Alliance Women in Media (2003, 2008); Alfred I. duPont-Columbia Award, Columbia University (2008); George Foster Peabody Award (2006); Headliner Award (2002); Edward R. Murrow Award, Radio Television Digital News Association (2002) **MEM:** Delta Delta Delta Fraternity

KOTCH, MARY, T: Global Chief Information Officer **I:** Technology **CN:** Aspen Insurance/Apollo Group **MS:** Married **CH:** Two Children **ED:** Master of Arts in Law, Temple University, Philadelphia, PA (1995); Bachelor of Science, Pennsylvania State University, University Park, PA (1992) **C:** Global Chief Information Officer, Apollo/Aspen Insurance, Global (2019-Present); Global Executive Vice President, Global Chief Information Officer, Validus Group/American International Group (2015-2019); Chief Information Officer, American International Group (2012-2015); Chief Technology Officer,

American International Group (2012-2015); Vice President of Technology, MetLife Investments, New York (2007-2012); Global Director, BioVail Pharmaceuticals (2004-2007); Global Director, Campbell Soup (2000-2004); Senior Principle Consultant, EDS (1993-2000) **CR:** Adjunct Professor, Pennsylvania State University, Muhlenberg College, Lehigh Carbon Community College, Pennsylvania (1993-2003); Advisory Board Member, Pillar Tech, RequirementOne, Aquiline Technology Investment Fund, Pharmaceutical IMPACC, ACORD Framework, and Behavioral Health Committee for Informatics **CIV:** Independent Board Member, Datacubes Inc. (2019-Present); Member, Advisory Board, Smartinsure (2018); Advisory Board Member, RequirementOne (2015-2016); Dress For Success; Girls Who Code; STEM & I-STEM Program; St. Joseph's University School of Insurance & Risk Management **CW:** Featured, Waters Technology Magazine and Executive Profile Magazine **AW:** Diversity & Inclusion Award, American International Group; Top 50 Women in Technology; 30 Most Influential Women in Business **AS:** Ms. Kotch attributes much of her success to her mother. Her mother initially thought that she would become a nurse but Ms. Kotch had plans of her own. When her mother found out about her passion for technology, she offered encouragement and support for her decision. **B/I:** Ms. Kotch became involved in her profession because her father owned a small service shop for cars, where she noticed a lack of usage for modern technology, which created inefficiencies. She found a way to help him create a simple database to collect information and keep track of important things. Eventually, Ms. Kotch attended Penn State University and Temple University, where she fell in love with technology and began her career as a consultant. She was able to travel around the world and work with major corporations, for which she transformed their business communications and distribution models. **AV:** Soccer coach; Mountain biking; Jeep riding; Mudding

KOUDELKA, GEORGE, T: Retired Music Educator **I:** Education/Educational Services **DOB:** 02/27/1945 **PB:** Hallettsville **SC:** TX/USA **PT:** John William Koudelka; Hilda Barbara (Stavinoha) Koudelka **ED:** MEd, Prairie View A&M University (1972); Bachelor of Music Education, Southwest Texas State University (1968) **CT:** Certified Teacher, Music and Band, Texas **C:** Retired (1998); Director, Bands and Music, Moulton Independent School District (1982-1998); Director, Bands and Music, Flatonia Independent School District (1969-1982); Instructor of Percussion and Music, Southwest Texas State University (1967-1969) **CR:** Lecturer, Czech Music Symposium, University of Texas (2000); Lecturer, U.S. Presidents, Texas Polka Music History **CIV:** Donnie Wavra Orchestra (1972-1994, 2003-Present); Knights of Dixie Orchestra, Sugar Land, TX (1996-2005); Gil Baca Orchestra (1997-2003); President, Parent-Teacher Association (1972-1973) **CW:** Contributing Author, "A Passion for Polka" (1992); Contributing Author, Church Cookbook (1985) **AW:** Flatonia Citizen of the Year (2000) **MEM:** Grand Knight, Knights of Columbus (1971-1973); Texas Music Education Association; Music Education National Conference **MH:** Albert Nelson Marquis Lifetime Achievement Award; Marquis Who's Who Top Professional **B/I:** As a young child, Mr. Koudelka was exposed to dance bands. His parents were avid dancers, oftentimes bringing him to dances and picnics. He watched these bands, which inspired him to play the drums. He played his first job when he was 10 years old, and, one year later, he went full time with a Country Polk Band. He started with the drums and went on to learn 15 other instruments. **AV:** Collecting records, stamps, old books and comic books

KOUDOU, AHILE NICOLAS, T: Professor of Business Administration **I:** Education/Educational Services **CN:** Nicolas Koudou **DOB:** 01/01/1958 **PB:** Doukouyo **SC:** Ivory Coast **PT:** Zaza Digbeu Koudou; Marceline Deh Koessehi-Koudou **MS:** Married **SPN:** Laurence Toilehi-Koudou **CH:** Pacome Euloge Koudou; Odio Sandrine Koudou; Sika Bassou Koudou; Nade SD Koudou; Nainon Rosa Koudou; Nicolas Ahile Koudou; Nicolord Ligba Koudou **ED:** Doctoral Coursework, Louisiana State University (1995-1998) **C:** Initiator, Global Executive MBA Programs (2013); Leader, MBA Program (2012); Reviewer, MBA Program, Accreditation Council for Business Schools and Programs **CR:** Associate Editor, African Journal of Business and Management; Co-founder, American University of the Ivory Coast **CW:** Contributor, Several National and International Conference Presentations; Contributor, Numerous Refereed Full-Length Articles **AW:** President's Award for Teaching Excellence (2015); Fulbright Research Award (2011); MBA Distinguished Professor Award (2009); Outstanding Faculty Award (2008); Fulbright Scholar, University d'Abomey-Calavy, Cotonou, Bénin (2004-2005); National Recognition as Who's Who Among America's Teachers (2002); National Recognition as Who's Who Among America's Teachers (2000); National Recognition as Who's Who Among America's Teachers (1996); Gamma Sigma Delta (1996) **MEM:** Academy of World Business, Marketing and Management Development Conference; International Academy of African Business and Development Conference; International Academy of Business and Public Affairs Discipline Conference; Parkville Rotary Club; Vice President, Board of Directors, IvoirEspoir; Planning Committee, St. Luke's Hospital Northland Board, Kansas City, MO; Louisiana State University Chapter of the Honor Society of Agriculture **AS:** Mr. Koudou attributes his success on hard work, courage, determination, drive, perseverance, and a strong desire to succeed. **RE:** Catholic

KOUFAX, SANDY, T: Professional Baseball Player (Retired) **I:** Athletics **DOB:** 12/30/1935 **PB:** Brooklyn **SC:** NY/USA **PT:** Jack Braun (Father); Evelyn (Litchenstein) Braun; Irving Koufax (Stepfather) **MS:** Married **SPN:** Jane Purucker Clarke (2010); Kimberly Francis (1985, Divorced 1998); Anne Koufax (1969, Divorced 1982) **ED:** Coursework, University of Cincinnati **C:** Special Advisor, Los Angeles Dodgers, Major League Baseball (2013); Minor League Pitching Instructor, Los Angeles Dodgers (1979-1990); Broadcaster, NBC Sports (1966-1973); Pitcher, Los Angeles Dodgers, Major League Baseball (1958-1966); Pitcher, Brooklyn Dodgers, Major League Baseball (1955-1957) **CIV:** Member, Advisory Board, Baseball Assistance Team **AW:** Named, One of the Four Best Living Players, Major League Baseball Fans (2015); Named, One of Baseball's 100 Greatest Players, Sporting News (1999); Inductee, Baseball Hall of Fame (1972); Hutch Award (1966); Named, National League Pitcher of the Year, Sporting News (1963-1966); Cy Young Award (1963, 1965, 1966); Winner, National League Triple Crown for Pitchers (1963, 1965, 1966); Inductee, National League All-Star Team (1961-1966); Babe Ruth Award, Major League Baseball (1963, 1965); Named, World Series MVP (1963, 1965); Named, Major League Player of the Year (1963, 1965); Winner, Los Angeles Dodgers, World Series Championships (1959, 1963, 1965); Named, National League MVP (1963)

KOUM, JAN BORIS, T: CO-Founder, Chief Executive Officer, Entrepreneur, Computer Engineer **I:** Technology **CN:** WhatsApp Inc. **DOB:** 02/24/1976 **SC:** Kiev/Ukraine **ED:** Coursework, San Jose University (1994-1997) **C:** Co-Founder, Chief Executive Officer, WhatsApp Inc., Santa Clara, CA (2009-Present); Infrastructure Engineer, Yahoo! Inc., Sunnyvale, CA (1997-2007); Security Tester, Ernst & Young **CR:** Board of Directors, Facebook, Inc. (2014-Present) **CIV:** Donor, The FreeBSD Foundation (2014, 2016); Donor, Silicon Valley Community Foundation (2014) **AW:** Listee, Forbes 400: Richest Americans, Forbes Magazine (2014-Present); Listee, 40 Under 40, Fortune Magazine (2014) **RE:** Jewish

KRAFKA, MARY BAIRD JD, T: Lawyer **I:** Law and Legal Services **DOB:** 01/04/1942 **PB:** Ottumwa **SC:** IA/USA **PT:** Glenn Leroy; Alice Erna (Krebill) Baird **MS:** Married **SPN:** Jerry Lee Krafka (10/14/1962) **CH:** Lisa Krafka Piper; Gregory D.; Jeffrey A.; Amy Krafka Pittman **ED:** Doctor of Jurisprudence, University of Iowa (1993); Bachelor of Arts in English and Human Relations, William Penn College, Oskaloosa, IA (1990) **C:** Private Practice, Ottumwa, IA (1994-Present); Volunteer Lawyer, Legal Services Corporation, Ottumwa, IA (1993-1994) **MEM:** Iowa Chapter, PEO Sisterhood (1973); American Association of University Women; Iowa Bar Association; Wapello County Bar Association **BAR:** Iowa (1993) **MH:** Albert Nelson Marquis Lifetime Achievement Award; Marquis Who's Who Top Professional **B/I:** Ms. Krafka became involved in her profession after working in a factory for several years. Following the birth of her children, she reconnected with several old friends, one of whom encouraged her to write a novel in which the characters would have to leverage their professional knowledge to survive on a deserted island. Deciding to insert herself as a character, she resolved that she would represent the legal profession, after which she resolved to live this experience, rather than merely write about it. **AV:** Reading; Running; People **RE:** Lutheran

KRAFT, ROBERT KENNETH, T: Principal Owner, Chairman, Chief Executive Officer; Professional Sports Team Executive **I:** Athletics **CN:** The Kraft Group, New England Patriots **DOB:** 07/05/1941 **PB:** Brookline **SC:** MA/USA **PT:** Harry Kraft; Sarah Bryna (Webber) Kraft **MS:** Divorced **SPN:** Myra (Hiatt) Kraft (1963, Deceased 2011) **CH:** Jonathan; Daniel; Joshua; David **ED:** Honorary Doctorate, Yeshiva University (2015); MBA, Harvard University (1965); BA, Columbia University, New York, NY **C:** Owner, Boston Uprising (2017-Present); Owner, New England Revolution, Major League Soccer (MLS) (1996-Present); Principal Owner, Chairman, Chief Executive Officer, New England Patriots, National Football League (NFL) (1994-Present); Owner, San Jose Clash (Now San Jose Earthquakes), Major League Soccer (MLS) (1998-2000); President, New England TV Corporation (1986-1991); Founder, International Forest Products (1972); Chairman, Carmel Container Systems, Ltd., Israel; President, International Forest Products Group Companies; With, Rand-Whitney Group, Inc., Worcester, MA; Chairman, Chestnut Hill Management; Owner, Gillette Stadium; Owner, Foxboro Stadium, Foxborough, MA **CR:** Board of Directors, Viacom Inc. (2006-Present); Chairman, Finance Committee, National Football League (NFL) (1998-Present); Board of Directors, Federal Reserve Bank of Boston **CIV:** Board of Overseers, Boston Symphony Orchestra and Museum of Sciences, Boston, MA; Board of Trustees, Boston College; Trustee Emeritus, Columbia University; Member, Executive Committee, Dana-Farber Cancer Institute **AW:** Named One of the Forbes 400:

Richest Americans, Forbes Magazine (2006-Present); Genesis Prize (2019); Carnegie Hall Medal of Excellence Award (2013); George S. Halas Courage Award (2012); Named One of the 50 Most Influential People in Sports Business, Street & Smith's SportsBusiness Journal (2007-2009); Named One of the Most Influential People in the World of Sports, Business Week (Now Bloomberg Businessweek) (2007, 2008); Theodore Roosevelt Award, NAACP (2006); Alexander Hamilton Award, Columbia University (2004); John Jay Award, Columbia University (1987); Six-Time Super Bowl Champion (as Owner of New England Patriots) **MEM:** American Academy of Arts & Sciences **AV:** Playing golf; Playing tennis **RE:** Jewish

KRAMER, CARL EDWARD, PHD, T: Historian, Urban Planner **I:** Education/Educational Services **CN:** Kramer Associates, Inc. **DOB:** 05/22/1946 **PB:** New Albany **SC:** IN/USA **PT:** Douglas Manuel Kramer; Jane Anastasia (Markert) Kramer Pitman **MS:** Married **SPN:** Mary Elizabeth Kagin (06/16/1990) **ED:** PhD, University of Toledo (1980); MS, University of Louisville (1972); MA, Roosevelt University, Chicago, IL (1970); BA, Anderson University, Indiana (1968) **C:** Vice President, Kramer Associates, Inc. (1997-Present); Adjunct Lecturer, Adjunct Assistant Professor of History, Indiana University Southeast, New Albany, IN (1978-2012); Adjunct Lecturer, University of Louisville School Urban Policy and Department of History (1976-1991); Executive Director, Clark County Planning, Zoning and Building Commission, Jeffersonville, IN (1991-1997);President, Kentuckiana Historical Services, Jeffersonville, IN (1981-1997); Architectural Historian, Louisville Historical Landmarks & Preservation Districts Commission (1977-1979); Research Planner, Louisville-Jefferson County Planning Commission (1971-1972); Population Analyst, U.S. Bureau Census, Jeffersonville, IN (1970-1971); Elementary Teacher Intern, Chicago Public Schools (1968-1970) **CR:** Member, Louisville-Jefferson County Planning Commission Cornerstone (2020); Ohio River Bridges Project Indiana Historic Preservation Advisory Team (2008-2016); Member, Louisville Mayor's Millennium Commission, Historic Preservation Committee (1999-2000); Chair, Southern Indiana Transit Advisory Group (1998-1999); Chair, Ohio River Major Investment Study Committee (1996-1997); Member, Operating Committee, Louisville-Jefferson County Planning Commission Cornerstone (1993-1997); Member, Transportation Technical Coordination Committee, Kentuckiana Regional Planning and Development Agency (1992-1997); Chair, Kentuckiana Regional Planning and Development Agency (1994, 1996); Member, Advisory Committee, Falls of Ohio Interpretive Center (1991-1994); Member, Education Committee, Historic Southern Indiana, Inc., Evansville, IN (1991-1993) **CIV:** Indiana Lewis and Clark Expedition Commission (2015-Present); Board of Directors, Clark County Museum (2009-Present); Board of Directors, Center for Cultural Resources at Indiana University Southeast (2008-2014); Chair, Center for Cultural Resources at Indiana University Southeast (2012-2013); Member, Council Advisory Board, Lincoln Heritage Council (1993-2009); Member, Board of Trustees, Historic Hoosier Hills Resource Conservation and Development, Inc. (2001-2005); Board of Directors, Falls of the Ohio Lewis and Clark Expedition Bicentennial Planning Committe (2002-2003); Assistant Governor, Rotary District 6580 (2001-2002); President, Rotary Club of Jeffersonville (1997-1998); Board of Trustees, Falls of the Ohio Lewis and Clark Expedition Bicentennial Planning Committee (1997-2003); Chairman, Clark County Chapter, American Red Cross (1994-1997); Board of Directors, Clark County

Chapter, American Red Cross (1991-1997); Secretary, Clark County Emergency Shelter (1987-1995); Vice Chairman, Clark County Chapter, American Red Cross (1992-1994); Assistant Council Commissioner, Lincoln Heritage Council (1993-1994); Member, Indiana State Service Council, American Red Cross (1992-1994); Board of Directors, Plymouth Community Renewal Center, Louisville, KY (1988-1994); Secretary, Board of Trustees, Methodist Evangelical Hospital Foundation Louisville, KY (1987-1994); Member, Executive Board, George Rogers Clark Council, Boy Scouts of America (1976-1992); Secretary, Leadership Southern Indiana Foundation (1987-1988); Program Chairman, Clark County Youth Shelter (1986-1988); Board of Directors, Leadership Southern Indiana Foundation (1984-1988); Board of Directors, Clark County Youth Shelter (1984-1988); President, Kentuckiana Association, United Church of Christ (1985-1986); Delegate, Indiana Governor's Conference on Small Business, Indianapolis (1984); Vice President, George Rogers Clark Council, Boy Scouts of America (1977-1978, 1981-1983); District Chair, George Rogers Clark Council, Boy Scouts of America (1979-1981) **CW:** Author, "Rivers of Time: A History of American Commercial Lines" (2015); Author, "Building on a Century of Commitment: A History of Whayne Supply Company" (2013); Editorial Advisory Board, Kentucky Historical Society (2010-2012); Author, "The Brandeis Century: Constant Values in Changing Times" (2008); Author, "This Place We Call Home: A History of Clark County, Indiana" (2007); Author, "It's Gooo-od: The History of the F. B. Purnell Sausage Company" (2005); Author, "The Corps of Discovery and the Falls of the Ohio" (2003); Author, "Visionaries, Adventurers, and Builders, Historical Highlights of the Falls of the Ohio" (2000); Author, "Sellersburg: A Century of Change" (1990); Co-editor, "Louisville's Olmstedian Legacy" (1988); Author, "Capital on the Kentucky: A 200-Year History of Frankfort and Franklin County" (1986); Author, "The Rieth-Riley Story,100 Years of Construction, 1916-2016"; Author, "Pride in the Past, Faith in the Future: A History of Michigan Livestock Exchange, 1922-1997"; Author, "Drovers, Dealers and Dreamers: 150 Years at Bourbon Stock Yards, 1834-1984"; Contributor, Articles and Book Reviews, Professional Journals and Reference Works **AW:** Captain Donald T. Wright Award for Maritime Journalism, Herman T. Pott National Inland Waterways Library (2019); Bales Humanitarian Award, American Red Cross (2018); Founders Award, Louisville Historical League (2018); Centurion Award, Order of Arrow (2015); Margaret Read Lifetime Volunteer Achievement Award, Clark County American Red Cross (2014); Sagamore of the Wabash, State of Indiana (2013); Dorothy Riker Hoosier Historian Award, Indiana Historical Society (2012); Cliff Dochterman Award, International Fellowship of Scouting Rotarians (2006); Silver Creek High School Outstanding Alumnus Award (2000); Rotary District 6580 Club President of the Year (1997-1998); W. Fred Hale Leadership Award, Clark County American Red Cross (1997); Certificate for Excellence in Writing, International Association Business Communicators (1985); Indiana University Southeast Outstanding Part-time Teacher Award (1983); Silver Beaver Award, Boy Scouts of America (1981); Kentucky Colonel, State of Kentucky (1978); District Award of Merit (1976); National Distinguished Service Award (1973); Vigil Honor (1964); Eagle Scout (1961) **MEM:** Board of Directors, Louisville Historical League (2016-Present); Board of Directors, Urban History Association (2011-2013); Best Dissertation in Urban History Committee, Urban History Association (2006); Historian, Indiana Planning Association (1996-2005); President, Louisville Agricultural Club (2004); Best Article in Urban History Committee, Urban History Association (2001); Francoise August de Montequin Prize Jury, Society of American City & Regional Planning History (1999); John W. Reps Prize Committee, Society of American City & Regional Planning History (1997); Otto Rothert Award Committee, Filson Historical Society (1991-1992); National Conference Local Publicity Committee, Organization of American Historians (1991); Publication Advisory Board, Filson Historical Society (1990-1993); President, Sunnyside Toastmasters (1990); Indiana Historical Society; Kentucky Historical Society; Historical Society of the Church of God, Anderson, IN; Phi Alpha Theta; Phi Kappa Phi; Alpha Chi; Pi Gamma Nu; Alpha Phi Gamma; Phi Eta Sigma; Alpha Phi Omega **MH:** Albert Nelson Marquis Lifetime Achievement Award **AS:** Dr. Kramer attributes his success to strong educational preparation, setting a goal to become a historian and writer, and working hard to overcome obstacles that appeared in the path to that goal. **B/I:** Dr. Kramer's father loved history and he encouraged his son to read about history. He did a lot reading at the library and his father would often quiz him on certain historical topics. Mr. Kramer soon came to love history. His interest in urban affairs and community development was sparked by his experiences in Chicago. Coming from a small company town, he became fascinated with urban living, politics, and transportation patterns. **AV:** Fishing; Travel **PA:** Democrat **RE:** United Church of Christ

KRAMER, REBECCA ANN, T: Artist **I:** Fine Art **CN:** Kramer Art **DOB:** 06/28/1953 **PB:** Adrian **SC:** MN/USA **PT:** Aloys Riesselman; Bette Riesselman **MS:** Divorced **ED:** MFA, University of Montana (1991); BS, SDSU (1977); AA, Minnesota West Community & Technical College (1972); BA, SDSU **C:** Artist; Sculptor; Medical Technologist **CR:** Arts Missoula, Neckergemund, Germany (1994); Curator, Missoula Cultural Exchange (1992-1994); Exhibition Curator, Greater Missoula Visual Artists Gallery Tours (1989-1994); Board Member, Women's Caucus for Art **CIV:** Vice President, Board of Directors, Bitterroot Homeowner's Association (1985-1992); News Editor, Missoula MS Healthy Active Lifestyle Support Group; Regional Vice President, Women's Caucus for Art; Exchange Coordinator, Friendship Force International **CW:** Exhibition, Art & History Museums Maitland (2004); Exhibition, Brewery Art Walk, L.A. Artcore (1999); Exhibition, Taos Gallery Association (1996, 1998); Exhibition, Eastern Washington University (1994); Exhibition, Alt Rathaus Museum (1994); Exhibition, Missoula Cultural Council (1994); Exhibition, Seattle Pacific Art Center, Seattle Pacific University (1993); Exhibition, Montana State University (1992); Exhibition, Ruggero Maggi (1992); Exhibition, Missoula Museum of Arts (1992-1993); Exhibition, Gallery of Visual Arts, School of Art, University of Montana (1991); Exhibition, Allister Gold Gallery (1991) **AW:** Senator Pat Williams/Fell-Oskins Grantee, University of Montana (1990) **MEM:** Vice President, Rocky Mountain Chapter, Women's Caucus for Arts (2002-2006); Member, National Board, Women's Caucus for Arts (2001-2006); Founder, Montana Chapter, Women's Caucus for Art (1994); Member, Steering Committee, Greater Missoula Visual Artists (1989-1991) **MH:** Albert Nelson Marquis Lifetime Achievement Award; Marquis Who's Who Top Professional **B/I:** Ms. Kramer became involved in her profession because she always wanted to paint. **AV:** Traveling; Making art; Reading; Cooking

KRAMER, RICHARD J., T: Chairman, President, Chief Executive Officer **I:** Manufacturing **CN:** The Goodyear Tire & Rubber Company **DOB:** 10/30/1963 **PB:** Cleveland **SC:** OH/USA **ED:** BS in Business Administration, John Carroll University (1986) **CT:** Certified Public Accountant **C:** Chairman, President, Chief Executive Officer, The Goodyear Tire & Rubber Company (2010-Present); President, Chief Executive Officer, The Goodyear Tire & Rubber Company (2010); Chief Operating Officer, The Goodyear Tire & Rubber Company (2009-2010); President, North American Tire, The Goodyear Tire & Rubber Company (2007-2009); Executive Vice President, Chief Financial Officer, The Goodyear Tire & Rubber Company (2004-2007); Senior Vice President of Strategic Planning and Restructuring, The Goodyear Tire & Rubber Company (2003-2004); Vice President of Finances, North American Tire, The Goodyear Tire & Rubber Company (2002-2003); Vice President of Corporate Finance, The Goodyear Tire & Rubber Company (2000-2003); With, PricewaterhouseCoopers (1987-2000); Partner, PricewaterhouseCoopers **CR:** Board of Directors, The Sherwin-Williams Company (2012-Present); The Goodyear Tire & Rubber Company (2010-Present)

KRANZ, PETER LEWIS, PHD, T: Professor **I:** Education/Educational Services **CN:** University of Texas Rio Grande Valley **PB:** Brooklyn **SC:** NY/USA **PT:** Rose Iranz; Ben Iranz **MS:** Single **CH:** Zoe Greenemeyer **ED:** Fellow, American Board of Examiners in Psychodrama, Sociometry and Group Psychotherapy (1991); PhD in Child Psychology, College of Agriculture and Applied Sciences, Utah State University (1969); Clinical Psychology Internship, Oklahoma Medical Center (1967-1968); Graduate, Psychology, Utah State University (1966-1967); Graduate, Psychology, Duquesne University, Pittsburgh, PA (1965-1966); Graduate, Merrill-Palmer Institute, Detroit, MI (1964-1965); MS in Psychology, College of Agriculture and Applied Sciences, Utah State University (1965); BA in Psychology, Grinnell College, Grinnell, IA (1963) **CT:** Psychology Licenses, Florida, Colorado, California, American Board of Examiners in Psychodrama, Sociometry and Group Psychotherapy **C:** Professor in Educational Psychology, University of Texas Rio Grande Valley (Formally University of Texas–Pan American), Edinburg, TX (2013-Present); Associate Professor in Educational Psychology, University of Texas Rio Grande Valley (Formally University of Texas–Pan American), Edinburg, TX (2007-Present); Assistant Professor in Educational Psychology, University of Texas Rio Grande Valley (Formally University of Texas–Pan American), Edinburg, TX (2002-2007); Director, Counseling Center, Northern Campus, Florida Atlantic University (2000-2002); Director of Counseling and Associate Adjunct Professor, School Services, Personnel and Psychology, Tennessee Tech University (1993-2000); Associate Professor, Director of Counseling Center, Eckerd College, St. Petersburg, FL (1988-1993); Associate Professor, Lock Haven University, Lock Haven, PA (1987-1988); Assistant Professor, Lock Haven University, Lock Haven, PA (1985-1987); Mental Health Work, Colorado (1983-1985); Associate Professor, University of North Florida, Jacksonville, FL (1962-1972); Psychologist, Mental Health Clinic, Bakersfield, CA **CR:** Speaker, Author, Contributor, More Than 90 Professional Presentations and Publications **CIV:** Santa Clause, Migrant Children (2018) **CW:** Subject, Book on her Race Relations Work, "An Arena of Truth Conflict in Black and White" by Terrance Clarke **AW:** Grinnell College Outstanding Alumni Award (2017); College of Education Distinguished Research Award, University of Texas Pan-American (2015); Utah State University Alumni Merit Award (2012); Winifred Overholser Prize Second Place (1980) **MEM:** American Psychological Association (APA); SEPA; Rocky Mountain Psychological Association;

Financial Planning Association **MH:** Albert Nelson Marquis Lifetime Achievement Award **AS:** Dr. Kranz attributes his success to being in the right place at the right time, with people who were supportive and willing to give him a chance to do what he has done. He was very fortunate at the University of North Florida to have a very progressive administration that would let him do what he did. Additionally, he attributes his success to growing up with a very supportive mother and father who valued education, and being blessed that folks trusted that he could perform at that level and give back the way he did and does. It is a combination of a lot of things; he feels family played a big part. **B/I:** Dr. Kranz became involved in his profession because his older brother went into medicine and psychology, which seemed interesting, so he decided to major in psychology and pursue the field. He didn't know when he selected it that it would be so rewarding.In addition, he became involved in teaching goes back with growing up in the family where the emphasis was giving back and trying to make the world a better place in general. His older brother was in medicine. Psychology sounded interesting, so he decided to major in that. However, he started in mental health and decided he wanted to teach and that was what transferred him into the teaching realm. **THT:** Dr. Kranz teaches in the counseling program, which is made up of graduate students who are looking forward to become either school counselors or mental health counselors. He teaches two graduate classes a semester, and is also responsible for doing research, professional presentations, and being involved in activities through the university serving on committees.

KRASINSKI, JOHN BURKE, T: Director, Actor **I:** Media & Entertainment **DOB:** 10/20/1979 **PB:** Boston **SC:** MA/USA **PT:** Ronald Krasinski; Mary Clare (Doyle) Krasinski **MS:** Married **SPN:** Emily Blunt (7/10/2010) **CH:** Hazel; Violet **ED:** Honorary DFA, Brown University (2019); BA in English Literature, Brown University, Providence, RI (2001); Graduate, National Theater Institute **C:** Script Intern, "Late Night with Conan O'Brien" **CW:** Actor, Executive Producer, "Jack Ryan" (2018-Present); Executive Producer, "Dream Corp, LLC" (2016-Present); Co-Creator, Executive Producer, Appearance, "Lip Sync Battle" (2015-Present); Actor, Director, Writer, Producer, "A Quiet Place Part II" (2020); Actor, Director, Writer, Executive Producer, "A Quiet Place" (2018); Voice Actor, "Next Gen" (2018); Narrator, "Born in China" (2017); Voice Actor, "Animal Crackers" (2017); Actor, "Detroit" (2017); Actor, "13 Hours: The Secret Soldiers of Benghazi" (2016); Executive Producer, "Manchester by the Sea" (2016); Actor, Director, Producer, "The Hollars" (2016); Guest Appearance, "Robot Chicken" (2016); Actor, Short Film, "Past Forward" (2016); Actor, "Aloha" (2015); Guest Appearance, "Bojack Horseman" (2014-2015); Voice Actor, "The Prophet" (2014); Voice Actor, "Monsters University" (2013); Guest Appearance, "Arrested Development" (2013); Voice Actor, "The Wind Rises" (2013); Actor, Producer, Director, "The Office" (2005-2013); Actor, "Nobody Walks" (2012); Actor, "Big Miracle" (2012); Guest Appearance, "30 Rock" (2012); Narrator, "Head Games" (2012); Actor, Writer, Producer, "Promised Land" (2012); Actor, "Something Borrowed" (2011); Cameo, "The Muppets" (2011); Actor, Director, Writer, Producer, "Brief Interviews with Hideous Men" (2009); Voice Actor, "Monsters vs. Aliens" (2009); Actor, "Away We Go" (2009); Actor, "It's Complicated" (2009); Actor, "Leatherheads" (2008); Actor, "Smiley Face" (2007); Voice Actor, "Shrek the Third" (2007); Actor, "License to Wed" (2007); Voice Actor, "Doogal" (2006); Actor, "A New Wave" (2006); Actor, "For Your Consideration" (2006); Actor, "The Holiday" (2006); Actor, "Dreamgirls" (2006); Guest Appearance, "American Dad!" (2006); Guest Appearance, "Without a Trace" (2005); Guest Appearance, "CSI: Crime Scene Investigation" (2005); Actor, "Duane Hopwood" (2005); Actor, "Jarhead" (2005); Actor, "Kinsey" (2004); Actor, "Taxi" (2004); Guest Appearance, "Law & Order: Criminal Intent" (2004); Guest Appearance, "Ed" (2003); Actor, Short Film, "Fighting Still Life" (2002); Actor, "Alma Mater" (2002); Cameo, "State and Main" (2000) **AW:** People's Voice for Video - Variety, "Notes on a Scene," Webby Awards (2019); Best Writing, "A Quiet Place," Saturn Awards (2019); Best Sci-Fi/Horror Movie, "A Quiet Place," Critics' Choice Awards (2019); People's Choice Award for Best Director, "A Quiet Place," IGN Awards (2018); Outstanding Variety or Game Show - (Series or Special), "Lip Sync Battle," NAACP Image Awards (2018); Vanguard Award for Career Achievement, Savannah College of Art and Design (2018); American Ingenuity Award - Visual Arts, "A Quiet Place," Smithsonian Institution (2018); Named, 100 Most Influential People of 2018, TIME 100 (2018); Best Original Screenplay, "A Quiet Place," Los Angeles Online Film Critics Society Awards (2018); Co-Recipient, Future Classic Award, Entertainment Weekly (2018); Vince Koehler Award, "A Quiet Place," Kansas City Film Critics Circle (2018); Best Ensemble, "Detroit," African American Film Critics Association (2017); Outstanding Debut Performance, "Dry Powder," Theatre World Awards (2016); Best Acting by an Ensemble, "It's Complicated," National Board of Review (2009); Future Classic Award, "The Office," TV Land Awards (2008); Outstanding Performance by an Ensemble in a Comedy Series, "The Office," Screen Actors Guild Awards (2007-2008); Ensemble of the Year, "The Office," Gold Derby Awards (2007); Best Ensemble in a Comedy Series, "The Office," Online Film and Television Association Awards (2007); Best Supporting Actor in a Comedy Series, "The Office," Online Film and Television Association Awards (2006-2007)

KRAVITZ, ZOË ISABELLA, T: Actress **I:** Media & Entertainment **DOB:** 12/01/1988 **PB:** Los Angeles **SC:** CA/USA **PT:** Lenny Kravitz; Lisa Bonet; Jason Momoa (Stepfather) **MS:** Married **SPN:** Karl Glusman (06/29/2019) **ED:** Diploma, Rudolf Steiner School, New York, NY (2007); Coursework, State University of New York at Purchase **CR:** Spokesmodel, Alexis Bittar (2015); Launched, Jewelry Line, Swarovski (2013); Spokesmodel, "Preppy Princess," Vera Wang (2011); Spokesmodel, Alexander Wang (2010); Spokesmodel, "Princess," Vera Wang (2009); Model, Jalouse, Venus Zine, Elle **CW:** Actress, "High Fidelity" (2020-Present); Actress, "Big Little Lies" (2017-2019); Voice Actress, "Spider-Man: Into the Spider-Verse" (2018); Guest Appearance, "Anti-Social Smokers Club" (2018); Guest Appearance, "Screwed" (2018); Actress, "Fantastic Beasts: The Crimes of Grindelwald" (2018); Actress, "Kin" (2018); Actress, "Rough Night" (2017); Guest Appearance, "Passionfruit" (2017); Musician, "Baby I'm Dyin'" (2017); Actress, "Gemini" (2017); Voice Actress, "The Lego Batman Movie" (2017); Cameo, "Fantastic Beasts and Where to Find Them" (2016); Guest Appearance, "Portlandia" (2016); Actress, "Adam Green's Aladdin" (2016); Actress, "Vincent N Roxxy" (2016); Musician, "Teardrop" (2016); Actress, "The Divergent Series: Allegiant" (2016); Actress, "Mad Max: Fury Road" (2015); Actress, "The Divergent Series: Insurgent" (2015); Actress, "Dope" (2015); Actress, "Good Kill" (2014); Actress, "The Road Within" (2014); Musician, "Calm Down" (2014); Musician, EP, "Lolawolf" (2014); Actress, "Pretend We're Kissing" (2014); Musician, "Summertime" (2014); Actress, "Divergent" (2014); Actress, "After Earth" (2013); Actress, "Treading Water" (2013); Actress, "Californication" (2011); Actress, "X-Men: First Class" (2011); Actress, "Yelling to the Sky" (2011); Actress, "It's Kind of a Funny Story" (2010); Actress, "Beware the Gonzo" (2010); Actress, "Twelve" (2010); Actress, "The Greatest" (2009); Actress, "Birds of America" (2008); Actress, "Assassination of a High School President" (2008); Actress, "The Brave One" (2007); Actress, "No Reservations" (2007) **AW:** Listee, Best Dressed Women, Net-a-Porter (2018)

KREIMER, HERBERT FREDERICK, T: Professor Emeritus **I:** Education/Educational Services **DOB:** 02/19/1936 **PB:** Cincinnati **SC:** OH/USA **PT:** Herbert Frederick Kreimer; Virginia Ann (Newstedt) Kreimer **MS:** Married **SPN:** Sarah Jane Klein (06/10/1961) **CH:** Caroline Louise; Herbert Frederick III **ED:** PhD, Yale University (1962); BS, Yale University, Summa Cum Laude (1958) **C:** Professor Emeritus, Florida State University (1995); Professor, Florida State University (1976-1995); Associate Professor, Florida State University (1965-1976); Visiting Professor, Northwestern University (1965-1966); Assistant Professor, Florida State University, Tallahassee (1962-1965) **CR:** Faculty Senate President, Florida State University (1982-1983, 1984-1985) **CIV:** Senior Warden, St. John's Episcopal Church (1984, 2008); Junior Warden, St. John's Episcopal Church (1979) **CW:** Contributor, Articles, Professional Journals **AW:** Grant, National Science Foundation (1965-1966, 1968-1973); Fellowship, National Science Foundation (1958-1962); Honorary Woodrow Wilson Foundation Fellowship (1958) **MEM:** Chapter Secretary, The Phi Beta Kappa Society (1988-1989); Chapter President, The Phi Beta Kappa Society (1982-1983) **MH:** Albert Nelson Marquis Lifetime Achievement Award **B/I:** Mr. Kreimer became involved in his profession because of his aptitude for the subject. **RE:** Episcopalian

KREITZER, LOIS M., T: Investor **I:** Financial Services **PT:** Franklin Maroney; Helen Katherine (Leyda) Maroney **MS:** Married **SPN:** William Emil Kreitzer (11/14/1962) **ED:** BS, Pennsylvania State University, University Park, PA (1955) **C:** Personal Investor, Pittsburgh, PA (1975-Present); Shareholder Activist, Pittsburgh, PA (1970-Present); Executrix of Estates, Pittsburgh, PA (1968-1982); Consultant, Pittsburgh, PA (1962-1968); Stockbroker, Janney Montgomery Scott LLC and Predecessor Firms, Pittsburgh, PA (1955-1962) **MEM:** President, Pennsylvania State Club of Allegheny County (1963); Life Member, Junior Secretary, Vice President, President, American Association of University Women (1960-1962); Life Member, Vice President, Pittsburgh Chapter, Soroptimist International (1961); Life Member, Junior Vice President, President College Club Pittsburgh (1959-1960); Junior Treasurer-Secretary, Vice President, President, Daughters of the American Revolution (1957-1960); Life Member, National Association Investors Corp.; Life Member, Pennsylvania State University Alumni Association; Charter Treasurer, Colonial Dames of the 17th Century; Pittsburgh Athletic Association **MH:** Albert Nelson Marquis Lifetime Achievement Award **B/I:** Growing up, Ms. Kreitzer was surrounded by finance professionals. Her mother was a bank teller and her father specialized in municipal bonds. After graduating from high school, she got a job at Janney Montgomery Scott LLC in Pittsburgh, Pennsylvania. This led her to become the first female stockbroker in the city. **AV:** Cooking; Baking; Watching theater; Traveling; Walking **PA:** Republican **RE:** Presbyterian

KREMENSKY, KENNETH, T: Fire Chief **I:** Civil Service **CN:** Barona Fire Department **MS:** Widowed **CH:** Three Children **C:** Fire Chief, Barona Fire Department, CA (2012-Present); Division Chief, Barona Band of Mission Indians (2009-2012); Division Chief, Lakeside Fire Protection District, CA (1981-2007); Seasonal Firefighter, California Division of Forestry (Now Department of Forestry and Fire Protection) (1976-1977) **CIV:** Federal Incident Management Team; Zone Coordinator; Chairman, Firefighter's Training Facility **AW:** Named Volunteer of the Year, The Burn Institute, San Diego County, CA **MEM:** International Fire Chief's Association (Now International Association of Fire Chiefs); California Fire Chiefs Association; San Diego County Fire Chiefs Association; California State Firefighters' Association (CSFA) **AS:** Mr. Kremensky believes that because he empowers and give his employees the tools they need to do the job, it helps him be a successful leader. He attributes his success to hard work integrity and honesty. "Life begins at the end of your comfort zone..." **B/I:** As a child, Mr. Kremensky grew up next to the fire marshall in his community. He was always adventurous and it seemed like something that would intrigue him. While in high school, he worked as a seasonal firefighter with the California Division of Forestry. From there, after graduating high school on Thursday, he began his full-time work as a firefighter on Monday. In addition, growing up as a kid in Southern California, there was a lot of wildfires with open country. He was fascinated by the engines, helicopters, etc. and it looked like exciting work as well as hard work. Furthermore, one of his friend's dad was a fire chief in the city and Mr. Kremensky grew up in that environment; it always looked challenging with something new everyday, and he liked that. But, his family didn't have an influence on his career choice, although his father gave him advice that he took to heart. His father wanted him to chose a career that he would be happy in because he would do the job for a long time, as well as being able to support himself financially. So, he is glad he followed his father's advise. **THT:** Unfortunately, Mr. Kremensky lost his wife in a battle to cancer, and has since taken over to raise his three children.

KRENZLER, BRANDON, T: Chief Executive Officer, Founder, Journalist **I:** Business Management/Business Services **CN:** Kind Leaf Pendleton, White Door Properties LLC, Mindful Soul, Men's Health & Wellness **MS:** Partner **SPN:** Erin Purchase **CH:** Shaiden; Ryleigh; Mykayla **ED:** Coursework, University **CT:** Oregon Marijuana Retail License, Oregon Liquor Control Commission (2017); CPR, First Aid, State of Oregon **C:** Managing Partner, White Door Properties LLC (2018-Present); Chief Executive Officer, Kind Leaf Pendleton (2016-Present); Contributing Author, Cannabis Now Magazine (2014-2017); Social Media Director, Sales Associate, SKUNK Magazine, Portland, OR (2013-2017); General Manager, Budtender, Canna and the City, Portland, OR (2015-2016); Blog Author, Cannadad's Blog (2013-2016); Freelance Journalist, Blogger, Photographer (2006-2016); Feature Writer, DOPE Magazine, Portland, OR (2015); Marketing Director, Sirius Extracts, Portland, OR (2014-2015); Contributing Writer, Ladybud Magazine (2013-2015) **CIV:** Executive Director, Parents 4 Pot **AW:** Budtender of the Year, DOPE Industry Award (2016); Best of the Valley **MH:** Marquis Who's Who Top Professional **AS:** Mr. Krenzler attributes his success to his wife and partner, Erin, as well as his children for inspiring him to provide a comfortable life for them and their futures. **B/I:** Mr. Krenzler built his own business off of his passions. He wants to better humanity in any small way that he can. He learned at an early age that cannabis can help people through various ailments, which is why he got involved in the industry. Likewise, seeing his daughter suffer from leukemia inspired him to make her hurt less, and medical cannabis could help. **THT:** Mr. Krenzler is mostly known for being a journalist in the cannabis industry. He's written with many famous related publications, such as "High Times," "SKUNK Magazine," and many others to name. He began a business for marketing and brand management where he now helps over 30 cannabis start-up companies venture into the recreational and medicinal side of the industry.

KRIEGEL, CHARLIE, T: Founder, Chief Executive Officer, Owner **I:** Real Estate **CN:** Winhill Advisors - Kirby **CH:** One Daughter **ED:** BA in Marketing, University of Houston (2002) **CT:** International Certifications **C:** Founder, Chief Executive Officer, Owner, WinHill Advisors - Kirby (2015-Present); Owner, Charlie Kriegel Properties (2012-2015) **CR:** Speaker in Field **CIV:** President, Federation International Real Estate (FIABCI), State of Texas (Present) **AW:** Voted One of Houston's Top Up and Coming Realtors; Ranked Number 6 Team, Houston, Texas **AS:** Mr. Kriegel attributes his success to always learning more. He has coaches, mentors, he goes to all types of conferences and reads all the time. He also listens to mentor box, and credits the consent learning and gaining of knowledge. He thinks because things change so rapidly in any industry, you need to make sure you're staying on top. Knowledge is power. **B/I:** Mr. Kriegel has always had a passion for real estate, the architectural design. He was also passionate about flipping homes and the investment side. While in college he played football and his coach got him involved with a gentlemen that did rehab work on homes. To see something that was in terrible shape and then seeing it completed was always a passion. It was always something he was really intrigued with. **AV:** Exercise; Running; Christian music; Hillsongs; Listen to mentors; Enjoying nature (detoxing on a daily bases)

KRISHNAMOORTHI, SUBRAMANIAN, "RAJA" RAJA, T: U.S. Representative from Illinois **I:** Government Administration/Government Relations/Government Services **CN:** U.S. House of Representatives **DOB:** 07/19/1973 **PB:** New Delhi **SC:** India **MS:** Married **SPN:** Priya Krishnamoorthi **CH:** Vijay; Vikram; Sonia **ED:** Doctor of Jurisprudence, Harvard Law, with Honors (2000); Bachelor of Arts in Mechanical Engineering, Princeton University, Summa Cum Laude (1995) **C:** Member, U.S. House of Representatives from Illinois' Eighth Congressional District (2017-Present); Deputy State Treasurer, State of Illinois (2008-2009); Campaign Staff, Barack Obama (2004, 2008); Illinois Special Assistant Attorney General (2006-2007); Staff, Illinois Housing Development Authority (2005-2007); Clerk, United States District Court for the Northern District of Illinois (2000-2002); Member, Committee on Education and the Workforce; Member, Committee on Oversight and Government Reform; Partner, Kirkland & Ellis; President, Sivananthan Laboratories Inc.; President, Episolar Inc. **CIV:** Vice Chairperson, Illinois Innovation Council; President, Director, Co-founder, InSPIRE

KROENKE, STANLEY, T: Professional Sports Team Owner **I:** Athletics **CN:** Kroenke Sports & Entertainment **DOB:** 07/29/1947 **PB:** Cole Camp, Missouri, July 29, 1947 **PT:** Married Ann Walton, 1974; children: Whitney, Josh. **ED:** Master of Business Administration, University of Missouri (1973); Bachelor of Science in Business, University of Missouri (1969) **C:** Majority Shareholder, Arsenal F.C., London, England (2007-Present); Owner, Colorado Rapids, Major League Soccer (2003-Present); Owner, Colorado Mammoth, National Lacrosse League (2002-Present); Owner, Colorado Avalanche, National Hockey League (2000-Present); Owner, Denver Nuggets, National Basketball Association (2000-Present); Owner, Pepsi Center, Denver, CO (2000-Present); Owner, Kroenke Sports & Entertainment (1999-Present); Vice Chairperson, Co-owner, St. Louis Rams, National Football League (1995-Present); Owner, Colorado Crush (2002-2009); Co-owner, Dick's Sporting Goods, CO; Chairperson, THF Realty; Chairperson, Owner, The Kroenke Group, Columbia, MO **CR:** Co-owner, Screaming Eagle Vineyard, Napa Valley, CA (2006-Present); Board of Directors, Community Investment Partnership Funds I and II, St. Louis, MO; Board of Directors, Boone County National Bank, Columbia, MO; Board of Directors, Central Bancompany, Jefferson City, MO **CIV:** Trustee, College of the Ozarks; Board Member, Greater St. Louis Area Council, Boy Scouts of America; Board Member, St. Louis Art Museum **AW:** Named, One of the Forbes 400: Richest Americans, Forbes Magazine (2006-Present); Named, One of the Most Influential People in the World of Sports, Bloomberg Businessweek (2008)

KRONEN, JERILYN, T: Psychologist **I:** Medicine & Health Care **DOB:** 07/17/1947 **PB:** New York **SC:** NY/USA **PT:** Morris Levy; Hester (Engel) Levy **MS:** Married **SPN:** Kenneth Kronen (4/11/1976) **CH:** Ari; Joshua **ED:** PhD, Yeshiva University (1982) **CT:** Certified in Psychotherapy & Psychoanalysis, New York University (1988); Licensed Psychologist, New York **C:** Private Practice, New York (1982-Present); School Psychologist, Board Cooperative Education Service, New York, NY (1972-1982); Teacher, Public School 119, New York, NY (1969-1972) **CR:** Member, Faculty Resolve, New York, NY (1989-Present); Adjunct Clinical Supervisor, Ferkauf-Yeshiva University, New York, NY (1989-Present); Lecturer in Field; Expert Witness in Specific Cases **CIV:** Adoption Resource Person, Couples Club Kehilat Jeshurun Synagogue, New York, NY (1990-Present); Liaison Member, Lower School Ramaz, New York, NY (1990-1992); Board of Directors, Couples Club Kehilat Jeshurun Synagogue, New York, NY (1989-1991); Board Member, Resolution Committee, Harbor Housing **MEM:** Division 39 Psychoanalysis, American Psychological Association; Chair, Friends of the Bipolar Center **B/I:** Dr. Kronen became involved in her profession because of her mother's mental health. She was not well psychologically and Dr. Kronen did not understand how people could not think clearly. It came from a passion of trying to figure out how to understand people with whom she could not understand. The other aspect was to make an enormous impact in the world which was to make people get better mentally.

KRUGMAN, PAUL ROBIN, PHD, T: 1) Professor 2) Columnist **I:** Education/Educational Services **CN:** 1) The Graduate Center, City University of New York 2) The New York Times **DOB:** 2/28/1953 **PB:** Albany **SC:** NY/USA **PT:** David Krugman; Anita (Alman) Krugman **MS:** Married **SPN:** Robin Wells; Robin L. Bergman (Divorced) **ED:** Doctor Honoris Causa, University of Oxford (2016); Honorary Doctor of Law, University of Toronto (2013); Doctor Honoris Causa, Universidade de Lisboa (2012); Doctor Honoris Causa, Universidade Técnica de Lisboa (2012); Doctor Honoris Causa, Universidade Nova de Lisboa (2012); Honorary Doctor of Humane Letters, Haverford College (2004); Doctor Honoris Causa in Economics, Free University of Berlin (1998); Doctor of Philosophy, Massachusetts Institute of Technology (1977); Bachelor of Arts, Yale University, New Haven, CT

(1974) **C:** Distinguished Scholar, LIS Cross-National Data Center in Luxemberg, City University of New York, NY (2014-Present); Distinguished Professor of Economics, The Graduate Center, City University of New York, NY (2014-Present); Professor of Economics and International Affairs, Princeton University, NJ (2000-2015); Professor of Economics, Stanford University, CA (1994-1996); Professor of Economics, Massachusetts Institute of Technology, Cambridge, MA (1983-1994); Associate Professor, Massachusetts Institute of Technology (1979-1983); Assistant Professor, Yale University, New Haven, CT (1977-1979) **CR:** Columnist, New York Times (2000-Present); Member, Board of Advisors, Peterson Institute for International Economics, Washington, DC (1986-Present); Research Associate, National Bureau of Economic Research (1979-Present); Columnist, Fortune Magazine (1997-1999); Columnist, Slate Magazine (1996-1999); International Policy Economist, Council of Economic Advisers, Washington, DC (1982-1983) **CW:** Author, "Arguing with Zombies: Economics, Politics, and the Fight for a Better Future" (2020); Author, "End This Depression Now!" (2012); Appearance, "Get Him to the Greek" (2010); Author, "The Return of Depression Economics and the Crisis of 2008" (2008); Author, "The Conscience of a Liberal" (2007); Author, "The Great Unraveling: Losing Our Way in the New Century" (2003); Author, "Fuzzy Math: The Essential Guide to the Bush Tax Plan" (2001); Editor, "Currency Crises" (2000); Author, "The Return of Depression Economics" (1999); Author, "The Spatial Economy - Cities, Regions and International Trade" (1999); Author, "The Accidental Theorist and Other Dispatches from the Dismal Science" (1998); Author, "The Self Organizing Economy" (1996); Author, "Pop Internationalism" (1996); Author, "Development, Geography, and Economic Theory," Ohlin Lectures (1995); Author, "Foreign Direct Investment in the United States" (1995); Author, "EMU and the Regions" (1995); Editor, "Trade with Japan: Has the Door Opened Wider?" (1995); Author, "Peddling Prosperity: Economic Sense and Nonsense in an Age of Diminished Expectations" (1995); Co-editor, "Empirical Studies of Strategic Trade Policy" (1994); Author, "World Savings Shortage" (1994); Author, "What Do We Need to Know About the International Monetary System?" (1993); Author, "Currencies and Crises" (1992); Author, "The Risks Facing the World Economy" (1991); Author, "Has the Adjustment Process Worked?" (1991); Author, "Geography and Trade," Gaston Eyskens Lecture Series (1991); Co-editor, "Exchange Rate Targets and Currency Bands" (1991); Author, "Rethinking International Trade" (1990); Author, "The Age of Diminished Expectations: US Economic Policy in the 1990s" (1990); Author, "Trade Policy and Market Structure" (1989); Author, "Exchange-Rate Instability," Lionel Robbins Lectures (1988); Author, "Adjustment in the World Economy" (1987); Editor, "Strategic Trade Policy and the New International Economics" (1986); Co-author, "Market Structure and Foreign Trade: Increasing Returns, Imperfect Competition, and the International Economy" (1985); Author, Co-author, Numerous Economics Textbooks; Contributor, Articles to Professional Journals **AW:** James Joyce Award, Literary and Historical Society (2013); Named, One of the 50 Most Influential People in Global Finance, Bloomberg Markets (2011-2013); Named, One of the Top Global Thinkers, Foreign Policy (2012); EPI Distinguished Economist Award (2011); Gerald Loeb Award for Commentary (2011); Named, One of the 50 Highest-Earning Political Figures, Newsweek (2010); Named, One of the Top 25 Market Movers, U.S. News & World Report (2009); Named, One of the World's Most Influential People, TIME Magazine (2009); Named, One of the 100 Agents of Change, Rolling Stone Magazine (2009); Nobel Prize in Economics, Royal Swedish Academy of Sciences (2008); National Journalism Award for Commentary, Scripps Howard Foundation (2008); Princess of Asturias Award (2004); Alonso Prize, RSAI - The Regional Scientific Association International (2002); Co-recipient, Nikkei Prize (2001); John Bates Clark Medal, American Economic Association (1991); Eccles Prize for Excellence in Economic Writing (1991) **MEM:** Fellow, American Academy of Arts & Sciences; Fellow, The Econometric Society; Group of Thirty

KRUSZYNSKI, TIMOTHY EDWARD, T: Protective Services Official, Poet (Retired) **I:** Civil Service **DOB:** 09/21/1949 **PB:** Chicago **SC:** IL/USA **PT:** Edward Michael; Dorothy Viola (Freske) K. **MS:** Single **ED:** Bachelor of Science in Psychology, DePaul University (1971) **CT:** Certified Deputy Sheriff, Cook County (1978) **C:** Retired (1999); Sergeant, Cook County, Chicago, IL (1992-1999); Corrections Officer, Cook County, Chicago, IL (1978-1999); Messenger, Ernst & Co. Chicago, IL (1976-1978); General Duties Clerk, Continental Bank, Chicago, IL (1971-1976); Dishwasher, Marshall Fields, Chicago, IL (1967-1971) **CR:** Poet (1989-Present); Author of Poetry, Franciscan Health Center, Olympia Fields, IL **CIV:** Supporter, Democratic National Committee (1999-2000) **CW:** Author of Poetry (1989) **AW:** Named, International Poet of Merit, International Society Poets (2000) **MH:** Albert Nelson Marquis Lifetime Achievement Award **B/I:** Mr. Kruszynski became involved in his profession because law enforcement intersected well with his background in psychology. **AV:** Writing poetry **RE:** Roman Catholic

KRZYZEWSKI, MIKE, T: College Basketball Coach **I:** Athletics **CN:** Duke University **DOB:** 02/13/1947 **PB:** Chicago **SC:** IL/USA **PT:** William Krzyzewski; Emily M. (Pituch) Krzyzewski **MS:** Married **SPN:** Carol Mickie Marsh **CH:** Debbie Savarino; Linda Frasher; Jamie Spatola **ED:** BS, United States Military Academy, West Point, NY (1969) **C:** Head Basketball Coach, Duke University Blue Devils, Durham, NC (1980-Present); Head Basketball Coach, United States Military Academy, West Point, NY (1975-1980); Assistant Coach, Indiana University (1974-1975); Head Basketball Coach, United States Military Academy Prep School, Fort Belvoir, VA (1972-1974) **CR:** Head Coach, U.S. Men's National Basketball Team (2006, 2008, 2012, 2016); Assistant Coach, U.S. Men's National Basketball Team (1979, 1984, 1992) **CIV:** Chairman, Children's Miracle Network Telethon; Board of Directors, V Foundation; With, Comprehensive Cancer Center, NABC Coaches Versus Cancer; Board of Directors, K Lab Human Performance; Fundraising Leader, Emily Krzyzewski Center, Immaculate Conception Catholic Church, Durham, NC; Board of Advisers, Code of Support Foundation **MIL:** Retired Captain, U.S. Army (1974); Officer, U.S. Army (1969-1974); With, U.S. Army (1967-1969) **CW:** Author, "The Gold Standard: Building a World-Class Team" (2009); Co-Author, with Jamie Krzyzewski Spatola, "Beyond Basketball: Coach K's Keywords for Success" (2006); Author, "5 Point Play: Duke's Journey to the 2001 National Championship" (2001); Co-Author, with Donald T. Phillips, "Leading with the Heart: Coach K's Successful Strategies for Basketball, Business and Life" (2000); Co-Author, with Bill Brill, "A Season is a Lifetime: The Inside Story of the Duke Blue Devils and Their Championships Seasons" (1993) **AW:** Gold Medal, Summer Olympics, Rio de Janeiro, Brazil (2016); Award, The Lincoln Academy of Illinois (2014); Order of Lincoln, The Lincoln Academy of Illinois (2014); Making History Award, Chicago History Museum (2013); Gold Medal, Summer Olympics, London, England, United Kingdom (2012); Wayman Tisdale Humanitarian Award, U.S. Basketball Writers Association (2012); Sportsman of the Year, Sports Illustrated (2011); Sportsman of the Year, Sports Illustrated (2011); United States Military Academy Sports Hall of Fame (2009); United States Olympic Hall of Fame (2009); Amos Alonzo Stagg Coaching Award, United States Sports Academy (1991, 2008); Gold Medal, Summer Olympics, Beijing, China (2008); Named America's Best Coach, Time Magazine (2001); Named to Naismith Memorial Basketball Hall of Fame (2001); America's Best Coach, Cable News Network (2001); Victor Award (2001); Coach of the Year, Atlantic Coast Conference (1984, 1986, 1997, 1999, 2000); District Coach of the Year, National Association of Basketball Coaches (1977, 1984, 1992, 1994, 1999, 2000); National Coach of the Year, CBS/Chevrolet (1986, 2000); Wooden Award, Legends of Coaching (2000); GTE (Now Verizon) Reads with the NABC Literacy Champion Award (2000); Naismith College Coach of the Year Award (1989, 1992, 1999); National Coach of the Year, National Association of Basketball Coaches (NABC) (1991, 1999); National Coach of the Year, Basketball Times (1997); Sportsman of the Year, Sporting News (1992); National Coach of the Year, Sporting News (1992); Inductee, National Polish American Sports Hall of Fame (1991); Coach of the Decade, National Association of Basketball Coaches (1990); National Coach of the Year, United Press International (1986); Metropolitan New York Basketball Writer's Coach of the Year (1977); Third Best Coach of All-Time, CBS Show **MEM:** President, National Association of Basketball Coaches (1998-1999); Basketball Issues Committee, NCAA

KUDLOW, LAWRENCE ALAN, T: Director, Former Financial News Correspondent, Economist **I:** Financial Services **CN:** National Economic Council **DOB:** 09/20/1947 **PB:** Englewood **SC:** NJ/USA **PT:** Irving Howard Kudlow; Ruth (Grodnick) K. Kudlow **MS:** Married **SPN:** Judy (Pond) Kudlow (07/11/1986); Susan Cullman Sicher (1981, Divorced); Nancy Ellen Gerstein (1974, Divorced 1975) **ED:** Honorary Doctor of Laws, Monmouth University (2009); Bachelor of Arts in History, University of Rochester (1969); Postgraduate Coursework, Princeton University School of Public and International Affairs (1971-1973) **C:** Director, National Economic Council, Office of the White House, Washington, DC (2018-Present); Chief Economist, Senior Managing Director, Chairperson, Investment Policy Committee, Bear Stearns & Co. Inc., New York, NY (1986-1994); President, Chief Executive Officer, Lawrence Kudlow & Associates, Washington, DC (1983-1986); Associate Director, Economics and Planning, Office of Management and Budget, Executive Office of the President, Washington, DC (1982-1983); Assistant Director, Economic Policy, Office of Management and Budget, Executive Office of the President, Washington, DC (1981-1982); Chief Economist, Bear Stearns & Co., New York, NY (1979-1981); Corporate Vice President, Chief Economist, Paine Webber, Jackson and Curtis, New York, NY (1975-1979); Staff Economist, Federal Reserve Bank of New York, New York, NY (1973-1975); Economic Counsel, Laffer Associates, San Diego, CA **CR:** Distinguished Scholar, Mercatus Center, George Mason University **CIV:** Board of Directors, American Council on Germany; Board of Directors, Institute Educational Affairs; Board of Directors, Change New York; Board of Directors, Empire Foundation; Board of Directors, Madison Center for Educational Affairs; Board of Directors, Emergency Shelter, Inc.; Former Member, Board of Governors, Smith Richardson Foundation; Member, Catholic Advisory Board, Ave Maria Mutual Funds; Board of Trustees, Fordham University; Member,

Advisory Committee, Kemp Institute, Pepperdine University School of Public Policy **CW:** Economics Editor, National Review Online (NRO) (2001-Present); Co-author, "JFK and the Reagan Revolution: A Secret History of American Prosperity" (2016); Host, "The Kudlow Report," CNBC (2009-2018); Host, "Kudlow & Company," CNBC (2005-2008); Author, "Tide: Why Tax Cuts are the Key to Prosperity and Freedom" (2005); Co-host, "Kudlow & Cramer," CNBC (2002-2005); Co-host, "America Now," CNBC (2001-2002); Author, "American Abundance: The New Economic and Moral Prosperity" (1998); Founder, Chief Executive Officer, Kudlow & Co., LLC; Co-host, "The Call," CNBC; Host, "The Larry Kudlow Show," 77 WABC Radio; Commentator, "MacNeil/Lehrer Report" and "Nightly Business Report," PBS; Commentator, "Crossfire," CNN; Commentator, "Business World," ABC; Network Appearances Including "This Week with David Brinkley," "Nightline," "60 Minutes" and "Larry King Live"; Regular Panelist, "Strictly Business," CNBC; Contributor, Op-ed Articles, The Wall Street Journal, New York Times, The Washington Times and Other Journals **AW:** Named, One of the Top 25 Market Movers, U.S. News & World Report (2009) **MEM:** Fiscal Policy Studies Advisory Council; American Enterprise Institute; New York State Legislative Committee on Private-Public Co-operation; U.S. Chamber of Commerce; Hudson Institute Inc.; The Heritage Foundation; Cato Institute; Union League Club; Capitol Hill Club; Princeton Club of New York; The Women's National Republican Club Inc. **AV:** Tennis; Golf **PA:** Republican **RE:** Roman Catholic

KUHN, JAMES E., JD, T: Judge **I:** Law and Legal Services **DOB:** 10/31/1946 **PB:** Hammond **SC:** LA/USA **PT:** Eton Percy Kuhn; Mildred Louise (McDaniel) Kuhn **MS:** Married **SPN:** Cheryl Aucoin (Kuhn) **CH:** James M.; Jennifer L. **ED:** JD, Loyola University New Orleans (1973); BA, Southeastern Louisiana University (1968); US Army War College **C:** Judge, Louisiana Court of Appeal, First Circuit, Baton Rouge, LA (1995-Present); Judge, Twenty-First Judicial District (1990-1995); Assistant District Attorney, Twenty-First Judicial District (1980-1990); Trial Attorney, Private Practice (1973-1980) **CR:** Member, Louisiana Board of Parole (2018-Present); Member, Louisiana Board of Pardons (2018-Present); History and Political Science Instructor, Southeastern Louisiana University (1991-2009); Member, Quality of Life, Insurance, Negligence and Workers' Compensation Committees, Louisiana State Bar Association (1983-1990); Member, Education Board, Southeastern Louisiana University; Former Member, Appellate Court Performance and Standards Committee, Louisiana Supreme Court **CIV:** Louisiana Association of Defense Counsel **MIL:** United States National Guard (1969-1974) **AW:** Volunteer of the Year, Ponchatoula Chamber of Commerce (2015); Good Citizen Award, Sixth District, Louisiana Chapter, The American Legion (2015); Poetry Service Award (2014-2015); Awards, Rotary International (2014-2015); Alumni Associate, Southeastern Louisiana University (2012); American Jurisprudence Award, Loyola Law School (2011); Distinguished Service Award, Southeastern Louisiana University (2011); Man of the Year, The Ancient Order of Hibernians (2011); Alumnus of the Year, College of Arts, Humanities and Social Sciences, Southeastern Louisiana University (2010) **MEM:** Continuing Education Legal Committee, Louisiana State Bar Association; American Bar Association; Colorado Bar Association; American Judicature Society; American Judges Association; New Orleans Bar Association; Baton Rouge Bar Association; Covington Bar Association; The Florida Parishes of Louisiana American Inn of Court; Delta Theta Phi; The Honor

Society of Phi Kappa Phi; Rotary International **BAR:** Colorado Bar Association (1995); Supreme Court of the United States (1980); Louisiana State Bar Association (1973) **MH:** Albert Nelson Marquis Lifetime Achievement Award; Marquis Who's Who Top Professional **B/I:** Mr. Kuhn became involved in his profession because it afforded him a great opportunity to help people. As for becoming a judge, he pursued it for the intellectual challenge.

KULENOVIC, MUSTAFA PHD, T: Mathematics Professor **I:** Education/Educational Services **DOB:** 06/23/1951 **PB:** Sarajevo **SC:** Bosnia-Herzegovina **PT:** Resad; Sadeta Kulenovic **MS:** Married **SPN:** Senada Kulenovic (02/15/1980) **CH:** Resad; Ema **ED:** Doctor of Philosophy, University of Sarajevo (1981) **C:** Assistant Professor to Professor, University of Rhode Island, Kingston, RI (2000-2006); Assistant Professor to Professor, University of Sarajevo (1981-1994) **MIL:** With, Bosnian Army (1992-1994) **CW:** Contributor, Scientific Papers; Contributor, 170 Papers, 2 Books **AW:** Grant, World University Service, Austria (2004-2008); Fellowship, University of Sarajevo (1981-1990); Fellowship, University of Ioannina, Greece (1979) **MEM:** ISDE; AMS; Academy of Science of Bosnia, Herzegovina **MH:** Albert Nelson Marquis Lifetime Achievement Award **AV:** Soccer; Tennis; Yoga; Visiting art museums **PA:** Democrat **RE:** Muslim

KULIK, TOM A., JD, T: Partner **I:** Law and Legal Services **CN:** Scheef & Stone, LLP **ED:** JD, Elisabeth Haub School of Law at Pace University **C:** Partner, Scheef & Stone, LLP **AW:** Best Lawyers in Dallas, D Magazine (2016, 2017, 2018) **MEM:** Texas Bar Association; Dallas Bar Association; International Trademark Association (INTA) **B/I:** After completing law school, Mr. Kulik began a judicial clerkship in New Jersey. It was a phenomenal experience, which led him to take on a position at a small law firm, Gilmore and Monahan. There, he gained experience in litigation, transactions, and working with clients. He later gained experience working on the EZ Pass Project, which consisted of long hours. It was hard work but it ultimately got him recruited to Texas.

KUMAR, TOBI J., T: Photographer; Poet (Retired) **I:** Fine Art **PB:** Long Beach **SC:** CA/USA **PT:** John Stewart O'Denny; Helen Ruth (Thompson) Denny **MS:** Single **SPN:** Prem Kumar Mago (07/01/1973) **ED:** Coursework, The Art Students League of New York (1965-1966); BA in Social Sciences, Kent State University (1963) **CT:** Certified in Photography, New York Institute of Photography (1973) **C:** Freelance Oil Painter, "Let There Be Dragons," Fairport, NY (1991-2016); Air Brush Artist, Leichtner's Photograph Studios, Rochester, NY (1978); Freelance Artist, India (1976-1977); Photo Colorist, American Photograph Corporation, New York, NY (1973-1975); Artist, Karl Mann Associates, New York, NY (1966-1967) **CIV:** Active, The Peace and Freedom Party, San Francisco, CA (1968); N.S.M. Martin Luther King Jr. Congress of Racial Equality, New York, NY and Baltimore, MD (1963); Tutor, News Manager, Harlem Education Project, New York, NY (1963); Co-sponsor, Martin Luther King Jr. Memorial Statue, Washington, DC **CW:** Artist, Photography Exhibited, 41 Union Square, West Sixth Avenue, Open Studios, New York, NY (1990-Present); Author, "Unfold the Sky," New Freedom, PA (2012); Author, Cassette, "Outstanding Poets of 1994, The Sounds of Poetry"; Author, Cassettes, National Library of Poetry; Author, Haiku, "Fudo's Anger" (1987); Contributor, Anthologies, Eber & Wein Publishing, New Freedom, PA; Author, Permanent Collection, Poets House, New York, NY; Author, CD, "Expressions," Sounds of Poetry **AW:** International Who's Who in Poetry Award, Eber

& Wein Publishing (2012); Third Prize, National Poetry Contest (2010); Three Golden Poet Awards, World of Poetry (1989-1991); First Prize in a Photo Contest, Rochester, NY **MEM:** The Statue of Liberty-Ellis Island Foundation, Inc.; Academy of American Poets; The National Library of Poetry on Cassettes; The Metropolitan Museum of Art, New York, NY **MH:** Albert Nelson Marquis Lifetime Achievement Award; Marquis Who's Who Top Professional **AS:** Ms. Kumar attributes her success to her determination and enjoyment of the process. **B/I:** Ms. Kumar became involved in her profession because of her love of humanity and the thrill of capturing a moment in time. **AV:** Painting; Collecting art; Writing; Biking; Photography **PA:** Democrat **RE:** Christianity and Beyond **THT:** Ms. Kumar observed the Sputnik satellite in the night sky after its launch. She said it looked like a manta ray gliding through the ocean depths. Her ancestors arrived from Europe in 1749 on the ship "Patience," landing in Philadelphia.

KUNDERA, MILAN, T: Author **I:** Writing and Editing **DOB:** 04/01/1929 **PB:** Brno **SC:** Czech Republic **PT:** Ludvik Kundera; Milada (Janosikova) Kunderova **MS:** Married **SPN:** Vera Hrabankiva (1967) **ED:** Doctor Honoris Causa, University of Michigan (1983); Diploma, Film Faculty, Academy of Performing Arts, Prague, Czech Republic (1952); Coursework, Charles University, Prague, Czech Republic **C:** Professor, Ecole des Hautes Etudes en Sciences Sociales, Paris, France (1980-1994); Professor, University of Rennes, France (1975-1980); Assistant Professor, World Literature, Film Faculty, Academy of Performing Arts, Prague, Czech Republic (1958-1969) **CW:** Author, "The Festival of Insignificance" (2014); Author, "L'Ignorance" (2000); Author, "Identity" (1998); Author, "Slowness" (1996); Author, "Testaments Betrayed" (1996); Author, "Immortality" (1991); Author, "The Art of the Novel" (1987); Author, "The Unbearable Lightness of Being" (1984); Author, "The Book of Laughter and Forgetting" (1980); Author, "Life is Elsewhere" (1974); Author, "Laughable Loves" (1974); Author, "The Farewell Waltz" (1973); Author, "Jacques and His Master" (1971); Author, "The Joke" (1969); Author, Poetry, Essays and Books **AW:** Ovid Prize (2011); Honorary Citizen, City of Brno, Czech Republic (2010); Prix Mondial Cino Del Duca (2009); Independent Award for Foreign Fiction (1991); Acadmie Francaise Critics' Prize (1987); Nell Sachs Prize (1987); Osterichischeve State Prize (1987); Austrian State Prize for European Literature (1987); Jerusalem Prize (1985); Los Angeles Times Book Prize for Fiction (1984); Prix Europa for Literature (1982); Commonwealth Award for Distinguished Service in Literature (1981); Premio Letterario Mondello (1978); Prix Medicis (1973); Czech Writers' Publishers House Prize (1969); Czech Writers' Union Prize (1968)

KURFEHS, HAROLD, "HAL" CHARLES, T: Vice President **I:** Real Estate **CN:** Coldwell Banker Commercial, Scalzo Group **DOB:** 12/10/1939 **PB:** Jersey City **SC:** NJ/USA **PT:** Harold Charles Kurfehs; Matilda Gertrude (Ruschman) Kurfehs **MS:** Married **SPN:** Linda Roberta Lepis (08/01/1964) **CH:** Harold Charles III; Diane E.; Robert C. **ED:** MBA, The Wharton School, The University of Pennsylvania, Philadelphia, PA (1964); BS, Saint Peter's College (Now Saint Peter's University), Jersey City, NJ **C:** Vice President, Coldwell Banker Commercial Scalzo Group, Bethel, CT (1996-Present); Senior Commercial-Investment Broker, William Raveis Commercial Real Estate, Danbury, CT (1985-1996); Director of Advertising & Public Relations, Board of Directors, Member, Marketing Planning Board, Ethan Allen, Inc., Danbury, CT (1983-1985); President, Chief Executive Officer, Fairfield Book Company, Inc., Harlin House, Ltd., Brookfield, CT (1977-1983); Vice President, General Manager, Fabric Division (Reed National Drapery Co. and Sanderson Fabrics), Toronto, Canada (1975-1977); Vice President, General Manager, Retail/Franchise Division, North America Operations, Reed Ltd., Toronto, Canada (1975-1977); Director of Advertising, Ethan Allen, Inc., New York, NY and Danbury, CT (1971-1975); Senior Accountant Executive, (American Cyanamid), McCaffrey & McCall, Inc., New York, NY (1970-1971); Vice President, Director of Marketing, Meta-Language Products, Inc., New York, NY (1969-1970); Account Manager, (Philip Morris Non-tobacco Products, Royal Crown Cola), Wells, Rich, Greene, Inc., New York, NY (1969); Account Executive, (General Foods, Procter & Gamble, Texaco), Benton & Bowles Advertising, New York, NY (1966-1968); Assistant Product Manager, then to to Product Manager, Lucky Strike, Carlton & Montclair Cigarettes, American Tobacco Company, New York, NY (1964-1966); Sales Administration, American Tobacco Company, New York, NY (1958-1962) **CR:** Chairman & Developed Regional Comprehensive Economic Development Strategy (CEDS), Western Connecticut Economic Development Alliance (WCEDA) (2011-2016); Economic Advisory Board, Western Connecticut Council of Governments (2015-Present); Board of Directors, The Greater Danbury Chamber of Commerce, (2019-Present); Board of Directors, Cultural Alliance of Western Connecticut, (2017-Present); Corporator, Advisory Board Member, Fairfield County Bank (2007-Present); President & Director of Commercial-Investment Division (CID), Connecticut Association of Realtors (1998-1990) President of Western CT CID (1996-1998); Headed Celebrate Connecticut! Annual Industry Awards for Western Region (2013-2018); Chair, Brookfield Economic Development Commission (2007-2017); Vice Chair, Brookfield Planning Commission (1994-2014); Speaker, Economic Development and Commercial Real Estate Conferences, Comcast Appearances (2009-2010); Stamford Chamber of Commerce, Connecticut Business & Industry Association, University of Connecticut, Construction Institute (2008-2015); Member, Policies and Procedures Committee, Lead Management, that founded Connecticut Economic Resource Center (1995-1996); Chairman, Real Estate, United Way (1990-91); Adjunct Professor, Ancell School of Business, Western Connecticut State University (1985-1986) **CIV:** Member, Republican Town Committee (2005-2006); Delegate, Republican State Convention, CT (2004); Economic Board, Western Connecticut Council of Governments; Chairman, Brookfield Economic Development Commission; Board of Directors, Cultural Alliance of Western Connecticut; Executive, "Celebrate Connecticut!" Statewide Annual Industry Awards for Western CT; Steering Committee to establish Connecticut Economic Resource Center (CERC); Chairman for Real Estate, United Way of Northern Fairfield County; Board of Directors, Greater Danbury Chamber of Commerce **CW:** Contributor, Numerous Articles, Professional Journals; Contributor, Columns, Hearst Media Newspapers **AW:** Named to Crandall Challenge Honor Roll, Wharton Graduate Emeritus Society (WGES) (2018); Coldwell Banker Commercial Circle of Distinction Award (2006, 2011); Costar Power Broker Award for the Westchester/ Southern Connecticut Market (2009-2010); Broker of the Year, Coldwell Banker Commercial (2002-2003, 2006-2011, 2013); Scholar, Oaklawn Foundation (1962); Listed, Who's Who in Aviation & Aerospace (1982); First Listed, Who's Who in America in 1997; First Listed, Who's Who in the World in 1982; First Listed in Who's Who in Finance & Industry in 1975; First Listed in Who's Who in the East

in 1974; Listed, Who's Who Among Students in American Universities & College (1962); Named to Honor Society, The Wharton School, The University of Pennsylvania (1964) **MEM:** State Director, Commercial Investment Division (CID), Connecticut Association of Realtors, Inc. (1998); State President, Commercial Investment Division (CID), Connecticut Association of Realtors, Inc. (1997); Regional President, Commercial Investment Division (CID), Connecticut Association of Realtors, Inc. (1995-1996); State Vice President, Commercial Investment Division (CID), Connecticut Association of Realtors, Inc. (1995); State Director, Commercial Investment Division (CID), Connecticut Association of Realtors, Inc. (1993-1994); President, Greater Danbury CID; National Rifle Association; Wharton Club of New York; Pi Sigma Phi; The Wharton Emeritus Society, University of Pennsylvania **MH:** Marquis Who's Who Top Professional; Marquis Real Estate "Expert Resource" **AS:** Mr. Kurfehs attributes his success to wanting to make a difference in the world and do something important. **B/I:** Mr. Kurfehs always sought challenges and was more interested in being happy at what he was doing rather than trying to amass a fortune. One thing led to another. He finally found his way to commercial real estate, which is always interesting and always changing. Equally important is the freedom that being an independent contractor allows. Currently he is doing development which provides a high level of satisfaction. **AV:** Travel; Art; History **RE:** Roman Catholic

KURZMAN, STEPHEN, T: Lawyer, Government Official (Retired) **I:** Law and Legal Services **DOB:** 03/25/1932 **PB:** New York **SC:** NY/USA **PT:** Albert W. Kurzman; Ceyl (Taylor) Kurzman **MS:** Married **SPN:** Patricia A. Goldman (05/20/1990); Ellen Goldberg (09/05/1955, Deceased 06/14/1978) **CH:** Charles T. Kurzman; George M. Kurzman **ED:** Doctor of Jurisprudence, Harvard University (1956); Bachelor of Arts, Harvard University, Summa Cum Laude (1953) **C:** With, Stephen Kurzman PC, Washington, DC (1993-2007); Of Counsel, Nixon, Hargrave, Devans & Doyle, Washington, DC (1991-1993); Partner, Nixon, Hargrave, Devans & Doyle, Washington, DC (1976-1991); Assistant Secretary for Legislation, U.S. Department of Health, Education and Welfare (1971-1976); Partner, Kurzman & Goldfarb, Washington, DC (1966-1971); Minority Counsel, Committee on Labor and Public Welfare, U.S. Senate (1965-1966); Legislative Assistant & Counsel, U.S. Sen. Jacob K. Javits (1961-1965); Assistant U.S. Attorney, Southern District New York, New York, NY (1959-1961) **CR:** Director, Office of Intergovernmental Affairs, White House Conference on Children and Youth (1970-1971); Consultant, Committee on Grants & Benefits, Administrative Conference of the U.S. (1969-1971); Consultant, Senate Committee Labor & Public Welfare (1969-1970); Consultant, U.S. Department of the Treasury (1969-1970); Special Counsel, Urban Coalition Action Council (1969-1970); Professorial Lecturer, George Washington University Law School (1969); Consultant, Republican Task Force on Urban Affairs, U.S. House of Representatives (1968); Consultant, Deputy Director for Operations, National Advisory Commission on Civil Disorders (1967-1968) **CIV:** Board Member, Dumbarton Concerts, InnerCity-Inner Child; Board Member, Chesapeake Legal Alliance; Former Elected Member, Vice Chairperson and Treasurer, DC Republican Committee; Former President, Citizens Association of Georgetown; Former Member, DC Advisory Committee, U.S. Civil Rights Commission; Former Member and Officer, American Jewish Committee **MIL:** U.S. Army (1957-1959); Legal Advisor in the Courts of the Republic of Panama **CW:** Reviser,

Gordon's Modern Annotated Forms of Agreement, Prentice-Hall (1970) **AW:** Community Service Award, American Jewish Committee (1988); Distinguished Service Award, U.S. Department of Health, Education & Welfare (1976); Secretary's Special Citation, U.S. Department of Health, Education & Welfare (1975) **MEM:** American Law Institute; Phi Beta Kappa; Harvard Club of DC; Cosmos Club of Washington, DC **BAR:** District of Columbia (1966-2007); New York (1959-2007) **PA:** Republican **RE:** Jewish

KUSHAR, KENT, T: Information Technology Executive; Executive Coach; Business Advisor **I:** Information Technology and Services **CN:** K2 Innovation **DOB:** 02/12/1944 **SC:** MT/USA **MS:** Married **CH:** Three Children **ED:** Postgraduate Coursework in Business and Technology, Kellogg School of Management at Northwestern University, Chicago, IL; Postgraduate Coursework in Advanced Business and Technology, Harvard Business School; BS in Business Administration, University of Montana **C:** Founder, K^2 Innovation (2015-Present); Vice President, Chief Information Officer, E&J Gallo Winery, Modesto, CA (1995 - 2015); Managing Principal, Unisys International Services Group; General Manager, IBM-ROLM; Director, IBM Consulting; Senior Technical Consultant, Ernst & Young (CITAS) Center for Information Technology and Strategy; Vice President of Technology, Citicorp **CR:** Director, IT Operations; Apple Computer; Vice President of Systems and Communications, Wells Fargo Bank **CIV:** Former Advisory Board Member, Eller College at the University of Arizona; Former Advisory Board Member, Walton School at the University of Arkansas; Former Advisory Board Member, California State University **MIL:** U.S. Army **AW:** Inductee, Chief Information Officer Hall of Fame, CIO Magazine (2013); Ranked #1 IT Organization in the United States, E&J Gallo Winery (2004) **MH:** Albert Nelson Marquis Lifetime Achievement Award; Marquis Who's Who Top Professional **AS:** Mr. Kushar attributes his success to his faith in Jesus Christ. Likewise, he credits his strengths in discipline, courage, continuous learning, persistence, hard work, and listening, as well as the powerful encouragement and mentoring he received over the years. **B/I:** Mr. Kushar has an interesting story as to how he became involved in his profession. He has been involved in information technology since 1963. His mother introduced him to a family friend who had a "new" available position in "computers" – because at the time, no one else wanted to do it. She convinced him to take the role as a night computer operator, running IBM tabulating equipment on swing shift. Mr. Kushar believes he got it because he was the only one who wanted it. He tried it, liked it, and he was good at it. This inspired him to pursue the field. The rest is history. **AV:** Restoring automobiles **THT:** Mr. Kushar is thankful for technology because it allows individuals to take advantage of the improvements it brings. Intelligence is knowing, wisdom is applying. Results count. He believes in changing the way one looks at the world and always listening. He makes his own luck and never surrenders.

KUSHNER, EVA, T: Academic Administrator, Educator; Author **I:** Education/Educational Services **DOB:** 06/18/1929 **PB:** Prague **SC:** Czechoslovakia **PT:** Josef Dubsky; Anna (Kafkova) Dubsky **MS:** Married **SPN:** Mutch Bruce (09/20/2005, Deceased 2013); Donn Jean Kushner (09/15/1949, Deceased 2001) **CH:** Daniel Peter; Roland Joseph **ED:** Honorary Doctorate, Victoria University, University of Toronto, Canada (2006); Honorary Doctorate, University of Szeged (1997); Honorary Doctorate, University of Western Ontario (Now Western University), Canada (1996); Honorary Doctorate, Saint Michael's University (1993); Honorary Doctorate, United Theological College (1992); Honorary Doctorate, Acadia University (1988); PhD in French Literature, McGill University (1956); MA, McGill University (1950); BA, McGill University (1948); PhB, College International Marie de France, Montreal, Canada (1946) **C:** Mary Rowell Jackman Professor, Victoria University (2001-Present); Visiting Professor, Princeton University (2000); Director, Center of Comparative Literature, University of Toronto (1994-1995); President, Vice Chancellor, Victoria University, University of Toronto (1987-1994); Professor, French Language and Literature, McGill University (1976-1987); Chair, Department of French, McGill University (1976-1980); Instructor, French, McGill University (1956, 1958, 1961-1962, 1967-1969); Lecturer, French, McGill University (1952-1955) **CR:** George R. Gardiner Museum of Ceramic Arts (Gardiner Museum) (1990-1994); Vice President, Social Science and Humanities Research Council, Canada (1983-1986); Member, Executive Committee, Canadian Council (1975-1981); Adjunct Professor, Literature (1976-1979); Chairman, Comparative Literature (1965-1969, 1970-1972, 1975-1976); Professor (1969-1976); Vice Chairman, Social Science and Humanities Research Council, Canada (1970-1972); Associate Professor (1965); Assistant Professor, French and Comparative Literature (1963); Lecturer, Carleton University (1961); Lecturer, University College London (1958-1959); Sessional Lecturer, Philosophy, Sir George Williams University (1952-1953); Member, Advisory Board, President, National Library of Canada **CW:** Author, "Mantice" (2014); Author, "Le Second Curieux" (2013); Author, "Maturations et Mutations (1520-60)" (2011); Co-author, Anthology of Quebec Poetry, Portuguese translation, Brazil (2010); Author, "Volume 4 Le Premier Curieux" (2010); Author, "Northrop Frye, the Critical Path and Other Writings on Critical Theory" (2008); Author, Homilies and Other Works (2007); Author, "De la Droite Imposition des Noms, Volume 7" (2007); Author, "Le Dialogue à la Renaissance: Histoire et Poetique" (2004); Author, Critical Edition, "Complete Works of Pontus de Tyard, Volume 1, Oeuvres Potiques" (2004); Author, "The Living Prism Itineraries in Comparative Literature" (2001); Author, "Pontus de Tyard et son Oeuvre Potique" (2001); Author, "Crises et Essors Nouveaux (1560-1610)," (2000); Author, "Histoire des Potiques" (1997); Editor, Co-author, "La Problematique du Sujet chez Montaigne" (1995); Co-editor, Volume X, International Comparative Literature Association (1995); Co-editor, Volume IX, International Comparative Literature Association (1994); Co-editor, Volumes VII-VIII, International Comparative Literature Association (1993); Co-editor, Volume VI, International Comparative Literature Association (1992); Co-editor, Procedures of the 7th, 9th, 11th ICLA Congress, Volumes IV-V, International Comparative Literature Association (1991); Member, International Advisory Board, Synthesis Literature Research (1990-1995); Author, "Thorie Literaire: Problmes et Perspectives" (1989); Co-editor/Co-author, "L'Avnement de l'Esprit Nouveau (1400-80)" (1988); Co-author, Anthology of Quebec Poetry, Polish Translation (1985); Co-author, Anthology of Quebec Poetry, Hungarian Translation (1978); Author, "Francois Mauriac," Japanese Translation (1976); Author, "Francois Mauriac" (1972); Author, "Saint-Denys Garneau" (1967); Author, "Poètes d'Aujourd'hui" (1969); Author, "Rina Lasnier, Collection Ecrivains Canadiens d'Aujourd'hui" (1964); Author, "Chants de Boheme" (1963); Author, "Le Mythe d'Orphée dans la Literature Francaise Contemporaine" (1961); Author, "Patrice de La Tour du Pin" (1961); Editor, "Renewals in the Theory of Literary His-

tory"; Director of Research, Renaissance Volumes, "Histoire Comparée des Littératures de Langues Européennes"; Author, "De la Droite Imposition des Noms, Volume 6"; Member, Editorial Committee, Canada Comparative Literature Review, Dalhousie French Studies, Etudes Montaignistes; Contributor, Articles to Professional Publications **AW:** Named Officer, Order of Canada (1997) **MEM:** Board Member, Académie Européenne des Lettres, des Sciences et des Arts (2012); Vice President, International Council for Philosophy and Humanistic Studies (Now International Council for Philosophy and Human Sciences (ICPHS/CIPSH) (2006-2010); Co-chair, Ontario Coalition of Senior Citizens' Organizations (OCSCO) (2003-2004); President, International Federation for Modern Languages and Literatures (FILLM) (1996-1999); Discipline Representative for French Studies, The Renaissance Society of America (1996-1999); Vice President, International Federation for Modern Languages and Literatures (FILLM) (1987-1993); Nominating Committee, Modern Language Association (1986-1988); Executive Council, Modern Language Association (1983-1986); Vice President, Royal Society Canada (1980-1982); President, International Comparative Literature Association (1979-1982); Vice President, Association Canadienne de Littérature Comparée (1969-1971); Fellow, Royal Society Canada; Modern Language Association; Delegate, Assembly, Chairman, 16th Century French Literature Division, Modern Language Association; Association Internationale des Etudes Francaises (AIEF); Association Canadienne de Littérature Comparée; Académie Européenne des Lettres, des Sciences et des Arts; American Comparative Literature Association (ACLA); Advisory Board, American Comparative Literature Association (ACLA); International Comparative Literature Association; International Federation for Modern Languages and Literatures (FILLM); International Council for Philosophy and Humanistic Studies (Now International Council for Philosophy and Human Sciences (ICPHS/CIPSH)); International Association for Neo-Latin Studies, Société Canadienne d'Etudes de la Renaissance; Association des Littératures Canadienne et Qubecoise, The Renaissance Society of America; Association des Professeurs de Francais des Universities Canadiennes (APFUCC); The Renaissance Society of America; National Board, Canada Pensioners Concerned; Ontario Coalition of Senior Citizens' Organizations (OCSCO) **MH:** Albert Nelson Marquis Lifetime Achievement Award

KUSHNER, JARED COREY, T: Senior Advisor to the President; Director; Real Estate Executive **I:** Government Administration/Government Relations/Government Services **CN:** Office of American Innovation **DOB:** 10/10/1981 **PB:** Livingston **SC:** NJ/USA **PT:** Charles B. Kushner; Seryl (Stadtmauer) Kushner **MS:** Married **SPN:** Ivanka Marie Trump (10/25/2009) **CH:** Arabella Rose; Joseph Frederick; Theodore James **ED:** Intern, Square Mile Capital; Intern, Paul, Weiss, Rifkin, Wharton & Garrison LLP; MBA, New York University Leonard N. Stern School of Business (2007); JD, New York University School of Law (2007); BA in Government, Harvard University (2003) **C:** Senior Advisor to the President, The White House, Washington, DC (2017-Present); Director, Office of American Innovation, The White House, Washington, DC (2017-Present); Owner, PoliticsNJ.com (2007-2017); Owner, Publisher, New York Observer (2006-2017); Principal, Kushner Companies **CW:** Appearance, "Gossip Girl" (2010) **AW:** Awarded Sash, Order of the Aztec Eagle, Mexico (2018); Named One of the 100 Most Influential People, TIME Magazine (2017) **PA:** Republican **RE:** Jewish

KUSHNER, TONY ROBERT, T: Playwright, Scriptwriter **I:** Media & Entertainment **DOB:** 07/16/1956 **PB:** New York **SC:** NY/USA **PT:** William David Kushner; Sylvia (Deutscher) Kushner **MS:** Married **SPN:** Mark Harris (2008) **ED:** Honorary LittD, Ithaca College (2015); Honorary Doctorate, The New School (2011); Honorary Doctorate, John Jay College of Criminal Justice, CUNY (2011); Honorary LittD, Purchase College, State University of New York (2008); Honorary Doctorate, Brandeis University (2006); Honorary Doctorate, Columbia College Chicago (2003); Diploma, New York University Tisch School of the Arts (1984); BA in Medieval Studies, Columbia University (1978) **CR:** Guest Artist, Graduate Theater Program, Yale University, New York University and Princeton University (1989-Present); Playwright-in-residence, Juilliard School of Drama (1990-1992); Director, Literary Services, Theatre Communications Group, New York, NY (1990-1991); Associate Artistic Director, New York Theatre Workshop (1987) **CW:** Screenwriter, "West Side Story" (2020); Screenwriter, "Lincoln" (2012); Playwright, "The Intelligent Homosexual's Guide to Capitalism and Socialism with a Key to the Scriptures" (2009); Playwright, "Tiny Kushner" (2009); Playwright, "Mother Courage and Her Children (Bertolt Brecht)" (2006); Writer "Munich" (2005); Playwright, "Only We Who Guard the Mystery Shall Be Unhappy" (2004); Playwright, "Caroline, or Change" (2003); Writer, Television Miniseries, "Angels in America" (2003); Playwright, "Brundibar (Operas)" (2003); Playwright, "Homebody/Kabul" (2001); Playwright, "Death and Taxes" (2000); Playwright, "Good Person of Setzuan (Bertolt Brecht)" (1999); Playwright, "Dybbuk and Other Tales of the Supernatural" (1997); Playwright, "Slavs!: Thinking About the Longstanding Problems of Virtue and Happiness" (1995); Playwright, "A Dybbuk (S.Y. Ansky)" (1995); Playwright, "Angels in America: A Gay Fantasia on National Themes, Part Two: Perestroika" (1992); Playwright, "Angels in America: A Gay Fantasia on National Themes, Part I: Millenium Approaches" (1991); Playwright, "A Bright Room Called Day" (1990); Playwright, "The Illusion (Pierre Corneille)" (1988); Director, Author, "In Great Eliza's Golden Time" (1986); Director, Author, "Yes Yes No No: The Solice of Solstice, Apogee/Perigee, Bestial/Celestial Holiday Show" (1985); Author, Playwright, Plays, Books **AW:** Award for Best Screenplay, National Society Film Critics (2013); Award for Best Adapted Screenplay, Critics Choice Awards (2013); Award for Best Screenplay, New York Film Critics Circle Awards (2013); Award for Best Screenplay, Boston Society of Film Critics (2012); Paul Selvin Award (2012); National Medal of Arts, National Endowment for the Arts (2012); Puffin/Nation Prize (2011); Steinberg Distinguished Playwright Award (2008); Laurence Olivier Award for Best New Musical (2007); Obie Award (2004); Emmy Award for Outstanding Writing for a Miniseries, Movie or a Dramatic Series, Academy of Television Arts & Sciences (2004); PEN/Laura Pels International Foundation for Theater Award, PEN America (2002); Lambda Literary Award (1996); Tony Award for Best Play (1993, 1994); Drama Desk Award for Outstanding Play (1993, 1994); American Academy of Arts and Letters Award (1994); Pulitzer Prize for Drama (1994); Grantee, National Education Association (1985, 1987, 1993); London Evening Standard Award (1992); Will Glickman Playwriting Prize (1992); Kesserling Award, National Arts Club (1992); John Whiting Award, Arts Council of Great Britain (1990); Whiting Award (1990); Princess Grace Award (1986); Cultural Achievement Award, National Foundation of Jewish Culture; Lila Wallace/Reader's Digest Fellowship **MEM:** American Academy of Arts and Letters; American Philosophical Society

KUSTER, ANN L., T: U.S. Representative from New Hampshire; Lobbyist **I:** Government Administration/Government Relations/Government Services **DOB:** 09/05/1956 **PB:** Concord **SC:** NH/USA **PT:** Malcolm McLane; Susan (Neidlinger) McLane **MS:** Married **SPN:** Brad Kuster **CH:** Zach; Travis **ED:** JD, Georgetown University Law Center (1984); BS in Environmental Policy, Dartmouth College (1978) **C:** Member, U.S. House of Representatives from New Hampshire's Second Congressional District, United States Congress, Washington, DC (2013-Present); Member, U.S. House Committee on Veterans' Affairs (2013-Present); Member, U.S. House Small Business Committee (2013-Present); Member, U.S. House Committee on Agriculture (2013-Present); Owner, Consultant, Newfound Strategies, LLC (2001-Present); Staff Member to Representative Pete McCloskey, U.S. House of Representatives, Washington, DC (1978-1981); Of Counsel, Rath Young Pignatelli P.C. **CR:** Delegate, Democratic National Convention (2004, 2008); Member, New Hampshire Steering Committee, Barack Obama's Presidential Campaign (2007-2008); New Hampshire Delegation, Boston, MA (2004); Member, John Kerry's Presidential Campaign (2003-2004); Founder, Women's Fund of New Hampshire; Co-chair, New Hampshire Women for Obama **CW:** Co-author with Susan McLane, "The Last Dance: Facing Alzheimer's with Love and Laughter" (2006) **AW:** Rainbow Award, Riverbend Community Mental Health Center (2008); Marilla M. Ricker Achievement Award, New Hampshire Women's Bar Association (NHWBA) (2004) **MEM:** American Academy of Adoption Attorneys (Now Academy of Adoption and Assisted Reproduction Attorneys) **PA:** Democrat

KUSTOFF, DAVID FRANK, T: U.S. Representative from Tennessee; Lawyer **I:** Government Administration/Government Relations/Government Services **DOB:** 10/08/1966 **PB:** Memphis **SC:** TN/USA **MS:** Married **SPN:** Roberta Kustoff **CH:** Maggie **ED:** JD, The University of Memphis Cecil C. Humphreys School of Law (1992); BBA, The University of Memphis (1989) **C:** Member, U.S. House of Representatives from Tennessee's Eighth District (2017-Present); United States Attorney, Western District of Tennessee, U.S. Department of Justice, Memphis, TN (2006-2008); Republican Study Committee; Partner, Kustoff & Strickland PLLC, Memphis, TN **CR:** Board of Directors, Bank of Tennessee; Tennessee Higher Education Commission **CIV:** Head, Bush-Cheney Election Effort, TN (2000, 2004); Chairman, Shelby County Republican Party, TN **BAR:** State of Tennessee (1992) **RE:** Jewish

LA BARGE, WILLIAM JOSEPH, T: Tutor, Researcher **I:** Education/Educational Services **DOB:** 06/27/1943 **PB:** Portis **SC:** KS/USA **PT:** Louis Joseph La Barge; Mary Genevieve (Colton) La Barge **ED:** Postgraduate Coursework, Cloud County Community College, Concordia, KS (1984); Postgraduate Coursework, Fort Hays State University, Hays, KS (1980); AB, Fort Hays State University, Hays, KS (1966); Military Education and Training **CT:** Certified Teacher, Kansas **C:** Private Tutor, World, American, Ancient History (1988-Present); Independent Study, Downs, KS (1983-1988); Production Worker, Becker Manufacturing Co., Downs, KS (1978-1979); Correctional Officer, Kansas Department of Corrections, Hutchinson, KS (1977); Depot Agent, Missouri Pacific R.R., Lenora, KS (1971-1977) **CR:** Systems Analyst, Global Societal Dynamics; Templemore Research in Various Topics **MIL:** Ed. Naval Intelligence (U.S.S. Oriskany: CVA-34) (1967-1970); U.S. Navy (1966-1970); Operations & Intelligence, Combat Information Center, Classified Material **AW:** Golden Fleece Pendent **MEM:** Association for Supervision and Curriculum Development; Archaeological Institute of America; U.S. Naval Institute **MH:** Albert Nelson Marquis Lifetime Achievement Award **B/I:** Mr. La Barge became involved in his field after attending a general meeting of the Archeological Institute of America during his time in the United States Navy. He ended up joining the institute and proceeded to specialize in operations and intelligence; his career naturally progressed from there. **AV:** Researching archaeology and history; Collecting toy soldiers; Traveling **PA:** Independent **RE:** Roman Catholic

LA ROSA, FRANCISCO G., MD, T: Pathologist, Researcher, Educator **I:** Education/Educational Services **CN:** University of Colorado, Anschutz Medical Campus **DOB:** 01/17/1949 **PB:** Lima **SC:** Peru **PT:** Aníbal La Rosa; María del Carmen (de la Pascua) La Rosa **MS:** Married **SPN:** Clara Ann Dufficy-La Rosa **CH:** David; Anamaria; Joseph; Marie-Carmen **ED:** Training, Heart Transplant Pathology, Department of Pathology, Cell Biology, College of Physicians & Surgeons, Columbia University (2015); Postgraduate Coursework, Renal Biopsy in Medical Diseases of the Kidneys, College of Physicians and Surgeons, Columbia University, New York, NY (2011); Graduate, Fundamentals of Health Information Technology Management, University of Colorado Denver (2004); Fellow, Urologic Pathology, Health Science Center, University of Colorado (2002-2004); Fellow, Lung Pathology, Health Science Center, University of Colorado, Denver (1995-1996); Resident, Anatomic, Clinical Pathology, Health Science Center, University of Colorado, Denver (1992-1995); Postdoctoral Fellow, Immunology, University of Colorado, Denver (1981-1985); Resident, Clinical Pathology, Universidad de San Marcos, Lima, Peru (1977-1979); MD, School of Medicine, National University of Federico Villarreal, Lima, Peru (1975); BS, School of Medicine, National University of Federico Villarreal, Lima, Peru (1975); Intern, Surgery, Internal Medicine, Arzobispo Loayza Hospital, Lima, Peru (1974); Intern, Obstetrics, Gynecology, Maternity Hospital, Lima, Peru (1974); Intern, Pediatrics, Childrens Hospital, Lima, Peru (1974) **CT:** Medical License, States of Oregon, Montana, Wyoming, New Mexico, Colorado; American Board Certified, Pathologist (1995); Federal Licensing Examination (1993); Educational Commission for Foreign Medical Graduates (1991) **C:** Medical Staff, University of Colorado Hospital (2005-Present); Associate Professor, Pathology Department, Health Science Center, University of Colorado, Denver (2001-Present); Laboratory Consultant, Miners Colfax Medical Center, Raton, NM (1996-2000); R&D Medical Consultant, REAADS Medical Products, Incorporated, Denver (1991); Instructor, Microbiology, Immunology, Health Science Center, University of Colorado, Denver (1985-1987); Consultant, Ortho Pharmaceutical, Lima, Peru (1979-1981); Private Practice, Clinical Pathology, Cytopathology, Family Practice, Lima, Peru (1978-1981); Instructor, Microbiology, National University of Federico Villarreal, Lima, Peru (1973-1979) **CR:** Honorary Professor, National University of Federico Villarreal, Lima, Peru (2003-Present); Teaching Scholar, Teaching Scholar's Program, Health Science Center, University of Colorado School of Medicine (2005-2007); Invited Professor, National University of Federico Villarreal, Lima, Peru (1999-2003); Clinical Assistant Professor, Pathology Department, Health Science Center, University of Colorado, Denver, Ad Honorem (1996-2002); Assistant Professor, Microbiology, Immunology, Health Science Center, University of Colorado, Denver (1987-1992); Supervisor, Histopathology Core, Barbara Davis Center, Webb-Waring Institute, Health Science Center, University of Colorado (1986-1992); Assistant Professor, Immunology Department, National University of Federico Villarreal, Lima, Peru (1979-1982); Apprentice Instructor, Histology, Embryology, School of Medicine, National University of Federico Villarreal, Lima, Peru (1968-1969); Telepathology Moderator, PathoIndia; Adviser, Informatics, Hipólito Unanue Medical School, National University of Federico Villarreal, Lima, Peru; Webmaster, Medical School "Hipólito Unanue", National University "Federico Villarreal", Lima, Peru; Grant Reviewer, Fundación Española para la Ciencia y la Tecnología; Founder, Chief-Editor, Revista Asociación Peruana de Telesalud y Telemedicina; Founder, Chief Editor, Journal of the Asociación Iberoamericana de Telesalud y Telemedicina **CIV:** Editorial Board, Medical and Surgical Urology Journal (2016-Present); Editorial Board, Clinics in Surgery Journal (2016-Present); Editorial Board, Austin Surgery Case Reports Journal (2015-Present); Member and Study Coordinator, Southwest Oncology Group (2012-Present); Leader, Organizer, Medical Mission Trips, Peru, Christian Life Movement (2006-Present); Editorial Board, International Journal of Clinical and Experimental Pathology (2005-Present); Director, Communications, Christian Life Movement, Denver, CO (2005-Present); Webmaster, Promoción 63, Colegio San Agustín (2002-Present); Webmaster, "Christian Life Movement, USA," Denver, CO (2001-Present); Webmaster, Club Peru Denver, Denver, CO (2000-Present); Reviewer, BMJ Case Reports Journal (2017); Faculty Senator, Pathology Department, Health Science Center, University of Colorado (2014-2016); Peer Reviewer, Abstracts, American Telemedicine Association (2009-2011); Medical Coordinator, Medical Mission Trip, Lima, Peru (2010); Webmaster, Catholic Youth Recreation Association, Colorado (2002-2010); Medical Coordinator, Medical Mission Trip, Lima, Peru (2009); Webmaster, Pathology Department, Health Science Center, University of Colorado (2005-2009); Medical Coordinator, Volunteer, Medical Mission Trips, Chincha, Peru (2008); Medical Adviser, Board Member, Salud y Vida For the Latino Community (2006); Volunteer, Denver Museum of National History, Exhibit, "Body Worlds 2" (2006); Informatics Consultant, Webmaster, School of Medicine, National University of Federico Villarreal, Lima, Peru (2001-2015); Scientific Peer Advisory, Review Services, The American Institute of Biological Sciences, Sterling, VA (2000-2002); Director, Animal Care Facility, Web-Waring Lung Institute, Health Science Center, University of Colorado (1989-1991); Co-Editor, Journal, Revista Asociación Peruana de Telesalud y Telemedicina; Grant, Project Reviewer, U.S. Army Medical Research, Materiel Command **CW:** Contributor, Chapters, Books; Contributor, Reviews; Contributor, More Than 95 Professional Journals **AW:** Inspector Excellence, College of American Pathologists (2018); Numerous Excellence in Teaching Awards, Pathology, University of Colorado Medical School (1994-2009); Honorary Professor, University of Federico Villarreal, Lima, Peru (2003); Fellowship Award, National Cancer Institute, Program of Oncology Research Excellence (1996); Scholarship, College of American Pathology (1994); Fellowship Awards, Diabetes Research and Education Foundation (1987-1988); Fellowship Awards, Juvenile Diabetes Foundation (1986-1987); Various Fellowship Awards, Krock Foundation (1983-1984); Enrique Leon García Award, Best Thesis in Pediatrics, Peruvian Pediatrics Society (1975); Certificate of Appreciation, Associate Dean of Education, Health Science Center, University of Colorado **MEM:** Faculty Sponsor, Students for Life, Anschutz Medical Campus, University of Colorado (2018-Present); Faculty Sponsor, Anschutz Medical Campus (2015-Present); Genitourary Committee, Southwest Oncology Group (2012-Present);

Leader, College of American Pathologists, Accreditation andLaboratory Improvement (2008-Present); Board, Catholic Medical Association (2007-Present); Scientific Committee, II Ibero-American Congress of Telehealth and Telemedicine (2015); President, Asociación Iberoamericana de Telesalud y Telemedicina (2013-2015); Vice Secretary, Asociación Iberoamericana de Telesalud y Telemedicina (2011-2015); Executive President, I International Congress of Telehealth and Telemedicine, Lima, Peru (2014); President, Congress, Asociación Iberoamericana de Telesalud y Telemedicina, Lima, Peru (2014); Scientific Committee, International Congress, Salud Conectada (2012); Asociación Iberoamericana de Telesalud y Telemedicina (2011); Scientific Committee, X Hispanic-American Virtual Congress of Anatomic Pathology (2009); Vice Chair, American Telemedicine Association, Latin-American, Carribean Chapter (2007-2009); Chair, Pathology Informatics Committee, Pathology Department, Health Science Center, University of Colorado (2006-2009); The American Urological Association (2008); ATA Special Interest Group, Telepathology, American Telemedicine Association (1999); PathoIndia (1996); American Medical Association (1996); Peruvian American Medical Society (1995); Honorary Member, Peruvian Society of Immunology and Allergy (1994); College of American Pathologists (1993); Colorado Society of Clinical Pathologists (1993); American Society of Clinical Pathologists (1993); The Peruvian Society of Clinical Pathology (1980); Pathology Grand Rounds Committee; Asociación Iberoamericana de Telesalud y Telemedicina; Denver Guild; American Telemedicine Association; Sociedad Latino, Americana de Patológica; Peruvian Society of Clinical Pathology **BAR:** Colorado **MH:** Albert Nelson Marquis Lifetime Achievement Award **AS:** Dr. La Rosa attributes his success to the inspiration and schooling of two of his high school teachers, Fathers Lucio Fernandez and Gaspar Vega. He additionally gives credit to his professors in medical school, Dr. Manasses Fernandez Lancho, Dr. David W. Talmage, and Dr. Bette K. DeMasters. **B/I:** Dr. La Rosa became involved in his profession because it gave him the opportunity to use his knowledge of medical science to help people live longer and stay healthy. **AV:** Photography; Videotaping; Web page designing; Movie editing; Graphic designing **PA:** Conservative **RE:** Roman Catholic

LA RUSSA, TONY JR., T: Senior Advisor of Baseball Operations; Former Professional Baseball Manager; Former Professional Baseball Player **I:** Athletics **CN:** Los Angeles Angels **DOB:** 10/04/1944 **PB:** Tampa **SC:** FL/USA **PT:** Anthony La Russa; Olivia (Cuervo) La Russa **MS:** Married **SPN:** Elaine Coker (12/31/1973); Luzette Sarcone (Divorced 1973) **CH:** Andrea; Averie; Bianca; Devon **ED:** JD, Florida State University College of Law (1978); BA in Industrial Management, University of South Florida (1969); Coursework, University of Tampa **C:** Senior Advisor, Baseball Operations, Los Angeles Angels, MLB (2019-Present); Manager, St. Louis Cardinals, MLB (1996-2011); Manager, Oakland Athletics, MLB (1986-1995); Manager, Chicago White Sox, MLB (1979-1986); Minor League Manager, Iowa Oaks, American Association (1979); Coach, Chicago White Sox, MLB (1978); Minor League Manager, Knoxville Sox, Southern League (1978); Coach, St. Louis Cardinals, MLB (1977); Infielder, Chicago Cubs, MLB (1973); Infielder, Atlanta Braves, MLB (1971); Infielder, Oakland Athletics, MLB (1968-1971); Infielder, Kansas City Athletics, MLB (1963) **CR:** Manager, National League All-star Team (2005); Manager, American League All-star Team (1988) **CIV:** Co-founder, Tony La Russa's Animal Rescue Foundation (1991-Present) **CW:** Author, "One Last Strike: Fifty Years in Baseball, Ten and a Half Games Back, and One Final Championship Season" (2012) **AW:** Named to St. Louis Cardinals Hall of Fame (2014); Named to Baseball Hall of Fame (2013); Ellis Island Family Heritage Award (2012); C.I. Taylor Award, Negro League Hall of Fame (2004); Named to Hispanic Heritage Baseball Museum Hall of Fame (2010); Named to Missouri Sports Hall of Fame (2006); Named National League Manager of Year, MLB (2002); Named to National Italian American Sports Hall of Fame (1998); Named American League Manager of the Year, MLB (1983, 1988, 1992) **BAR:** Florida (1979)

LACHER, MIRIAM BROWNER, PHD, T: Clinical Neuropsychologist (Retired) **I:** Medicine & Health Care **DOB:** 12/30/1942 **PB:** Bronx **SC:** NY/USA **PT:** Philip; Ruth Frieda (Rabinowitz) Browner **MS:** Married **SPN:** Maury Lacher **ED:** Postgraduate Coursework, Columbia University (1981-1982); Doctor of Philosophy, University of Michigan (1970); Bachelor of Arts, Cornell University (1963) **CT:** Licensed Psychologist, New York **C:** Retired (2018); Private Practice, Poughkeepsie, NY (1984-2018); Allied Health Professional, Vassar Brothers Hospital (1985-2016); Consultant, Vassar College Counseling Service, Poughkeepsie, NY (1984-1990); Consultant, First Step Nursery School, Hyde Park, NY (1988); Chief, Cognitive Rehabilitation, Children's Specialized Hospital, Westfield, NJ (1982-1984); Consultant, New York State Psychiatric Institute, New York, NY (1981); Associate of Neuropsychology, New York-Presbyterian/Columbia University, New York, NY (1980-1981); Visiting Lecturer, Vassar College, Poughkeepsie, NY (1978-1979); Visiting Research Associate, University of California Berkeley (1976-1977); Assistant Professor of Psychology, Carleton College, Northfield, MN (1970-1977) **CR:** Alternate Representative of the Hudson Valley Psychological Association to the New York State Psychological Association's Representative Council (2020); Council Representative, Hudson Valley Psychological Association to New York State Psychological Association (2014-2019) **CIV:** Science Advisor, Board of Directors, Mid-Hudson Chapter, Children and Adults with Attention Deficit Disorders (1989-1999); Mid-Hudson Association for the Learning Disabled (1992-1996); Vassar Brothers Hospital Support Group for Patents of Children with Attention Deficit Hyperactivity Disorder and Autistic Spectrum Disorders **CW:** Contributor, Articles to Professional Journals **AW:** Woodrow Wilson Fellow, University of Michigan (1963-1964); Nelson Lifetime Achievement Award **MEM:** Neuropsychology Division, American Psychological Association; International Neuropsychological Society; Secretary, Hudson Valley Psychological Association; Program Chairperson, Hudson Valley Psychological Association; Distinguished Fellow, New York State Psychological Association; Member at Large, Neuropsychology Division, New York State Psychological Association; New York Neuropsychological Group, American Association for the Advancement of Science; American Academy of Clinical Neuropsychology **AS:** Dr. Lacher attributes her success toward good education, hard work and the influence of excellent advisors. **B/I:** Dr. Lacher became involved in her profession out of her interest in intellectual questions, as well as a desire to leverage the science of psychology in a helpful manner. **AV:** Nature; Bird-watching; Hiking

LADD, CULVER S., PHD, MA, T: Secondary School Educator **I:** Education/Educational Services **DOB:** 11/15/1929 **PB:** Bismarck **SC:** ND/USA **PT:** Culver Sprogle Ladd; Eleanor (Pearson) Ladd **MS:** Single **ED:** PhD, American University (1984); MA, American University (1978); Postgraduate Coursework, Oxford University, England (1975-1976); Certificate, ICAF, National Defense University, Thailand (1972); Postgraduate Coursework, Harvard University (1963); MA, American University (1963); BS, University of Maryland (1953) **C:** Special Lecturer, Payap University, Chiang Mai, Thailand (2000-2001); Teacher, District of Columbia Public Schools (1978-2000); Special Lecturer, Payap University, Chiang Mai, Thailand (1974-1975); Project Director, Business Research Ltd., Thailand (1966-1967, 1972-1974); Lecturer, University of Maryland, Thailand (1966-1967, 1971-1974); Project Director, Research Associate, Developmental Education & Training Research Institute, American University (1968-1970); Teacher, International School, Bangkok, Thailand (1964-1966); Assistant Office Manager, Covington & Burling, Washington, DC (1956-1962); Photographer, United States Department of Justice, FBI, Washington, DC (1946-1954) **CR:** Board of Directors, Chesapeake Water Association (2002-Present); Lecturer, Ladd Legacy Symposium, North Dakota State University (2011); Master Teacher, Woodrow Wilson Fellowship Foundation (1989); Visiting Scientist, Brookhaven National Laboratories, Long Island, NY (1988); Consultant, United States Agency for International Development, Thailand (1973-1974) **CIV:** Representative Candidate, Maryland Senate 29th Legislative District (1998) **MIL:** Captain, United States Air Force Reserve (1953-1972); Intercept Controller, Department of Defense, United States Air Force (1954-1956) **CW:** Author, "Thailand Transformed" (1950-2012); Author, "Pure Food Crusader, Edwin Fremont Ladd, Chemist 1859-1925" (2006) **AW:** Appreciation Award, Payap University (1987) **MEM:** Middle States Council for Social Studies; National Council of Teachers of Mathematics; National Capital Area Political Science Association; Mid-Atlantic Region Association of Asian Studies; Experimental Aviation Association; Aircraft Owners and Pilots Association; Pi Sigma Alpha; Omicron Delta Kappa **MH:** Albert Nelson Marquis Lifetime Achievement Award; Marquis Who's Who Top Professional **B/I:** Dr. Ladd became involved in his profession after responding to his church's search for volunteer teachers in Thailand. **AV:** Gardening; Flying **PA:** Republican **RE:** Presbyterian **THT:** Dr. Ladd became an integral part of economic development in Thailand. Dr. Ladd's longevity was recognized at a recent conference.

LADENHEIM, JULES, T: Neurosurgeon **I:** Medicine & Health Care **DOB:** 04/21/1923 **PB:** Union Hill **SC:** NJ/USA **PT:** Solomon Ladenheim; Miriam (Preminger) Ladenheim **MS:** Widowed **SPN:** Janet Bloom (02/15/1959) **CH:** Eric; Fred (Deceased); Karen **ED:** Intern, Queens General Hospital, New York, NY (1947-1948); MD, New York Medical College (1947); AB, Harvard University (1944) **C:** Private Practice, Hackensack, NJ (1960-Present); Resident, Neurosurgery, Mary Hitchcock, Hanover, NH (1958-1960); Resident, Neurosurgery, Neurology Institute of New York (1957-1958); Resident, Neurosurgery, Medical College of Virginia, Richmond, VA (1956-1957); Resident, Neurosurgery, Serafimer Hospital, Stockholm, Sweden (1954-1956); Resident, General Surgery, Mount Sinai, Cleveland, OH (1953-1954); Resident, General Surgery, Pittsburgh Medical Center (1952-1953); Resident, General Surgery, New York Medical College (1948-1950) **CR:** Neurosurgeon, St. Mary Hospital, Hoboken, NJ (1987-Present); Neurosurgeon, Meadowland Hospital, Secaucus, NJ (1987-Present); Staff Neurosurgeon, Hackensack University Hospital (1960-Present); Neurosurgeon, Holy Name Hospital, Teaneck, NJ (1960-Present) **MIL:** Lieutenant, United States Naval Reserve (1950-1952) **CW:** Author, "Grant's Keeper" (2011); Author, "Abe Lincoln Afloat"

(2009); Author, "The Jarrett-Palmer Express of 1876" (2008); Author, "Custer's Thorn" (2007); Author, "Alien Horseman" (2003); Author, "Firearms and Ballistics" (1996); Author, "Leonardo Bertapaglia" (1991); Co-author, "Arteriovenous Aneurysm" (1956); Author, "Intraventric Meningiomas" **AW:** Decorated Navy Medal; Marine Corps Medal **MEM:** President, Abraham Lincoln Society (1993-1994); American Association of Neurologic Surgeons; Congress of Neurosurgery; Nordiska Neurokirugiska Forening; U.S. Ship Columbus Veterans Association; Harvard Club of New York **MH:** Albert Nelson Marquis Lifetime Achievement Award

LADMAN, JERRY R., PHD, I: Education/Educational Services **CN:** Professor Emeritus **DOB:** 12/30/1935 **PB:** Sioux City **SC:** IA/USA **PT:** Harry L.; Amy I. (Swearingen) L **MS:** Married **SPN:** Carmen Aida (12/15/1990) **CH:** Jeffrey; James; Michael (Deceased); Stephanie **ED:** Doctor of Philosophy, Iowa State University (1968); Bachelor of Science, Iowa State University (1958) **C:** Retired (2007); Associate Provost, International Affairs, Ohio State University (2000-2007); Professor of Agricultural Economics, Ohio State University, Columbus, OH (1990-2007); Director, Latin America Studies Program, Ohio State University, Columbus, OH (1998-2001); Director, Ohio LEAD Program, Columbus, OH (1997-2000); Professor of Economics, Arizona State University (1979-2000); Assistant Director, Ohio LEAD Program, Columbus, OH (1995-1997); Director, Center for Latin American Studies, Arizona State University (1976-1990); Associate Professor, Arizona State University (1972-1978); Assistant Professor, Arizona State University (1967-1972); Research Assistant, College of Agriculture, Iowa State University, Ames, IA (1965-1967); Placement Officer, College of Agriculture, Iowa State University, Ames, IA (1963-1965) **CR:** Principal Investigator, Numerous Research Grants in Bolivia, Central America and Mexico, U.S. Department of State (1969-2012); Chief of Party, University of Agriculture Business Partnership Project, Institute Superior de Agricultura, Santiago, Dominican Republic (1990-1995); Participant, U.S.-U.S.S.R. Cultural Exchange (1986); Honorary Professor, Catholic University of Bolivia (1986); Visiting Professor, Ohio State University (1979); Scholar, Diplomat, U.S. Department of State (1977); Visiting Scholar Stanford University (1975); Program Assistant, Ford Foundation, Mexico City (1971-1972); Visiting Professor, National School of Agriculture, Chapingo, Mexico (1965-1967, 1971-1972); Consultant, Numerous Organizations Including World Bank, U.S. Agency for International Development, U.S. Information Agency, U.S. Department of Agriculture and Others **CIV:** Docent, Columbus Museum of Art (2013-Present); Member, Columbus Council on World Affairs (2000-Present); Board of Directors, Columbus Council on World Affairs (2001-2016); Board Director, Friends of Mexican Art (1977-1986); Chairman, Troop Committee, Boy Scouts of America, Tempe, AZ (1976-1984) **MIL:** Captain, U.S. Army Reserve (1958-1965) **CW:** Author, "Mexico: A Country in Crisis" (1987); Author, "Modern Day Bolivia: The Legacy of the Revolution and Prospects for the Future" (1982); Author, "United States-Mexican Energy Relationships: Realities and Prospects" (1981); Author, "The Development of Mexicali Regional Economy" (1975); Contributor, Articles to Professional Journals, Chapters to Books **AW:** Fulbright Lecturer, Ecuador (1974) **MEM:** Board of Directors, PROFMEX (1983-1990); Board Director, Phoenix Committee on Foreign Relations, Arizona-Mexico Commission (1982-1990); Board Director, Rocky Mountain Council on Latin American Studies (1976-1990); Treasurer, Pacific Coast Council on Latin American Studies (1987); Vice President, Pacific Coast Council on Latin American Studies (1986); President, Pacific Coast Council on Latin American Studies (1977-1986); President, Association of Borderlands Scholars (1983-1985); American Agricultural Economic Association; Latin American Studies Association **MH:** Albert Nelson Marquis Lifetime Achievement Award **B/I:** Prof. Ladman became involved in his profession because his faculty advisor at Iowa State University, Louis M. Thompson, was promoted to associate dean at the same time he graduated. He was offered a position and, having been very involved in campus leadership as an undergraduate, eagerly accepted. **AV:** Reading; Exercise **PA:** Democrat **RE:** Catholic

LAENUI, POKA, T: Human Rights Advocate/Lawyer **I:** Law and Legal Services **CN:** Poka Laenui (Hayden F. Burgess) **DOB:** 05/05/1946 **PB:** Honolulu **SC:** HI/USA **YOP:** 1976 **PT:** Ned E. Burgess; Nora (Lee) Burgess **MS:** Married **SPN:** Puanani Sonoda Burgess (08/28/1968) **CH:** Pua'ena; Pohaokalani; La'ameaomauna'ala **ED:** JD, University of Hawai'i at Manoa William S. Richardson School of Law, Honolulu, Hawaii (1976); BA in Political Science, University of Hawaii at Manoa, Hawaii (1968) **CT:** Individual Study Under Tutorship of Pilahi Paki on Fundamental Hawaiian Beliefs (1980-1982); Thought Field Therapy Under Caroline Sakai, PhD, International Clubhouse Training, Greenville, SC **C:** Chairman, Native Hawaiian Convention (Aha Hawai'i 'Oiwi) (2002-Present); President, Hawaiian National Broadcast Corporation (1993-Present); Attorney at Law, Private Practice (1976-Present); Hale Na'au Pono (The Wai'anae Coast Community Mental Health Center, Inc.) (1997-2014); Executive Director, Waianae Coast Community Alternative Development Corporation (2000-2005); President, Pacific and Asia Council of Indigenous Peoples (PACIP); President, Hawaii Council; Director, Institute for the Advancement of Hawaiian Affairs (IAHA); Member, Na'i Aupuni Congregation **CR:** Chairman of the Convention, Native Hawaiian Convention (2002-Present); Chairperson, International Relations Committee, Native Hawaiian Convention (1999-Present); Instructor, Practitioner, Tai Chi Chuan (Young & Chuk Kai Style) (1971-Present); Council Member, Hawaiian Sovereignty Elections Council (1994); Appointed Commissioner by Governor John Waihe'e, Hawaiian Sovereignty Advisory Commission (1993); Organizer, Hawaiian Sovereignty Economic Symposium, University of Hawai'i at Manoa William S. Richardson School of Law (1993); Representative, Pacific Asia Council of Indigenous Peoples, U.N. Working Group on Indigenous Populations (1992); Vice President, World Council of Indigenous Peoples (WCIP) (1984-1990); Expert, "Effects of Racism and Racial Discrimination on the Social and Economic Relations Between Indigenous Peoples and States on Behalf of the World Council of Indigenous Peoples," United Nations' Seminar (1989); Co-instructor, "The Indigenous Pacific: Sovereignty, Independence and Then?," Political Science Department, University of Hawai'i at Manoa; Essayist, Science, Technology and Human Rights, Self-determination, Decolonization and Indigenous Peoples, Deep Cultures of Society; Behavioral Health and Community Cultures, Peace, Equity and Justice, Environmental Practice from the Perspective of Family Relationships and Fundamental Spiritual Characteristics **CIV:** Convener, Hawaii National Transitional Authority (HNTA) (2016-Present); President, Pacific Asia Council of Indigenous Peoples (1992-Present); Trustee, Office of Hawaiian Affairs (OHA), Honolulu, Hawaii (1982-1986); Vice President, World Council of Indigenous Peoples (1984); Leader, Hawaiian Independence Movement; Member, Hawaiian Sovereignty Elections Council (HSEC); Chair, Native Hawaiian Convention **MIL:** Honorably Discharged, United States Air Force (1969-1973) **CW:** Television Host, "A Second Glance," Olelo Public Access Television (1999-Present); Radio Host, "Hawaiian Potpourri," KWAI 1080AM (1996-2017); Speaker, Keynote Speaker, Numerous Presentations and Lectures (1992-2007); Radio Host, "A Second Glance," Hawaiian National Broadcast Corporation (HNBC) (1993-2000); Author, Numerous Papers, Monograms, and Articles to Professional Publications; Publication, "The 2016 Na'i Aupuni Congregation: A Brief Study in a Practice of Indigenous Self-Determination," In "Hulili Multidisciplinary Research on Hawaiian Well-Being, Volume II, No. 1" **AW:** Native Hawaiian Health Award for Ongoing Dedication to Improving the Health and Well-being of Kanaka Maoli and Advocating for their Rights as the Indigenous Peoples of Ka Pae Aina O Hawaii, Papa Ola Lokahi, Native Hawaiian Convention (2012); Named Executive of the Year, Mental Health Association of America in Hawaii (2006) **MEM:** Hawaii State Bar Association; American Bar Association (ABA); American Trial Lawyers Association; International Association of Democratic Lawyers; Union of Third World Journalists **BAR:** Hawaii, (1976); United States Tax Court; United States Court of Appeals for the Ninth Circuit **MH:** Albert Nelson Marquis Lifetime Achievement Award; Marquis Who's Who Top Professional; Marquis Who's Who Humanitarian Award **AS:** Mr. Laenui attributes his success to curiosity, challenge, fearlessness, acceptance of success and failure as learning experiences, tenaciousness, commitment to Aloha and Pono, and study. **B/I:** Mr. Laenui became involved in law as a means to make social and political changes, especially to address the colonization existing in Hawaii and to struggle for decolonization. In regards to the practice of Tai chi, Chi kung, the study of Buddhism and other religions, including Christianity, Islam, Judaism, Daoism, Lama-ism, he got involved because these are the studies necessary to understand world cultures and events which have such great influences in the world. **AV:** Practicing forms of Tai chi Chuang and Chi Kung and sharing such practice with others; Consult on a wide variety of issues in the analysis of cultures and its applicability in social services, on Hawaiian history and lore, in behavioral health and substance treatment, in human rights and fundamental freedoms, in indigenous peoples' rights both domestically and internationally, on peace approaches and methodologies, on international political and social concerns, on development of national and community economic approaches; Writing on a wide variety of topics **THT:** Mr. Laenui says, "Among the most important and yet least understood aspects in life is the flow and affect of a people's deep culture. One reason for the lack of understanding is because culture runs so deep that people are often not even aware of its existence, like a fish not knowing of the existence of the water in which it has swam in all its life. There are cultural codes in the collective subconscious of all societies which defines within that society what is right or wrong, moral and natural, and what forms of behavior is appropriate in given circumstances. These codes derive from the myths and legends, deep national memories, environmental conditions, internal conflicts and from a multitude of other processes which have taken place over long periods of time in a society. These codes are generally unwritten. They do not form a constitutive document or are in some explicit statement. They are generally unspoken. But they are so ingrained in a society that they become the driving force. You can often see them in the routines and habits, fears and pleasures of a people, in their dreams, expectations and the systems of reasoning. The deep culture lies at the foundation of a society. Sitting immediately upon that deep culture is a wide social system including economic relations, health care, families, shelter and clothing practices, food and eating customs, education forms and environmental attitudes. A political system develops upon and protects the social system and a military system upon that, protecting, of course, the political system. In the U.S., for example, the prevailing deep culture I have called DIE for Domination Individualism and Exclusion. These values sit so deep within that society that it is expressed in its economic system, social policy, environmental policies, judiciary system, education system, even its expression of its Christian religion. To bring about a change, it's not merely a matter of passing new laws or adopting new policies. It must come about first by an awareness of these motivating driving forces and the introduction of an alternative deep culture which must pervade the society. An alternative to the DIE culture could be one which is more compatible and accepting of differences and respect for a plethora of differing views. In Hawaii, I call that value by a cultural word, "'olu'olu." Rather than the value of individualism, an alternative could be "lokahi," which speaks of group and broad common society interest. Rather than the value of exclusion, an alternative would be "aloha," to not only be inclusive but to be loving, caring and respectful of the humanity in all beings. This is what I know as the "OLA" deep culture, a word which also means life and health. This alternative culture is not particularly Hawaiian; it can also be found in early U.S. history among the environmentalists, poets and philosophers of America, as well as many communities today across America and the world, of people struggling to express this alternate deep culture in new approaches to the environment, economy, social patterns, political expressions, international relations, religious practices, family relations and everything else which affects the quality of our lives today and into the future. I believe that awareness is the first step to change. By an appreciation of the impact upon us which a deep culture has, we can then move to examine the elements of that culture which moves us and search for values which would express alternate preferred cultures. Aloha."

LAFITTE, JACQUELINE, T: Youth Mentor **I:** Education/Educational Services **CN:** Cherryland Elementary **DOB:** 01/25/1954 **PB:** Lacombe **SC:** LA/USA **PT:** Miller Jack Lafitte; Celina Ducre Lafitte **MS:** Married **SPN:** Ronald Tutson **CH:** Danielle; Gabrielle; Aaliyah (Grandchild); Mariama (Grandchild); Solomom (Grandchild); Zachary (Grandchild) **ED:** BA in Business and Arts, Holy Name College, Oakland, CA (1989); AA, Miss Wades Fashion and Merchandising College, Dallas, TX (1982) **CT:** Certified, Landmark Education' Self Expression and Leadership Program (2020); Certified, TRIBES Trainer (1999); Teaching Credentials, Holy Names University, Oakland, CA (1997); Real Estate License (1994); Certified, Landmark Education's Forum (1992) **C:** Garden Club After School Program (2012-Present); Drama Club After School Program (1999-Present); Teacher, 4th and 5th Grade, Cherryland Elementary, Hayward Unified School District (1996-Present); Teacher, 4th Grade, St. Elizabeth Elementary, Diocese of Oakland (1991-1996) **CR:** Landlord, Triplex; Real Estate Loan Agent; Costumier, Mills College Drama Department, Oakland, CA (1989); Belt Designer, Manufacturing Company, Los Angeles, CA (1983); Accessories Designer's Product Manager, Dallas, TX (1980); Chuck E Cheese Prototypes, Sunnyvale, CA (1979); Mardis Gras Costumes, New Orleans,

LA (1978); Pocket Setter, Just Jeans Manufacturing Company, Pearl River, MS (1977); Alterations, Army Clothing Sales Store, Fort Sill, OK (1974) **CIV:** Founder, Clean Water Education (2020-Present); Cherryland's Earth Day Celebration (2020) **CW:** Director, "Cherryland Friendship Quilt Mural"; "Sound of Great Voices," Cherryland's Drama Club; "Kids and Parents," Cherryland's Drama Club; Cherryland's Dramatic Chorus Production, "One People"; Succulent and Rock Garden, Victorian Triple; Clean Water Education **MEM:** Arts Is Education; Alameda County Integrated Arts; Red Hats Society; UC Berkeley Botanical Garden; Oakland Community Organization; Diocese of Oakland Deacon's Wives; Landscape Committee; Site Base Decision Making; Instructional Leadership Team **AS:** Ms. Lafitte attributes her success to God's divine design. If she gets stuck in any situation she doesn't know how to get out of, she prays. She is a witness with grateful praise to miracles of so many answered prayers. Perseverance and making deadlines are important to her. Taking responsibility to do what it takes to move forward in the moment. Share God's abundant blessings. Love others unconditionally. **B/I:** God called her to the teaching profession in her late 30's. She kept running towards clothing design. When Mills College closed the Drama Department, she said, "Yes, God I will teach." She was in a classroom within months. She is grateful for every child she is blessed to mentor. It is pure joy to meet them as adults. **AV:** Family radio; Bikram yoga; Connecting with nature; Meditating in a garden; Mindful spiritual exercise; Watching every plant grow; Collecting succulents; U.C. Berkeley's Botanical Garden; Walking or bike riding along the beach in Alameda; Driving Volvo convertible on streets lined with oak trees or crossing bridges over Bay Area waterways; Dancing **RE:** Catholic **THT:** God's divine design to create global literacy. The evolution of Human Beings communicating from a place of love. Public Education will teach creative thinkers to do what works to make a difference today.

LAFLEUR, GUY, T: Retired Professional Hockey Player **I:** Athletics **DOB:** 09/20/1951 **PB:** Thurso **SC:** Quebec/Canada **PT:** Rejean Lafleur; Pierrette Lafleur **MS:** Married **SPN:** Lise Barre (06/16/1973) **CH:** Martin; Mark **ED:** Coursework, Public Schools **C:** Director of Corporate Affairs, Quebec Nordiques, National Hockey League (NHL) (1992-1993); Right Wing, Quebec Nordiques, National Hockey League (NHL) (1989-1991); Right Wing, New York Rangers, National Hockey League (NHL) (1988-1989); Right Wing, Montreal Canadiens, National Hockey League (NHL) (1971-1985); Right Wing, Quebec Remparts, Quebec Major Junior Hockey League (1969-1971) **CR:** Owner, Guy LaFleur Mike's Signature, Berthierville, Quebec, Canada (2002-Present); Owner, Bleu Blanc Rouge, Rosemere, Quebec, Canada (2008-2012); Vice President, Public Relations, Titrex (1993); Owner, Helicopter Rental Company **MIL:** Honorary Colonel, 3 Wing Bagotville, Quebec, Canada (2013); Honorary Colonel, 12 Radar Squadron, Bagotville, Quebec, Canada (2005-2008) **AW:** Listee, 100 Greatest NHL Players in History (2017); Knight, National Order of Quebec (2005); Inductee, Canada Sports Hall of Fame (1996); Officer, Order of Canada (1980); Winner, Montreal Canadiens, Stanely Cup (1973, 1976-1979); NHL Player of the Year, Sporting News (1977, 1978); Hart Memorial Trophy (1977, 1978); Lester B. Pearson Award (1976-1978); Art Ross Trophy (1976-1978); Lou Marsh Trophy (1977); Conn Smythe Trophy (1977)

LAGASSE, EMERIL JOHN III, T: Chef; Restaurateur; Television Show Host **I:** Food & Restaurant Services **DOB:** 10/15/1959 **PB:** Fall River **SC:** MA/

USA **PT:** John Lagasse; Hilda Medeiros Lagasse **MS:** Married **SPN:** Alden Lovelace (05/13/2000); Tari Hohn (1989, Divorced 1996); Elizabeth Kief (1978, Divorced 1986) **CH:** Jessica; Jillian; Emeril John Lagasse IV; Meril Lovelace **ED:** BS in Culinary Arts, Johnson & Wales University, Providence, RI (1978); Honorary Doctorate, Johnson & Wales University, Providence, RI; Coursework, Culinary Arts, France **C:** Owner, Chef, Burgers and More by Emeril, Sands Casino Resort, Bethlehem, PA (2009-Present); Owner, Chef, Lagasse's Stadium, Las Vegas, NV (2009-Present); Owner, Chef, Emeril's Chop House, Sands Casino Resort, Bethlehem, PA (2009-Present); Owner, Chef, Delmonico Steakhouse Restaurant, Las Vegas, NV (1999-Present); Owner, Chef, Delmonico Restaurant and Bar, New Orleans, LA (1998-Present); Owner, Chef, Emeril's New Orleans Fish House Restaurant, Las Vegas, NV (1995-Present); Owner, Chef, NoLA Restaurant, New Orleans, LA (1992-Present); Owner, Chef, Emeril's Restaurant, New Orleans, LA (1990-Present); Owner, Chef, Emeril's Orlando, Orlando, FL (1999-2018); Owner, Chef, Tchoup Chop Restaurant, Orlando, FL (2003-2017); Owner, Chef, Emeril's Italian Table, Sands Casino Resort, Bethlehem, PA (2011-2016); Owner, Chef, e2 Emeril's Eatery, Charlotte, NC (2011-2015); Owner, Chef, Emeril's Miami Beach (2003-2011); Owner, Chef, Table 10, Las Vegas, NV (2008-2010); Owner, Chef, Emeril's Gulf Coast Fish House, Gulfport, MS (2007-2010); Owner, Chef, Emeril's Atlanta, GA (2003-2008); Executive Chef, Commander's Palace, New Orleans, LA (1982-1990); Executive Chef, Dunfey's Hyannis Resort (1979-1982) **CR:** Partner, T-fal to Develop Emerilware Fryer, Grill/Panini Maker and Steamer (2006-Present); Partner, All-Clad Metalcrafters for Emerilware (1999-Present); Emeril Professional Stoneware (2005-Present); Emerilware Cookware and Gourmet Kitchen Tools, HSN (2007); Creator, Emeril's Gourmet Produce with Pride of San Juan (2004); Creator, Emerilware Electric Appliance Collection and Emerilware Cast Iron Cookware (2004); Creator, Emeril's Gourmet Meats with Sara Lee Foods (2004); Introduced Clog Line, Emeril by Sanita (2003); Creator, California Wines Line, Emerils' Classics with Fetzer Vineyards (2002); Launched, Emerilware Knives with Wusthof-Trident (2002); Creator, Gourmet Food Line of Seasonings, Salad Dressing, Pasta Sauces, and More, Emeril's Original (2000) **CIV:** Dedicated the Emeril Lagasse Foundation Culinary Arts Studio (2011-Present); Established, Emeril Lagasse Foundation (2002-Present) **CW:** Host, "The Originals with Emeril, Cooking Channel (2011-Present); Host, "Fresh Food Fast," Cooking Channel (2010-Present); Host, Live Call-in Radio Program, "Cooking with Emeril," Martha Stewart Living Radio on SIRIUS XM (2009-Present); Food Correspondent, "Good Morning America," ABC (1998-Present); Host, "Emeril's Florida," Cooking Channel (2013-2017); Author, "Essential Emeril: Favorite Recipes and Hard-Won Wisdom from My Life in the Kitchen" (2015); Mentor, "On the Menu" (2014); Author, "Emeril's Cooking with Power: 100 Delicious Recipes Starring Your Slow Cooker, Multi Cooker, Pressure Cooker, and Deep Fryer" (2013); Author, "Emeril's Kicked-Up Sandwiches: Stacked with Flavor" (2012); Appearance, "Treme" (2012); Author, "Sizzling Skillets and Other One-Pot Wonders" (2011); Judge, "Top Chef" (2011); Host, "Emeril's Table," Hallmark Channel (2011); Host, "The Emeril Lagasse Show," Ion Television (2010); Competitor, "Super Chef Battle, Iron Chef America" (2010); Author, "Farm to Fork: Cooking Local, Cooking Fresh" (2010); Host, "Essence of Emeril," Fine Living Network (2008-2010); Author, "Emeril 20-40-60: Fresh Food Fast" (2009); Guest Appearances, "Jon & Kate Plus 8" (2009); Voice Actor, "The Princess and the Frog"

(2009); Author, "Emeril at the Grill: A Cookbook for All Seasons" (2009); Host, "Essence of Emeril," Food Network (1994-1996, 2000-2007); Host, Cooking Show, "Emeril Live," Food Network (1997-2007); Appearance, "Last Holiday" (2006); Author, "There's a Chef in My World" (2006); Author, "Emeril's Delmonico: A New Orleans Restaurant with a Past" (2005); Author, "There's a Chef in My Family" (2004); Author, "Emeril's Potluck: Comfort Food with a Kicked-Up Attitude" (2004); Author, "From Emeril's Kitchens: Favorite Recipes from Emeril's Restaurants" (2003); Author, "There's a Chef in My Soup" (2002); Author, "Prime Time Emeril: More TV Dinners from America's Favorite Chef" (2001); Actor, "Emeril" (2001); Author, "Every Day's a Party" (1999); Author, "Emeril's TV Dinners" (1998); Author, "Emeril's Creole Christmas" (1997); Author, "Louisiana Real and Rustic" (1996); Author, "Emeril's New New Orleans Cooking" (1993); Host, "Emeril Green," Planet Green; Co-Columnist, Everyday Food Magazine **AW:** Emmy Award for Outstanding Culinary Program, The National Academy of Television Arts and Sciences (2017); Lifetime Achievement, Taste Awards (2014); Inductee, Taste Hall of Fame (2013); Honoree for Dedicated Efforts to Further the Culinary Arts in America and Work through the Emeril Lagasse Foundation, James Beard Foundation (2011); Lifetime Achievement Award, Food Network's South Beach Wine & Food Festival (2009); Inductee, Gaming Hall of Fame (2008); Restaurateur of the Year, New Orleans CityBusiness (2007); Inductee, MenuMasters Hall of Fame (2006); Distinguished Service Award, Wine Spectator Magazine (2005); Executive of the Year, Restaurants & Institutions Magazine (2004); Grand Award, Wine Spectator Magazine (1999); Salute to Excellence Award, National Restaurant Association (1998); Chef of the Year, GQ Magazine (1998); Listee, Most Intriguing People of the Year, People Magazine (1998); Cable ACE Award for Best Informational Series for "Emeril Live" (1997); Inductee, American Express for Fine Dining Hall of Fame (1994); Ivy Award for Restaurants and Institutions (1994); Best Esquire Award for Restaurant of the Year (1993); Best Chef Southeast, James Beard Foundation (1991); Esquire Award for Restaurant of the Year (1991); Listee, America's Top Twenty-Five New Chefs, Food & Wine (1991)

LAHAM, MICHEL, MD, T: Physician **I:** Medicine & Health Care **DOB:** 09/07/1946 **PB:** Jacksonville **SC:** FL/USA **MS:** Married **SPN:** Hala (1976) **CH:** Rima; Tarik **ED:** Specialty Training in Clinical Immunology, University of Florida (1976); Residency in Internal Medicine, University of Florida (1974); Internship in Straight Medicine, University of Florida (1972); Doctor of Medicine, University of Florida (1971); Bachelor of Arts in History and Pre-Med, University of Florida, Cum Laude (1967) **CT:** American Board of Allergy and Immunology (1979); American Board of Internal Medicine (1977) **C:** Courtesy Staff, Department of Medicine, Metropolitan Methodist Hospital (1990-Present); Physician, Private Practice (1982-Present); Courtesy Staff, Department of Medicine, Santa Rosa Medical Center (1982-Present); Staff, Department of Medicine, Metropolitan Methodist Hospital (1982-Present); Chief, Department of Medicine, Brooke Army Medical Center (1978-1985); Assistant Chief, Allergy Service, Brooke Army Medical Center (1976-1978) **CR:** Associate Clinical Professor, Department of Medicine, University of Texas Health Science Center at San Antonio (1992-Present); Associate Clinical Professor, Department of Pediatrics, University of Texas Health Science Center at San Antonio (1983-1992); Assistant Clinical Professor, Department of Medicine, University of Texas Health Science Center at San Anto-

nio (1982-1983) **CIV:** Co-Chairman, Institutional Review Board, Humana Hospital Metropolitan (1984-1994) **MIL:** Lieutenant Colonel, U.S. Army, Allergy Immunology Service Center, Brooke Army Medical Center (1979-1982) **CW:** Senior Year Thesis, "Neapolitan the Third and the Advent of the Modern Police State" **AW:** Listee, Texas Super Doctors (2004-2019); Special Research Fellowship Award, National Cancer Institute (1974-1976) **MEM:** President, San Antonio Allergy Society (1991); Vice President, San Antonio Allergy Society (1990); Secretary-Treasurer, San Antonio Allergy Society (1989); Fellow, American College of Physicians; Fellow, American College of Allergy, Asthma and Immunology; Fellow American Academy of Allergy, Asthma and Immunology; American Association of Certified Allergists; Joint Council of Allergy and Immunology; Bexar County Medical Society; Texas Medical Association; Texas Allergy, Asthma & Immunology Society; Phi Alpha Theta **MH:** Marquis Who's Who Top Professional **AS:** Dr. Laham attributes his success to persistence and determination. **AV:** Fishing; Exercising at the gym

LAHEY, BONITA LOUISE, T: Business and Market Development Projects Consultant **I:** Business Management/Business Services **PT:** Walter D. Lahey; Josephine (Moomwa) Lahey **MS:** Single **ED:** MBA, University of Denver (1977); Postgraduate Coursework, University of Colorado; MS in Geology, Colorado School of Mines, CO; BS, Colorado College **C:** Tour Guide, Dinosaur Ridge, Morrison, CO (2012-Present); Geology Research Associate, Denver Museum of Nature & Science, Denver CO (2000-Present); President, B.L. Lahey Consulting, Inc., Denver, CO (2002-2012); Chief Operating Officer, Chief Marketing Officer, CH2MHill Companies, Ltd. (Now Jacobs), Englewood, CO (2000-2002); Assistant General Manager, Los Angeles Department of Water and Power (1998-1999); Vice President, Sempra Energy, Los Angeles, CA (1995-1997); Executive, US West, Inc. (Now CenturyLink), Denver, CO (1977-1995) **CIV:** President, South City Park Neighborhood Association (2015-Present); Chair, Networks Committee, Women's Vision Foundation, Denver, CO (2001-2012); Vice Chair, Mile High Area, The American National Red Cross, Denver, CO (2001-2010) **CW:** Contributor, Scientific Journals **AW:** Virginia Oredson Memorial Award, Inter-Neighborhood Cooperation™, Inc., Denver, CO (2012); Service Award, Denver Museum of Nature & Science **MH:** Albert Nelson Marquis Lifetime Achievement Award **B/I:** Ms. Lahey became involved in her career when she switched areas of study while at Colorado College. Originally a history major, she was fascinated by the rocks in Colorado, and she decided to study a much older history: geology. Specifically, Ms. Lahey pursued petrology between undergraduate and graduate school, but upon receiving her degree, saw that geology was not a women-friendly field. She changed her area of expertise and entered the engineering field. Now retired, Ms. Lahey has returned to her love of geology. **AV:** Singing

LAHOOD, DARIN MCKAY, T: U.S. Representative from Illinois; Lawyer **I:** Government Administration/Government Relations/Government Services **DOB:** 07/05/1968 **PB:** Peoria **SC:** IL/USA **PT:** Ray LaHood; Kathy LaHood **MS:** Married **SPN:** Kristen LaHood **CH:** McKay; Lucas; Teddy **ED:** JD, University of Illinois at Chicago John Marshall Law School (1997); Bachelor in Political Science, Loras College, Dubuque, Iowa **C:** Member, Committee of Ways and Means (2018-Present); Member, U.S. House of Representatives from Illinois' 18th District, United States Congress, Washington, DC (2015-Present); Attorney, Miller, Hall & Triggs, LLC, Peoria, IL (2006-Present); Member, District 37, Illi-

nois State Senate, Springfield, IL (2011-2015); Lead Terrorism Prosecutor, District of Nevada, Office of U.S. Attorney (2005-2006); Federal Prosecutor, Office of U.S. Attorney, Las Vegas, NV (2001-2005); Assistant State's Attorney, Cook County, Tazewell County, IL (1997-2001); Legislative Assistant, Appropriations Committee Assistant, U.S. House of Representatives, Washington, DC (1990-1994); Member, Committee on Natural Resources; Member, Committee on Science, Space, and Technology; Member, U.S. Joint Economic Committee; Member, U.S.-Cuba Working Group; Co-chair, U.S.-China Working Group; Co-chair, U.S.-Brazil Caucus; Co-chair, Digital Trade Caucus; Co-chair, U.S.-Lebanon Friendship Caucus; Co-chair, Congressional Soccer Caucus **CR:** Adjunct Professor of Criminal Law, University of Nevada Las Vegas (2003-2005) **CIV:** Board of Directors, Center for Prevention of Abuse (2006-2010); Member, St. Vincent de Paul Parish, IL; Former Board Member, The Salvation Army USA; Former Board Member, Big Brothers Big Sisters of America **AW:** Edgar Fellow (2013); Named One of Peoria's 40 Under 40 **BAR:** State of Illinois (1997) **AV:** Running **PA:** Republican

LAMALFA, DOUGLAS LEE, T: U.S. Representative from California; Farmer **I:** Government Administration/Government Relations/Government Services **DOB:** 07/02/1960 **PB:** Oroville **SC:** CA/USA **MS:** Married **SPN:** Jill LaMalfa **CH:** Kyle; Allison; Sophia; Natalie **ED:** BS, California Polytechnic State University, San Luis Obispo, CA (1982); AA, Butte College (1980) **C:** Member, U.S. House of Representatives from California's First Congressional District, United States Congress, Washington, DC (2013-Present); Member, U.S. House Committee on Foreign Affairs (2013-Present); Member, U.S. House Financial Services Committee (2013-Present); Owner, Manager, Dsl Lamalfa Family Partnership (1990-Present); Member, District Four, California State Senate (2010-2012); Member, District Two, California State Assembly (2002-2008); Vice Chairman, Butte County Republican Central Committee (1992-2002) **CR:** Founding Director, California Rice Commission **CIV:** Past Chairman, Richvale Foundation Boosters **PA:** Republican **RE:** Christian

LAMANDA, AL, T: Author **I:** Writing and Editing **ED:** College Coursework **C:** Author (2004-Present); Private Investigator, NY and FL (1980-2004); Loss Prevention (1980-2004) **CW:** Author, "Assassin's Creed: Book Three: Revenant" (2019); Author, "Assassin's Creed: Book One: The Ruling Class" (2019); Author, as Ethan J. Wolfe, "The Cattle Drive" (2018); Author, as Ethan J. Wolfe, "The Devil's Waltz" (2018); Author, as Ethan J. Wolfe, "Comanche Sunrise" (2018); Author, as Ethan J. Wolfe, "The Reckoning" (2018); Author, "The Theory of Everything" (2018); Author, "Who Killed Joe Italiano?" (2018); Author, "Once Upon a Time in Puerto Rico" (2018); Author, as Ethan J. Wolfe, "One If By Land" (2017); Author, "Assassin's Creed: Book Two: Adjudicated"; Author, "With Six You Get Wally"; Author, "Jack"; Author, "This Side of Midnight"; Author, "Checkmate"; Author, "Shades of Gotham"; Author, "Lollypops"; Author, "Running Homeless"; Author, "Walking Homeless"; Author, "Dunston Falls"; Author, "Sunrise"; Author, "Sunset"; Author, "First Light"; Author, "For Better or Worse"; Author, as Ethan J. Wolfe, "The Last Ride"; Author, as Ethan J. Wolfe, "The Regulator"; Author, as Ethan J. Wolfe, "The Range War of 82"; Author, as Ethan J. Wolfe, "Murphy's Law"; Author, as Ethan J. Wolfe, "All the Queen's Men"; Author, as Ethan J. Wolfe, "Lawman"; Author, as Ethan J. Wolfe, "Baker's Dozen"; Author, as Ethan J. Wolfe, "The Illinois Detective Agency"; Screenwriter, "Two: A Horror Story"; Screenwriter, "American Violence" **AW:** Nero Award for Best Mystery, The

Wolfe Pack (2017); Named Best Crime Novel for "Sunrise," Maine Writers and Publishers Alliance (2013); The Edgar Award for Best Novel for "Sunset" (2012) **MEM:** Mystery Writers of America **AS:** Mr. Lamanda attributes his success to hard work, perseverance, a thick skin. a good imagination and luck. **B/I:** In his heart, Mr. Lamanda always wanted to be a storyteller. It's something he thinks that no writer can explain. **THT:** Mr. Lamanda's motto is, "Live it."

LAMB, CONOR JAMES, T: U.S. Representative from Pennsylvania **I:** Government Administration/Government Relations/Government Services **DOB:** 06/27/1984 **PB:** Washington, DC **SC:** DC/USA **PT:** Thomas F. Lamb Jr.; Katie Lamb **MS:** Married **SPN:** Hayley Haldeman (2019) **ED:** JD, University of Pennsylvania Carey Law School; BA, University of Pennsylvania **C:** Member, U.S. House of Representatives from Pennsylvania's 17th Congressional District (2019-Present); Member, U.S. House of Representatives from Pennsylvania's 18th Congressional District (2018-Present); Assistant U.S. Attorney, U.S. Department of Justice, Pittsburgh, PA (2014-2018) **PA:** Democrat **RE:** Catholic

LAMB, ROBERT, T: Diplomat (Retired); Professional Society Administrator **I:** Civil Service **DOB:** 11/17/1936 **PB:** Atlanta **SC:** GA/USA **PT:** Toker E. Lamb; Lois (Harris) Lamb **MS:** Married **SPN:** Lucille Trujillo (01/13/1962) **CH:** Robert Jr.; Anne Gretchen Beyer; Michael D. Lamb **ED:** BA in International Relations, University of Pennsylvania (1962) **C:** Executive Director, American Philatelic Society, State College, PA (1994-2006); Special Cyprus Coordinator (1993-1994); United States Ambassador to Cyprus, Cyprus (1990-1993); Assistant Secretary of State, Diplomatic Security, Washington, DC (1985-1989); Assistant Secretary of State for Administration, U.S. Department of State, Washington, DC (1983-1985); Administrative Counselor, United States Embassy, Bonn, Germany (1979-1983); Director of Passport Office, U.S. Department of State, Washington, DC (1977-1979); Director of Financial Services, U.S. Department of State, Washington, DC (1975-1977); Joined Foreign Service, U.S. Department of State, Washington, DC (1963) **MIL:** With, United States Marine Corps (1958-1961) **CW:** Publisher, "Index of American Philatelic Literature" (1999-2001) **MEM:** Former Member, Governing Board, American Foreign Service Association (1999-2001); Former, Board of Directors, Bellefonte Intervalley Chamber of Commerce; Rotary Club of Bellefonte; Former Board Member, YMCA; **MH:** Albert Nelson Marquis Lifetime Achievement Award; Marquis Who's Who Top Professional **B/I:** Mr. Lamb became involved in his profession because he always wanted to be a diplomat. He prepared for it and enjoyed every minute of it. In high school, one of Mr. Lamb's teachers had a brother who worked as a diplomat and the stories she told about him made him very interested. In addition, he thinks his stamp collecting may have lead him into diplomacy. He started collecting in the 5th grade. It gave him an interest in geography and politics. But, again, when he was in school, he had a substitute teacher whose brother was a very distinguished diplomate. She used to tell the students about his job. That is when he learned there was a career in the diplomat world and that is when he wanted to become a diplomat and in fact, he didn't want to do anything else. As he looks back on it, he took the foreign service exam and didn't do much else to find a job when he graduated from college. He passed the exam the first time and all the hurdles, which was very difficult. He went into the foreign service and never looked back. **AV:** Traveling; Stamp collecting **THT:** After college, Mr. Lamb joined the United

States Foreign Service beginning a career as a foreign service officer. A career diplomat, he rose through the ranks of the United States Department of State to become director of the United States Passport Office in the Bureau of Consular Affairs and Director of Financial Services. In 1983, President of the United States Ronald Reagan nominated Mr. Lamb as Assistant Secretary of the State for Administration, and he held this office from December 19, 1983 until July 1, 1985. He then became Director of the Bureau of Diplomatic Security. In 1987, the head of the Bureau of Diplomatic Security was elevated to the rank of Assistant Secretary and President Reagan named Mr. Lamb as the first Assistant Secretary of State for Diplomatic Security. He held this office from June 19, 1987 until August 9, 1989. President George H. W. Bush then nominated Mr. Lamb as United States Ambassador to Cyprus, with Mr. Lamb presenting his credentials on November 30, 1990 and serving as ambassador to Cyprus until October 24, 1993. He retired from the Foreign Service in 1994. Mr. Lamb then became Executive Director of the American Philatelic Society in State College, Pennsylvania. He retired from that position in 2006. Under his administration, the Society moved its headquarters to an historic, former Match Factory in Bellefonte, Pennsylvania. Upon his retirement, the Society named the executive wing of the headquarters complex in Mr. Lamb's honor.

LAMB, TOMMY, T: President **I:** Health, Wellness and Fitness **CN:** Attentive Health & Wellness **MS:** Married **CH:** Three Children **ED:** MD, New Orleans Baptist Theological Seminary, New Orleans, LA (1997); MS, New Orleans Baptist Theological Seminary, New Orleans, LA (1994); BS in Developmental Psychology, Western Carolina University, Cullowhee, NC (1991) **C:** Chief Broker, Development Officer, True Plan Performance Group (2017-Present); President, Attentive Health & Wellness (2016-Present) **CW:** Author, Article, "Riding the Wave to Affordable Healthcare," Heartandsoul.com; Contributor, Fox Fire Magazine **AW:** Cecil W. Man Senior Psychology Award **MEM:** Phi Kappa Phi National Honor Society; Psi Chi National Honor Society in Psychology **AS:** Dr. Lamb attributes his success to hard work, dedication, and passion. He inherited a strong work ethic from his parents, for which he is endlessly grateful. **B/I:** Dr. Lamb became involved in his profession because he has always been conscious of other people's emotions and their affections. He is a fixer and is always looking for a solution. He has wanted to be able to make other people's lives better for a long time, and he is now grateful to do so professionally. **THT:** Dr. Lamb's motto is, "Always better your best."

LAMBERT, MIRANDA LEIGH, T: Singer, Songwriter **I:** Media & Entertainment **DOB:** 11/10/1983 **PB:** Longview **SC:** TX/USA **PT:** Richard Lee Lambert; Beverly June (Hughes) Lambert **MS:** Married **SPN:** Brendan McLoughlin (01/26/2019); Blake Tollison Shelton (05/14/2011, Divorced 07/2015) **C:** Member, Pistol Annies (2011-Present); Solo Artist (2001-Present) **CIV:** Founder, Owner, Redemption Ranch, Tishomingo, OK (2014-Present); Co-founder, MuttNation Foundation (2009-Present) **CW:** Singer, "The Weight of These Wings" (2016); Singer, with Carrie Underwood, "Somethin' Bad" (2014); Singer, with Little Big Town, "Smokin' and Drinkin'" (2014); Singer, "Automatic" (2014); Singer, "Hush Hush" (2013); Singer, with Keith Urban, "We Were Us" (2013); Actress, "Law & Order: Special Victims Unit" (2012); Appearance, "The Voice" (2011); Singer, "Over You" (2011); Singer, "Mama's Broken Heart" (2011); Singer, with Pistol Annies, "Hell on Heels" (2011); Singer, "Four

the Record" (2011); Singer, "The House That Built Me" (2010); Singer, "White Liar" (2009); Singer, "Revolution" (2009); Singer, "Crazy Ex-Girlfriend" (2007); Appearance, "CMT Cross Country" (2007); Singer, "Kerosene" (2005); Contestant, "Nashville Star" (2003); Singer, "Miranda Lambert" (2001); Appearances, Television Shows **AW:** Milestone Achievement Award, Academy of Country Music Awards (2019); Awards for Song of the Year, Female Vocalist of the Year, Academy of Country Music Awards (2018); Named, Vocal Event of the Year, Academy of Country Music Awards (2016); Awards for Female Vocalist of the Year, Academy of Country Music Awards (2010-2016); Grammy Award for Best Country Album, The Recording Academy (2015); Award for Album of the Year, Academy of Country Music Awards (2015); CMT Music Award for Collaborative Video of the Year, Country Music Television Inc. (2015); Milestone Award (2015); Award for Song of the Year, Academy of Country Music Awards (2015); CMA Awards for Female Vocalist of the Year, CMA Country Music Association Inc. (2010-2015); CMA Awards for Album of the Year, CMA Country Music Association Inc. (2010, 2014, 2015); Award for Single Record of Year, Academy of Country Music Awards (2014); CMA Award for Single of the Year, CMA Country Music Association Inc. (2014); Award for Vocal Event of the Year, Academy of Country Music Awards (2014); CMA Award for Musical Event of the Year, CMA Country Music Association Inc. (2014); Platinum Award (2014); CMT Music Awards for Female Video of the Year, Country Music Television Inc. (2013, 2014); Awards for Song of the Year, Single Record of the Year, Academy Country Music Awards (2013); CMT Music Award for Performance of the Year, Country Music Television Inc. (2013); CMT Music Awards for Female Video of the Year, Song of the Year, Country Music Television Inc. (2012); Award for Album of the Year, Academy Country Music Awards (2012); Grammy Award for Best Female Country Vocal Performance, The Recording Academy (2011); Awards for Single Record of the Year, Video of the Year, Song of the Year, Academy of Country Music Awards (2011); CMT Music Award for Female Video of the Year, Country Music Television Inc. (2011); CMA Awards for Music Video of the Year, Song of the Year, CMA Country Music Association Inc. (2010); Award for Video of the Year, Academy of Country Music Awards (2010); CMT Music Award for Female Video of the Year, Country Music Television Inc. (2010); Awards for Album of the Year, Academy Country Music Awards (2008, 2010); Award for Top New Female Vocalist, Academy of Country Music Awards (2007); Cover Girl Fresh Face of Country Music Award (2005); Third Place, "Nashville Star" (2003); Numerous Awards

LAMBERT, RENE, T: Executive Director **I:** Other **CN:** Opportunity Works Connecticut **ED:** Diploma, RHAM High School (1987) **C:** Executive Director, Co-Founder, Opportunity Works Connecticut (2010-Present);Hiring Agent, Sunrise Northeast, Inc. (1990-2007) **CIV:** Vice President, Board, Rockville Downtown Association **AW:** Liberty Bell Award, 2017; **MH:** Marquis Who's Who Top Professional; Marquis Who's Who Humanitarian Award **AS:** Ms. Lambert attributes her success to her hard work. The smile and joy of the people's faces make everything worth it. **B/I:** Ms. Lambert became involved in her profession because her mother worked as a nurse at a training school. At the time, hey were just starting to depopulate those and putting people into group homes and other living arrangements. She got her foot in the door when group homes were just starting. **THT:** Ms. Lambert's daughter followed in her foot steps.

She is a counselor at a camp with special needs children. Her motto is "You need to change something to get a different outcome."

LAMBORN, DOUGLAS, "DOUG" LAWRENCE, T: U.S. Representative from Colorado; Lawyer **I:** Government Administration/Government Relations/Government Services **DOB:** 05/24/1954 **PB:** Leavenworth **SC:** KS/USA **MS:** Married **SPN:** Jeanie Lamborn (1977) **CH:** Luke; Eve; Will; Nathan; Mark **ED:** JD, The University of Kansas School of Law (1985); Bachelor in Journalism, The University of Kansas (1978) **C:** Member, U.S. House of Representatives from Colorado's Fifth Congressional District, United States Congress (2006-Present); Private General Practice Attorney, Colorado Springs, CO (1987-Present); Member, District Nine, Colorado State Senate, Denver, CO (1997-2006); Republican Whip, Colorado House of Representatives (1997); Member, Colorado House of Representatives (1995-1997); Member, Committee on Education and the Workforce; Member, Committee on Natural Resources; Member, Committee on Rules; Member, Committee on Natural Resources; Member, Committee on Veterans' Affairs; Member, Committee on Armed Services; President Pro-tempore, Chairman of State, Committee on Veterans and Military Affairs, Colorado State Senate **CR:** Member, Western States Republican Leadership Conference (1989, 1993) **CIV:** Former Member, Citizen's Advisory Committee; Former Member, Pikes Peak Area Council of Governments; Member, Principal's Advisory Council, Antelope Trails Elementary School, Colorado Springs, CO **PA:** Republican

LAMONT, EDWARD, "NED" MINER JR., T: Governor of Connecticut **I:** Government Administration/Government Relations/Government Services **DOB:** 01/03/1954 **PB:** Washington **SC:** DC/USA **PT:** Edward Miner Lamont; Camille Helene (Buzby) Lamont **MS:** Married **SPN:** Ann Greenlee Huntress (09/10/1983) **CH:** Emily; Lindsay; Teddy **ED:** MBA, Yale School of Management (1980); BA in Sociology, Harvard University (1976) **C:** Governor, State of Connecticut (2019-Present); Founder, President, Chairman, Lamont Digital Systems, Greenwich, CT (1984-Present); Founder, Campus Televideo (1984-2015); Project Director, Cablevision, Fairfield, CT (1980-1984) **CR:** Adjunct Faculty, Chair, Arts and Sciences Public Policy Committee, Central Connecticut State University; Teaching Fellow, Harvard Institute of Politics; Teaching Fellow, Yale School of Management **CIV:** Selectman, Town of Greenwich, CT (1987-1995); Board of Trustees, Conservation Services Group; Board of Trustees, Mercy Corps; Board of Trustees, Norman Rockwell Museum; Board of Trustees, YMCA; Board of Trustees, YPO; Advisory Board, Yale School of Management; Advisory Board, Brookings Institution; Volunteer, Warren Harding High School, Bridgeport, CT **CW:** Editor, Black River Tribune, Ludlow, VT (1977) **AW:** Distinguished Professor of Political Science and Philosophy, Central Connecticut State University **MEM:** Council on Foreign Relations; Harvard Club; Round Hill Club **PA:** Democrat **RE:** Episcopalian

LAMPE, DAVID ELWOOD, T: Professor of English Emeritus **I:** Education/Educational Services **CN:** State University of New York College at Buffalo **DOB:** 01/18/1941 **PB:** Storm Lake **SC:** IA/USA **PT:** Elwood Carl Lampe; Verna Marcella (Peterson) Lampe **MS:** Widowed **SPN:** Ruth Elaine Eickstaedt, (02/01/1963, Deceased, 08/08/2015) **CH:** Jeffrey; Paul **ED:** PhD, University of Nebraska (1969); MA, University of Nebraska (1964); BA, Buena Vista College, Cum Laude (1962) **C:** Professor Emeritus, State University of New York College at Buffalo (2006-Present); Professor, State University of New York College at Buffalo (1969-2006); Associate

Professor, State University of New York College at Buffalo (1973-1976); Assistant Professor, State University of New York College at Buffalo (1969-1973); Instructor, University of Nebraska, Lincoln (1966-1969); Instructor, Buena Vista College, Storm Lake, IA (1965-1966); Instructor, Bemidji State College (1964-1965) **CR:** Founder, Director, Poets and Writers State University of New York College at Buffalo (1978-Present); Board of Directors, Faculty-Student Association (1984-2010); Founder, Director, Western New York Medievalists, Buffalo, NY (1974-2004); Board of Directors, White Pine Press, Fredonia, NY (1985-1995) **CIV:** Member, Parkside Community Association; Delaware Park Steering Committee **CW:** Editor, "Mortals & Immortals Birchfield-Kenney Art Center Poetry Series 35th Anniversary Anthology" (2014); Editor, "Celtic Connections" (1993); Editor, "Voices and Myths" (1993); Editor, "An Occasion of Sin" (1992); Editor, "Born in Brooklyn" (1991); Editor, "Five Irish Poets" (1990); Editor, "The Legend of Being Irish" (1989); Editor, "The 15th Century" (1989); Contributor, 25 Articles, Professional Journals **AW:** Research Grant, National Endowment of the Humanities, Duke University (1978); Summer Research Grant, State University of New York (1970) **MEM:** Medieval Academy of America; American Conference on Irish Studies; New Chaucer Society; J.F. Cooper Society **MH:** Albert Nelson Marquis Lifetime Achievement Award; Marquis Who's Who Top Professional **B/I:** Mr. Lampe was influenced by a lifelong love affair with books. Mr. Lampe began reading before he even attended school. His mother was a teacher and his father was a farmer. Both of them loved reading as well. **AV:** Golf; Travel; Photography **PA:** Democrat **RE:** Lutheran

LAMPERT, EDDIE, T: Chief Executive Officer (Retired) **I:** Retail/Sales **CN:** Sears Holdings Corporation **DOB:** 07/19/1962 **PB:** Roslyn **SC:** NY/USA **ED:** Bachelor of Science in Economics, Yale University **C:** Founder, ESL Partners LP (1989-Present); Chairperson, Chief Executive Officer, Founder, ESL Investments Inc. (1988-Present); Chief Executive Officer, Sears Holdings Corporation (2013-2018)

LANCE, RYAN MICHAEL, T: Chairperson, Chief Executive Officer **I:** Oil & Energy **CN:** Conocophillips Inc. **PB:** Butte **SC:** MT/USA **ED:** Bachelor of Science in Petroleum Engineering, Montana Technological University, Butte, MT (1984) **C:** Chairperson, Chief Executive Officer, ConocoPhillips, Houston, TX (2012-Present); Senior Vice President, Exploration and Production, International, ConocoPhillips, Houston, TX (2009-2012); President, Exploration and Production, Europe, Asia, Africa and the Middle East, ConocoPhillips (2007-2009); Senior Vice President, Technology, ConocoPhillips (2007); Senior Vice President, Technology and Major Projects, ConocoPhillips (2006-2007); President, Strategy, Integration and Specialty Business, ConocoPhillips (2005-2006); President, Exploration and Production, Asia Pacific, ConocoPhillips (2003-2005); Vice President, United States, ConocoPhillips, Houston, TX (2002-2003); General Manager, United States and Canada, Phillips Petroleum, Houston, TX (2001-2003); Vice President, Western North Slope, ARCO, Alaska (1998-2001); Planning Manager, Vaster Resources, Houston, TX (1996-1998); Exploration Engineering Manager, ARCO, Alaska (1994-1996); Supervisor, Coalbed Methane Operations, ARCO, Midland, TX (1992-1994); Operations, ARCO, Bakersfield, CA (1989-1992); Engineer, ARCO, Alaska (1984-1989) **CR:** President, Board of Trustees, Spindletop International Board of Directors, ConocoPhillips (2012-Present) **CIV:** Advisory Board Member, Montana Tech Foundation; Board of Directors,

Independent Petroleum Association of America; Board of Directors, American Petroleum Institute **MEM:** Society of Petroleum Engineers

LANDMAN, JONATHAN I., T: Managing Editor **I:** Writing and Editing **CN:** Bloomberg Opinion **DOB:** 11/14/1952 **PB:** New York **SC:** NY/USA **MS:** Married **SPN:** Bonnie Van Gilder **CH:** Two Children **ED:** MS in Journalism, Columbia Journalism School (1978); BA in History, Amherst College, Magna Cum Laude (1974) **C:** Managing Editor, Bloomberg Opinion (2009-Present); Deputy Managing Editor, Digital Journalism, The New York Times Company (2005-2009); Culture Editor, The New York Times Company (2004-2005); Enterprise Editor, The New York Times Company (2003-2005); Metropolitan Editor, The New York Times Company (1999-2003); Week in Review Editor, The New York Times Company (1994-1999); Deputy Editor, The New York Times Company (1992-1994); Assistant Editor, The New York Times Company (1991-1992); Assistant Metropolitan Editor, The New York Times Company (1990-1991); Assistant National Editor, The New York Times Company (1989-1990); Deputy City Editor, New York Daily News (1985-1987); Reporter, Newsday (1984-1985); Reporter, Assistant City Editor, Chicago Sun-Times (1979-1984); Assistant Editor, Scholastic Magazines (1975-1977) **CR:** Member, Faculty, The Writer's Institute, The Graduate Center, The City University of New York **CIV:** Assistant to Program Adviser of Communications, Ford Foundation (1978-1979); Board of Trustees, Amherst College **AW:** Alfred I. duPont-Columbia Award, Columbia University (2007)

LANE, NATHAN, T: Actor **I:** Media & Entertainment **DOB:** 02/03/1956 **PB:** Jersey City **SC:** NJ/USA **PT:** Daniel Lane; Nora Lane **MS:** Married **SPN:** Devlin Elliott (11/17/2015) **C:** With, Second Stage Theater, Roundabout Theatre and Manhattan Theatre Club, NY; Stand-up Comedian, NY **CW:** Actor, "Penny Dreadful: City of Angels" (2020-Present); Actor, "Gary: A Sequel to Titus Andronicus" (2019); Actor, "Angels in America" (2017, 2018); Actor, "The Blacklist" (2018); Actor, "Sidney Hall" (2017); Actor, "White Rabbit, Red Rabbit" (2016); Actor, "The Front Page" (2016); Actor, "No Pay, Nudity" (2016); Actor, "Carrie Pilby" (2016); Actor, "American Crime Story: The People v. O.J. Simpson" (2016); Actor, "Difficult People" (2016); Actor," Maya & Marty" (2016); Actor, "The Iceman Cometh" (2015); Actor, "It's Only a Play" (2014-2015); Actor, "The Money" (2014); Actor, "The Odd Couple" (2013); Actor, "The Nance" (2013); Actor, "The English Teacher" (2013); Actor, "The Good Wife" (2012-2014); Actor, Executive Producer, "Local Talent" (2012); Actor, "Mirror Mirror" (2012); Actor, "The Good Wife" (2012); Actor, "Modern Family" (2010-2015); Actor, "The Addams Family" (2010); Voice Actor, "The Nutcracker in 3D" (2010); Actor, "Waiting for Godot" (2009); Voice Actor, "Astro Boy" (2009); Actor, "November" (2008); Appearance, "A Muppets Christmas: Letters to Santa" (2008); Actor, "Swing Vote" (2008); Actor, "30 Rock" (2007); Actor, "Butley" (2006-2007); Voice Actor, "Stuart Little 3: Call of the Wild" (2006); Actor, "A Midsummer Night's Dream" (2005); Actor, "Dedication or the Stuff of Dreams" (2005); Actor, "The Producers" (2005); Actor, "The Frogs" (2004); Actor, "Win a Date with Tad Hamilton!" (2004); Voice Actor, "The Lion King 1 1/2" (2004); Actor, "Absolutely Famous" (2004); Actor, "The Producers" (2001-2002, 2003); Actor, "Trumbo: Red, White and Blacklisted" (2003); Actor, Executive Producer, "Charlie Lawrence" (2003); Actor, "Nicholas Nickelby" (2002); Voice Actor, "Stuart Little 2" (2002); Actor, "Austin Powers in Goldmember" (2002); Actor, "Sex and the City" (2002); Actor, "Laughter on the 23rd Floor" (1993-1994, 2001); Actor, "Teacher's Pet" (2000-2002); Actor, "The Man Who Came to Dinner" (2000); Actor, "Isn't She Great?" (2000); Actor, "Trixie" (2000); Actor, "Love's Labour's Lost" (2000); Voice Actor, "Titan A.E." (2000); Actor, "George and Martha" (1999); Actor, "The Best Man" (1999); Actor, "At First Sight" (1999); Voice Actor, "Stuart Little" (1999); Actor, "Encore! Encore!" (1998-1999); Voice Actor, "The Lion King II: Simba's Pride" (1998); Actor, "Merry Christmas, George Bailey" (1997); Actor, "One Saturday Morning" (1997); Actor, "Mousehunt" (1997); Actor, "Mad About You" (1997); Actor, "A Funny Thing Happened on the Way to the Forum" (1996-1998); Actor, "The Boys Next Door" (1996); Actor, "The Birdcage" (1996); Performer, "The Wizard of Oz in Concert: Dreams Come True" (1995); Actor, "Love! Valour! Compassion!" (1995); Voice Actor, "Timon and Pumbaa" (1995); Actor, "Frasier" (1995); Voice Actor, "The Lion King" (1994); Actor, "Merlin" (1993); Actor, "Life with Mikey" (1993); Actor, "Addams Family Values" (1993); Actor, "Guys and Dolls" (1992-1995); Actress, "The Last Mile" (1992); Actor, "On Borrowed Time" (1991-1992); Actor, "The Days and Nights of Molly Dodd" (1989, 1990, 1991); Actor, "Lips Together, Teeth Apart" (1991); Actor, "He Said, She Said" (1991); Actor, "Frankie and Johnny" (1991); Actor, "The American Experience" (1991); Actor, "Some Americans Abroad" (1990); Actor, "Bad Habits" (1990); Actor, "The Lemon Sisters" (1990); Actor, "Joe Versus the Volcano" (1990); Actor, "The Lisbon Traviata" (1989); Actor, "A Pig's Valise" (1989); Actor, "Uncounted Blessings" (1988); Actor, "The Film Society" (1988); Actor, "Ironweed" (1987); Actor, "Claptrap," New York, NY (1987); Actor, "The Common Pursuit" (1986-1987); Actor, "A Backer's Audition," New York, NY (1985); Actor, "The Wind in the Willows" (1985); Actor, "Measure for Measure" (1985); Actor, "Walls of Glass" (1985); Actor, "Miami Vice" (1985); Actor, "The Common Pursuit" (1984-1985); Actor, "Raving," New York, NY (1984); Actor, "She Stoops to Conquer," New York, NY (1984); Actor, "One of the Boys" (1982); Actor, "Present Laughter" (1982-1983); Actor, "The Valley of the Dolls" (1981); Actor, Theater, Television Shows, Films **AW:** Drama Desk Award for Outstanding Featured Actor in a Play (1990, 1995, 2018); Tony Award for Best Performance by an Actor in a Featured Role in a Play (2018); Distinguished Achievement in Musical Theatre Award, The Drama League (2010); Named to American Theatre Hall of Fame (2008); Human Rights Campaign Equality Award (2007); Trevor Project Hero Award (2007); Recipient, Star, Hollywood Walk of Fame (2006); American Theatre Wing Honor (2006); Olivier Award for Best Actor in a Musical (2005); National Board of Review Award for Best Ensemble Performance (2002); Vito Russo Award, GLAAD (2002); People's Choice Award for Favorite Male Performer in a New Television Series (1999); Outer Critics Circle Awards (1992, 1995, 1996); Tony Award for Best Actor in Musical (1996, 2001); Drama Desk Award for Outstanding Actor in a Musical (1996, 2001); Daytime Emmy Award for Outstanding Performer in an Animated Program, Academy of Television Arts & Sciences (1996, 2001); SAG Award for Outstanding Performance by a Cast, SAG-AFTRA (1996); American comedy Award for Best Performance by an Actor in a Motion Picture - Musical or Comedy (1996); Obie Award for Ensemble Acting (1995); Drama Desk Award for Outstanding Actor in a Musical (1992); Obie Award for Sustained Excellence of Performance (1992); Lucille Lortel Award (1990); St. Clair Bayfield Award for Shakespearean Performance (1986)

LANG, GEORGE RUSSELL JR., T: Oil Company Executive (Retired) **I:** Oil & Energy **CN:** Exxon Mobil Corporation **DOB:** 06/13/1952 **PB:** Corinth **SC:** MS/ USA **PT:** Harold Minter; Manelle (Johnson) Blackwood **MS:** Married **SPN:** Cecilia Anne Hoffpauir Lang **CH:** Ashley Elizabeth; Taylor Nelle; Morgan Katherine; George Russell III; William Hunter **ED:** Pursuing Master of Legal Studies, Washington University in St. Louis (2019-Present); MBA, Tulane University (1989); Master in Structural Engineering, The University of Tennessee (1976); BS in Civil Engineering, The University of Tennessee (1975) **CT:** Registered Professional Engineer, States of Texas and Louisiana **C:** Construction Manager, Esso Exploration & Production Chad, Incorporated, Kome, Chad (2008-2012); Construction Manager, Mobil Equatorial Guinea, Incorporated, Malabo, Equatorial Guinea (2007-2008); Construction Advisor, Africa Project Services, Exxon Mobil Production Company (Now Exxon Mobil Corporation), Houston, Texas (2005-2007); Orlan Platform Deputy Site Manager, Exxon Neftegas Limited, Komsomolsk, Russia (2004-2005); Offshore Fabrication Advisor, ExxonMobil Development Corporation, Houston, Texas (2000-2004); Construction Manager, Mobil Research and Development Corporation, Dallas, Texas (1992-2000); Senior Marine Civil Engineering Advisor, Mobil Exploration & Producing U.S., Inc., New Orleans, LA (1990-1992); Civil Engineering Supervisor, Mobil Exploration & Producing U.S., Inc., New Orleans, LA (1985-1990); Civil Engineering Supervisor, Mobil Exploration & Producing U.S., Inc., Morgan City, LA (1981-1985); Structural Engineer, Mobil Research and Development Corporation, Dallas, Texas (1979-1981); Civil Engineer, Mobil Oil Exploration and Producing Southeast, Inc., New Orleans, LA (1977-1979) **CIV:** Advancement Coordinator, Boy Scouts of America, Troop 471, Tomball, Texas (2012-Present); Advisor, Junior Achievement USA, New Orleans, LA (1978) **CW:** Author, "Structural Design, Fabrication and Installation of Offshore Conductor Pipe", OTC No. 7453. (1994); Author, "Analysis, Prediction and Repair of Vertical Wave Fatigue Damage of Conductor Guide Bracing", OTC No. 6653 (1991); Author, "Predicting the Drivability of Large Diameter Offshore Piling", OTC No. 3827 (1980); Sole or Lead Author of Offshore Technology Conference Papers **MEM:** Fellow, American Society of Civil Engineers; The Honor Society of Phi Kappa Phi; The Tau Beta Pi Association, Inc.; Chi Epsilon, Inc.; Beta Gamma Sigma; Sons of the American Revolution (National Society of the Sons of the American Revolution); Sons of the Union Veterans of the Civil War; Sons of the Confederate Veterans of the Civil War **MH:** Albert Nelson Marquis Lifetime Achievement Award; Marquis Who's Who Top Professional **AS:** Mr. Lang has a strong belief in education. He believes in a foundation of education, hard work, perseverance and planning for alternate outcomes. He further believes that if you build on this foundation a long-range vision of success and a relentless pursuit of excellence, you will have a very high probability of a successful career. **B/I:** Mr. Lang had a strong interest in mathematics and science in high school. This led him to an interest in engineering at the University of Tennessee and he became a civil engineer. His interest in the analytical side of civil engineering led to his concentration in structural engineering. He received bachelor's and master's degrees in civil engineering before accepting a position with Mobil Oil. **AV:** Genealogical research; Reading; Hunting **PA:** Conservative **RE:** Christian **THT:** Mr. Lang is very proud of his family, especially his five children who are all college educated. He is particularly proud of his two sons who both became Eagle Scouts and had leadership training beyond the Eagle rank. Additionally, both sons went on to earn every merit badge available in the Scouts USA program. Specific pdfs for his sons are: http://meritbadgeknot.com/scoutbios/lang-george.pdfhttp://meritbadgeknot.com/scoutbios/lang-william.pdf

LANGE, JESSICA PHYLLIS, T: Actress **I:** Media & Entertainment **DOB:** 04/20/1949 **PB:** Cloquet **SC:** MN/USA **PT:** Albert John Lange; Dorothy Florence (Sahlman) Lange **MS:** Divorced **SPN:** Francisco Paco Grande (07/29/1971, Divorced 1981) **CH:** Aleksandra Lange Baryshnikov; Hannah Jane Shepard; Samuel Shepard **ED:** Coursework in Mime with Etienne DeCroux, Paris, France; Coursework, University of Minnesota **C:** Model, Wilhelmina Agency, New York, NY; Dancer, Opera Comique, Paris, France **CR:** Model, Marc Jacobs Beauty (2014) **CIV:** Ambassador, Save the Children (2008-Present); Goodwill Ambassador, UNICEF **CW:** Actress, "Wild Oats" (2016); Actress, "Long Day's Journey into Night" (2016); Actress, "Horace and Pete" (2016); Actress, "American Horror Story" (2011-2015); Photographer, Exhibiton, Multimedia Art Museum, Russia (2014); Actress, "The Gambler" (2014); Author, "It's About a Little Bird" (2013); Actress, "In Secret" (2013); Actress, "The Vow" (2012); Photographer, Exhibition, George Eastman Museum (2009); Actress, "Grey Gardens" (2009); Author, Photographer, "50 Photographs" (2008); Actress, "The Glass Menagerie," London, England (2007); Actress, "Sybil" (2007); Actress, "Bonneville" (2006); Actress, "The Glass Menagerie," NY (2005); Actress, "Broken Flowers" (2005); Actress, "Don't Come Knocking" (2005); Actress, "Neverwas" (2005); Actress, "Normal" (2003); Actress, "Masked and Anonymous" (2003); Actress, "Big Fish" (2003); Actress, "Prozac Nation" (2001); Actress, "Titus" (1999); Actress, "Cousin Bette" (1998); Actress, "Hush" (1998); Actress, "A Thousand Acres" (1997); Actress, "Losing Isaiah" (1995); Actress, "Rob Roy" (1995); Actress, "A Streetcar Named Desire" (1995); Actress, "Blue Sky" (1994); Actress, "O'Pioneers!" (1992); Actress, "A Streetcar Named Desire" (1992); Actress, "Night and the City" (1992); Actress, "Cape Fear" (1991); Actress, "Men Don't Leave" (1990); Actress, "Music Box" (1989); Actress, "Far North" (1988); Actress, "Everybody's All American" (1988); Actress, "Crimes of the Heart" (1986); Actress, "Sweet Dreams" (1985); Actress, Producer, "Country" (1984); Actress, "Cat on a Hot Tin Roof" (1984); Actress, "Tootsie" (1982); Actress, "Frances" (1982); Actress, "The Postman Always Rings Twice" (1981); Actress, "Angel on My Shoulder," NC (1980); Actress, "How to Beat the High Cost of Living" (1980); Actress, "All That Jazz" (1979); Actress, "King Kong" (1976) **AW:** Tony Award for Best Leading Actress in a Play (2016); Critics' Choice Award for Best Television Movie/Miniseries Actress (2014); Emmy Award for Outstanding Lead Actress in a Limited Series or Movie, National Academy of Television Arts & Sciences (2014); Emmy Award for Outstanding Supporting Actress in a Limited Series or Movie, National Academy of Television Arts & Sciences (2012); SAG Award for Outstanding Performance by a Female Actor in a Drama Series, SAG-AFTRA (2011); Golden Globe Award for Best Supporting Actress in a Series, Miniseries or Motion Picture Made for Television, Hollywood Foreign Press Association (2011); Emmy Award for Outstanding Lead Actress in a Limited Series or Movie, National Academy of Television Arts & Sciences (2009); George Eastman Museum Honors Award (2009); Golden Globe Award for Best Actress in a Miniseries or Motion Picture – Television, Hollywood Foreign Press Association (1995); Golden Globe Award for Best Actress in a Miniseries or Motion Picture - Drama, Hollywood Foreign Press Association (1994); Academy Award for Best Actress, Academy of Motion Picture Arts and Sciences (1994); Academy Award for Best Supporting Actress, Academy of Motion Picture Arts and Sciences (1982); Golden Globe Award for Best Supporting Actress - Motion Picture, Hollywood Foreign Press Association (1982); Golden Globe Award for New Star of the Year - Actress, Hollywood Foreign Press Association (1976); Recipient, Numerous Awards

LANGE, NICHOLAS THEODORE, PHD, T: Biostatistician, Educator **I:** Sciences **DOB:** 03/18/1952 **PB:** Valparaiso **SC:** IN/USA **PT:** Lester Henry Lange; Anne Marie (Pelikan) Lange **MS:** Divorced **SPN:** Dorothy Cresswell (09/06/1976, divorced 1982); Louise Marie Ryan, (12/15/1984, Divorced 1986) **CH:** Sarah Elisabeth; Nicholas Cresswell **ED:** ScD, Harvard University (1986); ScM, University of Massachusetts (1981);ScB, Northeastern University (1976) **C:** Associate Professor of Biostatistics, Harvard University (2000-Present);Chief Biostatistician, Director of Statistical Neuroimaging, McLean Hospital (1996-Present);Associate Professor of Psychiatry, Harvard University, Cambridge, MA (1996-Present); Specialist in Neuroimaging, National Institutes of Health, Bethesda, MD (1993-1996);Assistant Professor, Medical Statistics, Brown University, Providence, RI (1987-1993); Instructor, Applied Mathematics, Massachusetts Institute of Technology, Cambridge, MA (1986-1987) **CR:** Co-Investigator, National Institutes of Health (1996-Present); Co-Investigator, NINDS (1998); Co-Investigator, Human Brain Project (1995-1997); Consultant, Radiology Massachusetts General Hospital, Charlestown, Boston, MA (1994-1996, 1998-1999); National Institute on Aging (1997-1999); Expert Witness, McGovern, Noel & Benik, Providence, RI (1991-1993, 1997); Expert Witness, M. Scherzer, New York, NY (1993) **CW:** Associate Editor, Journal of the American Statistical Association (1993-1997); Guest Editor, Statistics in Medicine (1992); Editor, "Case Studies in Biometry" (1991-1994); Member, Editorial Board, Human Brain Mapping, NeuroImage, State Rev. Board, American Journal of Psychiatry, Arch Gen Psychiatry **AW:** Grantee, American Cancer Society (1991-1993); Robert Reed Prize, Harvard University (1986) **MEM:** American Association for the Advancement of Science; American Statistical Association; Biometric Society; Bernoulli Society; Honorary Member, International Society for Optical Engineering **MH:** Albert Nelson Marquis Lifetime Achievement Award **B/I:** Dr. Lange became involved in his profession because his father was a mathematician. He started out in chemistry but then switched to mathematics after his freshman year. He then got a master's degree in computer science and applied to Harvard University, where he ultimately obtained a PhD in 1986. At Harvard, he set up a lab of biostatistics that brings together labs and medicine, which was a partially missing piece that was needed in the world of research. He then jumped into genetics and imaging, where he flourished. When he completed that, he focused his lab on autism research.

LANGENBACH, RANDOLPH, T: Sole Practitioner **I:** Consulting **CN:** Conservationtech Consulting **ED:** Master of Architecture, Harvard Graduate School of Design, Cambridge, MA (1982); Diploma in Conservation Studies, Institute of Advanced Architectural Studies, York, England (1977); Bachelor of Arts, Harvard College, Cambridge, MA (1968) **C:** International Consultant in Historic Preservation Design & Building Construction Technology, Oakland, CA (1984-Present); Visiting Lecturer, Institution of Civil Engineers, London (2019); Visiting Lecturer, Universities of Roma Tre, Calabria, Pescara, and Trento, Italy (2013, 2014, 2017, 2019); Visiting Lecturer, Oxford and Cambridge Universities, England (2012, 2019); Visiting Lecturer, NED University of Engineering and Technology & Dawood University of Engineering and Technology, Karachi, Pakistan (2019); Visiting Lecturer, Colorado School of Mines (2017); Visiting Lecturer, Universities and National Institutes of Technology throughout India, including New Delhi, Mumbai, Ahmedabad, Kanpur, Hyderabad, and others (1981, 1989-2016); Visiting Lecturer, Institution of Structural Engineers, London (2012); Visiting Lecturer, University of Haifa (2012); Visiting Lecturer, Texas A&M University (2012); Building Conservation Consultant & Post Earthquake Reconnaissance Team Leader, Consultant to World Monuments Fund & Fondation Connaissance et Liberté, Haiti (2010); Member, UNESCO Expert Team to Pakistan (2010); Visiting Professor, University of Brescia, Brescia, Italy (2008); Visiting Specialist, Lecturer, U.S. Speaker and Specialist Program, U.S. Department of State, Portugal and Dominican Republic (1989, 2007); Building Conservation Educator, International Centre for the Study of the Preservation and Restoration of Cultural Property (2004, 2006); Building Conservation Consultant, Turquoise Mountain Foundation, Kabul, Afghanistan (2006); Consultant on Conservation Education for Federal Preservation Officers, Federal Preservation Institute, National Park Service, Washington, DC (2005); Visiting Lecturer, Iranian Institute of Technology, Tehran, Iran (2004); Building Conservation Consultant, UNESCO Division of Cultural Heritage (2001, 2003, 2004); Senior Analyst, Building Construction Technology Specialist, Response and Recovery Directorate, Infrastructure Support Division, Federal Emergency Management Agency, San Francisco, CA (1992-2004); Building Conservation Educator, UNESCO, Tbilisi, Georgia (2002); Building Conservation Consultant, Kathmandu Valley Preservation Trust International (2000); Assistant Professor of Architecture, University of California, Berkeley, Berkeley, CA (1984-1991); Specialist in New England Historic Industrial Buildings and Cities, Architectural Historian and Preservation Planning Consultant, Cambridge, MA (1968-1984); Principal, Moore-Heder Team, Architects and Planners (1978); Historian, Preservation Planner, Lowell National Historical Park on the Lowell Team, Architects and Planners, Massachusetts (1975); Historical Planning Consultant, Benjamin Thompson and Associates, Architects (1970) **CW:** Speaker, Keynote Speaker, Lecturer, Numerous Invited Keynote Addresses and Invited Lectures in Many Countries Around the World (2000-Present); Author and Photographer, "ROME WAS! The Eternal City from Piranesi to the Present," ORO Editions, (2019); Filmmaker, "ROME WAS! Ruins Eternal" (2015); Co-Author and Principle Photographer, "Preserving Haiti's Gingerbread Houses" (2010); Author and Photographer, "Don't Tear It Down! Preserving the Earthquake Resistant Vernacular Architecture of Kashmir," UNESCO (2009); Co-Author and Photographer, "Amoskeag, Life and Work in an American Factory-City" (1978); Author and Photographer, "A Future From the Past: The Case for the Conservation and Reuse of Old Buildings in Industrial Cities" (1978); Co-Author and Photographer, "Satanic Mills, The Conservation of the Pennine Textile Mills" (1978); Museum Exhibition Producer, Designer and Photographer, "A Sense of Place, the Milltown in England and New England," Boston City Hall Main Gallery, Boston, MA (1976); Museum Exhibition Producer, Designer and Photographer, "A Sense of Place, a Way of Life," Currier Gallery of Art, Manchester, NH (1975); Author, Approximately Peer-Reviewed 100 papers On the Preservation of Historic Industrial Buildings, and Preservation and Engineering Analysis of Traditional Construction in Earthquake Areas; Contributor, Author, Co-Author, 12 Book Chapters, Traditional Construction in Earthquake Areas **AW:** Best Animation Award for "ROME WAS! Ruins Eternal, 7th International Filmmaker Film Festival of World Cinema in London (2015); Selectee, Heritage and Vernacular Building Construction Expert, PBS NOVA (2015); Rome Prize in Historic Preservation, National Endowment for the Arts, American Academy in Rome (2002-2003); Director's Award and Meritorious Service Award, Federal Emergency Management Agency (1999); Oliver Torrey Fuller Award, for the Best Article for the Year in the APT Bulletin, "Bricks, Mortar, and Earthquakes, Historic Preservation vs. Earthquake Safety," Association for Preservation Technology International (1989); Indo-American Exchange Fellowship, American Academy in Rome (1981); Progressive Architecture Design Award, Lowell National Cultural Park, Lowell, MA (1976); Citation for Historic Preservation, for New England Textile Mills, American Society of Registered Architects (1975); Annual Award for Conservation, New England Chapter, The Victorian Society of America (1975); Research Grant, for Documentary Research on the History and Architecture of the Amoskeag Mills, National Endowment for the Humanities (1972); David McCord Book Prize, Harvard College (1968) **MEM:** Board of Directors, US/ICOMOS (1996-2002); ICOMOS International Scientific Committee, International Scientific Committee on the Analysis and Restoration of Structures of Architectural Heritage; ICOMOS International Scientific Committee, International Committee on Risk Preparedness; Earthquake Engineering Research Institute; National Trust for Historic Preservation; Society of Architectural Historians **MH:** Albert Nelson Marquis Lifetime Achievement Award

LANGERMAN, DUANE LEE, T: Construction Executive **I:** Architecture & Construction **DOB:** 02/04/1943 **PB:** Ellsworth **SC:** KS/USA **PT:** Dell Miles Langerman; Irma Alice Langerman **MS:** Married **SPN:** Linda Ruth Wilson (12/27/1962) **CH:** Scott Miles; Craig James **ED:** Coursework, Morningside College, Sioux City, IA (1976-1980); Coursework, Brown-Mackie College, Salina, KS (1961-1962) **C:** Consultant, Harper Construction, San Diego, CA (2002-2007); Director, Internal Auditing, Dillingham Construction Corporation, Pleasanton, CA (1994-2002); Vice President, Administration, Green Alaska, Inc., Anchorage (1989-1993); Administrative Manager, Construction, Green Holdings, Dallas, TX (1986-1989); Administrative Manager, Green Construction Company, Anchorage (1983-1986); Controller, N.L. Cole Construction Company, Lincoln, NE (1980-1982); Chief Accountant, Western Contracting Corporation, Sioux City, IO (1971-1980); Accountant, Internal Auditor, University Computing, Riverton, WY (1969-1971); Project Accountant, Western Contracting Corporation, Sioux City, Iowa (1965-1969); Assistant Retail Manager, School Specialty Supply, Salina, KS (1964-1965); Office Manager, Wells Department Store, Salina, KS (1963-1964); Accountant, James & Beckman Construction, Sylvan Grove, KS (1962-1963) **CR:** Board of Directors, Executive Board, Alaska Support Alliance (1991-1993); Member, Steering Committee, Green Holdings, Inc., Denver (1989-1993); Elder, Building Chair, First Presbyterian Church (1976-1979); Member, Steering Committee, The Alliance Organization; Chair, Pacific Northwest Congressional Delegate Subcommittee, The Alliance **CIV:** Active Member, Arctic National Wildlife Refuge Committee **MEM:** Elks **B/I:** Mr. Langerman became involved in his profession because, although he comes from a farming family, he decided to look into a different career as the family farm wasn't large enough to support two families. He started in construction at James & Beckman, which introduced him to project type accounting. However, he left construction for a brief period and entered into retail, but returned to his interest in construction accounting as a career. **AV:** Fishing; Cross-country skiing

LANGEVIN, JAMES, "JIM" R., T: U.S. Representative from Rhode Island **I:** Government Administration/Government Relations/Government Services **DOB:** 04/22/1964 **PB:** Providence **SC:** RI/USA **PT:** Richard Raymond Langevin; June Katherine (Barrett) Langevin **ED:** MPA, Harvard Kennedy School, John F. Kennedy School of Government (1994); BA, Rhode Island College (1990) **C:** Member, U.S. House of Representatives from Rhode Island's Second Congressional District, United States Congress, Washington, DC (2001-Present); Secretary of State, State of Rhode Island, Providence, RI (1995-2001); Member, District 29, Rhode Island House of Representatives, Providence, RI (1988-1994); Member, Committee on Armed Services; Member, Committee on Homeland Security **CIV:** Board of Directors, Rhode Island Shelter; Board of Directors, Big Brothers Big Sisters of Rhode Island; Board of Directors, Pari Independent Living Center, Pawtucket, RI; Board of Directors, Hope Alzheimers Center, Cranston, RI **AV:** Reading; Public speaking; Participating in community activities **PA:** Democrat **RE:** Roman Catholic

LANGFORD, ROLAND EVERETT, T: Owner **I:** Environmental Services **CN:** Langford Consulting **DOB:** 04/11/1945 **PB:** Owensboro **SC:** KY/USA **PT:** John Roland Langford; Mary Helen (Cockriel) Langford **MS:** Married **SPN:** Cecilia Son-Hee Shin (12/18/1971) **CH:** John Everett (Deceased); Lee Shin **ED:** PhD, University of North Carolina (1996); PhD, University of Georgia (1974);MS, University of Georgia (1971); BS, Georgia Southern College (1967); AA, Armstrong State College (1965) **CT:** Certified Hazardous Materials Professional, National Environmental Health Association (1990); Certification, American Academy of Sanitarians; Certified, American Industrial Hygiene Association (1988); Certified Environmental Scientist, American Academy of Environmental Engineers and Scientists; Registered Professional Engineer, Texas; Hazardous Substances Professional; Registered Sanitarian, National Environmental Health Association; Certified Professional Environmental Auditor; Certified Industrial Hygienist; Certified Safety Professional; Diplomate, American Academy of Sanitarians, Inc. **C:** Owner, Langford Consulting, Harker Heights, TX (2016-Present); Chief, Environmental Division USAG Red Cloud, Uijeongbu, South Korea (2009-2015); Industrial Hygiene Engineer, Huntsman Advanced Technology Center, The Woodlands, TX (2008-2009); EHSS Manager, Shanghai Lianheng Isocyanate Co. Ltd. (2004-2007); Manager, industrial Hygiene and Product Stewardship, Huntsman Corporation, Houston, TX (2000-2004); Superintendent, Health and Safety, Huntsman Corporation, Jefferson County Operations, Port Neches, TX (1998-2000);Chief, abiotic processes branch, Robert S. Kerr Laboratory of U.S. EPA, Ada, OK (1998); Commander, Medical Research Detachment for Toxicology, Walter Reed Army Institute Research, Wright-Patterson Air Force Base, Ohio (1992-1998); Preventive Medicine and Public Health Officer, NATO/IFOR, Zagreb, Croatia, Sarajevo, Bosnia-Herzegovina (1996-1997); Chief, Occupational Health Research, U.S. Army Biomed. R&D Laboratory, Fort Detrick, MD (1991-1992); Environmental Science Officer, Fort Huachuca, AZ (1984-1988);Commander, Environmental Sanitation Detachment, Taegu, South Korea (1981-1983); Sanitary Engineer, U.S. Army Environmental Hygiene Agency, Aberdeen Proving Ground, MD (1979-1981); Chief, Chemistry Section, U.S. Army Academy of Health Sciences, Fort Sam Houston, TX (1978-1979);

Assistant Professor, Georgia Southern College, Statesboro, GA (1977-1978); Assistant Professor of Chemistry, Georgia Military College, Milledgeville, GA (1975-1977); Instructor, Bainbridge State College, Bainbridge, GA (1973-1974); Instructor, Savannah Science Museum, Savannah, GA (1971-1972) **CR:** Chair, Science Review Panel, Hazardous Substances Data Bank, National Institutes of Health (2007-Present); Member, Science Review Panel, Hazardous Substances Data Bank, National Institutes of Health (1986-Present); Member, Emergency Response Planning Guidelines Committee Panel, American Industrial Hygiene Association (1999-2019); Adjunct Faculty, Purdue University (1995-2019) Adjunct Faculty, Air Force Institute of Technology (1993-1998); Member, U.S. Air Force Women in the Cockpit (1993-1995); Member, U.S. Navy Submarine Atmosphere Health Assessment (1993-1994); Adjunct Faculty, University of Maryland, Taegu and Pusan, Korea (1981-1983); Judge, International Science Fair, San Antonio, TX (1979); Adjunct Faculty, St. Leo's College, San Antonio, TX (1978-1979); Member, Panel, Comprehensive Assistance to Undergraduate Science Education, National Science Foundation (1975-1977) **CIV:** Lay Minister, Wright-Patterson Air Force Base Chapel (1992-1998); Lay Minister, St. Thomas More Church (1988-1991); Adviser, Medical Explorer Post, Fort Huachuca, AZ (1986-1988); Member, Parish Council, Lay Minister, Holy Family Parish, Fort Huachuca, AZ (1985-1988); Active Member, Boy Scouts of America, Fort Sam Houston, TX (1978-1979) **MIL:** U.S. Naval Reserve (1994); Advanced Through Grades to Lt. Col., U.S. Army (1992); Lt. Col., Environmental Science Officer, U.S. Army (1978-1998); Commission Captain, U.S. Army (1978) **CW:** Author, "Introduction to Weapons of Mass Destruction" (2004); Author, "International Book of Units and Measurement Systems" (1999); Co-Author, "Substance Abuse in the Workplace" (1994); Co-Author, "Fundamentals of Hazardous Materials Incidents" (1990); Co-Author, "Hazardous Materials Training Program for International Union of Operating Engineers" (1988); Contributor, Articles, Professional Journals **AW:** Garrison Support Executive of Year, U.S. Army Installation Management Command (2014); Numerous Military Awards, Including Legion of Merit **MEM:** Board of Directors, Royal Asiatic Society (1982-1983); Fellow, American Institute of Chemists; American Institute of Chemical Engineers; American Society of Safety Engineers; American Industrial Hygiene Association; American Chemical Society; National Environmental Health Association; Korean Chemical Society; Association of Military Surgeons of the United States; American Academy of Sanitarians; American Industrial Hygiene Association **AS:** Dr. Langford attributes his success to hard work with a firm foundation of experience and education. **B/I:** Dr. Langford became involved in his profession to help others. **AV:** Amateur radio; Asian studies; Photography **PA:** Republican **RE:** Roman Catholic

LANGLEY, LESTER D., PHD, T: Historian, Author **I:** Education/Educational Services **DOB:** 08/07/1940 **PB:** Clarksville **SC:** TX/USA **PT:** Lona Jane Clements (1898-1996); Lester L. Langley (1899-1994) **MS:** Married **SPN:** Wanda Dickson Langley **CH:** Charles H. Langley; Jonathan J. Langley **ED:** PhD, The University of Kansas (1965); MA, West Texas A&M University (1962); BA, West Texas A&M University (1961) **C:** Visiting Professor, Spring Semester, Texas A&M University (2002); Visiting Professor, Fall Semester, University of Texas (2000); Professor Emeritus (2000); Research Professor (1988-2000); Assistant to Full Professor, University of Georgia (1970-1987); Assistant Professor, Central Washington University (1967-1970);

Assistant Professor, Texas A&M University (1965-1967) **CW:** Author, "The Long American Revolution and Its Legacy" (2019); Author, "America and the Americas: The United States in the Western Hemisphere" (2010); Author, "The Americas in the Modern Age" (2003); Author, "The Americas in the Age of Revolution: 1750-1850" (1996) **MEM:** The Historical Society; American Historical Association; CLAH; The Society for Historians of American Foreign Relations; The Phi Beta Kappa Society **MH:** Albert Nelson Marquis Lifetime Achievement Award **AS:** Dr. Langley attributes his success to his determination, opportunity and God's help. **B/I:** Dr. Langley became involved in his profession because in Spring of 1961 he was admitted to the University of Texas' School of Law. **AV:** Golfing **PA:** Independent **RE:** Methodist **THT:** Dr. Langley states, "Never believe anyone who tells you that 'you are all you will ever be.'"

LANKFORD, JAMES PAUL, T: U.S. Senator from Oklahoma **I:** Government Administration/Government Relations/Government Services **DOB:** 03/04/1968 **PB:** Dallas **SC:** TX/USA **PT:** James Wesley Lankford; Linda Joyce (House) Lankford **MS:** Married **SPN:** Cindy Hennessey (1992) **CH:** Hannah; Jordan **ED:** MDiv, Southwestern Baptist Theological Seminary, Fort Worth, Texas (1994); BS in Secondary Education, The University of Texas (1990) **C:** Chair, Senate Ethics Committee, Washington, DC (2019-Present); U.S. Senator, State of Oklahoma (2015-Present); Chairman, U.S. House Republican Policy Committee, Washington, DC (2013-2015); Chairman, U.S. House Subcommittee on Energy, Policy, Health Care, and Entitlements, Washington, DC (2013-2015); Member, U.S. House Committee on Oversight and Government Reform, Washington, DC (2011-2015); Member, U.S. House Budget Committee, Washington, DC (2011-2015); Member, U.S. House of Representatives from Oklahoma's Fifth Congressional District, United States Congress, Washington, DC (2011-2015); Member, U.S. House Committee on Transportation and Infrastructure, Washington, DC (2011-2013); Director, Falls Creek Summer Youth Camp, Davis, OK (1996-2009); Staff Member, Baptist General Convention of Oklahoma (1996-2009) **MEM:** National Rifle Association of America; The Heritage Foundation; Edmond Area Chamber of Commerce; Deer Creek Chamber of Commerce **PA:** Republican **RE:** Christian

LAPIERRE, WAYNE R. JR., T: Chief Executive Officer **I:** Business Management/Business Services **CN:** National Rifle Association of America **DOB:** 11/08/1949 **PB:** Schenectady **SC:** NY/USA **PT:** Wayne Robert LaPierre Sr.; Hazel (Gordon) LaPierre **MS:** Married **SPN:** Susan LaPierre **ED:** MA in Government, Boston College; BA in Education, Siena College, Loudonville, NY (1971) **C:** Chief Executive Officer, Executive Vice President, Chief, National Spokesperson, National Rifle Association of America, Fairfax, VA (1991-Present); Executive Director, National Rifle Association of America, Institute for Legislative Action, Fairfax, VA (1986-1991); Director, Federal Affairs, National Rifle Association, Fairfax, VA (1981-1986); Director, State and Local Affairs, National Rifle Association of America, Fairfax, VA (1979-1980); State Liaison, National Rifle Association of America, Institute for Legislative Action, Fairfax, VA (1978-1979) **CR:** Board of Trustees, National Rifle Association Foundation; President, National Firearms Museum Fund **CIV:** Board of Directors, National Fish and Wildlife Foundation; Board of Directors, American Association of Political Consultants; Board of Directors, American Conservative Union **CW:** Author, "America Disarmed: Inside the U.N. and Obama's Scheme to Destroy the Second Amendment"

(2011); Author, "The Essential Second Amendment Guide" (2007); Author, "The Global War on Your Guns: Inside the UN Plan To Destroy the Bill of Rights" (2006); Author, "Corporate Fascism: How America's Companies are Butting into the Private Lives of Their Employees" (2005); Author, "Guns, Freedom, and Terrorism" (2003); Co-author with James Jay Baker, "Shooting Straight: Telling the Truth About Guns in America" (2002); Author, "Guns, Crime, and Freedom" (1994); Host, Syndicated TV Series, "Crime Strike" **AW:** Named One of the 100 Most Influential People in the World, Time Magazine (2013); Named One of the 25 Most Influential Republicans, Newsmax Magazine (2008); Named One of the 50 Most Powerful People in D.C., GQ Magazine (2007) **RE:** Roman Catholic

LAQUERCIA, THOMAS MICHAEL, T: Trial Lawyer for Personal Injury Cases **I:** Law and Legal Services **CN:** Laquercia LLP **DOB:** 04/22/1945 **PB:** Brooklyn **SC:** NY/USA **PT:** Antonio Salvatore Laquercia; Josephine Maria-Grazia (Livolsi) Laquercia **MS:** Married **SPN:** Susan (Antonicelli) Laquercia; Evelyn Margaret Fernandez (11/02/1943, Deceased) **CH:** Thomas Peter; Marc Anthony; Justin Gregory **ED:** JD, St. John's University, Queens, NY (1969); BA in English, St. Francis College, Brooklyn, NY (1966) **C:** Managing Partner, Laquercia LLP, New York, NY (1980-Present); Associate, Abrams & Martin, Professional Corporation, New York, NY (1974-1980); Associate, Litigation Department, Post DeMott & Grow, New York, NY (1971-1974); Staff Trial Attorney, Kings County Civil Court (1970-1971); General Accident Group, New York, NY (1970-1971); Office of Thomas V. Kingham **CR:** Arbitrator, Small Claims Night Court, Civil Court of the City, NY **CIV:** President, Board of Directors, Strong Place Day Care Center, Inc. **MIL:** Honorable Discharge, Staff Sergeant, United States Air Force (1979); With, United States Army Reserve (1969-1975) **AW:** Alumni Achievement Award, St. Francis College, Brooklyn, NY (2011); Arbitrator of the Year Award, Association of Arbitrators (2009); Scholarship, Regents College, University of the State of New York (1962-1966) **MEM:** New York County Bar Association; New York State Bar Association; New York County Lawyers Association; Board of Directors, Defense Association of New York, Inc.; Association of Arbitrators of the Civil Court of the City of New York; Columbian Lawyers of Brooklyn; Board of Directors, The Columbian Lawyers of the First Judicial Department; Charter Member, National Italian American Bar Association; Alpha Phi Delta Fraternity **BAR:** Supreme Court of the United States (1974); United States District Court for the Southern District of New York (1971); United States District Court for the Eastern District of New York (1971); United States Court of Appeals for the Second Circuit (1971); New York (1970) **MH:** Albert Nelson Marquis Lifetime Achievement Award **B/I:** Mr. Laquercia became involved in his profession because it was at the height of the Vietnam war and if he had gone on to study English he would have been drafted out. So he chose law, which was the deciding factor, and was admitted to practice law and never looked back. **AV:** Reading; Listening to music; Going to the opera **RE:** Roman Catholic **THT:** Mr. Thomas Michael Laquercia joined St. Francis College in 1962, after graduating from St. Francis Preparatory School. A Regent's College scholarship recipient, Thomas wrote for the "Voice" and "Sillion," acted in the "Troupers," sang in the Glee Club and was a member of the Beta Sigma Chapter of Alpha Phi Delta, St. Thomas More Law Society and Student Council. Upon graduation from the college with a Bachelor of Arts in English, he entered St. John's University School of Law, and in 1967, while a law student, married his college sweetheart, Evelyn Fernandez, whom he met at a Beta Sigma fraternity party. Mr. Laquercia graduated from St. John's Law School in 1969, and was admitted to the New York Bar, then, in 1971, to the bar of the United States District Courts for the Southern and Eastern Districts and the U.S. Circuit Court for the Second Circuit. He soon joined Friend, Post & Hopkins, and while there, was admitted to practice before the United States Supreme Court. During law school, Mr. Laquercia joined the U.S. Army Reserve and in 1975, received an honorable discharge with the rank of Staff Sergeant. In 1980, he founded the firm of Smith & Laquercia with Edwin L. Smith, where he has been practicing for over 30 years. Besides being a member of the New York State Bar Association, he is a member of the Board of Directors of the Columbian Lawyers Association, First Judicial Department and a charter member of the National Italian American Bar Association. He has been cited for his work sitting as a pro bono arbitrator in the Small Claims Part for over 30 years by both the New York County Bar Association and the Association of Arbitrators of the Civil Court of the City of New York. In 2009, he received the Arbitrator of the Year Award, New York County, from the Association of Arbitrators. At the College, Mr. Laquercia has served on the Alumni Board of Directors, and has endowed a medal in memory of Brothers Camillus Casey, O.S.F. for excellence in the humanities. He also endowed two three-year scholarships for academically gifted students. One bears his name and the other is known as the 17th of June Scholarship in memory of his late wife, Evelyn, who died in 2005 from complications of multiple sclerosis. Mr. Laquercia is the proud father of Thomas Peter, March Anthony, and Justin Gregory, and proud grandfather of Shane.

LARKIN, MICHAEL, T: Choral and Orchestral Conductor, Composer, Educator **I:** Fine Art **DOB:** 04/10/1951 **PB:** Cumberland **SC:** MD/USA **PT:** William James Larkin; Carolyn Maxine (Crouse) Larkin **MS:** Married **SPN:** Eileen Larkin (04/12/2014); Linda Jean Taylor (11/29/1986, Deceased 12/2011); Kathleen Winchell (05/11/1979, Divorced 10/1986) **CH:** Amy; Daniel; Jon **ED:** MusD, Temple University (1985); MusM, Catholic University (1975); MusB, University of Delaware (1973) **C:** Conductor, Music Director, Brandywine Pops Orchestra, Wilmington, DE (2014-Present); Director of Music Ministry, St. Barnabas' Episcopal Church, Wilmington, DE (2004-Present); Founder, Music Director, New Ark Chorale (1977-Present); Chairman, Vocal Music Department, Artist, Voice Teacher, Wilmington Music School (Now School of Delaware) (1986-2015); Director of Music, Second Baptist Church, Wilmington, DE (1996); Assistant Professor of Music, Misericordia University, Dallas, PA (1985-1986); Programmer, Consultant, Plato Project, University of Delaware (1981-1985); Minister of Music, White Clay Creek Presbyterian Church (1981-1985); Chairman, Music Department, Sanford School (1979-1981); Music Instructor, Wesley College (1975-1979) **CIV:** Owner, Therapy Dog, Dementia Patients, Reading-Challenged Children and Children with Cancer; Pastoral Musician **CW:** Composer, More Than 320 Publications; Choir Conductor, Seven States; Vocal, Choral, Piano and Orchestral Music Composer **AW:** Fellowship, Temple University (1982-1985); Fourth Place Award, Llangollen International Musical Eisteddfod Solo Competition (1972); Numerous Awards, ASCAP **MEM:** Music Educators National Conference; American Choral Directors Association; The Delaware Music Educators Association; American Guild of Organists; Association of Anglican Musicians **MH:** Albert Nelson Marquis Lifetime Achievement Award **AS:** Dr. Larkin attributes his success to his hard work, God-given talent, love of what he does and a little bit of luck. **B/I:** Dr. Larkin became involved in his profession because music was the only subject he ever wanted to pursue. **AV:** Reading; Building model railroads; Computing; Golfing **RE:** Episcopalian

LARRIMORE, JUDITH, "JUDY" RUTLEDGE, RN, T: Administrative Nursing **I:** Medicine & Health Care **CN:** Thomasville Hospital **DOB:** 09/06/1943 **PB:** Jackson **SC:** AL/USA **PT:** Kirxie Eugene Rutledge; Frankie Jewel (Walters) Rutledge **MS:** Married **SPN:** Lennox Wilson Larrimore (11/27/1969) **CH:** Jonathan; Jason; Jennifer; Julie **ED:** Coursework, University of Alabama (1989); BA, University of South Alabama (1966) **CT:** RN Certification, Alabama and Florida **C:** Patient Advisor, Board of Directors, Visiting Nurse Association (1990-1995); Patient Education, Social Services, Advocacy, Volunteer Services Coordinator, Thomasville Hospital (1990-1995); Obstetrics/Surgery, Nurse, Thomasville Hospital (1989-1990); School Nurse, Thomasville City School Systems (1988-1990); Charge Nurse, Thomasville Hospital (1986-1989); Patient Advocate, Thomasville Mental Health Rehabilitation Center (1987-1988); Clinical Instructor, Hobson State Technical Schools; Licensed Practical Nurse, School of Nursing (1986); School Nurse, Thomasville City School Systems (1969-1971); Charge Nurse, Escambia General Hospital, Pensacola, Florida (1967-1968); Charge Nurse, Thomasville Hospital (1966-1967) **CR:** Manager, Thomasville Hospital (1989-1995) **CIV:** Board of Directors, Thomasville Hospital Visiting Nurses **MIL:** Lieutenant, U.S. Air Force (1968-1970) **AW:** Best Bedside Nurse Award (1963-1964) **MEM:** Active Member, Alabama State Nurses Association (1966-1995); Continuing Education Presentation **MH:** Albert Nelson Marquis Lifetime Achievement Award **B/I:** When she was a child, Ms. Larrimore's sister ran over her doll with a tricycle. Ms. Larrimore repaired the toy and took care of it. Through a lot of make-believe, she cultivated a fascination with medical work. She characterizes herself as a people person who always wanted to look after folks. **AV:** Reading; Playing piano; Researching genealogy; Volunteer teaching; Working at Southern Baptist Church **PA:** Republican **RE:** Baptist

LARSEN, KIMBERT E., T: Journalist **I:** Writing and Editing **DOB:** 06/14/1941 **PB:** Boulder **SC:** CO/USA **PT:** Junius Larsen; Dorothy May (Cavanaugh) Larsen **ED:** AA, Idaho State University (1963) **C:** News Editor, The Harvest (1999-2005); Freelance Writer, Billings (1990-2005); Reporter, Editor, The Billings Gazette, Billings, MT (1970-1990); National Affairs Staff Writer, National Catholic News Service, WA (1969-1970); Associate Editor, Register Systems of Newspapers, Denver, CO (1963-1964, 1966-1969); Editor, Western Montana Register (1965-1966); City Hall Reporter, Indiana-Record, Helena, MT (1964); Bureau Reporter, Salt Lake Tribune, Salt Lake City, Utah (1960-1963); Bureau Reporter, Deseret News, Salt Lake City, Utah (1959-1960) **CIV:** Delegate, Montana Association of Churches (2004-2020); Parish Pastoral Council, Holy Rosary Church, Billings, MT (1994-1997, 2000-2003, 2006); Vice President, Montana Catholic Conference (MAC) (2001-2005); Board of Directors, Montana Catholic Conference (1999-2005); Secretary-treasurer, Montana Catholic Conference (1999-2001); Chairman, Diocesan Pastoral Council, Diocese of Great Falls-Billings, MT (1995-1999); President, Idaho Young Democrats, Pocatello, Idaho (1963); Member, Montana Human Rights Network; Member, Oblates of St. Benedict, Saint Benedict's Monastery **CW:** Author, "From Age to Age: A History of the Catholic Church in Eastern Montana" (2004); Member, Editorial Board, The Billings Gazette (1983-1985); Contributor, Ecotage! (1972);

Author, "The Case for Rimrocks National Monument" (1970) **AW:** Travel Grantee, Norwegian Royal Ministry of Foreign Affairs, Oslo, Norway (1980) **MEM:** Yellowstone Valley Audubon Society; Sierra Club **MH:** Albert Nelson Marquis Lifetime Achievement Award **B/I:** Mr. Larsen became involved in his profession because he always wanted to write. **AV:** Books; Classical music; Travel; Hiking **PA:** Independent **RE:** Roman Catholic

LARSEN, RICHARD, "RICK" RAY, T: U.S. Representative from Washington **I:** Government Administration/Government Relations/Government Services **DOB:** 07/15/1965 **PB:** Arlington **SC:** WA/USA **MS:** Married **SPN:** Tiia Karlen (1994) **CH:** Robert; Per **ED:** MPA, University of Minnesota; BA, Pacific Lutheran University, Tacoma, WA **C:** U.S. House of Representatives from Washington's Second Congressional District, United States Congress (2001-Present); Chair, Snohomish County Council, WA (1999); Member, Committee on Armed Services; Member, Committee on Transportation and Infrastructure; Co-Chair, Congressional Methamphetamine Caucus, United States Congress, Second Washington District; Councilman, Snohomish County Council, WA; Economic Development Official, Port of Everett, WA; Director of Public Affairs, Washington State Dental Association **AW:** Friend of the National Parks, National Parks Conservation Association **PA:** Democrat

LARSON, BRIE, T: Actress **I:** Media & Entertainment **DOB:** 10/01/1989 **PB:** Sacramento **SC:** CA/USA **PT:** Sylvain Desaulniers; Heather (Edwards) Desaulniers **CW:** Actress, "Captain Marvel" (2019); Actress, "Avengers: Endgame" (2019); Actress, "Just Mercy" (2019); Appearance, "Between Two Ferns" (2019); Appearance, "Carpool Karaoke: The Series" (2019); Appearance, "Running Wild with Bear Grylls" (2019); Actress, "Free Fire" (2016); Actress, "Basmati Blues" (2017); Actress, "Kong: Skull Island" (2017); Actress, "The Glass Castle" (2017); Actress, "Unicorn Store" (2017); Host, "Saturday Night Live" (2016); Actress, "Digging for Fire" (2015); Appearance, "Comedy Bang! Bang!" (2015); Actress, "Trainwreck" (2015); Actress, "Room" (2015); Actress, "The Gambler" (2014); Actress, "Community" (2013-2014); Actress, "The Spectacular Now" (2013); Actress, "Don Jon" (2013); Actress, "Short Term 12" (2013); Actress, "21 Jump Street" (2012); Actress, "Entry Level" (2012); Actress, "The League" (2011); Actress, "The Trouble with Bliss" (2011); Actress, "Rampart" (2011); Actress, "Treatment" (2011); Actress, "Greenberg" (2010); Actress, "Our Town" (2010); Actress, "Scott Pilgrim Versus the World" (2010); Actress, "United States of Tara" (2009-2011); Actress, "Just Peck" (2009); Actress, "Tanner Hall" (2009); Actress, "House Broken" (2009); Actress, "Ghost Whisperer" (2008); Actress, "Madison" (2005); Singer, "Finally Out of P.E." (2005); Actress, "13 Going on 30" (2004); Actress, "Sleepover" (2004); Actress, "Right on Track" (2003); Actress, "Hope & Faith" (2003); Actress, "Raising Dad" (2001-2002); Actress, "Schimmel" (2000); Actress, "Special Delivery" (1999); Actress, Music Videos, Television Shows and Film **AW:** Academy Award for Best Actress, Academy of Motion Picture Arts and Sciences (2016); Golden Globe Award for Best Performance by an Actress in a Motion Picture - Drama, Hollywood Foreign Press Association (2016); Critics' Choice Award for Best Actress (2016); Screen Actors Guild Award for Outstanding Performance by a Female Actor in a Leading Role, SAG-AFTRA (2016); BAFTA Award for Best Actress (2016); Numerous Awards

LARSON, DAVID, "DAVE" ROYAL PHD, MATHEMATICS DEPARTMENT, T: Mathematics Educator, Researcher **I:** Education/Educational Services **CN:** Texas A&M University **DOB:** 12/05/1942 **PB:** Superior **SC:** WI/USA **PT:** Royal Oliver Larson; Margaret Berget (Pederson) Larson **MS:** Widower **SPN:** Sunday Harriet Raygor (08/22/1968, Deceased, 12/12/2018) **CH:** April; Lisa **ED:** PhD in Mathematics, University of California Berkeley (1976); BS in Mathematics and Chemistry, University of Wisconsin (1965) **C:** Professor, Texas A&M University (1987-Present); Visiting Professor, University of Pennsylvania (1986); Visiting Scholar, University of Leeds (1984); Professor, University of Nebraska (1984-1986); Associate Professor, University of Nebraska (1981-1983); Assistant Professor, University Nebraska (1976-1980) **CR:** Chair, Steering Committee, Great Plains Operator Theory Symposium (1981-2013); Associate Head for Undergraduate Studies, Mathematics Department, Texas A&M University (2001-2005, 2007-2011); Editor, Numerous Articles, Professional Publications **CIV:** American Legion **MIL:** United States Air Force (1968-1972) **CW:** Contributor, Over 100 Refereed Research Articles, Numerous Journals **AW:** Elected Fellow, American Math Society (2015); Grantee, Texas A&M University (1986-2005); Grantee, National Science Foundation, University of Nebraska (1976-1986); S.E.R.C. Grantee, University of Leeds (1984) **MEM:** American Mathematics Society; Mathematics Association of America **MH:** Albert Nelson Marquis Lifetime Achievement Award **AS:** Dr. Larson credits his wife, Sunday, for inspiring him to find success. She played an instrumental role in not only his personal life but his professional life as well. After her unfortunate passing, Dr. Larson's PhD advisor, William Arveson, became an important part of his life. He was additionally inspired by his friend and mentor, Richard "Dick" Kadison of the University of Pennsylvania. Likewise, all of his former PhD students remain in his good graces. **B/I:** Dr. Larson always wanted to be a professor and receive a PhD. He started off being interested in chemistry, physics, and mathematics. However, he realized that what he really was attracted to was the mathematics part of the sciences, so he decided to get a PhD in mathematics. Later, Dr. Larson earned a position at the University of Nebraska. When he got there, he loved the environment. Additionally, his family was happy with his decision. He felt that his work in mathematics and research was important, which made it all the more rewarding. **AV:** Coin collecting and stamp collecting; Archery and firearm target shooting; Playing games with family and friends; Traveling **PA:** Democrat **RE:** Christian **THT:** Dr. Larson believes everyone should work hard for their success.

LARSON, JOHN BARRY, T: U.S. Representative from Connecticut; Insurance Company Executive **I:** Government Administration/Government Relations/Government Services **DOB:** 07/22/1948 **PB:** Hartford **SC:** CT/USA **PT:** Raymond Larson; Pauline (Nolan) Larson **MS:** Married **SPN:** Leslie Best (10/20/1981) **CH:** Carolyn; Laura; Raymond **ED:** BS in Education, Central Connecticut State University (1971) **C:** Member, U.S. House Committee on Ways and Means (2005-Present); Member, U.S. House of Representatives from Connecticut's First Congressional District, United States Congress (1999-Present); President Pro Tempore, Connecticut State Senate (1987-1995); Member, Connecticut State Senate (1983-1994); Partner, Larson & Lysik Insurance (1977-1990); High School Teacher (1972-1977); Member, U.S. House Select Committee on Energy Independence and Global Warming **CR:** Chairman, U.S. House Democratic Caucus (2009-2013); Vice Chairman, U.S. House Democratic Caucus (2007-2009); Founder, Chair, ConneCT96 Project (1996); Member, East Hartford Town Council (1979-1983); Member, East Hartford Board of Education (1978-1979) **AW:** Child Advocacy Legislative Leadership Award, Connecticut Coalition for Children (1991); Appreciation Award, Connecticut AIDS Consortium/United Way of Connecticut Award (1991); Recognition Award, Alzheimer's Association (1991); Named Man of the Year, United Irish Societies (1990); Legislator of the Year, Catholic Charities/Catholic Family Services (1989); Legislator of the Year, Connecticut Valley Girl Scout Council, Girl Scouts of the United States of America (1989); Legislator of the Year, Junior League of Connecticut (1988); Distinguished Alumni Award, Central Connecticut State University (1987); Legislative Leadership Award, Connecticut Association for Human Services (1987); Outstanding Alumni Award, East Hartford HS National Honor Society (1985); Fellow, Yale Bush Center in Child Development (Now Edward Zigler Center in Child Development) **MEM:** The Hartford Club **PA:** Democrat **RE:** Roman Catholic

LARSON, MARILYN J., T: Music Educator (Retired) **I:** Education/Educational Services **DOB:** 07/20/1933 **PB:** Lindstrom **SC:** MN/USA **PT:** Reuben Larson; Dorothy (Holm) Larson **MS:** Divorced **CH:** Paul; Morrie (Deceased); Robert (Deceased) **ED:** MA in Music History, University of Minnesota, with Honors (1957); BS in Music Education, University of Minnesota (1955) **CT:** Certificate in Kodaly Concept Level 1, Hamline University (1987); Accreditation, Minnesota Music Teachers Association (1967); National Certified Music Teacher; Certified Teacher, State of Minnesota; Licensed Realtor; Specialist, Certificate in Educational Administration **C:** General Music Teacher in Preschool, Elementary, and Junior High, St. Paul Public Schools, St. Paul, MN (1978-1997); Teacher, Minneapolis Public Schools, Minneapolis, MN (1976-1978); Teacher, Minneapolis Junior High School, Minneapolis, MN (1957-1960); Teacher, Music Appreciation, University of Minnesota, Minneapolis, MN (1955-1957); Piano Teacher, Private Studio **CR:** Accompanist, Adult Day Care, St. Mary's Home (2001-2004); Member, INS Roundtable (2000-2004); Accompanist, Tanglewood Chorus, Berkshire Music Center, Massachusetts; Designer, Music Curriculum, Minneapolis Public Schools **CIV:** Director of Talent Shows, Phillips Junior High School (1959); Singer, Salem Lutheran Church (1954) **CW:** Accompanist, Chorus, University of Minnesota (1953-1956); Pianist, Department of Music, University of Minnesota (1955); Pianist, "In A Garden," Nicholson Hall **AW:** Scholarship, Berkshire Music Center, Tanglewood, MA (1953); Tozer Foundation Graduate Scholarship; William Lindsey Piano Scholarship; Laura E. Cassidy Scholarship; Dean's Honor Roll; Award, Sigma Alpha Iota; Award, Pi Lambda Theta; Who's Who of American Women; Who's Who in America; Who's Who in the World; International Who's Who of Professionals **MEM:** Founder, Executive Director, Minnesotans for Immigration Reform (1999-Present); Music Teachers National Association; Federation for American Immigration Reform **MH:** Albert Nelson Marquis Lifetime Achievement Award; Marquis Who's Who Top Professional **AV:** Reading; Listening to music **PA:** Independent **RE:** Lutheran **THT:** Ms. Larson states, "We are all called upon by life itself to honor our human potential. The question is not what life has in store for us, but what we bring to life. With faith in God, we will find meaning and purpose in our lives as we learn and grow; take responsibility for our own actions and conduct; and show loving kindness to others - and the greatest of these is love."

LASORDA, TOMMY CHARLES, T: Former Professional Baseball Manager **I:** Professional Training & Coaching **CN:** Los Angeles Dodgers **DOB:** 09/22/1927 **PB:** Norristown **SC:** PA/USA **PT:** Sam Lasorda; Carmella (Covatto) Lasorda **MS:** Married **SPN:** Joan (Miller) Lasorda (04/14/1950) **CH:** Laura; Tom Charles (Deceased) **ED:** Coursework, Public Schools, Norristown, PA **C:** Senior Advisor to Chairman, Los Angeles Dodgers, MLB (2004-Present); With, Los Angeles Dodgers, MLB (1956-Present); Senior Vice President, Los Angeles Dodgers, MLB (1998-2004); Interim General Manager, Los Angeles Dodgers, MLB (1998); Vice President of Finance, Los Angeles Dodgers, MLB (1996-1998); Manager, Los Angeles Dodgers, MLB (1976-1996); Coach, Los Angeles Dodgers, MLB (1973-1976); Manager, Minor League Clubs, Los Angeles Dodgers, Pocatello, Idaho, Ogden, Utah, Spokane, WA, and Albuquerque, NM (1965-1973); Pitcher, Kansas City Athletics, MLB (1956); Pitcher, Brooklyn Dodgers, MLB (1954-1955) **CR:** Coach, USA Men's Baseball Team, Summer Olympics (2000) **CW:** Co-author with Bill Plaschke, "I Live for This!: Baseball's Last True Believer" (2007); Co-author with David Fisher, "The Artful Dodger" (1985) **AW:** Amos Alonzo Stagg Coaching Award, United States Sports Academy (2000); Named to Baseball Hall of Fame (1997); Winner, Los Angeles Dodgers, National League Pennant (1977, 1978, 1981, 1988); Named National League Manager of the Year, Baseball Writers' Association of America (1983, 1988); Winner, Los Angeles Dodgers, World Series (1981, 1988); Named Manager of the Year, Baseball America (1988); Named Co-manager of the Year, Sporting News (1988); Named National League Manager of the Year, Sporting News (1988); Milton Richman Memorial Award, Association Professional Ballplayers of America (APBPA) (1986); Named National League Manager of the Year, The Associated Press (1977); Named National League Manager of the Year, United Press International (1977); Named Pitcher of the Year, International League (1958) **MEM:** Association of Professional Ball Players of America (APBPA); Vice President, Variety Club of California **RE:** Roman Catholic

LATTA, GEORGE H. III, MD, MBA, FAAP, FACHE, CPE, T: Physician **I:** Health, Wellness and Fitness **DOB:** 09/04/1960 **PB:** Chattanooga **SC:** TN/USA **PT:** George Haworth Latta, Jr.; Charlotte (Major) Latta **MS:** Married **SPN:** Teresa Latta **ED:** MBA, University of Colorado at Denver (2011); MD, East Tennessee State University, Johnson City, TN (1986); BS in Applied Physics, Georgia Institute of Technology, Atlanta, GA (1982) **CT:** Licensure, State of Wisconsin (2020); Licensure, State of Idaho (2006); Licensure, State of California (2001); Licensure, State of Utah (2000); Licensure, State of Tennessee (1989); Board Certified in Neonatology and Medical Management **C:** Associate Chief Medical Officer, Children's Wisconsin, Neenah, WI (2020-Present); Staff Neonatologist, Timpanogos Regional Hospital, Orem, UT (2017-2020); Chair of Pediatrics, Medical Director, Senior Partner, Kaweah Delta (2007-2016); Staff Neonatologist, Perinatal Medical Group (2006-2007); Staff Neonatologist, Utah Valley Hospital (2000-2005); Senior Partner, Director of Neonatal Intensive Care Unit Research, Methodist Le Bonheur Healthcare (1995-1999); Staff Neonatologist, Forrest General Hospital (1994-1995); Staff Neonatologist, Rose Medical Center (1992-1994); Neonatology Fellow, The University of Tennessee Health Science Center, Memphis, TN (1990-1992); Neonatology Fellow, Vanderbilt University Medical Center, Nashville, TN (1989-1990); First- and Second-Year Pediatric Intern and Resident, Dartmouth-Hitchcock, Lebanon, NH (1986-1988) **CR:** Associate Chief Medical Officer, Children's Wisconsin (2020-Present); Chair

of Pediatrics, Kaweah Delta (2012-2016); Neonatal Intensive Care Unit Medical Director, Kaweah Delta (2006-2016) **CIV:** Medical Volunteer, Salt Lake City Medical Corps (2018-Present); Medical Volunteer, Salt Lake City Olympics (2002); Volunteer, Medical Corps, California; Volunteer, Best Friends Animal Sanctuary; Volunteer Usher, Egyptian Theatre, Park City, UT **AW:** National Institutes of Health Pulmonary Trainee Grantee, Vanderbilt University (1989); March of Dimes Scholar, East Tennessee State University (1984); Johnny J. Jones Scholar (1981) **MEM:** ATA (2010); American College of Healthcare Executives (2010); California Association of Neonatologists (2008); American Association for Physician Leadership (2005); Undersea & Hyperbaric Medical Society (2005); International Society of Travel Medicine (2004); Wilderness Medical Society (2000); National Perinatal Association (1996); American Academy of Pediatrics (1987); Phi Eta Sigma **MH:** Albert Nelson Marquis Lifetime Achievement Award **AS:** Dr. Latta attributes his success to being raised in an achievement-oriented military family that exposed him to many cultures. **B/I:** Dr. Latta became involved in his profession because he was a biophysics major at Georgia Tech and his best friend in college was premed; he was interested in genetic engineering because of his major and it tied into the medical background his friend was doing. That led him to apply for medical school instead of the PhD program. Dr. Latta thought he was going to follow a genetic background and do academic medicine but what he found was the neonatal intensive care unit had the highest complex of medicine in pediatrics, which really interested him. **AV:** Camping; Hiking; Kayaking; Canoeing; Mountain and road banking; Fly fishing; Scuba diving; Playing chess **RE:** Roman Catholic **THT:** Dr. Latta states, "the future depends on what we do in the present" and "children are out best investment in the future."

LATTA, ROBERT, "BOB" EDWARD, T: U.S. Representative from Ohio **I:** Government Administration/Government Relations/Government Services **DOB:** 04/18/1956 **PB:** Bluffton **SC:** OH/USA **PT:** Delbert Leroy Latta; Rose Mary (Kiene) Latta **SPN:** Marcia Sloan (1986) **CH:** Elizabeth; Maria **ED:** JD, The University of Toledo College of Law (1981); BA, Bowling Green State University (1978) **C:** Member, U.S. House of Representatives from Ohio's Fifth Congressional District, United States Congress (2007-Present); Member, District Six, Ohio House of Representatives (2001-2007); Member, District Two, Ohio State Senate, Columbus, Ohio (1997-2000); Wood County Commissioner, Bowling Green, Ohio (1991-1996); Associate Counsel, TrusCorp International Co., Ltd. (1983-1989); Attorney, Cheetwood & Davies, Bowling Green, Ohio (1982-1983); Attorney, Marshall & Melhorn, LLC, Toledo, Ohio (1981-1982); Member, Committee on Energy and Commerce; Member, Republican Study Committee; Chair, Criminal Justice Committee, Ohio House of Representatives **CIV:** Member, Wood County Historical Society **AW:** Distinguished Legislative Award, Ohio Economic Development Association (2007); Watchdog of Treasury Award, United Conservatives of Ohio (1998, 2000, 2005); Patriot Award, U.S Sportsmen's Alliance (2002); Named Legislator of the Year, League of Ohio Sportsmen (2000); Named Legislator of the Year, Ohio Farmers Union (2000); Major General Charles Dick Award for Legislative Excellence, Ohio National Guard Association (1999); Legislative Appreciation Award, Ohio Association of Alcohol Drug Addiction and Mental Health Services (ADAMHSCC) **MEM:** Trustee, Wood County Bar Association (1991-1995); President, Kiwanis International (1991-1992); Vice President, Kiwanis International (1990-1991); National Rifle Associa-

tion of America; National Federation of Independent Business; Ohio Rifle and Pistol Association; Wood County Historical Society (Wood County Museum); Kiwanis International; Omicron Delta Kappa **BAR:** State of Ohio (1981) **PA:** Republican

LAUDADIO, FRED, EDD, T: Executive Director of Learning Services and Technology **I:** Education/Educational Services **CN:** McHenry School District 15 **DOB:** 11/07/1980 **PB:** Chicago **SC:** IL/USA **MS:** Married **SPN:** Christine **CH:** Logan; Eli **ED:** EdD in Educational Leadership and Administration, Aurora University (2015); MEd in Education Leadership and Administration, Aurora University (2008); MEd in Secondary Education and Teaching, Roosevelt University (2004); BBA, Columbia College (2002); AAS in Management Systems, Business Administration, Management, and Computer Operations, McHenry County College (2001) **CT:** Chief School Business Official, Education/Finance, Concordia University of Chicago (2019) **C:** Executive Director of Learning Services and Technology, McHenry School District 15 (2008-Present); Business and Technology Teacher, Johnsburg School District 12 (2004-2008); Computer Technician, Webster University (2001-2006) **CR:** Athletic Director; Coach; Mentor Leader **CIV:** Community Leader; Volunteer, Local Causes **AW:** National STEM Excellence Winner Award, Future of Education Technology Conference (FETC) (2020); SETDA Digital Learning Award Finalist, State Educational Technology Directors Association, Washington, DC (2019); ISTE Technology Coordinator PLN Award, International Society for Technology in Education (2019); National STEM Excellence Finalist Award, Future of Education Technology Conference (FETC) (2019); International Recipient, Making IT Happen Award, International Society for Technology in Education (2018); National Recipient, Tech Excellence Award, District Administration Journal (2018); National Recipient, Digital Content and Curriculum Achievement Award, Center for Digital Curriculum; Common Core Standards Implementation Award, Center for College & Career Readiness; Golden Achievement Award in Communications and Digital Curricular Design, National School Public Relations Association **MEM:** International Society for Technology in Education (ISTE); Individuals with Disabilities Education Act (IDEA); Future of Education Technology Conference (FETC); Illinois Association of School Business Officials (IASBO); International Accounting Standards Board (IASB); IPA **AS:** Dr. Laudadio enjoys seeing things change in real-time. He is inspired by the look of a child's face when they enter a new learning space that is different, where they are able to be innovative in a non-traditional school setting. **B/I:** Inspiration comes from the team you surround yourself with, according to Dr. Laudadio. He always had a desire to create something bigger than one could imagine. **AV:** Running; Playing baseball and basketball; Practicing comedy; Partaking in trying foods/restaurants of any kind **RE:** Catholic **THT:** Mr. Laudadio dedicates his life to working hard and developing his passions. He believes teaching and learning are the gateways to allow the next generations to succeed.

LAUPER, CYNDI ANN STEPHANIE, T: Singer; Actress **DOB:** 06/20/1953 **PB:** Queens **SC:** NY/USA **PT:** Fred Lauper; Catrine (Gallo) Lauper **MS:** Married **SPN:** David Thornton (11/24/1991) **CH:** Declyn Wallace **ED:** Honorary LittD, Northern Vermont University (2019); Studied with Katie Agresta, New York, NY (1974); Coursework, Johnson State College **C:** Solo Artist (1981-Present); Member, Blue Angel (1978-1980); Member, Flyer; Member, Doc West; Singer, Night Clubs, NY

CIV: Board of Directors, Co-founder, True Colors Fund (2008-Present); Founder, True Colors United (2012); Honorary Chair, Co-founder, True Colors Residence; Supporter, LGBT Rights CW: Voice Actress, "Bubble Guppies" (2020); Voice Actress, "Young Sheldon" (2020); Actress, "Magnum P.I." (2018); Actress, "Bones" (2009-2015, 2017); Composer, Song, Broadway, "SpongeBob SquarePants" (2017); Singer, "Detour" (2016); Host, "BrainSurge" (2015); Appearance, "Front and Center" (2014); Actress, "Henry & Me" (2014); Featured, Executive Producer, "Cyndi Pauper: Still So Unusual" (2013); Composer, Music and Lyrics, Broadway, "Kinky Boots" (2013); Author, "Cyndi Lauper: A Memoir" (2012); Actress, "Happily Divorced" (2012); Voice Actress, "Bob's Burgers" (2012); Actress, "Dirty Movie" (2011); Singer, "Memphis Blues" (2010); Appearance, "30 Rock" (2009); Appearance, "Gossip Girl" (2008); Singer, "Bring Ya to the Brink" (2008); Actress, "Threepenny Opera" (2006); Voice Actress, "The Backyardigans" (2006); Singer, "The Body Acoustic" (2006); Actress, "That's So Raven" (2005); Appearance, "The Naked Brothers Band: The Movie" (2005); Singer, "Shine" (2004); Singer, "The Essential Cyndi Lauper" (2003); Singer, "At Last" (2003); Singer, "Feels Like Christmas" (2001); Actress, "Christmas Dream" (2000); Performer, "Matters of the Heart" (2000); Actress, "The Opportunists" (2000); Voice Actress, "The Simpsons" (1999); Actress, "The Happy Prince" (1999); Singer, "Merry Christmas...Have a Nice Life" (1998); Singer, "Sisters of Avalon" (1996); Appearance, "Sesame Street Elmocize" (1996); Singer, "Twelve Deadly Cyns...and Then Some" (1995); Appearance, "Mrs. Parker and the Vicious Circle" (1994); Actress, "Mad About You" (1993-1999); Actress, "Life with Mikey" (1993); Singer, "Hat Full of Stars" (1993); Contributor, "A Very Special Christmas, Volume 2" (1993); Contributor, "A Very Special Christmas" (1992); Actress, "Off and Running" (1991); Actress, "Mother Goose Rock n' Rhyme" (1990); Singer, Song and Album, "A Night to Remember" (1989); Actress, "Vibes" (1988); Singer, "True Colors" (1986); Singer, Co-writer, Song, "Goonies R Good Enough" (1985); Appearance, "Prime Cuts" (1984); Singer, Co-writer, Song, "She Bop" (1984); Singer, Co-writer, Song, "Money Changes Everything" (1984); Singer, Co-writer, Song, "Time After Time" (1984); Singer, "She's So Unusual" (1983); Singer, Co-writer, Song, "Girls Just Want to Have Fun" (1983); Singer with Blue Angels, "Blue Angels" (1980); Actress, Appearances, Television Shows, Films; Singer, Songwriter, Songs, Albums; Performer, Music Videos, Concert Tours, Worldwide Including United States, Japan, Australia, Hawaii and England, United Kingdom AW: Named to the National Recording Registry, Library of Congress (2019); Recipient, Star, Hollywood Walk of Fame (2016); Named to Songwriters Hall of Fame (2015); Grammy Award for Best Musical Theater Album, The Recording Academy (2014); Tony Award for Best Original Score, Kinky Boots (2013); Emmy Award for Outstanding Guest Actress, Academy of Television Arts & Sciences (1995); Award for Favorite Pop/Rock Female Video Artist, American Music Awards (1986); Award for Favorite Pop/Rock Female Artist, American Music Awards (1985); Grammy Awards for Best New Artist, Best Album Package, The Recording Academy (1985); Award for Best Female Video, MTV Video Music Award (1984); Named to 500 Greatest Albums of All Time, Rolling Stone Magazine; Named to 100 Best Songs of the Past 25 Years, VH1; Named One of the Greatest Women of Rock & Roll, VH1; Numerous Awards

LAUREN, RALPH, T: Fashion Designer, Fashion Company Executive **I:** Apparel & Fashion **CN:** Polo Ralph Lauren Corp. (Formerly Polo Fashions, Inc.) **DOB:** 10/14/1939 **PB:** Bronx **SC:** NY/USA **PT:** Frank Lifshitz; Fraydl (Kotlar) Lifshitz **MS:** Married **SPN:** Ricky Low-Beer (12/30/1964) **CH:** Andrew; David; Dylan **ED:** Honorary LHD, Brandeis University (1996); Honorary DFA, Pratt Institute (1988); Coursework in Business, Baruch College, The City University of New York **C:** Executive Chairman, Chief Creative Officer, Polo Ralph Lauren (Formerly Polo Fashions, Inc.), Ralph Lauren Corporation (2015-Present); Launched, Ralph Lauren Home Collection, Ralph Lauren Corporation (1983-Present); Launched, Polo/Ralph Lauren Luggage, Ralph Lauren Corporation (1982-Present); Launched, Fragrances, Polo for Men, Lauren for Women, Others, Ralph Lauren Corporation (1979-Present); Launched, Polo Leather Goods, Polo/Ralph Lauren for Boys, Ralph Lauren Corporation (1978); Launched, Ralph Lauren Womenswear, Ralph Lauren Corporation, New York, NY (1971-Present); Established, Various Lines Including Polo Men's Wear Co., Ralph Lauren Corporation, New York, NY (1968-Present); Founder, Chief Executive Officer, Chairman, Polo Ralph Lauren Corp. (Now Ralph Lauren Corporation), New York, NY (1967-2015); Neckwear Designer, Polo Division, Beau Brummel, New York, NY (1967-1969); Representative, Rivetz Necktie Manufacturers, New York, NY; Assistant Buyer, Allied Stores, New York, NY; Salesperson, Brooks Brothers Group, Inc., New York, NY **CR:** Opened, RL Restaurant, Ralph Lauren, Chicago, IL (1999-Present); Designer, Sportswear for Team USA, Opening and Closing Ceremonies, Winter Olympics, Sochi, Russia (2014); Designer, Sportswear for Team USA, Opening and Closing Ceremonies, Summer Olympics, London, England (2012) **MIL:** With, United States Army (1962-1964) **AW:** Named One of the World's Richest People, Forbes Magazine (2001-Present); Named to the Forbes 400: Richest Americans (1999-Present); Named One of the Top 25 Highest Paid Executives in Fashion, WWD (2018); Named Knight Commander, Order of the British Empire (2017); James Smithson Bicentennial Medal, Smithsonian Institution (2014); Named Chevalier de la Legion d'Honneur, Paris, France (2010); Key to the City of New York, Mayor Michael Bloomberg (2010); American Fashion Legend Award, CFDA Fashion Awards (2007); Menswear Designer of the Year Award (1996, 2007); Named One of the World's 100 Most Influential People, TIME Magazine (2006); Named Man of the Year, GQ Magazine (2002); VH1/Vogue Lifetime Achievement Award, VH1/Vogue Fashion Awards (2002); Inductee, Fashion Walk of Fame (2000); Humanitarian Award, Breast Cancer Research Foundation (1998); Humanitarian Leadership Award, CFDA Fashion Awards (1997); Dom Perignon Award (1997); Named Menswear Designer of the Year, CFDA Fashion Awards (1996); Humanitarian Award, Nina Hyde Center for Breast Cancer Research (1996); Named Womenswear Designer of the Year, CFDA Fashion Awards (1995); Lifetime Achievement Award (1991); Inductee, Coty American Fashion Critics' Hall of Fame (1977); American Fashion Award (1975); Winnie Award (1974); Neiman Marcus Distinguished Service Award (1973); Tommy Award, American Printed Fabrics Council (1971); Menswear Award (1970); Numerous Awards

LAURENCE, PETER, "PETE" A., BROKER EMERITUS, T: Real Estate Broker **I:** Real Estate **CN:** RE/MAX/ACCORD **PT:** Al Laurence; Beth Laurence **MS:** Married **SPN:** Sheryll **CH:** One son; Two daughters **ED:** AA in Business, Diablo Valley College, CA (1968) **CT:** Five Star Professional; Certified Distressed Property Expert; Certified Residential Specialist; Graduate Realtor Institute; REALTORS Political Action Committee; Short Sales and Foreclosure Resource Certification; Seniors Real Estate Specialist; Seller Representative Specialist; Brokerage License; Series 8 Securities License **C:** Three-Term Mayor, Clayton, CA; Member, City Council, CA; Real Estate Broker, RE/MAX/ACCORD **CIV:** President, Local Chamber of Commerce; Donor, Scholarship, Local High School Wrestling Program **MIL:** Active Combatant, Vietnam, U.S. Army Special Forces (1966-1967); Military Policeman (1965-1966) **AW:** Realtor Emeritus, Contra Costa Board of Realtors (2017); Realtor of the Year, Better Homes Realty; Realtor Emeritus, National Association of Realtors **MEM:** Emeritus Member, National Association of Realtors; Veterans of Foreign Wars; The American Legion; Special Forces Association **AS:** Mr. Laurence attributes his success to his competence, sincerity and friendliness. **B/I:** Mr. Laurence became involved in his profession because when he returned from active duty in Vietnam, his great training led him to enroll in Diablo Valley College. With the funds he accumulated during his service, he was able to buy two cheap houses, but sold one and made $1,000 profit. At the time, $1,000 was a lot of money, and the transaction got him attention from others in the industry. He decided that he would pursue real estate as a career while also attending law school. After finishing his associate degree, he planned to spend only a year working in real estate before finishing his schooling. After learning more about the law field, becoming a lawyer became less interesting to him. He realized that real estate is what he loved. Mr. Laurence loves helping others achieve the American dream within their price range. It is what keeps him motivated, and helping others, rather than just retiring and doing nothing. **AV:** Traveling; Staying abreast of current events and politics **PA:** Conservative **RE:** Christian **THT:** Mr. Laurence states "I've learned that life can be very difficult, but it's important to never give up. Always try to do your best no matter what you do. Also, treat everyone with respect and friendliness whether anyone is watching or not."

LAWRENCE, BRENDA LULENAR, T: U.S. Representative, Former Mayor **I:** Government Administration/Government Relations/Government Services **DOB:** 10/18/1954 **PB:** Detroit **SC:** MI/USA **MS:** Married **SPN:** McArthur Lawrence (1976) **CH:** Michael; Michelle **ED:** BS in Public Administration, Central Michigan University (2005) **C:** U.S. Representative, Michigan's 14th Congressional District, United States Congress, Washington, DC (2014-Present); Mayor, City of Southfield, MI (2001-2015); President, City of Southfield, MI (1999-2001); Councilman, City of Southfield (1997-1999); From Letter Carrier to Human Resources Management, USPS (1978-2008) **CR:** Member, School Board, City of Southfield, MI (1992-1996) **AW:** Distinguished Leadership and Future Leaders Award for Exemplary Leadership, Leadership Oakland (2004); Woman of the Year Award, Millennium Chapter, ABWA; Brotherhood Award, Department of Michigan, Jewish War Veterans of the United States of America; Black Woman Achiever Award **PA:** Democrat

LAWRENCE, JENNIFER SCHRADER, T: Actress **I:** Media & Entertainment **DOB:** 08/15/1990 **PB:** Indian Hills **SC:** KY/USA **PT:** Gary Lawrence; Karen Lawrence **MS:** Married **SPN:** Cooke Maroney (10/2019) **C:** Founder, Production Company, Excellent Cadaver (2018-Present) **CIV:** Founder, Jennifer Lawrence Foundation (2015-Present); Supporter, Planned Parenthood, Feeding America, Time's Up Initiative; Board Member, Represent Us **CW:** Actress, "X-Men: Dark Phoenix" (2019); Actress, "Mother!" (2018); Actress, "Red Sparrow" (2018); Guest Host, "Jimmy Kimmel Live!" (2017); Narrator, "A Beautiful Planet" (2016);

Actress, "X-Men: Apocalypse" (2016); Actress, "Passengers" (2016); Actress, "The Hunger Games: Mockingjay - Part 2" (2015); Actress, "Joy" (2015); Actress, "X-Men: Days of Future Past" (2014); Actress, "Serena" (2014); Actress, "The Hunger Games: Mockingjay - Part 1" (2014); Actress, "The Hunger Games: Catching Fire" (2013); Actress, "American Hustle" (2013); Host, "Saturday Night Live" (2013); Actress, "Devil You Know" (2012); Actress, "The Hunger Games" (2012); Actress, "House at the End of the Street: (2012); Actress, "Silver Linings Playbook" (2012); Actress, "Like Crazy" (2011); Actress, "The Beaver" (2011); Actress, "X-Men: First Class" (2011); Actress, "Winter's Bone" (2010); Actress, "The Bill Engvall Show" (2007-2009); Actress, "The Burning Plain" (2008); Actress, "Garden Party" (2008); Actress, "The Poker House" (2008); Actress, "Cold Case" (2007); Actress, "Not Another High School Show" (2007); Actress, "Company Town" (2006); Actress, "Monk" (2006) **AW:** Golden Globe Awards for Best Actress in a Motion Picture - Musical or Comedy, Hollywood Foreign Press Association (2013, 2016); Teen Choice Award for Choice Movie Actress: Sci-Fi/Fantasy (2012, 2013, 2014, 2015); Named Favorite Action Movie Actress, People's Choice Awards (2013, 2015); Named One of the Best Dressed Women, Glamour Magazine (2013-2015); Named Highest-grossing Action Heroine, Guinness World Records (2015); Named One of the 100 Most Powerful Women in Entertainment, The Hollywood Reporter (2012-2014); Golden Globe Award for Best Supporting Actress - Motion Picture, Hollywood Foreign Press Association (2014); BAFTA Award for Best Supporting Actress (2014); Critics Choice Award for Best Actress in a Comedy (2013); Screen Actors Guild Award for Outstanding Performance by a Female Actor in a Leading Role, SAG-AFTRA (2013); Academy Award for Best Actress, Academy of Motion Picture Arts & Sciences (2013); Named One of the 10 Most Fascinating People of 2013, Barbara Walters Special (2013); Named One of the 100 Most Influential People in the World, TIME Magazine (2013); Critics Choice Award for Best Actress in an Action Movie (2013); MTV Movie Award for Best Female Performance (2012); Named One of the Top 10 Actors to Watch, Variety Magazine (2010); Award for Best Breakthrough Performance, National Board of Review (2010); Numerous Awards

LAWRENCE, LU, T: Photographer, Educator **I:** Media & Entertainment **PB:** Massillon **SC:** OH/USA **PT:** Carl W. Lawrence; Ruth W. Lawrence **MS:** Married **SPN:** Altus Leon Simpson (12/20/1970) **CH:** Candace; Susan **ED:** BA, MA, California State University, Fullerton, CA (1968) **C:** Aerial Photographer (1995-2010); Adjunct Faculty, University of Puget Sound, Tacoma, WA (1984-1994); Professor, Cypress College (1967-1984); Training Consultant, Host International, Los Angeles, CA (1961-1977); Training Consultant, Western Airlines, Los Angeles, CA (1961-1967) **CR:** Lecturer, 114 International Cruises (1984-2004) **CW:** Author, "A Bird's Eye View of Bainbridge Island" (1989, 1993, 1998); Author, "Airline and Travel Career" (1979); Contributor, Articles, Photographs, Professional Publications; Patentee in Field **MH:** Albert Nelson Marquis Lifetime Achievement Award **B/I:** Ms. Lawrence became involved with photography when she bought her house; she planted hundreds of tulips, all of which were so beautiful, inspiring her to take photos of them. Her photographs gained widespread attention, consequently inspiring her to pursue a career in the field.

LAWRENCE, MERLOYD, T: Editor **I:** Writing and Editing **DOB:** 08/01/1932 **PB:** Pasadena **SC:** CA/USA **PT:** Nicholas Saltus; Mary Lloyd (Macy) Ludington

MS: Married **SPN:** John M. Myers (1985); Seymour Lawrence (June 21, 1952, Divorced 1984) **CH:** Macy; Nicholas **ED:** MA, Radcliffe College (1957); AB, Radcliffe College (1954) **C:** President, Merloyd Lawrence, Inc., Boston, MA (1983-Present); Editor, Treasurer and Vice President, Seymour Lawrence Inc., Boston, MA (1965-1983); Freelance Translator (1957-1965); With, Houghton Mifflin Co. (1955-1957) **CIV:** Board Member, Orion Society Magazine (2018-Present); Honorary Director, NE Wilderness Trust (2019-Present); Board of Directors, NE Wilderness Trust (2002-2018); Board of Directors, Island Press (2005-2017); Board of Directors, Woods Hole Research Center (1998-2015); Member, Advisory Board, World Land Trust (2006-2013); Member, Committee for Clinical Investigations, Beth Israel/Deaconess Hospital (1986-2007); Trustee, Milton Academy, Massachusetts (1974-1982); Treasurer, Vice President, Milford House Properties, Ltd., Canada (1975-1980); Executive Committee Member, Island Press; Member, Advisory Board, Non-human Rights Project **CW:** Translator, Various Works of Flaubert and Balzac; Translator, Modern French Fiction, German and Swedish Children's Books **MEM:** Director, New England Forestry Foundation (1989-2008); Executive Board Officer, New England Forestry Foundation (1990-2007); Director, Massachusetts Audubon Society (1974-2001); Executive Committee Member, Massachusetts Audubon Society (1992-2001); Honorary Director, Massachusetts Audubon Society (2001-Present); Tavern Club; Phi Beta Kappa

LAWSON, ALFRED, "AL" JAMES JR., T: 1) U.S. Representative from Florida 2) Insurance Company Executive **I:** Government Administration/Government Relations/Government Services **CN:** 1) U.S. House of Representatives 2) Lawson and Associates Inc. **DOB:** 9/21/1948 **PB:** Tallahassee **SC:** FL/USA **MS:** Married **SPN:** Delores Brooks (1975) **CH:** Alfred III; Shani **ED:** Master of Public Administration, Florida State University (1973); Bachelor of Science in Political Science, Florida A&M University (1970) **C:** Member, U.S. House of Representatives from Florida's Fifth Congressional District (2017-Present); President, Lawson and Associates Inc. (1984-Present); Insurance Agent, Northwestern Mutual Life Insurance Co. (1976-Present); Minority Leader, Florida State Senate (2008-2010); Member, District Sixth, Florida State Senate, Tallahassee, FL (2000-2010); Member, District Eighth, Florida House of Representatives, Tallahassee, FL (1982-2001); Member, Banking and Insurance Committee, Florida State Senate; Member, Committee on Governmental Oversight and Accountability, Florida State Senate; Member, Committee on Health Regulation, Florida State Senate; Member, Committee on Reapportionment, Florida State Senate; Member, Rules Committee, Florida State Senate; Vice Chair, General Government Appropriations Committee, Florida State Senate; Vice Chair, Select Committee on Florida's Inland Waters, Florida State Senate; Member, Committee on Agriculture, United States Congress; Member, Committee on Small Business, United States Congress **CIV:** Board Member, Tallahassee Chamber of Commerce; Boy Scouts of America **AW:** Leadership Award (1996); Rosewood Award (1996); National Sales Achievement Award (1977-1993); Named to Million Dollar Round Table (1975-1993); Outstanding Legislature Service Award, Sierra Club (1990); Environmental Leadership Award, The Nature Conservancy (1990); Legislature Service Award, Organized Fisherman of Florida (1989-1990); Inductee, Florida A&M University Sports Hall of Fame (1989); Distinguished Alumni Award, Florida State University (1989); Meritorious Award, Florida A&M University (1989); National Alumni Outstanding Service Award, Florida A&M

University Alumni (1985); Outstanding Community Leadership Award, Tallahassee Urban League Inc. (1985); Legislator of the Year, Florida Student Association (1985); Named, Florida Insurance Agent of the Year (1979) **MEM:** National Association for the Advancement of Colored People; National Association of Life Underwriters; Florida A&M University Booster Club; Florida A&M University National Alumni Association; Advisory Committee, Florida State University Alumni Club; Board Member, Tallahassee Urban League **PA:** Democrat **RE:** Episcopalian

LAWSON, H. BLAINE JR., PHD, T: Mathematician, Educator **I:** Education/Educational Services **DOB:** 01/04/1942 **PB:** Norristown **SC:** PA/USA **PT:** Herbert Blaine; Mary Louise (Corson) Lawson **MS:** Married **SPN:** Carolyn Elaine Pieroni (6/6/1964, Divorced 1977); Marie-Louise Michelsohn **CH:** Christina Corson; Heather Brooke **ED:** Doctor of Philosophy in Mathematics, Stanford University (1968); Master of Science in Mathematics, Stanford University (1966); Bachelor of Arts, Bachelor of Science in Applied Mathematics and Russian Literature, Brown University (1964) **C:** Distinguished Professor, Chairman, State University of New York, Stony Brook (1978-Present); Professor, University of California Berkeley (1974-1980); Assistant Dean, University of California, Berkeley (1975-1977); Associate Professor, University of California Berkeley (1971-1974); Lecturer of Mathematics, University of California Berkeley (1968-1970) **CR:** Member, Institute for Advanced Study, Princeton, NJ (2009); Visiting Professor, Institute des Hautes Etudes Scientifiques, Bures-sur-Yvette, France (1977-1978, 1993, 1999-2000, 2007); Member, Institut Henri Poincar, Paris, France (2003-2004); Chairperson, National Committee of Mathematics, National Academy of Sciences, Washington, DC (1995); Member, Mathematical Sciences Research Institute, Berkeley, CA (1993-1994); Visiting Professor, Tata Institute for Fundamental Research, Mumbai, India (1986-1987); Visiting Professor, Research Institute for Math Sciences, Kyoto, Japan (1986); École Polytechnique, Palaiseau, France (1983-1984); Member, Institute for Advanced Study, Princeton, NJ (1972-1973); Visiting Assistant Professor, The Instituto Nacional de Matemática Pura e Aplicada, Rio de Janeiro, Brazil (1970-1971); Board Director, U.S.-Brazilian Mathematics Exchange, Stony Brook, NY and Rio de Janeiro, Brazil; Trustee, Mathematical Sciences Research Institute, Berkeley, CA **CW:** Co-author, "Spin Geometry," with M.L. Michelsohn, Princeton University Press (1989); Author, "The Theory of Gauge Fields in 4 Dimensions" (1985); Author, "The Quantitative Theory of Foliations," Proceedings for the CBMS Regional Conference Series in Mathematics, Volume 27, American Mathematical Society, Providence, RI (1977); Author, "Lectures on Minimal Submanifolds," IMPA Press, Rio de Janeiro, Brazil (1973); Editor, Journal of Differential Geometry, Topology; Editor, Journal of the American Mathematical Society; Editor, The Princeton Mathematical Series; Contributor, Articles to Professional Journals **AW:** Fellow, American Academy of Arts and Sciences (2013); Fellow, Brazilian Academy of Sciences (1999); Addresses to the International Congress of Mathematicians (1974, 1994); Hardy Lectureship, London Mathematical Society (1991); Fellow, Guggenheim Foundation (1983); Fellow, Sloan Foundation (1971); Leroy P. Steele Prize, American Mathematical Society; Aisenstadt Chair at Centre De Recherches Mathematiques, Montreal **MEM:** American Mathematical Society; National Academy of Sciences; Brazilian Academy of Sciences; American Academy of Arts and Science **MH:** Albert Nelson Marquis Lifetime Achievement Award; Marquis Who's Who Top

Professional; Marquis Who's Who Humanitarian Award **B/I:** Prof. Lawson became involved in his profession during his studies in graduate school, when he realized his interest in education. Initially specializing in physics, he eventually focused on mathematics.

LAWSON, JACK W., I: Law and Legal Services **DOB:** 09/23/1935 **PB:** Decatur **SC:** IN/USA **PT:** Alva W. Lawson; Florence C. (Smitley) Lawson **MS:** Married **SPN:** Sarah J. Hibbard (12/28/1961) **CH:** Mark; Jeff **ED:** JD, Valparaiso University (1961); BA in Political Science, Valparaiso University (1958) **C:** Senior Partner, Beckman, Lawson LLP, Fort Wayne, IN (1984-Present); Partner, Beckman, Lawson LLP, Fort Wayne, IN (1961-1984) **CR:** Seminar Presenter, Writer, Independent Continuing Legal Education Forum, Indianapolis, IN (1970-Present); National Health Lawyers Association, Washington, DC (1986) **CIV:** Fort Wayne Chamber of Commerce (1975-Present); Small Claims Court Judge, Allen County, IN (1963-1967) **CW:** Editor-in-Chief, Indiana Real Estate Transactions; Contributor, Articles, Professional Journals **AW:** AV Preeminent Rating, Martindale-Hubbell (2007-Present); Sagamore Wabash Award, Governor of the State of Indiana (2001) **MEM:** American College of Real Estate Lawyers **BAR:** U.S. District Court for the Northern District of Indiana (1991); U.S. District Court for the Southern District of Indiana (1991); U.S. Court of Appeals for the 7th Circuit (1991); U.S. Supreme Court (1970); Indiana (1961) **B/I:** Mr. Lawson became involved in his profession after studying engineering at Purdue University. Though he initially wanted to become an engineer, he changed his mind after witnessing a jury trial. It inspired him to become a lawyer. **AV:** Sailing; Teaching religious seminars; Antique consulting **PA:** Republican **RE:** Lutheran

LAYTON, DONALD HARVEY, T: Chief Executive Officer **I:** Financial Services **CN:** Freddie Mac **DOB:** 05/09/1950 **PT:** Irving Layton; Charlotte (Bell) Layton **MS:** Married **SPN:** Sandra Lynn Lazo (06/01/1974) **CH:** Todd Samuel; Ross Charles **ED:** MBA, Harvard University (1974); MS in Economics, Massachusetts Institute of Technology (1972); BS in Economics, Massachusetts Institute of Technology (1972) **C:** Chief Executive Officer, Freddie Mac, Federal Home Loan Mortgage Corporation, McLean, VA (2012-Present); Chief Executive Officer, E*TRADE Financial Corporation (2008-2009); Chairman, E*TRADE Financial Corporation (2007-2009); Vice-Chairman, JPMorgan Chase & Co. (1995-2004); Senior Executive Vice President, Chemical Banking Corporation (Now JPMorgan Chase & Co.) (1992-1995); Trainee to Senior Managing Director, Manufacturer's Hanover Trust Company (Now JPMorgan Chase & Co.), New York, NY (1975-1991); Research Assistant, Harvard Business School, Boston, MA (1974-1975) **CR:** Board of Directors, Freddie Mac, Federal Home Loan Mortgage Corporation (2012-Present); American International Group, Inc. (AIG) (2010-2012); Assured Guaranty Ltd. (2005-2012); Senior Adviser, Securities Industry and Financial Markets Association (SIFMA) (2006-2008) **CIV:** Chair Emeritus, The Partnership for the Homeless, New York, NY (2015-Present); Chairman, Board of Directors, The Partnership for the Homeless, New York, NY (2005-2015); Board of Directors, Foreign Policy Association (1998-2006) **AW:** George F. Baker Scholar, Harvard Business School (1974) **MEM:** Chair Emeritus, The Harbor Club, New York, NY; Harvard Club of New York City, NY **MH:** Albert Nelson Marquis Lifetime Achievement Award; Marquis Who's Who Top Professional

LAZERWITZ, MILES, DDS, T: Owner, Principal **I:** Medicine & Health Care **CN:** Miles Lazerwitz, DDS **PT:** Max; Alma **CH:** Michael; Larry; Allison **ED:** Doctoral Degree, The University of Pennsylvania School of Dental Medicine (1951-1955) **C:** Owner, Principal, Miles Lazerwitz, DDS **MEM:** Principal, Martin M Keets Study Club, New York, NY **MH:** Marquis Who's Who Top Professional **B/I:** Dr. Lazerwitz became involved in dentistry because of Dr. Cott, a dentist who helped him get past his fear of the dentist.

LAZO, WALEUSKA, T: President **I:** Writing and Editing **CN:** DreamCatcher Print **DOB:** 05/08/1971 **SC:** Nicaragua **MS:** Single **CH:** Victoria; Emma **ED:** Master of Arts in Criminal Justice, University of Toronto, Toronto, Ontario, Canada (1995); Bachelor of Arts in Criminal Justice, University of Toronto, Toronto, Ontario, Canada **CT:** HeartMath **C:** President, DreamCatcher Print (2011-Present); Co-Founder, Magnum Opus Development Group (2008-Present); Founder, Corban, Cigar Company (2009-Present); Co-Founder, Embanet (1995-2007) **CR:** Transformational Gratitude Coach and Expert; Leader, Online Course, The Gratitude Experiment **CW:** Author, "The Gift of Bravery: The Story of Eli Cohen" (2019); Author, "Confessions from a Mom to her Child" (2019); Author, The Best Worst Thing That Happened to Me" (2018); Write-Ups, Canadian-Jewish News **AW:** Numerous Awards Through Former Online Company **AS:** Ms. Lazo attributes her success to the notions of altruism and perseverance. **B/I:** Ms. Lazo became involved in her profession after reaching a nadir in her life. Unhappy and depressed, but determined to remain strong for her family, she began taking five minutes out of every day to give thanks for all the things she had, which helped immensely. She began blogging about her experiences, and resolved to follow a life of service so that she could inspire and transform the lives of others. **AV:** Movies; Novella soap operas; Family **THT:** "The best way to live your life is to have no regrets... Do what is right and not what is easy..."

LE GRAND, CHARLES HEYWARD SR., CIA, CISA, T: Chief Executive Officer **I:** Writing and Editing **CN:** CHL Global Associates, LLC. **DOB:** 01/09/1949 **PB:** Jacksonville **SC:** FL/USA **PT:** Walter Heyward Le Grand; Evelyn Hazel (Thomas) Le Grand **MS:** Married **SPN:** Janet Susan Johns (06/01/2019) **CH:** Abbi Le Grand Ross; Christen E. Le Grand; Charles H. Le Grand II; Paul Thomas Le Grand; Robert Joseph Le Grand; Robin Christine Devor **ED:** BS in Aviation Management, Auburn University, Auburn, AL (1972) **CT:** Certified in Data Processing (CDP); Certified Internal Auditor (CIA), Institute of Internal Auditors; Certified Information Systems Auditor, Cybersecurity and Infrastructure Security Agency, ISACA **C:** Chief Executive Officer, CHL Global Associates, LLC, Longwood, FL (2005-2019); Director of Research, IIA Research Foundation, Institute of Internal Auditors, Inc., Altamonte Springs, FL (1989-2005); Manager, Advanced Technology, Institute of Internal Auditors, Inc., Altamonte Springs, FL (1981-1989); Electronic Data Processing Audit Officer, Barnett Banks of Florida, Inc., Jacksonville, FL (1978-1981); Manager of Electronic Data Processing Audit, Blue Cross/Blue Shield of Colorado, Denver, CO (1976-1977); Senior Electronic Data Processing Auditor, Blue Cross/Blue Shield of Florida, Jacksonville, FL (1974-1976); Programming Technician, Prudential Insurance Co. of America, Jacksonville, FL (1972-1974); Consultant, Information Security, Internal Controls, Compliance Management, and Auditing **CR:** Lecturer, Business Data Processing, Jacksonville University (1973-1976) **MIL:** U.S. Naval Reserve (1967-1971); Naval Reserve Officers Train-

ing Corps (ROTC) **CW:** Author, "Lexisnexis: Handbook For Internal Auditors"; Author, "Bank Internal Control Manual"; Author, "Bank Holding Company Compliance Manual" **MEM:** Institute of Internal Auditors (IIA); Information Systems Audit and Control Association (ISACA) **MH:** Albert Nelson Marquis Lifetime Achievement Award; Marquis Who's Who Top Professional **AS:** Mr. Le Grand's passion for successfully completing tasks served him well in information technology. However, in auditing, the equation was adjusted to factor in the cost of doing enough to avoid being identified as wrong. He attributes much of his success to his devotion to positive change, which allowed him to direct numerous projects addressing the benefits of ethics in decision making and managing business and technology risks. Now that Mr. Le Grand is retired, he has shifted his attention to focus on family, friends, art, music, and making the world a better place. **B/I:** An exceptionally strong programmer, Mr. Le Grand was teaching data processing at Jacksonville University in the evenings. One of his students was the director of finance for the local post office and asked Mr. Le Grand for help with a systems upgrade. He was able to help the post office, and shortly thereafter, the postmaster's secretary was requesting Mr. Le Grand's resume. This is how he became an EDP auditor. He spent the rest of his career advocating for effective controls, management, governance, auditing, and security of information. **AV:** Surfing; Windsurfing; Snow and water skiing; Playing acoustic guitar; Completing triathlons; Traveling; Collecting miniature wire puzzles **PA:** Independent **RE:** Christian

LE GUIN, URSULA KROEBER, T: Author **I:** Writing and Editing **DOB:** 10/21/1929 **PB:** Berkeley **SC:** CA/USA **PT:** Alfred Louis Kroeber; Theodora (Kracaw) Kroeber **MS:** Married **SPN:** Charles A. Le Guin (12/22/1953) **CH:** Elisabeth; Caroline; Theodore **ED:** MA, Columbia University, New York, NY (1952); BA in Renaissance French and Italian Literature, Radcliffe College, Cambridge, MA (1951) **CIV:** Member, Planned Parenthood Federation of America, Environmental Defense Fund, and Oregon Nature Conservancy **CW:** Author, "Lavinia" (2008); Author, "Powers" (2007); Author, "Voices" (2006); Author, "Incredible Good Fortune" (2006); Author, "The Wave in the Mind" (2004); Author, "Gifts" (2004); Author, "Changing Planes" (2003); Translator, "Kalpa Imperial" by Angelica Gorodischer (2003); Translator, Selected Poems of Gabriela Mistral (2003); Author, "Tom Mouse" (2002); Author, "The Birthday of the World" (2002); Author, "Tales from Earthsea" (2001); Author, "The Other Wind" (2001); Author, "The Telling" (2000); Author, "Jane on Her Own" (1999); Author, "Sixty Odd" (1999); Author, "Steering the Craft" (1998); Author with Diana Bellessi, "The Twins, The Dream" (1997); Translator, "Lao Tzu: Tao Te Ching: A Book About the Way and the Power of the Way" (1997); Author, "Unlocking the Air" (1996); Author, "Four Ways to Forgiveness" (1995); Author, "Wonderful Alexander and the Catwings" (1994); Author, "Going Out with Peacocks" (1994); Author, "A Fisherman of the Inland Sea" (1994); Author, "Blue Moon Over Thurman Street" (1993); Author, "Fish Soup" (1992); Author, "A Ride on the Red Mare's Back" (1992); Author, "The Language of the Night, Revised Edition" (1992); Author, "Searoad" (1991); Author, "Tehanu" (1990); Author, "Fire and Stone" (1989); Author, "Catwings Return" (1989); Author, "Dancing at the Edge of the World" (1989); Author, "Wild Oats and Fireweed" (1988); Author, "A Visit from Dr. Katz" (1988); Author, "Catwings" (1988); Author, "Solomon Leviathan" (1988); Author, "Buffalo Gals" (1987); Author, "Always Coming Home" (1985); Author, "King Dog" (1985); Author, "The Eye of the Heron" (1983); Author, "Cobbler's Rune" (1983); Author, "The Compass Rose" (1982); Author, "Hard Words" (1981); Author, "The Beginning Place" (1980); Author, "Leese Webster" (1979); Author, "Malafrena" (1979); Author, "The Language of the Night" (1979); Author, "Very Far Away from Anywhere Else" (1976); Author, "Orsinian Tales" (1976); Author, "The Word for World is Forest" (1976); Author, "The Wind's Twelve Quarters" (1975); Author, "The Dispossessed" (1974); Author, "The Farthest Shore" (1972); Author, "The Lathe of Heaven" (1971); Author, "The Tombs of Atuan" (1970); Author, "The Left Hand of Darkness" (1969); Author, "A Wizard of Earthsea" (1968); Author, "City of Illusion" (1967); Author, "Rocannon's World" (1966); Author, "Planet of Exile" (1966); Contributor, Articles, Professional Journals; Author, Short Stories, Numerous Poems, Screenplays **AW:** Medal for Distinguished Contribution to American Letters (2014); Gallun Award for Outstanding Contribution to the Genre of Science Fiction (2007); Maxine Cushing Gray Award for Literary Achievement (2006); CES Wood Distinguished Writers Award (2006); Literary Award, PEN Center USA (PEN America) (2005); PEN/USA Award (2005); Named Arbuthnot Lecturer, American Library Association (2004); Margaret A. Edwards Award (2004); Damon Knight Memorial Grand Master Award, Science Fiction Writers Association (SFWA) (2003); Locus Readers Award for Story (1995, 2002, 2003); Endeavor Award (2001, 2003); Asimov's Reader's Award (1995, 2003); Willamette Writers Lifetime Achievement Award (2002); PEN/Malamud Award for Short Fiction, PEN America (2002); World Fantasy Award (2002); Locus Readers Award for Story and Novel (2001); Lifetime Achievement Award, Pacific Northwest Booksellers Association (2001); Robert Kirsch Award for Lifetime Achievement, Los Angeles Times (2000); Named Living Legend, Library of Congress (2000); Bumbershoot Arts Award, Seattle, WA (1998); James Tiptree Junior Award (1995, 1997); Locus Readers Award for Collection (1984, 1996); Nebula Award for Story (1975, 1996); Retrospective Award (1996); Hubbub Annual Poetry Award (1995); Theodore Sturgeon Award for Story (1995); H.L. Davis Award, Oregon Institute of Literary Arts (1992); Howard D. Vursell Award, American Academy of Arts and Letters (1991); Pushcart Prize (1991); Nebula Award for Novel (1969, 1975, 1990); Hugo Award for Story (1974, 1988); International Fantasy Award (1988); Prix Lectures-Jeunesse Award (1987); Kafka Award (1986); Gandalf Award (1979); Lewis Caroll Shelf Award (1979); Jupiter Award (1975-1976); Hugo Award for Novel (1969, 1975); Locus Readers Award for Novel (1973); Newbery Honor Medal (1972); National Book Award (1972); Boston Globe-Hornbook Award for Excellence in Juvenile Fiction (1968) **MEM:** PEN America; Science Fiction Writers Association (SFWA); Science Fiction Research Association; Amnesty International; The Phi Beta Kappa Society

LE VINE, DUANE GILBERT, T: Petroleum Company Executive **I:** Oil & Energy **DOB:** 07/05/1933 **PB:** Baltimore **SC:** MD/USA **PT:** Frances Annette (Culleton) Le Vine; Harry B. Le Vine **MS:** Married **SPN:** Patricia J. Allman (08/10/1957) **CH:** Duane Gilbert, Michele P.; William A.; James D., Erin A.; Megan K. **ED:** MS in Engineering, Johns Hopkins University (1958); BSChemE, Johns Hopkins University (1956) **CT:** Risk Analysis Environmental Health, Harvard University (1985); Science and Policy of Global Change, Massachusetts Institute of Technology (MIT) (1980s); Executive Management Program, The Pennsylvania State University (1975) **C:** Manager, Science and Strategy Development, Exxon Mobil Corporation, Dallas, Texas (1990-1998); Manager, Corporations Office of Worldwide Environmental Affairs, Exxon Mobil Corporation,

New York, NY (1984-1990); Senior Director, Exxon's Corporate Science Laboratories, Exxon Mobil Corporation, Clinton, NJ (1979-1984); General Manager, Exxon's Baytown, Texas Research Center (1976-1979); Manager, Gasoline/Lubes Process Engineering Division, Florham Park, NJ (1974-1976); Director, Fuels Product Laboratory, Linden, NJ (1971-1974); Researcher, Combustion, Electrochemistry, Petroleum Products/Processes, Numerous Senior Executive Assignments, Exxon Mobil Corporation; Numerous Positions, Fuels Product Quality, Gasoline and Lubes Process Engineering, Synthetic Fuels Research and Development, Corporate Science Research, ExxonMobil Research and Engineering Company **CR:** Advisor, Coal International Board, International Energy Agency (IEA) (1980s, 1990s); Member, U.S. National Air Pollution Research Advisory Committee (1971-1974); Member, Advisory Council Board, Johns Hopkins University Whiting School of Engineering; Member, Chemistry/Chemical Engineering Advisory Board, California Institute of Technology **CW:** Co-author, "Critical Issues in the Economics of Climate Change" (1997); Author, "The City as a Human Environment" (1994); Co-author, "Management of Hazardous Agents" (1992); Author, "The Potential Enhanced Greenhouse Effect," IEA/OECD Seminar (1989) **MEM:** Vice Chairman, Chairman, Chief Officer, International Petroleum Industry Environmental Conservation Association (IPIECA) (1997, 1998); Fellow, American Institute of Chemists; Society of Automotive Engineers (SAE International); American Institute of Chemical Engineers; American Chemical Society; American Petroleum Institute (API); International Combustion Institute; The New York Academy of Sciences; American Association for the Advancement of Science; Sigma Xi, The Scientific Research Honor Society, The Johns Hopkins University; The Tau Beta Pi Association, Inc., The Johns Hopkins University; Phi Lambda Upsilon, The Johns Hopkins University **MH:** Albert Nelson Marquis Lifetime Achievement Award; Who's Who in Engineering; Who's Who in Technology; Who's Who in America; Who's Who in the World **B/I:** Mr. Le Vine became involved in his profession because of the educational process. He attended schools that were strong in the areas of science. **AV:** Reading history; Coaching football and lacrosse **THT:** Mr. Le Vine's favorite memories have been his five years of interactions with five Nobel Laureates in physics, chemistry and biology on the nature of science and related research programs between 1979 and 1984. Another was hosting Prime Minister Margaret Thatcher's visit to Exxon's Corporate Research Science Laboratories to discuss Exxon's programs, circa 1982/1983.

LEAF, DAN, T: CEO **I:** Business Management/Business Services **CN:** Leaf Communications **MS:** Married **CH:** Two daughters; Two sons **ED:** Attended, Northwest Nazarene University (2002) **C:** Chief Executive Officer, L5 Engineering (2015-Present); Co-Founder, Chairman, Dalt Communications International (2014-Present); Owner, Leaf Investment Holdings, LLC (2014-Present); Chief Executive Officer, President, Disabled Veteran Business Enterprise (2013-Present); Vice President of DAS and Small Cell Division, Tempest Telecom Solutions (2011-2014); Founder, Chief Executive Officer, President, Leaf Communication Services (2004-2011) **CIV:** Human Options; National Meningitis Association **MIL:** U.S. Air Force (2000-2004) **AW:** Excellence in Entrepreneurship (2018); Family-Owned Business Award (2018); Fastest Growing Company, U.S. Business Journal (2016-2018) **AS:** Mr. Leaf attributes his success to his relentless drive, as well as his family. **B/I:** Mr. Leaf became

involved in his profession because he wanted to go into business for himself and excel like no one else could.

LEAHY, PATRICK JOSEPH, T: U.S. Senator from Vermont **I:** Government Administration/Government Relations/Government Services **DOB:** 03/31/1945 **PB:** Montpelier **SC:** VT/USA **PT:** Howard Leahy; Alba (Zambon) Leahy **MS:** Married **SPN:** Marcelle Pomerleau (08/25/1962) **CH:** Kevin; Alicia; Mark **ED:** JD, Georgetown University Law Center (1964); BA in Political Science, Saint Michael's College (1961) **C:** President Pro Tempore Emeritus (2015-Present); U.S. Senator, State of Vermont (1975-Present); President Pro Tempore (2012-2015); Chairman, U.S. Senate Judiciary Committee (2001-2003, 2007-2015); Chairman, U.S. Senate Committee on Agricultural Nutrition and Forestry Committee (1987-1995); State's Attorney, Chittenden County, VT (1966-1975) **CR:** U.S. Representative, General Assembly of the United Nations (2004) **CIV:** Board of Visiting, National District Attorneys Association (1971-1974); Board of Visiting, National College for the Deaf, Washington, DC; Board of Visitors, Gallaudet University, Washington, DC; Board of Visitors, United States Military Academy, West Point, NY; Board of Regents, Smithsonian Institute, Washington, DC **AW:** John Heinz Award for Greatest Public Service by Elected or Appointed Official (2013); Robert Vaughn FOIA Legend Award, American University Washington College of Law (2009); Listee, 50 Most Powerful People in DC, GQ Magazine (2007); Champion for Real and Lasting Change Award, Save the Children (2005); Award for Distinguished Public Service, Medical Library Association (2003) **MEM:** Vice President, National District Attorneys Association (1971-1974) **BAR:** District of Columbia (1979); Supreme Court of the United States (1968); United States Court of Appeals for the Second Circuit (1966); Vermont Federal District Court (1965); State of Vermont (1964) **PA:** Democrat **RE:** Roman Catholic

LEAR, NORMAN MILTON, T: Producer, Writer, Director **I:** Media & Entertainment **DOB:** 07/27/1922 **PB:** New Haven **SC:** CT/USA **PT:** Hyman "Herman" Lear; Jeanette (Seicol) Lear **MS:** Married **SPN:** Lyn Davis (09/05/1987); Frances Loeb (12/07/1965, Divorced 1986); Charlotte Rosen (1943, Divorced 1956) **CH:** Ellen; Kate Breckir LaPook; Maggie Beth; Benjamin Davis; Madeline Rose; Brianna Elizabeth **ED:** Honorary Doctorate, Emerson College, Boston, MA (1968); Coursework, Emerson College, Boston, MA (1940-1942) **C:** Founder, Act III Communications (1986-Present); Engaged in Public Relations (1945-1949) **CIV:** President, ACLU of Southern California (1973-Present); Founder, Business Enterprise Trust (1989-1998); Trustee Emeritus, Museum of Broadcasting (Now the Paley Center for Media); Board of Directors, People for the American Way; Member, National Advisory Board, Young Storytellers **MIL:** Radio Operator/Gunner, United States Army Air Forces (1942-1945) **CW:** Producer, Writer, "American Divided" (2016); Featured, "Norman Lear: Just Another Version of You" (2016); Author, "Even This I Get to Experience" (2014); Producer, Writer, "American Masters" (2008); Executive Producer, "Pete Seeger: The Power of Song" (2007); Executive Producer, "Way Past Cool" (2003); Director, Executive Producer, "Maggie Bloom" (2000); Executive Producer, "Way Past Cool" (2000); Executive Producer, "Channel Umptee-3" (1997); Executive Producer, Creator, "704 Hauser" (1994); Producer, Director, Creator, "The Powers That Be" (1992); Producer, "Sunday Dinner" (1991); Executive Producer, "Fried Green Tomatoes" (1991); Executive Producer, "Princess Bride" (1987); Executive Producer, "Stand by Me"

(1986); Creator, "The Jeffersons" (1975-1985); Executive Producer, "Heartsounds" (1984); Executive Producer, "a.k.a. Pablo" (1984); Executive Producer, Creator, "One Day at a Time" (1975-1984); Producer, "The Baxters" (1979); Producer, "All That Glitters (1977); Producer, "A Year at the Top" (1977); Creator, "Fernwood 2-Night" (1977); Writer, "The Little Rascals" (1977); Executive Producer, "The Nancy Walker Show" (1976); Producer, "Hot L Baltimore" (1975); Executive Producer, Creator, "Good Times" (1974-1979); Producer, Director, Creator, "All in the Family" (1971-1979); Executive Producer, Creator, "Maude" (1972-1978); Executive Producer, Creator, "Sanford and Son" (1972-1977); Producer, Director, Writer, "Cold Turkey" (1971); Producer, "Start the Revolution Without Me" (1970); Producer, Writer, "The Night They Raided Minsky's" (1968); Producer, Writer, "Divorce American Style" (1967); Producer, Writer, "Never Too Late" (1965); Producer, Writer, "Come Blow Your Horn" (1963); Executive Producer, "The Andy Williams Show" (1962); Comedy Writer (1950-1954); Writer, "Scared Stiff" (1953); Director, Writer, Television Shows and Films; Contributor, Articles to Professional Publications **AW:** Britannia Award, BAFTA Los Angeles (2019); Named One of the Eight Over Eighty, The New Jewish Home (2017); Honoree, Kennedy Center Honors, John F. Kennedy Center for the Performing Arts (2017); Woody Guthrie Prize, Woody Guthrie Center (2017); Achievement Award in Television, Producers Guild of America (2006); National Medal of Arts (1999); National Arts Medal (1992); International Award of the Year, National Association of Television Program Executives (NATPE) (1987); Mass Media Award, American Jewish Committee, Institute of Human Relations (1986); Distinguished American Award (1984); Named to Academy of Television Hall of Fame (1984); Gold Medal, International Radio and Television Society (IRTS Foundation) (1981); Named First Amendment Lecturer, Ford Hall Forum (1981); William O. Douglas Award, Public Counsel (1981); Mark Twain Award, Platform - The International Platform Association (1977); Valentine Davies Award, Writers Guild of America (1977); Peabody Award (1977); Named Showman of the Year, Publicists Guild (Now International Cinematographers Guild (ICG) Local 600) (1971-1977); Humanitarian Award, National Conference of Christians and Jews (1976); Named Man of the Year, Hollywood Chapter, National Academy of Television Arts & Sciences (1973); Named Broadcaster of the Year, International Radio and Television Society (Now IRTS Foundation) (1973); Four Emmy Awards, Academy of Television Arts & Sciences (1970-1973); Named Broadcaster of the Year, Association of Business Managers (1972); Named One of the Top Ten Motion Picture Producers, Motion Picture Exhibitors (1963, 1967, 1968); Decorated Air Medal with Four Oak Leaf Clusters **MEM:** American Federation of TV and Radio Artists (Now SAG-AFTRA); Caucus for Producers, Writers & Directors; Directors Guild of America (DGA); Writers Guild of America

LEAVITT, RANDY T, ATTORNEY, T: Owner **I:** Law and Legal Services **CN:** Law Office of Randy T. Leavitt **DOB:** 04/24/1954 **PB:** Stamford **SC:** TX/USA **PT:** Jerry Leavitt; Tommye Martin **MS:** Married **SPN:** Karen **CH:** Carley; Kinsey; Cade **ED:** Doctor of Jurisprudence, Texas Tech University School of Law, Lubbock, TX (1980); Bachelor of Science in Education, Texas State University, San Marcos, TX (1977) **CT:** Board Certified, Criminal Law, Texas Board of Legal Specialization (1987-Present); Mediator, Qualified Pursuant to 154.052 Texas Civil Practice Remedies **C:** Owner, Private Practice, Law Office of Randy T. Leavitt (2009-Present); First Assistant, Travis County Attorney (2004-

2009); Partner, Minton, Burton, Foster & Collins PC (1982-2002); Associate, Law Office of Herman Gotcher (1980-1982) **CR:** Planning Committee, Advanced Criminal Law Seminar, State Bar of Texas (2008-2018); Course Director, Handling your First (Or Next) DWI Case, State Bar of Texas (2013); Course Director, Making/Breaking Your Case: The Role of Forensic Evidence, TexasBar-CLE, Dallas, TX (2011); Course Director, Advanced Criminal Law Course, San Antonio, TX (2008) **CIV:** Review Committee, Capital Area Private Defenders Service (2016-2020); Board of Directors, Austin Young Lawyers Association; Task Force On Habeas Counsel Training and Qualifications, State Bar of Texas; Former Member, College State Bar of Texas; Board of Directors, Western Hills Little League **CW:** Texas Tech Law Review (1978-1980) Staff & Associate Editor, Numerous Publications, Including the Fifth Circuit Survey, Criminal Law Procedure and Texas Tech Law Review **AW:** Selected, "Texas Super Lawyer" by Texas Monthly Magazine (2003-2020); Presidential Award, Texas Criminal Defense Lawyers Association (2012); AV Preeminent Rating, Martindale-Hubbell **MEM:** Board of Directors, Texas Criminal Defense Lawyers Association (1993-1999); Fellow, Texas Bar Foundation; Founding Member, Austin Criminal Defense Lawyers Association; Former President, Travis County Criminal Law & Procedure Section; Austin Bar Association; Texas District and County Attorneys Association; Board of Directors, Austin Young Lawyers Association **BAR:** State Bar of Texas (1980); U.S. District Court for the Western District of Texas; U.S. District Court for the Southern District of Texas; U.S. Court of Appeals for the Fifth Circuit **AS:** Mr. Leavitt attributes success to hard work and loving what he does. Likewise, he built his reputation for integrity and excellence early on, which proved essential to the longevity of his career. **B/I:** Mr. Leavitt became involved in his profession because he had an interest in the criminal justice system from an early age. He believed there were injustices in this world and felt he could contribute to reducing some of those injustices in the criminal justice system. **PA:** Democrat **RE:** Christian

LEE, BARBARA JEAN, T: U.S. Representative from California **I:** Government Administration/Government Relations/Government Services **CN:** U.S. House of Representatives **DOB:** 7/16/1946 **PB:** El Paso **SC:** TX/USA **PT:** Garvin Alexander Tutt; Mildred Adaire (Parish) Tutt **MS:** Divorced **SPN:** Micharl Millben **CH:** Tony; Craig **ED:** Master of Social Work, University of California Berkeley (1975); Bachelor of Arts, Mills College, CA (1973) **C:** Member, U.S. House of Representatives from California's 13th District, United States Congress (2013-Present); Member, U.S. House of Representatives from California's Ninth District, Washington, DC (1998-2013); Member, California State Senate (1996-1998); Member, District 16, California State Assembly (1992-1996); Member, District 13, California State Assembly (1990-1992); Chief of Staff to Representative Ron Dellums, U.S. House of Representatives (1976-1986); Northern California Presidential Campaign Coordinator (1972); Member, U.S. House Budget Committee; Member, U.S. House Appropriations Committee **CR:** Chair, Congressional Black Caucus (2009-2011); Member, California Defense Conversion Council; Member, California Commission on the Status of Women and Girls; California State Coastal Conservancy/District Export Council; Co-chair, Congressional Progressive Caucus; Founder, California Commission on the Status of African American Males; Chair, California Rainbow Coalition **CIV:** Board of Directors, Bay Area Black United Fund; Member, Advisory Board, Alameda Boys & Girls Club **AW:**

Named to the Power 150 (2008); Named, One of the Most Influential Black Americans, Ebony Magazine (2006) **MEM:** League of Women Voters; Black Women Organized for Political Action; Founder, Ronald V. Dellums Democratic Club; John George Democratic Club **PA:** Democrat **RE:** Baptist

LEE, HELEN, T: Music Educator **I:** Education/Educational Services **PT:** Chin Din Lee; Yueh Yin Lin **MS:** Married **SPN:** Mingyee Richard Lee (12/12/1969) **CH:** Felix; Eileen **ED:** MusM in Vocal Performance, University of Nevada (1976); BA in Vocal Performance, Chinese Culture University (1969) **C:** Voice Instructor, University of Nevada, Reno (1980-Present); Graduate Teaching Assistant Music, Brigham Young University, Provo, Utah (1969-1971); Resident Solo Artist, BCC Network, Taipei, Taiwan (1967-1969) **CR:** Music Director, Sierra Youth Choir, Reno, NV (1997-2000); Music Adviser, Melodia Sinica Choir, Northridge, CA (1993-1997); Sierra Nevada Chorale, Reno, NV (1979) **CIV:** Patroness, Sigma Alpha Iota International Music Fraternity (1995-Present) **CW:** Musician, Solo album, Solo Performances; Musician, Solo Television Performance, Skating Music for Olympic Gold Medalist Figure Skater, Katarina Witt (1996); Performer, Concert Tour to Japan **AW:** University Service Award (2016); Named Distinguished Alumna, Chinese Culture University Alumni, San Francisco, CA (1993); District Winner, Metropolitan Opera Co., Reno, NV (1976); National Winner in Singing, National Department of Education, Taipei, Taiwan (1965) **MEM:** Chapter President, International Honor Society for International Scholars (Now Phi Beta Delta Honor Society for International Scholars) (1998-2001); American University Professors Association (AUPA); North America Taiwanese Women's Association (NATWA); Music Adviser, North America Taiwanese Women's Association (NATWA) (1997-Present); International Honor Society for International Scholars (Now Phi Beta Delta Honor Society for International Scholars); Sigma Alpha Iota International Music Fraternity **B/I:** Mrs. Lee became involved in her profession because she was discovered by her high school teachers in a vocal competition. At first, she won locally, and then they sent her to Taipei, the capital of Taiwan, for the national competition, which she won. She always loved to sing and would sing herself to sleep everyday. She sang for fun so there was no pressure in doing something she loved.

LEE, MARGARET, T: Music Educator **I:** Education/Educational Services **DOB:** 10/11/1942 **PB:** Williamsport **SC:** PA/USA **PT:** Roscoe Brown Kendig; Margaret Bunnell (Creamer) Kendig **MS:** Widow **SPN:** M. Howard Lee (02/26/1967, Deceased) **CH:** Jennifer Katharine **ED:** MA in Musicology, University of Georgia (1977); MEd, University of Pennsylvania (1965); AB in Music, University of Pennsylvania (1964) **CT:** Certified, Georgia Music Teachers Association; Certified, Music Teachers National Association **C:** Private Music Instructor, Athens, GA (1973-Present); Music Teacher, Newton Public Schools (1969-1972); Music Teacher, Edmonton Public Schools (1967-1969); Teacher, Upper Darby Public Schools (1965-1967) **CIV:** President, National Association of Music Parents, Athens, GA (1984-1985) **CW:** Author, "Vihuela Music" (1977) **MEM:** Coordinator, Vice President of Auditions, Georgia Music Teachers Association (2005-Present); Vice President, President, Treasurer, Athens Music Teachers Association (1987-Present); Music Teachers National Association **MH:** Albert Nelson Marquis Lifetime Achievement Award **B/I:** Ms. Lee was inspired by her mother, an excellent pianist, to pursue a career in music. Her mother was also a respected teacher, which further influenced Ms. Lee's career. **AV:** Gourmet cooking; Reading; Playing the piano

LEE, MICHAEL, "MIKE" SHUMWAY, T: U.S. Senator from Utah; Lawyer **I:** Government Administration/Government Relations/Government Services **DOB:** 06/04/1971 **PB:** Mesa **SC:** AZ/USA **PT:** Rex E. Lee; Janet (Griffin) Lee **MS:** Married **SPN:** Sharon Burr **CH:** John Davis; James Rex; Eliza Rose **ED:** JD, Brigham Young University, Provo, UT, Magna Cum Laude (1997); BA in Political Science, Brigham Young University, Provo, UT, Cum Laude (1994) **C:** Chairman, Joint Economic Committee (2019-Present); Chairman, U.S. Senate Republican Steering Committee (2015-Present); U.S. Senator, State of Utah, Washington, DC (2011-Present); Member, Committee on Armed Services (2011-Present); Member Joint Economic Committee (2011-Present); Member, U.S. Senate Committee on Foreign Relations, Washington, DC (2011-Present); Member, U.S. Senate Committee on Energy and Natural Resources, Washington, DC (2011-Present); Member, U.S. Senate Judiciary Committee, Washington, DC (2011-Present); Member, U.S. Congressional Joint Economic Committee, Washington, DC (2011); Partner, Howrey LLP, Salt Lake City, UT (2007-2010); Law Clerk to the Honorable Samuel A. Alito, Supreme Court of the United States, Washington, DC (2006-2007); General Counsel to Governor Jon Huntsman, State of Utah, Salt Lake City, UT (2005-2006); Assistant U.S. Attorney, District for Utah, U.S. Department of Justice, Salt Lake City, UT (2002-2005); Partner, Sidley Austin LLP, Washington, DC (2000-2002); Law Clerk to the Honorable Samuel A. Alito, United States Court of Appeals for the Third Circuit, Newark, NJ (1998-1999); Law Clerk to the Honorable Dee V. Benson, United States District Court of Utah (1997-1998) **CW:** Author, "Our Lost Constitution: The Willful Subversion of America's Founding Document" (2015); Author, "The Freedom Agenda: Why a Balanced Budget Amendment is Necessary to Restore Constitutional Government" (2011) **AW:** Named One of the "Politics 40 Under 40," Time Magazine, TIME USA, LLC (2010) **MEM:** The Federalist Society for Law and Public Policy Studies (The Federalist Society) **BAR:** District of Columbia (1999); State of Utah (1998) **PA:** Republican **RE:** The Church of Jesus Christ of Latter-day Saints

LEE, RICHARD, "RICH" HOYT, T: Microscopist; Analyst (Retired) **I:** Research **DOB:** 12/21/1941 **PB:** Rochester **SC:** NY/USA **PT:** Daniel Hoyt Lee; Doris Manhold Lee **MS:** Married **SPN:** Barbara (Friedly) Lee (06/26/1965) **CH:** Deborah; Heidi **ED:** AAS, Milwaukee School of Engineering (1961) **C:** Analyst, Micro-analysis, Part-time BP Research, Naperville, IL (2006-2016); Microscopist, Argonne National Laboratory, IL (1962-2002) **CR:** Owner, S.P.A.M. (Scientific, Photography, Analysis, and Metallurgy) **CIV:** Former President, Archivist, Lemont Area Historical Society, IL (1990-1991); President, LAHS (2010-2011); Advisor, Canal Communications I & M, Lemont, IL (1988-1992); Archivist, LAHS; Historian, Argonne National Laboratory, LUMC **CW:** Scientific Art Exhibit, Chicago Academy of Science (1994); Author, Historical Stories, Lemont Area Historical Society; Showcasing "Lemont Then and Now Number 2" **AW:** First Prize, Black and White Division, ASM International (1992); Competent Toastmaster Award, Argonne Toastmasters (1991); Third Place, Kodak Industrial Applied Impact Division (1991); First Prize, Nikon Instruments Small World Division (1990); Awards, ASM International Contests **MEM:** Vice President, President, State Microscopical Society of Illinois (1995-Present); Vice President, President, Argonne Toastmasters (1995-Present); Vice President, President, Lemont Area Historical Society (1990-1991); State Microscopical Society of Illinois; Argonne Toastmasters; ASM International; American Association for the Advancement of Science **MH:** Albert Nelson Marquis Lifetime Achievement Award; Marquis Who's Who Top Professional **AS:** Mr. Lee attributes his success to his love of science and the Bible. **B/I:** Mr. Lee's career started when he was in college and he was studying metallurgy. Argonne National Laboratory was looking for someone who knew metallurgy to come and help them on a special project. They recruited him to come down from Milwaukee, Wisconsin and join them to help with the big project, which was to find better material for coolant tubes in nuclear reactors. They wanted to find the best material, and as he was doing this for several years, along the way, he captured some wonderful color photographs of the materials in various conditions. He began taking pictures of the material through the microscope. Starting in 1978, he began entering the photographs in contests and wining prizes. In 1980, he entered the Nikon Small World competition; he came in second place and won a Nikon camera. **AV:** Photography; Bible study; Writing; Hiking and climbing; Steam trains **PA:** Democrat **RE:** Methodist **THT:** Mr. Lee is currently an Archivist for the historical society. His work involves taking the actual images and digitizing them for easier retrieval; he stores a copy in the computer and on a backup drive for security and safekeeping. He does a similar activity for his church. For more information on his work at the historical society, please visit: www.lemonthistorical.org/

LEE, RUTH DAVIDSON, T: Tax Collector (Retired) **I:** Financial Services **DOB:** 07/15/1935 **PB:** Jackson County **SC:** IN/USA **PT:** Miles Davison; Elsie M. (George) Davidson **MS:** Married **SPN:** Robert Alexander Lee (09/08/1956) **CH:** Joan Rene Weeks; Robyn Ann Lorenz; Robert Anthony **ED:** Coursework, Jacksonville University (1989-1990); Coursework, Florida Junior College (1979, 1980, 1982) **CT:** Tax Collector **C:** Tax Collector, Clay County (1985-Present); Assistant Tax Collector, Clay County Tax Collector's Office (1959-1984); Office Staff, Green Cove Hosiery Co., Green Cove Springs, FL (1956-1959); Clerk, Prudential Insurance Co., Jacksonville, FL (1955-1956) **CIV:** American Cancer Society, Orange Park, FL (1992-Present) Clay County Community Services (1992-Present); Board of Directors, Area Council Aging (1991-Present); Penney Retirement Community, Penney Farms, FL (1992); Former Board of Directors, Green Cove Business Council; Chair, Precinct, Clay County Democratic Executive Committee; 4-H "500" Club, Clay County 4-H Club Foundation, Green Cove Springs, FL; Patron Life Member, Clay County Fair Board **AW:** Super Server Award, Leukemia Society of America (1991); Celebrity Waiters Award, American Cancer Society (1988); Presidential Award, Green Cove Business Council (1985) **MEM:** Past Director, Past Vice President, Orange Park Chamber of Commerce **MH:** Albert Nelson Marquis Lifetime Achievement Award **B/I:** Ms. Lee became involved in her profession because she enjoyed helping people. When her boss retired, she decided to step up and take on a leadership role. **AV:** Cooking; Gardening; Painting; Crafting **RE:** Baptist

LEE, SPIKE, T: Film Producer, Director, Screenwriter **I:** Media & Entertainment **DOB:** 03/20/1957 **PB:** Atlanta **SC:** GA/USA **PT:** William James Edwards; Jacqueline (Shelton) L. **SPN:** Tonya Lewis (10/02/1993) **CH:** Satchel; Jackson **ED:** MFA, New York University (1982); BA, Morehouse College (1979) **CR:** Chairman, Spike/DDB (1996-Present); Owner, Spike's Joint (1994-Present); Owner, 40 Acres & A Mule Filmworks (1986-Present); Moderator, Black Athletes Forum, Morehouse College (2007); Owner, 40 Acres & A Mule Musicworks (1987-1994) **CIV:** Trustee, Morehouse College (1992-Present) **CW:** Director, "Black Klansman" (2018); Director, "Brave Visions for Moncler" (2017); Director, Producer, "She's Gotta Have It" (2017); Director, "Rodney King" (2017); Director, "2 Fists Up" (2016); Director, "Michael Jackson's Journey from Motown to Off the Wall" (2016); Director, Producer, Writer, " Chi-Raq" (2015); Director, Producer, Writer, "Da Blood of Jesus" (2014); Producer, "Mania Days" (2014); Director, Producer, "Katt Williams Priceless Afterlife" (2014); Director, Producer, "Jerrod Carmichael Love at the Store" (2014); Director, "Oldboy" (2013); Director, Producer, "Mike Tyson: Undisputed Truth" (2013); Actor, Director, Producer, Writer, "Red Hook Summer" (2012); Director, Executive Producer, "Da Brick" (2011); Director, Producer, "If God is Willing and Da Creek Don't Rise" (2010); Director, Producer, "Kobe Doin' Work" (2009); Director, Producer, "M.O.N.Y." (2008); Director, Producer, "Miracle at St. Anna" (2008); Director, "Lovers & Haters" (2007); Director, Producer, "When the Levees Broke: A Requiem in Four Acts" (2006); Director, "Inside Man" (2006); Director, "Shark (Pilot)" (2006); Director, Producer, "Jesus Children of America" (2005); Director, Producer, "All the Invisible Children" (2005); Co-Author, with Kaleem Aftab, "That's My Story and I'm Sticking to It" (2005); Director, Producer, Writer, "She Hate Me" (2004); Director, Producer, "Sucker Free City" (2004); Director, Producer, "Jim Brown: All American" (2002); Co-Author, with Tonya Lewis Lee, "Please, Baby Please" (2002); Director, Producer, "25th Hour" (2002); Actor, Producer, "3 A.M." (2001); Director, Producer, "A Huey P. Newton Story" (2001); Executive Producer, "Home Invaders" (2001); Director, Producer, "Original Kings of Comedy" (2001); Actor, Director, Producer, "The Original Kings of Comedy" (2000); Producer, "Love and Basketball" (2000); Director, Producer, Writer, "Bamboozled" (2000); Actor, Director, Producer, Writer, "Summer of Sam" (1999); Producer, "The Best Man" (1999); Director, Producer, Writer, "He Got Game" (1998); Director, Producer, "Freak" (1998); Director, Producer, "4 Little Girls" (1997); Co-Author, with Ralph Wiley, "Best Seat in the House" (1997); Actor, Director, Producer, "Girl 6" (1996); Director, Producer, "Get on the Bus" (1996); Actor, Director, Producer, Writer, "Clockers" (1995); Executive Producer, "New Jersey Drive" (1995); Executive Producer, "Tales from the Hood" (1995); Executive Producer, "Drop Squad" (1994); Actor, Director, Producer, Writer, "Crooklyn" (1994); Actor, Director, Producer, Writer, "Malcolm X" (1992); Author, " "By Any Means Necessary: The Trials and Tribulations of the Making of 'Malcolm X'" (1992); Appearance, "Into the Comics: Part 1" (1992); Actor, Director, Producer, Writer, "Jungle Fever" (1991); Actor, Director, Producer, Writer, "Mo' Better Blues" (1990); Author, "Mo' Better Blues" (1990); Actor, Director, Producer, Writer, "Do The Right Thing" (1989); Author, "Do the Right Thing: A Spike Lee Joint" (1989); Actor, Director, Producer, Writer, "School Daze" (1988); Author, "Uplift the Race: The Construction of School Daze" (1988); Author, "Spike Lee's Gotta Have It: Inside Guerilla Filmmaking" (1987); Actor, Director, Producer, Writer, "She's Gotta Have It" (1986); Director, Producer, Writer, "Joe's Bed-Stuy Barbershop: We Cut Heads" (1983); Director, "Sarah" (1981); Director, "The Answer" (1980); Director, "Last Hustle in Brooklyn" (1977) **AW:** Best Adapted Screenplay, BAFTA Film Awards (2019); Best Adapted Screenplay, Academy Awards (2019); Honorary Academy Award, Governors Awards (2015); Image Award, NAACP (2015);

Dorothy & Lillian Gish Prize (2013); Wexner Prize, Wexner Center Foundation (2008); The Power 150, Ebony Magazine (2008); Special Achievement Award, African-American Film Critics Association (2006); Ossie Davis Humanitarian Award, Black Movie Awards (2006); Filmmaker Trumpet Award (2003); French Academy Cinema Award (2002); President's Award, NAACP **MEM:** Fellow, American Academy of Arts and Sciences

LEE, SUZANNE MARIE, T: U.S. Representative from Nevada **I:** Government Administration/Government Relations/Government Services **CN:** U.S. House of Representatives **DOB:** 11/7/1966 **PB:** Canton **SC:** OH/USA **PT:** Warren Kelley; Joan Kelley **MS:** Married **SPN:** Dan Lee **CH:** Two Children **ED:** Master of Science, Carnegie Mellon University; Bachelor of Arts, Carnegie Mellon University **C:** Member, U.S. House of Representatives from Nevada's Third Congressional District (2019-Present); President, Communities in Schools of Nevada (2010-Present); Founding Director, After-school All-stars (1993) **PA:** Democrat

LEE, WILLIAM, "BILL" BYRON, T: Governor of Tennessee **I:** Government Administration/Government Relations/Government Services **DOB:** 10/09/1959 **PB:** Franklin **SC:** TN/USA **MS:** Married **SPN:** Maria Lee (2008); Carol Ann (Deceased 2000) **CH:** Four Children **ED:** Bachelor of Science in Mechanical Engineering, Auburn University (1981) **C:** Governor, State of Tennessee (2019-Present); Chairperson, Lee Company (2016-2017); Chief Executive Officer, Lee Company (1992-2016) **CIV:** Board of Trustees, Belmont University; Chairman, YMCA of Middle Tennessee; Board Member, Hope Clinic for Women; Board Member, Men of Valor Prison Ministry **MEM:** President, Associated Builders and Contractors; Kappa Alpha Order **PA:** Republican

LEECH, MICHAEL J., T: Principal Lawyer **I:** Law and Legal Services **CN:** Talk Sense Mediation **ED:** JD, University of Virginia School of Law (1976); BA in History, University of Virginia School of Law, with Distinction (1973) **CT:** Certified Mediator, Circuit Court of Cook County, IL (2005-Present) **C:** Principal, Michael J. Leech, P.C. (2012-Present); Founder, Principal, Talk Sense Arbitration (2012-Present); Partner, Hinshaw & Culbertson LLP (1983-2011); Associate, Hinshaw & Culbertson LLP (1978-1983); Associate, Chapman and Cutler LLP (1976-1978) **CW:** Author, "Partners and Minority Shareholders" (2011); Author, "How Did You Do that? Trade Secrets of a Mediator" (2004); Author, "Abolishing Employment Discrimination Laws: A Foolish and Dangerous Policy" (1996); Author, Legal Textbook, "Employment Termination: Rights and Remedies" (1985) **AW:** Brusche Award, Association of Attorney-Mediators (2017); Named to Top 100 Illinois Super Lawyers (2011-2013) **MEM:** Illinois Super Lawyers and Leading Lawyers (2005-Present); Immediate Past President, Association of Attorney-Mediators (2015); American Law Institute (2013); Distinguished Fellow, International Academy of Mediators (2011); Fellow, American Bar Foundation (2011); Fellow, The College of Labor and Employment Lawyers Inc. (1997); Mediator, Arbitrator, Panelist, American Arbitration Association; Liaison, The College of Labor and Employment Lawyers, Inc., American Law Institute Restatement of Employment Law Project **BAR:** Commonwealth of Pennsylvania (2015) **MH:** Marquis Who's Who Top Professional **B/I:** Mr. Leech was a trial lawyer for about 30 years, handling employment cases. About 25 years ago, he started doing work as a mediator and most recently as an arbitrator, in which it consumed his whole practice, so he left the law firm he was in and had been

doing it full-time ever since. Mr. Leech thought law used the best skills that he had, being writing, speaking, thinking and analyzing. No one in his family went into law. During his first semester, he really paid attention and realized he truly enjoyed it. Mr. Leech has been interested in mediation since the first time he was in one back in 1979, but it took a long time for the legal profession to catch up. He feels it is a better way of looking at problems and very solution-oriented, which is the way he helps people the most. Being a peacemaker is the highest calling a lawyer can have and is truly rewarding.

LEFKOWITZ, ROBERT JOSEPH, MD, T: Physician; Professor **I:** Medicine & Health Care **CN:** Duke University School of Medicine **DOB:** 04/15/1943 **PB:** New York **SC:** NY/USA **PT:** Max Lefkowitz; Rose (Levine) Lefkowitz **MS:** Married **SPN:** Lynn (Tilley) Lefkowitz (05/26/1991); Arna Brandel (Divorced) **CH:** Five Children **ED:** Resident in Medicine, Massachusetts General Hospital (1970-1971); Resident in Medicine, Columbia University (1967-1968); Intern in Medicine, Columbia University (1966-1967); MD, Columbia University Vagelos College of Physicians and Surgeons, New York, NY (1966); BA in Chemistry, Columbia College, Columbia University, New York, NY (1962) **CT:** Diplomate, American Board of Internal Medicine **C:** Professor of Biochemistry, Duke University Medical Center, Durham, NC (1985-Present); James B. Duke Professor of Medicine, Duke University Medical Center, Durham, NC (1982-Present); Professor of Medicine, Duke University Medical Center, Durham, NC (1977-Present); Associate Professor of Medicine, Duke University Medical Center, Durham, NC (1973-1977) **CR:** Investigator, Howard Hughes Medical Institute (HHMI), Durham, NC (1976-Present); Visiting Professor, New York University (1996); Established Investigator, American Heart Association, Inc. (1973-1976) **CW:** Author, "Principles of Biochemistry" (1983); Author, "Receptor Regulation" (1981); Author, "Receptor Binding Studies in Adrenergic Pharmacology" (1978) **AW:** Golden Plate Award, American Academy of Achievement (2014); Co-recipient, Nobel Prize in Chemistry, Royal Swedish Academy of Sciences (2012); Kober Medal, AAPS - Association of American Physicians and Surgeons (2012); Achievement Award, Society for Biomolecular Sciences (SBS) (2011); Norman Weiner Award, American Society for Pharmacology and Experimental Therapeutics (2011); BBVA Frontiers of Knowledge Award (2009, 2010); Research Achievement Award, American Heart Association Inc. (2009); Steven's Triennial Prize, Columbia University Vagelos College of Physicians and Surgeons (2009); Distinguished Lecture Award for Basic Sciences, Heart Failure Society of America (2007); Shaw Prize, Life Science and Medicine, Shaw Prize Foundation (2007); National Medal of Sciences, The White House (2007); Herbert Tabor Lecture Award, American Society for Biological Chemistry and Molecular Biology (2004); Bio/Technical Winter Symposia Feodor Lynen Award (2003); Medal of Merit, International Academy of Cardiovascular Sciences (2003); IPSEN Endocrinology Prize, Fondation IPSEN, Paris, France (2003); Fondation Lefoulon-Delalande Grand Prize for Science Award, Institute of France (2003); Founding Distinguished Scientist Award, American Heart Association,Inc. (2003); 15th Annual Pasarow Cardiovascular Research Award, Robert J. & Claire Pasarow Foundation (2002); Award, International Academy of Cardiovascular Sciences (2002); Francis Gilman Blake Award, Association of American Physicians (2001); F.E. Shideman-Sterling Award, University of Minnesota (2001); Louis & Artur Lucian Award for Research in Circulatory Disease (2001); Jessie Stevenson Kovalenko

Medal, National Academy of Sciences (2001); Fred Conrad Koch Award, Endocrine Society (2001); Peter Harris Distinguished Scientist Award, International Society for Heart Research (2001); Novartis/Drew Award in Biomedical Research (2000); Glorney-Raisbeck Award in Cardiology, New York Academy of Medicine (1997); J. David Gladstone Institutions Distinguished Lecture Award (1996); CIBA Award (1996); Hypertension Research Award (1996); Endocrine Society Gerald D. Aurbach Lecturer Award, Institute of Medicine, National Academy of Sciences (1995); Joseph Mather Smith Prize (1993); Alumnus Award for Distinguished Achievement in Cardiovascular Research, Columbia University Valegoes College of Physicians and Surgeons (1992); The Giovani Lorenzini Prize for Basic Biomedical Research (1992); City of Medecin Award, State of North Carolina (1991); Novo Nordsk Biotechnology Award (1990); Basic Research Prize (1990); Biomedical Research Award, Association of American Medical Colleges (AAMC) (1990); International Award, Gairdner Foundation (1988); North Carolina Award in Science (1987); H.B. Van Dyke Award, Columbia University Vagelos College of Physicians and Surgeons (1986); Steven C. Beering Award, Indiana University School of Medicine (1986); Goodman and Gilman Award, American Society for Pharmacology and Experimental Therapeutics (1986); Lita Annenberg Hazen Award (1983); Outstanding Research Award, International Society of Health Research (1985); Gordon Wilson Medal, American Clinical and Climatological Association (1982); Oppenheimer Award (1982); George Thorn Award, Howard Hughes Medical Institute (1979); Young Scientist Award, Passano Foundation (1978); John J. Abel Award, American Society for Pharmacology and Experimental Therapeutics (1978) **MEM:** Treasurer, Association of American Physicians (1989-1994); President, The American Society for Clinical Investigation (1987-1988); President-Elect, The American Society for Clinical Investigation (1986-1987); Counselor, The American Society for Clinical Investigation (1982-1985); Secretary-treasurer, American Federation for Clinical Research (Now American Federation for Medical Research) (1980-1983); National Council, American Federation for Clinical Research (Now American Federation for Medical Research) (1978-1983); National Academy of Sciences; Institute of Medicine; American Heart Association Basic Research Society; American Academy Arts & Sciences; American Federation for Clinical Research (Now American Federation for Medical Research); Endocrine Society; American Society for Pharmacology and Experimental Therapeutics; Association of American Physicians; The American Society for Clinical Investigation; American Society of Biological Chemists; Honorary Member, Japanese Biochemical Society

LEGGETT, ANTHONY, "TONY" JAMES, T: Professor Emeritus; Physics Researcher **I:** Education/Educational Services **CN:** University of Illinois at Urbana-Champaign **DOB:** 03/26/1938 **PB:** Camberwell, London **SC:** United Kingdom **MS:** Married **SPN:** Haruko Kinase, PhD (06/1973) **CH:** Asako **ED:** Honorary DLitt, University of Oxford (2005); Honorary Doctorate, University of Sussex; Honorary Doctorate, The University of British Columbia; Honorary Doctorate, University of St. Andrews; Honorary Doctorate, University of Tokyo; Honorary Doctorate, Universidad Complutense de Madrid, Spain; PhD in Theoretical Physics, Merton College, University of Oxford, United Kingdom (1964); BA in Physics, Merton College, University of Oxford, United Kingdom, First Class Honors (1961); Coursework, Balliol College, University of Oxford, United Kingdom; Coursework, Beaumont College; Coursework, Wimbledon College

C: Professor Emeritus, University of Illinois, Urbana-Champaign (2020-Present); John D. and Catherine T. Macarthur Professor, University of Illinois, Urbana-Champaign (1983-2019); Professor, University of Sussex, United Kingdom (1978-1983); Reader, University of Sussex, United Kingdom (1971-1978); Member, Faculty, University of Sussex, United Kingdom (1967-1971) **CR:** Researcher, Urbana, IL and Kyoto, Japan; Lecturer in Field **CW:** Author, "Quantum Tunneling in Condensed Media" (1992); Author, "The Problems of Physics" (1987); Contributor, Articles to Professional Journals **AW:** Named to Engineering at Illinois Hall of Fame, University of Illinois (2015); Distinguished Service Medallion, University of Illinois (2009); Named Knight Commander, Order of the British Empire (2004); Nobel Prize in Physics (2003); Wolf Prize in Physics, Wolf Foundation, Israel (2003); Eugene Feenberg Memorial Medal (1999); John Bardeen Prize (1994); Paul Dirac Medal and Prize, Institute of Physics, United Kingdom (1992); Fritz London Memorial Award (1981); Simon Memorial Prize, Institute of Physics, United Kingdom (1981); James Clerk Maxwell Medal and Prize (1975) **MEM:** Foreign Fellow, Indian National Science Academy (2011); Fellow, American Physical Society; Honorary Fellow, Institute of Physics, United Kingdom; Fellow, The Royal Society, United Kingdom; Russian Academy of Sciences; Associate Member, National Academy of Sciences; American Academy of Arts & Sciences; American Philological Society (Now Society for Classical Studies)

LEGRANGE, ULYESSE J., CPA, T: Oil Company Executive **I:** Oil & Energy **DOB:** 06/06/1931 **PB:** Gibson **SC:** LA/USA **PT:** Treville J. LeGrange; Marion (Broussard) LeGrange **MS:** Married **SPN:** Barbara Elaine Perry (08/20/1949) **CH:** Deborah; Michael; Brian **ED:** BS in Accounting, Louisiana State University, Magna Cum Laude (1951) **CT:** Certified Public Accountant, State of Louisiana **C:** Retired (1991); Chief Financial Officer, Senior Vice President, Exxon Mobil Corporation, Houston, TX (1983-1991); Vice President, Controller, Exxon Mobil Corporation (1977-1983); President, ExxonMobil Pipeline Company (1975-1977); Deputy Controller, Exxon Mobil Corporation, New York, NY (1973-1975); Assistant Controller, Esso Europe Inc. (1969-1970) **CR:** Representative, International Accounting Standards Board, Association of International Certified Professional Accountants **CIV:** Chairman, Business Arts Fund, Houston, TX (1986); Board of Directors, Houston Symphony (1985); Vice Chairman, Business Arts Fund, Houston, TX (1985); Treasurer, Business Arts Fund, Houston, TX (1984); Member, Advisory Board, Tepper School of Business, Carnegie Mellon University (1983-1986); Member, Advisory Board, School of Business, Columbia University (1983); Board of Directors, Business Arts Fund, Houston, TX (1983); Vice Chairman, Board of Trustees, Paper Mill Playhouse, Millburn, NJ (1982); Vice Chairman, Citizens Budget Committee, Millburn, NJ (1979); Louisiana State University Foundation; Member, Advisory Board, Leonard N. Stern School of Business, New York University; Member, Advisory Board, Department of Accounting, Louisiana State University; Boy Scouts of America; Little League; Junior Achievement; United Way; President, Houston Symphony Endowment Fund; Treasurer, Taping for the Blind **MIL:** Corporal, Korean War, U.S. Army (1951-1953) **AW:** National Accountant of the Year, Beta Alpha Psi (1980); Inductee, Hall of Fame, Financial Executives International; Inductee, Business School Hall of Distinction, Louisiana State University; President's Award for Grand Benefactor, Louisiana State University; Pacesetter of the Year, Cancer League; Ovations for Excellence Award, Houston Symphony; Out-

standing Leader in the Arts Award, School of Music, University of Houston **MEM:** Chairman, Audit Committee, American Institute of Certified Public Accountants (1987-Present); President, Houston Chapter, Financial Executives Institute (1987); Mission Committee, Board of Directors, American Institute of Certified Public Accountants (1986); Chairman, Tax Research Association of Houston (1987); Vice Chairman, Tax Research Association (1986); Director, Tax Research Association (1984-1986); Council-at-Large, American Institute of Certified Public Accountants (1984-1986); Director, Houston Chapter, Financial Executives Institute (1984); Business Committee for the Arts, Houston Chamber of Commerce (1983-1984); National Board of Directors, Beta Alpha Psi (1983-1984); Chairman, National Advisory Forum, Beta Alpha Psi (1983-1984); Chairman, Finance Division, American Petroleum Institute; River Oaks Country Club; Task Force Member, Securities and Exchange Commission; Task Force Member, Financial Accounting Standards Board **MH:** Albert Nelson Marquis Lifetime Achievement Award; Marquis Who's Who Top Professional **B/I:** Mr. LeGrange became involved in his profession because he grew up in Baton Rouge, Louisiana and began with Exxon shortly after graduating. **PA:** Republican **RE:** Roman Catholic

LEHAN, RICHARD D., T: English Language Educator, Writer **I:** Education/Educational Services **DOB:** 12/23/1930 **PB:** Brockton **SC:** MA/USA **PT:** Ralph A Lehan; Mildred Lehan **MS:** Married **SPN:** Ann Evans (06/11/1960) **CH:** Edward Scott (Deceased) **ED:** PhD, University of Wisconsin (1958); MA, Boston College (1953); BA, Stonehill College (1952) **C:** Professor Emeritus, UCLA (1994-Present); Member, Faculty, Department of English, UCLA (1992-Present); Professor of English, UCLA (1962-1994); Chairman, Department of English, UCLA (1971-1973); Member, Faculty, University of Texas at Austin (1958-1962); Member, Faculty, Teaching Assistant, University of Wisconsin-Madison (1953-1957) **CR:** Fulbright Exchange Professor, Moscow State University (Lomonosov Moscow State University) (1974-1975) **CW:** Author, "Quest West" (2014); Author, "Modernism and Beyond" (2014); Author, "Realism and Naturalism" (2005); Author, "Sister Carrie Critiques" (2000); Author, "The City in Literature" (1998); Author, "The Great Gatsby: The Limits of Wonder" (1990); Author, "Literary Existentialism" (1973); Author, "Theodore Dreiser: His World and His Novels" (1969); Author, "F. Scott Fitzgerald: The man and his works" (1966) **AW:** President's Research Fellow, University of California (1988-1989); Guggenheim Fellow (1978-1979); Fulbright Award (1975); Distinguished Teaching Award, UCLA (1970); Distinguished Teaching Award, University of Texas (1961) **MH:** Albert Nelson Marquis Lifetime Achievement Award **B/I:** Dr. Lehan became involved in his profession because he wanted to transmit the various thoughts that he had about the academic life to other people. He has been proud of communicating the things he thought were important to others who would be interested in his form of enthusiasm.

LEIBOVITZ, ANNA-LOU, "ANNIE", T: Photographer **I:** Media & Entertainment **CN:** Leibovitz Studio Inc. **DOB:** 10/02/1949 **PB:** Waterbury **SC:** CT/USA **CH:** Sarah Cameron; Susan Anna; Samuelle Edith **ED:** Honorary DFA, Rhode Island School of Design (2018); BFA, San Francisco Art Institute (1971) **C:** Photographer, Vogue, Condé Nast (1998-Present); Photographer, Vanity Fair, Condé Nast (1980-Present); Chief Photographer, Rolling Stone (1973-1983); Photographer, Rolling Stone (1970-1983); Proprietor, Annie Leibovitz Studio,

Inc., New York, NY **CW:** Author, "Annie Leibovitz Portraits 2005-2016" (2017); Author, "Pilgrimage" (2011); Author, "Annie Leibovitz at Work" (2008); Author, "A Photographer's Life: 1990-2005" (2006); Author, "American Music" (2003); Author with Essay by Susan Sontag, "Annie Leibovitz: Women" (1999); Exhibit, The Corcoran Gallery (1999); Author, "Olympic Portraits" (1996); Creator, Official Portfolio for 26th Olympic Games, Atlanta, GA (1995); Author, "Photographs: Annie Leibovitz 1970-1990" (1992); Exhibit, National Portrait Gallery, Washington, DC (1991); Works Exhibited in Various Galleries and Museums **AW:** Paez Medal of Art, Venezuelan American Endowment for the Arts (VAEA) (2015); Prince of Asturias Award for Communication (2013); Wexner Prize, Wexner Center for the Arts (2012); Centenary Medal and Honorary Fellowship (HonFRPS) in Recognition of a Sustained, Significant Contribution to the Art of Photography, The Royal Photographic Society (2009); Named One of the 50 Most Powerful Women in New York City, New York Post (2008); Ordre des Arts et des Lettres, Commandeur French Government (2006); Medal of Distinction, Barnard College (2000); Named Living Legend, Library of Congress (2000); Named One of the Top 10 Living Artists, ARTnews Magazine (1999); Named to Art Directors Club (ADC) Hall of Fame (1999); Infinity Award for Applied Photography, International Center for Photography (1990); Clio Award (1987); Campaign of the Decade Award, Advertising Age Magazine (1987); Innovation in Photography Award, American Society of Magazine Photographers (1987); Photographer of the Year Award, American Society of Magazine Photographers (1984) **RE:** Jewish

LEMAHIEU, DAVID, "D.J." JOHN, T: Professional Baseball Player **I:** Athletics **CN:** New York Yankees **DOB:** 07/13/1988 **PB:** Visalia **SC:** CA/USA **MS:** Married **SPN:** Jordan LeMahieu (2014) **ED:** Coursework, Louisiana State University; Diploma, Brother Rice High School, Bloomfield Township, MI **C:** Professional Baseball Player, New York Yankees (2019-Present); Professional Baseball Player, Colorado Rockies (2012-2018); Professional Baseball Player, Chicago Cubs (2011) **AW:** Silver Slugger Award (2019); All-MLB First Team (2019); Three-Time All-Star (2015, 2017, 2019); Three-Time Gold Glove Award (2014, 2017-2018); Three-Time Wilson Defensive Player of the Year Award (2013, 2017-2018); Fielding Bible Award (2017)

LEMANN, THOMAS B., T: Retired Lawyer **I:** Law and Legal Services **CN:** Liskow & Lewis **DOB:** 01/03/1926 **PB:** New Orleans **SC:** LA/USA **ED:** MCL, Tulane University School of Law (1953); LLB, Harvard University School of Law (1952); AB, Harvard University, Summa Cum Laude (1949) **C:** Of Counsel, Liskow & Lewis, New Orleans, LA (1998-2016); Partner, Monroe & Lemann, New Orleans, LA (1958-1998); Associate, Monroe & Lemann, New Orleans, LA (1953-1958) **CIV:** Board Member, Zemurray Foundation, Hever Foundation, Hawkins Foundation, Parkside Foundation, Azby Fund, Azby Art Fund, Greater New Orleans Foundation (1996-2005); Trustee, New Orleans Museum of Art (1986-1992); President, Arts Council of New Orleans (1975-1980); Visiting Committee, Harvard University Art Museums (1974-1980); Board Member, New Orleans Philharmonic Symphony Society (1956-1978); President, Louisiana Civil Service League (1974-1976); Chairman, Mayor's Cultural Resources Committee (1970-1975); Board Member, Metairie Park Country Day School (1956-1971); Chairman, Metairie Park Country Day School (1967-1970); Board Member, Flint-Goodridge Hospital (1960-1970); Musica da Camera; Council, Louisiana State Law Institute; Secretary, Trust Advisory Committee **MIL:** U.S. Army (1944-

1946) **MEM:** Board of Governors, Louisiana Bar Association (1977-1978); American Bar Association; New Orleans Bar Association; New York City Bar Association; American Law Institute; Bartolus Society; New Orleans Country Club; Wyvern Club, New Orleans, LA; Phi Beta Kappa **RE:** Jewish

LEMMA, MULATU, "MULLE", PHD, T: Distinguished Professor of Mathematics **I:** Graphic Design **CN:** Savannah State University **DOB:** 03/01/1949 **PB:** Sagure **SC:** Arisi/Ethiopia **PT:** Lemma Beshae; Mamite Mariame **MS:** Married **SPN:** Aster Debebe **CH:** Samera Mulatu; Abyssinia Mulatu **ED:** PhD, Kent State University (1994); MA in Pure Mathematics, Kent State University (1993); MA in Applied Mathematics, Ethiopia (1982); BA, Ethiopia (1977) **C:** Distinguished Professor of Mathematics, Savannah State University (1994-Present) **CR:** Chair of Mathematics, Savannah State University **CW:** Published 116 Papers **AW:** Named One of the Most Awarded Professors, State of Georgia (2015); Named Georgia Professor of the Year (2013); Board of Regents' Teaching Excellence Award for Faculty in Regional and State Universities, University System of Georgia (2012); Named Distinguished Professor, Savannah State University (2010) **MH:** Marquis Who's Who Top Educator **AS:** Dr. Lemma attributes his success to his professor, John Friday, who was a professor at Kent State University. **B/I:** Dr. Lemma became involved in his profession because he liked mathematics and his passion started when he was in fifth grade. His dream was to be a teacher when he was in elementary school and that was why he became a teacher. **THT:** Dr. Lemma was inspired in his research by Professors John Friday, Chellu Chetty, Jonathan Lambright and Mohammed Mustafa.

LENARD, MARY JANE, T: Accounting Educator **I:** Education/Educational Services **CN:** Meredith College **DOB:** 07/08/1955 **PB:** York **SC:** PA/USA **PT:** Martin Kondor; Anne Ruth (Zimmerman) Kondor **MS:** Married **SPN:** Robert Louis Lenard (7/9/1977, Divorced 2004) **CH:** Kevin; Kelsey **ED:** PhD in Business Administration, Kent State University (1995); MBA in Finance, University of Akron (1982); BS in Economic and Administrative Science, Carnegie Mellon University (1977) **CT:** Certified Management Accountant; Certified Fraud Examiner **C:** Professor, Meredith College, Raleigh, NC (2014-Present); Associate Professor, Meredith College, Raleigh, NC (2005-2014); Assistant Professor, University of North Carolina, Greensboro, NC (2001-2005); Associate Professor, Barton College, Wilson, NC (1997-2001); Member, Adjunct Faculty, Cleveland State University (1994-1997); Instructor, University of Akron (1986-1993); Accountant, Auditor, Goodyear Tire and Rubber Co., Akron, OH (1978-1986); Management Trainee, Equibank, NA, Pittsburgh, PA (1977-1978) **CIV:** Member, Meredith College General Education Committee (2017-2019); Member, Meredith College Benefits Committee (2014-2016); Member, Meredith College Strongpoints Advisory Committee (2014-2016); Member, Bryan School, UNC Greensboro Undergraduate Programs Committee (2004-2005); Member, Bryan School, UNC Greensboro Faculty Development Committee (2002-2005); Member, Bryan School, UNC Greensboro Planning Committee (2002-2005); Member, Chair, IT Committee for Accounting Department at UNC (2001-2005); Member, Wakefield HS PTSA (2002-Present); Active, Revere Schools Computer Curriculum Committee (1994-1995); Coordinator, Volunteer Income Tax Assistance, Barton College, Wilson (1998-2001); Member, Newsletter Director, Wakefield Middle School PTSA (2000-2002); Vice President, Summit County PTA, Akron, OH (1994-1996); President, Hillcrest Elementary PTA, Richfield, OH (1992-1993) **CW:** Author, Proceedings; Contributor, Articles, Professional Journals, Journal of Management Information Systems, Decision Sciences, The Journal of Emerging Technologies in Accounting, Managerial Auditing Journal, Managerial Finance **AW:** Meredith College School of Business Scholar of the Year (2008, 2013, 2017); Laura Harrill Presidential Award, Meredith College (2014); Meredith College of Instructional Technology Grant (2012); Featured in Meredith College Endeavors of Excellence (2006); Grantee, Faculty Development Grant, Barton College (1999, 1997); Best Paper Award, American Accounting Association (1998) **MEM:** Director, Member, Retention Institute of Management Accountants (1994-1996); Association of Certified Fraud Examiners; Decision Sciences Institute; Akron Women's Network; Association for Information Systems; American Accounting Association; Beta Gamma Sigma **MH:** Albert Nelson Marquis Lifetime Achievement Award **B/I:** Dr. Lenard became involved in her profession because after practicing in the field for a while she decided that she wanted to give back and become a teacher. Her mother, Anne Ruth (Zimmerman) Kondor, inspired her to do that because she was a teacher and later on became a professor.

LENDARIS, GEORGE GREGORY, T: Professor Emeritus of Systems Science and of Electrical & Computer Engineering **I:** Education/Educational Services **CN:** Portland State University **DOB:** 04/02/1935 **PB:** Helper **SC:** UT/USA **PT:** Gregory George Lendaris; Argie (Xenakis) Lendaris **MS:** Widowed **SPN:** Irene Kokinos (06/26/1958, Deceased 07/29/1988) **CH:** Miriam Vareldzis; Dorothy Kemp **ED:** PhD in Electrical Engineering, University of California Berkeley (1961); MSEE, University of California Berkeley (1958); BSEE, University of California Berkeley, Cum Laude (1957) **CT:** Registered Professional Engineer, States of California and Oregon (Now Retired) **C:** Professor of Systems Science and of Electrical & Computer Engineering, Portland State University, OR (1971-2011); Director, Systems Science Program, Portland State University, OR (2001-2011); Associate Professor of Systems Science, Chairman of Faculty, Oregon Graduate Center for Studies & Research, Beaverton, OR (1969-1971); Senior Research Engineer, Program Manager, General Motors, Defense Research Laboratories, Santa Barbara, CA (1961-1969) **CR:** Board of Directors, Accurate Automation Corp., Chattanooga, TN (1994-Present); President, International Neural Network Society (INNS) (1999-2002); Member, Board of Governors, International Neural Network Society (INNS) (1996-1999); Presiding Officer, Faculty Senate, Portland State University, OR (1995-1996); General Chair, International Joint Conference on Neural Networks (IJCNN), OR (1991-1993); Consultant, Various Businesses **CIV:** Member, Justice and Human Rights Committee, Local Church, Portland, OR (1974-Present); Chairman, Various Church Community Committees (1962-Present); Member, Advisory Panel, Portland Energy Commission, Inc. (Now PECI) (1980); Oregon State Senate Task Force on Economic Development (1972-1973); Member, Governor's Technical Advisory Committee, OR (1970-1972); Choir Director, Greek Orthodox Churches, Santa Barbara, CA and Portland, OR (1962-1973); President, Parish Council **CW:** Editorial Board, International Journal of General Systems, Gordon & Breach (1974-2004); Editorial Board, IEEE Transactions on Neural Networks (1991-2001); Editorial Board, Systems Research Journal (1985-1994); Author, Over 75 Publications **AW:** Life Fellow, IEEE (2005); Fellow, International Neural Network Society (INNS) (2001); Fellow, Institute of Electrical and Electronics Engineers (IEEE) (1981); Fellow, National Academy of Sciences (1974) **MEM:** Institute of Electrical and Electronics Engineers (IEEE); International Neural Network Society (INNS); Systems, Man and Cybernetics Society (SMC) of IEEE; American Association for the Advancement of Science (AAAS); International Society of Knowledge Engineers; Institute of Noetic Sciences (IONS); American Hellenic Education Progressive Association (AHEPA); Sigma Xi, The Scientific Research Honor Society; The Tau Beta Pi Association, Inc.; IEEE-Eta Kappa Nu **MH:** Albert Nelson Marquis Lifetime Achievement Award; Marquis Who's Who Top Professional **AS:** Dr. Lendaris attributes his success to being passionate in his work and church community, along with raising and enjoying his family. He also credits taking things as they come. **B/I:** Due to his dad being in a business he owned, Dr. Lendaris originally intended to pursue a business school education. However, while he was a high school junior, he felt a calling to go into engineering. Because the university he hoped to attend, UC Berkeley, had a prerequisite of mechanical drawing for engineering applicants, he found himself taking mechanical drawing as a senior in high school (along with a "bunch of sophomores"). He was accepted into UC Berkeley, and upon completing his lower-division engineering courses, he applied and was accepted into the Electrical Engineering Department in the College of Engineering for his upper-division program. He earned the BS in Electrical Engineering with honors, and went on to earn MS and PhD degrees in Electrical Engineering as well. When he expressed to his academic advisor that he wanted to become an engineering professor, he received the following advice: "If you want to be a good engineering professor, you should spend 10 years in the industry first." He took this advice to heart, and after receiving his PhD, he went to work for the General Motors Defense Research Laboratory (GMDRL) in Santa Barbara, CA. He spent eight years there, and then transitioned into higher education, first at the Oregon Graduate Center for Study & Research (1969-1971), and then to Portland State University in Portland Oregon (1971-2011). Dr. Lendaris retired in 2011. **AV:** Woodworking; Folk dancing instructor; Church choir director; Active participation in leading and design-review of beautification projects at local Greek Orthodox Cathedral (40 years and counting) **PA:** Democrat **RE:** Greek Orthodox **THT:** Dr. Lendaris' motto is, "Life is good, especially when one follows his/her dreams."

LENK, CARLA, T: President **I:** Business Management/Business Services **CN:** Lenk and Associates, LLC **DOB:** 09/25/1938 **PB:** Milwaukee **SC:** WI/USA **PT:** Chester Paul Dombrowski; Dorothy Marie Dombrowski **MS:** Widowed **CH:** Elizabeth; Jeanette; Andrew **ED:** MS in Adult Education, University of Wisconsin-Milwaukee, WI (1975); BS in Education, English, University of Wisconsin-Milwaukee (1975) **C:** Jobs & Business Development Coordinator, North Central Community Action Program, Wisconsin Rapids, WI (2012-Present); Owner, President, Lenk & Associates, LLC (2004-Present); Director, Small Business Development Center, Whitewater, WI (1987-2004); Chief Executive Officer, Forward Services Corporation, Madison, WI (1994); President, Wisconsin Business Procurement Association, Wisconsin Rapids, WI (1981-1988) **CIV:** Member, SCORE Counseling (2005-Present); Member, Stateline World Trade Association (1986-2012); Director, USDA Emerging Market Grant (2001-2004); Director, SBDC & Small Business Institute (1987-2003) **AW:** Director **B/I:** Ms. Lenk says that she got into her profession due to survival. Her husband had passed away, leaving her with their three children and the need to figure out an efficient way to provide for them.

LENO, JAY DOUGLAS MUIR, T: Comedian; Former Television Personality **I:** Media & Entertainment **DOB:** 05/28/1950 **PB:** New Rochelle **SC:** NY/USA **PT:** Angelo Leno; Catherine (Muir) Leno **MS:** Married **SPN:** Mavis Nicholson (11/20/1980) **ED:** Honorary LHD, Emerson College, Boston, MA (2014); BA in Speech Therapy, Emerson College, Boston, MA (1972) **C:** Comedian, Actor (1976-Present); Television Personality (1992-2014); Owner, Comedy Club (1973); Auto Mechanic, Rolls-Royce; Deliveryman **CW:** Voice Actor, "Mickey Mouse Mixed-Up Adventures" (2017-Present); Appearance, "The Price Is Right" (2019); Voice Actor, "Mickey and the Roadster Racers" (2017); Appearance, "The Muppets" (2015); Actor, "Last Man Standing" (2015); Appearance, "Ted 2" (2015); Voice Actress, "Elf: Buddy's Musical Christmas" (2014); Executive Producer, Host, "Jay Leno's Garage: The Ultimate Car Week" (2014); Appearance, "Episodes" (2014); Voice Actor, "Phineas and Ferb" (2014); Voice Actor, "The 7D" (2014); Host, Producer, Writer, "The Tonight Show" (1992-2009, 2010-2014); Appearance, "Delivery Man" (2013); Appearance, "Real Husbands of Hollywood" (2013); Appearance, "Louie" (2012); Appearance, "I'm Still Here" (2010); Host, Producer, Writer, "The Jay Leno Show" (2009-2010); Appearance, "Entourage" (2009); Voice Actor, "Unstable Fables: Tortoise vs. Hare" (2008); Voice Actor, "Igor" (2008); Appearance, "The Great Buck Howard" (2008); Appearance, "The Astronaut Farmer" (2006); Voice Actor, "Ice Age: The Meltdown" (2006); Voice Actor, "Cars" (2006); Voice Actor, "Robots" (2005); Appearance, "Joey" (2005); Author, "How to Be the Funniest Kid in the Whole Wide World (or Just in Your Class)" (2005); Author, "If Roast Beef Could Fly" (2004); Appearance, "Mr. 3000" (2004); Appearance, "Stuck on You" (2003); Appearance, "The Bernie Mac Show" (2003); Appearance, "John Q" (2002); Appearance, "Space Cowboys" (2000); Appearance, "The Birdcage" (1996); Author, "Leading with my Chin" (1996); Appearance, "Major League II" (1994); Actor, "The Flintstones" (1994); Voice Actor, "We're Back! A Dinosaur's Story" (1993); Appearance, "Dave" (1993); Appearance, "Wayne's World 2" (1993); Guest Host, "The Tonight Show" (1987-1992); Actor, "Collision Course" (1989); Host, "Jay Leno's Family Comedy Hour" (1987); Producer, Host, "Jay Leno and the American Dream" (1986); Appearance, "Saturday Night Live" (1986); Voice Actor, "What's Up Hideous Sun Demon?" (1983); Actor, "Americathon" (1979); Writer, "Good Times" (1974-1979); Actor, "American Hot Wax" (1978); Actor, "Fun with Dick and Jane" (1977); Appearances, "Late Night with David Letterman"; Stand-up Comedian, Carnegie Hall, Caesar's Palace, Others; Actor, Appearances, Television Shows and Films **AW:** Mark Twain Prize for American Humor, John F. Kennedy Center for the Performing Arts (2014); Named to Television Hall of Fame (2014); Primetime Emmy for Outstanding Short Format Nonfiction Program, Television Academy (2011); Named Hasty Pudding Man of the Year, Hasty Pudding Theatricals Society (2011); Named One of the World's Most Influential People, TIME Magazine (2009); Named One of the 100 Most Powerful Celebrities, Forbes.com (2007, 2008); People's Choice Award for Favorite Late Night Talk Show Host (2006); Recipient, Star, Hollywood Walk of Fame (2000); Emmy Award for Outstanding Variety, Music or Comedy Series, Academy of Television Arts & Sciences (1995)

LENTZ, JACEK, T: Asset Forfeiture Attorney **I:** Law and Legal Services **CN:** The Lentz Law Firm, P.C. **MS:** Married **CH:** One Daughter **ED:** JD, Hastings College of Law, University of California (2000); Coursework in Philosophy of Law and European Union Law, Oxford University, Trinity College, England (2000); BA in Literature and American Studies, University of California, Santa Cruz, CA, With Honors (1990); Coursework in English Literature, University of California Los Angeles (1987) **C:** Owner, The Lentz Law Firm, PC (2008-Present); Partner, Shevin & Lentz, Attorneys at Law (2005-2007); Associate, Steefel Levitt & Weiss (2003-2004); Associate, Nixon Peabody (aka Lillick & Charles) (2000-2003) **AS:** Mr. Lentz is dedicated to his craft and is passionate about representing his clients who are underdogs when their property is seized by local, state or federal law enforcement. Mr. Lentz approaches his work with a strong sense of public responsibility and mission and invests a considerable amount of his time advising and counseling often underprivileged young people about understanding and following the law and making better choices in their lives. **B/I:** Mr. Lentz has a diverse practice, which started with his work as an associate attorney in several prestigious corporate law firms in San Francisco and Los Angeles. He then started his own practice as a criminal defense and notable medical marijuana trial attorney in 2005. As a young mid-level associate, Mr. Lentz decided that a big law firm civil practice was not the optimal route for him to develop his talent and legal skills. He saw early on that he needed to practice law with a high level of independence and freedom, and that he could thrive only in a practice that was consistent with his moral and philosophical views. To date, he has represented hundreds of claimants asserting their property rights in numerous state and federal jurisdictions across the U.S., including in cases heard in front of the California Supreme Court. Further, Mr. Lentz is very well known among his peers for the fact that he practices civil asset forfeiture exclusively. He owes his success in great part to a significant number of cases referred to him by his fellow attorneys, all of whom keep showing a great deal of trust in Mr. Lentz' ability to competently and successfully represent clients. While there are several excellent and prominent fellow forfeiture attorneys in the United States, Mr. Lentz is not aware of anyone who practices forfeiture law exclusively on the scale that he does. **AV:** Camping; Hiking; Traveling, DJ-ing; Listening to podcasts **THT:** Mr. Lentz's practice is rooted in and driven by his sense of public mission. He strives to provide high-quality advice, counsel, and representation consistently, regardless of whether a case is small or large. Mr. Lentz prides himself on his commitment to find the right and affordable legal solution to anyone who faces the awesome power and resources of state, local, and federal law enforcement and governments.

LEON, RIGO, T: Artist **I:** Fine Art **CN:** 2500 Biscayne Blv #609 **PB:** Havana **SC:** Cuba **CH:** Vincenzo; Dante **C:** Artist **CIV:** Volunteer, Habitat for Humanity; Donor, Paintings Monthly **AS:** He attributes his success to consistency and hard work. **B/I:** Mr. Leon had a passion for art and was afraid to stay in Cuba and not be able to express his love for art. His mom won the visa lottery so he was able to come to the United States and his entire family was involved in sports and art. His mom was a model back in the early 50s for Coca Cola and Crystal Beer. He expressed himself by painting and in 2006 he had an opportunity to do a show and after that it was show after show. Everything he did was in relation to communication and social problems. He did a little bit more abstract and for the past few years he had been doing paper boats and tribal things. He went back to Cuba after 20 years and took his son so he could see where he came from and the history of his country. He took his art very seriously and saw it as a lifestyle and not a job. The paper boats were hard to do because it was so connected to his environment as he was in Cuba at the worst time of the countries history. His process was personal including the commercial pieces and his requirement was that it had to be unique and his own work. If the customers say no to his requirement then he won't do it not even if he was paid a lot of money. He wants his art to be of a certain standard. He believed that art was a responsibility to society which means that as an artist they have a responsibility to spread art positively or negatively. In his case he does not want to change the world but wants people to think before they act.

LEONARD, ETHAN G., T: Chief Medical Officer; Professor of Pediatrics **I:** Medicine & Health Care **CN:** University Hospitals Rainbow Babies and Children's Hospital; Case Western Reserve University School of Medicine **PT:** Irvin; Elin **MS:** Married **SPN:** Holly Dickert-Leonard, MD **CH:** Joshua; Andrew **ED:** Fellowship, Pediatric Infectious Diseases, Case Western Reserve University Hospitals of Cleveland (2000-2003); Residency in Pediatrics, Chief Resident, Case Western Reserve University Hospitals of Cleveland (1999-2000); Residency in Pediatrics, Case Western Reserve University Hospitals of Cleveland (1997-1999); Internship in Pediatrics, Case Western Reserve University Hospitals of Cleveland (1996-1997); MD, Case Western Reserve University School of Medicine (1996); MBA, Case Western Reserve University Weatherhead School of Management; Bachelor's Degree, University of Michigan (1991) **CT:** Medical License, State of Ohio; Pediatrics, The American Board of Pediatrics; Pediatric Infectious Disease, The American Board of Pediatrics **C:** Chief Medical Officer and Vice Chair for Clinical Operations, University Hospitals Rainbow Babies and Children's Hospital (2019-Present); Chief Medical Officer, University Hospitals Rainbow Babies and Children's Hospital (2014-Present); Vice Chair for Quality, University Hospitals Rainbow Babies and Children's Hospital (2012-2019); Associate Chief Medical Office and Medical Director of Quality, University Hospitals Rainbow Babies and Children's Hospital (2013-2014); Associate Vice Chair for Quality, University Hospitals Rainbow Babies and Children's Hospital (2011); Director of Pediatric Medication Safety Practices, University Hospitals Rainbow Babies and Children's Hospital (2010); Associate Director, Residency Training Program: Pediatrics, University Hospitals Rainbow Babies and Children's Hospital (2004-2010) **CR:** Professor of Pediatrics, Case Western Reserve University School of Medicine (2019-Present); Associate Professor of Pediatrics, Case Western Reserve University School of Medicine (2003-2019); Assistant Professor of Pediatrics, Case Western Reserve University School of Medicine (2004-2010) **CW:** Contributor, Articles to Professional Journals; Speaker in Field **AW:** Named to Best Doctors (2008-Present); Named One of America's Top Doctors, Castle Connolly (2012-2014); Best Practice Award Acute Care, Ohio Patient Safety Institute (2013); Rainbow Trustees Award for Clinical Excellence, Rainbow Babies and Children's Hospital Foundation (2012); Named Top Doctor, Pediatric Infectious Disease, Castle Connolly **MEM:** Co-lead, Ventilator Associated Pneumonia, National Children's Hospital Solutions for Patient Safety (2013-Present); Fellow, American Academy of Pediatrics; Fellow, Infectious Disease Society of America (IDSA); Clinical Affairs Committee, Ohio Hospital Association; American College of Healthcare Executives; Ohio Hospital Association; National Children's Hospital Solutions for Patient Safety; Alpha Omega Alpha Honor Medical Society **AS:** Dr. Leonard has been fortunate to have had good mentors. There have been different people at different times that have encouraged him to do different things at different times. **B/I:** Dr. Leonard knew when he was doing his undergraduate degree that he wanted to work in pediatrics. As he did his residency, he enjoyed the rigor of infectious disease and the fact that they got to see patients in different settings, including outpatient settings, intensive care units, different inpatient settings, and that they were isolated to a given specific organ system.

LEONARD, GILBERT STANLEY, BS, MS, T: Oil Company Executive **I:** Oil & Energy **DOB:** 09/03/1941 **PB:** Kingsport **SC:** TN/USA **PT:**RobertSpencerLeonard;Hope(Palmer)Leonard **MS:** Married **SPN:** Linda Marie Gremillion (10/27/1984); Barbara Ann Bell (06/12/1965, Divorced 1982) **ED:** MS in Business, The University of Kansas (1970); BS in Industrial Management, Purdue University (1964) **C:** Academic and Work-Force Advisor - II Division-1, Lone Star College-CyFair (2015-Present); Academic and Work-Force Advisor - I, Lone Star College-CyFair (2011-2014); Senior Systems Supervisor, Center of Expertise Client/Server Systems, Exxon Co., USA (1996-Present); Adjunct Professor of Business, Lone Star College-CyFair (2003-2013); Lecturer, Executive Residence, Mays School of Business, Texas A&M University (2001); Instructor of Operations Management, Mays School of Business, Texas A&M University (2000); Lecturer, Graduate Coursework in Logistics, Mays School of Business, Texas A&M University (2000); Infrastructure Services Manager, Exxon Mobil Co. USA (1998-1999); Supervisor of Network and Telecommunication Division, Exxon Computing Service Corp. (1994-1996); Systems Supervisor, Exxon Card Center, Houston, TX (1990-1995); Supervisor of Applications Development, Exxon Co., USA, Houston, TX (1986-1989); Strategic Systems Planner, Exxon Co., USA, Houston, TX (1984-1985); Group Supervisor of Applications Support, Exxon Co., USA, Houston, TX (1982-1984); Staff Systems Analyst, Exxon Co., USA, Houston, TX (1979-1981); Distribution Specialist, Exxon Co., USA, Houston, TX (1975-1978); Marketing Analyst, Exxon Co., USA, Houston, TX (1970-1974); Production Planner, Tennessee Eastman Co., Kingsport, TN (1966-1968); Summer Trainee, Tennessee Eastman Co., Kingsport, TN (1963) **CR:** Instructor, Facilitator Quality Forum (1990-1994); Instructor, Facilitator, Team Leadership Forum, Exxon Co., USA, Houston, TX (1988); Advisor, Consultant, National Junior Achievement, Houston, TX (1972-1974) **CIV:** Member, Choir (Tenor), St. Mary's Episcopal Church, Cypress, TX (2007-Present); Worship Leader, St. Mary's Episcopal Church, Cypress, TX (2003-Present); Eucharistic Minister, St. Mary's Episcopal Church, Cypress, TX (2002-Present); Member of Vestry Committee, Finance Leader, St. Mary's Episcopal Church, Cypress, TX (2006-2007); Vestry Committee (Overall Leadership of Church), St. Mary's Episcopal Church, Cypress, TX (2004-2007); Teacher of Religious Education for Teens, St. Mary's Episcopal Church, Cypress, TX (2004-2006); President, Forrest Lake Townhome Association, Houston, TX (1988-1989); Treasurer, Forrest Lake Townhome Association, Houston, TX (1987-1988); Lay Reader, Episcopalian Church, Good Shepherd, Kingwood, TX (1975-1982) **MIL:** Lieutenant, United States Naval Reserve (1964-1966); Active Duty, United States Navy (1964-1966); Gunnery Officer, United States Navy, Destroyer USS Charles R. Ware (DD-865) **AW:** Exxon Quality Tiger Award (1991); Recognition for Excellence in Naval ROTC Chicago Tribune (1963) **MEM:** President, Quarterdeck Society (1962-1963); Quarterdeck Society; Beta Gamma Sigma **MH:** Albert Nelson Marquis Lifetime Achievement Award; Marquis Who's Who Top Professional **B/I:** Lt. Leonard became involved in his profession because his father wanted him to be an engineer and then his uncle, who was a naval aviator, influenced him to go to Naval RTC, which he did. He had a devastating day at Pensacola, FL, but it was a change of life experience because he wanted to fly an airplane that could not fly. However, Lt. Leonard learned command control and leadership on the deck of a destroyer. which was called the USS Charles. R. Ware (DD865). Then, he had a tough decision to make in regards with his career in the U.S. Navy. Lt. Leonard chose to end his career with the navy because the price he would have had to pay would have been too high. The price was that he would have to serve three more years for every year they gave him an education, which added up to another nine more years in total, so he left and pursued the things he wanted to do. **AV:** Private pilot; Golf; Running; Teaching **RE:** Episcopalian

LEONARD, KAWHI ANTHONY, T: Professional Basketball Player **I:** Athletics **CN:** Los Angeles Clippers **DOB:** 06/29/1991 **PB:** Los Angeles **SC:** CA/USA **PT:** Mark Leonard; Kim (Robertson) Leonard **MS:** Life Partner **SPN:** Kishele Shipley **CH:** One daughter; One son **ED:** Coursework, San Diego State University (2009-2011); Diploma, Martin Luther King High School, Riverside, CA; Student, Canyon Springs High School, Moreno Valley, CA **C:** Professional Basketball Player, Los Angeles Clippers (2019-Present); Professional Basketball Player, Toronto Raptors (2018-2019); Professional Basketball Player, San Antonio Spurs (2011-2018) **AW:** NBA All-Star Game MVP (2020); Four-Time NBA All-Star (2016-2017, 2019-2020); All-NBA Second Team (2019); Two-Time NBA Champion (2014, 2019); Two-Time NBA All-Defensive Second Team (2014, 2019); Two-Time NBA Finals MVP (2014, 2019); Inductee, Martin Luther King Hall of Fame (2018); Two-Time All-NBA First Team (2016-2017); Three-Time NBA All-Defensive First Team (2015-2017); Two-Time NBA Defensive Player of the Year (2015-2016); NBA All-Rookie First Team (2012); All-Mountain West Defensive Team (2011); NABC All-American Third Team (2011); Two-Time First-team All-Mountain West (2010-2011); Two-Time All-Mountain West All-Tournament Team (2010-2011); Mountain West Freshman of the Year (2010); Mountain West Tournament MVP (2010); California Mr. Basketball (2009)

LEONE, DOUGLAS M., T: Global Managing Partner **I:** Financial Services **CN:** Sequoia Capital **DOB:** 07/04/1957 **PB:** Genoa **SC:** Italy **MS:** Married **SPN:** Patricia Perkins-Leone **CH:** Four Children **ED:** MS in Management, MIT Sloan School of Management (1988); MS in Industrial Engineering, Columbia University (1986); BS in Mechanical Engineering, Cornell University (1979) **C:** Global Managing Partner, Sequoia Capital (2012-Present); Managing Partner, Sequoia Capital (1996-2012); With, Sequoia Capital (1988-1996); With, Sales and Management, Sun Microsystems, Inc., Hewlett-Packard Company and Prime Computer, Inc. **AW:** Named One of the Top 10 Investors, Forbes Magazine (2017); Named One of the World's Billionaires, Forbes Magazine (2017)

LERMAN, CATHY JACKSON, T: Lawyer **I:** Law and Legal Services **CN:** Cathy Jackson Lerman PA **DOB:** 04/12/1956 **PB:** Norfolk **SC:** VA/USA **MS:** Married **SPN:** Steven Lerman **CH:** Candace Lerman; Ryan Lerman **ED:** MBA, Regis University (1998); Doctor of Jurisprudence, Nova University (1981); BA in English, Old Dominion University (1978) **CT:** Supreme Court of the United States (1986); Florida (1982); U.S. District Court for the Southern District of Florida (1982); United States Court of Appeals for the Eleventh Circuit (1982) **C:** Private Practice (2011) **CR:** Adjunct Professor, Nova University Law Center, Fort Lauderdale, FL; Teacher of Business Law, University of Miami **AW:** Named, Outstanding Young Women of Year, Outstanding Young Women in America (1981); Public Service Award, Contractors License Board, Broward County, Florida; Meritorious Public Service Award, Florida Bar; Recognition Award, Broward County Trial Lawyers Association; Outstanding Service Award, Academy of Florida Trial Lawyers; Outstanding Service Award, Broward County Bar Association **MEM:** Chairperson, Amicus Committee, Florida Justice Association (1986-Present); Newsletter Editor, Broward County Trial Lawyers Association (1985-Present); Chairperson, Family Law Section, Florida Justice Association (1985-Present); Board of Governors, Broward County Trial Lawyers Association (1984-Present); Chairperson, Appellate Advocacy Committee, American Bar Association (1986); Editor, Appellate Advocacy Newsletter, American Bar Association (1986); Health Law Committee, Florida Bar Association; Business Law Section, Florida Bar Association; Elder Law Section, Florida Bar Association; American Association for Justice; Rules and Procedure Committee, American Bar Association; Legislative Committee, Broward County Trial Lawyers Association **B/I:** Ms. Lerman became involved in her profession out of a long-standing fascination with the field of legal service. After finishing college, she decided to save money and was offered a partial scholarship by Nova University. **AV:** Running

LERNER, NORMAN CONRAD PHD, PE, T: Professor, President **I:** Military & Defense Services **CN:** U.S. Naval Academy/Transcomm, Inc. **DOB:** 02/13/1936 **PB:** New York **SC:** NY/USA **YOP:** 1990 - Ina Lerner (Wife) **PT:** Irving Lerner; Florence Lerner **MS:** Married **SPN:** Doris Austin (5/22/2014) **CH:** Sheila Allen; Julie Lerner **ED:** PhD in Business/Economics, American University (1968); MBA, Columbia University (1961); BS in Electrical Engineering, Massachusetts Institute of Technology (1957) **CT:** Registered Professional Engineer, New York, Virginia, Hawaii; Industrial College of the Armed Forces, US Army Artillery & Missile School **C:** Professor, Economics, U.S. Naval Academy, Annapolis, MD (2014-Present); President, Transcomm Inc., Falls Church, VA (1971-Present); Consultant, Executive Office of the President, Office Telecommunications Policy, Washington, DC (1971-1973); Associate Professor, George Washington University (1971-1973); Director, Computer Sciences. Corp., Falls Church, VA (1968-1978); Project Manager, MITRE Corp., Arlington, VA (1965-1968); Program Manager, ITT, Arlington, VA (1962-1965); Assistant to President, Associated Testing Laboratories, Wayne, NJ (1961-1962); Manager Field Engineering, Merit Light & Power Co., Mt. Vernon, NY (1958-1961); Design Engineer, RCA Corp. (1957-1958) **CR:** Senior Advisor, InterAmerican Telecommunications Commission, Organization of American States and Special Representative to Caribbean Members (2010-2011); Consultant, Executive Office of the President, White House Office of Telecommunications Policy (1971-1973); Member, Cable Television Advisory Grouop, Federal Communications Commission; Member, Advisor Group for Landmobile World Administrative Radio Conference, Federal Communications Commission. **CIV:** President Lyndon B. Johnson Task Force on Communications Policy; Selected U.S. Representative to International Telecommunications Union; Guest Lecturer, InterAmerican Defense College; Study Group Member, Application of Satellite Communications for Underdeveloped Nations, National Aeronautics and Space Administration; Adjunct Professor, U.S. Naval Academy; Adjunct Professor, George Washington University; Adjunct Professor, University of Maryland; Member, U.S. Government Protocol Mission to the Peoples Republic of China; Member, Working Groups for Communications Common Carriers and International Communication, Office of Technology Assessment, U.S. Congress; Member, U.S. Interdepartmental Committee on Atmospheric Sciences **MIL:** Captain, U.S. Army (1957-1968) **CW:** Continuing Author, Articles, "Todays Engineer" (2011); Contributing Author, "Engineering for the Americas: The Organization of American States Program", Education Committee, IEEE (2011); Contributing Author, Erlbaum Associates (2004); Contributing Author, Frequencia (1997); Contributing Author, TelePress LatinoAmerica (1995); Contributing Author, RNT (1995); Contributing Author, Telephone Engineering & Management (1992); Contributing Author, International Telecommunications Union Journal (1991); Contributing Author, Telecommulnications (1990); Contributing Author, Via Satellite (1991); Contributing Author, Network World (1990); Author, "Benefits of Satellite Communications", Global Change Agents, Book Ed. J. Pelteon and J. Oslund; Continuing Contributor, Numerous Articles, Professional Journals, Related Publications **AW:** Post-Doctoral IEEE Diplomatic Fellowship, US Department of State/Organization of American States (2010-2011); Fellow, Columbia University (1958-1959) **MEM:** Life Member, Institute of Electrical and Electronic Engineers (IEEE); Life Member, National Society of Professional Engineers; Life Member, National Association of Business Economists; Life Member, American Economic Association **MH:** Albert Nelson Marquis Lifetime Achievement Award **B/I:** Engineering and science were always fascinating for Dr. Lerner. This was reinforced by being president of the high school chemistry club and studying electrical engineering at MIT. As a result, he initially worked on some fascinating projects, including the first successful Atlas missile launch and the electron microscope at RCA. After serving in the Army, he acquired an MBA, forgoing the MSEE. The move into financial-economics eventually led to being the Project Manager for the Initial Defense Communications Satellite at ITT and completion of the PhD in Mathematical Economics at American University. These both stimulated interest in working on combined techno-economic problems, both foreign and domestic. This interest and experience was instrumental in contributing to various projects at ITT/Computer Sciences and the Federal Government which, in turn, initiated the broader activities leading to the founding of Transcomm, Inc., specializing in engineering-finance-economics in the U.S. and internationally. **AV:** Sailing; Skiing; Classical music; Painting

LESKO, DEBRA, "DEBBIE" KAY, T: U.S. Representative from Arizona **I:** Government Administration/Government Relations/Government Services **DOB:** 11/14/1958 **PB:** Sheboygan **SC:** WI/USA **PT:** Don Lorenz; Delores Lorenz **MS:** Married **SPN:** Joe Lesko **CH:** Three Children **ED:** BA in Business, University of Wisconsin-Madison **C:** Member, U.S. House of Representatives from Arizona's Eighth Congressional District, United States Congress, Washington, DC (2018-Present); Member, District 21, Arizona State Senate (2015-2018); Member, U.S. House of Representatives from Arizona's 21st Congressional District, United States Congress, Washington, DC (2013-2015); Member, U.S. House of Representatives from Arizona's Ninth Congressional District, United States Congress, Washington, DC (2009-2013); Vice Chair, Committee of Ways and Means, United States Congress; Member, Public Employees, Retirement and Entitlement Reform, United States Congress; Owner, Construction Sales Business **CR:** Voter Registration Chairman; Representative, Maricopa County Republican Party; Chairman, Legislative District Nine Officer, State and County Republican Party **CIV:** Board Member, Arizona Federation of Taxpayers (2005-2008); Neighborhood Leader, Glendale Community Partnership Program; Treasurer, PUSD Community Committee; Hearing Officer, North Valley Justice Court; Member, Glendale Fire Department Community Emergency Response Team; Advisory Board Member, Eve's Place **MEM:** Arizona Citizens Defense League, Inc.; Parent Teacher Association; First Vice President, Arrowhead Republican Women's Club; Ironwood High School Booster Club **PA:** Republican

LESLIE, W. BRUCE, PHD, T: Distinguished Service History Professor **I:** Education/Educational Services **CN:** The College at Brockport State University of New York **DOB:** 07/21/1944 **PB:** Orange **SC:** NJ/USA **PT:** William; Annette (Riedell) L. **CH:** William Andrew; Sarah Acton **ED:** Doctor of Philosophy in History of Education, Johns Hopkins University (1971); Bachelor of Arts in History, Princeton University (1966) **C:** Distinguished Service Professor, The College at Brockport State University of New York (2013-Present); Professor of History, The College at Brockport State University of New York, Brockport, NY (1970-2013); Visiting Professor, Jordanhill College, Scotland (1972) **CR:** Visiting Fellow, University of Cambridge (2011); Visiting Scholar, University of Cambridge (2003, 2005, 2007-2008); Co-Director, State University of New York Social Science Program, London, England (1978-1979, 1982-1983, 1989) **CW:** Editorial Board, "History of Higher Education" (1991-Present); Editorial Board, "History Education Quarterly" (2006-2012); Editor, "State University of New York at Sixty" (2010); Author, "State University of New York Brockport" (2006); Author, "Gentlemen and Scholars" (1993, 2005); Contributor, Articles and Reviews to Professional Journals **AW:** Fulbright Scholar, Denmark (1996-1997) **MEM:** The Nassau Club of Princeton; Organization of American Historians; Princeton Club of New York **MH:** Albert Nelson Marquis Lifetime Achievement Award **PA:** Democrat **RE:** Episcopalian

LESTER, GILLIAN L.L., T: Dean, Professor **I:** Education/Educational Services **CN:** Columbia Law School **PB:** Maple Ridge **SC:** Canada **PT:** Richard Egerton Matheson Lester; Lois (Jensen) Lester **MS:** Married **SPN:** Eric Talley **CH:** Two Children **ED:** JSD, Stanford Law School (1998); LLB, University of Toronto Faculty of Law (1990); BSc, The University of British Columbia (1986) **C:** Dean, Faculty of Law, Columbia Law School (2015-Present); Werner and Mimi Wolfen Research Professor, School of Law, University of California Berkeley (2014-Present); Acting Dean, School of Law, University of California Berkeley (2013-2014); Acting Dean, School of Law, University of California Berkeley (2012-2013); Professor-in-Residence, The University of Chicago Law School (2011); Associate Dean, JD Program and Curricular Planning, School of Law, University of California Berkeley (2010-2013); Co-Director, Berkeley Center for Health, Economic and Family Security (2010-2012); Alexander F. and May T. Morrison Professor of Law, School of Law, University of California Berkeley (2006-2015); Professor of Law, School of Law, UCLA (1999-2006); Acting Professor, School of Law, UCLA (1994-1999); Teaching Fellow, Stanford Law School (1992-1993); Consultant on Health Legislation, World Health Organization, Geneva, Switzerland (1993-1994); Intern, Health Legislation Unit, World Health Organization, Geneva, Switzerland (1991); Judicial Clerkship to Chief Justice of Ontario Charles Dubin, Supreme Court of Ontario, Court of Appeal (1990-1991); Summer Associate, Banking Group, Goodman & Goodman, Toronto, Canada (1989); Summer Associate, Labour Group, Campney & Murphy, Vancouver, Canada (1988); Lab Technician, Department of Psychology, The University of British Columbia (1986-1987); Teaching Assistant, Department of Psychology, The University of British Columbia (1984-1987) **CR:** Visiting Professor, Radzyner School of Law, Interdisciplinary Center, Herzliya, Israel (2013); Sidney Austin Visiting Professor of Law, Harvard Law School (2008-2009); Distinguished Visiting Professor, University of Southern California Gould School of Law (2008); Visiting Professor of Law, Sloan Fellow, Georgetown Law (2000) **CIV:** Adviser, Restatement of Employment Law, American Law Institute **CW:** Co-Author, "Employment Law Cases and Materials, Fifth Edition" (2012); Co-Author, "Employment Law: Selected Federal and State Statutes" (2012); Author, "Family Security Insurance: A New Foundation for Economic Security" (2010); Co-Author, "Employment Law (Concepts and Insights)" (2008); Co-Author, "Employment Law Stories" (2006); Co-Author, "Jumping the Queue: An Inquiry into the Legal Treatment of Students with Learning Disabilities" (2002); Contributor, Chapters to Books, Articles to Professional Journals **MEM:** American Law Institute

LESTER, JONATHAN TYLER, T: Professional Baseball Player **I:** Athletics **CN:** Chicago Cubs **DOB:** 01/07/1984 **PB:** Tacoma **SC:** WA/USA **MS:** Married **SPN:** Farrah Stone Johnson **CH:** Hudson; Walker; Cy Elizabeth **ED:** Coursework, Bellarmine Preparatory School, Tacoma, WA **C:** Professional Baseball Player, Chicago Cubs (2015-Present); Professional Baseball Player, Oakland Athletics (2014); Professional Baseball Player, Boston Red Sox (2006-2014) **CIV:** Partner, Charity Wines, Hutchinson Cancer Research Center and Jimmy Fund (2011); Co-Founder, NVRQT (2011) **AW:** Five-Time All-Star (2010-2011, 2014, 2016, 2018); NLCS MVP (2016); Three-Time World Series Champion (2007, 2013, 2016); Gatorade State Player of the Year (2000) **AV:** Hunting; Drinking wine

LETTERMAN, DAVID MICHAEL, T: Talk Show Host (Retired); Producer; Comedian; Writer **I:** Media & Entertainment **DOB:** 04/12/1947 **PB:** Indianapolis **SC:** IN/USA **PT:** Harry Joseph Letterman; Dorothy Marie (Hofert) Letterman Mengering **MS:** Married **SPN:** Regina Lasko (03/19/2009); Michelle Cook (07/02/1968, Divorced 1977) **CH:** Harry Joseph **ED:** Diploma in Telecommunications, Ball State University (1969) **C:** Founder, Worldwide Pants Incorporated (1991-Present); Radio Talk Show Host, WNTS AM (1974-1975); Weatherman and Television Announcer, WTHR (1970-1974) **CR:** Co-owner, Rahal Letterman Racing **CIV:** Founder, The Letterman Foundation for Courtesy and Grooming (1993-Present) **CW:** Host, "My Next Guest Need No Introduction with David Letterman" (2018-Present); Appearance, "Between Two Ferns" (2019); Host, Writer, Executive Producer, "The Late Show with David Letterman," CBS (1993-2015); Co-author, "This Land Was Made for You and Me (But Mostly Me)" (2013); Actor, "I'm Still Here" (2010); Executive Producer, "Coming Home: Military Families Cope with Change" (2009); Executive Producer, "Families Stand Together: Feeling Secure in Tough Times" (2009); Executive Producer, "The Youngest Candidate" (2008); Co-author, "Late Night Fun Facts" (2008); Executive Producer, "Knights of Prosperity" (2007); Executive Producer, "Late Late Show with Craig Ferguson" (2005); Executive Producer, "Late Late Show with Craig Kilborn" (1999-2005); Executive Producer, "Everybody Loves Raymond" (1996-2005); Executive Producer, "Ed" (2000-2004); Executive Producer, "Welcome to New York" (2000-2001); Actor, "Man on the Moon" (1999); Executive

Producer, "The Late Late Show With Tom Synder" (1995-1999); Actor, "Cosby" (1998); Actor, "Private Parts" (1997); Actor, "Seinfeld" (1996); Actor, "Eddie" (1996); Executive Producer, "The High Life" (1996); Executive Producer, "The Bonnie Hunt Show" (1995-1996); Actor, "The Nanny" (1995); Actor, "Cabin Boy" (1994); Actor, "Murphy Brown" (1993); Host, "Late Night with David Letterman," NBC (1982-1993); Co-author, "An Altogether New Book of Top Ten Lists" (1991); Co-author, "The Late Night with David Letterman Book of Top Ten Lists" (1990); Co-author, "Late Night with David Letterman: The Book" (1985); Host, "The David Letterman Show" (1980); Actor, "Mork & Mindy" (1979); Announcer, Actor, "Mary" (1978); Actor, "Mary" (1978); Announcer, Actor, "The Starland Vocal Band Show" (1977); Performer, The Comedy Store, Los Angeles, CA (1975); Actor, Appearances, Numerous Television Shows and Films **AW:** Mark Twain Prize for American Humor (2017); Peabody Award (2015); Honoree, Kennedy Center Honors, John F. Kennedy Center for the Performing Arts, Washington, DC (2012); Johnny Carson Award for Comedic Excellence, The Comedy Awards (2011); Named One of the 100 Most Powerful Celebrities, Forbes.com (2007, 2008); People's Choice Award for Favorite Late Night Talk Show Host (2005); Named One of the 50 Greatest TV Shows of All Time, TV Guide (2002); Emmy Award for Outstanding Variety, Music or Comedy Program, Academy of Television Arts & Sciences (1994, 1998, 1999, 2000, 2001, 2002); Emmy Award for Outstanding Writing in a Variety or Music Program, Academy of Television Arts & Sciences (1984, 1985, 1986, 1987); Emmy Award for Outstanding Host or Hostess in a Variety Series, Academy of Television Arts & Sciences (1981); Numerous Awards **MEM:** Sigma Chi Fraternity

LEVENDOGLU-TUGAL, OYA, T: Professor, Medical Director **I:** Medicine & Health Care **CN:** New York Medical College; Boston Children's Health Physicians **ED:** MD, Hacettepe Üniversitesi Tip Fakültesi, Turkey (1974) **C:** Medical Director of Ambulatory Pediatric Hematology Oncology & Stem Cell Transplantation, Director of Pediatric Thrombosis, Hemostasis Program, Professor of Clinical Pediatrics, New York Medical College, NY (1987-present); Residency, Westchester Medical Center, NY, (1985-1987); Pediatric Oncology Hematology Fellowship, Mount Sinai Hospital, NY (1985-1987); Chief Resident, Pediatrics, Westchester Medical Center, NY (1984-1985); Nephrology Researcher, New Jersey College of Medicine & Dentistry (1981-1982); Assistant Professor, Ondokuz Mayis University (1978-1981) **CIV:** Volunteer, Lecturer **AW:** Teaching Award for Pediatric Residence, Excellence in Teaching (1997); Honorary Guest & Merit Award, Children's Cancer Research Fund (1994); Four-Time Recipient, Patients Choice Award; Castle Connolly Award; Westchester Top Doctors Award **MEM:** American Society of Pediatric Hematology Oncology; Pediatric Cancer Foundation; Histiocytosis Association; Thrombosis & Hemostasis Society **B/I:** Dr. Levendoglu-Tugal became involved in her profession because has always loved medicine in all areas. However she decided to focus on pediatrics and hematology.

LEVIN, ANDREW, "ANDY" SAUL, T: U.S. Representative from Michigan **I:** Government Administration/Government Relations/Government Services **CN:** U.S. House of Representatives **DOB:** 08/10/1960 **PB:** Berkley **SC:** MI/USA **PT:** Sander Levin; Vicki Schlafer **MS:** Married **SPN:** Mary (Freeman) Levin **CH:** Four Children **ED:** Doctor of Jurisprudence, Harvard Law School; Master of Arts, University of Michigan; Bachelor of Arts, Williams College **C:** Member, U.S. House of Representatives from Michigan's Ninth Congressional District (2019-Present); Chief Workplace Officer, Michigan Department of Energy, Labor and Economic Growth (2009-Present); Deputy Director, Michigan Department of Energy, Labor and Economic Growth (2007-Present); Acting Director, Michigan Department of Energy, Labor and Economic Growth (2010-2011) **PA:** Democrat

LEVIN, MICHAEL, "MIKE" TED, T: U.S. Representative from California **I:** Government Administration/Government Relations/Government Services **CN:** U.S. House of Representatives **DOB:** 10/20/1978 **PB:** Inglewood **SC:** CA/USA **MS:** Married **SPN:** Chrissy Levin **CH:** Two Children **ED:** Doctor of Jurisprudence, Duke University School of Law; Bachelor of Arts, Stanford University **C:** Member, U.S. House of Representatives from California's 49th Congressional District (2019-Present); Director, Government Affairs, FuelCell Energy Inc. (2014-2017); Vice President, Better Energy Systems; Co-founder, Sustain SoCal **CR:** Board of Directors, Center for Sustainable Energy **CIV:** Executive Director, Democratic Party of Orange County; Member, National Finance Committee, Hillary Clinton's 2016 Presidential Campaign **AW:** Listee, 40 Under 40, OC Metro Magazine **PA:** Democrat

LEVINE, ADAM NOAH, T: Singer, Musician **I:** Media & Entertainment **DOB:** 03/18/1979 **PB:** Los Angeles **SC:** CA/USA **PT:** Fredric Levine; Patsy (Noah) Levine **MS:** Married **SPN:** Behati Prinsloo (07/19/2014) **CH:** Dusty Rose; Gio Grace **ED:** Coursework, Five Towns College, Dix Hills, NY **C:** Co-founder, 222 Records (2012-Present); Singer, Musician, Maroon 5 (2002-Present); Signed to Octone Records (2001-Present); Signed to Reprise Records (1997-1999); Singer, Kara's Flowers (1994-2002) **CW:** Vocal Coach, Judge, "The Voice" (2011-2019); Actor, "Fun Mom Dinner" (2017); Singer, Musician with Maroon 5, "Red Pill Blues" (2017); Actor, "The Clapper" (2017); Actor, "Popstar: Never Stop Never Stopping" (2016); Actor, "Pitch Perfect 2" (2015); Actor, "Unity" (2015); Actor, "Klown Forever" (2015); Singer, Musician with Maroon 5, "V" (2014); Actor, "Begin Again" (2013); Singer, Musician with Maroon 5, "Overexposed" (2012); Singer, Musician with Maroon 5, "Hands All Over" (2010); Singer, Musician with Maroon 5, "It Won't Be Soon Before Long" (2007); Singer, Musician with Maroon 5, "Makes Me Wonder" (2007); Singer, Musician with Maroon 5, "This Love" (2004); Singer, Musician with Maroon 5, "Songs About Jane" (2002); Singer, with Kara's Flowers, "The Fourth World" (1997); Singer, Musician, Various Songs; Appearances, Television Shows and Film **AW:** Star, Hollywood Walk of Fame (2017); Award for Favorite Group, People's Choice Awards (2015); Named, Sexiest Man Alive, People Magazine (2013); Award for Top Hot 100 Artist, Billboard Music Awards (2013); Award for Favorite Adult Contemporary Artist, American Music Awards (2013); Award for Favorite Band, People's Choice Awards (2012, 2013); Award for Favorite Pop/Rock Band, Duo or Group, American Music Awards (2011, 2012); Grammy Award for Best Pop Performance by a Duo or Group with Vocals, The Recording Academy (2006, 2008); Grammy Award for Best New Artist, The Recording Academy (2005); Award for Best New Artist, MTV Video Music Awards (2004); Award for Best New Group, World Music Awards (2004)

LEVINE, ALAN HILLEL, T: Chief Executive Officer **I:** Business Management/Business Services **CN:** Powerhouse **DOB:** 03/03/1937 **PB:** Jersey City **SC:** NJ/USA **PT:** Robert Harry Levine; Bertha (Allen) Levine **MS:** Married **SPN:** Priscilla Reinhart (09/24/1961) **CH:** Victoria Anne; Jason Harris **ED:** MS, Columbia University Graduate School Business Administration (1959); BS, Rutgers, The State University of New Jersey (1958) **C:** Chief Executive Officer, PowerHouse, (Formerly Team Levine LLC DBA PowerHouse) (2012-Present); Senior Vice President, Morgan Stanley (1996-2012); Vice President, Smith Barney, Bethesda, MD (1986-1996); Financial Consultant, Merrill Lynch, Washington D.C. (1983-1986); Executive Vice President, Energy Futures Group, Bethesda, MD (1981-1983); Senior Analyst, Resource Planning Associate, Washington D.C. (1979-1981); Vice President, Energy Decisions, Incorporated, Washington D.C. (1976-1979); Senior Analyst, Petroleum Industry Research Foundation, New York, NY (1976); Senior Analyst, W.J. Levy Consultant Corporation, New York, NY (1969-1976); Manager, Economics, Johnson & Johnson, New Brunswick, NJ (1964-1969) **CIV:** Chairman Traffic & Transportation Commission, Rockville, MD (1991-2014) **MIL:** Lieutenant, U.S. Naval Reserve (1959-1964) **CW:** Contributor, Articles, Professional Journals **AW:** Mark Lively Award, National Capital Area Chapter, U.S. Association for Energy Economics (2019); Award, International Association of Energy Economists **MEM:** Chapter President, International Association Energy Economics (1980); Founder, International Association Energy Economics (1978) **MH:** Albert Nelson Marquis Lifetime Achievement Award; Marquis Who's Who Top Professional **B/I:** Mr. Levine went into his profession by way of fate and good luck. He was working for Johnson and Johnson and an opportunity to work in petroleum arose; he took the job.

LEVITT, STEPHAN HILLYER, T: Anthropologist, Indologist **I:** Research **DOB:** 02/09/1943 **PB:** Brooklyn **SC:** NY/USA **PT:** Abraham Levitt; Ida (Harlick) Levitt **MS:** Single **ED:** PhD in Oriental Studies, University of Pennsylvania (1973); BA in Anthropology, Columbia University (1964) **C:** Consultant, Penn Libraries, University of Pennsylvania (1978-Present); Consultant, The Burke Library, Union Theological Seminary (1989, 1999); Dropsie College for Hebrew and Cognate Learning (1981-1982, 1987-1989); Tutor, English Department, Queensborough Community College (1977-1978); Visiting Assistant Professor of Anthropology, University of Denver (1974-1976); Research Assistant, University of Pennsylvania (1972-1974); Cataloguer, Indic MSS, Penn Libraries, University of Pennsylvania (1971-1972); Consultant, Herbert D. Katz Center for Advanced Judaic Studies, University of Pennsylvania **CW:** Author, "The Patityagramanirnaya, A Puranic History of Some Brahman Communities: Includes Introduction, the Text of Patityagramanirnaya, Sahyadrikhanda, Skandapurana, Translation and Critical Apparatus" (2017); Author, "Verri Verkai, or The Hand with a Victorious Spear: A Popular Book of Maxims Attributed to the 16th Century South Indian King Ativirarama Pantiyan" (2015); Author, "Explanations of Misfortune in the Buddha's Life: The Buddha's Misdeeds in His Former Human Lives and Their Remnants" (2010); Author, "Stories of the Enlightenment Being, Jatakas 101-150, Jatakas 151-200, Jatakas 201-250" (2007-2011); Co-Author, "A Descriptive Catalog of the Indian Manuscripts in the Library of the University of Pennsylvania" (1977); Contributor, Numerous Articles, Professional Journals **AW:** Faculty Research Grant, University of Denver (1975); Travel Study Award, American Institute of Indian Studies (1974); Fellowship, American Council of Learned Societies (1967) **MEM:** American Oriental Society; The Bhandarkar Oriental Research Institute; Dravidian Linguistics Association **MH:** Albert Nelson Marquis Lifetime Achievement Award **AV:** Stamp collecting **RE:** Jewish

LEVKOVA-LAMM, INNESSA, T: Art Critic, Writer, Curator **I:** Fine Art **DOB:** 08/21/1939 **PB:** Moscow **SC:** Russia **PT:** Efim Levkov; Irine Nikitina **MS:** Widowed **SPN:** Leonid Lamm (01/09/1969) **CH:** Olga **ED:** Postgraduate Studies, The Maurice Thorez Institute of Foreign Languages, Moscow State Linguistic University (1966-1968); Degree in Film Engineering, Leningrad Institute of Motion Picture Engineers (1965) **CT:** Diploma **C:** Freelance Writer, Art Critic, Associated Press, New York, NY (1992-Present); Freelance Writer, Art Critic, Panorama City, Los Angeles, CA (1984-Present); President, Imago Fine Art & Design Inc. (1999-2014); Freelance Writer, Art Critic, Novoe Russkoe Slovo, New York, NY (1983-1995); Chief Curator, Eduard Nakhamkin Fine Arts, New York, NY (1989-1991); Freelance Writer, Art Critic, Contemporania International, Flash Art, New York and Milan (1988-1990); Freelance Writer, Art Critic, Voice of America, Liberty Radio, New York, NY (1983-1990); Freelance Writer, Art Critic, Lit. Rev., Moscow, Russia (1967-1982); Freelance Writer, Art Critic, Books' World, Literary Russia, Moscow, Russia (1977-1981) **CR:** Independent Curator, Berman Gallery, New York, NY (1991); Independent Curator, The Artis House, Moscow, Russia (1990); Independent Curator, The Russian State Museum, Leningrad, Russia (1990); Independent Curator, Baruch College Mishkin Gallery, New York, NY (1987) **CW:** Author, "Moscow Conceptualism in Context" (2011); Author, "Face of Square: Mystery of Kazimir Malevich" (2004); Author, "Kulturim Stalinism" (1994); Author, "Back to Square One" (1991); Co-Author, "Transit: Russian Art Between East and West" (1989) **MEM:** National Writers Union; International Association of Art Critics (Association Internationale des Critiques d'Art, AICA) **MH:** Albert Nelson Marquis Lifetime Achievement Award **B/I:** Ms. Levkova-Lamm became involved in her profession because she was participating in the creation of a Russian video writer when she was a student. They asked her to get her license for the production but when she realized it was not possible, she decided to not move forward. At the same time, she got married to her husband, who was a great artist, but she already had a background from the jobs she did. She was interested in providing the integration between art and science, which she did. **AV:** Traveling

LEWIN, SHARYN, T: Director of Gynecologic Oncology **I:** Medicine & Health Care **CN:** Holy Name Medical Center **CH:** One Child **ED:** Resident, Obstetrics & Gynecology Residency Program, Washington University, St. Louis, MO (2005); MD in Medicine, University of Kansas School of Medicine, Lawrence, KS (2001); BA in Biochemistry, University of Kansas, Lawrence, KS (1997) **CT:** Board-Certified Gynecologic Oncologist **C:** Assistant Clinical Professor, Icahn School of Medicine at Mount Sinai, New York, NY (2015-Present); Medical Director, Gynecologic Oncology Division, Holy Name Medical Center, New Jersey (2014-Present); President, Executive Director, Founder, The Lewin Fund to Fight Women's Cancers (2013-Present); Fellowship, Gynecologic Oncology, Memorial Sloan Kettering Cancer Center, New York, NY (2009); Assistant Clinical Professor, Member, Division of Gynecologic Oncology, Department of Obstetrics and Gynecology, Columbia University Medical Cancer, New York-Presbyterian Hospital **CW:** Author, Co-Author, More Than 100 Articles, Abstracts, Book Chapters, Presentations, and Scholarly Conferences **AW:** President's Award, Society of Gynecologic Oncology; Physician of the Year Award, New York-Presbyterian; PGO Excellence in Teaching Award; Merit Award; President's Award **MEM:** Society of Gynecologic Oncology; American Society of Clinical Oncology; American College of Surgeons; American College of Obstetrics and Gynecology; Alpha Omega Alpha Honor Medical Society (AOA) **MH:** Marquis Who's Who Top Professional; Marquis Who's Who Humanitarian Award **AS:** Dr. Lewin attributes her success to her hard work and passion for the field. She also has good mentors and a strong family base. Her life motto is to "be kind and treat others how they want to be treated." **B/I:** Dr. Lewin became involved in her profession because her grandmother, Gerda Bruno, was a gynecologist, so she followed in her footsteps. She had always been interested in women's health care and has wanted to be a physician since the third grade. She has not looked back and has a real passion for what she does. **THT:** Dr. Lewin noted, "Body surface area predicts plasma oxaliplatin and pharmacokinetic advantage in hyperthermic intraoperative intraperitoneal chemotherapy; Quantitative X-ray computed tomography peritoneography in malignant peritoneal mesothelioma patients receiving intraperitoneal chemotherapy; Comparative performance of the 2009 International Federation of Gynecology and Obstetrics' staging system for uterine corpus cancer; Comparative performances of the 2009 FIGO staging system for uterine corpus cancer Resource utilization for ovarian cancer patients at the end of life: How much is too much?"

LEWIS, BILLIE JEAN, T: Retired Library Director **I:** Library Management/Library Services **PB:** Eden **SC:** NC/USA **PT:** William G. Manns; Darnella Worthington; Vincent Worthington (Stepfather) **MS:** Married **SPN:** Jerome M. Lewis (08/06/1966) **CH:** Jerome Vincent; Jill Renee; Kristina Lewis Dickerson (Grandchild); Jessica Ortman (Grandchild); Victoria Lewis (Grandchild); Justyn Lewis (Grandchild); Jaylen Lewis Douglas (Grandchild); Jenna Lewis (Grandchild); Michael Wronikowski (Grandchild); Timbre Dickerson (Great-grandchild); Treble Dickerson (Great-grandchild); Tenor Dickerson (Great-grandchild); Justyn J. Lewis (Great-grandchild) **ED:** MLS, University of Michigan, Ann Arbor, MI (1988); BA, Florida A&M University, Tallahassee, FL, Summa Cum Laude (1987); AAS, Corning Community College, New York (1983); Certificate of Industrial and Labor Relations, Cornell University **CT:** Certified Professional Librarian, State of Kentucky (2000); Certified Professional Librarian, Commonwealth of Virginia (1999); Librarians Professional Certificate, Library of Michigan **C:** Library Director, Robert L.F. Sikes Public Library, Crestview, FL (2003-2015); Library Manager, Technical Services Librarian, Eglin Air Force Base Library, Eglin Air Force Base, Florida (2002-2003); Manager, H.C. Downing Branch Library, Norfolk Public Library, Norfolk Virginia (1999-2000); Assistant Branch Manager, Adult Reference Library, Shawnee Branch Library, Louisville Free Public Library. Louisville, KY (1995-1998); Assistant Branch Manager, Children's Library, Bowen Branch, Detroit Public Library, Detroit, MI (1993-1995); Children's Library, Detroit Public Library, Detroit, MI (1989-1990) **CIV:** Active, Velma K. Conyers #7 Order of the Eastern Star P.H.A., Crestview, FL (2004-Present); Volunteer, Childrens Reading Program, Mt. Zion Methodist AME Episcopal Church **AW:** Listed, Whos Who Among Black Americans; Whos Who in America **MEM:** BCALA (Black Caucus of the American Library Association); American Library Association; Velma Conyers #7 Order of the Eastern Stars; Florida A&M University National Alumni Association; MUMSI Alumni Association **MH:** Albert Nelson Marquis Lifetime Achievement Award **AS:** Ms. Lewis understood the need for young African American children to see people that looked like them in leadership positions. She wanted to become a role model for children of color and in the library is where she saw young children come in from daycare and school settings and they were able to see her. **B/I:** Ms. Lewis became involved in her profession because as a child, her go to place was always the library. She lived in a small African American community and her fondest memories were of the time she spent reading at home or at the Library, which was entertaining and educational. Later on in life, she pursued a degree in Business Administration but thought that was not what she wanted to do, so she enrolled in a Library Science program and received a MIS degree in Library and Information Science. **AV:** Reading; Travel; Exercise; Crafting **PA:** Democratic **RE:** Methodist

LEWIS, CARL, T: Track and Field Athlete (Retired), Assistant Coach **I:** Athletics **CN:** University of Houston **DOB:** 07/01/1961 **PB:** Birmingham **SC:** AL/USA **PT:** William McKinley Lewis Jr.; Evelyn (Lawler) Lewis **ED:** Coursework, University of Houston **C:** Assistant Track Coach, University of Houston (2018-Present); Member, U.S. Men's Track and Field Team, Summer Olympics (1980, 1984, 1988, 1992, 1996) **CR:** Owner, Marketing and Branding Company, C.L.E.G. **CIV:** Founder, Carl Lewis Foundation **CW:** Musician, "Break it Up" (1986); Appearances, Television Shows and Films Including "Perfect Stranger," "Speed Zone," "Alien Hunter," "Material Girls" and "The Weakest Link" **AW:** Inductee, Texas Track and Field Coaches Association Hall of Fame (2016); Inductee, New Jersey Hall of Fame (2010); Olympian of the Century, Sports Illustrated (2000); 1980's World Athlete of the Decade, Track & Field News (2000); Gold Medal, Long Jump, Summer Olympics, Atlanta, GA (1996); Bronze Medal, 200 Meter, World Championships, Stuttgart, Germany (1993); Gold Medal, Long Jump, 4X100 Meter Relay, Summer Olympics, Barcelona, Spain (1992); U.S. Athlete of the Year (1981-1984, 1987, 1988, 1991); Gold Medal, 100 Meter, 4X100 Meter Relay, World Championships, Tokyo, Japan (1991); Silver Medal, Long Jump, World Championships, Tokyo, Japan (1991); Gold Medal, 100 Meter, Long Jump, Summer Olympics, Seoul, South Korea (1988); Silver Medal, 200 Meter, Summer Olympics, Seoul, South Korea (1988); Gold Medal, Long Jump, Pan American Games, Indianapolis, IN (1987); Gold Medal, 100 Meter, Long Jump, 4X100 Meter Relay, World Championships, Rome, Italy (1987); Inductee, U.S. Olympic Hall of Fame (1985); Male Athlete of the Year, The Associated Press (1983, 1984); Athlete of the Year, United Press International (1983, 1984); Gold Medal, 100 Meter, 200 Meter, Long Jump, 4X100 Meter Relay, Summer Olympics, Los Angeles, CA (1984); Gold Medal, 100 Meter, Long Jump, 4X100 Meter Relay, World Championships, Helsinki, Finland (1983); Athlete of the Year, Track & Field News (1982-1984); Jesse Owens Award (1982); James E. Sullivan Award for Best Amateur Athlete (1981)

LEWIS, PERRY, T: Investment Banker **I:** Financial Services **DOB:** 02/11/1938 **PB:** San Antonio **SC:** TX/USA **PT:** Perry Joshua Lewis; Zelime L. Lewis **MS:** Divorced **CH:** Perry Joshua, IV; Memrie Fraser Kelly **ED:** BA, Princeton University, Princeton, NJ (1959); Phillips Academy, Andover, MA (1955) **C:** Senior Managing Director, Heartland Industrial Partners, Greenwich, CT (2006-2010); Senior Managing Director, Heartland Industrial Partners, Greenwich, CT (2000-2001); Partner, Morgan Lewis Githens & Ahn, Connecticut (1982-2004); President, MacKay-Lewis Inc., New York, NY (1980-1981); Senior Vice President, Manager, Division of Corporation Finance, Smith Barney, Harris Upham & Co. Inc., New York, NY (1967-1979); Commercial Project Manager, Parsons & Whittemore, Inc., New York, NY (1964-1967); Registered Rep.,

Lee Higginson Corporation, New York, NY (1960-1963) **CR:** Director, Clear Channel Communications Inc. (2000-2008); Director, Superior Essex Inc. (2000-2008); Chairman, Haynes International Corporation (1989-1997); Chairman, Ecusta Corporation (1985-1989); Director, Tyler Corporation (1980-1994); Director, Aon Corp. (1972-2003) **CIV:** Member, Board, New York City Center; Chairman, Board, Academy Festival Theatre Company, Lake Forest, IL; Member, Board, Chicago Ballet, Chicago, IL; Member, Board, The Joyce Theater, New York, NY; Chairman, Board, The Performing Arts Center at SUNY Purchase, New York; Member, Board, The Aldrich Contemporary Art Museum, Ridgefield, CT **MIL:** U.S. Army (1961-1962, 1959-1960) **MEM:** Knickerbocker of New York **MH:** Albert Nelson Marquis Lifetime Achievement Award

LEWITT, MILES, T: Engineer, Patented Inventor & Vice President **I:** Engineering **DOB:** 07/14/1952 **PB:** New York **SC:** NY/USA **PT:** George Herman Lewitt; Barbara (Lin) Lewitt **MS:** Married **SPN:** Susan Beth Orenstein (06/24/1973) **CH:** Melissa; Hannah **ED:** MS, Arizona State University (1976); BS, City College of New York Engineering, Summa Cum Laude (1973) **C:** Vice President, Technology Group, Intuit, Inc., Mountain View (2010-2013); Vice President, Technology Group, Intuit, Inc., San Diego (2001-2010); Vice President, Tax Engineering, Intuit Inc., San Diego (2003-2004); General Manager, Dealer Solutions, Automatic Data Processing, Inc., Houston, TX (1999-2001); Vice President, Research and Development, Automatic Data Processing, Portland, OR (1991-1999); Vice President, Engineering, Cadre Technologies, Inc., Beaverton, OR (1989-1991); Engineering Manager, Intel, Hillsboro, OR (1978-1989); Corporate Strategic Staff, Intel, Hillsboro, OR (1981-1982); Engineering Manager, Intel, Israel (1980-1981); Architect, iRMX Line Operating Systems and the x86 Line Microprocessors, Intel, Santa Clara, CA (1978); Software Engineer, Honeywell, Phoenix, AZ, Los Angeles, CA (1973-1978) **CR:** Instructor, Maricopa Technical College (Now GateWay Community College), Phoenix, AZ (1974-1975); Speaker, Professional Conferences, Published in Professional Magazines **CIV:** Executive Committee, American Electronics Association (1995-1999); Customer Advisory Board for Initiate (1991-1999); Board of Directors, Portland Computer Training Institute (1995-1998); Oregon Graduate Institute; Technical Advisory Board, Data Initiative Systems Center; Customer Advisory Board, Digital Equipment Corporation **CW:** Inventor, Patent, Virtual Environment for Data-Described Applications (2014) **AW:** Career Achievement Award, City College of New York (2013); Product of the Year Award, Electronic Products Magazine (1980); Advanced Engineering Program Award, Honeywell (1976); Engineering Alumni Award, City College of New York (1973); Eliza Ford Prize, City College of New York (1973); Presidents Award of Excellence, Automatic Data Processing, Inc.; Excellence in Leadership Award, Chief Executive Officer, Intuit **MEM:** Senior Member, IEEE; Voting Member, IEEE Computer Society; Voting Member, Association of Computing Machinery; Voting Member, American Electronics Association; Senior Member, American Society for Quality **MH:** Albert Nelson Marquis Lifetime Achievement Award; Marquis Who's Who Top Professional **B/I:** Mr. Lewitt became involved in his profession because he was fortunate that he was able to take a class in computing at his high school. While still in high school, he participated in National Science Foundation computing classes at New York University and at the Grove School of Engineering at the City College of New York. When the computing teacher at his high school had to leave, he taught the computing class while training

a teacher so that the class could continue after his High School graduation. He fell in love with computing and he knew he had to pursue it. Additionally, Mr. Lewitt was mentored by several exceptional leaders, including Andy Grove, Gary Butler, and Steve Bennett. **AV:** Photography; International travel; Walking **PA:** Democrat **RE:** Jewish **THT:** Throughout his career, Mr. Lewitt has emphasized the importance of defect-free software, speaking on the subject in presentations titled "Passion for Excellence." He fought back against the popular perception that building high quality software was very expensive and was a vocal proponent that software could be engineered with exceptional levels of quality. Celebrated for his expertise, on this and other topics, Mr. Lewitt has spoken at professional conferences and published in technical magazines. Mr. Lewitt and Watts Humphrey were both keynote presenters at a conference in 2005 sponsored by the Software Engineering Institute of Carnegie Mellon University. Other conference presentations include the Workshop on Performance and Reliability and STAREAST, a software testing and quality assurance conference. Mr. Lewitt met Bill Gates multiple times; one topic of discussion was the advantages and disadvantages of a segmented memory architecture.

L'HEUREUX, RICHARD JOSEPH, T: Volunteer Advocate **I:** Nonprofit & Philanthropy **CN:** Senior Companion Program **DOB:** 04/05/1932 **PB:** Manchester **SC:** NH/USA **PT:** Arthur L'Heureux; Lilian Daigle L'Heureux **MS:** Single **ED:** Coursework, North Hollywood College **CT:** Certification in CPR and First Aid, State of New Hampshire; Community Emergency Response Team (CERT); Certification, Visiting Nurse Association; Certification, Hospice Senior Companion Program of New Hampshire **C:** Lifetime Sales Specialist (1987-1994) **CR:** Owner, Extra Special Memories Creations **CIV:** Visiting Hospice Patient Program, Visiting Nurse Association of Manchester & Southern New Hampshire, Elliot Hospital (2000-Present); Volunteer, Recreation Department, Hillsborough County Nursing Home (HCNH), Goffstown, NH (1987-Present); Volunteer (1987-Present); Volunteer, Down Syndrome and Mental Clients, Local Group Home; Volunteer, The Moore Center; Volunteer, Elliot Hospital; Volunteer, Community Emergency Respond Team (CERT); Volunteer, Bi-Weekly Senior Dinners, Senior Companion Program, Saint Anthony's Church; Court Appointed Special Advocate for Abused Children; Neighborhood Watch; Retired Senior Volunteer Program; Confraternity of Christian Doctrine, St. Theresa **MIL:** United States Marine Corps (1952) **CW:** Author, "Home Sweet Home Poem"; Author, "Lovingly Peace Poem"; Author, "Romancing Moon, Ladders of Bravery"; Creator, Bi-monthly Newsletter, Hillsborough County Nursing Home (HCNH) **AW:** Spirit of New Hampshire Award; CYO Man of the Year **MEM:** The American Legion; International Society of Poets; Global Directory of Who's Who; Children's Lobby, Remington, NY; Founder, Mens Club, Hillsborough County Nursing Home (HCNH) **MH:** Albert Nelson Marquis Lifetime Achievement Award **B/I:** Mr. L'Heureux became involved in his profession because his community needed someone to make a difference by helping the less fortunate. **AV:** Writing poetry; Bowling; Golfing; Reading **RE:** Catholic

LI, SHINHWA, PHD, ME, MS, T: Product Manager **I:** Engineering **CN:** Kurt. J. Lesker Company **DOB:** 04/08/1958 **PB:** Taipei **SC:** Taiwan/ROC **PT:** WeiWen Li; Yuan Li **MS:** Married **SPN:** Yina Gan (07/10/1983) **CH:** Crystal; Jason **ED:** PhD in Materials Science, University of Utah (1990); ME in Materials Science, University of Utah (1988); MS in Chemical Engineering, University of South-

west Louisiana (1985); BS in Chemical Engineering, National Central University, Taiwan (1980) **C:** Product Manager, Kurt. J. Lesker Company, Jefferson Hill, PA (2013-Present); Program/Product Manager, Heraeus, Chandler, AZ (2005-2013); Continuous Improvement Manager, Novellus, Chandler, AZ (2002-2004); Process Support Engineer, Applied Materials (1999-2002); Applications Engineer, EKC Technology, Hayward, CA (1999); Process Engineer, STMicroelectronics, Phoenix, AZ (1994-1998); Research Associate, University of Michigan (1991-1994); Research Assistant, University of Utah (1985-1991); Research Assistant, University of Southwest Louisiana, Lafayette, LA (1983-1985); Quality Control Engineer, Ko-Shen Enterprises, Ltd., Taipei, Taiwan (1982-1983) **CR:** Instructor, ITT Technical Institute, Tempe, AZ (2004); Chair, Phoenix Chapter, Chinese American Semiconductor Professional Association (2000-2002); Instructor, Gateway Community College, Phoenix, AZ (1999) **CIV:** President/Deacon, Chinese School, Greater Phoenix Chinese Christian Church (2005-2007) **MIL:** Liaison Officer, Marine Corps, Taiwan, Republic of China (1980-1982) **CW:** Author, "Chemical Mechanical Polishing in Silicon Processing" (2000); Patentee, 13 Patents in Field; Author, 56 Technical Papers **AW:** CMP Productivity Appreciation, Applied Materials (2001); Technical Excellence, STMicroelectronics (1997); Best Student Paper, Electronic Materials Conference (1991) **MEM:** Institute of Electrical and Electronics Engineers (IEEE); Minerals Metals Materials Society; Chinese American Semiconductor Professional Association **MH:** Albert Nelson Marquis Lifetime Achievement Award **B/I:** Dr. Li was always interested in physics. In high school, he quickly found a natural aptitude for the field. Though he initially planned to pursue chemical engineering, he switched to semiconductor materials research, which is where he truly began to thrive. **AV:** Hiking; Playing basketball; Practicing photography **PA:** Republican **RE:** Christian

LICK, DALE WESLEY, PHD, T: Chairperson **I:** Education/Educational Services **CN:** HyLighter LLC **DOB:** 01/07/1938 **PB:** Marlette **SC:** MI/USA **PT:** John R. Lick; Florence M. (Baxter) Lick **MS:** Married **SPN:** Marilyn K. Foster (09/15/1956) **CH:** Lynette (Deceased); Kitty (Deceased); Diana; Ronald **ED:** Doctor of Philosophy in Mathematics, University of California Riverside (1965); Master of Science in Mathematics, Michigan State University, East Lansing (1959); Bachelor of Science, Michigan State University, East Lansing, with Honors (1958) **CT:** Certificate, Training; Certificate, Consulting; Certificate, Managing Organizational Change **C:** Emeritus President, Professor, Florida State University (2008-Present); Chairperson of the Board of Directors, HyLighter LLC (2006-Present); Board of Trustees, Graceland University (2016-2020); University Professor, Learning Systems Institute and Department Education Leadership, Florida State University, Tallahassee (1993-2008); President, Professor of Mathematics, Florida State University, Tallahassee (1991-1993); President, Professor of Mathematics, University of Maine, Orono (1986-1991); President, Professor of Mathematics and Computer Science, Georgia Southern College, Statesboro (1978-1986); Professor of Mathematics and Computing Sciences and Dean, School of Sciences and Health Professions, Old Dominion University, Norfolk, VA (1974-1978); Vice President, Academy Affairs, Russell Sage College, Troy, NY (1972-1974); Adjunct Associate Professor, Department of Pharmacology, Medical School, Temple University, Philadelphia, PA (1969-1972); Associate Professor, Head, Department of Mathematics, Drexel University, Philadelphia, PA (1969-1972); Associate Professor, University of Tennessee (1968-1969); Postdoctoral Fellow, Brookhaven National Laboratory, Upton, NY (1967-1968); Assistant Professor of Mathematics, University of Tennessee, Knoxville (1965-1967); Teaching Assistant, Mathematics, University of California Riverside (1964-1965); Instructor, University of Redlands (1961-1963); Assistant to Comptroller, Michigan Bell Telephone Company, Detroit (1961); Instructor, Chairperson, Department of Mathematics, Port Huron Junior College (1959-1960); Teaching Assistant, Mathematics, Michigan State University (1959); Research Assistant, Physics, Michigan State University, East Lansing (1958) **CR:** Consultant, Atomic Energy Commission, Oakridge, TN (1965-1967) **CIV:** Member, High Priest, Community of Christ (1995-Present); Chairperson, Higher Education Advisory Board, Community of Christ (1986-2004); United Way of The Big Bend (1992-1998); Katalidin Council (1986-1991); Vice President, Coastal Empire Council, Boy Scouts of America (1982-1986); Planning Committee, Bulloch Memorial Hospital (1979-1986); Board of Directors, Health Care Centers of America, Virginia Beach, VA (1978); Chairperson, Board of Directors, Assembly Against Hunger and Malnutrition (1977-1978); Board of Directors, Eastern Virginia Health Systems Agency (1976-1978); Statewide Health Coordinating Council, Virginia (1976-1978); Volunteer, Salvation Army **CW:** Author, "Schools Can Change: A Step-by-Step Change Creation System for Building Innovative Schools and Increasing Learning" (2013); Co-Author, "Schoolwide Action Research for Professional Learning Communities" (2008); Co-Author, "The Whole-Faculty Study Groups Field Book: Improving Schools and Enhancing Student Learning" (2006); Author, "Whole-Faculty Study Groups: Creating Professional Learning Communities That Target Student Learning" (2005); Co-Author, "Whole-Faculty Study Groups: Creating Student-Based Professional Development" (2001); Co-Author, "New Directions in Mentoring: Creating a Culture of Synergy" (1999); Co-Author, "Whole-Faculty Study Groups: A Powerful Way to Change Schools and Enhance Learning" (1998); Author, "Fundamentals of Algebra" (1970); Contributor, Over 100 Published Research and Professional Articles in Mathematics, Leadership and Change; Contributor, 285 Newspaper Columns; Contributor, Chapters, Books **AW:** International Peace Prize, United Cultural Convention (2010); Prize Winner, United Cultural Convention (2010); Distinguished Alumni Award, Michigan State University (2006); Listee, 40 Alumni Who Make a Difference, University of California Riverside (1994) **MEM:** Chairperson, Committee on Agricultural Resources and Rural Development, American Association of State Colleges and Universities (1981-1986); Governing Council, Pi Mu Epsilon (1972-1977); American Association of University Professors; American Association for the Advancement of Science; American Mathematics Society; Mathematics Association of America; American Association of University Administrators; American Society of Allied Health Professions; American Association for Higher Education; National Staff Development Council; Sigma Xi; Phi Kappa Phi; Beta Gamma Sigma; Pi Sigma Epsilon **B/I:** Dr. Lick decided to pursue mathematics at an early age, as he enjoyed it and it came easily to him. Throughout his childhood, his mother emphasized the importance of pursuing an education. Dr. Lick's brother earned a Doctor of Philosophy in mathematics from Michigan State University, which inspired him to follow in his footsteps. This decision led to a prosperous career in teaching, research and, subsequently, administration. **AV:** Square dancing; Volunteer work; Assisting other professionals in their careers **RE:** Community of Christ

LICKONA, THOMAS, PHD, T: Director, Professor Emeritus **I:** Education/Educational Services **CN:** State University of New York at Cortland **ED:** Doctor of Philosophy in Psychology, State University of New York at Albany, Albany, NY (1970); Master of Arts in English, Ohio University, Athens, OH (1965); Bachelor of Arts in English, Siena College, Loudonville, NY (1964) **C:** Founder, Director, Center for the 4th and 5th Rs, State University of New York College at Cortland (1994-Present); Childhood and Early Childhood Education Department, State University of New York College at Cortland (1970-Present); Visiting Professor, School of Education, Boston University, Boston, MA (1978-1980); Visiting Professor, Graduate School of Education, Harvard University, Cambridge, MA (1978-1979); Psychology Department, State University of New York at Albany (1968-1970); Professor Emeritus of Education, State University of New York College at Cortland **CIV:** Board, Adoption Agency; Board Member, Newman Center; Board, Character.org **CW:** Editor, Periodical, "Excellence & Ethics" (2007-Present); Author, Book, "How to Raise Kind Kids: And Get Respect, Gratitude, and a Happier Family in the Bargain" (2018); Co-Author, Book, "Smart & Good High Schools: Integrating Excellence and Ethics for Success in School, Work, and Beyond" (2005); Author, Book, "Character Matters: How to Help Our Children Develop Good Judgment, Integrity, and Other Essential Virtues" (2004); Co-Author, Book, "Character Quotations: Activities That build Character and Community" (2004); Video, "Eleven Principles of Effective Character Education" (1998); Video, "Character Education: Restoring Respect and Responsibility in Our Schools" (1996); Co-Author, Book, "Sex, Love and You: Making the Right Decisions" (1994); Video, 4-Part Series, "Character Education Strategies" (1994); Co-Author, Book, "Character Development in Schools and Beyond" (1992); Author, Book, "Educating for Character: How Our Schools Can Teach Respect and Responsibility" (1991); Author, Book, "Raising Good Children: From Birth Through the Teenage Years" (1983); Author, Book, "Moral Development and Behavior: Theory, Research, and Social Issues" (1976) **AW:** Iowa Governor Robert D. Ray Pillar of Character Award (2010); President's Award for Funded Research, SUNY Cortland (2005); SUNY Research Foundation Award for Outstanding Research (2004); "Sandy" Award for Lifetime Achievement in Character Education, Character Education Partnership (2001); Distinguished Alumni Award, SUNY Albany (1996); Award for Outstanding Achievement in Moral Education, University of San Francisco (1994); Christopher Award for Educating for Character, The Christopher Society (1992); 1st Place Distinguished Achievement Award for Excellence in Education, American Association of Colleges for Teacher Education (1973) **AS:** Dr. Lickona attributes his success to his Christian faith. **B/I:** Dr. Lickona became involved in psychology because he wanted to contribute to a better world. In order to do that, one must understand the nature of people and their behaviors. To Mr. Lickona, psychology was the best career path to pursue. **THT:** Do your best and let God do the rest.

LIEBERMAN, DOUGLAS LIONEL, T: Instructional Designer, Screenwriter, Playwright **I:** Fine Art **DOB:** 12/14/1946 **PB:** Detroit **SC:** MI/USA **PT:** Barnard Leon Lieberman; Mary Elizabeth McKinney Lieberman **MS:** Married **SPN:** Beverly Anne Berneman Lieberman **CH:** Alexander Barnard Lieberman; Victoria Rose Lieberman **ED:** Master of Adult Education, National Louise University (2006); Master of Fine Arts, Art Institute of Chicago (1972) **CT:** Project Management Institute (2001) **C:** Thought Leader, IBM (2007-Present); Instructional Designer,

HSBC Holdings PLC (2002-2007); Associate, Hewitt Associates, Lincolnshire, IL (1998-2001); Adjunct Faculty, Loyola University, Chicago, IL (1984-1986); Adjunct Faculty, Northwestern University, Evanston, IL (1978-1986); Faculty, Cranbrook School, Bloomfield Hills, MI (1968-1970); Screen Writer, Playwright **CR:** With, Center for Advanced Learning **CIV:** Board of Directors, Illinois School District 69 Board of Education; Halevi Chorus; Sounds Good Chorus; Good Memories Chorus **CW:** Playwright, "Contemporary Children's Theatre," Avon Books; Editor, "Pre-Med: Foundation of a Medical Career," McGraw-Hill; Screenwriter, Documentaries for National Geographic Educational Films; Screenwriter, Encyclopaedia Britannica, PBS **AW:** Best in Talent Development, Associate for Talent Development; Excellence in Practice, Associate for Talent Development; Best Unique or Innovative Learning and Development Program, Brandon Hall; Best Use of Video for Learning, Brandon Hall; Editor's Choice Award for Learning Strategy, Magazine; Emmy Award for Outstanding Achievement for Documentary of Cultural Significance as a Screenwriter; Gold Hugo, Chicago International Film Festival as a Screenwriter; International Gold CINDY, International Gold Quill **MEM:** Dramatists Guild of America **MH:** Albert Nelson Marquis Lifetime Achievement Award; Marquis Who's Who Top Professional **B/I:** Mr. Lieberman became involved in his profession due to his passion for working in theater, particularly regarding document film writing and adult education. He came to appreciate the educational and cultural content of his work. **AV:** Choral composer; Playwright

LIEBMANN, GEORGE, T: Lawyer **I:** Law and Legal Services **DOB:** 06/20/1939 **PB:** New York **SC:** NY/USA **PT:** William Liebmann; Margaret (Hirschman) Cook Liebmann **MS:** Married **SPN:** Anne-Lise Grimstad (4/29/1967) **CH:** Pamela; George; Franklin **ED:** JD, University of Chicago (1963); AB, Dartmouth College (1960) **C:** Principal, George W. Liebmann, P.A., Baltimore, MD (1980-Present); Executive Assistant, Governor of Maryland, Annapolis, MD (1979-1980); Assistant Attorney General, State of Maryland, Baltimore, MD (1967-1969); Frank, Bernstein, Conaway and Goldman, Baltimore, MD (1964-1979); Law Clerk to Chief Judge, Court of Appeals of Maryland (1963-1964); Chaucer, Head Book Shop, Inc., New York, NY (1958-1959) **CR:** Panelist, United States Bankruptcy Trustee (1980-Present); Visiting Fellow, Wolfson College, Cambridge (1998-present); General Counsel, Maryland Economic Development Corporation (1985-2011); Visiting Fellow, University of Salford, England (1996); Lecturer, Johns Hopkins University (1991-1992); Chairman, Governor's Commission of Health Care Providers' Professional Liability Insurance (1983-1984); Governor's Task Force, Local Government Antitrust Liability (1982-1983); Alternate Member, State Planning Council on Radioactive Waste Management (1980-1982); Governor's Commission to Revise Annotated Code, Maryland (1974-1983); Lecturer, University of Maryland Law School (1977-1978) **CIV:** Executive Director, Calvert Institute of Policy Research (2001-Present); Republican Primary Candidate, U.S. Senate (1998); Trustee, Historic Annapolis Foundation (1991-1999); Secretary, Coalition Against the SST (1969) **MIL:** U.S. Army (1965); U.S. Naval Reserve-JAG (Inactive) (1966-1969) **CW:** Author, "Maryland Civil Practice Forms, Fourth Edition" (2019); Author, "America's Political Inventors: The Lost Art of Legislation" (2018); Author, "The Fall of the House of Speyer" (2015); Author, "The Last American Diplomat: John D Negroponte and the Changing Face of US Diplomacy" (2012); Editor, "Prohibition in Maryland: A Collection of Documents" (2011); Author, "Diplomacy Between the Wars: Five Diplomats and the Shaping of the Modern World" (2008); Editor, "The Trimmer's Almanac: Ten Years of the Calvert Institute" (1996-2007); Author, "The Common Law Tradition: A Collective Portrait of Five Legal Scholars" (2005); Reprint, "Neighborhood Futures" (2004); Author, "Six Lost Leaders: Prophets of Civil Society" (2001); Author, "Solving Problems Without Large Government" (1999); Author, "The Gallows in the Grove: Civil Society in American Law" (1997); Author, "The Little Platoons: Sub-Local Governments in Modern History" (1995); Author, "Maryland Civil Practice Forms, Two Volumes" (1984); Author, "Maryland District Court Law and Practice, Two Volumes" (1976); Managing Editor, "University of Chicago Law Review" (1962-1963) **AW:** Simon Industrial and Professional Fellow, University of Manchester, England (1993-1994) **MEM:** President, Baltimore Bar Library (2006-Present, 1975-1977); Board of Directors, Baltimore Bar Library (1967-Present); Life Member, American Law Institute; Permanent Member, Federal Judicial Conference of the Fourth Circuit; Associate, Engineering Society of Maryland; 14 West Hamilton Street Club **BAR:** Maryland (1964); Illinois (1964) **MH:** Albert Nelson Marquis Lifetime Achievement Award **AV:** Reading; Writing; Walking **PA:** Republican **RE:** Episcopalian

LIEN, ERIC JUNGCHI, PHD, T: Professor Emeritus, Pharmacy **I:** Biotechnology **CN:** University of Southern California **DOB:** 11/30/1937 **PB:** Kaohsiung **SC:** Taiwan **MS:** Married **SPN:** Linda L. Chen (10/02/1965) **CH:** Raymond; Andrew **ED:** Postdoctoral Fellow in Bio-Organic Chemistry, Pomona College, Claremont, CA (1967-1968); PhD in Pharmaceutical Chemistry, University of California San Francisco (1966); BS in Pharmacy, National Taiwan University (1960) **C:** Professor Emeritus, School of Pharmacy, University of Southern California (2003-Present); Retired, Professor, University of Southern California (1976-2003); Coordinator of Section on Biomedicinal Chemistry, University of Southern California (1975-1984); Coordinator of Sections Biomedicinal Chemistry and Pharmacies, University of Southern California (1975-1978); Associate Professor, University of Southern California (1972-1976); Assistant Professor of Pharmaceutics and Biomedicinal Chemistry, University of Southern California, Los Angeles, CA (1968-1972); Hospital Pharmacist, 862 Hospital, Republic of China (1960-1961); Pharmacist, Teaching Assistant, National Taiwan University **CR:** Consultant, National Institutes of Health (2003); Consultant, Arizona Disease Control Research Commission (1986-2003); Consultant, National Institutes of Health (1994); Executive, Yuan, China, Department of Health, Taipei, Taiwan (1992-1994); Consultant, National Institutes of Health (1992); Consultant, EPA (1989); Consultant, EPA (1985); Consultant, National Institutes of Health (1982-1987); Consultant, International Medication Systems, Ltd. (1978); Consultant, Institute Drug Design, Inc., California (1971-1973); Consultant, Allergan Pharmacy, Inc. (1971-1972); Consultant, National Institutes of Health (1971); Referee, Journal on Pharmacokinetics and Biopharmaceutics; Referee, Journal on Medicinal Chemistry; Referee, Journal on Food Agriculture Chemistry; Referee, Journal on Pharmaceutical Science; Referee, Pesticide Biochemistry and Physiology; Referee, Chemical Review; Referee, Journal on Organic Chemistry; Referee, Pharmaceutical Research; Referee, Journal of Drug Targeting; Referee, International Journal of Oriental Medicine; Referee, American Journal on Pharmaceutical Education; Referee, Journal on Inorganic Medical Chemistry; Science Advisor of National Laboratories, Department of Health, Foods and Drugs **CIV:** Deed Holder, Culver City Senior Center **MIL:** Army Hospital 862, Taiwan

(1960-1961) **CW:** Editorial Board, Chinese Pharmaceutical Journal (2001-Present); Editorial Board, Acta Pharmaceutica (1992-Present); Editorial Board, International Journal on Oriental Medicine, Medical Chemical Research (1991-Present); Editorial Board, Journal on Clinical Pharmacy and Therapeutics (1979-2003); Author, "Modern Chemical and Medical Interpretations of Ancient Yin-Yang Theory" (1995); Editorial Board, Chinese Pharmaceutical Journal (1991-1993); Contributor, 235 Publications, Professional Journals; Author, Four Books; "Lien's Eight Rules in Ancient Chinese Medicine" (1991) **AW:** Grantee, H&L Foundation (1989-2006); Grantee, IMS (1979); Grantee, National Science Foundation (1976-1977); Grantee, National Science Foundation (1972-1974); Grantee, Abbott Laboratories (1971-1972); Grantee, Merck Foundation (1970); Frank Shu China Science Scholarship, National Taiwan University (1960) **MEM:** Fellow, AAPS; American Association for the Advancement of Science; Louis Pasteur Foundation; American Association for Cancer Research; Academy of Pharmaceutical Sciences; American Chemical Society; American Association of Pharmaceutical Scientists; International Union of Pure and Applied Chemistry; Sigma Xi; Rho Chi; Phi Kappa Phi; NA Chinese Writers Association of Southern California; Honorary Member, P.R. China; Honorary Professor, Shandong Academy of Medical Sciences **MH:** Albert Nelson Marquis Lifetime Achievement Award **AS:** Dr. Lien has a keen interest in chemistry, mathematics, and biological science, all to which he attributes his success. **B/I:** Dr. Lien was always interested in mathematics, biological science and chemistry, and for that reason, he chose to pursue a PhD in pharmaceutical chemistry. **AV:** Practicing photography; Appreciating Chinese poetry; Gardening **THT:** Dr. Lien believes life is to be cherished and enjoyed.

LIESCH, BARRY W., PHD, T: Music Educator **I:** Education/Educational Services **DOB:** 05/21/1943 **SC:** Vancouver/Canada **PT:** Jacob Liesch; Corena Walker Liesch **CH:** Jesse David **ED:** PhD in Music Research, University of California San Diego (1979); MusM, State University of New York at Binghamton (1967); MusB, University of British Columbia, Vancouver, Canada (1964) **C:** Music Professor, Biola University, La Mirada, CA (1974) **CIV:** Creator, The Jacob Liesch Composition Scholarship, The Jacob Liesch Worship Scholarship, Biola University; Supporter, Vikasitha Children's Home, India **CW:** Author, "The New Worship" (2001); Author, "People in Presence of God" (1988) **MH:** Albert Nelson Marquis Lifetime Achievement Award; Marquis Who's Who Top Professional **AS:** Dr. Liesch attributes his success to his mentor, Dr. Marquis. **B/I:** Dr. Liesch came from a very poor family. When he was graduating, the head of the music department, Dr. Marquis, asked him if he had ever thought about graduate school, and he replied that he didn't know if he was capable of that. His teacher said that he could do well and that and he should apply to a lot of schools. Dr. Marquis encouraged him to talk to his parents about it, and then he started filling out applications for him. He was offered a full scholarship to the State University of New York at Binghamton and then he went on to go to college for about 12 years. He went to four different universities. **AV:** Writing

LIEU, TED W., T: U.S. Representative from California **I:** Government Administration/Government Relations/Government Services **DOB:** 03/29/1969 **PB:** Tapei **SC:** Taiwan **MS:** Married **SPN:** Betty Lieu **CH:** Brennan; Austin **ED:** JD, Georgetown University Law Center, Magna Cum Laude (1994); BA in Political Science, Stanford University (1991); BS in

Computer Science, Stanford University (1991) **C:** Member, U.S. House of Representatives from California's 33rd Congressional District (2015-Present); Member, District 28, California State Senate (2010-2015); Member, District 53, California State Assembly (2005-2010); Law Clerk, Judge Thomas Tang, United States Court of Appeals for the Ninth Circuit; Member, Committee on Appropriations; Attorney, U.S. Air Force; Attorney, Judge Advocate General's Corps; Member, Torrance Environmental Quality and Energy Conservation Commission; Member, Torrance City Council **MIL:** Colonel, U.S. Air Force Reserve (2015-Present); With, U.S. Air Force Reserve (2000-Present); With, U.S. Air Force (1995-1999) **CW:** Editor-in-Chief, Georgetown Law Journal **AW:** Four-time Recipient, American Jurisprudence Awards **PA:** Democrat

LIGGINS-ROGERS, SHARRON E., EDD, T: 1) Founder, Chief Executive Officer 2) Consulting Executive Director **I:** Consulting **CN:** 1) Liggins & Associates, Inc. 2) Continuum of Care Network of NWI **DOB:** 02/08/1944 **PB:** Gary **SC:** IN/USA **PT:** Joseph Benjamin Hightower; Rubye Mae (Whitehurst) Hightower **MS:** Married **SPN:** James Liggins Jr. **CH:** Jamya L. Liggins-Fisher; Jenaya L. Liggins-Taylor **ED:** EdD in Organizational Leadership, Graduate School of Business and Management, Argosy University, Chicago, IL (2015); MS in Nursing, Indiana Dabney University (2013); Honorary PhD in Human Services, GMOR Theological Institute of America (2004); MS in Administration and Health/Non-Profit, Notre Dame University (1985); BA in Psychology, Minor in Clinical Counseling, Purdue University (1981); Diploma of Nursing, St. Margaret School of Nursing/St. Joseph's College (1965) **CT:** Registered Nurse, State of Indiana; Parenting Leader Trainer Certification; Not-for-Profit Institution "Legal Aspect" Certification; Balancing Healing Mission with Business Ethics Certification; Substance Abuse Prevention Specialist Certification; Train the Trainer; Substance Abuse Prevention Specialist **C:** Consulting Executive Director, Continuum of Care Network of NWI, Drug Free Gary Coalition, Gary, IN (2003-Present); Founder, Chief Executive Officer, Liggins & Associates, Inc. (1998-Present); Instructor, Indiana Dabney University, Hammond, IN (2010-2013); Managing Director, Workforce Department Empowerment Zone, Gary, East Chicago, Hammond, IN (2000-2003); Administrative Director, Nursing Rehabilitation Institute, Methodist Hospital, Gary, IN (1989-1998); Administrative Director, Rehabilitation Institute, Methodist Hospital, Gary, IN (1989-1998); Inpatient Director, Methodist Hospital, Gary, IN (1985-1986); Nursing Services Coordinator, Methodist Hospital, Gary, IN (1984-1985); Patient Educator, Special Projects Coordinator, St. Mary Medical Center, Gary, IN (1980-1983); Supervisor, Industrial Hospital, American Bridge, Gary, IN (1972-1980); Critical Care/Cardiovascular Surgery, St. Catherine's Hospital, East Chicago, IN (1966-1971); Substitute School Nurse, Gary, IN (1967-1969); Staff Nurse, Medical Surrogate, Methodist Hospital, Gary, IN (1965-1966); Registered Nurse, Open Heart Surgery, Nurse Educator, Supervisor, Director of Nursing Services, St. Catherine Hospital, American Bridge, St. Mary Hospital, Methodist Hospital, Health South Rehab Hospital, Indiana Dabney University (1965); Founding Member, Governing and Advisory Boards, Indiana Balance of State Continuum of Care/Continuum of State Steering Committee; Oversight Administrator, Rapid Re-Housing Administrator, Homelessness Prevention & Rapid Re-Housing Program/Emergency Solution Program (HPRP/ESG); Nursing Instructor for BA of Nursing Program; Instructor, Pharmacology and Basic Principles of Nursing **CIV:** Former Liaison for Education, St. Mark's Church, Gary, IN; Volunteer,

Community Organization, Urban League **AW:** Gale C. Corley Award for "Remarkable Service to Community Mental Health," Porter Starke Services (2018); Most Influential Woman In NWI, Non-Profit Influential Women (2016); Commonweal Award for "Personal and Professional Leadership," Edgewater (2016); Alfred P. Davis Award, Pubic Policy & Health Award, Porter Starke Services (2016); Community Recognition IHCDA Magazine Front Cover & Feature Story, IHCDA (2014); Community Leadership Pearl Award, Sigma Gamma Rho (2013); Community Leadership/Advocate Award, IHCDA/CSH (2012); Community Leadership Award, National Black Women's Hook-Up (2011); Community Service Award, CR Works (2008); Delegate- Elected for Indiana Business and Professional Women/ District 1, Lake County (2006-2008); Women of the NAACP Award, Women of Action (2007); Hisorial Achievement, Salvation Army (2007); Leader of the Year, State of Indiana, Michael Carroll Leadership for Economic & Community Development Award (2006); Board Chair, Drifting Dunes Girl Scout Council Leadership Award (2006); Keeper of the Dream, Housing Summit Conference Award (2006); Delegate- Elected for Drifting Dunes Girl Scout Council in Atlanta (2005-2006); Keeper of the Dream Fair Housing Partner Award (2004); Outstanding Member/Parent of the Year, Alpha Kappa Alpha (1990); Citizen of the Month, Midtown Registered Nurses Association, City of Gary, IN (1987); Fundraiser of the Year Award, Indiana State Nursing Association, District 2 (1986); Named Citizen of Gary, National Association Black Women/Gary Civic Community **MEM:** Board Member–Community Investment Funding Indiana (CIFI) (2018-Present); Board Member, Vice President, Community Advocates of Northern Indiana (2017-Present); Alpha Kappa Alpha Sorority, Incorporated Sigma Phi Omega Chapter (2016-Present); Board Member, Porter Starke Services (Mental Health & Marram/FQHC) (2016-Present); Board Member, Secretary, Indiana Minority Health Coalition (2016-Present); Board Member, Gary Neighborhood Services (2016-Present); Board Member, Balance of State/Continuum of Care (2013-Present); Board Member, President, Broadway Area Community Development Company (2012-Present); Board Member, South Shore Leadership Council/ Leadership Northwest Indiana (2012-Present); Chairman, Regional Planning Council, Region 1-A, Lake County, IL (2010-Present); Board Chairperson, Serenity House (2006-Present); Board Member, Veterans Life Changing Service (2011-2015); Board Member, The Grant Incorporated (South Shore GRANTS) (2010-2013); Trustee, Pentecostal Church of God's Love (2003-2012); Board Member, Vice President, CBK Performing Arts Center (2010-2012); Nomination Committee Chairperson, District 1, State committee Representative, GBPW (2006-2008); Board Member, Vice President, Gary Business and Professional Women (GBPW) District 1 (2006-2007); Board Member, Drifting Dunes Girl Scout Council (2002-2007); Board Chairperson, Drifting Dunes Girl Scout Council (2004-2006); Charter Member, NWI Chapter, Black National Nurses Association (2000-2005); Board Member, Midtown Registered Nurses (1984-2000); Board Chair, President, Midtown Registered Nurses (1985-1989); President, Midtown Registered Nurses (1985-1988) **MH:** Albert Nelson Marquis Lifetime Achievement Award **AV:** Reading; Traveling **PA:** Democratic **RE:** Catholic **THT:** As Founder and Chief Executive Officer of Liggins & Associates, Dr. Liggins-Rogers began her second career in 2003. She is now the Consulting Executive Director of the Continuum of Care Network of Northwest Indiana and Drug Free Gary Coalition (CoC/DFGC), which includes more than 60 community organizations. She is an advocate for issues around safe/affordable housing and homelessness and promotion of health. She has aided community partners through creating strategic, innovative, and collaborative models that have yielded over $22 million in HUD financing for the Gary, East Chicago, and Hammond region, which included $2.5 million for the Homelessness Prevention and Rapid Re-Housing Program, as well as spearheaded the largest Region-Wide Housing Summit Conference in the state of Indiana for five years. She heads the Point-in-Time Count for Lake County, which is a national requirement for procuring the unduplicated count of the local homeless population. She has facilitated the process of Permanent Supportive Housing for the homeless (men, women, children, families, veterans and special populations) in Lake County with an accumulation of over 300+ apartments/housing including 44 units for homeless veterans, 60 units for mentally ill with disabilities and 40 more units for homeless families. She received on behalf of the Continuum of Care the donation of four homes from the City of Gary and facilitated the process and wrote the grant, which allowed for donated property by Wells Fargo to the Continuum. Between 2003 and 2018, she facilitated through the Continuum of Care Network of NWI, Inc. (CoC) as the Consulting Executive Director guiding and directing, and/or aiding the writing and acquiring of grants for organizations that serve the homeless. The Continuum of Care has approximately 60 organization that provide direct and indirect services to the homeless populations throughout Lake County, Indiana. The facilitation and guidance have aided in the accumulation of approximately 300 units of permanent housing for the homeless including those living with AIDS.

LIGHT, JUDITH ELLEN, T: Actress **I:** Media & Entertainment **DOB:** 02/09/1949 **PB:** Trenton **SC:** NJ/USA **PT:** Sidney Light; Pearl Sue (Hollander) Light **MS:** Married **SPN:** Robert Desiderio (1/1/1985) **ED:** Bachelor of Fine Arts, Carnegie Mellon University (1970) **CIV:** Former Board Member, Matthew Shepard Foundation, Point Foundation **CW:** Actress, "Before You Know It" (2019); Actress, "Escaping the Madhouse: The Nellie Bly Story" (2019); Guest Appearance, "The Politician" (2019); Guest Appearance, "Queen America" (2018-2019); Actress, "Transparent" (2014-2019); Guest Appearance, "The Good Fight" (2018); Guest Appearance, "The Assassination of Gianni Versace: American Crime Story" (2018); Actress, "Hot Air" (2018); Actress, "Ms. White Light" (2018); Voice Actress, "Penn Zero: Part-Time Hero" (2017); Actress, "I'm Sorry" (2017); Actress, "Doubt" (2017); Actress, "God Looked Away," Pasadena Playhouse (2017); Actress, "All the Ways to Say I Love You," MCC Theater (2016); Actress, "Digging for Fire" (2015); Actress, "We'll Never Have Paris" (2015); Actress, "Thérèse Raquin," Roundabout Theater at Studio 54 (2015); Guest Appearance, "The Exes" (2012-2015); Guest Appearance, "Raising Hope" (2014); Actress, "Last Weekend" (2014); Actress, "The Winklers" (2014); Actress, "Dallas" (2013-2014); Actress, "The Assembled Parties," Samuel J. Friedman Theatre (2013); Actress, "Other Desert Cities," Booth Theatre (2011-2012); Narrator, "Scrooge & Marley" (2012); Appearance, "Rhymes with Banana" (2012); Guest Appearance, "Nurse Jackie" (2011); Actress, "Other People's Kids" (2011); Actress, "Lombardi," Circle in the Square Theatre (2010-2011); Actress, "Ugly Betty" (2006-2010); Actress, "Law & Order: Special Victims Unit" (2002-2010); Actress, "Save Me" (2007); Actress, "A Broken Sole" (2006); Guest Appearance, "Twenty Good Years" (2006); Actress, "Colder Than Here," Lucille Lortel Theatre (2005); Actress, "Ira & Abby" (2005); Actress, "The Stones" (2004); Guest Appearance, "Spin City" (2002); Actress, "Sorrows and Rejoicings," Second Stage Theatre (2002); Actress, "Hedda Gabler," Shakespeare Theatre Company (2001); Actress, "Born in Brooklyn" (2001); Voice Actress, "Joseph: King of Dreams" (2000); Actress, "Wit," Union Square Theatre (1999-2000); Actress, "The Simple Life" (1998); Actress, "Carriers" (1998); Voice Actress, "Cow & Chicken" (1997); Actress, "Too Close to Home" (1997); Guest Appearance, "Duckman" (1996-1997); Actress, "Murder at My Door" (1996); Actress, "A Strange Affair" (1996); Actress, "A Step Toward Tomorrow" (1996); Appearance, "Paul Monette: The Brink of Summer's End" (1996); Actress, "Lady Killer" (1995); Actress, "Against Their Will: Women in Prison" (1994); Actress, "Betrayal of Trust" (1994); Actress, "Phenom" (1993-1994); Actress, "Men Don't Tell" (1993); Actress, "Who's the Boss?" (1984-1992); Actress, "Wife, Mother, Murderer" (1991); Actress, "In Defense of a Married Man" (1990); Actress, "My Boyfriend's Back" (1989); Actress, "The Ryan White Story" (1989); Actress, "Stamp of a Killer" (1987); Guest Appearance, "Charmed Lives" (1986); Guest Appearance, "You Are the Jury" (1984); Guest Appearance, "Remington Steele" (1984); Guest Appearance, "The Mississippi" (1984); Guest Appearance, "Family Ties" (1983); Guest Appearance, "St. Elsewhere" (1983); Actress, "Intimate Agony" (1983); Actress, "One Life to Live" (1977-1983); Guest Appearance, "Kojak" (1977); Actress, "Herzi," Palace Theatre (1976); Actress, "Measure for Measure," Delacorte Theater (1976); Actress, "A Doll's House," Vivian Beaumont Theater (1975); Actress, "Tick Tick... Boom!" **AW:** Isabelle Stevenson Award, Tony Awards (2019); Outstanding Featured Actress in a Play, "Thérèse Raquin," Outer Critics Circle Awards (2016); Outstanding Featured Actress in a Play, "The Assembled Parties," Drama Desk Awards (2013); Best Featured Actress in a Play, "The Assembled Parties," Tony Awards (2013); Outstanding Featured Actress in a Play, "Other Desert Cities," Drama Desk Awards (2012); Best Featured Actress in a Play, "Other Desert Cities," Tony Awards (2012); Best Performance in a Comedy Series, "Ugly Betty," Prism Awards (2007); Vision Award, GLAAD Media Awards (1998); Outstanding Lead Actress in a Drama Series, "One Life to Live," Daytime Emmy Awards (1980-1981); Outstanding Actress, "One Life to Live," Soapy Awards (1979-1980) **RE:** Jewish

LIGHTHIZER, ROBERT EMMET, T: United States Trade Representative **I:** Business Management/ Business Services **DOB:** 10/11/1947 **PB:** Ashtabula **SC:** OH/USA **PT:** Orville James Lighthizer; Michaelene Lighthizer **CH:** Robert; Claire **ED:** JD, Georgetown Law (1973); BA, Georgetown University (1969) **C:** United States Trade Representative, Washington, DC (2017-Present); Deputy United States Trade Representative, Washington, DC (1983-1985); Practice Leader, Legislative/Lobbying, Skadden, Arps, Slate, Meagher & Flom, LLP, Washington, DC; Partner, Practice Leader, International Trade and Transactions, Skadden, Arps, Slate, Meagher & Flom, LLP, Washington, DC; Associate Attorney, Covington & Burling LLP, Washington, DC **CR:** Rank of Ambassador Treasurer, Republican Presidential Campaign (1996); Chief of Staff, Committee of Finance, United States Senate (1981-1983); Vice Chairman, Board of the Overseas Private Investment Corporation; Speaker on Trade and Tax Issues, Politics and Other Developments, Washington, DC; Board Director, Several Charitable and Political Groups **CW:** Contributor, Articles, Professional Publications; Contributor, Journals **MEM:** International Bar Association (IBA) **BAR:** The District of Columbia Bar (1973)

LIGHTNER, JAMES EDWARD, PHD, T: Mathematics Educator **I:** Education/Educational Services **DOB:** 08/29/1937 **PB:** Frederick **SC:** MD/USA **PT:** Norman Edward Lightner; Lydia Irene (Biddle) Lightner **MS:** Single **ED:** Honorary LittD, McDaniel College (2017); PhD, The Ohio State University (1968); MA, Northwestern University (1962); BA, Western Maryland College (Now McDaniel College) (1958) **C:** Emeritus Professor of Mathematics (1998-Present); Director of Mathematics Proficiency, Western Maryland College (Now McDaniel College), Westminster, MD (1982-1995); Professor of Mathematics, Western Maryland College (Now McDaniel College), Westminster, MD (1977-1998); Associate Professor of Mathematics, Western Maryland College (Now McDaniel College), Westminster, MD (1968-1977); Assistant Professor of Mathematics, Western Maryland College (Now McDaniel College), Westminster, MD (1965-1968); Mathematics Instructor, Western Maryland College (Now McDaniel College), Westminster, MD (1962-1965); Mathematics and English Teacher, Frederick County Public Schools (1958-1962) **CR:** Reader, Advanced Placement Calculus Testing Service, Princeton, NJ (1980-1988); Consultant, Maryland State Department of Education, Baltimore, MD (1975-1998); Speaker in Field **CIV:** Historical Society of Carroll County (2011-Present); Board of Trustees, McDaniel College (2010-Present); Westminster Rotary Club (1974-Present); Board Chair, Historical Society of Carroll County (2015-2017); Former President, Former Secretary, Westminster Rotary Club; Carroll Arts Council; Boys and Girls Club of Westminster **CW:** Author, "Fearless and Bold: A History of McDaniel College, 1866-2002" (2008); Co-Author, "Geometry" (1980, 1984); Contributor, Articles, Professional Journals; Contributor, Biography, Alumni Magazine, "The Hill" **AW:** John Hope Franklin Award, The Phi Beta Kappa Society (2015); Distinguished Service Award, Kappa Mu Epsilon (1993); Outstanding Maryland Mathematics Educator, Maryland Council of Teachers of Mathematics (1986) **MEM:** Secretary, Westminster Rotary Club (2008-2018); Senator, The Phi Beta Kappa Society (2006-2012); Secretary, Treasurer, Local Chapter, The Phi Beta Kappa Society (1980-1998); Paul Harris Fellow, Westminster Club (1990); Executive Secretary, Maryland Council of Teachers of Mathematics (1988-1994); President, Maryland Council of Teachers of Mathematics (1982-1983); President, Westminster Rotary Club (1980-1981); National President, Kappa Mu Epsilon (1977-1981); National Council of Teachers of Mathematics; Phi Delta Kappa; Sigma Xi, The Scientific Research Honor Society; Phi Delta Theta **MH:** Albert Nelson Marquis Lifetime Achievement Award **B/I:** Dr. Lightner became involved in his profession because math was an easy subject for him. He taught in high school for four years and was subsequently invited to teach at his college, Western Maryland College, in 1962. Additionally, he became a historian in order to study the history of the college itself. **AV:** Traveling; Listening to music; Singing; Reading **PA:** Independent **RE:** Lutheran

LILIEN, ELLIOT, T: Secondary School Educator **I:** Education/Educational Services **PB:** Maplewood **SC:** NJ/USA **PT:** Bernard Banner; Judith Batson (Mulally) Lilien **MS:** Married **SPN:** Nancy Goddard Pierce (07/21/1985); Louise Anne Hoehl (01/29/1965, Divorced 07/1968) **ED:** Master of Arts in Teaching, Harvard University (1965); Doctor of Jurisprudence, Columbia University (1964); Bachelor of Arts, University of Chicago (1961) **C:** Retired (2000); Head Coach of Tennis, Concord-Carlisle High School, Concord, MA (1989-Present); Teacher, Concord-Carlisle Schools, Concord, MA (1965-Present); Chairper-

son of Social Studies, Concord-Carlisle Schools, Concord, MA (1987-2000); Tournament Director, Dave Mason Tennis Tournament (2000-2015); Curriculum Coordinator, Social Studies K-12, Concord-Carlisle Schools, Concord, MA (1997-2000); Head Coach of Fencing, Concord-Carlisle Schools, Concord, MA (1965-1985) **CR:** Director, Concord-Academy Fencing Camp (1975-Present); Fencing Coach, Harvard University (2000); Head Coach of Fencing, Brown University, Providence, RI (1987-1993) **CIV:** Chairperson, Board Director, Conifer Maintenance Corporation (2015-Present); President, Concord Teachers Association (1994); Commissioner, Northeast Fencing Conference, Boxboro, MA (1993); President, Conifer Maintenance Corporation (1985-1993); Founder, Four School History Consortium (1990) **CW:** Author, "Water is Rising in the Classroom: True Teacher Terror Dreams" (2004); Author, "Competition Experiment" (1986); Author, "History of Greece and Rome" (1979); Author, "German History 1815-1945" (1972) **AW:** Inductee, Concord-Carlisle Athletic Hall of Fame (1996); Grantee, Council for Basic Education (1983); Sabre Champion, New England; National Humanities Award **MEM:** President, Concord-Carlisle Teachers (1972-1994); Founder, President, Four School Consortium (1987) **MH:** Albert Nelson Marquis Lifetime Achievement Award **B/I:** Mr. Lilien became involved in his profession due to the influence of his parents, who wanted him to attend law school. After realizing that he did not enjoy the prospect of such an occupation, he transferred to Harvard and received a degree in education. **AV:** Tennis; WW1 poster collecting; Swords; Beer steins; Autographs

LILLIS, PATRICIA PROPHIT, DSN, PHD, T: Professor Emeritus **I:** Education/Educational Services **DOB:** 05/06/1941 **PB:** Monroe **SC:** LA/USA **PT:** Clarence Alston Prophit; Hortense (Callahan) Prophit **ED:** DSN, PhD, University of Alabama, Birmingham (1985); MS, University of California, San Francisco (1972); BSN, Northwestern State University (1963) **CT:** Registered Nurse, Louisiana, California, Georgia **C:** Professor Emeritus, Medical College of Georgia; Chair, Department of Adult Nursing, Medical College of Georgia (1990-1999); Associate Professor, School of Graduate Studies, Medical College of Georgia (1989-1999); Instructor, Department of Adult Nursing to Associate Professor, Medical College of Georgia, Augusta, GA (1972-1989); Graduate Research Associate, University of Alabama, Birmingham (1982-1984); Clinical Instructor, DeAnza College, Cupertino, CA (1971-1972); Medical Nurse Specialist, Hematology-oncology and Neurology, Stanford University Medical Center, Palo Alto, CA (1965-1971); Staff Nurse, Assistant Head Nurse, St. Francis Medical Center, Monroe (1963-1965) **CR:** Chairman, PhD Comprehensive Exam Committee, Medical College of Georgia (1990-1996) **CW:** Contributor, Articles, Professional Publications; Contributor, Chapters, Books **AW:** Nutrition Project Award, American Cancer Society (1994); Excellence in Writing Award, Adria Oncology Nursing Society (1991); Fellow in Oncology Nursing Education, National Cancer Institute (1981-1982); Research Grantee, American Cancer Society; MCG Center for Nursing Research Grantee, Surgikos/Johnson and Johnson Co.; **MEM:** Board of Directors, Marriotts Harbour Club (2012); President, Sigma Theta Tau (1989-1993, 2001-2003); President, Continuing Education, Approver Committee, Education Committee, Membership Committee, Scholarship, Oncology Nursing Society (1999); Multimedia Awards Committee Chair, Sigma Theta Tau (1994); Counselor, Sigma Theta Tau (1987-1989); Chair, Chapter Research Committee, Sigma Theta Tau (1985-1989); Chair, Professional Education Committee, Board of Directors, Vice President,

Medical, Project Steering Committee, American Cancer Society; Adria Oncology Nursing Society; Sigma Xi; Omicron Delta Kappa **MH:** Albert Nelson Marquis Lifetime Achievement Award **PA:** Republican **RE:** Presbyterian

LIM, HENRY CHOL, T: Biochemical Engineering Educator, Researcher **I:** Engineering **DOB:** 10/24/1935 **PB:** Seoul **SC:** South Korea **PT:** Kwang Un Lim; Chang (Soon) Lim **MS:** Married **SPN:** Sun Boo Lee (12/11/1959) **CH:** David; Carol; Michael **ED:** PhD, Northwestern University (1967);MS in Engineering, University of Michigan (1959); BSChE, Oklahoma State University (1957) **C:** Professor of Chemical Biochemical Engineering, University of California, Irvine (1998-Present); Professor, Chair of Department, Biochemical engineering and Materials Science, University of California, Irvine (1995-1997); Professor, Chair of Department, Chemical and Biochemical Engineering, University of California, Irvine (1993-1995); Professor, Chair, Biochemical Engineering Department, University of California, Irvine (1987-1993); Professor, Chemical Engineering, Purdue University, West Lafayette, IN (1974-1987); Associate Professor, Chemical Engineering, Purdue University, West Lafayette, IN (1970-1974); Assistant Professor, Chemical Engineering, Purdue University, West Lafayette, IN (1966-1970); Research and Development Engineer, Pfizer, Inc., Groton, CT (1959-1963) **CR:** Consultant, Lucky Biotech, Emeryville, CA (1988-1991); Adjunct Professor Purdue University (1987-1990); Consultant, Monsanto Company, St. Louis, MO (1987-1990); Consultant, Eli Lilly and Company, Indianapolis, IN (1982-1984); Consultant, Novo Enzyme Corporation, Mamaroneck, NY (1973-1977) **CW:** Co-Author, "Fed-Batch Cultures: Principles and Applications of Semi-Batch Bioreactors" (2013); Co-Author, "Biological Waste Water Treatment (1999) **AW:** American Institute of Chemical Engineers Award; Numerous Teaching Awards, Purdue University **MEM:** American Institute of Chemical Engineers; American Chemical Society; American Society for Microbiology; Society for Industrial Microbiology and Biotechnology; Korean Academy of Science and Engineering; Sigma Xi; Phi Kappa Phi; Phi Lambda Upsilon **MH:** Albert Nelson Marquis Lifetime Achievement Award **B/I:** Dr. Lim became involved in his profession because his father was in the Korean War and he encouraged him to go into chemical engineering. During that time, everything was destroyed and his father thought that would be a good career.

LIMBAUGH, RUSH HUDSON III, T: Radio Talk Show Host **I:** Media & Entertainment **DOB:** 01/12/1951 **PB:** Cape Girardeau **SC:** MO/USA **YOP:** 2021 **PT:** Rush Hudson Limbaugh Jr.; Mildred Carolyn (Armstrong) Limbaugh **MS:** Married **SPN:** Kathryn Rogers (06/05/2010); Marta Fitzgerald (05/27/1994, Divorced 12/21/2004); Michelle Sixta (12/19/1982, Divorced 1990); Roxy Maxine McNeely (09/24/1977, Divorced 07/10/1980); **ED:** Diploma, Elkins Institute of Radio and Technology; Coursework, Southeast Missouri State University **C:** Radio Talk Show Host, "The Rush Limbaugh Show," New York, NY (1988-Present); Host, "Rush Limbaugh," Syndicated Television Show (1992-1996); Radio Talk Show Host, KFBK-AM Radio, Sacramento, CA (1984-1988); Political Commentator, KMBZ-FM Radio, Kansas City, KS (1983-1984); Director of Group Sales to Director of Sales and Special Events, Kansas City Royals, MLB (1979-1983); Disc Jockey, WHB-AM Radio, Kansas City, KS (1975-1978); Disc Jockey, KQV-AM Radio, Pittsburgh, PA (1971) **CR:** Publisher, "The Limbaugh Letter" (1995-Present); Co-founder, Two if by Tea, KARHL Holdings **CIV:** Fundraiser,

EIB Cure-a-thon, Leukemia & Lymphoma Society; Supporter, Tunnel to Towers Foundation, Marine Corps-Law Enforcement Foundation **CW:** Author, "Rush Revere and the Presidency" (2016); Author, "Rush Revere and the Star-Spangled Banner: Time-Travel Adventures with Exceptional Americans" (2015); Author, "Rush Revere and the First Patriots: Time-Travel Adventures with Exceptional Americans" (2014); Author, "Rush Revere and the Brave Pilgrims: Time Travel Adventures with Exceptional Americans" (2013); Weekly Analyst, "ESPN's Sunday NFL Countdown" (2003); Appearance, "The Drew Carey Show" (1998); Appearance, "Forget Paris" (1995); Appearance, "Hearts Afire" (1994); Author, "See, I Told You So" (1993); Author, "The Way Things Ought to Be" (1992); Appearances, Television Shows **AW:** Presidential Medal of Freedom, The White House (2020); Named, One of the 50 Highest-earning Political Figures, Newsweek (2010); Named, One of the World's Most Influential People, TIME Magazine (2009); Named, One of the 10 Most Fascinating People of 2008, Barbara Walters' Special (2008); Named, One of the 100 Most Powerful Celebrities, Forbes.com (2008); Named, Man of the Year, Human Events Magazine (2007); William F. Buckley Jr. Award for Media Excellence, Media Research Center (2007); Marconi Radio Award for Syndicated Radio Personality of the Year, National Association of Broadcasters (1992, 1995, 2000, 2005); Named, Greatest Radio Talk Show Host of All Time, Talkers Magazine (2002); Inductee, National Association of Broadcasters Hall of Fame (1998); Inductee, National Radio Hall of Fame (1993) **PA:** Republican

LIN, JENNY, T: Chief Operating Officer, Board Director **I:** Pharmaceuticals **CN:** CMIC Inc. **CH:** Hanna **ED:** Master of Science in Medicinal Chemistry, University of Connecticut, Storrs, CT (1994); Bachelor of Science in Analytical Chemistry, Peking University, Beijing, China (1989) **C:** Board Member, CMIC Incorporated, Hoffman Estates, IL (2018-Present); Chief Operating Officer, CMIC Incorporated, Hoffman Estates, IL (2015-Present); Vice President, Operations and CSO, JCL Bioassay USA, Incorporated, CMIC Incorporated, Hoffman Estates, IL (2009-2015); Director, Vice President, Analytical Chemistry, deCODE Chemistry (1994-2009) **CR:** Chairperson, International Conferences **CW:** Author, Co-Author, Approximately 40 Publications, White Papers, and Presentations; Member, Editorial Board, Peer-Reviewed Journal **AW:** Most Influential Women Award, Inside Success Magazine (2019); Woman of the Year, National Association of Professional Women (2012, 2013) **MEM:** American Society of Mass Spectrometry; American Association of Pharmaceutical Scientists; American Chemical Society; National Association of Professional Women; Global CRO Council; Global Bioanalysis Consortium **AS:** Ms. Lin attributes her success to her sensitivity to new developments in the industry, as well as business integrity, which is very important to her. The ethics and business integrity is critically important to her. **B/I:** Ms. Lin was always interested in business. She felt that she would need a good technical background and solid foundation in order to support her interests. Chemistry degrees were important pursuits for her to be well versed in the pharmaceutical business.

LIN, KENNETH C., T: Chief Executive Officer **I:** Financial Services **CN:** Credit Karma, Inc. **SC:** China **ED:** BA in Economics and Mathematics, Boston University (1998) **C:** Founder, Chief Executive Officer, Credit Karma, Inc. (2007-Present); President, Multilytics Marketing, Inc. (2006-2008); Director of Analytics, Research and Cross Sell, E-LOAN (2004-2006); Principal, Founder, Adren-

aline Group, LLC (2001-2005); Senior Marketing Analyst, UPromise (2003-2004); Manager of Business Consulting, FairMarket (2000-2002); Analyst, Partners First (1998-2000) **CR:** Henry Crown Fellow, The Aspen Institute (2018-Present)

LINCECUM, TIM LEROY, T: Professional Baseball Player (Retired) **I:** Athletics **DOB:** 06/15/1984 **PB:** Bellevue **SC:** WA/USA **PT:** Chris Lincecum; Rebecca Lincecum **ED:** Coursework, University of Washington, Seattle, WA (2003-2006) **C:** Pitcher, Texas Rangers, MLB (2018); Pitcher, Los Angeles Angels, MLB (2016); Pitcher, San Francisco Giants, MLB (2007-2015) **CR:** Coach, Giants Challenger Clinic (2007) **AW:** Winner, San Francisco Giants, World Series Championship (2010, 2012, 2014); National League All-Star Team, MLB (2009-2011); Babe Ruth Award (2010); National League Cy Young Award, Baseball Writers' Association of America (2008, 2009); Graduate of the Year, National Baseball Congress (2009); National League Pitcher of the Year, Sporting News (2009); National League Outstanding Pitcher, Major League Baseball Players Association (MLBPA) (2008); Harry S. Jordan Award, San Francisco Giants (2007); First Team All-American, Collegiate Baseball (2006); Golden Spikes Award, USA Baseball (2006); Named Pitcher of the Year (2004); Freshman of the Year, PAC-10 Conference (2004); National Freshman of the Year (2004)

LINDBLAD, RICHARD ARTHUR, DRPH, T: Public Health Officer **I:** Medicine & Health Care **CN:** National Institute on Drug Abuse, National Institutes of Health **DOB:** 07/15/1937 **PB:** Atlantic **SC:** IA/USA **PT:** Clifford Robert Lindblad; Emma Ruth (Dunham) Lindblad **MS:** Married **SPN:** Lona; Jerri Lee (Divorced) **CH:** Julie; Richard; Mark **ED:** DrPH, Johns Hopkins University (1974); MPH, Johns Hopkins University (1971);MS, University of Colorado (1965); BS, San Jose State University (1961) **C:** Retired (1994); Captain (06), U.S. Public Health Service Commissioned Corps (1964-1994); Director, International Program Branch, National Institute on Drug Abuse, National Institutes of Health (1987-1993); Associate Institute Director for Policy and Program Planning, National Institute on Drug Abuse, National Institutes of Health (1981-1987); Director, Program Development and Analysis Branch, National Institute on Drug Abuse, National Institutes of Health (1976-1981); Regional Director, Division of Narcotic Addiction and Drug Abuse, National Institute on Mental Health (NIMH) (1967-1970); Treatment Supervisor, U.S. Public Health Service Commissioned Corps Narcotic Treatment Hospital, Fort Worth, TX (1966-1967); Hospital, Fort Worth, TX, NIMH Regional Office, Denver, CO (1964) **CR:** Director, South American Epidemiology Study, World Health Organization; Director, International Drug Abuse Assessment Program (IDAAS), United Nations **MIL:** Commissioned Officer (Retired), Grade 06, U.S. Public Health Service Commissioned Corps; Captain (Colonel), U.S. Public Health Service Agency **CW:** Designer, Funding, Supervisor, Development, Hubert Humphrey International Visiting Scientist and Technical Exchange Program, National Institute on Drug Abuse; Contributor, Author, Numerous Books and Articles Relating to Drug Abuse Treatment and Epidemiology, Professional Journals **AW:** Three Special Promotions in Military Rank Based on his Meritorious Performance as a Commissioned Officer **MEM:** American Public Health Association; Maryland Public Health Association; Commissioned Officers Association of the USPHS Inc.; National Association for Uniformed Services (NAUS) **MH:** Albert Nelson Marquis Lifetime Achievement Award **AS:** Dr. Lindblad attributes his success to a sincere interest in the public health issue of substance abuse, the association

with many talented researchers and experts, and a tenacity to address many challenges. **B/I:** Dr. Lindblad became involved in his profession as part of his military obligation; he was first assigned to the U.S. Public Health Service Narcotic Treatment Hospital in Fort Worth, Texas, and later assigned to the National Institute on Drug Abuse in Washington, D.C.. He went on to become a specialist in substance abuse treatment, epidemiology, and research.

LINDNER, CYNTHIA MS., T: Certified Hypnotherapist **I:** Health, Wellness and Fitness **CN:** Advanced Hypnotherapy **MS:** Married **SPN:** Frank Lindner **ED:** MS in Counseling Psychology, Columbia State University (1998); BS in Liberal Arts, New York Regents College (1993) **CT:** Certified Hypnotherapist; Master NLP Practitioner; Certified NLP Instructor **C:** NLP Trainer, NLP Long Island (1998-Present); Counselor/Hypnotherapist, Advanced Hypnotherapy (1993-Present); Therapy Assistant, Pilgrim Psychiatric Center (1991-1992); Therapy Assistant, Kings Park Psychiatric Center (1983-1992) **CIV:** Past President, American Psychotherapy and Medical Hypnosis Association (2002-2004) **CW:** Contributor, Articles, Professional Journals **AW:** Dans Papers Best of the Best in Addiction Therapy (2019); VIP Woman of the Year Circle (2014); NGH Order of Braid (2014); Lisee, Best of Long Island Hypnotherapist Category (2009-2011, 2013); Leadership Award, American Psychotherapy and Medical Hypnosis Association (2002); NBHA Pen and Quill Award (2000); NBHA Faculty Award (1999); NGH Exceptional Performance Recognition (1998); Listee, Sterling Who's Who (1994) **MEM:** National Guild of Hypnotists **AS:** Ms. Lindner attributes her success to her people skills, as it is easy for her to communicate, which yields positive results often. She has a genuine desire to help people. **B/I:** As a counseling student in college, Ms. Lindner was introduced to guided imagery, visualization, and hypnosis. It appeared to be a quick, effective way to change her clients' behavior, for which she is ever-thankful.

LINDSEY, SETH MARK, T: Lawyer (Retired) **I:** Law and Legal Services **DOB:** 10/18/1947 **PB:** Los Angeles **SC:** CA/USA **PT:** Seth Rankin Lindsey; Lela Belle Lindsey **MS:** Widowed **SPN:** Susan Adelaide Badger **CH:** Samantha Lindsey **ED:** JD, Yale University (1971); BA, University of Southern California Los Angeles (1968) **C:** Chief Counsel, Federal Railroad Administration, Washington, DC (1986-2010); Acting Administrator, Federal Railroad Administration, Washington, DC (2001); Acting Administrator, Federal Railroad Administration, Washington, DC (1993); Assistant Chief Counsel, Federal Railroad Administration, Washington, DC (1976-1986); Attorney, Housing and Urban Development, Washington, DC (1972-1976); Honors Attorney, Housing and Urban Development, Washington, DC (1971-1972) **CR:** Special Counsel for Conrail and Union Station Redevelopment Federal Railroad Administration (1984-1986) **AW:** Presidential Rank Award (2003); Gold Medal (1984); Silver Medal, Department of Transportation (1983, 1977) **BAR:** Supreme Court of the United States (1984); California (1972); Washington, DC **MH:** Albert Nelson Marquis Lifetime Achievement Award; Marquis Who's Who Top Professional **B/I:** Mr. Lindsey was influenced by his father to get into the law profession. He was also influenced by his desire to help society change in a positive way and he felt that being a lawyer could allow him to do so. **AV:** Hunting; Shooting; Researching astronomy and theology **PA:** Republican **RE:** Christian

LINNEY, LAURA LEGGETT, T: Actress **I:** Media & Entertainment **DOB:** 02/05/1964 **PB:** Manhattan **SC:** NY/USA **PT:** Romulus Zachariah Linney IV; Miriam Anderson "Ann" (Leggett) Perse **MS:** Married **SPN:** Marc Schauer (05/02/2009); David Adkins (09/02/1995, Divorced 2000) **CH:** Bennett Armistead **ED:** Honorary DFA, The Juilliard School (2009); Honorary DFA, Brown University (2003); Diploma, The Juilliard School (1989); BFA, Brown University (1986) **CW:** Actress, "The Little Foxes" (2017); Actress, "Red Nose Day Actually" (2017); Appearance, "Last Week Tonight with John Oliver" (2017); Actress, "Ozark" (2017); Actress, "Sink Sank Sunk" (2017); Actress, "The Dinner" (2017); Actress, "Inside Amy Schumer" (2016); Actress, "Genius" (2016); Actress, "Teenage Mutant Ninja Turtles: Out of the Shadows" (2016); Actress, "Sully" (2016); Actress, "Nocturnal Animals" (2016); Actress, "Mr. Holmes" (2015); Actress, "The Fifth Estate" (2013); Actress, "Hyde Park on Hudson" (2012); Actress, "The Details" (2011); Voice Actress, "Arthur Christmas" (2011); Actress, Producer, "The Big C" (2010-2013); Actress, "Time Stands Still" (2010); Actress, "Sympathy for Delicious" (2010); Actress, "Morning" (2010); Actress, "The City of Your Final Destination" (2009); Actress, "Les Liaisons Dangereuses" (2008); Actress, "John Adams" (2008); Actress, "The Other Man" (2008); Actress, "Breach" (2007); Actress, "The Nanny Diaries" (2007); Actress, "The Savages" (2007); Actress, "Driving Lessons" (2006); Actress, "Jindabyne" (2006); Actress, "The Hottest State" (2006); Actress, "Man of the Year" (2006); Actress, "American Dad" (2006); Actress, "The Squid and the Whale" (2005); Actress, "The Exorcism of Emily Rose" (2005); Actress, "P.S." (2004); Actress, "Kinsey" (2004); Actress, "Sight Unseen" (2004); Actress, "Frasier" (2003-2004); Actress, "The Life of David Gale" (2003); Actress, "Mystic River" (2003); Actress, "Love Actually" (2003); Actress, "The Laramie Project" (2002); Actress, "The Mothman Prophecies" (2002); Actress, "The Crucible" (2002); Actress, "King of the Hill" (2002); Featured, Sandra Boynton's "Philadelphia Chickens" (2002); Actress, "Wild Iris" (2001); Actress, "You Can Count on Me" (2000); Actress, "The House of Mirth" (2000); Actress, "Running Mates" (2000); Actress, "Maze" (2000); Actress, "Uncle Vanya" (2000); Actress, "Lush" (1999); Actress, "Love Letters" (1999); Actress, "Honour" (1998); Actress, "The Truman Show" (1998); Actress, "Absolute Power" (1998); Actress, "More Tales of the City" (1998); Actress, "Primal Fear" (1996); Actress, "Congo" (1995); Actress, "Holiday" (1995); Actress, "A Simple Twist of Fate" (1994); Actress, "Hedda Gabler" (1994); Actress, "Tales of the City" (1993); Actress, "Searching for Bobby Fischer" (1993); Actress, "Blind Spot" (1993)' Actress, "Dave" (1993); Actress, "Lorenzo's Oil" (1992); Actress, "Sight Unseen" (1992); Actress, "The Seagull" (1992); Actress, "Six Degrees of Separation" (1990) **AW:** Outer Critics Circle Award for Outstanding Solo Performance (2020); Outer Critics Circle Award for Outstanding Actress in a Play (2017); Drama Desk Award for Outstanding Actress in a Play (2017); Emmy Award for Outstanding Lead Actress in a Miniseries or Movie, Academy of Television Arts & Sciences (2002, 2008, 2013); Golden Globe Award for Best Performance by an Actress in a TV Series-Comedy or Musical, Hollywood Foreign Press Association (2011); Golden Globe Award for Best Performance by an Actress in a Miniseries or Motion Picture Made for TV, Hollywood Foreign Press Association (2009); SAG Award for Outstanding Performance by a Female Actor in a TV Movie or Miniseries, SAG-AFTRA (2009); Emmy Award for Outstanding Guest Actress in a Comedy Series, Television Academy of Arts & Sciences (2004); Award for Best Supporting Actress, National Board of Review (2004); Numerous Awards

LINNINGTON, MICHAEL S., T: Chief Executive Officer **I:** Nonprofit & Philanthropy **CN:** Wounded Warrior Project **ED:** MS in Applied Mathematics, Rensselaer Polytechnic Institute (1990); BS in General Engineering, U.S. Military Academy, West Point, NY (1980) **C:** Chief Executive Officer, Wounded Warrior Project (2016-Present); Director, Defense POW/MIA Accounting Agency, Arlington, VA (2015-2016); Military Deputy, Under Secretary of Defense (Personnel and Readiness), U.S. Department of Defense, Washington, DC (2013-2015); Commanding General, Joint Force Headquarters National Capital Region and U.S. Army Military District of Washington, Fort McNair, Washington, DC (2011-2013)

LIPINSKI, DANIEL WILLIAM, PHD, T: U.S. Representative from Illinois **I:** Government Administration/Government Relations/Government Services **DOB:** 07/15/1966 **PB:** Chicago **SC:** IL/USA **PT:** William Lipinski; Rose Marie (Lapinski) Lipinski **MS:** Married **SPN:** Judy Lipinski **ED:** Doctor of Philosophy in Political Science, Duke University (1998); Intern, Representative George E. Sangmeister (1993-1995); Intern, United States Department of Labor (1992); Master of Arts in Engineering Economic Systems, Stanford University (1989); Bachelor of Science in Mechanical Engineering, Northwestern University (1988) **C:** Member, U.S. House of Representatives from Illinois' Third District, United States Congress (2005-Present); Associate Professor, The University of Tennessee (2001-2004); Associate Professor, Notre Dame University (2000-2001); Legislative Staff Member, Representative Jerry Costello (1995-1996); With, State Attorney Richard A. Devine's Campaign and Transition Team, Cook County, IL (1995-1996); Member, Representative Rod Blagojevich's Staff; Communication Staff Aide, House Minority Leader Richard Gephardt; Member, Committee on Transportation, United States Congress; Member, Committee on Science, Space and Technology, United States Congress **PA:** Democrat **RE:** Roman Catholic

LIPINSKI, TARA KRISTEN, T: Professional Figure Skater (Retired), Sportscaster **I:** Athletics **DOB:** 06/10/1982 **PB:** Philadelphia **SC:** PA/USA **PT:** Jack Lipinski; Patricia (Brozyniak) Lipinski **MS:** Married **SPN:** Todd Kapostasy (06/2017) **C:** Fashion, Lifestyle and Social Media Correspondent, NBC Sports (2017-Present); Commentator, NBC Sports (2011); Commentator, Universal Sports (2010); Professional Figure Skater **CIV:** National Spokesperson, Campaign for Tobacco-Free Kids; National Spokesperson, Childhood Leukemia Foundation; National Spokesperson, Boys and Girls Clubs of America; National Spokesperson, National Youth Anti-Drug Media Campaign; Supporter, Texas Children's Hospital; Supporter, Make-a-Wish Foundation; Supporter, Candie's Foundation; Supporter, St. Jude Children's Research Hospital **CW:** Appearance, "Superstore" (2016); Actress, "Malcolm in the Middle" (2006); Actress, "Still Standing" (2005); Actress, "What's New, Scooby-Doo?" (2005); Actress, "The Metro Chase" (2004); Actress, "7th Heaven" (2003); Appearance, "The Wayne Brady Show" (2003); Actress, "Generation Jets" (2003); Performer, "Stars on Ice" (1998-1999); Author, "Totally Tara; An Olympic Journey" (1998); Author, "Tara Lipinski: Triumph on Ice" (1998); Actress, Appearances, Television Shows **AW:** Inductee, United States Figure Skating Hall of Fame (2006); First Place, Champion Series Final (1997, 1998); Gold Medal, Winter Olympics (1998); First Place, Rattle and Roll (1998); Second Place, National Championship (1998); First National Senior (1997); Female Athlete of the Year, U.S. Olympic Committee (1997); First Place, World Championships (1997); First Place, Hershey's Kisses Challenge (1997); Third Place, Trophy Lalique (1996); Second Place, Nations Cup (1996); Second Place, Skate Canada (1996); Mary Lou Retton Award, U.S. Olympic Festival (1994) **AV:** Reading; Cooking; Playing tennis

LIPSKY, LESTER, T: Professor Emeritus **I:** Education/Educational Services **CN:** University of Connecticut **DOB:** 12/04/1933 **PB:** New York **SC:** NY/USA **PT:** Morris Lipsky; Ray (Polonsky) Lipsky **MS:** Married **SPN:** Sue Marie (Basinet) (05/04/1996) **CH:** Ian Paul; Eric Mitchell; Tonya; Sylvie **ED:** Postdoctorate Coursework, University of London (Royal Holloway College) (1966-1968); PhD in Physics, University of Connecticut (1965); Coursework in Physics, Brandeis University (1958); BME, City College of New York (1956); Postdoctorate Coursework, National Bureau of Standards **C:** Professor Emeritus, Department of Computer Science and Engineering, University of Connecticut (2007-Present); Professor, Department of Computer Science and Engineering, University of Connecticut, Storrs, CT (1987-2007); Professor, Department of Computer Science and Physics, University of Nebraska-Lincoln (1976-1987); Professor, University of Nebraska-Lincoln (1968-1987); Visiting Professor of Informatics, Radboud University, Nijmegen, Netherlands (1976-1977); Associate Professor, University of Nebraska-Lincoln (1973-1976); Assistant Professor, Department of Computer Science, University of Nebraska-Lincoln (1968-1973); Research Fellow, University of London (1966-1968); Research Fellow, National Bureau of Standards, Washington, DC (1965-1966); Research Physicist, United Aircraft, Middletown, CT (1958-1961) **CR:** Consultant in Field **CW:** Author, "Monograph Queuing Theory: A Linear Algebraic Approach, Second Edition" (2009); Author, "Monograph Queuing Theory-A Linear Algebraic Approach" (1992); Contributor, Numerous Articles, Professional Publications; Contributor, American Physical Review, Internal of Physics in Great Britain; Contributor, Nuclear and Atomic Tables, Performance Evaluation Review, Journal of Applied Probability **AW:** Recipient, National Science Foundation Fellowship, NBS (1965-1966) **MEM:** Institute of Electrical and Electronics Engineers (IEEE); Association for Computing Machinery; American Physical Society; Sigma Xi; Sigma Pi Sigma; Upsilon Pi Epsilon **MH:** Albert Nelson Marquis Lifetime Achievement Award; Marquis Who's Who Top Professional **B/I:** Dr. Lipsky entered his profession because he was led by Einstein when he was an undergraduate. He decided that he would try to understand what the incredible scientist accomplished. **AV:** Singing in chorus; Bicycling; Collecting stamps; Playing bridge **PA:** Democrat **RE:** Jewish

LISSKA, ANTHONY JOSEPH, PHD, T: Maria Theresa Barney Chair in Philosophy, Professor **I:** Education/Educational Services **CN:** Denison University **DOB:** 07/23/1940 **PB:** Columbus **SC:** OH/USA **PT:** Joseph Anthony Lisska; Florence (Wolfel) Lisska **MS:** Married **SPN:** Marianne Hedstrom (03/16/1968) **CH:** Megan Catherine; Elin Elizabeth **ED:** PhD in Philosophy, The Ohio State University (1971); MA in Philosophy, St. Stephen's College, Dover, MA (1967); BA in Philosophy, Providence College, Cum Laude (1963) **CT:** Certificate, Institute for Educational Management, Harvard University (1979) **C:** Maria Theresa Barney Chair in Philosophy, Denison University (2004-Present); Professor of Philosophy, Denison University (1981-Present); Department Chair, Denison University (2008-2009); Charles and Nancy Brickman

Distinguished Service Chair, Denison University (1998-2001); Director, Honors Program, Denison University (1987-2002); Department Chair, Denison University (1984-1987); Dean, Denison University (1978-1983); Associate Professor, Denison University (1976-1981); Department Chair, Denison University (1973-1978); Assistant Professor, Denison University (1969-1976) **CR:** Consultant, Kenyon College (2008); Consultant, Luther College (2005); Consultant, Hampden-Sydney College (1998); Member, Scholarship Committee, Sherex Chemical Company (1984-1992); Consultant, Franklin Pierce University (1991); Consultant, Defiance College (1987); Visiting Scholar, University of Oxford, England (1984); Consultant, St. Joseph College (1980, 1982); Evaluator, Advisory Board, Midwest Faculty Seminar, The University of Chicago (1981-1990); Project Reviewer, National Endowment of the Humanities (1979-1990); Referee, Various Philosophy Journals; Lecturer in Field **CIV:** Precinct Representative, Democratic Party (1994-Present); Vice President, Granville Community Foundation (2003-2009); President, Granville Community Foundation (2004, 2008); Acting President, Granville Community Foundation (2007); Member, Granville Bicentennial Commission (1996-2006); Board Management, The Granville Historical Society (1987-2002); Convener, Civil War Roundtable (1989-1995) **CW:** Co-Editor, "Aquinas's Theory of Perception: An Analytic Reconstruction" (2016); Co-Editor, "Jacob Little's History of Granville" (2009); Author, "Illustrated History of Buckeye Lake Yacht Club" (2007); Co-Editor, "Bicentennial History of Granville" (2004); Author, "Aquinas's Theory of Natural Law, Paperback Edition" (1997, 2002); Author, "Aquinas's Theory of Natural Law" (1996); Co-Editor, "The Historical Times" (1988-2010); Author, "Philosophy Matters" (1977); Contributor, Numerous Articles, Professional Journals; Contributor, Chapters, Books **AW:** Eponym, Lisska Center for Scholarly Achievement (2016); R.C. Good Fellow (1990, 1996, 2002, 2009); Historian of the Year Award (2005); Carnegie Professor of the Year, Carnegie Foundation (1994); Teaching Award, American Philosophical Association (1994); Teaching Award, Sears Foundation (1990); Grant, National Endowment of the Humanities (1973, 1977, 1985) **MEM:** Executive Council, American Catholic Philosophical Association (2004-2007); President, American Catholic Philosophical Association (2005-2006); Vice President, American Catholic Philosophical Association (2004-2005); Program Committee, American Philosophical Association (2003); National Collegiate Honors Council; The Society for Ancient Greek Philosophy; The Society for Medieval and Renaissance Philosophy; St. Thomas Aquinas Society; New England Political Science Association; The Phi Beta Kappa Society **MH:** Albert Nelson Marquis Lifetime Achievement Award; Marquis Who's Who Top Professional **AV:** Studying; Taking photographs; Walking; Golfing **PA:** Democrat **RE:** Roman Catholic

LISTON, JEFFERSON, T: Lawyer **I:** Law and Legal Services **DOB:** 04/11/1954 **PB:** Troy **SC:** OH/USA **PT:** George Edward Liston; Jane Britannia Liston **MS:** Married **SPN:** Teresa Liston **CH:** Jane Elizabeth Liston; Scott Crowder **ED:** Doctor of Jurisprudence, Case Western Reserve University, Cleveland, OH (1978); Bachelor of Arts in Government, Otterbein College, Westerville, OH (1975) **C:** Solo Practioner (2016-Present); Partner, Tyack, Blackmore, Liston & Nigh, Columbus, OH (2010-2015); Partner, Tyack, Blackmore & Liston, Columbus, OH (1993-2009); Associate, Tyack & Blackmore, Columbus, OH (1990-1993); Court Magistrate, Franklin County Juvenile Court, Columbus, OH (1985-1990); Attorney, Bureau of Support, Franklin County Domestic Court, Columbus, OH (1984-

1985); Private Practice, Columbus, OH (1978-1984) **CR:** Commission on the Appointment of Counsel in Capital Cases (2018-2019); Chairman, Ohio Public Defender Commission (2013-2016); Member, Ohio Public Defender Commission (2006-2013); Government's Task Force, MR/DD Victims of Crime (2002-2003); Investigation and Prosecution of Child Abuse (2001-2003); Juvenile Justice Advisory Committee, Franklin County (2001); Advisory Board, Franklin County Juvenile Court (2001); Founding President, Central Ohio Association of Juvenile Lawyers (1997); Board of Trustees Juvenile Justice Coalition (1994); Ohio Magistrates Association (1989-1990); Speaker in Field **CIV:** Board of Trustees, St. Joseph Montessori School (1990-1997); Advisory Board, Central Juvenile Defender Center; Past Member, Juvenile Justice Advocacy Group; League Against Child Abuse; Community Advisory Board, Children's Hospital; Founding Member, Chemical Assessment Referral, Evaluation Services Advisory Board **CW:** Co-author, "Justice Cut Short: An Assessment of Access to Counsel and Quality of Representation in Delinquency Proceedings in Ohio" (2003) **AW:** Attorney of the Year (2016); Award of Distinction, National Juvenile Defender Center (2004); Community Service Award, Columbus Bar Association (1988); Ohio Association of Criminal Defense Lawyers **MEM:** Board of Directors, President, Ohio Association Criminal Defense Lawyers (2001-2002); American Bar Association; Columbus Bar Association; Ohio State Bar Association **BAR:** Supreme Court of the United States (1987); United States District Court for the Southern District of Ohio (1987); Ohio (1987) **MH:** Albert Nelson Marquis Lifetime Achievement Award **B/I:** Mr. Liston became involved in his profession due to the influence of his parents, who were both educators in their own right. He saw the law as an avenue to create a successful career and make a positive impact on the lives of others. **AV:** Enjoying family; Travel

LITHGOW, JOHN ARTHUR, T: Actor **I:** Media & Entertainment **DOB:** 10/19/1945 **PB:** Rochester **SC:** NY/USA **PT:** Arthur Lithgow; Sarah Jane (Price) Lithgow **MS:** Married **SPN:** Mary Yeager (1981); Jean Taynton (09/10/1966, Divorced 1980) **CH:** Ian; Phoebe; Nathan **ED:** Honorary Degree, Harvard University (2005); Postgraduate Coursework, London Academy of Music and Dramatic Art (1967-1969); BA in History and Literature, Harvard University, Magna Cum Laude (1967) **C:** Printmaker, Founder, Lithgow Graphics **CW:** Actor, "Late Night" (2019); Actor, "The Tomorrow Man" (2019); Actor, "Pet Sematary" (2019); Actor, "Bombshell" (2019); Voice Actor, "The Simpsons" (2019); Voice Actor, "Unikitty!" (2018-2019); Actor, "Beatriz at Dinner" (2017); Actor, "Trial & Error" (2017); Actor, "Daddy's Home 2" (2017); Actor, "Pitch Perfect 3" (2017); Actor, "The Crown" (2016-2019); Actor, "Miss Sloane" (2016); Actor, "The Accountant" (2016); Actor, "Louie" (2015); Narrator, "Best of Enemies" (2015); Actor, "Drunk History" (2014); Actor, "Love is Strange" (2014); Actor, "The Homesman" (2014); Actor, "Interstellar" (2014); Actor, "Once Upon a Time in Wonderland" (2013-2014); Actor, "The Magistrate" (2013); Actor, "Timms Valley" (2013); Actor, "The Campaign" (2012); Actor, "This is 40" (2012); Actor, "Rise of the Planet of the Apes" (2011); Actor, "The Columnist" (2011); Author, "Drama: An Actor's Education" (2011); Actor, "Leap Year" (2010); Actor, "Confessions of a Shopaholic" (2009); Actor, "Mr. & Mrs. Fitch" (2009); Actor, "Dexter" (2009); Actor, "The Macabre World of Lavender Williams" (2009); Actor, "Classical Baby (I'm Grown Up Now): The Poetry Show" (2008); Actor, "Paloozaville" (2008); Actor, "All My Sons" (2008); Actor, "John Lithgow: Stories by Heart" (2008); Actor, "Twenty Good

Years" (2006-2008); Actor, "Dreamgirls" (2006); Actor, "E=mc²" (2005); Actor, "Dirty Rotten Scoundrels" (2005); Actor, "The Retreat from Moscow" (2004); Author, "Carnival of the Animals" (2004); Actor, "The Life and Death of Peter Sellers" (2004); Actor, "Kinsey" (2004); Author, "I'm a Manatee" (2003); Actor, "Orange County" (2002); Voice Actor, "Shrek" (2001); Author, "Marsupial Sue" (2001); Actor, "Sweet Smell of Success" (2000-2003); Voice Actor, "Rugrats in Paris: The Movie" (2000); Actor, "C-Scam" (2000); Author, "The Remarkable Farkle McBride" (2000); Singer, "Singing in the Bathtub" (1999); Actor, "Portofino" (1999); Actor, "Don Quixote" (1999); Actor, "Officer Buckle and Gloria" (1998); Actor, "Johhny Skidmarks" (1998); Actor, "Homegrown" (1998); Actor, "A Civil Action" (1998); Actor, "3rd Rock from the Sun" (1996-2001); Actor, "Christmas in Washington" (1996); Actor, "Cosby" (1996); Narrator, "Special Effects: Anything Can Happen" (1996); Actor, "Hollow Point" (1995); Actor, "The Tuskegee Airmen" (1995); Actor, "My Brother's Keeper" (1995); Actor, "Redwood Curtain" (1995); Actor, "Good Man in Africa" (1994); Actor, "Then There Were Giants" (1994); Actor, "American Cinema" (1994); Actor, "World War II: When Lions Roared" (1994); Actor, "Silent Fall" (1994); Actor, "Princess Caraboo" (1994); Actor, "The Pelican Brief" (1993); Actor, "Cliffhanger" (1993); Actor, "The Wrong Man" (1993); Actor, "Love, Cheat and Steal" (1993); Actor, "Raising Cain" (1992); Actor, "At Play in the Fields of the Lord" (1991); Actor, "Ricochet" (1991); Actor, "The Boys" (1991); Actor, "Memphis Belle" (1990); Actor, "Ivory Hunters" (1990); Actor, "Out Cold" (1989); Actor, "Tales from the Crypt" (1989); Actor, "Traveling Man" (1989); Actor, "Distant Thunder" (1988); Actor, "Harry and the Hendersons" (1987); Actor, "Baby Girl Scott" (1987); Actor, "Resting Place" (1986); Actor, "Mesmerized" (1986); Actor, "The Manhattan Project" (1986); Actor, "Santa Claus: The Movie" (1985); Appearance, "Amazing Stories" (1985); Actor, "The Glitter Dome" (1984); Actor, "2010: The Year We Make Contact" (1984); Actor, "Footloose" (1984); Actor, "Adventures of Buckaroo Banzai Across the 8th Dimension" (1984); Actor, "Twilight Zone: The Movie" (1983); Actor, "Terms of Endearment" (1983); Actor, "Mom, the Wolfman and Me" (1983); Actor, "The Day After" (1983); Actor, "Not in Front of the Children" (1982); Actor, "I'm Dancing as Fast as I Can" (1982); Actor, "The World According to Garp" (1982); Actor, "Blow Out" (1981); Actor, "Rich Kids" (1979); Actor, "All That Jazz" (1979); Actor, "The Big Fix" (1978); Actor, "Obsession" (1976); Actor, Plays, Television Shows and Film; Author, Books **AW:** Screen Actors Guild Award for Outstanding Performance by a Male Actor in a Drama Series, SAG-AFTRA (2017); Emmy Award for Outstanding Supporting Actor in a Drama Series, Academy of Television Arts & Sciences (2017); Harvard Arts Medal (2017); Golden Globe Award for Best Performance by a Supporting Actor in a Series, Mini-Series, or Motion Picture Made for TV, Hollywood Foreign Press Association (2010); Emmy Award for Outstanding Guest Actor in a Drama Series, Academy of Television Arts & Sciences (2010); Inductee, Theater Hall of Fame (2005); Tony Award for Best Male Actor in a Musical (2002); Star, Hollywood Walk of Fame (2001); Emmy Award for Outstanding Lead Actor in a Comedy Series, Academy of Television Arts & Sciences (1996, 1997, 1999); Screen Actors Guild Awards for Outstanding Performance by a Male Actor in a Comedy Series, SAG-AFTRA (1997, 1998); Golden Globe Award for Best Actor in a TV Series Musical and Comedy, Hollywood Foreign Press Association (1996); Emmy for Outstanding Guest Performer in a Drama Series, Academy of Television Arts & Sciences (1986); Drama Desk

Award for Outstanding Actor in a Play (1985); Tony Award for Best Featured Actor in a Play (1973); Numerous Awards

LITTLE, BRADLEY, "BRAD" JAY, T: Governor of Idaho **I:** Government Administration/Government Relations/Government Services **DOB:** 02/15/1954 **PB:** Emmett **SC:** ID/USA **MS:** Married **SPN:** Teresa Soulen (05/1978) **CH:** Adam; David **ED:** BS in Agri-Business, University of Idaho (1977) **C:** Governor, State of Idaho (2019-Present); Lieutenant Governor, State of Idaho (2009-2019); Majority Caucus Chairman, Idaho State Senate (2003-2009); Member, District 11, Idaho State Senate (2002-2009); Member, District 8, Idaho State Senate (2001-2002) **CR:** Manager, Little Land and Livestock; Head, Little Enterprises, Inc.; Board of Directors, Performance Design Inc. **CIV:** Vice-Chair, The Idaho Community Foundation (2004); Vice-Chair, Emmett Public School Foundation (2004) **AW:** Honorary Lifetime Membership Award, Boise State University Alumni Association **MEM:** Phi Delta Theta Fraternity, Idaho Alpha Chapter **PA:** Republican **RE:** Episcopalian

LITTLE, R. JOHN JOHN, PHD, T: President, Botanist **I:** Environmental Services **CN:** Sycamore Environmental Consultants, Inc. **DOB:** 07/08/1946 **PB:** Oceanside **SC:** CA/USA **PT:** Robert Little; Ruth Little **MS:** Married **SPN:** Cynthia Little **CH:** Jeff Little; Branden Little **ED:** PhD in Botany, Claremont Graduate University (1980); MA in Biology, California State University, Fullerton, CA (1977); BS in Botany, The University of Utah (1968) **CT:** California Community Colleges, Instructor Credential (1979); Valid for Life: Biological & Botanical Sciences **C:** President, Sycamore Environmental Consultants Inc., Sacramento, CA (1991-Present); Director of Environmental Services, Envirosphere Company, Sacramento, CA (1980-1991); Instructor of Biology, Sierra College, Auburn, CA (1992); Lecturer of Botany, California State University, Fullerton, CA (1977-1980); Instructor of Biology, Saddleback College, Mission Viejo, CA (1977-1980) **CR:** Reviewer, National Science Foundation (NSF) Graduate Research Fellowship Program (GRFP) (2019-Present); Certified Arborist, International Society of Arboriculture (1992-2014); President, California Botanical Society (1997-2000); Council Member, California Botanical Society (1993-1997); Board of Directors, Southern California Botanists (1979-1985); President, Orange County Chapter, California Native Plant Society (1983-1984); Research Associate and Visiting Scholar, Herbarium, University of California Berkeley; Reviewer, Research Papers and Books, American Journal of Botany, Biotropica, Ecosphere (Online), Madroño, Oikos, and Plant Science Bulletin **CIV:** Trustee, Greenhaven Neighborhood Church (2019-2021); Presenter, Seminar on Nyctinasty in Viola Banksii, Queensland Herbarium, Brisbane, Australia (2017); Invited Speaker, Seminar Course for Second Year Masters Students in Biological Sciences, "What is Environmental Consulting?" (2008, 2014); Invited Speaker, Workshop on How to Identify Viola Species, Consortium of Pacific Northwest Herbaria (2005) **MIL:** Commissioned Officer, United States Navy, Three Tours of Vietnam (1968-1972); Midshipman, United States Navy (1964-1968) **CW:** Author, "Violaceae Treatment in Flora of Oregon" (2018); Senior Author, "Violaceae Treatment in Flora North America" (2015); Author, "Hybanthus Treatment in Flora North America" (2015); Author, "Violaceae in Jepson Manual, Higher Plants of California" (1993, 2012); Author, "Violaceae Family Treatment," The Jepson Desert Manual (2002); Author, "Violaceae Family Treatment in Vascular Plants of Arizona" (2001); Co-editor, "Handbook of Experimental Pollination of Biology" (1983); Senior

Author, "A Dictionary of Botany" (1980); Author, "A Flora of Starr Ranch" (1978); Author, "Violaceae Family Treatment in Flora of the Four Corners Region, Vascular Plants of the San Juan River Drainage: Arizona, Colorado, New Mexico, and Utah"; Author, "An Eighty-year Index to Madroño (1916-1996)," West American Journal of Botany **AW:** Recognition as Senior Ecologist, The Ecological Society of America (2012-Present); Listee, Who's Who in Frontiers of Science and Technology, Second Edition (1985); Research Grantee, Audubon Society (1975-1977); Navy ROTC Scholarship (1964-1968) **MEM:** The Botanical Society of America; American Society of Plant Taxonomists; Ecological Society of America (ESA); California Botanical Society; California Native Plant Society; Society for Ecological Restoration; California Invasive Plant Council **MH:** Albert Nelson Marquis Lifetime Achievement Award; Marquis Who's Who Top Professional; Marquis Who's Who Humanitarian Award **AS:** Dr. Little attributes his success to hard work, fear of failure, and the desire to help others, especially those in need. **B/I:** Dr. Little was always interested in science as far back as he can remember, everything from astronomy, chemistry, birds, bees, lizards, plants, etc. Growing up, he had fruit trees and a vegetable garden, and he was always amazed when those tiny seeds germinated and became a mature plant. For a book report assignment at Carlsbad High School at age 15, he read a biography on Luther Burbank, a pioneer horticulturist. He never realized plants could do so many fascinating things. He started taking classes in horticulture and learning scientific names of plants. It was very cool, and he found he had a knack for remembering scientific names. From then on, Dr. Little wanted to know the name of every plant he saw. In 1970, the federal National Environmental Policy Act (NEPA) was signed into law. A short time later, also in 1970, the California Environmental Policy Act (CEQA) was passed. In order to comply with federal and state requirements for conducting environmental studies and impact analyses, scientists were suddenly needed who actually knew how to identify the plants and animals in given project area. It took responsible agencies years to figure out what information needed to be collected to evaluate the impacts of a project on the environment. Eventually, it was determined that at a bare minimum, lists of all plant and wildlife species observed in the project area needed to be prepared. While in graduate school in 1976, he was asked to conduct several botanical surveys in southern CA and AZ for NEPA and/or CEQA projects. After receiving his PhD in 1980, he was unable to obtain a teaching position at a four-year university due to the limited number of open positions. However, with his background in plant taxonomy, several degrees in botany, and recent experience with several botanical consulting projects, he soon learned there were numerous agencies and private firms seeking to hire people with his experience as a result of the NEPA and CEQA legislation. In over 44 years as a consulting botanist, Dr. Little has worked on hundreds of different types of projects, culminating in over a thousand reports. Projects have been conducted in 13 states (AK, AZ, CA, CO, CT, GA, MA, MT, NV, NM, NY, OR and WA), and include high-voltage transmission lines, water, wastewater, and gas pipelines, flood control, fiber optic, energy generation (biomass, cogeneration, solar, wind), railroads, airports, highway and bridge projects, military bases, air quality effects on vegetation, and design and implementation of habitat restoration projects for wetlands, plants, and wildlife. **AV:** HO model railroading; Collecting native plant species and pressing them (for deposit in an herbarium); Taxonomy and biology of Australian species of

Viola in section Erpetion; Conducting research on floral nyctinasty **RE:** Mennonite **THT:** Dr. Little says, "'Life' didn't begin in a drop of primordial ooze; that's an absurd assumption."

LITTLEFIELD, CHRISTINA, T: Attorney **I:** Law and Legal Services **CN:** Littlefield Law and Mediation Office **CH:** One Daughter **ED:** JD, University of California, Davis (1982); MA, University of Maryland, College Park (1979); BA, Mills College (1974) **CT:** Certified Family Law Specialist **CIV:** Arbitrator, Alameda County Fee Arbitration program; Past Coordinator, Southern Alameda County Domestic Violence Law Project; Judge Pro Tem, Alameda County Court **AW:** Super Lawyer, San Francisco Magazine; Top Women Attorneys in Northern California **MEM:** Delegate, Collaborative Practice California; Board Member, Northern California Collaborative Practice Public Education Committee; Past Board member: Mills College Alumnae Board, Women Lawyers of Alameda County and Alameda County Bar; Association Juvenile Court Appointed Board; Past Delegate to California State Bar Conference of Delegates **BAR:** California **MH:** Marquis Who's Who Top Professional **AS:** Ms. Littlefield attributes her success to curiosity. **B/I:** Ms. Littlefield became involved in her profession because she thought she was going to save the world.

LITVAK, MARVIN MARK, PHD, T: Physicist **I:** Sciences **DOB:** 10/20/1933 **PB:** Newark **SC:** NJ/USA **PT:** Bernard Litvak **MS:** Married **SPN:** Marilyn Patricia Canney (03/09/1963) **CH:** Stephanie; David **ED:** PhD, Cornell University (1960); Bachelor Degree, Cornell University (1956) **C:** Chief Scientist, Technology Research Associates, Palos Verdes, CA (1993-2019); Senior Scientist, TRW, Redondo Beach, CA (1985-1993); Technology Staff Member, Jet Propulsion Laboratory, California Institute Technology, Pasadena, CA (1978-1985); Assistant Group Leader, Lincoln Laboratory, Massachusetts Institute of Technology, Lexington, MA (1983-1985); Radio Astronomer, Center for Astrophysics, Cambridge, MA (1971-1978); Assistant Group Leader, Lincoln Laboratory, Massachusetts Institute of Technology, Lexington, MA (1963-1970); Senior Staff Member, Avco-Everett Research Laboratory, Everett, MA (1960-1963) **CR:** Consultant in Field **CW:** Contributor, Articles to Physical Revision Astrophysics Journal, Proceedings of SPIE, Chapter to Annual Revisions of Astronomy Astrophysics **AW:** Fellow, National Science Foundation (1952, 1954, 1955); Fellow, Cornell University (1951) **MEM:** Fellow, American Physical Society; American Association for the Advancement of Science; International Astronomical Union; American Astronomical Society **MH:** Albert Nelson Marquis Lifetime Achievement Award

LIU, PAUL Y., T: Plastic Surgeon, Educator **I:** Medicine & Health Care **DOB:** 07/18/1960 **PB:** Fort Collins **SC:** CO/USA **PT:** Hsin-Kuan (Deceased 1960); Esther T.C. Liu (Deceased 2010) **MS:** Married **SPN:** SallyAnne Lund, MD (06/19/1988) **CH:** Christian A.; Meredith G. **T: ED:** MD, Harvard Medical School (1987); MA, University of Oxford (1983); BA, Colorado College (1981) **CT:** Diplomate, American Board of Plastic Surgery (2000, 2009) **C:** Founder, Chief Executive, Pax Therapeutics, Inc. (2017-Present); Chairman, Department of Plastic Surgery, Lifespan (2012-Present); Professor of Surgery, Alpert Medical School, Brown University (2012-Present); Program Director, Residency in Plastic Surgery, Brown University (2012-2017); Associate Professor of Surgery, School of Medicine, Boston University (2006-2012); Chairman of Surgery, Roger Williams Medical Center (2002-2012); Director, Roger Williams Medical Center (2004-2007); Senior Staff Surgeon, Lahey

Health System, Inc. (1998-2002); Assistant Professor of Surgery, School of Medicine, Tufts University (1998-2002); Assistant Professor of Surgery, Miller School of Medicine, University of Miami (1996-1998) **CIV:** Elder, Christ Church Evangelical Covenant (2009-2011); Sunday School Teacher, Christ Church Evangelical Covenant (2007-2009) **AW:** Dean's Award for Teaching, Alpert Medical School, Brown University (2016); Founder's Award, New England Society of Plastic Surgeons (2013); Patient's Choice Award (2011); Grantee, Marshall Scholarship, British Government (1981) **MEM:** Fellow, American College of Surgeons; The Phi Beta Kappa Society; The Aesculapian Club, Harvard University **MH:** Albert Nelson Marquis Lifetime Achievement Award **AS:** Dr. Liu attributes his success to fellow physicians, Dr. John Mulliken and Dr. Elof Eriksson. **B/I:** Dr. Liu became involved in his profession because of his experiences at Boston Children's Hospital; it was there that he learned the depths of what he could study as a plastic surgeon. **AV:** Playing violin with the Warwick Symphony Orchestra **RE:** Protestant

LOCKWOOD, FRANCES MANN PHD, T: Clinical Psychologist **I:** Medicine & Health Care **DOB:** 06/20/1946 **PB:** Washington **SC:** DC/USA **PT:** Ernest Daniel Mann; Thelma Gertrude (Gheen) Hubert **MS:** Widowed **SPN:** Bruce Robert Lockwood (05/10/1975) **CH:** Kathleen Gail; Karen Ann **ED:** PhD, University of Tennessee (1973); MA, University of Tennessee (1971); BA, University of Richmond (1968) **C:** Retired (2015); Private Practice, Jackson, TN (2007-2015); Staff Psychologist, Charter Lakeside, Jackson, TN (1999-2007); Staff Psychologist, Pathways, Inc. (1993-1999); Private Practice as Clinical Psychologist, Jackson, TN (1982-1993); Private Practice as Clinical Psychologist, Arlington, Alexandria, VA (1978-1981); Staff Psychologist, Assistant Director of Psychology, Commonwealth Psychiatric Center, Richmond, VA (1975-1977); Staff Psychologist, Children's Youth Program, Helen Ross McNabb Center, Knoxville, TN (1973-1975); Intern, VA Hospital, Memphis, TN (1971-1972) **CR:** Board of Directors, Montessori Center of Jackson (1991-Present); Coordinator, Children's and Youth Services West Tennessee Behavioral Center (1993-1995); Board of Directors, In-Home Care Planning, Inc. (1987-1989) **CIV:** Chairman, Rutherford County Board of Elections (2017-Present); Rutherford County Guardian Ad Liter (2016-Present); Red Bow Tie Volunteer, (2016-Present); Member, Child Protection Investigative Team (1994-Present); Leadership Rutherford, (2017-2018); Citizen Police Academy Alumni Association (2014-2016); Property Master, Jackson Theatre Guild (2014-2016); Jackson Citizen Police Academy (2014); Member, Child Abuse Review Team, Madison County, TN (1985-1990); Secretary, Andrew Jackson PTA, President, Jackson Business and Professional Women (1986-1987, 1987-1988); Member, Steering Committee, Jackson Chapter, Association for Children with Learning Disabilities (ACLD) (1985); Member, Leadership Jackson (1985) **AW:** Book Award, Psi Chi (1968) **MEM:** Leadership Conference, Tennessee Psychological Association (1990-1991); Second Vice President, Jackson Business & Professional Women's Club (1986-1987); Insurance Committee, Tennessee Psychological Association (1984-1985); Southeastern Psychological Association; American Psychological Association; Psi Chi **MH:** Albert Nelson Marquis Lifetime Achievement Award **B/I:** Dr. Lockwood became involved in her profession because she started undergraduate school with the notion of going into journalism. She had worked on a small time paper and enjoyed writing very much and had done some reporting. When she got to college and took her first psychology course because it

was a requirement at the time. She shortly thereafter became hooked and she became fascinated. So that became her major.In addition, what inspired Dr. Lockwood to get involved as a clinical psychologist is that again she just became fascinated with the classes that she was taking. She also fascinated by the human mind, brain, how it works, and plays out in peoples lives.Dr. Lockwood's private practice first occurred because they had made a move, her husband was a psychologist also, and they moved to Jackson, Tennessee, to join a practice there, but things didn't work out. She had just had their second child and was not ready to go back to work until after six months were she would work part-time. Her husband had signed a no compete and he couldn't open a practice. In fact neither one had a job for about six months, which put them in a bad situation until her husband got a job at a state mental hospital. A few months after that she took a loan to open a practice. She bought in a business plan and a female loan officer gave it to her. She started off with a card table, folding chairs, and an answering machine. It gradually grew and after a year she was able to pay off the loan. That is how the private practice business started kind of out of necessity. There was really no other place to practice other than another community mental health center, but the director didn't get along with many, so she couldn't go to work there, and so she opened the practice where her husband joined her. **AV:** Hiking; Visiting waterfalls; Walking; Outdoor activities

LODI, UMBREEN S., T: Assistant Professor **I:** Education/Educational Services **CN:** Emory University **MS:** Married **SPN:** Afzal **CH:** One Daughter **ED:** Fellowship in Allergy and Clinical Immunology, University of Alabama (1993-1995); Residency in Internal Medicine, Saint Louis University Hospital (Now SSM Health) (1991-1993); Internship in Internal Medicine, Sinai Samaritan Medical Center (Now Aurora Sinai Medical Center), University of Wisconsin (1990-1991); Foreign Medical Graduates Examination (1989); MBBS, Sindh Medical College (Now Jinnah Sindh Medical University), Karachi, Pakistan (1986) **CT:** Medical License, State of Georgia (1998-2019); American Board of Allergy and Immunology (ABAI) **C:** Assistant Professor of Medicine, Emory School of Medicine (2006-Present); Allergist, Peachtree Allergy & Asthma Clinic (2003-2014); Medical Director, Grady Clinic (Now Grady Health System) (2006-2007); Assistant Professor, Medicine, Division of Pulmonary, Allergy, Critical Care and Sleep Medicine, Emory School of Medicine (2000-2003); Internist, Allergist, Nathan Segall, MD, PC (1998-2000); Internist, American Family Care and Decatur Primary Care, Birmingham, AL (1997-1998); Clinical Instructor, Division of Allergy and Immunology, University of Alabama School of Medicine (1995-1997); Research Assistant, Hematology/Oncology, Department of Internal Medicine, Indiana University School of Medicine (1988-1989) **CIV:** Vice Chair, Health Fair Committee, Georgia Chapter, APPNA, Atlanta, GA (2012-Present) **CW:** Contributor, Articles, Professional Journals; Contributor, Lectures **AW:** Named Top Doctor of Atlanta (2012-Present); Named to America's Most Honored Professionals, American Registry (2018); Named Top 1%, American Registry (2018); Named to Top Doctors, Regional, Castle Connolly Medical Ltd. (2017, 2018); Named Women of Excellence in Medicine (2016) **MEM:** American Academy of Allergy, Asthma & Immunology; American College of Allergy, Asthma & Immunology **AS:** Dr. Lodi attributes her success to honesty, hard work and earning her living the right way. She firmly believes that treating the patient the right way is the only way. **B/I:** Dr. Lodi has wanted to be a doctor since childhood, as her

father and grandmother always wanted a physician in the family. Her family saw potential in her from the beginning and never stopped encouraging her. As Dr. Lodi grew up, her drive to do good only became stronger, and she chose medicine as a way to serve humanity. She ultimately became an allergist with inspiration from her father, who had asthma that was never properly treated. Dr. Lodi's father was her role model. A self-established man, he moved from Pakistan to America in 1915, and always impressed upon his family the importance of humility, hard work and pursuing the impossible. Dr. Lodi has always closely followed her father's advice, which also includes the significance of karma and giving to charity. **THT:** Dr. Lodi's strong belief in God has guided her; through prayer, forgiveness and a listening ear are always in reach. On a daily basis, she pursues strength, motivation and persistence and prioritizes taking the best of any situation, accepting anything she cannot change. Dr. Lodi values honesty and keeping a clear conscience.

LOEBSACK, DAVID, "DAVE" WAYNE, PHD, T: U.S. Representative from Iowa; Former Political Science Professor **I:** Government Administration/Government Relations/Government Services **DOB:** 12/23/1952 **PB:** Sioux City **SC:** IA/USA **MS:** Married **SPN:** Terry Loebsack **CH:** Jennifer; Sarah; Marcos Melendez (Stepchild); Madeleine Melendez (Stepchild) **ED:** PhD in Political Science, University of California Davis (1985); MA in Political Science, Iowa State University (1976); BS in Political Science, Iowa State University (1974) **C:** Member, U.S. House of Representatives from Iowa's Second Congressional District, United States Congress, Washington, DC (2007-Present); Professor, Political Science, Cornell College (1982-2006); Committee on Armed Services, United States Congress; Committee on Education and Labor, United States Congress **CR:** Board Member, United Nations Ambassador; Former President, Iowa Conference of Political Scientists; Former Chairman, Politics Department, Cornell College **CIV:** Chair, Linn Phoenix Club (2002-2005); Local Leader, Bill Bradley Presidential Campaign (2000); Linn County Coordinator, Howard Dean for President (2000) **MEM:** Humanities Iowa Speakers Bureau **PA:** Democrat **RE:** Methodist

LOEWENHARDT, PAULINE MARIA, MSN, T: Community Nursing Coordinator **I:** Health, Wellness and Fitness **CN:** James A. Haley Veterans Hospital **DOB:** 01/18/1934 **PB:** Detroit **SC:** MI/USA **PT:** Herman Josef Loewenhardt (Deceased); Elizabeth Henrietta Ring (Deceased) **MS:** Divorced **SPN:** Henry M. Klobucar (Divorced 1974) **CH:** Morgan Wolf; Joseph Michael; Peter Anthony **ED:** MSN, Marquette University (1973); BSN, Mercy College (1955) **CT:** Certified in Nursing Administration, American Nurses Association **C:** Freelance Writer (1997-Present); Retired Community Nursing Coordinator (2000); Community Nursing Coordinator, James A. Haley Veterans Hospital, Tampa, FL (1992-2000); Co-Investigator, Ergonomics, Evaluating and Modifying Nursing Tasks and the Workplace to Prevent Injuries (1994-1995); Co-Investigator, Long Range Planning Initiative, American Association of Spinal Cord Injury Nurses (AASCIN) (1991-1992); Nurse Manager, Spinal Cord Unit James A. Haley Veterans Hospital, Tampa, FL (1987-1992); Instructor, Medical College of Georgia, Augusta, GA (1986-1987); Executive Director, Visiting Nurse Association of Coastal Georgia, Savannah, GA (1985-1987); Director, Home Care Department, Trinity Memorial Hospital, Milwaukee, WI (1982-1985); Assistant Professor, Division of Nursing, Alverno College, Milwaukee, WI (1978-1982); Pediatric Clinical Specialist, Visiting Nurse

Association, Milwaukee, WI (1973-1976); Clinical Instructor, Charge Nurse, Milwaukee Children's Hospital (1968-1970); Instructor, Lamaze Method of Prepared Childbirth, Detroit, MI (1965-1966); Various Nursing Positions (1955-1961) **CR:** Consultant, Human Resources, Medical Foster Care Program, Tampa, FL (1989); DePaul-Bellevue Rehabilitation Hospital, Milwaukee, WI (1982); Next Door Foundation, Milwaukee, WI (1980-1982); Coordinator, Department of Continuing Education, Marquette University, Milwaukee, WI (1978-1980); Instructor, Department of Continuing Education, Marquette University, Milwaukee, WI (1978-1980); High Risk Infant Follow-up Program, Milwaukee, WI (1973-1975) **CIV:** Member, Unitarian Universalist Congregation of Ann Arbor, MI (2010-Present); Group Facilitator, Athens Mothers' Center, Athens, GA (1988); Board of Directors, Women's Crisis Line, Milwaukee, WI (1980-1985); President, Women's Crisis Line, Milwaukee, WI (1982-1984); Board of Directors, Wisconsin Alliance for School-Age Parents, Milwaukee, WI (1975-1977); Member, Gaia Women of the Great Lakes Basin **CW:** Author, Memoir, "Almost Lost: Detroit Kids Discover Holocaust Secrets and Family Survivors," Fifth Avenue Press, Ann Arbor, MI (2019); Author, "Developing Administrative Standards for Nursing Service," The Florida Nurse (1991); Co-author, Chapter on "Video," "Innovative Teaching-Learning Strategies in Nursing, Second Edition," Aspen(1989); Author, "Assuring Successful Home Enteral Feedings," Home Health Care Nursing (1989); Co-author, Home Health Resource Manual (1989); Contributor, Georgia Infection Control Network, Atlanta, GA; Contributor, Bylaws, Annual Reports, and Peer-reviewed Articles, Local Magazines and Newspapers **AW:** Research Certificate for Contributions to Ongoing Research Projects in the Spinal Cord Injury Program, James A. Haley Veterans Hospital (1995) **MEM:** Director, Bylaws Committee, District Four, Florida Nurses Association; Program Committee, Florida League for Nursing; American Nurses Association; American Association of Spinal Cord Injury Nurses; National League for Nursing; Sigma Theta Tau International Honor Society of Nursing **MH:** Albert Nelson Marquis Lifetime Achievement Award **AS:** Ms. Loewenhardt's parents, Herman and Elizabeth, set a fine example for all their children. They emigrated from Germany in the 1920s, met in Detroit, Michigan at a singing society and worked hard to raise their four children. They both suffered many traumas in their younger years and put that behind them as they focused on their family and earning a livelihood. She wrote several chapters about them in her memoir and dedicated the book to them. Ms. Loewenhardt attributes her success in her career to their example, and her resolve to always work hard, to take care of details in every situation, foster relationships in life and work with honesty and forthrightness, and maintain personal and professional integrity. She cared deeply for the people she took care of, and those she worked with in any capacity. **B/I:** Ms. Loewenhardt decided to become a nurse during the time she was hospitalized with polio at Herman Kiefer Hospital. An epidemic was raging throughout the country in 1944. She was completely paralyzed and could not speak or swallow for six weeks. She gradually recovered and learned to walk, eat and talk again with the help of many nurses, physical therapists, speech and occupational therapists. She recovered well enough that she was admitted to a four-year nursing program at Mercy College in Detroit in 1951. There is a chapter in her memoir about her experience with polio. By the time Ms. Loewenhardt entered her nursing program, there were still polio patients, though the vaccine had been discovered by Jonas Salk in 1953, and the live, attenuated vaccine by Albert Sabin in 1956.

AV: Writing; Singing **PA:** Independent/Democrat **RE:** Unitarian Universalist **THT:** Ms. Loewenhardt has always loved to write and began as a reporter for her Mackenzie High School newspaper. She enjoyed writing during her career as a nurse doing such tasks as program development, writing bylaws, annual reports, and peer-reviewed articles, etc. As she approached retirement from nursing, she began her freelance writing career and has been doing this for two decades. She has been published in local magazines and newspapers. In 2019, her memoir was published by the Fifth Avenue Press of Ann Arbor, Michigan. The heart of the story is finding lost relatives of her Jewish father in the Netherlands. Ms. Loewenhardt is a member of the Gaia Women of the Great Lakes Basin, a group of women from two countries, Canada and the USA, who sing love songs to Earth. Their mission is to raise awareness of the dire plight of planet Earth and many people who lack the necessities of life. She has three children and four grandchildren. Morgan Wolf is married to Terese Wolf, Joseph Michael married Linda Stingl and has two sons, Casey Joseph and Ryan Francis, and Peter Anthony is married to Martha Davis, and has two daughters, Shelby Lorraine and Sydne Kim. She has lived a long life and is grateful for each and every moment, even the difficult ones. They say adversity makes you stronger. She has had her share of adversity and it has strengthened her. To quote from the epilogue in her memoir, "I have learned to love, deeply and fiercely, all those in my circle of family and friends, and to love our beautiful, broken blue planet home with all its many creatures and different people. Love, respect, honesty and integrity are of prime importance to me, above all else. I have learned to forgive myself first, and then others for misdeeds. I live with a light footprint so as to do what I can to help with climate change. I work toward peace so that all people may live together in justice and peace." Her memoir is available on Amazon, or on her website, http://www.paulineloewenhardt.com

LOFGREN, SUSAN, "ZOE" ELLEN, T: U.S. Representative from California **I:** Government Administration/Government Relations/Government Services **DOB:** 12/21/1947 **PB:** Palo Alto.**SC:** CA/USA **PT:** Milton R. Lofgren; Mary Violet Lofgren **MS:** Married **SPN:** John Marshall Collins (10/22/1978) **CH:** Sheila Zoe; John Charles **ED:** JD, Santa Clara Law, University of Santa Clara, Cum Laude (1975); BA in Political Science, Stanford University (1970) **C:** Member, U.S House of Representatives, California's 19th Congressional District, United States Congress (2013-Present); Chair, U.S. House Standards of Official Conduct Committee (2009-2011); Member, U.S House of Representatives, California's 16th Congressional District, United States Congress (1995-2013); Member, Santa Clara County Board of Supervisors (1981-1994); Partner, Webber & Lofgren (1978-1980); Administrative Assistant to Representative Don Edwards, U.S. House of Representatives, San Jose, CA (1970-1978) **CR:** Adjunct Professor, Immigration Law, Santa Clara Law, University of Santa Clara (1981-1994); Founding Executive Director, Community Housing Developers, Santa Clara County, CA (1978-1981); Law Teacher, Santa Clara Law, University of Santa Clara (1976-1978) **CIV:** Board of Trustees, San Jose Evergreen Community College District (SJECCD) (1979-1981); Active Member, PACT: People Acting in Community Together **AW:** Bancroft-Whitney Award for Excellence in Criminal Procedure (1973) **MEM:** President, Santa Clara Law School Alumni Association (1978); Vice President, Santa Clara Law School Alumni Association (1977); The Bar Asso-

ciation of DC; Santa Clara County Bar Association **BAR:** State of California; Washington, DC **PA:** Democrat **RE:** Lutheran

LOGAN, THOMAS, T: Computer Scientist, Consultant **I:** Technology **CN:** Logatron Services **DOB:** 06/16/1949 **PB:** Bronxville **SC:** NY/USA **PT:** Thomas Logan; Anne (Gunther) Logan **SPN:** Janie Divid **ED:** Graduate Coursework, Advanced Computer Program, Columbia University (1996); Postgraduate Coursework, Pace University (1994); AAS in Electrical Technology, Westchester Community College, Valhalla, NY (1986); BSBS in Business Administration, Finance, New Hampshire College (1973); AAS in Marketing, Grahm Junior College, Boston, MA (1970) **CT:** MCSF Implementation; Windows 2000; OS Essential; Supporting Windows 2000 Network Infrastructure **C:** Consultant, Owner, Logatron Services, Tuckahoe, NY (1988-Present); Scribitur Information Services, White Plains, NY (1986-1988); Programmer, IBM, Yorktown, NY (1984-1986); Independent Contractor, Crigal Chemical Company, Boston, MA (1981-1983); Management Analyst, Program Administrator, County of Westchester, White Plains, NY (1978-1981) **CR:** Laboratory Supervisor, CTA Program, Columbia University (1995); Tutor, Electrical Technology, Westchester Community College (1983-1985); Tutor, College Math, Westchester Community College; Tutor, Computer Languages, Columbia University; Tutor, Mathematics, New Hampshire College **CIV:** Organizer, Community Youth Basketball League (1991); Assistant Football Coach, Roosevelt High School, Pop Warner Football, Eastchester, NY (1975-1977); Organizer, Community Program, Summer Lunch Program, New York, NY (1976); Tutor for Disadvantaged Children **CW:** Author, TLJ Process Specifications for Medical Authors; Author, Various Research Manuals; Author, Numerous Healthcare Issues Records; Author, "Math Understanding, A Manual on People with Disabilities" **AW:** Listee, Who's Who of Entrepreneurship (2003-2004); IEEE Service Award, Institute of Electrical and Electronics Engineers (IEEE) (1985-1986); Listee, Most Outstanding College Athletes in America (1972); Award of Excellence for Information Technology; Listee, Who's Who In America; Listee, Who's Who in the Media and Communication; Listee, Who's Who International; Listee, Who's Who of Information Technology; Editor Choice Award for Poetry Published on Poetry.Com; Listee, The Library of Poetry International **MEM:** Institute of Electrical and Electronics Engineers (IEEE); American Management Association; Masons; Kappa Sigma Beta **MH:** Albert Nelson Marquis Lifetime Achievement Award; Marquis Who's Who Top Professional **B/I:** When Mr. Logan was in high school, IBM visited one of his classes to advertise their services. They administered aptitude tests to the students, and Mr. Logan scored perfectly on each test. Hoping to travel and see the world as a professional, he enrolled in classes at BOCES (Boards of Cooperative Educational Services) to hone his skills prior to enrolling in college. **AV:** Appreciating theater; Traveling; Reading; Camping; Building robotics; Passing on knowledge; Walking in the first snow; Sitting by the fireplace; Playing with water **RE:** Baptist

LOMBARDI, FREDERICK, T: Lawyer **I:** Law and Legal Services **DOB:** 04/01/1937 **PB:** Akron **SC:** OH/USA **PT:** Leonard Anthony Lombardi; Dorothy (McKean) Lombardi **MS:** Married **SPN:** Margaret J. (Gessler) Lombardi (03/21/1962) **CH:** Marcus M.; David G.; John A.; Joseph F. **ED:** LLB, Case Western Reserve University (1962); BA, University of Akron (1960) **C:** Principal, Shareholder, Buckingham, Doolittle & Burroughs, Akron, OH (1962-2018);

Chairman, Commercial Law and Litigation Department, Buckingham, Doolittle & Burroughs, Akron, OH (1989-1999) **CIV:** Trustee, Executive Committee, Vice President, Ohio Ballet (1985-1993); Trustee, Walsh Jesuit High School (1987-1990); Life Trustee, Akron Golf Charities, NEC World Series of Golf; Board Member, Summa Health Systems Foundation, Downtown Akron Partnership; Board Member, President, St. Hilary Parish Foundation **CW:** Board of Editors, Western Reserve Law Review (1961-1962) **AW:** Lawyer of the Year, Akron Banking and Financial Law (2015); Akron Litigation Real Estate (2014); Listee, Best Lawyers in America (2010-2014); Ohio Super Lawyer (2004-2008) **MEM:** Board Member, Case Western Reserve University Law Alumni Association (1995-1998, 2003-2006); Trustee, Akron Bar Association (1991-1994, 1997-2000); Council of Delegates, Ohio Bar Association (1995-1997); Case Western Reserve Society Benchers; Past President, Fairlawn Swim and Tennis Club; Portage Country Club; Pi Sigma Alpha **BAR:** U.S. Court Appeals for the 6th Circuit (1966); U.S. District Court for the Northern District of Ohio (1964); U.S. District Court for the Northern District of Ohio (1964); Ohio (1962) **MH:** Albert Nelson Marquis Lifetime Achievement Award; Marquis Who's Who Top Professional **B/I:** Mr. Lombardi's father was a lawyer and a judge. He served as Mr. Lombardi's inspiration to pursue the field. **PA:** Democrat **RE:** Roman Catholic **THT:**

LONCHYNA-LISOWSKY, MARIA, MMUS, MUSIC EDUCATOR, PIANIST, T: Music Educator **I:** Education/Educational Services **CN:** The Piano Nook **DOB:** 09/26/1945 **PB:** Munich **SC:** Germany **PT:** Bohdan Ivan Lonchyna; Irene Lonchyna **MS:** Married **SPN:** Bohdan Lisowsky (05/31/1969) **CH:** Mykola Lisowsky; Danylo Lisowsky; Taras Lisowsky; Petro Lisowsky **ED:** MMus, Wayne State University (1969); BA, University of Detroit Mercy (1967); Diploma of Artistic Merit, Ukrainian Music Institute of America, Detroit, MI (1967) **CT:** Permanent Professional Certified Teacher of Music in Piano, Music Teachers National Association (2015-Present); Emeritus Certificate, Michigan Music Teachers Association (2015-Present); Certified Teacher of Music in Piano (2005); Certified Teacher of Music in Piano, Michigan Music Teachers Association (2001) **C:** President, Ukrainian Music Institute of America, Detroit, MI (2016-Present); Director, Ukrainian Music Institute of America (2001-2016); Piano Teacher, Ukrainian Music Institute of America (1967-Present); Piano Soloist, Collaborative Artist, Various Venues (1960) **CR:** Collaborative Artist, Others (2004-Present); Solo and Ensemble Festivals, Michigan School Band and Orchestra Association (1989-1998, 2004-2009); Artist, Troy, MI (1984-1998); With, Suzuki Workshops, Troy, MI (1984-1998); Music Director, Collaborative Artist Luna Ensemble, Warren, MI (1977-1983); With, Trembita Chorus, Detroit, MI (1975-1977); Pianist, Ukrainian Music Institute Trio, Detroit, MI (1965-1967); Collaborative Artist, National Education Committee, Ukrainian National Women's League of America (UNWLA) Accompanist, Immaculate Conception Ukrainian Catholic High School Chorus and Orchestra, Hamtramck, MI (1959-1964) **CIV:** Librarian, Detroit Symphony Civic Orchestra, Detroit, MI (1996-1998) **CW:** Musician, Recordings, "Listen and Sing Along-Ukrainian Christmas Carols" (1981); Musician, Recordings, "Listen and Sing Along" (1979); Musician, "Ukrainian Stories for Children" (1976) **AW:** Michigan International Professional Award, Cultural Bridge Ambassador, International Institute of Metropolitan Detroit (2017); Named Teacher of the Year, Metropolitan Detroit Musicians League (2003-2004, 2015-2016); Recognition Award, Ukrainian National Women's League of America

(UNWLA) (1998-2011, 2013); Recognition Award, Plast, Inc. (1999); Alumna of the Year Award, Parents Club of Immaculate Conception Ukrainian Catholic High School (1991) **MEM:** Treasurer, Metropolitan Detroit Musicians League (2018-Present); Eastern District Semi-finals Chair, Michigan Music Teachers Association (2009-Present); Student Achievement Testing Committee, Metropolitan Detroit Musicians League (2005-Present); President, Ukrainian Arts Society (1996-Present); Piano Testing Revision Committee, Michigan Music Teachers Association (2012-2018); Student Achievement Testing Chair, Metropolitan Detroit Musicians League (2008, 2012-2013, 2014-2015); Certification Committee, Michigan Music Teachers Association (2009-2015); President, Metropolitan Detroit Musicians League (2005-2007, 2011-2012); Member, Audit Committee, Ukrainian National Women's League of America (UNWLA) (2005-2009); Detroit Regional Council Correspondence Secretary, Ukrainian National Women's League of America (UNWLA) (2004-2005); Correspondence Secretary Regional Council, Ukrainian National Women's League of America (UNWLA) (2004-2005); Detroit Regional Council, Correspondence Secretary, Ukrainian National Women's League of America (UNWLA) (1997-1999, 2004-2005); Press Secretary, Ukrainian Language, Ukrainian National Women's League of America (UNWLA) (2003-2005); Secretary, Metropolitan Detroit Musicians League (2001-2004); President, Ukrainian National Women's League of America (UNWLA) (1995-1997); Treasurer, Ukrainian Educational Association (1985-1986, 1992-1997); Subscriptions, Plast, Inc. (1992-1996); President, Ukrainian Educational Association (1986-1992); Dues, Senior Division, Plast, Inc. (1984-1992); Subscription Chair, Senior Division, Plast, Inc. (1984-1992); Correspondence Secretary, Ukrainian National Women's League of America (UNWLA) (1980-1984); Recording Secretary, Ukrainian National Women's League of America (UNWLA) (1978-1980); Chapter 53, Educational Committee Chair, Ukrainian National Women's League of America (UNWLA) (1976-1978); Correspondence Secretary, Plast, Inc., Detroit Region, MI (1964-1969); Music Teachers National Association; Metropolitan Detroit Musicians League; Tuesday Musicale of Detroit; Ukrainian National Women's League of America (UNWLA); National Federation of Music Clubs **MH:** Albert Nelson Marquis Lifetime Achievement Award **AS:** Mrs. Lonchyna-Lisowsky attributes her success to hard, consistent work. **B/I:** Mrs. Lonchyna-Lisowsky became involved in her profession because her piano teacher encouraged her to teach. **THT:** Mrs. Lonchyna-Lisowsky motto is, "Always remember to thank God for all His Blessings, Grace and His Protection."

LONG, DAVID H., T: Chairman, President, and Chief Executive Officer **I:** Insurance **CN:** Liberty Mutual Group **C:** Chairman, Liberty Mutual Group, Inc., Boston, MA (2013-Present); President, Chief Executive Officer, Liberty Mutual Group, Inc., Boston, MA (2011-Present); President, International, Liberty Mutual Group, Inc., Boston, MA (2009-Present); President, Liberty Mutual Group, Inc., Boston, MA (2010-2011); Various Management Positions through Executive Vice President National Market & President Commercial Business Insurance Unit, Liberty Mutual Group, Inc., Boston, MA (1985-2008)

LONG, DONLIN MARTIN, PHD, T: Surgeon; Researcher; Educator **I:** Medicine & Health Care **DOB:** 04/14/1934 **PB:** Rolla **SC:** MO/USA **PT:** Donlin M. Long; Davene E. (Johnson) Long **MS:** Married **SPN:** Harriett Page (06/13/1959) **CH:** Kimberley Page; Elisabeth Merchant; David Bradford **ED:** Res-

ident in Neurological Surgery, Peter Bent Brigham and Children's Hospital Medical Center (Now Brigham and Women's Hospital), Boston, MA (1965); PhD in Neuroanatomy, University of Minnesota (1964); Resident in Neurological Surgery, University of Minnesota Health Science Center, Minneapolis, MN (1960-1964); Intern, University of Minnesota Hospitals, Minneapolis, MN (1959-1960); MD, University of Missouri (1959); Undergraduate Diploma, University of Missouri (1955); Coursework, Jefferson City Junior College (Now Jefferson College) (1951-1952) **CT:** Diplomate, America Board for Neurological Surgery **C:** Professor of Neurosurgery-Distinguished Service Emeritus (2010-Present); Practice of Medicine, Specializing in Neurosurgery, Baltimore, MD (1973-Present); President, Neuroscience Consultants (2010); Professor of Neurosurgery-Distinguished Service (2000-2010); Member, Principal of Staff, Applied Physics Laboratory, Johns Hopkins University (1976-2010); Professor, Chairman, Department of Neurosurgery, Johns Hopkins University (1973-2000); Neurosurgeon-in-chief, Department of Neurosurgery, Johns Hopkins Hospital (1973-2000); Associate Professor, University of Minnesota Hospitals (1970-1973); Neurosurgeon, University of Minnesota Hospitals (1967-1973); Assistant Professor, Department of Neurosurgery, University of Minnesota Hospitals (1967-1970) **CR:** With, John F. Kennedy Institute (1977); With, Baltimore City Hospital (1973); Consultant in Neurosurgery, Minneapolis VA Hospital (1967-1973) **CIV:** Medical Advisor, Bobby Jones Chiari & Syringomyelia Foundation (2015-Present); Served, U.S. Public Health Service (1965-1967); Co-founding Member, International Society for Study of Pain and Cervical Spine Research Society **CW:** Contributor, Numerous Articles on Neuropathology and Surgery to Professional Journals; Contributor, Book Chapters in Field; Co-developed with North and Fischell, First Rechargeable, Programmable, Implantable Drug In-fusion Pumps and Electrical Neural Stimulators; Founding Editor of Journal Spine (with collaborators); Basic Research Publications on Steroid Effects on Brain Edema **AW:** Dandy Society Medal for Distinguished Achievement (2018); Jamieson Medal, Australian Neurosurgery Society; Beks Medal, Dutch Neurosurgery Society; Ginde Medal, Indian Neurosurgery Society; Distinguished Service Award, International Federation of Neurosurgery Societies **MEM:** Society for Neuroscience; American Association of Neuropathologists; Society of Neurological Surgeons; American Association for the Advancement of Science; American Medical Association; Baltimore Neurological Society; International Association Study of Pain; International Society for Pediatric Neurosurgery; William T. Peyton Society; Congress of Neurological Surgeons; Johns Hopkins Medical and Surgical Association; Electron Microscopy Society of America; Maryland Neurosurgical Society (MNS); American Academy of Neurological Surgery; American Association of Neurological Surgeons; Neurological Society American (Now American Neurological Association); Cajal Club; Sigma Xi, The Scientific Research Honor Society; Omicron Delta Kappa; Alpha Omega Alpha Honor Medical Society; Phi Eta Sigma National Honor Society, Inc.; Pi Mu Epsilon; Mystical Seven **MH:** Albert Nelson Marquis Lifetime Achievement Award; Marquis Who's Who Top Professional; Marquis Who's Who Humanitarian Award **B/I:** Dr. Long started his education without any thought of being a physician. He was planning on being a chemical engineer; he had a dual major additionally in physics and mathematics and he was not interested in medicine at all. Towards the end of college, he saw that most of his friends were attending medical school and he decided to explore it also. He decided medical school was a good idea, so Dr. Long attended. The neurosurgery was straight forward; in medical school, his favorite class was the anatomy of the brain and when Dr. Long was looking for an internship, he went to the University of Minnesota and saw a young neurosurgeon there who was the best technical surgeon. His name was Dr. Lyle French and he was the ultimate surgeon. Dr. Long watched him operate and said he wanted to be able to do that, so he chose neurosurgery. **AV:** Fly fishing; Military history; Philosophy of medicine; Gardening **RE:** Christian

LONG, MICHAEL J., T: Chairman, President, and Chief Executive Officer **I:** Technology **CN:** Arrow Electronics, Inc. **ED:** Student, Milwaukee School of Engineering; BBA, University of Wisconsin **C:** Chairman, president, Chief Executive Officer, Arrow Electronics, Inc. (2009-Present); President, Chief Executive Officer, Arrow Electronics, Inc. (2009);President, Chief Operating Officer, Arrow Electronics, Inc. (2008-2009); Senior Vice President, President, Global Components, Arrow Electronics, Inc. (2006-2008); President, North America and Asia/Pacific components, Arrow Electronics, Inc. (2006); President, Chief Operating Officer, North American Computer Products (Now Arrow ECS (Enterprise Computing Solutions)), Arrow Electronics, Inc. (1998-2005); President, Gates/Arrow Distributing, Arrow Electronics, Inc. (1995-1999); President, Capstone Electronics, Arrow Electronics, Inc. (1994); Joined, Arrow Electronics, Inc. (1991); Numerous Leadership Positions, Schweber Electronics (1983-1990) **CR:** Board of Directors, AmerisourceBergen **CIV:** Board of Directors, Denver Zoo **AW:** Named One of Top 25 Executives, Computer Reseller News (2002, 2004)

LONG, THAD GLADDEN, T: Lawyer **I:** Law and Legal Services **CN:** Thad Long Legal Services **DOB:** 03/09/1938 **PB:** Dothan **SC:** AL/USA **PT:** Lindon Alexander Long; Della Gladys (Pilcher) Long **MS:** Married **SPN:** Carolyn Wilson Long (08/13/1966) **CH:** Louisa Frances Stockman; Wilson Alexander (Deceased) **ED:** JD, University of Virginia (1963); BA, Columbia University (1960) **CT:** Registered Member, Patent Bar **C:** Principal, Thad Long Legal Services (2011-2020); Partner, Bradley Arant Boult Cummings LLP (1970-2011); Associate Attorney, Bradley Arant Cummings LLP (1963-1970) **CR:** Private Practice (1963-Present); Adjunct Professor, Cumberland Law School (1999-2002); Samford University (1988-2002) **CIV:** Trustee, Birmingham Music Club Endowment (1995-Present); Secretary, Canterbury United Methodist Foundation (1993-Present); Trustee, Oscar Wells Trust for Museum Art (1983-Present); Trustee, President, Birmingham Music Club (2000-2003); Vice Chairman, Trustee, Sons of the American Revolution Foundation (1994-2002); Chairman, Secondary Schools Committee, Alabama Area, Columbia University (1975-2000); President, Jefferson County Historical Association (1995-1997); Chairman, Entrepreneurship Institute (1989); President, Chairman, Greater Birmingham Arts Alliance (1977-1979) **MIL:** Captain, Judge Army General's Corps, U.S. Army **CW:** Contributing Author, "Reflections" (2017); Editorial Board Member, "The Trademark Reporter" (1994-2007); Co-Author, "Unfair Competition Under Alabama Law" (1990); Co-Author, "Protecting Intellectual Property" (1990); Contributor, Articles, Professional Journals **AW:** Best Lawyers in America; Alabama Super Lawyers; Special Service Award, Alabama Association for Retarded Children, Great Communicator Award, International Trademark Association; Omicron Delta Kappa; The Raven Society; American Law Institute; Alabama Law Foundation **MEM:** Secretary, BIO Alabama (1998-2001); Chairman, Bir-

mingham Chapter, Alumni Association, School of Law, University of Virginia (1984-1989); Fellow, Alabama Law Foundation; Patent Bar; International Trademark Association; American Law Institute; Alabama Law Institute; Alabama Bar Association; Legal Aid Society of Birmingham; SASMS; Omicron Delta Kappa **BAR:** Alabama State Bar (1963); United States District Court Northern District of Alabama; United States District Court Southern District of Alabama; United States District Court Middle District of Alabama; United States Court of Appeals for the Eleventh Circuit; United States Court of Appeals for the Fifth Circuit; Supreme Court of the United States **MH:** Albert Nelson Marquis Lifetime Achievement Award; Marquis Who's Who Top Professional **AS:** Mr. Long attributes his success to his never-give-up attitude, hard work, optimism and his faith in the legal system. **B/I:** Mr. Long became involved in his profession because he used to read Earl Stanley Gardner and Perry Mason books as a high school student. After losing both of his parents, he received a scholarship to Columbia University and he has never looked back. **AV:** Traveling the world; Writing; Playing table tennis; Studying history and historical architecture **PA:** Republican **RE:** Methodist

LONG, WILLIAM B., T: Administrator **I:** Government Administration/Government Relations/Government Services **CN:** FEMA **DOB:** 04/06/1975 **PB:** Newton **SC:** NC/USA **ED:** MPA, Appalachian State University; BS, Appalachian State University **C:** Administrator, FEMA (2017-Present); Executive Vice President, Hagerty Consulting (2011-2017); Head, Alabama Emergency Management Agency (2008-2011); Southeast Regional Director, Beck Disaster Recovery (2007-2008); Hurricane Program Manager, FEMA (2001-2006); Statewide Planner, School Safety Coordinator, Georgia Emergency Management Agency (1999-2001)

LONG, WILLIAM, "BILLY" HOLLIS II, T: U.S. Representative from Missouri **I:** Government Administration/Government Relations/Government Services **DOB:** 08/11/1955 **PB:** Springfield **SC:** MO/USA **MS:** Married **SPN:** Barbara Long (1984) **CH:** Two Children **ED:** Diploma, Missouri Auction School, Kansas City; Coursework, University of Missouri **CT:** Certified Auctioneer, National Auctioneers Association **C:** Member, U.S. House of Representatives from Missouri's Seventh Congressional District, Washington, D.C (2011-Present); Member, U.S. House Homeland Security Committee, Washington, DC (2011-Present); Member, U.S. House Committee on Transportation and Infrastructure Committee, Washington, DC (2011-Present); Member, Committee on Energy and Commerce; Owner, Billy Long Auctions, LLC **CW:** Former Talk Radio Show Host, KWTO AM 560, Springfield, MO **MEM:** National Rifle Association of America; Greater Springfield Board of Realtors; Missouri Professional Auctioneers Hall of Fame; Former President, Missouri Professional Auctioneer Association; Member, National Board of Directors, National Auctioneers Association; National Association of Realtors; Springfield Area Chamber of Commerce; Rotary Club of Southeast **PA:** Republican **RE:** Presbyterian

LOOMIS, JAMES COOK, T: Mathematician; Cyberneticist; Writer; Educator; Navigator **I:** Education/Educational Services **DOB:** 09/22/1935 **PB:** Long Beach **SC:** CA/USA **PT:** Joseph Gray Loomis; Elizabeth Cook Loomis **CH:** Gannon Joseph; Megan Leslie Loomis Powers **ED:** Postgraduate Coursework, University of Michigan (1962); MA, University of California (1961); BS, University of California (1958) **C:** Director, Planetary Healing Pageants, Maui, Hawaii (1976-2005); Director,

Cetacean Relations Society, Maui, Hawaii (1976-1998); Department Head Mathematician, Culver City High School, CA (1962-1970) **CR:** Y2Kaper FOANA-TUNUP-HAS Flags of All Nations and The United Nations Underwater Parade Honoring All Species for the Global Millennium Television Network, 24 Hour Broadcast (2001); First Global Peace Research Conference (1994); SHE PEACE: A World Peace Beadgame Creating Future Friendly Eco-Geo-Chief Executive Officer's Captain, Project Jonah Grant (1976); PhD Fellow, Mental Health Research Institute; Prisoner's Dilemma, Under Dr. Merril Flood; Genetic Algorithms, Under John Holland and Director J.G. Miller; Living Systems Speaker, University of Hawaii The Matsunaga Institute for Peace; Deep Breathold Diving Dolphin Entertainer Creator; Stem Teacher, Haiku School; Creator and Teacher, Course, Sacred Geometry of the Holoversse, The University of Hawaii Maui College, Kahului, Hawaii **CW:** Creator, US-UP-UC, United Species Underwater Parade Uniting Civilizations (2007); Author, "Saving the Cosmos ('Til Tuesday)" (1995); Author, "Strange Fluke" (1990); Featured, Life Magazine Centerfold (1979); Featured, Surfer Magazine Painting John Severson, Merry Eco-prankster Saving (1979); Exhibitions Include New York, The Museum of Contemporary Art, PAiA, The Puka **AW:** First Prize, Maui Writers Conference (1994); Two-time Grant Recipient, National Science Foundation; Named Captain, Dolphin Research Vessel TUTUNUI **MH:** Albert Nelson Marquis Lifetime Achievement Award **B/I:** Mr. Loomis says being tall, strong and brilliant in a two pier town in Long Beach, California, inspired him. Also another inspiration came after swimming in the beaches of California. He has hitchhiked across the United States. By his writings, Mr. Loomis wanted to be one of those people who kept the great poetic works alive. **AV:** Deep breath hold diver (108 feet); Memorized eight hours of poetry; Quoted four chapters of The Prophet to Vice President Nixon in White House **PA:** Democrat **RE:** Poetry of Science

LOPEZ, JENNIFER, "J.LO." LYNN, T: Actress, Singer, Dancer **I:** Media & Entertainment **DOB:** 07/24/1969 **PB:** Bronx **SC:** NY/USA **PT:** David Lopez; Guadalupe (Rodriguez) Lopez **MS:** Divorced **SPN:** Marc Anthony (06/05/2004, Divorced 06/2014); Cris Judd (09/29/2001, Divorced 01/26/2003); Ojani Noa (02/22/1997, Divorced 01/01/1998) **CH:** Emme Maribel; Maximilian David **ED:** Coursework, Baruch College; Diploma, Preston High School **CR:** Launched, Shoes Collection, DSW, Designer Brands (2020); Launched, Shoes and Jewelry Collection, Giuseppe for Jennifer Lopez, Giuseppe Zanotti (2017); Launched, Fragrance, Sunkissed Glow (2009); Launched, Fragrance, My Glow (2009); Launched, Fragrance, Deseo (2008); Launched, Fragrance, Glow After Dark (2007); Launched, Fragrance, Love at First Glow (2006); Launched, Fragrance, Live Luxe (2006); Launched, Fragrance, Miami Glow (2005); Launched, Fragrance, Live Jennifer Lopez (2005); Launched, Fragrance, Still (2004); Launched, Lingerie Line (2004); Owner, Madre's Restaurant, Pasadena, CA (2002-2008); Launched, Signature Fragrance, Glow (2002); Launched, Clothing Line, J-Lo by Jennifer Lopez (2001) **CW:** Executive Producer, "Good Trouble" (2019-Present); Judge, "World of Dance" (2017-Present); Performer, "One World: Together at Home" (2020); Appearance, "Dear Class of 2020" (2020); Appearance, "One World: Together at Home" (2020); Actress, Producer, "Hustlers" (2019); Performer, Super Bowl LIV Halftime Show (2019); Actress, Producer, "Second Act" (2018); Appearance, "One Voice Somos Live: A Concert for Disaster Relief" (2017); Actress, Executive Producer, "Shades of Blue" (2016-

2018); Voice Actress, "Ice Age: Collision Course" (2016); Actress, Producer, "The Boy Next Door" (2015); Actress, "Lila & Eve" (2015); Voice Actress, "Home" (2015); Judge, "American Idol" (2010-2012, 2014-2016); Executive Producer, "The Fosters" (2013-2015); Singer, "A.K.A." (2014); Author, "True Love" (2014); Actress, "Parker" (2013); Executive Producer, "South Beach Tow" (2011-2013); Actress, "What to Expect When You're Expecting" (2012); Singer, "Dance Again: The Hits" (2012); Co-creator, "Q'Viva!: The Chosen" (2012); Voice Actress, "Ice Age: Continental Drift" (2012); Singer, "Love?" (2011); Actress, "The Back-up Plan" (2010); Actress, "How I Met Your Mother" (2010); Producer, "Feel the Noise" (2007); Actress, Producer, "El Cantante" (2007); Actress, "Bordertown" (2007); Singer, "Como Ama Una Mujer" (2007); Singer, "Brave" (2007); Singer, "Rebirth" (2005); Actress, "Monster-in-Law" (2005); Actress, "An Unfinished Life" (2005); Actress, "Jersey Girl" (2004); Actress, "Shall We Dance?" (2004); Actress, "Gigli" (2003); Singer, "J to Tha L-O!: The Remixes" (2002); Singer, "This Is Me...Then" (2002); Actress, "Enough" (2002); Actress, "Maid in Manhattan" (2002); Singer, "J.Lo" (2001); Actress, "The Wedding Planner" (2001); Actress, "Angel Eyes" (2001); Actress, "The Cell" (2000); Singer, "On the 6" (1999); Voice Actress, "Antz" (1998); Actress, "Out of Sight" (1998); Actress, "Anaconda" (1997); Actress, "Selena" (1997); Actress, "U-Turn" (1997); Actress, "Jack" (1996); Actress, "Blood and Wine" (1996); Actress, "My Family" (1995); Actress, "Money Train" (1995); Actress, "South Central" (1994); Actress, "Hotel Malibu" (1994); Actress, "Second Chances" (1993-1994); Back-up Dancer, Music Video for Janet Jackson, "That's the Way Love Goes" (1993); Dancer, "In Living Color" (1991-1993); Backup Dancer, New Kids on the Block Performance, "18th Annual American Music Awards" (1991); Singer, "Por Primera Vez"; Actress, Appearances, Producer, Television Shows, Films AW: Michael Jackson Video Vanguard Award, MTV Video Music Award (2018); Telemundo Star Award (2017); Award for Favorite TV Crime Drama Actress, People's Choice Award (2017); Icon Award, Billboard Music Awards (2014); Ally for Equality Award, Human Rights Campaign (2013); Star, Hollywood Walk of Fame (2013); Award for Favorite Latin Artist, American Music Awards (2007, 2011); One of the Women of the Year, Glamour Magazine (2011); World's Most Beautiful Woman, People Magazine (2011); One of the 10 Most Fascinating People, Barbara Walters' Special (2010); Legend Award, World Music Awards (2010); Award for Latin Pop Album of the Year, Billboard Latin Music Awards (2008); One of the 100 Most Powerful Celebrities, Forbes.com (2008); Artists for Amnesty Award, Berlin International Film Festival/Amnesty International (2007); One of the 100 Most Influential Hispanics (2007); Crystal Award, Women in Film, Los Angeles, CA (2006); One of the 50 Most Beautiful People, People en Español (2006); One of the 25 Most Influential Hispanics, Time Magazine (2005); Children's Humanitarian Award, Children's Hospital Los Angeles (2004); Award for Favorite Hip-Hop/R&B Female Artist, American Music Awards (2003); Award for Female Star of the Year, ShoWest Awards/National Association of Theatre Owners (2002); Award for Bestselling Latin Female Artist, World Music Awards (2002); Most Influential Artist (2002); Voted Number One, 100 Sexiest Women list, FHM Magazine (2000, 2001); Female Entertainer of the Year, American Latino Media Arts Awards (2000); Award for Outstanding Actress, American Latino Media Arts Awards (1998, 1999); Most Fashionable Female Artist, VH1/Vogue Fashion Awards (1999); One of the 50 Most Beautiful People in the World, People Magazine (1997); Numerous Awards

LOREN, SOPHIA, T: Actress **I:** Media & Entertainment **DOB:** 09/20/1934 **PB:** Rome **SC:** Italy **PT:** Riccardo Scicolone; Romilda Villani **MS:** Widowed **SPN:** Carlo Ponti (04/09/1966, Deceased 01/09/2007) **CH:** Carlo Jr.; Edoardo **ED:** Coursework, L'Istituto Magistrali Superiori **CW:** Featured, "Sophia Loren: Live from the TCM Classic Film Festival" (2016); Actress, "La Voce Umana" (2013); Voice Actress, "Cars 2" (2011); Actress, "My House is Full of Mirrors" (2010); Actress, "Nine" (2009); Actress, "Too Much Romance...It's Time for Stuffed Peppers" (2004); Actress, "Lives of the Saints" (2004); Actress, "Between Strangers" (2002); Actress, "Francesca and Nunziata" (2001); Actress, "Destinazione Verna" (1999); Actress, "Soleil" (1997); Actress, "Messages" (1996); Actress, "Grumpier Old Men" (1995); Actress, "Ready to Wear (Prêt-à-Porter)" (1994); Actress, "La Ciociara" (1989); Actress, "Running Away" (1989); Actress, "The Fortunate Pilgrim" (1987); Actress, "Courage" (1986); Actress, "Aurora" (1984); Actress, "Blood Feud" (1981); Featured, "Sophia Loren: Her Own Story" (1980); Actress, "Brass Target" (1979); Actress, "Firepower" (1978); Actress, "Angela" (1978); Actress, "The Cassandra Crossing" (1977); Actress, "A Special Day" (1977); Actress, "Brief Encounter" (1974); Actress, "The Verdict" (1974); Actress, "The Voyage" (1973); Actress, "Man of La Mancha" (1972); Actress, "White Sister" (1971); Actress, "The Priest's Wife" (1970); Actress, "Lady Liberty" (1970); Actress, "Sunflower" (1969); Actress, "Ghosts - Italian Style" (1968); Actress, "More Than a Miracle" (1968); Actress, "Happily Ever After" (1967); Actress, "Arabesque" (1966); Actress, "A Countess from Hong Kong" (1966); Actress, "Operation Crossbow" (1965); Actress, "Lady L" (1965); Actress, "Judith" (1965); Actress, "The Fall of the Roman Empire" (1964); Actress, "Marriage Italian Style" (1964); Actress, "Yesterday, Today and Tomorrow" (1963); Actress, "Bocaccio '70" (1962); Actress, "The Condemned of Altona" (1962); Actress, "Five Miles to Midnight" (1962); Actress, "El Cid" (1961); Actress, "Madame" (1961); Actress, "It Started in Naples" (1960); Actress, "A Breath of Scandal" (1960); Actress, "The Millionaires" (1960); Actress, "Two Women" (1960); Actress, "Heller in Pink Tights" (1960); Actress, "That Kind of Woman" (1959); Actress, "Black Orchid" (1959); Actress, "Desire Under the Elms" (1958); Actress, "Houseboat" (1958); Actress, "The Key" (1958); Actress, "Pride and Passion" (1957); Actress, "Boy on a Dolphin" (1957); Actress, "Legend of the Lost" (1957); Actress, "Lucky to Be a Woman" (1956); Actress, "The Sign of Venus" (1955); Actress, "The Miller's Beautiful Wife" (1955); Actress, "Scandal in Sorrento" (1955); Actress, "Miseria e Nobilta" (1954); Actress, "Gold of Naples" (1954); Actress, "Woman of the River" (1954); Actress, "Too Bad She's Bad" (1954); Actress, "Aida" (1953); Actress, "Tempi Nostri" (1953); Actress, "Ci Troviamo in Gellera" (1953); Actress, "La Domenica della Buona Genti" (1953); Actress, "Il Paese dei Campanelli" (1953); Actress, "Un Giorno in Pretura" (1953); Actress, "Due Notti con Cleopatra" (1953); Actress, "Pelegrini d'Amore" (1953); Actress, "Attila" (1953); Actress, "Carosello Napoletano" (1953); Actress, "Africa Sotto i Mari" (1952); Actress, "La Favorita" (1952); Actress, "La Tratta delle Bianche" (1952); Actress, "E Arrivato L'Accordatore" (1951); Actress, Numerous Films; Singer, Several Singles **AW:** David di Donatello Award for Best Actress (1959, 1962, 1963, 1964, 1969, 1973, 1978, 1984, 1999, 2014); Cecil B. DeMille, Golden Globe Awards, Hollywood Foreign Press Association (1995); Recipient, Star, Hollywood Walk of Fame (1994); Honorary Academy Award, Academy of Motion Picture Arts & Sciences (1991); Award for Best Actress of the Year for TV Miniseries (1987); Golden Globe Award for World Film Favorite, Hollywood Foreign Press Association (1964, 1965, 1969, 1977); Ramo d'Oro Award, Italy (1968); Best Foreign Actress Diploma, USSR (1967); Alexander Korda Award, British Film Institute (1964); Academy Award for Best Actress in a Leading Role, Academy of Motion Picture Arts & Sciences (1962); Award for Best Actress, Rapallo Festival, Italy (1960); Award for Best Actress, Venice Film Festival (1959); Victoire Popularity Award, France (1959); Best Actress Award, Japan (1958); Award for Best Actress, Buenos Aires Festival (1954); Named Most Popular Actress in Italy; Nastro d'Argento, Italy; 14 Bambi and Bravo Popularity Awards, Federal Republic of Germany; Three Prix Uilenspiegoel Fiamingo Awards, Belgium; Popularity Awards, The American Legion, Texas Cinema Exhibitors; Four Snosiki Popularity Awards, Finland; Two Best Actress Awards, Bengal Film Journalists Association, India; Box-Office Favorite Medal, Italy; Helene Curtis Award, United States; Simpatia Popularity Award, Italy; Rudolph Valentino Screen Services Award, Italy; Award for Best Actress, Moscow Film Festival; Numerous Best Actress Awards Including, Hollywood, Cannes Film Festival, New York Critics, British Film Academy, Awards from Ireland, Japan, Belgium, Spain, France, Others

LORENZEN, ROBERT FREDERICK, MD, T: Ophthalmologist **I:** Medicine & Health Care **DOB:** 03/20/1924 **PB:** Toledo **SC:** OH/USA **PT:** Martin Robert Lorenzen; Pearl Adaline (Bush) Lorenzen **MS:** Married **SPN:** Lucy Logsdon (02/14/1970) **CH:** Roberta Jo; Richard Martin; Elizabeth Anne **ED:** MS, Tulane University (1953); Resident, Tulane Graduate School (1951-1953); Resident, Duke University Medical Center (1949-1951); Intern, Presbyterian Hospital, Chicago, IL (1948-1949); MD, Duke University (1948); BS, Duke University (1948) **C:** Practice, Medicine Specializing in Ophthalmology, Phoenix, AZ (1953-Present) **CR:** Chairman, Board of Trustees, Rockefeller and Abbe Prentice Eye Institute of St. Luke's Hospital (1975); President, Ophthalmic Sciences Foundation (1970-1973); Board of Directors, St. Vincent de Paul Eye Clinic; Member, Staff, St. Joseph's Hospital; Member, Staff, St. Luke's Hospital; Member, Staff, Good Samaritan Hospital; Member, Staff, Surgical Eye Center of Arizona **CW:** Editor-in-Chief, Arizona Medicine (1963-1966, 1969-1970) **AW:** Gold Headed Cane Award (1974); Named to Honorable Order of Kentucky Colonel **MEM:** President, Phoenix, Rotary (1984); Trustee, American Association of Ophthalmology (1973-1976); Secretary, House of Delegates, American Association of Ophthalmology (1972-1973); Board of Directors, Arizona Medical Association (1963-1966, 1969-1970); President, Arizona Ophthalmology Society (1966-1967); Fellow, American College of Surgeons; Fellow, International College Surgeons; Fellow, American Academy Ophthalmology; Fellow, Pan American Association Ophthalmology; Royal Society Medicine; Pan American Association Ophthalmology **MH:** Albert Nelson Marquis Lifetime Achievement Award **B/I:** Dr. Robert Lorenzen's father, Martin Robert Lorenzen was a cardiologist, and Dr. Lorenzen knew he was going to be a doctor at a young age because he would follow his father around at hospitals and spend sometime in his office and Dr. Lorenzen thought that it was a very fine profession and he decided to be a doctor specializing in ophthalmology. **AV:** Painting; Music **PA:** Republican **RE:** Roman Catholic

LORING, JOHN, T: Design Director Emeritus; Artist; Author **I:** Luxury Goods & Jewelry **CN:** Tiffany & Co. (T&Co.) **DOB:** 11/23/1939 **PB:** Chicago **SC:** IL/USA **PT:** Edward D'Arcy Loring; China

Robbins (Logeman) Loring **ED:** Honorary ArtsD, Pratt Institute, Brooklyn, NY (1996); Postgraduate Coursework, Ecole Beaux Arts, Paris, France (1960-1964); BA in English Literature, Yale University, New Haven, CT (1960) **C:** Design Director Emeritus, Tiffany & Co. (T&Co.) (2009-Present); Design Director, Tiffany & Co. (T&Co.) (1979-2009) **CR:** Member, Acquisitions Committee Department, Prints and Illustrated Books, The Museum of Modern Art, New York, NY (1990-1999); Bureau Chief, Architectural Digest Magazine, New York, NY (1977-1978); Distinguished Visiting Professor, University of California Davis (1977) **CW:** Author, "Tiffany Time" (2015); One-man Show, Sarah Gavlak Gallery (2012); One-man Show, Holden Luntz Gallery, Palm Beach, FL (2011); Contributing Editor, Architectural Digest Magazine (2000-2010); Author, "Tiffany Style" (2008); Author, "Tiffany Colored Gems" (2007); Author, "Tiffany Pearls" (2006); Author, "Tiffany's Palm Beach" (2005); Author, "Tiffany Diamonds" (2005); Author, "Greetings from Andy" (2004); Author, "Tiffany Timepieces" (2004); Author, "Tiffany in Fashion" (2003); Author, "Tiffany Flora & Fauna" (2003); Author, "Louis Comfort Tiffany at Tiffany & Co." (2002); Author, "Magnificent Tiffany Silver" (2001); Author, "Paulding Farnham: Tiffany's Lost Genius" (2000); Author, "Tiffany Jewels" (1999); Author, "Tiffany's 20th Century" (1997); Author, "Tiffany Christmas" (1996); Author, "The Tiffany Gourmet Cookbook" (1992); Author, "Tiffany Parties" (1989); Author, "The Tiffany Wedding" (1988); Author, "Tiffany's 150 Years" (1987); Author, "Tiffany Taste" (1986); Author, "The New Tiffany Table Settings" (1981); One-man Show, Pace Editions, Galerie de Marignan, Paris, France (1973, 1977); Exhibited in Group Shows, Biennale Graphic Art, Ljubljana, Yugoslavia (1977); One-man Show, ADI Gallery, San Francisco, CA (1976); Exhibit, Group Show, Rhode Island School of Design (1976); One-man Show, Long Beach Museum of Art (1975); Exhibit, Group Show, Art Institute of Chicago (1975); Exhibit, Group Show, Intergrafia, Krakow, Poland (1974); Contributing Editor, Arts Magazine (1973-1979); Exhibit, Group Shows, Biennale Graphic Art, Ljublijana, Yugoslavia (1973); One-man Show, Baltimore Museum of Art (1972); One-man Show, Hundred Acres Gallery, NY (1972); Exhibit, Group Show, New York Cultural Center (1972); Exhibit, Group Shows, Philadelphia Museum of Art (1971); Represented in Permanent Collections, The Museum of Modern Art, New York, NY, Whitney Museum of American Art, Art Institute Chicago, Museum of Fine Arts, Boston, Rhode Island School of Design, Yale University Art Gallery, Kalamazoo Institute of Arts and Boston Museum of Art; Principle Works, U.S. Alexander Hamilton Custom House, New York, NY, The Metropolitan Museum of Art, Prudential Insurance Co. (Prudential Financial, Inc.), Woodbridge, NJ and Scranton, PA, City of Scranton, PA, Western Saving Fund Society, Philadelphia, PA, and Tivoli Gardens, Copenhagen, Kingdom of Denmark (20 Years); Author, "Joseph Urban"; One-man Show, Galerie Verkauf, Vienna and Gallery Barozzi, Venice and Milan, Italy **AW:** Artistic Achievement Award, American Cancer Society, Inc. (2010); Lifetime Achievement Award, Museum of Arts and Design, New York, NY (2005); Dallas Fashion Award (2004); Legend Award, Pratt Institute, Brooklyn, NY (2002); Distinction in Design Award, The Fashion Group International, Inc. (1996); Edith Wharton Award, Design & Art Society (1988) **MEM:** Chelsea Arts Club, Chelsea, London, United Kingdom **MH:** Albert Nelson Marquis Lifetime Achievement Award; Marquis Who's Who Top Professional **B/I:** Mr. Loring became involved in his profession because of a lifelong love of art. As a child, he gravitated to the field; his father was a talented painter, so he was exposed to art around the house. At Yale University, he majored in literature with minors in art and art history. Then he decided to do postgraduate work to get himself into Ecole Beaux Arts in Paris, France, where he was one of two Americans out of 3,000 students. The job at Tiffany & Co. was offered to him while he was working at a gallery in New York. **THT:** Mr. Loring designed the whole look of Tiffany & Co., from the stores and its windows to advertising and merchandise.

LORNE, SIMON M., T: Vice Chairman, Chief Legal Officer **I:** Law and Legal Services **CN:** Millennium Management LLC **DOB:** 02/01/1946 **PB:** Hampton **SC:** England **PT:** Henry Thomas Lorne; Daphne Mary (Brough) Lorne **CH:** Christopher; Michele; Allison; Nathan James; Katrina **ED:** JD, University of Michigan Law School, Magna Cum Laude (1970); AB in Economics and Psychology, Occidental College, Cum Laude (1967) **C:** Chairman, AIMA (The Alternative Investment Management Association) (2016-Present); Board of Directors, Council (2014-Present); AIMA (The Alternative Investment Management Association) (2014-Present); Vice Chairman, Chief Legal Officer, Millennium Management LLC (2004-Present); Partner, Munger, Tolles & Olson LLP (1999-2004); Managing Director, Salomon Brothers, Inc. (1996-1999); General Counsel, U.S. Securities and Exchange Commission (1993-1996); Partner, Munger Tolles & Olson, LLP, LA (1972-1993); Associate Firm, Munger Tolles & Olson, LLP, LA (1970-1972) **CR:** Lecturer in Law, Corporate Finance, University of Southern California (1986-1988); Acting Director, Center of Study of Finance Institutions (1977-1978); Visiting Associate Professor, Law, University of Pennsylvania (1977-1978); Adjunct Faculty, New York University Law School and New York University Stern School of Business **CIV:** Board of Directors, Chairman, Audit Committee, Teledyne Technologies Incorporated (2004-Present); Vice Chairman, Director, DeAnza Land & Leisure (1996-Present); Member, Board of Directors, Chairman, Investment Committee, National Center for State Courts (2012-2018); Co-Director, Stanford Law School Directors' College (1999-2016); Visiting Fellow, University of Oxford, Centre for Corporate Reputation (2009-2013); New York Area Chairman, Appleseed Foundation (2006-2009); Chairman, Alternative Industry Management Association, London; Board Member, Irish Rep Theatre Company, New York **MIL:** U.S. Marine Corps Reserve (1967-1968) **CW:** Author, Book, "Acquisitions and Mergers: Negotiated and Contested Transactions" (1985); Author, Multiple Series; Contributor, 20 Articles, Professional Journals **AW:** One of the 100 Influential People in Corporate Governance, National Association of Corporate Directors **MEM:** Executive Committee, Business and Corps. Law Section, Chairman, L.A. County Bar Association; California (1984-1985); Leadership Mission to People's Republic of China, L.A. Area Chamber of Commerce (1980); Former Chairman, American Bar Association; Executive Committee, International Commerce Committee, L.A. Area Chamber of Commerce; Jonathan Club **BAR:** California (1971) **AS:** He attributes his success to hard work. **B/I:** Mr. Lorne thought that a law profession provided him with more options in life, more ability to do different things. He didn't think he was going to be practicing law, but turned out he enjoyed practicing law. He thought the legal back ground would provide flexibility and optionality. **PA:** Republican **RE:** Roman Catholic

LOTT, DOLORES M., EDD, T: School System Administrator (Retired) **I:** Education/Educational Services **DOB:** 07/17/1930 **PB:** Rockdale **SC:** TX/USA **PT:** Isaac Hanibal Woods; Ada (Green) Woods **MS:** Widowed **SPN:** Rufus Lott (07/25/1956, Deceased); Frank White II (02/12/1951, Divorced 09/1955) **CH:** Rufus Lott Jr.; Vernon Lott; David Lott; Lorenzo (Stepson); Freddie (Stepson); Magauret Maxine (Stepdaughter) **ED:** EdD, Nova University (1986); EdM, Our Lady of the Lake University, San Antonio, Texas (1963); BA, Prairie View A&M University, Texas (1951) **CT:** Teacher; Counselor; Administrator **C:** Retired (1989); Director, Program Coordination, San Antonio Independent School District (1983-1989); Personnel Director, San Antonio Independent School District (1973-1983); Counselor, Thomas Jefferson High School, San Antonio, Texas (1971-1973); Counselor, J.W. Riley Middle School (Now Martin Luther King Jr. Academy), San Antonio, Texas (1965-1971); Librarian, Counselor, J.W. Riley Elementary Junior High School (Now Martin Luther King Jr. Academy), San Antonio, Texas (1957-1965); From Procurement Clerk to Assistant Supervisor, Kelly AFB, San Antonio, Texas (1951-1957) **CR:** Lecturer, Our Lady of the Lake University, Summers (1971, 1972); District 2 Council Woman **CIV:** Precinct Chairman, San Antonio Democratic Party (1988-Present); President, Saturday Morning Breakfast Club (1986-Present); Member, San Antonio City Council, Texas (1996-1997); Mayor Pro-tem, San Antonio City Council, Texas (1996); Commissioner, Civil Service, City of San Antonio, Texas (1993-1996); Member, National Coalition of 100 Black Women, Inc. **CW:** Author, Biography, "Ada, Journey of a Post Slavery Negro Woman of Valor," iUniverse (2012); Author, Director, 21 Christian Plays, Presentation in Church Sanctuary **AW:** Community Service Award, Prairie View A&M University National Alumni Association (1982); Fellow, Our Lady of the Lake University (1963, 1965) **MEM:** Texas State Teachers Association (TSTA); Texas Retired Educators Deferred Dividend Association (TREDDA); San Antonio Area Retired Teachers Association **MH:** Albert Nelson Marquis Lifetime Achievement Award **B/I:** Dr. Lott became involved in her profession because she wanted to be a teacher but her first two positions were a library and counselor, and she had to go back to school to get those certifications to enable her to be qualified to be in the job that she was in. Then she became an administrator and went on to central administration so she had been working in the district for 32 years. Her entire first institution for education were catholic schools and her first public school was at college, which she began when she was 15 years old. **AV:** Reading; Motivational speaking; Teaching church school; Playing bridge; Dance; Writing **PA:** Democrat **RE:** Baptist

LOUDERMILK, BARRY DEAN, T: U.S. Representative from Georgia **I:** Government Administration/Government Relations/Government Services **CN:** U.S. House of Representatives **DOB:** 12/22/1963 **PB:** Riverdale **SC:** GA/USA **MS:** Married **SPN:** Desiree Loudermilk (1983) **CH:** Three Children **ED:** Bachelor of Arts in Occupational Education and Information Systems Technology, Wayland Baptist University, Plainview, TX **C:** Member, U.S. House of Representatives from Georgia's 11th Congressional District, United States Congress, Washington, DC (2014-Present); Co-owner, President, Innovative Network Systems Inc., Cartersville, GA (1995-Present); Member, District 14, Georgia State Senate (2013); Member, District 52, Georgia State Senate (2011-2013); Member, District 14, Georgia House of Representatives (2005-2011); Member, Committee on Financial Services; Member, Committee on Science, Space and Technology; Member, Committee on House Administration **CR:** Chairperson, Bartow County Republican Party (2000-2004) **AW:** Named, One of the 50 Most Influential Georgians, James Magazine (2008); Named, Public Servant of the Year, Advocates for Children (2006); Named,

National Legislator of the Year, Civil Air Patrol (2006); Named, Legislator of the Year, State of Georgia (2006) **PA:** Republican

LOUGANIS, GREG EFTHIMIOS, T: Former Professional Diver **I:** Automotive **DOB:** 01/29/1960 **PB:** San Diego **SC:** CA/USA **PT:** Peter E. Louganis (Adoptive Father); Frances I. (Scott) Louganis (Adoptive Mother); Fouvale Lutu (Father) **MS:** Married **SPN:** Johnny Chaillot (10/12/2013) **ED:** BA in Drama, University of California (1983); Coursework, University of Miami (1978-1980) **C:** Retired Professional Diver (1989); Former Member, U.S. National Diving Team **CR:** Hill-Nickleodeon Sport Theater (1997); Color Commentary, U.S. Diving Nationals (1990); Participant, U.S. Diving Championships (1985); Participant, U.S. Olympic Festival (1985); Motivational Speaker; Dog Agility Expert Judge; Mentor, Red Bull Cliff Diving Tour; Coach, U.S. Olympic Diving Team **CIV:** Board of Directors, Princess Charlene of Monaco Foundation; Supporter, Human Rights Campaign **CW:** Appearance, "Entourage" (2015); Actor, "Sabre Dance" (2015); Featured, "Back on Board" (2014); Trainer, "Celebrity Splash" (2013); Trainer, "Splash" (2013); Appearance, "Portlandia" (2012); Author, "For the Life of Your Dog" (1999); Actor, "Just Say No" (1999); Actor, "Nunsense A-Men" (1999); Host, "Where are They Now?" (1997); Actor, "Touch Me" (1997); Actor, "It's My Party" (1995); Actor, "The Only Thing Worse You Could Have Told Me..." (1995); Author, "Breaking the Surface" (1995); Actor, "Jeffrey" (1994); Actor, "Mighty Ducks II" (1992); Actor, "The Boyfriend" (1990); Actor, "Object of Desire" (1990); Actor, "Cinderella" (1989); Actor, "Dance Kaliedescope" (1987); Actor, "Hollywood Squares" (1986); Performer, "Circus of the Stars" (1986); Actor, "16 Days of Glory" (1985); Actor, "Dirty Laundry" (1985); Contestant, "The Brain" (1985); Contestant, "NBC Superstars" (1985); Contestant, "Battle of the Network Stars" (1985); Actor, "Equus" (1980); Contestant, "Battle of the Sexes" (1979); Actor, "Working" (1978); Actor, "Camelot" (1978); Actor, "Carousel" (1978); Producer, Narrator, "Breaking the Surface"; Actor, Appearances, Television Shows, Documentaries **AW:** Bonham Centre Award, The Mark S. Bonham Centre for Sexual Diversity Studies, University of Toronto (2015); Inductee, California Sports Hall of Fame (2013); Inductee, National Gay and Lesbian Sports Hall of Fame (2013); Robert J. Kane Award, U.S. Olympic Committee (1994); Inductee, International Swimming Hall of Fame (1993); Spirit Award, Maxwell House/U.S. Olympic Committee (1988); Gold Medal, Platform and Springboard, Summer Olympics, Seoul, South Korea (1988); Gold Medal, Pan American Games (1979, 1983, 1987); Jesse Owens Award (1987); Winner, Platform and Springboard, World Diving Championships (1986); Inductee, U.S. Olympic Hall of Fame (1985); James E. Sullivan Award, Amateur Athletic Union (1984); Two Gold Medals, Summer Olympics, Los Angeles, CA (1984); Silver Medal, 10 Meter Platform, Summer Olympics, Montreal, Canada (1976); Five-Time U.S. Olympic Festival Titles; Recipient, Four-Time Gold Medalist, FINA World Cup; Three-Time NCAA Champion; Winner, 47 U.S. National Diving Titles

LOUIS-DREYFUS, JULIA SCARLETT ELIZABETH, T: Actress; Comedian **I:** Media & Entertainment **DOB:** 01/13/1961 **PB:** New York **SC:** NY/USA **PT:** Gérard Louis-Dreyfus; Judith (LeFever) Louis-Dreyfus **MS:** Married **SPN:** Brad Hall (06/25/1987) **CH:** Henry; Charles **ED:** Honorary ArtsD, Northwestern University (2007); Coursework, Northwestern University (1980-1982) **C:** Member, Second City and Practical Theatre Company, Chicago, IL **CW:** Voice Actress, "Onward" (2020); Actress, "Downhill" (2020); Actress, Producer, Executive Producer, "Veep" (2012-2019); Appearance, "Inside Amy Schumer" (2015); Producer, "Generosity of Eye" (2015); Actress, "Enough Said" (2013); Voice Actress, "Planes" (2013); Actress, "Web Therapy" (2012); Actress, "30 Rock" (2010); Actress, "The New Adventures of Old Christine" (2006-2010); Appearance, "Curb Your Enthusiasm" (2000, 2001, 2009); Actress, "Arrested Development" (2002, 2004, 2005); Actress, Producer, "Watching Ellie" (2002-2003); Voice Actress, "The Simpsons" (2001); Actress, "Gepetto" (2000); Actress, "Speak Truth to Power" (2000); Actress, "Gilligan's Island" (1999); Voice Actress, "Animal Farm" (1999); Voice Actress, "A Bug's Life" (1998); Actress, "Seinfeld" (1989-1998); Actress, "Father's Day" (1997); Actress, "Deconstructing Harry" (1997); Voice Actress, "Hey Arnold!" (1997); Actress, "London Suite" (1996); Actress, "The Single Guy" (1995); Actress, "North" (1994); Actress, "Jack the Bear" (1993); Actress, "Dinosaurs" (1991); Actress, "National Lampoon's Christmas Vacation" (1989); Actress, "Family Ties" (1988); Actress, "Day by Day" (1986-1989); Actress, "The Art of Being Nick" (1986); Actress, "Soul Man" (1986); Actress, "Troll" (1986); Actress, "Hannah and Her Sisters" (1986); Performer, "Saturday Night Live" (1982-1985); Actress, Appearances, Television Shows, Films **AW:** Mark Twain Prize for American Humor (2018); Emmy Award for Outstanding Comedy Series, Academy of Television Arts & Sciences (2012, 2013, 2015, 2016, 2017); Emmy Award for Outstanding Lead Actress in a Comedy Series, Academy of Television Arts & Sciences (2006, 2012, 2013, 2014, 2015, 2016, 2017); Screen Actors Guild Award for Outstanding Performance by an Ensemble in a Comedy Series, SAG-AFTRA (1994, 1996, 1997, 2017); Named One of the 100 Most Influential People in the World, TIME Magazine (2016); Named One of the 100 Most Powerful Women in Entertainment, The Hollywood Reporter (2014); Award for Outstanding Individual Achievement in Comedy, Television Critics Association Awards (2014); Named to Television Academy Hall of Fame (2014); Screen Actors Guild Award for Outstanding Performance by a Female Actor in a Comedy Series, SAG-AFTRA (1997, 1998, 2014); Recipient, Star, Hollywood Walk of Fame (2010); American Comedy Award for Best Supporting Actress (1993, 1994, 1995, 1997, 1998); Emmy Award for Best Supporting Actress in a Comedy Series, Academy of Television Arts & Sciences (1996); Golden Globe Award for Best Supporting Actress, Hollywood Foreign Press Association (1994)

LOVATO, DEMI DEVONNE, T: Singer, Actress **I:** Media & Entertainment **DOB:** 08/20/1992 **PB:** Albuquerque **SC:** NM/USA **PT:** Patrick Martin Lovato; Diana (Lee Smith) De La Garza **ED:** High School Diploma **CR:** Spokesperson, Ember (2018); Brand Ambassador, JBL Audio Company (2017); Launched, Workout Collection, Fabletics (2017); Spokesperson, Sketchers (2014-2016); Brand Ambassador, N.Y.C. (2015) **CIV:** Spokesperson, PACER (2010); Honorary Ambassador of Education, American Partnership For Eosinophilic Disorders (2009); Spokesperson, Join the Surge Campaign!, DoSomething.org **CW:** Performer, "The Star-Spangled Banner," Super Bowl LIV, NFL (2020); Voice Actress, "Charming" (2018); Voice Actress, "Smurfs: The Lost Village" (2017); Featured, "Demi Lovato: Simply Complicated" (2017); Appearance, "Project Runway" (2017); Singer, "Tell Me You Love Me" (2017); Appearance "The Voice of Germany" (2017); Appearance, "Victoria's Secret Swim Special" (2016); Appearance, "RuPaul's Drag Race" (2015); Actress, "From Dusk Till Dawn: The Series" (2015); Appearance, "We Day" (2015); Singer, "Confident" (2015); Actress, "Matador" (2014); Author, "Staying Strong: A Journal" (2014); Actress, "Glee" (2013-2014); Author, "Staying Strong: 365 Days a Year" (2013); Singer, "Demi" (2013); Judge, "The X Factor" (2012-2014); Featured, "Demi Lovato: Stay Strong" (2012); Singer, "Unbroken" (2011); Actress, "Camp Rock 2: The Final Jam" (2010); Actress, "Grey's Anatomy" (2010); Appearance, "Extreme Makeover: Home Edition" (2010); Actress, "Sonny with a Chance" (2009-2011); Actress, "Princess Protection Program" (2009); Performer, "Jonas Brothers: The 3D Concert Experience" (2009); Singer, "Here We Go Again" (2009); Singer, "Don't Forget" (2008); Actress, "Camp Rock" (2008); Actress, "As the Bell Rings" (2007-2008); Actress, "Just Jordan" (2007); Actress, "Prison Break" (2006); Actress, "Barney & Friends" (2002-2003) **AW:** One of the 100 Most Influential People, Time Magazine (2017); Vanguard Award, GLAAD Media Awards (2016); Favorite Female Artist, People's Choice Awards (2014); Grand Marshal, LA Pride Parade (2014); Favorite Celebrity Judge, People's Choice Awards (2013); Choice Summer Female Music Star, Teen Choice Awards (2012); Favorite Pop Artist, People's Choice Awards (2012); Favorite TV Guest Star, People's Choice Awards (2011); Award for Choice TV Breakout Star: Female, Teen Choice Awards (2009); Numerous Awards **AV:** Practicing Brazilian jiu-jitsu

LOVELL, JAMES ARTHUR JR., T: Astronaut (Retired) **I:** Aviation **DOB:** 3/25/1928 **PB:** Cleveland **SC:** IL/USA **PT:** James A. Lovell; Blanch Lovell **MS:** Married **SPN:** Marilyn Gerlach (06/06/1952) **CH:** Barbara Lynn; James Arthur; Susan Kay; Jeffrey C. **ED:** Graduate, Advanced Management Program, Harvard Business School (1971); Graduate, Aviation Safety School, University of Southern California (1961); Bachelor of Science, U.S. Naval Academy (1952); Coursework, University of Wisconsin (1946-1948) **C:** Senior Vice President of Administration, Executive Vice President, Centel Corp., Chicago, IL (1980-1991); President, Fisk Telephone Systems (1977-1981); Chief Executive Officer, Bay-Houston Towing Co. (1975); With, Bay-Houston Towing Co. (1973); Retired (1973); Deputy Director, Science and Applications, Directorate Manned Spacecraft Center, National Aeronautics and Space Administration (1971-1973); Spacecraft Commander, Apollo 13 (1970); Backup Commander, Apollo 11 (1969); Command Module Pilot, Apollo 8 (1968); Commander, Gemini XII (1966); Pilot, Gemini VI (1965); Astronaut, Manned Spacecraft Center, National Aeronautics and Space Administration (1962); Flight Instructor, Safety Officer, Fighter Squadron 101, Naval Air Station, Oceana, VA; Backup Pilot, Gemini IV **MIL:** Advanced through Grades to Captain, U.S. Navy (1965); Test Pilot, U.S. Naval Test Pilot School, Patuxent River, MD (1958-1961); Enlisted, U.S. Navy (1952); Served in, Korean War **CW:** TV Appearance, "The Colbert Report" (2007); Cameo, TV Series, "Situation Critical" (2007); Cameo, Film, "In the Shadow of the Moon" (2007); Speaker, TV Series, "Pritzker Military Library Presents" (2006); Cameo, Film, "The American Experience" (2005); Cameo, Film, "Conquering Space: The Moon and Beyond" (2005); Speaker, "Failure is Not an Option" (2003); Speaker, "AFI Life Achievement Award: A Tribute to Tom Hanks" (2002); Cameo, TV Series, "Modern Marvels" (2001); Cameo, TV Series, "Lateline" (1998); Cameo, Film, "Apollo 13: For the Record" (1995); Technical Consultant, Cameo, Film, "Apollo 13" (1995); Co-author, "Lost Moon: The Perilous Voyage of Apollo 13," with Jeffrey Kluger (1994); Cameo, "Apollo 13: To the Edge and Back" (1994); Cameo, TV Series, "Spaceflight" (1985); Cameo, TV Series, "VIP Schaukel" (1977); Cameo, Film, "The Man Who Fell to Earth" (1976); TV Appearance, "The Tonight Show Starring Johnny Carson" (1970) **AW:** Silver Buffalo, Boy Scouts of America (1992); Distinguished Eagle Scout Award (1976); Grand Medallion Award, Aero Club France (1972); Congressional Space Medal of Honor (1970); Robert H. Goddard Memorial Trophy (1969); H.H. Arnold Trophy (1969); General Thomas D. White U.S. Air Force Space Trophy (1969); Robert J. Collier Trophy (1968); Named, Man of the Year, Time Magazine (1968); Harmon International Trophy (1966-1967); Decorated Naval Aviator Badge, National Aeronautics and Space Administration (1965); Naval Astronaut Wings, National Aeronautics and Space Administration (1965); National Defense Service Medal, National Aeronautics and Space Administration (1965); Navy Commendation Medal, National Aeronautics and Space Administration (1965); Air Medal, National Aeronautics and Space Administration (1965); Distinguished Flying Cross with Gold Service Star, National Aeronautics and Space Administration (1965); Exceptional Service Medal, National Aeronautics and Space Administration (1965); Distinguished Service Medal, National Aeronautics and Space Administration (1965); Presidential Medal of Freedom; Hubbard Medal, National Geographic Society; FAI De Laval Medal; Gold Space Medals; Légion d'honneur **MEM:** Fellow, American Astronautical Society; Fellow, Society of Experimental Test Pilots; Past President, National Eagle Scout Association; Board of Governors, National Space Society; Board of Directors, Lindbergh Foundation; Association of Space Explorers; Golden Eagles; Toastmasters; Alpha Phi Omega

LOW, GILBERT IRVINE, T: Lawyer **I:** Law and Legal Services **CN:** Orgain Bell & Tucker, LLP **DOB:** 07/14/1933 **PB:** Geneva **PT:** William Elzie Low; Gertrude (Matthews) Low **MS:** Divorced **CH:** Rachael Low Roane; Mark Matthews; Courteney Lynn **ED:** JD, The University of Texas (1960); BS, Stephen F. Austin State University (1954) **C:** Partner, Orgain, Bell & Tucker, LLP, Beaumont, Texas (1966-1986) **CR:** Vice Chairman, Texas Supreme Court Advisory Committee (2000-Present); Member, Texas Supreme Court (1978-Present); Chairman, Professional Ethics Committee, Beaumont, Texas (1986) **CIV:** Honorary Member, Beaumont Police Department; Member, Foundation Board, All Saints' Episcopal School; Past President, School Board, All Saints' Episcopal School **MIL:** With, United States Army **AW:** Outstanding Alumni Award, The University of Texas School of Law (2012) **MEM:** Fellow, American Bar Foundation; Texas Bar Foundation; American Board of Trial Advocates; American Board of Professional Liability Attorneys; Association Trial Lawyers America (Now American Association for Justice); Texas Association of Defense Counsel (TADC, Inc.); Jefferson County Bar Association; Littlefield Society; The International Academy of Trial Lawyers; International Society of Barristers; Sons of the Republic Texas, Inc.; Texas State Historical Association (TSHA); Philosophical Society of Texas **BAR:** United States District Court for the Southern District of Texas (1970); United States Court of Appeals for the Fifth Circuit (1962); United States District Court for the Eastern District of Texas (1961); Texas (1960) **MH:** Albert Nelson Marquis Lifetime Achievement Award; Marquis Who's Who Top Professional **B/I:** After graduating college with a degree in teaching, a close friend of Mr. Low's was drafted into the Army but did not want to go alone. Being the loyal and dedicated friend he is, he volunteered to join the United States Army to accompany his friend. After returning from the Army, Mr. Low received a job working as a teacher for a year. His sister wanted him to go to law school and signed him up to take

the law school entrance exam. He ended up taking the exam and shortly after enrolled in law school full-time.

LOWENTHAL, ALAN STUART, T: U.S. Representative from California **I:** Government Administration/Government Relations/Government Services **DOB:** 03/08/1941 **PB:** New York **SC:** NY/USA **MS:** Married **SPN:** Deborah Malumed **CH:** Daniel; Joshua **ED:** PhD, The Ohio State University (1967); MA, The Ohio State University (1965); BA, Hobart College (Now Hobart and William Smith College) (1962) **C:** Member, U.S. House of Representatives from California's 47th Congressional District, Washington, DC (2013-Present); Member, U.S. House Committee on Natural Resources (2013-Present); Member, U.S. House Committee on Foreign Affairs (2013-Present); Member, District 27, California State Senate (2004-2012); Professor, Community Psychology, California State University, Long Beach (1969-2008); Member, District 54, California State Assembly (1998-2004); City Councilman, City of Long Beach, CA (1992-1998); Human Relations Commission (1990-1992); Committee on Transportation and Infrastructure; Republican Study Committee **CIV:** Advisory Board, St. Mary's Medical Center (1992-1998) **AW:** Legislator of the Year, California State Firefighters' Association (CSFA) (2002); Award, League of California Cities (2001) **PA:** Democrat **RE:** Jewish

LOWEY, NITA SUE, T: U.S. Representative from New York; Chair of the House Committee on Appropriations **I:** Government Administration/ Government Relations/Government Services **DOB:** 07/05/1937 **PB:** Bronx **SC:** NY/USA **PT:** Jack Melnikoff; Beatrice (Fleisher) Melnikoff **MS:** Married **SPN:** Stephen Lowey (1961) **CH:** Dona; Jacqueline; Douglas **ED:** BA in Marketing, Mount Holyoke College, MA (1959) **C:** Chair, House Committee on Appropriations (2017-Present); Member, U.S. House of Representatives from New York's 17th Congressional District, United States Congress, Washington, DC (2013-Present); Member, U.S. House of Representatives from New York's 18th Congressional District, United States Congress, Washington, DC (1993-2013); Member, U.S. House of Representatives from New York's 20th Congressional District, United States Congress, Washington, DC (1989-1992); Assistant Secretary of State, State of New York (1985-1987); Assistant to Secretary of State for Economic Development and Neighborhood Preservation, Director, Division of Economic Opportunity, State of New York, Albany, NY (1975-1985); Community Activist **CIV:** Board of Directors, The Windward School; Board of Directors, Effective Parenting Information for Children; Board of Directors, Close-Up Foundation **AW:** Named One of the Most Powerful Women in New York City, New York Post (2007); Congressional Leadership Award, Coalition to Stop Gun Violence (2001); Named One of the 10 Women's Health Heroes, Reader's Digest (1999); Excellence in National Pubic Leadership Award, National Assembly of Health and Human Service Organizations (1999); Herbert Tenzer Award for Public Service, Five Towns Jewish Council (1999); Named Legislator of the Year, MADD; Responsible Choices Award, Planned Parenthood Federation of America **MEM:** Women's Network of YWCA **PA:** Democrat **RE:** Jewish

LOWRIE, YVONNE, T: Artist, Educator, Volunteer **I:** Consulting **DOB:** 03/04/1936 **PB:** Knoxville **SC:** TN/USA **PT:** Clarence F. Coleman; Helen Black Coleman **MS:** Married **SPN:** Max Lowrie (12/18/1962) **ED:** MEd, Southwestern Baptist Theological Seminary, Fort Worth, TX (1962); BA, Carson-Newman College (Now Carson-Newman University), Jeffer-

son City, TN (1959) **CT:** Certification, American Business Women's Association Leadership Conference (2010); Certified, Fund Development, Girl Scouts of the United States of America, Edith Macy Conference Center, NY (2010); Certified Teacher, S-T-R-E-T-C-H and Sew Teachers School, Eugene, OR (1975); Certified in Working with Adolescents, YWCA, Michigan State University, East Lansing, MI (1961); Training School Graduate Certificate, YWCA, Lake Erie College, Ohio (1959) **C:** Sales Consultant, Tole Etc., Fort Worth, TX (1985-1988); Sewing Teacher and Sales, S-T-R-E-T-C-H and Sew Fabric Center, Arlington, TX (1975-1977); Teen Program Director, YWCA, Fort Worth and Tarrant County, Texas (1959-1968); Assistant Executive Director, YWCA, Fort Worth and Tarrant County, Texas (1959-1968) **CR:** Girl Scouts of the United States (1956) **CIV:** Volunteer, World Association of Girl Guides and Girl Scouts of America; Volunteer, Girl Scouts of Texas Oklahoma Plains; Highland Church of Christ **CW:** Exhibitor, Arlington Public Library, Arlington County Government (1989-Present); Exhibitor, Bob Duncan Community Center, Arlington CVB, Arlington, TX (1989-Present); Exhibitor, Fort Worth Regional Library, Fort Worth, TX (1986-Present); Exhibitor, Fort Worth Community Arts Center (2004); Artist, Painted Wall, Cancer Care Services, Children's Area, Fort Worth, TX; Artist, Painted Wall, Woman's Haven Children's School (Now Safehaven of Tarrant County), Fort Worth, TX; Artist, Painted Wall, Arlington Life Shelter; Artist, Painted Wall, Welcome House Youth Center, Mission Arlington; Artist, Painted Wall, Dallas Outdoor Fence Enclosure, Family Gateway; Artist, Painted Wall, Fielder House Museum, Arlington Historical Society; Artist, Painted Wall, Thistle Hill House Museum; Exhibitor, Permanent Collection, White House; Exhibitor, Permanent Collection, Library of Congress; Exhibitor, Permanent Collection, Blair House; Exhibitor, Permanent Collection, Number One Observatory Circle; Exhibitor, Permanent Collection, Smithsonian Institute; Exhibitor, Permanent Collection, Anatole Hotel, Dallas, TX; Exhibitor, Permanent Collection, State Capitol of Texas, Austin, TX **AW:** Honor, 60-Year Pin, School Grades 2-11, Girl Scouts of the United States of America, Knoxville, TN (2018); Award, 50-Year Volunteer, Girl Scouts of the United States of America, Fort Worth, TX (2018); Hall of Fame, Knoxville East High School Alumni Association (2016); Lifetime Achievement Award, Girl Scouts of Texas Oklahoma Plains (2015); Woman of District Award (2015); Appreciation Award, 100th Anniversary Task Group (2012); Centenary Appreciation Recognition Award, World Foundation for Girl Guides and Girl Scouts (2012); Volunteer Service Award, President's Council on Service and Civic Participation (2009); Lone Star Legend Award, Volunteer Center, Texas (2009); Council Award, Girl Scouts Alumnae Association (2008); Thanks Badge, Girl Scouts Circle T Council (2005); Outstanding Member Star Award, Fort Worth Decorative Painters (2005); Outstanding Chapter Service Award, Bluebonnet Tole and Decorative Painters, Inc. (2003); Dedicated Service Award, National Society of Tole and Decorative Painters (2003); Scholar, Funding Information Center, Fort Worth, TX (2002); Outstanding Chapter Service Award, Fort Worth Decorative Painters (2001-2003); Juliette Low World Friendship Medal, Girl Scouts of the United States of America (1997); Outstanding Woman of the Year in the Arts, Fort Worth Mayor's Commission on the Status of Women (1996); Volunteer Service Award, Trinity Meadows Community, Girl Scouts Circle T Council (1992); Appreciation Pin (1986); Thanks Badge (1978); Inductee, Hall of Fame, Knoxville East High School Alumni Association (1952-1968); Grantee, Juliette Low World Friendship Fund, Girl Scouts of the United States, Sangam, India; Lifetime Achievement Award, World Foundation for Girl Guides and Girl Scouts **MEM:** National Society Committee Member, Bluebonnet Tole and Decorative Painters, Inc. (1988-Present); Fundraiser, Sangam, World Centre, World Association of Girl Guides and Girl Scouts, India (1986-Present); Committee Member, Fort Worth Decorative Painters (1985-Present); Committee Member, National Society of Tole and Decorative Painters (1985-Present); Committee Member, American Business Women's Association (ABWA Management, LLC) (1961-Present); Instructor, Silk Scarf Painting, Girl Scout Alumnae Association (2018); Leadership, Gift Committee Member, World Foundation for Girl Guides and Girl Scouts (2014); Vice President, Tarrant County ABWA Friends Council (2011), Board Secretary, World Foundation for Girl Guides and Girl Scouts (2009-2013); Founding Chairman, Friends of Pax Lodge, World Foundation for Girl Guides and Girl Scouts (1991-2009); Founding Chair, Girl Scouts Alumnae Association (2007); Invited, 32nd World Conference, World Foundation for Girl Guides and Girl Scouts (2005); National Division Board Director, National Society of Tole and Decorative Painters (1992-1994); Committee Member, World Foundation for Girl Guides and Girl Scouts (1986); President-Elect, Forth Worth Charter - Six Flags Chapter, American Business Women's Association (ABWA Management, LLC); Chapter President, American Business Women's Association (ABWA Management, LLC); Vice President, American Business Women's Association (ABWA Management, LLC); Secretary, American Business Women's Association (ABWA Management, LLC); Treasurer, American Business Women's Association (ABWA Management, LLC); League of Women Voters of Tarrant County, Texas; Executive Board Member, Girl Scouts Alumnae Association; National Society of Tole and Decorative Painters; Founder, Fort Worth Decorative Painters; President, Fort Worth Decorative Painters; Vice President, Fort Worth Decorative Painters; Christmas Party Chair, Fort Worth Decorative Painters; SDP Chapter, Bluebonnet Tole and Decorative Painters, Inc; Olave Baden-Powell Society; Attendee, Annual Gathering of Girl Scout Committee Members, Edith Macy Conference Center, World Foundation for Girl Guides and Girl Scouts, New York; Founding Chair, PAX LODGE, World Centre in North London, World Association of Girl Guides and Girl Scouts, United Kingdom; Founding Chair, World Association of Girl Guides and Girl Scouts, United States **MH:** Albert Nelson Marquis Lifetime Achievement Award; Marquis Who's Who Top Professional; Marquis Who's Who Humanitarian Award **AV:** Painting; Travel; Volunteering; Acting; Sewing **PA:** Independent

LOWRY, EUGENE L., T: Theological Educator **I:** Education/Educational Services **DOB:** 09/07/1933 **PB:** Meade **SC:** KS/USA **PT:** Austin Lynn Lowry; Myrtle Louise (Jordan) Lowry **MS:** Married **SPN:** Sarah Cheatum (10/03/1976) **CH:** Mark; Diane; Jill **ED:** EdD, University of Kansas, Lawrence, KS (1972); MA, Columbia University, New York, NY (1958); Master of Divinity, Drew Theological Seminary, Madison, NJ (1958); BA, Southwestern College, Winfield, KS (1955) **CT:** Ordained to Ministry, United Methodist Church (1956) **C:** Professor, Preaching and Communication, Saint Paul School of Theology (1979-Present); Interim Academy Dean, Saint Paul School of Theology (1984-1985); Director, Doctoral Studies, Saint Paul School of Theology (1974-1981); Associate Professor, Saint Paul School of Theology (1973-1979); Assistant Professor, Saint Paul School of Theology (1968-1973); Pastor, College Heights United Methodist Church, Kansas City, MO (1964-1968); Lecturer, Saint Paul School of Theology (1962-1968); Associ-

ate Pastor, Country Club United Methodist Church, Kansas City, MO (1962-1964); Associate Pastor, 1st Methodist Church, Wichita, KS (1959-1962); Pastor, St. Paul Methodist Church, West New York, New Jersey (1955-1959) **CR:** Guest Lecturer, Over 50 Higher Learning Institutions (1980-Present); Lyman Beecher Lecturer, Yale Divinity School, New Haven, CT (2009); Guest Professor, Princeton Theological Seminary (1999); President, Academy of Homiletics (1992) **CIV:** President, Board of Trustees, Kansas City Public Library (1993-2009); President, Human Relations Commission of City, Kansas City, MO (1967-1971) **CW:** Author, "The Homiletical Beat: Why All Sermons Are Narrative" (2012); Featured, "Great North America Preachers/Odyssey," Cable Network (2000); Author, "The Sermon: Dancing the Edge of Mystery" (1997); Author, "Living with the Lectionary: Preaching Through the Revised Common Lectionary" (1992); Author, "How to Preach a Parable: Designs for Narrative Sermons" (1989); Author, "Doing Time in the Pulpit" (1985); Author, "The Homiletical Plot: The Sermon as Narrative Art Form" (1980) **AW:** Masterbuilder Award, Southwestern College, Winfield KS (1955) **MEM:** American Academy of Homiletics; American Federation of Musicians; Kansas City Theological Studies; American Academy of Religion **MH:** Albert Nelson Marquis Lifetime Achievement Award; Marquis Who's Who Top Professional **AS:** Dr. Lowry attributes his success to his father, who had the biggest influence on his work ethic, and his mother, who had an influence on his empathetic nature. More broadly, ambiguity is key to everything, he says. One must leave things open to interpretation and let people connect the dots themselves. **B/I:** Dr. Lowry's career involvement comes from his affiliation with the church. In the life of the church, one listens to what one thinks one is hearing of the infinite of the world, life, and history. Dr. Lowry was more broadly fascinated by preachers, being particularly intrigued by the structure of preaching, narrative, and plot, which is extremely useful in capturing people's hearts and minds. **AV:** Listening to music; Appreciating vintage cars; Playing jazz piano **RE:** Methodist

LOWRY, GLENN DAVID, T: Director **I:** Fine Art **CN:** Museum of Modern Art **DOB:** 09/28/1954 **PB:** New York **SC:** NY/USA **PT:** Warren Lowry; Laure (Lynn) Lowry **MS:** Married **SPN:** Susan Chambers (08/24/1974) **CH:** Nicholas; Alexis; William **ED:** Honorary PhD, Pennsylvania Academy of the Fine Arts (2000); PhD, Harvard University (1982); MA, Harvard University (1978); BA, Williams College (1976) **C:** Director, The Museum of Modern Art, New York, NY (1995-Present); Director, Art Gallery of Ontario, Toronto, ON, Canada (1990-1995); Curator, Near Eastern Art, Arthur M. Sackler and the Freer Gallery Art, Smithsonian Institution, Washington, DC (1984-1990); Curatorial Coordinator, Arthur M. Sackler and the Freer Gallery Art, Smithsonian Institution, Washington, DC (1987-1989); Director, Joseph and Margaret Muscarelle Museum Art, Williamsburg, VA (1982-1984); Curator, Oriental Art, Museum of Art, Rhode Island School of Design, Providence, RI (1981-1982); Research Assistant, Archaeological Survey of Mediterranean Town of Amalfi, Italy (1980); Assistant Curator, Fogg Art Museum, Harvard University, Cambridge, MA (1978-1980) **CR:** Advisory Council, Department of Art History and Archaeology, Columbia University; Smithsonian Council Steering Committee, Aga Kahn Architect Award; Fellow, American Academy of Arts and Sciences **CIV:** Trustee, The Toronto Convention and Visitors Association **CW:** Co-Author, "Europe and the Arts of Islam: The Politics of Taste" (1991); Co-Author, "Timur and the Princely Vision: Persian Art and Culture in the Fifteenth Century" (1989);

Co-Author, "An Annotated and Illustrated Checklist of the Vever Collection" (1988); Co-Author, "A Jeweler's Eye: Art of the Book from the Vever Collection" (1988); Co-Author, "From Concept to Context: Approaches to Asian and Islamic Calligraphy" (1986); Co-Author, "Fatehpur-Sikri: A Source Book" (1985) **AW:** Named, Power 100, ArtReview (2018); Officer, Order of Arts & Letters Award, Government of France (2004); Scholarly Studies Award (1990); Special Exhibitions Award (1987); Travel Award, Institute of Turkish Studies, Smithsonian Institution (1980) **MEM:** Association of Art Museum Directors; College Art Association of America, Inc.

LUCAS, FRANK DEAN, T: U.S. Representative from Oklahoma **I:** Government Administration/Government Relations/Government Services **DOB:** 01/06/1960 **PB:** Cheyenne **SC:** WY/USA **MS:** Married **SPN:** Lynda L. Bradshaw (1988) **CH:** Three Children **ED:** BS in Agricultural Economics, Oklahoma State University (1982) **C:** Member, U.S. House of Representatives from Oklahoma's Third Congressional District, United States Congress, Washington, DC (2003-Present); Vice Chairman, U.S. House Science Committee (2015); Chairman, U.S. House Committee on Agriculture, Washington, DC (2011-2015); Member, U.S. House of Representatives from Oklahoma's Sixth Congressional District, U.S. Congress, Washington, DC (1994-2003); Member, Oklahoma House of Representatives (1989-1994); Member, Committee on Financial Services; Member, Committee on Science, Space, and Technology **AW:** Named a Property Rights Champion, League of Property Voters (Now Vote Smart) (2002); Congressional Conservation Champion (2001); Champion of Small Business Award, Small Business Survival Committee; Guardian of Small Business Award, National Federation of Independent Business; Staff of Life Award, Oklahoma Wheat Commission; Friend of the Farm Bureau Award, American Farm Bureau Federation; Wheat Champion Award, National Association of Wheat Growers **MEM:** Oklahoma Cattlemens Association; Oklahoma Farmers Union; Oklahoma Farm Bureau **PA:** Republican **RE:** Baptist

LUCAS, LENELL JR., OWNER, T: Accountant (Retired); Inventor **I:** Media & Entertainment **CN:** LL Overlord Enterprises **DOB:** 11/05/1954 **PB:** Brooklyn **SC:** NY/USA **PT:** Lenell Lucas; Anne Small **MS:** Divorced **ED:** BBA, Baruch College, NY (1982); Coursework, Rutgers, The State University of New Jersey (1985-1987); Coursework, Chaminade University (1977-1978); Coursework, Howard University (1972-1974) **CT:** Certified Defense Financial Management, American Society of Military Comptrollers **C:** Consultant, Herdt Consulting, Inc. (2011); Consultant, Federal Government (2008-2011); Financial Analyst, Delta Resources, Inc. (2009); Staff Accountant, FUTREND Technology, Inc. (2008); Operations Accountant, Defense Information System Agency (2004-2007); Accountant, Federal Government, U.S. Department of the Army and Navy (1986-2007); Staff Accountant, Equal Employment Opportunity Commission (2001-2004); Instructor, Business Schools (1989, 1997) **MIL:** Petroleum Supply Specialist, United States Army (1976-1979) **CW:** Inventor, FruitSuit Card Game(2005-Present); Professional Disk Jockey (1988-Present) **AW:** Awards, Certified Defense Financial Manager (2006-2011) **MEM:** National Association for the Advancement of Colored People (NAACP) **MH:** Who's Who Inventing/Gambling Games **AS:** Mr. Lucas attributes his success to listening and learning, as well as having the desire to be the best he could be in his career. **B/I:** Mr. Lucas always enjoyed mathematics. He went to Brooklyn Tech High School, which is where his passion began. Mr. Lucas went to college for a few years and then worked at the post office. He then went to the Army, and on the GI Bill, he went back to school and obtained a bachelor's degree. After getting his degree, he took some accounting courses at Rutgers University. Those courses helped him to qualify for the accounting position he had with the federal government. **AV:** Cello; Disc jockey; Travel; Photography; Videography; Chess; Sports; Music; Electronics; Board games; Card games **PA:** Democrat **RE:** Christian **THT:** Mr. Lucas' motto is, "Beware, yet be aware."

LUCAS, ROBERT EMERSON JR., PHD, T: Economist; Professor Emeritus **I:** Education/Educational Services **CN:** The University of Chicago **DOB:** 09/15/1937 **PB:** Yakima **SC:** WA/USA **PT:** Robert Emerson Lucas; Jane Templeton Lucas **ED:** Honorary DSc, Technion-Israel Institute of Technology (1996); Honorary PhD, University of Montréal (1998); Honorary PhD, Athens University of Economics and Business (1994); Honorary PhD, University of Paris-Dauphine (1992); PhD in Economics, The University of Chicago (1964); BA in History, The University of Chicago (1959) **C:** John Dewey Distinguished Service Professor Emeritus in Economics, The University of Chicago (1980-Present); Chairman, Department of Economics, The University of Chicago (1986-1988); Vice Chairman, Department of Economics, The University of Chicago (1975-1983); Professor of Economics, The University of Chicago (1975-1980); Ford Foundation Visiting Research Professor of Economics, The University of Chicago (1974-1975); Professor, Carnegie Mellon University (1970-1974); Associate Professor, Carnegie Mellon University (1967-1970); Assistant Professor of Economics, Carnegie Mellon University (1963-1967) **CR:** Visiting Professor of Economics, Northwestern University (1981-1982) **CW:** Editor, Journal of Political Economy (1988-Present); Associate Editor, Journal of Monetary Economics (1977-Present); Author, "Lectures on Economic Growth" (2001); Author, "Recursive Methods in Economic Dynamics" (1989); Author, "Models of Business Cycles" (1985); Author, "Studies in Business-Cycle Theory" (1981); Co-Editor, "Rational Expectations and Econometric Practice" (1981); Associate Editor, Journal of Economic Theory (1972-1978); Contributor, Articles, Professional Journals **AW:** Nobel Prize in Economics (1995); Fellow, John Simon Guggenheim Memorial Foundation (1981-1982); Fellow, The Brookings Institution (1961-1962); Grantee, Woodrow Wilson Fellowship (1959-1960) **MEM:** President, The Econometric Society (1997); Council Member, American Academy of Arts & Sciences (1991-1995); Vice President, American Economic Association (1987); Member, Executive Committee, American Economic Association (1980-1982); Fellow, American Academy of Arts & Sciences; Fellow, The Econometric Society; National Academy of Sciences; American Economic Association; American Philosophical Society; European Academy of Arts, Sciences and Humanities; Phi Beta Kappa

LUCERO, CHELSEA R., LPCC, LADAC, NCC, T: Behavioral Health Manager **I:** Medicine & Health Care **CN:** El Centro Family Health **DOB:** 04/17/1989 **SC:** CO/USA **PT:** Alfred Stoinski; Patricia Stoinski **MS:** Married **SPN:** Kevin Lyle Lucero **ED:** PsyD in Psychology, California Southern University, Costa Mesa, CA (2022); MS in Clinical and Counseling Psychology, New Mexico Highlands University, Las Vegas, NM (2014); BA in Psychology and Sociology, New Mexico Highlands University, Las Vegas, NM (2010) **CT:** Licensed Substance Abuse Associate, National Certified Counselor (2018); Certification in "Best Practices to Stop Sexual Harm by Youth,"

New Mexico Coalition of Sexual Assault Programs (2017); New Mexico Licensed Professional Clinical Counselor; Licensed Professional Clinical Counselor; Clinical Certified Trauma Professional; Anger Management Trauma Professional; QPR Certified Instructor; Eye Movement Desensitization and Reprocessing (EMDR) Certification **C:** Behavioral Health Manager, El Centro Family Health (2019-Present); Behavioral Health Manager, Pecos Valley Medical Center, Pecos, NM (2018-2019); Behavioral Health Therapist, CARE/NMBHI, Las Vegas, NM (2016-2018); Interim Program Director, Behavioral Health Therapist, CARE/New Mexico Behavioral Health Institute, Las Vegas, NM (2017); Behavioral Health Therapist, Community Based Services (CBS)/New Mexico Behavioral Health Institute, Las Vegas, NM (2015-2016); Treatment Planning Coordinator, Behavioral Health Therapist, New Mexico Behavioral Health Institute, Las Vegas, NM (2014-2015) **CR:** Adjunct Instructor of Abnormal Psychology, Luna Community College, Las Vegas, NM (2013-Present); Adjunct Instructor, Introduction to Psychology, Luna Community College, Las Vegas, NM (2013-Present); Thesis: "Performance on Standardized Field Sobriety Tests (SFSTs): Effects of Anxiety, Stress, and Attitudes toward Authority Figures" (2012-2014); Intelligence Testing Graduate Teaching Assistant (2013); Psychology and Society 101 Teaching Assistant (2012-2013); Junior Teaching Assistant, Introductory Psychology, UCCS (2010) **CIV:** Co-Leader, 100% Community Initiative Behavioral Health Action Team; Regional Vice President, NAADAC of New Mexico; Habitat for Humanity, Las Vegas, NM; President, NMHU Chapter, Psi Chi National Honors Society **MEM:** American Psychology Association (APA); American Counseling Association (ACA); Association for the Addicted Professional (NADAC); American Association for Marriage and Family Therapy (AAMFT); Eye Movement Desensitization and Reprocessing International Association (EMDRIA); Psi Chi National Honors Society; Phi Kappa Phi Honors Society; Delta Kappa Honor Society **AS:** Ms. Lucero attributes her success to the guidance of supervisors and mentors she had at New Mexico Highlands University. She believes it was very beneficial for the school to be in such a rural community. **B/I:** Ms. Lucero became involved in her profession because of her passion to help people. Her curiosity to work with different types or people has kept her moving forward. **THT:** Ms. Lucero likes the Socrates quote: "The more I know, the more I realize I know nothing."

LUCIANO, JUAN RICARDO, T: Chairman, President, Chief Executive Officer **I:** Food & Restaurant Services **CN:** ADM **PB:** San Nicolas **SC:** Argentina **ED:** MS in Industrial Engineering, The Buenos Aires Institute of Technology (1985); BS in Industrial Engineering, The Buenos Aires Institute of Technology (1983) **C:** Chairman, President, Chief Executive Officer, ADM (2016-Present); President, Chief Executive Officer, ADM (2015-Present); President, Chief Operating Officer, ADM (2014); Executive Vice President, Chief Operating Officer, ADM, Decatur, IL (2011-2014); Executive Vice President, President's Performance Division, Dow (2010-2011); Senior Vice President of Hydrocarbons and Energy, Basic Plastics and Joint Ventures, Dow (2008-2010); Business Group President of Hydrocarbons and Energy, Dow (2007-2008); Global Business Vice President of Olefins and Aromatics, Dow (2006-2007); Business Vice President of Engineering Polymers, Dow (2004-2006); Global Business Director for Polypropylenes, Dow (2001-2004); Global Business Director, LDPE/PRIMACOR/SARAN/Slurry PE, Dow (2000-2001); Business Director of Chelants and Specialty Chemicals, Dow (1999-2000); Senior Marketing Manager of Polygly-

cols and Specialty Chemicals for the Americas, Dow (1996-1999); Sales and Marketing Manager of Specialty Chemicals, Dow (1994-1996) With, Dow (1985) **CR:** Board of Directors, ADM (2014-Present); Board of Directors, Wilmar International Ltd (2012-Present) **CIV:** Governor, Boys & Girls Clubs of America

LUETKEMEYER, WILLIAM, "BLAINE" BLAINE, T: U.S. Representative **I:** Government Administration/Government Relations/Government Services **DOB:** 05/07/1952 **PB:** Jefferson City **SC:** MO/USA **MS:** Married **SPN:** Jackie Luetkemeyer (1976) **CH:** Nicole; Brandy; Trevor **ED:** BA, Lincoln University (1974) **C:** U.S. Representative, Missouri's Third Congressional District, United States Congress (2013-Present); U.S. Representative, Missouri's Ninth Congressional District, United States Congress (2009-2013); Insurance Agent, Owner, Luetkemeyer Insurance Agency (1988-2009); Vice President, Loan Officer, Bank of St. Elizabeth (1976-2009); District 115, Missouri House of Representatives (1999-2004); Bank Examiner, State of Missouri (1974-1976); Farmer (1968-1988); Member, Financial Services Committee; Member, Republican Study Committee **CR:** Board of Governors, Capital Region Medical Center (1990-1993, 2002-Present) **CIV:** Member, Board of Trustees, Village of St. Elizabeth, MO (1978-1987) **MEM:** American Family Insurance Agents' Association **PA:** Republican **RE:** Roman Catholic

LUJAN, BEN RAY JR., T: U.S. Representative from New Mexico; Assistant Speaker of the U.S. House of Representatives **I:** Government Administration/Government Relations/Government Services **DOB:** 07/07/1972 **PB:** Santa Fe **SC:** NM/USA **PT:** Ben Lujan; Carmen Lujan **MS:** Married **ED:** Coursework, The University of New Mexico, Albuquerque, NM (1997-1999); BBA, New Mexico Highlands University, Las Vegas, NM **C:** Chairman, Democratic Congressional Campaign Committee (DCCC) (2015-Present); Member, U.S. House of Representatives from New Mexico's Third Congressional District (2009-Present); Commissioner, District Three, State Public Regulation Commission, NM (2005-2009); Deputy State Treasurer, State of New Mexico (2003-2005); Director, Administration Service, Chief Financial Officer, New Mexico Department of Cultural Affairs **PA:** Democrat **RE:** Roman Catholic

LUJÁN, BEN RAY SR., T: Former U.S. Representative from New Mexico **I:** Government Administration/Government Relations/Government Services **DOB:** 07/12/1935 **PB:** Nambe Pueblo **SC:** NM/USA **PT:** Celedon Lujan; Nestora Lujan **MS:** Married **SPN:** Carmen Ray Lujan (1959) **CH:** Ben Jr.; Jerome; Shirley; Jackie **ED:** Coursework, College of Santa Fe **C:** Member, U.S. House of Representative from New Mexico's Third Congressional District (2009-2012); Member, District 46, New Mexico House of Representatives (1975-2012); Member, Committee on Energy and Commerce; Speaker of the House, New Mexico House of Representatives (2001-2009); Majority Leader, New Mexico House of Representatives (1999-2001); Democratic Whip, New Mexico House of Representatives (1983-1999); Member, Santa Fe County Commission (1970-1974); Contractor, Iron Worker, Los Alamos National Laboratory; Iron Worker, Zia Company, Los Alamos, NM **PA:** Democrat

LUNSFORD, RACHEL, T: Partner **I:** Law and Legal Services **CN:** Barnett, Bolt, Kirkwood, Long, Koche & Foster, P.A. **PT:** Dallas Albritton; Anne Albritton **MS:** Married **CH:** Two Children **ED:** LLM in Taxation, University of Florida Levin College of Law (2001); JD, University of Florida Levin College of

Law (1999); BA, International Studies, University of South Florida (1994) **CT:** Graduate, Florida Fellows Institute, American College of Trust and Estate Counsel (ACTEC); Board Certified, Wills, Trusts and Estates, The Florida Bar **C:** Estate Planning, Probate and Tax Attorney, Barnett, Bolt, Kirkwood, Long, Koche & Foster, P.A., Tampa/St. Petersburg, FL (2013-Present); Estate Planning, Probate and Tax Attorney, Trenam Kemker (Now Trenam), Tampa, FL (2008-2013); Estate Planning, Probate and Tax Attorney, Albritton & Lunsford Lawyers, PA, Tampa, FL (2003-2008); International Tax Attorney, Sharp, Smith & Harrison, PA, Tampa/St. Petersburg, FL (2001-2002) **CIV:** WEDU Professional Advisory Group Continuing Education Committee (2009-2016); Co-chair, Hillsborough County Bar Association (2007-2010); Member, Inaugural Class, Leadership Institute, (2008); Co-chair, Community Service Committee, The Leadership Institute (2004-2007); Real Property, Probate and Trust Law Section, The Florida Bar; Tax Section, The Florida Bar; Tax Section, American Bar Association (ABA); Real Property Probate and Trust Section, American Bar Association (ABA); Women in Leadership & Philanthropy, USF Foundation, Inc.; Tampa Bay Estate Planning Council (TBEPC) **CW:** Author, "Celebrity Wills," Crisis Center of Tampa Bay Legacy Council CE Course, North Suncoast Estate Planning Council, Estate Planning Council of Polk County, Community Foundation of Tampa Bay Legacy Luncheon, Tampa Bay Paralegal Association, and Partnership for Philanthropic Planning of Tampa Bay (2008-2017); Author, "Same-Sex Couples Married in Florida," Planning Panel Discussion for Suncoast Hospice Foundation (2016); Author, "Biel and Statute of Limitations for Proceedings Supplementary," Asset Protection Committee, Real Property, Probate and Trust Law Section, The Florida Bar (2015); Author, "Disposition of Assets upon the Death of the Child," The Lawyer, Hillsborough County Bar Association (2009); Co-author, "Practice Pointer: Residuary Homestead Devise," The Lawyer, Hillsborough County Bar Association (2008); Co-author, "U.S. Tax Information Exchange Agreements A Comparative Analysis," Tax Notes International (2002); Co-author, "Settling IRS Examinations and Tax Court Cases," Tax Notes International (2002); Author, "Planning and Probate Practice Pointer: Adopted and Emancipated Heirs in Intestate Estates," The Lawyer, Hillsborough County Bar Association; Author, "A Comparative Analysis of the Channel Islands and Isle of Man TIEAs," Tax Notes International **AW:** Named to Best Lawyers in America, Trusts & Estates (2016-2018); Named to Top 100 Lawyers in Florida, Super Lawyers (2017); Named to Top 50 Lawyers in Tampa Bay (2017); Named to Top 50 Women Lawyers in Florida (2015-2017); Named to Estate Planning and Probate (2014-2017); Named to Florida Trend Legal Elite, Wills, Trusts & Estates (2013-2014, 2016-2017); Named "Up & Comer" (2012); Named "Rising Star" (2009-2012); Named "Up and Comer," Tampa Bay Business Journal (2009); James M. "Red" McEwen Award for Outstanding Service to the Bar and the Community, Hillsborough County Bar Association (2006); AV Preeminent Peer-review Rated, Martindale Hubbell **MEM:** Florida Bar Association (The Florida Bar); American Bar Association (ABA) **BAR:** Florida; United States Tax Court **AS:** Mrs. Lunsford attributes her success to putting her clients' needs first. **B/I:** Mrs. Lunsford was inspired to become a lawyer by her father, who was a practicing lawyer for over 50 years in Tampa, Florida.

LUPONE, PATTI ANN, T: Actress; Singer **I:** Media & Entertainment **DOB:** 04/21/1949 **PB:** Northport **SC:** NY/USA **PT:** Orlando Joseph LuPone; Angela Louise (Patti) LuPone **MS:** Married **SPN:** Matthew Johnston (12/12/1988) **CH:** Joshua Luke **ED:** BFA, The Juilliard School (1972) **C:** Actress, Broadway, Television, Films (1976-Present); Actress, Theater Touring Company, The Acting Company (1972-1976) **CIV:** Volunteer, Craft and Folk Art Museum (1999-2000) **CW:** Actress, "Penny Dreadful" (2015, 2016, 2020); Actress, "Hollywood" (2020); Actress, Broadway, "Company" (1993, 2020); Voice Actress, "Steven Universe: The Movie" (2019); Actress, "Pose" (2019); Voice Actress, "The Simpsons" (2019); Actress, "Last Christmas" (2019); Actress, "Cliffs of Freedom" (2019); Actress, "War Paint" (2017); Actress, "Crazy Ex-Girlfriend" (2017); Actress, "BoJack Horseman" (2017); Voice Actress, "Steven Universe" (2016-2020); Actress, "The Comedian" (2016); Actress, Broadway, "Shows for Days" (2015); Actress, "Dinner with Family with Brett Gelman and Brett Gelman's Family" (2015); Actress, "Law & Order: Special Victims Unit" (2015); Actress, "Girls" (2014); Actress, "American Horror Story" (2013-2014); Actress, "Parker" (2013); Actress, "People in New Jersey" (2013); Actress, Broadway, "The Anarchist" (2012); Actress, "Army Wives" (2012); Actress, "Company" (2011); Actress, "Union Square" (2011); Actress, "The Miraculous Year" (2011); Featured, Broadway, "An Evening with Patti LuPone & Mandy Patinskin" (2011); Actress, "Open Books" (2010); Author, "Patti Lupone: A Memoir" (2010); Actress, "30 Rock" (2009-2010); Actress, Broadway, "Gypsy" (2008); Actress, "Ugly Betty" (2007); Actress, Regional Productions, "Rise and Fall of the City of Mahogany" (2007); Actress, Regional Productions, "Anyone Can Whistle" (2005); Actress, Regional Productions, "The Little Foxes" (2005); Appearance, "Will & Grace" (2005); Actress, Broadway, "Children & Art" (2005); Actress, Broadway, "Sweeney Todd" (2005); Actress, Regional Productions, "The Lady with the Torch" (2004); Actress, "Strip Search" (2004); Actress, "Cold Blooded" (2003); Actress, "Oz" (2003); Actress, "City by the Sea" (2002); Actress, "Life at Five Feet" (2002); Actress, "Monday Night Mayhem" (2002); Actress, Broadway, "Anything Goes" (2002); Actress, Broadway, "Noises Off" (2001); Actress, "The Victim" (2001); Actress, "Heist" (2001); Actress, "Touched by an Angel" (2001); Performer, "Sweeney Todd: The Demon Barber of Fleet Street in Concert" (2001); Actress, "Bad Faith" (2000); Actress, "Falcone" (2000); Actress, "State and Main" (2000); Actress, "State and Maine" (1999); Actress, "Just Looking" (1999); Actress, "Bad Faith" (1999); Actress, "The 24 Hour Woman" (1999); Actress, "Summer of Sam" (1999); Actress, "Bonanno: A Godfather's Story" (1999); Appearance, "Saturday Night Live" (1998); Actress, "Family Brood" (1998); Actress, Broadway, "The Old Neighborhood" (1997); Actress, "Remember WENN" (1996); Actress, "Her Last Chance" (1996); Actress, "The Song Spinner" (1995); Actress, Broadway, "Master Class" (1995); Actress, "Family Prayers" (1993); Actress, "Frasier" (1993); Actress, "Sunset Boulevard," London, England (1993); Actress, "Family Prayers" (1993); Actress, "The Water Engine" (1992); Actress, "Law & Order" (1990); Actress, "Life Goes On" (1989-1993); Actress, "Driving Miss Daisy" (1989); Actress, Broadway, "Anything Goes" (1987); Actress, "LBJ: The Early Years" (1987); Actress, "Wise Guys" (1986); Actress, "Les Miserables," London, England, Untied Kingdom (1985); Actress, "Witness" (1985); Actress, Broadway, "Oliver!" (1984); Actress, Broadway, "Accidental Death of an Anarchist" (1984); Actress, "Fighting Back" (1982); Actress, "1941" (1979); Actress, "King of the Gypsies" (1978); Actress, Broadway, "Evita" (1979); Actress, Broadway, "The Water Engine" (1978); Actress, Broadway, "Working" (1978); Actress, "The Time of Your Life" (1976); Actress, Broadway, "The Three Sisters" (1973, 1975); Actress, Broadway, "The Robber Bridegroom" (1975); Actress, Broadway, "Edward II" (1975); Actress, Broadway, "The Time of Your Life" (1975); Actress, Broadway, "Next Time I'll Sing to You" (1974); Actress, Broadway, "The Beggar's Opera" (1973); Actress, Broadway, "Measure For Measure" (1973); Actress, Broadway, "Scapin" (1973); Actress, Off-Broadway, "Into the Woods," "School for Scandal," "The Lower Depths," "Stage Directions"; Singer, "Patti LuPone Live"; Singer, "Matters of the Heart"; Singer, "The Lady with the Torch"; Singer, "The Lady with the Torch...Still Burning"; Actress, Performer, Theater, Television, Films **AW:** Laurence Olivier Award for Best Actress in a Supporting Role in a Musical (2019); Honoree, "Patti's Turn," The Acting Company, Kaye Playhouse (2012); Grammy Awards for Best Classical Album, Best Opera Recording, The Recording Academy (2009); Drama Desk Awards for Outstanding Actress in a Musical (1980, 1987, 2008); Tony Award for Best Performance by a Leading Actress (2008); Named One of the 50 Most Powerful Women in New York City, New York Post (2008); Named to Theater Hall of Fame (2007); John Houseman Award (2006); Tony Award for Best Actress in a Musical (1980); Numerous Awards

LURIA, ELAINE, T: U.S. Representative from Virginia **I:** Government Administration/Government Relations/Government Services **DOB:** 08/15/1975 **PB:** Birmingham **SC:** AL/USA **MS:** Married **SPN:** Robert Blondin **CH:** Three Children **ED:** MS, Old Dominion University (2004); Coursework, United States Naval Nuclear Power School (2000); BS in Physics and History, United States Naval Academy (1997) **C:** Member, U.S. House of Representatives from Virginia's Second Congressional District (2019-Present) **CIV:** Active Member, Ohef Sholom Temple, URJ, Norfolk, VA **MIL:** With, United States Navy (1997-2017); Commander, Assault Craft Unit Two (2014-2017) **PA:** Democrat **RE:** Jewish

LUTHER, DAVID B., T: Management Consultant (Retired) **I:** Business Management/Business Services **CN:** Corning Incorporated **DOB:** 05/26/1936 **PB:** Utica **SC:** NY/USA **PT:** Everett David Luther; Mary (Brown) Luther **SPN:** Geraldine Frost **ED:** MBA, Syracuse University (1961); BS, Syracuse University (1958) **C:** Founder, Principal, Luther Quality Associates (1994-Present); Senior Vice President, Corporate Director of Quality, Corning Glass Works (Now Corning Incorporated) (1985-1994); Vice President of Quality, Corning Glass Works (Now Corning Incorporated) (1983-1985); Vice President of Personnel, Corning Glass Works (Now Corning Incorporated) (1980-1983); Director of Information Services, Corning Glass Works (Now Corning Incorporated) (1979-1980); Director of Corporate Planning, Corning Glass Works (Now Corning Incorporated) (1978-1979); Assistant Corporate Controller, Corning Glass Works (Now Corning Incorporated) (1976-1978); Director of Personnel Resources, Corning Glass Works (Now Corning Incorporated) (1974-1976); Manufacturing Manager, Corning Glass Works (Now Corning Incorporated) (1962-1974); Customer Service Representative, New York Telephone (1959-1961); Field Advertising Representative, Procter and Gamble (1958-1959) **CR:** Board of Trustees, SUNY Corning Community College (1993-1994); Board of Trustees, College Center of the Finger Lakes (1992-1993); Member, Judging Panel, Malcolm Baldrige National Quality Award (1988-1991); National Chairman, Koalty Kid Education Project; Conference Board Member, Total Quality Management Center; Co-Founder, Conference Board Quality Council; Former Chair, Excelsior Incorporated, New York State Quality Award; Executive-in-Residence, Whitman School of Management, Syracuse

University; Member, Visions for Governance Effort, Harvard John F. Kennedy School of Government; National Science Foundation Advisory Committee on Quality Organization Research **MIL:** Lieutenant Commander, Ordinance Ammunition, U.S. Army **AW:** Founders' Medal, National Academy for Quality **MEM:** Archaeological Institute of America (1995-Present); Chairman, American Society for Quality (1995-1996); President, American Society for Quality (1994-1995); Member Emeritus, International Academy for Quality; Trustee, Arnot Art Museum **MH:** Albert Nelson Marquis Lifetime Achievement Award **AV:** Reading; Exercising

LUTTRELL, CYNTHIA, "CYNDI" R.F., T: IT Specialist **I:** Technology **CN:** Census Bureau **MS:** Divorced **CH:** One Child **ED:** BS in Information Technology, American Intercontinental University (2008) **C:** Business and Systems Analyst, IT Specialist, App/Web Developer, U.S. Census Bureau (2009-Present); Information Technology Specialist, U.S. Census Bureau, National Processing Center (2008-2009); Statistical Assistant, US Census Bureau, National Processing Center (2007-2008); Lead Peripheral Equipment Operator, U.S. Census Bureau, National Processing Center (1991-2003) **CIV:** Executive Vice President, AFGE Council 241 (2011); Executive Vice President, AFGE Local 1438 (2007, 2011); Treasurer, AFGE Local 1438 (2003) **AW:** Bronze Medal Award, U.S. Census Bureau (2019); Vision Award (2016) **AS:** Ms. Luttrell attributes her success to her persistence, education, excellent communication skills, and her positive attitude. **B/I:** Ms. Luttrell has always had an interest in computers and information technology; it began in high school. At the time, computers were just starting to become popular. She was fascinated by them. To her, it was the way of the future. This was what motivated her to pursue a career in computer technology. Though her career was paused after having children, Ms. Luttrell later returned to work and earned a degree in information technology in 2008. From there, she became a software application and web developer. Today, Ms. Luttrell is a well-versed computer systems professional. **AV:** Traveling; Ballroom dancing; Hiking in the woods; Taking outdoor adventures; Living sustainably; Completing home improvement projects; Practicing agriculture **THT:** Ms. Luttrell's motto is, "Hold on loosely; nothing lasts forever."

LYNCH, BOB DAVID, T: Retired Business Agent **I:** Business Management/Business Services **DOB:** 04/04/1931 **PB:** Columbus **SC:** MO/USA **PT:** Henry David Lynch; Opal Blanche (Horn) Lynch **MS:** Married **SPN:** Muriel Nadine (Hale) (6/18/1979); Bertha Louise Kassner (1/13/1952, Deceased 9/29/1977) **CH:** Ronnie David; Michael Alan; Steven Leroy Lynch; Marilyn Kay (Stepchild); Michael Lee (Stepchild); Susan Elizabeth Stinnett (Stepchild) **ED:** Coursework, Central Missouri State University (1950-1951) **CT:** Business Agent, Kansas **C:** Retired (1993); Board of Directors, Institute of Labor Studies, Kansas City, MO (1983-1993); Vice President, Allied Services Division, Transportation Communications Union, Kansas City, MO (1980-1993); Local Chairman, Lodge 26, Brotherhood Railway and Airline Clerks, Kansas City, MO (1968-1993); Regional Representative, Allied Services Division, Transportation Communications Union, Kansas City, MO (1975-1980); Senior Vice Chairman, Brotherhood Railway and Airline Clerks, Kansas City, MO (1970-1975); Coach, American Junior Bowling Congress, Kansas City, MO (1965-1975); Neighborhood Commissioner, Boy Scouts of America, Kansas City, MO (1966-1974) **CIV:** Board of Directors, Barry Harbor Homes Association, Kansas City, MO (1995-Present); Board of Directors, Wedgewood Homes Association,

Independence, MO (1959-1962) **MIL:** Corporal, United States Army (1952-1954) **AW:** Inductee, Missouri State Hall of Fame (1992); All-City Bowling Team, Independent Examiner Paper (1968-1977); Inductee, Bowling Hall of Fame, Kansas City Bowling Association (1972) **MEM:** Tribe of Mic-O-Say; Boy Scouts of America **MH:** Albert Nelson Marquis Lifetime Achievement Award **B/I:** Mr. Lynch won the regional and national Scholastic Art Contest when he was in high school. Two of his paintings were displayed in seven national art galleries for a year after he won the contest. As a result, he received several scholarships around the country. When it came time for him to attend college, he knew he wanted to become an art teacher. He also played the cornet in various bands, orchestras, and the Sedalia Symphony. Mr. Lynch later became affiliated with the Kansas City Terminal Railroad. He then got married but, shortly afterward, he was drafted into the U.S. Army and spent 18 months in Korea. **AV:** Researching genealogy; Traveling; Camping in 5th Wheel; Model railroading; Researching computers; Teaching computer classes and genealogy classes; Making music discs **PA:** Democrat **RE:** Assembly of God

LYNCH, DAVID KEITH, T: Film Producer; Director; Screenwriter **I:** Media & Entertainment **DOB:** 01/20/1946 **PB:** Missoula **SC:** MT/USA **PT:** Donald Walton Lynch; Edwina "Sunny" (Sundholm) Lynch **MS:** Married **SPN:** Emily Stofle (2009); Mary Sweeney (05/2006, Divorced 07/2006); Mary Fisk (06/21/1977, Divorced 1987); Peggy Reavey Lentz (1967, Divorced 1974) **CH:** Jennifer; Austin Jack; Riley; Lula Boginia **ED:** Coursework, Tufts University School of the Museum of Fine Arts, Boston, MA (1964); Coursework, The George Washington University Corcoran School of the Arts & Design, Washington, DC; Coursework, Pennsylvania Academy of the Fine Arts, Philadelphia, PA **CR:** Launched, David Lynch Signature Cup Coffee **CIV:** Eagle Scout, Boy Scouts of America **CW:** Artist, Exhibitions, Paintings, Drawings and Photography, Kayne Griffin Corcoran, Los Angeles, CA (2011-Present); Co-Author, "Room to Dream" (2018); Artist, "The Unified Field," Pennsylvania Academy of the Fine Arts, Philadelphia, PA (2014-2015); Director, "Duran Duran Unstaged" (2014); Co-Designer, Silencio Nightclub, Paris, France (2011); Singer, "Crazy Clown Time" (2011); Actor, "The Cleveland Show" (2010-2011); Voice Actor, "Family Guy" (2010); Singer, "Good Day Today" (2010); Singer, "I Know" (2010); Author, "Catching the Big Fish: Meditation, Consciousness, and Creativity" (2006); Director, Writer, Producer, Editor, Sound Designer, Cinematographer, "Inland Empire" (2006); Director, Composer, "Rabbits" (2002); Director, "Darkened Room" (2002); Creator, "Dumbland" (2002); Director, Writer, Sound Designer, "Mulholland Drive" (2001); Director, Sound Designer, "The Straight Story" (1999); "Driven to It" (1999); Director, Co-writer, Sound Designer, "Lost Highway" (1997); Co-Director, "Lumiere et Compagnie" (1995); Director, "Hotel Room" (1993); Director, "On the Air" (1992); Director, Co-Writer, Executive Producer, Sound Designer, "Twin Peaks: Fire Walk with Me" (1992); Actor, Creator, "Twin Peaks" (1990-1991); Creator, "American Chronicles" (1990); Director, Writer, "Wild at Heart" (1990); Artist, Performance Piece, "Industrial Symphony #1" (1989); Screenwriter, Director, "Blue Velvet" (1986); Director, Writer, "Dune" (1984); Director, Writer, Sound Designer, "The Elephant Man" (1980); Co-Writer, Director, Producer, Editor, Sound Designer, "Eraserhead" (1978); Creator, "David Lynch - Daily Weather Report," YouTube; Director, Writer, Composer, Music Videos, Television and Films **AW:** Honorary Academy Award, Academy of Motion Picture Arts

& Sciences (2019); Award for Best Guest Performance TV Series, Saturn Awards (2018); Co-Recipient, Special Distinction Award, Independent Spirit Awards (2007); Future Film Festival Digital Award, Venice Film Festival (2006); Career - Golden Lion Award, Venice Film Festival (2006); Co-Recipient, Award for Best Director, Cannes Film Festival (2001); Life Career Award, Saturn Awards (1993); Palme d'Or, Cannes International Film Festival (1990); Grantee, American Film Institute **MEM:** Directors Guild of America (DGA)

LYNCH, STEPHEN, T: Editor-in-Chief **I:** Publishing **CN:** New York Post **C:** Editor-in-Chief, New York Post (2016-Present); General Assignment Business Writer, Sunday Editor, New York Post (2003-2016)

LYNCH, STEPHEN FRANCIS, T: U.S. Representative from Massachusetts **I:** Government Administration/Government Relations/Government Services **DOB:** 03/31/1955 **PB:** Boston **SC:** MA/USA **PT:** Frances Lynch; Anne (Havlin) Lynch **MS:** Married **SPN:** Margaret Shaughnessy **CH:** Victoria Bailey **ED:** MPA, Harvard University (1999); JD, Boston College Law School (1991); BS in Construction Management, Wentworth Institute of Technology, Cum Laude (1988); Coursework, University of Wisconsin-Madison **C:** Member, U.S. House of Representatives from Massachusetts' Eighth Congressional District, United States Congress (2013-Present); Member, U.S. House of Representatives from Massachusetts' Ninth Congressional District, United States Congress (2001-2013); Member, First Suffolk District, Massachusetts State Senate, Boston, MA (1996-2001); Member, Fourth Suffolk District, Massachusetts House of Representatives, Boston, MA (1994-1996); Ironworker, General Dynamics Shipyard (Now General Dynamics NASSCO) (1973-1991); Member, Financial Services Committee; Member, Committee on Oversight and Government Reform Committee; Private Law Practice; Ironworker, General Motors (GM); Ironworker, US Steel Plant **CR:** Co-founder, Congressional Labor and Working Families Caucus **MEM:** President, Local Seven, US Ironworkers Union, Boston, MA **PA:** Democrat **RE:** Roman Catholic

LYNN, LORETTA WEBB, T: Singer **I:** Media & Entertainment **DOB:** 04/14/1935 **PB:** Butcher Hollow **SC:** KY/USA **PT:** Ted Webb; Clara (Butcher) Webb **MS:** Widow **SPN:** Oliver V. Lynn Junior (01/10/1948, Deceased 1996) **CH:** Betty Sue Lynn Markworth (Deceased); Jack Benny (Deceased); Clara Lynn Lyell; Erne **ED:** Student, Public Schools **CR:** Secretary-Treasurer, Loretta Lynn Enterprises; Vice President, United Talent, Inc; Honorary Chairman, Board, Loretta Lynn Western Stores **CIV:** Honorary Representative, United Giver's Fund (1971) **CW:** Singer, "Wouldn't It Be Great" (2018); Singer, "Full Circle" (2016); Singer, "You're Cookin' It Country" (2004); Singer, "Van Lear Rose" (2004); Singer, "Still Woman Enough" (2002); Singer, "Still Country" (2000); Singer, "All Time Gospel Favorites" (1997); Singer, "Making More Memories" (1994); Singer, "Country's Favorite Daughter" (1993); Singer, "Greatest Hits Live" (1992); Singer, "Loretta Lynn: The Seasons of My Life" (1992); Singer, "Who Was That Stranger" (1988); Singer, "Just a Woman" (1985); Singer, "Lyin', Cheatin', Woman Chasin', Honky Tonkin', Whiskey Drinkin' You" (1983); Singer, "Making Love from Memory" (1982); Singer, "I Lie" (1981); Singer, "Loretta" (1980); Singer, "Lookin' Good" (1980); Singer, "We've Come a Long Way Baby" (1979); Co-Singer, "Diamond Duet" (1979); Singer, "Out of My Head and Back in Bed" (1978); Co-Singer, "Honky Tonk Heroes" (1978); Singer, "I Remember Patsy" (1977); Co-Singer, "Dynamic Duo" (1977); Singer, "When the Tingle Becomes a Chill" (1976);

Co-Author, "United Talent" (1976); Singer, "Somebody, Somewhere" (1976); Co-Singer, "Country Partners" (1974); Singer, "Back to the Country" (1975); Co-Singer, "Feelin's" (1975); Singer, "Home" (1975); Singer, "They Don't Make 'em Like My Daddy" (1974); Singer, "Entertainer of the Year - Loretta" (1973); Co-Singer, "Louisiana Woman, Mississippi Man" (1973); Singer, "Love is the Foundation" (1973); Co-Singer, "Lead Me On" (1972); Singer, "One's on the Way" (1972); Singer, "Here I Am Again" (1972); Singer, "Coal Miner's Daughter" (1970); Singer, "I Wanna Be Free" (1971); Singer, "We Only Make Believe" (1971); Singer, "You're Lookin' At Country" (1971); Singer, "Wings Upon Your Horns" (1970); Singer, "Loretta Lynn Writes 'em & Sings 'em" (1970); Singer, "Your Squaw is on the Warpath" (1969); Co-Singer, "If We Put Our Heads Together" (1969); Singer, "Woman of the World/ To Make a Man" (1969); Singer, "Singin' With Feelin'" (1967); Singer, "Fist City" (1968); Singer, "Who Says God is Dead!" (1968); Singer, "Don't Come Home a Drinkin'" (1967); Singer, "Ernest Tubb & Loretta Lynn Singin' Again" (1967); Singer, "I Like Em' Country" (1966); Singer, "You Aint Woman Enough" (1966); Singer, "Songs from My Heart" (1965); Singer, "Hymns" (1965); Singer, "Blue Kentucky Girl" (1965); Co-Singer, "Mr. & Mrs. Used to Be" (1965); Singer, "Loretta Lynn Sings" (1963); Singer, "Before I'm Over You" (1964) **AW:** Kris Kristofferson Lifetime Achievement Award (2019); Grammy for Best Country Album (2017); Inductee, Nashville Music City Walk of Fame (2015); Academy of Country Music Awards (2014); Crystal Milestone, Americana Music Association Awards (2014); Presidential Medal of Freedom, The White House (2013); Grammy for Presidents Merit Award (2010); Grammy for Lifetime Achievement (2010); Inductee, Songwriter's Hall of Fame (2008); Recording Academy Honor Award (2007); Johnny Cash Visionary Award; Country Music Television Music Award (2005); Kennedy Center Honors, John F. Kennedy Center for the Performing Arts (2003); Pioneer Award, Academy of County Music (1995); Inductee, Country Music Hall of Fame (1988); Entertainer of the Decade, Academy of Country Music (1980); American Music Award (1978); Top Duet (1972, 1973, 1974, 1975); Country Music Association Female Vocalist of Year (1967, 1972, 1973); Entertainer of the Year (1972)

LYTLE, MICHAEL A., T: Forensic Criminologist, Consultant **I:** Biotechnology **DOB:** 10/22/1946 **PB:** Salina **SC:** KS/USA **PT:** Milton Earl Lytle; Geraldine Faye (Young) Lytle **MS:** Divorced **CH:** Eric Alexander **ED:** Graduate Certificate, University of California Riverside, Riverside, CA (2007); Diploma, U.S. Army Command and General Staff College, Leavenworth, KS (1992); Diploma, National Defense University, Washington, DC (1988); Postgrad Study, Texas A&M University System, College Station, TX (1978-1980); MEd, Texas A&M University System, College Station, TX (1978); Graduate Certificate, Sam Houston State University, Huntsville, TX (1977); BA, Indiana University Bloomington, Bloomington, IN (1973) **CT:** Licensed Police Training Instructor, Texas Commission on Law Enforcement **C:** Consulting Criminologist (2017-Present); Principal, Michael A. Lyte & Associates (2017-Present); Coordinator, Forensic Investigation Program, University of Texas Rio Grande Valley (2015-2017); Coordinator, Forensic Investigation Program, University of Texas at Brownsville (2008-2015); Assistant Professor, Criminal Justice, University of Texas at Brownsville (2006-2008); Deputy Manager, Tech. Services Division, Science Applications International Corporation (2000-2006); Adjunct Professor, Criminal Justice, Marymount University and Lutheran Colleges Washington Consortium (1999-2005); Senior Research

Associate, Science Applications International Corporation (1997-1999); Research Fellow, Office of the Under Secretary of Defense (1997); Senior Lecturer, Criminal Justice, University of Texas at Brownsville (1995-1997); Executive Director, Institutional Devel., University of Texas at Brownsville (1993-1995); Principal and Senior Counsel, The Erik Alexander Group (1992-1993); Adjunct Professor, International Business Studies, Syracuse University, New York (1990-1992); Director, Federal Relations, Syracuse University, New York (1988-1992); Adjunct Senior Research, Associate Tech. and Information Policy Program, Maxwell School Citizenship and Public Affairs, Syracuse University, New York (1987-1992); Executive Director, Government Relations, Syracuse University, New York (1988-1989); Director, Research Development and Special Assistant to Vice President for Research and Grad. Studies, Syracuse University, New York (1987); Special Assistant to Chancellor for Federal Relations, Texas A&M University System, (1984-1987); Assistant Director, Government Relations, Texas A&M University System (1983-1984); Assistant to Chancellor, Texas A&M University System (1981-1983); Staff Associate, Office Chancellor, Texas A&M University System (1980-1981); Intern Administrative Assistant, Office Vice Chancellor, Legal Affairs and General Counsel, Texas A&M University System (1980); Teaching Assistant, Texas A&M University (1977-1980); Adjunct Instructor, Criminal Justice, University of Tennessee, Chattanooga, TN (1975-1976); Instructor, Criminal Justice, Cleveland State Community College, Cleveland, TN (1974-1977); Substitute, High School Teacher, Butler County, KS (1969) **CR:** Office for Victims of Crime (2002-Present); Consultant, National Institute of Justice (2000-Present); Member, U.S. Mexico Committee Philanthropy and the Border (1994-1995); Member, Secretary of the Army, Adv. Panel in ROTC Affairs (1988-1992); Advisory Board, International Business Studies, Texas A&M University (1986-1987); Res. Assistant Army Attache to Rep. of Ireland (1986-1987); Rep. Council on Federal Relations; Association of American Universities Institutional Rep. Research Univs. Network; Militarily Critical Techs. Adv. Committee, U.S. Department Commerce, Secretary Army Advisory Panel ROTC Affairs; Member, Executive Committee, Northeast Parallel Architectures Center (1990-1992) **CIV:** Executive Director, Texas Committee for Employer Support of the Guard and Reserve (1994-1996): Board of Directors, Historic Brownsville Museum (1993-1997); Board of Directors, Veterans Outreach Center of Central New York (1988-1993); Endowment Scholarship Benefactor, LTC Michael A Lytle Academic Prize in Forensic Science, Sam Houston State University **MIL:** U.S. Army Reserve Service, Vietnam and Bosnia **CW:** Member, Editorial Board, Journal of Technology Transfer (1987-1995); Contributor, Numerous Articles to Professional Journals; Principal Investigator on Multiple Research Grants and Contracts **AW:** Distinguished Alumni Award, Sam Houston State University (2003); Decorated Legion of Merit; Bronze Star; Purple Heart; Meritorious Service Medal with 2 Oak Leaf Clusters; Joint Service Commendation Medal; Army Commendation Medal with 4 Oak Leaf Clusters; Individual Foreign Decorations; RVN Staff Service Honor Medal 1st Class; RVN Civil Action Medal 1st Class **MEM:** Fellow, Inter-Univ. Seminar Armed Forces and Society; American Association for the Advancement of Science; Executive Committee Section, Past Chair on National Security and Defense Analysis, American Society for Public Administration; Veteran Affairs and National Service Committee, National Association of State Universities and Land-Grant Colleges; Councilor, Atlantic Council; Chartered Society of Forensic Sciences; Academy of Criminal

Justice Sciences; International Association for the Study of Organized Crime; International Association of Chiefs of Police; International Association for Identification; International Association of Law Enforcement Intelligence Analysts; Army and Navy Club; Capitol Hill Club; Sigma Xi; Phi Delta Kappa; Alpha Phi Sigma; Lambda Alpha Epsilon; Zeta Beta Tau **MH:** Albert Nelson Marquis Lifetime Achievement Award **PA:** Independent **RE:** Episcopalian

MA, ALAN W. C. JD, MBA, T: Lawyer **I:** Law and Legal Services **DOB:** 04/20/1951 **SC:** Hong Kong **PT:** Pak Ping Ma; Qi Quon (Hung) Ma **ED:** JD, Golden Gate University (1983); MBA, Chaminade University (1981); BBA, University of Hawaii (1975) **C:** Principal, Law Offices of Alan W.C. Ma (1999-Present); Counsel, Goodsill Anderson Quinn & Stifel, Honolulu, HI (1995-1999); Principal, Law Offices of Alan W.C. Ma, Honolulu, HI (1990-1995); Partner, Oldenberg & Ma, Honolulu, HI (1984-1990) **CR:** Adjunct Professor of Law, University of Hawaii, Honolulu, HI (1988-1995) **CIV:** Trade Representative, Hong Kong (1995); Trade Representative, State of Hawaii **CW:** Co-Author, "Real Estate Investment and Practices in the USA" (2007); Co-Editor, "New Waves for Foreign Investors" (1990); Author, Screenplay; Author, Short Stories **AW:** Listee, Best Lawyers in America (1993-Present); Outstanding Volunteer Award, Hawaii Community Service Council (1990) **MEM:** Board of Directors, U.S. Japan Volunteer Association (1989-Present); Board of Directors, Overseas Chinese American Association (1993-1994); Chapter Chair, American Immigration Lawyers Association (1993-1994); American Bar Association; International Bar Association; Inter-Pacific Bar Association **BAR:** U.S. Supreme Court (1989); U.S. Court Appeals for the 9th Circuit (1986); Hawaii (1984); U.S. District Court of Hawaii (1984) **MH:** Albert Nelson Marquis Lifetime Achievement Award; Marquis Who's Who Top Professional **B/I:** Mr. Ma is a first-generation immigrant. Although he was born in Hong Kong, he grew up in Hawaii. There, Mr. Ma witnessed a lot of unfairness and recognized that people needed the legal system. He decided to study the law, winning a scholarship that was funded by congress. Selected in 1980, he was the only individual chosen from the state of Hawaii. Once he was selected, he received scholarship funding and was sent to a training program to ensure that he would get through. The training that Mr. Ma received benefited him, as he was able to finish law school quickly and earned an MBA. **AV:** Dancing; Playing tennis

MA, SHAN-LYN, T: Chief Executive Officer **I:** Business Management/Business Services **CN:** Zola **ED:** MBA, General Management, Stanford University Graduate School (2006); Bachelor of Commerce, University of New South Wales **C:** Chief Executive Officer, Founder, Zola (2013-Present); Chief Product Officer, Chlo + Isabel (2012-2013); General Manager, Founder, Gilt Group (2010-2012); Senior Director of Product Management, Gilt Group (2008-2010)

MACARTHUR, THOMAS, "TOM" CHARLES, T: Former U.S. Representative **I:** Government Administration/Government Relations/Government Services **DOB:** 10/16/1960 **PB:** Hebron **SC:** CT/USA **MS:** Married **SPN:** Debbie MacArthur (1983) **CH:** Grace (Deceased); David; Isabella **ED:** BA, Hofstra University (1982) **C:** U.S. Representative, New Jersey's Third Congressional District, United States Congress (2015-2019); Mayor, City of Randolph, NJ (2013-2014); Deputy Mayor, City of Randolph, NJ (2012-2013); Councilman, Randolph Township, NJ (2010-2013); Chairman, Chief Executive Officer, York Risk Services Group, Inc., NJ (1999-2010);

Insurance Adjuster, New York, NY; Member, Committee on Financial Services CIV: Co-Founder, St. Peter's Sandy Relief Fund; Co-Founder, In God's Hands PA: Republican

MACCRACKEN, THOMAS GREGG, PHD, T: Musicologist, Independent Scholar **I:** Writing and Editing **DOB:** 05/15/1951 **PB:** Norwalk **SC:** CT/USA **PT:** Constable MacCracken; Eleanor (Dickson) MacCracken **MS:** Married **SPN:** Alexandra Jane (Moore-Robinson) MacCracken (05/28/1988) **ED:** Doctor of Philosophy, University of Chicago (1985); Bachelor of Arts, Yale University (1973) **C:** Independent Scholar (1993-Present); Research Fellow, Smithsonian Institution (1991-1993); Assistant Professor of Music, University of Virginia, Charlottesville, VA (1986-1990) **CR:** Trustee, Kinhaven Music School (1974-1980, 1993-1998) **CW:** Editorial Board, Viola da Gamba Society of America (1996-Present); Editor, American Musical Instrument Society (1996-2006); Review Editor, Southeastern Historical Keyboard Society (1991-1996); Editor, Jean Mouton Opera Omnia; Co-editor, Mathurin Forestier Opera Omnia; Editor, Database of Historical Viols; Musician, Pour 2 Clavecins; Concert Performer, Historical Instruments; Contributor, Articles, Professional Journals **MEM:** Board Member, Early Music America (1990-1994); American Musical Instrument Society; American Musicological Society; American Recorder Society; Galpin Society; Historical Keyboard Society of North America; Viola da Gamba Society of America **MH:** Albert Nelson Marquis Lifetime Achievement Award **RE:** Episcopalian

MACDIARMID, ALAN GRAHAM, PHD, T: Chemist; Professor **I:** Education/Educational Services **CN:** University of Pennsylvania **DOB:** 04/14/1927 **PB:** Masterton **SC:** New Zealand **MS:** Widowed **SPN:** Gayl Gentile (2005, Deceased 2014); Marian MacDiarmid (1954, Deceased 1990) **CH:** Heather; Dawn; Gail; Duncan **ED:** Honorary Doctorate, Victoria University of Wellington (1999, 2001); PhD in Chemistry, University of Cambridge (1955); PhD in Chemistry, University of Wisconsin - Madison (1953); MS, University of Wisconsin - Madison (1952); MSc, Victoria University of Wellington (1950); BSc, Victoria University of Wellington, New Zealand (1948) **C:** Blanchard Professor of Chemistry, University of Pennsylvania, Philadelphia, PA (1998-2007); Professor of Chemistry, University of Pennsylvania, Philadelphia, PA (1964-2007); Sloan Fellowship, University of Pennsylvania, Philadelphia, PA (1959-1963); From Instructor to Associate Professor, University of Pennsylvania, Philadelphia, PA (1955-1964); Assistant Lecturer in Chemistry, St. Andrews University (1955) **CR:** Member, Faculty, The University of Texas at Dallas; Visiting Professor, Kyoto University, Japan; Speaker in Field **CW:** Contributor, Articles, Professional Journals **AW:** Friendship Award, Republic of China (2004); Named to Order of New Zealand, New Year Honours (2002); Rutherford Medal, Royal Society of New Zealand (2000); Co-recipient, Nobel Prize in Chemistry (2000); Award in Materials Chemistry, American Chemistry Society (1999); Francis J. Clamer Medal, Franklin Institute (1993); Chemical Pioneer Award (1984); Doolittle Award (1982); Marshall Award (1982); Frederic Stanley Kipping Award (1970); Royal Society of Chemistry Centenary Medal **MEM:** Fellow, Royal Society; Royal Society of Chemistry; American Chemical Society

MACDONALD, KAREN, T: Occupational Therapist, Geriatrics Services Professional **I:** Medicine & Health Care

MACHANN, CLINTON J., T: English Educator **I:** Education/Educational Services **DOB:** 07/18/1947 **PB:** Bryan **SC:** TX/USA **PT:** J.W. Machann; Sophie E. Machann **MS:** Married **SPN:** Virginia Brown **CH:** Alena; Theresie; Sarah **ED:** PhD, University of Texas (1976); BA, Texas A&M University (1969) **C:** Emeritus Professor of English (2017); Professor English, Texas A&M University, College Station, TX (1976-2017); Teaching Assistant, University of Texas at Austin (1971-1976); Teacher, Texas Public Schools, Houston, TX (1969-1971) **CR:** Chairman, Board of Directors, Czech Educational Foundation of Texas (1995-2019); Fulbright Lecturer, Charles University, Prague, Czech Republic (1990) **CW:** Editor, Kosmas: Czechoslovak and Central European Journal (2000-2012); Editor, Czech-Americans in Transition (1999); Author, "Matthew Arnold: A Literary Life" (1998); Author, "The Genre of Autobiography in Victorian Literature" (1994); Author, "Masculinity in Four Victorian Epics" **MEM:** Modern Language Association **MH:** Albert Nelson Marquis Lifetime Achievement Award; Marquis Who's Who Top Professional **B/I:** Mr. Machann became involved in his profession after majoring in journalism in college and working for a newspaper. He became interested in writing at an early age and his high school English teacher inspired him to pursue a career in the field, motivating his decision to attend college. **AV:** Writing novels and poems; Songwriting

MACK, KHALIL DELSHON, T: Professional Football Player **I:** Athletics **CN:** Chicago Bears **DOB:** 02/22/1991 **PB:** Fort Pierce **SC:** FL/USA **PT:** Sandy Mack Sr.; Yolanda Mack **MS:** Single **ED:** Coursework, State University of New York at Buffalo; Diploma, Fort Pierce Westwood High School, Fort Pierce, FL **C:** Professional Football Player, Chicago Bears (2018-Present); Professional Football Player, Oakland Raiders (2014-2017) **AW:** Five-Time Pro Bowl Champion (2015-2019); Butkus Award (Pro) (2016, 2018); Three-Time First-team All-Pro Champion (2015-2016, 2018); NFL Defensive Player of the Year (2016); MAC Defensive Player of the Year (2013)

MACKEY, AARON K., MED, T: Superintendent (Retired) **I:** Education/Educational Services **DOB:** 06/05/1948 **PB:** Glendale **SC:** OH/USA **PT:** Norman T. Mackey; Wanda I. (Cunningham) Mackey **MS:** Married **SPN:** Karen M. (Lachowski) Mackey (11/09/1985) **CH:** Kayla M. Mackey **ED:** MEd in Administration, Xavier University (1978); BS in Education, University of Cincinnati (1970) **CT:** Certified Teacher, Supervisor and Administrator **C:** Superintendent, Princeton City School District (2004-2008); Associate Superintendent, Princeton City School District (2001-2004); Principal, Princeton Junior High School, Princeton City Schools (1990-2001); Principal, Springdale Elementary School, Princeton City Schools (1989-1990); Principal, Glendale Elementary School, Princeton City Schools (1982-1989); Assistant Principal, Princeton Junior High School, Princeton City Schools (1978-1982); Teacher, Princeton City Schools (1970-1978) **CR:** Adjunct Professor, Wright State University (2009-Present) **CIV:** Council President, City of Sharonville (1983-1985); At-Large Council Member, City of Sharonville (1980-1983); Ward Council Member, City of Sharonville (1976-1980) **CW:** Developer, Success Team **AW:** Three-Time Winner, Award of Excellence, U.S. Department of Education; Princeton Emeritus Career Award **MEM:** Buckeye Association of School Administrators **MH:** Albert Nelson Marquis Lifetime Achievement Award **AS:** Mr. Mackey attributes his success to his drive to ensure the best possible education for his students. **B/I:** Mr. Mackey became involved in his profession because he was inspired by childhood teachers and had a desire to foster the next generation of students. **AV:** Traveling the United States and Europe; Reading; Watching movies; Engaging in politics **PA:** Conservative **RE:** Methodist **THT:** Mr. Mackey states, "There is nothing more important than devoting the energy, interest, support and the resources to a child throughout their educational years to prepare them for the decisions effecting their life."

MACKEY, JOHN P., T: Chief Executive Officer **I:** Retail/Sales **CN:** Whole Foods Market Inc. **DOB:** 08/15/1953 **PB:** Houston **SC:** TX/USA **PT:** Bill Mackey; Margaret Mackey **ED:** Coursework, University of Texas, Austin, TX; Coursework, Trinity College, San Antonio, TX **C:** Chief Executive Officer, Whole Foods Inc. (2017-Present); Co-Chief Executive Officer, Whole Foods Market Inc., Austin, TX (2010-2016); Chief Executive Officer, Whole Foods Market Inc., Austin, TX (1980-2010); Co-founder, Chairman, Whole Foods Market Inc., Austin, TX (1978-2009); President, Whole Foods Market Inc., Austin, TX (2001-2004); Owner, Safer Way Natural Foods, Austin, TX (1978-1980) **AW:** Named, Overall National Entrepreneur of Year, Ernst & Young (2003) **AV:** Yoga; Meditation; Scuba diving

MACKEY, WILLIAM ARTHUR GODFREY, T: Director of Finance & Administration **I:** Manufacturing **CN:** Advanced Adhesive Systems, Inc. **DOB:** 03/23/1946 **PB:** Glasgow, Scotland **SC:** U.K. **PT:** William Arthur Mackey; Joan Margaret (Sykes) Mackey **ED:** MBA, Harvard University (1972); MSc in Engineering, Imperial College London (1970); BSc in Mechanical Engineering, Imperial College London (1968); The Glasgow Academy (1951-1964) **C:** Director of Finance & Administration, Advanced Adhesive Systems, Newington, CT (2018-Present); Director of Finance, Advanced Adhesive Systems, Newington, CT (2014-2017); Manager of Administration, Advanced Adhesive Systems, Newington, CT (2004-2014); Financial Advisor, Financial Services Industry (2002-2004); Adjunct Professor, School of Engineering, Science and Technology, Central Connecticut State University, New Britain, CT (2001-2002); President, Axiom Laboratories, Inc., Bloomfield, CT (1998-2001); President, Signum Microsystems, Inc., Bloomfield, CT (1991-1997); Senior Consultant, PricewaterhouseCoopers LLP (Pwc), Hartford, CT (1988-1991); Worldwide Manager Remote Elevator Monitoring, Otis Elevator Company, Farmington, CT (1985-1987); President, Signum Microsystems, Inc., Bloomfield, CT (1983-1984); Corporate Productivity Improvement Manager, Henkel Corporation, Newington, CT (1980-1983); Operations Manager, Systems Division, Henkel Corporation, Newington, CT (1978-1980); Manufacturing Controller, Americas Group, Henkel Corporation, Newington, CT (1976-1978); Special Projects Engineer, Fafnir Bearings Division, The Timken Company, New Britain, CT (1974-1976); Financial Analyst, RBC Wealth Management, Boston, MA (1972-1974); Manufacturing Engineer, Aero Engine Division, Rolls-Royce plc, Glasgow, Scotland (1969-1970); Engineering Student Apprentice, Aero Engine Division, Rolls-Royce plc, Glasgow, Scotland (1964-1965) **CR:** Board of Directors, Axiom Laboratories, Inc., Bloomfield, CT (1998-2002); Non-Executive Chairman, Association Promoting Education and Conservation in Amazonia, Inc., West Hartford, CT (1997-2002); Chapter Chair, Society of Manufacturing Engineers, Hartford Chapter 7 (1996-1997); Board of Directors, Signum Microsystems, Inc., Bloomfield, CT (1983-1997) **CIV:** Scoutmaster, BSA Troop 12, West Hartford, CT (2018-Present); Member, Community Partners, Harvard Business School Club of Connecticut (2017-Present); Chartered Organization Representative, BSA Troop 12,

West Hartford, CT (2016-2017); Volunteer Member Classical Music Staff, WWUH 91.3 FM, West Hartford, CT (2002-Present); Reading Committee Chair, Simsbury Light Opera Co. (2014-2015); Board of Directors, West Hartford Taxpayers Association, CT (1995-1996); Board of Directors, World Affairs Council of Connecticut (1992-1998); Vice Chairman, Connecticut Committee, Newcomen Society of the United States, Exton, PA (1980-1998); Volunteer, Wadsworth Atheneum Capital Development Program (1978); Volunteer, Junior Achievement USA, New Britain, CT (1975-1976); Assistant Scoutmaster, Scouts Scotland, 183rd Glasgow (Bearsden) Scout Group (1964-1965) **AW:** BSA, Connecticut Rivers Council, Wood Badge N2-66-18 (2019); Legion of Honor, DeMolay International (2016); Knight Commander of the Temple, Grand Encampment, Knights Templar (2015); Commissioned a Kentucky Colonel, Commonwealth of Kentucky (2002); President's Award, Society Manufacturing Engineers (SME) (1992 & 1998); Chief of Staff, City of New Haven Blue Ribbon Commission (1990); Post-Graduate Scholarship, Rolls-Royce plc (1970-1972); Engineering Student Scholarship, Rolls-Royce plc (1964-1969); The Duke of Edinburgh's Award, Gold Standard (1964); Flying Scholarship, Royal Air Force (1963); Queen's Scout Award, The Scout Association (1963) **MEM:** Harvard Business School Club of Connecticut; Imperial College London in Boston; Presidents' College University of Hartford; MIT Enterprise Forum of Connecticut; American Mensa, Ltd.; Masons; St. Andrew's Society of Connecticut **MH:** Albert Nelson Marquis Lifetime Achievement Award; Marquis Who's Who Top Professional **AS:** Mr. Mackey attributes the foundation of his success to the generosity and support of his late parents. Business mentors also helped him in the early stages of his career. At the start of his career, Mr. Mackey's training manager at Rolls-Royce plc played an essential role in providing him with constructive career guidance. At Loctite Corporation, the chief executive officer was a valued mentor. **B/I:** Mr. Mackey has enjoyed a lifelong interest in science, technology, and engineering. During his teenage years, Mr. Mackey was influenced by Project Mercury, which put Col. John H. Glenn, Jr. into orbit around the earth. While Mr. Mackey was still in high school, his father drew his attention to Imperial College London and the Harvard Business School. His father felt they would be a natural fit, as Mr. Mackey wished to pursue a career in engineering and business. Mr. Mackey's career interests have always been business-related. He harbors hope of pursuing more new ventures. **AV:** Books; Dance; Fine Arts; Music; Radio Broadcasting; Motorcycles; Volunteering; Fitness; Camping; Hiking; Sailing; Swimming **PA:** Independent **RE:** United Church of Christ **THT:** Looking back on his early years, Mr. Mackey has come to appreciate the many acts of kindnesses shown to him by his parents and the parents of childhood friends. To express his gratitude, he now pays it forward by acts of kindness in helping others and mentoring young people. Mr. Mackey's intent is to make a positive difference wherever possible.

MACLAINE, SHIRLEY, T: Actress **I:** Media & Entertainment **DOB:** 04/24/1934 **PB:** Richmond **SC:** VA/USA **PT:** Ira Owens Beaty; Kathlyn Corinne (MacLean) Beaty **MS:** Divorced **SPN:** Steve Parker (09/17/1954, Divorced 1982) **CH:** Stephanie Sachiko **ED:** Diploma, Washington-Lee High School **CW:** Actress, "Noelle" (2019); Voice Actress, "Jim Button and Luke the Engine Driver" (2019); Actress, "The Little Mermaid" (2017); Actress, "Wild Oats" (2016); Actress, "A Heavenly Christmas" (2016); Author, "Above the Line: My Wild Oats" (2016); Actress, "The Last Word" (2016); Actress, "Elsa & Fred" (2014); Actress, "Glee"

(2014); Actress, "The Secret Life of Walter Mitty" (2013); Author, "What If...A Lifetime of Questions, Speculations, Reasonable Guesses and a Few Things I Know for Sure" (2013); Actress, "Downton Abbey" (2012-2013); Actress, "Bernie" (2011); Author, "I'm All Over That: And Other Confessions" (2011); Actress, "Valentine's Day" (2010); Actress, "Anne of Green Gables: A New Beginning" (2008); Actress, "Coco Chanel" (2008); Actress, "Closing the Ring" (2007); Author, "Sage-ing While Ageing" (2007); Actress, "Bewitched" (2005); Actress, "In Her Shoes" (2005); Actress, "Rumor Has It..." (2005); Actress, "Carolina" (2003); Author, "Out on a Leash: Exploring the Nature of Reality and Love" (2003); Actress,"Hell on Heels: The Battle of Mary Kay" (2002); Actress, "Salem Witch Trials" (2002); Actress, "These Old Broads" (2001); Author, "The Camino: A Journey of the Spirit" (2000); Directorial Debut, Actress, "Bruno" (2000); Actress, "Joan of Arc" (1999); Actress, "Mrs. Winterbourne" (1996); Actress, "Evening Star" (1995); Actress, "The West Side Waltz" (1995); Author, "My Lucky Stars: A Hollywood Memoir" (1995); Actress, "Guarding Tess" (1994); Actress, "Wrestling Ernest Hemingway" (1993); Actress, "Used People" (1992); Actress, "Defending Your Life" (1991); Author, "Dance While You Can" (1991); Actress, "Waiting for the Light" (1990); Featured, Stage Musical, "Out There Tonight," U.S. Tour (1990); Actress, "Postcards from the Edge" (1990); Author, "Going Within: A Guide for Inner Transformation" (1989); Actress, "Steel Magnolias" (1989); Actress, "Madame Sousatzka" (1988); Author, "It's All in the Playing" (1987); Actress, "Out on a Limb" (1987); Author, "Dancing in the Light" (1985); Actress, "Cannonball Run II" (1984); Actress, "Terms of Endearment" (1983); Author, "Out on a Limb" (1983); Actress, "A Change of Seasons" (1980); Actress, "Loving Couples" (1980); Appearance, "Shirley MacLaine...Every Little Movement" (1980); Actress, "Being There" (1979); Appearance, "Shirley MacLaine at the Lido" (1979); Actress, "The Turning Point" (1977); Actress, "Where Do We Go from Here?" (1976-1977); Actress, "Gypsy in My Soul" (1975-1976); Actress, "The Other Half of the Sky: A China Memoir" (1975); Co-director, Documentary, "China: The Other Half of the Sky" (1975); Author, "You Can Get There from Here" (1975); Appearance, "Shirley MacLaine: If They Could See Me Now" (1974-1975); Author, "The New Celebrity Cookbook" (1973); Actress, "The Possession of Joel Delaney" (1972); Editor, "McGovern: The Man and His Beliefs" (1972); Appearance, "Shirley's World" (1971-1972); Actress, "Desperate Characters" (1971); Author, "Don't Fall Off the Mountain" (1970); Actress, "The Bliss of Mrs. Blossom" (1969); Actress, "Sweet Charity" (1969); Actress, "Two Mules for Sister Sara" (1969); Actress, "Gambit and Woman Times Seven" (1967); Actress, "John Goldfarb Please Come Home" (1965); Actress, "What a Way to Go" (1964); Actress, "The Yellow Rolls Royce" (1964); Actress, "Irma La Douce" (1963); Actress, "Two for the Seesaw" (1962); Actress, "Ask Any Girl" (1959); Actress, "Career" (1959); Actress, "Can-Can" (1959); Actress, "The Apartment" (1959); Actress, "Some Came Running" (1958); Actress, "Hot Spell" (1957); Actress, "The Matchmaker" (1957); Actress, "The Sheepman" (1957); Actress, "Around the World in 80 Days" (1955-1956); Actress, "Pajama Game" (1954); Actress, "The Trouble with Harry" (1954); Actress, "Artists and Models" (1954); Actress, "Me and Juliet" (1953) **AW:** "Movies for Grown-ups" Lifetime Achievement Award, AARP Magazine (2019); Honoree, Kennedy Center Honors, John F. Kennedy Center for the Performing Arts, Washington, DC (2013); Lifetime Achievement Award, American Film Institute (2012); Named Chevalier, Legion d'Honneur (2011); Honorary Golden Bear,

49th Berlin International Film Festival (1999); Cecil B. DeMille Award, Hollywood Foreign Press Association (1998); Golden Globe Award for Best Actress, Hollywood Foreign Press (1984, 1989); Emmy Award for Outstanding Special: Comedy-Variety or Music, Academy of Television Arts & Sciences (1976); Golden Globe Awards for Best Actress - Motion Picture Comedy or Musical, Hollywood Foreign Press Association (1964); Golden Globe Award for Best Actress - Motion Picture Comedy or Musical, Hollywood Foreign Press Association (1961); Recipient, Star, Hollywood Foreign Press Association (1960); Golden Globe Award for Most Promising Newcomer - Female, Hollywood Foreign Press Association (1956)

MACLIN, ARLENE PAIGE, T: Program Director **I:** Technology **CN:** Howard University **DOB:** 06/07/1945 **PB:** Rawlings **SC:** VA/USA **PT:** Otis Armstead Maclin; Alice Matthews Maclin **MS:** Widowed **SPN:** Donald P. Addison (Deceased) **ED:** PhD in Theoretical Condensed Matter Physics, Howard University, Washington, DC (1974); MS in Theoretical Nuclear Physics, University of Virginia (1971); Post-Baccalaureate Fellow, Haverford College, Bryn Mawr, PA (1968); BS in Engineering Physics, North Carolina Agricultural and Technical University (1967) **C:** Program Director, Howard University Partnership for Design & Development, Howard, Washington, DC (2016-Present); Executive Director, Mid Atlantic Consortium-Center for Academic Excellence (2011-2016); Program and Adjunct Professor of Physics, Morgan State University, Baltimore, MD (2011-2016); Adjunct Professor, Physics, Morgan State University (2009-2011); Delta Sigma Theta Distinguished Professor, Division of Natural Science and Mathematics, Bennett College for Women (2009-2011); Professor of Optical Engineering, Director, Intelligence Community-Center for Academic Excellence, Norfolk State University (2002-2009); Technical Consultant, Dean of the College of Arts and Sciences, Howard University, Washington, DC (1998-2002); Senior Business Developer, Mnemonic Systems, Washington, DC (1996-1998); Guest Scientist, NASA Langley Research Center, Hampton, VA (1994-1995); Director, Research, Professor, Physics, Hampton University, Hampton, VA (1992-1994); Associate Professor, Electrical Engineering, Howard University, Washington, DC (1988-1992); Program Staff Officer, National Research Council, Washington, DC (1985-1988); Congressional Fellow, United States Congressional Office of Technology Assessment, Washington, DC (1978-1980); Associate Dean, Associate Professor, Physics, Morgan State University, Baltimore, MD (1976-1978); Research Physicist, MIT Lincoln Laboratory, Lincoln, MA (1975-1976); Lecturer, Associate Director, Comprehensive Sciences Program, Howard University, Washington, DC (1971-1975) **CR:** Mentor in Field **CIV:** Board Member, The History Makers (2014-Present); Board Member, Center for Innovative Technology in the State of Virginia (1988-1993); Primary Program Staff, Materials Science and Engineering Report; Primary Program Staff, International Survey of Atomic and Molecular Science; Board Member, Washington Baltimore Hampton Roads, Alexander Program, Howard University **CW:** Over 50 Refereed Journal Articles, Technical Journals; Speaker, 250 International Invited Talks **AW:** Optical Society of America, Inaugural Diversity and Inclusion Award (2018); Listee, The History Makers (2013); Super Professor, Faculty Row (2012); Listee, International Who's Who of Women (1982, 1987); Listee, Who's Who Among Black Americans (1978) **MEM:** American Physical Society; Institute of Electrical and Electronics Engineers; Materials Research Society; National Society of Black Physicists; American Association of

Imaginative Sciences **AS:** Dr. Maclin attributes her success to her work ethic; she has a strong work ethic, which she got from her mother. Growing up on the farm, she had a lot of chores and she had to schedule a time to read and time to play. She has been very diligent about doing that throughout her entire career. She loves a challenge. **B/I:** Dr. Maclin had a marvelous math teacher in high school. She was a wonderful mentor and is now the reason why she is a physicist. During her years in high school, the Sputnik race was happening. It was quite an experience to be able to see, consequently inspiring her to pursue her field. **AV:** Golfing **RE:** Traditional Anglican **THT:** Dr. Maclin takes care of herself.

MACNEIL, ROBERT, "ROBIN" BRECKENRIDGE WARE, T: Journalist, Writer (Retired) **I:** Writing and Editing **DOB:** 01/19/1931 **PB:** Montreal **SC:** Quebec/Canada **PT:** Robert A.S. MacNeil; Margaret Virginia (Oxner) MacNeil **MS:** Widower **SPN:** Donna P. Richards (10/20/1984, Deceased 2015); Jane J. Doherty (05/29/1965, Divorced 1983); Rosemarie Anne Copland (1956, Divorced 1964) **CH:** Catherine Anne; Ian B.; Alison N.; William H. **ED:** Honorary LHD, Dalhousie University (2000); Honorary LHD, Mount Allison University (1998); Honorary LHD, University Toronto (1997); Honorary LHD, The Cooper Union (1996); Honorary LHD, Princeton University (1995); Honorary LHD, Columbia University (1995); Honorary LHD, Long Island University (1995); Honorary LHD, University of Miami (1994); Honorary LHD, University of Western Ontario (1992); Honorary LHD, Kenyon College (1990); Honorary LHD, Nazareth College (1988); Honorary LHD, Franklin and Marshall College (1987); Honorary LHD, University of South Carolina (1985); Honorary LHD, Brown University (1984); Honorary LHD, George Washington University (1983); Honorary LHD, Bucknell University (1982); Honorary LHD, Lawrence University (1980); Honorary LHD, Beaver College, Bates College (1979); Honorary LHD, William Patterson College (1977); BA, Carleton University (1955); Coursework, Dalhousie University (1949-1951); Coursework, Ashbury College, Ottawa, Canada (1944-1945); Coursework, Rothesay Collegiate School (1944-1945) **C:** Host, "America At A Crossroads," PBS (2006-Present); Host, "Do You Speak American?" (2003); Retired, Macneil/Lehrer News Hour, PBS (1995); Executive Editor, Co-Anchor, Macneil/Lehrer News Hour, PBS (1983-1995); Executive Editor, Co-Anchor, Macneil/Lehrer Report, Station WNET-TV, New York, NY (1975-1995); Host, "The Story Of English" (1986); Correspondent, Panorama Program BBC (1967-1975); Senior Correspondent, National Public Affairs Center For TV (1971-1973); News Correspondent, NBC, New York, NY (1965-1967); News Correspondent, NBC, Washington, DC (1963-1965); News Correspondent, NBC, London, England (1960-1963); Sub-Editor to Filing Editor, Reuters News Agency (1955-1960); Radio/Television Announcer, Canadian Broadcasting Company (1954-1955); Announcer, News Writer, Station CFRA, Ottawa, Canada (1952-1954); Announcer, Station-CJCH (1951-1952); Radio Actor, Canadian Broadcasting Company, Halifax, Canada (1950-1952) **CR:** Partner, MacNeil-Lehrer Productions, Arlington, VA **CIV:** Trustee, Emeritus Freedom Forum Newseum **CW:** Author, "Portrait of Julia" (2013); Co-Author, "Do You Speak American?" (2005); Author, "Looking For My Country" (2003); Author, "Breaking News" (1998); Author, "The Voyage" (1995); Author, "Burden of Desire" (1992); Author, "Wordstruck" (1989); Editor, "The Way We Were" (1988); Co-Author, "The Story of English" (1986); Author, "The Right Place at the Right Time" (1982); Author, "The People Machine, The Influence of Television on American Poli-

tics" (1968); Editor, "The Way We Were" (1963) **AW:** Honoree, Giants Broadcasting (2012); Catto Fellow, The Aspen Institute, Canadian Journalism Foundation Honorary Tribute (2011); Inductee, Television Academy Hall of Fame (1999); Decorated Officer, Order of Canada (1998); Lifetime Achievement Award, Overseas Press Club (1995); Broadcaster of the Year, International Radio and Television Society (1991); Paul White Award, Radio and Television News Directors Association (1990); Medal of Honor, University of Missouri School of Journalism (1980) **MEM:** The MacDowell Colony (1993-2010); Chairman, Fellow, American Association for the Advancement of Science; American Federation of Television and Radio Artists; Association of Radio and TV News Analysts; Writers Guild of America; Century Club, New York, NY **MH:** Albert Nelson Marquis Lifetime Achievement Award; Marquis Who's Who Top Professional **B/I:** Mr. MacNeil initially thought that he would be an actor. He later ventured into play-writing; however, his plays were not selling. This prompted him to pursue journalism. He additionally began working in the radio industry by doing reports for the Centers for Disease Control, which led to him receiving a job at NBC in London, England. Some of his most notable projects were his work on the John F. Kennedy assassination and the Cuban Missle Crisis. **THT:** In 1954, Mr. MacNeil was the first television announcer on the first television station (CBOT) in Ottawa, Canada.

MACY, WILLIAM HALL JR., T: Actor **I:** Media & Entertainment **DOB:** 03/13/1950 **PB:** Miami **SC:** FL/USA **PT:** William Hall Macy Sr.; Lois (Overstreet) Macy **MS:** Married **SPN:** Felicity Huffman (09/06/1997) **CH:** Sofia Grace; Georgia Grace **ED:** Diploma, Goddard College (1972); Coursework, HB Studio; Coursework in Veterinary Medicine, Bethany College **CR:** Founding Member, Atlantic Theatre Company, New York, NY; Founding Member, St. Nicholas Theater, Chicago, IL **CIV:** National Ambassador, United Cerebral Palsy Association **CW:** Actor, "Shameless" (2011-Present); Actor, "The Unit" (2017); Actor, "The Layover" (2017); Actor, "Krystal" (2017); Actor, "Blood Father" (2016); Actor, "Walter" (2015); Actor, "Blood Father" (2015); Actor, "Room" (2015); Actor, "Stealing Cars" (2015); Actor, "Dial a Prayer" (2015); Actor, "Two-Bit Waltz" (2014); Actor, "Cake," (2014); Actor, Director, Executive producer, Writer, "Rudderless" (2014); Actor, "A Single Shot" (2013); Actor, "Trust Me" (2013); Actor, "The Surrogate" (2012); Actor, "The Sessions" (2012); Actor, "The Lincoln Lawyer" (2011); Actor, "Marmaduke" (2010); Actor, "Dirty Girl" (2010); Actor, "Speed-the-Plow" (2009); Actor, "Shorts" (2009); Actor, "Bart Got a Room" (2008); Actor, "The Deal" (2008); Voice Actor, "The Tale of Despereaux" (2008); Actor, Executive Producer, Writer, "Family Man" (2008); Actor, "The Unit" (2007); Actor, "He Was a Quiet Man" (2007); Actor, "Wild Hogs" (2007); Actor, "Thank You for Smoking" (2006); Voice Actor, "Doogal" (2006); Actor, "Bobby" (2006); Actor, "Inland Empire" (2006); Voice Actor, "Everyone's Hero" (2006); Voice Actor, "The Simpsons" (2006); Actor, "Sahara" (2005); Actor, "Edmond" (2005); Executive Producer, "Transamerica" (2005); Actor, "The Wool Cap" (2004); Actor, "Cellular" (2004); Actor, "Reversible Errors" (2004); Actor, "The Cooler" (2003); Actor, "Seabiscuit" (2003); Actor, "Out of Order" (2003); Actor, "It's a Very Merry Muppet Christmas Movie" (2002); Actor, "Door to Door" (2002); Writer, "Just a Walk in the Park" (2002); Actor, "Welcome to Collinwood" (2002); Actor, "Jurassic Park III" (2001); Actor, "Focus" (2001); Actor, "Panic" (2000); Actor, "State and Main" (2000); Actor, "The Night of the Headless Horseman" (1999); Actor, "Batman

Beyond" (1999); Actor, "Happy, Texas" (1999); Actor, "Mystery Men" (1999); Actor, "Magnolia" (1999); Actor, "A Slight Case of Murder" (1999); Actor, Writer, "The Con" (1998); Actor, "Hercules" (1998); Actor, "Jerry and Tom" (1998); Actor, "Pleasantville" (1998); Actor, "Psycho" (1998); Voice Actor, "The Secret of National Institute of Mental Health 2: Timmy to the Rescue" (1998); Actor, "A Civil Action" (1998); Actor, "Sports Night" (1998); Actor, "The Lionhearts" (1998); Actor, "ER" (1994-1998); Voice Actor, "King of the Hill" (1997); Actor, "Air Force One" (1997); Actor, "Boogie Nights" (1997); Actor, "Wag the Dog" (1997); Actor, "Superman" (1996); Actor, "Andersonville" (1996); Actor, "Down Periscope" (1996); Actor, "Fargo" (1996); Actor, "Hit Me" (1996); Writer, "Every Woman's Dream" (1996); Actor, "Ghosts of Mississippi" (1996); Actor, "Mr. Holland's Opus" (1995); Actor, "Colin Fitz" (1996); Actor, "In the Shadow of Evil" (1995); Actor, "Above Suspicion" (1995); Actor, "Murder in the First" (1995); Actor, "Roommates" (1995); Actor, "Tall Tale" (1995); Actor, "Evolver" (1995); Actor, "The Client" (1994); Actor, "Oleanna" (1994); Actor, "Texan" (1994); Actor, "The Writing on the Wall" (1994); Actor, "The Heart of Justice" (1993); Actor, "Bakersfield P.D." (1993); Actor, "Frasier" (1993); Actor, "Benny & Joon" (1993); Actor, "Searching for Bobby Fischer" (1993); Actor, "Twenty Bucks" (1993); Actor, "Being Human" (1993); Actor, "Shadows and Fog" (1992); Actor, "In the Line of Duty: Siege at Marion" (1992); Actor, "A Private Matter" (1992); Actor, "The Water Engine" (1992); Actor, "Homicide" (1991); Actor, "Civil Wars" (1991); Actor, "Law & Order" (1990); Actor, Director, "Lip Service" (1988); Actor, "Things Change" (1988); Actor, "L.A. Law" (1986); Actor, "Spenser: For Hire" (1985-1988); Actor, "The Murder of Mary Phagan" (1988); Actor, "thirtysomething" (1987); Actor, "Radio Days" (1987); Actor, "House of Games" (1987); Actor, "The Equalizer" (1985); Actor, "The Last Dragon" (1985); Actor, "Kate & Allie" (1984); Actor, "The Boy Who Loved Trolls" (1984); Actor, "The Dining Room" (1984); Actor, "The Cradle Will Fall" (1983); Actor, "Without a Trace" (1983); Actor, "Foolin' Around" (1980); Actor, "Somewhere in Time" (1980); Actor, "The Awakening Land" (1978); Actor, "American Buffalo" (1975); Actor, Television Shows and Films **AW:** Screen Actors Guild Award for Outstanding Performance by a Male Actor in a Comedy Series, SAG-AFTRA (2015, 2017, 2018); Star, Hollywood Walk of Fame (2012); Screen Actors Guild Award for Outstanding Performance by a Male Actor in a TV Movie or Miniseries, SAG-AFTRA (2003); Emmy Award for Best Actor in a TV Movie, Academy of Television Arts & Sciences (2003); Emmy Award for Best Writing for a TV Movie, Academy of Television Arts & Sciences (2003); Numerous Awards **AV:** Playing ukulele; Woodturning

MADDEN, JOHN, T: Lawyer **I:** Law and Legal Services **DOB:** 05/27/1946 **PB:** New York City **SC:** NY/USA **PT:** John L. Madden; Bertha M. Madden **MS:** Married **SPN:** Mary A. Madden (06/19/1976) **CH:** Elisabeth; Samuel **ED:** JD, Fordham University, Cum Laude (1975); BA, University of Pennsylvania (1968) **CT:** Avocat a la cour de Paris (1994) **C:** Of Counsel, Shearman & Sterling LLP (2011-Present); Partner, Shearman & Sterling LLP, New York, NY (1983-2011); Firm Managing Partner, Shearman & Sterling LLP (2004-2009); Head, Mergers and Acquisitions Group, Shearman & Sterling LLP, New York, NY (1995-2001); Managing Partner, European Offices, Shearman & Sterling LLP, Paris, France (1991-1995); Co-Head, Mergers and Acquisitions Group, Shearman & Sterling LLP, New York, NY (1987-1991); Associate, Partner, Shearman & Sterling LLP, New York, NY (1975-1983) **CIV:** Trustee, St. David's School, New York, NY (1981-

1991) **MIL:** 1st Lieutenant, Infantry Platoon Leader, 101st Airbourne Division, U.S. Army (1969-1971) **CW:** Articles Editor, Law Review, Fordham Law School **MEM:** Board of Advisors, World Policy Institute (2004-Present); American Bar Association; New York Bar Association; Association Bar City of New York; International Bar Association; Cercle de l'Union Interalliee **BAR:** New York (1976); U.S. District Court for the Southern District of New York (1976) **MH:** Albert Nelson Marquis Lifetime Achievement Award

MADDEN, JOHN EARL, T: Former Sportscaster; Former Professional Football Coach **I:** Athletics **DOB:** 04/10/1936 **PB:** Austin **SC:** TX/USA **PT:** Earl Madden; Mary O'Flaherty Madden **MS:** Married **SPN:** Virginia (Fields) Madden (12/26/1959) **CH:** Michael; Joseph **ED:** MA, California Polytechnic State University (1961); BS, California Polytechnic State University (1959) **C:** Special Advisor to Commissioner, NFL (2009-Present); Sports Commentator, Football Analyst, "NBC Sunday Night Football" (2006-2009); Sports Commentator, Football Analyst, "Monday Night Football," ABC (2002-2006); Sports Commentator, Football Analyst, Fox Sports (1994-2002); Sports Commentator, Football Analyst, CBS Sports (1979-1993); Head Football Coach, Oakland Raiders, American Football League (Now American Football Conference, NFL) (1969-1979); Linebackers Coach, Oakland Raiders, American Football League (Now American Football Conference, NFL) (1967-1969); Defensive Coordinator, California State University, San Diego, CA (1964-1966); Head Football Coach, Hancock Junior College (Now Allan Hancock College), Santa Maria, CA (1962-1964); Assistant Coach, Hancock Junior College (Now Allan Hancock College), Santa Maria, CA (1960-1962); Professional Football Player, Philadelphia Eagles, NFL (1959) **CR:** Head Coach, Pro Bowl Team, American Football Conference (1971-1975) **CW:** Co-Author, "John Madden's Heroes of Football" (2006); Co-Author, "John Madden's Ultimate Tailgating" (1998); Co-Author, "All Madden: Hey, I'm Talking Pro Football" (1996); Developer, Software, "John Madden Football II" (1993); Author, "One Size Doesn't Fit All" (1993); Developer, Software, "John Madden Football" (1988); Author, "One Knee Equals Two Feet (and Everything Else You Wanted to Know About Football" (1987); Author, "Hey, Wait a Minute (I Wrote a Book!) (1984) **AW:** Inductee, California Hall of Fame (2009); Listee, Top 50 Sportscasters, American Sportscasters Association (2009); Listee, Most Influential People in the World of Sports, Bloomberg BusinessWeek (2007, 2008); Inductee, Pro Football Hall of Fame (2006); Pete Rozelle Radio-TV Award (2002); Sports Personality of the Year, American Sportscasters Association (1985, 1992); Emmy Awards for Sports Broadcasting, Academy of Television Arts & Sciences (1982, 1983, 1985-1988); Winner (As Head Coach), Oakland Raiders, Super Bowl XI (1977); Inductee, NSSA Hall of Fame (1984); NFL Coach of the Year, American Football League (1969); NFL Coach of the Year, Pro Football Weekly (1969)

MADDON, JOE JOHN JR., T: Professional Baseball Manager **I:** Athletics **CN:** Los Angeles Angels **DOB:** 09/19/1954 **PB:** West Hazleton **SC:** PA/USA **MS:** Married **SPN:** Jaye Sousoures (11/08/2008); Betty (Stanton) Maddon (1981, Divorced 1999) **CH:** Sarah; Joey **ED:** Honorary Doctor of Letters, Lafayette College, Easton, PA (2010); Bachelor of Science in Economics, Lafayette College, Easton, PA (1976) **C:** Manager, Los Angeles Angels, MLB (2020-Present); Manager, Chicago Cubs, MLB (2015-2019); Manager, Tampa Bay Devil Rays, MLB (2005-2014); Bench Coach, Los Angeles Angels, MLB (1996, 2000-2005); Interim Manager,

Los Angeles Angels, MLB (1996, 1999); First Base Coach, Los Angeles Angels, MLB (1995); Bullpen Coach, Los Angeles Angels, MLB (1994); Director of Player Development, Los Angeles Angels, MLB (1994); Roving Hitting Instructor, Los Angeles Angels, MLB (1987-1993); Coordinator, Los Angeles Angels, Arizona Instructional League (1984-1993); Manager, Midland Minor League Baseball (1985-1986); Manager, Idaho Falls, Minor League Baseball (1981); Manager, Peoria Minor League Baseball; Manager, Salem Minor League Baseball **CIV:** Founder, Respect 90 Foundation **AW:** Winner, Chicago Cubs, World Series (2016); Named, American League Manager of the Year, Baseball Writers' Association of America (2008, 2011, 2015); Named, Manager of the Year, Sporting News (2008); Winner, Los Angeles Angels, World Series (2002)

MADDUX, GREG ALAN, T: Professional Sports Team Executive; Professional Baseball Player (Retired) **I:** Athletics **DOB:** 04/14/1966 **PB:** San Angelo **SC:** TX/USA **MS:** Married **SPN:** Kathy Maddux **CH:** Amanda Paige; Chase Alan **ED:** Diploma, Valley High School, Las Vegas, NV **C:** Assistant Baseball Coach, Pitching Coach, Rebels, University of Nevada, Las Vegas (2016-Present); Special Assistant to President of Baseball Operations, Los Angeles Dodgers, MLB (2016); Special Assistant to the General Manager, Texas Rangers, MLB (2012); Assistant to the General Manager, Chicago Cubs, MLB (2010-2011); Retired, MLB (2008); Pitcher, Los Angeles Dodgers, MLB (2006, 2008); Pitcher, San Diego Padres, MLB (2007-2008); Pitcher, Chicago Cubs, MLB (1986-1992, 2004-2006); Pitcher, Atlanta Braves, MLB (1993-2003) **CR:** Pitching Coach, USA Team, World Baseball Classic (2013) **CIV:** Co-Founder, Maddux Foundation (1993-Present) **AW:** Inductee, Baseball Hall of Fame (2014); William J. Slocum Award, Baseball Writers' Association of America, New York Chapter (2009); All-Time Rawlings Gold Glove Team (2007); Gold Glove Award (1990-2002, 2004-2008); National League All-Star Team, MLB (1988, 1992, 1994-1998, 2000); One of the 100 Greatest Baseball Players, Sporting News (1999); National League Outstanding Pitcher, Major League Baseball Players Association (1994, 1995, 1998); MLB ERA Leader (1993-1995, 1998); MLB Wins Leader (1992, 1994, 1995); Winner, Atlanta Braves, World Series Champion (1995); National League Pitcher of the Year, Sporting News (1992-1995); Cy Young Award, Baseball Writers' Association of America (1992-1995); Inductee, Braves Hall of Fame

MADERO, BLANCHE VERGOBBI, T: Retired Nurse, Administrator **I:** Medicine & Health Care **PB:** Jerome **SC:** AZ/USA **ED:** MA in Health Systems, University of San Francisco, CA (1987); BS in Nursing Education, Holy Names University, Oakland, CA (1973) **CT:** Licensed Nurse Practitioner **C:** Retired (1999); Assistant Medical Group Administrator, Director, Ambulatory Nursing/Administration, Kaiser-Permanente Medical Center, Oakland, CA (1999); Director, Ambulatory Nursing Services, Assistant Medical Group Administrator, Kaiser-Permanente Medical Center, Oakland, CA (1988-1999); Acting Director, Nurses, Medical Office of Nursing, Kaiser-Permanente Medical Center, Oakland, CA (1987-1988); Assistant Director, Medical Office of Nursing, Kaiser-Permanente Medical Center, Oakland, CA (1982-1987); Supervising Nurse Instructor, Practitioner, Kaiser-Permanente Medical Center, Oakland, CA (1968-1982); Nurse-Preceptor, Kaiser-Permanente Medical Center, Oakland, CA (1968-1981); Float Nurse, Kaiser-Permanente Medical Center, Oakland, CA (1963-1968); Staff Nurse, Head Nurse, Herrick Memorial Hospital, Berkeley, CA (1957-1963) **CR:** Consultant, Veterans Administration Hospital; Nurse Practitioner **CIV:** Pastoral

Council, St. Ambrose Catholic Church; Singer, Local Church Choir **CW:** Hypertension Patient Education, American Nursing Journal; Contributor, Articles, Professional Journals; Guest Lecturer **AW:** Flagship Award, Kaiser-Permanente Medical Center **MEM:** Sigma Theta Tau **MH:** Albert Nelson Marquis Lifetime Achievement Award; Marquis Who's Who Top Professional **AS:** Ms. Madero attributes her success to growth in her career. She started as an RN in the pediatric ward at Herrick Hospital and then moved to Kaiser-Permanente Medical Center. Throughout her career, she has upheld titles such as assistant director of nurses, director of nurses, and assistant administrator to nurses. **B/I:** Ms. Madero always wanted to be a nurse. As a child, while playing with friends, she would insist they play "nurse". Later, she taught an acupressure class to the department of medicine at Kaiser-Permanente Medical Center in Oakland, California. **AV:** Quilting; Cross-stitching; Collecting miniatures; Painting; Drawing **RE:** Catholic

MADIRAJU, DURGA, SENIOR SOFTWARE ENGINEER, T: Senior Software Engineer **I:** Information Technology and Services **CN:** Health Care Industry **PB:** Hyderabad, Andhra Pradesh **SC:** India **PT:** Dr. Chinta Chidananda Rao; Chinta Visalakshi **MS:** Married **SPN:** Srinivas Madiraju **CH:** Anika Anandita Madiraju **ED:** MBA in Accounting and Finance, Eastern Michigan University; Master in Information Systems, Eastern Michigan University; Master in Economics, University of Hyderabad, India; BS in Accounting, Osmania University **CT:** Certified in Executive Leadership, Cornell University; Certified in High Performance Leadership, Cornell University; Certified Scrum Master; Lean Certified; Certified Six Sigma Green Belt; Certified Six Sigma Orange Belt; Certified Six Sigma Yellow Belt **C:** Senior Software Engineer, Healthcare Industry (2017-Present); Senior Software Engineer, AT&T Mobility (1994-2017) **CR:** Worked with Databases Including MS SQL Server (2008-2014); Senior Software Engineer/Project Manager,Extensive Programming Experience Using ASP.NET 2.0, Visual Basic 6, Microsoft Azure, VB.NET, C#, HTML/HTML5.0, CSS 3.0, MVC, AngulasJS, Responsive Web Design, XML, APIs, and Cloud Deployments; Worked with Databases Including MS Access, DB2, IDMS, Oracle 10g Platforms, Windows 2000/NT/XP, OS/390/MVS, DOS, Cloud Software Visual Studio. NET, MS Office Suite; Worked with Project Management Tools Including JIRA, Rally, TDP (Technology Delivery Platform), Data Modeling: Visio, Erwin Model, Camunda Data Modeler, and Quickstack; Repository Administrator, SVN, and CVS **CIV:** St. Jude's Children's Research Hospital **CW:** Contributor, "Seasonal Woods Collection of Poems, Volume One"; Contributor, "Summer Woods Collection of Poems, Volume Two"; Contributor, "Autumn Woods Collection of Poems, Volume Three"; Contributor, "Winter Woods Collection of Poems, Volume Four"; Contributor, "Springtime Woods Collection of Poems, Volume Five"; Contributor, "Mid-Summer Woods Collection of Poems, Volume Six"; Contributor, "Woods a Summer Weave, Collection of Poems, Volume Seven"; Contributor, "Woods an Autumn Weave Gold, Collection of Poems, Volume Eight"; Author, "Scrum Art Handbook"; Contributor, "An Artsy Life, Collection of Short Stories"; Artist, Piano Classic Music Album, "Summer's Way," CD Baby; Artist, "Seasons Summers," CD Baby; Interviewed, Books on Authors; Interviewed, Radio Show; Author, Poetry **AW:** President's Voluntary Service Award (2014-2016): IT Wall of Stars Award; Recipient, IT Rewards; IT Professional Growth Award **MEM:** Mentor, Judge, APCA Scholarship Program; OASIS, Atlanta, GA; WOA, Atlanta, GA; Scrum Alliance **MH:** Albert Nelson Marquis Lifetime

Achievement **AS:** Mrs. Madiraju attributes her success to her father, Dr. Chinta Chidananda Rao, who is the Chief Medical Officer at South Central Railway in India, her mother, Chinta Visalakshi, her spouse, Srinivas Madiraju, and her daughter, Anika Madiraju. **B/I:** Mrs. Madiraju has a background in software engineering/business and information systems. She has an MA in economics, and an MBA and MS in information systems. Her background and qualifications are a fit for the IT industry. She enjoys software, design and programming. She has 15 years experience as a software engineer in the telecom, insurance, and health care industry. She learned new technologies and support and contributes to technological and project management inventions and innovations. She has received the IT Wall of Stars Award, and the IT Technology Award at AT&T. **AV:** Writing poetry classics and piano classics; Cooking; Art (painting and jewelry work) **RE:** Hindu **THT:** Mrs. Madiraju's book, "Autumn Woods," was showcased at the Frankfurt Book Festival in October, 2018. Her book, "Mid-Summer Woods," was showcased at the Miami Book Festival, Nov 14-16, 2019. Her books were reviewed by U.S. Book Review and Pacific Book Review, and received an 8.34/10. Her interview with Fox News was for "Autumn Woods." Her press release was published in all major newspapers and her radio show with Susanna Harris is available on webtalk radio.

MAGILL, MARY, "M." ELIZABETH, T: Executive Vice President, Provost, Professor of Law **I:** Education/Educational Services **CN:** University of Virginia School of Law **PB:** Fargo **SC:** ND/USA **PT:** Frank John Magill; Mary Louise (Timlin) Magill **MS:** Married **SPN:** Leon Francis Szeptycki **CH:** Alexander Magill Szeptycki; Claire Magill Szeptycki **ED:** JD, University of Virginia School of Law, Charlottesville, VA (1995); BA in History, Yale University, New Haven, CT (1988) **C:** Executive Vice President, Provost, David and Mary Harrison Distinguished Professor of Law, University of Virginia School of Law (2019-Present); Richard E. Lang Professor of Law, Dean, Stanford Law School, CA (2012-2019); Elizabeth D. and Richard A. Merrill Professor, University of Virginia School of Law (2011-2012); Vice Dean, University of Virginia School of Law (2009-2012); Joseph Weintraub-Bank of America Distinguished Professor of Law, University of Virginia School of Law (2006-2012); Professor, University of Virginia School of Law (2002-2012); Horace W. Goldsmith Research Professor, University of Virginia School of Law (2007-2010); John V. Ray Research Professor, University of Virginia School of Law (2003-2006); Associate Professor of Law, University of Virginia School of Law (1997-2002); Law Clerk to Honorable Ruth Bader Ginsburg, Supreme Court of the United States, Washington, DC (1996-1997); Law Clerk to Honorable J. Harvie Wilkinson III, United States Court of Appeals for the Fourth Circle (1995-1996); Summer Associate, Covington & Burling LLP, Washington, DC (1994); Senior Legislative Assistant for Energy and Natural Resources to Senator Kent Conrad, United States Senate, Washington, DC (1988-1992) **MEM:** Vice-chair, Judicial Review Subcommittee, ABA; Associate Reporter, Administrative Procedure Act Project, ABA; ABA **BAR:** Maryland (1997)

MAGSIG, JUDITH A, T: Retired Primary School Educator **I:** Education/Educational Services **DOB:** 11/09/1939 **PB:** Saginaw **SC:** MI/USA **PT:** Harold Howard Gay; Catherine Louise (Barstow) Gay **MS:** Married **SPN:** George Arthur Magsig (6/22/1963) **CH:** Amy Catherine; Karl Joseph **ED:** BA, Alma College (1961) **CT:** Certified Teacher, Early Childhood Teacher, Michigan (1961) **C:** Retired, Violin Teacher, Concord Academy Antrim, Mancelona,

MI (2003-2004); Kindergarten Teacher, Gaylord Schools (1968-1999); Special Education Teacher, Gaylord Schools (1965-1967); First Grade Teacher, Gaylord Schools (1961-1964) **CR:** Private Violin Instructor **CIV:** Gaylord Chamber Orchestra (2001-Present); Great Lakes Chamber Orchestra (2001); Cadillac Symphony Orchestra (1999-2000); Instructor, Suzuki Violin Method, Second Violinist Traverse Symphony Orchestra (1985-1992) **MEM:** Chaplain, Warder, Electa, Order Eastern Star (1997-Present); President, Treasurer, Beta Rho, Alpha Delta Kappa (1980-2000); Historian, Gaylord Education Association (1997-1999); National Education Association; Association for Supervision and Curriculum Development; Music Teachers National Association; American String Teachers Association; Suzuki Association American; Association for Childhood Education International; Association for Education of Young Children; Spirits of the North **MH:** Albert Nelson Marquis Lifetime Achievement Award **AS:** Mrs. Magsig attributes her success to her parents and college education. **B/I:** Mrs. Magsig always loved working with children, which motivated her desire to be a teacher. She was also inspired by her mother, a teacher at the local hospital. In regard to her musical endeavors, Mrs. Magsig began playing the violin in fifth grade; her mother was a piano teacher, which was inspiring to watch. Mrs. Magsig continues to teach piano today. **AV:** Cross-stitching; Camping; Canoeing; Sewing; Quilting; **RE:** Methodist

MAGUIRE, JOSEPH, T: Acting Director of National Intelligence; Director of the National Counterterrorism Center **I:** Government Administration/Government Relations/Government Services **DOB:** 08/14/1951 **PB:** Brooklyn **SC:** NY/USA **MS:** Married **CH:** Two Children **ED:** MS in Scientific and Technical Intelligence, Naval Postgraduate School (1985); BS, Manhattan College (1974) **C:** Acting Director of National Intelligence, Washington, DC (2019-Present); Director, National Counterterrorism Center, Washington, DC (2018-Present); Vice President, Booz Allen Hamilton Inc. (2010); Deputy Director, Strategic Operational Planning, National Counterterrorism Center (2007-2010) **CR:** National Security Fellow, Harvard University (1994-1995) **CIV:** President, Chief Executive Officer, Special Operations Warrior Foundation (2013) **MIL:** Vice Admiral, U.S. Navy (2010); Commander, Naval Special Warfare Command, U.S. Navy (2004-2007); Commanding Officer, Naval Special Warfare Center, U.S. Navy (1997-1999); Commanding Officer, SEAL Team Two, U.S. Navy (1993-1994); Naval Special Warfare's Assignment Officer and Community Manager, Bureau of Naval Personnel, Washington, DC (1989-1993); Flag Lieutenant, Commander Amphibious Forces Seventh Fleet, U.S. Navy (1979-1981) **AW:** Navy Distinguished Service Medal; Two Defense Superior Service Medals; Two-Time Recipient, Legion of Merit; Defense Meritorious Service Medal; Two Meritorious Service Medals; Three Navy and Marine Corps Commendation Medals; Navy and Marine Corps Commendation Medal; Navy Achievement Medal; Joint Meritorious Award; Navy Unit Commendation; National Defense Service Medal with Bronze Service Star; Humanitarian Service Medal with Bronze Service Stars; Navy Sea Service Deployment Ribbon with Three Bronze Service Stars; Navy and Marine Corps Overseas Service Ribbon with Three Bronze Service Stars; Navy Rifle Markmanship Badge; Navy Pistol Markmanship Badge; SEAL Trident; Navy and Marine Corps Parachutist Insignia

MAGUIRE, TOBEY VINCENT, T: Actor **I:** Media & Entertainment **DOB:** 06/27/1975 **PB:** Santa Monica **SC:** CA/USA **PT:** Vincent Maguire; Wendy (Brown) Maguire **MS:** Divorced **SPN:** Jennifer

Meyer (09/03/2007, Divorced 2017) **CH:** Ruby Sweetheart; Otis Tobias **ED:** General Educational Diploma (2000) **CW:** Producer, "The Violent Heart" (2020); Producer, "Boyz in the Wood" (2019); Producer, "The Best of Enemies" (2019); Producer, "Brittany Runs a Marathon" (2019); Voice Actor, "The Boss Baby" (2017); Producer, "The 5th Wave" (2016); Producer, "The 5th Wave" (2016); Producer, "Z for Zachariah" (2015); Producer, "Good People" (2014); Actor, "Labor Day" (2014); Actor, "The Spoils of Babylon" (2014); Actor, Producer, "Pawn Sacrifice" (2014); Actor, "The Great Gatsby" (2013); Actor, "Life of Pi (2012); Producer, "Rock of Ages" (2012); Actor, "The Details" (2011); Producer, "Seeking Justice" (2011); Producer, "Country Strong" (2010); Actor, "Brothers" (2009); Participant, World Series of Poker Main Event Championship (2005, 2006, 2007); Actor, "Spider-Man 3" (2007); Actor, "The Good German" (2006); Actor, "Spider-Man 2" (2004); Actor, Executive Producer, "Seabiscuit" (2003); Producer, "Whatever We Do" (2003); Actor, "Spider-Man" (2002); Producer, "25th Hour" (2002); Actor, "Don's Plum" (2001); Voice Actor, "Cats & Dogs" (2001); Actor, "Wonder Boys" (2000); Host, "Saturday Night Live" (2000); Actor, "The Cider House Rules" (1999); Actor, "Ride with the Devil" (1999); Actor, "Fear and Loathing in Las Vegas" (1998); Actor, "Pleasantville" (1998); Actor, "Deconstructing Harry" (1997); Actor, "The Ice Storm" (1997); Actor, "Joy Ride" (1996); Actor, "Seduced by Madness: The Diane Borchardt Story" (1996); Actor, "Tracey Takes On" (1996); Actor, "Revenge of the Red Baron" (1994); Actor, "SFW" (1994); Actor, "Healer" (1994); Actor, "Spoils of War" (1994); Actor, "A Child's Cry for Help" (1994); Actor, "Walker, Texas Ranger" (1994); Actor, "This Boy's Life" (1993); Actor, "Wild & Crazy Kids" (1992); Actor, "Great Scott!" (1992); Actor, "Blossom" (1991); Actor, "Roseanne" (1991); Actor, "Eerie, Indiana" (1991); Actor, "Tales from the Whoop: Hot Rod Brown Class Clown" (1990); Actor, "The Wizard" (1989); Actor, Producer, Television Shows, Films **AW:** Award for Best Actor, International Competition, CinEuphoria Awards (2011); Saturn Award for Best Actor (2005); Award for Choice Movie: Liplock, Teen Choice Awards (2002); Award for Choice Movie Actor: Drama/Action-Adventure, Teen Choice Awards (2002); Award for Best Supporting Performance – Male, Toronto Film Critics Association Awards (2000); Saturn Award for Best Younger Actor (1999) **AV:** Poker

MAHER, BILL, T: Political Commentator; Television Personality: Comedian **I:** Media & Entertainment **DOB:** 01/20/1956 **PB:** New York **SC:** NY/USA **PT:** William Aloysius Maher Jr.; Julie (Berman) Maher **ED:** BA in English and History, Cornell University, New York, NY (1978) **C:** Minority Owner, New York Mets, MLB (2012-Present); Host, "Real Time with Bill Maher," HBO (2003-Present); Creator, Host, "Politically Incorrect," ABC (1996-2002); Creator, Host, "Politically Incorrect," Comedy Central, New York, NY (1993-1996); Host, "Catch a Rising Star," Comedy Club, New York, NY (1979) **CIV:** Board of Directors, PETA; Advisory Board Member, The Reason Project **CW:** Performer, Stand-up, "Live from Oklahoma," HBO (2018); Performer, Stand-up, "Live from DC," HBO (2014); Author, "The New New Rules: A Funny Look at How Everybody But Me Has Their Head Up Their Ass" (2011); Performer, Stand-up, "... But I'm Not Wrong," HBO (2010); Actor, "Swing Vote" (2008); Appearance, Producer, "Religulous" (2008); Performer, Stand-up, "The Decider," HBO (2007); Author, "New Rules: Polite Musings from a Timid Observer" (2005); Performer, Stand-up, "I'm Swiss," HBO (2005); Actor, "The Aristocrats" (2005); Author, "Keep the Statue of Liberty Closed:

The New Rules" (2004); Author, "When You Ride Alone You Ride With Bin Laden: What the Government Should Be Telling Us to Help Fight the War on Terrorism" (2003); Performer, Stand-up, "Victory Begins at Home," HBO (2003); Actor, "Tomcats" (2001); Performer, Stand-up, "Be More Cynical," HBO (2000); Actor, "EDtv" (1998); Author, "Does Anybody Have a Problem with That? The Best of Politically Incorrect" (1997); Actor, "Bimbo Movie Bash" (1997); Performer, Stand-up, "The Golden Goose Special," HBO (1997); Actor, "Don't Quit Your Day Job" (1996); Author, "Does Anybody Have a Problem with That? Politically Incorrect's Greatest Hits" (1996); Appearance, "The Weinerville Election Special: From Washington British Columbia" (1996); Performer, Stand-up, "Stuff that Struck Me Funny," HBO (1995); Author, "True Story: A Novel" (1994); Actor, "Married with Children" (1993); Actor, "Roseanne" (1993); Actor, "DC Cab" (1993); Actor, "The Jackie Thomas Show" (1993); Performer, Stand-up, "One Night Stand," HBO (1989, 1992); Actor, "Say What?" (1992); Actor, "Charlie Hoover" (1991); Actor, "Pizza Man" (1991); Actor, "The Midnight Hour" (1990); Actor, "Murder, She Wrote" (1989-1990); Actor, "Cannibal Women in the Avocado Jungle of Death" (1989); Actor, "Newhart" (1988); Actor, "Out of Time" (1988); Actor, "Max Headroom" (1987); Actor, "Rags to Riches" (1987); Actor, "Hard Knocks" (1987); Actor, "House II: The Second Story" (1987); Actor, "Ratboy" (1986); Actor, "Club Med" (1986); Actor, "Alice" (1985); Actor, "Sara" (1985); Performer, Stand-up, "The Bob Monkhouse Show," "Late Night with David Letterman," "The Tonight Show" **AW:** Award for Best Social - Content - Entertainment, Davey Awards (2017); Award for Best Comedy/Variety - Talk Series, Writers Guild of America (2016); Emmy Award for Outstanding Informational Series or Special Vice, Academy of Television Arts & Sciences (2014); Listee, 50 Highest-Earning Political Figures, Newsweek (2010); Star, Hollywood Foreign Press Association (2010); Johnny Carson Producer of the Year Award, Producers Guild of America (2007); President's Award for Championing Free Speech, LA Times Press Club (2002); CableAce Awards for Best Talk Show Series, National Academy of Cable Programming (1995, 1996); CableACE Award for Best Talk Show Host, National Academy of Cable Programming (1995); Listee, Comedy Central's 100 Greatest Stand-Ups of All Time **PA:** Democrat

MAHMUD, SHIREEN D., T: Photographer/Photojournalist **I:** Media & Entertainment **DOB:** 10/04/1949 **PB:** Chittagong **SC:** Bangladesh **PT:** Mohammed Mazhurul Qudus; Mumtaz Mahal Begum **MS:** Divorced **SPN:** Abdul Wazed Mahmud (04/10/1966, Divorced 1996) **CH:** Sharmin; Shahnaz **ED:** BA in Mass Communications, University of Hartford, Magna Cum Laude (1982) **CT:** Federal Communications Commission (FCC) License **C:** Freelance Photographer, Middletown, CT (1985-Present); Typist, Aetna Insurance Co., Middletown, CT (1983); Part-time Medical Secretary, Middletown, CT (1979-1982) **CR:** Member, Bridgeport Regional Business Council (BRBC) (1997); Realtor, Buyer's Capital **CIV:** Literacy Volunteer, Russell Library, Middletown, CT; CPTV Volunteer, Hartford, CT; Volunteer, Middlesex Memorial Hospital **CW:** Producer/Host, Feature Program, Storer Cable Communications, Clinton, CT (1985-1995); Photography Exhibitions, Various Galleries, Libraries, CT **AW:** Award, International Society of Poets Hall of Fame (1997); Recipient, Many Awards, Local Photography Contest **MEM:** American Association of University Women (AAUW); National League of American Pen Women (NLAPW); International Society of Poets; Connecticut Society Poets; Connecticut Songwriters Association; The International Platform Association **MH:** Albert Nelson Marquis Lifetime Achievement Award **AS:** Mrs. Mahmud was passionate about photography, art and traveling. She always wants to capture the moment of her being there and express it to the world. Also, she credits her background of being the granddaughter of a famous poet, Mozammel Haque, and her mother. Her mother was very artistic and a creative person; being around her, Mrs. Mahmud was inspired. She is an outgoing person and loves people. The loving energy that she receives from being around people of the world, she thinks, is the key to her success. **B/I:** Mrs. Mahmud became involved in her photography profession because she loved the world, nature and people around her. She wanted to document everything she saw and put it into her own perspective. She just loved photography. **AV:** Photography; Reading; Traveling; Poetry **THT:** Mrs. Mahmud says, "There is no creative future without the creative people. The world enjoys and appreciates the contribution of creative people."

MAHOMES, PATRICK LAVON II, T: Professional Football Player **I:** Athletics **CN:** Kansas City Chiefs **DOB:** 09/17/1995 **PB:** Tyler **SC:** TX/USA **PT:** Patrick Mahomes; Randi Mahomes **ED:** Coursework, Texas Tech University (2016) **C:** Quarterback, Kansas City Chiefs (2017-Present) **AW:** NFL Most Valuable Player (2018); NFL Offensive Player of the Year (2018); Sammy Baugh Trophy (2016); Male Athlete of the Year, MaxPreps (2016)

MAIN, AMANDA M., PHD, T: Associate Professor of Management and Academic Program Coordinator for Social Entrepreneurship, Social Innovation and Business Administration **I:** Education/Educational Services **CN:** Lynn University **PT:** Maria V. Hammack; David R. Wolcott **MS:** Married **SPN:** Eric B. Main **ED:** PhD in Industrial and Organizational Psychology, University of Central Florida (2017); MS in Industrial and Organizational Psychology, University of Central Florida (2014); BS in Psychology, University of North Georgia (2011); AA in General Transfer, Palm Beach State College (2008) **CT:** Certified Professional Coach; Apple Teacher Certification **C:** Associate Professor of Management, Lynn University; Academic Program Coordinator of Social Entrepreneurship, Social Innovation, and Business Administration, Lynn University; Lecturer of Management, University of Central Florida; Lecturer of Psychology, Florida Institute of Technology; Lecturer of Psychology, University of Central Florida; Instructional Specialist, University of Central Florida; Organization Consultant, Gallaher Edge **CW:** Co-Author, "A Quantitative Analysis of the Relationship Between Work-Life Balance and Individual and Organizational Outcomes" (2020); Author, "Utilizing Team-Based Learning in Any Classroom for Student Engagement" (2020); Author, "Let's Get Creative! Infusing Imagination and Innovation Into Your Curriculum" (2020); Co-Author, "Do You Only Have Yourself to Blame? A Meta-Analytic Test of the Victim Precipitation Model" (2019); Co-Author, "Perceptions of Service-Learning in the Sunshine State (2019); Co-Author, "The Nonprofit Sector: Charity and Chicanery" (2019); Author, "Strategic Planning for Wellbeing and Engagement" (2019); Co-Author, "Is it the Person or the Place? A Meta-Analytic Test of the Antecedents of Workplace Incivility" (2019); Co-Author, "A Faculty Development Program/SOTL Project to Improve Students Approaches to Learning" (2019); Co-Author, "Integrating Contemplative and Well-being Practices for Student Success" (2019); Author, "Improving Perceived Organizational Support for Full-Time, Non-Tenure-Track Faculty" (2019); Co-Author, "Is it the Person or is it the Place? A Meta-Analytic Test of the Antecedents of Experienced Workplace Incivility" (2019); Interviewee, "Workplace Hacks," Boca Raton Observer (2019); Author, "Strategic Planning for Wellbeing and Engagement" (2019); Author, "Glass Slippers to Glass Ceilings: The Realities of Being Female in the Modern Workplace" (2019); Author, "Banter, Business & Beers: Becoming a Networking Pro" (2019); Author, "Instructor's Resource Manual for Organizational Behavior Second Edition," John Wiley & Sons (2019); Author, "Student Development Through Contemplative Pedagogy: Mindfulness Based Stress Reduction" (2018); Author, "Females in STEM Field: Is Equality Part of the Problem? A Conversation" (2018); Author, "The Role of Emotional Intelligence in Workplace Humor" (2018); Co-Author, "Secrecy and Transparency in Nonprofit Organizations: If a Nonprofit Prefers Secrecy, What Does it Want to Hide?" (2018); Co-Author, "A Meta-Analysis of the Antecedents and Outcomes of Workplace Incivility" (2018); Co-Author, "Asset Mapping for Women in Leadership" (2018); Co-Author, "Innovative Techniques to Improve Student Learning Approaches" (2018); Co-Author, "Facilitating Faculty Development to Promote Self-Directed Learning" (2018); Co-Author, "Leader-Member Exchange and Higher Education Leadership: A Relationship-Building Tool for Department Chairs" (2017); Author, "An I/Opening Perspective on Faculty Development" (2017); Author, "Not Woman Enough Harassment: An Integrated Model" (2017); Author, "Fixed Mindset vs. Growth Mindset: What is it and Can You Change It?" (2017); Author, "The Relationship of Safety Climate and Behaviors with Organizational Commitment" (2017); Co-Author, Measurement Equivalence of the Organizational Tolerance for Sexual Harassment Inventory" (2017); Co-Author, "Modifying the Teaching Squares Model for a Collaborative Workshop" (2017); Interviewee, "The Psychology of Political Ideology" (2017); Author, "Supporting the Three Pillars of Academic Achievement in a Diverse Classroom" (2017); Author, "Flipping for Teams: How to Apply Team-Based Learning to Your Course Regardless of Size" (2017); Interviewee, "Meet Professor Amanda Wolcott," HerCampus (2016); Co-Author, "Transparency in Nonprofit Organizations: Public Access to Minutes of Board Meetings" (2015); Co-Author, "Increasing Task Elaboration During Team Debriefs using Team Dimensional Training" (2015); Co-Author, "Measurement Equivalence in Ethnic Harassment Across Minority and Majority Groups" (2015); Co-Author, "A Comprehensive Meta-Analysis of Workplace Mistreatment" (2015); Co-Author, "Just Kidding: The Role of Emotional Intelligence and Sense of Humor in the Interpretation of Ambiguous Humor in the Workplace" (2015); Author, "Newcomer Helping Behaviors in an NBA Context" (2015) **AW:** Academic and Creative Excellence Award, Lynn University (2019, 2020); Best Paper, Academy of Management (2019); Best Paper Award, Academy of Business Research Conference (2018); Distinguished Young Alumnus, University of North Georgia (2018) **MEM:** Omicron Delta Kappa; Pi Gamma Mu Honor Society; Psi Chi International Honor Society in Psychology; Phi Sigma Pi National Honor Fraternity; Golden Key International Honour Society; Delta Epsilon Iota Academic Honor Society **AS:** Dr. Main attributes her success to her perseverance and having a passion for what she does. She believes, "it's not always knowing the right answers, but having the willingness to go out and find the right answers. I wake up excited to go into work, to see what I can learn and how I can help people." **B/I:** Dr. Main became involved in her profession by first pursuing clinical psychology. Just before graduate school applications were due, she learned about industrial and organizational psychology, which really spoke to her. As part of her graduate work, she was required to do research or teach for the university. She had hoped for a research position but was assigned a 7 AM statistics course instead. She walked into the classroom afraid that she was in way over her head, but 15 minutes into the class, a student asked her a math question that she had struggled with growing up. Being able to help that student from her own experience made her realize she was in the right place and there would be no going back. She had found her calling in classroom teaching. **THT:** Dr. Main's teaching philosophy resembles her coaching philosophy: she believes that everyone has unlimited potential waiting to be unlocked, and she can help unlock it. Her mission is to inspire others to see their potential and, through teaching, guided reflection, and reinforcing the power of choice, to facilitate their development into the best possible versions of themselves.

MAITLAND, GARY, T: Partner **I:** Law and Legal Services **CN:** Kreisberg & Maitland, LLP **ED:** JD, Boston University (1978); BA, Vassar College (1977) **C:** Partner, Kreisberg & Maitland, LLP (1987-Present); Assistant District Attorney, Brooklyn, NY (1978-1987) **CIV:** Manager, RA Training, Vassar College (1974); Tutor, Local High School; Assistant Scout Leader, Cub Scouts of America; Volunteered, Clinical Instructor, ICAP **AW:** Super-Lawyer (2013-Present) **MEM:** National Association of Defense Lawyers; New York State Analog **BAR:** New York (1978); U.S. Supreme Court; U.S. Court of Appeals for the 2nd Circuit; U.S. District Court for the Eastern District of New York; U.S. District Court for the Southern District of New York; U.S. Tax Court **AS:** Mr. Maitland attributes his success to his passion and dedication to his work. **B/I:** Mr. Maitland was inspired by his family members, many of whom were law professionals, to pursue a career in law. He wanted to continue the family legacy in the field. **THT:** Mr. Maitland's motto is, "The truth will prevail."

MAKRIDES, LYDIA, MCSP, BPT, MSC, PHD, T: President, Blogger; Global Wellness Head **I:** Health, Wellness and Fitness **CN:** Evexia Inc.; Toyaja Inc **SC:** Cyprus **PT:** Dr. Diomedes Isaia; Evangelia Isaia **MS:** Single **SPN:** Andreas Makrides **CH:** Carl Makrides **ED:** PhD in Cardiovascular Physiology, McMaster University, Hamilton, Ontario, Canada; MSc in Kinanthropology, University of Ottawa, Ontario, Canada; BSc in Physiotherapy, University of Saskatchewan, Saskatoon, SK, Canada; MCSP, School of Physiotherapy, London, United Kingdom **CT:** Canadian Physiotherapy Association (1975-2018); ACSM Program Director, CSEP (1988-1996); Chartered Society of Physiotherapists, United Kingdom **C:** President, Chief Executive Officer, Evexia Inc., Global Wellness Head, Toyaja Inc. (2018-Present); Consultant, Educator, Researcher; Founder, President, Creative Wellness Solutions Incorporated (CWS) (2005-2018); Adjunct Professor (2006-2016); Professor, Director, School of Physiotherapy, Dalhousie University (1994-2005); Lecturer, Assistant Professor, Associate Professor, Professor, Dalhousie University (1975-2005); Director, Dalhousie University, International Services (Now International Centre) (2001); Founder, Director, Dalhousie Cardiac Rehab Program (1981-1996); Board of Trustees, Husson College (Now Husson University), Bangor, Maine **CW:** Global Health and Wellness Portal, Evexia Website (2012-Present); Atlantic Health and Wellness Institute, Atlantic Health Care (1997-2005); Cardiac Prevention Research Center (1993-1996); Elderfit Videos, Accompanying Booklets, Broadcasted Nationally through Television, Ontario, Canada (1990-1992) **AW:** Special Award, N.S. Division, Canadian Physiotherapy Association

(1997); Honorary Member, Canadian Physiotherapy Association (1993); Progress Women of Distinction Award in the Health and Education Area (1990); First Prize Research Award, Exercise Physiology, International Sports Medicine Symposium, Master Athlete (1985); Silver Quill Award (1981) **MEM:** Fitness Center **AS:** Dr. Makrides attributes her success to her steadfast belief in what she does. **B/I:** Dr. Makrides is particularly interested in health and science; she believes people can become self-leaders and take charge of their own health if they are supported by their governments, employers and health care systems. Much of the chronic diseases that affect people globally can be prevented and better managed with a healthier lifestyle and appropriate community resources. She sees the emphasis on treatment with much less emphasis on prevention and helping people stay well, a major flaw that drives the rising costs and incidence of preventable chronic diseases. **AV:** Hiking; Yoga; Fitness; Kayaking; Swimming; Blogging on corporate wellness issues **THT:** Dr. Makrides' father, a prominent Cypriot physician, taught her the importance of education and hard work. Her mother taught her the importance of being independent, in both thought and life. And there was one special university mentor who showed her the importance of physical activity in health and disease.

MALAIHOLLO, NATASIA, T: Head of Business Development; Co-founder, Former Chief Executive Officer **I:** Technology **CN:** PopCom; Wyzerr, Inc. **ED:** BA in Legal Studies, University of California Berkeley (2008) **C:** Head of Business Development, PopCom (2020-Present); Co-founder, Chief Executive Officer, Wyzerr, Inc. (2014-2020); Events Associate, Vator (2014-2015); Chief Executive Officer, Sooligan (2011-2014); Patent Specialist, Sughrue Mion PLLC (2011-2012); Intellectual Property Specialist, The Patel Law Firm (2008-2011); Law Clerk, National Center for Youth Law (2007-2008); Tutor, Making Waves Education Program (2006-2007) **CIV:** Board Member, Cincinnati Reds, MLB (2017-Present); With, Hilary Clinton for President (2007-2008) **CW:** Editor, Writer, Researcher, KOBA Institute (2011-2012)

MALASPINA, ALEX, PHD, T: Soft Drink Company Executive **I:** Food & Restaurant Services **DOB:** 01/04/1931 **PB:** Athens **SC:** Greece **PT:** Spiros Malaspina; Mary (Souyiouljoglou) Malaspina **MS:** Married **SPN:** Doris Woodruff Gould (09/25/1954) **CH:** Spiros (Deceased 2014); Ann; Paul; Mark **ED:** Honorary Degree, Universidad Del Salvador, Buenos Aires, Argentina (1996); PhD, Massachusetts Institute of Technology, Cambridge, MA (1955); B, Massachusetts Institute of Technology, Cambridge, MA (1952) **C:** Vice President, British Industrial Biological Research Association, London, England (1991-Present); Vice President, Toxicology Forum, Washington, DC (1979-Present); President, International Technical Caramel Association, Washington, DC (1977-Present); President, International Life Sciences Institute, Washington, DC (1978-2001); Senior Vice President, The Coca-Cola Company, Atlanta, GA (1986-1998); Vice President, The Coca-Cola Company, Atlanta, GA (1978-1986); Vice President, The Coca-Cola Export Corporation, New York, NY (1969-1978); Manager, Quality Control, The Coca-Cola Export Corporation, New York, NY (1961-1969); Coordinator for New Products, Pfizer Inc., New York, NY (1955-1961) **CIV:** Board, Overseers, School of Medicine, Tufts University (1995-Present) **AW:** Medal for the People's Health, Minister of Health in Vietnam (2006); Foreign Correspondent Award, Royal Academy of Medicine, Cadiz, Spain (1998); International Award, Institute of Food Technologists (1994); Toxicology Award,

International Society of Regulatory Toxicology and Pharmacology (1992) **MEM:** American Association for the Advancement of Science; New York Academy of Sciences; American Institute of Chemists; Institute of Food Technologists; American Chemical Society; Board of Trustees, Forsythe Institute, Cambridge, MA; Board of Directors, Forsythe Institute, Cambridge, MA **MH:** Albert Nelson Marquis Lifetime Achievement Award; Marquis Who's Who Top Professional; Marquis Who's Who Humanitarian Award **B/I:** Dr. Malaspina became involved in his profession after he came to the United States in 1948. He grew up in Greece during World War II; his aunt Nellys was a famous Greek photographer, and she was working in America and could not get back to Greece because of the war. She asked Dr. Malaspina to come to the United States, which he eventually did in 1948. He thought he would go back to Greece to help the economy there, but he wound up getting a job with Pfizer, Inc., got married, and decided not to go back. His mission has been to help people in the world, one he inherited from his father, a member of Parliament in Greece, and has passed down to his children. **RE:** Greek Orthodox

MALEK, MARLENE, T: Foundation Administrator **I:** Nonprofit & Philanthropy **CN:** Friends of Cancer Research **PT:** William McArthur; Yolanda (Stella) McArthur **MS:** Married **SPN:** Frederic Malek **CH:** Frederic William; Michelle A. Olson **ED:** Degree in Nursing, Marymount University **C:** President, Friends Cancer Research, Washington, DC (2000) **CR:** Vice Chairman, Board of Directors, Marymount University, Arlington, VA; Vice Chairman, Board of Directors, International Committee, J.F. Kennedy Center Performing Arts; Board of Directors, Fords Theatre; Board of Directors, National Museum of Women in Arts; Board of Directors, Vital Voices Global Partnership, MD Anderson Cancer Center, Houston, TX; Board of Overseers, Duke University Cancer Center; Member, National Dialogue Cancer; Board of Directors, Virginia Museum of Fine Arts **MH:** Albert Nelson Marquis Lifetime Achievement Award **AV:** Cross country skiing; Bicycling; Hiking

MALININ, THEODORE, T: Professor Emeritus of Orthopaedics **I:** Education/Educational Services **DOB:** 09/13/1933 **PB:** Krasnodar **SC:** Russia **PT:** Ivan M. Malinin; Olga A. (Senitzkaya) Malinin **MS:** Married **SPN:** Dorothy A. Rearick **CH:** Ellen M.; Alexander T.; Catherine T. Malinin-Dunn; Michael T. Malininn **ED:** Honorary DSc, The University of Scranton (1990); MD, The University of Virginia (1960); MS, The University of Virginia (1958); BS, Concord College (Now Concord University) (1955) **C:** Professor Emeritus, University of Miami (Present); Professor of Orthopedics, University of Miami (1979-Retirement); Professor of Surgery, University of Miami, FL (1970-1979); Associate Professor, Georgetown University, Washington, DC (1968-1970); Assistant Professor, Georgetown University, Washington, DC (1964-1968) **CIV:** Active, National Representative Committee, Washington, DC (1964-Present); Vice President, Mannheimer Foundation, Inc. **MIL:** Medical Director, U.S. Public Health Service (1964-2015); Surgeon, U.S. Public Health Service (Reserve) (1962-1964) **CW:** Author, "Cancer Merchants: (2008); Author, "Surgery and Life" (1978); Editor, Three Books; Contributor, Over 200 Articles to Professional Journals **AW:** Named Distinguished Rotarian, Rotary International (1994); Recipient, Orden, University of Javeriana (Now Pontificia Universidad Javeriana) (1992); Order of Merit, Republic of Colombia (1992); George Hyde Award, American Association of Tissue Banks (AATB) **MEM:** American Medical Association; American Academy of Orthopaedic

Surgeons; Orthopaedic Research Society; Southern Medical Association; American Association for Cancer Research (AACR); American Association of Tissue Banks (AATB); Cell Transplantation Society (The Transplantation Society); American Society for Investigative Pathology (ASIP); The Royal Society of Medicine; Rotary International **MH:** Albert Nelson Marquis Lifetime Achievement Award **B/I:** Dr. Malinin was inspired by studying biology in college; also, his father was a doctor. Dr. Malinin was working at the National Cancer Institute in the biology division and there were a lot of people there who were originally working on polio, and that translated into ecology. He was fortunate enough in his life to become associated with Dr. Frank Gollan, who was a great scientist and the first to isolate the poliovirus.

MALINOWSKI, TOMASZ, "TOM" P., T: U.S. Representative from New Jersey **I:** Government Administration/Government Relations/Government Services **DOB:** 09/23/1965 **PB:** Slupsk **SC:** Poland **PT:** Blair Clark (Stepfather); Joanna Malinowski **ED:** MPhil in Political Science, St. Antony's College, University of Oxford (1991); BA in Political Science, University of California Berkeley (1987) **C:** Member, U.S. House of Representatives from New Jersey's Seventh Congressional District (2019-Present); Assistant Secretary of States, Democracy, Human Rights and Labor, U.S. Department of State, Washington, DC (2014-2017); Washington Director, Human Rights Watch (2001-2013); Senior Director for Foreign Policy, National Security Council (1998-2001); Member, Policy Planning Staff, Speechwriter, U.S. Department of State (1994-1998); Research Assistant, Ford Foundation (1992-1993); Special Assistant to Senator Daniel Patrick Moynihan, U.S. Senate **AW:** Rhodes Scholar, University of Oxford **PA:** Democrat

MALKOVICH, JOHN GAVIN, T: Actor **I:** Media & Entertainment **DOB:** 12/09/1953 **PB:** Christopher **SC:** IL/USA **PT:** Daniel Leon Malkovich; Joe Anne (Choisser) Malkovich **MS:** Life Partner **SPN:** Nicoletta Peyran (1989); Glenne Headly (1982, Divorced 1988) **CH:** Amandine; Loewy **ED:** Coursework, Illinois State University; Coursework, Eastern Illinois University; Coursework, William Esper Studio **CR:** Founder, Mrs. Mudd (2002-Present); Launched, Technobohemian (2010); Launched, Menswear, Uncle Kimono (2003); Co-founder, Steppenwolf Theatre, Chicago, IL (1976) **CW:** Actor, "Space Force" (2020-Present); Actor, "Arkansas" (2020); Actor, "The New Pope" (2020); Narrator, "Matchday: Inside FC Barcelona" (2019); Actor, "Valley of the Gods" (2018); Actor, "The Wilde Wedding" (2017); Actor, "I Love You, Daddy" (2017); Actor, "About Love. Only for Adults" (2017); Actor, "Bullet Heads" (2017); Actor, "Zoolander 2" (2016); Actor, "Dominion" (2016); Actor, "Deepwater Horizon" (2016); Actor, "Psychogenic Fugue" (2016); Actor, "Unlocked" (2016); Actor, "Chavez" (2014); Actor, Executive Producer, "Cesar Chavez" (2014); Actor, "Cut Bank" (2014); Actor, "The Casanova Variations" (2014); Voice Actor, "Penguins of Madagascar" (2014); Actor, "Crossbones" (2014); Actor, "Warm Bodies" (2013); Actor, "Educazione Siberiana" (2013); Actor, "Red 2" (2013); Actor, "The Perks of Being a Wallflower" (2012); Actor, "Lines of Wellington" (2012); Actor, "Drunkboat" (2011); Actor, "The Infernal Comedy: Confessions of a Serial Killer" (2011); Actor, "Transformers: Dark of the Moon" (2011); Executive Producer, "Young Adult" (2011); Executive Producer, "Abel" (2010); Actor, "Jonah Hex" (2010); Actor, "Secretariat" (2010); Actor, "Red" (2010); Actor, "Burn After Reading" (2008); Actor, "Changeling" (2008); Actor, "Juno" (2007); Actor, "Drunkboat" (2007); Actor, "Gardens of the Night" (2007); Actor, "In

Tranzit" (2007); Voice Actor, "Beowulf" (2007); Actor, "Klimt" (2006); Actor, "The Call" (2006); Actor, "Eragon" (2006); Actor, "Kill the Poor" (2006); Actor, "Art School Confidential" (2006); Actor, "The Hitchhiker's Guide to the Galaxy" (2005); Actor, "Colour Me Kubrick" (2005); Actor, "The Libertine" (2004); Actor, "Johnny English" (2003); Actor, "A Talking Picture" (2003); Actor, "Johnny English" (2003); Actor, "Ripley's Game" (2002); Actor, "The Dancer Upstairs" (2002); Actor, Director, Co-producer, "The Dancer Upstairs" (2002); Actor, "Ripley's Game" (2002); Actor, "Napoleon" (2002); Producer, "The Loner" (2001); Producer, "Found in the Street" (2001); Actor, "Les Ames Forte" (2001); Actor, "Knockaround Guys" (2001); Actor, "Je Rentre a la Maison" (2001); Actor, "Hotel" (2001); Executive Producer, "Somewhere Else" (2000); Producer, "Ghost World" (2000); Actor, "Les Miserables" (2000); Actor, "Shadow of the Vampire" (2000); Actor, "Le Temps Retrouvé" (1999); Actor, "The Libertine" (1999); Actor, "Ladies Room" (1999); Actor, "Joan of Arc" (1999); Actor, "Being John Malkovich" (1999); Actor, "RKO 281" (1999); Actor, "The Man in the Iron Mask" (1998); Actor, "Rounders" (1998); Actor, "Primary Colors" (1997); Actor, "Con Air" (1997); Actor, "Mulholland Falls" (1996); Actor, "Der Unhold" (1996); Actor, "The Portrait of a Lady" (1996); Actor, "Touchstone" (1994); Actor, "Para De La Nuages" (1994); Actor, "Heart of Darkness" (1994); Actor, "Mary Reilly" (1994); Actor, "Libra" (1994); Actor, "Steppenwolf" (1994); Actor, "In the Line of Fire" (1993); Actor, "States of Shock" (1993); Actor, "Alive" (1993); Actor, "Shadows and Fog" (1992); Actor, "Jennifer 8" (1992); Actor, "Of Mice and Men" (1992); Actor, "Queen's Logic" (1991); Actor, "The Object of Beauty" (1991); Actor, "Old Times" (1991); Actor, "The Sheltering Sky" (1990); Actor, "Miles from Home" (1988); Actor, "Dangerous Liaisons" (1988); Executive Producer, "The Accidental Tourist" (1988); Actor, "Making Mr. Right" (1987); Actor, "Glass Menagerie" (1987); Actor, "Empire of the Sun" (1987); Actor, "Santabear's High Flying Adventure" (1987); Actor, "Burn This" (1987); Actor, "Rocket to the Moon" (1986); Actor, "The Caretaker" (1986); Actor, "Death of a Salesman" (1985); Actor, "Eleni" (1985); Actor, "Arms and the Man" (1985); Actor, "Coyote Ugly," Chicago, IL and John F. Kennedy Center for the Performing Arts, Washington, DC (1985); Director, "Balm in Gilead" (1984-1985); Actor, "Places in the Heart" (1984); Actor, "The Killing Fields" (1984); Actor, "Death of a Salesman" (1984); Actor, Theatrical Debut, "True West," NY (1982); Actor, "Word of Honor" (1981); Actor, "American Dream" (1981); Actor, Voice Actor, Producer, Appearances, Television Shows, Video Games, Films **AW:** Order of Merit, Ukraine (2018); Globe de Cristal Award for Best Play (2008); St. Louis Gateway Film Critics Association Award for Best Actor (2008); American Comedy Award (2000); New York Film Critics Circle Award for Best Supporting Actor (1999); Emmy Award for Outstanding Supporting Actor in a Miniseries or a Special, Academy of Television Arts & Sciences (1986); Obie Award (1982); Clarence Derwent Award (1982); Numerous Awards

MALONE, JOHN D., MD, MPH, T: Infectious Diseases Physician Scientist **I:** Sciences **DOB:** 06/21/1953 **PB:** Cleveland **SC:** OH/USA **MS:** Married **SPN:** Eleanor Jones Smith, PharmD (1991) **ED:** MPH, Uniformed Services University (2005); MD, The Ohio State University Medical School (1978); BA, Ohio Northern University (1975) **CT:** American Board of Internal Medicine in Infectious Diseases and Internal Medicine **C:** Professor of Medicine, Uniformed Services University (2009Present); Head, Clinical Investigations Department, Naval Medical Center San Diego/Research Program

Manager Navy Medicine West Region (2011-2018); Infectious Diseases Staff Physician, Naval Medical Center San Diego (2010-2018); Center for Disaster and Humanitarian Assistance Medicine, Uniformed Services University (2008-2010); Center for Biological Monitoring and Modelling, Pacific Northwest National Laboratory (2006-2008) **MIL:** Retired Captain (O6), Medical Corps, U.S. Navy (2004); Commanding Officer, Medical Treatment Facility, USNS MERCY Hospital Ship (2001-2004); Medical Corps Officer, U.S. Navy (1974-2004); Director, Medical Services, Internal Medicine Department, Naval Medical Center San Diego (2000-2003); Chairman, Naval Medical Center San Diego (1998-2000); Head, Infectious Diseases Division, National Naval Medical Center (1994-1998); Head of HIV Unit, National Naval Medical Center, Bethesda, MD, (1989-1994) **CW:** Lecturer, 90 Lectures Covering Topics in Infectious Disease, Including Work with the Center for Disaster and Humanitarian Assistance Medicine in Africa on influenza; Author, 55 Publications **AW:** Legion of Merit, U.S. Navy; Defense Meritorious Service Medal, U.S. Navy; Three Meritorious Service Medals, U.S. Navy; Navy Commendation Medal, U.S. Navy; Joint Service Achievement Medal, U.S. Navy; Navy Achievement Medal, U.S. Navy; Humanitarian Service Medal, U.S. Navy; Sea Service Ribbon, U.S. Navy; Navy and Marine Corps Commendation Medal **MEM:** Fellow, Infectious Diseases Society of America; Fellow, American College of Physicians; Fellow, American College of Physicians Executives (Now American Association for Physician Leadership) **MH:** Albert Nelson Marquis Lifetime Achievement Award **B/I:** Dr. Malone became involved in his profession because he was from Garfield Heights, a working class neighborhood outside of Cleveland, Ohio. His father was a third-class hospital corpsman in the U.S. Navy. He was a great student and enjoyed sciences. At 16, he began working for Cleveland Barrel & Drum and was able to make enough money in the summer to pay his way through Ohio Northern University. **AV:** Going to the gym; Exercising, Yard work; Reading; Great Courses educational videos

MALONE, KARL ANTHONY, T: Professional Basketball Coach; Former Professional Basketball Player **I:** Athletics **CN:** Utah Jazz **DOB:** 07/24/1963 **PB:** Summerfield **SC:** LA/USA **PT:** Shedrick Hay; Shirley Malone **MS:** Married **SPN:** Kay Kinsey (12/24/1990) **ED:** Coursework, Louisiana Tech University, Ruston, LA (1981-1985) **C:** Assistant Coach, Utah Jazz, NBA (2013-Present); Director, Basketball Promotions, Assistant Strength and Dieting Coach, Louisiana Tech University Bulldogs (2007-2011); Power Forward, Los Angeles Lakers, NBA (2004-2005); Power Forward, Utah Jazz, NBA, Salt Lake City, Utah (1985-2003) **CR:** Member, U.S. National Team, Summer Olympic Games, Atlanta, GA (1996); Member, U.S. National Team, Summer Olympic Games, Barcelona, Spain (1992) **CIV:** With, Utah Special Olympics; Founder, Karl Malone Foundation for Kids **AW:** Named to Naismith Memorial Basketball Hall of Fame (2010); Named to Western Conference All-star Team, NBA (1988-1998, 2000-2002); Named NBA Most Valuable Player (1997, 1999); Named to First Team All-defense, NBA (1997-1999); Named One of the 50 Greatest Players in NBA History (1996); Gold Medal, Men's Basketball, Atlanta Olympic Games (1996); Named Most Valuable Player, NBA All-star Game (1989, 1993); Gold Medal, Men's Basketball, Barcelona Olympic Games (1992); Named to First Team All-NBA (1989-1999); Named to First Team All-rookie (1986)

MALONEY, CAROLYN JANE, T: U.S. Representative from New York **I:** Government Administration/Government Relations/Government Services **DOB:** 02/19/1948 **PB:** Greensboro **SC:** NC/

USA **PT:** R.G. Bosher; Christine (Clegg) Bosher **MS:** Widowed **SPN:** Clifton H.W. Maloney (1976, Deceased 09/25/2009) **CH:** Christina; Virginia **ED:** BA, Greensboro College (1968) **C:** Chair, U.S. House Committee on Oversight and Government Reform (2019-Present); Member, U.S. House of Representatives from New York's 12th Congressional District, United States Congress (2013-Present); Chair, U.S. Congressional Joint Economic Committee (JEC) (2007-Present); Chair, U.S. House Democratic Caucus Task Force on Homeland Security (2003-Present); Ranking Member, Joint Economic Committee (2005-2007); Member, U.S. House of Representatives from New York's 14th Congressional District, United States Congress (1993-2013); City Councilwoman, District 8, New York, NY (1983-1993); Director of Special Projects, Office of New York State Senate Minority Leader Manfred Ohrenstein (1980-1982); Executive Director, Advisory Council, Office of New York State Senate Minority Leader Manfred Ohrenstein (1979-1982); Senior Progressive Analyst Cities Committee, New York State Assembly (1977-1979); Legislative Aide, Housing Committee, New York State Assembly (1977); Special Assistant, Center for Career and Occupational Education, New York City Board of Education (1975-1976); Community Affairs Coordinator, Welfare Education Progressive, New York City Board of Education, New York, NY (1972-1975); Member, U.S. House Financial Services Committee **CR:** Member, U.S. Delegate, International Conference on Population and Development, The Hague, Netherlands; Member, Fourth World Conference on Women, Beijing, China; Founder, Chair, House Caucus on Hellenic Issues **CIV:** Active Member, Association for a Better New York; Active Member, Women's Political Caucus, Manhattan, NY **CW:** Author, "Rumors of Our Progress Have Been Greatly Exaggerated: Why Women's Lives Aren't Getting Any Easier and How We Can Make Real Progress for Ourselves and Our Daughters" (2008) **AW:** Named One of 21 Leaders for the 21st Century, Women's eNews (2017); Named One of 50 Women Who Made a Difference, Ms. Magazine (2003); Women's Leadership Award, United Nations Family Planning (2002); Special Impact Award, Healthy Mothers, Healthy Babies (2000); Decorated Military Order of the Purple Heart; Queens Women of Distinction Award, Women's Political Caucus, Queens, NY; Global Peace Award, Peace Action; Ellis Island Medal of Honor; Distinguished Public Service Award, National Family Planning & Reproductive Health Association; Myrtle Wreath Award, Hadassah; Outstanding Service Award, Manhattan Chamber of Commerce; CUNY Women's Leadership Award; Eleanor Roosevelt Trailblazer of Democracy Award, Eleanor's Legacy; Humane Advocate Award, The Humane Society of the United States; Outstanding Legislator Award, National Federation of Business and Professional Women's Club, NY Chapter; Jessie Bernard Wise Women's Award, Center for Women's Policy Studies; Planned Parenthood Responsible Choices Award **MEM:** Hadassah, The Women's Zionist Organization of America, Inc.; National Organization of Women, NAACP; Council on Foreign Relations; Women's City Club; Alice Paul Institute; Eleanor Roosevelt Legacy; Financial Women's Association; New York Landmarks Conservancy; CIVITAS; The Junior League of the City of New York **PA:** Democrat **RE:** Presbyterian

MALONEY, SEAN PATRICK, T: U.S. Representative from New York; Lawyer **I:** Government Administration/Government Relations/Government Services **DOB:** 07/30/1966 **PB:** Sherbrooke, Quebec **SC:** Canada **PT:** James Francis Maloney; Joan Caroline (Daley) Maloney **MS:** Married **SPN:** Randy Gene Florke (06/21/2014) **CH:** Jesus (Adopted); Daley (Adopted); Essie (Adopted) **ED:** JD, University of Virginia School of Law (1992); BA, University of Virginia (1988); Coursework, Georgetown University Walsh School of Foreign Service, Washington, DC (1984-1986) **C:** Member, U.S. House of Representatives from New York's 18th Congressional District, Washington, DC (2013-Present); Member, U.S. House Committee on Transportation and Infrastructure (2013-Present); Member, U.S. House Committee on Agriculture (2013-Present); Partner, Orrick Herrington & Sutcliffe LLP (2011-2012); First Deputy Secretary to Governor, State of New York, Albany, NY (2007-2009); Associate, Willkie Farr & Gallagher LLP, New York, NY (1992-1997, 2003-2007); Chief Operating Officer, Kiodex, Inc., New York, NY (2000-2003); Vice President, General Counsel, Kiodex, Inc., New York, NY (2000); Assistant to President, Staff Secretary, The White House, Washington, DC (1997-2000) **AW:** Grantee, Next Generation Leadership Fellowship, The Rockefeller Foundation (2002-2003) **BAR:** Washington, DC (1994); State of New York (1993) **AV:** Soccer; Running **PA:** Democrat

MANCHIN, JOSEPH, "JOE" III, T: U.S. Senator from West Virginia; Former Governor of West Virginia **I:** Government Administration/Government Relations/Government Services **DOB:** 08/24/1947 **PB:** Farmington **SC:** WV/USA **PT:** John Manchin; Mary Manchin **MS:** Married **SPN:** Gayle Conelly (1967) **CH:** Heather; Joseph IV; Brooke **ED:** BS in Business and Economics, West Virginia University (1970) **CT:** Certified Pilot **C:** Ranking Member, Senate Energy Committee (2019-Present); U.S. Senator, State of West Virginia, Washington, DC (2010-Present); Member, U.S. Senate Select Committee on Aging, Washington, DC (2010-Present); Member, U.S. Senate Committee on Energy and Natural Resources, Washington, DC (2010-Present); Member, U.S. Senate Armed Services Committee, Washington, DC (2010-Present); Chairman, National Governors Association (2010); Governor, State of West Virginia (2005-2010); Secretary of State, State of West Virginia, Charleston, WV (2001-2005); Member, West Virginia State Senate (1986-1992); Member, West Virginia House of Delegates (1982-1986); Operator, Manchin's Carpet Center, Marion County, WV (1970) **CW:** Co-host, "No Labels Radio: A Town Hall with America," Sirius XM Radio (2013-Present) **MEM:** National Rifle Association of America **PA:** Democrat **RE:** Catholic

MANHOLD, JOHN H., T: Dental Educator, Consultant **I:** Medicine & Health Care **DOB:** 08/20/1919 **PB:** Rochester **SC:** NY/USA **PT:** John Henry Manhold; Helen Martha (Shulz) Manhold **MS:** Married **SPN:** Enriqueta Manhold (3/20/1971); Beverly Schecter (1953, Divorced 1969) **ED:** MA, Washington University (1956); MD, Harvard University (1944); BA, University of Rochester (1940) **C:** Retired (1989); Medical Director, Woog International (1987-1989); Assistant Professor, Professor, Chairman, Department of General and Oral Pathology, Seton Hall College of Medicine and Dentistry (Now University of Medicine and Dentistry New Jersey), Newark, NJ (1956-1987); Assistant Professor, Chairman, General and Oral Pathology College of Dentistry, University of Washington, St. Louis, MO (1954-1956); Instructor, College of Medicine, Tufts University, Boston, MA (1948-1950) **CR:** Lecturer in Field, Consultant, Consumer Communications Network (1990-2008); Consumer Communications Network (1990-2005); Health Care Development Group (1990-2005); Richardson-Vicks, Shelton, CT (1981-1987); Los Produits Associes, Geneva, Switzerland (1965-1987); Johnson & Johnson, New Brunswick, NJ (1960-1970) **MIL:** Korean War (1950-1955); World War II (1944) **CW:** Author, "El Tigre II" (2011); Author, "Lobo" (2009); Author, "The Elymais Coin" (2008); Author, "El Tigre" (2007); Editor, "Clinical Preventive Dentistry Journal" (1979-1992); Co-Author, "Handbook of Pathology" (1987); Author, "Illustrated Dental Terminology: A Lexicon for the Dental Profession" (1985); Author, "Practical Dental Management: Patients and Practice" (1984); Author, "Tissue Respiration and Oxigenating Agents" (1977); Editor, "Clinical Oral Diagnosis" (1965); Author, "Outline of Pathology" (1960); Author, "Introductory Psychosomatic Dentistry" (1956); Contributor, Articles, Professional Journals **AW:** Honorary Mention Award, Paris Book Festival (2013); Western Fiction Book Award (2012); Book Award, National Indie Excellence (2010); Suspense Category Book Award (2009); Lifetime Achievement Award (2009); Best Book Award (2008); Western Category Book Award (2008); Historical Category Book Award (2008); Distinguished Alumni, Harvard University (1989); Listee, Senior Society Harvard School of Dental Medicine (1984); Letter of Appreciation, Asara Mihara (1980); President Award, Alumni Association, University of Medicine and Dentistry (1980); Certificate of Achievement, University of Maryland (1965) **MEM:** Secretary, Treasurer, President, Fellow, Academy Psychosomatic Medicine (1975-1978); International College of Dentists; American College of Dentists; American Psychological Association; AZ Authors; Florida Writers Association; Western Writers of America; International Association Dental Research; American Society of Clinical Pathologists; Sarasota Yacht Club; Sigma Xi **MH:** Albert Nelson Marquis Lifetime Achievement Award **B/I:** Dr. Manhold was interested in research, teaching, and problem solving throughout his entire life. He went to Harvard to get a dual degree so that he could have a wide variety of activities to pursue. **AV:** Making sculpture; Boating; Golfing; Shooting

MANILLA, JACK, T: Author, Contractor, Entrepreneur, Educator **I:** Other **CN:** Portofino Pools **DOB:** 07/17/1941 **PB:** Sharon **SC:** PA/USA **PT:** Vito John; Helen Elizabeth (Papai) Manilla **MS:** Married **SPN:** Paula Gale Jurko (1960) **CH:** Jacqueline Lee; John Paul; Paul Allan; Bradley James **ED:** MS in Management, Aquinas College (1984); Postgraduate Coursework, Duquesne University (1967-1968); BS, Youngstown State University (1966) **C:** Founder, President, Chief Executive Officer, Portofino Pools (1996-Present); Executive Vice President, Hayworth Dealer, Wagner Office Furniture, Inc. (1991-1995); Executive Vice President, Lubin Business Interiors, Milford, CT (1990-1991); Senior Vice President of Sales and Marketing, General Office Equipment Company, Incorporated (1989-1991); Vice President of Sales and Marketing, General Office Equipment Company, Incorporated (1987-1989); Director of Sales and Marketing, General Office Equipment Company, Incorporated (1984-1986); Director of Corporation Distribution Resources, Herman Miller, Inc. (1984); Director of Marketing, Herman Miller, Inc. (1981-1984); Group Marketing Manager, Herman Miller, Inc. (1981); Manager of Strategic Programs, Herman Miller, Inc. (1981); National Field Sales Manager, Elevator Company, Westinghouse Electric Corporation (1979-1981); Regional Architectural Manager, Furniture System Division, Elevator Company, Westinghouse Electric Corporation (1977-1979); District Manager, Elevator Company, Westinghouse Electric Corporation (1973-1977); Salesman II, Elevator Company, Westinghouse Electric Corporation (1971-1972); Vice President, Yankee Lake Amusement Company (1970-1971); Salesman I, Elevator Company, Westinghouse Electric Corporation (1968-1970); Staff Assistant, Elevator Company, Westinghouse Electric Corporation (1966-1968); Vice President, Yankee Lake Amusement Company (1961-1966)

CR: Author, Speaker, Consultant, Blue Diamond Consulting, LLC (2017-Present); Architect, Engineering and Facilities Management Consultant (1970) CIV: Action Council Member, Seniors on a Mission, Inc. (2019-Present); Chairman of the Board, World of Recreational Water Foundation (2017-2018); Master's Program Scholarship Fund Committee, Aquinas College (1983-1984); Consultant, Financial and Building Fund, St. Mary Magdalen Parish (1984); Co-Chairman, Capital Endowment Campaign, Continuing Education Division, Aquinas College (1982); President, Princeton Estates Homeowners Association (1982); Active Member, Diocese of Grand Rapids (1982); Grand Rapids Arts Council (1980); President, Board of Education, Our Lady of Mount Carmel School (1973-1976); Carmel Dad's Club (1973); Assistant, Boy Scouts of America (1973); Assistant Scoutmaster, Boy Scouts of America (1971-1972); Junior High School Principal, Instructor, Saint Sebastian Parish (1970); Junior High School Principal, Instructor, Church of St. Ursula (1968-1970) CW: Author, "Secrets of the Pink House: From Saltwater to Holy Water" AW: Performance Award, Westinghouse Electric Corporation (1972); 120 Club Honor Roll Award (1968-1972) MEM: Education Committee, Board of Directors, FRLA (2016-Present); Former Chair, Chair-Elect, Secretary, Treasurer, Board of Directors, Association of Pool and Spa Professionals (2011-2019); Executive Committee, Board of Directors, North Florida Hotel & Lodging Association (2010-2016); President, Water Sky Club (1990-1991); Trustee, Sparta Commons Condominium Association (1989-1991); Vice President, New Jersey State Water Ski Federation (1988-1991); Assistant Chairman, New Jersey Garden State Games (1988-1991); NAUI Worldwide; President, Local Chapter, Rotary International; MWSA; Tournament Official, American Water Ski Association; Association General Contractors Indiana; Construction Specifications Institute; Building Owners and Managers Association B/I: Mr. Manilla became involved in his profession after losing a large amount of wealth. He centered himself and readjusted his mentality before seeking out employment once again. Eventually, he received a call from a contracting business and his career has grown ever since. AV: Reading; Spending time with family; Judging sports competitions

MANLEY, EDWARD, "ED" HARRY JR., T: Owner, Food Safety and Management Trainer; Professional Association Administrator; Veteran's Charity Founder I: Food & Restaurant Services CN: E. H. Manley and Associates DOB: 09/12/1941 PB: Staten Island SC: NY/USA PT: Edward H. Manley; Ruth V. Manley MS: Divorced SPN: Judith Harvey Manley (Divorced); Jane Hopkins Manley (Deceased); Geraldine Crawford Gann Manley (Deceased) CH: Deborah Szymchack; Michael E. ED: Doctorate of Food Service, NAFEM (2019); MS, Rollins College (1978); BS in Hotel Management, Cornell University (1975) CT: Master Certified Food and Beverage Director (MCFBD) (2010); Master Certified Foodservice Professional (MCFP) (2010); Certified HACCP Professional (CHP) (2010); Certified Beverage Professional (CBP) (2010); Certified Professional Food Manager (2010); Certified in Culinary Nutrition (CCN) (2010); Certified Culinary Professional, ServSafe Alcohol (2010); Certified HACCP Manager (CHM) (2003); Master Certified Food Executive (1985); Certified Food Executive (1978) C: Founder, Workaholics International Network (1999-Present); Founding President, Veterans' Support Network (2012); Founder, Global Food Service Institute (2009); Professional Association Administrator, International Food Service Executives Association (IFSEA) (1989-2008); Founder, Military Culinary Competition and Enlisted Aide of the Year Award (2003); Food Safety and Management Trainer, Creative Cuisine Catering (1987-1990); Food Service Director, North Broward Hospital, Broward Health, Pompano Beach, FL (1981-1989); Lieutenant Commander, Hospital Food Service Director, United States Navy (1970-1980); Retired, Naval Regional Medical Center (1980); Food Service Director, Naval Regional Medical Center, Orlando, FL (1975-1980); Food Service Director, Naval Hospital, Annapolis, MD (1972-1973); Assistant Food Service Director, National Naval Medical Center, Bethesda, MD (1971-1972); Hospital Corpsman, United States Navy (1959-1970); Founder, Military Hospitality Alliance; President, VIP Food Safety; President, Creative Food Concepts, Incorporated CR: Chairman, Skill Standard Board for Hospitality and Tourism (2012); Presenter in Field (2012); Atlantic Vo-Tech Dietetic Program (1981-1989); Member, Advisory Board, Technical Food Service Program, Mid-Florida (1978-1980) CIV: Member, Advisory Board, Broward College (1985-Present); Pro Bono Teacher of $2000 Certification Program to Homeless Veterans (2015); Member, Evaluation Team, Hennessey Award, United States Air Force (1982) MIL: Advanced Through Grades to Lieutenant Commander, United States Navy (1980); Commissioned Ensign, United States Navy (1970); Joined, United States Navy (1959) CW: Author, "The 5 Second Rule and Other Kitchen Do's and Don'ts" (2017); Author, "Food Safety 101" (2009); Author, "Restaurant Manager's Guide" (2007); Editor/Publisher, "HACCP Implementation Manual" (2006) AW: Chairman Award, International Food Service Executives Association (IFSEA) (2003, 2005, 2006, 2008); Chairman Military Award, International Food Service Executives Association (IFSEA) (2008); Named to Dignified Order of Dinner Gong, International Food Service Executives Association (IFSEA) (2001, 2006); Peter Gust Economou Award (1987); Named Distinguished Health Care Food Service Administrator (1985); Ed Manley Scholarship Fund Established (1984); Distinguished Service Award, International Food Service Executives Association (IFSEA) (1984); Named Member of the Year, International Food Service Executives Association (IFSEA), South Florida Branch, FL (1984); Named Member of the Year, International Food Service Executives Association (IFSEA), Orlando Branch, FL (1978) MEM: Chairman, International Food Service Executives Association (IFSEA) (2008); President, International Food Service Executives Association (IFSEA) (1989-2008); Treasurer, Cornell Hotel Society (CHS), Las Vegas, NV (2001-2003); Chairman, Board, International Food Service Executives Association (IFSEA) (1988-1989); International Secretary Treasurer, International Food Service Executives Association (IFSEA) (1986-1987); President, International Food Service Executives Association (IFSEA), South Florida Branch (1983-1984); Board Director, Florida Restaurant Association (Now FRLA) (1980); President, International Food Service Executives Association (IFSEA), Orlando Branch, FL (1979-1980); President, Naval Training Center Officers Club (1978-1980); President, Cornell Hotel Society (CHS), Central Florida Chapter (1976-1980); International Food Service Executives Association (IFSEA); Cornell Hotel Society (CHS); Florida Restaurant Association (Now FRLA); American Society Hospital Food Service Administration (ASHFSA); Secretary, American Society Hospital Food Service Administration (ASHFSA), South Florida Chapter; Cornell of Central Florida Club; Naval Training Center Officers Club; Founder, Pompano Square Mall Walkers Club MH: Albert Nelson Marquis Lifetime Achievement Award; Marquis Who's Who Top Professional AS: Networking has been the key element of Mr. Manley's success. He has always been involved in activities which had him meeting people in his area, both in and after the Navy. When he saw something that needed to get done and he felt he could do it, he did. He was never afraid to try, never afraid to say "I can do that at least as well and probably better than the people before." And at this point, he tells people, "I don't THINK I change lives, I KNOW I change lives by getting people education and certifications, which help them to get better jobs and pay raises." B/I: Mr. Manley fell into his profession solely by pure interest he's always had, even as a boy. In addition, what attracted Mr. Manley to his career is that he got commissioned in the military. He was told that if he got into food service the military would send him to Cornell. So, he got into food service and they sent him to Cornell. AV: Attending shows; Concerts; Plays; Volunteering; Walking PA: Democrat RE: Roman Catholic THT: Mr. Manley says, "My core theory in life is to be better than the person that did it before."

MANN, NOEL R., PHD, T: Professor I: Education/Educational Services CN: William Carey University PT: Robert; Elizabeth MS: Married CH: Three Children ED: PhD in Environmental Science, The University of Southern Mississippi (1980); MS in Chemistry, Physics, Math, Delta State University; BS in Chemistry, Physics, and Math, Delta State University CT: Engineering Certification, United States Army C: Professor of Chemistry and Physics, William Carey University (2013-Present); Teacher, Presbyterian Christian School (2008-2013); Researcher, Science Department, The University of Southern Mississippi (2003-2008) CIV: Pastor (Off and On), Local Churches (30 Years) MIL: Retired, Lieutenant Colonel, United States Army (1996); With, United States Army (25 Years) CW: Author, Laboratory Manuals, Study Guides, Published In-house AW: HEADWAE (Higher Education Appreciation Day Working for Academic Excellence), Mississippi State Legislature (2016); Named Mississippi State Teacher of the Year, National Association of Independent Schools (2013); Named Teacher of the Year, Presbyterian Christian High School (2013); Cold War Medal, United States Army (2013); Award, NISOD (National Institute for Staff and Organizational Development) (1997); Named National Instructor of the Year (1996); Armed Forces Retired Medal, United States Army (1996); Honorable Discharge Medal, United States Army (1996); Named Outstanding Teacher in America (1995); Named Instructor of the Year, Mississippi Gulf Coast Community College (1994); Patent for Developing Acoustical Coupler for Ultrasound Identification of Chemical Agents, United States Army (1992); Meritorious Service Medal, Desert Storm, United States Army (1991); National Defense Service Medal, United States Army, Desert Storm (1991); Named One of the Outstanding Young Men in America (1985); Army Achievement Medal, Second Army NBC School, Admin Log Officer (1983); Army Achievement Medal, First Army NBC School, Admin Log Officer (1982); Humanitarian Service Medal for Hurricane Frederick, United States Army (1979); National Defense Service Medal, United States Army, Vietnam (1971) MH: Marquis Who's Who Top Professional; Marquis Who's Who Humanitarian Award AS: Dr. Mann attributes his success to his parents. They didn't have a college degree but they always encouraged them to read, study, and work hard. B/I: Dr. Mann went into education because he enjoyed learning and being in education afforded him the opportunity to continue learning. In addition, what got him interested in his career was his high school teacher who taught him chemistry and that was what ignited his interests in chemistry in college. He never had physics in high school, but when he took it in college, he got interested in that as well, and ended up with a double major in chemistry and physics. **AV:** Reading; Running for Senior Olympics

MANNICK, JOHN, MD, T: Surgeon **I:** Medicine & Health Care **DOB:** 03/24/1928 **PB:** Deadwood **SC:** SD/USA **PT:** Alfred Mannick; Catherine Elizabeth (Schuster) Mannick **MS:** Married **SPN:** Alice Virginia Gossard (06/09/1952) **CH:** Catherine Virginia; Elizabeth Eleanor; Joan Barbara **ED:** Resident in Surgery, Massachusetts General Hospital, The General Hospital Corporation (1956-1960); Intern, Massachusetts General Hospital, The General Hospital Corporation (1953-1954); MD, Harvard University (1953); BA, Harvard University (1949) **CT:** Diplomate, American Board of Surgery, Inc. **C:** Moseley Distinguished Professor of Surgery, Harvard University (1994-2008); Director of Educational Programs, Harvard Medical International (1994-1996); Chairman, Department of Surgery, Peter Bent Brigham Hospital and Brigham and Women's Hospital, Boston, MA (1976-1994); Moseley Professor of Surgery, Harvard University (1976-1994); Chairman, Division of Surgery, Boston University (1973-1976); Associate Professor to Professor of Surgery, Boston University (1964-1976); Instructor in Surgery to Assistant Professor, Medical College Virginia (Now Virginia Commonwealth University School of Medicine) (1960-1964) **CR:** Member, Surgery, Anesthesiology and Trauma Study Section, National Institutes of Health (1978-1982); Research Committee, Medical Foundation, Inc. (1970-1976); Member, Medicine Study Section, National Institutes of Health (1967-1970) **MIL:** Served to Captain, Medical Corps, United States Air Force (1954-1956) **CW:** Member, Editorial Board, Shock (1997-Present); Member, Editorial Board, Advances in Surgery (1979-Present); Associate Editor, Journal of Vascular Surgery (1990-1997); Member, Editorial Board, Journal of Vascular Surgery (1984-1997); Member, Editorial Board, Surgery (1982-1997); Member, Editorial Board, European Journal of Vascular Surgery (1988-1996); Member, Editorial Board, British Journal of Surgery (1982-1992); Co-author, "The Cause and Management of Aneurysms" (1990); Editor, Advances in Surgery (1984-1986); Member, Editorial Board, American Medical Association Archives of Surgery (1973-1984); Member, Editorial Board, Clinical Immunology and Immunopathology (1972-1984); Co-author, "Core Textbook of Surgery" (1972); Co-author, "Surgery of Ischemic Limbs" (1972); Co-author, "Modern Surgery" (1970); Contributor, Articles to Professional Journals **AW:** Scientific Leadership Award, Surgical Infection Society (2008); Lifetime Achievement Award, Society of University Surgeons (2005); Distinguished Service Award, International Cardiovascular Society (2002); Science Achievement Award, Shock Society (2000); Nathan Smith Distinguished Service Award, New England Surgical Society (1999); Markle Scholar, Academy of Medicine (1961-1966) **MEM:** Honorary Member, Dr. Military Medicine and Surgery, Uniformed Services University of Health Sciences (2003); President, Lifeline Foundation (1997-2002); President, New England Society for Vascular Surgery (1994-1995); International Vice President, International Cardiovascular Society (1993); President, International Cardiovascular Society, North America Chapter (1991-1992); President, American Surgical Association (1989-1990); President, Society of Surgical Chairs, American College of Surgeons (1987-1988); Secretary, Society of Surgical Chairs, American College of Surgeons (1985-1987); President, Society for Vascular Surgery (1981); Director, American Board of Surgery, Inc. (1971-1977); Recorder, International Cardiovascular Society, North America Chapter (1973-1976); Fellow, Governor, American College of Surgeons; Honorary Member, The Royal College of Surgeons of England; Honorary Member, The Royal College of Surgeons of Edinburgh; Honorary Member, RCSI Royal College of Surgeons in Ireland; Honorary Member, The Vascular Society for Great Britain and Ireland; American Federation for Clinical Research (AFCR); The American Association of Immunologists, Inc.; American Society for Experimental Pathology; Society for Clinical Investigation (Now The American Society for Clinical Investigation); Society of Clinical Surgery; Society of University Surgeons; Society of Surgical Chairs, American College of Surgeons; American Surgical Association; International Cardiovascular Society; Society for Vascular Surgery; Northeast Surgical Society; New England Society for Vascular Surgery; Honorary Member, Royal Australasian College of Surgeons; Southern Surgical Association; Honorary Member, Southern Society for Vascular Surgery; Surgical Infection Society; The Halsted Society; Lifeline Foundation; Shock Society; Uniformed Services University of Health Sciences; The Phi Beta Kappa Society **MH:** Albert Nelson Marquis Lifetime Achievement Award **B/I:** Dr. Mannick became involved in his profession because of the popularity of Freudian psychiatry at that time. He thought he would be a psychiatrist but after spending some time in medical school, he realized psychiatry was not for him and the rest evolved after that for him. He became involved in academia because he did a research fellowship during his residency. His fellowship was done with a remarkable man by the name of Dr. Edward Donald Thomas, who won the Nobel prize in 1990.

MANNING, JOHN F., T: Dean; Professor **I:** Education/Educational Services **CN:** Harvard Law School **DOB:** 04/11/1961 **PB:** Los Angeles **SC:** CA/USA **ED:** JD, Harvard University, Magna Cum Laude (1985); AB in History, Harvard University, Summa Cum Laude (1982) **C:** Morgan and Helen Chu Dean, Harvard Law School, Cambridge, MA (2013-Present); Professor, Law, Harvard Law School (2004-Present); Deputy Dean, Harvard Law School (2013-2017); Bruce Bromley Professor of Law, Harvard Law School (2013-2017); Professor, Columbia Law School, New York, NY (1994-2004); Assistant to U.S. Solicitor General (1991-1994); Associate, Gibson, Dunn & Crutcher LLP, Washington, DC (1989-1991); Law Clerk to Justice Antonin Scalia, Supreme Court of the United States (1988); Attorney-advisor, Office of Legal Counsel, U.S. Department of Justice (1986-1988); Law Clerk to Judge Robert H. Bork, United States Court of Appeals for the District of Columbia Circuit (1985) **CW:** Co-author, "Legislation and Regulation" (2010); Co-author, "Hart and Wechsler's Federal Courts and the Federal System, Sixth Edition" (2009); Contributor, Articles, Professional Journals **MEM:** American Academy of Arts & Sciences (2013) **BAR:** California (1990); Pennsylvania (1986)

MANNING, PEYTON WILLIAMS, T: Former Professional Football Player **I:** Athletics **DOB:** 03/24/1976 **PB:** New Orleans **SC:** LA/USA **PT:** Archie Manning; Olivia (Williams) Manning **MS:** Married **SPN:** Ashley Thompson (03/17/2001) **CH:** Mosley Thompson; Marshall Williams **ED:** BA in Speech Communications, University of Tennessee (1998) **C:** Quarterback, Denver Broncos, National Football League (NFL) (2012-2016); Quarterback, Indianapolis Colts, National Football League (NFL) (1998-2012) **CR:** Founder, The Peyback Foundation (1999-Present) **CW:** Host, ESPY Awards (2017); Voice Actor, "Ferdinand" (2017); Appearance, "Saturday Night Live" (2008, 2015); Co-Author (with Archie Manning and Eli Manning), "Family Huddle" (2009); Voice Actor, "The Simpsons" (2009); Host, "Saturday Night Live" (2007); Co-Author (with Archie Manning), "Manning: A Father, His Sons and a Football Legacy" (2000) **AW:** Inductee, Indianapolis Colts Ring of Honor (2017); ESPY Icon Award (2016); Winner, Denver Broncos, Super Bowl 50 (2015); Winner, Pro Bowl (2014); Named to American Football Conference Pro-Bowl Team, NFL (1999, 2000, 2002-2010, 2012-2014); Named to First Team All-Pro (2003-2005, 2008, 2009, 2012, 2013); Named NFL MVP (2003, 2004, 2008, 2009, 2013); Named NFL Passing Yard Leader of the Year (2004, 2013); Named NFL Offensive Player of the Year, The Associated Press (2004, 2013); Bert Bell Award, Maxwell Football Club (2003, 2004, 2013); Named Sportsman of the Year, Sports Illustrated (2013); Named NFL Comeback Player of the Year, The Associated Press (2012); Named NFL Athlete of the Decade: 2000s, Sporting News (2009); Named One of the Most Influential People in the World of Sports, Business Week (Now Bloomberg Businessweek) (2007, 2008); Named NFL Player of the Year (2003, 2004, 2008); Named Super Bowl XLI MVP, NFL (2007); Winner, Indianapolis Colts, Super Bowl Champion XLI (2007); ESPY Award for Best Championship Performance, ESPN (2007); Named Pro Bowl MVP (2005); Walter Payton Man of the Year Award (2005); Byron "Whizzer" White Humanitarian Award (2005); ESPY Award for Best NFL Player (2004); John Wooden Trophy, Athletes for a Better World (2004); Henry P. Iba Citizen Athlete Award (2002); American Dream Award, Hudson Institute (2001); Johnny Unitas Award (1997); Davey O'Brien Award, Davey O'Brien Foundation (1997); Maxwell Award, Maxwell Football Club (1997)

MANSELL, KEVIN B., T: Chairman, President, and Chief Executive Officer **I:** Retail/Sales **CN:** Kohl's Corporation **PB:** St. Louis **SC:** MO/USA **ED:** Coursework, University of Missouri **C:** Chairman, President, Chief Executive Officer, Kohl's Corporation, Menomonee Falls, WI (2009-2018); President, Chief Executive Officer, Kohl's Corporation, Menomonee Falls, WI (2008-2009); President, Kohl's Corporation, Menomonee Falls, WI (1999-2008); Senior Executive Vice President of Merchandising and Marketing, Kohl's Corporation, Menomonee Falls, WI (1998-1999); General Merchandise manager, Kohl's Corporation, Menomonee Falls, WI (1987); Divisional Merchandise Manager, Kohl's Corporation, Menomonee Falls, WI (1982-1987); With, Venture Store Division, May Department Stores (1975); Positions in Merchandising and Buying, May Department Stores **CR:** Board of Directors, Kohl's Corporation (1999-Present)

MANSFIELD, WILLIAM A., T: Lawyer **I:** Law and Legal Services **DOB:** 10/23/1929 **PB:** Redmond **SC:** OR/USA **PT:** Ellithorpe Garrett Mansfield; Constance G. (Loney) Mansfield **CH:** Johnathan E.; Frederick W.; Paul F. **ED:** JD, University of Oregon (1953); BS in Economics, University of Oregon (1951) **C:** Private Practice (1965-Present); City Attorney, Medford, OR (1962-1964); Staff Attorney, General Counsel, U.S. Bureau of Public Roads (1961); Assistant Attorney General, Salem, OR (1955-1960) **CIV:** Planning Committee, City of Medford (2012-Present); Chairman, Rogue Valley Symphony (1992-Present); City Council Member, Medford, OR (1985-1996); Chairman, Southern Oregon Child and Family Council (1991); Board of Directors, Southern Oregon Child and Family Council (1989-1991); Board of Directors, Rogue Valley Transportation District (1976-1981); Chairman, Rogue Valley Transportation District (1977-1978); Board of Directors, American Civil Liberties Union (1971-1977); Trustee, Trillium Family Services (1970-1976); Board of Directors, Britt Music & Arts Festival (1963-1965); Board of Directors, Teacher, Osher Lifelong Learning Institute

MIL: First Lieutenant, U.S. Air Force (1953-1955) **BAR:** United States Court of Appeals for the Ninth Circuit (1982); U.S. District Court District of Oregon (1966); Oregon State Bar (1953); Supreme Court of the United States **MH:** Albert Nelson Marquis Lifetime Achievement Award **B/I:** Mr. Mansfield became involved in his profession because of his interest in social sciences, which led to his interest in law. **AV:** Listening to classical music; Gardening **PA:** Democrat **RE:** Congregationalist

MANSOLILLO, CHARLES RONALD, ESQ., T: Lawyer **I:** Law and Legal Services **DOB:** 03/08/1949 **PT:** Nicholas William Mansolillo; Adeline Ann Marie (Marcello) Mansolillo **MS:** Single **ED:** Postgraduate Coursework, Weston Jesuit School of Theology and Ministry (1997-1999); JD, Suffolk University (1985); BA, Saint Michael's College (1971); Classic High School (1967) **C:** City Solicitor Emeritus, City of Providence, RI (2003-Present); City Solicitor, City of Providence, RI (1992-2003); Deputy City Solicitor, City of Providence, RI (1991-1992); Director, Governor's Policy Office (1990-1991); Director of Governors, Office of Housing, Energy and Intergovernmental Relations (1989-1990); Legal Counsel, Department of Children and Families, State of Rhode Island (1987-1988); Chief of Staff, Mayor's Office, City of Providence, RI (1983-1984); City Councilman, City of Providence, RI (1975-1983); Member, House of Representatives, State of Rhode Island, Providence, RI (1973-1975) **CR:** Member, Narragansett Bay Commission (1980-1983); Member, Executive Board, Rhode Island League Cities and Towns (1979-1984); Providence Home Rule Charter Commission (1979-1980) **CIV:** Trustee, Providence Public Library (1979-1987); Nominee, Republican Mayor, Providence, RI (1986); Chairman, Board of Directors, Providence Community Action Program, Inc., Community Action Partnership of Providence (1975-1984); Board of Directors; Providence Industrial Development Corporation; Lectern, St. Pius V Catholic Church, Providence, RI **MH:** Albert Nelson Marquis Lifetime Achievement Award; Marquis Who's Who Humanitarian Award **B/I:** Mr. Mansolillo was young when he became involved in politics in college. He requested to run for state legislature in 1973 in Providence because the former legislature passed away and had to be replaced; he was drafted to run in 1973. Mr. Mansolillo was teaching school in Worcester, Massachusetts and commuting to Providence every day. As time went by, he left the legislature to run for city council in Providence because he was dealing with more matters on the municipal side. He was elected to the city council when the famous Buddy Cianci approached him to keep his status as a Democrat to support him. After some long soul searching from Mr. Monsolillo, he decided to support Mr. Cianci as a better candidate. When Mayor Cianci became elected, Mr. Mansolillo became like a surrogate. After working with the mayor in 1986, Mr. Mansolillo started to lose his passion for public service and being rather a faithful Christian, he thought he could be doing some better things in the ministry. Mayor Cianci decided to run for mayor again and he won in 1994; at that time he was employed by the governor office. Mr. Monsolillo left the office to become appointed City Solicitor by Mayor Cianci. **THT:** Mr. Mansolillo has four brothers, Robert, John, Nicholas, and James.

MANTEL, LINDA HABAS, PHD, I: Education/Educational Services **DOB:** 05/12/1939 **PB:** Brooklyn **SC:** NY/USA **PT:** Eugene J. Habas; Sylvia (Seltzer) Habas **MS:** Married **SPN:** Kenneth H. Mantel (06/25/1966) **ED:** PhD, University of Illinois (1965); MS, University of Illinois (1962); BA, Swarthmore College, Swarthmore, PA (1960) **C:** Associate

Research Professor, Portland State University, Portland, OR (2004-present); Assistant Vice President for Technology Services, University of Portland, Portland, OR (1999-2002); Vice President, Academic Administration, Willamette University, Salem, OR (1998-1999); Dean, Faculty, Professor, Biology, Reed College, Portland, OR (1993-1998); Chairman, Biology Department, City College of New York, New York, NY (1987-1993); Professor, City College of New York, New York, NY (1985-1993); Research Associate, American Museum of Natural History (1968-1993); Assistant Provost, Research and Graduate Studies, City College of New York, New York, NY (1982-1987); Associate Professor, City College of New York, New York, NY (1975-1984); Extramural Associate, National Institutes of Health, (1982); Assistant Professor, Biology, City College of New York, New York, NY (1968-1975); NICHHD Post-Doctoral Research Fellow, American Museum of Natural History, New York, NY (1965-1968) **CR:** Co-Chair, Leadership Council, Senior Adult Learning Center, Portland State University (2020); Higher Education and Community Liaison, Pacific Northwest Louis Stokes Alliance for Minority Participation (2009-2019); President, Board of Directors, Sigma Xi of the Columbia-Willamette (2008-2019); Regional Director, Northwest Region, Sigma Xi (2009-2015); Judging Advisory Committee, Society for Science and the Public (2010-2015); Review Panelist, NSF Louis Stokes Alliance for Minority Participation (2004-2015); Executive Director, Intel Northwest Science Expo System (2004-2012); President, Board of Directors, Museum of Contemporary Craft (2004-2008); Secretary, Board of Directors, Sigma Xi of the Columbia-Willamette (2004-2008); Member, Diversity Committee, Strategic Planning Committee (2003-2008); Consultant on Intel ISEF Categories for Science Service (2005); Co-Chair, Higher Education Program, Intel ISEF (2003-2004); President, Past President, Association for Women in Science (1999-2003); Member, Education Council, Society for Integrative and Comparative Biology (1999-2003); Leader, Diversity Strand, Oregon Collaborative for Excellence in Preparation of Teachers (OCEPT) (2000-2002); Member, Editorial Board, Physiological Zoology (1991-1995); Director, Undergraduate Program in Biological Sciences, Howard Hughes Institute (1989-1993); Visiting Professor, Autonomous University of Santo Domingo (1991); Chair, Dioxin Advisory Panel, New Jersey Department of Environmental Protection (1989-1991); Consultant, Columbia University Press (1984-1988); Consultant, Educational Testing Service, Princeton, NJ (1984-1987) **CIV:** Development Chair, League of Women Voters of Portland, (2020-Present); Member, Board of Directors, League of Women Voters of Portland, (2019-Present); Member, Council on Presidential Initiatives, Swarthmore College, (2018-Present); Portland Art Museum, Contemporary Art Council Board (2010-2018); Participant, Renaissance Weekend (2017); Board of Directors, Downtown Neighborhood Association (2005-2010) **CW:** Contributor, Articles to Professional Journals; Presentations on Many Topics in Physiology, Women in Science, Higher Education (1965-present); Editor, "Kaleidoscope" (1984-1987); Author, Editor, "The Biology of Crustacea" (1984-1986); Co-Author, "The Balance of Living" (1971) **AW:** Evan Ferguson Award for Service to Sigma Xi, (2019); Legacy Award, Pacific Northwest Louis Stokes Alliance for Minority Participation, University of Washington, (2019); Fellow, Association for Women in Science (2002); Faculty Service Award, Alumni Association of City College (1992); Citywoman of the Year, City College (1990); Outstanding Woman Scientist Award, New York Metropolitan Chapter of the Association for Women in Science (1988); Elected Fellow, Ameri-

can Association for the Advancement of Science (AAAS) (1984); Elected Fellow, New York Academy of Sciences (NYAS), (1983) **MEM:** Fellow, American Association for the Advancement of Science; New York Academy of Sciences; Association for Women in Science; Crustacean Society; Society for Integrative and Comparative Biology; Council of Graduate Schools; Sigma Xi; Mensa; Association of American Museums; Numerous Environmental Organizations; Numerous Women's Organizations; Numerous Museums and Gardens **MH:** Albert Nelson Marquis Lifetime Achievement Award **AS:** Dr. Mantel's parents were her first mentors and encouraged her in any activities she chose to undertake. She was never told "girls can't do that". She also admired her uncle, who was an engineer and gave her scientific books to read. Inspiring science teachers in sixth and twelfth grades, and supportive and encouraging professors in college and graduate school were important to keeping her on track. **B/I:** She was always curious about how things worked in the world. She asked a lot of questions, read a lot, and had many explorative toys: a tinker toy, an Erector set, a microscope, a chemistry set, and more, all provided by her parents to encourage her curiosity. She was never hesitant to try something new. When offered something to do, her motto is to "say yes and worry later." When in college, she had many interests, including languages and music, as well as science. She toyed with going to graduate school in music, but she was happy to choose science as a vocation and music as an avocation. **AV:** Music; Listening; Attending concerts; Playing chamber music; Singing; Traveling; Historical and cultural outdoor gardens; Art museums; Collecting art works by local artists **THT:** Family is a life-line, Long-time friends are priceless, Don't be afraid to take a risk, Take advantage of serendipity, Give back to those who have given to you, Be a good spotter of talent, Give a hand to those who need it to move up, Know the Golden Rule: She who has the gold makes the rules, Have confidence in yourself, and others will too, Always know your goals and several ways to get there. Have your ducks in a row.

MANTERFIELD, ERIC A., T: Banker; Law Educator; Lawyer (Retired) **I:** Law and Legal Services **DOB:** 10/02/1947 **PB:** New York **SC:** NY/USA **PT:** Erskine Walker Manterfield; Louise Ruth (Wild) Manterfield **MS:** Divorced **SPN:** Susan Jennings Manterfield (1991, Divorced 2011); Valerie Jane Siegel (07/18/1969) **CH:** Brian W.; Elyse A.; Wesley A.; Sean P. **ED:** JD, University of Michigan (1972); BA, Denison University (1969) **C:** Retired (2012); Partner, Krieg DeVault, LLC, Indianapolis, IN (1996-2012); Adjunct Professor of Law, Indiana University Maurer School Law, Bloomington, IN (1977-2003); Manager, Personal Trust Division, American Fletcher National Bank, North America (1982-1986); Manager, Probate Department, American Fletcher National Bank, North America (1976-1982); Trust Officer, American Fletcher National Bank, North America, Indianapolis, IN (1975-1976); Associate, Barnes & Thornburg LLP (Formerly Barnes, Hickam, Pantzer & Boyd), Indianapolis, IN (1972-1974); Trust Officer, Bank One (Now JPMorgan Chase & Co.), Indianapolis, IN **CR:** Fellow, Indiana State Chair, The American College of Trust and Estate Counsel **CIV:** Docent, Indiana Landmarks (2015-Present); Board of Directors, Indianapolis Symphony Orchestra (1997-2009); Indiana Delegate, North Central Regional Heart Committee, American Heart Association, Inc., Dallas, Texas (1981-1986); Member, Deferred Giving Committee, Crossroads Rehabilitation Center, Indianapolis, IN (1984-1985); Chairman of the Board, Festival Music Society, Indianapolis, IN (1982); Chairman, Board, American Heart Association, Inc., Indiana Affiliate,

Indianapolis, IN (1978-1982); Buy-Sell Agreements; Estate Planning for Second Marriages **CW:** Author, "Critical Elements of Estate Planning with Forms, Fourth Edition" (2009); Author, "Fundamentals of Estate Planning" (1982); Author, "Estate Planning for Married Couples" (1982); Author, "Basic Estate Planning" (1980); Contributor, Articles to Professional Journals **AW:** Named Best Article, Library of Congress (2009); Named Excellence in Estate Planning, Indianapolis Bar Association (2006) **MEM:** President, Estate Planning Council of Indianapolis, Inc., National Association of Estate Planners & Councils (1986-1987); Vice President, Estate Planning Council of Indianapolis, Inc., National Association of Estate Planners & Councils (1985-1986); Secretary, Estate Planning Council of Indianapolis, Inc., National Association of Estate Planners & Councils (1984-1985); Treasurer, Executive Committee, Estate Planning Council of Indianapolis, Inc., National Association of Estate Planners & Councils (1983-1984); Indianapolis Bar Association, Indiana State Bar Association; Estate Planning Council of Indianapolis, Inc., National Association of Estate Planners & Councils; The Phi Beta Kappa Society; American Bar Association (ABA) **BAR:** United States Tax Court (1979); United States District Court for the South District of Indiana (1972); Indiana State Bar Association (1972); Indianapolis Bar Association; American Bar Association (ABA) **MH:** Albert Nelson Marquis Lifetime Achievement Award; Marquis Who's Who Top Professional **B/I:** Mr. Manterfield had a desire to help other people as a lawyer.

MARCHANT, KENNY EWELL, T: U.S. Representative **I:** Government Administration/Government Relations/Government Services **DOB:** 02/23/1951 **PB:** Bonham **SC:** TX/USA **MS:** Married **SPN:** Donna Marchant **CH:** Luke; Matthew; Kenny; Dallas **ED:** Honorary DHL, Southern Nazarene University, Bethany, OK (1999); BA, Southern Nazarene University, Bethany, OK (1974); Coursework, Nazarene Theological Seminary, Kansas City, MO **C:** U.S. Representative, Texas' 24th Congressional District, United States Congress, Washington, DC (2005-Present); Chair, House Republican Caucus, Texas House of Representatives, Austin, Texas (1999-2003); Member, Texas House of Representatives, Austin, Texas (1987-2004); Mayor, City of Carrollton, Carrollton City Council (1984-1987); Councilman, Carrollton City Council, Texas (1980-1984); Member, Committee on Ways and Means, United States Congress; Member, Committee on Ethics, United States Congress; Member, Republican Study Committee, United States Congress **AW:** One of the Top Ten Legislators, Texas Monthly Magazine; Top Pro-Family Legislator of the Year, American Family Association; Legislator of the Year, Texas Municipal League; Citizen of the Year, Metrocrest Chamber of Commerce **PA:** Republican **RE:** Nazarene

MARCU, LEN, T: Owner **I:** Business Management/Business Services **CN:** Lens Remodeling & Contracting Services **MS:** Married **CH:** Three Stepchildren; Two Children **ED:** BA in Business Administration, Temple University (1979) **C:** Owner, Lens Remodeling and Contracting Services (2003-Present); Regional/Store Manager, CompUSA (1992-2003) **AW:** Best of Professionals, The Bath Outlet (2018); Best of Houzz, Service (2016-2018); Super Service Award, Angie's List (2015-2018); Top 500, Qualified Remodeler **MEM:** Business Association; National Kitchen and Bath Association **AS:** Mr. Marcu is always thinking of ways to improve himself and his team. They have weekly production meetings in which the company tries to make corrections and find areas to improve upon. **B/I:** Mr. Marcu loves leaving people satisfied. It is

a big thrill to improve someone's life. He is always excited to work. **AV:** Walking the dog; Boating; Fishing **THT:** Mr. Marcu's motto is "Do the right thing."

MARGULIES, JULIANNA LUISA, T: Actress **I:** Media & Entertainment **DOB:** 06/08/1966 **PB:** Spring Valley **SC:** NY/USA **PT:** Paul Margulies; Francesca (Gardner) Margulies **MS:** Married **SPN:** Keith Lieberthal (11/10/2007) **CH:** Kieran Lindsay **ED:** BA, Sarah Lawrence College (1989) **CW:** Actress, "Billions" (2020); Actress, "The Hot Zone" (2019); Actress, "Dietland" (2018); Appearance, "Nightcap" (2017); Actress, "Three Christs" (2017); Actress, "The Upside" (2017); Actress, "The Good Wife" (2009-2016); Author, "Three Magic Balloons" (2015); Actress, "Stand Up Guys" (2012); Actress, "City Island" (2009); Actress, "The Sopranos" (2006, 2007, 2009); Actress, "Canterbury's Law" (2008); Actress, "The Darwin Awards" (2006); Actress, "Festen" (2006); Actress, "Snakes on a Plane" (2006); Actress, "Beautiful Ohio" (2006); Actress, "Slingshot" (2005); Actress, "Scrubs" (2004); Actress, "The Grid" (2004); Actress, "Hitler: The Rise of Evil" (2003); Voice Actress, "Love Gets You Twisted" (2002); Actress, "Ghost Ship" (2002); Actress, "Evelyn" (2002); Actress, "Ten Unknowns" (2001); Actress, "The Mists of Avalon" (2001); Actress, "Jenifer" (2001); Actor, "The Man from Elysian Fields" (2001); Actress, "What's Cooking" (2000); Voice Actress, "Dinosaur" (2000); Actress, "ER" (1994-2000); Actress, "The Vagina Monologues" (1999); Actress, "The Big Day" (1999); Actress, "The Newton Boys" (1998); Actress, "Traveller" (1997); Actress, "Paradise Road" (1997); Actress, "A Price Above Rubies" (1997); Actress, "Philly Heat" (1994); Actress, "Homicide: Life on the Street" (1994); Actress, "Law & Order" (1993); Actress, "Murder, She Wrote" (1993); Actress, "Out for Justice" (1991); Actress, Theater, Television Shows, Films **AW:** Listee, 100 Most Influential People in the World, Time Magazine (2015); Listee, 100 Most Powerful Women in Entertainment, The Hollywood Reporter (2014); Emmy Award for Outstanding Lead Actress in a Drama Series, Academy of Television Arts & Sciences (2011, 2014); SAG Award for Outstanding Performance by a Female Actor in a Drama Series, SAG-AFTRA (1998, 1999, 2009, 2010); Golden Globe Award for Best Performance by an Actress in a TV Series - Drama, Hollywood Foreign Press Association (2010); SAG Award for Outstanding Performance by an Ensemble in a Drama Series, Academy of Television Arts & Sciences (1996, 1997, 1998, 1999); Emmy Award for Best Supporting Actress - Drama, Academy of Television Arts & Sciences (1995); Star, Hollywood Walk of Fame

MARGULIES, STANLEY IRA, T: Radiologist **I:** Medicine & Health Care **DOB:** 01/06/1935 **PB:** Baltimore **SC:** MD/USA **PT:** Oscar Margulies; Anne (Hendin) Margulies **MS:** Married **SPN:** Jenny Cohen Pardo (11/27/1994); Karen Mintz (02/13/1962, Divorced 1991) **CH:** Robin Juenger **ED:** Fellow in Academy Radiology, National Institute of General Medical Sciences, U.S. Department of Health and Human Services (1966-1967); Fellow in Academy Radiology, Johns Hopkins Hospital and Johns Hopkins University, Baltimore, MD (1966-1967); Assistant Resident and Fellow in Radiology, Johns Hopkins Hospital and Johns Hopkins University, Baltimore, MD (1964-1967); Assistant Resident in Surgery, University Hospital Cleveland, Ohio (1961-1962); Intern, University Hospital Cleveland, Ohio (1960-1961); MD, Johns Hopkins University (1960); MA, Johns Hopkins University (1956); AB, Johns Hopkins University (1956) **CT:** Diplomate, American Board of Nuclear Medicine (ABNM), American Board of Radiology **C:** Retired (2002); Vice Presi-

dent of Radiology, InPhyNet Medical Management, Inc., Fort Lauderdale, FL (1995-1997); Radiologist, Memorial Hospital West (1992-1997); Radiologist, Memorial Hospital Pembroke, Pembroke Pines, FL (1975-1997); Radiologist, Chief of Radiology, Memorial Hospital and Memorial Healthcare Systems, Hollywood, FL (1972-1997); Radiologist, Hollywood Medical Center, FL (1974-1996); Clinical Associate Professor of Radiology, University of Miami Miller School of Medicine (1972-1974); Associate Professor of Radiology, Johns Hopkins Hospital, Baltimore, MD (1970-1972); Radiologist, Johns Hopkins Hospital, Baltimore, MD (1967-1972); Assistant Professor of Radiology, Johns Hopkins Hospital, Baltimore, MD (1969-1970); Instructor of Radiology, Johns Hopkins University School Medicine, Baltimore, MD (1967-1968) **CR:** Board of Governors, Florida Patient's Compensation Fund (1983-Present); Chair, Florida Patient's Compensation Fund (1996-2000); Vice Chair, Florida Patient's Compensation Fund (1990-1996); Member, Medical Radiation Advisory Committee, U.S. Department of Health & Human Services, Washington, DC (1982-1986); Medical Malpractice Insurance Advisory Council, State of Florida (1982-1983) **CIV:** Member, DPR's Volunteer Expert Witness Program (1993-Present); Board of Directors, Member, National Executive Committee, American Associates of Ben-Gurion University of the Negev, New York, NY (1979-Present); Broward Regional Health Planning Council, Inc., FL (1982-1993); District Representative for National Elections, Political Education Committee, Florida Medical Political Action Committee (1981-1992); Board of Directors, Statewide Health Council of Florida (1982-1990); Board of Directors, Jewish Federation of South Broward (1975-1988); Holocaust Memorial Center (1982-1987); Executive Committee, National Committee, American Israel Public Affairs Committee, Washington, (1981-1986); South Florida Blood Service (1982-1985); Campaign Cabinet, National Jewish Appeal (1976-1978) **MIL:** With, United States Navy (1962-1964) **MEM:** Chairman, Board of Directors, Cypress Savings Association (1981-1987); Fellow, American College of Radiology, Florida Chapter; American Medical Association; Radiological Society of North America; Radiological Alumni Association Johns (Now Johns Hopkins Alumni Association); Johns Hopkins Medical and Surgical Association (JHM&SA); Florida Medical Association; Cypress Savings Association; Board, Baptist Health System; Board, Florida Keys Jewish Community Center **MH:** Albert Nelson Marquis Lifetime Achievement Award **B/I:** Dr. Margulies became involved in his profession because from the time he was a child he always marveled at how important it was to provide healthcare for others and for oneself. As he became older, it became obvious to him that there was a way to do that and that was to be a participant in medical care, and because of that, he decided to go to medical school. He started off in surgery and then he began to look at what he wanted to do in his professional life; it became apparent to him that one of the great progresses in medicine was being made in radiological science. He decided he wanted to become a radiologist. In 1971, he started off in academics by taking a position as chief of radiology at Memorial Healthcare system. **RE:** Jewish

MARINO, THOMAS, "TOM" ANTHONY, T: Former U.S. Representative from Pennsylvania; Former Federal Prosecutor **I:** Government Administration/Government Relations/Government Services **DOB:** 08/13/1952 **PB:** Lycoming County **SC:** PA/USA **MS:** Married **SPN:** Edie Marino **CH:** Two Children **ED:** JD in Dickinson Law, The Pennsylvania State University, Carlisle, PA (1988); BA in Political Science and Education, Lycoming College, Williamsport, PA, Magna Cum Laude (1985); AA, Williamsport Area Community College (1983) **C:** Member, U.S. House of Representatives from Pennsylvania's 10th Pennsylvania Congressional District, U.S. Congress, Washington, DC (2011-2019); Member, U.S. House Judiciary Committee, Washington, DC (2011-2019); Member, U.S. House Homeland Security Committee, Washington, DC (2011-2019); Member, U.S. House Committee on Foreign Affairs, Washington, DC (2011-2019); Business Law Attorney, DeNaples Management (2007-2009); United States Attorney for the Middle District of Pennsylvania, U.S. Department of Justice, Philadelphia, PA (2002-2007); District Attorney, Lycoming County, PA (1996-2002); Associate, McNerney, Page, Vanderlin & Hall, Williamsport, PA (1988-1996) **PA:** Republican **RE:** Roman Catholic

MARK, ARTHUR, T: Emeritus Professor of Teacher Education **I:** Education/Educational Services **DOB:** 05/30/1930 **PB:** Boston **SC:** MA/USA **PT:** Charles Markovitz; Eva Markovitz **MS:** Married **SPN:** Cecile Druss Mark **CH:** Bonnie Eve Mark; Carolyn Mark **ED:** EdD, Teachers College, Columbia University (1973); MA, Teachers College, Columbia University (1956); BS in Education, University of Massachusetts Boston (1952) **CT:** Certified in Early Childhood and Elementary Education, Supervisor, Speech and Drama Programs, Grades Kindergarten Through Twelfth; Certified, Director, Administrator Kindergarten Through Ninth **C:** Professor Emeritus, East Stroudsburg University of Pennsylvania (1971-1989); Headmaster, The Long Ridge School (1969-1971); Director of Gifted and Talented Programs for Grades Four Through Nine, Elementary and Junior High Schools, Greenwich, CT (1953-1969) **CR:** Founder, President, Business and Industry for Arts in Education, New York, NY (1986-2000); Art Education Action; Association for Supervision and Curriculum Development; International Presentations on Arts in Education, Egypt, Japan, Netherlands; Founder, Pocono Arts Center **CIV:** Founder, Pocono Arts Council (1979-Present); Founder, President, Monroe County Museum Association (1977-1979); School Board Candidate, Democratic Party, Westport, CT (1968) **MIL:** Active Member, Active Reserve Member, United States Army (1948-1954) **CW:** Author, "Two Libertarian Educators: Elizabeth and Alexis Ferm" Teachers College, Columbia University (1973); Author, "Integrating Arts into K-6 Curriculum"; Author, "Architecture Field Trips in the Community"; Creator, International Symposium, The Renaissance of Cities, Royal Society of Arts **AW:** Honorary Mayor, State of Louisiana Governor's Award for Business and Industry for the Arts in Education, City of Baton Rouge, LA **MEM:** Founder, Arts in Education Network, Association for Supervision and Curriculum Development (1979-Present); International Chair, Project Milestone, Teachers College, Columbia University (1971-1972); World Council for Curriculum and Instruction; Association of Pennsylvania State College and University Faculties; American Association of College and University Professors; Brown University Faculty Club; Westminster Unitarian Church Congregation **MH:** Albert Nelson Marquis Lifetime Achievement Award; Marquis Who's Who Top Professional **B/I:** Dr. Mark became involved in his profession because of his love of theater. After the sudden death of his father, he put his dreams of being an actor to the side and began focusing on teaching instead. **AV:** Singing; Painting; Acting; Reading poetry; Writing **PA:** Democrat **RE:** Unitarian Universalist

MARKEY, EDWARD, "ED" JOHN, T: U.S. Senator from Massachusetts **I:** Government Administration/Government Relations/Government Services

DOB: 07/11/1946 **PB:** Malden **SC:** MA/USA **PT:** John E. Markey; Christine M. Markey **MS:** Married **SPN:** Susan J. Blumenthal (1988) **ED:** JD, Boston College Law School (1972); BA, Boston College (1968) **C:** Member, U.S. Senate Environment and Public Works Committee (2014-Present); U.S. Senator, Commonwealth of Massachusetts (2013-Present); Member, U.S. Senate Small Business and Entrepreneurship (2013-Present); Member, U.S. Senate Foreign Relations Committee (2013-Present); Member, U.S. Senate Commerce, Science and Transportation Committee (2013-Present); Member, U.S. House of Representatives from Massachusetts' Fifth Congressional District, United States Congress (2013); Member, U.S. House of Representatives from Massachusetts' Seventh Congressional District, United States Congress (1976-2013); Chairman, U.S. House of Energy, Independence and Global Warming Committee (2007-2011); Member, District 16, Massachusetts House of Representatives (1973-1976) **CIV:** With, United States Army Reserve (1968-1973) **CW:** Member, Editorial Staff, Boston College Law Review **AW:** Named Massachusetts Legislator of the Year, Massachusetts Bar Association (1975) **MEM:** Massachusetts Bar Association; Knights of Columbus **BAR:** Commonwealth of Massachusetts **PA:** Democrat **RE:** Roman Catholic

MARONE, RICHARD ANTHONY, ESQ., T: Partner **I:** Law and Legal Services **CN:** Murtha Cullina LLP **DOB:** 05/08/1956 **PB:** New York **SC:** NY/USA **PT:** Anthony V. Marone; Jean H. (Schmidt) Marone **MS:** Married **SPN:** Sandra J. Marone **CH:** Katherine L. Marone; Elizabeth A. Marone **ED:** LLM in Taxation, Boston University (1990); JD, College of William and Mary (1981); BA in Politics, Fairfield University, Magna Cum Laude (1978) **C:** Chair, Trusts and Estates Department, Murtha Cullina LLP (2015-Present); Partner, Murtha Cullina LLP (2000-Present); Principal, Marone & Messina, P.C.(1988-2000); National Design Attorney, CIGNA Corporation (1985-1988); Associate Attorney, Pullman & Comley LLC (1981-1985) **CR:** Fellow, The American College of Trust and Estate Counsel (2001-Present); Connecticut State Chair, The American College of Trust and Estate Counsel (2010-2015); Connecticut Bar Association; High Net Worth Individual, Chambers & Partners; AV-Preeminent Rating, Martindale-Hubbell; Connecticut Super Lawyer; Best Lawyers in America in Trusts and Estates **CIV:** Finance Council, Holy Family Passionist Retreat Center; Former Chair, Library Board, Town of West Hartford; Former Member, , West Hartford Library Foundation; Former President, The Church of St. Timothy; Former Co-Chair, The Church of St. Timothy; Former Grand Knight, Council 3,600, Knights of Columbus; Former President, Rotary Club of Farmington; Former Member, Rotary Club of West Hartford; Former Member, Professional Advisory Committee, Hartford Foundation for Public Giving **CW:** Speaker, "What Are We Doing in Response to the American Taxpayer Relief Act?" New England Regional Meeting, The American College of Trusts and Estates Counsel (2013); Author, "Firms Turn To Video To Tout Practice Areas," Connecticut Law Tribune (2013); Author, Chapter, "Life Insurance and Estate Planning," "A Practical Guide to Estate Planning in Connecticut, Volume II of II," MCLE New England (2013) **MEM:** Former Director, Limestone Trout Club; Former President, Alumni Club of Hartford, Fairfield University **BAR:** Connecticut Bar Association; Massachusetts Bar Association; United States Court of Federal Claims; United States Tax Court; United States District Court District of Connecticut **AS:** Mr. Marone attributes his success to his ability to listen very well and advise his clients holistically. **B/I:** Mr. Marone became involved in

his profession because he enjoyed the impact that kind of work had on clients. He enjoys helping his clients take care of their families. **AV:** Singing in chorus; Playing guitar; Trout fishing; Cycling; Running; Taking photographs; Woodworking; Grilling **RE:** Roman Catholic **THT:** Mr. Marone believes, "Respect everyone and don't assume you have the only point of view on everything."

MARQUIS, BARBARA S., RN, BS, T: Maternal and Women's Health Nurse **I:** Medicine & Health Care **DOB:** 11/11/1937 **PB:** Benton **SC:** IL/USA **PT:** Haskell C. Boaz; Zetta Ruth (Martin) Boaz **MS:** Married **SPN:** Paul R. Marquis (09/06/1958) **CH:** Michael; Carol; Lisa **ED:** BS, University of St. Francis (1980); Diploma, DePaul Hospital, SSM Health (1958) **CT:** Registered Nurse **C:** Prior Authorization Case Manager, Health Choice Arizona (1994-Present); MCH Coordinator, Health Choice Arizona (1990-1994); Home Perinatal Nurse, CareLink Corporation (1989-1990); Maternal Transport Nurse, Head Nurse of Labor and Delivery, St. Joseph's Hospital and Medical Center (1984-1989); Head Nurse for Labor and Delivery, Obstetrics and Gynecological Surgery Division, Maricopa Medical Center, Maricopa Integrated Health System (1977-1983); Night Supervisor, Maricopa Medical Center, Maricopa Integrated Health System (1975-1977); Night Staff Nurse, Night Charge Nurse for Labor and Delivery, Maricopa Medical Center, Maricopa Integrated Health System (1973-1975); Staff Nurse for Labor and Delivery, Naval Medical Center Camp Lejeune (1971-1973); Staff Nurse, Relief Charge Nurse for Labor and Delivery, St. Joseph's Hospital (1968-1969); Staff Nurse for Labor and Delivery, Naval Medical Center Camp Lejeune (1963-1967); Staff Nurse, Relief Evening Supervisor, Franklin Hospital (1961-1962); Various Nursing Positions (1958-1960) **CR:** Consultant in Field; Expert Witness in Field; Case Reviewer **MEM:** Vice Chairman, District VIII, Nurses Association, American College of Obstetricians and Gynecologists (1985-Present); Chairman, Arizona Section, Nurses Association, American College of Obstetricians and Gynecologists (1981-1983); Vice Chairman, Arizona Section, Nurses Association, American College of Obstetricians and Gynecologists (1979-1980); Publicity Conference Chairman, District VIII, Nurses Association, American College of Obstetricians and Gynecologists (1976); Arizona League for Nursing; Advisory Board Member, Healthy Mothers Healthy Babies **MH:** Albert Nelson Marquis Lifetime Achievement Award; Marquis Who's Who Top Professional; Marquis Who's Who Humanitarian Award **B/I:** Ms. Marquis became involved in her profession because of her lifelong desire to be a nurse. At the age of 5, she would stand in the kitchen with her mother and father pretending to make medicine. **AV:** Walking with her husband; Going to the gym; Staying active; Collecting brand name beverage merchandise

MARROW, TRACY, "ICE-T" LAUREN, T: Rap Artist; Actor **I:** Media & Entertainment **DOB:** 02/16/1958 **PB:** Newark **SC:** NJ/USA **PT:** Solomon Morrow; Alice Morrow **MS:** Married **SPN:** Nicole "Coco" Austin (12/31/2005) **CH:** Chanel Nicole; Tracy Jr.; Letesha **MIL:** 25th Infantry Division, United States Army (1977-1979) **CW:** Actor, "Law and Order: Special Victims Unit" (2000-Present); Rap Artist, "Carnivore" (2020); Appearance, "Celebrity Ghost Stories" (2020); Voice Actor, "Ugly Dolls" (2019); Appearance, Executive Producer, "Public Enemy Number One" (2019); Appearance, "Golden Revenge" (2019); Appearance, "Saturday Night Live" (2019); Rap Artist, "Criminal Vortex" (2018); Actor, "Bloodrunners" (2017); Rap Artist, "Bloodlust" (2017); Actor, "How We Met" (2016); Actor, "What Now" (2015); Co-Host, Executive Producer, "Ice and Coco" (2015); Actor, "The Ghetto" (2015); Actor, "Chicago P.D." (2014-2015); Rap Artist with Body Count, "Manslaughter" (2014); Actor, "Crossed the Line" (2014); Actor, "Santorini Blue" (2013); Actor, "Once Upon a Time in Brooklyn" (2013); Co-Author, "Mirror Image" (2013); Actor, "The Passions of Jesus Christ" (2012); Executive Producer, "Something from Nothing: The Art of Rap" (2012); Executive Producer, "Iceberg Slim: Portrait of a Pimp" (2012); Actor, "30 Rock" (2011-2013); Reality TV Personality, Executive Producer, "Ice Loves Coco" (2011-2013); Executive Producer, "Planet Rock: The Story of Hip-Hop and the Crack Generation" (2011); Author, "Ice: A Memoir of Gangster Life and Redemption: From South Central to Hollywood" (2011); Actor, "Good Hair" (2009); Executive Producer, "25 to Life: Ice T Presents" (2008); Rap Artist, "Urban Legends" (2008); Rap Artist, "Murder 4 Hire" (2006); Rap Artist, "Gangsta Rap" (2006); Rap Artist, "Repossession" (2004); Rap Artist, "Gang Culture" (2004); Actor, "On the Edge" (2002); Actor, "Tracks" (2002); Actor, "Stranded" (2001); Actor, "Kept" (2001); Actor, "Crime Partners" (2001); Actor, "3000 Miles to Graceland" (2001); Actor, "Point Doom" (2001); Rap Artist, "Greatest Hits: The Evidence" (2001); Actor, "Deadly Rhapsody" (2001); Actor, "'R Xmas" (2001); Actor, "Ticker" (2001); Actor, "Out Kold" (2001); Actor, "Ablaze" (2001); Actor, "Guardian" (2000); Actor, "Gangland" (2000); Actor, "Luck of the Draw" (2000); Actor, "The Alternates" (2000); Rap Artist, "Pimp to Eat" (2000); Rap Artist, "WWW Aggression" (2000); Actor, "The Disciples" (2000); Actor, "Final Voyage" (1999); Rap Artist, "The Seventh Deadly Sin" (1999); Actor, "Corrupt" (1999); Actor, "The Wrecking Crew" (1999); Actor, "Sonic Impact" (1999); Actor, "The Heist" (1999); Actor, "Frezno Smooth" (1999); Actor, "Urban Menace" (1999); Actor, "Stealth Fighter" (1999); Actor, "Exiled" (1998); Actor, "Crazy Six" (1998); Actor, "Players" (1997-1998); Rap Artist, "$port Ya Vest in the West" (1997); Rap Artist with Body Count, "Violent Demise: The Last Days" (1997); Actor, "Mean Guns" (1997); Actor, "The Deli" (1997); Actor, "Beyond Utopia" (1997); Rap Artist, "Ice-T VI: Return of the Real" (1996); Rap Artist, "Murder Squad Nationwide" (1995); Actor, "Tank Girl" (1995); Actor, "Johnny Mnemonic" (1995); Actor, "Surviving the Game" (1994); Author, "The Ice Opinion" (1994); Rap Artist with Body Count, "Born Dead" (1994); Rap Artist, "Home Invasion" (1993); Actor, "Trespass" (1992); Actor, "Why Colors?" (1992); Rap Artist with Body Count, "Body Count" (1992); Rap Artist with King Tee, "Havin' a T Party" (1991); Actor, "New Jack City" (1991); Actor, "Ricochet" (1991); Rap Artist, "O.G. Original Gangster" (1991); Rap Artist, "The Iceberg/Freedom of Speech...Just Watch What You Say" (1989); Author, "The Iceberg/Freedom of Speech, Just Watch What You Say" (1989); Rap Artist, "Power" (1988); Rap Artist, "Rhyme Syndicate Comin' Through" (1988); Rap Artist, "Rhyme Pays" (1987); Actor, "Breakin'" (1984); Actor, "Breakin' 2" (1984); Rap Artist, "Breaking and Entering" (1983); Rap Artist, Milutiple Solo and Collaborative Albums **AW:** Awards for Outstanding Supporting Actor in a Drama Series, NAACP Image Awards (1996, 2002); Grammy Award for Best Rap Performance by a Duo or Group, The Recording Academy (1991)

MARS, BRUNO, T: Singer, Songwriter, Music Producer **I:** Media & Entertainment **DOB:** 10/08/1985 **PB:** Honolulu **SC:** HI/USA **PT:** Peter Hernandez; Bernadette (San Pedro Bayot) Hernandez **C:** Member, Production Team, The Smeezingtons (2009-2015) **CIV:** Established, Grammy Camp Scholarship Fund, Hawaii Community Foundation and Grammy Foundation (2014); Performer, Benefit Concerts **CW:** Singer with Cardi B, "Finesse" (2018); Singer, "24K Magic" (2016); Singer, "That's What I Like" (2016); Singer with Mark Ronson, "Uptown Funk" (2014); Voice Actor, "Rio 2" (2014); Performer, Super Bowl XLVIII Half-time Show (2014); Singer, "Locked Out of Heaven" (2013); Singer, "Treasure" (2013); Singer, "Unorthodox Jukebox" (2012); Singer, "The Lazy Song" (2011); Singer, "Let It Rain" (2011); Singer with Various Artists, "The Twilight Saga: Breaking Dawn - Part 1 Original Motion Picture Soundtrack" (2011); Singer, "Doo-Wops & Hooligans" (2010); Singer, "Just the Way You Are" (2010); Singer, "Grenade" (2010); Co-writer, Guest Vocalist with B.o.B, "Nothin' on You" (2010); Co-writer, Guest Vocalist with Travie McCoy, "Billionaire" (2010); Appearance, "Honeymoon in Vegas" (1992); Appearances, Television Shows; Singer, Songwriter, Solo and Collaborations **AW:** Named to Celebrity 100 List, Forbes Magazine (2018, 2019); Award for Favorite Song - Soul/R&B, American Music Awards (2018); Awards for Artist of the Year, Favorite Pop/Rock, Favorite Soul/R&B, Favorite Pop/Rock Song, Favorite Soul/Rock, Video of the Year, American Music Awards (2017); Awards for Best Male R&B/ Pop Artist, Video of the Year, BET Awards (2017); Winner, 14 ASCAP Pop Music Awards (2011-2017); Grammy Awards for Record of the Year, Best Pop Duo/Group Performance, Best Remixed Recording, Non-Classical, The Recording Academy (2016); Award for Best Male Video, MTV Video Music Awards (2015); Grammy Award for Best Pop Vocal Album, The Recording Academy (2014); Awards for Best Male Video, Best Choreography, MTV Video Music Awards (2013); Named Favorite Male Artist, People's Choice Awards (2012); Award for Favorite Pop/Rock Male Artist, American Music Awards (2011); Named One of the 100 Most Influential People in the World, TIME Magazine (2011); Grammy Award for Best Male Pop Vocal Performance, The Recording Academy (2011); Award for Top Radio Song, Billboard Music Awards (2011); Award for Song of the Year, Soul Train Music Awards (2010); Numerous Awards

MARSH, ROBERT BUFORD, T: Chemical Engineer, Consultant **I:** Engineering **DOB:** 11/16/1946 **PB:** Chicago **SC:** IL/USA **PT:** Ivar Buford Marsh; Blanche Julien (Morrisette) Marsh **MS:** Married **SPN:** Claudia Ann Werner (2/14/1970) **CH:** Julie Ann; Kristy Louise **ED:** BSChemE, Michigan Technological University (1968) **CT:** Registered Professional Engineer, Massachusetts **C:** President, Marsh Engineer, Inc., Andover, MA (1992-2019); Worldwide Plasticizer Technology Expert, Engineering Specialist, Monsanto, Everett, Indian Orchard, MA (1992-1993); Manufacturing Technology Specialist, Monsanto, Everett, MA (1986-1991); Environmental Engineer, Monsanto, Everett, MA (1984-1985); Manufacturing Supervisor, Monsanto, Everett, MA (1978-1983); Lustrex Supervisor, Monsanto, Long Beach, CA (1973-1978); Technology Service Engineer, Chevron Research, Richmond, CA (1970-1973); Engineer 1 Design Engineer, Chevron Research, Richmond, CA (1968-1970) **CR:** Consultant, Shawsheen Environmental Action (2005-Present); Compliance Coordinator, Board of Directors, Shawsheen River Watershed Association (1999-Present); Toxic Use Reduction Planner (1994-2005); Environmental Instructor, University of Massachusetts (1994); Consultant, EPA Research Grant (1994); Consultant, Massachusetts Department of Environmental Protection, Lowell, MA (1993-1994); Chairman, Footbridge Committee, Shawsheen Flooding Committee, Andover Trails Committee **CIV:** President, Shawsheen River Watershed Association (2018-Present); Board of Directors, Shawsheen River Watershed Association (2005-Present); Compliance Director, Shawsheen River Watershed Association (2004-Present); Shawsheen River Watershed Association (2003-Present); Volunteer, Lawrence School System (2019-2020); Election Committee, State Senator, L'ltalien (2012-2018); Election Committee, State Senator Tucker (2010-2018); Election Committee, State Senator O'Brien Committee (2000-2010); Compliance Contact, Shawsheen River Watershed Association (1994-2007); Volunteer, Chicopee River Watershed Association, Springfield, MA (2004); Advisory Committee, Leady Junior Achievement, Long Beach, CA (1975-1977) **MEM:** Shawsheen River Watershed Association; Andover Village Improvement Society **AS:** Mr. Marsh attributes his success to his high school teacher, Mr. Fruicci, who taught chemistry. Another positive influence was Charles Weingartner, Mr. Marsh's boss at Monsanto. He inspired Mr. Marsh to have confidence. **B/I:** When Mr. Marsh was a teenager, his father got laid off, and his family was worried about the future. Mr. Marsh decided then that he would become an engineer because it paid well. He didn't want to be a lawyer because of the ethical dilemma or a doctor because of the long hours. He chose chemical engineering because his favorite course in high school was chemistry. He loved working with chemicals and completing experiments. **PA:** Independent **RE:** Methodist

MARSHALL, ROGER WAYNE, MD, T: U.S. Representative from Kansas **I:** Government Administration/Government Relations/Government Services **CN:** U.S. House of Representatives **DOB:** 08/09/1960 **PB:** El Dorado **SC:** KS/USA **MS:** Married **SPN:** Laina Marshall (1983) **CH:** Four Children **ED:** Doctor of Medicine, University of Kansas School of Medicine (1987); Bachelor of Science in Biochemistry, Kansas State University; Associate of Science, Butler Community College (1980); Resident in Obstetrics and Gynecology, Bayfront Medical Center, St. Petersburg, FL **C:** Member, U.S. Representative from Kansas' First Congressional District (2017-Present); Member, Committee on Agriculture; Member, Committee on Science, Space and Technology; Member, Committee on Small Business **CIV:** Chairperson, Board of Directors, Great Bend Regional Hospital **MIL:** Advanced through Grades to Captain, United States Army Reserve (1984-1991) **MEM:** District Governor, Rotary International

MARSHALL, VINCENT DEPAUL, PHD, T: Microbiologist **I:** Sciences **DOB:** 04/05/1943 **PB:** Washington **SC:** DC/USA **PT:** Vincent dePaul Marshall Sr.; Mary Frances (Bach) Marshall **MS:** Married **SPN:** Sylvia Ann Kieffer (11/15/1986) **CH:** Vincent dePaul III; Amy **ED:** PhD, University of Oklahoma Health Sciences Center, Oklahoma City, OK (1970); MS, University of Oklahoma Health Sciences Center, Oklahoma City, OK (1967); BS, Northeastern State College (Now Northeastern State University), Tahlequah, OK (1965) **C:** Senior Scientist, The Upjohn Company (Upjohn Pharmacia), Kalamazoo, MI (1991-2000); Senior Research Scientist, The Upjohn Company, Kalamazoo, MI (1976-1991); Research Head, The Upjohn Company, Kalamazoo, MI (1975); Research Scientist, The Upjohn Company, Kalamazoo, MI (1973-1974); Postdoctoral Fellow, University of Illinois at Urbana-Champaign (1971-1973); Research Associate, University of Illinois at Urbana-Champaign (1970) **MIL:** Served, United States Army National Guard (1960-1965) **CW:** Member, Editorial Board, Journal of Antibiotics (1990-2001); Member, Editorial Board, Journal of Industrial Microbiology (1989-2001); Member, Editorial Board, Developments in Industrial Microbiology (1990); Contributor, Numerous Articles to Professional Journals; Contributor, Chapters to Books; Patentee in Field **AW:** National Institutes of Health Postdoctoral Fellow (1971-1973); National

Institutes of Health Predoctoral Fellow (1967-1970) **MEM:** Nominating Committee, Society for Industrial Microbiology & Biotechnology (1999-2000); Co-chair, Program Committee, Society for Industrial Microbiology & Biotechnology; Director, Society for Industrial Microbiology & Biotechnology (1994-1996); Local Sections Committee, Society for Industrial Microbiology & Biotechnology (1991-1996); President, Southern Great Lakes Section, Society for Industrial Microbiology & Biotechnology (1992-1995); Industrial Microbiology & Biotechnology (1993-1994); Chair, Nominating Committee, Society for Industrial Microbiology & Biotechnology (1993-1994); Membership Committee, Society for Industrial Microbiology (Now Society for Industrial Microbiology & Biotechnology) (1988-1990); Fellow, The American Academy for Microbiology; American Society for Microbiology; American Society for Biochemistry and Molecular Biology; Science Advisory Board, International Society for Antimicrobial Activity of Non-Antibiotics; Sigma Xi, The Scientific Research Honor Society **MH:** Albert Nelson Marquis Lifetime Achievement Award **B/I:** Dr. Marshall is a first-generation scientist; he was interested in going to medical school and then he became more interested in science, so he attended undergraduate school at Northeastern State College. From there, he attended Oklahoma Health Science in Oklahoma City to receive his master's degree and PhD in science. **PA:** Republican **RE:** Lutheran

MARTER, JOAN M., PHD, T: Distiguished Professor Emerita, Art Critic and Curator **I:** Education/Educational Services **CN:** Rutgers, The State University of New Jersey **DOB:** 08/13/1946 **PB:** Philadelphia **SC:** PA/USA **MS:** Married **SPN:** Walter Marter **CH:** Julia M. Collision **ED:** PhD, University of Delaware, Newark, DE (1974); MA, University of Delaware, Newark, DE (1970); BA in Art History, Temple University, Philadelphia, PA, Magna Cum Laude (1968) **C:** Distinguished Professor Emerita, Rutgers, the State University of New Jersey, New Brunswick, NJ (2016-Present); Distinguished Professor, Rutgers, The State University of New Jersey, New Brunswick, NJ (2000-2016); Director, Curatorial Studies Program, Rutgers, the State University of New Jersey, New Brunswick, NJ (1990-2016); Professor II, Department of Art History, Rutgers, the State University of New Jersey, New Brunswick, NJ (2000-2012); Director, Graduate Studies, Rutgers, the State University of New Jersey, New Brunswick, NJ (1994-1997); Professor of Art History, Rutgers, the State University of New Jersey, New Brunswick, NJ (1980-1989); Assistant Professor of Art History, Rutgers, the State University of New Jersey, New Brunswick, NJ (1977-1989); Assistant Professor, Sweet Briar College, Virginia (1974-1977); Instructor, Pennsylvania State University, University Park, PA (1970-1973) **CR:** Editor-in-Chief, Woman's Art Journal (2006-Present); Guest Curator, Numerous Exhibitions, Museums and Institutions **CIV:** President, Dorothy Dehner Foundation **CW:** Editor, Woman's Art Journal (2006-Present); Author, "Women Artists on the Leading Edge: Visual Arts at Douglass College" (2019); Guest Curator, "Abstract Expressionism Revisited," Guild Hall Museum, East Hampton, NY (2019); Editor, Essayist, "Women of Abstract Expressionism" (2016); Author, "Der Abstrakte Expressionismus und seine eruopaischen Wurzeln," Phanomen Expressionismus (2012); Author, "Nancy Holt and the '90s Reclamation Revival," The New Earthwork, Art, Agency, Action (2012); Editor-in-Chief, "Grove Encyclopedia of American Art" (2011); Author, "Artist-Endowed Foundations: Archives, Access, and Scholarship," The Artist as Philanthropist (2010); Author, "Critical Writing on Feminist Topics," Blaze: Discourse on Art, Women,

and Feminism (2008); Editor, "Abstract Expressionism, The International Context" (2007); Author, "Arcadian Nightmares: The Evolution of David Smith and Dorothy Dehner's Work in Bolton Landing," Reading Abstract Expressionism: Context and Critique (2005); Contributor, "American Sculpture in The Metropolitan Museum of Art, Volume II" (2001); Editor, Principal Essayist, "Off Limits: Rutgers University and the Avant-Garde, 1957-1963" (1999); Author, "Theodore Roszak, The Drawings" (1992); Author, "Alexander Calder" (1991); Co-Organizer, "Design in America, The Cranbrook Vision 1925-1950," National Endowment for the Humanities, National Endowment for the Arts, The Detroit Institute of Arts (1983-1984); Author, "Jose de Rivera Constructions" (1980); Co-Author, "Vanguard American Sculpture 1913-1939" (1979); Author, Co-Author, Numerous Chapters and Essays, Books; Author, Co-Author, Numerous Essays, Museum Publications; Author, Co-Author, Contributor, Numerous Professional Journals; Author, Co-Author, Contributor, Numerous Book and Exhibition Reviews; Presenter, Contributor, Numerous Selected Public Lectures; Author, Contributor, Numerous Chapters and Essays, Books; Author, Essays, Numerous Museum Publications; Organizer, Numerous Exhibitions **AW:** Distinguished Feminist Award, College Art Association of America (2017); Outstanding Reference Source Award for "Grove Encyclopedia of American Art," American Library Association: Reference and User Services Association (2011); Lifetime Achievement Award, National Women's Caucus for Art (2011); Joseph G. Astman Distinguished Symposium Scholar, Hofstra University, Hempstead, NY (2009); Research Council Grants, Rutgers University (2002-2006); University of Delaware Alumni Wall of Fame for Distinguished Graduates (2004); Library Research Grant, The Getty Research Institute (2002); Graduate Teaching Award, Northeastern Association of Graduate Schools (1999); Research Council Grants, Rutgers University (1977-1999); Graduate Teaching Excellence Award, Rutgers, The State University of New Jersey (1998); Jane and Morgan Whitney Senior Fellowship, Metropolitan Museum of Art (1997-1998); Diamond Achievement Award in the Humanities, Temple University (1993); John Sloan Foundation Grant (1989-1990); George Wittenborn Award, Art Libraries Society of North America (1985); Charles F. Montgomery Prize, Decorative Arts Society of the Society of Architectural Historians (1984); Research Council Summer Fellowship, Rutgers University (1978); Research Council Summer Fellowship, Rutgers University (1978); Travel Grant, National Endowment for the Humanities (1976); Chester Dale Fellowship, National Gallery of Art, Washington, DC (1973-1974); Unidel Fellowship, University of Delaware (1969-1972) **MEM:** Art Table (2000-Present); American Section, International Association of Art Critics (1981-Present); National Member, Women's Caucus for Art (1970-Present); College Art Association of America (1969-Present); National Advisory Board, Women's Caucus for Art (1984-1987); New Jersey Chapter Advisory Board, Women's Caucus for Art (1982-1983); Member, New York Chapter Advisory Board, Women's Caucus for Art (1978-1981) **MH:** Albert Nelson Marquis Lifetime Achievement Award **B/I:** Dr. Marter became involved in her profession because, despite being an art student, she had never studied art history until she discovered it while attending Temple University. She quickly realized that she had a passion for the field and decided to pursue teaching art history instead of art classes. Her studies coincided with the transformative feminist movement.

MARTIN, CALIA MARSAI, T: Producer, Actress **I:** Media & Entertainment **DOB:** 08/14/2004 **PB:** Little Elm **SC:** TX/USA **PT:** Joshua Martin; Carol Martin **MS:** Single **CW:** Actress, "Black-ish" (2014-Present); Actress, "DreamWorks Dragons: Rescue Riders" (2019-2020); Guest Appearance, "Vampirina" (2019); Guest Appearance, "Mixed-ish" (2019); Actress, Executive Producer, "Little" (2019); Voice Actress, "Elena of Avalor" (2016-2019); Guest Appearance, "Unbreakable Kimmy Schmidt" (2018); Actress, "Lemonade Mafia" (2017); Actress, "Fun Mom Dinner" (2017); Actress, "An American Girl Story - Melody 1963: Love Has to Win" (2016); Actress, "Nina" (2016); Guest Appearance, "The Mr. Peabody and Sherman Show" (2016); Actress, "Goldie & Bear" (2015-2016); Actress, "Amari and the Night Brothers" **AW:** NAACP Image Award for Outstanding Supporting Actress in a Motion Picture, Outstanding Breakthrough Performance in Motion Picture, "Little," NAACP Image Awards (2020); Outstanding Supporting Actress in a Comedy Series, Outstanding Performance by a Youth (Series, Special, Television Movie or Mini-series), "Black-ish," NAACP Image Awards (2019-2020); Phenom Award - Entertainment, Shorty Awards (2019); YoungStars Award, BET Awards (2019); Best Acting, "Melody 1963: Love Has to Win," Kidscreen Awards (2018); Outstanding Supporting Actress in a Comedy Series, "Black-ish," NAACP Image Awards (2016, 2018); Outstanding Performance by a Youth (Series, Special, Television Movie or Mini-series), "Black-ish," NAACP Image Awards (2017); Best Performance in a TV Series - Supporting Young Actress, "Black-ish," Young Artist Awards (2016)

MARTIN, GEORGE RAYMOND RICHARD, T: Author **I:** Writing and Editing **DOB:** 09/20/1948 **PB:** Bayonne **SC:** NJ/USA **PT:** Raymond Collins Martin; Margaret (Brady) Martin **MS:** Married **SPN:** Parris McBride (02/15/2011); Gale Burnick (11/15/1975, Divorced 1979) **ED:** Journalism Intern, Medill News Service, Washington, DC (1971); MS in Journalism, Northwestern University, Cum Laude (1971); BS in Journalism, Northwestern University, Summa Cum Laude (1970) **C:** Writer-in-Residence, Clarke College (Now Clarke University), Dubuque, Iowa (1978-1979); Instructor of Journalism, Clarke College (Now Clarke University), Dubuque, Iowa (1976-1978); Founder, Chairman, Windy City Science Fiction Writers' Workshop, Chicago, IL (1972-1976); Communications & Education Coordinator, Cook County Legal Assistance Foundation, Chicago, IL (1972-1974); Sportswriter, Public Relations Officer, New Jersey Department of Parks, Bayonne, NJ (1971) **CIV:** Established, The Miskatonic Scholarship (2017); Fundraiser, Wild Spirit Wolf Sanctuary, Food Depot of Santa Fe (2014) **CW:** Editor, Contributor, Numerous Volumes, Science Fiction and Superhero Anthology Series, "Wild Cards" (1987-Present); Writer, Producer, Co-Creator, "Game of Thrones," HBO (2011-2019); Author, "Fire & Blood" (2018); Executive Producer, "Nightflyers" (2018); Author, "The Sons of the Dragon" (2017); Author, "A Knight of the Seven Kingdoms" (2015); Co-Editor, "Rogues" (2014); Author, "Feast Crows" (2014); Author, "The World of Ice & Fire: The Untold History of Westeros and the Game of Thrones" (2014); Author, "A Dance with Dragons" (2011); Author, "Starlady/Fast-Friend" (2008); Author, "Hunter's Run" (2008); Author, "Dreamsongs: A Retrospective" (2007); Author, "The Ice Dragon" (2006); Author, "Shadow Twin" (2005); Author, "A Feast for Crows" (2005); Author, "GRRM: A RRetrospective" (2003); Author, "Quartet" (2001); Author, "A Storm of Swords" (2000); Author, "A Clash of Kings" (1998); Author, "A Game of Thrones: A Song of Ice and Fire" Series (1996); Co-Author, "Dead Man's Hand" (1990); Writer, Producer, "Beauty and the Beast" (1987-1990); Author, "Tuf Voyaging" (1987); Author, "Portraits of His Children" (1987); Writer, Story Editor, "The Twilight Zone" (1986); Author, "Nightflyers" (1985); Author, "Songs the Dead Men Sing" (1983); Author, "The Armageddon Rag" (1983); Author, "Fevre Dream" (1982); Author, "Windhaven" (1981); Author, "Sandkings" (1981); Author, "Songs of Stars and Shadows" (1977); Author, "Dying of the Light" (1977); Author, "A Song for Lya" (1976); Contributor, Numerous Works, Short Fiction and Essays, Anthologies, Science Fiction and Fantasy Publications; Appearances, Television Shows and Films **AW:** Inductee, New Jersey Hall of Fame (2019); Post International Recognition Award (2019); Primetime Emmy for Outstanding Drama Series, Academy of Television Arts & Sciences (2015-2016, 2018); Listee, 10 Most Fascinating People of 2014, Barbara Walters Special (2014); Hugo Awards (1975, 1980, 1997, 2012, 2013); World Fantasy Award for Life Achievement (2012); Listee, 100 Most Influential People in the World, Time Magazine (2011); Premio Ignotus Awards (2003, 2004, 2006); Locus Fantasy Award (1997, 1999, 2001); Recipient, Numerous Awards **MEM:** Vice President, Science Fiction & Fantasy Writers of America, South Central (1996-1998); Regional Director, Science Fiction & Fantasy Writers of America, South Central (1977-1979); Writers' Guild of America West; Science Fiction & Fantasy Writers of America, South Central

MARTIN, HULBERT, "HUGH", T: Author, Educator, Investment Advisor, Life Guide **I:** Education/Educational Services **CN:** Hugh Martin & Co.; Animal Kingdom (AK) Language Arts; Skirvana Crossword Games; The Human Odyssey Counseling; Hugh4Success, Your Other Dad **DOB:** 08/31/1939 **PB:** Chicago **SC:** IL/USA **PT:** Charles Francis Martin; Elizabeth Louise (Wyant) Martin **MS:** Married **SPN:** Bonita Jean Felgenhauer (06/1967, Divorced 08/1972); Susan Preston Martin (06/1962, Divorced 08/1966) **CH:** Jennifer Andrea Martin Borja; Naomi Elizabeth Martin Johnson; Amalia Jude Martin Dobbins; Rebecca Celeste Martin; Joshua James Martin; Samuel Wyant Martin; Olivia Gabrielle Martin **ED:** Degree in Teaching Elementary Education, University of California Berkeley (1969); Doctorate, Indiana University (1964); MA, University of Pennsylvania (1962); BA, Swarthmore College (1961) **CT:** Certified Life and Success Coach; Certified Financial Planner **C:** President, Chief Executive Officer, 'Hugh4Success' & 'YourOtherDad': Success and Life Counseling (2006-Present); President, Chief Executive Officer, Animal Kingdom Language Arts (2002-Present); President, Chief Executive Officer, Hugh Martin Securities (FINRA), San Anselmo, CA (1978-2013); President, Chief Executive Officer, Hugh Martin Investment Advisory (SEC), San Anselmo, CA (1978-2013); Financial Authority, Numerous Television and Radio Talk Programs (1972-1999); Featured Speaker, Conferences of the International Association of Financial Planners (1978-1987); Instructor, Investment Finance, Foothill and DeAnza Colleges, Palo Alto, CA (1974-1987); Accountant Executive, Blyth Eastman Dillon, San Francisco, CA (1976-1978); Accountant Executive, Reynolds Securities, Oakland, CA (1974-1976); Master Teacher, Demonstration Classroom, Oakland Public Schools, Oakland, CA (1970-1974); Primary Grade Teacher, Oakland Public Schools, Oakland, CA (1969-1974); Initial Development, Animal Kingdom Language Arts Curriculum, Berkeley, CA (1966-1974); Primary Grade Teacher, Administrator, Magic Child Charter School, Kensington, CA (1966-1968); Writing and Critical Thinking Instructor, Indiana University, Bloomington, IN (1962-1964); Civil Rights Voter Registration Coordinator, Congress on Racial Equality, Plaquemine, Los Angeles, CA (1963) **CR:**

Author, Educator, Integral Theorist, Life Guide (2002-Present); Investment Advisor, Financial Authority (1972-2013); Teacher (1961-1974); Professor Investment Finance Foothill, DeAnza Colleges, IAFP Finance Conferences, Featured Speaker Guest **CIV:** Advocate, Peace Through Strength; Disentanglement from Unnecessary Foreign Wars **CW:** Author, Composer, "The Human Odyssey: Our Journey of Life from Infancy to Eternity"; Author, Composer, "Ken Wilber, Joseph Campbell, and the Meaning of Life"; Author, Composer, "The Fundamental Ken Wilber"; Author, Composer, "The Processes of Human Development"; Author, Composer, "The Processes According to Esalen"; Author, Composer, "Arrays of Light: Ken Wilber's Tables of Correspondence"; Originator, Developer, "The Animal Kingdom Book"; Originator, Developer, "The Peaceable Kingdom Book"; Originator, Developer, "The Kingdom of Cats"; Originator, Developer, "My Alpha-Sound Animals"; Originator, Developer, "Alpha-Sound Animal Adventures"; Originator, Developer, "Silly Stories for Alpha-Sounds"; Originator, Developer, "The Big Cats Book"; Originator, Developer, "The Six Wild Cats Book"; Originator, Developer, "Star Power for Big Cats"; Originator, Developer, "The Alpha-Babies Alpha-Sound Animals"; Originator, Developer, "The 279,000 Syllables of Phonetic Blocks"; Originator, Developer, "The Phonetic Blocks Playing Mat"; Originator, Developer, "The Miniature Economy"; Originator, Developer, "The Skirvana Tiles and Playing Board"; Originator, Developer, "The Hidden Wisdom of Skirvana: Secrets of Becoming a Skirvana Grand Master"; Originator, Developer, "Skirvana in a Nutshell: All the Essentials of the World's Greatest Word Game"; Author, Composer, "The Whole Story of Christmas: Everything the Bible Tells Us about the Nativity of Jesus Christ"; Author, Composer, "The Whole Story of Easter: "Everything the Bible Tells Us about the Sacrificial Death and Resurrection of Jesus Christ" **AW:** Who's Who Lifetime Achievement Award **MEM:** International Coach Federation (ICF); International Association of Financial Planners (IAFP); Mensa International **AS:** Mr. Martin attributes his success to his loving and caring parents, Charles and Elizabeth, as well as to his spirited and steadfast wife, Kaye. Along with his seven creative and individualistic, loyal, and devoted, caring and compassionate children, he additionally credits his willingness to grow, transform, and reinvent himself over the course of a lifetime. Above all, he credits his all-knowing and all-loving Creator, who has orchestrated all things in his life for good. **B/I:** Mr. Martin became involved in his profession because he has engaged in his profession to help people lead fuller, more productive, and more successful lives. **AV:** Exotic traveling; Home exchanging; Wilderness backpacking; Mountain biking; Long-distance swimming; Natural medicine; Health and wellness processes; Life extension technologies **PA:** Culturally-Liberal, Economically-Conservative, Entrepreneurial Individualist; A synthesis from the best of Liberal, Conservative, Libertarian **RE:** Biblically-based, diversity-tolerant, spirit-filled Christian

MARTIN, JERRY WAYNE, T: Family Physician (Retired) **I:** Medicine & Health Care **DOB:** 11/28/1935 **PB:** Providence **SC:** RI/USA **PT:** Charles Martin Jr.; Rosena (Playl) Martin **MS:** Married **SPN:** Jimmie D. Hobgood (12/18/1955) **CH:** Melissa Martin Johnson; Charles Stanley; Mary Elizabeth; Jerry Wayne Martin Jr. (Deceased) **ED:** Rotating Internship, University of Louisville Affiliated Hospitals (1963-1964); MD, University of Louisville (1963); BS, Western Kentucky University (1958) **CT:** Founding Diplomate, Diplomate, American Board of Family Practice (American Board of Family

Medicine) **C:** Private Practice, Bowling Green, KY (1964-2002); Analytical Chemist, Spencer Chemical Company, Henderson, KY (1958-1959) **CR:** Board of Trustees, KMA Sixth District (1987-1993); Board of Directors, KEMPAC (1987-1992); Alternate Delegate, AAFP Congress of Delegates (1987-1992); Ad-hoc Advisory Planning Committee for Family Medicine Review, University of Kentucky (1985); Board of Directors, Warren County Chapter, American Heart Association, Inc. (1981-1997); Chairman, Board of Trustees, Greenview Hospital (Now TriStar Greenview Regional), C-HCA, Inc. (1978-1979); President, Staff, Greenview Hospital (Now TriStar Greenview Regional), C-HCA, Inc. (1976-1977); Team Physician, Bowling Green High School Basketball (1975-1984); Warren County Board of Health (1973-1984); President, Chief of Staff, Bowling Green-Warren County Community Hospital (1970-1971); Team Physician, All Sports, Western Kentucky University (1965-2002); Parliamentarian, Speaker, Lecturer, Presenter, Various Engagements, Clubs and Conferences **CIV:** Deacon, First Baptist Church, Bowling Green, KY (1968-Present); Chairman, Committee, History and Archive, Church **MIL:** With, 18th Surgical Hospital (MA), MASH Unit, Pleiku Province (Central Highlands), Republic of Vietnam (1966-1967) **CW:** Author, "Soldiers Saving Soldiers: Vietnam Remembered, A History of the 18th Surgical Hospital, Second Edition" (2016); Author, "Symbols and Myths of Medicine: Staff of Asclepius/Staff of Hermes/Mercury (Caduceus), First Edition" (2016); Author, "Soldiers Saving Soldiers: Vietnam Remembered, A History of the 18th Surgical Hospital" (2011) **AW:** Summit Award, College Heights Foundation, Western Kentucky Foundation (2008); Physicians Recognition Award (1970-2006); Summit Award, Lancaster-Puckett Lectureship Society (2004); Certificate of Appreciation, University of Louisville Health Science Center (2002); Certificate of Appreciation, Kansas Academy of Family Physicians-Foundation (KAFP-F) (1994-1995, 1997-1998); Award of Merit, ABFP (Now American Board of Family Medicine) (1996); Certificate of Appreciation, American Heart Association, Inc. (1990); NCAA Commemorative Sports Award (1987, 1988); Certificate of Recognition, Family Health Foundation of America (1987); Century Club Award, Boy Scouts of America, Audubon Council (1970-1979); Certification of Appreciation, WKU Athletics Director (1973); Republic of Vietnam Gallantry Cross with Bronze Palm **MEM:** EQB Literary Club (1982-Present); Kentucky Ornithological Society (1971-Present); Warren County Historical Society (1969-Present); Kentucky Historical Society (1969-Present); Filson Club (1969-Present); Fellow, American Academy of Family Physicians; Fellow, The Royal Society of Medicine; American Board of Family Practice (Now American Board of Family Medicine); Fellow, American College of Emergency Physicians; Kentucky Academy of Family Physicians; American Academy of Family Physicians; American Medical Association; Kentucky Medical Association; World Organization of National Colleges and Academies of Family Physicians; Sigma Nu Fraternity, Inc.; Alpha Kappa Kappa; Pan American Medical Association; American Physicians Art Association; American Geriatrics Society; American College Health Association; The American Medical Society for Sports Medicine **MH:** Albert Nelson Marquis Lifetime Achievement Award; Marquis Who's Who Top Professional; Marquis Who's Who Humanitarian Award **B/I:** Dr. Martin had a great grandfather who was a physician; he never knew him or knew much about him, but for some reason, as a young kid, he liked nature. As he got older, if he found an animal that had been hit by a car and it was still fresh, he would dissect it. He loved chemistry and biology and just followed his desires and went into medicine. **AV:** Photography; History; Beekeeping; Reading and writing; Ornithology **PA:** Republican **RE:** Baptist **THT:** Dr. Martin is the author of "Soldiers Saving Soldiers: Vietnam Remembered, A History of the 18th Surgical Hospital, Second Edition" in 2016. It was written for the 50th anniversary commemorative edition; there are about 500 of his photographs in the book.

MARTIN, JOSEPH LEONARD, T: Business, Real Estate Investor, Educator **I:** Business Management/Business Services **PB:** Denville **SC:** NJ/USA **PT:** Leonard Martin; Dorothy Martin **MS:** Married **SPN:** Pam **CH:** Joseph **ED:** MEd in Sports Management and Leisure Studies, Temple University, Philadelphia, PA (1995); BS in Management, Fairleigh Dickinson University, Teaneck, NJ (1989) **CT:** Certified, Volleyball, NJSIAA, State of New Jersey (2018-Present); NCAA Certified, Volleyball (2017-Present); NCAA Certified, Basketball (2013-Present); NCAA Certified, Soccer (2010-Present); NCAA Certified, Baseball (2005-Present); NCAA Certified, Softball (2004-Present); Certified, Soccer, State of New Jersey (2001-Present); Certified, Basketball, State of New Jersey (1988-Present); Certified, Baseball, State of New Jersey (1988-Present); Certified, Softball, NJSIAA, State of New Jersey (1988-Present); Certified in Grades K-8, Special Education; Certified Sports Official; Certified Mediator, Somerset County, New Jersey **C:** Assigner of Umpires, Morris Majors (2018-Present); WG Contracting (2018-Present); Wine Distributor, Argentina, Italy, Spain (2014-Present); Adjunct Professor, Physical Education/Health, Essex County College (2014-Present); Property Manager, Residential and Commercial Buildings (2006-Present); Assigner of Basketball Referees, Burnham Park Men's Basketball League, Morristown, NJ (1998-2000); Certified Sports Official, Five Sports NCAA – Volleyball, Soccer, Men's Basketball, Baseball, Softball; Certified Sports Official, Six High School Sports – Volleyball, Soccer, Basketball, Baseball, Softball, Football; Certified Teacher, Grades K-8, Special Education, Business Administrator, Principal, Driver Education, Highly Qualified Mathematics; Somerset County Certified Mediator, New Jersey **CR:** State Soccer Tournament, NJSIAA (2010-Present); CBUAO (2010-Present); State Basketball Tournament, NJSIAA (1999-Present); Sectional Finals, Basketball, NJSIAA (2019); Softball, CACC (2019); Eighth Grade Basketball, Freshman Finals, CYO Finals (2019); Women's Final, Soccer, Conference Postseason (2018); Volleyball High School State Tournament, NJSIAA (2018); NISOA Clinic (2018); Group State Semi-finals, Basketball, NJSIAA (2018); Sectional State Semi-finals, Soccer NJSIAA (2017-2018); Region 19 Men's Semi-finals, Soccer, Conference Postseason (2017-2018); Sectional Finals, Baseball (2017-2018); Baseball Camp (2017); ASA National Softball Clinic (2016); Group State Baseball Finals (Plate) (2016); ASA 16U Gold, Softball (2016); PSAC (2014); Softball, Centennial Conference (2014); PSAC (2014); Softball, Centennial Conference (2014); Soccer Postseason, NCAA (2013-2018); Group State Semi-finals, Baseball (2013-2015); Group State Semi-finals, Baseball (2013-2015); County Semi-finals, Softball (2013); NISOA Camp (2011); Basketball County Finals (2010); Softball, Eastern College Athletic Conference (ECAC) (2009); High School State Baseball Tournament, NJSIAA (2008-2018); NCAA Baseball Clinic (2008-2014); NCAA Softball Clinic (2008-2014); Semi-Finals, Basketball County Tournament (2008-2009); ASA 18U Nationals, Softball (2007-2008); Basketball County Finals (2007); ASA National Softball Clinic (2007); Region 19 Semi-finals, Softball, Conference Postseason (2007); Semi-Finals, Basketball County Tournament (2004); Jim Evans Camp (2003-2004); Athletic Director/Head Soccer Coach/Head Softball Coach/Physical Education/Health Instructor, Lacordaire Academy, Upper Montclair, NJ (1999-2005); Basketball County Finals (1999); Softball Pitching Instructor, Starmaker (1996-2010); Recreation/Pool Director, Mendham Township, NJ (1996-1998); Ticketing Intern, USTA (1995); Athletic Director/Head Boy's Basketball Coach, St. Jude CYO (1994-2001); Sports Information Intern, The Philadelphia 76ers (1993-1996); Private School Educator; Public School Educator; Assistant/Softball Pitching Coach, Division I, Lafayette College; Head, Division III Softball/Pitching Coach, St. Elizabeth College; NIKE EYBL; West 4th Street Basketball League; Diamond Jacks Summer League, Baseball, Somerville, NJ; Summer/Fall College Showcases, Bridgewater/Edison, NJ; Sub-varsity Assignments, Football; Varsity Clock Operator, Football **CIV:** Coach, Soccer, Basketball, Baseball, and Softball, Recreation Sports (2012); Chairman, Fundraising, Philadelphia Boys' and Girls' Basketball Championships (1993-1995); Chairman, Phi Sigma Kappa 24-hour Marathon (1987); Participant, 24-Hour Softball Marathon, Valerie Fund (1987) **AW:** Indicator Award (2016); Champions, Boys Basketball Team, Paterson Diocese (1999); Xerox Gold Award for Perfect Attendance Award (1992); Level Five Review (Highest), Xerox President's Club (1991); Xerox Par Club (1990); Dean's List (1987-1988) **MEM:** Vice President, High School Baseball Chapter (2016-2018); Commissioner, Babe Ruth Softball (1998-2000); Xerox President's Club (1991); Xerox Par Club (1990); Student Council President and Vice President, Fairleigh Dickinson University (1987-1989); NCAA; NJSIAA; The International Association of Approved Basketball Officials, Inc. (IAABO); USSF; ASA; National Association of Sports Officials (NASO); Metropolitan Approved Girls Basketball Officials (MAGBO); CBOA; NJ Real Estate Salesperson; CBUAO, ECUA; KRVA, CSUA, Eastern College Athletic Conference (ECAC); Phi Sigma Kappa **MH:** Marquis Who's Who Top Professional **AS:** Mr. Martin attributes his success to four key components. They are commitment, communication, trust and hard work. Additionally, he treats people the way he wants to be treated. Last but not least, he makes sure to under promise and over deliver. He goes above and beyond what is required and never settles for mediocrity or complacency. **B/I:** Mr. Martin became involved in his professions because his mother was an educator. He completed an undergraduate degree in business and worked in the corporate world for a while, but he didn't like it. He always liked teaching, coaching and athletic directing. He found that teaching was the entry point to all of that and was able to put everything together and make a nice career out of it. **AV:** Sports memorabilia; Ticket stubs **RE:** Roman Catholic **THT:** Additional bio information available at:http://www.linkedin.com/in/jmartin95

MARTIN, MIRTA MARURI, T: President **I:** Education/Educational Services **CN:** Fairmont State University **PB:** Havana **SC:** Cuba **MS:** Married **SPN:** John Newton Martin Jr., P.E. **CH:** Katherine Blair Martin, PhD; Patrick Newton Martin, MSM, MSREI **ED:** Doctor of Philosophy in Strategy and Leadership, Virginia Commonwealth University; Master of Business Administration, University of Richmond, Robins School of Business; Bachelor of Science in Psychology, Political Science, Duke University; Coursework on Spanish, French and Portuguese Languages **CT:** Federal Bureau of Investigation Citizens Academy (2019); Governors Education Retreat, Advancing Cross-State Conversations (2019); Harvard Institute for Higher Education for Presidential Leadership (2018); Spectrum Executive Leadership Fellow, American Council on Education (2013); Advancing Women's Leadership, 80th National Women's Leadership Forum, American Council on Education, (2012); Virginia Network for Women in Higher Education, American Council on Education; Senior Leadership Seminar (2010); Future Presidents Institute, Hockaday-Hunter and Associates, Center for School Leadership Development, University of North Carolina at Chapel Hill (2007); Advancing to the Presidency, American Council on Education (2006) **C:** President, Fairmont State University (2017-Present); Managing Director, Kirchner Group (2017-Present); Senior Education Adviser to former President Vicente Fox, Centro Fox (2017-2019); Senior Fellow, American Association of State Colleges and Universities (2016-2018); Presidential Adviser, Kansas Board of Regents and Fort Hays State University (2016-2017); President, Fort Hays State University (2014-2016); Dean, School of Business, Virginia State University (2009-2014); Special Assistant to Chancellor, Virginia Community College System (2009); Special Assistant to the President, Executive Vice President and Executive Director, John Tyler Community College Foundation (2005-2009); Education and Executive Consultant, Consulting Alliance Group, Inc. (2004-2005); Executive Director, Management Institute (2000-2003); Associate Dean, University of Richmond, Robins School of Business (2000-2003); Associate Professor, Averett University (1992-2001); Interim Dean, Regional Director, Averett University (1995); Senior Vice President, First Union National Bank (1993-1994); Vice President, Dominion Bank (1991-1993); Assistant Vice President, Dominion Bank (1988-1991); Branch Manager and Banking Officer, First Virginia Bank Colonial (1985-1988); Assistant Branch Manager, First Virginia Bank Colonial (1984-1985); Management Associate, First Virginia Bank Colonial (1982-1984) **CR:** Appointee, Blue Ribbon Commission on Four-Year Higher Education, West Virginia (2018); Co-chairperson, Personnel Committee, State Board for Community Colleges, Virginia (2013); Chairperson, Audit Committee, State Board for Community Colleges, Virginia (2012); Appointee, State Board for Community Colleges, Virginia (2011); Chairperson, Academic, Student Affairs and Workforce Development Committee, State Board for Community Colleges, Virginia (2011); Appointee, Governor's Commission on Higher Education, Reform, Innovation and Investment, Virginia (2010); Appointee, Latino Advisory Board, Ex-Officio representing the Office of the Secretary of Education, Virginia (2010); Appointee, Council on the Status of Women, Virginia (2009); Board Liaison, J. Sargeant Reynolds Community College and John Tyler Community College;Appointee, Finance Sub-Committee, Ex-Officio Governance Committee **CIV:** Advisory Committee, Governor's Cyber Security (2018-Present); Member, Rotary of South Fairmont (2018-Present); Director, Marion County Chamber of Commerce (2018-Present); Director, United Way of Marion County (2018-Present); Anti-Terrorism Advisory Council, Northern District of West Virginia (2018-Present); Managing Director, Kirchner Group (2017-Present); Honorary Campaign Chair, United Way (2019, 2020); Director, Advisory Board, Racing Toward Diversity Magazine (2012-Present); Director, Board of Advisers, Fairmont Regional Medical Center (2018-2019); Named to the Anti-Terrorism Advisory Council in the Northern District of West Virginia (2018); Director, Valley Hope Association (2015-2017); Board Member, Fundraising Committee, Housing Opportunities Made Equal (2010-2014); Board Member, REDC Community Capital Group (2010-2014); Board Member, Fundraising and Finance Committee, Safe Harbor (2010-2014); Board Member, Greater Richmond Chamber of Commerce (2009-2014); Board Member, Metropolitan Business League (2009-2014); Executive Leadership Team, Fundraising Committee, Go Red for Women, American Heart Association (2009-2014); Founding Member, Council 4611, League of United American Citizens **AW:** West Virginia Inspiring Women (2020); West Virginia Educator of the Year (2019); Recognized, Talent Transplant, West Virginia Executive Magazine (2019); Named, Woman of Distinction, NCWV Life Magazine (2018); National Outstanding New Program Award, Student Affairs Administrators in Higher Education, Hispanic College Institute, National Association of Student Personnel Administrators (2017); Partner of the Year, Sigma Phi Epsilon Fraternity (2016); Best Paper in Session Award, Self-Determination's Intrinsic Value of Post-Exile Cuban-American Women. The Clute Institute International Business Conference (2015); Finalist, Innovation in Education Educator of the Year Award, Richmond, VA (2014); Named, Most Influential Women, Chesterfield County, VA (2013); Humanitarian Award for Educational Excellence, Metropolitan Business League (2013); Technology Innovation Deployment Award, RichTech (2012); Alumni Inductee, Phi Kappa Phi (2012); Best Business Program in the Nation, Reginald F. Lewis College of Business (2012); Governor's Award for Technology in Innovation in Higher Education (2011); Finalist, Administrator of the Year, HBCU Faculty (2010); Legacy Award, Hispanic College Fund (2010); Most Inspiring Dean Award (2010-2012); The President of the United States' Volunteer Service Award, President's Council on Service and Civic Participation (2009); Inductee, Beta Gamma Sigma (2009); Inductee, Phi Theta Kappa (2006); Outstanding Faculty of the Year, Averett University (1999, 2001); Inductee, Phi Alpha Alpha Honor Society (1996); Inductee, Phi Kappa Phi (1995) **MEM:** Governor's Cyber Security Workforce Advisory Council (2018-Present); President, West Virginia Council of Presidents (2018-Present); Member, West Virginia Council of Presidents (2017-Present); Director Representing the Americas, International Association of Universities (2015-Present); President, President Emeritus and Founding Director, Virginia Latino Higher Education Network (2006-Present); Council of Presidents, American Association of State Colleges and Universities (2014-2018); Director, BizEd Advisory Council, Association to Advance Collegiate Schools of Business (2009-2018); Director, Kansas Council on Economic Education (2014-2017); Director at Large, American Association of Community Colleges (2014-2017); Member, Regents Institutions Council of Presidents (2014-2016); Chair, Regents Institutions Council of Presidents (2015); Women Executives in Virginia Higher Education (2009-2014); Association to Advance Collegiate Schools of Business (2009-2014); Co-Chair, New Deans Affinity Group, Association to Advance Collegiate Schools of Business (2009-2014); Southern Business Administration Association (2009-2014) **AS:** Dr. Martin attributes her success to her family, as well as her Christian faith. Likewise, she credits her perseverance and grit, and the wise counsel of numerous mentors. **B/I:** After distinguishing herself as the first member of her family to attend college, Dr. Martin immersed herself in corporate America, and saw the need to expand access and create avenues toward higher education. **THT:** Always remember to pay it forward.

MARTIN, PAULA J., T: Executive Director **I:** Education/Educational Services **CN:** Harlem Center for Education **PB:** New York **SC:** NY/USA **ED:** MA in Developmental Psychology, Teachers College, Columbia University (1968-1978); BA in Psychology, Syracuse University (1964-1968) **C:** Executive Director, Harlem Center for Education (1985- Present); Director, Columbia University (1973-1985) **CIV:** Association for Equality & Excellence in Education (AEEE); Board Member, Council for Opportunity in Education; Training, United States Department of Education **AW:** Walter O. Mason Award, Council for Opportunity in Education (2011); Award for Excellence, Association for Equality & Excellence in Education (AEEE) **AS:** Ms. Martin attributes her success to her mother, Frances Martin, a World War II veteran who knew the importance of having an education, especially as an African American woman in America. She made sure Ms. Martin always did her best. Her mother was also a community activist, which led Ms. Martin to develop a passion for community responsibility. **B/I:** Ms. Martin became involved in education after becoming an adjunct teacher of child psychology. At the end of her teaching term, she was asked to fill the newly open academic counselor position. Ms. Martin accepted and later became the assistant director. Slowly but surely, she fell in love with working in education, leading to her multitude of professional success. **AV:** Drawing; Painting; Appreciating art, ballet, and theatre

MARTIN, STEVE GLENN, T: Actor; Comedian; Musician **I:** Media & Entertainment **DOB:** 08/14/1945 **PB:** Waco **SC:** TX/USA **PT:** Glenn Vernon Martin; Mary Lee (Stewart) Martin **MS:** Married **SPN:** Anne Stringfield (07/28/2007); Victoria Tennant (11/20/1986, Divorced 1994) **CH:** One Child **ED:** Honorary LHD, California State University, Long Beach (1989); Coursework, University of California Los Angeles (1967); Coursework, Long Beach State College (Now California State University, Long Beach); Coursework, Santa Ana College **CIV:** Trustee, Los Angeles Museum of Art **CW:** Appearance, "Saturday Night Live" (1998, 2012, 2015, 2019); Performer, "An Evening You Will Forget for the Rest of Your Life" (2018); Appearance, "Oh, Hello on Broadway" (2017); Actor, "Billy Lynns's Long Halftime Walk" (2016); Appearance, "Maya & Marty" (2016); Host, "Saturday Night Live" (1976, 1977, 1978, 1979, 1980, 1986, 1987, 1989, 1991, 1994, 2006, 2009, 2015); Voice Actor, "Home" (2015); Actor, "Love the Coopers" (2015); Musician with Edie Brickell, "Love Has Come for You" (2013); Musician, "Rare Bird Alert" (2011); Actor, "The Big Year" (2010); Author, "An Object of Beauty" (2010); Author, "Late for School" (2010); Host, Academy Awards (2001, 2003, 2010); Musician, "The Crow: New Songs for the Five-String Banjo" (2009); Actor, "It's Complicated" (2009); Actor, Writer, "The Pink Panther 2" (2009); Actor, "Baby Mama" (2008); Appearance, "30 Rock" (2008); Writer, "Traitor" (2008); Author, "Born Standing Up: A Comic's Life" (2007); Author, "The Alphabet from A To Y with Bonus Letter Z!" (2007); Actor, Writer, "The Pink Panther" (2006); Actor, "Cheaper by the Dozen 2" (2005); Actor, Writer, Producer, "Shopgirl" (2005); Actor, "Jiminy Glick in La La Wood" (2004); Actor, "Cheaper by the Dozen" (2003); Author, "The Pleasure of My Company" (2003); Actor, "Looney Tunes: Back in Action" (2003); Actor, "Bringing Down the House" (2003); Actor, "Rutles 2: Can't Buy Me Lunch" (2002); Actor, "Novocaine" (2001); Actor, "Joe Gould's Secret" (2000); Author, Novel, "Shopgirl" (2000); Actor, "Bowfinger" (1999); Writer, "Bowfinger" (1999); Author, "Pure Drivel" (1998); Actor, "The Spanish Prisoner" (1998); Actor, "Sergeant Bilko" (1995); Actor, "A Simple Twist of Fate" (1994); Actor, "Mixed Nuts" (1994); Appearance, "And the Band Played On" (1993); Playwright, "Picasso at the Lapin Agile" (1993); Actor, "Leap of Faith" (1993); Actor, "Housesitter" (1992); Actor, Writer, Executive Producer, "L.A. Story" (1991); Actor, "Grand Canyon" (1991); Actor, "Father of the Bride" (1991); Actor, "My Blue Heaven" (1990); Actor, "Parenthood" (1989); Actor, "Dirty Rotten Scoundrels" (1988); Actor, "Waiting for Godot" (1988); Actor, "Planes, Trains and Automobiles" (1987); Actor, Writer, Executive Producer, "Roxanne" (1987); Actor, Writer, Executive Producer, "Three Amigos" (1986); Actor, "Little Shop of Horrors" (1986); Executive Producer, "Domestic Life" (1984); Actor, "The Lonely Guy" (1984); Actor, "All of Me" (1984); Actor, Writer, "The Man with Two Brains" (1983); Writer, "Easy Money" (1983); Actor, Writer, "Dead Men Don't Wear Plaid" (1982); Performer, "The Steve Martin Brothers" (1982); Actor, Writer, "Pennies from Heaven" (1981); Performer, "Steve Martin's Best Show Ever" (1981); Performer, Television Special, "Comedy is Not Pretty" (1980); Performer, Album, "Comedy is Not Pretty" (1979); Actor, Writer, "The Jerk" (1979); Actor, "The Muppet Movie" (1979); Actor, "The Kids are Alright" (1979); Performer, "A Wild and Crazy Guy" (1978); Actor, "Sergeant Pepper's Lonely Hearts Club Band" (1978); Performer, "Steve Martin: A Wild and Crazy Guy" (1978); Author, "Cruel Shoes" (1977); Performer, "Let's Get Small" (1977); Actor, Writer, "The Absent-Minded Waiter" (1977); Writer, "Van Dyke and Company" (1976); Appearance, "The Smothers Brothers Show" (1975); Writer, "Sonny and Cher Comedy Hour" (1971-1973); Writer, "The Ray Stevens Show" (1970); Writer, "The Smothers Brothers Comedy Hour" (1967-1969); Writer, Pat Paulsen, John Denver and "The Glen Campbell Comedy Hour"; Comedian, Night Clubs; Playwright, Plays; Actor, Comedian, Television Shows and Films; Musician, Albums **AW:** Co-recipient, Drama Desk Award for Outstanding Music (2016); Life Achievement Award, American Film Institute (2015); Honorary Academy Award, Academy of Motion Picture Arts and Sciences (2013); Grammy Award for Best American Roots Song, The Recording Academy (2014); Entertainer of the Year Award, International Bluegrass Music Awards (2011); Grammy Award for Best Bluegrass Album, The Recording Academy (2010); Award for Best Cast, National Board of Review (2009); Honoree, Kennedy Center Honors, John F. Kennedy Center for the Performing Arts (2007); Named One of the 50 Most Powerful People in Hollywood, Premiere Magazine (2006); Mark Twain Prize for American Humor (2005); Named Disney Legend (2005); Co-recipient, Grammy Award for Best Country Instrumental Performance, The Recording Academy (2001); Film Excellence Award, Boston Film Festival (2001); Lifetime Achievement Award in Comedy, American Comedy Awards (2000); Grand Jury Award - Comedy Performance, The Comedy Festival (1998); Award for Favorite Actor in a Comedy Motion Picture, People's Choice Awards (1992, 1993); Named Man of the Year, Hasty Pudding Theatricals (1988); National Society of Film Critics Award for Best Actor (1984, 1987); New York Film Critics Circle Award for Best Actor (1984); Award for Variety, Musical or Comedy, Writers Guild of America (1981); Grammy Award for Best Comedy Album, The Recording Academy (1978, 1979); Georgie Award, American Guild of Variety Artists (1977, 1978); Co-recipient, Emmy Award for Outstanding Writing for a Variety Series, Academy of Television Arts & Sciences (1969)

MARTIN, THOMAS J., MD, T: Pediatrician **I:** Medicine & Health Care **CN:** Geisinger Commonwealth School of Medicine **DOB:** 07/04/1934 **PB:** Greensburg **SC:** PA/USA **PT:** John William Martin; Mary DeTar Martin **MS:** Married **SPN:** Lois Darlene Miller (06/20/1992) **CH:** Jack T.; Susan L. O'Malley; James S.; David S. **ED:** Pediatrics Resident, Children's Hospital of Pittsburgh, UPMC (1965-1967); MD, University of Pittsburgh (1960); BS, Franklin and Marshall College, Lancaster, PA (1956)

CT: The American Board of Pediatrics C: Professor, Geisinger Commonwealth School of Medicine, Geisinger Health (2012-2019); Director of Pediatrics Education, Geisinger Commonwealth School of Medicine, Geisinger Health (2010-2019); Vice Chairman of Pediatrics, Geisinger Commonwealth School of Medicine, Geisinger Health (2008-2019); Professor of Pediatrics, Milton S. Hershey Medical Center, Penn State Health (2014-2018); Clinical Professor of Pediatrics, Milton S. Hershey Medical Center, The Pennsylvania State University, (2005-2014); Professor Emeritus, Department of Orthopedic and Rehabilitation, Milton S. Hershey Medical Center, Penn State Health (2005-2013); Associate Program Director, Family Practice Residency, The Williamsport Hospital, UPMC, PA (2004-2013); Director of Pediatrics, Hospital Level II Nursery Service, Geisinger Commonwealth School of Medicine, Geisinger Health (2004-2013); Clinical Professor, Geisinger Commonwealth School of Medicine, Geisinger Health (2008-2012); Director of Inpatient Pediatrics, Aultman Hospital, Canton, Ohio (1995-1997); Chairman of Pediatrics, Geisinger Medical Center (1975-1995); Associate in Pediatrics, Geisinger Medical Center, Danville, PA (1967-1975); General Practice Medicine, Slippery Rock, PA (1961-1962, 1964-1965) CR: With, Nittery Medical Center (Now Mount Nittery Medical Center), Mount Nittany Health System, State College, PA (1997-2005); Team Physician, Football, Wrestling, The Pennsylvania State University, University Park, PA (1997-2005); Courtesy Staff, Lewistown Hospital (Now Geisinger Lewistown Hospital, Geisinger Health (1999-2004); Active Staff, Children's Hospital Medical Center of Akron, Ohio (1995-1997); Chairman of Pediatrics, Geisinger Medical Center (1975-1995); With, Neonatal Unit, Geisinger Medical Center (1973); Adjunct Clinical Associate Professor, Jefferson Medical College (Now Sidney Kimmel Medical College), Philadelphia, PA; Lecturer in Field MIL: Captain, United States Army (1962-1964) CW: Writer, Primary Care Sports Medicine and Pediatric Exam; Author, 34 Peer-reviewed Articles AW: Thomas E. Schiffer Award, American Academy of Pediatrics (2014); Named First Emeritus Professor, Geisinger Commonwealth School of Medicine, Geisinger Health (2019); Best Teaching Award (2009); Named to Geisinger's Pediatrics Wall of Fame (2005); Named Citizen of the Year, BPO Elks (1995); Honors for Exceptional Service to Children and Youth, National Child Labor Committee, New York, NY (1995); Franklin Marshall Lifetime Achievement Award; Lifetime Achievement Award for Sports Medicine, American Academy of Pediatrics MEM: Committee on Sports Medicine and Fitness, American Academy of Pediatrics (1998-2004); Executive Committee, Section on Sports Medicine, American Academy of Pediatrics (1997-2003); Continuing Medical Education Accreditation Surveyor, Pennsylvania Medical Society (1988-1993); Chapter Chairman, American Academy of Pediatrics (1980-1982); American Medical Association; National Wrestling Coaches Association; Pennsylvania Medical Society; American College of Sports Medicine (ACSM); American Academy of Pediatrics; Lycoming County Medical Society; The American Board of Pediatrics MH: Albert Nelson Marquis Lifetime Achievement Award; Marquis Who's Who Top Professional AS: Dr. Martin has attributes his success to being persistent. B/I: Dr. Martin was influenced by many factors. First, by his previous ancestors, who were in medicine; also, his father drove an ambulance that he spent high school years working in. His college, Franklin Marshall, emphasized medicine. Dr. Martin's mother's cousin was the first gynecologist in Pittsburgh. There were many doctors in the family. Pursuit of a medical career seemed like an easy decision for Dr. Martin. AV: Running;

Skiing; Swimming RE: Lutheran THT: Dr. Martin planned and directed the construction of the first children's hospital ever to be built in a rural area in the United States. The students, residents and medical students have shown a great appreciation for Dr. Martin's teaching. Patients he has taken care of remain in contact with him to this day as well; Dr. Martin says that God has been good to him. He has led him to interesting places through interesting times.

MARTINEZ, DAVE, T: Manager I: Athletics CN: Washington Nationals DOB: 09/26/1964 PB: Brooklyn SC: NY/USA MS: Married SPN: Lisa CH: Josh; Jagger; Dalton; Angelica ED: Coursework, Valencia Community College; Diploma, Lake Howell High School, Winter Park, FL C: Manager, Washington Nationals (2018-Present); Coach, Chicago Cubs (2015-2017); Coach, Tampa Bay Rays (2008-2014); Professional Baseball Player, Atlanta Braves (2001); Professional Baseball Player, Toronto Blue Jays (2000); Professional Baseball Player, Texas Rangers (2000); Professional Baseball Player, Chicago Cubs (2000); Professional Baseball Player, Tampa Bay Devil Rays (1998-2000); Professional Baseball Player, Chicago White Sox (1995-1997); Professional Baseball Player, San Francisco Giants (1993-1994); Professional Baseball Player, Cincinnati Reds (1992); Professional Baseball Player, Montreal Expos (1988-1991); Professional Baseball Player, Chicago Cubs (1986-1988) AW: World Series Champion (2016, 2019)

MARTINEZ, PEDRO JAIME, T: Sportscaster; Former Professional Baseball Player I: Athletics DOB: 07/25/1971 SC: Manoquayabo/Dominican Republic PT: Paolino Martinez; Leopoldino Martinez MS: Married SPN: Carolina Cruz de Martinez CH: Pedro Jr.; Pedro Isaias; Enyol; Nayla ED: Coursework, Ohio Dominican College (Now Ohio Dominican University) C: Studio Analyst, MLB Network (2015-Present); Special Assistant to General Manager, Boston Red Sox, MLB (2013); Pitcher, Philadelphia Phillies, MLB (2009); Pitcher, New York Mets, MLB (2005-2008); Pitcher, Boston Red Sox, MLB (1998-2004); Pitcher, Montreal Expos, MLB (1994-1997); Pitcher, Los Angeles Dodgers, MLB (1992-1993); Studio Analyst, "MLB on TBS" CW: Co-Author, "Pedro" (2015) AW: Inductee, Canadian Baseball Hall of Fame (2018); Inductee, National Baseball Hall of Fame (2015); Invited, National League All-Atar Team (1996, 1997, 2005, 2006); Winner, Boston Red Sox, World Series Championship (2004); Invited, American League All-Star Team (1998-2000, 2002); Pitcher of the Year, Sporting News (1997, 1999, 2000); Cy Young Award, America League (1999, 2000); All-Star Game MVP, MLB (1999); Cy Young Award, National League (1997); Named Minor League Player of the Year (1991)

MARTINEZ, ROMAN IV, T: Investment Banker, Board Member (Retired) I: Financial Services DOB: 12/29/1947 PB: Santiago SC: Cuba PT: Roman Martinez; Virginia (Gomez) Martinez MS: Married SPN: Helena Hackley Martinez (12/20/1974) CH: Roman Martinez V; Helena M. Cornell ED: MBA, University of Pennsylvania (1971); BS, Boston College (1969) C: Retired, Lehman Brothers (Formerly Lehman Brothers, Kuhn, Loeb, Inc./Shearson Lehman Brothers, Inc.), New York, NY (2003); Managing Director, Lehman Brothers (Formerly Lehman Brothers, Kuhn, Loeb, Inc./Shearson Lehman Brothers, Inc.), New York, NY (1978-2003); Corporate Vice President, Lehman Brothers (Formerly Lehman Brothers, Kuhn, Loeb, Inc./Shearson Lehman Brothers, Inc.), New York, NY (1977); Vice President, Kuhn, Loeb & Co., New York, NY (1974-1977); Associate, Kuhn, Loeb & Co.,

New York, NY (1971-1973) CR: Board of Governors, United States Postal Service (USPS) (2019-Present); Board of Directors, Cigna Corp. (2005-Present); Board of Directors, Orbital ATK, Inc. (Now Northrop Grumman Corporation) (2004-2019); Board of Directors, Bacardi Ltd. (2008-2014) CIV: Board of Trustees, New York-Presbyterian Hospital (1996-Present); Board of Directors and Overseers, International Rescue Committee (1996-Present); Board of Trustees, The German Marshall Fund of the United States (2005-2017); Former Vice Chairman, Investment Advisory Council, State of Florida (2005-2009) MEM: Council on Foreign Relations PA: Republican RE: Roman Catholic

MARTINSON, DORIS ANN, T: Archivist, Manger I: Government Administration/Government Relations/Government Services CN: Knox County Government Archives DOB: 06/27/1939 PB: Knoxville SC: TN/USA PT: Howard Carlton; Hazel Owen Moore Rivers MS: Divorced SPN: Fred H. Martinson (06/10/1961, Divorced 1996) CH: Matthew; Christopher; Eric ED: Master in Information Sciences, University of Tennessee (1996); MFA, Chicago Art Institute (1964); BFA, University of Tennessee (1961) CT: Certified Archivist, Academy of Certified Archivists C: Manager, County Archivist, Knox County Archives, Knoxville, TN (1986) CIV: President, Knox County League of Women Voters (1983-1985); Teacher, Genealogy Class Sessions on Saturdays, East Tennessee History Center, East Tennessee Counties CW: Contributor, Articles, Professional Journals AW: Scholarship, Colonel Dames Chapter, Society of American Archivists (1988) MEM: President, University of Tennessee Graduate School Information Science Alumnus (1999-2000); President, Society of Tennessee Archivists (1998-1999); Society of American Archivists; Association of Records Managers and Administrators; National Association of Government Archivists and Records Administrators; Academy of Certified Archivists; East Tennessee Historical Society; Washington County Historical Society; Knox County Government Archivist; Knox County Tennessee Public Records Commission MH: Albert Nelson Marquis Lifetime Achievement Recipient B/I: Ms. Martinson had an interest in history for much of her life. She enjoys people, working with them and helping. Her motto is "Do not leave this earth until you know how you got here." She was born and raised in Tennessee, so it was natural for her curiosity to explore her roots. AV: Geneology; History; Painting; Creative writing RE: Methodist

MARTY, SANDRA JOY DEL CORSO, T: Nursing Administrator I: Medicine & Health Care DOB: 07/20/1948 PB: Paterson SC: NJ/USA PT: Nichols R. Del Corso; Margaret B. (Conrad) Del Corso MS: Married SPN: Daniel K. Marty, Junior (10/5/1979) ED: BS, William Patterson College (1983); Diploma, St. Joseph's School of Nursing, Paterson, NJ (1968); Postgraduate Coursework, St. Joseph's College CT: RN, New Jersey; Certified Operating Room Nurse C: Manager, Ambulatory Surgery, Clara Maass Hospital, Belleville, NJ (2013-2017); Director, Christ Hospital, Jersey City, NJ (2010-2013); Manager, Director, Ambulatory Surgery, St. Clare's Hospital, Dover, NJ (2001-2009); Perioperative Director, Nursing, Beth Israel Hospital, Passaic, NJ (1991-2001); Supervisor, Operating Room, Montclair Community Hospital (1981-1991); Supervisor, Operating Room, St. Joseph's Hospital and Medical Center, Paterson, NJ (1974-1981); Perioperative Nurse, St. Joseph's Hospital and Medical Center, Paterson, NJ (1968-1974) CR: Clinical Consultant, Free-Standing Ambulatory Center (1995) CW: Contributor, Research, Professional Journals **AW:** Listee, Who's Who in American Nursing, Society of Nursing Professionals (1990-1991); Best Scholastic Award; Grantee, Nursing Grant **MEM:** Association of Operating Room Nurses; Alpha Kappa Delta; Aspan; National Association for Female Executives **AS:** Ms. Marty attributes her success to her ability to lead others. She additionally enjoys researching in her field, which keeps her motivated. For 43 of her 49 years as a nurse, she upheld leadership positions. This is a direct result of her compassion for others. **B/I:** Ms. Marty became involved in her profession because she wanted to take care of people and excel in a healing role. She ended up in the operating room, which she found to be exciting work. **AV:** Fostering felines **THT:** Ms. Marty will never forget how she obtained her success.

MARVIN, KAREN, T: Owner **I:** Business Management/Business Services **CN:** South Shore Paddleboards **MS:** Married **CH:** Two Children **ED:** Coursework in Business Retail Management, Visual Merchandising, and Store Design, Fashion Institute of Technology (1991) **C:** Owner, South Shore Paddleboards, Babylon, NY (2013-Present) **AW:** Stewardship Award, South Shore Estuary Reserve Council (2019); #2 Paddle-Board Shop in the World (2018); #1 Paddle-Board Shop in the World (2017); Paddle-Board Shop of the Year **MEM:** Board of Directors, Save the Great South Bay; Ambassador, Sea Paddle, Surfers Environmental Alliance **AS:** Ms. Marvin's success is based on her honesty and a true passion for what she does. She tells her story as it is and expresses who she is, as she is. She loves paddle-boarding and loves sharing it with others. She also enjoys introducing people to something they have never tried before. Her motto is, "Never give up. Just keep paddling." **B/I:** For 16 years, Ms. Marvin was a residential house painter. When she grew tired of painting, she began to explore the possibility of pursuing her dream of opening a paddleboard shop. An opportunity arose in 2014, and she knew she could not ignore it. She was inspired to share her passion for paddleboarding with others.

MASKIN, ERIC STARK, PHD, T: Professor of Economics and Mathematics **I:** Education/Educational Services **CN:** Harvard University **DOB:** 12/12/1950 **PB:** New York **SC:** NY/USA **ED:** Honoris Causa Professor, HEC Paris (2017); Honorary Doctorate in Economics, University of Cambodi (2010); PhD in Applied Mathematics, Harvard University (1976); AM in Applied Mathematics, Harvard University (1974); AB in Mathematics, Harvard University (1972) **C:** Adams University Professor, Professor of Economics and Mathematics, Harvard University, Cambridge, MA (2012-Present); Visiting Lecturer of Economics, Princeton University (2000-Present); Albert O. Hirschman Professor, Social Science, Institute of Advanced Study, Princeton, NJ (2000-2011); Professor of Economics, Adams University, Cambridge, MA (1985-2000); Professor, Massachusetts Institute of Technology, Cambridge, MA (1981-1984); Associate Professor, Massachusetts Institute of Technology, Cambridge, MA (1980-1981); Assistant Professor of Economics, Massachusetts Institute of Technology, Cambridge, MA (1977-1980); Research Fellow, Jesus College, University of Cambridge (1976-1977); Visiting Professor of Economics, Massachusetts Institute of Technology, Cambridge, MA **CR:** Visiting Fellow, Hong Kong University of Science and Technology (2010-Present); Visiting Professor, Covenant University, Nigeria (2014); Overseas Fellow, St. John's College (1987-1988); Overseas Fellow, Churchill College, University of Cambridge (1980-1982) **CW:** Associate Editor, B.E. Journal of Theoretical Economics (2000-Present); Associate Editor, Games

and Economic Behavior (1988-Present); Associate Editor, Review of Economic Design (1993-Present); Associate Editor, International Journal of Game Theory (2003-2007); Associate Editor, Journal of Economic Perspectives (2001-2004); Associate Editor, Social Choice and Welfare (1983-2007) **AW:** Louise Blouin Foundation Award (2013); Jean Jacques Laffont Prize (2013); Gabarron Foundation International Economics Award (2011); Centennial Medal, Harvard University (2010); Co-recipient, Nobel Prize in Economics (2007); Kempe Award (2007) **MEM:** Game Theory Society (2010-2012); President, Econometric Society (2003); Fellow, Society for Advancement of Economic Theory; Fellow, Royal Academy of Economic Sciences and Finances, Spain; Fellow, American Academy of Arts & Sciences; Fellow, Econometric Society; Fellow, European Economic Association; Fellow, Correspondent, British Academy; National Academy of Sciences; Society of Social Choice and Welfare; American Economic Association **AV:** Music

MASLAND, LYNNE, T: University Official (Retired) **I:** Education/Educational Services **DOB:** 11/18/1940 **PB:** Boston **SC:** MA/USA **PT:** Keith Arnold; Camilla (Puleston) Shangraw **MS:** Married **SPN:** Steven Alan Mayo (07/01/1995); Edwin Grant Masland (09/19/1960, Divorced 1975) **CH:** Mary Conklin; Molly Allison **ED:** Doctor of Philosophy, University of British Columbia, Vancouver, Canada (1994); Master of Arts, University of California Riverside (1971); Bachelor of Arts, University of California Riverside (1970); Coursework, Mount Holyoke College, South Hadley, MA (1958-1960) **C:** Retired (2006); Director, University Communications, Western Washington University (1988-2006); Adjunct Assistant Professor, Comparative Literature, Fairhaven College (1994-2006); Media Specialist, Western Washington University (1984-1988); Executive Editor, Northwest Happenings Magazine, Greenbank, WA (1980-1984); Project Director, Consultant, Washington Commission for the Humanities, Seattle, WA (1976-1980); Instructor of English, University of Nebraska (1972-1974); Assistant to Director of Elementary Education, Government of American Samoa (1966-1968); Assistant to Public Relations Director, Inter-American University, San German, Puerto Rico (1963-1964) **CR:** Instructor, Western Washington University (1977-1986, 2000); Consultant, William O. Douglas Institute, Seattle, WA (1978); With, Whatcom Museum History and Art, Bellingham, WA (1977); Instructor, University of Nebraska (1972-1974) **CIV:** Board of Directors, Whatcom Community College Foundation (2006-Present); Board of Directors, Station KZAZ, National Public Radio, Bellingham, WA (1992-1993); Board of Directors, Washington State Folklife Council (1985-1990); Board of Directors, Northwest Concert Association (1981-1983); President, League of Women Voters, Whatcom County, Bellingham, WA (1977-1979); Docent, National Gallery, Washington, DC (1969); Board of Directors, Mt. Baker Planned Parenthood **CW:** Author, "A Century of Challenge and Change: Whatcom Women and the YWCA"; Author, "A Cup of Tea: Collected Poems"; Author, "Island Reflections: Poems and Paintings"; Editor, "Western at 100"; Editor, "Folklore of the Northwest Corner: The Human Touch" **AW:** University Graduate Fellow, University of British Columbia (1990-1994); Paul Harris Award, Rotary International; Case District VIII Gold Award for Media Relations, Council for Advancement and Support Education **MEM:** Board of Directors, Rotary International (2008-Present); Board of Directors, Downtown Renaissance Network (2004-2007); District VII Board of Directors, Council for Advancement and Support Education (2003-2005); Paul Harris Fellow, Rotary International (1999); Board of

Directors, Rotary International (1992-1994); Board of Directors, Bellingham City Club **MH:** Albert Nelson Marquis Lifetime Achievement Award **AV:** Boating; Gardening; Travel; Painting **PA:** Democrat **RE:** Episcopalian

MASSIE, THOMAS HAROLD, T: U.S. Representative from Kentucky; Farmer **I:** Government Administration/Government Relations/Government Services **DOB:** 01/13/1971 **PB:** Huntington **SC:** WV/USA **MS:** Married **SPN:** Rhonda Massie **CH:** Four Children **ED:** MS in Electrical Engineering, Massachusetts Institute of Technology (1996); BS in Electrical Engineering, Massachusetts Institute of Technology (1993) **C:** Member, U.S. House of Representatives from Kentucky's Fourth Congressional District, United States Congress, Washington, DC (2013-Present); Member, U.S. House Committee on Transportation and Infrastructure (2013-Present); Member, U.S. House Science, Space and Technology Committee (2013-Present); Member, U.S. House Committee on Oversight and Government Reform (2013-Present); Judge-Executive, Lewis County, KY (2011-2012); Co-Founder, Chairman, Chief Technology Officer, SensAble Technologies, Inc. (Formerly SensAble Devices Inc.) (1993-2003); Owner, Cattle Farm, Garrison, KY **AW:** Lemelson-MIT Student Prize (1995) **PA:** Republican **RE:** Methodist

MAST, BRIAN JEFFERY, T: U.S. Representative from Florida **I:** Government Administration/Government Relations/Government Services **CN:** U.S. House of Representatives **DOB:** 7/10/1980 **PB:** Grand Rapids **SC:** MI/USA **PT:** James Mast; Tixomena Trujillo **MS:** Married **SPN:** Brianna Mast **CH:** Madalyn; Maverick; Magnum; Major **ED:** Bachelor of Liberal Arts, Harvard Extension School (2016); Coursework, American Military University (2008-2010) **C:** Member, U.S. Representative from Florida's 18th Congressional District (2017-Present); Explosive Specialist, U.S. Department of Homeland Security (2012-2015); Analyst, National Nuclear Security Administration (2011-2012); Member, Committee on Transportation and Infrastructure; Member, Committee on Foreign Affairs **CIV:** Volunteer, Israel Defense Forces (2015); Member, Evangelical Calvary Chapel **MIL:** With, United States Army Reserve (2000-2001) **AW:** Named, One of the 10 House Freshmen to Watch, The Hill (2016); Bronze Medal Star; Purple Heart; Defense Meritorious Service Medal; Army Commendation Medal with "V" **PA:** Republican

MATHAS, THEODORE A., T: Chairman, President, Chief Executive Officer **I:** Insurance **CN:** New York Life Insurance Company **DOB:** 04/04/1967 **ED:** JD, University of Virginia (1992); BA, Stanford University (1989) **C:** Chairman, President, Chief Executive Officer, New York Life Insurance Company (2009-Present); President, Chief Executive Officer, New York Life Insurance Company (2008-2009); President, Chief Operating Officer, New York Life Insurance Company (2007-2008); Vice Chairman, Chief Operating Officer, Member, Executive Management Committee, New York Life Insurance Company (2006-2007); Executive Vice President, Co-Head of Life and Annuity, New York Life Insurance Company (2004-2006); Chief Operating Officer, Life and Annuity Division, New York Life Insurance Company (2001-2004); Senior Vice President, New York Life Insurance Company (1998-2004); Chief Operating Officer, Agency Department, New York Life Insurance Company (1999-2001); President of NY Life Securities, New York Life Insurance Company (1997-1999); President, Eagle Strategies Corporation, New York Life Insurance Company (1996-1999); Corporate Vice President, New York Life Insurance Company (1995-1998); Attorney,

Debevoise & Plimpton LLP **CR:** Chairman, American Council of Life Insurers (2012-Present); Board of Directors, American Council of Life Insurers (2007-Present); Board of Directors, New York Life Insurance Company (2006-Present); Haier New York Life Insurance Ltd. **CW:** Member, The University of Virginia Law Review **MEM:** Order of the Coif

MATHER, JOHN CROMWELL, PHD, T: Senior Scientist; Astrophysicist **I:** Sciences **CN:** NASA/Goddard Space Flight Center **DOB:** 08/07/1946 **PB:** Roanoke **SC:** VA/USA **PT:** Robert Eugene Mather; Martha Belle (Cromwell) Mather **MS:** Married **SPN:** Jane Anne Hauser (11/22/1980) **ED:** Honorary DSc in Physics, University of Notre Dame, South Bend, IN (2011); Honorary DSc in Physics, University of Maryland, College Park, MD (2008); Honorary DSc in Physics, Swarthmore College (1994); PhD in Physics, University of California Berkeley (1974); BA in Physics, Swarthmore College, PA (1968) **C:** Senior Scientist, NASA/Goddard Space Flight Center (1993-Present); Project Scientist, COBE, NASA/Goddard Space Flight Center, Greenbelt, MD (1982-Present); Principal Investigator, FIRAS on COBE, NASA/Goddard Space Flight Center, Greenbelt, MD (1976-Present); Astrophysicist, NASA/Goddard Space Flight Center, Greenbelt, MD (1976-Present); Head, Office of Chief Scientist, NASA, Washington, DC (2007-2008); Senior Project Researcher, James Webb Space Telescope (2002); Researcher, Next Generation Space Telescope (1995-2002); Head, Infrared Astrophysics Branch, NASA/Goddard Space Flight Center (1988-1989, 1990-1993); Senior Scientist, NASA/Goddard Space Flight Center, Greenbelt, MD (1989-1990); Study Scientist, Cosmic Background Explorer Satellite, NASA/Goddard Space Flight Center, Greenbelt, MD (1976-1982); Lecturer, Astronomy, Columbia University, New York, NY (1975-1976); NAS/NRC Research Associate, NASA/Goddard Institute of Space Studies, New York, NY (1974-1976) **CR:** Astrophysics Subcommittee, NASA Advisory Council (2006-2007); National Research Council Board of Physics and Astronomy (1998-2001); Chairman, External Advisory Board, Research in the Antarctic, The University of Chicago Center for Astronomy and Astrophysics (1992-1995); NASA Lunar Astrophysics Management Operations Working Group, Washington, DC (1992) **CIV:** President, John and Jane Mather Foundation for Science and the Arts (2007-Present) **CW:** Co-Author, "The Very First Light: The True Inside Story of the Scientific Journey Back to the Dawn of the Universe" (1996); Contributor, Articles, Professional Journals **AW:** Award, New Jersey Educational Association (2010); Gold Medal, Prime Minister of India (2009); Robinson Prize, Newcastle University (2008); Presidential Rank Award, NASA (2003, 2008); Antoinette de Vaucouleurs Medal, The University of Texas at Austin (2007); Listee, World's Most Influential People, Time Magazine (2007); Co-Recipient, Nobel Prize in Physics (2006); Cosmology Prize, Peter Gruber Foundation (2006); George W. Goddard Award, SPIE (2005); Inductee, Newton High School Hall of Fame, NJ (2003); Benjamin Franklin Medal in Physics, Franklin Institute (1999); Marc Aaronson Memorial Prize (1998); Inductee, Aviation Week & Space Technology Hall of Fame (1997); Rumford Prize, American Academy of Arts & Sciences (1996); John Scott Award, City of Philadelphia, PA (1995); Goddard Fellow (1994); Dannie Heineman Prize for Astrophysics, American Astronomical Society (1994); American Institute of Aeronautics and Astronautics Space Science Award (1993); Laurels Award for Space/Missiles, Aviation Week & Space Technology (1992); National Space Achievement Award, Rotary Club (1991); National Air & Space Museum Trophy (1991); Fellowship, Hertz Foundation (1970-1974); Fellowship, National Science Foundation (1968-1970); Honorary Woodrow Wilson Fellowship (1968-1970); Recipient, Numerous Other Prizes and Medals **MEM:** Councilor, American Astronomical Society (1998-2001); Fellow, American Physical Society; American Institute of Aeronautics and Astronautics; National Academy of Sciences; American Academy of Arts & Sciences; SPIE; International Astronomical Union; American Astronomical Society; The Phi Beta Kappa Society; Sigma Xi **PA:** Democrat **RE:** Unitarian Universalist

MATHERNE, RAY, "DOC" JOSEPH, T: Educational Administrator; Real Estate Developer **I:** Real Estate **CN:** RJM Enterprises, Inc. **DOB:** 06/17/1945 **PB:** Des Allemands **SC:** LA/USA **PT:** Victor Joseph Matherne; Edna (Dufrene) Matherne **MS:** Married **SPN:** Dr. Elsa Martinez Matherne (06/19/2004); Carolyn Danos (02/19/1966) **CH:** Scott; Ron; Monique **ED:** Postdoctorate Coursework, Harvard University, Cambridge, MA (1990); Postdoctorate Coursework, Université Laval, Quebec, Canada (1978); PhD, The University of Southern Mississippi, Hattiesburg, MS (1975); MEd, Nicholls State University, Thibodaux, LA (1974); BS, Nicholls State University, Thibodaux, LA (1968) **CT:** Certified Administrator, Superintendent, Evaluator, Supervisor, Principal, Teacher, State of Louisiana **C:** Owner, President, RJM Enterprise, Inc., Des Allemands, LA (1969-Present); Assistant Executive Director, St. Charles Parish Public Schools, Luling, LA (1990-2002); Supervisor of Teacher Recruitment, St. Charles Parish Public Schools, Luling, LA (1997); Principal, Luling Elementary School, St. Charles Parish Public Schools, Luling, LA (1986-1990); Executive Director, South Louisiana Port Commission (Port of South Louisiana), LaPlace, LA (1983-1985); Principal, Allemands Elementary School, St. Charles Parish Public Schools, Des Allemands, LA (1979-1983); Bilingual Director, St. Charles Parish Public Schools, Luling, LA (1977-1979); Public Schools, Luling, LA (1975-1977); Science Teacher, J. B. Martin Junior High School (Now J.B. Martin Middle School), St. Charles Parish Public Schools, Paradis, LA (1971-1974) **CR:** Owner, President, RJM Enterprises, Paradis, LA (1969-Present); State Department of Education Teacher Certification Advisory Board, LA (1992-2000); Owner, President, Realtors of St. Charles (Now St. Charles Realtors Association); Educational Evaluator, State Department of Education, Baton Rouge, LA **CIV:** St. Charles Civic Alliance, Hahnville, LA (1988-Present); Vice President, Coastal Commission, Hahnville, LA (1983-Present); President, Port Association of Louisiana, Baton Rouge, LA (1984-1985); President, Citizen Action Committee, Bayou Gauche, LA (1975-1985); Founder, Port Association of Louisiana **CW:** Author, Children's Book, "T-Jacque Le Piegier" (1981) **AW:** Support Award, Boy Scouts of America (1989); Outstanding Leadership Award, Allemands Parent Association (1982) **MEM:** Board of Directors, Louisiana Education Priorities for Future (1982); Board of Directors, Louisiana Education Research Association; Board Member, River Road Historical Society **MH:** Albert Nelson Marquis Lifetime Achievement Award **B/I:** Dr. Matherne became involved in his profession because he came from an impoverished community and struggling parents. His father was a commercial fisherman and trapper. He felt the need to improve himself and his future family in whatever capacity that he could. The first thing he saw was the importance of an excellent education. That is the reason he pursued education to the degree that he did. He was trying to improve himself and provide for his family in the most comprehensive fashion possible while still being dedicated to the mission of helping others in rural areas that are impoverished. **AV:** Diving; Fishing; Hunting; Sports; International traveler **PA:** Democrat **RE:** Roman Catholic **THT:** Dr. Matherne said, "Once you get past that burden of going to school to achieve an education, it gets to the point that it becomes an exciting adventure of learning, hence, the completion of the doctorate and studies in Quebec, Harvard, and Paris." This process led him to interacting with different people in different fields, which led to the port activity and the real estate development activity.

MATHERS, MARSHALL (EMINEM), T: Rap Artist; Producer **I:** Media & Entertainment **DOB:** 10/17/1973 **PB:** St. Joseph **PT:** Marshall Bruce Mathers Jr.; Deborah R. (Nelson) Mathers-Briggs **MS:** Married **SPN:** Kimberly Anne Scott (06/14/1999, Divorced 10/11/2001, Remarried 2006, Divorced April 2006) **C:** Founder, Producer, Shady Records, New York, NY (1999-Present); Performer, D12 (1996-Present); Solo Artist (1992) **CIV:** Founder, The Marshall Mathers Foundation **CW:** Performer, Album, "Music to be Murdered by" (2020); Performer, Album, "Revival" (2017); Actor, "Bodied" (2017); Himself, "The Defiant Ones" (2017); Himself, "Stretch and Bobbito: Radio That Changed Lives" (2015); Himself, "Not Afraid: The Shady Records Story" (2015); Actor, "The Interview" (2014); Performer, Album, "The Marshall Mathers LP" (2013); Himself, "Detroit Rubber" (2013); Himself, "How to Make Money Selling Drugs" (2012); Himself, "Something from Nothing: The Art of Rap" (2012); Performer, Album, "Recovery" (2010); Actor, "Entourage" (2005, 2010); Himself, "Saturday Night Live" (1999, 2000, 2002, 2004, 2010); Performer, Album, "Relapse" (2009); Actor, "Funny People" (2009); Author, "The Way I Am" (2008); Performer, Album, "The Re-Up" (2006); Producer, Album, "Second Round's on Me," Obie Trice (2006); Performer, Album, "Curtain Call" (2005); Producer, Album, "The Massacre," 50 Cent (2005); Performer, Album, "D12 World" (2004); Performer, Album, "Encore" (2004); Producer, Album, "Get Rich or Die Tryin'," 50 Cent (2003); Producer, Album, "Cheers," Obie Trice (2003); Himself, "50 Cent: The New Breed" (2003); Performer, Album, "The Eminem Show" (2002); Actor, "8 Mile" (2002); Performer, Album, "Devil's Night" (2001); Performer, Album, "The Marshall Mathers LP" (2000); Performer, Album, "The Slim Shady LP" (1999); Performer, Album "Infinite" (1997) **AW:** Top Rap Artist, Billboard (2011, 2014); Favorite Hip-Hop Artist, Billboard (2010, 2011, 2012); Favorite Hip-Hop Artist, People's Choice Awards (2010, 2011, 2012); Top Male Artist, Billboard (2011); Named Top Artist, Billboard Music Awards (2011); Favorite Male Artist, People's Choice Awards (2011); Favorite Hip Hop/R&B Male Artist, American Music Awards (2003, 2005, 2006, 2010); Artist of the Decade, Billboard (2009); Favorite Male Musical Performer, People's Choice Awards (2003, 2005); Best Selling Rap/Hip-Hop Artist, World Music Awards (2005); Best Selling Pop/Rock Artist, World Music Awards (2005); Best American Male Artist, World Music Awards (2003); Favorite Pop/Rock Male Artist, American Music Awards (2003); Named One of the 100 Greatest Artists of All Time, Rolling Stone Magazine, VH1; Five Source Hip Hop Music Awards; Seven Teen Choice Awards; Twelve MTV Video Music Awards; Twelve Detroit Music Awards; Numerous Grammy Awards

MATHES, EDWARD C., T: Chairman **I:** Architecture & Construction **CN:** Mathes Breirre Architects **DOB:** 03/10/1943 **PB:** New Orleans **SC:** LA/USA **PT:** Earl L. Mathes; Margaret (Gash) Mathes **MS:** Divorced **SPN:** Anne M. Ergenbright (03/1964, Divorced 06/2000) **CH:** Margaret (Megby) Elizabeth Hughes; Anne Catherine Aboud **ED:** BArch, University of Louisiana at Lafayette (1968) **CT:** Registered

Architect, States of Louisiana, Mississippi, Florida, Texas, Alabama, Georgia, Tennessee, Kentucky, North Carolina, South Carolina, West Virginia and Connecticut **C:** Chairman, Mathes Breirre Architects (2001-Present); President, The Mathes Group, New Orleans, LA (1982-2000); President, Mathes, Bergman & Associates, Inc., New Orleans, LA (1969-1982); Assistant to Managing Architect, Rogers, Taliaferro, Kostritsky & Lamb, Baltimore, MD (1969); Institute Scholar, AIA (1968-1969) **CR:** Visiting Committee, College of Business, Loyola University New Orleans (2008-Present); Dean's Adviser Council, College of the Arts, University of Louisiana at Lafayette (2004-2008); The President's Council, Loyola University (1989-1999); National President, Association of Student Chapters, AIA (1967-1968) **CIV:** Board Member, Alabama Contemporary Art Center (2008-Present); American Red Cross (1989-2007); Board of Directors, City Park Improvement Association (1993-1994, 1996-2003); Participant, Institute of Politics, Loyola University (1971); Session, St. Charles Avenue Presbyterian Church **CW:** National World War II Museum Capital Expansion Projects (2004-Present); New Orleans Center for Creative Arts (1999) **AW:** Spark Lifetime Achievement Award, University of Louisiana at Lafayette (2018); Recognition of Design Excellence, National Organization of Minority Architects (2002); People's Choice Award for University Library (2000); Chief Executive Officer's Award, Southeast Louisiana Chapter, American Red Cross (1998); People's Choice Award for Communications, Music and Theater, Loyola University New Orleans (1989); American School and University Award (1983, 1985) **MEM:** President, New Orleans Chapter, AIA (1989); President, Construction Industry Association (1984-1985); City Energy Club; Metairie Country Club; Pickwick Club **MH:** Albert Nelson Marquis Lifetime Achievement Award **B/I:** Mr. Mathes became involved in his profession because his father was an architect, so he always had an interest in the field. **AV:** Collecting stamps; Playing tennis; Traveling **PA:** Republican **RE:** Presbyterian

MATSUI, DORIS KAZUE, T: U.S. Representative **I:** Government Administration/Government Relations/Government Services **DOB:** 09/25/1944 **PB:** Dinuba **SC:** CA/USA **MS:** Widowed **SPN:** Robert Takeo Matsui (09/17/1966, Deceased 01/01/2005) **CH:** Brian **ED:** BA in Psychology, University of California Berkeley (1966) **C:** U.S. Representative, California's Sixth Congressional District, United States Congress (2013-Present); U.S. Representative, California's Fifth Congressional District, United States Congress (2005-2013); Government Relations Adviser, Collier, Shannon & Scott PLLC, Washington, DC (1999-2005); Senior Adviser to President, The White House, Washington, DC (1993-1999); Member, Committee on Budget; Member, Committee on Natural Resources **CR:** Member, Clinton-Gore Transition Team (1992-1993) **CIV:** Board of Regents, Smithsonian Institute; Former Member, Board of Trustees, Sacramento Children's Home; Former Member, Board of Trustees, Arena Stage; Former Member, Board of Trustees, Crocker Art Museum; Board of Trustees, Meridian International Center; Board of Trustees, Woodrow Wilson Center **AW:** Rosalie Stern Award, Alumni Association, University of California Berkeley; Newmyer Award, Sidwell Friends School; Mentor Award, Sacramento School for Public Administration, University of Southern California (Now USC Price School in Sacramento); Advocates Award, National Association for Mental Health; Action for Breast Cancer Awareness Award **MEM:** Junior League of Sacramento; Women's Club of Sacramento **PA:** Democrat **RE:** Methodist

MATTHEW, THOMAS LEWIS, MD, T: Director **I:** Medicine & Health Care **CN:** Suburban Hospital **PT:** Dr. Thomas William Matthew **MS:** Married **SPN:** Dr. Dayna Matthews **CH:** Sarah Griffin Mueller; Thomas William; Marion Lewis **ED:** MD, Columbia University College of Physicians and Surgeons (1985); Bachelor's Degree, Harvard College (1981); Research Fellowship, Ford Foundation Grant, University of Virginia; Resident, General Surgery, University of Virginia **CT:** Thoracic and Cardiac Surgery, American Board of Thoracic Surgery (1995); Surgery, American Board of Surgery (1993) **C:** Director, Johns Hopkins Cardio-thoracic Surgery Program, Suburban Hospital (2017-Present); Resident, Chief Resident, Thoracic Cardiovascular Surgery, University of Virginia (1993-1994); Co-director, Cardiovascular and Thoracic Surgical Services, Boulder Community Hospital; Co-director, Cardiovascular Service Line, Medical Center of the Rockies; Founder, Bolder Valley Thoracic and Cardiovascular Surgery; Founder Program, Longmont United Hospital, Bolder, CO; Chief, Medical Staff, Medical Director, Progressive Open Heart Unit, Audubon Hospital, Louisville, KY; Director, Cardiac Intensive Care Unit; Partner, Louisville Heart Surgery, Louisville, KY **CR:** Perioperative Governance Committee; Director, CV Quality Committee; Board Member, Jewish Hospital Cardiovascular Institute; Board Member, American Heart Association of Louisville, Kentucky; Vice President, Falls City Medical Society **CIV:** Volunteer, Open Heart Surgeon, King Faisal Hospital, Rwanda (2013-2015); Volunteer, Medical Mission, Youth with a Mission, Mexico, Honduras; Team Heart Surgical Mission Development Team, Kigali, Rwanda **CW:** Co-Author, "Ethical precepts for medical volunteerism: including local voices and values to guide RHD surgery in Rwanda" (2015) **AW:** Ford Foundation Fellowship for Research; America's Top Doctors, Castle Connolly; Regional Top Doctor, Castle Connolly; Multicultural Award, Bolder, CO **MEM:** Fellow, American College of Surgeons; Fellow, American College of Cardiology; National Medical Association; Society of Thoracic Surgeons **MH:** Albert Nelson Marquis Lifetime Achievement Award; Marquis Who's Who Top Professional **B/I:** Dr. Matthew was inspired by his father; he was a highly successful neurosurgeon. In fact, Dr. Matthew's father was the first black neurosurgeon trained in the United States. Additionally, he founded a non-profit organization dedicated to helping poor African Americans in Harlem develop job skills and find employment. Another way Dr. Matthew's father helped people was by employing them at the construction company and hospital with which he worked. Dr. Matthew is proud of his father; he wanted to emulate his dedication to helping people, so he worked hard to get where he is today.

MATTHEWS, CHRIS JOHN, T: Former Political Commentator; Author **I:** Media & Entertainment **DOB:** 12/17/1945 **PB:** Philadelphia **SC:** PA/USA **PT:** Herbert Charles Matthews; Mary Teresa (Shields) Matthews **MS:** Married **SPN:** Kathleen Ann (Cunningham) Mattews (1980) **CH:** Michael; Thomas; Caroline **ED:** Honorary Doctorate, Pierce College, PA (2015); Honorary Doctorate, Merrimack College, MA (2015); Honorary Doctorate, La Salle University, PA (2014); Honorary LittD, University of Rochester (2014); Honorary LLD, Suffolk University, MA (2013); Honorary DHL, Howard University, Washington, DC (2012); Honorary Doctor of Communications, Saint Joseph's University, PA (2009); Honorary DHL, Washington University in St. Louis, MO (2008); Honorary DHL, Temple University, PA (2008); Honorary DHL, Old Dominion University, VA (2008); Honorary Doctorate, Fordham University, NY (2006); Honorary DHL, Quinnipiac University, CT (2005); Honorary Doctorate, Hobart and William Smith Colleges, NY (2004); Honorary Doctorate, College of the Holy Cross, MA (2003); Honorary Doctorate, Drexel University, PA (2003); Honorary Doctorate, College of the Holy Cross, Worcester, MA (2003); BA in Economics, College of the Holy Cross, Worcester, MA (1967); Honorary Doctorate, Chesnut Hill College; Honorary Doctorate, Anna Maria College, MA; Honorary Doctorate, New England Law, MA; Honorary Doctorate, Beaver College (Now Arcadia University); Honorary Doctorate, Fontbonne College (Now Fontbonne University); Honorary Doctorate, Niagara University, NY; Honorary Doctorate, Loyola College Maryland (Now Loyola University Maryland); Honorary Doctorate, Saint Leo University, FL **C:** Host, "The Chris Matthews Show" (2002-2013); Host, "Hardball with Chris Matthews," MSNBC (1999-2020); Host, "Hardball with Chris Matthews," CNBC (1997-2002); Bureau Chief, Columnist, San Francisco Examiner, WA (1987-2000); Political Analyst, "CBS This Morning," WA (1987); Aide to Speaker Tip O'Neill, U.S. House of Representatives, Washington, DC (1981-1987); Speechwriter to President Jimmy Carter, The White House, Washington, DC (1977-1979); Staff Assistant, U.S. Senate Budget Committee, Washington, DC (1974-1977); Staff Member to Senator Edward Muskie, U.S. Senate, Washington, DC (1973-1974;) Legislative Assistant to Senator Frank Moss, U.S. Senate, Washington, DC (1971-1973); Former National Syndicated Columnist, San Francisco Chronicle **CIV:** Trade Development Advisor, U.S. Peace Corps, Swaziland (1968-1970) **CW:** Author, "Bobby Kennedy: A Raging Spirit" (2017); Author, "Tip and the Gipper: When Politics Worked" (2013); Author, "Jack Kennedy: Elusive Hero" (2011); Author, "Life's a Campaign: What Politics Has Taught Me About Friendship, Rivalry, Reputation and Success" (2007); Actor, "Man of the Year" (2006); Author, "American: Beyond Our Grandest Notions" (2002); Author, "Now, Let Me Tell You What I Really Think" (2001); Author, "Hardball: How Politics is Really Played- Told By One Who Knows the Game" (1999); Author, "Kennedy & Nixon: The Rivalry That Shaped Postwar America" (1996); Contributor, Articles, Professional Journals **AW:** Tip O'Neill Irish Diaspora Award (2016); Listee, 50 Highest-Earning Political Figures, Newsweek (2010); Gold Medal for Distinguished Achievement, The Pennsylvania Society (2005); David Brinkley Award for Excellence in Broadcast Journalism; John F. Kennedy Memorial Award; Abraham Lincoln Award, The Union League of Philadelphia **PA:** Democrat **RE:** Roman Catholic

MATTHIAS, JOHN, EMERITUS PROFESSOR, AMERICAN POET, T: English Literature Educator **I:** Education/Educational Services **CN:** University of Notre Dame **DOB:** 09/05/1941 **PB:** Columbus **SC:** OH/USA **PT:** John Marshall Matthias; Lois (Kirkpatrick) Matthias **MS:** Married **SPN:** Diana Clare Jocelyn (12/27/1967) **CH:** Cynouai; Laura **ED:** Postgraduate, University of London, London, England (1967); MA, Stanford University, Stanford, CA (1966); BA, Ohio State University, Columbus, OH (1963) **C:** Emeritus Professor, University of Notre Dame, IN (2000-Present); Retired, Professor, University of Notre Dame, IN (1980-2000); Associate Professor, University of Notre Dame, IN (1973-1980); Assistant Professor, Department of English, University of Notre Dame, IN (1967-1973) **CR:** Life Member, Clare Hall, University of Cambridge, Cambridge, England (1985-Present); Visiting Professor, Department of English, University of Chicago, Chicago, IL (1980); Associate, Clare Hall, University of Cambridge, Cambridge, England (1977); Visiting Fellow, Clare Hall, University of Cambridge, Cambridge, England (1966-1977); Visiting Professor, Department of English, Skidmore College, Saratoga

Springs, NY (1975) **CW:** Author, "Acoustic Shadows" (2019); Co-Author, "Regrounding a Pilgrimage" (2018); Co-Author, "Revoloutions: A Collaboration" (2017); Playwright, "Six Short Play" (2016); Author, "Complayntes for Doctor Neuro & Other Poems" (2016); Author, "At Large" (2016); Author, "Different Kinds of Music" (2014); Author, "Collected Shorter Poems, Vol. 1, 1961-1995" (2013); Author, "Collected Longer Poems" (2012); "The Salt Companion to John Matthias" (2011); Author, "Collected Shorter Poems, Vol. 2, 1995-2011" (2011); Author, "Who Was Cousin Alice? and Other Questions" (2011); Author, "Trigons" (2010); Interview, "Samizdat" (2010); Author, "Kedging" (2007); Author, "New Selected Poems" (2004); Author, "Working Progress, Working Title" (2002); Subject, "Word Play Place: Essays On The Poetry Of John Matthias" (1998); Author, "Swimming at Midnight: Selected Shorter Poems" (1995); Author, "Beltane at Aphelion" (1995); Author, "Reading Old Friends" (1992); Author, "A Gathering of Ways" (1991); Author, "Northern Summer: New and Selected Poems" (1984); Author, "Introducing David Jones" (1980); Author, "Bathory & Lermontov" (1980); Author, "Crossing" (1979); Author, "Turns" (1975); Author, "Bucyrus" (1970) **AW:** Ohio Library Association Poetry Award (1996); Grantee, Lily Endowment (1991-1992); George Bogin Memorial Award, Poetry Society of America (1990); Ingram Merrill Foundation Award (1984, 1990); Slobadan Jovanovic Literary Prize (1989); Society for the Study of Midwestern Literature Poetry Prize (1986); Society of Midland Authors Poetry Award (1984); Columbia University Translation Center Award (1979) **MEM:** American Association of University Professors; PEN America; Poets & Writers; Poetry Society of America **MH:** Albert Nelson Marquis Lifetime Achievement Award **B/I:** Mr. Matthias became involved in his profession because of the teachers he had in high school.

MATTOS, DANA JON, T: Owner, Manager **I:** Consumer Goods and Services **CN:** Hawaii Coffee Connection **DOB:** 07/21/1961 **PB:** Newark **SC:** NJ/USA **PT:** Dennis Mattos; Doris Mattos **MS:** Married **SPN:** Laurie Mattos **CH:** Joshua Jon Mattos; Kamariya Rose Mattos; Kaleia Francis Mattos **ED:** Associate of Arts in Criminal Justice, Sierra College (1981) **CT:** Certified Coroner **C:** Owner, Hawaii Coffee Connection (2001-Present); Police Officer (1990-1997) **CIV:** President, Kona Dance and Performing Arts **MIL:** Military Police School, U.S. Army (1981-1983) **CW:** Owner, Lead Instructor, KunTao Silat **MH:** Albert Nelson Marquis Lifetime Achievement Award **AS:** Mr. Mattos attributes his success to his strong work ethic and soft politics. **B/I:** Mr. Mattos became involved in his profession because his parents asked him to help expand their business. **AV:** Weightlifting; Barbecue cooking **PA:** Republican **RE:** Humanist

MATTSON, JANET MARIE, T: Contracting Officer, Microbiologist **I:** Sciences **DOB:** 03/21/1947 **PB:** Bozeman **SC:** MT/USA **PT:** Howard Lawrence; Lucille Irene (Cloninger) **MS:** Married **SPN:** Harry Franklin Baker (05/23/1981) **CH:** Matthew; David **ED:** MGA, University of Maryland, College Park (1984); Postgraduate Coursework, Georgetown University, Washington, DC (1977); MS in Biology, South Dakota State University, Brookings, SD (1972); BS in Microbiology, Montana State University, Bozeman, MT (1969) **CT:** National Cancer Institute Quality Council Certificate of Commendation (1996); FAC-C Level III Contracting Officer; Certified Professional Contracts Manager (CPCM); NCMA Fellow **C:** Retired (2018); Branch Chief Contracting Officer, National Heart, Lung, and Blood Institute/NIH, Rockville, MD (2012-2018); Contracting Officer Team Leader, Department of Health & Human Services, Substance Abuse and Mental Health Services Administration (2005-2012); Contracting Officer, National Institute of Allergy & Infectious Diseases/NIH, Rockville, MD (2000-2005); Contracting Officer, National Cancer Institute/NIH, Rockville, MD (1993-2000); Contracting Officer, Division Procurement, National Institutes of Health, Bethesda, MD (1990-1993); Contract Specialist, Goddard Space Flight Center, Greenbelt, MD (1986-1989); Presidential Management Intern, Goddard Space Flight Center, Greenbelt, MD (1984-1986); Technical Information Specialist, National Library Medicine/NIH, Bethesda, MD (1980-1984); Virologist, National Institute of Neurological and Communicable Diseases and Stroke/NIH, Bethesda, MD (1975-1980); Microbiologist, Microbiology Associates, Inc., Bethesda, MD (1974-1975); Microbiologist, Meloy Laboratories, Inc., Springfield, VA (1973-1974); Virologist, Veterinary Research Diagnostic Laboratory, South Dakota State University, Brookings, SD (1970-1973); NASA/Goddard Space Flight Center **CIV:** Volunteer, Habitat for Humanity, New Orleans, LA **CW:** Co-Author, Scholarly Article, "Isolation, Identification and Characterization of Six Bovine Picornavirus Isolates" (1974); Co-Author, Scholarly Article, "Pathogenic Properties of Six Bovine Picornavirus Isolates in Mice" (1974); Exhibitions, Friendship Heights, Kensington, Glen Echo, Brookside Gardens, Maryland **AW:** NIH Director's Award, National Heart, Lung, and Blood (2015); National Institutes of Health (NIH) Honor Award (2014); National Achievement Award, National Contract Management Association (NCMA) (2012); Quality of Work Life HHS/SAMHSA Partnership Award (2011); Superior Internal Service Award (2008); Secretary's Award for Distinguished Service (2006); NCMA Arthur G. Miller Volunteer Award (2006); NCMA Mid-Atlantic Region Member of the Year Award (2001); NCMA Fellow Designation (2000); Gamma Sigma Delta Scholastic Honorary (1971); Sigma Xi Research Proposal Award (1971); American Cancer Society Fellowship (1965) **MEM:** National Contract Management Association, Sigma Xi; Gamma Sigma Delta; Montgomery County Art Association **MH:** Albert Nelson Marquis Lifetime Achievement Award; Marquis Who's Who Top Professional **B/I:** Ms. Mattson became involved in her profession because of high school. She had a fabulous high school teacher, and when she was a junior in high school, she got a grant to go work in a microbiology lab at the university during the summer. In contracting, she was still involved in science, so she never left science - that has always been her passion. **AV:** Travel; Artist (oil, acrylics, water color painting) **THT:** In November 2006, Ms. Mattson worked for Habitat for Humanity after Hurricane Katrina in New Orleans, Louisiana.

MATTSON, MAUREEN, "MO", T: Physical Education Teacher **I:** Education/Educational Services **CN:** Pittsburg High School **PB:** Hollister **SC:** CA/USA **PT:** Robert Mattson, Sr. (Deceased); Diane Mattson **ED:** MS in Physical Education, California State University, East Bay, Hayward, CA (1992); BA in Physical Education, University of California, Berkeley (1984) **CT:** Sudden Cardiac Arrest, NFHS (2018); Registered Athletic Administrator, NIAAA (2012); Fundamentals of Coaching and the California State Component, NFHS (2012); Sportmanship Certification, NFHS (2012); The Role of the Parent in Sports-Positive Sport Parenting, NFHS (2012); Bullying, Hazing and Inappropriate Behaviors Course, NFHS (2012); Certification, NIAAA; Certification, NFHS **C:** Physical Education Instructor, Pittsburg High School, Pittsburg, CA (1986-Present); Assistant Athletic Director, Pittsburg High School, Pittsburg, CA (2010-2012); Physical Education Instructor, Diablo Valley College, Pleasant Hill, CA (2004-2010); Assistant Principal, Pittsburg High School, Pittsburg, CA (1998-1999); Aquatics Program Manager, Swim Instructor, Parks and Recreation Department, City of Hollister (1981-1985) **CR:** Unified Sports Coach, Pittsburg High School, Pittsburg, CA (2015-Present); Coach, Varsity Girls Volleyball, Pittsburg High School, Pittsburg, CA (2010-2011); Head Coach, Women's Basketball, Diablo Valley College, Pleasant Hill, CA (2004-2010); Coach, Varsity Girls Basketball, Pittsburg High School, Pittsburg, CA (1989-2004); Coach, Varsity Boys Volleyball, Pittsburg High School, Pittsburg, CA (1986-1994); Coach, Girls Freshman Basketball, Pittsburg High School, Pittsburg, CA (1986-1989); Coach, Varsity Girls Basketball, San Benito High School, Hollister, CA (1984-1986); Coach, Junior Varsity Volleyball, San Benito High School, Hollister, CA (1984-1986); Coach, Varsity Softball, San Benito High School, Hollister, CA (1984-1985) **CIV:** Special Olympics Mentor (2019-Present); Special Olympics North America Unified Champion Schools Academic Practitioners Network (2018-Present); Western Association of Schools and Colleges Leadership Team, Pittsburg High School (2006, 2009); Board Member, Friends of the Pirate Bingo Board, Pittsburg High School (1992-2006); Basketball Advisory Committee, State CIF (1995-1997); Attendance and Tardy Committee, Pittsburg High School (1995); North Coast Section Basketball Management Committee (1994-1995) **CW:** Author, "Unified Bowling-Bonding Experience for Everyone at California School" (2019) **AW:** Teacher of the Year, Contra Costa County (2019-2020); Teacher of the Year, Pittsburg Unified School District (2019-2020); Coach of the Year, BVAL (2017-2018); Equity Award, Pittsburg Unified School District (2017); Volunteer of the Year, Northern California Schools Partnership Program, Special Olympics (2015) **MEM:** California Association for Health, Physical Education, Recreation and Dance; Women's Basketball Coaches Association; California Coaches Association; CSADA; NIAAA **MH:** Marquis Who's Who Top Professional; Marquis Who's Who Humanitarian Award **AS:** Ms. Mattson attributes her success to listening, learning and collaborating with other educators and coaches. She also attributes her success to being active within her community and school. She enjoys teaching and coaching and is proud of her work in unifying the general and special education students through unified sports. **B/I:** Ms. Mattson was influenced by her father, who was a physical education teacher and coach for 38 years at San Benito High School. Additionally, her father was the athletic director and physical education department chair. He coached her high school basketball team and then mentored her in coaching basketball while she was student teaching at San Benito High School. Her father's mentoring along with her master teacher, Jackie Vosbrink, helped shape her into the teacher and coach she is today.

MATTY, VERA ANNA, T: Public Speaker in Washington Senate **I:** Government Administration/Government Relations/Government Services **CN:** United Nations UNSCO **SC:** Budapest/Hungary **PT:** Veronica (Vera) Beslic; Imre Buzogany **ED:** MA, Arizona State University (1979); ABD, Arizona State University; BS in English, University of Wisconsin-Madison **C:** Vice President, Charles Rutenberg Realty (2007-2011);Executive Assistant to Chief Executive Officer, BMG Entertainment (1993-2002); Assistant to President, New York Unemployment Project; Advocacy and Communications Officer, United Nations UNSCO; Self-Employed **CR:** Principle Speaker, U.S. Senate (2000) **CIV:** Volunteer, Community Church **CW:** Painter, International Painting Exhibitions **AW:** Humanitarian Award, Humanitarian Foundation (2013); Humanitarian Award (2003); Painting Award, International Exhibition, Europe (1986) **AS:** Ms. Matty attributes her success to her faith. With hard work and dedication, success is imminent and achievable. Likewise, she thanks her mother for her endless support. **B/I:** Ms. Matty is a humanitarian. Currently, she is working on a book, which she hopes to publish this year. It is about creating a better, happier life on earth. Ms. Matty knew she wanted to pursue work in her field since high school. **AV:** Reading; Listening to classical and modern music **THT:** Ms. Matty tries to enjoy her life and help others all the while.

MAURER, FRANK W., PHD, T: Land Trust Administrator **I:** Environmental Services **DOB:** 08/25/1941 **PB:** Boston **SC:** MA/USA **PT:** Frank W Senior; Elizabeth M. Maurer **ED:** Doctor of Philosophy in Vertebrate Zoology and Ecology, Cornell University, Ithaca, NY (1968); Bachelor of Arts in Biology, Antioch College, Yellow Springs, OH (1964) **CT:** Licensed Vessel Operator, California **C:** Executive Director, President, Environmental Education Farm Foundation, Davis, CA (1993-Present); Executive Director, President, Quail Ridge Wilderness Conservancy, Davis, CA (1989-Present); Organic Farmers Market Producer (1978-Present); Owner, Operator, Director, Research Farm, Davis, CA (1978-Present); Interviewer, 13 Countries in Asia (1978); Research Associate, Swedish University Agricultural Scis., Uppsala, Sweden (1977); Lecturer in Zoology, National University of Lesotho (1971-1976); Assistant Professor of Biology, University of the Bosphorus, Istanbul, Turkey (1968-1971) **CR:** Owner, Deer Canyon Preserve, New Mexico (2006-Present); Founder, Children's Program on Fluorescent Rocks and Invertebrates (2015); Conservator, Sundance Ranch, Rawlins, WY (2011); Consultant, Open Space and Conservation Models for Small Landowners, Nevada (2007-Present); Consultant, Open Space and Conservation Models for Small Landowners, Wyoming (2004-Present); Lecturer in Field **CIV:** Activist, Californians for Electoral Reform, Sacramento, CA (2004-Present); Activist, Center for Voting and Democracy, Takoma Park, MD (2004-Present); Registered Pacifist, U.S. Draft Board (1966) **CW:** Carved Petroglyphs, Tartan Stones for Various Buildings and Organizations, Including the California State Archives, the Assembly of Wales, Parliament of Scotland, Idaho State Historical Society, New Mexico State Records Center & Archives and the Newton North High School Building, Among Many Others (2000-2016); Author, Facilitator, Wyoming State Grass Bill (2007); Producer, Photobook, "Portraits of a Vanishing Landscape A Pictorial Interpretation of the Western Sagebrush Steppe" (2006); Author, Legislation, California State Grass Bill (2004); Producer, CD, Scottish Poetry (2003); Producer, Educational Videos, "Reflections" (2000); Producer, Educational Videos, Quail Ridge Reserve (1998); Contributor, Articles to Professional Publications **AW:** The President's Volunteer Service Award (2016); Recognition Award, University of California Natural Reserve Systems (2009); Conservation Achievement Recognition, Napa County Land Trust (1990); John Muir Award, Davis Farmer's Market (1989) **MEM:** Lifetime Member, Society Conservation Biology; Lifetime Member, Society for the Study of Evolution; Lifetime Member, American Society of Mammalogy; Dixon Scottish Cultural Association, Sacramento Caledonian Club **MH:** Albert Nelson Marquis Lifetime Achievement Award **AV:** Travel; Hiking; Birdwatching; Photography **PA:** Green Party **THT:** Always among his goals are human rights, education, promoting environmental and open space programs, interwoven with artistic expression. In addition to starting an educational teaching farm in Davis, CA in 1978, he and his wife worked over 25 years to create a 2000 acre native habitat and wildlife reserve in Napa County by purchasing, via innovative fundraising strategies, land destined for development. He led the initiative to incorporate this reserve into the University of California's Natural Reserve System. Today's activities focus on public speaking, voting reform, habitat restoration, creating openspace and conservation models for small landowners and using photography and the art of hand-carved petroglyphs for teaching and commemorations.

MAY, JOSEPH, "JACK" L., T: Lawyer, Manufacturer of Socks **I:** Law and Legal Services **DOB:** 05/27/1929 **PB:** Nashville **SC:** TN/USA **PT:** Daniel May; Dorothy (Fishel) May **MS:** Married **SPN:** Lynn Hewes Lance (06/10/1994); Natalie McCuaig (04/12/1957, Deceased 1990) **CH:** Benjamin; Andrew; Joshua May; Maria TeSelle; Tom Lance (Stepson); Rob Lance (Stepson) **ED:** Postgraduate Coursework, Harvard Business School, Harvard University (1969); JD, New York University (1958); BA, Yale University (1951) **C:** Director, Private Practice Law, Nashville, TN (1984-Present); Secretary, Yale Class of 1951 (2013); Vice President, Wayne-Gossard Corporation, Chattanooga, TN (1972-1983); President, Athens Hosiery Mills (1966-1983); President, May Hosiery Mills, Nashville, TN (1960-1983); President, Nuweave Socks, Inc., New York, NY (1955-1959); CIA (1951-1955); Producer, Candied Yam Jackson Show (1947-1951) **CR:** Founding Director, Truxton Trust (2003); Director, Merrill Lynch Investment Management (1987-2002); Chairman, Guardianship and Trust Corporation (1994-1996); Advisory Board, Asian Strategies Group (1994) **CIV:** Collectors Circle, Frist Art Museum (2004-Present); Chairman, Campus for Human Development (2000-2002); Board of Directors, Vanderbilt Cancer Center (1994-1999); President, Jewish Community Center (1969) **MIL:** U.S. Army (1954); U.S. Navy (1947-1953) **CW:** Author, "Vestigial Organ" (2015); Author, "The Rest" (2013); Author, "An Alphabet of Letters" (2010); Author, "A Confetti of Papers" (2008); Author, "Walking Around the House" (2007) **MEM:** President, Tennessee Historical Society (2000-2002); President, Nashville Chapter, Rotary International (1971); Tennessee Bar Association; Nashville Bar Association; Panel of Neutrals, American Arbitration Association; Eagle Scout Association; Belle Meade Country Club; Shamus Club; Old Oak Club; Old Goats; Zodiac; Group of Six; Yale Club New York; Trustee, Tennessee Historical Society **BAR:** Tennessee (1959) **MH:** Albert Nelson Marquis Lifetime Achievement Award; Marquis Who's Who Top Professional; Marquis Who's Who Humanitarian Award **B/I:** Mr. May became involved in his profession after returning from the Korean War and attending New York University School of Law. After graduating, Mr. May went to work at a local law firm with some of his friends. **PA:** Republican **RE:** Jewish **THT:** Mr. May worked in his family's sock manufacturing business for 30 years before selling the company. He comes from a long line of Republicans. Additionally, he has served on some the New York Stock Exchange's corporate boards including Merrill Lynch Asset Management and many charitable boards. In 2003, he helped start a bank that is now called The Truxton Trust. He writes essays and memoirs. Mr. May has been a country music disc jockey and collects art prints.

MAY, REBECCA, "BECKY" SHRUM, NCTM, ACM, T: Piano Educator **I:** Education/Educational Services **CN:** Rebecca S. May Piano Studio **DOB:** 10/20/1947 **PB:** Shreveport **SC:** LA/USA **PT:** Bailey Everett Shrum; Ada Elizabeth (Dacus) Shrum **MS:** Married **SPN:** Roy Louis May Sr. **CH:** Susan- nah Abbott; Amanda Coussoule; Roy L. May Jr. **ED:** BMus, University North Texas (1973) **CT:** Certified, Music Teachers National Association; Certified, National Guild of Piano Teachers **C:** Teacher, Piano, Spring, Texas (1980-Present); Teacher, Piano, Various Locations (1973-1980) **CIV:** Leader, Girl Scouts of the United States of America, Spring (1982-1985) **AW:** Named Member of the Year, Cypress Creek Music Teachers Association (CCMTA) (1989, 1990, 1995, 2003); Named to National Guild of Piano Teachers Honor Roll **MEM:** Convention Committee, Texas Music Teachers Association; Music Teachers National Association; National Guild of Piano Teachers; Cypress Creek Music Teachers AssociationPresident, Cypress Creek Music Teachers Association (CCMTA) (1988-1990, 2002-2005); **MH:** Albert Nelson Marquis Lifetime Achievement Award **AS:** Mrs. May attributes her success to a passion for music. **B/I:** Mrs. May became involved in her profession because she always loved the piano and started piano lessons when she was 5 years old. She always admired her piano teacher, Mrs. Elizabeth Turner, and loved her dearly, so that was when she decided she wanted to be like her. Her mother, Ada Elizabeth, was a singer and she taught her the love of music. **AV:** Reading; Cooking **PA:** Republican **RE:** Christian

MAYER, DANIELLA, T: Partner **I:** Law and Legal Services **CN:** Cohen Clair Lans Greifer Thorpe & Rottenstreich Ll **PT:** Garry Mayer; Nicole Mayer **MS:** Married **SPN:** Martin Laguerre **CH:** Gabriel; Lucas **ED:** Doctor of Jurisprudence, Northwestern University School of Law (2000); Bachelor of Arts, Brown University (1995) **C:** Partner, Cohen Clair Lans Greifer Thorpe & Rottenstreich Ll (2018-Present); Senior Counsel, Cohen Clair Lans Greifer Thorpe & Rottenstreich Ll (2004-2018); Associate in Commercial Litigation, Kirkland & Ellis LLP (2000-2004) **CIV:** Pro Bono Legal Work **AW:** "Super Lawyer" by Super Lawyers Magazine (2014-Present); Rising Star (2012-2013); Justice John Paul Stevens Fellowship **MEM:** New York State Bar; New York City Bar **MH:** Marquis Who's Who Top Professional **AS:** Ms. Mayer attributes her success on her innate diligence and compassionate nature. She is able to resolve complex problems and devise plans for her clients to achieve their goals. **B/I:** Ms. Mayer became involved in her profession due to her lifelong interest in legal service. After observing how slow change is affected in the halls of power, she joined the local district attorney's office, during which time she worked in the fields of domestic violence and child abuse, where she observed the impact that lawyers can have on concrete problems in people's lives. **PA:** Family Law Section and Women in Law Sections, New York State Bar Association

MAYER, MARION SIDNEY, PHD, T: Research Entomologist **I:** Sciences **CN:** U.S. Department of Agriculture **DOB:** 07/25/1935 **PB:** New Orleans **SC:** LA/USA **PT:** Marion Sidney Mayer; Jewel (Colvin) Mayer **MS:** Married **SPN:** Anne M. Mayer **CH:** Melissa; Ellen **ED:** PhD, Texas A&M University (1963); MS, Texas A&M University (1961); BS, Louisiana State University (1957) **C:** Research Entomologist, ARS, U.S. Department of Agriculture, Gainesville, FL (1963) **MIL:** U.S. Army Reserve (1958-1964) **CW:** Author, "Insect Pheromones and Sex Attractants" (1990) **MH:** Albert Nelson Marquis Lifetime Achievement Award **AS:** Dr. Mayer attributes much of his success to Professor James R. Brazzel, a WWII hero who gave him a chance to further his education at Texas A&M University. Dr. Mayer was consistently inspired by Professor

Brazzel's drive, professionalism, honesty, care, and intelligence. He has always strived to emulate these values in his professional life.

MAYES, GLENN HOWARD, LCSW, ACSW, QCSW, DCSW, BCD, CPHQ,, T: Licensed Clinical Social Worker **I:** Health, Wellness and Fitness **DOB:** 08/23/1955 **PT:** Johnny Mayes; Lillie (Hopper) Mayes **MS:** Married **SPN:** Marjorie Mayes **CH:** Melissa Wallace; Michelle Hudson; Misty Tardiff; Nicole Hill **ED:** MSW, University of Oklahoma (1984); BS, Cameron University (1977) **CT:** Certified Professional Healthcare Quality; Academy of Certified Social Workers, National Association of Social Workers; Diplomate Clinical Social Worker; LCSW Oklahoma; Board Certified Diplomate **C:** Licensed Clinical Social Worker, U.S. Department of Veterans Affairs (2006-2020); Quality Improvement Director, Jim Taliaferro Community Mental Health Center Lawton, OK (1986-2006); With, Jim Taliaferro Community Mental Health Center Lawton, OK (1976-2006) **CIV:** Creating Partnerships to Access Housing and Urban Development Continuum of Care Grant, presented this proposal to he Lawton, OK City Council receiving $25,000 in funding from them to assist in funding housing for homeless mentally ill and substance abuse clients **CW:** Developed and Implemented with Team Support a Medication Error Improvement Project, Seclusion and Restraint Use Improvement Project, Intake and Evaluation Unit Project, Critical Incident Reporting Project, Inpatient Documentation Improvement Project, Staff Injury Reduction Improvement Project, and Clinical Record Improvement Project, Jim Taliaferro Community Mental Health Center **AW:** Governor's Commendation for 30 Years of Service for the "Ability to Get the Job Done, Commitment and Dedication," Jim Taliaferro Community Mental Health Center, State of Oklahoma (2006); Governors Commendation Award for Submitted Agency Quality Improvement Projects, Quality Oklahoma Team Days (1999-2005); Red Tape Reduction Award (2004); Quality Crown Award (1999); Continuum of Care (CoC) Grant, US Department of Housing and Urban Development (1999); Recipient, Specialty Awards, Quality Oklahoma Team Days **MEM:** Member, National Association of Social Workers; National Association Healthcare Quality **MH:** Albert Nelson Marquis Lifetime Achievement Award **AS:** Mr. Mayes attributes her success to dedication and hard work. **B/I:** Mr. Mayes became involved in his profession because he always wanted to work in the medical field. He always had the desire to be a doctor but he did not have the money or time to go to medical school. He started working at nights at the mental health center when he was 19-years-old and attending Cameron University in the day. He worked as a patient care assistant at Taliaferro Community Mental Health Center with psychiatric patients. **AV:** University of Oklahoma sport activities **THT:** Mr. Mayes wrote and received a Housing and Urban Development Continuum of Care (CoC) Grant for over $450,000 to house homeless mentally ill and substance abuse clients in 1999.

MAYNE, THOM, T: Principal; Architect **I:** Architecture & Construction **CN:** Morphosis Architects **DOB:** 01/19/1944 **PB:** Waterbury **SC:** CT/USA **PT:** Walter Mayne; Bernice (Gornall) Mayne **MS:** Married **SPN:** Blythe Alison Mayne (08/08/1981); Susan Burnham (09/10/1964, Divorced 1970) **CH:** Richard; Sam; Cooper **ED:** MArch, Harvard University (1978); BArch, University of Southern California (1968) **C:** Architect, Morphosis, Santa Monica, CA (1972-Present); Member, Faculty, UCLA School of the Arts and Architecture, Santa Monica, CA (1972-Present) **CR:** Member, Visiting Faculty, Hochschule für Angewandt Kunst, Vienna, Austria

(1991, 1993); Adjunct Professor, University of California Los Angeles (1986, 1993); Member, Visiting Faculty, Technical University (Now TU Wien), Vienna, Austria (1993); Member, Visiting Faculty, Berlage Institute, Amsterdam, Netherlands (1993); Member, Visiting Faculty, University of Illinois at Urbana-Champaign (1992-1993); Member, Visiting Faculty, Clemson University (1991); Member, Visiting Faculty, Yale University" (1991); Member, Visiting Faculty, Harvard University (1988); Member, Visiting Faculty, Columbia University, New York, NY (1986); Member, Visiting Faculty, University of Pennsylvania (1985); Member, Visiting Faculty, Washington University in St. Louis (1984); Member, Visiting Faculty, The University of Texas at Austin (1984); Member, Visiting Faculty, Miami University, Ohio (1982); Member, Visiting Faculty, California State College, Pomona, CA (1971); Lecturer in Field; Adjudicator, Numerous Awards **CIV:** Trustee, Board of Directors, Southern California Institute of Architecture, Santa Monica, CA (1983-Present); Member, President Barack Obama's Committee on Arts and Humanities (2009) **CW:** Architect, Emerson College Los Angeles Center, Los Angeles, CA (2014); Architect, Bill & Melinda Gates Hall, Cornell University, Ithaca, NY (2013); Architect, Perot Museum of Nature and Science, Victory Park, Dallas, Texas (2012); Architect, Cahill Center for Astronomy and Astrophysics, California Institute of Technology, Pasadena, CA (2009); Architect, New Academic Building, 41 Cooper Square, The Cooper Union for the Advancement of Science and Art, NY (2009); Architect, National Oceanic Atmospheric Administration Satellite Operations Facility, Suitland, MD (2007); Architect, University of Cincinnati Student Recreation Center, Cincinnati, Ohio (2006); Architect, Public Housing, Madrid, Spain (2006); Architect, Wayne Lyman Morse United States Courthouse, Eugene, OR (2006); Architect, San Francisco Federal Building, San Francisco, CA (2006); Architect, Caltrans District 7 Headquarters, Los Angeles, CA (2004); Architect, Dr. Theodore T. Alexander Jr. Science Center School, LAUSD, Los Angeles, CA (2004); Architect, Hypo Alpe-Adria Center, Klagenfurt, Austria (2002); Architect, University of Toronto Graduate House, Toronto, Ontario, Canada (2000); Architectural One-man Exhibition, Diane Farris Gallery (1993); Architect, Cranbrook Academy Gatehouse Competition (1993); Architect, Spreebogen Master Plan, Berlin, Germany (1993); Architect, Check Point Charlie Office Building, Berlin, Germany (1993); Architectural One-man Exhibition, I Space Gallery, Chicago, IL (1992); Architectural One-man Exhibition, Sadock & Uzzan Galerie, Paris, France (1992); Group Exhibition, ROM Galleri for Arkitektur, Oslo, Norway (1992); Group Exhibition, 65 Thompson Street Gallery, New York, NY (1992); Architectural One-man Exhibition, Laguna Art Museum, CA (1991); Architectural One-man Exhibition, G201 Gallery, Ohio (1991); Group Exhibition, Sadock & Uzzan Galerie (1991); Group Exhibition, Bannatyne Gallery, Santa Monica, CA (1991); Architect, Higashi Azabu Tower, Tokyo, Japan (1991); Architect, Yuzen Vintage Car Museum, Los Angeles, CA (1991); Architect, Disney Institute and Town Center Competition, Orlando, FL (1991); Architectural One-man Exhibition, San Francisco Museum of Modern Art (1990); Architectural One-man Exhibition, Graham Foundation, Chicago, IL (1990); Architectural One-man Exhibition, Aedes Galerie and Architecture Forum, Berlin, Germany (1990); Architectural One-man Exhibition, Fenster Architektur Galerie, Frankfurt, Germany (1990); Architectural One-man Exhibition, Gallery MA, Toyko, Japan (1990); Group Exhibition, Gwenda Jay Gallery (Now Addington Gallery), Chicago, IL (1990); Architect, Politix (1990); Architect, Salick Health Care Corporate Headquarters (1990);

Architect, Visual Performing Arts School at Thomas More College (Now Thomas More University), Crestview, KY (1990); Architect, MTV Studios, Los Angeles, CA (1990); Group Exhibition, G.A. Gallery, Tokyo, Japan (1985, 1987, 1990); Group Exhibition, U.S. Information Agency, Moscow, Russia (1989-1990); Group Exhibition, Kirsten Kiser Gallery (1988, 1989); Architectural One-man Exhibition, Cheney Cowles Museum, Spokane, WA (1989); Architectural One-man Exhibition, Walker Arts Center, Minneapolis, MN (1989); Architectural One-man Exhibition, Gallery of Architecture, Los Angeles, CA (1989); Architectural One-man Exhibition, Contemporary Arts Center, Cincinnati, Ohio (1989); Group Exhibition, Gallery of Functional Art, Santa Monica, CA (1989); Group Exhibition, Deutsches Architekturmuseum, Frankfurt, Germany (1989); Group Exhibition, Laumeier Sculpture Park, St. Louis, MO (1989); Architect, Expo '90 Folly, Osaka, Japan (1989); Architect, The Emery Center for the Performing Arts (1989); Architect, Temple University Commodity Credit Corporation, Philadelphia, PA (1989); Architectural One-man Exhibition, 2 AES Gallery, San Francisco, CA (1988); Group Exhibition, Axis Gallery, Tokyo, Japan, Milan, Italy and Paris, France (1988); Group Exhibition, Pacific Design Center, Los Angeles, CA (1988); Group Exhibition, Australia Center for Contemporary Arts, Victoria, Australia (1988); Group Exhibition, Cooper-Hewitt Museum, New York, NY (1988); Group Exhibition, Aedes Galerie für Architektur und Raum, Berlin, Germany (1988); Group Exhibition, Visual Arts Ontario, Toronto, Canada (1988); Architect, Cedar Sinai Comprehensive Cancer Center (Cedars-Sinai), Los Angeles, CA (1988); Architect, Artspark Performing Arts Pavilion (1988); Architect, Leon Max Showroom, Los Angeles, CA (1988); Architect, Club Post Nuclear, Laguna Beach, CA (1988); Architect, Berlin Wall Competition (1988); Group Exhibition, Max Protech Gallery, New York, NY (1985, 1986); Group Exhibition, I.D.C., New York, NY (1986); Group Exhibition, California Museum of Science and Industry (Now California Science Center) (1984); Architect, Hermosa Beach Central Business District (1984); Architect, Bergren Residence (1984); Group Exhibition, Institute of Contemporary Arts, London, England, United Kingdom (1983); Group Exhibition, Architectural Association, London, England, United Kingdom (1983); Group Exhibition, National Academy of Design, New York, NY (1983); Group Exhibition, 88, San Francisco Museum of Modern Art (1983); Architect, 72 Market Street Restaurant (1983); Group Exhibition, La Jolla Museum of Contemporary Art, CA (1982); Architect, Western Melrose Office Building (1981); Architect, Sedlak Residence (1980); Group Exhibition, The Architectural Gallery, Venice, CA (1979); Architect, Flores Residence (1979); Group Exhibition, Umwelt Galerie, Stuttgart, Germany (1978); Architect, Sequoyah Education and Research Center, Santa Monica, CA (1977); Contributor, Articles to Professional Journals; Architect, Numerous Projects **AW:** AIA Gold Medal (2013); Neutra Medal for Professional Excellence (2011); Edward MacDowell Medal (2008); Top Ten Green Project Award, AIA Committee on the Environment (2007); Pritzker Architecture Prize, The Hyatt Foundation (2005); Chrysler Design Award of Excellence (2001); American Institute of Architects Award, AIA (1981, 1985, 1986, 1988, 1990, 1992, 1993); CCAIA Award (1986, 1989, 1990, 1993); Pilkington Planar Prize (1993); Architecture Award, American Academy of Arts and Letters (1992); Architectural Record Interior Award (1990); Progressive Architecture Award (1974, 1980, 1982, 1984, 1987, 1989); Rome Prize Fellow, American Academy in Rome (1987); Numerous

Awards **MEM:** Fellow, American Academy of Arts & Sciences; AIA; American Academy of Design **AV:** Skiing; Traveling **PA:** Democrat

MAYOPOULOS, TIMOTHY J., T: Chief Executive Officer, President **I:** Business Management/Business Services **CN:** Fannie Mae **DOB:** 03/07/1959 **PB:** Reading **PT:** Harry B. Mayopoulos; Eleanor Ida (Raifsnider) Mayopoulos **SPN:** Amy F. Lefkof (04/28/1990) **CH:** Philip Alexander **ED:** JD, New York University, Cum Laude (1984); AB, Cornell University, With Distinction (1980) **C:** President, Chief Executive Officer, Fannie Mae (Federal National Mortgage Association), Washington, DC (2012-Present); Executive Vice President, General Counsel, Corporate Secretary, Chief Administrative Officer, Fannie Mae (Federal National Mortgage Association), Washington, DC (2009-2012); Executive Vice President, General Counsel, Bank of America Corporation, Charlotte, NC (2004-2008); Managing Director, General Counsel, Deutsche Bank AG (2002-2004); Associate General Counsel, Donaldson, Lufkin & Jenrette (1996); Associate Counsel, Office of Independent Counsel Kenneth Starr (1994-1996); Associate, Davis, Polk & Wardwell, New York, NY (1986-1994); Law Clerk, Hon. William C. Conner, U.S. District Court for the Southern District of New York (1984-1986); Managing Director, Credit Suisse First Boston **MEM:** Federal Bar Council; Association of the Bar of the City of New York; New York State Bar Association; Securities Industry Association; Order of the Coif **BAR:** U.S. Court of Appeals for the Eighth Circuit (1995); U.S. District Court for the Eastern District of Arkansas (1994); U.S. District Court for the Western District of Arkansas (1994); U.S. Court of Appeals for the Second Circuit (1993); U.S. Supreme Court (1993); U.S. District Court for the Southern District of New York (1987); U.S. District Court for the Eastern District of New York (1987); New York (1985)

MAYS, WILLIE HOWARD JR., T: Former Professional Baseball Player **I:** Athletics **DOB:** 05/6/1931 **PB:** Westfield **SC:** AL/USA **PT:** William Howard Mays; Ann M. Mays **MS:** Married **SPN:** Mae Louise Allen (11/27/1971); Margherite Wendell Chapman (1956, Divorced 1961) **CH:** Michael (Adopted) **ED:** Honorary LHD, San Francisco State University (2009); Honorary Doctorate, Dartmouth College (2007); Honorary LHD, Yale University (2004) **C:** Special Assistant to the President, Team Emissary, San Francisco Giants (1986-Present); Special Assistant to the President, Bally's Atlantic City Hotel and Casino, Atlantic City, NJ (1979-1985); Retired, Major League Baseball (MLB) (1973); Outfielder, New York Mets, MLB (1972-1973); Outfielder, San Francisco Giants, MLB (1958-1972); Outfielder, New York Giants, MLB (1951-1957); Outfielder, Minneapolis Millers, American Association (1951); Outfielder, Trenton Inter-State League (1950-1951); Outfielder, Birmingham Black Barons (1948-1950) **CIV:** With, Army of the United States (1952-1954) **CW:** Author, "Willie Mays: The Life, The Legend" (2010); Author, "Say Hey: The Autobiography of Willie Mays" (1988); Author, "Willie Mays: My Life In and Out of Baseball" (1966) **AW:** Presidential Medal of Freedom, The White House (2015); Named to African American Ethnic Sports Hall of Fame (2010); Beacon of Life Award, MLB (2010); Named to California Hall of Fame (2007); Named to Rawlings All-time Gold Glove Team (2007); Lifetime Achievement Award, Bobby Bragan Youth Foundation (2005); Named Sportsman of the Decade, Congress of Racial Equality (1991); Spirit of Life Award, City of Hope (1988); Named to Baseball Hall of Fame (1979); Golden Plate Award to America's Captains of Achievement, American Academy of Achievement (1976); Named to Alabama Sports Hall of Fame (1973); Named to Black Hall of Fame (1973); Roberto Clemente Award (1971); First Commissioner's Award (1970); Named Baseball Player of the Decade (1970); Named National League MVP (1954, 1965); Gold Glove Award (1957-1968); Named to National League All-star Team (1954-1973); Hickok Belt (1954); Named Male Athlete of the Year, The Associated Press (1954); Named Player of the Year, Sporting News (1954); Winner, New York Giants, World Series Championship (1954); Named National League Rookie of the Year (1951); Legendary Star Award, HBO Video; Golden Bat Award to Commemorate 600 Home Runs

MAYTHAM, THOMAS, T: Art and Museum Consultant **I:** Fine Art **DOB:** 07/30/1931 **PB:** Buffalo **SC:** NY/USA **PT:** Thomas Edward; Margaret (Northrup) M. **MS:** Married **SPN:** Gloria Goode Evans (6/11/1994, Deceased); Daphne Chace (12/30/1960, Divorced) **CH:** T.F. Gifford **ED:** Certification in German, Colby College (1954); Master of Art in Art History, Yale University (1956); Bachelor of Art in Art History, Williams College, Williamstown, MA (1954) **C:** Art Consultant, Publisher, ART Advisors LLC, Denver, CO (1983-Present); Director, Denver Art Museum (1974-1983); Associate Director, Acting Director, Seattle Art Museum (1967-1974); Head, Department of Paintings, Boston Museum of Fine Arts (1957-1967); Research Assistant, Yale University (1956); Intern, Wadsworth Atheneum (1955) **CR:** Past Trustee, American Association of Museums; American Federation of Arts; Grants Reviewer, National Endowment for the Arts; Washington Reviewer, National Endowment for the Humanities; Policy Panel and Advisor Committee, Smithsonian Institution; Colorado Council on the Arts and Humanities; Co-founder, Consortium of Rocky Mountain Regional Conservation Center, University of Denver; Founder, Directors Association of Denver Cultural Agencies; Delegate, Inter-American Museums Conference, Oaxaca, Mexico; Co-founder, United Arts Fund; Art Advisor, Airport Art Advisory Committee; President's Leadership Class, University of Colorado; Consultant, Aspen Center Visual Arts; Sangre De Cristo Arts Center; Pueblo, Western States Arts Foundation Santa Fe **CIV:** Trustee, International Exhibitions Foundation, Washington **CW:** Organizer, Exhibition, American Painting from the Boston and Metropolitan Museums, National Gallery, St. Louis and Seattle Museums (1970-1971); Organizer, Exhibition, Ernst Ludwig Kirchner Retrospective, Seattle, Pasadena and Boston Museums (1968-1969); Contributor, Articles to Professional Journals; Presenter, TV Programs on Collections and Exhibitions, Boston Public TV **AW:** Downtown Denver Awards, Denver Art Museum (1978); Governor's Arts Award, Seattle Airport Art Program (1972) **MEM:** Officer, Trustee, Operations Committee Secretary, Future Directions Committee Chairman, Association of Art Museum Directors **MH:** Albert Nelson Marquis Lifetime Achievement Award

MAZIE, DEONKA, T: Coordinator **I:** Human Resources **CN:** Marine Corps Toys for Tots **MS:** Married **CH:** 10 Children **ED:** Master's Degree in Human Resources, University of Phoenix (2004); Bachelor of Science in Business administration, University of Phoenix (2001) **C:** Human Resource Specialist, Department of Veteran Affairs (2011-Present); Quality Assurance Manager, City of New Orleans (2008-2011); Operations Manager, University of Phoenix (1999-2008) **CR:** Sales Director, Mary Kay Cosmetics (2018-Present) **CIV:** Coordinator, Marine Corps Toys for Tots (2015-Present); Board of Directors, Crescent City Family Services (2009-Present) **MIL:** U.S. Navy **MH:** Marquis Who's Who Humanitarian Award **AS:** Ms. Mazie attributes her success to her Christian faith, her patients and the ability to make an impact on her community. **B/I:** Ms. Mazie was attracted to her profession because she is a disabled veteran, having served in the United States Navy for more than a decade. After trying for more than 20 years, she was able to join the Department of Veterans Affairs.

MAZO, ROBERT MARC, T: Professor Emeritus **I:** Education/Educational Services **CN:** University of Oregon **DOB:** 10/03/1930 **PB:** Brooklyn **SC:** NY/USA **PT:** Nathan Mazo; Rose Marion Mazo **MS:** Married **SPN:** Joan Spector Mazo (09/05/1994) **CH:** Ruth Karras; Jeffrey Mazo; Daniel Mazo **ED:** PhD, Yale University (1955); MS, Yale University (1953); BA, Harvard University (1952) **C:** Professor Emeritus, University of Oregon, Eugene, OR (1996); Professor of Chemistry, University of Oregon, Eugene, OR (1965-1995); Director, Institute for Theoretical Science, University of Oregon, Eugene, OR (1964-1967, 1984-1987); Head, Chemistry Department, University of Oregon, Eugene, OR (1978-1981); Program Director, National Science Foundation (1977-1978); Associate Dean, University of Oregon Graduate School, Eugene, OR (1967-1971); Associate Professor, University of Oregon, Eugene, OR (1962-1965); Assistant Professor, California Institute of Technology (1958-1962); Research Associate, The University of Chicago (1956-1958) **CR:** University of New South Wales, Australia (1989); Visiting Professor, Technische Hochschule Aachen, Weizmann Institute, Rehovoth, Israel (1981-1982); Senior Postdoctoral Fellow, Visiting Professor, University Libre de Bruxelles, Belgium (1968-1969); Alfred P. Sloan Fellow, National Science Foundation **CW:** Author, "Brownian Motion" (2002); Author, "Statistical Mechanical Theories of Transport Processes" (1967); Author, Research Articles **AW:** National Science Foundation Postdoctoral Fellow, University of Amsterdam, Netherlands (1955-1956) **MEM:** Fellow, American Physical Society **MH:** Albert Nelson Marquis Lifetime Achievement Award **AS:** Dr. Mazo attributes his success to lucky genetics, plus a supportive family. **B/I:** Dr. Mazo was a teenager and his friends had a chemistry set and so he saved some money and got his own; he was hooked from there.

MAZUR, SHERRI, T: Attorney **I:** Law and Legal Services **CN:** The Mazur Law Firm **ED:** JD, Promise Goode Jones School of Law, Magna Cum Laude (2014); MBA, Troy University, Troy, AL, Magna Cum Laude (2012); BS, Troy University, Troy, AL, Magna Cum Laude (2010) **C:** Attorney, The Mazur Law Firm (2017-Present); Deputy District Attorney, Montgomery AL (Five Years); Adjunct Professor, Promise Goode Jones School of Law **CR:** Member, Editorial Board, Promise Goode Jones Law Review **AW:** Award for Probono Work/Criminal Defense, Alabama Access to Justice Commission (2018); Walter J. Knobe Memorial ScholarNational Runner up, Top Gun (2014); Regional Champion, National Trial Advocacy Competition, Opening Statement (2013); National Champion, National Trial Advocacy Competition (2013); National Champion of the Lonestar Classical Trial Competition (2012); Best of Greece Award, American Bar Association Appellate Completion **MEM:** Alabama State Bar Association; Montgomery County Bar Association; American Bar Association; Alabama Criminal Defense Lawyers Association **BAR:** Court of Appeals for the Eleventh Circuit; U.S. District Court; Alabama **AS:** Ms. Mazur attributes her success to hard work, perseverance, and a great deal to the advocacy education at her law school. **B/I:** Ms. Mazur became involved in her law profession because she wanted to help people. Being a prosecutor really took it a step further and inspired her to do criminal defense work.

MCADAM, LOWELL CLAYTON, T: Chairman and Chief Executive Officer (Retired) **I:** Telecommunications **CN:** Verizon Communications Inc. **DOB:** 05/28/1954 **PB:** Buffalo **SC:** NY/USA **ED:** MBA, University of San Diego (1983); BS in Engineering, Cornell University (1976) **CT:** EIT **C:** Chief Executive Officer, Verizon Communications (2012-2018); Chairman, Cellco Partnership (2010-2018); Chairman, Verizon Wireless, Inc. (2010-2018); President, Chief Operating Officer, Verizon Communications, Inc. (2010-2011); President, Chief Executive Officer, Verizon Wireless, Inc. (2007-2010); Executive Vice President, Chief Operating Officer, Verizon Wireless, Inc. (2000-2007); Executive Director, International Applications and Operations, AirTouch Communications (Now Verizon) (1993); With, Pacific Bell (1983-1993); President, Chief Executive Officer, PrimeCo Personal Commission; Chief Operating Officer, PrimeCo Personal Commission; Vice President, International Operations, AirTouch Communications (Now Verizon); General Manager, South Bay Customer Services, Pacific Bell; Vice President, Bay Area Marketing, Pacific Bell **CR:** Board of Directors, Verizon Communications, Inc. (2011-Present); Board of Directors, Verizon Wireless, Inc. (2003-Present); Board of Directors, Cellular Telecommunications & Internet Association (CTIA)

MCADAMS, BENJAMIN, "BEN" MICHAEL, T: U.S. Representative from Utah **I:** Government Administration/Government Relations/Government Services **DOB:** 12/05/1974 **PB:** West Bountiful **SC:** UT/USA **MS:** Married **SPN:** Julie McAdams **CH:** Four Children **ED:** JD, Columbia Law School, with Honors; BA in Political Science, The University of Utah **C:** Member, U.S. House of Representatives from Utah's Fourth Congressional District (2019-Present); Mayor, Salt Lake County, Utah (2013-Present); Member, District Two, Utah State Senate (2009-2012); Senior Adviser, Mayor Ralph Becker, Salt Lake City, Utah; Associate, Dorsey & Whitney, Salt Lake City, Utah; Member, Committee on Science, Space and Technology; Member, Committee on Financial Services **CIV:** Member, The Church of Jesus Christ of Latter-day Saints; Volunteer Adjunct Faculty Member, The University of Utah S.J. Quinney College of Law **CW:** Member, Columbia Human Rights Law Review **AV:** Hiking; Soccer; Baseball; Cultural Activities **PA:** Democrat

MCBATH, LUCIA, "LUCY" KAY, T: U.S. Representative from Georgia **I:** Government Administration/Government Relations/Government Services **DOB:** 06/01/1960 **PB:** Joliet **SC:** IL/USA **PT:** Lucien Holman; Wilma Holman **MS:** Married **SPN:** Curtis McBath; Ronald Davis (Divorced) **CH:** Two Sons (Deceased) **ED:** Intern, Governor Lawrence Douglas Wilder; BA in Political Science, Virginia State University (1982) **C:** Member, U.S. House of Representatives from Georgia's Sixth Congressional District (2019-Present); National Spokeswoman, Moms Demand Action for Gun Sense in America (2012-Present); Flight Attendant, Delta Air Lines, Atlanta, GA **CIV:** Founder, Champion in the Making Legacy Foundation **CW:** Appearance, Documentary, "3 1/2 Minutes, 10 Bullets" (2015); Appearance, Documentary, "The Armor of Light" (2015) **MEM:** Delta Sigma Theta Sorority, Inc. **PA:** Democrat

MCBRIDE, MARTINA MARIEA, T: Singer, Songwriter **I:** Media & Entertainment **DOB:** 07/29/1966 **PB:** Sharon **SC:** KS/USA **PT:** Daryl Schiff; Jeanne (Clark) Schiff **MS:** Married **SPN:** John McBride (05/15/1988) **CH:** Delaney Katherine; Emma Justine; Ava Rose Kathleen **C:** Solo Artist, Singer, Songwriter (1992-Present); Backup Singer, Garth Brooks (1992-1993); Member, Lotus (1987); Vocalist, Keyboard Player, Schiffters (1975-1986); Member, The Penetrators, Wichita, KS; Vocalist, Assorted Bands, Wichita, KS **CW:** Singer, "It's the Holiday Season" (2018); Singer, "Reckless" (2016); Author, "Around the Table: Recipes and Inspiration for Gatherings Throughout the Year" (2015); Singer, "Everlasting" (2014); Singer, "The Classic Christmas Album" (2013); Singer, "Eleven" (2011); Singer, "Shine" (2009); Singer, "Martina McBride: Live in Concert" (2008); Singer, "Waking Up Laughing" (2007); Singer, "Timeless" (2005); Singer, "Martina" (2003); Singer, "Greatest Hits" (2001); Singer, "Girls Night Out" (1999); Singer, "Emotion" (1999); Singer, "White Christmas" (1999); Singer, "Martina McBride Christmas" (1998); Singer, "Evolution" (1997); Singer, "Wild Angels" (1995); Singer, "The Way That I Am" (1993); Singer, "The Time Has Come" (1992); Singer, Solo and Various Artists, Songs, Albums, Tours **AW:** Icon Award, Academy of Country Music (2019); Honorary Award, Academy of Country Music (2011); BMI Award for Most Played Song of the Year (2007); Named Top Country Grossing Tour of the Year, Billboard Music Awards (2007); Named Female Song of the Year, ASCAP (2007); CMA Award for Female Vocalist of the Year, CMA Country Music Association Inc. (1999, 2002, 2003, 2004); Award for Top Female Vocalist, Academy of Country Music (2001, 2002, 2003); Award for Female Video of the Year, Flameworthy Awards (2001, 2003); Humanitarian of the Year Award, Academy of Country Music (2003); Award for Favorite Country Female Artist, American Music Awards (2003); Named Favorite Female Artist, Country Weekly (2003); Founding President's Award, CMA Country Music Association Inc. (1999); Award for Best Female Artist, Country Radio Music Awards (1996); Named Video of the Year, Nashville Music Awards (1996); Named Music Video of the Year, TNN/Music City News (1995); Gold Clio for Country Music Video of the Year, Clio Awards (1995); CMA Award for Music Video of the Year, CMA Country Music Association Inc. (1994); Named Video of the Year, Nashville Music Awards (1995); Named Best Video of the Year, Great Britain Music Awards (1994); Named Breakthrough Artist, Music Row Independent Summit Awards (1994)

MCCARTHY, KEVIN BART, T: Lawyer **I:** Law and Legal Services **CN:** Kevin B. McCarthy, Attorney **DOB:** 05/07/1948 **PB:** Washington, DC **SC:** DC/USA **PT:** Frank Jeremiah McCarthy; Frances Patricia (Bilderback) McCarthy **MS:** Married **SPN:** Patrice Borders (04/03/1971) **CH:** Kevin Patrick; Charles Ryan; Molly Virginia; Bridget Louise; Moira Patrice **ED:** Licentiate in Sacred Theology, University of St. Thomas Aquinas, (The Angelicum), Rome, Italy (2013); Diploma, University of St. Thomas Aquinas, Rome, Italy (2008); JD, Indiana University, Indianapolis, IN (1973); BBA, University of Notre Dame (1970) **C:** U.S. Trustee, United States Department of Justice, Indianapolis, IN (1988); Acting U.S. Trustee, United States Department of Justice, Springfield, IL (1987-1988); Private Practice, Law, Springfield, IL (1982-1987); Counsel, Committee on Public Works and Transportation, House of Representatives, Washington, DC (1982); Assistant Counsel, Committee on Public Works and Transportation, House of Representatives, Washington, DC (1979-1982); Counsel, Committee on Interstate and Foreign Commerce, Subcommittee on Transportation and Commerce, House of Representatives, Washington, DC (1977-1979); First Assistant, Chief Counsel, Illinois Department of Transportation, Springfield, IL (1975-1977); Assistant Regional Counsel, Federal Highway Administration, Homewood, IL (1973-1975); Bail Commissioner, Municipal Court of Marion County, Indianapolis, IN (1972-1973) **CR:** Private Practice, Indianapolis and Springfield, IL **CIV:** Member, Illinois State Board of Agricultural Advisors (1987-1988) **CW:** Author, Law Review Articles (1985, 1986); Author, Articles on Transportation Law, Association of Interstate Commerce Commission and Practitioners Journal; Pending Publishing, Theological Journal **BAR:** U.S. Court of Appeals for the Sixth Circuit (1985); U.S. District Court for the Central District of Illinois (1985); Illinois (1976); U.S. Court of Appeals for the Seventh Circuit (1974); U.S. District Court for the Southern District of Indiana (1973); Indiana (1973) **B/I:** Mr. McCarthy became involved in his profession because of his father, Frank Jeremiah, who went back to law school as a young railroad executive. After that, he became the Resident Vice President and General Counsel of the Pennsylvania Railroad Company in Washington DC. He was the Washington lawyer and representative at that time of the largest industrial corporation in the world. Mr. McCarthy chose his career because it was by discernment of interest and abilities. The best path to love thy neighbor is to use your gifts to help other people.

MCCARTHY, KEVIN OWEN, T: U.S. Representative from California, House Minority Leader **I:** Government Administration/Government Relations/Government Services **CN:** U.S. House of Representatives **DOB:** 1/26/1965 **PB:** Bakersfield **SC:** CA/USA **PT:** Owen McCarthy; Roberta Darlene (Palladino) McCarthy **MS:** Married **SPN:** Judy Wages (1992) **CH:** Connor; Meghan **ED:** Master of Business Administration, California State University, Bakersfield Business and Public Administration (1994); Bachelor of Science in Marketing, California State University, Bakersfield (1989); Coursework, Bakersfield College **C:** House Minority Leader (2019-Present); Member, U.S. House of Representatives from California's 23rd Congressional District, United States Congress, Washington, DC (2013-Present); House Majority Leader (2014-2019); Assistant Majority Leader (2011-2014); Member, U.S. House of Representatives from California's 22nd Congressional District, United States Congress, Washington, DC (2007-2013); Chief Deputy Whip (2009-2011); Assistant Whip (2006-2009); Minority Leader, California State Assembly (2004-2006); Member, District 32, California State Assembly (2002-2007); District Director to Representative Bill Thomas, U.S. House of Representatives; Owner, Kevin O's Deli; Owner, Bakersfield Batting Range **CR:** Chairperson, Young Republican National Federation (1999-2001) **CIV:** Board of Directors, First Book (2001-Present); Executive Director, McCarthy Foundation (2000-Present); Coach, YMCA (1999-Present); Member, Kern County Republican Central Committee (1992-Present); Trustee, District Board, Kern Chamber of Commerce (2000-2002); Board of Directors, Head Start; Former Board Member, Community Action Partnership of Kern **CW:** Co-author, with Eric Cantor and Paul Ryan, "Young Guns: A New Generation of Conservative Leaders" (2010) **AW:** Named, One of the 10 Members to Watch in the 112th Congress, Roll Call (2011); Named, One of the 50 Politicos to Watch, Politico (2010) **MEM:** Rotary International **PA:** Republican **RE:** Baptist

MCCARTHY, MELISSA ANN, T: Actress **I:** Media & Entertainment **DOB:** 08/26/1970 **PB:** Plainfield **SC:** IL/USA **PT:** Michael McCarthy; Sandra McCarthy **MS:** Married **SPN:** Ben Falcone (10/08/2005) **CH:** Vivian; Georgette **ED:** Coursework, Fashion Institute of Technology; Coursework in Textiles, Southern Illinois University **C:** Co-founder, On the Day Productions (2013-Present); Stand-up Comedian, NY; With, The Groundlings, Los Angeles, NY; Costumer, Dance Company **CR:** Launched,

Fashion Line, Seven7 (2015-Present) **CW:** Actress, Executive Producer, Writer, "The Boss" (2016); Actress, "Bridesmaids" (2011); Actress, "Mike & Molly" (2010-2016); Actress, "Ghostbusters" (2016); Actress, "Spy" (2015); Actress, "St. Vincent" (2014); Actress, Producer, Writer, "Tammy" (2014); Actress, "Identity Thief" (2013); Actress, "The Hangover Part III" (2013); Actress, "The Heat" (2013); Actress, "This is 40" (2012); Actress, "The Back-up Plan" (2010); Actress, "Life as We Know It" (2010); Actress, "Private Practice" (2010); Actress, "Rita Rocks" (2009); Actress, "Samantha Who?" (2007-2009); Actress, "Just Add Water" (2008); Actress, "Pretty Ugly People" (2008); Actress, "The Nines" (2007); Actress, "The Captain" (2007); Actress, "Gilmore Girls" (2000-2007); Actress, "Cook-Off!" (2006); Actress, "Kim Possible" (2002-2005); Actress, "Curb Your Enthusiasm" (2004); Actress, "The Life of David Gale" (2003); Actress, "Pumpkin" (2002); Actress, "The Third Wheel" (2002); Actress, "White Oleander" (2002); Appearance, "The Lost World" (2001); Actress, "Drowning Mona" (2000); Actress, "Charlie's Angels" (2000); Appearance, "D.C." (2000); Actress, "Go" (1999) **AW:** Emmy Award for Outstanding Guest Actress in a Comedy Series, Academy of Television Arts & Sciences (2017); Named Favorite Comedic TV Actress, People's Choice Awards (2016); Named Favorite Comedic Movie Actress, People's Choice Awards (2015, 2016); Recipient, Star, Hollywood Walk of Fame (2015); Named One of the 100 Most Powerful Women in Entertainment, The Hollywood Reporter (2011, 2013); Best Supporting Actress Award, Boston Society of Film Critics (2011); Emmy Award for Outstanding Lead Actress in a Comedy Series, Academy of Television Arts & Sciences (2011); Numerous Awards

MCCARTNEY, JAMES ROBERT, MD, T: Psychiatrist **I:** Medicine & Health Care **DOB:** 01/06/1932 **PB:** Elmira **SC:** NY/USA **PT:** James L. McCartney; Edith T. (Tufs) McCartney **MS:** Married **SPN:** Lois McCartney **CH:** Four Children **ED:** Honorary MA, Brown University (1989); Resident in Psychiatry, Institute of Living, Hartford HealthCare, Hartford, CT (1959-1961); Resident in Psychiatry, Saint Elizabeth's Hospital, Washington, DC (1958-1959); Intern, Boston City Hospital for Medicine (1955-1956); MD, Columbia University (1955); BA, Ohio Wesleyan University (1952) **CT:** Diplomate, National Board of Medical Examiners (NBME); Diplomate, American Board of Psychiatry and Neurology, Inc.; Diplomate, American Board of Geriatric Psychiatry **C:** Staff, Butler Hospital, Care New England Health System (1980-Present); Director of Geropsychiatry, Life Span Academy Medical Center (Now Academy for Health & Lifespan Research), Providence, RI (1998); Psychiatrist-in-chief, The Miriam Hospital, Lifespan, Providence, RI (1980-1997); Associate Director, North Shore University Hospital (Now Northwell Health) (1978-1980); Chief of Liaison Services, North Shore University Hospital (Now Northwell Health) (1973-1980); Director of Training and Education Department, Psychiatry, North Shore University Hospital (Now Northwell Health) (1972-1979); Associate Attending Psychiatrist to Attending Psychiatrist, North Shore University Hospital (Now Northwell Health) (1964-1980); Associate Attending Psychiatrist, Nassau Hospital (Now Nassau University Medical Center), NuHealth (1964-1971); Attending Psychiatrist, Meadowbrook Hospital (Now Nassau University Medical Center), NuHealth (1961-1964) **CR:** Associate Professor Emeritus, Brown University, Providence, RI (1998); Associate Professor, Brown University, Providence, RI (1988-1998); Consultant, Impaired Physician Committee, Rhode Island Medical Society (RIMS) (1981); Assistant Professor of Psychiatry, Brown University, Prov-

idence, RI (1980-1988); Advisory Board, Mental Health Association of Nassau County (1972-1980); Fellow, American College of Physicians; Fellow, American Psychiatric Association; Fellow, Academy of Psychosomatic Medicine **CIV:** Alzheimer's Support Group (2014-Present) **MIL:** Captain, United States Army (1956-1958) **CW:** Contributor, Articles to Professional Journals **MEM:** Rhode Island Medical Society (RIMS); Association for Academic Psychiatry; Providence Medical Associate; American Association of General Hospital Psychiatrists, American Psychiatric Association **MH:** Albert Nelson Marquis Lifetime Achievement Award **AS:** Dr. McCartney attributes his success in life to his marriage and his wife.

MCCAUL, MICHAEL THOMAS SR., T: U.S. Representative from Texas; Lawyer **I:** Government Administration/Government Relations/Government Services **DOB:** 01/14/1962 **PB:** Dallas **SC:** TX/USA **PT:** James Addington McCaul, Jr.; Frances Jane (Lott) McCaul **MS:** Married **SPN:** Linda Mays **CH:** Caroline; Jewell; Lauren; Michael; Avery **ED:** Diploma, Senior Executive Fellowship, Harvard Kennedy School, John F. Kennedy School of Government (1987); JD, St. Mary's School of Law, St. Mary's University (1987); BA in History, Trinity University (1984) **C:** Ranking Member, House Committee on Foreign Affairs (2019-Present); Chairman, U.S. House Homeland Security Committee (2013-Present); Member, U.S. House of Representatives from Texas' 10th Congressional District, United States Congress (2005-Present); Chief, Terrorism and National Security Section, State of Texas (2002); Deputy Attorney General, State of Texas (2000-2002); Special Assistant Attorney General, State of Texas (1999-2000); Federal Prosecutor, Public Integrity Section, U.S. Department of Justice, Washington, DC (1990-1999); Deputy Attorney General, State of Texas, Austin, Texas (1987-1990); Member, U.S. House Committee on Ethics (Formerly House Standards of Official Conduct Committee) **CR:** Vice Chairman, US-Mexico Interparliamentary Group (2005) **PA:** Republican **RE:** Roman Catholic

MCCLANAHAN, JUDY CAROL, T: County Administrator **I:** Government Administration/Government Relations/Government Services **DOB:** 01/17/1945 **PB:** Paris **SC:** TN/USA **PT:** Lewis Lee Jackson; Madge Irene (Smith) Jackson **MS:** Widowed **SPN:** LeRoy McClanahan (06/10/1962, Deceased 04/1989) **CH:** James Lee **ED:** Certificate, Public Administrator Institute Public Service, The University of Tennessee **C:** Trustee, Tax Collector, Collector Revenue State and County, Henry County Government, Paris, TN (1982-Present); Bookkeeper, Henry County Highway Department, Paris, TN (1977-1982); Secretary, Department of Maintenance, Henry County General Hospital, Paris, TN (1975-1977) **CIV:** Member, Church of Christ **MEM:** Henry County Democratic Women; West Tennessee Trustee Association; Tennessee State Trustee's Association; County Officials Association of Tennessee; Henry County Democratic Party; Quota Club **MH:** Albert Nelson Marquis Lifetime Achievement Award **AV:** Horseback riding; Walking; Yard work

MCCLEARY, MONICA JEAN, RN, CNM, MSN, T: Certified Nurse Midwife (Retired) **I:** Medicine & Health Care **DOB:** 08/21/1952 **PB:** St. Paul **SC:** MN/USA **PT:** Robert Thomas Jackels; Lois Elizabeth (Tiling) Jackels **MS:** Married **SPN:** Mark Edward (03/03/1978) **ED:** MS, University of Minnesota (1978); BA, College of St. Catherine (Now St. Catherine University) (1974) **CT:** Registered Nurse, Minnesota; Certified Nurse-Midwife **C:** Retired; Certified Nurse Midwife, Health Partners,

St. Paul, (1976-2016); Preterm Birth Instructor, Group Health Incorporated, St. Paul, MN (1988-1992); Certified Nurse Midwife, Family Tree Clinic, St. Paul, MN (1978-1987); Nurse, St. Joseph's Hospital, St. Paul, MN (1975-1976); Nurse, Divine Redeemer Hospital, South St. Paul, MN (1974-1975) **CR:** Adjunct Clinical Instructor, University of Minnesota (1978-2016); Clinical Instructor, Frontier Nursing Service, Hayden, KY (1985-1989) **MEM:** Chapter Vice Chairman, American College Nurse Midwives (1986-1988) **MH:** Albert Nelson Marquis Lifetime Achievement Award; Marquis Who's Who Top Professional **B/I:** Ms. McCleary became involved in her profession because of an article she once read. She was in a summer speed-reading class when she read a story about Mary Breckenridge, a nurse-midwife. Breckenridge was 27 when her husband and child died, leading her to become a midwife. She found out that the highest rate of infant mortality was found in Hardin County, Kentucky, so she went to study in England and came back to the United States to work in Hardin County. Because of her work there, the rate of infant mortality dropped; it was now even with the rest of the country. This inspired Ms. McCleary to become a nurse-midwife. **AV:** Physical Fitness; Traveling (mostly places in the US); Her and her husband Mark likes classic cars; Time with Friends; Enjoying life **PA:** Democrat **RE:** Roman Catholic

MCCLINTOCK, THOMAS, "TOM" MILLER II, T: U.S. Representative from California **I:** Government Administration/Government Relations/Government Services **DOB:** 7/10/1956 **PB:** Bronxville **SC:** NY/USA **PT:** Thomas Miller McClintock; Marianne (Christy) McClintock **MS:** Married **SPN:** Lori McClintock (1987) **CH:** Justin; Shannah **ED:** BA, University of California Los Angeles (1978) **C:** Member, U.S. House of Representatives from California's Fourth Congressional District, United States Congress, Washington, DC (2009-Present); Member, District 19, California State Senate (2000-2008); Member, District 38, California House of Representatives (1996-2000); Republican Whip, California House of Representatives (1984-1989); Member, District 28, California House of Representatives (1982-1992); Chief of Staff to U.S. Senator Ed Davis, California State Senate (1980-1982); Member, Committee on Transportation and Infrastructure **CR:** Director, Economic and Regulatory Affairs, National Tax Limitation Foundation (1995-1996); Director, Golden State Center for Policy Studies, Claremont Institute (1995-1996); Director, Center for the California Taxpayer (1992-1994); Resolution Chairman, California State Republican Central Committee (1985-1992); Chairman, Ventura County Republican Party (1979-1981); Local Government Consultant, Conejo Simi Moorpark Association of Realtors (1975-1976); Member, California State Republican Central Committee (1973-2001); Charter State President, California State Republican Organization (1973-1974) **CW:** Political Columnist, Thousand Oaks News Chronicle (1976-1980) **AW:** Medal of Merit, Peace Officers Association of Ventura County ; Benjamin Franklin Award, California Printing Industry **PA:** Republican

MCCLURE, ALVIN BRUCE, T: President **I:** Information Technology and Services **CN:** Reality Bytes, Inc. **DOB:** 03/02/1953 **PB:** Cincinnati **SC:** OH/USA **PT:** Alphonso Bruce McClure; Jewel Lee (Smith) Yates **MS:** Married **SPN:** Penny Bliss (07/07/2000); Katherine Shenkar (11/07/1979) **CH:** Jaina; Randi **ED:** Coursework, Saint Paul College (2005-2006); Coursework, College of St. Thomas (1989-1991); Coursework, University of Michigan (1971-1973, 1976-1977); Coursework, Fanshawe College, London, Ontario, Canada (1974-1975) **C:** President, Reality Bytes, Inc., Elk River, MN

(2001-Present); Watchmaker, Ben Bridge Jeweler, Inc., Edina, MN (2007-2009); Data Management Engineer, Kroll Ontrack, Inc. (Now KLDiscovery Ontrack, LLC), Eden Prairie, MN (2002-2003); Technical Consultant, Productive Solutions Group, Minneapolis, MN (2000-2001); Senior Technical Consultant, Database/Network/WEB Lawson Software, St. Paul, MN (1999-2000); Information System Manager, Van Wagenen Co. (Now van Wagenen Financial Services, Inc), Eden Prairie, MN (1998-1999); Network Manager, Minnesota Department of Health, Minneapolis, MN (1998); Local Area Network Administrator, Minnesota Pollution Control Agency, St. Paul, MN (1997-1998); Programmer/Analyst, Minnesota Department Natural Resources (Minnesota DNR), St. Paul, MN (1985-1997); Software Systems Support Programmer, INTRAN Corporation of Minnesota, Bloomington, MN (1984-1985); Systems Analyst, NCR Comten, Inc., Roseville, MN (1981-1984); Systems Software Specialist, Minneapolis Star and Tribune (Now StarTribune) (1979-1981); Programmer, Manufacturing Data Systems, Ann Arbor, MI (1978-1979) CR: Member, Technical Committee, Management Information Services, St. Paul, MN (1987-1997) CIV: Member, Otsego Police Commission (2003-2005); Member, Community Advisory Board, Station 91.9FM WCAL (1988-1990); Chairman, Watchmaking Program Advisory Committee, Saint Paul College MEM: IEEE; AWI; American Institute of Physics; Audio Engineering Society; The International Platform Association; Management Information Services; American Watchmakers-Clockmakers Institute; National Association of Watch and Clock Collectors, Inc.; Fifth Degree Black Belt, Head Instructor, Aikido Yoshinkai, Minneapolis-St. Paul, MN MH: Albert Nelson Marquis Lifetime Achievement Award AV: Chess; Photography; Sailing

MCCOLLOUGH, CAROL KEENEY, T: Academic Administrator **I:** Education/Educational Services **DOB:** 08/04/1937 **PB:** Dallas **SC:** TX/USA **PT:** D. L. Keeney, Jr.; H. Adelle (Fogle) Bowsher **MS:** Married **SPN:** Charles Randolph McCollough (06/02/1959) **CH:** Colin Kean; Wendy Lynne; Timothy Randolph **ED:** Postgraduate Coursework, Princeton Theological Seminary (1979-1981); MA, Southern Methodist University (1960); BA, Southern Methodist University (1959) **CT:** Certification in Secondary School Teaching; Marriage Enrichment Trainer; Christian Education Lay Worker, United Church of Christ **C:** Academic Administrator; Assistant to President, Mercer County Community College, West Windsor, NJ (1991-2000); Assistant, Director of Planning, Assistant Dean of Engineering School, Manager of the Department of History, Princeton University, Princeton, NJ (1981-1991); Director, Resource Center, Central Atlantic Conference, Montclair, NJ (1975-1981); Instructor, English, Eastern College, Villanova University, St. Davids, PA (1968-1973); Teacher, English, Barrington College, Barrington, RI (1966-1970); Teacher, English, Mountain Lakes High School, Mountain Lakes, NJ (1960-1964) **CIV:** Trainer, Association for Couples in Marriage Enrichment (ACME), Winston-Salem, NC (1980-Present); Board of Directors, Princeton Pro Musica (1985-1990); Singer, Singing City Choir, Philadelphia, PA (1978-1988); Founder, Chairperson, Network of Directors of Resource Centers in the United Church of Christ (1977-1979); Board of Directors, Central Atlantic Conference United Church of Christ **CW:** Co-Author, "Lifestyles of Faithfulness: Resources for Outdoor Ministry"; Co-Author, "The Morality of Power: A Notebook on Christian Education for Social Change"; Co-Author, "Heads of Heaven, Feet of Clay"; Co-Author, "to Love the Earth"; Co-Author, "Resolving Conflict with Justice and Peace"; Co-Author, "Faith Made Visible: Shaping the Human Spirit in Sculpture and Word"; Co-Author, "The Art of Parables: Reinterpreting the Teaching Stories of Jesus in Word and Sculpture"; Co-Author, "The Non-Violent Radical: Seeing and Living the Wisdom of Jesus"; Editor, Nine Books **AW:** "M" Award; President's Award for Service and Scholarship, Southern Methodist University; Inductee, Sigma Delta Pi Hispanic Honorary Society **MEM:** The Church and Ministry Commission of the New Jersey Association of the United Church of Christ; The Women's International League for Peace and Freedom; The Association of United Church Educators; American Federation of Teachers; New Jersey American Council on Education; Gamma Phi Beta **AS:** Ms. McCollough attributes her success to her loving mother, as well as her family. She also credits the loving support and encouragement of her husband of 61 years. **B/I:** Ms. McCollough became involved in her profession because she had aunts who were teachers; she was inspired by their success. Likewise, she had many good teachers who were influential in her life. They set a good model for how education can enrich someone's life. She enjoys relating to people alongside helping them grow and expand their horizons through education. **AV:** Singing with Princeton Pro Musica; Gardening; Playing the piano and violin; Leading in her local church **PA:** Democrat **RE:** United Church of Christ

MCCOLLUM, BETTY LOUISE, T: U.S. Representative from Minnesota **I:** Government Administration/Government Relations/Government Services **DOB:** 07/12/1954 **PB:** Minneapolis **SC:** MN/USA **MS:** Married **SPN:** Douglas McCollum **CH:** Two Children **ED:** BS in Education, College of St. Catherine (Now St. Catherine University) (1987) **C:** Member, U.S. House of Representative from Minnesota's Fourth Congressional District, U.S. Congress, Washington, DC (2001-Present); Member, Minnesota House of Representatives (1992-2000); Member, Committee on International Relations; Member, Education and Workforce Committee; Member, Resources Committee; Member, Appropriations Committee; Member, Committee on Rules and Administrative Legislation, Minnesota House of Representatives; Chair, Legislative Commission on Economic Status of Women, Minnesota House of Representatives; Assistant Majority Leader, Minnesota House of Representatives; Member, Transportation and Transit Committee, Minnesota House of Representatives; Member, General Legislative Committee, Veteran Affairs and Elections Committee, Minnesota House of Representatives; Member, Education Committee, Minnesota House of Representatives; Member, Committee on Environmental and Natural Resources, Minnesota House of Representatives; Retail Store Manager, MN **CIV:** Member, Girl Scout Council of St. Croix Valley **MEM:** American Legion Auxiliary; VFW Auxiliary **PA:** Democrat

MCCONATHY, WALTER JAMES, PHD, T: Biochemist **I:** Sciences **DOB:** 11/03/1941 **PB:** McAlester **SC:** OK/USA **PT:** Edward William McConathy; Irene Amelia (Stark) McConathy **MS:** Married **SPN:** Linda K. McConathy (07/12/1966) **CH:** Jonathan Edward MD, PhD; Suzy Lapi, PhD **ED:** PhD in Biochemistry, Molecular Biology, University of Oklahoma, Oklahoma City, OK (1971) **C:** President, LipoMedics, Ltd. Co., Fort Worth, TX (2002-2014); Professor, Department of Internal Medicine, Texas Tech University Health Sciences Center, Permian Basin (2007-2011); Associate Professor, Director, Division of Clinical Research, Department of Medicine, Adjunct Associate Professor, Department of Biochemistry and Molecular Biology, University of North Texas Health Science Center, Fort Worth, TX (1992-2007); Acting Chairman, Department of Biochemistry and Molecular Biology, University of North Texas Health Science Center, Fort Worth, TX (1993-1995); Adjunct Associate Professor, Department of Biochemistry and Molecular Biology, University of Oklahoma College of Medicine, Oklahoma City, OK (1985-1992); Associate Member, Lipoprotein/Atherosclerosis Research Program, Oklahoma Medical Research Foundation (OMRF), (1978-1991); Assistant Member, Lipoprotein Laboratory, Oklahoma Medical Research Foundation (OMRF), (1975-1981); Staff Scientist, Lipoprotein Laboratory, Oklahoma Medical Research Foundation (OMRF), (1974-1975); Postdoctoral Fellow, Lipoprotein Laboratory, Oklahoma Medical Research Foundation (OMRF), (1971-1974); Predoctoral Fellow, Cardiovascular Section, Oklahoma Medical Research Foundation (OMRF), Oklahoma City, OK (1966-1971) **CIV:** Participant, USA-USSR Health Professional Exchange Program, USSR (1979) **CW:** Contributor, Over 200 Articles, Professional Publications **MEM:** Fellow, Council on Arteriosclerosis, American Heart Association; American Association for the Advancement of Science; American College of Surgeons; American Society for Biochemistry and Molecular Biology; American Federation for Clinical Research; Sigma Xi **MH:** Albert Nelson Marquis Lifetime Achievement Award; Marquis Who's Who Top Professional; Distinguished Humanitarian **B/I:** Dr. McConathy became involved in his profession because of an early curiosity for academics alongside his passion for the field. Likewise, the fellow he was working with was well-known internationally, so his initial involvement was an opportunity to gather strength and skills.

MCCONAUGHEY, MATTHEW DAVID, T: Actor **I:** Media & Entertainment **DOB:** 11/04/1969 **PB:** Uvalde **SC:** TX/USA **PT:** Jim McConaughey; Kay McConaughey **MS:** Married **SPN:** Camila Alves (06/09/2012) **CH:** Levi; Vida; Livingston **ED:** BA in Film Production, The University of Texas at Austin (1993) **CR:** Professor of Practice, Department of Radio-Television-Film, The University of Texas at Austin Moody College of Communication (2019-Present); Minority Owner, Austin FC, MLS (2019-Present); Visiting Instructor, The University of Texas at Austin (2015-2019) **CIV:** Co-founder, Just Keep Livin' Foundation (j.k.livin' Foundation) **CW:** Actor, Co-producer, "The Gentlemen" (2019); Appearance, "Between Two Ferns: The Movie" (2019); Actor, "The Beach Bum" (2019); Actor, "Serenity" (2019); Actor, "White Boy Rick" (2018); Actor, "The Dark Tower" (2017); Voice Actor, "Gold" (2016); Voice Actor, "Sing" (2016); Voice Actor, "Kubo and the Two Strings" (2016); Actor, "Free State of Jones" (2016); Actor, "The Sea of Trees" (2015); Actor, Executive Producer, "True Detective" (2014-2015); Actor, "Interstellar" (2014); Actor, "The Wolf of Wall Street" (2013); Actor, "Dallas Buyers Club" (2013); Actor, "Mud" (2012); Actor, "Magic Mike" (2012); Actor, "The Paperboy" (2012); Actor, "The Lincoln Lawyer" (2011); Actor, "Bernie" (2011); Actor, "Killer Joe" (2011); Actor, "Eastbound & Down" (2010-2012); Actor, "Ghosts of Girlfriends Past" (2009); Actor, "Fool's Gold" (2008); Actor, Producer, "Surfer, Dude" (2008); Actor, "Failure to Launch" (2006); Actor, "We Are Marshall" (2006); Actor, Executive Producer, "Sahara" (2005); Actor, "Absolute Evel: The Evel Knievel Story" (2005); Actor, "Two for the Money" (2005); Actor, "Freedom: A History of Us" (2003); Actor, "How to Lose a Guy in 10 Days" (2003); Actor, "Tiptoes" (2003); Actor, "Reign of Fire" (2002); Actor, "The Wedding Planner" (2001); Actor, "Thirteen Conversations About One Thing" (2001); Actor, "Frailty" (2001); Actor, "U-571" (2000); Actor, "Sex and the City" (2000); Actor, "South Beach" (1999); Actor, "Last Flight of the

Raven" (1999); Actor, "Edtv" (1999); Voice Actor, "King of the Hill" (1999); Actor, "The Rebel" (1998); Actor, "The Newton Boys" (1998); Actor, "Making Sandwiches" (1998); Actor, "Scorpion Spring" (1997); Actor, "Amistad" (1997); Actor, "Contact" (1997); Actor, "Lone Star" (1996); Actor, "A Time to Kill" (1996); Actor, "Larger than Life" (1996); Actor, "Glory Daze" (1996); Actor, "Submission" (1995); Actor, "Judgement" (1995); Actor, "Boys on the Side" (1995); Actor, "The Return of The Texas Chainsaw Massacre" (1994); Actor, "Angels in the Outfield" (1994); Actor, "My Boyfriend's Back" (1993); Actor, "Dazed and Confused" (1993); Appearance, "Unsolved Mysteries" (1992); Actor, Appearances, Television Shows, Films **AW:** Creative Conscience Award, Unite4:Humanity (2016); Named One of the 100 Most Influential People in the World, TIME Magazine (2014); Recipient, Star, Hollywood Walk of Fame (2014); Golden Globe Award for Best Performance by an Actor in a Motion Picture - Drama, Hollywood Foreign Press Association (2014); Critics' Choice Award for Best Actor (2014); Screen Actors Guild Award for Outstanding Performance by a Male Actor in a Leading Role, SAG-AFTRA (2014); Academy Award for Best Actor in a Leading Role, Academy of Motion Picture Arts and Sciences (2014); National Society Film Critics Award for Best Supporting Actor (2013); New York Film Critics Circle Award for Best Supporting Actor (2012); Award for Favorite Male Action Star, People's Choice Awards (2006); Named Sexiest Man Alive, People Magazine (2005); Numerous Awards

MCCONKIE, GEORGE WILSON, PHD, T: Professor Emeritus **I:** Education/Educational Services **CN:** University of Illinois **DOB:** 07/15/1937 **PB:** Holden **SC:** UT/USA **PT:** G. Wilson McConkie; Mabel (Stephenson) McConkie **MS:** Married **SPN:** Orlene Carol Johnson (09/06/1962) **CH:** Lynnette Mooth; Heather Usevitch; April Rhiner; Faline Coffelt; George Wilson McConkie; Bryce Johnson McConkie; Camille Howard; Elissa McConkie; Esther Ostler; Bryna Burton; Ruth Olsen; Anna Cooke; Cynthia Lau; Thomas McConkie **ED:** PhD, Stanford University, Stanford, CA (1966); MS, Brigham Young University, Provo, Utah (1961); BS, Brigham Young University, Provo, Utah (1960); AA, Dixie Junior College (Now Dixie State University), St. George, Utah (1957) **C:** Professor Emeritus, University of Illinois at Urbana-Champaign (2003-Present); Professor, University of Illinois at Urbana-Champaign (1978-2003); Chairman, Department of Educational Psychology, University of Illinois at Urbana-Champaign (1995-1997); Acting Chairman, Department of Education Psychology, University of Illinois at Urbana-Champaign (1993-1994); Chairman, Department of Education, Cornell University (1977-1978); Professor, Cornell University (1975-1978); Associate Professor, Cornell University (1970-1975); Assistant Professor of Education, Cornell University (1964-1970) **CR:** Senior Scientist, Beckman Institute for Advanced Science & Technology, University of Illinois (1989-2004); Visiting Professor, Beijing Normal University, Beijing, China (1999); Visiting Professor, National Yang-Ming University, Taipei, Taiwan (1998); Senior Scientist, Center for the Study of Reading, University of Illinois at Urbana-Champaign (1978-1995); Research Fellow, Université Catholique de Louvain, Belgium (1991-1992) **CIV:** Missionary, The Church of Jesus Christ of Latter-day Saints (1957-1959) **CW:** Contributor, Articles, Professional Journals **AW:** Grantee, General Motors (2002-2004); Grantee, National Science Foundation (1989-1991, 2000-2003); Grantee, Research Laboratory, United States Army (1996-2001); Senior Scholarship, Chiang Chung Kuo Foundation (1998-1999); Fulbright Scholarship,

Taiwan (1998); Grantee, Yamaha Motor Corporation, USA (1997-1999); Grantee, Central Intelligence Agency (CIA) (1991-1997); Grantee, National Institute of Child Health and Human Development (Now Eunice Kennedy Shriver National Institute of Child Health and Human Development), National Institutes of Health (1983-1989, 1991-1995); Fogarty International Fellowship, National Institutes of Health (1991-1992); Outstanding Scientific Contribution Award, Society for the Scientific Study of Reading (SSSR) (1995); Grantee, AT&T (1986-1989); Grantee, National Institute of Mental Health, National Institutes of Health (1974-1984); Grantee, National Institute of Education, National Institutes of Health (1974-1977); Grantee, U.S. Office of Education (1970-1973); Special Fellowship, National Institute of Mental Health, National Institutes of Health (1971-1972); Inductee, Reading Hall of Fame **MEM:** Psychonomic Society; Cognitive Science Society (CSS); Society for the Scientific Study of Reading (SSSR) **MH:** Albert Nelson Marquis Lifetime Achievement Award; Marquis Who's Who Top Professional **AS:** Dr. McConkie attributes his success to hard work and divine inspiration. **B/I:** Dr. McConkie became involved in his profession because he was fascinated by the possibility of being able to major in aspects of the mind. As a graduate student, he found that it was possible to study mental processes. **AV:** Fishing; Reading; Playing the harmonica **RE:** Christian

MCCOURT, PETER J. II, DEACON, T: President, Chief Executive Officer **I:** Education/Educational Services **CN:** Cristo Rey Richmond High School Inc. **PB:** Scranton **SC:** PA/USA **PT:** Peter W. McCourt; Rose Ann (Bicking) McCourt **MS:** Married **SPN:** Loriann M.C. McCourt **CH:** Daniel; Erin **ED:** Ministerial Studies, Deacon Formation Program, Saint Leo University; Professional Studies, Executive Integral Leadership Program, University of Notre Dame; Professional Certificate, Leadership/Management, University of Notre Dame; Postgraduate Studies, Systematic Theology-Moral, Washington Theological Union, Washington DC; Master of Arts, Master of Theological Studies in Theology-Word and Worship, Washington Theological Union, Washington, DC; Bachelor of Arts in History and Political Science, Virginia Polytechnic Institute **CT:** Ordained Deacon, Roman Catholic Church **C:** President, Chief Executive Officer, Cristo Rey Richmond CWSP Inc. & Cristo Rey Richmond High School Inc.; Vice President, Mission & Ethics, Bon Secours Virginia Medical Group, Bon Secours Health System; Vice President of Mission, Bon Secours St. Mary's Hospital; Administrative Director of Mission & Spiritual Care, Bon Secours Richmond Health System; Adjunct Professor of Religious Studies and Catholic Studies, Virginia Commonwealth University; Catholic Campus Minister, Virginia Commonwealth University, Catholic Diocese of Richmond; Director of Music, Sacred Heart Catholic Church, Richmond, Virginia; Associate Campus Minister, Director of Music, Virginia Tech Newman Community, Catholic Diocese of Richmond **CR:** Lecturer on Religion, University of Oxford, England; Lecturer, Ministry Leadership, Loyola University Chicago, Executive Leadership Program; Active in Pastoral Ministry, Catholic Diocese of Richmond **CIV:** Board of Directors, Bon Secours Ambulatory Surgery Center, Suffolk, VA; Board of Directors, Bon Secours Ambulatory Surgery Center, Virginia Beach, VA; Third Degree Knight, Knights of Columbus; Second Degree Member, Ancient Order of Hibernians; Active in Church Service, St. Mary's Catholic Church, Richmond, VA **AW:** Eagle Scout, Boy Scouts of America **MEM:** American Academy of Religion; National Association of Pastoral Musicians; College Theology Society; National Eagle Scout Association;

American College of Healthcare Executives **AS:** Mr. McCourt was blessed with a strong, supportive family that valued faith and education highly together with civic engagement and community service. His parents instilled within him a strong work ethic and moral code. **B/I:** Mr. McCourt became involved in his profession due to the influence of his parents, both of whom were educators. He was blessed to grow up in a faith-filled home where religious values and service to others were held as expectations. **AV:** Singer; Pianist; Guitarist; Pipe organist **RE:** Roman Catholic **THT:** Injustice anywhere is a threat to justice everywhere.

MCCRACKEN, ROBERT DALE, T: Anthropologist, Writer **I:** Sciences **CN:** RDM Associates **DOB:** 08/08/1937 **PB:** Fairplay **SC:** CO/USA **PT:** Robert Gerald McCracken; Martha Lucile (Grice) McCracken Foster **MS:** Divorced **SPN:** Susan (Shihadeh) McCracken Cline (06/24/1967, Divorced 10/1974) **CH:** Bambi Michelle McCracken Metscher **ED:** Postgraduate Coursework, Washington University at St. Louis (1972); Postdoctoral Fellow, Department of Psychology, Washington University at St. Louis (1971-1972); PhD in Anthropology, University of Colorado (1968); MA in Anthropology, University of Colorado (1965); BA in Psychology, University of Colorado (1962) **C:** Independent Social Science Consultant, RDM Associates, Las Vegas, NV (1980-Present); Assistant Professor, University of Tennessee, Knoxville, TN (1978-1979); Assistant Professor, Memphis State University (1976-1978); Director, Research, Colorado Migrant Council, Denver, CO (1974-1976); Freelance Writer (1972-1974); Assistant Professor, School of Public Health, UCLA (1969-1971); Assistant Professor, Anthropology, California State University, Long Beach (1968-1969); Instructor, Colorado Women's College, Denver, CO (1966-1967); Instructor, Department of Anthropology, Metropolitan State College, Denver, CO (1966); Instructor, Extension Center, University of Colorado, Grand Junction, CO (1965) **CR:** Director, Research and New Programs, Colorado Migrant Council (1974-1975); Navajo Reservation (1966-1971); Research and Field Experience at Navajo Urban Relocation Project, University of Colorado, Boulder, CO (1964-1967); Consultant, Researcher, Presenter in Field **CIV:** Active with Sioux, Ute, Hopi, Shoshoni, Navajo Native Americans (1965-Present); Director, Nye County Nevada Town Historical Project (1987-1996); Active with Migrant Farm Workers, Colorado (1974-1976) **CW:** Western American History Research (1987-Present); Author, 25 Books; Contributor, Articles, Professional Publications **MEM:** Board Member, Pahrump Valley Museum, Nevada **MH:** Albert Nelson Marquis Lifetime Achievement Award **AS:** Dr. McCracken attributes his success to his education. **B/I:** He became involved because of his love of studying human beings and their societies. **AV:** Hiking; Study of humanity's future

MCCRAY, MARK, T: Vice President of Programming and Operations **I:** Corporate Communications & Public Relations **CN:** Urban One **ED:** Coursework in Communications/Radio-TV, Southern Illinois University (1995) **C:** Vice President of Programming and Operations, Urban One, Dallas, Texas (2017-Present); Operations Manager/Program Director/On-Air, Radio One, Urban One (2011-Present); Operations Manager/Program Director/Mornings, CBS Radio (2001-2011); PD/APD/MD/On-Air Talent, CBS Radio (1998-2001) **AW:** Named Personality of the Year; Named Program Director of the Year; Named One of the Best Program Directors in America, Radio Inc.; Named African American Leaders, Radio Inc.; Crystal

Award for Community Service **AS:** Mr. McCray attributes his success to his work ethic and passion. He believes certain traits can be taught but passion can not. **B/I:** Mr. McCray stumbled upon radio accidentally as a teenager. He started college at age 16 and the summer prior his mom told him that he needed to find a hobby to pass the time. So they found a program in Columbia College in Chicago that was giving high school kids college credit. After the very first class of TV/Radio, he knew he wanted to do this for the rest of his life; he found his passion that summer. **THT:** Mr. McCray's motto is, "Passion Wins."

MCCULLAGH, GRANT GIBSON SR., T: Managing Director **I:** Consulting **CN:** GIBS Consulting LLC **DOB:** 04/18/1951 **PB:** Cleveland **SC:** OH/USA **PT:** Robert Ernest McCullagh (Deceased); Barbara Louise (Grant) McCullagh **MS:** Married **SPN:** Suzanne Dewar Folds (09/13/1975) **CH:** Charles Weston Folds; Grant Gibson Jr. **ED:** Master of Business Administration in Finance, University of Chicago, Chicago, IL; Master of Architecture, University of Pennsylvania, Philadelphia, PA; Bachelor of Science in Architecture, University of Illinois at Urbana-Champaign, Champaign, IL **C:** Managing Director, TTWiiN 1, LLC (2016-Present); Executive Chairperson, BEK Building Group (2015-2019); Executive Vice President, Pernix Group (2015-2019); Chief Executive Officer, LTC (2012-2014); Chairperson, Chief Executive Officer, GIBS LLC (2004-2015); Group Executive, DMJM/Holmes & Narver/McClier Group, AECOM, Los Angeles, CA (1999-2000); President, Chief Executive Officer, Holmes & Narver, AECOM, Orange, CA (1997-2000); Vice Chairperson, Executive Vice President, AECOM, Los Angeles, CA (1996-2004); Chairperson, Chief Executive Officer, Co-Founder, McClier Corporation, Chicago, IL (1988-2000); Corporate Vice President, District Manager, The Austin Company, Chicago, IL (1977-1988) **CR:** Director, Hill International (2019-Present); Director, Thornton Tomasetti (2015-Present); Director, OnScale (2016-2018); Director, Weidlinger Association (2013-2015); Director, WSP Global (2011-2015); Director, Screampoint, Sequoia Capital (2008-2011); Director, RCMS Inc. (2008-2010) **CIV:** Trustee, Brookfield Zoo - Chicago Zoological Society (2004-2013); Trustee, Newberry Library (1982-2013) **CW:** Contributor, Articles to Numerous Industrial Publications **AW:** Entrepreneur of the Year, Ernst & Young **MEM:** American Institute of Architects College of Fellows; Past Director, Chairperson, Design-Build Institute of America; Indian Hills Country Club; University Club Of New York; Casino Club; Lyford Cay Club **PA:** Republican **RE:** Episcopalian

MCCURDY, ROBERT LAYTON, MD, T: Dean Emeritus **I:** Education/Educational Services **CN:** Medical University of South Carolina **DOB:** 08/20/1935 **PB:** Florence **SC:** SC/USA **PT:** William Barclay McCurdy; Catherline (Layton) McCurdy **MS:** Married **SPN:** Gwendolyn A. McCurdy (08/18/1958) **CH:** Robert L. McCurdy Jr.; David Barclay McCurdy **ED:** Psychoanalytic Trainee, Columbia University Psychoanalytic Clinic Atlanta Branch (1967-1968); Resident in Psychiatry, North Carolina Memorial Hospital, Chapel Hill, NC (1961-1964); Rotating Internship, Medical University of South Carolina (1960-1961); MD, Medical University of South Carolina (1960); Coursework, University of North Carolina (1953-1956) **CT:** Certified in Psychiatry, American Board of Psychiatry and Neurology (1968); License to Practice Medicine; Certified in Psychiatry, State of South Carolina **C:** Distinguished Professor, Medical University of South Carolina (2004-Present); Dean Emeritus, Medical University of South Carolina (2001); Professor of Psychiatry, Medical University of South Carolina (1990-2004); Psychiatrist-in-Chief, Institute of Pennsylvania Hospital, Philadelphia, PA (1982-1990); Professor of Psychiatry School of Medicine, University of Pennsylvania, Philadelphia, PA (1982-1990); Adjunct Professor of Behavioral Sciences, College of Dental Medicine, Medical University of South Carolina (1973-1982); Professor, Chairman of Department of Psychiatry and Behavioral Sciences, Medical University of South Carolina (1968-1982); Visiting Professor, Institute of Psychiatry, University of London (1974-1975); Assistant Professor, Department of Psychiatry School of Medicine, Emory University, Atlanta, GA (1966-1968); With, Psychiatry Training Branch, National Institute of Mental Health, Bethesda, MD (1964-1966) **CR:** Appointed, Pennsylvania Advisory Committee for Mental Health and Mental Retardation (1984-1987); National Advisory Mental Health Council, National Institute of Mental Health (1980-1983); Visiting Colleague, Institute of Psychiatry, University of London (1974-1975); Visiting Professor; Lecturer in Field **MIL:** Commissioned Officer, Lieutenant, United States Public Health Service (1966-1968) **CW:** Editorial Board Member, Psychiatry Digest (Europe), Clinical Advances in the Treatment of Depression, Dissociation: Progress in the Dissociative Disorders, American Journal of Drug and Alcohol Abuse, Academic Psychiatry; Invited Reviewer, Southern Medical Journal, American Journal of Psychiatry, Archives of General Psychiatry, Journal of Neuropsychopharmacology, Academic Medicine, Academic Psychiatry; Contributor, Articles to Numerous Journals **AW:** Humanitarian Award, La Societe Francaise (2002); Earl B. Higgins Diversity Achievement Award, Medical University of South Carolina (1999); Bowis Award, American College of Psychiatrists (1997); Distinguished Alumnus Award, George C. Ham. Society (1990); Distinguished Alumnus Award (1988) **MEM:** Chairman, South Carolina Commission on Higher Education (2005-Present); President, Waring Library Society (2004-2005); Lifetime Member, Waring Library Society (1998); President, American College of Psychiatrists (1993-1994); American Board of Psychiatry and Neurology (1993); Chairman, Committee on Diagnosis and Assessment, American Psychiatric Association (1988-1994); Joint Commission on Public Affairs, American Psychiatric Association (1981-1984); President, Waring Library Society (1979-1980); Executive Council, Waring Library Society (1977-1982); Secretary-Treasurer, Waring Library Society (1977-1978); Association for Academic Psychiatry (1970-1971); Royal College of Psychiatrists, United Kingdom; Cosmos Club; Fellow, American College of Psychiatrists **MH:** Albert Nelson Marquis Lifetime Achievement Award **B/I:** Dr. McCurdy was initially inspired to go to medical school because at the time of his upbringing in South Carolina, becoming a doctor was seen as one of the most prestigious professions. Also, his family encouraged him to follow that path as well. **AV:** Tennis; Fly fishing; Scuba diving; Reading; International travel, especially to China

MCCURRY, MARGARET I., FAIA, FIIDA, T: Architect, Furniture & Interior Designer; Educator **I:** Architecture & Construction **CN:** Tigerman McCurry Architects **DOB:** 09/26/1942 **PB:** Chicago **SC:** Il/USA **PT:** Paul D. McCurry; Irene B. McCurry **MS:** Married **SPN:** Stanley Tigerman (03/17/1979) **ED:** Diploma in Advanced Environmental Studies, Harvard Graduate School of Design, Cambridge, MA (1987); BA in Art History, Vassar College (1964) **CT:** Registered Architect; Licensed, States of Illinois and Michigan; Licensed, NCARB - National Council of Architectural Registration Boards; Registered Interior Designer, State of Illinois **C:** Member, Woman's Board, The University of Chicago (2013-Present); Partnership, Tigerman McCurry Architects, Chicago, IL (1982-Present); Member, Visiting Committee, The University of Chicago Divinity School (2013-2016); Private Practice Architect, Margaret I McCurry Ltd., Chicago, IL (1977-1982); Senior Interior Designer, Skidmore, Owings & Merrill, Chicago, IL (1966-1977); Design Coordinator, The Quaker Oats Company, Chicago, IL (1964-1966) **CR:** Peer Reviewer, Design Excellence Program, U.S. General Services Administration (GSA) (1992-Present); Visiting Studio Critic, Art Institute Chicago (1985-1986, 1988, 1998); Lecturer, Art Institute Chicago (1988, 1998); American Institute of Architects (AIA) Students Design Competition (1993); National Education Association Challenge Design Review (1992); Visiting Studio Critic, University of Illinois Chicago and Miami University, Oxford, Ohio (1990); Juror, Advertising Awards (1988); Juror, International Furniture Awards, Progressive Architecture Magazine, New York, NY (1986); Juror, Design Grants, National Endowment for Arts, Washington, DC (1983); Juror, American Institute of Architects (AIA), WI, MN, CA, VA, WA, Pittsburgh, PA, KY, GA, Connecticut Society of Architects, Detroit, MI, New York, NY, Memphis, TN, Austin, Texas, LA, Toledo, Ohio and Jacksonville, FL Chapters; American Wood Council **CIV:** Board of Directors, Architecture and Design Society, Art Institute Chicago (1988-1997, 2010-Present); Board of Directors, Textile Department (1995-Present); President, Alumni Council, Graduate School of Design, Harvard University (1997-2000); Chairman, Furniture Section, Fundraising Auction, Station WTTW-TV, PBS, Chicago, IL (1975-1976); Member, Chicago Beautiful Committee (1968-1970); Member, Textile Advisory Board, Textile Department; Board Member, Chicago's Women Network; Board Member, International Women's Forum; Board Member, Architecture and Design Committee, Art Institute of Chicago; Board Member, Textile Committee, Art Institute of Chicago **CW:** Author, "Distillations: The Architecture of Margaret McCurry" (2011); Designer, Contributor, Architectural Exhibit, Art Institute Chicago (1983-1985, 1993,1999, 2005); Author, "Margaret McCurry: Constructing 25 Short Stories" (2000); Artist, Women of Design Traveling Exhibition (1992-1996); Exhibit, Gwenda Jay Gallery (Now Addington Gallery) (1992); Exhibit, The Chicago Athenaeum (1990); Exhibit, Calouste Gulbenkian Foundation, Lisbon, Portugal (1989); Exhibit, Chicago Historical Society (Now Chicago History Museum) (1984); Contributor, Chicago Architectural Club Journal; Architectural Drawings and Models in Permanent Collection, Art Institute Chicago and Deutsches Architekturmuseum, Frankfurt, Germany **AW:** Accepted, International Women's Forum (2018); First Place, ASID Design Excellence Award, American Society of Interior Designers (2010, 2011); AD 100 Award (1991, 2000, 2002, 2007, 2010); Best of Show Award, American Society of Interior Designers Chapter (2008, 2010); American Library Association Design Excellence Award, ALA/IIDA (2009); Excellence Design Award, American Society of Interior Designers (ASID) (1994, 2005, 2008); Design Excellence Award (2008); Interior Design Magazine Best of Year Award, IL (2006); Named a Dean of Design, Architectural Digest (2005); Design Excellence Award, American Society of Interior Designers (2005); Design Excellence Award in History Preservation, American Society of Interior Designers (ASID) (2005); Award in Corporate Interiors, American Society of Interior Designers (ASID) (2005); Silver Medal Design Award, Association of Licensed Architects (2003); Designer of Distinction Award, American Society of Interior Designers (2002); Distinguished Building Award, AIA, Chicago Chapter,

IL (1984, 1986, 1991, 1994, 1999-2000); National Interior Architecture Award, AIA (1992, 1998); Gold Award, Best of Neocon, AIA (1998); Distinguished Interior Architecture Award, AIA (1981, 1983, 1988, 1991, 1997); National Design Award, American Society of Interior Designers (ASID), Illinois Chapter (1992, 1994); Inductee, Interior Design Hall of Fame, Interior Design Magazine, (1990); Dean of Architecture Award, Chicago Design Source and the Merchandise Mart (Design Center at the Merchandise Mart), Chicago, IL (1989); Product Display Neocon Award, AIA (1985, 1988); Loeb Fellow, Harvard University (1986-1987); Builders Choice Grand Award, Builders Magazine (1985); National Honor Award, AIA (1984); Interior Design Award, Interiors Magazine (1983) **MEM:** Board of Directors, Harvard Alumni Association (2008-Present); President, The Harvard Club of Chicago (2006-2008); Director, Harvard Alumni Association (2000-2006); Vice President, The Harvard Club of Chicago (2004-2006); National Convention, AIA (1988, 1997-1998); Chair, National Design Committee, AIA (1993); Monterey Design Conference, AIA (1989); Washington Design Center, AIA (1989); Vice President, Board of Directors, American Institute of Architects (AIA), Chicago Chapter (1984-1989); Lecturer, AIA, Colorado Chapter (1985); Fellow, American Institute of Architects (AIA); Fellow, International Interior Design Association (IIDA); The Chicago Network; American Society of Interior Designers (ASID); Vice President, Board of Directors, American Society of Interior Designers (ASID), Chicago Chapter, IL; Chicago Architectural Club; The Arts Club of Chicago; Harvard Alumni Association; The Harvard Club of Chicago **MH:** Albert Nelson Marquis Lifetime Achievement Award; Marquis Who's Who Top Professional **B/I:** Mrs. McCurry's father was an architect and her mother was an artist and an art teacher, so she grew up in that environment. She was always taken to job sites by her father to watch construction. She was an art history major at Vassar and became licensed under the apprentice system for the American Institute of Architects after eleven years at Skidmore, Owings & Merrill, which is one of the largest architectural firms in the country. So, it was natural, it was the world she grew up in and she wanted to make a difference. **AV:** Writing; Travel; Golf; Gardening; Drawing **RE:** Episcopalian **THT:** Mrs. McCurry's husband, Stanley Tigerman, is a renowned architect and a documentary movie is being done on him at Columbia College Chicago.

MCCUTCHEON, STEVEN C., PHD, T: Ecological and Environmental Engineer, Hydrologist **I:** Sciences

MCDANIEL, RONNA, T: Chair **I:** Media & Entertainment **CN:** Republican National Committee **DOB:** 01/19/1973 **PB:** Austin **SC:** TX/USA **PT:** Scott Romney; Ronna (Stern) Romney **MS:** Married **SPN:** Patrick McDaniel **CH:** Two Children **ED:** BA, Brigham Young University **C:** Chair, Republican National Committee (2017-Present); Chair, Michigan Republican Party (2015-2017); Delegate, Republican National Convention for Donald Trump (2016); Michigan Representative, Republican National Committee (2014); Staff, Mitt Romney's Presidential Campaign (2012) **CR:** Michigan Board of Marriage and Family Therapy (2013); Manager, Ajilon; Business Manager, Mills James; Production Manager, SRCP Media

MCDONOUGH, JOHN R., T: Retired Cardiologist **I:** Medicine & Health Care **DOB:** 08/25/1928 **PB:** Tacoma **SC:** WA/USA **PT:** John Francis McDonough; Gladys Ferne (Corington) McDonough **MS:** Married **SPN:** Jane Loretta Landolt (11/20/1954) **CH:** John R. Junior; Stephen G.; Patrick K.; Catherine A.; Thomas G.; James M.; Mark F. **ED:** MPH in Epidemiology, University of California Berkeley (1959); MD, Creighton University (1954); MS in Physiology, Creighton University (1953); BS, Seattle College (1952) **CT:** Diplomate, American Board of Preventive Medicine; Diplomate, American Board Internal Medicine; Diplomate, American Board of Cardiovascular Disease **C:** Clinical Associate Professor of Medicine, University of Washington, Seattle, WA (1975-Present); Retired, Allenmore Medical Center, Tacoma, WA (1998); Private Practice, Allenmore Medical Center, Tacoma, WA (1975-1998); Associate Professor, Medical Cardiology, University of Washington, Seattle, WA (1970-1975); Senior Fellow, Cardiology, University of Washington, Seattle, WA (1968-1970); Resident in Medicine, U.S. Public Health Service Hospital, New Orleans, LA (1966-1968); Chief, Hypertension Section, U.S. Public Health Service, Washington, DC (1964-1966); Assistant Professor, Epidemiology, University of North Carolina, Chapel Hill, NC (1962-1964); Project Director, CV Field Study Heart Disease Control, U.S. Public Health Service, Claxton, GA (1959-1962); Rheumatic Fever Program, Heart Disease Control, U.S. Public Health Service (1956-1958) **CW:** Author, "Beatitude" (2018); Author, "Angels and Other Stories" (2017); Author, "The Good Doctor" (2016); Author, "Writer Sun" (2015); Author, "The Open Door" (2014); Author, "Casting About 100 Lyric Poems From the Heart" (2013); Author, Seven Books; Contributor, 37 Publications, Professional Journals **AW:** Research Grant, National Institutes of Health (1970-1975); Inductee, Alpha Epsilon Delta, Seattle University; Inductee, Alpha Omega Alpha, Creighton University **MEM:** Fellow, American College of Physicians, American Heart Association; American College of Cardiology **MH:** Albert Nelson Marquis Lifetime Achievement Award **B/I:** Dr. McDonough suffered the loss of two women in his life when he was young. The first was his aunt, who took sick and passed away of Rheumatic Heart Disease. Later, his grandmother died of recurrent breast cancer. Those tragic events helped shape the course of life. He wanted to be able to help people, which inspired him to pursue medicine. Further, Dr. McDonough had a teacher in high school, Jesuite Novice, who taught him about the beauty of words. Through writing essays and short stories, he found his love for words, writing, and learning. **AV:** Fishing; Boating; Jogging; Reading; Swimming; Writing **RE:** Catholic

MCDORMAND, FRANCES LOUISE, T: Actress **I:** Media & Entertainment **DOB:** 06/23/1957 **PB:** Chicago **SC:** IL/USA **PT:** Vernon W. McDormand; Noreen E. (Nickleson) McDormand **MS:** Married **SPN:** Joel Coen (1984) **CH:** Pedro (Adopted) **ED:** MFA, Yale School of Drama (1982); BA, Bethany College (1979) **CW:** Voice Actress, "Good Omens" (2019); Actress, "Isle of Dogs" (2018); Actress, "Three Billboards Outside, Ebbing, Missouri" (2017); Actress, "Hail, Caesar!" (2016); Voice Actress, "The Good Dinosaur" (2015); Actress, "Olive Kitteridge" (2014); Actress, Executive Producer, "Olive Kitteridge" (2014); Actress, "Moonrise Kingdom" (2012); Voice Actress, "Madagascar 3: Europe's Most Wanted" (2012); Actress, "Promised Land" (2012); Actress, "Good People" (2011); Actress, "This Must Be the Place" (2011); Actress, "Transformers: Dark of the Moon" (2011); Actress, "The Country Girl," New York, NY (2008); Actress, "Miss Pettigrew Lives for a Day" (2008); Actress, "Burn After Reading" (2008); Actress, "Friends with Money" (2006); Voice Actress, "The Simpsons" (2006); Actress, "North Country" (2005); Actress, "Aeon Flux" (2005); Actress, "Last Night" (2004); Actress, "Something's Gotta Give" (2003); Actress, "City by the Sea" (2002); Actress, "Laurel Canyon" (2002); Actress, "To You, the Birdie!" (2002); Actress, "Far Away" (2002); Actress, "Man Who Wasn't There" (2001); Narrator, "Precinct Hollywood" (2005); Actress, "State of Grace" (2001); Actress, "Almost Famous" (2000); Actress, "Wonder Boys" (1999); Actress, "Johnny Skidmarks" (1998); Actress, "Madeline" (1998); Actress, "Talk of Angels" (1998); Actress, "Paradise Road" (1997); Actress, "Plain Pleasures" (1996); Actress, "Fargo" (1996); Actress, "Lone Star" (1996); Actress, "Primal Fear" (1996); Actress, "Hidden in America" (1996); Actress, "Palookaville" (1996); Actress, "Good Old Boys" (1995); Actress, "Beyond Rangoon" (1995); Actress, "The Swan," New York, NY (1993); Actress, "Sisters Rosensweig," New York, NY (1993); Actress, "Short Cuts" (1993); Actress, "Moon for the Misbegotten" (1992); Actress, "Passed Away" (1992); Actress, "Crazy in Love" (1992); Actress, "Three Sisters," NJ (1991); Actress, "The Butcher's Wife" (1991); Actress, "Chattahoochee" (1990); Actress, "Darkman" (1990); Actress, "Miller's Crossing" (1990); Actress, "Hidden Agenda" (1990); Actress, "A Streetcar Named Desire," New York, NY (1988); Actress, "Mississippi Burning" (1988); Actress, "Raising Arizona" (1987); Actress, "Legwork" (1986-1987); Actress, "All My Sons," New Haven, CT (1986); Actress, "The Twilight Zone" (1986); Actress, "Vengeance: The Story of Tony Cimo" (1986); Actress, "Crime Wave" (1986); Actress, "Scandal Sheet" (1985); Actress, "The Three Sisters," Minneapolis, MN (1985); Actress, "The Equalizer" (1985); Actress, "Spencer: For Hire" (1985); Actress, "Hill Street Blues" (1985); Actress, "Hunter" (1985); Actress, "Awake and Sing!," New York, NY (1984); Actress, "Painting Churches," New York, NY (1984); Actress, "Blood Simple" (1984); Actress, Plays, Television Shows, Films **AW:** Screen Actors Guild Award for Best Actress, SAG-AFTRA (1997, 2006, 2015, 2018); Award for Best Actress in a Leading Role, Academy of Motion Picture Arts and Sciences (1997, 2018); Golden Globe Award for Best Actress, Hollywood Foreign Press Association (2018); Emmy Award for Outstanding Lead Actress in a Miniseries or Movie, Academy of Television Arts and Sciences (2015); Tony Award for Best Performance by an Actress in a Leading Role in a Play (2011); Broadcast Film Critics Association Award for Best Supporting Actress (1997, 2001); Boston Society Film Critics Award for Best Supporting Actress (2000); American Comedy Award for Funniest Actress in a Motion Picture (1997); National Board of Review Award for Best Actress (1996); Golden Globe Award for Best Ensemble Cast, Hollywood Foreign Press Association (1994); National Board Review Award for Best Supporting Actress (1988); Numerous Awards

MCEACHIN, ASTON, "DONALD" DONALD, T: U.S. Representative from Virginia **I:** Government Administration/Government Relations/Government Services **CN:** U.S. House of Representatives **DOB:** 10/10/1961 **PB:** Nuremberg **SC:** West Germany **MS:** Married **SPN:** Colette McEachin (1986) **CH:** Three Children **ED:** Master of Divinity, Samuel Dewittt Proctor School of Theology at Virginia Union University (2008); Doctor of Jurisprudence, University of Virginia School of Law (1986); Bachelor of Science, American University (1982) **C:** Member, U.S. House of Representatives from Virginia's Fourth Congressional District (2017-Present); Member, Ninth District, Virginia Senate (2008-2017); Member, 74th District, Virginia House of Delegates (1996-2002, 2006-2008); Member, Committee on Armed Services; Member, Committee on Natural Resources; Partner, McEachin and Gee **MEM:** Lifetime Member, Kappa Alpha Psi.; Lifetime

Member, National Association for the Advancement of Colored People; Virginia Trial Lawyers Association; Virginia State Bar

MCELVEEN, JOSEPH JAMES JR., T: Journalist, Writer, Newscaster, Educator **I:** Education/Educational Services **DOB:** 02/23/1939 **PB:** Sanford **SC:** FL/USA **PT:** Joseph James McElveen Sr.; Genevieve (Stoll) McElveen **MS:** Married **SPN:** Mary Louise Young (08/18/1979) **CH:** Ryan Leighton **ED:** MA, University of South Carolina (1968); BA, Furman University (1961) **C:** English Teacher, Fairfax County Public Schools, Vienna, VA (2002-Present); Consultant in Media Communications, Vienna, VA (1999-Present); Senior Program Officer, Corporation for Public Broadcasting, Washington, DC (1996-1999); Director of Program Administration, Corporation for Public Broadcasting, Washington, DC (1992-1996); Director of Internal Communications, Corporation for Public Broadcasting, Washington, DC (1987-1992); Director of Public Affairs Administration, NCTA, Washington, DC (1981-1987); Senior Public Affairs Specialist, Federal Communications Commission, Washington, DC (1979-1981); Professor of Journalism, University of South Carolina (1968-1979); Director of Information, Professor of Journalism, Columbia College (1965-1968); English and Journalism Teacher, St. Andrew's Parish High School, Charleston, SC (1961-1965); Reporter, Photographer, The Post and Courier (1955-1957); Editor, Publisher, West Ashley News, Charleston, SC (1951-1957); Newsman, WSAV Radio-TV (1959); Newsman, WSAV Radio-TV, Savannah, GA (1950) **CR:** President, McElveen Seminars, Vienna, VA (2000-Present); Columnist, Alexandria Gazette (1981-1988); Ombudsman **CW:** Author, "Effective Writing and Editing" (2000); Author, "1940s: Decade on the Threshold" (2000); Author, "Words, Words, Words: A Journalist's Memoir" (1997); Author, Chapter, "Dictionary of Literary Biography" (1986); Author, "Modern Communications" (1964); Author, "Introduction to Creative Writing" (1963) **MEM:** Organization of News Ombudsmen; Society of Professional Journalists; The Mencken Society **MH:** Albert Nelson Marquis Lifetime Achievement Award; Marquis Who's Who Top Professional **B/I:** Mr. McElveen became involved in his profession because of his lifelong interest in reading and writing. At 8 years old, he got his first printing press, and began publishing a local newspaper as a teenager. **AV:** Taking photographs; Reading **RE:** Episcopalian

MCENROE, JOHN PATRICK JR., T: Former Professional Tennis Player **I:** Athletics **DOB:** 02/16/1959 **PB:** Wiesbaden **SC:** Germany **PT:** John Patrick McEnroe; Kathy McEnroe **MS:** Married **SPN:** Patty Smyth (1997); Tatum O'Neil (08/01/1986, Divorced 1994) **CH:** Kevin; Sean; Emily; Anna; Ava; Ruby (Stepchild) **ED:** Coursework, Stanford University; Diploma, Trinity School, New York, NY (1977) **C:** Member, Coaching Staff for Milos Raonic (2016); Captain, U.S. Davis Cup (1999-2000); Member, Johnny Smyth Band (1995-1997); Tennis Sportscaster, USA Network (1993); Professional Tennis Player (1978-1994) **CR:** Owner, John McEnroe Gallery (1993) **CIV:** Player, Benefit Exhibition Tennis Matches; Co-chair, Annual Tennis Fundraiser, City Parks Foundation **CW:** Host, "McEnroe," CNBC (2004); Author, "Serious" (2003); Host, "The Chair," ABC and BBC One (2002); Co-author with James Kaplan, "You Cannot Be Serious" (2000); Appearance, Numerous Television Shows and Films Including "30 Rock," "Curb Your Enthusiasm," and "You Don't Mess with the Zohan" **AW:** Davis Cup Commitment Award, International Tennis Federation (2013); Co-winner with Jonas Bjorkman, Doubles Title, SAP Open (2006); Inductee, Tennis Hall of Fame (1999); Winner, U.S. Davis Cup (1978,

1979, 1981, 1982, 1992); Winner, Doubles, Wimbledon (1992); International Tennis Federation World Champion (1981, 1983, 1984); Winner, Singles, Wimbledon (1981, 1983, 1984); Named ATP Player of the Year (1981, 1983, 1984); Winner, Men's Singles Championship, U.S. Open (1979, 1980, 1981, 1984); Winner, Tournament of Champions (1981, 1983); Winner, World Championship Tennis (1979, 1983); Winner, Grand Prix Masters Tournament, New York, NY (1979); Named ATP Most Improved Player (1978); Winner, Intercollegiate U.S. Men's Singles, National College Athletic Association (NCAA) (1978); Winner, Junior Titles, French Junior Singles (1977); Winner, Junior Titles, French Mixed Doubles (1977); Named World Number One Male Player; Winner, Numerous U.S. Junior Singles and Doubles Titles **MEM:** Men's Seniors Tour Circuit (1994)

MCENTIRE, REBA NELL, T: Singer; Musician; Actress **I:** Media & Entertainment **DOB:** 03/28/1955 **PB:** McAlester **SC:** OK/USA **PT:** Clark Vincent McEntire; Jacqueline (Smith) McEntire **MS:** Divorced **SPN:** Narvel Blackstock (06/03/1989, Divorced 10/2015); Charlie Battles (06/21/1976, Divorced 1987) **CH:** Shelby Steven McEntire Blackstock; Cassidy Blackstock (Stepchild); Shawna Blackstock (Stepchild); Brandon Blackstock (Stepchild) **ED:** Diploma in Elementary Education and Music, Southeastern State University, Durant, OK (1976) **C:** Recordin Artist, Universal Music Group Nashville (2020-Present); Recording Artist, Valory Music Co. (2008-2020); Recording Artist, MCA Records (1984-2008); Recording Artist, Mercury Records (1978-1983) **CIV:** National Spokesperson, American Lung Association (1990-1991); Spokesperson, Middle Tennessee United Way (United Way of Greater Nashville) (1988); National and State 4-H Alumni; Bob Hope's Hope for a Drug-Free America **CW:** Actress, "Young Sheldon" (2020); Singer, "Stronger Than the Truth" (2019); Voice Actress, "Spies in Disguise" (2019); Singer, "Sing It Now: Songs of Faith and Hope" (2017); Singer, "My Kind of Christmas" (2016); Voice Actress, "The Land Before Time: Journey of the Brave" (2016); Actress, "Last Man Standing" (2016); Appearance, "America's Got Talent" (2016); Actress, "Romances of the Republics" (2015); Singer, Album and Song, "Love Somebody" (2015); Actress, "Baby Daddy" (2015); Appearance, "Best Time Ever with Neil Patrick Harris" (2015); Appearance, "Disney Parks Christmas Day Parade" (2015); Appearance, "The Voice" (2015); Singer, "Icon" (2014); Appearance, "Kelly Clarkson's Cautionary Christmas Music Tale" (2013); Actress, "Malibu Country" (2012-2013); Appearance, "One Life to Live" (2011); Actress, "Working Class" (2011); Singer, "All the Women I Am" (2010); Singer, "Keep on Loving You" (2009); Singer, "Love Revival" (2008); Singer, "50 Greatest Hits" (2008); Singer, "Reba Duets" (2007); Singer, "The Best of Reba McEntire" (2007); Voice Actress, "The Fox & the Hound 2" (2006); Voice Actress, "Charlotte's Web" (2006); Actress, "South Pacific" (2006); Singer, "Reba #1s" (2005); Host, "Academy of Country Music Awards" (2004-2012); Singer, "The Christmas Collection: The Best of Reba" (2003); Singer, "Room to Breathe" (2003); Actress, Co-executive Producer, "Reba" (2001-2007); Singer, "Greatest Hits Volume III: I'm a Survivor" (2001); Actress, "Annie Gets Your Gun" (2001); Actress, "One Night at McCool's" (2001); Singer, "I'll Be" (2000); Author, "Comfort from a Country Quilt" (2000); Singer, "The Secret of Giving: A Christmas Collection" (1999); Singer, "So Good Together" (1999); Singer, "Star Profile" (1999); Singer, "Moments and Memories: The Best of Reba" (1998); Singer, "Forever Reba" (1998); Actress, Television Film, "Secret of Giving" (1999); Voice Actress, "Hercules" (1998);

Appearance, "The Roseanne Show" (1998); Actress, "Forever Love" (1998); Singer, "If You See Him" (1998); Singer, "What If It's You" (1996); Singer, "Starting Over" (1995); Co-Author, "Reba: My Story" (1995); Actress, "Buffalo Girls" (1995); Actress, "The Little Rascals" (1994); Actress, "North" (1994); Actress, "Frasier" (1994); Singer, "Oklahoma Girl" (1994); Singer, "Read My Mind" (1994); Actress, Executive Producer, "Is There Life Out There?" (1994); Singer, "Greatest Hits Volume 2" (1993); Actress, "The Man from Left Field" (1993); Actress, "Evening Shade" (1993); Singer, "It's Your Call" (1992); Appearance, "Wrestlemania VIII" (1992); Singer, "Forever in Your Eyes" (1992); Singer, "For My Broken Heart" (1991); Actress, "The Gambler Returns: The Luck of the Draw" (1991); Singer, "Rumor Has It" (1990); Actress, "Tremors" (1990); Singer, Reba Live" (1989); Singer, "Sweet 16" (1989); Singer, "Reba" (1988); Singer, "The Last One to Know" (1988); Singer, "Merry Christmas to You" (1987); Appearance, "Bob Hope Winterfest Christmas Show" (1987); Singer, "Greatest Hits" (1987); Singer, "What am I Gonna Do About You" (1987); Singer, "Whoever's in New in England" (1986); Singer, "Reba Nell McEntire" (1986); Singer, "The Best of Reba McEntire" (1985); Singer, "Have I Got a Deal for You" (1985); Singer, "My Kind of Country" (1984); Singer, "Just a Little Love" (1984); Singer, "Behind the Scene" (1983); Performer, "Country Gold" (1982); Singer, "Unlimited" (1982); Singer, "Heart to Heart" (1981); Singer, "Feel the Fire" (1980); Singer, "Out of a Dream" (1979); Singer, "Reba McEntire" (1977) **AW:** Horatio Alger Award (2018); Honoree, Kennedy Center Honors, John F. Kennedy Center for the Performing Arts (2018); Grammy Award for Best Roots Gospel Album, The Recording Academy (2018); Milestone Award (2015); Inductee, Country Music Hall of Fame (2011); Golden Note Award, ASCAP (2008); Woman of the Year, Billboard Magazine (2007); Inductee, Music City Walk of Fame (2006); Special Award for Most Female Vocalist Wins (2005); Awards for Favorite Female Country Artist, American Music Awards (1988, 1990-1994, 1998, 2004); International Artist Achievement Award (2004); Leading Lady Award (2003); Award for Favorite Female Performer in a New Television Series, People's Choice Awards (2002); Home Depot Humanitarian Award (2002); Star, Hollywood Walk of Fame (1999); Awards for Favorite Female Country Performer, People's Choice Awards (1992, 1994, 1995); Awards for Favorite Country Album, American Music Awards (1991,1993, 1995); Award for Favorite Female Vocalist, People's Choice Awards (1995); Awards for Top Female Vocalist of the Year, Entertainer of the Year, Academy of Country Music Awards (1995); Award for Favorite Female Vocalist, TNN Viewer's Choice Awards (1995); Awards for Top Female Vocalist, Academy of Country Music (1984-1987, 1991, 1994); Grammy Award for Best Country Vocal Collaboration, The Recording Academy (1994); Awards for Entertainer of the Year, Female Vocalist Award, Country Radio Awards (1994); Award for Favorite Female Country Artist, Billboard Music Awards (1994); Award for Favorite Female Musical Performer, People's Choice Awards (1992, 1993); TNN Viewer's Choice Award (1993); Awards for Female Vocalist of the Year, Academy of Country Music (1984-1987, 1992); Grammy Award for Best Country Vocal Performance, The Recording Academy (1987); Award for Favorite Country Female Video Artist, American Music Awards (1987); Award for Entertainer of the Year, CMA Country Music Association (1986); Named to Grand Ole Opry (1986); CMA Awards for Female Vocalist, CMA Country Music Association, Inc. (1984-1987); Distinguished Alumni Award, Southeastern State University; Recipient, Numerous Awards **MEM:** CMA Country Music Association

Inc.; Academy of County Music; National Academy of Recording Arts and Sciences (Now The Recording Academy); Grand Ole Opry; American Federation of Television and Radio Artists (Now SAG-AFTRA); Nashville Songwriters Association International

MCEWIN, AARON, T: Director of Sustainability **I:** Engineering **CN:** Jordan & Skala Engineers **MS:** Married **SPN:** Valerie **CH:** Nathan; Elliott **ED:** BSME, Texas A&M University (2002-2007) **C:** Director of Sustainability, Jordan & Skala Engineers (2016-Present); Mechanical Engineer, Jordan & Skala Engineers (2011-Present); Engineering Analysis and Commissioning, Jordan & Skala Engineers (2007-Present); Lead Project Designer, Green Squared (2010-2011); Warehouse/Counter Sales, Barsco (1999-2004) **CIV:** Volunteer, Church of the Cross; Volunteer, Covenant Christian School **AW:** National Green Building Standard **MEM:** ASHRAE; U.S. Green Building Council; National Eagle Scout Association **AS:** Mr. McEwin attributes his success to his parents. **B/I:** Mr. McEwin became involved in his profession because of the challenges and uniqueness of it.

MCFADDEN, DANIEL LITTLE, PHD, T: Professor Emeritus; Professor of Economics **I:** Education/Educational Services **CN:** University of California Berkeley; University of Southern California **DOB:** 07/29/1937 **PB:** Raleigh **SC:** NC/USA **PT:** Robert S. McFadden; Alice (Little) McFadden **MS:** Married **SPN:** Beverlee Tito Simboli (12/15/1962) **CH:** Nina; Robert; Raymond **ED:** Honorary Doctor of Philosophy, North Carolina State University (2006); Honorary Doctorate, University College London (2003); Doctor of Laws, The University of Chicago (1992); Doctor of Philosophy in Economics, University of Minnesota (1962); Bachelor of Science in Physics, University of Minnesota (1957) **C:** Presidential Professor of Health Economics, University of Southern California (2011-Present); Professor Emeritus, University of California Berkeley (2006-Present); Director, Econometrics Laboratory, University of California Berkeley (1996-2006); E. Morris Cox Professor and Chair, Economics, University of California Berkeley (1990-2006); Chairman, Department of Economics, University of California Berkeley (1995-1996); Director, Econometrics Laboratory, University of California Berkeley (1991-1995); James R. Killian Chair, Massachusetts Institute of Technology (1984-1991); Professor of Economics, Massachusetts Institute of Technology (1979-1991); Director, Statistics Research Center, Massachusetts Institute of Technology (1986-1988); Professor of Economics, University of California Berkeley (1968-1979); Associate Professor, University of California Berkeley (1966-1968); Assistant Professor of Economics, University of California Berkeley (1963-1966); Assistant Professor of Economics, University of Pittsburgh, PA (1962-1963) **CR:** Sherman Fairchild Distinguished Scholar, California Institute of Technology (1990); Board of Directors, National Bureau of Economic Research (1976-1977, 1980-1983); Irving Fisher Research Professor, Yale University, New Haven, CT (1977-1978); Member, Executive Committee, Transportation Research Board (1975-1978); Member, Economics Advisory Panel, National Science Foundation (1969-1971); Visiting Associate Professor, The University of Chicago (1966-1967) **CIV:** Member, Advisory Committee, City of Berkeley Coordinated Transit Project (1975-1976) **CW:** Member, Advisory Committee, Journal of Applied Economics (1996-Present); Co-author, "Handbook of Econometrics Volume IV" (1994); Co-author, "Preferences, Uncertainty, and Optimality" (1990); Co-author, "Microeconomic Modeling and Policy Analysis" (1984); Co-author, "Structural Analysis of Discrete Data with Econometric Applications" (1981); Member, Editorial Board, Transportation Research (1978-1980); Co-author, "Production Economics, Volumes I and II" (1978); Associate Editor, Journal of Econometrics (1977-1978); Member, Editorial Board, Journal of Mathematical Economics (1973-1977); Co-author, "Urban Travel Demand: A Behavioral Analysis" (1975); Co-editor, "Essays on Economic Behavior Under Uncertainty" (1974); Member, Editorial Board, American Economic Review (1971-1974); Editor, Journal of Statistical Physics (1968-1970); Contributor, Articles to Professional Journals **AW:** Richard Stone Prize in Applied Economics, Journal of Applied Econometrics (2000-2001); Co-recipient, Nobel Prize in Economics, The Nobel Foundation (2000); Nemmers Prize in Economics, Northwestern University (2000); Frisch Medal, The Econometrics Society (1986); Outstanding Teacher Award, Massachusetts Institute of Technology (1981); Fisher-Schultz Lecturer, The Econometrics Society (1979); John Bates Clark Medal, American Economic Association (1975); Ford Faculty Research Fellow (1966-1967); Earhart Fellow (1960-1961); Behavioral Science Fellow, Ford Foundation (1958-1962) **MEM:** President-elect, American Economic Association (2004); Vice President, American Economic Association (1994); Executive Committee, American Economic Association (1985-1987); President, The Econometrics Society (1985); Vice President, The Econometrics Society (1984); Fellow, The Econometrics Society (1969); National Academy of Sciences; American Philosophical Society; Mathematical Association of America; American Statistical Association; American Economic Association; American Academy Arts & Sciences **AV:** Bicycling; Tennis; Squash; Sailing; Skiing **PA:** Democrat

MCGARRY, MICHAEL, T: Chairman, Chief Executive Officer **I:** Business Management/Business Services **CN:** PPG Industries Inc. **ED:** BA, The University of Texas at Arlington **C:** Chairman, PPG Industries Inc. (2016-Present); Chief Executive Officer, PPG Industries Inc. (2015-Present); President, Chief Operating Officer, PPG Industries Inc. (2015) **MEM:** Board Member, Pittsburgh Glass Works LLC

MCGEACHIN, ROBERT BRUCE, T: Academic Librarian, Educator **I:** Education/Educational Services **CN:** Texas A&M University **DOB:** 06/20/1951 **PT:** Robert L. McGeachin; Margaret DeLong McGeachin **MS:** Married **SPN:** Leila Payne (1978) **CH:** Tavis Payne **ED:** MLIS, University of Texas at Austin (1992); PhD in Wildlife and Fisheries Sciences, Texas Agricultural and Mechanical University (Now Texas A&M University), College Station, TX (1980); MS in Wildlife and Fisheries Sciences, Texas Agricultural and Mechanical University (Now Texas A&M University), College Station, TX (1977); BA in Biology and Anthropology, University of Louisville, Louisville, KY (1973) **C:** Agriculture and Digital Services Librarian, Texas A&M University Libraries, Texas A&M University, College Station, TX (2010-Present); Agriculture and Life Sciences Librarian, Texas A&M University Libraries, Texas A&M University (2007-2010); Coordinator for Agricultural Library Services, Medical Sciences Library, Texas A&M University, College Station, TX (2004-2006); Head, Director for Business and Agriculture Services, West Campus Library, Texas A&M University, College Station, TX (1999-2003); Interim Head, Interim Director for Business and Agriculture Services, West Campus Library, Texas A&M University, College Station, TX (1998-1999); Agriculture Reference Librarian, West Campus Library, Texas A&M University, College Station, TX (1994-1998); Science Reference Librarian, Sterling C. Evans Library, Texas A&M University, College Station, TX (1993-1994); Reference Librarian, Visiting Lecturer, Sterling C. Evans Library, Texas A&M University, College Station, TX (1992-1993); Technician, Poultry Science Department, Texas A&M University, College Station, TX (1987-1993); Consultant, Clean Livin' Fish Farms, Houston, TX (1987-1988); Research Scientist, Caribbean Marine Research Center, Lee Stocking Island, Exuma Cays, Bahamas (1985-1986); Research Associate, Department of Wildlife and Fisheries Sciences, Texas A&M University, College Station, TX (1983-1984); Research Assistant, Department of Wildlife and Fisheries Sciences, Texas A&M University, College Station, TX (1983); Technician, Department of Wildlife and Fisheries Sciences, Texas A&M University, College Station, TX (1981-1983); Technician, LGL Ecological Research Associates, Bryan, TX (1981); Instructor, Department of Wildlife and Fisheries Sciences, Texas A&M University, College Station, TX (1981) **CR:** Chair, AgNIC (2004-2005, 2015-2016) **CIV:** Finance Chair, Unitarian Universalist Church of Brazos Valley (2005-2008, 2012-2020); Troop Committee Member, Troop 102, Boy Scouts of America (2001-2019); President, Board of Trustees, Unitarian Universalist Church of Brazos Valley (2009-2010); Assistant Scout Master, Troop 102, Boy Scouts of America, College Station, TX (1993-2000); Treasurer, Unitarian Universalist Church of Brazos Valley, College Station, TX (1993-1995); President, International Folk Dancers, Texas A&M University (1975-1980); Eagle Scout, Boy Scouts of America (1966) **CW:** Author, Article, Numerous Refereed Publications (1977-2018); Author, Numerous Monographs (1977-2001); Co-Author, Book Chapters, Proceedings and Essays (1987-1995); Author, Invited Publications, Including Journal Articles, Book Chapters, Proceedings and Essays (1986-1993); Presenter, Numerous Juried Regional, National and International Presentations **AW:** Distinguished Service Award, AgNIC (2013, 2019); Texas Digital Library Award for Excellence in Digital Libraries (2014); H.W. Wilson Co. Scholarship, Graduate School of Library and Information Sciences, University of Texas at Austin (1990-1991) **MEM:** American Library Association; International Association of Agricultural Information Specialists; United States Agricultural Information Network; World Aquaculture Society; Life Member, American Fisheries Society; Beta Phi Mu-The International Library and Information Studies Honor Society; Sigma Xi, The Scientific Research Honor Society; Phi Sigma Biological Sciences Honor Society; The Honor Society of Phi Kappa Phi **MH:** Albert Nelson Marquis Lifetime Achievement Award; Marquis Who's Who Top Professional **B/I:** Dr. McGeachin became involved in his profession because he wanted to start his career in fish farming research, so he spent a year in the Bahamas pursuing it. When he returned to the United States, he could not find a full time position; he then started doing research in poultry nutrition. Later, he switched his focus to being a librarian focusing on agriculture and has never looked back. **AV:** Reading; Swimming; Sculpting; Bicycling; Folk dancing; Planting trees **RE:** Unitarian Universalist

MCGINNIS, RICHARD PROVIS, PHD, T: Chemical Educator **I:** Sciences **DOB:** 12/24/1941 **PB:** Woodland **SC:** CA/USA **PT:** Richard Adams McGinnis; Olive Verna Ruth (Provis) McGinnis **MS:** Married **SPN:** Jacqueline Dedeaux-McGinnis **CH:** Brian (Stepson); Monique (Stepdaughter); Deirdre (Stepdaughter) **ED:** Woodrow Wilson Teaching Intern (1969-1972); PhD in Chemistry, Harvard University (1971); AM in Chemistry, Harvard University (1965); BS in Basic Chemistry, University of California Berkeley, with Honors (1963) **C:** Chair, Chemistry Department, Tougaloo College, MI

(1978-1979, 1981-1982, 1996-Present); Professor, Tougaloo College, MI (1977-Present); Chair, Natural Science Division, Tougaloo College, MI (1979-1981, 1989-1991); Acting Vice President, Academic Affairs, Tougaloo College, MI (1985); Member, Chemistry Faculty, Tougaloo College, MI (1969-1977) **CR:** Project Director, Health Career Opportunity Program, Pre-Health Program (1973-1976, 1977-Present); Ran Summer Science Program for Entering Freshmen, Tougaloo College (1972-2016); Coordinator, Title III Program, Tougaloo College (1987-1988); Visiting Scientist, Joint Institute Laboratory Astrophysics National Bureau of Standards and University of Colorado (1982-1983); Visiting Professor, Brown University (1978); Head Tutor, Health Careers Summer Program and Intensive Summer Studies Program, Harvard University (1969); Tutor, Summers (1966-1969); Teaching Fellow in Chemistry (1963-1967); Head, Teaching Assistant, Summer (1965); Pre-med Advisor **CIV:** President/Co-founder, Mississippi Academy of Ancient Music (MAAM) (1982-Present); Principal Investigator, Alabama Alliance for Minority Participation (Now Alabama Louis Stokes Alliance for Minority Participation (LSAMP)) (1991-1998) **CW:** Contributor, Articles to Professional Journals **AW:** Distinguished Service Award, National Association of Medical Minority Educators, Inc. (1985); Award, Tougaloo College Alumni (1979); Named Professor of the Year, Phi Beta Sigma Fraternity, Inc., Tougaloo Chapter (1977); Named Pre-Medical Adviser of the Year, Minority Medical Education Foundation (1976) **MEM:** American Chemical Society **MH:** Albert Nelson Marquis Lifetime Achievement Award **AS:** Dr. McGinnis attributes his success to a variety of interests including writing grants for chemistry and science education at the college level with special focus on African Americans. After building a harpsichord while finishing college, he began to promote early music performances by local and international performers through the Mississippi Academy of Ancient Music (MAAM) which they started. **B/I:** Dr. McGinnis wasn't really sure what he wanted to do. His father had went to college and majored in English, but wound up playing piano for silent movies. When he went to Hollywood for a while, he got fascinated on how they made film. So, he went back to college and got a PhD in chemistry from Berkley. Once he got the degree, he started a research department for a sugar company in California and he devised better methods of purifying the sugar. His father was a big inspiration for him. He always wanted to teach more than do research. He got involved in a program that Harvard, Yale, and Columbia were running to involve students from historically black colleges. He really enjoyed it and did it for two of three summers. They came to him and offered him a chance to recruit students to the program, so Dr. McGinnis went to visit some of the schools. One of the schools he visited was Tougaloo; his host was a fascinating character. He had been a judge in Germany, he was Polish by background. He had a broad background and a deep commitment for the people that had been denied opportunities. Dr. McGinnis thought that Tougaloo would be a nice place to spend some time until he figured out what he wanted to do, and he has never left. **AV:** Singing; Keyboard (harpsichord) **PA:** Democrat **RE:** Christian

MCGOVERN, ALICIA, T: Financial Adviser **I:** Financial Services **CN:** Edward Jones **MS:** Married **CH:** Two Daughters **ED:** BBA, Cleary University (2000) **CT:** Accredited Asset Management Specialist (2012-Present) **C:** Financial Adviser, Edward Jones (2007-Present); Financial Relationship Manager, First Horizon Home Loans (2003-2007) **CIV:** Past President, Greater Belleville Chamber of Commerce **AW:** 5 Star Wealth Manager, Detroit Magazine (2018); Awards for Asset Sharing Programs; Awards for Training Programs **MEM:** Women's Council of Muskegon Community College **AS:** Ms. McGovern attributes her success to caring and never giving up. **B/I:** Ms. McGovern became involved in her profession because she feels the need to educate the employee body and equip the surrounding areas and community with the tools to be solid self-advocates–whether they work with her or not. She wants to make sure people are headed in the right direction. **THT:** Ms. McGovern says, "Let go, Let God."

MCGOVERN, GAIL J., T: President, Chief Executive Officer **I:** Nonprofit & Philanthropy **CN:** American Red Cross **PB:** Springfield **SC:** NJ/USA **MS:** Married **SPN:** Donald E. McGovern **CH:** One Child **ED:** MBA, Columbia University (1987); BA in Quantitative Sciences, Johns Hopkins University (1974) **C:** President, Chief Executive Officer, American Red Cross, Washington, DC (2008-Present); MBA Class Of 1966 Professor of Management Practice, Harvard Business School, Boston, MA (2002-Present); President, Personal Investments, Fidelity Investments, Boston, MA (2001-2002); President, Distribution and Services, Fidelity Investments, Boston, MA (1998-2001); Executive Vice President, Business Markets Division, AT&T Corp., Basking Ridge, NJ (1996-1998); Vice President, General Manager, Business Services, AT&T Corp., Basking Ridge, NJ (1994-1996); Vice President, Strategic Planning For Communications Services Group, AT&T Corp., Basking Ridge, NJ (1993); Division Manager, Industry Marketing, AT&T Corp., Basking Ridge, NJ (1987-1989); Branch Manager, AT&T Corp., New York, NY (1987); District Sales Manager, AT&T Corp., New York, NY (1984-1987); District Manager, Long Range System Planning, AT&T Corp., Basking Ridge, NJ (1980-1984); Computer Programmer, Bell Telephone Co., Pennsylvania (1974-1980) **CR:** Board of Directors, Digitas, Inc., Boston, MA (2004-Present); Board of Directors, DTE Energy Co. (2003-Present); Board of Directors, Hartford Finance Services Group, Inc. (2003-Present) **CIV:** Board of Trustees, Boston Children's Hospital; Board of Trustees, Teach for America Foundation; Board of Trustees, Johns Hopkins University **AW:** Named, 100 Most Powerful Women in DC, Washingtonian Magazine (2009); Named, 50 Most Powerful Women in Corporate America, Fortune Magazine (2001); Named, 50 Most Powerful Women in Corporate America, Fortune Magazine (2000); Alumna Award, Johns Hopkins University (2000); Distinguished Citizens Award, Boy Scouts of America (1997); Distinguished Alumna Award, Columbia Graduate School of Business (1997); Named, 25 Most Influential Working Mothers, Working Mother Magazine (1995)

MCGOVERN, JAMES, "JIM" PATRICK, T: U.S. Representative from Massachusetts **I:** Government Administration/Government Relations/Government Services **CN:** U.S. House of Representatives **DOB:** 11/20/1959 **PB:** Worcester **SC:** MA/USA **PT:** Walter McGovern; Mindy McGovern **MS:** Married **SPN:** Lisa Murray **CH:** Patrick George; Molly Ginette **ED:** Master of Public Administration, American University (1984); Bachelor of Arts in History, American University (1981) **C:** Member, U.S. House of Representatives from Massachusetts' Second Congressional District, United States Congress, Washington, DC (2013-Present); Member, U.S. House of Representatives from Massachusetts' Third Congressional District, United States Congress, Washington, DC (1997-2013); Staff Positions, Including Spokesman, Legislative Director and Senior Aide to Representative Joe Moakley, U.S. House of Representatives (1981-1996); Aide to Senator George McGovern, U.S. Senate (1977-1980); Member, House Rules Committee **CR:** Leader, Congressional Investigation on El Salvador (1989); Delivered McGovern Presidential Nomination Speech, Democratic National Convention, San Francisco, CA (1984); Manager, George McGovern for President (1984) **CIV:** Candidate for U.S. Congress (1996); Volunteer, Mount Carmel House; Board of Directors, Jesuit International Volunteers **PA:** Democrat **RE:** Roman Catholic

MCGOWAN, JON G., PHD, T: Mechanical Engineer, Educator **I:** Engineering **DOB:** 05/03/1939 **PB:** Lockport **SC:** NY/USA **PT:** Gerald F. McGowan; Xenia W. (Guenther) McGowan **MS:** Married **SPN:** Suzanne Jessop (9/25/1965) **CH:** Gerald; Edward **ED:** PhD in Mechanical Engineering, Carnegie Institute of Technology (1965); MS in Mechanical Engineering, Stanford University (1962); BS in Mechanical Engineering, Carnegie Institute of Technology (1961) **C:** Consultant, Alden Research Laboratory (2000-Present); Consultant, United States Bureau of Standards, Washington, DC (1978-Present); Consultant, Combustion Engineering, Inc., Windsor, CT (1970-Present); Professor, Mechanical Engineering, University of Massachusetts, Amherst, MA (1967-Present); Development Engineer, E. I. DuPont de Nemours, Wilmington, DE (1965-1967) **CIV:** Trustee, Dickensen Memorial Library, Northfield, MA (1975-Present) **CW:** Contributor, Articles, Professional Journals **MEM:** International Hydrogen Energy Association; Air Pollution Control Association; International Solar Energy Society; Fellow, American Society of Mechanical Engineers **MH:** Albert Nelson Marquis Lifetime Achievement Award **B/I:** Dr. McGowan was always fascinated by how mechanical products worked. Naturally, mechanical engineering was the perfect fit for his interests. **AV:** Restoring vintage and sports care; Building tin plate electric trains; Skiing **PA:** Republican **RE:** Congregationalist

MCGRAW, TIM, T: Musician; Actor **I:** Media & Entertainment **DOB:** 05/01/1967 **PB:** Start **SC:** LA/USA **PT:** Frank Edwin "Tug" McGraw; Elizabeth "Betty" Ann D'Agostino **MS:** Married **SPN:** Faith Hill (10/06/1996) **CH:** Gracie Katherine; Maggie Elizabeth; Audrey Caroline **ED:** Coursework, Florida Community College, Jacksonville, FL **CW:** Singer, Musician, "The Rest of Our Life" (2017); Appearance, "The Voice" (2016); Actor, "The Shack" (2016); Appearance, "Repeat After Me" (2015); Singer, Musician, "Damn Country Music" (2015); Actor, "Tomorrowland" (2015); Singer, Musician, "Humble and Kind" (2015); Singer, Musician, "Sundown Heaven Town" (2014); Co-Musician, "Highway Don't Care" (2013); Appearance, "Cake Boss" (2013); Singer, Musician, "Two Lanes of Freedom" (2013); Singer, Musician, "Emotional Traffic" (2012); Musician with Kenny Chesney, "Feel Like a Rock Star" (2012); Appearance, "Who Do You Think You Are" (2011); Actor, "Dirty Girl" (2010); Singer, Musician, "Number One Hits" (2010); Actor, "Country Strong" (2010); Singer, Musician, "Here On Earth" (2010); Actor, "The Blind Side" (2009); Singer, Musician, "Southern Voice" (2009); Appearance, "Saturday Night Live" (2008); Singer, Musician, "Greatest Hits: Limited Edition" (2008); Singer, Musician, "Collector's Edition" (2008); Singer, Musician, "Greatest Hits Volume Three" (2008); Singer, Musician, "Limited Edition: Greatest Hits: Volumes 1, 2 & 3" (2008); Actor, "Four Christmases" (2008); Musician with Tracy Lawrence and Kenny Chesney, "Find Out Who Your Friends Are" (2007); Singer, Musician, "Let It Go" (2007); Singer, Musician, "Tim McGraw Reflected Greatest Hits Volume Two" (2006); Actor, "Flicka" (2006); Actor, "Black Cloud" (2004); Actor, "Friday Night Lights" (2004); Singer, Musician, "Live Like You Were

Dying" (2004); Singer, Musician, "Tim McGraw and the Dancehall Doctors" (2002); Singer, Musician, "Grown Men" (2001); Musician with Faith Hill, "Let's Make Love" (2001); Singer, Musician, "Set the Circus Down" (2001); Appearance, "Sesame Street" (2000); Singer, Musician, "Tim McGraw Greatest Hits" (2000); Singer, Musician, "A Place in the Sun" (1999); Appearance, "The Jeff Foxworthy Show" (1997); Singer, Musician, "It's Your Love" (1997); Singer, Musician, "Everywhere" (1997); Singer, Musician, "All I Want" (1995); Singer, Musician, "Not a Moment Too Soon" (1994); Singer, Musician, "Tim McGraw," (1993); Appearances, Television Shows, Films **AW:** CMT Music Award for Video of the Year, CMA Country Music Association Inc. (2016); Award for Video of the Year, Academy Country Music Awards (2014); Favorite Country Music Icon, People's Choice Awards (2014); Musical Event of Year, Music Video of Year, CMA Country Music Association Inc. (2013); Musical Event of the Year, Country Music Association Awards (2007, 2012); Vocal Event of the Year, Academy Country Music Awards (2008); Awards for Favorite Male Country Artist, American Music Awards (2001, 2002, 2003, 2005, 2007); Award with Faith Hill, Best Country Collaboration with Vocals (2006); Award for Favorite Country Album, American Music Awards (2006); Grammy Award for Best Country Collaboration, The Recording Academy (2006); Favorite Male Performer, People's Choice Awards (2004, 2006); Grammy Award for Best Male Country Vocals, The Recording Academy (2005); CMT Music Award for Most Inspiring Video of the Year, CMA Country Music Association Inc. (2005); Awards for Single Record of the Year, Song of the Year, Favorite Country Album, Academy Country Music Awards (2005); CMT Music Award, Single of Year, Song of Year, CMA Country Music Association Inc. (2004); Country Male Artist, Radio Music Awards (2003); Award for Best Country Album, American Music Awards (2002); Favorite Male Artist, Blockbuster Awards (2001); Entertainer of the Year, CMA Country Music Association Inc. (2001); Named Single of the Year, Radio Music Association (2001); Grammy Award for Vocal Collaboration, The Recording Academy (2001); Named Male Vocalist of Year (1999, 2000); Male Artist of the Year, TNN/Music City News (1999);CMT Music Award for Album of the Year, CMA Country Music Association Inc. (1998, 1999); Top Male Vocalist, Academy of County Music Awards (1994, 1998, 1999); Award for Single of the Year, Song of Year, Academy Country Music Awards (1998); Awards, Academy of County Music Awards (1997, 1998); Award for Vocal Event of the Year (1997); Award for Favorite New Artist, American Music Award (1995); Triple-Platinum, Album of the Year, Academy of County Music Awards (1994); Recipient, Numerous Awards

MCGREGOR, CONOR ANTHONY, T: Professional Boxer, Former Professional Mixed Martial Artist **I:** Athletics **DOB:** 07/14/1988 **PB:** Crumlin **SC:** Ireland **PT:** Anthony McGregor; Margaret McGregor **CH:** Conor Jack Jr.; Croia **C:** Professional Boxer (2017-Present); Professional Mixed Martial Artist, Ultimate Fighting Championship (2013-2020) **CW:** Boxer, "The Money Fight" (2017); Featured, "Conor McGregor: Notorious" (2017); Appearances, Television Specials, Fighting Matches **AW:** Named, One of the 100 Most Influential People, TIME Magazine (2017); ESPY Award for Best Fighter (2016); Named Fighter of the Year, Bleacher Report (2015, 2016); Named, Fighter of the Year, ESPN (2015); Winner, Numerous Fighting Matches and Titles **RE:** Catholic

MCGREGOR, EWAN GORDON, T: Actor **I:** Media & Entertainment **DOB:** 03/31/1971 **PB:** Perth **SC:** Scotland **PT:** James McGregor; Carol Diane (Lawson) McGregor **MS:** Married **SPN:** Eve Mavrakis (07/22/1995) **CH:** Jamyan (Adopted); Anouk (Adopted); Clara Mathilde; Esther Rose **ED:** Doctor of Law, University of Ulster (2001) **C:** Co-founder, with John Lee Miller, Sean Pertwee, Jude Law, Sadie Frost, Production Company, Natural Nylon (1996-2002) **CW:** Appearance, "Long Way Up" (2020); Actor, "Birds of Prey" (2020); Actor, "Star Wars: The Rise of Skywalker" (2019); Actor, "Doctor Sleep" (2019); Actor, "Zoe" (2018); Actor, "Christopher Robin" (2018); Actor, "T2 Trainspotting" (2017); Actor, "Beauty and the Beast" (2017); Actor, "Fargo" (2017); Actor, "Our Kind of Traitor" (2016); Narrator, "Highlands: Scotland's Wild Heart" (2016); Actor, "American Pastoral" (2016); Actor, "Mortdecai" (2015); Actor, "Last Days in the Desert" (2015); Actor, "Miles Ahead" (2015); Actor, "Jane Got a Gun" (2015); Appearance, "Doll & Em" (2015); Actor, "Son of a Gun" (2014); Actor, "The Real Thing" (2014); Actor, "The Corrections" (2013); Narrator, "Hebrides: Islands on the Edge" (2013); Actor, "Jack the Giant Slayer" (2013); Actor, "August: Osage County" (2013); Actor, "Haywire" (2012); Actor, "Salmon Fishing in the Yemen" (2012); Actor, "The Impossible" (2012); Actor, "The Corrections" (2012); Appearance, "Ewan McGregor: Cold Chain Mission" (2012); Appearance, "Bomber Boys" (2012); Co-executive Producer, "Marley Africa Roadtrip" (2011); Actor, "Perfect Sense" (2011); Actor, "I Love You Phillip Morris" (2010); Actor, "The Ghost Writer" (2010); Actor, "Nanny McPhee Returns" (2010); Appearance, "The Battle of Britain" (2010); Actor, "Beginners" (2010); Actor, "Angels & Demons" (2009); Actor, "Amelia" (2009); Actor, "The Men Who Stare at Goats" (2009); Actor, "Incendiary" (2008); Actor, "Deception" (2008); Appearance, Executive Producer, Writer, "Long Way Down" (2007); Actor, "Cassandra's Dream" (2007); Actor, "Star Wars: Episode III - Revenge of the Sith" (2005); Actor, "The Island" (2005); Voice Actor, "Robots" (2005); Actor, "Guys and Dolls" (2005); Actor, "Valiant" (2005); Actor, "Stay" (2005); Actor, "Motor Bike: Round the World Trip" (2004); Appearance, Executive Producer, Writer, "Long Way Round" (2004); Actor, "Down with Love" (2003); Actor, "Young Adam" (2003); Actor, "Big Fish" (2003); Actor, "Star Wars: Episode II - Attack of the Clones" (2002); Appearance, "The Polar Bears of Churchill with Ewan McGregor" (2002); Actor, "Moulin Rouge" (2001); Actor, "Black Hawk Down" (2001); Actor, Co-producer, "Nora" (2000); Actor, "Eye of the Beholder" (1999); Actor, "Star Wars: Episode I - The Phantom Menace" (1999); Actor, "Velvet Goldmine" (1998); Actor, "Little Voice" (1998); Actor, "A Life Less Ordinary" (1997); Actor, "Emma" (1996); Actor, "Trainspotting" (1996); Actor, "Brassed Off" (1996); Actor, "Karaoke" (1996); Actor, "Blue Juice" (1995); Actor, "Kavanagh QC" (1994); Actor, "ER" (1994); Actor, "Doggin' Around" (1994); Actor, "The Pillow Book" (1994); Actor, "Shallow Grave" (1994); Actor, "Being Human" (1993); Actor, "Lipstick on Your Collar" (1993); Actor, "Tales from the Crypt" (1989); Actor, Plays, Television Shows and Film **AW:** Award for Best Actor in a Movie Made for Television or Limited Series, Critics Choice Television Awards (2018); Golden Globe for Best Actor in a Miniseries Television Film, Hollywood Foreign Press Association (2017); Humanitarian Award, Britannia Awards, BAFTA Los Angeles (2016); Named, Knight, Order of the Arts and Letters, France (2010); Named, Officer, Order of the British Empire (2013); Icon Award, Empire Awards (2008); Named, One of British Culture's Top 50 Movers and Shakers, BBC 3 (2004); Award for Best Dance Sequence, MTV Movie and TV Awards (2002);

Award for Best Actor, Empire Awards (1996, 1997, 1998, 2002); Named, One of the 100 Top Movie Stars of All Time, Empire Magazine (1997); ALFS Award (1997); Numerous Awards

MCGREGOR, JOHN M., MD, T: Associate Professor **I:** Education/Educational Services **CN:** The Ohio State University **MS:** Married **CH:** Four Children **ED:** MD, Roy J. and Lucille A. Carver College of Medicine, University of Iowa (1984) **C:** Associate Professor of Clinical Neurosurgery, Department of Neurological Surgery, The Ohio State University Wexner Medical Center; Associate Professor of Clinical Neurosurgery, Department of Radiology, The Ohio State University Wexner Medical Center; Associate Professor of Clinical Neurosurgery, Department of Otolaryngology, The Ohio State University Wexner Medical Center **CIV:** CISV USA, CISV International Ltd. **CW:** Contributor, Articles, Professional Journals; Author, Chapters, Professional Journals **AW:** Fellow, American College of Surgeons; Fellow, American Association of Neurological Surgeons **MEM:** American College of Surgeons; American Association of Neurological Surgeons **AS:** Dr. McGregor attributes his success to many great mentors who set the groundwork for him and his career. **B/I:** Dr. McGregor became involved in his profession in order to use the biology skills that he learned to help patients on a day-to-day basis, providing care and comfort to them when their medical conditions call for his expertise. Neurology became the most interesting and rewarding part of that journey. Dr. McGregor was challenged by neurology, a field that has changed dramatically over time. There was always something new to learn. To his involvement in this profession, he also cites his commitment to always be extraordinary in what he learns and how he works. **AV:** Outdoor activities; National parks

MCHARGUE, CARL J., PHD, T: Educator **I:** Education/Educational Services **DOB:** 01/30/1926 **SC:** KY/USA **PT:** John David McHargue; Virginia (Thomas) McHargue **MS:** Widower **SPN:** Betty F. McHargue (09/30/1960, Deceased 06/01/2019); Edith Trovillion (08/28/1948, Deceased) **CH:** Anne Odell McHargue Diegel; Carol Virginia Hornberger; Margaret Katherine McHargue **ED:** PhD, University of Kentucky (1953); MS, University of Kentucky (1951); BS in Metallurgical Engineering, University of Kentucky (1949) **C:** Retired, Research Professor, University of Tennessee (2013-Present); Professor of Materials Science and Engineering, University of Tennessee, Knoxville, TN (1991-2018); Director of Center Materials Processing, University of Tennessee, Knoxville, TN (1991-2012); Senior Research Staff, Oak Ridge National Laboratory (1980-1990); Oak Ridge National Laboratory (1953-1990); Program Manager for Materials Sciences, Oak Ridge National Laboratory (1961-1988); Section Head, Oak Ridge National Laboratory (1960-1980); Instructor, University of Kentucky, Lexington, KY (1949-1953) **CR:** Adjunct Professor, Vanderbilt University (1988-Present); Board of Directors, Accreditation Board for Engineering and Technology (1998-2004); Visiting Professor, University of Newcastle, Newcastle upon Tyne, England (1987); Board of Directors, The Minerals, Metals, and Materials Society **MIL:** Infantry, U.S. Army (1944-1946) **CW:** Contributor, Numerous Articles, Professional Journals; Editor, Eight Books **AW:** Inductee, Hall of Fame, College of Engineering, University of Tennessee (2018); Honorary Member, Ordem dos Engenheiros, Portugal (2011); Ferris Award, University of Tennessee College of Engineering (2010); REI Medal for Radiation Effects in Insulators (2005); Distinguished Service Award, The Minerals, Metals, and Materials Society (2001); Engineering Hall of Distinction, University of Kentucky (1995); Fellowship, Minerals, Metals, and Materials Society; Fellowship, ASM International, ABET Inc.; Fellowship, University of Kentucky **MEM:** Fellow, Metallurgical Society; American Institute of Mining; American Society for Metals; Accreditation Board Engineering Technology; Materials Research Society; Lifetime Member, Optimist International; Sigma Xi; Tau Beta Pi **MH:** Albert Nelson Marquis Lifetime Achievement Award; Marquis Who's Who Top Professional **B/I:** Dr. McHargue became involved with his profession because he lived with his grandparents for many years; they were insistent that all the children attend college. After he left the Army, he received an opportunity for a funded education through the GI Bill. His aunt and uncle were school teachers, and his aunt married a chemical engineer, so it was apparent that Dr. McHargue was going to study science. **AV:** Practicing photography; Traveling **PA:** Republican

MCHENRY, DEBRA COLLEEN, T: Ironworker **I:** Architecture & Construction **CN:** Ironworkers Union Local #433 **MS:** Divorced **CH:** Kira **CT:** Ironworkers Certificate **C:** Ironworker, Ironworkers Union Local #433 (2008-Present); Hotel Front Desk Clerk, Marriott Hotel, Las Vegas, NV **CIV:** Volunteer, Miss Nevada Competition; Clown, Special Olympics (Five Years); Volunteer, St. Viator Catholic Church, Las Vegas, NV; Teacher, Fifth Grade, Sunday School **AW:** Ironworker Working Woman of the Year, Harry Bridges Institute (2016) **MEM:** Catholic Daughters of the Americas **AS:** Ms. McHenry attributes her success to many people. It's not easy being a woman in her trade. She cried every day and didn't think she was going to make it, but there were a few people in her union that made sure she finished and had the tools and knew how to do the work. She did not do this on her own; there were a few people who have helped her the entire way. **B/I:** Ms. McHenry became involved in her profession because of her daughter, who has always been an inspiration to her. She needed to see that "when you get out there and work as hard as you can, the benefits come." Her daughter was 2018 Miss Nevada and has received her Girl Scout Gold Award.

MCHENRY, PATRICK TIMOTHY, T: U.S. Representative from North Carolina **I:** Government Administration/Government Relations/Government Services **DOB:** 10/22/1975 **PB:** Gastonia **SC:** NC/USA **MS:** Married **SPN:** Giulia Cangiano **ED:** BA in History, Belmont Abbey College (1999); Coursework, North Carolina State University **C:** Member, U.S. House of Representatives from North Carolina's 10th Congressional District, United States Congress (2005-Present); Chief Deputy Whip, North Carolina's 10th District, United States Congress (2014-2019); Member, North Carolina State House of Representatives (2003-2005); Special Assistant to Secretary Elaine L. Chao, U.S. Department of Labor, Washington, DC (2000); Member, Committee on Financial Services; Member, Committee on Government Reform; Member, Republican Study Committee; Owner, Broker, McHenry Real Estate, Gastonia, NC; Executive, DCI/New Media, Inc., Washington, DC **CIV:** Board of Directors, Success by Six, United Way; Board of Directors, Youth Progressive **AW:** Named One of the Politics 40 Under 40, TIME Magazine (2010); Named a Protector of Property Rights, Property Rights Alliance; Named Hero of the Taxpayer, Americans for Tax Reform; Named Small Business Champion, Small Business and Entrepreneurship Council; Spirit of Enterprise Award, United States Chamber of Commerce **MEM:** Gaston Chamber of Commerce; National Rifle Association of America; Rotary Club of Gastonia **PA:** Republican **RE:** Roman Catholic

MCHUGH, PETER CHADWICK, ACADEMIC/ RESEARCH CONSORTIUM, T: Director, FAA and Aeronautics Programs **I:** Aviation **CN:** National Institute of Aerospace **DOB:** 08/08/1944 **PB:** Vancouver **SC:** BC/Canada **PT:** John Lawrence McHugh **MS:** Married **SPN:** Dee Jean **CH:** John; Christopher; Kevin; Sean; Adrianna **ED:** MS in Systems Management, University of Southern California (1974); Rotary Wing Instrument Examiner Course, Ft. Rucker, AL (1973); BS in Aeronautical Science, Embry-Riddle Aeronautical University, Daytona, FL, Summa Cum Laude (1972); Rotary Wing Aviator Qualification Course, Ft. Rucker, AL (1970); U.S. Army Initial Entry Fixed-Wing Course, Ft. Rucker, AL (1967); Postgraduate Cousework in Human Factors, University of Michigan; Executive Development Program, U.S. Department of Agriculture Graduate School; Coursework, Joint Combined Warfighter School, National Defense University, Joint Forces Staff College, Norfolk, VA; Air Carrier Operations Inspector Course, FAA Academy, Oklahoma City, OK; Federal Aviation Administration, Accident Investigators Courses, Washington, DC; Accident Investigation Course, National Transportation Safety Board, Washington, DC **CT:** Boating Safety Instructor, Virginia Department of Game and Inland Fisheries (2007-Present); Aviation Safety Investigator, Federal Aviation Administration (1987-2014); Air Traffic Control Evaluator, Federal Aviation Administration Programs (1986-2014); Bow Hunting/Safety Instructor, Alabama Department of Natural Resources (1972); Commercial SEMEL and SE Seaplane, Rotorcraft, Instrument, Federal Aviation Administration (1967) **C:** Director, Federal Aviation Administration and Aeronautics Programs, National Institute of Aerospace (2016-Present); Aviation Technical Specialist, Federal Aviation Administration (2014-Present); Manager, National Security Professional Development (NSPD) and Civilian Response Corps (CRC) Programs, Office of the Secretary of Transportation and the Office of Intelligence, Security and Emergency Response (2008-2011); Academic Chair, Federal Aviation Administration, Department of Transportation, National Defense University (NDU), Joint Forces Staff College (2006-2008); Counselor, Senior Consultant, Senior Aviation Advisor, Federal Aviation Administration/Department of Transportation, Department of State, US Embassy, Baghdad, Iraq (2005-2006); FAA Program Manager, NASA Small Aircraft Transportation System, Federal Aviation Administration (1999-2005); FAA Division Manager, Flight Operations and Maintenance Division, Cabin Safety Division, Office of Aviation Safety (1988-1999); Alternate U.S. Member, Air Navigation Commission, International Civil Aviation Organization, Montreal, QC, Canada (1986-1988); U.S. Army Aviation, CW4 Viet Nam, Panama, Germany (1967-1984); U.S. Army Infantry, E5 Panama, Canal Zone (1963-1967) **CIV:** Staff and Leadership Experience, Local, District, and National Levels, U.S. Coast Guard Auxiliary (1981-Present); President, 16th Cavalry Association (2015) **MIL:** LNO to U.S. Air Force, Air Combat Command (ACC), Federal Aviation Administration, Department of Transportation, Langley Air Force Base (2011-2014); Academic Chair, Joint Forces Staff College, Norfolk Navy Base (2006-2008); Infantryman/Master Aviator, U.S. Army (1963-1984) **AW:** FIA Collier Team Award; Two-Time Recipient, NASA Turning Goals Into Reality (TGiR) Team Award; Air Traffic Control Association Chairman's Commendation; Recipient, FAA Performance Awards; Secretary of Transportation War on Terror Medal; DOT New Dawn Award; Legion of Merit, United States Army; Bronze Star, United States Army; Meritorious Service Medal, United States Army; 38 Air Medals, United States Army; Army Commendation Medal,

United States Army; Vietnamese Cross of Gallantry; Expert Infantryman Badge, United States Army; Master Army Aviator Badge, United States Army **MEM:** Vice President, Aircraft Owners and Pilot Association (1984-1986); American Institute of Aeronautics and Astronautics **AS:** Mr. McHugh attributes his success to the love and support of his wife, as well as to having had excellent mentors. **B/I:** Mr. McHugh's father had an extraordinary work ethic. Inspired by him, Mr. McHugh saw a clear, consistent career path for himself in the United States Military. He was additionally inspired by his neighbor, John Glenn, a United States Marine Corps aviator and Mercury Astronauts. **THT:** Mr. McHugh believes mentoring is a critical skill only a few leaders have; however, all should try to exercise.

MCILROY, RORY, MBE, T: Professional Golfer **I:** Athletics **DOB:** 05/04/1989 **PB:** Holywood **SC:** Northern Ireland **PT:** Gerry McIlroy; Rosie (McDonald) McIlroy **MS:** Married **SPN:** Erika Stoll **ED:** Student, Sullivan Upper School **C:** Professional Golfer (2007-Present) **CR:** European Team, Ryder Cup (2010, 2012); Great Britain and Ireland Team, Vivendi Trophy (2009) **CIV:** Ambassador, UNICEF Ireland **AW:** Winner, WGC-HSBC Champions (2019); Winner, RBC Canadian Open (2019); Winner, Players Championship (2019); Winner, Tour Championship (2016, 2019); Winner, Arnold Palmer Invitational (2018); Winner, Ryder Cup (2010, 2012, 2014, 2016, 2018); Winner, Dubai Duty Free Irish Open (2016); Winner, Deutsche Bank Championship (2012, 2016); Winner, Wells Fargo Championship (2015); Winner, WGC-Cadillac Match Play (2015); Winner, Omega Dubai Desert Classic (2015); Winner, DP World Tour Championship, Dubai (2015); Winner, BMW PGA Championship (2014); Winner, PGA Championship (2012, 2014); Winner, WGC-Bridgestone Invitational (2014); Winner, Open Championship (2014); Winner, Emirates Australian Open (2013); Winner, BMW Championship (2012); Winner, Honda Classic (2012); Winner, DP World Tour Championship, Dubai (2012); Winner, Lake Malaren Shanghai Masters (2011); Winner, UBS Hong Kong Open (2011); Winner, U.S. Open (2011); Winner, World Cup (2009, 2011); Winner, Quail Hollow Championship (2010); Winner, Dubai Desert Classic (2009); Winner, Seve Trophy (2009); Winner, European Amateur Team Championship (2007); Winner, Walker Cup (2007); Winner, West of Ireland Championship, Irish Amateur Close Championship, European Amateur Championship (2006); Winner, Bonallack Trophy (2006); Winner, Eisenhower Trophy (2006); Winner, St Andrews Trophy (2006); Winner, West of Ireland Championship, Irish Amateur Close Championship (2005); Winner, Junior Ryder Cup (2004)

MCINTOSH, CAROLYN, T: Librarian (Retired) **I:** Library Management/Library Services **CN:** California State University, Los Angeles **MS:** Single **ED:** MLIS in Library & Information Science, Indiana University, Bloomington, IN (1974); BA in Sociology, Clark College (1964); Master's Degree in Liberal Arts, Cambridge University **C:** Retired, California State University (2011-Present); Librarian, California State University (1995-2011); Ethnic Studies Bibliographer, University of Southern California (1975-1992); Neighborhood Information Specialist, Cleveland Public Library (1972-1973); Social Worker, Cleveland, OH **CIV:** Volunteer, Mission Society **AW:** Historic Preservation Award, City of Jacksonville Historic Preservation Commission; Gamma Rho Omega Story Award **MEM:** Black Caucus of the American Library Association; Alpha Kappa Alpha **AS:** Ms. McIntosh attributes her success to her dedication to helping those who cannot help themselves.

B/I: At one point in Ms. McIntosh's career, she was working as a social worker. One day her father suggested she look for a new career. From there, she became the coordinator for a neighborhood information center at a local library. Her career naturally progressed from that point forward. **AV:** Collecting dolls of all cultures; Collecting owls

MCKECHNIE, C. LOGAN, T: Lawyer **I:** Law and Legal Services **CN:** Law Offices of C. Logan McKechnie, Inc. **DOB:** 09/29/1942 **PB:** Monticello **SC:** KY/USA **PT:** Glenn Logan McKechnie; Jean Alva (Eads) McKechnie **MS:** Single **CH:** Amanda J. **ED:** JD, LLB, Western State University, San Diego, CA (1977); BA, Goethe Institute, Bad Aibling, Germany (1964-1967); ABA, Amarillo College, Amarillo, TX (1961); Coursework, LLM Program, University of Denver **C:** Private Legal Practice, San Diego, CA (1995-Present); Contract Public Defender, Merced County, CA (1994-1995); Office of the Alternate Public Defender, San Diego, CA (1991-1992); Private Practice, San Diego, CA (1980-1994); Special Assistant to the District Attorney, San Diego, CA (1972-1980); Investigative Reporter, The Arizona Republic, Phoenix, AZ (1967-1972); Reporter, Editor, The Evening Tribune, San Diego, CA; Editor, San Diego Business Magazine; Anchor, KTAR-TV, Phoenix, AZ **CR:** Adjunct Professor of Law, University of Houston (1982-Present); Adjunct Professor of Law, National District Attorneys College (1982-Present); Adjunct Professor of Law, Merced College (1982-Present); Adjunct Professor of Law, Western State University (1982-Present); Adjunct Professor of Law, San Diego State University (1982-Present); Commissioner, Central Valley Conference (1994-2018); Chairman, CCCAA Disabilities Board (1996-2018); Board of Directors, California Commission on Athletics (2010-2016); Council Chairman, Multiple District Four, Lions Clubs International (1991-1992); District Governor, District 4-L6, Lions Clubs International (1990-1991); Newsman, The News-Texan, Grand Prairie, TX (1959-1961) **CIV:** Board of Directors, East County Business Council, Board of Directors, Lakeside Cityhood Committee (1987-Present); Advisor, California Legislative Sports Law Committee (1983-Present); Life Member, Advisor, Counsel, Tierrasanta Friends Libr., San Diego, CA (1979-Present); Board of Directors Boys and Girls Clubs of San Diego and Merced (1986-2000); Advisor, Mudd Judge Campaign, San Diego, CA (1984); President, Tierrasanta Community Council, San Diego, CA (1974) **MIL:** Public Information and Public Affairs Officer, U.S. Army (1961-1967) **CW:** Contributor, Articles, International Magazines; Publisher, Community Newspapers; Editorial Cartoonist; Professional Sports Agent; Auctioneer; Commercial Sign Painter; Court-Certified Expert, U.S. Coins and Stamps; Magazine Feature Writer; Professional Political Campaign Chairman; Elected Chairman, Community Council, San Diego, CA **AW:** Recipient, 14 National Awards for Writing and Reporting; Recipient, Over 100 Service Awards; The Ambassador of Good Will Award for International Humanitarian Service, Lions Clubs International **MEM:** Legal Ethics Committee, Client Dispute Resolution Committee, San Diego Bar Association; Vice-Chairman, General Practice Sections Criminal Justice Committee, American Bar Association; Sports and Entertainment Law Section; California Public Defenders Association; California Attorneys for Criminal Justice; Merced County Bar Association; California and National District Attorneys Association **MH:** Albert Nelson Marquis Lifetime Achievement Award **B/I:** Mr. McKechnie became a reporter because his family owned a Newspaper in Kentucky. In this role, he was assigned to cover the courts in Amarillo, Texas. Shortly thereafter, he went to law school, which lead him to work in sports law. He later became a criminal lawyer, resulting in him working on a death penalty case. **AV:** Coin collecting **PA:** Republican

MCKENZIE, KEVIN PATRICK, T: Artistic Director **I:** Media & Entertainment **CN:** American Ballet Theatre **DOB:** 04/29/1954 **PB:** Burlington **SC:** VT/USA **PT:** Raymond James McKenzie; Ruth (Davison) McKenzie **MS:** Married **SPN:** Martine van Hamel **ED:** Honorary Doctor of Arts, Adelphi University, Garden City, NY (2019); Honorary Doctor of Arts, Saint Michel's College, Colchester, VT (1993); Coursework, Washington School of Ballet **C:** Artistic Director, American Ballet Theatre, New York, NY (1992-Present); Artistic Associate, The Washington Ballet (1991-1992); Principal Dancer, American Ballet Theatre, New York, NY (1979-1991); Permanent Guest Artist, The Washington Ballet (1989); Principal Dancer, Joffrey Ballet, New York, NY (1974-1978); Member, Corps de Ballet, National Ballet of Washington (1972-1974); Associate Artistic Director and Choreographer, New Amsterdam Ballet **CR:** Founding Board Member, Kaatsbaan International Dance Center, Tivoli, NY (1991-Present); President, Board of Directors, Ballet Theatre Foundation Inc. (1982-1989) **CW:** Choreographer, Metropolitan Opera House (2001); Choreographer, "Swan Lake" Ballets, American Ballet Theatre (2000); Choreographer, "Don Quixote" (1995); Choreographer, "The Nutcracker" (1993); Choreographer, "Lucy and the Count" (1992); Choreographer, "Liszt Etudes" (1991); Appearance with Martine Van Hamel, "Swan Lake," National Ballet of Cuba, Havana, Cuba (1986); Appearance with Merrill Ashley, "Tchaikowsky Pas de Deux," Bolshoi Theatre, Moscow, Russia (1986); Created Roles, "Adrienne Dellos' The Blind Man's Daughter," Seoul, South Korea (1986); Dancer, Spoleto Festival (1980, 1984); Choreographer, Groupo Zambaria Ballet (1984); Dancer, Asami Maki Ballet Co., Tokyo, Japan (1983); Producer, Director, "The Party of the Year" (1982); Dancer, Aspen Festival (1982); Dancer, Theatre des Champs Elysees, Paris, France (1981); Dancer, Sadler's Wells Theatre, London, England, United Kingdom (1981); Dancer, Houston Ballet (1978); Performer, "Unicorn" (1971); Dancer, "La Bayadere," "Carmen," "Cinderella," "Coppelia," "Dim Lustre," "Don Quixote," "Giselle," "The Garden of Villandry," "Jardin aux Lilas," "The Leaves Are Fading," "Pillar of Fire," "Raymonda," "Requiem," "Rodeo," "Romeo and Juliet," "The Sleeping Beauty," "Swan Lake," "La Sylphide," "Paquita," "Sylvia Pas de Deux," "Theme and Variations"; Dancer, "Amnon V'Tamar," SPEBSQSA; Dancer, Numerous Productions **AW:** Dance Magazine Award (1999); Performing Arts Award, American Ireland Fund (1994); Artistic Achievement Medal, Mayor of Burlington, VT (1984); Award, U.S. Department of State, United States Government (1972); Silver Medal, Varna International Ballet Competition, Bulgaria (1972)

MCKINLEY, DAVID BENNETT, T: U.S. Representative, Civil Engineer **I:** Government Administration/Government Relations/Government Services **DOB:** 05/28/1947 **PB:** Wheeling **SC:** WV/USA **MS:** Married **SPN:** Mary Gerkin **CH:** Four children **ED:** BS in Engineering, Purdue University, West Lafayette, IN (1969) **C:** Member, House Committee on Energy and Commerce, U.S. House of Representatives (2011-Present); U.S. Representative, West Virginia's First Congressional District, United States Congress (2011-Present); Founder, Principal, McKinley & Associates (Now McKinley Architecture and Engineering), Wheeling, WV (1981-Present); Member, District Three, West Virginia House of Delegates (1981-1994); Member, Republican Study Committee **CIV:** Chairman, West Virginia Republican Party (1992-1996) **AW:** One of the 50 Most Influential People in West Virginia, West Virginia Executive Magazine **MEM:** National Society of Professional Engineers **PA:** Republican **RE:** Episcopalian

MCKISSICK, MICHAEL LANDON, T: Transportation Consultant (Retired) **I:** Consulting **DOB:** 06/12/1950 **PB:** Clearfield **SC:** PA/USA **PT:** Robert Charles; Ruby Delores (Landon) McKissick **MS:** Single **ED:** Associate of Science in Computer System Management, Pittsburgh Technical Institute (1985); Associate of Science in Mechanical Design, Pittsburgh Technical Institute (1979) **C:** Retired (2010-Present); CADD Manager, Pennsylvania Department of Transportation, Montoursville, PA (1987-2010); Consultant, Pennsylvania Department of Transportation, Montoursville, PA (1985-1987); Vice President, Pittsburgh Technical Institute (1982-1985); Instructor, Carnegie Mellon University, Pittsburgh, PA (1981-1982); Instructor, Pittsburgh Technical Institute (1980-1982); Proposal Engineer, Blaw Knox F&MM Company, Pittsburgh, PA (1979-1980); Drafter, Bearings Division TRW, Falconer, New York, NY (1979); Owner, Operator, Northern Photographic Services, Warren, PA (1975-1977); Inventory Control Coordinator, Aerotech, Incorporated, Pittsburgh, PA (1974-1975) **CR:** Member, Board of Advertising, Pittsburgh Technical Institute (1985-Present); Speaker in Field **CW:** Author, "Computer Aided Drafting and Design" (1987) **AW:** Distinguished Alumnus, Pittsburgh Technical Institute (2007) **MEM:** Intergraph Users Group; Pennsylvania College of Technology; Civil Engineering Advisory Board **MH:** Albert Nelson Marquis Lifetime Achievement Award **B/I:** Mr. McKissick became involved in his profession due to the influence of his father and grandfather, who both found success in technical engineering in their own right. **AV:** Music; Photography; Scale modeling; Acoustic guitar

MCLARTY, GREG, T: Drama Instructor **I:** Fine Art **CN:** Wharton County Junior College **MS:** Married **SPN:** Andra **ED:** MS in Theater and Speech, Texas A&M University (1994); BS in Theater and Speech, Texas A&M University (1985) **CT:** Texas Teaching Certification, Middle and High School Theatre Arts and Speech (1986) **C:** Instructor of Drama/Theatre, Wharton County Junior College (2011-Present) **CIV:** "Ghost Along the Brazos"; "Shattered Dreams" **CW:** Stage Direction, Scenic Design, Lighting Design, Sound Design, Makeup Design, Numerous Stage Productions **AW:** Awards for Play Direction and Design, Numerous University Interscholastic League One-Act Play Contests; Acting and Design/Technical Awards for Plays, American College Theater Festival; Direction and Design Awards, Texas Community College Speech and Theatre Association **MEM:** Texas Educational Theater Association; Texas Theater Adjudicators Association; Past President, Texas Community College Speech and Theater Association; Association for Theatre in Higher Education **AS:** Mr. McLarty attributes his success to his students. "This is where I acquire my greatest feeling of accomplishment. When I see the light bulb go off over a student's head, that's when I derive the most satisfaction in teaching," he says. **B/I:** Mr. McLarty has always enjoyed theatre, both in front of the curtain and backstage. He went into college and decided he wanted to teach theatre, passing on his love of the profession to the future actors and technicians. Two of his professors, Dr. Kay Cougenhour and Dr. John Hanners, were very influential in passing on their knowledge and helping him along his path in educational theater.

MCLEAN, CARI, T: Dance Studio Owner, Competition Judge, Master Teacher **I:** Fine Art **CN:** MantyDance **DOB:** 09/21/1984 **PB:** Manitowoc **SC:** WI/

USA **ED:** BA in Exercise Science, Lakeland College **C:** Dance Studio Owner, Competition Judge, Master Teacher, MantyDance (2003-Present) **AW:** Studio Spirit Award; Best Choreography; 30th Year Plaque; Numerous Competition Awards; Best Studio on the Lakeshore (WI) **AS:** Ms. McLean attributes her success to the people who have supported her and given her a chance in life. **B/I:** Ms. McLean became involved in her profession because her parents told her that, at the age of two, she told them that she was going to be a dance teacher. They took her to dance class and she continued throughout the years. Her dance teacher had to move and was going to sell the studio. At age 18, she started traveling and teaching at different dance studios. When she turned 20, she really wanted to open her own studio, which she did. She has since networked with professionals in the industry from all over the world. She travels as a competition judge and master teacher and brings the love of the art to numerous people a year. **THT:** Ms. McLean's motto is, "If you're going through hell, keep on going." Her mentor is dance teacher Kristine Bremmer.

MCLELLAN, JOHN SIDNEY, T: Judge **I:** Law and Legal Services **DOB:** 01/16/1946 **PB:** Kingsport **SC:** TN/USA **PT:** John Sidney McLellan Jr.; Opal Lee (Poe) McLellan **SPN:** Wanda Ruth (Gulley) McLellan (06/05/1966) **CH:** John Richardson; Jason Ray **ED:** JD, The University of Tennessee (1970); BS, The University of Tennessee (1968) **C:** Circuit Court Judge, Second Judicial District (1994-Present); Attorney, McLellan Law Offices, Kingsport, TN (1971-1994) **CR:** County Attorney, Sullivan County, Blountville, TN (1978-1994) **AW:** Honor for Support Award, Tennessee Paralegal Association, Tri-cities Chapter (1994) **MEM:** M.M. Martin Lodge #547, Scottish Rite of Freemasonry 32 Degree (2015-Present); Junior Warden, Free and Accepted Masons (2019); President, Tennessee Judicial Conference (2004-2005); President-elect, Tennessee Judicial Conference (2003-2004); Executive Committee, Tennessee Judicial Conference (1997-2002); Vice President, Tennessee Trial Judges Association (1996-1997); Secretary, Tennessee Judicial Conference (1995-1996); Fellow Tennessee Bar Foundation; American Judges Association; Tennessee Judicial Conference; Tennessee Trial Judges Association; Kingsport Bar Association; Court of the Judiciary, Tennessee Bar Association; Bristol County Bar Association **BAR:** United States Court of Appeals for the Sixth Circuit (1972); United States District Court for the District of Tennessee (1971); Tennessee (1971) **MH:** Albert Nelson Marquis Lifetime Achievement Award **B/I:** Judge McLellan's father was an attorney and inspired him to enter the same field. **AV:** Gardening **PA:** Democrat **RE:** Episcopalian

MCLEOD, JAMES R., T: Language Educator (Retired) **I:** Education/Educational Services **DOB:** 01/08/1942 **PB:** Spokane **SC:** WA/USA **PT:** Richard Leland; Bernice Lola (Smith) McLeod **MS:** Married **SPN:** Judith Ann Osterberg Sylte (06/11/1982) **CH:** Brock; Rory; Anne (Stepdaughter); John (Stepson) **ED:** MA in English, Eastern Washington University, with Honors (1969); BA in English, University of Washington (1966) **CT:** Certified Teacher, State of Washington **C:** Associate Professor of English, Chapman University, Oak Harbor, CA (2002-2008); Associate Professor of English, North Idaho College, Coeur d'Alene, Idaho (1970-2001); Director, Scottish Studies Program, North Idaho College (1982-1990); Teacher, Central Valley School District, Spokane, WA (1966-1969); Psychiatric Group Worker, Ryther Child Center, Seattle, WA (1961-1963); Teacher, University of Idaho; Teacher, Lewis-Clark State College, Lewiston, Idaho **CR:** Coordinator, Two-year College Programs, Member, Executive Committee, Associated Writing Programs (1974-1975); Co-leader, Tours through Scotland and Turkey **CIV:** Elevator, Oral History of Coeur d'Alene Indian Project, Idaho Humanities Council (1992-1993); Coordinator, Kootenai County Centennial Committee, Fort Sherman Day, Coeur d'Alene, Idaho (1988-1990); Member-at-large, United Ministries in Higher Education, Seattle, WA (1979-1985); Cub Master, Kootenai County Council, Boy Scouts of America (1983-1984); Board of Directors, Kootenai County Council on Alcoholism, Coeur d'Alene, Idaho (1977-1980) **CW:** Author, "Making the Arrows: Poems" (2015); Author, "Mysterious Lake Pend Oreille and Its Monster" (1987); Author, "Theodore Roethke: A Bibliography" (1973); Author, "Theodore Roethke: A Manuscript Checklist" (1971); Poems Featured in Anthology, "Deep Down Things: An Anthology of Inland Northwest Poetry"; Contributor, Scholarly Publications; Author, Numerous Poems **AW:** Named Undergraduate Instructor of the Year, Chapman University (2006); Director's Special Award, Chapman University (2004); Award for Outstanding Contributions to North Idaho College (2002); Named Honored Author, Idaho State Library, Boise, Idaho (1976); Named Honored Author, Washington State Arts Commission (1972); Outstanding Undergraduate Professor Award, Chapman University **MEM:** Advisor, North Idaho College Rowing Club (Coeur d'Alene Rowing Association) (1988-1992); Treasurer, The Piobaireachd Society, Spokane, WA (1983-1991); National Vice President, Clan MacLeod Society USA (1982-1986); Board of Directors, Washington Poets Association (1973-1976); Former Member, Community College Humanities Association; Former Member, National Trust for Scotland; Clan MacLeod Society USA; Former Member, Washington Poets Association; Former Member, The Piobaireachd Society, Spokane, WA; Former Member, North Idaho College Rowing Club (Coeur d'Alene Rowing Association); Former member, North Idaho College Cryptozoology Club **MH:** Albert Nelson Marquis Lifetime Achievement Award **B/I:** Mr. McLeod was initially a history major but switched to English because he went into education. He has taught at every level. **AV:** Racquetball (30 Years); Travel; Genealogy; Poetry; Scottish music; Family history he put together (1000 Pages); Scottish history **PA:** Democrat **RE:** Episcopalian

MCLEOD, WALTON JAMES III, T: Lawyer; Former State Legislator; Businessman **I:** Law and Legal Services **CN:** McLeod Law Office **DOB:** 06/30/1937 **PB:** Walterboro **SC:** SC/USA **PT:** Walton James McLeod Jr.; Rhoda Lane (Brown) McLeod **MS:** Married **SPN:** Julie Edwina Hamiter (02/15/1969) **CH:** Walton James **ED:** Postgraduate Coursework, University of Minnesota Public Health School (1972); LLB, University of South Carolina (1964); BA, Yale University (1959) **C:** Special Counsel, South Carolina Department of Health and Environmental Control, Columbia, SC (1994-1996); General Counsel, South Carolina of Department Health and Environmental Control, Columbia, SC (1968-1994); Deputy South Carolina Attorney General, Columbia, SC (1987-1988); Assistant United States Attorney, Columbia, SC (1967-1968); Associate, Pope and Schumpert, Newberry, SC (1965-1967); Law Clerk, Chief Judge Clement Haynsworth, United States Court of Appeals for the Fourth Circuit, Richmond, VA (1964-1965) **CR:** State Representative, District 40, South Carolina House of Representatives (1996-2016); Mayor, Town of Little Mountain (1983-1989, 1993-1996); Municipal Judge (1981-1983); Magistrate Judge, Newberry County (1973-1981) **CIV:** Board Member, South Carolina Alzheimer's Association (2007-Present); Board Member, Newberry College Foundation (2005-Present); Board Member, Newberry County Council on Aging (2001-Present); Assistant House Democratic Leader (2013-2016); South Carolina State House Committee (2010-2016); South Carolina Legislative Audit Council (2008-2016); Board Member, South Carolina Humanities Council (2008-2014); Board Member, Southeastern Institute for Women in Politics (2007-2012); First Vice-Chair, House Judiciary Committee (2006-2008); Chair, Central Midlands Council of Governments, Columbia, SC (2001-2003); Board Member, South Carolina Housing Finance and Development Authority, Columbia, SC (1977-1996); Trustee, South Carolina State Museum, Columbia, SC (1981-1985); President, Newberry Jaycees, SC (1967) **MIL:** United States Navy Reserve (1961-1992); Lieutenant Junior Grade to Captain, United States Navy (1961-1992); Active Duty, US Navy (1959-1961,1963, 1990) **CW:** Co-Author, "Hospital Franchising Law and Regulation" (1979); Co-Author, "Environmental Quality Law" (1975); Author, "Legal Perspectives of Environmental Health" (1973) **AW:** Legislator of the Year Award, South Carolina Human Service Providers Association (2008); Legislative Appreciation Award, South Carolina Association of Conservation Districts (2006); Outstanding Service Award, South Carolina American Legion (2006); Outstanding Legislator Award, Gift of Life Trust Fund (1999); Reserve Officer of the Year (1998); Outstanding Freshman Representative of the Year, South Carolina Historical Foundation Society, Inc. (1997); Howell Excellence Award, Naval Reserve Law Program, Washington, DC (1991); Distinguished Judicial Service Award (1975); Outstanding Jaycee Award, Newberry Jaycees (1967) **MEM:** President, South Caroliniana Society, University of South Carolina (1990-1993); National President, Judge Advocates Committee (1991-1992); State President, Reserve Officers Association, South Carolina (1981-1982); President, South Carolina Magistrates Association (1976-1977); Fellow, South Carolina Bar Foundation; President, Clariosophic Society, University of South Carolina **BAR:** Supreme Court of the United States (1974); South Carolina (1964) **AV:** Reading; Maintaining physical fitness **PA:** Democrat **RE:** Protestant (Lutheran)

MCMAHON, LINDA MARIE, T: Administrator (Retired) **I:** Business Management/Business Services **CN:** Small Business Administration **DOB:** 10/04/1948 **PB:** New Bern **SC:** NC/USA **PT:** Henry Edwards; Evelyn Edwards **MS:** Married **SPN:** Vincent Kennedy McMahon (1966) **CH:** Shane; Stephanie **ED:** BA in French, East Carolina University (1969) **C:** Administrator, Small Business Administration, Washington, DC (2017-2019); Co-founder, Board of Directors, World Wrestling Entertainment, Inc., Stamford, CT (1980-2017); Chief Executive Officer, World Wrestling Entertainment, Inc. (1997-2009); President, World Wrestling Entertainment, Inc. (1993-2000); Paralegal, Covington & Burling LLP **CR:** Member, International Advisory Council, APCO Worldwide LLC (2013-Present) **CIV:** Member, Connecticut Board of Education (2009-Present); Board of Trustees, Sacred Heart University (2004-Present) **CW:** Producer, TV Series, "WWE: Smackdown!" (1999-Present); Producer, TV Series, "WWE: Sunday Night Heat" (1998-Present); Producer, TV Series, "WWE: Raw is War" (1997-Present); Executive Producer, TV Series, "WWE Experience" (2004) **AW:** Dedication of Linda E. McMahon Commons Building, Sacred Heart University, Fairfield, CT (2012); Corporate Patriot Award, GI Film Festival (2008); Secretary of Defense Exceptional Public Service Award, USO, Inc. (2007); Legacy of Hope Award, USO, Inc. (2007); Named One of the Wonder Women, Multichannel News (2007); Arthur M. Sackler Award, Connecticut Grand Opera and Orchestra (2005) **PA:** Republican **RE:** Roman Catholic

MCMANUS, JOHN WILLIAM, T: Associate Professor **I:** Education/Educational Services **CN:** Randolph-Macon College **DOB:** 08/24/1961 **PT:** Vincent Joseph McManus; Maryelaine Ramey McManus **MS:** Married **SPN:** Mary Loving McManus **ED:** PhD in Computer Science and Philosophy, William & Mary (1992); MS in Computer Science, William & Mary (1986); BA in English, Randolph-Macon College (1984) **CT:** Advanced Certificate in Executives in Management, Innovation, Technology (2013); Executive Certificate in Technology, Operations, Value Chain Management (2013); Executive Certificate in Management Leadership (2013) **C:** Associate Professor, Artificial Intelligence, Robotics, Randolph-Macon College (2020-Present); Assistant Professor, Artificial Intelligence, Robotics, Randolph-Macon College (2014-2020); President, Founder, Blue Skies Solutions, LLC (2013-Present); Chief, Cyber Security Architect, Concentric Advisors (2013-2017); Chief, Information Officer, Chief Technology Officer, Watermark Estate Management Services, LLC (2007-2013); Deputy Chief Information Officer, Chief Technology Officer, United States Department of Commerce (2006-2007); Deputy Chief Information Officer, Chief Technology Officer, National Aeronautics and Space Administration (NASA) (2003-2007); Vice President, Software Technology Center, Bell Labs, Lucent Technologies (2000-2003); Vice President of Research, Cigital, Reliable Software Technologies (1999-2000); Assistant Branch Head, Simulation Systems Branch, NASA Langley Research Center (1992-1999); Adjunct Professor, Applied Physics and Computer Science, Christopher Newport University, Newport News, Virginia (1998); Adjunct Professor, Applied Physics and Computer Science, Christopher Newport University (1998); Research Engineer, Aircraft Guidance and Control Branch, NASA Langley Research Center (1987-1992); Systems Analyst, PRC, Kentron Inc. (1986-1987); Systems Analyst, Office of Management and Budget (1984-1985) **CR:** The EDGE AdvantEdge Student Mentoring Program (2016-Present); Computer Science Department Liaison, Bassett Academic Internship Program (2014-Present); Independent Cybersecurity Consultant (2014-Present); Lead, Alumni Engagement, Computer Science Department (2014-Present); Reviewer, National Science Foundation Computer and Network System Program (2019); Student Conduct Board (2018- 2019); Reviewer, Consortium for Computing Sciences, Colleges Eastern Region Conference (2017-2019); Reviewer, Proceedings, ACM SIGSE Conference (2017-2019); Reviewer, Proceedings, National Conference on Undergraduate Research (2016-2019); Assistant Faculty Marshall (2015-2019); Representation, Randolph-Macon College, Metro Richmond STEM Science Fair (2014-2019); Interviewer, The EDGE Boot Camp (2014-2019); Reviewer, National Science Foundation CISE Research Infrastructure Program (2018); Senior Faculty Marshall (2017-2018); Reviewer, Consortium for Computing Sciences, Colleges Southeastern Region Conference (2017-2018); Reviewer, Consortium for Computing Sciences in Colleges Northeastern Region Conference (2017); National Conference, Undergraduate Research (2016-2017); Associate Faculty Marshall (2016-2017); Volunteer Faculty Marshall (2015); Invited Reviewer, IEEE Software (2003) **CIV:** Class Agent, Class of 1984 (2017-Present); Co-Chair, Annual Faculty, Staff Campaign (2014-Present); Advisor, Legendary Llamas Lego First Robotics League (2018-2019); Volunteer, Ashland Museum (2014-2017); Volunteer, Saint James the Less Free Clinic (2016); Vol-

unteer, Ashland Community Emergency Services (2016); Board of Directors, At Home in Ashland (2016) **CW:** Speaker, "Using Three-Dimensional Terrain Models to Measure Terrain Change," The Consortium for Computing Sciences in Colleges, Eastern Region 35th Annual Regional Conference (2019); Speaker, "Project-Based Learning in Computer Science: A Student and Research Advisor's Perspective," The Consortium for Computing Sciences in Colleges, Eastern Region 34th Annual Regional Conference (2017); Speaker, "Security by Design: Teaching Secure Software Design and Development Techniques," The Consortium for Computing Sciences in Colleges, Eastern Region 33rd Annual Regional Conference (2017); Speaker, "Cyber Security and the Internet of Things," The American Society for Nondestructive Testing, Old Dominion Section Meeting (2015); Speaker, "Artificial Intelligence (AI) Based Tactical Guidance for Fighter Aircraft," AIAA Guidance, Navigation, and Control Conference (1990); Speaker, Over 15 Professional Presentations **AW:** Thomas Branch Award, Excellence in Teaching (2018, 2020); R-MC Student Life Will Schick Outstanding Fraternity Advisor Award (2018, 2019); Student Life Commitment to Fraternal Relevance Award, Phi Delta Theta Fraternity (2017); The Federal Computer Week Federal 100 Award (2005, 2007); Federal Chief Information Officers Council Leadership Award (2006); NASA Exceptional Achievement Medal (2005); NASA Group Achievement Award (2005); NASA Langley Research Center Group Achievement Award (1998); Grantee, NASA Director's Discretionary Fund, PI John McManus (1993-1994); U.S. Army Official Commendation (1993); Special Act Award, U.S. Army Rotorcraft Pilots Associate Program (1993); NASA Certificate of Significant Accomplishment **MEM:** Faculty Development Committee (2018-Present); The Edge Faculty Advisory Committee (2016-Present); Faculty Advisor, Phi Delta Theta Fraternity (2016-Present); American Association for the Advancement of Science (2016-Present); RMC Coastal Climate Change Initiative (2016-Present); Technology Advisory Committee (2014-Present); Association for Computer Machinery (1999-Present); Randolph-Macon College Society of Alumni Board of Directors (2013-2018); Bridging RVA (2014-2015); American Institute of Aeronautics and Astronautics (1987-2007); Institute of Electrical and Electronics Engineers (1997-2003); Association for Computing Machinery **AS:** Mr. McManus attributes his success to his parents. They placed a great value on education and attending an undergraduate institution, as it would ensure he had the skills to be a lifelong learner. **B/I:** Mr. McManus received the best advice of his life when he was an undergraduate, "Major in something that you love and minor in something you plan to do for a living." He was an undergraduate English major; he loved it. He feels it prepared him to have better education skills. He minored in computer sciences and went on to graduate school. He knew at that point that he was going to focus on computer science rather than his love for English. He loves challenges and problem-solving, and computer science is a discipline that continues to evolve and change. Mr. McManus is thankful that his life doesn't get stale. He focuses on artificial intelligence and cooperating systems, working with small robots to solve problems. His profession is exciting. To this day, he works hard to keep up with the ever-changing atmosphere. **THT:** Mr. McManus' motto is, "To do what ought to be done."

MCMANUS, RICHARD P., T: Lawyer, Agricultural Products Executive **I:** Financial Services **CN:** Household Finance Corp, Security Pacific Corp., Bank America Corp. & Mosamac Co. Inc.

DOB: 10/20/1929 **PB:** Keokuk **SC:** IA/USA **PT:** Edward William McManus; Kathleen (OConnor) McManus **MS:** Married **SPN:** Marjorie Theresa Mullaney (11/5/1955) **CH:** Michael L.; Mark J.; Matthew A. **ED:** MBA, Roosevelt University, with Honors, Chicago, IL (1965); JD, University of Michigan (1952); BA, St. Ambrose University, Davenport, IA (1949) **C:** Retired (2018); President, Chairman, Board of Directors, Mosamac Co., Inc. (1992-2018); General Counsel, Bank of America Financial Services (1991-1992); Executive Vice President, Secretary, Bank of America Financial Services, San Diego CA (1991-1992); General Counsel, Security Pacific Financial Services, Inc. (1982-1991); Executive Vice President, Secretary General Counsel, Security Pacific Financial Services, Inc., San Diego, CA (1981-1991); Vice President, Director, Law, Household Financial Corp., Chicago, IL (1966-1981); Division Counsel, U.S. Navy Facility Engineering Command, Great Lakes, IL (1963-1966); Partner, McManus & McManus, Keokuk (1953-1963) **CR:** Member, Advisory Board, Hostler Institute of International Affairs, San Diego State University (2005-2008); Member, General Committee, Conference of Consumer Finance Law, Chicago, IL (1975-1992) **CIV:** Board Director, Charles Hostler Institute of World Affairs, San Diego State University (2004-2007); Board Director, Treasurer, Attorney, Tijuana/San Diego Habitat for Humanity, Inc. (1992-1995); Trustee, Village of Lake Bluff, Illinois (1974-1978) **MIL:** First Lieutenant, JAGD, U.S. Air Force (1952-1953) **CW:** Contributor, Articles, Professional Journals **AW:** San Diego Volunteer Lawyer Distinguished Service Award (1995-2010); Named, San Diego Pro Bono Attorney of the Year (2005); President California Bar Pro Bono Services Award (1998); Distinguished Service Award, American Financial Services Association (1990) **MEM:** Chairman, Law Committee, California Financial Services Association (1981-1992); Chairman, Law Forum, American Financial Services Association (1980-1981); California Bar Association; Lions; Elks; Knights of Columbus; Beta Gamma Sigma **BAR:** California (1982); Illinois (1958); Iowa (1952) **MH:** Albert Nelson Marquis Lifetime Achievement Award; Marquis Who's Who Top Professional **AS:** Mr. McManus attributes his success to God, family, hard work and luck. **B/I:** His father, Edward W McManus, and brothers, Neil E and Edward J, were lawyers and together were the largest family law firm in Iowa. His father died in 1954 and Edward J was appointed U.S. District Judge in 1959. The firm dissolved in 1960. **AV:** Golf; Flying; Sailing; Woodworking **PA:** Democrat **RE:** Roman Catholic

MCMASTER, HENRY DARGAN, T: Governor of South Carolina **I:** Government Administration/Government Relations/Government Services **DOB:** 05/27/1947 **PB:** Columbia **SC:** SC/USA **PT:** John Gregg McMaster; Ida Bacot (Dargan) McMaster **MS:** Married **SPN:** Peggy Jean McAbee Anderson (03/18/1978) **ED:** JD, University of South Carolina School of Law (1973); BA in History, University of South Carolina (1969) **C:** Governor, State of South Carolina (2017-Present); Lieutenant Governor, State of South Carolina (2015-2017); Attorney General, State of South Carolina (2003-2011); Partner, Tompkins & McMaster, Columbia, SC (1985-2003); Head, Law Enforcement Coordinating Committee, District of South Carolina (1981-1985); U.S. Attorney, District of South Carolina, Columbia, SC (1981-1985); Partner, Tompkins & McMaster, Columbia, SC (1974-1981); Attorney, Legislative Assistant to Representative Strom Thurmond, U.S. Senate, Washington, DC (1973-1974) **CR:** Chairman, South Carolina Republican Party (1994-2002); Board of Directors, South Carolina Policy Council (1991-2003); Member, South Carolina

Commission on Higher Education (1991-1994) **CIV:** Council Member, The Humane Society of the United States **CW:** Contributor, Articles, Legal Publications **AW:** Named National Law Enforcement Officer of the Year, The Humane Society of the United States (2005); Public Servant of the Year, Sierra Club (2004); Order of the Palmetto (1996) **MEM:** Province Commander, Kappa Alpha Order (1975-1991); Deputy Province Commander, Kappa Alpha Order (1974-1975); ABA; South Carolina Bar; Richland County Bar Association; Centurion Society; Caroliniana Ball Club; The International Legal Honor Society of Phi Delta Phi; Saint Andrew's Society **BAR:** Supreme Court of the United States (1978); U.S. Court of Appeals for the Fourth Circuit (1976); U.S. Court of Federal Claims (1974); U.S. District Court for District of South Carolina (1973); State of South Carolina (1973) **PA:** Republican **RE:** Presbyterian

MCMASTER, HERBERT, "H.R." RAYMOND, T: United States National Security Adviser (Retired) **I:** Government Administration/Government Relations/Government Services **DOB:** 07/24/1962 **PB:** Philadelphia **SC:** PA/USA **PT:** Herbert McMaster; Marie C. (Curcio) McMaster **MS:** Married **SPN:** Kathleen Trotter (1985) **CH:** Three children **ED:** BS, United States Military Academy, West Point, NY (1984); PhD in American History, The University of North Carolina at Chapel Hill; MA in American History, The University of North Carolina at Chapel Hill **C:** United States National Security Adviser (2017-2018); Director, U.S. Army Capabilities Integration Center, U.S. Army Training and Doctrines Command (2014-2017); Commanding General, Maneuver Center of Excellence, Fort Benning, GA (2012-2014); Director, Concept Development and Learning, U.S. Army Training and Doctrine Command, Fort Monroe, VA (2008-2010); Special Assistant to the Commander, Multinational Force-Iraq (2007-2008); Director, Commander's Advisory Group, U.S. Central Command (2003-2004); National Security Affairs Fellow, Hoover Institution (2002-2003); Assistant Professor of History, United States Military Academy, West Point, NY (1994-1996) **MIL:** Lieutenant General, U.S. Army (1984-2018) **CW:** Author, "Dereliction of Duty" (1997) **AW:** Army Distinguished Service Medal with Two Oak Leaf Clusters; Silver Star; Defense Superior Service Medal; Legion of Merit with Oak Leaf Cluster; Purple Heart; Bronze Star Medal with Oak Leaf Cluster; Defense Meritorious Service Medal with Oak Leaf Clusters; Army Meritorious Service Medal with Four Oak Leaf Clusters; Joint Service Commendation Medal; Army Commendation Medal with Three Oak Leaf Clusters; Army Achievement Medal with Three Oak Leaf Clusters; Various Unit Award; Various Other Awards

MCMILLAN, ROBERT WALKER, PHD, T: Physicist; Consultant **I:** Sciences **DOB:** 04/18/1935 **PB:** Sylacauga **SC:** AL/USA **PT:** Robert Thomas McMillan; Alma (Bush) McMillan **MS:** Married **SPN:** Ann Simmons (09/11/1955) **CH:** Marisa Ann; Robert Murray; Natalie June **ED:** PhD, University of Florida (1974); MS, Rollins College (1966); BS, Auburn University (1957); Diploma, Sylacauga High School (1953) **CT:** Private Pilot (2004); Open Water Diver (1980) **C:** Senior Research Scientist, U.S. Army Space and Missile Defense Command (1998-2011); Intergovernmental Personnel Act Appointee from Georgia Institute of Technology as Senior Scientist, United States Air Force Research Laboratory, Rome Research Site, Rome, NY (1994-1998); Principal Research Scientist, Georgia Tech Research Institute, Georgia Institute of Technology (1976-1998); Staff Engineer, Martin Marietta Aerospace (Now Lockheed Martin Corporation) (1961-1976); Engineer, Westinghouse

Electric Corporation (1960-1961); **CR:** Chairman, Conferences; Consultant in Field **CIV:** Fresh Start Tutor, Franklin County Jail (2018-Present); Visiting Evangelist, Elementary and High Schools, Zambia and Malawi (2009); Board Member, President, Homeowners Association, FL; Volunteer Tutor, Local High School **MIL:** Lieutenant, Communications Officer, United States Air Force (1958-1960) **CW:** Contributor, Articles, Professional Journals and Conference Digests; Contributor, Chapters to Books **AW:** Meritorious Presidential Rank Award (2005); Outstanding Performance in Research Award, Georgia Tech Research Institute, Georgia Institute of Technology (1985); Sigma Pi Sigma, The Physics Honor Society, American Institute of Physics; Pi Mu Epsilon; Arnold Air Society & Silver Wings **MEM:** Life Fellow, IEEE; Senior Member, The Optical Society of America (Now The Optical Society); Senior Member, The Society of Photo Optical Instrumentation Engineers (Now SPIE) **MH:** Albert Nelson Marquis Lifetime Achievement Award **AS:** Dr. McMillan attributes his success to the unwavering support of his wife, Ann, and children, Marisa, Robert, and Natalie, while he studied for three technical degrees. His parents, Alma and Robert McMillan, were perfect nurturers and perfect adult examples for him while growing up. **B/I:** Dr. McMillan has always been interested in technology; he was very fortunate to choose the field that provided a measure of success for him. **AV:** Flying; Exercise; Three marathons; Many half-marathons, 5K and 10K races and several dozen triathlons of various lengths **PA:** Republican **RE:** Baptist **THT:** Throughout Dr. McMillan's life, he has relied on his Christian faith to help him through the difficult times and as a source of great joy and thanksgiving in the many joyful times. He could have accomplished nothing without it. As one who has benefitted beyond reasonable measure from education, he has come to believe that education is an important factor in a happy life and an important partial solution to the problem of income inequality and poverty in our country. To this end, he has resolved to use every possible opportunity to share his knowledge of science and mathematics whenever he has a suitable forum such as the Franklin County Jail Fresh Start program and serving as a volunteer tutor.

MCMILLON, CARL, "DOUG" DOUGLAS, T: Retail Company Executive **I:** Other **CN:** Walmart Inc. **DOB:** 10/12/1966 **PB:** Memphis **SC:** TN/USA **PT:** Morris McMillon; Laura McMillon **MS:** Married **SPN:** Shelley McMillon **CH:** Blake; Spencer **ED:** MBA in Finance, University of Tulsa (1991); BA in Business Administration, University of Arkansas (1989) **C:** President, Chief Executive Officer, Walmart Inc. (2014-Present); President, Chief Executive Officer, Walmart International (2009-2014); President, Chief Executive Officer, Sam's Club (2005-2009); Executive Vice President, Walmart Inc. (2005-2009); Executive Vice President, Merchandising & Replenishment, Sam's Club (2002-2005); Senior Vice President, General Merchandise Manager, Walmart Inc. (1999-2002); Buyer Trainee in Sporting Goods, Walmart Inc. (1991-1999); Summer Associate, Walmart Inc. (1984) **CR:** Board of Directors, Walmart Inc. (2013-Present); Board of Directors, Consumer Goods Forum; Board of Directors, US-China Business Council; Advisory Board, American Workforce Policy **CIV:** Director Emeritus, The Sunshine School (Now Sunshine School & Development Center), Bentonville, AR; Member, Executive Board, Center for Retailing Excellence, The Sam M. Walton College of Business, University Arkansas; Board of Advisers, National Council of La Raza (Now UnidosUS); Advisory Board, Tsinghua University School of Economics and Management, Beijing, China; Board of Directors, Crystal

Bridges Museum of American Art **AW:** Named One of the Top 25 Highest Paid Executives in Fashion, WWD (2018); Named One of the World's Most Powerful People, Forbes Magazine (2014)

MCMORRIS RODGERS, CATHY ANNE, T: U.S. Representative from Washington **I:** Government Administration/Government Relations/Government Services **DOB:** 05/22/1969 **PB:** Salem **SC:** OR/USA **PT:** Wayne McMorris; Corrine (Robinson) McMorris **MS:** Married **SPN:** Brian Rodgers (08/05/2006) **CH:** Cole McMorris; Grace Blossom; Brynn Catherine **ED:** MBA, Foster School of Business, University of Washington (2002); BA, Pensacola Christian College, FL (1990) **C:** Chair, U.S. House Republican Conference (2013-Present); Member, U.S. House of Representatives from Washington's Fifth Congressional District (2005-Present); Vice Chair, U.S. House Republican Conference (2009-2012); Member, District Seven, Washington State House of Representatives (1995-2005); Minority Leader, Washington State House of Representatives (2002-2003); Member, Committee on Energy and Commerce **AW:** Named One of the 100 Most Powerful Women in DC, Washingtonian Magazine (2009); Named Legislator of the Year, Washington Farm Bureau (1997); Gold Medal, Independent Business Association (1996); Guardian of Small Business Award, National Federation of Independent Business (1996); Sentinel Award, Washington State Law Enforcement Association (1996); Cornerstone Award, Association of Washington Business (1995-1996) **MEM:** Washington Women for Survival of Agriculture; Washington Rural Health Association; Washington State Farm Bureau; Washington Cattlemen's Association **PA:** Republican **RE:** Christian

MCNAB, BRIAN K., PHD, T: Professor Emeritus **I:** Education/Educational Services **CN:** Department of Biology, University of Florida **DOB:** 09/26/1932 **PB:** Chicago **SC:** IL/USA **PT:** Gordon; Herta **MS:** Widowed **SPN:** Greta (07/1960, Deceased 2014) **CH:** Roan; Derrick **ED:** PhD in Zoology, University of Wisconsin-Madison, WI (1961); BSBA, Oregon State University, OR (1954); Postgraduate Coursework, University of California, Berkley, CA **C:** Professor Emeritus, Department of Biology, University of Florida (2002-Present) **CW:** Author, "Extreme Measures: The Energetics of Birds and Mammals" (2012); Author, "A General Analysis of Comparative Physiology of Vertebrae (2002) **AW:** Nominee, Japanese Prize in Biology **B/I:** Dr. McNab became involved in his profession after going on a bird walk at the Washington Park Zoo. It piqued his curiosity and felt compelled to pursue a career in zoology. **AV:** Bird Watching; Painting **THT:** Dr. McNab has been very much concerned about climate change and the environment. In fact, some of the organisms he's worked on have changed their distribution area due to climate change. For example, living in north Florida, he now sees birds that were once native to the Florida Keys, meaning that populations are beginning to move north.

MCNAIR, ROBERT, "BOB" C., T: Chairman, Chief Executive Officer, Owner, Entrepreneur **I:** Athletics **CN:** Houston Texans **DOB:** 01/01/1937 **PB:** Tampa **SC:** FL/USA **MS:** Married **SPN:** Janice (Suber) McNair **CH:** Four children **ED:** Honorary LHD, University of South Carolina, Columbia, SC (1999); BS, University of South Carolina, Columbia, SC (1958) **C:** Chairman, Chief Executive Officer, Houston Texans, NFL (1999-2018); Founder, Houston NFL Holdings (1998); Chairman, Chief Executive Officer, RCM Wealth Advisors; Chairman, Chief Executive Officer, Palmetto Partners, Ltd.; Chairman, The McNair Group; Founder, Chief Executive Officer, Cogen Technologies Energy Group, Houston, TX; Chairman, U.S. Telesystems, Inc.; Chairman, Cypress Telecommunications Corporation **CR:** Member, Audit, Finance, Stadium and Expansion Committees, NFL; Chairman, Investment Committee, NFL; Chairman Emeritus, The Texas Bowl; Board of Directors, Mosher, Inc.; Board of Directors, Federal Reserve Bank of Dallas and Houston; Owner, Thoroughbred Horse Farm, Stonerside Stable, KY; Speaker in Field **CIV:** Co-Founder, Robert and Janice McNair Foundation (2015); Co-Founder, Robert and Janice McNair Educational Foundation (1989); Chairman, Board of Trustees, McNair Foundation and Free Enterprise Institute; President, Houston Grand Opera; Board of Trustees, Baylor College of Medicine, Houston, TX; Board of Trustees, Sigma Chi Foundation; Board of Trustees, Museum of Fine Arts; Board of Trustees, Center for the American Idea; Board of Trustees, Greater Houston Partnership; Board of Trustees, Greater Houston Convention Center and Visitors Bureau; Board of Governors, Rice University; Founder, Cotswold Project, Houston Elder Memorial Drive Presbyterian Church, Houston, TX **AW:** The Richest People in America, The Forbes 400 (2006-2018); Entrepreneur of the Decade, Houston Technology Center (2009); Inductee, Texas Business Hall of Fame; President and Mrs. George H.W. Bush Community Impact Award; Award, Fellowship of Christian Athletes; National Patriotism, Responsible Citizenship and Community Involvement Award, Freedoms Foundation at Valley Forge; Denton A. Cooley Leadership Award, Texas Heart Institute; Trailblazer Award, Houston Advertising Federation; City Builder Award, South Main Center Association; Distinguished Citizen Award, Sam Houston Area Council, Boy Scouts of America; Award, Rotary Club of Houston; Distinguished American Award, National Football Foundation, Houston Chapter, TX; Herman W. Lay Memorial Award, The Association of Private Enterprise Education; Outstanding Business Leader Award, Northwood University; Torch of Liberty Award, Anti-Defamation League

MCNEALL, PETER IAN, T: Systems Engineer (Retired) **I:** Engineering **DOB:** 03/18/1940 **PB:** Kenley, Surrey **SC:** England **PT:** Leslie Alfred McNeall; Vera Lois (Dark) McNeall **MS:** Single **ED:** BS in Physics, University College London (UCL) (1961) **C:** Senior Instrumentation Engineer, Ultra-Systems, Irvine, CA (1992-1993); Senior Instrumentation Engineer, Jacobs Engineering, Houston, TX (1991); Senior Instrumentation Engineer, CPI Plants, Indianapolis, IN (1990-1991); Senior Instrumentation Engineer, Lummus Crest, Houston, TX (1990); Senior Instrumentation Engineer, CRS Sirrine, Raleigh, NC (1989); Senior Instrumentation Engineer, Barnard and Burk, Baton Rouge, LA (1987-1988); Instrument Engineer, Ford, Bacon, and Davis, Richardson, TX (1985-1986); Instrument Engineer, International Paper Company, Mobile, AL (1984-1985); Instrument Engineer, Ralph M. Parsons Company, Pasadena, CA (1981-1982); Instrument Engineer, Badger America, Inc., Houston, TX (1981); Instrument Engineer, Howe-Baker Houston, TX (1980-1981); Instrument Engineer, C.E. Lummus, Houston, TX (1980); Engineer, Numerous Positions (1961-1980) **CW:** Author, "The Theory of Gravitation" (1995); Co-Inventor, Design Patent for "Space Age" House; Screenwriter **MEM:** Senior Member, Instrument Society of America **MH:** Albert Nelson Marquis Lifetime Achievement Award **AV:** Playing tennis; Swimming **PA:** Republican

MCNERNEY, GERALD, "JERRY" MARK, T: U.S. Representative from California; Engineer **I:** Government Administration/Government Relations/Government Services **DOB:** 06/18/1951 **PB:** Alburquerque **SC:** NM/USA **PT:** Colonel John E. McNerney; Rosemary (Tischhauser) McNerney **MS:** Married **SPN:** Mary Martine (1977) **CH:** Michael; Windy; Gregory **ED:** PhD in Engineering and Mathematics, The University of New Mexico (1981); MS, The University of New Mexico (1975); BS, The University of New Mexico (1973); Coursework, United States Military Academy, West Point, NY **C:** Member, U.S. House of Representatives from California's Ninth Congressional District (2013-Present); Member, U.S. House of Representatives from California's 11th Congressional District (2007-2013); Chief Executive Officer, Hawt Power Inc. (2003-2004); Senior Engineer, Field Manager, Wind Turbine Co. (1999-2003); Energy Consultant, Various Companies (1994-1998); Senior Engineer, U.S. Windpower/Kenetech Windpower Inc. (1985-1994); Contractor, Sandia National Laboratories, Kirkland Air Force Base **MEM:** American Mathematical Society; The American Society of Mechanical Engineers **AV:** Reading; Hunting; Running; Hiking **PA:** Democrat **RE:** Roman Catholic

MCNULTY, KATHLEEN A., PHD, T: Clinical Psychologist, Teacher, Mentor **I:** Social Work **DOB:** 10/06/1958 **PB:** Hackensack **SC:** NJ/USA **MS:** Married **SPN:** Henry Stanislaw Kowel (09/16/1988) **CH:** Eryn; Kelsey; Shawn **ED:** Postgraduate Coursework, Fielding Graduate Institute (2001-2009); MSW, Smith College (1984); BA, Rutgers, the State University of New Jersey (1980) **CT:** Licensed Clinical Social Worker, Psychologist (1998); Licensed Marriage and Family Therapist **C:** Private Practice, Teaching, Fairleigh Dickinson University Integrated Healthcare (2012-Present); Private Practice, Ridgewood, NJ (1999-Present); Private Practice, Rutherford, NJ (1987-1999); Clinical Social Worker, Cliffwood Mental Health Center, Englewood, NJ (1986-1987); Clinical Social Worker, Family Guidance Bergen, Hackensack, NJ (1986-1987); Clinical Social Worker, Albert Einstein College of Medicine, Bronx, NY (1984-1986); Mental Health Aide, Belleville Mental Health Clinic, New Jersey (1980-1982); Director, Residential Program, St. Joseph Hospital Medical Center; Clinical Psychologist, Teacher, Mentor **CR:** Consultant, Meadowlands Weight Control, Rutherford, NJ (1988-Present); Consultant, St. Luke's-Roosevelt Hospital Center, New York, NY (1988); Contract, Rutgers, the State University of New Jersey **CIV:** President, Ambulance Corp Emergency Medical Technician **CW:** Contributor, Articles, Professional Journals **MEM:** American Orthopsychiatry Association; Academy of Certified Social Workers; National Association of Social Workers; New Jersey Psychological Association **MH:** Albert Nelson Marquis Lifetime Achievement Award **AS:** Dr. McNulty attributes her success to her passion for helping people and her strong work ethic. **B/I:** Dr. McNulty became involved in her industry when she was 13 years old. She was always a compassionate child and her classmates always came to her to talk. In eighth grade, she witnessed a teacher bully her peers. Since then, she always wondered what motivated humans to hurt one another. Later, she transitioned to studying human nature and after that, she researched how to heal human disease. **AV:** Painting; Singing; Sports; Poetry

MCREYNOLDS, JOHN W., T: President **I:** Oil & Energy **CN:** Energy Transfer LP **C:** President, Energy Transfer LP (2013-Present); President, Chief Financial Officer, Energy Transfer Equity, LP (2005-2013); Partner, Hunton & Williams LLP (1979-2005); Attorney, Hunton & Williams LLP (1978) **CR:** Board of Directors, Energy Transfer Partners, LP (2004-Present); LE GP LLC (2004-Present)

MCSALLY, MARTHA ELIZABETH, T: U.S. Senator from Arizona **I:** Government Administration/Government Relations/Government Services **DOB:** 03/22/1966 **PB:** Providence **SC:** RI/USA **PT:** Bernard McSally; Eleanor McSally **MS:** Single **SPN:** Donald Frederick Henry (1997, Annulled 1999) **ED:** BS, United States Air Force Academy (1988); Honorary LLD in Civil Law, Rhode Island College; MS in Strategic Studies, Air War College; Master's Degree in Public Policy, John F. Kennedy School of Government, Harvard Kennedy School **C:** U.S. Senator, State of Arizona (2019-Present); Member, U.S. House of Representatives from Arizona's Second Congressional District, Washington, DC (2014-2019); Committee on Armed Services; Committee on Homeland Security; Advisor on National Security Issues to Senator Jon Kyl, U.S. Senate **CR:** Professor, George Marshall European Center for Security Studies, Garmisch-Partenkirchen, Germany (2011-Present) **MIL:** Retired, United States Air Force (2010); United States Air Force (1988-2010); Commander, 354th Fighter Squadron, Davis-Monthan Air Force Base (2004-2006); Advanced Through Grades to Colonel, United States Air Force (1988); Flight Commander, Director of Operations, 612 Combat Operations Squadron, 12th Air Force Headquarters, Davis-Monthan Air Force Base **AW:** "A Woman Who Leads," University of Arizona Women's Studies Advisory Council (2005); David C. Shilling Award, Air Force Association (2005); Al Neuharth Free Spirit Award (2002); Lifetime Achievement Award, National Center for Women in Policing; Woman on the Move Award, Tucson YWCA **PA:** Republican

MCSHANE, LAWRENCE EDWARD, I: Advertising & Marketing **DOB:** 07/28/1952 **PB:** Waukegan **SC:** IL/USA **PT:** Edgar Leon McShane; Betty Lucile (Riehl) McShane **MS:** Married **ED:** ABA approved Paralegal Studies Program, Graduate Degree in Litigation and Legal Research, Roosevelt University, Chicago, IL (1984); Graduate Coursework, Northern Baptist Theological Seminary, Lombard, IL (1979); BA, Carthage College, Kenosha, WI (1975) **CT:** Summation, Concordance and Case-Map/TextMap/TimeMap, Roosevelt University, Chicago, IL (2010); Conversational Spanish, Marketing and Managment, College of Lake County, Grayslake, IL (1986, 2010); Certified University of Chicago Mini-Medical School (1997) **C:** Progressive Political Campaign Consultant, Lake County, IL (2017-Present); Marketing Specialist, Bird Dog Media, Arlington Heights, IL (2012-2017); Civil Service Commission Administrator, City of Waukegan, Waukegan IL (2011-2015); Community Services Liaison, Illinois State Representative Eddie Washington, Waukegan, IL (2009-2010); Paralegal Advocate, Prairie State Legal Services, Waukegan, IL (1987-2009); Sales Representative, Focal Point Fotographics, Waukegan, IL (1985-1987); Sales Representative, Dun & Bradstreet, Glen Ellyn, IL (1983-1984) **CR:** National Democratic Training Committee, VoteBuilder Training (2019) **CIV:** Lion's Club, Membership Committee Co-Chair (2018-Present); Democratic Party Leadership Circle (2018-Present); Publicly Elected, Democratic Precinct Committeeman (2017-Present); Board of Trustees, Waukegan Public Library (2017-Present); Tenth District Democrats (2016-Present); Church Clerk, First Congregational Church United Church of Christ, Waukegan, IL (2013-Present); Publicly Elected, Regional Board of School Trustees of Lake County (1994-Present); Former Chair, Waukegan Democrats (1996-2000) **MEM:** Democratic Party Leadership Circle; Democratic Senatorial Campaign Committee; Democratic Congressional Campaign Committee; Democratic National Committee; Tenth District Democrats; Lake County Democrats; Waukegan Democrats; WTTW (PBS educational/

cultural TV broadcasting for Chicago); WFMT (fine arts radio broadcasting for Chicago); Sierra Club; Environmental Defense Fund; Lion's Club; Waukegan Historical Society; First Congregational Church United Church of Christ, Waukegan, IL **MH:** Albert Nelson Marquis Lifetime Achievement Award **B/I:** Mr. McShane's parents were very well read, and he attended a church, that was very aware of the needs of others and they believed in getting involved with the community, helping the less fortunate and getting involved with community projects. Mr. McShane got involved with that as a young person and he got to see the needs and issues and he wanted to be a part of trying to make it better for people. He then went to college and he thought about going into ministry but he found it to be limiting so he actually received his bachelors degree in political science. He started thinking that elections and campaigns were a great way to make a difference, shortly after he volunteered at a campaign here or there and it seemed to go well, people liked him and it was fun and exciting and it manifested from there to people saying that he should run for something himself as oppose to helping every one, shortly after, he ran for public office and he was elected. **AV:** Current events; Progressive political campaigns; Piano performance; American Civil War history/re-enacting; Hiking; Walking; Reading; Writing **PA:** Democrat **RE:** United Church of Christ

MEADOR, JO, T: Author; Teacher; Speaker **I:** Writing and Editing **PT:** James Andrew Guasasco; Dorothy Marie McCarthy **SPN:** Edward J. Meador (1984) **CH:** Kathryn Croom Boaz **ED:** MFA, Northwest Institute of Literary Arts (2007); BA in English, California State University (1970); AA in Music, College of San Mateo, CA (1965) **CT:** Certificate in Mystery Writing (2000); Certificate in Advanced Commercial Fiction (1999); Certified in Fiction Writing, University of Washington (1991-1992); Certified Teacher, State of California (1971) **C:** Author, Teacher, Speaker, Langley, WA (2001-Present); Executive Consultant, Information Systems Strategy for Corporate Information Resource Policy (1996-2001); Manager, Data Resource, Defense and Space Finance (1993-1996), Corporate Data Resource Management Plan, Boeing Company, Seattle, WA (1989-1993); Information System Architect and Analyst, US West, Denver, CO (1988-1989); Data and Database Administration Network Systems, Incorporated, Bellevue, WA (1986-1987); Database Applications Consultant, McRoberts, Meador & Associate, Issaquah, WA (1984-1986); Data Administrator, Seattle First National Bank (1983-1984); Database and Data Administrator, Federal Home Loan Bank, San Francisco, CA (1978-1983); Senior Systems Analyst, Bank of America Corporation, San Francisco, CA (1975-1978); Secondary School Teacher in English and Music, Academy of the Presentation, San Francisco, CA (1973-1974); Secondary School Teacher in English and Music, Mitchell Middle School (Mitchell Intermediate School), Atwater, CA (1971-1973); Freelance Writer, Newsletters, Websites, Programs; Speaker, Conferences and Library Talks; Leader on Writing Workshops **CR:** Volunteer Speaker, Host, Workshop Leader, Pacific Northwest Writer's Conferences (PNWC) (1998-2018); Instructor, Data Resource Management Program University of Washington, Seattle, WA (1990-2000); Workshop Leader, Write on the Sound Writers' Conferences, Edmonds WA (2003-2004); Consultant, National Focus Information Systems Architecture (1984-1998); Deputy Project Manager in Data Administration, SHARE Users Group, IBM International, Poughkeepsie, NY (1986-1993); Member, Task Force in Application Development Management, Share International, San Jose, CA (1990-1992);

Speaker, Zachman Information Sys-Architecture Forums, Washington, DC (1990-1991); Instructor, University of California San Francisco (1980-1982) **CIV:** Ambassador, Greater Issaquah Chamber of Commerce (1986-1994); Girl Scout Leader, Girl Scouts of the United States of America (1976-1978); Contributor, Whidbey Island Orchestra; Contributor, South Whidbey Senior Center Workshops; National Genealogical Society **CW:** Author, "There is Love" (2017); Co-editor, Quarterly DRM Journal (1988-1994); Co-editor, "DRM Journal" (1990-1993); Co-author, "Handbook of Systems Management" (1989); Contributor, In-house and Trade Publications, Newsletters; Contributor, Handbooks on Systems and Data Management; Contributor, Numerous Writing Conferences **AW:** Soundings Literary Journal Publication Award for First Poem, "Awakening" (2010); Volunteer of the Year Family Award, Greater Issaquah Chamber of Commerce (1993); Individual Achievement Award, Data Administration Management Association International (DAMA International, Inc.) (1991); Honors Award for Boeing Integration Systems, Advanced Technologies, Inc. (1990) **MEM:** Genealogical Society of South Whidbey Island; Whidbey Island Writers Association and Conference; Seattle Freelancers; Pacific Northwest Writer's Association; Whidbey Island Writers Conference (WIWC); Northwest Institute of Literary Arts (NILA); Data Management Resource Association, Seattle, WA; Data Administration Management Association, International (DAMA International, Inc.) **MH:** Albert Nelson Marquis Lifetime Achievement Award **AS:** Mrs. Meador attributes her success to a strong faith in God and love as the central force of life, as well as the cadre of mentors and allies who have guided her path, be they teachers, leaders, friends or adversaries, young or old. The religion that forced her to sit in a golden-shaft of light in an empty pew waiting for confession, to the writing teacher who commanded his students to examine their lives daily in journal form, and to the neighbor who shed light into the chaos and drama of her family home; all along the path, have been leaders who encouraged and bosses who disparaged, yet all had lessons to teach and gifts to give. Mrs. Meador said, "To know yourself is to accept that gift with gratitude." Mrs. Meador is grateful for the generous community that offered many experiences in the arts, as well as sports and sciences, where every child and adult had opportunities to learn, perform, and play with public funding, where public libraries, civic auditoriums and sports grounds were available to the community at-large. Public education systems extended through four years of college allowed Mrs. Meador a low-cost way to fulfill dreams of college and a teaching career, and adapted to the disrupted time frame forced by life changes. In times she was not enrolled, she studied voraciously using the public library as a key resource and taking advantage of workshops and classes run by communal organizations offering classes in reading, study, and writing in focused topics. **B/I:** Reading and writing have been the foundational skills of Mrs. Meador's work, no matter what career path she was in. At 13, she began a journal of self-examination, a work still active today, following Socrates' edict that an "unexamined life" is not worth living. Each move in her life has been considered through observation, testing, and risking. Teaching offered the best path for carrying along her love of music and writing, but in 1970, a future promised only a string of pink slips and repeated first-years. As the teaching field was drying up, the burgeoning computer field was facing scarcity in skilled workers. Through leg work, networks, and retooling of some basic skills, she earned a starting position in a training program at Bank of America. Despite

this detour, writing and teaching kept a prominent place in her tool box, evaluating her own development and then helping others to do the same, going on to teach managers and directors, and introducing executives to the burgeoning "data processing" function and its effect on businesses. She then designed training programs and helped develop curricula for specialized functions, such as finance, engineering and education. **AV:** Writing; Art; History; Music; Playing the French horn **PA:** Conservative Liberal Democrat **RE:** New Age Teachings and Practice/Culturally Catholic **THT:** Every shift that Mrs. Meador takes in her life is a shift forward. It is not defined by a line but by circles arcing into spirals, creating shifts that follow a pattern of exploring, learning and teaching. She believes that what she learns is stronger and more useful when she passes it on through some kind of instructional offering. Her motto is, "Explore, evaluate, learn, reach out, teach."

MEADOWS, GRADY MILLIDGE, T: President **I:** Business Management/Business Services **CN:** Step Up Bisbee-Naco **PB:** San Jose **SC:** CA/USA **PT:** Weaver Meadows; Edith Meadows **MS:** Married **SPN:** Mary Catherine Kate Bishop **CH:** Marina Velez **ED:** BS in Political Science, University of San Francisco (1972); Graduate Coursework, University of San Francisco **CT:** Licensed General Building Contractor, Northern California **C:** Co-Founder, President, Step Up Bisbee-Naco (2014-Present); General Building Contractor, San Francisco, CA **CIV:** Teacher, Furniture Building, Bisbee, AZ (2005-2017); Volunteer, Rebuilding Together (2004-2014); Cofounder, Construction Technology Program, Marin County, CA (1995-2005); Volunteer, Habitat for Humanity; Volunteer Teacher, Construction and Engineering, Haiti **MIL:** Medical Department, United States Navy (1965-1967) **AW:** Best Nonprofit of the Year Award (2017) **B/I:** Mr. Meadows lived in the San Francisco Bay area, which is very crowded, so he and his wife felt if they moved to the Bisbee-Naco area they could retire early and spend more time traveling. It is an interesting community because it is an art town; there are many creative people. Mr. Meadows knew he could make a lot of difference in the area. **AV:** Sailing; Travel; Furniture building

MEADOWS, MARK RANDALL, T: U.S. Representative from North Carolina **I:** Government Administration/Government Relations/Government Services **DOB:** 07/28/1959 **SC:** Verdun/France **MS:** Married **SPN:** Debbie Meadows (1979) **CH:** Blake; Haley **ED:** BS in Business Management, University of South Florida (1981) **C:** Owner, Highland Properties (1990-Present); Chair, House Freedom Caucus (2017-2019); Member, U.S. House of Representatives from North Carolina's 11th Congressional District, United States Congress (2013-2019); Member, U.S. House Committee on Transportation and Infrastructure (2013-2019); Member, U.S. House Committee on Oversight and Government (2013-2019); Member, U.S. House Committee on Foreign Affairs (2013-2019); Chairman, Macon County Republican Party (2002); Owner, Sandwich Shop (1986-1990); Director of Customer Relations and Public Safety, Tampa Electric (1983-1986) **PA:** Republican **RE:** Evangelical Christian

MEARS, RICK RAVON, T: Professional Race Car Driver (Retired) **I:** Athletics **DOB:** 12/03/1951 **PB:** Wichita **SC:** KS/USA **PT:** Bill Ravon Mears; Mae Louise (Simpson) Mears **MS:** Married **SPN:** Christyn Bowen (11/28/1986) **CH:** Clint Ravon; Cole Ray **ED:** Coursework, Public Schools **C:** Consultant, Penske Racing Team (1993-Present); Retired, Professional Race Car Driver (1992); Member, Penske Racing Team (1978-1992); Professional

Race Car Driver (1973-1992) **AW:** Penske Hall of Fame (2017); Inductee, Motorsports Hall of Fame of America (1998); Inductee, International Motorsports Hall of Fame (1997); One of the 10 Champions for Life, Driver of the Year Awards (1992); Winner, Indianapolis 500 (1979, 1984, 1988, 1991); Winner, Michigan 500 (1991); Winner, Phoenix Race (1989, 1990); Winner, Milwaukee Indy Car Race (1988, 1989); Winner, Laguna Seca Race (1989); Driver of Decade, The Associated Press (1989); Winner, Pocono 500 (1985, 1987); Winner, Triple Crown Championship (1983, 1984); Second Place, Indy 500 (1984); Winner, Michigan 200 Indy Car Race (1983); Winner, National Championship Auto Racing Team (1979, 1981, 1982); Four-Time Winner, Indy Car Races (1982); Two-Time Winner, Atlanta Races (1981); Winner, Riverside Race (1981); U.S. Driver of the Year Jerry Titus Memorial Trophy (1981); Winner, Michigan Race (1981); Winner, Watkins Glen Race (1981); Winner, Mexico City Race (1980-1982); Winner, Trenton Race (1979); Winner, Atlanta Race (1979); Rookie of the Year, American Auto Racing Writers & Broadcasters Association (1979); Auto Racing All American (1979); Winner, National Championship (1979); Co-Rookie of the Year, Indianapolis 500 (1978); Rookie of the Year, Championship Division, U.S. Auto Club (1976); Third Place, Sprint Buggy Open-Wheel Pikes Peak Hill Climb (1976); Winner, Third Annual Firecracker 250, Japan Grand Prix Off-Road Race (1973, 1974); Winner, NorCal 100 (1974); Winner, Several Regional and National Formula Vee and Super Vee Races (1974); Winner, 29 National Championship Races in 203 Career Starts

MEAUX, ALAN, T: Facilities Technician, Artist, Bronze Sculptor, Rare Japanese Book Dealer **I:** Fine Art **CN:** Ronin Art Productions **DOB:** 09/10/1951 **PB:** Joliet **SC:** IL/USA **PT:** Berry Lee Meaux; Luella Ann (Ferguson) Meaux **MS:** Married **SPN:** Letta Sue Nygaard (09/15/1984) **CH:** Ashley Meaux Ovalle; Lacey Marie Meaux **ED:** Coursework, Skagit Valley College, Oak Harbor, WA (1983-1985); Coursework, U.S. Department Agriculture Graduate School, Washington DC (1972); Coursework, Bradley University, Peoria, IL (1971-1972); Coursework, Joliet Junior College, Joliet, IL (1969-1971); Diplopma, Kailua High School, Kailua, HI (1967-1969) **CT:** Certified Specialist, Water Distribution, Washington (2013) **C:** Facilities Technician, Island County Government, Coupeville, WA (1987-2009); Maintenance Technician, Troubleshooters Inc., Oak Harbor, WA (1986-1987); Property Manager, Olympic Builders, Oak Harbor, WA (1979-1986); Carpenter, Klappenbach Construction Co., Moscow, ID (1975-1979); Auto Mechanic, Calvin Ford and Hoffman Olds and Rolls Royce, Hartford, CT (1974-1975); Auto Mechanic, Pohanka Olds and Fiat, Hillcrest Heights, MD (1972-1974); Bolling Air Force Base Gas Station, Washington DC (1971-1972); Photographer, J.J.C. Blazer, Joliet Herald News, Joliet, IL (1969-1971) **CR:** Board of Directors, North West Token Kai, University of Washington, Seattle, WA (1989-Present); Appraiser, Class A, Mid-American Appraisers Association, Springfield, MO (1986-Present); Contributor, Nanka Token Kai, Los Angeles, CA (1985-Present); Bronze Sculptor, Ronin Art Productions, Oak Harbor, WA (1979-Present); Chairman, Safety Committee, Island County Government (1997-2000, 2003); Lecturer, University of Washington, Seattle, WA (1985) **CIV:** Safety Committee Chairman, Island County Government (1998-2003); Assistant Coach, Whidbey Islanders Soccer League (1997-1999) **CW:** Sculptor, Bronze Limited Editions of Samurai Related Subjects (1981-Present); Author, "Japanese Samurai Weapons and Rare Books Collector and Seller" (1989); Exhibitor, Principal Works, Worldfest/Ethnic Heritage Council, Seattle, WA (1988-1990); Exhibitor,

Principal Works, Stanwood Invitational Art Show (1988); Exhibitor, Principal Works, Mini Guild Children's Orthopedic Show, Ballard, WA (1986) **MEM:** President, Leisure Acres Water Association (1998-2000); Assistant Coach, Girls under 12, Whidbey Islanders Futbol Club (1997-1999); Charter, Board of Directors, Northwest Token Kai (1989-1991); Life Member, National Rifle Association; Life Member, Law Enforcement Alliance of America; Life Member, Citizens Committee For The Right To Keep And Bear Arms; Life Member, Japanese Sword Society U.S.; Western Museum Conference; Washington Museum Association; Ethnic Heritage Council; Nanka Token Kai; Japan Society; Washington Arms Collectors Association; Chairman, Range Committee, Trustee, North Whidbey Sportmen's Association; International Defensive Pistol Association; Central Whidbey Sportmen's Club **MH:** Albert Nelson Marquis Lifetime Achievement Award **AV:** Hunting; Fishing; Woodworking; Reading; Collecting Japanese antiques; Target shooting

MEDIN, JULIA A., PHD, T: Mathematics Professor, Researcher **I:** Education/Educational Services **DOB:** 01/16/1929 **PB:** Dayton **SC:** OH/USA **PT:** Caroline (Feinberg) Levitt **MS:** Married **SPN:** A. Louis Medin (12/24/1950) **CH:** Douglas; David; Thomas; Linda **ED:** PhD in Counseling and Mathematics Education, American University (1985); MA in Higher Education, The George Washington University (1977); BS in Mathematics Education, The Ohio State University (1951) **CT:** Certified Teacher, States of Maryland and Florida **C:** Senior Associate, Management and Educational Technology Associates (1999-Present); Senior Educational Technology, School of Modeling, Simulation, and Training, University of Central Florida (1990-1999); Assistant Professor of Mathematics, University of Central Florida (1988-1990); Mathematics Teacher, Montgomery County Public Schools (1973-1988); Research Engineer, Sun Oil Company (Now Sunoco) (1951-1953); Mathematics Teacher, Highland Park School District (1951-1953) **CR:** Senior Mathematics Educator, Researcher, School of Modeling, Simulation, and Training (1988-1990); Adviser, Title II Steering Committee, U.S. Department of Education (1985-1989) **CIV:** Religious School Director, Beth Tikvah Congregation (1971); Democratic Committee Woman, Town of Monroeville, PA (1962); Consultant, Monroeville Mental Health (1960) **CW:** Author, "Single-Sex Public Schools - Who Needs Them and Why" (2005); Contributing Author, "Math for 14 & 17 Year Olds" (1987); Editor, "Simulation and Computer-Based Technology for Education"; Contributor, Articles, Professional Journals **MEM:** Task Force on Minorities in Mathematics, Mathematical Association of America; National Council of Teachers of Mathematics; Women and Mathematics Education; National Coalition for Technology in Education & Training; Phi Delta Kappa; Kappa Delta Pi **MH:** Albert Nelson Marquis Lifetime Achievement Award

MEDVECKY, ROBERT S., ESQ., T: Lawyer **I:** Law and Legal Services **DOB:** 02/12/1931 **PB:** Bridgeport **SC:** CT/USA **PT:** Stephen Medvecky; Elizabeth (Petro) Medvecky **MS:** Married **SPN:** Ellen R. Munt **CH:** Allison L.; Beth A.; Craig R. **ED:** JD, Harvard University (1955); AB, Dartmouth University (1952) **C:** Partner, Reid & Priest, New York, NY (1978-1987); Partner, Lord, Bissell & Brook, Washington, DC (1975-1978); Vice President, General Counsel, Secretary, Amtrak, Washington, DC (1971-1975); General Attorney, Southern New England Telephone Co., New Haven, CT (1957-1971); Associate, Lord, Bissell & Brook, Chicago, IL (1955-1957) **MEM:** Harvard Club; Fiddlesticks Country Club **BAR:** Florida (1989); District of Columbia (1972); Con-

necticut (1958); Illinois (1955) **MH:** Albert Nelson Marquis Lifetime Achievement Award; Marquis Who's Who Top Professional **B/I:** Mr. Medvecky became involved in his profession because, when he finished his studies at Dartmouth University, he had no specific plan. He decided to go to Harvard Law School to see if he could handle the challenge, and he continued to practice law from there.

MEEKS, DONNA M., T: Professor and Chair **I:** Education/Educational Services **CN:** Lamar University **PB:** Louisville **SC:** KY/USA **ED:** Master's Degree, University of Wisconsin, Milwaukee, WI (1984-1986) **C:** Professor and Chair, Lamar University **AW:** Award, Axis Gallery Exhibition (2017); Visiting Artist Award, University of Texas of the Permian Basin (2012) **AS:** Ms. Meeks attributes her success to her persistence in her work. **B/I:** Ms. Meeks became involved in her profession because she was passionate about art from a young age.

MEEKS, GREGORY WELDON, T: U.S. Representative from New York **I:** Government Administration/Government Relations/Government Services **DOB:** 09/25/1953 **PB:** New York **SC:** NY/USA **PT:** James Weldon; Mary (McNeal) Weldon **MS:** Married **SPN:** Simone-Marie Meeks **CH:** Ebony Renee; Aja J.; Nia-Aiyana **ED:** JD, Howard University School of Law, Washington, DC (1978); BA in History, Adelphi University, Garden City, NY (1975) **C:** Member, U.S. House of Representatives from New York's Fifth Congressional District, United States Congress (2013-Present); Member, U.S. House of Representatives from New York's Sixth Congressional District, United States Congress (1998-2013); Member, New York State Assembly (1993-1998); Supervising Judge, New York State Workers' Compensation Board (1987-1993); Judge, New York State Workers' Compensation Board (1985-1987); Hearing Officer, New York Family Court (1984-1985); Assistant Counsel, State Investigations Commission (1983-1984); Assistant Special Narcotics Prosecutor, Office of Special Narcotics Prosecutor, New York, NY (1981-1983); Assistant District Attorney, Queens District Attorney's Office (1978-1981); Member, Committee on Financial Services; Member, Committee on Foreign Affairs **CIV:** Board of Directors, Peninsula Nursing and Rehabilitation Center (Formerly Peninsula General Hospital) (1989-Present); Chairman, Board, Joseph P. Addabbo Family Health Care Center (1990-1992); Board of Directors, Rockaway Peninsula Civic Association (1983-1991); Member, Allen AME Church (Now The Greater Allen A.M.E. Cathedral of New York), St. Albans, NY **AW:** Named to the Power 150, Ebony Magazine (2008); Congressional Leadership Award, National Urban League (2006); Named One of the Most Influential Black Americans, Ebony Magazine (2006); William Garvin Public Service Award (2004); Community Leader Award, Boy Scouts of America (1992); Outstanding Volunteer Mentor Award, New York Mentoring (1990); Political Leadership Award, NAACP, Far Rockaway Chapter (1989) **MEM:** ABA; Vice President, Macon B. Allen Black Bar Association; Queens County Bar Association; NAACP, Far Rockaway Chapter; Alpha Phi Alpha Fraternity, Inc.; Macon B. Allen Black Bar Association **PA:** Democrat **RE:** Baptist

MEIER, DEBORAH, I: Education/Educational Services **DOB:** 04/19/1931 **PT:** Joseph Willen; Pearl Willen **MS:** Married **SPN:** Fred Meier (1952) **CH:** Becky; Nicky; Roger **ED:** Honorary Degree, Columbia Teachers College; Honorary Degree, Brown University; Honorary Degree, Yale University; Honorary Degree, Harvard University; Master's Degree in History, University of Chicago **C:** Co-Founder, Principal, Central Park East I Elementary School (1974-Present); Co-Principal,

Mission Hill Elementary School (1997-2004) **CIV:** Trustee, Educational Alliance; Trustee, Educators for Social Responsibility; Board Member, Fairtest; Board Member, Panasonic Foundation; Board Member, Center for Collaborative Education Boston; Board Member, National Academy Education **CW:** Author, "These Schools Belong to You and Me" (2019); Author, "In Schools We Trust" (2002); Author, "Will Standards Save Public Education" (2000); Author, "The Power of Their Ideas: Lessons to America from a Small School in Harlem" (1995); Author, "Creating Communities of Learning in an Era of Testing and Standardization"; Editorial Board, The Nation; Editorial Board, Dissent and the Harvard Education Letter; Contributor, Articles, Professional Journals **AW:** Senior Annenberg Fellow (1994-1997); MacArthur Award **MEM:** Coalition of Essential Sciences; Founding Member, National Board for Professional Teaching Standards; Board Member, Vice-Chair, Carnegie Foundation for Advancement in Education **MH:** Albert Nelson Marquis Lifetime Achievement Award **B/I:** Mrs. Meier was always a writer; however, she wasn't inspired to teach, so she became a substitute teacher, which would allow her to spend ample time with her children. In this role, she inevitably became interested in teaching. Later, she was offered a position as a kindergarten teacher. In that class, she fell in love with education. The rest of her career has since progressed naturally. **AV:** Reading; Talking with friends **PA:** Democratic Socialist of America **RE:** Jewish

MEISELS, GERHARD GEORGE, PHD, T: Academic Administrator, Chemist, Educator **I:** Education/Educational Services **DOB:** 05/11/1931 **PB:** Vienna **SC:** Austria **PT:** Leo Meisels; Adele Josefa Maria (Seehofer) Meisels **MS:** Married **SPN:** Gerry Meisels **CH:** Laura Germaine Meisels Brown **ED:** Doctor of Philosophy, University of Notre Dame, Indiana (1955-1956); Master of Science, University of Notre Dame, Indiana (1952); Coursework, University of Vienna (1949-1952) **C:** Director, Coalition for Science Literacy (1994-Present); Director, Suncoast Area Center for Educational Enhancement (1996-1999); Provost and Academic Vice President, University of South Florida, Tampa, FL (1988-1994); Dean, College of Arts and Sciences, University of Nebraska, Lincoln, NB (1981-1988); Professor, Department of Chemistry, University of Nebraska, Lincoln, NB (1975-1981); Chairperson, Department of Chemistry, University of Nebraska, Lincoln, NB (1975-1981); Chairperson, Chemistry Department, University of Houston (1973-1975); Professor, University of Houston (1970-1975); Associate Professor, University of Houston (1965-1970); Assistant Group Leader, Union Carbide Corporation (1964-1965); Chemist Nuclear Division, Union Carbide Corporation, Tuxedo, NY (1959-1963); Chemist, Gulf Oil Corporation, Pittsburgh (1956-1959); Part-time Instructor, Carnegie Institute of Technology, Pittsburgh, PA (1956-1958); Postdoctoral Research Associate, University of Notre Dame (1955-1956) **CIV:** Chairperson, Florida Coalition for Improving Mathematics and Science Education (1998-2010); Interim Executive Director (1998-2008); Secretary, President, Ramsey Junior Chamber of Commerce (1959-1964); Board Member, National Club **CW:** Editor, Journal of Radiation Physics and Chemistry (1980); Contributor, Writings in Field to Professional Publications; Contributor, Articles for Dog Magazines **AW:** Senior Fellow, Science Research Council, England (1976); Fulbright Fellow (1951-1952); Smith-Mundt Fellow (1951-1952) **MEM:** Board of Directors, Triangle Coalition STEM (2011-Present); Vice President, National Alliance State Science and Math (2007-Present); Board of Directors, National Alliance State Science and Math (1999-Present); Del-

egate to American Kennel Club, St. Peters Dog Fanciers Association (1998-Present); Central Steering Committee, Florida Higher Education Consortium Mathematics and Science (1995-Present); President, St. Peters Dog Fanciers Association (2012-2018); Board of Directors, West Highland White Terrier Club (2008-2012); President, Lakeland-Winter Haven Kennel Club (2006-2009); Secretary, St. Peters Dog Fanciers Association (2000-2004); President, Conformation Judges Association of Florida (1996-2004); Chairperson, Florida Higher Education Consortium Mathematics and Science (1998-2000); Secretary, St. Peters Dog Fanciers Association (1996-1998); Executive Board, Council Science Society (1989-1992); Chairperson, Council Science Society (1991); Chairperson Elect, Council Science Society (1990); Board of Directors, American Society for Mass Spectrometry (1988-1990); President, American Society for Mass Spectrometry (1986-1988); Delegate to American Kennel Club, Cornhusker Kennel Club (1976-1988); Vice President, American Society for Mass Spectrometry (1984-1986); Board of Directors, Council for Chemical Research (1982-1985); Board of Directors, Houston Kennel Club (1968-1970); Chairperson, Committee on Science Priorities, Council Science Society; President, Council Science Society; Committee Chairperson, American Chemical Society; Committee Chairperson, American Society for Mass Spectrometry; Florida Academy Sciences; American Association for the Advancement of Science; American Physical Society; President, Cornhusker Kennel Club; Board of Directors, Cornhusker Kennel Club; Florida Stem Council; Sigma Xi **MH:** Albert Nelson Marquis Lifetime Achievement Award **B/I:** Dr. Meisel became involved in his profession as an academic administrator, chemical educator because he has always liked chemistry in high school and working in the lab. He rose to become an administrator after having served as a faculty member, and he was the logical choice for the position. His career in high academic leadership naturally unfolded from there. **AV:** Writing; Dog breeding and exhibiting at conformation shows for the American Kennel Club; Photography **RE:** Episcopalian

MELIN, ARTHUR, "ART" WALDEN, INCOME MAINTENANCE SPECIALIST, T: Auditor, Income Maintenance Specialist **I:** Social Work **CN:** Milwaukee Enrollment Services **DOB:** 12/23/1972 **PB:** Gaborone **SC:** Botswana **PT:** Robert Arthur Melin; Mary Magdalene (O'Brien) Melin **MS:** Single **ED:** Bachelor of Science in Accounting and German, Valparaiso University (1996) **C:** Income Maintenance Specialist, Wisconsin Department of Health Services, (2013-Present); Field Auditor, Department of Revenue, State of Wisconsin (1999-Present); Controller, Accountant, Professionally Speaking Inc., Milwaukee, WI (1997-1999) **CR:** Award for Exceeding Standards, Milwaukee Enrollment Services (2019) **AW:** National Letter of Intent, National Collegiate Athletic Association (1991-1995) **MEM:** Academic Officer, Lambda Chi Alpha (1993-1994); Lifetime Member, Valparaiso Varsity Club; Alpha Lambda Delta; Delta Phi Alpha **MH:** Albert Nelson Marquis Lifetime Achievement Award; Marquis Who's Who Humanitarian Award **AV:** Coaching; Weightlifting; Sports; Internet **PA:** Republican **RE:** Roman Catholic

MENDES, SHAWN PETER RAUL, T: Singer **I:** Media & Entertainment **DOB:** 08/08/1998 **PB:** Pickering **SC:** Ontario/Canada **PT:** Manuel Mendes; Karen (Rayment) Mendes **ED:** Diploma, Pine Ridge Secondary School, Canada (2016) **C:** Recording Artist, Island Records (2014-Present) **CR:** Wilhelmina International, Inc. (2016-Present); Brand Ambassador, Calvin Klein (2019); Ambas-

sador, Emporio Armani Watch Collection (2018-2019) **CIV:** Founder, Shawn Mendes Foundation (2018-Present); Participant, Global Citizen Festival (2018); Co-Founder, Mexico Earthquake Relief Fund, The American National Red Cross (2017); Notes from Shawn Campaign, DoSomething.org (2014-2016); Pencils of Promise; Performer, Benefit Songs, Concerts **CW:** Performer, "Saturday Night Live" (2016, 2019); Singer, "Shawn Mendes" (2018); Appearance, "Drop the Mic" (2018); Singer, "Illuminate" (2016); Singer, "Handwritten" (2015); Actor, "Yo Quisiera" (2015); Singer, Numerous Songs; Appearances, Television Shows **AW:** Juno Award for Single of the Year, Artist of the Year (2020); Awards for Choice Summer Male Artist, Teen Choice Awards (2017, 2019); Award for Collaboration of the Year, American Music Awards (2019); Awards for Favorite Adult Contemporary Artist, American Music Awards (2017, 2018); Listee, 100 Most Influential, Time Magazine (2018); Awards for Choice Web Star: Music, Teen Choice Awards (2014, 2015); Recipient, Numerous Awards

MENDIOLA, PATRICIA, T: Associate Professor in Practice **I:** Education/Educational Services **CN:** The University of Texas **MS:** Married **SPN:** Enrique **CH:** Three Children **ED:** MS in Mathematics, The University of Texas-Pan American, Texas (2012); MA in Supervision, The University of Texas-Pan American, Texas (1990); BS in Mathematics, Fitchburg State College (Now Fitchburg State University), MA (1982) **C:** Associate Professor in Practice, University of Texas (2012-Present); High School Math Teacher, Campus Administrator, Central Office Coordinator, Public School System (30 Years) **CIV:** Sunday School Teacher; Volunteer, World Birding Center **MEM:** National Council of Teacher of Mathematics; National Science Teachers Association (NSTA); Rio Grande Valley Council of Teachers of Mathematics (RGVCTM) **AS:** Mrs. Mendiola was given the understanding of how important different teaching styles are to engage students very early in her life. She feels that knowledge was a gift and it is her duty to continue to spread her gift. Colossians 3:23 "Whatever you do, work at it with all your heart, as working for the Lord, not for human masters..." **B/I:** Mrs. Mendiola had always known that she would be a teacher. She feels fortunate to have had mostly great teachers throughout high school. The one teacher that she recalls that she disliked is the one that inspired her to teach geometry in a different style.

MENEAR, CRAIG ALBERT, T: Chief Executive Officer and President **I:** Retail/Sales **CN:** The Home Depot Inc. **PB:** Flint **SC:** MI/USA **ED:** BA in Business, Michigan State University Eli Broad College of Business (1979) **C:** President, Chief Executive Officer, The Home Depot Inc. (2014-Present); President, U.S. Retail, The Home Depot, Inc., Atlanta, GA (2014); Executive Vice President of Merchandising, The Home Depot, Inc., Atlanta, GA (2007-2014); Senior Vice President of Merchandising, The Home Depot, Inc., Atlanta, GA (2003-2007); Joined, The Home Depot, Inc. (1997); Merchandising Vice President of Hardware, The Home Depot, Inc., Atlanta, GA; Merchandising Vice President, Southwest Division, The Home Depot, Inc., Atlanta, GA; Division Merchandise Manager, The Home Depot, Inc., Atlanta, GA; With, Montgomery Ward; With, Grace Home Centers; With, Builders Emporium; With, IKEA Wholesale, Inc. **CR:** Board of Directors, The Home Depot, Inc. (2014-Present); Chairman, The Home Depot Foundation

MENEFEE, SAMUEL P., JD, T: Lawyer, Academic **I:** Education/Educational Services **CN:** University of Virginia **DOB:** 06/08/1950 **PB:** Denver **SC:** CO/USA **PT:** George Hardiman Menefee; Martha Elizabeth (Pyeatt) Menefee MS: Married SPN: Mary W. (04/21/2000) CH: Mary Elizabeth ED: MPhil in International Relations, University of Cambridge (1995); SJD, University of Virginia (1993); LLM in Ocean Law, University of Virginia (1982); JD, Harvard University (1981); BLitt, University of Oxford (1975); Diploma in Social Anthropology, University of Oxford (1973); BA in Anthropology, Yale University, Summa Cum Laude (1972) C: Advisory Board, School of Law , University of Virginia (1997-Present); Maury Fellow, School of Law, University of Virginia (1989-Present); University of Virginia (2013-2017); Senior Associate, Center for National Security Law, School of Law, University of Virginia (1985-2017); Of Counsel, Barham & Churchill PC, New Orleans, LA (1985-1988); Associate, Phelps Dunbar (1983-1985); Fellow, Center for Oceans Law and Policy, School of Law, University of Virginia (1982-1983) CR: Member, Consultative Task Force on Commercial Crime, Interstate Commerce Commission (1996-Present); Professor, Regent University (1998-2003); Scholar-at-Large, Regent University (1997-2003); Adviser, Hellenic American Maritime Forum (1997-1999); Visiting Professor, Regent University (1996-1997); Law Clerk, Honorable Pasco M. Bowman, United States Court of Appeals for the Eighth Circuit (1994-1995); Visiting Assistant Professor, University of Missouri-Kansas City (1990); Visiting Lecturer, University of Cape Town (1987); Lecturer, Various National and International Organizations CW: National Editor, "Association Research on Peasant Diaries" (1996-Present); Editorial Board Member, International Journal of Marine and Coastal Law (1997-2003); Author, "Trends in Maritime Violence: A Special Report from Jane's Intelligence Review and Jane's Sentinel" (1996); Author, "Contemporary Piracy and International Law" (1995); Co-Editor, "Materials on Ocean Law" (1982); Author, "Wives for Sale: Ethnographic Study of British Popular Divorce" (1981); Contributor, Articles, Professional Journals AW: Piracy Reporting Center Fellowship, Kuala Lumpur (1993-Present); Fellowship, Interstate Commerce Commission, International Maritime Bureau (1991-Present); Huntington Fellowship, The Mariners' Museum and Park (1997); Katharine Briggs Prize, American Folklore Society (1992); Cosmos Fellowship, School of Literatures, Languages and Cultures, The University of Edinburgh (1991-1992); Rhodes Scholarship, Yale University (1972); Scholar of House Fellowship, Yale University (1972); Bates Traveling Fellowship, Yale University (1971) MEM: United Nations Educational Study Group, The Maritime Law Association of the United States (1998-Present); Chairman, Law of Sea Committee, Subcommittee on Naval Warfare, Maritime Terrorism and Piracy, American Bar Association (1989-Present); Chairman, Marine Security Committee, Marine Technology Society (1991-2004); Co-Chairman, Marine Security Committee, Marine Technology Society (1991-2004); Chairman, Committee of International Law of Sea, The Maritime Law Association of the United States (1999-2003); Chair, Working Group of Piracy, The Maritime Law Association of the United States (1992-2003); Rapporteur, Joint International Working Group on Uniformity of Law of Piracy, International Law Association (1998-2001); Chairman, Committee on Law of Sea, American Branch, International Law Association (1996-2001); Co-Chairman, Committee on Law of Sea, American Branch, International Law Association (1996-2001); Law of Sea Steering Committee, American Bar Association (1996-1999); Vice Chairman, Committee of International Law of Sea, The Maritime Law Association of the United States (1991-1999); Observer, Convention on Law of Sea Meeting of States Parties, United Nations (1996); Rapporteur, Committee on Maritime Neutrality,

American Branch, International Law Association (1992); Chairman, Subcommittee on Law of Sea, The Maritime Law Association of the United States (1988-1991); Proctor, Subcommittee on Law of Sea, The Maritime Law Association of the United States (1988-1991); Committee Member, Subcommittee on Law of Sea, The Maritime Law Association of the United States (1988-1991); Rapporteur, Committee EEZ, American Branch, International Law Association (1988-1990); Vice Chairman, Marine Resources Committee, American Bar Association (1987-1990); Fellow, Royal Anthropological Institute; American Anthropological Association; Royal Asiatic Society; Society of Antiquaries of Scotland; Royal Geographical Society; Maritime International Committee, ASIS International; U.S. Naval Institute; Navy League of the United States; American Folklore Society; The Royal Celtic Society; International Studies Association; Royal Scottish Geographical Society; Royal African Society; Egypt Exploration Society; Arctic Institute of Northern America; The American Society of International Law; American Historical Society; Working Group on Terrorism, American Bar Association; Committee Member, Southeastern Admiralty Law Institute; Society for the History of Discoveries; The Society for Nautical Research; National Eagle Scout Association; Raven Society, Alumni Association, University of Virginia; The Jefferson Literary and Debating Society; Mory's Association; The Elizabethan Club of Yale; Yale Political Union; Leander Club; The Cambridge Union; Oxford and Cambridge Club; The Yale Club New York; Paul Morphy Club; Round Table Club; The Phi Beta Kappa Society; Omicron Delta Kappa The National Leadership Honor Society BAR: Maine State Bar Association (1986); Pennsylvania Bar Association (1986); United States Court of Appeals District of Columbia Circuit (1986); Supreme Court of the United States (1985); The District of Columbia Bar (1985); Nebraska State Bar Association (1985); The Florida Bar (1985); United States Court of Appeals for the First, Third, Fourth, Fifth, Sixth, Seventh, Eighth and Ninth Circuits (1984); The Virginia Bar Association (1983); United States Court of Appeals for the Armed Forces (1983); United States Court of International Trade (1983); United States Court of Federal Claims (1983); The United States Court of Appeals for the Tenth Circuit (1983); Louisiana State Bar Association (1983); United States Court of Appeals for the Eleventh Circuit (1982); State Bar of Georgia (1981) MH: Albert Nelson Marquis Lifetime Achievement Award; Marquis Who's Who Top Professional; Marquis Who's Who Humanitarian Award AV: Anthropology; Archaeology; Hiking PA: Republican

MENENDEZ, ROBERT, "BOB", T: U.S. Senator from New Jersey; Lawyer I: Government Administration/Government Relations/Government Services DOB: 01/01/1954 PB: New York SC: NY/USA PT: Mario Menendez; Evangelina (Lopez) Menendez MS: Divorced SPN: Jane Jacobsen (06/05/1976, Divorced 2005) CH: Alicia (Stepdaughter); Robert ED: JD, Rutgers Law School (1979); BA in Political Science and Urban Studies, Saint Peter's College (Now Saint Peter's University) (1976) C: Ranking Member, U.S. Senate Committee on Foreign Relations (2018-Present); U.S. Senator, State of New Jersey (2006-Present); Chairman, U.S. Senate Committee on Foreign Relations (2013-2015); Chairman, Democratic Senatorial Campaign Committee (DSCC) (2009-2011); Chairman, U.S. House Democratic Caucus (2003-2006); Member, U.S. House of Representatives from New Jersey's 13th Congressional District, U.S. Congress (1993-2006); Member, District 33, New Jersey State Senate (1992-1993); Mayor, City of Union City, NJ (1986-1992); Attorney, Diaz & Menendez, Union City, NJ (1980-1992);

Member, District 33, New Jersey General Assembly (1987-1991) CR: Co-Chair, Hillary Rodham Clinton Presidential Campaign (2007-2008) CIV: Member, Government's Hispanic Advisory Committee, Trenton, NJ (1984-Present); Member, Alliance Civic Association (1982-1992); Member, Government's Ethnic Advisory Committee, Washington, DC (1985); Chief Financial Officer, Union City Board of Education (1978-1982); President, Alliance Civic Association (1981); Trustee, Union City Board of Education (1974-1978) AW: Named Man of the Year, Armenian National Committee of New Jersey (2007); Paraskevaides Award, 16th Annual Cyprus Conference (2005); Capital Award, National Council of La Raza (Now UnidosUS) (2003); Excellence in Education Award, Ana G. Mendez University System (2003); Lifetime Achievement Award, Hispanic Business Roundtable (2000); Public Service Achievement Award, American Hellenic Institute (1997); Justice of Cyprus Award, Cyprus Federation of America (1995); Man of the Year Award, Kiwanis International (1994); Distinguished Citizen Award, University of Medicine and Dentistry of New Jersey (1994); Award, U.S. Conference of Mayors (1987, 1988, 1991); Outstanding Community Service Award, Revista Actualidades en Educacion (1982); Outstanding Service Award, Hispanic Law Enforcement (1981); Community Service Award, Gran Logia del Norte (1981) MEM: American Bar Association; Federal Bar Association; New Jersey Bar Association; Hispanic National Bar Association; Hudson County Bar Association; New Jersey Employment and Training Commission; New Jersey Mayors Coalition; Chairman, New Jersey Hispanic Leadership Opportunities Program; Chairman, Hispanic Elected and Appointed Officials Organization (Now NALEO); Chairman, Hoboken Elks Lodge; Chairman, North Hudson Lawyers Club; New Jersey Hispanic Leadership Opportunities Program; Hispanic Elected and Appointed Officials Organization (Now NALEO); Hoboken Elks Lodge; North Hudson Lawyers Club BAR: State of New Jersey (1980) AV: Playing chess; Playing racquetball PA: Democrat RE: Roman Catholic

MENG, GRACE, T: U.S. Representative from New York; Lawyer I: Government Administration/Government Relations/Government Services DOB: 10/01/1975 PB: Queens SC: NY/USA PT: Jimmy K. Meng; Shiao-Mei Meng MS: Married SPN: Wayne Kye (2005) CH: Tyler; Brandon ED: JD, Yeshiva University Benjamin N. Cardozo School of Law (2002); BA, University of Michigan (1997) C: Vice Chair, Democratic National Committee (2017-Present); Member, U.S. House of Representatives from New York's Sixth Congressional District, United States Congress, Washington, DC (2013-Present); Member, U.S. House Small Business Committee (2013-Present); Member, U.S. House Committee on Foreign Affairs (2013-Present); Member, District 22, New York State Assembly, Flushing, NY (2009-2013); Campaign Worker, Barack Obama's Presidential Campaign (2008); Campaign Worker, Hillary Rodham Clinton Senatorial Campaign (2006); Campaign Worker, Lieutenant Governor David Paterson (2006); Campaign Worker, New York State Governor Eliot Spitzer (2006); Campaign Worker, Fernando Ferrer (2005); Campaign Manager, Assemblyman Jimmy K. Meng, New York State Assembly; District Office Administrator, Counsel, Assemblyman Jimmy K. Meng, New York State Assembly; Partner, Yoon & Kim, LLP CIV: Pro Bono Attorney, Sanctuary for Families, New York, NY AW: Named One of the 40 Under 40, Crain's New York Business (2013) PA: Democrat

MENZIES, CARL S., PHD, T: Agriculturist, Researcher, Nutritionist **I:** Agriculture **DOB:** 03/06/1932 **PB:** Menard **SC:** TX/USA **PT:** Alex L. Menzies; Marguerite (Watson) Menzies **MS:** Married **SPN:** Shirley W. Martin (09/02/1952) **CH:** John S.; Linda D. **ED:** PhD, University of Kentucky (1965); MS, Kansas State University (1956); BS, Texas Tech College (1954) **C:** Professor Emeritus, Texas A&M University (1997); Resident, Director of Research, Professor of Animal Science, Texas Agricultural Experiment Station, San Angelo, TX (1971-1996); Head, Animal Science Department, Professor, South Dakota State University, Brookings, SD (1969-1971); Associate Professor, Kansas State University, Manhattan, KS (1965-1969); Assistant Professor, Kansas State University, Manhattan, KS (1958-1965); Research Assistant, Animal Science, University of Kentucky, Lexington, KY (1961-1962); Instructor, Animal Science, Kansas State University, Manhattan, KS (1955-1958) **CR:** Member, Fiber Advisory Committee, Texas Department of Agriculture (1999-Present); Member, Advisory Board, Agricultural Program, Angelo State University (1986-Present); Member, Advisory Committee Research Station, U.S. Department of Agriculture, Dubois, ID (1985-Present); Consultant, Pakistan Project King Ranch, Kingsville, TX (1975); Board of Directors, Sml. Ruminant, Cooperative Research Support Program Project, U.S. Agency for International Development, Davis, CA **CIV:** Chairman, Livestock Committee, Goals for San Angelo (1988-1990) **CW:** Contributor, Articles, Professional Journals **AW:** Distinguished Alumnus, College of Agriculture Texas Technology University (1993); Silver Ram Award, American Sheep Producers Council (1988); Inductee, Manard School Hall of Fame; Texas A&M University Deputy Chancellor for Agriculture Award for Distinguished Performance in Administration (1983); Appreciation for Service Award, Kansas, Purebreed Sheep Breeders Association (1968); American Sheep Industry Award for Contradictions to the Wool Industry **MEM:** Board of Directors, San Angelo Chamber of Commerce (1990-1993); Fellow, American Society of Animal Science; CAST; Rotary International; Past President, Texas Sheep and Goat Raisers Association; Sigma Xi; Gamma Sigma Delta; Phi Kappa Phi; Alpha Zeta; Farm House Frat **MH:** Albert Nelson Marquis Lifetime Achievement Award **B/I:** Dr. Menzies became involved in his profession because he grew up on a ranch; his family was mainly involved with livestock. He traveled with Panam's judging team and they were a 4h judging team. He was inspired to go to the university and study agriculture. **AV:** Ranching; Producing registered sheep; Outdoor activities; Playing golf **PA:** Republican **RE:** First United Methodist Church **THT:** Earlier in his career, around the time he got his PhD, Dr. Menzies went into administration research, specifically with sheep nutrition.

MERCER, EVELYN LOIS ROBINSON, T: Counseling Administrator **I:** Education/Educational Services **DOB:** 04/25/1934 **PB:** Ellensboro **SC:** NC/USA **PT:** Milton Bernadine Robinson Senior; Lois Lenora Robinson **MS:** Divorced **SPN:** Theodore Roosevelt Mercer Senior (Divorced, June 1978) **CH:** Theodore Roosevelt Junior; Brian Vincent; David Lemuel **ED:** Coursework, Miami University, Oxford, OH (1973-1975);Coursework, University of Akron (1973-1974); MEd in Guidance and Counseling, University of Cincinnati (1972); BS in Mathematics, Livingstone College (1957) **CT:** Professional Counselor, Ohio Counselor and Social Worker Board (1984); Guidance Counselor, Ohio (1972); Mathematics Teacher, Ohio (1963) **C:** Retired, Winton Woods City School District (1994); Guidance Counselor, Winton Woods City School District, Cincinnati, OH (1973-1994); Guid-

ance Counselor, Cincinnati Public Schools (1972-1973); Math Teacher, Cincinnati Public Schools, Cincinnati, OH (1963-1972); Math Teacher, Jackson County Public Schools, Gumberry, NC (1957-1960) **CR:** Director, School of Counseling Consultant Service, Cincinnati, OH (1994-Present); Nursing School Advisory Board, Deaconess Hospital School of Nursing, Cincinnati, OH (1983-1988); Admissions Advisory Board, The Ohio State University, Columbus, OH (1982-1985); Cincinnati Technical College, Cincinnati, OH (1975-1981); Advisory Committee, Counselor, Education University of Cincinnati (1975-1976) **CIV:** Democratic Precinct Executive, Hamilton County Board Elections, Cincinnati, OH (1974-1996); Housing Commission, City of Forest Park, Cincinnati, OH **AW:** Outstanding Counselor of Year, Inroads of Cincinnati (1984) **MEM:** American President, Charlotte Branch, Association of University Women (2001-2003); Founder, President, Les Birdies Golf Club Charlotte (1999-2001); National Education Association; Past State Vice President, American Association of University Women of North Carolina; American Association of College Admissions Counselors; Ohio Association of College Admissions Counselors; Ohio School Counselors Association; Ohio Education Association; Livingstone College Alumni Association; University of Cincinnati Alumni Association; National Association for the Advancement for Colored People; Order of Eastern Star; Zeta Phi Beta **MH:** Albert Nelson Marquis Lifetime Achievement Award **B/I:** Ms. Mercer's father believed in the importance of education. This value stuck with her throughout her entire life, inspiring her to further her education after high school by earning a degree in mathematics. This jumpstarted her career as a teacher, which later morphed into counseling. **AV:** Golfing; Traveling; Playing bridge; Volunteering; Gardening; Singing **PA:** Independent **RE:** Methodist

MERCER, REBEKAH, T: Foundation Director **I:** Nonprofit & Philanthropy **CN:** Mercer Family Foundation **DOB:** 12/06/1973 **PB:** Yorktown Heights **SC:** NY/USA **PT:** Robert Mercer; Diana Lynne (Dean) Mercer **MS:** Married **SPN:** Sylvain Mirochnikoff (2003) **CH:** Four Children **ED:** MA in Management Science and Engineering, Stanford University; BS, Stanford University **C:** Director, Mercer Family Foundation; Trader, Renaissance Technologies; Co-owner, Ruby et Violette; Co-owner, Breitbart; With, Emerdata **CIV:** Member, Board of Directors, American Museum of Natural History (2013-2020) **CW:** Author, "Clinton Cash" (2015)

MERKLEY, JEFFREY, "JEFF" ALAN, T: U.S. Senator from Oregon **I:** Government Administration/Government Relations/Government Services **DOB:** 10/24/1956 **PB:** Mystic Creek **SC:** OR/USA **PT:** Darrell Philip Merkley; Betty Lou (Collins) Merkley **MS:** Married **SPN:** Mary Sorteberg **CH:** Jonathan; Brynne **ED:** MA in Public Affairs, Princeton University Woodrow Wilson School of Public and International Affairs (Now Princeton School of Public and International Affairs) (1982); BA in International Relations, Stanford University (1979) **C:** U.S. Senator, State of Oregon, Washington, DC (2009-Present); Member, U.S. Senate Committee on Health, Education Labor and Pensions, Washington, DC (2009-Present); Member, U.S. Senate Committee on Environment and Public Works, Washington, DC (2009-Present); Member, U.S. Senate Committee on Banking, Housing and Urban Affairs, Washington, DC (2009-Present); Member, U.S. Senate Budget Committee, Washington, DC (2009-Present); Speaker, Oregon House of Representatives, Salem, OR (2007-2009); Member, District 46, Oregon House of Representatives, Salem, OR (1999-2009); Minority Leader, Oregon

House of Representatives, Salem, OR (2003-2007); Executive Director, World Affairs Council of Oregon (1996-2003); Director of Housing Development, Human Solutions (1995-1996); Executive Director, Habitat for Humanity, Portland/Metro East, OR (1991-1994); Managing Partner, Computer Medics (1989-1991); Analyst, Congressional Budget Office (1985-1989); Presidential Intern (1982-1985) **CIV:** Board of Trustees, WorldOregon (World Affairs Council of Oregon) **PA:** Democrat **RE:** Protestant

MERLO, LARRY J., T: Chief Executive Officer and President **I:** Pharmaceuticals **CN:** CVS Health Corporation **PB:** Pittsburgh **SC:** PA/USA **ED:** Bachelor's Degree, University of Pittsburgh School of Pharmacy **C:** President, Chief Executive Officer, CVS Health Corporation (formerly CVS Caremark Corporation), Woonsocket, RI (2011-Present); President, Chief Operating Officer, CVS Caremark Corporation, Woonsocket, RI (2010-2011); Executive Vice President, CVS Caremark Corporation, Woonsocket, RI (2007-2010); President, CVS Pharmacy Inc., Woonsocket, RI (2007-2011); Executive Vice President, Stores, CVS Corporation, Woonsocket, RI (2000-2007); Executive Vice President, Stores, CVS Pharmacy, Inc., Woonsocket, RI (1998-2000); Senior Vice President, Stores, CVS Pharmacy, Inc., Woonsocket, RI (1994-1998) **CR:** Board of Directors, CVS Caremark Corp. (2010-Present); Former Chairman, Vice Chairman, National Association Chain Drug Stores (NACDS) (2009-2010); Member, Business Roundtable, Member, Board, Executive Committee, National Association Chain Drug Stores (NACDS) **CIV:** Board Trustee, University of Pittsburgh

MERRELL, RICHARD G., T: Electronics Systems Engineer (Retired) **I:** Engineering **DOB:** 01/16/1937 **PB:** Bald Knob **SC:** AR/USA **PT:** Leroy G. Merrell; Callie I. (Beavers) Merrell **MS:** Married **SPN:** Aprildawn D. Messerschmidt (06/22/1963) **CH:** Christopher G.; Kelly E. **ED:** MSEE, Illinois Institute of Technology, Chicago, IL (1974); BSEE, Illinois Institute of Technology, Chicago, IL, With Distinction (1970); BSEE, Valparaiso Technical Institute, Valparaiso, IL (1962) **C:** Electronic Engineer, GFI Genfare (1999-2003); Electronic Systems Engineer, Baxter Healthcare Corp., Round Lake, IL (1997-1998); Technical Recruiter, TSC Management Services Group (1993-1996); Technical Recruiter, Executive Search Network, Arlington Heights, IL (1991-1992); Electronic Engineering Manager, Zenith Electronics Corp., Glenview, IL (1981-1991); Electronic Engineering Manager, Oak Industries, Crystal Lake, IL (1978-1981); Senior Consultant Engineer, Zenith Electronics Corp., Glenview, IL (1968-1978); Electronic Engineer, Motorola, Inc., Chicago, IL (1962-1968) **CR:** Part-Time Instructor, Illinois Institute of Technology, Chicago, IL (1974-1982) **CIV:** Member, Illinois District 19 Board of Education, Hebron, IL (1995-1997, 1985-1993); Vice President, Illinois District 19 Board of Education, Hebron, IL (1991-1993); Coach, Girls' Softball and Little League Baseball, Hebron, IL (1984-1991); Volunteer, McHenry County Conservation Group **MIL:** Ranked SA for Seaman Apprentice, U.S. Navy (1954-1955) **CW:** Contributor, Articles, Professional Journals; Co-Author, Numerous Technical Papers; 28 Patents in the Field **AW:** "Best Paper" Award for the Year, Paper, Digital Vertical Sync System **MEM:** Former Senior Member, IEEE (Institute of Electrical and Electronic Engineers); Former Member, Adcom (Administrative Committee) of the Consumer Electronics Group of IEEE **MH:** Albert Nelson Marquis Lifetime Achievement Award **B/I:** Mr. Merrell became involved in his profession because one of his high school teachers was an electrical engineer and influenced him to go down that path. **AV:** Camping; Fishing; Traveling; Spectator sports; Exercising **RE:** Lutheran

MERRITT, MARYTHERESE, T: Geologist; Industry Analyst **I:** Sciences **DOB:** 07/21/1933 **PB:** Detroit **SC:** MI/USA **PT:** James F. William; Berenice Columbia (Franchere) Best **MS:** Divorced **SPN:** Z.S. Merritt (07/12/1956, Divorced 12/1978, Deceased 2020) **CH:** Aline Elizabeth; Dennis Samuel **ED:** BS in Geology, University Wyoming, with Honors (1956) **CT:** Registered Geologist, State of Wyoming **C:** Consultant (2001-2004); Retired (2001); Industry Analyst, International, Marathon Oil Co., Houston, Texas (1993-2001); Industry Analyst, Continental Division, Marathon Oil Company, Houston, Texas (1991-1993); Continental Regional Scout, Marathon Oil Company, Houston, Texas (1987-1990); Rocky Mountain Regional Analyst, Marathon Oil Company, Casper, WY (1980-1987); Geologist, Assistant Manager, Chief Scout, Hotline Energy Reports, Casper, WY (1978-1980); Consultant Landman, Inexco, Casper, WY (1968-1970); Geologist, Wolf Ridge Minerals, Glenwood Springs, CO (1967-1968); Geologist, GeoScout Petroleum Service, Salt Lake City, Utah (1964-1966) **CIV:** Numerous Memberships, Museums and Organizations **MEM:** Executive Vice President, International Oil Scouts Association (1989-1991); Vice President, International Oil Scouts Association (1986-1989); Board of Directors, International Oil Scouts Association; American Association of Petroleum Geologists; Wyoming Association of Petroleum Geologists; Rocky Mount Association Geologists; The Phi Beta Kappa Society **AV:** Archeology; Camping **PA:** Independent **RE:** Roman Catholic

MERSHON, JERRY L., T: Retired Judge **I:** Law and Legal Services **DOB:** 09/25/1933 **PB:** Oakley **SC:** KS/USA **PT:** Louis Mershon; Edith Mershon **MS:** Married **SPN:** Jacqueline L. Page (04/21/1957) **CH:** Diane; Michelle; Daniel **ED:** JD, Washburn University (1961); BS, Kansas State University (1955) **C:** Retired (1997); Administrative Judge, 21st Judicial District of Kansas, Riley County Court, Manhattan, KS (1982-1997); District Judge, 21st Judicial District of Kansas, Riley County Court, Manhattan, KS (1978-1997); Associate District Judge, 21st Judicial District of Kansas, Riley County Court, Manhattan, KS (1977-1978); Probate Judge, 21st Judicial District of Kansas, Riley County Court, Manhattan, KS (1965-1976); Private Practice, Manhattan, KS (1961-1965) **CR:** Appointed Member, District Magistrate Manual and Certification Committee, Kansas Supreme Court (1977-1978); District Court Records Committee, Kansas Judicial Council (1977-1978); Kansas Delegate, National Conference of Special Court Judges (1973); Business Law Instructor, Kansas State University (1963-1964); Standing Family Law Advisory Committee; Past Member, Governor's Committee on Criminal Administration; Lecturer, Various Summer Colleges and Training Sessions **CIV:** Board Fellows, National Center For Juvenile Justice, Pittsburgh, PA (1996); Board of Directors, Kansas Corporation for Change-Children's Issues, Riley County Family Services Council, Riley County Community; Past President, Advisor, Manhattan Unit National Council on Alcoholism and Drug Education; Past Member, Past Vice-Chairman, Board of Directors, Memorial Hospital, Manhattan, KS **MIL:** 1st Lieutenant, U.S. Air Force (1955-1958) **CW:** Contributor, Articles, Washburn Law Journal; Contributor, Articles, Juvenile and Family Court Journal; Contributor, National Council of Juvenile and Family Court Judges Textbook; Contributor, Articles, Kansas Family Law Quarterly **AW:** Kansas Supreme Court Justice Award (1996); Faculty Meritorious Service Award, National College of Juvenile and Family

Law (1995); Service to Children Award, Governors Conference for the Prevention of Child Abuse (1987); Lawyers Helping People Award, Kansas Trial Lawyers (1986); Outstanding Participant Award, Summer College II, National College of Juvenile Justice, Reno, NV (1975); Listee, Outstanding Young Men in America (1967); Distinguished Service Award, City of Manhattan (1967); Outstanding Young Man Award (1967) **MEM:** The Kansas Advisory Group on Juvenile Justice and Delinquency Prevention (2004-2007); Executive Committee, Secretary-Treasurer, President Kansas District Judges Association (1987-1989); Judicial Administration Division, Juvenile and Family Law Committee, American Bar Association; Publications Policy Group, National Council of Juvenile and Family Court Judges; National Conference of State and Trial Court Judges; National College of Probate Judges; National Association of Probate Judges; International Association of Probate Judges; Kansas Bar Association; Kansas Council on Crime and Delinquency; Past President, Kansas Probate, County, and Juvenile Court Judges Association; Past President, Riley County Bar Association; Clay County Bar Association; Masons; Shriners; Lions; Elks; Phi Alpha Delta **BAR:** Kansas (1961); U.S. District Court of Kansas (1961); American Bar Association **MH:** Albert Nelson Marquis Lifetime Achievement Award **B/I:** Mr. Mershon got involved in his field as a result of his gift for talking to others. He started his career in journalism and then switched to pre-law, which inspired him to pursue a career in the field. **AV:** Playing sports; Listening to music; Taking photographs; Improving home and yard **RE:** First United Methodist Church

MERTON, ROBERT COX, PHD, T: Economist, Professor **I:** Education/Educational Services **CN:** MIT Sloan School of Management **DOB:** 07/31/1944 **PB:** New York **SC:** NY/USA **PT:** Robert K. Merton; Suzanne (Carhart) Merton **MS:** Divorced **SPN:** June Rose (1966, Divorced) **CH:** Two sons; One daughter **ED:** Honorary PhD in Business Administration, University of Macau (2014); Honorary DSc, The Chinese University of Hong Kong (2014); Honorary PhD, Pontifical Catholic University of Chile (2014); Honorary PhD, University National Mayor San Marcos, Peru (2004); Honorary PhD, Universidad Nacional Federico Villarreal, Lima, Peru (2004); Honorary Doctorate, Paris Dauphine University (1997); Honorary DSc, Claremont Graduate University (2008); Honorary DSc, Athens University of Economics and Business (2003); Honorary DSc, National Sun Yat-Sen University, Taiwan (1998); Honorary DSc, University of Lausanne, Switzerland (1996); Honorary LLD, The University of Chicago (1991); Honorary MA, Harvard University (1989); PhD in Economics, Massachusetts Institute of Technology (1970); MS in Applied Mathematics, California Institute of Technology (1967); BS in Engineering Mathematics, Columbia University, NY (1966) **C:** Professor of Finance, MIT Sloan School of Management (2010-Present); University Professor Emeritus, Harvard University (2010-Present); Resident Scientist, Dimensional Holdings, Inc. (2009-Present); Distinguished Professor of Finance, MIT Sloan School of Management (2010-Present); Honorary Professor, Saint-Petersburg University of Management and Economics, Russia (2011); John & Natty McArthur University Professor, Harvard University, Boston, MA (1998-2010); Honorary Professor, HEC (1995); George Fisher Baker Professor, Business Administration, Harvard University (1988-1998); Visiting Professor of Finance, Harvard University (1987-1988); J.C. Penney Professor of Management, MIT Sloan School of Management (1980-1988); Professor, MIT Sloan School of Management (1974-1980); Associate Professor, MIT Sloan School of

Management (1973-1974); Assistant Professor of Finance, MIT Sloan School of Management (1970-1973); Research Assistant, Economics Instructor, Massachusetts Institute of Technology, Cambridge, MA (1968-1970) **CR:** Chairman, Board of Directors, Daedalus Software, Inc. (2008-Present); Member, Competitive Markets Advisory Council, Chicago Mercantile Exchange (CME Group, Inc.) (2004-Present); Board of Directors, Vical Inc. (Now Brickell Biotech, Inc.) (2002-Present); Research Associate, National Bureau of Economic Research (1979-Present); Board of Directors, Dimensional SmartNest LLC (2010-2014); Senior Adviser, Platinum Grove Asset Management, LP (2008); Board of Directors, Trinsum Group (2007-2008); Board of Directors, Peninsula Banking Group (2003-2010); Board of Directors, Community First Financial Group (2003-2010); Board of Directors, Dimensional Funds (2003-2009); Co-Founder, Chief Scientific Officer, Board of Directors, Integrated Finance, Ltd. (2002-2007); Board of Directors, MF Risk, Inc. (2001-2009); Member, Advisory Board, nuServe (2001-2004); Member, Advisory Board, eCredit. com (2000-2002); Senior Adviser, J.P. Morgan & Company, Inc. (1999-2000); Co-Founder, Member, Management Committee, Long-term Capital Management, L.P., Greenwich, CT (1993-1999); Senior Adviser, Salomon Inc. (1988-1992); Board of Directors, Travelers Investment Management Company (1987-1991); Board of Directors, Nova Fund (1980-1988) **CIV:** Member, International Advisory Board, Middle East Science Fund (2008-Present); Board of Advisers, Santa Clara University Center of Innovation in Finance and Investment (2008-Present); Honorary Member, Board of Directors, Angelo Roncalli International Committee (2003-Present); Honorary Member, Board of Directors, International Raoul Wallenberg Foundation (2003-Present); Board of Trustees, College Retirement Equities Fund (1988-1996) **CW:** Advisory Editor, Review of Developmental Finance (2009-Present); Co-Editor, Annual Review of Financial Economics (2007-Present); Author, "Teacher's Manual for Cases in Financial Engineering: Applied Studies of Financial Innovation" (1996); Co-Author, "Cases in Financial Engineering: Applied Studies of Financial Innovation" (1995); Author, "The Global Financial System: A Functional Perspective" (1995); Associate Editor, Journal of Banking and Finance (1977-1979, 1992-2003); Associate Editor, Journal of Fixed Income (1991-2012); Author, "Continuous-Time Finance" (1990); Associate Editor, Geneva Papers Risk and Insurance (1989-1996); Associate Editor, Journal of Financial Economics (1977-1983); Associate Editor, Journal of Money, Credit and Banking (1974-1979); Associate Editor, Journal of Finance (1973-1977); Associate Editor, International Economic Review (1972-1977); Editor, "The Collected Scientific Papers of Paul A. Samuelson" (1972); Contributor, Numerous Articles to Professional Journals **AW:** Finance Diamond Prize, Fundacion de Investigacion IMEF, Mexico (2017); Lifetime Achievement Award, Financial Intermediation Research Society (2014); Excellence Award, World Federation Exchanges (2013); Group Melamed-Arditti Innovation Award, CME Group, Inc. (2011); Hamilton Medal, Royal Irish Academy (2010); Kolmogorov Medal, University of London (2010); Robert A. Muh. Award, Massachusetts Institute of Technology (2009); Excellence Award, Hastings on Hudson High School (2009); Tjailing C. Koopmans Asset Award, Tilburg University (2009); Distinguished Finance Educator Award, Finance Education Association (2008); One of the 40 People of Power and Influence in Finance, Institutional Investor Magazine (2007); PRIMIA Higher Standard Award, Professional Risk Managers' International Association (2006); Nicholas Molodovsky Award, Association for Investment Management & Research

(Now CFA Institute) (2003); Lifetime Achievement Award, Risk Magazine (2003); Risk Hall of Fame, Risk Magazine (2002); Lifetime Achievement Award, Boston University (1999); Distinguished Alumni Award, California Institute of Technology (1999); Inductee, Derivatives Hall of Fame, Derivatives Strategy Magazine (1998); Michael I. Pupin Medal, Columbia University (1998); Co-Recipient, Nobel Prize in Economics (1997); FORCE Award for Financial Innovation, Duke University's Fuqua School of Business (1993); Senior Financial Engineer of the Year Award, International Association of Financial Engineers (Now International Association for Quantitative Finance) (1993); International INA-Academia Nazionale dei Lincei Prize, National Academy of Lincei, Rome, Italy (1993); Distinguished Scholar Award, Eastern Finance Association (1989); Roger Murray Prize, Institute of Quantitative Research in Finance (Now Q Group) (1985, 1986); Leo Melamed Prize, The University of Chicago (1983); Salgo-Noren Award for Excellence in Teaching, Massachusetts Institute of Technology (1971-1972) **MEM:** President, Society for Financial Studies (1993); Board of Directors, American Finance Association (1982-1984, 1987-1988); President, American Finance Association (1986); Fellow, The Econometric Society; Fellow, American Academy of Arts & Sciences; Fellow, Financial Management Association International; Fellow, American Finance Association; Fellow, International Association of Financial Engineers (Now International Association for Quantitative Finance); National Academy of Sciences; Society for Financial Studies; Honorary Member, Bachelier Finance Society; The Tau Beta Pi Association, Inc.; Sigma Xi, The Scientific Research Honor Society

MESSENGER, TONY, T: Columnist **I:** Writing and Editing **CN:** St. Louis Post-Dispatch **PB:** Littleton **SC:** CO/USA **ED:** Coursework, Loyola University Chicago **C:** Metro Columnist, St. Louis Post-Dispatch (2016-Present); Editorial Page Editor, St. Louis Post-Dispatch (2012-2016); Capital Correspondent, Political Columnist, Jefferson City Bureau, St. Louis Post-Dispatch (2008-2012); Editorial Page Editor, Springfield News-Leader (2006-2008); Columnist, Editor, Columbia Daily Tribune (1999-2006); Journalist, Yuma Pioneer, Yuma, CO **AW:** Pulitzer Prize for Commentary (2019); Missouri Honor Medal for Distinguished Service in Journalism, University of Missouri School of Journalism (2016); Co-Finalist, Pulitzer Prize for Commentary (2015); Sigma Delta Chi Award for Editorial Writing (2014); Burl Osborne Editorial Leadership Award, American Society of News Editors (2014); Co-Recipient, Walker Stone Editorial Writing Award, Scripps Howard Foundation (2014) **MEM:** Society of Professional Journalists; American Society of New Editors; Scripps Howard Foundation

MESSIER, MARK DOUGLAS, T: Retired Professional Hockey Player **I:** Athletics **DOB:** 01/18/1961 **PB:** St. Albert **SC:** Alberta/Canada **PT:** Doug Messier; Mary-Jean (Dea) Messier **MS:** Married **SPN:** Kim Clark **CH:** Lyon; Douglas; Paul; Jacqueline Jean **C:** Spokesperson, NHL Coverage, Rogers Communications (2014-Present); Special Assistant to President, New York Rangers, NHL (2009-2013); Center, Captain, New York Rangers, NHL (2000-2005); Center, Captain, Vancouver Canucks, NHL (1997-2000); Center, Captain, New York Rangers, NHL (1991-1997); Captain, Edmonton Oilers, NHL (1988-1991); Center, Edmonton Oilers, NHL (1979-1991); Center, Cincinnati Stingers, World Hockey Association (1979); Center, Indianapolis Racers, World Hockey Association (1978); Hockey Analyst, "NHL on Versus"; Guest Commentator, "NHL on NBC" **AW:** Named One of the 100 Greatest NHL

Players in History (1998, 2017); Named to Order of Hockey in Canada (2013); Named Officer, Order of Canada (2017); Inaugural Legends of the Game Inductee, World Hockey Association Hall of Fame (2010); Lester Patrick Trophy (2009); Named to Hockey Hall of Fame (2007); Named to NHL All-star Game (1982-1984, 1986, 1988-1992, 1994, 1996-1998, 2000, 2004); Winner, New York Rangers, Stanley Cup (1994); Winner, Edmonton Oilers, Stanley Cup (1984, 1985, 1987, 1988, 1990); Hart Memorial Trophy (1990, 1992); Named NHL Player of Year, Sporting News (1990, 1992); Named to Sporting News All-Star Team (1981-1982, 1982-1983, 1989-1990, 1991-1992); Lester B. Pearson Award (1989-1990, 1991-1992); Conn Smythe Trophy (1984)

MESSING, DEBRA LYNN, T: Actress **I:** Media & Entertainment **DOB:** 08/15/1968 **PB:** Brooklyn **SC:** NY/USA **PT:** Brian Messing; Sandra (Simons) Messing **MS:** Divorced **SPN:** Daniel Zelman (09/03/2000, Divorced 03/01/2016) **CH:** Roman Walker **ED:** MFA, New York University; BA in Theater, Brandeis University, Summa Cum Laude (1990) **CW:** Actress, "Irresistible" (2020); Appearance, "Project Runway All Stars" (2014, 2016, 2019); Actress, "Searching" (2018); Actress, "Will & Grace" (1998-2006, 2017-2020); Actress, "Dirty Dancing" (2017); Appearance, "Match Game" (2016); Appearance, "Nightcap" (2016); Appearance, "Jeopardy!" (2015); Actress, "The Mysteries of Laura" (2014-2016); Actress, "Like Sunday, Like Rain" (2014); Executive Producer, "The Mysteries of Laura" (2014); Actress, "Outside Mullingar" (2014); Actress, "It Could Be Worse" (2013); Actress, Co-executive Producer, "Mother's Day" (2013); Actress, "Smash" (2012-2013); Appearance, "Project Runway" (2006, 2012); Actress, "Wright versus Wrong" (2010); Executive Producer, "Smash" (2012); Actress, "Law & Order: Special Victims Unit" (2011); Actress, "The Starter Wife" (2008); Actress, "The Women" (2008); Actress, "Nothing Like the Holidays" (2008); Actress, "Purple Violets" (2007); Actress, "Lucky You" (2007); Voice Actress, "Open Season" (2006); Actress, "The Wedding Date" (2005); Actress, "Along Came Polly" (2004); Voice Actress, "Garfield" (2004); Voice Actress, "King of the Hill" (2002); Actress, "The Mothman Prophecies" (2002); Actress, "Hollywood Ending" (2002); Actress, "Prey" (1998); Actress, "Celebrity" (1998); Actress, "McHale's Navy" (1997); Actress, "Prey" (1997); Actress, "Seinfeld" (1996-1997); Actress, "Partners" (1995); Actress, "Ned and Stacey" (1995); Actress, "Walk in the Clouds" (1995); Actress, "NYPD Blue" (1994-1995) **AW:** Recipient, Star, Hollywood Walk of Fame (2017); Excellence in Media Award, GLAAD (2017); Gracie Allen Award (2008); Lucy Award, Women in Film Crystal + Lucy Awards (2005); Emmy Award for Outstanding Lead Actress in a Comedy Series, Academy of Television Arts & Sciences (2003); SAG Award for Outstanding Performance by an Ensemble in a Comedy Series, SAG-AFTRA (2001); Numerous Awards

METAFERIA, GETACHEW, PHD, T: Political Science Educator **I:** Education/Educational Services **CN:** Morgan State University **DOB:** 07/16/1949 **PB:** Gore **SC:** Illubabor, Ethiopia **MS:** Married **SPN:** Maigenet Shifferraw **CH:** Tigist; Helina; Kaleb **ED:** PhD, Howard University, Washington, DC (1983); MA, University of New Orleans, New Orleans, LA (1977); BA, University of Nebraska, Lincoln, NE (1975) **C:** Professor, Morgan State University, Baltimore, MD (1995-Present); Lecturer, University of Maryland Eastern Shore, Princess Anne, MD (1983-1995) **CR:** Senior Scholar, Fulbright Fellow, Telaviv University, Israel (2018) **CIV:** Board of Directors, Ethiopian Community Center, Washington, DC (1997-2000) **CW:** Author, Numerous

Books, Articles, and Book Chapters; Comments of African, Ethiopian, and American Politics on TV and Media **AW:** Fulbright-Hay Fellow, Namibia; Thailand and Myanmar; China and Peru. **MEM:** American Association of University Professors; American Political Science Association; African Studies Association; African Association of Political Science **MH:** Albert Nelson Marquis Lifetime Achievement Award; Marquis Who's Who Top Professional **B/I:** Dr. Metaferia became involved in his profession because he was born in Ethiopia and grew up in the 1960s during the height of the Cold War. He became interested in political science after witnessing several movements around the world, some of which being the civil rights movement and the student uprisings in Africa and Latin America. He came to the University of Nebraska and completed an undergraduate degree in two and a half years; in the following years, he earned a master's at the University of New Orleans, and PhD in political science from Howard University, Washington, DC. His dissertation was carried out in Zambia, Africa and focused on human resource development; especially the training of civil servants for national development. **AV:** Reading

METCALF, LAURIE ELIZABETH, T: Actress **I:** Media & Entertainment **DOB:** 06/15/1955 **PB:** Carbondale **SC:** IL/USA **PT:** James Metcalf; Libby Metcalf **MS:** Divorced **SPN:** Matt Roth (1993, Divorced 2014); Jeff Perry (1983, Divorced 1992) **CH:** Zoe; Mae Akins; Donovan (Adopted) **ED:** BA in Theatre, Illinois State University (1976) **C:** Founding Ensemble Member, Steppenwolf Theatre, Chicago, IL **CW:** Actress, "The Conners" (2018-Present); Voice Actress, "Toy Story 4" (2019); Actress, "Roseanne" (1988-1997, 2018); Actress, "Three Tall Women" (2018); Actress, "Supergirl" (2018); Voice Actress, "American Dad!" (2018); Actress, "Portlandia" (2017); Actress, "Playing House" (2017); Actress, "Lady Bird" (2017); Actress, "A Doll's House Part 2" (2017); Actress, "Horace and Pete" (2016); Actress, "Misery" (2015-2016); Actress, "The McCarthys" (2014-2015); Actress, "Getting On" (2013-2015); Actress, "The Big Bang Theory" (2007-2015); Actress, "The Other Place" (2013); Actress, "Domesticated" (2013); Actress, "The Goodwin Games" (2013); Actress," A Long Day's Journey into Night" (2012); Voice Actress, "Toy Story 3" (2010); Actress, "Strange Brew" (2010); Actress, "Brighton Beach" (2009); Actress, "The Farm" (2009); Actress, "November" (2008); Actress, "Stop-Loss" (2008); Actress, "Easy Money" (2008); Voice Actress, "Meet the Robinsons" (2007); Actress, "Georgia Rule" (2007); Actress, "The Virgin of Akron, Ohio" (2007); Actress, "Rains" (2007); Actress, "All My Sons" (2006); Actress, "Steel City" (2006); Actress, "Beer League" (2006); Actress, "Monk" (2006); Actress, "Grey's Anatomy" (2006); Actress, "Desperate Housewives" (2006); Actress, "My Boys" (2006); Actress, "Without a Trace" (2005); Actress, "Malcolm in the Middle" (2004); Actress, "Frasier" (2004); Actress, "Phil at the Gate" (2003); Actress, "Charlie Lawrence" (2003); Actress, "Treasure Planet" (2002); Actress, Two Families (2002); Actress, "The Norm Show (1999, 2001); Actress, "God, the Devil and Bob" (2000); Voice Actress, "Toy Story 2" (1999); Actress, "Ball on Farm" (1999); Actress, "Bulworth" (1998); Actress, "Always Outnumbered" (1998); Actress, "The Long Island Incident" (1998); Actress, "3rd Rock from the Sun" (1998); Actress, "Hellcab" (1997); Actress, "U-Turn" (1997); Actress, "Scream 2" (1997); Actress, "Dharma & Greg" (1997); Voice Actress, "King of the Hill" (1997); Actress, "Dear God" (1996); Voice Actress, "Toy Story" (1995); Actress, "My Thing of Love" (1995); Actress, "Leaving Las Vegas" (1995); Actress, "Blink" (1994); Actress, "The Secret Life of Houses" (1994);

Actress, "A Dangerous Woman" (1993); Actress, "Mistress" (1992); Actress, "Frankie and Johnny" (1991); Actress, "JFK" (1991); Actress, "Pacific Heights" (1990); Actress, "Uncle Buck" (1989); Actress, "Internal Affairs" (1989); Actress, "Killers" (1988); Actress, "Stars and Bars" (1988); Actress, "The Appointments of Dennis Jennings" (1988); Actress, "Candy Mountain" (1988); Actress, "Miles from Home" (1988); Actress, "Little Egypt" (1987); Actress, "Educating Rita" (1987); Actress, "Making Mr. Right" (1987); Actress, "Bodies, Rest, and Motion" (1986); Actress, "The Equalizer" (1986); Actress, "Coyote Ugly" (1985); Actress, "Desperately Seeking Susan" (1985); Actress, "Execution of Raymond Graham" (1985); Actress, "Balm in Gilead" (1984); Actress, "Who's Afraid of Virginia Woolf?" (1982); Appearance, "Saturday Night Live" (1981); Actress, Theater, Television Shows, Films **AW:** Tony Award for Best Performance by an Actress in a Featured Role in a Play (2018); Outer Critics Circle Award for Best Featured Actress in a Play (2018); Tony Award for Best Lead Actress in a Play (2017); Lucille Lortel Award (2011); LA Ovation Award for Best Lead Actress in a Play (2006); Emmy Awards for Outstanding Supporting Actress in a Comedy Series, Academy of Television Arts & Sciences (1992, 1993, 1994); Joseph Jefferson Award for Best Performance by a Principal Actress in a Play (1987); Theatre World Award; Numerous Awards

METER, KAREN, T: Music Educator (Retired); Veterans Advocate **I:** Education/Educational Services **DOB:** 06/04/1946 **PB:** Crawford **SC:** NE/USA **PT:** Alfred Arnold Thompson; Betty Jean (Connell) Thompson **MS:** Married **SPN:** Charles Louis Meter (04/19/1980) **CH:** Christopher Vincent **ED:** BS, North Dakota State University (1971) **CT:** Certificate, Secondary Teacher, State of North Dakota **C:** Owner, Burley Hollow, Crystal Lake, IL (1995-Present); Organist, St. Thomas the Apostle Catholic Church, Crystal Lake, IL (1987-1994); Owner, Music Par Elegance, Crystal Lake, IL (1980-1995); Singer, Chicago Symphony Chorus (Chicago Symphony Orchestra Association) and Chicago Chamber Choir (1974-1976); Teacher of Choral Music, Watford City High School, ND (1971-1973) **CR:** Illinois Department of Veterans' Affairs (1997-2007); American Legion Service Officer VA Medical Center, North Chicago, IL (1994-1997); Member, Women's Veteran's Committee (1995-1996); Commander, The American Legion, Crystal Lake, IL (1993-1995); Chairman, School Lobbyist LINK, Public School District 47, Crystal Lake, IL (1988-1991) **CIV:** Member, Vestry, Deanery Delegate, St. Mary Episcopal Church (2003-Present); Stakeholders Committee, Standdown VAMC, North Chicago, IL (1999-Present); Member, Rosebud Episcopal Mission (1998-Present); Veterans Service Officer, Illinois Department of Veterans Affairs (1997-Present); Standdown VAMC, North Chicago, IL (1995-Present); President, McHenry Country Veterans Assistance Commission (VAC), Crystal Lake, IL (1996-1997); Senior Vice President, McHenry Country Veterans Assistance Commission (VAC), Crystal Lake, IL (1995-1997); Treasurer, Democratic Party of McHenry County (1994-1996); Chairman, Chicago Standdown, IL (1994-1996); Junior Vice President, McHenry Country Veterans Assistance Commission (VAC), Crystal Lake, IL (1994-1995) **MIL:** Enlisted, United States Navy (1965-1973); Stationed, Beaufort Naval Hospital, United States Navy, SC (1965-1968) **MEM:** Senior Vice Commander, The American Legion (1997-Present); Post 171 Crystal Lake Service Officer, The American Legion (1995-Present); Executive Board, The American Legion (1995-Present); The American Legion Evanston Post 42 (2018); Junior Vice Chair, The American Legion (1999-

2000); Sergeant-at-arms, The American Legion (1998-1999); McHenry County Sergeant-at-arms, The American Legion (1996-1997); First Vice Regent, National Society Daughters of the American Revolution (NSDAR) (1993); National Society Daughters of the American Revolution (NSDAR); American Guild of Organists; The American Legion **MH:** Albert Nelson Marquis Lifetime Achievement Award; Marquis Who's Who Humanitarian Award **AS:** Mrs. Meter attributes her success to her independence and persistence. **B/I:** Mrs. Meter became involved in her profession because when she was 4 years old, she sang at church productions and that was how she got started. Also, her family on her father's side was very musical. She played the piano, pipe organ and guitar, and was a vocal major at Northwestern University from 1973 until 1976. **AV:** Quiltmaking; Floral designing; Freelance writing **PA:** Democrat **RE:** Episcopal

METZGER, JAMES BORCHARD, T: Partner **I:** Government Administration/Government Relations/Government Services **CN:** Metzger Associates **DOB:** 08/16/1938 **PB:** New York **SC:** NY/USA **PT:** H.A. Metzger; Evelyn (Borchard) Metzger **MS:** Married **SPN:** Agnes Hoffman Metzger **CH:** James; Elizabeth **ED:** MBA, Columbia University, New York, NY (1964); BA in Economics, Cornell University, New York, NY (1962) **C:** U.S. Representative of Sodiga (Spain), New York, NY (1986); Senior Vice President, General Manager, U.S. and Grand Cayman Branches of Banco de Bilbao, BBVA (1981-1982); Vice President, Deputy Manager (1979-1981); Money Market Manager, Banco de Bilbao, New York, NY (1977-1979); Vice President, Treasurer, Borchard Management Corp., New York, NY (1975-1977); U.S. Government, Washington, DC(1973-1975); Mini-Institutional Sales, International Business Development Staff, Laird, Inc. (1973); Manager, Foreign Department, Paribas Corp., New York, NY (1970-1971); Vice President, Treasurer, Overseas Ventures, Inc., New York, NY (1966-1970); Portfolio Manager, Investment Department, Chase Manhattan Bank, New York, NY (1964-1966); Special Assistant to Director, Office of Policy Development, U.S. Department Commerce, Washington, DC; Business Development for Overseas Private Investment Corp., OPIC., El Salvador, Costa Rica, Guatemala; Assistant Director, Office of Foreign Direct Investments, Washington, DC; Partner, Metzger Associates **CR:** Member, Dean's Council, Harvard Kennedy School; Former Member, Dean's International Council, Harris School of Public Policy, University of Chicago; Member, SELA Advisory Committee, Yale Law School **AW:** Centre College Associate of the Year (2011) **MEM:** Metropolitan Club, New York, NY **MH:** Albert Nelson Marquis Lifetime Achievement Award **B/I:** Mr. Metzger became involved in his profession because he was an electrical engineering for two years and then switched to economics because he was interested in finance. He earned his MBA in finance at Columbia University. **AV:** Photography; Duplicate Bridge

MEUSER, DANIEL, "DAN" P., T: U.S. Representative from Pennsylvania **I:** Government Administration/Government Relations/Government Services **DOB:** 02/10/1964 **SC:** NY/USA **MS:** Married **SPN:** Shelley Van Acker Heuser **CH:** Caroline; Jacqueline; Daniel **ED:** BA, Cornell University; Coursework, Maritime College, State University of New York **C:** Member, U.S. House of Representatives from Pennsylvania's Ninth District (2019-Present); Secretary, Pennsylvania Department of Revenue (2011-2015); Executive, Pride Mobility Products Corp. (1998-2008); Member, Committee on House Budget; Member, Committee on Veterans' Affairs; Member, Committee on Edu-

cation and Labor **CR:** Board of Directors, Pride Mobility Products Corp. **CIV:** Board Member, Greater Pittston Chamber of Commerce; Board of Trustees, Misericordia University; Board Member, Greater Pittston YMCA; Donor, United Way, Make-A-Wish Foundation, National Multiple Sclerosis Society, St. Jude Children's Research Hospital and St. Joseph's Hospital **AW:** HomeCaring Award, HomeCare Magazine (2006) **PA:** Republican

MEYER, BENNY LEE, T: Systems Engineer, Manager **I:** Military & Defense Services **CN:** Lockheed Martin Federal Systems **DOB:** 09/07/1939 **PB:** Redding **SC:** CA/USA **PT:** Chester Bryant Meyer; Evlyn May (Lord) Meyer **MS:** Married **SPN:** Marguerite M. Meyer (05/29/1983); Darleen Ellen Bauer (07/18/1959) **CH:** Kimberley May; Lance Allen **ED:** BA in Mathematics, California State University, Chico, CA (1961) **C:** Senior Systems Engineer, Lockheed Martin Federal Systems, Boulder, CO (1988-1998); Site Manager, The Aerospace Corporation, Buckley, CO (1972-1988); Systems Analyst, Program Manager, Mellonics Division, Litton Industries, Inc., Sunnyvale, CA (1966-1972); Systems Analyst, Ames Research Center, NASA, Moffett Field, CA (1961-1966) **CR:** Chair, SHARE, Peripheral Computer Group, IBM Users (1964) **CIV:** Volunteer, Colorado Division of Wildlife (1989-Present) **AW:** Aerospace Corporation Award for Team Leadership; Golden Circle Award, IBM; Numerous Awards, U.S. Air Force **MEM:** Aurora Stamp Club **MH:** Albert Nelson Marquis Lifetime Achievement Award **B/I:** Mr. Meyer became involved in his profession after college, when he was hired by NASA. He was placed in a special category, computer programming, because there was a shortage of scientists and engineers. **AV:** Collecting stamps; Hunting; Fishing **PA:** Republican

MEYER, DANNY, T: Founder, Chief Executive Officer, Restaurateur **I:** Food & Restaurant Services **CN:** Union Square Hospitality Group **DOB:** 03/14/1958 **PB:** St. Louis **SC:** MO/USA **MS:** Married **SPN:** Audrey Rayelyn Hefferman (1988) **CH:** Hallie; Charles; Gretchen; Peyton **ED:** Bachelor of Arts in Political Science, Trinity College, Hartford, CT (1980) **C:** Founder, Marta (2014-Present); Founder, The Modern (2013-Present); Founder, Untitled, Whitney Museum of American Art (2011-Present); Founder, Maialino (2010-Present); Founder, Hospitality Quotient (2010-Present); Founder, Union Square Events (2005-Present); Founder, Shake Shack (2004-Present); Founder, Blue Smoke and Jazz Standard (2002-Present); Founder, Chief Executive Officer, Union Square Hospitality Group (1998-Present); Founder, Grammercy Tavern (1994-Present); Founder, Union Square Cafe (1985-Present); Founder, North End Grill (2012-2018); Founder, Eleven Madison Park (1998-2011); Founder, Tabla (1998-2010); Assistant Manager, Pesca, New York, NY (1984-1985); Cook County Field Director, Representative John Anderson's Presidential Campaign, Chicago, IL (1980); Founder, Cafe 2 and Terrace 5, The Museum of Modern Art **CR:** Conti Professor, School of Hospitality Management, Pennsylvania State University College of Health and Human Development (2013) **CIV:** Co-chair, Union Square Partnership; Member, Executive Committee, Madison Square Park Conservancy; Member, Executive Committee, NYC & Company Inc.; Board of Directors, City Strength Pty Ltd.; Member, Board of Directors, Share Our Strength; Member, Board of Directors, City Harvest **CW:** Author, "Setting the Table" The Transforming Power of Hospitality in Business" (2006); Co-author, "Second Helpings from Union Square Cafe" (2001); Co-author, with Michael Romano, "Union Square Cafe Cookbook" (1994) **AW:** Workplace Legacy Award (2018);

Julia Child Award, International Association of Culinary Profiles (2017); Named, One of the 100 Most Influential People, TIME Magazine (2015); Preston Robert Tisch Award in Civic Leadership, The Aspen Institute (2012); Lewis Rudin Award for Exemplary Service to New York, New York University (2011); Named, One of the 25 Leaders Reshaping New York, Crain's New York Magazine (2008); Outstanding Restaurant Award for Gramercy Tavern, James Beard Foundation (2008); Outstanding Restaurateur, James Beard Foundation (2005); IFMA Gold Plate Award (2000); Winner, with Union Square Hospitality Group, 28 James Beard Foundation Awards **RE:** Jewish

MEYER, DARLA A., CPA, T: Accountant **I:** Financial Services **CN:** Darla A. Meyer, CPA **DOB:** 09/24/1964 **PB:** Dallas **SC:** TX/USA **PT:** Charles Robert Smith; Carol Jean Mims Smith **MS:** Married **SPN:** Tim Martin Meyer (05/26/1984) **CH:** Robert Terry **ED:** BBA in Accounting, Computer Science and Mathematics, The University of Texas at Tyler, Summa Cum Laude (1994) **CT:** Certified Professional Accountant, Texas State Board of Public Accountancy (2003) **C:** Private Practice (2007-Present); Certified Professional Accountant, Darla A. Meyer, CPA, Grapeland, TX (2007-Present); Accountant, Bolton, Sullivan, Taylor & Weber, L.L.P., Palestine, TX (2002-2006); Computer Operator, Citizens National Bank, Crockett, TX (2000-2001); Computer Operator, Moody National Bank, Galveston, TX (1990-1992); Teller, Plains National Bank, Lubbock, TX (1984-1986) **CIV:** Treasurer, East Texas Tres Dias, Grapeland, TX (2004-2009); Houston County Republican Women, Crockett, TX (1995-2005); Houston County Career Women, Crockett, TX (1998-2002); Treasurer, Grace Bible Church, Grapeland, TX (1997-2002); Treasurer, Christian Women Association, Crockett, TX (1996-2000) **AW:** Rookie of Year, Houston County Career Women (1999) **MEM:** TXCPA; Association of International Certified Professional Accountants **MH:** Albert Nelson Marquis Lifetime Achievement Award **AS:** Ms. Meyer attributes her success to God, as well as her honesty, integrity and hard work. **B/I:** Ms. Meyer became involved in her profession because of her love of computer science and mathematics. After her children were in middle school, she returned to school and pursued a career in accounting. **AV:** Spending time with grandchildren; Reading; Attending church activities; Doing puzzles; Playing hidden object games **PA:** Conservative **RE:** Protestant

MEYER, EDMOND, PHD, T: Professor Emeritus of Chemistry; Academic Administrator **I:** Education/Educational Services **DOB:** 11/02/1919 **PB:** Albuquerque **SC:** NM **PT:** Leopold Meyer; Beatrice (Ilfeld) Meyer (Deceased) **MS:** Widowed **SPN:** Betty F. Knobloch (07/04/1941, Deceased) **CH:** Lee Gordon; Terry Gene; David Gary **ED:** PhD, The University New Mexico (1950); MS, Carnegie Mellon University (1942); BS, Carnegie Mellon University (1940) **C:** Chief Executive Officer, Advanced Coal to Chemicals Technologies LLC (1999-Present); Professor and Dean, University of Wyoming (1989-Present); Professor of Energy and Natural Resources, University of Wyoming (1981-1989); Vice President of Research, University of Wyoming (1974-1980); Dean, University of Wyoming College of Arts and Sciences (1963-1975); Director, Institute for Scientific Research, Dean, Graduate School, New Mexico Highlands University (1953-1963); Head, Department of Chemistry, New Mexico Highlands University (1952-1959); Head, Department Science, University of Albuquerque (1950-1952); Chemist, Research Division, New Mexico Institute of Mining and Technology (1946-1948); Assistant Physical Chemist, United States

Bureau of Mines (1942-1943); Instructor, Carnegie Mellon University (1941-1942); Chemist, Harbison Walker Refractories Co., Harbison Walker International (1940-1941) **CR:** President, Coal Tech. Corp. (1981-Present); Scientific Adviser to Governor of Wyoming (1964-1990); Executive Consultant, Diamond Shamrock Corp. (1980); Fulbright Exchange Professor, University of Concepcion, Chile (1959); Consultant, Los Alamos National Laboratory, NFS, Department of Health and Human Services, General Accounting Office, Tennessee Valley Authority, Wyoming Bancorp (Now Wyoming Bank & Trust); Contractor, Investigator Research Corp. (Investigators Research Group, LLC), U.S. Department of the Interior, United States Atomic Energy Commission, National Institutes of Health, National Science Foundation, United States Department of Energy, United States Department of Education **CIV:** Member, Laramie Regional Airport Board (1989-2014); Vice Mayor, Laramie City Council (1998-2001); Laramie City Council (1997-2001); Chair, Laramie Regional Airport Board (1992-1997); Treasurer, Laramie Regional Airport Board (1989-1992); Board Member, Ivinson Manor - Laramie Plains Museum, Territorial Prison, Chamber of Commerce, University of Washington College of Arts and Sciences Visitors, American Chemical Society; Founder, American Chemical Society, Rocky Mountain Region **MIL:** Naval Officer, US Naval Research Laboratory (1943-1946); Retired Lieutenant Commander, United States Navy Reserve **CW:** Co-author, "Industrial Research & Development Management" (1982); Co-author, "Legal Rights of Chemists and Engineers" (1977); Co-author, "Chemistry - Survey of Principles" (1963); Contributor, Articles to Professional Journals; Patentee in Field **AW:** Centennial Symposium, American Chemical Society (2019); Gold Medal, American Institute of Chemists (2018); Honorary Recognition, New Mexico Highlands University (2017); Distinguished Faculty Award, University of Wyoming (2009); Volunteer Service Award, American Chemical Society, Mountain Region (2008); Volunteer Service Award, American Chemical Society (2006); Research Fellow, The University of New Mexico (1948-1950); Distinguished Service Award, Jaycees; Record Holder, 100m, 200m, 400m Dashes for Age 100+, National Senior Games **MEM:** Fellow, American Chemical Society; American Association for the Advancement of Science; American Chemical Society; Chairman, American Chemical Society, Rocky Mountain Region (1972-1988, 2000, 2009-Present); Chairman, American Chemical Society, Wyoming Section (1997, 2002); Chairman, American Institute of Chemists (1994-1995); Honorary President, American Institute of Chemists (1992-1993); Councilor, American Chemical Society (1962-1990); President, Laramie Chamber of Commerce (1984); Secretary-treasurer, Council of Colleges of Arts and Sciences (1972-1975); Chairman, Association of Western University (1972-1974); Director, Washington Office, Council of Colleges of Arts and Sciences (1973); President, Council of Colleges of Arts and Sciences (1971); Senior Member, American Institute of Chemical Engineers; AIC; Biophysical Society; Association of Western University; Laramie Chamber of Commerce **AS:** Dr. Meyer attributes his success to hard work and being at the right place at the right time. **B/I:** Dr. Meyer has loved science and engineering since childhood. **AV:** Art collecting

MEYER, JACK E., MD, T: Radiologist, Educator **I:** Education/Educational Services **DOB:** 10/21/1939 **PB:** Davenport **SC:** IA/USA **PT:** Russell Meyer; Ellen Meyer **MS:** Married **SPN:** Mary Jean **CH:** Heather; Hilary **ED:** MS (Honorary), Harvard University (1991); Resident in Radiology, Massachusetts General Hospital, Boston, MA (1969-1971);

Resident in Radiology, University of Michigan, (1968-1969); Intern, San Francisco General Hospital (1965-1966); MD, Cornell University (1965); BA, Grinnell College (1961) **CT:** Diplomate, American Board of Radiology; Licensed Physician, Massachusetts **C:** Member, Harvard Medical School Admissions Committee (2015-Present); Director, Breast Imaging, Brigham and Women's Hospital & Dana-Farber Cancer Institute, Boston, MA (1999-2017); Director of Diagnostic Radiology, Brigham and Women's Hospital, Boston, MA (1989-1999); Acting Director, Diagnostic Radiology, Brigham and Women's Hospital, Boston, MA (1987-1988); Professor, Chairman, Department of Radiology, University of Louisville (1985-1987); Director of Oncologic Diagnostic Radiology, Massachusetts General Hospital, Boston, MA (1979-1985); Chief of Radiology, Chief of Staff, Pondville Cancer Hospital, Walpole, MA (1978-1979); Chief of Diagnostic Radiology, Pondville Cancer Hospital, Walpole, MA (1972-1978); Assistant in Radiation Medicine, Massachusetts General Hospital, Boston, MA (1971-1972) **CR:** Professor Emeritus of Radiology, Harvard Medical School (2017-Present); Professor of Radiology, Harvard Medical School (1991-2017); Professor of Radiology, University of Louisville (1985-1987); Assistant Professor of Radiology, Harvard Medical School, Boston, MA (1979-1982); Assistant Professor of Radiology, Harvard Medical School, Boston, MA (1979-1982); Assistant Professor, University of Massachusetts (1976-1977); Associate Clinical Professor, Boston University (1974-1979); Assistant Professor of Radiology, Boston University (1972-1974) **CIV:** Examiner, American Board of Radiology (1992-2005) **MIL:** Captain, U.S. Air Force (1966-1968) **CW:** Co-Author, "Lymphatic Imaging" (1985); Co-Author, "Cancer: A Manual for Practitioners" (1982); Co-Author, "Interventional Radiology" (1981); Consultant, Editorial Board Journals; Contributor, More Than 120 Peer-Reviewed Articles, Professional Journals **AW:** Brigham and Women's Hospital Diagnostic Radiology George Marina Teaching Award (1991, 2011); Leadership Award, Brigham and Women's Hospital Department of Radiology (1995); Outstanding Administrator Award, University of Louisville (1986) **MEM:** Fellow: Society of Breast Imaging; American College of Radiology; Radiological Society of North America; Massachusetts Medical Society **MH:** Albert Nelson Marquis Lifetime Achievement Award **B/I:** Dr. Meyer became involved in his profession because his father was ill with cancer when he was in his teenage years, and he suffered considerably and didn't last long. Seeing this made him want to go into medicine to help people. **AV:** Sports; History

MEYER, MARA, T: Educational Consultant **I:** Consulting **CN:** Self-Employed **DOB:** 10/28/1952 **PB:** Chicago **SC:** IL/USA **PT:** David; Harriett (Lazar) Einhorn **MS:** Married **SPN:** Leonard X. Meyer (07/20/1986) **CH:** Hayley Rebecca; David Joseph **ED:** EdD in Educational Policy and Leadership, National Louis University, Chicago, IL (2010); Postgraduate Studies, University of Illinois (1990-1995); MS in Speech and Language Pathology, University of Illinois (1975); BS in Speech and Hearing Science, University of Illinois (1974) **CT:** Certified Speech and Language Pathologist, Special Education Teacher, Reading Teacher, General Education Teacher, Reading, Language Arts; Licensed Professional Educator **C:** Speech and Language Pathologist, Lincolnshire-Prairie View School District (2007-2009); Speech and Language Pathologist, Adlai Stevenson High School, Lincolnshire, IL (2006-2007); Reading Specialist, Learning Disabilities Coordinator, Community Consolidated School District #59 (1976-1987); Speech and Language Pathologist, Macon-Piatt Special Education District, Decatur, IL (1975-1976); Speech and Language Pathologist, Community Consolidated School District #59, Arlington Heights, IL **CR:** Adjunct Professor, National Louis University (1985-1987, 2003-Present); Consultant, Special Education District, Lake County (1995-Present); Private Practice Educational Consultant, Deerfield, IL (1994-Present); Principal educational Consultant, Illinois State Board of Education (2004-2006); Special Consultant, Avoca School District 37, Wilmette, IL (2003-2005); Special Education Administrator, Wilmette Schools (2001-2003); Assistant Principal, Inclusion Coordinator Mundelein School District, Illinois (1999-2001); Consultant, Lake Zurich Public Schools (1996-1998); Consultant Waukegan Public Schools, Illinois (1997); Project Director, Riverside Pub. Company, Chicago, IL (1993-1994); Educational Consultant, American Guidance Service, Circle Pines, MN (1989-1994); Educational Consultant, Psychological Corporation (1987-1989); Test Consultant (1987-1989) **CIV:** Area Coordinator, Democratic Party, Lake County, IL (1978-Present); Principle Committee Woman, West Deerfield Township (2016); Member, Advisory Council, Headstart, Department of Human Services, Chicago, IL (1990-1999); President, Park West Condo Association, Lake County, IL (1983-1988); Chair, West Deerfield Township Democratic Organization; Chair, Combined Community Consolidated High School District **AW:** National Distinguished Service Award, Speech and Hearing Science **MEM:** National Education Association; Association for Supervision and Curriculum Development; National Association of Elementary School Principals; National Family Partnership Network; American Speech-Language and Hearing Association; Illinois Speech-Language-Hearing Association; Illinois Principals Association; International Reading Association; Council on Exceptional Children **MH:** Marquis Who's Who Top Professional **AS:** Ms. Meyer attributes her success to her ability to work together with people for a common purpose. **B/I:** Ms. Meyer became involved in her profession because of the children. She wanted to ensure that they got the services and education they needed to survive. She started out as a speech and language pathologist in the school and became a reading specialist. She also continued her education in administration. **AV:** Serving as a swimming official; Leisure reading; Technical reading; Playing golf

MEYER, PAUL J., T: Owner **I:** Business Management/Business Services **CN:** Woodstock Woodworks & Studio, LTD **DOB:** 03/22/1958 **PB:** Fairbury **SC:** IL/USA **PT:** Marlin Henry Meyer; Jean Ellyn Meyer **MS:** Married **SPN:** Cindy (Cynthia) **CH:** Phillip; Wyatt **ED:** AOS in Furniture Design and Construction, Wendell Castle Workshop (1985); MEd in Vocational and Technical Education, University of Illinois at Urbana-Champaign (1981); BS in Occupational and Practical Art Education, University of Illinois at Urbana-Champaign, with Highest Honors (1980) **CT:** General Administrative Certificate, Type 75, State of Illinois (1983); Teaching Certificate for Grades 6-12, State of Illinois (1980); Endorsed, Cooperative Vocational Education Director, State of Illinois; Professional Education License **C:** Owner, Designer, Craftsman, Woodstock Woodworks & Studio, LTD (2015-Present) **CR:** Instructor, Woodworking Classes, Bull Valley Hardwoods (2016-Present); Woodworking/Drafting Instructor, Harvard High School, Harvard, IL (2008-2016); Interim Administrator and Director of Christian Education, Grace Lutheran Church, Woodstock, IL (1997-2002); Vocational System Director, McHenry County Cooperative for Employment Education, Woodstock, IL (1990-1994); Vocational System Director, Delabar Vocational Educa-

tion System, Monmouth, IL (1987-1990); Furniture Maker, Plant Manager, California Manufacturing/Agati Design, Chicago, IL (1985-1987); Furniture Maker, Wendell Castle, Inc., Scottsville, NY (1984-1985); Industrial Education Instructor, Highland High School, Highland, IL (1980-1982) **CIV:** Grace Lutheran Church, Woodstock, IL (1992-Present); Community Unit 200 Board of Education, Woodstock, IL (2001-2016); Vice President, Community Unit 200 Board of Education, Woodstock, IL (2014-2015); President, Community Unit 200 Board of Education, Woodstock, IL (2005-2014); Little League Coach, Assistant Coach, Woodstock Boys Basketball (2005-2009); Soccer Coach, Assistant Coach, WAYSO (1998-2009); Groundhog Day Committee, Woodstock, IL (2000-2008); Leadership of Greater McHenry County (2007); Assistant Coach of Boys Basketball, Woodstock Boys Basketball (2004-2006); Council Member, Grace Lutheran Church, Woodstock, IL (2003-2006); Friends of Woodstock Public Library Board (2000-2006); President, Friends of Woodstock Public Library Board (2004-2005); Vice President, Community Unit 200 Board of Education, Woodstock, IL (2003-2005); Treasurer, Groundhog Day Committee, Woodstock, IL (2002-2005); Call Committee Chair for Assistant Pastor, Grace Lutheran Church, Woodstock, IL (2003); Vice President, Friends of Woodstock Public Library Board (2001-2003); State Vocational Education Representative, State Superintendent's Recognition Process Committee (1990-1993); Board of Directors, West Central Community Services, Inc., Monmouth, IL; Education Committee Chairperson, Board of Directors, Monmouth Chamber of Commerce, Monmouth, IL; Community Development Vice President, Monmouth Jaycees, Monmouth, IL; Former Vice President of Individual Development, Monmouth Jaycees, Monmouth, IL; Construction Referendum Committee; Facilities Study Task Force Committee; Dual Language Committee, SEDOM; Board of Directors, Co-Curricular Committee, Architectural Firm Selection Committee; Operation and Maintenance Referendum Committee; D200 Education Foundation; Community Unit 200 Board of Education, Woodstock, IL; Woodstock District 200 Committee on Finance; Woodstock District 200 Committee on Construction Management Firm Selection; Woodstock District 200 Committee on Community Survey Development/Selection; WACEP; Former Member, McHenry County Industrial Council and the Business/Education Partnership Council **AW:** Excellence Award, Illinois State Superintendent (2016); Award of Excellence, Illinois State Board of Education (2016); LeaderShop Academy Fellowship, Illinois School Board (2016) **MEM:** Woodstock Woodworking Club **AS:** Mr. Meyer attributes his success to having a strong background in both woodworking and education. Education gave him the background to work well with others and also teach others how to do things. The Wendell Castle Workshop strengthened Mr. Meyer's woodworking knowledge. **B/I:** Since Mr. Meyer graduated from the Wendell Castle Workshop in 1985, he had wanted to be a full-time designer and woodworker. He started working at a woodworking shop in Chicago, Illinois, after graduating. The business closed after two years and he was unable to find a good woodworking business at that time, so he went back into education. After Mr. Meyer's sons graduated from high school, he was able to do more woodworking in addition to his teaching job. After they attended college, he was able to quit teaching at a high school and start his own woodworking business. Mr. Meyer became involved with this since it is the one thing that he has always enjoyed and wanted to do full time. **AV:** Singing in Grace Lutheran Church Choir **RE:** Lutheran **THT:** As Mr. Meyer works, he feels that

he can always learn more about woodworking. In his mind, one can always learn something new and then use that to make projects better. Mr. Meyer watches some videos, talks with other woodworkers, and reads a majority of the woodworking magazines for information. Although Mr. Meyer has a strong background in using woodworking hand tools, he has observed that woodworking machines have improved dramatically. At some point, using machines will produce similar quality as hand tools. As this continues to advance, it may decrease the amount of time needed to make the projects.Wendell Castle was a huge inspiration for Mr. Meyer when he attended school in the 1980s. He had a strong background and made incredible projects. Stephen Proctor, from England, worked with Wendell Castle and was another inspiration for Mr. Meyer. Mr. Meyer enjoys having people thoroughly enjoy what he has made for them. His advice to others in the field is as follows: "Make sure that you have a strong background in using hand tools. They will help you to concentrate more on your projects and also make them look much nicer. In addition, that will help you be safer using any power tool."

MEYER, STEVEN JOHN, T: Development and Investments Officer **I:** Military & Defense Services **CN:** Naval Air Warfare Center Weapons Division **DOB:** 03/17/1961 **PB:** Glendale **SC:** CA/USA **PT:** Albert John Meyer; Diane (Whitehead) Meyer **MS:** Married **SPN:** Wendy Dawn (Fullmer) Meyer **CH:** Joshua Steven; Trevor John; Sarah Diane; Rebecca Celeste; Victoriah Dawn; Jeremiah EliasIn **ED:** Coursework, Executive Leadership Program, Graduate School of the USA, Washington DC (2019); MSEE, California State University, Northridge (1991); BSEE, Brigham Young University (1987) **CT:** Engineering, Level 3 **C:** Electrical Engineer, Weapons Division, Naval Air Warfare Center, China Lake, CA (1987-Present); Electrical Engineering Intern, Radio Free Europe, Radio Liberty, Lisbon, Portugal (1984) **CR:** Telemetry Design Engineer; Systems Engineering; Project Management; Supervisor; Development and Investments Officer **CIV:** Boy Scouts of America (1987-2019); Varsity Coach, Crew Advisor, Committee Chairman, Advancement Chairman, Ridgecrest, CA **CW:** Contributor, Articles, Professional Journals; Patentee, 5 Patents in Field **MEM:** Institute of Navigation; Mercury Amateur Radio Association; Sierra Amateur Radio Club; National Rifle Association; International Test and Evaluation Association; Icelandic National League of the United States **MH:** Albert Nelson Marquis Lifetime Achievement Award **AS:** Mr. Meyer attributes his success to his wanting to understand how things work and make them better. He tends to be resistant to change. He has had to push through that resistance at times to be able to move forward. He additionally credits his ability to understand his own weaknesses. **B/I:** Mr. Meyer became involved in his profession after being introduced to the radio industry during his time as a boy scout. Ever since then, he has been intrigued by the radio and television industry. He wrote his Master's degree thesis on digitizing video and adding telemetry data into the video data stream. Likewise, his dad encouraged him to pursue the field, which only further motivated him to succeed. **AV:** Practicing amateur radio; Shooting; Camping; Fishing; Staying outdoors; Gardening; Genealogy **PA:** Republican **RE:** The Church of Jesus Christ of Latter-Day Saints **THT:** The most important part of Mr. Meyer's life is his family. Mr. Meyer and his wife have been foster parents and have had over 60 foster children come through their home.

MEYERS, DAVID W., T: Lawyer, Writer, Educator **I:** Law and Legal Services **DOB:** 07/19/1942 **PB:** Hobart **SC:** Tasmania/Australia **PT:** Philip T. Meyers; Margaret M. Meyers **MS:** Married **SPN:** Jane Arthur Meyers (12/27/1969) **CH:** Duncan; Vanessa **ED:** LLM, University of Edinburgh, Scotland (1968); JD, University of California, Berkeley (1967); BA, University of Redlands, Magna Cum Laude (1964) **C:** Of Counsel, Dickenson, Peatman, Fogarty, Napa, CA (2008-2015); Partner, Dickenson, Peatman, Fogarty, Napa, CA (1972-2008); Associate, Rutan & Tucker, Santa Ana, CA (1968-1971); Tutor, Department of Comparative Law, University of Edinburgh, Scotland (1967-1968) **CR:** Visiting Fellow, University of Tasmania (2000-2010); Visiting Fellow, University of Edinburgh, Scotland (1999, 2004); Adjunct Lecturer, University of California Medical School, San Francisco, CA (1985-1987) **CIV:** Emeritus (2019-Present); Petaluma Gap Winegrowers Alliance (2019-Present); Board Member, Napa Valley Vine Trail Coalition (2009-2019); Board Member, Napa Valley Vintners Auction Board (2008-2013); Board Director, Community Foundation Napa Valley (2003-2008); President, Napa Valley College Foundation (1997-1999); Trustee, Queen of the Valley Hospital (1987-1993); Secretary, Chair, Grants Committee **CW:** Author, Revised Edition, "Human Body and the Law" (1990); Author, "Human Body and the Law" (1970) Author, "Medical-Legal Implications of Death & Dying" (1981); Contributor, Chapters, Books; Contributor, Articles, Professional Journals **AW:** AV Rated, Martindale-Hubbell; Listee, Super Lawyers, San Francisco Magazine **MEM:** Former Member, President, Napa County Bar Association (1986); State Bar of California **BAR:** U.S. Court of Appeals for the 10th Circuit (1994); Supreme Court of the United States (1976); U.S. District Court for the Northern District of California (1971); State of California (1968) **B/I:** Mr. Meyers became involved in his profession because he originally thought he wanted to be an orthodontist. However, he changed his mind because he was not interested in the required math or science courses. After some thought, he decided to go into law. His mother had suggested the profession as well. Spending a year at the University of Edinburgh really solidified his thinking that he had made the right decision in going to law school. He has enjoyed his experiences practicing and teaching law. **AV:** Bicycling; Travel; Skiing; Sailing; Writing; Wine tasting **PA:** Democrat

MEYERS, MARK, T: Executive Director **I:** Agriculture **CN:** Peaceful Valley Donkey Rescue **C:** Executive Director, Peaceful Valley Donkey Rescue; Owner, General and Electrical Contracting Company, Los Angeles, CA **CW:** Author, "America's Wild Burros" (2019); Author, "Donkeys of the Caribbean" (2017); Author, "Talking with Donkeys," Volumes One Through Four (2005-2014); Filmmaker, "Without a Voice" **AW:** Named, Top 10 CNN Heroes (2019) **AV:** Photography; Filmmaking

MEYERS, SETH ADAM, T: Television Host; Actor; Writer, Television Producer; Comedian **I:** Media & Entertainment **CN:** NBC Universal **DOB:** 12/28/1973 **PB:** Evanston **SC:** IL/USA **PT:** Laurence Meyers Jr.; Hilary Claire (Olson) Meyers **MS:** Married **SPN:** Alexi Ashe (09/01/2013) **CH:** Ashe Olson; Axel Strahl **ED:** Diploma, Northwestern University, Evanston, IL (1996) **C:** Host, "Late Night with Seth Meyers" (2014-Present); Head Writer, "Saturday Night Live" (2006-2014); Co-head Writer with Tina Fey and Andrew Steele, "Saturday Night Live" (2006-2007); Writing Supervisor, "Saturday Night Live" (2005-2006); Cast Member, "Saturday Night Live" (2001); Member, Preponderate, ImprovOlympic, Chicago, IL; Member, Boom Chicago, Amsterdam, Netherlands **CR:** Keynote Speaker, White House Correspondents' Association Dinner (2011); Host, Webby Awards (2008, 2009); Host, Microsoft Company Meeting, Seattle, WA (2009) **CW:** Executive Producer, "A.P. Bio" (2018-Present); Host, "Late Night with Seth Meyers" (2014-Present); Performer, "Seth Meyers: Lobby Baby" (2019); Appearance, "Late Night" (2019); Host, "Saturday Night Live" (2018); Host, 75th Golden Globe Awards (2018); Appearance, "This is Us" (2016); Appearance, "Lady Dynamite" (2016); Actor, "Portlandia" (2015): Actor, "Difficult People" (2015); Creator, Voice Actor, Writer, Executive Producer, "The Awesomes" (2013-2015); Actor, "The Interview" (2014); Host, 66th Primetime Emmy Awards (2014); Co-anchor with Cecily Strong, Weekend Update, "Saturday Night Live" (2013-2014); Head Writer, Performer, "Saturday Night Live" (2001-2014); Appearance, "The Office" (2013); Solo Anchor, Weekend Update, "Saturday Night Live" (2008-2013); Appearance, "The Mindy Project" (2012); Head Writer, Performer, "Saturday Night Live: Weekend Update Thursday" (2008-2012); Host, ESPY Awards (2010, 2011); Actor, "I Don't Know How She Does It" (2011); Actor, "New Year's Eve" (2011); Producer, "MacGruber" (2010); Actor, "Spring Breakdown" (2009); Actor, "Spring Breakdown" (2009); Actor, "Journey to the Center of the Earth" (2008); Actor, "Nick and Norah's Infinite Playlist" (2008); Co-anchor with Amy Poehler, Weekend Update, "Saturday Night Live" (2006-2008); Co-producer, "Hot Rod" (2007); Actor, "American Dreamz" (2006); Actor, "Perception" (2005); Actor, "See This Movie" (2004); Actor, Host, Writer, Performer, Television Shows, Award Shows, Comedy Specials, Films **AW:** Critics' Choice Television Award for Best Talk Show (2020); Writers Guild of America Award for Comedy/Variety – Sketch Series (2017); Writers Guild of America Award for Comedy/Variety (Music, Awards, Tributes) – Specials (2015); Named One of the 100 Most Influential People in the World, TIME Magazine (2014); Primetime Emmy for Outstanding Original Music and Lyrics, Academy of Television Arts & Sciences (2011); Writers Guild of America Award for Comedy/Variety Series (2007, 2009, 2010); Peabody Award (2009); Winner, "Bravo's Celebrity Poker Showdown" **MEM:** Phi Gamma Delta

MICHAEL, GEORGE C, T: Advertising and Public Relations Executive **I:** Advertising & Marketing **DOB:** 07/06/1941 **PB:** Waukegan **SC:** IL/USA **PT:** Christ Michael; Tessie G. (Pilafas) Michael **MS:** Married **SPN:** Elizabeth Baly (06/20/1965) **CH:** Stacey Elizabeth; Christopher Basil; William Baly **ED:** PhD, Northwestern University (1969); MBA, Northwestern University (1965); BS in Mechanical Engineering, Northwestern University (1963) **C:** Independent Consultant (2008-Present); Chairman, Michael & Partners Public Relations (2004-2008); President, Michael & Partners Public Relations (1998-2004); Managing Director, Evans MBRK Advertising & Public Relations, Dallas, Texas (1997-1998); President, MBRK Advertising & Public Relations, Dallas, Texas (1992-1997); President, Michael & Partners Advertising and Public Relations, Dallas, Texas (1983-1992); Senior Vice President, General Manager, Bozell & Jacobs (Now Bozell), Dallas, Texas (1980-1982); Senior Vice President, Director of Account Services, Bozell & Jacobs (Now Bozell), Dallas, Texas (1979-1980); Vice President, Director of Marketing Services, Bozell & Jacobs (Now Bozell), Dallas, Texas (1977-1979); Lecturer, Loyola University, Chicago, IL (1969-1976); Director of Marketing Services, United Airlines, Inc., Chicago, IL (1968-1977); Consultant, Chicago, IL (1967-1968); Venture Analyst, Standard Oil, Chicago, IL (1965-1966); Lecturer, Northwestern University, Evanston, IL (1965-1966) **CR:** Adjunct Professor, Southern Methodist University, Dallas, Texas (1978-1982) **CIV:** Active, Public Relations Campaigns, Various Civic Organizations Including Dallas Symphony Orchestra, Holy Trinity Church, McKinney Avenue Transit Authority, March of Dimes, Dallas Museum of Art **CW:** Contributing Author, "Handbook of Modern Marketing" (1986) **AW:** Citation of Merit Award, American Marketing Association (1969) **MEM:** Founder, Dallas Assembly, Marketing Advisory Board, The University of Texas at Dallas; Board, USA Film Festival; Board, Texas Institute of Sustainable Technologies; Board, The Institute for Innovation and Entrepreneurship, The University of Texas at Dallas **MH:** Albert Nelson Marquis Lifetime Achievement Award **RE:** Greek Orthodox

MICHAEL, MAGGIE, T: Journalist **I:** Writing and Editing **SC:** Cairo/Egypt **AW:** Pulitzer Prize for International Reporting (2019); Michael Kelly Award (2019)

MICHAELIS, KAREN L., PHD, JD, T: Law Educator **I:** Law and Legal Services **DOB:** 03/30/1950 **PB:** Milwaukee **SC:** WI/USA **PT:** Donald Lee Michaelis; Ethel Catherine (Stevens) Michaelis **MS:** Married **SPN:** Dan T. Giernoth **CH:** Quinn A. Michaelis **ED:** JD, University of Wisconsin-Madison (1989); PhD, University of Wisconsin-Madison (1988); MS, University of Wisconsin-Madison (1985); MA, California State University, Los Angeles, CA (1979); BS, University of Wisconsin-Madison (1974); BA, University of Wisconsin-Madison (1972) **C:** Private Practice, Kenosha, WI (2018-2019); Private Practice, Kenosha, WI (2006-2013); Private Practice, Madison, WI (2003-2006); Associate Professor, Washington State University, Pullman, WA (1995-2002); Associate Professor, Illinois State University, Normal, IL (1993-1995); Assistant of Professor Law, Hofstra University, Hempstead, NY (1990-1993) **CW:** Author, "From Indifference to Injustice: The Politics of School Violence" (2004); Author, "Student as Enemy: A Legal Construct of the Other" (1999); Member, Editorial Board, Journal on School Leadership (1991-1999); Author, "Postmodern Perspectives and Shifting Legal Paradigms: Searching for a Critical Theory of Juvenile Justice" (1998); Author, "Theories of Liability for Teacher Sexual Misconduct" (1996); Member, Editorial Board, National Council of Professors of Educational Administration (Now International Council of Professors of Educational Leadership (ICPEL)) (1994-1995); Member, Editorial Board, "People & Education: The Human Side of Education" (1991-1996); Member, Editorial Board, "Planning and Changing" (1993-1995); Editor, "Illinois School Law Quarterly" (1993-1995); Author, "Reporting Child Abuse: A Guide to Mandatory Requirements for School Personnel" (1993) **MEM:** Co-chair, Publications Committee, Education Law Association (1998-Present); Board of Directors, Education Law Association (1998-2000); Program Committee, Education Law Association (1995); Publications Committee, Education Law Association (1993-2001); Morphet Fund Committee, National Council of Professors of Educational Administration (Now International Council of Professors of Educational Leadership (ICPEL)) (1993-2000); ABA; Executive Board, Education Law Association; State Bar of Wisconsin; Program Committee, National Council of Professors of Educational Administration (Now International Council of Professors of Educational Leadership (ICPEL)) **BAR:** United States District Court for the Western District of Wisconsin (1990) **MH:** Albert Nelson Marquis Lifetime Achievement Award **B/I:** Dr. Michaelis started out as a pre-school teacher and ended up working her way through public middle schools and then she went back to school and received her degree in educational administration. At the University of

Wisconsin-Madison, they don't focus on preparing students to be principals and superintendents, they focused on training them to be professors. She then went off to graduate school to work as her profession. Dr. Michaelis went to Hofstra University as a professor of the School of Law in the education department. She was not a professor of law in that sense, but she was a professor of education administration with a focus on school law. **AV:** Gardening; Crochet; Traveling

MICHAELS, LORNE, T: Television Producer **I:** Media & Entertainment **DOB:** 11/17/1944 **PB:** Toronto **SC:** ON/CAN **PT:** Henry Abraham Lipowitz; Florence (Becker) Lipowitz **MS:** Married **SPN:** Alice Barry (1991); Susan Forristal (09/13/1981, Divorced 1987); Rosie Schuster (1973, Divorced 1980) **CH:** Henry; Edward; Sophie **ED:** Diploma, University College, University of Toronto (1966); Honorary Doctorate, Ryerson University **C:** Chairman of the Board, Founder, Broadway Video, New York, NY (1979-Present); Writer, "Rowan & Martin's Laugh-In" and "The Beautiful Phyllis Diller Show," NBC, Los Angeles, CA (1968-1975); Former Producer, CBC, Toronto, Canada **CW:** Executive Producer, "Documentary Now" (2015-Present); Executive Producer, "The Tonight Show Starring Jimmy Fallon" (2014-Present); Executive Producer, "Late Night with Seth Meyers" (2014-Present); Writer, Executive Producer, "Saturday Night Live" (1975-1980, 1985-Present); Producer, "Sandy Wexler" (2017); Executive Producer, "Maya & Marty" (2016); Executive Producer, "Michael Che Matters" (2016); Producer, "Whiskey Tango Foxtrot" (2016); Producer, "Masterminds" (2016); Producer, "Brother Nature" (2015); Executive Producer, "Man Seeking Man" (2015); Executive Producer, "Mulaney" (2014); Executive Producer, "The Maya Rudolph Show" (2014); Producer, "The Guilt Trip" (2012); Executive Producer, "Portlandia" (2011-2014); Executive Producer, "Up All Night" (2011-2013); Producer, "MacGruber" (2010); Executive Producer, "Late Night with Jimmy Fallon" (2009-2014); Producer, "Baby Mama" (2008); Producer, "Hot Rod" (2007); Executive Producer, "30 Rock" (2006-2013); Producer, "Mean Girls" (2004); Executive Producer, "Late Night with Conan O'Brian: 10th Anniversary Special" (2003); Executive Producer, "Night of Too Many Stars" (2003); Executive Producer, "The Rutles 2: Can't Buy Me Lunch" (2002); Producer, "Enigma" (2001); Producer, "The Ladies Man" (2000); Producer, "Superstar" (1999); Executive Producer, "Saturday Night Live: 25th Anniversary" (1999); Producer, "A Night at the Roxbury" (1998); Producer, "Black Sheep" (1996); Producer, "Kids in the Hall: Brain Candy" (1996); Producer, "Tommy Boy" (1995); Producer, "Stuart Saves His Family" (1995); Executive Producer, "The Vacant Lot" (1994); Executive Producer, "Late Night with Conan O'Brien" (1993-2009); Producer, "Wayne's World II" (1993); Writer, Producer, "Wayne's World" (1992); Executive Producer, "The Kids in the Hall" (1989-1994); Executive Producer, "Sunday Night" (1988); Co-Executive Producer, "Rolling Stone Presents Twenty Years of Rock & Roll" (1987); Writer, Producer, "Three Amigos" (1986); Writer, Producer, "Nothing Lasts Forever" (1984); Producer, "The New Show" (1984); Producer, "Coneheads" (1983); Executive Producer, "Simon and Garfunkel: The Concert in Central Park" (1982); Writer, Producer, "Steve Martin's Best Show Ever" (1981); Co-Writer, "Gilda Live" (1980); Executive Producer, "Mr. Mike's Mondo Video" (1979); Executive Producer, "The Rutles: All You Need is Cash" (1978); Producer, "Things We Did Last Summer" (1977); Writer, Producer, "The Paul Simon Special" (1977); Writer, Producer, "Lily Tomlin" (1975); Writer, Producer, "The Hart and Lorne Terrific Hour" (1970);

Producer, Television Shows, Specials and Films **AW:** Companion of the Order of Canada (2018); Presidential Medal of Freedom, The White House (2016); Queen Elizabeth II Diamond Jubilee Medal (2012); Personal Peabody Award (2012); Danny Thomas Producer of the Year Award in Episodic TV-Comedy, Producers Guild of America (2009, 2010); Award for Best Comedy/Variety-Series, Writers Guild of America (2009); Primetime Emmy for Outstanding Comedy Series, Academy of Television Arts & Sciences (2007, 2008); Webby Film & Video Lifetime Achievement, International Academy of Digital Arts and Sciences (2008); One of the 100 Most Influential People in the World, Time Magazine (2008); Herb Sargent Award for Comedy Excellence, Writers Guild of America (2007); Governor General's Performing Arts Award for Lifetime Artistic Achievement (2006); Mark Twain Prize for American Humor, John F. Kennedy Center for the Performing Arts (2004); Star, Canada Walk of Fame (2003); Order of Canada (2002); Queen Elizabeth II Jubilee Medal (2002); Inductee, Television Academy Hall of Fame (1999); Star, Hollywood Walk of Fame (1999); Broadcaster of the Year, International Radio and TV Society (1992); George Foster Peabody Award for "Saturday Night Live" (1990); 11 Emmy Awards; Numerous Awards

MICHALSKI, PATTY, T: Executive Editor **I:** Publishing **CN:** USA Today **ED:** BA in Journalism and Art History, University of St. Thomas (1995) **C:** Executive Editor, Digital USA Today (2017-Present); Director, Audience, USA Today Network (2017-Present); Interim Editor-in-Chief, USA Today (2016-2017); Managing Editor, USA Today (2013-2017); Editorial Mobile Manager, USA Today (2010-2013); News Director, USA Today (2003-2010); Night News Director, USA Today (2002-2003); Content Developer, Homefront, USA Today (2000-2002)

MICHELSON, LOUIS, T: Attorney **I:** Law and Legal Services **CN:** Louis E. Michelson, A Professional Corporation **DOB:** 11/24/1956 **PB:** Los Angeles **SC:** CA/USA **PT:** Irving Michelson; Sonia Michelson **MS:** Married **SPN:** Judy Michelson **CH:** Shoshana Helen; Miriam Regina; Aaron Noam; Renina Aliza **ED:** JD, University of California Los Angeles (1988); MA, DePaul University, Chicago, IL (1982); BA, The University of Chicago (1977) **CT:** CPA (1984) **C:** Private Practice (2000-2007); Tax Partner, Grobstein Horwath & Co. LLP, Los Angeles, CA (1997-2000); Attorney, Sanders, Barnet, Goldman, Simons & Musk, PC, Los Angeles, CA (1993-1997); Attorney, Loch & Loeb, Los Angeles, CA (1988-1993); Senior Accountant, PriceWaterhouse (Now PwC), Los Angeles, CA (1982-1985) **CR:** Appointed Nonprofit Director, Superior Court, California Attorney General (2003); Appointed Permanent Receiver, United States District Court, Federal Trade Commission (FTC) (1997-1999) **CIV:** Vice President, Young Israel of Century City, Los Angeles, CA (2005-2007) **CW:** Editor, Los Angeles Lawyer Magazine (1993-1995) **AW:** Chancellor's Marshall Award (1988); American Juris Prudence Award, UCLA Law (1987, 1988); AV Rating, Martindale-Hubbell **MEM:** Chair-elect, Taxation Section, Los Angeles County Bar Association (2006-2007); Co-chair, Nonprofit Organization Committee, Business Law Section, The State Bar of California (2000-2006); The State Bar of California; Los Angeles County Bar Association **BAR:** United States District Court for the Central District of California (1988); California (1988) **AS:** Mr. Michelson attributes his success to staying current in the field and keeping up with the latest developments. He is also willing to tackle difficult issues and difficult client situations, and help them get through what can be a daunting process dealing with government agencies. Mr. Michelson looks at the challenge and the opportunities

to provide a service. Mr. Michelson's motto is, "Do as much as needed and as little as possible." **B/I:** Mr. Michelson worked at a law firm and there were certain areas that were considered bearable and there were areas that the partners did not want to work on. One of the areas that they found not interesting and he did was the nonprofit area. He started in the nonprofit area; it gave him an avenue to use his skills in more than one way. When Mr. Michelson started doing his development work, he gravitated to the area that he was most interested in. He developed his talent as a speaker and the more he spoke, people became interested, and he found out that it was possible to develop work in his area.

MICKEL, EMANUEL JOHN, PHD, T: Professor Emeritus **I:** Education/Educational Services **CN:** Indiana University **DOB:** 10/11/1937 **PB:** Lemont **SC:** IL/USA **PT:** Emanuel John Mickel; Mildred (Newton) Mickel **MS:** Married **SPN:** Kathleen Russell (05/31/1959) **CH:** Jennifer; Chiara; Heather **ED:** PhD, University of North Carolina (1965); MA, University of North Carolina (1961); BA, Louisiana State University (1959) **C:** Professor Emeritus, Indiana University Bloomington, IN (2015-Present); Retired (2015); Professor, Indiana University Bloomington (1973-2015); Chairman, Department of French and Italian, Indiana University Bloomington (2009-2015); Chairman, Department of French and Italian, Indiana University Bloomington (1984-1995); Director, Medieval Studies Institute, Indiana University Bloomington (1976-1991); Associate Professor, Indiana University Bloomington (1968-1973); Associate Professor, University of Nebraska–Lincoln (1967-1968); Assistant Professor, University of Nebraska–Lincoln (1965-1967) **CR:** Advisory Board Member, Nineteenth Century French Studies (1995-Present); Advisory Board Member, Mediaevalia (2007); Visiting Scholar, University of Cambridge (2006); French Advisor, Société Rencesvals (1995-1998); Consultant, National Endowment for the Humanities; Evaluator, ALVS Fellowship; Visiting Scholar, Pembroke College **MIL:** Captain, United States Army (1963-1965) **CW:** Author, "Les Enfances Godefroi and Le Retour de Cornumarant" (1999); Author, "Jules Vernes' Complete Twenty Thousand Leagues Under the Sea" (1992); Author, "Ganelon, Treason, and the 'Chanson de Roland'" (1989); Author, "Eugene Fromentin" (1982); Co-editor, "Old French Crusade Cycle, Volume 10," The University of Alabama (1977-2003); Author, "Marie de France" (1974) **AW:** Promoted to Officier, L'Ordre des Palmes Academiques (2011); Named Chevalier, L'Ordre des Palmes Académiques (1997); Lilly Open Fellow, Lilly Endowment Inc., Indianaoplis, IN (1981-1982); Grantee, National Endowment for the Humanities, Washington, DC (1978-1984) **MH:** Albert Nelson Marquis Lifetime Achievement Award **B/I:** What inspired Professor Mickel to get involved in his career of teaching was having a wonderful high school teacher in history and Latin. He was a good lecturer and taught as if he was a professor. He lectured about world history and Latin well, which was an inspiration for him and an interest for him to go into academics. Also, an inspiration was starting in Latin, French, and Spanish in high school. When he went on to grad school, he thought about the research and decided he would do something in North African/ French literature, so, he learned Arabic. **AV:** Music; Theater; Sports; Travel; Ancient literature

MIDDLETON, REECE MA, T: Addictions Treatment Executive, Retired **I:** Health, Wellness and Fitness **DOB:** 10/05/1935 **PB:** McCaysville **SC:** GA/USA **PT:** Frank Leon Senior; Thelma Reece Middleton **MS:** Married **SPN:** Marshall Boudreaux; Janet

Carolyn Wilkins (10/19/1957, Divorced 11/1969) **CH:** Lindsey Middleton Baccino; Reece Disney **ED:** MA in Counseling, Louisiana Technical University (1983); BA, Davidson College (1957) **CT:** Board-Certified Substance Abuse Counselor; Certified Compulsive Gambling Counselor **C:** Executive Director, Louisiana Association on Compulsive Gambling, Shreveport, LA (1996-2014); Executive Director, CORE-South, Center of Recovery Gambling Treatment Center, New Orleans, LA (1999-2005); Referrals Director, Charter Medical Corporation, Shreveport, LA (1979-1989, 1994-1996); Program Director, Community Psychiatric Centers (1992-1994); Program Director, Parkside Medical Service Corporation (1989-1992) **CR:** Board of Directors, Northwest Louisiana Human Services District (2017-Present); Consultant, Louisiana Office of Alcohol and Drug Abuse (1997-Present); Former Executive Vice President, National Council on Problem Gambling (2010); Host, 11th National Conference on Gambling Behavior, New Orleans, LA (1997); Board of Directors, Baton Rouge Commissioner Governor's Commission on Alcohol & Drug Abuse, Baton Rouge, LA (1993-1996); Board of Directors, Louisiana State University Gambling Advisory Board; Presenter in Field **CIV:** Steering Committee, Clinton/Gore Campaign (1992-Present); Vestry Member, Senior Warden Episcopal Church, Shreveport, LA (1983-Present); Alternate Delegate, General Convention, The Episcopal Church, Washington, DC (1999-2000); Board of Directors, Rescue Mission, Shreveport, LA (1993-1996); Board of Directors, Shreveport Little Theatre (1990-1996) **MIL:** Captain of Artillery, U.S. Army (1976-1978) **CW:** Contributor, Articles, Professional Journals **AW:** Special Designation, State of Louisiana House of Representatives (2015); The Goldman Award, National Council Of Problem Gambling (2006); First Place Award, Louisiana Association of Community Theaters (1997); Times Drama Award, "Big Daddy and Cat on A Hot Tin Roof" (1996); Times Drama Award, Gannet News (1994-1995) **MEM:** Board of Directors, National Council on Problem Gambling (1996-Present); Former Member, Committee Chairman, Shreveport Rotary Club (1985-Present); Former Member, Vice President, Substance Abuse Counselor Organization (1979-Present); Former Member, National Association Substance Abuse Counselors; Louisiana Association of Substance Abuse Counselors and Trainers; Employee Assistance Professionals Association **MH:** Albert Nelson Marquis Lifetime Achievement Award **B/I:** Mr. Middleton became involved in his profession because he was a recovering alcoholic. Since 1976, he has felt compelled to help others suffering from addiction. **AV:** Watching community theater and sports; Listening to music; Reading **PA:** Democrat **RE:** Episcopalian

MIDLER, BETTE, T: Singer, Actress **I:** Media & Entertainment **DOB:** 12/01/1945 **PB:** Honolulu **SC:** HI/USA **PT:** Fred Miller; Ruth (Schindel) Midler **MS:** Married **SPN:** Martin von Haselberg (1984) **CH:** Sophie **ED:** Coursework in Drama, University of Hawaii **C:** Singer (1972-Present); Actress (1966-Present) **CIV:** Founder, New York Restoration Project (1995-Present) **CW:** Actress, "The Glorias" (2020); Actress, "The Politician" (2019-2020); Voice Actress, "The Addams Family" (2019); Actress, "Hello Dolly" (2017-2018); Actress, "Freak Show" (2017); Appearance, "The Voice" (2016); Singer, "It's the Girls!" (2014); Performer, "Bette Midler: One Night Only" (2014); Performer, "I'll Eat You Last: A Chat with Sue Mengers" (2013); Actress, "Parental Guidance" (2012); Co-producer, "Priscilla: Queen of the Desert" (2011); Performer, "The Showgirl Must Go On," HBO (2010); Appearance, "Paul O'Grady's Christmas" (2010);

Voice Actress, "Cats & Dogs: The Revenge of Kitty Galore" (2010); Performer, "Bette Midler: The Showgirl Must Go On," Las Vegas, NV (2008-2010); Appearance, "Kathy Griffin: My Life on the D-List" (2009); Actress, "The Women" (2008); Actress, "The Woman" (2008); Actress, "Then She Found Me" (2007); Actress, "Then She Found Me" (2007); Singer, "Cool Yule" (2006); Singer, "Bette Midler Sings the Peggy Lee Songbook" (2005); Actress, "The Stepford Wives" (2004); Actress, "The Stepford Wives" (2004); Singer, "Bette Midler Sings the Rosemary Clooney Songbook" (2003); Executive Producer, "Divine Secret of the Ya-Ya Sisterhood" (2002); Executive Producer, "Some of My Best Friends" (2001); Singer, "Bette" (2000); Executive Producer, Composer, "Bette" (2000); Actress, "Drowning Mona" (2000); Actress, "Get Bruce" (1999); Actress, "Isn't She Great" (1999); Singer, "Bathhouse Betty" (1998); Actress, "That Old Feeling" (1997); Actress, "The First Wives Club" (1996); Singer, "Bette of Roses" (1995); Actress, "Get Shorty" (1995); Actress, "Hocus Pocus" (1993); Appearances, "Gypsy" (1993); Actress, "Scenes from a Mall" (1991); Actress, "For the Boys" (1991); Singer, "Some People's Lives" (1990); Actress, "Stella" (1990); Singer, "Beaches" (1989); Voice Actress, "Oliver and Company" (1988); Actress, "Big Business" (1988); Actress, "Beaches" (1988); Appearance, "Bette Midler's Mondo Beyondo," HBO (1988); Actress, "Outrageous Fortune" (1987); Actress, "Down and Out in Beverly Hills" (1986); Actress, "Ruthless People" (1986); Singer, "Mud Will Be Flung Tonight" (1985); Singer, "No Frills" (1984); Author, "The Saga of Baby Divine" (1984); Actress, "Jinxed" (1982); Author, "A View from a Broad" (1981); Singer, "Divine Madness" (1980); Performer:, "Divine Madness," (1980); Performer, "Bette! Divine Madness" (1979-1980); Actress, "The Rose" (1979); Singer, "The Rose" (1979); Singer, "Songs for the New Depression" (1979); Singer, "Thighs and Whispers" (1979); Singer, "Broken Blossom" (1977); Singer, "Live at Last" (1977); Performer, "Bette Midler's Clams on the Half Shell Revue" (1975); Performer, Special Concert, "Bette Midler" (1973); Singer, "Bette Midler" (1973); Singer, "The Divine Miss M" (1972); Actress, "Tommy," Seattle Opera Company (1971); Actress, "Salvation" (1970); Actress, "Hawaii" (1966); Actress, "Fiddler on the Roof" (1964-1972) **AW:** Tony Award for Best Actress (2017); Drama Desk Award for Outstanding Actress in a Musical (2017); Sammy Cahn Lifetime Achievement Award, Songwriters Hall of Fame (2012); Emmy Award for Outstanding Performance in a Variety or Music Program, Academy of Television Arts & Sciences (1997); Golden Globe Award for Best Actress in a Miniseries or Movie Made for Television, Hollywood Foreign Press Association (1994); Golden Globe Award for Best Actress in a Motion Picture - Comedy or Musical, Hollywood Foreign Press Association (1980, 1992); Emmy Award for Outstanding Individual Performance in a Variety or Music Program, Academy of Television Arts & Sciences (1992); Grammy Award for Record of the Year, The Recording Academy (1990); Awards for Lifetime Achievement in Comedy, Funniest Female Performer of the Year, American Comedy Awards (1987); Recipient, Star, Hollywood Walk of Fame (1986); Jack Oakie Comedy Award, Women in Film Crystal + Lucy Awards (1985); Grammy Award for Best Female Pop Performance, The Recording Academy (1981); Golden Globe Award for New Star of the Year in a Motion Picture – Female, Hollywood Foreign Press Association (1980); Emmy Award for Outstanding Special – Comedy-Variety or Music, Academy of Television Arts & Sciences (1978); Named Woman of the Year, Hasty Pudding Theatrical Society (1976); Grammy Award for Best

New Artist, The Recording Academy (1974); Special Tony Award (1974); After Dark Ruby Award (1973); Numerous Awards

MIDYETT, SARAH OVERSTREET, OWNER, T: Author (Retired) **I:** Education/Educational Services **CN:** Bible Discoveries **DOB:** 06/04/1927 **PB:** Tampa **SC:** FL/USA **PT:** Rev. Leroy Blan Overstreet; Aldah Myrick Overstreet **MS:** Widowed **SPN:** James Thomas Midyett (Deceased) **CH:** None **ED:** Graduate Coursework, Wheaton College, Wheaton, IL (1967); MA in Biblical Education, Columbia Bible College, Columbia, SC (1954); BA in Biblical Education, Columbia Bible College, Columbia, SC (1949) **C:** Author (2010-Present); Homemaker, Caregiver (1993-2010); Missionary to Australia and India (1976-1993); Mostly Self-employed Author (1965-1976); Professor's Assistant, Columbia Bible College, Columbia, SC (1951-1965); Owner, Bible Discoveries; Developer, Bible Curriculum for Christian schools and Home Schools, United States and Other Countries; Creator, Biblical Instruction and Bible Teacher Training Material; Marketer, Christian Curriculum, Internationally **CIV:** Former Member, Edmond Road Baptist Church, Edmond, OK; Charter Member, St. Andrews Evangelical Church, Columbia, SC (now Hope Church) **CW:** Author, 12 Bible Discovery Guides Covering the Entire Bible; Author, Three Bible Teacher Training Books; Author, "A song summary of My Life," Not Published Yet; Contributor, Book, "J.T. Another Mighty Midyett" **MEM:** Association of Mature American Citizens (Amac) **MH:** Albert Nelson Marquis Lifetime Achievement Award; Marquis Who's Who Top Professional **AS:** Ms. Midyett attributes her success to having been reared in a godly Christian home, where they had Bible reading and family prayers every evening we were not in church. The conviction of God's Holy Spirit, which led her at age 12 to turn in repentance toward God and faith toward our Lord Jesus Christ, accepting Him as her personal Savior and the Lord of her life. Beginning at age 14 to read through the Bible once each year until I went to Bible college at age 18, and reading through the Bible many times since then. Having a personal quiet time for Bible reading, prayer, and personal communion and fellowship with her Lord nearly every day of her life since age 14. Having memorized more than 2400 Bible verses and longer passages by age 72—one or two each week for many years. Having the privilege of studying under godly professors at Columbia Bible College, who taught her much about the Bible and Christian living, not only through their classes but also through the examples of their personal lives. Having been mentored for many years by one of them, Miss Sara Petty. Having continued to ask for and follow God's leading every step of the way throughout her life. **B/I:** Because as she sought the Lord about what she should do, He definitely led her into that field of service. **AV:** Writing poetry and songs; Singing hymns and spiritual songs **RE:** Evangelical **THT:** If you want a life that is truly blessed and satisfying, turn it over to the Lord, by turning in repentance toward God for all your sins, and in faith toward out Lord Jesus Christ, accepting Him as your personal Savior and the Lord of your life.

MIGNONE, MADELINE, T: Biology Professor **I:** Education/Educational Services **DOB:** 03/17/1951 **PB:** New York **SC:** NY/USA **PT:** Joseph John Micceri; Estelle Lucia Micceri **MS:** Married **SPN:** Nino Antonio Mignone (12/13/1975) **CH:** Roberto Joseph; Joseph Antonio; Francesco Matthew; Stefania Angela **ED:** Doctor of Philosophy in Biology, City University of New York Graduate Center (2001); Master of Philosophy in Biology, City University of New York Graduate Center (1994); Bachelor of Science in Biology, Pace University, White Plains, NY (1973); Master of Science in Education with a Concentration in Biology, Iona College **CT:** Licensed New York City Teacher, New York City Board of Education (2000); Permanent New York State Teaching Certification, New York State Education Department (1975) **C:** Associate Professor, Chairman, Dominican College, Orangeburg, NY (2007-2012); Assistant Professor of Biology, Dominican College, Orangeburg, NY (2001-2007); Teacher, Bronx High School of Science (1999-2001); Teacher, Roosevelt High School, Yonkers, NY (1998-1999); Adjunct Lecturer, City University of New York Lehman College, Bronx, NY (1993-1994); Teacher, Mount Vernon High School (1988-1989); Coordinator, Earth Science Program, A.B. Davis Middle School, Mount Vernon, NY (1985-1986); Teacher, Humanities Program, A. B. Davis Middle School, Mount Vernon, NY (1982-1986); Adjunct Teacher of Genetics, Mercy College, Dobbs Ferry, NY (1985); Teacher, Gifted Program, Mount Vernon High School Annex, Mount Vernon, NY (1975-1976); Teacher, Nichols Junior High School, Mount Vernon, NY (1973-1975) **CR:** Outside Reviewer, PSC-CUNY Grants, City University of New York Research Foundation, New York, NY (2003-Present); Thesis Advisory and Examination Committee Member, George Tsalakostas City University of New York Graduate Center, New York, NY (2002-Present); Dissertation Examination Committee Member, Sandy Hecht Thesis (2003); Reviewer, Prentice Hall, New York, NY (2003) **CIV:** Chairman, Respect Life Society, St. Eugene's Roman Catholic Church, Yonkers, NY (2002-2005); Delegate to Representative, New York Republican Party, Yonkers, NY (1988); Ward Co-leader, Yonkers Republican Party (1986-1988); Cub Scout Den Leader, Boy Scouts of America, Yonkers, NY (1983-1988); Vice President, Yonkers Philharmonics Orchestra **CW:** Author, Review, "Moss Protonema Differentiation by Satish Bhatla," American Society of Plant Taxonomists Association Newsletter (1994); Author, Research, "Evidence for the Interrelated Actions of Auxin, Ethylene and Arabinogalactan-proteins on the Transition from Non Apical to Apical Growth of Physcomitrella Patens Hedw.(Funariaceae)"; Co-author, "Arabinogalactan-proteins, Place-dependent Suppression, and Plant Morphogenesis **AW:** Eponym, Laboratory, Dominican College, Orangeburg, NY (2014); Education and Community Service Award, American Committee on Italian Migration (1994) **MEM:** Council Member, Torrey Botanical Society (1995-2000); Secretary, Sigma Xi (1997-1999); New York Biology Teacher Association; National Association of Biological Teachers; National Science Teachers Association; American Association for the Advancement of Science; Sigma Xi **MH:** Albert Nelson Marquis Lifetime Achievement Award **B/I:** Dr. Mignone became involved in her profession due to the influence of her ninth grade science teacher. She greatly enjoyed watching how her students, who often hailed from a variety of strong backgrounds, advanced through their studies. **AV:** Travel; Piano; Reading; Gardening **PA:** Conservative **RE:** Roman Catholic

MIHALIK, COLIN, DDS, MS, T: Board-Certified Orthodontist **I:** Medicine & Health Care **CN:** CC Braces **MS:** Married **SPN:** Kim **ED:** MS in Dentistry, University of North Carolina at Chapel Hill School of Dentistry (Now the UNC Claude A. Adams Jr. and Grace Phillips Adams School of Dentistry), Chapel Hill, NC (2002); DDS, University of Texas Health Science Center at Houston (UTHealth), San Antonio, TX, Magna Cum Laude (1994); BS in Mathematics, Creighton University, Omaha, NE (1986) **CT:** Diplomate, American Board of Orthodontics (2010); Board Certified, American Board of Orthodontics

(2005); Certificate in Orthodontics, University of North Carolina at Chapel Hill School of Dentistry (Now the UNC Claude A. Adams Jr. and Grace Phillips Adams School of Dentistry), Chapel Hill, NC (2002); Certified in Advanced Cardiac Life Support and Intravenous Sedation (1994-1995); Licensure, Texas (1994); Honor Graduate, Ordnance Maintenance Management Officer Basic Course, Aberdeen Proving Grounds, MD (1986) **C:** Private Practice, Star Orthodontics, Corpus Christi, TX (2014-2017); Associate Professor, Tri-Service Orthodontic Residency Program (TORP), Orthodontic Program for U.S. Army, Navy, and Air Force Dental Officers, Associate Professor, Uniformed Services University of Health Sciences (USUHS) (2012-2014); Orthodontic Instructor, Advanced Education in General Dentistry (AEGD) Residency, U.S. Air Force, Part-Time Clinical Instructor, Tri-Service Orthodontic Residency Program (TORP) (2010-2012); Orthodontic Element Chief, Clinical Flight Commander, AEGD Orthodontic Instructor, Scott Air Force Base, St. Clair County, IL (2006-2010); Orthodontic Element Chief, Ramstein Air Base, Germany (2002-2006); Orthodontic Residency, University of North Carolina at Chapel Hill, Chapel Hill, NC (1999-2002); Assistant Director, Dental Services, Goodfellow Air Force Base, San Angelo, TX (1997-1999); Officer in Charge, General Dentistry Element, Reese Air Force Base, Lubbock, TX (1995-1997) **CR:** Presenter, "Orthodontic Appliances: Applications and Limitations," Area Dental Lab, Peterson Air Force Base (2008); Presenter, "Eruption Complication," St. Clair District Dental Society (2007); Presenter, "Orthodontic Tidbits for the General Dentist," Garmisch Dental Conference, U.S. Air Force (2006); Presenter, "C1 II Camouflage Versus Surgical Advancement," Ramstein Air Base, Germany (2005); Curriculum in Military Leadership and Tactical Organization of the Armed Services, Air Command and Staff College (ACSC), U.S. Air Force (1998); Study of Protocols for Squadron Level Military Operations, Squadron Officer School, U.S. Air Force (1996); Presenter, "Table Clinic on Stabident," Davis Month Regional Dental Meeting (1995); Advanced Education in General Dentistry (AEGD) Residency, Davis Monthan Air Force Base, Tucson, AZ (1994-1995) **CIV:** Volunteer, Emergency Room, St. Anthony's Hospital; Volunteer, Emergency Room, AMC Cancer Research Hospital; Chairman, Little Sisters Committee, Pi Kappa Alpha Fraternity, Creighton University **MIL:** Commissioned Officer, Dental Officer, U.S. Air Force (1994-2014); Commissioned Officer, U.S. Army Reserve (1990-1994); Commissioned Officer, U.S. Army (1986-1990); Platoon Leader, Battalion Adjutant and Headquarters Detachment Commander (1986-1990) **CW:** Co-Author, "Comparison of Self-limiting and Traditional Etchant Systems on Composite Resin Bond Strength," Journal of the World Federation of Orthodontists (2016); Co-Author, "Long-term follow-up of Class II adults treated with orthodontic camouflage: A comparison with orthognathic surgery outcomes," American Journal of Orthodontics and Dentofacial Orthopedics (ORTHO) (2003) **AW:** Company Grade Officer of the Year, Reese Air Force Base (1996); Company Grade Officer of the Year, 64th Medical Group (1996); First Place, Dental Students Category for Table Clinics, Texas Dental Association Meeting (1994); Air Force Meritorious Service Medal with Three Oak Leaf Clusters, U.S. Air Force; Army Commendation Medal, U.S. Army; Army Achievement Medal with Oak Leaf Cluster, U.S. Army; Military Orders of World Wars Award of Merit, U.S. Army; Army ROTC Three-Year Full Tuition Scholarship Award; Scholarship in Basic Science Award; Achievement on the National Boards Part I Award; Achievement on the National Boards Part II Award; International Congress of

Oral Implantologists Predoctoral Achievement Award; Achievement Award, American Equilibration Society **MEM:** Mu Nu Chapter, Omicron Kappa Upsilon Honorary Dental Society (1994); American Association of Orthodontists; Southwest Society of Orthodontists; American Association of Military Orthodontists; American Dental Association; American Student Dental Association; Nueces County Distract Dental Society **AS:** Dr. Mihalik attributes his success to hard work, family, and following Dr. Profit, who was a great instructor while he was in the Air Force and practicing his residency. **B/I:** Dr. Mihalik became involved in his profession because, after a year of his residency in advanced education in general dentistry, he rotated through all the different dental professions before realizing that he liked orthodontics. This was because it was an elective treatment for patients and granted him the opportunity to work with a lot of children. He has enjoyed changing their smiles and giving them a better outlook on life. **AV:** Enthusing about Acura NXS vehicle; Water and snow skiing; Traveling; Boating; Spending time with wife and daughter

MIKES, JUDITH PAULINE, MED, T: Director **I:** Other **CN:** 1) Sto-Notes 2) Western Reserve Community Band **DOB:** 12/04/1949 **PB:** Winnipeg **SC:** Manitoba/Canada **PT:** Austen Geoffrey Trevallyn-Jones; Alfea Louisa Jones **MS:** Married **SPN:** Loniel Jerry Mikes (08/02/1975) **CH:** Heather Autumn; Steven Loniel **ED:** MEd, Kent State University (1974); MusB in Music Education, Miami University, Oxford, OH (1972) **CT:** National Board, Early-Middle Childhood Music Professional Teaching Standards (2002); Permanent Teaching, Special Education, Ohio Department of Education (1985); Music K-12 Teaching, Ohio Department of Education (1984) **C:** Music Teacher, Stow-Munroe Falls City Schools, Stow-Munroe Falls, OH (1977-2011); Special Education Teacher, Stow-Munroe Falls City Schools (1974-1977); Music Teacher (1972-1974) **CR:** Western Reserve Community Band (2009-Present); Sto-Notes, Stow, OH (1982-Present); Clarinetist, Stow Chamber Orchestra (1998-2018); Director, Stow Youth Symphony (1987-2015); Practice Assessor, State of Ohio; Presenter in Field **CIV:** Reflection's Contest Adjudicator, Parent–Teacher Association (1997-2011); Parent–Teacher Association, Stow-Munroe Falls, OH (1972-2011) **CW:** Presenter, Conference, Greater Akron Mathematics Educators Society (2004); Presenter, Conference, National Board for Professional Teaching Standards, Washington DC (2003); Selected Exhibitor, "Music, Math, and Graphing with Technology," Student Achievement Fair, Capital Conference (2003); Selected Exhibitor, "Teaching Music Literacy with Recorders," Student Achievement Fair, Capital Conference (2002) **AW:** Grantee, Impact II Disseminator Grant Award, Summit Education Initiative (2003-2004); Governors Educational Leadership Award, Ohio (2003); Recognition of Excellence Award, Ohio Coalition of Board Certified Teachers (2003); Outstanding Educator of the Year, Fishcreek Elementary PTA (2003); Master Cadre, Teachers Technology, Summit Education Initiative (2003); 25 Years of Service Award, Ohio Music Educators Association (2001); Golden Rule Award, JC Penny (1996); Distinguished Alumni Award, Exceptionally Talented Children All-American Youth Show Choir (1992) **MEM:** Program Instructor, Planning Committee, Residential Camp Design Team (2005-Present); Master Cadre, Steering Committee, Teachers in Technology (2004-Present); College Liaison, North Coast Kodaly Association (2002-Present); Building Representative, Stow Teachers Association (2003-2005); Second Vice President, Parent Teacher Association (1976-1977); Building Representative, Stow Teachers

Association (1975-1977); National Education Association; Ohio Music Educators Association; North Eastern Ohio Education Association; Ohio Education Association; Organization of American Kodaly Educators; Midwest Kodaly Music Educators Association **MH:** Albert Nelson Marquis Lifetime Achievement Award; Marquis Who's Who Top Professional **B/I:** Ms. Mikes became involved in her industry because her family members played music and inspired her to do the same. Her father played the banjo, and both her mother and father sang in the church choir, which she eventually joined with them. **AV:** Traveling; Playing in band and orchestra; Sto-Notes singing group

MIKKELSON, RUTH LYNN, PHD, T: Mathematics Educator (Retired) **I:** Education/Educational Services **CN:** University of Wisconsin, Milwaukee **DOB:** 12/15/1946 **PB:** Duluth **SC:** MN/USA **PT:** Harold Louis Larson; Margaret (Chapman) Larson **MS:** Married **SPN:** Dennis John Mikkelson (06/10/1950) **CH:** Christopher (Math and Computers) **ED:** PhD in Mathematics, University of Wisconsin-Milwaukee (1977); MS in Mathematics, University of Wisconsin-Milwaukee (1970); BS in Mathematics, University of Minnesota Duluth (1968); BS in Chemistry, University of Minnesota Duluth (1968) **C:** Scientific Data Analysis, Spallation Neutron Source, Oakridge, TN (2009-2013); Scientific Data Analysis, Argonne National Labs (2000-2008); Professor, University of Wisconsin, Stout, Menomonie, WI (1994-2006); Associate Professor, University of Wisconsin, Stout, Menomonie, WI (1990-1994); Assistant Professor of Mathematics, University of Wisconsin-Stout, Menomonie, WI (1983-1990); Lecturer, University of Wisconsin, Menomonie, WI (1980-1981, 1982-1983); Lecturer, University of Wisconsin-Eau Claire (1981-1982); Lecturer, University of Wisconsin, Milwaukee, WI (1977-1980) **CIV:** Treasurer, Faith Lutheran Church, Menomonie, WI (1984-1988) **CW:** Contributor, Articles, Professional Journals **MEM:** Former Member, American Mathematical Society **MH:** Albert Nelson Marquis Lifetime Achievement Award **AS:** Dr. Mikkelson attributes her success to coming from a family of farmers and educators. **B/I:** Dr. Mikkelson became involved in her profession because she always loved math and sciences. Her education was always priority. Dr. Mikkelson's husband is also involved with the sciences, scientific computing especially, with which she helped him.

MILES, BRADLEY ROBERT, T: Rancher, Construction and Design Consultant **I:** Agriculture **DOB:** 01/28/1944 **PB:** Modesto **SC:** CA/USA **PT:** Harold Bradley; Claire (Widmer) Miles **MS:** Married **SPN:** Emily Brown (11/23/1971) **CH:** Rebekah Emilia; Wesley Berrien **ED:** Bachelor of Fine Arts, Master of Fine Arts, Otis Art Institute, Los Angeles, CA (1972); Coursework, Edinburgh College of Art, The University of Edinburgh, Edinburgh, Scotland (1967-1968); Associate of Arts, Santa Barbara City College (1967); Coursework, Northrop Institute of Technology, Los Angeles, CA (1963-1964) **CT:** Lifetime Credential in Fine and Applied Arts in Photography, California **C:** Owner, Ranchito Coletero, Production Manager, Board Director, California Tropics, Carpinteria, CA (1981-2005); Commercial Fisherman, F/V Havana (1980); Builder of Custom Homes, Santa Barbara, CA (1975-1980); Shipwright, Santa Barbara, CA (1972-1975) **CR:** Advisory Board Member, Santa Barbara Community Agricultural Commission (2009-Present); Consultant, Superintendent, Private Restoration, Carpinteria, CA (1988-Present); Board Member, California Avocado Commission (2002-2012); Chairperson, Carpinteria Historical Society (1985-2005); Teacher of Tractor Restoration, Carpinteria High School **CIV:** Vice President, President,

Board of Directors, Carpinteria Historical Society (1987-Present); Vice Chairperson, Carpinteria Architectural Review Board (1991-2001); Docent, Carpinteria Schools (1985-1989); Chairperson, Site Council, Carpinteria Schools (1981-1989) **MIL:** California National Guard (1960-1961) **CW:** Designer, Subtropical Pulping Operation (1990); Designer, Subtropical Packing Plant (1987); Designer, First Cherimoya Packing Operation (1983) **AW:** Carpinterian of the Year (2009); Certificate of Appreciation, U.S. Department of Agriculture (1990) **MEM:** Backcountry Horsemen of California **MH:** Albert Nelson Marquis Lifetime Achievement Award **B/I:** Mr. Miles became involved in his profession after having grown up among lemon and avocado orchards, through which he learned to graft avocado trees. After conducting his college studies in the United States and abroad, he married his wife and they ended up returning to his hometown, where they began farming. **AV:** Pack mules and horses in High Sierra; Photography; Mexican folk history; Designer and planner for buildings and homes; Writing **PA:** Democrat **RE:** Methodist

MILLER, CAROL, T: U.S. Representative from West Virginia **I:** Government Administration/Government Relations/Government Services **CN:** U.S. House of Representatives **DOB:** 11/4/1950 **PB:** Columbus **SC:** OH/USA **PT:** Samuel L. Devine; Betty Devine **MS:** Married **SPN:** Matt Miller **CH:** Two Children **ED:** Bachelor of Arts in History and Political Science, Columbia College (1972) **C:** Member, U.S. House of Representatives from West Virginia's Third Congressional District (2019-Present); Member, District 16, West Virginia House of Delegates (2013-Present); Owner, Swann Ridge Bison Farm (1994-Present); Member, District 15, West Virginia House of Delegates (2007-2013); Member, Committee on Agriculture Committee; Member, Committee on Energy, Industry and Labor; Member, Committee on Economic Development and Small Business; Member, Committee on Health and Human Resources Committee, West Virginia House of Delegates; Ranking Minority Member, Committee on Business, West Virginia House of Delegates; Ranking Minority Member, Committee and Government Organization Committee, West Virginia House of Delegates **PA:** Republican **RE:** Baptist

MILLER, DEANNA, T: Superintendent **I:** Education/Educational Services **CN:** Fulton Independent School **MS:** Married **SPN:** Sam Miller **CH:** Jordan; Mary Kathryn; Behr; Carson **ED:** PhD, North Central University (2016); MS in Library Information Science, Western Kentucky University (2004); BS in Psychology, University of Tennessee at Martin (1993) **C:** Superintendent, Fulton Independent School District (2016-Present); Instructional Supervisor, Director of Pupil Personnel, Fulton Independent School District (2010-2016); Assistant Principal, Fulton Independent School District; School Librarian, Fulton Independent School District; Gifted and Talented Teacher, Fulton Independent School District **CR:** Adjunct Professor, Library Information, Syracuse University; Adjunct Professor, Education, Department for Gifted and Talented, Georgetown College; Adjunct Professor, Education Department, University of the Cumberlands **CIV:** Troop Leader, Girl Scouts of America (2013-Present); Foster Parent (2006-2012); Volunteer, Juvenile Diabetes Foundation; State Advisory Council, Gifted and Talented Education **CW:** Author, "Gifted Learners in the Education Accountability Era" (2016) **AW:** Paul Harris Fellow, Rotary (2019); Michael Caudill Distinguished Educator Award, Kentucky Association for Gifted Education (2019) **MEM:** Kentucky Association of

School Administrators; Kentucky Association of School Superintendents; Kentucky Association of Gifted Education; National Association of Gifted Education; Wall Counsel for Gifted Education; Rotary; Alpha Gamma Delta **AS:** Dr. Miller attributes her success to the community she works in and her school family. They do great work on a daily basis, which pushes her to want to be a better person. She is also motivated to support her family. **B/I:** Dr. Miller's husband was an educator and she saw how much satisfaction he got from helping children. The more she became involved with education, the greater her need to work with children became. She lives in a high poverty area and prioritizes helping at-risk students. **THT:** Dr. Miller celebrates the good and deals with the bad.

MILLER, DWIGHT MERRICK, T: Senior Archivist, Historian **I:** Civil Service **CN:** Herbert Hoover Presidential Library **DOB:** 07/25/1932 **PB:** Keosauqua **SC:** IA/USA **PT:** Leo Albert Miller; Beryl Irene Miller **MS:** Married **SPN:** Pauline K. Leaverton (1999); Judith Spencer, (1979, Divorced, 1988); Frances Florine Olney, (1961, Deceased, 1977) **CH:** Dianne **ED:** Postgraduate Coursework, The American University (1963-1964); MA in History, Truman State University (1961); BA, University of Iowa (1959) **C:** Senior Archivist, Herbert Hoover Presidential Library, West Branch (1964-1999); Assistant Archivist, Manuscript Division, Library of Congress, Washington, DC (1961-1964) **CIV:** Co-Chairman, Iowa Sesquicentennial Commission, Cedar County, Tipton (1995-1997) **MIL:** 7th Infantry Division, Korea (1952-1954) **CW:** Author, "175th Anniversary History of the First Presbyterian Church" (2015); Editor, "Laura Ingalls Wilder and The American Frontier: Five Perspectives" (2002); Co-Editor, "Herbert Hoover and Franklin D. Roosevelt: A Documentary History" (1998); Co-Editor, "Historical Materials in the Herbert Hoover Presidential Library" (1996); Co-Editor, "Herbert Hoover And Harry S. Truman: A Documentary History" (1992); Compiler, Assistant Editor, "The Public Papers Of The Presidents: Herbert Hoover; 1929-1933 (6 Vols.)" (1974-1977) **MEM:** Advisory Board, Fort Ticonderoga Association (1991-1999); Advisory Board, Friends of the University of Iowa Libraries (1976-1981); Herbert Hoover Presidential Library Association **MH:** Albert Nelson Marquis Lifetime Achievement Award **B/I:** Mr. Miller began his career at the Library of Congress in the manuscript division. He was assigned to a project consisting of indexing the 23 presidential collections, all of which are held in the library. Mr. Miller has spent his entire career with the presidential papers. **AV:** Book collecting; Appreciating historical Iowa pottery **RE:** Presbyterian

MILLER, E. JOAN, PHD, T: Geography Educator **I:** Education/Educational Services **DOB:** 03/02/1923 **PB:** Wednesbury, England **SC:** United Kingdom **PT:** Arthur Wilson; Edith (Cliff) Wilson **MS:** Widowed **SPN:** George J. Miller (06/04/1958, Deceased 1973) **ED:** PhD, University of North Carolina at Chapel Hill (1965); MA, University of Cambridge, England, United Kingdom (1947); Graduate Certificate in Education (1945); BA in Geography, University of Cambridge, England, United Kingdom, with Honors (1944) **C:** Professor Emerita, Illinois State University, Normal, IL (1993-Present); Professor, Department of Geography, Geology, and the Environment, Illinois State University, Normal, IL (1962-1993); Lecturer, Department of Geography, Indiana University Bloomington (1957-1962); Head of Geography Department, Notting Hill and Ealing High School, Girls' Day School Trust (GDST), London, England, United Kingdom (1947-1957); Head of Geography Department, Girls' Grammar School, Batley, England, United Kingdom (1945-1947)

CR: Invited Ridgley Lecturer of Arts and Sciences (2003); Invited Arts and Science Lecturer (1975); Instructor, Graduate Courses, Cultural Geography and Life and Landscape; Director, Three Graduate Theses **CIV:** Contributor, The Salvation Army USA **CW:** Author, "An English Geographer Remembers, Part One: The War Years 1939-1945"; Author, "Atlas of Friendly Footmaps in London and Train Trips in England"; Author, "Local Geography"; Author, Articles, Annals of the American Association of Geographers, The Geographical Review, The Professional Geographer, The Journal of Geography, and Others; Presenter, Local Papers; Contributor, Articles and Book Reviews to Professional Publications **AW:** Inductee, Hall of Fame, Illinois State University College of Arts and Sciences (2009); Award for Ozark Studies, Society of Woman Geographers (1961) **MEM:** Fellow, Society of Woman Geographers; American Association of Geographers; National Council for Geographic Education; American Geographical Society **MH:** Albert Nelson Marquis Lifetime Achievement Award **AS:** Dr. Miller attributes her success to her mentors, Dr. George J. Miller and Dr. Doug Eyre. **B/I:** Dr. Miller became involved in her profession because she enjoyed teaching girls. **AV:** Gardening; Traveling; Drawing; Music **PA:** Democrat **THT:** Dr. Miller's motto is, "Just keep going."

MILLER, JEFF, T: Chairman, President, and Chief Executive Officer **I:** Oil & Energy **CN:** Halliburton Company **ED:** MBA, Texas A&M University; BA, McNeese State University **CT:** CPA **C:** Chairman, Halliburton Company (2019-Present); President, Chief Executive Officer, Halliburton Company (2017-Present); President, Halliburton Company (2014-2017); Executive Vice President, Chief Operating Officer, Halliburton Company (2012-2014); Senior Vice President, Global Business Development and Marketing, Halliburton Company (2011-2012) **MEM:** Board Member, Halliburton Company (2014-Present); Board Member, Atwood Oceanics (2013-Present)

MILLER, LINDA B., PHD, T: Political Scientist **I:** Education/Educational Services **DOB:** 08/07/1937 **PB:** Manchester **SC:** NH/USA **PT:** Louis; Helene (Chase) Miller **ED:** Doctor of Philosophy, Columbia University (1965); Master of Arts, Columbia University (1961); Bachelor of Arts, Radcliffe College, Cum Laude (1959) **C:** Professor of Political Science, Wellesley College (1975-2004); Chairperson, Political Science Department, Wellesley College (1985-1989); Research Associate, Harvard University (1967-1971, 1976-1981); Associate Professor, Wellesley College (1969-1975); Lecturer of Political Science, Harvard University (1968-1969); Research Associate, Princeton University (1966-1967); Assistant Professor, Barnard College (1964-1967) **CR:** Adjunct Professor of International Relations, Watson Institute, Brown University (1998-2000, 2003-2011, 2012-Present); Visiting Fellow, Watson Institute, Brown University (2011-2012); Senior Fellow, Watson Institute, Brown University (2000-2003); Visiting Professor of Research, Watson Institute, Brown University (1997) **CW:** Co-author, Co-editor, "New Directions in US Foreign Policy," Second Edition (2014); Co-author, Co-editor, "New Directions in US Foreign Policy" (2009); Co-author, Co-editor, "Argentina" (2007); Editor, International Studies Review (1999-2002); Co-author, Co-editor, "Ideas and Ideals: Essays on Politics in Honor of Stanley Hoffmann (1993); Author, "Cyprus: The Law and Politics of Civil Strife" (1968); Author, "Dynamics of World Politics: Studies in the Resolution of Conflicts" (1968); Author, "World Order and Local Disorder: The United Nations and Internal Conflicts" (1967); Contributor, Articles to Professional Journals **AW:** Social Science Research Fellow, North Atlantic Treaty Organization (1982-1983); Senior Fellow, Oceanographic Institution (1979-1980, 1982-1983); Fellow, Rockefeller Foundation (1976-1977); International Affairs Fellow, Council on Foreign Relations (1973-1974) **MEM:** Institute for Strategic Studies; British International Studies Association; Council on Foreign Relations; Scholars Strategy Network; Phi Beta Kappa **MH:** Albert Nelson Marquis Lifetime Achievement Award **B/I:** Ms. Miller was initially inspired to enter her profession due to the influence of Stanley H. Hoffmann, who served as her professor of government at Harvard University.

MILLER, LINDA ELLEN, T: Museum Administrator; Education Expert **I:** Museums & Institutions **DOB:** 08/31/1947 **PB:** Paterson **SC:** NJ/USA **PT:** Edward E. Douglas; Flora M. (Christen) Douglas **MS:** Married **SPN:** Philip R. Miller (09/19/ 1970) **CH:** Douglas Scott **ED:** MS in Museum Leadership and Education, Bank Street College of Education (1992); BA in Human Resource Management, Upsala College (1983) **CT:** Certificate of Accomplishment, Rutgers Cooperative Research and Extension Master's Gardener Program (2005) **C:** Curator, Administrator, Vernon Township Historical Museum, NJ (1995-2015); Curator of Education, Clinton Historical Museum, NJ (1993-1995); Educator, Kaleidoscope Kids Program, New Jersey State Museum, Trenton, NJ (1992-1993); Curator of Education, Old Barracks, Trenton, NJ (1989-1992) **CR:** Retired; Gardening; Disability Coordinator, First Reformed Church of Hawthorne **MEM:** Vice President, League of Historical Societies of New Jersey (1997-Present); Chairman, Education Committee, Trustee, League of Historical Societies of New Jersey (1994-1997); Steering Committee, New Jersey Studies Academic Alliance (NJSAA) (1993-1994); National Education Committee, American Association of Museums; Museum Education Roundtable (MER); New Jersey Association of Museums, League of Historical Societies of New Jersey **MH:** Albert Nelson Marquis Lifetime Achievement Award **AV:** Artist; Naturalist

MILLER, MELODY JEAN, T: Senior Aide, Kennedy Family Spokesperson (Retired) **I:** Government Administration/Government Relations/Government Services **DOB:** 02/19/1945 **PB:** Seattle **SC:** WA/USA **PT:** Peter Miller; Dorothy Jean (Chittenden) Miller **MS:** Widowed **SPN:** William P. Wilson (Deceased 2014) **CH:** Eliza **ED:** BA in Secondary Education Social Studies, Pennsylvania State University, University Park, PA (1967); Diploma, Yorktown High School, Arlington, Virginia (1963) **C:** Member, U.S. Senate Staffs, Senators Robert and Edward M. Kennedy (1966-2005); Deputy Press Secretary and Senior Aide (1981-2005); Assistant Press Secretary, Senator Ted Kennedy Presidential Campaign (1980); Press Assistant, Senator Robert F. Kennedy Presidential Campaign (1968); Receptionist, Office of Senators Robert & Edward Kennedy (1967-1969); Member, Washington Senate Staff, Senator Robert F. Kennedy (1967); Intern, Office of Senator Robert Kennedy (1965,1966); Intern, Office for Jacqueline Kennedy (1964); Senior Aide and Spokesperson for the Kennedy Family, Senator Edward M. Kennedy; Point Person, Long-Range Media Projects; Official Spokesperson for the Kennedy Family; Liaison for Numerous Kennedy Family Members; Speechwriter **CR:** Guest Speaker, Penn State Forum; Guest Speaker, Texas State University; Panelist, Renaissance Weekend; Manager, EMK Events and Kennedy Family Press Needs at Democratic National Conventions; Intern, Office of Congressman Joseph Montoya Mex **CIV:** Panelist, Renaissance Weekend; Trustee, Wilson Legal Support Trust; Legislative Assistant for Reauthorization of the Endangered Species Act, and Saving the Redwoods **CW:** Production Consultant, Films and Television Shows Specializing in Politics (1971-2015); Consultant, Film, "Fair Game" (2010); Writing Consultant, Commercial Spots in Support of Barack Obama (2008); Speaker, Penn State Forum (2003); Profiled in Newspapers, Magazines, and on Television **AW:** 22 Outstanding Alumni of the College of Education, The Pennsylvania State University (1988); Most Outstanding Senior Girl, Yorktown High School (1963); Inductee, Yorktown High School Hall of Fame **MEM:** President, Friday Night Dinner Club; Kappa Alpha Theta; Library and Development Advisory Board, The John F. Kennedy Library, The Pennsylvania State University; The Edward M. Kennedy Institute for the Study of the Senate **AS:** Ms. Miller attributes her success to her mother and father, as well as her college adviser, Dr. John E. Searles, and a teacher and friend by the name of Sarajane Knight. She also credits her RFK and EMK colleagues and President Kennedy's White House staff. **B/I:** Ms. Miller became involved in her profession after President Kennedy was elected. She began racing home in time to see his press conferences and began volunteering at the 10th District Democratic Headquarters. Soon after, she began canvassing neighborhoods in Northern Virginia and obtained an internship. Upon graduating, she volunteered at the Democratic National Committee and was devastated when she heard about the President's assassination. When she received the opportunity to work in Jacqueline Kennedy's office, she began her lifelong career in service to the Kennedy family. **AV:** Gardening; Taking photographs; Rescuing animals; Mentoring family members **PA:** Democrat **RE:** Protestant

MILLER, MICHAEL G., T: Purchasing Management **I:** Manufacturing **CN:** Clarks Shoe Company/ Philips Lighting International **DOB:** 06/08/1951 **PB:** Hanover **SC:** PA/USA **PT:** Reginald E. Miller; Mary Miller **MS:** Married **SPN:** Elaine Miller **CH:** Stacey Fox; Cynthia Leonard **ED:** Bachelor of Science **CT:** Certified Purchasing Manager; Certification in Teaching **C:** Teacher, Secondary Education; Purchasing Manager, Clarks Shoe Company; Director, Purchasing Philips Lighting **AW:** CPM; Teaching Certificates Football Coaching Awards **MEM:** CPM; Central Pennsylvania Purchasing Organization; Notre Dame Club of Gettysburg **MH:** Albert Nelson Marquis Lifetime Achievement Award **AS:** Mr. Miller attributes his success to his catholic educational background, as well as the support he received from his wife and his parents. **B/I:** Mr. Miller started his career as a teacher, though he quickly discovered he longed for the challenges of professional business. **AV:** Gardening; Golfing; Exercising **PA:** Republican **RE:** Catholic

MILLER, PHILIP NICHOLSON, T: Engineering and Technology Educator; Consultant **I:** Education/Educational Services **DOB:** 02/22/1947 **PB:** Providence **SC:** RI/USA **PT:** Arthur Phillip Miller; Mildred May (Brown) Miller **MS:** Married **SPN:** Sandra Veronica Green **CH:** Stephanie; Spencer; Erik; Brian; Philip; Adrian; Vonya **ED:** PhD in Industrial and Manufacturing Engineering, University of Rhode Island (2004); MS in Industrial Engineering, University of Rhode Island (1986); MBA, Providence College (1976); BS in Industrial Technology, Roger Williams College (1970); AS in Mechanical Engineering Technology, Roger Williams College (1968) **C:** Professor, Engineering and Technology, Community College of Rhode Island, Warwick (1999-2018); Associate Professor, Engineering, Community College of Rhode Island, Warwick, RI (1992-1999); Assistant Professor, Engineering, Community College of Rhode Island, Warwick, RI

(1986-1992); Manager, Training and Development, Stanley-Bostitch (Now Stanley Back & Decker, Inc.), East Greenwich, RI (1985-1986); Industrial Engineer, Bostitch Textron (Now Stanley Back & Decker, Inc.), East Greenwich, RI (1980-1985); Senior Management Engineer, Roger Williams Hospital, Providence, RI (1979-1980); Manufacturing Cost Engineer, Submarine Division, Raytheon Technologies Corporation, Portsmouth, RI (1974-1979); Standards Engineer, Kaiser Aluminum, Bristol, RI (1973); Methods Engineer, Raytheon Technologies Corporation, North Dighton, MA (1970-1972); Process Engineer, Corning Glass Works, Providence, RI (1970) **CR:** Consultant, Antaya Inc. (Now Antaya Technologies), Providence, RI (1991) **CIV:** Volunteer, Times Square Organization (STEM School) **AW:** Excellence Award, National Institute for Staff and Organizational Development (NISOD) (2005); Minority Mentoring Program CCRI (2005); Teacher Excellence Award, Community College of Rhode Island (1994); Teacher Excellence Award, Community College of Rhode Island (1993) **MEM:** Order of Engineer Institute of Industrial Engineers; American Society for Engineering Education (ASEE); American Society for Quality; Society of Manufacturing Engineers (SME) **MH:** Who's Who in Science and Engineering (1996, 1997); Who's Who Among America's Teachers (1994) **B/I:** When Dr. Miller was in junior high school, he wrote a paper on electrical engineering. He was drawn to the topic and since he was always good in math, he gravitated toward it. Dr. Miller participated in the work study program, which ran at the community college. It was a program that consisted of attending school for one semester and working in the next one. Dr. Miller really enjoyed it. After working for some time, one of his professors from Roger Williams University called to see if he would like to teach a course in quality control and quality engineering. Dr. Miller enjoyed his work, so he took the opportunity to enlighten students with open arms. **RE:** Pentecostal

MILLER, PRINGL LEE, MD, FACS, T: General Surgeon, Hospice and Palliative Medicine Specialist, Clinical Medical Ethicist **I:** Medicine & Health Care **CN:** DOB: 08/24/1964 **PB:** New York **SC:** NY/USA **PT:** Earl B. Miller; Marion W. Miller **CH:** MiEstrella "Mia" Miller-Cruz **ED:** Senior Clinical Medical Ethics Fellowship, The MacLean Center, The University of Chicago (2018-2020); Fellowship in Clinical Medical Ethics, The MacLean Center, The University of Chicago (2017-2018); Fellowship, Hospice and Palliative Medicine (2016-2017), Residency in General Surgery, Santa Barbara Cottage Hospital (1997-2002); MD, Pritzker School of Medicine, The University of Chicago (1997); BS in Biology and General Studies, University of Illinois at Chicago (1993) **CT:** Certified in Hospice and Palliative Medicine (2018-Present); Certified, American Board of Surgery (2004-Present); Medical License, State of California (1999-2021); Medical License, State of Illinois (2016-2020); Medical License, State of Washington (2004-2019); Medical License, State of Vermont (2013); Medical License, State of Montana (2006) **C:** Assistant Professor, Section of Palliative Medicine, Department of Surgery and Medicine, Rush University Medical Center, Rush Medical College, Rush University (2017-2020); Associate Medical Director, Ada F. Addington Inpatient Hospice Care Center, Rush Medical Center, Chicago, IL (2017-2020); Clinical Instructor, Acute Care Surgery, Department of Surgery, University of California San Francisco (2011-2012); Clinical Instructor, Attending Academic Surgeon, Department of Surgery, Contra Costa Health Services (2007-2012); President, Chief Executive Officer, Pringl Miller, MD, FACS, PC (2002-2007) **CR:** Acute Care Surgery, El Centro Regional Medical

Center, El Centro, CA (2018-Present); Acute Care Surgery, Yakima Regional Medical Center, Yakima, WA (2017-2018); Franciscan Acute Surgery Team, CHI Franciscan Health, Tacoma, WA (2013-2016); Acute Care Surgery, Dartmouth Hitchcock, Southwestern Vermont Medical Center, Bennington, VT (2013); Acute Care Surgery, Mendocino Coast District Hospital, Fort Bragg, CA (2013); Acute Care Surgery, Tri-State Memorial Hospital, Clarkston, WA (2012-2013); Acute Care Surgery, Mammoth Lakes Hospital, Mammoth Lakes, CA (2012-2013); Presenter in Field **CIV:** Founder, Physician Just Equity (2020-Present); Volunteer, Time's Up Healthcare (2018-Present); Founder, #WoSurgMeToo (2018-Present); Volunteer, Operation Giving Back, American College of Surgeons, Puerto Rico (2019); Operation Access (2002-2007); World Surgical Foundation (2006) **CW:** Reviewer, Annals of Surgery (2020); Guest Editor, "Surgical Clinics of North America," "Practicing Primary Palliative Care" (2019); Contributor, "Supportive Care in Cancer" (2018); Editor, "Me Too In Surgery, Narrative by Women Surgeons" **AW:** Associate Member, Academy of Master Surgeon Educators, American College of Surgeons (2019); Nominee, #IStandWithHer Award, Women in Medicine (2019); Hearst Leadership Scholarship, American Academy of Hospice and Palliative Medicine (2019); Best Surgical Consultant, Contra Costa Regional Medical Center (2009); Golden Scalpel Award, Contra Costa Regional Medical Center (2009); Teaching Excellence Award, Contra Costa Regional Medical Center (2008); Resident Achievement Award, Society of Laparoscopic Surgeons (2002); Merit Award, British Journal of Surgery (2001) **MEM:** American College of Surgeons (1997-Present); American Academy of Hospice and Palliative Medicine (2016-Present); Acting Chair, Surgical and Perioperative Committee, American Academy of Hospice and Palliative Medicine (2018-2021); Awards Committee, American Academy of Hospice and Palliative Medicine (2019-2021); Complaints Sub-Committee, ACGME (2020); Committee on Palliative Care, American College of Surgeons (2020); Women's Leadership Council, Rush University Medical Center (2019-2020); Steering Committee, Women in Medicine Summit (2019-2020); Ethics Committee, Rush University Medical Center (2018-2020); Communities Committee, American Academy of Hospice and Palliative Medicine (2017-2018); Graduate Medical Education Committee, Palliative Care and Anesthesia Committee, The University of Chicago (2016-2017); Board of Trustees, Pierce County Medical Society, Tacoma, WA (2016); Medical Executive Committee, CHI Franciscan Health, Tacoma, WA (2014-2016); American Society of Bioethics and Humanities (2011-2012); Surgeon Liaison, Resident Leadership Group, Chair of Bioethics Committee, Contra Costa Regional Medical Center (2010-2012); Tumor Board, Cancer Committee, Contra Costa Regional Medical Center (2007-2012); Board of Directors, Marin Medical Society (2004-2006); Gastrointestinal and Breasts Tumor Board, Marin General Hospital, Greenbrae, CA (2002-2006); Medical Executive Committee, Bioethics Committee, Critical Care Committee, Surgical and Tissue Committee, Tumor Board, Novato Community Hospital, Novato, CA (2002-2006) **AS:** Dr. Miller attributes her success to the strength, creativity, intelligence, and generosity of her parents, brother, daughter and ex-husband. Furthermore, she credits her professional mentors, sponsors, collaborators, patients, friends, and other family members who have provided inspiration, encouragement, support, and opportunities during her life and career. **B/I:** Dr. Miller became involved her profession because she felt called to help others. She always knew that she had the capacity to do so and could connect with people in intimate vul-

nerable health related settings. She wanted the opportunity to be impactful in helping to restore the health and wellness of others. **AV:** Traveling; Hiking; Spending time with her dogs; Meditating **THT:** Dr. Miller lives by the Maya Angelou quote, "I've learned that people will forget what you said, people will forget what you did, but people will never forget how you made them feel."

MILLER, ROBERT G., T: Chief Executive Officer **I:** Business Management/Business Services **CN:** Albertsons Companies LLC **PB:** Louisville **SC:** MS/USA **ED:** Coursework, Executive Management Program, Stanford University, California;Coursework, Orange Coast College, Costa Mesa, CA **C:** Chairman, SuperValu, Inc., Eden Prairie, MN (2013-Present); President, Chief Executive Officer, AB Acquisition, LLC (2013-Present); Chief Executive Officer, Albertsons Companies LLC (2006-Present); Chief Executive Officer, Albertson's Inc. (2006-2013); Chairman, Rite Aid Corp., Camp Hill, PA (1999-2007); Chairman, Wild Oats Markets, Boulder, CO (2004-2006); Chief Executive Officer, Rite Aid Corp., Camp Hill, PA (1999-2003); Vice Chairman, Chief Operating Officer, Kroger Co., Cincinnati, OH (1999); Vice Chairman, Board, Chief Executive Officer, Fred Meyer Inc. (1998-1999); Chairman, Board, President, Chief Executive Officer, Fred Meyer Inc., Portland, OR (1991-1998); Executive Vice President, Retail Operations, Albertson's Inc. (1989-1991); With, Albertson's Inc. (1961-1989) **CR:** Director, Food Marketing Institute (2008-Present); Director, Nordstrom Inc. (2005-Present); Director, Harrah's Entertainment Inc. (1999-Present); Director, Rite Aid Corp. (1999-2011); Director, Non-executive Chairman, Wild Oats Markets Inc. (2004-2006); Chairman, Distribution Trucking Co. Inc.

MILLER, SARABETH, T: Secondary School Educator (Retired) **I:** Education/Educational Services **DOB:** 04/06/1927 **PT:** Clayton Everett Reif; Eva Margaret (Noland) Reif **MS:** Married **SPN:** Lloyd Melvin Miller (12/02/1944) **CH:** Virginia; Shirley (Deceased 2018); Judith; John; Nola; Steven **ED:** Postgraduate Coursework, Saint Joseph's University, Philadelphia, PA (1998); Postgraduate Coursework, Indiana State University, Terre Haute, IN (1996, 1997); Postgraduate Coursework, Art Institute of Fort Lauderdale, Fort Lauderdale, FL (1992); Postgraduate Coursework, Indiana University Bloomington, Bloomington, IN (1991, 1986); Postgraduate Coursework, Purdue University, West Lafayette, IN (1983); MA in Liberal Studies, Valparaiso University, Valparaiso, IN (1977); BA, Valparaiso University, Valparaiso, IN (1972) **CT:** Certified in Data Processing; Licensed in Teaching, Indiana **C:** Retired (2010); Teacher, Art, Kankakee Valley High School, Wheatfield, IN (1976-2010); Teacher, Art, DeMotte Elementary School, IN (1972-1976); Office Employee, Hannon's, Valparaiso, IN (1969-1972); Office Employee, Jasper County Co-op, Tefft, IN (1965-1969); Office Employee, Little Company of Mary Hospital and Home, San Pierre, IN (1960-1965); Office Employee, Porter County Herald, Hebron, IN (1954-1955) **CR:** Participant, Lilly Creative Teacher's Workshop **CIV:** Participant, North Central Regional Forum (1991-1993); Participant, Archaeological Gig, K.V. Historical Society and Notre Dame; Leader, 4-H Club, Kouts, IN; Member, Elder, First Presbyterian Church, Kouts, IN **CW:** Participant, Art and Literary Magazine, Mirage, Northern Region Artists Invitational; Contributor, Numerous Articles and Photographs to Local Newspapers **AW:** Lilly Endowment Fellow, Lilly Extending Teacher Creativity Institute (1987, 1994, 1995, 1996, 2002, 2003, 2004, 2005, 2007-2008); Gainer Bank Calendar Award, Photography Award, Porter County Fair (1989, 1996, 1998, 2000,

2001, 2004); 4-H Alumni Award (2002); 4-H 53-Year Leader Tenure Award (1994); Grantee, National Gallery of Art (1993); Various Prizes, Lake Central Fair, IN (1975, 1980); Indiana Department of Tourism (1976) **MEM:** Archaeological Institute of America; Near East Area Renewal (NEAR); ISTAR; Evaluation Team Member, North Central Association of Colleges and Schools (Now Higher Learning Commission (HLC); KVTAR; Smithsonian Institution; Kankakee Valley Historical Society **MH:** Albert Nelson Marquis Lifetime Achievement Award; Marquis Who's Who Top Professional **B/I:** Mrs. Miller became involved in her profession because of her mother, Eva Margaret. She was a boarding school and public school teacher and Mrs. Miller wanted to follow in her footsteps. Furthermore, she always wanted to pass on her knowledge to the students and make their world a little happier. **AV:** Church work **RE:** Presbyterian

MILLER, STEPHEN, T: Senior Adviser to the President **I:** Government Administration/Government Relations/Government Services **DOB:** 08/23/1985 **PB:** Santa Monica **SC:** CA/USA **ED:** BA, Duke University **C:** Senior Adviser to the President, Washington, DC (2017-Present);Director of Speechwriting, The White House, Washington, DC (2017-Present); Press Secretary to Representative John Shadegg, U.S. House of Representatives, Washington, DC (2009-2010) **PA:** Republican

MILLER, VEL, T: Artist **I:** Fine Art **DOB:** 01/22/1936 **PB:** Nekoosa **SC:** WI/USA **PT:** Clarence Alvin Krause Clark; Celia Mae (Houston) Clark **MS:** Married **SPN:** Warren Eugene Miller (04/30/1955) **CH:** Jennifer; Andrea; Matthew; Stuart **ED:** Student, Los Angeles Art League; Teacher, Los Angeles Art League; Student, Valley College **C:** Artist, Art Teacher, Participant, Art Shows (Mostly Western Themed) **CW:** Artist, Exhibitions include Stamford (Texas) Art Foundation, Haley Memorial Library, Midland, TX, Peppertree Ranch, Santa Ynez, CA, Mountain Oyster Club, Tucson, AZ, Cowboy Gathering, Paso Robles, CA, Cattlemans Show, San Luis Obispo, CA, Judith Hale Gallery, Los Olivos, CA, Western Interpretations Gallery, Atascadero, CA; Artist, Represented in Permanent Collections at Home Savings and Loan L.A., Glendale (Arizona) College, Cavalry Museum, Samore, France, Lawrence Gallery Scottsdale, Cowgirl Up! Show, Wickenburg; Artist, Private Collections, Cowgirl Up! Show, Wickenburg **AW:** Best of Show Award, San Fernando Valley Art Club, San Gabriel Art Association, Death Valley Invitational Show, Numerous Others **MEM:** Founder, American Women Artists **MH:** Albert Nelson Marquis Lifetime Achievement Award **THT:** Ms. Miller raises Texas longhorns and has eight grandchildren; her seventh great-grandchild is on the way.

MILLS, DAVID L., PHD, T: Electrical Engineer **I:** Law and Legal Services **DOB:** 06/06/1938 **PB:** Oakland **SC:** CA/USA **PT:** Richard A. Mills; Adele E. Mills **MS:** Married **SPN:** Beverly J. Csizmadia (02/28/1965) **CH:** Eileen Elizabeth Mills; Keith Daniel Mills **ED:** PhD in Computer Science, University of Michigan, Ann Arbor, MI (1971); MS in Communications Sciences., University of Michigan, Ann Arbor, MI (1964); MS in Electrical Engineering, University of Michigan, Ann Arbor, MI (1962); BS in Engineering Mathematics, University of Michigan, Ann Arbor, MI (1961); BS in Engineering Science, University of Michigan, Ann Arbor, MI (1960) **C:** Retired, Full Professor, Computer and Information Science, University of Delaware (1986-2008); Senior Scientist, M/A-COM Linkabit, Inc., Vienna, VA (1977-1986); Assistant Professor, University of Maryland, College Park, MD (1972-1977); Lecturer, University of Edinburgh (1971-1972) **MEM:** Fellow,

Institute of Electrical and Electronics Engineers (IEEE); Fellow, Association Computing Machinery (ACM); ALM; National Academy of Engineering; Sigma Xi **MH:** Albert Nelson Marquis Lifetime Achievement Award **AV:** Researching archaeology; Exploring ham radio; Listening to audiobooks

MILLS, JANET TRAFTON, T: Governor of Maine **I:** Government Administration/Government Relations/Government Services **DOB:** 12/12/1947 **PB:** Farmington **SC:** MN/USA **PT:** Sumner Peter Mills Jr.; Katherine Louise (Coffin) Mills **MS:** Widowed **SPN:** Stanley Kuklinski (1985, Deceased 2014) **CH:** Five Stepchildren **ED:** JD, University of Maine School of Law; BA, University of Massachusetts Boston; Coursework, Colby College **C:** Governor, State of Maine (2019-Present); Attorney General, State of Maine (2009-2011, 2013-2019); Of Counsel, Litigation Group, Preti, Flaherty, Beliveau & Pachios, LLP (2011-2012); Member, District 78, Maine House of Representatives (2002-2008); Attorney, Wright & Mills, PA, Skowhegan, Maine (1995-2008); District Attorney, Third Judicial District of Maine (1980-1995); Assistant Attorney General, State of Maine (1976-1980) **CR:** Vice Chair, Maine Democratic Party; Professor, Justice Studies Program, University of Maine at Augusta **MEM:** Board of Directors, National Association of Criminal Defense Lawyers (1996); Maine Trial Lawyers Association (1996); President, Maine Prosecutors Association (1984, 1988-1992); Maine Prosecutors Association (1980-1994); Maine Humanities Council; ACLU of Maine (1978-1980); League of Women Voters; National Association of Criminal Defense Lawyers **AV:** Poetry; Fishing; Cooking; Reading **PA:** Democrat

MILNER, CHARLES, "MONTY" FREMONT JR., T: Manufacturing Executive **I:** Apparel & Fashion **CN:** CM Industries, Inc. **DOB:** 07/21/1942 **PB:** Durham **SC:** NC/USA **PT:** Charles Fremont Milner; Eloyse Sargent Milner **MS:** Married **SPN:** Molly (Wakefield) Milner (1965) **CH:** Bernadette Gardener; Eloyse Ellerman **ED:** MBA, Harvard University (1965); BA, Guilford College (1963) **C:** With, CM Industries, Inc., Denver, PA (1983-Present); President, Chief Executive Officer, Hope Hosiery Mills, Denver, PA (1983-2018); Vice President, Genesco Inc. (1981-1982); General Manager, Shoe Company Division, Johnston & Murphy (1979-1982); General Manager, Footwear Marketing and Manufacturing, Genesco Inc. (1980-1981); President, Chief Executive Officer, BBC, Inc. and Camp Industry Divisions, Genesco Inc. (1976-1980); Vice President, Apparel Group, M. Lowenstein & Sons, Inc., New York, NY (1975-1976); President, Division of NCC Industries, Rudin & Roth, Inc., New York, NY (1974-1975); Executive Vice President, Parklane Hosiery Co., Inc., New Hyde Park, NY (1971-1974); Assistant Vice President, Burlington Hosiery Company, Division of Burlington Industries, NC (1970-1971); With, Burlington Hosiery Company, Division of Burlington Industries, NC (1966-1971); Instructor, Northeastern University, Boston, MA (1965-1966); Assistant to Comptroller, Harvard University (1965-1966) **CIV:** Co-chairman, 25th and 40th Reunion, Harvard Business School (2005); Alumni Board, Harvard Business School (1992-2001); Past President, Harvard Business School (1999-2001); President, Harvard Business School (1997-1999); Vice President, Harvard Business School (1995-1997); Chairman, Guilford College (1990-1997); Trustee, Guilford College (1982-1997); Member, Class Chief Fund Agent, Harvard Business School (1986-1991); Vice Chairman, Guilford College (1989); Trustee, Friends Academy, Locust Valley, NY (1974-1979) **MIL:** First Lieutenant, United States Army Reserve **MEM:** President, Hourglass Foundation (2010-Present); Executive Committee, National Associ-

ation of Hosiery Manufacturers (1989-1993, 1999-2013); Director, National Association of Hosiery Manufacturers (1978-1982, 1987-2013); Board of Governors, Lancaster Country Club (2004-2010); Vice President, Hourglass Foundation (2008-2009); Chairman, National Association of Hosiery Manufacturers (1993); Vice-chairman, National Association of Hosiery Manufacturers (1992); Second Vice-chairman, National Association of Hosiery Manufacturers (1991-1992); National Association of Hosiery Manufacturers; Hourglass Foundation; Lancaster Country Club; Hamilton Club of Pennsylvania; Moselem Springs Golf Club **MH:** Albert Nelson Marquis Lifetime Achievement Award **B/I:** Attending Guilford and receiving his undergraduate in economics, Mr. Milner's career goals led him to be a manufacturing executive. His aunt was a professor of the school and his uncle was the president, so they entertained most of the visitors that came to the college. Mr. Milner had the opportunity to meet many CEOs that came to contribute to the college.

MILONAS, HERODOTOS MINOS, MFA, T: Artist, Poet **I:** Fine Art **DOB:** 04/28/1936 **PB:** Heraklion **SC:** Crete/Greece **PT:** Stavros Milonas; Maria (Kaplantzis) Milonas **MS:** Married **SPN:** Elaine Mauceli (05/26/1988); Sarah Brown (12/1973, Divorced 1974); Arlene Watson (12/23/1963, Divorced 1970) **ED:** MFA, University of Washington (1972); BA, California State University (1970) **C:** Artist, Studio Milonas, New York, NY (1977-Present); Textile Designer, Studio Milonas, New York, NY (1984-1994); Instructor, Studio Milonas, Seattle, WA (1972-1976); Instructor, University of Washington (1971-1972); Artist, Los Angeles, CA (1964-1966); Writer, Athens, Greece (1960-1964) **CIV:** Donor, Poetry Books, 28 Public Libraries, Greece; Donor, Books, Five Public Libraries, Cyprus; Donor, Three-Piece Sculpture, California State University Northridge; Donor, Large Sculpture, St. Demetrios Church, Seattle, WA; Donor, Painting, Central Park Conservancy, New York, NY; Donor, Two Paintings, St. Luke's-Roosevelt Hospital, New York, NY; Donor, Two Paintings, New York City Fire Department; Donor, Painting, Cypriot Consulate, New York, NY; Donor, Two Paintings, National Archaeological Museum, Heraklion, Crete; Donor, Three Paintings, Bikelaia Public Library, Heraklion, Crete; Donor, Three Paintings, Artemisia Cultural Center, Heraklion, Crete **CW:** Author, "Tropic Rhapsodies," Poems in English (2017); Author, "Florida," Bilingual Poems in English and in Greek (2006); Author, "For Her," Bilingual Poems in English and Greek (2005); Author, "Poems from April," Bilingual Poems in English and Greek (2005); Author, "Autobiography at 66" (2005); Author, "Look At Manhattan," Poems in English (2004); Author, "From A to Z", Poems in English (2003); Exhibitions in Group Shows, Melina Merkouri Cultural Center, Athens, Greece (2003); One-Man Show, Hellenic Cultural Center, New York, NY (1990, 1993); Video: "500 Definitions - Art Is" (1991); One-Man Show, Cypriot Consulate, New York, NY (1990); Exhibitions in Group Shows, Morin-Miller Galleries, New York, NY (1989-1990); Exhibitions in Group Shows, Ball State University, Muncie, IN (1989); Exhibitions in Group Shows, Greek Cultural Center, Springfield, MA (1987, 1989); One-Man Show, Doma Gallery, New York, NY (1988); Video: "Multimedia Artist" (1988); Exhibitions in Group Shows, University of North Dakota, Grand Forks, ND (1987); Exhibitions in Group Shows, Del Bello Gallery, Toronto, Ontario, Canada (1987); Exhibitions in Group Shows, Haggin Museum, Stockton, CA (1985-1986); One-Man Show, Kreonides Gallery, Athens, Greece (1983, 1984); One-Man Show, Heraklion Art Gallery, Crete, Greece (1983); Exhibitions in Group Shows, Bowes Museum, Barnard Castle, England

(1982); Exhibitions in Group Shows, International Drawing Biennale, Cleveland, England (1981-1982); One-Man Show, West Broadway Gallery, New York, NY (1979, 1981, 1982); One-Man Show, Stavrakakis Gallery, Crete, Greece (1977); Exhibitions in Group Shows, Cretan Artists, Stavrakakis Gallery, Heraklion, Crete (1977); Exhibitions in Group Shows, Bellevue Art Museum, Bellevue, WA (1976); Exhibitions in Group Shows, Sunne Savage Gallery, Boston, MA (1976); Exhibitions in Group Shows, University District Arts Festival, Seattle, WA (1976); One-Man Show, Polly Friedlander Gallery, Seattle, WA (1973); Exhibitions in Group Shows, Panaca Gallery, Bellevue, WA (1973); Exhibitions in Group Shows, Mercer Island Art Gallery, Seattle, WA (1973); One-Man Show, Henry Art Gallery, Seattle, WA (1972); Exhibitions in Group Shows, University of Washington Library (1971, 1972); One-Man Show, Second Story Gallery, Seattle, WA (1971); Exhibitions in Group Shows, Municipal Art Gallery, Los Angeles, CA (1969); Exhibitions in Group Shows, California State University Northridge (1968-1969); Author, "The Small Caravan" Short Stories in Greek (1962); Author, 41 Books of Poetry in Greek and English **AW:** Two Merit Awards, Greek Cultural Center, Springfield, MA (1987); Four Sculpture Awards, Summer Art Festivals (1970-1976); Scholar, University of Washington (1971); Grantee, University of Washington (1970) **MEM:** Poets House; Greek-American Writers Association **MH:** Albert Nelson Marquis Lifetime Achievement Award; Marquis Who's Who Top Professional **AS:** Mr. Milonas attributes his success to his ambition, dedication, and love of languages and color. In art, he attributes his success to striving to create prototypical work; in poetry, he makes realistic poems that touch the emotions with their content. **B/I:** Mr. Milonas became involved in his profession because, when he was in Greece, he was writing short stories and poems; he had his first book of short stories published there. When he came to the United States, he didn't speak enough English to continue his writing, so he focused on art and earned a Master of Fine Arts degree in sculpture. Since moving to New York City in 1977, a lack of studio space led Mr. Milonas to devote himself to two-dimensional art, such as painting, drawing, and collage. **PA:** Democrat

MINAJ, NICKI, T: Rap Artist **I:** Media & Entertainment **DOB:** 12/08/1984 **PB:** St. James, Port of Spain **SC:** Trinidad and Tobago **PT:** Robert Maraj; Carol Maraj **MS:** Married **SPN:** Kenneth Petty (10/21/2019) **C:** Artist, Young Money Entertainment (2009) **CR:** Co-Owner, Tidal (2015-Present); Owner, Trini Girl (2016); Fragrance Line, Minajesty (2013); Fragrance Line, Pink Friday (2012); Collaborator, MAC Cosmetics; Collaborator, OPI Products; Collaborator, Addidas; Collaborator, H&M; Collaborator, Fendi **CW:** Voice Actress, "The Angry Birds Movie 2" (2019); Rap Artist, "Queen" (2018); Actress, "Barbershop: The Next Cut" (2016); Actress, "The Other Woman" (2014); Rap Artist, "The Pink Print" (2014); Rap Artist, "Anaconda" (2014); Judge, "American Idol" (2013); Voice Actress, "Ice Age: Continental Drift" (2012); Rap Artist, "Pink Friday: Roman Reloaded" (2012); Rap Artist, "Starships" (2012); Rap Artist, "Super Bass" (2011); Rap Artist, "Pink Friday" (2010); Rap Artist, Numerous Collaborations **AW:** Game Changer Award, Billboard Women in Music (2019); Listee, 100 Most Influential People in the World, Time Magazine (2016); Award for Favorite Hip-Hop Artist, People's Choice Awards (2013, 2016); Award for Best Hip-Hop Video, MTV Video Music Awards (2015); Awards for Favorite Rap/Hip-Hop Album, Favorite Rap/ Hip Hop Artist, American Music Awards (2011, 2012, 2015); Awards for Top Rap Album, Top Streaming Artist, Top Rap Artist,

Billboard Music Awards (2013); Award for Top Streaming Song-Video, Billboard Music Awards (2012); Award for Best Female Video, MTV Video Music Awards (2012); Award for Best Female Hip-Hop Artist, BET Awards (2010-2015); Award for Best New Artist, BET Awards (2010); Recipient, Numerous Awards

MINGE, JOAN A., T: Senior Project Manager **I:** Oil & Energy **DOB:** 06/12/1949 **PB:** Knoxville **SC:** TN/USA **PT:** James Howard Minge; Helen Regene (Ellenburg) Minge **MS:** Divorced **SPN:** Charles Emerson Jones (05/12/1979, Divorced 1981) **ED:** Coursework, Xavier University (1982-1985); Coursework, The University of Tennessee at Chattanooga (1969-1978); Coursework, The University of Tennessee at Knoxville (1967-1968) **CT:** Certified in Data Processing, Tennessee College Automation (1968) **C:** Senior Project Manager, Pilot Flying J (Pilot Travel Centers LLC), Knoxville, TN (1996-2018); Systems Manager, Mobil Chemical Company (Now Exxon Mobil Corporation), Rochester, NY (1990-1994); Supervisor, Planning Technical Operations, Mobil Mining and Minerals Company, Richmond, VA (1989-1990); Senior System Analyst, Mobil Mining and Minerals Company, Richmond, VA (1987-1989); Senior System Analyst, Nerco Coal Corporation, St. Louis, MO (1985-1987); Senior System Analyst, Nerco Coal Company, Cincinnati, Ohio (1982-1985); Systems Analyst, Nerco Eastern Mining Division, Chattanooga, TN (1981-1982); Client Consultant, Datalogic Incorporated (Now Datalogic S.p.A.), Chattanooga, TN (1976-1981); Programmer, Analyst, Ernest Holmes Company, Chattanooga, TN (1974-1976); Programmer, Analyst, Pioneer Bank, Chattanooga, TN (1969-1972) **CR:** Network Distributor, National Pet Protection (1996); Systems Consultant, Truckload Solutions (1995) **CIV:** Founding Member, Steering Committee, Women in the Next Generation, United Way of Greater Knoxville **MH:** Albert Nelson Marquis Lifetime Achievement Award **AV:** Travel; Cooking **PA:** Democrat **RE:** Protestant

MINKEL, HERBERT P. JR., T: Lawyer **I:** Law and Legal Services **DOB:** 02/11/1947 **PB:** Boston **SC:** MA/USA **PT:** Herbert Philip Minkel; Helen (Sullivan) Minkel **ED:** JD, New York University (1972); BA, Holy Cross College (1969) **CT:** United States District Court Southern District of New York (1978); New York State Bar Association (1976); United States District Court District of Massachusetts (1973); Massachusetts Bar Association (1973) **C:** Senior Partner, Minkel & Associates (1994-2018); Partner, Fried, Frank, Harris, Shriver & Jacobson LLP (1979-1994); Member, Advisory Committee on Bankruptcy Rules, Judicial Conference of the United States (1987-1993); Associate, Milbank LLP (1973-1979); Law Clerk, United States District Court District of Massachusetts (1972-1973) **CR:** Adjunct Associate Professor, New York University School of Law (1987-1994) **CW:** Contributing Editor, "Collier on Bankruptcy, 15 Edition" (1979-1996); Contributing Author, Bankruptcy Manual, American Bankers Association (1979) **AW:** Root-Tilden Scholar, New York University (1969-1972) **MEM:** American Bar Association; National Bankruptcy Conference; The Association of the Bar of the City of New York **MH:** Albert Nelson Marquis Lifetime Achievement Award; Marquis Who's Who Top Professional **B/I:** Mr. Minkel became involved in his profession after spending time working for the Worcester and Boston re-development authorities, which piqued his interest in city planning. From there, a professor suggested he pursue a career in law. **AV:** Sailing; Golfing; Cooking

MINNELLI, LIZA MAY, T: Singer; Actress **DOB:** 03/12/1946 **PB:** Los Angeles **SC:** CA/USA **PT:** Vincente Minnelli; Judy (Garland) Minnelli **MS:** Divorced **SPN:** David Gest (03/16/2002, Divorced 04/2007); Mark Gero (12/04/1979, Divorced 01/1992); Jack Haley Jr. (09/15/1974, Divorced 04/1979); Peter Allen (03/03/1967, Divorced 07/24/1972) **ED:** Honorary Doctorate, Mercy College (2007) **CIV:** Board of Directors, IAHP; Supporter, amfAR **CW:** Singer, "Confessions" (2010); Actress, "Drop Dead Diva" (2009); Singer, "Liza's at the Palace" (2008); Actress, "The Oh in Ohio" (2006); Actress, "Law & Order: Criminal Intent" (2006); Actress, "The Oh in Ohio" (2006); Singer with Herbie Hancock, Johnny Mathis, and Donna Summer, "Liza's Back!" (2003); Singer, "Minnelli on Minnelli" (2000); Actress, "Jackie's Back!" (1999); Appearance, "My Favorite Broadway: The Leading Ladies" (1999); Actress, "Arrested Development" (2003-2005, 2013); Actress, "Victor Victoria" (1997); Singer, "Maybe This Time" (1996); Singer, "Gently" (1996); Actress, "The West Side Waltz" (1995); Actress, "Parallel Lives" (1994); Actress, "Love Letters" (1994); Appearance, "A Century of Cinema" (1994); Actress, "Stepping Out" (1991); Featured, "Liza Minnelli Live from Radio City Music Hall" (1990); Featured, "The Wonderful World of Oz: 50 Years of Magic" (1990); Singer, "Results" (1989); Actress, "Rent A Cop" (1988); Appearance, "Sam Found Out" (1988); Singer, International Tour with Frank Sinatra and Sammy Davis Jr. (1988); Actress, "Arthur on the Rocks" (1988); Singer, "Liza Minnelli at Carnegie Hall" (1987); Appearance, "A Time to Live" (1985); Actress, "The Rink" (1984); Appearance, "The Princess and the Pea" (1983); Appearance, "Showtime" (1983); Actress, "Arthur" (1981); Featured, "Goldie and Liza Together" (1980); Appearance, "Baryshnikov on Broadway" (1980); Actress, "The Owl and the Pussycat" (1978-1979); Actress, "The Act" (1977-1978); Singer, "Tropical Nights" (1977); Actress, "New York, New York" (1977); Actress, "A Matter of Time" (1976); Actress, "Silent Movie" (1976); Actress, "Chicago" (1975); Actress, "Lucky Lady" (1975); Actress, "That's Entertainment" (1974); Actress, "Liza" (1974); Singer, "The Singer" (1973); Featured, "Liza with a Z" (1972); Actress, "Cabaret" (1972); Actress, "Tell Me That You Love Me, Junie Moon" (1970); Singer, "New Feelin'" (1970); Singer, "Come Saturday Morning" (1969); Actress, "The Sterile Cuckoo" (1969); Actress, "Charlie Bubbles" (1967); Actress, "The Pajama Game" (1966); Singer, "There is a Time" (1966); Singer, "Liza Minnelli" (1966); Actress, "Flora, the Red Menace" (1965); Singer, "It Amazes Me" (1965); Actress, "Carnival!" (1964); Actress, "Time Out for Ginger" (1964); Singer, "Liza! Liza!" (1964); Actress, "The Fantasticks" (1964); Actress, "Best Foot Forward" (1963); Actress, "The Diary of Anne Frank" (1961-1962); Actress, "Wish You Were Here" (1961); Actress, "Take Me Along" (1961); Actress, "Flower Drum Song" (1961) **AW:** Special Drama Desk Award (2009); Tony Award for Special Theatrical Event (2009); Inductee, Grammy Hall of Fame, The Recording Academy (2008); Vanguard Award, GLAAD (2005); Grammy Living Legend Award, The Recording Academy (1990); Tony Award for Best Leading Actress in a Musical (1965, 1978); Special Tony Award (1974); Woman of the Year, Hasty Pudding Theatricals Society (1973); Emmy Award for Outstanding Variety Special, Academy of Television Arts & Sciences (1973); Golden Globe Award for Best Actress - Miniseries or Motion Picture Made for Television, Hollywood Foreign Press Association (1972); Academy Award for Best Actress, Academy of Motion Picture Arts & Sciences (1972); BAFTA Award for Best Actress in a Leading Role (1972); Two-Time Recipient, David di Donatello Awards, Italy; Valentino Award; Recipient, Numerous Awards

MINOR, ROBERT LYNN, T: Lawyer, Military Officer, Court Executive **I:** Law and Legal Services **DOB:** 06/24/1952 **PB:** Marceline **SC:** MO/USA **PT:** William Henry Minor; Lois Marie (Kosman) Minor **MS:** Married **SPN:** Bridget Mary McCabe (09/10/1976) **CH:** Erin Eileen; Kelley Elizabeth **ED:** Graduate Coursework, U.S. Army Command and General Staff College (1986); Graduate Coursework, U.S. Army Judge Advocate General School (1983); JD, University of Notre Dame (1980); BS, U.S. Military Academy (1974) **C:** Staff Judge Advocate, U.S. Army Reserve Command, Fort McPherson, GA (2002-Present); Staff Judge Advocate, U.S. Army, Fort Gillem, GA (1999-2002); Staff Judge Advocate, Recruiting Command (1996-1999); Staff Judge Advocate, Fort Sam, Houston, TX (1994-1996); Chief, General Litigation, U.S. Department of the Army, Washington, DC (1992-1994); Deputy Staff Judge Advocate, 3rd Infantry Division, Wuerzburg, Germany (1990-1992); Litigation Attorney, U.S. Department of the Army, Washington, DC (1986-1989); Chief, Administrative Law and Claims, Chief Prosecutor, Judge Advocate, Berlin, Germany (1983-1986); Senior Trial Counsel, Office Staff Judge Advisory, Fort Riley, KS (1981-1982); Assistant Staff Judge Advocate, U.S. Army, Fort Riley, KS (1980-1981); Chief Deputy, U.S. District Court for the Northern District of Georgia **CR:** U.S. District Court for the Southern District of Georgia (1988-1990); Magistrate, U.S. Command, Berlin, Germany (1983-1986); Special Assistant, U.S. Attorney, U.S. District Court for the Eastern District of Arkansas **MIL:** Commissioned 2nd Lieutenant, U.S. Army (1974); Colonel, U.S. Army **MEM:** American Bar Association; Chair, Military Law Committee, Federal Bar Association; Association of Trial Lawyers in America; Indiana State Bar Association; Berlin Judicature Society (1984-1986); VFW, Military Law Section, State Bar of Texas; San Antonio Bar Association **BAR:** U.S. Court of Claims (1988); U.S. District Court of Maryland (1987); U.S. District Court for the Eastern District of Texas (1987); U.S. Supreme Court (1984); Indiana (1980); U.S. Court of Military Appeals (1980); U.S. Court of Appeals for the 4th Circuit; U.S. Court of Appeals for the 5th Circuit; U.S. Court of Appeals for the 8th Circuit; U.S. Court of Appeals for the 11th Circuit; U.S. Court of Appeals for the District of Columbia; U.S. Court of Appeals for the Federal Circuit **MH:** Albert Nelson Marquis Lifetime Achievement Award; Marquis Who's Who Top Professional **B/I:** Mr. Minor became involved in his profession because he grew up in a patriotic family, as his father and uncles had all served in World War II. He decided early on that he was going to serve in the military. He applied for West Point and was accepted to the U.S. Military. **AV:** Traveling; Farming; Spending time with family **RE:** Roman Catholic

MINSHEW, KATHRYN, T: Founder, Chief Executive Officer **I:** Other **CN:** The Muse **DOB:** 10/30/1985 **SC:** NJ/USA **ED:** BA in Political Science and French, Duke University; Coursework in International Relations, Institut d'Etudes Politiques de Strasbourg **C:** Founder, Chief Executive Officer, The Muse (2011-Present); Business Analyst, McKinsey & Company (2008-2010); Regional Security Officer, U.S. Embassy, Nicosia, Cyprus (2007) **CIV:** With, HPV Vaccine Introduction Global Team, Clinton Health Access Initiative (2010-2011); External Relations Intern, Health Action in Crises, World Health Organization (2006) **CW:** Author, "The New Rules of Work" (2017); Appearances, "The Today Show," Bloomberg Television, Fox, MSNBC; Contributor, Articles to Professional Journals **AW:** One Young World Entrepreneur of the Year (2019); Game Changer, Workforce Magazine (2016); New York Future 50 Award, SmartCEO Magazine (2016); Silicon Alley 100 (2012, 2015); One of the 30 Under 30 in Media, Forbes (2011, 2012); One of the 15 Women to Watch in Tech, Inc.com (2012)

MINYARD, BLAIR, T: Mechanical Engineer **I:** Engineering **CN:** BL Harbert International LLC **ED:** BS in Civil Engineering/Mechanical Engineering, The University of Alabama at Birmingham (2008); High School Diploma, E.B. Erwin High School, AL (2001) **CT:** CPD, American Society of Plumbing Engineers (ASPE); Society Board of Directors, American Society of Plumbing Engineers (ASPE) **C:** Vice President of Education, American Society of Plumbing Engineers (ASPE) (2018-Present); Virtual Design and Construction Engineer, BL Harbert International LLC (2016-Present); Adjunct Professor, The University of Alabama at Birmingham (2016-Present); Mechanical Coordinator/Piping Specialist, BL Harbert International LLC (2015-2016); Discipline Engineer, Robins & Morton (2014-2015); Adjunct Instructor, Jefferson State Community College (2011-2015); Plumbing Designer, CRS Engineering Inc. (2008-2012); Fire Designer/Clerical Assistant, Central Station, Inc. (2000-2008); Construction Documents Technology Certificate (CDT), Construction Specifications Institute **CIV:** Youth Leader, Southern Baptist Church (7 Years) **AW:** Named Millennial on the Move, Plumbing Design Industry (2019); Autodesk Building Performance Analysis Certificate; Named One of the Up & Comers (Ins and Outs), 40 Under 40 **MEM:** American Society of Plumbing Engineers (ASPE); American Society of Plumbing Engineers (ASPE), Alabama Chapter; ASHRAE - North Alabama; JSCC-Industrial Advisory Committee (Building & Construction Science Technology) **AS:** Ms. Minyard attributes her success to her dedication and her strive for perfection. **B/I:** Ms. Minyard became involved in her profession because she was curious on how things worked and how she could make them better. **THT:** Ms. Minyard's motto is, "Don't give up!"

MIRANDA, LIN-MANUEL, T: Composer, Actor, Producer, Playwright **I:** Media & Entertainment **DOB:** 01/16/1980 **PB:** New York **SC:** NY/USA **PT:** Luis A. Miranda Jr.; Luz Towns-Miranda **MS:** Married **SPN:** Vanessa Adriana Nadal (2010) **CH:** Sebastian; Francisco **ED:** Honorary Doctor of Arts, University of Pennsylvania (2016); Honorary Doctor of Humane Letters, Yeshiva University (2009); Bachelor of Arts, Wesleyan University (2002) **CR:** Member, New York City Theater Subdistrict Council (2015); Board Member, Young Playwrights Inc. **CIV:** Performer, Benefit Songs, Concerts **CW:** Actor, Writer, Composer, Producer, Film, "Hamilton" (2020); Appearance, "Some Good News" (2020); Actor, "Star Ears: The Rise of Skywalker" (2019); Appearance, "One Day at a Time" (2020); Appearance, "Sesame Street: Elmo's Playdate" (2020); Actor, "Brooklyn Nine-Nine" (2019); Co-author, "Gmorning, Gnight!: Little Pep Talks for Me & You" (2018); Actor, "Mary Poppins Returns" (2018); Actor, "My Brother, My Brother and Me" (2017); Actor, "Bojack Horseman" (2017); Appearance, "The Magic School Bus Rides Again" (2017); Appearance, "Curb Your Enthusiasm" (2017); Voice Actor, "Duck Tales" (2017); Actor, "Speech and Debate" (2017); Composer, "The Hamilton Instrumentals" (2017); Appearance, "Last Week Tonight with John Oliver" (2016); Appearance, "Drunk History" (2016); Composer, Lyricist, Singer, "The Hamilton Mixtape" (2016); Actor, "Speech & Debate" (2016); Actor, "Hamilton's America" (2016); Voice Actor, Composer, "Moana" (2016); Co-author, "Hamilton: The Revolution" (2016); Composer, Lyricist, Performer, "Hamilton" (2015-2016); Appearance, "Tick, Tick...Boom!" (2014); Narrator, Audiobook, "The Brief Wondrous Life of Oscar Wao" (2013); Narrator, Audiobook, "Aristotle and Dante Discover the Secrets of the Universe" (2013); Actor, "Looking for Maria Sanchez" (2013); Co-composer, Lyricist, "Bring it On: The Musical" (2012); Appearance, "Merrily We Roll Along," City Center Encores! (2012); Actor, "The Odd Life of Timothy Green" (2012); Actor, "Freestyle Love Supreme" (2012); Composer, Lyricist, Performer, Broadway Play, "In the Heights" (2008-2011); Spanish Translations, "West Side Story" (2009); Appearance, "The Electric Company"; Actor, "The Sopranos"; Actor, "House"; Appearance, "Modern Family" Actor, "Do No Harm"; Actor, "How I Met Your Mother"; Actor, Appearances, Theater, Television Shows, Films **AW:** Portrait of a Nation Prize, Smithsonian National Portrait Gallery, Smithsonian Institution (2019); Honoree, Kennedy Center Honors, John F. Kennedy Center for the Performing Arts (2018); Grammy Award for Best Song Written for Visual Media, The Recording Academy (2018); Pulitzer Prize (2016); American Ingenuity Award, Smithsonian Magazine (2016); Named, One of the 100 Most Influential People in the World, TIME Magazine (2016); Grammy Award for Best Musical Show Album, The Recording Academy (2009, 2016); Oliver Award for Outstanding Achievement in Music for Original London Production (2016); Tony Award for Best Book of a Musical, Best Original Score, Best Book of a Musical (2016); MacArthur Foundation Award (2015); New York Drama Critics' Circle Award for Best Musical (2015); Drama Desk Awards for Outstanding Music, Outstanding Lyrics, Outstanding Book of a Musical (2015); Lucille Lortel Award for Outstanding Lead Actor in a Musical (2015); Outer Critic Circle Awards for Outstanding New Score, Outstanding Book of a Musical (2015); Drama Desk Awards for Outstanding Music, Outstanding Lyrics, Outstanding Book of a Musical (2015); New York Drama Critics Circle Award for Best New Musical (2015); OBIE for Best New American Play (2015); Edward M. Kennedy Prize for Drama Inspired by American History (2015); Primetime Emmy Award for Outstanding Original Music, American Academy of Television Arts & Sciences (2014); Named, One of the 40 Under 40, Crain's New York Business (2009); Tony Awards for Best Musical, Best Score, Best Orchestrations, Best Choreography (2008); Clarence Derwent Award for Most Promising Male Performance, Actors' Equity Foundation (2007); Theatre World Award for Outstanding Debut Performance (2007); Drama Desk Award for Outstanding Ensemble Performance (2007); Outer Critics Circle Award for Outstanding Musical (2007); Lucille Lortel Award for Outstanding Musical (2007); Obie Award for Music and Lyrics (2007); National Arts Club Medal of Honor, The ASCAP Foundation; Richard Rodgers New Horizons Award; Numerous Awards **MEM:** Council Member, Dramatists Guild of America Inc.

MIRIPOL, JERILYN, T: Poet, Writer, Writing Therapist; Pianist **I:** Writing and Editing **CN:** AMITA Saint Francis Hospital Evanston **PB:** Chicago **SC:** IL/USA **PT:** Albert Miripol; Janice (Tuchin) Miripol **SPN:** Richard Palmer Van Duyne (12/30/1986) **ED:** BA in English Literature, Northeastern Illinois University (1974) **C:** Writing Therapist, St. Francis Hospital (Now AMITA Saint Francis Hospital Evanston, AMITA Health, IL (1989-2015); Creative Writing Teacher, Oakton Community College, Evanston, IL (1985-1989); Writing Therapist, Friendly Visitor, Advocate, Nursing/Retirement Home, North Shore Retirement Hotel (Now The Merion), Evanston, IL (1982-1983) **CR:** Writing Facilitator for Individual Students, Chicago, IL (1987-Present); National

Association for Poetry Therapy (NAPT), Chicago, IL (1991); Presenter, Writing Therapy Workshop (1990); Teacher, Writing Therapy to Mental Health Professionals and Caregivers, University of Wisconsin-Milwaukee (1989); Artist-in-residence, Evanston Township High School (1988); Artist/Writer-in-residence, Dawes School, Evanston, IL (1985) **CIV:** Volunteer, Ridgeview Nursing Home, Evanston, IL (1982-1983); Advocate, Children of Abuse, Human and Civil Rights **CW:** Author, "Discovering Self-Awareness Through Poetry" (1987); Author, "The Sounds Were Distilled" (1977); Author, Poetry, "A Complete Mute Light"; Keynote Speaker, 11th Annual Poetry Therapy Conference; Author, Numerous Poems; Contributor, Articles to Professional Journals **AW:** Grantee to Teach 10-Year-Olds, District 12, Dawes School, Evanston, IL (1987); Fellow Scholar, Radgale Foundation (1985); Named Talent Scholar in Creative Writing, Northeastern Illinois University (1980); Named Squaw Valley Community Writers Scholar (1980); Named Breadloaf Writers Conference Scholar, Aspen Writer's Workshop, Aspen Words; Danforth Fellow Nominee **MEM:** National Organization for Women; PEN America; UNICEF; American Civil Liberties Union; National Association of Poetry Therapy; Women's International League for Peace & Freedom (WILPF); Human Rights Committee, Humanitas International Foundation; Amnesty International, American Academy of Poets; Illinois Alliance of Arts (Now Arts Alliance Illinois); Vice President, Pan-Pacific & Southeast Asia Women's Association; Greenpeace International; Death Penalty Foes **MH:** Albert Nelson Marquis Lifetime Achievement Award **B/I:** What initially inspired Mrs. Miripol to become involved in her profession is that she was artistic as a child and she was in the LA Company. She always had piano; when she went to college she played the flute but she wanted to go back to playing the piano. She returned to the piano because she loves it. She went to four workshops. The Valley Community of Writers paid for her tuition via scholarship and then a Pulitzer Prize winning poet, Lisel Mueller, asked to work with her at the University of Indiana in Bloomington. Mrs. Miripol was then accepted to the Bredlow Feeders Conference, where she worked with other writers in Middlebury, Vermont. She was at the Aspen Writers Workshop and they only accepted six people there. Everyone put in recommendations to be accepted but she just put her poetry in and was accepted. **AV:** Music; Dance; Art; Reading; Drama; Films

MISIEK, DALE J., DMD, T: Professor **I:** Medicine & Health Care **CN:** LSU Health School of Dentistry **DOB:** 12/10/1952 **PB:** Hartford **SC:** CT/USA **PT:** Jadwiga (Jennie) Magdelena (Wojtowicz) (Deceased 2005); Joseph John (Deceased 1974) **MS:** Married **SPN:** Holly Elizabeth Kirby Pisarello (10/29/2016); Patricia Ann Munson (06/28/1975, Deceased 12/25/2011) **CH:** Matthew Bryan; Stacey Lynne; Michael Stephen **ED:** Certified Advanced Training, Oral and Maxillofacial Surgery, Louisiana State University (1982); Resident, Oral Surgery, LSU Division, Charity Hospital of Louisiana at New Orleans (1978-1982); DMD, University of Connecticut (1978); BA, University of Connecticut, Magna Cum Laude (1974) **CT:** Diplomate, American Board of Oral and Maxillofacial Surgery (ABOMS) (1984) **C:** Professor, Program Director, Department of Oral and Maxillofacial Surgery, School of Dentistry, Louisiana State University, New Orleans, LA (2020); Private Practice, Oral and Maxillofacial Surgeon, Charlotte, NC (1998-2019); Professor, Department of Oral and Maxillofacial Surgery, School of Dentistry, Louisiana State University, New Orleans, LA (1994-1998); Associate Professor, Department of Oral and Maxillofacial Surgery, School of Den-

tistry, Louisiana State University, New Orleans, LA (1987-1994); Assistant Professor Department of Oral and Maxillofacial Surgery, School Dentistry, Louisiana State University, New Orleans, LA (1984-1987); Practice, Dentistry Specializing in Oral Surgery, New Orleans, LA (1982-1984); Member, Numerous Committees, School of Dentistry, Louisiana State University, New Orleans, LA **CR:** Member, Medical Staffs, Numerous Hospitals, New Orleans, Metairie, Kenner, LA, Charlotte, Concord, Huntersville, Matthews, NC **CIV:** Director, Oral and Maxillofacial Surgery Foundation (2018-Present); Director, William F. Harrigan Society (2015-Present); Vice President, Jack Kent Oral & Maxillofacial Surgery Foundation (2011-Present); President, Jack Kent Oral & Maxillofacial Surgery Foundation (2007-2011) **CW:** Contributor, Articles and Abstracts, Professional Journals; Author, Textbook Chapters; National and International Lecturer **AW:** C.V. Mosby Book Award; Arnold K. Maislen Award, NYU National Honor Society **MEM:** Consultant Commission on Dental Accreditation, American Association of Oral and Maxillofacial Surgeons (1986-2000); Regional Adviser, District III, American Association of Oral and Maxillofacial Surgeons (1996-1999); Advisory Committee, American Association of Oral and Maxillofacial Surgeons (1990-1995); Special Committee on Oral and Maxillofacial Surgery Self-Assessment Program, American Association of Oral and Maxillofacial Surgeons (1990); Special Committee for Development Standards and Criteria for Care, American Association of Oral and Maxillofacial Surgeons (1986); Fellow, American Association of Oral and Maxillofacial Surgeons; American College of Oral and Maxillofacial Surgeons; American Dental Association; American Board of Oral and Maxillofacial Surgery; American Academy of Cosmetic Surgery; Numerous Positions, Louisiana Society of Oral & Maxillofacial Surgeons; International Association of Oral and Maxillofacial Surgery; Academy of Osseointegration; Charlotte Dental Society; Second District Dental Society, North Carolina Dental Society; North Carolina Society of Oral and Maxillofacial Surgeons; LDA; NODA; NCDA; CDA; Louisiana Society of Oral & Maxillofacial Surgeons; SESOMS; AO; American Dairy Science Association; American Association of Cosmetology Schools; Jack Kent Oral and Maxillofacial Surgery Foundation; WFHS; Phi Beta Kappa; Phi Kappa Phi; Omicron Kappa Upsilon **MH:** Albert Nelson Marquis Lifetime Achievement Award **AS:** Dr. Misiek attributes his success to hard work and proper positioning during his career, meeting and working with influential people, and rising to the occasion when faced with challenges. **B/I:** Dr. Misiek became involved in his profession because of conversations he had with his father in the year between graduating from high school and going to college. His father never pushed him to make any decision, but gently guided him and allowed him to make his own choices. **AV:** Baseball; CrossFit training; Fishing **PA:** Independent **RE:** Roman Catholic **THT:** Dr. Misiek said, "When you choose to put your needs second to those entrusted to your care, and you always put forward your best effort, you will be rewarded in ways you never would have imagined."

MITCHELL, PAUL III, T: U.S. Representative from Michigan **I:** Government Administration/Government Relations/Government Services **CN:** U.S. House of Representatives **DOB:** 11/14/1956 **PB:** Boston **SC:** MA/USA **MS:** Married **SPN:** Sherry Mitchell (2008) **CH:** Six Children **ED:** Bachelor of Arts, Michigan State University (1978) **C:** Member, U.S. House of Representatives from Michigan's 10th District (2017-Present); Chairperson, Faith & Freedom Coalition, Michigan (2013-Present); Owner,

Ross Medical Education Center (2004-Present); Member, Committee on Education and the Workforce; Member, Committee on Oversight and Government Reform; Member, Committee on Transportation

MITCHELL, ROBERT, T: Founder **I:** Health, Wellness and Fitness **CN:** Safe Harbour Wellness **MS:** Married **ED:** Coursework, University of Louisiana at Lafayette **C:** Founder, Chief Wellness Officer, Safe Harbour Wellness (2018-Present); Model, Click Model Management (Click Model NYC) (2016-Present); President, Safe Harbour, Inc., (2012-Present); Actor, J Pervis Talent Agency (2009-Present); President, Greenovation Specialists, LLC (2004-Present); President of Sales, Castle Medical, LLC (2012-2015); President and Chief Executive Officer, Coastal Disaster Solutions (2010-2012) **CIV:** President, Giving Hands, Inc. (2008-Present) **AW:** Named to People on the Move in Birmingham, AL, Birmingham Business Journal, American City Business Journals (2018); Named Number One Fastest Growing Healthcare Company, Number Four Fastest Growing Company Overall, Inc., 5000 List, Mansueto Ventures (2015); Named to People on the Move in Atlanta, GA, Atlanta Business Journal, American City Business Journals (2014) **AS:** Mr. Mitchell attributes his success to his unwavering commitment to challenge himself beyond perceived limitations. He gives himself permission both to dream and to fail, which has been key to his uncommon success. Further, Mr. Mitchell believes success is a team effort and thus strives to assemble teams of smart and talented individuals to collaborate with and grow in success together. **B/I:** Mr. Mitchell's fascination with wellness led him to his industry. He is moved to help optimize individual wellness through scientific innovation and nature's FARMaceuticals. **THT:** Mr. Mitchell's believes one should always stretch their perceived limits, live outside of the box and constantly challenge the status quo.

MITTY, HAROLD A. MD, T: Radiologist **I:** Medicine & Health Care **DOB:** 02/20/1933 **PB:** New York **SC:** NY/USA **MS:** Widower **SPN:** Ethel Mitty, RN (Deceased) **CH:** Roger; Emily **ED:** Resident Radiologist, Mount Sinai Hospital, New York, NY (1962-1965); Resident Internal Medicine, Maimonides Hospital, Brooklyn, NY (1961-1962); Intern, Mount Sinai Hospital, New York, NY (1958-1959); MD, State University of New York Downstate (1958) **CT:** Certified, CAQ-diagnostic and Interventional Radiology (1995); Certified Radiologist (1966) **C:** Retired (2013); Professor, Radiology, Mount Sinai School Medicine; MD, Mount Sinai Hospital, New York, NY **MIL:** U.S. Navy (1959-1961) **CW:** Author, "Radiology of the Adrenals: with Sonography and CT" (1982); Author, 190 Peer Reviewed Articles; Author, 25 Chapters, Books **AW:** Gold Medal of the Society of Interventional Radiology; Lifetime Achievement Award, Society of Uroradiology; Master Teaching Award, State University College of Medicine; Jacobi Medal, Mount Sinai Hospital **MEM:** Fellow, American College Radiology (FACR); Fellow, Society of Interventional Radiology (FSIR); Founding Member, FSIR; American Roentgen Ray Society; Radiology Society of North America; Past President, New York Roentgen Society **MH:** Albert Nelson Marquis Lifetime Achievement Award **AS:** Dr. Mitty attributes his success to right place, right time, hard work. **B/I:** Dr. Mitty liked biology and other sciences in high school. He was the oldest of five children and the first in his family to attend college. With limited financial resources, Dr. Mitty attended Queens College, which was tuition free, majoring in biology and chemistry. Following college graduation, he entered the State University College of Medicine at New York City, graduating in 1958. **AV:** Amateur radio; Travel: Europe, Africa, Japan, China, Vietnam, Cambodia, Galapagos Islands **THT:** It is at the end of one's life that you realize how important the decisions were at the beginning.

MIYAMOTO, RICHARD T., MD, T: Otolaryngologist **I:** Medicine & Health Care **DOB:** 02/02/1944 **PB:** Zeeland **SC:** MI/USA **PT:** Dave Norio Miyamoto; Haruko (Okano) Miyamoto **MS:** Married **SPN:** Cynthia VanderBurgh (06/17/1967) **CH:** Richard Christopher; Geoffrey Takashi **ED:** Honorary Degree in Engineering, Rose Hulman Institute of Technology (2001); MS in Otology, University of Southern California (1978); MD, University of Michigan (1970); BS, Wheaton College, Cum Laude (1966) **CT:** Otolaryngology (1976); Neurotology **C:** Professor Emeritus, Indiana University School of Medicine (2018-Present); Arilla Devault Professor Emeritus, Otolaryngology, Indiana University School of Medicine (1991-Present); Professor, Indiana University School of Medicine (1988-2018); Chairman, Department of Otolaryngology, Indiana University School of Medicine (1987-2014); Chief, Otology and Neurotology, Department of Otology, Head and Neck Surgery, Indiana University School of Medicine (1982-2014); Chief, Otolaryngology, Head and Neck Surgery, Wishard Memorial Hospital (1979-2002); Associate Professor, Indiana University School of Medicine (1983-1988); Assistant Professor, Indiana University School of Medicine (1978-1983); Fellow in Otology and Neurotology, St. Vincent Hospital, Otologic Medical Group (1977-1978); Resident in Otolaryngology, Indiana University School of Medicine (1972-1975); Resident in Surgery, Butterworth Hospital, Grand Rapids, MI (1971-1972); Intern, Butterworth Hospital, Grand Rapids, MI (1970-1971) **CIV:** Advisory Council, National Institute of Deafness and Other Communication Disorders (2002-Present); Advisory Council, National Institute of Deafness and Other Communication Disorders (1989-1994); Chairman, Advisory Board, St. Joseph Institute for the Deaf; Advisory Board, The Ear Foundation; Advisory Board, Alexander Graham Bell Association for the Deaf; Advisory Board, National Institutes of Health **MIL:** Major, U.S. Air Force (1975-1977) **CW:** Editorial Board, Laryngoscope; Editorial Board, American Journal of Otology; Editorial Board, Associate Editor, Otolaryngology-Head and Neck Surgery; Editorial Board, European Archives of Oto-Rhino-Laryngology; Editorial Board, Anales de Otorhinolaryngology Mexicana; Editorial Board, Auris Nasus Larynx; Editorial Board, World Journal of Otorhinolaryngology-Head and Neck Surgery; Editorial Board, Cochlear Implants international; Contributor, Articles, Professional Journals **AW:** Ritchey Emeriti Faculty Service Award (2018); President's Medal, Indiana University (2018); Award of Merit, American Otological Society (2014) **MEM:** President, Indiana Chapter, Alpha Omega Alpha (2003-Present); President, Association of Research Otolaryngology (2001-Present); Otosclerosis Study Group (1993-Present); Governor, President, American Academy of Otolaryngology-Head And Neck Surgery (1982-Present); Secretary-Treasurer, President-Elect, President, Association Academy Departments In Otolaryngology-Head And Neck Surgery (2002-2008); Vice-President, Middle Section, American Otological, Rhinological, and Laryngological Society (2002-2003); Fellow, Executive Committee, American College Of Surgeons; American Auditory Society (1985-2003); President, American Neurotology Society (2000-2001); Council Member, American Otolaryngology Society (1992-1994); Board of Directors, President Centurion Group, Deafness Research Institute; Institute of Medicine of National Academy of Sciences; Collegium Oto-Rhino-Laryngologicum Amicitiae

Sacrum; Royal Society of Medicine of London; New York Academy of Sciences; American Academy of Pediatricians; Marines Memorial Association; Cosmos Club Of Washington; Wheaton College Scholastic Honor Society; Psi Iota Xi **MH:** Albert Nelson Marquis Lifetime Achievement Award; Marquis Who's Who Top Professional **AS:** Dr. Miyamoto has had tremendous support from his family every step of the way on his journey to success. He married his wife, Cynthia, during his freshman year of medical school. She has been supportive from the very beginning of his career, for which he is ever-grateful. **B/I:** It was not Dr. Miyamoto's upbringing or family history that attracted him to his profession but, as a medical student, he found a specialty in the pre-dental program when he attended Wheaton College. Most of his classes overlapped with pre-med courses, so, after his freshman year, he decided to take on the pre-med program. Dr. Miyamoto then went to the University of Michigan, where he got to work with their excellent staff. There, he became more exposed to otolaryngology and microsurgery, finding these fields to be his primary interests. **AV:** Golfing **RE:** Presbyterian

MOBLEY, JONNIEPAT, PHD, T: Theater Director, Professor **I:** Education/Educational Services **DOB:** 08/01/1932 **PB:** Detroit **SC:** MI/USA **PT:** John Patrick Moore; Charlotte Pauline (Tillman) Moore **MS:** Widowed **SPN:** J. Dwight Mobley **CH:** Eve Stanlyn Mobley **ED:** PhD in English, Concentration in Drama, University of Southern California (1974); MA in English, Cal State LA (1964); BA in English, Mount Saint Mary College (1962) **CT:** Certified English, Speech and Theater Teacher, State of California **C:** Retired, Theater Director, Professor, Theater Department Chair, Cuesta College (1996); Speech Instructor, Cuesta College (1985-1996); Director, Mission Players (1983); Director, Parish Players (1981-1982); Professor, West Los Angeles College (1969-1978); Lecturer, Mount Saint Mary College (1962-1967) **CR:** Guest Poet, Read Together Los Angeles (2018); Central Coast Theatre (2017); St. Peter's Readers Theatre (1990, 2015); Director, Cuesta College Players (1990, 1996) **CIV:** National Right to Life; PETA; Secretary, Friends of the Los Osos Library Board; Former President, Meals on Wheels of Morro Bay; Liturgist, Pastoral Council Member, St. Elizabeth Ann Seton Catholic Church **CW:** Editor, Woods Newsletter (1995-Present); Author, "Access to Shakespeare" (1995); Author, "Play Production Today!" (1995); Author, "Dictionary of Theater and Drama" (1992); Writer, Director, "The Orange Grove" (1990); Director, Workshop Production, "Two Stars Evenly Placed," Edward Albee Workshop Summer Arts Festival (1987); Writer, Director, "Murder at Maywood" (1983); Writer, Director, Radio Play, "Nursery Crimes" (1981); Writer, Director, Radio Play, "Snug Harbor" (1981) **AW:** Outstanding Young Women of America (1965) **MEM:** Alpha Mu Gamma; Lambda Iota Tau; Bound and Determined Book Discussion Club; Melrose Actors Theater **MH:** Albert Nelson Marquis Lifetime Achievement Award; Marquis Who's Who Top Professional **B/I:** Dr. Mobley became involved in her profession because of her long-standing interest in the theater and entertainment, as well as her father's encouragement and influence. **AV:** Growing roses; Writing; Playing bridge; Reading; Baking **RE:** Roman Catholic

MOCK, ROBERT CLAUDE, T: Architect **I:** Architecture & Construction **DOB:** 05/03/1928 **PB:** Baden **SC:** Germany **PT:** Ernest Mock; Charlotte (Geismar) Mock **MS:** Married **SPN:** Marjorie Reubenfeld (12/20/1964); Belle Carol Bach (12/23/1952, Divorced) **CH:** John Bach; Nicole Louise **ED:** MArch, Harvard University (1953); BArch, Pratt

Institute (1950) **C:** Founder, Robert C. Mock & Associates, New York, NY (1960-1994); Director Facility Design, American Airlines, New York, NY (1955-1960); Architectural Critic, Columbia School of Architecture, New York, NY (1953-1954); Architect, George C. Marshall Space Center, Huntsville, AL (1950-1951) **CR:** Mayor's Panel of Architects, New York, NY **CW:** Residencies, Bethesda, MD (1993, 1997, 1998, 1999); Residencies, Potomac Falls, MD (1995); Residencies, Fenwick Island, DE (1994); Residences, Palm Beach, FL (1989-1992); Flight Kitchen Buildings, Ogden Food Corporation, Kennedy Airport (1984, 1988); Restaurants, La Guardia Airport (1987); Passenger Terminal Extension, Varig Brazilian Airlines (1985); Greenwich Association of Retarded Citizens School (1983); Cargo Terminal, Air India, Flying Tiger, Kennedy Airport (1982); Corporate Headquarters, Bankers Trust Company, New York, NY (1980); Norel-Ronel Industrial Park, Hollywood, FL (1979); North American Headquarters, Irish International Airlines, New York, NY (1979); Corporate Headquarters, American Airlines (1977); North American Headquarters, Varig Brazilian Airlines, New York, NY (1977); Passenger Terminal, Aerolineas, Argentina (1974); North American Headquarters, Aerolineas Argentinas, New York, NY (1974); Cargo Terminals, El Al Israel Airline Cargo Terminal, Kennedy Airport (1972); FAA-National Prototype Air Traffic Control Tower (1966); Happyland School, New York, NY (1965); Cargo Buildings, Alitalia Airlines, Lufthansa German Airlines, Kennedy Airport (1965); Ambassador Club, La Guardia Airport, New York, NY (1964); Terminal Buildings, Eastern Air Lines, Trans World Airlines, La Guardia Airport, New York, NY (1963); Eastern Air Lines Medical Center, Kennedy Airport (1962); Ticket Office, Trans World Airlines, New York, NY (1962); Shine Motor Inn, Queens, NY (1961); Temporary Terminal Building, Eastern Air Lines, La Guardia Airport, New York, NY (1961); Cargo Buildings, United Airlines, Trans World Airlines (1961); Swiss Air Cargo Terminal, Lufthansa German Airlines **AW:** Volunteer of Year Award, United Way (1984) **MEM:** American Arbitration Association; Harvard Club; Admirals Cove Club **MH:** Albert Nelson Marquis Lifetime Achievement Award **B/I:** From a young age, Mr. Mock was a talented mathematician and artist. After reading Ayn Rand's book, "The Fountainhead," which was about a young architect, he knew what he wanted to do with his life. After serving in the military, Mr. Mock was able to fully dedicate himself to his career in architecture.

MODICA, IPPOLITO, T: Site Director of Anatomic Pathology **I:** Medicine & Health Care **CN:** Mount Sinai West **SC:** Italy **PT:** Salvatore Modica; Grace Modica **ED:** Fellowship in Gynecologic Pathology, Memorial Sloan Kettering Cancer Center; Fellowship in Ontological Surgical Pathology, Memorial Sloan Kettering Cancer Center; Residency, St. Vincent's Hospital; Residency in Anatomic Pathology, Università Degli Studi di Genova; MD, Università Degli Studi di Genova **C:** Site Director of Anatomic Pathology, Mount Sinai West (2011-Present); Postdoctoral Research Scientist, Memorial Sloan Kettering Cancer Center **CIV:** College of American Pathologists; United States & Canadian Academy of Pathology; American Society for Clinical Pathology **AW:** Nevil Coleman Award; Pozzallo United Award **MEM:** Society of The Citizens of Pozzallo United **B/I:** Dr. Modica became involved in his profession because of his lifelong interest in biology and science.

MOESSNER, DAVID P., DR.THEOL, T: A.A. Bradford Chair of Religion **I:** Education/Educational Services **CN:** Texas Christian University **PB:** Lincoln **SC:** NE/USA **PT:** Samuel F. Moessner; Helen L. Moessner; **MS:** Married **SPN:** The Rev. Dr. Jeanne

Stevenson-Moessner CH: David Stevenson; Jean McCarley **ED:** Doctor of Theology, University of Basel, Switzerland, Insigni Cum Laude (1983); MA, University of Oxford; BA, University of Oxford (1976); MDiv, Princeton Theological Seminary, NJ, Summa Cum Laude (1975); BA in Pre-Med, Religion, Princeton University, NJ, with High Honors (1971) **CT:** SNTS (International Society of New Testament Studies) (1989-Present); NAPS - The North American Patristics Society (2004); Chicago Society of Biblical Research (CSBR) (1997); Library Committee for Eastern Europe, SNTS (1996); Society of Biblical Literature (1985); Ordained as Minister of Word and Sacrament (Teaching Elder) in the Presbyterian Church, (PC (USA) **C:** A. A. Bradford Chair of Religion in Biblical Studies, Texas Christian University (2012-Present); Faculty Associate, Department of Theology, Radboud University, Nijmegen, Netherlands (2011-Present); Honorary Faculty, Associate, New Testament Faculty, Theology, University of Pretoria, South Africa (2009-Present); Professor of Biblical Theology, University of Dubuque Theological Seminary, Iowa (1997-2012); Associate and Full Professor of New Testament, Columbia Theological Seminary, Decatur, GA (1984-1995, 1996-1997); Assistant Professor, New Testament, Yale Divinity School, New Haven, CT (1983-1984); Instructor of Biblical Studies, Louisiana State University, Baton Rouge, LA (1982-1983) **CR:** Belhar Special Committee General Assembly, Presbyterian Church (PC(USA)), Louisville, KY (2009-Present); President, Southwest Region, Society of Biblical Literature, Dallas/Fort Worth, Texas (2017-2018); Special Session, Featuring Career Work as "Premier Scholar of the Lukan Writings," Gospel of Luke and Acts of the Apostles, Annual North American Meeting, Society of Biblical Literature and American Academy of Religion, San Antonio, Texas (2016); Guest Professor of New Testament, Eberhard Karls Universität, Tübingen, Germany, Winter Semester (1993-1994); Member, Greek Education Ministries International, Professional Consultant Scholars Program **CIV:** Board of Directors, Rotary Club of Dubuque (2002-2006); Board of Directors, Dubuque Rescue Mission, Iowa (2001-2008); Volunteer, Charitable Fund Drives, Including The Salvation Army USA, The American National Red Cross, March of Dimes, Others **CW:** Editorial Board, Sacra Scripta, Kluj-Napoca, Romania (2006-Present); Editorial Board, New Testament Studies (2003-2006); Editorial Board, Novum Testamentum (1991-Present); Executive Editor, Supplements to Novum Testamentum; Book Editor, New Revision of the NRSV2 (Gospel of Luke); Author, "Lord of the Banquet. The Literary and Theological Significance of the Lukan Travel Narrative," Two Editions; Author, "Luke the Historian of Israel's History, Theologian of Israel's Christ. A New Reading of the Gospel Acts of Luke"; Author/Editor, "Luke the Historian of Israel," Two Volumes, "Jesus and the Heritage of Israel" and "Paul and the Heritage of Israel"; Editor, "Re-examining Paul's Letters"; Contributor, Nearly 100 Articles, Professional Peer-reviewed Journals **AW:** John Knox Coit Prize in Teaching Excellence, University of Dubuque Board of Trustees (2010); E.S.I. Research Fellowship, The Pew Charitable Trusts (1993-1994); Karl Barth Prize, Presbytery of Chicago (1978); Named to The Phi Beta Kappa Society, Princeton University, NJ (1971); Most Valuable Student Award, International Order of Elks (1967); Named to Hall of Fame, University of Dubuque Board of Trustees; Named to Top 2000 Intellectuals of 21st Century; Named to Outstanding Young Men of America; Viva Voce for First Class Honors **MEM:** Rotary International; The Phi Beta Kappa Society; Professional Guilds **MH:** Albert Nelson Marquis Lifetime Achievement Award **AS:** Dr. Moessner attributes his success to a loving God, caring

parents, committed wife-life partner, devoted children, remarkable colleagues, and hard work! **B/I:** Dr. Moessner is committed to loving God and loving people; one way to follow this ambition was to become a biblical scholar and teach others about the Jewish and Christian Bibles that together form the greatest salutary influence upon civilization than any other literature in world history. **AV:** Travel; Music; History, especially World War II **RE:** Christian **THT:** Dr. Moessner's wife, Rev. Dr. Jeanne Stevenson-Moessner, is from Southern Methodist University. His work with the Library Committee for Eastern Europe, at SNTS in 1996, was supporting the re-establishing of departments and libraries for religious studies at the universities of Sophia, Bulgaria, St. Petersburg, Russia, and Clug-Napoca, Romania. Dr. Moessner's motto is, "Never be jealous of those smarter and more gifted than myself; such an attitude only makes one even less smart and lacking even more in one's ability to achieve in one's profession."

MOGUL, HARRIETTE ROSEN, BA, MD, MPH, T: Endocrinologist; Author **I:** Medicine & Health Care **PB:** Newark **SC:** NJ/USA **PT:** Emanuel P. Rosen; Pearl P. Rosen **MS:** Widowed **SPN:** Malcolm D. Mogul (07/12/1964, Deceased 2019) **CH:** Jennifer Mogul; Fred Mogul; Douglas Mogul **ED:** MPH, Columbia University Mailman School of Public Health, New York, NY (1991); MD, Albert Einstein College of Medicine, Bronx, NY (1965); BA, Bryn Mawr College, PA, Cum Laude (1961) **CT:** Board Eligible, Endocrinology, Westchester Medical Center (1996) **C:** Associate Professor in Endocrinology, New York Medical College, Valhalla, NY (1992-2018); Founder, Director, Institute of Women's Medical Research, Barnard College, Columbia University (1985-1991); Director of Health Services, Barnard College, Columbia University, New York, NY (1971-1991) **CR:** Principal Investigator, Student Suicide Prevention Program, Pew Charitable Trust, Collaborative College, New York, NY (1988-1990) **CIV:** President, National Board of Governors, Alumni Association, Albert Einstein College Medicine, Bronx, NY (1998-2000) **CW:** Author, "Syndrome W, A Woman's Guide to Reversing Midlife Weight Gain" (2005, 2010) **AW:** Lifetime Achievement Award, Albert Einstein College of Medicine (2019); Named Woman of Distinction, Women's Division, Albert Einstein College for Women (Now Albert Einstein College of Medicine) (2005) **MH:** Albert Nelson Marquis Lifetime Achievement Award **B/I:** Dr. Mogul became involved in her profession because her father was a physician and her great aunt on her father's side was also a well-known female physician. On her mother's side of the family, her first cousin was a well-known pathologist who made some major discoveries. Her familial inspirations were her main influence in deciding to pursue medicine. In addition, she knew that she was going to pursue her profession. **AV:** Writing; Photography; Cooking; Gardening; Opera; Movies; Family time **PA:** Democrat

MOHAMMED WOODS, MARIO, T: Founder, Chief Executive Officer **I:** Leisure, Travel & Tourism **CN:** Oceanwide Travel Services LLC **DOB:** 10/09/1980 **PB:** Saint Croix, Virgin Islands **PT:** Mario Augustin Mason; Rhonda Leatrice Woods **MS:** Divorced **SPN:** Ricky Lynn Tate Jr. **CH:** Samuel McNeal Gonzalez; Donnie Haywood; Lawrence Gaston **ED:** Bachelor of Applied Science in Business Administration and Management, Ashley University (2000) **C:** Founder, Chief Executive Officer, Tempo Records, Florida (2019-Present); Founder, Chairperson, Chief Executive, Visionary Officer, Oceanwide Travel Services LLC, Florida (2013-Present) **CIV:** Donor, Covenant House Florida **MIL:** Honorary Colonel of the Royal Guard of

the Former Grand Dukedom of Pomerania and Livonia and Knight of the Sacred and Military Order of Merit of Livonia **AW:** Best Travel Agency in Florida (2015, 2016) **AS:** H.S.H. Prince Mohammed attributes his success to perseverance. **B/I:** H.S.H. Prince Mohammed worked in call centers for different travel agencies and began to take an interest in the industry. He eventually progressed to the role of a supervisor of vacation planning, and eventually directed operations. Once he spent some time in this position, he began to realize that he was practically running the business himself and that he could handle such a venture on his own.

MOIR, RALPH WAYNE, T: Physicist **I:** Sciences **DOB:** 01/21/1940 **PB:** Bellingham **SC:** WA/USA **PT:** Francis LeRoy Moir; Florence Augusta (Hershey) Moir **MS:** Married **SPN:** Elizabeth Grace Branstead (06/09/1963); Maryann Brent (06/01/2001) **CH:** Sara Louise; Steven Hershey; Christina Elizabeth **ED:** ScD, Massachusetts Institute of Technology (1967); BS, University of California Berkeley (1962) **CT:** Registered Professional Nuclear Engineer, California **C:** Group Leader in Magnetic and Inertial Fusion Energy, Lawrence Livermore National Laboratory (1968-2009); Head Fusion Breeder Program, Lawrence Livermore National Laboratory (1979-1988); Postdoctoral Researcher, Center Nuclear Studies, Atomic Energy Commission, Fontenay-Aux-Roses, France (1967-1968) **CR:** Development and Commercializing Molten Salt Fission Power **CIV:** Board of Directors, Interfaith Housing, Inc., Livermore (1985-Present); President, Interfaith Housing, Inc., Livermore (1991-1994) **CW:** Member, Editorial Board, Journal of Fusion Energy (1984-1993); Contributor, Articles, Professional Journals and Books; Patentee in Field **AW:** Atomic Energy Commission Fellow (1962-1965); Named Eagle Scout, Boy Scouts of America (1958) **MEM:** Chairman, Fusion Energy Division, American Nuclear Society (1993-1994); Fellow, American Physical Society (1981); Fellow, American Nuclear Society (1989); World Future Society; Negative Population Growth Society; Americans for Energy Independence; Americans for Nuclear Energy; Scientists and Engineers for Secure Energy; Sigma Xi; Delta Chi **MH:** Albert Nelson Marquis Lifetime Achievement Award; Marquis Who's Who Top Professional **B/I:** Mr. Moir liked science and the practical stuff, building things with his hand so practical science. He had a relative Harold Hershey Hall, who was a physicist and was very inspiring. **PA:** Republican **RE:** Unitarian Universalist

MOLIÈRE, JOHN, T: Chairman **I:** Telecommunications **CN:** Standard Communication Inc. **DOB:** 07/05/1942 **PB:** Jersey City **SC:** NJ/USA **PT:** Carl A. Molière (Deceased); Margaret Mary (Maher) Molière (Deceased) **MS:** Married **SPN:** Susanne (1992) **CH:** Five Children **ED:** Postgraduate Studies, University of Virginia (1988); BS in Computer Science and Mathematics, Boston University (1986) **C:** President, Standard Communications Inc. (2001-Present); President, Sherikon Inc. (1996-2001) **CIV:** Donator, Numerous Nonprofit and Charitable Organizations **AW:** Fed 100 Award, 100 Most Influential People in the Greater Washington Area; John K. Lopez Lifetime Achievement Award, National Veterans Business Owners Association; Gordon H. Mansfield Award, National Veterans Small Business Coalition; Legionnaire of the Year, American Legion; Entrepreneur of the Year, Sherikon Inc.; Don Quixote Award, Cimcon Systems; KPMG Entrepreneur Award; Fairfax County Chamber of Commerce Award **MEM:** Disabled American Veterans; The American Legion **AS:** Mr. Molière attributes his success to having a great deal of perseverance and not believing in quitting. He said, "In the pursuit of perfection, if you can achieve excellence along the way, you've done a great job." Additionally, he attributes his success to leadership and training, noting, "Leadership is an element of management that can't be taught, but rather improved upon. From the time of childhood, you are always in a position of leadership because people gravitate toward leaders." Believing in many cases, his success was at the expense of his competitors; he simply outworked, outsmarted, and outhustled them. **B/I:** Mr. Molière became involved in his profession because his mother and sister died the same year; his grandmother stepped up and became his surrogate mother afterward. His upbringing revolved around his French heritage, which led him to speak French growing up in his household. When he joined the military, and they knew of his ability to speak the language, they sent him to Vietnam. While working on a ship, he discovered that there were man more ways to communicate than he had previously knew. He became fascinated with communications, especially in the medical field due to how rapidly they must communicate in emergencies. As a service disabled he did rehab at Brockton VA Hospital. He enrolled in Boston College on the GI Bill. He developed an appreciation for veterans and the work they had done. When he had the chance he started to serve disabled veterans through a small business. Then, with a colleague, he established a veterans' government wide acquisition contract. **THT:** Mr. Molière's words to live by are "Non sibi sed patriae," which means "Not for self, but country"; "be prepared"; and "do a good turn daily."

MOLLIGAN, PETER NICHOLAS, T: Lawyer **I:** Law and Legal Services **DOB:** 03/08/1938 **PB:** New Orleans **SC:** LA/USA **PT:** Peter Nicholas Molligan; Violet Augusta (Scheeler) Molligan **MS:** Married **SPN:** Paula Peterson Molligan (12/23/1999) **CH:** Liza J.; Jessica L.; Rene J. **ED:** Doctor of Jurisprudence, San Francisco Law School (1970); Bachelor of Arts, Louisiana State University (1960) **CT:** Recognition of Experience Certificate in Trial Law, Personal Injury, Product Liability Professional Negligence and Insurance Bad Faith, California Trial Lawyers Association (1975) **C:** Retired (1999); Chief Executive Officer, Molligan, Cox & Moyer, San Francisco, CA (1970-1999); Claims Manager, Government Employees Insurance Company, San Francisco, CA (1963-1970) **CR:** Marin Superior Court, Alameda Superior Court (1989-2000); Judge Pro Tempore, San Francisco Superior Court **MIL:** Lieutenant Junior Grade, U.S. Navy (1960-1965); Officer Training Command, Officer Candidate School, U.S. Navy (1960) **AW:** Best Lawyers in America or Settlements in Major Verdicts in Medical and Legal Malpractice, Products Liability, Insurance Excess Liability, Multi State Toxic Torts, Bencate and DBCP; Highest Possible Rating by Martindale-Hubbell **MEM:** Fellow, American College Trial Lawyers; American Board of Trial Advocates; National Board of Trial Advocates **BAR:** California (1970) **MH:** Albert Nelson Marquis Lifetime Achievement Award **B/I:** Mr. Molligan became involved in his profession because he knew he would make great strides in trial law. He transitioned from the insurance industry to the legal field at the age of 33. **AV:** Tennis; Chess; Hunting; Skeet shooting; Sporting clays **PA:** Independent

MOLNAR, ROBYN L., T: Registered Nurse **I:** Medicine & Health Care **CN:** Self Employed **ED:** BS in Nursing, William Paterson University (1997); AS in Applied Science, Passaic County Community College (1995) **C:** Hospice Nurse, Vitas (2018-Present); Oncology Nurse, Osceola Regional Medical Center **CW:** Profiled as a Photographer, Cloud Appreciation Society (2014-Present); Author, Poetry, The International Who's Who of Poetry (2009) **AW:** Spirits of Nursing Award, U.S. Army (1995) **MEM:** Cloud Appreciation Society **AS:** Ms. Molnar has a lot of energy; she enjoys what she does. **B/I:** Ms. Molnar's cousin on her mother's side was a nurse for 35 years, and a great aunt on her father's side was a nurse as well. These individuals inspired her to become a nurse. She was also attracted to the field because of the variety of positions. **AV:** Taking photographs of clouds

MOLTON, PETER M., PHD, T: Waste Conversion Researcher, Consultant **I:** Consulting **DOB:** 08/21/1943 **PB:** Wolverhampton **SC:** England **PT:** Cuthbert Joseph Molton; Fay (Hudson) Molton **MS:** Single **SPN:** Elizabeth Eirwen Carrington (11/17/1964, Divorced 02/1971); Marion Elizabeth Glock (02/25/1971, Divorced 06/1995) **CH:** Sharon Elizabeth; Ivan Robert; Kerrin Amy **ED:** Diploma in Space Physics, University of London (1971); MPhil in Microbiology, University of London (1971); PhD in Organic Chemistry, University of London (1967); BSc, The University of Manchester, With Honors (1964) **C:** Retired (2005); Senior Research Scientist, Battelle Pacific Northwest National Laboratory (1975-2005); Research Associate, University of Maryland, College Park, MD (1972-1974); National Academy of Sciences Postdoctoral Fellow, NASA (1971-1972) **CIV:** Ward Treasurer, Chiswick Conservative Party, London (1969-1970) **CW:** Contributor, Articles, Professional Journals; Author, Articles on Extraterrestrial Life; Inventor, Sludge to Oil Reactor System; Patentee, Tritum Polymer Lights **AW:** Research and Development 100 Award, Research and Development World (1988); Excellence in Technology Transfer Award, Federal Laboratory Consortium for Technology Transfer (1988) **MEM:** Fellow, The British Interplanetary Society; American Chemical Society; International Society for the Study of the Origin of Life; Alpha Chi Sigma **MH:** Albert Nelson Marquis Lifetime Achievement Award; Marquis Who's Who Top Professional; Marquis Who's Who Humanitarian Award **B/I:** Dr. Molton became involved in his profession because he was always interested in space and the post doctoral fellowship at NASA was the scientific study of extraterrestrial lives. **AV:** Gardening; Camping; Studying amateur astronomy; Teaching **PA:** Republican **RE:** Spiritualist

MOMJIAN, MARK ALBERT, T: Lawyer **I:** Law and Legal Services **CN:** Momjian Anderer, LLC **DOB:** 10/09/1961 **PB:** Philadelphia **SC:** PA/USA **PT:** Albert Momjian; Esther (nee Gostigian) Momjian **MS:** Married **SPN:** Melineh V. Momjian **CH:** David V. Momjian; Gregory V. Momjian **ED:** JD, Columbia University School of Law, Columbia University, New York, NY (1986); BA, Columbia College, Columbia University, New York, NY (1983) **C:** Shareholder, Momjian Anderer, LLC (2010-Present) **CR:** Associate/Partner, Schnader Harrison Segal & Lewis LLP (1988-2010); Adjunct Professor of Law, Villanova University School of Law; Adjunct Professor of Psychiatry, Drexel University College of Medicine **CIV:** Chair, Armenian Center at Columbia University; Chair, Alumni Representative Committee of Philadelphia for Columbia College and School of Engineering and Applied Science; Former President, Current Member of the Executive Committee, Columbia University Club of Philadelphia; Goodwill Ambassador, Aurora Forum; Former Board Member, International House Philadelphia; Armenian Assembly of America; Armenian Missionary Association of America; Radnor Memorial Library **CW:** Co-Author, Momjian & Momjian, Pennsylvania Family Law Annotated, Thomson Reuters (2019); Author, Contributor, Articles on Family Law, Journals and Newspapers, Including the National Law Journal, the American Journal of Family Law, Divorce Litigation, the Matrimonial Strategist, and the Pennsylvania Bar Association Quarterly; Lecturer on Family Law, Numerous Institutions, Princeton University, the University of Pennsylvania, Temple University, Rutgers University, Widener University, and on behalf of the Pennsylvania Bar Institute, Numerous State and Local Bar Associations, including the American Bar Association **AW:** Inductee, Alumni Representative Committee Hall of Fame, Columbia University, New York (2017); Alumni Medal for Distinguished Service, Columbia University, New York (2011); Outstanding Advocate Award, SeniorLAW Center (2006); Earl G. Harrison Award for Pro Bono Service (2006); Cheryl Ingram Advocate for Justice Award, Philadelphia Bar Association (2004); Pro Bono Attorney of the Year, Center for Lesbian and Gay Civil Rights (2002); Certificates for Pro Bono Service, First Judicial District, Philadelphia County Court of Common Pleas; Homeless Advocacy Project; Legal Aid of Southeastern Pennsylvania **MEM:** Union League of Philadelphia; Philadelphia, Delaware, and Montgomery County Bar Associations; Pennsylvania, American and Armenian Bar Associations; The Collector's Club (New York); Armenian Philatelic Association (Los Angeles) **BAR:** U.S. Supreme Court (2006); U.S. Court of Appeals for the Third Circuit (1989); U.S. District Court for the Eastern District of Pennsylvania (1987); Supreme Court of Pennsylvania (1986) **MH:** Who's Who in American Law; Who's Who in American Education

MOMOA, JOSEPH JASON, T: Actor **I:** Media & Entertainment **DOB:** 08/01/1979 **PB:** Nanakuli **SC:** HI/USA **PT:** Joseph Momoa; Coni (Lemke) Momoa **MS:** Married **SPN:** Lisa Bonet (10/2017) **CH:** Lola Iolani; Nakoa-Wolf; Zoë Kravitz (Stepdaughter) **C:** Owner, Producer, Pride of Gypsies **CW:** Actor, "See" (2019-Present); Actor, "Dune" (2020); Guest Appearance, "The Simpsons" (2019); Voice Actor, "The Lego Movie 2: The Second Part" (2019); Producer, Actor, "Braven" (2018); Actor, "Aquaman" (2018); Host, "Saturday Night Live" (2018); Executive Producer, Actor, "Frontier" (2016-2018); Actor, "Once Upon a Time in Venice" (2017); Actor, "The Bad Batch" (2017); Actor, "Justice League" (2017); Cameo, "Batman v Superman: Dawn of Justice" (2016); Actor, "Sugar Mountain" (2016); Actor, "The Red Road" (2014-2015); Guest Appearance, "Drunk History" (2014-2015); Director, Producer, Co-Writer, Actor, "Road to Paloma" (2014); Actor, "Debug" (2014); Actor, "Wolves" (2014); Actor, "Bullet to the Head" (2012); Actor, "Game of Thrones" (2011-2012); Actor, "Conan the Barbarian" (2011); Actor, "The Game" (2009); Actor, "Stargate Atlantis" (2005-2009); Actor, "Pipeline" (2007); Actor, "North Shore" (2004-2005); Actor, "Johnson Family Vacation" (2004); Actor, TV Film, "Baywatch: Hawaiian Wedding" (2003); Actor, TV Film, "Tempted" (2003); Actor, "Baywatch: Hawaii" (1999-2001); Actor, "Sweet Girl" **AW:** CinemaCon Award for Male Rising Star, "Game of Thrones" (2012); CinemaCon Award for Male Rising Star, "Conan the Barbarian" (2011); Hawaii's Model of the Year (1999)

MONDALE, WALTER, "FRITZ" FREDERICK, T: Former Vice President of the United States; Lawyer **I:** Government Administration/Government Relations/Government Services **DOB:** 01/05/1928 **PB:** Ceylon **SC:** MN/USA **PT:** Theodore Sigvaard Mondale; Claribel Hope (Cowan) Mondale **MS:** Widowed **SPN:** Joan Adams (12/27/1955, Deceased 02/03/2014) **CH:** Theodore; Eleanor Jane (Deceased); William **ED:** LLB, University of Minnesota, Cum Laude (1956); BA, University of Minnesota, Cum Laude (1951) **C:** Senior Counsel, Dorsey

& Whitney LLP, Minneapolis, MN (1997-Present); Presidential Envoy to Indonesia, U.S. Department of State (1998); U.S. Ambassador to Japan, U.S. Department of State, Tokyo, Japan (1993-1996); Partner, Dorsey & Whitney LLP, Minneapolis, MN (1987-1993); Democratic Nominee, Presidential Election, United States (1984); Partner, Winston & Strawn LLP (1981-1987); National Security Council (1977-1981); Vice President of the United States (1977-1981); U.S. Senator, State of Minnesota (1964-1977); Attorney General, State of Minnesota (1960-1964); Private Practice, Law, Minneapolis, MN (1956-1960); Law Clerk to Justice Thomas F. Gallagher, Minnesota Supreme Court, Minneapolis, MN (1956) **CR:** Chairman, National Democratic Institute for International Affairs (1986-1993) **CW:** Co-Author, "Twelve Years and Thirteen Days: Remembering Paula and Sheila Wellstone" (2003); Author, "The Good Fight: A Life in Liberal Politics" (2010); Co-Author, "Crisis and Opportunity in a Changing Japan" (1999); Author, "The Accountability of Power Toward a Responsible Presidency" (1975) **AW:** Lifetime Achievement Award, The American Lawyer Magazine (2011); Distinguished University Fellow in Law & Public Affairs, University of Minnesota Hubert H. Humphrey Institute of Public Affairs **BAR:** Minnesota (1956) **PA:** Democrat **RE:** Presbyterian

MONDELLO, MARK T., T: Chief Executive Officer **I:** Business Management/Business Services **CN:** Jabil Inc. **ED:** BSME, University of South Florida **C:** Chief Executive Officer, Jabil Circuit, Inc. (2013-Present); Chief Operating Officer, Jabil Circuit, Inc. (2002-2013); Senior Vice President, Jabil Circuit, Inc. (1999-2002); Vice President, Jabil Circuit, Inc. (1997-1999); Project Manager, Jabil Circuit, Inc. (1993-1997); Production Line Supervisor, Jabil Circuit, Inc., St. Petersburg, FL (1992-1993); Former Project Manager, Commercial and Def.-Related Aerospace Programs, Moog, Inc. **CIV:** Board of Directors, All Children's Hospital

MONTANA, JOE CLIFFORD JR., T: Former Professional Football Player **I:** Athletics **DOB:** 06/11/1956 **PB:** New Eagle **SC:** PA/USA **PT:** Joseph C. Montana Sr.; Theresa M. Montana **MS:** Married **SPN:** Jennifer Wallace (1985); Cass Castillo (1981, Divorced 1984); Kim Moses (1975, Divorced 1978) **CH:** Alexander Whitney; Elizabeth Jean; Nathaniel Joseph; Nicholas Alexander **ED:** BBA in Marketing, University of Notre Dame (1978) **C:** Member, New Business Development Department, Viking Components, Inc., Rancho Santa Margarita, CA (1999-2000); Retired Professional Football Player, NFL (1995); Quarterback, Kansas City Chiefs, NFL (1993-1995); Quarterback, San Francisco 49ers, NFL (1979-1993) **CR:** Founder, Montagia (2016) **CW:** Co-Author, With Alan Steinberg, "Cool Under Fire" (1989) **AW:** Named Number One Clutch Quarterback of All Time, Sports Illustrated (2006); Named to Pro Football Hall of Fame (2000); Named Greatest Athlete of the 20th Century (1999); Named to National Football Conference Pro Bowl Team, NFL (1982, 1984-1986, 1988, 1990, 1991, 1994); Named to First Team All-pro (1987, 1989, 1990); Winner, San Francisco 49ers, Super Bowl Championships (1982, 1985, 1989, 1990); Named Male Athlete of the Year, The Associated Press (1989, 1990); Named AP Athlete of the Year, The Associated Press (1989, 1990); Named Super Bowl MVP, NFL (1982, 1985, 1990); Named Man of the Year, Sporting News (1989); Named Player of the Year (1989); Named Offensive Player of the Year, The Associated Press (1989); Named NFL MVP (1989); Named NFL Comeback Player of the Year, The Associated Press (1986); Named to NFL 75th Anniversary All-time Team; Named to NFL Super Bowl Silver Anniversary Team; Named to NFL All-Decade Team (1980s) **AV:** Winemaking

MONTGOMERY, DENISE KAREN RN, RN, T: Nurse, Office Administration **I:** Medicine & Health Care **DOB:** 12/23/1951 **PB:** New York **SC:** NY/USA **PT:** Thomas Cornell; Dorothy Marie (Castine) Simons **MS:** Married **SPN:** Joseph Samuel Montgomery (08/20/1983); Timothy Bruce Montgomery (07/19/1974, Divorced 02/1981) **CH:** Elizabeth; Joshua **ED:** Associate in Nursing, San Jacinto College (1971) **CT:** Registered Nurse, Texas **C:** Office Manager, Supervisor, Dr. J.S. Montgomery III (1987-Present); Office Manager, Supervisor, Dr. Samuel Law, Houston, TX (1983-1984); Nurse, Dr. Eric J. Haufrect, Houston, TX (1982-1983); Program Coordinator, Population Control Program, Baylor College Medicine, Houston, TX (1979-1981); Nursing Supervisor, Baylor College Medicine, Houston, TX (1979-1981); Research Assistant, Department of Obstetrics-gynecology, Baylor College Medicine, Houston, TX (1977-1981); Charge Nurse, Aarons Womens Clinic, Houston, TX (1977) **CW:** Contributor, Articles, Professional Journals **AW:** Distinguished Public Service Award, American Heart Association (1976); Numerous Research Grants **MEM:** National Association of College Obstetricians and Gynecologists **MH:** Albert Nelson Marquis Lifetime Achievement Award; Marquis Who's Who Top Professional **AS:** Her determination to do what she wanted to do no matter what obstacles crossed her path. **B/I:** Ms. Montgomery became involved in her profession because when she was 14 years old she started out as a candy striper. She volunteered at the hospital and one day a nurse came to her and told her to go down to the emergency room. When she went down she saw her father having a heart attack and it suddenly hit her that's what she wanted to do for the rest of her life. **AV:** Sewing; Beading; Ballroom dancing **PA:** Republican **RE:** Christian Church

MOOK, SARAH, T: Chemist (Retired) **I:** Sciences **DOB:** 10/29/1929 **PB:** Brooklyn **SC:** NY/USA **PT:** Wong Mook; Lie Won (Woo) Mook **ED:** Postgraduate Coursework, Columbia University (1954-1957, 1962-1965); Postgraduate Coursework, University of Hartford (1958-1959); BA, Hunter College (1952) **CT:** Diplomate, Citizens Police Academy Program, The City of New York (2001) **C:** Principal Chemist, Bellevue Hospital Center, The City of New York, NY (1989-1995); Associate Chemist, Bellevue Hospital Center, The City of New York, NY (1984-1989); Clinical Chemist, Coney Island Hospital, The City of New York, NY (1974-1984); Community Board, Coney Island Hospital, The City of New York, NY (1978-1980); Senior Chemist, Nuclear Research Associates, Inc., New Hyde Park, NY (1964-1975); Chemist, Marks Polarized Corporation (1962-1964); Research Scientist, Radiation Applications, Inc. (1959-1962); Analytical Chemist, Nuclear Division, Combustion Engineering, Inc. (Now ALSTOM) (1957-1959); Research Assistant, Mineral Beneficiation Laboratory, Columbia University (1954-1957); Cartographic Aide, United States Geological Survey, U.S. Department of the Interior (1952-1954) **CR:** Member, Patient Safety Committee, Coney Island Hospital, The City of New York, NY (2007-Present); Instructor in English as a Second Language, Jay-Harama Senior Center, The City of New York, NY (2006-Present); Community Advisory Board, Coney Island Hospital, The City of New York, NY (2004-Present); Staff, Homecrest Community Services (1999-2005) **CIV:** Member, By-laws Committee, Coney Island Hospital, The City of New York, NY (2009-Present); Member, Community Advisory Board, Coney Island Hospital, The City of New York, NY (2004-Present); Member, Neighborhood Advisory Board, Department of Youth & Community Development, The City of New York, NY (1996-Present); Elder, Women's Christian Fellowship (1982-Present); Chair, Legislative Committee, Coney Island Hospital, The City of New York, NY (2011-2013); Member, Membership Committee, Coney Island Hospital, The City of New York, NY (2011-2012); Member, Community Board, Department of Youth & Community Development, The City of New York, NY (2002-2004); Chair, Neighborhood Advisory Board, Department of Youth & Community Development, The City of New York, NY (2000-2002); Secretary, Neighborhood Advisory Board, Department of Youth & Community Development, The City of New York, NY (1996-1999); Chair, Board of Trustees, Park Avenue Christian Church (1981-1982); Trustee, Park Avenue Christian Church (1973-1982); Vice Chair, Park Avenue Christian Church (1980-1981); Secretary, Park Avenue Christian Church (1973-1980); Member, Advisory Committee to State Assemblyman, State of New York (1970-1972); President, Women's Christian Fellowship (1962-1965) **CW:** Contributor, Articles, Professional Journals **AW:** Certificate of Recognition, Coney Island Hospital, The City of New York, NY (2012); Marjorie Matthews Community Advocate Recognition Award, Health & Hospital Committee, The New York City Council (2008); Woman of the Year Humanitarian Award, New York State Senate (2004); Honoree, Woman of the Year, New York City Council (2004); Margaret M. McCord Woman of the Year Memorial Award, Brooklyn Historical Society (Now Center for Brooklyn History), Brooklyn Public Library (2004); Distinguished Leadership In Community Award, Office of the New York City Comptroller **MEM:** Publicity Committee, National Citizens Police Academy Association (NCPAA) (2004-Present); Secretary, New York Metropolitan Section, American Association for Clinical Chemistry (AACC) (1999-2008); American Association for the Advancement of Science; American Chemical Society; The New York Academy of Sciences; Van Slyke Society; Nuclear Research Associates, Inc. **MH:** Albert Nelson Marquis Lifetime Achievement Award; Marquis Who's Who Top Professional; Marquis Who's Who Humanitarian Award **B/I:** Ms. Mook always wanted to be in medicine. However, she eventually found that she was better suited for a career in chemistry and pursued that. **AV:** Playing the piano; Playing the violin; Basketball; Fencing; Music **PA:** Republican **THT:** Ms. Mook's parents are very progressive; they believed that she should learn as much as possible. Her mother knew both English and Latin at the time she came to America. Music has been an ever-present aspect in her life. This is why she continues to meet with the city board to help raise money for charities associated with music.

MOOLENAAR, JOHN ROBERT, T: U.S. Representative from Michigan **I:** Government Administration/Government Relations/Government Services **DOB:** 05/08/1961 **PB:** Midland **SC:** MI/USA **MS:** Married **SPN:** Amy Moolenaar **CH:** Ben; Isaac; Sarah; Maggie; Audrey; Ann Marie **ED:** MPA, Harvard University (1989); BS, Hope College (1983) **C:** Member, U.S. House of Representatives from Michigan's Fourth Congressional District (2015-Present); Member, District 36, Michigan State Senate (2010-2015); Member, District 98, Michigan House of Representatives (2002-2008); Member, Committee on Appropriations; Member, Republican Study Committee;" Councilman, Midland City Council, MI; Director of Business Development, MITECH+; Lecturer, Saginaw Valley State University; Former Administrator, Midland Academy of Advanced and Creative Studies; Director, Small Business

Center, Midland Michigan Development Corporation; Product Market Developer, Dow Chemical **PA:** Republican

MOON, PETER S., T: Librarian (Retired) **I:** Library Management/Library Services **DOB:** 02/22/1953 **PB:** Washington, DC **SC:** USA **PT:** Alfred Evans Moon; Doris (Pender) Moon **MS:** Married **SPN:** Mary "Dottie" Gemmel (05/26/1979) **ED:** Master of Library Science, Syracuse University (1980); Bachelor of Science, Syracuse University (1977) **CT:** Certified Librarian, State University of New York (1980) **C:** Manager, Technical Resource Center, Hartford Steam Boiler Inspection and Insurance Co. (1988-2016); Reference Librarian, Aetna Life & Casualty, Hartford, CT (1988); Information Professor, Donahue & McCaughtry Inc., Wethersfield, CT (1987-1988); Reference Librarian, Health Center, University of Connecticut, Farmington, CT (1987); Library Services Coordinator, New England Journal of Medicine, Waltham, MA (1985-1986); Reference Librarian, Countway Library Medical, Harvard University, Boston, MA (1980-1985) **CR:** Library Professional, Governor's Conference on Library and Information Services, Waterbury, CT (1990) **CIV:** County Committee, 19th Election District of Oyster Bay, New York (1971) **CW:** Contributing Writer, TRC Column, "The Esch." (1990-Present); Associate Editor, Newsletter, "The Pulse" (1985-1986); Editor, "Countway Mini-Guide" (1983-1984); Compiler, Bibliography, "Countway Mini-Guide" (1982) **MEM:** Chapter President, Special Librarians Association (1993-1994); Program Chair, President-elect, Special Librarians Association (1992-1993); Chairman, Employment Committee, Connecticut Valley Chapter, Special Librarians Association (1989-1992); American Library Association; American Society for Information Science; New England Online Users Group; Strategic and Competitive Intelligence Professionals **MH:** Albert Nelson Marquis Lifetime Achievement Award **B/I:** Mr. Moon's interest in library science came about during the time he spent in public libraries as he came of age. However, he initially wanted to be an architect. After his first year in the architecture program at Syracuse University, Mr. Moon knew he needed to do something different. Marta Dosa, a library science advisor at Syracuse University, helped him navigate his way to the Ernest Stevenson Berg Library; he worked in the catalog section. From there, his career in library science grew. **AV:** Travel

MOONEY, ALEXANDER, "ALEX" XAVIER, T: U.S. Representative from West Virginia **I:** Government Administration/Government Relations/Government Services **CN:** U.S. House of Representatives **DOB:** 06/07/1971 **PB:** Washington **SC:** DC/USA **PT:** Vincent Mooney; Lala Mooney **MS:** Married **SPN:** Grace Gonzalez (2002) **CH:** Three Children **ED:** Bachelor of Arts in Philosophy, Dartmouth College (1993) **C:** Member, U.S. House of Representatives from West Virginia's Second Congressional District (2015-Present); Chairperson, Republican Party of Maryland (2011-2013); Director, National Journalism Center (2005-2012); Member, District Three, Maryland State Senate (1999-2011); Vice President, Legislative Analysis, CNP Action Inc. (1995-1998); Legislative Analyst, U.S. House Republican Conference (1995); Staff Assistant to Representative Roscoe G. Bartlett, U.S. House of Representatives (1993-1995); Member, House Committee on Financial Services; Member, Republican Study Committee **MEM:** Knights of Columbus **PA:** Republican **RE:** Roman Catholic

MOORE, ALECIA, "PINK" BETH, T: Singer **I:** Media & Entertainment **DOB:** 09/08/1979 **PB:** Doylestown **SC:** PA/USA **PT:** James Moore; Judith (Kugel)

Moore **MS:** Married **SPN:** Carey Hart (01/07/2006) **CH:** Jameson Moon Hart; Willow Sage Hart **C:** Solo Artist; Member, Choice; Member, Basic Instinct **CR:** Model, Spokesperson, CoverGirl (2012-Present) **CW:** Singer, "Hurts 2B Human" (2019); Singer, "Walk Me Home" (2019); Singer with Cash Cash, "Can We Pretend" (2019); Singer with Chris Stapleton, "Love Me Anyway" (2019); Singer, "A Million Reasons" (2018); Singer, "Beautiful Trauma" (2017); Appearance, "Popstar: Never Stop Never Stopping" (2016); Appearance, "Billy on the Street" (2015); Actress, "Janis: Little Girl Blue" (2015); Actress, "Thanks for Sharing" (2012); Singer, "The Truth About Love" (2012); Voice Actress, "Happy Feet II" (2011); Appearance, "Get Him to the Greek" (2010); Singer, "Greatest Hits...So Far!!!" (2010); Singer, "Raise Your Glass" (2010); Singer, "F**kin' Perfect" (2010); Singer, "Please Don't Leave Me" (2009); Singer, "Sober" (2008); Singer, "Funhouse" (2008); Singer, "So What" (2008); Appearance, "Catacombs" (2007); Singer, "Stupid Girls" (2006); Singer, "Who Knew" (2006); Singer, "Ur + Ur Hand" (2006); Singer, "I'm Not Dead" (2006); Singer, "Try This" (2003); Singer, "Trouble" (2003); Singer, "God Is a DJ" (2003); Appearance, "Charlie's Angels: Full Throttle" (2003); Appearance, "Rollerball" (2002); Singer, "Don't Let Me Get Me" (2002); Singer, "Just Like a Pill" (2002); Singer, "Family Portrait" (2002); Singer with Mya, Lil' Kim, and Christina Aguilera, "Lady Marmalade" (2001); Singer, "You Make Me Sick" (2001); Singer, "Get the Party Started" (2001); Singer, "M!ssundaztood" (2001); Singer, "There U Go" (2000); Singer, "Most Girls" (2000); Appearance, "Ski to the Max" (2000); Singer, "Can't Take Me Home" (2000) **AW:** Recipient, Star, Hollywood Walk of Fame (2019); Michael Jackson Video Vanguard Award, MTV Video Music Award (2017); Emmy Award for Outstanding Promotional Announcement - Image, Academy of Television Arts & Science (2016); BMI President's Award (2015); Co-recipient, Best Collaboration with Nate Ruess, MTV Video Music Awards (2013); Named One of the World's Most Powerful Celebrities, Forbes Magazine (2010); Two BMI Pop Awards, Broadcast Music, Inc. (2008); Award for Best Pop Video, MTV Video Music Awards (2006); Grammy Award for Best Female Rock Vocal Performance, Recording Academy (2004); Award for Best International Female Solo Artist, Brit Awards (2003); Award for Best Selling American Pop Female Artist, World Music Awards (2003); Grammy Award for Best Pop Collaboration with Vocals, Recording Academy (2002); Awards for Best Female Video, Best Dance Video, MTV Video Music Awards (2002); Award for Favorite Song, Nickelodeon Kids' Choice Awards (2002); Award for Favorite Female Artist, Nickelodeon Kids' Choice Awards (2002); Named One of the 100 Sexiest Artists, VH1 (2002); Awards for Video of Year, Best Video from a Film, MTV Video Music Awards (2001); Award for Favorite Female - New Artist, Blockbuster Entertainment Awards (2001); Award for Best Pop New Artist, Billboard Music Awards (2000); Named One of the Top Accomplished Women Entertainers, CEOWORLD Magazine; Recipient, Numerous Awards

MOORE, DAVID LOWELL, T: Dental Professor (Retired) **I:** Education/Educational Services **DOB:** 04/03/1930 **PB:** Hartshorne **SC:** OK/USA **PT:** David Lee Moore; Zula (Winslow) Moore **MS:** Married **SPN:** Mary Janell Stewart (09/07/1962) **CH:** David Lee; Andrew Stewart **ED:** MS, MA, University of Missouri at Kansas City (1964); DDS, University of Missouri at Kansas City School of Dentistry (1955); BS, Oklahoma State University, Stillwater, OK (1949) **C:** Retired Professor, Chairman, Department of Restorative Dentistry, University of Missouri at Kansas City (UMKC) School of Dentistry, Kansas City, MO (1964-2008); Associate Professor,

University of Missouri at Kansas City (UMKC) School of Dentistry, Kansas City, MO (1963-1964); Teaching Fellow, University of Missouri at Kansas City (UMKC) School of Dentistry, Kansas City, MO (1961-1963); Assistant Professor, Dentistry, University of Missouri at Kansas City (UMKC) School of Dentistry, Kansas City, MO (1958-1961) **CR:** Faculty Fellow, University of Kansas City Trustees (1982-1983);Consultant, Veterans Administration (VA) Hospitals; Faculty, VA Physician and Dentist in Residence Program; Test Construction Committee; National Board of Dental Examination; Presenter, Continuing Education Courses, 43 States; Faculty Practice, University of Missouri at Kansas City (UMKC) School of Dentistry **CIV:** Deacon, Nall Avenue Baptist Church, Shawnee, KS (1970) **MIL:** U.S. Air Force (1955-1958) **CW:** Author, Numerous Articles, Professional Journals; Author, Chapter, Textbook; Editorial Review Board, Journal of Prosthetic Dentistry **AW:** UMKC Dental Alumnus of the Year (2008); Certificate of Appreciation, Department of Veterans Affairs (1995); UMKC Elmer Pearson Outstanding Teacher Award (1989); Instructor of the Year Award (1989); Certificate of Appreciation for Contribution to Continuing Education, University of Pittsburg School of Dental Medicine (1986-1987); Outstanding Contribution to Continuing Education, Century Club, University of Southern California (1984); Distinguished Alumni Award (1984); Certificate of Appreciation, American Dental Association (1981); Outstanding Instructor Award (1971, 1973, 1976, 1977); Instructor of the Year Award (1965); Award of Merit, Florida Dental Society (1965); Instructor of the Year Award (1959); University Alumni Achievement Award **MEM:** Chairman, Operative Dentistry Section, American Association of Dental Schools (1985-1986); Century Club, University of Southern California (1984); Royal Order of Golden Tongue Orators, Fort Campbell, KY (1980); Exam Review Committee, Central Regional Dental Testing Service (1979); President, UMKC Dental Alumni Association (1977); Phi Kappa Phi (1976); Omicron Delta Kappa; Psi Omega; Dental Association **MH:** Albert Nelson Marquis Lifetime Achievement Award; Marquis Who's Who Top Professional **AS:** Dr. Moore attributes his success to persistence. **B/I:** Dr. Moore made the choice to become a dentist when he was 9 years old after being impressed by his dentist, Dr. Turner, who had a practice in his home. He additionally served three years in the Air Force, which he also loved. **AV:** Gardening, Writing **PA:** Republican **RE:** Christian **THT:** Dr. Moore believes life is all about love, family, and relationships. He additionally prioritizes making the right choices.

MOORE, GORDON EARLE, PHD, T: Co-founder, Chairperson Emeritus **I:** Technology **CN:** Intel Corporation **DOB:** 01/03/1929 **PB:** San Francisco **SC:** CA/USA **PT:** Walter Harold Moore; Florence Almira (Williamson) Moore **MS:** Married **SPN:** Betty I. Whittaker (09/09/1950) **CH:** Kenneth; Steven **ED:** Doctor of Philosophy in Chemistry and Physics, California Institute of Technology, Pasadena, CA (1954); Bachelor of Science in Chemistry, University of California Berkeley (1950); Coursework, San Jose State University **C:** Chairman Emeritus, Intel Corporation, Santa Clara, CA (1997-2006); Chairman, Intel Corporation (1979-1997); Chief Executive Officer, Intel Corporation (1979-1987); President, Chief Executive Officer, Intel Corporation (1975-1979); Co-founder, Executive Vice President, Intel Corporation (1968-1975); Director, Research and Development, Fairchild Semiconductor Corporation, Mountain View, CA (1959-1968); Co-founder, Manager, Engineering Department, Fairchild Semiconductor Corporation (1957-1959); Member, Technical Staff, Shockley

Semiconductor Laboratory, Palo Alto, CA (1956-1957); Postdoctoral Research, Applied Physics Laboratory, Johns Hopkins University (1953-1956) **CR:** Board of Directors, Gilead Sciences, Inc. (1996-Present); Member, Business Advisory Board, Gilead Sciences Inc. (1991-1996); Board of Directors, Transamerica Corporation; Board of Directors, Varian Associates Inc. **CIV:** Senior Trustee, California Institute of Technology (2001-Present); Co-founder, Chairman, Gordon and Betty Moore Foundation (2000-Present); Chairman, California Institute of Technology (1995-2001) **AW:** Inductee, National Inventors Hall of Fame (2009); Medal of Honor, Institute of Electrical and Electronics Engineers (2008); Nierenberg Prize (2006); Perkin Medal, Society of Chemical Industry (2004); Bower Award for Business Leadership, Franklin Institute, Philadelphia, PA (2002); Presidential Medal of Freedom, The White House (2002); Named, One of the World's Richest People, Forbes Magazine (2001); Named, One of Forbes Richest Americans (1999); Fellow Award, Computer History Museum (1998); John Fritz Medal, American Association of Engineering Societies (1993); National Medal of Technology (1990); Founders Medal, Institute of Electrical and Electronics Engineers (1977); Distinguished Alumnus Award, California Institute of Technology; Advancement of Research Medal, ASM International; Computer Pioneer Medal, IEEE **MEM:** Fellow, American Association for the Advancement of Science; Fellow, Institute of Electrical and Electronics Engineers; Fellow, Royal Society of Engineering; National Academy of Engineering; American Physical Society **AV:** Fishing; Golf

MOORE, GWENDOLYNNE, "GWEN" SOPHIA, T: U.S. Representative from Wisconsin **I:** Government Administration/Government Relations/Government Services **DOB:** 04/18/1951 **PB:** Racine **SC:** WI/USA **CH:** Three Children **ED:** BA in Political Science, Marquette University, Milwaukee, WI (1978) **C:** Caucus Whip, Congressional Black Caucus, 115th United States Congress (2016-Present); Vice Chair, Congressional Women's Caucus, Fourth United States Congress (2009-Present); Member, U.S. House of Representatives from Wisconsin's Fourth Congressional District, United States Congress (2005-Present); Member, District Four, Wisconsin State Senate (1993-2004); Member, Wisconsin State Assembly (1989-1992); Member, Committee on the Budget; Member, Committee on Financial Services **CR:** Neighborhood Development Strategist, City of Milwaukee, WI (1985-1989); With, State Department of Employment Relations and Health and Social Services, WI; Housing Officer, Wisconsin Housing and Economic Development Authority (WHEDA) **CIV:** Organizer, Volunteers in Service to America (Now AmeriCorps VISTA (Volunteers in Service to America)) **AW:** Named to the Power 150 (2008); Named One of the Most Influential Black Americans, Ebony Magazine (2006); VISTA Volunteer of the Decade from (1976-1986) Award, AmeriCorps VISTA (Volunteers in Service to America) **PA:** Democrat

MOORE, JAMES D., JD, T: Lawyer **I:** Law and Legal Services **CN:** Ryan, Moore, Cook, Triplett & Albertson LLP **DOB:** 06/03/1952 **PB:** Danville **SC:** IL/USA **PT:** Harry Dalton Moore; Margaret Katherine (Sandy) Moore **MS:** Married **SPN:** Diana P. Moore (03/28/1981) **CH:** Adam Dalton Moore **ED:** JD, Indiana University, Magna Cum Laude (1977); BA, DePauw University, with High Distinction (1974) **C:** Partner, Ryan, Moore, Cook, Triplett & Albertson, LLP, Frankfort, IN (1982-Present); Associate, Ryan, Hartzell & Ryan, Frankfort (Now Ryan, Moore, Cook, Triplett & Albertson, LLP), IN (1981-1982); Associate, Barnes, Hickam, Pantzer & Boyd (Now Barnes & Thornburg LLP), Indianapolis, IN (1977-1981) **CIV:** President, Clinton County Board of Elections (1992-2017); Board of Directors, Frankfort Mainstreet, Inc. (1985-1995); City Attorney (1983-1984); Assistant City Attorney, Frankfort, IN (1981-1982) **CW:** Assistant Articles Editor, Indiana University Law Journal (1976-1977) **AW:** William Wallace Carson Award Depauw University (1973) **MEM:** Board of Directors, The Farmers Bank, Frankfort, IN (2014-Present); Chairman, St. Vincent Frankfort Hospital (2015-2016); Board of Trustees, St. Vincent Frankfort Hospital (2014-2016); Board of Directors, Clinton County Hospital Foundation and St. Vincent Frankfort Hospital Foundation (1993-2009); House of Delegates, Indiana State Bar Association (1983-1999); Ethics Subcommittee, Indiana State Bar Association (1982-1994); President, Clinton County Bar Association (1984-1985); Secretary, Clinton County Bar Association (1983-1984); American Bar Association (ABA); Indiana State Bar Association; Clinton County Bar Association; Order of the Coif **BAR:** Indiana (1977); United States District Court for the Southern District of Indiana (1977) **MH:** Albert Nelson Marquis Lifetime Achievement Award **B/I:** Mr. Moore became involved in his profession because the profession fit well with his interest and academic skills. His interest were in where he thought his abilities would glide. His family does not have a background in practiced law; no family member was a lawyer. **PA:** Republican

MOORE, JAMES R., T: Lawyer **I:** Law and Legal Services **DOB:** 09/14/1944 **PB:** Longview **SC:** WA/USA **PT:** James Carlton Moore; Virginia (Rice) Moore **MS:** Married **SPN:** Kathryn Lindquist (8/26/1996); Christine M. Monkman (7/14/1979, Divorced 1996); Patricia Riley (8/25/1967, Divorced 1978) **CH:** Katherine M.; Amy McKenna (Stepchild); John McKenna (Stepchild); Matthew Elggren (Stepchild); Adam Elggren (Stepchild); Erin Koerselman (Stepchild); David Heilner (Stepchild); Zia Sunseri (Foster Child) **ED:** JD, Duke University (1969); BA, Whitman College (1966) **C:** Senior Fellow, University of Utah S.J. Quinney College of Law (2013-Present); Executive Vice President, Huntsman International LLC, Salt Lake City, UT (2010-2013); Secretary, Huntsman International LLC, Salt Lake City, UT (2010-2013); General Counsel, Huntsman International LLC, Salt Lake City, UT (2010-2013); Corporate Compliance, Huntsman International LLC, Salt Lake City, UT (2009-2013); Vice President, Huntsman International LLC, Salt Lake City, UT (2002-2009); Deputy General Counsel, Huntsman International LLC, Salt Lake City, UT (2002-2009); Senior Environmental Counsel, Huntsman International LLC, Salt Lake City, UT (1998-2002); Vice President, Huntsman International LLC, Salt Lake City, UT (1998-2002); Partner, Perkins Coie (1989-1998); Counsel, Perkins Coie (1987-1988); Regional Counsel, Region Ten, United States Environmental Protection Agency (1982-1987); Assistant United States Attorney, United States Attorney's Office, Seattle, WA (1974-1982); Trial Attorney for Pollution Control, Land/Natural Resources Division, United States Department of Justice, Washington, DC (1970-1974); Law Clerk to the Honorable J. Stanley Barnes, United States Court of Appeals for the Ninth Circuit (1969-1970) **CR:** Speaker in the Field **CIV:** Trustee, Whitman College (2013-Present); Senior Fellow, School of Law, The University of Utah (2013-Present); Member, Athlete's Hall of Fame Committee, Whitman College (2003-Present); President, W Club, Whitman College (2008-2010); Board of Overseers, Whitman College (2003-2013); Chairman of Audit Committee, Whitman College (1994-2007; 2017-present); Board of Directors, Environmental Law Institute (1995-2000) **CW:** Contributor, Articles, Professional Journals **AW:** Recipient, Distinguished Service Award, Whitman College (2016) **MEM:** Chairman, In-house Counsel Committee, ABA (2004-2006); Vice Chairman, In-house Counsel Committee, ABA (2003-2004); Special District Council, Washington State Bar Association (1988-1995); Section on Environmental, Energy and Resources, ABA (1987-2013); Environmental and Land Use Section, Washington State Bar Association (1974-2013) **BAR:** Utah (2008); Washington, DC (1995); United States Court of Appeals for the Ninth Circuit (1974); Supreme Court of the United States (1973); United States Court of Appeals for the Fourth Circuit (1972); Washington (1970) **MH:** Albert Nelson Marquis Lifetime Achievement Award; Marquis Who's Who Top Professional **AS:** Mr. Moore attributes his success to good parents, hard work and good luck. **B/I:** Mr. Moore didn't know whether he really wanted to be a lawyer or not, but he thought law school would help him develop his analytical. He wound up being a lawyer as a result. **AV:** Golf, baseball, football, and basketball. Mr. Moore also enjoys working on his model railroad. **THT:** Mr. Moore's motto for the legal department when he was General Counsel of Huntsman Corporation was "Do the right thing in the right way."

MOORE, JULIANNE, T: Actress **I:** Media & Entertainment **DOB:** 12/03/1960 **PB:** Fort Bragg **SC:** NC/USA **PT:** Peter Moore Smith; Anne (Love) Smith **MS:** Married **SPN:** Bart Freundlich (08/23/2003); John Gould Rubin (05/03/1986, Divorced 08/25/1995) **CH:** Live; Caleb **ED:** BFA in Theater, Boston University (1983) **C:** With, The Guthrie Theater (1988-1989) **CW:** Actress, "After the Wedding" (2019); Actress, "The Staggering Girl" (2019); Actress, "Gloria Bell" (2018); Actress, "Bel Canto" (2018); Appearance, "Nightcap" (2017); Actress, "Wonderstruck" (2017); Actress, "Suburbicon" (2017); Actress, "Kingsman: The Golden Circle" (2017); Actress, "Inside Amy Schumer" (2016); Actress, "Difficult People" (2016); Actress, "Freeheld" (2015); Actress, "The Hunger Games: Mockingjay-Part 2" (2015); Actress, "Non-Stop" (2014); Actress, "Maps to the Stars" (2014); Actress, "Still Alice" (2014); Actress, "The Hunger Games: Mockingjay-Part 1" (2014); Actress, "Seventh Son" (2014); Actress, "Don Jon" (2013); Actress, "Carrie" (2013); Author, "My Mom is a Foreigner, But Not to Me" (2013); Actress, "Being Flynn" (2012); Actress, "The English Teacher" (2012); Actress, "What Maisie Knew" (2012); Actress, "Game Change" (2012); Actress, "Game Change" (2012); Voice Actress, "A Child's Garden of Poetry" (2011); Author, "Freckleface Strawberry: Best Friends Forever" (2011); Actress, "Crazy, Stupid, Love" (2011); Actress, "The Kids Are All Right" (2010); Actress, "As the World Turns" (1985-1988, 2010); Actress, "6 Souls" (2010); Actress, "30 Rock" (2009-2013); Actress, "A Single Man" (2009); Author, "Freckleface Strawberry and the Dodgeball Bully" (2009); Actress, "Chloe" (2009); Actress, "Blindness" (2008); Actress, "Next" (2007); Author, "Freckleface Strawberry" (2007); Actress, "I'm Not There" (2007); Actress, "Savage Grace" (2007); Actress, "Freedomland" (2006); Actress, "The Vertical Hour" (2006); Actress, "Children of Men" (2006); Actress, "The Prize Winner of Defiance, Ohio" (2005); Actress, Executive Producer, "Marie and Bruce" (2004); Actress, "Laws of Attraction" (2004); Actress, "The Forgotten" (2004); Actress, "Far from Heaven" (2002); Actress, "The Hours" (2002); Actress, "Hannibal" (2001); Actress, "Evolution" (2001); Actress, "The Shipping News" (2001); Actress, "Map of the World" (1999); Actress, "Magnolia" (1999); Actress, "Cookie's Fortune" (1999); Actress, "An Ideal Husband" (1999); Actress, "The End of the Affair" (1999); Actress,

"Chicago Cab" (1998); Actress, "The Big Lebowski" (1998); Actress, "Psycho" (1998); Actress, "The Myth of Fingerprints" (1997); Actress, "The Lost World: Jurassic Park" (1997); Actress, "Hellcab" (1997); Actress, "Boogie Nights" (1997); Actress, "Surviving Picasso" (1996); Actress, "Roommates" (1995); Actress, "Nine Months" (1995); Actress, "Safe" (1995); Actress, "Assassins" (1995); Actress, "Vanya on 42nd Street" (1994); Actress, "Body of Evidence" (1993); Actress, "Benny & Joon" (1993); Actress, "The Fugitive" (1993); Actress, "Short Cuts" (1993); Actress, "The Hand That Rocks the Cradle" (1992); Actress, "The Gun in Betty Lou's Handbag" (1992); Actress, "Lovecraft" (1991); Actress, "The Last to Go" (1991); Actress, "Cast a Deadly Spell" (1991); Actress, "Ice Cream with Hot Fudge" (1990); Actress, "Money, Power, Murder" (1989); Actress, "Bone-the-Fish" (1988); Actress, "Serious Money" (1987); Actress, "The Edge of Night" (1984); Actress, Plays, Television Shows and Films **AW:** Golden Globe Award for Best Actress in a Motion Picture-Drama, Hollywood Foreign Press Association (2015); Critics' Choice Award for Best Actress (2015); Screen Actors Guild Award for Outstanding Performance by a Female Actor in a Leading Role, SAG-AFTRA (2015); BAFTA Award for Best Leading Actress (2015); Academy Award for Best Actress, Academy of Motion Picture Arts & Sciences (2015); Award for Best Actress, National Board of Review (2002, 2014); Golden Globe Award for Best Performance by an Actress in a Miniseries or Motion Picture Made for TV, Hollywood Foreign Press Association (2013); Screen Actors Guild Award for Outstanding Performance by a Female Actor in a TV Movie or Miniseries, SAG-AFTRA (2013); Star, Hollywood Walk of Fame (2013); Emmy Award for Outstanding Lead Actress in a Miniseries or Movie, Academy of Television Arts & Sciences (2012); Award for Best Supporting Actress, National Board of Review (1994); Emmy Award for Outstanding Ingenue in Daytime Drama Series, Academy of Television Arts & Sciences (1988); Numerous Awards

MOORE, NANCY M., EDD, T: Secondary School Educator **I:** Education/Educational Services **SC:** IL/USA **PT:** Frederick Miller; Barbara Miller **ED:** PhD, Capella University (2005) **C:** Teacher, Nassau County Schools, Callahan, FL (1999-2019); Adjunct Instructor, Florida State College at Jacksonville, Jacksonville, FL (2001-2008) **MH:** Albert Nelson Marquis Lifetime Achievement Award; Marquis Who's Who Top Professional **B/I:** Ms. Moore became involved in her profession because she liked working with children. She was very involved in her school's Parent-Teacher Association as well, and she did a lot of community work.

MOORE, PAMELA R., T: Master of Specific Learning Disabilities **I:** Education/Educational Services **DOB:** 02/22/1959 **PB:** Paulding **SC:** OH/USA **PT:** Loren J. Thomas; Louella I. Thomas **MS:** Married **SPN:** Chet (12/10/1977) **CH:** Amy Renae; Cheryl Kae **ED:** MS, St. Francis University, Fort Wayne, IN (1995); BS, Defiance College (1990) **C:** Middle School English Language Arts (ELA) Teacher (2014-Present); Middle School Reading Teacher, Paulding, GA (1999-Present); High School Learning Disabilities Teacher, Paulding, GA (1991-1999); Master of Specific Learning Disabilities **MH:** Albert Nelson Marquis Lifetime Achievement Award; Marquis Who's Who Top Professional **B/I:** Ms. Moore became involved in her profession because of her desire to work with youth and students. She also wanted to share her love of reading with students. In addition, Ms. Moore chose her career because she wanted to be involved with something that would have a positive impact on today's youth. **AV:** Grandchildren; Pets; Gardening; Reading; Being outside, especially in the summer weather; Being with friends **RE:** Methodist **THT:** Ms. Moore said, "It has definitely been a pleasure to have benefited or influenced as many students as I have..."

MOORE, SAMUEL DAVID, T: Vocalist **I:** Media & Entertainment **DOB:** 10/12/1935 **PB:** Miami **SC:** FL/USA **C:** Solo Musician (1990-Present); Musician, Sam & Dave (1961-1981) **CW:** Musician, "Overnight Sensational" (2006); Musician, "This Christmas" (1998); Musician, "Papa Soul's Christmas" (1998); Featured Musician, "Rainy Night in Georgia" (1994) **AW:** Lifetime Achievement Award, Grammy Awards (2019); Music of Black Origin Lifetime Achievement Award (2006); Inductee, Rock & Roll Hall of Fame (1992); Rhythm and Blues Foundation Pioneer Award for Individual Artist (1991)

MORA, JUANITA, T: MD, Chief Executive Officer **I:** Medicine & Health Care **CN:** Chicago Allergy Center **PT:** Samuel Mora; Maria Mora **ED:** Fellowship in Allergy and Immunology, Rush University Medical Center, Chicago, IL (2009); Residency in Pediatrics and Internal Medicine, Rush University Medical Center, Chicago, IL (2007); MD, University of Illinois College of Medicine (2003); BS in Chemistry, University of Chicago **C:** MD, Chief Executive Officer, Physician, Chicago Allergy Center (2014-Present) **CR:** Advocate, Various Causes **CIV:** Board Member, Catholic Charities of Chicago **CW:** Author, Clinical Research; Contributor, Articles, Professional Journals **AW:** National Spokesperson, American Lung Association (2018-Present); Clinic Partner, American Lung Association (2015-Present); Inspiration for the Recognizing Excellence in Diagnostics, RED Award, Vasculitis Foundation (2017); VIP Woman of the Year Circle (2017) **MEM:** American Academy of Allergy and Immunology; American Lung Association **AS:** Dr. Mora is surrounded by good people at all times, which allows her to be an advocate on top of her role as a doctor. She attributes her success to being humble and having the ability to relate to her patients. As a physician, she is always in a partnership with her patients. **B/I:** Dr. Mora came from humble beginnings. She is a first-generation Mexican-American. Her father was a butcher. Dr. Mora is the oldest of five children; she always dreamt of becoming a doctor. Unfortunately, her mother had kidney failure when she was young, which inspired Dr. Mora to accompany her at the doctor. There, she saw the need for Spanish-speaking doctors and wanted to bridge the gap. Since achieving her dreams, Dr. Mora loves to be able to touch lives and make her own schedule.

MORALES, JESUS, T: Chef, Owner **I:** Food & Restaurant Services **CN:** La Bella Managua **CH:** 2 Children **ED:** Associate's Degree **C:** Chef, Owner, General Manager, La Bella Managua (2005-Present); Sous-chef, Hot House Café (1989-2003) **AW:** Urban Spoon; Talk of the Town **AS:** Mr. Morales attributes his success on his upbringing in Toronto, where he greatly enjoyed sharing food with people. **B/I:** Mr. Morales became involved in his profession after having spent much of his childhood cooking with his mother. He became interested in cuisine after moving to Montreal, and his love for food grew from there.

MORAN, GERALD, "JERRY" WESLEY, T: U.S. Senator from Kansas; Lawyer **I:** Government Administration/Government Relations/Government Services **DOB:** 05/29/1954 **PB:** Great Bend **SC:** KS/USA **PT:** Raymond Edwin Moran; Madeline Eleanor (Fletcher) Moran **MS:** Married **SPN:** Robba A. Moran **CH:** Kelsey; Alex **ED:** JD, The University of Kansas School of Law (1981); BS in Economics, The University of Kansas (1976); Coursework, Fort Hays State University **C:** Chair, Senate Veterans Affairs Committee (2020-Present); U.S. Senator, State of Kansas (2011-Present); Member, U.S. Senate Committee on Veterans' Affairs (2011-Present); Member, U.S. Senate Appropriations Committee (2011-Present); Member, U.S. Senate Committee on Banking, Housing, and Urban Affairs (2011-Present); Chairmen, National Republican Senatorial Committee (2013-2015); Member, U.S. Senate Special Committee on Aging (2011-2013); Member, U.S. Senate Committee on Small Business and Entrepreneurship (2011-2013); Member, U.S. Senate Committee on Homeland Security and Governmental Affairs (2011-2013); Member, U.S. House of Representatives from Kansas' First Congressional District, United States Congress (1997-2011); Majority Leader, Kansas State Senate (1995-1996); Member, District 37, Kansas State Senate (1989-1996); Deputy Attorney, Rooks County, KS (1987-1995); Partner, Jeter & Moran (1983-1987); Special Assistant Attorney General, State of Kansas, Topeka, KS (1982-1985); With, Stinson, Mag & Fizzell, Kansas City, Kansas; Adjunct Professor of Political Science, Fort Hays State University **CIV:** Board of Directors, Kansas Chamber of Commerce & Industry (Now The Kansas Chamber of Commerce) (1996-1997); President, The University of Kansas School of Law (1994-1995); Vice President, The University of Kansas School of Law (1993-1994); Board of Governors, The University of Kansas School of Law **AW:** Named a Guardian of Small Business, National Federation of Independent Business (2008, 2010); Distinguished Leadership Award, American Association for Marriage and Family Therapy (2007); Wheat Leader of the Year Award, National Association of Wheat Growers & U.S. Wheat Associates (2004); Small Business Advocate Award, Small Business Survival Committee (2004); Intergovernmental Leadership Award, League of Kansas Municipalities (2003); Jim Edwards Alumnus of the Year Award, Leadership Kansas (2003); Legislative Award, National Rural Health Association (1999); Named Home Care Hero of the Year, Kansas Home Care Association (Now Kansas Home Care & Hospice Association) (1998) **PA:** Republican **RE:** Methodist

MORAN, JASON, T: Jazz Pianist, Composer, Educator **I:** Fine Art **DOB:** 01/21/1975 **PB:** Houston **SC:** TX/USA **PT:** Andy Moran; Mary Moran **MS:** Married **SPN:** Alicia Hall **CH:** Two children **ED:** MusB, Manhattan School of Music, New York, NY (1997); Diploma, High School for the Performing and Visual Arts (1993) **C:** Artistic Adviser for Jazz, John F. Kennedy Center for the Performing Arts (2014-Present); Musical Adviser for Jazz, John F. Kennedy Center for the Performing Arts (2011-Present); Faculty, New England Conservatory Music, Boston, MA (2010-Present) **CR:** Honorary Professor, Rhythmic Music Conservatory, Copenhagen, Denmark (2015); Organizer, Very Very Threadgill (2014); Artist-in-Residence, Juilliard and Molde Jazz Festival, San Francisco Jazz Organization (2013); Organizer, "713–>212: Houstonians in NYC" (2011); MacArthur Fellow (2010); USA Prudential Fellow, U.S. Artists (2007) **CIV:** Supporter, Justice for Jazz Artists, American Federation of Musicians (2013); Organizer, Mary Lou Chester Moran Foundation (2005); Grant Manager, Moran Scholarship Award, HSPVA (1994) **CW:** Musician, "Music for Joan Jonas" (2018); Musician, "Looks of a Lot" (2018); Musician, "MASS (Howl, eon)" (2017); Musician, "Bangs" (2017); Musician, "Thanksgiving at the Vanguard" (2017); Musician, "The Armory Concert" (2016); Composer, "13th" (2016); Musician, "All Rise: A Joyful Elegy for Fats Waller" (2014); Composer, "Selma" (2014); Musician, "Ten" (2010); Composer, "RFK in the Land of Apartheid" (2009); Composer, "Stutter" (2007); Musician, "Artist in Residence" (2006); Musician, "Same Mother" (2005); Composer, "All We Know of Heaven" (2004); Composer, "Five Deep Breaths" (2003); Musician, "The Bandwagon" (2003); Composer, "Two Three Time" (2002); Musician, "Modernistic" (2002); Musician, "Black Stars" (2001); Musician, "Facing Left" (2000); Musician, "Soundtrack to Human Motion" (1999); Sideman, Numerous Albums **AW:** Museum Survey, Cultured Magazine, Walker Art Center (2018); Pianist of the Year, Expanded Critics' Poll (2011); Second Place for Artist of the Year, Expanded Critics' Poll (2011); Album of the Year, Village Voice Jazz Critics' Poll (2010); Jazz Artist of the Year, Playboy (2005); Rising Star Jazz Artist, Rising Star Pianist, Rising Star Composer, Down Beat (2003-2005); Up-n-Coming Jazz Musician Award, Jazz Journalists Association (2003)

MORAVA, ALICE J., T: Corporate Executive **I:** Business Management/Business Services **DOB:** 10/07/1930 **PB:** Fond du Lac **SC:** WI/USA **PT:** Sidney George; Nina Mary (Ottery) Crofts **MS:** Single **SPN:** Robert Theodore Morava (09/30/1954, Deceased August 1987) **CH:** Robert Theodore Jr; Catherine Ann **ED:** MEd, University of Wisconsin, Whitewater (1979); BA, Carroll College (1952) **C:** Chief Executive Officer, Stuart W. Johnson & Company, Incorporated, Lake Geneva, WI (1987-Present); Teacher, Title I Reading, Fontana Public Schools (1967-1969); Teacher, Primary School, William Bay Public School (1954-1957); Teacher, Primary School, Waukesha Public Schools (1952-1954) **CR:** Member, Aurora University/George Williams College, William Bay, WI (1996-Present); Member, Advisory Board, Firstar Bank Walworth County, Lake Geneva, WI (1995-Present); Secretary, Board of Trustees, Carroll College, Waukesha, WI (1990-2018); Secretary, Board of Trustees, Gateway Technical College, Kenosha, Racine, Walworth County, WI (1993-2007) **CIV:** Charter Member, Aurora/Lakeland Medical Center Foundation, Elkhorn, WI (1993); Member, United Church of Christ **MEM:** President, Williams Bay Lioness Club (1982); President, Geneva Lake Branch, American Association of University Women (1973-1975); Big Foot Country Club; Vice President, Friends of Kishwauketoe; President, Geneva Lake Water Safety Patrol **MH:** Albert Nelson Marquis Lifetime Achievement Award **B/I:** Ms. Morava initially started out as a teacher. After meeting her husband, eventually she began working for a company her husband worked for. In about 1960, Ms. Morava and her husband purchased the business from the original owner and continued to run it for years until in 1987, her husband Robert passed and left her the business. The business has since continued as a successful family business. **AV:** Golf; Boating; Bridge; Family; Travel **PA:** Independent **RE:** Protestant

MORAYTIS, LOUIS J., JD, T: Lawyer **I:** Law and Legal Services **CN:** Eckert Seamans Cherin & Mellott, LLC **DOB:** 06/21/1947 **PB:** Pittsburgh **SC:** PA/USA **PT:** John N. Moraytis; Maria J. (Andriotis) Moraytis **MS:** Married **SPN:** Patricia J. Sonntag (11/28/1970) **CH:** Catherine M.; Annamarie J. **ED:** JD, Rutgers, The State University of New Jersey (1981); BCE, Bucknell University (1969) **C:** Partner, Eckert Seamans Cherin & Mellott, LLC, Pittsburgh, PA (1988-2013); Associate, Eckert Seamans Cherin & Mellott, LLC, Pittsburgh, PA (1981-1987); Engineer, Manager, ExxonMobil Research and Engineering, Florham Park, NJ (1976-1981) **CIV:** Parish Council Member, Officer, Holy Cross Church, Pittsburgh, PA (1984-1985); Board of Directors, Juvenile Diabetes Research Foundation (JDRF), International Western Pennsylvania Chapter **MIL:** Lieutenant Commander, United States Naval Reserve

(1969-1975); Civil Engineer Corps, United States Navy (1969-1975) **MEM:** Past Member, American Bar Association (ABA); Pennsylvania Bar Association; Allegheny County Bar Association **BAR:** Pennsylvania Bar (1981); United States Court of Appeals for the Third Circuit (1981) **MH:** Albert Nelson Marquis Lifetime Achievement Award **B/I:** Mr. Moraytis became involved in his profession because he had an interest in math and science and also the ability to communicate with people. He always wanted to be an attorney. **AV:** Reading; Golf; Gardening **RE:** Greek Orthodox

MOREHOUSE, KRISTI KAY, T: Elementary School Educator (Retired) **I:** Education/Educational Services **DOB:** 07/09/1962 **PB:** Greenfield **SC:** IA/USA **PT:** Dennis Ray Tietz; Eleanor Kay (Bissell) **MS:** Married **SPN:** William J. Morehouse **CH:** Michael; Kira **ED:** Gifted Endorsement, University of Iowa (2007); Master of Science in Learning Disabilities, Creighton University (1992); Bachelor of Arts in Elementary Education and Special Education, University of Northern Iowa (1984) **C:** Gifted and Talented Teacher, Kindergarten through Grade 5, Lewis Central School District (2006-2017); Fourth and Fifth Grade Teacher, Lewis Central School District, Council Bluffs, IA (1997-2006); Elementary Special Education Teacher, Lewis Central School District, Council Bluffs, IA (1985-1997); Junior High School Resource Teacher, Clarinda Community School District, Iowa (1984-1985) **CR:** Past Member, Social Studies District Committee, Lewis Central School District; Past Member, Talented and Gifted District Committee, Lewis Central School District; Past Cadre Member, Kreft Elementary School, Lewis Central School District **CIV:** Junior Treynor Women (1995-2004); Church Board (2000-2006); Omaha Coalition of Citizen Patrols-Florence Citizen Patrol **AW:** Exemplary, Sat-Ra Temple # 59 Daughters of Nile (1996) **MEM:** Former Member, National Education Association; Iowa Education Association; Lewis Central Education Association, Cognitive Coaching; Sat-Ra Temple # 59 Daughters of Nile; Iowa Talented and Gifted Association; Iowa Iota Chapter, Alpha Delta Kappa **MH:** Albert Nelson Marquis Lifetime Achievement Award; Marquis Who's Who Top Professional **AS:** Ms. Morehouse attributes his success to her passion for working with children, especially in helping them learn and grow. **B/I:** Ms. Morehouse became involved in her profession after having taught preschool Sunday school classes, during which time she developed an interest in working with children. She went on to specialize in special education. **AV:** Reading; Traveling; Family; Games **RE:** United Church of Christ

MOREL, MARILYN ANNE, T: Dietitian (Retired) **I:** Health, Wellness and Fitness **CN:** Natural Housebuilders & Terry Davenport Design **DOB:** 11/29/1947 **PB:** Queens Village **SC:** NY/USA **PT:** Alfred Francis Morel; Charlotte Adelaide Ward **MS:** Married **SPN:** Terry Del Davenport (09/10/1995); John Howard Pearson (06/27/1981, Divorced 07/1989) **ED:** MS in Nutrition and Computers in Nutrition, University of Massachusetts Amherst (1975); BS in Mathematics and Secondary Education, University of Massachusetts Amherst (1969); AA in Liberal Arts, Southern Seminary Junior College (Now Southern Virginia University), Buena Vista, VA (1967) **C:** Administrative Consultant, Bookkeeper, Natural Housebuilders & Terry Davenport Design, Victor, MT (1995-Present); Nursing Home Consultant, Powell County Nursing Home, Deerlodge, MT (1989-1994); Head Clinical Dietitian, St. Mary's Hospital and Medical Center, Grand Junction, CO (1978-1982); Head Clinical Dietitian, Cabell Huntington Hospital, WV (1977-1978); Clinical Dietitian, Aspen Valley Hospital, CO

(1974-1975); Mathematics Teacher, Highland Falls High School (Now James I. O'Neill High School), NY (1969-1971) **CW:** Author, "Earthero: Stabilizing Victimization" (2000); Author, "Earthero" **MEM:** Montana Dietetic Association; American Dietetic Association **MH:** Albert Nelson Marquis Lifetime Achievement Award **B/I:** Mrs. Morel was trying to control her weight but in reality it was more than that. It became a whole experience of trying to coordinate all forms of diet with regard to behavioral health, addiction, and mental health. She was oriented more towards establishing diseases versus any new event that might occur after she had been trained. It was her sports nutrition and her substance abuse training that really propelled her for this. She is very well read in the addiction area; the wellness really came from her sports nutrition. **AV:** Walking

MORELLE, JOSEPH D., T: U.S. Representative from New York **I:** Government Administration/Government Relations/Government Services **CN:** U.S. House of Representatives **DOB:** 04/29/1957 **PB:** Utica **SC:** NY/USA **MS:** Married **SPN:** Mary Beth (Bauer) Morelle (1984) **CH:** Lauren; Joseph Jr.; Nicholas **ED:** Bachelor of Arts in Political Science, State University of New York Geneseo **C:** Member, U.S. House of Representatives from New York's 25th Congressional District (2018-Present); Interim Speaker, New York State Assembly (2015); Majority Leader, New York State Assembly (2013-2018); Member, New York State Assembly (1991-2018); Member, Monroe County Legislature, New York (1983-1990); President, Chief Executive Officer, MMI Technologies Inc.; Former Sales Representative, Project Manager and Financial Analyst, Cooper-Schuler **PA:** Democrat

MORELLO, DANIEL C. MD, T: Plastic Surgeon **I:** Medicine & Health Care **CN:** Daniel C. Morello **DOB:** 11/12/1943 **PB:** Vineland **SC:** NJ/USA **PT:** John B. Morello; Mina M. (Conway) Morello **MS:** Married **SPN:** Mona L. Comras Morello **CH:** Amy Leahy; Kate Kusner; Elise Vinci **ED:** Doctor of Medicine, Georgetown University, Washington, DC (1969); Bachelor of Science, University of Notre Dame, Notre Dame, IN, Dean's Honor List (1965) **CT:** Diplomate, American Board of Plastic Surgery (1977); American Board of Surgery (1975); National Board of Medical Examiners (1970); Certificate of Advanced Education in Cosmetic Surgery; Licensed, States of New York, Florida **C:** Consultant, Jupiter Medical Center, Jupiter, FL (2010-Present); Attending Surgeon, Aqua Plastic Surgery (2010-Present); Attending Surgeon, Mank Eye, Ear and Throat Hospital (1999-Present); Emeritus Chief of Plastic Surgery, White Plains Hospital Medical Center, New York (1999-Present); Private Practice in Plastic Surgery, White Plains, NY (1976-Present); Attending Surgeon, White Plains Hospital Medical Center, New York (1976-Present); Attending Surgeon, Jupiter Outpatient Surgery Center (2008-2016); Attending Surgeon, Jupiter Medical Center (2008-2010); Attending Surgeon, Lenox Hill Hospital (2005-2012); Attending Surgeon, Manhattan Eye, Ear & Throat Hospital (2001-2012); Chief Emeritus, Plastic Surgery, White Plains Hospital, White Plains, NY (1998-2012); Attending Surgeon, St. Agnes Hospital, White Plains, NY (1987-2003); Chief of Plastic Surgery, White Plains Hospital Medical Center, New York (1992-1998); Clinical Assistant Professor, Plastic Surgery, New York University School of Medicine, New York, NY (1978-1986); Plastic Surgery Resident to Chief Resident, New York University Medical Center Institute for Reconstructive Plastic Surgery, New York, NY (1974-1976); Intern, Surgery Residency, Hahnemann University Hospital (1974-1976); Resident, Plastic Surgery, Institute for Reconstructive Plastic Surgery, New York University Medical Center (1974-1976); Surgery Resident to Chief Resident, Hahnemann Medical College Hospital (1970-1974); Intern, Hahnemann Medical College Hospital, Philadelphia, PA (1969-1970) **CR:** Attending Surgeon, Northern Westchester Hospital Center (1976-Present); Attending Surgeon, White Plains Hospital (1976-2012); Attending Surgeon, Northern Westchester Hospital Center (1976-2012); Attending Surgeon, United Hospital (1976-2005); Clinical Assistant Professor, Plastic Surgery (1978-1986); Assistant Attending Surgeon, Bellevue Hospital, Manhattan VA Hospital, Manhattan Eye, Ear and Throat Hospital, New York, NY (1976-1985); Assistant Attending Surgeon, Bellevue Hospital (1976-1985); Assistant Attending Surgeon, Manhattan Veteran's Administration Hospital (1976-1985); Consultant, Burke Rehabilitation Center (1977-1981); Clinical Instructor, Plastic Surgery, New York University School of Medicine, New York, NY (1974-1978); Clinical Instructor, Plastic Surgery, New York University School of Medicine (1974-1978); Assistant Instructor of Surgery, Drexel University College of Medicine, Philadelphia, PA (1973-1974); Staff Privileges, Manhatten Eye Ear and Throat Hospital; Staff Privileges, Lenox Hill Hospital; Staff Privileges, Northern Westchester Hospital Center; Staff Privileges, St. Agnes Hospital; Staff Privileges, Putnam Community Hospital; Staff Privileges, United Hospital; Staff Privileges, White Plains Hospital; Staff Privileges, Jupiter Medical Center; Staff Privileges, Jupiter Outpatient Surgery Center **CIV:** Chair, 50th Anniversary Celebration, Member, Heritage Committee, Jupiter Hills Club (2017-Present); House Committee, Jupiter Hills Club (2010-2017); Golf Chairman, Board of Directors, Whippoorwill Club (1989-1995) **CW:** Contributor, Numerous Articles to Professional Journals, Chapters to Books; Presenter in the Field, Numerous Presentations and Exhibits **AW:** Best Panel Moderator Award, Annual Meeting of the American Society for Aesthetic Plastic Surgery, New York (2001); AMA Physicians Recognition Award (1981-1998) **MEM:** Nominating Committee, Board of Directors, Aesthetic Surgery Education & Research Foundation (2003-2009); Board of Governors, National Endowment for Plastic Surgery, Inc. (2003-2006); Board of Directors, American Society for Aesthetic Plastic Surgery (1991-2004); Strategic Planning Committee, American Society for Aesthetic Plastic Surgery (1992, 1995-2003); Executive Director Search Committee, American Society of Plastic & Reconstructive Surgeons (2001-2002); President, Chair of Board of Trustees, American Society for Aesthetic Plastic Surgery (2000-2002); Board of Directors, Aesthetic Surgery Education & Research Foundation (1998-2001); Medical-Legal Relations Committee, Westchester County Medical Society (1986-1999); Treasurer, American Society for Aesthetic Plastic Surgery (1995-1998); President, American Association for Accreditation of Ambulatory Surgery Facilities (1994-1998); Public Education Committee, American Society of Plastic & Reconstructive Surgeons (1994-1996); Treasurer, American Association for Accreditation of Ambulatory Surgery Facilities (1991-1994); Board of Directors, New York Regional Society of Plastic Surgery (1988-1991); Educational Research Committee, American Society for Aesthetic Plastic Surgery (1989-1990); Secretary, New York Regional Society of Plastic Surgery (1988-1990); Program Chairman, New York Regional Society of Plastic Surgery (1987-1988); Board of Directors, Westchester County Medical Society (1986-1988); Peer Review Committee, Westchester County Medical Society (1979-1986); Fellow, American College of Surgeons; American Association for Hand Surgery; American Burn Association; American Trauma Society; Association for Academic Surgery; International Society for Aesthetic Plastic Surgery; Medical Society of the State of New York; New York Society for Surgery of the Hand **MH:** Albert Nelson Marquis Lifetime Achievement Award **AS:** Dr. Morello credits his success on persistence, hard work and dedication. Additionally, he attributes it to standing on the shoulders of giants. **B/I:** Dr. Morello became involved in his profession because he knew he wanted to be a doctor since he was 10 years old. He was the first member of his family to be a physician. **AV:** Golf; Travel; Reading

MORENO, PEDRO, T: Professor, Director of Quality Assurance and Promotions **I:** Medicine & Health Care **CN:** Mount Sinai Hospital **PT:** Rasal Moreno Pena **ED:** MD in Internal Medicine, Pontifical Xavierian University, Bogata Columbia; Coursework/Trained, Harvard Medical School, Massachusetts General Hospital and Brigham and Women's Hospital **CT:** American Board of Internal Medicine; Certified in Cardiovascular Disease **C:** Professor of Medicine, Cardiology, Mount Sinai St. Luke's (Now Mount Sinai Morningside), Icahn School of Medicine at Mount Sinai (10 Years); Director, Cardiac Cath Lab, Mount Sinai St. Luke (Now Mount Sinai Morningside), Icahn School of Medicine at Mount Sinai **CIV:** Works with Underserved Areas of NY **MEM:** New York Philharmonic (1997-Present) **AS:** Dr. Moreno attributes his success to hard work and dedication. He is trying to find the root of the problems of health. **B/I:** Dr. Moreno's family is full of physicians. He was inspired by understanding the path of physiology, being around Nobel Prizes, and real pioneers that created a pathway for treatment. His uncle was the Dean at Harvard, and was a cardiologist; he gave him the support to do research at Harvard University. Dr. Moreno now has been a pioneer in the understanding of inflammation and acute coronary syndromes. In addition, he knew that he wanted to be involved in his profession since the age of 13. His father was a physician along with his uncle. So, when he was age 13 he was trying to understand the electrocardiograms and felt like being a physician was the right profession for him. **AV:** New York Philharmonic (classical music); Self-motivation Books

MORENO, RITA, T: Actress **I:** Media & Entertainment **DOB:** 12/11/1931 **PB:** Humacao **SC:** Puerto Rico **PT:** Francisco José "Paco" Alverió; Rosa María (Marcano) Alverió Moreno **MS:** Widowed **SPN:** Leonard I. Gordon (06/18/1965, Deceased 06/30/2010) **CH:** Fernanda Luisa **CW:** Actress, "Bless This Mess" (2019-Present); Actress, "One Day at a Time" (2017-Present); Voice Actress, "Carmen Sandiago" (2019); Actress, "Jane the Virgin" (2015-2019); Actress, "Remember Me" (2016); Actress, "A Gift of Miracles" (2015); Actress, "Old Soul" (2014); Actress, "Nicky Deuce" (2013); Voice Actress, "Rio 2" (2014); Actress, "Six Dance Lessons in Six Weeks" (2014); Author, "Rita Moreno" (2013); Actress, "Happily Divorced" (2011-2013); Actress, "In Plain Sight" (2010); Actress, "Cane" (2007); Actress, "Law & Order: Criminal Intent" (2006-2007); Actress, "Lolo's Cafe" (2006); Actress, "Play It By Ear" (2006); Actress, "Law and Order: Trial by Jury" (2005); Actress, "Copshop" (2004); Actress, "King of the Corner" (2004); Actress, "The Guardian" (2003); Actress, "Strong Medicine" (2003); Actress, "Open House" (2003); Actress, "Oz" (1997-2003); Actress, "American Family" (2002); Actress, "Pinero" (2001); Actress, "Blue Moon" (2000); Actress, "Carlo's Wake" (1999); Actress, "The Rockford Files: If It Bleeds...It Leads" (1999); Actress, "Slums of Beverly Hills" (1998); Actress, "The Spree" (1998); Actress, "Sunset Boulevard" (1996); Actress, "After Play" (1995); Actress, "Angus" (1995); Actress, "The Wharf Rat" (1995); Actress, "Best Defense" (1995); Voice Actress, "Where on Earth is Carmen Sandiego?" (1994-1999); Actress, "I Like It Like That" (1994); Actress, "Top of the Heap" (1991); Actress, "B.L. Stryker" (1989-1990); Actress, "Miami Vice" (1989); Actress, "The Odd Couple" (1985); Actress, "The Love Boat" (1983); Actress, "Portrait of a Showgirl" (1982); Actress, "Wally's Cafe" (1981); Actress, "Evita Peron" (1981); Actress, "The Four Seasons" (1981); Actress, "Anatomy of a Seduction" (1979); Actress, "The Electric Company" (1971-1977); Actress, "The Muppet Show" (1976); Actress, "The Ritz" (1975); Actress, "The Rockford Files" (1974); Actress, "The National Health" (1974); Actress, "Dominic's Dream" (1974); Actress, "Out to Lunch" (1974); Actress, "Carnal Knowledge" (1971); Actress, "The Last of the Red Hot Lovers" (1970-1971); Actress, "Gantry" (1969-1970); Actress, "Night of the Following Day" (1968); Actress, "The Sign in Sidney Brustein's Window" (1964-1965); Actress, "West Side Story" (1961); Actress, "The King and I" (1956); Actress, "Singin' in the Rain" (1952); Spanish Dancer, Night Club Entertainer; Actress, Theater, Television Shows, Film **AW:** Career Achievement Peabody Award (2019); Ellis Island Medal of Honor (2018); Honoree, Kennedy Center Honors, John F. Kennedy Center for the Performing Arts, Washington, DC (2015); Lifetime Achievement Award, SAG-AFTRA (2014); National Medal of Arts Award, National Endowment for the Arts (2010); Named to California Hall of Fame (2007); Presidential Freedom Medal, The White House (2005); Award, National Osteoporosis Foundation (NOF) (2000); Recipient, Star, Hollywood Walk of Fame (1995); Emmy Award for Outstanding Lead Actress for a Single Appearance in a Drama or Comedy Series, Academy of Television Arts & Sciences (1978); Emmy Award for Outstanding Individual Performance in a Variety or Music Program, Academy of Television Arts & Sciences (1977); Antoinette Perry (Tony) Award for Best Supporting Actress in a Broadway Play (1975); Grammy Award for Best Recording, The Recording Academy (1973); Academy Award for Best Supporting Actress, Academy of Motion Picture Arts and Sciences (1961); Golden Globe Award for Best Supporting Actress in a Motion Picture, Hollywood Foreign Press Association (1961); Numerous Awards

MORÉTEAU, OLIVIER, PHD, T: Law Educator **I:** Education/Educational Services **MS:** Married **SPN:** Maria Antonia "Marie-Antoinette" Moréteau **CH:** Alexandre; Viviane **ED:** PhD, Jean Moulin University Lyon 3, Summa Cum Laude (1990); Diplôme d'études approfondies in French Private Law, Jean Moulin University Lyon 3 (1981); Diplôme d'études approfondies in Comparative Law, Jean Moulin University Lyon 3 (1978) **C:** Professor of Law, Russell B. Long Eminent Scholars Academic Chair, Director of Center of Civil Law Studies, Louisiana State University, Baton Rouge, LA (2005-Present); Professor of Comparative Law, Jean Moulin University Lyon 3, Lyon, France (2000-2005); Director, Jean Moulin University Lyon 3, Lyon, France (2000-2005); Professor of Private Law, Universite Pierre Mendes, Grenoble, France (1998-2000); Associate Director, Edouard Lambert Institute of Comparative Law, Jean Moulin University Lyon 3, Lyon, France (1985-2000); Vice President, International Relations, Jean Moulin University Lyon 3, Lyon, France (1997-1999); Associate Professor, Jean Moulin University Lyon 3, Lyon, France (1990-1998); Director of International Relations, Jean Moulin University Lyon 3, Lyon, France (1993-1995); Teaching and Research Assistant, Jean Moulin University Lyon 3, Lyon, France (1980-1990) **CR:** Visiting Professor, University of Nantes (2018); Visiting Professor, Jean Moulin University Lyon 3 (2012-2018); Visiting Professor, University of Luxembourg (2014-2015); Visiting Professor, University of Nantes (2013); Visiting Professor, University of Melbourne (2004); Visiting Professor, Boston University (2002-2004); Visiting Professor, University of Melbourne (2002); Visiting Professor, Boston University (1993-2000); Visiting Professor, University of Minnesota (1992) **CW:** Editor-in-Chief, Journal of Civil Law Studies (2008-Present); Contributor, Articles, Professional Journals; Principal Editor, Comparative Legal History **AW:** John Ashby Hernandez III Memorial Francophone Leadership Award, Louisiana State Bar Association (2014); Official Des Palmes Academic **MEM:** American Law Institute; Societe de Legislation Comparee; European Centre of Tort and Insurance Law; European Group on Tort Law; International Academy of Comparative Law; President, Juris Diversitas; Louisiana Bar Foundation **MH:** Albert Nelson Marquis Lifetime Achievement Award **AS:** Dr. Moréteau attributes his success to his mentor and inspiration, Dr. H.A. Schwarz-Liebermann von Wahlendorf. He would additionally like to highlight his wife, Marie A. Moréteau. She is inspiring, patient, and kind. He is eternally grateful for her patience, love, and support. **B/I:** Dr. Moréteau's main source of inspiration was his discovery of comparative law. He enjoyed studying and comparing various legal systems of the world. When he was in law school in the late 1970s, the development of the European Union began. It was an opportune time for his studies. He thought receiving a PhD in comparative law would be a great start, and then he discovered teaching. Once he discovered teaching, it clearly was the perfect fit for his skills. He decided that he would teach law with the intent of introducing students to other international legal systems.

MORGAN, DENNIS BRENT, T: Minister, Psychologist, Psychoanalyst, Psychiatrist (Retired) **I:** Medicine & Health Care **CN:** Psychoanalysis P.C. **DOB:** 12/28/1949 **PT:** Ira Pershing Morgan; Josephine (Langworthy) Morgan **MS:** Widowed **SPN:** Ann **CH:** Tamara; Erika; Brent; Troy **ED:** Doctor of Psychology, Western Colorado University (1978); Postgraduate Doctoral Coursework, The University of Kansas (1976-1978); MS, Pittsburgh State University, Kansas (1976); BA, Pittsburgh State University, Kansas (1971); Coursework in Theology, Pasadena, CA; Doctoral Coursework **CT:** Continuing Medical Education, University of Missouri (1990); Ordained to Ministry, International Ministerial Fellowship, Minneapolis, MN (1989); World Congress of Professional Hypnotists (1982); American National Board of Psychiatry (1978); National Honor Society in Psychology (1977); Psychiatric Medication Coursework, Menninger School of Psychiatry (1977); Diplomate, American Board of Psychotherapy; Certified Health Service Provider; Diplomate in Psychopharmacology; FPPR; FACAPP **C:** Founder, Owner, Psychanalysis P.C. (2000-2019); Chief Psychologist, Professional Psychological Services, Kansas City, MO (1976-1998); Senior Pastor, Heartland Community Church Inc., Kansas City, MO (1989-1991); Partner, Christian Psychiatric Associates of Los Angeles (1985); Chief Psychologist, HSA Heartland Hospital, NV, MO (1983-1984); Psychological Assistant, Center for Active Psychology, Riverside, CA (1981-1983); Chief Psychologist, Sierra Vista Psychiatric Hospital (Now Sierra Vista Behavioral Health Center, Genesis HealthCare), Highland, CA (1980) **CR:** Charter Baywood Hospital, College Hospital, Cerritos, CA (1981-1983); Vice President, Psychological Services Group Dynamics, Dallas, Texas (1978-1980); Staff, Kellogg Psychiatric Hospital, Corona, CA; Staff, Long Beach Neuropsychiatric Institute; Faculty, Crystal Cathedral Lay Ministry Training Center, Mini-Seminary, San Juan Capistrano Community Church, San Juan Capistrano, CA **MIL:** Major, U.S. Army (1971-1989) **CW:** Author, "Manage Your Stress Before It Manages You" (1983) **AW:** Twentieth-century award for achievement International Biographical Centre, Cambridge, England (1999); International Man of the Year, International Biographical Centre, Cambridge, England (1992-1993); Honoree, 35 Years of Practice, State Psychiatric Association **MEM:** Board of Directors, American Board of Psychotherapy (1982-Present); The New York Academy of Sciences (1985); Lifetime National Psychiatric Association; American Association of Christian Counselors; National Association of Disability Examiners (NADE); Missouri Association of Disability Examiners; Missouri Psychological Association (MOPA); Retired Officers Association, U.S.A. (Now Military Officers Association of America); Navy League of the United States; Kansas City Club; University Club of Kansas City; Psi Chi, The International Honor Society in Psychology; Lambda Chi Alpha; C.F. Menninger Society; Military Order of the World Wars; American Legion **AS:** Dr. Morgan attributes his success to education, hard work, and a few mentors along the way. **AV:** Collecting; Gardening **PA:** Republican **RE:** Episcopalian

MORGAN, JENNIFER, T: Co-Chief Executive Officer **I:** Business Management/Business Services **CN:** SAP SE **DOB:** 03/13/1971 **PB:** Fairfax **SC:** VA/USA **MS:** Married **SPN:** Michael Morgan **CH:** Two Children **ED:** Graduate Coursework in Business, Finance, and French, James Madison University **C:** Co-Chief Executive Officer, SAP SE (2019-Present); Various Leadership Roles, SAP SE (2004-2019); Business Development, Siebel (2000-2004); Client Manager, Accenture (1993-2000) **CIV:** Board of Directors, BNY Mellon (2016-Present); Board Member, NAF (2015-Present); Advisory Board Member, College of Business, James Madison University (2014-Present); Board Member, GEN-YOUth Foundation (2015-2018) **AW:** Listee, 50 Most Powerful Women in Business, Fortune Magazine (2019); Listee, Most Powerful Women in the World, Forbes (2018-2019); Distinguished Leadership Award, New York Hall of Science (2017)

MORIARTY, RICHARD GRAHAM, T: City Retirement System Manager **I:** Government Administration/Government Relations/Government Services **DOB:** 04/07/1938 **PB:** Lecompte **SC:** LA/USA **PT:** Donald Peter Moriarty, Sr.; Catherine Graham (Stafford) Moriarty **MS:** Married **SPN:** Janet Mott Moriarty (07/28/1990); Lydia Lawler Kramer (12/13/1969, Deceased 1985) **CH:** Richard Graham, Jr.; Mary Catherine; Cullen Kramer; Richard Travis Odom (Stepson); Jennifer O. White (Stepdaughter) **ED:** BBA, Louisiana Tech University, Ruston, LA (1960); Law Coursework, Louisiana State University, Baton Rouge, LA (1960) **C:** Secretary-Treasurer, City of Alexandria Employee Retirement System (1969-Present); Director, Personnel, City of Alexandria, LA (1969-1990); Budget Director, City of Alexandria, LA (1969); Assistant Secretary-Treasurer, City of Alexandria, LA (1963-1969); Accountant, City of Alexandria, LA (1960-1963) **CIV:** Secretary-Treasurer, Trinity Episcopal Church, Cheneyville, LA (1994-Present); President, Lecompte Rotary Club (2001-2002); Senior Warden, St. James Episcopal Church, Alexandria, LA (1991-1994); Vestry, St. James Episcopal Church, Alexandria, LA (1973); Division Chairman, Alexandria United Way (1972) **MIL:** Served to Sergeant, U.S. Army Reserve (1966-1969); U.S Army Reserve (1962-1968) **CW:** Author, "Rivers of Time" (2012); Author, "My Early Years: Richard Graham Moriarty"; Author, "A History: 150 Years of Service: Trinity Episcopal Church, Cheneyville, LA"; Author, "The Wells Brothers of Rapides Parish, Breeders of Champion Horses" **AW:** Service Above Self Award, Lecompte Rotary Club (2004-2005); Charles E. Dunbar Career Service Award, Louisiana Civil Service League (1972, 1969); Listee, Who's Who in Finance & Industry; Listee, Who's Who in Government **MEM:** Board of Directors, Alexandria Club, Kiwanis (1965-Present); Vice President, Kiwanis (1982); Municipal Personnel Officers Association; Louisiana Association of Public Employees' Retirement Systems (LAPERS); Louisiana Civil Service League; International Personnel Management Association For Human Resources **MH:** Albert Nelson Marquis Lifetime Achievement Award **B/I:** Mr. Moriarty became involved in his profession because his father was originally associated with the city; he attended law school, however, he did not graduate and grew up around city hall. His father set an example for him and he was truly inspired by him; he followed in his footsteps. Mr. Moriarty graduated from Louisiana Tech University with a degree in accounting and then needed a job. He believed in community service, so he was able to get a job as an accountant for the City of Alexandra in Louisiana. He believes in public employment because it's a service that people do not always understand. Mr. Moriarty grew up in church and believes in serving God, life, people, and his country; he's a service-oriented person. **AV:** Hunting; Fishing; Painting; Writing **PA:** Republican **RE:** Episcopalian **THT:** Mr. Moriarty believes life is what one makes it. His grandfather always told him, "I cried because I had no shoes, until I met a man who had no feet." This saying sticks with Mr. Moriarty to this day.

MORITZ, MICHAEL JONATHAN, T: Chairman; Venture Capitalist **I:** Financial Services **CN:** Sequoia Capital **DOB:** 09/12/1954 **PB:** Cardiff **SC:** Wales/United Kingdom **PT:** Ludwig Alfred Moritz; Doris (Rath) Moritz **MS:** Married **SPN:** Harriet Heyman **CH:** Two Children **ED:** Doctor Honoris Causa, Hong Kong University of Science and Technology (2014); MBA, The Wharton School, University of Pennsylvania (1978); MA in History, University of Oxford (1976) **C:** Chairman, Sequoia Capital (2012-Present); General Partner, Managing Director, Sequoia Capital (1986-2012); Correspondent, TIME Magazine (1979); Founder, Technologic Partners; With, Time Warner **CR:** Board of Directors, LinkedIn Corporation (2011-Present); Board of Directors, Klarna Bank AB (2010-Present); Board of Directors, Kayak.com (2007-Present); Board of Directors, 24/7 Customer (2003-Present); Board of Directors, Sugar Inc. (2007); Board of Directors, Google, Inc., (1999-2007); Board of Directors, Flextronics International, LTD. (1993-2005); Board of Directors, Green Dot Corporation (2003); Board of Directors, Yahoo! Inc. (1995-2003); Board of Directors, PayPal, Inc. (1999-2002) **CIV:** Co-Sponsor, Booker Prize (2019-2024); Participant, The Giving Pledge; Donor, Christ Church, Juilliard School's Music Advancement Program, University of California, San Francisco, The University of Chicago **CW:** Author, "The Little Kingdom: The Private Story of Apple Computer" (1986); Co-Author, "Going for Broke: The Chrysler Story" (1986) **AW:** Fellow, Aberystwyth University (2014); Named Knight Commander, Order of the British Empire (2013); Honorary Fellowship, Cardiff University (2010); Named One of the Forbes 400: Richest Americans (2009); Named to Midas List, Forbes Magazine (2008, 2009); Named One of the Richest People in Britain, London's Sunday Times (2007); Named One of the 50 Who Matter Now, Business 2.0 (2007); Named One of the Most Influential People in the World, TIME Magazine (2007)

MORITZ, MILTON, "MICK" E., CPP, T: Security Consultant **I:** Consulting **DOB:** 09/05/1931 **PB:** Reading **SC:** PA/USA **PT:** Edward Raymond Moritz; Anna May Moritz **SPN:** Pamela Wand; Elizabeth Ann (Deceased 2007) **CH:** Stephen Edward; Sandra E; Betsy Ann Moritz Koppenhaver; Tracey Mowery; Peyton Felts; Tammy Barnwell **ED:** Florida State University (1959-1960); University of Maryland (1950-1951) **CT:** Certified Protection Professional (1985-Present) **C:** Principal, Moritz Associates, Harrisburg, PA (1994-2005); Security Manager, Sprint, Carlisle, PA (1972-1994); Safety and Security Director, Harrisburg Hospital, Harrisburg, PA (1970-1972) **CR:** Lecturer, Instructor, Harrisburg Area Community College; Industrial Security Advisory Council **CIV:** President, Greater Harrisburg Crime Clinic (1974) **MIL:** Chief Warrant Officer 3, U.S. Army (1968); U.S. Army (1949); Special Agent, Military Intelligence, U.S. Army **CW:** Associate Editor, Protection of Assets Manual **AW:** Decorated Bronze Star, Oak Leaf Cluster **MEM:** Board Chairman, American Society of Industrial Security (1987); Board Member, American Society of Industrial Security (1982-1987); President, American Society of Industrial Security (1986); Association of Former Intelligence Officers; International Narcotic Enforcement Officers Association; Board of Directors, Pennsylvania Crime Prevention Officers' Association **MH:** Albert Nelson Marquis Lifetime Achievement Award **B/I:** Mr. Moritz became involved in his profession because he knew that the security field would expand in the future. **AV:** Walking; Hiking **PA:** Republican **RE:** Lutheran

MORNINGSTAR, ROBERT D., T: Computer Company Executive **I:** Human Resources **CN:** M.A.R.S. **DOB:** 10/18/1948 **PB:** Bluefields **SC:** Nicaragua **PT:** Captain Ludovico Bottner; Ines (Gomez) Echeverri; Rodolfo Echeverri (Stepfather) **MS:** Domestic Partnership **SPN:** Jill Benzer **ED:** Graduate, Power Memorial Academy (1967-1972); Degree in Psychology, Fordham University (1969) **CT:** Certified Novell Engineer (1992); Instrument Ground Instructor, Federal Aviation Administration (1991); Certified Pilot, Federal Aviation Administration (1990) **C:** President, M.A.R.S. (1986-Present); Department of Homeland Security (2002); Adjunct Lecturer, Department of Dance and Music, Hunter College (1994-1995); Psychotherapist, Behavioral Medicine, Department, International Center for the Disabled (1992-1993); Tai Chi Instructor for Physical Therapy Staff, International Center for the Disabled (1985-1986); Dance Critic, "In-Step: The New York Dancer (1983-1984); Guest Lecturer, Department of East Asian Studies, Oberlin College (1980-1981); Tai Chi Master, Instructor, New York State Office of Parks, Recreation and Historic Preservation (1980-1981); Director of Dance and Movement Research, Metaphorms (1977-1980); Bilingual Instructor, China Institute America (1977-1978); Assistant Manager, Wittenberg Surgical Supply Company (1970-1973) **CR:** Coach, Lifesport Gymnastics (1983) **CIV:** Gymnastics Instructor, Bank Street College of Education (1990-1991); Founding Member, Challenger Foundation (1988) **MIL:** Air Force Reserve (1986) **CW:** Appearance, "ETs, CIA & the Death of JFK" (2020); Appearance, "ETs Among Us 2: Our Alien Origins, Antarctica, Mars and Beyond" (2017); Appearance, "The Professor: Tai Chi's Journey West (2016); Featured Speaker, Secret Space Program Conference (2015); Work Cited, "The Assassination of America"; Work Cited, "Assassination Science"; Publisher, Editor, "UFO Digest" **AW:** Commendation, CG Unit, Department of Homeland Security (2010-2011); Medal for Contributions to American History, Harbor Defense Museum at Fort Hamilton (1994); Regent's Scholar, Fordham University (1967-1974) **MEM:** Aircraft Owners and Pilots Association; Former Member, Air Force Association; Aerospace Education Foundation; Associate Member, New York Federation of Police; Association, New York State Association of Chiefs of Police; U.S Naval Institute; National Space Society **MH:** Albert Nelson Marquis Lifetime Achievement Award **AS:** Mr. Morningstar attributes his success to his wonderful parents, his brothers, Louis and Rudy, his amazing partner, Jill Benzer, and countless mentors, including John F. Kennedy, Robert F. Kennedy, Mickey Mantle, Roger Maris and Buster Crabbe. Additionally, he notes his dedication to truth and excellence, and his lifelong practice of Jungian and Gestalt psychology as reasons for his success. **B/I:** Mr. Morningstar became involved in his profession because of his innate curiosity. **AV:** Researching aeronautics, astronautics, human body mechanics and kinesiology; Practicing martial arts **PA:** Republican **RE:** Roman Catholic

MORRIS, DOLORES O., PHD, ABPP, T: Psychologist, Psychoanalyst **I:** Health, Wellness and Fitness **PT:** Joseph Morris; Gertruda Stokes Morris **MS:** Divorced **ED:** Certificate in Psychoanalysis and Psychotherapy, New York University (1980); PhD in Clinical Psychology,, Yeshiva University, NY (1974); MS in Clinical School Psychology, College of the City of New York (1960); Rotating Psychology Internship, New York State (1958-1959); Coursework in Experimental Psychology, Tufts University (1956-1957); BS, Morgan State College (Now Morgan State University, Baltimore, MD (1956) **CT:** Certified in Psychoanalysis, American Board of Professional Psychology (1996) Certificate in Psychoanalysis, American Board of Professional Psychology (1996); Permanent Certification, School District Administrator, New York State (1988); Certified Supervisor of School Psychologists, New York, NY (1987); Permanent Certification, School Administrator and Supervisor, New York State (1981); Licensed Psychologist, New York State (1980); Licensed Psychologist, New Jersey State (1980); Certified School Psychologist, New York, NY (1963); Permanent Certification, School Psychologist, New York State (1961) **C:** Supervisor, Postdoctoral Program in Psychotherapy and Psychoanalysis, Interpersonal Track, New York University (1992-Present); Psychologist, Private Practice, New York, NY (1980-Present); National Examination Coordinator, Specialty Board for Psychoanalysis (2008-2015); Representative, Council of Representatives for Division 39, Treasurer, Women's and Ethnic Minority Caucuses (2006-2012); Chairperson, Multicultural Concerns Committee (2000-2005) **CR:** Supervisor, Postdoctoral Program in Psychotherapy and Psychoanalysis, New York University (1990-Present); Presenter in Field **CIV:** NAACP; New York Urban League; The Children's Art Carnival, New York, NY **CW:** Editorial Board, Journal of Infant, Child and Adolescent Psychotherapy (2000-Present); Co-author, "Specialty Competencies in Psychoanalysis in Psychology," In A. Nezu and C. Nezu, (Eds.), "Specialty Competencies in Professional Psychology Series," Oxford University Press, NY (2014); Contributor, "Race in the Analytic Situation: Reflections of an African American Therapist," In A. Roland, B. Ulanov and C. Barbre, (Eds.), "Creative Dissent: Psychoanalysis in Evolution," Praeger, Westport, CT (2003); Contributor, "The Supervision of Psychotherapy for African American and Culturally Diverse Patients," In R.A. Javier and W.G. Herron, (Eds.), "Personality Development and Psychotherapy in Our Diverse Society: A Source Book," NY (1998); Contributor, "African American Students and Their Families," In M. Procidano and C. Fischer, (Eds.), "A Handbook for School Professionals," Teacher's College Press, Columbia University (1992) **AW:** Diversity Award, Division 39, American Psychological Association (2011) **MEM:** President, New York University Chapter, Psychoanalytic Society of the Postdoctoral Program (1998-2001); Advisory Board Member, Adolescent Unit Regent Hospital (1990-1994); Founding Member of Eastern Region, Treasurer, The Association of Black Psychologists (ABPsi) (1965-1974); Divisions 5, 9, 12, 16, 39, 42, American Psychological Association; New York State Psychological Association (NYSPA); Inactive, Specialty Board on Psychoanalysis, American Board of Professional Psychology; National Register of Health Service Psychologists **MH:** Albert Nelson Marquis Lifetime Achievement Award **AS:** Dr. Morris attributes her success to her determination to help others and make a difference. She was fortunate to meet mentors that understood and guided her. **B/I:** Dr. Morris' curiosity about herself and others motivated her to major in psychology when she went to college. She continued to pursue the clinical aspect of the profession, which included a receiving a certificate in the specialty in psychoanalysis from the American Board of Professional Psychology. **AV:** Gardening; Travel; Poetry **RE:** Protestant Christian **THT:** Dr. Morris strongly values her privilege to vote. Her motto is, "Life is challenging - meet it with a sense of humor and humility."

MORRIS, GORDON J., PRESIDENT, T: Emeritus Financial Company Executive, Consultant, Investor **I:** Financial Services **CN:** Beacon Wealth Management **DOB:** 10/06/1942 **PB:** Mount Vernon **SC:** OH/USA **PT:** Hugh Morris; Betty Jane (Roberts) Morris **MS:** Divorced **SPN:** Nancy Joan Meyfarth (7/26/1975, Divorced 1998); Janet Ann Swanson (8/28/1965, Divorced 1971) **CH:** Lawrence Hugh; Married Phyllis Hersha (Deceased) **ED:** Postgraduate Coursework, Institute of Certified Fund Specialists (1991); Postgraduate Coursework, College of Financial Planning, Denver, CO (1983-1990); Postgraduate Coursework in Law, Capital University, Bexley, OH (1967-1968); BA, Otterbein College (1966); Coursework, Ohio State University (1960-1961) **CT:** Life Licensed, Florida (1974-2017); Security License, FINRA (1976-2017); Real Estate License, Florida (1986-2011); Registered Investment Advisor; Certified Financial Planner; Certified Fund Specialist; Licensed Loving Trust Advisor; Certified Divorce Planner **C:** Retired (2017); President, Beacon Wealth Management (Formerly Morris & Associates, P.A.), Sarasota, FL (1981-2017); Co-General Partner, Beacon Bridge Loan Pool, Ltd. (1994-1997); Representative, Equitable Financial Services, Sarasota, FL (1974-1981); Assistant to President, Jaeger Machine Company, Columbus, OH (1968-1973); Emeritus Financial Company Executive, Consultant, Investor; Vice President, Treasurer, Homeowners Association Country Place, Inc. **CR:** Seminar Lecturer, High Mark Insurance Services, Inc., Beacon Wealth Management (2003-2009); Radyx Capital Partner, Tampa, FL (1999-2003); Board of Directors, Vice President, Soccer Resource Group, Sarasota, FL (1997-1999); Co-Owner, U.S.I.S.L. West Florida Fury Soccer Team (1996-1998); Chairman, Board of Directors MAP Financial Group, Inc., Sarasota, FL (1985-1989) **CIV:** Vice President, All School Kids, Inc. (1998-1999); Past Chairman, Board of Directors, West Coast Chapter, March of Dimes, Bradenton, FL (1986-1988); President, Epilepsy Foundation of Southwest Florida, Incorporated (1986-1987) **MIL:** ROTC, U.S. Air Force (1960-1961) **CW:** Past Columnist, The Creative News **MEM:** President, Local Club, Institute of Certified Financial Planners, Million Dollar Roundtable, Sertoma, FL (1979-1980) **MH:** Albert Nelson Marquis Lifetime Achievement Award; Marquis Who's Who Top Professional **B/I:** After moving from Ohio to Florida, Mr. Morris was promised a position at a company. However, he decided to turn the position down and seek new opportunities for himself. Mr. Morris resorted to his background in law and used it to change career routes. **PA:** Independent **RE:** Methodist

MORRIS, J.W. JR., T: Materials Science Educator; Consultant **I:** Education/Educational Services **CN:** University of California Berkeley **DOB:** 06/07/1943 **PB:** Birmingham **SC:** AL/USA **PT:** John William Morris; Lillian Lucille (Burnette) Morris **MS:** Married **SPN:** Naomi Naito (01/16/1994); Pamela Mary Dryer (12/30/1966, Divorced 1978) **CH:** McKinley Lee; John Takeshi **ED:** ScD in Materials Science, Massachusetts Institute of Technology, (1969); BS in Metallurgical Engineering, Massachusetts Institute of Technology (1964) **C:** Professor, Graduate School (2011-Present); Professor of Metallurgy, Materials Science and Mineral Engineering, University of California Berkeley (1977-2011); Senior Science Faculty Member, Lawrence Berkeley National Laboratory (1971-2011); Miller Research Professor, University of California Berkeley (1976-1977); Associate Professor, University of California Berkeley (1974-1977); Assistant Professor, Department of Materials Science and Mineral Engineering, University of California Berkeley (1971-1974); Manager of Materials Science, Bell Aerospace Co., Buffalo, NY (1970-1971); Research Scientist, Bell Aerospace Co., Buffalo, NY (1968-1970) **CR:** Program Leader, Advanced Metals, Lawrence Berkeley Laboratory (1985-2005); Lecturer, Chairman, Various Technical Conferences; Owner, J.W. Morris LLC, Consulting Business **CW:** Author, "The Structure and Properties of Dual Phase Steels" (1979); Patentee, Various Steels and Alloys; Contributor Articles to Professional Journals **AW:** Changzu Shi Lectureship Award, Chinese Academy of Sciences (2018); Named Honorable Professor, Xi'an Jiaotong University (2014); John Bardeen Award, The Materials Society (2012); NIMS Award, National Institute for Materials Science (NIMS), Japan (2012); Berkeley Citation, University of California Berkeley (2011); Charles Barrett Silver Medal, ASM International (2009); Fellow, Materials Research Society (2008); Lee Hsun Memorial Lecturer, Institute Metals Research (Now Institute of Metal Research Chinese Academy of Sciences), China (2002); Fellow, The Materials Society (TMS) (Now The Minerals, Metals & Materials Society) (2001); Japanese Government Research Award (1990); AT&T Foundation Award, American Society for Engineering Education (ASEE) (1989); Distinguished Teaching Award, University of California Berkeley (1988); Fellow, American Society of Metals (ASM International) (1987); Distinguished Exchange Scholar, People's Republic of China (1985); Technology 100 Citation for Advancement Technology, U.S. Technology Magazine (1981); Materials Research Award, U.S. Department of Energy (1981); Bradley Stoughton Teaching Award, American Society of Metals (ASM International) (1975); Robert Lansing Hardy Gold Medal, American Institute of Mining, Metallurgical, and Petroleum Engineers (1972) **MEM:** Honorary Member, Japan Institute of Metals and Materials (2011-Present); Honorary Member, Iron and Steel Institute of Japan (2011); Chairman, Golden Gate Chapter, American Society of Metals (ASM International) (1979-1980); Chairman, Chemistry and Physics of Metals Committee, American Institute of Mining, Metallurgical, and Petroleum Engineers (1978-1980); Chairman, Publications Committee, American Institute of Mining, Metallurgical, and Petroleum Engineers (1978-1979); Education Committee, American Society of Metals (ASM International) (1975); Fellow, American Society of Metals (ASM International); Elected Member, National Academy of Engineering; The Minerals, Metals & Materials Society (TMS); American Institute of Mining, Metallurgical, and Petroleum Engineers; Heat Treatment Committee, American Institute of Mining, Metallurgical, and Petroleum Engineers; Materials Research Society; American Physical Society; American Society for Engineering Education (ASEE); Board of Directors, International Cryogenic Materials Conference (CEC-ICMC); Phi Delta Theta Fraternity **MH:** Albert Nelson Marquis Lifetime Achievement Award **B/I:** Dr. Morris had applied to MIT for mathematics and during the summer, before he went, he did construction work that involved metals and then changed to metallurgy. Also, during the summer, he started to read about metallurgy and he found it interesting and decided to pursue a career. **AV:** Golf **PA:** Republican **RE:** Roman Catholic **THT:** Dr. Morris' group did research for a number of years on steels that would be tough over cryogenic temperatures or very low temperatures, liquid nitrogen, liquid helium temperatures; in a more scientific perspective, sorting out or understanding the complicated micro structure of what is called dislocated Martensitic steels.

MORRIS, JAMES MALACHY, ATTORNEY AT LAW, T: Executive Assistant, Counsel to the Chairman **I:** Law and Legal Services **CN:** Farm Credit Administration, Farm Credit System Insurance Corporation (FCSIC) **DOB:** 06/05/1952 **PB:** Champaign **SC:** IL/USA **PT:** Walter Michael Morris; Ellen Frances (Solon) Morris **MS:** Married **SPN:** Mary Delilah Baker (10/17/1987) **CH:** James Malachy Jr.; Elliot Rice Baker; Walter Michael; Nicholas Aidan **ED:** JD, University of Pennsylvania (1977); BA, Brown University (1974); Coursework, University of Oxford, England (1972) **C:** Executive Assistant and Counsel to the Chairman, Farm Credit Administration, Farm Credit System Insurance Corporation (FCSIC); Counsel, FCA Bank Regulation (2018-Present); Sole Practice, FCS Insurance Corporation (FCSIC), McLean, VA (2013-2017); General Counsel, FCS Insurance Corporation (FCSIC), McLean, VA (2006-2013); Executive Assistant, Board Chairman, FCS Insurance Corporation (FCSIC), McLean, VA (2005-2006); Acting Secretary, General Counsel, FCS Insurance Corporation (FCSIC), McLean, VA (1990-1998); Counsel, Farm Credit Administration, Washington, DC (1987-2006); Sole Practice, New York, NY (1983-1987); Associate, Carter, Ledyard & Milburn, LLP, New York, NY (1981-1983); Senior Law Clerk, Illinois Supreme Court, Springfield, IL (1980-1981); Associate, Reid & Priest, New York, NY (1977-1980) **CR:** Consultant, Herbert Oppenheimer, Nathan & Van Dyke, London, England, United Kingdom (1985-2004); With, Pritzker Architecture Prize Foundation, The Hyatt Foundation (1981-2002); With, International Awards Foundation, Zurich, Switzerland (1981-2002) **CW:** Contributor, Articles, Professional Journals **AW:** Funding Award, FCS Insurance Corporation (FCSIC) (2012); Trust Award, Farm Credit Administration Trust (2001) **MEM:** American Bar Association (ABA); Illinois State Bar Association; New York State Bar Association; New York County Lawyers Association; Association of the Bar of the City of New York; British Institute of International and Comparative Law (BIICL); American Institute of Parliamentarians; Brown University 1764 Society; Brown University Association of Class Leaders; Lansdowne Club, London, England, United Kingdom; The Penn Club of New York; Brown Club of DC; New York Athletic Club **BAR:** Barristers' Chambers, Manchester, England, United Kingdom (1987); Supreme Court of the United States (1983); United States Tax Court (1982); Illinois (1980); New York (1978); United States District Court for the Southern District of New York (1978); United States District Court for the Eastern District of New York (1978) **MH:** Albert Nelson Marquis Lifetime Achievement Award; Marquis Who's Who Top Professional **AV:** Reading

MORRIS WINSTON, ALYCE A., T: Founder, Chief Executive Officer **I:** Nonprofit & Philanthropy **CN:** The Jeffrey Foundation **MS:** Married **CH:** One Son (Deceased) **ED:** BS in Social Work, University of Wisconsin **C:** Founder, Chief Executive Officer, The Jeffrey Foundation **CW:** Author, "To Jeffrey with Love: A Heartwarming Story of a Mother and Her Special Needs Son" **AW:** Named Child Care Innovator of the Year; Named California Community Foundation Unsung Hero; Named Susan B. Anthony Professional Woman of the Year; Named American Mothers, Inc. California Mother of the Year; Sybil Brand Humanitarian Award; Children, Youth & Families Angels Over LA Award; National Philanthropy Day Founder Award; Commendation, Mayor Antonio Villaraigoisa , City of Los Angeles, CA (2006); Commendation, Mayor Michael D. Antonovich, County of Los Angeles, CA (2003); Open House & First Year Celebration of Child Care Center, County of Los Angeles, CA (2003); City of Los Angeles Award for Outstanding Service, Councilman Martin Ludlow, CA (2003); Appreciation Award, Association of Fundraising Professional, Greater Los Angeles Chapter, CA (2002); Certification of Appreciation, City of Los Angeles, CA (2002); Grand Opening Award, County of Los Angeles, CA (2002); Pioneer Award, California Community Foundation (2001); Unsung Heroes Award, California Community Foundation (2000); Children Youth & Families Angels Over LA Award (1999); Commendation, City of Los Angeles (1999); State of California Award the Great Seal-Bill Jones (1999) **AS:** Mrs. Morris Winston attributes her success to her mother. **B/I:** Mrs. Morris Winston was very angry that there was a divorce because her ex-husbands family could not accept Jefferey and his disabilities. She was angry because she couldn't continue her career. She decided that she wasn't going to stop; she wanted to make difference for her son and others with the disabilities.

MORRISETT, LLOYD N., PHD, T: Retired Foundation Executive **I:** Education/Educational Services **DOB:** 11/02/1929 **PB:** Oklahoma City **SC:** OK/USA **PT:** Lloyd N. Morrisett; Ruth (Watson) Morrisett **MS:** Married **SPN:** Mary Morrisett **CH:** Sarah; Julie **ED:** Honorary Degree, Frederick S. Pardee RAND Graduate School, Santa Monica, CA (1995); Honorary Degree, Northwestern University, Evanston, IL (1975); Honorary LHD, Oberlin College, Oberlin, OH (1971); PhD, Yale University, New Haven, CT (1956); Postgraduate Coursework, University of California Los Angeles (1951-1953); BA, Oberlin College, Oberlin, OH (1951) **C:** President, Markle Foundation (1969-1998); Vice President, Carnegie Foundation for Advancement Teaching (1965-1969); Vice President, Carnegie Corporation of New York (1965-1969); Executive Associate and Assistant to President, Carnegie Corporation of New York (1963-1965); Executive Associate, Carnegie Corporation of New York (1961-1963); Executive Assistant, Carnegie Corporation of New York (1959-1961); Staff Member, Social Science Research Council (1958-1959); Assistant Professor, University of California Berkeley (1957-1958); Instructor, University of California Berkeley (1956-1957) **CR:** Trustee, Sesame Workshop (2000-Present); Chairman, Board of Trustees, Children's TV Workshop (1970-2000); Overseers, Geisel School of Medicine, Dartmouth College, Hanover, NH (1995-1998); Board Member, WEBS (1996); Advisory Board, Walt Whitman Center, Rutgers University (1993); Trustee, Oberlin College (1972-1988); Trustee, Systems Development Foundation (1970-1988); Trustee, Educational

Testing Service (1983-1987); Trustee, Research Triangle Institute (1970-1979); Trustee, New York City RAND Institute (1969-1975); Trustee, Riverside Research Institute (1971-1974); Director, Infonautics, Tucows, Inc., Toronto, Canada **CIV:** Co-Founder, Children's Television Workshop (Sesame Workshop), New York, NY, (1968-Present); Council on Foreign Relations (1968-1998); Steering Committee, National Research Council (1994-1995); American Council on Germany (1975-1979); Visiting Committee, Department of Information Technology, Harvard University (1974-1980); Board of Directors, Haskins Laboratories (1976); New York State Commission on Quality, Cost, and Financing Elementary and Secondary Education (1969-1972); Board of Directors, Systems Development Corp. (1966-1970) **CW:** Co-Creator, Developer, "Sesame Street" (1969-Present) **AW:** Honoree, Kennedy Center Honors (2019); Co-Recipient, LA Press Club Distinguished Storyteller Award (2017); Hall of Fame Award, ACT Children's Television (1988); Golden Plate Award, American Academy of Achievement (1971) **MEM:** Fellow, National Science Foundation (1953-1956); Fellow, American Psychological Association; American Association for the Advancement of Science; New York Academy of Sciences; Sigma Xi **MH:** Albert Nelson Marquis Lifetime Achievement Award **B/I:** In college, Dr. Morrisett discovered his passion for psychology. After graduating, he began teaching at the University of California Berkley, where he gained early experience. From there, Dr. Morrisett brought his skills to the Social Science Research Council and then to the Carnegie Foundation for the Advancement of Teaching. There, Dr. Morrisett became responsible for the department's ventures into childhood education. He and his team completed important research covering special education and how to help children who were deficient in skills. Dr. Morrisett got results and then sought out children to teach. At the time, he knew Joan Cooney, a television executive, and she was able to give him the opportunity to start the Children's Television Workshop. This later became known as the Sesame Workshop.

MORRISON, FREDERICK FOSTER, T: Mathematician, Writer, Editor **I:** Research **DOB:** 07/20/1939 **PB:** Philadelphia **SC:** PA/USA **PT:** Frederick Foster Morrison; Virginia Pearl (White) Morrison **MS:** Married **SPN:** Nancy Lewis Morrison (1970) **ED:** Postgraduate Coursework, Yale University (1964-1965); AB, Wesleyan University, Middletown, CT (1961) **C:** President, Turtle Hollow Associates, Inc., Gaithersburg, MD (1986-2015); Mathematician, National Ocean Service, Rockville, MD (1965-1985); Mathematician, Army Map Service, Washington, DC (1961-1964) **CR:** Teacher, USDA Graduate School, Washington, DC (1994-1997); Visiting Scholar, Stanford University (1977-1978) **CW:** Author, "The Art of Modeling Dynamic Systems" (1991); Editor, "Geodesy, Mapping & Photogrammetry" (1973-1979); Associate Editor, "Reviews of Geophysics and Space Physics" (1977-1979); Author, "Satellite Geodesy" **AW:** Book of the Year Award, International Institute for Advanced Studies in Systems Research and Systems Research Foundation, Baden-Baden, Germany (1992) **MEM:** Board of Directors, International Association Business Forecasting (1989-1990); President, DC Chapter, Sigma Xi (1985-1987); Translation Board, American Geophysical Union (1976-1978); Former Member, Turtle Hollow Alliance **MH:** Albert Nelson Marquis Lifetime Achievement Award **B/I:** After finishing college, Mr. Morrison found a position in the Army map service as a mathematician. He enjoyed working with computers, which eventually led him to predict orbits for the satellites the Army was using in order to determine positions

on the Earth. **AV:** Practicing photography; Hiking; Appreciating wine and gourmet food; Traveling by rail transportation; Skiing **PA:** Republican

MORRISON, TONI, T: Literature and Language Professor (Retired), Writer, Educator **I:** Education/Educational Services **DOB:** 02/18/1931 **PB:** Lorain **SC:** OH/USA **PT:** George; Ella Ramah (Willis) Wofford **MS:** Divorced **SPN:** Harold Morrison (1958, Divorced 1964) **CH:** Harold Ford; Slade Kevin **ED:** Honorary Degree, Princeton University, Princeton, NJ (2013); Honorary LittD, University of Geneva, Geneva, Switzerland (2011); Honorary LittD, Rutgers, The State University of New Jersey, New Brunswick, NJ (2011); Honorary LittD, University of Oxford (2005); MA in American Literature, Cornell University, New York, NY (1955); BA in English, Howard University, Washington, DC (1953); Honorary Degree, University of Paris; Honorary Degree, Oberlin College, Oberlin, OH; Honorary Degree, Sarah Lawrence College, Yonkers, NY; Honorary Degree, Dartmouth College, Hanover, NH; Honorary Degree, University of Michigan, Ann Arbor, MI; Honorary Degree, Brown University, Providence, RI; Honorary Degree, Georgetown University, Washington, DC; Honorary Degree, Yale University, New Haven, CT; Honorary Degree, Columbia University, New York, NY; Honorary Degree, University of Pennsylvania, Philadelphia, PA **C:** Director, Princeton Atelier, Princeton University (1994-2006); Robert F. Goheen Chair of Humanities, Princeton University, Princeton, New Jersey (1989-2006); Andrew D. White Professor-at-Large, Cornell University (1997-2003); Albert Schweitzer Professor of Humanities, University at Albany (1984-1989); Senior Editor, Random House, New York, NY (1967-1983); Associate Professor of English, Purchase College, State University of New York (1971-1972); Associate Editor, Random House, Syracuse, NY (1965-1967); Instructor of English, Howard University (1957-1964); Instructor of English, Texas Southern University, Houston, TX (1955-1957); Professor Emeritus, Princeton University, Princeton, NJ **CR:** International Cordorcet Chair, Ecole Normale Superieure & College, France (1994); Presenter, Massey Lecturers, Harvard University, Cambridge, MA (1990); Presenter, Clark Lecturers Trinity College, Hartford, CT (1990); Jeannette K. Watson Distinguished Professor, Syracuse University, Syracuse, NY (1988); Obert C. Tanner Lecturer, University of Michigan, Ann Arbor, MA (1988); Visiting Lecturer, Bard College, Annadale-On-Hudson, NY (1986-1988); Yale University, New Haven (1976-1977) **CW:** Author, "God Help the Child" (2015); Author, "Home" (2012); Author, "What Moves at the Margins: Selected Essays, Reviews and Speeches" (2008); Author, "A Mercy" (2008); Writer, Opera, Libretto, "Margaret Garner" (2005); Author, "Remember: The Journey to School Integration" (2004); Author, "Love" (2003); Co-Author, "The Lion or the Mouse?" (2003); Co-Author, "The Ant or the Grasshopper?" (2003); Co-Author, "The Poppy or the Snake?" (2003); Co-Author, "The Big Box" (2002); Co-Author, "The Book of Mean People" (2002); Author, "Paradise" (1999); Co-Editor, "Birth of a Nation'hood: Gaze, Script, Spectacle in the O.J. Simpson Case" (1997); Author, "The Dancing Mind" (1996); Editor, "To Die for the People: The Writings of Huey P. Newton" (1995); Editor, "Race-ing Justice, En-Gendering Power: Essays on Anita Hill, Clarence Thomas, and the Construction of Social Reality" (1992); Author, "Playing in the Dark: Whiteness and the Literary Imagination" (1992); Author, "Jazz" (1992); Author, "Beloved" (1987); Author, "Dreaming Emmett" (1986); Author, "Tar Baby" (1981); Author, "Song of Solomon" (1977); Author, "Sula" (1974); Author, "The Black Book" (1974); Author, "The Bluest Eye" (1970) **AW:** The Thomas Jefferson Medal,

The American Philosophical Society (2018); The Edward MacDowell Medal, The MacDowell Colony (2016); The Charles Eliot Norton Professorship in Poetry, The Norton Lectures, Harvard University (2016); PEN/Saul Below Award for Achievement in American Fiction (2016); Ivan Sandrof Lifetime Achievement Award given by the National Book Critics Circle (2014); The Nichols-Chancellor's Medal, Vanderbilt University (2013); Presidential Medal of Freedom (2012); Library of Congress Creative Achievement Award for Fiction (2011); Officier de la Légion d'Honneur (2010); Norman Mailer Prize, Lifetime Achievement (2009); Inductee, New Jersey Hall of Fame (2009); Nominee, Best Spoken Word Album for Children Grammy Award (2008); Best American Novel Published in Previous 25 Years, New York Times Book Review (2006); Coretta Scott King Award, American Library Association (2005); Golden Plate Award, Academy Achievement (2005); 100 Greatest African Americans, Molefi Kete Asante (2002); One of The 30 Most Powerful Women in America, Ladies' Home Journal (2001); Recipient, National Humanities Medal (2000); Living Legends Award, Library of Congress (2000); National Humanities Medal (2000); Medal for Distinguished Contribution to American Letters, National Book Foundation (1996); Jefferson Lecture (1996); Rhegium Julii Prize for Literature (1994); Condorcet Medal, Paris, France (1994); Commander of the Arts and Letters, Paris, France (1993); Nobel Prize for Literature, Swedish Academy (1993); Robert F. Kennedy Memorial Book Award (1988); Anisfield-Wolf Book Award (1988); Frederic G. Melcher Book Award, Unitarian Universalist Association (1988); New York State Governor's Art Award (1986); Medal of Distinction, Barnard College (1979) National Book Critics Circle Award (1977); Ohioana Book Award (1975); Pulitzer Prize for Fiction (1988); Elizabeth Cady Stanton Award, National Organization of Women **MEM:** American Academy of Arts and Letters; National Council on the Arts; Authors Guild

MORRIS-SMITH, TIM, T: Finance Company Executive **I:** Financial Services **DOB:** 05/16/1965 **PB:** Northampton **SC:** England **PT:** Richard Morris-Smith; Beryl Morris-Smith **MS:** Married **SPN:** Bernadette M.A. Howard (08/02/1997) **CH:** Daniel; Isaac **ED:** Graduate Diploma in Education, University of the Sunshine Coast, Australia (2016); BA in Economics, Geography, Economic Geography and Quantitative Techniques, Hull University, England, With Honors (1987); Vincent Fairfax Fellowship, Ethical Leadership, Melbourne Business School **CT:** Chartered Accountant, England and Wales (1991) **C:** Managing Director, Shared Adviser (2014-2019); Chief Financial Officer, Mission Australia (2008-2014); Director, Finance Integration and Program Office, UTC Fire and Security (2004-2008); General Manager, Finance Australia and Pacific, TNT Express (2002-2004); Director, Global Business Services for Pacific Region, Honeywell (2000-2002); Director, Operations, Finance JAPA/Director Project and Process Management, American Express (1995-2000); Group Finance Director, Computer Answers International (Crauford Group PLC) (1994-1995); Finance Director/Group Finance Director, Oakley Investments Group (1991-1994) **CIV:** Member, Parish Council, St. Matthews Manly, Sydney; Board Finance Committee, Arrow Leadership; Director, 106.5 FM Sunshine Coast; Director, Trinity Youth and Community Services/Skate Aid Australia; Director, Walk A While Foundation **MIL:** With, Royal Air Force (RAF) Cadets (1980-1983) **MEM:** ACA, Institute of Chartered Accountants in England and Wales (ICAEW) **MH:** Albert Nelson Marquis Lifetime Achievement Award **B/I:** Mr. Morris-Smith became involved in his profession because he was always unusual.

They had a real calling to go to Australia, they kept visiting and going back. Every time they visited there, they left a piece of him there when they left. In 1999, they moved there to make a difference. He worked in finance and made a difference in that area but deep down inside he could see that there was this area that was not being addressed. It was the area of the minorities, the underprivileged. He worked on Mission Australia with people who were homeless, women and children who needed help, drug addicts, human beings who needed someone to listen to them to help them to give them a voice. They moved out of Sydney and he wanted to teach to spend time with his children. Mrs. Morris-Smith went back to work full time to support the family when he did this. This is when the consulting opened and the doors opened up to help with skate charity, for young kids in school so they don't drop out they drop in. It was were people with mental health issues could reach out and talk. They realized if you don't invest in the young people today there wont be a tomorrow. If you give people the tools to get them through some of their difficulties and challenges it will pay off. He was also involved in meeting teaching and training young leaders in schools, they have a scholarship in his honor. He believed in young leaders, he believed in you people to make a difference, you just have to invest in them. He was so invested in this he took eight projects off. When he died he had so much calling of him. He was a not for profit guru who believed in helping people and investing in young people. **RE:** Christian

MORS, MATTHEW, T: President **I:** Corporate Communications & Public Relations **CN:** MIX Public Relations **CT:** Security Certification, Master's Level in Social Engineering, Social-Engineer.org (2017); Security Certification, Advanced Practical Social Engineering Training, Social-Engineer.org (2015) **C:** Principal, MIX Public Relations (2010-Present); Owner, Square One Books (2002-2010); Principal, MMPR (2009-2010); Technology Public Relations Rock Star, Text 100 Public Relations (2006-2009); Media Relations, Children's Hospital and Regional Medical Center (2005-2006); Media Relations, Starbucks Coffee Company (1997-2005) **CR:** Guest Lecturer on Public Relations Issues, University of Washington Foster School of Business (2015); Guest Lecturer on Marketing and Public Relations, University of Dar es Salaam, Tanzania (2008); Past Advisor, Department of Journalism, Western Washington University (2008) **CIV:** Volunteer Consultant, Technoserve (2008) **AW:** PR News' Data Dynamo (2018); Agency "Awe" Professional Award, PR News Agency Elite Awards (2018)

MORTENSEN, GORDON LOUIS, T: Artist, Printmaker **I:** Fine Art **DOB:** 04/27/1938 **PB:** Arnegard **SC:** ND/USA **PT:** Gunner Mortensen; Otillia Ernestine (Reiner) Mortensen **MS:** Married **SPN:** Linda Johanna Sisson (12/7/1969) **ED:** Postgraduate Coursework, University of Minnesota (1969-1972); BFA, Minneapolis College Art and Design (1964) **C:** Artist, Printmaker **MIL:** Served with U.S. Marine Corps (1957-1960) **CW:** Exhibitor, Group Show, Boston Printmakers National Exhibition (1977, 1979-1981, 1983, 1997, 2003); Exhibitor, Group Show, 12th National Silvermine Guild Print Exhibition, New Canaan, CT (1976, 1978, 1980, 1983, 1986, 1994, 1996); Solo Exhibtor, C.G. Rein Galleries, Minneapolis, MN (1978, 1980, 1985, 1989, 1991, 1993); Solo Exhibitor, Concept Art Gallery, Pittsburgh, PA (1981, 1983, 1985, 1987, 1989, 1991, 1993); Exhibitor, Group Show, Rockford International (1981, 1985); Solo Exhibitor, Minnesota Museum, St. Paul, MN (1967); Exhibitor, Group Show, Miami University, Oxford, OH; Exhibitor, Group Show, Philadelphia Print Club;

Exhibitor, Group Show, 4th Miami International Print Biennial; Exhibitor, Permanent Collections, Achenbach Foundation Graphic Arts at Palace Legion of Honor, San Francisco, CA; Exhibitor, Permanent Collections, Brooklyn Museum, Philadelphia Museum Art, Library of Congress, Minnesota Museum of Art, Metropolitan Museum and Art Center, Miami, FL, Museum of American Art, Washington, Art Institute of Chicago, Museum of Art at Carnegie-Mellon Institute, Pittsburgh, PA, Walker Art Center, Minneapolis, MN, Dulin Gallery Art, Knoxville, TN, Philadelphia Museum of Art, Tokyo Fuji Art Museum; Exhibitor, Numerous Corporate Collections; Profiled in Numerous Art Journals **AW:** Juror's Accommodation (2007); Purchase Award (1983, 1986); Purchase Award (1977, 1979, 1983); Juror's Award (1981); 4th Place Award (1980); Hearsch Magazine Award (1978); 1st Place Award (1977); George Bunker Award (1977); **MEM:** Boston Printmakers (1972-Present); Philadelphia Print Center; LA Printmaking Society; Albany Print Club; American Print Alliance **MH:** Albert Nelson Marquis Lifetime Achievement Award; Marquis Who's Who Top Professional **B/I:** Mr. Mortensen became involved in his profession because he grew up in an area that did not have any art and so he decided that art was what he wanted to do.

MOSCHINI, SILVINA, T: Co-founder, President **I:** Business Management/Business Services **CN:** TransparentBusiness **PB:** Azul **SC:** Argentina **MS:** Married **SPN:** Alex Konanykhin **ED:** Coursework, Latino Growth Leadership Program, Stanford University (2016-2020); Coursework, Endeavor Strategic Growth Program, Stanford University (2016); Master's Degree in Public Relations, The University of Houston, Texas; BA in Marketing, New York University; BA in Public Relations, Universidad Argentina de la Empresa **C:** Chief Executive Officer, Founder, SheWorks! (2016-Present); Founder, Yandiki (2014-Present); Co-founder, President, TransparentBusiness (2013-Present); Internet and Technology Contributing Expert, Various Networks Including Cable News Network, (CNN) (2012-Present); Founder, Intuic (2008-2014); Vice President, Corporate Communications, Patagon.com International Ltd. (2001-2002); Head of International Public Relations, Compaq Computer Corporation (1999-2001); Public Relations Manager, Compaq Computer Corporation, Latin America and Caribbean Region (1998-2001) **CR:** Mentor, Launchpad and AI for Impact Accelerator, Google, Inc. (2017-Present); Speaker in the Field **CIV:** Volunteer, Miami Dade Animal Services (2016-Present); With, Endeavor Miami, FL (2015-Present); Chairwoman, TransparentBusiness (2013-Present); Executive Board Member, KMGi Group (2003-Present) **CW:** Columnist, La Vanguardia; Contributor, Articles for Professional Journals Including Voxxi, El Universal, and Thrive Global

MOSER, JEFFERY RICHARD, T: English Literature Educator; Writer; Political Advocate; Party Leader **I:** Education/Educational Services **DOB:** 02/08/1961 **PB:** Miller **SC:** SD/USA **PT:** Richard Moser; Ardessa Joan (Yost) Moser **ED:** PhD/ABD in English with Concentration in Literary Studies, University of Denver, Denver, CO; MA in English with Concentration in Literary Studies, University of Denver, Denver, CO (2010); BA in English with Concentration in Textual Studies, University of Denver, Denver, CO, with Department Honors (2008) **CT:** Member and Minister, Open Ministry; Certificate in Lay Ministry, Presbytery of South Dakota and Presbyterian Church, U.S.A. (PC(USA)); Certificate in Public Finance, Northwestern University; Certificate in Public Policy, Duke University; CPR Certificate, The American National Red Cross **C:** English Adjunct, Aims

Community College, Greeley and Fort Lupton, CO (2018-Present); Adjunct Faculty Instructor, Department of English, University of Northern Colorado, Greeley, CO (2016-Present); Chair, House District 41 Democrats, Aurora, CO (2016-2019); Mail Processing Clerk, U.S. Postal Service (USPS), Denver, CO (2014-2016); Assistant to Director of Graduate Studies, Department of English, University of Denver, Denver, CO (2013); Academic Writing Tutor for ESL Graduate Students (2012); Language Tutor, Conversation Partners Program, University of Denver English Language Center (2011); Grammar Tutor to NCAA Division I Student-Athletes, Athletics & Recreation Program, University of Denver (2011); GTA Instructor in English, University of Denver (2011-2013); Writing Center Consultant, University of Denver (2010-2011); Circulation Desk Assistant, University of Denver Penrose Library (2007-2008); National Director of Co-op & Economic Development, National Farmers Union (1999-2009); Deputy State Treasurer, Pierre, SD (1995-1999); Democratic Nominee and Candidate for Congress, South Dakota At-Large (1998); Alternate Delegate Pledged to Bill Clinton, Democratic National Convention, Chicago, IL (1998); Democratic Nominee for State Auditor, SD (1994); State Executive Director, South Dakota Association of Towns and Townships (1989-1995); Small Business Owner and Independent Contractor, Wessington, SD (1986-1989) **CR:** Contributing Member, Peninsula Poets, Long Beach, WA (2019-Present); Participant, 4-H/UN/USAID Presidential Young Adult Exchange Program to Kenya and Botswana, Africa (1985) **CIV:** County Credentials Committee, Arapa-Member, National Association of Parliamentarians and Colorado Association of Parliamentarians (2015-Present); Member, Sierra Club (1985-Present); Member, Colorado Democratic Party State Executive Committee, Twice Elected to 2-year Term (2017-2021); County Credentials Committee, Arapahoe County Democratic Party (2016, 2020); Bylaws Revision Committee, Progressive Democrats of Colorado State Initiative (2017-2020); Precinct Committee Person, Precinct 438, House District 41, Arapahoe County, CO (2010-2020); Vice Chair, Sixth Congressional District, Colorado Democratic Party (2017-2019); Omega Gaveliers Unit Secretary, Colorado Association of Parliamentarians (2017-2019); Board of Directors, Farmers Union Federal Credit Union (2008-2009) **CW:** Author, Book Chapter, "'Each Toy Seems Prologue to Some Great Amiss' So the 'Readiness is All' – Alan Isler's Postmodern Appraisal of Modern Ill Accounts and Illusory Aesthetics," In (Eds.) Sunita Sinha and Carole Rozzonelli, "Shakespeare: A Reappraisal, Volume Two," New Delhi: Atlantic (2015); Assistant Editor, Restoration and Eighteenth-Century Theatre Research (RECTR), Peer-reviewed Journal (2011-2012); Co-editor, The Rustler, High School Yearbook, Miller High School, Miller, SD (1979); Author, Co-author, Contributor, Numerous Peer-reviewed Articles, Book Chapters, Conference Papers, Selected Book and Film Reviews, and Selected Published Poems; Contributor, Numerous Invited Readings **AW:** Certificate of Recognition as Most Helpful Faculty/Staff Member, Presented by Office of Enrollment Management & Student Access, University of Northern Colorado (2016); Lane Alton Nusz Award for Genealogical Research and Submission of Pedigree Chart (2016); Named Volunteer of the Year, Arapahoe County Democratic Party, Aurora, CO (2016); Book Selected, Shakespeare Society of Eastern India (2015-2016); Named Reader, Folger Shakespeare Library, Washington, DC (2015); Named Best Book of the Year, 39th International Kolkata Book Fair (2015); Selected for "Re-imagining Topicality" Seminar, Trustees of Shakespeare Association of America (2014); All-state Honors, South Dakota High School

Activities Association (1979); Book Selected, Shakespeare Society of Eastern India (2015-2016); Named Best Book of the Year, 39th International Kolkata Book Fair (2015); Selected by Trustees of Shakespeare Association of America (SAA) for "Re-imagining Topicality" Seminar (2014); All-state Honors, South Dakota High School Activities Association (1979); **MEM:** Board of Directors, Rocky Mountain Medieval & Renaissance Association (2017-2020); Shakespeare Association of America; Renaissance English Text Society (RETS); Renaissance Society of America; Bibliographic Society of America; Modern Language Association of America; Rocky Mountain Modern Language Association; American Film Institute; Academy of American Poets; College Honor Societies: Sigma Tau Delta; Delta Epsilon Iota Academic Honor Society; Golden Key International Honour Society; Mortar Board; Omicron Delta Kappa; The Phi Beta Kappa Society **MH:** Albert Nelson Marquis Lifetime Achievement Award **B/I:** Dr. Moser became involved in his profession because it was important for him to complete his bachelor's degree that he began 29 years earlier. He was always interested in history and politics, and these led him onto his academic pursuits. His doctoral concentration was in literary studies with an emphasis in renaissance poetry and drama. His doctoral dissertation was on Shakespeare's published poems and early modern print culture. As much as he teaches his students, he says they are also teaching and informing him. **AV:** Piano; Painting and drawing; Poetry; Writing; Genealogy; Theater; Coin and stamp collecting **PA:** Democrat **RE:** Presbyterian

MOSES, RONALD ELLIOT, T: Toiletries Products Executive (Retired), Chemist **I:** Sciences **DOB:** 12/29/1930 **PB:** Chelsea **SC:** MA/USA **PT:** Isadore Philip Moses; Ida (Finstein) Moses **MS:** Widowed **SPN:** Eleanor Antoinette Vitale (06/22/1952, Deceased 2018) **CH:** Judith Jeanne (Deceased, 4/2018); Thomas Charles **ED:** MS in Chemistry, Northeastern University, Boston, MA (1959); AB, Harvard University, Cambridge, MA (1952) **C:** Vice President, Research and Development, Toiletries Technologies Laboratory, Gillette North Atlantic, Boston, MA (1991-1993); Director, Research and Development, Shaving and Personal Care Group, Gillette North Atlantic, Boston, MA (1990-1991); Vice President, Research and Development, Personal Care Group, Gillette North Atlantic, Boston, MA (1987-1990); Vice President, Research and Development, Personal Care Division, Gillette Safety Razor Co., Boston, MA (1983-1987); Director, Product Development, Personal Care Division, Gillette Safety Razor Co., Boston, MA (1978-1983); Director, Product Development Toiletries Division, Gillette Safety Razor Co., Boston, MA (1973-1978); Senior Manager, Research Toiletries Division, Gillette Safety Razor Co., Boston, MA (1970-1973); Project Chemist, Toiletries Division, Gillette Safety Razor Co., Boston, MA (1965-1970); Senior Chemist, Gillette Safety Razor Co., Boston, MA (1960-1965); Chemist, General Foods Corp., Woburn, MA (1954-1960) **CIV:** Board Member, Producer, Winthrop Community Access TV, Inc. (1993-Present); Member, Producer, Winthrop Public Access TV Station (1992-Present); President, Winthrop Community Access TV, Inc. (1993-2016); Election Volunteer; Town of Winthrop Financial Advisory Committee; Winthrop Rotary Club; Rotary Club of Belle Isle; Rotary Club of Bell Isle Foundation, Inc. **MIL:** Honorable Discharge (1963); U.S. Naval Reserve (1948-1963); Lieutenant Junior Grade, USS Woodson, U.S. Navy (1952-1954) **CW:** Co-Patentee, Five Patents Dealing with Gelatin Fining and Preparation, Shaving Product Composition, and Hair Conditioning Composition; Producer, More Than 700 Programs, Winthrop Public Access TV Station **AW:** Winthrop Chamber of Commerce Awards, Lifetime Achievement (2011); Winthrop Chamber of Commerce Awards, Community Service (2002) **MEM:** Fellow, American Institute of Chemists; Member Emeritus, American Chemical Society; American Society of Cosmetic Chemists; Winthrop Golf Club; Rotary Club of Belle Isle **MH:** Albert Nelson Marquis Lifetime Achievement Award; Marquis Who's Who Top Professional **B/I:** Mr. Moses became involved in his profession early on because when he was a teenager, he and his friend had a miniature laboratory in his basement. The real inspiration he had was when he read a book by Paul DeKiuif; it was a series of stories about famous scientists. When Mr. Moses first got into the Navy, he wanted to go into cancer research, but most were headed by medical doctors. The pay wasn't enough to support his family, so that is how he ended up at General Foods. **AV:** Classical music; Reading; Golf; Model ships; Computer programming **PA:** Republican **RE:** Jewish

MOSKOVITZ, DUSTIN AARON, T: Co-founder; Entrepreneur; Social Networking Company Executive **I:** Internet **CN:** Asana **DOB:** 05/22/1984 **PB:** Gainesville **SC:** FL/USA **PT:** Richard A. Moskovitz; Nancy Siegel **MS:** Married **SPN:** Cari Tuna **ED:** Coursework in Economics, Harvard University (2002-2004) **C:** Co-founder, Asana, CA (2008-Present); Vice President of Engineering, Facebook, Inc., Palo Alto, CA (2004-2008); Co-founder, Facebook, Inc., Palo Alto, CA (2004) **CIV:** Co-founder, Open Philanthropy Project (2014-Present); Co-founder, Good Ventures (2011-Present) **AW:** Named One of the Forbes 400: Richest Americans, Forbes Magazine (2011-Present); Named One of the Richest in Tech, Forbes Magazine (2017); Named One of America's Richest Entrepreneurs Under 40, Forbes Magazine (2016)

MOSLEY, CLINT JR., T: Professional Football Player **I:** Athletics **CN:** New York Jets **DOB:** 06/19/1992 **PB:** Mobile **SC:** AL/USA **PT:** Clinton Mosley; Tracy Mosley **MS:** Single **ED:** Coursework, University of Alabama; Diploma, Theodore High School **C:** Linebacker, New York Jets (2019-Present); Linebacker, Baltimore Ravens (2014-2018) **AW:** 4-Time Pro Bowl Champion (2014, 2016-2018); PFWA All-Rookie Team (2014); Butkus Award (2013); SEC Defensive Player of the Year (2013); 2-Time Consensus All-American (2012-2013); SEC Champion (2012); 2-Time BCS National Champion (2011-2012)

MOSS, BILL RALPH, T: Lawyer **I:** Law and Legal Services **DOB:** 09/27/1950 **PB:** Amarillo **SC:** TX/USA **PT:** Ralph Voniver Moss; Virginia May (Atkins) Moss **CH:** Brandon Price **ED:** Certificate in Regulatory Studies, Michigan State University (1981); JD, Baylor University (1976); MA, West Texas A&M University (1974); BS, West Texas A&M University, With Honors (1972) **C:** Attorney at Law (2011-Present); Assistant Attorney General, Antitrust and Civil Medicaid Fraud Division, Office of the Attorney General (2004-2011); Assistant General Counsel, Texas Ethics Commission, Austin, TX (1997-2004); Founder, Owner, Price & Co. Publications, Austin, TX (1987-1997); Assistant General Counsel, State Bar of Texas, Austin, TX (1983-1987); Hearings Examiner, Public Utility Commission of Texas, Austin, TX (1981-1983); Associate, Culton, Morgan, Britain & White, Amarillo, TX (1977-1980); Briefing Attorney, Court of Appeals for the Seventh Supreme Judicial District of Texas, Amarillo, TX (1976-1977) **CR:** Instructor, Lecturer, Eastern New Mexico University (1977-1980); Instructor, Lecturer, West Texas State University; Speaker in Field **MEM:** Panel Director, Issues Facing Profession, American Bar Association; American Association of Individual Investors; Democratic National Committee; Federal Bar Association; Member Emeritus, State Bar of Texas; National Organization of Bar Counsel; National Council of Prescription Drug Programs; International Platform Association; Capitol of Texas Rotary Club; Nature Conservancy; Alpha Chi; Lambda Chi Alpha; Omicron Delta Epsilon; Phi Alpha Delta; Sigma Tau Delta; Pi Gamma Mu **BAR:** U.S. District Court for the Western District of Texas (2005); U.S. Court of Appeals for the Fifth Circuit (1983); U.S. Tax Court (1979); Texas (1976); U.S. District Court for the Northern District of Texas (1976) **RE:** Episcopalian

MOSS, ELISABETH SINGLETON, T: Actress **I:** Media & Entertainment **DOB:** 7/24/1982 **PB:** Los Angeles **SC:** CA/USA **PT:** Ron Moss; Linda Moss **MS:** Divorced **SPN:** Fred Armisen (10/25/2009, Divorced 05/13/2011) **CW:** Actress, "The Handmaid's Tale" (2017-Present); Actress, "The Invisible Man" (2020); Actress, "Shirley" (2020); Actress, "The Kitchen" (2019); Actress, "Us" (2019); Actress, "Her Smell" (2018); Actress, "The Seagull" (2018); Actress, "The Old Man and the Gun" (2018); Actress, "The Square" (2017); Actress, "The Free World" (2016); Actress, "The Bleeder" (2016); Actress, "The Seagull" (2016); Actress, "Mad to Be Normal" (2016); Actress, "Meadowland" (2015); Actress, "Truth" (2015); Actress, Producer, "Queen of Earth" (2015); Actress, "High-Rise" (2015); Actress, "Mad Men" (2007-2015); Actress, "Listen Up Philip" (2014); Actress, "The One I Love" (2014); Actress, "The Simpsons" (2013); Actress, "Top of the Lake" (2013); Actress, "Smoking/Non-Smoking" (2012); Actress, "Darling Companion" (2012); Actress, "On the Road" (2012); Actress, "A Buddy Story" (2010); Actress, "The Pack" (2010); Actress, "Get Him to the Greek" (2010); Actress, "Did You Hear About the Morgans?" (2009); Actress, "The Attic" (2008); Actress, "New Orleans, Mon Amour" (2008); Actress, "El Camino" (2008); Actress, "The Pack" (2008); Actress, Broadway, "Speed-the-Plow" (2008); Actress, "They Never Found Her" (2007); Actress, "Day Zero" (2007); Actress, "Honored" (2007); Actress, "Invasion" (2005-2006); Actress, "The West Wing" (1999-2006); Actress, "Bittersweet Place" (2005); Actress, "Heart of America" (2003); Actress, "Temptation" (2003); Actress, "Virgin" (2003); Actress, "The Missing" (2003); Actress, "West of Here" (2002); Actress, "Spirit" (2001); Actress, "Earthly Possessions" (1999); Actress, "The Joyriders" (1999); Actress, "Mumford" (1999); Actress, "Anywhere But Here" (1999); Actress, "Girl, Interrupted" (1999); Actress, "Angelmaker" (1998); Actress, "A Thousand Acres" (1997); Actress, "Separate Lives" (1995); Actress, "The Last Supper" (1995); Actress, "Escape to Witch Mountain" (1995); Actress, "Naomi & Wynonna: Love Can Build a Bridge" (1995); Actress, "Picket Fences" (1992-1995); Actress, "Imaginary Crimes" (1994); Actress, "Gypsy" (1993); Actress, "Once Upon a Forest" (1993); Actress, "Midnight's Child" (1992); Actress, "Frosty Returns" (1992); Actress, "It's Spring Training, Charlie Brown!" (1992); Actress, "Suburban Commando" (1991); Actress, "Bar Girls" (1990); Actress, "Lucky Chances" (1990); Dancer, Ballet, "Sleeping Beauty," New York City Ballet, NY; Dancer, Ballet, "The Nutcracker," Joffrey Ballet; Actress, Plays, "Sound of Music," "Christmas Dragon," "Big Tush/Little Tush," and "Franny's Way"; Actress, Appearances, Television Shows, Films **AW:** Golden Globe Award for Best Performance by an Actress in a Television Series Drama, Hollywood Foreign Press Association (2018); Critics' Choice Award for Best Actress in a Drama Series (2018); Primetime Emmy Award for Outstanding Lead Actress in a Drama Series, Academy of Television Arts & Sciences (2017);

Primetime Emmy Award for Outstanding Drama Series, Academy of Television Arts & Sciences (2017); Golden Globe Award for Best Performance by an Actress in a Miniseries or Motion Picture Made for TV, Hollywood Foreign Press Association (2014); Award for Outstanding Actress in a Mini-Series, Monte-Carlo Television Festival Awards (2014); Critics' Choice Award for Best Actress in a Movie or Miniseries (2013); Awards for Outstanding Performance by an Ensemble in a Drama Series, Screen Actors Guild - American Federation of Television and Radio Artists (2009, 2010)

MOSSINGHOFF, GERALD JOSEPH, T: Lawyer, Educator **I:** Law and Legal Services **CN:** Oblon, McClelland, Maier & Neustadt, L.L.P.; George Washington University **DOB:** 09/30/1935 **PB:** St. Louis **SC:** MO/USA **MS:** Married **SPN:** Jeanne Carole Jack (12/29/1958) **CH:** Pamela Ann Jennings; Gregory Joseph; Melissa M. Ronayne **ED:** JD, George Washington University, With Honors (1961); BSEE, Saint Louis University (1957) **CT:** Admitted to Practice, U.S. Patent and Trademark Office **C:** Senior Counsel, Oblon, McClelland, Maier & Neustadt, L.L.P., Arlington, VA (1997-Present); Cifelli Professor, Intellectual Property Law, George Washington University, Washington, DC (1996-Present); President, Pharmaceutical Research and Manufacturers of America, Washington, DC (1985-1996); Assistant Secretary of Commerce, Commissioner, United States Patent and Trademark Office (1981-1985); Deputy General Counsel, Congressional Liaison, Director, National Aeronautics and Space Administration, Washington, DC (1967-1973); Project Engineer, Sachs Electric (1954-1957) **CR:** Ambassador, Paris Convention Diplomatic Conference **CW:** Contributor, "Reagan Remembered" (2011) **AW:** Honoree, Best in Intellectual Property Law, Best Lawyers in America (2012-2018); Giles S. Rich American Inn of Court Fellow (2011-2012); Inductee, Intellectual Property Hall of Fame (2007); Listee, Who's Who in Intellectual Property, Legal Times (2001); Jefferson Medal (2000); Distinguished Alumnus, George Washington University (1996); Roger W. Jones Award for Executive Leadership, American University (1984); Distinguished Public Service Award, Secretary of Commerce (1982); Outstanding Leadership Medal, National Aeronautics and Space Administration (1981); Honoree, Old Master, Purdue University (1980); President Rank of Meritorious Executive (1980); Distinguished Service Medal, National Aeronautics and Space Administration (1980); Exceptional Service Medal, National Aeronautics and Space Administration (1972) **MEM:** Fellow, National Academy of Public Administration; Board of Directors, Reagan Alumni Association; Cosmos Club; Knights of Malta; The Order of the Coif; Pi Mu Epsilon; Eta Kappa Nu; American Bar Association; American Intellectual Property Law Association; Federal Bar Association; International Intellectual Property Institute **BAR:** Virginia State Bar (1981); The District of Columbia Bar (1965); The Missouri Bar (1957) **MH:** Albert Nelson Marquis Lifetime Achievement Award

MOSTOFI, HORMOZ, T: Owner **I:** Financial Services **CN:** HM & Associates **MS:** Widowed **SPN:** Marguerite **ED:** MS in Management, Northrop University (1975); BS in Iranian Advanced Accounting **CT:** Enrolled Agent **C:** Owner, HM & Associates (1983-Present); Accountant (1966-1983) **AS:** Mr. Mostofi attributes his success to hard work and caring about people. He didn't have proper guidance when he came to the United States, and he realized how important it was for people new to the country to have that. **B/I:** Mr. Mostofi became involved in his profession because his father was an accountant, so he followed in his footsteps.

MOTT, PEGGY LAVERNE, PHD, T: Instructor of Sociology (Retired) **I:** Education/Educational Services **DOB:** 03/23/1930 **PB:** Stephenville **SC:** TX/USA **PT:** Artemis "Temis" Victor Dorris (Deceased 1986); Tempie Pearl (Price) Hickman (Deceased 2005) **MS:** Widowed **SPN:** J.D. Mott (09/11/1947, Deceased 04/1988) **CH:** Kelly A. Wilcoxson; Kimberly S. Mott **ED:** Master of Arts in Teaching, Southwest Texas State University (Now Texas State University) (1982); Bachelor of Applied Arts and Sciences, Southwest Texas State University, (Now Texas State University) (1980); PhD in Comparative Religions, Southwest Texas State University (Now Texas State University) (1995) **CT:** Certified Instructor of Ceramic Arts, National Ceramic Art Institute (1986) **C:** Instructor of Sociology, Palo Alto College, San Antonio, Texas (1991-2010); Assistant Instructor, Southwest Texas State University (Now Texas State University), San Marcos, Texas (1980-1982); Director of Sales, Arts & Crafts Center, Lackland AFB (Air Force Base), San Antonio, Texas (1972-1977); Instructor of Ceramics, Arts & Crafts Center, Lackland AFB (Air Force Base), San Antonio, Texas (1969-1972) **CIV:** Parliamentarian Artistic Expressions (1996); Volunteer Coordinator, Fisher Houses, Inc., Lackland AFB (Air Force Base) (1992-1994) **CW:** Author, "Hwap, Patchwork Poems" (1995); Author, "Lucidity, The T.O.P. Hwupp" (1994-1995); Author, "Inkwell Echos" (1989-1995); Author, "Screaming Silences" (1994); Author, Poem, "Concho River Review" (1993); Co-author, Activities, Field Studies for Students **AW:** Named Volunteer of the Quarter, Lackland Air Force Base (1976, 1977, 1978, 1984); Named Volunteer of the Year, Lackland Air Force Base (1980); Named Volunteer of the Year, Air Training Command (1980); Named Volunteer of the Month, Lackland Air Force Base (1976, 1977, 1978) **MEM:** Poet Laureate, San Antonio Poets Association (1994-1995); President, San Antonio Poets Association (1992-1993); Vice President, San Antonio Poets Association (1991-1992); International Society of Poets; Clipper Ship Poets; San Antonio Poets Association; San Antonio Ethnic Art Society; San Antonio Poetry Festival; Alamo Area Poets of Texas **MH:** Albert Nelson Marquis Lifetime Achievement Award **B/I:** Dr. Mott became involved in her profession because she wanted a degree in cultural anthropology but none of the universities at that time had such a degree, so it ended up being sociology. She did sociology because she wanted to know why people did what they did but did not want to do psychology. **AV:** Reading; Writing; Needlecrafts **PA:** Independent

MOTTA, DICK, T: Former Professional Basketball Coach **I:** Athletics **DOB:** 09/03/1931 **PB:** Midvale **SC:** UT/USA **MS:** Married **SPN:** Janice Motta **CH:** Three Children **ED:** Diploma, Utah State Agricultural College (Now Utah State University) **C:** Coach, Denver Nuggets, National Basketball Association (NBA) (1996-1997); Coach, Dallas Mavericks, National Basketball Association (NBA) (1980-1987, 1994-1996); Coach, Sacramento Kings, National Basketball Association (NBA) (1990-1991); Coach, Washington Bullets (Now Washington Wizards), National Basketball Association (NBA) (1976-1980); Coach, Chicago Bulls, National Basketball Association (NBA) (1968-1976); Coach, Weber State Wildcats (1962-1968) **AW:** NBA All-Star Game Head Coach (1979); NBA Coach of the Year (1971); Big Sky Champion (1965, 1966, 1968); Big Sky Coach of the Year (1965)

MOULTON, SETH WILBUR, T: U.S. Representative from Massachusetts **I:** Government Administration/Government Relations/Government Services **DOB:** 10/24/1978 **PB:** Salem **SC:** MA/USA **PT:** Wilbur Thomas Moulton; Lynn Alice (Meader) Moulton **MS:** Married **SPN:** Liz Boardman (09/22/2017) **CH:** Emmy **ED:** MBA, Harvard Business School (2011); MA in Public Policy, Harvard Kennedy School, John F. Kennedy School of Government (2011); BA in Physics, Harvard University (2001) **C:** Member, U.S. House of Representatives from Massachusetts' Sixth Congressional District, United States Congress, Washington, DC (2014-Present); Candidate, Democratic Nominee, 2020 Presidential Election (2019); Managing Director, Texas Central Railway (2011-2012); Co-founder, Eastern Healthcare Partners (2011); Member, Budget Committee; Member, Committee on Armed Services; Member, Committee on Small Business **MIL:** Advanced through Grades to Captain, United States Marine Corps (2001-2008) **CW:** Appearance, Documentary, "No End in Sight" (2007); Co-Host, "Moulton and Mohammed" (2003); Appearance, CNN; Appearance, MSNBC; Appearance, "Morning Edition," NPR; Appearance, "All Things Considered," NPR **AW:** Decorated Commendation Medal, U.S. Marine Corps; Bronze Star, U.S. Marine Corps **PA:** Democrat

MOUSER, BARBARA CHRISTINE, RNC, MSN, T: Family Nurse Practitioner **I:** Medicine & Health Care **DOB:** 03/13/1939 **PB:** Flint **SC:** MI/USA **PT:** Hubert Fontaine; Hattie Christine (Palmer) Doyle **MS:** Married **SPN:** Hugh Allen Mouser **CH:** Tracie Lynn Grimes; Lance Allen Mouser; Jay Marvin Mouser **ED:** Family Nurse Practitioner, CSUB (1999); MS in Nursing, California State University (1992); BSN, California State University Bakersfield (1979); AARN, Bakersfield College (1959) **CT:** CQI, Rehabilitation Nursing, Coronary Care, Pediatric Assessment, California State University Long Beach **C:** Lecturer in Nursing, California State University Bakersfield (1993-1998); Nurse Practitioner, Kings View Clinic, Hanford CA (1990-1992); Migrant Nurse, Director of Nurses, Westside Hospital, Taft, CA (1988-1992); Educator, Bakersfield College (1989-1990); Educator, Taft College (1979-1988); Public Health Nurse, Kern County Health Department, Bakersfield, CA (1981-1983); School Nurse, Bakersfield-Kern County School District (1971-1976); Staff Nurse, Hanford Community Hospital (1965-1970); Staff Nurse, Neurology, Valley Medical Center, Fresno, CA (1961-1962); Staff Nurse, St. Peters Hospital, Olympia, WA (1959-1961) **CR:** PMPI Contracted FNP (2008-2014); Kings View Clinic (2003-2012); Bakersfield Rehab-Director, CQI, Education, Faculty, CSU Bakersfield (1993-2000); Mercy Hospital Home Health Supervisor (1993) **CW:** Artist, Stained Glass Works **AW:** Mental Health Professional of the Year (2012); Volunteer of the Year, American Cancer Society (1987); Inductee, Sigma Theta Tau; Inductee, Phi Kappa Phi **MEM:** President, American Association Infection Control Practitioners (1992); Vice President, Nursing Honor Society (1989-1991); Fellow, Nightingale Society; Kern Council of Nursing Administrators **MH:** Albert Nelson Marquis Lifetime Achievement Award **AV:** Playing piano; Skiing; Making stained glass; Running; Biking competitively **PA:** Democrat **RE:** Protestant

MOYER, NANCY JAN, PHD, T: Professor Emerita of Art **I:** Education/Educational Services **DOB:** 01/24/1938 **PB:** Los Angeles **SC:** CA/USA **PT:** Vernon Moyer; Leila Mae (Sturges) Moyer **MS:** Single **ED:** PhD, Southern Illinois University (1970); MA, Louisiana State University (1963); BA, University of Southwestern Louisiana (Now University of Louisiana at Lafayette) (1960) **C:** Chair, Art

Department, University of Texas - Pan American, Edinburg, Texas (1994-2003); Chair, Art Department, Pan American University, Edinburg, Texas (1972-1980); Art Professor, University of Texas - Pan American, Edinburg, Texas (1969-1994); Head, Art Department, St. Francis Academy (Now Joliet Catholic Academy), Joliet, IL (1966-1967); Art Instructor, Southwest Texas State University (Now Texas State University), San Marcos, Texas (1964-1966) **CR:** Art Critic, The Monitor (2003-Present) **CIV:** Committee Chair, McAllen Public Art (2014-2018); Chair, McAllen Arts Council (2010-2012); Committee Member, GSA Project, Pharr Bridge Public Art (1996); Board of Trustees, McAllen International Museum (Now IMAS International Museum of Arts & Science) (1994-1996); Board of Directors, KZLN-TV (1981); Board of Directors, Texas Consumer Development and Educational Corporation (1975-1980) **CW:** Artist, "Jackrabbit," Public Sculpture (2010) **AW:** Citation for Comment and Criticism, Texas Associated Press Managing Editors (2018); Outstanding Faculty Award (1990); Distinguished Faculty Achievement Award, University of Texas - Pan American (1989-1990); Named Profesora Visitante, University de las Americas (1989); Named to One Hundred Women of the Rio Grande Valley (1983) **MEM:** Professional Guidelines Board, Society of North American Goldsmiths (2009-Present); Board of Directors, National Council of Arts Administrators (2001-2003); Society of North American Goldsmiths **MH:** Albert Nelson Marquis Lifetime Achievement Award **AS:** Dr. Moyer attributes her success to satisfaction. **B/I:** Dr. Moyer was always interested in art. As an undergraduate, she looked at the faculty and admired their lifestyle; she knew that she wanted to be like them, so she went in the professional direction of art and teaching. When Dr. Moyer decided to get her doctorate, she looked at degrees and she realized that being a women in the higher education field would give her an edge in the job market. She wrote her first theoretical dissertation at the Department of Secondary Education at Southern Illinois University.

MOYERS, BILL DON, T: White House Press Secretary (Retired), Journalist, Writer **I:** Writing and Editing **DOB:** 06/05/1934 **PB:** Hugo **SC:** OK/USA **PT:** John Henry Moyers; Ruby (Johnson) Moyers **MS:** Married **SPN:** Judith Suzanne Davidson (12/18/1954) **CH:** William Cope; Suzanne; John **ED:** Honorary LHD, Whittier College (2011); MDiv, Southwestern Baptist Theological Seminary (1959); Graduate Coursework, University of Edinburgh, Scotland (1956-1957); BJ, University of Texas, With Honors (1956); Honorary DFA, American Film Institute **C:** Anchor, Writer, Bill Moyers Journal (2006-Present); Founder, Public Affairs Programming, Inc. (1986-Present); Anchor, Writer, National Organization of Women With Bill Moyers (2002-2004); Senior News Analyst, CBS News, CBS-TV (1981-1986); Editor-in-Chief, Bill Moyers Journal (1971-1976, 1978-1981); Chief Correspondent, CBS Reports, CBS-TV (1976-1978); Public, Newsday, Garden City, NY (1967-1970); Press Secretary, The White House (1965-1967); Special Assistant to President, The White House (1963-1967); Department Director, Peace Corps (1963); Associate Director of Public Affairs, Peace Corps (1961-1962); Personal Assistant to Sen. Lyndon B. Johnson, US Senate (1960-1961) **CIV:** President, The Florence and John Schumann Foundation (1991-Present) **CW:** Author, "Bill Moyers Journal: The Conversation Continues" (2011); Author, "Moyers on Democracy" (2008); Author, "Moyers on America: A Journalist and His Times" (2004); Author, "Fooling with Words: A Celebration of Poets and Their Craft" (1999); Author, "Sister Wendy in Conversation With Bill Moyers: The Complete Conversation" (1997); Author, "Gene-

sis: A Living Conversation" (1996); Author, "The Language of Life" (1995); Author, "Healing and the Mind" (1993); Author, "A World of Ideas II: Public Opinions from Private Citizens" (1990); Author, "A World of Ideas: Conversations With Thoughtful Men and Women About American Life Today and the Ideas Shaping Our Future" (1989); Host, "The Power of Myth" (1988); Co-Author, "The Secret Government: The Constitution in Crisis: With Excerpts from an Essay on Watergate" (1988); Author, "Listening to America: A Traveler Rediscovers His Country" (1971) **AW:** Lifetime Emmy Award (2006); Walter Cronkite Award for Excellence in Journalism (1995); Inductee, Television Hall of Fame (1995); Three George Polk Career Awards; Lifetime Peabody Award; Gold Baton, Alfred I. duPont-Columbia University Awards; Lifetime Achievement Award, National Academy of Television Arts and Sciences; More Than 30 Emmy Awards **MEM:** President, Schumann Center for Media and Democracy (1990-Present); Director, Council on Foreign Relations (1967-1974); Fellow, American Association for the Advancement of Science; American Philosophical Society; Organization of American Historians; Bilderberg Group; American Academy of Arts and Letters **PA:** Independent **RE:** Protestant

MOYLAN, SUSAN NELIS, T: Business and Industry Center Director **I:** Business Management/Business Services **DOB:** 11/23/1941 **PB:** Evergreen Park **SC:** IL/USA **PT:** William M. Nelis Jr.; Rosemary (Luken) Nelis **MS:** Widowed **SPN:** William D. Moylan Jr. (07/10/1965, Deceased 11/27/2019) **CH:** Elizabeth; Catherine; Rosemary; Martha **ED:** MA, Northern Illinois University, DeKalb, IL (1999); BS, Loyola University (1964) **C:** Director, Business and Industry Training Center, Elgin Community College, Elgin, IL (1979-2004) **CR:** Borden Gail Borden Public Library Board; Board, Gail Borden Library Foundation; Board, Pads of Elgin, Elgin, IL **CIV:** Gail Borden Public Library Board (2009-Present); President, United Way of Elgin (1990-Present); President, St. Joseph Hospital Foundation (1993-1995); Board of Directors, St. Edward High School Foundation (1986-1993); Councilwoman, City of Elgin (1985-1993); Former Member, St. Joseph Hospital Foundation (1991); Former Member, Ethics Committee, St. Joseph Hospital, Elgin, IL (1988); President, Dukane Council, Geneva, IL (1989-1983); Renz Addiction Counseling Center, United Way of Elgin; Elected Library Trustee, Gail Borden Public Library, Elgin, IL **AW:** Political Leader of the Year, Association for Individual Development (1988) **MEM:** President, Rotary International (2002); Chair, Women's Council, Elgin Chamber of Commerce (1984-1985); Elgin Chamber of Commerce **MH:** Albert Nelson Marquis Lifetime Achievement Award **B/I:** Ms. Moylan became involved in her profession because she saw an ad in the newspaper for a part-time local government training coordinator at Elgin Community College in 1979; she applied for the job, which had a three-year part-time grant, and got it. By the time the grant expired, she had been there three years, working successfully with local government training and she was then moved to business training at Elgin Community College and eventually went full-time. She then became the director of corporate sales, working with businesses. **AV:** Quilting; Gardening tomatoes **PA:** Democrat **RE:** Roman Catholic

MOYNIHAN, BRIAN THOMAS, T: Chairman, President, Chief Executive Officer **I:** Financial Services **CN:** Bank of America **DOB:** 10/09/1959 **PB:** Marietta **SC:** OH/USA **MS:** Married **SPN:** Susan Berry **CH:** Three Children **ED:** JD, University of Notre Dame Law School (1984); BA, Brown University (1981) **C:** Chairman, President, Chief Executive

Officer, Bank Of America Corporation (2014-Present); President, Chief Executive Officer, Bank Of America Corporation (2010-2014); Head Consumer Banking, Bank Of America Corporation (2009-2010); President Global Banking, Global Wealth & Investment Management, Bank Of America Corporation (2009); Chief Executive Officer, Merrill Lynch, Bank Of America Corporation (2009); Executive Vice President, General Counsel, Bank Of America Corporation (2008-2009); President Global Corporate & Investment Banking, Bank Of America Corporation (2007-2009); President Global Wealth & Investment Management, Bank Of America Corporation, Charlotte, NC (2004-2007); Executive Vice President, Brokerage & Wealth Management, Fleetboston Financial Corporation (2000-2004); Executive Vice President, Fleetboston Financial Corporation (1999-2000); Managing Director Corporate Strategy & Development, Fleetboston Financial Corporation (1994-2000); Senior Vice President, Fleetboston Financial Corporation (1998-1999); Deputy General Counsel, Fleetboston Financial Corporation (1993-1994); Partner, Edwards & Angell LLP (1991-1993); Associate, Edwards & Angell LLP (1984-1991) **CR:** Board of Directors, Bank of America Corp. (2010-Present) **CIV:** Past Chairman, Providence Haitian Project, Inc.; Past Chairman, Travelers Aid Society, Rhode Island; Board of Directors, Boys & Girls Clubs of Boston; Board of Directors, YouthBuild Boston

MUCARSEL-POWELL, DEBBIE JESSIKA, T: U.S. Representative from Florida **I:** Government Administration/Government Relations/Government Services **CN:** U.S. House of Representatives **DOB:** 01/18/1971 **PB:** Guayaquil **SC:** Ecuador **PT:** Guido Mucarsel Yunes; Imelda Gil **MS:** Married **SPN:** Robert Powell **CH:** Two Children **ED:** Master of Arts, Claremont Graduate University; Bachelor of Arts, Pitzer College **C:** Member, U.S. House of Representatives from Florida's 26th Congressional District (2019-Present); Associate Vice President for Advancement, Florida International University Herbert Wertheim College of Medicine (2007-2011); Director of Development, Florida International University (2003-2007) **CIV:** With, Hope Center; With, Zoo Miami Foundation; With, Coral Restoration Foundation; Volunteer, John Kerry Presidential Campaign; Volunteer, Barack Obama Presidential Campaign **PA:** Democrat

MUCEDOLA, MICHAEL S., T: Department Chair **I:** Education/Educational Services **CN:** Longwood University **DOB:** 04/13/1981 **PB:** Auburn **SC:** NY/USA **PT:** Felix Mucedola; Mary Ann Mucedola **MS:** Single **ED:** PhD in Public Health, Walden University, Minneapolis, MN (2012); MS in Health Education, State University of New York at Cortland, Cortland, NY (2007); BS in Physical Education, Ithaca College, Ithaca, NY (2004); Coursework in Sport and Hotel Management, Webber International University, Babson Park, FL (1999-2001); Coursework in Nutritional Sciences (15 Credits), Cayuga Community College, Auburn, NY **CT:** Master Certified Health Education Specialist, National Commission for Health Education Credentialing, Inc. (NCHEC) (2014); Certificate in Plant-based Nutrition, T. Colin Campbell Foundation and eCornell (2013); Health Education Professional Teacher Certification, New York State Education Department (2009); Physical Education Professional Teacher Certification, New York State Education Department (2009) **C:** HARK Department Chair, Tenured Associate Professor, Longwood University (2018-Present); Part-time Health Education Faculty, Trident University International (2011-Present); HPE Graduate Program Director, Longwood University (2014-2018); Student Teacher Supervisor, Part-time Faculty, State University of New York

(2012-2013); Heath Education Teacher, Cayuga-Onondaga BOCES (2008-2013); Tenured Health and PE Teacher, Elmira City School District (2008-2011); Alternative Education Teacher, Auburn Enlarged City School District (2005-2007); Substitute Teacher, Auburn Enlarged City School District (2004-2005); Teaching Assistant, Cayuga Community College (2004) **CR:** Public School Teacher, At-risk Youth, Auburn/Elmira, NY **CIV:** Donner, "Multicultural Gala and Donning of the Kente" Ceremony, NAACP: Youth and College Division and the Office of Citizen Leadership and Social Justice Education (2017, 2018); Breast Cancer Research Foundation; Roswell Park Cancer Institute; Piedmont Community Health Coalition **CW:** Author, Book, "Culture-Based Differentiated Instruction: Connecting Schools with Their Communities" (2021); Author, "Teaching the Domino Effect to Combat the Rise in Unintentional Injuries," Journal of Physical Education, Recreation and Dance (2019); Author, "Addressing Dietary Habits with Elementary School Students in Physical Education Class," Journal of Physical Education, Recreation and Dance (2018); Author, "Integrating Presidential History in Middle School Physical Education Class," Journal of Physical Education, Recreation and Dance (2018); Author, "Applying Health and Physical Education Teacher Pedagogy in a Community Setting," Strategies: A Journal for Physical and Sport Educators (2018); Author, "Second Language Acquisition in High School Physical Education Archery Class," Journal of Physical Education, Recreation and Dance (2018); Author, "Intrinsic Motivation Paired with Community Outreach Strategies to Improve Learning and Academic Success," The Clearing House: A Journal of Educational Strategies, Issues and Ideas (2018); Author, "Community Resource Mapping: An Interactive Health Education Lesson," Journal of Physical Education, Recreation and Dance (2018); Author, "Behavioral Classroom Management for Impoverished At-risk Youth," International Journal of Learning, Teaching and Educational Research (2018); Author, "Health and Physical Education Advocacy Efforts with At-risk Youth," Strategies: A Journal for Physical and Sport Educators (2018); Author, "Preparing Traditional Health Education Teachers to Work Outside the Classroom," The Virginia Journal (2018); Author, "Developing Citizen Leaders Through Community Outreach Strategies in School-based Physical Education," Journal of Physical Education, Recreation and Dance (2017); Author, "Addressing Physical Inactivity in Impoverished Communities Through School-based Physical Education," Journal of Physical Education, Recreation and Dance (2017); Author, "Utilizing the Theory of Planned Behavior and Active Learning Strategies to Combat Designer Drug Use with College Students," The Virginia Journal (2017); Interviewed for Feature on Scholars, "Once Upon a Dime," Virginia's Public Colleges and Universities, Charlottesville, VA (2017); Featured for Program Designed on Culture-based Differentiate Instruction, Ithaca College Alumni Magazine (2017); Featured, "2017's Best Places to Raise a Family in Virginia," WalletHub (2017); Featured, "Auburn Native Winning Awards and Touching Lives at Longwood University, Site of VP Debate," The Citizen (2016); Author, "Canvas Learning Management System for Online Health Education University Courses to Improve Performance and Enhance the Learning Experience," The Virginia Journal (2016); Author, "Empowering Impoverished Youth Through Autonomous Community Outreach Strategies to Improve Learning and Academic Success," National Youth At-Risk Journal (2016); Author, "A Culture-based Differentiated Instruction Model: Addressing School, Community, and Health Related Behaviors Through Health Education," The Virginia Journal (2016); Author, "Nutrition Guidelines: A Healthy Eating Spectrum," Journal of Health Education Teaching Techniques (2015); Author, "Connecting Health Education and Health Promotion Through Community Outreach to Bridge PreK-12 School Health Programs and Corresponding Communities," The Virginia Journal (2015); Author, "Depression, Suicide, and Maslow's Hierarchy of Needs: A Preventive Approach," Journal of Health Education Teaching Techniques (2015); Appearance in "The Rotunda", "The Pillar" and "New Lancer Days," Longwood University (2015); Featured as a Public Relations Pitch to Multiple Local and State News Outlets to Promote Longwood University, "The Healthy Eating Spectrum" (2014); Featured, "Nutrition 335 Class," Longwood University Alumni Magazine (2014); Appearance in "The Rotunda", "The Pillar" and "New Lancer Days," Longwood University (2014); Author, Peer-reviewed Publications **AW:** Graduate Research Award, Longwood University (2019); Maude Glenn Raiford Award for Excellence in Teaching, Longwood University (2019); Nominated for Graduate Teaching and Mentoring Award, Longwood University (2019); Nominated for Maria Bristow Starke Award, Longwood University (2019); Nominated for Provost's Scholarship Award, Longwood University (2019); Nominated as a Donner for the NAACP: Youth and College Division and the Office of Citizen Leadership and Social Justice Education's "Multicultural Gala and Donning of the Kente" Ceremony (2017, 2018); "With Good Reason Radio Show"- Nominated, Longwood University (2017); Maude Glenn Raiford Junior Faculty Teaching Award, Longwood University (2017); Student Faculty Recognition Award in Recognition for Professional Excellence and Devoted Service to Students, Longwood Commencement (2016); Nominated for Faculty Citizen Leader Award, Longwood University (2016); Nominated for Trident Teaching Excellence Award (2016); Named Outstanding First Year Student Advocate (2015); Named Outstanding First Year Student Advocate (2014); Presidential Scholarship, Webber International University (1999) **MEM:** American Public Health Association; T. Colin Campbell Center for Nutrition Studies; National Commission for Health Education Credentialing; Ithaca College Alumni Association; SUNY Cortland Alumni Association; NutritonFacts.org; The Honor Society of Phi Kappa Phi; Virginia Association for Health, Physical Education, Recreation, and Dance **AS:** Dr. Mucedola attributes his success to his faith and his family. **B/I:** Dr. Mucedola became involved in his profession because his parents were teachers. His father taught high school English and his mother taught middle school math. He saw their selfless act of helping others every day and it inspired him to go into the field. His father advised him to go into physical education and once he got started, Dr. Mucedola liked it and wanted to go into the health aspect of it. That is where a light bulb clicked for him. He tells his students that as an undergraduate student he could have earned B's and been fine, but when he went on to get his master's degree, something clicked and he wanted to actually learn as opposed to just getting by. From then on, he became a voracious reader with a desire to learn and be better each day. **AV:** Buying, selling, and collecting rare coins; Reading presidential history; Gardening **RE:** Catholic **THT:** Dr. Mucedola's motto is, "A good plan today is better than a perfect plan tomorrow."

MUCHA, JOHN III, JD, T: Attorney **I:** Law and Legal Services **DOB:** 01/28/1955 **PB:** Flint **SC:** MI/USA **PT:** John Mucha Jr.; Mary Mucha **ED:** JD, University of Michigan (1987); Master in Public Policy, University of Michigan (1979); AB, University of Michigan, Cum Laude (1977) **C:** Partner, Dawda, Mann, Mulcahy & Sadler, Bloomfield Hills, MI (1995-Present); Associate, Pepper, Hamilton & Scheetz, Detroit, MI (1987-1995); Associate/Clerk, Lord Bissell & Brook, Chicago, IL (1986) **CR:** Speaker Institute for Continuing Legal Education (2000) **CW:** Contributing Author, Business Opportunities in the United States (1992) **AW:** Distinguished Volunteer Legal Services Award, Detroit Bar Association (1994) **MEM:** Birmingham Rotary Club **BAR:** Council Litigation Section, Chair, State Bar of Michigan (1995-Present); United States Court of Appeals for the 6th Circuit (1990); United States District Court for the Eastern District of Michigan (1987) **MH:** Albert Nelson Marquis Lifetime Achievement Award **B/I:** Mr. Mucha was inspired by a teacher at the University of Michigan who was a lawyer by trade. This teacher enlightened him on how exactly to apply the legal skills to succeed. **AV:** Bicycle riding; Playing music

MUDD, DOUGLAS A., T: Curator/Museum Director **I:** Research **DOB:** 03/23/1963 **PB:** Washington **SC:** DC/USA **PT:** Donald Eugene Mudd; Carol Lynn Mudd **MS:** Married **SPN:** Patricia Lynn Costello (12/30/1995) **CH:** Loren Carol **ED:** MA in American History, George Mason University, Fairfax, VA (2004); BA in International Relations, William & Mary, Williamsburg, VA (1985) **C:** Curator, Museum Director, Money Museum, American Numismatic Association, Colorado Springs, CO (2013-Present); Curator, Money Museum, American Numismatic Association, Colorado Springs, CO (2004-2013); Collection Manager, National Numismatic Collection, Smithsonian Institution, Washington, DC (1991-2004); Museum Technician, Smithsonian Institution, Washington, DC (1985-1989) **CR:** Teacher, American Numismatic Association's Summer Seminar, Digital Numismatic Photography for Collectors (2015-Present); Instructor, American Numismatic Association, Colorado Springs, CO (2001-Present); Teacher, American Numismatic Association's Summer Seminar, Coinage of the Late Roman Empire (2018); Teacher, Evening Mini-Seminars, American Numismatic Association's Summer Seminar, Numismatics of World War I (2017-2018); Teacher, American Numismatic Association's Summer Seminar, Coinage of the Roman Republic (2016); Teacher, American Numismatic Association's Summer Seminar, Finances of the American Civil War (2014-2015); Teacher, American Numismatic Association's Summer Seminar, Ancient Greek Coinage: An Overview of the World's First Coins (2013-2015); Teacher, American Numismatic Association's Summer Seminar, Numismatics for Museum Professionals (2011, 2007, 2004-2005, 2002); Teacher, Evening Mini-Seminars, American Numismatic Association's Summer Seminar, Editing Digital Images 101 (2010-2016); Teacher, American Numismatic Association's Summer Seminar, Money of the World (2009-2010); Teacher, Evening Mini-Seminars, American Numismatic Association's Summer Seminar, Coinage of the English Civil Wars (2008) **CW:** Curator, Numerous Exhibits (1998-2019); Guest, "Mysteries in the Museum" (2016, 2013); Co-Author, "Money & Sovereignty as Expressed in Gold Coinage" (2008); Author, "All the Money in the World" (2006); Contributor, IMF at IMF Headquarters, Washington, DC (2002-2003); Contributor, Permanent Display on the Ancient Silk Road, IMF at IMF Headquarters, Washington, DC (2001); Co-Author, "Money & Sovereignty - As Expressed in Gold Coinage"; Designer, Editor, Photographer, "Life in Republican Rome on Its Coinage"; Author, Monthly Column on Numismatics and the ANA Money Museum Collection, Numismatic Magazine; Author, "Plastic Cash: A History of Money and the Credit Card in America"; Author, Article, "Money & Sovereignty," ANA Journal; Contributor, "100 Greatest 100 Error Coins"; Writer, Designer, Creator of Image, National Numismatic Collection Website; Contributor, Numerous Lectures; Public Speaker, Radio and TV Programs; Guest Speaker, Television Shows **AW:** Best Numismatic Book on World Paper Money Award, Numismatic Literary Guild (2007) **MEM:** Classical and Medieval Numismatic Society; Ancient Coin Collector's Guild; Russian Numismatic Society; American Numismatic Association; Phi Alpha Theta **MH:** Albert Nelson Marquis Lifetime Achievement Award **B/I:** Mr. Mudd became involved in his profession because he grew up all over the world. His parents were interested in archaeology, so they would often visit old ruins and museums, which initially piqued his interest in the field. **AV:** Playing soccer and frisbee; Bicycling; Playing war games; Researching the military history

MUEGGE, G. PAUL, T: State Legislator, Farmer (Retired) **I:** Government Administration/Government Relations/Government Services **DOB:** 09/28/1936 **PB:** Lamont **SC:** OK/USA **PT:** George A. Muegge; Estellee B. Muegge **MS:** Married **SPN:** Nancy (Voorhees) **CH:** Tim; Jeff; Shawn; Amy **ED:** Bachelor of Science in Agriculture Economics, Oklahoma State University **CT:** Georgetown University, Harrison Institute of Democracy and Trade; State Governance 21st Century Promoting Civil Society, Security & Economic Prosperity **C:** Center for Rural Development, Northeastern University, Tahlequah, OK (2003-2008); Member, Oklahoma State Senate (1991-2002) **CR:** Member, Agriculture and Rural Development Committee, Oklahoma State Senate (1994-2002); Member, Energy Environmental Resources and Regulatory Affairs, Oklahoma State Senate (1992-2002); Appropriations, Business and Labor, Oklahoma State Senate; Financial Committee, Oklahoma State Senate **MIL:** ROTC, Oklahoma State University (1955-1956) **CW:** Board of Directors, Organization for Competitive Markets (2019); Bavarian-American State Legislators Conference (2002) **AW:** Lifetime Achievement, Humane Society of the United States (2016); Carrie Dickerson Lifetime Achievement Award (2008); John F. Kennedy Profile in Courage Award, John Fitzgerald Kennedy Library Foundation (2004); Governor's Conservation Award (2003); Citizen of the Year (2002); Public Official of the Year, Governing Magazine Publication (1998); Tonkawa Chamber of Commerce **MEM:** Oklahoma Academy of Physicians Assistants; Federation of Independent Businessmen **MH:** Albert Nelson Marquis Lifetime Achievement Award; Marquis Who's Who Top Professional **B/I:** Senator Muegge became involved in his profession due to his experiences as the parent of a handicapped child. Seeing that there were no special education programs in his state, he sought public office in order to address this deficiency. **AV:** Political consulting; Public relations and human resources consulting **PA:** Democrat **RE:** Methodist

MUEHLBAUER, JAMES H., T: Manufacturing and Distribution Executive **I:** Manufacturing **DOB:** 11/13/1940 **PB:** Evansville **SC:** IN/USA **PT:** Herman Joseph Muehlbauer; Anna Louise (Overfield) Muehlbauer **MS:** Married **SPN:** Mary Kay Koch (06/26/1965) **CH:** Stacey; Brad; Glen; Beth; Katy **ED:** MS in Industrial Administration, Purdue University, West Lafayette, IN (1964); BSME, Purdue University, West Lafayette, IN (1963) **CT:** Registered Professional Engineer, Indiana (1970) **C:** Vice Chairman, Koch Enterprises, Inc. (2012-Present); Executive Vice President, Board of Directors, Koch Enterprises, Inc. (1999-Present); President, Koch Air LLC (2003-2011); Chairman, George Koch Sons, LLC (2003-2004); President, George Koch Sons, LLC (1999-2003); Executive Vice President, George Koch Sons, Inc. (Now George Koch Sons, LLC) (1982-1998); Vice President, George Koch Sons, Inc. (Now George Koch Sons, LLC) (1975-1981); Chief Engineer, George Koch Sons, Inc. (Now George Koch Sons, LLC) (1973-1974); Chief Estimator, George Koch Sons, Inc. (Now George Koch Sons, LLC) (1968-1972); Engineer, George Koch Sons, Inc. (Now George Koch Sons, LLC) (1966-1967); Manufacturing and Distribution Executive **CR:** Board of Directors, Anchor Industries, Inc., Evansville, IN (2006-Present); Board of Directors, South Western Communications, Inc., Evansville, IN (2006-2012); Board of Directors, George Koch Sons LLC, Koch Air LLC, Evansville, IN (1999-2012); Board of Directors, Fifth Third Bank, Southern Indiana (1995-2012); Vice President, Board of Directors, Brake Supply Company (1985-2012); Board of Directors, Gibbs Die Casting Corporation, Henderson, KY (1981-2012); Board of Directors, Uniseal, Inc., Evansville, IN (1984-2012); Board of Directors, George Koch Sons Europe Ltd., Lichfield, England (1991-2004); George Koch Sons de México, Monterrey, Mexico, Koch Air, LLC, Evansville, IN (1980-2004) **CIV:** Junior Achievement Instructor (2015-Present); Equestrian Order of the Holy Sepulcher of Jerusalem (1996-Present); Director, Board of Advisors, University of Southern Indiana Business School (1997-Present); Board of Directors, Past President, Past Campaign Chairman, United Way of Southwestern Indiana, Evansville, IN (1983-Present); Board of Directors, Past President, Evansville Industrial Foundation (1980-Present); Board of Trustees, Saint Meinrad Archabbey (2018); Board of Directors, Welborn Baptist Foundation (2012-2017); Board of Overseers, Saint Meinrad Seminary and School of Theology (2014); Member, Financial Council, Evansville Catholic Diocese (2008-2011); Board of Directors, Deaconess Hospital, Evansville, IN (1986-2007); Board of Directors, Indiana United Ways (2000-2006); Board of Directors, Catholic Foundation of Southwestern Indiana (1998-2004); Board of Directors, Alliance Indianapolis (1993-2004); Vice-Chairman, Deaconess Hospital, Evansville, IN (1999-2003); Chairman, Board of Advisors, University of Southern Indiana Business School (2001-2002); Board of Directors, Past Vice-Chairman, University of Southern Indiana Foundation, Evansville, IN (1988-2001); President, Alliance Indianapolis (1999); Treasurer, Deaconess Hospital, Evansville, IN (1991-1996) **MIL:** Lt., U.S. Army (1964-1966) **CW:** Co-Author, "Tool & Manufacturing Engineering Handbook" (1976); Patentee in Paint Finishing Equipment **AW:** United Way of Southwestern Indiana President's Award (2018); United Way of Southwestern Indiana Community Service Award (2015); Boy Scouts Buffalo Trace Council Distinguished Citizen Award (2015); Inductee, Evansville Business Hall of Fame (2012); Tri-State Multiple Sclerosis Association Spirit Award (2008); United Way of Southwestern Indiana Spirit Award (2000); Named to Catholic Diocese Evansville Brute Society (1997); Purdue Alumni Association Citizenship Award (1991); Technological Achievement Award Tri-State Council for Science and Engineering, Evansville, IN (1984); Engineer of the Year, Southwest Chapter, Indiana Society of Professional Engineers (1983); Vietnam Campaign Medal; Army Commendation Medal **MEM:** Board of Directors, Evansville Kennel Club (1997-2001); Past National Chairman, Finishing and Coating Technology Division, Society of Manufacturing Engineers (SME); American Society of Mechanical Engineers; American Society of Heating; National Society of Professional Engineers; Evansville Country Club **MH:** Albert Nelson Marquis Lifetime Achievement Award; Marquis Who's Who Top Professional **B/I:** Mr. Muehlbauer became involved in his profession because of the encouragement he received from his father and his high school counselors; it wasn't a very hard decision for him to take the path of engineering. In addition to Mr. Muehlbauer's father, Herman Joseph also encouraged him. He also gravitated toward becoming a manufacturing and distribution executive because his father, too, was an executive. His father also coached him and kept him out of trouble. So, it boiled down to his upbringing and his family history. **AV:** Boating **PA:** Republican **RE:** Roman Catholic

MUELLER, ROBERT SWAN III, T: Special Counsel; Lawyer **I:** Law and Legal Services **CN:** U.S. Department of Justice **DOB:** 08/07/1944 **PB:** New York **SC:** NY/USA **PT:** Robert Swan Mueller Jr.; Alice C. (Truesdale) Mueller **MS:** Married **SPN:** Ann (Standish) Mueller (09/03/1966) **CH:** Cynthia; Melissa **ED:** JD, University of Virginia School of Law (1973); MA in International Relations, New York University (1967); BA in Politics, Princeton University (1966) **C:** Partner, Wilmer Cutler Pickering Hale and Dorr LLP (2014-2017, 2019-Present); Special Counsel, U.S. Department of Justice (2017-2019); Director, Federal Bureau of Investigation, U.S. Department of Justice (2001-2013); Acting Deputy Attorney General, U.S. Department of Justice (2001); U.S. Attorney, Northern District of California, U.S. Department of Justice (1998-2001); Senior Litigator, Homicide Section, DC U.S. Attorney's Office, U.S. Department of Justice, Washington, DC (1995-1998); Partner, Hale & Dorr LLP (Now Wilmer Cutler Pickering Hale and Dorr LLP, Washington, DC (1993-1995); Assistant Attorney General, Criminal Division, U.S. Department of Justice, Washington, DC (1990-1993); Assistant to Attorney General for Criminal Matters, U.S. Department of Justice, Washington, DC (1989-1990); Partner, Hill & Barlow, Boston, MA (1988-1989); Deputy U.S. Attorney, U.S. Department of Justice, Boston, MA (1987-1988); U.S. Attorney, U.S. Department of Justice, Boston, MA (1986-1987); First Assistant U.S. Attorney, U.S. Department of Justice, Boston, MA (1985); Chief, Criminal Division, Massachusetts District, U.S. Department of Justice, Boston, MA (1982-1985); Chief, Criminal Division, U.S. Department of Justice, San Francisco, CA (1981-1982); Chief, Unit of Special Prosecutions, U.S. Department of Justice, San Francisco, CA (1980-1981); Assistant U.S. Attorney, Northern District of California, U.S. Department of Justice, San Francisco, CA (1976-1980); Associate, Pillsbury, Madison & Sutro (Now Pillsbury Winthrop Shaw Pittman LLP), San Francisco, CA (1973-1976) **CR:** Lead Investigator, Independent Investigation into National Football League's Handling of Ray Rice Domestic Violence Incident (2014) **MIL:** Captain, United States Marine Corps, Vietnam (1968-1971) **AW:** Thomas Jefferson Foundation Medal in Law, University of Virginia (2013); Listee, 50 Most Powerful People in DC, GQ Magazine (2009); Decorated Bronze Star with Combat V; Purple Heart; Vietnamese Cross of Gallantry; Navy & Marine Corps Commendation Medal with Combat V and Service Star; Combat Action Ribbon; Meritorious Unit Commendation; National Defense Service Medal; Vietnam Service Medal with Four Bronze Campaign Stars; Civil Action Medal, Republican of Vietnam; Vietnam Campaign Medal; Marksmanship Badge; Expert Marksmanship Badge; Ranger Tab; Parachutist Badge **MEM:** American College of Trial Lawyers; California Bar Association; Massachusetts Bar Association **BAR:** Commonwealth of Massachusetts; United District Court for the District of Massachusetts; United States Court of Appeals for the First Circuit; State of California; United States District Court for the Northern District; United States Court of Appeals for the Ninth Circuit

MUHAMMAD, IBTIHAJ, T: Fencer **I:** Athletics **DOB:** 12/04/1985 **PB:** Maplewood **SC:** NJ/USA **PT:** Eugene Muhammad; Denise Muhammad **ED:** Bachelor's Degree in International Relations and African American Studies, Duke University (2007) **C:** Co-Founder, Louella (2014-Present); Member, United States Fencing Team **CIV:** Sports Ambassador, Empowering Women and Girls Through Sport Initiative, U.S. Department of State **CW:** Author, "Proud: My Fight for an Unlikely American Dream" (2018); Author, "Proud: Living My American Dream" (2018); Author, "The Proudest Blue: A Story of Hijab and Family" (2018) **AW:** Bronze Medal in Fencing, Summer Olympics (2016); Junior Olympic Champion (2005); Three-Time All-American

MUILENBURG, DENNIS A., T: Chairman, President, and Chief Executive Officer **I:** Engineering **CN:** The Boeing Company **PB:** Orange City **SC:** IA/USA **ED:** MS in Aeronautics & Astronautics, University of Washington, Seattle; BS in Aerospace Engineering, Iowa State University (1986) **C:** Chairman, President, Chief Executive Officer, The Boeing Company (2016-Present); Various Engineering and Program Management Positions, The Boeing Co. (1985-Present); President, Chief Executive Officer, The Boeing Company (2015-2016); Vice Chairman, President, Chief Operating Officer, The Boeing Co. (2013-2015); President, Chief Executive Officer, Boeing Defense, Space & Security (2009-2013); Executive Vice President, The Boeing Company (2009-2013); President, Global Services & Support, The Boeing Company (2008-2009); General Manager, Combat Systems Division & Progressive Manager, Future Combat Systems, The Boeing Company (2003-2008); Vice President, Programs & Engineering, Boeing Air Traffic Management, The Boeing Company (2001-2003); Director, Weapon Systems Joint Strike Fighter Progressive, The Boeing Co. **CR:** Executive Committee Member, Business Roundtable Board of Directors, Caterpillar Inc. (2011-Present) **CIV:** Board of Directors, St. Louis Sports Commission; Board Trustee, Washington University at St. Louis; Board Trustee, National World War II Museum; Board of Trustees, St. Louis Science Center **MEM:** Fellow, Associate, American Institute of Aeronautics and Astronautics; Fellow, Royal Aeronautical Society; Chairman, Board of Governors, Member, Executive Committee, Aerospace Inductries Association; Vice President, Community Relations, Gateway Chapter, Association of the US Army

MUIR, DAVID JASON, T: News Correspondent; Anchor **I:** Media & Entertainment **CN:** ABC News **DOB:** 11/08/1973 **PB:** Syracuse **SC:** NY/USA **ED:** Honorary Doctor of Media, Northeastern University (2015); Honorary LittD, Ithaca College (2015); Coursework, University of Salamanca, Spain; Coursework, Institute of Political Journalism, Georgetown University; BA, Ithaca College, Magna Cum Laude, NY (1995) **C:** Anchor, "World News Tonight with David Muir," ABC News (2015-Present); Co-anchor, "20/20," ABC (2013-Present); Reporter, Anchor, ABC News, New York, NY (2003-Present); Weekend Anchor, "ABC World News" (2007-2015); Anchor, "World News with David Muir," ABC News (2011-2013); Co-anchor, "Primetime," ABC News (2004-2011); Anchor, "World News Now," ABC News (2003-2004); Reporter, Anchor, WCVB-TV, Boston, MA; Reporter, Anchor, WTVH-TV, Syracuse, NY **AW:** CINE Golden Eagle Award (2016); Jessica Savitch Award of Distinction for Excellence in Journalism, Ithaca College (2015); Edward R. Murrow Award for Investigative Reporting (2013); Named One of 12 to Watch in TV News (2013); Best Enterprise

Reporting Award, The Associated Press; National Headliner Award, TV Week; Named One of Syracuse's Best News Anchors, Syracuse New Times

MULLALLY, MEGAN, T: Actress **I:** Media & Entertainment **DOB:** 11/12/1958 **PB:** Los Angeles **SC:** CA/USA **PT:** Carter Mullally Jr.; Martha (Palmer) Mullally **MS:** Married **SPN:** Nick Offerman (09/20/2003); Michael A. Katcher (1992, Divorced 1996) **ED:** Coursework, Northwestern University **C:** Band Member, Nancy and Beth (2012-Present); Band Member, Supreme Music Program **CW:** Actress, "Will and Grace" (1998-2006, 2017-2020); Actress, "Lemon" (2017); Actress, "Infinity Baby" (2017); Actress, "The Disaster Artist" (2017); Actress, "Why Him" (2016); Actress, "Life in Pieces" (2016); Actress, "Annapurna" (2015); Voice Actress, "Hotel Transylvania 2" (2015); Actress, "You, Me and the Apocalypse" (2015); Voice Actress, "Randy Cunningham: 9th Grade Ninja" (2012-2015); Voice Actress, "Bob's Burgers" (2011-2015); Actress, "Parks and Recreation" (2009-2015); Actress, "It's Only a Play" (2014); Actress, "Date and Switch" (2014); Actress, "Apartment Troubles" (2014); Actress, "Alexander and the Terrible, Horrible, No Good, Very Bad Day" (2014); Actress, "Trophy Wife" (2014); Actress, "Out There" (2013); Actress, "The Kings of Summer" (2013); Actress, "G.B.F." (2013); Actress, "Web Therapy" (2013); Actress, "Axe Cop" (2013); Voice Actress, "Sofia the First" (2013); Voice Actress, "Axe Cop" (2012-2013); Actress, "Happy Endings" (2011-2013); Actress, "Children's Hospital" (2008-2013); Actress, "Breaking In" (2012); Actress, "Smash" (2012); Actress, "Somebody Up There Likes Me" (2012); Actress, "Up All Night" (2012); Actress, "Party Down" (2010); Actress, "In the Motherhood" (2009); Actress, "Fame" (2009); Actress, "Bad Mother's Handbook" (2008); Actress, "Young Frankenstein" (2008); Actress, "30 Rock" (2008); Voice Actress, "Bee Movie" (2007); Host, Talk Show, "Megan Mullally Show" (2006-2007); Actress, "Rebound" (2005); Voice Actress, "Teacher's Pet" (2004); Actress, "The Pact" (2002); Actress, "Stealing Harvard" (2002); Actress, "King of the Hill" (2002); Actress, "Monkey Bone" (2001); Actress, "Speaking of Sex" (2001); Actress, "Everything Put Together" (2000); Actress, "Everything Put Together" (2000); Actress, "3rd Rock from the Sun" (2000); Actress, "Anywhere But Here" (1999); Actress, "Best Man in Grass Creek" (1999); Actress, "Winchell" (1998); Actress, "Just Shoot Me!" (1998); Actress, "Frasier" (1997); Actress, "Mad About You" (1997); Actress, "Caroline in the City" (1997); Actress, "How to Succeed in Business Without Really Trying" (1995-1996); Actress, "Grease" (1994); Actress, "Seinfeld" (1993); Actress, "Fish Police" (1992); Actress, "Rachel Gunn, RN" (1992); Actress, "My Life and Times" (1991); Actress, "Herman's Head" (1991); Actress, "Rainbow Drive" (1990); Actress, "Wings" (1990); Actress, "China Beach" (1989); Actress, "Murder, She Wrote" (1988); Actress, "Last Resort" (1986); Actress, "About Last Night" (1986); Actress, "Once Bitten" (1985); Musician with Supreme Music Program, "The Sweetheart Break-In," "Big as a Berry," and "Free Again!"; Actress, Theater, Television Shows, Films **AW:** Emmy Award for Supporting Actress in a Comedy Series, Academy of Television Arts & Sciences (2000, 2006); Award for Outstanding Actress in a Comedy Series, Screen Actors Guild - American Federation of Television and Radio Artists (2001, 2002, 2003, 2004); American Comedy Award (2001); Emmy Award for Outstanding Comedy Series, Academy of Television Arts & Sciences (2000)

MULLEN, ELAINE H., T: Research Scientist **I:** Sciences **DOB:** 08/08/1944 **PB:** Richmond **SC:** VA/USA **PT:** Morgan Milton Hull; Helen Schuyler Bailey

MS: Divorced **SPN:** Saba Shami (1982, Divorced 1990); John Mullen (1969, Divorced 1980) **ED:** BS in Biology, Virginia Commonwealth University, Richmond, VA (1970) **C:** Research Scientist, The MITRE Corporation (2000-Present); Scientific Illustrator, The MITRE Corporation, McLean, VA (1979-1999) **CR:** Curation, SugarBind Database **CW:** U.S. Patent, Glycoprotein Vesicles and Their Methods of Use (2014); U.S. Patent, Sequestering of Glycoprotein Molecules and Oligosaccharide Moieties in Lipo-glycoprotein Membranes and Micelles (2010); U.S. Patent, Sequestering of Glycoprotein Molecules and Oligosaccharide Moieties in Lipo-glycoprotein Membranes and Micelles (2006); U.S. Patent, Synthetic Membranes and Micelle-like Structures Comprising Lipo-glycoprotein Membranes (1999); U.S. Patent, Synthetic Membranes Forming Micelles and Micelle-like Structures Comprising Lipo-glycoprotein Membranes (1998) **AW:** Best Paper Award, IEEE Sensors Journal (2010); Ronald Fante Best Paper Award, The MITRE Corporation (2010) **MEM:** Society for Glycobiology (SFG); Consortium for Functional Glycomics; International Society for Biocuration **MH:** Albert Nelson Marquis Lifetime Achievement Award; Marquis Who's Who Top Professional **AS:** Ms. Mullen attributes her success to her mentors, including a chemist at MITRE, James Ellenbogen, who gave her great advice. **B/I:** Ms. Mullen became involved in her profession because she worked as a lab technician but didn't like what they were doing with animals, so she quit. She then needed a job and got one as an illustrator at the Medical College of Virginia. Based on that experience, she got her job at MITRE as an illustrator. She had been doing scientific illustrations for the medical college and she just switched to a different kind of science. She was working as a medical illustrator in Richmond for the Medical College. She had done an illustration on how to dye a slide and in the process she noticed one of those glycoprotein films. She was trying to get a dye to stick and it wouldn't, so in her attempt she put some chemicals together and noticed a film that she later patented. She spent years researching it. She was fascinated by it. **AV:** Writing children's stories; Printing watercolor on paper from carved styrofoam sheets coated with glycoprotein film; Illustrating and Teaching relationships among Middle Eastern musical modes **RE:** Lutheran Christian

MULLER, RICHARD, "DICK" LOUIS SR., T: Retired Government Executive **I:** Government Administration/Government Relations/Government Services **CN:** United States Department of Defense **DOB:** 01/26/1935 **PB:** Chicago **SC:** IL/USA **PT:** Ludwig Oboe Muller; Lilyan (Gershon) Muller **MS:** Married **SPN:** Norma **CH:** Richard Louis Muller, Jr. **ED:** Coursework, University of Maryland (1966); MEd, John Hopkins University (1965); Postgraduate Coursework, Peabody College (1963); BS in Biology, University of Central Arkansas, AK, With Highest Honors (1961) **C:** Director of Manpower, Personnel and Training, Naval Sea Systems Command, Washington DC (1980-1993); Director of Curriculum, Chief of Naval Education and Training, Pensacola, FL (1973-1980); Education Specialists, Fleet Training Facility, Key West, FL (1971-1973); Training Specialist, Department of Army, Aberdeen Proving Grounds, MD (1966-1971); High School Educator (1961-1966); Owner, Muller Fine Arts, Pensacola, FL **CR:** LEGIS Fellows Program (1985); Civilian Personnel Management Field Seminar (1978); Seminar for Advancing Managers (1976) **CIV:** Nominating Caucus School Board, Harford County, MD; Board of Directors, Friendship Fire Department, Marion County, FL; Mission Programs, Local Churches; Board of Trustees, Charles Couty Nursing Home and Rehabilitation Center, Charles County, MD; Board of Directors, Habitat for Humanity, Charles County, MD; SMASH, Charles County, MD; Representative Payee, Charles County, MD; Citizen Goals for Maryland; Council for the Elderly; Past President, Junior Chamber of Commerce, Edgewood, MD; Board of Directors, Military Testing Association; American Research Association; Fleet of the Chesapeake **MIL:** United States Navy (1953-1958) **CW:** Presenter, Annual Convention, National Science Teachers Association (1977); Author, "The Symbolic Integrated Maintenance Manual Concept Study"; Author, "Project INSTRUCT" **AW:** Plaque of Appreciation for Service, Charles County Nursing Home & Rehabilitation Center, Charles County, MD (1996); Numerous Certificates, Plaques of Achievement, United States Army, United States Navy, United States Congress (1967-1993); Numerous Performance Awards (1967-1992); Meritorious Civilian Service Medal, United States Military (1990); Listee, International Who's Who in Community Service (1972); Presidential Award of Honor, Edgewood, MD (1969); Listee, Outstanding Men of Maryland (1968) **MEM:** Phi Delta Kappa; Alpha Chi Honor Society; Kiwanis; Fellow, National Science Foundation; National Science Teachers Association; American Education Research Association; Congressional Fellow; Gilman Fellow; American Medical Technologist; American Legion **AS:** Mr. Muller attributes his success to hard work. Also, as an Orthodox Jewish man, he follows the path that God has put his feet upon. **B/I:** Mr. Muller became involved in his field after speaking with his neighbor, who was involved in the United States Army. Mr. Muller had previously worked with the military, but he became involved once again due to his neighbor's influence. **RE:** Jewish

MULLIN, MARKWAYNE, T: U.S. Representative from Oklahoma; Plumber; Rancher **I:** Government Administration/Government Relations/ Government Services **DOB:** 07/26/1977 **PB:** Tulsa **SC:** OK/USA **MS:** Married **SPN:** Christie Mullin (1998) **CH:** Ivy; Jim; Larra; Lynette; Andrew **ED:** AAS in Construction Technology, Oklahoma State University Institute of Technology (2010); Coursework, Missouri Valley College (1996) **C:** Member, U.S. House of Representatives from Oklahoma's Second District, United States Congress (2013-Present); Member, U.S. House Committee on Natural Resources (2013-Present); Member, U.S. House Committee on Transportation and Infrastructure (2013-Present); Owner, Mullin Plumbing, Mullin Farms, Mullin Properties, Mullin Services (1997-Present); Member, Republican Study Committee **CW:** Radio Host, "House Talk," KFAQ **MEM:** Cherokee Nation **PA:** Republican **RE:** Pentecostal

MULLIS, KARY BANKS, PHD, T: Biochemist **I:** Sciences **DOB:** 12/28/1944 **PB:** Lenoir **SC:** NC/USA **PT:** Cecil Banks Mullis; Bernice Alberta (Barker) Fredericks **MS:** Married **SPN:** Nancy Lier Cosgrove (1988); Cynthia Gibson (Divorced); Richards Mullis (Divorced) **CH:** Louise; Christopher; Jeremy **ED:** Doctor Honoris Causa in Biological Sciences, Masaryk University, Czech Republic (2010); Honorary Doctorate in Pharmaceutical Biotechnology, University of Bologna, Italy (2004); Honorary DSc, University of South Carolina (1994); PhD in Biochemistry, University of California Berkeley (1973); BS in Chemistry, Georgia Institute of Technology (1966) **C:** Founder, Chief Scientific Officer, Altermune LLC, Newport Beach, CA (2003-2019); Distinguished Researcher, Children's Hospital, Oakland Research Institute, CA (2003-2019); Vice President, Molecular Biology, Burstein Technologies, Irvine, CA (1999-2003); Private Consultant, Nucleic Acid Chemistry, CA (1987-2002); Vice President, Molecular Biology, Vyrex Inc., La Jolla, CA (1997-1998);

Vice President, Research, Atomic Tags, Inc., La Jolla, CA (1992-1993); Director, Molecular Biology, Xytronyx, Inc., San Diego, CA (1986-1988); Scientist, Cetus Corporation, Emeryville, CA (1979-1986); Postdoctoral Fellow, University of California San Francisco (1977-1979); Postdoctoral Fellow, University of Kansas Medical School, Kansas City, KS (1973-1976); Lecturer, Biochemistry, University of California Berkeley (1962) **CR:** Distinguished Visiting Professor, University of South Carolina College of Science and Mathematics (1994-2019) **CIV:** Board of Directors, National Organization for the Reform of Marijuana Laws (NORML) (2000) **CW:** Author, Autobiography, "Dancing Naked in the Mind Field" (1998); Author, "The Polymerase Chain Reaction" (1994); Author, "The Unusual Origin of the Polymerase Chain Reaction" (1990); Contributor, Articles, Professional Journals **AW:** Ronald H. Brown American Innovator Award (1998); Inductee, National Inventors Hall of Fame (1998); Nobel Prize in Chemistry (1993); Japan Prize, Japan Science and Technology Foundation (1993); Chiron Corporation Biotechnology Research Award, American Society of Microbiology (1992); Robert Koch Award (1992); California Scientist of the Year (1992); Scientist of the Year, R&D Magazine (1991); National Biotechnology Award (1991); Gairdner Foundation International Award (1991); Allan Award, German Society of Clinical Chemistry (1990); Preis Biochemische Analytik Award (1990) **MEM:** American Academy of Achievement; American Chemical Society **AV:** Researching astrology; Surfing

MULVANEY, JOHN, "MICK" MICHAEL, T: Acting White House Chief of Staff **I:** Government Administration/Government Relations/Government Services **DOB:** 07/21/1967 **PB:** Alexandria **SC:** VA/USA **PT:** Michael Mulvaney; Kathleen Mulvaney **MS:** Married **SPN:** Pamela West (1998) **CH:** Caroline; James; Finnegan **ED:** Diploma, Owners and Presidents Management Program, Harvard Business School (2006); Doctor of Jurisprudence, University of North Carolina at Chapel Hill (1992); Bachelor of Science, Georgetown University School of Foreign Service, with Honors (1989) **C:** Acting White House Chief of Staff, Washington, DC (2019-Present); Director, Office of Management and Budget, Washington, DC (2017-Present); Member, United States House Budget Committee, Washington, DC (2011-Present); Director, Consumer Financial Protection Bureau (2017-2018); Member, United States House of Representatives, United States Congress, South Carolina's Fifth District (2011-2017); Member, United States House Small Business Committee, Washington, DC (2011-2017); Member, District 16, South Carolina State Senate, Columbia, SC (2009-2011); Member, District 45, South Carolina House of Representatives, Columbia, SC (2007-2009); Attorney, Mulvaney & Fisher PA, Charlotte, NC (1997-2000); Attorney, James, McElroy & Diehl, PA, Charlotte, NC (1992-1997) **CR:** Franchise Owner, Operator, Salsarita's Fresh Cantina (2009-Present) **CIV:** Board of Visitors, University of South Carolina, Lancaster, SC; Youth Baseball Coach; Lancaster County Parks and Recreation, South Carolina **MEM:** Founding Member, Indian Land Rotary, Carolina Lakes Golf Club **PA:** Republican **RE:** Roman Catholic

MUNDEY, PAUL ESTON, T: Minister **I:** Religious **CN:** Church of the Brethren **DOB:** 08/20/1951 **PB:** Hagerstown **SC:** MD/USA **PT:** Eston George Mundey; Anna Rebecca (Harne) Mundey **MS:** Married **SPN:** Robin Risser Mundey (06/29/1980) **CH:** Peter John Mundey; Sarah Elizabeth Mundey Dorsey **ED:** Certificate, Bowen Family Theory, Rutgers University School of Social Work, New Brunswick, NJ (2018); DMin,

Princeton Theological Seminary, Princeton, NJ (2008); Certificate in Business Administration for Nonprofit Organizations, University of Illinois at Chicago, Chicago, IL (1990); MDiv, Fuller Theological Seminary, Pasadena, CA (1977); BS, Towson University, Towson, MD, Magna Cum Laude (1973) **CT:** Clinical Certificate, Bowen Family Systems Theory, Rutgers School of Social Work, Rutgers, New Brunswick, NJ (2018); Certificate in Business Administration for Nonprofit Organizations, University of Illinois at Chicago, Chicago, IL (1990) **C:** Moderator, Church of the Brethren (2019-Present); Moderator-elect, Church of the Brethren (2018-2019); Visiting Scholar, Princeton Theological Seminary (2016-2017); Senior Pastor, Frederick Church of the Brethren, Frederick, MD (1996-2016); Director of Evangelism and Congregational Growth, Parish Ministries Commission, Church of the Brethren General Board (1983-1996); Pastor, Friendship Church of the Brethren, Linthicum Heights, MD (1977-1983); Pastor, Fairview Church of Brethren, New Market, VA (1974-1976) **CR:** Leadership Team, Church of the Brethren, Inc. (2018-Present); Annual Conference Officers, Church of the Brethren, Inc. (2018-Present); Program and Arrangements Committee, Annual Conference, Church of the Brethren, Inc. (2018-Present); Board of Trustees, Bridgewater College, Bridgewater, VA (2017-Present); Accredited Visitor, World Council of Churches Assembly, Canberra, ACT, Australia (1991); Advisory Board, Religion in American Life, Princeton, NJ (1990); Board, National Leadership Institute, Lubbock, TX (1990); Commission on Worship and Evangelism, National Council of Churches of Christ (1989); Consultant, Conference on World Mission and Evangelical World Council of Churches, San Antonio, TX (1989); Fellow, Organizational and Community Systems, Johns Hopkins University, Baltimore, MD (1982-1983) **CIV:** Rotary International (1996-2001); Founding Member, Habitat for Humanity, Frederick County, MD **CW:** Featured, "Paul Mundey Steps into Role of Moderator," Frederick News Post (2019); Featured, "Heeding The Call, Longtime Church of the Brethren Pastor Leaves Post to Pursue Other Paths of Service," Frederick News-Post (2016); Producer, Host, Weekly Radio Program, "A Time of Challenge," WFMD (1996-2016); Featured, "Non-Traditional Churches Grow Most. Faith Flourishes in Frederick County," The Gazette Newspaper (2009); Author, "Unlocking Church Doors," Abingdon Press, Nashville, TN (1997); Co-author, "Including and Involving New People," Church of the Brethren General Board, Elgin, IL (1989); Co-author, "New Life for All," Church of the Brethren General Board, Elgin, IL (1987); Contributor, Articles and Essays to Professional Journals **AW:** Visiting Scholar, Princeton Theological Seminary (2016-2017); Elected Chaplain, Maryland House of Delegates (1998-1999) **MEM:** Rotary International (1996-2001) **MH:** Albert Nelson Marquis Lifetime Achievement Award **AS:** Dr. Mundey attributes his success, overall, to the grace, wisdom and courage of God.Dr. Mundey contends that perseverance is central to achievement; accomplishment is seldom attained quickly, but rather, through a long obedience in the same direction. As Dr. Mundey reflects in his forthcoming book, In God's Good Time. Navigating the Painful, Slow Seasons of Life "... though God does not respond immediately to every petition, God does answer-over time-our requests, through billions of particulars that seldom provide all we want, but all that is wise." **B/I:** Dr. Mundey was inspired and mentored by Dr. DeWitt L. Miller, senior pastor of the Hagerstown Church of the Brethren in Hagerstown, Maryland. Overall, the ministry of the Hagerstown Church of the Brethren was formative in his life, calling out his gifts, along with giving him early opportunities to serve in ministry. The Church of the Brethren's national, global expanse also had a profound impact on him, giving him access to life-changing ministries, along with exposure to the breadth and depth of the trans-local arena. **AV:** Hiking; Photography; Reading **PA:** Independent **RE:** Protestant **THT:** Dr. Mundey reflects, "It is God's dependability and accuracy that charts our course. Much rattles and disrupts; we have our doubts and are afraid. Yet we press on toward God's adventurous future, drawing on the endurance of God. For "The Lord [our] God is in [our] midst, a mighty one who will save; he will rejoice over [us] with gladness; he will quiet [us] by his love; he will exult over [us] with singing" (Zephaniah 3:17 ESV). Our calling, then, is to allow God's divine decibel to captivate us, invading our apprehension, stirring us to trek onward–nevertheless–toward God's new creation in Jesus. For "What no eye has seen, nor ear heard, nor the human heart conceived, [is] what God has prepared for those who love him" (1 Corinthians 2:9, NRSV)."

MUNDT, BARRY M., T: Management Consultant **I:** Consulting **PT:** Kenneth Francis Mundt; Janet (Doughty) Mundt **MS:** Married **SPN:** Sally Hanscom Mundt (06/13/1960) **CH:** Kevin Warren; Trevor Stevens; Stacey Corbin **ED:** MBA, Santa Clara University (1964); BS in Industrial Engineering, Stanford University (1959) **CT:** Registered Industrial Engineer, State of California **C:** Principal, The Strategy Facilitation Group, Asheville, NC (1995-2017); Management Consultant, Partner, KPMG Peat Marwick U.S. (Now KPMG LLP), Montvale, NJ (1992-1995); International Management Consultant Partner, KPMG International Limited, New York City and Amsterdam, The Netherlands (1988-1992); Partner-in-charge, Operations Management Consultant, KPMG Peat Marwick Main & Co. (Now KPMG LLP), New York, NY (1984-1988); Manager, Principal, Peat, Marwick, Mitchell & Co. (KPMG LLP), Atlanta, GA (1968-1984); Senior Consultant, Peat, Marwick, Livingston & Co. (Now KPMG LLP), Los Angeles, CA (1965-1968); Management Engineer, CEIR, Inc., Los Altos, CA (1961-1965); Reliability Engineer, Lockheed Missiles, Sunnyvale, CA (1959-1961); Statistician, Aerojet-General Corporation, Sacramento, CA (1957-1958) **CR:** Board of Directors, Mosaic Accounting, Inc. (2005-Present); Board of Directors, Adjusters International, Inc., Rising Phoenix Holdings Corporation (2005-2017) **CIV:** Chairman, Member, Steering Council, Osher Lifelong Learning Institute (2007-2017); Board Chairman, Member, Brandon Hall School, Atlanta, GA (1980, 2002); Delegate to Assembly, United Way of Metropolitan Atlanta (1974-1984); Member, Annual Campaign, Atlanta Symphony Orchestra (1974-1982); Member, Atlanta Arts Alliance (1976-1981) **CW:** Author/Editor, "Managing Professional Service Delivery" (2014); Member, Editorial Board, Contributing Author, "Handbook of Industrial Engineering, Third Edition" (2001); Co-author, "Il Manager Pubblico," Italy (1986); Author/Editor, "Managing Public Resources" (1982); Contributor, Articles to Professional Journals **MEM:** Former Member, Country Club of Asheville; Chair, "Leadership Asheville Forum," Asheville, NC (2014-2017); Assistant Treasurer, Institute of Industrial Engineers (1985-1992); President, Institute of Industrial Engineers (1982-1983); Treasurer, Institute of Industrial Engineers (1976-1981); Fellow, Institute of Industrial Engineers **MH:** Albert Nelson Marquis Lifetime Achievement Award **B/I:** Mr. Mundt became involved in his profession because his father, Kenneth Francis, was a civil engineer and he followed in his footsteps. **AV:** Golf; Travel **PA:** Independent

MUNSON, VIRGINIA A., T: Interior Designer, Decorator **I:** Retail/Sales **CN:** Virginia Munson Interiors **DOB:** 10/10/1932 **PB:** Evanston **SC:** IL/USA **PT:** Jefferson Elliott Aldrich; Catherine (Stinson) Aldrich **MS:** Married **SPN:** Samuel McTier (1997); John Chester Munson (02/04/1956, Divorced) **CH:** Catherine; John C. Munson Jr.; Laura Munson **ED:** AA, Bennett Junior College (1952) **C:** Owner, President, Virginia Munson Interiors, Lake Forest, IL (1967) **CIV:** Women's Board, Northwestern Lake Forest Hospital (1977-Present); Altar Guild, Church of the Holy Spirit, Lake Forest, IL (1970-2020); Board of Directors, National Headquarters for The National Society of The Colonial Dames of America, Washington, DC (2006-2019); Chairman, Dining Services Committee (2009-2012); Finance Commission (2003-2012); Lake Forest Historic Preservation Society (2005-2011); Chairman, Landscape and Grounds (2004-2008); Resident Advisory Council (2000-2006); Illinois Regent, Gunston Hall, Lorton, VA (1997-2005); Guild of Chicago Historical Society (1990-2000); Associate Trustee, Friends of Sulgrave Manor, Sulgrave, England (1994-1996); Board of Directors, Infant Welfare Society, Chicago, IL (1957-1993); Committee Candidates Caucus, Lake Forest, IL (1984-1987); President, National Society of The Colonial Dames of America in the State of Illinois (1982-1984); President, Infant Welfare Society of Chicago, Lake Forest, IL (1978-1980) **AW:** Inaugural Recipient, The National Society of The Colonial Dames of America in the State of Illinois' Special Recognition Citation (2012); Inductee, Roll of Honor, National Society of the Colonial Dames of American in the State of Illinois **MEM:** Allied Member, American Society of Interior Designers (1978-2014); Society of Mayflower Descendants; Onwentsia Club; Contemporary Club of Chicago **MH:** Albert Nelson Marquis Lifetime Achievement Award **AS:** Ms. Munson attributes her success to hard work. **B/I:** Ms. Munson became involved in her profession because she always loved the practice of design. **AV:** Playing tennis; Practicing needlepoint; Researching genealogy **PA:** Republican **RE:** Episcopalian

MUNYON, MARVIN L., T: Cultural Organization Administrator **DOB:** 10/25/1940 **PB:** Omaha **SC:** NE/USA **PT:** Rex Munyon; Elizabeth Ellen (Bryant) Bailey **MS:** Married **SPN:** Sandra June Johnson Munyon (07/24/1960) **CH:** Rex Duane; Tod Michael **ED:** BA, Maranatha Baptist Bible College (Now Maranatha Baptist University), Watertown, WI (1977) **C:** Founding Director, Treasurer, Secretary, Rock River Patriots (2010-Present); President, Director, Family Research Institute of Wisconsin (Now Wisconsin Capitol Watch), Madison, WI (1986-Present); President, Director, Wisconsin Capitol Watch (2000-2013); Administrator, Calvary Baptist Christian School, Watertown, WI (1980-1986); Field Engineer, Burroughs Corp., Madison, WI (1973-1980); Field Engineer, Burroughs Corp., Pueblo, CO and Casper, WY (1964-1973) **CR:** Commission on Families and Children (1991); Commission on Schools for 21st Century (1990); Member, Governor's Task Force on Children and Families, State of Wisconsin, Madison, WI (1989-1990); Speaker, Lecturer, Wisconsin Parents Association, Christian Home Educators Association (CHEA) (8-10 Years) **CIV:** Jefferson County Representatives (1992-1997); Member, Dodge County Representatives, Beaver Dam, WI (1988-1992) **MH:** Albert Nelson Marquis Lifetime Achievement Award; Marquis Who's Who Top Professional **B/I:** Mr. Munyon became involved in his profession because when he went to college he had a big picture in his mind of what was going on in today's society. He felt there was a need for a spokesman for family values, and to speak up and be involved; the more he looked at that, the more he got involved. **AV:** Hunting; Fishing **PA:** Republican **RE:** Baptist

MURAI, KEVIN M., T: Director, President, Chief Executive Officer **I:** Information Technology and Services **CN:** Synnex Corporation **ED:** Bachelor of Science in Electrical Engineering, University Waterloo, Ontario **C:** Chairperson, Chief Executive Officer, Rite Aid Corporation, Camp Hill, PA (2012-Present); President, Chief Executive Officer, Director, Synnex Corporation, Fremont, CA (2008-Present); President, Chief Executive Officer, Rite Aid Corporation, Camp Hill, PA (2010-2013); President, Chief Operating Officer, Rite Aid Corp., Camp Hill, PA (2008-2010); Co-chief Executive Officer, Synnex Corporation, Fremont, CA (2008); Chief Executive Officer, Pathmark Stores Inc. (2005-2008); President, Chief Operating Officer, Ingram Micro Inc. (2005-2007); President, Chief Operating Officer, Ingram Micro North America (2002-2005); Chief Operating Officer, Ingram Micro U.S. (2000-2002); President, Ingram Micro U.S. (2000-2001); Executive Vice President, Ingram Micro Inc., Santa Ana, CA (2000-2005); Senior Vice President, Ingram Micro Inc. (1997-2002); President, Ingram Micro Canada (1997-2000); Vice President, Operations, Ingram Micro Canada (1993-1997); Joined, Ingram Micro Inc. (1988); Manager, Management Information Services, Verifact Inc., Canada

MURAKAMI, HARUKI, T: Author, Professor **I:** Education/Educational Services **DOB:** 01/12/1949 **PB:** Kyoto **SC:** Japan **MS:** Married **SPN:** Yoko Murakami (1971) **ED:** Honorary Doctorate, Tufts University (2014); Honorary Doctorate, Princeton University (2008); Honorary Doctorate, University of Liege (2007); Diploma in Theater Arts, Waseda University, Tokyo, Japan **C:** Associate Professor, William Howard Taft University, Santa Ana, CA (1993-2001); Associate Professor, Princeton University, NJ (1992-1993); Associate Researcher, Princeton University (1991-1992); Co-Owner, Peter Cat Jazz Bar, Tokyo, Japan (1974-1981) **CW:** Author, "South of the Border, West of the Sun" (2000); Author, "Killing Commendatore" (2017); Author, "Colorless Tsukuru Tazaki and His Years of Pilgrimage" (2014); Author, "IQ84" (2011); Author, "Blind Willow, Sleeping Woman" (2006); Author, "Kafka on the Shore" (2005); Author, "After the Quake" (2003); Author, "Sputnik Sweetheart" (2002); Author, "Underground" (1997); Author, "Wind-up Bird Chronicle" (1996); Author, "Dance Dance Dance" (1994); Author, "The Elephant Vanishes" (1993); Author, "Norwegian Wood" (1987); Author, "Hard-Boiled Wonderland and End of the World" (1985); Author, A Wild Sheep Chase" (1982); Author, "Pinball" (1980); Author, "Hear the Wind Sing," (1979); Author, Short Stories, Books **AW:** Hans Christian Anderson Literature Award (2016); Hans Christian Andersen Literature Award (2016); One of the 100 Most Influential People, Time Magazine (2015); Welt-Literaturpreis (2014); International Catalunya Prize (2011); Jerusalem Prize (2009); Frank O'Connor International Short Story Award (2006); World Fantasy Award (2006); Yomiuri Literature Award (1996); Junichi Tanizaki Award (1985); Noma Literature Award for New Writers (1982); Gunzo New Writer Award (1979)

MURDOCH, JAMES, T: Chairman (Retired) **I:** Telecommunications **CN:** Sky Plc **DOB:** 12/13/1972 **PB:** Wimbeldon, London **SC:** England/United Kingdom **PT:** Rupert Murdoch; Anna Maria (Torv) Murdoch **ED:** Coursework, Harvard University (1991-1995) **C:** Chief Executive Officer, 21st Century Fox Inc. (Now Disney) (2015-2019); Chairman, Sky PLC (2016-2018); Co-chief Operating Officer, 21st Century Fox, Inc. (Now Disney) (2014-2015);

Deputy Chief Operating Officer, 21st Century Fox, Inc. (Now Disney) (2013-2014); Chairman, Supervisory Board, Sky Deutschland AG, Frankfort, Germany (2013); Deputy Chief Operating Office, News Corporation, New York, NY (2011-2013); Executive Chairman, News Corporation International, London, England, United Kingdom (2011-2012); Chairman, British Sky Broadcasting Group Plc (2007-2012); Chairman, Chief Executive Officer, News Corporation International, New York, NY (2011); Chairman, Chief Executive Officer, Europe & Asia, News Corporation, London, England, United Kingdom (2007-2011); Chief Executive Officer, British Sky Broadcasting Group PLC (BSkyB), Middlesex, England, United Kingdom (2003-2007); Chairman, Chief Executive Officer, Star TV, Hong Kong (2000-2003); Executive Vice President, News Corporation, New York, NY (1996-2000); Chairman, Festival Records (1996); Founder, Rawlus Entertainment LLC (1995) **CR:** Member, Board of Directors, Tesla (2017-Present); Board of Advertising, True[X] Media (2014-Present); Member, Board of Directors, Sky Deutschland AG (2013-Present); Member, Board of Directors, British Sky Broadcasting Group PLC (BSkyB) (2003-Present); Member, Board of Directors, News Corporation (2000-2003, 2007-2020); Member, Board of Directors, Sotheby's Holding, Inc. (2010-2012); Member, Board of Directors, GlaxoSmithKline plc (2009-2012)

MURDOCH, ROBERT W., ESQ, FSA SCOT, T: Lawyer **I:** Law and Legal Services **DOB:** 03/21/1937 **PB:** Pittsburgh **SC:** PA/USA **PT:** Thomas Murdoch; Julia (Whitten) Murdoch **MS:** Married **SPN:** Eleanore L. (Uram) Murdoch (09/26/1967) **CH:** Robert John Murdoch, Esq. **ED:** Private Law Study (1963-1966); Coursework, Duquesne University (1961-1963); BA in Pre-law and Sociology, University of Pittsburgh (1960); Diploma, Munhall High School (1955) **C:** Sole Practitioner (2011-Present); Of Counsel, Rawle & Henderson, LLP (2004-2011); Of Counsel, Zimmer Kunz PLLC (1998-2004); Shareholder, Grogan, Graffam, McGinley & Lucchino, Professional Corporation, Pittsburgh, PA (1985-1998); Partner, Jones, Gregg, Creehan & Gerace, LLP, Pittsburgh, PA (1967-1985) **CR:** Zoning Hearing Board, Borough of Whitehall, PA (1976-1991); Former Chairman, Scottish National Room, University of Pittsburgh (17 Years) **CIV:** National Chairman Emeritus, National Tartan Day (2013-Present); Board of Trustees, Caledonian Foundation USA, Inc. (1999-2013); National Chairman, National Tartan Day (1999-2013); Former President, Caledonian Foundation USA, Inc. (2011-2012); Tenor Soloist, 250th Anniversary Celebration, Saint Andrew's Society of the State of New York (2006); Member-at-large, The Scottish Coalition, USA **MIL:** Second Lieutenant of Military Intelligence, United States Army Reserve (1961-1968); United States Army (1960-1961) **CW:** Performer, Tartan Tenor (1970-2020); Author, "The Economic Expert in Litigation" (1984); Author, "Pfeifer: The Supreme Court on the Longshoremen's and Harbor Workers Compensation Act and Inflation" (1983-1984); Author, Articles about the Nationality Room, Society of Antiquaries in Scotland and Various Scottish Periodicals **AW:** Scottish Heritage Center Service Award, St. Andrews Presbyterian College, NC (2010); Personal Coat of Arms Granted by the Court of the Lord Lyon, Scotland (2009); Honored Guest, Grandfather Mountain Highland Games, NC (2007); National Tartan Day Award, The Scottish Coalition, USA (2007); Distinguished Service Medal, Clan Donald (2004); Citation, House of Representatives, Commonwealth of Pennsylvania (1999, 2002); AV Rating, Martindale-Hubbell; Named, Proctor in Maritime Law, Maritime Law Association of the United States (MLAUS) **MEM:** Academy of Trial Lawyers of Allegheny County

(1974-Present); An Ceud Fear (2002); Fellow, Society of Antiquaries of Scotland; National Society of the Sons of the American Revolution; Gaelic Arts Society of Pittsburgh; Council of Scottish Clans & Associations; The American Legion; The Society of Scottish Armigers; American College of Legal Medicine; Allegheny County Bar Association; Pennsylvania Bar Association; Pitt Varsity Letter Club; The Plymouth Hereditary Society; Secretary, Charter Member, Saint Andrews Society of Pittsburgh; Pittsburgh Golden Panthers; Sons of Union Veterans of the Civil War; Descendants of the Colonial Clergy; National Society of the Sons of Colonial New England; Clan Donald USA, Inc.; Continental Society of the Sons of Indian Wars; Advisory Board, The Scottish Coalition, USA; Phi Alpha Delta; Scottish Heritage Society of North Central West Virginia; Scottish American Military Society, Ltd.; 65 Roses Club, Cystic Fibrosis Foundation **BAR:** United States Court of Appeals for the Eleventh Circuit (1986); United States Court of Appeals for the Eighth Circuit (1984); United States Court of Appeals for the Third Circuit (1979); Supreme Court of the United States (1978); Commonwealth Court of Pennsylvania (1970); Supreme Court of Pennsylvania (1968); United States District Court for the Western District of Pennsylvania (1967); Superior Court of Pennsylvania (1967); Court of Common Pleas of Allegheny County (1967) **MH:** Albert Nelson Marquis Lifetime Achievement Award **AS:** Although hard work has been at the core of any success Mr. Murdoch achieved, that would not have been possible without the aid and friendships of his family and the co-workers he encountered in his 53 years of being an attorney. The song, "No Man is an Island," has been one of his favorite songs over the years, and it is so true that what any person acquires as he or she goes through life, no one can do it by themselves. **B/I:** Mr. Murdoch became involved in his profession because he wanted to be an FBI agent growing up; he felt that he had to be an attorney to become an FBI agent, so he became an attorney. His family knew an attorney who was local, and eventually, Mr. Murdoch decided not to pursue his goals of being an FBI agent, but to become an attorney instead. Although he did not complete law school, he read law to qualify to take the bar exam with the help and sponsorship of fellow attorney, Thomas Lewis Jones. After he passed the bar, he went to work with Thomas Lewis Jones as a partner in his law firm. The study of law led to his decision to continue in that profession and be involved helping persons who required the help of an attorney. The challenge of being a trial attorney was satisfying and at the same time rewarding. **AV:** Genealogy; Golf; Singing **PA:** Republican **RE:** Presbyterian **THT:** Mr. Murdoch's father, a native Scot, performed as Pittsburgh's Scottish Tenor from 1925 till 1970 and Robert performed as the Tartan Tenor from his father's retirement until 2020, a period of 95 years. Mr. Murdoch's motto is, "Whether you deal with a friend or an adversary, do so with grace and a smile. Accept the fact that the other person may not respond to you with the same type of courtesy immediately, but in the long run, you will see the benefit."

MURDOCH, RUPERT, T: Broadcast Executive **I:** Media & Entertainment **CN:** FOX News Network, LLC **DOB:** 03/11/1931 **SC:** Melbourne/Australia **PT:** Sir Keith Arthur Murdoch; Dame Elisabeth Joy (Greene) Murdoch **MS:** Married **SPN:** Jerry Hall (03/04/2016); Wendi Deng (06/25/1999, Divorced 11/20/2013); Anna Maria Torv (04/28/1967, Divorced 06/08/1999); Patricia Booker (1956, Divorced 1960) **CH:** Prudence; Elisabeth; Lachlan; James; Grace Helen; Chloe **ED:** MA, Worcester College, Oxford, England (1953); BA, University

of Oxford; BS, University of Oxford **C:** Chairman, Chief Executive Officer, Fox News Network, LLC (2016-Present); Executive Co-Chairman, 21st Century Fox (2015-Present); Chairman, Chief Executive Officer, 21st Century Fox (2013-Present); Executive Chairman, News Corporation, New York, NY (2013-Present); Chairman, Chief Executive Officer, 21st Century Fox, Disney (2013-2015); Chairman, Chief Executive Officer, News Corporation, New York, NY (1991-2013); Chairman, DirecTV Group (Now AT&T Intellectual Property) (2003-2007); Chairman, British Sky Broadcasting Group PLC (BSkyB) (Now Sky UK) (1999-2007); Publisher, New York Post (1976-1986, 2005); Chief Executive Officer, News Corporation (1979-1991) **CR:** Board of Directors, British Sky Broadcasting Group PLC (BSkyB) (Now Sky UK) (1999-2007); Board of Directors, China Netcom Group Corporation, Ltd. (2001-2005); Board of Directors, Philip Morris Companies, Inc. (Now Altria Group, Inc.) (1989-2002); Chairman, STAR Group Ltd. (1993-1998); Owner, Publisher, Numerous International Newspapers, Magazines, TV Operations **AW:** Listee, Forbes 400: Richest Americans (1999-Present); Listee, World's Richest People, Business Insider (2019); Listee, World's Most Powerful People, Forbes Magazine (2009-2014); Listee, Top 25 Market Movers, U.S. News & World Report (2009); Listee, Global Elite, Newsweek Magazine (2008); Listee, Most Influential People in the World of Sports, Business Week (2007, 2008); Listee, 100 Most Influential People in the World, TIME Magazine (2004, 2005, 2008); Listee, 25 Most Powerful People in Business, Fortune Magazine (2007); Listee, 50 Who Matter Now, CNNMoney.com Business 2.0 (2006, 2007); Knighted, Order of St. Gregory the Great (1998); Companion, Order of Australia (1984) **AV:** Sailing

MURKOWSKI, LISA ANN, T: U.S. Senator for Alaska; Lawyer **I:** Government Administration/Government Relations/Government Services **DOB:** 05/22/1957 **PB:** Ketchikan **SC:** AK/USA **PT:** Frank Hughes Murkowski; Nancy (Gore) Murkowski **MS:** Married **SPN:** Verne Martell (08/22/1987) **CH:** Nicholas; Matthew **ED:** JD, Willamette University College of Law (1985); BA in Economics, Georgetown University (1980) **C:** Chairman, Senate Energy Committee (2015-Present); Member, U.S. Senate Appropriations Committee (2009-Present); U.S. Senator, State of Alaska (2002-Present); Vice Chairman, U.S. Senate Republican Conference (2009-2010); Majority Leader, Alaska House of Representatives, Anchorage, Alaska (2002); Member, District 18, Alaska House of Representatives, Anchorage, Alaska (2000-2002); Member, District 14, Alaska House of Representatives, Anchorage, Alaska (1998-2000); Private Law Practice (1989-1996); Attorney, Hoge & Lekisch (1989-1996); Attorney, Anchorage District Court, Anchorage, Alaska (1987-1989) **CR:** Citizens' Advisory Board, Joint Committee on Military Bases in Alaska (1998-Present); Commissioner, Anchorage Equal Rights Commission (1997-2002); Republican Chair, District 14, State Central Committee (1993-1998); Member, Mayor's Task Force for the Homeless (1990-1991); Director, First Bank **CIV:** Trustee, Catholic Services; President, Government Hill Elementary; PTA Director, Alaskan Drug Free Youth; Member, YWCA Arctic Power **AW:** Food Safety Award, National Food Processors Association (2003); Outstanding Volunteer Award, Alaska School District (1998, 2000); Community Leadership Award, FBI Director (1993) **MEM:** Alaska Bar Association; Anchorage Bar Association; Board of Directors, Alaska Federation of Republican Women; Anchorage Republican Women's Club; Midnight Sun Republican Women; Alaska Federation of Republican Women **PA:** Republican **RE:** Roman Catholic

MURPHY, BOBBY CORNELIUS, T: Co-founder I: Information Technology and Services CN: Snap Inc. DOB: 07/19/1988 PB: Berkeley SC: CA/USA MS: Married SPN: Kelsey Bateman ED: BS in Mathematical and Computational Science, Stanford University (2010) C: Co-founder, Snap Inc. (2016-Present); Co-founder, Chief Technology Officer, Snapchat (2011-Present) CIV: Co-founder, Snap Foundation (2017-Present) AW: Named Second Youngest Billionaire, Forbes (2015); Named One of the 100 Most Influential People, TIME Magazine (2014)

MURPHY, CHRISTOPHER, "CHRIS" SCOTT, T: U.S. Senator from Connecticut; Lawyer I: Government Administration/Government Relations/ Government Services DOB: 08/03/1973 PB: White Plains SC: NY/USA PT: Scott L. Murphy; Catherine A. (Lewczyk) Murphy MS: Married SPN: Catherine (Holahan) Murphy (08/18/2007) CH: Owen; Rider ED: Honorary LHD, University of New Haven (2013); JD, University of Connecticut School of Law (2002); BA in History and Political Science, Williams College, With Honors (1996); Coursework, Exeter College, University of Oxford, England C: U.S. Senator, State of Connecticut (2013-Present); U.S. Congressional Joint Economic Committee (JEC) (2013-Present); Member, U.S. Senate Committee on Foreign Relations (2013-Present); Member, U.S. Senate Committee on Health, Education, Labor and Pensions (2013-Present); Member, U.S. House of Representatives from Connecticut's Fifth Congressional District, United States Congress (2007-2013); Member, District 16, Connecticut State Senate (2003-2007); Attorney, Ruben, Johnson & Morgan, P.C. (Now Ruben/ Horan, P.C.), Hartford, CT (2002-2006); Member, District 81, Connecticut House of Representatives (1998-2002) CR: Planning and Zoning Commission, Southington, CT (1997-1999); Staff Member, Connecticut State Senate Majority Caucus (1996-1998) PA: Democrat

MURPHY, EDDIE REGAN, T: Actor; Comedian I: Media & Entertainment DOB: 04/03/1951 PB: Brooklyn SC: NY/USA PT: Charles Edward Murphy; Lillian (Laney) Murphy; Vernon Lynch (Stepfather) MS: Divorced SPN: Nicole Mitchell (03/18/1993, Divorced 04/17/2006) CH: Angel Iris Murphy Brown; Max Charles; Izzy Oona; Bria; Myles Mitchell; Shayne Audra; Zola Ivy; Bella Zahra; Eric; Christian ED: Coursework, Public School, Brooklyn, NY C: Performer, The Comic Strip, New York, NY; Performer, Richard M. Dixon's White House, New York, NY; Performer, Various Comedy Clubs CW: Actor, "Dolemite is My Name" (2019); Host, "Saturday Night Live" (1982, 1984, 2019); Actor, "Mr. Church" (2016); Actor, Executive Producer, "Beverly Hills Cop" (2015); Actor, "A Thousand Words" (2012); Actor, Producer, "Tower Heist" (2011); Voice Actor, "Donkey's Christmas Shrektacular" (2010); Voice Actor, "Shrek Forever After" (2010); Actor, "Imagine That" (2009); Actor, "Meet Dave" (2008); Voice Actor, "Shrek the Third" (2007); Voice Actor, "Shrek the Halls" (2007); Actor, Writer, Producer, "Norbit" (2007); Actor, "Dreamgirls" (2006); Voice Actor, "Shrek 2" (2004); Actor, "Daddy Day Care" (2003); Actor, "The Haunted Mansion" (2003); Actor, "Showtime" (2002); Actor, "The Adventures of Pluto Nash" (2002); Actor, "I Spy" (2002); Voice Actor, "Shrek" (2001); Actor, "Dr. Dolittle 2" (2001); Voice Actor, Executive Producer, "The PJ's" (1999-2001); Actor, Executive Producer, "The Nutty Professor II: The Klumps" (2000); Actor, Producer, "Life" (1999); Actor, "Bowfinger" (1999); Voice Actor, "Mulan" (1998); Actor, "Dr. Dolittle" (1998); Actor, "Holy Man" (1998); Actor, "Metro" (1997); Actor, "The Nutty Professor" (1996); Actor, Producer, "Vampire in Brooklyn" (1995); Actor,

"Beverly Hills Cop III" (1994); Singer, "Love's Alright" (1993); Actor, "The Distinguished Gentleman" (1992); Actor, Writer, "Boomerang" (1992); Actor, Writer, "Another 48 Hrs." (1990); Singer, "So Happy" (1989); Actor, Executive Producer, "Harlem Nights" (1989); Actor, Writer, "Coming to America" (1988); Actor, Writer, "Beverly Hills Cop II" (1987); Featured, "Eddie Murphy Raw" (1987); Actor, Executive Producer, "The Golden Child" (1986); Singer, "How Could It Be" (1985); Actor, "Best Defense" (1984); Actor, "Beverly Hills Cop" (1984); Actor, Writer, "Saturday Night Live" (1980-1984); Host, 14th Annual NAACP Image Awards (1983); Host, 35th Annual Emmy Awards (1983); Actor, "Trading Places" (1983); Featured, "Eddie Murphy: Delirious" (1983); Actor, "48 Hrs." (1982) AW: Mark Twain Prize for American Humor, John F. Kennedy Center for the Performing Arts (2015); Critics Choice Award for Best Supporting Actor (2007); Golden Globe Award for Best Performance by an Actor in a Supporting Role in a Motion Picture, Hollywood Foreign Press Association (2007); Screen Actors Guild Award for Outstanding Performance by a Male Actor in a Supporting Role, SAG-AFTRA (2007); Award for Best Supporting Actor, Broadcast Film Critics Association (2007); Award for Best Supporting Actor, African-American Film Critics Association (2006); Star, Hollywood Walk of Fame (1996); NAACP Image Award for Entertainer of the Year (1990); NAACP Image Award for Outstanding Lead Actor in a Motion Picture (1983); Recipient, Numerous Awards

MURPHY, GREGORY, "GREG" FRANCIS, MD, T: U.S. Representative from North Carolina; Physician I: Medicine & Health Care DOB: 03/05/1963 PB: Raleigh SC: NC/USA MS: Married SPN: Wendy Murphy CH: Three Children ED: BS, Davidson College, Magna Cum Laude (1985); MD, University of North Carolina at Chapel Hill School of Medicine, With Honors C: Member, U.S. House of Representatives from North Carolina's Third Congressional District, United States Congress, Washington, DC (2019-Present); Member, House Committee on Science and Technology, United States Congress, Washington, DC (2019-Present); Member, House Committee on Education and Labor, United States Congress, Washington, DC (2019-Present); Member, District Nine, North Carolina House of Representatives (2015-2019); Residency in Urology and Renal Transplantation, University of Kentucky, Lexington, KY; President, Eastern Urological Associates, Greenville, NC; Chief, Division of Urology, East Carolina University Brody School of Medicine; Chief of Staff, Vidant Medical Center, Vidant Health CIV: Former President, Davidson College Alumni Association; Board of Trustees, Davidson College Alumni Association; Medical Missionary, Third World Countries Including India, Africa, Nicaragua and Haiti; Board Member, North Carolina Urological Association (NCUA); Board of Directors, Southeastern Section of the AUA, Inc.; Executive Board, Judicial and Ethics Committee, American Urological Association, Member, By-Laws Committee, American Urological Association MEM: AOA; North Carolina Institute of Medicine (NCIOM)

MURPHY, PHILIP, "PHIL" DUNTON, T: Governor of New Jersey I: Government Administration/Government Relations/Government Services DOB: 08/16/1957 PB: Needham SC: MA/USA PT: Walter F. Murphy; Dorothy Louise (Dunton) Murphy MS: Married SPN: Tammy Snyder (1994) CH: Emma; Josh; Charlie; Sam ED: MBA, The Wharton School, The University of Pennsylvania, Philadelphia, PA (1983); AB in Economics, Harvard University, Cambridge, MA (1979) C: Governor, State of New Jersey, Trenton, NJ (2018-Present); Principal Owner, Sky Blue FC, Somerset, NJ (2009-Present);

United States Ambassador to Germany, United States Department of State, Berlin, Germany (2009-2013); Principal, Murphy Endeavors, LLC, Red Bank, NJ (2009); National Finance Chair, Democratic National Committee, Washington, DC (2006-2009); Senior Director, Goldman Sachs Group, Inc. (2003-2006); Summer Associate, Numerous Positions of Increasing Responsibility, Goldman Sachs Group, Inc., United States, Europe, and Asia (1982-2006); Co-head, Investment Management Division, Goldman Sachs Group, Inc. (1999-2003); President, Goldman Sachs Asia, Goldman Sachs Group, Inc. (1997-1999); Head, German Region, Goldman Sachs Group, Inc., Frankfurt, Germany (1993-1997) CR: Member, Management Committee, Goldman Sachs; Sponsor, Women's Network CIV: Member, Bid Committee, USA Soccer; Member, Huntsman Program Advisory Board; Member, University of Pennsylvania; Member, Board of Directors, US Soccer Foundation; Board President, US Soccer Foundation; Member, 180 Turning Lives Around, Inc.; Board of Trustees, Center for American Progress; Chairman, Executive Committee, Local Initiatives Support Corporation; Board of Trustees, Special Contribution Fund, NAACP; President, Chief Executive Officer, Search Committee, NAACP; Former Co-chair, Renewing Our Schools, Securing Our Future: A Task Force on Public Education for the 21st Century; Former Chair, Benefits Review Task Force, State of New Jersey; Former Trustee, The Goldman Sachs Foundation; Former Trustee, Prosperity New Jersey; Former Member, Graduate Executive Board, Asian Advisory Board, The Wharton School, The University of Pennsylvania AW: Named Business Leader of the Year, American Women's Economic Development Corporation (2003) PA: Democrat

MURPHY, RYAN PATRICK, T: Screenwriter, Director, Producer I: Media & Entertainment DOB: 11/30/1965 PB: Indianapolis SC: IN/USA PT: J. Andy Murphy MS: Married SPN: David Miller (07/02/2012) CH: Logan Phineas; Ford ED: Coursework in Journalism, Indiana University Bloomington C: Former Journalist, Entertainment Weekly, Knoxville News Sentinel, New York Daily News, Los Angeles Times, Miami Herald CIV: Founder, HALF Initiative (2017); National Advisory Board, Young Storytellers Foundation CW: Creator, Writer, Executive Producer, "9-1-1: Lone Star" (2020-Present); Creator, Director, Writer, Executive Producer, "The Politician" (2019-Present); Creator, Writer, Executive Producer, "9-1-1" (2018-Present); Creator, Director, Writer, Executive Producer, "Pose" (2018-Present); Writer, Executive Producer, "American Crime Story" (2016-Present); Creator, Director, Writer, Executive Producer, "American Horror Story" (2011-Present); Creator, Executive Producer, "Hollywood" (2020); Executive Producer, "Ratched" (2020); Producer, "The Boys in the Band" (2020); Director, Producer, "The Prom" (2020); Executive Producer, "Inside Look: The Assassination of Gianni Versace - American Crime Story" (2017-2018); Executive Producer, "Inside Look: Feud - Bette and Joan" (2017); Producer, "Inside Look: The People v. O.J. Simpson - American Crime Story" (2016); Creator, Director, Writer, Executive Producer, "Scream Queens" (2015-2016); Creator, Director, Writer, Executive Producer, "Feud" (2017); Creator, Director, Writer, Executive Producer, "Glee" (2009-2015); Director, Writer, Executive Director, "Open" (2014); Director, "American Horror Story Freak Show: Extra-Ordinary-Artists" (2014); Director, Executive Producer, TV Film, "The Normal Heart" (2014); Producer, "The Town That Dreaded Sundown" (2014); Creator, Director, Writer, Executive Producer, "The New Normal" (2012-2013); Executive Producer, "The Glee Project" (2011-2012); Producer, Documentary, "Glee: The 3D Concert Movie" (2011); Director, Writer, "Eat Pray Love" (2010); Creator, Director, Writer, Executive Producer, "Nip/Tuck" (2003-2010); Director, Writer, Executive Producer, "Pretty/Handsome" (2008); Director, Writer, Producer, "Running with Scissors" (2006); Director, Executive Producer, "St. Sass" (2002); Creator, Director, Writer, Executive Producer, "Popular" (1999-2001); Writer, Short Film, "The Furies" (1999); Executive Producer, "Halston" **AW:** Tony Award for Best Revival of a Play, "The Boys in the Band" (2019); Emmy Awards for Outstanding Limited Series, Outstanding Directing for a Limited Series, Movie, or Dramatic Special, "The Assassination of Gianni Versace: American Crime Story," The Television Academy (2018); Emmy Award for Outstanding Limited Series, "The People v. O. J. Simpson: American Crime Story," The Television Academy (2016); Emmy Award for Outstanding Short Form Nonfiction or Reality Series, "Inside Look: The People v. O. J. Simpson: American Crime Story," The Television Academy (2016); Award of Inspiration, amfAR, the Foundation for AIDS Research (2015); Emmy Award for Outstanding Television Movie, "The Normal Heart," The Television Academy (2014); Emmy Award for Outstanding Directing for a Comedy Series, "Glee," The Television Academy (2010) **RE:** Catholic

MURPHY, STEPHANIE, T: U.S. Representative from Florida **I:** Government Administration/Government Relations/Government Services **CN:** U.S. House of Representatives **DOB:** 09/16/1978 **PB:** Ho Chi Minh City **SC:** Vietnam **MS:** Married **SPN:** Sean Murphy **CH:** Two Children **ED:** Master of Science in Foreign Service, Georgetown University (2004); Bachelor of Arts in Economics, College of William & Mary (2000) **C:** Member, U.S. House of Representatives from Florida's Seventh Congressional District, United States Congress, Washington, DC (2017-Present); Professor, Business, Rollings College (2014-2016); National Security Specialist, United States Department of Defense (2004-2008); Strategy Consultant, Deloitte Consulting; Executive, Investment Efforts and Government Affairs Initiatives, Sungate Capital, Winter Park, FL; Member, Committee on Armed Services, United States Congress; Member, Committee on Small Business, United States Congress **AW:** Secretary of Defense Medal for Exceptional Civilian Service **PA:** Democrat **RE:** Protestant

MURRAY, BILL JAMES, T: Actor, Writer **I:** Media & Entertainment **DOB:** 09/21/1950 **PB:** Evanston **SC:** IL/USA **PT:** Edward Murray; Lucille (Collins) Murray **MS:** Divorced **SPN:** Jennifer Butler (07/04/1997, Divorced 06/2008); Margaret Kelly (01/25/1981, Divorced 01/1994) **CH:** Homer; Luke; Jackson; Caleb; Cooper; Lincoln **ED:** Honorary HHD, Regis University (2007); Coursework, Regis College, Denver, CO; Studied, Second City Workshop, Chicago, IL **CR:** Co-Owner, "Team Psychologist," St. Paul Saints Baseball Club (2014-Present); Co-Owner, Caddyshack Restaurant, Jacksonville, FL (2001-Present); Co-Owner, Charleston River-Dogs; Co-Owner, St. Paul Saints; Co-Owner, Hudson Valley Renegades; Co-Owner, Brockton Rox, Minor League Baseball **CW:** Actor, "The Dead Don't Die" (2019); Appearance, "Zombieland: Double Tap" (2019); Actor, "Isle of Dogs" (2018); Featured, "Bill Murray and Brian Doyle-Murray's Extra Innings" (2017); Actor, "Angela Tribeca" (2016); Actor, "Vice Principals" (2016); Voice Actor, "The Jungle Book" (2016); Actor, "Ghostbusters" (2016); Executive Producer, Writer, Actor, "A Very Murray Christmas" (2015); Guest Host, "Saturday Night Live" (2015); Actor, "Parks and Recreation" (2015); Actor, "A Very Murray Christmas" (2015); Actor, "Aloha" (2015); Actor, "Rock the Kasbah" (2015); Actor,

"Olive Kitteridge" (2014); Actor, "The Monuments Men" (2014); Actor, "The Grand Budapest Hotel" (2014); Actor, "St. Vincent" (2014); Actor, "Dumb and Dumber To" (2014); Actor, "Moonrise Kingdom" (2012); Actor, "Hyde Park on Hudson" (2012); Actor, "A Glimpse Inside the Mind of Charles Swan III" (2012); Actor, "Passion Play" (2010); Actor, "The Limits of Control" (2009); Actor, "Get Low" (2009); Appearance, "Zombieland" (2009); Voice Actor, "Fantastic Mr. Fox" (2009); Actor, "Get Smart" (2008); Actor, "City of Ember" (2008); Actor, "The Darjeeling Limited" (2007); Voice Actor, "Garfield: A Tail of Two Kitties" (2006); Actor, "Broken Flowers" (2005); Actor, "The Lost City" (2005); Voice Actor, "Garfield: The Movie" (2004); Actor, "The Life Aquatic with Steve Zissou" (2004); Actor, "Coffee and Cigarettes" (2003); Actor, "Lost in Translation" (2003); Actor, "The Sweet Spot" (2002); Actor, "Speaking of Sex" (2001); Actor, "The Royal Tenenbaums" (2001); Actor, "Osmosis Jones" (2001); Actor, "Charlie's Angels" (2000); Actor, "The Cradle Will Rock" (1999); Actor, "Scout's Honor" (1999); Actor, "Hamlet" (1999); Actor, "Company Man" (1999); Author, "Cinderella Story: My Life in Golf" (1999); Voice Actor, "Stories from My Childhood" (1998); Actor, "With Friends Like These" (1998); Actor, "Veeck as in Wreck" (1998); Actor, "Rushmore" (1998); Actor, "Wild Things" (1998); Actor, "The Man Who Knew Too Little" (1997); Actor, "Kingpin" (1996); Actor, "Larger Than Life" (1996); Actor, "Space Jam" (1996); Actor, "Ed Wood" (1994); Actor, "Groundhog Day" (1993); Actor, "Mad Dog and Glory" (1993); Actor, "What About Bob?" (1991); Actor, Director, Producer, "Quick Change" (1990); Actor, "Ghostbusters II" (1989); Actor, "Scrooged" (1988); Actor, "Little Shop of Horrors" (1986); Actor, "Nothing Lasts Forever" (1984); Actor, "The Razor's Edge" (1984); Actor, "Ghostbusters" (1984); Actor, "Tootsie" (1982); Actor, "Stripes" (1981); Actor, "Loose Shoes" (1980); Actor, "Caddyshack" (1980); Actor, "Where the Buffalo Roam" (1980); Actor, Writer, "Saturday Night Live" (1977-1980); Actor, "Mr. Mike's Mondo Video" (1979); Actor, "Meatballs" (1979); Actor, "The Rutles: All You Need is Cash" (1978); Actor, "Next Stop, Greenwich Village" (1976); Voice Actor, National Lampoon Radio Hour (1975); Performer, Second City Comedy Troupe (1973-1975) **AW:** Mark Twain Prize for American Humor (2016); Primetime Emmy Award for Supporting Actor in a Limited Series or Movie, Academy of Television Arts & Sciences (2015); Inductee, Class A South Atlantic League Hall of Fame (2012); Golden Globe for Best Actor in a Motion Picture Musical or Comedy, Hollywood Foreign Press Association (2004); BAFTA Award for Best Actor in a Leading Role (2004); Primetime Emmy Award for Writing for a Variety Series, Academy of Television Arts & Sciences (1977); Recipient, Numerous Awards

MURRAY, FRED F., T: Attorney **I:** Law and Legal Services **CN:** Murray Attorney **DOB:** 08/01/1950 **PB:** Corpus Christi **SC:** TX/USA **MS:** Married **ED:** JD, University of Texas (1974); BA, Rice University (1972) **CT:** Certified Public Accountant, Maryland (2004); Certified Public Accountant, Texas (1975); Board Certified in Tax Law, Texas **C:** Special Counsel, Professor in Residence, Office of the Chief Counsel for the Internal Revenue Service (2019-Present); Director, Graduate Tax Program and Professor of Tax Practice (2017-2019); Managing Director, Tax Practice Policy and Quality, Grant Thornton LLP (2007-2017); Deputy Assistant Attorney General, Tax Division, U.S. Department of Justice (2006); General Counsel, Director, Tax Affairs, Tax Executives Institute, Inc. (2002-2004); Vice President, Tax Policy, National Foreign Trade Council (1996-2002); Special Counsel, Legislation, U.S. Department of Treasury, IRS, Washington,

DC (1992-1996); Partner, Chamberlain, Hrdlicka, White, Williams & Martin, Professional Corporation, Houston, TX (1985-1992) **CR:** Member, Internal Revenue Service Advisory Council (2019-Present); Member, U.S. International Advisory Board (2011-Present); Faculty Lecturer, Graduate Tax Progressive, New York University (2008-Present); Member, Taxpayer Advisory Council, New York Commissioner of Taxation and Finance (2002-Present); Member, Internal Revenue Service Information Reporting Advisory Committee (2018); Adjunct Professor, Georgetown University Law Graduate Tax Program (2005-2017); Chair, Internal Revenue Service Advisory Council (2015); Member, Internal Revenue Service Advisory Council (2011-2015); Member, Bureau of National Affairs, Tax Management Advisory Board (2002-2004); Member, Tax Law Advisory Commission, Texas Board of Legal Specialization (1984-1999); Member, Commission of Tax Law Examiners (1984-1999); Vice Chairman, Tax Law Advisory Commission, Texas Board of Legal Specialization (1987-1992); Vice Chairman, Commission of Tax Law Examiners (1987-1992); Faculty Lecturer, Rice University Jones Graduate School Administration (1987-1992); Member, Board of Advisors, Houston Journal of International Law (1986-1992); Adjunct Professor, University of Houston Law Center (1984-1992); Chairman, Board of Advisors, Houston Journal of International Law (1987-1991); Adjunct Professor, University of Texas School of Law (1987); Speaker, Various Associations and Universities **CIV:** Member, Red Mass Committee, Archdiocese of Washington (1993-Present); Chairman, Pilgrimage Committee, Member, Finance Council, St. Matthew's Cathedral, Archdiocese of Washington (2003-2010); Parish Council, Chair, Social Justice Committee, Archdiocese of Washington (2006-2009); Board of Directors, John Carroll Society, Archdiocese of Washington (1996-2005); Member, Fund Council, Rice University (1987-1996); Chairman, Major Gifts Committee, Rice University (1988-1992); Executive Committee, Fund Council, Rice University (1988-1992); Member, Red Mass Steering Committee (1986-1992); Chairman, Government and Public Affairs Committee, Houston Symphony Society (1988-1991); Member, Executive Committee, Board of Directors, Red Mass Steering Committee (1987-1991); Co-trustee, Houston Symphony Society Endowment Fund (1987-1991); Chairman, Parish Council, Sacred Heart Cathedral, Catholic Diocese of Galveston-Houston (1979-1981, 1989); Chairman, Deferred Giving Committee, Houston Symphony Society (1987-1988); Delegate, Bishop's Diocesan Pastoral Council (1979-1980); General Counsel, Board of Directors, Committee on Finance and Administration, Southeast Texas Chapter, National Multiple Sclerosis Society **CW:** Author, Various Publications **AW:** Knighted Equestrian Order of the Holy Sepulchre of Jerusalem (1998-Present); Knight Commander, Equestrian Order of the Holy Sepulchre of Jerusalem (2005) **MEM:** Vice Chair, Continuing Legal Education for the Tax Section, American Bar Association (2017-Present); Member, Council on Tax Section, Federal Bar Association (1995-Present); Tax Advisory Group, American Law Institute (1990-Present); Panels Commercial and International Arbitrators, American Arbitration Association (1980-Present); Council Director, American Bar Association (2012-2013); Chairman, Admin Practice Communications, American Bar Association (2009-2011); Board of Directors, American Tax Policy Institute (2000-2003); Chairman, Tax Section, Federal Bar Association (1998-1999); Chairman, Formation Tax Policy Committee, American Bar Association (1998-2004); President, International Tax Forum of Houston (1984-1992); Secretary, International Tax Forum of Houston

(1981-1984); Fellow, American College Tax Counsel; American Institute of Certified Public Accountants; International Bar Association; Houston Bar Association; Various Committees, State Bar of Texas; New York State Bar Association; District of Columbia Bar Association; Texas Society of CPAs; International Fiscal Association; American Society of International Law; American Foreign Law Association **BAR:** United States Court of Appeals for the Second Circuit (2005); Maryland (2004); United States District Court for the Eastern District of Texas (1987); New York (1987); District of Columbia (1987); Supreme Court of the United States (1978); U.S. Court of International Trade (1985); U.S. Court of Claims (1976); U.S. Tax Court (1976); United States Court of Appeals for the Fifth Circuit (1976); United States Court of Appeals for the District of Columbia Circuit (1976); United States Court of Appeals for the Federal Circuit (1976); United States District Court for the Southern District of Texas (1976); Texas (1975)

MURRAY, KATHLEEN PAULA, T: Client Advocate, Claims Specialist **I:** Insurance **CN:** Capstone Brokerage **DOB:** 06/04/1948 **PB:** Sharon **SC:** PA/USA **ED:** BA in Music, Baldwin-Wallace College (Now Baldwin-Wallace University), Berea, Ohio (1977); AA in Journalism, University of California Los Angeles, CA; Certificate in Legal Studies, Penn State Shenango, The Pennsylvania State University, Sharon, PA **C:** Client Advocate, Claims Specialist, Capstone Brokerage (2006-Present); Account Executive, Caputo Insurance Agency, Beaver Falls, PA (2004-2006); Independent Agent Lead, Abraham & Petrini Insurance Agency, Sharon, PA (2002-2004); Administrator, Commercial Loans, First National Bank of Pennsylvania, F.N.B. Corporation, Hermitage, PA (1998-2002); Department Administrator, Trinity Industries, Inc., Greeneville, PA (1995-1997) **CW:** Author, "Monthly Safety Newsletter," Capstone Brokerage **AW:** Client Advocacy Award, State of Nevada; Certificate of Commendation, Recognition of Service in Client Advocacy in the State of Nevada, U.S. Senator Catherine Cortez Masto; Certificate of Special Congressional Recognition, Outstanding Service and Excellence in Client Advocacy, Nevada House of Representatives; Leadership Award, Most Promising Law Student, Penn State Shenango, The Pennsylvania State University, Sharon, PA **MEM:** AMWA; National Federation of Paralegal Associations, Inc. **MH:** Marquis Who's Who of Professional Women (2020-2021) **AS:** Ms. Murray attributes her success to passion, determination, dedication, intelligence and a refusal to give up. She also credits her grandfather, who was a major influence, because he always allowed her to simply be herself. She lives by a quote from "Hamlet" by William Shakespeare, "to thine own self be true." **B/I:** Ms. Murray became involved in her profession because of her aptitude for writing. When she worked in public relations for a medical company, a doctor commended her abilities, and assisted in promoting her to the workers' compensation department to fill a writing position. Ms. Murray loved her role there, and continued to progress as a writer over the course of her career. This path led her to claims, where she works today. **AV:** Playing piano **THT:** Ms. Murray is fluent in French, Italian, German and Korean.

MURRAY, MICHAEL W., T: Owner **I:** Financial Services **CN:** Murray Insurance and Financial Services, Inc. **MS:** Married **SPN:** Kathy (1991) **ED:** BBA, Sam Houston State University, Huntsville, Texas (1970) **C:** Owner, Murray Insurance and Financial Services, Inc., Houston, Texas (1982-Present); Principal, WhitetailDomains.com (2004-2012); Vice President, Policy Owners Services, Great Southern Life Insurance Company, Americo Life, Inc., Hous-

ton, Texas (1971-1980) **AW:** Service Award, Alumni Association, Sam Houston State University (2007); Inductee, Hall of Honor, Athletics, Sam Houston State University (1993); National Quality Award, NAIFA **MEM:** Life Member, Court of the Table and Top of the Table, Million Dollar Round Table **AS:** Mr. Murray attributes his success to advice from his father, and entered the insurance business with a set of important principles already in place. He is driven to do what is right and take care of his clients, trusting that meeting his clients' needs will take care of his back pocket. **B/I:** Mr. Murray was exposed to his profession from an early age, as his father was in the life insurance business from the 1930s until the 1970s. In an effort to replicate the lifestyle his father's career provided for his family, Mr. Murray followed in his footsteps, even working for the same company, Great Southern Life Insurance. **THT:** Mr. Murray has worked in the life, health and financial planning business for 32 years, and in the insurance business for 45 years.

MURRAY, PATRICIA, "PATTY" LYNN, T: U.S. Senator from Washington **I:** Government Administration/Government Relations/Government Services **DOB:** 10/11/1950 **PB:** Bothell **SC:** WA/USA **PT:** David L. Johns; Beverly A. (McLaughlin) Johns **MS:** Married **SPN:** Robert R. Murray (06/02/1972) **CH:** Randy P.; Sara A. **ED:** BA, Washington State University (1972) **C:** Senate Assistant Democratic Leader (2017-Present); Member, Senate Health Committee (2015-Present); Member, U.S. Senate Rules and Administration Committee (2007-Present); U.S. Senator, State of Washington (1993-Present); Ranking Member, Senate Health Committee (2015); Chairwoman, U.S. Senate Budget Committee (2013-2015); Chairwoman, U.S. Senate Committee on Veterans' Affairs (2011-2013); Co-Chair, Joint Select Committee on Deficit Reduction (2011); Secretary of the Senate Democratic Conference (2007-2017); Member, Washington State Senate, Seattle, WA (1989-1992); Instructor, Shoreline Community College, Seattle, WA (1984-1988); Citizen Lobbyist, Various Educational Groups, Seattle, WA (1983-1988); Legislative Lobbyist, Organization for Parent Education, Seattle, WA (1977-1984); Secretary, Various Companies, Seattle, WA (1972-1976) **CR:** Secretary, U.S. Senate Democratic Conference (2007-Present); Chairwoman, Democratic Senatorial Campaign Committee (DSCC) (2001-2003, 2011-2013) **CIV:** Member, Board, Shoreline School, Seattle, WA (1985-1989); Member, Steering Committee, Demonstration for Education, Seattle, WA (1987); First Congressional Representative, Washington Women United (1983-1985); Founder, Chairman, Organization of Parenting Education Programs, Washington, DC (1981-1985) **CW:** Co-Author, with Catherine Whitney, "Nine and Counting: The Women of the Senate" (2000) **AW:** Named One of the 10 Members to Watch in the 112th Congress, Roll Call (2011); Person of the Year Award, Washington State VFW (2004); George Falcon Spike Award, National Association of Railroad Passengers (Now Rail Passengers Association) (2003); Washington State Legislator of the Year (1990); Golden Acorn Service Award, (1989); Outstanding Service to Public Education Award, Citizens Educational Center Northwest, Seattle, WA (1987); Outstanding Service Award, Washington Women United (1986); Recognition of Service to Children Award, Shoreline PTA Council (1986); Outstanding Award, Washington Women United (1986) **AV:** Fishing; Exploring Washington State's outdoors; Spending time with family **PA:** Democrat **RE:** Roman Catholic

MURRAY, THOMAS VEATCH, T: Lawyer **I:** Law and Legal Services **CN:** LathropGPM LLP **DOB:** 07/17/1947 **PB:** Phoenix **SC:** AZ/USA **PT:** Robert Morrison Murray, Jr.; Jane Veatch (Murray) Barber; Richard A. Barber **MS:** Married **SPN:** Emilie H. Murray (11/14/2015); Cynthia Ann Burnett (06/02/1971, Deceased 2012) **CH:** Anne Caroline Emert; Thomas Veatch Murray, Jr. **ED:** JD, University of Michigan (1972); BA, University of Kansas (1969) **C:** Of Counsel, LathropGPM LLP, Overland Park, KS (2004-Present); Member, Barber, Emerson, Springer, Zinn & Murray, L.C., Lawrence, KS (1976-2003); Associate, Barber, Emerson, Six, Springer & Zinn, Lawrence, KS (1972-1976) **CR:** Director, The Reuter Organ Company (1991-2016); Director, The First National Bank of Lawrence, Kansas (1980-1991); Adjunct Professor, University of Kansas School of Law (1990-1991); Instructor, Kansas University Bar Review Course (1975-1982); Adjunct Professor, Western Civilization, University of Kansas (1975-1977) **CIV:** Member, Advisory Board, Hall Center for the Humanities (1988-2017); Chairman, Kansas Board Law Examiners (2006-2013); Member, Kansas Board Law Examiners (1995-2013); Member, Lawrence Emergency Services Council (1998-2002); Director, Lawrence Chamber of Commerce (1993-1995); Member, Board of Education, Unified School District 497, Lawrence, KS (1991-1995); Member, Advisory Board, Station KANU, Lawrence, KS (1975-1980); Member, Advisory Board, Lawrence Consumer Affairs Association (1974-1977); Trustee, First Presbyterian Church (1975-1976); Treasurer, Louie Holcom Baseball Association (1972-1973) **CW:** Contributor, Articles, Professional Journals **AW:** Named, Missouri/Kansas Super Lawyers (2013-2019); Elected to Lawrence High School Alumni Hall of Honor (2016) **MEM:** Trustee, Kansas Bar Foundation (1999-2005); Director, Federation Defense and Corporation Counsel (1997-1999); Regional Vice President, Federation Defense and Corporation Counsel (1994-1997); Director, Kansas Association Defense Counsel (1993-1997); President, Corporation, Banking and Business Law Section, Kansas Bar Association (1983); Fellow, American Bar Foundation; American Bar Association; Defense Research Institute; Johnson County Bar Association; Douglas County Bar Association; Lawrence Lions Alumni Association; Supreme Court Historical Society; Nelson Gallery Advisors; The River Club; Lawrence Country Club; Fortnightly Club (Lawrence) **BAR:** United States District Court for the Western District of Missouri (2014); United States Court of Appeals for the Tenth Circuit (1983); Supreme Court of the United States (1976); United States District Court for the District of Kansas (1972) **MH:** Albert Nelson Marquis Lifetime Achievement Award **AV:** Classical and operatic music; Philately **PA:** Republican **RE:** Presbyterian

MURREN, JAMES JOSEPH, T: Chief Executive Officer **I:** Leisure, Travel & Tourism **CN:** MGM Resorts **DOB:** 10/05/1961 **PB:** Bridgeport **SC:** CT/USA **PT:** John Murren; Jean-Marie Murren **MS:** Married **SPN:** Heather Hay (1990) **CH:** Two Children **ED:** BA in Art History & Urban Studies, Trinity College (1983); Diploma, Roger Ludlowe High School; Coursework, Cesare Barbieri Center, Rome, Italy **CT:** Chartered Financial Analyst (1991) **C:** Chairman, Corporate Responsibility Officers Association (2013-Present); Chairman, Chief Executive Officer, MGM Resorts International, Las Vegas, NV (2008-Present); President, Chief Operating Officer, MGM Mirage, Las Vegas, NV (2007-2008); Treasurer, MGM Mirage (2001-2007); President, Chief Financial Officer, MGM Mirage (1999-2007); Executive Vice President, Chief Financial Officer, MGM Mirage, Las Vegas, NV (1998-1999); Managing Director, Director Research, Deutsche Bank (1994-1998); Various Positions, Deutsche Morgan Grenfell (1984-1994) **CR:** Board of Directors, Delta Petroleum Corp. (2008-Present); Board of Directors, MGM Mirage (2000-Present); Board of Directors, Cyrus J. Lawrence **CIV:** Co-Founder, Board of Directors, Nevada Cancer Institute (2005-Present); Trustee, University of Nevada Reno Foundation; Trustee, University of Nevada Las Vegas Foundation; Executive-in-Residence, Johns Hopkins University Carey Business School; Co-Founder, Murren Family Foundation **AW:** Distinguished Leader Award, University of Massachusetts Isenberg School of Management (2015); Responsible CEO of the Year Award, Corporate Responsibility Magazine (2013); Named, 40 Best Companies for Diversity, Black Enterprise Magazine; Named, Top 10 Companies for Latinos, DiversityInc Magazine; Named, Best Places to Work for LGBT Equality, Human Rights Campaign Foundation; Named, Top 10 Regional Companies, DiversityInc; Named, Top 100 Companies for MBA Students, Universum Global; Named, Top Corporation for Women's Business Enterprises, Women's Business Enterprise National Council; Named, World's Most Admired Companies, Fortune Magazine **MEM:** Former Member, National Honor Society

MUSGRAVES, KACEY LEE, T: Musician **I:** Media & Entertainment **DOB:** 08/21/1988 **PB:** Golden **SC:** TX/USA **CW:** Musician, Album, "Golden Hour" (2018); Musician, Television, Hollywood Medium with Tyler Henry (2017); Musician, Television, Nashville (2017); Musician, Album, "A Very Kacey Christmas" (2016); Musician, Album, "Pageant Material" (2015); Musician, Television, CMT Crossraods (2014); Musician, Song, "Follow Your Arrow" (2013); Musician, Album, "Same Trailer Different Park" (2013); Musician, Song, "Merry Go Round" (2013); Musician, Album, "Kacey Musgraves" (2007); Musician, Television, Nashville Star (2007); Musician, Album, "Wanted: One Good Cowboy" (2003); Musician, Album, "Movin' On" (2002) **AW:** Grammy for Golden Hour, Album of the Year (2018); Grammy Award, Best Country Solo of the Year, "Butterflies" (2018); Grammy for Best Country Song, "Space Cowboy" (2018); Grammy Award for Best Country Album (2014); Grammy Award for Best Country Song (2014); Country Music Association Award for Song of the Year (2014); Academy Country Music Award for Album of the Year (2014); Named New Artist of the Year, Country Music Association Awards (2013); Album of the Year, Country Music Association

MUSIHIN, KONSTANTIN K., T: Senior Engineer, Electrical Engineer (Retired) **I:** Engineering **DOB:** 06/17/1927 **PB:** Harbin **SC:** China **PT:** Konstantin N. Musihin; Alexandra A. (Lapitsky) Musihin **MS:** Married **SPN:** Natalia Krilova (10/18/1964) **CH:** Nicholas **ED:** Degree in Electrical Engineering, Harbin Polytechnic (Now Harbin Institute of Technology) (1948); Coursework, North Manchurian University (1945); Coursework, YMCA Institute (1942) **CT:** Registered Professional Engineer, States of California, New York, Pennsylvania and Washington **C:** Electrical Engineer (1948-2000); Senior Engineer, Bechtel Corporation, San Francisco, CA (1989); Consultant Engineer, Pacific Gas and Electric Company, San Francisco, CA (1986-1989); Principal Engineer, Brown and Caldwell, Pleasant Hill, CA (1984-1985); Principal Engineer, Morrison–Knudsen, San Francisco, CA (1979-1984); Chief Electrical Engineer, L.K. Comstock, San Francisco, CA (1978-1979); Supervisor of Power and Control, San Francisco Bay Area Rapid Transit District (1976-1978); Senior Engineer, Bechtel Corporation, San Francisco, CA (1973-1975); Senior Engineer, Kaiser Engineering

Building, Oakland, CA (1967-1973); Project Engineer, ABB, São Paulo, Brazil (1965-1967); Chief of Works, Vidrobras, St. Gobain, Brazil (1962-1964); Mechanical Engineer, Matarazzo Industries, São Paulo, Brazil (1961-1962); Construction Project Manager, Caterpillar Brasil, São Paulo, Brazil (1960-1961); Electrical Engineer, Moinho Santista, São Paulo, Brazil (1955-1960); Assistant Professor in High Frequency Communications, Harbin Polytechnic Institute (Now Harbin Institute of Technology) (1950-1953); Electrical Engineer, Changchun Railway Station (1949-1950) **MEM:** Life Member, Senior, IEEE; National Society of Professional Engineers; NSPE-CA **MH:** Albert Nelson Marquis Lifetime Achievement Award; Marquis Who's Who Top Professional **B/I:** Mr. Musihin became involved in his profession because of his lifelong interest in electrical products. **AV:** Reading technical publications **RE:** Christian Orthodox

MUSK, ELON REEVE, T: Founder, Chief Executive Officer; Technology Entrepreneur; Engineer **I:** Engineering **CN:** SpaceX; Tesla **DOB:** 06/28/1971 **PB:** Pretoria **SC:** South Africa **PT:** Errol Musk; Maye (Halderman) Musk **MS:** Divorced **SPN:** Talulah Riley (2013, Divorced 2016); Talulah Riley (09/25/2010, Divorced 2012); Justine Wilson (2000, Divorced 2008) **CH:** Seven Children **ED:** BA in Physics, University of Pennsylvania (1997); BS in Economics, The Wharton School, University of Pennsylvania (1997); Coursework, Stanford University (1995); Coursework, Queen's University, Kingston, Ontario, Canada (1989); Coursework, University of Pretoria **C:** Chief Executive Officer, Founder, The Boring Company (2016-Present); Chief Executive Officer, Co-founder, Neuralink (2016-Present); Co-founder, OpenAI (2015-Present); Product Architect, Chief Executive Officer, Tesla Motors, Inc. (2008-Present); Co-founder, Tesla Motors, Inc., Palo Alto, CA (2003-Present); Chief Executive Officer, Chief Technology Officer, Founder, SpaceX (Space Explorations Technologies Corp.), Hawthorne, CA (2002-Present); Chief Executive Officer, Co-founder, PayPal (Merger of X.com and Confinity Inc., Acquired by eBay Inc.) (2001-2002); Chief Executive Officer, Co-founder, X.com (1999-2001); Chief Technology Officer, Chief Executive Officer, Co-founder, Zip2 (Acquired by Compaq Computer Corp.) (1995-1999); Software Developer, Microsoft, Redmond, WA; Software Developer, Rocket Science; With, Pinnacle Research **CR:** Chairman, Board of Directors, SolarCity (Now Tesla), Foster City, CA (2006-Present); Chairman, Tesla Motors, Inc. (Now Tesla) (2003-2008, 2008-2018); Board of Directors, The Planetary Society, Pasadena, CA (2003); Chairman, PayPal (2001-2002); Chairman, X.com (1999-2001); Chairman, Zip2 (1995-1999); Past Member, Aeronautics and Space Engineering Board, National Academy of Sciences **CIV:** Member, Engineering Advisory Board, Stanford University; Chairman, Board of Directors, Musk Foundation; Board Trustee, XPRIZE Foundation **CW:** Appearance, "Why Him?" (2016); Voice Actor, "South Park" (2016); Voice Actor, "The Simpsons" (2015); Appearance, "The Big Bang Theory" (2015); Featured, "Racing Extinction" (2015); Appearance, "Iron Man 2" (2010); Actor, Appearances, Television Shows, Films **AW:** Named One of the Most Innovative Leaders, Forbes Magazine (2019); Stephen Hawking Medal for Science Communication, Starmus International Festival (2019); Named to Order of the Direkgunabhorn, King of Thailand (2019); Named One of the World's Richest People, Business Insider (2019); Named One of the Top 50 Best CEOs of Large Companies, Comparably (2018); Fellow, The Royal Society (2018); Oslo Business for Peace (2017); Named One of the 10 Most Fascinating People of 2014, Barbara Walters Special (2014); Edison Achievement Award

(2014); Named One of the 50 Most Influential People in Global Finance, Bloomberg Markets (2013-2014); Named One of the World's Most Powerful People, Forbes Magazine (2012-2014); Named One of the CNN 10: Thinkers (2013); Named Businessperson of the Year, Fortune Magazine (2013); Named One of the 100 Most Influential People in the World, TIME Magazine (2010, 2013); Gold Medal, Royal Aeronautical Society (2012); Named One of America's 20 Most Powerful CEOs 40 and Under (2012); Named One of the 40 Under 40, Fortune Magazine (2010); Named a Living Legend in Aviation, Kitty Hawk Foundation (2010); Von Braun Trophy, National Space Society (2009); Named One of the 100 Agents of Change, Rolling Stone Magazine (2009); National Conservation Achievement Award, National Wildlife Federation (2008); Named One of the 75 Most Influential People of the 21st Century, Esquire Magazine (2008); Named Aviation Week 2008 Laureate (2008); George Low Award, American Institute of Aeronautics & Astronautics (2007-2008); Named One of the 50 Who Matter Now, Business 2.0 (2007); INDEX Design Award (2007); Innovator of the Year Award, R&D Magazine (2007); Entrepreneur of the Year Award, Inc. Magazine (2007); Product Design Award, Global Green USA (2006); Numerous Awards **MEM:** Fellow, The World Technology Network; Honorary Member, IEEE

MUZINICH, JUSTIN GEORGE, T: United States Deputy Secretary of the Treasury **I:** Government Administration/Government Relations/Government Services **CN:** U.S. Department of the Treasury **DOB:** 11/05/1977 **PB:** New York **SC:** NY/USA **PT:** George M. Muzinich; Camille Muzinich **MS:** Married **SPN:** Eloise Davis Austin (2008) **ED:** Doctor of Jurisprudence, Yale Law School (2007); Master of Business Administration, Harvard Business School (2005); Bachelor of Arts, Harvard University, Magna Cum Laude (2000) **C:** Deputy Secretary, United States Treasury (2018-Present); Professor, Columbia Business School (2014-2016); President, Muzinich and Company; With, Mergers and Acquisitions Group, EMS Capital and Morgan Stanley **CIV:** Member, Board of Trustees, NewYork-Presbyterian Hospital **AW:** Olin Fellow; Baker Scholar

MYERS, GREGORY E., T: Aerospace Engineer **I:** Engineering **DOB:** 01/01/1960 **PB:** Harrisburg **SC:** PA/USA **PT:** Bernard Eugene Myers; Joyce (Calhoun) Myers **MS:** Divorced **SPN:** Susan Ann Hayslett (12/30/1983, Divorced 1999) **CH:** Kimberly; Benjamin **ED:** MS in Aerospace Engineering, Air Force Institute of Technology (1982); BS in Aerospace Engineering, University of Michigan (1981) **CT:** Software Safety Engineer (2011) **C:** Senior Principal Software Engineer, Orbital Sciences Corporation, Chandler, AZ (1999-Present); Principal Software Engineer, Orbital Sciences Corporation, Chandler, AZ (1997-Present); Principal Engineer, Honeywell International, Inc., Phoenix, AZ (1993-1997); Senior Project Engineer, Air Transport Systems, Honeywell International, Inc., Phoenix, AZ (1992-1993); Senior Project Engineer, Satellite Systems Operations, Honeywell International, Inc., Glendale, AZ (1990-1992); Aerospace Engineer, Sperry Commercial Flight Systems Group, Honeywell International, Inc., Phoenix, AZ (1987-1990); Space Shuttle Operations Manager, United Stated Air Force, Vandenberg AFB (1983-1986) **CR:** Presenter in Field **CIV:** Pre-school Oversight Committee (2009); President, Bethlehem Lutheran Church, Mesa, AZ **MIL:** Captain, United States Air Force (1981-1986) **CW:** Contributor, Articles to Professional Journals; Contributor, AAS Advances in Astrodynamics, 37th International Instrument Symposium **AW:** Orbital ATK Star Award (Above and

Beyond) (2017); Turning Goals into Reality" Award (Hyper-X Program Team), NASA Administrators (2005); Group Achievement Award (Hyper-X Flight 3 Team), NASA Langley Research Center (2004); Certificate of Appreciation, Instrument Society of America (1991); Recipient, Certificates of Recognition and Appreciation, Lompoc Valley Festival Association, Inc. (1983) **MEM:** Instrument Society of America (1991-1992); Active, Aviation Week Research Advisory Panel (1990-1991); University of Michigan Commander, James Van Veen Squadron, Arnold Air Society (1979); Senior Member, American Institute of Aeronautics and Astronautics **MH:** Albert Nelson Marquis Lifetime Achievement Award; Marquis Who's Who Top Professional **AV:** Softball; Tennis; Reading; Computer programming **RE:** Lutheran

MYTELKA, ARNOLD K., T: Lawyer **I:** Law and Legal Services **CN:** Kraemer, Burns, PA **DOB:** 07/24/1937 **PB:** Jersey City **SC:** NJ/USA **PT:** Herman Donald Mytelka; Jeannette (Krieger) Mytelka **MS:** Married **SPN:** Rosalind Marcia Kaplan (12/17/1961) **CH:** Andrew Charles; Daniel Sommer **ED:** Frank Knox Memorial Fellow, Harvard University (1961-1962); Frank Knox Memorial Fellow, London School of Economics and Political Science (1961-1962); Postgraduate Coursework, London School of Economics (1961-1962); LLB, Harvard University, Cum Laude (1961); AB, Princeton University (1958) **C:** Principal, Kraemer, Burns, PA, Springfield, NJ (1994-Present); Partner, Clapp & Eisenberg, Newark, NJ (1968-1994); Associate, Clapp & Eisenberg, Newark, NJ (1963-1968); Law Secretary, Chief Justice Joseph Weintraub, New Jersey Supreme Court, Newark, NJ (1962-1963) **CR:** American Law Institute, Philadelphia, PA (1990-Present); Trustee, Legal Services Foundation of Essex County (1982-2019); ALI Advisory Council, Restatement of Law Governing Lawyers (1990-1999); President, Legal Services Foundation of Essex County (1990-1992); Chairman, District V Ethics Committee, Supreme Court of New Jersey (1983-1984); District V Ethics Committee, Supreme Court of New Jersey (1981-1984); Trustee, Education Law Center (1974-1975); Lecturer, Rutgers Law School, Newark, NJ (1973); Founding Trustee, Newark Legal Services Project (1965-1968); Lecturer, Land Use Law **CIV:** Mediator, Chancery Division, New Jersey Superior Court (1990-Present); Mediator, Early Settlement Program, Chancery Division, Superior Court (1990-2013); Special Fiscal Agent, Chancery Division, Superior Court (2009-2010); Receiver, Chancery Division, Superior Court (2004-2007); Trustee, Chancery Division, New Jersey Superior Court (2003-2006); Merit Selection Panel, U.S. District Court for Appointment of Magistrate Judge (2005); Special Fiscal Agent, Chancery Division, Superior Court (2004-2005); Mediator, Chancery Division, Superior Court (2004); Liquidating Trustee, Chancery Division, Superior Court (2001-2002); Special Counsel, City of Englewood Board of Education (1985-2002); Special Counsel, Borough of Paramus (1985-2002); Special Counsel, Township of Harding (2001); Receiver, Chancery Division, Superior Court (2000-2001); Discovery Master, Law Division, Superior Court (2000); Special Master, Chancery Division, New Jersey Superior Court (1999-2000); Trustee, Chancery Division, New Jersey Superior Court (1998-2000); Special Fiscal Agent, Chancery Division, Superior Court (1997); Chairman, Board of Trustees, Ramapo College (1979-1980); Board of Trustees, Ramapo College (1975-1980) **CW:** Editorial Board, New Jersey Law Journal (1991-Present); Contributor, Legal Articles, Professional Journals **AW:** Alfred C. Clapp Award, New Jersey Law Journal (2008); Frank Knox Memorial Fellowship (1961-1962) **MEM:** American Law Institute (1990-Present); Board of Directors, Land Use Law Section, New Jersey State Bar Association (1981-2002); Chairman, Land Use Law Section, New Jersey State Bar Association (1984-1985); Co-Chairman, Appellate Practices Study Committee, New Jersey State Bar Association (1977-1979); Litigation Section, American Bar Association **BAR:** U.S. District Court for the Southern District of New York (1983); U.S. District Court for the Eastern District of New York (1983); U.S. Court of Appeals for the Third Circuit (1978); Supreme Court of the U.S. (1970); U.S. District Court for the State of New Jersey (1963); New Jersey (1961) **MH:** Albert Nelson Marquis Lifetime Achievement Award **AS:** Mr. Mytelka attributes his success to hard work and good luck.

N. (NESRALLAH) TANNIS, WINSTON, "W.G." GEORGE, ESQ., T: Founding Executive Chair, Author-Artist, Publisher/Producer-Financier, Jurist-Mediator, Arbitrator, Consultant, Editor, Entrepreneur, Singer-Songwriter, Actor, Former Tennis Wear Runway Model & Director, Major Motion Picture Filmmaker **I:** Law and Legal Services **CN:** Winston Tannis International/WG & Beacon Groups **DOB:** 07/19/1966 **SC:** ON/Canada **PT:** Sana T. Nesrallah Tannis; George N. Tannis **MS:** Single **SPN:** Alexandra Cork (Divorced 1997) **ED:** LLD (Law & Sociology, ADR), Beacon Institute for Advanced Studies, Ottawa, ON, Canada (2000); Barrister at Law Degree, Ontario, Canada (1996); LLB, JD, Queens University Law School, Kingston, ON, Canada, Scholarship, Honors in Corporate Governance & Tax Policy (1994); BA in Philosophy & Political Science, Western University, London, ON, Canada, Gold Medallist, With Honors (1989); Coursework, Ivey School of Business & UWO Economics **C:** Founding Publisher/Contributing Editor, The Tannis Report (2020-Present); Founding Publisher/Contributing Editor, WG FASHION (2018-Present); Founding Publisher/Contributing Editor, The Neo-Republican (2015-Present); Founding Publisher/Contributing Editor, WG Magazine (2015-Present); Founding Publisher/Contributing Editor, New America Today & Tomorrow (2014-Present); Founder, EchoEternity Entertainment & Publishing (2014-Present); Founding Chair, Distinguished Professor, Beacon Institute for Advanced Studies (2008-Present); Founding Chair & Creator, Winston Tannis International, Ottawa, ON, Canada (2003-Present); Founder, The Beacon Letters/Les Lettres du Balise (2002-Present); Founding Director, Tannis & Associates International, Toronto-Ottawa, ON, Canada (1997-Present); Counsel, Davies Ward, Toronto, ON, Canada (1993-Present); Associate Counsel, Stikeman Elliott, Toronto, ON, Canada (1994-1997); Co-Founder, Queen's Annual Business Law Symposium (1993-1997); Law Clerk to Chief Justice Barry L. Strayer, Federal Court of Canada (Trial & Appeal Divisions), Court Martial Appeal Court of Canada, Supreme Court of Canada, Ottawa, ON, Canada (1994-1995); Corporate Development Director & Editor, Cast Communications/Ontario Design, Toronto, ON, Canada (1990-1991); Assistant Investment Advisor, HSBC Securities, Toronto, ON, Canada (1989-1990); Marketing, Fashion Show & Conference Planning Director, The Inn at Manitou, Toronto, ON, Canada (1987-1990); Student Police Officer, Residence Advisor, Tennis Professional, Western University, Ontario, ON, Canada (1987-1989); Tennis Professional, The Inn at Manitou, McKellar, Toronto, ON, Canada (1987-1988); Commentator, Writer, Glebe Report, Ottawa, ON, Canada (1984-1985); Restaurant Executive, Worker, McDonald's Restaurants, Pepper's, Ottawa, ON, Canada (1983-1985); Club Supervisor, Tennis Professional, St James Tennis Club, Ottawa, ON, Canada (1983-1985); Child Program Supervisor, Planner, St. James Community Center, Ottawa, ON, Canada (1983-1985); Kitchen, Cafeteria Assistant, Carleton University, Ottawa, ON, Canada (1970); Newspaper Distributor, Ottawa Journal, Ottawa Citizen, Globe and Mail (1970); Founder, The Winston George School of Advanced Business Studies; Global & Environmental Studies, Turbulence Equilibrium Centers; New Americana Studies Center; Tannis and Einstein Peace Studies Institute; The Winston George School of Phoenician Studies; The Nesrallah Institute of Mid-East and Arab Studies; Tannis & Machiavelli Ethics Institute; The Winston George Film & Music Analysis Center; Founding Managing Director, Creator, The WG Group - WG Design, WGT Capital Wealth Associates & Real Estate **CR:** Founding Chair & Counsel, Beacon Library of Heritage & Civilization (2012-Present); Winston George Foundation (2006-Present); Beacon Watch International (BWI) (1989-Present); Founding President, Queens Annual Business Law Symposium, Queen's University (1993-1998); Director and Contributing Editor In Chief, Queens Annual Business Law Symposium, Queen's University (1993-1998); Law Clerk, Chief Justice Barry L. Strayer, Federal Court of Canada, Court-Martial, Appeal Court of Canada at the Supreme Court of Canada; Tennis Professional (Tennis Canada, Manitou/Peter Burwash International); Co-Author, Works on Corporate Governance, Sen. Trevor Eyton, Stanley Hartt and Bill Braithwaite; Editor, Over 70 Works on Business, Securities, Finance, Corporate Restructurings & Insolvency Law, Public/Administrative Law & Banking Law; Law Clerk, Somalia Inquiry Cases, Chief Justice of Court Martial, Appeals Court of Canada; Co-Preparer, Canadian Military Law Manual for the Chief Justice **CIV:** Commander-in-Chief (De Jure Coup in Effect), New America (2005-Present); Chair & Counsel, Winston George Foundation (Global) & BWI - BeaconWatch International (2002-Present); Pro Bono Work, Tannis & Associates International (1990-Present); Founding Chair, Beacon Institute For Advanced Studies (2000); Secretary-Treasurer, Queens Law '94 (1994); Executive Member, UWO Entrepreneurs & Philosophy Club (1985-1989); President, Graduating Class, Glebe Collegiate Institute (1984-1985) **CW:** Founding Publisher & Author-Artist, The Neo-Republican (2015-Present); Founding Publisher & Author-Artist, WG FASHION and MAGAZINE (2015-Present); Founding Publisher & Author-Artist, New America Today & Tomorrow (2014-Present); Founding Publisher & Author-Artist, The Beacon Letters (2002-Present); Editor-in-Chief, Queens Annual Business Law Symposium, Queen's University (1993-1998); Contributor, Articles, Professional Journals; Pianist; Musician; Lyricist; Vocalist, Composer, Singer-Songwriter, Over 100 Songs, 10 Publicly Released Recordings and Music Videos; Co-Author, "Corporate Governance Reform"; Author, "The Pillars of Justice & Law"; Author, "The Columns of America, The Americas"; Author, "The Bridges To The Spirit"; Author, "Landmarks Ottawa: New York: Montreal: Toronto: Kingston: Sao Paulo"; Author, "WG Selections – Kate Upton"; Author, "WG Selections – Jennifer Aniston"; Author, "Trump as Unconstitutional: Legal Checks"; Author, "Media Checks in America"; Author, "Joining the Neo Republican Movement & Constituting New America Today & Tomorrow"; Author, "WG Magazine Special Edition"; Author, Over 500 Globally Published Articles on Politics, Finance, Philosophy, Diplomacy, Business, Peacemaking, International Affairs, Corporate Governance, Economics & Diplomacy, Arts & Culture; Creator, Artist, Over 200 Works of WG PedART Including Bedouin Hospitality, BeaconWatch, Najla My Love, Self Portrait: Rain, Recreation & Dreams, Autumn **AW:** International Recognition Award, Wikipedia (2005-Present); Platinum Pen for Professional & Scholastic Leadership, Beacon Institute for Advanced Studies (2000); Platinum Pen, Queens Annual Business Law

Symposium (1998); David Sabbath Tax Policy Award, Queens University Faculty of Law (1994); Queen's Law Scholarship (1991); National Silver Medal, Canadian Corporate Securities, Toronto, ON, Canada (1994); Offer of Admittance, Osgoode Hall Law School (1991); Gold Medal in Political Science & Philosophy, Western University, Ontario, Canada (1989); Offer of Admittance, Masters in Political Science, University of Toronto, UWO & York University (1989); Bilingual & Ontario Scholarship, Glebe Collegiate (1980-1985); Winner, Nominee, Athlete of the Year (1980, 1982); Listee, American Registry of Top Executives **MEM:** Former Lawyer Member, Law Society of Ontario (2018); Founder, WGT Real Estate & Finance; IMDB; St. James Tennis Club; Yahoo.ca; The Beacon Society **BAR:** Ontario Bar (1996) **MH:** Marquis Who's Who Top Professional **AS:** Mr. Tannis attributes his success to hard and intelligent work, commitment and inspiration. **B/I:** Mr. Tannis credits his passion for justice, equity, innovation, skilled leadership and compassion. **AV:** Athletics; Weightlifting; Travel; Reading; Architecture **THT:** Mr Tannis has stated, "I am not simply a political, business, economics and business scientist. I am a communications and leadership specialist and good teacher of ideas. There are no moral vacuums in this life."Mr. Tannis has worked as an environmental and finance lawyer, and consultant on environmental products and services; he possesses a doctorate in the sociology of law and conflict resolution. He offered to run as leader of the Conservative Party of Canada and for American president as leader of the New America Party (as created by him).

NADAL, RAFAEL, "RAFA", T: Professional Tennis Player **I:** Athletics **DOB:** 06/03/1986 **PB:** Manacor **SC:** Spain **PT:** Sebastián Nadal Homar; Ana María Parera **MS:** Married **SPN:** María Francisca (Xisca) Perelló (2019) **C:** Professional Tennis Player, ATP Tour (2001) **CR:** Spanish National Team, Davis Cup (2004, 2008-2009, 2011); Spanish National Team, Summer Olympic Games, Beijing, China (2008); Spanish National Team, Summer Olympic Games, Athens, Greece (2004) **CIV:** Founder, Fundación Rafa Nadal (2007-Present) **CW:** Co-Author, "Rafa" (2011) **AW:** Winner, Grand Slam Singles, U.S. Open (2010, 2013, 2017, 2019); ATP Player of the Year (2008, 2010, 2013, 2017, 2019); ITF World Champion (2008, 2010, 2017, 2019); Winner, Grand Slam Singles, French Open (2005-2008, 2010-2014, 2017-2019); Winner, Davis Cup (2004, 2008-2009, 2011, 2019); Gold Medal, Doubles, Men's Tennis, U.S. Olympics, Rio de Janeiro, Brazil (2016); Winner, Tour Finals (2010, 2013); Winner, Grand Slam Singles, Wimbledon (2008, 2010); Winner, Grand Slam Singles, Australian Open (2009); Gold Medal, Singles, Men's Tennis, U.S. Olympics, Beijing, China (2008); Semi-Finalist, Grand Slam Doubles, U.S. Open (2004)

NADER, RALPH, T: Advocate; Lawyer; Author **I:** Law and Legal Services **DOB:** 02/27/1934 **PB:** Winsted **SC:** CT/USA **PT:** Nathra Nader; Rose (Bouziane) Nader **ED:** LLB, Harvard University, with Distinction (1958); AB, Princeton University, Magna Cum Laude (1955) **C:** Founder, Center for Justice & Democracy (1998-Present); Founder, Center for Study of Responsive Law (1969-Present); Founder, Numerous Nonprofit Organizations (1969-Present); Founder, Center for Insurance Research (1995); Founder, Center for Women Policy Studies (1972); Founder, Director, Public Citizen, Washington, DC (1971-1980); Staff Member to Assistant Secretary, U.S. Department of Labor, Washington, DC (1964); Professor, History and Government, University of Hartford (1961-1963); Private Law Practice, Hartford, CT (1959-1961) **CR:** Candidate for Independent Party, U.S. Presidential Election (2004, 2008); Candidate for Green Party, U.S. Presidential Election (1996, 2000) **CIV:** Founder, American Museum of Tort Law, Winsted, CT (2015-Present) **MIL:** With, United States Army **CW:** Co-host, "Ralph Nader Radio Hour" (2014-Present); Author, "Animal Envy" (2016); Author, "Breaking Through Power: It's Easier Than We Think" (2016); Featured, Cover, Pacific Standard (2016); Author, "Return to Sender: Unanswered Letters to the President" (2015); Author, "Unstoppable: The Emerging Left-Right Alliance to Dismantle the Corporate State" (2014); Author, "The Seventeen Solutions: New Ideas for Our American Future" (2012); Author, "Getting Steamed to Overcome Corporatism: Build It Together to Win" (2011); Featured, "The Greatest Movie Ever Sold" (2011); Author, "Only the Super Rich Can Save Us!" (2009); Author, "The Seventeen Traditions: Lessons from an American Childhood" (2007); Featured, "An Unreasonable Man" (2006); Appearance, "Fun with Dick and Jane" (2005); Author, "In Pursuit of Justice: Collected Writing" (2004); Author, "The Good Fight: Declare Your Independence and Close the Democracy Gap" (2004); Author, "Civic Arousal" (2004); Author, "Crashing the Party: Taking on the Corporate Government in an Age of Surrender" (2002); Author, "The Ralph Nader Reader" (2000); Author, "No Contest: Corporate Lawyers and the Perversion of Justice in America" (1996); Co-author with Wesley J. Smith, "Collision Course: The Truth About Airline Safety" (1993); Author, "Winning the Insurance Game" (1990); Author, "The Big Boys" (1986); Co-editor, "Who's Poisoning America" (1981); Author, "The Lemon Book" (1980); Co-author with John Abbots, "Menace of Atomic Energy" (1979); Co-editor, "Verdicts on Lawyers" (1976); Author, "Taming the Giant Corporation" (1976); Author, "The Consumer and Corporate Accountability" (1973); Co-editor, "Corporate Power in America" (1973); Author, "You and Your Pension" (1973); Editor, "Whistle Blowing: The Report on the Conference on Professional Responsibility" (1972); Author, "Working on the System: A Manual for Citizen's Access to Federal Agencies" (1972); Author, "Action for a Change" (1972); Featured, Cover, Esquire (1971); Featured, Cover, TIME Magazine (1969); Featured, Cover, Newsweek (1968); Author, "Unsafe at Any Speed" (1965); Appearance, Television Shows Including "Saturday Night Live," "The Daily Show," "The O'Reilly Factor," "Real Time with Bill Maher," "Meet the Press," "Democracy Now!," "The Late Show with David Letterman," "Late Night with Conan O'Brien," and "Sesame Street" **AW:** Ghandi Peace Award, Promoting Enduring Peace (2016); Named to Automotive Hall of Fame (2016); Named One of the 100 Most Influential Americans, Britannica Guide to 100 Most Influential Americans (2008); Named One of the 100 Most Influential Americans, The Atlantic (2006); Named One of the 100 Most Influential Americans of the 20th Century, TIME Magazine (1999); Named One of the 100 Most Influential Americans of the 20th Century, Life Magazine (1990); Named One of the 10 Outstanding Young Men of the Year, U.S. Junior Chamber of Commerce (1967); Nieman Fellows Award (1965-1966) **MEM:** American Association for the Advancement of Science; ABA; The Phi Beta Kappa Society **BAR:** Supreme Court of the United States (1959); Massachusetts (1959); Connecticut (1958) **PA:** Independent **RE:** Maronite Catholic

NADLE, MARLENE MS., T: Reporter **I:** Media & Entertainment **DOB:** 10/20/1938 **PB:** Buffalo **SC:** NY/USA **PT:** Pincus Nadle; Beulah Nadle **MS:** Single **ED:** BA in English, University of Buffalo, New York (1961); Graduate Coursework in English, Columbia University; Coursework, Student Camp, Ghana, Africa **C:** Journalist, Village Voice (1963-1975); Staff Reporter, Newark News (1965-1966); Journalist, International Media Coverage **CR:** Seminar Participant, Transregional Center for Democratic Studies, New School, New York, NY (1990-Present); Director, COFY (Organization Supporting Independent Media in Former Yugoslavia) (1991-1993); Research Associate, Council of Hemispheric Affairs, Washington, DC (1973-1990) **CIV:** Chair, Housing Committee; Save the Hospital Committee **AW:** Fellowship, MacDowell Artists Colony (1977, 1978) **MEM:** American Society of Journalists and Authors **MH:** Albert Nelson Marquis Lifetime Achievement Award **AV:** Observing politics; Appreciating theater and films; Writing a memoir **PA:** Independent

NADLER, JERROLD, "JERRY" LEWIS, T: U.S. Representative, Lawyer **I:** Government Administration/Government Relations/Government Services **DOB:** 06/13/1947 **PB:** Brooklyn **SC:** NY/USA **PT:** Emanuel "Max" Nadler; Miriram (Schreiber) Nadler **MS:** Married **SPN:** Joyce L. Miller (1976) **CH:** Michael **ED:** JD, School of Law, Fordham University (1978); BA in Government, Columbia University (1969) **C:** U.S. Representative, New York's 10th Congressional District, United States Congress (2013-Present); Member, U.S. House Subcommittee on Construction (1997-2006); Ranking Minority Member, U.S. House Subcommittee on Commercial/Administrative Law (1997-2000); U.S. Representative, New York's Eighth Congressional District, United State Congress (1993-2013); Member, U.S. House Subcommittees on Surface Transportation, Water Resources and Environment (1993-1994); Member District 67, New York State Assembly (1983-1992); Member, District 69, New York State Assembly (1977-1982); Law Clerk, Morgan, Finnegan, Pine, Foley and Lee (1976); Democratic District Leader, 69th Assembly District Part A (1973-1977); Executive Director, Community Free Democrats (1972); Democratic Leader, 67th Assembly District Part C (1969-1971); Member, Community Planning Board Number 7, Manhattan, NY (1967-1971); Member, Committee on the Judiciary; Member, Committee on Transportation and Infrastructure **CR:** Chairman, Assembly Committee on Corps, Authorities and Commission (1991-1992); Chairman, Assembly Consumer Affairs and Protection Committee (1987-1990); Chairman, Assembly Committee on Ethics and Guidance (1985-1986); Chairman, Assembly Subcommittee on Mass Transit and Rail Freight (1979-1986) **CIV:** Founder, Chairman, West Side Peace Committee (1969-1971) **AW:** Legislator of the Year Award, International Association of Fire Fighters (2003); Distinguished Service Award, Coalition on Domestic Violence (1989); Recognition Award, New York State Nurses Association (1982); Assembly Member of the Year, National Organization for Women, New York Chapter (1980); Honor Roll, New York Civil Liberties Union; Pulitzer Scholar, Columbia University **MEM:** Board of Directors, Americans for Democratic Action; Vice President, Americans for Democratic Action; National Organization for Women; NAACP; New York State Bar Association; New York Civil Liberties Union; Citizens Union; League of Conservation Voters; New Democrat Coalition **PA:** Democrat

NAFZIGER, RALPH H., PHD, T: Research Chemist, Research Supervisor **I:** Sciences **DOB:** 08/09/1937 **PB:** Minneapolis **SC:** MN/USA **PT:** Ralph Otto Nafziger; Charlotte Monona (Hamilton) Nafziger **ED:** PhD, Pennsylvania State University (1966); BS, University of Wisconsin (1960) **CT:** Registered Geologist, Oregon **C:** Consultant (1996-2000); Retired (1996); Research Supervisor, U.S. Bureau Mines, Albany, OR (1981-1996); Research Supervisor, U.S. Bureau Mines, Minneapolis, MN (1979-1981); Research Chemist, U.S.

Bureau Mines, Albany, OR (1967-1979); Research Associate, Pennsylvania State University, University Park, PA (1966-1967); Field Assistant, U.S. Geological Survey, Denver, CO (1963) **CR:** Key Reader, Metallurgical Transactions, Pittsburgh, PA (1980-Present) **CIV:** Board of Directors, President, Albany Concert Band (1970-Present); Western Oregon State College Summer Band, Monmouth, OR (1975-1994); Salem Concert Band (1981-1983); Salem Pops Orchestra (1969-1979); North Albany Sewer District Board; Volunteer, American Red Cross; Volunteer, United Way; Minerals, Metals, and Materials Society **MIL:** U.S. Army Medical Service Corps (1960) **CW:** Patentee, Four U.S. Patents; Author, 67 Professional Publications; Speaker, 37 Professional Formal Presentations; Contributor, Articles, Professional Journals **AW:** Outstanding Performance Award, U.S. Bureau Mines (1973, 1977, 1984-1986); U.S. Department of Interior Meritorious Service Award; Award of Scientific Merit, American Foundry Society; Best Paper, American Foundry Society **MEM:** Physical Chemistry Committee, Copper, Nickel, Cobalt, Precious Metals Committee, Vice Chairman, American Society of Metals (1980-Present); Fuels Committee, Charge Materials Committee, Cupola Committee, American Foundry Society (1980-Present); Abstractor, Mineralogical Society America (1977-Present); Vice President-Treasurer, Chemeketans Club (1975-1978); Vice President, President Sigma Xi (1972-1973); Desert Trail Association; Geological Society of America; Oregon Academy of Science; Geological Society of Oregon Country; International Horn Society; Mazamas Club; Obsidians Club; Buick Club of America; Nine Philatelic Society; Sierra Club; Member, Numerous Professional Committees; Chair, Several Organizations in Field **MH:** Albert Nelson Marquis Lifetime Achievement Award **B/I:** Mr. Nafziger became involved in his profession because, in high school, he discovered his love for chemistry. When combined with his love for nature, geology became the perfect field for Mr. Nafziger to dedicate himself. He later earned a PhD in geochemistry, the combination of his favorite sciences. **AV:** Taking photos; Astronomy; Playing sports; Appreciating automobiles; Appreciating music; Philately; Hiking; Traveling

NAKAMURA, SHUJI, T: Professor of Engineering **I:** Education/Educational Services **CN:** University of California, Santa Barbara **DOB:** 05/22/1954 **PB:** Ikata **SC:** Ehime/Japan **ED:** Honorary DEng, Hong Kong University of Science and Technology (2008); DEng, University of Tokushima, Japan (1994); MEE, University of Tokushima, Japan (1979); BEE, University of Tokushima, Japan (1977) **C:** CREE Distinguished Professor, Materials, University of California, Santa Barbara (2008-Present); Professor of Materials, Electrical and Computer Engineering Department, University of California, Santa Barbara (1999-2008); Senior Researcher, Department of Research and Development, Nichia Chemical Industry, Ltd. (Now Nichia Corporation) (1993-1999); Group Head, Research and Development Second Section, Nichia Chemical Industry, Ltd. (Now Nichia Corporation) (1989-1993); Group Head, Research and Development First Section, Nichia Chemical Industry, Ltd. (Now Nichia Corporation) (1985-1988); Research and Development Staff, Nichia Chemical Industry, Ltd. (Now Nichia Corporation) (1979-1984); Director, Solid State Lighting & Display Center, University of California, Santa Barbara **CR:** Visiting Research Associate, Electronic Engineering, University of Florida (1988-1989) **CW:** Member, Editorial Board, Applied Physics Society (1998-2000); Author, Several Scientific Papers **AW:** Zayed Future Energy Prize (2018); Mountbatten Medal (2017); Draper Prize, National Academy of Sciences (2015); Named to

National Inventors Hall of Fame (2015); Co-recipient Nobel Prize in Physics, Royal Swedish Academy of Sciences (2014); Named Inventor of the Year, Silicon Valley Intellectual Property Law Association (2012); Technological & Engineering Emmy Award, National Academy of Television, Arts & Sciences (2012); Harvey Prize, Technion Israeli Institute of Technology (2009); Prince of Asturias Prize for Technical and Scientific Research (2008); Czochralski Award (2007); Millennium Technology Prize for Inventions in Light and Laser Technology, Millennium Prize Foundation (2006); Benjamin Franklin Medal in Engineering, Franklin Institute (2002); Named CREE Professor in Solid State Light and Display Endowed Chair (2001); LEOS Distinguished Lecturer Award (2001); OSA Nick Holonyak Jr. Award, The Optical Society (2001); Asahi Award (2001); Crystal Growth and Crystal Technology Award (2000); Honda Award (2000); Carl Zeiss Research Award (2000); Takayanagi Award (2000); Julius-Springer Prize for Applied Physics (1999); British Rank Prize (1998); Jack A. Morton Award, IEEE (1998); Innovation in Real Materials Award (1998); C&C Award (1998); Best Paper Award, Japanese Applied Physics Society (1994, 1997); Society Medal Award, Materials Research Society (1997); Okochi Memorial Award (1997); Engineering Award, Nikkei Business Publications (1994, 1996); Nishina Memorial Award (1996); Engineering Achievement Award, IEEE Lasers and Electro-Optics Society (1996); Special Recognition Award, Society for Information Display (SID) (1996); Sakurai Award (1995) **MEM:** National Academy of Sciences

NAPOLITANO, GRACIELA, "GRACE" FLORES, T: U.S. Representative from California **I:** Government Administration/Government Relations/Government Services **DOB:** 12/04/1936 **PB:** Brownsville **SC:** TX/USA **PT:** Miguel Flores; Maria Alicia (Ledezma) Flores **MS:** Married **SPN:** Frank Napolitano (1982) **CH:** Yolando; Fred; Edward; Michael; Cynthia **ED:** Coursework, Texas Southmost College; Coursework, Los Angeles Trade Technical College; Coursework, Cerritos College **C:** Member, U.S. House of Representatives from California's 32nd Congressional District, United States Congress (2013-Present); U.S. House of Representatives from California's 38th Congressional District, United States Congress (2003-2013); U.S. House of Representatives from California's 34th Congressional District, United States Congress, Washington, DC (1999-2003); California State Assembly (1993-1998); City Councilwoman, City of Norwalk, CA (1986-1992); Mayor, City of Norwalk, CA (1989-1990); Committee on Financial Services; Committee on Foreign Affairs **CIV:** Active Member, Cerritos College Foundation **MEM:** US/Mexico Sister Cities Association; Veterans of Foreign Wars; Lions Club **PA:** Democrat **RE:** Roman Catholic

NARVAEZ, BERNICE MARIE, T: Principal Systems Engineer **I:** Engineering **CN:** Raytheon **DOB:** 06/07/1956 **PB:** Houston **SC:** TX/USA **PT:** Ella Mae Williams **MS:** Married **SPN:** Raymond Narvaez (1999) **CH:** Alexis Appollonia Robinson **ED:** Master of Science in Management Information Systems, George Washington University (1994); Bachelor of Science in Mechanical Engineering, Massachusetts Institute of Technology (1978) **CT:** Information Systems Security Professional, International Information System Security Certification Consortium; Capability Maturity Model Integration, Carnegie Melon Software Engineering Institute; Agile Certifications; Assisted Living Manager License; CPR; First Aid; Emergency/Disaster; Medication Technician; Continuing Education Certificate, Cryptology; Continuing Education Certificate, Project Management; Continuing Education Cer-

tificate, Cloud Technology; Continuing Education Certificate, Cloud Security; Continuing Education Certificate, Web Development **C:** Principal Systems Engineer, Raytheon, McLean, VA (2017-Present); IT Program Manager, Raytheon, Reston, VA (2015-2017); Principal Systems Engineering, Raytheon, Annapolis Junction, MD (2015-2017); Lead Senior Systems Engineer, Software Development Department, Praxis Engineering Technologies, Annapolis Junction, MD (2009-2015); Senior Business Process Consultant II, SAIC, Columbia, MD (2004-2006); Business Process Re-Engineering Specialist, SAIC, Baltimore, MD (2000-2004); Senior Consultant, Comsys Technical Services, Arlington, VA (1999-2000); Technical Staff, IBM Global Services, Tampa, FL (1997-1999); Senior Consultant, Comsys Technical Services, Arlington, VA (1994-1997); System Analyst, MCI Communication, Arlington, VA (1990-1994); Computer Programmer, Ciber Consultants/MCI, Arlington, McLean, State of Virginia (1989-1990); Computer Programmer, University of Texas, Houston, TX (1985-1989); Engineer, Shell Oil, Houston, TX and Ventura, CA (1978-1981) **CR:** President, Golden Sunset Services (2010); President, Co-Founder, Online Retail Store, GS4LESS; President, Co-Founder, Online Retail Store, DealHawks **CIV:** International Council Systems Engineering (2003-2006); Volunteer, Industry Advisor Board, Public Schools; Process Improvement Committee, Science Applications International Corporation; Watchtower Society; Habitat for Humanity International; Contributor, MIT Alumni Fund **MH:** Albert Nelson Marquis Lifetime Achievement Award; Marquis Who's Who Top Professional **AS:** Ms. Narvaez is as successful as she is because of the people who believed in her. She has always wondered how things work, and she has always liked technology. **B/I:** Ms. Narvaez became involved in her profession after having taken care of her grandmother, who passed of cancer, which led to her interest in senior care. As a child, she often wondered how things work, but as she became older she aspired to become more impactful, which led to her interest in facility management. **AV:** Tennis; Piano; Art collecting; Traveling; Grandparenting; Senior care **RE:** Christian

NASH, DONALD R., PHD, T: Immunologist, Bacteriologist (Retired) **I:** Sciences **DOB:** 11/15/1938 **PB:** Pittsfield **SC:** MA/USA **PT:** Joseph Nash; Bernadette K. (Valley) Nash **MS:** Married **SPN:** Mary B. Campbell (06/23/1963) **CH:** Brendon A. **ED:** PhD, University of North Carolina (1967); MS, Boston College (1963); BA, American International College (1961) **C:** Retired (1999); Associate Director, Center of Pulmonary Infectious Disease Control, The University of Texas Health Science Center at Tyler, Texas (1992-1999); Professor, The University of Texas Health Science Center at Tyler (1992-1999); Director, Hybridoma Core, The University of Texas Health Science Center at Tyler (1985-1992); Associate Professor, The University of Texas Health Science Center at Tyler (1972-1992); Senior Research Scientist, World Health Organization (WHO), Lausanne, Switzerland (1971-1972); Associate Professor, John A. Burns School of Medicine University of Hawai'i at Manoa, Honolulu, Hawaii (1970-1971); Postdoctoral Fellow, University of Louvain, Belgium (1968-1970); Postdoctoral Fellow, The University of North Carolina at Chapel Hill (1967-1968) **CR:** Adjunct Professor, The University of Texas Health Science Center at Tyler (1975-Present) **MH:** Albert Nelson Marquis Lifetime Achievement Award; Marquis Who's Who Top Professional **B/I:** Dr. Nash became involved in his profession because he found the process of immunology very exciting and it was a lot of work to get done to find out what was going on. At the time in the late 60s, immunology was an important subject that had crept back from the 30s. He wanted to proceed and find out more about it and how it affected people.

NASH, SEYMOUR C., MD, FACS, T: Urological Surgeon **I:** Medicine & Health Care **DOB:** 11/18/1931 **PB:** New York **SC:** NY/USA **PT:** Annette (Gersten) Cook **MS:** Widowed **SPN:** Sally Anne Kugler, (08/06/1958, Deceased 2015) **CH:** Allison; Elizabeth; Gregory **ED:** Surgical Resident, Yale Medical Center, New Haven, CT (1957-1959); Surgical Intern, Yale Medical Center, New Haven, CT (1956-1957); MD, Washington University of St. Louis (1956); BS in Biology, Chemistry, Political Science, University of Florida (1952) **CT:** Diplomate, American Board of Urology; Fellow of American College of Surgeons **C:** Retired; Private Practice in Urology, Miami Beach, FL (1964-2014); Chairman, Department of Urology, Mount Sinai Hospital, Miami Beach, FL (1989-2014); Associate Clinical Professor, University of Miami Medical School (1964-1994); Urology Resident, Georgetown University Hospital, Washington DC (1961-1964); Clinical Associate, National Cancer Institute, Bethesda, MD (1959-1961) **CR:** Mentor, Residency Program, Mount Sinai **CIV:** Chairman, Hosted Numerous Community Lectors on Prostate Cancer; Medical Director, Fundraiser, Cancer Lifeline, Mount Sinai Hospital (Mount Sinai Medical Center); Lifelong Medical Trustee, Mount Sinai Hospital **MIL:** Captain, U.S. Public Health Service (1959-1961) **CW:** Co-author, "Prostate Cancer Making Survival Decisions" (1994); Speaker, Delivered Paper, Sloan Kettering Memorial Hospital, "Cancer Cells in Postoperative Wound Drainage" (1964); Contributor, Articles, Medical Journals; Wrote Six Papers, Published Five Papers, Cancer Institute; Pathological Features of Cryosurgery for Cancer Prostate **AW:** Fellow, American College of Surgeons; American Medical Association; American Association of Clinical Urologists; Florida Medical Association; Dade County Medical Association; Phi Beta Kappa; Washington University, St. Louis, AOA Honor Society **MH:** Albert Nelson Marquis Lifetime Achievement Award **B/I:** Dr. Nash always wanted to be a surgeon, even when he was in medical school. During the summers he would volunteer at a hospital in Pennsylvania to work with a surgeon. Dr. Nash had an uncle who was a dentist, originally that is what he wanted to do but he eventually decided being a surgeon was a better fit. In addition, he became involved in urology because he was in the surgical training program at Yale in New Haven and then he went to the Cancer Institute in Bethesda for two years doing research and surgery. He liked doing diagnostic work, doing surgery, and treating patients, and that encouraged him to be an urologist. **AV:** Tennis; Travel, Watching sports; Concerts; Plays; Meeting people in Miami; Basketball; Reading nonfiction historical books; Former golf and tennis player; Family time **PA:** Republican **RE:** Jewish

NASH, WILLIAM D., T: Chief Executive Officer, President **I:** Automotive **CN:** Carmax Inc. **ED:** Bachelor in Business Accounting, James Madison University **C:** President, Chief Executive Officer, CarMax, Inc., CarMax Business Services, LLC (2016-Present); Executive Vice President, CarMax, Inc., CarMax Business Services, LLC (2012-2016); Senior Vice President, Merchandising, CarMax, Inc., CarMax Business Services, LLC (2010-2011); Vice President, Merchandising, CarMax, Inc., CarMax Business Services, LLC (2007-2010); Auction Manager, CarMax, Inc., CarMax Business Services, LLC (1997); Auction Director, Assistant Vice President, Auction Services and Vice President,

Auction Services, CarMax, Inc., CarMax Business Services, LLC; Various Positions, Public Accounting, Circuit City, Circuit City Corporation, Inc.

NASHIF, TAYSIR N., T: Researcher, Writer **I:** Research **DOB:** 03/22/1940 **PB:** Tayyiba **SC:** Jerusalem/Israel **PT:** Najm A. Nashif; Aisha A. Nashif **MS:** Married **SPN:** Mayyada I. Nashif (04/15/1968) **CH:** Fawz; Fayruz; Hanin **ED:** PhD in Political Science, Binghamton University State University of New York (1974); MA in Islamic Studies, University of Toronto (1969); MA in International Relations, Hebrew University of Jerusalem (1968); BA in Political Science/Arabic Language & Literature, Hebrew University of Jerusalem (1964) **C:** Chief, Arabic Verbatim Reporting Section, United Nations, New York, NY (1996-2002); Reviser, Editor, United Nations, New York, NY (1982-1996); Political Affairs Officer, United Nations, New York, NY (1980-1981); Professor, United Nations, New York, NY (1976-1977); Professor, University of Oran, Algeria (1974-1976) **CW:** Author, "The Arabs and the World in the Next Century" (1999); Author, "Nuclear Weapons in Israel" (1996); Author, "Nuclear Warfare in the Middle East" (1984); Author, "The Palestine Arab and Jewish Political Leaderships" (1979); Author, "Government, the Intellectual, and Society in the Third World"; Contributor, Articles on Strategic, Political, and Cultural Issues, Professional Journals **AW:** Grantee, State University of New York (1971-1973) **MEM:** Association of Third World Studies, Inc.; American Translators Association; Middle East Studies Association; American Political Science Association **MH:** Albert Nelson Marquis Lifetime Achievement Award **AV:** Sea cruising; Fishing; Mountain climbing

NASSETTA, CHRISTOPHER J., T: President, Chief Executive Officer **I:** Leisure, Travel & Tourism **CN:** Hilton **MS:** Married **SPN:** Paige Nassetta **CH:** Six Children **ED:** BS in Finance, University of Virginia (1984) **C:** Chairman, World Travel & Tourism Council (2018-Present); President, Chief Executive Officer, Hilton Worldwide Holdings Inc., Beverly Hills, CA (2007-Present); President, Chief Executive Officer, Host Hotels & Resorts Inc., Bethesda, MD (2000-2007); Chief Operating Officer, Host Hotels & Resorts Inc. (1997-2000); Executive Vice President, Host Hotels & Resorts Inc. (1995-1997); Co-Founder, President, Bailey Realty Corp. (1991-1995); Various Positions Including Chief Development Officer, Oliver Carr Co. (1984-1991) **CR:** Board of Directors, Hilton Worldwide Holdings inc. (2007-Present); Board of Directors, Costar Group Inc. (2002-Present); Host, Hotels & Resorts Inc. (1999-2007); Trustee, Prime Group Realty Trust (1997-2005) **CIV:** Vice Chairman, Corporate Fund, John F. Kennedy Center for the Performing Arts; Federal City Council, Board of Directors, The Real Estate Roundtable; Board of Directors, Wolf Trap Foundation for the Performing Arts; Advisory Board, University of Virginia McIntire School of Commerce **AW:** Cornell Hospitality Icon of the Industry Award, Cornell University School of Hotel Administration (2019); Hospitality Property Executive of the Year, Commercial Property Executive (2016); Hospitality Industry Hall of Honor, University of Houston Conrad N. Hilton College of Hotel and Restaurant Management (2015); Stephen W. Brener Silver Plate Award, Lodging Hospitality Marketing (2015); Albert E. Koehl Award for Lifetime Achievement in Hospitality Marketing, Hospitality Sales and Marketing Association International (2014); CEO of the Year, Washington Business Journal (2014); Corporate Hotelier of the World, HOTELS Magazine (2014); Virginia Business Person of the Year, Virginia Business Magazine (2014); International Hotelier of the Year, HVS/China Hotel Investment Conference Awards (2011)

MEM: Arlington Free Clinic; Independent Director, CoStar Group; Economic Club of Washington, DC; Federal City Council; Former Chairman, Real Estate Roundtable; Vice Chairman, Corporate Fund, John F. Kennedy Center for the Performing Arts; Chairman, World Travel and Tourism Council

NATALICIO, DIANA SIEDHOFF, PHD, T: President Emeritus **I:** Education/Educational Services **CN:** The University of Texas at El Paso **DOB:** 08/25/1939 **PB:** St. Louis **SC:** MO/USA **PT:** William Siedhoff; Eleanor Jo (Biermann) Siedhoff **ED:** Honorary LHD, Georgetown University (2011); Honorary PhD, Smith College (2001); PhD in Linguistics, The University of Texas at Austin (1969); MA in Portuguese Language, The University of Texas at Austin (1964); BS in Spanish, St. Louis University, Summa Cum Laude (1961); Honorary PhD, Universidad Autonoma de Nuevo Leon **C:** President Emeritus, The University of Texas at El Paso, Texas (2019-Present); President, The University of Texas at El Paso, Texas (1988-2019); Vice President of Academy Affairs, The University of Texas at El Paso (1984-1988); Dean, College of Liberal Arts, The University of Texas at El Paso (1980-1984); Acting Dean, College of Liberal Arts, The University of Texas at El Paso (1979-1980); Associate Dean, College Liberal Arts, The University of Texas at El Paso (1977-1979); Chairman, Department of Modern Languages, The University of Texas at El Paso (1973-1977) **CR:** Board of Directors, U.S.-Mexico Commission for Educational and Cultural Exchange (1994-Present); Board of Directors, National Action Council for Minorities in Engineering (1993-Present); Board Chair, American Association for Higher Education (1995-1996); Member, National Science Board (1994-2006); Member, Advisory Council, NASA (1994-1996); Board Member, Fund for Improvement of Post-Secondary Education (1993-1997); Board of Directors, Fogarty International Center, National Institutes of Health (1993-1996); Member, Presidential Advisory Commission on Educational Excellence for Hispanic Americans (1991); Chairman, Federal Reserve Board of Dallas, El Paso Branch, Texas (1989); Board of Directors, Federal Reserve Board of Dallas, El Paso Branch, Texas; Board of Directors, Sandia Corporation; Board of Directors, Trinity Industries, Inc. **CIV:** Chairperson, ORAU HBCU/MEI Council (1991-1993); Chairman, Quality Education for Minorities Network in Mathematics, Science and Engineering (1991-1992); Board of Directors, United Way of El Paso (1990-1993); Chairman, Needs Survey Committee, United Way of El Paso (1990-1991); Chairperson, Class 12, Leadership El Paso (1989-1990); Chairman, Education Division, United Way of El Paso (1989); Member, Advisory Council, Class 12, Leadership El Paso (1987-1990); Participant, Class 12, Leadership El Paso (1980-1981); Member, Historically Black Colleges and Universities/Minority Institutions Consortium on Environmental Technologies; Trustee, Rockefeller Foundation; Board Member, American Council on Education; Board of Directors, Hispanic Scholarship Fund; Principal Investigator, National Science Foundation **CW:** Co-Author, "Sounds of Children" (1977); Contributor, Articles to Professional Journals **AW:** One of the Top 50 World Leaders, Fortune Magazine (2017); One of the 100 Most Influential People in the World, Time Magazine (2016); Carnegie Corporation of New York Academic Leadership Award (2015); Hesburgh Award, TIAA-CREF (2013); Order of the Aztec Eagle (2011); Distinguished Alumnus Award, The University of Texas at Austin (2006); Inductee, Texas Women's Hall of Fame (1998); Harold W. McGraw Junior Prize in Education (1997); Torch of Liberty Award, Anti-Defamation League of B'nai B'rith (Now Anti-Defamation League) (1991); Conquistador Award, City of El

Paso, TX (1990); Humanitarian Award, National Conference of Christians and Jews, El Paso Chapter, TX (1990); Inductee, El Paso Women's Hall of Fame (1990); Hispanic Heritage Award in Science, Technology, Engineering and Math **MEM:** Philosophical Society of Texas **AV:** Hiking; Bicycling; Skiing; Skating

NATION, DAVID, T: Computer Scientist (Retired), Sculptor **I:** Technology **DOB:** 08/23/1947 **PB:** Waterloo **SC:** IA/USA **PT:** Harold Stanley Nation; Martha Elizabeth (Loonan) Nation **MS:** Married **SPN:** Rebecca L. Johnson (10/27/1979); Jean Lee Bielefeldt (08/09/1969, Divorced 1979) **CH:** Justin David **ED:** Studied at Maryland Institute College of Art, Baltimore, MD (1996); MS, Johns Hopkins University, Baltimore, MD (1979); BS in Computer Science, Iowa State University, Ames, IA (1970) **C:** Systems Engineer, Contractor, MCI Information Systems (2004-2015); Computer scientist, U.S. Government, Washington, DC (1975-2001) **CIV:** Paint Branch Unitarian Universalist Church, Adelphi, MD (2013-Present); Treasurer, Emmanuel United Methodist Church, Dorsey, MD (1987-2006) **MIL:** Staff Sergeant, U.S. Air Force (1970-1973) **CW:** Solo Show, "Dave Nation's Art Gallery" (1995-Present); Sculpture in Resident Art Shows at Riderwood Village, Calverton, MD (2013-2018); Solo Show, "Bay Country Art Guild Member Show" (2008, 2000); Author, Mapping Software, Pattern Classification Software, Web Software, Information Visualization Software; Sculptor **MEM:** SAG-AFTRA (Formerly the Screen Actors Guild) (2000-Present); President, Riderwood Genealogy Club (2015) **MH:** Marquis Who's Who Top Professional **B/I:** Mr. Nation became involved in his profession after studying architecture, math, art, and psychology in college. He later transferred to Iowa State University and was the first graduating class in computer science. Mr. Nation became interested in art in high school during an art course. He started making sculptures with clay and fire, and just progressed from there. Mr. Nation was an art major for a semester at the University of Iowa, and has also taken other sculpture classes at community colleges, with his most formal one at Maryland Institute College of Art in Baltimore, Maryland, in 1996. **AV:** Sculpting; Birdwatching; Genealogy; Photography; Community Theater **PA:** Democrat **RE:** Unitarian Universalist

NAVRATILOVA, MARTINA, T: Former Professional Tennis Player **I:** Athletics **DOB:** 10/18/1956 **PB:** Prague **SC:** Czech Republic **PT:** Miroslav Navratil; Jana Navratilova **MS:** Married **SPN:** Julia Lemigova (12/15/2014) **ED:** Honorary Doctorate, The George Washington University (1996); Coursework, Schools, Czech Republic **C:** Member, Coaching Staff of Agnieszka Radwanska (2014-2015); Professional Tennis Player (1973-1994, 2003-2006); Tennis Commentator, Broadcaster, HBO Sports (1995-1999) **CR:** Member, World Team Tennis (2009); Member, U.S. Fed Cup Team (1982, 1986, 1989, 1995, 2003); Member, Czech Federal Cup Team (1975) **CIV:** Co-founder, Rainbow Card; Health and Fitness Ambassador, AARP **CW:** Columnist; Contestant, "Dancing with the Stars" (2012); Author, "Shape Your Self: My 6-Step Diet and Fitness Plan to Achieve the Best Shape of Your Life" (2006); Co-author with Liz Nickles, "Killer Instinct" (1997); Co-author with Liz Nickles, "Breaking Point" (1996); Co-author with Liz Nickles, "The Total Zone" (1995); Co-author with George Vecsey, "Martina" (1985); Featured, "Unmatched"; Appearance, Television Shows Including "Hart to Hart," "Portlandia," and "The Politician" **AW:** Named to National Gay and Lesbian Sports Hall of Fame (2013); Named One of the 30 Legends of Women's Tennis: Past, Present and Future, TIME Magazine (2011); Eugene L. Scott Award, International

Tennis Hall of Fame (2010); Winner, Mixed Doubles, U.S. Open (1987, 2006); Czech Sport Legend Award (2006); Winner, Mixed Doubles, Wimbledon (1985, 1993, 1995, 2003); Winner, Mixed Doubles, Australian Open (2003); BBC Lifetime Achievement Award (2003); BBC Sports Personality of the Year Lifetime Achievement Award (2003); Named to International Tennis Hall of Fame (2000); National Equality Award, Human Rights Campaign (2000); Martina Navratilova Day Proclaimed, City of Chicago, IL (1992); Winner, Virginia Slims Championship (1978, 1983-1986, 1991); Winner, Singles, Wimbledon (1978, 1979, 1982-1987, 1990); Winner, Doubles, U.S. Open (1977, 1978, 1980, 1983, 1984, 1987, 1990); Co-winner with Pam Shriver, Roland Garros (1985, 1987, 1989); Co-winner with Pam Shriver, Doubles, Australian Open (1982, 1984, 1985, 1987-1989); Winner, Singles, U.S. Open (1983, 1984, 1986, 1987); Co-winner with Gabriela Sabatini, Italian Open (1987); Winner, Triple Crown, U.S. Open (1987); Flo Hyman Award, Women's Sports Foundation (1987); Winner, Women's Doubles, Wimbledon (1976, 1979, 1981-1984, 1986); Winner, Singles, Australian Open (1981, 1983, 1985); Winner, Singles, French Open (1982, 1984); Winner, Grand Slam (1983); Named Honorary Citizen, City of Dallas, Texas (1983); Named Female Athlete of the Year, The Associated Press (1983); International Tennis Federation World Champion (1979, 1982-1986); Named WTA Player of Year (1978-1979, 1982-1986); Named Sportswoman of the Year, Women's Sports Foundation (1982-1984); Co-winner with Pam Shriver, COREL WTA Tour Doubles Team of the Year (1981-1989); Co-winner with Betsy Nagelsen, Doubles, Australian Open (1980); Winner, Czechoslovak National Singles (1972-1974); Named Female Athlete of the Decade (1980s), National Sports Review, United Press International, and The Associated Press; Numerous Awards **MEM:** President, Women's Tennis Association Tour Players Association (Now WTA Tour, Inc. (1979-1980, 1983-1984, 1994-1995); President, Women's Tennis Association (WTA Tour, Inc.); Director, Executive Committee, Women's Tennis Association (WTA Tour, Inc.)

NAZAIRE, MICHEL HARRY, T: Surgeon **I:** Medicine & Health Care **DOB:** 09/29/1939 **PB:** Jérémie **SC:** Haiti **PT:** Joseph Nazaire; Hermance Nazaire **MS:** Divorced **SPN:** Nicole Lamarque (12/28/1968, Divorced) **CH:** Hanick; Carline **ED:** MD in Medicine and Pharmacology, State University of Haiti (1966); BS, Port-Au-Prince, Haiti (1959) **C:** Physician, Pneumo-Physiology, Port-Au-Prince, Haiti (1966-2016); Fellow, Klinik Havelhohe and Heckeshorn, Berlin (1989-1991); Attending Physician, Sanitarium, Port-Au-Prince, Haiti (1976-1991); Fellow, Klinik Havelhohe and Heckeshorn, Berlin (1969-1970); Physician, Pneumology (1966-1968); Resident Physician, Sanitarium, Port-Au-Prince, Haiti (1966-1968); Intern, State University Hospital, Port-Au-Prince, Haiti (1965-1966) **CR:** Deputy Member, International Parliament for Safety and Peace; Envoy-at-Large, International State Parliament; Global Environmental Technological Network, World Health Organization **CW:** Contributor, Articles, Professional Journals **AW:** Physician's Recognition Award, American Medical Association (2002, 2005); Inductee, American Medical Association (2002) **MEM:** Fellow, International Society for Respiratory Protection; American College of Chest Physicians; American Medical Association; American Public Health Association; American Conference Governmental Industrial Hygienists; International Union Against Tuberculosis; International Platform Association; Physicians for Social Responsibility; European Respiratory Society **MH:** Albert Nelson Marquis Lifetime Achievement Award **RE:** Catholic

NEAL, RICHARD EDMUND, T: U.S. Representatives **I:** Government Administration/Government Relations/Government Services **DOB:** 02/14/1949 **PB:** Worcester **SC:** MA/USA **PT:** Edmund J. Neal; Mary H. (Garvey) Neal **MS:** Married **SPN:** Maureen (Conway) Neal (12/20/1975) **CH:** Rory Christopher; Brendan Conway; Maura Katherine; Sean Richard **ED:** Postgraduate Coursework, University of Massachusetts Amherst, MA (1982); MPA, University of Hartford, CT (1976); BS, American International College, Springfield, MA (1972); Coursework, Holyoke Community College **C:** Chair, House Ways and Means Committee (2019-Present); Member, House Ways and Means Committee (2013-2019); U.S. Representative, Massachusetts' First Congressional District, United States Congress (2013-Present); U.S. Representative, Massachusetts' Second Congressional District, United States Congress (1989-2013); Mayor, City of Springfield, MA (1984-1988); City Councilman, City of Springfield, MA (1978-1983); Administrative Aide to Mayor, City of Springfield, MA (1973-1978) **CR:** Lecturer in Business and Government, Western New England University, Springfield, MA (1979-1982); Project Director, Springfield Technical Community College, MA (1979-1982); Lecturer in History and Politics, Springfield Technical Community College, MA (1973-1983); Instructor, University of Massachusetts Amherst; Instructor, Cathedral High School, Springfield, MA **CIV:** Trustee, The American National Red Cross; Trustee, YMCA, Springfield, MA; Trustee, Springfield Library and Museums Association **AW:** International Leadership Award, American Ireland Fund (2002); Alumni Achievement Award, American International College Alumni Association (1980); Outstanding Young Men in America, US Junior Chamber of Commerce, Springfield, MA; John F. Kennedy Award, Holyoke, MA; Ambassador's Award, Holyoke, MA; Award, St. Patrick's Day Committee **MEM:** President, Alumni Association, American International College (1980); Springfield Library and Museums Association; Valley Press Club/John Boyle O'Reilly Club, Springfield, MA **PA:** Democrat **RE:** Roman Catholic

NEECE, OLIVIA H., T: Investment Company Executive, Consultant **I:** Financial Services **CN:** Neece Associates **DOB:** 01/03/1948 **PB:** Los Angeles **SC:** CA/USA **PT:** Robert Ernst; Beatrice Pearl Ernst **MS:** Married **SPN:** Anthony Ray Neece (03/20/1976); Huntley Lee Bluestein (1967, Divorced 1974) **CH:** Melissa Dawn; Brendon Wade **ED:** Postgraduate Coursework, Peter F. Drucker Institute of Management, Claremont Graduate University (1998-2004); MBA, University of California, Los Angeles (1993); BSBA, University of Southern California (1990) **CT:** Certified Interior Designer, California Council for Interior Design, University of California, Los Angeles (1975); Licensed General Contractor, Real Estate Broker, State of California (1972) **C:** Board of Directors, The Ernst Group (2005-Present); President, Neece Associates (2003-Present); Treasurer-secretary, EON Corporation, Los Angeles, CA (1980-Present); Director of Operations, The Ernst Group, Los Angeles, CA (1989-2005); Owner, Olivia Neece Planning & Design, Tarzana, CA (1989-1990); Vice President, Project Administration, Hirsch-Bedner Associate, Santa Monica, CA (1987-1989); Vice President, Project Development, Design Service/Aircoa, Englewood, CO (1986-1987); Owner, Olivia Neece Planning & Design, Tarzana, CA (1977-1986); Project Designer, Yates Silverman Incorporated, Los Angeles, CA (1974-1977); Staff Designer, Frances Lux Designs, Los Angeles, CA (1974) **CR:** University Assistant Professor, Peter F. Drucker School of Management, Claremont Academic Research (2000-2009); Academy Researcher, Jet Propulsion Laboratory (2000-2002); Associate Professor,

California State University, Northridge, CA (1994-1999); Instructor, Extension Program, University of California, Los Angeles (1981-1983); Speaker in Field CIV: Member, Choir, Los Angeles County Museum of Art, Donor, Los Angeles County Museum Art (2007-Present); Founder, Los Angeles Music Center (2002-Present); Patron, Los Angeles County Museum of Art (2002-Present); Board Member, Music Center Club 100 (2000-Present); Board Director, Historian, Master Choral Associate (1995-2005); Co-Chair, Los Angeles Master Chorale Gala (1993-1997); Volunteer, Restoration, San Diego Railroad Museum (1985-1992); Patron, Inner Circle, Center Theatre Group; Patron, Los Angeles Opera Council, Patron Laos Angeles Philharmonic; Member, Hollywood Bowl Society; Deacon, First Presbyterian Church, Anacin, California CW: Co-Author, "A Step by Step Approach to Hotel Development" (1988); Contributor, Chapters, Books; Contributor, Articles, Professional Journals AW: Albert Nelson Marquis Lifetime Achievement (2018), Best Paper Award, American Conference On Information Systems (2002); Holiday Inn Development Award, Warwick, RI (1988); First and Second Place Awards, Lodging Hospitality Designers Circle (1987); Gold Key Award, Russell Street Inn (1986); Holiday Inn Development Award, Foster City, CA (1986); First Place, Portfolio Competition, American Society of Interior Designers (1974) MEM: American Society of Interior Designers; Academy Management; Financial Management Association; Professional, Vice President, Board Director, International Institute of Designers & Architect; Association for Information Systems; Institute of Operations Research and Management Sciences; Beta Gamma Sigma MH: Albert Nelson Marquis Lifetime Achievement Award B/I: Ms. Neece became involved in her profession because she has had a multifaceted career. She started off as a designer designing hotels in the 1970s. She then opened her own design company and held it until the late 1980s. Ms. Neece then transitioned to investments by way of her family's company. AV: Art; Painting

NEEDELMAN, MARTIN SEIDEL, T: Attorney **I:** Law and Legal Services **CN:** Law Office of Martin S. Needelman Esq. PC **DOB:** 04/21/1946 **PB:** Brooklyn **SC:** NY/USA **PT:** Joseph Needelman; Sarah (Seidel) Needelman **MS:** Married **SPN:** Carlota America Ruiz (07/02/1981) **CH:** Joseph Lee Needelman- Ruia; Laura Jenny Friedenberg **ED:** LLM, New York University Law School (1978); JD, Boston University Law School (1969); BA, Brooklyn College (1966) **C:** Private Practice, Law Office of Martin S. Needelman Esq. PC (2019-Present); Project Director, Chief Counsel, Brooklyn Legal Services Corp. "A" (1984-2018); Staff Attorney, Brooklyn Legal Services Corp. A. (1971-1984); Vista (Volunteers in Service to America) Attorney, Southside Community Mission, Brooklyn, NY (1969-1971) **CIV:** President, Congregation Beth Jacob Ohev Sholom (2014-Present); Board of Directors, Nuestros Ninos Child Development School, Brooklyn, NY (1989-Present); Former Chair, Housing Resources Committee, Southside United Housing Development Fund, Brooklyn, NY; Member Community Board #1, Brooklyn, NY **AW:** Louis Lefkowitz Award, Fordham Law School Public Interest Center (2010); Risk Taker of the Year Award, Jews for Racial and Economic Justice (1998); Pro Bono Award, Brooklyn Bar Association (1992) **MEM:** Brooklyn Bar Association; Brooklyn Bar Association Volunteer Lawyers Project, Inc; Association of Bar of City of New York; New York State Bar Association; National Lawyers Guild **BAR:** New York (1970); United States District Court for the Southern District of New York; United States District Court for the Eastern District of New York; United States Court of Appeals for the Second Circuit; Supreme Court of the United States **MH:** Albert Nelson Marquis Lifetime Achievement Award; Marquis Who's Who Top Professional **B/I:** No one in Mr. Needelman's family was a lawyer, the reason why he attended law school was he graduated from Brooklyn College in 1966 and it was the Vietnam era days and one of the reason he went to graduate school was to avoid the draft, a war he was opposed of. He could not decide what to do, he majored in political science and urbanization yet he still could no decide what to do for graduate school, after some thinking he realized that law school did not require him to make a decision because law is so very broad. He saw that as an opportunity not to mention the fact that he did well on the Law Board exam and got into a better law school. He attended Boston University. **PA:** Democrat **RE:** Jewish

NEESON, LIAM JOHN, T: Actor **I:** Media & Entertainment **DOB:** 06/07/1952 **PB:** Ballymena **SC:** Northern Ireland **PT:** Bernard "Barney" Neeson; Katherine "Kitty" (Brown) Neeson **MS:** Widowed **SPN:** Natasha Richardson (07/03/1994, Deceased 03/18/2009) **CH:** Michael Richard Antonio; Daniel Jack **ED:** Honorary PhD, Queen's University, Belfast, Northern Ireland, United Kingdom (2009); Coursework, Teacher Training College, Newcastle upon Tyne, England, United Kingdom; Coursework in Physics and Computer Science, Queen's University, Belfast, Northern Ireland, United Kingdom **C:** With, Lyric Players' Theatre, Belfast, Northern Ireland, United Kingdom (1976-1978) **CR:** Various Roles Including Forklift Operator and Truck Driver, Guinness Brewery **CIV:** Goodwill Ambassador, UNICEF (2011); Patron, CineMagic Film Festival **CW:** Actor, "Ordinary Love" (2019); Actor, "Men in Black: International" (2019); Actor, "Cold Pursuit" (2019); Actor, "The Commuter" (2018); Actor, "Widows" (2018); Actor, "The Ballad of Buster Scruggs" (2018); Actor, "Hard Powder" (2018); Actor, "Mark Felt: The Man Who Brought Down the White House" (2017); Actor, "Red Nose Day Actually" (2017); Actor, "The Orville" (2017); Actor, "Operation Chromite" (2016); Actor, "A Monster Calls" (2016); Actor, "Silence" (2016); Actor, "Inside Amy Schumer" (2016); Actor, "Dream Corp" (2016); Actor, "Taken 3" (2015); Actor, "Run All Night" (2015); Actor, "Ted 2" (2015); Actor, "A Christmas Star" (2015); Voice Actor, "Family Guy" (2014-2015); Actor, "Rev" (2014); Actor, "Key & Peele" (2014); Actor, "Wild Japan" (2014); Actor, "Breadwinners" (2014); Voice Actor, "The Nut Job" (2014); Voice, Actor, "The Lego Movie" (2014); Actor, "Non-Stop" (2014); Voice Actor, "Kahlil Gibran's The Prophet" (2014); Actor, "A Million Ways to Die in the West" (2014); Actor, "A Walk Among the Tombstones" (2014); Voice Actor, "Khumba" (2013); Actor, "Third Person" (2013); Actor, "Anchorman 2: The Legend Continues" (2013); Actor, "The Grey" (2012); Actor, "Wrath of the Titans" (2012); Actor, "Battleship" (2012); Actor, "The Dark Knight Rises" (2012); Actor, "Taken 2" (2012); Actor, "The Gentleman Prizefighter" (2012); Voice Actor, "Star Wars: The Clone Wars" (2011-2014); Producer, "James-X" (2011); Actor, "Unknown" (2011); Actor, "Life's Too Short" (2011); Actor, "The Big C" (2010); Actor, "Clash of the Titans" (2010); Actor, "The A-Team" (2010); Actor, "Five Minutes of Heaven" (2009); Actor, "Chloe" (2009); Voice Actor, "The Chronicles of Narnia: Prince Caspian" (2008); Voice Actor, "Ponyo on the Cliff" (2008); Actor, "The Other Man" (2008); Actor, "Taken" (2008); Actor, "Kingdom of Heaven" (2005); Actor, "Batman Begins" (2005); Actor, "Breakfast on Pluto" (2005); Voice Actor, "The Chronicles of Narnia: The Lion, the Witch, and the Wardrobe" (2005); Voice Actor, "The Simpsons" (2005); Actor, "Patrick" (2004); Actor, "Kinsey" (2004); Actor, "Love Actually" (2003); Actor, "K-19: The Widowmaker" (2002); Actor, "Gangs of New York" (2002); Actor, "Liberty's Kids" (2002); Actor, "Evolution" (2001); Actor, "Gun Shy" (2000); Actor, "Empires: The Greeks" (2000); Actor, "Star Wars: Episode I-The Phantom Menace" (1999); Actor, "The Haunting" (1999); Actor, "Les Miserables" (1998); Actor, "The Judas Kiss" (1998); Actor, "The Great War of the Shaping of the 20th Century" (1996); Actor, "Before and After" (1996); Actor, "Michael Collins" (1996); Actor, "Rob Roy" (1995); Actor, "Nell" (1994); Actor, "Schindler's List" (1993); Actor, "Anna Christie" (1993); Actor, "Shining Through" (1992); Actor, "Under Suspicion" (1992); Actor, "Husbands and Wives" (1992); Actor, "Leap of Faith" (1992); Actor, "Ethan Fromme" (1992); Actor, "Ruby Cairo" (1991); Actor, "Darkman" (1990); Actor, "Crossing the Line" (1990); Actor, "Next of Kin" (1989); Actor, "Satisfaction" (1988); Actor, "The Good Mother" (1988); Actor, "Screen Two" (1988); Actor, "A Prayer for the Dying" (1987); Actor, "Suspect" (1987); Actor, "The Mission" (1986); Actor, "Miami Vice" (1986); Actor, "Hold the Dream" (1986); Actor, "Duet for One" (1986); Actor, "Lamb" (1986); Actor, "A Woman of Substance" (1985); Actor, "Arthur the King" (1985); Actor, "The Innocent" (1984); Actor, "The Bounty" (1984); Actor, "Krull" (1983); Actor, "Excalibur" (1981); Actor, "BBC2 Playhouse" (1980); Actor, "Play for Today" (1978) **AW:** Distinguished Service for the Irish Abroad Award, President Michael D. Higgins, Ireland (2018); ALOS Award for Best Supporting Actor (2018); Named One of the 200 Most Influential Philanthropists and Social Entrepreneurs Worldwide, Richtopia (2017); Outstanding Contribution to Cinema Award, Irish Film and Television Academy (2016); Performing Arts Award, American Ireland Fund (2016); Award for Best Actor, Irish Film and Television Academy (2004); Award for Best Actor, Los Angeles Film Critics Association (2004); Named Officer of the Order of the British Empire (OBE), Her Majesty Queen Elizabeth II (1999); Theatre World Award (1993); Award for Best Actor, Chicago Film Critics Association (1993)

NEGISHI, EI-ICHI, PHD, T: Chemistry Professor **I:** Education/Educational Services **CN:** Purdue University **DOB:** 07/14/1935 **ED:** PhD in Organic Chemistry, University of Pennsylvania (1963); BS in Organic Chemistry, The University of Tokyo (1958) **C:** Herbert C. Brown Distinguished Chemistry Professor, Purdue University, West Lafayette, IN (1999-Present); Professor, Purdue University (1979-1999); Associate Professor, Syracuse University (1976-1979); Assistant Professor, Syracuse University (1972-1976); Assistant to Herbert C. Brown, Purdue University (1968-1972); Postdoctoral Associate, Purdue University (1966-1968); Research Chemist, Teijin Limited (1963-1966, 1958-1960) **CR:** Consultant in Field, National University of Singapore (2000); Lecturer in Field, National University of Singapore (2000); Visiting Professor, National University of Singapore (2000); Consultant in Field, University of California Santa Cruz (1980); Lecturer in Field, University of California Santa Cruz (1980); Visiting Professor, University of California, Santa Cruz (1980) **CW:** Author, "Handbook of Organopalladium Chemistry for Organic Synthesis," Wiley-Interscience (Now John Wiley & Sons, Inc.) (2002); Contributor, Several Articles, Publications **AW:** Co-recipient, Nobel Prize in Chemistry, The Nobel Foundation, Nobel Prize Outreach (2010); ACS Award for Creative Work in Synthetic Organic Chemistry (2010); Yamada-Koga Prize, Japan Research Foundation of Optically Active Compounds (2007); Gold Medal, Charles University, Prague, Czech Republic (2007); Professional/Scholarly Publishing Division Award, Chemistry, Japan Research Foundation of Optically Active Compounds (2003); Sir Edward Frankland Prize Lectureship, Royal Society of Chemistry (2000); Humboldt Researcher Award, Alexander von Humboldt-Stiftung/Foundation (1998-2001); Organometallic Chemistry Award, American Chemical Society (1998); Award, The Chemical Society of Japan (1996-1997); A.R. Day Award (1996); Fellow, John Simon Guggenheim Memorial Foundation (1987); Harrison Fellow (1962-1963); Fulbright Scholar (1960-1963) **MEM:** American Association for the Advancement of Science; Royal Society of Chemistry; The Chemical Society of Japan; American Chemical Society; Sigma Xi, The Scientific Research Honor Society; Phi Lambda Epsilon **MH:** Albert Nelson Marquis Lifetime Achievement Award; Marquis Who's Who Top Professional; Marquis Who's Who Humanitarian Award

NEGUSE, JOSEPH, "JOE" D., T: U.S. Representative from Colorado **I:** Government Administration/Government Relations/Government Services **DOB:** 05/13/1984 **PB:** Bakersfield **SC:** CA/USA **MS:** Married **SPN:** Andrea Neguse **CH:** One Child **ED:** JD, University of Colorado Law School, Boulder, CO (2009); BA in Political Science, University of Colorado Boulder (2005) **C:** Member, U.S. House of Representatives from Colorado's Second Congressional District (2019-Present); Executive Director, Colorado Department of Regulatory Agencies (2015-2017); Regent, University of Colorado Boulder (2008-2015); With, Snell & Wilmer L.L.P.; Assistant to Representative Andrew Romanoff, Colorado House of Representatives; Founder, New Era Colorado **PA:** Democrat

NEIDORFF, MICHAEL F., T: Chairperson, President, Chief Executive Officer **I:** Insurance **CN:** Centene Corporation **DOB:** 11/19/1942 **PB:** Philadelphia **SC:** PA/USA **PT:** A. Harvey; Shirley R. (Rubin) N. **MS:** Married **SPN:** Noemi Karpati **ED:** Master of Arts, St. Francis College (1966); Bachelor of Science, Trinity University (1965) **C:** Chairperson, President, Chief Executive Officer, Centene Corporation, St. Louis, MO (2004-Present); President, Chief Executive Officer, Centene Corporation, St. Louis, MO (1996-2004); Treasurer, Centene Corp., St. Louis, MO (1996-2001); President, Chief Executive Officer, Group Health Plan Inc., St. Louis, MO (1995-1996); President, Chief Executive Officer, Physician Health Plan (1985-1995); Manager, Miles Laboratories Ltd. (1969-1975) **CR:** Board of Directors, Miles Laboratories Ltd. (1967-1985); Board of Directors, Mark Twain Bank, St. Louis, MO; Board of Directors, Brown Shoe Co. Inc. **CIV:** Board of Trustees, St. Louis Symphony Orchestra; Board of Directors, St. Louis Area Council, Boy Scouts of America, Grand Center **MEM:** Missouri Managed Healthcare Association

NEJEDLO, DEREK K., T: Senior Applications Consultant **I:** Oil & Energy **CN:** WEC Energy Group **PB:** Green Bay **SC:** WI/USA **PT:** Scott Nejedlo; Debby Nejedlo **MS:** Married **SPN:** Jennifer Nejedlo **CH:** Aurora Nejedlo **ED:** BS in Computer Science, Minor in Business, University of Wisconsin-Green Bay (2005) **C:** Senior Applications Consultant, WEC Energy Group, Integrys Energy Group, Wisconsin Public Service Corporation; Application Architect, WEC Energy Group, Integrys Energy Group, Wisconsin Public Service Corporation; Senior Programmer Analyst, WEC Energy Group, Integrys Energy Group, Wisconsin Public Service Corporation; Programmer Analyst, WEC Energy Group, Integrys Energy Group, Wisconsin Public Service Corporation; Associate Programmer Analyst, WEC Energy Group, Integrys Energy Group,

Wisconsin Public Service Corporation; Web Programmer, Engineer, University of Wisconsin-Green Bay; Technology Consultant, University of Wisconsin-Green Bay; Computer Consultant, University of Wisconsin-Green Bay; Information Technology Helpdesk, University of Wisconsin-Green Bay; Enumerator, United States Census Bureau **CIV:** Supporter, March of Dimes; Donor, Numerous Charities **AW:** ICE Project Recognition (2013-2014); Nominee, Employee of the Year, University of Wisconsin-Green Bay (2005); Listed, National Who's Who College Students (2004); Academic Symposium, VirtuTech, Academic Symposium HipCubed (2004) **MH:** Marquis Who's Who Top Professional **AS:** Mr. Nejedlo attributes his success to his desire to ensure issues are addressed in a timely manner. He sets deadlines for himself to make sure things do get done and he doesn't get lost in detail. **B/I:** Mr. Nejedlo was inspired to pursue his career path by the idea and concept of game design. When it came time for him to go to college, he second guessed that particular path, but knew he wanted to continue to work with computers. Ultimately, he decided to pursue utilities so that he could help the largest amount of people. **AV:** Playing board, strategy and video games; Reading; Watching Netflix; Playing with his dog

NELSON, JEFFREY, T: Neurosurgeon **I:** Medicine & Health Care **CN:** University Hospitals of Cleveland, Case Western Reserve University School of Medicine **ED:** MD, The University of Texas Medical School at Houston (2011); BA in Molecular and Cell Biology, University of California Berkley (2006) **C:** Neurosurgery Resident, University Hospitals of Cleveland, Case Western Reserve University School of Medicine (2011-Present); Research Assistant, University of Texas Medical School at Houston (2009-2011) **CIV:** Tutor, Making Waves Foundation (2004-2006) **MEM:** Congress of Neurological Surgeons; American Association of Neurological Surgeons; Society of NeuroInterventional Surgery; Ohio State Neurosurgical Society; American Academy of Neurological Surgeons **AS:** Dr. Nelson attributes his success to both dedication and looking to the future. He could not have become so successful without hard work and the support around him. He is especially grateful for his family and mentors. **B/I:** Dr. Nelson decided to pursue his career as a direct result of his fascination with the human brain and how it worked. Likewise, he always wanted to help people. By pursuing medicine, he could do everything he wanted.

NELSON, JERRY R., PHD, SM(AAM), T: Microbiologist, Educator, Inventor **I:** Education/Educational Services **DOB:** 04/22/1947 **PB:** Payson **SC:** UT/USA **PT:** Rees William Nelson; Fern Nelson **MS:** Married **SPN:** Lynda Smith (06/08/1967) **CH:** Jeffery; Amanda **ED:** PhD, University of Utah (1976); MS, University of Utah (1974); BS, University of Utah (1969); AS, Dixie College, St. George, UT (1967) **CT:** Regulatory Affairs Certified; Specialist Microbiologist, American Academy of Microbiology **C:** Chief Executive Officer, Power Wiper (2014-Present); Associate Professor, Bio-Engineering, University of Utah, Salt Lake City, UT (1991-Present); Adjunct Professor, Brigham Young University (2019); Chief Science Officer, Nelson Laboratories (1991-2014); Laboratory Director, Nelson Laboratories Inc., Salt Lake City, UT (1985-1991); Section Manager, Utah Biomedical Test Laboratory, Salt Lake City, UT (1984-1985); Laboratory Director, Microbiology Development, Salt Lake City, UT (1974-1984); Principle Ambit Holdings LLC **CR:** Inventor, Power Wiper **CIV:** Eastside Community Council, Salt Lake City, UT (1974); Chairman, Legislature District 2, Salt Lake City Democratic Committee (1972) **CW:** Contributor, Articles, Journal of Biomedical Mate-

rials Research; Proceedings, Kilmer Conference; Contributor, Articles, AIDS Research and Human Retrovirus; Contributor, Articles, American Journal of Infection Control; Contributor, Articles, Numerous Professional Journals **MEM:** American Society for Testing and Materials; American Society of Microbiology; American Society of Quality Control; Parenteral Drug Association; American Academy of Microbiology **MH:** Albert Nelson Marquis Lifetime Achievement Award **B/I:** Dr. Nelson fell in love with microbiology in school. One specific class directed his career, encouraging him to become a microbiologist. He is also an educator and an inventor. **AV:** Collecting stamps; Operating ham radio **RE:** Church of Latter-Day Saints

NELSON, W. JOHN, T: Geologist **I:** Sciences **CN:** Illinois State Geological Survey **DOB:** 05/22/1949 **PB:** Middlebury **SC:** VT/USA **PT:** Walter J. Nelson; Marjorie (Bishop) Nelson **MS:** Single **ED:** MS in Geology, University of Illinois (1973); BS in Geology, Williams College (1971) **C:** Geologist, Illinois State Geological Survey, Champaign, IL (1974-Present) **CW:** Contributor, Over 150 Scientific Articles, Professional Journals **MEM:** Geological Society of America **MH:** Albert Nelson Marquis Lifetime Achievement Award **B/I:** Mr. Nelson has always had an interest in the outdoors and science, especially astronomy. He took geology courses in college and became passionate about the work, deciding to pursue a career in the field. **PA:** Libertarian

NELSON, WARREN B., T: Commodity Trader (Retired) **I:** Consumer Goods and Services **DOB:** 09/29/1922 **PB:** Manhattan **SC:** KS/USA **YOP:** 2020 **PT:** Oscar Nelson; Eda Nelson **MS:** Married **SPN:** Betty Lou Wiley (12/24/1944) **CH:** Barbara Ann; David William (Deceased); Marcia Lynn; Robert Warren **ED:** Bachelor of Science in Agricultural Economics, Kansas State University, Cum Laude (1942) **C:** Chairman, Clayton Brokerage Co. (1986-1992); Vice Chairman, Clayton Brokerage Co. (1977-1986); President, Clayton Brokerage Co. (1979-1981); President, Clayton Brokerage Co. (1972-1977); Vice President, Clayton Brokerage Co. (1969-1972); Secretary, Clayton Brokerage Co. (1959-1969); Partner, Longstreet Abott & Co. (1959-1960); Price Analyst, Longstreet Abott & Co. (1951-1959); Statistician, U.S. Crop Reporting Service USDA, Topeka, KS (1948-1950); Statistician, Agriculture Division Census Bureau (1945-1948) **CIV:** Trinity Lutheran Church, Kirkwood, MO (1953-Present) **MIL:** First Lieutenant, U.S. Air Force (1942-1945) **CW:** Author, "My Life"; Author, "My War"; Author, Biographies of Grandparents, Parents and Other Family **AW:** Distinguished Flying Cross, U.S. Air Force; Air Medals, U.S. Air Force **MEM:** Chicago Board of Trade; Chicago Mercantile Exchange **MH:** Albert Nelson Marquis Lifetime Achievement Award **PA:** Republican **RE:** Lutheran

NELSON, WILLIE HUGH, T: Musician **I:** Media & Entertainment **DOB:** 4/30/1933 **PB:** Abbott **SC:** TX/USA **CH:** Jacob; Lukas; Paula Carlene; Amy; Lana; Susie; Billy **ED:** Honorary Doctor of Music, Berklee College of Music (2013); Coursework, Baylor University **C:** Personal Appearances, throughout the U.S. (1964-Present); Personal appearances, Grand Ole Opry, Nashville, TN (1964-Present); Founder, Pedernales Records, Austin, TX (2007); Owner, Pedernales Golf Club/Willie Nelson's Cut-N-Putt; Founder, Pedernales Studios, Spicewood, TX; Recording Artist, RCA Records; Recording Artist, Columbia; Recording Artist, Atlantic; Bass Player, Ray Price's Band; Announcer, Host, Country Music Shows, Local Texas Stations; Salesman **CR:** Co-founder, Willie Nelson's Biodiesel **CW:** Musician, Album, "Summertime: Willie

Nelson Sings Gershwin" (2016); Musician, Album, with Merle Haggard, "Django & Jimmie" (2015); Musician, Album, "Band of Brothers" (2014); Musician, Album, "2012, Let's Face the Music and Dance" (2013); Musician, Album, "Heroes" (2012); Musician, Album, with Wynton Marsalis, "Here We Go Again: Celebrating the Genius of Ray Charles" (2011); Musician, Album, "Country Music" (2010); Musician, Album, "I Let My Mind Wander: The Best of Willie Nelson" (2010); Musician, Album, "Naked Willie" (2009); Musician, Album, "Moment of Forever" (2008); Musician, Album, "Last of the Breed" (2007); Musician, Album, "Willie Nelson Christmas" (2007); Musician, Album, "Gravedigger" (2007); Musician, Album, "You Don't Know Me" (2006); Musician, Album, "Just a Couple of Outlaws" (2006); Musician, Album, "All American Country" (2006); Musician, Album, "Songs for Tsunami Relief" (2005); Musician, Album, "Countryman" (2005); Actor, Film, "The Dukes of Hazzard" (2005); Actor, Film, "The Big Bounce" (2004); Musician, Album, "Live in Amsterdam" (2004); Musician, Album, "Music Legends: The Best of Willie Live" (2004); Musician, Album, "Live at Billy Bob's Texas" (2004); Musician, Album, "It Always Will Be" (2004); Musician, Album, "Honky Tonk Heroes" (2003); Musician, Album, "Broken Promises" (2003); Musician, Album, "Reunion - Can't Get the Hell Out of Texas" (2003); Musician, Album, "Willie Nelson and Friends: Live and Kickin'" (2003); Musician, Album, "Standard Time" (2003); Musician, Album, "Keepsake" (2003); Musician, Album, "Run That By Me One More Time" (2003); Musician, Album, "I Just Don't Understand" (2003); Musician, Album, "The Great Divide" (2002); Musician, Album, "Home is Where You're Happy" (2002); Musician, Album, "All of Me Live...in Concert" (2002); Musician, Album, "Stars & Guitars" (2002); Musician, Album, "Night Life, 2002, Country Willie" (2002); Musician, Album, "Is There Something in Your Mind" (2002); Musician, Album, "On the Road Again" (2002); Musician, Album, "Tales Out of Luck" (2001); Musician, Album, "Rainbow Connection" (2001); Musician, Album, "Clean Shirt" (2000); Musician, Album, "Outlaws" (2000); Musician, Album, "Memories of Hank Williams, Senior" (2000); Musician, Album, "2000, Me and the Drummer" (2000); Musician, Album, "Milk Cow Blues" (2000); Musician, Album, "Good Ol' Country Singin'" (2000); Actor, Film, "The Journeyman" (2001); Actor, Film, "Stardust" (2000); Musician, Album, "Night and Day" (1999); Appearance, Film, "Dill Scallion" (1999); Appearance, Film, "Austin Powers: The Spy Who Shagged Me" (1999); Musician, Album, "Teatro" (1998); Musician, Album, "Life's Railway to Heaven" (1998); Musician, Album, "Back to Back: Willie Nelson and Patsy Cline" (1998); Actor, Film, "Gone Fishin'" (1997); Actor, Film, "Wag the Dog" (1997); Appearance, Film, "Anthem" (1997); Musician, Album, "Christmas with Willie Nelson" (1997); Musician, Album, "Hill Country Christmas" (1997); Musician, Album, "Just One Love" (1996); Musician, Album, "Spirit" (1996); Musician, Album, "How Great Thou Art" (1996); Actor, Film, "Starlight" (1996); Musician, Album, "Pancho, Lefty and Rudolph" (1995); Musician, Album, "Six Hours at Pedernales" (1995); Musician, Album, "Moonlight Becomes You" (1994); Musician, Album, "Healing Hands of Time" (1994); Musician, Album, "The IRS Tapes: Who'll Buy My Memories?, Willie Nelson" (1993); Musician, Album, "Across the Borderline" (1993); Musician, Album, "Born for Trouble" (1990); Musician, Album, "Horse Called Music" (1989); Musician, Album, "What a Wonderful World" (1988); Musician, Album, "Island in the Sea" (1987); Musician, Album, "Seashores of Old Mexico" (1987); Musician, Album, "Partners" (1986); Musician, Album, "The Promiseland" (1986); Actor, Film, "Red-

Headed Stranger" (1986); Musician, Album, "Me and Paul" (1985); Musician, Album, "Half Nelson" (1985); Musician, Album, "Brand on My Heart" (1985); Musician, Album, "Funny How Time Slips Away" (1985); Musician, Album, "Portrait in Music" (1984); Musician, Album, "Music from Songwriter" (1984); Musician, Album, "Angel Eyes" (1984); Musician, Album, "City of New Orleans" (1984); Actor, Film, "Songwriter" (1984); Musician, Album, "Tougher Than Leather" (1983); Musician, Album, "Pancho & Lefty" (1983); Musician, Album, "Without a Song" (1983); Musician, Album, "Take It to the Limit" (1983); Musician, Album, "Old Friends" (1982); Musician, Album, "Always on My Mind" (1982); Actor, Film, "Barbarosa" (1982); Musician, Album, "Blue Skies" (1981); Actor, Film, "Thief" (1981); Musician, Album, "Somewhere over the Rainbow" (1981); Musician, Album, "Honeysuckle Rose" (1980); Actor, Film, "Honeysuckle Rose" (1980); Musician, Album, "The Electric Horseman" (1979); Musician, Album, "Sings Kris Kristofferson" (1979); Actor, Film, "The Electric Horseman" (1979); Musician, Album, "One for the Road" (1979); Musician, Album, "Pretty Paper" (1979); Musician, Album, "Stardust" (1978); Musician, Album, "Waylon & Willie" (1978); Musician, Album, "Willie and Family Live" (1978); Musician, Album, "To Lefty from Willie" (1977); Musician, Album, "Willie Nelson Live" (1976); Musician, Album, "The Sound in Your Mind" (1976); Musician, Album, "The Troublemaker" (1976); Appearance, with Waylon Jennings, "Wanted: The Outlaws" (1976); Musician, Album, "Red Headed Stranger" (1975); Musician, Album, "Phases and Stages" (1974); Musician, Album, "Shotgun Willie" (1973); Musician, Album, "The Willie Way" (1972); Musician, Album, "The Words Don't Fit the Picture" (1972); Appearance, Album by Waylon Jennings, "Good Hearted Woman" (1972); Musician, Album, "Willie Nelson & Family" (1971); Musician, Album, "Laying My Burdens Down, Yesterday's Wine" (1971); Musician, Album, "Both Sides Now" (1970); Musician, Album, "My Own Peculiar Way" (1969); Musician, Album, "Good Times" (1968); Musician, Album, "Texas in My Soul" (1968); Musician, Album, "Make Way for Willie Nelson" (1967); Musician, Album, "Live Country Music Concert" (1966); Musician, Album, "Country Favorites: Willie Nelson Style" (1966); Musician, Album, "Country Willie: His Own Songs" (1965); Musician, Album, "Here's Willie Nelson" (1963); Musician, Album, "And Then I Wrote" (1962); Musician, Album, "Love & Pain" (1961); Actor, Film, "Half Baked, Beerfest" AW: Grammy for Best Traditional Pop Vocal Album, "My Way" (2018); Kris Kristofferson Award, Nashville Songwriters Association International (2013); Grammy Award, Best Country Vocal Collaboration, for "Last of the Breed" (2008); Grammy Award, with Lee Ann Womack, Best Country Collaboration With Vocals for "Mendocino County Line" (2002); Inductee, Country Music Hall of Fame (1993); Grammy Lifetime Achievement Award (1989); Special Humanitarian Award, National Farmers Organization (1986); Vocal Duo of the Year, with Julio Iglesias, for "Half Nelson," Country Music Association Awards (1984); Vocal Duo Year, with Merle Haggard, for "Pancho & Lefty," Country Music Association Awards (1983); Grammy Award, Best Country Vocal Performance for "Always On My Mind" (1982); Country Music Association Awards, "Always on My Mind" (1982); Single of the Year, "Always On My Mind" (1982); Grammy Award, Best Country Song, for "On The Road Again" (1980); Named, Entertainer of the Year, Country Music Association (1979); Grammy Award Best Country Vocal Performance for song "Georgia on My Mind" (1978); Grammy Award, Best Country Vocal Performance by a Duo or Group for "Mammas Don't Let Your Babies Grow

Up to Be Cowboys" (1978); Citation for Top Album Artist, Billboard Magazine (1976); Single of the Year, with Waylon Jennings, for "Good Hearted Woman," Country Music Association Awards (1976); Vocal Duo of the Year, with Waylon Jennings, for "Wanted: The Outlaws," Country Music Association Awards (1976); Album of the Year, with Waylon Jennings, Tompall Glaser and Jessi Colter, Country Music Association Awards (1976); Grammy Award Best Country Vocal Performance for song "Blue Eyes Crying In The Rain" (1975); Inductee, Nashville Songwriters Association International Hall of Fame (1973)

NERUD, ANTHONY FRANCIS, T: Lawyer I: Law and Legal Services **DOB:** 09/10/1951 **PB:** Dodge Center **SC:** MN/USA **PT:** Benjamin R. Nerud; Anna D. (Tupy) Nerud **MS:** Married **SPN:** Kathleen D. Bruns (10/4/1980); Melanie R. Cear (02/16/1974, Divorced 10/1979) **CH:** Margaret Ann (Deceased); Deborah; Amanda **ED:** JD, William Mitchell College (1979); BS, University of Minnesota, Cum Laude (1973) **C:** Private Practice, Arlington, MN (1984-Present); Assistant, 1st District Public Defender (1984-2017); Partner, McCarthy-Nerud, Winthrop, MN (1982-1984); Assistant, County Attorney, Sibley County Attorney's Office, Gaylord, MN (1980-1984) **CR:** President, Winthrop Community Theatre (1984-1986); Government's Select Commission for Child Protection Laws, Rules, Procedures (1984-1985); Secretary, Sibley County Democratic-Farmer-Labor Party (1983-1985) **AW:** Jack Durfee Award, Distinguished Career Service as Assistant District Public Defender, Office of Minnesota State Public Defender (2017) **MEM:** Minnesota Trial Lawyers Association; Minnesota Bar Association; American Bar Association **BAR:** State of Minnesota (1980) **MH:** Albert Nelson Marquis Lifetime Achievement Award **B/I:** Mr. Nerud was always fascinated by American history, politics, and economics. His family, though, was incredibly economically disadvantaged. This caused Mr. Nerud to worry that the application of the law was unequal for everyone. With this in mind, Mr. Nerud was drawn to the public defender's office. During his time working there, he became responsible for handling many serious cases. He was appointed to over a dozen sexually psychopathic personality cases. The issue was not to prove the individuals innocent but to uphold the fundamental fairness of the practice of law. This is exactly why Mr. Nerud was drawn to the law in the first place. **AV:** Fishing; Reading; Gardening **PA:** Democrat **RE:** Christian

NEUKOM, WILLIAM, "BILL" HORLICK, T: Founder and Chief Executive Officer; Professional Sports Team Executive (Retired); Lawyer **I:** Law and Legal Services **CN:** World Justice Project **DOB:** 11/07/1941 **PB:** Chicago **SC:** IL/USA **PT:** John Goudey Neukom; Ruth (Horlick) Neukom **MS:** Married **SPN:** Sally Neukom; Diane McMakin (12/28/1963, Divorced 06/1977) **CH:** Josselyn; Samantha; Gillian; John **ED:** LLB, Stanford University (1967); BA, Dartmouth College (1964); Honorary Degree, Dartmouth College; Honorary Degree, Gonzaga University; Honorary Degree, University of Puget Sound; Honorary Degree, University of South Carolina **C:** Managing General Partner, Chief Executive Officer, San Francisco Giants (2008-2011); Chair, Preston Gates & Ellis LLP (Now K&L Gates LLP), Seattle, WA (2004); Partner, Business Practice Group, Preston Gates & Ellis LLP (Now K&L Gates LLP), Seattle, WA (2002); Executive Vice President, Law & Corporate Affairs, Secretary, Microsoft Corporation, Redmond, WA (1994-2002); Vice President, Law, Corporate Affairs, Microsoft Corporation, Redmond, WA (1985-1993); Partner, Preston, Gates & Lucas (Formerly Shidler,

McBroom, Gates & Lucas), Seattle, WA (1978-1985); Attorney, MacDonald, Hoague & Bayless, Seattle, WA (1968-1977) **CR:** Founder, Chief Executive Officer, World Justice Project (2006-Present); Policy Consensus Center (2004-Present); Board of Directors, Pacific Council International Policy (2002-Present); Washington State Delegate, House of Delegates (1999-2005); Chair, Decennial Governance Commission **CIV:** Dean's Council, Stanford Law School (1999-Present); Board of Trustees, Seattle Metropolitan Chamber of Commerce (1987-Present); Chair, Board of Trustees, Dartmouth College (2004-2007); Chair, Gates Challenge Endowment Campaign, United Way King County, WA (2002-2007); Member, Board of Trustees, Dartmouth College (1996-2007); Board of Directors, YMCA of Greater Seattle (1988-2007); Member, Board of Trustees, University of Puget Sound (1995-2006); Chair, Board of Trustees, Seattle Metropolitan Chamber of Commerce (2001-2002); Trustee, Seattle Art Museum (1993-1999); Board of Directors, Oregon Shakespeare Festival (1993-1999); Chairman, Board of Directors, Business Software Alliance (1995-1996); Co-Founder, Neukom Family Foundation (1995); Board of Directors, University of Washington Foundation; Board of Directors, Corporate Council for the Arts (1988); Board of Directors, Business Software Alliance; Executive Committee, Preston Gates & Ellis LLP (Now K&L Gates LLP), Seattle, WA **MEM:** President, American Bar Association (2007-2008); House of Delegates, American Bar Association (1978-1980, 1983-1998); Secretary, American Bar Association (1983-1987); Chairman, Young Lawyers Division, American Bar Association (1977-1978); Chairman, Young Lawyers Division, King County Bar Association, Seattle, WA (1972-1973); Washington State Trial Lawyers Association; Washington State Bar Association; King County Bar Association, Seattle, WA **BAR:** Supreme Court of the United States (1974); United States Court of Appeals for the Ninth Circuit (1968); State of California; State of Washington; United States District Court for the Western District of Washington; United States Court for the Northern District of California **AV:** Fly fishing; Skiing; Running; Golfing; Appreciating jazz

NEUWIRTH, STEPHEN R., T: Lawyer **I:** Law and Legal Services **CN:** Quinn Emanuel Urquhart & Sullivan, LLP **MS:** Married **CH:** Four Children **ED:** JD, Yale Law School, New Haven, CT (1987); BS, Yale College, Summa Cum Laude, New Haven, CT (1984) **C:** Partner, Quinn Emanuel Urquhart & Sullivan, LLP, New York, NY (2006-Present); Partner, Boies, Schiller & Flexner (1997-2005); Associate Counsel to President, The White House, Washington, DC (1993-1996); Associate, Wachtell, Lipton, Rosen & Katz (1988-1993); Law Clerk to Honorable Peter K. Leisure, U.S. District Court for the Southern District of New York (1987-1988) **AW:** Named as One of Five Antitrust "MVPs" Nationwide, Corporate LiveWire (2018); Named to Law360 (2017); Named, U.S. Antitrust and Competition Lawyer of the Year, National Law Journal (2015); Antitrust Trailblazer, Law360 (2014); Titan of the Plantiff's Bar; Ranked Legal 500 in Tier 1 **MEM:** Phi Beta Kapa **BAR:** The State Bar of New York; Supreme Court of the United States; United States Court of Appeals: District of Columbia Circuit, Second Circuit, Third Circuit, Fourth Circuit, Sixth Circuit, Ninth Circuit, Tenth Circuit, Eleventh Circuit; United States District Court: Southern District of New York, Eastern District of New York **MH:** Albert Nelson Marquis Lifetime Achievement Award **B/I:** Mr. Stephen Neuwirth wanted the opportunity to be in a profession where he could make a difference in peoples live and also to be in a position to help others.

NEVILLE, NANCY MARIE, T: Aerospace Engineer **I:** Engineering **DOB:** 05/08/1937 **PB:** Portsmouth **SC:** NH/USA **PT:** Edward Joseph Neville; Margaret Frances (Holden) Neville **MS:** Single **ED:** MA in Mathematics, Boston College, Chestnut Hill, MA (1961); BS in Mathematics, Boston College, Chestnut Hill, MA (1959) **C:** Senior Staff Member, Charles Stark Draper Laboratory, Inc., Cambridge, MA (1973-2001); Staff Member, Instrumentation Laboratory (Subcontracted from Systems Development), Massachusetts Institute of Technology, Cambridge, MA (1966-1973); Senior Operations Research Analyst, System Development Corp., Lexington, MA (1962-1971); Science Programmer, RCA, Burlington, MA (1961-1962) **AW:** Apollo Achievement Award, NASA (National Aeronautics and Space Administration) (1969); Certificate of Commendation, Massachusetts Institute of Technology, Cambridge, MA (1969) **MEM:** American Institute of Aeronautics and Astronautics; Portsmouth Country Club **MH:** Albert Nelson Marquis Lifetime Achievement Award; Marquis Who's Who Top Professional **AS:** Ms. Neville attributes her success to a mentor she in college, the head of the math department, and when she went into the industry if she had a question she would ask him and he would go get her the right book; it helped. **B/I:** Ms. Neville became involved in her profession because, since high school, she has loved mathematics and wanted to teach the subject. After she went to college, she found that there was a lot more than algebra, geometry and trigonometry. Additionally, Ms. Neville earned a master's degree and was accepted into a doctorate program but she had been in school for quite a few years and thought she would like to get into industry. **AV:** Playing golf **RE:** Roman Catholic **THT:** Ms. Neville was subcontracted from Systems Development for six years and during that time she worked out in Colorado Springs, Colorado, on a project that consisted of space detection tracking. At that time, Massachusetts Institute of Technology didn't need mathematicians they needed people to program the system development corporation at their computer house. It was a machine that they used to track UFOs. "It was fun," Ms. Neville said.

NEWHOUSE, DANIEL, "DAN" MILTON, T: U.S. Representative, Farmer **I:** Government Administration/Government Relations/Government Services **DOB:** 07/10/1955 **PB:** Sunnyside **SC:** WA/USA **PT:** Irv Newhouse; Ruth Newhouse **MS:** Married **SPN:** Joan Gavin (2018); Carol Newhouse (1982, Deceased 2017) **CH:** Jensena; Devon **ED:** BS in Agriculture Economics, Washington State University (1977); Diploma, Washington Agriculture and Forestry Leadership Program **C:** U.S. Representative, Washington's Fourth Congressional District, U.S. House of Representatives (2015-Present); State Representative, District 15, Washington, DC (2003-Present); Member, Republican Study Committee; Farmer, Sunnyside Area; Member, Committee on Financial Insights and Insurance; Member, Judiciary Committees; Member, Capital Budget **MEM:** Hop Growers of America; Hop Growers Washington; Washington State Farm Bureau **PA:** Republican **RE:** Presbyterian

NEWSOM, GAVIN CHRISTOPHER, T: Governor of California **I:** Government Administration/Government Relations/Government Services **DOB:** 10/10/1967 **PB:** San Francisco **SC:** CA/USA **PT:** William Newsom; Tessa (Menzies) Newsom **MS:** Married **SPN:** Jennifer Siebel (07/26/2008); Kimberly Guilfoyle (12/08/2001, Divorced 2006) **CH:** Montana Tessa; Hunter Siebel; Brooklynn; Dutch **ED:** BA in Political Science, Santa Clara University (1989) **C:** Governor, State of California (2019-Present); Lieutenant Governor, State of California, Sacramento, CA (2011-2019); Mayor, City of San Francisco, CA (2004-2010); Supervisor, District 2, San Francisco Board of Supervisors, San Francisco, CA (1997-2004); President, San Francisco Parking and Traffic Commission, San Francisco, CA (1996-1997); Founder, PlumpJack Winery Management Group, San Francisco, CA (1992-2004) **CW:** Co-author with Lisa Dickey, "Citizenville: How to Take the Town Square Digital and Reinvent Government" (2013) **AW:** Named a Young Global Leader, World Economic Forum (2005); Named One of the 17 People Who Matter, TIME Magazine (2004) **PA:** Democrat **RE:** Roman Catholic

NEWTON, ELIZABETH DEANE, T: Elementary Music Teacher (Retired) **I:** Education/Educational Services **CN:** Chesterfield County Public Schools **DOB:** 09/29/1951 **PB:** Chattanooga **SC:** TN/USA **PT:** Talbert Swanson; Grace Stryker Deane **MS:** Married **SPN:** Dr. Scott Howard Newton (07/22/1989); Ronald Steve Gallimore (Divorced) **CH:** Grace Medora Stryker, RN **ED:** MA, Trenton State College (1975); Bachelor in Music Education, Greensboro College (1973) **CT:** Certified Music Teacher Grades K-12, Commonwealth of Virginia **C:** Retired (2014); Elementary Music Teacher, Chesterfield County Public Schools, VA (1987-2014); Elementary Summer School Site Coordinator, Chesterfield County Public Schools, VA (2004, 2005); Elementary Music Teacher, Richmond Public Schools, VA (1986-1987); Teacher, Adult Basic Education, GED, English as Second Language, Richmond Public Schools, VA (1979-1986); Teacher, Adult Basic Education, United States Army, Fort Dix, NJ (1974-1978) **CR:** Owner, Sycamore Grove RV Park, LLC (2015-Present); Professional Dog Breeder (Labrador Retrievers, Poochons, MaltiPoos, Labradoodles) (2003-Present); Private Voice and Piano Teacher, Richmond, VA (1979-2018); Director, Crestwood Celebration Singers (1990-2014) **CIV:** Oakwood United Methodist Church, Columbia, VA (2005-Present); Deacon and Elder, Forest Hill Presbyterian Church, Richmond, VA (1980-2005); Choir Member, Soloist, Forest Hill Presbyterian Church, Richmond, VA (1957-2005); Early Contemporary Service Music Director, Forest Hill Presbyterian Church, Richmond, VA (1998-2004) **AW:** Award, The Golden Rule Foundation (1999); Special Church Stewardship Award, Forest Hill Presbyterian Church (1998) **MEM:** Cartersville Garden Club (2013-Present); President, Cartersville Garden Club (2018-2019); Secretary, Cartersville Garden Club (2016-2017); National Education Association; Virginia Music Educators Association; Music Educators National Conference (Now Music Supervisors National Conference), National Association for Music Education; Virginia Education Association; Virginia Museum of Fine Arts; Lewis Ginter Botanical Gardens **MH:** Albert Nelson Marquis Lifetime Achievement Award; Marquis Who's Who Top Professional **B/I:** Mrs. Newton started playing the piano that she had in her home when she was 5 or 6 years old, and singing along. She has loved music ever since. Between singing in the church children's choir and taking early piano lessons, it just carried through.She knew early on she wanted to be a teacher and once when got into high school choirs, she knew she wanted to be a music teacher. **AV:** Breeding and raising registered yellow Labrador retrievers; Gardening; Boating; Fishing; Reading **PA:** Liberal **RE:** Presbyterian/Methodist

NÉZET-SÉGUIN, YANNICK, T: Music Director **I:** Media & Entertainment **CN:** The Metropolitan Opera; The Philadelphia Orchestra; Montreal's Orchestre Métropolitain **DOB:** 03/06/1975 **PB:** Montreal **SC:** Quebec/Canada **PT:** Serge P. Séguin, PhD; Claudine Nézet **ED:** Doctorate Honoris Causa in Music, McGill University (2017); Doctorate Honoris Causa, Université du Québec à Montréal (2011); Coursework, Rider University Westminster Choir College; Coursework, Conservatoire de Musique et D'Art Dramatique, Quebec, Canada; Coursework, Collège Bois-de-Boulogne **C:** Music Director Designate, The Metropolitan Opera, NY (2018-Present); Honorary Conductor, Rotterdam Philharmonic Orchestra (2018-Present); Music Director, The Philadelphia Orchestra, PA (2010-2012, 2012-Present); Artistic Director, Principal Conductor, Montreal's Orchestre Métropolitain (2000-Present); Principal Guest Conductor, London Philharmonic Orchestra (2008-2010, 2010-2014); Music Director, Rotterdam Philharmonic Orchestra (2008-2018); Music Advisor, Assistant Conductor, Chorus Master, Opera de Montreal (1998-2002) **CW:** Conductor, "Fantasy - A Night at the Opera" (2010); Conductor, "Tenor Arias" (2010); Conductor, "Brahms - A German Requiem" (2010); Conductor, "Charles Gounod Roméo et Juliette" (2009); Conductor, "Beethoven, Korngold Violin Concertos" (2009); Conductor, "Bruckner 8" (2009); Conductor, "Ravel" (2009); Conductor, "Beethoven Symphony No. 3 'Eroica - Strauss Death and Configuration'" (2008); Conductor, "Bruckner 9" (2008); Conductor, "Bruckner 7" (2007); Conductor, "La Mer Debussy Britten Mercure" (2007); Conductor, "Pierre LaPointe en Concert Dans La Foret des Mal-Aimés Avec L'Orchestre Métropolitain de Grand Montréal Dirige par Yanick-Nézet-Séguin" (2007); Conductor, "Camille Saint-Saens, Symphony No. 3" (2006); Conductor, "Weill Rota" (2006); Conductor, "Kurt Weill" (2005); Conductor, "Arianna a Naxos" (2004); Conductor, "Mahler 4" (2004); Conductor, "Flemish Connexion Volume 5" (2004); Conductor, "Nino Roto" (2003); Conductor, "Pianist Conversations" (2003); Conductor, Numerous Symphonies and Operas **AW:** Named Companion, Order of Canada (2012); Prix Denise-Pelletier, Government of the Province of Quebec, Canada (2011); National Arts Center Award, Governor General for Performing Arts Awards (2010); Royal Philharmonic Society Award (2009); Prix Opus, Conseil Québécois de la Musique (2005); Virginia Parker Award, Canada Council for the Arts (2000)

NIBLOCK, ROBERT A., T: Chairman, President, Chief Executive Officer (Retired) **I:** Business Management/Business Services **CN:** Lowe's Companies Inc. **SC:** FL/USA **ED:** BA in Accounting, University North Carolina **C:** Chairman, President, Chief Executive Officer, Lowe's Companies, Inc., Mooresville, NC (2011-2018); Chairman, Chief Executive Officer, Lowe's Companies, Inc., Mooresville, NC (2005-2011); President, Lowe's Companies, Inc., Mooresville, NC (2003-2006); Executive Vice President, Chief Financial Officer, Lowe's Companies, Inc., Mooresville, NC (2001-2003); Senior Vice President, Chief Financial Officer, Lowe's Companies, Inc., Mooresville, NC (2000-2001); Senior Vice President of Finance, Lowe's Companies, Inc., Mooresville, NC (1999-2000); Vice President, Treasurer, Lowe's Companies, Inc., Mooreville, NC (1997-1999); Accountant, Ernst & Young LLP (1986-1993); Senior Director of Tax, Lowe's Companies, Inc., Mooreville, NC; Director of Tax, Lowe's Companies, Inc., Mooresville, NC **CR:** Vice-Chairman, Board of Directors, ConocoPhillips (2010-Present); Lowe's Companies Inc. (2004-Present); Chairman, Retail Industry Leaders Association (2008-2009)

NICHOLS, JOHN D., CPCU, LUTCF, ARE, T: Insurance Agent, Insurance Broker, Business Owner **I:** Insurance **CN:** Nichols Pond Insurance Agency **DOB:** 03/18/1948 **PB:** Oneonta **SC:** NY/USA **PT:** Sidney N. Nichols; Emily M. (Clark) Nichols **MS:** Married **SPN:** Annemarie **CH:** David; Christine; James **ED:** BA, Muskingum College (1971); Coursework, The Institutes, American College, National Alliance **CT:** Life Underwriter Fellow, Life Underwriter Training Council (1992); Chartered Property Casualty Underwriter, The American Institute for Property Casualty Underwriters (1992); License, New York; Certified Insurance Broker, Insurance P&C Agent; Life Insurance Agent; License, Federal Communications Commissions; Amateur Extra **C:** Owner, Nichols Pond Insurance Agency, Walton, NY (2003-Present); New York State Insurance Broker, Insurance Agent, Walton, NY (1996-Present); Principal, Business Insurance and Risk Management Services (1994-2000); Underwriter, Broker, Sieger & Smith, Inc., Scarsdale, NY (1996); Commercial Underwriter, Utica First Insurance Co., Peekskill, NY (1994-1996); District Agent, Regional Representative, Prudential Insurance Co., Yorktown Heights, NY (1992-1993); Manager of Directors and Officers, Liability Insurance Department, Interstate Risk Placement, Inc., Interstate Coverage Corp., Bedford, NY (1990-1992); Analyst, Interstate Risk Management Corp., Bedford, NY (1990-1992); Accountant Executive, Walter Kaye Associates, Inc., New York, NY (1988-1990); Associate Accountant Executive, A. Matarasso & Co., Inc., White Plains, NY (1985-1988); Senior Casualty Underwriter, North America Managers, American International Group, New York, NY (1984-1985); Associate Account Executive, Murray, Schoen & Homer, Inc., Bronxville, NY (1981-1984); Senior Casualty Underwriter, The Hartford Insurance Group, Mount Kisco, NY (1977-1981); Supervising Underwriter, United States Fidelity & Guaranty, Toledo, OH (1976-1977); Underwriter, U.S. Fidelity & Guaranty, Baltimore, MD (1973-1976); Underwriter Trainee, United States Fidelity and Guaranty, Scranton, PA (1972-1973) **CIV:** Free and Accepted Masons; Lions; American Radio Relay League; Amateur Radio Emergency Service; Treasurer, Past President, Rotary Club; Past President, Walton Lions Club **MEM:** American Institute for Chartered Property and Casualty Underwriters Society **MH:** Albert Nelson Marquis Lifetime Achievement Award **B/I:** Mr. Nichols became involved in his profession because of two influential people, John C. Howley from Pennsylvania and Douglas Perry, a former supervisor and underwriter. **AV:** Playing outdoor sports; Completing home projects; Exploring amateur radio **PA:** Republican **RE:** Episcopalian

NICHOLS, NANCY, T: Business Executive, Financial Consultant **I:** Business Management/Business Services **DOB:** 12/01/1939 **PB:** Monroe **SC:** MI/USA **PT:** Joseph William; Eva Arlene Smith **MS:** Married **SPN:** Raymond Arlyn Nichols (01/17/1959) **CH:** Anita Marie Nichols Baran; Amy Beth Nichols Gilhouse **ED:** Coursework, Siena Heights College (1983); Coursework, University of Michigan (1972) **C:** Owner, Captain, Anywhere Sports Fishing (1978-Present); Corporate Vice President, Stauder Barch & Associates, Inc. (1989-2010); Associate, Consultant, Stauder, Barch & Associate, Inc., Ann Arbor, MI (1985-1989); Acting Director, Lenawee Health Department (1975-1978); Manager, Bennett Ambulance, Tecumseh, MI (1972-1975); Sales Staff, Glover Real Estate, Adrian, MI (1972-1975); Speaker, Numerous Seminars **CR:** Private Consultant for Business (2010-2018) **CIV:** Rollin Township Palling Commission (2008-Present); Chairman, St. Mary on the Lake Catholic Church, Finance Council (2008-Present); Chairman, Lenawee County Health Board (1992-Present); Executive Board, Tecumseh Housing Commission (1975-Present); Chairperson, Lenawee County Democratic Party (1972-Present); Advisory Committee, Great Lakes Fishery (1986-1988); Chairman, Lenawee County Democratic Party (1985-1988); Industry Coordinating Council (1983-1985); Board of Directors, University of Michigan School of Public Health (1980-1985); Candidate for State Representative, Lenawee County (1984); Candidate for State Representative, State Health Coordinating Council (1980-1984); Chairman, Lenawee County Health Board (1976-1984); Chairman, Executive Committee, South Central Substance Abuse Commission (1976-1984); Candidate for State Representative, Michigan Association Boards of Health (1976-1984); Board of Directors, Community Mental Health Board Lenawee County (1975-1984); Lenawee County Commissioner (1974-1984); County Commissioner, Lenawee County (1974-1984); Board of Directors, Michigan Mid-South Health Systems Agency (1976-1983); Candidate for State Representative, Selection Committee, State Director of Public Health (1981); President, Michigan Mid-South Health Systems Agency (1981); Chairman, Lenawee County Energy Task Force (1980-1981); Candidate for State Representative, State Michigan Committee Unification of Public Mental Health System (1979); President, Chairperson, Human Service Board (1976-1978); Candidate for State Representative, State Michigan Substance Abuse Consolidation Task Force (1975-1976) **AW:** Women Making History Award, Zonta Club of Lenawee County (1994); Democrat of the Year, Lenawee Democratic Party (1985); Michigan Legislative Certificate Tribute (1983, 1985); Namesake, Nancy Nichols Award (1983); Michigan Minuteman Citation Honor (1979) **MEM:** Past Matron, Order of the Eastern Star; Michigan Municipal League; Municipal Financial Officers Association; Michigan Association Counties, Business, and Professional Women; Safari Club; Detroit Bond Club **B/I:** Ms. Nichols was happy being a wife and a mother. It wasn't until after her grandfather passed away that decided to pursue a career in real estate. Prior to this venture, she worked in the ambulance industry. **AV:** Reading; Cooking; Decorating **PA:** Democrat **RE:** Catholic

NICHOLSON, JACK, T: Actor **I:** Media & Entertainment **DOB:** 04/22/1937 **PB:** Neptune **SC:** NJ/USA **PT:** June Frances Nicholson (Mother) **MS:** Divorced **SPN:** Sandra Knight (06/17/1962, Divorced 08/08/1968) **CH:** Jennifer; Honey Hollman; Lorraine Broussard; Raymond Broussard **ED:** Honorary DFA, Brown University (2011); Studied, Players Ring Theater **C:** With, William Hanna and Joseph Barbera, MGM Studios (1955) **MIL:** With, California Air National Guard (1957-1962) **CW:** Actor, "How Do You Know" (2010); Actor, "The Bucket List" (2007); Actor, "The Departed" (2006); Actor, "Anger Management" (2003); Actor, "Something's Gotta Give" (2003); Actor, "About Schmidt" (2002); Actor, "The Pledge" (2001); Actor, "As Good as It Gets" (1997); Actor, "Mars Attacks!" (1996); Actor, "The Evening Star" (1996); Actor, "Blood and Wine" (1996); Actor, "The Crossing Guard" (1995); Actor, "Wolf" (1994); Actor, "A Few Good Men" (1992); Actor, "Hoffa" (1992); Actor, "Man Trouble" (1991); Actor, Director, "The Two Jakes" (1990); Actor, "Batman" (1989); Actor, "The Witches of Eastwick" (1987); Actor, "Broadcast News" (1987); Actor, "Ironweed" (1987); Actor, "Heartburn" (1986); Actor, "Prizzi's Honor" (1985); Actor, "Terms of Endearment" (1983); Actor, "The Border" (1982); Actor, "The Postman Always Rings Twice" (1981); Actor, "Reds" (1981); Actor, "The Shining" (1980); Actor, Director, "Goin' South" (1978); Actor, "The Missouri Breaks" (1976); Actor, "The Last Tycoon" (1976); Actor, "Tommy, The Passenger" (1975); Actor, "The Fortune," (1975); Actor, "One Flew Over the Cuckoo's Nest" (1975); Actor, "Chinatown" (1974); Actor, "The Last Detail" (1974); Actor, "Carnal Knowledge" (1971); Actor, "A Safe Place" (1971); Director, "Drive, He Said" (1971); Actor, "Five Easy Pieces" (1970); Actor,

"Easy Rider" (1969); Producer, "Head" (1968); Actor, "The Trip" (1967); Producer, "The Shooting" (1966); Producer, "Ride the Whirlwind" (1965); Actor, "Ensign Pulver" (1964); Actor, "Studs Lonigen" (1960); Actor, "Little Shop of Horrors" (1960); Actor, "Cry-Baby Killer" (1958); Actor, Debut, Hollywood Stage Production, "Tea an Sympathy" **AW:** Named to New Jersey Hall of Fame (2010); Named to California Hall of Fame (2008); MTV Movie Award for Best Villain (2007); Golden Globe Award for Best Actor, Hollywood Foreign Press Association (1975, 1976, 1998, 2003); Cecil B. DeMille Award, American Film Institute (1999); Academy Award for Best Actor, Academy of Motion Picture Arts and Sciences (1975, 1998); Screen Actors Guild Award for Best Actor, SAG-AFTRA (1998); Life Achievement Award, American Film Institute (1994); Co-recipient with Bobby McFerrin, Grammy Award for Best Recording for Children, The Recording Academy (1987); BAFTA Award for Best Actor (1977, 1984); Academy Award for Best Supporting Actor, Academy Motion Picture Arts and Sciences (1984); BAFTA Award for Best Supporting Actor (1983); New York Film Critics Circle Award for Best Actor (1974, 1975); Two BAFTA Awards for Best Actor (1975)

NIELSEN, KIRSTJEN MICHELE, T: Former United States Secretary of Homeland Security, Lawyer **I:** Government Administration/Government Relations/Government Services **DOB:** 5/14/1972 **PB:** Colorado Springs **SC:** CO/USA **PT:** James McHenry; Phyllis Michele **ED:** Doctor of Jurisprudence, University of Virginia School of Law (1999); Bachelor of Science, Georgetown University Walsh School of Foreign Service **C:** United States Secretary of Homeland Security (2017-2019); Principal Deputy Chief of Staff, White House, Washington, DC (2017); Chief of Staff to the Secretary of Homeland Security (2017); Founder, Sunesis Consulting (2008) **CR:** Member, National Infrastructure Advisory Council (2019-Present); Senior Member, Resilience Task Force, Center for Cyber & Homeland Security Committee, The George Washington University; Advisory Board, World Economic Forum

NIXON, CYNTHIA ELLEN, T: Actress **I:** Media & Entertainment **DOB:** 04/09/1966 **PB:** New York **SC:** NY/USA **PT:** Walter Elmer Nixon Jr.; Anne Elizabeth (Knoll) Nixon **MS:** Married **SPN:** Christine Marinoni (05/27/2012) **CH:** Samantha Mozes; Charles Ezekiel Mozes; Max Ellington Nixon-Marinoni **ED:** BA in English, Barnard College (1988); Coursework, Semester at Sea (1986) **C:** Founding Member, The Drama Dept. (1996) **CR:** Gubernatorial Candidate, State of New York (2018) **CW:** Actress, "Stray Dolls" (2019); Actress, "The Parting Glass" (2018); Actress, "The Only Living Boy in New York" (2017); Actress, "The Little Foxes" (2017); Actress, "A Quiet Passion" (2016); Actress, "Broad City" (2016); Actress, "Killing Reagan" (2016); Actress, "Stockholm, Pennsylvania" (2015); Actress, "The Affair" (2015); Actress, "James White" (2015); Actress, "The Adderall Diaries" (2015); Actress, "Hannibal" (2014); Actress, "5 Flights Up" (2014); Actress, "Hannibal" (2014); Actress, "Alpha House" (2013-2014); Actress, "Alpha House" (2013); Actress, "World Without End" (2012); Actress, "30 Rock" (2012); Actress, "Wit" (2011); Actress, "Rampart" (2011); Actress, "Too Big to Fail" (2011); Actress, "Law & Order: Criminal Intent" (2011); Actress, "The Big C" (2010-2011); Actress, "Sex and the City 2" (2010); Actress, "An Englishman in New York" (2009); Actress, "Sex and the City: The Movie" (2008); Actress, "Lymelife" (2008); Actress, "Rabbit Hole" (2006); Actress, "The Prime of Miss Jean Brodie" (2006); Actress, "Warm Springs" (2005); Actress, "Tanner on Tanner" (2004); Actress, "Sex and the City" (1998-2004); Actress, "The Paper Mache Chase" (2003); Actress, "Stage on Screen: The Women" (2002); Actress, "Igby Goes Down" (2002); Actress, "Sex and the Matrix" (2000); Actress, "Papa's Angels" (2000); Actress, "The Out-of-Towners" (1999); Actress, "Advice from a Caterpillar" (1999); Actress, "Indiscretions" (1996); Actress, "Marvin's Room" (1996); Actress, "'M' Word" (1996); Actress, "Baby's Day Out" (1994); Actress, "Addams Family Values" (1993); Actress, "The Pelican Brief" (1993); Actress, "Through an Open Window" (1992); Actress, "Kiss-Kiss, Dahlings!" (1992); Actress, "Face of a Stranger" (1991); Actress, "Love, Lies and Murder" (1991); Actress, "Women & Wallace" (1990); Actress, "The Love She Sought" (1990); Actress, "Let It Ride" (1989); Actress, "Tanner '88" (1988); Actress, "The Murder of Mary Phagan" (1988); Actress, "O.C. and Stiggs" (1987); Actress, "The Manhattan Project" (1986); Actress, "The Real Thing" (1984); Actress, "Hurlyburly" (1984); Actress, "Amadeus" (1984); Actress, "I am the Cheese" (1983); Actress, "Rascals and Robbers: The Secret Adventures of Tom Sawyer and Huck Finn" (1982); Actress, "My Body, My Child" (1982); Actress, "Fifth of July" (1982); Actress, "The Private History of a Campaign That Failed" (1981); Actress, "Tattoo" (1981); Actress, "Prince of the City" (1981); Actress, "The Philadelphia Story" (1980); Actress, "Little Darlings" (1980); Actress, "The Seven Wishes of a Rich Kid" (1979); Actress, Theater, Television Shows, Film **AW:** Tony Award for Best Featured Actress in a Play (2017); Drama Desk Award for Outstanding Featured Actress in a Play (2017); Award for Outstanding Female Actor in a Supporting Role – Drama, Gracie Allen Awards (2016); Faith Hubley Memorial Award, Provincetown International Film Festival (2016); Vito Russo Award, GLAAD Media Awards (2010); Grammy Award for Best Spoken Word Album, The Recording Academy (2009); Muse Award, New York Women in Film & Television (2008); Tony Award for Best Performance by a Leading Actress in a Play (2006); Emmy Award for Outstanding Supporting Actress in a Comedy Series, Academy of Television Arts & Sciences (2004); Theatre World Award (1981); Numerous Awards **THT:** Ms. Nixon made theatrical history by simultaneously appearing in two hit Broadway plays directed by Mike Nichols, "The Real Thing" and "Hurlyburly."

NOAH, TREVOR, T: Television Personality, Comedian **I:** Media & Entertainment **DOB:** 02/20/1984 **PB:** Johannesburg **SC:** South Africa **PT:** Robert Noah; Patricia Nombuyiselo Noah **C:** Host, "The Daily Show with Trevor Noah" (2015-Present); Contributor, "The Daily Show with Jon Stewart" (2014-2015) **CIV:** Founder, Trevor Noah Foundation (2018-Present) **CW:** Writer, Executive Producer, Personality, "Loud and Clear" (2019); Contributor, "The Donald J. Trump Presidential Twitter Library" (2018); Voice Actor, "Black Panther" (2018); Appearance, "American Vandal" (2018); Writer, Executive Producer, Personality, "Trever Noah: Afraid of the Dark" (2017); Writer, Executive Producer, Personality, "Nashville" (2017); Writer, Executive Producer, Personality, "The Opposition with Jordan Klepper" (2017); Appearance, "Nashville" (2017); Author, "Born a Crime" (2016); Writer, Executive Producer, Personality, "Trevor Noah: The Nationwild Comedy Tour" (2015); Writer, Executive Producer, "The Daily Show with Trevor Noah" (2015); Writer, Executive Producer, Personality, "Trevor Noah: Lost in Translation" (2015); Writer, Executive Producer, Personality, "Trevor Noah: African American" (2013); Writer, Executive Producer, Personality, "Trevor Noah: It's My Culture" (2013); Actor, "Mad Buddies" (2012); Writer, Executive Producer, Personality, "Trevor Noah: The Racist" (2012); Featured, "You Laugh But It's True" (2012); Writer, Executive Producer, Personality, "Trevor Noah: Crazy Normal" (2011); Actor, "Taka Takata" (2011); Writer, Executive Producer, Personality, "Trevor Noah: The Daywalker" (2009); Actor, "Isidingo" (2002); Host, "Noah's Ark"; Co-Host, Various Television Shows; Opening Act, Various Comedians Including Gabriela Iglesias and Russell Peters **AW:** Emmy Award for Outstanding Short Form Variety Series, Academy of Television Arts & Sciences (2018); Awards for Outstanding Literary Work, Biography/Autobiography, NAACP Image Awards (2017); Outstanding Literary Work, Debut Author, NAACP Image Awards (2017); Thurber Prize for American Humor, Thurber House (2017); Personality of the Year, MTV Africa Music Awards (2015); Comic of the Year, South African Comics' Choice Awards (2012)

NOBLE, TAL D., T: Founder, Director **I:** Corporate Communications & Public Relations **CN:** American Communication Arts **SC:** CT/USA **PT:** Daniel E. Noble **MS:** Married **C:** Founder, Director, American Communication Arts (1964-Present) **CIV:** Honorary Trustee, Parents Television Council **CW:** Author, "Goodbye America?" (1999); Featured, "Byte Magazine" (1985); Artist, Virtual Reality Abstracts **AW:** Special Commendation Award, San Diego City Council (1993); Bicentennial Award, American Revolution (1976) **MEM:** National Membership, Library of Congress **MH:** Marquis Who's Who Top Professional **AS:** Mr. Noble attributes his success to his stubbornness. For any new idea, thought, or direction, he has an automatic opposing response to question it, like most other humans. Mr. Noble believes that when presenting new ideas, such as his, to the world, one must be stubborn to face the immense opposition one will meet like all other pioneers. His motto is as follows: "I have a good mind, and I am not afraid to use it." **B/I:** Mr. Noble has felt the biggest problem that humans have with one another is communication at any level. Most of the time, communication between people is not on the level it should be. He felt that "the fine art of human communication" needs a lot of work. When Mr. Noble founded his company more than 50 years ago, as time progressed, he began to learn many new things that sparked his curiosity along the way. Specifically, computers were of interest to him. At the time, computers were in their infancy and used the CPM Operating system, which he described as primitive. Even then, Mr. Noble thought graphics were possible and that there would be changes to the storage capacity of data in the future. Eventually, his career path led him to create the first graphic software for computers. **AV:** Ice skating; Traveling **THT:** Mr. Noble's father, Daniel E. Noble, was the inventor of the portable communicator known as the "Walkie Talkie."

NODEEN, JANEY PRICE, T: President **I:** Business Management/Business Services **CN:** Burke Consortium, Inc. **MS:** Married **SPN:** Thomas Nodeen **ED:** Graduate Coursework, Owner President's Program, Harvard Business School (2003); Graduate Coursework, Advanced Management Program, National Defense University (1995); Graduate Coursework, Defense Systems Management College (1994); BS in Information Science, Christopher Newport College (1987) **C:** President, Burke Consortium, Inc., Springfield, VA (1997-Present); Deputy Program Executive Officer, Submarines for Acquisition, Department of the Navy, Washington, DC (1996-1997); Executive Development Program, Department of the Navy, Washington, DC (1993-1996); Senior Staff, Navy Acquisition Reform Executive, Department of the Navy, Washington, DC (1995); Manager, Submarine Information Resources and Computer Operations, Department of the Navy, Washington, DC (1986-1993); Engineering Analyst, Newport News Shipbuilding (1978-1986) **CR:** Military, Legislative Fellow, Congressman Sam Gejdenson (1994); Senior Executive Fellow, John F. Kennedy School of Government, Harvard University (1994)

NODINE, MARTHA, "MARTI" LOCKHART, T: Writer, Educator **I:** Education/Educational Services **DOB:** 01/03/1940 **PB:** Corpus Christi **SC:** TX/USA **PT:** Hugh Rairdon Lockhart; Amelia Virginia (McRee) Lockhart **MS:** Married **SPN:** Col. Wright Anderson Nodine Jr.; William M. Stephens **ED:** BFA in Drawing, University of Texas, San Antonio, TX (1989); MA in English Literature, University of Arizona (1967); BA in English Literature, Minors in Art, History, and Government, Colorado College (1961) **CT:** Certified Teacher of English, Colorado, California, and Texas **C:** Art Teacher and Department Head, North East Independent School District, San Antonio, TX (1986-1996); Art, Creative Writing and Spanish Teacher, NEISD, San Antonio, TX (1981-1985); Level Chairman English, NEISD, San Antonio, TX (1974-1982); English Teacher, NEISD, San Antonio, TX (1972-1982); Chairman, English Literature, Selection Committee, NEISD, San Antonio, TX (1977); English Teacher, San Antonio Independent School District (1968-1972); English Teacher in Colorado, Alabama, New York, Virginia and California Public Schools (1961-1968) **CR:** Captain, TAEA Region V (1991-1993); Representative for Region 10, Texas Art Education Association (TAEA) (1989-1993); Advisory Board, San Antonio Art Education Association (1988-1993); President, San Antonio Art Education Association (1990-1992); Educational Consultant, McNay Art Museum, San Antonio, TX (1987); Consultant, Tour Guide for the David Smith Retrospective, San Antonio Museum of Art (1983-1986); Presenter for Workshops on Cubist Sculpture, Drawing and Design, Gallery Tour Guide (1983); Feature Writer, "Lively Arts," San Antonio Express-News (1981-1982); Advisory Board, San Antonio Council of Teachers of English (1980); President, San Antonio Council of Teachers of English (1980) **CIV:** Board Member, Food Policy Council of San Antonio (2016-Present); Reading Buddy, San Antonio Youth Literacy, SAYL (2015-Present); Membership Council Representative, Christian Assistance Ministry (CAM) for St. George Episcopal Church (2015-Present); CAM Food Pantry Volunteer, (2005-Present); Lay Eucharistic Minister; Community of Hope (2020); FPCSA Secretary, (2017-2019) **CW:** Researcher, Author, "Resilience: The Life and Work of Artist Dorothy Dehner" (1994-2002); Artist, Solo Show, Art Center Gallery, San Antonio, TX (1989); Artist, Group Show, Northeast Independent School District Exhibit (1986); Artist, Group Exhibit, University of Texas at San Antonio, (1986); Artist, Texas Society of Sculptors Exhibit, United Bank of Austin (1985); Artist, Group Show, Alternate Space Gallery, San Antonio (1983); Artist, Group Art Exhibit, National Organization of Women Convention, San Antonio, TX (1980); Artist, Two-Women Show, Chapman Graduate Center, Trinity University (1979) **AW:** Personal Service Award, Texas Art Education Association (1993); Gold Crown Award, Columbia School Press Association for "Bullseye," Student Publication (1992); State Champion Award for "Bullseye," Texas High School Press Association (THSPA) Teacher/Sponsor (1990-1992); Citation for Excellence, Scholastic Art And Writing Awards for Student Publication, Texas High School Press Association (1992); TAEA Merit Award, Personal, (1986); Teacher/Sponsor for "Bullseye"; Teacher/Sponsor, for "Bullseye" **MEM:** Biographers International Organization (2015-Present); Member and Presenter, Society of German American Studies (1997, 2004-2005); National Education Association;

Texas State Teachers Association; National Association of Teachers of English; Presenter, North East ISD Teachers Association; National Art Education Association; Texas Art Education Association; San Antonio Art Education Association **MH:** Albert Nelson Marquis Lifetime Achievement Award **AS:** Ms. Nodine attributes her success to a privileged background afforded by her family, which led to educational and professional opportunities. In childhood, she was encouraged to read widely, draw consistently, listen to classical music and jazz, sing choral music, and make friends with children of different races. Although Texans, her parents encouraged her to respect Hispanics and Black people. This mindset later enabled her, as a military wife, to communicate with students in Colorado, Alabama, New York, Virginia, and Texas. **B/I:** Ms. Nodine became involved in her profession because of her love of expressive language and aptitude in English, both of which led to her profession as an educator. As a high school senior, because she scored in the 98th percentile in English vocabulary and usage, it seemed natural for her to become a teacher of literature and composition. Meanwhile, she took drawing and sculpture courses at night and over the summer for years. As a teacher of English and art, she enjoyed working with teenagers because of their intensity and evolving intelligence. That realization led to her sponsoring student art and writing publications for the last 10 years of her career, while she also wrote about art for the San Antonio Express-News and designed student and adult tours for the San Antonio Museum of Art. After her retirement from teaching, those activities led to a second career as the biographer of artist Dorothy Dehner. **AV:** Painting; Sculpture; Writing (Biography and Poetry); Choral singing; Reading **PA:** Democrat **RE:** Episcopalian (Lay Eucharistic Minister, Community of Hope Chaplain, Choir Member) **THT:** Ms. Nodine has said, "'Embrace chance' is my credo. Every time I dared to enter a new field—to hone a new skill or to embrace an unfamiliar opportunity—I have experienced a burst of excitement and joy in discovering the New. Sometimes, my decisions made no sense at the time, but my curiosity is constantly rewarded. As I embrace a second career as the biographer of artist Dorothy Dehner, I participate in conferences sponsored by BIO (Biographers International Organization), while forming relationships with encouraging and like-minded people who seek excellence."

NOEL, DON O., T: Editor, Author, Columnist (Retired) **I:** Other **DOB:** 11/27/1931 **PB:** Elizabeth **SC:** NJ/USA **PT:** Don O. Noel; Catherine (Pyle) Noel **MS:** Widowed **SPN:** Elizabeth Brad Noel (Married 08/29/1953, Deceased 01/23/2019) **CH:** Emily R. Noel; Ken Eric Noel (Deceased 1978) **ED:** MFA in Creative Writing, Fairfield University (2013); BA in American Studies, Cornell University (1954) **C:** Political Columnist, Op-ed Page, Hartford Courant (1984-1997); Senior Correspondent, Host, Face the State, Post-Newsweek Stations, WFSB-TV (1975-1984); Editor-in-Chief, The Hartford Times (1974-1975); Editorial Page Editor, The Hartford Times (1969-1975); Assistant Managing Editor, The Hartford Times (1968-1969); Reporter, The Hartford Times (1958-1968) **CR:** Author, Tabloid, "The Negro in Hartford," The Hartford Times (1963) **CIV:** President, Residents' Council, Seabury (2020-Present); Member, Board of Directors, ACLU of Connecticut (1998-Present); Chair, Board of Directors, ACLU of Connecticut (2005-2010); Secretary of the Board, BHCA (1988-2005); Chair, Blue Hills Cub Pack (1968-1972) **MIL:** American Friends Service Committee, Tokyo, Japan (1954-1956) **CW:** Author, More Than 60 Short Stories, Literary Magazines, Anthologies (2014-2019); Author, Book, "Near A

Far Sea: A Jamaican Odyssey" (2006) **AW:** National Journalism Award, American Society of Planning Officials (1972, 1974); National Journalism Award, American Medical Association (1972); Sevellon Brown Memorial Award, New England Associated Press (1964); Finalist, Pulitzer Prize for Non-Deadline Reporting (1964) **MH:** Albert Nelson Marquis Lifetime Achievement Award; Marquis Who's Who Top Professional; Marquis Who's Who Humanitarian Award **AS:** Mr. Noel attributes his success to what he suspects is generation-skipping DNA. His paternal grandfather, whom he never knew, was editor of the Butte Miner, and his father, Don O., was a pioneering powder metallurgist with minimal writing urges but a hugely positive influence. His mother, a coloratura soprano, studied in Leipzig, Germany, but her budding operatic was cut short by his arrival. Thanks to her, he was steeped in music; he became an all-state trombonist in high school and a part-time music critic during his first decade as a journalist. He absorbed from both parents a passion for contributing to society. **B/I:** Mr. Noel became involved in his profession when he began covering his Boy Scout troop for the West Orange Chronicle in New Jersey in seventh grade. By the time of his high school graduation, he was the principal sports reporter and covered many town events. His involvement in his profession has been supported by both his parents and his wife. **AV:** Attending concerts, plays, and operas; Bird watching; Writing fiction and non-fiction; Videotaping events for the Seabury Retirement Community; Editing and publishing videos online **PA:** Democrat **RE:** Quaker

NOEM, KRISTI LYNN, T: Governor of South Dakota **I:** Government Administration/Government Relations/Government Services **DOB:** 11/30/1971 **PB:** Watertown **SC:** SD/USA **PT:** Ron Arnold; Corinne (Bergan) Arnold **MS:** Married **SPN:** Bryon Noem **CH:** Kassidy; Kennedy; Booker **ED:** BA in Political Science, South Dakota State University (2012); Coursework, Northern State University, Aberdeen, SD (1990-1992); Coursework, Mount Marty College, Watertown, SD **C:** Governor, State of South Dakota (2019-Present); Member, U.S. House Armed Services Committee (2013-2019); Member, U.S. House Agricultural Committee (2011-2019); Member at-Large, U.S. Congress from South Dakota, Washington, DC (2011-2019); Member, Committee on Ways and Means (2015); Member, U.S. House Natural Resources Committee, Washington, DC (2011-2012); Member, U.S. House Committee on Education and the Workforce, Washington, DC (2011-2012); Assistant Majority Leader, South Dakota House of Representatives (2009-2010); Member, District Six, South Dakota House of Representatives (2006-2010); Co-Owner, Racota Valley Ranch, Hazel, SD **AW:** Named One of the Heroes on the Hill, Indian Country Today Media Network (2011); Named One of the Politics 40 Under 40, TIME Magazine (2010); Named One of the 50 Politicos to Watch, Politico (2010); Named a South Dakota Outstanding Young Farmer (2007) **PA:** Republican **RE:** Evangelical Christian

NOHRIA, NITIN, PHD, T: Dean **I:** Education/Educational Services **CN:** Harvard Business School **DOB:** 02/09/1962 **PB:** New Delhi **SC:** India **MS:** Married **SPN:** Monica Nohria **CH:** Two Daughters **ED:** PhD in Management, Massachusetts Institute of Technology Sloan School of Management (1988); Bachelor of Technology in Chemical Engineering, Indian Institute of Technology, Bombay, India (1984) **C:** Dean, Harvard Business School, Boston, MA (2010-Present); Co-Chair, Leadership Initiative, Harvard Business School (2009-Present);Richard P. Chapman Professor, Business Administration, Harvard Business School (1999-Present); Senior

Associate Dean, Faculty Development, Harvard Business School (2006-2009); Director, Research Division, Harvard Business School (2003-2004); Chair, Organizational Behavior Unit, Harvard Business School (1998-2002); Associate Professor, Harvard Business School (1993-1999); Assistant Professor, Harvard Business School (1988-1993) **CR:** Co-founder, The Smart Manager (2002); Visiting Faculty Member, London Business School (1996) **CW:** Co-Author, "Handbook of Leadership and Theory Practice" (2010); Co-Author, "Entrepreneurs, Managers, and Leaders: What the Airline Industry Can Teach Us About Leadership" (2009); Co-Author, "Paths to Power: How Insiders and Outsiders Shaped American Business Leadership" (2006); Co-Author, "In Their Time: The Greatest Business Leaders of the 20th Century" (2005); Co-Author, "What Really Works: The 4+2 Formula for Sustained Business Success" (2003); Co-Author, "Master Passions: The Interplay of Anxiety, Ambition, and Envy" (2002); Co-Author, "Changing Fortunes: The Rise and Fall of the Industrial Corporation" (2002); Co-Author, "Driven: How Human Nature Shapes Our Choices" (2001); Co-Author, "The Arc of Ambition: Defining the Leadership Journey" (2000); Co-Author, "Breaking the Code of Change" (2000); Co-Author, "The Portable MBA Desk Reference" (1998); Co-Author, "The Differentiated Network: Organizations Knowledge Flows in Multinational Corporations" (1997); Co-Author, "The Best Ideas on Managing Business Change" (1996); Co-Author, "Building the Information-Age Organization: Structure, Control, and Information Technologies" (1994); Co-Editor, "Networks and Organizations: Structure, Form, and Action" (1992); Co-Author, "Beyond the Hype: Rediscovering the Essence of Management" (1992); Contributor, Articles, Professional Journals **AW:** Distinguished Alumnus Medal, Indian Institute of Technology (2007)

NOLAN, CHRISTOPHER EDWARD, T: Film Director, Producer, Writer **I:** Media & Entertainment **DOB:** 07/30/1970 **PB:** London **SC:** United Kingdom **PT:** Brendan Nolan; Christina (Jensen) Nolan **MS:** Married **SPN:** Emma Thomas (1997) **CH:** Flora; Rory; Oliver; Magnus **ED:** Bachelor of Arts in English Literature, University College London **C:** Co-founder, Syncopy Films Inc. **CW:** Director, Writer, Producer, "Tenet" (2020); Executive Producer, "The Doll's Breath" (2019); Executive Producer, "Justice League" (2017); Director, Writer, Producer, "Dunkirk" (2017); Executive Producer, "Batman v Superman: Dawn of Justice" (2016); Director, Producer, Editor, "Quay" (2015); Director, Co-writer, Producer, "Interstellar" (2014); Executive Producer, "Transcendence" (2014); Co-writer, Producer, "Man of Steel" (2013); Director, Co-writer, Producer, "The Dark Knight Rises" (2012); Director, Writer, Producer, "Inception" (2010); Director, Co-writer, Producer, "The Dark Knight" (2008); Director, Writer, Producer, "The Prestige" (2006); Director, Co-writer, "Batman Begins" (2005); Director, "Insomnia" (2002); Director, Writer, "Memento" (2000); Director, Writer, Cinematographer, Editor, Producer, "Following" (1998); Director, Writer, "Doodlebug" (1997) **AW:** Named, Commander of the Order of the British Empire (2019); Named Movie of the Year, American Film Institute (2008, 2010, 2010, 2012, 2014, 2017); Inductee, Top Ten Films, National Board of Review (2001, 2008, 2010, 2017); Named, One of the 100 Most Influential People in the World, TIME Magazine (2015); Award for Best Original Screenplay, Writers Guild of America (2010); Named Screenwriter of the Year, American Film Institute (2001); Awards for Best Feature, Best Director and Best Screenplay, Independent Spirit Awards (2001); Numerous Awards

NORCROSS, DONALD W., T: U.S. Representative from New Jersey **I:** Government Administration/ Government Relations/Government Services **DOB:** 12/13/1958 **PB:** Camden **SC:** NJ/USA **PT:** George E. Norcross Jr. **MS:** Married **SPN:** Andrea (Doran) Norcross; Nancy Norcross (Divorced) **CH:** Three Children **ED:** AS in Criminal Justice, Camden County College, NJ **C:** Member, U.S. House of Representatives from New Jersey's First Congressional District (2015-Present); Vice-Chair, Committee on Transportation, New Jersey State Senate (2010-2015); Vice-Chair, Committee on Law and Public Safety, New Jersey State Senate (2010-2014); Member, District Five, New Jersey State Senate (2010-2014); Member, District Five, New Jersey General Assembly (2010); President, South Jersey AFL-CIO Central Labor Council; Assistant Business Manager, IBEW Local 351 **CIV:** Executive Board, United Way **PA:** Democrat

NOREEN, TERRY GENE SR., I: Insurance **CN:** Health and Safety Consultant **DOB:** 05/21/1946 **PB:** Walla Walla **SC:** WA/USA **PT:** Arthur Sanford Noreen; Norma Jean (Slater) Noreen **MS:** Married **SPN:** Cindra L. Starmer; Linda Lou Mays (05/02/1965, Divorced 1982) **CH:** Jennifer; Ryan; Erin; Jenice; Scott; Holly; Tina; Terry Gene Jr, **ED:** MS, Portland State University (1980); BA, San Diego State University (1976); AS, Grossmont College (1974) **CT:** Licensed Tankerman, U.S. Merchant Marine; Certified Hazard Control Manager **C:** Health and safety Consultant, Marine and General Industry (1982-Present); Retired (2014); AIG Insurance Home Office Reinspector (1994-2014); Reliance Insurance Senior Appraiser (1987-1993); Health and Safety Specialist, Tidewater Barge Lines, Vancouver, WA (1976-1982); Data Communications Equipment, Naval Commnunications. Station, San Diego, CA (1972-1976) **CIV:** Leader, Boy Scouts of America (1981-2020); Active, Clark County Sheriff Reserve (1981) **MIL:** Retired PDRL (1973); With, U.S. Navy (1963-1971) **CW:** Contributor, Articles, Professional Journals **MEM:** Co-director, Chapter, Auto Body Craftsmen's Society (1984-1986); Program Director, Auto Body Craftsmen's Society (1983-1985); Program Director, Southwest Washington Chapter, Auto Body Craftsmen's Society (1983-1984); Health and Safety Steward, Oil Chemical and Atomic Workers Union (1979-1982); Shop Steward, Oil Chemical and Atomic Workers Union (1978-1980); Secretary, Columbia River Boatman's Union (1977-1978); National Safety Management Society; American Public Health Association; National Fire Protection Association; American Society of Safety Engineers; Portland Shipyard Safety Council; Lions **MH:** Albert Nelson Marquis Lifetime Achievement Award **B/I:** He was going to San Diego State University when OSHA just came out. He took a course with the OSHA program and San Diego State had a major called health science and safety so he did triple major there in health science and safety, business administration, and industrial technology. He then became interested in health and safety in marine industry. **PA:** GOP **RE:** LDS Church

NORIEGA, NORMAN J., T: Minister **I:** Religious **CN:** Interdenominational Pentecostal Fellowship and Church **DOB:** 08/28/1942 **PB:** Wareham **SC:** MA/USA **PT:** Anthony Noriega; Irene E. (Grace) Noriega **ED:** Honorary Diploma, Zion Bible Institute, Barrington, RI (1987); Intern, Classes, Inter-Church Council of Greater New Bedford; New Testament Content and Value, Inter-Church Council of Greater New Bedford, RI (1963); Diploma, Choral Conducting, Inter-Church Council of Greater New Bedford (1962); Diploma, Salvation Army (1961) **CT:** Ordained to Ministry, Pentecostal Church (1977-2011); Ordained, Gospel Temple

(1977) **C:** Founder, Interdenominational Pentecostal Fellowship and Church, New Bedford, MA (1974-Present); Pastor, Interdenominational Pentecostal Fellowship and Church, New Bedford, MA (1974-Present); Fellow, Zion Gospel Ministerial (1977) **CR:** Publisher, "Our Portuguese Evangelical Heritage" (2007); Author, "Our Portuguese Evangelical Heritage" (2007) **MIL:** U.S. Army, Honorable Discharge (1967) **AW:** American Registry of Outstanding Professionals (2002); American Registry of Outstanding Professionals (1993); Men of Achievement (1993) **MH:** Albert Nelson Marquis Lifetime Achievement Award **B/I:** Mr. Noriega became involved in the ministry because as a young boy, he always watched and admired the minister at Church and felt that he was going to be a preacher. Mr. Noriega only thought of being a minister and never thought of any other profession. **AV:** Music; Piano; Organ; Coin collecting **PA:** Republican **RE:** Christian

NORMAN, RALPH WARREN JR., T: U.S. Representative from South Carolina; Real Estate Executive **I:** Government Administration/Government Relations/Government Services **DOB:** 06/20/1953 **PB:** Rock Hill **SC:** SC/USA **PT:** Warren Norman **MS:** Married **SPN:** Elaine (Rice) Norman **CH:** Warren III; Caroline; Anne; Mary Catherine **ED:** BS, Presbyterian College (1973) **C:** Member, U.S. House of Representatives from South Carolina's Fifth Congressional District (2017-Present); Member, District 48, South Carolina House of Representatives (2009-2017); Member, South Carolina House of Representatives (2004-2006); Committee on Science, Space and Technology; Committee on Small Business; Real Estate Developer, Warren Norman Company **CIV:** Board of Visitors, Medical University of South Carolina **MEM:** Board of Directors, YMCA

NORTHAM, RALPH SHEARER, T: Governor of Virginia **I:** Government Administration/ Government Relations/Government Services **DOB:** 09/13/1959 **PB:** Nassawadox **SC:** VA/USA **PT:** Wescott B. Northam; Nancy B. (Shearer) Northam **MS:** Married **SPN:** Pam Northam **CH:** Wes; Aubrey **ED:** Child Neurology Fellowship, Walter Reed Army Medical Center, Washington, DC and Johns Hopkins Hospital, Baltimore, MD; Pediatric Resident, Brooke Army Medical Center, San Antonio, Texas; MD, Eastern Virginia Medical School (1984); BS in Biology, Virginia Military Institute (1981) **C:** Governor, Commonwealth of Virginia, Richmond, VA (2018-Present); Pediatric Neurologist, Children's Hospital of the King's Daughters, Norfolk, VA (1992-Present); Lieutenant Governor, Commonwealth of Virginia, Richmond, VA (2014-2018); Member, District Six, Virginia State Senate (2008-2014); Assistant Professor of Neurology, Eastern Virginia Medical School **MIL:** Major, United States Army (1992); Medical Officer, United States Army (1984-1992) **AV:** Working on classic cars; Running **PA:** Democrat **RE:** Baptist

NORTON, EDWARD HARRISON, T: Actor **I:** Media & Entertainment **DOB:** 08/18/1969 **PB:** Boston **SC:** MA/USA **PT:** Edward Mower Norton Jr.; Lydia Robinson "Robin" (Rouse) Norton **MS:** Married **SPN:** Shauna Robertson (04/2012) **CH:** Atlas **ED:** BA in History, Yale University (1991) **CIV:** UN Goodwill Ambassador for Biodiversity (2010-Present); Member, President Barack Obama's Committee on Arts and Humanities (2009); President, Maasai Wilderness Conservation Trust, American Branch; Member, Board of Trustees, Enterprise Community Partners **CW:** Actor, Writer, Producer, "Motherless Brooklyn" (2019); Actor, "Alita: Battle Angel" (2019); Voice Actor, "Isle of Dogs" (2018); Actor, "Little Door Gods" (2016); Actor, "Sausage Party" (2016); Actor, "Collateral Beauty" (2016); Actor,

"Stella" (2015); Appearance, "Last Week Tonight with John Oliver" (2015); Actor, "The Grand Budapest Hotel" (2014); Actor, "Birdman (The Unexpected Virtue of Ignorance)" (2014); Executive Producer, "My Own Man" (2014); Guest Host, "Saturday Night Live" (2013); Featured, "Salinger" (2013); Voice Actor, "The Simpsons" (2000-2013); Executive Producer, "Thanks for Sharing" (2012); Actor, "Moonrise Kingdom" (2012); Actor, "The Bourne Legacy" (2012); Actor, "Stone" (2010); Actor, Producer, "Leaves of Grass" (2009); Actor, "Leaves of Grass" (2009); Actor, "Modern Family" (2009); Actor, "Pride and Glory" (2008); Actor, Writer, "The Incredible Hulk" (2008); Actor, "Kingdom of Heaven" (2005); Executive Producer, "Dirty Work" (2004); Actor, "The Italian Job" (2003); Actor, "Death to Smoochy" (2002); Actor, "Red Dragon" (2002); Actor, "Frida" (2002); Actor, Co-producer, "25ᵗʰ Hour" (2002); Actor, "The Score" (2001); Director, Producer, "Keeping the Faith" (2000); Actor, "Fight Club" (1999); Actor, "Rounders" (1998); Actor, "American History X" (1998); Actor, "The People versus Larry Flynt" (1996); Actor, "Everyone Says I Love You" (1996); Actor, "Primal Fear" (1996) AW: SAG Award for Outstanding Performance by a Cast in a Motion Picture, SAG-AFTRA (2015); National Board of Review Award for Best Supporting Actor (1996, 2014); Golden Globe Award for Best Performance by an Actor in a Supporting Role in a Motion Picture, Hollywood Foreign Press Association (1996); Numerous Awards

NOVAK, JOSEPH, T: Professor Emeritus of Plant Biology and Science Education I: Education/Educational Services DOB: 12/02/1930 PB: Minneapolis SC: MN/USA PT: Joseph Daniel Novak; Anna (Podnay) Novak MS: Married SPN: Joan Owen (07/18/1953) CH: Joseph Mark; Barbara Joan; William John ED: Honorary Doctor, University of Urbino, Italy (2006); Honorary Doctor, Public University of Navarre, Spain (2002); Honorary Doctor, Universidad Nacional del Comahue, Neuquen, Argentina (1998); PhD, University of Minnesota (1958); MA, University of Minnesota (1954); BS, University of Minnesota (1952) C: Professor Emeritus of Plant biology and Science Education, Cornell University, Ithaca, NY (1995-Present); Retired, Senior Research Scientist Emeritus, Institute for Human & Machine Cognition (IHMC), Pensacola, FL (1995); Professor, Cornell University, Ithaca, NY (1967-1995); Associate Professor, Purdue University, West Lafayette, IN (1962-1967); Assistant Professor, Purdue University, West Lafayette, IN (1959-1962); Assistant Professor, Kansas State Teachers College (Now Emporia State University) (1957-1959); Instructor, University of Minnesota, Minneapolis, MN (1956-1957); Teaching Assistant, University of Minnesota, Minneapolis, MN (1952-1956); President, Joseph D. Novak Knowledge Consultants, Inc. CR: Senior Research Scientist, Institute of Human & Machine Cognition (IHMC), FL (1996-Present); Visiting Professor, University of South Florida (1995); Consultant, Over 400 Schools and Colleges (1975-1995); Distinguished Visiting Professor, University of West Florida (1987-1988); Distinguished Visiting Professor, University of North Carolina, Wilmington, NC (1980); Visiting Fellow, Harvard University (1965-1966); Knowledge Construction and Organization Consultant, Procter & Gamble and Other Companies CIV: Volunteer, Workshops, Public Schools and Universities CW: Author, "Learning, Creating and Using Knowledge," Routledge (2010); Author, "Errores Conceptuales: Diagnosis, Tratamientoy Reflexiones" (2001); Author, "Assessing Science Understanding" (2000); Author, "Una Aportacion a la Mejora de la Calidad de la Docentia Universitaria: Los Mapas Conceptuales" (2000); Author, "Learning, Creating and Using Knowledge: Con-

cept Maps as Facilitative Tools for Schools and Corporations" (1998); Author, "Teaching Science for Understanding" (1998); Author, "Aprendizaje Significativo: Techieas y Aplicaciones" (1997); Author, "Learning How to Learn," in 10 Languages (1984-1996); Author, "Learning How to Learn" (1984); Author, "Educational Psychology: A Cognitive View" (1978); Author, "A Theory of Education" (1977); Author, 22 Others; Contributor, Over 40 Chapters to Books; Contributor, Over 130 Articles to Professional Journals AW: Charles E. Bessey Award, The Botanical Society of America (2003); First Honorable Award for Research in Science Education, Council of Scientific Society Presidents (1998); Outstanding Contributions in Science Teaching through Research Award, National Association for Research in Science Teaching (NARST) (1990); Fulbright-Hays Senior Scholar, Australia (1980); Research Associate, Harvard University (1965-1966); Lydia and Alexander Anderson Summer Fellow, Tozer Foundation (1955-1956); Distinguished Alumni Award, University of Minnesota; Honorable Member Award, National Association of Biology Teachers MEM: President, National Association for Research in Science Teaching (NARST) (1968); Fellow, American Association for the Advancement of Science; Secretary, Section Q, American Association for the Advancement of Science; National Science Teaching Association; Council of Scientific Society Presidents; National Association of Biology Teachers; National Association for Research in Science Teaching (NARST); Sigma Xi, The Scientific Research Honor Society MH: Albert Nelson Marquis Lifetime Achievement Award B/I: Dr. Novak was the son of immigrants that came over from Karparthia, Russia. Dr. Novak was disappointed with the school he attended growing up; he promised that if he were to ever be involved with schools, he would find a better way to teach people, which persisted throughout his career. Dr. Novak was torn between doing botanical research and doing research for advance learning and teaching; he chose to go with the latter of the two. He thought he could do more for the world as an educator than a botanist. AV: Hiking; Swimming; Dance; Music

NOVAKOVIC, PHEBE N., T: Chairman, Chief Executive Officer I: Military & Defense Services CN: General Dynamics Corporation ED: MBA in Strategic Planning and Finance, The Wharton School, The University of Pennsylvania (1988); BS, Smith College, Northampton, MA (1979) C: Chairman, Chief Executive Officer, General Dynamics Corporation (2013-Present); President, Chief Operating Officer, General Dynamics Corporation (2012); Executive Vice President of Marine Systems, General Dynamics Corporation (2010-2012); Senior Vice President of Planning and Development, General Dynamics Corporation (2005-2010); Vice President of Strategic Planning, General Dynamics Corporation (2002-2005); Director of Strategic Planning and Development, General Dynamics Corporation, Falls Church, VA (2001-2002); Special Assistant to Secretary and Deputy Secretary, U.S. Department of Defense (1997-2001); Deputy Associate Director of Office Management and Budget, Executive Office of the President, Washington, DC (1992-1997) CR: Board of Directors ,General Dynamics Corporation (2013-Present); Board of Directors, Abbott Laboratories (2010-Present) AW: The 50 Most Powerful Women in Business, Fortune Magazine (2010-2015); One of The 100 Most Powerful Women, Forbes Magazine (2013-2014)

NOVÁNYÓN IDIZOL, ANGÉLÁ, T: Olori Erelu Gro Mambo/Head of Religious Order, Writer I: Religious DOB: 06/09/1953 PB: Philadelphia SC: PA/USA PT: Joseph Smith; Bertha (Hack)

Smith MS: Married SPN: Ahmed Lewis (12/2/1977) CH: Ahmed Junior; Angela Novanyon ED: Coursework Under Hungan Lieonells, Haiti (1978-1983); Coursework Under Hungan Marcell, Mais Jace, Haiti (1978-1983); Coursework Under Hungan Daniel, St. Louis, Haiti (1978-1983); Coursework Under Hungan Rejje', Kenscoff, Haiti (1978-1983); Coursework Under Mambo Josephine, Delmas, Haiti (1978-1983); Coursework in Voodoo Religion Under Papa Hilaire Michel, Mariane, Haiti (1978-1983); Coursework in Akan Religion Under Nana Parabia (1977-1978); Coursework in Business, Community College of Philadelphia (1971-1972); Coursework in Dance, Arthur Hall Dance Ensemble, Philadelphia, PA (1971) CT: Certified Master Dancer C: Founder, High Priestess, Leperistyle Haitian Sanctuary, Philadelphia, PA (1982-Present); Founder, Director, Spirit Cultural Dance Ensemble, Philadelphia, PA (1975-Present); Instructor, Arthur Hall Dance Ensemble, Philadelphia, PA (1973-1977); Founder, Leperistyle Haitian Sanctuary CR: Center for African Culture, Philadelphia, PA (1991-Present); Board Director, Le Peristyle Sanctuary, Mariane (1990-Present); Founder, Chairman, National African Religion Congress (1999); Founder, Voodoo Sanctuary, Sao Paulo, Brazil (1999); Director, African Dance Department, Lacher Latari (1976); Dance Instructor, Various Colleges and Universities; Expert Witness in Field CIV: Tour Conductor, Lecturer, Ile Ife Museum (1974) CW: Public Voodoo Ceremonies, Afro-American Historical and Cultural Museum, Philadelphia, PA (1992, 1993, 1994); Author, "The African Way" (1992); Appearance, Aqua Suite, The Play Germantown Friends Theatre (1991); Author, "Divine Messages of the Loas" (1990); Appearance, Aqua Suite, Robin Hood, Dell Theatre (1982); Presenter, Dance Recitals, Walnut St. Theatre (1976); Appearance, Ayida, Academy of Music, Philadelphia, PA (1974); Editor, "National African Religion Congress"; Featured, "Search of History: Voodoo"; Featured, "Ancient Mysteries: Voodoo" AW: Honorary Citizen, Mayor March. H. Morial (1998); Choreographer Grantee, Pennsylvania Council of the Arts (1991); J.J. Desslaine Award, J.J. Desslaine Society (1990); Special Achievement Award, Level Movement (1990) MH: Albert Nelson Marquis Lifetime Achievement Award B/I: Ms. Idizol suffered from illness for much of her life. After many tests, a doctor informed her that her brain was affected in the section that deals with human spirituality. At the time, she was not religious. However, it quickly became clear to her that the reason she fell ill in the first place was because the spirits were calling her to begin working with them. After Ms. Idizol accepted the calling, she was miraculously healed of her illness within seven days.

NOWIERSKI, ROBERT M., PHD, T: Entomologist, National Program Leader for Bio-Based Pest Management I: Sciences CN: National Institute of Food and Agriculture, U.S. Department of Agriculture DOB: 01/31/1951 PB: Boise SC: ID/USA PT: Leon W. Nowierski; Mary Ellen Nowierski MS: Married SPN: Kathy Diane Johnson (08/30/1975) CH: Lukas James; Ryan Hays ED: Coursework, Brookings Institution, Washington, DC (2012); Coursework, National Research Initiative Competitive Grants Program Workshop (1993); PhD in Entomology, Biological Control, Insect Ecology and Integrated Pest Management, University of California Berkeley, Berkeley, CA (1979); MS in Entomology and Systematics, University of Idaho, Moscow, ID (1975); BS in Pre-Dentistry, University of Idaho, Moscow, ID, Cum Laude (1973) C: National Program Leader for Bio-Based Pest Management, U.S. Department of Agriculture National Institute of Food and Agriculture (NIFA), Washington, DC (2002-Present); Assistant, Associate and Full Professor, Montana State University (1982-2002); IPM Systems Analyst, University of California Berkeley (1980-1982); Postdoctoral Research, University of California Berkeley (1979-1980); Research Assistant, Department of Entomology, University of California Berkeley (1975-1979); Research Assistant, Department of Entomology, University of Idaho, Moscow, ID (1973-1975) **CR:** Research Design Consultant, Graves and Klein, Pensacola, FL (1995-1996); National Research Initiative Competitive Grants Program Panel Member, Biological Control Section, Washington, DC (1995); Permitting Board of Advisors, APHIS-PPQ; Co-Chair, Integrated Pest Management Training Consortium; Co-Chair, Control and Management Subcommittee, National Invasive Species Management Plan; Cooperative State Research, Education and Extension Service, U.S. Department of Agriculture; Representative, Management of Invasive Terrestrial Animals and Pathogens, Cooperative State Research, Education and Extension Service, U.S. Department of Agriculture; Representative, Federal Interagency Committee, Management of Noxious and Exotic Weeds, Federal Integrated Pest Management Coordinating Committee, Forest Health Steering Committee; Technical Advisory Group, Biological Control of Weeds, Cooperative State Research, Education and Extension Service, U.S. Department of Agriculture; Design Consultant, USDA-ARS Insect Quarantine Laboratory, Fort Lauderdale, FL; Invited Participant, Invitational Workshop on USDA Activities in Biological Control **CIV:** Biocontrol Symposium Steering Committee, Shepherdstown, WV (2010); Organizing Committee, International Symposium, IOBC-NRS and ESCOP-WGBC, Bozeman, MT (2001); Co-Chairman, IOBC-NRS/ESCOP-WGBC International Symposium on Biological Control, Bozeman, MT (2001); Chair, Microbial U.S. Chairman, Toadflax Consortium (1998-2001); Management Committee, Plant Growth Center, Montana State University (1989-2001); USDA-ARS National Program Weed Science Workshop, Dulles, VA (2000); Co-Chairman, Xth International Symposium for the Biological Control of Weeds, Bozeman, MT (1999); Montana Schools Advisory Committee (1989); Planning Committee, Plant Growth Center and Insect Quarantine Facility, Montana State University (1985-1985); Participant, Several Other Committees, Montana State University **CW:** Editorial Board, "Biological Control: Theory and Applications in Pest Management" (2000-2006); Keynote Speaker, Leafy Spurge Symposium, Dickinson, ND (1984); Invited Lecturer, International Course on Biological Control, Division of Biological Control, Berkeley, CA (1982); Invited Presenter, International Congress of Entomology, Japan (1980); Contributor, 50 Articles, Refereed Journals, Chapters to Books; Co-Author, 85 Technical Publications; Invited Speaker in Field **AW:** International IPM Award of Recognition, Grower Incentives for an IPM Team Project, Sixth International IPM Symposium (2009); American Planning Association's (APA) Award in the Federal Planning Division (FPD) for Environmental Planning Excellence for "A National Early Detection and Rapid Response System for Invasive Plants in the United States-Conceptual Design" (2004); DuPont Grant in Aid for Teaching (1983); H.C. Manis Award for Excellence in Entomological Research, Department of Entomology, University of Idaho (1975); Grantee, Over 100 Research Grants, Montana State University **MEM:** Chair, ITAP Invertebrates Subcommittee, Interagency Committee for the Management of Invasive Terrestrial Animals and Pathogens (2015-Present); NIFA Representative, Interagency Committee for the Management of Invasive Terrestrial Animals and Pathogens (2004-Present); NIFA Representative, Technical Advisory Group, Biological Control of Weeds (2002-Present); NIFA Rep-

resentative, Federal IPM Coordinating Committee (2002-Present); NIFA Representative, Federal Interagency Committee for the Management of Noxious and Exotic Weeds (2002-Present); NIFA Representative, USDA Invasive Species Working Group (2002-Present); Recruitment Committee, Research Leader Position, USDA-ARS, Northern Plains Agricultural Research Laboratory, Sidney, MT (2007); Lead21 Program (2005-2006); Secretary-Elect to Chairman, Section C, Entomological Society of America (2002-2004); Steering Committee, Topics and Breakout Sessions Committee, Local Arrangements Committee, Fourth National IPM Conference, Indianapolis, IN (2003); Experiment Station Committee on Organization and Policy, Working Group on Biological Control (1999); Secretary, Biological Control, Entomological Society of America, Las Vegas, NV (1998); Invited Participant, Bureau of Indian Affairs, U.S. Department of Interior, Okanogan County, WA (1985); Invited Member, Program Review, USDA/ARS European Parasite Laboratory, Paris, France (1983); Secretary and Chairman, Subsection on Cabiocontrol, Entomological Society of America; Phi Gamma Delta; Ecological Society of America; Entomological Society of America; Entomological Society of Canada; International Organization for Biological Control; Sigma Xi; Gamma Sigma Delta; Weed Science Society of America **MH:** Albert Nelson Marquis Lifetime Achievement Award; Marquis Who's Who Top Professional **B/I:** Dr. Nowierski became involved in his profession because, when he was 4 years old, his father was called into the Korean War and was an on-call surgeon. The house that they rented had a vacant lot across from them, and Dr. Norwierski would go and collect black widow spiders and put them in jars and then feed them bugs. He would collect them from the gopher holes, and not once was he ever bitten. He was fascinated with them, which is what led him to his profession.

NUMBERE, AROLOYE, T: Lecturer **I:** Education/Educational Services **CN:** University of Port Harcourt **DOB:** 05/05/1972 **PB:** Port Harcourt **SC:** Rivers State/Nigeria **MS:** Married **SPN:** Salome **CH:** Eliatha; Elias; Eliel; Elidad **ED:** PhD in Biology, Saint Louis University, St. Louis, MO (2014); MSc in Environmental Management, University of Science and Technology, Nigeria (2006); BSc in Zoology, University of Port Harcourt, Nigeria (1996) **CT:** Certificate in University Teaching Skills, Saint Louis University, St. Louis, MO (2012); OCP (Oracle Certified Professional), Oracle University, Port Harcourt Centre, Nigeria (2005) **C:** Lecturer, Department of Animal and Environmental Biology, University of Port Harcourt, Nigeria (2008-Present); Research/Teaching Assistant, Department of Biology, Saint Louis University, St. Louis, MO (2009-2013); Lecturer, Science Laboratory Technology, Polytechnic, Port Harcourt, Nigeria (2006-2008); Instructor, Environmental Safety, University of Science and Technology, Nigeria (2003-2006); Teacher, High Schools and Colleges, Nigeria (1997-2003) **CW:** Author, "Comparison of Microbial and Heavy Metal Contents in Soils and Roots Under Mangrove Forests Stands with Different Levels of Pollution," American Journal of Applied Sciences (2017); Co-author, "Mangrove Leaf Litter Decomposition Under Mangrove Forest Stands with Different Levels of Pollution in the Niger River Delta, Nigeria," African Journal of Ecology (2016); Co-author, "Long Term Changes in Mangrove Landscape of the Niger River Delta, Nigeria," American Journal of Environmental Sciences (2016); Co-author, "Reciprocal Transplant of Mangrove (Rhizophora racemosa) and Nypa palm (Nypa fruticans) Seedlings in Soils with Different Levels of Pollution in the Niger River Delta, Nigeria," Global Journal of Environmental Research (2016); Co-author, "Effect

of Temperature on Global Mangrove Rhizophora Species Distribution," American Journal of Environmental Sciences (2016) **AW:** Certificate of Achievement in Research Excellence, Saint Louis University Graduate Student Association (2012); GSA-Brennan 2012 Summer Fellowship Award, Saint Louis University Graduate Student Association (2012); PhD Scholarship, Niger Delta Development Commission, Nigeria (2011); Educational Trust Fund PhD Scholarship, University of Port Harcourt, Nigeria (2010); Edward L. and Rhelda Marbry Morgan PhD Endowed Book Fund, Saint Louis University, St. Louis, MO (2009) **MEM:** Ecological Society of America (ESA); Coastal Education and Research Foundation (CERF); Missouri Botanical Garden; International Society Mangrove Ecosystems (ISME) **AS:** Dr. Numbere attributes his success to hard work and determination. **B/I:** Dr. Numbere became involved in his profession because while growing up in Nigeria, he was passionate about nature; his community was by a river and it always inspired him. **AV:** Soccer; Reading; Traveling; Field work **RE:** Christianity **THT:** Dr. Numbere's mission is to help others no matter where they come from.

NUNES, DEVIN GERALD, T: U.S. Congressman from California **I:** Government Administration/Government Relations/Government Services **DOB:** 10/01/1973 **PB:** Tulare **SC:** CA/USA **PT:** Antonio L. Nunes Jr.; Toni Diane (Enas) Nunes **MS:** Married **SPN:** Elizabeth (Tamariz) Nunes (2003) **CH:** Three Daughters **ED:** MS in Agriculture, California Polytechnic State University (1996); BS in Agricultural Business, California Polytechnic State University (1995); AA, College of the Sequoias **CT:** Certified, California Agricultural Leadership Fellowship (2000) **C:** Ranking Member, House Intelligence Committee (2019-Present); Member, U.S. House of Representatives from California's 22nd Congressional District, United States Congress, Washington, DC (2013-Present); Chairman, U.S. House Permanent Select Committee on Intelligence (2015-2019); Member, U.S. House of Representatives from California's 21st Congressional District, United States Congress, Washington, DC (2003-2013); California State Director, U.S. Department of Agriculture (2001); Farmer, Manager, Nunes Dairy (1998-2000); Ranking Member, Subcommittee on Health, Committee of Ways and Means; Member, Committee of Ways and Means **CIV:** Member, Board of Trustees, College of the Sequoias (1996-2002) **CW:** Author, Foreword, "Home Is an Island," Revised Edition (2012); Author, "Restoring the Republic: A Clear, Concise and Colorful Blueprint for America's Future" (2010) **AW:** Named Commander, Order of the Star of Romania (2017); Named Grand Officer, Order of Prince Henry, Portugal (2013); Named to the Politics 40 Under 40, TIME Magazine (2010) **PA:** Republican **RE:** Roman Catholic

NUTTER, DAVID, T: Director **I:** Media & Entertainment **PB:** Dunedin **SC:** FL/USA **MS:** Widowed **SPN:** Birgit Nutter (1987, Deceased 2019) **CH:** Zoe K.; Ben **ED:** Diploma, Dunedin High School (1978); Graduate Coursework in Music, University of Miami **CW:** Director, "Game of Thrones" (2012-2019); Director, Short Film, "Rising" (2018); Pilot Director, "Lost in Space" (2018); Pilot Director, "Deception" (2018); Director, "Untitled Paranormal Project" (2016); Director, "Shameless" (2011-2016); Pilot Director, "Containment" (2016); Guest Director, "The Flash" (2014); Director, TV Film, "The Advocates" (2013); Guest Director, "Homeland" (2013); Pilot Director, "Arrow" (2012); Director, TV Film, "The Doctor" (2011); Director, "Entourage" (2005-2011); Pilot Director, "Chase" (2010); Guest Director, "The Pacific" (2010); Guest Director, "Eastwick" (2009); Guest Director, "The Mentalist"

(2008); Guest Director, "Terminator: The Sarah Connor Chronicles" (2008); Pilot Director, "Traveler" (2007); Guest Director, "Dr. Vegas" (2004-2006); Guest Director, "The Sopranos" (2006); Guest Director, "Nip/Tuck" (2005); Guest Director, "Supernatural" (2005); Guest Director, "Jack & Bobby" (2004); Guest Director, "Without a Trace" (2002-2003); Guest Director, "Tarzan" (2003); Guest Director, "The West Wing" (2002); Director, "ER" (1996-2002); Guest Director, "Smallville" (2001); Guest Director, "Band of Brothers" (2001); Pilot Director, "Dark Angel" (2000); Guest Director, "Roswell" (1999); Director, "Disturbing Behavior" (1998); Pilot Director, "Sleepwalkers" (1997); Guest Director, "Millennium" (1996-1997); Director, "The X-Files" (1993-1995); Guest Director, "Space: Above and Beyond" (1995); Director, "Trancers 5: Sudden Deth" (1994); Guest Director, "M.A.N.T.I.S." (1994); Director, "Trancers 4: Jack of Swords" (1994); Guest Director, "The Commish" (1992); Guest Director, "Bill & Ted's Excellent Adventure" (1992); Director, "Superboy" (1989-1992); Guest Director, "P.S.I. Luv U" (1991); Guest Director, "Broken Badges" (1991); Director, "The 100 Lives of Black Jack Savage" (1991); Guest Director, "Super Force" (1990); Guest Director, "Booker" (1990); Guest Director, "21 Jump Street" (1987-1990); Director, "Cease Fire" (1985)

NYQUIST, CORINNE, PHD, T: Librarian **I:** Library Management/Library Services **CN:** State University of New York **DOB:** 11/01/1935 **PB:** Minnesota Falls **SC:** MN/USA **PT:** Clair Francis Johnson; Ebba Ingeborg Johnson **MS:** Married **SPN:** Thomas Eugene Nyquist (12/22/1956) **CH:** Jonathan Eugene; Lynn Marie **ED:** Honorary PhD, University at Albany, State University of New York (2004); MALS, University of Minnesota (1971); BA, Macalester College, Cum Laude (1956) **C:** Faculty Senator, State University of New York (2012-Present); Assistant Librarian, Librarian, State University of New York at New Paltz (1968-2018); Ombudsman, State University of New York at New Paltz (1983-1985); Assistant Librarian, Research Assistant, Rhodes University, Grahamstown, Republic of South Africa (1967); Assistant Librarian, Skokie Public Library (1965-1966); Assistant Librarian, Evanston Public Library (1962-1964); Assistant Librarian, University of Minnesota (1959-1960) **CR:** Co-Project Director, Human Rights Documentation Project, Ford Foundation (1986-1988); Chairman, International Libraries Committee, State University of New York (1984-1986); Consultant, New York State Education Department, Albany, NY (1980-1982) **CIV:** Chairman, Town Democratic Committee, New Paltz, NY (1984-1986, 2007-2012); Advisory Committee on Awards, State University of New York (1989-1994) **CW:** Author, "Resource Sharing Today" (2014); Contributor, Articles, Professional Journals **AW:** Chancellor's Award (1986); Grantee, Ford Foundation (1986); Grantee, State University of New York Research Foundation (1975, 1984-1986) **MEM:** American Library Association (1989-Present); Director Secretariat, New York African Studies Association (2008); Board of Directors, Sojourner Truth Institute (1997-2001); Co-Editor, Newsletter, Vice President, President, New York African Studies Association (1974-1999); Executive Committee, Ulster County Libraries Association (1984-1994); African Studies Association; State University of New York Libraries Association; Beta Phi Mu **MH:** Albert Nelson Marquis Lifetime Achievement Award **B/I:** Dr. Nyquist became involved in her profession because she initially wanted to be a violinist but eventually realized she was better suited in other fields. When she went to college, her mother suggested she think about becoming a librarian. Dr. Nyquist took her mother's advice and has since found consistent success. **AV:** Reading; Hiking; Cross country skiing; Traveling

NZEWI, UGOCHUKWU-SMOOTH C., PHD, T: Artist, Curator **I:** Fine Art **CN:** Museum of Modern Art **SC:** Enugu/Nigeria **ED:** PhD in Art History, Emory University (2013); Postgraduate Diplomate, Museum and Heritage Studies, University of Western Cape/University of Cape Town (2006); BA in Fine and Applied Art, University of Nigeria, Nsukka, Nigeria (2001) **C:** Steven and Lisa Tananbaum Curator in Painting and Sculpture, Museum of Modern Art (2019-Present); Visual Artist (2001-Present); Curator of African Art, Cleveland Museum of Art (2017-2019); Curator of African Art, Hood Museum, Dartmouth College, Hanover, NH (2013-2017) **CR:** Co-Conspirator, 1RoomShack Collective, Lagos, Nigeria (2005-Present); Curator, High Museum, Atlanta, GA (2009) **CW:** Contributor, "Anthropology of Practice: Artists of Africa and the Ethnographic Field in Contemporary Art," Alternative Art and Anthropology: Global Encounters (2017); Curator, "Eric van Hove: The Craft of Art" (2016); Curator, "Inventory: New Works and Conversations Around African Art" (2016); Contributor, "A Nigerian Tradition of Independent Art Spaces/Initiatives," New Spaces for Negotiating Art and Histories in Africa (2015); Curator, "Ukwara: Ritual Cloth of the Ekpe Secret Society" (2015); Curator, "The Art of Weapons: Selections from the African Collection" (2014)

OAKES, ANDRA NAN, T: Lawyer **I:** Law and Legal Services **DOB:** 11/22/1946 **PB:** New York **SC:** NY/USA **PT:** John Bertram Oakes; Margery Hartman Oakes **MS:** Married **SPN:** Edwin Emmett Huddleson III (07/08/1978) **CH:** Michael Alexander Oakes Huddleson; Jonathan Edwin Huddleson **ED:** Doctor of Jurisprudence, The University of Chicago (1971); Bachelor of Arts, Bryn Mawr College, Cum Laude, with Honors (1968) **C:** Counsel, Bernabei & Katz, Washington, DC (1997-1998); Program Director, Emeritus Foundation, Washington, DC (1995-1997); Partner, Dobrovir, Oakes and Gebhardt, Washington, DC (1980-1984); Associate, Law Firm of Wm. A. Dobrovir, Washington, DC (1971-1979); Summer Investigator, Center for the Study of Responsive Law, Washington, DC (1970); Summer Researcher, Senate Foreign Relations Committee, Washington, DC (1967) **CR:** Board Director, Washington Council of Lawyers (1979-1985); Member, District of Columbia Employment Discrimination Complaint Service (1997-1979); Government Accountability Project, Whistleblower Advisory Council (1977-1979); Testified Before the DC City Council on Behalf of the Washington Council of Lawyers in Support of the DC Family and Medical Leave Act **CIV:** Volunteer, You Can Vote, Charlotte, NC (2020); Capital Campaign Solicitor, Parent Host, Georgetown Day School, Washington, DC (1990-2000); Board of Trustees, St. John's Community Services, Washington, DC (1993-1996); Capital Campaign Solicitor, Alumna Interviewer, Bryn Mawr College (1993); Capital Campaign Committee, Development Committee, Burgundy Farm Country Day School, Alexandria, VA (1989-1991); Treasurer, Ladies Board, St. John's Community Services, Washington, DC (1988-1990) **CW:** Author, "Protecting the Rights of Whistleblowers and the Accused in Federally Supported Biomedical Research," President's Commission for the Study of Ethical Problems in Biomedical and Behavioral Research (1982); Co-author, "The Offenses of Richard M. Nixon: A Guide to His Impeachable Crimes" (1973) **MEM:** American Civil Liberties Union; Sierra Club; National Lawyers Guild; The District of Columbia Bar; Animal Legal Defense Fund; The Bryn Mawr Club of Washington, DC

BAR: District of Columbia; Supreme Court of the United States; U.S. Court of Appeals for the District of Columbia Circuit; U.S. Court of Appeals for the Federal Circuit; U.S. District Court for the District of Maryland; U.S. District Court for the District of Columbia **MH:** Albert Nelson Marquis Lifetime Achievement Award **AV:** Travel; Reading; Gardening; Art; Progressive politics; DC voting rights **PA:** Democrat **RE:** Jewish

OATES, JOHN ALEXANDER III, MD, MACP, T: Physician, Medical Educator and Biomedical Scientist **I:** Medicine & Health Care **DOB:** 04/23/1932 **PB:** Fayetteville **SC:** NC/USA **PT:** John Alexander Oates; Isabelle (Crowder) Oates **MS:** Married **SPN:** Meredith Stringfield (06/12/1956) **CH:** David Alexander; Christine Larkin; James Caldwell **ED:** MD, Bowman Gray School of Medicine of Wake Forest College, Wake Forest, NC (1956); BS, Wake Forest College, Wake Forest, NC, Magna Cum Laude (1953) **CT:** Board Certified, Sub-Specialty of Hypertension (1999); Diplomat, American Board of Internal Medicine (1963); License to Practice Medicine, Tennessee (1964); License to Practice Medicine, North Carolina (1956) **C:** Thomas F. Frist Senior Professor of Medicine, Vanderbilt University School of Medicine, Nashville, TN (1988-Present); Professor of Medicine and Pharmacology, Vanderbilt University School of Medicine, Nashville, TN (1969-Present); Faculty, Vanderbilt University School of Medicine, Nashville, TN (1963-Present); Chairman, Department of Medicine, Vanderbilt University School of Medicine, Nashville, TN (1983-1997); Joe and Morris Werthan Professor of Investigative Medicine, Vanderbilt University School of Medicine, Nashville, TN (1974-1984); Clinical Associate, Senior Investigator, National Heart Institute, Bethesda, MD (1958-1963); Intern, Assistant Resident Medicine, New York Hospital, Cornell University Medical Center, New York, NY (1961-1962, 1956-1958) **CR:** Advisory Council, National Heart, Lung and Blood Institute (1985-1989); Drug Research Board, National Academy of Sciences (1967-1971); Chairman, Pharmacology and Toxicology Training Committee, National Institute of General Medical Sciences (1969-1970) **CIV:** Scientific Advisor, Board of Cumberland Pharmaceuticals **MIL:** U.S. Public Health Service Commissioned Corps (1958-1962) **CW:** Co-Author, "Triamterene Enhances the Blood Pressure Lowering Effect of Hydrochlorothiazide in Patients with Hypertension," Journal of General Internal Medicine (2016); Co-Author, "Cyclooxygenase-2 Promotes Early Artherosclerotic Lesion Formation in LDL Receptor-Deficient Mice" (2002); Presenter, "The Pharmacology of Prostaglandin E2: Actions in Human Diseases Involving the Mast Cells in: Eicosanoids, Aspirin, and Asthma." (1998); Author, "Introduction: Misoprostol and Eicosanoid Symposium" (1995); Presenter, "Antagonism of Antihypertensive Drug Therapy by Nonsteroidal Anti-Inflammatory Drugs," NHLBI Workshop on Drug Side Effects, Drug Interactions, Drug Resistance, and the Management of Hypertension (1986); Co-Author, "Presidential Address: Clinical Investigation: A Pathway to Discovery," Transactions of the Association of American Physicians (1982); Author, "Prostaglandins as Mediators of the Hypercalcemia Associated with Certain Human Cancers," Biochemical Aspects of Prostaglandins and Thromboxane (1977); Author, "The Carcinoid Syndrome," Harrison's Principles of Internal Medicine (1971); Author, Co-Author, Articles, Numerous Professional Journals; Author, Co-Author, Numerous Book Chapters; Presenter, Numerous Published Presentations **AW:** Earl Sutherland Award for Achievement in Research (2010); Novartis Award Council for High Blood Pressure Research (2010); Award of Excellence in

Clinical Research, The General Clinical Research Centers Program, NIH (2004); Distinguished Achievement Award, New York Hospital-Cornell Medical Center (1986); Award of Merit, American Heart Association (1985); Oscar B. Hunter Award, American Society for Clinical Pharmacology and Therapeutics (1980); Harry Gold Award for Clinical Pharmacology, American Society for Pharmacology and Experimental Therapeutics (1979); Wake Forrest College's Distinguished Alumnus Award (1976); Bowman Gray School of Medicine's Distinguished Alumnus Award (1971); American Society for Pharmacology and Experimental Therapeutics Award for Experimental Therapeutics for "Outstanding Basic Pharmacologic Investigations in Man" (1969) **MEM:** President, American Clinical and Climatological Association (2010-2011); American Association for the Advancement of Science (1998); American Academy of Arts and Sciences (1996); National Academy of Medicine (1994); American Clinical and Climatological Association (1982); President, Association for American Physicians (1981-1982); Vice President, American Society for Clinical Investigation (1976-1977); New York Academy of Science (1975); President, American Federation for Medical Research (1970-1971); Chairman, Executive Committee, Division of Clinical Pharmacology, American Society for Pharmacology and Experimental Therapeutics (1967-1969); Council for High Blood Pressure Research of the American Heart Association (1968); Association of American Physicians (1968); American Society for Clinical Investigation (1965); American Society for Pharmacology and Experimental Therapeutics (1965); Southern Society for Clinical Investigation (1964); American Federation for Clinical Research (1962); Master, American College of Physicians; Fellow, American Academy of Arts and Sciences; American Association for the Advancement of Science **MH:** Albert Nelson Marquis Lifetime Achievement Award; Marquis Who's Who Top Professional; Distinguished Humanitarian Award **B/I:** Dr. Oates became involved in his profession because of his interest in research, which was driven by the mentors he had in medical school, such as chemistry professor Camilo Arton.

OATES, JOYCE CAROL, T: Author; Professor Emerita **I:** Writing and Editing **DOB:** 06/16/1938 **PB:** Lockport **SC:** NY/USA **PT:** Frederic James Oates; Caroline (Bush) Oates **MS:** Widowed **SPN:** Charles Gross (2009, Deceased 2019); Raymond Joseph Smith (01/23/1961, Deceased 02/18/2008) **ED:** Honorary ArtsD, University of Pennsylvania (2011); Honorary LHD, Mount Holyoke College (2006); MA, University of Wisconsin-Madison (1961); BA, Syracuse University (1960) **C:** Visiting Professor, University of California Berkeley (2016-Present); Roger S. Berlind '52 Professor Emerita, Princeton University (2014-Present); Roger S. Berlind '52 Professor, Humanities and Creative Writing, Princeton University (2008-2014); Professor, Princeton University (1987-2008); Professor, English, University of Windsor, Canada (1967-1987); Writer-in-residence, Princeton University (1978-1981); Assistant Professor, University of Detroit (1965-1967); Instructor, English, University of Detroit (1962-1965); Teacher, Beaumont, TX (1961) **CIV:** Board of Trustees, John Simon Guggenheim Memorial Foundation (1997-2016); Honorary Member, Simpson Literary Project **CW:** Author, "Night. Sleep. Death. The Stars" (2020); Author, "The Pursuit" (2019); Author, "My Life as a Rat" (2019); Author, "Hazards of Time Travel" (2018); Author, "A Book of American Martyrs" (2017); Author, "The Man without a Shadow" (2016); Author, "The Doll Master and Other Tales" (2016); Author, "The Sacrifice" (2015); Author, "Jack of Spades" (2015); Author, "The Lost Land-

scape" (2015); Author, "Carthage" (2014); Author, "High Crime Area: Tales of Darkness and Dread" (2014); Author, "Lovely, Dark, Deep" (2014); Author, "Daddy Love" (2013); Author, "Evil Eye: Four Novellas of Love Gone Wrong" (2013); Author, "The Accursed" (2013); Author, "Mudwomen" (2012); Author, "Two or Three Things I Forgot to Tell You" (2012); Author, "Black Dahlia & White Rose" (2012); Author, "A Widow's Story: A Memoir" (2011); Author, "Blonde" (2009); Author, "Wild Nights!" (2008); Author, "My Sister, My Love" (2008); Author, "The Museum of Dr. Moses: Tales of Mystery and Suspense" (2007); Author, "The Gravedigger's Daughter" (2007); Author, "The Female of the Species: Tales of Mystery and Suspense" (2006); Author, "High Lonesome: New and Selected Stories" (2006); Author, "After the Wreck, I Picked Myself Up, Spread My Wings, and Flew Away" (2006); Author, "Blood Mask" (2006); Author, "Black Girl/White Girl" (2006); Author, Under Pseudonym Lauren Kelly, "Blood Mask" (2006); Author, "The Corn Maiden: A Love Story" (2005); Author, "Missing Mom" (2005); Author, "The Stolen Heart" (2005); Author, "Sexy" (2005); Author, "I Am No One You Know: Stories" (2004); Author, "Dr. Magic: Six One Act Plays" (2004); Author, "The Falls" (2004); Author, "Small Avalanches and Other Stories" (2003); Author, "Freaky Green Eyes" (2003); Author, "Where is Little Reynard?" (2003); Author, Under Pseudonym Lauren Kelly, "Take Me, Take Me with You" (2003); Author, "The Tattooed Girl" (2003); Author, "Rape: A Love Story" (2003); Author, "Beasts" (2002); Author, "I'll Take You There" (2002); Author, "Big Mouth & Ugly Girl" (2002); Author, "The Barrens" (2001); Author, "Middle Age: A Romance" (2001); Author, "Faithless: Tales of Transgression" (2001); Author, "Blonde" (2000); Author, "Starr Bright Will Be with You Soon" (1999); Author, "Broke Heart Blues" (1999); Author, "My Heart Laid Bare" (1998); Author, "Come Meet Muffin!" (1998); Author, "New Plays" (1998); Author, "The Collector of Hearts: New Tales of the Grotesque" (1998); Author, "Double Delight" (1997); Author, "Man Crazy" (1997); Author, "We Were the Mulvaneys" (1996); Author, "Demon and Other Tales" (1996); Author, "Tenderness" (1996); Author, "Will You Always Love Me? And Other Stories" (1996); Author, "First Love: A Gothic Tale" (1996); Author, "The Perfectionist and Other Plays" (1996); Author, "You Can't Catch Me" (1995); Author, "Zombie" (1995); Author, "Haunted: Tales of the Grotesque" (1994); Author, "What I Lived For" (1994); Author, "Where are You Going, Where Have You Been?: Selected Early Stories" (1993); Author, "Foxfire: Confessions of a Girl Gang" (1993); Author, "Where is Here?" (1992); Author, "Snake Eyes" (1992); Author, "Black Water" (1992); Author, "The Rise of Life on Earth" (1991); Author, "Heat and Other Stories" (1991); Author, "In Darkest America" (1991); Author, "I Stand Before You Naked" (1991); Author, "Twelve Plays" (1991); Author, "Nemesis" (1990); Author, "Because It is Bitter, and Because It is My Heart" (1990); Author, "I Lock My Door Upon Myself" (1990); Author, "Oates in Exile" (1990); Author, "Soul/Mate" (1989); Author, "The Assignation: Stories" (1989); Author, "The Time Traveler" (1989); Author, "American Appetites" (1989); Author, "You Must Remember This" (1987); Author, Under Pseudonym Rosamond Smith, "Lives of the Twins" (1987); Author, "Raven's Wing: Stories" (1986); Author, "Marya: A Life" (1986); Author, "Solstice" (1985); Author, "Mysteries of Winterthurn" (1984); Author, "Last Days: Stories" (1984); Author, "Wild Saturday" (1984); Author, "Invisible Woman: New and Selected Poems" (1982); Author, "A Bloodsmoor Romance" (1982); Author, "Angel of Light" (1981); Author, "Bellefleur" (1980); Author, "Three Plays" (1980); Author, "A Sentimental Education:

Stories" (1980); Author, "All the Good People I've Left Behind" (1979); Author, "Cybele" (1979); Author, "Unholy Loves" (1979); Author, "Women Whose Lives are Food, Men Whose Lives are Money" (1978); Author, "Son of the Morning" (1978); Author, "Night-Side" (1977); Author, "The Triumph of the Spider Monkey" (1976); Author, "Crossing the Border: Fifteen Tales" (1976); Author, "Childwold" (1976); Author, "The Poisoned Kiss and Other Stories from the Portuguese" (1975); Author, "The Assassins: A Book of Hours" (1975); Author, "The Seduction and Other Stories" (1975); Author, "The Fabulous Beasts" (1975); Author, "Miracle Play" (1974); Author, "The Goddess and Other Women" (1974); Author, "Angel Fire" (1973); Author, "Do with Me What You Will" (1973); Author, "Marriages and Infidelities" (1972); Author, "Wonderland" (1971); Author, "Love and Its Derangements" (1970); Author, "The Wheel of Love and Other Stories" (1970); Author, "Anonymous Sins & Other Poems" (1969); Author, "Them" (1969); Author, "Women in Love and Other Poems" (1968); Author, "Expensive People" (1968); Author, "A Garden of Earthly Delights" (1967); Author, "Upon the Sweeping Flood and Other Stories" (1966); Author, "With Shuddering Fall" (1964); Author, "By the North Gate" (1963); Contributor, Numerous Essays, Short Stories, Plays, Works of Criticism, Books **AW:** Prix Mondial Cino Del Duca (2020); Jerusalem Prize for Lifetime Achievement (2019); Bram Stoker Award (1996, 2012, 2013); Norman Mailer Prize for Lifetime Achievement (2012); Stone Award for Lifetime Literary Achievement, Oregon State University (2012); Inductee, New Jersey Hall of Fame (2012); World Fantasy Award for Best Short Fiction (2011); Ivan Sandorf Lifetime Achievement Award, National Book Critics Circle (2010); Fernanda Pivano Award (2010); National Humanities Medal (2010); Humanist of the Year, American Humanist Association (2007); Chicago Tribune Literature Prize (2006); Prix Femina Etranger, France (2005); Kenyon Review Award for Literary Achievement (2003); Peggy V. Helmerich Distinguished Author Award (2002); Golden Plate Award, American Academy of Achievement (1997); Fisk Fiction Prize, Boston Book Review (1996); PEN/Malamud Award for Excellence in Art of Short Story (1996); Rea Award for Short Story (1990); Heidemann Award (1990); St. Louis Literary Award, Saint Louis University Library Association (1988); O. Henry Award (1967, 1973); National Book Award (1970); Grantee, National Education Association (1966, 1968); M.L. Rosenthal Award, National Institute of Arts & Letters (1968); Scholastic Art & Writing Award (1955, 1956) **AV:** Running

OBAMA, BARACK HUSSEIN II, T: 44th President of the United States **I:** Government Administration/Government Relations/Government Services **DOB:** 08/04/1961 **PB:** Honolulu **SC:** HI/USA **PT:** Barack Obama Sr.; Shirley Ann (Dunham) Obama **MS:** Married **SPN:** Michelle (LaVaughn Robinson) Obama (10/18/1992) **CH:** Malia Ann; Natasha ("Sasha") **ED:** Honorary LLD, Hampton University (2010); Honorary LLD, University of Michigan, Ann Arbor, MI (2010); Honorary LLD, University of Notre Dame (2009); Honorary LLD, Wesleyan University (2008); Honorary LLD, Harvard University (2007); Honorary LLD, Southern New Hampshire University (2007); Honorary LLD, Xavier University, (2006); Honorary LLD, University of Massachusetts (2006); Honorary LLD, Northwestern University (2005); Honorary LLD, Knox College (2005); JD, Harvard Law School, Magna Cum Laude (1991); BA in Political Science, Columbia University (1983); Coursework, Occidental College, Los Angeles, CA (1979-1981) **C:** 44th President of the United States, Washington, DC (2009-2017); Member, U.S. Senate Committee on Homeland

Security and Governmental Affairs (2007-2009); Member, U.S. Senate Committee on Health, Education, Labor and Pensions (2007-2009); U.S. Senator, State of Illinois (2005-2008); Member, U.S. Senate Committee on Environment and Public Works (2006-2007); Member, U.S. Senate Committee on Veterans' Affairs Committee (2005-2006); Member, U.S. Senate Committee on Foreign Relations (2005-2006); Member, District 13, Illinois State Senate, Springfield, IL (1997-2005); Of Counsel, Davis, Miner, Barnhill & Galland, Professional Corporation (Now Miner, Barnhill & Galland, P.C.) (1996-2004); Associate, Davis, Miner, Barnhill & Galland, Professional Corporation (Now Miner, Barnhill & Galland, P.C.) (1993-1996); Executive Director, PROJECT VOTE!, Chicago, IL (1992); Director, Developing Communities Project (1985-1988); Writer, Financial Analyst, Business International Corporation (1984-1985) CR: Keynote Speaker, Democratic National Convention, Boston, MA (2004); Senior Lecturer, The University of Chicago Law School (1996-2004); Lecturer, Constitutional Law, The University of Chicago Law School (1992-1996) CIV: Board of Directors, The Joyce Foundation (1994-2002); Board of Directors, Woods Fund Chicago (1993-2001); Founding President, Chairman, Chicago Annenberg Challenge (1995-1999); Board of Directors, Chicago Annenberg Challenge (1995-1999); Board of Directors, Chairman, Chicago Lawyers' Committee for Civil Rights Under the Law (Now Chicago Lawyers' Committee for Civil Rights) (1995); Co-founder, Lugenia Burns Hope Center (1994) CW: Author, "Of Thee I Sing: A Letter to My Daughters" (2010); Appearance, Television Series, "Mythbusters" (2010); Appearance, Documentary, "By the People: The Election of Barack Obama" (2009); Author, "Change We Can Believe In: Barack Obama's Plan to Renew America's Promise" (2008); Author, "Audacity of Hope: Thoughts on Reclaiming the American Dream" (2006); Author, "Dreams from My Father: A Story of Race and Inheritance" (1995); Editor-in-Chief, Harvard Law Review (1990-1991) AW: Listee, 100 Most Influential People in the World, Time Magazine (2005, 2007-2014); Presidential Medal of Distinction, Government of Israel (2013); Person of the Year, Time Magazine (2008, 2012); Listee, 50 Highest-earning Political Figures, Newsweek (2010); Listee, World's Most Powerful People, Forbes Magazine (2009-2014); Listee, 100 Agents of Change, Rolling Stone Magazine (2009); Listee, Top 25 Market Movers, U.S. News & World Report (2009); Nobel Peace Prize, Norweigan Nobel Committee (2009); Most Fascinating Person of 2008, Barbara Walters Special (2008); Listee, Global Elite, Newsweek Magazine (2008); Grammy Award for Best Spoken Word Album, Recording Academy (2008); Best Literary Work in Nonfiction, NAACP (2007); Listee, 50 Most Powerful People in DC, GQ Magazine (2007); Grammy Award for Best Spoken Word or Non-Musical Album, Recording Academy (2006); Listee, Most Influential Black Americans, Ebony Magazine (2006); Congressional Leadership Award, National Urban League (2006); Lifetime Achievement Award, NAACP, Detroit, MI Chapter (2005); Howard Blake Walker Award, Christopher House (2005); Award, Harvard Law School Association (2005); Chairman's Award, NAACP (2005); Legislative Award, Associated Fire Fighters of IL (AFFI) (2004); Outstanding Legislator Award, Campaign for Better Health Care, Illinois Primary Health Care Association (1998); Freshman Legislative Award, IVI-IPO (1997); "Legal Eagle" Award for Litigation, IVI-IPO (1995); Monarch Award for Outstanding Public Service (1994); Listee, 40 Under 40, Crain's Chicago Business (1993) MEM: Illinois State Bar Association; Cook County Bar Association AV: Golfing PA: Democrat RE: Christian

O'BRIEN, CONAN CHRISTOPHER, T: Talk Show Host; Writer **I:** Media & Entertainment **DOB:** 04/18/1963 **PB:** Brookline **SC:** MA/USA **PT:** Thomas Francis O'Brien; Ruth (Reardon) O'Brien **MS:** Married **SPN:** Liza Powel (01/12/2002) **CH:** Neve; Beckett **ED:** Bachelor of Arts in American History and Literature, Harvard University (1985) **CR:** Talk Show Host (1983-Present); President, The Harvard Lampoon (1983, 1984); Staff Member, The Harvard Lampoon (1981-1985) **CW:** Host, "Conan" (2010-Present); Appearance, "Dads" (2019); Voice Actor, "The Lego Batman Movie" (2017); Appearance, "Sandy Wexler" (2017); Actor, "Mi Adorable Maldicion" (2017); Appearance, "One More Happy Ending" (2016); Actor, "Gute Zeiten, Schlechte Zeiten" (2016); Appearance, "Ground Floor" (2015); Actor, "Stranger's Soul" (2015); Actor, "Clipped" (2015); Appearance, "ArmComedy" (2015); Host, "MTV Movie Awards" (2014); Appearance, "The Comeback" (2014); Appearance, "Sharktopus vs Pteracude" (2014); Voice Actor, "Family Guy" (2013, 2014); Executive Producer, Appearance, "Eagleheart" (2011-2014); Appearance, "Clear History" (2013); Voice Actor, "Batman: The Dark Knight Returns Part 2" (2013); Appearance, "Now You See Me" (2013); Appearance, "The Secret Life of Walter Mitty" (2013); Host, White House Correspondents' Dinner (2013); Appearance, "Arrested Development" (2013); Appearance, "Nashville" (2013); Appearance, "It's Always Sunny in Philadelphia" (2013); Appearance, "Real Husbands of Hollywood" (2013); Appearance, "Brody Stevens: Enjoy It!" (2013); Actor, "How I Met Your Mother" (2012); Voice Actor, "The Penguins of Madagascar" (2012); Appearance, "Web Therapy" (2011); Host, "Christmas in Washington" (2011); Appearance, "Eagleheart" (2011); Featured, "Conan O'Brien Can't Stop" (2011); Host, Writer, Executive Producer, "The Tonight Show with Conan O'Brien" (2009-2010); Writer, Producer, Host, "Late Night with Conan O'Brien" (1993-2009); Appearance, "The Great Buck Howard" (2008); Appearance, "The Great Buck Howard" (2008); Voice Actor, "Robot Chicken" (2005); Appearance, "Queer Duck: The Movie" (2006); Appearance, "Pittsburgh" (2006); Appearance, "Bewitched" (2005); Appearance, "Bewitched" (2005); Appearance, "End of the Century: The Story of the Ramones" (2003); Appearance, "Pootie Tang" (2001); Appearance, "Vanilla Sky" (2001); Appearance, "Storytelling" (2001); Host, "Saturday Night Live" (2001); Appearance, "Vanilla Sky" (2001); Appearance, "Barenaked in America" (1999); Appearance, "LateLine" (1999); Appearance, "Space Ghost Coast to Coast" (1999); Voice Actor, "Futurama" (1999); Actor, "Tomorrow Night" (1998); Appearance, "Veronica's Closet" (1998); Appearance, "Spin City" (1998); Appearance, "Tomorrow Night" (1998); Voice Actor, "Dr. Katz, Professional Therapist" (1997); Actor, "The Single Guy" (1996); Appearance, "Arli$$" (1996); Voice Actor, "The Simpsons" (1994); Writer, Producer, "The Simpsons" (1991-1993); Writer, "Lookwell" (1991); Writer, "Saturday Night Live" (1988-1991); Writer, Performer, "The Happy Happy Good Show," Los Angeles, CA and Chicago, IL (1988); Writer, Producer, "The Wilton North Report" (1987); Stage Appearances, The Groundlings, Los Angeles, CA (1985-1987); Writer, "Not Necessarily the News," HBO (1985-1987) **AW:** iHeartRadio Podcast Awards for Best Comedy Podcast, Best Ad Read (2020); Primetime Emmy Award for in Interactive Media - within an Unscripted Program, Academy of Television Arts & Sciences (2018); Primetime Emmy Award for Outstanding Creative Achievement in Interactive Media - Enhancement to a Television Program or Series, Academy of Television Arts & Sciences (2012); Named Favorite Talk Show Host, People's Choice Awards (2011); Named One of the 100 Most Influential People in the World, TIME Magazine (2010); Primetime Emmy Award for Outstanding Writing for a Variety, Music or Comedy Series, Academy of Television Arts & Sciences (2007); Award for Best Writing in Comedy/Variety Show, Writers Guild of America (1997, 2000, 2002, 2003, 2005, 2006); Emmy Award for Outstanding Writing in Comedy Series, Academy of Television Arts & Sciences (1989) **PA:** Democrat **RE:** Catholic

O'BRIEN, JOAN SUSAN, T: Lawyer, Educator **I:** Law and Legal Services **DOB:** 04/14/1946 **PB:** New York **SC:** NY/USA **PT:** Edward Vincent O'Brien; Joan Therese (Kramer) Quinn **MS:** Married **SPN:** Michael P. Wilpan (05/27/1979, Divorced) **CH:** Edward B Wilpan; Anabel T. Wilpan **ED:** JD, Georgetown University (1970); BA, New York University (1967) **C:** Trial Attorney, Grey & Grey, LLP (1997-2008); Appellate Attorney, Fusco, Brandenstein, & Rada (1993-1997); Administrative Law Judge, New York State Workers Compensation Board (1990-1993); Assistant Professor, St. John's University (1984-1990); Trial Attorney, Mendes & Mount LLP (1979-1984); Private Practice, New York (1976-1979); Assistant U.S. Attorney, Office of the U.S. Attorney, U.S. District Court Eastern District of New York (1972-1976); Law Clerk, Honorary Frank J. Murray, United States District Court District of Massachusetts (1970-1971) **CIV:** Mentor for Incarcerated Juveniles, Nassau County Juvenile Detention Center, Leadership Training Institute (2012-Present); Leader Girl Scouts of Nassau County (1990-1993); President, Women's Caucus, Nassau County Democratic Committee (1988-1990) **CW:** Editor, Georgetown Law Journal (1968-1970) **MEM:** Vice-President, The Italian Cultural Society of Washington, DC, Inc. (2017); Farmingdale-Bethpage Historical Society **BAR:** United States District Court Eastern District of New York (1972); United States District Court Southern District of New York (1972); New York State Bar Association (1971); Massachusetts Bar Association (1971); United States Court of Appeals for the Second Circuit (1971) **MH:** Albert Nelson Marquis Lifetime Achievement Award **AS:** Ms. O'Brien attributes her success to ignoring prejudice against her while fighting it in regard to others. **B/I:** Ms. O'Brien became involved in her profession because of her lifelong desire to be a lawyer; she used to watch Perry Mason a lot as a child. **AV:** Mahjong **PA:** Democrat **RE:** Catholic; Unitarian-Universalism

O'BRIEN, ROBERT CHARLES, T: United States National Security Advisor **I:** Government Administration/Government Relations/Government Services **DOB:** 06/18/1966 **PB:** Los Angeles **SC:** CA/USA **PT:** Robert Charles O'Brien; Judith Lorie O'Brien **MS:** Married **SPN:** Louisa Maria Thuynsma (05/09/1988) **CH:** Margaret Elizabeth; Robert Christopher; Lauren Marie **ED:** JD, University of California Berkeley School of Law (1991); BA, University of California Los Angeles (1988) **C:** United States National Security Advisor (2019-Present); Founding Partner, Larson O'Brien LLP (2016-2019); United States Special Presidential Envoy for Hostage Affairs (2018-2019); Advisor, Ted Cruz's Presidential Campaign (2015); Advisor, Foreign Policy and National Security Affairs, Wisconsin Governor Scott Walker's Presidential Campaign (2015); Co-chair, International Organizations Work Group, Mitt Romney Advisory Team (2011); Managing Partner, Arent Fox LLP, Los Angeles, CA (2006-2012); United States Alternate Representative to UN General Assembly, United States Department of State, New York, NY (2005-2006); Partner, O'Brien Abeles LLP, Los Angeles, CA (1999-2006); Legal Officer, United Nations Compensation Commission (UNCC), Geneva, Switzerland (1996-1998) **CIV:** Member, National Steering Committee, United

States Cultural Advisory Committee (2008-2011); Member, National Steering Committee, Lawyers for Mitt Romney, Boston, MA (2007-2008); Co-chair, United States Department of State Public-Private Partnership for Justice Reform, Afghanistan (2007); Co-chairman, Lawyers for Bush-Cheney, CA (2004) **MIL:** Major, United States Army Reserve **CW:** Author, "While America Slept: Restoring American Leadership to a World in Crisis" (2016) **MEM:** Chairman, Los Angeles Chapter, J. Reuben Clark Law Society (2003-2005); Executive Committee, International Law Section, The State Bar of California (1999-2002); The State Bar of California; J. Reuben Clark Law Society **BAR:** The State Bar of California (1991) **RE:** Church of Jesus Christ of Latter-day Saints

OBST, NORMAN P., PHD, T: Economist; Educator **I:** Consulting **DOB:** 05/25/1944 **PB:** Brooklyn **SC:** NY/USA **PT:** Joseph J. Obst; Pearl L. (Newmark) Obst **MS:** Married **SPN:** Barbara E. Brudevold (12/23/1970) **CH:** Lindora; Jannise; Laara; Benjamin **ED:** PhD in Economics, Purdue University (1970); MS in Economics, Purdue University (1967); BA, Binghamton University, State University of New York (1965) **C:** Professor Emeritus, Michigan State University, East Lansing, MI (2017-Present); Professor of Economics, Michigan State University, East Lansing, MI (1992-2017); Director of Undergraduate Programs, Michigan State University, MI (2000-2003); Associate Professor, Michigan State University, East Lansing, MI (1977-1992); Assistant Professor, Michigan State University, East Lansing, MI (1973-1977); Assistant Professor, University of Washington (1970-1973) **CR:** Consultant in Field **CIV:** Co-chair, Government Committee, Ingham County Drain Commission, MI (1996); Strategic Economic Plan, Lansing Area Business Leaders (1990); Board of Determination, Ingham County Drain Commission, MI (1989); Supervisor, Assessor, Williamstown Township, MI (1988-2000); Secretary, Board of Appeals, Williamstown Township, MI (1988-2000); Chief Administrative Officer, Williamstown Township Budget, MI (1989-2000); Central Administrator, Williamstown Township Sewer System, MI (1988-2000); Vice Chairman, Williamstown Township, MI (1985-1988); Planning Commission Member, Williamstown Township, MI (1974-1988); Served as an Elected Republican Public Official **CW:** Referee, American Economic Review, International Economic Reviews, Journal of Money, Credit and Banking, Eastern Economic Journal, Journal of Economic Issues, Journal of Macroeconomics, Journal of Economics and Business, Zentralblatt fur Mathematik; Contributor, Articles to Professional Journals **MH:** Albert Nelson Marquis Lifetime Achievement Award **AV:** Financial markets; Table tennis including Oculus Quest Eleven Table Tennis; Chess **THT:** Dr. Obst uses knowledge of the financial markets, in the process of creating and managing a hedge fund. The goal is to use a significant portion of the resulting profits to contribute to worthy causes.

OCASEK, RIC, T: Rock Vocalist, Songwriter, Guitar Player, Producer **I:** Medicine & Health Care **DOB:** 03/23/1944 **PB:** Baltimore **SC:** MD/USA **MS:** Married **SPN:** Paulina Porizkova (08/23/1989); Suzanne Otcasek (1971, Divorced 1988); Constance (Divorced 1971) **CH:** Christopher; Adam; Eron; Derek; Jonathan Raven; Oliver **ED:** Diplomate, Maple Heights High School, Maple Heights, Ohio (1963); Coursework, Bowling Green State University, Bowling Green, Ohio; Coursework, Antioch College, Yellow Springs, Ohio **C:** Founder, The Cars (1976-1988); Co-founder, ID Nirvana (1968); Co-founder, Milkwood; Founder, Richard and the Rabbits; Band Member, Cap'n Swing; Solo Artist **CR:** Producer, Weezer, Hole, Bad Religion, Nada Surf, Cakelike, Black 47, Mercury Rev **CW:** Member, The Cars, Album, "Move Like This" (2011); Solo Artist, Album, "Nexterday" (2005); Solo Artist, Album, "Troublizing" (1997); Author, "Negative Theatre" (1993); Solo Artist, Album, "Fireball Zone" (1991); Film Appearance, "Hairspray" (1988); Solo Artist, Album, "This Side of Paradise" (1987); Film Appearance, "Made In Heaven" (1987); Member, The Cars, Album, "Door to Door" (1987); Member, The Cars, Album, "Heartbeat City" (1984); Solo Artist, Album, "Beatitude" (1982); Member, The Cars, Album, "Shake It Up" (1981); Member, The Cars, Album, "Panorama" (1980); Member, The Cars, Album, "Candy-O" (1979) **AW:** Inductee, Rock and Roll Hall of Fame (2018)

O'CONNELL, FINNEAS, T: Singer, Songwriter, Record Producer, Musician, Actor **I:** Media & Entertainment **DOB:** 07/30/1997 **PB:** Los Angeles **SC:** CA/USA **PT:** Patrick O'Connell; Maggie Baird **MS:** Single **CR:** Singer, Songwriter, The Slightlys **CW:** Writer, Producer, "No Time to Die" (2020); Writer, Producer, "I Hate Everybody" (2020); Writer, Producer, "Passion and Pain Taste the Same When I'm Weak" (2020); Writer, Producer, "Bikini Porn" (2020); Producer, "First Man" (2019); Writer, Producer, "Used to This" (2019); Producer, "Lose You to Love Me" (2019); Producer, "If the World Was Ending" (2019); Writer, Producer, "Everything I Wanted" (2019); Writer, Producer, "When We All Fall Asleep, Where Do We Go?" (2019); Writer, Producer, "Moral of the Story" (2019); Writer, Producer, "When I Was Older" (2019); Musician, EP, "Blood Harmony" (2019); Musician, "Angel" (2019); Musician, "Claudia" (2019); Musician, "Luck Pusher" (2018); Musician, "College" (2018); Actor, "Confessions of a Teenage Jesus Jerk" (2018); Musician, "Hollywood Forever" (2018); Musician, "Landmine" (2018); Featured Musician, "The Ending" (2018); Musician, "Life Moves On" (2018); Musician, "Heaven" (2018); Musician, "Break My Heart Again" (2018); Writer, Producer, "Come Out and Play" (2018); Writer, Producer, EP, "Don't Smile at Me" (2017); Writer, Producer, "Satellite" (2017); Writer, Producer, "Lost My Mind" (2017); Writer, Producer, "Bored" (2017); Producer, "Filthy Rich" (2017); Writer, "Your Eyes" (2017); Musician, "I'm in Love Without You" (2017); Featured Musician, "Come to Think" (2017); Featured Musician, "Evermore" (2016); Writer, Producer, "Six Feet Under" (2016); Writer, Producer, "Come to Think" (2016); Featured Musician, "Goodnews Bay" (2016); Musician, "New Girl" (2016); Featured Musician, "Your Mother's Favorite" (2015); Featured Musician, "Maybe I'm Losing My Mind" (2015); Featured Musician, "Call Me When You Find Yourself" (2015); Guest Appearance, "Aquarius" (2015); Guest Appearance, "Glee" (2015); Actor, Short Film, "happySADhappy" (2014); Guest Appearance, "Modern Family" (2013-2014); Actor, Short Film, "Tomorrow" (2013); Actor, "Life Inside Out" (2013); Actor, "Bad Teacher" (2011) **AW:** Producer, of the Year, Non-Classical, Grammy Awards (2020); Best Engineered Album, Non-Classical, Grammy Awards (2020); Best Pop Vocal Album, Grammy Awards (2020); Album of the Year, Grammy Awards (2020); Song of the Year, Grammy Awards (2020); Songwriter of the Year, Apple Music Awards (2019); Vanguard Award, ASCAP Pop Music Awards (2019)

O'CONNOR, JOHN ARTHUR, T: Artist, Educator, Director **I:** Education/Educational Services **DOB:** 01/23/1940 **PB:** Twin Falls **SC:** ID/USA **PT:** John Francis O'Connor; Laurie (Ostrander) O'Connor **MS:** Married **SPN:** Mallory McCane (1/19/1963) **CH:** Christopher Sean Deigh **ED:** MAA in Art, University of California Davis (1963); BA in Art, University of California Davis, with Honors (1961) **C:** Professor Emeritus, University of Florida (2005-Present); Director, MBA Degree Program in Arts Administration, College of Fine Arts, University of Florida, Gainesville, FL (1993-2005); Director, Center for Arts and Public Policy, University of Florida, Gainesville, FL (1988-2005); Professor, University of Florida, Gainesville, FL (1985-2005); Acting Chair, Department of Art, University of Florida, Gainesville, FL (1987-1988); Associate Professor, University of Florida, Gainesville, FL (1975-1985); Assistant Professor of Art, University of Florida, Gainesville, FL (1969-1975); Art Instructor, Ohio University, Athens, OH (1965-1969); Art Instructor, Blake College (1964-1965); Art Instructor, University of California Santa Barbara (1963-1964) **CR:** Executive Director, Florida Higher Education Arts Network, Gainesville, FL (1985-2005); Consultant on Arts, Florida Board of Regents, Tallahassee, FL (1983-1995); Director, Appalachian Center for Crafts, Smithville, TN (1980-1982) **CIV:** Florida Cultural Action Alliance (1993-2003); Coordinator, United Way Campaign, University of Florida (1991); Arts Council of Alachua County, Gainesville, FL (1985-1990); Florida Cultural Action Alliance (1985-1988); Board of Directors, Florida Arts Celebration, Gainesville, FL (1985-1988) **CW:** One Man Show, Schmidt Gallery, Florida Atlantic University, Boca Raton, FL (1999-Present); Retrospective, News-Journal Center, Daytona Beach, FL (2015); Retrospective, Thrasher-Horne Center for the Arts, Orange Park, FL (2012); One Man Show, University of Florida Gallery (2005); One Man Show, Thomas Center Gallery (2005); Group Show, University of Florida Art Faculty Exhibition (1970-2005); One Man Show, Pensacola Museum of Art, University of West Florida (2003); One Man Show, Cornell Fine Arts Museum, Rollins College, Winter Park, FL (1998); One Man Show, Bender Fine Art, Atlanta, GA (1997); One Man Show, Capital Gallery, Tallahassee, FL (1992); Group Show, Florida Fellowship Exhibition, Center Contemporary Art, North Miami, FL (1992); Group Show, University Gallery, University of Florida, Gainesville, FL (1992); Group Show, Tallahassee Florida National, Florida State University Fine Art Gallery (1991); Group Show, Cheekwood National, Nashville, TN (1991); One Man Show, Capricorn Galleries, Maryland (1989, 1986, 1982); One Man Show, The John and Mable Ringling Museum of Art (1972); One Man Show, Santa Barbara Museum of Art (1963); Featured, Over 200 Group Shows; Featured, 36 Solo Exhibitions; Contributor, Articles, Essays, Monographs, Professional Publications **AW:** Lifetime Achievement Award, Florida Higher Education Arts Network (2005); Individual Artists Fellow, Division of Cultural Affairs, State of Florida (2002); Regional Fellow, Southern Arts Federation (Now South Arts), National Endowment for the Arts (1992-1993); Individual Artists Fellow, Division of Cultural Affairs, State of Florida (1991); Grantee, U.S. Air Force, University of Florida (1974) **MH:** Albert Nelson Marquis Lifetime Achievement Award; Marquis Who's Who Top Professional **B/I:** From the time Mr. O'Connor was three years old, he knew he wanted to be an architect. He focused his attention on that until he ran out of architectural engineering classes in college. Mr. O'Connor then decided to take some art courses and found he really enjoyed it. He ended up deciding to pursue art professionally, though it was a long process. He went to five different colleges and universities, ending with the University of California Davis. **AV:** Appreciating opera; Cooking; Wine tasting; Gardening

O'CONNOR, MALLORY, T: Curator, Art Historian, Author **I:** Fine Art **DOB:** 02/15/1943 **PB:** Decatur **SC:** IL/USA **PT:** Kenneth Everette McCane; Lela

Mildred (Day) McCane **MS:** Married **SPN:** John A. O'Connor (01/19/1963) **CH:** Christopher Sean **ED:** MFA in Art History, Ohio University (1970);MA in History, Ohio University (1968); BFA in Art, Ohio University (1966) **C:** Professor Emeritus, Santa Fe College, Gainesville, FL (2005-Present); Author (1982-Present); Associate Professor, Art History, Santa Fe College, Gainesville, FL (1999-2005); Curator, Instructor, Santa Fe College, Gainesville, FL (1994-1999); Curator, Thomas Center Gallery, City of Gainesville (1985-1994); Freelance Writer, Tallahassee, FL (1983-1984); Instructor, Art History, University of Florida, Gainesville, FL (1969-1977) **CR:** Exhibit Designer Florida Museum of Natural History, Gainesville, FL (1997-Present); Board of Directors, Southeastern Women's Caucus for Art, Gainesville, FL (1978-1981) **CIV:** Member, Cultural Advisory Board, City of Gainesville (1996-1997); Member, Executive Committee, Alachua County Democratic Party, Gainesville, FL (1993-1995); Board of Directors, Dance Alive (1989-1993); Member, Planning Committee, Florida Arts Celebration (1986-1987) **CW:** Author, "Key to Eternity" (2020); Author, "Epiphany's Gift" (2019); Author, "The American River Trilogy" (2017, 2018); Author, Florida's American Heritage River," University Press of Florida (2009); Author, "Lost Cities of the Ancient Southeast," University Press of Florida (1995); Feature Writer, Business to Business Magazine, Tallahassee (1981-1983) **AW:** Grantee, Florida Humanities Council (1991, 1993, 1996, 1999, 2000, 2002); Design Award, "Lost Cities of the Ancient Southeast" (1996); Grantee, Southern Arts Federation (1980, 1987, 1989); Grantee, Ulrich Bay Foundation, Tallahassee, FL (1979); First Prize in Fiction, Northern California Publishers & Authors; Silver Medal, President's Award for Fiction, Florida Authors **MEM:** College Art Association; Native American Art Studies Association; Florida Writers Association; Northern California Publishers & Authors; Writers Alliance of Gainesville; Historical Novel Society **MH:** Albert Nelson Marquis Lifetime Achievement Award; Marquis Who's Who Top Professional **AS:** Ms. O'Connor attributes her success to enthusiasm and just being really eager to take the next step, go further, and learn more. **B/I:** Ms. O'Connor became involved in her profession because she grew up in northern California, which is such a beautiful area full of nature; she grew up on a ranch. Her parents were also very nurturing in terms of getting her interested in art and music. She started taking piano lessons when she was 4 years old, and her mother always took her to art classes and music classes and everything else she could. So, even though she lived in a rural area and grew up on a ranch, she had a very broad cultural education as well. Her grandfather was also a violinist and composer. He was also a big influence in her interest in music. She is passionate about art, music, and nature. Those are really the three pillars of her career; her interest in art and classical music, in particular, as well as environmental and social justice issues. Growing up in Northern California on the American river where gold was discovered was a really kind of a key to everything that followed because so many people flocked to that particular small area and the cultural diversity in the area where she grew up is one of the most culturally diverse in the country. So, from a very early age, she was fascinated by and exposed to people from other countries, other cultures, which made a lasting impression on her that cultural differences were fascinating and something she wanted to know more about. **AV:** Gardening; Hiking; Horseback riding; Traveling **THT:** Ms. O'Connor's son, Christopher Sean, is an educator with a master's degree in sports administration. He and his wife moved to the West Coast and he became the athletic direc-

tor at Portland Community College in Portland, Oregon. His wife was the senior auditor for the North West area with an insurance corporation, but they realized that they were in a field that was not them, so they sold their house and moved to Tennessee and became middle school teachers. Now they do environmental work. Her son and his wife are also looking into adoption because they are environmentally conscious.

O'CONNOR, MARILYN, T: Paralegal **I:** Law and Legal Services **DOB:** 09/17/1947 **PB:** Reno **SC:** NV/USA **PT:** William James Weiss; Elizabeth Lillian (Gordon) Weiss **MS:** Divorced **SPN:** Dennis Lindley O'Connor (05/18/1969, Divorced 01/20/1984) **CH:** John Kelley; Stephanie Lynne **CT:** Certified in Paralegal Studies, University of Nevada, Reno (2003) **C:** Associate, Access to Healthcare Network (2011-2017); Associate, Fullerton Design Co. (2009-2011); Associate, Ajilon Legal (2006-2008); Complex Litigation Specialist (1980-2006); Document Review, Content Acquisition Specialist, Ajilon Legal **CIV:** Member, National Women's History Museum **CW:** Contributor, Court Case Reviews and Summaries, Reno Legal Digest **MH:** Albert Nelson Marquis Lifetime Achievement Award **B/I:** Mrs. O'Connor and her husband had a pizza place in Nevada and wanted to put in a casino in the pizza place. The city attorney did not want them to have the casino, so he tried to block it at every turn. She had to self-teach herself to counter what the city attorney was doing. She started winning case after case and case. **THT:** For more information on Mrs. O'Connor's Supreme Court case, please see: https://www.nytimes.com/1994/07/01/us/2-nevada-women-battle-for-seats-on-a-bench-marked-lawyers-only.html

O'CONNOR, OTIS, T: Lawyer, Director (Retired) **I:** Law and Legal Services **DOB:** 07/06/1935 **PB:** Charleston **SC:** WV/USA **PT:** Robert Emmett O'Connor; Julia Elizabeth (Autlz) O'Connor **MS:** Married **SPN:** Elizabeth Frances Morris (08/07/1965) **CH:** Otis Leslie; James M. **ED:** MA, Trinity Theological Seminary (2003); MBA, West Virginia College Graduate Studies (1979); JD, Harvard University (1963); AB, Princeton University (1957) **C:** Lawyer, Director (Retired); Partner, Steptoe & Johnson, Charleston, SC (1969-2008); Associate, Steptoe & Johnson, Charleston, SC (1963-1969) **CR:** President, Daymark, Inc. (1981-1982) **MIL:** Commander Judge Advocate General Corps, US Naval Reserve (1960-1981); With, US Navy (1957-1960) **MEM:** Board Member, Union Mission Ministries (1987-Present); American Bar Association; West Virginia Bar Association; Kanawha County Bar Association; Reserve Officers Association; Rotary International Club; Board member, Kanawha Valley Senior Services; President, Springhill Cemetery Commission; First Presbyterian Church Session; Secretary, Treasurer, Princeton Alumni Association of West Virginia; Board of Directors, Harvard Club of West Virginia **MH:** Albert Nelson Marquis Lifetime Achievement Award; Marquis Who's Who Top Professional; Marquis Who's Who Humanitarian Award **B/I:** Mr. O'Connor became involved in his profession because his father, Robert Emmett O'Connor, was a lawyer and he wanted to follow in his footsteps by becoming a lawyer also. He was the same type of lawyer as his father. **AV:** Violin; Tennis **PA:** Republican **RE:** Presbyterian

O'CONNOR, SANDRA, T: Chancellor (Retired), Associate Justice of the Supreme Court (Retired) **I:** Government Administration/Government Relations/Government Services **DOB:** 03/26/1930 **PB:** El Paso **SC:** TX/USA **PT:** Harry A. Day; Ada Mae (Wilkey) Day **MS:** Widowed **SPN:** John Jay O'Connor III (12/20/1952, Deceased 11/11/2009)

CH: Scott; Brian; Jay **ED:** LLB, Stanford University (1952); BA, Stanford University, with Great Distinction (1950) **C:** Chancellor, College of William & Mary, Williamsburg, VA (2005-2012); Associate Justice, Supreme Court of the United States, Washington, DC (1981-2006); Judge, Arizona Court Appeals (1979-1981); Judge, Maricopa County Superior Court, Phoenix, AZ (1975-1979); Majority Leader, Arizona State Senate (1972-1975); Member, Arizona State Senate (1969-1975); Chairman, Committee on State, County and Municipal Affairs, Arizona State Senate (1972-1973); Assistant Attorney General, State of Arizona (1965-1969); Private Law Practice, Maryvale, AZ (1958-1960); Civilian Attorney, Q.M. Market Center, Frankfurt am Main, Germany (1954-1957); Deputy County Attorney, San Mateo, CA (1952-1953) **CR:** Harry Rathbun Visiting Fellow, Office of Religious Life, Stanford University (2008); Member, Iraq Study Group (2006); Vice Chair, Arizona Select Law Enforcement Review Commission (1979-1980); Chair, Maricopa County Superior Court Judges Training and Education Committee (1977-1979); Member, National Defense Advisory Committee on Women in Services (1974-1976); Chair, Arizona Criminal Code Commission (1974-1976); Chair, Arizona Supreme Court Committee to Reorganize Lower Courts (1974-1975); Chair, Visiting Board, Maricopa County Juvenile Detention Home (1963-1964); Chair, Maricopa County Board of Adjustments and Appeals (1963-1964) **CIV:** Member, Advisory Board, Smithsonian National Museum of Natural History (2006-Present); Co-Chair, National Advisory Council, Campaign for Civic Mission of Schools (2005-Present); Member, Selection Committee, Oklahoma City National Memorial & Museum (2005-Present); Member, Cathedral Chapter, Washington National Cathedral (1991-1999); Trustee, The Rockefeller Foundation; Trustee, National Constitution Center **CW:** Author, "Out of Order: Stories from the History of the Supreme Court" (2013); Author, "Finding Susie" (2009); Developer, Video Game, "Our Courts" (2008); Author, Children's Book, "Chico: A True Story from the Childhood of the First Woman Supreme Court Justice" (2005); Author, "The Majesty of the Law: Reflections of a Supreme Court Justice" (2005); Co-Author with H. Alan Day, Memoir, "Lazy B: Growing Up on a Cattle Ranch in the American Southwest" (2002) **AW:** Margaret Chase Smith American Democracy Award, National Association of Secretaries of State (2009); Presidential Medal of Freedom, The White House (2009); Harry F. Byrd Junior '35 Public Service Award, Virginia Military Institute (2008); One of the World's Most Powerful Women, Forbes Magazine (2005); American Bar Association Medal (1997); Sara Lee Frontrunner Award (1997); Inductee, National Women's Hall of Fame (1995); Fordham-Stein Ethics Prize, Fordham University (1992); Ohio State Law Award, The Ohio State University (1992); Award of Merit, Stanford Law School (1990); William Green Award for Professional Excellence, University of Richmond (1990); Achievement Award, AAUW (1988); Thomas Jefferson Award of Law, University of Virginia (1987); Elizabeth Blackwell Award, Hobart & William Smith College (1985); Gimble National Award, Gimble Philadelphia Awards Committee (1982); Distinguished Achievement Award, Arizona State University (1980); Annual Award, National Conference of Christians and Jews (1975); Woman of the Year, Phoenix Advertising Club (1972) **MEM:** Advisory Board, Stanford Center of Ethics (Now McCoy Family Center for Ethics in Society), Stanford University (2005-Present); Commission on Civic Education and Separation of Powers, American Bar Association (2005-Present); Advisory Commission, Standing Committee on Law, Library of Congress, American Bar Association (2002-Present); Advisory Committee, The American Society of International Law (2001-Present); Executive Committee, Museum Law, American Bar Association (2000-Present); Executive Board, Central European and Eurasian Law Initiative, American Bar Association (1990-Present); Chair, Lawyer Referral Service, Maricopa County Bar Association (1960-1962); Fellow: American Academy of Arts & Sciences; Anglo-American Exchange; Arizona State Personnel Commission; Arizona Women Lawyers Association; National Association of Women Judges; Honorary Member, Advisory Committee, Judiciary Leadership Development Council; Arizona Judges Association; California Bar Association; Former Member, Committee on Legal Aid, Arizona Bar Association; Former Member, Committee on Public Relations, Arizona Bar Association; Former Member, Committee on Lower Court Reorganization, Arizona Bar Association; Former Member, Committee on Continuing Legal Education, Arizona Bar Association; American Bar Association **BAR:** State Bar of Arizona; The State Bar of California

ODEGARD, MARK E., T: 1) Chief Geoscientist 2) Chief Technology Officer and Director **I:** Oil & Energy **CN:** 1) Grizzly Geosciences 2) Messinian Energy **DOB:** 11/01/1940 **PB:** Plentywood **SC:** MT/USA **PT:** Harold Theodore Odegard; Edna Marcella (Jacobsen) Odegard **SPN:** Elisabeth Snow (06/17/1967) **CH:** Liv **ED:** Doctor of Philosophy in Geology and Geophysics, University of Hawaii (1975); Master of Science in Physics, Oregon State University (1965); Bachelor of Arts in Physics, University of Montana (1962); Bachelor of Arts in Mathematics, University of Montana (1962); Associate of Arts in Pre-engineering, Dawson Community College, Glendive, Montana (1960); Coursework, University of Maryland; Coursework, Yale University; Coursework, Navy War College **C:** Director, Messinian Energy, Denver, CO (2017-Present); Chief Technology Officer, Messinian Energy, Denver, CO (2017-Present); Chief Geoscientist, Grizzly Geosciences, Missouri City, TX (2004-Present); Chief Technology Officer, Denver, CO (2015-2017); Director, Insight Energy, Denver, CO (2015-2017); President, Madison Valley Energy Company, Ennis, MT (2005-2008); Vice President, GETECH Inc., Stafford, TX (1998-2004); Technical Manager, GETECH Inc., Stafford, TX (1998-2004); Supervisor, Unocal Potential Fields Group, Sugar Land, TX (1993-1998); Research Associate, Unocal Science & Technology, Brea, CA (1988-1993); Senior Advising Geophysicist, Unocal Applied Exploration Tech., Anaheim, CA (1988-1993); Principal Scientist, Basalt Waste Isolation Program, Westinghouse Hanford Corporation, Richland, WA (1986-1988); Staff Research Geophysicist, Sohio Petroleum Co., Dallas, TX (1983-1986); Associate Professor, Department of Physics, New Mexico State University (1981-1983); Associate Professor, Department of Earth Sciences, New Mexico State University (1981-1983); Director, Geology and Geophysics Program, Office of Naval Research, Arlington, VA (1978-1981); Assistant Geophysicist, Hawaii Institute of Geophysics (1974-1978); Assistant Professor, University of Hawaii (1974-1978); Geophysicist, Alpine Geophysical Associates, Norwood, NJ (1966-1967); Alpine Party Chief, United States Naval Ship Eltanin T-AGOR-8 (1965-1966); Group Leader, Geology and Geophysics Program, Geophysics Division, Office of Naval Research; Acting Director, Geophysics Division, Office of Naval Research **CR:** Integrated Interpretation Committee, American Association of Petroleum Geologists-Society of Exploration Geophysicists; Chairman, Technical Committee, Society of Exploration Geophysicists; With, Joint Society of Exploration Geophysicists-American Geophysical Union Coordination Committee; Office of Naval Research

Coordinator, National Academies for Science and Engineering; Office of Naval Research Coordinator, U.S.-U.S.S.R. Joint Geosciences Program **CIV:** Madison River Negotiated Rulemaking Committee, State of Montana (2018-Present); Vice Chairman, Zoning Commission, Ennis, MT (2016-Present); Zoning Commission, Ennis, MT (2016-Present); Vice Chairman, Chino Hills Planning Commission (1992-1993); Co-founder, City of Chino Hills, CA (1991); Municipal Advisory Council, Chino Hills Planning Commission (1990-1991); Chairman, Advisory Commission to the County Supervisor, Service Area 48, County of San Bernardino, CA (1989-1991); Integrated Interpretation Committee, Society of Exploration Geophysicists with American Association of Petroleum Geologists; Chairman, Technical Committee, Annual Meetings, Society of Exploration Geophysicists; Coordination Committee, Exploration Geophysicists with American Association of Petroleum Geologists; Coordinator, National Academies for Science and Engineering; Coordinator, U.S.-U.S.S.R. Joint Geosciences **CW:** Contributor, More Than 200 Scientific Publications **AW:** Antarctica Service Medal, U.S. Congress (1966); Top 10 Poster, American Association of Petroleum Geologists **MEM:** President, Math-Physics Club, University of Montana; President, Geophysical Society, Oregon State University; Master Councilor, DeMolay; Chevalier of the DeMolay; Senior Patrol Leader, Boy Scouts of America; Junior Assistant Scout Master, Boy Scouts of America; Crew Leader, Explorers; State Representative, Key Club; Head Beaver, Friends of the Beaver, Oregon State University; Society of Exploration Geophysicists, American Geophysical Union, American Association of Petroleum Geologists; Sociedade Brasileira de Geofísica; Sociedad Española de Psicología Experimental; Houston Geological Society; Geophysical Society of Houston, Southeast Asia Petroleum Exploration Society; Seismological Society of America; Sigma Xi **MH:** Albert Nelson Marquis Lifetime Achievement Award **AS:** Dr. Odegard attributes his success to the exemplary education he received at state universities, as well as hard work. **AV:** Golf; Running; Fishing; Camping; Skiing; Hunting

O'DONNELL, BRENDAN JAMES, T: Captain (Retired) **I:** Military & Defense Services **CN:** United States Navy **DOB:** 09/07/1949 **PB:** Detroit **SC:** MI/USA **PT:** John James O'Donnell; Margaret Mary (Shupe) O'Donnell **MS:** Married **SPN:** Barbara Jean Frinder (06/12/1971) **CH:** Brendan Neil; Sean Michael; Daniel James **ED:** Engineer, Aeronautical Engineering, The George Washington University (1998); Coursework, National War College (1990); Coursework, Naval War College (Non-resident) (1987); MS in Aeronautical Engineering, Naval Postgraduate School, with Distinction (1978); AB in French and Russian, Holy Cross College, Cum Laude (1971) **CT:** Project Management Professional; Certified Scrum Master; Radio Frequency Identification **C:** Vice President, Programs & Business Development, RF Logistics, LLC (2011-Present); DOD Program Manager, Computer Systems Corporation (2006-2011); Vice President, Corporate Development, Anvicom (2002-2006); Federal & Navy Marketing Manager, Lockheed Martin Systems Integration Owego (1998-2002); Deputy Director, Naval Aviation Science and Technology Office (1996-1998); Director of Inspections and Information Technology Manager, Naval Inspector General (1993-1996); Divison Chief, Joint Staff C4 Directorate, Washington (1990-1993); Commanding Officer, Training Squadron Two, Milton, FL (1988-1989); Executive Officer, Training Squadron Two, Milton, FL (1987-1988); Staff Officer, Commander, Patrol Wings Atlantic, Brunswick, ME (1985-1987); Maintenance, Safety Officer, Patrol

Squadron Eight, Brunswick, ME (1983-1985); Evaluation Department Head, Air Test and Evaluation Squadron One, Patuxent River, MD (1980-1982); Anti-Sub. Warfare Officer, United States Ship John F. Kennedy, Norfolk, VA (1978-1980); Standardization Officer, Patrol Squadron 46, Mountain View, CA (1973-1976) **CIV:** Historian, Editor, College of the Holy Cross, O'Callahan Society (2011-Present); Treasurer, Boy Scouts of America Troop 1544, Burke, VA (1991-1996); Assistant Scoutmaster, Boy Scouts of America Troop 1544, Burke, VA (1989-1996); Den Leader, Cub Scouts of America Pack 648, Brunswick, Maine (1985-1987) **MIL:** Commissioned, United States Navy (1971); Captain, United States Navy **CW:** Author, "History of the Naval ROTC Program at the College of Holy Cross" (2016); Author, Published Magazine Articles, "Strategic Review," "Naval War College Review," "Naval History," "New England Historical & Genealogical Register," "New Jersey Genealogy Society," and "Approach" **AW:** Distinguished Essayist, Chairman of the Joint Chiefs of Staff (1990); Defense Superior Service Medal; Legion of Merit; Meritorious Service Medal **MEM:** American Institute of Aeronautics and Astronautics; Armed Forces Communications and Electronics Association; Association of Naval Aviation; U.S. Naval Institute; National Defense Industrial Association; Navy League of the United States; Air Force Association; Association of the United States Army; Naval Historical Foundation; Air Force Historical Foundation; The Army Historical Foundation; Military Officers Association of America; National Eagle Scout Association; Sigma Xi, The Scientific Research Honor Society; Alpha Sigma Nu; Phi Sigma Iota **MH:** Albert Nelson Marquis Lifetime Achievement Award **B/I:** Mr. O'Donnell's decision to join the military was a natural one. He was a child of the World War II generation, so almost every adult he knew growing up partook in some sort of military service. There was also the advantage of going to college on an NROTC scholarship. He had no plan on making the Navy a career and, before he got commissioned, he had applied to half a dozen graduate schools to attend after he completed his obligated service. He stayed on active duty because of the opportunity to be a part of history. Additionally, he couldn't resist the ability to travel so easily. Mr. O'Donnell's family was never stationed overseas; however, he did spend a lot of time there because of the United States Navy being an expeditionary force. **AV:** Family history **RE:** Roman Catholic

OELMAN, BRADFORD COOLIDGE, T: Senior Vice President of Government and Public Affairs, Retired **I:** Government Administration/Government Relations/Government Services **CN:** Owens-Corning **DOB:** 01/21/1938 **PB:** Dayton **SC:** OH/USA **PT:** Robert Schantz Oelman; Mary Elizabeth (Coolidge) Oelman **MS:** Married **SPN:** Elizabeth Jean Cammet (09/01/1968); Julie Garrow Hutcheson (Divorced, 1968) **CH:** Kristen; David; Cammett; Bradford; Kimberly **ED:** MA in International Law and Diplomacy, Fletcher University (1961); AB in International Relations, Stanford University (1960); Diploma, Deerfield Academy (1956) **CT:** Confirmed as Foreign Service Officer, United States Senate (1961-1963) **C:** Retired, Senior Vice President, Government and Public Affairs, Owens-Corning (1986-1998); Vice-President of National Affairs, Owens-Corning, Washington, DC (1976-1986); Manager, Government Affairs, Armco Steel, Washington, DC (1974-1976); Manager, Armco Steel, Middletown, OH (1965-1974); Foreign Service Officer, United States State Department, Bordeaux, France (1963-1965); Foreign Service Officer, United States State Department, Washington, DC (1961-1963) **CR:** Chief Operating Officer, Civil Justice Reform Group (1998-2000); Chairman,

Budget Control Working Group, Washington, DC (1985-1987); Chairman, Energy Users Forum (1981-1987); Trustee, North American Insulation Association; Fiscal/ Monetary Committee, National Association of Manufacturers; Chairman, Owens Corning Contributions Committee **CIV:** President, Ridge Cove Condominium Association, Chatham, MA (2016-2019); President, Landings Condominium Association, Delray Beach, FL (2004-2009); President, Oelman Foundation; Juror, Coolidge Foundation; Volunteer, Habitat for Humanity **MIL:** Military Liaison Officer, United States Armed Forces, Bordeaux, France (1963-1965) **CW:** Producer, "Count Down to Start-Up" (1968-1969) **AW:** President, United Way, Middletown, OH; Featured, WSJ Front-Page Story (1988); Steel Fellow, American Iron and Steel Institute (1970-1973) **MEM:** Alpha Delta Phi; Stanford University; Dayton Polo Club; Brown's Run Country Club, Middletown, OH; Country Club of Florida; Village of Golf; Ocean Club, Ocean Ridge, FL; Gulfstream Bath and Tennis, Delray Beach, FL; Stone Horse Yacht Club, Harwich Port, MA **MH:** Albert Nelson Marquis Lifetime Achievement Award **AV:** Gardening **PA:** Independent **RE:** Episcopalian

OERTER, AL ADOLPH JR., T: Former Professional Discus Throw Athlete **I:** Athletics **DOB:** 09/19/1936 **PB:** Queens **SC:** NY/USA **PT:** Alfred Adolph Oerter; Mary (Strup) Oerter **MS:** Married **SPN:** Cathy Jo Carroll (07/23/1983); Corinne Benedetto (10/1958, Divorced 05/1975) **CH:** Crystiana; Gabrielle **ED:** Coursework, The University of Kansas (1954-1959) **C:** Motivational Speaker (1984-2007); Computer Manager, Grumman Data Systems, Bethpage, NY (1959-1984) **CIV:** Founder, Art of the Olympians (2006) **CW:** Artist, Exhibitions, Art of the Olympians (2006) **AW:** Named to Nassau County Sports Hall of Fame (2005); Named to Suffolk Sports Hall of Fame (1990); Four-time Gold Medalist, Summer Olympics (1956, 1960, 1964, 1968); Named to U.S. Olympic Hall of Fame; Named to IAAF Hall of Fame; Recipient, Olympic Order **MEM:** Delta Tau Delta

OH, SANDRA MIJU, T: Actress **I:** Media & Entertainment **DOB:** 07/20/1971 **PB:** Nepean **SC:** ON/Canada **PT:** Jun-su Oh; Jeon Young-nam **MS:** Divorced **SPN:** Alexander Payne (1/1/2003, Divorced 12/21/2006) **ED:** Graduate, National Theatre School of Canada (1993) **CW:** Actress, "Killing Eve" (2018-Present); Voice Actress, "She-Ra and the Princesses of Power" (2018-Present); Voice Actress, "Invincible" (2020); Co-Host, 76th Golden Globe Awards (2019); Host, "Saturday Night Live" (2019); Guest Appearance, "American Crime" (2017); Actress, "Meditation Park" (2017); Actress, "Catfight" (2017); Producer, Voice Actress, "Window Horses" (2016); Voice Actress, "Peg + Cat" (2016); Guest Appearance, "Shitty Boyfriends" (2015); Actress, Short Film, "The Scarecrow" (2015); Guest Appearance, "Betas" (2014); Actress, "Grey's Anatomy" (2005-2014); Actress, "Tammy" (2014); Voice Actress, "American Dad!" (2005-2013); Voice Actress, "Phineas and Ferb" (2008-2012); Guest Appearance, "Sesame Street" (2011); Guest Appearance, "Micheal: Every Day" (2011); Guest Appearance, "Thorne" (2010); Voice Actress, "Quantum Quest: A Cassini Space Odyssey" (2010); Actress, "Ramona and Beezus" (2010); Actress, "Rabbit Hole" (2010); Actress, "Defendor" (2009); Voice Actress, "Robot Chicken" (2009); Appearance, Documentary, "The People Speak" (2009); Actress, "Blindness" (2008); Voice Actress, "The Land Before Time XIII: The Wisdom of Friends" (2007); Actress, Short Film, "Falling" (2007); Voice Actress, "American Dragon: Jake Long" (2006-2007); Actress, "The Night Listener" (2006); Guest Appearance, "Odd Job Jack" (2006); Actress, "For Your Consideration" (2006); Actress,

"Hard Candy" (2005); Actress, "Break a Leg" (2005); Voice Actress, Short Film, "Stationery" (2005); Actress, "Cake" (2005); Actress, "3 Needles" (2005); Actress, "Sorry, Haters" (2005); Actress, "Kind of a Blur" (2005); Actress, "Sideways" (2004); Actress, "Wilby Wonderful" (2004); Voice Actress, "Mulan II" (2004); Actress, Short Film, "8 Minutes to Love" (2004); Actress, "Under the Tuscan Sun" (2003); Cameo, "Owning Mahowny" (2003); Actress, "Big Fat Liar" (2002); Actress, "Full Frontal" (2002); Actress, "Rick" (2002); Actress, "Long Life, Happiness & Prosperity" (2002); Actress, Short Film, "Barrier Device" (2002); Voice Actress, "The Proud Family" (2001-2002); Actress, "Arliss" (1996-2002); Actress, "The Princess Diaries" (2001); Actress, Short Film, "Date Squad" (2001); Appearance, Documentary, "The Frank Truth" (2001); Actress, TV Miniseries, "Further Tales of the City" (2001); Guest Appearance, "Six Feet Under" (2001); Guest Appearance, "Judging Amy" (2001); Guest Appearance, "Popular" (2000); Actress, "Waking the Dead" (2000); Actress, "Dancing at the Blue Iguana" (2000); Narrator, Short Film, "Three Lives of Kate" (2000); Actress, "Guinevere" (1999); Voice Actress, "Happily Ever After: Fairy Tales for Every Child" (1999); Actress, "Last Night" (1998); Actress, "The Red Violin" (1998); Actress, "Permanent Midnight" (1998); Actress, "Bean" (1997); Actress, "Bad Day on the Block" (1997); Actress, Short Film, "Cowgirl" (1996); Guest Appearance, "Kung Fu: The Legend Continues" (1996); Guest Appearance, "If Not for You" (1995); Guest Appearance, "Lonesome Dove: The Outlaw Years" (1995); Actress, TV Film, "Cagney & Lacey: The View Through the Glass Ceiling" (1995); Actress, Short Film, "Prey" (1995); Actress, "Double Happiness" (1994); Actress, TV Film, "The Diary of Evelyn Lau" (1994); Cameo, "Degrassi High: School's Out" (1992); Actress, TV Film, "Denim Blues" (1989); Actress, Short Film, "The Journey Home" (1989) **AW:** Actress in a Leading Role - Drama, "Killing Eve," Gracie Awards (2019); National Arts Centre Award, Governor General's Performing Arts Awards (2019); Best Actress - Television Drama Series, "Killing Eve," Golden Globe Awards (2019); Best Actress in a Television Series Drama, "Killing Eve," Critics' Choice Awards (2018); Outstanding Performance by a Female Actor in a Drama Series, "Killing Eve," Screen Actors Guild Awards (2018); TV Performance of the Year - Actress, "Killing Eve," Dorian Awards (2018); Best Actress in a Short, "The Scarecrow," Hollywood Reel Independent Film Festival (2016); Favorite TV Character We Miss Most, "Grey's Anatomy," People's Choice Awards (2015); Star, Canada's Walk of Fame (2011); Best Cast - Television Series, "Grey's Anatomy," Satellite Awards (2006); Outstanding Performance by an Ensemble in a Drama Series, "Grey's Anatomy," Screen Actors Guild Awards (2006); Outstanding Motion Picture Ensemble, "Sideways," Satellite Awards (2004); Best Supporting Actress - Series, Miniseries or Television Film, "Grey's Anatomy," Golden Globe Awards (2005); Outstanding Performance by a Female Actor in a Drama Series, "Grey's Anatomy," Screen Actors Guild Awards (2005); Best Acting by an Ensemble in a Movie, "Sideways," Critics' Choice Awards (2004); Best Cast, "Sideways," Boston Society of Film Critics Awards (2004); Best Cast, "Sideways," Phoenix Film Critics Society Awards (2004); Outstanding Performance by a Cast in a Motion Picture, "Sideways," Screen Actors Guild Awards (2004); Best Performance by an Actress in a Leading Role, "Last Night," Genie Awards (1998); Actress in a Comedy Series, "Arliss," CableACE Awards (1997); Fiction: Actress, "The Diary of Evelyn Lau," Festival International de Programmes Audiovisuels (1995); Best Performance by an Actress in a Leading Role, "Double Happiness," Genie Awards (1994)

O'HALLERAN, THOMAS, "TOM" CHARLES, T: U.S. Representative from Arizona **I:** Government Administration/Government Relations/Government Services **DOB:** 01/24/1946 **PB:** Chicago **SC:** IL/USA **MS:** Married **SPN:** Pat O'Halleran **CH:** Sean; Casey; Katie **ED:** Coursework, DePaul University (1991-1992); Coursework, Lewis University (1965-1966) **C:** Member, U.S. House of Representatives from Arizona's First Congressional District (2017-Present); Member, Arizona State Senate (2007-2017); State Representative, District One, Arizona House of Representatives (2002-2007); State Representative, District Two, Arizona House of Representatives (2001-2002); Vice Chairman, Committee on Agriculture; Vice Chairman, Environmental Committee; Member, Environmental Committee; Member, County and Municipal Committee; State Senator, District One, Arizona House of Representatives; House Representative, Arizona House of Representatives **AW:** Recognition Award, Arizona Department of Veterans' Services (AZDVS) (2006); Leadership Award, Arizona Commission on Indian Affairs (2005); Children and Youth Champion Award, Arizona School Age Coalition (2004); Outstanding Leadership Award (2003-2005); Public Policy Award, Mental Health Association Arizona (2003) **MEM:** Blue Dog Coalition **PA:** Democrat **RE:** Catholic

OHMER, STEVEN RUSSELL, T: Judge **I:** Law and Legal Services **DOB:** 04/18/1954 **PB:** St. Louis **SC:** MO/USA **PT:** Russell Joseph Ohmer; Patricia Ann Ohmer **MS:** Married **SPN:** Roberta Marie Ohmer (12/29/1976) **CH:** Rachel Caroline; Rebecca Anne; Brian Meyers **ED:** JD, Creighton University (1979); BS, Florida State University (1975) **C:** Circuit Judge, 22nd Judicial Circuit State Of Missouri, St. Louis, MO (2000-Present); Associate Circuit Judge, 22nd Judicial Circuit, State of Missouri, St. Louis, MO (1994-2000); Assistant Circuit Attorney, Chief Warrant Officer, Circuit Attorney Office for St. Louis (1987-1994); Attorney, Ohmer & Ohmer, Professional Corporation, St. Louis, MO (1983-1987); Assistant Circuit Attorney, Circuit Attorney Office for St. Louis (1979-1983) **CR:** Legal Advocates of Abused Women (1995); Lecturer, St. Louis Police Department (1993-1995); Missouri Association of Prosecuting Attorneys (1991-1992) **CIV:** Chairman, Supreme Court, Circuit Court Budget Committee (1999-Present); Chair, St. Pius V Parish Council (2003-2005); President, St. Pius V Sponsor's Club, St. Louis, MO (1992-1994); Supreme Court Family Court Committee **CW:** Author, "Missouri Judges Handbook" (2000); Contributor, Articles, Professional Journals **MEM:** Missouri Bar Association; Illinois Bar Association; Bar Association of Metropolitan St. Louis; Lawyers Association of St. Louis **BAR:** Missouri (1979); Illinois (1980) **MH:** Albert Nelson Marquis Lifetime Achievement Award **B/I:** Mr. Ohmer played baseball in college; however, he ultimately decided to pursue a career in a more reliable industry. After considering various options, Mr. Ohmer decided to enroll in law school. He was inspired by his cousin, who was a respected lawyer. **AV:** Golfing; Reading; Gardening **RE:** Roman Catholic

OHNO, APOLO ANTON, T: Former Olympic Speed Skater **I:** Athletics **DOB:** 05/22/1982 **PB:** Seattle **SC:** WA/USA **PT:** Yuki Ohno; Jerrie Lee **C:** Commentator, Winter Olympics, NBC (2014, 2018); Member, U.S. Elite Short Track Speedskating Team **CIV:** Founder, Apolo Anton Ohno Foundation (2010-Present); Global Ambassador, Special Olympics; With, Product Red; With, RMHC (Ronald McDonald House Charities); With, The Salvation Army USA **CW:** Host, "Spartan: Ultimate Team Challenge" (2017); Appearance, "Superstore" (2016); Performer, "Dancing with the Stars" (2007);

Actor, Appearances, Television Shows **AW:** Named to U.S. Olympic Hall of Fame (2019); Silver Medal, Men's 1500 Meter Short Track, Winter Olympics (2010); Bronze Medal, Men's 1000 Meter Short Track, Winter Olympics (2010); Bronze Medal, Men's 5000 Meter Relay, Winter Olympics (2010); Named Male Athlete of the Month, U.S. Olympic Committee (2003, 2008); Champion, "Dancing with the Stars" (2007); Named to Asian-American Hall of Fame (2007); Gold Medal, Men's 500 Meter, Winter Olympics (2006); Bronze Medal, Men's Short Track Relay, Winter Olympics (2006); Bronze Medal, Men's 1000 Meter, Winter Olympics (2006); Named Speedskating Athlete of the Year (2003); Named U.S. Champion (1997, 1999, 2001, 2002); Silver Medal, Men's 1000 Meter, Winter Olympics (2002); Gold Medal, Men's 1500 Meter, Winter Olympics (2002); Named 1500 Meter Champion (2001); Named 1000 Meter Champion (2001); Named 500 Meter Champion (2001); Named World Cup Overall Champion (2001); Named World Junior Short Track Champion (1999) **AV:** Music; Badminton; Basketball; Breakdancing

OHOTNICKY, STEPHEN THADDEUS, T: Engineering Executive **I:** Engineering **DOB:** 12/22/1943 **PB:** Torrington **SC:** CT/USA **PT:** Stephen Edward Ohotnicky; Emily C. (Wilczek) Ohotnicky **MS:** Married **SPN:** Barbara Marie Shay (06/11/1966) **CH:** Peter; Susan **ED:** MBA, Eastern Michigan University (1973); MSE, University Michigan University (1971); BS, U.S. Military Academy (1966) **CT:** Professional Engineer, Michigan **C:** Quality Assurance Manager, Scroll Compressor Operation Carrier, United Technologies, Arkadelphia, AR (1990-Present); Retired (2013); Manager, Quality Assurance, Alco Controls Division, Emerson Electric, Wytheville, VA (1987-1990); Supplier, Quality, Hydra-Matic Division, General Motors Corporation, Ypsilanti, MI (1986-1987); Staff Engineer, Hydra-Matic Division, General Motors Corporation, Ypsilanti, MI (1980-1986); Supervisor, Quality Control, Hydra-Matic Division, General Motors Corporation, Ypsilanti, MI (1977-1980); Materials and Project Engineer, Hydra-Matic Division, General Motors Corporation, Ypsilanti, MI (1971-1977) **CIV:** Parks and Recreation Committee, City of Arkadelphia (1992); Chairman, Recreation Commission, Wytheville, VA (1990); Scouting Coordinator, Washtenaw County Explorer Post 400, Ypsilanti, MI (1983-1987); Chairman, Parks and Recreation Commission, Superior Township, MI (1976-1979); Catholic Social Services **MIL:** Resigned, U.S. Army (1970); Captain, U.S. Army (1968); Commissioned, Second Lieutenant, U.S. Army (1966) **AW:** Trainee, National Science Foundation (1970-1971) **MEM:** Secretary, West Point Society (1984-1987); American Society for Metals; American Society for Quality Control; Engineering Society of Detroit; Elks **MH:** Albert Nelson Marquis Lifetime Achievement Award **B/I:** Mr. Ohotnicky became involved in his profession because he liked science and engineering. He got to fully explore these fields with General Motors, all the while trying to get the local children interested in the subjects. Later, while working with Whirlpool, Mr. Ohotnicky got to travel the world, which was a great side of his business. **AV:** Golfing; Fishing; Running **PA:** Republican **RE:** Roman Catholic

OKAFOR, TOCHUKWU, T: Chief Executive Officer **I:** Health, Wellness and Fitness **CN:** Lintoc Care, LLC **DOB:** 12/02/1974 **SC:** Nigeria **PT:** Chief J.U. Okafor (Deceased); Mrs. J. U. Okafor **MS:** Married **SPN:** Linda Okafor **CH:** Four Children **ED:** MPA, Walden University (2012); BS, New Jersey City University (2004) **C:** President, Chief Executive Officer, Lintoc Care, LLC (2015-Present) **CIV:** First Care Charity Foundation **CW:** Author, "Surviving

in a Dangerous World" (2014); Author, "The Joy of Success: What It Means to Transform Success Into Excellence" (2013) **AW:** Named to Best of 2019, Mesa, AZ (2019) **AS:** Mr. Okafor attributes his success to his integrity and desire for excellence. **B/I:** Mr. Okafor loves to see smiles on people's faces. **AV:** Traveling **PA:** Democrat **RE:** Christian **THT:** Mr. Okafor says, "Life is good when you are doing what you are called to do. Being able to discover your purpose in life gives you an edge to a challenge against the impediments of life as well as the precarious predicaments of life. In every life-struggle of man, God still exists, and He is there to give you an expected end."

OKAMOTO, JEFFREY K. MD, T: Developmental-Behavioral Pediatrician **I:** Medicine & Health Care **CN:** John A. Burns School of Medicine, University Of Hawaii at Manoa **PT:** Nancy Okamoto; Henry Okamoto **MS:** Married **SPN:** Alison Uyeda **CH:** Andrew Okamoto **ED:** Public Policy, Joseph Kennedy Jr., Foundation, California (2011); Fellowship, Children's Hospital Los Angeles, Developmental Pediatrics (1993); Residency, Pediatrics, Kaiser Los Angeles Medical Center (1991); MD, John A. Burns School of Medicine, University of Hawai?i at Manoa (1988); BS, University of Hawai?i at Manoa (1984) **CT:** Medical License, State of Hawaii (1995); Medical License, State of California (1990); Board-Certified, Developmental-Behavioral Pediatrics, American Board of Pediatrics; Board Certified, General Pediatrics, American Board of Pediatrics; Diplomate, National Board of Medical Examiners **C:** Developmental-Behavioral Pediatrician, Kapiolani Medical Center for Women and Children, Hawaii (1995-Present); Medical Director and Acting Administrator, State of Hawaii Developmental Disabilities Division (2007-2018); Assistant Professor, University of Hawaii, John A. Burns School of Medicine, Hawaii **CIV:** Past Chairman, Council of School Health, American Academy of Pediatrics; Former President, Healthy Mother's Healthy Babies; Board Member, Hawaii International Child **AW:** Professional of the Year, Special Parent Information Network (2018); Faculty Excellence in Preceptor Teaching Award, Pediatrics Department, John A. Burns School of Medicine (2018); Manager of the Year, State of Hawaii Department of Health (2015); Superior Performance Award, State of Hawaii Department of Health (2015); Outstanding Community Contribution to Persons with Disabilities, Center on Disability Studies, University of Hawaii at Manoa (2006); Excellence in Teaching Award for Pediatrics, John A. Burns School of Medicine (1999); Inductee, Alumnus Member, Alpha Omega Alpha (1999); Bernard Goldberg Memorial Award, Los Angeles Kaiser Permanente (1991) **MEM:** Society for Developmental and Behavioral Pediatrics (1995-Present); Fellow, American Academy of Pediatrics (1992); American Academy of Developmental Medicine and Dentistry **AS:** Dr. Okamoto attributes his success to his good mentors and his supportive family. His community of scientists and clinicians have been very important in his career as well. **B/I:** Dr. Okamoto became involved in his profession because he volunteered at a local hospital and could see that there was room for a lot of different adventures in medicine. A lot of people had wants and needs. As a volunteer, he could see that another professional that can coach people through things would be necessary. He also had a strong science background and loves to work with people. He likes understanding different cultures as well, so his international work has been an exciting part of his career. **THT:** Dr. Okamoto is a specialist in autism, intellectual and other developmental disabilities. He has also been a leader in the American Academy of Pediatrics in School

Health. His interests include the interaction between clinical care and educational systems for children with special health care needs.

OKINAKA, ALTON M. PHD, PHD, T: Associate Professor **I:** Education/Educational Services **CN:** University of Hawai'i at Hilo **DOB:** 12/25/1957 **PB:** Honolulu **SC:** HI/USA **PT:** Harold Tsuneo Okinaka; Kikuye Matsui Okinaka **MS:** Single **ED:** PhD in Sociology, Indiana University Bloomington (1991); MA in Sociology, Indiana University Bloomington (1984); BA in Sociology and Mathematics, University of Hawaii, Honolulu, HI (1979) **C:** Associate Professor, Sociology, University of Hawai'i at Hilo (1993-Present); Chair, Education Department, University of Hawai'i at Hilo (2004-2007); Chair, Social Sciences Division, University of Hawai'i at Hilo (2003-2006); Chair, Social Sciences Division, University of Hawai'i at Hilo (2003-2006); Chair, Sociology Department, University of Hawai'i at Hilo (1999-2003); Director of Institutional Research, University of Hawai'i at Hilo (1992-1994); Assistant Professor, University of Hawai'i at Hilo (1988-1993); Visiting Assistant Professor, University of Hawai'i at Hilo (1987-1988) **CR:** Consultant in Field **CIV:** Friends of Liliuokalani Board (2016-Present); Local School Board, Ke Ana La'ahana Public Charter School (2014-Present); Hawaii Historic Places Review Board (2015-2019); Executive Committee, Hui Kaua, Hilo, HI (2006-2014); Governors Council of Advisors, Hilo, HI (2004-2012); Task Force, Strategic Vision for Downtown Hilo (2005-2006); Hawaii Island Chamber of Commerce Sustainability Task Force (2004-2005); Hawaii Island United Way Strategic Management Committee (1995-1998) **AW:** Outstanding Advisor/Mentor, University of Hawai'i at Hilo (2005); Service Award (2003); Service to Student Life Award (2003) **MEM:** Executive Board for Race, Class, and Gender Section, Mathematical Sociology Section, American Sociological Association (1994-1999); Vice President, Treasurer, Hawaii Sociological Association; American Educational Research Association **MH:** Albert Nelson Marquis Lifetime Achievement Award; Marquis Who's Who Top Professional **AS:** Dr. Okinaka's family grew up during the Great Depression. His grandfather immigrated to the United States and made a deal with the local school to become their handyman in exchange for English lessons, hoping to obtain his contractor's license. Never forgetting his grandfather's hard-working nature, Dr. Okinaka and his family were always community-oriented. They did everything in their power to help those around them. In his community, everyone depended on one another for survival. This left a lasting impression on Dr. Okinaka. **B/I:** Dr. Okinaka chose to become an educator because it was a family tradition. His mother was a school teacher, as were several of his aunts. In later years, many more individuals in his family pursued a career in education. Dr. Okinaka additionally was inspired to become a teacher after his time as a Boy Scout. Through his time leading his fellow scouts, he found that he loved educating others.

OLAJUWON, HAKEEM ABDUL, T: Former Professional Basketball Player **I:** Athletics **DOB:** 01/21/1963 **PB:** Lagos **SC:** Nigeria **PT:** Salaam Olajuwon; Abike Olajuwon **MS:** Married **SPN:** Dalia Asafi (08/08/1996) **CH:** Rahmah; Aisha; Abisola **ED:** Coursework, University of Houston (1980-1984) **C:** Co-Founder, Islamic Da'wah Center, Houston, Texas (2002-Present); Retired, Professional Basketball Player, NBA (2002); Center, Toronto Raptors, NBA (2001-2002); Center, Houston Rockets, NBA (1984-2001) **CR:** Founder, Big Man Camp (2006-Present) **AW:** Named to FIBA Hall of Fame (2016); Named to Naismith Memorial Basketball

Hall of Fame (2008); Named to Western Conference All-Star Team, NBA (1985-1990, 1992-1997); Gold Medal, Men's Basketball, Summer Olympics (1996); Named One of the 50 Greatest Players in NBA History (1996); Winner, Houston Rockets, NBA Championships (1994, 1995); Named NBA Finals MVP (1994, 1995); Named NBA MVP (1994); Named NBA Defensive Player of the Year (1993, 1994); Named to First Team All-defensive, NBA (1987-1988, 1990, 1993-1994); Named to First Team All-NBA (1987-1989, 1993-1994); Named to NBA All-Rookie Team (1985); Named to First Team All-American, Sporting News (1984)

OLALDE, JOSH, T: Photographer **I:** Media & Entertainment **CN:** Josh Olalde **MS:** Married **C:** Media Production Director, No Label Brewing & Hart Plumbing (2020-Present); Photographer, Strawbridge Studios Inc. (2018-Present); Videographer & Photographer, Josh Olalde Photography & Video (2017-Present); Photographer, Houston Beer Chronicle (2018); Production Technician II, Toshiba International **CIV:** Community Photographer, Houstonia Magazine **AS:** Mr. Olalde attributes his success to his passion for photography. He loves his ability to transform something from bland to grand and make it aesthetically pleasing. **B/I:** Photography came at Mr. Olalde out of nowhere. After graduating from high school, he thought he wanted to work in the fitness industry or the medical field but he quickly found that he would be better suited elsewhere. Eventually, Mr. Olalde found himself working on a video podcast, which was his first real interaction with a camera. He became interested in the technical side of videography, later venturing off into the photography world and making his name known throughout the beer and bar community in Houston. Mr. Olalde currently works at No Label Brewing and Hart Plumbing as their media production director. **THT:** Mr. Olalde's motto is, "Don't talk about it, just do it."

OLDMAN, GARY LEONARD, T: Actor **I:** Media & Entertainment **DOB:** 03/21/1958 **PB:** London **SC:** United Kingdom **PT:** Leonard Bertram Oldman; Kathleen (Cheriton) Oldman **MS:** Married **SPN:** Gisele Schmidt (08/2017); Alexandra Edenboroug (12/31/2008, Divorced 09/2015); Donya Fiorentino (02/16/1997, Divorced 04/13/2001); Uma Thurman (10/01/1990, Divorced 04/30/1992); Lesley Manville (1987, Divorced 1990) **CH:** Alfie; Gulliver; Charlie **ED:** BA, Rose Buford College of Theatre & Performance (1979) **CW:** Actor, "The Courier" (2019); Actor, "The Laundromat" (2019); Actor, "Mary" (2019); Actor, "Killers Anonymous" (2019); Voice Actor, "Tau" (2018); Actor, "Hunter Killer" (2018); Actor, "The Hitman's Bodyguard" (2017); Actor, "Darkest Hour" (2017); Actor, "Criminal" (2016); Actor, "The Space Between Us" (2016); Actor, "Child 44" (2015); Actor, "Man Down" (2015); Actor, "RoboCop" (2014); Actor, "Dawn of the Planet of the Apes" (2014); Actor, "Paranoia" (2013); Actor, "Lawless" (2012); Actor, "The Dark Knight Rises" (2012); Actor, "Red Riding Hood" (2011); Voice Actor, "Kung Fu Panda" (2011); Actor, "Harry Potter and the Deathly Hallows: Part 2" (2011); Actor, "Tinker Tailor Soldier Spy" (2011); Actor, "The Book of Eli" (2010); Voice Actor, "Planet 51" (2009); Actor, "The Dark Knight" (2008); Actor, "Batman Begins" (2005); Actor, "Harry Potter and the Goblet of Fire" (2005); Actor, "Harry Potter and the Prisoner of Azkaban" (2004); Actor, "Who's Kyle" (2004); Actor, "Sin" (2003); Actor, "Interstate 60" (2002); Actor, "The Hire: Beat the Devil" (2002); Actor, "Greg the Bunny" (2002); Actor, "Friends" (2001); Actor, "Nobody's Baby" (2001); Actor, "Hannibal" (2001); Actor, Executive Producer, "The Contender" (2000); Actor, "Jesus," (1999); Actor, "Lost in Space," (1998); Actor, "Quest for Camelot (aka Magic Sword)" (1998); Director, Writer, Producer, "Nil By Mouth" (1997); Actor, "The Fifth Element" (1997); Actor, "Air Force One" (1997); Actor, "Basquiat" (1996); Actor, "Murder in the First" (1995); Actor, "The Scarlet Letter" (1995); Actor, "The Professional" (1994); Actor, "Immortal Beloved" (1994); Actor, "Romeo is Bleeding" (1993); Actor, "Fallen Angels: Dead End for Delia" (1993); Actor, "True Romance" (1993); Actor, "Bram Stoker's Dracula" (1992); Actor, "Who Was Lee Harvey Oswald" (1992); Actor, "JFK" (1991); Actor, "Heading Home" (1991); Actor, "Henry & June" (1990); Actor, "State of Grace" (1990); Actor, "Rosencrantz and Guildenstern Are Dead" (1990); Actor, "Paris by Night" (1989); Actor, "Chattahoochee" (1989); Actor, "Track 29" (1988); Actor, "We Think the World of You" (1988); Actor, "Criminal Law" (1988); Actor, "The Firm" (1988); Actor, "Prick Up Your Ears" (1987); Actor, "Serious Money" (1987); Actor, "Sid and Nancy" (1986); Actor, "Women Beware Women" (1986); Actor, "Real Dreams" (1986); Actor, "The War Plays" (1985); Actor, "The Desert Air" (1985); Actor, "Honest, Decent and True" (1985); Actor, "Rat in the Skull" (1984); Actor, "The Pope's Wedding" (1984); Actor, "Meantime" (1984); Actor, "Remembrance" (1982); Actor, "Summit Conference" (1982); Actor, "Massacre at Paris" (1980); Actor, "Chinchilla" (1980); Actor, "Desperado Corner" (1980); Actor, "A Waste of Time" (1980); Actor, Television Shows, Music Videos, Video Games and Films **AW:** Academy Award for Best Actor, Academy of Motion Picture Arts and Sciences (2018); Golden Globe Award for Best Actor, Hollywood Foreign Press Association (2018); Screen Actors Guild Award for Best Actor, SAG-AFTRA (2018); Award for Best Actor in a Leading Role, BAFTA Awards (2018); Awards for Best Original Screenplay, Best British Film, BAFTA Awards (1998); Fringe Best Newcomer Award (1985-1986); Drama Magazine Best Actor Award (1985); Numerous Awards

OLESEN, MICHAEL D., T: Owner **I:** Food & Restaurant Services **CN:** Stockholm's Vardshus, Inc. **CH:** Brittni L. Nix **ED:** BA in Economics, University of Illinois **CT:** Series 4, Series 7, Series 24, Series 66, Securities Licenses **C:** Owner, Stockholm's Vardshus, Inc. (2002-Present); Owner, Geneva Investment Group (1991-Present) **CIV:** Board Member, Geneva Chamber of Commerce (2011-Present); Financial Supporter, Former Board Member, Geneva Community Chest; Contributor, Volunteer, Various Community Organizations **AW:** Member of the Year, Geneva Chamber of Commerce (2016) **MH:** Albert Nelson Marquis Lifetime Achievement Award; Marquis Who's Who Top Professional **AS:** Mr. Olesen attributes his success to hard work and persistence. **B/I:** Mr. Olesen was mentored by a local small business owner, Bill Briner, as a teenager. He learned about cash flow management and its importance for a business. With his tutelage and natural talent, Mr. Olesen understood how money worked for its direct relationship to investments. While in college at the University of Illinois, he discovered that he wanted to be self-employed. After graduating, he looked at a number of bars and restaurants to buy. Unfortunately, he did not find one right away. In 1987, he decided to go into the investment business full time and opened his own firm, Geneva Investment Group, in 1991. In 2002, a restaurant became available for purchase, and Mr. Olesen bought it.

OLIPHANT, THOMAS J., T: Executive Vice President, President, Entrepreneur, Business Owner, International Business Partner **I:** Business Management/Business Services **CN:** Sound Ideas Music LLC, DBA Ventura Guitars **DOB:** 05/28/1948 **PB:** Wichita **SC:** KS/USA **PT:** Joseph J. Oliphant; Bonnie (Knight) Oliphant **MS:** Married **SPN:** Lily Oliphant **CH:** Yvonne; Michelle; Jerry **ED:** MBA in Business Administration, University of Texas at Arlington, Arlington, TX (1979); BBA in Economics, Wichita State University, Wichita, KS, Summa Cum Laude (1973) **CT:** Certified Purchasing Manager, National Association of Purchasing Management (NAPM) **C:** Partner, 26 International English Schools, China (2018-Present); Owner, Sound Ideas Music LLC, McKinney, TX (2001-Present); President, M&M Merchandisers, Fort Worth, TX (1998-2001); Senior Vice President, Tucker-Rocky Distributing Incorporated, Irving, TX (1981-1998); Materials Manager, NCH Corporation, Irving, TX (1974-1981) **CIV:** Vice President, Purchasing Management Association of Dallas; Board of Directors, Purchasing Management Association; Founder, Dallas Branch, Materials Management Association; National Board, National Material Management Association; Charitable Activities; Various Organizations, Local Church **MIL:** Department of Classification and Reassignment, Headquarters, U.S. Army, Heidelberg, Germany (1967-1969) **CW:** Researcher, Participating Writer, "How to Conduct a Land Use Study" (1973-1974) **AW:** Certified Purchasing Manager **MEM:** National Purchasing Management Association; National Materials Management Association; Purchasing Management Association of Dallas; National Association of Music Merchants **AS:** Mr. Oliphant attributes his success to feeling that his life has been his work. He has made a total commitment and his life is consumed by his work, although he has also had a great family life. He attributes most of his success to his absolute and total involvement in his work. He always felt that he had to be the hardest worker in order to serve as an example to the people that are working for him. **B/I:** Mr. Oliphant became involved in his profession because he has spent a great deal of time traveling, visiting customers, and establishing relationships with them. Music store owners have always been his favorite people with whom to work. He admires their desire to keep real music alive and in the hands of the youth. Mr. Oliphant always felt they had a great business model, which attracted him to working with them. **AV:** Golfing; Fishing; Reading; Extensive world traveling **PA:** Independent **RE:** Christian **THT:** Mr. Oliphant would advise the importance of travel and developing an understanding of other cultures and how they teach us of the many approaches to life and life's problems.

OLIVER, DAVID BURDETTE, T: Communications Company Executive (Retired) **I:** Publishing **CN:** Knight Ridder, Inc. **DOB:** 10/21/1940 **PB:** Versailles **SC:** OH/USA **PT:** Orlan Eugene; Dorothy Emma (Schilling) Oliver **MS:** Married **SPN:** Joan Oliver (11/02/1974) **CH:** Gary Alan Hewetson; James Bruce Hewetson; Jan Feasel **ED:** MBA, University Miami, Coral Gables, FL (1964); BBA, Wittenberg University (1962) **C:** Manager, Data Analysis Department, Knight Ridder, Inc., Miami, FL (1975-1998); Assistant to the President, Miami Herald Publishing Co. (1967-1975); Manager, Marketing Research, Miami Herald Publishing Co. (1964-1967); Assistant Buyer, Wren's Department Store, Springfield, OH (1961-1962) **CIV:** Member, Fundraiser Committee, United Way of Miami-Dade (1970-Present); Member, Biscayne Gardens Civic Association (1985) **AW:** Inductee, Miami Lakes Sports Hall of Fame (2019); Named One of the Outstanding Young Men in America, Coral Gables Jaycees (1970) **MEM:** Economic Society of South Florida Clubs, University of Miami; President, Miami Lakes Loch Isle Homeowners Association; President, Miami Lakes Duplicate Bridge Club; Vice Chairman, Miami Lakes Elderly Affairs Committees

MH: Albert Nelson Marquis Lifetime Achievement Award **B/I:** Mr. Oliver became involved in his profession because initially, when he was in college, he was assistant buyer of infants wear at Wren's Department Store. He was going into department store retailing and he did his thesis at the university of Miami in conjunction with the local department stores. It was all about the impact of night openings and one of his questions was if you knew then what you know now regarding night openings would you still enter that as your profession. Ninety percent of them said no but by virtue of doing that research study he found out that research was fun. So he applied at the Miami herald store which was opening up for the first time a marketing research department for the position and got that position. That's how he got into it. **AV:** Softball; Basketball; Reading; Theater; Working out at Shula's Athletic Club **PA:** Republican **RE:** Lutheran **THT:** Alvah Herman Chapman Jr. was an American newspaper publisher who served at the helm of The Miami Herald and as chairman of the Knight Ridder newspaper division.

OLIVER, JOHN WILLIAM, T: Comedian; Television Host **I:** Media & Entertainment **DOB:** 04/23/1977 **PB:** Erdington **SC:** Birmingham/United Kingdom **PT:** Jim Oliver; Carol Oliver **MS:** Married **SPN:** Kate Norley (10/2011) **CH:** Two Sons **ED:** Diploma in English, Christ's College, University of Cambridge (1998) **C:** Stand-up Comedian, Night Clubs, NY; Comedy Group, Chocolate Milk Gang **CW:** Host, "Last Week Tonight with John Oliver" (2014-Present); Actor, "Amusement Park" (2019); Voice Actor, "The Lion King" (2019); Executive Producer, "Wyatt Cenac's Problem Areas" (2018-2019); Voice Actor, "Bob's Burgers" (2017); Actor, "The Detour" (2017); Voice Actor, "Danger Mouse" (2016); Performer, Writer, "The Daily Show" (2006-2017); Voice Actor, "The Simpsons" (2014); Voice Actor, "Robot Chicken" (2014); Actor, "Community" (2009-2014); Actor, "Rick and Morty" (2013); Actor, "The Smurfs 2" (2013); Actor, "The Smurfs: The Legend of Smurfy Hollow" (2013); Performer, "John Oliver's New York Stand-Up Show" (2010-2013); Actor, "Gravity Falls" (2012); Actor, "Randy Cunningham: 9th Grade Ninja" (2012); Actor, "Moves: The Rise and Rise of the New Pornographers" (2011); Actor, "The Smurfs" (2011); Performer, "Important Things with Demetri Martin" (2009); Actor, "The Love Guru" (2008); Performer, "John Oliver: Terrifying Times" (2008); Actor, "The Comic Side of 7 Days" (2005); Actor, "Mock the Week" (2005); Actor, "Green Wing" (2004); Actor, "Gash" (2003); Actor, "People Like Us" (2001); Actor, "My Hero" (2001); Comedian, The Comedy Zone, Edinburgh Festival Fringe (2001); Actor, "Bleak House" (1985); Actor, Performer, Television Shows, Films **AW:** Producers Guild of America Award for Outstanding Producer of Live Entertainment and Talk Television (2016-2020); Writers Guild of America Award for Comedy/Variety – Talk Series (2015, 2017-2020); Primetime Emmy Awards for Outstanding Writing for a Variety, Music or Comedy Series, Academy of Television Arts & Sciences (2009-2011, 2016-2017, 2019); Primetime Emmy Award for Outstanding Variety, Music, or Comedy Series, Academy of Television Arts & Sciences (2011, 2016-2019); Primetime Emmy Award for Outstanding Interactive Program, Academy of Television Arts & Sciences (2015, 2017); Numerous Awards **MEM:** Vice President, Cambridge Footlights, University of Cambridge

OLSHAKER, MARK BRUCE, T: Author, Filmmaker **I:** Writing and Editing **DOB:** 02/28/1951 **PB:** Washington **SC:** DC/USA **PT:** Bennett Olshaker; Thelma A. (Abramson) Olshaker **MS:** Married **SPN:** Carolyn M. Clemente (8/28/1977) **ED:** BA, George Washington University, Washington, DC (1972) **C:** Writer, Author, Film Maker, Washington, DC (1972-Present); Special Correspondent, St. Louis Post Dispatch, Washington Bureau (1974-1975) **CR:** Mindhunters, Inc. Vienna, VA (1995-Present); Vice President, Unicorn Projects, Inc., Washington, DC (1983-Present) **CIV:** Judge, Helen Hays Theater Awards (2007-2009); Media Advisor, National Endowment of the Humanities, Corp. Public Broadcasting, Washington, DC (1984, 1989, 1991, 1998); Communications Arts and Humanities Hearing Committee, DC Court of Appeals Board on Professional Responsibility (1988-1991) **CW:** Author, "The Killer's Shadow" (2020); Author, "The Killer Across the Table" (2019); Co-Author, "Deadliest Enemy: Our War Against Killer Germs" (2017); Screenwriter, "Who Killed Lindbergh's Baby?" (2013); Author, "Law and Disorder" (2013); Screenwriter, "Anatomy of a Pandemic" (2009); Screenwriter, "Flashpoints USA: God and Country" (2004); Screenwriter, "Avoiding Armageddon" (2003); Screenwriter, "Mill Times" (2001); Screenwriter, "Bioterror: Dealing with a New Reality" (2001); Author, "The Cases That Haunt Us" (2000); Author, "The Anatomy of Motive" (1999); Author, "Mindhunters: Broken Wings" (1999); Screenwriter, "Bridge" (1998); Author, "Obsession" (1998); Co-Author, "Virus Hunter" (1997); Author, "Journey into Darkness" (1997); Author, "Unabomber: On the Trail of America's Most-Wanted Serial Killer" (1996); Author, "Unusual Suspects" (1996); Screenwriter, "The Edge" (1996); Co-Author, "Mindhunter" (1995); Screenwriter, "Stormchasers" (1995); Screenwriter, "Roman City" (1994); Author, "The Edge" (1994); Screenwriter, 'Mind of a Serial Killer" (1992); Screenwriter, "What's Killing the Children?" (1990); Screenwriter, "Discovering Hamlet" (1990); Author, "Blood Race" (1989); Screenwriter, "Pyramid" (1988); Author, "Unnatural Causes" (1986); Screenwriter, "Cathedral" (1985); Screenwriter, "Castle" (1983); Author, "Einstein's Brain" (1981); Screenwriter, 'Lewis Mumford: Toward Human Architecture" (1979); Author, "The Instant Image" (1978); Screenwriter, "A Moment in Time" (1975); Screenwriter, "Patent Pending" (1975); Screenwriter, "We All Came to America" (1974); Contributor, 'Forensic Emergency Medicine"; Contributor, "Norman Mailer in Context"; Co-Author, "The Mailer Review"; Contributor, Numerous Articles, Professional Publications **AW:** IP Champion, Global Innovations Police Center (2019); National Emmy (1994-1995); National Emmy Nomination (1992-1993) **MEM:** Writers Guild of American East; The Cosmos Club; Past Chairman, Cosmos Club Foundation; Past President, Norman Mailer Society; Board of Directors, Rod Serling Memorial Foundation; Authors Guild; Mystery Writers of America; International Thriller Writers Inc. **MH:** Albert Nelson Marquis Lifetime Achievement Award **THT:** The Netflix series, "Mindhunter," is based on Mr. Olshaker's novel.

OLSON, DONALD B., PHD, T: Professor **I:** Education/Educational Services **CN:** University of Miami **DOB:** 05/28/1952 **PB:** Greybull **SC:** WY/USA **PT:** Donald Henry Olson; Dawn Beverly (Van Winkle) Olson **MS:** Married **SPN:** Margaret Isobel Wanner (05/18/1974) **CH:** Wendy; Bryan; Elizabeth; Aaron **ED:** PhD, Texas A&M University (1979); MS, Texas A&M University (1976); BS, University of Wyoming (1974) **C:** Assistant Professor, Professor, University of Miami (1979-Present); 3rd Engineer, Houston Barge Lines (1971-1974) **CR:** Chairman, Committees for Thesis & Dissertation Advising, University of Miami Rosenstiel School of Marine and Atmospheric Science (1982-Present); Instructor, Physical Oceanography; Instructor, Ocean Circulation; Instructor, Atmospheric and Oceanic Turbulence; Instructor, Models in Fluid Dynamics and Ecology; Senior Professor, Ecosystem Science and Policy; Instructor, Field Methods **CW:** Associate Editor, Journal of Marine Research (2000-2010); Editor, Geophysical Research Letters-Oceans (1999-2003); Associate Editor, Oceanography Magazine (1988-1994); Contributor, Over 150 Publications **AW:** Grantee, Office of Naval Research; Grantee, National Science Foundation; Grantee, NASA; Distinguished Alumni Award, University of Wyoming **MEM:** American Meteorological Society; American Geophysical Union; American Association for the Advancement of Science; Oceanographic Society; American Fisheries Society; Sigma Xi **MH:** Albert Nelson Marquis Lifetime Achievement Award; Marquis Who's Who Top Professional **B/I:** Dr. Olson was always interested in science. He grew up on a small ranch farm in Wyoming where the hills were covered with marine fossils. His family used to irrigate, and he loved to watch the water flow to try to understand the process of nature. He decided in the 8th grade to be a physical oceanographer, as it could enable him to learn how the ocean flows. **AV:** Drawing; Painting

OLSON, PETER, "PETE" GRAHAM, T: U.S. Representative **I:** Government Administration/Government Relations/Government Services **DOB:** 12/09/1962 **PB:** Fort Lewis **SC:** WA/USA **MS:** Married **SPN:** Nancy Olson **CH:** Kate; Grant **ED:** JD, School of Law, The University of Texas at Austin (1988); BA in Computer Science, Rice University, Houston, TX (1985) **C:** U.S. Representative, Texas' 22nd Congressional District, United State Congress, Washington, DC (2009-Present); The House Committee on Transportation and Infrastructure, Washington, DC (2009-Present); U.S. House of Representatives Committee on Science, Space and Technology (2009-Present); Committee on Homeland Security, U.S. House of Representatives (2009-Present); Member, Energy and Commerce Committee, Washington, DC (2011-2019); Chief of Staff to Senator John Cornyn, U.S. Senate, Washington, DC (2002-2007); Legislative Aide to Senator Phil Gramm, U.S. Senate, Washington, DC (1998-2002); Naval Liaison Officer, U.S. Senate (1995-1998) **AW:** Decorated Joint Service Commendation Medal; Joint Service Achievement Medal; Navy and Marine Corps Achievement Medal; Armed Forces Expeditionary Medal; Southwest Asia Service Medal; Joint Chiefs of Staff Badge **MEM:** NRA; The Texas State Society; R Association, Rice University; Director, The Texas Lyceum; Littlefield Society **PA:** Republican **RE:** Methodist

OLSON, WALTER J. JR., T: Sole Proprietor **I:** Financial Services **CN:** Walter J. Olson & Associates **DOB:** 07/27/1941 **PB:** Paterson **SC:** NJ/USA **PT:** Walter Justus Olson; Viola Patricia (Trautvetter) Olson **MS:** Single **ED:** MBA, Columbia University (1967); BS, BA, Brown University (1964) **CT:** Certified Public Accountant (CPA), Virginia **C:** Sole Proprietor, Principal, Walter J. Olson & Associates (Present); Principal, Walter J. Olson & Associates, Washington, DC (1986-Present); Senior Research Analyst, U.S. House Select Committee on Technology Transfer to PRC, Washington, DC (1998-1999); Deputy Assistant Secretary for Export Administration, U.S. Department of Commerce, Washington, DC (1983-1986); Principal, Walter J. Olson & Associate, McLean, VA (1982-1983); Corporate Planning Coordinator, Washington Gas Light Company, Washington, DC (1978-1982); Senior Consultant, Booz, Allen and Hamilton, Inc., Washington, DC (1973-1978); Management Officer, CIA, Washington, DC (1969-1973); Design Engineer, Rockwell International, Inc., Downey, CA (1964-1965) **CIV:** Vice-Chairman, Committee on Finance, Fairfax County Representatives, Virginia (1982-1983)

MIL: Served to 1st Lt., U.S. Air Force (1967-1969) **MEM:** President, Washington Chapter, Strategic Leadership Forum (1990-1991); American Institute of Certified Public Accountants; Greater Washington Society of CPAs **MH:** Albert Nelson Marquis Lifetime Achievement Award **B/I:** Mr. Olson has been a Certified Public Accountant since 1967 because he used to work for Booz Allen and was always encouraged to get whatever license he can. He decided to get his CPA license even though he doesn't work as a CPA; it just evolved that way. He worked for the government and companies. **PA:** Republican **RE:** Episcopalian

O'MALLEY, MICHELLE, DSCHEME, T: Associate Professor **I:** Education/Educational Services **CN:** University of California Santa Barbara **ED:** DSChemE, University of Delaware (2009); BSChemE in Biomedical Engineering, Carnegie Mellon University (2004); USDA-NIFA Postdoctoral Fellowship, Massachusetts Institute of Technology **C:** Colburn Lecturer, Department of Chemical and Biomolecular Engineering, University of Delaware (2016) **CW:** Co-author, "A Parts List for Fungal Cellulosomes Revealed by Comparative Genomics," Nature Microbiology (2017); Co-author, "Early-branching Gut Fungi Possess a Large, Comprehensive Array of Biomass-degrading Enzymes," Science (2016); Co-patentee, "Novel Proteins from Anaerobic Fungi and Uses Thereof" **AW:** Biochemical Technology Division Young Investigator Award, American Chemical Society (2018); Camille Dreyfus Teacher-Scholar Award (2017); CAREER Award, National Science Foundation (2016); Presidential Early Career Award for Scientists and Engineers (2016); Named to 35 Innovators Under 35, MIT Technology Review (2015)

O'MALLEY, SEAN PATRICK, PHD, T: Cardinal; Archbishop of Boston **I:** Religious **DOB:** 06/29/1944 **PB:** Lakewood **SC:** OH/USA **PT:** Theodore O'Malley; Mary Louise (Reidy) O'Malley **ED:** PhD in Spanish and Portuguese, The Catholic University of America (1979); MA in Spanish, Capuchin College, Washington, DC (1972); MA in Religious Education, Capuchin College, Washington, DC (1971); BA in Theology, Capuchin College, Washington, DC (1971); Diploma, Saint Fidelis Seminary, Herman, PA (1967) **CT:** Ordained Priest **C:** Cardinal-Priest, Santa Maria della Vittoria (2006-Present); Archbishop, Boston, MA (2003-Present); Elevated to Cardinal (2006); Bishop, Palm Beach, FL (2002-2003); Bishop, Fall River, MA (1992-2002); Bishop, Saint Thomas (1985-1992); Coadjutor Bishop, Saint Thomas (1984-1985); Ordained Priest, Saint Thomas (1984); Episcopal Vicar of Priests, Serving Portuguese, Haitian and Hispanic Communities, Washington, DC (1978-1984); Executive Director, Centro Catolico Hispano, Washington, DC (1973-1978); Professor, The Catholic University of America, Washington, DC (1969-1973); Ordained Priest, Order of Friars Minor Capuchin (1970); Ordained Priest, Roman Catholic Church (1970) **CR:** Presidential Council of the Pontifical Council for the Family (2009-Present); Congregation for the Clergy (2006-Present); Congregation for Institutes of Consecrated Life and Societies of Apostolic Life in the Roman Curia (2006-Present); Chairman, Committee on Consecrated Life, United States Conference of Catholic Bishops **AW:** Grand-Cross, Order of Prince Henry, Portugal (2016); Honorary Chaplain, Sovereign Military Order of Malta (1991); Knight Commander of the Order of Infante D. Henrique, Government of Portugal (1985) **RE:** Roman Catholic

OMAR, ILHAN ABDULLAHI, T: U.S. Representative from Minnesota **I:** Government Administration/Government Relations/Government Services **CN:** U.S. House of Representatives

DOB: 10/04/1981 **PB:** Mogadishu **SC:** Somalia **PT:** Nur Omar Mohamed; Fadhuma Abukar Haji Hussein **MS:** Divorced **SPN:** Ahmed Abdisalan Hirsi (2018, Divorced 2019); Ahmed Nur Said Elmi (2009, Divorced 2017) **CH:** Three Children **ED:** Bachelor of Arts in Political Science and International Studies, North Dakota University (2011) **C:** Member, U.S. House of Representatives from Minnesota's Fifth Congressional District (2019-Present); Member, Minnesota House of Representatives, 60B District (2017-Present); Director of Policy Initiatives, Women Organizing Women Network (2015); Senior Policy Aide, Andrew Johnson (2013-2015); Manager, City Council Campaign for Andrew Johnson, Minneapolis, MN (2013); Campaign Manager, Kari Dziedzic's (2012); Community Nutrition Educator, University of Minnesota (2006-2009) **CW:** Featured, Documentary, "Time for Ilhan" (2018); Appearance, Music Video, Maroon 5, "Girls Like You" (2018) **AW:** Named, Progressive Rising Star, Roll Call (2018); Named to "Firsts: Women Who are Changing the World," TIME Magazine (2017); Named, One of "Five Families Who are Changing the World as We Know It," Vogue (2017); Community Leadership Award, Mshale (2015); Policy Fellow, University of Minnesota Humphrey School of Public Affairs **PA:** Democrat

OMIDYAR, PIERRE M., T: Internet Company Executive; Film Company Executive **I:** Other **CN:** eBay Inc., First Look Media **DOB:** 06/21/1967 **PB:** Paris **SC:** France **MS:** Married **SPN:** Pam Kerr **CH:** Three Children **ED:** Honorary Doctor of Public Service, Tufts University (2011); BS in Computer Science, Tufts University (1988) **C:** Launched, First Look Media (2013-Present); Founder, Chairman, eBay Inc. (1998-Present); Co-Founder, Ink Development Corporate (1991); Software Developer, Claris (Subsidiary of Apple Computer) (1988-1991); With Developer Relations, General Magic, Inc. **CR:** Trustee, Santa Fe Institute; Member, Administration and Finance Committee, Tufts University; Member, Committee on Trusteeship, Tufts University **CIV:** Co-Founder, Chair, Board of Directors, Omidyar Foundation (1998-Present); Co-Founder, Chief Executive Officer, Omidyar Network; Board of Directors, Meetup.com **CW:** Producer, "Spotlight" (2015); Producer, "Merchants of Doubt" (2014) **AW:** Named One of Forbes 400: Richest Americans (2006-Present); Named One of the Top 25 Players Who Can Actually Get an Independent Movie Made, The Hollywood Reporter (2018); Named One of the World's Richest People, Forbes (1999-2007); Named One of the 50 Most Generous Philanthropists, Fortune Magazine (2005); Ernst & Young Entrepreneur of the Year (1999); Co-Recipient (with Pam Omidyar), Light on the Hill Award, Tufts University

O'NEAL, SHAQUILLE, "SHAQ" RASHAUN, T: Sportscaster, Professional Basketball Player (Retired) **I:** Athletics **DOB:** 03/06/1972 **PB:** Newark **SC:** NJ/USA **PT:** Joe Tony (Father); Lucille O'Neal; Philip A. Harrison (Stepfather) **MS:** Divorced **SPN:** Shaunie Nelson (12/26/2002, Divorced 2011) **CH:** Shareef Rashaun; Amira Sanaa; Shaquir Rashuan; Me'arah Sanaa; Taahirah **ED:** EdD, Barry University (2012); Coursework in Broadcasting, Sportscaster University at Syracuse University (2009); Coursework in Broadcasting, Staten Island Newhouse School of Public Communications, NY (2009); MBA, University of Phoenix (2005); BS, Louisiana State University, Baton Rouge, LA (2000) **C:** Minority Owner, Sacramento Kings, NBA (2013-Present); Sportscaster, "Inside the NBA," TNT (2011-Present); NBA Analyst, Turner Sports (2011-Present); Retired, Professional Basketball Player, NBA (2011); Center, Boston Celtics, NBA (2010-2011); Center, Cleveland Cavaliers, NBA (2009-2010);

Center, Phoenix Suns, NBA (2008-2009); Center, Miami Heat, NBA (2004-2008); Center, Los Angeles Lakers, NBA (1996-2004); Center, Orlando Magic, NBA (1992-1996) **CR:** Owner, Spokesperson, Nine Restaurants, Papa John's (2019-Present); Owner, Krispy Kreme (2016-Present); Investor, Loyale3 Holdings Inc. (2015); Member, U.S. Men's Basketball Team, Summer Olympics, Atlanta, GA (1996); Member, U.S. Men's Basketball Team, World Championships, Toronto, Canada (1994); Owner, Clothing Line, Record Label, TWIsM, Real Estate Properties; Investor, NRG Esports **CIV:** Special Deputy, Colonel, Maricopa County Sheriff's Department, AZ (2006-2008); Reserve Deputy Officer, Bedford County Sheriff's Department, VA (2004-2007); Volunteer, Tempe Police Department, AZ; Reserve Officer, Miami Beach Police Department, FL **CW:** Appearance, "Graduate Together: America Honors the High School Class of 2020" (2020); Appearance, "Rock & Roll Road Trip with Sammy Hagar" (2020); Appearance, "What Men Want" (2019); Actor, "Uncle Drew" (2018); Voice Actor, "Show Dogs" (2018); Voice Actor, "The Lego Movie" (2014); Voice Actor, "The Smurfs 2" (2013); Co-Author, "Shaq Uncut: My Story" (2011); Actor, "Scary Movie 4" (2006); Actor, "After the Sunset" (2004); Actor, "The Year of the Yao" (2004); Rap Artist, "Shaquille O'Neal Presents His Superfriends, Volume I" (2002); Actor, "The Wash" (2001); Actor, "Steel" (1997); Rap Artist, "The Best of Shaquille O'Neal" (1996); Actor, "Kazaam" (1996); Rap Artist, "You Can't Stop the Reign" (1995); Rap Artist, "Shaq Fu: Da Return" (1994); Actor, "Blue Chips" (1994); Rap Artist, "Shaq Diesel" (1993); Actor, Appearances, Wrestling Events, Music Festivals, Television Shows, Films **AW:** Inductee, FIBA Hall of Fame (2017); Inductee, Naismith Basketball Hall of Fame (2016); Western Conference All-Star Team (1997, 1998, 2000-2004, 2009); NBA All-Star Game Co-MVP (2009); Inductee, New Jersey Hall of Fame (2009); One of the 100 Most Powerful Celebrities, Forbes.com (2008); One of the Most Influential People in the World of Sports, Business Week (Now Bloomberg Businessweek) (2007); Eastern Conference All-Star Team (1993-1996, 2005-2007); Winner, Miami Heat, NBA Championship (2006); NBA Player of the Year, Sporting News (2000, 2005); NBA All-Star Game MVP (2000, 2004); NBA Finals MVP (2001, 2002); All-NBA First Team (1998, 2000-2006); Winner, Los Angeles Lakers, NBA Championship (2000-2002); NBA MVP (2000); All-NBA Second Team (1995, 1999); One of the 50 Greatest Players in NBA History (1996); Gold Medal, Men's Basketball, Summer Olympics, Atlanta, GA (1996); Gold Medal, Men's Basketball, World Championships (1994); NBA Rookie of the Year (1993); First Team All-American, Sporting News (1991, 1992)

O'NEILL, EDWARD LEONARD, T: Actor **I:** Media & Entertainment **DOB:** 04/12/1946 **PB:** Youngstown **SC:** OH/USA **PT:** Edward Phillip O'Neill; Ruth Ann (Quinlan) O'Neill **MS:** Married **SPN:** Cathy Rusoff (02/1986) **CH:** Claire; Sophia **ED:** Coursework, Youngstown State University; Coursework, The Ohio State University **CW:** Actor, "Modern Family" (2009-2020); Actor, "The Last Shift" (2020); Actor, "Weird City" (2019); Voice Actor, "Ralph Breaks the Internet" (2018); Actor, "Sun Dogs" (2017); Voice Actor, "Finding Dory" (2016); Voice Actor, "Family Guy" (2015); Actor, "Real Husbands of Hollywood" (2013); Voice Actor, "Wreck-It Ralph" (2012); Voice Actor, "The Penguins of Madagascar" (2012); Actor, "Handy Manny" (2011); Actor, "Kick Buttowski: Suburban Daredevil" (2011); Actor, "WordGirl" (2009); Actor, "Redbelt" (2008); Actor, "John from Cincinnati" (2007); Actor, "Twenty Good Years" (2006); Actor, "Inseparable" (2006); Actor, "The Unit" (2006); Actor, "8 Simple Rules" (2005); Actor, "The West Wing" (2004-2005); Actor, "Spartan" (2004); Actor, "In the Game" (2004); Actor, "L.A. Dragnet" (2003-2004); Actor, "Big Apple" (2001); Actor, "Nobody's Baby" (2001); Actor, "Lucky Numbers" (2000); Actor, "The 10th Kingdom" (2000); Actor, "The Bone Collector" (1999); Actor, "Prefontaine" (1997); Actor, "The Spanish Prisoner" (1997); Actor, "W.E.I.R.D. World" (1995); Actor, "Little Giants" (1994); Actor, "In Living Color" (1994); Actor, "Blue Chips" (1993); Actor, "Wayne's World" (1992); Actor, "Top of the Heap" (1991); Actor, "Dutch" (1991); Actor, "The Whereabouts of Jenny" (1991); Actor, "Sibling Rivalry" (1990); Actor, "The Adventures of Ford Fairlane" (1990); Actor, "Disorganized Crime" (1989); Actor, "K-9" (1989); Actor, "Midnight Caller" (1988); Actor, "Married...with Children" (1987-1997); Actor, "Right to Die" (1987); Actor, "Popeye Doyle" (1986); Actor, "Spenser: For Hire" (1986); Actor, "A Winner Never Quits" (1986); Actor, "Androcles and the Lion" (1986); Actor, "Hunter" (1985); Actor, "The Equalizer" (1985); Actor, "Elm Circle" (1984); Actor, "Of Mice and Men" (1984); Actor, "Miami Vice" (1984); Actor, "Lakeboat" (1983); Actor, "When Your Lover Leaves" (1983); Actor, "Farrell for the People" (1982); Actor, "Another World" (1981); Actor, "The Day the Women Got Even" (1980); Actor, "Cruising" (1980); Actor, "Dogs of War" (1980); Actor, "Knockout" (1979); Actor, "Deliverance" (1972) **AW:** SAG Award for Outstanding Performance by an Ensemble in a Comedy Series, SAG-AFTRA (2010, 2011, 2012); Star, Hollywood Walk of Fame (2011); Emmy Award for Best Actor in a Comedy Series, Academy of Television Arts & Sciences (2010); Innovator Award, TV Land Awards (2009)

OPDAHL, VIOLA ELIZABETH, T: Secondary School Educator **I:** Education/Educational Services **DOB:** 01/06/1925 **PB:** Watervliet **SC:** NY/USA **PT:** Leslie Rouse Woodruff; Violetta Frances (O'Bryon) Woodruff **MS:** Widowed **SPN:** Robert Clarence Opdahl (08/04/1956, Deceased) **ED:** Postgraduate Studies, State University of New York at Albany (1959-1961); MS in Education, Cornell University (1951); BA, Skidmore College (1945) **CT:** Certified Social Studies Teacher; Certified Guidance Counselor **C:** College Student Technology Supervisor, SUNY New Paltz (1989-1994); Social Studies Teacher, Kingston City School District (1962-1986); Social Studies Teacher, Kingston City School District (1956-1958); Social Studies Teacher, Selkirk School District (1955-1956); Social Studies Teacher, Patchogue-Medford High School (1951-1955); Social Studies Teacher, New Lebanon Central School District (1945-1950) **CR:** Adjunct Instructor of Psychology, Marist College (1972-1986); Ad Hoc Syllabi and Testing Committees, New York State Education Department (1967-1982) **CIV:** Special Activities Organizer, Special Events Committee, Town of Hurley (1988) **CW:** Co-Author, "A Shaker Musical Legacy" (2004); Author, Articles on Hurley, New York, as the 1870s Venue of Selected Winslow Homer Rural Paintings, Local Museum **AW:** Dean's Award, SUNY New Paltz (1989); Outstanding Social Studies Teacher, Mid-Hudson Society, New York State Council (1986); President Award, Marist College (1986) **MEM:** League of Women Voters; American Association of University Women; Hurley Heritage Society; Friends of Senate House **MH:** Albert Nelson Marquis Lifetime Achievement Award **B/I:** Ms. Opdahl became involved in her profession because her mother was a teacher. **AV:** Reading; Writing poetry and prose; Enjoying nature **PA:** Democrat

OPFER, NEIL DAVID, PHD, T: Construction Educator; Consultant **I:** Education/Educational Services **CN:** University of Nevada **DOB:** 06/01/1954 **PB:** Spokane **SC:** WA/USA **PT:** Gus Chris Opfer; Alice Anna (Nibbe) Opfer **ED:** PhD in Engineering, University of Wisconsin (2003); MS in Management, Purdue University (1982); BA in Business, Washington State University, Cum Laude (1977); BA in Economics, Washington State University, Cum Laude (1977); BS in Building Theory, Washington State University, Cum Laude (1976) **CT:** Certified, General Industry Safety, University of California (2012); Certified, Construction Safety, University California, San Diego, CA (2011); Licensed General Contractor, OSHA; General Industry Training, Professional Constructor, Project Manager; Construction Trainer, Estimating Professional, Scheduling Professional; Certified Safety & Health Manager **C:** Associate Professor of Construction and Construction Management, University of Nevada, Las Vegas (1995-Present); Assistant Professor of Construction and Construction Management, University of Nevada, Las Vegas (1989-1995); Assistant Professor of Construction and Construction Management, Western Michigan University (1987-1989); Senior Engineer, Inland Steel Corp. (1984-1987); Project Engineer, Inland Steel Corp. (1982-1984); Field Engineer, Inland Steel Corp. (1979-1982); Millwright Supervisor, Inland Steel Corp., East Chicago, IL (1978-1979); Associate Engineer, Inland Steel Corp., East Chicago, IL (1977-1978); General Carpenter Foreman, Opfer Construction Corp., Spokane, WA (1976); Estimator, Standard Oil, Richmond, CA (1975) **CIV:** Board of Directors, Habitat for Humanity International (1991-Present); Board of Directors, Christmas in April (1993-1998) **CW:** Contributor, Articles, Professional Journals; Contributor, Chapters, Books **AW:** International Charles V. Keane Award, American Association of Cost Engineers (Now AACE International) (2009); Silver Member Award, American Welding Society (2006); International Brian Dunfield Academic Award, American Association of Cost Engineers (Now AACE International) (2004); Order of Engineer Award, American Association of Cost Engineers (Now AACE International) (1989) **MEM:** Nevada Board of Directors, American Association of Cost Engineers (AACE International) (1994-Present); National Board of Directors, American Association of Cost Engineers (AACE International) (1995-1997); Board of Directors, American Welding Society (1982-1987); Fellow, American Association of Cost Engineers (AACE International); American Welding Society; American Institute of Constructors (AIC); Project Management Institute, Inc.; Construction Management Association (CMAA); National Safety Council; American Society of Safety Engineers; American Society of Engineering Education (Now American Society of Safety Professionals); The Tau Beta Pi Association, Inc.; The Honor Society of Phi Kappa Phi **MH:** Albert Nelson Marquis Lifetime Achievement Award **B/I:** Dr. Opfer wanted to make a difference by helping students become their best selves within their career field. By doing this, he aims to contribute to improving the state of construction education. **AV:** Bicycling; Running **RE:** Methodist

OPLINGER, KATHRYN, T: President, Chief Executive Officer **I:** Manufacturing **CN:** Spring Valley Farm's Jamco Trailers NC **DOB:** 04/18/1951 **PB:** Wadsworth **SC:** OH/USA **PT:** Herman Carl Simshauser; Blanche Ruth (White) Simshauser **MS:** Married **SPN:** Douglas E. Oplinger (07/26/1986) **CH:** Raymond; Karla; Kathleen; Laura Dawn **ED:** Coursework, Kennesaw State University, Kennesaw, GA (1988-1989); Coursework, Washington College, Chestertown, MD (1969-1971) **CT:** CNEW **C:** President, Chief Executive Officer, Spring Valley Farm's Jamco Trailers NC (2019-Present); President, Chief Executive Officer, Dawn Enterprises, Inc. (1981-1997); President, Chief Executive Officer, CMAS (1981-1997); President, Chief Executive Officer, Tiller Stewart & Company (1981-1997) **CR:** Management Information Systems Consultant, Fortune 500 Corporations (1989-Present); Spokesperson, Designer, Saks Fifth Avenue (1981-1986); Software Expert, Programmer, Novell Network & Accounting **MEM:** Founder, Young Rider Advancement Program, United States Eventing Association (2001-2004); President, Georgia Chapter, Lions International (1986-1987); NAFE; ABWA Management LLC; Sponsor, Retired Racehorse Project; Sponsor, Carolina Horse Park **MH:** Albert Nelson Marquis Lifetime Achievement Award **AS:** Ms. Oplinger attributes her success to her wonderful, loving family. **B/I:** Ms. Oplinger became involved in her profession because she was a student of chemistry and was considered for a scholarship from Johns Hopkins University. **AV:** Golfing; Whitewater rafting; Hiking, Eventing **PA:** Republican **RE:** Protestant

OPP, CHRIS, T: Owner, Operator **I:** Fine Art **CN:** Chris Opp Art **DOB:** 04/01/1953 **PB:** Orange **SC:** CA/USA **PT:** Richard Opp; Shirlee Opp **MS:** Single **CH:** Shaun Christopher Opp; Melissa Ann Opp **CT:** UCLA "Construction and Teaching Techniques" Lifetime Teaching Credentials (Fine Arts, Design and Photography), State of California (1985) **C:** Owner, Operator, Chris Opp Art, Bossier City, LA (2006-Present); Owner, Operator, Opp Art Inc., (Chris Opp Art and Construction) (1975-2006); Instructor, Fine Art, Signage, Airbrushing, and Photography, Golden West College (1985-1988); Co-Owner, Operator, Vantage Creations (1973-1975) **CIV:** Volunteer, Samaritan's Purse; Volunteer, Children's Miracle Network; Volunteer, Pride Academy; Former President, "Keep Bossier Beautiful"; Lecturer at local schools; Mentored four Senior High Students with their Senior Art Projects **CW:** Custom Murals, Graphics, Signs, Faux Finishes and Wood Graining, Table Tops for these Casinos: Hollywood Casino/Hotel, Tunica, MS, Harrisburg, PA, Aurora, Il Shreveport, LA, Sunset Station Casino/Hotel, Las Vegas, NV, Boulder Station Casino/Hotel, Las Vegas, NV, Fiesta Casino/ Hotel, Las Vegas, NV, Paris Casino/Hotel/ Resort, Las Vegas, NV, Tropicana Casino/Hotel, Las Vegas, NV, Ameristar Casino/Hotel, Vicksburg, MS, Silverstar Casino/Hotel, Philadelphia, MS, Barley's Casino, Las Vegas, NV, Isle of Capri Casino/ Hotel, Biloxi, MS, Hard Rock Casino/Hotel, Biloxi, Mississippi, Beau Rivage Casino/Hotel, Biloxi, Mississippi, Sandia Casino/Hotel/Resort, Albuquerque, NM, Sky City Casino/Hotel, New Mexico, Santa Ana Star Casino/Resort, Bernalillo, NM, Route 66 Casino/Hotel, Rio Puerco, NM, Ohkay Casino/Hotel, Espanola, NM, Big Rock Casino, Espanola, NM, Eldorado Casino/Hotel, Shreveport, LA, Evangeline Downs Race Track/Casino/ Hotel, Opelousas, LA, Silver Legacy Casino/Hotel/ Resort, Reno, NV, Tamarack Casino, Reno, NV; Designed the Themed Interior of Sky City Casino's Travel Center, Graphics, Murals, Signage, 3D Sculptures; Designed the Themed Poker Room for Route 66 Casino, Wall Build-outs, Graphics, Murals, Signage, Special Finishes, Décor; Designed the Interiors (some Exteriors) completed Murals, Millwork, Logos, Signage, Graphics, Table Tops, Décor purchasing and Installation, Bar Tops, for these Restaurants: Gardunos Mexican Restaurant, Albuquerque, NM, Five locations, Yesterdave's Grill, Albuquerque, NM, Marco Pollo Restaurant, Albuquerque, NM, Mustang Café at Rich Ford, Albuquerque, NM, Sea Food Show Restaurant, Torrance, California, Scarpas Restaurant (San Antonio), Albuquerque, NM, Bob's Burger (Fourth Street), Albuquerque, NM, Cajun Kitchen, Albuquerque, NM, Pinon Tree Coffee Café, Sky City, NM, Cosmic Café/Bar, Santa Ana Casino, Bernalillo, NM; Designed, Demo & Built a 2,000 sq. ft.

Show Room for Branton Indoor/Outdoor, Bossier City, LA, Installed 2,000 ft. of Cypress T&G Pine on the Walls, all Electrical, Slant Wall, Paint, Finishes, Mill Work, Free Standing Podium, 1,500 Flooring; Designed and Built a 150 sq. ft. Custom kitchen and a 350 sq. ft. Employees Lounge, to match the Show Room; Designed and Built 2 11 Foot Trees that surrounded Support Columns in the Branton Conference Big Game Room, Sonotubes, Lath, Concrete, Finishes, Vines & Leaves; Route 66 Casino's "Poker Pub", Rio Puerco, New Mexico, Built the Exterior and Interior, Mill Work (except the Bar OGB), Tin Type Metallic Ceiling Tiles, Wall Finishes, Murals, Irish Signage (from Ireland), and 90 sq. ft. of Concrete Counter Tops, Completed all the Brick Façade, Paint & Stain; Route 66 Casino's Themed "Thunder Road Restaurant", Restored two 1950 Ford Coupes (one a Police Car) Installed one on the second floor wall and the other on a Hydraulic lift on top of the Bar, all the Stone & Brick Work, Finishes, Murals on the Garage doors, Faux Finishes, Wall Décor; Designed and Built the new Daycare for Calvary Baptist Church, Shreveport, Louisiana. Completed 3,500 sq. ft. of Wainscot stacked Stone, Crown Molding, Wall Texturing & Faux Finishes, Wood front Entrance Arch, 2,000 sq. ft. of Metallic painted Tintype Ceiling panels, Painted 10 Class rooms and three Offices **AW:** Numerous Awards **MH:** Marquis Who's Who Top Professional **AS:** Mr. Opp attributes his success to his God-given gift and the belief that he was put on this Earth to bring color and images into this gray world. **B/I:** Mr. Opp became involved in his profession as young as he can remember; born in California, he didn't have computers and everything was done by hand. He considers himself an 'old school sign painter,' adding that "there are not many of us around these days!" He has been an artist and a carpenter since 1975. Before that, he was printing t-shirts out of his garage and brushing murals on motorcycles and cars for people like Burt Reynolds, Carrol Shelby, the Beach Boys and others over the years. From there, he started doing restaurants. He has since contributed his art to more than 300 restaurants across the United States. From there, he worked in more than 20 casinos and then locally more than 350 projects in Louisiana, and more than 1,600 public art projects across the country. He and artisans spent a year and a half on Don & Diedre Imus Ranch in New Mexico and finished on the Interior & Exterior of 21 Buildings. He was given a gift; he has a picture of him drawing at his parents' table when he was 5 years old. He has lived and traveled throughout the United States and experienced many things and opportunities that God has given him. He feels God gave him a gift and he is fortunate to make a living doing what he loves. **PA:** Republican **RE:** "Follower of the Way" **THT:** Mr. Opp said of himself: "I'm the Artist that throws a pebble across the lake of life, if I cause you to look at what I've created and painted with my God given gift, then I have done what God intended me to do with my gift! In the many schools that I have completed artwork I tell the students, that God gave you a gift, you just have to find it and use it to make this world a better place! Additionally, he said he got his education from the school of life! You just have to look at what other people do, and create and learn and give a better response! My father said, 'Son, if you hammer a nail, paint a wall, or rake leaves, at the end of your day, if you can say, 'I did my best', then it was a good day!'"

ORDÓÑEZ, ANDRÉS, T: Chief Creative Officer **I:** Advertising & Marketing **CN:** FCB Chicago **SC:** Colombia **CH:** Mia; Sol **ED:** Coursework in Art Direction, Miami Ad School (1998-2000); Coursework, Florida International University **C:** Chief Creative Officer, FCB Chicago, FCB Worldwide, Inc., Chicago, IL (2019-Present); Chief Creative Officer, Energy BBDO, Chicago, IL (2016-2019); Executive Vice President, Executive Creative Director, Energy BBDO, Chicago, IL (2014-2016); Senior Vice President, Creative Director, Energy BBDO, Chicago, IL (2014-2016); Vice President, Creative and Managing Director, Bravo Group, Inc., Chicago, IL (2011-2013); Vice President, Creative Director, Zubi Advertising, Miami, FL (2007-2011); Vice President, Creative Director, BBDO, San Juan, Puerto Rico (2001-2007) **CR:** With, Ruiz Nicoli, Spain **AW:** Named, Most Awarded CCOs in the World, The Drum's Big Won Rankings (2018); Named, Top 20 Most Celebrated Campaigns of the Year, "Prescribed to Death," National Safety Council (2018); Numerous Other Awards

ORLEANS, CAROLE TRACY, T: Senior Scientist **I:** Sciences **CN:** Robert Wood Johnson Foundation **ED:** BA, Wellesley College (1970); PhD in Clinical Psychology, University of Maryland; Internship, Duke University Medical Center, NC **C:** Senior Scientist, Robert Wood Johnson Foundation, NJ (1995-Present); National Researcher (1979-Present) **CIV:** U.S. Preventative Services Task Force **AW:** Outstanding Contributions, U.S. Preventative Services Task Force (1998, 2003); Joseph W. Collin Memorial Award, American Society of Preventative Oncology (1994); Award, Agency for Healthcare Research & Quality; Distinguished Scientist Award, Society of Behavioral Medicine; Meritorious Research Service Award, American Psychological Association; Distinguished Service Award, Society of Behavioral Medicine **MEM:** Society of Behavioral Medicine **AS:** Dr. Orleans attributes much of her success to her mother's influence and the passion that she has for her work. Finding solutions for healthcare problems and public health problems has become a driving force behind Dr. Orleans' work. **B/I:** Dr. Orleans became involved in her profession because her mother always wanted her to be a doctor. Although she wasn't inclined to be a physician, she wanted to make a difference at the societal level.

ORMAN, SUZE LYNN, T: Financial Consultant; Writer; Columnist **I:** Financial Services **DOB:** 06/05/1941 **PB:** Chicago **SC:** IL/USA **PT:** Morry Orman; Ann Orman **MS:** Married **SPN:** Kathy Travis (2010) **ED:** Honorary Doctorate in Commercial Science, Bentley University (2010); Honorary LHD, University of Illinois at Urbana-Champaign (2009); BA in Social Work, University of Illinois at Urbana-Champaign (1976) **CT:** Certified Financial Planner **C:** Director, Suze Orman Financial Group (1987-1997); Vice President of Investments, Prudential Bache Securities (1983-1987); Account Executive, Merrill Lynch (1980-1983) **CR:** Motivational Speaker **MIL:** United States Army Reserve (2016); Personal Finance Educator, United States Army **CW:** Author, "The Ultimate Retirement Guide for 50+: Winning Strategies to Make Your Money Last a Lifetime" (2020); Author, "The Adventures of Billy & Penny" (2017); Host, National Syndicated Radio Talk Show, "The Suze Orman Show" (2001-2015); Author, "Suze Orman's Money Class" (2011); Author, "The Money Class: Learn to Create Your New American Dream" (2011); Author, "Suze Orman's 2010 Action Plan" (2010); Author, "Suze Orman's 2009 Action Plan" (2009); Author, "Women and Money: Owning the Power to Control Your Destiny" (2007); Author, "The Money Book for the Young, Fabulous & Broke" (2005); Author, "The Nine Steps to Financial Freedom" (2004); Author, "The Laws of Money, the Lessons of Life: Keep What You Have and Create What You Deserve" (2003); Author, "The Road to Wealth: Suze Orman's Complete Guide to Your Money" (2001); Co-Producer, Host, "The Courage to Be Rich," PBS (1999); Author, "The Courage to Be Rich: Creating a Life of Material and Spiritual Abundance" (1999); Co-Author, "You've Earned It, Don't Lose It: Mistakes You Can't Afford to Make When You Retire" (1995); Host, "Financial Essentials Hour," QVC Network; Contributing Editor, "O: The Oprah Magazine"; Columnist, "Money Matters," Yahoo! Finance, Costco Connection Magazine; Appearances, Various Television Shows; Host, Podcast, "Suze Orman Women & Money Podcast"; Contributor, Articles, Professional Journals **AW:** Gracie Allen Awards for Outstanding Talk Show, American Women in Radio and Television (AWRT) (2007, 2008, 2009, 2013); Ranked 10th, List of the Most influential Celebrities (2013); Listee, 100 Most Powerful Women, Forbes Magazine (2010); Gracie Allen Tribute Award, American Women in Radio and Television (AWRT) (2010); Touchstone Award, Women in Cable Telecommunications (2010); Visionary Award, Council for Economic Education (2009); Ranked 18th, List of the Most Influential Women in Media, Forbes Magazine (2009); Listee, World's Most Influential People, Time Magazine (2008, 2009); CableFAX Program Award for Best Show or Series in Talk Show/ Commentary (2008); Amelia Earhart Award (2008); National Equality Award, Human Rights Campaign (2008); Top Female Motivational Speaker in the World, Bloomberg Businessweek (2007); Gracie Allen Award for Individual Achievement-Program Host, American Women in Radio and Television (AWRT) (2005, 2006); Emmy Award for Outstanding Service Show Host, Academy of Television Arts & Sciences (2004, 2006); Multiple Sclerosis Society Spirit Award (2006); Crossing Borders Award, Feminist Press (2003); Gracie Allen Award for National/ Network/Syndication Talk Show, American Women in Radio and Television (AWRT) (2003); Inductee, Books for a Better Life Hall of Fame (2003); TJFR Group News Luminaries Award (2002); Listee, "Who Have Revolutionized the Way America Thinks About Money," Worth Magazine, 100th Issue (2001); Motivational Book Award, Books for a Better Life (1999); Listee, Top 30 Power Brokers Who Most Influenced Mutual Fund Industry and Affected Money, Smart Money Magazine (1999) **PA:** Democrat

OROSZ, JOEL J., PHD, T: Philanthropist, Educator **I:** Education/Educational Services **CN:** Grand Valley State University **DOB:** 03/15/1957 **PB:** Kalamazoo **SC:** MI/USA **PT:** Joseph Frank Orosz; Caroline Mae Orosz **MS:** Married **SPN:** Florence Upjohn Orosz **CH:** Caroline Elizabeth; Anita Jane; Marianna Margaret; Andrew Joel **ED:** PhD in American Social History, Case Western Reserve University (1986); MA in History and Museum Studies, Case Western Reserve University (1981); BA in American History, Kalamazoo College (1979) **C:** Founding Director, The Grantmaking School (2004-2009); Distinguished Professor of Philanthropic Studies, Dorothy A. Johnson Center for Philanthropy and Nonprofit Leadership, Grand Valley State University, Grand Rapids, MI (2001-2010); Executive Assistant, Program Director, W.K. Kellogg Foundation, Battle Creek, MI (1986-2001); Curator of Interpretation, Kalamazoo Valley Museum (1983-1986) **CR:** Principal, Inside Philanthropy Consulting, Kalamazoo, MI (2001-2011); Commissioner, Michigan Community Service Commission, Lansing, MI (1991-2000); Chair, Committee on Legislation and Regulations, Council on Foundations (1993-1997) **CIV:** Kalamazoo Advisory Council, Turn 2 Foundation (2017-Present); Board Member, Lakeside for Children Foundation (2011-Present); Burton H. and Elizabeth S. Upjohn Charitable Trust (1999-Present); Board Member, Guido and Elizabeth Binda Foundation (1997-Present); Board Chair, Lakeside for Children

Foundation (2013-2019); Board Member, Guido and Elizabeth Binda Foundation **CW:** Author, "1792: Birth of a Nation's Coinage" (2017); Author, "Truthseeker: The Life of Eric P. Newman" (2016); Author, "The Secret History of the First United States Mint" (2011); Author, "Effective Foundation Management" (2007); Author, "The Insider's Guide to Grantmaking" (2000); Editor, "For the Benefit of All: A History of Philanthropy in Michigan" (1996); Author, "Curators and Culture: A History of the Museum Movement in America, 1740-1870" (1990); Author, "The Eagle That Is Forgotten: Pierre Eugene Du Simitiere, Founding Father of American Numismatics" (1989) **AW:** Book of the Year, Numismatic Literary Guild (2012, 2017, 2018); Heath Literary Award, American Numismatic Association (2000, 2010, 2017) **MEM:** Fellow, American Numismatic Society; Board of Trustees, Historian, Archivist, Numismatic Bibliomania Society; Attinelli Fellowship; American Numismatic Association **MH:** Albert Nelson Marquis Lifetime Achievement Award **AS:** Dr. Orosz attributes his success to the self-discipline and work ethic instilled by his parents, Caroline and Joseph Orosz. **B/I:** Mr. Orosz has always had an intense interest in the past, he has always been interested in history, history is generalized through philanthropy and numismatics and book collecting but there is a common thread of history that runs through everything he has done professionally and in terms of his avocation. His family was more interested in the present and he was always interested in the past. His parents Joseph and Caroline Orosz were very adamant about him pursuing higher education so he could transcend the hard blue-collar jobs they had to do all their lives. It was his parents' determination and their encouragement that helped him appreciate his education. **AV:** Coin collecting/numismatics; Book collecting; Biographical writing; Conservation of historical objects **PA:** Democrat **THT:** The Buddha was correct: there are many different paths to enlightenment. Also, karma is real, and consequential. At the end of the day, only kindness matters.

O'ROURKE, JAMES, T: Attorney **I:** Law and Legal Services **CN:** Law Offices of James L. O'Rourke **PT:** James G. O'Rourke; Margaret Elizabeth (Fesco) O'Rourke **MS:** Married **SPN:** Margaret C. DiCicco (09/18/1994) **ED:** JD, University of Bridgeport (1987); BS, University of Bridgeport (1984) **C:** Private Practice, Stratford, CT (1987) **MIL:** With, United States Navy (1976-1979) **AW:** Named to Directory of Distinguished Attorneys, Martindale-Hubbell **MEM:** Association of Trial Lawyers of America (Now American Association for Justice); American Bar Association (ABA); Greater Bridgeport Bar Association; Connecticut Bar Association; Connecticut Trial Lawyers Association **BAR:** Supreme Court of the United States (1998); Mashantucket Pequot Tribal Bar (1995); United States District Court for the District of Connecticut (1989); Connecticut (1988) **AV:** Boating; Gardening; Fishing; Bicycling; Swimming **RE:** Roman Catholic

O'ROURKE, ROBERT, "BETO" FRANCIS, T: Former U.S. Representative **I:** Government Administration/Government Relations/Government Services **DOB:** 09/26/1972 **PB:** El Paso **SC:** TX/USA **PT:** Pat Francis O'Rourke; Melissa Martha (Williams) O'Rourke **MS:** Married **SPN:** Amy Hoover Sanders (09/24/2005) **CH:** Three Children **ED:** BA in English Literature, Columbia University (1995) **C:** Candidate, Democratic Nominee, 2020 U.S. Presidential Election (2019); U.S. Representative, Texas' 16th Congressional District, United States Congress, Washington, DC (2013-2019); Member, U.S. House Committee on Veterans' Affairs (2013-2019); Member, Committee on Armed Services (2013-2019); Member, U.S. House Committee on Homeland Security (2013-2019); City Councilman, District Eight, City of El Paso, TX (2005-2011); Co-Founder, Stanton Street Technology Group, El Paso, TX (1999-2017); Singer, Guitarist, Los Dregtones; Singer, Guitarist, Foss; Singer, Guitarist, Swipe **CIV:** Board Member, El Paso Hispanic Chamber of Commerce; Board Member, Institute for Policy and Economic Development, The University of Texas at El Paso **CW:** Co-Author, "Dealing Death and Drugs: The Big Business of Dope in the U.S. and Mexico" (2011); Singer, Guitarist, "Fewel St." (1994); Singer, Guitarist, Albums with Foss, "The El Paso Pussycats" (1993); Proofreader, H.W. Wilson Company **AW:** Civility in Public Life Award, Allegheny College (2018) **MEM:** Rotary Club International; United Way; Center Against Sexual & Family Violence **PA:** Democrat **RE:** Roman Catholic

ORSINI, PAUL V. JR., T: Music Educator **I:** Education/Educational Services **DOB:** 10/04/1955 **PB:** Albany **SC:** NY/USA **PT:** Paul Vincent Orsini Sr.; Lucia (Rutolo) Orsini **MS:** Married **SPN:** Lisa **ED:** MusM in Performance, Syracuse University, Syracuse, NY (1979); MusB in Music Education, State University of New York at Potsdam, Potsdam, NY (1977) **CT:** Certified, K-12 Music Teacher, State of New York **C:** Teacher, Shenendehowa Central School District, Clifton Park, NY (1987-Present); Teacher, Corinth Central School District, NY (1986-1987); Substitute Teacher, Suburban Council Schools, Albany, NY (1983-1986); Freelance Entertainer, Albany, NY (1983-1986); Entertainer, "The Carmen Canavo Show," Tampa, FL (1979-1983); Musician, The Mirage (1978-1979) **CR:** Owner, Leader, High Society Big Band, Clifton Park, NY (1988-1991) **CIV:** Principal, Trumpet South Colonie Memorial Wind Ensemble (2000-Present); With, Dominant Five Brass Quintet (2005-2006); Lead Trumpet, Georgie Wonders' Big Band (Georgie Wonders Orchestra (Swing Band)) (2004-2006); Lead Trumpet, The Starliters Big Band (2002-2004); Lead Trumpet, Greg Nazarian Big Band (1998-2002); Representative, Unified Arts, Shenendehowa, NY (1999); Active Shenendehowa Partnership Team (1995-1997); Faculty Representative, Executive Board, Friends of Music, Shenendehowa, Clifton Park, NY (1993); Advisor, Shenendehowa Crisis Intervention Team, Clifton Park, NY (1988-1993) **CW:** Premiered Trumpet Compositions, Dr. Brian Israel, Syracuse University (1977-1979); Premiered Trumpet Compositions, Dr. Earl George (1977-1979) **MEM:** Albany Musicians' Association, American Federation of Musicians, Local 14; International Trumpet Guild; Honorary Life Member, New York State Congress of Parents and Teachers; Phi Mu Alpha (Now Phi Mu Alpha Sinfonia Fraternity of America) **MH:** Albert Nelson Marquis Lifetime Achievement Award **AS:** Mr. Orsini attributes his success to his parents, his teachers and professors, his wife and his students. They include John Johnson from elementary school, Gene Falcone from middle school, Henry Carr from high school and Patrick Renzi from middle and high school. In high school, he performed with Louis Belson, Clark Terry, and Urbie Green, conducted by Dr. William Ravelli. In 1973, he was selected to study at the School of Orchestral Studies in Saratoga, NY. He was blessed to study with Eugene Ormandy, Gil Johnson, Seymore Rosenfeld and Mason Jones. More inspirations came from Dr. Gordon Mathie and Dr. John Schorge from college, Dr. James Mosher from Onondaga CC/Syacuse University College of Visual and Performing Arts, and Dr. Brian Israel of Syracuse University, College of Visual and Performing Arts, as well as road musician, Mr. Carmen Cannavo. Other people of note are Mr. Paul V. Orsini Sr., Mrs. Lucia Orsini, Mrs. Lisa Orsini, Mr. Patrick Renzi, Mr. Henry Carr, and the toughest trumpet teacher he ever had, Dr. James Mosher. He thanks Dr. Mosher, and misses and loves all his mentors. He was taught by all of them that nothing is given to us. To truly appreciate what we have, it has to to be earned! **B/I:** Mr. Orsini became involved in his profession because he had a neighbor who played the trumpet, and one night, he came out in a suit and tie; he was dressed for a concert. Mr. Orsini asked if he could try his trumpet, and so he did. At the young age of 8, he decided then that music would be his life. **AV:** Fishing; Sports; Travel; Reading; Jazz **PA:** Independent **RE:** Catholic **THT:** Mr. Orsini plays a total of 13 instruments, including brass, woodwind, and percussion. He says, "Embrace every moment in life, 'cause you don't know what you've got till it's gone." I did embrace those moments, and it's been a wonderful voyage. Honor, honesty, integrity, and love are what shape a person's life. Always be true to yourself. It's always worked for me."

ORTEGA PERRIER, RICARDO, T: Entrepreneur **I:** Military & Defense Services **DOB:** 09/18/1951 **PB:** Iquique **SC:** Chile **PT:** Ricardo Rolando Ortega **MS:** Married **SPN:** Denise Ximena del Carmen Denise Benard Shand (2/11/1977) **CH:** Francisca; Ricardo; Rodrigo; Martin **ED:** MBA, Chilean Air Force Academy, Santiago (1971); MA in Political Science, Chilean Air Force Academy, Santiago **CT:** Aeronautical System Engineer, Air Force War College **C:** President, LATAM, Kallman Worldwide, Santiago (2011); Russian Defense Agency; Teacher, War College of Santiago (2011-2013); Board of Directors, Codelco Norte; Director, Corporacion Nacional del Cobre de Chile **CIV:** Air Force Retired Generals Association, Santiago, Chile (2010-2014); COAR Supporter Charity, Un Techo Para Chile **MIL:** Major General, Commander in Chief, Chile Air Force, Santiago, Chile (2006-2010) **AW:** Decorated Legion of Merit in the Grade of Commander, Governments of USA, Brazil, Spain, France, Bolivia, Ecuador, Venezuela, Argentina, Colombia **MEM:** Associate, Retired Armed Forces Generals **MH:** Albert Nelson Marquis Lifetime Achievement Award **AS:** General Perrier attributes his success to achieving his goals. He has always valued fairness and he loves a challenge. He knew he was successful when he felt at peace with himself. **B/I:** General Perrier's father was a general in the air force; he worked as the undersecretary. His example inspired General Perrier to follow the same path. Entry into the field was natural for him. **AV:** Playing tennis; Practicing yoga **PA:** Independent **RE:** Roman Catholic

ORTIZ TAYLOR, SANDRA, T: Artist, Educator **I:** Education/Educational Services **CN:** IRS **DOB:** 04/27/1936 **PB:** Los Angeles **SC:** CA/USA **PT:** John Santry Taylor; Juanita Loretta (Shrode) Taylor **MS:** Single **ED:** MA in Fine Arts, Iowa State University (1962); BA in Art, University of California Los Angeles (1958) **C:** Instructor of Art, City College of San Francisco (1966-2001); Instructor of Art, Indian Valley College (Now College of Marin), Marin County, CA (1973-1974); Instructor of Art, Iowa State University, Iowa City, Iowa (1961-1962) **CR:** Chair, All-media National Exhibit, Fine Arts Gallery, Broward College, Davie, FL (1994); Seminar Guest Speaker, National Book Conference (1991); Chair, Humanities Art Gallery, Palm Beach State College **CW:** Group Show, Exhibit, Bedford Gallery, Walnut Creek, CA (1996); Group Show, Exhibit, San Francisco Open Studios (1996); Group Show, Exhibit, ACCI Gallery, Berkeley, CA (1995-1996); Group Show, Exhibit, Moreau Galleries, St. Mary's College, Notre Dame, IN (1995); Group Show, Exhibit, California Museum of Art, Santa

Rosa, CA (1991-1995); Group Show, Exhibit, San Francisco Airport Committee & Corporation of Fine Arts Museum of San Francisco (1994); Group Show, Exhibit, Women Artists Gallery, San Francisco, CA (1994); Group Show, Exhibit, San Jose Institute of Contemporary Art, CA (1993-1994); Group Show, Exhibit, Falkirk Center, San Rafael, CA (1992, 1993); Group Show, Exhibit, Gallery Route One, Point Reyes Station, CA (1993); Commissioned for Graduate Program, Chicano and Latino Studies, University of California Irvine (1992); Group Show, Exhibit, University of Hawai'i at Manoa, Hawaii; Group Show, Exhibit, Austin Museum of Art, Texas; Group Show, Exhibit, San Mateo County Arts Council, Belmont, CA; Group Show, Exhibit, San Jose Contemporary Art & Performance Gallery; Work Reviewed in Various Publications **AW:** Jurors Award, California Museum of Art (1992); Scholar, Anderson Ranch Art Center, Snow Mass, CO (1991) **MH:** Albert Nelson Marquis Lifetime Achievement Award **B/I:** Ms. Taylor became involved in her profession because her father was a musician and he always loved art and drew a lot but her mother was not inclined to draw. He encouraged them to draw and whenever someone had a birthday, he would take them to buy art supplies. She also had an undying interest in art and used paint, acrylic and oil. She started drawing when she was a kid and her family were very supportive as she showed early talent. She draws with colored pencil a lot.

OSAKA, NAOMI, T: Professional Tennis Player **I:** Athletics **DOB:** 10/16/1997 **PB:** Chuo-Ku, Osaka **SC:** Japan **AW:** Winner, Grand Slam Single, Australian Open (2019); Winner, Grand Slam Single, U.S. Open (2018)

OSBORNE, THOMAS, T: Oral and Maxillofacial Surgery **I:** Medicine & Health Care **CN:** Thomas E. Osborne Oral and Facial Surgery **DOB:** 11/25/1954 **PB:** Santa Barbara **SC:** CA/USA **PT:** Thomas Osborne; Inez (Terres) Osborne **MS:** Married **SPN:** Joan Boubek **CH:** Elisabeth; Tommy **ED:** Certified in Oral and Maxillofacial Surgery, Johns Hopkins University (1983-1987); Doctor of Dental Surgery, Loyola University, Chicago, IL (1982); Bachelor of Arts, University of California Santa Barbara (1978) **CT:** Diplomate, American Board of Oral and Maxillofacial Surgery **C:** Retired (2019); Private Practice in Oral Surgery, Tucker, GA (1991-2019); Chief Executive Officer, Benchmarq Educational Systems, Atlanta, GA (1999-2017); President, Executive Council, Chief Operating Officer, Board of Directors, Benchmarq Healthcare Systems, Atlanta, GA (1995-1997); Assistant Chief of Oral and Maxillofacial Surgery, Grady Memorial Hospital, Atlanta, GA (1987-1991); Assistant Professor, School of Dentistry, Emory University, Atlanta, GA (1987-1991); Assistant Chief of Services, Johns Hopkins Hospital, Baltimore, MD (1986-1987) **CR:** Chairperson, Continuing Education Committee, North District Dental Society, Atlanta, GA (1993-1994); Instructor, Oral and Maxillofacial Surgery, Emory University (1987-1992); Founder, Director, Atlanta Center for Advance Dental Study; Director, Atlanta Dental Implant Institute **CIV:** Cub Scout Leader, Boy Scouts of America, Tucker, GA (1994-Present); Volunteer, World Relief; Volunteer, Various Organization for Refugees; Volunteer, Various Educational Societies **CW:** Author, "Hospital Dentistry" (1992); Contributor, Articles to Professional Journals; Author, Chapter in Book **AW:** Fellowship in Oral and Maxillofacial Surgery, The John Hopkins School of Medicine; Most Outstanding Teacher, Educator, Oral and Maxillofacial Surgery, Emory College **MEM:** Fellow, American Board of Oral and Maxillofacial Surgery; Fellow, Hinman Dental Society; American Dental Associ-

ation; American Association of Oral and Maxillofacial Surgery; Georgia Society of Oral and Maxillofacial Surgery; Georgia Dental Association; Johns Hopkins Medical and Surgical Society; Xi Psi Phi; Seattle Study Club Society **AS:** Dr. Osborne attributes his success to his innate compassion for his patients. **B/I:** Dr. Osborne became involved in his profession due to his longstanding interest in science and teaching. Upon attending dental school, he began to specialize in the maxillofacial aspects of the field. **AV:** Skiing; Writing; Running; Rollerblading; Weightlifting

OSMAN, HENRY P., T: President, Chief Executive Officer **I:** Business Management/Business Services **CN:** Marine Toys for Tots Foundation **ED:** Graduate, Old Dominion University (1969) **C:** President, Chief Executive Officer, Marine Toys for Tots Foundation (1989-Present) **MIL:** Lieutenant General, U.S. Marine Corps (1967-2006) **AW:** Defense Superior Service Medal, U.S. Marine Corps; Legion of Merit, U.S. Marine Corps

OSTEEN, JOEL SCOTT, T: Minister **I:** Religious **CN:** Lakewood Church **DOB:** 03/05/1963 **PB:** Houston **SC:** TX/USA **PT:** John Osteen; Dolores "Dodie" (Pilgrim) Osteen **MS:** Married **SPN:** Victoria Iloff (1987) **CH:** Jonathan; Alexandria **ED:** Coursework, Oral Roberts University (1981-1982) **CT:** Ordained (1992) **C:** Senior Pastor, Lakewood Church, Houston, TX (1999-Present); President, Co-Owner, Station KTBU-TV 55, Houston, TX (1998-2006); Producer, Creator, John Osteen TV Program (1982-1999) **CW:** Author, "Next Level Thinking: 10 Powerful Thoughts for a Successful and Abundant Life" (2018); Author, "Blessed in the Darkness: How All Things Are Working for Your Good" (2017); Author, "Think Better, Live Better: A Victorious Life Begins in Your Mind" (2016); Author, "The Power of I Am: Two Words That Will Change Your Life Today" (2015); Author, "Fresh Start: The New You Begins Today" (2015); Author, "You Can You Will: 8 Undeniable Qualities of a Winner" (2014); Author, "Break Out!: 5 Keys to Go Beyond Your Barriers and Live an Extraordinary Life" (2013); Author, "I Declare: 31 Promises to Speak Over Your Life" (2012); Author, "Every Day a Friday: How to Be Happier 7 Days a Week" (2011); Author, "It's Your Time: Activate Your Faith, Achieve Your Dreams and Increase in God's Favor" (2009); Author, "Your Best Life Begins Each Morning: Devotions to Start Every New Day of the Year" (2008); Author, "Become a Better You: 7 Keys to Improving Your Life Every Day" (2007); Author, "Scriptures and Meditations for Your Best Life Now" (2006); Co-Author, "Choosing Life: One Day at a Time" (2006); Author, "Living the Joy Filled Life (Six Easy Steps to Living a Life of Victory Abundance and Blessing" (2005); Author, "Your Best Life Now: 7 Steps to Living at Your Full Potential" (2004); Featured, Several Compact Discs Titles and Journals/Devotional Books **AW:** Most Influential Christian, Church Report Magazine (2006); One of Barbara Walters' 10 Most Fascinating People (2006)

OSTERBERG, JAMES NEWELL JR., T: Composer, Singer, Musician **I:** Media & Entertainment **DOB:** 04/21/1947 **PB:** Muskegon **SC:** MI/USA **PT:** James Newell Osterberg; Louella Kristine (Christensen) Osterberg **MS:** Married **SPN:** Nina Alu (2008); Suchi Asano (1984, Divorced 1999); Wendy Weissberg (1968, Annulled) **CH:** Eric Benson **ED:** Coursework, University of Michigan (1963-1964) **C:** Solo Artist (1975-Present); Lead Singer, Composer, The Stooges (1967-1974); Drummer, Lead Singer, Composer, The Iguanas (1966-1967) **CW:** Musician, "Free" (2019); Cameo, "The Dead Don't Die" (2019); Voice Actor, Short Film, "ALT-J - In Cold Blood" (2017); Appearance, "Song

to Song" (2017); Actor, "Gutterdammerung" (2016); Actor, "Blood Orange" (2016); Musician, "Post Pop Depression" (2016); Guest Appearance, "Sheriff Callie's Wild West" (2016); Guest Appearance, "Mr. Pickles" (2014); Appearance, "Asthma" (2014); Voice Actor, "Once Upon a Time in Wonderland" (2013-2014); Appearance, TV Shorts, "Iggy Pop and the Stooges Scarecrow," "Iggy Pop Has His Fortune Told" (2013); Musician, "Ready to Die" (2013); Musician, "Après" (2012); Appearance, "L'étoile du jour" (2012); Appearance, "Iggy and the Stooges Live at Academy of Music New York City" (2011); Voice Actor, "Arthur 3: The War of the Two Worlds" (2010); Actor, "Art House" (2010); Actor, "Suck" (2009); Voice Actor, Video Game, "Grand Theft Auto IV: The Lost and Damned" (2009); Musician, "Préliminaires" (2009); Voice Actor, Video Game, "Grand Theft Auto IV" (2008); Voice Actor, "Lil' Bush: Resident of the United States" (2007-2008); Voice Actor, "Persepolis" (2007); Guest Appearance, "American Dad!" (2007); Musician, "The Weirdness" (2007); Appearance, "Wayne County Ramblin'" (2006); Voice Actor, Video Game, "Driv3r" (2004); Appearance, "Coffee and Cigarettes" (2003); Musician, "Skull Ring" (2003); Guest Appearance, "Fastlane" (2002); Musician, "Beat 'Em Up" (2001); Actor, "Snow Day" (2000); Musician, "Avenue B" (1999); Voice Actor, "The Rugrats Movie" (1998); Guest Appearance, "Star Trek: Deep Space Nine" (1998); Appearance, "The Brave" (1997); Appearance, "Private Parts" (1997); Musician, "Naughty Little Doggie" (1996); Appearance, "The Crow: City of Angels" (1996); Actor, "The Adventures of Pete & Pete" (1994-1996); Actor, "Atolladero" (1995); Actor, "Dead Man" (1995); Actor, "Tank Girl" (1995); Appearance, "Coffee and Cigarettes III" (1993); Musician, "American Caesar" (1993); Actor, "Hardware" (1990); Guest Appearance, "Tales from the Crypt" (1990); Guest Appearance, "Shannon's Deal" (1990); Musician, "Brick by Brick" (1990); Actor, "Cry-Baby" (1990); Musician, "Instinct" (1988); Appearance, "The Color of Money" (1986); Musician, "Blah-Blah-Blah" (1986); Appearance, "Sid and Nancy" (1986); Voice Actor, "Rock & Rule" (1983); Guest Artist, "Hold Tight!" (1982); Musician, "Zombie Birdhouse" (1982); Musician, "Party" (1981); Musician, "Soldier" (1980); Musician, "New Values" (1979); Musician, "Lust for Life" (1977); Musician, "The Idiot" (1977); Musician, With James Williamson, "Kill City" (1977); Musician, "Raw Power" (1973); Musician, "Fun House" (1970); Musician, "The Stooges" (1969) **AW:** Grammy Lifetime Achievement Award (2020); Co-Recipient, Best Video, "Bells & Circles," Q Awards (2018); Commander of the Ordre des Arts et des Lettres (2017); Most Compelling Living Subject of a Documentary, "Gimme Danger," Critics' Choice Documentary Awards (2016); Icon Award, GQ Men of the Year Awards (2014); Inductee, Rock and Roll Hall of Fame (2010); Integrated Wood Pencil, "Together Incredible," D&AD Awards (2010); Living Legend, Classic Rock Roll of Honour Awards (2009); Wood Pencil for Direction, "Kick It," D&AD Awards (2004); Punk of the Year - No. 1, Creem Magazine Awards (1980); Comeback of the Year - No. 1, Creem Magazine Awards (1977)

OSTRIKER, JEREMIAH PAUL, PHD, T: Astrophysicist; Professor **I:** Education/Educational Services **CN:** Columbia University **DOB:** 04/13/1937 **PB:** New York **SC:** NY/USA **PT:** Martin Ostriker; Jeanne (Sumpf) Ostriker **MS:** Married **SPN:** Alicia Suskin (12/01/1958) **CH:** Rebecca; Eve; Gabriel **ED:** MA, University of Cambridge, England, United Kingdom (2002); Honorary PhD, The University of Chicago (1992); Honorary DSc, The University of Chicago (1992); PhD in Astrophysics, The University of Chicago (1964); AB in Physics and Chemistry, Harvard University (1959) **C:** Professor,

Department of Astronomy, Columbia University (2012-Present); Charles A. Young Professor Emeritus of Astronomy, Princeton University (2012-Present); Director, Institute of Computational Science and Engineering, Princeton University (2005-2009); Distinguished Visiting Professor, Institute of Advanced Study, Princeton University (2004-2005); Plumian Professor, Astronomy and Experimental Philosophy, University of Cambridge (2001-2004); Provost, Princeton University (1995-2001); Charles A. Young Professor of Astronomy, Princeton University (1982-2002); Chairman, Department of Astrophysical Sciences, Director, Princeton University Observatory, Princeton University (1979-1995); Professor, Princeton University (1971-2012); Associate Professor, Princeton University (1968-1971); Assistant Professor, Princeton University (1966-1968); Research Associate, Lecturer of Astrophysics, Princeton University (1965-1966); Postdoctoral Fellow, University of Cambridge, England, United Kingdom (1964-1965) **CR:** Visiting Miller Professor, University of California, Berkeley (1990); Visiting Professor, Harvard University (1987) **CIV:** Honorary Trustee, American Museum of Natural History (2007-Present); Trustee, American Museum of Natural History (1997-2006) **CW:** Author, "Heart of Darkness: Unraveling the Mysteries of the Invisible Universe" (2013); Author, "Development of Large-Scale Structure in the Universe" (1991); Member, Editorial Board, Princeton University Press (1982-1984, 1986); Contributor, Articles to Professional Journals **AW:** Gruber Prize in Cosmology (2015); Named Champions of Charge, The White House (2013); Gruber Cosmology Prize (2015); James Craig Watson Medal (2012); Catherine Wolfe Bruce Gold Medal (2011); Associate Gold Medal, Royal Astronomical Society (2004); Golden Plate Award, American Academy of Achievement (2001); National Medal of Science (2000); Karl Schwarzschild Medal, German Astronomical Society (1999); Vainu Bappu Memorial Award, Indian National Science Academy (1993); Regents Fellow, Smithsonian Institute, (1984-1985); Henry Norris Russell Prize, American Astronomical Society (1980); Sherman Fairchild Fellowship, California Institute of Technology (1977); Helen B. Warner Prize, American Astronomical Society (1972); Alfred P. Sloan Foundation (1970-1972); Fellow, National Science Foundation (1960-1965) **MEM:** Board of Governors, National Academy of Sciences (1993-1995, 2008-Present); Treasurer, National Academy of Sciences (2008-Present); Fellow, Royal Society (2007); Councilor, National Academy of Sciences (1992-1995); Councilor, American Astronomical Society (1978-1980); Fellow, American Association for the Advancement of Science; National Academy of Sciences; American Academy of Arts & Sciences; American Philosophical Society; International Astronomical Union; American Astronomical Society; Foreign Member, Royal Society; Foreign Member, Royal Netherlands Academy of Arts & Sciences; Royal Astronomical Society

OSTROW, ALEC PAUL, T: Lawyer **I:** Law and Legal Services **DOB:** 05/04/1956 **PB:** New Hyde Park **SC:** NY/USA **PT:** Harold; Sylvia (Altman) Ostrow **MS:** Married **SPN:** Elizabeth **CH:** Kayla; Amelia **ED:** JD, New York University School of Law (1980); AB, Dartmouth College (1977) **C:** Partner, Becker, Glynn, Muffly, Chassin & Hosinski LLP, New York, NY (2010-Present); Shareholder, Stevens & Lee, New York, NY (2005-2010); Partner, Salomon Green & Ostrow PC, New York, NY (1986-2004); Associate, Chester B. Salomon PC, New York, NY (1980-1985) **CR:** Adjunct Professor, School of Law, St. John's University, Queens, NY (1999-Present) **CW:** "Situation Comity: Something Familiar, Something Peculiar; Nothing That's Formal, Nothing That's Normal," "Norton Annual Survey of Bankruptcy Law" (2018); "Doubting the Indubitable: Can a Partial 'Dirt for Debt' Plan Supported by a Contested Appraisal Constitute [the] Indubitable Equivalent of a Secured Claim?," American Bankruptcy Institute Journal," Volume XXXVII, No. 3 (2018); "Due Process and the Denial of the Opportunity to Negotiate: The Innovation of the Second Circuit's GM Ignition Switch Case," "Norton Annual Survey of Bankruptcy Law" (2017); "Classification of Core Proceedings for Purposes of Determining the Authority of Bankruptcy Judges and the Enforceability of Arbitration Clauses: The 'Hard Core' and the 'Soft Core'," "Norton Annual Survey of Bankruptcy Law" (2013); "Nondisclosure as a Basis for Judicial Estoppel in Bankruptcy, or Estop Me If You Haven't Heard This Before," "Norton Annual Survey of Bankruptcy Law" (2011); "We Don't Need the Case Law to Turn the DIP's Attorney into a Court Informant," "American Bankruptcy Institute Law Review," Volume XXVII, No. 4 (2008); "The 'Animal Farm' of Administrative Insolvency," "American Bankruptcy Institute Law Review" (2003); Author, "Constitutionality of Core Jurisdiction," "American Bankruptcy Law Journal" (1994) **AW:** Philip F. Cohen Award for Meritorious Service, Annual Survey of American Law, New York University School of Law (1980) **MEM:** Fellow, American College of Bankruptcy (2005); American Bankruptcy Institute; New York State Bar Association; New York County Lawyers Association **BAR:** United States District Court for the District of Connecticut (2015); United States District Court for the Western District of New York (2007); United States Court of Appeals for the Second Circuit (1983); United States District Court for the Eastern District of New York (1981); United States District Court for the Southern District of New York (1981); State of New York (1981) **MH:** Albert Nelson Marquis Lifetime Achievement Award; Marquis Who's Who Top Professional **B/I:** Mr. Ostrow became involved in his profession as a matter of urgency, as his father's business went bankrupt during his first year of law school. Effectively becoming the family's bankruptcy attorney, he had no choice but to learn quickly. After graduating, Mr. Ostrow briefly considered a career in academia. Ultimately, he joined up with a small law firm that specialized in heavy bankruptcy, and whose practitioner offered to officially represent Mr. Ostrow's parents, free of charge. **AV:** Baseball; Languages; Literature; Traveling; Multicultural cuisine

OSTROY, JOAN PATSY, T: Lawyer, Mediator **I:** Law and Legal Services **CN:** Law and Meditation Offices of Joan Patsy Ostroy **DOB:** 07/21/1942 **PB:** New York **SC:** NY/USA **PT:** Leo Sternberg; Lillie (Sichel) Sternberg **MS:** Married **SPN:** Joseph Martin Ostroy (05/24/1964) **CH:** Alexander Morris; Lee Rachel **ED:** Doctor of Jurisprudence, Loyola University School of Law, Los Angeles, CA, Cum Laude (1976); Coursework, London School of Economics and Political Science, London, England (1972-1973); Bachelor of Arts, University of Pennsylvania, Philadelphia, PA, With Honors (1964); Coursework, Paris-Sorbonne University, Paris, France (1962-1963) **CT:** Certified Fellow, American Academy of Matrimonial Lawyers (1991-Present); Certificate, Study, London School of Economics and Political Science, London, England (1963); Certified Family Law Specialist, State Bar of California Board of Legal Specialization **C:** Principal, Law Offices of Joan Patsy Ostroy, Los Angeles, CA (1991-2020); Partner, Ostroy & Truby, Los Angeles, CA (1984-1991); Private Practice, Los Angeles, CA (1980-1984); Associate, Bersch & Kaplowitz, Los Angeles, CA (1977-1980); Of Counsel, Law Offices of Jams R. Eliaser **CIV:** Chair, Conference of Delegates, State Bar of California (1988); Member, Governing Board, Steppingstone Youth Crisis Shelter (1984-1986); Co-Founder, Attorneys Against Discrimination (1980); Volunteer Mediator, Family Law Division, Los Angeles Central and West Los Angeles Superior Courts; Member, L.A.S.C. Domestic Violence Task Force; Co-Founder, Volunteer Attorney, Member, Advisory Council, Harriett Buhai Center for Family Law; Volunteer, Black/Jewish Justice Alliance **CW:** Editor, Publication, "HFH v. Superior Court: Another Perspective on the Dilemma of the Downzoned Property Owner," Loyola Law Review (1977); Frequent Seminar Lecturer **AW:** Distinguished Service Award, Women Lawyers Association of Los Angeles; Assembly Resolution for Extraordinary Contributions to the People of her Community and Throughout the State, California Legislature; Alumnae of the Year Award, Executive Committee, State Bar of California, Conference of Delegates; Resolution, Commendation for Integrity and Commitment to Justice Los Angeles City Council **MEM:** National Public Relations and Marketing Committee, Mediation Committee, American Academy of Matrimonial Lawyers (1998-Present); Fellow, American Academy of Matrimonial Lawyers (1991-Present); Advisory Board, Women Lawyers' Association of Los Angeles (1983-Present); Volunteer Mediator, Judge Pro Tem in the Santa Monica Superior Court (1979-Present); Chair and Member, National Mediation Committee, American Academy of Matrimonial Lawyers (1999-2007); National Newsletter Committee, American Academy of Matrimonial Lawyers (1991-2001); Chair and Member, National Committee on Racial and Ethnic Bias in the Profession, American Academy of Matrimonial Lawyers (1993-1999); Chair, Officer, Member, Executive Committee of the Family Law Section, Los Angeles County Bar Association (1983-1997); Chair, National Pro-Bono Committee, American Academy of Matrimonial Lawyers (1994-1996); Vice President and Member, Board of Directors, Southern California Chapter, American Academy of Matrimonial Lawyers (1992-1996); Member, National Committee on Gender Bias, American Academy of Matrimonial Lawyers (1991-1993); Ad Hoc Committee on Association and Section Finances, Los Angeles County Bar Association (1991-1992); Judicial Evaluation Committee, Los Angeles County Bar Association (1983-1987); Executive Committee of the Trial Lawyers Section, Los Angeles County Bar Association (1981-1985); President, Women Lawyers' Association of Los Angeles (1982-1983); Founding Board Member, Los Angeles Collaborative Family Law Association; Beverly Hills Bar Association **BAR:** U.S. Court of Appeals for the Ninth Circuit (1978); California (1977); U.S. District Court for the Central District of California (1977) **AS:** Ms. Ostroy attributes her success to the fact that she was a people person. She liked talking to people and hearing what was going on in their lives and helping to find a solution. **B/I:** Ms. Ostroy became involved in her profession because she was a social worker and her husband was getting his doctorate, as well as a job, at the University of California Los Angeles. She became involved in the women's movement, which made her consider that, by entering law, she could perpetuate change in peoples lives. She felt that, as a social worker, she was mostly helping people adjust to the status quo rather than affecting change. **AV:** Community activism; Tennis; Swim; Reading; Music

OSWALD, JAMES MARLIN, EDD, T: Educator, Researcher, Agriculturalist **I:** Education/Educational Services **DOB:** 08/17/1935 **PB:** Plainview **SC:** TX/USA **PT:** James Buchanan Oswald; Eula Bea (Marlin) Oswald **MS:** Widowed **SPN:** Dorothy Ann Veigel (12/27/1956, Deceased 08/15/2018) **CH:** Richard; Ramona; Roberta **ED:** EdD, Stanford University (1970); Internship for Educational Leadership, Washington, DC (1968-1969); MA, West Texas State College (1958); BS, West Texas State College (1957) **CT:** Administrative Certification, University of Utah, Brigham Young University **C:** Energy Conservation Consultant (1959-Present); Instructional Development Specialist, Community College of Philadelphia (1980-1996); Field Coordinator, Pennsylvania, Delaware and New Jersey Citizen Education, Research for Better Schools, Philadelphia, PA (1978-1980); Assistant Superintendent of Instruction, East Pennsylvania School District, Emmaus, PA (1975-1978); Research Writer, Director of Global Cultural Studies Education Projects, American University Field Staff (1972-1975); Assistant Professor of Social Studies and Social Sciences Education, Syracuse University, New York (1969-1972); Staff Associate, National Council for Social Studies (1968-1969); Curriculum Specialist, American Institutes for Research (1966-1968); Teacher, Supervisor, Salt Lake City Public Schools (1958-1966) **CR:** Career Mentor, Life Coach (2002-Present); Consultant, DudeSpa (2002-Present); Nutrition Educator (1997-Present); Co-Founder, President, Institute for Plant-Based Nutrition (1996-Present); Consultant, Macro/Micro Agro (1992-Present); Financial and Retirement Planning Consultant (1980-Present); Proprietor, Energy Consultant, Main Line Stoves (1972-Present); President, New York State Council on Social Studies (1971-1972); Physical Fitness Trainer; Consultant in Diverse Fields **MIL:** Captain, Infantry, United States Army Reserve (1958-1968); Training Officer, Fort Leonard Wood, MO (1958); Infantry Officer Training, Fort Benning, GA (1957-1958); United States Army (1957-1958); ROTC, West Texas State College (1953-1957) **CW:** Editor, Quarterly Newsletter, "Plant-Based Nutrition" (1997-Present); Co-Author, "Commemoration of Heroic Produce Grower Sacrifices, Death and Survival on September 11" (2001); Co-Author, "Ferdinand Magellan Vegan Cuisine" (2000); Co-Author, "Criteria for Nutritional Guidelines for Century 21" (1999); Co-Author, "Christopher Columbus Vegan Cuisine" (1999); Co-Author, "Marco Polo Vegan Cuisine" (1998); Co-Author, "Our Home, the Earth" (1980); Co-Author, "Planet Earth" (1976); Co-Author, "Earthship" (1974); Co-Author, "Global Cultural Studies" (1972-1974); Researcher, Social Studies and Social Science Education (1972); Author, "The Monroe Doctrine: Does It Survive?" (1969); Contributor, Articles, Professional Journals **AW:** Henry Newell Fellowship, Stanford University (1966-1968); Fulbright-Hays Fellowship, Southeast Asia University Singapore Study Program (1967); Sertoma Service to Mankind Award, Salt Lake City, UT (1966); Grantee, Stanford University, National Science Foundation, United States Office Education, Institute of International Studies **MEM:** Lifetime Member, American Vegan Society; Vegan Organic Network Horticulture-Agriculture; Board Advisor, Institute of Nutrition Education and Research; Lifetime Member, Institute for Plant-Based Nutrition; Lifetime Member, North America Vegetarian Society; Toronto Vegetarian Association; Founder, Main Line Vegan Society; Hindu Temple Society of America; International Society for Krishna Consciousness; Food for Life International; Archaeology Conservancy; The Army Historical Foundation; Emeritus, Social Science Education Consortium; Lifetime Member, Texas Panhandle-Plains Historical Society; Lifetime Member, Utah Historical Society; Lifetime Member, Descendant Founders of Ancient Windsor; Lifetime Member, Windsor Historical Society; St. Lawrence County Historical Society; Colonial Williamsburg Foundation; Jenkins Arboretum; Marshall Steam Museum; Lower Merion Historical Society; Montgomery County Historical Society; Pennsylvania Historical Society; Henry Foundation of Botanical Research; Pennsylvania Forestry Association; Pennsylvania Vegetable Growers Association; Lifetime Member, Pennsylvania Nut Growers Association; Heritage Foundation; Lifetime Member, Stanford University Alumni Association; Sons of the American Revolution; Pennsylvania Sons of the American Revolution; Philadelphia Sons of the American Revolution; Antique Automobile Association of America; Antique Automobile Museum Association; Arbor Day Foundation Hazelnut Project; National Wildlife Certified Demonstration Site Project; Emeritus, Phi Delta Kappa; Sons of Utah Pioneers **MH:** Albert Nelson Marquis Lifetime Achievement Award; Marquis Who's Who Top Professional **AS:** Dr. Oswald attributes his success to his unwavering optimism and following and completing his assignments from God. He believes helping one another is a criterion of professionalism and is essential for success. Happiness brings success and power; money does not. **B/I:** Dr. Oswald entered his profession because he had a great, supportive family. He doesn't quite understand why but everything in his life has felt magical. He believes that "everything is by God's arrangement." **AV:** Gardening; Writing; Practicing photography; Researching genealogy; Researching nutrition **THT:** Dr. Oswald praises God and expresses gratefulness for his blessings.

OUBOU, IMAN, T: Founder, Chief Executive Officer **I:** Media & Entertainment **CN:** Swaay Media **ED:** MS in Biomedical Engineering, University of Colorado Denver (2013); BS in Biochemistry/Molecular Biology, Colorado State University (2011) **CT:** Certificate of Bio-innovation Entrepreneurship **C:** Founder, Chief Executive Officer, SWAAY Media (2016-Present); Regional Director, Gen Next (2015-2016); Account Executive, Science Communications, The Ruth Group (2014-2015); Research Scientist, Siva Therapeutics Inc. (2013-2014); Research Associate, Barbara Davis Center of Diabetes, University of Colorado) (2008-2012); Research Associate, Nanotemper Technologies, Gmbh (2011) **CIV:** Project Coordinator, Mission to Heal (2011-2014) **CW:** Contributor, Articles to Professional Journals

OWEN, WENDY, T: Lead Designer, Owner **I:** Fine Art **CN:** Wendy Owen Design **C:** Owner, Wendy Owen Design (1999-Present); Chief Executive Officer, Custom Drapery, Connecticut (1989-1999) **MEM:** Interior Design Society **AS:** Ms. Owen attributes her success to the love of her work, and to the respect with which she treats her clients. **B/I:** Ms. Owen gleans inspiration for her work from looking at nature and being outdoors. Her design has much to do with the late Michael Taylor's influence of indoor-outdoor living. Likewise, her father was an artist, painter and decorator in England, which is where she believes she inherited her artistic abilities.

OWENS, CYNTHIA DENISE, DO, T: Physician **I:** Medicine & Health Care **CN:** Digestive Health Center **DOB:** 03/14/1952 **PB:** Detroit **SC:** MI/USA **PT:** Jimmie Edwards Owens, Jr.; Anne Elizabeth (King) Owens **MS:** Divorced **CH:** Lucious; Hendrix **ED:** DO, Michigan State University (1979); BA, Wayne State University (1975); AD, Highland Park Junior College (1973) **CT:** Internal Medicine; Geriatric Medicine; Hospital Medicine **C:** Locum Hospitalist (2005-Present); Internist, Digestive Health Center, Pascagoula, MS (1996-2001); Internist, Prevention Health Physicians, Biloxi, MS (1994-1996); Internist, Geriatric Health, Pascagoula, MS (1986-1994); Internist, Private Practice, Quincy, FL (1984-1986) **CR:** Fellow, American College of Physicians; Fellow, American Diabetes Association; Assistant Professor of Medicine; Wayne State University Physicians Group; Fellow, American College of Osteopathic Internists; American Diabetes Association; Society of Hospital Medicine; American Osteopathic Association; American Medical Association; American Geriatrics Society **CW:** Author, "The Triangle" (Unpublished) **MEM:** Board of Directors, American Cancer Society (1996); National Association for the Advancement of Colored People; American College of Osteopathic Internists; American Osteopathic Association; American Geriatric Association; Mississippi State Medical Association; American Medical Association; Society of Hospital Medicine **MH:** Albert Nelson Marquis Lifetime Achievement Award; Marquis Who's Who Top Professional **B/I:** Dr. Owens became involved in her profession because she always wanted to help people and make a difference. For her, this profession was a dream come true. **AV:** Listening to music; Playing the piano; Jogging; Body sculpting; Spending time with family **RE:** Baptist

OWENS, DANA, "QUEEN LATIFAH", T: Rapper, Singer, Songwriter, Actress, Producer **I:** Media & Entertainment **DOB:** 03/18/1970 **PB:** Newark **SC:** NJ/USA **PT:** Lancelot Amos Owens; Rita Lamae (Bray) Owens **ED:** Coursework, Borough of Manhattan Community College **C:** Co-founder, Chief Executive Officer, Flavor Unit Entertainment (1993-Present); Launched, Perfume Line, Queen; Spokeswoman, CoverGirl; Spokeswoman, Revlon; Spokeswoman, Jenny Craig **CW:** Actress, "Hollywood" (2020); Actress, "The Little Mermaid Live!" (2019); Executive Producer, "Scream" (2019); Actress, "Star" (2016-2019); Actress, "Empire" (2017); Actress, "Flint" (2017); Actress, "Girls Trip" (2017); Actress, "Miracles from Heaven" (2016); Voice Actress, "Ice Age: Collision Course" (2016); Voice Actress, "Ice Age, The Great Egg-Scapade" (2016); Featured, "The Art of Organized Noize" (2016); Executive Producer, "The Secrets of Emily Blair" (2016); Executive Producer, "The Perfect Match" (2016); Executive Producer, "November Rule" (2015); Actress, "Bessie" (2015); Executive Producer, "Brotherly Love" (2015); Actress, "The Wiz Live!" (2015); Voice Actress, "Hot in Cleveland" (2014); Host, Executive Producer, "The Queen Latifah Show" (1999-2001, 2013-2014); Actress, "Let's Stay Together" (2011-2014); Actress, "House of Bodies" (2013); Actress, "Percentage" (2013); Actress, "Steel Magnolias" (2012); Actress, "Joyful Noise" (2012); Voice Actress, "Ice Age: Continental Drift" (2012); Actress, "The Dilemma" (2011); Actress, "Valentine's Day" (2010); Actress, "Just Wright" (2010); Appearance, "Entourage" (2010); Rap Artist, "Persona" (2009); Voice Actress, "Ice Age: Dawn of the Dinosaurs" (2009); Actress, Producer, "Mad Money" (2008); Actress, Producer, "The Secret Life of Bees" (2008); Actress, "Who's Your Caddy?" (2007); Voice Actress, "Arctic Tale" (2007); Actress, "Hairspray" (2007); Actress, "Wifey" (2007); Singer, "Trav'lin' Light" (2007); Actress, Producer, "The Perfect Holiday" (2007); Actress, "Life Support" (2007); Voice Actress, "Ice Age: The Meltdown" (2006); Actress, "Stranger Than Fiction" (2006); Actress, "Last Holiday" (2006); Author, "Queen of the Scene" (2006); Actress, "The Muppets' Wonderful Wizard of Oz" (2005); Actress, Producer, "Beauty Shop" (2005); Actress, Producer, "The Cookout" (2004); Singer "The Dana Owens Album" (2004); Actress, "Eve" (2004); Actress, "Scary Movie 3" (2004); Actress, "Barbershop 2: Back in Business" (2004); Actress, "Taxi" (2004); Voice Actress, "The Fairly Odd Parents" (2004); Voice Actress, "Crash Nebula" (2004); Actress, Executive Producer, "Bringing Down the House" (2003); Actress, "Kung Faux" (2003); Actress, "Living with the Dead" (2002); Actress, "Chicago" (2002); Actress, "The Country Bears"

(2002); Actress, "Brown Sugar" (2002); Voice Actress, "Pinocchio" (2002); Rap Artist, "She's the Queen: A Collection of Hits" (2002); Actress, "Spin City" (2001); Author, "Ladies First: Revelations of a Strong Woman" (1999); Voice Actress, "Bringing Out the Dead" (1999); Actress, "The Bone Collector" (1999); Actress, "Mama Flora's Family" (1998); Rap Artist, "Order in the Court" (1998); Actress, "The Wizard of Oz" (1998); Actress, "Living Out Loud" (1998); Actress, "Sphere" (1998); Actress, "Living Single" (1993-1998); Appearance, "Mad TV" (1997); Actress, "Hoodlum" (1997); Composer, "Girls Town" (1996); Rap Artist, "Black Reign" (1994); Actress, "My Life" (1993); Actress, "Who's the Man" (1993); Actress, "Juice" (1992); Actress, "Sister in the Name of Rap" (1992); Rap Artist, "X-tra Naked" (1992); Composer, "White Man Can't Jump" (1992); Rap Artist, "The Nature of Sista" (1991); Actress, "In Living Color" (1991); Actress, "Fresh Prince of Bel Air" (1991); Composer, "New Jack City" (1991); Actress, "House Party 2" (1991); Actress, "Jungle Fever" (1991); Rap Artist, "All Hail the Queen" (1990) **AW:** Emmy Award, as Producer, for Outstanding Television Movie, Academy of Television Arts & Sciences (2016); SAG Award for Outstanding Performance by a Female Actor in a TV Movie or Mini-series, Screen Actors Guild - American Federation of Television and Radio Artists (2016); People's Choice Award for Favorite New Talk Show Host (2014); Inductee, New Jersey Hall of Fame (2011); Lifetime Achievement Award, BET Awards (2010); Listee, Power 150, Ebony Magazine (2008); Golden Globe Award for Best Performance by an Actress in a Mini-Series or Motion Picture Made for TV, Hollywood Foreign Press Association (2008); Award for Outstanding Performance by a Female Actor in a TV Movie or Miniseries, NAACP Image Awards (2008); Named, Woman of the Year, Glamour Magazine (2006); Recipient, Star, Hollywood Walk of Fame (2005); Named, One of the 50 Most Influential African Americans, Ebony Magazine (2004); Award for Outstanding Actress in a Motion Picture, NAACP Image Awards (2004); Artist of the Year Award, Harvard Foundation (2003); SAG Award for Outstanding Performance by a Cast, Screen Actors Guild - American Federation of Television and Radio Artists (2002); Named, Best Actress, American Black Film Festival (1997); Award for Best Actress, NAACP Image Awards (1997); Soul Train Music Award (1995); Sammy Davis Junior Award (1995); Entertainer of the Year Award (1995); Grammy Award for Best Rap Solo Performance, The Recording Academy (1995); Named, Best Female Rapper, Rolling Stone Readers' Poll (1990); Named, Best New Artist, New Music Seminar (1990); Numerous Awards

OXLEY, MARGARET STEWART, T: Elementary School Educator **I:** Education/Educational Services **DOB:** 04/01/1930 **PB:** Petaluma **SC:** CA/USA **PT:** James Calhoun Stewart; Clara Thornton (Whiting) Bomboy **MS:** Widow **SPN:** Joseph H. Oxley (08/25/1951) **CH:** Linda Margaret Oxley; Carolyn Blair Oxley Greiner; Joan Claire Oxley Willis; Joseph Stewart Oxley; James Harmon Oxley; Laura Marie Oxley **ED:** Coursework, The Ohio State University (1985, 1988, 1992, 2003-2008); MA in Language Arts Literature, Reading, The Ohio State University (1984); BS, The Ohio State University, Summa Cum Laude (1973); Coursework, University of California Berkeley (1949-1951) **CT:** Certified Teacher, Ohio **C:** 2nd Grade Teacher, St. Paul School, Westerville, OH (1973-2016) **CR:** Member, Advisory Board, Language Arts (2006-2007); Presenter in Field **CIV:** Active, Akita Child Conservation League, Columbus, OH (1968-1970) **CW:** Member, Editorial Board, Journal of Children's Literature (1996-2007); Co-author, "Children's Literature Remembered, Issues, Trends, and

Favorite Books" (2004); Co-author, "Adventuring With Books, Volume 13" (2002); Co-author, "Adventuring With Books, Volume 12" (2000); Co-author, "Teaching with Children's Books, Path to Literature-Based Instruction" (1995); Member, Editorial Board, Reading Teacher, Volume 47-48 (1993-1994); Co-author, "Reading and Writing, Where it All Begins" (1991) **AW:** Nominee, Distinguished Teacher Award, National Catholic Education Association, Department of Elementary Schools (2011); Outstanding Work in Literacy Education Citation, Pi Lambda Theta (2004); Mary Karrer Award, The Ohio State University (1994); Exemplary Service in Promotion of Literacy Award, International Reading Association (1991); Outstanding Educator, Ohio Council Teachers English Language Arts (1990); Named, Columbus Diocesan Teacher of the Year (1988); Phoebe A. Hearst Scholar (1951); Rose Sterheim Memorial Scholar (1951) **MEM:** Endowment Commission, Children's Literature Assembly, National Council of Teachers of English (2008-2012); Co-chair, Excellence in Poetry for Children Committee, National Council of Teachers of English (2003-2006); Co-chair, Fall Breakfast Children's Literature Assembly, National Council of Teachers of English (2000-2003); Treasurer, Children's Literature Assembly Board of Directors, National Council of Teachers of English (1996-1999); Chair, National Council of Teachers of English (1995-1996); Notable Children's Books in the Language Arts Committee, National Council of Teachers of English (1993-1994); International Reading Association; Ohio Council International Reading Association; President, Literacy Connection; Children's Literature Assembly; Ohio Council Teachers English Language Arts; Phi Kappa Phi; Honorary Member, Vice President, Local Chapter, Pi Lambda Theta **MH:** Albert Nelson Marquis Lifetime Achievement Award **AV:** Reading; Writing; Travel; Gardening; Working with children **PA:** Democrat **RE:** Roman Catholic

PACIFICO, JOSEPH C., T: Counselor (Retired) **I:** Social Work **CN:** Christian Counseling Associates, Inc **DOB:** 06/10/1950 **PB:** Grosse Ile Township **SC:** MD/USA **PT:** Carl Richard Pacifico; Mary Milano Pacifico Campbell **MS:** Married **SPN:** Claire Lee (Schlauch) Pacifico **CH:** Mark Joseph; David Joseph **ED:** MS in Counseling Psychology, Loyola College, Baltimore, MD (1998); MBA in Marketing, University of Maryland (1975); BS in Psychology, University of Maryland (1972) **CT:** Trained Instructor, Couple Communications Program (2007); Licensed Clinical Professional Counselor, MD (2002) **C:** Retired, Licensed Clinical Professional Counselor, Christian Counseling Associates, Inc., Columbia, MD (2002-2013); Master's Level Therapist, Christian Counseling Associates, Inc., Columbia, MD (1999-2002); Master's Level Therapist, Family and Marriage Therapy Center, Burtonsville, MD (1998-2002); Account Representative, Wallace Computer Services, Inc., Rockville, MD (1975-1999) **CR:** Board Member, President, Director of Development, Christian Counseling Associates, Inc., Columbia, MD (2013-2020); Leader, Anger Management Expert, Christian Counseling Associates, Inc. (2001-2012) **CIV:** President of the Board, Christian Counseling Associates, (2020-2023); Worship Assistant, Lay Leader, Elder, Our Shepherd Lutheran Church, Columbia, MD (1998-2013); Board Member, Care Team, CrossWalk Lutheran Church; National Alliance on Mental Illness, Howard County **CW:** Author, "Anger Prevention and Management- Breaking the Cycle" (2009); Author, "Responding to an Angry Child" (2007); Author, "Anger Management" (2003); Author, "Taming Anger in Schools" (2000) **AW:** Sales, Millionaire's Club (1997) **MEM:** North American Nature Photography Association

MH: Albert Nelson Marquis Lifetime Achievement Award; Marquis Who's Who Top Professional **AS:** Mr. Pacifico attributes his success to focusing on doing his best every day. He is consistently motivated to help others reduce their pains. **B/I:** Mr. Pacifico, unfortunately, had a troublesome childhood. However, this only motivated him to work hard and provide a better life for his children. He has since made the decision to dedicate himself completely to cultivating healthy relationships and helping those with mental illness. **AV:** Taking photos of nature; Hiking; Biking; Golfing **PA:** Democrat **RE:** Lutheran **THT:** Mr. Pacifico believes in listening often, putting oneself aside, and having empathy for others.

PACIFICO, LARRY, T: Chief Executive Officer, President, Owner **I:** Athletics **CN:** Pacifico Power Systems **CH:** Theresa; Patrick; James **C:** Founder, Owner, Chief Executive Officer, Pacifico Sports Enhancement New Life, Vice President 20 years **CR:** Weight Management; Over 6,000 Clients **CIV:** Suicide Prevention Hotline, Dayton, OH **CW:** Author, "Champion of Champions" **AS:** Personality, you can know everything about lifting, you can know everything about fitness, you can know everything about nutrition, but if you can't project that to the clients because you just don't have that smile, that outgoing personality, that greeting that hand shake, when your meet them and eye contact, you are not going to make it **B/I:** Mr. Pacifico, was always a great athlete in high school, he was fast, strong, he could always do things beyond his friends and contemporaries he decided to see how far he could go and how strong he can get, he won nine consecutive world titles, traveled the world and hit 54 world records. After high school, Mr. Pacifco graduated 1964 he came to Dayton, Ohio with the Idea of going to the University of Dayton once he arrived he joined a local health club and decided the moment he walked through the health club that he would be in it forever. He was 18 then and currently he is 73, He opened 21 facilities around Ohio and Indiana, He worked with and organization called New Life fitness centers as vice president for 20 years. The owner Of New Life Fitness sold the Company to Mr. Pacifico's Brother and Mr. Pacifico subsequently followed suit and open up his own facility Pacifico sport Enhancement. **THT:** Networking is important

PACINO, AL JAMES, T: Actor **I:** Media & Entertainment **DOB:** 04/25/1940 **PB:** Harlem **SC:** NY/USA **PT:** Salvatore Pacino; Rose (Gerardi) Pacino **CH:** Julie Marie; Anton James; Olivia Rose **ED:** Coursework, Actors Studio; Coursework, High School of Performing Arts, New York, NY **C:** Co-president, The Actors Studio (2010); Co-artistic Director, The Actors Studio, New York, NY (1982-1984); Former Messenger, Movie Theatre Usher, Building Superintendent; Former Mail Deliverer, Editorial Offices, Commentary Magazine **CW:** Actor, "Hunters" (2020); Actor, "Once Upon a Time in Hollywood" (2019); Actor, "The Irishman" (2019); Actor, Executive Producer, "Untitled Joe Paterno Film" (2018); Actor, "The Pirates of Somalia" (2017); Actor, "Hangman" (2017); Actor, "Misconduct" (2016); Actor, "Danny Collins" (2015); Actor, "Manglehorn" (2014); Actor, Producer, "The Humbling" (2014); Actor, "Salomé" (1992, 2013); Actor, "Stand Up Guys" (2013); Voice Actor, "Despicable Me 2" (2013); Actor, Executive Producer, "Phil Spector" (2013); Actor, "Glengarry Glen Ross" (2012); Actor, "The Son of No One" (2011); Actor, "Jack and Jill" (2011); Actor, "The Merchant of Venice" (2011); Actor, Writer, Director, "Wilde Salome" (2011); Appearance, "I Knew It Was You: Rediscovering John Cazale" (2010); Actor,

"You Don't Know Jack" (2010); Actor, "Righteous Kill" (2008); Actor, "88 Minutes" (2007); Actor, "Ocean's Thirteen" (2007); Actor, "Two for the Money" (2005); Actor, "The Merchant of Venice" (2004); Actor, "The Recruit" (2003); Actor, "Gigli" (2003); Actor, "Angels in America" (2003); Actor, "People I Know" (2002); Actor, "Simone" (2002); Actor, "Insomnia" (2002); Actor, Director, "Chinese Coffee" (2000); Actor, "The Insider" (1999); Actor, "Any Given Sunday" (1999); Actor, "Donnie Brasco" (1997); Actor, "Devil's Advocate" (1997); Appearance, "Looking for Richard" (1996); Actor, "City Hall" (1996); Actor, "Hughie" (1996); Actor, "Two Bits" (1995); Actor, "Heat" (1995); Actor, "Carlito's Way" (1993); Actor, "Glengarry Glen Ross" (1992); Actor, "Scent of a Woman" (1992); Actor, "Chinese Coffee" (1992); Appearance, "Madonna: Truth or Dare" (1991); Actor, "Frankie and Johnny" (1991); Actor, "Dick Tracy" (1990); Actor, "The Godfather, Part III" (1990); Director, "The Local Stigmatic" (1990); Actor, "Sea of Love" (1989); Actor, "Revolution" (1985); Actor, "Scarface" (1983); Actor, "American Buffalo" (1983); Actor, "Author! Author!" (1982); Actor, "Cruising" (1980); Actor, "King Richard III" (1979); Actor, "And Justice for All..." (1979); Actor, "Bobby Deerfield" (1977); Actor, "The Basic Training of Pavlo Hummel" (1977); Actor, "Dog Day Afternoon" (1975); Actor, "The Godfather, Part II" (1974); Actor, "Scarecrow" (1973); Actor, "Serpico" (1973); Actor, "The Godfather" (1972); Actor, "The Panic in Needle Park" (1971); Actor, "Camino Real" (1970); Actor, Broadway, "Does a Tiger Wear a Necktie?" (1969); Actor, "Me, Natalie" (1969); Actor, One-act Play, Off-Broadway, "The Indian Wants the Bronx," Astor Place Theater (1968); Actor, Theater, Television and Films **AW:** Honoree, American Icon Awards (2019); Honoree, Kennedy Center Honors, John F. Kennedy Center for the Performing Arts (2016); Golden Globe Awards for Best Actor in a Miniseries or Motion Picture - Television, Hollywood Foreign Press Association (2004, 2011); SAG Awards for Outstanding Performance by a Male Actor in a Television Movie of Miniseries, SAG-AFTRA (2004, 2011); National Medal of Arts (2011); Emmy Awards for Outstanding Lead Actor in a Limited Series or Television Movie, Academy of Television Arts & Sciences (2004, 2010); Internet Award, Variety Club (2008); Marcus Aurelius Lifetime Achievement Award, Rome Film Festival (2008); Lifetime Achievement Award, American Film Institute (2007); American Cinematheque Lifetime Achievement Award (2006); Cecil B. DeMille Award, Golden Globe Awards, Hollywood Foreign Press Association (2001); Award for Outstanding Documentary Directorial Achievement, Directors Guild of America (1997); Lifetime Achievement Award, Independent Feature Project, Gotham Awards (1996); Career Golden Lion, Venice International Film Festival (1994); Golden Globe Awards for Best Actor in a Motion Picture - Drama, Hollywood Foreign Press Association (1974, 1993); Academy Award for Best Actor, Academy of Motion Picture Arts & Sciences (1993); Tony Award for Best Leading Actor in a Play (1977); Drama Desk Award for Best Leading Actor in a Play (1977); Two BAFTA Awards for Best Actor (1976); Award for Best Actor, National Society of Film Critics (1972); Tony Award for Best Featured Actor in a Play (1969); Drama Desk Award for Best Performance (1969); Obie Award for Best Actor in an Off-Broadway Production (1968); Numerous Awards

PAGE, JIMMY PATRICK, T: Singer, Musician **I:** Media & Entertainment **DOB:** 01/09/1944 **PB:** Heston, England **SC:** United Kingdom **PT:** James Patrick Page; Patricia Elizabeth Gaffikin **MS:** Divorced **SPN:** Jimena Gómez-Paratcha (1995, Divorced 2008); Patricia Ecker (1986, Divorced 1995) **CH:** Ashen Josan; Zofia Jade; Jana (Adopted);

James Patrick III; Scarlet Lilith Eleida **ED:** Honorary Doctorate, Berklee College of Music (2014) **C:** Guitarist, Solo and Collaborations (1986-Present); Guitarist, The Firm (1984-1986); Guitarist, Led Zeppelin (1968-1980); Guitarist, The Yardbirds (1966-1968); Guitarist, Carter-Lewis & the Southerners (1964); Guitarist, Neil Christian & the Crusaders (1961-1962) **CIV:** Active Member, Action for Brazil's Children Trust (1998-Present) **CW:** Artist with Led Zeppelin, "Celebration Day" (2012); Appearance, "It Might Get Loud" (2009); Artist with Led Zeppelin, "Definitive Collection" (2008); Artist with Led Zeppelin, "Mothership" (2007); Artist with Led Zeppelin, "How the West Was Won" (2003); Artist with Led Zeppelin, "Latter Days: The Best of Led Zeppelin, Volume Two" (2002); Artist with Led Zeppelin, "Early Days: The Best of Led Zeppelin, Volume One" (2000); Artist with The Black Crowes, "Live at the Greek" (2000); Artist with Robert Plant, "Walking into Clarksdale" (1998); Artist with Led Zeppelin, "BBC Sessions" (1997); Performer, "Unledded" (1994); Artist with Robert Plant, "No Quarter: Jimmy Page and Robert Plant Unledded" (1994); Artist with David Coverdale, "Coverdale/Page," (1993); Artist with Led Zeppelin, "Remasters" (1990); Solo Artist, "Outrider" (1988); Artist with The Firm, "Mean Business" (1986); Artist with Roy Harper, "Whatever Happened to Jugula?" (1985); Artist with The Firm, "Firm" (1985); Artist with The Honeydrippers, "The Honeydrippers: Volume One" (1984); Artist with Led Zeppelin, "Coda" (1982); Composer, "Death Wish II" (1982); Artist with Led Zeppelin, "In Through the Out Door" (1979); Artist with Led Zeppelin, "Presence" (1976); Artist with Led Zeppelin, "The Song Remains the Same" (1976); Performer, "The Song Remains the Same" (1976); Artist with Led Zeppelin, "Physical Graffiti" (1975); Artist with Led Zeppelin, "Houses of the Holy" (1973); Artist with Led Zeppelin, "Led Zeppelin IV" (1971); Artist with Led Zeppelin, "Led Zeppelin III" (1970); Artist with Led Zeppelin, "Led Zeppelin II" (1969); Artist with Led Zeppelin, "Led Zeppelin" (1968); Guitarist with The Yardbirds, "Little Games" (1967) **AW:** Grammy Award for Best Rock Album, Recording Academy (2014); Honoree, Kennedy Center Honors, John F. Kennedy Center for the Performing Arts, Washington, DC (2012); Polar Music Prize, Royal Swedish Academy of Music (2006); Named to United Kingdom Music Hall of Fame (as Member of Led Zeppelin) (2006); Named Honorary Citizen, City of Rio de Janiero, Brazil (2005); Co-recipient, Lifetime Achievement Award, Grammy Awards, Recording Academy (2005); Named Officer of the Most Excellent Order of the British Empire (OBE), Her Majesty Queen Elizabeth II (2005); Named One of the 100 Greatest Guitarists of All Time, Rolling Stone Magazine (2003); Named London's Greatest Guitarist, Total Guitar Magazine (2001); Grammy Award for Best Hard Rock Performance, Recording Academy (1999); Named to Rock & Roll Hall of Fame (as Member of Led Zeppelin) (1995); Named to Rock & Roll Hall of Fame (as Member of The Yardbirds) (1992); Numerous Awards

PAGE, LAWRENCE, "LARRY" EDWARD, T: Information Technology Officer **I:** Information Technology and Services **CN:** Alphabet Inc. **DOB:** 03/26/1973 **PB:** Lansing **SC:** MI/USA **PT:** Carl Victor Page; Gloria Page **MS:** Married **SPN:** Lucinda Southworth (12/08/2007) **CH:** Two Children **ED:** Honorary Master of Business Administration, IE Business School, Madrid, Spain (2003); Bachelor of Science in Computer Engineering, University of Michigan (1995); Master of Science in Computer Science, Stanford University, CA **C:** Chief Executive Officer, Alphabet Inc., Mountain View, CA (2011-Present); President of Products, Google Inc., Mountain View, CA (2001-2011);

Co-president, Google Inc., Mountain View, CA (1998-2001); Co-founder, Google Inc., Mountain View, CA (1998) **CR:** Board of Directors, Google Inc. (1998-Present); Speaker, Wall Street Journal Technology Summit, Technology, Entertainment & Design Conference, World Economic Forum **CIV:** Board Trustee, X Prize (2005-Present); Member, National Advisory Committee, University of Michigan College of Engineering **AW:** Named, One of the Forbes 400: Richest Americans (2006-Present); Named, One of the World's Richest People (2006-Present); Named, One of the World's Richest People, Business Insider (2019); Awarded Honorary Citizenship, Agrigento, Italy (2017); Named, Businessperson of the Year, Fortune Magazine (2014); Named, One of the World's Most Powerful People (2009-2014); Named, One of America's 20 Most Powerful CEOs 40 and Under, Forbes Magazine (2012); Named, One of the 40 Under 40, Fortune Magazine (2009-2012); Named, One of the 100 Most Influential People in the World, TIME Magazine (2004, 2005, 2011); Named, One of the 100 Agents of Change, Rolling Stone Magazine (2009); Named, a Power Player, Advertising Age (2009); Named, One of the 25 Most Powerful People in Business, Fortune Magazine (2007); Named, One of the 50 Most Important People on the Web, PC World (2007); Named, One of the 50 Who Matter Now, CNNMoney.com Business 2.0 (2006, 2007); Named, Business Leader of the Year, Scientific American Magazine (2005); Named, Persons of the Week with Sergey Brin, "ABC World News Tonight" (2004); Golden Plate Award, Academy of Achievement (2004); Co-recipient, with Sergey Brin, Marconi Prize (2004); Named, Innovator of the Year, R&D Magazine (2002); Global Leader for Tomorrow, World Economic Forum (2002); Named, Young Innovator Who Will Create the Future, Massachusetts Institute of Technology Technology Review; Engineering Graduate Award, University of Michigan Alumni Society **MEM:** Fellow, American Academy of Arts & Sciences; National Academy of Engineering; Eta Kappa Nu; Institute of Electrical and Electronics Engineers

PAGELS, ELAINE HIESEY, PHD, T: Professor; Author **I:** Education/Educational Services **CN:** Princeton University **DOB:** 02/13/1943 **PB:** Palo Alto **SC:** CA/USA **PT:** William McKinley Hiesey; Louise Sophia (van Druten) Hiesey **MS:** Divorced **SPN:** Kent Greenwalt (1995, Divorced 2005); Heinz Pagels (06/07/1969, Deceased 07/1988) **CH:** Sarah Marie; David van Druten; Mark (Deceased) **ED:** PhD, Harvard University (1970); MA, Stanford University (1965); BA, Stanford University (1964) **C:** Harrington Spear Paine Professor of Religion, Princeton University, NJ (1982-Present); From Associate Professor to Professor, Chair, Department of Religion, Barnard College, Columbia University, NY (1974-1982); Assistant Professor, History Religion, Barnard College, Columbia University (1970-1974) **CW:** Author, "Why Religion?: A Personal Story" (2018); Author, "Revelations: Visions, Prophecy, and Politics in the Book of Revelation" (2012); Author, "Reading Judas: The Gospel of Judas and the Shaping of Christianity" (2007); Author, "Beyond Belief: The Secret Gospel of Thomas" (2003); Author, "The Origin of Satan: How Christians Demonized Jews, Pagans, and Heretics" (1995); Author, "Adam, Eve and the Serpent" (1988); Author, "The Gnostic Gospels" (1979); Author, "The Gnostic Paul" (1975); Author, "The Johannine Gospel in Gnostic Exegesis" (1973) **AW:** MacArthur Fellow (1981-1987); Fellow, John Simon Guggenheim Memorial Foundation (1979-1980); National Book Award (1979); National Book Critics Circle Award (1979); Fellow, Rockefeller Foundation (1978-1979); Hazen Fellow (1975); Mellon Fellow, Aspen Institute of Humanistic Studies, The Aspen Institute (1974); Grantee, National Endowment for the Humanities (1973) **MEM:** American Academy of Religion; Society of Biblical Literature; Biblical Theologians Club **RE:** Episcopalian

PAI, AJIT VARADARAJ, T: Chairman; Lawyer **I:** Law and Legal Services **CN:** Federal Communications Commission **DOB:** 01/10/1973 **PB:** Buffalo **SC:** NY/USA **PT:** Varadaraj Pai, MD; Radha Pai, MD **MS:** Married **SPN:** Janine Van Lancker (2010) **CH:** Two Children **ED:** JD, The University of Chicago Law School (1997); AB in Social Studies, Harvard University, Cambridge, MA, with Honors (1994) **C:** Chairman, Federal Communications Commission, Washington, DC (2017-Present); Commissioner, Federal Communications Commission, Washington, DC (2012-2017); Partner, Jenner & Block LLP, Washington, DC (2011-2012); Special Advisor to the General Counsel, Federal Communications Commission (2010-2011); Deputy General Counsel, Federal Communications Commission, Washington, DC (2007-2010); Associate General Counsel, Federal Communications Commission, Washington, DC (2007); Chief Counsel, U.S. Senate Judiciary Subcommittee on the Constitution, Civil Rights and Property Rights (2005-2007); Senior Counsel, Office of Legal Policy, U.S. Department of Justice (2004-2005); Deputy Chief Counsel, U.S. Senate Committee on Administrative Oversight and the Courts, Washington, DC (2003-2004); Associate General Counsel, Verizon Communications Inc. (2001-2003); Law Clerk to the Honorable Martin L.C. Feldman, United States District Court for the Eastern District of Louisiana (1997-1998); Honors Program Trial Attorney, Antitrust Division, Telecommunication Task Force, U.S. Department of Justice, Washington, DC **CW:** Editor, University of Chicago Law Review; Contributor, Articles to Professional Journals **AW:** Named One of the 100 Most Influential People in Healthcare, Modern Healthcare (2019); Thomas J. Mulroy Prize **MEM:** Board Member, South Asian Bar Association of Washington, DC (SABA-DC) (2002-2003); The Bar Association of DC; Federal Communications Bar Association; Network Indian Professionals (NetIP); The Federalist Society **BAR:** State of Kansas; District of Columbia **PA:** Republican

PAISLEY, BRAD DOUGLAS, T: Singer, Songwriter, Musician **I:** Media & Entertainment **DOB:** 10/28/1972 **PB:** Glen Dale **SC:** WV/USA **PT:** Douglas Edward Paisley; Sandra Jean (Jarvis) Paisley **ED:** BBA in Music Business, Belmont University Mike Curb College of Entertainment & Music Business, Nashville, TN (1995); Coursework, West Liberty University **C:** With, Arista Nashville (1999-Present); With, EMI Music Publishing (1995) **CR:** Launched, DB4 Guitar, Dr. Z Amplification (2016); Launched, Paisley Drive, Wampler Pedals (2010) **CIV:** Founder, The Brad Paisley Foundation (2001-Present) **CW:** Judge, "America's Got Talent" (2019); Judge, "The Gong Show" (2018); Appearance, "Hard Knocks" (2018); Singer, "Love and War" (2017); Appearance, "Repeat After Me" (2015); Appearance, "The Voice" (2015); Judge, Reality Television Competition, "Rising Star" (2014); Singer, "Moonshine in the Trunk" (2014); Singer, "Wheelhouse" (2013); Author, "Diary of a Player: How My Musical Heroes Made a Guitar Man Out of Me" (2011); Singer, "This is Country Music" (2011); Singer with Carrie Underwood, "Remind Me" (2011); Singer, "Hits Alive" (2010); Singer, "American Saturday Night" (2009); Singer, "Cluster Pluck" (2009); Singer, "Play" (2008); Singer with Keith Urban, "Start a Band" (2008); Singer, "5th Gear" (2007); Singer, "Throttleneck" (2007); Singer, "Letter to Me"

(2007); Singer, "Online" (2007); Singer with Andy Griffith, "Waitin' on a Woman" (2007); Singer, "A Brad Paisley Christmas" (2006); Singer, "Time Well Wasted" (2005); Singer with Dolly Parton, "When I Get Where I'm Going" (2005); Singer, "Mud on the Tires" (2003); Singer, "Celebrity" (2003); Singer with Alison Krauss, "Whiskey Lullaby" (2003); Singer, "I'm Gonna Miss Her" (2001); Singer with Chely Wright, "Hard to be a Husband, Hard to be a Wife" (2001); Singer, "Part II" (2001); Singer, "Who Needs Pictures" (1999); Singer, "He Didn't Have to Be" (1999); Singer, Songwriter, Musician, Solo and Collaboration Songs and Albums; Appearances, Television Shows **AW:** Award for Collaborative Video of the Year, CMT Music Awards (2012); Award for Favorite Male Country Artist, American Music Awards (2008, 2010); Entertainer of the Year Award, CMA Country Music Association Inc. (2010); Grammy Award for Best Male Country Vocal Performance, The Recording Academy (2009); Grammy Award for Best Country Instrumental Performance, The Recording Academy (2008, 2009); Awards for Video of the Year, Vocal Event of the Year, Academy of Country Music (2006, 2009); Award for Comedy Video of the Year, Country Music TV (2008); CMA Award for Music Video of the Year, CMA Country Music Association Inc. (2008); Award for Video of the Year, Academy of Country Music (2008); Award for Top Male Vocalist, Academy of Country Music (2007-2011); CMA Awards for Male Vocalist of the Year, CMA Country Music Association Inc. (2000-2003, 2007-2009); CMA Award for Music Video of the Year, CMA Country Music Association Inc. (2007); Awards for Inspiring Video of the Year, Country Music TV (2006); CMA Awards for Musical Event of the Year, Album of the Year, CMA Country Music Association (2006); Award for Album of the Year, Academy of Country Music Awards (2006); Awards for Video of the Year, Event of the Year, Academy of Country Music (2005); Award for Collaborative Video of the Year, Country Music TV (2005); CMA Awards for Video of the Year, Event of the Year, CMA Country Music Association Inc. (2004); CMA Awards for Song of the Year, Single of the Year, Video of the Year, CMA Country Music Association Inc. (2000, 2002, 2003); Grammy Award for Best Male Country Vocal Performance, The Recording Academy (2003); CMA Award for Vocal Event of the Year, CMA Country Music Association Inc. (2001); Named to the Jamboree USA Hall of Fame; Numerous Awards **MEM:** Freemason

PALADINO, CONSTANCE, T: President **I:** Other **CN:** Language Exchange International **MS:** Married **CH:** Two Children **ED:** MA in French Language and Literature, Middlebury College (1995); BA in French and Spanish, Montclair State University (1964) **C:** Chair, French Department, American Heritage School (2007-Present); President, Language Exchange International (1983-Present) **CIV:** Volunteer, Lilian & Julian Greene Wellness Center **AW:** Teacher of the Year, Rotary International; William P. Dwyer Award for Excellence; Business Woman of the Year, Boca Raton Chamber of Commerce **MEM:** American Association of Teachers of French **MH:** Marquis Who's Who Top Professional **AS:** Ms. Paladino attributes her success to her love and passion for her work. "If you love what you do, you'll do it well." **B/I:** Ms. Paladino became involved in her profession because of her proficiency for language. She speaks five languages and has aspirations to become a United Nations translator. She began her career as a language educator. As time progressed, more parents and other people requested lessons. She did not want to tutor privately because she enjoys teaching in groups. As word continued to spread, her husband brought it to her attention that she had

a thriving business. Her husband worked a local hotel and she began a successful club for teaching in a hotel conference room. As it continued to expand, she eventually rented out her own large space, received her national accreditation and despite ups and downs, the business is still thriving today. **AV:** Traveling; Boating; Cruising

PALAZZO, STEVEN MCCARTY, T: U.S. Representative from Mississippi **I:** Government Administration/Government Relations/Government Services **DOB:** 02/21/1970 **PB:** Gulfport **SC:** MS/USA **MS:** Divorced **SPN:** Lisa M. (Belvin) Palazzo (1996, Divorced 2016) **CH:** Barrett; Aubrey; Bennett **ED:** MPA, The University of Southern Mississippi (1996); BA in Accounting, The University of Southern Mississippi (1994) **CT:** Certified Public Accountant (CPA) **C:** Member, U.S. House of Representatives from Mississippi's Fourth Congressional District, U.S. Congress (2011-Present); Member, U.S. House Committee on Armed Services (2011-Present); Member, U.S. House Committee on Science, Space and Technology (2011-Present); Chairman, House Aerospace Caucus (2016); Member, District 116, Mississippi House of Representatives (2007-2011); Member, House Appropriations Committee; Chairman, House National Guard Caucus **MIL:** With, Mississippi Army National Guard (1997-Present); With, U.S. Marine Corps Reserve (1989-1996) **MEM:** National Rifle Association of America; American Institute of Certified Public Accountants (AICPA); Mississippi Society of CPAs; Marine Corps Association & Foundation; Rotary International; Sigma Chi Fraternity **PA:** Republican **RE:** Roman Catholic

PALAZZOLO, ANGIE, T: Managing Broker, Owner **I:** Real Estate **CN:** RE/MAX Destiny **CH:** Two Daughters **ED:** High School Diploma **C:** Broker, Owner, RE/MAX Destiny; Real Estate Agent, RE/MAX, LLC **CIV:** Volunteer, Homeless Shelters; 40 Acts of Kindness; Board Member, The Will B. Foundation Inc. **AW:** Platinum Club Award, RE/MAX LLC; Chairman's Club Award, RE/MAX LLC; Above the Crowd Award, RE/MAX LLC **AS:** Ms. Palazzolo attributes her success to consistency and persistence. She believes that if you want something, you must work at it; nothing will fall in your lap. **B/I:** Ms. Palazzolo became involved in her profession because she has always been committed to helping people and giving. It is a wonderful feeling for her to facilitate for others the process of building a home and living out the "American Dream." **THT:** Ms. Palazzolo's motto is, "be honest, be yourself and everything else will fall into place."

PALLONE, FRANK JOSEPH JR., T: U.S. Representative from New Jersey; Ranking Member of Committee on Energy and Commerce; Lawyer **I:** Government Administration/Government Relations/Government Services **DOB:** 10/31/1951 **PB:** Long Branch **SC:** NJ/USA **MS:** Married **SPN:** Sarah Hospodor (1992) **CH:** Rose Marie; Celeste Teresa; Frank Andrew **ED:** JD, Rutgers Law School, NJ (1978); MA in International Relations, The Fletcher School - Tufts University, MA (1974); BA in History and French, Middlebury College, Cum Laude, VT (1973) **C:** Ranking Member, U.S. House Committee on Energy and Commerce (2015-Present); Member, U.S. House of Representatives from New Jersey's Sixth Congressional District, U.S. Congress, Washington, DC (1993-Present); Member, U.S. House of Representatives from New Jersey's Third Congressional District, U.S. Congress, Washington, DC (1988-1993); Member, District 11, New Jersey State Senate (1984-1988); Councilman, Town of Long Branch, NJ (1982-1988); Maritime Attorney, New York, NY (1982-1984); Assistant Professor, Sea Grant Extension Progressive, George

H. Cook Campus, Rutgers, The State University of New Jersey (1980-1981); Coastal Law Specialist, New Jersey Marine Advanced Science (1980-1981); Instructor, Monmouth County Community College (Now Brookdale Community College); Counsel, Monmouth County Protective Services for the Elderly, New Jersey **AW:** Named Outstanding Legislator of the Year, VFW (1999); Named Legislator of the Year, The New Jersey Academy of Ophthalmology (1998); International Year of the Ocean Award, Clean Ocean Action (1998); Cancer Advocacy Award, Rutgers Cancer Institute of New Jersey (1998); Named Consumer Hero, Consumer Federation of America (1997) **BAR:** States of New York, New Jersey and Florida; Commonwealth of Pennsylvania **PA:** Democrat **RE:** Roman Catholic

PALMER, GARY JAMES, T: U.S. Representative from Alabama; Public Policy Research and Education Executive **I:** Government Administration/Government Relations/Government Services **DOB:** 05/14/1954 **PB:** Haleyville **SC:** AL/USA **PT:** J.C. Palmer; Mae (Lacy) Palmer **MS:** Married **SPN:** Marjorie Ann Cushing (11/19/1983) **CH:** Claire Elaine; Kathleen Corrie; Robert William **ED:** BS in Operations Management/Management Science, The University of Alabama (1977) **C:** Member, U.S. House of Representatives from Alabama's Sixth Congressional District (2015-Present); President, Alabama Policy Institute (1993-2015); Executive Director, Alabama Policy Institute (1990-1993); Co-founder, State Coordinator, Alabama Policy Institute, Birmingham, AL (1989-1990); Cost Engineer, Project Control Engineer, Rust International, Inc., Birmingham, AL (1981-1989); Cost Engineer, Combustion Engineering, Birmingham, AL (1980-1981); Business Manager, Bradford and Company, Birmingham, AL (1979-1980); General Manager, Palmer Truss Company, Hodges, AL (1977-1978); Member, Committee on Ways and Means; Member, Committee on Intelligence **CR:** Speaker in Field; Writer in Field **CIV:** President, State Policy Network (1996-1998); Board of Directors, State Policy Network (1992-1998); Member, Briarwood Presbyterian Church, Birmingham, AL **CW:** Contributor, Articles, Professional Journals **AW:** Roe Award, State Policy Network (2002); Named to Outstanding Young Men of America (1989) **MEM:** Rotary International **AV:** Hunting; Fishing; Golf; History; Skiing **RE:** Presbyterian

PALTROW, GWYNETH KATE, T: Actress **I:** Media & Entertainment **DOB:** 09/28/1972 **PB:** Los Angeles **SC:** CA/USA **PT:** Bruce Paltrow; Blythe Danner **MS:** Married **SPN:** Brad Falchuk (2018); Chris Martin (12/05/2003, Divorced 07/2016) **CH:** Apple Blythe Alison Martin; Moses Bruce Anthony Martin **ED:** Coursework, University of California Santa Barbara **CR:** Designer, ZOE Tee's Loves Gwyneth (2009-Present); Launched, Weekly Lifestyle Newsletter, Goop (2008-Present); Spokesmodel, Coach, Estee Lauder (2005-Present) **CIV:** Board Member, Robin Hood Foundation **CW:** Actress, "The Politician" (2019-Present); Host, Executive Producer, "The Goop Lab" (2020); Actress, "Avengers: Endgame" (2019); Author, "The Clean Plate: Eat, Reset, Heal." (2019); Actress, "Avengers: Infinity War" (2018); Actress, "Spider-Man: Homecoming" (2017); Appearance, "Planet of the Apps" (2017); Actress, "Man in Red Bandana" (2017); Appearance, "Justin Timberlake + The Tennessee Kids" (2016); Appearance, "Nightcap" (2016); Author, "It's All Easy: Delicious Weekday Recipes for the Super-Busy Home Cook" (2016); Actress, "Mortdecai" (2015); Actress, "Web Therapy" (2014); Actress, "Glee" (2010-2014); Actress, "Iron Man 3" (2013); Author, "It's All Good: Delicious, Easy Recipes That Will Make You Look Good and Feel Good" (2013); Executive Producer, "Stand Up to

Cancer" (2012); Actress, "The Avengers" (2012); Actress, "The New Normal" (2012); Actress, "Thanks for Sharing" (2012); Actress, "Glee: The 3D Concert Movie" (2011); Actress, "Contagion" (2011); Author, "My Father's Daughter: Delicious, Easy Recipes Celebrating Family and Togetherness" (2011); Appearance, "Who Do You Think You Are?" (2011); Actress, "Iron Man 2" (2010); Actress, "Country Strong" (2010); Actress, "Iron Man" (2008); Co-author with Mario Batali, "Spain...A Culinary Road Trip" (2008); Host, "Spain...On the Road Again" (2008); Actress, "Two Lovers" (2008); Actress, "The Good Night" (2007); Actress, "Infamous" (2006); Actress, "Love and Other Disasters" (2006); Actress, "Running with Scissors" (2006); Actress, "Proof" (2005); Actress, "Sky Captain and the World of Tomorrow" (2004); Actress, "View from the Top" (2003); Actress, "Sylvia" (2003); Actress, "Possession" (2002); Actress, "The Anniversary Party" (2001); Actress, "The Royal Tenenbaums" (2001); Actress, "Shallow Hal" (2001); Actress, "The Intern" (2000); Actress, "Duets" (2000); Actress, "Bounce" (2000); Actress, "The Talented Mr. Ripley" (1999); Voice Actress, "Out of the Past" (1998); Actress, "Great Expectations" (1998); Actress, "Sliding Doors" (1998); Actress, "Hush" (1998); Actress, "A Perfect Murder" (1998); Actress, "Shakespeare in Love" (1998); Actress, "Hard Eight" (1996); Actress, "The Pallbearer" (1996); Actress, "Emma" (1996); Actress, "Jefferson in Paris" (1995); Actress, "Se7en" (1995); Actress, "Moonlight and Valentino" (1995); Actress, "Mrs. Parker and the Vicious Circle" (1994); Actress, "Malice" (1993); Actress, "Flesh and Bone" (1993); Actress, "Deadly Relations" (1993); Actress, "Cruel Doubt" (1992); Actress, "Hook" (1991); Actress, "Shout" (1991); Actress, "Picnic," "The Adventures of Huck Finn," "Sweet Bye and Bye," "The Seagull," "Proof"; Actress, Plays, Television Shows, Music Videos, and Films **AW:** Named World's Most Beautiful Woman, People Magazine (2013); Named World's Best Dressed Woman, People Magazine (2012); Emmy Award for Outstanding Guest Actress in a Comedy Series, Academy of Television Arts & Sciences (2011); Recipient, Star, Hollywood Walk of Fame (2010); Named One of the 100 Most Powerful Celebrities, Forbes.com (2008); Academy Award for Best Actress, Academy of Motion Picture Arts & Sciences (1998); Golden Globe Award for Best Actress in a Motion Picture - Musical or Comedy, Hollywood Foreign Press Association (1998); Screen Actors Guild Awards for Outstanding Performance by a Female Actor in a Leading Role in a Motion Picture, Outstanding Performance by an Ensemble Cast in a Motion Picture, SAG-AFTRA (1998) **MEM:** SAG-AFTRA

PANETTA, JAMES, "JIMMY" VARNI, T: U.S. Representative from California; Lawyer **I:** Government Administration/Government Relations/Government Services **DOB:** 10/1/1969 **PB:** Washington **SC:** D.C. **PT:** Leon Panetta **MS:** Married **SPN:** Carrie (McIntyre) Panetta **CH:** Siri; Gia **ED:** JD, Santa Clara University School of Law; BA in International Relations, University of California Davis; Coursework, Monterey Peninsula College **C:** Member, U.S. House of Representatives from California's 20th Congressional District (2017-Present); Member, Committee on Agriculture; Member, Committee on Armed Services; Deputy District Attorney, District Attorney's Office, Monterey County, CA; With, Prosecutor's Office, Alameda County, CA **CIV:** Board Member, Veterans Transition Center **MIL:** Intelligence Officer, Joint Special Operations Command, United States Navy Reserve (2007); With United States Navy Reserve **AW:** Named Monterey County Veteran of the Year (2015); Bronze Star

PAO, ELLEN KANGRU, T: Investor, Activist, Co-Founder **I:** Nonprofit & Philanthropy **CN:** Project Include **SC:** NJ/USA **PT:** Young-Ping Pao; Tsyh-Wen Pao **MS:** Married **SPN:** Buddy Fletcher (2007); Roger Kuo (Divorced) **CH:** One Daughter **ED:** MBA, Harvard Business School (1998); JD, Harvard Law School (1994); BSEE, Princeton University (1991); Certificate, Wilson School of Public and International Affairs, Princeton University; Crown Fellow, Aspen Institute **C:** Chief Executive Officer, Project Include, Oakland, CA (2015-Present); Chief Diversity and Inclusion Officer, Venture Partner, Kapor Center/Kapor Capital, Oakland, CA (2017-2018); Interim Chief Executive Officer, Reddit, San Francisco, CA (2014-2015); Business Development and Strategic Partner, Reddit, San Francisco, CA (2013-2014); Partner, Kleiner Perkins Caufield & Byers (2005-2012); Senior Director, Corporate Business Development, BEA Systems (2001-2005); Business Development, Tellme Networks, MyCFO, Danger Research (1999-2001); Business Development, Microsoft/WebTV (1998-1999); Corporate Attorney, Cravath, Swaine & Moore (1994-1996) **CR:** Board Member, Datameer (2011-2012); Board Member, Flipboard Inc. (2010-2012); Board Member, Lehigh Technologies (2008-2012); Sponsor, Sunfire (2009-2011); Teaching Assistant, Wilson School of Public and International Affairs, Princeton University **CW:** Managing Editor, The Daily Princetonian

PAPPAS, CHRISTOPHER, "CHRIS" CHARLES, T: U.S. Representative from New Hampshire **I:** Government Administration/Government Relations/Government Services **CN:** U.S. House of Representatives **DOB:** 06/04/1980 **SC:** NH/USA **PT:** Arthur Pappas; Dawn Pappas **ED:** Bachelor of Arts in Government, Harvard University (2002) **C:** Member, U.S. House of Representatives from New Hampshire's First District (2019-Present); Member, District Four, New Hampshire Executive Council (2012-2019); Treasurer, Hillsborough County, NH (2006-2010); Member, New Hampshire House of Representatives (2002-2006) **CIV:** Volunteer, Jeanne Shaheen Governor Campaign (1996); Board Member, Southern New Hampshire Services; Board Member, Manchester Historic Association **CW:** Contributing Author, The Harvard Crimson

PAPPONI, PAULA LUMETTA, T: Superintendent **I:** Education/Educational Services **DOB:** 12/18/1943 **PB:** New York **SC:** NY/USA **PT:** Joseph LuMetta; Lillian (Savoca) LuMetta **MS:** Married **SPN:** Gabriel Papponi (06/10/1962) **CH:** Louis Gabriel; Janice Michelle; Adrienne Elizabeth **ED:** EdD, New Mexico State University, Las Cruces, NM (1999); MA, New Mexico State University, Las Cruces, NM (1986); BA, Dowling College, Oakdale, NY, Summa Cum Laude (1979); AA, Suffolk County Community College, with Distinction (1977) **CT:** Certified Administrator, New Mexico **C:** Superintendent, Jemez Valley Public Schools, Jemez Pueblo, NM (1998-Present); Superintendent, Carrizozo Municipal School District, Carrizozo, NM (1995-1998); Principal, Ruidoso Middle Schools, NM (1990-1995); Assistant Principal, Los Alamitos Middle School, Grants, NM (1988-1990); Teacher, Grants High School, Grants, NM (1984-1988); Teacher, Los Alamitos Middle School, Grants, NM (1980-1984) **CIV:** Crimestoppers, Ruidoso, NM (1991); Board of Directors, Cibola Arts Council, Grants, NM (1983-1986) **CW:** Contributor, Poems to Professional Publications; Artist, Works in Oils, Watercolor, Pen and Ink; Exhibited in Galleries, Ruidoso, Albuquerque, NM **AW:** National Leadership Award, National Republican Congressional Committee (2006); Certificate of Appreciation (2004); Cooperative Leadership Award, National School Development

Council (2002); Recognition Certificate, Education Outreach Department, Sandia National Laboratories (1994); Honorary State FFA Degree, State of New Mexico (1994); Heritage Preservation Award, State of New Mexico (1994); Award, Edward A. Tallot National Poetry Competition (1982) **MEM:** New Mexico Association of Elementary School Principals (NMAESP); New Mexico Association of Secondary School Principals; New Mexico School Superintendents Association (NMSSA); Peking University, China; University of Oxford, England; Columbia University, New York, NY **MH:** Albert Nelson Marquis Lifetime Achievement Award; Marquis Who's Who Top Professional **B/I:** Dr. Papponi became involved in her profession because when she was very little, she went to kindergarten and she would come home and play school with her sister. She loved being the teacher. **AV:** Art; Poetry **PA:** Republican **RE:** Roman Catholic

PARCAK, SARAH HELEN, T: Egyptologist **I:** Sciences **PB:** Bangor **SC:** ME/USA **MS:** Married **SPN:** Greg Mumford **CH:** One Son **ED:** BA in Egyptology and Archaeological Studies, Yale University (2001); PhD, University of Cambridge **C:** Professor of Anthropology, University of Alabama at Birmingham; Teacher, Egyptian Art and History, University of Wales, Swansea, Wales **CR:** Co-Director, Survey and Excavation Projects, Fayoum, Sinai, Egypts East Delta; Founder, The Laboratory for Global Observation at the University of Alabama at Birmingham **CW:** Author, "Archaeology from Space: How the Future Shapes Our Past" (2019); Author, "Satellite Remote Sensing for Archaeology" (2009) **AW:** TED Prize (2016); Ingenuity Award, Smithsonian Magazine (2016)

PARCELLS, BILL, T: Professional Sports Executive; Sportscaster; Former Professional Football Coach **I:** Athletics **DOB:** 08/22/1941 **PB:** Englewood **SC:** NJ/USA **PT:** Charles Parcells; Ida (Naclerio) Parcells **MS:** Divorced **SPN:** Judith (Goss) Parcells (1962, Divorced 01/16/2002) **CH:** Suzy; Jill; Dallas **ED:** BA, Wichita State University (1964) **C:** Courtesy Consultant, Cleveland Browns, NFL (2014-Present); Studio Analyst, "Sunday NFL Countdown," ESPN (2011-Present); Team Consultant, Miami Dolphins, NFL (2010); Executive Vice President, Football Operations, Miami Dolphins, NFL (2007-2010); Radio Co-host, ESPN Radio (2007); Studio Analyst, "Monday Night Countdown," ESPN (2007); Head Coach, Dallas Cowboys, NFL (2003-2007); Studio Analyst, "NFL Pregame Show," ESPN (2002); Chief, Football Operations, New York Jets, NFL (2000-2001); Head Coach, New York Jets, NFL (1997-2000); Head Coach, New England Patriots, NFL (1993-1997); Studio Analyst, NBC Sports (1991-1992); Head Coach, New York Giants, NFL (1983-1991); Defensive Coordinator, Linebackers Coach, New York Giants, NFL (1981-1982); Linebackers Coach, New England Patriots, NFL (1980-1981); Defensive Coordinator, New York Giants, NFL (1979-1980); Head Coach, U.S. Air Force Academy Falcons, Colorado Springs, CO (1978-1979); Linebackers Coach, Texas Tech University Red Raiders, Lubbock, Texas (1975-1977); Linebackers Coach, Vanderbilt University Commodores, Nashville, TN (1973-1974); Linebackers Coach, Florida State University Seminoles, Tallahassee, FL (1970-1972); Defensive Coordinator, United States Military Academy Black Knights, West Point, NY (1968-1969); Linebackers Coach, United States Military Academy Black Knights, West Point, NY (1966-1967); Linebackers Coach, Wichita State University Shockers, KS (1965); Linebackers Coach, Hastings College Broncos, NE (1964) **CW:** Co-Author, With Nunyo Demasio, "Parcells: A Football Life" (2014); Co-Author with Will McDonough, "The Final Season: My Last

Year as Head Coach in the NFL" (2000); Co-Author with Jeff Coplon, "Finding a Way to Win: The Principles of Leadership, Teamwork and Motivation" (1995) **AW:** Named to Pro Football Hall of Fame (2013); Named NFL Coach of the Year, Pro Football Weekly (1994, 1996); Named NFL Coach of the Year, The Associated Press (1986, 1994); Named NFL Coach of the Year, United Press International (1986, 1994); Named NFL Coach of the Year, Maxwell Football Club (1994); Winner (As Coach), New York Giants, Super Bowl (1986, 1990); Named NFL Coach of the Year, Sporting News (1986); Named to NFL 1990s All-Decade Team

PARENT, MARY CAMPBELL, T: Film Producer; Studio Executive **I:** Media & Entertainment **CN:** Disruption Entertainment **C:** Office of the Chief Executive Officer, Metro-Goldwyn-Mayer Inc., Los Angeles, CA (2009-Present); Chairperson, Worldwide Motion Picture Group, Metro-Goldwyn-Mayer Inc., Los Angeles, CA (2008-Present); Producer, Universal Pictures, Universal City, CA (2006-2008); Vice Chairperson, Worldwide Production, Universal Pictures, Universal City, CA (2003-2005); Co-President of Production, Universal Pictures, Universal City, CA (2001-2003); Executive Vice President of Production, Universal Pictures, Universal City, CA (2000-2001); Senior Vice President of Production, Universal Pictures, Universal City, CA (1997-2000); Director of Development to Vice President of Production, New Line Cinema (1994-1997); Agent Trainee, ICM **CW:** Producer, "Dune" (2020); Producer, "Enola Holmes" (2020); Producer, "Godzilla vs. Kong" (2020); Guest Appearance, "Wonder Pets!" (2019); Producer, "Godzilla: King of the Monsters" (2019); Producer, "Detective Pikachu" (2019); Producer, "Pacific Rim: Uprising" (2018); Producer, "Same Kind of Different as Me" (2017); Producer, "Kong: Skull Island" (2017); Producer, "Monster Trucks" (2016); Producer, "The Revenant" (2015); Producer, "The SpongeBob Movie: Sponge Out of Water" (2015); Producer, "Godzilla" (2014); Producer, "Noah" (2014); Producer, "Pacific Rim" (2013); Producer, "Role Models" (2008); Executive Producer, "Welcome Home, Roscoe Jenkins" (2008); Executive Producer, "The Kingdom" (2007); Producer, "You, Me and Dupree" (2006); Executive Producer, "Pleasantville" (1998); Executive Producer, "Trial and Error" (1997); Production Manager, "Dangerous Ground" (1997); Executive Producer, "Set It Off" (1996) **AW:** Named, 50 Women to Watch, Wall Street Journal (2008); Named, 100 Most Powerful Women in Entertainment, Hollywood Reporter (2004)

PARÉS-MATOS, ELSIE I., T: Professor **I:** Education/Educational Services **CN:** University of Puerto Rico at Mayagüez **ED:** PhD in Biochemistry, Purdue University, West Lafayette, IN (2000); MS in Bio-Organic Chemistry (1990) **C:** Professor, University of Puerto Rico at Mayagüez (1990-Present) **CW:** Contributor, Numerous Articles, Professional Journals **MEM:** American Chemical Society; Eli Lilly and Company **MH:** Marquis Who's Who Top Professional **AS:** Dr. Parés-Matos attributes her success to the result of good intentions, and a genuine love and enjoyment for what she does. **B/I:** Dr. Parés-Matos became involved in her profession because of her innate curiosity. **AV:** Enjoying movies; Shopping; Traveling; Spending time with family and friends **THT:** Dr. Parés-Matos states, "Everything I do is with good intention."

PARK, CHUI SUH, "CHRIS", BS, MS, RPH, T: Pharmacist (Retired) **I:** Pharmaceuticals **DOB:** 08/26/1941 **SC:** Korea **PT:** Seung Ryong Park; Jong Nam (Kim) Park **MS:** Married **SPN:** Youn Jin Kim (05/04/1968) **CH:** Clara; Sharon **ED:** Non-Tradi-

tional Doctor of Pharmacy Program, School of Pharmacy and Allied Health Professions, Creighton University, Omaha, NE (1995); BS, University of Utah (1976); MS in Biopharmaceutics/Pharmacokinetics, Purdue University (1972); MS in Industrial Pharmacy, Seoul National University (1967); BS in Pharmacy, Seoul National University (1964) **CT:** Registered Pharmacist, South Korea, California, Nevada, Colorado **C:** Pharmacist, Rite Aid Pharmacy (2008-2010); Pharmacist, CVS Pharmacy, Los Angeles, CA (1980-2007); Pharmacist, Disco Drugs, Riverside, CA (1979-1980); Pharmacist, De Jay Drugs, Los Angeles, CA (1976-1979); Pharmacist, Hanil Pharmaceutical Industrial Co., Ltd., Seoul, South Korea (1966-1969) **CIV:** Contributor, Saint Thomas Korean Catholic Center (1991-1993); Head, Subdivision, 2-2 Districts of Church, California **CW:** Author, Memoir, "An Unfinished Finish" (To Be Completed in 2021, Published Afterward) **AW:** International Scholarship, Research Assistantship, Teaching Assistantship; Research Assistantship, Purdue University **MEM:** President, Seoul National University College of Pharmacy Alumni Association (1994-1995); American Pharmaceutical Association; California Employee Pharmacist Association; California Korean Pharmacist Association **MH:** Albert Nelson Marquis Lifetime Achievement Award **AS:** Mr. Park attributes his success to being a community pharmacist in Southern California and serving all kinds of people for more than 40 years. **B/I:** Mr. Park became involved in his profession because his father asked for him to pursue the career. His father noticed that, in his own home town, a pharmaceutical career was very stable and that if he opened up his own pharmacy, he would be able to make good money. **AV:** Reading; Traveling; Playing the game of Go **PA:** Democrat **RE:** Roman Catholic **THT:** "After receiving my BS and MS degrees at Seoul National University in 1964 and 1967, I came to USA to finish up my PhD in industrial pharmacy, go back to my home country, and become a professor; that was the original American dream when I left my home country on February 3, 1969. I got another MS degree at Purdue University in 1972 and BS degree at University of Utah in 1976 and ended up becoming a registered pharmacist. When I work as a community pharmacist, the customers called me a pill pusher. I have been a pill pusher for a long time, now retired, and thanks to Purdue University, University of Utah, and customers whom I have served. Even though I have not achieved the original American Dream, I have been happy being a pill pusher and very thankful to God and the United States."

PARKER, DOUG, T: Chief Executive Officer **I:** Leisure, Travel & Tourism **CN:** American Airlines Group Inc. **PB:** New York **SC:** NY/USA **ED:** MBA, Vanderbilt University, Nashville, TN (1986); BA in Economics, Albion College, Michigan (1984) **C:** Chief Executive Officer, American Airlines, Inc., Fort Worth, TX (2013-Present); Chief Executive Officer, American Airlines Group, Inc., Fort Worth, TX (2013-Present); Chairman, Chief Executive Officer, US Airways Group, Inc., Tempe, AZ (2005-2013); President, US Airways/US Airways Group Inc., Tempe, AZ (2005-2006); Chairman, President, Chief Executive Officer, America West Airlines (2001-2005); President, Chief Operating Officer, America West Airlines (2000-2001); Executive Vice President, America West Airlines (1999-2000); Senior Vice President, Chief Financial Officer, America West Airlines (1995-1999); Various Financial Management Positions, American Airlines, Inc. (1986-1991); Vice President, Financial Planning & Analysis, Assistant Treasurer, Northwest Airlines **CR:** Board of Directors, American Airlines Group, Inc. (2013-Present); Board of Directors,

Pinnacle West Capital Corp. (2007-2012); Board of Directors, Clear Channel Outdoor Holdings Inc. (2005-2008) **AW:** Distinguished Alumnus Award, Vanderbilt University Owen Graduate School of Management (2004) **PA:** Republican **RE:** Methodist

PARKER, SARAH JESSICA, T: Actress; Producer **I:** Media & Entertainment **DOB:** 03/25/1965 **PB:** Nelsonville **SC:** OH/USA **PT:** Stephen Parker; Barbara Parker **MS:** Married **SPN:** Matthew Broderick (05/19/1997) **CH:** James Wilkie; Marion Loretta Elwell; Tabitha Hodge **CR:** Spokesmodel, Garnier Nutrisse Products, L'Oréal (2003-Present); Launched, Fragrance Line, Dawn, Endless and Twilight (2009); Designer, Clothing Line, Exclusive to Steve & Barry's, Bitten (2007-2008); Launched, Fragrance Line, Covet (2007); Launched, Fragrance Line, Lovely (2005); Spokesmodel, The Gap (2004-2005) **CIV:** Member, President Barack Obama's Committee on Arts and Humanities (2009); National Ambassador, U.S. Fund for UNICEF **CW:** Actress, Producer, "Here and Now" (2018); Actress, "Best Day of My Life" (2017); Actress, "Divorce" (2016-2019); Actress, "All Roads Lead to Rome" (2016); Appearance, "Nightcap" (2016); Actress, "The Commons of Pensacola" (2013); Voice Actress, "Escape from Planet Earth" (2013); Actress, "Lovelace" (2013); Producer, "Pretty Old" (2013); Actress, "Glee" (2012); Actress, "I Don't Know How She Does It" (2011); Actress, "New Year's Eve" (2011); Actress, Producer, "Sex and the City 2" (2010); Actress, "Did You Hear About the Morgans?" (2009); Actress, "Smart People" (2008); Actress, Producer, "Sex and the City: The Movie" (2008); Actress, "Spinning into Butter" (2007); Appearance, "Project Runway" (2007); Appearance, "Sesame Beginnings: Moving Together" (2007); Actress, "Failure to Launch" (2006); Actress, "Strangers with Candy" (2005); Actress, "The Family Stone" (2005); Actress, Co-executive Producer, "Sex and the City" (1998-2004); Actress, "Life Without Dick" (2001); Actress, "State and Main" (2000); Actress, "Sex and the Matrix" (2000); Host, "MTV Movie Awards" (2000); Actress, "Isn't She Great" (1999); Actress, "Dudley Do-Right" (1999); Actress, "'Til There Was You" (1997); Voice Actress, "A Life Apart: Hasidism in America" (1997); Actress, "Once Upon a Mattress" (1996); Actress, "If Lucy Fell" (1996); Actress, "Mars Attacks!" (1996); Actress, "The First Wives Club" (1996); Actress, "Extreme Measures" (1996); Actress, "The Substance of Fire" (1996); Actress, "Miami Rhapsody" (1995); Actress, "The Sunshine Boys" (1995); Actress, "Ed Wood" (1994); Actress, "Hocus Pocus" (1993); Actress, "Striking Distance" (1993); Actress, "Honeymoon in Vegas" (1992); Actress, "In the Best Interest of the Children" (1992); Actress, "L.A. Story" (1991); Actress, "Equal Justice" (1990-1991); Actress, "The Heidi Chronicles" (1989); Actress, "The Ryan White Story" (1989); Actress, "Twist of Fate" (1989); Actress, "Dadah is Death" (1988); Actress, "A Year in the Life" (1987-1988); Actress, "The Room Upstairs" (1987); Actress, "Terry Neal's Future" (1986); Actress, "Flight of the Navigator" (1986); Actress, "A Year in the Life" (1986); Actress, "The Alan King Show" (1986); Actress, "Girls Just Want to Have Fun" (1985); Actress, "Going for the Gold: The Bill Johnson Story" (1985); Actress, "Firstborn" (1984); Actress, "Footloose" (1984); Actress, "To Gillian on Her 37th Birthday" (1983-1984); Actress, "Somewhere Tomorrow" (1983); Actress, "Square Pegs" (1982-1983); Actress, "The Death of a Miner" (1982); Actress, "My Body, My Child" (1982); Actress, "The War Brides" (1981); Actress, "Rich Kids" (1979); Actress, "The Sound of Music" (1977); Actress, "The Innocents" (1976); Actress, Theater, Television Shows, Films **AW:** Named One of the 100 Most Powerful Women, Forbes Magazine (2010); Named One of the 100 Most Powerful Celebrities (2008); Named One of the 50 Most Powerful Women in New York City, New York Post (2008); Vanguard Award, ShoWest (2008); Screen Actors Guild Awards for Outstanding Performance by an Ensemble in a Comedy Series, SAG-AFTRA (2002, 2004); Golden Globe Awards for Best Supporting Actress, Hollywood Foreign Press Association (2000, 2001, 2002, 2004); Emmy Award for Outstanding Lead Actress in a Comedy Series, Academy of Television Arts & Sciences (2004); Named Woman of the Year, Hasty Pudding Theatricals (2002); Screen Actors Guild Award for Outstanding Performance by a Female Actor in a Comedy Series, SAG-AFTRA (2001); American Civil Liberties Union Award (1995); Numerous Awards

PARKER, SEAN, T: Venture Capitalist, Entrepreneur **I:** Business Management/Business Services **DOB:** 12/03/1979 **PB:** Herndon **PT:** Bruce Parker; Diane Parker **C:** Co-Founder, Airtime (2010-Present); Co-Founder, Chairman, Causes, San Francisco (2007-Present); Managing Partner, Founders Fund, San Francisco (2006-Present); Founding President, Facebook, Inc., Palo Alto, CA (2004-2005); Adviser, Facebook, Inc., Palo Alto, CA (2004); Co-Founder, President, Plaxo (2001-2004); Co-Founder, Napster, Inc. (1999-2001) **CR:** Board Member, Votizen (2009-Present); Board Member, Spotify (2009-Present); Board Member, Yammer (2009-Present) **AW:** One of The World's Richest People, Forbes Magazine (2011-Present); Richest Americans, Forbes 400 (2011-Present)

PARKER, STUART BLAIN, T: Chief Executive Officer **I:** Automotive **CN:** United Services Automobile Association **ED:** Master of Business Administration, St. Mary's University, San Antonio; Master of Arts in Political Science, Midwestern University; Bachelor of Business Administration in Management, Valdosta State University, Georgia **CT:** Chartered Life Underwriter; Chartered Financial Consultant **C:** Chief Executive Officer, United Services Automobile Association (2015-Present); Chief Operating Officer, United Services Automobile Association (2014); Chief Financial Officer, United Services Automobile Association (2012-2014); President, Financial Planning Services, United Services Automobile Association (2004); Certified Financial Planner Practitioner, United Services Automobile Association, San Antonio, TX (1998); President, Property and Casualty Insurance Group, United Services Automobile Association; Vice President, Financial Planning Services, United Services Automobile Association **MIL:** Pilot, U.S. Air Force **MEM:** Financial Planning Association

PARKER-CONRAD, JANE E., RN, PHD, T: Nursing Consultant **I:** Medicine & Health Care **YOP:** Dec 18, 2019 **PT:** Vinson Van Fleet; Helen Trezona **MS:** Married **SPN:** Daniel E. Conrad, MD **ED:** PhD, Loyola University Chicago (1987); MS, University of Wisconsin (1976); BSN, University of Wisconsin (1969) **CT:** RN, Methodist Hospital School of Nursing **C:** Educational Consultant, Conrad & Conrad Consultants (1996-Present); Dean, Health Programs Division, Walters State Community College (1994-1996); Joanna Johnson Chair in Occupational Health Nursing, University of Wisconsin (1990-1992); Acting Assistant Dean, Office of International Studies, College of Nursing, University of Illinois (1984-1986); Program Director of Occupational Health Nursing, University of Illinois (1979-1986); Deputy Director, Occupational Health Section, Division of Health, State of Wisconsin (1975-1979); Chief Occupational Health Nurse Consultant, Division of Health, State of Wisconsin (1975-1979) **CIV:** Choir Member, Church of the Good Samaritan **CW:** Contributor, Articles, Professional Journals **AW:** Schering Award for Excellence in Occupational Health Nursing **MEM:** Fellow, AAOHN, Inc.; American Nurses Association; ICOH – International Commission on Occupational Health; Phi Delta Gamma **MH:** Albert Nelson Marquis Lifetime Achievement Award **B/I:** Dr. Parker-Conrad became involved in her profession because she was inspired by a close cousin, who works as a nurse. **RE:** Episcopalian

PARRELLA, SUSAN IRENE, EDD, T: Superintendent of Schools, Special Educator, Adjunct Professor, Consultant **I:** Education/Educational Services **DOB:** 08/15/1951 **PB:** Waltham **SC:** MA/USA **PT:** Louis Joseph Parrella; Ursula Helena (Colella) Parrella **MS:** Single **ED:** EdD, Boston College (1990); MA in Special Education, Regis College (1977); BA in English, Regis College (1973) **CT:** Superintendent of Schools; Director of Special Education; Principal, High School, Middle School and Elementary School; English teacher **C:** 35 years in Waltham Public Schools: Superintendent of Schools, (1998-2008); Acting Superintendent of Schools (1997-1998); Director, Special Education, (1994-1998); Director, Chapter I/Title I (1993-1994); Assistant Director, Special Education (1988-1993); Generic Specialist, High School Special Education Coordinator (1981-1988); Teacher, English (1973-1981) **CR:** Adjunct Professor, University of Massachusetts Boston (1991-1996); Consultant in the Field; Adjunct Professor, Bridgewater State University; Adjunct Professor, American International University; Developer, Teacher-Friendly Website **CIV:** Active Member, Waltham Partnership for Youth (1988-2008); Board Member, Waltham Education and Beyond Foundation; Board Member, Friends of the Library; Board Member, Opportunities for Inclusion; Contributor, Statewide Scholarship Commission, Order Sons of Italy; Guest Speaker, Award Banquet, Order Sons of Italy **CW:** Co-Author, Presenter, "The Clock Keeps Ticking: An Ecological Approach to Learning," Council for Exceptional Children Conference, California **AW:** Outstanding Public Service Award in Recognition of Outstanding Dedication to the Citizens of Waltham (2003, 2004, 2008) **MEM:** Massachusetts Association of School Superintendents; National Association of State Directors of Special Education; Massachusetts Teachers Association; Founder, Renaissance Lodge, Order Sons of Italy; Phi Delta Kappa **MH:** Albert Nelson Marquis Lifetime Achievement Award **AS:** Dr. Parrella attributes her success to her parents, who were models for her work ethic and instilled in her that she could accomplish anything if she put her mind to it. She also attributes it to listening and working with staff to implement changes needed. She understood the difficulty in learning as she was diagnosed with dyslexia. **B/I:** Dr. Parrella became involved in her profession because she was inspired by her mother, Ursula Parrella, who was bilingual. When she first attended school, she did not speak English; however, she learned it so well that she received a double promotion later in life. It was important to her for both of her children to receive a good education and achieve more than she could. Her mother helped her to realize that a learning disability does not define her but helped her understand ways and tools one can use to enhance their skills and knowledge. **AV:** Traveling and volunteering to help children in education; Spending quality time with her family and friends **RE:** Catholic **THT:** Dr. Parella has said, "Life is a constant education." In 1973, she began her career with the Waltham Public school as a High School English teacher before transitioning to become a learning specialist and special education coordinator in 1981. She later found success as the district's assistant director of Special Education in 1988. Where she was able to expand the Special Education Pre-School Program by having students attend on a low cost as role models. She moved into Chapter 1/Title 1 for a short time before going back into special education as the director, where she developed and enhanced programs. She expanded the Language Based Programs through out the system, developed programs for students with autism, and a Deaf Program. She then became the acting Superintendent at the request of the School Committee. A year later, she became Superintendent where she remained for 10 years until her retirement in 2008.

PARROTT, BILLY JAMES, T: Film Director, Communications Executive **I:** Media & Entertainment **DOB:** 05/09/1935 **PB:** Bolton **SC:** MS/USA **PT:** Benny James Parrott; Ethel (Seyton) Hobson Parrott **MS:** Married **SPN:** Geraldine Meik (12/22/1964) **CH:** Michael S.; Stephanie **ED:** BS, Oregon State University (1962) **C:** Owner, President, Chief Executive Officer, Roanoke Valley Cellular Telephone Company, Virginia (1986-Present); Film Director, Chief Executive Officer, Parrott and People Communications Inc., New York, NY (1969-Present); Copy Group Head, Creative Supervisor, Benton and Bowles Advertising, New York, NY (1968-1969); Copywriter, McCann Erickson Advertising, New York, NY (1965-1966); Mail Boy, McCann Erickson Advertising, New York, NY (1964-1965) **CR:** Columbia Pictures, Burbank, CA (1984-1986); Cox Broadcasting, Atlanta, GA (1985); Director, International Emmy Awards, New York, NY (1980); Founder, Board of Directors, Executive Committee, XM Radio; Consultant, Chief Executive Officer Private Networks, Inc., Time, Inc., New York, NY; Nightcore **CIV:** Chairman, Hastings Tax Payers Committee; Board of Directors, Genelux Corporation **MIL:** U.S. Air Force (1952-1956) **CW:** Author, Television Film, "The Lady and the Lynching"; Author, Television Film, "On Account of Sex: The Grimke Sisters"; Author, Director, Television Documentary, "From King to Congress"; Director, "Gladys Knight and the Pips"; Director, "The Boy King" **AW:** Peabody Foundation Award (1987); Clio Award (1973); American Institute Graphic Arts Awards (1969); Numerous Addy Awards; Guggenheim Award for "The Boy King"; Eagle Award **MEM:** Directors Guild of America; Board of Directors, American Youth Hostels; Board of Directors, American Mobile Satellite Corporation **MH:** Albert Nelson Marquis Lifetime Achievement Award **B/I:** Mr. Parrott became involved in his profession because he was born in Southern Mississippi, which was segregated at the time. To get out of the hostile environment, he volunteered for the Air Force. After he finished his time there, he was accepted to Oregon State University with a full football scholarship. However, Mr. Parrott had always wanted to be a writer. He wanted to get to New York to pursue those dreams, so he accepted a job as a mail boy for a writing agency there. Mr. Parrott used his writing as the tool to get him out of the mailroom. In his first year there, he won awards for his writing and was also published in several notable magazines. This catapulted him into the world of advertising. After five successful years working in advertising, Mr. Parrott decided he wanted to be a director. **PA:** Liberal **RE:** Christian

PARSON, MICHAEL L., T: Governor of Missouri **I:** Government Administration/Government Relations/Government Services **DOB:** 09/17/1955 **PB:** Wheatland **SC:** MO/USA **MS:** Married **SPN:** Teresa Parson (1985) **CH:** Two Children **ED:** Coursework, University of Hawaii; Coursework, University of Maryland **C:** Governor, State of Missouri (2018-Present); Lieutenant Governor,

State of Missouri (2017-2018); Member, District 28, Missouri State Senate (2011-2017); Member, District 133, Missouri House of Representatives (2004-2010); Sheriff, Polk County, MO (1992-2004); Cattle Farmer, Bolivar, MO **CR:** Former Commissioner, Missouri Emergency Response; Commission Member, Missouri State Employee's Retirement Board **MIL:** Sergeant, Two Tours in Military Police, United States Army (1975-1981) **MEM:** Polk County Cattlemen's Association; National Sheriffs' Association; Missouri Sheriffs' Association; Missouri Farm Bureau; Missouri Cattlemen's Association; The American Legion **PA:** Republican

PARSONS, DAVID STANLEY, MD, FAAP, FACS, T: Otolaryngologist, Pediatrician (Retired); Professor; Missionary **I:** Education/Educational Services **DOB:** 12/09/1944 **PB:** Washington, DC **SC:** DC/USA **PT:** James Robert Parsons; Barbara Gail (Beans) Parsons **MS:** Married **SPN:** Barbara Jean Parsons **CH:** Julie Ann Reed; Stephen Corey Parsons; Laura Kathryn Gallimore **ED:** Fellowship in Pediatric Head and Neck Surgery, Hospital for Sick Children (Now Great Ormond Street Hospital Children's Charity), London, United Kingdom (1987); Fellowship in Pediatric Facial Plastics (Cleft Lip and Palate), University of Colorado (1986-1987); Fellowship in Pediatric Bronchoesophagology, Sydney, Australia (1986); Residency in Otolaryngology/Head and Neck Surgery, University of Colorado (1983-1986); Residency in General Surgery, Saint Luke's Hospital (Now Presbyterian St. Luke's Medical Center), C-CHCA, Inc., Denver, CO (1982-1983); Diploma, United States Air Force School of Aerospace Medicine, with Honors, Brooke Air Force Base, Texas (1981); Residency in Pediatrics, Wilford Hall United States Air Force Medical Center, Lackland Air Force Base, Texas (1977-1980); MD, University of Texas Medical School (The University of Texas Health Science Center at Houston (UTHealth)), Houston, Texas, with Honors (1977); BA, Texas Christian University (1967) **CT:** Diplomate, American Board of Otolaryngology; Diplomate, The American Board of Pediatrics **C:** Clinical Professor, University of North Carolina (1999-Present); Clinical Professor, University of South Carolina (1998-Present); Retired Otolaryngologist, Pediatrician (2013); Professor of Surgery and Pediatrics, University of Missouri School of Medicine (1993-1998); Pediatric Head and Neck Surgeon, Great Ormond Saint Hospital Sick Children (Now Great Ormond Street Hospital Children's Charity), London, England, United Kingdom; Pediatric Facial Plastic Surgeon, Children's Hospital Colorado, Denver, CO **CR:** Clinical Professor, The University of Texas at San Antonio (1988-1993); Clinical Professor, University of Colorado (1988-1993); Clinical Assistant Professor, The University of New Mexico, Albuquerque, NM (1980-1983); Clinical Professor, University of North Carolina; Clinical Professor, University of South Carolina; Clinical Professor, Uniformed Services University **CIV:** Christian Society of Otolaryngology/Head & Neck Surgeons (CSO) (1996-Present); Board of Directors, Comcare Christian Mission for Hearing Impaired (Christian Mission for the Deaf) (1994-Present); Mexico Medical Missions (1989-Present); Consultant Surgeon, TIME for Christ, Cuba (1996-2018); Resources Exchange International, Vietnam, House of David, Israel (2005-2006) **MIL:** Colonel, United States Air Force (1985-1993); With, United States Air Force (1967-1993); Chairman, Department of Otolaryngology/Head and Neck Surgery), United States Air Force, Desert Storm (1991-1992); Fighter Pilot, United States Air Force, Vietnam (1969-1974); Commissioned Second Lieutenant, United States Air Force (1967); Vice Chairman, Department of Otolaryngology, United States Air Force **CW:** Editor, "Otolaryn-

gologic Clinics of North America" (1996); Contributor, Over 130 Articles to Professional Journals, Chapters to Books **AW:** Named, Best Doctors in America (1992-Present); Named, Humanitarian of the Year, Society of Ear, Nose and Throat Advances in Children (SENTAC) (2006); Sylvan Stool Award as an Outstanding Global Professor for Children (2006); Named, Humanitarian of the Year, American Academy of Otolaryngology - Head and Neck Surgery (2002); Distinguished Award, American Academy of Otolaryngology - Head and Neck Surgery (2002); Decorated, Three Distinguished Flying Crosses; Decorated, 13 Air Medals, United States Air Force **MEM:** Fellow, American Academy of Pediatrics; American Academy of Otolaryngology - Head and Neck Surgery; American Society of Pediatric Otolaryngology (ASPO); Society for Ear, Nose and Throat Advances in Children (SENTAC) **MH:** Albert Nelson Marquis Lifetime Achievement Award; Marquis Who's Who Top Professional; Marquis Who's Who Humanitarian Award **AS:** Dr. Parsons attributes his success to his mentor, Dr. Bruce Benjamin, who was based in Sydney, Australia, back when Dr. Parsons was the first American to do a fellowship in Australia. He changed the way he looked at everything and was such a grand person and grand doctor. Another mentor, John Evans, was in London, England, when Dr. Parsons did his next fellowship and he was monumental in his life. **B/I:** Dr. Parsons wanted to become an astronaut when he returned from Vietnam, most combat pilots wanted to do that. He enrolled in medical school instead because there were so many applicants for astronaut training, but he still became involved with NASA and met many astronauts. In fact, the Mercury and Apollo 13 astronauts convinced Dr. Parson to stick with medical school. He decided to focus on children as a doctor. In addition, he wanted to be a teacher his entire life. **AV:** Golf; Travel **RE:** Follower of Jesus **THT:** Dr. Parsons retired from medicine in April 2013. In 2019 he and his wife planned to go on another mission to Cuba and Honduras for two weeks teaching modern surgical techniques to these and other third world countries. Over his career, Dr. Parsons has designed 46 surgical instruments for otolaryngology surgeries. He returned from a trip to Washington, DC, where he had a fifth reunion of his pilot training class who were all Vietnam veterans. Dr. Parsons served in Vietnam and flew in the invasion of Cambodia as a fighter pilot. When he came back from the war, he continued to instruct much higher-ranking men in combat tactics. When a man arrived in Vietnam, Dr. Parsons got him ready for combat status. His goal was to be able to save soldiers' lives on the ground. Dr. Parsons felt that if he went to medical school it would give him an edge over competitors. During his time in medicine, he became involved with NASA and the Mercury and Apollo astronauts. They convinced Dr. Parsons not to become an astronaut. It changed his attitude and he decided to be a surgeon for children. Then, 30 years ago, Dr. Parsons had another change of life and got involved with doing medical mission work. He loves that. For 2-3 months a year, he does medical mission work in third-world countries. Dr. Parsons is still very active in teaching third-world doctors what's happening in current surgery. Along the way, some wonderful people challenged Dr. Parsons to study and read the bible. He studied it the way he did with medicine. About 30 years ago, Dr. Parsons became a strong believer. The work that he does in third-world countries is to not only teach modern surgery but to engage the people.

PARSONS, JIM JOSEPH, T: Actor **I:** Media & Entertainment **DOB:** 03/24/1973 **PB:** Houston **SC:** TX/USA **PT:** Milton Joseph Parsons Jr.; Judy

Ann (McNight) Parsons **MS:** Married **SPN:** Todd Spiewack (2017) **ED:** MA in Dramatic Arts, University of San Diego (2001); BA in Theater, University of Houston (1996) **C:** Founding Member, Infernal Bridegroom Productions, Houston, Texas **CW:** Actor, "Young Sheldon" (2017-Present); Voice Actor, "The Simpsons" (2020); Actor, "Hollywood" (2020); Actor, "Extremely Wicked, Shockingly Evil and Vile" (2019); Actor, Broadway, "The Boys in the Band" (2018); Actor, "A Kid Like Jake" (2018); Host, "Jim Parsons is Too Stupid for Politics," Sirius XM (2017); Actor, "Hidden Figures" (2016); Actor, "Supermansion" (2016); Actor, "An Act of God" (2015); Voice Actor, "Home" (2015); Actor, "Visions" (2015); Actor, "The Big Bang Theory" (2007-2015); Actor, Film, "The Normal Heart" (2014): Voice Actor, "Elf: Buddy's Musical Christmas" (2014); Actor, "Wish I Was Here" (2014); Actor, "Sunset Stories" (2012); Actor, "Harvey" (2012); Actor, "The Big Year" (2011); Actor, "The Muppets" (2011); Actor, Broadway, "The Normal Heart" (2011); Actor, "Glenn Martin, DDS" (2010); Voice Actor, "Family Guy" (2009-2012); Actor, "On the Road with Judas" (2007); Actor, "Gardener of Eden" (2007); Actor, "10 Items or Less" (2006); Actor, "School for Scoundrels" (2006); Actor, "The King's Inn" (2005); Actor, "The Great New Wonderful" (2005); Actor, "Heights" (2005); Actor, "Judging Amy" (2004-2005); Actor, "Garden State" (2004); Actor, "Nowhere to Go But Up" (2003); Actor, Plays, Television Shows and Film; Appeared in Television Commercials for Quiznos, Stride Gum, FedEx, Others **AW:** Stephen F. Kolzak Award, GLAAD Media Awards (2018); SAG Award for Outstanding Performance by a Cast in a Motion Picture, SAG-AFTRA (2017); People's Choice Award for Favorite Comedic TV Actor (2016); Recipient, Star, Hollywood Walk of Fame (2015); Emmy Award for Outstanding Lead Actor in a Comedy Series, Academy of Television Arts & Sciences (2010, 2011, 2013, 2014); Golden Globe Award for Best Performance by an Actor in a TV Series - Comedy or Musical, Hollywood Foreign Press Association (2011); TV Chairman's Award, National Association of Broadcasters (2010); TV Critics Association Award for Individual Achievement in Comedy (2009); Numerous Awards

PARSONS, LORRAINE LEIGHTON, T: Nurse; Preschool Administrator **I:** Medicine & Health Care **DOB:** 02/07/1939 **PB:** Albany **SC:** ME/USA **PT:** Alfred Elmer Leighton; Arlene Rachael Winslow **MS:** Widowed **SPN:** Jack Arnol Greig (Divorced 07/1982) **CH:** Scotty; Kim **CT:** Licensed in Special Education, University of Maine (1965); RN, Central Maine General Hospital (Now Central Maine Medical Center) (1960) **C:** Child Care Professional, Marwin Consultant Co., Raymond, Maine (1996-Present); Nurse, Central Maine Medical Center, Lewiston, Maine (1980-1996); Nurse, Ledgeview Nursing Home, West Paris, Maine (1979-1980); Teacher, Reading and Math, Buckfield School, Maine (1974-1978); Teacher of Special Education, West Paris School, Maine (1969-1973); With, Stephens Memorial Hospital, Norway, Maine (1964-1969); Office Nurse, Charles Hannigan, MD, Auburn, Maine (1961-1964) **CIV:** Program Chairwoman, Hartford Bicentennial (1997-1998); President, Founder, Hartford Heritage Society, Maine (1976) **CW:** Author, "Rokomeko Indians Native Americans" (2002); Author, "Rokomeko-Native Americans" (2002); Author, "Winslow Home" (2001); Author, "The Alfred E. Leighton Family" (2001); Author, "Town of Hartford" (2000); Author, "Military Service" (2000); Author, "Marston Homestead" (2000); Author, "Crazy Quilt" (2000); Author, "Quilting is Qumforting" (1999); Author, "Families of the Fox and Geese Quilt" (1997); Author, "Homesteads of Hartford" (1997); Co-author, "Hartford

in Pictures" (1984); Author, "Life - 1870, 1879 & 1881" **AW:** Double-Trouble Award, Nature Category, International Library of Photography (2000); Certificate of Honor, Bicentennial, State of Maine (1998); Grantee, Maine Arts Commission (1998); Town of Hartford Annual Report of the Municipal Officers Dedicated in Her Honor **MH:** Albert Nelson Marquis Lifetime Achievement Award **AV:** Collecting dolls; Stamps; Local town history

PARTON, DOLLY REBECCA, T: Singer, Songwriter; Actress **I:** Media & Entertainment **DOB:** 01/19/1946 **PB:** Pittman Center **SC:** TN/USA **PT:** Robert Lee Parton Sr.; Avie Lee Caroline (Owens) Parton **MS:** Married **SPN:** Carl Thomas Dean (05/30/1966) **ED:** Honorary LHD, The University of Tennessee, Knoxville, TN (2009) **C:** Recording Artist, Mercury, Monument, RCA, CBS Records **CR:** Founder, Owner, Dixie Pixie Productions (2015-Present); Co-Founder, Co-Owner, Entertainment Park, Dollywood (1985-Present); Founder, Dollywood Splash Country (2001); Founder, Dixie Stampede (1988); Owner, Southern Light Productions; Co-Owner, Sandollar Productions; Established, Velvet Apple Music, BMI; Owner, Blue Eye Records **CIV:** Co-Founder, Dollywood Foundation (1988-Present) **CW:** Singer, "Pure & Simple" (2016); Actress, "Dolly Parton's Christmas of Many Colors: Circle of Love" (2016); Actress, "Dolly Parton's Coat of Many Colors" (2015); Singer, "Blue Smoke" (2014); Actress, "A Country Christmas Story" (2013); Author, "Dream More: Celebrate the Dreamer in You" (2012); Actress, "Joyful Noise" (2012); Voice Actress, "Gnomeo & Juliet" (2011); Singer, "Better Day" (2011); Actress, "Hannah Montana" (2006-2010); Author, Music and Lyrics, Broadway Musical, "9 to 5" (2009); Singer, "Backwoods Barbie" (2008); Author, "Dolly's Dixie Fixin's: Love, Laughter and Lots of Good Food" (2006); Actress, "Reba" (2005); Singer, "Those Were the Days" (2005); Singer (With Norah Jones), "Creepin' In" (2004); Singer, "Live and Well" (2004); Singer, "For God and Country" (2003); Singer, "Makin' Believe" (2003); Actress, "Frank McKlusky, C.I." (2002); Singer, "Halos and Horns" (2002); Actress, "Blue Valley Songbird" (1999); Singer, "Grass is Blue" (1999); Singer, "Best of the Best - Porter & Doll" (1999); Singer, "Hungry Again" (1998); Singer, "Trio II" (1998); Actress, "Mindin My Own Business" (1996); Actress, "Unlikely Angel" (1996); Singer, "Just the Way I Am" (1996); Singer, "Super Hits" (1996); Singer, "I Will Always Love You & Other Greatest Hits" (1996); Singer, "The Essential Dolly Parton" (1995); Actress, "Heavens to Betsy" (1994); Author, "Dolly" (1994); Author, "My Life and Other Unfinished Business" (1994); Singer (With Tammy Wynette and Loretta Lynn), "Honky Tonk Angels" (1994); Singer, "Slow Dancing with the Moon" (1993); Actress, "Wild Texas Wind" (1991); Actress, "Straight Talk" (1991); Singer, "Eagle When She Flies" (1991); Singer, "Home for Christmas" (1990); Actress, "Steel Magnolias" (1989); Singer, "White Limozeen" (1989); Singer, "Heartbreaker" (1988); Singer, "Great Balls of Fire" (1988); Singer, "Rainbow" (1988); Singer with Emmylou Harris, Linda Ronstadt, "Trio" (1987); Singer, "Portrait" (1986); Singer, "Think About Love" (1986); Actress, "A Smoky Mountain Christmas" (1986); Singer, "Just the Way I Am" (1986); Singer, "Real Love" (1985); Actress, "Rhinestone" (1984); Actress, "The Best Little Whorehouse in Texas" (1982); Singer, "9 to 5" (1982); Actress, "Nine to Five" (1980); Singer, "Here You Come Again" (1979); Appearance, "Porter Wagoner Show" (1967); Appearance, "Cass Walker Program," "Bill Anderson Show," "Wilburn Brothers Show," "Barbara Mandrell Show"; Appearances, Various Television Shows and Films; Composer, Numerous Songs **AW:** Tex Ritter Award for "Coat of Many Colors" (2016); Inductee, National Hall of

Fame for Mountain Artisans (2014); Grammy Lifetime Achievement Award, The Recording Academy (2011); Inductee, Country Gospel Music Hall of Fame (2010); Jim Reeves International Award (2009); Inductee, Gospel Music Hall of Fame (2009); Inductee, Music City Walk of Fame (2009); Cliffie Stone Pioneer Award, Academy of Country Music Awards (2008); Johnny Mercer Award, Songwriters Hall of Fame (2007); Honoree, Kennedy Center Honors, John F. Kennedy Center for the Performing Arts (2006); Co-Recipient with Brad Paisley, CMT Award for Most Inspiring Video of the Year, Country Music Television, Inc. (2006); Awards for Video of the Year, Vocal Event of Year, Academy of Country Music Awards (2006); National Medal of Arts, National Endowment for the Arts (2005); Living Legend Award, United States Library of Congress (2004); Icon Award, Broadcast Music, Inc. (2003); Inductee, National Academy of Popular Music Songwriters Hall of Fame (2001); Grammy Award for Best Bluegrass Album, The Recording Academy (1999); Inductee, Country Music Hall of Fame (1999); Inductee, Small Town of America Hall of Fame (1988); Inductee, East Tennessee Hall of Fame (1988); Grammy Award for Best Country Vocal Performance with Group, The Recording Academy (1987, 1988); Recipient, People's Choice Awards (1980, 1988); Co-Recipient, Academy of Country Music Award for Album of the Year (1987); Co-Recipient, Best Duo Performance, American Music Award (1984); Star, Hollywood Walk of Fame (1984); Grammy Awards for Best Country Vocal Performance, Female, Best Country Song, The Recording Academy (1982); Grammy Award for Best Country Song, The Recording Academy (1981); Grammy Awards for Best Female Country Vocalist, The Recording Academy (1978, 1981); Female Vocalist of the Year, Academy Country Music Awards (1980); Nashville Metronome Award (1979); Grammy Award for Best Country Vocal Performance, Female, The Recording Academy (1979); Country Star of the Year, Sullivan Productions (1977); Entertainer of the Year, CMA Country Music Association Inc. (1978); Female Vocalist of the Year (1975, 1976); Vocal Duo of the Year Award, All Country Music Association (1970, 1971); Co-Recipient, Vocal Group of the Year Award (1968); Recipient, Numerous Awards

PARTON STANARD, SUSAN LORANE, MA, T: Director of Choral Ensembles and Vocal Studies **I:** Education/Educational Services **CN:** Lewis and Clark Community College **PB:** Alton **SC:** IL/USA **PT:** Raymond Hay Parton; Dorothy J. (Kaus) Parton **MS:** Divorced **CH:** Raymond Harris Stanard **ED:** MA in Teaching Music Education, Jacksonville University (1988); BM in Voice and Opera, Jacksonville University (1979); Postgraduate Coursework in Diaconal Ministry, United Methodist Church, Asbury Theological Seminary, Orlando, FL; Postgraduate Coursework in Choral Conducting and Literature, Illinois State University **CT:** Nationally-Certified Voice and Piano Teacher, Music Teachers National Association (2009-Present); Charter Certification in Contemporary Commercial Music Levels 1-3, "Jeanette Lo Vetri Method of Somatic Voiceworks," Shenandoah Conservatory **C:** Director of Choral Ensembles & Vocal Studies, Lewis and Clark Community College (2002-Present); Professor of Music, Lewis & Clark Community College (2002-Present); Performer, Opera, Concerts, Recitals (1982-Present); Music Program Coordinator, Lewis & Clark Community College (2003–2010); Adjunct Professor of Voice, Florida State College at Jacksonville (1999-2002); Adjunct Professor of Music, Jacksonville University (1983-1995); Orchestra, Choral Director, Mayport Junior High School (Now Mayport Coastal Sciences Middle School) (1985-1987) **CR:** Director of Music,

Evangelical United Church of Christ (2010-Present); Preparatory Music Coordinator, Evangelical United Church of Christ (2007-Present); Operatic and Concert Artist, Evangelical United Church of Christ(1980-Present); Director of Music, Organist, Godfrey First United Methodist Church (2007-2011); Director of Music, Organist, 12th Street Presbyterian Church (2004-2007); Director of Music and Worship, Organist, Isle Faith UMC (1995-2002); Organist, St. Paul United Methodist Church (1983-1995); Co-Director of Vocal and Choral Education, Douglas Anderson High School for the Performing Arts (Now Douglas Anderson School of the Arts); Vocal Coach; Lecturer in Field **CIV:** President, Board of Directors, Greater Alton Concert Association; Treasurer, Board of Directors, Advisory Committee, Alton Little Theater; Board of Directors, Alton Youth Symphony; Representative of Western Opera, Sister City Festivities with Chinese National Opera, Beijing, China and Jacksonville, FL **CW:** Singer, Musician, Verdi's "Requiem"; Singer, Musician, Mozart's "Requiem"; Singer, Musician, Handel's "Messiah"; Singer, Musician, Vivaldi's "Gloria"; Singer, "Carmen"; Singer, "Cavalleria Rusticana"; Singer, "Tosca"; Singer, "Don Giovanni"; Singer, "Tannhauser"; Singer, "Manon Lescaut"; Singer, "Suor Angelica" **AW:** Woman of Distinction, YWCA (2009); Excellence in Teaching Award, Emerson Electric Co. (2008); Outstanding Teacher of the Year, Mayport Junior High School (Now Mayport Coastal Sciences Middle School) (1985-1986); Outstanding Artist of Northeast Florida, Cummer Gallery Art (Now Cummer Museum) (1982); First Place Winner, Metropolitan Opera Auditions, Florida Eastern Regional (1981-1982); Outstanding Artist of the Year Award, New Jersey State Opera (1981); Award Recipient, Competition, Palm Beach Opera; Award Recipient, Competition, Florida Atlantic University; Grantee, Various Organizations **MEM:** Illinois Articulation Incentive Music Advisory Panel, Illinois Board of Higher Education; Associate Member, Fine Arts Steering Committee, Illinois Board of Higher Education; American Guild of Organists; Music Teachers National Association; Music Educators National Conference (Now National Association for Music Education); American Choral Directors Association; National Association of Teachers of Singing, Inc.; National Archive Committee, The Fellowship of United Methodists in Music and Worship Arts; Illinois Music Education Association; Advisory Board, Southern Illinois Young Artist Organization **MH:** Albert Nelson Marquis Lifetime Achievement Award; Marquis Who's Who Top Professional **AS:** Ms. Parton Stanard attributes her success to her honor, kindness and her faith. **B/I:** Ms. Parton Stanard became involved in her profession because music isn't what she does, it's who she is. **AV:** Collecting antiques and collectibles; Genealogy research **RE:** United Methodist

PASCRELL, WILLIAM, "BILL" JAMES JR., T: U.S. Representative **I:** Government Administration/Government Relations/Government Services **DOB:** 01/25/1937 **PB:** Paterson **SC:** NJ/USA **PT:** William James Pascrell; Roffie J. (Loffredo) Pascrell **MS:** Married **SPN:** Elsie Marie (Botto) Pascrell (1962) **CH:** William III; David; Glenn **ED:** MA in Philosophy, Fordham University, NY (1961); BA in Journalism, Fordham University, NY (1959); Postgraduate Coursework, Fairleigh Dickinson University **C:** U.S. Representative, New Jersey's Ninth Congressional District, United States Congress (2013-Present); U.S. Representative, New Jersey's Eighth Congressional District, United States Congress (1997-2013); Mayor, City of Paterson, NJ (1990-1996); Member, District 35, New Jersey General Assembly (1987-1990); Director of Policy, Planning and Development, City of Paterson, NJ (1979-1987); President, Board of Educa-

tion, City of Paterson, NJ (1979-1982); Member, Paterson Planning Board, NJ (1975-1977); Director of Public Works, City of Paterson, Paterson, NJ (1974-1977); Adult School Teacher, Dwight Morrow High School, Englewood, NJ (1969-1970); Ophthalmic Technician, Seymour Pollack Opticians (1968-1974); Adjunct Professor, Fairleigh Dickinson University, Madison, NJ (1964-1969); Teacher, Paramus High School, NJ (1962-1974); Teacher, Junior High School, Clifton, NJ (1962); Member, Committee on the Budget, Committee on Ways and Means; Member, Committee on Ways and Means; Member, Committee on Homeland Security, United States Congress; Co-Chair, Congressional Brain Injury Task Force **CIV:** Member, Boys & Girls Club in New Jersey (1975-Present); Chairman, Passaic County Democrats, NJ (1982-1990); Active Member, County Chairmen for Senator Frank Lautenberg, New (1982); Regional Coordinator, James Florio for Governor, Hudson County, NJ (1981); Campaign Coordinator, Robert A. Roe for Governor, NJ (1977); Board of Directors, Passaic County Community College (1973-1979) **MIL:** Sergeant, U.S. Army Reserve (1962-1967); With, U.S. Army (1961-1962) **AW:** Congressional Recognition Award, International Association of Fire Fighters (2001); Man of the Year, Passaic County Young Democrats (1983); Award, American Legion 438-John Raad Post (1983); Award, Unico Passaic County (1982); Award, Federation of Italian Societies (1981); Award, Mother Cabrini Society (1979) **MEM:** Pat Mone Association; Charles Alfano Association; Riverside Veterans; Knights of Columbus; Alumni Association, Fordham University; American Cancer Society, Inc.; The National Italian American Federation; Paterson Taxpayers Association; Elks **PA:** Democrat **RE:** Roman Catholic

PASIK-DUNCAN, BOZENNA, PHD, DSC, T: Mathematics Professor, Researcher **I:** Education/Educational Services **DOB:** 06/30/1947 **PB:** Radom **SC:** Warsaw/Poland **PT:** Janina Pasik; Antoni Pasik **SPN:** Tyrone Edward Duncan (05/21/1983) **CH:** Dominique Duncan **ED:** Doctor of Science, University of Warsaw (1986); Doctor of Philosophy, University of Warsaw (1978); Master of Science, University of Warsaw (1970) **C:** Professor, Mathematics, University of Kansas, Lawrence, KS (1993-Present); Associate Professor, University of Kansas, Lawrence, KS (1989-1993); Assistant Professor, University of Kansas, Lawrence, KS (1987-1989); Instructor, University of Kansas, Lawrence, KS (1984-1987); Assistant Professor, Warsaw School of Economics (1970-1984) **CR:** Lecturer, Warsaw Technical University (1973-1975); Professor of Electrical Engineering, Computer Science and Aerospace, Kansas University; Investigator, Information and Telecommunication Technology Center **CIV:** Board of Governors, Control Systems Society, Institute of Electrical and Electronics Engineers, Piscataway, NJ (1996-2002); Technical Board, International Federation of Accountants **CW:** Contributor, Scientific Papers, Professional journals **AW:** Research Grantee, National Science Foundation (1987-Present); Fellow, International Research & Exchanges Board (1982-1983); Excellence in Research and Teaching, Ministry of Higher Education and Science (1975) **MEM:** Vice President, Institute of Electrical and Electronics Engineers (1999); Board of Governors, Institute of Electrical and Electronics Engineers (1996); American Association of the University Women; International Statistics Institute; Society of Industrial and Applied Mathematics; Bernoulli Society; American Mathematics Society; Polish Mathematics Society; Association Women in Mathematics; Mathematics Association of America **MH:** Albert Nelson Marquis Lifetime Achievement Award **B/I:** Dr. Pasik-Duncan became involved in her profession

due to the influence of her mother, who encouraged her to become and teacher and develop her expertise with mathematics. She loves teaching her students; whenever she walks in a classroom and starts discussing mathematics with her students, all problems seem to be minor in comparison to the equations they are solving. **AV:** Travel; Music; Poetry

PASTIAN, ALAN D., T: Pastor **I:** Religious **CN:** River Valley Church **MS:** Married **SPN:** Heidi Pastian **CH:** Anja; Magnus **ED:** BA in Pastoral Studies, North Central University, Minneapolis, MN (1999); BS in Communications and Public Relations, St. Cloud State University (1995) **C:** Pastor, NextGen Leader, Author, River Valley Church, Woodbury, MN, (2015-Present); Creative Director, Young Adults Pastor, Desert Springs Church, Phoenix, AZ (2014-2015); Campus Pastor, National Community Church, Washington, DC (2011-2014); Family Life, Youth Pastor, River Valley Church, St. Paul, MN (2003-2012) **CW:** Author, "Blunt: 7 Brutally Honest Perspectives On Your Spiritual Life" **MEM:** Theta Chi; Save the Storks **AS:** Pastor Pastian attributes his success to his devotion to and compassion for his work. He has the ability to see a better future for others and an insight on how to guide them to it. **B/I:** Pastor Pastian visited the United Kingdom when he was 22 years old. While he was there, he connected with a group of homeless teenagers living out of an abandoned building. He bought them food and spoke with them about having hope for their futures. They all received his words well. This inspired Pastor Pastian to divert his career path from advertising and business into something service-based and compassionate. After completing studies in communications, he attended theology school and became a pastor. Since then, Pastor Pastian has devoted his career to the youth; he additionally works with families. **AV:** Writing; Traveling

PATE, J'NELL LAVERNE, T: History and Government Educator (Retired), Writer **I:** Education/Educational Services **DOB:** 07/31/1938 **PB:** Jacksboro **SC:** TX/USA **PT:** Vernon Leon Rogers; Berta May (Riggs) Rogers **MS:** Married **SPN:** Fred Barnes (05/14/2016); Kenneth Doyle Pate (06/03/1960, Deceased 03/08/2013) **ED:** PhD in History, University of North Texas (1982); MA in History, Texas Christian University (1964); BA in Journalism, Texas Christian University (1960) **CT:** Certified Teacher, Texas **C:** Professor of Texas History, Texas Government, and American History and Government, Tarrant County College, Fort Worth, TX (1968-2000); Teacher of Social Studies, Fort Worth Independent School District (1960-1967) **CIV:** Secretary, Azle Republican Club (1990-2000); Sponsor, Student Newspapers, Fort Worth Public Schools (1960-1967) **CW:** Columnist, The Azle News (1968-2018); Author, "Images of America Texas Sesquicentennial Wagon Trail" (2011); Author, "Arsenal of Defense Fort Worth's Military Legacy" (2011); Author, "Images of America Fort Worth Stockyards" (2009); Author, "America's Historic Stockyards Livestock Hotels" (2005); Author, "Hazel Vaughn Leigh and the Fort Worth Boys' Club" (2000); Author, "Ranald Slidell Mackenzie Brave Cavalry Colonel' (1994); Author, "North of the River" (1994); Compiler, Texas and the Southwest in U.S. History (1991); Author, "Livestock Legacy" (1988); Contributor, Articles, Professional Journals **AW:** Outstanding Graduate, University of North Texas (1990); Excellence in Teaching Award, Northeast Campus Tarrant County College (1986) **MEM:** Fellow, Texas State Historical Association (1989); Western History Association; North Fort Worth Historical Society; Vice President, Secretary, Azle Historical Museum Society (1989-2016);

West Texas Historical Association; Board of Directors, Westerners International; Phi Kappa Phi **MH:** Albert Nelson Marquis Lifetime Achievement Award; Marquis Who's Who Top Professional **AS:** Dr. Pate attributes her success to hard work. **B/I:** Dr. Pate became interested in writing at a young age. In middle school, she joined the student newspaper, proceeding to remain involved all throughout high school. In college, she continued to study writing. While writing her dissertation, Dr. Pate realized that she could publish her work if she wanted to. She did, and her dissertation became her first book, "The Live Stock Legacy: History of the Fort Worth Stock Yards." **AV:** Reading; Sewing; Knitting; Traveling **PA:** Republican **RE:** Church of Christ **THT:** Dr. Pate feels that she has lived a fortunate life.

PATRICK, CARLIANNE, T: Assistant Professor **I:** Education/Educational Services **CN:** Georgia State University **MS:** Married **CH:** Patrick **ED:** PhD, The Ohio State University (2012); MSc, LSE, with Merit (2001); BA, University of West Georgia Honors College, Magna Cum Laude (2000) **C:** Assistant Professor, Department of Economics, Georgia State University (2012-Present) **CR:** Research Affiliate, W.E. Upjohn Institute for Employment Research; Center for State and Local Government Excellence; Andrew Young School of Policy Studies, Georgia State University; Fiscal Research Center, Andrew Young School of Policy Studies, Georgia State University; Affiliate, Real Estate Center, Department of Real Estate, J. Mack Robinson College of Business, Georgia State University **CIV:** Norwich Church **AW:** The William H. Miernyk Research Excellence Medal (2016); Lincoln Institute Scholar (2015); Dean's Early Career Award, Andrew Young School of Policy Studies (2014); Regional Science Association International Dissertation Award (2012); Susan L. Huntington Dean's Distinguished University Fellowship (2008-2012); 26th Charles M. Tiebout Prize in Regional Science (2012); Barry M. Moriarty Prize for Best Graduate Research Paper in Regional Science (2011); Honorable Mention, 25th Competition for the Charles M. Tiebout Prize (2011); Helen Jackson Award for Best Undergraduate Research Paper (2000); Presidential Scholar (1996-2000); Advanced Academy of Georgia (1996-2000); Sullivan Scholarship for Economics (1999); Hirsch Award for Psychology (1999); American Scholar (1998) **MEM:** Urban Economics Association; National Tax Association; The Regional Science Association International; American Real Estate and Urban Economics Association **AS:** Ms. Patrick attributes her success to hard work and putting in a lot of hours. She has had great mentors along the way. **B/I:** Ms. Patrick became involved in her profession because her initial inspiration was a desire to do meaningful work. She found herself drawn to messes and thought of economics as an important framework for thinking about the world. Ms. Patrick could see that this particular line of work would let her engage in making the world a better place.

PATTON, FITZ, T: Sound Designer **I:** Media & Entertainment **CW:** Sound Designer, "The Rose Tattoo" (2019); Sound Designer, "Choir Boy" (2019); Sound Designer, "Bernhardt/Hamlet" (2018); Sound Designer, "Three Tall Women" (2018); Sound Designer, "Meteor Shower" (2017); Sound Designer, "The Little Foxes" (2017); Sound Designer, "Present Laughter" (2017); Sound Designer, "An Act of God" (2016); Sound Designer, "The Father" (2016) **AW:** Outstanding Music in a Play, "Choir Boy," Drama Desk Awards (2019); Best Sound Design of a Play, "Choir Boy," Tony Awards (2019); Outstanding Sound Design of a Play, "The

Humans," Drama Desk Awards (2016); Outstanding Sound Design of a Play, "When the Rain Stops Falling," Drama Desk Awards (2010)

PAUL, CHRIS EMMANUEL, T: Professional Basketball Player **I:** Athletics **CN:** Oklahoma City Thunder **DOB:** 05/06/1985 **PB:** Winston-Salem **SC:** NC/USA **PT:** Charles Edward Paul; Robin Jones **MS:** Married **SPN:** Jada Crowley (09/10/2011) **CH:** One Son; One Daughter **ED:** Coursework, Wake Forrest University, NC (2002-2005) **C:** Guard, Phoenix Suns, NBA (2020-Present); President, National Basketball Players Association (2013-Present); Guard, Oklahoma City Thunder, NBA (2019-2020); Guard, Houston Rockets, NBA (2017-2019); Guard, Los Angeles Clippers, NBA (2011-2017); Guard, New Orleans Hornets, NBA (2005-2011) **CR:** Member, U.S. National Team, Summer Olympic Games, London, England, United Kingdom (2012); Member, U.S. National Team, Summer Olympic Games, Beijing, China (2008) **AW:** Named to All-NBA Second Team (2008, 2015, 2016); Named to All-NBA First Team, NBA (2008, 2012, 2013, 2014); Named to All-defensive First Team (2009, 2012, 2013); Named All-star Game MVP, NBA (2013); Gold Medal, U.S. National Men's Basketball, Summer Olympic Games (2008, 2012); Named NBA All-star (2008-2016); Named to Western Conference All-star Team (2008-2013); Named to All-rookie First Team (2006); Named Rookie of Year, NBA (2006); Named Player of the Year, Atlantic Coast Conference (2004-2005); Named Male Athlete of the Year, USA Basketball (2004); Named Rookie of the Year, Atlantic Coast Conference (2003-2004); Named North Carolina Mr. Basketball, The Charlotte Observer (2003); Named First-team, Parade All-American (2003)

PAUL, M. LEE EDD, T: Professor of Psychology, Psychotherapist **I:** Education/Educational Services **DOB:** 07/13/1951 **PB:** Shreveport **SC:** LA/USA **PT:** Francis Malcolm Paul; Ava Aileen (Boyles) Paul **MS:** Married **SPN:** Stephanie Maxfield (07/23/1994) **CH:** Ryan Lee Paul; Cameron Scott Paul; Blake Wayne Paul **ED:** EdD, Nova Southeastern University, Broward County, FL (1986); MS, Abilene Christian University, Abilene, TX (1977); BS, Abilene Christian University, Abilene, TX (1974) **CT:** Certified Family Life Educator, National Council on Family Relations; Psychotherapist, Licensed Professional Counselor, Texas; Licensed Marriage and Family Therapist, Texas **C:** Associate Professor of Psychology, Southwestern Christian College, Terrell, TX (1991-Present); Professor of Psychology, Amberton University, Garland, TX (1980-Present); Vice president for Psychological Services, Security Research Consultant, Dallas, TX (1980-1982); Director, University Services and Research, Abilene Christian University, Dallas, TX (1977-1982); Entertainer, Six Flags Over Texas, Arlington, TX (1965-1978) **CR:** Private Practice, Psychotherapy, Dallas, TX (1982-Present); Member, Ethics Committee, Baylor Hospital, Garland, TX; Member, Advisory Board, RFD Television Network **CIV:** Deacon, Saturn Road Church of Christ **CW:** Lecturer, "Anxiety and Anxiety Disorders," Gilmer, TX (2019); Lecturer, "Depression," Gilmer, TX (2018); Co-Author, "The Parable of a Man" (1980) **AW:** Who's Who In Medicine And Healthcare (2000); Distinguished Alumnus Dallas Christian School (1998); Outstanding Young Men Of America (1979) **MEM:** American Psychological Association; American Counseling Association; American Association of Marriage and Family Therapy **MH:** Albert Nelson Marquis Lifetime Achievement Award **B/I:** Dr. Paul became involved in his profession while he was a student at Abilene Christian Univer-

sity; there was nobody in his family in the field of psychology. **AV:** Scuba diving; Hunting; Music **PA:** Independent **RE:** Member, Church of Christ

PAUL, RANDAL, "RAND" HOWARD, MD, T: U.S. Senator from Kentucky; Ophthalmologist **I:** Government Administration/Government Relations/Government Services **DOB:** 01/07/1963 **PB:** Pittsburgh **SC:** PA/USA **PT:** Ronald Ernest Paul; Carol Wells Paul **MS:** Married **SPN:** Kelley (Ashby) Paul (1991) **CH:** William; Duncan; Robert **ED:** Resident in Ophthalmology, Duke University Medical Center (1990-1993); Intern in Surgery, Georgia Baptist Medical Center (1989); MD, Duke University School of Medicine (1988); BS, Baylor University **C:** Member, U.S. Senate Committee on Foreign Relations, Washington, DC (2013-Present); U.S. Senator, Commonwealth of Kentucky, Washington, DC (2011-Present); Member, U.S. Senate Committee on Health, Education, Labor, and Pensions, Washington, DC (2011-Present); Member, U.S. Senate Committee on Small Business and Entrepreneurship, Washington, DC (2011-Present); Member, U.S. Senate Committee on Homeland Security and Governmental Affairs, Washington, DC (2011-Present); Private Practice, Bowling Green, KY (1993-Present); Member, U.S. Senate Committee on Energy and Natural Resources, Washington, DC (2011-2013); Ophthalmologist, Graves Gilbert Clinic; Staff Member, T.J. Samson Hospital, Glasgow, KY; Staff Member, Logan Memorial Hospital, Russellville, KY; Staff Member, Bowling Green Medical Center (Med Center Health); Staff Member, TriStar Greenview Regional Hospital, Bowling Green, KY **CR:** Founder, Chairman, Kentucky Taxpayers United (KTU) (1994-Present); Candidate, Republican Party Presidential Nomination (2016) **CIV:** Founder, Southern Kentucky Lions Eye Clinic (1995) **CW:** Author, "The Tea Party Goes to Washington" (2011) **AW:** Named One of the 100 Most Influential People in the World, TIME Magazine (2013, 2014); Outstanding Service and Commitment to Seniors, Twilight Wish Foundation (2002); Melvin Jones Fellow Award for Dedicated Humanitarian Services, Lions Clubs International; Lion of the Year Award, Bowling Green Lions, Lions Clubs International; Fines E. Davis Fellow Award for Dedicated Humanitarian Service, Lions Clubs International; Governors' Appreciation Award for Sight Conservation, Lions Clubs International **MEM:** Former President, Lions Clubs International **PA:** Republican **RE:** Presbyterian

PAUL, RONALD, "RON" EARNEST, MD, T: Former U.S. Representative from Texas; Physician **I:** Government Administration/Government Relations/Government Services **DOB:** 08/20/1935 **PB:** Pittsburgh **SC:** PA/USA **PT:** Howard Caspar Paul; Margaret Dumont Paul **MS:** Married **SPN:** Carolyn (Wells) Paul (1957) **CH:** Ronald; Lori; Randal; Robert; Joy **ED:** Resident, Obstetrics-gynecology, UPMC Magee-Womens Hospital, University of Pittsburgh Medical Center (1965-1968); Intern, Henry Ford Hospital, Detroit, MI (1961-1962); MD, Duke University Medical Center, Durham, NC (1961); BA in Biology, Gettysburg College, PA (1957) **C:** Member, U.S. House of Representatives from Texas' 14th Congressional District, United States Congress, Washington, DC (1997-2013); Member, U.S. House of Representatives from Texas' 22nd Congressional District, United States Congress, Washington, DC (1976-1977, 1979-1985); Private Medical Practice, Brazoria County, Texas (1968) **CR:** Republican Candidate, U.S. Presidential Election (2012); Libertarian Candidate, U.S. Presidential Election (2008); Libertarian Candidate, U.S. Presidential Election (1988) **MIL:** Flight Surgeon, United States Air National Guard (1965-1968); Flight Surgeon, United States Air Force (1963-1965) **CW:** Author, "Liberty Defined: 50 Essential Issues That Affect Our Freedom" (2011); Author, "End the Fed" (2009); Author, "Pillars of Prosperity" (2008); Author, "The Revolution: A Manifesto" (2008); Author, "A Foreign Policy of Freedom: Peace, Commerce, and Honest Friendship" (2007); Author, "The Case for Defending America" (2002); Author, "A Republic, If You Can Keep It" (2000); Author, "The Ron Paul Money Book" (1991); Author, "Challenge to Liberty: Coming to Grips with the Abortion Issue" (1990); Author, "Freedom Under Siege: The U.S. Constitution After 200 Years" (1987); Author, "Mises and Austrian Economics: A Personal View" (1984); Author, "Texas: Foundation for Rational Economics and Education" (1983); Author, "Ten Myths About Paper Money: And One Myth About Paper Gold" (1983); Author, "The Case for Gold: A Minority Report of the U.S. Gold Commission" (1982); Author, "Gold, Peace, and Prosperity: The Birth of a New Currency" (1981); Author, "The School Revolution: A New Answer for our Broken Education System" **AW:** Named One of the 100 Most Influential People in the World, TIME Magazine (2012); Taxpayer's Best Friend Award, National Taxpayers Union; Torch Freedom Award, Young Conservatives of Texas; Leadership Award, National Coalition for Peace through Strength **PA:** Republican **RE:** Baptist

PAULEY, BRUCE, T: Professor Emeritus **I:** Education/Educational Services **DOB:** 11/04/1937 **PB:** Lincoln **SC:** NE/USA **PT:** Carroll Righter Pauley; Blanche Marie (Hulsebus) Pauley **MS:** Married **SPN:** Marianne Barbara Utz (12/21/1963) **CH:** Mark Allan; Glenn Hamilton **ED:** PhD, University of Rochester (1966); MA, University of Nebraska (1961); BA, Grinnell College (1959) **C:** From Associate Professor to Professor of History, University of Central Florida, Orlando, FL (1971-2006); Professor Emeritus, University of Central Florida (2006); Chairman, Faculty Senate, University of Central Florida (1978-1979); Assistant Professor of History, University of Wyoming (1966-1971);Instructor, History, University of Nebraska–Lincoln (1965-1966); Instructor of History, College of Wooster (1964-1965) **CR:** Visiting Professor of History, University of Nebraska–Lincoln (2002, 2006); Consultant, Expert Witness, Consultant, Expert Witness, War Crimes Division Department of Justice Canada (1998-1999) **CIV:** Pauley Family Speaker Series on Global Affairs, University of Central Florida (2000); Established Carroll R. Pauley Lecture Series, University of Nebraska-Lincoln (1997); Chairman, Parents Advisory Committee, Oviedo High School, Florida (1981-1982) **CW:** Author, "Pioneering History on Two Continents: An Autobiography" (2014); Author, "Hitler, Stalin and Mussolini: Totalitarianism in the Twentieth Century" (1997, 2014); Author, "Eine Geschichte des österreichischen Antisemitismus: Von der Ausgrenzung zur Auslöschung" (1993); Author, "From Prejudice to Persecution: A History of Austrian Anti-Semitism" (1992); Author, "Der Weg in den Nationalsozialismus: Ursprünge und Entwicklung in Österreich" (1988); Author, "Hitler and the Forgotten Nazis: A History of Austrian National Socialism" (1981); Author, "The Habsburg Legacy, 1867-1939" (1972); Author, "Hahnenschwanz und Hakenkreuz: Steirischer Heimatschutz und österreichischer Nationalsozialismus, 1918-1934" (1972) **AW:** Alumni Achievement Award, Grinnell College (2019); Honor Cross Scholarship, Government of Austria (2010); Lifetime Achievement Award, University of Nebraska- Lincoln (2005); Named Distinguished Alumnus, University of Nebraska-Lincoln (1996); Best Brook, Austrian Studies, Austrian Cultural Institute (1993); Charles Smith Prize for "Best Book on European History," "From Prejudice to Persecution: A History of Austrian Anti-Semitism,"

Southern Historical Association (1992); Research Fellow, National Endowment of the Humanities (1972, 1987); Fulbright Fellow (1963-1964) **MEM:** Society for Austrian and Habsburg History **AS:** Dr. Pauley attributes his success to inspiration from his father, Carroll Pauley, and mother, Blanche Pauley. In addition, he is grateful for the help of his wife, Marianne Pauley, and tenacity in completing major research projects. **B/I:** Dr. Pauley became involved in his profession because of vacations with his parents to historic sites in Europe from 1954 to 1955, a trip abroad to Vienna during his junior year from 1957 to 1958, and the inspiration he received from history professors at Grinnell College. **AV:** Traveling to historical sites in more than 80 countries; Photography; Playing golf **THT:** Dr. Pauley is currently working on a book about everyday life in the United States at the turn of the 20th century.

PAULEY, JANE, T: Newscaster; Journalist **I:** Media & Entertainment **CN:** CBS News **DOB:** 10/31/1950 **PB:** Indianapolis **SC:** IN/USA **PT:** Richard Pauley; Mary Pauley **MS:** Married **SPN:** Garry Trudeau (1980) **CH:** Three Children **ED:** Honorary Doctor of Journalism, DePauw University (1978); Bachelor of Arts in Political Science, Indiana University (1971) **C:** Host, "CBS Sunday Morning" (2016-Present); Correspondent, Substitute Host, "CBS This Morning" (2014-2016); Host, Monthly Segment, "Your Life Calling," "The Today Show," NBC, New York, NY (2009-2013); From Co-anchor to Correspondent, NBC News, New York, NY (1976-2013); Host, "The Jane Pauley Show" (2004-2005); Anchor, "Time & Again," MSNBC (1999-2003); Principal Anchor, "Dateline NBC," New York, NY (1999-2003); Substitute Anchor, "NBC Nightly News," NY (1990-2003); Co-anchor, "Dateline NBC," New York, NY (1992-1999); Principal Correspondent, "Real Life with Jane Pauley," NBC (1991); Co-anchor, "The Today Show," NBC, New York, NY (1976-1990); Co-anchor, "Early Today," NBC (1982-1983); Principal Writer, Reporter, "NBC Nightly News," NY (1980-1982); Co-anchor, WMAQ-TV News, Chicago, IL (1975-1976); Reporter, Station WISH-TV, Indianapolis, IN (1972-1975) **CIV:** Board of Directors, The Mind Trust, Indianapolis, IN (2009-Present); Chairperson, Advisory Board, Board of Directors, Children's Health Fund, New York, NY; Board of Directors, Public Education Needs Civic Involvement in Learning; Member, Advisory Board, International Council, Freedom from Hunger; Ambassador of "Your Life Calling", AARP **CW:** Author, "Your Life Calling: Re-imagining the Rest of Your Life" (2014); Author, "Skywriting: A Life Out of the Blue" (2004) **AW:** Emmy Awards for Outstanding Morning Program, Academy of Television Arts & Sciences (2015, 2019); Emmy Award for Best Report in a News Magazine, Academy of Television Arts & Sciences (2002); Named to Broadcasting and Cable Hall of Fame (1998); Named, Best in the Business, Washington Journalism Review (1990); Named Broadcaster of the Year, International Radio and TV Society (1986); Paul White Award, NTNDA; Leonard Zeidenberg First Amendment Award, Radio Television Digital News Association; Salute to Excellence Award, National Association of Black Journalists; Wilbur Award, Religion Communicators Council; Clarion Award, Association for Women in Communications; Gracie Allen Award; Commendation Award, American Women in Radio and Television; Humanitas Award; Maggie Award; Nancy Susan Reynolds Award; Gabriel Award; Edward R. Murrow Award; Matrix Award, Association for Women in Communications; Walter Cronkite Award for Excellence in Journalism **MEM:** Fellow, Society of Professional Journalists; Honorary Chair, Jane Pauley Task Force on Mass Communications Education

PAULSEN, LISA, T: Chief Nursing Officer **I:** Medicine & Health Care **CN:** Audubon County Memorial Hospital **MS:** Married **SPN:** William **CH:** Dakota; Madaline; Dane **ED:** Master's Degree in Healthcare Administration, Southern New Hampshire University (2018); Bachelor's in Nursing Degree, Mercy College of Health Sciences, Des Moines IA (2008); Associate Degree, Mercy College of Health Sciences, Des Moines IA (2002); **CT:** Registered Nurse, Mercy College of Health Sciences, Iowa (2002); Certified Perioperative Nursing (CNOR); Certified Surgical Services Management (CSSM) **C:** Chief Nursing Office (CNO), Audubon County Memorial Hospital (2018-Present); Director of Surgical and Outpatient Services, Audubon County Memorial Hospital (2013-2018); House Supervisor, Mercy West Lakes Hospital, Des Moines, IA (2009-2013); Staff Nurse, Audubon County Memorial Hospital (1997-2009) **CIV:** Volunteer, Numerous Community Activities **MEM:** Exira Community Club **MH:** Marquis Who's Who Top Professional **AS:** Ms. Paulsen attributes her success to being tenacious and persistent when she sets a goal; she doesn't quit until she is done with it. As much as she likes taking care of patients, she has always had a vision of teaching newer staff to be a strong caregiver and confident in that they do. She spends a lot of time trying to educate and mentor her staff so they are the best they can be. **B/I:** Ms. Paulsen became interested in her profession because her mother was a nurse, so watching her taking care of people was very interesting to her as a child. **THT:** Ms. Paulsen oversees a staff of 35.

PAULSON, SARAH CATHARINE, T: Actress **I:** Media & Entertainment **DOB:** 12/17/1974 **PB:** Tampa **SC:** FL/USA **PT:** Douglas Lyle Paulson II; Catharine Gordon (Dolcater) Paulson **MS:** Partner **SPN:** Holland Taylor (2015); Cherry Jones (2004-2009) **ED:** Coursework, American Academy of Dramatic Arts **CW:** Actress, "Mrs. America" (2020); Actress, "The Goldfinch" (2019); Actress, "Katrina: American Crime Story" (2019); Actress, "Abominable" (2019); Voice Actress, "Family Guy" (2019); Actress, "Glass" (2019); Actress, "American Horror Story: Apocalypse" (2018); Actress, "American Horror Story: Apocalypse" (2018); Actress, "Rebel in the Rye" (2017); Actress, "The Post" (2017); Actress, "Feud: Bette and Joan" (2017); Actress, "American Horror Story: Cult" (2017); Actress, "American Horror Story: Roanoke" (2016); Actress, "American Crime Story: The People v. O.J. Simpson" (2016); Actress, "Blue Jay" (2016); Actress, "American Horror Story: Hotel" (2015-2016); Actress, "Carol" (2015); Actress, "The Runner" (2015); Actress, "American Horror Story: Freak Show" (2014-2015); Actress, "American Horror Story: Coven" (2013-2014); Actress, "Twelve Years a Slave" (2013); Actress, "Talley's Folly" (2013); Actress, "American Horror Story: Asylum" (2012-2013); Actress, "Mud" (2012); Actress, "Fairhaven" (2012); Actress, "The Time Being" (2012); Actress, "Stars in Shorts" (2012); Actress, "Blue" (2012); Actress, "Game Change" (2012); Actress, "Martha Marcy May Marlene" (2011); Actress, "Untitled Kari Lizer Project" (2011); Actress, "American Horror Story: Murder House" (2011); Actress, "New Year's Eve" (2011); Actress, "Collected Stories" (2010); Actress, "Law & Order: Special Victims Unit" (2010); Actress, "Grey's Anatomy" (2010); Actress, "November Christmas" (2010); Actress, "Cupid" (2009); Actress, "The Spirit" (2008); Actress, "Pretty/Handsome" (2008); Actress, "Puppy Love" (2008); Actress, "Desperate Housewives" (2007); Actress, "Studio 60 on the Sunset Strip" (2006-2007); Actress, "Diggers" (2006); Actress, "A Christmas Wedding" (2006); Actress, "Griffin & Phoenix" (2006); Actress, "The Glass Menagerie" (2005);

Actress, "Swimmers" (2005); Actress, "Deadwood" (2005); Actress, "Piccadilly Jim" (2005); Actress, "Serenity" (2005); Actress, "The Notorious Bettie Page" (2005); Actress, "The D.A." (2004); Actress, "Down with Love" (2003); Actress, "Bug" (2002); Actress, "Path to War" (2002); Actress, "Leap of Faith" (2002); Actress, "Touched by an Angel" (2001); Actress, "Jack & Jill" (1999-2001); Actress, "What Women Want" (2000); Actress, "Metropolis," (2000); Actress, "The Other Sister" (1999); Actress, "Held Up" (1999); Actress, "The Long Way Home" (1998); Actress, "Real Life" (1998); Actress, "Cracker: Mind Over Murder" (1997); Actress, "Levitation" (1997); Actress, "Shaughnessy" (1996); Actress, "American Gothic" (1995-1996); Actress, "Friends at Last" (1995); Actress, "Law & Order" (1994) **AW:** SAG Award for Outstanding Performance by a Female Actor in a Miniseries or Television Movie, SAG-AFTRA (2018); Golden Globe Award for Best Actress - Miniseries or Television Film, Hollywood Foreign Press Association (2017); Named One of the 100 Most Influential People in the World, TIME Magazine (2017); Satellite Award for Best Actress - Miniseries or Television Film (2017); Emmy Award for Outstanding Lead Actress in a Limited Series or a Movie, Academy of Television Arts & Sciences (2016); Primetime Emmy Award for Outstanding Lead Actress in a Miniseries, Academy of Television Arts & Sciences (2016); Critics' Choice Award for Best Actress in a Miniseries (2016); Award for Individual Achievement in Drama, Television Critics Association Awards (2016); Dorian Award for TV Performance of the Year - Actress (2016); Critics' Choice Awards for Best Supporting Actress in a Movie or Miniseries (2013, 2015); Fangoria Chainsaw Award for Best Supporting Actress (2015); Satellite Award for Best Supporting Actress – Series, Miniseries or Television Film (2014); Award for Best Ensemble, Black Film Critics Circle Awards (2013); Independent Spirit Robert Altman Award (2013)

PAVELKA, ELAINE B., PHD, T: Emeritus Mathematics Professor **I:** Education/Educational Services **PB:** Chicago **SC:** IL/USA **PT:** Frank Joseph Pavelka; Mildred Bohumila (Seidl) Pavelka **ED:** PhD, University of Illinois; MS, Northwestern University; BA, Northwestern University **C:** Emeritus Mathematics Professor, Morton College; Teacher, Leyden Community High School, Franklin Park, IL; Northwestern University Aerial Measurements Laboratory, Evanston, IL **CR:** Invited Professor, International Congress on Mathematics Education, Karlsruhe, Germany (1976) **AW:** Listee, International Who's Who of Professional Business Women (2000); Science Talent Award, Westinghouse Electric Co. **MEM:** American Education Research Association; American Mathematics Association of Two-Year Colleges; American Mathematics Society; Association of Women in Math; Canadian Society of History and Philosophy of Mathematics; Illinois Council of Teachers of Mathematics; Illinois Mathematics Association of Community Colleges; American Mathematics Action Group; Georgia Center for Assessment; National Council of Teachers of Mathematics; School Science and Mathematics Association; Northwestern University Alumni Association; University of Illinois Alumni Association; American Mensa, Ltd.; Intertel; Sigma Delta Epsilon; Pi Mu Epsilon **MH:** Albert Nelson Marquis Lifetime Achievement Award **AV:** Traveling

PAYNE, DONALD MILFORD, T: Former U.S. Representative from New Jersey **I:** Government Administration/Government Relations/Government Services **DOB:** 07/16/1934 **PB:** Newark **SC:** NJ/USA **PT:** William Evander Payne; Norma (Garrett) Payne **MS:** Widowed **SPN:** Hazel (Johnson)

Payne (06/18/1958, Deceased 1963) **CH:** Donald Milford Jr.; Wanda **ED:** Honorary Doctorate, William Paterson University; Honorary Doctorate, Essex County College; Honorary Doctorate, Drew University; Honorary Doctorate, Chicago State University; BA in Social Studies, Seton Hall University, NJ (1957); Postgraduate Coursework, Springfield College, MA **C:** Member, U.S. House of Representatives from New Jersey's Tenth District, United States Congress (1989-2012); Member, Newark Municipal Council (1982-1988); Member, Essex County Board of Chosen Freeholders (1972-1978); Vice President, Urban Data Systems, Inc. (1969); Executive, Prudential Insurance Company, Prudential Financial, Inc. (1964-1969); Teacher, Pulaski Elementary School, Passaic, NJ (1959-1964); Teacher, Robert Treat Junior High School (Now Robert Treat Academy Charter School, Inc., Newark, NJ (1957-1959); Teacher, South Side High School, Newark, NJ (1957) **CR:** Chairman, Essex County Democratic Committee (2003-2004); Member, Congressional Black Caucus (1995-1997) **CIV:** Member, Congressional Delegate, United Nations (2003, 2005); Chairman, World YMCA Refugee & Rehabilitation Committee (1973-1981); National President, YMCA (1970-1973); Board of Directors, EnterpriseWorks/VITA; Board of Directors, Congressional Award Foundation; Board of Directors, Discovery Channel Global Education Fund; Board of Directors, TransAfrica; Board of Directors, National Endowment for Democracy; Board of Directors, YMCA of Newark and Vicinity, NJ; Board of Directors, Fighting Back Initiative; Board of Directors, The Newark Day Center; Member, U.S. Committee for UNICEF **AW:** Named to the Power 150 (2008); Named One of the People to Watch, Sunday Star Ledger (2007); Africa Grand Leadership Prize Award, Celebrate Africa Foundation (2007); Named One of the Most Influential Black Americans, Ebony Magazine (2006); Bishop John T. Walker Distinguished Humanitarian Service Award, Africare (2004); Humanitarian Service Award, Isaac Hayes Foundation (2004); Visionaries for Africa Award, The Africa Society (2004); Leadership Award, Urban League of Hudson County, NJ (2003) **MEM:** Life Member, NAACP; Council on Foreign Relations; National Council of Negro Women, Inc. **PA:** Democrat **RE:** Baptist

PAYNE, DONALD MILFORD JR., T: U.S. Representative from New Jersey **I:** Government Administration/Government Relations/Government Services **DOB:** 12/16/1958 **PB:** Newark **SC:** NJ/USA **PT:** Donald Milford Payne; Hazel (Johnson) Payne **MS:** Married **SPN:** Beatrice Payne **CH:** Donald III; Jack; Yvonne **ED:** Coursework, Kean University **C:** Member, U.S. House of Representatives from New Jersey's 10th Congressional District, United States Congress, Washington, DC (2013-Present); Member, Congressional Black Caucus (2013-Present); Member, U.S. House Small Business Committee (2013-Present); Member, U.S. House Committee on Homeland Security (2013-Present); Council President, City of Newark, NJ (2010-2012); Member-At-Large, Essex County Board of Chosen Freeholders (2006-2012); City Councilman, At-Large District, City of Newark, NJ (2006-2012); Supervisor, Student Transportation, Essex County Educational Services Commission (1996); Staff, New Jersey Highway Authority (Now New Jersey Turnpike Authority) (1990-1996) **CIV:** Founder, President, Newark South Ward Junior Democrats **PA:** Democrat

PAYNE, PHILIP H., T: Founder, Chief Executive Officer **I:** Medicine & Health Care **CN:** Apportis **MS:** Married **SPN:** Carol (1996) **CH:** Cosette **ED:** Master of Business Administration, University of Pennsylvania, The Wharton School (2008);

Bachelor's Degree in Business and Marketing, Baldwin Wallace University (1990) **CT:** Customer Centric Selling (2008); Pragmatic Marketing Certified, Pragmatic Marketing, Product Management Certification (2008); Information Mapping Professional (1995) **C:** Founder, President, APPORTIS (2014-Present); Vice President of Marketing, AutoSweet (2012-2014); Senior Vice President of Sales & Marketing, BCSG-Business Centric Services Group (2010-2012); Director of Marketing, MindLeaders, ThirdForce PLC (2006-2010); Creative Director, Lead Instructional Designer, MindLeaders (1994-2006); President, Scioto Valley RFC (2003-2004); Marketing Director, Case Management Services (1993-1994); Marketing Manager, Arrow Industrial Supply (1991-1993); Creative Services-Intern, Kitchum (1990-1991) **CR:** Head Coach, Director of Rugby, The Columbus Rugby Club-Men's Division 1 (2016-Present); Speaker in the Field **CIV:** Head Coach, Women's Rugby Team, The Ohio State University (2005-2015); Board Member, Ohio Rugby Classic (2004-2015); Volunteer, Mid-Ohio Food Bank

PAZ, JESSICA, T: Sound Designer **I:** Media & Entertainment **CW:** Sound Co-designer, "Hadestown" (2019); Sound Designer, "Kiss My Aztec" (2019); Sound Designer, "Coriolanus" (2019); Sound Designer, "Much Ado About Nothing" (2010, 2019); Sound Designer, "Othello" (2019); Student Advisor, Sound Design, "Next to Normal" (2018); Sound Designer, "Public Works: Twelfth Night" (2018); Sound Designer, "Miss You Like Hell" (2018); Sound Designer, "Welcome to Fear City" (2018); Sound Designer, "Public Works: As You Like It" (2017); Sound Designer, "Julius Caesar" (2017); Sound Designer, "A Midsummer Night's Dram" (2017); Associate Sound Designer, "Bandstand" (2017); Associate Sound Designer, "Dear Evan Hansen" (2016); Sound Designer, "Ugly Lies the Bone" (2015); Associate Sound Designer, "Fela! The Concert" (2015); Associate Sound Designer, "Disaster! the Musical" (2015); Sound Designer, "A Sucker EmCee" (2014); Sound Designer, "The Muscles in Our Toes" (2014); Sound Designer, "Fable" (2014); Sound System Designer/Engineer, Actor's Studio Drama School (2009-2014); Sound Designer, "Becoming Dr. Ruth" (2013); Sound Designer, "The King's Whore" (2013); Sound Designer, "This is a Play About Artists" (2013); Sound Designer, "Scott and Hem... Garden of Allah" (2013); Associate Sound Designer, "The Assembled Parties" (2013); Associate Sound Designer, "Fela!" (2009, 2011, 2013); Sound Designer, "See How They Run" (2012); Sound Designer, "9 to 5 the Musical" (2012); Sound Designer, "Legally Blonde" (2011); Sound Designer, "SCKBSTD" (2011); Assistant Sound Designer, "A Life in the Theater" (2010); Sound Designer, "DOT" (2010); Sound Designer, "Veritas" (2010); Sound Designer, "The Threepenny Opera" (2009); Sound Designer, "And Her Hair Went With Her" (2008); Sound Designer, "Stretch: A Fantasia" (2008); Sound Designer, "Looking for the Pony" (2007); Sound Designer, "Minstrel Show" (2007); Sound Designer, "BookEnds" (2007); Sound Designer, "TempOdyssey" (2007); Sound Designer, "Way to Go!" (2007); Sound Designer, "Charm of Preparedness" (2007) **AW:** Tony Award for Best Sound Design of a Musical, "Hadestown" (2019); Drama Desk Award for Best Sound Design of a Musical, "Hadestown" (2019); Outstanding Ensemble, Fringe NYC Awards (2010); Tony Award for Best Sound Design of a Musical, "Fela!" (2009)

PEACE, H.W. II, T: Small Business Owner, Retired Oil Industry Executive **I:** Oil & Energy **DOB:** 05/21/1935 **PB:** Clinton **SC:** OK/USA **PT:** Herman Wilbern Peace; Bernice (Mitchell) Peace **MS:** Married **SPN:** Norma June Williams **CH:** Hugh William;

Susannah Lee **ED:** Postgraduate Coursework, University of Southwest Louisiana (1968); MS in Geology, University of Oklahoma (1964); BS in Geology, University of Oklahoma (1959) **C:** Owner, EXAD (2006-Present); President, Chief Executive Officer, Wood Oil Company Subsidiary Panhandle Royalty Company (2001-2006); President, Chief Executive Officer, Director, Panhandle Royalty Company, Oklahoma City (1991-2006); Managing Partner, EXAD, Oklahoma City, OK (1988-1991); Executive Vice President, Chief Operating Officer, Anadarko Supply Company, Oklahoma City, OK (1986-1988); Executive Vice President, Chief Operating Officer, Mosswood Oil and Gas Company, Oklahoma City, OK (1985-1988); Executive Vice President, Chief Operating Officer, Hadson Petroleum Company, Oklahoma City, OK (1985-1988); Vice President of Exploration, Hadson Petroleum Company, Oklahoma City, OK (1983-1985); Manager of Division Exploration, Cotton Petroleum Company, Tulsa, OK (1980-1983); Manager, Rocky Mountain Exploration, Union Oil Company California, Casper, WY (1977-1980); Geologist, District Exploration, Union Oil Company California, Oklahoma City, OK (1970-1977); Area Geologist, Union Oil Company California, Lafayette, LA (1965-1970); Junior Geologist, Union Oil Company California, Houston, TX (1964-1965); Board of Directors, Anadarko Supply Company, Oklahoma City, OK; Board of Directors, Hadson Petroleum Corporation, Oklahoma City, OK **CR:** Chairman, Farmers Royalty Company (2014-Present); Board of Directors, Advisory Director, Energy Library Online (2009-Present); Oil Law Records Corporation (2006-2012); Board of Directors, Management Committee, PLC Energy Data, LLC (1994-2001) **CIV:** Director, School of Geology, Advisory Committee, University of Oklahoma (1984-Present) **MIL:** Retired (1985); Captain, U.S. Naval Reserve (1963-1982); Lieutenant, U.S. Navy (1959-1963) **MEM:** Rotary Club (2007-Present); Board of Directors, Associate, Oklahoma National Royalty Owners (2006-Present); Royalty Advisory Committee, Oklahoma Corporation Commission (1998-Present); Chairman, Professional Affairs, Oklahoma City Geological Society (1976-2020); Secretary, Mid-Continent Section, President, American Association of Petroleum Geologists (2011-2017); Representative Delegate, Mid-Continent Section Board Secretary, Vice President, American Association of Petroleum Geology (1984-2015); President, Fieldstone Homeowners Association (1983); Vice President, Petroleum Association of Wyoming (1979-1980); President, Cherokee Hills Homeowners Association (1971-1973); Society of Exploration Geophysicists; Society of Economic Paleontologists and Mineralogists; Tulsa Geological Society; Naval Reserve Association; Navy League **MH:** Albert Nelson Marquis Lifetime Achievement Award **B/I:** Mr. Peace grew up in the country and always enjoyed being outdoors. He became fascinated by the rocks he would encounter and grew an immense love for nature. **AV:** Golfing; Swimming; Hiking **PA:** Republican **RE:** Disciples of Christ

PEASE, DONALD E., PHD, T: Humanities Educator **I:** Education/Educational Services **PT:** Donald Eugene Pease; Marie Theresa Pease **SPN:** Patricia Ann Mckee (06/07/1985) **ED:** Doctorate Honoris Causa, Uppsala University The Faculty of Languages, Sweden (2011); PhD, The University of Chicago (1973) **C:** Chair, Masters, Liberal Studies, Dartmouth College (1999-Present); Founding Director, Futures American studies, Dartmouth College (1996-Present); Avalon Chair Humanities, Dartmouth College, Hanover, NH (1995) **CR:** Dru Heinz Professor of American Literature, University of Oxford (2001-2002); Board of Governors, Clinton Institute, Dublin, Ireland, United Kingdom; Distinguished Visiting Professor, University of Würzburg, Würzburg, Germany **CIV:** Co-director, Dartmouth 250th Anniversary (2019) **CW:** Author, Book, "Visionary Compacts: American Renaissance Writings in Cultural Context"; Author, "Unacknowledged Legislators: State Fantasies from the Persian Gulf War to Barack Obama"; Editor, "Cultures of US Imperialism," 14 Volumes; Editor, "Future of American Studies, American Democratic Cultures"; Editor, "Revisionist Interventions into the Canon"; Editor, "American Renaissance Reconsidered"; Editor, "Futures of American Studies"; Editor, "Theodore SEUSS Geisel"; Editor, 10 Books **AW:** Selected Faculty Member, Dartmouth Society of Fellows (2014); Carl Bode-Norman Holmes Pearson Prize for Outstanding Contributions to American Studies, American Studies Association (ASA) (2012); Teaching Fellowship, National Endowment of the Humanities (1990, 1993); Guggenheim Fellowship (1989, 1990); Mark Ingaham Best Book Prize (1987); Named Distinguished Visiting Professor, University of Würzburg, Würzburg, Germany; Named Druheinz Professor **MH:** Albert Nelson Marquis Lifetime Achievement Award **B/I:** The professors who Dr. Pease learned American literature from in college were the most imaginative and the most inspiring. He wanted to continue in that tradition. He wanted to discover as much as he could, what might be called the imaginative foundations of the United States, by studying authors for whom the imagination was the preeminent instrument for exploration.

PECK, ART, T: Chief Executive Officer **I:** Retail/Sales **CN:** Gap Inc. **ED:** MBA, Harvard Business School;BA in Economics, Occidental College, Los Angeles, CA (1977) **C:** Chief Executive Officer, Gap Inc. (2015-Present); President Growth, Innovation and Digital (GID) Division, Gap Inc. (2012-2015); President, Gap North America, Gap Inc. (2011-2012); President, Gap Outlet, Gap Inc., San Francisco, CA (2008-2011); Executive Vice President, Strategy and Operations, Gap Inc., San Francisco, CA (2005-2011);Director, Boston Consulting Group, Inc. (1988-2005); Senior Vice President, Boston Consulting Group Inc. (1982-2005); Financial and Marketing Positions, Avery Denison, Pasadena, CA **CR:** Board of Directors Gap Inc. (2015-Present); Trustee, The Gap Foundation (2008-Present) **AW:** Named One of The 100 Most Creative People in Business, Fast Company (2013)

PEELE, JORDAN HAWORTH, T: Actor, Comedian, Director, Producer **I:** Media & Entertainment **DOB:** 02/21/1979 **PB:** New York **SC:** NY/USA **PT:** Hayward Peele; Lucinda Williams **MS:** Married **SPN:** Chelsea Peretti (04/2016) **CH:** Beaumont **ED:** Coursework, Lawrence College **C:** Performer, The Second City, Chicago, IL; Founder, Performer, Comedy Duo, Boom Chicago, Amsterdam, The Netherlands **CW:** Producer, "Hunters" (2020-Present); Host, Writer, Producer, "The Twilight Zone" (2019-Present); Writer, Producer, "The Last O.G." (2018-Present); Producer, "Lovecraft Country" (2020); Writer, Producer, "Candyman" (2020); Writer, Producer, "Weird City" (2019); Producer, "Lorena" (2019); Featured, "Horror Noire: A History of Black Horror" (2019); Voice Actor, "Toy Story 4" (2019); Actor, "The Shivering Truth" (2018); Producer, "BlacKkKlansman" (2018); Appearance, "The Daily Show" (2017); Actor, "Big Mouth" (2017); Actor, Director, Writer, Producer, "Us" (2017); Actor, Director, Writer, Producer, "Get Out" (2017); Voice Actor, "Captain Underpants: The First Epic Movie" (2017); Appearance, "The Muppets" (2016); Voice Actor, "American Dad!" (2016); Actor, Writer, Producer, "Keanu" (2016); Voice Actor, "Storks" (2016); Actor, "Life in Pieces" (2015); Voice Actor, "Rick and Morty" (2015); Actor, "Wet Hot American Summer: First Day of Camp" (2015); Voice Actor, "Trip Tank" (2015); Voice Actor, "Supermansion" (2015); Voice Actor, "Bob's Burgers" (2014-2016); Actor, "Fargo" (2014); Actor, "Drunk History" (2014); Voice Actor, "Robot Chicken" (2014); Actor, "The Mindy Project" (2013); Actor, "Workaholics" (2013); Actor, "Comedy Bang! Bang!" (2013); Voice Actor, "Axe Cop" (2013); Actor, "Modern Family" (2013); Actor, "Kroll Show" (2013); Actor, "The Sidekick" (2013); Actor, Writer, Producer, "Key and Peele" (2012-2015); Actor, "Wanterlust" (2012); Actor, "Love Bites" (2011); Actor, "Children's Hospital" (2010-2015); Actor, "Little Fockers" (2010); Actor, "3B," (2010); Voice Actor, "Supernews!" (2009-2010); Actor, "Reno 911" (2009); Actor, "The Station" (2009); Actor, "Chocolate News" (2008); Actor, "Boner Boyz!" (2008); Actor, Writer, "Mad TV" (2003-2008) **AW:** John Schlesinger Britannia Award for Excellence in Directing (2019); Academy Award for Best Original Screenplay, Academy of Motion Picture Arts and Sciences (2018); Award for Outstanding Directing - First-Time Feature Film, Directors Guild of America (2018); Award for Best Original Screenplay, Writers Guild of America (2018); One of the 100 Most Influential People, Time Magazine (2017); Emmy Award for Outstanding Variety Sketch Series, Academy of Television Arts & Sciences (2016); Peabody Award (2013); Numerous Awards

PEGULA, TERRY MICHAEL, T: Professional Sports Team Executive; Former Gas Industry Executive **I:** Athletics **CN:** Pegula Sports and Entertainment, LLC **DOB:** 03/27/1951 **PB:** Carbondale **SC:** PA/USA **MS:** Married **SPN:** Kim Kerr (1993) **CH:** Michael; Laura; Jessica; Kellie; Matthew **ED:** BS in Petroleum and Natural Gas Engineering, The Pennsylvania State University (1973) **C:** Owner, Buffalo Beauts, NWHL (2017-Present); Owner, Buffalo Bills, NFL (2014-Present); Owner, Buffalo Sabres, NHL (2011-Present); Owner, Buffalo Bandits, National Lacrosse League (2011-Present); Co-founder, Pegula Sports and Entertainment, LLC (2011-Present); Founder, President, Chief Executive Officer, East Resources Inc. (1983-2010); With, Felmont Oil; With, Getty Oil **CR:** Operator, First Niagara Center (Now KeyBank Center), Buffalo, NY; With, IMPACT Sports Performance; Co-owner, Black River Music (Black River Entertainment), Nashville, TN; Launched, Craft Beer, One Buffalo, Southern Tier Brewing Company **PA:** Republican

PEI, I.M., T: Architect **I:** Architecture & Construction **DOB:** 4/26/1917 **PB:** Canton **SC:** China **PT:** Tsu Yee Pei; Lien Kwun Chwong; **MS:** Married **SPN:** Eileen Loo (6/20/1942) **CH:** Ting Chung; Chien Chung; Li Chung; Liane **ED:** Honorary Doctor of Fine Arts, Dartmouth College (1991); Honorary Doctor of Humane Letters, American University, Paris, France (1990); Honorary Doctor of Humane Letters, University of Hong Kong (1990); Honorary Doctor of Humane Letters, University of Rochester (1982); Honorary Doctor of Humane Letters, University of Colorado (1982); Honorary Doctor of Humane Letters, Columbia University, New York, NY (1980); Honorary Doctor of Fine Arts, New York University (1980); Honorary Doctor of Fine Arts, Brown University (1980); Honorary Doctor of Fine Arts, University of Massachusetts (1980); Honorary Doctor of Fine Arts, Carnegie Mellon University (1980); Honorary Doctor of Fine Arts, Rensselaer Polytechnic Institute (1978); Honorary Doctor of Law, Chinese University, Hong Kong (1970); Honorary Doctor of Fine Arts, University of Pennsylvania (1970); Master of Architecture, Harvard University (1946); Bachelor of Architecture, Massachusetts Institute of Technology (1940); Honorary Doctor of Law, Pace University; Honorary Doctor of Fine Arts, University of Rochester; Honorary Doctor of

Fine Arts, Harvard University; Honorary Doctor of Fine Arts, Northeastern University **C:** Independent Architect, New York, NY (1990-2019); Founding Partner, Pei Cobb Freed & Partners, New York, NY (1955-1990); Director, Architectural Division, Webb & Knapp Inc. (1948-1955); Assistant Professor, Harvard Graduate School of Design (1945-1948); With, National Defense Research Committee (1943-1945); Architect, New York, NY (1939-1942) **CIV:** National Council on Arts (1981-1984); National Council on the Humanities (1966-1970) **CW:** Architect, Planned Project, Macao Science Center (2009); Architect, Planned Project, Museum of Islamic Art (2008); Architect, Planned Project, Embassy of the People's Republic of China to the United States of America (2006); Architect, Planned Project, Suzhou Museum (2006); Architect, Planned Project, MUDAM-Musée d'Art Moderne Grand-Duc Jean (2006); Architect, Planned Project, Zeughaus Wing at Deutsches Historisches Museum (2003); Architect, Planned Project, Republic of Korea Permenant Mission to the United Nations (2000); Architect, Planned Project, Essensa Condiminum (2000); Architect, Planned Project, Bank of China Head Office Building (1999); Architect, Planned Project, Miho Museum (1997); Architect, Planned Project, Buck Institute on Aging (1996); Architect, Planned Project, Rock and Roll Hall of Fame (1995); Architect, Planned Project, Louvre Pyramid (1993); Architect, Mile High Center, Denver, CO; Architect, National Center Atmospheric Research, Boulder, CO; Architect, Dallas City Hall; Architect, John Fitzgerald Kennedy Library, Boston, MA; Architect, Canadian Imperial Bank Commerce Complex, Toronto, Canada; Architect, Overseas Chinese Banking Corporate Center, Singapore; Architect, Dreyfus Chemistry Building, Massachusetts Institute of Technology; Architect, East-West Center University Hawaii, Honolulu, HI; Architect, Mellon Art Center and Choate Rosemary Hall Science Center, Wallingford, CT; Architect, University Plaza, New York University; Architect, Johnson Museum Art Cornell University, Ithaca, NY; Architect, Washington Square East, Philadelphia, PA; Architect, Everson Museum Art, Syracuse, NY; Architect, National Gallery Art, East Building, Washington, DC; Architect, Wilmington Tower, Raffles City, Singapore; Architect, West Wing Museum of Fine Arts, Boston, MA; Architect, Expansion and Modernization, Louvre Museum, Paris, France; Architect, Expansion and Modernization, Morton H. Meyerson Symphony Center, Dallas, TX; Architect, Expansion and Modernization, Massachusetts Institute of Technology Arts and Media Center; Architect, Expansion and Modernization, Jacob K. Javits Convention Center, New York, NY; Architect, Expansion and Modernization, Fragrant Hill Hotel, Beijing, China; Architect, Expansion and Modernization, Texas Commerce Tower, Houston, TX; Architect, Expansion and Modernization, Bank of China, Hong Kong; Architect, Expansion and Modernization, Creative Artists Agency, Beverly Hills, CA; Architect, Expansion and Modernization, Guggenheim Pavilion; Architect, Expansion and Modernization, Mount Sinai Medical Center, New York, NY; Architect, Expansion and Modernization, Rock n' Roll Hall of Fame and Museum, Cleveland, OH; Architect, Expansion and Modernization, Museum of Modern Art, Athens, Greece; Architect, Expansion and Modernization, Miho Museum of Art, Shiga, Japan; Architect, Expansion and Modernization, Bilbao Estuary Project, Spain; Architect, Expansion and Modernization, Four Seasons Hotel, New York, NY **AW:** Oreint und Okzident Preis, Erwin Wickert Foundation (2006); Legion of Honor, France (2006); Thomas Jefferson Medal for Distinguished Achievement in the Arts, Humanities or Social Sciences, American Philosophical Society (2001); Freedom Medal (1993);

Presidential Medal of Freedom (1992); Excellence 2000 Award (1991); First Award for Excellence, Colbert Foundation (1991); Gold Medal, University of California Los Angeles (1990); Praemium Imperiale, Japan Art Association (1989); National Medal of Art (1988); Medal of French Legion of Honor (1988); Medal of Liberty (1986); Pritzker Architecture Prize (1983); La Grande Medaille D'or L'Académie d'Architecture (1981); Mayor's Award of Honor for Art and Culture, New York, NY (1981); Gold Medal of Honor, National Arts Club (1981); Gold Medal, American Institute of Architects (1979); Gold Medal for Architecture, American Academy of Arts and Letters (1979); Thomas Jefferson Memorial Medal for Architecture (1976); Medal of Honor, New York Chapter, American Institute of Architects (1963); Arnold Brunner Award, American Academy of Arts and Sciences, National Institute of Arts and Letters (1961); Wheelwright Fellow, Harvard University (1951); Traveling Fellowship, Massachusetts Institute of Technology (1940) **MEM:** Chancellor, American Academy and Institute of Arts and Letters (1978-1980); Fellow, American Institute of Architects; American Society of Interior Designers; National Academy of Design; Urban Design Council; Royal Institute of British Architects; American Academy of Arts and Sciences; National Institute of Arts and Letters

PELLETIER, NANCY A., T: Obstetrical and Gynecological Nurse; Educator (Retired) **I:** Medicine & Health Care **DOB:** 06/16/1951 **PB:** St. Louis **SC:** MO/USA **PT:** David Cooper Hill; C. Lorraine Gore **MS:** Married **SPN:** Russell Dean Pelletier (6/16/1972) **CH:** Kyle; Lindsay; Bradley **ED:** AAS Magna Cum Laude, Northern Virginia Community College (1984); Certified in Health Education, University of Maryland (1973); Certified in Practical Nursing, Alexandria Hospital School of Practical Nursing (1971) **CT:** Certified Childbirth Educator (1989); Registered Nurse, VA (1984); Licensed Practical Nurse, VA (1971) **C:** Lead OBGYN Nurse, Kaiser Permanente of Mid-Atlantic Region, Woodbridge, VA (1991-2017); Nurse Post Partum and Float Pool, Alexandria Hospital (1984-1993); Lead Nurse, OBGYN Associates of Northern Virginia, Alexandria (1984-1991); Childbirth Educator, Alexandria Hospital (1978-1993); Licensed Practical Nurse in Post Partum and Intensive Care Nursery, Alexandria Hospital (1977-1984); School Nurse, Teacher, Health Education, Alexandria City Public Schools (1973-1976); Licensed Practical Nurse in Medications, Alexandria Hospital (1972-1973); Licensed Practical Nurse in Pediatrics, Alexandria Hospital (1971-1972) **CR:** Advisor, Vocational Industrial Clubs of America, Washington DC (1974) **CW:** Author, "A Nurse Discusses Your Cesarean Delivery"; Author, "Test Your Pregnancy Knowledge" **AW:** Healthcare Employee/Nurse of Year, Kaiser-Permanente (2003); Meade Johnson Award (1997); Nurse Educator of the Year, Alexandria Hospital (1983); Recipient Nurse of Year, Kaiser Woodbridge **MEM:** Nurses Association of the American College of Obstetrics and Gynecology; American Society for Psychoprophylaxis in Obstetrics; Phi Theta Kappa **MH:** Marquis Lifetime Achievement Award **B/I:** Mrs. Pelletier became involved in her profession because her mother was mentally ill most of her life. In her mother's darkest moments, she wasn't able to function correctly. Mrs. Pelletier would go on to adopt a nurturing type of behavior, as she would also need to take care of herself and be independent. **AV:** Interior Design; Reading; Children's Interests

PELLETIER, PAUL, T: Scottsdale Boxing Club **I:** Other **CN:** Owner **PB:** , **CT:** Athletics and Fitness Association of America (2004) **C:** Owner, Scottsdale Boxing Club (2017-Present); Owner, Personal

Training Studio (2005-2017); Owner, Scottsdale Moving Service; Owner, OG Boxing **CIV:** Sponsor, Youth Boxing Tournaments; Volunteer **MIL:** Naval Amphibious Base Coronado, USS Squall; U.S. Navy **AW:** Best of Scottsdale, Physical Fitness Program (2015, 2016-2018); Spectrum Award (2016); Best Place to Take a Fitness Class, E-Essentials (2015); Best Customer Service **AS:** Mr. Pelletier attributes his success to his people skills. He treats people how he would like to be treated. Every relationship he is in he tries to give more than he takes. **B/I:** Mr. Pelletier became involved in his profession because of a series of fortunate circumstances. **AV:** Spending time with his dogs; Cooking **THT:** Mr. Pelletier states, "I don't lie about anything, you're going to get 100% of the truth all the time."

PELLI, CESAR, T: Architect **I:** Architecture & Construction **DOB:** 10/12/1926 **PB:** San Miguel de Tucuman **SC:** Argentina **PT:** Victor V. Pelli; Teresa S. Pelli **MS:** Married **SPN:** Diana Balmori **CH:** Dennis G.; Rafael A. **ED:** MS in Architecture, University of Illinois (1954); BArch, National University of Tucuman, Cum Laude (1949) **C:** Associate, Pelli Clarke Pelli Architects (Formerly Cesar Pelli & Associates), New Haven, CT (1977-2019); Dean, Yale University School of Architecture, New Haven, CT (1977-1984); Associate, Gruen Associates, Los Angeles, CA (1968-1977); Associate, Daniel, Mann, Johnson & Mendenhall (DMJM) (1964-1968); Associate, Eero Saarinen & Associates (1954-1964) **CW:** Architect, Louis Armstrong International Airport, New Terminal, New Orleans, LA (2018); Architect, Transbay Transit Center, San Francisco, CA (2017); Architect, Indiana University School of Informatics and Luddy Hall, IN (2017); Architect, McKinney & Olive, Mixed-use Development, Dallas, Texas (2016); Architect, Hancher Auditorium, University of Iowa, Iowa City, Iowa (2016); Architect, The Cabin Stack Prefabricated House (2016); Architect, Eccles Theater, Performing Arts Center, Salt Lake City, Utah (2016); Architect, Cameron and Edward Lanphier Center, Choate Rosemary Hall, Wallingford, CT (2015); Architect, Torre Mitikah, Mexico City, Mexico (2014); Architect, Banco Macro Tower, Buenos Aires, Argentina (2013); Architect, Torre Sofia, San Pedro Garza García, Mexico (2013); Architect, The Landmark, Abu Dhabi, United Arab Emirates (2013); Architect, The Theatre School at DePaul University, Chicago, IL (2013); Architect, St. Katharine Drexel Chapel, Xavier University of Louisiana, New Orleans, LA (2012); Architect, Unicredit Tower, Master Plan and Mixed-use Development, Milan, Italy (2012); Architect, Cira Center South, Philadelphia, PA (2012); Architect, Sidra Medical Center, Qatar (2012); Architect, Cajasol Tower, Office Building, Seville, Spain (2012); Architect, Maral Explanada, Mar del Plata, Argentina (2012); Architect, Iberdrola Tower, Office Building, Bilbao, Spain (2011); Author, "Observations for Young Architects" (1999); Editor, Yale Seminars on Architecture (1981-1982); Architect, Pacific Design Center and Expansion, Los Angeles, CA, U.S. Embassy, Tokyo, Japan, The Museum of Modern Art Expansion, New York, NY, World Finance Center and Winter Garden, New York, NY, Cleveland Clinic, Herring Hall, Rice University, Houston, Texas, Carnegie Hall Tower, New York, NY, Boyer Center of Molecular Medicine, Yale University, Bank of America Corporation Center, Charlotte, NC, One Canada Square, London, England, United Kingdom, NTT Corporation Headquarters, Tokyo, Japan, Terminal B/C, Reagan National Airport, Washington, DC, Aronoff Center for the Arts, Cincinnati, Ohio, Petronas Towers, Kuala Lumpur, Malaysia, The Frances Lehman Loeb Art Center, Vassar College, Poughkeepsie, NY, International Finance Center, Hong Kong, National Museum of

Art, Osaka, Japan, Overture Center for the Arts, Madison, WI, Cira Center, Philadelphia, PA, The Solaire, NY, Carnival Center for the Performing Arts, FL, Minneapolis Central Library, Bloomberg Tower, NY, Orange County Performing Arts Center, Costa Mesa, CA, Bank of Oklahoma Center, Tulsa, OK, Connecticut Science Center, Hartford, CT, Torre de Cristal, Madrid, Spain, Torre Libertad, Mexico City, Mexico, South Station Air Rights Development, Boston, MA, Torre Iberdrola, Bilbao, Spain, Paradise Street Development and One Park West, Liverpool, England, United Kingdom, Gran Torre Costanera, Santiago, Chile, Project City Center Hotel and Casino, Las Vegas, NV, Torre Puerto Triana, Seville, Spain, Winnipeg Airport Terminal, National Children's Museum, Washington, DC, Repsol YPF Headquarters, Buenos Aires, Argentina, Transby Terminal and Tower, San Francisco, CA; Architect, Numerous Buildings **AW:** Lynn S. Beedle Lifetime Achievement Award (2008); Design Award, AIA Connecticut (1991, 1996-1999, 2005-2007); American Architecture Award (2006); Urban Land Institute Award for Excellence (2005); Aga Khan Award, Aga Khan Trust for Culture (2004); Design for Transportation Award (2000); NE Design Award (1999, 2000); Honor Award, AIA (1976, 1984, 1986, 2000); USITT Honor Award (1996); AIA Gold Medal, AIA (1995); Bard Award (1992); Named One of the 10 Most Influential Living American Architects, AIA (1991); Firm Award, AIA (1989); Arnold M. Brunner Memorial Prize, National Academy of Design (1978); LEED Gold **MEM:** Fellow, AIA; National Academy of Design; Academician, American Academy of Arts and Letters; Academician, International Academy of Architecture

PELOSI, NANCY PATRICIA, T: Speaker of the House **I:** Government Administration/Government Relations/Government Services **CN:** U.S. House of Representatives **DOB:** 03/26/1940 **PB:** Baltimore **SC:** MD/USA **PT:** Thomas J. D'Alesandro Jr.; Annunciata M. Lombardi D'Alesandro **MS:** Married **SPN:** Paul Pelosi (1963) **CH:** Nancy Corinne; Christine; Jacqueline; Paul; Alexandra **ED:** Honorary LLD, Mount Holyoke College (2018); Honorary LLD, Mills College (2010); AB in Political Science, Trinity College (1962) **C:** Speaker of the House, U.S. House of Representatives (2007-2011, 2019-Present); U.S. House of Representatives from California's 12th Congressional District, U.S. Congress (2013-Present); Chair, U.S. House Democratic Steering and Policy Committee (2003-Present); Minority Leader, U.S. House of Representatives (2003-2007, 2011-2019); U.S. House of Representatives from California's Eighth Congressional District, U.S. Congress (1993-2013); Assistant Minority Leader (Minority Whip), U.S. House of Representatives (2002-2003); U.S. House of Representatives from California's Fifth Congressional District, U.S. Congress (1987-1993); Finance Chairman, Democratic Senatorial Campaign Committee (1987); Committeewoman, Democratic National Committee (1976, 1980, 1984); Chairman, California State Democratic Committee (1981-1983); Chair, Northern California Democratic Party (1977-1981) **CIV:** Board Member, National Organization of Italian American Women; Board Member, National Italian American Foundation **CW:** Co-Author, "Know Your Power: A Message to America's Daughters" (2008) **AW:** Named, World's 100 Most Powerful Women, Forbes Magazine (2019); Foremother Award, National Center for Health Research (2016); Grand Cordon, Order of the Rising Sun (2015); Named, 100 Most Powerful Women, Forbes Magazine (2005-2014); Inductee, National Women's Hall of Fame (2013); Named, 10 Most Powerful Women in Washington, Fortune Magazine (2009-2010); Named, 100 Most Influential People in the World,

TIME Magazine (2007, 2010); Named, 100 Most Powerful Women in DC, Washingtonian Magazine (2009); Named, 50 Most Powerful People in DC, GQ Magazine (2007, 2009); Named, Global Elite, Newsweek Magazine (2008); Named, America's Best Leaders, U.S. News & World Report (2007); Knight Grand Cross, Order of the Merit of the Italian Republic (2007); Special Achievement Award for Public Advocacy, National Italian American Foundation (2007); Barbara Walters' Most Fascinating Person of the Year (2006); Golden Plate Award, Academy Achievement (2006); National Legislative Award, League of United Latin American Citizens (2004); Legacy Award, Cesar E. Chavez Foundation (2003); Alan Cranston Peace Award, Global Security Institute (2003); Congressional Service Award, American Council for Voluntary International Action (1999); Public Service Award, Federation of American Societies for Experimental Biology (1997) **PA:** Democrat **RE:** Roman Catholic

PELTON, JOSEPH NEAL, PHD, T: Executive Board **I:** Sciences **CN:** International Association for the Advancement of Space Safety (IAASS) **DOB:** 10/29/1943 **PB:** Tulsa **SC:** OK/USA **PT:** Irmal Walker Pelton; Flora Elizabeth (Buser) Pelton **MS:** Married **SPN:** Eloise Christine (Eloise C. Janssen) Pelton (09/10/1965) **CH:** Emily Daniele Pelton; Elaine Gabrielle Pelton; Alexander Joseph Pelton **ED:** PhD in International Relations, Georgetown University, Washington, DC (1972); MA in Political Science, New York University, New York (1969); BS in Physics, University of Tulsa, Oklahoma (1965) **C:** Director of Research, Planet Defense LLC (2018-Present); Director, Academic Programs, International Association for the Advancement of Space Safety (IAASS) (2009-Present); Principal, Pelton Consulting International (2008-Present); Professor and Director, Space & Advanced Communications Research Institute, George Washington University, Washington, DC (1998-2007); Vice President of Academic Programs and Dean, International Space University, Illkirch-Graffenstaden, France (1996-1997); Chairman of the Board of Trustees, International Space University, Illkirch-Graffenstaden, France (1993-1996); Professor and Director, Interdisciplinary Telecommunications Program, University of Colorado at Boulder, Boulder, CO (1987-1996); Director, Strategic Policy, Intelsat Global Satellite Organization, Washington, DC (1983-1986); Executive Assistant to Director General, Intelsat Global Satellite Organization, Washington, DC (1974-1983); Manager, Intelsat Affairs, Communications Satellite Corporation, Washington, DC (1969-1973) **CR:** IT Advisory Commission, Arlington County, VA (2008-2017); President, International Space Safety Foundation, Washington, DC (2007-2009); Chairman, Reach to Space Conference, Washington, DC (2007); President, Global Legal Information Network (GLIN) Foundation, Law Library of the Library of Congress, Washington, DC (2005-2007); Board of Directors, Japan-U.S. Science Technology and Space Applications Program (2004-2006); External Review Committee, National Space and Development Agency (NASDA) of Japan (Now JAXA) (2001-2002); Board of Directors, International Information Institute, London, England (1983-1985, 1997-1999); Executive Director, Arthur C. Clarke Foundation (1986-1996); Founding President, Society of Satellite Professionals International, Washington, DC (1983-1985); Managing Director, World Communications Year-USA (1983) **CIV:** Vice President, National, International Space Safety Foundation (2007-Present); Chairman, Local, Information Technology Advisory Commission, Arlington, VA (2006-Present); Board of Directors, National, President, Global Legal Information Network (GLIN) Foundation, Law Library, Library of Congress, Washington, DC (2005-2007)

CW: Editor, Journal of Space Safety Engineering (2017-Present); Editorial Board of Room Space Journal (2017-Present); Editorial Board of Space Policy (1989-Present); Author, "Space 2.0: The Revolution in the Space Industry" (2019); Author, "Preparing for the Next Cyber Revolution" (2019); Author, "Smart Cities for Today and Tomorrow" (2019); Author, "The Oracle of Colombo: How Arthur C. Clarke Revealed the Future" (2015, 2019); Author, "The Farthest Shore: A 21st Century Guide to Space" (2018); Handbook of Cosmic Hazards and Planetary Defense Global Space Governance: An International Study" (2017); Author, "Handbook of Satellite Applications" (2012, 2017); Author, "The New Gold Rush: The Riches of Space Beckon" (2016); Author, "Space Mining and its Regulation" (2016); Author, "New Solutions for Orbital Debris Removal" (2016); Author, "Digital Defense: A Primer in Cyber Security" (2015); Author, "Handbook of Cosmic Hazards and Planetary Defense" (2014); Author, "Launching into Commercial Space" (2013); Author, "Space Debris and Other Threats from Outer Space" (2013); Author, "The Safe City" (2013); Author, "Small Satellites and their Regulation" (2013); Author, "Space Safety Regulations and Standards" (2010); Author, "License to Orbit: The Future of Commercial Space Travel" (2009); Author, "Future Cities" (2009); Author, "Space Exploration and Astronaut Safety" (2006); Author, "Basics of Satellite Communications" (2003, 2006); Author, "Satellite Communications: Global Change Agent" (2005); Author, "e-Sphere" (2000); Author, "Future Talk" (1992); Informatics Editor, Ad Astra, Executive Editor, International Journal of Space Communications (1986-1994); Author, "Global Talk" (1983-1984); Contributor to Scientific American, Science, Space News, Space Safety Magazine, Journal of Space Safety Engineering, Space Policy, and Numerous Other Journals; Author, More Than 50 Books on Space, Satellites and Telecommunications, Futurism, and the Impact of Science and Technology on Society **AW:** Leonardo da Vinci Prize, International Association for the Advancement of Space Safety (2017); Arthur C. Clarke International Achievement Award in the United Kingdom, British Interplanetary Society (2014); Arthur C. Clarke Lifetime Achievement Award (2001); Arthur C. Clarke Award, Government of Sri Lanka (1999); Outstanding Educator Award (1996); Distinguished Alumnus Award, University of Tulsa (1986); Senior Executive Top Productivity Award, INTELSAT (1985); Pulitzer Nomination for "Global Talk" (1982); Literary Award, American Astronaut Society (1982); Author, "Global Talk" (1981); Named Arlington Citizen of the Year, Washington Star, Journal/Newspaper (1977); Global Development Award, Miami Children's Hospital; H. Rex Lee Award for Directing Intelsat's Project Share **MEM:** Associate Fellow, American Institute of Aeronautics and Astronautics (2012-Present); Vice President, Global Legal International Network) (2008-Present); Board of Directors, International Association for the Advancement of Space Safety (2005-Present); Awards Committee, Society of Satellite Profiles (2003-Present); Cosmos Club (1984-1988, 1999-2014); International Academy of Astronautics (2001-2012); Vice President, International Space Safety Foundation (2008); President, Global Legal International Network (2007-2008); Trustee, International Institute of Communications (1987-1990, 1996-1998); Co-Chairman, International Advisory Board, Society of Satellite Profiles (1985-1996); Founding President, Society of Satellite Profiles (1983-1984); American Institute of Aeronautics and Astronautics; World Future Society; International Academy of Astronautics; Cosmos Club **AV:** Traveling; Playing tennis; Stamp collecting/Philately **PA:** Democrat **RE:** Unitarian

PEMBERTON, CHARLES EDWARD, BS, MS, T: Chief Executive Officer, Primary Instructor **I:** Business Management/Business Services **CN:** AdventureSwim.com **DOB:** 12/28/1942 **PB:** Covington **SC:** KY/USA **PT:** Charles Edward Pemberton; Marjorie Evelyn (Smallwood) Pemberton **MS:** Single **SPN:** Nancy Young (08/13/1977-1982); Cassandra Marie Underhill (04/03/1965-1970) **CH:** Charles Edward (Deceased); Jonathan Robert **ED:** Doctoral Coursework in Human Anatomy and Mechanical Aspects of Motion, University of Iowa (1970); MS in Physical Education, University of Kentucky (1969); BS in Mathematics and Physical Education, Eastern Kentucky University (1965) **CT:** Instructor Course Director, PADI; Adapted Aquatics Water Safety Instructor Trainer, American Red Cross; Water Safety Instructor Trainer, American Red Cross; Private Pilot, FAA **C:** President and Chief Executive Officer, Pemberton & Associates Inc. (1984-Present); Consultant, Teacher, Knoxville Pediatric Associates, Knoxville, TN (1981-Present); Health Teacher, Farragut Middle School, Knoxville, TN (1992-2005); Aquatics Teacher, Clinton City School District, Clinton, TN (1978-1985); Industrial Graphics, Minneapolis, MN (1972-1979); Director, Hydro Help-Handicapped Swim Program, The University of Tennessee, Knoxville (1977-1978); District Manager of Industrial Graphics, 3M, Bloomington, IL (1976-1977); Advertising Manager, District Director, Dacor, Inc., Chicago, IL (1969-1972, 1973-1976); Aquatics Director, UNC Charlotte (1970-1973); Health Teacher, Alice Lloyd College, Pippa Passes, KY (1967-1968); Mathematics Teacher, Conner Middle School, Hebron, KY (1965); Chief Executive Officer, Primary Instructor, AdventureSwim.com, Knoxville, TN **CIV:** Council Member, Assistant Training Instructor, Camp Buck Toms, Boy Scouts of America **MIL:** First Lieutenant, First Infantry Division, U.S. Army (1965-1967) **CW:** Contributor, Articles, Professional Journals **AW:** National Outstanding Swim Teacher (1990-1992); Outstanding National Swim Instructor; Bronze Star, U.S. Army; Army Commendation Medal, U.S. Army **MEM:** Aquatics Chairman, TAHPERD (1980-1982); Master Instructor, Course Director, Tennessee District Director, PADI; National Swim School Association, Inc.; Undersea & Hyperbaric Medical Society **MH:** Albert Nelson Marquis Lifetime Achievement Award **B/I:** Mr. Pemberton became involved in his profession because he taught himself to swim at a young age and started teaching swimming at the age of 12. Swimming is Mr. Pemberton's passion. In college, he pursued health, physical education, and recreation - an extension of his great love for swimming. While he did not have a professional swim career, Mr. Pemberton is proud of having swum competitively in high school, during which time he won several medals. While studying at Eastern Kentucky University, he swam and taught university students on a part-time basis. Mr. Pemberton has used his love for swimming to work with children and adults of all ages and abilities, including handicapped swimmers. **PA:** Republican **RE:** Baptist

PENCE, GREGORY, "GREG" JOSEPH, T: U.S. Representative from Indiana **I:** Government Administration/Government Relations/Government Services **CN:** U.S. House of Representatives **DOB:** 11/14/1956 **PB:** Columbus **SC:** IN/USA **PT:** Ed Pence; Nancy Pence **MS:** Married **SPN:** Denise Pence **CH:** Nicole; Lauren; Emily; John **ED:** Master of Business Administration, Loyola University Chicago Quinlan School of Business (1983); Bachelor of Arts in Theology and Philosophy, Loyola University Chicago **C:** Member, U.S. House of Representatives from Indiana's Sixth Congressional District (2019-Present); Finance Chairperson, U.S. House Representative Luke Messer Campaign (2018); President, Kiel Brothers Oil Company (1998-2004); Owner, Antique Malls, IN **CR:** Board of Directors, Home Federal Bancorp; Board of Directors, Home Federal Savings Bank **MIL:** Advanced through Grades to Lieutenant, United States Marine Corps (1979-1984) **PA:** Republican

PENCE, MICHAEL, "MIKE" RICHARD, T: Vice President of the United States **I:** Government Administration/Government Relations/Government Services **DOB:** 07/07/1959 **PB:** Columbus **SC:** IN/USA **PT:** Edward Joseph Pence Jr.; Nancy Jane (Cawley) Pence **MS:** Married **SPN:** Karen Pence (06/08/1985) **CH:** Michael; Charlotte; Audrey **ED:** JD, Indiana University Robert H. McKinney School of Law (1986); BA in History, Hanover College (1981) **C:** Vice President of the United States (2017-Present); Governor, State of Indiana, Indianapolis, IN (2013-2016); Member, U.S. House Committee on Foreign Affairs Committee (2007-2013); Member, U.S. House of Representatives from Indiana's Sixth Congressional District (2003-2013); Chairman, U.S. House Republican Conference (2009-2011); Chairman, U.S. House Republican Study Committee (2005-2007); Member, U.S. House of Representatives from Indiana's Second Congressional District (2001-2003); President, Indiana Policy Review Foundation (1991); Attorney (1986-1991); Admissions Counselor, Hanover College (1981-1983) **CR:** Candidate, Republican Party Nominee for Vice President of the United States (2016) **CIV:** State Policy Network (1991-1993) **CW:** Host, Television Show, "The Mike Pence Show," WNDY, Indianapolis, IN (1995-1999); Host, Radio Show, "The Mike Pence Show," WRCR-FM, Rushville, IN (1992-1999); Host, Radio Show, "Washington Update with Mike Pence," WRCR-FM, Rushville, IN (1988) **MEM:** Phi Gamma Delta **PA:** Republican

PENN, SEAN, T: Actor, Director **I:** Media & Entertainment **DOB:** 08/17/1960 **PB:** Santa Monica **SC:** CA/USA **PT:** Leo Penn; Eileen (Ryan) Penn **MS:** Divorced **SPN:** Robin Wright (04/27/1996, Divorced 2010); Madonna Louise Ciccone (08/16/1985, Divorced 1989) **CH:** Dylan Frances; Hopper Jack **C:** Founder, CORE (Formerly J/P Haitian Relief Organization) (2010) **CIV:** Aided Hurricane Katrina Victims (2005); Special Guest, PDA - Progressive Democrats of America; Advocate, Numerous Political and Social Causes **CW:** Guest Appearance, "Curb Your Enthusiasm" (2020); Actor, "The Professor and the Madman" (2019); Actor, "The First" (2018); Actor, Short Film, "Sound of Sun" (2016); Voice Actor, "Family Guy" (2016); Voice Actor, "The Angry Birds Movie" (2016); Director, "The Last Face" (2016); Co-director, Music Video, ""I Forgive It All," Mudcrutch (2016); Actor, "The Gunman" (2015); Guest Appearance, Music Video, "On the Run," Jay-Z Featuring Beyoncé (2014); Actor, "The Secret Life of Walter Mitty" (2013); Actor, "Gangster Squad" (2013); Actor, Short, "Americans" (2012); Actor, "This Must Be the Place" (2011); Actor, "The Tree of Life" (2011); Guest Appearance, "I'm Still Here" (2010); Actor, "Fair Game" (2010); Actor, "Milk" (2008); Guest Appearance, "What Just Happened" (2008); Narrator, Documentary, "Witch Hunt" (2008); Director, Screenwriter, "Into the Wild" (2007); Voice Actor, "Persepolis" (2007); Narrator, Documentary, "War Made Easy" (2007); Actor, "All the King's Men" (2006); Actor, "The Interpreter" (2005); Guest Appearance, "Two and a Half Men" (2004); Actor, "The Assassination of Richard Nixon" (2004); Actor, "21 Grams" (2003); Actor, "Mystic River" (2003); Guest Appearance, "Pauly Shore Is Dead" (2003); Actor, "It's All About Love" (2003); Director, Music Video, "The Barry Williams Show," Peter Gabriel (2002); Director, Segment, "September 11" (2002); Director, "The Pledge" (2001); Actor, "I Am Sam" (2001); Narrator, Documentary, "Dogtown and Z-Boys" (2001); Actor, "Friends" (2001); Actor, "The Weight of Water" (2000); Actor, "Before Night Falls" (2000); Appearance, Documentary, "A Constant Forge" (2000); Actor, "Up at the Villa" (2000); Actor, "Sweet and Lowdown" (1999); Guest Appearance, "Being John Malkovich" (1999); Actor, "The Thin Red Line" (1998); Actor, "Hurlyburly" (1998); Guest Appearance, "The Larry Sanders Show" (1998); Actor, "Hugo Pool" (1997); Guest Appearance, "Ellen" (1997); Actor, "The Game" (1997); Actor, "U Turn" (1997); Actor, "She's So Lovely" (1997); Actor, "Loved" (1997); Director, Music Video, "You Were Meant for Me," Jewel (1996); Actor, Screenwriter, Director, "The Crossing Guard" (1995); Actor, "Dead Man Walking" (1995); Actor, "Carlito's Way" (1993); Director, Music Video, "Dance with the One That Brought You," Shania Twain (1993); Appearance, Documentary, "The Last Party" (1993); Director, Music Video, "North Dakota," Lyle Lovett (1992); Actor, Short, "Cruise Control" (1992); Director, Screenwriter, "The Indian Runner" (1991); Actor, "State of Grace" (1990); Actor, "Cool Blue" (1990); Actor, "We're No Angels" (1989); Actor, "Casualties of War" (1989); Actor, "Judgement in Berlin" (1988); Actor, "Colors" (1988); Narrator, Documentary, "Dear America: Letters Home from Vietnam" (1987); Actor, "Shanghai Surprise" (1986); Actor, "At Close Range" (1986); Actor, "The Falcon and the Snowman" (1985); Actor, "Racing with the Moon" (1984); Actor, "Crackers" (1984); Actor, "Risky Business" (1983); Actor, "Summerspell" (1983); Actor, "Bad Boys" (1983); Actor, Theater, "Slab Boys" (1983); Actor, "Fast Times at Ridgemont High" (1982); Director, Music Video, "Highway Patrolman," Bruce Springsteen (1982); Actor, Theater, "Heartland" (1981); Actor, "The Beaver Kid 2" (1981); Actor, "The Killing of Randy Webster" (1981); Actor, "Hellinger's Law" (1981); Actor, "Barnaby Jones" (1979); Actor, "Little House on the Prairie" (1975, 1974); Executive Producer, Producer, Numerous Films and Documentaries **AW:** Peace Summit Award, World Summit of Nobel Peace Laureates (2012); International Humanitarian Service Award, The American Red Cross (2012); Named Ambassador-at-Large to Haiti, Haiti's Ministry Foreign & Religious Affairs (2012); Stanley Kramer Award, Producers Guild of America (2011); Named One of the 100 Agents of Change, Rolling Stone Magazine (2009); Desert Palm Achievement Award, Palm Springs International Film Society (2009); Academy Award for Best Performance by an Actor in a Leading Role, "Milk," Academy of Motion Picture Arts & Sciences (2009); Christopher Reeve First Amendment Award, The Creative Coalition (2006); Academy Award for Best Actor in a Leading Role, "Mystic River," Academy of Motion Picture Arts & Sciences (2004); Golden Globe Award for Best Performance by an Actor in a Motion Picture - Drama, "Mystic River," Hollywood Foreign Press Association; (2004); John Steinbeck Award, San Francisco Chronicle (2004)

PÉPIN, JACQUES, T: Chef, Television Personality **I:** Food & Restaurant Services **DOB:** 12/18/1935 **SC:** Bourg-en-Bresse/France **PT:** Jean-Victor Pépin; Jeannette Pépin **MS:** Married **SPN:** Gloria **CH:** Claudine **ED:** Honorary LHD, Columbia University (2017); Honorary LHD, Boston University (2011); MA, Columbia University (1972); BA, Columbia University (1970) **C:** Chef, The French Culinary Institute (1990-Present) **CR:** Executive Culinary Director, Honorary Commodore, Oceania Cruises (2010); Chef, Hôtel Plaza Athénée, Le Pavillon, Howard Johnson's, La Potagerie **CW:** Host, "Jacques Pepin: Heart & Soul" (2015-2016); Author, "Jacques Pépin: Heart & Soul in the Kitchen" (2015); Author, "New Complete Techniques" (2012); Author, "Essential Pepin"

(2011); Author, "More Fast Food My Way" (2008); Co-Author, "Chez Jacques: Traditions and Rituals of a Cook" (2007); Host, "The Complete Pépin" (1997, 2007); Author, "Fast Food My Way" (2004); Author, "The Apprentice: My Life in the Kitchen" (2003); Author, "Jacques Pépin Celebrates" (2001); Co-Author, "Julia and Jacques: Cooking at Home" (1999); Author, "Jacques Pépin's Kitchen: Encore with Claudine" (1998); Co-Author, "The French Culinary Institute's Salute to Healthy Cooking" (1998); Author, "Jacques Pépin's Kitchen: Cooking with Claudine" (1996); Author, "Jacques Pepin's Simple and Healthy Cooking" (1994); Author, "Today's Gourmet II" (1992); Author, "Cuisine Economique" (1992); Author, "Today's Gourmet" (1991); Author, "Short-Cut Cook" (1990); Author, "The Art of Cooking, Vol 2" (1988); Author, "The Art of Cooking, Vol 1" (1988); Author, "Everyday Cooking With Jacques Pepin" (1982); Author, "La Methode" (1979); Author, "La Technique" (1976); Author, "Jacques Pépin: A French Chef Cooks at Home" (1975); Author, "The Other Half of the Egg" (1967); Host, "Fast Food My Way," "More Fast Food My Way" AW: Inaugural Tribute Dinner, New York Food and Wine Festival (2011); Legion d'Honneur (2004); L'Ordre des Arts et des Lettres (1997); L'Ordre du Mérite Agricole (1992); 24 James Beard Foundation Awards; Co-Recipient, Daytime Emmy Award

PERA, ROBERT J., T: Communications Company Executive, Professional Sports Team Owner **I:** Athletics **DOB:** 03/10/1978 **SC:** USA **ED:** MS in Electrical Engineering, University of California San Diego; BS in Electrical Engineering, University of California San Diego; BA in Japanese Language, University of California San Diego; Coursework, Japanese Language Institute, Tokyo, Japan **C:** Owner, Memphis Grizzlies, National Basketball Association (NBA) (2012-Present); Founder, Chief Executive Officer, Ubiquiti Networks, Inc. (2005-Present); Hardware Engineer, Apple, Inc. (2003-2005) **CIV:** Supporter, Grizzlies Foundation **AW:** Listed, "10 Youngest Billionaires in the World," Forbes (2014); Named One of "America's 20 Most Powerful CEOs 40 and Under," Forbes (2012) **MEM:** Phi Beta Kappa

PERDUE, DAVID ALFRED JR., T: U.S. Senator from Georgia; Management Consultant **I:** Government Administration/Government Relations/Government Services **DOB:** 12/10/1949 **PB:** Macon **SC:** GA/USA **PT:** David A. Perdue; Gervaise (Wynn) Perdue **MS:** Married **SPN:** Bonnie (Dunn) Perdue (08/26/1972) **CH:** David Alfred III; Blake R. **ED:** MS in Operations Research, Georgia Institute of Technology (1975); BS in Industrial Engineering, Georgia Institute of Technology (1972) **CT:** Registered Securities Principal; Certified Financial Planner; Certified Management Consultant **C:** U.S. Senator, State of Georgia (2015-Present); Member, U.S. Senate Special Committee on Aging (2015-Present); Member, U.S. Senate Judiciary Committee (2015-Present); Member, U.S. Senate Committee on Foreign Relations (2015-Present); Member, U.S. Senate Budget Committee (2015-Present); Member, U.S. Senate Committee on Agricultural Nutrition and Forestry (2015-Present); Partner, Perdue Partners, LLC, Atlanta, GA (2011-2015); Senior Consultant, Gujarat Heavy Chemicals Lt (GHCL Limited), New Delhi, India (2007-2011); Chairman, Chief Executive Officer, Dollar General Corporation, Nashville, TN (2003-2007); Chairman, Chief Executive Officer, Pillowtex Corporation, Kannapolis, NC (2002-2003); President, Chief Executive Officer, Reebok Brand, Reebok International Ltd. (2001-2002); Executive Vice President, Global Supply Chain, Reebok International Ltd. (2001-2002); Executive Vice President, Global Operations Units, Reebok International Ltd. (1999-

2001); Senior Vice President Global Supply Chain, Reebok International Ltd. (1998-1999); Senior Vice President, Haggar Inc. (1994-1998); Senior Vice President, Operations, Sara Lee Corporation, Hong Kong, China (1992-1994); President, Westar Holding Company (1987-1992); Vice President, Paul R. Ray & Company (1986-1987); Vice President, Professional Planning Associates (1983-1986); Partner, Kurt Salmon Associates (1976-1983); Staff Consultant, Kurt Salmon Associates (1972-1975) **CR:** Board of Directors, Alliant Energy Corp. (2001-Present); Board of Directors, BRG Sports Inc. (2011-2014); Board of Directors, Cardlytics, Inc. (2010-2014); Board of Directors, Liquidity Services, Inc. (2009-2014); Board of Directors, Jo-Ann Stores, LLC (2008-2011); Board of Directors, Dollar General Corporation (2003-2007) **CIV:** Atlanta Care Advisory Board (1983-1985); Georgia Council on Youth, Atlanta, GA (1972) **MEM:** Mortgage Bankers Association; Institute Certified Financial Planners; Institute of Management Consultants USA; Atlanta Athletic Club **AV:** Playing tennis and golf; Sailing; Reading **PA:** Republican **RE:** Baptist

PERDUE, SONNY III, T: United States Secretary of Agriculture **I:** Government Administration/ Government Relations/Government Services **DOB:** 12/20/1946 **PB:** Perry **SC:** GA/USA **PT:** Ervin Perdue; Ophie Perdue **MS:** Married **SPN:** Mary Ruff (1972) **CH:** Leigh; Lara; Jim; Dan **ED:** DVM, University of Georgia College of Veterinary Medicine (1971) **C:** United States Secretary of Agriculture, United States Department of Agriculture, Washington, DC (2017-Present); Governor, State of Georgia, Atlanta, GA (2003-2011); President Pro Tempore, Georgia General Assembly (1997); Member, District 18, Georgia General Assembly, Atlanta, GA (1990-2002); Co-chair, Joint Committee on Legislative Information Management, Georgia General Assembly; Chairman, Higher Education Committee, Defense Conversion Committee, Georgia General Assembly; Majority Leader, Georgia General Assembly; Member, Houston County Planning & Zoning Board; Former Veterinarian **MIL:** Captain, United States Air Force, Vietnam (1971-1974) **MEM:** Beta-Lambda Chapter, Kappa Sigma Fraternity **AV:** Fishing; Flying **PA:** Republican **RE:** Baptist

PEREDNEY, CHRISTINE, T: Social Worker, Educator, Community Volunteer **I:** Social Work **DOB:** 09/12/1944 **PB:** Athens **SC:** GA/USA **PT:** James Henry; Dorothy Elizabeth (Isbell) Booth **MS:** Widow **SPN:** Michael Stanley James Peredney, (01/24/1970, Deceased 09/30/2017) **CH:** Christopher Lee **ED:** Certificate, Georgia State University (1979); MS, University of Georgia (1971); Postgraduate, LaSalle Extention University (1971); Student, US Air Force Administrative School (1969); BS, University of Georgia (1966) **CT:** Certified, Elementary Teacher, GA; Administrator, Gifted Education Teacher, GA; Department of Children-Family Services-Food Stamps, TANF, PEACH **C:** PEACH Case Manager, Gwinnett Co. Family and Children Services (2000-2002); PEACH Case Manager, DeKalb County Family and Children Services (1994-2000); Principal Caseworker, Walton County Family and Child Service, Monroe, GA (1992-1994); Senior Caseworker, Walton County Family and Child Service, Monroe, GA (1987-1991); Teacher, Gwinnett Board Education, Lawrenceville, GA (1976-1986); Preschool Teacher, Playcare at Tucker (1972-1974); Teacher, Dekalb Board Education, Decatur, GA (1967-1968); Psychometrist, University of Georgia Guidance Center, Athens, GA (1966-1967) **CR:** Agency Representative, Georgia County Welfare Association, Monroe, GA (1988-1990); Teacher Advisory Committee, Gwinnett Board Education (1982, 1983, 1985); School Coordinator, Tapestry Art Festival (1984-1986); Speaker in the Field

CIV: Children's Choir Director (2002-Present); Choir Leader, Smoke Rise Baptist Church, Stone Mountain, GA (1990-Present); International Outreach Chairman (2015-2017); Children's Sunday School Teacher (2002-2017); President, Lilburn Woman's Club (2003); President, Sunday School (1992-1993); Choir, Section Leader (1992-1993); Chairman, Lilburn Daze Costumes and Youth Volunteers (1986); Honors Program Committee, University of Georgia (1982-1983) **MIL:** Administrative Officer, United States Air Force (1968-1970) **AW:** Lilburn Woman's Club Lifetime Achievement Award, 2012 **MEM:** Lilburn Woman's Club (Club Woman of Year, 1988-2004, Secretary, 1989-1990, Education Chairman, 1984-1986, Chairman Conservation, 1990-1991, Co-Chairman, Home Life Department, 1995); Alpha Delta Kappa; Phi Beta Kappa; Phi Kappa Phi **MH:** Albert Nelson Marquis Lifetime Achievement Award **B/I:** Ms. Peredney initially pursued teaching because her mother was a teacher and her aunts were teachers. In the 60s there were not many opportunities, as the options were teaching, clerical and the Air Force. When she returned the Air Force, she went back to teaching but wanted more. Essentially, she decided to pursue a career in social work. **AV:** Sewing; Photography; Gardening; Interior Decorating; Shopping; Walking; Traveling **PA:** Democrat **RE:** Baptist

PEREIRA, ARMANDO M., T: Principal, Designer **I:** Architecture & Construction **CN:** CDBS Comprehensive Design/Build Services **MS:** Married **SPN:** Elizabeth Ferrera **CH:** Victoria Ana Dumas **ED:** Bachelor of Science in Architectural Preservation, Roger Williams University (1989) **C:** Principal, Designer, CDBS Comprehensive Design/Build Services (1992-Present) **CR:** Educator, Owner, Integrated Houserights LLC **MEM:** American Institute of Architects; Prince Henry Society, New Bedford Chapter; Knights of Columbus; Pico, Holy Ghost Organization; American Institute of Building Designers **B/I:** Mr. Pereira was attracted to his industry because of its structure and due to his acknowledgement of the need for human habitation, as well as the need for creativity in lodging.

PERETZ, DAVID, MD, T: Staff Member **I:** Media & Entertainment **CN:** Columbia University Center for Psychoanalytic Training and Research **DOB:** 09/17/1933 **PB:** New York **SC:** NY/USA **PT:** Bernard Louis Peretz; Rose (Schiff) Peretz **MS:** Married **SPN:** Eileen Peretz **CH:** Deborah Peretz; Adam Peretz **ED:** Psychiatric Resident, Presbyterian Hospital, New York State Psychiatric Institute, Columbia University (1960-1963); BA, The City College of New York (1954); Intern, Montefiore Hospital (Montefiore Medical Center (1959-1960); MD, New York University (1959); MA, Columbia University (1955) **CT:** Certified in Psychoanalytic Medicine, Columbia University (1967); Certified in Medicine, State of New York; Board Certified, Psychiatry **C:** Staff Member, Psychoanalytic Center for Training and Research, Columbia University, New York, NY (1968-Present); Private Practice (1963-Present); Faculty, Department of Psychiatry, Columbia University (1963-2017); Lecturer, Psychology and Philosophy, Hunter College, New York, NY (1960-1963) **CR:** Consultant in Field **CW:** Editor-in-chief, Advances in Thanatology (1979-1987); Editor, 15 Books; Author, Articles on Loss, Grief, Death, Dying, Bereavement; Author, "The Mosel Legacy"; Author, "The Broderick Curse"; Author, "Vengeance Out of the Shadows"; Author, "Sex and Murder in Paris"; Author, Screenplay, "The Auction House"; Author, Screenplay, "One for All"; Member, Various Editorial Boards **AW:** Rose Gullo Humanitarian Award, American Institute of Life Threatening Illness and Loss (1992); Herman Wortis Neuropsychiatric Prize for Excellence in Psychiatry,

Neurology and Medicine, New York University Grossman School of Medicine (1959); Fellow in Behavioral Science, Ford Foundation (1955) **MEM:** Founder, Chairman, Board of Advisors, American Institute of Life Threatening Illness and Loss (1995); Fellow, American Psychiatric Association; American Academy of Psychoanalysis (Now The American Academy of Psychodynamic Psychiatry and Psychoanalysis); Founding Member, Foundation of Thanatology; The Phi Beta Kappa Society; Alpha Omega Alpha Honor Medical Society **MH:** Albert Nelson Marquis Lifetime Achievement Award **B/I:** Dr. Peretz has always known that he wanted to be a physician. Dr. Peretz became a novelist after writing his first book at 17-years-old. **AV:** Creative Writing; Travel; Theater; Exercise

PEREZ, JORGE LUIS, T: Manufacturing Executive **I:** Manufacturing **DOB:** 11/29/1945 **PB:** Jaguey Grande **SC:** Cuba **PT:** Adalberto Aquileo Perez; Esther Mireya (Haedo) Perez **CH:** Jorge Alejandro; Ricardo Javier; Ruben Luis **ED:** MBA, Drexel University (1981); BS in Commerce & Engineering Science, Drexel University (1969) **C:** Program Manager, IBM, Boca Raton, FL (1988-1992); Project Manager, IBM, Boca Raton, FL (1986-1988); Manager, Production Control, IBM, Boca Raton, FL (1983-1985); Finance Program Administrator, IBM, Franklin Lakes, NJ (1980-1982); Operations Research Analyst, IBM, Princeton, NJ (1977-1980); Staff Industrial Engineer, IBM, East Fishkill, NY (1976-1977); Senior Associate Industrial Engineer, IBM, East Fishkill, NY (1972-1975); Associate Industrial Engineer, IBM, East Fishkill, NY (1970-1971); Junior Industrial Engineer, IBM, East Fishkill, NY (1969-1970); Former Owner, Wee Bee Tots; Former Owner, Little Learners; Former Owner, Small World Preschools; Former Owner, Academy for Child Enrichment; Former Owner, Noah's Ark Academy **CR:** Consultant, Eclipse Group; Sponsor, Child Care Food Program of Florida **CIV:** Chair, Board of Directors, Transitions Elementary Charter School (2013); Executive Committee, Palm Beach County Republican Party (1989); President, Board of Directors, Palm Beach Farm Workers Council (1989) **CW:** Author, "Machine Tooling"; Author, "Transportation Forecasting"; Author, "Workload Planning"; Author, "Measurement" **AW:** Excellence Award, Institute of Industrial Engineers (1975) **MEM:** Board Member, Florida Association of Child Care Management (2010-2015); President, Palm Beach County Child Care Director's Association (2010); Vice President, Membership Committee, American Production and Inventory Control Society (1984-1985); President, Institute Industrial Engineers (1974-1975); American Production and Inventory Control Society; Senior Member, Institute Industrial Engineers **MH:** Albert Nelson Marquis Lifetime Achievement Award **AV:** Boating; Fishing; Reading; Watching movies **PA:** Republican **RE:** Roman Catholic

PEREZ, THOMAS EDWARD, T: Chairman **I:** Government Administration/Government Relations/Government Services **CN:** Democratic National Committee **DOB:** 10/07/1961 **PB:** Buffalo **SC:** NY/USA **PT:** Dr. Rafael Antonio de Jesus Perez Lara; Grace (Altagracia Brache Bernard) Perez **MS:** Married **SPN:** Ann Marie Staudenmaier **CH:** Amalia; Susana; Rafael **ED:** Honorary HHD, Oberlin College (2014); Honorary LLD, Drexel University School of Law (2014); Honorary LLD, Brown University (2014); MPP, Harvard Kennedy School, John F. Kennedy School of Government (1987); JD, Harvard Law School, Cum Laude (1987); AB in International Relations and Political Science, Brown University (1983) **C:** Chair, Democratic National Committee (2017-Present); Secretary, U.S. Department of Labor, Washington, DC (2013-

2017); Assistant Attorney General, Civil Rights Division, U.S. Department of Justice, Washington, DC (2009-2013); Secretary, Department of Labor, Licensing and Regulation (DLLR), State of Maryland, Annapolis, MD (2007-2009); Assistant Professor, Director of Clinical Law Office, University of Maryland School of Law, Baltimore, MD (2001-2007); Director, Office of Civil Rights (OCR), U.S. Department of Health and Human Services (1999-2002); Deputy Assistant Attorney for Civil Rights, U.S. Department of Justice (1998-1999); Special Counsel to Senator Edward M. Kennedy, U.S. Senate (1995-1998); Deputy Chief, Criminal Section, Civil Rights Division, U.S. Department of Justice (1994-1997); Trial Lawyer, Criminal Section, Civil Rights Division, U.S. Department of Justice (1989-1994); Law Clerk to Honorable Zita L. Weinshienk, United States District Court for the District of Colorado (1987-1989); Law Clerk, Attorney General Edwin Meese (1986) **CR:** Consultant, Vera Institute of Justice, New York, NY (1997-1999); Teacher, Stanford University, WA (1994-1996); Part-time Faculty Member, The George Washington University Milken Institute School of Public Health **CIV:** Member, Montgomery County Council (2002-2006); President, Montgomery County Council (2005) **MEM:** Board of Directors, Hispanic National Bar Association **BAR:** The District of Columbia (1998); State of New York (1988) **PA:** Democrat

PERKIN, RONALD MURRAY, T: Pediatrician, Educator **I:** Medicine & Health Care **DOB:** 07/31/1948 **PB:** Denver **SC:** CO/USA **PT:** Robert Murray Perkin; Marion Kathryn (Thompson) Perkin **MS:** Married **SPN:** Susan Renee Sheer **CH:** Matthew Murray; Jeffrey Jay; Nickolas James; Thomas Mitchell; Benjamin Sheer; Savannah Paige **ED:** MA, Loma Linda University (1997); MD, University of South Florida (1976); Postgraduate Coursework, Johns Hopkins University (1970-1971); BS in Engineering, University of Colorado (1970) **CT:** Diplomate, American Board of Pediatrics **C:** Research Professor, Department of Pediatrics, Brody School of Medicine at East Carolina (2015-Present); Professor, Chair Emerita, Pediatrics, Brody School of Medicine at East Carolina University (2015-Present); Attending Physician, Vidant Sleep Center, Greenville, NC (2001-Present); Adjunct Professor, Department of Bioethics and Interdisciplinary Studies, Brody School of Medicine, East Carolina University (2011-2015); Professor, Chairman, Department of Pediatrics. Brody School Medicine, East Carolina University, Greenville, NC (2000-2015); Attending Physician, PICU (2000-2012); Professor, Pediatrics, Loma Linda University (1990-2000); Director of Pediatrics, Critical Care Division, Loma Linda University Children's Hospital (1988-2000); Associate Professor, Pediatrics, Loma Linda University (1988-1990); Attending Physician, Newborn ICU, St. Joseph's Hospital (1984-1988); Director, Pediatric ICU, Children's Hospital (1984-1988); Co-Director, Pediatric Intensive Care, University of California School Medicine, San Diego, CA (1982-1984); Assistant Adjunct Professor, Pediatrics, University of California School of Medicine, San Diego, CA (1982-1984); Clinical Assistant Professor, Pediatrics, University of Texas Health Science Center, Southwestern Medical School, Dallas, TX (1981); Assistant Director of Pediatric Intensive Care, Children's Medical Center, Dallas, TX (1981); Fellow in Pediatric Intensive Care, Children's Medical Center, Dallas, TX (1979-1981); Resident in Pediatrics, Children's Medical Center, Dallas, TX (1976-1979) **CR:** James And Connie Maynard Professor of Pediatrics (2011-2015); Board Member, North Carolina Respiratory Care (2010-2014); Associate Chair, Department of Pediatrics, Loma Linda University School of Medicine (1993-2000); Emergency Department Committee, Ethics Com-

mittee, Ethics Consultant Service, Critical Care Committee, Resident Evaluation Sub-Communications, Respiratory Care Director of Pediatrics, Loma Linda University Children's Hospital (1990-2000); Assistant Adjunct Professor, Pediatrics, University of California Irvine (1984-1988); Director, Pediatrics Intensive Care Fellowship Program, University California Irvine (1984-1988); Consultant, Naval Hospital, San Diego, CA (1983-1984); Critical Care Committee, Critical Care Council, Extra Corporeal Membrane Oxygenation Foundation **CIV:** Board of Directors, Community Shelter **MIL:** U.S. Navy (1971-1973) **CW:** "The PICU Book" (2012); "Pediatric Emergency Medicine Manual" (2007); "Primer on Pediatric Palliative Care" (2005); "Pediatric Hospital Medicine: A Textbook of Inpatient Care" (2003); Reviewer, Capistrano Press, Ltd. (1982-1984); Co-Editor, "Brain Insults in Infants and Children: Pathophysiology and Management; Emergency Management of the Critically Ill Child"; Contributor, Articles, Professional Journals; Contributor, Chapters, Books **AW:** Listee, Best Doctors (1995-2018); James R. Talton, Jr. Award, East Carolina University (2012); Women Faculty Advocacy Award, Brody School of Medicine (2010); Teaching Excellence Award, Emergency Medicine Residents (1995, 1997, 1998, 1999); Outstanding Physician in the Inland Empire (1998); Clinical Faculty Award of Excellence, Loma Linda University (1989-1990); Faculty Awards, Multiple Institutions (1984-1985); Outstanding Resident Award, Dallas Children's Hospital (1979); Inductee, Alpha Omega Alpha (1976); Student Awards, University South Florida College Medicine **MEM:** California Children Services (1986-2000); Fellow, American Academy Pediatrics; American College of Critical Care Medicine; American Academy of Sleep Medicine; Society of Critical Care Medicine **MH:** Albert Nelson Marquis Lifetime Achievement Award **B/I:** Dr. Perkin's goal was to be an admiral and a pilot in the U.S. Navy. During the Vietnam War, he ended up getting injured, and, while he was recovering, he began to consider medicine as a career path. Dr. Perkin was in the astronaut program as well prior to being injured, and one of his instructors helped him through the difficult times recovering physically and mentally from what he suffered. When he was honorably discharged, he decided to actually pursue medicine, which he did and loved.

PERKINS, EDWARD JOSEPH, PHD, T: U.S. Ambassador (Retired) **I:** Government Administration/Government Relations/Government Services **DOB:** 06/08/1928 **PB:** Sterlington **SC:** LA/USA **MS:** Married **SPN:** Lucy Liu (Deceased 2009) **CH:** Katherine; Sarah **ED:** Honorary Degree, University of Southern California (1995); Honorary Doctor of Humane Letters, Bowie State College (1993); Honorary Degree, St. Augustine College (1991); Honorary Degree, Beloit College (1990); Honorary Doctor of Humane Letters, Winston-Salem State University (1990); Honorary Doctor of Humane Letters, St. John's University (1990); Honorary Doctor of Humane Letters, University of Maryland (1990); Honorary Doctor of Humane Letters, Lewis and Clark College (1988); Coursework in French, Foreign Service Institute (1983); Doctor in Public Administration, University of Southern California (1978); Master of Public Administration, University of Southern California (1972); Bachelor of Arts, University of Maryland University College (1967); Coursework, Lewis and Clark College; Coursework, University of California **C:** U.S. Ambassador to Australia, U.S. Department of State, Canberra, New South Wales, Australia (1993-1996); U.S. Ambassador to U.N., U.S. Department of State, New York, NY (1992-1993); Director General, Director of Personnel, Foreign Service, U.S. Department of State, Washington, DC

(1989-1992); U.S. Ambassador to South Africa, U.S. Department of State (1986-1989); U.S. Ambassador to Liberia, U.S. Department of State (1985-1986); Director, Office of West African Affairs, Bureau of African Affairs, U.S. Department of State (1983-1985); Deputy, Chief of Mission, U.S. Department of State, Monrovia, Liberia (1981-1983); Counselor, Political Affairs, U.S. Department of State, Accra, Ghana (1978-1981); Officer, Management Analysis, Office of Management Operations, U.S. Department of State (1975-1978); Administrative Officer, Bureau of Near Eastern Affairs, U.S. Department of State (1974-1975); Administrative Officer, Bureau of South Asian Affairs, U.S. Department of State (1974-1975); Personnel Officer, Office of the Director General of Foreign Service (1972-1974); Staff Assistant, Office of the Director General of Foreign Service (1972); Assistant Director for Management, United States Operations Mission, Thailand (1970-1972); Management Analyst, United States Agency for International Development (1969-1970); Assistant General Services Officer, Bureau for Asia, United States Agency for International Development (1967-1969); Chief of Personnel and Administration, Army and Air Force Exchange Service, Okinawa, Japan (1964-1966); Deputy Chief, Army and Air Force Exchange Service, Okinawa, Japan (1962-1964); Chief of Personnel, Army and Air Force Exchange Service, Taipei, Taiwan (1958-1962) **CR:** White House Advisory Committee on Trade Policy and Negotiations (2003-Present); Advisory Board, Institute of International Public Policy (1997-Present); Professor and Executive Director, William J. Crowe International Programs Center, University of Oklahoma, Norman, OK (1996-Present); Advisory Council, University Office of International Programs, The Pennsylvania State University (1997) **CIV:** President, Association of Black American Ambassadors (2017-Present); Board of Visitors, National Defense University (2002-Present); Trustee, Woodrow Wilson National Fellowship Foundation (1999-Present); Steering Committee, Center for Australian and New Zealand Studies, Georgetown University (1996-Present); Trustee, Lewis and Clark College (1994-Present); Board of Governors, Joint Center for Political and Economic Studies (1996-2003); Board, Cranlana Programme **CW:** Co-editor, "Mr. Ambassador: Warrior for Peace" (2008); Co-editor, "Democracy, Morality, and the Search for Peace in America's Foreign Policy" (2002); Co-editor, "Middle East Peace Process: Vision Versus Reality" (2002); Co-editor, "Palestinian Refugees: Traditional Positions and New Solutions" (2001); Co-editor, "Preparing American's Foreign Policy for the 21st Century" (1999); Contributor, Articles, Professional Publications **AW:** Award for Outstanding Contribution and Dedication to Foreign Service, Hakka Association in Washington Metropolitan Area (2014); Special Citation Award for a Book of Distinguished Writing on the Practice of American Diplomacy, American Academy of Diplomacy (2006); Director, General's Cup, U.S. Department of State (2001); Honoree, Beta Gamma Sigma, University of Oklahoma (1998); Laurel Wreath Award, Kappa Alpha Psi Fraternity, Inc. (1993); Statesman of the Year Award, The George Washington University (1992); Distinguished Alumni Award, University of Southern California (1991); Achievement Award, Southern University (1991); C. Rodger Wilson Leadership Conference Award (1990); Award for Outstanding Service as Foreign Service Officer, Una Chapman Cox Foundation (1989); Living Legend Award, The Links Inc. (1989); Presidential Distinguished Service Award (1989); Presidential Meritorious Service Award (1987); Outstanding Achievement Award for Foreign Service (1986); Superior Honor Award, U.S. Department of State (1983); Meritorious Honor Award, United States Agency for International Development (1967); International Career Advancement Program Diversity Award; Diplomatic Award, University of Maryland **MEM:** Board of Directors, Association for Diplomatic Studies & Training (1998-Present); Fellow, National Academy of Public Administration; Veterans of Foreign Wars; The American Society for Public Administration; Navy League of the United States; American Political Science Association; Ambassadorial Fellow, Foreign Policy Association; International Studies Association; Council on Foreign Relations; The American Academy of Diplomacy; American Consortium for International Public Administration; American Foreign Service Association; The American Legion; Center for the Study of the Presidency; Chester A. Arthur Society; Public Service Communications; World Affairs Councils Oklahoma; World Affairs Councils, Washington; Pacific Council on International Policy; The Honor Society of Phi Kappa Phi; Kappa Alpha Psi Fraternity Inc. **MH:** Albert Nelson Marquis Lifetime Achievement Award; Marquis Who's Who Top Professional **B/I:** Dr. Perkins became interested in international affairs when several foreign service officers visited his school to discuss their careers, after which he became intrigued by how much diplomacy can affect a country. After graduating from high school, he secured a trial position, during which time he met Vice President Henry Wallace, who encouraged Dr. Perkins to apply for a job as a foreign service officer.

PERKINS, MARIAN E., T: Judge **I:** Law and Legal Services **CN:** Circuit Court of Cook County **MS:** Married **SPN:** Reverend Terrell Phillips **CH:** Four Children **ED:** JD, School of Law, Howard University (1985); BBA in Business Marketing, School of Business, Howard University **C:** Circuit Court Judge of Cook County, Chancery Division/Mortgage Foreclosure Section, IL (2018-Present); Judge of the Circuit Court of Cook County, First Municipal District, Illinois (2017-2018); Attorney, Counselor-at-Law, The Law Offices of Marian E. Perkins, PC (1998-2017); Staff Attorney, Illinois Department of Professional Regulation, Health Related Prosecutions Unit (1996-1998); Assistant State's Attorney, Senior Trial Supervisor, The Cook County State Attorney's Office, Child Support Enforcement Division (1989-1991); Assistant Appellate Defender of Illinois, The Office of the State Appellate Defender, First District, Chicago, IL (1987-1989) **CIV:** Former Board Member, Southside Community Arts Center; Art Institute of Chicago; DuSable Museum of African American History **AW:** Exceptional Service to the Community, Black Women Lawyer's Association of Greater Chicago, Inc. (2017); John C. McMahon Pro Bono Service Award, Illinois State Bar Association; Outstanding Recognition Award, Institute for Social Justice; William R. Meem Jr. Award; Women of Excellence Award **MEM:** Past President, Cook County Bar Association; Judicial Council, American Bar Association; Judicial Council, National Bar Association; Illinois Judges Association; Illinois Judicial Council; National Association of Women Judges; Delta Sigma Theta **AS:** Ms. Perkins attributes her success to the many people who helped her on her journey to success. She was also taught great reading, writing and critical thinking skills. Ms. Perkins lives by the motto, "Try and try again. Don't give up." **B/I:** Ms. Perkins was inspired by the late United States Congresswoman, Barbra Jordan, to seek the fair administration of justice in the court system. She was inspired by those who came before her and laid the foundation.

PERKINS, MATTHEW, T: Chief Executive Officer **I:** Business Management/Business Services **CN:** Service Coordination Unlimited, Inc. **MS:** Married **SPN:** Jessica **CH:** Eric; Ariel; Andrew; Zayne **ED:** MS in Health Science, Slippery Rock University; BS in Health Services Administration, Slippery Rock University (1997) **C:** Chief Executive Officer, Service Coordination Unlimited Incorporated (2013-Present); Program Director, Service Coordination Unlimited Incorporated (2008-2013) **CIV:** Past President, Pennsylvania Provider Coalition Association; Board Member, Pennsylvania Provider Coalition Association **AW:** Community Base Service Award, Community Care Connections; Home and Community Based Services Excellence Award, PA Provider Coalition Association; Community Service Award, DHS Butler County **MEM:** Past President, Pennsylvania Provider Coalition Association **AS:** Mr. Perkins attributes his success to his faith, his dedication to hard work, networking and developing relationships and working collaboratively with others has been a major part of his success as well as his agency's. "Take each day as a new day, and do your best..." **B/I:** When Mr. Perkins was growing up, his parents would take care of elderly people that had disabilities, that weren't able to live by themselves. That inspired him to get into the social service field.

PERLMAN, ITZHAK, T: Violinist **I:** Fine Art **DOB:** 08/31/1945 **PB:** Tel Aviv **SC:** Israel **PT:** Chaim Perlman; Shoshana Perlman **MS:** Married **SPN:** Toby Lynn Friedlander **CH:** Noah; Navah; Miriam; Leora; Ariella **ED:** Degree in Music (Honorary), Tufts University (1986); Degree (Honorary), Hebrew University; Degree (Honorary), Yeshiva University; Degree (Honorary), Roosevelt University; Degree (Honorary), Brandeis University; Degree (Honorary), Yale University; Degree (Honorary), Harvard University; Student, Meadowmount School of Music; Studied with Ivan Galamian & Dorothy DeLay, Juilliard School; Student, Samuel Rubin Israeli Academy of Music Tel Aviv University **C:** Dorothy Richard Starling Foundation Chair in Violin Studies, Juilliard School (2003); Faculty Post, Conservatory of Music, Brooklyn College (1975); Instructor, Perlman Music Program, Long Island, NY; Artistic Director, Principal Conductor, Westchester Philharmonic; Principal Guest Conductor, Detroit Symphony Orchestra **CR:** Founder, Perlman Music Program, New York, NY (1998-Present); Music Adviser, St. Louis Symphony (2002-2004); Principal Guest Conductor, Detroit Symphony (2001-2005); Appeared with Numerous Orchestras, including New York Philharmonic, Cleveland Orchestra, Philadelphia Orchestra, National Symphony Orchestra, Berlin Royal Philharmonic, English Chamber Orchestra, London Symphony, London Philharmonic, Royal Philharmonic, BBC Orchestra, Vienna Philharmonic, Israel Philharmonic; Participant, Numerous Music Festivals, including Ravinia Festival, Tanglewood Music Festival, Aspen Music Festival, Israel Festival, Wolf Trap Summer Festival Participant, Numerous Recital Tours, United States, Canada, South America, Europe, Israel, Australia, Far East; Recorded for Angel, London, RCA Victor, DG, Telarc, Teldec, Sony **CW:** Subject, Documentary, "Itzhak" (2017); Musician, Album, "The Perlman Sound" (2015); Musician, Album, "Violin Sonatas" (2015); Musician, Album, "Eternal Echoes: Songs and Dances for the Soul" (2012); Musician, Album, "The Essential Itzhak Perlman" (2009); Violinist, "Air and Simple Gifts" by John Williams, 2009 Inauguration Ceremony for Barack Obama (2009); Musician, Album, "Dvořák in Prague: A Celebration" (2007); Violin Soloist, Film Score, "Memoirs of a Geisha" (2005); Musician, Album, "Concertos from My Childhood" (1999); Guest Appearance, "Fantasia 2000" (1999); Musician, Album, "Holiday Tradition" (1998); Musician, Album, "The American Album" (1995); Musician, Album (with Oscar Peterson), "Side by Side" (1994); Violin Soloist, Film Score,

"Schindler's List" (1993); Musician, Album, "Vivaldi: The Four Seasons/3 Violin Concertos" (1992); Musician, Album, "Duos" (1987); Musician, Album, "Tradition" (1987); Musician, Album (with Andre Previn), "It's a Breeze" (1981); Musician, Album (with Andre Previn), "A Different Kind of Blues" (1980); Musician, Album (with Andre Previn), "The Easy Winners" (1975); Musician, Numerous Performances and TV Appearances **AW:** Genesis Prize, Prime Minister of Israel (2016); Presidential Medal of Freedom, President Barack Obama (2015); Grammy Lifetime Achievement Award, Grammy Awards (2008); Golden Plate Award of the American Academy of Achievement (2005); Honoree, Kennedy Center Honors (2003); National Medal of Arts, President Bill Clinton (2000); Emmy Award for Outstanding Classical Music-Dance Program, "Itzhak Perlman: Fiddling for the Future" (1999); Emmy Award for Outstanding Cultural Music-Dance Program, "Itzhak Perlman: In the Fiddler's House" (1996); Grammy Award for Best Instrumental Soloist(s) Performanc (with orchestra), "The American Album - Works of Bernstein, Barber, Foss" (1995); Emmy Award for Outstanding Individual Achievement: Cultural Programming (1994); Emmy Award for Outstanding Classical Program in the Performing Arts, "Perlman in Russia" (1992); Grammy Award for Best Instrumental Soloist(s) Performance (with orchestra), "Shostakovich Violin Concerto No. 1 in A Minor/GlazunovL Violin Concerto in A Minor" (1990); Honoree, Medal of Liberty, President Ronald Reagan (1986); Winner, Levenritt Competition (1964); 16 Grammy Awards; Four Emmy Awards

PERLMUTTER, EDWIN, "ED" GEORGE, T: U.S. Representative from Colorado; Lawyer **I:** Government Administration/Government Relations/Government Services **DOB:** 05/01/1953 **PB:** Denver **SC:** CO/USA **PT:** Leonard Michael Perlmutter; Alice Love (Bristow) Perlmutter **MS:** Married **SPN:** Nancy (Henderson) Perlmutter (2010); Deana M. Perlmutter (1981, Divorced 2008) **CH:** Alexis; Abbey; Zoey **ED:** JD, University of Colorado Law School (1978); BA, University of Colorado Boulder (1975) **C:** Member, U.S. House of Representatives from Colorado's Seventh Congressional District (2006-Present); Attorney, Berenbaum, Weinshienk & Eason, Professional Corporation, Denver, CO (1978-Present); President, Pro Tempore, Colorado State Senate, Denver, CO (2001-2003); Member, District 20, Colorado State Senate, Denver, CO (1994-2002); Member, Committee on Financial Services; Member, Committee on Science, Space, and Technology; Member, Committee on Financial Services; Member, Committee on Homeland Security; Member, Public Policy and Planning Committee, Joint Legal Services Committee, Colorado State Senate **CR:** Chair, First Judicial Performance Commission (1991-1993); Board of Trustees, First Judicial Performance Commission (1989-1991); Financial Chair, Jefferson County Democrats **CIV:** Active Member, American Heart Association, Inc.; Active Member, Girl Scouts of the United States of America; Active Member, Thomas Jefferson Foundation, Inc.; Trustee, Midwest Research Institute (Now MRIGlobal); Member, PTA; Maple Grove Elementary School, Golden, CO; Member, Applewood Community Church; Past Board of Directors, National Jewish Medical and Research Center **MEM:** ABA; Commercial Law League of America; University of Colorado Alumni Association; Colorado Trial Lawyers Association; Colorado Oil & Gas Association; Associated General Contractors Colorado, Applewood Business Association, American Judicature Society; American Bankruptcy Institute; Golden Chamber of Commerce; West Metro Chamber of Commerce; Northwest Metro Chamber of Commerce; Denver Bar Association; Board of Governors, Colorado Bar Association; Arvada Soccer Association; Table Mountain Soccer Association; Wheat Ridge Soccer Association **PA:** Democrat

PERLOFF, JEAN, T: Property Manager, Lawyer (Retired) **I:** Other **DOB:** 06/25/1942 **PB:** Lakewood **SC:** OH/USA **PT:** John Solomon; Marcella Catherine (Borngen) Marcosson **MS:** Widowed **SPN:** Lawrence Storch (08/1991) **ED:** JD, The College of Law Ventura, Magna Cum Laude (1976); MA in Italian, UCLA (1967); BA, Lake Erie College, Magna Cum Laude (1965) **CT:** United States District Court Central District of California (1978); The State Bar of California (1976) **C:** Retired (2013); Commercial Property Manager, Santa Barbara, CA (1997-2013); Retired (1997); Senior Judicial Attorney to Presiding Justice, Sixth Division, Second District Court of Appeals (1982-1997); Co-Principal, Clabaugh & Perloff, A Professional Corporation (1979-1982); Private Practice (1976-1979); Law Clerk, Paralegal, County of Ventura Public Defender (1975); Associate in Italian, UC Santa Barbara (1967-1970) **CR:** Instructor, The College of Law Ventura (1976-1979) **CIV:** Trustee, Lake Erie College (1993-Present); Board of Directors, Montecito Community Foundation (1999-2016); Member, 19th Agricultural District Board (2001-2007); President, Board of Directors, Santa Barbara Zoo (1987-1988) **AW:** Sesquicentennial Fellow, Lake Erie College (2001); Distinguished Alumnae Award, Lake Erie College (1996); Woman of the Year, 18th Senatorial District, California Legislature (1993); Woman of the Year, 35th Assembly District, California Legislature (1993) **MEM:** Appellate Court Committee, The State Bar of California (1993-1995); Kappa Alpha Sigma **MH:** Albert Nelson Marquis Lifetime Achievement Award **B/I:** Ms. Perloff became involved in her profession after meeting her husband. **AV:** Reading; Listening to music; Hiking **PA:** Democrat

PEROT, ROSS, T: Data Processing Executive, Real Estate Company, Investment Company **I:** Other **DOB:** 06/27/1930 **PB:** Texarkana **SC:** TX/USA **YOP:** 2019 **PT:** Gabriel Ross; Lulu May Perot **MS:** Married **SPN:** Margot Birmingham (1956) **CH:** Ross Jr. Nancy; Suzanne; Carolyn; Katherine **ED:** U.S. Naval Academy (1949-1953); Coursework, Texarkana Junior College (1947-1949); Diplomate, Texas High School, Texarkana, TX (1947); Diplomate, Patty Hill, Texarkana, TX **C:** Chairman Emeritus, Perot Systems Corporation, Plano, TX (2004); Chairman, Perot Systems Corporation, Plano, TX (2000-2004); Board Member, Perot Systems Corporation, Plano, TX (1997); Board Member, Perot Systems Corporation, Dallas, TX (1988-1994); Chairman, Perot Systems Corporation, Dallas, TX (1988-1992); Founder, Perot Systems Corporation, Washington, DC (1988); Founder, The Perot Group, Dallas, TX (1986); Chairman, CEO, Director, Electronic Data Systems Corporation, Dallas, TX (1986); Sold to GM, Electronic Data Systems Corporation, Dallas, TX (1984); Founder, Electronic Data Systems Corporation, Dallas, TX (1962-1984); Data Processing Salesman, IBM Corporation (1957-1962) **CR:** Reform Party Candidate, U.S. Presidential Election (1996); Independent Presidential Candidate (1992) **CIV:** Testified in Support of Proposals to Extend Technology to Students, Texas Legislature (2005); Pro-Choice Activist; Supporter, Planned Parenthood **MIL:** Serviceman, U.S. Navy (1953-1957) **CW:** Author, "The Dollar Crisis: A Blueprint to Help Rebuild the American Dream" (1996); Author, "Ross Perot: My Life & the Principles for Success" (1996); Author, "Preparing Our Country for the 21st Century" (1995); Author, "Intensive Care: We Must Save Medicare and Medicaid Now" (1995); Co-Author (with Pat Choate), "Save Your Job, Save Our Country: Why NAFTA Must Be Stopped-Now!" (1993); Author, "Not for Sale at Any Price: How We Can Save America for Our Children" (1993); Author, "United We Stand: How We Can Take Back Our Country" (1992) **AW:** Honorary Marine, U.S. Marine Corps (2017); Boots on the Ground Award, Army Heritage Center Foundation (2011); Distinguished Leadership Award, Command and General Staff College Foundation Inc., Fort Leavenworth, KS (2010); William J. Donovan Award, OSS Society (2010); Honorary Chairman, OSS Society (2009); Sylvanus Thayer Award, U.S. Military Academy (2009); Honorary Green Beret, US Army (2009); Named, Distinguished Alumni, Texarkana Independent School District (2009); Named, One of of Forbes 400: Richest Americans (1999); Named, World's Richest People, Forbes Magazine (1999); International Distinguished Entrepreneur Award, University Manitoba (1988); Inductee, Junior Achievement U.S. Business Hall of Fame (1988); Winston Churchill Award (1986); S. Roger Horchow Award for the Greatest Public Service by a Private Citizen (1986); Raoul Wallenberg Award, Jefferson Award; Patrick Henry Award; National Business Hall of Fame Award; Sarnoff Award; Eisenhower Award; Smithsonian Computerworld Award; Horatio Alger Award **PA:** Republican

PERRY, JAMES, "RICK" RICHARD, T: Former United States Secretary of Energy **I:** Government Administration/Government Relations/Government Services **DOB:** 03/04/1950 **PB:** Haskell **SC:** TX/USA **PT:** Joseph Ray Perry; Amelia June (Holt) Perry **MS:** Married **SPN:** Anita Thigpen (11/06/1982) **CH:** Griffin; Sydney **ED:** BS in Animal Science, Texas A&M University (1972) **C:** United States Secretary of Energy, Washington, DC (2017-Present); Governor, State of Texas, Austin, Texas (2000-2015);Lieutenant Governor, State of Texas, Austin, Texas (1999-2000); Commissioner Agricultural, State of Texas, Austin, Texas (1991-1999); Member, District 64, Texas House of Representatives, Austin, Texas (1985-1991); Farmer/Rancher **CR:** Candidate, Republican Party Nomination for President (2012, 2016); Chairman, Republican Governors Association (2007-2008, 2010-2011); United States Presidential Election Finance Chairman, Republican Governors Association (2008-2009) **MIL:** Captain, United States Air Force (1972-1977) **CW:** Author, "Fed Up!: Our Fight to Save America from Washington" (2010); Author, "On My Honor: Why the American Values of the Boy Scouts Are Worth Fighting For" (2008) **AW:** Named an Outstanding Tex Leader, John Ben Shepperd Public Leadership Institute (1996); Distinguished Eagle Scout Award, Boy Scouts of America (1992); Named Man of the Year in Texas Agricultural, Texas County Agricultural Agents Association (1990); Named One of the Most Effective Legislators, Dallas Morning News (1989); Gerald W. Thomas Outstanding Agriculturist Award **MEM:** Texas and Southwestern Cattle Raisers Association; Life Member, Texas Firemen & Fire Marshals Association; National Future Farmers of America Alumni Association (Now National FFA Alumni and Supporters, National FFA Organization); Life Member, The American Legion Post #75; Eagle Scouts **PA:** Republican **RE:** Methodist

PERRY, KATY, T: Singer **I:** Media & Entertainment **DOB:** 10/25/1984 **PB:** Santa Barbara **SC:** CA/USA **PT:** Keith Hudson; Mary (Perry) Hudson **MS:** Married **SPN:** Orlando Bloom (2019); Russell Brand (10/23/2010, Divorced 2012) **C:** Spokesmodel, CoverGirl (2013) **CIV:** Goodwill Ambassador, UNICEF (2013-Present); Co-Chair, 25th Annual Elton John's AIDS Foundation Academy Award Party (2017); Donor, "Make Roar Happen,"

Staples Inc. (2014); Designer, Clothing, "Fashion Against AIDS" Campaign, H&M (2009); Donor, Musi-Cares; Donor, Children's Health Fund (CHF); Host, Performer, We Can Survive Concert; Supporter, Keep a Breast Foundation; Supporter, Numerous Children's Organizations; Advocate, LGBT Rights **CW:** Judge, "American Idol" (2018-Present); Guest Appearance, "The Rookie" (2020); Singer, "Witness" (2017); Guest Appearance, "Popstar: Never Stop Never Stopping" (2016); Guest Appearance, "Zoolander 2" (2016); Herself, "Jeremy Scott: The People's Designer" (2015); Performer, "Katy Perry: The Prismatic World Tour" (2015); Singer, "Prism" (2013); Voice Actress, "The Smurfs 2" (2013); Herself, "Katy Perry: Part of Me" (2012); Guest Appearance, "Raising Hope" (2012); Voice Actress, "The Smurfs" (2011); Singer, "Teenage Dream" (2010); Singer, "MTV Unplugged" (2009); Singer, "One of the Boys" (2008); Singer, "Katy Hudson" (2001); Performer, Numerous TV Appearances; Singer, Numerous Tracks; Herself, Numerous Music Videos **AW:** National Equity Award, Human Rights Campaign Gala (2017); Best Female Video, "Bon Appétit," MTV Video Music Awards Japan (2017); Audrey Hepburn Humanitarian Award, UNICEF (2016); Most Performed Song, "Black Widow," ASCAP Pop Music Awards (2015); Woman of the Year, Elle Style Awards (2014); Most Performed Song, "Roar," ASCAP Pop Music Awards (2014); Single of the Year, "Dark Horse," American Music Awards (2014); Favorite Adult Contemporary Artist, American Music Awards (2014); Favorite Pop/Rock Female Artist, American Music Awards (2014); Top Female Artist, Top Digital Songs Artist, Billboard Music Awards (2014); Best Female Video, "Dark Horse," MTV Video Music Awards (2014); Most Performed Song, "Wide Awake," ASCAP Pop Music Awards (2013); Most Performed Song, "Part of Me," ASCAP Pop Music Awards (2013); Favorite Female Singer, Nickelodeon Kids Choice Awards (2013); Woman of the Year, Billboard Women in Music (2012); Billboard Spotlight Award, Billboard Music Awards (2012); Favorite Pop/Rock Female Artist, American Music Awards (2012); Trevor Hero Award, Trevor Project Awards (2012); Video of the Year, "Firework," MTV Video Music Awards (2011); Best Collaboration, "E.T.," MTV Video Music Awards (2011); International Album of the Year, "Teenage Dream," Juno Awards (2011); Top Digital Songs Artist, Billboard Music Awards (2011); Favorite Female Singer, Nickelodeon Kids Choice Awards (2011); Special Achievement Award, American Music Awards (2011); Fashion Icon, red! Star Awards (2010); Most Played Artist on British Radio, Radio Academy (2011); International Female Solo Artist, Brit Awards (2009); Newcomer of the Year, Glamour Awards (2009); Best-Selling Album in Poland, "One of the Boys," Eska Music Awards (2009); Best Breakthrough, MTV Australia Awards (2009); Best Pop Video, "I Kissed a Girl," MTV Video Music Awards Japan (2009); Numerous Honors, Guinness World Records; Numerous BMI Awards; Most Performed Song, Numerous Songs, ASCAP Pop Music Awards; Recipient, Numerous Awards and Accolades

PERRY, REGINALD, T: President, Chief Executive Officer **I:** Aviation **CN:** Barbers Point Aviation Services **SC:** HI/USA **MS:** Married **SPN:** Michelle **CH:** Three Children **ED:** BS in Aeronautics, Embry-Riddle Aeronautical University (1993) **C:** President, Chief Executive Officer, Barbers Point Aviation Services, Barbers Point Flight School (2010-Present); Pilot, Air Molokai, Scenic Air Tours, Polynesian Airways, Mahalo Airlines, Corporate Air, Ryan International Airlines (1993-2011) **CIV:** Volunteers, Aircraft's **MIL:** Mr. Perry, Hawaii Army National Guard (1987-2013); Major, United States Army **AW:** Named Hawaii's Small Business Person of the Year (2018) **MEM:** NDAA; NAPA; EAA **AS:** Mr. Perry attributes his success to his initiative and tenacity; he doesn't take no for an answer. There is always one more call he can make, one more effort he can make to get the answer he wants. "Don't take no for an answer." **B/I:** Mr. Perry wanted to fly from the time he was in the first grade. He thinks it is because he grew up right outside of the naval base. He would sit on his roof and watch the planes come right over his house. His father took him to the Branas Headquarters and he got to sit in the co-pilot set and he took a photo of it, which was on the wall his whole life. That reinforced the idea of what he wanted to do. When he came back home from Iraq when he was deployed with the Army, there was an opportunity at a local air field to manage a fuel concession for the state of Hawaii. This was in 2010. That lead him to buying his first fuel truck, and it just went from there.

PERRY, SCOTT GORDON, T: U.S. Representative from Pennsylvania **I:** Government Administration/Government Relations/Government Services **DOB:** 05/27/1962 **PB:** San Diego **SC:** CA/USA **MS:** Married **SPN:** Christy Perry **CH:** Ryenn; Mattea **ED:** MA in Strategic War Planning, United States Army War College (2012); BS in Business Administration, The Pennsylvania State University (1991) **C:** Member, U.S. House of Representatives from Pennsylvania's Fourth Congressional District, United States Congress, Washington, DC (2013-Present); Member, U.S. House Committee on Transportation and Infrastructure (2013-Present); Member, U.S. House Committee on Homeland Security (2013-Present); Member, U.S. House Committee on Foreign Affairs (2013-Present); Founder, Hydrotech Mechanical Services, Inc., Dillsburg, PA (1993-Present); Member, District 92, Pennsylvania House of Representatives (2007-2012) **CIV:** Chairman, Dillsburg Area Wellhead Protection Advisory Committee; Member, Dillsburg Revitalization Committee; Active Member, Pennsylvania Jaycees; Regional Director, Pennsylvania Jaycees **MIL:** Brigadier General, Pennsylvania Army National Guard (1980-2019) **AW:** Bronze Star Medal; Meritorious Service Medal with Bronze Oak Leaf Cluster; Joint Service Commendation Medal; Army Commendation Medal with Bronze Oak Leaf Cluster; Army Achievement Medal with Two Bronze Oak Leaf Clusters; Army Reserve Components Achievement Medal with Silver Oak Leaf Cluster and Three Bronze Oak Leaf Clusters; National Defense Service Medal with Bronze Service Star; Armed Forces Expeditionary Medal; Armed Forces Reserve Medal with Gold Hour Glass, "M" Device, and "2" Device Army Service Ribbon; Army Reserve Components Overseas Training Ribbon with "4" Device; Iraq Campaign Medal; Global War on Terrorism Service Medal; Overseas Service Ribbon; NATO Medal; Pennsylvania 20 Year Service Medal with Two Silver Stars; MG T.R. White Medal; General T.J. Stewart Medal; Master Army Aviator Badge **MEM:** Dillsburg VFW Post #6671 (South Mountain Post 6771); Northern York County Republican Club; Republican Club of York County; Dillsburg American Legion Post #26; Lions Clubs International; National Rifle Association of America; Army Aviation Association of America (AAAA) **PA:** Republican **RE:** Christian

PERRY, TYLER A., T: Playwright, Actor, Film Director, Producer **I:** Media & Entertainment **DOB:** 09/14/1969 **PB:** New Orleans **SC:** LA/USA **PT:** Emmitt R. Perry Sr.; Willie Maxine (Campbell) Perry **SPN:** Gelila Bekele (2009) **CH:** Aman **C:** Founder, Tyler Perry Studios **CW:** Director, Writer, Producer, "Tyler Perry's Young Dylan" (2020-Present); Director, Writer, Producer, Actor, "House of Payne" (2007-2012, 2020-Present); Director, Writer, Producer, "The Oval" (2019-Present); Director, Writer, Producer, "Sistas" (2019-Present); Director, Writer, Producer, "If Loving You is Wrong" (2014-Present); Director, Writer, Producer, "The Haves and Have Nots" (2013-Present); Director, Writer, Producer, "Ruthless" (2020); Director, Writer, Producer, "Bruh" (2020); Director, Writer, Producer, Actor, "A Fall from Grace" (2020); Actor, "Those Who Wish Me Dead" (2020); Director, Writer, Producer, Actor, "Madea's Farewell" (2019); Director, Writer, Producer, Actor, "A Madea Family Funeral" (2019); Director, Writer, Producer, "Acrimony" (2018); Director, Writer, Producer, "Nobody's Fool" (2018); Actor, "Vice" (2018); Director, Writer, Producer, "The Paynes" (2018); Author, "Higher is Waiting" (2017); Voice Actor, "The Star" (2017); Director, Writer, Producer, Actor, "Boo 2! A Madea Halloween" (2017); Director, Writer, Producer, "Too Close to Home" (2016-2017); Director, Writer, Producer, Actor, "Love Thy Neighbor" (2013-2017); Director, Writer, Producer, "For Better or Worse" (2011-2017); Actor, "Teenage Mutant Ninja Turtles: Out of the Shadows" (2016); Actor, "Brain on Fire" (2016); Director, Writer, Producer, Actor, "Boo! A Madea Halloween" (2016); Producer, Actor, "Madea's Tough Love" (2015); Director, Writer, Producer, Actor, "Madea on the Run" (2015); Director, Writer, Producer, "Hell Hath No Fury Like a Woman Scorned" (2014); Director, Writer, Producer, Actor, "The Single Moms Club" (2014); Actor, "Gone Girl" (2014); Director, Writer, Producer, "Temptation: Confessions of a Marriage Counselor" (2013); Producer, "Peeples" (2013); Director, Writer, Producer, Actor, "Madea's Neighbors from Hell" (2013); Director, Writer, Producer, Actor, "A Madea Christmas" (2011, 2013); Director, Writer, Producer, Actor, "The Haves and Have Nots" (2012); Director, Writer, Producer, Actor, "Madea Gets a Job" (2012); Director, Writer, Producer, Actor, "Good Deeds" (2012); Director, Writer, Producer, Actor, "Madea's Witness Protection" (2012); Actor, "Alex Cross" (2012); Director, Writer, Producer, Actor, "Madea's Big Happy Family" (2011); Director, Writer, Producer, "Aunt Bam's Place" (2011); Director, Writer, Producer, "I Don't Want to Do Wrong" (2011); Director, Writer, Producer, "Meet the Browns" (2005, 2009-2011); Director, Writer, Producer, Actor, "Why Did I Get Married Too?" (2010); Director, Writer, Producer, Actor, "Madea's Big Happy Family" (2010); Director, Writer, Producer, "For Colored Girls" (2010); Actor, "Star Trek" (2009); Director, Writer, Producer, Actor, "I Can Do Bad All by Myself" (2009); Director, Writer, Producer, "Laugh to Keep From Crying" (2009); Producer, "Precious" (2009); Director, Writer, Producer, Actor, "Madea Goes to Jail" (2006, 2009); Director, Writer, Producer, Actor, "Meet the Browns" (2008); Director, Writer, Producer, Actor, "The Family That Preys" (2008); Director, Writer, Producer, "The Marriage Counselor" (2008); Director, Writer, Producer, "What's Done in the Dark" (2007); Director, Writer, Producer, "Daddy's Little Girls" (2007); Director, Writer, Producer, Actor, "Why Did I Get Married?" (2007); Author, "Don't Make a Black Woman Take Off Her Earrings: Madea's Uninhibited Commentaries on Love and Life" (2006); Director, Writer, Producer, Actor, "Madea's Family Reunion" (2002, 2006); Writer, Producer, Actor, "Diary of a Mad Black Woman" (2001, 2005); Director, Writer, Producer, "Why Did I Get Married?" (2004); Director, Writer, Producer, Actor, "Madea's Class Reunion" (2003); Director, Writer, Producer, "Behind Closed Doors" (2000); Director, Writer, Producer, Actor, "Woman, Thou Art Loosed!" (1999); Director, Writer, Producer, Actor, "I Can Do Bad All by Myself" (1999); Director, Writer, Producer, Actor, "I Know I've Been Changed" (1998) **AW:** Ultimate Icon Award, BET Best Movie Awards (2019); Best Supporting Actor, "Gone Girl," African-American Film Critics

Association (2014); Outstanding Motion Picture, Outstanding Directing for a Motion Picture/Television Movie, "For Colored Girls," NAACP Image Awards (2011); Best Cast, "Star Trek," Boston Society of Film Critics (2009); Outstanding Writing for Theatrical Film, Outstanding Actor in a Theatrical Film, "Diary of a Mad Black Woman," BET Comedy Awards (2005)

PESCI, JOE, T: Actor **I:** Media & Entertainment **DOB:** 02/09/1943 **PB:** Newark **SC:** NJ/USA **PT:** Angelo Pesci; Mary Pesci **SPN:** Angie Everhart (Partnered 2000, Separated 2008); Claudio Haro (1988, Divorced 1992) **CH:** Tiffany **CW:** Actor, "The Irishman" (2019); Singer, Album, "Pesci... Still Singing" (2019); Actor, Commercial, "Google Assistant: Home Alone Again" (2018); Voice Actor, "A Warrior's Tail" (2015); Actor, "Love Ranch" (2010); Actor, "The Good Shepherd" (2006); Singer, Album, "Vincent LaGuardia Gambini Sings Just for You" (1998); Actor, "Lethal Weapon 4" (1998); Actor, "Gone Fishin'" (1997); Actor, "8 Heads in a Duffel Bag" (1997); Actor, "Casino" (1995); Actor, "With Honors" (1994); Actor, "Jimmy Hollywood" (1994); Actor, "A Bronx Tale" (1993); Host, "Saturday Night Live" (1992); Actor, "Home Alone 2: Lost in New York" (1992); Actor, "The Public Eye" (1992); Actor, TV Series, "Tales from the Crypt" (1992); Actor, "Lethal Weapon 3" (1992); Actor, "My Cousin Vinny" (1992); Actor, "JFK" (1991); Actor, "The Super" (1991); Actor, "Home Alone" (1990); Actor, "Goodfellas" (1990); Actor, "Betsy's Wedding" (1990); Actor, "Catchfire" (1990); Actor, "The Legendary Life of Ernest Hemingway" (1989); Actor, "Lethal Weapon 2" (1989); Actor, Music Video, "Smooth Criminal" by Michael Jackson (1988); Actor, "Moonwalker" (1988); Actor, "Man on Fire" (1987); Actor, TV Series, "Half Nelson" (1985); Actor, TV Film, "Half Nelson" (1985); Actor, "Tutti dentro" (1984); Actor, "Once Upon a Time in America" (1984); Actor, "Easy Money" (1983); Actor, "Eureka" (1983); Actor, "Dear Mr. Wonderful" (1982); Actor, "I'm Dancing as Fast as I Can" (1982); Actor, "Raging Bull" (1980); Actor, "Short Eyes" (1977); Actor, "The Death Collector" (1976); Singer, Album, "Little Joe Sure Can Sing!" (1968); Actor, "Hey, Let's Twist!" (1961) **AW:** Best Supporting Actor, "The Irishman," New York Film Critics Circle (2020); Co-Honoree, Best Movie Cast, "The Irishman," Critics' Choice Awards (2020); Best Supporting Actor, "Goodfellas," 20/20 Awards (2011); Outstanding Artistic Contribution, "The Good Shepherd," Berlin International Film Festival (2007); Funniest Lead Actor in a Motion Picture, "My Cousin Vinny," American Comedy Awards (1993); Best Supporting Actor, "Goodfellas," Boston Society of Film Critics (1991); Best Supporting Actor, "Goodfellas," Chicago Film Critics Association (1991); Best Supporting Actor, "Goodfellas," Dallas-Fort Worth Film Critics Association (1991); Best Supporting Actor, "Goodfellas," National Board of Review (1991); Best Supporting Actor, "Goodfellas," Kansas City Film Critics Circle Awards (1990); Best Supporting Actor, "Goodfellas," Los Angeles Film Critics Association (1990); Best Supporting Actor, "Goodfellas," Academy Awards (1990); Best Film Newcomer, "Raging Bull," British Film Academy Awards (1982); Best Supporting Actor, "Raging Bull," National Board of Review (1981); Best Supporting Actor, "Raging Bull," National Society of Film Critics (1981); Best Supporting Actor, "Raging Bull," New York Film Critics Circle (1980)

PESSINA, STEFANO, T: Vice Chairperson, Chief Executive Officer **I:** Retail/Sales **CN:** Walgreens Boots Alliance Inc. **DOB:** 06/04/1941 **PB:** Pescara **SC:** Italy **MS:** Partnered **SPN:** Ornella Barra; Barbara Pessina (Divorced) **CH:** Two Children

ED: Honorary Doctorate in Science, Nottingham Business School, Nottingham University (2013); Honorary Doctor of Business Administration, Nottingham Business School, Nottingham Trent University (2012); Honorary Doctor of Science, University of Cardiff (2009); Degree in Nuclear Engineering, Polytechnic University of Milan **C:** Chief Executive Officer, Executive Vice Chairperson, Director, Walgreens Boots Alliance Inc. (2015-Present); Acting Chief Executive Officer, Walgreens Boots Alliance Inc. (2015); Executive Chairperson, Alliance Boots (2007-2014); Chief Executive Officer, Alliance UniChem (2001-2004); Executive Deputy Chairperson, Alliance Boots; Executive Deputy Chairman, Alliance UniChem; Founder, Alliance Santé, Italy; Joined, ACNielsen **CR:** Member, Board of Directors, Galencia AG (2000-2017); Member, Board of Directors, Alliance UniChem (1997); Member, Board of Directors, Numerous Privately-Held Companies; Director, Consumer Goods Forum **AW:** Named, One of "The World's Richest People," Forbes (2006-Present); Inductee, World Retail Hall of Fame (2018); Golden Plate Award, American Academy of Achievement (2017); Special Achievements Award in Business, National Italian American Foundation (2016); International Executive of the Year, Executives' Club of Chicago (2016); Retailer of the Year, Chain Drug Review (2016); Grande ufficiale dell'Ordine della stella d'Italia (2013); Retailer of the Year, Chain Drug Review (2013); Retail Leader of the Year, Clarity Search (2013); Alkemeon International Prize, Rome, Italy (2012); Global Retailer of the Year, Chain Drug Review (2010); Keynes-Sraffa Award (2009); William L. Ford International Award (2006)

PETERS, BERNADETTE, T: Actress **I:** Media & Entertainment **DOB:** 02/28/1948 **PB:** Queens **SC:** NY/USA **PT:** Peter Lazzara; Marguerite (Maltese) Lazzara **MS:** Married **SPN:** Michael Wittenberg (07/20/1996, Deceased 2005) **ED:** Honorary Doctor of Philosophy, Hofstra University, Hempstead, NY (2002) **C:** Actress (1958-Present) **CIV:** Patron, The Stephen Sondheim Society (2012); Participant, Annual Benefit, Drama League of New York (2010); Co-Founder, Broadway Barks; Host, Annual Broadway Barks Event, New York, NY; Member, Board of Trustees, Broadway Cares/Equity Fights AIDS; Participant, Numerous Events, Broadway Cares/Equity Fights AIDS **CW:** Voice Actress, "Animaniacs" (2020); Actress, "Zoey's Extraordinary Playlist" (2020); Actress, "Katy Kreene" (2020); Actress, Stage, "Hello Dolly!" (2018); Actress, "The Good Fight" (2017-2018); Actress, Singer, Numerous Plays (1958-2018); Actress, "Mozart in the Jungle" (2014-2018); Author, "Stella and Charlie: friends Forever" (2015); Actress, "Legends of Oz: Dorothy's Return" (2014); Author, "Smash" (2012-2013); Actress, Stage, "Follies" (2011); Actress, "Coming p Roses" (2011); Actress, Stage, "A Little Night Music" (2010); Author, "Stella is a Star!" (2010); Actress, "Ugly Betty" (2009); Actress, "Living Proof" (2008); Actress, "Grey's Anatomy" (2008); Author, "Broadway Barks" (2008); Actress, "Wine and Kisses" (2007); Actress, "Boston Legal" (2007); Actress, "Law & Order: Special Victims Unit" (2006); Actress, "Will & Grace" (2006); Actress, "Adopted" (2005); Voice Actress, "The Land Before Time X: The Great Longneck Migration" (2003); Actress, Stage, "Gypsy" (2003); Actress, "It Runs in the Family" (2003); Actress, "Bobbie's Girl" (2002); Actress, "Prince Charming" (2001); Actress, "Ally McBeal" (2001); Actress, "Frasier" (2001); Voice Actress, "Teacher's Pet" (2000); Actress, Stage, "Annie Get Your Gun" (1999); Actress, "Let It Snow" (1999); Voice Actress, "Animaniacs: Wakko's Wish" (1999); Actress, "The Closer" (1998); Actress, "Holiday in Your Heart" (1997); Actress, "What the Deaf Man Heard" (1997); Voice Actress,

"Anastasia" (1997); Voice Actress, "Beauty and the Beast: The Enchanted Christmas" (1997); Actress, "The Wonderful World of Disney" (1997); Actress, "The Odyssey" (1997); Voice Actress, "Animaniacs" (1993-1996); Actress, "The Larry Sanders Show" (1994); Actress, Stage, "The Goodbye Girl" (1993); Actress, "The Last Mile" (1992); Actress, "The Carol Burnett Show" (1991); Actress, "Impromptu" (1991); Actress, "American Playhouse" (1986, 1991); Actress, "Alice" (1990); Actress, "Carol & Company" (1990); Actress, "The Last Best Year" (1990); Actress, "Fall from Grace" (1990); Actress, "Pink Cadillac" (1989); Actress, "Slaves of New York" (1989); Actress, "David" (1988); Actress, Stage, "Into the Woods" (1987); Actress, Stage, "Song and Dance" (1985); Actress, Stage, "Sunday in the Park with George" (1984); Actress, "Faerie Tale Theatre" (1983); Actress, Stage, "Sally and Marsha" (1982); Actress, "Annie" (1982); Actress, "Baryshnikov in Hollywood" (1982); Actress, "Heartbeeps" (1981); Actress, "Pennies from Heaven" (1981); Actress, "Tulips" (1981); Actress, "The Martian Chronicles" (1980); Actress, "The Jerk" (1979); Actress, "The Islander" (1978); Actress, "All's Fair" (1976-1977); Actress, "Vigilante Force" (1976); Actress, "Silent Movie" (1976); Actress, "W.C. Fields and Me" (1976); Actress, "McCloud" (1976); Actress, "McCoy" (1976); Actress, "The Owl and the Pussycat" (1975); Actress, "All in the Family" (1975); Actress, "Maude" (1975); Actress, "The Longest Yard" (1974); Actress, Stage, "Mack & Mabel" (1974); Actress, "Love, American Style" (1973); Actress, "Ace Eli and Rodger of the Skies" (1973); Actress, "Once Upon a Mattress" (1972); Actress, Stage, "Tartuffe" (1972); Actress, "Great Performances" (1971); Actress, "George M!" (1958); Actress, "Kraft Theatre" (1958); Singer, Performer, Numerous Recordings **AW:** Prince Rainier III Award (2019); Brooke Astor Award, Animal Medical Center (2018); John Willis Award for Lifetime Achievement in the Theatre, Theatre World Awards (2016); Special Award of Distinguished Achievement in Musical Theatre Award (2013); Lifetime Achievement Award, New Dramatists (2012); Sondheim Award (2011); Artistic Honoree, National Dance Institute (2009); Inductee, Hollywood Bowl Hall of Fame (2002); Tony Award for Best Actress in a Musical, "Annie Get Your Gun" (1999); Drama Desk Award for Outstanding Actress in a Musical, "Annie Get Your Gun" (1999); Outer Critics Circle Award for Outstanding Actress in a Musical, "Annie Get Your Gun" (1999); Actors' Fund Artistic Achievement Medal (1999); Sarah Siddons Award (1994); Honoree, Star, Hollywood Walk of Fame (1987); Hasty Pudding Woman of the Year (1987); Tony Award for Best Actress in a Musical, "Song and Dance" (1986); Drama Desk Award for Outstanding Actress in a Musical, "Song and Dance" (1986); Golden Globe Award for Best Actress - Motion Picture Musical or Comedy, "Pennies from Heaven" (1981); Drama Desk Award for Outstanding Actress in a Musical, "Dames at Sea" (1968); Theatre World Award for Outstanding Broadway Debut, "George M!" (1968); Numerous Awards and Accolades

PETERS, GARY CHARLES SR., T: U.S. Senator from Michigan; Lawyer **I:** Government Administration/Government Relations/Government Services **DOB:** 12/01/1958 **PB:** Pontiac **SC:** MI/USA **PT:** Herbert Garrett Peters; Madeleine A. (Vignier) Peters **MS:** Married **SPN:** Colleen Ochoa **CH:** Gary Jr.; Madeleine; Alana **ED:** Diploma, College of Naval Command and Staff, U.S. Naval War College (2018); MA in Philosophy, Michigan State University, East Lansing, MI; JD, Wayne State University Law School (1989); MBA, University of Detroit Mercy (1984); BA, Alma College (1980) **C:** Ranking Member, Senate Homeland Security Committee (2019-Present); U.S. Senator, State of Michigan (2015-Present); Member, U.S. House of Representatives from Michigan's 14th Congressional District (2013-2015); Member, U.S. House of Representatives from Michigan's Ninth Congressional District, Washington, DC (2009-2013); Commissioner, Michigan State Lottery (2003-2008); Member, District 14, Michigan State Senate, Lansing, MI (1994-2002); Financial Consultant, Resident Manager, Assistant Vice President, Merrill Lynch, Pierce, Fenner & Smith, Incorporated, Rochester, MI (1980-1989); Vice President, Branch Manager, PaineWebber, Inc., Rochester, MI **CR:** Instructor, Wayne State University (1992-1994); Adjunct Professor, Oakland University, Rochester, NY (1991-1993); Securities Arbitrator, Mediator, National Association of Securities Dealers (NASD), New York Stock Exchange (NYSE), Intercontinental Exchange, Inc., American Arbitration Association **CIV:** Officer-at-large, Michigan Democratic Party (1996); Councilman, City of Rochester Hills, MI (1991-1993); Member, Zoning Board of Appeals, Paint Creek Trailways Commission (1992-1994) **MIL:** Officer, United States Navy Reserve (1993-2000, 2001-2005) **AW:** Decorated Military Outstanding Volunteer Service Medal; Navy and Marine Corps Achievement Medal **MEM:** Michigan Bar Association; Sierra Club; The Phi Beta Kappa Society **BAR:** State of Michigan (1990) **AV:** Hiking; Motorcycling; World travel; Soaring; Scuba diving **PA:** Democrat **RE:** Episcopalian

PETERS, SCOTT HARVEY, T: U.S. Representative from California; Lawyer **I:** Government Administration/Government Relations/Government Services **DOB:** 06/17/1958 **PB:** Springfield **SC:** OH/USA **MS:** Married **SPN:** Lynn E. (Gorgunze) Peters (1990) **CH:** Two Children **ED:** JD, New York University School of Law; BA in Economics and Political Science, Duke University, Magna Cum Laude **C:** Member, U.S. House of Representatives from California's 52nd Congressional District, United States Congress, Washington, DC (2013-Present); Member, U.S. House Committee on Science, Space and Technology (2013-Present); Member, U.S. House Committee on Armed Services Committee (2013-Present); Chairman, San Diego Unified Port Commission (2011); Commissioner, San Diego Unified Port Commission (2009-2012); President, San Diego City Council (2006-2007); Councilman, District One, San Diego City Council (2000-2008); Deputy Company Counsel, San Diego, CA (1991-1996); Partner, Peters & Varco LLP (1996-2000); Economist, U.S. Environmental Protection Agency (EPA), Washington, DC (1980-1981); Attorney, Baker & McKenzie, San Diego, CA; Attorney, Dorsey & Whitney LLP, Minneapolis, MN; Member, Committee on Education and the Workforce; Member, Committee on Transportation and Infrastructure; Member, U.S. House Committee on the Budget; Member, U.S. House Energy and Commerce Committee **PA:** Democrat **RE:** Lutheran

PETERSON, ADRIAN, T: Professional Football Player **I:** Athletics **CN:** Washington Redskins **DOB:** 03/21/1985 **PB:** Palestine **SC:** TX/USA **PT:** Nelson Peterson; Bonita Brown Peterson **MS:** Married **SPN:** Ashley Brown (2014) **CH:** Six Children **ED:** Coursework, University of Oklahoma, Norman, OK (2004-2006) **C:** Running Back, Washington Redskins, National Football League (2018-Present); Running Back, Arizona Cardinals, National Football League (2017); Running Back, New Orleans Saints, National Football League (2017); Running Back, Minnesota Vikings, National Football League (2007-2016) **AW:** NFL MVP, Associated Press (2012); NFL Offensive Player of the Year (2012); NFL MVP, Pro Football Writers America (2012); Named to The National Football Conference Pro Bowl Team, NFL (2012, 2007-2010); ESPY

Award for Best Breakthrough Athlete, ESPN (2008); NFL Pro Bowl MVP (2008); FedEx Ground Player of Year (2008, 2012); Bert Bell Award, Maxwell Football Club (2008, 2012); NFL Offensive Rookie of the Year (2007); Named, 1st Team All-Freshman, Associated Press (2004); 1st Team All-American (2004); Hall Trophy (2003)

PETERSON, COLLIN CLARK, T: U.S. Representative from Minnesota **I:** Government Administration/Government Relations/Government Services **DOB:** 06/29/1944 **PB:** Fargo **SC:** ND/USA **MS:** Divorced **CH:** Sean; Jason; Elliott **ED:** BA in Business Administration and Accounting, Minnesota State University Moorhead (1966) **CT:** Certified Public Accountant (CPA), Minnesota; Licensed Private Pilot **C:** Chairman, U.S. House Committee on Agriculture (2007-2011, 2019-Present); Member, U.S. House of Representatives from Minnesota's Seventh Congressional District, United States Congress, Washington, DC (1991-Present); Member, District 10, Minnesota State Senate (1976-1986) **CIV:** With, U.S. Army National Guard (1963-1969) **MEM:** The American Legion; Ducks Unlimited; Elks; Sportsmen's Club; Mainstream Forum; Cormorant Lakes Sportsmans Club; Congressional Sportsmen's Caucus; Congressional Rural Caucus **PA:** Democrat **RE:** Lutheran

PETERSON, DOUGLAS L., T: Chief Executive Officer **I:** Financial Services **CN:** S&P Global **PB:** Santa Fe **SC:** NM/USA **MS:** Married **SPN:** Teresa Aracama **CH:** Two sons **ED:** MBA, The Wharton School, The University of Pennsylvania (1985); BA in Mathematics and History, Claremont McKenna College, With Honors (1980) **C:** President, Chief Executive Officer, S&P Global (2016-Present); President, Chief Executive Officer, McGraw Hill Financial, New York, NY (2013-2016); President, Standard & Poor's, New York, NY (2011-2013); Chief Operating Officer, Citibank, North America (2010-2011); Chairman, President, Chief Executive Officer, Representative Director, Nikko Citi Holdings (2008-2010); Chief Auditor, Citigroup, Inc. (2000); Managing Director, Audit And Risk Review, Citigroup, Inc. (1998); Country Corporate Officer, Citigroup, Inc., Costa Rica (1991); Country Corporate Officer, Citigroup, Inc., Uruguay (1995-1988); Relationship Manager, Citigroup, Inc., Buenos Aires, Argentina (1985); Economics Department, Chevron Corporate, San Francisco, CA; Chief Executive Officer, Japan Holdings Ltd., Citigroup, Inc. **CR:** Board of Directors, McGraw Hill Financial, New York, NY (2013-Present) **CIV:** Board of Trustees, Paul Taylor American Modern Dance; Board of Trustees, Claremont McKenna College; Board of Advisers, Partnership for New York City; Board of Advisers, Kravis Leadership Institute; Board of Advisers, Wharton Financial Institutions Center

PETERSON, JEREMY, T: Chief Executive Officer **I:** Other **CN:** Erie Metropolitan Transit Authority **MS:** Married **SPN:** Leanne **CH:** Emma; Bryce **C:** Chief Executive Officer, Erie Metropolitan Transit Authority, PA (2018-Present); Director of Operations, Erie Metropolitan Transit Authority (2011-2018) **CIV:** Board Member, Sunflower Club **AW:** Award, Business Magazine; Award, Manufacturer & Business Association; 10,000 Friends of Pennsylvania, Manufacturer & Business Association **MEM:** Pennsylvania Public Transportation Association; American Public Transit Association **AS:** Mr. Peterson attributes his success to his staff. He has a great staff of hard working and dedicated people that he has the pleasure of working alongside daily, to achieve a common goal for the community. **B/I:** Mr. Peterson became involved in his profession because he always worked in public service and found pleasure in doing so.

PETERSON, JOHN, T: Civil Engineering Educator **I:** Education/Educational Services **DOB:** 07/27/1926 **PB:** Harrold **SC:** SD/USA **PT:** John Carl Peterson; Vera May (Krimble) Peterson **SPN:** Alberta Morton Curry **CH:** Margaret Ann; Charles Robert; Connie Jean **ED:** Doctor of Philosophy, University of Wisconsin (1964); Master of Science in Chemical Engineering, University of Illinois (1959); Bachelor of Science in Agricultural Engineering, South Dakota State College, Brookings, SD (1951) **C:** Associate Professor of Civil Engineering, Oregon State University, Corvallis, OR **CIV:** U.S. Navy (1945-1946) **MIL:** U.S. Navy (1945-1946) **AW:** Recycler of the Year Judges Award, State of Oregon (1997); L.J. Markwart Wood Engineering Research Award, Forest Products Society (1983) **MH:** Albert Nelson Marquis Lifetime Achievement Award

PETERSON, SOPHIA PHD, T: Political Scientist, Educator **I:** Education/Educational Services **DOB:** 11/24/1929 **PB:** Astoria **SC:** NY/USA **PT:** George Loizos Yimoyines; Caroline (Hofstetter) Yimoyines **MS:** Widow **SPN:** Virgil Allison Peterson (12/28/1951, Deceased 2001) **CH:** Mark Jeffrey; Lynn Marie **ED:** Honorary DHL, Wheeling Jesuit University (1997); PhD, UCLA (1969); MA, UCLA (1956); BA, Wellesley College, Massachusetts (1951) **C:** Professor Emerita, West Virginia University, Morgantown (1997-Present); With, West Virginia University, Morgantown (1966-Present); Director, International Studies Major, West Virginia University, Morgantown (1980-1992); Professor, West Virginia University, Morgantown (1979-1997); Associate Professor, West Virginia University, Morgantown (1972-1979); Instructor, Miami University, Oxford, OH (1961-1963) **CR:** Founding Director, West Virginia Consortium for Faculty & Course Development in International Studies, Morgantown (1997); Director, West Virginia Consortium for Faculty & Course Development in International Studies, Morgantown (1980-1997) **CW:** Author, Monograph Series in World Affairs (1979) **AW:** Finalist, Professor of Year Award, West Virginia Faculty Merit Foundation (1991); Outstanding Teacher Award, West Virginia University, West Virginia University College Arts and Sciences (1988); Professor of the Year Award, Council for Advancement and Support of Education (1987); Heebink Award for Distinguished State Service, West Virginia University (1984); Gold Medal Semi-finalist, CASE **MEM:** President, West Virginia Political Science Association (1984-1985) **MH:** Albert Nelson Marquis Lifetime Achievement Award **B/I:** Ms. Peterson became involved in her profession because initially she did not plan to teach but was inspired by her husband to do so. They were both university professors at the same university. **AV:** Sailing; Travel **PA:** Democrat

PETITTI, TONY, T: President of Sports and Entertainment; Former Chief Operating Officer **I:** Athletics **CN:** Activision Blizzard; Major League Baseball **ED:** JD, Harvard Law School, MA (1986); BA in Economics, Haverford College, PA (1983) **C:** President, Sports and Entertainment, Activision Blizzard (2020-Present); Deputy Commissioner, Business & Media, Major League Baseball (MLB) (2017-2020); Chief Operating Officer, Major League Baseball (MLB) (2014-2020); President, Chief Executive Officer, MLB Network (2008-2015); Executive Vice President, CBS Sports (2005-2008); Executive Producer, CBS Sports (2002-2008); Vice President, General Manager, Station WCBS-TV, New York, NY (1999-2002); Senior Vice President, Business Affairs and Programming, CBS Sports, New York, NY (1997-1999); Senior Vice President, Negotiations, NBC Sports, New York, NY (1996-1997); Vice President, Programming, ABC Sports (1994-1996); General Attorney, ABC Sports (1988); Attorney,

Cadwalader, Wickersham & Taft LLP (1986-1988); Special Adviser to the President, CBS Sports; Director, Programming, ABC Sports **AW:** Named One of "The Most Influential People in the World of Sports," Business Week (Now Bloomberg Businessweek) (2007); Lawrence Forman Award, Haverford College (2006); Named Among the "40 Under 40 Top Executives in the Industry," Sports Business Journal (2000); Five Emmy Awards

PETREQUIN, HARRY JOSEPH JR., T: Senior Foreign Service Officer (Retired) **I:** International Affairs/International Business **CN:** U.S. Agency for International Development **DOB:** 07/01/1929 **PB:** Ste. Genevieve **SC:** MO/USA **PT:** Harry Joseph Petrequin; Cresentia Ellen (Bechter) Petrequin **MS:** Married **SPN:** Katharine McDonnel Petrequin **CH:** John Andrew; Marc Christopher; Paul Nicholas **ED:** MA, The Fletcher School, Tufts University (1970); AB, Thunderbird School of Global Management (1954); AB, Westminster College (1950) **C:** Consultant, U.S. Agency for International Development (1990); Faculty, National Security Policy Department, National War College (1988-1989); U.S. Agency for International Development Representative, Industrial College of the Armed Forces (1987); Coordinator, Senior Management Course, U.S. Agency for International Development (1986); Deputy Director, Mission in Morocco, U.S. Agency for International Development (1981-1985);Director, Program Development and Evaluation Staff, Bureau of International Organization Affairs (IO), Department of State (1980-1981); Director, U.S. Agency for International Development Office of Indonesian, Korean, South Pacific and ASEAN Affairs (1977-1980); U.S. Coordinator, Senegal River Basin Development Authority, Dakar, Senegal (1975-1976); Deputy Director, Southeast Asia Regional Economic Development Office, Thailand (1970-1974) **CR:** Faculty, College for Seniors, University North Carolina (1998-1999); Adjunct Professor of Political Science, Warren Wilson College, Swannanoa, NC (1993-1994) **MIL:** U.S. Coast Guard Ready Reserve (1951-1979); Postings, Vietnam, Madagascar, Togo, Indonesia (1956-1970); Joined, U.S. Foreign Service, (1956); Deck Officer, Korea, Vietnam; Commander (Retired) **AW:** Commander of the Army Award for Service, National War College (1989); Westminster College Alumni Achievement Award (1989); American Graduate School of International Management Alumni Achievement Award (1986); State Department Superior Honor Award (1981); Superior Honor Award, U.S. Agency for International Development (1979); Southeast Asia Ministers of Education Organization (SEAMEO) Citation for Achievement (1974) **MEM:** Veterans for Peace; Citizens for Global Solutions; United Nations Association; Union of Concerned Scientists; Council for a Livable World; Amnesty International; Human Rights Watch; ACLU; NAACP; Southern Poverty Law Center; World Watch Institute; The Land Institute; Greenpeace; National Resources Defense Council; Ocean Conservancy; World Wildlife Fund; The Nature Conservancy; Coast Guard Combat Veterans Association; Destroyer Escort Sailors Association **MH:** Albert Nelson Marquis Lifetime Achievement Award **B/I:** Mr. Petrequin became involved in his profession because he was born and raised in the Midwest during events leading up to World War II and the formation of the United Nations thereafter. These historic episodes imparted an incentive to become a participant in international affairs. His initial service in the Coast Guard, which took him overseas during the Korean War, confirmed this desire. **THT:** Mr. Petrequin said, "During the last 50 years, we have entered the Anthropocene Geologic Epoch of Earth's history wherein the planet's fate will now be determined more by human activities rather than natural phenomena. This new classification was in recognition of the disruption and destruction of Earth's major life support systems caused by a global economy oblivious to the environmental damage it causes in pursuit of infinite growth. Human activities are closing down the basic life systems through abuse of the air, the oceans and waters, the soil and the vegetation, eliminating species at a rate never before known in historic time.. A great change in our stewardship of the Earth and life upon it is required if vast human misery is to be avoided and our global home on this planet is not to be irretrievably mutilated."

PETRICK, JOSEPH ANTHONY, T: Management Professor (Retired), Business Ethics Consultant, American Philosopher, Small Business Owner **I:** Education/Educational Services **DOB:** 12/31/1946 **PB:** Pueblo **SC:** CO/USA **PT:** Joseph John; Hermina Emma Petrick **MS:** Married **SPN:** Kimberly Marie Weber (09/22/1984) **ED:** MBA, University of Cincinnati (1990); PhD, Pennsylvania State University (1972); BA, Colorado State University (1968) **CT:** Senior Professional in Human Resources (SPHR), Human Resources Certification Institute, Washington, DC (1993-1998) **C:** Full Tenured Professor of Management & International Business, Wright State University, Dayton, OH (1989-2013); Field Service Professor, University of Cincinnati (1987-1989); Head, Off-Campus Department of Business & Economics, Wilmington College, Ohio (1984-1987); Assistant Dean, Southern Ohio College, Fairfield, OH (1982-1984); Tenured Associate Professor and Head of Philosophy Program, Northern Kentucky University, Highland Heights, KY (1975-1982); Assistant Professor of Philosophy, College of Charleston, SC (1972-1975) **CR:** Chief Executive Officer, Institute for Secular Wisdom, Cincinnati, OH (2014-Present); Chief Executive Officer, Integrity Capacity Associates, Cincinnati, OH (2002-Present); Chief Executive Officer, Performance Leadership Associates, Cincinnati, OH (1996-Present); Member, Board of Directors of the Human Resources Certification Institute (HRCI) **CIV:** Baldrige National Quality Award Examiner, U.S. Department of Commerce, Washington, DC; Ohio Baldrige Quality Award for Excellence Examiner, Dayton, OH; Volunteer, American Heart Association; Volunteer Security Patrol Driver, Sun City Center, Florida; Retirement Community Great Books Discussion Leader; Chief Executive Officer, Institute for Secular Wisdom (ISW) **CW:** Co-Author, "Managing Project Quality" (2002); Co-Author, "Management Ethics: Integrity at Work" (1997); Co-Author, "Total Quality and Organization Development" (1997); Co-Author, "Total Quality in Managing Human Resources" (1995); Author, Article, "Sustainable Stakeholder Capitalism," Corporate Citizenship **AW:** WSU Trustees' Award for Faculty Excellence; WSU Golding Distinguished Professor Research Award; WSU Innovation in Business Education Group Award, Midwestern Deans of U.S. Business Schools; Selected as Malone Arabic Studies Fellow by the U.S. Arab Relations Institute; Selected as a Woodrow Wilson Dissertation Fellow by the Woodrow Wilson National Foundation; Selected as a National Beta Gamma Sigma National Faculty Fellow **MEM:** Society for Business Ethics (1995-Present); President, International Business Honor Society (2006-2013); President, Midwestern Society for Human Resources and Industrial Relations (1996-1997); Vice President for Individual Entrepreneurship, U.S. Association for Small Business and Entrepreneurship (1994-1995); Academy of Management; American Philosophical Association; Society for Human Resource Management; Society for Business Ethics; Sigma Iota Epsilon; Beta Gamma Sigma (National Business Honorary Society) **MH:** Marquis Lifetime Achievement Award **B/I:** Mr. Patrick became involved in his profession because he was drawn to a higher education career as a university professor both by his love of ideas and his exposure to three positive professorial role models, including Dr. Theodore Scharle, Dr. Kenneth Kennard, and Dr. Henry Finch. All the role models conducted research to discover new knowledge, taught effectively to disseminate knowledge, and provided helpful institutional and community service, all of which added value to the world and provided modest lifetime financial remuneration. "Coming from a working class family, my exposure to them helped me concretely imagine a new future by investing my life energies into 25 years of formal education, 40 years of full-time career-related employment and 35 years of leisurely retirement." **AV:** Traveling; Reading; Book discussion groups; Films; Ballroom dancing; Fitness exercise; Playing tennis; Pickleball; Playing billiards; Playing table tennis; Music; In-depth conversations with family and friends **PA:** Democrat **RE:** Agnostic secular ecological humanist **THT:** Mr. Patrick's life motto is "Invest your life energies wisely and deserve to be happy. In my life I have looked at my years of formal education, full-time career-related employment and leisurely retirement as sound investments of my life energies so that in the short and long term I could make difficult decisions between have a good time and leading a good life. An essential part of leading a good life is the development of intellectual, moral, social, emotional and political virtue or the habitual readiness to act ethically rather than impulsively enjoying unethical or amoral pleasures. Wisdom is the preeminent intellectual virtue that integrates knowledge and experience so that individuals and collectives can deserve to be happy. I agree with Aristotle that happiness is the quality of a whole human life characterized by the maximization of six goods: health, wealth, knowledge, friendship, good luck and virtue, the last factor being the most important. The lifelong commitment to achieve and sustain a level of wisdom with which to honorably navigate the human predicament in order to deserve to be happy is a worthy challenge for a meaningful life."

PETRONE, JOHN R., T: Music Educator, Composer (Retired) **I:** Education/Educational Services **DOB:** 12/26/1932 **PB:** Youngstown **SC:** OH/USA **PT:** Angelo R. Petrone; Mary C. Petrone **SPN:** Diane Rupple Petrone (10/18/1987); Married Margaret Adams Petrone (04/12/1958) (Divorced 02/20/1986) **CH:** Nicolette; Jennifer; John; Margaret; Michael; Susan **ED:** PhD in Music Composition, Conservatoire de Lille, France (1982); MusM, Duquesne University (1963); MusB, Youngstown College (1958) **CT:** Certified Teacher, State of Ohio (1980) **C:** Retired (2005); Adjunct Faculty, Ursuline College (1986-2005); Retired (1984); Music Director, Specialist, Willoughby-Eastlake City Schools (1965-1984); Music Director, Cardinal Mooney High School (1960-1965); Elementary Music Supervisor, Catholic Diocese of Youngstown (1958-1960); Director of Music, St. Mary's High School (1957-1958) **CR:** Private Piano Teacher; Piano Player, Local Shows in Ohio **MIL:** Special Services, Korea, U.S. Air Force (1951-1954) **CW:** Composer, NASA/Higbees Christmas Show (1983); Composer, Arranger, Music Director, "Care Bears" (1982); Composer Arranger, Music Director, "Mr. Jingeling" (1981); Composer, Arranger, Music Director, "Augustine" (1980); Composer, Arranger, Conductor, "The Flight of Apollo Eleven" (1979); Composer, "Disco-Tinued" (1979); Composer, "Haydn Seek" (1979); Composer, "Goin' Baroque" (1977) **AW:** Martha

Holden Jennings Scholar (1975-1976); Outstanding Secondary Educator of America (1974) **MEM:** ASCAP; American Federation of Musicians; Kappa Delta Pi, International Honor Society in Education; Phi Mu Alpha Sinfonia Fraternity of America **MH:** Albert Nelson Marquis Lifetime Achievement Award; Marquis Who's Who Top Professional **B/I:** Dr. Petrone became involved in his profession because his high school band frequently ushered at the Stambaugh Auditorium, where famous musicians would play and rehearse. He heard a lot of music for free and was inspired by what he heard. Dr. Petrone enlisted in the Air Force and went into special services, where he performed a show called "Stars and Khaki and Blue" in Korea and Japan. Upon his return home, he decided to parlay his love of music to others as a teacher. **AV:** Racing cars **PA:** Republican **RE:** Roman Catholic

PETTY, BOB, T: News Reporter, Anchor **I:** Other **DOB:** 11/26/1940 **PB:** Memphis **SC:** TN/USA **MS:** Married **SPN:** Cora **CH:** Bobby; Cory **ED:** MA in Communications, Governors State University, University Park, IL (1979); BA, Arizona State University (1970) **C:** Anchor, Saturday Weekend News, WLS-TV (1983-2002); Producer, Host, Weekend Edition (1978-1983); Member, Action 7 News Team, WLS-TV (1975-1978); General Assignment Reporter, WLS-TV (1971-1975); News Writer, Reporter, Producer, KOOL-TV and Radio, Phoenix, AZ; With KPHO-TV **AW:** William Benton Fellow in Broadcast Journalism, University of Chicago (1987); Urban Journalism Fellowship, University of Chicago

PEW, ROBERT, T: Real Estate and Equipment Leasing Corporation Officer (Retired) **I:** Real Estate **DOB:** 08/22/1936 **PB:** Philadelphia **SC:** PA/USA **PT:** Arthur Edmond Pew; Mary Elizabeth (Elliot) Pew **MS:** Married **SPN:** Daria S. Decerio (06/19/1993) **CH:** Robert Anderson (Deceased); James Cunningham; Glenn Edgar; Joan Elliot; Richard Westeman Pew **ED:** Honorary LHD, Gettysburg College (1984); Honorary Doctor of Professional Studies, Temple University (1983); Honorary LLD, Widener University (1982); MS in Management, Massachusetts Institute of Technology (1970); BS, Temple University (1959); Coursework, Princeton University (1954-1956) **C:** Chairman, Glenmede Corporation, Philadelphia, PA (1997-2004); Chief Executive Officer, Radnor Corporation (1995-1996); President, Helios Capital Corp. (1977-1996); Corporate Secretary, Sun Oil Co. (Now Sunmarks, LLC), Philadelphia, PA (1974-1977); Secretary-treasurer, Manager, Financial Control of Products Group, Sun Oil Co. (Now Sunmarks, LLC), Philadelphia, PA (1971-1974); Assistant to Executive Vice President, Corporate Projects Group, Sun Oil Co. (Now Sunmarks, LLC), Philadelphia, PA (1970-1971); Staff Assistant, Treasury Department, Sun Oil Co. (Now Sunmarks, LLC), Philadelphia, PA (1965-1969); Auditor, Internal Audit Department, Sun Oil Co. (Now Sunmarks, LLC), Philadelphia, PA (1960-1965); Operations Assistant, Production Division, Sun Oil Co. (Now Sunmarks, LLC), Premont, Texas (1959-1960); Operations Assistant, Production Division, Sun Oil Co. (Now Sunmarks, LLC), Morgan City, LA **CR:** Board of Directors, Sunoco Inc. (Sunmarks, LLC), Philadelphia, PA (1978-2009); Board of Directors, Glenmede Corporation, Philadelphia, PA; With, Glenmede Trust Co., N.A., Philadelphia, PA; With, Academy of Music, Philadelphia, PA; With, The Pew Charitable Trusts, Philadelphia, PA **CIV:** Vice Chairman Emeritus, The Children's Hospital of Philadelphia, PA (2012-Present); Vice Chairman, The Children's Hospital of Philadelphia (1991-2010); Trustee, The Children's Hospital of Philadelphia **MIL:** Served,

Pennsylvania Air National Guard (1956-1959) **AW:** R. Kelso Carter Award, Widener University (1971); Alfred P. Sloan Fellow, Massachusetts Institute of Technology (1970) **MEM:** Trustee, Aircraft Owners and Pilots Association (1970-2014); Chairman, Aircraft Owners and Pilots Association (1974-1977, 1985-2002); President, Harbor Club (1992-1996); Vice Chairman, Aircraft Owners and Pilots Association (1979-1985); Honorary Member, American Hospital Association; The College of Physicians of Philadelphia; The Union League Club; Philadelphia Aviation Country Club (PACC); The Merion Cricket Club; Northeast Harbor Fleet; Seal Harbor Yacht Club **PA:** Republican **RE:** Presbyterian

PFEIFFER, MARY LOUISE, "MARY LOU", T: Artist, Educator **I:** Education/Educational Services **CN:** Florida International University **DOB:** 02/14/1944 **PB:** Troy **SC:** OH/USA **PT:** John Edward Dunnick; Helen Elizabeth Johnson-Dunnick **MS:** Married **CH:** William G. II; Scott Edward **ED:** MA in Religious Studies, Florida International University, Miami, FL (2004); LLM, St. Thomas University School of Law, Miami, FL (2002); BA, Florida International University, Miami, FL (1986); AS, Tidewater College, Virginia Beach, VA, Magna Cum Laude (1976) **C:** Retired (2018); Faculty, Fellow, The Honors College, Florida International University (2005-2018); Adjunct Professor, Department of Religious Studies, Florida International University (2002-2018); Owner, Operator, Pfeiffer Originals, Art Class Designs, Miami, FL (1976) **CR:** Board of Advisors, College of Arts, Sciences, and Education (CASE), Florida International University; President, Women's Studies Advisory Board, Florida International University **CIV:** Steering Committee, 5th-7th Tribal Symposia, St. Thomas University School of Law (2002-2006); Hospitality Coordinator, Performing Arts Community and Education, Miami, FL (1982-1984); POW-MIA Committee, Naval Air Station Oceana, Virginia Beach, VA (1970-1975); President, Secretary-Treasurer, Officers' Wives Club (1968-1969); Acting Chairman, Navy Relief Society, Meridian, MS (1968-1969) **CW:** Author, Technical Textbook, Basic Radiography, NCHS Monograph **AW:** Outstanding Service Award, Department Religious Studies, Florida International University (2000, 2002); Alumni Association Torch Award, Florida International University Alumni Association (2000) **MEM:** Phi Theta Kappa; Theta Alpha Kappa **B/I:** Ms. Pfeiffer was inspired to work in her field because of the opportunity to continue learning through her work. She wanted to retain as much knowledge as possible. **AV:** Swimming; Sailing; Golfing; Traveling

PFEIFFER, MICHELLE MARIE, T: Actress **I:** Media & Entertainment **DOB:** 04/29/1958 **PB:** Santa Ana **SC:** CA/USA **PT:** Richard Pfeiffer; Donna (Taverna) Pfeiffer **MS:** Married **SPN:** David E. Kelley (1993); Peter Horton (1981, Divorced 1990) **CH:** Claudia Rose (Adoptive Daughter); John Henry **ED:** Diploma, Fountain Valley High School (1976); Coursework, Golden West College **CR:** Launched, Fragrance Line, "Henry Rose" (2019); Spokesmodel, Giorgio Armani (2005) **CIV:** Board Member, Environmental Working Group, Washington, DC (2016); Attendee, Los Angeles Gala, Healthy Child Healthy World (2016); American Cancer Society; Humane Society **CW:** Actress, "French Exit" (2020); Actress, "Avengers: Endgame" (2019); Actress, "Maleficent: Mistress of Evil" (2019); Actress, "Ant-Man and the Wasp" (2018); Actress, "Where is Kyra?" (2017); Actress, "Mother!" (2017); Actress, "Murder on the Orient Express" (2017); Actress, TV Film, "The Wizard of Lies" (2017); Actress, "The Family" (2013); Actress, "Dark Shadows" (2012); Actress, "People Like Us"

(2012); Actress, "New Year's Eve" (2011); Actress, "Personal Effects" (2009); Actress, "Cheri" (2009); Actress, "I Could Never Be Your Woman" (2007); Actress, "Hairspray" (2007); Actress, "Stardust" (2007); Voice Actress, "Sinbad: Legend of the Seven Seas" (2003); Actress, "White Oleander" (2002); Actress, "I Am Sam" (2001); Actress, "What Lies Beneath" (2000); Actress, "The Deep End of the Ocean" (1999); Actress, "A Midsummer Night's Dream" (1999); Actress, "The Story of Us" (1999); Voice Actress, "The Prince of Egypt" (1998); Actress, "A Thousand Acres" (1997); Actress, "Up Close & Personal" (1996); Actress, "To Gillian on Her 37th Birthday" (1996); Actress, "One Fine Day" (1996); Guest Appearance, "Muppets Tonight" (1996); Guest Appearance, "Picket Fences" (1995); Actress, "Dangerous Minds" (1995); Actress, "Wolf" (1994); Actress, "The Age of Innocence" (1993); Guest Appearance, "The Simpsons" (1993); Actress, "Batman Returns" (1992); Actress, "Love Field" (1992); Actress, "Frankie and Johnny" (1991); Actress, "The Russia House" (1990); Actress, "The Fabulous Baker Boys" (1989); Actress, "Married to the Mob" (1988); Actress, "Tequila Sunrise" (1988); Actress, "Dangerous Liaisons" (1988); Actress, "The Witches of Eastwick" (1987); Appearance, "Amazon Women on the Moon" (1987); Guest Appearance, "Great Performances" (1987); Actress, "Sweet Liberty" (1986); Actress, "Into the Night" (1985); Actress, TV Special, "One Too Many" (1985); Actress, "Ladyhawke" (1985); Actress, "Scarface" (1983); Actress, "Grease 2" (1982); Actress, "Charlie Chan and the Curse of the Dragon Queen" (1981); Actress, TV Film, "The Children Nobody Wanted" (1981); Actress, TV Film, "Splendor in the Grass" (1981); Actress, TV Film, "Callie & Son" (1981); Guest Appearance, "Fantasy Island" (1978, 1981); Guest Appearance, "Enos" (1980); Actress, "B.A.D. Cats" (1980); Actress, "The Hollywood Knights" (1980); Actress, "Falling in Love Again" (1980); Guest Appearance, "CHiPs" (1979); Actress, "The Solitary Man" (1979); Actress, "Delta House" (1979) **AW:** Best Supporting Actress, "White Oleander," Kansas City Film Critics Circle Awards (2003); Best Supporting Actress, "White Oleander," San Diego Film Critics Society Awards (2002); Favorite Actress – Suspense, "What Lies Beneath," Blockbuster Entertainment Awards (2001); Favorite Actress – Comedy/Romance, "One Fine Day," Blockbuster Entertainment Awards (1997); Favorite Actress – Drama, "Dangerous Minds," Blockbuster Entertainment Awards (1996); Elvira Notari Prize, "The Age of Innocence," Venice International Film Festival (1993); Silver Bear for Best Actress, "Love Field," Berlin International Film Festival (1992); Best Actress in a Supporting Role, "Dangerous Liaisons," BAFTA Awards (1989); Best Actress in a Motion Picture – Drama, "The Fabulous Baker Boys," Golden Globe Awards (1989); Best Actress, "The Fabulous Baker Boys," Chicago Film Critics Association Awards, Los Angeles Film Critics Association Awards, National Board of Review Awards, National Society of Film Critics Awards, New York Film Critics Circle Awards (1989); Winner, Miss Orange County (1978) **MEM:** Alpha Delta Pi

PFLAUM, STEVEN FORBES, T: Partner, Co-Chair of Litigation Department, Chair of Pro Bono Committee **I:** Law and Legal Services **CN:** Neal, Gerber & Eisenberg, LLP **PB:** Chicago **SC:** Il/USA **MS:** Married **SPN:** Karen Robertson **CH:** Kimberlee Mott (Ryan Mott); Dr. Katharine Mershon (Kevin Mershon); Matthew Pflaum; Dr. Kevin Pflaum; Brian Pflaum (Jodie Pflaum); Krista LeRay (Andrew LeRay) **ED:** JD, University of Michigan Law School, Magna Cum Laude (1979); BA in Political Science, University of Illinois at Urbana-Champaign (1976) **C:** Co-Chair, Litigation Department (2017-Present);

Chair, Pro Bono Committee (2010-Present); Partner (2010-Present); Chair, General & Commercial Litigation Department (2015-2017); Neal, Gerber & Eisenberg LLP; Partner, McDermott, Will & Emery LLP (1988-2009); Partner, O'Donnell & Gordon (1984-1987); Associate, O'Donnell & Gordon (1982-1983); Associate, Beardsley, Hufstedler & Kemble (1979-1981); Hufstedler, Miller, Carlson & Beardsley (1981-1982) **CIV:** Chair, Illinois Judicial Ethics Committee (2013-Present); Founding Member, Illinois Judicial Ethics Committee (1992-Present); Member, Chair, Illinois Supreme Court Committee on Professional Responsibility; Chair, Illinois Statutory Court Fee Task Force **CW:** Co-Author, "Civil Appeals: State and Federal, Chapters on Direct Appeals to, and Original Actions in Illinois Supreme Court," IICLE (2018); Co-Author, "Rule 6.5 of the Illinois Rules of Professional Conduct: Empowering Lawyers to Provide More Pro Bono," 24 CBA Record 40 (2010); Co-Author, "New Focus on Lawyers' 'Reporting-Up' Responsibilities," Health Lawyers' Weekly, Vol. VII, no. 32 (2009); Co-Author, "Proposed Rule 225: Needed Guidance for Illinois Courts," 93 Ill. B.J. 203 (2005); Author, "Regulating Out-of-State Counsel a Welcome Step Forward," Chicago Lawyer (2004); Co-Author, "Limited Liability Legal Practice: New Opportunities and Responsibilities for Illinois Lawyers," 17 CBA Record 37 (2003); Co-Author, "Justice James D. Heiple: Impeachment and the Assault on Judicial Independence," 29 Loyola University Chicago Law Journal 741 (1998); Co-Author, "Should Justice Heiple Be Impeached?," Chicago Tribune (1997); Co-Author, "Successful Practice Under the New Illinois Civil Discovery Rules," 9 CBA Record 20 (1995); Co-Author, "Client Solicitation-What You Can Do and What to Do About It," 19 Litigation 31 (1993); Co-Author, "The Ethics of Solicitation of Business from Corporate Clients," 5 Georgetown J. Leg. Ethics 423 (1991) **AW:** Edward J. Lewis II Pro Bono Service Award, Chicago Bar Foundation (2019); Lawyer of the Year, Chicago Litigation–Regulatory Enforcement, Best Lawyers (2015, 2017, 2019); Amicus Award, Illinois Judges Association (2018) **MEM:** President, Illinois Appellate Lawyers Association (2014-2015); General Counsel, Chicago Bar Association, (1996-2009); Phi Beta Kappa; Order of the Coif; American Academy of Appellate Lawyers **BAR:** Illinois; California **MH:** Who's Who in American Law **AS:** He attributes his success to hard work, good fortune, and family support and guidance. **B/I:** Mr. Pflaum is the first lawyer in his family. He was struck, at a young age, by how the friends of his father's who were lawyers had a unique ability to help people. He was also inspired by Thurgood Marshall and the Civil Rights Movement. **THT:** Work hard, play hard, and hardly Sleep.

PHILBIN, GARY M., T: Chief Executive Officer, President **I:** Other **CN:** Dollar Tree, Inc. **ED:** MBA, Xavier University; BS in Accounting, Miami University **C:** Chief Executive Officer, President, Dollar Tree, Inc. (2017-Present); Chief Operating Officer, President, Dollar Tree, Inc. (2013-Present); Enterprise President, Dollar Tree, Inc. (2016-2017); Chief Operating Officer, President, Dollar Tree, Inc. (2013-2015); Chief Operating Officer, Dollar Tree, Inc. (2007-2013); Senior Vice President, Stores, Dollar Tree, Inc. (2001-2007); Numerous Executive Positions (1997-2001); Executive Vice President, Operations and Merchandising, Cub Foods (1996-1997); Senior Vice President, Merchandising, Waldbaums (1993-1996); Numerous Positions in Store Operations and Merchandising, Kroger Company (1973-1993)

PHILIPP, KARLA ANN, T: Musician, Educator, Conductor **I:** Media & Entertainment **DOB:** 09/12/1955 **PB:** Milwaukee **SC:** WI/USA **PT:** John William Philipp; Catherine Anne Philipp **ED:** MusM, Memphis State University (Now University of Memphis) (1979); MusB, University of Arizona (1977) **C:** Adjunct Instructor, University of Memphis, Memphis, TN (2009-2019); Conductor, Youth Sinfonia, Memphis Youth Symphony Program (1997-2019); Conductor, Youth String Ensemble, Memphis Youth Symphony Program (1997-2017); Teacher, Itinerant Strings, Memphis City Schools (1979-2009) **CR:** Section Member, Jackson Symphony Orchestra (2011-Present); Orchestra Director, Intermountain Suzuki String Institute (2011); Note-Reading Teacher, Intermountain Suzuki String Institute (2011); Orchestra Director, Summer String Camp, The University of Memphis (2006-2008); Orchestra Director, Intermountain Suzuki String Institute (2001-2008); Note-Reading Teacher, Intermountain Suzuki String Institute (1993-2008); Principal Bass Player, Memphis Symphony Orchestra (1989-2007); Conductor, American Suzuki Institute, Suzuki Association of the Americas (1993-2005); Section Bass Player, Memphis Symphony Orchestra (1979-1989); Member, Tucson Symphony Orchestra (1977-1978); Private Studio; Work with Bass Players, Collierville Public School; Presenter in Field **CIV:** Integrity, Memphis, TN (2003-Present) **AW:** Honoree, Amro Music Educator's Walk (2015); West Tennessee School Band and Orchestra Associated Hall of Fame (2013); Outstanding Teacher Award, Tennessee Governor's School for the Arts (2009-2010); Award For Teacher Excellence, Rotary Club of Memphis (1998); Grantee, Rotary Club of Memphis (1997); Outstanding Teacher Award, Tennessee Governor's School for the Arts (1994-1995); Outstanding Teacher Award, Tennessee Governor's School for the Arts (1991); Grantee, Rotary Club of Memphis (1991); Haldeman Scholarship, School of Music, University of Arizona (1974-1978) **MEM:** Vice President, West Tennessee Chapter, American String Teachers Association (1993-1995); International Society of Business Leaders; Tennessee Music Education Association; National Association for Music Education; Local 71; American Federation of Musicians **MH:** Albert Nelson Marquis Lifetime Achievement Award; Marquis Who's Who Top Professional **AV:** Reading; Traveling **RE:** Episcopalian

PHILIPSON, TOMAS, PHD, T: Acting Chairman, Vice Chair; Professor **I:** Government Administration/Government Relations/Government Services **CN:** Council of Economic Advisers **PB:** Uppsala **SC:** Sweden **PT:** Lennart Philipson; Malin Philipson **ED:** PhD, The Wharton School, The University of Pennsylvania (1989); MA in Economics, The Wharton School, The University of Pennsylvania; MA, Claremont Graduate University (1985); BSc, Uppsala University, East Orange, NJ (1984) **C:** Acting Chairman, Vice Chair, Council of Advisers (2019-Present); Member, Council of Economic Advisers (2017-2019); Professor, Harris School Public Policy Studies, The University of Chicago (1998-2017); Associate Professor, The University of Chicago (1996-1998); Visiting Assistant Professor, Yale University, New Haven, CT (1990-1995); Postdoctoral Fellow, The University of Chicago (1990); Senior Adviser, Vice President Biden's Cancer Moonshot Initiative, U.S. Congress; Scientific Adviser, 21st Century Cures Act, U.S. Congress; Appointed Member, Key Indicator Commission, Affordable Care Act; Senior Health Care Adviser, Senator John McCain's Presidential Campaign; Senior Economic Adviser, Centers for Medicare and Medicaid Services (CMS); Senior Economic Adviser, Food and Drug Administration (FDA) **CR:** Co-Founder, Precision Health Economics, Los Angeles, CA **CIV:** Board Member, National Bureau of Economic Research; Board Member, American Enterprise Institute; Chairman, Project FDA, Manhattan Institute for Policy Research, Inc.; Board Member, Heartland Institute; Board Member, Milken Institute; Board Member, RAND Corporation; Board Member, USC Leonard D. Schaeffer Center for Health Policy & Economics, The University of Chicago; With, John M. Olin Program of Law and Economics, George J. Stigler Center for the Study of the Economy and the State, Population Research Center, and National Opinion Research Center (NORC); Consultant, Private Corporations and Government Organizations, National and International **CW:** Founding Editor, Forums for Health Economics & Policy; Editorial Board, Health Economics and The European Journal of Health Economics; Contributor, Monthly Column, Forbes Magazine; Contributor, Articles, Professional Journals, including American Economic Review, Journal of Political Economy, Quarterly Journal of Economics, Journal of Economic Theory, Journal of Health Economics, Health Affairs, and Econometrica **AW:** Two-Time Recipient, Kenneth Arrow Award, International Health Economics Association; Garfield Award, Research America; Prêmio Haralambos Simeonidisand, Brazilian Economic Association; Distinguished Economic Research Award, Milken Institute

PHILLIPS, DEAN BENSON, T: U.S. Representative from Minnesota **I:** Government Administration/Government Relations/Government Services **CN:** U.S. House of Representatives **DOB:** 01/20/1969 **PB:** Saint Paul **SC:** MN/USA **PT:** Artie Pfefer (Deceased); Eddie Phillips; DeeDee (Cohen) Phillips **MS:** Married **SPN:** Karin (Einisman) Phillips **ED:** Master of Business Administration, University of Minnesota Carlson School of Management; Bachelor of Arts, Brown University **C:** Member, U.S. House of Representatives from Minnesota's Third Congressional District (2019-Present); President, Phillips Distilling Company; With, InMotion **PA:** Democrat **RE:** Jewish

PHILLIPS, KENNETH W., T: President and Chief Executive Officer **I:** Insurance **CN:** Kilpatrick Life Insurance Company **CH:** Two Children **ED:** Bachelor of Arts, The University of Texas at Austin (1964) **CT:** Fellow, Life Management Institute (1978); Chartered Life Underwriter; Data Processing **C:** President, Jefferson National Life Insurance Company of Indianapolis (1985-Present); Consultant, Piedmont & Mitchell (1969-Present); Chairperson, Chief Executive Officer, Radford National Life Insurance (1997); Actuary, Republic National Life Insurance Company (1964-1969); President, Chief Executive Officer, Kilpatrick Life Insurance Company; With, American Founders Life Insurance Company; President, First Continental Life Insurance Company; President, Union Life Insurance Company; President, Lomis Financial Group, Dallas, TX; Executive Vice President, Pilneck Company, TX; Chief Financial Officer, Pilneck Company, Waco, TX; Actuary, Chief Financial Officer, American Life Insurance Company, MS **CR:** President, 17 Companies **AS:** Mr. Phillips attributes his success to patience and hard work. **B/I:** Mr. Phillips became involved in his profession after graduating from the University of Texas with a degree in mathematics. He was presented with the opportunity to take an actuarial job, and worked in this capacity for several years. He found the work interesting and intriguing.

PHILLIPS, TODD, T: Director **I:** Media & Entertainment **DOB:** 12/20/1970 **PB:** Brooklyn **SC:** NY/USA **ED:** Coursework, New York University Film School **CR:** Kim's Video and Music **CW:** Director,

Writer, Producer, "Joker" (2019); Producer, "A Star is Born" (2018); Director, Writer, Producer, "War Dogs" (2016); Executive Producer, "Limitless" (2015-2016); Director, Writer, Producer, "The Hangover Part III" (2013); Producer, "Project X" (2012); Director, Producer, Commercial, "Matthew Broderick's Day Off" (2012); Director, Writer, Producer, "The Hangover Part II" (2011); Director, Writer, Producer, "Due Date" (2010); Director, Producer, "The Hangover" (2009); Director, Executive Producer, TV Film, "The More Things Change..." (2008); Story Writer, "Borat" (2006); Director, Writer, Producer, "School for Scoundrels" (2006); Producer, "All the King's Men" (2006); Director, Writer, "Starsky & Hutch" (2004); Director, Writer, Producer, "Old School" (2003); Director, Writer, "Road Trip" (2000); Director, Writer, Producer, Documentary, "Bittersweet Motel" (2000); Co-Director, Writer, Producer, Appearance, Documentary, "Frat House" (1998); Field Producer, "Taxicab Confessions" (1997); Director, Writer, Producer, Documentary, "Hated: GG Allin and the Murder Junkies" (1993) AW: Golden Lion, "Joker," Venice International Film Festival (2019); Director of the Year, ShoWest Convention (2010); Best Motion Picture – Musical or Comedy, "The Hangover," Golden Globe Awards (2009); Grand Jury Prize Documentary, "Frat House," Sundance Film Festival (1998); Certificate of Merit, "Frat House," San Francisco International Film Festival (1998); Best Documentary Film, "Hated: GG Allin and the Murder Junkies," New Orleans Film Festival (1994) RE: Jewish

PHIPPS, BENJAMIN K., T: Lawyer I: Law and Legal Services DOB: 01/16/1933 PB: Boston SC: MA/USA PT: Benjamin Kimball Phipps; Bertha Elizabeth (Forsyth) Phipps MS: Widow SPN: Phyllis Jarrett Anderson (1/10/1962, Deceased) CH: Lisa Jarrett; Christina Caroline (Deceased) ED: LLB, University of Virginia (1958); BS in Commerce, University of Virginia (1955) CT: Certified, Institute of Professionals in Taxation (2004) C: Private Practice, Tallahassee, FL (1965-Present); Chairman, Senior Partner, Phipps & Howell CR: Elected Director, Florida Council of Property Tax Lawyers (2003); Member, Legislative Task Force, Taxpayers' Bill Rights (1989-1991); Member, Advisory Committee, Finance & Tax Committee (1983-1984); Counsel to Speaker, Florida House of Representatives (1973-1974); Counsel, Tax Committee, Florida House of Representatives (1966-1972) CIV: Treasurer, Tallahassee Trust for Historic Preservation (1998-Present); Board, Tallahassee Trust for Historic Preservation (1997-Present); Chairman, Historic Tallahassee Preservation Board (1970-1991) MIL: Served to Captain, U.S. Army (1958-1964) CW: Contributor, Articles, Professional Journals; Columnist, Tallahassee Democrat; Publisher, Many Works, Newspapers AW: Named Best Lawyers in America; Preeminent, Martindale Hubbell; Historic Preservation Award; Outstanding Contribution Award; Legal Elite, Florida Trend Magazine MEM: Treasurer, Vice Chairman, Chairman, Tax Section, Florida Bar Association (1985-1986); President, St. Andrews Society (1978-1979); Editorial Board, Florida Bar Journal News, Chairman, Florida Bar Association (1975-1976); Tax Section, State and Local Tax Committee, American Bar Association; Board, Florida Heritage Foundation; Tallahassee Bar Association; Certified Member, Institute of Professionals Taxation (IPT); CMI; Gov.'s Club; University Center Club; Cosmos Club; Exchange Club; Director, Tiger Bay Club; Florida Economic Club; Sigma Alpha Epsilon; Phi Alpha Delta; Pi Delta Epsilon; Museum Art and History Foundation Board BAR: Florida (1964); United States District Court for the Northern District of Florida; U.S. Claims Court; United States Court of Appeals for the Fifth Circuit; United States Court of Appeals for the Eleventh Circuit; U.S. Tax Court MH: Albert Nelson Marquis Lifetime Achievement Award B/I: Mr. Phipps became involved in his profession because when he was 13 years old he made a decision that he wanted to be a lawyer and he chose taxation because he was very good with numbers. PA: Republican RE: Episcopalian

PICHAI, SUNDAR, T: Chief Executive Officer, Engineer I: Business Management/Business Services CN: Google LLC DOB: 06/10/1972 PB: Madurai SC: Tamil Nadu/India PT: Regunatha Pichai; Lakshmi Pichai MS: Married SPN: Anjali Pichai CH: Two Children ED: MBA, Wharton School, University of Pennsylvania; MS in Material Sciences and Engineering, Stanford University; BT, Indian Institute of Technology Kharagpur C: Chief Executive Officer, Google LLC, Mountain View, CA (2015-Present); Vice President, Product Management, Google LLC, Mountain View, CA (2014-Present); Senior Vice President, Android, Chrome & Apps, Google LLC, Mountain View, CA (2013-2014); Senior Vice President, Google Chrome & Apps, Google LLC, Mountain View, CA (2011-2013); Vice President, Product Management, Google LLC, Mountain View, CA (2004-2011); Management Consultant, McKinsey & Company; Various Engineering and Product Management Positions, Applied Materials, Inc. CR: Board of Directors, Jive Software (2011-2013) CW: Speaker, World Internet Conference, China (2017) AW: Listee, Top 50 Best CEOs of Large Companies, Comparably (2018); Inductee, Palmer Scholar, University of Pennsylvania; Siebel Scholar, University of Pennsylvania; Institute Silver Medal, Indian Institute of Technology Madras AV: Playing soccer and cricket

PICK, JAMES B., T: Business Professor, Writer I: Education/Educational Services CN: University of Redlands DOB: 07/29/1943 PB: Chicago SC: IL/USA PT: Grant Julius Pick; Helen (Block) Pick MS: Married SPN: Dr. Rosalyn Laudati ED: PhD, University of California, Irvine (1974); MS in Education, Northern Illinois University (1969); BA, Northwestern University (1966) C: Director, Center for Spatial Business (2011-2012, 2017-2019, 2020-Present); Professor, Business, University of Redlands (1995-Present); Chair, University Committee of Academic Planning & Standards (2010-2011, 2013-2015); Member, University Faculty Senate (2014-2015); Chair, Faculty Assembly, School of Business, University of Redlands (2001-2004); Associate Professor of Business, Director, Information Management Program, University of Redlands (1995-2001); Chair, Department of Management and Business, University of Redlands (1995-1999); Co-director, U.S. Mexico Database Project (1988-1991); Director, Computing, Graduate School of Management, University of California (1984-1991); Assistant Research Statistician, Lecturer, Graduate School of Management, University of California, Riverside (1975-1991) CR: Associate Editor, Senior Associate Editor, "European Journal Information Systems" (2010-Present); Senior Editor, Associate Editor, Information Technology for Development (2007-Present); Global Associate Editor, "Journal of Information Technology Case and Application Research" (2002-Present); Board, Professionals Advisors, Demographic Analysis, University of California, Irvine (2002-Present); Visiting Researcher, Department of Sociology, University of California Irvine (2005, 2009, 2013, 2016, 2020); Editorial Board Member, "Journal Borderlands Studies" (1999-2020); Visiting Professor, Esade, Barcelona (2019); Managing Guest Editor, "Decision Support Systems" (2016-2017); Chair, Special Interest Group inGIS, Association Information Systems (2013-2017); City University, Hong Kong, China (2012); External Faculty Research Associate, Center for Research Information Technology and Organizations, University of California, Irvine (2006-2012); Lingnan University, Hong Kong, China (2009); President, PCCLAS, Association for Borderlands Studies (2002-2003); Visiting Professor, University Iberoamericana, Mexico City, Mexico (1997, 2001); University Commission, Future Business Programs (1998-2000); National Curriculum Task Force (1997); Board of Governors (1989-1992); University Commons Board (1982-1986); President, Orange County Chapter, Association Systems Management (1978-1979); Consultant, International Division, United States Census Bureau (1978) CIV: Board of Directors, Northern Illinois University Foundation (2014-Present); Trustee, South California Public Radio (2014-Present); Trustee, Treasurer, Berkeley Art Museum and Pacific Film Archives (2003-Present); Trustee, Chairman, Collection Committee, Orange County Museum of Art (1996-Present); Regional Advisory Council, KPCC Public Radio (2009-2014); Board Advisors, Block Museum (2006-2012); External Committee, Block Museum, (1999-2001); Vice President, Newport Harbor Art Museum (1991-1996); Trustee, Newport Harbor Art Museum (1988-1996); Trustee, Newport Harbor Art Museum (1981-1987) CW: Author, "Renewable Energy, Problems and Prospects in Coachella Valley of California" (2017); Author, "The Global Digital Divides" (2015); Author, "Exploring the Urban Community: A GIS Approach, Second Edition" (2011); Author, "Geo-Business, GIS in the Digital Organization" (2008); Author, "Exploring the Urban Community: A GIS Approach, First Edition" (2005); Author, "Geographic Systems in Business" (2004); Author, "Mexico and Mexico City in the World Economy" (2001); Author, "Mexico Megacity" (1997); Author, "The Mexico Handbook" (1994); Author, "Atlas of Mexico" (1989); Author, "Computer Systems in Business" (1986); Author, "MicroManual" (1986); Author, "Geothermal Energy Development" (1982); Author, Numerous Articles, Professional Journals; Author, Book Chapters AW: Grantee, Co-Principal Investigator Grant, Esri Inc. (2018-2021), Distinguished Member, Association for Information Systems (2020); Best Conference Paper Runner Up Award, America's Conference on Information Systems (2016); Volunteer Spotlight Award, Association for Systems Management (2010); Grantee, Co-Principal Investigator Grant, U.S. Small Business Administration (2006-2008); Outstanding Alumnus Award, Northern Illinois University (2004); Senior Fulbright Scholar (2001); Ford Foundation Grantee (1998-1999); Thunderbird Award, Business Association of Latin American Studies (1993) MEM: American Association for the Advancement of Science; Association for Information Systems; Association of American Geographers; International Union Scientific Study of Population; Population Association of America; American Sociological Association; Association Computing Machinery; International Union Science Study Population; Population Association of America; American Sociological Association; Association of Computing Machinery MH: Albert Nelson Marquis Lifetime Achievement Award B/I: Dr. Pick became involved in his profession because of his interest in environmental problems and systems. His career began in the 1970s during the first wave of nation-wide environmental concerns. This interest led Dr. Pick to become interested in computer modeling, information systems applications, and geospatial analysis.

PIEGARI, JAMES, T: Psychologist I: Medicine & Health Care DOB: 08/04/1951 PB: Brooklyn SC: NY/USA PT: Vincent Piegari; Olympia Piegari ED: PhD in Psychology, Saybrook Graduate School and

Research Center (1999); MA in Psychology, New School Social Research (1995); MA in Psychology, Rutgers, The State University of New Jersey (1995); MA in Clinical Psychology, St. John's University (1975); BS in Psychology, Georgetown University (1972) **CT:** Certified in Primary and Advanced Training, Albert Ellis Institute (2006); Certified in Rational Emotive Behavior Theory and Techniques, Albert Ellis Institute, Primary and Advanced Training (2004); Certified in Mind, Body Meditation and Healing, Health Science Division, Columbia University College of Physicians and Surgeons (2001); Dispute Resolution Certificate Program, Cornell University (2000); Certified School Psychologist, New York; Licensed Psychologist, New York; Certified Mediator, Staten Island Community Dispute Resolution Center **C:** Private Practice Psychologist, Staten Island, NY (2002-2013); Psychologist, Terence Cardinal Cooke Health Care Center, New York, NY (2002-2013); Applied Behavioral Sciences Specialist, Terence Cardinal Cooke Health Care Center, New York, NY (1980-2001); Applied Behavioral Sciences Specialist, United Cerebral Palsy Associations of New York State, Staten Island, NY (1978-1980); Operations Research Analyst, United States Public Health Service Hospital, Staten Island, NY (1976-1978) **CR:** Superintendent Provider, Psychological Services, New York City Department of Education (2002-2010); Consultant, Vietnamese Refugee Program, Mission of Immaculate Virgin, Mount Loretto, Staten Island, NY (1986-1996); Associate Professor, Mercy College, Arthur Kill Correctional Facility, Staten Island, NY (1989-1990); Member, Publications Committee, Flower Hospital, New York, NY (1980-1981); Former Member, Alumni Admissions Program, Georgetown University **CIV:** Board of Directors, Friends of South Beach Psychiatric Center, Staten Island, NY (1980-1981); Chairman, Mental Health Symposium Committee, Friends of South Beach Psychiatric Center, Staten Island, NY (1980-1981); Charter Member, Friends of South Beach Psychiatric Center, Staten Island, NY (1980-1981); Member, Health and Hospitals Committee, New York City Community Board, Staten Island, NY (1979-1980); Former Member, Appellate Division Panel, Mental Health Professional Psychologist, New York State Supreme Court, New York **CW:** Contributor, Articles, Professional Journal; Contributor, Chapters, Books **AW:** Employee Recognition Award, Terence Cardinal Cooke Health Care Center (2001) **MEM:** American Psychological Association; New York State Psychological Association **MH:** Albert Nelson Marquis Lifetime Achievement Award **B/I:** Dr. Piegari felt that there was a great need for psychology in the world. Also a psychological point of view for conflict resolution was very important for international relations. Psychology was instrumental in every sector of society. People with mental illnesses are under served and he felt compelled to make a contribution. **AV:** Civil War artifacts; Photography; Travel; Motorcycle touring

PIERCE, FREDERICK, "FRED" WATSON IV, T: President, Chief Executive Officer **I:** Real Estate **CN:** Pierce Education Properties **PT:** Frederick W. Pierce, III; Diane T. Pierce **MS:** Married **SPN:** Christine Folsom Pierce **CH:** Peyton G. Pierce; Riley F. Pierce **ED:** MBA Program, Graduate Studies in Real Estate Finance, San Diego State University (1988); BS in Finance, San Diego State University, Cum Laude (1984) **C:** President, Chief Executive Officer, Pierce Education Properties (1995-Present); Senior Vice President, Chief Financial Officer, The Platt Companies (1993-1995); Regional Director of Real Estate Counseling, PwC (1988-1993); Manager of Real Estate Consulting, KPMG LLP (1988); Director of Real Estate Investment Consulting, The

Goodkind Group, LLC. (1983-1988); Appraiser, Bank of America (1983) **CIV:** Board Member, Beta Theta Pi Foundation (2019-Present); Chairman, Board of Trustees, Franklin Pierce University (2019-Present): Board Member, Franklin Pierce University (2017-Present); Chairman, Student Housing Research Fund Advisory Board, National Multifamily Housing Council (2017-Present); Board Member, The Aztec Club, San Diego State University (2015-Present); Board Member, Wine Business Institute, Sonoma State University (2011-Present); Executive Committee Member, Corky McMillin Center for Real Estate, San Diego State University (2009-Present); President, San Diego Region, Beta Theta Pi Alumni (1986-1987, 2009-Present); Chairman, Fowler College of Business Board, San Diego State University (2000-Present); Board Member, Alumni Association, San Diego State University (1992-Present); President, Poway Unified School District Foundation (2012-2015); Board Member, Poway Unified School District Foundation (2011-2015); Board Member, Marshall Faulk Foundation (2010-2015); Board Member, Aztec Warrior Foundation (2006-2009); Board Member, INVESCO Real Estate Fund (2003-2005); President, San Diego City Employees' Retirement System (1999-2005); Trustee, San Diego City Employees' Retirement System (1997-2005); Trustee Emeritus, Board of Trustees, The California State University (1999-2004); Board Member, Alumni Council, California State University (1991-2004); President, Alumni Council, California State University (1995-1996); President, Young Alumni, California State University (1991-1992); President, Beta Theta Pi House Corporation, San Diego State University (1988-1989); Chairman, Taxpayer's for Civic Responsibility (1988) **AW:** Distinguished Alumni Service Award, Alumni Association, San Diego State University (2020); Moving Forward San Diego Award, San Diego Regional Chamber of Commerce (2019); Top 25 Owners of Student Housing, Student Housing Business Magazine (2010-2019); Top 25 Managers of Student Housing, Student Housing Business Magazine (2010-2019); Finalist, Most Admired Chief Executive Officer, San Diego Business Journal (2018, 2019); San Diego 500 Influential Business Leaders, San Diego Business Journal (2018, 2019); America's 5000 Fastest Growing Private Companies, Inc. 5000 (2018, 2019); 50 Influence Leaders in San Diego, San Diego Daily Transcript (2017-2019); Certificate of Recognition, California Senator Joel Anderson (2018); Most Influential People in San Diego Development, Our City San Diego Magazine (2017); 100 Influential Leaders in San Diego, San Diego Daily Transcript (2016); Student Housing Pioneer, Rea Estate Forum (2013); Entrepreneur of the Year in Real Estate and Construction, San Diego Region, EY (2012); Biltmore Who's Who (2008-2009); Resolution of Commendation, California Legislature (2005); Resolution of Commendation, Academic Senate, California State University (2005); Toro Award for Recognition, Alumni Association, California State University, Dominguez Hills (2005); City of Villages Pilot Village Demonstration, The Paseo, City of San Diego (2004); Award of Excellence for Most Outstanding Project in the United States, Association of University Real Estate Officials (2003); Gold Nugget Award for Best Public/Private Special Use Facility (2003); International Beta of the Week, Beta Theta Pi Fraternity (2003); California State University Trustee of the Year, California State Student Association (2000-2001); Gold Nugget Award for Best Redevelopment Project (2000); Gold Nugget Award for Best Apartment Project (2000); Who's Who in Real Estate, San Diego Daily Transcript (1999); Congressional Award of Special Recognition, Congressman Brian Bilbray (1999); Distinguished Alumni Award, Fowler College of Business

Administration, San Diego State University (1999); Outstanding Alumni Award, Associated Students, San Diego State University (1996-1997); Outstanding Young Men of American (1990); Who's Who in Southern California Real Estate (1987); Who's Who in American Colleges and Universities (1984) **MEM:** Student Housing Council, National Multifamily Housing Council (2017-Present); Jamestowne Society (2011-Present); The Lincoln Club, San Diego, CA (2010-Present); The San Diego Colony of the Society of the Mayflower Descendants (2010-Present); Sons of the American Revolution (2010-Present); Association of University Real Estate Officials (2001-Present) **B/I:** Mr. Pierce became involved in his profession because of an internship opportunity he had at San Diego State University. It was there that he got "bit" by the real estate "bug."

PIERCE, ROGER A. II, T: Pharmacist, Director **I:** Pharmaceuticals **DOB:** 07/30/1948 **PB:** Dover **SC:** NH/USA **PT:** Roger A. Pierce; Helen A. Simmons Pierce **MS:** Married **SPN:** Doris M. Pierce (07/09/1977) **CH:** Michael R.; Jennifer C. **ED:** Master of Science in Health Services Administration, Central Michigan University, Mount Pleasant, MI (1988); Bachelor of Pharmacy, University of Rhode Island, Kingston, RI (1976); Bachelor of Arts in Zoology, University of New Hampshire, Durham, NH (1971) **CT:** Registered Pharmacist, Rhode Island; Registered Pharmacist, New Hampshire; Registered Pharmacist, Maine; Registered Pharmacist, Virginia; Registered Pharmacist, Illinois **C:** Director, U.S. Department of Veterans Affairs, Southwest CMOP, Tucson, AZ (2005-2011); Director, U.S. Department of Veterans Affairs Consolidated Mail Outpatient Pharmacy, Los Angeles, CA (1999-2005); Chief, Support Services Health Care Group, U.S. Department of Veterans Affairs Health Care System, Long Beach, CA (1997-1999); Chief, Pharmacy Service, U.S. Department of Veterans Affairs Medical Center, Long Beach, CA (1994-1997); Regional Clinical Pharmacy Manager, U.S. Department of Veterans Affairs Central Region Office, Ann Arbor, MI (1992-1994); Associate Chief, U.S. Department of Veterans Affairs Hospital, Hines, IL (1989-1992); Assistant Chief, Pharmacy Service, McGuire U.S. Department of Veterans Affair Medical Center, Richmond, VA (1987-1989); Pharmacy Management Trainee, Hospital Staff Pharmacist, McGuire U.S. Department of Veterans Affairs Medical Center, Richmond, VA (1985-1987); Retail Pharmacist, AARP Pharmacy Service, Virginia Retired Persons Pharmacy, Inc., Richmond, VA (1986); Hospital Staff Pharmacist, U.S. Department of Veterans Affairs Medical Center, Salem, VA (1982-1985); Hospital Staff Pharmacist, U.S. Department of Veterans Affairs Medical Center, Manchester, NH (1980-1982); Retail Pharmacist, State Pharmacy Inc., Manchester, NH (1977-1980); Pharmaceutical Manufacturer's Sales Representative, Division of Eli Lilly Co., Dista Products Company, Bristol, CT (1976-1977) **CR:** Chairperson, Department of Veterans Affairs, National Consolidated Mail Outpatient Pharmacy Network, Technicians Professional Standards Board, Leavenworth, KS (2005-Present); National Veterans Affairs Licensed Pharmacist Professional Standards Board, Washington, DC (2006-2011); Managing Projects, George Washington University School of Business, George Washington University (2009); Chairperson, Veterans Integrated Service Network 22 Licensed Pharmacist Professional Standards Board, U.S. Department of Veteran Affairs, Los Angeles, CA (1999-2005); Adjunct Assistant Professor, Pharmacy Practice, USC School of Pharmacy, Los Angeles, CA (1995-2005); Consultant to Board Directors, Central Region Consolidated Mail Outpatient Pharmacy Establishment Project, U.S. Department of Veteran Affairs, Leavenworth, KS (1992-1994); Clinical Assistant Professor, Pharmacy Practice, University of Illinois at Chicago, Chicago, IL (1990-1993); Chairperson, Central Region Licensed Pharmacists Professional Standards Board, Edward Hines, Jr. Veterans Hospital, U.S. Department of Veteran Affairs, Hines, IL (1991-1992); Affiliate Assistant Professor, Department of Pharmacy Practice, Purdue University, Chicago, IL (1990-1992); Chairperson, Licensed Pharmacist Professional Standards Board, Edward Hines, Jr. VA Hospital, Chicago, IL (1990-1992); Clinical Practitioner, Teacher, VCU School of Pharmacy, Richmond, VA (1988-1989); President, Central Virginia Chapter, Federal Pharmacist Association, Richmond, VA (1986-1988); Chairperson, Pharmacy & Nursing Committee, Salem VA Medical Center, Salem, VA (1985-1987) CIV: Certified Mentor, U.S. Department of Veterans Affairs CW: Co-Author, "VA CMOPs: producing a pattern of quality and efficiency in government," Journal of the American Pharmacists Association (2012); Co-Author, Publication, "Mil Med Tech." (2002); Presenter, Numerous Presentations (1983-2001); Co-Author, "Impact of therapeutic interchange from pravastatin to lovastatin in a veterans affairs medical center," American Journal of Managed Care: AJMC (1999); Co-Author, "A unique automated outpatient drug distribution system: VA central region cmop," Federal Practitioner (1996); Co-Author, "VA achieving cost control with prime vendor," Federal Practitioner (1995); Co-Author, "Prime vendor purchasing of pharmaceuticals in the veterans affairs health care system," American Journal of Health-System Pharmacy (1995); Co-Author, "Prime vendor: a prime plan for VA pharmacies," VA Practitioner (1993); Co-Author, "Pharmacy by mail: the CMOP initiative," VA Practitioner (1993); Co-Author, "Issues in VA procurement of pharmaceuticals," VA Practitioner (1992) AW: Executive Career Field Performance Award, Consolidated Mail Outpatient Pharmacy, U.S. Department of Veterans Affairs (2011); Special Contribution Award for Contributing as a Member/Subject Matter (2011); Executive Career Field Performance Award, Consolidated Mail Outpatient Pharmacy, U.S. Department of Veterans Affairs (2010); Executive Career Field Performance Award, Consolidated Mail Outpatient Pharmacy, U.S. Department of Veterans Affairs (2009); Executive Career Field Performance Award, Consolidated Mail Outpatient Pharmacy, U.S. Department of Veterans Affairs (2008); Executive Career Field Performance Award, Consolidated Mail Outpatient Pharmacy, U.S. Department of Veterans Affairs (2007); Special Contribution Award for Leadership Provided as Acting Director, Great Lakes U.S. Department of Veterans Affairs Consolidated Mail Outpatient Pharmacy (2007); Letter of Appreciation and Special Contribution Award for Providing Support for the Successful Completion of the One-Time Conversion of all U.S. Department of Veterans Affairs (2007); Executive Career Field Performance Award, Consolidated Mail Outpatient Pharmacy, U.S. Department of Veterans Affairs (2006); Special Contribution Award for Leadership Provided in Establishing the First National U.S. Department of Veterans Affairs CMOP Pharmacy Technician Professional Standards Board (2006); Executive Career Field Performance Award, Consolidated Mail Outpatient Pharmacy, U.S. Department of Veterans Affairs (2005); Performance Award for Sustained Superior Performance, U.S. Department of Veterans Affairs Consolidated Mail Outpatient Pharmacy (2004); Certificate of Appreciation for Dedication to the VA and Contributions to the Accomplishment of VISN, VA Desert Pacific Healthcare Network Director, U.S. Department of Veterans Affairs Desert Pacific Healthcare Network Office (2003); Special Contribution Award for Receiving JCHAO Accreditation Score of 99/100 and Having an Articles about the National CMOP Program Accepted for Publication in a Professional Journal, U.S. Department of Veterans Affairs Consolidated Mail Outpatient Pharmacy (2003); Special Contribution Award for a Unique Contribution to the VA CMOP Program, U.S. Department of Veterans Affairs CMOP LA (2002); Special Contribution Award for Receiving JCHAO Accreditation with Commendation, U.S. Department of Veterans Affairs CMOP LA (2000) MEM: President, Central Virginia Chapter, Federal Pharmacists Association (1986-1988); Patrolman, National Ski Patrol (1970-1976); Association of Military Surgeons of the United States; Federal Pharmacists Association; Virginia and Michigan Chapters; American Pharmacists Association; American Society Health-Systems; Life Pharmacist, Leadership Virginia Alumni Association; Kappa Psi Pharmaceutical Fraternity MH: Albert Nelson Marquis Lifetime Achievement Award B/I: Mr. Pierce became involved in his profession after trying to secure a job in zoology. Unable to do so, he went back to pharmacy school and further developed his expertise in the field of pharmaceuticals as the medical surgical warden at Elliot Hospital in New Hampshire. AV: Hiking; Hunting; Fishing; Golf; Skiing

PIERINO, THOMAS MICHAEL, EDD, T: School Psychologist, Vocational Evaluator, Counselor, Mathematics and Social Science Teacher, Adjunct Professor I: Education/Educational Services DOB: 08/18/1951 PB: Buffalo SC: NY/USA PT: Thomas Michael Pierino Sr.; Marie Clarine (Loffredo) Pierino MS: Married SPN: Karen Ann DiMuro (08/07/1981) CH: Marisa ED: Doctor of Education, State University of New York at Buffalo (1982); Master of Science, State University of New York at Buffalo (1980); Master of Arts, State University of New York at Buffalo (1979); Master of Science in Education, Buffalo State College (1976); Bachelor of Science in Education, Buffalo State College (1973) CT: Certified in Teaching Industrial Arts, Mathematics and Social Studies, State of New York; Certified School Counselor and School Psychologist, State of New York; National Certifications in Vocational Evaluation, School Counseling and Career Counseling; Master Career Counselor; National Counseling Certifications, National Board for Certified Counselors C: Counselor, Vocational Evaluator, School Psychologist, Counseling and Transitioning Team Coordinator, St. Mary's School for the Deaf, Buffalo, NY (1987-2013); Guidance Counselor, Math and Technology Teacher, St. Mary's High School, Lancaster, NY (1974-1987) CR: Graduate-Level Adjunct Faculty, Canisius College, Buffalo, NY (1992-2012); Adjunct Faculty, Daemen College, Amherst, NY (1987-1996); Private Educational Research and Testing Consultant. CIV: Former Republican Committeeman, Amherst, NY CW: Contributor, Various Publications on Transitioning and Career Counseling, "Odyssey," "Perspectives in Education and Deafness" AW: Epsilon Pi Tau Honorary Fraternity in Technology (1974); Kappa Delta Pi Honorary Fraternity in Education (1974) MEM: Former Member, American Counseling Association; Former Member, National Career Development Association; Former Member, American School Counselor Association; Former Member, American Rehabilitation Association; Former Member, Association for Measurement and Evaluation in Counseling; Former Member, American Educational Research Association; Former Member, National Employment Counselors Association; Former Member, American College Counseling Association; Former Member, American Mensa; Former Member, Buffalo State College Alumni Association; Former Member, University of Buffalo Alumni Association MH: Albert Nelson Marquis Lifetime Achievement Award AS: Dr. Pierino attributes his success to hard work and excellent guidance from his teachers, professors and parents. B/I: Dr. Pierino became involved in his profession because he always loved education and working with students; it was something he was able to do well, and he enjoyed doing it. AV: General athletics; Physical fitness; Sports memorabilia; History; Architecture; Social science research and statistics; Real estate investing PA: Independent RE: Roman Catholic THT: Find a career that you love and you will never have to work a day in your life.

PILKERTON, CHRISTOPHER MICHAEL, T: Acting Administrator, Genreal Counsel I: Business Management/Business Services CN: United States Small Business Administration MS: Married ED: JD, The Catholic University of America Columbus School of Law; MPA, Columbia University School of International and Public Affairs; Bachelor's Degree, Fairfield University CT: Certificate in Data Analytics, Cornell University SC Johnson College of Business C: Acting Administrator, General Counsel, United States Small Business Administration, Washington, DC (2019-Present); Compliance Director, JPMorgan Chase & Co.; Partner, Two Law Firms; Senior Counsel, U.S. Securities and Exchange Commission; Assistant District Attorney, Office of the Special Narcotics Prosecutor and Office of Money Laundering and Tax Crimes, New York, NY CR: Associate Director, Law and Public Policy Program, The Catholic University of America Columbus School of Law CIV: Board of Directors, NASDAQ Futures, Inc. AW: Listee, Heroes of the Fortune 500, Fortune Magazine; Fulbright Teaching Scholar, Poland

PILLAI, A.K.B., T: Chair I: Professional Training & Coaching CN: New York Institute of Integral Human Development, Inc. DOB: 05/09/1930 PB: Changanassery SC: India PT: Venkitachalam Potti (Deceased); Narayani Amma (Deceased) MS: Married SPN: Donna Pompa (1995) CH: Gita; Prita ED: PhD, Columbia University (1975); MPhil, MA, Columbia University (1972); MA, East Carolina University (1968); MA, Kerala University, India (1955) CT: Registered Yoga Practitioner C: Coach, Private Practice, Integral Development Therapist, Riverdale, New York (1986-Present); Research in Transcultural Psychiatry, Human Development (1975-Present); Professor, Chair, Anthropology, Ramapo College of New Jersey (1972-2001); Co-Chair, Asian Studies, Ramapo College of New Jersey (1988-2001); Director, Asian Studies, Hollywood College, Florida (1966-1967); Professor, Chair, Department of English, Sri Sankara College, University of Kerala, Kalady, India (1955-1966); Instructor, Columbia University, New York (1964) CR: Founder, Chair, New York Institute of Integral Human Development, Inc., Riverdale (1987-Present); Coach, Psychotherapist, Social Worker (1986-Present); Integral Development Consultant (1985-Present); Workshop Leader and Organizer, American Anthropological Association; Workshop Leader and Organizer, American Association of Asian Studies; Workshop Leader and Organizer, World Psychiatry Association; Founder, Integral Developmental Therapy, Developmental Transcultural Psychiatry, Integral Development System of Human Development CW: Author, Facebook Writings, "Encyclopedia of Humanistic Living" (2021); Author, "Integral Development Philosophy and Literature" (2021); Author, "Family Security" (2020); Author, "Women and Children: Sexual Abuse and Violence, With a Plan to Stop Now!" (2013); Author, "Transcendental Self" (1987); Author, "Culture of Social Stratification and Sexism: The Nayars"

(1987); Author, "King Lear: A Study of Human Order" (1985); Contributor, Numerous Scholarly Articles, Creative Writings, Stories and Poems **AW:** Predoctoral Fellowship, National Institute of Mental Health (1972-1975); Fellow, American Anthropological Association; Fellow, Diplomate, American Board of Medical Psychologists; Numerous Life Achievement Awards **MEM:** Chairperson, Various Committees, Seminars, Federation of Kerala Associations of North America (1983-1998); Executive Vice President, World Malayalee Council (1993-1995); American Association of Counseling and Human Development (1980-1995); Founding Executive Vice President, World Malayalee Convention (1993); Subcommittee Chair, Metropolitan Medical Anthropological Association (1980-1983); Founding Chairperson, New York Region, Federation of Kerala Associations in North America (1982); Fellow, American Anthropological Association; Chair, Ad Hoc Committee, Society of Indian Academics of America; International Association of Marriage and Family Counselors; Association of Multicultural Counseling and Development; Founder, Director, Ramapo Anthropology Society; Chair, India Development Institute; Academy of Anti-Aging Medicine; Associate, Academy of American Poets **MH:** Albert Nelson Marquis Lifetime Achievement Award **AS:** Dr. Pillai attributes his success to his passion for wisdom and humanistic services. **B/I:** Dr. Pillai became involved in his profession because of his passion for learning, creative writing abilities and drive to help others. **AV:** Traveling for field studies; Studying horticulture; Playing bridge; Reading poetry; Listening to music **PA:** Democrat **RE:** Universalistic Hinduism

PINEDA, ARNEL, T: Singer **I:** Media & Entertainment **DOB:** 09/05/1967 **SC:** Tonda/Phillappines **PT:** Restituto Lising Pineda; Josefina Manansala Companer **MS:** Married **SPN:** Cherry (2001) **CH:** Matthew; Angelo; Cherub; Thea Chenelle **C:** Singer, Journey (2007-Present); Singer, The Zoo (2006-2007); Singer, 9mm (2001-2002); Singer, Pineda, New Age (1990-2001); Solo Artist (1999); Singer, Intensity Five (1990); Singer, Amo (1986-1990); Singer, Ijos (1982-1986) **CW:** Singer, "AP" (2016); Performer, "Don't Stop Believin': Everyman's Journey" (2012); Singer (With Journey), "Eclipse" (2011); Singer, "Journey: Live in Manila" (2009); Singer (With Journey), "Revelation" (2008); Singer (With The Zoo), "Zoology" (2007); Guest Singer, "Looking Glass," "The Way We Do," Earl Romielle Salinas (2001); Singer, "Dayo" (2005); Singer, "Arnel Pineda" (1999); Singer, "Ang Tunay na Amo ("The Real Master")" (1990); Singer, Numerous Television Appearances **AW:** Outstanding Global Achievement by a Filipino Artist, GMMSF Box Office Entertainment Awards (2009); Best Vocalist Award, Yamaha World Band Explosion (1990); Winner, Philippines Section, Yamaha World Band Explosion (1988)

PINEDA, RAMIRO, I: Advertising & Marketing **ED:** Master of Science in Global Marketing, University of Liverpool, England (2014); Bachelor of Science in Communication Sciences, Instituto Technologico y de Estudios Superiores de Monterrey, Mexico (2003) **C:** E-Commerce Director, Latin America, The Estee Lauder Companies Incorporated (2017-2018); Sales & Marketing Director, Consumer Business Unit, Bridgestone, Nashville, TN (2017-2017); Marketing Director, Latin America, Bridgestone, Nashville, TN (2015-2017); Manager of Advertising & Digital Marketing, Latin America, Bridgestone, Nashville, TN (2010-2014); Marketing Analyst, Latin America, Bridgestone, Nashville, TN (2008-2010); Assistant Manager, Advertising & Promotion - Mexico, Bridgestone, Mexico City (2007-2008); Assistant Manager, Trade

Marketing of Mexico, Bridgestone, Mexico City (2007-2008); Marketing Coordinator of Mexico, Mexico City (2003-2006); Marketing Coordinator of Mexico, Grupo Comercial de Teotihuacan, Mexico City (2000-2003) **CIV:** Board Member, American Red Cross, Nashville, TN; Volunteer, Habitat for Humanity; Board Member, Conexion Americas; Guest Speaker, YMCA of Middle Tennessee **AW:** President's Award, Bridgestone Tire Company **AS:** Mr. Pineda attributes his success on his propensity for hard work, resourcefulness and creativity. He is great at improvising and working under pressure and uncertainty. **B/I:** Mr. Pineda began his career in insurance with aspirations to work in international affairs. He decided to switch majors to begin a career in the film industry, so he majored in mass communications, with an emphasis on marketing. With a passion toward brands and story telling, he elected to pursue marketing and advertising as the next step of his career.

PINGREE, CHELLIE MARIE, T: U.S. Representative from Maine **I:** Government Administration/ Government Relations/Government Services **DOB:** 04/02/1955 **PB:** Minneapolis **SC:** MN/ USA **PT:** Harry Johnson; Dorothy Johnson **MS:** Divorced **SPN:** Selwyn Donald Sussman (2011; Divorced 2016); Charlie Pingree (Divorced) **CH:** Hannah; Cecily; Asa **ED:** Coursework, Summer Fellows Program, Harvard Kennedy School, John F. Kennedy School of Government (1996); BA, College of the Atlantic (1976); Coursework, Outward Bound (1970); Coursework, University of Southern Maine **C:** Member, U.S. House of Representatives from Maine's First Congressional District, United States Congress, Washington, DC (2009-Present); Founder, Managing Partner, Nebo Lodge (2006-2009); President, Chief Executive Officer, Common Cause (2003-2007); Majority Leader, District 12, Maine State Senate (1996-2000); Member, District 12, Maine State Senate (1992-2000); Owner, Founder, North Island Designs (1981-1993); Farmer, North Island Farm (1977-1980); Committee on Appropriations **CR:** Board of Directors, Walmart Watch (2005-Present); Advisory Board, Main Businesses for Social Responsibility (2000-Present); North Haven Grange (1981-Present); Founder, President, North Haven Arts and Enrichment Fund (1999-2000) **CIV:** Co-Chair, Maine Economic Growth Council (1995-1998); Advisory Committee on Mental Retardation (1995-1996); Commission to Study Poverty Among the Working Poor (1995-1996); Special Committee to Study Nursing Home Rates (1995-1996); North Haven Planning Board (1989-1994); Chair, North Haven Tax Assessors (1980-1994); Former Chair, SAD 7 School Board **CW:** Author, "North Island Designs 5: A Scrapbook of Sweaters from a Maine Island" (1993); Author, "North Island Designs" (1992); Author, "Maine Island Classics" (1992); Author, "Sweaters from the Maine Islands" (1990); Author, "Maine Island Classics: Sweaters and Stories from Offshore" (1988); Author; Photography, Design, and Production Coordinator **PA:** Democrat **RE:** Lutheran

PINKETT SMITH, JADA, T: Actress **I:** Media & Entertainment **DOB:** 09/18/1971 **PB:** Baltimore **SC:** MD/USA **PT:** Robsol Pinkett Jr.; Adrienne Banfield-Jones Pinkett **MS:** Married **SPN:** Will Smith (12/31/1997) **CH:** Jaden Christopher Syre Smith; Willow Camille Reign Smith; Trey Smith (Stepson) **ED:** Degrees in Dance and Theater, Baltimore School for the Arts (1989) **C:** Co-Investor, Beauty Products, Carol's Daughter (2005); Founder, Music company, 100% Women Productions; Developer, Fashion Label, Maja **CIV:** Emcee, Million Woman March, Philadelphia, PA (1997); Co-Founder, Will and Jada Smith Family Foundation; Advocate, PETA **CW:** Actress, "The Matrix 4" (2021); Exec-

utive Producer, "King Richard" (2021); Executive Producer, "Charm City Kings" (2020); Actress, "Angel Has Fallen" (2019); Executive Producer, "Life in a Year" (2019); Executive Producer, One Episode, TV Series, "Red Table Talk" (2019); Executive Producer, "Hala" (2019); Actress, "Girls Trip" (2017); Actress, TV Series, "Gotham" (2014-2017); Actress, "Bad Moms" (2016); Actress, "Magic Mike XXL" (2015); Producer, "Annie" (2014); Executive Producer, TV Film Documentary, "Children for Sale: The Fight to End Human Trafficking" (2014); Voice Actress, "Madagascar 3: Europe's Most Wanted" (2013); Executive Producer, TV Series, "The Queen Latifah Show" (2013); Producer, "After Earth" (2013); Executive Producer, Documentary, "Rape For Profit" (2012); Executive Producer, Documentary, "Free Angela and All Political Prisoners" (2012); Actress, "Men in Black 3" (2012); Actress, Executive Producer, TV Series, "Hawthorne" (2009-2011); Producer, "The Karate Kid" (2010); Executive Producer, "The Secret Life of Bees" (2010); Voice Actress, "Madagascar: Escape 2 Africa" (2008); Actress, Director, Screenwriter, "The Human Contract" (2008); Actress, "The Women" (2008); Actress, Music Video, "Superwoman" by Alicia Keys (2008); Actress, "Reign Over Me" (2008); Executive Producer, 88 Episodes, TV Series, "All of Us" (2003-2007); Singer, Album, "Wicked Wisdom," Wicked Wisdom (2006); Voice Actress, "Madagascar" (2005); Actress, "Collateral" (2004); Actress, "The Matrix Revolutions" (2004); Executive Producer, "The Seat Filler" (2004); Author, Book, "Girls Hold Up This World" (2004); Executive Producer, Video, "Ride or Die" (2003); Voice Actress, Video Game, "Enter the Matrix" (2003); Actress, "The Matrix Reloaded" (2003); Narrator, TV Film, "Maniac Magee" (2003); Herself, Music Video, "1000 Kisses" by Will Smith Featuring Jada Pinktt Smith (2002); Actress, "Ali" (2001); Actress, "Kingdom Come" (2001); Actress, "Bamboozled" (2000); Guest Appearance, "Welcome to Hollywood" (1998); Actress, Executive Producer, Short Film, "Blossoms and Veils" (1998); Actress, "Return to Paradise" (1998); Actress, Music Video, "Just the Two of Us" by Will Smith (1998); Actress, TV Series, "Ellen" (1998); Actress, "Woo" (1998); Actress, "Scream 2" (1997); Voice Actress, "Princess Mononoke" (1997); Actress, "Set It off" (1996); Actress, TV Film, "If These Walls Could Talk" (1996); Actress, "The Nutty Professor" (1996); Actress, Music Video, "Temptations" by 2Pac (1995); Actress, "Tales from the Crypt: Demon Knight" (1995); Actress, "A Low Down Dirty Shame" (1994); Actress, "Jason's Lyric" (1994); Actress, "The Inkwell" (1994); Actress, "Menace II Society" (1993); Actress, TV Series, "A Different World" (1991-1993); Actress, TV Series, "21 Jump Street" (1991); Actress, TV Series, "Doogie Howser, M.D." (1991); Actress, TV Film, "Moe's World" (1990); Actress, TV Series, "True Colors" (1990); Director, Music Videos; Singer, Numerous Live Performances **AW:** NAACP Image Award for Outstanding Host in a Talk or News/Information (Series or Special) - Individual or Ensemble, "Red Table Talk" (2020, 2019); MTV Trailblazer Award (2019); Gracie for Outstanding Female Actor in a Supporting Role in a Drama Series, "Gotham," Gracie Allen Awards (2016); Vision Award for Best Performance - Drama, "Hawthorne," NAMIC Vision Awards (2012); NAACP Image Award for Outstanding Actress in a Drama Series, "Hawthorne" (2010); Honoree, Essence Black Women in Hollywood (2008); Co-Recipient, Award, 4th Annual Lupus Foundation of America Awards (2007); NAACP Image Award for Outstanding Literary Work - Children, "Girls Hold Up This World" (2006); Co-Recipient, David Angell Humanitarian Award, American Screenwriters association (2006); Interactive Achievement Award for Outstanding Achievement in Character Performance -

Female, "Enter the Matrix," Academy of Interactive Arts & Sciences (2004); Glow Award for Best Voice Performance - Female, "Enter the Matrix," G-Phoria Awards (2004); Chainsaw Award for Best Actress, "Tales from the Crypt: Demon Knight," Fangoria Chainsaw Awards (1996)

PINSKY, ROBERT NEAL, T: Poet, Educator **I:** Education/Educational Services **DOB:** 10/20/1940 **PB:** Long Branch **SC:** NJ/USA **PT:** Milford Simon Pinsky; Sylvia (Eisenberg) Pinksy **MS:** Married **SPN:** EllenJane Bailey (12/30/1961) **CH:** Nicole; Caroline; Elizabeth **ED:** Guggenheim Fellowship (1980); Doctor of Philosophy, Stanford University (1966); Bachelor of Arts, Rutgers University (1962) **C:** Professor of Creative Writing, Boston University (1989-Present); Poet Laureate (1997-2000); Professor, Boston University (1980-1989); Professor of English, University of California Berkeley (1980-1989); Member, English Faculty, Wellesley College (1968-1980); Member, English Faculty, University of Chicago (1967-1968); Poetic Adviser, Library of Congress **CR:** Poetry Editor, New Republic (1978); Visiting Lecturer, Harvard University; Hurst Professor Washington University, St. Louis, MO **CW:** Himself, Documentary, "Get Lamp" (2010); Author, "Gulf Music" (2007); Co-Author, "A Convergence of Birds: Original Fiction and Poetry Inspired by the Work of Joseph Cornell" (2001); Author, "Jersey Rain" (2000); Author, "Americans' Favorite Poems" (2000); Editor, Poetry, Slate Magazine (1994-2000); Author, "The Handbook of Heartbreak" (1998); Author, "The Sounds of Poetry" (1998); Author, "The Figured Wheel: New and Collected Poems 1966-1996" (1996); Author, "The Inferno of Dante" (1994); Author, "The Want Bone" (1990); Author, "Poetry and the World" (1988); Author, "History of My Heart" (1984); Author, Text Adventure, "Mindwheel," Synapse Software (1984); Author, "An Explanation of America" (1980); Author, "The Situation of Poetry" (1977); Author, "Sadness and Happiness" (1975); Author, "Landor's Poetry" (1968) **AW:** Premo Capri (2009); Manhae Foundation Prize (2006); PEN/Voelcker Award for Poetry (2004); Harold Washington Literary Award (1999); Appointed, U.S. Poet Laureate (1997); Shelley Memorial Award (1996); Los Angeles Times Book Prize for Poetry, "The Inferno of Dante" (1995); William Carlos Williams Prize (1984); Saxifrage Prize (1980); Artists Award, American Academy of Arts and Letters (1979) **MEM:** Elected Member, American Academy of Arts and Letters; Elected Member, American Academy of Arts and Sciences; American Association for the Advancement of Science; Poetry Society of America; PEN America

PINSON, WILLIAM MEREDITH JR., THD, I: Religious **CN:** Texas Baptist Heritage Center **DOB:** 08/03/1934 **PB:** Fort Worth **SC:** TX/USA **PT:** William Meredith Pinson; Ila Lee (Jones) Pinson **MS:** Married **SPN:** Bobbie Ruth Judd (06/04/1955) **CH:** Meredith Pinson Creasey; Allison Pinson Hopgood **ED:** Honorary LLD, Hardin-Simmons University (1999); Honorary LittD, Dallas Baptist University (1990); Honorary LHD, Howard Payne University (1986); Honorary DD, University of Mary Hardin-Baylor (1984); Honorary LittD, California Baptist University (1978); MDiv, Southwestern Baptist Theological Seminary (1973); ThD, Southwestern Baptist Theological Seminary (1963); BD, Southwestern Baptist Theological Seminary (1959); BA, University of North Texas (1955); Postgraduate Work, Columbia University; Postgraduate Coursework, The University of Edinburgh **CT:** Ordained to Ministry, Baptist Church (1955) **C:** Distinguished Visiting Professor, Baylor University (2001-Present); Distinguished Professor, Dallas Baptist University (2001-Present); Volunteer Director, Texas Baptist Heritage Center, Baptist General Convention of

Texas (2000-Present); President Emeritus, San Francisco Campus, Gateway Seminary (2000-Present); President, San Francisco Campus, Gateway Seminary (1977-1982); Pastor, First Baptist Church (1975-1977); Professor of Christian Ethics, Southwestern Baptist Theological Seminary (1963-1975); Associate Secretary, Christian Life Commission, Baptist General Convention of Texas (1957-1963) **CR:** Trustee, Baylor Scott & White Health (2010-Present); Baptist Heritage and Identity Committee, Baptist World Alliance (2010-Present); Executive Director Emeritus, Baptist General Convention of Texas (2000-Present); Member, Commission on Racism, Baptist World Alliance (1992-Present); Member, Policy and Heritage Committee, Baptist World Alliance (2000-2010); Member, Board of Directors, Baylor Scott & White Health (2002-2003); Centennial Committee Chair, Baylor Scott & White Health (2002-2003); Executive Director, Baptist General Convention of Texas (1982-2000); Member, Board of Directors, T.B. Maston Foundation (1986-1996); Member, Board of Directors, Stewardship Commission, Southern Baptist Convention (1986-1996); Member, Study Commission on Ethics (1990-1995); Member, National Task Force, Planned Growth in Giving (1984-1994); Chairman, Study Commission on Freedom, Justice and Peace (1975-1980); Speaker in Field, Baptist General Convention of Texas (1976-1977); Chairman, Resolutions Committee, Baptist General Convention of Texas (1976-1977); Chairman, Steering Committee, Good News Texas (1976-1977); Member, State Missions Commission (1976-1977); Adjunct Professor, Southwestern Baptist Theological Seminary (1976-1977); Vice Chairman, Urban Strategy Committee (1976); Chairman, Order of Business Committee (1976); Special Researcher, Home Mission Board, Member, Christian Life Commission, Baptist General Convention of Texas; Program Committee Chair, Christian Life Commission, Baptist General Convention of Texas **CIV:** Member, Advisory Committee on School Leadership, Dallas Baptist University (2003-Present); Member, Advisory Board, Baptist History and Heritage Society (2002-Present) **CW:** Contributor, Articles, Professional Journals; Contributor, Book Chapters; Author, Books on Ethics; Author, Books on History **AW:** Pinson Endowed Lectures Award (2000-Present); T.B. Maston Award (2015); Pro Ecclesia Award (2010); George W. Truett Award, Baylor University (2008); Elder Statesman Award, Independence Association (2005); Officers' Award, Baptist History and Heritage Society (2003); W. Winfred Moore Award For Lifetime Achievement in Ministry, Baylor University (2001); Pioneer Award, Baptist General Convention of Texas (2001); Texas Baptist Missions Award (2000); Spirit of Excellence Award, Houston Baptist University (2000); Parabolani Award, Texas Baptist Men (1999); Mosaic Missions Award, Home Mission Board, The National Baptist Convention, USA, Inc (1984); Distinguished Alumni Award, University of North Texas (1980); Distinguished Alumni Award, Southwestern Baptist Theological Seminary (1979); Lilly Foundation Scholarship, Southwestern Baptist Theological Seminary (1960-1962) **MEM:** President, Southern Baptist Association of State Executive Directors (1996-1997); Southern Baptist Association of Christian Schools **AV:** Traveling; Reading **RE:** Baptist

PIRCHER, LEO, T: Lawyer, Director **I:** Law and Legal Services **CN:** Pircher, Nichols & Meeks **DOB:** 01/04/1933 **PB:** Berkeley **SC:** CA/USA **PT:** Leo Charles Pircher; Christine (Moore) Pircher **MS:** Married **SPN:** Nina Silverman (06/14/1987); Phyllis McConnell (08/04/1956, Divorced 1981) **CH:** Christopher; David; Eric **ED:** JD, University of California, Berkeley (1957); BS, University of California, Berkeley (1954) **CT:** Certified California Board

Legal Specialization; Certified Specialist, Taxation Law **C:** Senior Partner, Pircher, Nichols & Meeks, Los Angeles, CA (1983-Present); Senior Partner, Lawler, Felix & Hall, Los Angeles, CA (1965-1983); Partner, Lawler, Felix & Hall, Los Angeles, CA (1962-1965); Associate, Lawler, Felix & Hall, Los Angeles, CA (1957-1962) **CR:** Secretary, American Metal Bearing Co., Gardena, CA (1975-Present); Adjunct Professor, Loyola University Law School (1959-1961); Speaker, Various Law Schools and Bar Associations Education Programs; Director, Varco International, Inc., Orange, CA **CIV:** Chairman, Public Finance and Taxation Section, California Town Hall, Los Angeles, CA (1970-1971) **CW:** Co-Author, "Definition and Utility of Leases" (1968) **MEM:** American Bar Association; National Association of Real Estate Investment Trusts; Executive Committee, Commercial Law Section, Los Angeles County Bar Association; New York State Bar; California State Bar **BAR:** New York (1985); California (1958) **MH:** Albert Nelson Marquis Lifetime Achievement Award **B/I:** Mr. Pircher became involved in his profession because he knew he wanted to be a lawyer since he was in eighth grade. He studied accounting in college and developed an interest in tax law. Eventually, he became an M&A lawyer doing mergers and acquisitions. Mr. Pircher now works in real estate law. **PA:** Republican

PIRKLE, GEORGE EMORY, T: Photographer, Instructional Media Producer **I:** Media & Entertainment **DOB:** 10/03/1947 **PT:** George Washington Pirkle; Glanna Adeline (Palmer) Pirkle **MS:** Married **SPN:** Karen Leigh Horn (10/23/1973) **CH:** Charity **ED:** MA, University of Georgia (1971); BA in Journalism, University of Georgia (1969); Coursework, North Georgia College (1965-1966) **CT:** Certified in Photography, University of North Georgia (2013) **C:** Owner, Talking Rock Productions, Cumming, GA (1989-Present); Producer, Production Works, Birmingham, AL (1984-1988); Executive Vice President, Management and Human Development Associates, Inc., Birmingham, AL (1984-1986); Coordinator, TV Production Services, Southern Co. Services, Inc., Birmingham, AL (1978-1988); Public Information Officer, Georgia Department of Revenue, Atlanta, GA (1973-1978); TV Producer, Director, Instructional Resources Center, Athens, GA (1969-1970); Radio Announcer, Sportscaster, Various Radio Stations, North Georgia Area (1968-1970) **CR:** Actor, Various Radio and TV Commercials, Corporation of TV Programs, Radio Dramas, Stage Plays (1968-Present); Adjunct Instructor, Computer Science, Lanier Technical College (2001); Anchor, This Week Banking Bankers, TV Network (1990-1992); Instructor, Cliff Osmond Acting Program (1989-1992); Commercial Acting Instructor, Elan Casablancas Modeling Career Center (1988-1992) **CIV:** Chair, Forsyth County Board of Ethics (2002-2012); Historian, Archivist, Historical Society of Forsyth County (2011); Communications Board of Directors, Bald Ridge Lodge (2005-2010); Board of Directors, Leadership Forsyth (2005-2008); Permanent Member, Allocations Committee, United Way Forsyth County (2000-2004); Board of Directors, United Way of Forsyth County (1995-2004); Vice President, Allocations, United Way of Forsyth County (2003); Volunteer, American Cancer Society Relay for Life (1996-2002); Member, City Parks Recreation Board (1996); Member, Technical Steering Committee, Forsyth Board of Education (1995); Commercial Acting Instructor, Elan/Casablancas Modeling/Career Center (1988-1992); Board of Directors, Birmingham International Educational Film Festival (1987-1991); Chairman, Sadie Award Committee, Director, Campaign Film, United Way, Pensacola, FL (1989); Member, Commissions Committee, Birmingham Area Councils, Boy Scouts of America (1983-1985); Master of Ceremonies, Government's Veterans Awards Presentation, World Peace Luncheon (1981, 1982, 1984); Director, Student Video Competition; Member, Advisory Board, Sawnee Mountain Preserve **MIL:** 1st Lieutenant, U.S. Army (1971-1973); 2nd Lieutenant, U.S. Army (1969) **CW:** Photographer; Instructional Media Producer; Editor, Newsletter Freeze Frame, International TV Association **AW:** Group Study Exchange Team Leader, Rotary (2011); Captained Winner (2004); Small Business Member of the Year, Cumming Forsyth County (2002); Business Member of the Year, Cumming/Forsyth Chamber of Commerce (2002); Birmingham International Educational Film Festival Battles Award (1988); Southern Superlative Outstanding Employee Award, Southern Co. Services (1986); International Television Association Paddlewheel Award (1986) **MEM:** District 6910 Literacy Chair, Rotary Club of Forsyth County (2013-Present); Rotary Club of Forsyth County (2012-Present); Paul Harris Fellow, Rotary Club of Forsyth County (2001, 2013); President, Historical Society Forsyth County (1996); Charter President, Birmingham Chapter, International TV Association (1984-1985); President, Pro Tempore, International TV Association (1984); Founding Member, Southern Electric Systems Visual Commissions Sub-committee; Georgia Historical Society; Cumming/Forsyth Chamber of Commerce **MH:** Albert Nelson Marquis Lifetime Achievement Award **B/I:** When Mr. George Pirkle was young, he would sit in front of the television watching the local programs in Atlanta, he was fascinated with the announcers and the people who were involved in the news and people who hosted various programs. His aunt, Hassie Palmer suggested to him that he should attend Journalism school, and he ended up going to the University of Georgia, his major was radio and broadcasting. **AV:** Photography; Astronomy; Genealogy; History; Archaeology; Model railroading

PISACANO, DON ARLIE, T: Attorney **I:** Law and Legal Services **CN:** Miller Griffin & Marks **DOB:** 08/28/1956 **PB:** Philadelphia **SC:** PA/USA **PT:** Nicholas Joseph Pisacano; Anna Mae Cunningham **SPN:** Margaret Mary Hornberger Pisacano **CH:** Anthony Dean; Dominic Joseph; Vincent Michael; Martha Rae **ED:** JD, College of Law, University of Kentucky (1990); Bachelor's Degree, University of Kentucky (1978) **C:** Attorney, Miller Griffin & Marks (2009-Present); Attorney, Miller Edwards Rambicure PLLC (1999-2009); Attorney, Stites & Harbison, PLLC (1990-2009) **CIV:** Fellowship of Christian Athletes; Fayette County Consumer Advocacy **MIL:** Commander, Surface Warfare Officer, U.S. Navy (1980-2003) **AW:** AV-Preeminent Rating, Martindale-Hubbell **MEM:** American Bar Association; Fayette County Bar Association; Kentucky Justice Association; Kentucky Defense Counsel; Defense Research Institute **BAR:** Fayette County Bar Association; Kentucky Bar Association; United States Court of Appeals for the Sixth Circuit; United States Court of Appeals for the Fifth Circuit **MH:** Marquis Who's Who Top Professional **AS:** Mr. Pisacano attributes his success to hard work. **B/I:** Mr. Pisacano became involved in his profession because he was inspired by his brother.

PITKIN, ROY MACBETH, T: Retired Obstetrician, Educator **I:** Medicine & Health Care **DOB:** 05/24/1934 **PB:** Anthon **SC:** IA/USA **PT:** Roy Pitkin; Pauline Allie (McBeath) Pitkin **MS:** Widowed **SPN:** Marcia Alice Jenkins (8/17/1957, Deceased 05/07/2019) **CH:** Barbara; Robert Macbeth; Kathryn; William Charles; **ED:** Resident in Obstetrics-gynecology, University of Iowa Hospitals and Clinics, Iowa City, IA (1960-1963); Intern, King County Hospital, Seattle, WA (1959-1960); MD, University of Iowa (1959); BA, University of Iowa, with Highest Distinction (1956) **CT:** Diplomate, American Board of Obstetrics and Gynecology **C:** Professor Emeritus, UCLA (1997-Present); Professor, UCLA (1987-1997); Chair, Department of Obstetrics-gynecology, UCLA (1987-1995); Head, Department of Obstetrics-gynecology, University of Iowa (1977-1987); Professor, University of Iowa (1972-1987); Associate Professor, Obstetrics-gynecology, University of Iowa, Iowa City (1968-1972); Assistant Professor, Obstetrics-gynecology, University of Illinois (1965-1968) **CR:** Director, American Board of Emergency Medicine (1990-1998); President, American Gynecological and Obstetrical Society (1995); Director, American Board of Obstetrics and Gynecology (1980-1988); Chairman (1985-1987); Member, Residency Review Committee, Obstetrics-gynecology (1981-1987); President, Society of Gynecologic Investigation (1985) **MIL:** Served to Lieutenant Commander, Medical Corps., U.S. Naval Reserve (1963-1965) **CW:** Author, "Whom the Gods Love Die Young: A Modern Medical Perspective on Illness that Caused the Early Death of Famous People" (2008); Author, "The Green Journal 50 Years On" (2003); Co-editor, "The Best of After Office Hours" (2003); Editor Emeritus, "Obstetrics and Gynecology" (2001); Editor, "Obstetrics and Gynecology" (1985-2001); Editor-in-Chief, "Clinical Obstetrics and Gynecology" (1979-2000); Editor-in-Chief, "Year Book of Obstetrics and Gynecology" (1975-1986); Contributor, Approximately 200 Articles, Medical Journals **AW:** Luella Klein Lifetime Achievement Award, American College of Obstetricians and Gynecologists (2017); Distinguished Alumni Achievement Award, University of Iowa (2002); Distinguished Service Award, Council of Science Editors (2002); National Institutes of Health Career Awardee (1972-1977); Joseph Goldberger Award in Nutrition, American Medical Association; Agnes Higgins Award in Nutrition, March of Dimes **MEM:** President, American Obstetricians and Gynecologists Society (1994-1995); President, Society of Gynecological Investigation (1985-1986); President, Society of Perinatal Obstetricians (1978-1979); Fellow, Ad Eundem, Royal College of Obstetrics and Gynecology; Council of Science Editors; National Academy of Medicine; National Academy of Sciences; Honorary Member, German Society of Obstetricians and Gynecologists; American College of Obstetricians and Gynecologists **MH:** Albert Nelson Marquis Lifetime Achievement Award; Marquis Who's Who Top Professional **AS:** Dr. Pitkin could not have chosen a more satisfying life in terms of family and career, which he attributes to a supportive family, a good education, and lots of luck. **B/I:** His father was a pharmacist and that triggered an interest in medicine. He was also attracted to it because of the opportunity to serve others. He found he enjoyed practicing medicine but was led to the academic aspect because he realized the personal satisfaction of teaching and doing research. **AV:** Wine and food; Tennis; Reading history; Writing; Finding the right way of expressing something **RE:** Presbyterian

PITMAN, KATHRYN ANNETTE, PHD, T: Mental Health Counseling Executive (Retired), Consultant (Retired) **I:** Health, Wellness and Fitness **CN:** Private Practice **DOB:** 08/01/1940 **PB:** Creswell **SC:** OR/USA **PT:** Henry Wilbur Monroe; Lake Ilene (Wall) Monroe **MS:** Widowed **SPN:** Gary Pitman (2012, Deceased 2015); Ray Ballinger (06/27/1998, Deceased 01/01/2003) **CH:** David Bryan (Deceased); Derek Alan; Darla Ailene **ED:** PhD, Columbia State University (1993); MSW, Columbia State University (1992); BS in Education, Western Oregon State College (Now Western Oregon University) (1962) **C:** Mental Health Counseling Executive, Consultant, Geriatric Psychiatric Facility, Coos Bay, OR (2002-2006); Mental Health Coordinator, Geriatric Psychiatric Facility, Coos Bay, OR (1999-2002); Specialist in Learning Disability Testing, Educational Consultant, Comprehensive Assessment Services, Eugene, OR (1995-1999); Chief Executive Officer, Comprehensive Assessment Services, LLC (1995-1997); Senior Executive Vice President, Comprehensive Assessment Services, The Focus Institute, Inc., Eugene, OR (1994); Therapist, Comprehensive Assessment Services, The Focus Institute, Inc., Eugene, OR (1994); Senior Executive Vice President, Education Director, Light Streams, Inc., Eugene, OR (1993); Counselor, Alcohol and Drug Abuse Prevention and Intervention in Teens (1990-1993); Counselor, Eugene, OR (1989-1994); Teacher, Germany (1962-1988); Teacher, Thailand (1962-1988); Mental Health Counselor, Private Practice; Weight-Loss Counselor; Accountant Executive, Insurance Industry; Mental Health Counselor, Chemical Dependency of Adults and Adolescents **CR:** Consultant, Consumer Education Member, Various Private Businesses; Teacher, GED Course, American Military Personnel, Germany; Teacher, English Course, Thai Royal Air Force Officers **CIV:** Hospice Volunteer (2007-2012); Volunteer, Mom/Baby Unit, 1336 Hours, PeaceHealth Hospital (2007-2012); Volunteer, Orphanages, Thailand (1954-1995); Volunteer, Orphanages, Germany (1954-1995); Volunteer, Orphanages, United States (1954-1995); Volunteer, Elderly Nursing Homes, Germany (1954-1995); Volunteer, Elderly Nursing Homes, Thailand (1954-1995); Volunteer, Elderly Nursing Homes, United States (1954-1995); Sunday School Teacher (1956-1990); Sponsor, Several Exchange Students (1984-1988); Guardian Job's Daughters (1980-1982); Member, Board of Directors, Den Mother, Cub Scouts, Boy Scouts of America, KS (1974-1982); Member, Board of Directors, Den Mother, Cub Scouts, Boy Scouts of America, OR (1974-1982); Coach, Girls Volleyball (1974-1980); Volunteer Singer, Various Church and Community Choirs, Worldwide; Volunteer to Establish Vacation Bible Schools, Many Military Bases, Stateside and Worldwide; Volunteer, Teaching, Cooking to Children and Adults, United States and Worldwide **CW:** Author, Book, "Easy Does It"; Author, Book, "Easy Does It 2"; Host, Weekly Television Cooking Segment, Portland, OR; Guest Speaker, Several Radio Shows; Guest Speaker, Several Professional Women's Groups **MEM:** American Board of Disability Analysts (ABDA; Order of the Eastern Star; National Association of Social Workers; American Counseling Association; Columbia State University Alumni Association; Women's International Bowling Conference **MH:** Albert Nelson Marquis Lifetime Achievement Award **AS:** Dr. Pitman accepted Christ as her Savior at 7 years of age and God has been her ever-present guide in life. He put a desire to help others and helped her fulfill this desire in many unexpected ways. Although life has thrown many hard events at her, she feels blessed for her family and friends. **B/I:** Dr. Pitman became involved in the teaching profession because it was always in her heart to do so and she felt that God put it there. **AV:** Cooking; Gardening; Reading; Walking; Car races; Bowling **PA:** Republican **RE:** Protestant **THT:** Dr. Pitman says, "When younger, I felt confident that I was "mature for my age!" Now, at 80 years of age, I feel confident that I don't know much! Throughout life, God provided many people to care for me and to mentor me so that I could walk through the many rough spots and rejoice in the many successes! Each day I'm grateful for a fresh beginning and to realize that even in my elderly years, I have much to contribute to make the world a better place."

PIZZO, JOSEPH FRANCIS, PHD, T: Physics Educator **I:** Education/Educational Services **DOB:** 10/30/1939 **PB:** Houston **SC:** TX/USA **PT:** Joseph Francis Pizzo; Irene Pizzo **MS:** Married **SPN:** Roberta Applegate (03/13/1991) **CH:** Stephen; Charlotte; Paul; Christopher; Francesca; Samuel **ED:** PhD, University of Florida (1964); BA, University of St. Thomas (1961) **C:** Visiting Professor, U.S. Military Academy West Point (1992-1993, 2002-2003); Research Participant, Oak Ridge National Laboratory (1965-1968); Professor, Department Head, Lamar University (1964-1992) **CR:** Regent's Professor, Lamar University (1993-Present) **CIV:** Board of Directors, Jason Project **CW:** Co-Author, "Collector's Guide to Bubble Bath Containers" (1999); Editor, Monthly Column, The Physics Teacher Journal (1989-1992); Author, "Interactive Hallway Demonstrations" **AW:** Distinguished Faculty Lecturer, Lamar University (1997); Piper Professorship, The Minnie Stevens Piper Foundation (1995); Distinguished Emeritus Professor of Physics, Lamar University; Robert N. Little Award, American Association of Physics Teachers; Distinguished Service Citation, American Association of Physics Teachers **MEM:** President, Texas Chapter, American Association of Physics Teachers (1984-1985); American Association of Physics Teachers; The Phi Beta Kappa Society **MH:** Albert Nelson Marquis Lifetime Achievement Award **AS:** Mr. Pizzo attributes his success to his parents and grandparents. **B/I:** Mr. Pizzo became involved in his profession because he was inspired by his teacher, Father Burbot. **AV:** Collecting bubble bath bottles; Reading

PLANT, ROBERT ANTHONY, T: Singer; Musician **I:** Media & Entertainment **DOB:** 8/20/1948 **PB:** Bromwich **SC:** Staffordshire/England **PT:** Robert C. Plant; Annie C. (Cain) Plant **MS:** Married **SPN:** Mareen Wilson (09/09/1969, Divorced 1983) **CH:** Carmen Jayne; Karac Pendragon (Deceased 1977); Logan Romero; Jesse Lee **C:** Singer, Solo Career (1982-Present); Lead Singer, Led Zeppelin (1968-1980); Lead Singer, Band of Joy (1966-1968); Lead Singer, Crawling King Snakes **CW:** Singer, Producer, Solo Album, "Carry Fire" (2017); Singer, Producer, Solo Album, "Lullaby and... The Ceaseless Roar" (2014); Singer, Live Album, "Robert Plants Presents: Sensational Space Shifters (Live in London July '12)" (2012); Singer, Concert Film, "Celebration Day" (2012); Singer, Producer, Solo Album, "Band of Joy" (2010); Singer, Album (With Alison Krauss), "Raising Sand" (2007); Singer, Producer, Compilation Album, "Nine Lives" (2006); Singer, Producer, Solo Album, "Mighty ReArranger" (2005); Singer, Producer, Compilation Album, "Sixty Six to Timbuktu" (2003); Singer, Live Album, "How the West Was Won," Led Zeppelin (2003); Singer, Producer, Solo Album, "Dreamland" (2002); Singer, Album (With Jimmy Page), "Walking into Clarksdale" (1998); Singer, Live Album, "No Quarter (Unledded)" (1994); Singer, Producer, Solo Album, "Fate of Nations" (1993); Singer, Producer, Solo Album, "Manic Nirvana" (1990); Singer, Producer, Solo Album, "Now and Zen" (1988); Singer, Producer, Solo Album, "Shaken 'n' Stirred" (1985); Singer, Collaborative Album, "The Honeydrippers: Volume One" (1984); Singer, Producer, Solo Album, "The Principle of Moments" (1983); Singer, Producer, Solo Album, "Pictures at Eleven" (1982); Singer, Compilation Album, "Coda," Led Zeppelin (1982); Singer, Album, "In Through the Out Door," Led Zeppelin (1979); Singer, Album, "Presence," Led Zeppelin (1976); Singer, Concert Film, "The Song Remains the Same," Led Zeppelin (1976); Singer, Live Album, "The Song Remains the Same," Led Zeppelin (1976); Singer, Album, "Physical Graffiti," Led Zeppelin (1975); Singer, Album, "Houses of the Holy," Led Zeppelin (1973); Singer, Album,

"Led Zeppelin IV," Led Zeppelin (1971); Singer, Album, "Led Zeppelin III," Led Zeppelin (1970); Singer, Album, "Led Zeppelin II," Led Zeppelin (1969); Singer, Album, "Led Zeppelin," Led Zeppelin (1969); Singer, Numerous Live and Compilation Albums; Singer, Performer, Numerous Live Performances **AW:** Honoree, Kennedy Center Honors (2012); One of the "50 Great Voices," National Public Radio (NPR) (2010); Grammy Award for Best Pop Collaboration with Vocals (2009, 2008); Grammy Award for Album of the Year, "Raising Sand" (2009); Grammy Award for Record of the Year, "Please Read the Letter" (2009); Grammy Award for Best Country Collaboration with Vocals, "Killing the Blues" (2009); Grammy Award for Best Contemporary Folk Album, "Raising Sand" (2009); Outstanding Contribution to Music Prize, Q Awards (2009); Voted "Greatest Voice in Rock," Planet Rock (2009); Named Among "Artists of the Century," Q Magazine (2009); Commander of the Most Excellent Order of the British Empire (CBE), Prince Charles of Wales (2009); CMA Award for Musical Event of hte Year (2008); Ranked #15, "100 Greatest Singers of All Time," Rolling Stone (2008); Grammy Award for Best Hard Rock Performance, "Most High" (1999); Inductee, Led Zeppelin, Rock and Roll Hall of Fame (1995); Knebworth Silver Clef Award (1990); NME Award for Best Male Singer (1976); NME Award for World Male Singer (1975)

PLASKETT, STACEY E., T: U.S. Representative from the Virgin Islands; Lawyer **I:** Government Administration/Government Relations/Government Services **DOB:** 05/13/1966 **PB:** New York **SC:** NY/USA **PT:** LeRoy Plaskett; Magdalene (Hendricks) Plaskett **MS:** Married **SPN:** Jonathan Buckney Small **CH:** Jeremiah; Christian; Ariel; Israel; Taliah **ED:** JD, American University Washington College of Law (1994); BS in History and Diplomacy, Georgetown University Walsh School of Foreign Service (1984) **C:** Member, U.S. House of Representatives from Virgin Island's At-Large Congressional District (2015-Present); Member-Elect, U.S. House of Representatives from Virgin Island's At-Large Congressional District (2014); General Counsel, United States Virgin Islands Economic Development Authority (2007-2014); Senior Counsel to Deputy Attorney General, U.S. Department of Justice (2002-2004); Consultant, Legal Counsel, The Mitchell Madison Group (1997-1999); Private Practice, The Plaskett Group LLC; Deputy General Counsel, Americhoice, UnitedHealth Group; Staff of Deputy Attorney General Larry Thompson, U.S. Department of Justice; Counsel, Assistant Attorney General for Civil Division, U.S. Department of Justice; Assistant District Attorney, Bronx, NY; Staff, Jones Day; Staff, Lobbying Division, American Medical Association **PA:** Democrat

PLODZIEN, CAROL ANNA, T: Retired Physical Education Teacher **I:** Education/Educational Services **CN:** William Fremd High School **DOB:** 10/07/1948 **PB:** Chicago **SC:** IL/USA **PT:** Joseph Thomas Plodzien; Elizabeth Ann (Hempel) Plodzien **ED:** MA, Roosevelt University (1989); MS, George Williams College (1979); BS, North Illinois University (1971) **CT:** Certified in K-12 Education **C:** Junior Varsity Head Girls Basketball Coach, Resurrection College Prep High School, Chicago, IL (2013-Present); Assistant Varsity Girls Basketball Coach, Saint Viator High School, Arlington Heights, IL (2011-2013); Assistant Varsity Girls Basketball Coach, Regina Dominican High School, Wilmette, IL (2008-2011); Head Girls Basketball Coach, Richmond Burton High School, Richmond, IL (2007-2008); Athletic Coordinator, William Fremd High School, Palatine, IL (1972-2008); Teacher, Physical Education, William Fremd High School, Palatine, IL (1971-2008); Head Basketball Coach, William Fremd

High School, Palatine, IL (1972-2006) **CR:** Girls Basketball Coach, Maine East High School, Park Ridge, IL (2018-Present); Substitute Teacher, St. Viator High School, Arlington Heights, IL (2008-Present) **CIV:** Chairperson, Hall of Fame Committee, Illinois Basketball Coaches Association (2004-Present); Girls Basketball Volunteer Worker, Illinois High School Association (1992-Present); All-State Selection Representative at Large, Illinois Basketball Coaches Association (1991-Present); Basketball Advisory Committee, Illinois High School Association (2003-2006); High School Panel Member, Illinois High School Association (2004); Executive Head Coach, Challenge West Clinic, Reebok Women's Sports Training (1995-1996); President, Illinois Girls Coaches Association (1991-1995); President, Illinois Girls Basketball Association (1986-1988) **CW:** Co-author, Book, "Excelling in Sports Through Thinking Straight: The Right Choices for Coaches and Athletes" (1988); Contributor, Article, "A multi-sensory approach to winning," National Federation Magazine (1984); Contributor, Article, "Motivating Positive Thinking," Athletic Journal (1984); Contributor, Article, "Viewpoint: Is the High School Bench Decorum Rule Needed," Pro-response for Coaching Women's Basketball Magazine; Lecturer, Many Clinics and Camps **AW:** A-E-O Meyer-Hart Award, Ray Meyer (2017); Named Coach of the Year, Mid-Suburban League North (1984, 1990, 1999, 2001-2004); 500 Victory Club Award, Women's Basketball Coaches Association (2003); District Coach of the Year, Illinois Girls Basketball Association (1990, 1991, 1998, 1999, 2001); District 6 Coach of the Year, Illinois Basketball Coaches Association (2001, 1999, 1998, 1991, 1990); 400 Victory Club Award, Women's Basketball Coaches Association (1998); Inductee, Illinois Girls Coaches Association Hall of Fame (1996); Inductee, Illinois Basketball Coaches Association Hall of Fame (1995); Citation, Illinois High School Association, AD HOC Committee for Restructuring of State Tournaments (1994); 300 Victory Club (1993); Certificate of Recognition for Outstanding Athletic Achievement, Illinois House of Representative (1990); Wall of Honor William Fremd High School; Oral History of Girls Basketball in Illinois, Abraham Lincoln Presidential Library; 200 Victory Club (1987); Awards, Women's Basketball Coaches Association **MEM:** President, Illinois Girls Basketball Association (1979-1980); Girls Representative, Hall of Fame Chair, Illinois Basketball Coaches Association; National Audubon Society; National Wildlife Federation; Former Member, Women's Basketball Coaches Association; Illinois Coaches Association Girls' and Women's Sports; The National WWII Museum; Special Olympics Partner; Association Of The Miraculous Medal **MH:** Albert Nelson Marquis Lifetime Achievement Award **AS:** Being knowledgeable, creative, flexible, doing the work to succeed, and the mentors in her life. Showing people that she cares about them as a person and helping others. **B/I:** Ms. Plodzien grew up in Chicago where the park districts had programs for girls. She participated in volleyball, softball, track and field, and speed skating. She went to high school and played basketball, and then went on to play basketball in college. She wanted to be a teacher and share with young students all she had learned during her great experiences in sports. In addition, Ms. Plodzien always had a passion for teaching and mentoring young people. **AV:** Title IX for girls and women's sports (1971-1974) **RE:** Roman Catholic **THT:** Knowledge is power acquired through reading and research, surrounding yourself with successful people and experiences. Use your knowledge and follow your heart to find your passion in life and live it fully. Develop values and principles to live by that will help you do good and the right things. Be who you are and be the best you. Serve others. Develop healthy relationships where you can love, have fun, and create memories. Show gratitude for all of your gifts and blessings. Worship God and know through Him all things are possible.

PLOWDEN, DAVID, T: Photographer; Writer **I:** Fine Art **DOB:** 10/09/1932 **PB:** Boston **SC:** MA/USA **PT:** Roger Plowden; Mary Russell (Butler) Plowden **MS:** Married **SPN:** Sandra Oakes Schoellkopf (07/08/1977); Pleasance Coggeshall (06/20/1962, Divorced 1976) **CH:** John; Daniel; Philip; Karen **ED:** BA in Economics, Yale University (1955); Private Coursework Studies with Minor White and Nathon Lyons, Rochester, NY (1959-1960); Coursework, The Putney School, VT (1948-1951) **C:** Photographer, Writer (1958-Present); Assistant, George Meluso Studio, New York, NY (1960-1962); Assistant, O. Winston Link Studio, New York, NY (1958-1959) **CR:** Visiting Professor, Grand Valley State University (1988-1990, 1991-2007); Artist-in-residence, University of Baltimore (1990-1991); Lecturer, The University of Iowa School of Journalism and Mass Communication (1985-1988); Associate Professor, Institute Design, Illinois Institute of Technology, Chicago, IL (1978-1986) **CW:** Artist, Numerous Exhibitions; Author, 22 Books, and Many Magazine Articles **AW:** Honored Imagemaker, Society for Photographic Education (2002); Subject of PBS Documentary, "David Plowden: Light, Shadow & Form" (2000); R.R. History Award (1989); Award, State Historical Society of Iowa (1987-1988); Award, Iowa Humanities Board (1987-1988); Award, Seymour H. Knox Foundation (1987); Award, Baird Foundation (1987); Grantee, New York State Council of Arts (1966, 1987); Award, Chicago Historical Society (1980-1984); Award, H. E. Butt Foundation (1977); Award, United Board for Homeland Ministries (1976); Award, Department of Transportation and Smithsonian Institute (1975-1976); Grantee, Smithsonian Institute (1970-1971); John Simon Guggenheim Fellowship (1968) **MEM:** American Society of Media Photographers, Inc. **MH:** Albert Nelson Marquis Lifetime Achievement Award **AS:** Mr. Plowden attributes his success to his love of photography and concern for what he saw changing in America. His success comes from 70 years of dedicated work in the field, in the darkroom, and devotion to his art. **B/I:** Mr. Plowden was seeing the disappearance of so many things that all of us took for granted. The first subjects he photographed were the steam locomotives on the railroads. That was a major undertaking. Mr. Plowden went to Canada twice to work with the Canadian Pacific Railway and he was there for the last run of the steam locomotives in regular service. In March 1960, he rode train #518, the last regularly scheduled steam powered train outside of the suburban community of Montreal. Mr. Plowden also worked for the railroad, the Great Northern Railway in 1955 and he was assigned to the regional division that had the last steam locomotives operating, so he had another chance to photograph steam locomotives. He loved these engines that were disappearing; they represented a different age in America. America was changing so rapidly, which was the reason he started to make photographs. He studied photography at the Putney School in Vermont, graduating in 1951. After he graduated from Yale University in 1955, he went to work for the Great Northern Railway. Many thought he was going to be a railroad executive, however not Plowden. He instead went back to New York and took a job with the American Express Company as a travel clerk for a brief moment. He finally went to work as a photographer's assistant for Winston Link, the railroad photographer. Shortly after, he went to work for photographer George Meluso, who he worked for until 1962 and then he went on his own. **AV:** Fly fishing **PA:** Democrat **RE:** Christian **THT:** For more information on Mr. Plowden's work, please visit: www.davidplowden.com/copy-of-small-town-1; www.davidplowden.com/about; www.mocp.org/detail.php?type=related&kv=7572&t=people; https://beinecke.library.yale.edu/collections/highlights/david-plowden; https://art.nelson-atkins.org/people/13927/david-plowden; jsessionid=AE80D0C96CB57F03E863DB-F7E7349C9B/objects

PLUMLEY, GERALDINE VIRGIL, T: Health Services Director, Training Coordinator **I:** Medicine & Health Care **CN:** International Paper Company **DOB:** 02/27/1942 **PB:** Cambridge **SC:** NY/USA **PT:** George Louis Virgil; Beatrice Geraldine (Brown) Virgil **MS:** Married **SPN:** Donald Thomas Plumley (09/09/1964) **ED:** BS, Professional Arts and Health Care Administration, St. Joseph's College, North Windham, ME (1984); Diploma in Nursing, Memorial Hospital, Albany, NY (1963); Regents Diploma, Indian Lake Central School, Indian Lake, NY (1959) **CT:** Certified, Community Health Nurse **C:** Occupational Health Nurse, International Paper Company, Ticonderoga, NY (1996-2001); Staff Nurse, Greater Adirondack Home Aides, Glens Falls, NY (1993-1995); Health Services Director, Training Coordinator, Mountain & Valley In-Home Services, Elizabethtown, NY (1992-1993); Health Services Director, Training Coordinator, Home Health Care, Indian Lake, NY (1984-1992); School Nurse Substitute, Minerva Central School, Olmstedville, NY (1978-1983); Occupational Health Nurse, NL Industries, Tahawus, NY (1973-1978); Private Practice (1967-1973); Operating Room Staff Nurse, Glens Falls Hospital, Glens Falls, NY (1963-1967) **CIV:** Instructor, CPR and Standard First Aid, American Red Cross, Glens Falls, NY (1976-2001) **AW:** Grantee, Health Agency, New York State Department of Health, Albany, NY (1987-1988, 1988-1989); Grantee, Home Health Agency, New York State Department of Social Services, Albany, NY (1984-1987) **MEM:** Retired Member, Minerva Rescue Squad, AEMT 3 **MH:** Who's Who in the East (1990); Who's Who Among Nurse Specialists (1988); Albert Nelson Marquis Lifetime Achievement Award **AS:** Ms. Plumley attributes her success to a lot of hard work and a supportive spouse. **B/I:** Ms. Plumley became involved in her profession because she wanted to be a nurse since she was 5 years old. **AV:** Singing; Reading **PA:** Democrat **RE:** Catholic

PLUMLEY, MICHAEL, "MIKE" A., T: Rubber Manufacturing Company Executive, Consultant to Industry **I:** Business Management/Business Services **DOB:** 12/18/1950 **PB:** Fort Wayne **SC:** IN/USA **PT:** Harold Johnson Plumley; Opal Aline (Beall) Plumley **MS:** Married **SPN:** Emily Jane Brewer (09/02/1972) **CH:** Christopher Michael; Matthew Alan; Michael Alan II **ED:** Graduate Coursework, Harvard Business School (1998); Coursework in Logistics, University of Tennessee (1989); Coursework, Institute for Productivity Through Quality, University of Tennessee (1988); Graduate Coursework, Advanced Executive Program, Vanderbilt University (1984); Graduate Coursework, Wabash College-Wabash Institute for Personal Development, Crawfordsville, IN (1978-1980); Coursework in Psychology, University of Tennessee, Martin, TN (1972-1973); Coursework in Business Administration, Ball State University (1969-1970); Graduate Coursework, Cowan High School, Cowan, IN (1969) **CT:** First Aid Instructor (2008-2010); American Red Cross Certification in CPR **C:** Board Member, Chairman, Plumley Properties of Tennessee (2001-Present); Independent Consultant, Investor (2000-Present); Owner, Cool Springs Thorough-breds (2003-2014); Senior Advisor, New German Land Industrial Investment Council, Berlin, Germany (2000-2005); Board Member, New River Cabinet & Fixture Company (2001-2005); Founder, Owner, Veritas Management & Investment, LLC (2001); President, Dana Industrial Group/Strategic Business Unit, Dana's Strategic Operating Committee (1998-2000); Vice President, Global Industrial Components Group, Dana Corporation (1997-1998); Core Product Parent for Industrial Products, Ex-Officio Member, World Operating Committee, Dana Corporation (1996-1997); Group Vice President, Industrial Products, North American Operating Committee, Dana Corporation (1996-1997); Chief Executive, General Manager, Plumley Division, Dana Corporation (1995-1996); Board of Directors, Plumley Companies (1974-1995); Chairman, Chief Executive Officer, Plumley Companies, Paris, TN (1988-1994); Vice Chairman, Plumley Companies, Paris, TN (1987); President Plumley Companies Paris, TN (1984-1987); Vice President, Sales and Marketing, Plumley Companies, Paris, TN (1982-1984); President, Plumley Rubber Company, Paris, TN (1980-1982); Vice President, Manufacturing, Plumley Rubber Company, Paris, TN (1977-1980); Vice President, Purchasing, Plumley Rubber Company, Paris, TN (1976-1977); General Manager, Crenshaw Division, Plumley Rubber Company, Crenshaw, MS (1974-1976); Safety Director, Plumley Rubber Company Paris, TN (1973-1974); Lab Technician, Plumley Rubber Company, Paris, TN (1972-1973) **CR:** Board of Directors, Warner Electric Europe (1996-2000); Board of Directors, Mohawk Plastics (1996-1997); Governor's Board of Directors (1992-1997); Auto Parts Advisory Committee, Department of Commerce (1990-1996); Board of Directors, Plumley-Marugo Limited (1989-1996); Advisory Board, Liberty Mutual Insurance Company (1992-1995); District Export Council, U.S Commerce Department of International Trade Administration (1990-1995); Automotive Sales Council (1989-1993); Board of Directors, Motor & Equipment Manufacturers Association, Englewood Cliffs, NJ (1986-1992); President, Tennessee Automotive Manufacturers Association (1991); Supplier Advisory Board, Fayette Tubular Products, Fayette, OH (1986-1989) **CIV:** Director, Friends of the Library (2016-2017); Board Member, Battle of Franklin Trust (2010-2017); Committee Chairman, Nominating Committee Chair, Finance Committee, Treasurer, The Trust (2010-2017); State Representative, Veterans Administration Voluntary Services, Tennessee Valley VA (2010-2016); Board of Trustees, Historic Carter House, Community of Franklin, TN (2009-2015); Commissioner, Battlefield Preservation (2009-2013); Advisory Council to the Dean, School of Business, University of Tennessee (2000-2004); Advisory Board, School of Business University of Tennessee at Martin (1993-1999); Chairman, Tennessee Quality Award (1994-1996); Development Committee, University Tennessee at Martin (1989-1992); Development Council, University of Tennessee (1990-1991); Founder, Plumley Family Scholarship Fund, Wabash College (1987); Executive Vice President, Paris Little League (1986-1987); Board of Directors, Junior Achievement, Paris, TN (1977-1986); Sons of the American Revolution; Lifelong Member, First Presbyterian Church **MIL:** US. Army Reserves (1972-1973); Active Duty, U.S. Army Medical Corps (1970-1971) **CW:** Subject, "Strategic Management," Stahl & Grigsby (1997); Subject, "Japanese Industry in the American South-Kim" (1995); Subject, "Total Quality Management-Wiley" (1994); Subject, "Improving Workforce Basic Skills," Dr. Larry Moore (1992); Guest Author, Chief Executive Magazine (1989); Author, "Staying Aloft in a Global Marketplace" **AW:** Legacy Award, Battle of Franklin Trust (2018); Star Award for VA Voluntary Service, Tennessee Valley Veterans Administration (2016); Meritorious Service Medal, Sons of the American Revolution (2016); Bronze Roger Sherman Medal, Sons of the American Revolution (2014); Service to Veterans Medal Awarded with Two Oak Leaf Clusters, Sons of the American Revolution (2012); Military Service Medal, Sons of the American Revolution (2009); George Washington Fellow (2009); Medal, Chamber of Commerce of Lyon, French Minister of Industry (1993); Executive of the Year, Rubber & Plastics News (1991); Executive of the Year, Professional Secretaries International (1991); Kentucky Colonel (1990); High-Performance Award, Society of Automotive Engineers (1989); Outstanding Young Man of America (1976); Good Conduct Medal, U.S. Army (1971); National Defense Medal, U.S. Army (1970); All-Star Baseball Batting Champion, Cowan High School, Cowan, IN (1969) **MEM:** Paris Elks Lodge #816 (1974-Present); General Society of the Sons of the American Revolution (2009-2014); Southern Rubber Group; Rotary Club (1990-1991); Crenshaw Mississippi Lions Club (1974-1976); Kiwanis, Paris, TN (1974); Battle of Franklin Trust; Randall McGavock Society; Old Hickory Chapter, Society of the War of 1812; Tennessee State Secretary, Society of Colonial Wars; Life Member, Tennessee Division, Sons of Confederate Veterans; Sons of Union Veterans of the Civil War; VLife Member, Vietnam Veterans of America; Society of Automotive Analysts; Automotive Hall of Fame; National Association of Manufacturers; Society of Automotive Engineers; Japan Society of Automotive Engineers; President's Association; Tennessee Business Roundtable **MH:** Albert Nelson Marquis Lifetime Achievement Award **AS:** Mr. Plumley attributes his success to hard work and strategic thinking alongside his commitment to excellence. **B/I:** Mr. Plumley's father started the Plumley Rubber Company. After finishing high school, Mr. Plumley was drafted into the U.S. Army. When he returned from service, his father encouraged him to take control of the company. **AV:** Preserving history; Studying Geneology; Coin collecting; Knife collecting; Treasure hunting; Arrowhead hunting; Horse racing **PA:** Republican **RE:** Presbyterian **THT:** Mr. Plumley believes in using one's brain to the fullest potential. He makes the right decisions and has a heart for those less fortunate than him. Likewise, he is mindful that his primary purpose in life is contributing to making things better.

PLUMMER, STEPHEN RAY, T: IT Project Manager **I:** Manufacturing **CN:** Marsh Furniture Company **DOB:** 10/18/1952 **PB:** High Point **SC:** NC/USA **PT:** Ray Craig Plummer; Rebecca Maye (Warden) Plummer **MS:** Married **SPN:** June Pinson (09/15/1979) **CH:** Meredith Annette; Andrew Ross; Richard Stephen **ED:** BS in FMM, North Carolina State University (1974) **C:** IT Project Manager, Marsh Furniture Co. (Now Marsh Cabinets), High Point, NC (2019-Present); IT Manager, Marsh Furniture Co. (Now Marsh Cabinets), High Point, NC (1982-2018); Production Control Manager, Marsh Furniture Co. (Now Marsh Cabinets), High Point, NC (1978-1981); Industrial Engineer, Marsh Furniture Co. (Now Marsh Cabinets), High Point, NC (1974-1977) **CIV:** President, Archdale-Trinity Jaycees, Archdale, NC (1978); Eagle Scout (1969); Local Board of Administration, Mt. Zion Wesleyan Church, Thomasville, NC **MEM:** President, Growth Power Regional User Group of the Carolinas (1993); President, High Point Administrative Management Society (1982-1983); National Beta Club **MH:** Albert Nelson Marquis Lifetime Achievement Award **B/I:** What inspired Mr. Plummer to become a project manager at Marsh Furniture Company

was his interest in engineering. **AV:** Reading; Gardening; Fishing; Camping; Personal computers **PA:** Republican **RE:** Wesleyan

PLUNKETT, MELBA KATHLEEN, T: Manufacturing Company Executive **I:** Manufacturing **DOB:** 03/20/1929 **PB:** Marietta **SC:** IL/USA **PT:** Lester George Bonnett; Florence Marie (Hutchins) Bonnett **MS:** Married **SPN:** James P. Plunkett (08/18/1951) **CH:** Gregory James Plunkett; Julie Marie Plunkett Hayden **C:** Secretary-treasurer, Director, Coils Inc.; Co-founder, Coils Inc., Huntley, IL (1961) **MEM:** Illinois Notary Association; Illinois Chamber of Commerce; US Manufacturing Association; US Chamber of Commerce; DAR (Daughters of American Revolution) **MH:** Albert Nelson Marquis Lifetime Achievement Award **B/I:** Ms. Plunkett became involved in her profession because she and her husband worked with the same company. They both met and were mentored by a great engineer in the department, Mr. Robert Bachi. **AV:** Travel; Singing; Reading (biographies); Barber shop quartet; Gardening **PA:** GOP **RE:** Roman Catholic

POCAN, MARK WILLIAM, T: U.S. Representative from Wisconsin **I:** Government Administration/Government Relations/Government Services **CN:** U.S. House of Representatives **DOB:** 08/14/1964 **PB:** Kenosha **SC:** WI/USA **MS:** Married **SPN:** Phillip Frank (2006) **ED:** Bachelor of Arts in Journalism, University of Wisconsin-Madison (1986) **C:** Member, U.S. House of Representatives from Wisconsin's Second Congressional District, United States Congress, Washington, DC (2013-Present); Member, U.S. House Committee on Oversight Reform (2013-Present); Member, U.S. House Committee on Budget (2013-Present); Member, District 78, Wisconsin State Assembly (1999-2013); Member, Dane County Board of Supervisors (1991-1996); Member, Committee on Urban and Local Affairs; Member, Committee on Colleges and Universities **AW:** Planned Parenthood Rebecca Young Leadership Award (2009); Fair Wisconsin Statewide Leader Award (2009); Named, Legislator of the Year, Professional Fire Fighters Wisconsin (2008); Voices of Courage Public Policy Award, Wisconsin Coalition Against Sexual Assault Inc. (2008); Inductee, Wisconsin League of Conservation Voters Honor Roll (2008); Public Policy Award, Wisconsin Library Association (2008); Outstanding Young Legislator Award, Wisconsin Counties Association (2006, 2008); Wisconsin AIDS Fund Award (2007); Conservative Champion, Wisconsin League of Conservation Voters (2006); Clean 16 Award, Clean Wisconsin (2000, 2002, 2004); Council Representative of the Year, American Federation of Teachers (2002, 2003); Special Recognition Award, American Civil Liberties Union (2001); Outreach Man of the Year (1999) **MEM:** American Civil Liberties Union **PA:** Democrat

PODESTA, ANTHONY, "TONY" THOMAS, T: Lobbyist (Retired) **I:** Government Administration/Government Relations/Government Services **DOB:** 10/24/1943 **PB:** Chicago **SC:** IL/USA **PT:** John David Podesta; Mary (Kokoris) Podesta **MS:** Divorced **SPN:** Heather (Miller) Podesta (2003, Divorced 2014) **ED:** Doctor of Jurisprudence, Georgetown University Law Center; Coursework in Political Science, Massachusetts of Institute; Bachelor of Arts in Political Science, The University of Illinois at Chicago **C:** Co-founder, President, Podesta Group, Washington, DC (2006-2017); Co-founder, PodestaMattoon (2001-2006); Co-founder, Podesta Associates (1988); With, Michael Dukakis' Presidential Campaign (1988); With, Walter Mondale's Presidential Campaign (1984); With, Ted Kennedy's Presidential Campaign (1980); With, George

McGovern's Presidential Campaign (1972); With, Ed Muskie's Presidential Campaign (1972); With, Joe Duffy's Senatorial Campaign, CT (1970); With, U.S. Senator Eugene McCarthy's Presidential Campaign (1968) **CR:** Visiting Professor, Georgetown University Law Center **CIV:** Founding President, People for the American Way (1981-1987) **AW:** Named, One of the 50 Most Powerful People in DC, GQ Magazine (2009); Named, One of the 50 Top Lobbyists, Washingtonian Magazine (2007); Named, Power Collector, The Washington Post **AV:** Art Collecting **PA:** Democrat

POE, LENORA MADISON, T: Psychotherapist, Author **I:** Health, Wellness and Fitness **DOB:** 01/03/1934 **PB:** New Bern **SC:** AL/USA **PT:** Tommy Madison; Carrie (Norfleet) Madison **MS:** Married **SPN:** Levi Mathis Poe (6/21/1957) **CH:** Michael DeWayne; Michaelle DaNita Burke **ED:** PhD, Center for Psychological Studies, Albany, CA (1991); MS, California State University, Hayward, CA (1980); MA, California State University, Hayward, CA (1972); BS, Stillman College, Tuscaloosa, AL (1956) **CT:** Licensed Marriage, Family and Child Therapist **C:** Psychotherapist, Private Practice, West Coast Children's Center, El Cerrito, CA (1982-Present); Psychotherapist, Private Practice, Berkeley, CA (1982-Present); Guidance Counselor, Berkeley Unified Schools (1969-1979); Classroom Teacher, Richmond Unified Schools (1962-1969); Classroom Teacher, Perry County Schools, Uniontown, AL (1956-1958) **CR:** Lecturer, "Grandparents as Parents" (1992-Present); Delegate, White House Conference on Aging, Washington, DC (1995); Part-Time Professor, John F. Kennedy University, Orinda, CA (1993); Consultant in Field, Staff Consultant, Community Adult Day Health Services, Highland General Hospital, Oakland, CA **CIV:** President, National Board of Directors, Stillman College; Mentor, Consultant, Black Women Organized for Educational Development, Oakland, CA (1994-Present); Advisory Board, National Black Aging Network, Oakland, CA (1992-Present); Founding Member, Advisor Realmindcas Civic Club, Richmond, CA (1976-Present); Families United Against Crack Cocaine; Oakland Board Directors Center For Elders For Independence, Oakland Trustee, Center for Psychological Studies, Albany, CA; Chairperson, Grandparents Caregivers Advocacy Task Force; Board of Education, Ministry of the Church by the Side of the Road, Berkeley, CA **CW:** Author, "Black Grandparents as Parents" (1992) **AW:** Trademark Women of Distinction Honor Award (2017); Outstanding Alumna of the Year Award, Center for Psychological Studies (1995); Appreciation Award for Excellence, Nystrom Elementary School, Richmond, CA (1994); President's Citation for Excellence, National Association for Equal Opportunity in Higher Education (1993); Excellence in Education Award, National Council of Negro Women (1993); Appreciation Certification, African American Historical and Cultural Society, San Francisco, CA (1992); S. Award, Stillman College **MEM:** Advisory Committee, National Coalition Grandparents as Parents (1992-Present); No. Coalition Grandparents as Parents (1991-1993); President, Stillman College National Alumni Association; Co-Chair, California Coalition Grandparent/Relative Caregivers; National Coalition Grandparent/Relative Caregivers **MH:** Albert Nelson Marquis Lifetime Achievement Award **B/I:** Dr. Poe graduated from Stillman College and became a classroom teacher. She then moved to California and continued to work as a classroom teacher. She got her degree in classroom psychology and wanted to do more outreach in the family structure, positive interventions, and early education for children, especially minority children. This is how she got into the field of psychology. Later, she pursued a PhD in clinical psychology; at that point, she wanted to further her research in family structure. By the grace of God, Dr. Poe was directed into the field of grandparents parenting grandchildren. She was not aware at the time, but the media got a hold of her research and realized what she was doing. She was sent an article from the research institute which stated that her research was the first research of its kind in the nation in the field. From there, she was inspired to keep going.

POEHLER, AMY, T: Comedienne, Actress **I:** Media & Entertainment **DOB:** 09/16/1971 **PB:** Newton **SC:** MA/USA **PT:** William Poehler; Eileen Poehler **SPN:** Will Arnett (08/23/2003, Divorced 2014) **CH:** Archie; Abel **ED:** Bachelor's Degree in Media and Communications, Boston College (1993) **C:** Performer, Second City Comedy Troupe, Chicago, IL (1993-1996); Co-Founder, Upright Citizens Brigade Theatre; Performer, Improv Olympic, Los Angeles, CA **CW:** Actress, "Duncanville" (2020); Actress, "A Parks and Recreation Reunion Special" (2020); Actress, "Wine Country" (2019); Actress, "Household Name" (2017); Narrator, "SMILF" (2017); Actress, "Wet Hot American Summer: Ten Years Later" (2017); Actress, "The House" (2017); Actress, "Unscripted" (2017); Actress, "Maya & Marty" (2017); Actress, "Sisters" (2015); Actress, "A Very Murray Christmas" (2015); Voice Actress, "Riley's First Date?" (2015); Actress, "Wet Hot American Summer: First Day of Camp" (2015); Voice Actress, "Inside Out" (2015); Co-Host, "The 72nd Golden Globe Awards" (2015); Voice Actress, "The Awesomes" (2014-2015); Actress, "Welcome to Sweden" (2014-2015); Actress, "Kroll Show" (2014, 2015); Actress, Writer, Producer, "Parks and Recreation" (2009-2015); Actress, "Half Sisters" (2014); Actress, "Broad City" (2014); Actress, "They Came Together" (2014); Co-Host, "The 71st Golden Globe Awards" (2014); Author, "Yes Please" (2014); Voice Actress, "The Simpsons" (2005, 2014); Actress, "Anchorman 2: The Legend Continues" (2013); Voice Actress, "Free Birds" (2013); Actress, "Are You Here" (2013); Actress, "The Greatest Event in Television History" (2013); Actress, "A.C.O.D." (2013); Co-Host, "The 70th Golden Globe Awards" (2013); Actress, "Louie" (2012); Actress, "30 Rock" (2012); Voice Actress, "Napoleon Dynamite" (2012); Voice Actress, "Alvin and the Chipmunks: Chipwrecked" (2011); Actress, "Broad City" (2011); Voice Actress, "Ho'odwinked Too! Hood vs. Evil" (2011); Actress, "UCB Comedy Originals" (2008-2011); Actress, "The Mighty B!" (2008-2011); Voice Actress, "The Secret World of Arrietty" (2010); Actress, "Freak Dance" (2010); Voice Actress, "Alvin and the Chipmunks: The Squeakquel" (2009); Actress, "The Mystery of Claywoman" (2009); Voice Actress, "Monsters vs. Aliens" (2009); Actress, "Spring Breakdown" (2009); Actress, "Baby Mama" (2008); Voice Actress, "Horton Hears a Who!" (2008); Actress, "Hamlet 2" (2008); Actress, "Cast Member, Writer, "Saturday Night Live" (2001-2008); Actress, "Wild Girls Gone" (2007); Actress, "Mr. Woodcock" (2007); Voice Actress, "Shrek the Third" (2007); Actress, "On Broadway" (2007); Actress, "Blades of Glory" (2007); Actress, "Girl Missing" (2007); Actress, "The Ex" (2006); Actress, "Tenacious D in the Pick of Destiny" (2006); Actress, "Man of the Year" (2006); Actress, "Southland Tales" (2006); Actress, "Wonder Showzen" (2006); Voice Actress, "O'Grady" (2006); Voice Actress, "SpongeBob SquarePants" (2005); Actress, "Soundtracks Live" (2004); Actress, "Envy" (2004); Actress, "Mean Girls" (2004); Actress, "Arrested Development" (2004, 2005); Actress, "Shortcut to Happiness" (2003); Actress, "Sick in the Head" (2003); Actress, "Martin & Orloff" (2002); Actress, "Undeclared"

(2001, 2002); Actress, "North Hollywood" (2001); Actress, "Late Friday" (2001); Actress, "Wet Hot American Summer" (2001); Actress, "ShortCuts" (2000); Actress, "Zoe Loses It" (2000); Actress, "Upright Citizens Brigade" (1998-2000); Actress, "Deuce Bigalow: Male Gigolo" (1999); Voice Actress, "Deer Avenger 2: Deer in the City" (1999); Actress, "Saving Manhattan" (1998); Actress, "Spin City" (1998); Actress, "Tomorrow Night" (1998); Actress, Performer, "Late Night with Conan O'Brien" (1997-1998); Actress, "Apt. 2F" (1997); Voice Actress, "Escape from It's a Wonderful Life" (1996); Executive Producer, Producer, Numerous Films, TV Series and TV Specials; Writer, Numerous Films, TV Series and TV Specials **AW:** Outstanding Guest Actress in a Comedy Series, "Saturday Night Live," Primetime Emmy Awards (2016); Blimp Award for Favorite Voice from an Animated Movie, "Inside Out," Kids' Choice Awards (2016); MTV Movie Award for Best Virtual Performance, "Inside Out," MTV Movie + TV Awards (2016); OFTA Film Award for Best Voice-Over Performance, "Inside Out," Online Film & Television Association (2016); Gold Derby TV Award for Comedy Lead Actress, "Parks and Recreation," Gold Derby Awards (2015); Woman of the Year, Hasty Pudding Theatricals (2015); Honoree, Star, Hollywood Walk of Fame (2015); Best Performance by an Actress in a Television Series - Comedy or Musical, "Parks and Recreation," Golden Globes (2014); Co-Honoree, Gold Derby TV Award for Variety Performer, "71st Golden Globe Awards" (2014); Co-Honoree, Gold Derby TV Award for Variety Performer, "70th Golden Globe Awards" (2013); Gold Derby TV Award for Comedy Lead Actress, "Parks and Recreation" (2013); Gracie Allen Award for Outstanding Female Actor in a Leading Role in a Comedy Series, "Parks and Recreation" (2013); Peabody Award, "Parks and Recreation" (2012); Best Actress in a Comedy Series, "Parks and Recreation," Critics' Choice Television Awards (2012); Gold Derby TV Award for Comedy Lead Actress, "Parks and Recreation" (2012); Gold Derby TV Award for Comedy Lead Actress, "Parks and Recreation" (2011); Ranked Among "The 100 Most Influential People in the World," Time Magazine (2011); Best Comedy Actress - TV, "Parks and Recreation," American Comedy Awards (2009); Webby Award for Best Actress, The Webby Awards (2009); Named a Maverick, Details Magazine (2008); Woman of the Year Award, Glamour Magazine (2009); Gold Derby TV Award for Variety Performer, "Saturday Night Live" (2006); Gold Derby TV Award for Variety Performer, "Saturday Night Live" (2005); Best Host or a Performer in a Variety, Musical, or Comedy Series, "Saturday Night Live" (2003)

POITIER, SIDNEY, T: Actor **I:** Media & Entertainment **DOB:** 02/20/1927 **PB:** Miami **SC:** FL/USA **PT:** Reginald Poitier; Evelyn (Outten) Poitier **MS:** Married **SPN:** Joanna Shimkus (01/23/1976); Juanita Hardy (04/29/1960, Divorced 1965) **CH:** Beverly; Pamela; Sherri; Anika; Sydney Tamilia **ED:** Coursework, The Bahamas **C:** Performer, American Negro Theater, New York, NY **CR:** Ambassador of the Bahamas to UNESCO (2002-2007); Ambassador to Japan from the Bahamas (1997-2007); Member, Board of Directors, Walt Disney Company (1995-2003) **MIL:** Honorably Discharged, Untied States Army (1944); Enlisted, United States Army (1943-1944); Assigned, Veteran's Administration Hospital, Northport, NY **CW:** Author, "Life Beyond Measure: Letters to My Great-Granddaughter" (2008); Subject, Documentary, "Sidney Poitier, an Outsider in Hollywood" (2008); Actor, TV Film, "The Last Brickmaker in America" (2001); Author, "The Measure of a Man: A Spiritual Autobiography" (2000); Subject, Documentary, "Sidney Poitier: One Bright Light" (2000); Actor, TV Film, "The Simple Life of

Noah Dearborn" (1999); Actor, TV Film, "David and Lisa" (1998); Actor, Executive Producer, TV Film, "Free of Eden" (1998); Actor, "The Jackal" (1997); Actor, TV Film, "Mandela and de Klerk" (1997); Actor, TV Film, "To Sir, with Love II" (1996); Actor, TV Miniseries, "Children of the Dust" (1995); Producer, "Summer Knowledge" (1993); Actor, "Sneakers" (1992); Actor, TV Miniseries, "Separate But Equal" (1991); Director, "Ghost Dad" (1990); Actor, "Little Nikita" (1988); Actor, "Shoot to Kill" (1988); Director, "Fast Forward" (1985); Director, "Hanky Panky" (1982); Director, "Stir Crazy" (1980); Author, "This Life" (1980); Actor, Director, "A Piece of the Action" (1977); Actor, Director, "Let's Do It Again" (1975); Actor, "The Wilby Conspiracy" (1975); Actor, Director, "Uptown Saturday Night" (1974); Actor, Theater, "Anna Lucasta" (1974); Actor, Director, "A Warm December" (1973); Actor, Director, Producer, "Buck and the Preacher" (1972); Actor, "The Organization" (1971); Actor, Executive Producer, "Brother John" (1971); Actor, "They Call Me Mister Tibbs!" (1970); Actor, "The Lost Man" (1969); Actor, "For Love of Ivy" (1968); Actor, "Guess Who's Coming to Dinner" (1967); Actor, "In the Heat of the Night" (1967); Actor, "To Sir, with Love" (1967); Actor, "Duel at Diablo" (1966); Actor, "A Patch of Blue" (1965); Actor, "The Slender Thread" (1965); Actor, "The Bedford Incident" (1965); Actor, "The Greatest Story Ever Told" (1965); Actor, "The Long Ships" (1964); Actor, "Lilies of the Field" (1963); Actor, "Pressure Point" (1962); Actor, "Pressure Point" (1962); Actor, "Paris Blues" (1961); Actor, "A Raisin in the Sun" (1961); Actor, "All the Young Men" (1960); Actor, Theater, "A Raisin in the Sun" (1959-1960); Actor, "Porgy and Bess" (1959); Actor, "Our Virgin Island" (1958); Actor, "The Defiant Ones" (1958); Actor, "The Mark of the Hawk" (1957); Actor, "Band of Angels" (1957); Actor, "Something of Value" (1957); Actor, "Edge of the City" (1957); Actor, "Good-bye, My Lady" (1956); Actor, TV Series, "The Philco Television Playhouse" (1955, 1952); Actor, TV Series, "Ponds Theater" (1955); Actor, "Blackboard Jungle" (1955); Actor, "Go Man Go" (1954); Actor, TV Series, "Omnibus" (1952); Actor, "Red Ball Express" (1952); Actor, TV Series, "CBS Television Workshop" (1952); Actor, "Cry, the Beloved Country" (1951); Actor, "No Way Out" (1950); Actor, "Sepia Cinderella" (1947); Actor, Theater, "Lysistrata" (1946) **AW:** Academy Fellowship, BAFTA Awards (2016); Icon Award, African American Film Critics Association (AAFCA) (2016); Career - Honorary Award, CinEuphoria Awards (2012); Gala Tribute, Film Society of Lincoln Center (2011); Inductee, Acting, OFTA Film Hall of Fame, Online Film & Television Association (2009); Britannia Award for Lifetime Contributions to International Film, BAFTA Los Angeles, CA (2006); Honorary Award, Academy Awards, Academy of Motion Picture Arts and Sciences (2002); Inductee, Hall of Fame, NAACP Image Awards (2001); Best Spoken Word Album, "The Measure of a Man," Grammy Awards (2001); Governors' Award, Society of Camera Operators (2001); Life Achievement Award, Screen Actors Guild Awards (2000); Outstanding Actor in a Television Movie/Miniseries/Dramatic Special, "The Simple Life of Noah Dearborn," Image Awards (NAACP) (2000); Golden Satellite Award for Best Actor in a Miniseries or a Motion Picture Made for Television, "Mandela and de Klerk," Satellite Awards (1998); Honoree, Kennedy Center Honors, John F. Kennedy Center for the Performing Arts, Washington, DC (1995); Career Achievement Award, National Board of Review (1994); Honoree, Star, Hollywood Walk of Fame (1994); Lifetime Achievement Award, American Film Institute (1992); Cecil B. DeMille Award, Golden Globes, Hollywood Foreign Press Association (1982); Best Director, "Let's Do It

Again," NAACP Image Awards (1976); Henrietta Award, World Film Favorite - Male, Golden Globes, Hollywood Foreign Press Association (1969); Best Foreign Performer, "Guess Who's Coming to Dinner," Fotogramas de Plata (1969); Best Actor, "For Love of Ivy," San Sebastian International Film Festival (1968); Male Star of the Year, Golden Apple Awards (1967); Academy Award for Best Actor in a Leading Role, "Lilies of the Field," Academy of Motion Picture Arts and Sciences (1964); Golden Globe Award for Best Actor - Drama, "Lilies of the Field," Hollywood Foreign Press Association (1964); Silver Berlin Bear for Best Actor, "Lilies of the Field," Berlin International Film Festival (1963); Best Foreign Actor, "The Defiant Ones," BAFTA Awards (1959); Silver Berlin Bear for Best Actor, "The Defiant Ones," Berlin International Film Festival (1958)

POLAN, DAVID R., T: Public Administration & Finance Executive (Retired) **I:** Government Administration/Government Relations/Government Services **DOB:** 03/18/1953 **PB:** Cleveland **SC:** OH/USA **PT:** Donald Byron Polan; Elvira (Giovannetti) Polan **MS:** Married **SPN:** Patricia Rose Dynski (12/26/1983); Debra Anne Dyason (06/25/1975, Divorced 04/1983) **CH:** Evangeline **ED:** MPA, University at Albany Rockefeller College (1986); AB, Colgate University (1975) **CT:** Certified in Advanced Study, State University of New York (University at Albany), Albany, NY (1995) **C:** Part-time, Civil Service Examiner and Adjunct Professor (2006-Present); Retired (2006); Commissioner of Management and Budget, Albany County, NY (2002-2006); Associate Budget Examiner, New York State Division of the Budget, Albany, NY (1986-2002); Contract Manager, New York State Department of Labor, Albany, NY (1980-1986); Public Administrator, Tompkins County Personnel Office, Ithaca, NY (1977-1980); Mental Health Counselor, Probation Officer, Madison County, Wampsville, NY (1975-1977) **CIV:** Member, St. Francis of Assisi Parish (Previously St. James Church), Albany, NY (1995-Present); Past President, Parish Council; Past Finance Chairman, Member, St. Vincent de Paul Society (Now National Council of the US Society of St. Vincent de Paul); Past President, Local Conference and District Council; Volunteer, The American National Red Cross **MH:** Albert Nelson Marquis Lifetime Achievement Award **AS:** Mr. Polan attributes his success to a strong Jesuit and liberal arts education. **B/I:** Mr. Polan always enjoyed being a volunteer. In college, he volunteered to work for the probation department in the county he was living in. After graduation, Mr. Polan was offered a job as a probation officer and began his career in public service. From then on, he saw the benefits of good government and continued to work his way through the ranks of the profession. **AV:** Golf; Travelling; Camping; Reading; Cruising; Music; Sailing; Kayaking; Cross country; Nordic skiing **PA:** Democrat **RE:** Roman Catholic **THT:** Mr. Polan's motto is, "What goes around, comes around."

POLIS, JARED SCHUTZ, T: Governor of Colorado **I:** Government Administration/Government Relations/Government Services **DOB:** 05/12/1975 **PB:** Boulder **SC:** CO/USA **PT:** Stephen Schutz; Susan (Polis) Schutz **MS:** Life Partner **SPN:** Marlon Reis **CH:** Caspian Julius; Cora Barucha **ED:** BA in Political Science, Princeton University, NJ (1996) **C:** Governor, State of Colorado (2019-Present); Member, Colorado's Second Congressional District, United States Congress, Washington, DC (2009-2019); Member, Committee on Rules, Committee on Education and the Workforce, Committee on Ethics, and House Democratic Steering and Policy Committee (2009-2019); Founder, TechStars

(2006); Founder, Sonora Entertainment Group (2001); Founder, Proflowers.com/Proflowers Inc., San Diego, CA (1998); Executive Director, Internet Startup, Dan's Chocolates; Executive Director, Internet Startup, FrogMagic; Executive Director, Internet Startup, BlueMountain.com; Sales Manager, Blue Mountain Arts **CR:** Executive Committee, Boulder County Democrats (2000-2007); Colorado Democratic Party (2000-2007); Colorado State Board of Education (2001-2006); Chairman, Colorado State Board of Education (2004-2005); Board Member, Colorado Conservation Voters; Board Member, Colorado Consumer Health Initiative; Board Member, Colorado Anti-Defamation League; Board Member, Latin American Research and Service Agency; Chair of Finance, Literacy Study Group; NASBE; Co-Chair, Colorado Commission HS Improvement **CIV:** Founder, Jared Polis Foundation (2000-Present); Co-Founder, Academy of Urban Learning, Denver, CO (2005); Founder, Superintendent, New America School, Thornton, CO (2004); Founder, Community Computer Connection, Aurora, CO; Board of Directors, Watershed School, Boulder, CO **AW:** Listee, Politics 40 Under 40, Time Magazine (2010); Listee, 50 Politicos to Watch, Politico (2010); Pacesetter Award in Education, Boulder Daily Camera (2007); Outstanding Philanthropist, State of Colorado (2006); Ernst & Young Entrepreneur of the Year (2000); Listee, 40 Under 40, Denver Business Journal (2000); Martin Luther King Junior Humanitarian Award; Community Award, Kauffman Foundation; Community Builder Award, Anti-Defamation League; Ohtli Award, Consul General of Mexico, Denver, CO; Outstanding Young Coloradoan, Colorado Jaycees **PA:** Democrat **RE:** Jewish

POLISI, JOSEPH WILLIAM, T: President Emeritus **I:** Education/Educational Services **CN:** The Juilliard School **DOB:** 12/30/1947 **PB:** New York **SC:** NY/USA **MS:** Married **SPN:** Elizabeth Polisi **CH:** Three Children **ED:** Honorary Doctor of Fine Arts, Fordham University, Bronx, NY (2006); Honorary Doctor of Humane Letters, The Juilliard School (2005); Doctor of Musical Arts, New England Conservatory of Music (2001); Honorary Doctor of Music, Curtis Institute of Music (1990); Honorary Doctor of Humane Letters, Ursinus College, Collegetown, PA (1986); Doctor of Musical Arts, Yale University (1980); Master of Museum Arts, Tufts University (1975); Master of Music, Tufts University (1973); Master of Arts in International Relations, Tufts University (1970); Bachelor of Arts in Political Science, University of Connecticut (1969) **C:** President Emeritus, The Juilliard School, New York, NY (2018-Present); Chief China Officer, The Tianjin Juilliard School (2018); President, The Juilliard School, New York, NY (1984-2018); Dean, College Conservatory of Music, University of Cincinnati (1983-1984); Dean of Faculty, Manhattan School of Music, New York, NY (1980-1983); Executive Officer, Yale School of Music, New Haven, CT (1976-1980) **CR:** Speaker in Field **CIV:** Director, Samuels Foundation; Director, Irene Diamond Fund; Director, Edward John Noble Foundation **CW:** Author, "American Muse: The Life and Times of William Schuman" (2008); Author, "The Artist as Citizen" (2005); Performances as Bassoonist throughout the United States; With, Juilliard Orchestra; Contributor, Articles to Various Publications, United States and France **AW:** Named, Educator of the Year, Musical American International Directory of the Performing Arts (2005) **MEM:** Fellow, American Academy Arts & Sciences; Honorary Member, Royal Academy of Music, London, United Kingdom

POLIZZI, JOSEPH, T: Social Scientist, Cultural Historian, Professor Emeritus, Author **I:** Education/Educational Services **DOB:** 11/08/1938

PB: Rochester **SC:** NY/USA **PT:** Russell A. Polizzi; Caroline (Antinoro) Polizzi **ED:** Postgraduate Coursework, University of Naples, Italy (1963-1964); Postgraduate Coursework, University of Perugia, Italy (1963); PhD, Cornell University (1967); MA, Fordham University (1962); BS, St. John Fisher College, Rochester, NY (1960) **C:** Publisher, Ausonia Press, Tallevast, FL (1988-Present); Professor Emeritus, St. John Fisher College (1986-Present); Professor, Department of Sociology, St. John Fisher College (1965-1986); Editorial Assistant, Center for International Studies, Cornell University, Ithaca, NY (1964) **CR:** President, Director of Cultural Affairs, The Ausonian Society Inc., Sarasota-Bradenton, FL (1993-2015); Executive Vice President, Ausonia Heritage Preservation Foundation, Scottsville, NY (1983-1985); Academy Advisory Committee, Center for Italian Studies, Nazareth College, Rochester, NY (1978-1980); Consultant, Sociological Associates, Rochester, NY (1973-1976); Adjunct Professor, Sociology, Rochester Institute of Technology (1972); College Liaison Officer, The Peace Corps, Rochester, NY (1967-1970); Policy Committee for Family Service, Rochester, NY (1965-1969); Participant, Giorgione Symposium, Oglethorpe University Museum **CIV:** Art Shows International, Sarasota, FL (1994); Designer, Curator, "Architect Palladio: His Life and Works" (1992); Designer, Curator, "Cameo of Women, as Artists and Subjects of Art" (1992); Ringling Museum Foundation; Assistant Curator, Leonardo Exhibit; Manatee Community College **CW:** Author, "Fanciful and Elegant Works of Art in Miniature" (2019); Author, "The Court of Winter Roses: A Children's Fairy Tale" (2018); Author, "Paintings, Photographs, Curiosities and Poetic Fragments" (2015); Author, "The New Flowering: A Cameo of Women in 19th Century Italian Art" (2012); Author, "The Golden Orrery: A Story of Love and Remembrance in Sicily and America" (2011); Author, "Illustrissimo Palladio: Architect of the Veneto and the World" (2007); Author, "Books on Italian Themes and More"; Co-Designer, Architecture of Andrea Palladio, Venice, Florida Arts Center (1992); Co-Designer, Italian Painters of the 19th Century, Florida State College, Bradenton (1992); Co-Designer, Architecture of Andrea Palladio, Lavery Library, St. John Fisher College (1992); Author, "Lady of Asolo: A Pictorial History of the Life and Times of Caterina Cornaro" (1985); Co-Designer, Commemorative on Leonardo da Vinci, The George Eastman International House of Photography, Rochester, NY (1985); Co-Designer, Engravings of Giovanbattista Piranesi, Hartness Gallery, University of Rochester (1983); Co-Author, "L 'Influsso Delle Idee Vichaiane Nell'Ispirazione Artistica Di Piranesi," Florence, Italy (1982); Author, "Word Paintings and Poetic Fragments" (1980); Co-Author, "The Golden Conch: An Anthology on the Splendid Isle of Sicily" (1975); Author, "We Remember: A Bicentennial Collection of 200 Years of Golden Sayings" (1975); Co-Author, 'Ghetto and Suburbia: An Urban Reference Guide" (1973); Co-Author, "My Grandmother Used to Say" (1972); Author, "Southern Italian Society: Its Peasantry and Change" (1968); Author, "Bel Giro: Italian Places in Rhapsodic Images, Odes"; Author, "In Praise of the Italian Pleasure Garden: An Essay with Antique Illustrations"; Author, "Societal Types and Development Strategies," Sociologia Ruralis, Journal of the European Society for Rural Sociology **AW:** Fullbright Scholar (1963-1964); Rochester Rotary United Nations Scholar (1958) **MEM:** Program Director, Cultural Affairs, President, Ausonian Society (1993-2015); Former Member, American Sociological Association; National Trust for Historic Preservation; Former Member, Fulbright Association; Sons of Italy; Vice-President, Italian American Club of Sarasota-Bradenton; Phi Kappa

Phi; Pi Gamma Mu; Delta Upsilon Sigma; Thomas Jefferson Monticello Foundation; The John and Marble Ringling Museum of Art Foundation; Sarasota Sisters Cities Association **MH:** Albert Nelson Marquis Lifetime Achievement Award; Marquis Who's Who Top Professional **B/I:** Intrigued by philosophy, Dr. Polizzi decided to pursue an education in the field after graduating from high school. However, as he pursued the field, he found that he was more interested in sociology. He then decided to attend Fisher College, where he met Dr. Edna O'Hern, an absolute inspiration. Dr. Polizzi then attended graduate school in New York City, which was an amazing experience for which he is endlessly grateful. There, he was inspired by Father Fitzpatrick, who made it possible for Dr. Polizzi to become an assistant at Fordham University. **AV:** Making art; Appreciating architecture; Traveling; Collecting antiques; Playing piano; Donating Pucciniopera Memorabilia to the Sibley Music Library **PA:** Democrat **RE:** Roman Catholic

POLLACK, MARSHA, T: Secondary School Educator **I:** Education/Educational Services **CN:** Solomon Schechter School of Queens **DOB:** 07/22/2020 **PT:** Harry Grunberg; Rose Grunberg **MS:** Married **SPN:** Bertram Pollack (07/15/1973) **CH:** Meredith Pollack-Richman **ED:** Specialist Diploma in Administration and Supervision, Queens College (2003); MS, Brooklyn College (1973); BA, Brooklyn College (1968) **CT:** Certified Teacher, National Board of Professional Teaching Standards (2001) **C:** Teacher, Solomon Schechter School of Queens (2006-Present); Teacher, Coach, Staff Development, New York City Department of Education, Queens, NY (2003-2006); Assistant Principal, New York City Department of Education, Queens, NY (2002-2003); Teacher, New York City Department of Education, Brooklyn and Queens, NY (1968-2002) **CR:** National Staff Developer, New York City Department of Education (2000-2006); Lesson Plan Abstract Evaluator, International Literacy Association (2003-2005); Professional Developer, Jericho Middle School (2003); L.E.A.D. Teacher (1998-2002) **AW:** CAL Grantee, Chase Manhattan (2001) **MEM:** Former Member, American Federation of Teachers; Former Member, NCTE; Former Member, Phi Delta Kappa; Former Member, International Literacy Association; Former Member, ASCD **MH:** Albert Nelson Marquis Lifetime Achievement Award; Marquis Who's Who Top Professional **AS:** Ms. Pollack attributes her success to loving what she does. **B/I:** Ms. Pollack became involved in her profession because she actually wanted to be a psychologist many years ago, but her mother talked her out of it, telling her that teaching was a good career. She loves to teach and likes children. She was also an assistant principal and hated it and thought the job was boring, one in which one either had a lot to do or nothing at all to do. He always had a passion to work with children. When she was a kid, she would take the other kids outside, open a little school, and teach them. She wanted to be so many different things but it all surrounded some form of teaching. It might have been older children; she wanted to work with convicts at one time. She was also supposed to go up to Brooklyn College to be part of a program that dealt with drug addicts, which her parents talked her out of. She was accepted for modeling when she was 17, but her mother decided it was a very bad profession. Teaching was the best, safest kind of profession and gave her summers off. **AV:** Law; Educational research; Writing; Online classes

POLLARD, HERSCHEL NEWTON, PHD, T: Artist, Psychologist **I:** Fine Art **DOB:** 04/06/1938 **PB:** Chadbourn **SC:** NC/USA **PT:** Herschel Newton; Lora Frances Pollard **MS:** Married **SPN:** Luz Mariela Gomez Bolanos (10/10/1997); Margaret Kathleen Innes (1962, Divorced 1972) **CH:** Joanna Sophia; Charles William; Steven Morton; Herschel III; Heather Dianne; Christopher Charles **ED:** Postgraduate Coursework, Chattanooga State Community College (1992-1994); PhD, Vanderbilt University (1964-1972); Postgraduate Coursework, Divinity School, Vanderbilt University (1963-1964); Postgraduate Coursework, University of Tennessee (1963-1964); Postgraduate Coursework, Georgia State University (1963); BA, Vanderbilt University (1960) **CT:** Licensed in Clinical, Consulting and Forensic Psychology, States of Alaska, Arkansas, Florida, Mississippi and Tennessee **C:** Lecturer, Ringling College of Art & Design (2007-Present); Lecturer, Renaissance Academy, Gulf Coast University (2007-Present); President, Art Institute of Florida (2006-Present); President, Corporacion Euanitos, S. A. (1996-Present); Private Practice Psychologist (1986-Present); Psychologist, Tennessee Valley Healthcare System (2009-2016); Clinical Director, Family Counseling and Recovery Centers (2008-2009); President, Board of Directors, Visual Arts Center, Punta Gorda, FL (2003-2007); Instructor, Cape Coral Arts Studio (2002-2004); Instructor, President, Board of Directors, Von Liebig Art Center (1990-2003); Instructor, Art League of Bonita Springs (1995-1998); Private Practice Clinical and Consulting Psychologist (1979-1989); Clinical Director, Anchorage Community Mental Health Services (1977-1979); Member, President's Commission on Mental Health (1976-1978); Director, Yukon-Kuskokwim Health Corporation (1976-1977); Clinical Director, Northwest Mississippi Regional Mental Health Systems (1975-1976); Private Practice Psychologist, Memphis, TN (1972-1974); Intern, Nashville Community Mental Health Center (1971-1972); Counselor, InterUniversity Psychological and Counseling Center (1964-1972); Officer Candidate, Officer, U.S. Navy (1956-1972); Adjunct Professor, St. Thomas Aquinas College (1970-1971); Contributing Researcher, President's Commission to Investigate Civil Disturbances (1970); Professor, Murray State University (1967-1969) **CR:** Founder, National Aviation Art Exhibition **CIV:** Art Therapy, Erlanger Hospital (2017-2018); President, Charlotte Artists Guild (2005-2007); Director, Charlotte Artists Guild (2004-2005); President, Center for the Visual Arts (2005); Representative, Southwest Florida Arts Council (2003-2004); Originator, Children's Art Exhibition, Early Education Project Policy Council (2002-2003) **MIL:** U.S. Navy Reserve (1962-1976); Junior Grade Lieutenant, United States Navy (1960-1962); Naval ROTC, Vanderbilt University (1956-1960) **CW:** Author, Director, Producer, "Dealing with Conflict" (1964); Author, "Vincent Van Gogh: Love, God and Art"; Author, "The Re-Emergence of a Noteworthy Baroque Painting"; Author, "The Madman of Arles"; Author, "Pollard's Brief Handbook for Painters"; Author, "Wait for the Thunder"; Author, "The Art of Frances Morton Pollard"; Co-Author, "A Life Remembered"; Author, "The Nineteen Friends of Robbie McNee"; Featured Exhibitions, Von Liebig Center for the Arts, Naples National Art Festival, Museum of the Everglades, Impac University, First Community National Bank, Alla Prima Pastel Invitational, Parthenon Museum, Larson Gallery, McCallie School; Represented, Permanent Collections **AW:** Artist of the Month, Charlotte County (2005); First Award, Commercial Aviation Division, National Aviation Art Exhibition (2005); Bowles Award for Portraiture (2005); First Judge's Award, Charlotte National Art Competition (2004); First Award, Visual Arts Center (2004); First Prize, Plein Aire Festival (2003); Teaching Fellowship, National Institute of Mental Health (1964-1972); First Award, Collier County Fair Art Competition (1970); First Award, Tennessee State Fair (1965); Mitchell Scholarship, Vanderbilt University (1956-1960) **MEM:** American Psychological Association; National Register of Health Service Psychologists; Arkansas Psychological Association; American Art Therapy Association; Professional Coin Grading Service; DAV **MH:** Albert Nelson Marquis Lifetime Achievement Award **AS:** Dr. Pollard attributes his success to God. **B/I:** Dr. Pollard became involved in his profession because he wanted to help others and foster his creative side. **AV:** Studying pre-Columbian archaeology; Collecting coins; Sailing; Preserving nature; Writing **PA:** Democrat **RE:** Protestant

POMPEO, MICHAEL, "MIKE" RICHARD, T: United States Secretary of State **I:** Government Administration/Government Relations/Government Services **DOB:** 12/30/1968 **PB:** Orange **SC:** CA/USA **PT:** Wayne Pompeo; Dorothy (Mercer) Pompeo **MS:** Married **SPN:** Susan Pompeo (2000); Leslie Libert (1986, Divorced) **CH:** Nicholas **ED:** JD, Harvard Law School (1994); BS in Engineering Management, United States Military Academy at West Point (1986) **C:** United States Secretary of State, Washington, DC (2018-Present); Member, United States House Energy & Commerce Committee, Washington, DC (2011-Present); Director, Central Intelligence Agency, Washington, DC (2017-2018); Member, United States House Select Committee on the Events Surrounding the 2012 Terrorist Attack in Benghazi (2014-2017); Member, United States House of Representatives from Fourth Kansas District, United States Congress, Washington, DC (2011-2017); President, Sentry International, Wichita, KS (2006-2017); Founder, Chief Executive Officer, Thayer Aerospace, Wichita, KS (1996-2006) **CIV:** National Committeeman, Republican National Convention (2008-Present); Board Member, YMCA; Board Member, Wichita Metro Chamber of Commerce **MIL:** United States Army (1986-1991) **PA:** Republican **RE:** Presbyterian

PORAT, RUTH M., T: Senior Vice President, Chief Financial Officer **I:** Business Management/Business Services **CN:** Alphabet Inc. **DOB:** 04/22/1957 **SC:** Sale/England **PT:** Dr. Dan I. Porat; Frieda Porat **MS:** Married **SPN:** Anthony Paduano (12/17/1983) **CH:** Three Children **ED:** MBA, University of Pennsylvania Wharton School, Philadelphia, PA (1987); AB in Economics, Stanford University, California (1979); MS in Economics, London School of Economics & Political Science **C:** CFO, Senior Vice President, Google, Inc. and Alphabet, Inc., Mountain View, CA (2015-Present); Executive Vice President, CFO, Morgan Stanley (2010-2015); Global Head, Financial Institutions Group, Morgan Stanley (2006-2009); Vice Chairman, Investment Banking Division, Morgan Stanley (2003-2009); Chairman, Financial Sponsors Group, Morgan Stanley (2004-2006); Smith Barney, New York, NY (1993-1996); Mergers & Acquisitions Department, Morgan Stanley, New York, NY (1987); Management Consultant, Yankelovich, Skelly & White, New York, NY; Fraud Investigations Unit, U.S. Department Of Justice; Co-Head, Global Technology Group, Morgan Stanley **CR:** Business Committee, Metropolitan Museum of Art **CIV:** Humanities and Science Council, Stanford University; Board of Trustee, Stanford University; Board of Directors, Stanford University Management Company; Borrowing Advisory Committee, U.S. Treasury; Board of Directors, Council on Foreign Relations; Board of Trustees, Economic Club of New York; Bretton Woods Committee; Advisory Council, Hutchins Center on Fiscal and Monetary Policy, Brookings Institution; Economic Strategy Group, Aspen Institute **AW:** 21st Most Powerful Woman in the World, Forbes Magazine (2018); Listee, 50 Most Powerful Women, Fortune Magazine (2015); Listee, 50 Most Influential People in Global Finance, Bloomberg

Markets (2012-2013); Listee, 25 Most Powerful Women in Finance, American Banker (2011-2012); Listee, 100 Most Powerful Women, Forbes Magazine (2011); Listee, 50 Most Powerful Women in New York, Crain's New York Business (2009, 2011); Listee, U.S. Banker (2010); Listee, 50 Women to Watch, The Wall St. Journal (2008)

PORTER, KATHERINE, "KATIE", T: 1) U.S. Representative from California 2) Educator **I:** Government Administration/Government Relations/Government Services **CN:** 1) U.S. House of Representatives 2) University of California Irvine School of Law **DOB:** 01/03/1974 **PB:** Fort Dodge **SC:** IA/USA **MS:** Divorced **SPN:** Matthew Hoffman (Divorced 2013) **ED:** Doctor of Jurisprudence, Harvard Law School, Magna Cum Laude (2001); Bachelor of Arts in American Studies, Yale University **C:** Member, U.S. House of Representatives from California's 45th District (2019-Present); Tenured Professor, University of California Irvine School of Law (2011-Present); Faculty Member, University of Iowa College of Law (2006) **CW:** Author, "Modern Consumer Law" (2016) **PA:** Democrat

PORTER, OTTO JR., T: Professional Basketball Player **I:** Athletics **CN:** Chicago Bulls **DOB:** 06/03/1993 **PB:** St. Louis **SC:** MO/USA **PT:** Otto Porter Sr.; Elnora (Timmons) Porter **MS:** Single **ED:** Coursework, Georgetown University (2011-2013); Diploma, Scott County Central High School, Sikeston, MO (2011) **C:** Professional Basketball Player, Chicago Bulls (2019-Present); Professional Basketball Player, Washington Wizards (2013-2019) **AW:** Consensus First-Team All-American (2013); Big East Player of the Year (2013); First-Team All-Big East (2013)

PORTMAN, NATALIE, T: Actress **I:** Media & Entertainment **DOB:** 06/09/1981 **PB:** Jerusalem **SC:** Israel **PT:** Avner Hershlag; Shelley Hershlag **MS:** Married **SPN:** Benjamin Millepied (08/04/2012) **CH:** Aleph; Amalia **ED:** BS in Psychology, Harvard University (2003) **C:** Founder, HandsomeCharlie Films (2008) **CR:** Spokesmodel, Dior (2010); Designer, Té Casan Vegan Shoe Collection (2008) **CIV:** Ambassador, WE Charity (2011-Present); Speaker, Women's March, Los Angeles, CA (2018); Donor, Time's Up (2018); Visiting Lecturer, Village Banking Campaign (2007); Ambassador of Hope, FINCA International (2004-2005); World Patrol Kids; One Voice Movement **CW:** Narrator, Documentary, "Dolphin Reef" (2020); Appearance, "Avenger: Endgame" (2019); Actress, "Lucy in the Sky" (2019); Actress, "Annihilation" (2018); Executive Producer, Actress, "Vox Lux" (2018); Actress, "The Death & Life of John F. Donovan" (2018); Host, "Saturday Night Live" (2006, 2018); Guest Appearance, "Angie Tribeca" (2017); Actress, "Song to Song" (2017); Appearance, "The Heyday of the Insensitive Bastards" (2017); Producer, Actress, "Jane Got a Gun" (2016); Producer, "Pride and Prejudice and Zombies" (2016); Actress, "Jackie" (2016); Actress, "Planetarium" (2016); Executive Producer, Documentary, "The Seventh Fire" (2015); Actress, "Knights of Cups" (2015); Director, Writer, Actress, "A Tale of Love and Darkness" (2015); Actress, "Thor: The Dark World" (2013); Actress, Short Film, "Illusions & Mirrors" (2013); Guest Appearance, "The Simpsons" (2007, 2012); Executive Producer, Actress, "No Strings Attached" (2011); Actress, "Your Highness" (2011); Actress, "Thor" (2011); Producer, Actress, "Hesher" (2010); Actress, "Black Swan" (2010); Executive Producer, Actress, "The Other Woman" (2009); Director, Writer, Appearance, "New York, I Love You" (2009); Actress, "Brothers" (2009); Actress, "The Other Boleyn Girl" (2008); Actress, "My Blueberry Nights" (2007); Actress, Short Film, "Hotel Chevalier" (2007); Cameo,

"The Darjeeling Limited" (2007); Actress, "Mr. Magorium's Wonder Emporium" (2007); Appearance, "Paris, je t'aime" (2006); Actress, "Goya's Ghosts" (2006); Narrator, Documentary, "The Armenian Genocide" (2006); Actress, "Star Wars: Episode III - Revenge of the Sith" (2005); Actress, "Free Zone" (2005); Actress, "V for Vendetta" (2005); Narrator, Documentary, "Hitler's Pawn: The Margaret Lambert Story" (2004); Actress, "Garden State" (2004); Actress, "Closer" (2004); Guest Appearance, "Sesame Street" (2003-2004); Actress, "Cold Mountain" (2003); Actress, "Star Wars: Episode II - Attack of the Clones" (2002); Appearance, "Zoolander" (2001); Actress, "Where the Heart Is" (2000); Actress, "Star Wars: Episode I - The Phantom Menace" (1999); Actress, "Anywhere but Here" (1999); Actress, "Beautiful Girls" (1996); Actress, "Everyone Says I Love You" (1996); Actress, "Mars Attacks!" (1996); Actress, Short Film, "Developing" (1995); Actress, "Heat" (1995); Actress, "Léon: The Professional" (1994) **AW:** The Genesis Prize, The Genesis Prize Foundation (2018); Ongoing Commitment Award, The Environmental Media Association (EMA) Awards (2017); Named Best Actress, "Jackie," Washington DC Area Film Critics Association Awards (2016); Named Best Movie Actress, Critics' Choice Awards (2010, 2016); Named Best Actress, Chicago Film Critics Association Awards (2010, 2016); Named Choice Movie Actress: Drama, "Black Swan," Teen Choice Awards (2011); Academy Award for Best Actress, "Black Swan," Academy of Motion Picture Arts and Sciences (2010); Best Film Actress in a Leading Role, "Black Swan," BAFTA Awards (2010); Golden Globe Award for Best Actress in a Motion Picture – Drama, "Black Swan," Hollywood Foreign Press Association (2010); Best Actress in a Film, "Black Swan," Saturn Awards (2010); Screen Actors Guild Award for Outstanding Performance by a Female Actor in a Leading Role in a Motion Picture, "Black Swan," SAG-AFTRA (2010); Named Best Actress, "Black Swan," Austin Film Critics Association Awards, Boston Society of Film Critics Awards (2010); Named Best Female Lead, "Black Swan," Independent Spirit Awards (2010); Named Best Actress in a Film, "V for Vendetta," Saturn Awards (2006); Golden Globe Award for Best Supporting Actress – Motion Picture, "Closer," Hollywood Foreign Press Association (2004); Named Best Ensemble Cast, "Closer," National Board of Review Awards (2004); Named Choice Movie Actress: Action, "Star Wars: Episode II - Attack of the Clones," Teen Choice Awards (2002) **PA:** Democrat **RE:** Jewish

PORTMAN, ROBERT, "ROB" JONES, T: U.S. Senator from Ohio; Lawyer **I:** Government Administration/Government Relations/Government Services **DOB:** 12/19/1955 **PB:** Cincinnati **SC:** OH/USA **PT:** William C. Portman; Joan (Jones) Portman **MS:** Married **SPN:** Jane Dudley (1986) **CH:** Jed; Will; Sally **ED:** JD, University of Michigan Law School (1984); BA, Dartmouth College (1979) **C:** Vice Chairman, Finance, National Republican Senatorial Committee (NRSC) (2013-Present); Member, U.S. Senate Committee on Finance Committee (2013-Present); U.S. Senator, State of Ohio (2011-Present); Member, U.S. Senate Committee on Budget (2011-Present); Member, U.S. Senate Committee on Homeland Security and Governmental Reform (2011-Present); Member, U.S. Senate Committee on Energy and Natural Resources Committee (2011-Present); Member, Joint Select Committee on Deficit Reduction, Washington, DC (2011); Member, U.S. Senate Committee on Armed Services, Washington,DC (2011-2012); Of Counsel, Squires Sanders & Dempsey LLP (Now Squire Patton Boggs), Cincinnati, Ohio and Washington, DC (2007-2009); Director, Office Management and

Budget, Executive Office of the President, Washington, DC (2006-2007); U.S. Trade Representative, Office of the United States Trade Representative, Executive Office of the President, Washington (2005-2006); Member, U.S. House of Representatives from Ohio's Second Congressional District, United States Congress, Washington, DC (1993-2005); Member, U.S. Delegate to United Nations' Subcommittee on Human Rights (1992); Deputy Assistant to President for Legislative Affairs, The White House, Washington, DC (1989-1991); Associate Counsel to President, The White House, Washington, DC (1989-1991); Partner, Graydon Head & Ritchey LLP, Cincinnati, OH (1986-1989, 1991-1993); Associate, Patton Boggs LLP (Now Squire Patton Boggs), Washington, DC (1984-1986) **CIV:** Member, Advisory Board, John Glenn College of Public Affairs, The Ohio State University (2008-Present); Vice Chairman, Hamilton County George Bush for President Campaign (1988, 1992); Delegate, Republican National Convention (1988, 1992); Chairman, Republican Early Bird Campaign Committee (1992); Board of Trustees, Springer School and Center; Board of Trustees, The United Way; Board of Trustees, Hyde Park Community United Methodist Church; Founding Trustee, Cincinnati-China Sister City Committee; Active Member, Hamilton County Republican Party Executive Committee; Active Member, Hamilton County Republican Party Finance Committee **CW:** Co-author with Cheryl Bauer, "Wisdom's Paradise: The Forgotten Shakers of Union Village" (2004) **AW:** Named One of the 10 Members to Watch in the 112th Congress, Roll Call (2011); National Leadership Award, Community Anti-drug Coalition of America (CDCA) (2008); Excellence in Public Service Award, John Glenn College of Public Affairs, The Ohio State University (2008); Albert Gallatin Award, Swiss-American Chamber of Commerce; Leadership on Alcohol & Other Drug Services Award, Hamilton County Mental Health & Recovery Services Board; PLANSPONSOR Magazine Legend Award; Nelson A. Rockefeller Distinguished Public Service Award, Nelson A. Rockefeller Center for Public Policy and the Social Sciences, Dartmouth College **MEM:** Cincinnati World Trade Association **PA:** Republican **RE:** Methodist

POSEY, WILLIAM, "BILL" JOSEPH, T: U.S. Representative from Florida; Real Estate Executive **I:** Government Administration/Government Relations/Government Services **DOB:** 12/18/1947 **PB:** Washington **SC:** DC/USA **PT:** Walter J. Posey; Beatrice (Tohl) Posey **MS:** Married **SPN:** Katie Ingram (11/23/1967) **CH:** Pamela J.; Catherine L. **ED:** AA, Brevard Community College (1969); Coursework, Stetson University (1978) **C:** Member, U.S. House of Representatives from Florida's Eighth Congressional District, United States Congress, Washington, DC (2013-Present); President, Chief Executive Officer, Posey & Company, Rockledge, FL (1978-Present); Member, U.S. House of Representatives from Florida's 15th Congressional District, United States Congress, Washington, DC (2009-2013); Member, District 24, Florida State Senate, Tallahassee, FL (2003-2009); Member, District 15, Florida State Senate, Tallahassee, FL (2001-2003); Member, District 32, Florida House of Representatives, Tallahassee, FL (1992-2000); Broker, Sherwood Realty Inc., Cocoa, FL (1974-1978); Manager, Gay & Taylor Inc., St. Petersburg, FL (1971-1974); President, Chief Executive Officer, Mid Florida Racing Inc., Melbourne, FL (1969-1971); Quality Assurance Representative, McDonnell Douglas, Cape Kennedy, FL (1966-1969); Member, Committee on Financial Services, Committee on Science, Space, and Technology **CR:** Founder, Florida Motorsports Hall of Fame (1986); Board of Directors, Cocoa-Rockledge Land Company; Board of Directors, Indian Oaks Corporation, Rockledge, FL; Board of Directors, Rockledge Realty Corporation; Board of Directors, National Racetrack Clearinghouse, Rockledge, FL CIV: Rockledge Economic Development Commission (1985-Present); Business and Industrial Task Force (1985-Present); Rockledge City Council (1976-1986); Rockledge Planning Commission (1974-1976) CW: Author, "Race Track Promoters Handbook" (1971) MEM: President, Cape Kennedy Area Board of Realtors (1987-Present); Board of Directors, Florida Association of Realtors (1986-Present); Committee 100, Cocoa Beach Area Chamber of Commerce (1974-Present); Brevard Country Club; Florida Association of Realtors; Cape Kennedy Area Board of Realtors; Cocoa Beach Area Chamber of Commerce; Kiwanis International; Masons PA: Republican RE: Methodist

POSNANSKY, MERRICK, PHD, T: HISTORY and Archaeology Educator I: Education/Educational Services DOB: 03/08/1931 PB: Bolton SC: Lancashire/England PT: Simon Posnansky; Dora (Cohen) Posnansky SPN: Eunice Sarah Lubega (02/10/1962, Deceased 2003) CH: Sheba; Tessa; Helen ED: Doctor of Philosophy, University of Nottingham, Nottingham, England (1956); Diploma in Archaeology, Peterhouse, Cambridge University, England (1953); Bachelor of Arts, University of Nottingham, Nottingham, England (1952) C: Retired (1994); Professor of History and Anthropology, University of California Los Angeles (1976-1994); Director, African Studies Center, University of California Los Angeles (1988-1992); Chairperson, Advisory Committee, James S. Coleman African Studies Center, University of California Los Angeles (1983-1988); Director, Cotsen Institute of Archaeology, University of California Los Angeles (1984-1987); Chairperson, Archaeology Program, University of California Los Angeles (1979-1981); Professor of Archaeology, University of Ghana (1967-1976); Assistant Director, British Institute in Eastern Africa, Kampala, Africa (1962-1964); Curator, Uganda Museum, Kampala (1958-1962); Warden of Prehistoric Sites, Royal National Parks, Nairobi, Kenya, Africa (1956-1958) CR: Chairperson, Historical Monuments Commission, Uganda (1964-1967) CIV: Keynote Speaker, Pan African Archaeological Studies (2010); Keynote Speaker, Black History Month, Howard University (2010); President, Society of Africanist Archaeologists (1992-1993) CW: Guest Editor, Africa and Archaeology: Empowering an Expatriate Life (2009); Guest Editor, Dutile, Moyo, Uganda (2008); Guest Editor, Reflecting on Begho and Hani (1970-1998); Editor, Proceedings of America-Japanese Cooperation on Africa UCLA (1994); Guest Editor, Journal of New World Archaeology (1982, 1986); Editor, Begho, Ghana's Earliest Town as Revealed by Archaeology and Ethno Archaeology (1984); Joint Editor, The Archaeological and Linguistic Reconstruction of African History (1982); Editor, Journal, Uganda Society (1962-1967); Editor, Prelude to East African History (1966); Editor, Nile Quest (1962); Founding Editor of Backdirt, Journal of Cotsen Institute of Archaeology; Contributor, over 240 Articles, Book Chapters, Reviews and Notes AW: Harrington Medal, Society for Historical Archaeology (2003); Leadership Award of the Arts, Council, African Studies Association (1998); Visiting Fellow, Clare Hall, Cambridge University (1974); Honorary Fellow, British Institute in Eastern Africa (1964); Grantee, United Nations Educational; Grantee, British Academy; Grantee, Leverhulme Trust; Grantee, L.S.B. Leakey Foundation; Grantee, Valco Foundation; Grantee, Wenner-Gren Foundation; Grantee, National Geographic Society; Grantee, Fulbright Program; Grantee, Rotary Foundation; Fellow, Society of Antiquaries of London

MEM: President, Uganda Society (1964); Founding President, Museum Association of Middle Africa (1959-1961); Fellow, Society of Antiquaries of London; Society for Historical Archaeology; African Studies Association; UCLA Friends of Archaeology MH: Albert Nelson Marquis Lifetime Achievement Award B/I: Dr. Posnansky became involved in his profession because, as a small child, he would follow grit cleaners around. They would occasionally come up with odd coins and, fascinated, he became a numismatist. AV: Philatelist; Gardening RE: Universalist

POST, AUSTIN, "POST MALONE" RICHARD, T: Rap Artist I: Media & Entertainment DOB: 07/04/1995 PB: Syracuse SC: NY/USA PT: Rich Post; Jodie Post (Stepmother) MS: Single ED: Coursework, Tarrant County College; Diploma, Grapevine High School CW: Actor, "Spenser Confidential" (2020); Featured Musician, "V12" (2020); Featured Musician, "It's a Raid" (2020); Featured Musician, "Forever" (2020); Featured Musician, "Writing on the Wall" (2019); Musician, "Hollywood's Bleeding" (2019); Featured Musician, "Celebrate" (2019); Musician, "Beerbongs & Bentleys" (2018); Voice Cameo, "Spider-Man: Into the Spider-Verse" (2018); Featured Musician, "All My Friends" (2018); Featured Musician, "What About Me" (2018); Featured Musician, "Jackie Chan" (2018); Featured Musician, "You" (2018); Musical Guest, "FishCenter Live" (2017); Featured Musician, "Too Late" (2017); Featured Musician, "Homemade Dynamite (Remix)" (2017); Featured Musician, "Burning Man" (2017); Featured Musician, "Notice Me" (2017); Musician, "Stoney" (2016); Musician, "August 26ᵗʰ" (2016); Featured Musician, "Malibu" (2016); Featured Musician, "Winner Time" (2016); Featured Musician, "Camera" (2016); Featured Musician, "BonBon (Remix)" (2016); Featured Musician, "OMG" (2016); Featured Musician, "The Meaning" (2016); Featured Musician, "Write Our Names" (2016); Featured Musician, "Fade" (2016); Featured Musician, "Embarrassed" (2015); Featured Musician, "Tryna Fuck Me Over" (2015); Featured Musician, "On God" (2015); Featured Musician, "Getcha Some" (2015); Featured Musician, "Came Up" (2015) AW: Best Hip-Hop/R&B Tour, Pollstar Awards (2020); Bronze Animation, "Sunflower," Clio Awards (2019); Favorite Album - Rap/Hip-Hop, "Hollywood's Bleeding," American Music Awards (2019); Three Winning Songs, ASCAP Pop Music Awards (2019); Winning Song, "Rockstar," ASCAP Rhythm & Soul Music Awards (2019); Three Winning Songs, iHeartRadio Titanium Awards (2019); International Album of the Year, "Beerbongs and Bentleys," Juno Awards (2019); Winning Video, "Sunflower," MTV Video Play Awards (2019); Favorite Male Artist - Pop/Rock, Favorite Album - Rap/Hip-Hop for "Beerbongs and Bentleys," American Music Awards (2018); Breakthrough Artist, Billboard Live Music Awards (2018); Top Rap Song, "Rockstar," Billboard Music Awards (2018); Song of the Year, "Rockstar," MTV Video Music Awards (2018); Winning Video, "Psycho," MTV Video Play Awards (2018); Top Package, Billboard Live Music Awards (2016)

POSTON, REBEKAH J., T: Senior Partner I: Law and Legal Services CN: Squire Patton Boggs DOB: 04/20/1948 PB: Wabash SC: IN/USA PT: Bob Poston; April (Ogle) Poston MS: Single ED: JD, School of Law, University of Miami, Coral Gables, FL (1974); BS, School of Law, University of Miami, Coral Gables, FL (1970) C: Partner, Squire Patton Boggs, Miami, FL (2006-Present); Partner, Steel Hector & Davis, Miami, FL (1994-2006); Partner, Fine, Jacobson, Schwartz, Nash & Block, Miami, FL (1978-1994); Special Attorney, Organized Crime and Racketeering Section, The United States

Department of Justice, Cleveland, OH (1976-1978); Assistant U.S. Attorney, The United States Attorney's Office, Southern District of Florida, The United States Department of Justice, Miami, FL (1974-1976) CR: Adjunct Professor, School of Law, University of Miami, Coral Gables, FL CIV: Vice Chair, Squire Patton Boggs Foundation CW: Speaker, Numerous Speaking Engagements (2014-2017); Co-Author, Book, "USCIS to Accept Cap-Subject H-1B Specialty Occupation Visa Petitions on April 3, 2017," Squire Patton Boggs Client Alert (2017); Co-Author, "New I-9 Form Released by USCIS," Squire Patton Boggs Client Alert (2016); Co-Author, "Changes to STEM OPT Extensions Lengthen Timeframe and Increase Employer Responsibilities," Squire Patton Boggs Client Alert (2016); Author, Editor, Book, "International White Collar Enforcement: Leading Lawyers on Preventative Measures, Regulatory Compliance, and Litigation" (2016); Co-Author, Book, "Global Business Fraud and the Law: Preventing and Remedying Fraud and Corruption" (2015) AW: Who's Who Legal 100 (2018) MEM: American Bar Foundation; Dade County Bar Association; American Immigration Lawyers Association; National Association Criminal Defense Attorneys; The Florida Bar BAR: The Florida Bar (1974); United States Court of Appeals for the Eleventh Circuit; United States District Court for the Southern District of Florida; United States District Court for the Middle District of Florida MH: Albert Nelson Marquis Lifetime Achievement Award AS: Ms. Poston attributes her success to the wonderful mentors she had when starting out. They set very high standards, academically and ethically, for her to follow. Additionally, a number of firms provided her with amazing opportunities. B/I: Ms. Poston became involved in her profession because of her undergraduate studies. At the University of Miami, she was afforded the opportunity to take a summer course at the renowned University of Miami School of Marine Atmospheric sciences. While there, she realized she could combine her love of the environment and the ocean with the law. AV: Powerboat racing; Swimming PA: Democrat RE: Lutheran

POTTENGER, MARK MCCLELLAND, T: Computer Programmer I: Technology DOB: 02/09/1955 PB: Tucson SC: AZ/USA PT: Henry Farmer Dobyns; Zipporah Herrick (Pottenger) Dobyns MS: Single ED: Honorary, DDiv, LA-CCRS (1998); BA, UCLA (1976) C: Programmer, Analyst Consultant, R. Gonzalez Management, Los Angeles, CA (1980-Present); Programmer, Analyst Consultant, Los Angeles and San Diego (1977-Present); Programmer, Analyst, LA-CCRS, Los Angeles, CA (1977-1980); Data Entry Operator, Astro Computing, Pelham, NY (1976-1977) CR: Research Director, International Society of Astrology Research, Los Angeles, CA (1985-1995) CIV: Member, Religious Science Church CW: Author, "Asteroid Ephemerides" (1994-Present); Editor, "The Mutable Dilemma" (1977-1999); Author, "Frequencies for Aspect Research" (1986-1992); Author, Computer Programs, "CCRS Horoscope Program" (1977-1992); Editor, "Astrological Research Methods" (1995); Co-author, "Tables for Aspect Research" (1986) AW: Jansky Award, Aquarius Workshops, Los Angeles, CA (1989) MEM: International Society of Astrological Research; National Council of Geocosmic Research MH: Albert Nelson Marquis Lifetime Achievement Award AV: Reading PA: Democrat

POWELL, COLIN LUTHER, T: Former U.S. Secretary of State; Strategic Advisor I: Government Administration/Government Relations/Government Services DOB: 04/05/1937 PB: NYC SC: NY/USA PT: Luther Powell; Maud Ariel (McKoy) Powell MS: Married SPN: Alma Vivian (Johnson) Powell

(08/25/1962) **CH:** Michael; Linda; Annemarie **ED:** Diploma, National War College (1976); MBA, The George Washington University School of Business (1971); BS in Geology, The City College of New York, The City University of New York (1958) **C:** Strategic Advisor, Kleiner Perkins Caufield & Byers (Now Kleiner Perkins), Menlo Park, CA (2005-Present); Secretary, U.S. Department of State, Washington, DC (2001-2005); Chairman, Joint Chiefs of Staff, U.S. Department of Defense, Washington, DC (1989-1993); Assistant to President, National Security Affairs, National Security Council, Washington, DC (1987-1989); Deputy Assistant to the President, National Security Affairs, National Security Council, Washington, DC (1987); Military Assistant to Secretary of Defense, U.S. Department of Defense, Washington, DC (1983-1986); Senior Military Assistant to Deputy Secretary, U.S. Department of Defense, Washington, DC (1979-1981); Executive Assistant to Secretary, U.S. Department of Energy, Washington, DC (1979); Assistant to Deputy Director, Office of Management and Budget, Washington, DC (1972-1973) **CR:** Founding Chair, America's Promise Alliance (1997-Present); Public Speaker, National and International **CIV:** Board of Trustees, Eisenhower Fellowships (2006-Present); National Board of Advisors, High Point University (2014); Honorary Board Member, Wings of Hope **MIL:** Advanced through Grades to General, United States Army (1989-1993); Commander-in-chief, United States Army Forces Command (FORSCOM), Fort McPherson, GA (1989); Assigned to U.S. V Corps, Europe (1986-1987); Assistant Division Commander, Fourth Infantry Division, U.S. Department of Defense, Fort Carson, CO (1981-1983); Commander, Second Brigade, 101st Airborne Division, Fort Campbell, KY (1976-1977); Battalion Commander, Republic of Korea (1973-1974); Commissioned Second Lieutenant, United States Army (1958) **CW:** Co-author with Tony Koltz, "It Worked for Me: In Life and Leadership" (2012); Co-author with Joseph E. Persico, Autobiography, "My American Journey" (1995) **AW:** Named One of the 50 Highest-earning Political Figures, Newsweek (2010); Legion of Honor, France (2006); Truman Peace Prize, Harry S. Truman Research Institute for the Advancement of Peace, The Hebrew University of Jerusalem (2006); Andrus Award, AARP (2006); Co-recipient, Woodrow Wilson Award for Public Service, Woodrow Wilson International Center for Scholars, Smithsonian Institution (2005); Ellis Island Family Heritage Award in Government Service, Statue of Liberty-Ellis Island Foundation, Inc. (2005); Bishop John T. Walker Distinguished Humanitarian Service Award, Africare (2005); Liberty Medal (2002); Named Honorable Knight Commander, Most Honorable Order of Bath, Queen Elizabeth II (1993); Ronald Reagan Freedom Award (1993); Spingarn Medal, NAACP (1991); Golden Plate Award, Academy of Achievement (1988); White House Fellow (1972-1973); Decorated Purple Heart; Air Medal; Bronze Star; Two Legion of Merits; Secretary of Energy Distinguished Service Medal; Secretary of State Distinguished Service Medal; Congressional Gold Medal; President's Citizens Medal; Two Presidential Medals of Freedom; Silver Buffalo Award, Boy Scouts of America; Several Schools and Other Institutions Named in His Honor **MEM:** Association of the United States Army; American Academy of Arts & Sciences **PA:** Republican **RE:** Episcopalian

POWELL, HEIDI, T: Fitness Trainer; Co-founder; Co-host **I:** Health, Wellness and Fitness **CN:** Transform HQ; Extreme Weight Loss **MS:** Married **SPN:** Chris Powell **CH:** Four Children **C:** Fitness Trainer, Transform HQ, Transform Management, LLC **CW:** Co-host, "Extreme Weight Loss" (2011-2015)

POWELL, ROBERT EUGENE, T: Computer Operator **I:** Information Technology and Services **DOB:** 03/31/1955 **PB:** Fairmont **SC:** WV/USA **PT:** Grover E. Powell; Mary Jo (Hart) Powell **ED:** BS, Kent State University (1980) **C:** Computer Operator, Greater Akron Right to Life (1997-2000); Computer Operator, Sage Computer Services (1989-1995); Clerk, Premier Screening, LLC (1987-1989) **CIV:** Candidate, National Hall of Fame for Persons with Adapted Abilities (2021); President's Trophy Candidate for Ohio (1992); Active, President's Committee on Employment for People with Disabilities; Founding Member, Treasurer, National Alliance for Mentally Ill of Portage County (NAMI) **AW:** Named International Man of the Year (1992-1993); Award of Excellence, Ohio Rehabilitation Association (1989, 1990) **MEM:** Knights of Columbus **MH:** Albert Nelson Marquis Lifetime Achievement Award **PA:** Democrat **RE:** Roman Catholic

POWER, SAMANTHA JANE, T: Former U.S. Ambassador; Public Policy Educator **I:** Government Administration/Government Relations/Government Services **CN:** United Nations **DOB:** 09/21/1970 **PB:** London **SC:** England/United Kingdom **PT:** Jim Power; Vera Delaney **MS:** Married **SPN:** Cass Robert Sunstein (07/04/2008) **CH:** Rian Power; Declan Power **ED:** JD, Harvard Law School, Cambridge, MA (1999); BA, Yale University, New Haven, CT (1993) **C:** Anna Lindh Professor, Practice of Global Leadership and Public Policy, Harvard Kennedy School, John F. Kennedy School of Government (2000-Present); United States Ambassador to the United Nations, U.S. Department of State, New York, NY (2013-2017); Director for Multilateral Affairs, National Security Council (2009-2013); Foreign Policy Adviser, Obama-Biden Presidential Transition Team (2008); Senior Foreign Policy Adviser, Barack Obama Presidential Campaign (2008); Foreign Policy Fellow to Senator Barack Obama, U.S. Senate (2005-2006); Founding Executive Director, Carr Center for Human Rights Policy, Harvard Kennedy School, John F. Kennedy School of Government (1998-2002); Political Analyst, International Crisis Group **CR:** Columnist, TIME Magazine (2007-Present) **CW:** Featured, Documentary, "Watchers of the Sky" (2014); Co-editor with Derek Chollet, "The Unquiet American: Richard Holbrooke in the World" (2011); Author, "Chasing the Flame: Sergio Vieira de Mello and the Fight to Save the World" (2008); Author, "A Problem from Hell: America and the Age of Genocide" (2003); Co-editor with Graham Allison, "Realizing Human Rights: Moving from Inspiration to Impact" (2000); Reporter Covering the Yugoslav Wars, U.S. News & World Report, The Boston Globe, The Economist and New Republic (1993-1996) **AW:** Henry A. Kissinger Prize (2016); Barnard Medal of Distinction (2015); Named the 41st Most Powerful Woman in the World, Forbes Magazine (2016); Named One of the 100 Most Powerful Women, Forbes Magazine (2014); Named One of the 100 Agents of Change, Rolling Stone Magazine (2009); National Magazine Award for Reporting (2005); Named One of the 100 Top Scientists and Thinkers of Year, TIME Magazine (2004); Pulitzer Prize for General Nonfiction (2003); National Book Critics Circle Award for General Nonfiction (2003); Arthur Ross Prize for Best Book in U.S. Foreign Policy (2003); J. Anthony Lukas Book Prize (2003) **PA:** Democrat **RE:** Roman Catholic

POWERS, KIRSTEN ANNE, T: Author, Columnist, Political Analyst **I:** Writing and Editing **CN:** USA Today, CNN **DOB:** 12/14/1967 **MS:** Engaged **SPN:** Robert Draper (11/16/2016); Marty Makary (2010, Divorced 2013) **ED:** Diploma, Monroe Catholic High School, Fairbanks, Alaska (1986); BJ, University of Maryland; Coursework, Georgetown University Law Center **C:** Political Analyst, CNN (2016-Present); Vice President, AOL Time Warner Foundation; Vice President for International Communications, America Online (Now Verizon Media); Deputy Assistant U.S. Trade Representative, Clinton Administration **CR:** Consultant, New York State Democratic Committee **CIV:** Consultant, Human Rights First, National Council for Research on Women (Now International Center for Research on Women (ICRW)) **CW:** Author, "The Silencing: How the Left is Killing Free Speech" (2015)

POYDASHEFF, ROBERT STEPHEN, T: Lawyer **I:** Law and Legal Services **DOB:** 02/13/1930 **PB:** New York **SC:** NY/USA **PT:** Stephen Alexander Poydasheff; Pauline M. Miller Poydasheff **MS:** Married **SPN:** Anastasia Catherine Latto (08/29/1954) **CH:** Catherine Alexandra (Deceased); Robert Stephen Jr. **ED:** Honorary PhD, ITEP (2008); Diploma, U.S. Army War College (1976); Diploma, U.S. Army Command and General Staff College (1969); MA, Boston University (1966); JD, Tulane University (1957); BA in Political Science, The Citadel, The Military College of South Carolina (1954) **C:** Attorney, Private Practice, Columbus, GA (1995-Present); Mayor, City of Columbus, GA (2003-2007); City Councilman, Columbus, GA (1996-2002); Senior Vice President, SunTrust Bank of West Georgia, Columbus, GA (1979-1995) **CR:** Executive Vice President, Allied Technologies International, Inc., Columbus, GA (1995-2003); Adjunct Professor, Troy University, Fort Benning, GA (1976-2003); Adjunct Professor, International Law, Extension Division, University of Maryland, Berlin, Germany (1964-1967); Adjunct Professor, American Government, Extension Division, University of Maryland, Berlin, Germany (1964-1967); Adjunct Professor, Business Law, Extension Division, University of Maryland, Berlin, Germany (1964-1967); Instructor, Business Law, Extension Division, American University, Fort Benning, GA (1961-1963); Consultant, Strayer University; Former Legal Adviser to Secretary of the Army; Former Legal Adviser to Secretary of Defense on Military Dependent School and Labor Relations **CIV:** Board of Directors, Springer Opera House Association (1998-Present); Trustee, Executive Committee, Georgia Humanities Council (1998-Present); Mayor, Columbus, GA (2003-2007); City Councilor, City of Columbus, GA (1996-2002); Board of Education, Fort Benning Schools (1976-1979); Chairman, Personnel Actions Committee, Fort Benning Schools (1976-1979); Trustee, Dr. Hospital; Board of Directors, Columbus Area United Way; RiverCenter for the Performing Arts; Former President, Chattahoochee Council, Boy Scouts of America, Columbus, GA; Former President, Chattahoochee Valley-Ft. Benning Chapter, Association of the United States Army; Anne Elizabeth Shepherd Home, Twin Cedars Youth and Family Services, Inc.; Columbus Symphony Orchestra; The American National Red Cross; Chairman, Board of Directors, Leadership Morality Institute; Chairman, Civilian Military Council; Georgia Governor's Commission on Transportation; Board of Trustees, Hughston Rehabilitation Hospital; Board of Visitors, Brookstone School; Notable Citadel Alumnus **MIL:** Retired Colonel, United States Army (1979); With, United States Army (1955-1979); Colonel, United States Army (1975); Colonel, United States Army, Vietnam War (1967-1968); Second Lieutenant, United States Army (1955) **CW:** Contributor, Commentaries, Articles, and Analyses, Professional Journals; Contributor, Tulane Law Review and Naval War College Review **AW:** Daniel Carter Beard Masonic Scouter Award (2015); Outstanding Alumnus, U.S. Army War College (2010); MLK Jr. Unity, Alpha Phi Alpha (2010); Outstanding Civilian Service Medal, United States Army (2004); Decorated Legion of Merit with Two

Oak Leaf Clusters; Bronze Star; Commendation Medal with Oak Leaf Cluster; Vietnam Service Medal with Four Bronze Stars; Honoree, Order of St. George Episcopal Church; Honoree, Infantry Order of Saint Maurice; Honoree, Cavalry Armor, Order of Noble Patron of Armor; Paratrooper Badge; Badge of the Army Secretariat; Georgia Governor's Humanities Award; St. Michael the Archangel Medal, Greek Orthodox Archdiocese of America; Clara Barton Award, The American National Red Cross; CSM Robert McLoy Service; Service to Mankind Award, Sertoma, Inc.; Named to Georgia Military Veterans Hall of Fame; Named to Army Ranger Hall of Fame, US Army Ranger Association **MEM:** Fellow, Leadership Morality Institute; Chairman of the Board, Leadership Morality Institute; Georgia Municipal Association; Columbus Bar Association; Board of Directors, Chamber of Commerce; Military Affairs Committee, Chamber of Commerce; The Army Historical Foundation; Kiwanis International; 33rd Degree, Masons; Scottish Rite KCCH, Masons; Columbus Sertoma Club; The International Legal Honor Society of Phi Delta Phi; Pi Sigma Alpha **BAR:** Admitted to Practice, United States District Court for the Federal District of South Carolina (1988); Admitted to Practice, United States District Court for the Federal District of Georgia (1987); Admitted to Practice, United States District Court for the Middle District of Georgia (1987); Admitted to Practice, State Bar of Georgia (1979); Admitted to Practice, Supreme Court of the United States (1964); Admitted to Practice, United States Court of Military Commission Review (1964); Admitted to Practice, South Carolina Bar (1958); Admitted to Practice, United States Court of Military Appeals (Now United States Court of Appeals for the Armed Forces) **AS:** Mr. Poydasheff attributes his success to the support of his wife, family, mentors, and all of the people working with him. **B/I:** Mr. Poydasheff became involved in his profession because he loves it. **AV:** Walking; Reading **PA:** Republican **RE:** Orthodox Christian **THT:** Mr. Poydasheff motto is, "Live it."

PRATA, ENRICO ALFONSO, T: Educational Administrator **I:** Education/Educational Services **DOB:** 07/22/1945 **PB:** Altavilla Irpina, Avellino **SC:** Italy **PT:** Angelantonio Prata; Margherita (Porcaro) Prata **MS:** Married **SPN:** Charlotte A. Prata (07/06/1968) **CH:** Carl Anthony Prata **ED:** Certificate in Management Lifelong Education, Harvard University (1990); MA, Montclair State College (Now Montclair State University) (1970); BA, Rutgers, The State University of New Jersey (1967) **CT:** Certified Secondary Teacher and School Administrator, State of New Jersey **C:** Director, Adult and Continuing Education, Caldwell-West Caldwell Board of Education (1984-Present); Supervisor, Adult and Continuing Education, Caldwell-West Caldwell Board of Education (1975-1984); Teacher, Biology, Caldwell-West Caldwell Board of Education (1971-1984); Teacher, Biology, Essex Catholic High School, Newark, NJ (1967-1971) **CIV:** Youth Employment Service of West Essex, West Caldwell, NJ (1990-Present); Board of Directors, Essex Literacy Consortium, Montclair, NJ (1988-Present); Chairman, Essex County, Adult Education Council (1987-1988); Program Director, Essex County Division of Parks and Recreation, Newark, NJ, Summers (1970-1982) **CW:** Contributing Editor, "Fishing in New Jersey" (1977); Author, Pamphlets; Contributor, Articles to Professional Journals **AW:** Award, Partnership Against Illiteracy (1992-1993); Grantee, New Jersey Department of Education (1986-1993); Award, United Way (1991, 1992) **MEM:** President, New Jersey Association Lifelong Learning (NJALL) (1991-1992); President-elect, New Jersey Association Lifelong Learning (NJALL)

(1990-1991); Vice President, New Jersey Association Lifelong Learning (NJALL) (1989-1990); West Essex Chamber of Commerce; New Jersey Association Lifelong Learning (NJALL); American Association for Adult and Continuing Education; Phi Delta Kappa (PDK International) **MH:** Albert Nelson Marquis Lifetime Achievement Award **B/I:** Mr. Prata became involved in his profession because he started doing science and decided eventually to go to school to help others. **AV:** Travel; Art; Archaeology; Cooking **RE:** Roman Catholic

PRATT, CHRIS, T: Actor **I:** Media & Entertainment **DOB:** 06/21/1979 **PB:** Virginia **SC:** MN/USA **PT:** Daniel C. Pratt; Kathleen (Indahl) Pratt **MS:** Married **SPN:** Katherine Schwarzenegger (06/08/2019); Anna Faris (07/09/2009, Divorced 2018) **CH:** Jack **CW:** Actor, "Guardians of the Galaxy, Vol. 3" (2021); Actor, "Jurassic World: Dominion" (2021); Actor, Executive Producer, "The Tomorrow War" (2021); Actor, "A Parks and Recreation Reunion Special" (2020); Voice Actor, "Onward" (2020); Actor, "Avengers: Endgame" (2019); Actor, "The Kid" (2019); Voice Actor, "The Lego Movie 2: The Second Part" (2019); Actor, "Jurassic World: Fallen Kingdom" (2018); Actor, "Avengers: Infinity War" (2018); Actor, "Guardians of the Galaxy Vol. 2" (2017); Actor, "Mom" (2017); Actor, "Passengers" (2016); Actor, "The Magnificent Seven" (2016); Actor, "Jem and the Holograms" (2015); Actor, "Jurassic World" (2015); Voice Actor, Video Game, "Lego Dimensions" (2015); Voice Actor, Video Game, "Lego Jurassic World" (2015); Actor, "Parks and Recreation" (2009-2015); Host, "Saturday Night Live" (2014); Actor, "Guardians of the Galaxy" (2014); Voice Actor, "The Lego Movie" (2014); Actor, "Delivery Man" (2013); Actor, "Her" (2013); Actor, "Movie 43" (2013); Actor, "Mr. Payback" (2013); Actor, "Zero Dark Thirty" (2012); Actor, "The Five-Year Engagement" (2012); Voice Actor, "Kinect Star Wars: Duel" (2012); Executive Producer, Documentary, "On the Mat" (2012); Actor, "What's Your Number?" (2011); Actor, "10 Years" (2011); Actor, "Take Me Home Tonight" (2011); Voice Actor, "Ben 10: Ultimate Alien" (2010-2011); Actor, "The Multi-Hyphenate" (2009); Actor, "Jennifer's Body" (2009); Actor, "Deep in the Valley" (2009); Actor, "Bride Wars" (2009); Actor, "Everwood" (2002-2009); Actor, "Wanted" (2008); Actor, "Wieners" (2008); Voice Actor, "The Batman" (2008); Actor, "Walk the Talk" (2007); Actor, "The O.C." (2006- 2007); Actor, "Path of Destruction" (2005); Actor, "Strangers with Candy" (2005); Actor, "The Extreme Team" (2003); Actor, "The Huntress" (2001); Actor, "Cursed Part 3" (2000) **AW:** Choice Summer Movie Star: Male, "Jurassic World: Fallen Kingdom," Teen Choice Awards (2018); Choice Movie Actor: Sci-Fi, "Guardians of the Galaxy Vol. 2," Teen Choice Awards (2017); Honoree, Star, Hollywood Walk of Fame (2017); MTV Movie Award for Best Action Performance, "Jurassic World" (2016); Best Actor, Academy of Science Fiction, Fantasy & Horror Films, "Guardians of the Galaxy" (2015); Man of the Year, Hasty Pudding Theatricals (2015); Jupiter Award for Best International Actor, "Guardians of the Galaxy" (2015); Best Breakthrough Performance - Male, Online Film & Television Association, "Guardians of the Galaxy" (2015); Shorty Award for Best Actor on Social Media (2015); CinemaCon Award for Breakthrough Performer of the Year (2014); Golden Schmoes Award for Breakthrough Performance of the Year, "Guardians of the Galaxy" (2014) **RE:** Non-Denominational Christian

PRATTE, PAUL ALFRED, T: Journalist **I:** Writing and Editing **DOB:** 06/06/1938 **PB:** Regina **SC:** SK/Canada **PT:** Joseph Louis Pratte; Olive Elizabeth (Fraser) Pratte **MS:** Married **SPN:** June E. (Turner)

Pratte (11/21/1962) **CH:** Derek; Mitchell; Christopher; Doran; Alison **ED:** Doctor of Philosophy in American Studies, University of Hawaii (1976); Master of Arts in Communications, Brigham Young University (1967); Bachelor of Science in Journalism, Brigham Young University (1962) **C:** Associate Professor, Brigham Young University, Provo, UT (1984-Present); Associate Professor, Shippensburg University (1981-1984); Coordinator, Marine Advisory Program, University of Hawaii, Honolulu, HI (1979-1981); Administrative Assistant, Senate Minority Office, Honolulu, HI (1969-1979); Reporter, Honolulu Star-Bulletin (1964-1969); Reporter, Provo Bureau, Deseret News, Salt Lake City, UT (1961-1964); Reporter, Lethbridge, Alberta, Canada Herald, Salt Lake Tribune, Provo Herald, Utah (1958-1959); Reporter, Utah County Journal, Lehi Free Press, Honolulu Star-Bulletin, Salt Lake Deseret News **CIV:** Secretary, Democratic Party Precinct, Provo, UT (1990); Administrative Assistant, Republican/Minority (1969-1979); Chairperson, Honolulu School District Advisory Council; Two-Time Candidate, State School Board, Hawaii State Adult Education Board; Shop Steward, Hawaii Newspaper Guild, AFL-CIO **CW:** Author, "The Strength of Their Partnership: An Examination of Collaborative Marriages and Their Contributions to American Journalism," Raymond F. Ida Lee Beckham Annual Lecture in Communication (2001); Author, "Gods Within the Machine: A History of the American Society of Newspaper Editors, 1923-1993" (1995) **AW:** Ford Foundation Fellow (1964); Honor, Urban School of Journalism, Northwestern University **MEM:** Historian, American Society of News Editors (1990-Present); Member, Annenberg Commission, Freedom of the Press (2003); President, American Journalism Historians Association (1994); Society of Professional Journalists; Board of Directors, Crandall Print Museum, Provo, UT; Sigma Delta Chi **MH:** Albert Nelson Marquis Lifetime Achievement Award **B/I:** Dr. Pratte became involved in his profession because, when he was very young, he was inspired by Clark Kent in the "Superman" comics, whose occupation was a mild-mannered reporter. So, from the very beginning, he was interested in journalism. He got his start writing columns about fellow students while in high school, some of which were published in Toronto, Ontario, and other places in Canada. When he moved to Lethbridge, Alberta, Canada, he began to work in the industry in earnest. **AV:** Jogging; Reading; Tai chi **PA:** Democrat **RE:** The Church of Jesus Christ of Latter-day Saints

PRAY, MERLE EVELYN, RN, APN, MS, T: Nurse Psychotherapist, Educator (Retired) **I:** Medicine & Health Care **DOB:** 04/19/1931 **PB:** Washington **SC:** DC/USA **PT:** Clifton Clough Pray; Dorothy (Wadleigh) Pray **ED:** Master of Science, University of Illinois, Chicago, IL (1983); Bachelor of Science in Nursing, Loyola University, Chicago, IL (1977); Diploma in Nursing, New Hampshire School Nursing, Concord, NH (1952) **CT:** Registered Nurse, Illinois; Certified in Addictions Nursing, International Nurses Society on Addictions; Certified Clinical Specialist in Adult Psychiatric and Mental Health Nursing, American Nurses Association **C:** Retired (2014); Nurse Psychotherapist, Clinical Specialist, VA West Side Medical Center, Chicago, IL (1986-2014); Advanced Practice Nurse, VA West Side Medical Center, Chicago, IL (1985); Head Nurse, VA West Side Medical Center, Chicago, IL (1984); Mental Health Administrator, Planning Area Coordinator, Illinois Department of Mental Health and Development Disability, Chicago, IL (1978-1981); Community Placement Coordinator, Illinois Department of Mental Health and Development Disability, Chicago, IL (1977); Head Nurse,

Michael Reese Psychosomatic Psychiatric Institute, Chicago, IL (1953-1964) **CR:** Adjunct Clinical Instructor of Psychiatric Nursing, University of Illinois (1986-1987) **CW:** Author, "Effectiveness of Day Treatment for Dual Diagnosis Patients with Severe Chronic Illness," Journal of Addictions (2008) **MEM:** American Nurses Association; International Nurses Society on Addictions; American Psychiatric Nurses Association; Illinois Nurses Association; Alpha Lambda Chapter, Sigma Theta Tau **MH:** Albert Nelson Marquis Lifetime Achievement Award; Marquis Who's Who Top Professional **B/I:** Ms. Pray became involved in her profession after having read about Clara Barton, the famous nurse who served during the American Civil War. Likewise, she drew from a family history of service in the field. **AV:** Collection of depression ware glass

PRESSLEY, AYANNA SOYINI, T: U.S. Representative from Massachusetts **I:** Government Administration/Government Relations/Government Services **DOB:** 02/03/1974 **PB:** Cincinnati **SC:** OH/USA **PT:** Martin Terrell; Sandra (Echols) Pressley **MS:** Married **SPN:** Conan Harris **CH:** One Stepdaughter **ED:** Coursework, Boston University College of General Studies (1992-1994); Coursework, Boston University Metropolitan College **C:** Member, U.S. House of Representatives from Massachusetts' Seventh Congressional District (2019-Present); Member, Boston City Council-at-large (2010-2019); Political Director, Senior Aide, U.S. Senator John Kerry (2009) **AW:** Named One of the 100 Most Influential People in Boston, Boston Magazine (2018); Named One of the 14 Young Democrats to Watch, The New York Times (2016); Gabrielle Giffords Rising Star Award, EMILY's List (2015); Named One of the 50 Most Powerful People, Boston Magazine (2015); Leadership Award, Victim Rights Law Center (2014); Named One of 10 Outstanding Young Leaders, Greater Boston Chamber of Commerce (2014); Named Truman National Security Project Partner (2012); Aspen-Rodel Fellow in Public Leadership, Class of 2012 (2012) **PA:** Democrat

PRESTON, DEAN LAVERNE, T: Theoretical Physicist **I:** Research **CN:** Los Alamos National Laboratory **DOB:** 02/04/1953 **PB:** Oswego **SC:** NY/USA **PT:** Verne Elmer Preston; Marjorie Alma (Connors) Preston **MS:** Married **SPN:** Sally E. (Archuleta) Preston (1983); Marsha Preston (Divorced) **CH:** Daniel N.; Matthew J.; Melissa; Christopher **ED:** PhD in Physics, Princeton University, Princeton, NJ (1980); BS in Physics, Rensselaer Polytechnic Institute, Troy, NY, Summa Cum Laude (1975); Diploma, Oswego High School, Oswego, NY (1971) **C:** Laboratory Associate Fellow, XCP-5, Materials and Physical Data, X Computational Physics Division, Los Alamos National Laboratory (2017-Present); LANL Fellow, XCP-5, Materials and Physical Data, X Computational Physics Division, Los Alamos National Laboratory (2016-Present); Scientist 5, XCP-DO, X Computational Physics Division Office, Los Alamos National Laboratory (2015-2016); Scientist 5, CXP-5, Materials and Physical Data, X Computational Physics Division, Los Alamos National Laboratory (2010-2015); Scientist 4, P-23, Physics Division, Los Alamos National Laboratory (2008-2010); Technical Staff Member, Scientist 4, P-22 Physics Division, Los Alamos National Laboratory (2004-2008); Technical Staff Member, X-DO and X-7, Applied Physics Division, Los Alamos National Laboratory (1998-2000); Cyril Stanley Smith Scholar, Center for Materials Science, MST Division, Los Alamos National Laboratory (1995-1996); Technical Staff Member, X-4, Primary Design and Assessment, Applied Physics Division, Los Alamos National Laboratory (1985-1998); Consultant, Los Alamos National Laboratory (1983-1985); Assistant Professor, Department of Physics, University of New Hampshire (1983-1985); Postdoc, T-8, Elementary Particles and Field Theory, Theoretical Division, Los Alamos National Laboratory (1980-1983); Researcher, Physics Department, Princeton University (1980) **CR:** Project Leader, ASC PEM Materials Project (2015-2017); Group Leader, X-7, Materials Science, Applied Physics Division, Los Alamos National Laboratory (2000-2004); Program Manager, Senior Project Leader, Weapon Physics and Physical Data, ASCI Program, Los Alamos National Laboratory (1997-1998); Project Leader for Primary Physics, Weapon Physics and Evaluation Program, Los Alamos National Laboratory (1995-1997); Project Leader, Weapon Physics Experiments, AGEX 1 Program, Los Alamos National Laboratory (1994-1997); Numerous Contributions to Laboratory Missions **CW:** Member, Review Committee, Caltech PSAAP (Predictive Science Academic Alliance Program) (2010); External Reviewer, Third Institutional Unclassified Computing Grand Challenge, Lawrence Livermore National Laboratory (2008); Organizer, Symposium on Solid-Solid Phase Transformations, Plasticity (2007); Principal Investigator, Institutional Computing Project: Quantum Molecular Dynamics Simulations of High-Pressure Melting (2006-2008); Co-organizer of Symposium on Phase Transformations, Plasticity (2006); U.S. Principal Investigator, Five Collaborations in Materials Physics between Russian Federal Nuclear Centers (VNIIEF and VNIITF) and Los Alamo National Laboratory (1997-2014); Contributor, Referee for Physical Review Letters, Physical Review B, International Journal of Plasticity, Journal of Applied Physics; Author, Contributor, More Than 80 Peer-reviewed Publications on Elementary Particle Theory, Dislocation Dynamics, and High-Rate Material Strength, Solid-Solid Phase Transformations, High-Pressure Melting, and Shear Moduli, Shock Wave Physics, and Plasma Theory; Contributor, Numerous Committee Papers and Reports, Los Alamo National Laboratory/Lawrence Livermore National Laboratory; Contributor, Numerous Selected Presentations; Contributor to Professional Articles **AW:** Appointed Fellow, Los Alamos National Laboratory (2016); Defense Programs Award of Excellence for Physical Uncertainty Bounds (PUB) (2014); Defense Programs Award of Excellence for Significant Contributions to the Stockpile (2012); ASC Certificate of Appreciation, Quantum MD Calculations of the Pu Phase Diagram, Signed, and Presented by Bob Meisner, ASC Director (2012); Los Alamos National Laboratory LAAP Award for Outstanding Technical Achievement for the Plutonium EOS Predictive Science Panel Review (2012); Los Alamos National Laboratory LAAP Award, Rayleigh-Taylor Strength Team (2010); Defense Program Award of Excellence for Significant Contribution to the Nuclear Weapons Program, Subcritical Experiment Rebound (1997); Named Valedictorian, Oswego High School, Oswego, NY (1971) **MEM:** Fellow, Member, American Physical Society **MH:** Albert Nelson Marquis Lifetime Achievement Award **B/I:** Dr. Preston became involved in his profession because he was very interested in physics from junior high school. He had an excellent teacher in junior high who exposed them to basic concepts of the theory of relativity. This really piqued his interest, and he continued from there. He was an unusual kid; during the summer he would stay in his room and read mathematics books. His mother would take him to the library to get these books. He started at Rensselaer as a mathematics major, but was told he wouldn't get a job so he switched to physics. In addition, Dr. Preston knew that he wanted to be a theoretical physicist when he was young, in early high school. And of course, being in school he was exposed to both experimental and theoretical work. He was okay with the experimental work, but it was the theoretical work that excited him. And that goes back to something else. When he was young, his first interest was mathematics. When he went to college his first year, he was a mathematics major, and math is your tool set for theoretical physics. And, in fact, there was an upperclassman who oversaw the freshman, and he told him one time that it was all well that he wanted to become a mathematician, but you will never get a job. You will end up driving a cab in Manhattan. This was back in the 1970s. Dr. Preston thought maybe there is some truth to what he was saying, so he transitioned into theoretical physics. **AV:** Travel; Building houses (contractor) **THT:** Dr. Preston is building another house in Sante Fe as a second home.

PRESTON, STEVEN C., T: President, Chief Executive Officer **I:** Nonprofit & Philanthropy **CN:** Goodwill Industries International **DOB:** 8/4/1960 **PB:** Janesville **SC:** WI/USA **MS:** Married **CH:** Five Children **ED:** Master of Business Administration, University of Chicago Booth School of Business (1985); Bachelor of Science in Political Science, Northwestern University (1982) **C:** President, Chief Executive Officer, Goodwill Industries International (2019-Present); Chief Executive Officer, Livingston International (2013); Executive Vice President, Chief Financial Officer, Waste Management Inc. (2011-2012); President, Chief Executive Officer, Oakleaf Waste Management LLC (2009-2011); President, Oakleaf Waste Management LLC (2009); Secretary, U.S. Department of Housing and Urban Development (2008-2009); Head, U.S. Small Business Administration (2006-2008); Administrator, Small Business Association (2006-2008); Executive Vice President, Strategic Services, Servicemaster Company (2004-2006); Executive Vice President, Chief Financial Officer, Servicemaster Company (1998-2004); Senior Vice President, Chief Financial Officer, Servicemaster Company (1997-1998); Senior Vice President, Treasurer, First Data Corporation (1985-1993) **CIV:** Board Member, Partnership for Public Service; Board of Visitors, Northwestern University; Sunshine Enterprises; Board of Trustees, Wheaton College

PREUSS, HARRY GEORGE, MD, MACN, CNS, T: Internist, Nephrologist, Nutritionist **I:** Medicine & Health Care **CN:** Gergetown University Medical Center **DOB:** 05/14/1934 **PB:** Binghamton **SC:** NY/USA **PT:** Harry George Junior Preuss; Mary Lillian (Kumpon) Preuss **SPN:** Veronica Marie Coleman (10/08/1960) **CH:** Mary Beth; Jeffrey; Christopher; Michael **ED:** MD, Cornell University (1959); BA, Cornell University (1956); Training, Vanderbilt Medical Center; Training, Cornell Medical Center; Training, Georgetown Medical Center **CT:** Certification, Board Nutrition Specialists (1998); Certified Nutrition Specialist **C:** Associate Professor, Professor, Biochemistry, Medicine, Physiology & Pathology, Georgetown University (1971-Present); Assistant Professor, Associate Professor, University of Pittsburgh (1966-1971); Fellow, Nephrology, Georgetown University, Washington, DC (1964-1966); Fellow in Renal Physiology, Cornell University Medical School, New York, NY (1962-1964); Resident in Medicine, Vanderbilt University Hospital, Nashville, TN (1960-1962); Intern, Vanderbilt University Hospital, Nashville, TN (1959-1960) **CR:** Lecturer, National Naval Medical Center, Bethesda, MD (1974-1978) **CIV:** Former Co-Chairman, Georgetown University Medical Center Internal Review Board; Advisory Council, National Institute on Aging; Advisory Council of the Director, National Institutes of Health; Advisory Council, Office of Alternative Medicine, National Institutes of Health; Research Review Committee, National

Institutes of Health; American Heart Association; National Cholesterol Education Program, NHLBI; Clinical Study Section JH-07, National Institutes of Health **CW:** Researcher, 600 Medical Articles; Author, "Geriatric Nephrology"; Author, "Management of Common Problems in Renal Disease"; Author, "The Clinical Practice of Nephrology"; Author, "Laboratory Evaluation of Renal, Electrolyte and Acid-Base Functions"; Author, "The Prostate Cure"; Author, "Maitake Magic"; Author, "Phytopharmaceuticals in Cancer Prevention and Therapy"; Author, "Obesity: Epidemiology, Pathophysiology, and Prevention"; Author, "The Natural Fat Loss Obesity: Epidemiology, Pathophysiology, and Prevention"; Author, "Nutraceuticals and Functional Foods in Human Health and Disease Prevention"; Author, "The Bitter Sweet: Recognizing and Resolving the Sugar Crisis"; Author, "Food Addiction: Assessment, Management, and Treatment"; Author, "Dietary Sugars, Salt and Fats in Human Health"; Patentee, Nine Patents **AW:** Charles E. Ragus Award (2006, 2016, 2018); Outstanding Senior Investigator in Nutrition Award (2010); Established Investigator, American Heart Association (1967-1971); Special Fellow, National Institutes of Health (1966); Special Research Fellow, National Institutes of Health (1962-1966); Fellow, National Institutes of Health (1962-1965); Fellow, American College of Nutrition (FACN); Harold Harper Lectureship Award, American College for Advancement in Medicine; William B. Peck Award; James Lind Award; Bieber Award; Three-Time Recipient, Jonathan Emord Award; Elected Membership, American Society for Clinical Investigation **MEM:** Fellow, Vice President, American College Nutrition (1997); American Federation of Clinical Research; International Society of Nephrology; American Society of Nephrology; American Society of Physiology; Society of Experimental Biology and Medicine; American Society of Clinical Investigation; American Society of Renal Biochemistry; Association Clinical Scientists; American Society of Hypertension; Alpha Omega Alpha **MH:** Albert Nelson Marquis Lifetime Achievement Award **AS:** Dr. Preuss attributes his success to his wife and family, as well as many of his former teachers. Specifically, he credits Henry Marean, Thomas Hannon, David E. Rogers, MD, Robert Pitts, George E. Schreiner, all of whom gave him free rein to investigate. **B/I:** Dr. Preuss' mother and aunt were nurses. Inspired by them but not convinced, he was not quite sure what to do after high school. Ultimately, he decided to follow in his brother's footsteps and pursue medicine. Dr. Preuss attended Cornell University on the pre-med track. He started performing clinical work initially, and after three years, he decided to focus on research. He returned to Cornell University in New York to work with Dr. Pitts. **AV:** Painting; Reading; Watching spectator sports **THT:** Dr. Preuss' motto is, "If you don't comply, don't complain."

PRICE, DAVID EUGENE, PHD, T: U.S. Representative, Professor **I:** Government Administration/Government Relations/Government Services **DOB:** 08/17/1940 **PB:** Erwin **SC:** TN/USA **PT:** Albert Lee Price; Elna (Harrell) Price **MS:** Married **SPN:** Lisa Beth (Kanwit) Price (07/27/1968) **CH:** Karen Elizabeth; Michael Edmond **ED:** PhD in Political Science, Yale University (1969); BD in Theology, Yale University (1964); BA in American History and Mathematics, The University of North Carolina at Chapel Hill (1961); Coursework, Mars Hill College, NC (1957-1959) **C:** U.S. Representative, North Carolina's Fourth Congressional District, United States Congress, Washington, DC (1987-1995, 1997-Present); Professor of Political Science and Public Policy, Duke University, Durham, NC (1973-1986); Legislative Aide, Staff of U.S. Senator Edward Lewis

Bartlett of Alaska (1963-1967); Co-Chair, Democratic Budget Group, North Carolina's Fourth Congressional District, United States Congress; Member, Democracy Assistance Commission, North Carolina's Fourth Congressional District, United States Congress; Chairman, Homeland Security Subcommittee, North Carolina's Fourth Congressional District, United States Congress; Member, Committee on Appropriations, North Carolina's Fourth Congressional District, United States Congress **CR:** Member, North Carolina Democratic Party, Raleigh, NC (1983-Present); Chairman, North Carolina Democratic Party, Raleigh, NC (1983-1984); Staff Director, National Committee on Presidential Nomination, Democratic Party (1981-1982); Executive Director, North Carolina Democratic Party, Raleigh, NC (1979-1980) **CW:** Author, "The Congressional Experience: A View from the Hill" (2000); Author, "Bringing Back the Parties" (1984); Author, "Policymaking in Congressional Committees" (1979); Author, "Who Makes the Laws" (1972) **AW:** Champion of Science, The Science Coalition (2002, 2004); Award, Engineering Deans Council, ASEE (2003); Hubert H. Humphrey Public Service Award, American Political Science Association; Charles Dick Medal of Merit, North Carolina National Guard **MEM:** American Political Science Association; Society for Values in Higher Education; The Phi Beta Kappa Society; The Dialectic and Philanthropic Societies; Kiwanis International **AV:** Jogging; Listening to music **PA:** Democrat **RE:** Baptist

PRICE, MORTON L., T: Lawyer, Partner **I:** Law and Legal Services **DOB:** 04/12/1935 **PB:** New York **SC:** NY/USA **PT:** David Price; Pearl B. (Edelman) Price **MS:** Married **SPN:** Merle Chait Price (09/11/1966) **CH:** Seth J.; Sharon L. Singer **ED:** LLB, Yale University (1959); BA, Bowdoin College, Cum Laude (1956) **C:** Senior Counsel, Price Benowitz LLP, Washington, DC (2014-Present); Partner, McLaughlin & Stern, LLP, New York, NY (2010-Present); Attorney, Cowan, Liebowitz & Latman, PC, New York, NY (1998-2010); Partner, Schwab Goldberg Price & Dannay, New York, NY (1972-1998); Associate, Schwab & Goldberg, New York, NY (1967-1972); Associate, Schur, Handler & Jaffin, New York, NY (1963-1967); Associate, Pomerantz, Levy, Haudek & Block, New York, NY (1961-1963); Law Clerk to Honorable Herbert B. Cohen, Pennsylvania Supreme Court, York, PA (1960-1961); Research Assistant to Professor Jack B. Weinstein, Columbia Law School, Columbia University, New York, NY (1960); Staff Attorney, New York Advisory Committee on Practice and Procedure, New York, NY (1960) **MIL:** U.S. Army Reserve (1959-1960) **MEM:** Committee on Legal Problems of the Aging, Transportation Committee, New York Bar Association (1989-1993); Transportation Committee, New York Bar Association (1982-1985); Administrative Law Committee, Transportation Committee, New York Bar Association (1979-1982); Chairman, Transportation Committee, New York Bar Association (1976-1979); Transportation Committee, New York Bar Association (1973-1979); Municipal Affairs Committee, New York Bar Association (1969-1972); Committee on Professional Responsibility, Transportation Committee, New York Bar Association; Estate Planning Council of New York City; American Bar Association; Trustee, Treasurer, City Club of New York; Phi Beta Kappa; Section on Trusts and Estates, Committee on Estate and Trust Administration; New York State Bar Association **BAR:** Supreme Court of the United States (1973); United States Court of Appeals for the Second Circuit (1971); United States District Court for the Southern District of New York (1962); United States District Court for the Eastern Dis-

trict of New York (1962); Pennsylvania (1961); New York (1960) **MH:** Albert Nelson Marquis Lifetime Achievement Award

PRIEBUS, REINHOLD, "REINCE" RICHARD, T: Former White House Chief of Staff; Lawyer **I:** Government Administration/Government Relations/Government Services **DOB:** 03/18/1972 **PB:** Dover SC: NJ/USA **MS:** Married **SPN:** Sally Priebus (1999) **CH:** Jack; Grace Avalyn **ED:** JD, University of Miami School of Law, Cum Laude, Coral Gables, FL (1998); BS, University of Wisconsin, Cum Laude, Whitewater, WI (1994) **C:** President, Chief Strategist, Michael Best & Friedrich LLP, Washington, DC (2017-Present); Chief of Staff, The White House, Washington, DC (2017); Chairman, Republican National Committee (RNC), Washington, DC (2011-2017); General Counsel, Republican National Committee (RNC), Washington, DC (2009-2010); Partner, Litigation Practice Group, Michael Best & Friedrich LLP, Milwaukee, WI (1998-2011); Law Clerk, NAACP Legal Defense and Educational Fund, Los Angeles, CA; Law Clerk, United States District Court for the Southern District of Florida; Law Clerk, Wisconsin Supreme Court; Law Clerk, Wisconsin Court of Appeals **CR:** Speaker, Washington Speakers Bureau **CIV:** Chairman, Republican Party of Wisconsin (2007-2011); Chair, Southeastern Wisconsin American Heart Association Heart Ball (2008); Co-chair, Southeastern Wisconsin American Heart Association Heart Ball (2007); Vice Chairman, Republican Party of Wisconsin (2006-2007); Treasurer, Republican Party of Wisconsin; Chairman, First District, Republican Party of Wisconsin; Vice Chairman First District, Republican Party of Wisconsin; Advisory Board Member, Past President, Kenosha Symphony Orchestra; Advisory Board Member, Care Net Crisis Pregnancy Center, Kenosha, WI; Archon, Greek Orthodox Church **MIL:** With, United States Navy Reserve (2019-Present) **AW:** Named One of the 100 Most Influential People, TIME Magazine (2017); Named One of Milwaukee's 40 Under 40, Milwaukee Business Journal (2008) **MEM:** ABA; Kenosha County Bar Association; Racine County Bar Association; Wisconsin Bar Association; Milwaukee Bar Association **BAR:** United States District Court for the Western District of Wisconsin (1998); United States District Court for the Eastern District of Wisconsin **PA:** Republican

PRINCE, ANNA, T: Composer, Music Publisher; Construction Executive **I:** Media & Entertainment **DOB:** 05/28/1935 **PB:** Isabella **SC:** TN/USA **PT:** Ulysses Gordon Prince; Della Carrie (Hawkins) Prince **MS:** Married **SPN:** Dr. Reverend Eddie Joe McCurry **CH:** Sandra; Teresa; Vandi **ED:** Diploma of Honors on International Affairs, Institute de Droit des Affaires Internationales, Paris, France (1994); Honorary PhD, Australian Institute Coordinator Research, Victoria, Australia (1993); Diplomatic Diploma, Academia Argentina de Diplomacia (1993); MusD, London Institute of Applied Research (1991); Coursework, United Christian Association (1976); Diploma, Southwest Technical College (1970); Zion Diploma, Israel Bible School, Jerusalem, Israel (1970); Diploma, Carolina School of Broadcasting (1966) **CT:** Licensed Bible Teacher, United Christian Academy **C:** Owner, Prince TV Co., Nashville, TN (1986-2003); Partner, Owner, Hands-on Builder and Supervisor, Grad Builders, Canton, NC (1982-1986); Entertainer, 1982 World's Fair, Knoxville, TN (1982); Partner, Prince Wholesale Bait Company, Canton, NC (1976-1982); Songwriter, Hank Locklin Music Co., Nashville, TN (1963-1970); Writer, Composer, Released Three International Hit Songs **CR:** Music Publishing, BMI (Broadcast Music, Inc.), Nashville, TN (1982-Present); Member, Production

Staff, Talent Coordinator, Television Series, "Down Home, Down Under" (1989-1990) **CIV:** American Registrar of Ohio Valley (2002-Present); Vice President, Macon County Taxpayers Association, Inc. (1984-1986); Candidate, County Commissioner, Democratic Party, Macon County, NC (1984); Board of Directors, Macon County Taxpayers Association, Inc. (1984); Board of Directors, Head Start, Topton, NC (1969-1973); Judge, Emmy Awards, Television Academy **CW:** Author, "Love Doctor of Nashville: God Created Sex" (2013, 2014); Author, "Anna from Prince Mountain" (2011); Author, "The Strange Life of Anna Prince" (2006); Executive Producer, Host, Television Talk Show, "Real Heroes of Country Music" (1997-2003); Singer, Composer, "I'm In Love with You" (1995); Interviewer, Country Music Celebrities, Weekly/Five-times per Week, Nashville Television (1993-2003); Appearance, Grand Ole Opry (1970); Composer, "Anna," RCA (1969); Composer, "I Feel a Cry Coming On," RCA (1965); Television Show Host, Nashville Television Interviews (17 Years); Composer, "Best Part of Loving You," RCA; Singer, Composer, Recording Artist, Over 40 Songs; Performer, "Prince Writes Hit Songs"; Singer, Composer, Writer, Numerous Songs; Creator, Host, Television Series, Nashville, TN **AW:** Nominee, Emmy Award, "Real Heroes of Country Music," Television Academy (1997); Named Outstanding Business Woman, Small Business Administration (1984); Nominee, Distinguished Women of North Carolina, North Carolina Council on Status of Women (1984); Song Ranked Hit, "Anna," Europe and New Zealand (1970); Song Ranked Number One, "I Feel a Cry Coming On," England, United Kingdom (1965); Song Ranked Number One, "Best Part of Loving You," England, United Kingdom; Jefferson Award, WYFF TV, American Institute for Public Service; Named to Outstanding Intellectuals of 20th Century; Named to International Biographical Centre, Cambridge, England, United Kingdom; Named Outstanding Intellectual, Maison International des Intellectuals; Named, "Creativity in International Music!" **MEM:** Moderator, Teacher, Nashville Songwriters Association International (1984-1986); BMI (Broadcast Music, Inc.); International Parliament for Safety and Peace; Life Member, Department of Foreign Affairs, Deputy Member Assembly, International Parliament for Safety and Peace; Nashville Songwriters Association International; CMA Country Music Association, Inc.; Reunion of Professional Entertainers (R.O.P.E.); Fraternal Order Police, Chamber of Commerce; Dame, Order of Knight of Templars; Dame, Lofsensic Order, Maison International des Intellectuals **MH:** Albert Nelson Marquis Lifetime Achievement Award **B/I:** Dr. Prince's father was a preacher, and he would use her on the revivals because she could sing and play the guitar. As a result, the children saw her singing and she would draw a crowd. Dr. Prince was a praying person, and when her father would have his roadside revival, she would get the children, gather them around and they would get away from the adults to go pray in the woods. She would pray that God would save every one of them and the crowd kept growing. She started teaching bible class at the age of 11, which she enjoyed because she was able to talk to the children one on one. That was an incentive for Dr. Prince to pursue her career. **THT:** Dr. Prince married her husband, Dr. Reverend Eddie Joe McCurry, on her television show in Nashville, TN in 2003. She is the composer of "Anna," a song recorded in Ireland in 1974. The song was performed by Hawk Locklin, on RCA Nashville, and was produced by Chet Atkins.

PRINGLE, PAUL, T: Staff Writer **I:** Media & Entertainment **CN:** Los Angeles Times **ED:** Master of Arts in Journalism, Pennsylvania State University (1979); Bachelor of Arts in Political Science and Journalism, California State University, Northridge (1978) **C:** Investigative Reporter and General Assignment Writer, Los Angeles Times (2001-Present); West Coast Bureau Chief, Dallas Morning News (1998-2001); Part-Time Journalism Instructor, California State University, Northridge (1986-2000); Los Angeles Bureau Chief, Copley News Service (1984-1998); Stringer, Los Angeles, Dallas Morning News and Tampa Tribune (1986-1997) **CW:** Columnist, Daily Collegian, Pennsylvania State University; Staff Writer, Daily Sundial, California State University, Northridge **AW:** Pulitzer Prize in Investigative Reporting (2019); Fraud Fighter Award, Los Angeles Chapter, Association of Certified Fraud Examiners (2017); Joseph L. Brechner Award, University of Florida (2015); First Amendment Award, California Newspaper Publishers Association (2014); Pulitzer Prize for Public Service (2011); Worth Bingham Prize for Investigative Journalism, Harvard University (2011); Distinguished Journalist, Society of Professional Journalists of Greater Los Angeles (2009); George Polk Award (2009); Pulitzer Prize Finalist in Investigative Reporting (2009); Pulitzer Prize in Breaking News (2004); Co-Recipient, Polk Award, Selden Ring Award, American Society of News Editors Distinguished Writing Award, Investigative Reporters and Editors Top Honor; Finalist, Goldsmith Prize, Harvard University

PRIOLEAU, DARWIN, T: Dance Educator, Choreographer **I:** Education/Educational Services **DOB:** 05/10/1949 **PB:** New York **SC:** NY/USA **PT:** E. L. Prioleau; Marietta Camilla Prioleau **MS:** Married **SPN:** Carl Victor Conrad (12/19/1992) **ED:** EdD, University of Massachusetts (1999); MA, New York University (1981); BA, Bennett College (1971) **C:** Dean, School of the Arts Humanities and Social Sciences, The College at Brockport, State University of New York (2010-Present); Professor, Dance, Kent State University (1995-Present); Chair, Dance Division, State University of New York, Brockport, NY (2004-2010); Assistant Dean, College of Fine & Professional Arts, Kent State University (2001-2002); Head, Dance Division, Kent State University (1988-1995); Associate Professor, Dance, Southern Methodist University, Dallas, TX (1981-1988); Artistic Director, Young Peoples Dance Co., New York, NY (1978-1981); Featured Dancer, Guest Artist, Various Dance Companies and off-Broadway Productions, New York, NY (1977-1981); Soloist, Dancer, National Horne Dance Co., New York, NY (1976-1979); Dancer, Ed Kresley Jazz Co., New York, NY (1974-1976) **CR:** Trustee, International 39th Bartholin Ballet Seminar, Copenhagen (2001); Trustee, American Dance Guild, New York, NY (1993-1995); Artistic Consultant, Dallas Black Dance Theatre (1983-1988); Dance Coordinator, International Center for Integrative Studies, New York, NY (1975-1981) **CIV:** Member, Ohio Arts Council (2000); Member, Arts Midwest (2000); Member, Columbus, OH (2000); Member, Pittsburgh on Tour (2000); Advisory Board, Cleveland School of the Arts (1994-1995); Quest Teacher, Urban League, Akron, OH (1994); Mentor, I Had A Dream Program, Dallas, TX (1986-1988) **CW:** Choreographer, Ashland Regional Ballet (2001); Choreographer, Opus II Dance Co. (1994); Choreographer, Dance Cleveland/Cain Park (1991); Choreographer, Commissioned Choreography, Dance Black Dance Theatre (1983, 1984, 1988, 1991); Solo Performer, Texas, New York, France (1985-1988); Choreographer, Dallas Theatre Center (1985, 1986); Member, Editorial Board, National Dance Education Journal; Contributor, Articles, Professional Journals **AW:** Ohio Joint Programs in the Arts, Columbus, OH (1995); Vira I. Heinz Endowment, Pittsburgh, PA (1994); Grantee, National Education Association Arts Expansion Program, Washington DC (1980) **MEM:** Past President, National Dance Education Organization (2013-Present); National Association of Schools of Dance; International Black Dance Association; Americas for the Arts; American Association of Higher Education **MH:** Albert Nelson Marquis Lifetime Achievement Award; Marquis Who's Who Humanitarian Award **B/I:** Mrs. Prioleau always danced, even in her living room when she was a little girl, but the real reason is actually seeing individuals dance on stage when she was young. One of those individuals was Rudolph Nureyev. One of the reasons is that he was not just beautiful in the sense of technique but his performance quality was just phenomenal to her, so she found that more interesting, than how he performs. And the other person is Judith Jameson. **AV:** Travel; Spas; Hiking; Jazz music; Watching movies from different countries; Reading

PRITZKER, JAY, "J.B." ROBERT, T: Governor of Illinois **I:** Government Administration/Government Relations/Government Services **DOB:** 1/19/1965 **PB:** Atherton **SC:** CA/USA **PT:** Donald Pritzker; Sue (Sandel) Pritzker **MS:** Married **SPN:** Mary Kathryn "M.K." Meunster (1993) **CH:** Two Children **ED:** Doctor of Jurisprudence, Northwestern University Pritzker School of Law; Bachelor of Arts in Political Science, Duke University **C:** Governor, State of Illinois (2019-Present); Delegate, Democratic National Convention (2008, 2016); National Co-chairperson, Hillary Clinton's Presidential Campaign (2008); Co-founder, Pritzker Group Private Capital; Co-founder, Chicago Ventures **CR:** Chairperson Emeritus, ChicagoNEXT, World Business Chicago **CIV:** Founder, 1871; Founder, Democratic Leadership for the 21st Century **AW:** Entrepreneurial Champion Award, Chicagoland Chamber of Commerce (2008) **MEM:** Illinois State Bar Association; The Chicago Bar Association **BAR:** State of Illinois

PROCTOR, MARK ALAN, T: Consultant; Elected Official; Real Estate Executive; Television Panelist; Commentator **I:** Real Estate **DOB:** 06/03/1948 **PB:** Daytona Beach **SC:** FL/USA **PT:** John George Proctor; Christine (Crosier) Proctor **MS:** Married **SPN:** Dr. Carolyn Louise Morgan (07/24/1982) **CH:** Morgan Alan **ED:** Postgraduate Coursework, Florida State University (1978); BA, Florida International University (1975); AA, Miami-Dade Community College (Now Miami Dade College), Miami, FL (1968) **CT:** Florida Real Estate Broker's License (1987) **C:** Chairman, Elected Countrywide, Hillsborough Soil and Water Conservation District, Plant City, FL (2014); Broker/Sales, The Bunkley Group, Inc., Brandon, FL (2012); President, Proctor Properties, Brandon, FL (1987-2012); Principal, MPA Consulting, Brandon, FL (2003); Broker/Salesman, Select Properties & Investment Corp., Tampa, FL (1983-1987); Sales Manager, General Development Corp., Tampa, FL (1981-1983); Communications Director, Florida Dental Association, Tampa, FL (1980-1981); Systems Consultant, Florida Game & Fish Commission (Now Florida Fish and Wildlife Conservation Commission), Tallahassee, FL (1977-1979); Sales Associate, R.C. Peacock & Co., Miami, FL (1975-1977); Director of Admission, World Jai-Alai, Inc., Miami, FL (1970-1975); Public Relations Assistant, Woody Kepner & Associate, Inc., Miami, FL (1968-1970) **CR:** President, District Six, Inc. (1994-Present); Member, Hillsborough County Public Safety Coordinating Council (PSCC) (1992-Present); Member, Hillsborough County Housing Resource Board (1989-Present); Member, Industrial Development Authority, Hillsborough County, Tampa, FL (1988-Present); Vice Chairman, Industrial Development Authority, Hillsborough County, Tampa, FL (1991-1992, 1993-1994); Participant, Joint Civil Orientation Conference, U.S. Department of Defense Governor's Appointee, State of Florida Growth Management Committee (1993); President, Hillsborough County Housing Resource Board (1991-1992, 1992-1993); Member, Policy Board, Tampa Committee of 100 (1988-1989); Board of Directors, Homes for Hillsborough, Inc. **CIV:** Chairman, Tampa Sports Authority, Tampa FL (2001-2009); Alumni Association Leadership Hillsborough (1994-1995); Church Moderator, United Church of Christ (1994); Brandon Balloon Festival and Marathon (1994); Co-chair, Highlighting Hillsborough "Paint Your Heart Out" (1992, 1993-1994); Arts & Crafts Community Education Services, Inc., Tampa, FL (1991-1992); Member, Presidents' Roundtable of Greater Brandon, FL (1989-1990); President, Hillsborough Association Chambers, Tampa, FL (1988-1989); President, Hillsborough County Republican Executive Commission, Tampa, FL (1984) **CW:** Regular Guest Analyst, Bayside, Station WTOG-Channel 44 (1994-Present); Regular Guest Analyst, Weekly Current Events Television Show, Tampa Bay Week, Station WEDU-Channel 3 (1993); Contributor, Florida Conservation News (1986); Contributor, Tampa Realtor (1986); Contributor, Articles to Florida Dental Journal (1980-1981); Editor, Contributor, Articles to Wildlife Inventory (1979) **AW:** Named Key Citizen of the Year, Greater Brandon Chamber of Commerce (2014); Award, President's Roundtable of Brandon (1994); W.H. Copeland Award for Outstanding Community Service, Greater Tampa Association of Realtors (1991); Civic Achievement Award, Greater Tampa Association of Realtors (1991); Community Service Award, Greater Brandon, FL (1989); Award, President's Council, University of South Florida Muma College of Business Administration, Tampa, FL (1989); Named Up & Comer of the Year, PricewaterhouseCoopers-Tampa Bay Business Journal (1988); Named Realtor of the Year, Greater Tampa Association of Realtors (1985); Named Outstanding Volunteer, Bay Area Youth Services, Inc., Tampa, FL (1984); Alice B. Tompkins Community Service Award **MEM:** District Vice President, Florida Association of Realtors (Florida Realtors) (1994); Issues Mobilization Committee, Florida Association of Realtors (Florida Realtors) (1991); Chairman, Executive Board, Greater Tampa Association of Realtors (1991); Political Affairs Committee, National Association of Realtors (1991); Chairman, Local Government Subcommittee, Florida Association of Realtors (Florida Realtors) (1990); President, Greater Tampa Association of Realtors (1990); Honor Society, Florida Association of Realtors (Florida Realtors) (1988-1990); State Director, Florida Association of Realtors (Florida Realtors) (1987-1990); Congressional Coordinator, National Association of Realtors (1987-1989); President, Real Estate Investment Council (REIC), Greater Brandon Chamber of Commerce (1988); Affiliate Member, Women's Council of Realtors **MH:** Albert Nelson Marquis Lifetime Achievement Award; Marquis Who's Who Top Professional **B/I:** Both parents of Mr. Proctor were in real estate. It was not something that he wanted to do at first, it was a means to an end. He went into real estate so he could get enough money to attend college and he has been in real estate ever since then. **AV:** Fishing; Hunting; Politics; Travel **PA:** Republican

PROST, MARY JANE, T: School Nurse **I:** Medicine & Health Care **PT:** George; Mary Anne (Zigon) Klobucher **MS:** Married **SPN:** William Andrew Prost (07/17/1954) **CH:** Willy; Peggy; Beth Ann **ED:** MA in Psychology, Washington & Jefferson College (1976); BS, California University of Pennsylvania (1973); Diploma, Canonsburg General Hospital,

(1953) **CT:** Certified School Nurse, State of Pennsylvania **C:** Retired (1997); School Nurse, Keystone Oaks School District (1973-1997); Mental Health Nurse, Washington Hospital Healthcare System (1971-1973); Medical-Surgical Nurse, Canonsburg Hospital (1953-1971) **CR:** Speaker, School Nurse Coordinator, Keystone Oaks School District (1993-1997); Teacher, Nursing Assistant Classes (1971-1973) **CIV:** Teacher, First Aid Classes, American Heart Association (1975-1990); Teacher First Aid Classes, American Red Cross (1975-1985) **AW:** School Nurse of Year, Pennsylvania Association of School Nurses and Practitioners (1995) **MEM:** Former President, Pennsylvania Association of School Nurses and Practitioners; National Association of School Nurses **MH:** Albert Nelson Marquis Lifetime Achievement Award **B/I:** Ms. Prost became involved in her profession because her mother died when she was 10 years old so her father could not come up for the money for college. However, he was able to come up with the money for nurses college at Canonsburg General Hospital. **AV:** Sewing; Dancing; Doing water aerobics **PA:** Democrat **RE:** Catholic

PROVENZANO, DOMINIC, T: Information Specialist **I:** Financial Services **CN:** Morgan Stanley Wealth Management **DOB:** 01/25/1951 **PB:** New York **SC:** NY/USA **PT:** Nicholas Patrick Provenzano; Evelyn Provenzano **CH:** Saverio; Carmela; James **ED:** MA, New York University (1987); MS, Long Island University (1978); MS in Foreign Service, Georgetown University (1976); BA, Hobart and William Smith Colleges (1972) **CT:** Certificate in Financial Planning; Certificate in Security Analysis **C:** Vice President, Morgan Stanley Wealth Management (2009-Present); Vice President, UBS (2008-2009); Account Vice President, UBS (2006-2008); Finance Adviser, UBS, Melville, NY (2003-2005); Finance Adviser, Prudential Financial, Inc., Melville, NY (1998-2003); Director of Research, D.S. Wolf Group International, LLC (1997-1998); Research Associate, Russell Reynolds Associates, New York, NY (1996-1997); Manager of Information Services, Wasserstein, Perella & Company, New York, NY (1994-1996); Research Specialist, Wasserstein, Perella & Company, New York, NY (1991-1993); Assistant Professor, Suffolk County Community College, Selden, NY (1987-1991); Researcher, Time, Inc., New York, NY (1982-1987); Researcher, The White House, Washington, DC (1981-1982) **CW:** Contributor, Articles, Professional Journals **AW:** Outstanding Young Men of America (1982) **MEM:** Head, Bay Club; Beta Phi Mu-The International Library and Information Studies Honor Society; Pi Gamma Mu Honor Society **MH:** Albert Nelson Marquis Lifetime Achievement Award **RE:** Roman Catholic

PRYCE, JONATHAN, CBE, T: Actor **I:** Media & Entertainment **DOB:** 06/01/1947 **PB:** Carmel **SC:** Wales **PT:** Isaac Pryce; Margaret Ellen (Williams) Pryce **MS:** Married **SPN:** Kate Fahy (2015) **CH:** Patrick; Gabriel; Phoebe **ED:** Honorary Doctorate, University of Liverpool (2006); Coursework, Edge Hill University, Ormskirk, England, United Kingdom; Fellow, Royal Welsh College of Music & Drama; Companion, Liverpool Institute for Performing Arts **CW:** Actor, "Tales from the Loop" (2020); Actor, "The Two Popes" (2019); Actor, "The Man Who Killed Don Quixote" (2018); Actor, "The Ghost and the Whale" (2017); Actor, "The Healer" (2017); Actor, "The Wife" (2017); Actor, "The Man Who Invented Christmas" (2017); Guest Appearance, "Taboo" (2017); Actor, "To Walk Invisible" (2016); Actor, "The White King" (2016); Actor, "Game of Thrones" (2015-2016); Actor, "Under Milk Wood" (2015); Guest Appearance, "Wolf Hall" (2015); Actor, "Woman in Gold" (2015); Actor, "Narcopo-

lis" (2015); Actor, "Dough" (2015); Actor, "Listen Up Philip" (2014); Actor, "The Salvation" (2014); Actor, "G.I. Joe: Retaliation" (2013); Actor, "Hysteria" (2011); Actor, "Echelon Conspiracy" (2009); Actor, "G.I. Joe: The Rise of Cobra" (2009); Guest Appearance, "Return to Cranford" (2009); Actor, TV Film, "My Zinc Bed" (2008); Guest Appearance, "Clone" (2008); Actor, "Leatherheads" (2008); Actor, "Bedtime Stories" (2008); Actor, "Pirates of the Caribbean: At World's End" (2007); Actor, "Sherlock Holmes and the Baker Street Irregulars" (2007); Actor, "Pirates of the Caribbean: Dead Man's Chest" (2006); Voice Actor, "Renaissance" (2006); Actor, "The Brothers Grimm" (2005); Actor, "The New World" (2005); Actor, "Brothers of the Head" (2005); Actor, "De-Lovely" (2004); Actor, "Pirates of the Caribbean: The Curse of the Black Pearl" (2003); Actor, "What a Girl Wants" (2003); Actor, "Unconditional Love" (2002); Guest Appearance, "The Wonderful World of Disney" (2002); Guest Appearance, "Victoria & Albert" (2001); Actor, "The Affair of the Necklace" (2001); Actor, "Bride of the Wind" (2001); Actor, "Very Annie Mary" (2001); Actor, "Stigmata" (1999); Actor, TV Short, "Doctor Who: The Curse of Fatal Death" (1999); Actor, "Deceit" (1999); Actor, "Ronin" (1998); Actor, "Regeneration/Behind the Lines" (1997); Actor, "David" (1997); Actor, "Tomorrow Never Dies" (1997); Actor, "Evita" (1996); Actor, "Carrington" (1995); Actor, "A Business Affair" (1994); Voice Actor, "A Troll in Central Park" (1994); Actor, "Deadly Advice" (1994); Actor, "Great Moments in Aviation" (1994); Actor, "Shopping" (1994); Actor, "Dark Blood" (1993); Guest Appearance, "Mr. Wroe's Virgins" (1993); Actor, "Barbarians at the Gate" (1993); Actor, "Thicker Than Water" (1993); Actor, "The Age of Innocence" (1993); Actor, "Glengarry Glen Ross" (1992); Voice Actor, "Freddie as F.R.O.7" (1992); Guest Appearance, "Selling Hitler" (1991); Guest Appearance, "Screen Two" (1990); Guest Appearance, "The Jim Henson Hour" (1990); Actor, "The Rachel Papers" (1989); Guest Appearance, "Whose Line Is It Anyway?" (1988-1989); Actor, "Consuming Passions" (1988); Guest Appearance, "Tickets for the Titanic" (1988); Guest Appearance, "The Storyteller" (1988); Actor, "The Adventures of Baron Munchausen" (1988); Actor, "Man on Fire" (1987); Actor, "Haunted Honeymoon" (1986); Actor, "Jumpin' Jack Flash" (1986); Actor, "Brazil" (1985); Actor, "The Doctor and the Devils" (1985); Actor, "Something Wicked This Way Comes" (1983); Actor, "The Ploughman's Lunch" (1983); Actor, "Martin Luther, Heretic" (1983); Actor, "Praying Mantis" (1982); Actor, "Murder is Easy" (1982); Actor, "Timon of Athens" (1981); Guest Appearance, "Roger Doesn't Live Here Anymore" (1981); Guest Appearance, "Theatre Box" (1981); Actor, "Loophole" (1981); Actor, "Breaking Glass" (1980); Actor, "The Day Christ Died" (1980); Guest Appearance, "Spine Chillers" (1980); Guest Appearance, "Play for Today" (1975-1979); Actor, "Daft as a Brush" (1975, 1978); Actor, "After the Boom Was Over" (1977); Actor, "Chalk and Cheese" (1977); Guest Appearance, "BBC2 Playhouse" (1976); Guest Appearance, "Bill Brand" (1976); Actor, "Voyage of the Damned" (1976); Actor, "Doomwatch" (1972) **AW:** Named Commander, Order of the British Empire (2009); Named Best Actor, "Carrington," Evening Standard British Film Awards (1996); Named Best Actor, "Carrington," Cannes Film Festival (1995); Tony Award for Best Actor in a Musical, "Miss Saigon" (1991); Named Best Actor - Musical, "Miss Saigon," Drama Desk Awards (1991); Named Best Actor - Musical, "Miss Saigon," Olivier Awards (1990); Named Most Promising Newcomer - Actor, Evening Standard British Film Awards (1981); Named Best Actor - Revival, "Hamlet," Olivier Awards (1980); Tony Award for Best Featured Actor in a Play, "Comedians" (1977)

PUCK, WOLFGANG, T: Chef **I:** Food & Restaurant Services **DOB:** 07/08/1949 **PB:** Sankt Veit an der Glan **SC:** Carinthia/Austria **MS:** Married **SPN:** Gelila Assefa (2007); Barbara Lazaroff (1983, Divorced 2003); Marie France Trouillot (1975, Divorced 1980) **CH:** Oliver; Alexander **ED:** Honorary Doctor of Culinary Arts, Johnson & Wales University, Providence, RI (1998); Apprentice, Raymond Thuillier, L'Oustau de Baumanière, Les Baux-de-Provence, Hôtel de Paris, Monte Carlo, Monaco **C:** Executive Chef, Partner, CUT, Beverly Hills, CA (2006-Present); Executive Chef, Partner, 20 21, Minneapolis, MN (2005-Present); Executive Chef, Partner, Wolfgang Puck Bar & Grill, Las Vegas, NV (2004-Present); Partner, Wolfgang Puck Worldwide, Inc. (2000-Present); Owner, Chef, Wolfgang Puck Catering (1998-Present); Owner, Wolfgang Puck Cafes (1993-Present); Executive Chef, Partner, Spago, Las Vegas, NV (1992-Present); Owner, Wolfgang Puck Express (1991-Present); Executive Chef, Partner, Trattoria del Lupo, Las Vegas, NV (1989-Present); Executive Chef, Partner, Postrio, San Francisco, CA (1989-2009); Executive Chef, Partner, Chinois on Main, Santa Monica, CA (1983-Present); Executive Chef, Partner, Spago (1982-Present); Chef, Part Owner, Ma Maison, Los Angeles, CA (1975-Present); Executive Chef, Partner, Postrio Las Vegas, NV (1998-2015); Executive Chef, Partner, Chinois, Las Vegas, NV (1998-2009); Executive Chef, Partner, Granita, Malibu, CA (1991-2005); Chef, La Tour, Indianapolis, IN (1973-1975); Owner, Wolfgang Puck Fine Dining Group; Executive Chef, Partner, Vert Brasserie, Hollywood, CA; Former Chef, L'Oustau de Baumanière, Provence, RI; Former Chef, Maxim's, Paris, France; Former Chef, Hôtel de Paris, Monte Carlo, Monaco **CR:** Official Caterer, Governors Ball, Academy of Motion Picture Arts and Sciences (1995-Present) **CIV:** Founder, Puck-Lazaroff Charitable Foundation (1982-Present); Honorary Chair Chef, "Give Star Sensation" Benefit, Cleveland, Ohio; Fundraising, Meals on Wheels America **CW:** Author, Newspaper Column, "Wolfgang Puck's Kitchen" (2003-Present); Guest, "Good Morning America" (1986-Present); Appearance, Television Series, "The Best Thing I Ever Ate" (2019); Author, "Wolfgang Puck Makes It Healthy: Light Delicious Recipes and Easy Exercises for a Better Life" (2014); Guest Appearance, Television Series, "90210" (2013); Voice Actor, Film, "The Smurfs" (2011); Guest Appearance, Television Series, "Die Erfolgsstory" (2009); Guest Appearance, Television Series, "Shark" (2006); Guest Appearance, Television Series, "Las Vegas" (2003, 2006); Guest Appearance, Film, "The Weather Man" (2005); Author, "Wolfgang Puck Makes It Easy" (2004); Guest Appearance, Television Film, "Just Desserts" (2005); Host, Chef, "Wolfgang Puck" (2000-2005); Voice Actor, Television Series, "The Simpsons" (2002); Author, "Live, Love, Eat! The Best of Wolfgang Puck" (2002); Guest Appearance, Television Series, "Frasier" (2000, 2002); Author, "Pizza, Pasta and More!" (2000); Guest Appearance, Film, "The Muse" (1999); Actor, Television Film, "Rhapsody in Bloom" (1998); Guest Appearance, Television Series, "Tales from the Crypt" (1992); Author, "Adventures in the Kitchen with Wolfgang Puck" (1991); Guest Appearance, Television Series, "Babes" (1991); Author, "The Wolfgang Puck Cookbook: Recipes from Spago and Chinois" (1986); Author, "Modern French Cooking for the American Kitchen" (1982); Producer, Instructional Cooking Video, "Spago Cooking with Wolfgang Puck"; Appearance, Numerous Cooking Shows, Including "Iron Chef America: Masters"; Appearance, Numerous Television Talk Shows **AW:** 2017 Gold Plate Winner, International Foodservice Manufacturers Association (IFMA) (2017); Recipient, Michelin Star, CUT, Marina Bay Sands, Singapore (2016); Recipient, Star, Hollywood Walk of Fame (2017); Recipient, Michelin Star, CUT, Beverly Hills, CA (2007); James Beard Foundation Outstanding Service Award (2005); Daytime Emmy Award for Outstanding Service Show, "Wolfgang Puck," The National Academy of Television Arts & Sciences (2002); James Beard Restaurant of the Year Award, Spago Hollywood (1994); Humanitarian of the Year, James Beard Foundation (1994); Inductee, Spago Hollywood, Nation's Restaurant News Fine Dining Hall of Fame (1993)

Puckett, Dale, T: Owner **I:** Architecture & Construction **CN:** Stonepuck, LLC **PT:** William Otis Puckett; Gloria Ann Puckett **MS:** Married **SPN:** Claudia P. Puckett **CH:** Travis; Casey Lee Trent; Juan david **C:** Owner, Stonepuck, LLC (2008-Present) **AS:** Mr. Puckett attributes his success to his dad who constantly encouraged him. **B/I:** Mr. Puckett became involved in his profession because his father ran a church furniture factory, where he would volunteer during the winters. He learned how to use every machine, load and unload the trucks as well as taking the machines apart and putting them back together. In the summer time, Mr. Puckett would go in the mountains and collect stones to create walls and fireplaces for people. **AV:** Carving; Hunting

PUGH, FLORENCE, T: Actress **I:** Media & Entertainment **DOB:** 1/3/1996 **PB:** Oxford **SC:** England **MS:** Single **SPN:** Clinton Pugh; Deborah Pugh **ED:** Student, Wychwood School and St. Edward's School, Oxford **CW:** Actress, "Black Widow" (2020); Actress, "Little Women" (2019); Actress, "Midsommar" (2019); Actress, "Fighting With My Family" (2019); Actress, "Malevolent" (2018); Actress, "Outlaw King" (2018); Actress, "The Commuter" (2018); Actress, TV Series, "The Little Drummer Girl" (2018); Actress, TV Film, "King Lear" (2018); Actress, "Lady Macbeth" (2016); Guest Appearance, "Marcella" (2016); Actress, "Studio City" (2015); Actress, "The Falling" (2014) **AW:** Breakthrough Award, Best Ensemble, Best Supporting Actress, "Little Women," Georgia Film Critics Association (2020); Best Breakthrough Performer, Gold Derby Awards (2020); Virtuoso Award, Santa Barbara International Film Festival (2020); Best Breakthrough Performance, Best Supporting Actress, "Little Women," Alliance of Women Film Journalists (2019); Breakthrough Artist Award, "Little Women," Austin Film Critics Association (2019); Best Ensemble Cast, "Little Women," Boston Society of Film Critics (2019); Chopard Trophy, Cannes Film Festival (2019); Best Supporting Actress, "Little Women," Chicago Film Critics Association (2019); Best Breakthrough Performance, "Little Women," Detroit Film Critics Society (2019); Rising Star of the Year, Dorian Awards (2019); Pauline Kael Breakout Award, Best Ensemble, "Little Women," Florida Film Critics Circle (2019); British/Irish Actress of the Year, "Little Women," London Film Critics' Circle (2019); Best Breakthrough Artist, "Little Women," San Diego Film Critics Society (2019); Best Performance by an Actress, "Lady Macbeth," British Independent Film Awards (2017); Best Actress, "Lady Macbeth," Dublin International Film Festival (2017); Breakthrough of the Year, "Lady Macbeth," Evening Standard British Film Awards (2017); Special Jury Prize, "Lady Macbeth," Montclair Film Festival (2017)

PULIDO, MAURICIO, T: Chief Executive Officer **I:** Oil & Energy **CN:** GBG Energy Management LLC **MS:** Married **SPN:** Paulina **CH:** Isabella **ED:** Bachelor of Science in Industrial Engineering, Finance, Marketing and Agroindustry, Universidad de los Andes, Bogota, Colombia (1994) **CT:** CSOC Supreme Regular Certification, Columbia Population Research Center (1994-2012) **C:** Chief Executive Officer, GBG Energy Management USA LLC, Jamaica (2012-Present); Transition Manager, Chevron (2010-2012); Portfolio Strategy Specialist, Chevron (2006-2011); Portfolio Strategy Specialist, Chevron (1994-2010); Underground Storage Tank Systems Coordinator, Chevron (2007-2008); Retail Venezuela Manager, Chevron (2003-2005); Regional Sales Manager, Chevron (2001-2002); Marketing Support Manager, Texaco (2000-2001); Fuel Revenues Manager, SORO (2000-2001); Planning Manager, Texaco (1998-1999); Senior Sales Representative, Medellin, Colombia (1995-1997); Market Analyst, Texaco Colombia (1994-1995); Planning Coordinator, Andean Region (1994-1995) **CIV:** Sponsor, Junior Achievement Jamaica (2016-Present); Vice President, Board of Directors, American Chamber of Commerce, Jamaica (2015-Present); Membership Committee, Energy Committee, Private Sector Organization of Jamaica, PSOJ (2015-Present) **MIL:** Served in Egypt and Israel, International Force and Observers, Colombian Army (1988) **AW:** President's Award, Champions for Youth, Junior Achievement Jamaica (2016, 2018); Pioneer Award, American Chamber of Commerce **MH:** Marquis Who's Who Top Professional **AS:** Mr. Pulido credits his success on his ability to manage people, as well as his propensity for maintaining an open door policy. **B/I:** Mr. Pulido became involved in his profession due to his interest in engineering. In this capacity, he leveraged his experience in marketing, finance, agriculture and business.

PUMA, GRACE M., T: Executive Vice President of Global Operations **I:** Business Management/Business Services **CN:** PepsiCo **ED:** BBA in Economics, Benedictine University, IL **C:** Executive Vice President of Global Operations, PepsiCo (2017-Present); Senior Vice President, Chief Supply Officer, PepsiCo (2015-2017); Senior Vice President, Chief Procurement Officer, PepsiCo (2010-2015); Senior Vice President, Strategic Sourcing, Chief Procurement Officer, United Airlines Inc., Elk Grove Village, IL (2007-2010); Vice President, Global Indirect Materials And Services Procurement, Kraft Foods (Now The Kraft Heinz Company) (1999-2007); Lead, International Strategic Sourcing Team, Motorola, Inc. (Now Motorola Mobility LLC); Lead, Procurement, BASF Corp. (BASF SE); Lead, Procurement, Gillette Co. **CR:** Board Member, Williams-Sonoma Inc. (2017-Present); Board Member, Marietta Corporation (2010-2015); Board Member, Institute for Supply Management; Former Board Member, Steppenwolf Theatre Company **AW:** Ranked #2 on the "Most Powerful Latina," Fortune Magazine and Association of Latino Professionals for America (ALPFA) (2018); Ranked #4 on the "Most Powerful Latina," Fortune Magazine and Association of Latino Professionals for America (ALPFA) (2017); Named Executive of the Year, Latina Style Magazine (2016); Ranked #4 CPO of 5,000 Global CPOs Across All Industries, ExecRank (2013); Named to Women to Watch, Crain's Chicago Business (2008)

PURVIN FOX, RONNIE ILAINE, T: Volunteer Educator **I:** Education/Educational Services **CN:** Densitometry Technician **DOB:** 08/11/1943 **PB:** Rochester **SC:** NY/USA **PT:** Lloyd Zultan Purvin; Alice (Temkin) Purvin **MS:** Married **SPN:** Melvin Fox, MD **CH:** Shari Charna Fox; Michele Askenazi; Jason Fox **ED:** Bachelor of Science in Education, The University of Texas at El Paso (1989); Diploma, Durham Business College, El Paso, TX (1962) **C:** Densitometry Technician, Beta Diagnostics, Incorporated, El Paso, TX (1983-1994); Substitute Teacher, El Paso Public School, Texas (1981-1982); Pathology Secretary, Assistant, Kaiser Foundation

Hospital, Hollywood, CA (1964-1968) **CR:** Chevra Kadisha Burial Committee **CIV:** President, Southwest Branch, Women's League for Conservative Judaism (1998-2000); Regional Board of Directors, United Synagogue Women's League (1992-1996); Drive-A-Meal Council (1980-1982); Active Member, El Paso Committee, Neighborhood Watch Board of El Paso; Texas Political Action Committee; Association for Retarded Citizens; Member, Advisory Council on Elder Abuse, El Paso Region, Texas **MEM:** President, National Council of Jewish Women (1992-1994); Chair Acculturation, Russian Resettlement in El Paso (1991-1993); Regional Director, B'nai Zion Sisterhood (1990-1992); President, B'nai Zion Sisterhood (1987-1989); Alumni President, Hadassah, Alpha Epsilon Phi (1974-1989); President, El Paso County Medical Society Auxiliary (1982-1983); Organization Rehabilitation through Training; University of Texas at El Paso Alumni Association; Lifetime Member, B'nai B'rith Women; Lifetime Member, Hadassah, Alpha Epsilon Phi; National Association of Female Executives; American Association of University Women **MH:** Albert Nelson Marquis Lifetime Achievement Award **B/I:** Ms. Fox entered her profession because her mother did a fair amount of volunteer work. They moved frequently due to her father, who served in the military, and she maintained a great deal of involvement whenever she was on base. When they arrived in El Paso, Texas, she joined other groups, and subsequently returned to volunteer work. **AV:** Golfing; Sewing; Traveling; Reading **PA:** Republican **RE:** Jewish

PUTH, CHARLIE OTTO JR., T: Singer **I:** Media & Entertainment **DOB:** 12/02/1991 **PB:** Rumson **SC:** NJ/USA **PT:** Charles Otto Puth Sr.; Debra Puth **MS:** Single **ED:** Degree in Music Production and Engineering, Berklee College of Music (2013); Diploma, Rumson-Fair Haven Regional High School (2010); Pre-College Coursework, Manhattan School of Music (2005-2010) **CR:** Endorser, Hollister Co. (2017-Present); Summer Youth Jazz Ensemble, Count Basie Theatre's Cool School, Red Bank, NJ (2003) **CW:** Musician, "Cheating on You" (2019); Musician, "Mother" (2019); Musician, "I Warned Myself" (2019); Featured Musician, "Easier (Remix)" (2019); Co-Writer, Co-Producer, "Why Do You Love Me" (2019); Co-Writer, Co-Producer, Contributing Musician, "Harleys in Hawaii" (2019); Co-Writer, Co-Producer, "Small Talk" (2019); Co-Writer, Co-Producer, "Easier" (2019); Co-Writer, "So Am I" (2019); Guest Appearance, "Songland" (2019); Advisor, Mentor Assistant, "The Voice" (2016, 2019); Co-Writer, Contributing Musician, "Love You Anymore" (2018); Co-Writer, "You Can Cry" (2018); Guest Appearance, "Sugar" (2018); Musician, "Voicenotes" (2018); Musician, EP, "Spotify Singles" (2017); Featured Musician, "Sober" (2017); Co-Writer, "Bedroom Floor" (2017); Co-Writer, Co-Producer, "Lips on You" (2017); Co-Writer, Co-Producer, "So Good" (2017); Guest Appearance, "Drop the Mic" (2017); Guest Appearance, "Life in Pieces" (2017); Guest Appearance, "Undateable" (2016); Co-Writer, "Cake" (2016); Co-Writer, Contributing Musician, "Trouble" (2016); Musician, "Nine Track Mind" (2016); Featured Musician, "Santa Claus is Coming to Town" (2016); Featured Musician, Co-Writer, Co-Producer, "Oops" (2016); Musician, Video Album, "Apple Music Festival: London 2015" (2015); Musician, EP, "Some Type of Love" (2015); Featured Musician, "Nothing but Trouble" (2015); Featured Musician, "See You Again" (2015); Co-Writer, "Working Class Heroes (Work)" (2015); Co-Writer, Co-Producer, "I See You" (2015); Co-Writer, Co-Producer, "Serve It Up" (2015); Co-Writer, Co-Producer, "Slow Motion" (2015); Co-Writer, "Bombastic" (2015); Co-Writer, Producer, "Broke" (2015); Co-Writer, Producer,

Contributing Musician, "Pull Up" (2015); Co-Producer, "Blue Sky" (2014); Co-Writer, Co-Producer, "How Long" (2014); Co-Writer, "California Winter" (2014); Co-Writer, "Celebrate" (2014); Musician, EP, "Ego" (2013); Creator, "Charlies Vlogs" (2009-2013); Contestant, "Can You Sing?" (2011); Featured Musician, "Break Again" (2011); Musician, EP, "The Otto Tunes" (2010) **AW:** Best Pop Artist, MBC Plus X Genie Music Awards (2018); International Rising Star of the Year, Gaon Chart Awards (2016); Top Rap Song, Top Hot 100 Song, "See You Again," Billboard Music Awards (2016); Best Collaboration, "See You Again," Nickelodeon Kid's Choice Awards (2016); Best Song, "See You Again," Critics' Choice Movie Awards (2016); Song – Feature Film, "See You Again," Hollywood Music in Media Awards (2015); Choice Music: TV or Movie Song, Choice Music: R&B/Hip-Hop Song, "See You Again," Teen Choice Awards (2015)

QUARNE, TRACEY J., T: Superintendent **I:** Education/Educational Services **CN:** Glenn County Office of Education **CH:** Ali **ED:** Bachelor of Science in Business Administration, United States University **C:** Superintendent, Glenn County Office of Education (2010-Present); Alternative Education Teacher, Orland Unified School District **CIV:** Member, City Council; Member, County Board of Supervisors; Director, Glen Corral Community Choir; Volunteer, National Coalition of Forests and Schools **AW:** Teacher of the Year; Volunteer of the Year **MEM:** Secessa California Superintendents Association; Phi Mu Alpha Symphonia; Orland's Patriots; Rotary Club **AS:** Mr. Quarne attributes his success to the people he has had around him. **B/I:** Mr. Quarne became involved in his profession due to the influence of his mother, who was also a teacher. Her example led Mr. Quarne to desire to be just like her. **AV:** Travel; Spending time with grandchildren **RE:** Lutheran

QUAYLE, JAMES, "DAN" DANFORTH, T: Former Vice President of the United States; Investment Company Executive **I:** Government Administration/Government Relations/Government Services **DOB:** 04/04/1947 **PB:** Indianapolis **SC:** IN/USA **PT:** James Cline Quayle; Corinne (Pulliam) Quayle **MS:** Married **SPN:** Marilyn (Tucker) Quayle (11/18/1972) **CH:** Tucker Danforth; Benjamin Eugene; Mary Corinne Berger **ED:** JD, Indiana University Robert H. McKinney School of Law (1974); BS in Political Science, DePauw University, Greencastle, IN (1969) **C:** Chairman, Global Investments, Cerberus Capital Management, LP (2000-Present); Founder, BTC Inc. (1994); Vice President of the United States, Washington, DC (1989-1993); U.S. Senator, State of Indiana, Washington, DC (1981-1989); Member, U.S. House of Representatives from Indiana's Fourth Congressional District, U.S. Congress, Washington, DC (1977-1981); Associate Publisher, General Manager, Huntington Herald-Press (Now The Herald-Press), IN (1974-1976); Teacher, Business Law, Huntington College (1975); Director, Indiana Inheritance Tax Division (1973-1974); Administrative Assistant to Governor, State of Indiana (1971-1973); With, Consumer Protection Division, Office of Attorney General, State of Indiana (1970-1971); Court Reporter, Pressman, Huntington Herald-Press (Now The Herald-Press), IN (1965-1969); President, Quayle & Associates, Phoenix, AZ **CR:** Board of Directors, Bell Automotive, Heckmann Corporation (Renamed Nuverra) (2007-Present); Board of Directors, IAP Worldwide Services, Inc. (2000-Present); Board of Directors, Aozora Bank Ltd. (2000-Present); Board of Directors, K-2, Inc. (2001-2007); Distinguished Visiting Professor, American Graduate School of International Management (Now Thunderbird Graduate School of Global Management), Arizona

State University (1997-1999); Consultant in Field **CIV:** Chairman, Campaign America (1995-1999); Honorary Trustee Emeritus, Hudson Institute, Inc. **MIL:** With, Indiana Army National Guard (1970-1976) **CW:** Author, "Worth Fighting For" (1999); Co-Author (with Diane Medved), "The American Family: Discovering the Values That Make Us Strong" (1996); Author, "Standing Firm: A Vice-Presidential Memoir" (1994) **BAR:** State of Indiana (1974) **PA:** Republican

QUESADA, GEORGE, T: Partner **I:** Law and Legal Services **CN:** Sommerman, McCaffity & Quesada **MS:** Married **CH:** Four Children **ED:** JD, School of Law, Baylor University School of Law (1986); BA, Baylor University (1983) **C:** Partner, Sommerman McCaffity, Quesada & Geisler, LLP (2002-Present); Supreme Court of Texas **CIV:** North Texas Tollway Authority **CW:** Author, "Evidence and Case Law Update for the 31st Annual Advanced Personal Injury Law Course"; Author, "Oilfield Litigation, Texas Trial Lawyers Association"; Author, "Once Bitten, Twice Shy: Knowing Your Expertise Daubert History"; Author, "Experts Who Travel With their Own Motion in Limine: Knowing The Daubert History"; Author, "Daubert- Proofing Your Experts" **AW:** Named, Super Lawyers, Thomson Reuters (2003-2018); Named, The Best Lawyers in America, 19th Edition, Best Lawyers (2013); Gene Cavin Award for Excellence in Continuing Legal Education, State Bar of Texas (2012); AV Preeminent Rating, Martindale-Hubbell **MEM:** American Association for Justice; Association of Plaintiff Interstate Trucking Lawyers of America; Past President, Dallas Trial Lawyers Association; Past President, Texas Trial Lawyers Association; New Mexico Trial Lawyers Association; Million Dollar Advocates Forum; Lifetime Member, Best Attorneys of America **BAR:** State of New Mexico (2004); Texas (1986); United States Court of Appeals for the Fifth Circuit; United States Court of Appeals for the Eighth Circuit; Supreme Court of Texas **AS:** Mr. Quesada attributes his success to the immense support of others. He has had the same legal assistant for 25 years and the same partners for more than 15 years. Mr. Quesada has gotten to where he is with the help of others and he is glad to assist as well.

QUIAMBAO STEVENSON, DALISAY LELAY, T: Dietitian; Consultant; Surveyor **I:** Health, Wellness and Fitness **DOB:** 07/10/1945 **PB:** Catanduanes **SC:** Phillipines **PT:** Patricio Lelay; Concepcion (Aldave) Lelay **MS:** Married **SPN:** John Stevenson (10/27/2010); Enrique Quiambao; (12/10/1967, Divorced 08/1989) **CH:** Larry; Edwin; Cheryl **ED:** Postgraduate Coursework, University of North Carolina Greensboro (1976-1978); BS in Nutrition, The Philippine Women's University, Manila, Philippines (1966) **CT:** Registered Dietitian; Licensed Dietitian **C:** Dietitian Consultant, Division of Facility Services, North Carolina Department of Human Resources (Now North Carolina Office of State Human Resources), Raleigh, NC (1988-Present); Dietitian Consultant, Gentiva, Kindred Healthcare, LLC (1995-2007); Director, Food Service, North Carolina Special Care Center, Wilson, NC (1986-1988); Dietitian Consultant, Granville Medical Center, Granville Health System, NC (1985-1986); Administrative Dietitian, Murdoch Developmental Center, Butner, NC (1984-1986); Clinical Dietitian, Murdoch Developmental Center, Butner, NC (1980-1984); Dietetic Technician, Murdoch Developmental Center, Butner, NC (1978-1980); Cafeteria Manager, Durham County Schools (Now Durham Public Schools), Durham, NC (1973-1978) **CR:** Dietary Consultant, Coordinating Council for Senior Citizens, Durham, NC (1990-1991); Interim Health Care Corporation Instructor,

Durham Technical Community College (1990); Food Service Consultant, Classic Food Services, Durham, NC (1989-1990); Dietitian Consultant, Meals on Wheels America **CIV:** Treasurer, Catholic Daughters of the Americas (2017-Present); Secretary, Philippine American Association of NC (PAANC) (2016); Chairman, Advisory Committee, Durham County Nursing Home (2014); Church Activities, Fundraising; School Lunch Program Initiative; Member, Charismatic Services in the Diocese of Raleigh, NC; Coordinator, Servants of God Ministry, Holy Infant Catholic Church; Co-founder, Santo Nino Devotee Ministry and Our Mother of Perpetual Help (Catholic Filipino Ministry and Evangelization) **AW:** Service Award, North Carolina Department of Human Resources (1988); Certificate for Public Manager Program, North Carolina Office of State Personnel (1987) **MEM:** Registered Member, American Dietetic Association; North Carolina Dietetic Association (Now North Carolina Academy of Nutrition and Dietetics (NCAND)); American Heart Association, Inc., Philippines; American Heart Association, Inc., NC; American Diabetics Association **MH:** Albert Nelson Marquis Lifetime Achievement Award **AS:** Mrs. Quiambao Stevenson attributes her success to her great faith in God. Faith has given her the strength to carry on through the challenges that she encountered throughout her life. The power of the Holy Spirit has sustained her, giving her courage to accept or face difficulties; even make things possible when it seems impossible. Her children and their family are her source of inspiration as they are her pride and joy. **B/I:** Mrs. Quiambao Stevenson came to the U.S. 49 years ago. At the time she entered her profession, she was a staff dietitian at Van Etten Hospital in New York City in 1970. She was not a registered dietitian until 1978, which gave her more opportunity to further her career. She has always wanted to help and the jobs she has always had had something to do with helping people - from school lunch program dealing with school children, dealing with residents with physical and developmental disabilities, dealing with elderly in nursing homes, and consulting in home health. The most fulfilling was working with the state of North Carolina inspecting long-term care services to make sure nursing homes are in compliance with federal regulations. **AV:** Reading; Baking; Arts and crafts; Developing recipes; Volunteering **RE:** Roman Catholic **THT:** Mrs. Quiambao Stevenson says, "Life is what we make of it. Just like plants, we plant the seeds, we water them, allowing that they get the sun, some rain, fertilizer, and allow them to grow, making sure there are no weeds that grow around them. We have to free ourselves of negativity, vices that could ruin our life. We need to stay focus. Sure, we run into many challenges and obstacles while we are trying to accomplish what we wanted to do, but if we stay on course, with God's grace, we could reach what we sought out to do. In the end, life is worth living."

QUIGLEY, MICHAEL, "MIKE" BRUCE, T: U.S. Representative from Illinois **I:** Government Administration/Government Relations/Government Services **DOB:** 10/17/1958 **PB:** Indianapolis **SC:** IN/USA **MS:** Married **SPN:** Barbara Quigley **CH:** Alyson; Meghan **ED:** JD, Loyola University Chicago School of Law (1989); MA in Public Policy, The University of Chicago (1985); BA in Political Science, Roosevelt University, Chicago, IL (1981) **C:** Member, U.S. House of Representatives from Illinois' Fifth Congressional District, United States Congress, Washington, DC (2009-Present); Representative, District 10, Cook County Board of Commissioners, Chicago, IL (1998-2009); Attorney, Law Offices of Michael B. Quigley (1990-2009);

Aide to Alderman Bernie Hansen, Chicago City Council (1983-1989); Intelligence Committee **CR:** Instructor, Political Science, Loyola University Chicago **AW:** Public Service Award, Chicago House (2008); Human Rights Award, Evangelical Catholic Church; Chicago Recycling Coalition Award; Distinguished Service Award, Illinois Committee for Honest Government; Audobon Leadership Award; Human Rights Campaign Equality Award; Community Advocate Award, Chicago Battered Women's Network; Legislator Award, Respiratory Health Association; Leon Despres Award, Independent Voters of Illinois/Independent Precinct Organization; Outstanding Public Servant Award, Lakeview Chamber of Commerce **MEM:** Lakeview Chamber of Commerce **PA:** Democrat

QUINCEY, JAMES ROBERT B., T: Chief Executive Officer, President **I:** Food & Restaurant Services **CN:** The Coca-Cola Company **DOB:** 01/08/1965 **PB:** London **SC:** England **MS:** Married **SPN:** Jacqui Quincey **CH:** Two children **ED:** BSEE, University of Liverpool; Coursework, King Edward's School, Birmingham, England **C:** Chairman, Chief Executive Officer, The Coca-Cola Company (2019-Present); President, Chief Executive Officer, The Coca-Cola Company (2017-2019); President, Chief Operating Officer, The Coca-Cola Company (2015-2017); President, Europe Group, The Coca-Cola Company (2013-2015); President, Northwest Europe and Nordics Business Unit, The Coca-Cola Company (2008-2012); President, Mexican Division, The Coca-Cola Company (2005-2008); President, South Latin Division, The Coca-Cola Company (2003-2005); General Manager, South Latin Division, The Coca-Cola Company (2003); Region Manager, The Coca-Cola Company, Uruguay (2000-2003); Region Manager, The Coca-Cola Company, Argentina (2000-2003); Deputy to Division President, The Coca-Cola Company, Mexico (1999-2000); Director of Learning Strategy, Latin American Group, The Coca-Cola Company (1996-1999); Partner, Strategy Consulting, The Kalchas Group **CR:** Board of Directors, Embotelladora Andina South America (2006-Present); Vice Co-Chair, The Consumer Goods Forum; Founding Member, Board Advisory Council, New York Stock Exchange; Director, Pfizer, Inc. **AW:** Executive of the Year, Dive Awards (2019)

QUINN, VIRGINIA LYNN, T: Paramedic **I:** Medicine & Health Care **CN:** Bayfront Health Port Charlotte **DOB:** 10/04/1960 **SC:** OH/USA **PT:** Robert Murphy; Lorietta Murphy **MS:** Married **SPN:** Thomas Patrick Quinn Jr. **CH:** Dakota M. Quinn (Firefighter/EMT); Hunter J. Quinn **ED:** Coursework in Emergency and Paramedic Technology, Edison Community College, Punta Gorda, FL (1995); Coursework, EMT School, City of Sarasota Fire Department (1985) **CT:** Certified Paramedic, State of Florida; ACLS Certified; EKG Certified; BLS Certified; CPR Certified; IV Certified; PALS Certified **C:** Paramedic, Emergency Room, Bayfront Health Port Charlotte (2020-Present); Paramedic, MST/Labor and Delivery, Sarasota Memorial Health Care System (2019-2020); Paramedic, Venice Regional Bayfront Hospital (2012-2019); Emergency Room Paramedic Technician, Venice Regional Bayfront Hospital (2012); Open-Heart Anesthesia Technician Paramedic, Peace River Bayfront Hospital (2012); Paramedic Supervisor, KBR, Inc., Iraq (2010-2011); Paramedic, KBR, Inc., Afghanistan (2007-2008); Paramedic, Ambitrans (2006-2007); Paramedic, Sarasota Cardiovascular Group (2000-2006); EMT-Paramedic, Charlotte County Fire/Emergency Medical Services (1988-1999); Dispatcher, Fire/EMS, City of Sarasota Dispatch (1981-1988) **CR:** Fire-EMS **MIL:** Contract, U.S. Army (2007-2011) **AW:** Recognized for "Contributions to Serve Charlotte County Citizens," Charlotte County Fire

& EMS; Five Phoenix Awards; Three Stork Awards **MH:** Marquis Who's Who Humanitarian Award **AS:** Ms. Quinn attributes her success to a very supportive family, which inspires her to be a better person. They motivate her every day. **B/I:** Ms. Quinn became involved in her profession because she loves to help people. She believes everyone is here for a reason and that if people can make a difference, they should. **PA:** Republican **RE:** Christian **THT:** Ms. Quinn's motto is as follows: "Live each day like it's your last. Help anybody you can and things will always work out the way they're supposed to...and just breathe. It will get better in the long run."

QUINTERO, YAMILE, T: District Family Facilitator/Homeless Liaison **I:** Social Work **CN:** Little Elm Independent School District **DOB:** 09/10/1967 **PB:** Macaravita Santander **SC:** Colombia **PT:** Isaias **MS:** Married **SPN:** Mauricio **CH:** Angel; Maripaz **ED:** MS in Human Development and Family Studies, University of North Texas; Post-Graduate Coursework in Learning Disabilities under a Neuropsychological Behavioral Analysis Approach, Konrad Lorenz University, Bogotá, Colombia; BS in Clinical Psychology, Konrad Lorenz University, Bogotá, Colombia **CT:** Teachers Certification in EC-4 & Bilingual Education; Certified Family Life Educator, National Council of Family Relations **C:** District Family Facilitator/Homeless Liaison, Little Elm Independent School District (2007-Present); Bilingual Pre-Kindergarten Teacher, Little Elm Independent School District (2006-2007); Bilingual Teacher, Head, Start Program, Denton Independent School District (2002-2006); Family Life Educator, Violence Intervention Crisis Specialist, Denton Family Resource Center; Family Coordinator, AVANCE-Dallas, Dallas Independent School District; Human Development and Family Science Department, University of North Texas; Assistant Professor, Psychology Faculty, Pontifical Bolivarian University, Colombia **CR:** Founder, Teacher, Parent Education Academy (2007-Present) **AW:** Triple E Award, Little Elm Independent School District Superintendent; Excellence Achievement in Launching The AVANCE Program, Dallas Independent School District **MEM:** National Council of Family Relations; National Association of Psychology in Colombia; Nu Delta Kappa Gamma Society International for Key Women Educators **AS:** Ms. Quintero attributes her success to her supportive father, husband, and children. She additionally credits her great work community, as well as the motivation from those families with whom she works. **B/I:** Ms. Quintero was inspired to pursue social work by her high school psychologist. In Columbia, she worked as a volunteer adult teacher in an underserved community. This is what motivated her to work with struggling families in her adult life. She is passionate about mental health. **RE:** Catholic **THT:** Ms. Quintero lives with a sense of purpose. She is happy to serve others with a kind heart and no judgment. Her mission is to serve and be there for every family in need.

RABOVITSER, IOSIF (JOSEPH) K., T: Director of R&D of Combustion Systems **I:** Research **CN:** Gas Technology Institute (GTI) **SC:** Russia **MS:** Widowed **SPN:** Tamara (Deceased 2018) **CH:** Anna **ED:** PhD, All-Russia Thermal Engineering Institute (1976); MS in Control and Information; MS in Power Engineering **C:** Director of R&D of Combustion Systems, Gas Technology Institute (GTI) (2008-2019) **CW:** Contributor, Chapters to Three Books; Author, Co-author, 28 Patents and More Than 300 Publications **AW:** Special Recognition Award (1995); Recipient, R&D 100 Awards **MEM:** Worldwide Gas Institute **AS:** Dr. Rabovitser's success really took place in America; in Russia there were some restrictions. His main success was the Super Boiler with thermal efficiency up to 93.5% HHV, and the another was the Partial Oxidation Gas Turbine (POGT). He developed POGT-based power system capable to achieve 65% electrical power to fuel input efficiency. **B/I:** Mr. Rabovitser's first research job started when he was a university student in 1960. This is when he published his first paper. He worked for All Thermal Engineering Institute in Russia for 32 years, from 1960 to 1992. At that time, he was invoked in many research and engineering projects in former Soviet Union. In 1992, he came to America and began to work for the Gas Technology Institute, where he retired from in 2019.

RACOMA, FAWN, T: Owner/Chef/Entrepreneur **I:** Food & Restaurant Services **CN:** Rootz Organic Cafe & Shop **CH:** One Daughter **ED:** AA in Culinary Arts **C:** Owner/Chef/Entrepreneur, Seedz Organic Cafe & Beverages (2017-Present); Owner/Chef/Entrepreneur, Rootz Organic Cafe & Shop (2013-Present) **CIV:** Participant, Local Buddha Center **AW:** Seven-time Named Best Vegetarian Restaurant for Rootz in Local Community **AS:** Ms. Racoma attributes her success to her support from her husband and her daughter. She also attributes it to her motivation to make strides within her community. **B/I:** Ms. Racoma grew up around food; her mother owned restaurants as she was growing up. Unfortunately, Ms. Racoma also grew up around a lot of sick people. She studied holistic health. She enjoyed that but it really came back to food and diet for her. She thought, 'what are we putting inside our bodies and how do we sustain our bodies?' At that time healthy food had a bad representation. It was about low fat cottage cheese and rice cakes. She wanted to be able to transform and change people's understanding of healthy food and delicious food and blend the two. **AV:** Snowboarding in the winter; Hiking in the summertime; Bicycling; Kayaking; Tubing; Anything in the river will be fun **THT:** Both of Ms. Racoma's businesses, Rootz and Seedz, include menus with fresh, organic choices. They sell food that she grew up eating but making them healthier, while having multiple options for people with dietary restrictions (such as, vegan, keto, paleo, etc). Rootz is more lunch based, and Seedz will sell breakfast specials. The shops at the locations sell local art and spiritual gifts. Ms. Racoma's motto is, "Food is fuel."

RADEFELD, MATTHEW, ESQ., T: Partner **I:** Law and Legal Services **CN:** Frank, Juengel & Radefeld, Attorneys at Law **MS:** Married **CH:** Three children **ED:** JD, School of Law, Saint Louis University (2000) **C:** Partner, Attorney, Frank, Juengel & Radefeld, Attorneys at Law **MIL:** Captain, Judge Advocate General Corps, U.S. Army Reserve (2002-2011); Corporal, U.S. Marine Corps (1993-2000) **CW:** "Gun Laws in America and Missouri: An Overview," The St. Louis Bar Journal (2016); Speaker, Mini-Law School, The Missouri Bar, School of Law, Saint Louis University (2015); Editor, DWI Manual, Missouri Bar Desk Reference Series (2014); Contributor, Lorman Education Services, CLE Webinars (2014); Presenter, Missouri State Legislature and Senate Joint Commission of Reformation of Sex Offender Registration Laws (2014); Speaker, Criminal Law 101, Annual Meeting, The Missouri Bar (2012) **MEM:** Fellow, The Missouri Bar Foundation (2015); Barrister, The Theodore McMillan American Inn of Court (2012-2014); Executive Council Member, St. Louis County Bar Association; Former Chair, Criminal Law Section, The Bar Association of Metropolitan St. Louis; Elected Delegate, Young Lawyer Council, The Missouri Bar; Military Law Commission, National Association of Criminal Defense Lawyers; MACDL; Criminal Justice Act Lead Panel, United States District Court Eastern District of Missouri **BAR:** United States Court of Appeals for the Armed Forces (2005); The Supreme Court of the United States (2004); United States District Court Southern District of Illinois (2003); Illinois State Bar Association (2001); The Missouri Bar (2000); United States District Court Eastern District of Missouri (2000); United States Court of Appeals for the Eighth Circuit (2000) **AS:** Mr. Radefeld attributes his success to hard work and dedication to the law. **B/I:** Mr. Radefeld became involved in his profession because he always wanted to be an FBI agent. He was told that one of the best ways to realize that dream was to go to law school and become an attorney. **THT:** Mr. Radefeld aims to be the best version of himself every day.

RADIL, GARY W., T: Of Counsel **I:** Law and Legal Services **CN:** Baird Holm LLP **DOB:** 12/09/1941 **PB:** Ord **SC:** NE/USA **PT:** Charles Radil; Harriet (Hrdy) Radil **MS:** Married **SPN:** Sara Ellen Coffee Radil (06/08/1969) **CH:** Amy; C. Buffington; Ann; Jennifer **ED:** LLB, Harvard University, Cambridge, MA (1967); BA, University of Nebraska–Lincoln, With High Distinction (1964) **C:** Partner, Baird Holm LLP (1972-Present); Of Counsel, Baird Holm LLP (2012); Associate, Baird, Holm, McEachem, Pedersen, Hamann & Strasheim, Omaha, NE (1968-1971) **CR:** Lecturer, Great Plains Federal Tax Institute, Inc.; Lecturer, American Hospital Association; Lecturer, Continuing Education Seminars, Nebraska State Bar Association; Teacher, United States National Guard **CIV:** Nebraska Children's Home Society (1987-Present); Nebraska Masonic Home Foundation (1987-Present); Trustee Emeritus, Omaha Home for Boys (1984-Present); President, Nebraska Children's Home Society (2005-2007); Omaha Symphony (1991-1999); Visiting Nurse Association, Omaha, NE (1987-1993); Board of Directors, Opera Omaha, Inc. (1980-1986) **MIL:** Captain, Judge Advocate General's Corps, Staff Judge Advocate, Nebraska National Guard (1970-1973) **AW:** Great Plains Super Lawyers List (2009-Present); One of Best Lawyers in America (1996-Present); Best Lawyer of Omaha in Tax Law and Non-Profit Organization in Employee Benefit **MEM:** Secretary, Nebraska State Bar Foundation (2006-Present); Board of Directors, Nebraska State Bar Foundation (1999-Present); President, Nebraska State Bar Foundation (2013-2014); President, Pro Tem Club (2000); Executive Committee, Real Property, Probate and Trust Law Section, Nebraska State Bar Association (1987-1992); Chairman, Real Estate, Probate and Trust Law Section, Nebraska State Bar Association (1990-1991); Fellow, American College of Trust and Estate Counsel; American College of Tax Counsel; American Bar Foundation; Personal Service Organizations Committee Section on Taxation, Exempt Organizations Committee, American Bar Association; Happy Hollow Club; The Phi Beta Kappa Society; Delta Sigma Rho **BAR:** United States Tax Court (1972); Nebraska State Bar Association (1967); United States District Court District of Nebraska (1967) **MH:** Albert Nelson Marquis Lifetime Achievement Award; Marquis Who's Who Top Professional **B/I:** Mr. Radil became involved in his profession because he always liked to understand the rules; if there's a game, he wants an explanation of the rules. Tax laws definitely have rules and what he likes about his practice has been helping people plan their affairs and realizing their objectives. In order to do that, they have to understand what the rules are and, more importantly, what the tax rules are. The ideals of planning have always appealed to Mr. Radil. **AV:** Fly fishing **PA:** Republican **RE:** Presbyterian

RAE, ISSA, T: Actress, Writer, Director **I:** Media & Entertainment **DOB:** 01/12/1985 **PB:** Los Angeles **SC:** CA/USA **MS:** Engaged **SPN:** Louis Diame **ED:** BA in African and African-American Studies, Stanford University (2007); Theater Fellowship, The Public Theater, New York, NY **CIV:** Advocate, Protesting Against Police Violence and Brutality Against Black Americans; Donor, Sterling Family Trust **CW:** Actress, "Vengeance" (2021); Actress, "#BlackAF" (2020); Actress, "The Photograph" (2020); Executive Producer, "The Lovebirds" (2020); Actress, Writer, Executive Producer, "Insecure" (2016-2020); Actress, Executive Producer, "A Black Lady Sketch Show" (2019); Voice Actress, "Hair Love" (2019); Actress, "Little" (2019); Voice Actress, "BoJack Horseman" (2018); Actress, "The Hate U Give" (2018); Actress, "Nice for What" by Drake (2018); Actress, "Moonlight" by Jay-Z (2017); Executive Producer, "Insecure: Due North" (2017); Producer, "Killing Lazarus" (2017); Author, "The Misadventures of Awkward Black Girl" (2016); Actress, "A Bitter Lime" (2015); Actress, "Protect and Serve" (2015); Executive Producer, "Get Your Life" (2015); Executive Producer, Short Film, "Protect and Serve" (2015); Episodes, Writer, Executive Producer, "The Choir" (2013-2015); Co-Executive Producer, Co-Producer, "First" (2014); Actress, TV Film, "Rubberhead" (2014); Writer, "Black Twitter Screening" (2014); Executive Producer, "Roomieloverfriends" (2013-2014); Director, Two Actress, "Little Horribles" (2013); Actress, "Happy" by Pharrell Williams (2013); Actress, "Instacurity" (2013); Actress, "My Roommate the" (2013); Actress, "Orange Is the New Black and Sexy" (2013); Actress, "True Friendship Society" (2013); Actress, Executive Producer, "Little Horribles" (2013); Executive Producer, "How Men Become Dogs" (2013); Executive Producer, "Inside Web Series" (2013); Actress, "The Number" (2012-2013); Actress, Writer, Director, Producer, "The Misadventures of Awkward Black Girl" (2011-2013); Actress, "The Couple" (2012); Executive Producer, TV Series, "M.O. Diaries" (2012) **AW:** Outstanding Actress, Comedy Series, "Insecure," Black Reel Awards for Television (2019); Best Actress in a Series, Comedy or Musical," Insecure," Satellite Awards (2019); Outstanding Actress, Comedy Series, "Insecure," Black Reel Awards for Television (2018); Outstanding Female Actor in a Leading Role in a Comedy or Musical, "Insecure," Gracie Allen Awards (2018); Best Drama Series, "Giants," The Streamy Awards (2018); Outstanding Actress, Comedy Series, "Insecure," Black Reel Awards for Television (2017); Vision Award, Best Performance - Comedy, "Insecure," NAMIC Vision Awards (2017); Cover, Essence Magazine (2015); Listee, "30 Under 30," Entertainment Section, Forbes (2012)

RAFFA, JEAN, T: Author; Educator **I:** Writing and Editing **DOB:** 04/23/1943 **PB:** Lansing **SC:** MI/USA **PT:** Ernest Raymond Benedict; Verna Lois (Borst) Benedict **MS:** Married **SPN:** Frederick Anthony Raffa (06/15/1964) **CH:** Juliette Louise; Matthew Benedict **ED:** EdD, University of Florida (1982); MS, Florida State University (1968); BS, Florida State University (1964) **C:** Writer, Orlando, FL (1989-Present); Instructor, Disney Institute, Orlando, FL (1996); Consultant of Education, Teacher Education Center, University of Central Florida, Orlando, FL (1980-1989); Coordinator, Children's Programming, WFTV, Orlando, FL (1978-1980); Teacher, Leon County School Systems, Tallahassee, FL (1964-1969) **CR:** Instructor, The Jung Center, Winter Park, FL (1997-Present); Visiting Assistant Professor, Stetson University, DeLand, FL (1988-1989); Adjunct Instructor, University of Central Florida (1977-1985); Consultant, Language Arts Curriculum Committee, Orange County Public

Schools (1983) **CIV:** President, Board of Directors, Canterbury Retreat and Conference Center, The Episcopal Diocese of Central Florida (1988-1990); Chair, Education Commission, Episcopal Church of the Good Shepherd (1986-1989); With, Seminole County Public Schools Literary Magazine (1985-1989); Consultant, Young Authors' Conference Orange and Seminole County Public Schools (1985-1989); Senior Warden, Vestry, Episcopal Church of the Good Shepherd (1988); President, Maitland Junior High School (Maitland Middle School) PTA (1986-1987); Mistress of Ceremonies, Young Authors' Conference, Orange County Public Schools and Volusia County Schools (1984-1985); Judge, Volusia County Schools Poetry Contest (1983, 1984) **CW:** Author, "Dream Theatres of the Soul: Empowering the Feminine Through Jungian Dreamwork" (1994); Author, "The Bridge to Wholeness: A Feminine Alternative to the Hero Myth" (1992); Author, "Introduction to Television Literacy" (1989); Author, "Healing the Sacred Divide: Making Peace with Ourselves, Each Other, and the World"; Author, "The Soul's Twins: Emancipate Your Feminine and Masculine Archetypes"; Contributor, Articles to Professional Journals, Articles and Meditations to Religious Journals **AW:** Wilbur Award for "Excellence in Communicating Religious Faith and Values to the Public Arena and for Encouraging Understanding Among Faith Groups on a National Level," Religion Communicators Council (2013); Nominee, Kimball Wiles Award for Best Dissertation, University of Florida College of Education (1982); Florida State Teacher's Scholarship (1961); Easterseals Award; Named to Kappa Delta Pi, International Honor Society in Education; Fellow, International Biographical Centre **MEM:** Kappa Delta Pi, International Honor Society in Education; Phi Delta Kappa (PDK International) **B/I:** Dr. Raffa became involved in her profession because when she went back to get her doctorate, she began to have a mid-life awakening of not having lived her true gift. She was disenchanted with her education career because she was not teaching things that she loved, she was teaching things that other people had written. After a few years, she had a new awakening of who she really was and what she felt, learning to be present to herself and attend to herself. She wanted to do what she loved and realized that after 10 years of soul searching that she loved to write and had some stories to tell. She resigned from teaching and started writing. She got her first book published and never looked back. **AV:** Antiques; Horseback riding; Travel; Reading **PA:** Democrat

RAGATZ, THOMAS, T: Lawyer **I:** Law and Legal Services **DOB:** 02/18/1934 **PB:** Madison **SC:** WI/USA **PT:** Wilmer Leroy Ragatz; Rosanna (Kindschi) Ragatz **MS:** Married **SPN:** Karen C. Ragatz (12/19/1965) **CH:** Thomas Rolf; William Leslie; Erik Douglas **ED:** Bachelor of Laws, University of Wisconsin–Madison, Madison, WI (1961); Bachelor of Business Administration, University of Wisconsin–Madison, Madison, WI (1957) **C:** Chairperson, Budget Committee, Foley & Lardner, Madison, WI (1994-2002); Partner, Foley & Lardner, Madison, WI (1978-2002); Managing Partner, Foley & Lardner, Madison, WI (1984-1993); Partner, Boardman Suhr Curry & Field, Madison, WI (1965-1978); Associate, Boardman Suhr Curry & Field, Madison, WI (1962-1964); Law Clerk, Wisconsin Supreme Court (1961-1962); Instructor, Wisconsin School of Business at University of Wisconsin-Madison, Madison, WI (1958-1960); Staff Accountant, Peat, Marwick, Mitchell & Co., Minneapolis, MN (1958); Former Lecturer in Accounting and Law, University of Wisconsin Law School **CR:** Lecturer, Seminars on Tax Subjects Board of Directors; President, Wisconsin Sports Development Corporation; President,

Courtier Foundation; Board of Directors, United Way Foundation; Board of Directors, Wisconsin Sports Foundation; Board of Directors, Norman Bassett Foundation; Board of Directors, Sub-Zero Freezer Co. Inc.; Board of Directors, Wolf Appliance Co. LLC **CIV:** Member, Board of Directors, Metropolitan YMCA, Madison, WI (1983-1990); President, Business and Education Partnership (1983-1989); Past President, Vice President, HospiceCare Foundation; Member, Board of Directors, Business and Education Partnership; Member, Board of Directors, Foundation for Madison's Public Schools; Past President, Past Moderator, 1st Congregational Church; Chairman Site Selection Committee, University Wisconsin Hospital Committee; Member, University Wisconsin Foundation; Formerly Director, United Way, Methodist Hospital Found; Panel Provision of Legal Services, University Wisconsin; Board Regents, University of Wisconsin-Madison, Madison, WI **MIL:** Captain, U.S. Army Reserve **CW:** Author, "The Ragatz History" (1989); Editor-in-Chief, Wisconsin Law Review (1960-1961); Chairperson, National Conference of Law Reviews (1960-1961); History of the Practice of Law in Dane County; Contributor, Numerous Articles to Professional Journals **AW:** Distinguished Alumni Award, Wisconsin School of Business, University of Wisconsin-Madison, Madison, WI (2019) **MEM:** Board of Directors, Madison Club House Corporation (1999-Present); President, Madison Club (1980-1981); President, Dane County Bar Association (1978-1979); Chairperson, Finance Committee, State Bar of Wisconsin (1975-1980); Board of Governors, State Bar of Wisconsin (1971-1975); Chairperson, Special Committee on Economics, State Bar of Wisconsin; Chairperson, Services for Lawyers Committee, State Bar of Wisconsin; Chairperson, Judicial Qualification Committee, Dane County Bar Association; Fellow, American Bar Foundation; American Bar Association; Wisconsin Bar Foundation; Seventh Circuit Bar Association; American Judicature Society; Order of Constantine; Bascom Hill Society; Wisconsin Institute of Certified Public Accountants (WICPA); Order of Coif; Beta Gamma Sigma; Sigma Chi **BAR:** Supreme Court of the United States (1968); U.S. Court of Appeals for the Seventh Circuit (1965); U.S. Tax Court (1963); U.S. District Court for the Eastern and Western Districts of Wisconsin (1961); Wisconsin (1961) **MH:** Albert Nelson Marquis Lifetime Achievement Award **B/I:** Mr. Ragatz became involved in his profession because he felt that he could enjoy it more than practicing accounting. **AV:** Sports; Spending time with grandchildren; Reading; Ancient archaeology **PA:** Republican **RE:** Presbyterian

RAIMONDO, GINA MARIE, T: Governor of Rhode Island **I:** Government Administration/Government Relations/Government Services **DOB:** 05/17/1971 **PB:** Smithfield **SC:** RI/USA **PT:** Joseph Raimondo; Josephine (Piro) Raimondo **MS:** Married **SPN:** Andrew Kind Moffit (11/01/2001) **CH:** Cecilia; Thompson **ED:** Honorary Doctorate, Bryant University (2012); JD, Yale Law School, New Haven, CT (1998); BS in Economics, Harvard University, Cambridge, MA, Magna Cum Laude (1993) **C:** Governor, State of Rhode Island, Providence, RI (2015-Present); Chair, Democratic Governors Association (2019); Vice Chair, Democratic Governors Association (2018); Governor-Elect, State of Rhode Island, Providence, RI (2014-2015); General Treasurer, State of Rhode Island, Providence, RI (2011-2015); Co-Founder, General Partner, Point Judith Capital (Now PJC) (2001-2010); Senior Vice President for Fund Development, Village Ventures (1999-2001); Law Clerk to Honorable Kimba Wood, United States District Court Southern District of New York (1998-1999) **CIV:** Trustee, Chair, Quality

Committee, Women & Infants Hospital, Care New England Health System; Vice Chair, Board of Directors, Crossroads Rhode Island; Member, Board Member, La Salle Academy and Family Service of Rhode Island **AW:** Fellow, Alumni Association, Yale University (2014); Rhodes Scholar, University of Oxford, England; Numerous Awards, Northern Rhode Island Chamber of Commerce; Numerous Awards, YWCA Rhode Island; Rodel Fellowship, The Aspen Institute **MEM:** Council on Foreign Relations **PA:** Democrat

RAJAKUMAR, CHARLES, PHD, T: Mechanical Engineer **I:** Engineering **DOB:** 04/12/1947 **PB:** Tamil Nadu **SC:** India **PT:** Charles Rajamony; Thangammal (Kumaradhas) **MS:** Married **SPN:** Lalitha Theresa Daniel (06/12/1975) **CH:** Vinod; Anita **ED:** PhD in Mechanical Engineering, Stevens Institute Technology (1985); MSc in Mechanical Engineering, Cranfield University, England (1974); MME, Indian Institute of Science (1971); BME, Annamalai University, Tamil Nadu, India (1969) **C:** Senior Technical Support, Alpha Omega Product Development Systems, (2018-Present); Consulting Engineer, CAE Engineers, LLC (2016-Present); Principal Engineer, Westinghouse Electric Company, PA (2010-2015); Senior Research Engineer, ANSYS, Inc. (1985-2010); Deputy Design Engineer, Hindustan Aeronautics, Ltd., Bangalore (1974-1981); Aeronautical Engineer, Hindustan Aeronautics, Ltd., Bangalore (1971-1973) **CIV:** Road to Recovery Volunteer Driver, American Cancer Society, Pittsburgh, PA (1988-Present); Council Member, Our Redeemer Lutheran Church, McMurray, PA (1988-1990) **CW:** Contributor, Articles, Professional Journals **MEM:** Secretary, Treasurer, Toastmasters International (1989); ASME; Sigma Xi, The Scientific Research Honor Society **MH:** Marquis Lifetime Achievement Award **B/I:** Dr. Rajakumar became involved in his profession after studying in India. He moved to the United States to further his career.

RALES, MITCHELL P., T: Co-founder **I:** Technology **CN:** Danaher Corporation **PB:** Pittsburgh **SC:** PA/USA **PT:** Norman Rales; Ruth (Abramson) Rales **MS:** Married **SPN:** Emily Wei; Lyn Goldthorp (Divorced) **CH:** Two Children **ED:** BBA, Miami University, Ohio (1978); Diploma, Walt Whitman High School (1974) **C:** Founder, Director, Colfax Corporation (1995-Present); Chairman Executive Committee, Danaher Corporation, Washington, DC (1990-Present); President, Danaher Corporation, Washington, DC (1984-Present); Partner, Equity Group Holdings, Washington, DC (1979-Present); Board Directors, Danaher Corporation, Washington, DC **CIV:** Trustees Council, National Gallery of Art; Board of Trustees, Hirshhorn Museum and Sculpture Garden; Advisory Council, Miami University, Ohio; Treasurer, Trustee, Chairman, Capital Campaign of Norwood School; Chairman, Capital Campaign for Hospital Sick Children **AW:** Named One of Forbes 400: Richest Americans (2006-Present); Named One of the Top 200 Collectors, ARTnews Magazine (2003-2012) **AV:** Collecting modern and contemporary art **RE:** Jewish

RAMOS, JESUS, "JESS" G., T: Sheriff **I:** Civil Service **CN:** Lampasas County Sheriff's Office **DOB:** 07/17/1962 **PB:** Killeen **SC:** TX/USA **PT:** Juan Ramos; Maria Ramos **MS:** Married **SPN:** Rebecca Dawn Ramos **CH:** Jessyn Rebecca **ED:** AS in Biomedical Technician Electronics, Texas State Technical College, Waco, TX (1983); Prerequisite Coursework, Central Texas College, Killeen, TX **C:** Sheriff, Lampasas County, TX (2017-Present); Criminal Investigator, Captain, Criminal Investigations Divisions, Horseshoe Bay Police Department (2012-2016); Texas Ranger, Cleburne, Lampasas, TX (2001-2012); Texas Ranger, Homicide and Major Investigations, Texas Department of Public Safety (1984-2012); Narcotics Sergeant, Texas Department of Public Safety (1996-2000); Sergeant, DPS Narcotics Service, College Station, TX; Texas Highway Patrol **CIV:** Organizer, Humanitarian Relief Coalition of Six Central Texas Rural County Sheriff's Offices, Aransas Pass, TX; Coach, Little League Sports; Executive Board Member, Past Chairman, Boys and Girls Club **AW:** Lumen Gentium Award (Light of the World Award), Austin Catholic Diocese **MEM:** Ex-Officio Board Member, Central Texas Counties Behavior and Development Board (2019); Board Member, Sheriff's Association of Texas (2018); Lampasas City Sports Recreation Committee; Committee Member, St. Mary Immaculate Conception Catholic Church Finance Committee **B/I:** Mr. Ramos became involved in his profession because he was interested in the state police; when he was in college, he and his twin brother were pulled over and, instead of getting a ticket, the state trooper handed them a job application. **THT:** Mr. Ramos encourages others to "Always do the right thing at all times, never compromise your integrity no matter what, love yourself and your family, and, most importantly, always center God in your every thought and action."

RAMOS, JORGE, T: Newscaster **I:** Media & Entertainment **DOB:** 03/16/1958 **PB:** Mexico City **SC:** Mexico **SPN:** Lisa Bolivar (1992, Divorced 2005); Gina Montaner (Divorced 1990) **CH:** Paola; Nicolas **ED:** DLitt (Honorary), University of Richmond (2007); Master's Degree in International Studies, University of Miami; Degree in Communications, Ibero-American University, Mexico City, Mexico **C:** Host, Fusion TV (2013-Present); Host, "Al Punto" (2007-Present); Co-Anchor, "Noticiero Univision" (1987-Present); Host, "Mundo Latino," KMEX (1986-1987); With, KMEX-TV (1984-1986); With, XEW-TV, Grupo Televisa, Mexico City, Mexico **CR:** Founder, Despierta Leyendo (Wake Up Reading) (2002) **CW:** Author, "Take a Stand: Lessons from Rebels" (2016); Author, "La Ola Latina (The Latino Wave): Como los Hispanos Estan Transformando la Politica en los Estados Unidos (How Hispanics Will Elect the Next American President)" (2016); Author, "A Country for All: An Immigrant Manifesto" (2009); Author, "The Gift of time: Letters from a Father" (2008); Author, "Dying to Cross: The Worst Immigrant Tragedy in American History" (2005); Author, "No Borders: A Journalist's Search for Home" (2003); Author, "No Borders: A Journalist's Search for Home" (2002); Author, "The Other Face of America" (2000); Contributor, Weekly Column, New York Times Syndicate **AW:** Ondas Award for International Career in Journalism (2015); Lifetime Achievement Award, National Academy of Television Arts and Sciences (2012); John F. Hogan Distinguished Service Award, Radio Television Digital News Association (2012); Sol Taishoff Award for Excellence, National Press Foundation (2012); Premio Internacional de Periodismo (International Journalism Award), Club de Periodistas de Mexico (Journalists' Club of Mexico) (2011); Named, One of "The 50 Highest-Earning Political Figures," Newsweek (2010); Distinguished Citizen Award, Commonwealth Club of California (2008); Listed, 25 Most Influential Hispanics, Time Magazine (2005); Humanitarian Award, Congressional Hispanic Caucus Institute (2004); Honors Award, American Association of Publishers (2004); Listed, "10 Most Admired Latinos," Latino Leaders Magazine (2004); David Brinkley Award for Journalistic Excellence, Barry University (2003); Maria Moors Cabot Journalism Award, Columbia University (2001); Eight Emmy Awards for "Excellence in Journalism" **PA:** Independent

RAMSEY, OCEAN, T: Shark Conservationist, Marine Biologist, Model **I:** Sciences **CN:** One Ocean Diving, LLC **PB:** Oahu **SC:** HI/USA **ED:** MA in Ethology; BA in Behavioral Sciences, Psychology, Marine Biology **C:** Operator, One Ocean Diving, LLC **CR:** Instructor, SCUBA; Instructor, PADI **CW:** Filmmaker, "Saving Jaws" (2020) **AV:** Traveling; Shopping; Listening to music

RANDALL, KAY TEMPLE, T: Accountant (Retired); Real Estate Agent **I:** Real Estate **DOB:** 09/23/1952 **PB:** Chattanooga **SC:** TN/USA **PT:** James H. Temple; Hortense N. (Dailey) Goodner Temple **MS:** Married **SPN:** Rodney B. Randall (1982); Gary F. Goodner (02/09/1968, Divorced 1972) **CH:** Jeffrey F. Goodner **ED:** Coursework, American Institute of Banking (1977-1979); Coursework, Chattanooga State College (1982-1983, 1970-1977) **CT:** Licensed Real Estate Agent, Tennessee (Retired); Notary Public, Tennessee **C:** Real Estate Agent, Chattanooga, TN (1989-2010); Accountant, Mr. Transmission of Chattanooga, Inc., Tennessee (1987-2009); Real Estate Appraiser, Agent, Chattanooga, TN (1983-1988); Insurance Representative, Colonial Life Accident and Health, Columbia, SC (1980-1982) **CR:** Administrative Assistant to Legal Profession, Chattanooga, TN (1972-1975) **CIV:** St. Peter's Episcopal Church (1989-Present); Fellow, Central Branch YMCA, Chattanooga, TN (1977-1997); Teacher, United Methodist Church, Chattanooga, TN (1979-1982); Advisory Board, United Methodist Church, Chattanooga, TN (1979-1982) **MH:** Albert Nelson Marquis Lifetime Achievement Award **AV:** Collecting art **PA:** Republican **RE:** Episcopalian

RANDOLPH, RICHARD RUTHERFORD III, T: Real Estate Executive **I:** Real Estate **DOB:** 09/07/1939 **PB:** Tulsa **SC:** OK/USA **PT:** Richard R. Randolph Jr.; Lillian Beverly (Fant) Randolph **MS:** Married **SPN:** Natalie "Natasha" Blinov Randolph (11/30/1963) **CH:** Richard IV; Ryland MacKenzie **ED:** BS in Finance, University of Alabama (1961); Coursework, University of the South (1957-1958); Coursework, Sewanee Military Academy, Sewanee, TN (1957); Coursework, Shades Valley High School, Birmingham, AL (1953-1955) **C:** General Partner, Recolonization, Blount Springs, AL (1988-Present); Vice President of Company Operations, Norville-Randolph Realtors (Now Lawrence-Arendall-Humphries Real Estate, Inc.), Birmingham, AL (1996-2001); Chief Financial Officer, Vice President, Treasurer, Co-Owner, Norville-Randolph Realtors (Now Lawrence-Arendall-Humphries Real Estate, Inc.), Birmingham, AL (1974-1996); President, Central Trane Air Conditioning Co., Birmingham, AL (1969-1974); Sales Representative, U.S. Pipe and Foundry Co., Atlanta, GA (1967-1969) **CIV:** Past President, St. Andrew's Society of the Middle South; Board of Trustees, Birmingham Historical Society; Vestry, St. Luke's Episcopal Church; Elder, Metropolitan Church of God; St. Peter's Anglican Church **MIL:** Honorably Discharged Captain, Flight Officer, Worldwide (1966); 63rd Military Airlift Wing, U.S. Air Force, Hunter Air Force Base, Savannah, GA (1961-1966) **MEM:** Birmingham Area Chamber of Commerce; Mensa; Downtown Club; Sewanee Club; Monday Morning Quarterback Club; Summit Club; Phi Delta Theta; Delta Kappa Epsilon; Birmingham Association of Realtors; Birmingham Association of Home Builders; Social Register; The Club; Past Director, Jefferson County Historical Association; Past Board Chairman, King's Ranch/Hannah Homes; Randolph Society; Family of Bruce International; Society of Descendants of the Order of Queen Boadicea; Newcomen Society of Alabama; First Families of Alabama; General Society of the War of 1812; English-Speaking Union; Jamestowne Society; Past President, Oak Hill Memorial

Association; Veterans of Foreign Wars; American Legion; Council, Society of Colonial Wars in the State of Alabama; Board of Managers, Society of the Revolution in the State of Alabama; General Society of the Sons of the Revolution; Bolling Family Association; National Society of Magna Charta Dames and Barons; Order of the Descendants of Ancient Planters; National Society of the Sons of the American Revolution; Order of First Families of Virginia of 1607-1624/5; Order of the First Families of the Alabama Territory **MH:** Albert Nelson Marquis Lifetime Achievement Award **AV:** Hiking; Researching genealogy; Traveling; Participating in Bible study **RE:** Anglican

RANSOM, CLIFTON LOUIS, T: Lawyer, Real Estate Investor **I:** Law and Legal Services **DOB:** 05/25/1935 **PB:** Houston **SC:** TX/USA **PT:** Clifton Louis Ransom; Birdelle (Wykoff) Ransom **MS:** Widowed **SPN:** Dorothy Ellen Peterson (12/25/1974, Deceased) **ED:** LLM in Taxation, Washington Law School, Salt Lake City, UT (1991); JD, Texas Southern University (1974); MA in Biblical Theology, St. Louis University (1970); BA in Philosophy, St. Joseph's College, Rensselaer, IN (1964); BS in Mathematics, Texas Southern University (1956) **CT:** Ordained Priest, Roman Catholic Church (1968) **C:** Attorney, Lone Star Legal Aid, Houston, TX (1980-Present); Attorney, Texas Welfare Department, Houston, TX (1975-1980); Priest, Diocese of Galveston-Houston (1968-1974) **CIV:** Board of Directors, Hope is Victory AIDS Foundation, Houston, TX (1993-1996) **MIL:** Lieutenant, U.S. Navy (1957-1960) **CW:** Author, "Uncertain Trumpet" (2011) **AW:** Lifetime Achievement Award, Orthodox Church (1996) **BAR:** U.S. Tax Court (1991); U.S. Court Appeals for the 5th Circuit (1980); U.S. Supreme Court (1980); U.S. District Court for the Southern District of Texas (1976); Texas (1974) **MH:** Albert Nelson Marquis Lifetime Achievement Award **B/I:** Mr. Ransom began his career as a Catholic priest, though it did not end up being the right path for him. He then pursued a career in law after the dean at his local school suggested he explore the field. **PA:** Democrat **RE:** Byzantine Catholic

RANSONE, ROBIN KEY, T: Proposals Consultant **I:** Technology **CN:** Ransone Associates, Inc. **DOB:** 03/28/1933 **PB:** Fort Worth **SC:** TX/USA **PT:** Reuben Key Ransone; Lilyan Paula (Hudzietz) Ransone **MS:** Married **SPN:** Paula Jane McBride (1/30/1959) **CH:** William Key; Cheryl Elizabeth Ransone Bafford **ED:** Postgraduate MBA Coursework, University of Texas (1979-1982); Postgraduate Coursework in Management of Research and Development Personnel, University of California Los Angeles (1963); Postgraduate Coursework in Executive Development, Texas A&M University (1963); BS in Aeronautical Engineering, Texas A&M University (1956) **CT:** Associate Fellow, American Institute of Aeronautics and Astronautics **C:** President, Ransone Associates, Incorporated, Chapel Hill, NC (1986-Present); Vice President of Systems Development, MJI Associates, Inc., Centerport, NY (1984-1986); Proposals Director, Fairchild Republic Company, Farmingdale, NY (1982-1984); Senior Specialist of Technical Communicating, Vought Corporation, Dallas, TX (1976-1982); Visiting Associate Professor, University of Virginia, Charlottesville, VA (1973-1976); Director of Aeronautical Operating Systems Office, NASA, Washington, DC (1972-1973); Developmental Engineer, American Airlines, Incorporated, New York, NY (1968-1972); Flight Test Program Manager, Air Force Flight Test Center, Edwards Air Force Base, California (1963-1968) **CR:** Invited Presenter, Lectures in Field **CIV:** Elder, First Presbyterian Church, Smithtown, NY (1984-1987); Founder, President, Huntington Park Homeowners Association, Duncanville, TX

(1981-1982); Chairman of Building Committee, Trinity United Methodist Church, Duncanville, TX (1981-1982); Trustee, Trinity United Methodist Church, Duncanville, TX (1979-1982) **MIL:** Civil Service GS-13 (1963-1968); Second Lieutenant, First Lieutenant, Captain, U.S. Air Force (1956-1963) **CW:** Author, "07HCRM-4"; Author, "Genesis Too"; Author, "How To Understand Federal Government Solicitations and Win Government Contracts"; Author, "Letters You Would Read If I Were Famous"; Author, "More Than An Engineer, Flight Testing Unusual Aircraft"; Author, "Our World"; Author, "So You Want To Be A Proposals Professional"; Author, "The Best of Internet Win & Wisdom"; Author, "The Patio"; Author, "The Road to Ben"; Author, "In an Alternate Universe"; Author, "I'd Rather Be a Texas Aggie" **AW:** Published in "SAE Transactions For 1976," "Chelsea STOLport - The Airline View" (1976); Three-Time Recipient, Consecutive Outstanding Officer Effectiveness Reports, U.S. Air Force; Superior Performance Award, Air Force Flight Test Center, Edwards Air Force Base, CA; Associate Fellow, American Institute of Aeronautics and Astronautics **MEM:** Research Advisory Panel, Aviation Week (1986); U.S. Air Force Scientific Advisory Board (1970); President of Edwards Air Force Base Chapter, Toastmasters International (1964-1968); Founder, President, Antelope Valley Photography Association, Lancaster, CA (1966-1967); Associate Fellow, Associate, Lifetime Member, American Institute of Aeronautics and Astronautics; Former Member, American Society of Automotive Engineers; Former Member, Technology, Marketing, Society of America; Association of Proposal Management Professionals; Lifetime Member, Flight Test Historical Society; Former Member, American Helicopter Society; Great Courses Advisory Panel, The Teaching Company **MH:** Albert Nelson Marquis Lifetime Achievement Award **AS:** Mr. Ransone attributes his success to his parents always supporting him. Additionally, he makes decisions based upon unbiased observations instead of wishes. He is not afraid to stand up for what he believes, even in the face of conflict, and he believes that it is easier to obtain forgiveness than permission. Mr. Ransone initiates solutions to problems. Although he often seeks to be in charge of projects, he relies upon the knowledge and contributions of others. Mr. Ransone addresses the project objectives and ignores personalities, never taking criticism personally. He seeks opposing viewpoints in order to fully understand all aspects of a problem. **B/I:** Mr. Ransone's interest in airplanes began in the sixth grade when he made airplane models out of balsa wood. Since then, he knew that he would work with airplanes. Later, when he was no longer involved directly with aircrafts, Mr. Ransone became proficient at helping aerospace, defense, and pharmaceutical companies sell their programs to the United States and foreign governments. **AV:** Restoring old houses; Eating; Drinking wine; Appreciating sports cars; Japanese gardening **PA:** Independent **RE:** Christian **THT:** Mr. Ransone's invited paper, "The Chelsea STOLport- the Airline View," presented at the SAE National Transportation Meeting in New York in 1976, was published in the prestigious SAE Transactions for 1976 for its "high quality, lasting value and contribution to the art." Only 10% of SAE papers presented each year are awarded that honor.

RAPINO, MICHAEL, T: Music Company Executive **I:** Media & Entertainment **CN:** Live Nation Entertainment **PB:** Thunder Bay **SC:** ON/Canada **MS:** Married **SPN:** Jolene Blalock (04/22/2003) **CH:** Three Sons **ED:** Honorary Doctorate of Commerce, Lakehead University, Thunder Bay, ON, Canada; BBA, Lakehead University, Thunder Bay, ON, Canada **C:** President, Chief Executive Officer, Live Nation Entertainment, Inc. (2010-Present); President, Chief Executive Officer, Live Nation, Inc. (2005-2010); Chief Executive Officer, President, Global Music, Clear Channel Music Group; Head, International Music Division, Clear Channel Entertainment, London, England; Partner, Core Audience Entertainment (Now SFX), Canada; Head, Marketing Brands, Labatt's Breweries Canada; Director, Entertainment & Sports, Labatt's Breweries Canada; Film Producer **CR:** Board of Directors, Sirius XM Radio Inc. (2018-Present) **CIV:** Co-Founder, Rapino Foundation **CW:** Executive Producer, Documentary, "Believer," HBO (2018); Executive Producer, Film, "A Star is Born" (2018) **AW:** Named, Power 100, Billboard (2018-2019); Diamond Honors Award, Clara Lionel Foundation (2015); Maverick, Details Magazine (2008)

RAPPACH, NORMA JEANNE, T: Nurse, Health Occupations Educator **I:** Medicine & Health Care **DOB:** 03/07/1938 **PB:** Hastings **SC:** PA/USA **PT:** James Eugene Fairbanks; Katherine Luella (Lear) Fairbanks **MS:** Married **SPN:** Ronald Rappach; James Davis Mrus (06/30/1959, Divorced 1978) **CH:** Timothy James; Susan Marie Mrus Dolgae (Deceased); Joseph Michael **ED:** BSN, Youngstown State University, Magna Cum Laude (1986); AAS, Kent State University, With Honors (1983); Diploma, Trumbull Memorial School of Nursing (1959) **CT:** Vocational Teacher Certification, Kent State University (1996); Certified EMT/Paramedic, Cuyahoga Community College (1978); RN, Ohio; Certified Diversified Health Occupations Instructor, Ohio **C:** Diversified Health Occupations Instructor, Gordon D. James Career Center, Lordstown Schools (1993-1999); School Nurse, Lordstown Local Schools (1978-1993); Certified Emergency Medical Instructor, Ohio Department of Education, Columbus, OH (1973-1978); Substitute School Nurse, Howland Local Schools (1972-1978); Substitute Industrial Nurse, Packard Electric Division GM (1974-1976); Part-Time Private Duty Nurse, Trumbull Memorial Hospital, Warren, OH (1969-1971); Geriatric Staff Nurse, Meadows Manor, Terre Haute, IN (1965-1966); Pediatric Staff Nurse, Trumbull Memorial Hospital, Warren, OH (1960-1962); Vocational Teacher **CR:** Instructor, Nurse Aid, Training Ohio Board of Nursing (1993-1998); Part-Time Geriatric Nurse, Gillette's Nursing, Warren, OH (1972-1974); Part-Time Nurse, Obstetrical Office, Warren, OH (1961-1973); Part-Time General Office Nurse, Warren, OH (1960-1972) **CIV:** Diversified Health Advisory Board (1990-1999); Volunteer Nurse, First Aid/CPR/HIV-AIDS Instructor, American Red Cross, Warren, OH (1990-1998); Parish Nurse, Blessed Sacrament Church, Warren, OH (1992-1994); HIV/AIDS Coordinator, Lordstown Local Schools (1985-1993); Advisor, Teen Institute for Alcohol Abuse, Warren, OH (1981); County Emergency Medical Coordinator, Trumbull County, Warren, OH (1976-1977); President, Trumbull County Emergency Medical Committee (1976-1977); Volunteer, Numerous Jobs, Catholic Church **AW:** Vocational Citizenship Award, Omicron Tau Theta (1995); Honorary Firewoman, Howland Township Fire Department (1978); Professional Woman of the Year, Trumbull County Fair (1977); Nursing Scholar, Warren Kiwanis Club (1956) **MEM:** Former Member, State Teachers of Ohio **MH:** Albert Nelson Marquis Lifetime Achievement Award **B/I:** For as long as she can remember, Ms. Rappach wanted to become a nurse. When she earned a Kiwanis Club scholarship in high school, she knew she would be able to attend nursing school. **AV:** Reading; Exploring computers; Making crafts; Playing the organ; Spending time with family; Attending church **RE:** Catholic

RASKIN, JAMIN, "JAMIE" BEN, T: U.S. Representative from Maryland **I:** Government Administration/Government Relations/Government Services **CN:** U.S. House of Representatives **DOB:** 12/13/1962 **PB:** Washington **SC:** DC/USA **PT:** Marcus Goodman Raskin; Barbara Judith (Bellman) Raskin **MS:** Married **SPN:** Sarah (Bloom) Raskin (08/11/1990) **CH:** Hannah Grace; Thomas Bloom; Tabitha Claire **ED:** Doctor of Jurisprudence, Harvard Law School (1987); Bachelor of Arts in Government, Harvard College (1983) **C:** Member, U.S. House of Representatives from Maryland's Eighth Congressional District (2017-Present); Professor of Law, American University Washington College of Law (1990-Present); Vice Ranking Member, House Judiciary Committee (2017-2019); Member, District 20, Maryland State Senate (2007-2017); Associate Dean, Faculty and Academy Affairs, American University Washington College of Law (1994-1996); Assistant Attorney General, MA (1987-1989); Member, Committee on House Administration; Member, Committee on the Judiciary; Member, Committee on Oversight and Government Reform **CR:** Visiting Professor, Sciences Po, Paris, France (2003-2004); Chairperson, Maryland State Higher Education Labor Relations Board **CIV:** Board of Directors, Washington Area National Rainbow Coalition (1992-Present); Member, 1992 Clinton-Gore Transition Team, Justice Department Civil Rights Cluster, Washington, DC (1992); Co-founder, Marshall-Brennan Constitutional Literacy Project **CW:** Author, "The Supreme Court versus the American People" (2003); Author, "We the Students, the Wealth Primary"; Contributor, Articles to Professional Journals; Featured Guest, National and Local TV and Radio Shows Including "Crossfire," "C-Span," "Diane Rehm Show," NPR and Others **AW:** Named, Scholar-Teacher of the Year, American University (2000-2001) **MEM:** Co-chair, Section on Administrative Law, Committee on Election Law, American Bar Association (1998-Present) **BAR:** Massachusetts (1987) **PA:** Democrat

RASMUSSEN, ROBERT, T: Chief Executive Officer **I:** Technology **CN:** Agile Six Applications, Inc. **ED:** MBA in Business Administration, National University (2004) **C:** Co-Founder, Digital Services Coalition (2019-Present);President, Chief Executive Officer, Agile Six Applications, Inc. (2015-Present); Senior Vice President, Three Wire Systems (2014-2015); Director, Government Operations (DefenseWeb Technologies), Humana (2012-2014); Program Director, Northern Europe, Netcracker Technology (2010-2011); Senior Project Manager - Norway, Devoteam / Mobile Norway (2009-2010); Operations Manager, Nordic & Baltics, Ericsson, Norway & Sweden (2001-2009); Senior System Administrator, IT Project Manager, Protocol Integrated Direct Marketing - MC Direct, California (1999-2001); Secure Network Manager, U.S. Navy, SAIC (1991-1999) **AW:** Honoree, "4th Fastest Growing Private Company in San Diego," San Diego Business Journal **MEM:** Digital Services Coalition; AGL Association

RASMUSSEN, STEPHEN SCOTT, T: Chief Executive Officer and President **I:** Insurance **CN:** Nationwide Mutual Insurance Company **ED:** BS in Business Administration, University of Iowa **C:** President, Chief Executive Officer, Nationwide Mutual Insurance Company, Columbus, Ohio (2009-Present); President, Chief Operating Officer, Property and Casualty Operations, Nationwide Mutual Insurance Company, Columbus, Ohio (2003-2009); President, Chief Operating Officer, CalFarm Insurance (2001-2003); Executive Vice President, Product Management, Allied Insurance (1998-2001); Vice President, Underwriting, Allied Insurance (1986-1998); Regional Vice President,

Pacific Coast Regional Office, Allied Insurance (1982-1986); Underwriting & Marketing, Allied Insurance, (1974-1982) **CIV:** Chair, Walk Corporation, Central Iowa Chapter (2002); Juvenile Diabetes Research Foundation; Trustee, Grand View College (Now Grand View University); Board Member, The Columbus Metropolitan Library; Board Member, Franklin County Convention Facilities Authority; Board Member, Insurance Institute for Highway Safety (IIHS); Board Member, National Urban League

RASMUSSON, BOBBY, T: Group Product Manager, Head of Core Consumer **I:** Business Management/Business Services **CN:** DoorDash **ED:** BS in Computational Informatics and Japanese Language, University of Michigan; Coursework in Engineering and Japanese, Nagoya University **C:** Group Product Manager, Head of Core Consumer, DoorDash, San Francisco, CA (2019-Present); Product Lead, Self-Driving Vehicle Experience, Lyft, Inc., San Francisco, CA (2017-2019); Product Manager, Enterprise, Lyft, Inc., San Francisco, CA (2016-2017); Product Manager, Payments, Lyft, Inc., San Francisco, CA (2015-2016); Product Manager, SigFig Wealth Management, San Francisco, CA (2014-2015); Product Manager, Search and Browse Experience, Groupon, Inc., Palo Alto, CA (2013-2014); Product Manager, Groupon Reserve, Groupon, Inc., San Francisco, CA (2012-2013) **CW:** Patents in Field **AW:** Listee, 40 Under 40 Tech CEOs and Founders, San Francisco Business Times (2019)

RASSEL, RICHARD E., T: Chairman **I:** Law and Legal Services **CN:** Butzel Long **DOB:** 01/10/1942 **PB:** Toledo **SC:** OH/USA **PT:** Richard Edward Rassel; Madonna Mary (Tuohy) Rassel **MS:** Married **SPN:** Dawn Ann Lynch-Rassel (09/17/1983); Elizabeth Ann Frederick (12/05/1967, Deceased 06/1977) **CH:** Richard III; Elizabeth; Lauren; Brian **ED:** JD, University of Michigan (1966); BA, University of Notre Dame (1964) **CT:** Certified Judge Advocate, U.S. Naval Justice School (1967) **C:** Chairman, Butzel Long, Detroit, MI (2010-Present); Director Global Client Relations, Butzel Long, Detroit, MI (2006-2010); Chairman, Chief Executive Officer, Butzel Long, Detroit, MI (1994-2006); Shareholder, Vice President, Butzel Long, Detroit, MI (1969-1994); Law Clerk, Michigan Court of Appeals, Detroit, MI (1966-1969) **CR:** Chairman, Detroit Public Television; Chairman, Metropolitan Affairs Coalition (MAC); Co-chair, Detroit Drives Degrees, Detroit Regional Chamber; Director & Secretary, Detroit Legal News; Vice Chair, Board, Detroit Regional Chamber of Commerce Foundation **CIV:** President, The Community House, Birmingham; Board of Advisors, University of Detroit; Board of Advisors, Mercy College School of Business; Board of Directors, Detroit Legal News; Detroit Police Athletic League (Detroit PAL); International Visitors Council; William Beaumont Hospital; Chair, Metropolitan Affairs Coalition, Oakland University College of Arts and Sciences; Past President, Past Board of Directors, Rosa Parks Scholarship Foundation; Foundation Trustee, Seed Foundation; Chairman, Board, Community House **MIL:** Lieutenant, United States Naval Reserve (1966-1969) **MEM:** Fellow, American College of Trial Lawyers; Vice Chairman, Media and Law Committee, American Bar Association (ABA); Chairman, Multidisciplinary Practice Law Committee, State Bar of Michigan; Birmingham Athletic Club; Detroit Athletic Club **BAR:** Michigan; District of Columbia **MH:** Albert Nelson Marquis Lifetime Achievement Award **B/I:** Mr. Rassel has always been curious about the law, so he decided to be a lawyer. **PA:** Independent **RE:** Catholic

RATCLIFFE, JOHN LEE, T: U.S. Representative, Lawyer **I:** Government Administration/Government Relations/Government Services **DOB:** 10/20/1965 **PB:** Mount Prospect **SC:** IL/USA **MS:** Married **SPN:** Michele (Addington) Ratcliffe **CH:** Two daughters **ED:** JD, SMU Dedman School of Law (1989); BA in Government and International Studies, University of Notre Dame (1987) **C:** U.S. Representatives, Texas Fourth Congressional District, United States Congress, Washington, DC (2015-Present); Partner, Ashcroft Sutton Ratcliffe LLC (2009-2014); Partner, Ashcroft (2009-2014); U.S. Attorney, Eastern District of Texas, The U.S. Department of Justice (2007-2008); Mayor, City of Heath, TX (2004-2012); Chief, Anti-Terrorism and National Security, The U.S. Department of Justice (2004-2007); Member, Judiciary Committee, Texas Fourth Congressional District, United States Congress, Washington, DC; Member, Committee on Homeland Security, Texas Fourth Congressional District, United States Congress, Washington, DC; Member, Republican Study Committee, Texas Fourth Congressional District, United States Congress, Washington, DC **CR:** Adjunct Professor of Law, Texas Wesleyan University; Adjunct Professor of Law, Southern Methodist University **PA:** Republican

RAY, RACHAEL DOMENICA, T: Cookbook Author, Television Personality **I:** Media & Entertainment **DOB:** 08/25/1968 **PB:** Glens Falls **SC:** NY/USA **PT:** James Claude Ray; Elsa Providenza Scuderi **MS:** Married **SPN:** John M. Cusimano (09/24/2005) **C:** Founder, Editorial Director, Magazine, Every Day with Rachael Ray (2005-Present); Buyer, Cowan & Lobel, Albany, NY; Manager, Mister Brown's Pub, The Sagamore, Lake George, NY **CR:** Designer, Rachael Ray Home Collection, Interior Design Division, PultreGroup (2016); Founder, "Nutrish" Pet Food (2008); Designer, Sheets, Blankets, and Coverlets, WestPoint Home (2007); Celebrity Endorser, Dunkin' Donuts (2007); Spokeswoman, Nabisco Crackers (2006) **CIV:** Founder, Nonprofit Organization, Yum-O! (2006-Present) **CW:** Host, "30 Minute Meals," Food Network (2001-2012, 2019-Present); Host, "Rachael Ray" (2006-Present); Author, "Rachael Ray 50: Memories and Meals from a Sweet and Savory Life: A Cookbook" (2019); Voice Actress, "Butterbean's Café" (2019); Guest Appearance, "Gilmore Girls: A Year in the Life" (2016); Author, "Everyone is Italian on Sunday" (2015); Author, "Comfort food: Rachael Ray's Top 30 30-Minute Meals" (2014); Author, "Kid Food: Rachael Ray's Top 30 30-Minute Meals" (2014); Author, "Guy Food: Rachael Ray's Top 30 30-Minute Meals" (2014); Team Captain, Rachael vs. Guy: Celebrity Cook-Off," Food Network (2012-2014); Author, "Week in a Day" (2013); Author, "My Year in Meals" (2012); Author, "The Book of Burger" (2012); Author, "Rachael Ray's Look and Cook" (2010); Author, "Rachael Ray's Book of 10: More Than 300 Recipes to Cook Every Day" (2009); Author, "Rachael Ray's Big Orange Book" (2008); Author, "Yum-O! The Family Cookbook" (2008); Host, "Rachael's Vacation," Food Network (2008); Executive Producer, "Viva Daisy!," Food Network (2008); Author, "Rachael Ray: Just in Time" (2007); Author, "Rachael Ray's Classic 30-Minute Meals: The All-Occasion Cookbook" (2006); Author, "Rachael Ray's Express Lane Meals" (2006); Author, "Rachael Ray 2, 4, 6, 8: Great Meals for Couples or Crowds" (2006); Author, "Rachael Ray's 30-Minute Get Real Meals: Eat Healthy Without Going to Extremes" (2005); Author, "Rachael Ray's 30-Minute Meals for Kids: Cooking Rocks!" (2004); Author, "Rachael Ray's 30-Minute Meals: Cooking 'Round the Clock" (2004); Author, "$40 a Day: Best Eats in Town" (2004); Author, "Cooking Rocks!: Rachael Ray 30-Minute Meals for

Kids" (2004); Author, "Get Togethers: Rachael Ray 30-Minute Meals" (2003); Author, "30-Minute Meals 2" (2003); Author, "Veggie Meals" (2001); Author, "Comfort Foods" (2001); Author, "Rachael Ray's Open House Cookbook" (2000); Author, "30 Minute Meals" (1999) **AW:** People's Choice Award for Favorite TV Cook (2011); Inaugural Honoree, Ride of Fame (2010); Named the "79th Most Powerful Celebrity in the World," Forbes (2009); Daytime Emmy Award for Best Outstanding Talk Show, "Rachael Ray" (2008); Daytime Emmy Award for Best Outstanding Service Show, "30 Minute Meals" (2006); Named One of the "100 Most Influential People," Time Magazine (2006)

RAYMOND, SUSAN GRANT, T: Sculptor **I:** Fine Art **DOB:** 05/23/1943 **PB:** Denver **SC:** CO/USA **PT:** Edwin Hendrie Grant; Mary Belle (McIntyre) Grant **MS:** Divorced **SPN:** Macpherson Raymond Jr. (08/18/1967, Divorced 03/1987) **CH:** Lance Ramsay Raymond (Deceased); Mariah McIntyre Raymond **ED:** MA in Anthropology, University of Colorado (1968); BA in English, Cornell University (1965) **C:** Instructor in Anthropology, United States International University, Steamboat Springs, CO (1971-1973); Contract Artist, Denver Museum of National History (Now Denver Museum of Nature & Science (1976-1977, 1979, 1981, 1983); Curator of Anthropology, Denver Museum of National History (Now Denver Museum of Nature & Science (1968-1971) **CIV:** Board of Directors, Tread of Pioneers Museum, Steamboat Springs, CO (1971-1987); Member, National Ski Patrol (1965-1975) **CW:** Exhibit, National Western Stock Show Art (1994-2006, 2017); Memorial Plaque, Teton Science School, Moose, WY (2018); Memorial Plaque in Murie Building, University of Arkansas Fairbanks, AR (2017); Artist, Honor the Mountain, Watertown, NY (2016); Artist, Fallen Warriors Monument, Fort Drum, NY (2013); Artist, Texas A&M University-Commerce, Texas (2009); Artist, Veterans Plaza, Fort Collins, CO (2008); Artist, Anchor Center for Blind Children, Denver, CO (2007); Artist, Colorado Academy, Denver, CO (2005); Exhibit, Colorado Governor's Invitational Art Show and Sale (2003-2005); Sculptor, Montauk State Park, MO (2003); Artist, Monument for Rigden Farm, Fort Collins, CO (2001); Artist, Monument for Wichita Strykers, KS (2000); Sculptor, Craig Hospital (1984, 1994, 1999); Commissioned Sculpture, Littleton Museum, CO (1999); Donor, Alliance Monument, Hudson Gardens & Event Center, Littleton, CO (1999); Exhibit, Memorial Wall for Kent Denver School (1998); Exhibit, Monument for City of Albuquerque (1998); Sculptor, Saint Joseph's Hospital, SCL Health, Denver, CO (1997); Sculptor, Zoo Atlanta, GA (1997); Sculptor, Ritchie Associates, Wichita, KS (1993-1994, 1996); Exhibit, Sculpture in the Park, Loveland, CO (1993, 1994); Sculptor, Tulsa Zoo, (1994); Sculptor, Ketring Park, Littleton, CO (1994); Sculptor, Denver Zoo (1993); Exhibit, Western Heritage Art Fair, Littleton, CO (1991); Sculptor, 10th Mountain Division Monument, Fort Drum, NY (1991); Sculptor, Stonegate Swimming Hole, Scottsdale, AZ (1989); Sculptor, Monumental Bronze Sculpture, Littleton, CO (1987); Sculptor, Vail, CO (1986); Sculptor, Lakewood Westernaires (1984); Artist, Diorama Figures for Denver Museum of Nature & Science (1971, 1976, 1977, 1979, 1981, 1983); Sculptor, University of Denver (1982); Sculptor, Inspirational Sculpture, Children's Hospital (1977); Sculptor, Sculptures, Routt Memorial Hospital (1977); Numerous Private Memorial Commissions **AW:** Anchor Center Volunteer of the Year Award (2011); Mary Belle Grant Award, Coors Art Show (2005); Named Honorable Member, 10th Mountain Division (1992); Winner, 10th Mountain Division, Monumental Sculpture at Fort Drum, Watertown, NY (1990); Summer Art Award, Steamboat Springs Arts and Humanities (1984); Maurice Hexter Award, National Sculpture Society (1984); Art Castings Award, North American Sculpture Exhibition (1982) **MH:** Albert Nelson Marquis Lifetime Achievement Award; Marquis Who's Who Top Professional **B/I:** Ms. Raymond, "drifted into" her profession. She was influenced during the time she volunteered as a student for the Natural History Museum. Her boss assigned her to do some exhibit work and she had an aptitude for it, and continued. In the process, she studied human anatomy, and progressed so much with her art, she began to accept commissions, and from there it blossomed into a career. **AV:** Skiing; Riding; Backpacking; Tennis; Silversmithing; Photography; Land preservation; Hiking; Spending time with friends; Horses

RAYNOR, PATRICIA HERBERT, T: Special Education Educator, K-12 Mild/Moderate Disabilities **I:** Education/Educational Services **CN:** Numerous School Districts **DOB:** 12/15/1949 **PB:** Oakland **SC:** CA/USA **PT:** Maurice Dooling H.; Audrey Claire (Olsen) H. **MS:** Married **SPN:** Gailen McArthur Raynor (06/23/1979); Steven Arthur Davis (06/20/1968, Divorced 1978) **CH:** David G. (Stepchild); Robin M. (Stepchild); William Tyler Watkins, PhD (Grandson) **ED:** M.S.Ed., Northwest Missouri State University (1989); AB, San Diego State University (1984);AA, San Diego Mesa College (1976) **CT:** Certified K-8 Teacher and K-12 Special Education Teacher, Iowa, Social Studies Endorsement **C:** Special Education Teacher, Essex Community School District, Iowa (1993-Present); Special Education Teacher, Bedford Community School District (1988-1993); Secretary, Transcriptionist, Waubonsie Mental Health Center & Farmer Assistance Project, Clarinda, IA (1985-1987); Administrative Secretary, Centre City Hospital, San Diego, CA (1976-1983); Legal Secretary, Smith, Biggins, Bollman & Mogilner, San Diego, CA (1976-1978); Legal Secretary, John Kosmas & John Greene, San Diego, CA (1974-1976) **CR:** Vice president, Owner, Clarinda Home Medical Inc. (1992-1994); Member, Iowa Behavior Initiative **CIV:** President, Essex Education Association (1998-Present); Co-Leader Clover K-9s 4-H Project Club, Page County, Iowa (1993-Present); Step Aerobics Instructor, Wellness Program, Essex Community school District (1997-1998) **AW:** Permanent Member, Whos Who Honors Edition **MEM:** Council for Exceptional Children, NEA & ISEA (Present); President, Essex Education Association (1998-1999); Vice President, Membership, American Association of University Women (1993-1995); Chairman, Grievance Committee, Bedford Community Education Association (1988-1993); National Education Association; Iowa Education Association **MH:** Albert Nelson Marquis Lifetime Achievement Award; Marquis Who's Who Top Professional **AS:** Ms. Raynor attributes her success to always having had a desire to learn as much as possible about the world and people around her, working with people, and helping students become contributing members of society. **B/I:** Ms. Raynor became involved in her profession because she made up her mind in the third grade, at eight years old, that she was going to be a teacher. She would do what she had to do to accomplish that made up her mind in 3rd grade (8 years old) that she was going to be a teacher and would do what she had to do to accomplish that goal. **AV:** Dog training/showing in conformation, obedience, and agility; Needlework; Sewing; Swimming; Collecting stuffed animals; Heisey crystal; Genealogy; History **PA:** Republican **RE:** Baptist **THT:** Ms. Raynor worked full-time throughout working toward her AB degree, had to complete one year of full-time student teaching at SDSU for 5th year education program and was a graduate assistant at Northwest Missouri State University

while working towards my Master of Science in Education degree. Additionally, taught Sunday School grades 4-8 for five years at Calvary Baptist Church in Clarinda, IA, as well as summer Vacation Bible School.

REA, ROGER, T: Chemistry Educator, Consultant **I:** Education/Educational Services **DOB:** 08/26/1944 **PB:** Newton **SC:** KS/USA **PT:** Harold Hugh Rea; Elinor Lucile (Uhl) Rea **MS:** Married **SPN:** Elizabeth Agnes Woerdeman **ED:** MNS, University of South Dakota (1973); BS, Kansas State University (1966) **CT:** Certified Teacher, State of Nebraska **C:** Chemistry Teacher, Omaha Public Schools (1966-2000) **CR:** Computer Programmer, Merrill Publishing Company (1983-1989); Driving Instructor, Dual Driving School, Omaha, NE (1979); Planner Assistant, Waccamaw Regional Council of Governments (1974); Consultant, Kiewit Corporation (1973) **CIV:** Trustee, Omaha School Employees' Retirement System (1987-1994, 2000-Present); Vice Chairman, First Nebraska Credit Union (1999-2019); Selection Committee, The Nebraska Christa McAuliffe Prize For Courage and Excellence in Education (1987-2012); Vice Chair, NPERS (2007-2008); Treasurer, Educators Credit Union (1978-1999); Delegate, Douglas County Representative Convention (1980-1995); President, Omaha Education Association (1984-1985); Vice President, OEA Senior Citizens Inc. (1983-1984) **CW:** Reviewer, Journal of Chemical Education (1984-1994); Author, Chemistry and Physics Software; Author, Chapter 14, "Points East: Selected Science Sites for Central and Eastern Europe," "Science History: A Traveler's Guide" **AW:** Big Apple Award, Nebraska Association of Retired School Personnel (2014); School Bell Award, Omaha Education Association (2005); Teacher of the Year Award, Nebraska Department of Education (1989); Presidential Award for Excellence, NSTA (1985); Grantee, NSTA (1983); Cooper Foundation Award for Excellence in Teaching (1981) **MEM:** Delegate, National Education Association (1981-Present); President, National Council on Teacher Retirement (2018-2019); Board Member, NIRS (2017-2019); President, Nebraska State Education Association (2008-2017); Trustee, Educators Health Alliance (1997-2015); Board of Directors, Nebraska State Education Association (1993-1999); Chairman, Teacher Welfare and Services Commission (1988-1994); Chairman, Nebraska Professional Practices Commission (1993-1994); Vice Chairman, Nebraska Professional Practices Commission (1992-1993); High School Examination Committee, American Chemical Society (1973-1991); Trustee, Omaha Education Association (1982-1986); President, Omaha Education Association (1984-1985) **MH:** Albert Nelson Marquis Lifetime Achievement Award **B/I:** Mr. Rea became involved in his profession because he was inspired by his mother, an elementary school teacher. Due to his interest in science, he pursued a career in scientific education. **AV:** Playing piano; Gardening; Attending sports car rallies; Taking photographs; Studying astronomy; Traveling **PA:** Republican

REAVES, CHARLES D., T: Investment Company Executive, Lawyer **I:** Law and Legal Services **CN:** Charles Durham Reaves **DOB:** 06/01/1935 **PB:** Florence **SC:** SC/USA **PT:** Howard Meacham Reaves; Kathleen (Durham) Reaves **MS:** Married **SPN:** Gretchen W. (05/04/1963) **CH:** Mark Charles **ED:** MBA, Emory University (1981); LLM, Georgetown University (1966); LLB, University of Alabama (1961); BA, Furman University, Magna Cum Laude (1956) **C:** Special Counsel, Apperson Cromp, PLC (2007-2016); Of Counsel, Armstrong Allen PLLC (2002-2006); Executive Vice President, General Counsel, Chief Compliance Officer, Longleaf Partners Funds (1993-2002); President, Southeastern

Asset Management Funds Trust, Memphis, TN (1986-1993); Senior Vice President of Finance, Secretary, Saunders Leasing System, Inc. (1981-1986); Vice President, Secretary, General Counsel, Saunders Leasing System, Inc., Birmingham, AL (1974-1980); Vice President, Secretary, General Counsel, Fidelity Investment Co. Group, Inc., Washington, DC (1970-1974); Secretary, Associate Counsel, Paul Revere Life Insurance Co., Worcester, MA (1967-1970); Legal Advisory to Chairman, Federal Trade Commission, Washington, DC (1963-1967) **CIV:** Board of Trustees, Memphis Opera (1993-Present); Captain, U.S. Army Reserve (1961-1966) **MIL:** Captain, Judge Advocate Generals Corps, U.S. Army (1961-1963); Lawyer, U.S. Court of Military Appeals, Washington, DC **AW:** Army Commendation Medal, U.S. Army **MEM:** Rotary Club (1981-Present); Director, Economic Club of Memphis (1993-1996, 2004); Director, Financial Executives Institute (1983-1984); President, Alabama Association of Corporate Counsel (1981-1982); American Bar Association; Federal Bar Association; Massachusetts Bar Association; DC Bar Association; Alabama Bar Association; Tennessee Bar Association; Rotary Club; Westwood Country Club, Vienna, VA; Southwind Country Club **BAR:** Tennessee (2003); Washington, DC (1970); Massachusetts (1967); Alabama (1961) **MH:** Albert Nelson Marquis Lifetime Achievement Award **B/I:** Mr. Reaves was always interested in the law.

RECKFORD, JONATHAN THOMAS MORE, T: Nonprofit Organization Administrator **I:** Nonprofit & Philanthropy **CN:** Habitat for Humanity International **DOB:** 08/31/1962 **PB:** Chapel Hill **SC:** NC/USA **PT:** Kenneth Reckford; Mary (Stevens) Reckford **MS:** Married **SPN:** Ashley Louise Richard (06/09/1990) **CH:** Three Children **ED:** Master of Business Administration, Stanford University (1989); Bachelor of Arts in Political Science, University of North Carolina at Chapel Hill (1984) **C:** Chief Executive Officer, Habitat For Humanity International Inc., Americus, GA (2005-Present); Executive Pastor, Christ Presbyterian Church, Edina, MN (2003-2005); President of Stores, The Musicland Group Inc. (2000-2002); President, Mall Stores Division, The Musicland Group Inc. (1999-2000); Senior Vice President, Corporate Planning and Communications, Circuit City Stores Inc. (1997-1999); Vice President, Circuit City Stores Inc. (1995-1997); Director, Business Planning and Development, Disney Design and Development, The Walt Disney Co. (1994-1995); Director, Finance and Business Planning, Disney's America, The Walt Disney Co. (1994); Marketing Manager, Disney Vacation Club, The Walt Disney Co. (1993); Manager, Business Planning, The Walt Disney Co. (1991-1992); Financial Analyst, Goldman, Sachs & Co. (1984-1986); Manager, Service Group, Strategy and Business Development, Host Marriott Corp. **AW:** Henry Luce Foundation Scholarship for Young American Leaders

REDFORD (CHARLES ROBERT REDFORD), ROBERT, T: Actor, Film Director, Producer **I:** Media & Entertainment **DOB:** 08/08/1937 **PB:** Santa Monica **SC:** CA/USA **PT:** Charles Robert Redford; Martha Redford **MS:** Married **SPN:** Sibylle Szaggars (07/11/2009); Lola Van Wagnenen (09/12/1958, Divorced 1985) **CH:** Shauna; James; Amy; Scott (Deceased) **ED:** DFA (Honorary), Brown University (2008); LHD (Honorary), Bard College (1995); LHD (Honorary), University of Colorado (1988); Student, American Academy of Dramatic Arts; Student, Painting, Pratt Institute, Brooklyn, NY; Student, University of Colorado Boulder **C:** Co-Founder, Sundance Film Festival; Founder, Sundance Institute; Founder, Sundance Cinemas; Founder, Sundance Catalog; Founder,

Sundance Channel; Co-Owner, Wildwood Enterprises, Inc.; Owner, Sundance Mountain Resort; Former Owner, Restaurant, Zoom **CIV:** Advocate, Environmentalism, Native American Rights, LGBT Rights, Arts; Advocate, Political Action Committee of the Directors Guild of America **CW:** Actor, "Omniboat: A Fast Boat Fantasia" (2020); Actor, "Avengers: Endgame" (2019); Narrator, "Buttons, A New Musical Film" (2018); Actor, "The Old Man & the Gun" (2018); Actor, "Our Souls at Night" (2018); Narrator, "Arena" (2017); Actor, "The Discovery" (2017); Actor, "Pete's Dragon" (2016); Actor, "One More Chance" (2016); Actor, "Truth" (2015); Voice Actor, "Nature Is Speaking" (2014); Narrator, "The Glove" (2014); Actor, "Captain America: The Winter Soldier" (2014); Actor, "Making a Scene" (2014); Director, "Cathedrals of Culture" (2014); Actor, "All Is Lost" (2013); Actor, Director, "The Company You Keep" (2012); Director, "The Conspirator" (2010); Actor, Director, "Lions for Lambs" (2007); Voice Actor, "Charlotte's Web" (2006); Actor, "Unfinished Life" (2005); Actor, "The Clearing" (2004); Actor, "Spy Game" (2001); Actor, "The Last Castle" (2001); Director, "The Legend of Bagger Vance" (2000); Actor, "The Horse Whisperer" (1998); Actor, Director, "The Horse Whisperer" (1998); Actor, "Up Close & Personal" (1996); Director, "Quiz Show" (1994); Actor, "Indecent Proposal" (1993); Narrator, Director, "A River Runs Through It" (1992); Actor, "Sneakers" (1992); Actor, "Havana" (1990); Director, "The Milagro Beanfield War" (1988); Actor, "Legal Eagles" (1986); Actor, "Out of Africa" (1985); Actor, "The Natural" (1984); Director, "Ordinary People" (1980); Actor, "Brubaker" (1980); Actor, "The Electric Horseman" (1979); Actor, "A Bridge Too Far" (1977); Narrator, "Nova" (1977); Actor, "All the President's Men" (1976); Actor, "Three Days of the Condor" (1975); Actor, "The Great Waldo Pepper" (1975); Actor, "The Great Gatsby" (1974); Actor, "The Sting" (1973); Actor, "The Way We Were" (1973); Actor, "The Candidate" (1972); Actor, "Jeremiah Johnson" (1972); Actor, "The Hot Rock" (1972); Actor, "The Hot Rock" (1972); Actor, "Little Fauss and Big Halsy" (1970); Actor, "Tell Them Willie Boy Is Here" (1969); Actor, "Downhill Racer" (1969); Actor, "Butch Cassidy and the Sundance Kid" (1969); Actor, "This Property Is Condemned" (1966); Actor, "The Chase" (1966); Actor, "Inside Daisy Clover" (1965); Actor, "Situation Hopeless – But Not Serious" (1965); Actor, "The Defenders" (1964); Actor, "The Virginian" (1963); Actor, "Breaking Point" (1963); Actor, "The Dick Powell Theatre" (1963); Actor, "The Alfred Hitchcock Hour" (1963, 1962); Actor, "The Untouchables" (1963); Actor, Theater, "Barefoot in the Park" (1963); Actor, "Alcoa Premiere" (1962); Actor, "Dr. Kildare" (1962); Actor, "War Hunt" (1962); Actor, "The Twilight Zone" (1962); Actor, "Alfred Hitchcock Presents" (1961); Actor, "The New Breed" (1961); Actor, "Bus Stop" (1961); Actor, "Route 66" (1961); Actor, "Whispering Smith" (1961); Actor, "The Americans" (1961); Actor, "Naked City" (1961); Actor, "Play of the Week" (1961, 1960); Actor, Theater, "Sunday in New York" (1961); Actor, "Our American Heritage" (1960); Actor, "The Iceman Cometh" (1960); Actor, "Perry Mason" (1960); Actor, "Tate" (1960); Actor, "Moment of Fear" (1960); Actor, "Playhouse 90" (1960); Actor, "The Deputy" (1960); Actor, "Tall Story" (1960); Actor, "Rescue 8" (1960); Actor, "Captain Brassbound's Conversion" (1960); Actor, "Maverick" (1960); Actor, Theater, "The Highest Tree" (1959); Actor, Theater, "Tall Story" (1959); Producer, Executive Producer, Numerous Films, Documentaries, and TV Series **AW:** Honorary César 44th César Awards (2019); Golden Lion for Lifetime Achievement, Venice Film Festival (2017); Presidential Medal of Freedom, President Barack Obama (2016); Tribute Award, Gotham Awards (2015); Named One of "The 100 Most Influential People in the World," TIME Magazine (2014); Jury Prize, Best Director, "The Conspirator," Global Nonviolent Film Festival (2012); Career Achievement Award, AARP Movies for Grownups Awards (2011); The Dorothy and Lillian Gish Prize (2008); Honoree, Kennedy Center Honors (2005); Honorary Award, Academy Awards (2002); Freedom in Film Award, Nashville Film Festival (2001); National Medal of Arts (1996); Cecil B. DeMille Award, Golden Globes (1994); Audubon Medal, National Audubon Society (1989); Oscar for Best Director, "Ordinary People," Academy Awards (1981); DGA Award for Outstanding Directorial Achievement in Motion Pictures, "Ordinary People," Directors Guild of America (1980); Golden Globe for Best Director - Motion Picture, "Ordinary People," Golden Globes (1980); Henrietta Award, World Film Favorite - Male, Golden Globes (1978); Henrietta Award, World Film Favorite - Male, Golden Globes (1977); Henrietta Award, World Film Favorite - Male, Golden Globes (1975); Best Actor, "Butch Cassidy and the Sundance Kid," "Tell Them Willie Boy Is Here," "Downhill Racer," BAFTA Awards (1971); Man of the Year, Hasty Pudding Theatricals (1970); Golden Globe for Most Promising Newcomer - Male, "Inside Daisy Clover," Golden Globes (1966); Named Officer of French Ordre des Arts et des Lettres; Numerous Other Awards and Accolades **MEM:** Fellow, American Academy Arts & Sciences; Advisory Committee, Land Trust of Napa County; Kappa Sigma, University of Colorado Boulder

REDMAN, ANN, T: President **I:** Education/Educational Services **CN:** Hispanic Organization for Progress and Education **PB:** Ledoux **SC:** NM/USA **PT:** Martin Esquibel; Gertrude Garcia Esquibel **MS:** Married **SPN:** Ralph Redman (08/1957) **CH:** Steve; Rob; Scott; Michael **ED:** Graduate Coursework, Leadership Wyoming (2013); Graduate Coursework, Parks Business College, Denver, CO (1956); Diploma, St. Mary's Catholic School, Cheyenne, WY (1954); Graduate Coursework, Our Lady of Sorrows Catholic Grade School, Las Vegas, NM (1950) **C:** Governor Dave Freudenthal's Transition Team (2002); State Planning Division, State of Wyoming Office of the Governor (1975-1995); State of Wyoming Personnel Division (1973-1975); Army and Air Force Exchange Service, Limestone Air Force Base (1959-1961); Davis Construction Company, Greenville, SC (1957-1958); Culbertson Law Firm, Greenville, SC (1957); Reibschied & Machol, Attorneys, Denver, CO (1955-1957); State Historian, Lola Homsher, Wyoming State Archives (1954-1955); Sky Trail Restaurant, Cheyenne, WY (1950-1955); Valencia Restaurant, Cheyenne, WY (1950) **CR:** Appointed Member, Industrial Siting Council, Governor Jim Geringer of Wyoming (1997); Appointed Head, State's Centennial Celebration (1990); Founder, Latina Youth Conference; Grants Review Coordinator, Office of Governor Ed Herschler; International Trade Assistant and Protocol Officer, Governor Mike Sullivan; Appointed Head, 50-50 QVC Tour, USS Wyoming Committee, Governor Jim Geringer of Wyoming; Two-Year Residency, Reibscheid and Machol, Denver, CO **CIV:** Founder, Honorary Chair, Wyoming Latina Youth Conference (2016-Present); Appointed Member, City of Cheyenne's Personnel Commission, Mayor Rick Kaysen (2009); Appointed Member, Wyoming Abraham Lincoln Bicentennial Commission, Governor Dave Freudenthal (2007); Governor's Task Force, U.S. Census (2000); Honorary Board Member, Foster Grandparents; Trustee, Wyoming Women's Foundation; Laramie County Community College Foundation Board; Former Board of Trustees, Seton Catholic High School; Former Board Member, United Way of Laramie County; Church Council, Holy Family and Cathedral of St. Mary, Cheyenne, WY; Cinco de Mayo Committee, Cheyenne, WY; Founding Member, Wyoming Latina/Latino Coalition; Founding Member, Cheyenne Hispanic Festival; Advisory Council, Foster Grandparent Program; Board of Trustees, PODER Academy; President, St. Mary's/Seton Catholic High School Alumni Association; St. Mary's School Foundation; President, Hispanic Organization for Progress and Education (HOPE); Trustee, Board Member, Professional Development Site Committee, University of Wyoming; Wyoming's Silent Witness Initiative; Selection Committee, Dick Cheney USS Wyoming Scholarship, Curt Kaiser Scholarship, HOPE Scholarship Committee; St. Mary's Cathedral Parish Council; Holy Family Youth Minister, Holy Family Parish Council, F.E. Warren Air Force; Curt Kaiser Scholarship Committee; Blue Federal Credit Union Foundation **AW:** Woman of Influence Lifetime Achievement Award, Wyoming Business Report (2017); Wyoming Council for Women's Issues (2016); MALCS Lifetime Achievement Award (2016); Woman of Distinction Award, Wyoming Student Leaders, University of Wyoming (2009); Wyoming Woman of Distinction Award (2009); Jesse Vialpando Spirit & Service Award, Cesar Chavez Banquet, Esperanza Por La Vida Marginal, University of Wyoming (2008); Volunteer of the Year, Cinco de Mayo Committee (2007); Athena Award, Greater Cheyenne Chamber of Commerce (2001); Honorary Queen, Cinco de Mayo Royalty Committee (2001); Governor's Service & Volunteer Award (2000); J.C. Penney Golden Rule Award (1999); Recognition of Dedicated Service, Hispanic Organization for Progress and Education (HOPE) (1998); Minority Advocate of the Year, Small Business Administration (1996); Award of Gratitude, Foster Grandparent Program (1995); SOMOS/HOPE Recognition for Service to Community (1994) **MEM:** NCO Wives Club, Aviano Air Force Base, Italy; Squadron Wives Club; Catholic Women of the Chapel, Aviano Air Force Base, Italy **B/I:** Once Ms. Redman noticed that people of color had very little voice in American society, she decided to take action to change this. She began her journey by joining many community activist organizations, all of which led to her current career today. **THT:** Ms. Redman's wish is to leave the world in a better state than it was when she entered it.

REED, DAVID GEORGE, T: Entrepreneur **I:** Business Management/Business Services **DOB:** 07/19/1945 **PB:** Alameda **SC:** CA/USA **PT:** David Francis Reed; Anna Amelia Vangeline (Paulson) Reed **MS:** Widower **SPN:** Michele Ann Hock (06/28/1989, Deceased 2017); Marianne Louise Watson (04/07/1971, Divorced 1975) **CH:** Casey Christine Michele **ED:** MBA in Marketing, San Francisco State University, San Francisco, CA (1969); BA in Design and Industry, San Francisco State University, San Francisco, CA (1967); AA in Business Administration, Diablo Valley College, Pleasant Hill, CA (1965) **CT:** Certified Member, Professional Ski Instructors of America (2002); Certified Reserve Police Officer, Los Medanos College, Pittsburg, CA (1977) **C:** Owner, Dave Reed & Co. Water Ski School, White Water Rafting, Chiloquin, OR (1987-Present); Owner, Dave Reed & Co., Design, Market, Manufacturing Contender boats, Chiloquin, OR (1976-Present); Manufacturing Engineer, Beckman Instruments, San Ramon, CA (1984-1990); Manufacturing Engineer, Systron Donner, Concord, CA (1982-1984); Management Consultant, Thomas-Ross Associates, Mercer Island, WA (1972-1982); Plant Manager, Bonner Packing, Morgan Hill, CA (1981); Management Consultant, Management Scheduling Systems, Houston, TX (1974-1976); Owner, Dave Reed's Texaco, Concord,

CA (1973-1976); Management Consultant, Controlled Interval Scheduling, Rolling Hills Estates, CA (1972-1973); Owner, Western Furs, Ltd., Walnut Creek, CA (1963-1972) **CR:** Design and Supply, Solar Electric Power System (1994-Present); Financial Manager, Japanese Investors, Dave Reed & Co., Chiloquin, OR (1986-Present); Lecturer, Management Seminars (1982-Present); Lecturer, Wildlife Management, Dave Reed & Co., Chiloquin, OR (1965-Present); Part-Time Snow Ski Instructor, Willamette Path (2003-2007); Factory Representative, Goode Ski Technologies, Space Age Carbon Fiber Snow Skis (2003-2007); Coach, Japanese Water Ski Team, Bluff Water Ski Club, Tokyo, Japan (1984) **CIV:** Reserve Deputy Sheriff, Contra Costa County Sheriff's Department, Martinez, CA (1977-1980) **MIL:** U.S. Army, Vietnam (1969-1971) **AW:** Champion, California State Water Ski (1977, 1986); Gold Medal, International Freestyle Wrestling Senior Olympics, Fullerton, CA (1983); Western Region Water Ski Champion (1977); Silver Medal, National Water Ski Championships (1977); Combat Soldier of the Month, 11th Aviation Battalion and 74th Aviation Company (1971) **MEM:** President, Klamath Solar Association, Inc. (2002-Present); Chairman, Bay Area Tournament Association (1968-Present); Board of Directors, Diablo Water Ski Club (1968-Present); American Water Ski Association **MH:** Albert Nelson Marquis Lifetime Achievement Award; Marquis Who's Who Top Professional **B/I:** Mr. Reed became involved in his profession because he feels he was born for the role; he is the second in his family to strike out on his own, the first being his grandfather. At a woodworking shop in school, he made gun racks for his father and many others, and, by high school, he was determined to be self-employed. **AV:** Water-skiing; Skiing; Surfing; Camping; Fly-fishing **PA:** Republican

REED, JEFFREY, "JEFF" GARTH, PHD, T: Organizational Psychologist (Retired); Educator (Retired) **I:** Health, Wellness and Fitness **DOB:** 03/28/1948 **PB:** Black Creek **SC:** WI/USA **PT:** George Edward Reed; Norma Groeling (Renneisen) Reed **MS:** Married **SPN:** Sylvia F. Kollasch (04/18/1981) **CH:** Daniel; Benjamin **ED:** PhD in Psychology, Kansas State University (1979); MA in Psychology, Towson University (1976); MLS in Library and Information Science, University of Maryland (1971); BA in Political Science, Muskingum College (Now Muskingum University) (1970) **CT:** PMP Certification, Project Management Association (1998-2008); Certificate in Business, New York University (1983); Certificate in Program Evaluation, University of Massachusetts (1977) **C:** Professor, Management, Marian College, Fond du Lac, WI (1998-2019); Dean, Marian University Byrum School of Business, Fond du Lac, WI (2008-2017); Director, Management Program, Marian College (Now Marian University), Fond du Lac, WI (1998-2008); Associate Professor, Management, Marian College (Now Marian University), Fond du Lac, WI (1998-2006); Interim Director, International Research, Marian College (Now Marian University), Fond du Lac, WI (2001-2002); Planning and Process Manager, Xerox Corporation (1996-1998); Manager, Scanning Requirements Strategies and Planning, Xerox Corporation (1995-1996); Process and Planning Manager, Xerox Corporation (1993-1994); Electronics and System Software Program Manager, Xerox Corporation (1991-1992); User Interface Software Design Manager, Xerox Corporation (1989-1990); User Interface Developer, Xerox Corporation, Webster, NY (1985-1988); Organizational Consultant, Rochester, NY (1983-1985); Assistant Professor, Industrial and Organizational Psychology, State University of New York, Geneseo, NY (1979-1983); Educational Researcher, Kansas State University, Manhattan,

KS (1975-1979); Research Assistant, Towson University, Baltimore, MD (1974-1975); Assistant, Reference Librarian, Bucknell University, Lewisburg, PA (1971-1973) **CR:** Interim Chair, Business Administration, Marian College (Now Marian University) (2007-2008); Honors Program Director, Marian College (Now Marian University) (2005-2007); Visiting Professor, Harlaxton College, Grantham, England, United Kingdom (2006); Co-chair, Strategic Planning, Marian College (Now Marian University) (2002-2006); Vice President, President, Faculty Senate, Marian College (Now Marian University) (2001-2003); Careers in Business, New York University (1983) **CIV:** Assistant Rotary Coordinator, Rotary International , Region 36 (2020-2021); District Governor, District 6270, Rotary International (2017-2018); Board of Directors, The Arc Fund du Lac (2004-2008); Diversity Director, Wisconsin State Council, Society for Human Resource Management (SHRM) (2003-2005); Co-executive Director, Marian College (Now Marian University) Center of Spirituality and Leadership (2003-2006); Chair, Board of Directors, Marian College (Now Marian University) Coffee House (1998-2001); Chair, Personnel Committee, Cobblestone School, Rochester, NY (1993-1998); Board Secretary, Webster Montessori School, Monroe County, NY (1987-1990); Trustee, Cobblestone School, Rochester, NY **CW:** Co-author, "Using Reference Databases," In "Handbook of Research Synthesis and Meta-Analysis" (2009); Co-author, "Bibliographic Research" In "Psychology Research Handbook" (2005); Co-author, "Preparing Undergraduate Students for Careers in Business" (1987); Author, Book, "Library Use: Handbook for Psychology" (1983); Author, "Dropping a College Course," Journal of Educational Psychology (1981); Co-author, "Development and Validation of a Set of University Involvement Scales," Measurement and Evaluation in Guidance (1980); Contributor, 15 Articles and Chapters; Contributor, 15 Conference Papers, Presentations **AW:** Named to Sigma Beta Delta (2008); Alliant Energy James R. Underkofler Award for Teaching Excellence (2003); Xerox Teamwork Award (1987, 1993, 1997); Xerox Production Systems Excellence Award (1995); Xerox Patent Award (1992); Xerox Special Merit Award (1989, 1991); Named, Outstanding Young Men of America (1984); National Institute of Mental Health Evaluation Research Institute Fellowship (1977); Siegel Memorial Scholarship in Applied Psychology, Towson University (1975); Named to Psi Chi, The International Honor Society in Psychology (1974); Named to Beta Phi Mu - The International Library and Information Studies Honor Society (1971); "Students to Dallas" Award, American Library Association (1971) **MEM:** President, Fond du Lac Morning Rotary Club (2009-2010); Board of Directors, Fond du Lac Area Human Resource Association (2001-2009); Secretary, Fond du Lac Morning Rotary Club (2006-2007); President, Board of Directors, Fond du Lac Area Human Resource Association (2005-2006); President, Secretary, Pittsford New York Homeowners' Association (1991-1994); American Psychological Association **MH:** Albert Nelson Marquis Lifetime Achievement Award; Marquis Who's Who Top Professional; Marquis Who's Who Humanitarian Award **B/I:** Dr. Reed became involved in his profession to follow in the footsteps of his mother. In addition, he got involved with Rotary to be of service, something he believes that he got from his parents; it has always been there. His mother was a teacher, his father was a minister, and they were helping in the same way when he was growing up. They had missionaries that came to visit them at their house from other countries, and he found it interesting, rewarding, neat and fun to meet and help people. Dr. Reed's father was a chaplain at a state

mental hospital. He started out as a parish minister at the Methodist church for about 20 years, went back for additional training, and became a hospital chaplain. His mother was a teacher for many years.

REED, JOHN, "JACK" FRANCIS, T: U.S. Senator **I:** Government Administration/Government Relations/Government Services **DOB:** 11/12/1949 **PB:** Cranston **SC:** RI/USA **PT:** Joseph Anthony Reed; Mary Louise (Monahan) Reed **MS:** Married **SPN:** Julia Hart (08/16/2005) **CH:** Emily **ED:** JD, Harvard Law School, Cum Laude (1982); MA in Public Policy, Harvard University (1973); BS in Engineering, United States Military Academy at West Point (1971) **C:** Ranking Member, Senate Committee on Armed Services (2015-Present); U.S. Senator, State of Rhode Island (1997-Present); U.S. Representative, Rhode Island's Second Congressional District, United States Congress, Washington, DC (1991-1997); Member, Rhode Island State Senate (1984-1990); Associate, Edwards & Angell, Providence, RI (1983-1989); Associate, Sutherland, Asbill & Brennan, Washington, DC (1982-1983); Assistant Professor, United States Military Academy, West Point, NY (1977-1979) **MIL:** With, 82nd Airborne Division, U.S. Army (1973-1977); With, U.S. Army (1967-1979) **CW:** Contributing Author, "American National Security" (1981) **AW:** Joan Gallagher Legislative Award, Massachusetts School Library Media Association (2003); Congressional Leadership Award, Coalition to Stop Gun Violence and Education Fund to Stop Gun Violence (2002); National Excellence in Public Health Award, Association of State and Territorial Health Officials (2002); Excellence in Immunization Award, National Partnership for Immunization (2001); Excellence in Public Service Award, American Academy of Pediatrics (1998); Crystal Apple Award, American Association of School Librarians, ALA (1994); John Fogarty Award (1990); Distinguished Service Award, AARP (1989); Distinguished Legislative Award, United Way of Southeastern New England (1988) **MEM:** American Bar Association; Rhode Island Bar Association; The District of Columbia Bar; Environmental and Energy Study Institute; The Phi Kappa Phi Society **BAR:** Rhode Island Bar Association (1983); The District of Columbia Bar (1982) **AV:** Reading; Hiking **PA:** Democrat **RE:** Roman Catholic

REED, JONATHAN, T: Founder, Chief Executive Officer **I:** Media & Entertainment **CN:** CS Global **ED:** BA in Economics, Swarthmore College, Swarthmore PA (1999) **C:** Co-founder, Chief Executive Officer, Jeffrey Dodd, New York, NY (2014-Present); Chief Executive Officer, SPEC Entertainment, CS Global, New York, NY (2004-Present); Production Director, Kevin Krier & Associates, New York, NY (1999-2004); Managing Director, Stephen Rivers & Associates, Los Angeles, CA (1996-1999) **CR:** Founder, CS Global, New York, NY (2004-Present) **MH:** Marquis Who's Who Top Professional **AS:** Mr. Reed attributes his success to passionate dedication and hard work. He additionally credits having a great business acumen as well as understanding the creative side of the business. **B/I:** Mr. Reed became involved in his profession after he began working as a college intern for Stephen Rivers & Associates. After graduating, he received a position at the company. That was his first exposure to brand communication and event production. He continued working with high end fashion brands and learning the business; five years later, he decided to open his own firm. **THT:** CS Global's formidable client roster includes AERIN, Amazon Fashion, Brooks Brothers, CFDA, Diane von Furstenberg, Estée Lauder, HBO, Hugo Boss, La Mer, La Perla, MoMA, Omega, Phillips, Tag Heuer, Tiffany & Co., TOM FORD, Veuve Clicquot, and Zac Posen. The company works with celebrated figures such as Jennifer Lopez, Beyoncé, Madonna, Nicki Minaj, Kate Hudson, Gwyneth Paltrow, Kim Kardashian, Katie Holmes, Kanye West, and Jay-Z.

REED, THOMAS, "TOM" W. II, T: U.S. Representative, Lawyer **I:** Government Administration/Government Relations/Government Services **DOB:** 11/18/1971 **PB:** Joliet **SC:** IL/USA **PT:** Tom Reed; Betty (Barr) Reed **MS:** Married **SPN:** Jean Reed (1996) **CH:** Autumn; Will **ED:** JD, Petit College of Law, Ohio Northern University (1996); BA in Political Science, Alfred University (1993) **C:** U.S. Representative, New York's 23rd Congressional District, United States Congress, Washington, DC (2013-Present); Member, Means and Ways Committee, U.S. House of Representatives (2011-Present); Member, House Committee on Rules (2011); Member, U.S. Representative, New York's 29th Congressional District, United States Congress, Washington, DC (2010-2013); Member, The House Committee on Transportation and Infrastructure (2010-2011); Member, U.S. House Committee On The Judiciary (2010-2011); Mayor, City of Corning, NY (2008-2009); Private Practice, Law Office of Thomas W. Reed, Corning, NY (1999-2014); Attorney, Litigation Department, Gallo & Iacovangelo, LLP., Rochester, NY (1997-1999) **BAR:** New York State Bar Association (1997) **PA:** Republican **RE:** Roman Catholic

REEVES, KEANU CHARLES, T: Actor **I:** Media & Entertainment **DOB:** 09/02/1964 **PB:** Beirut **SC:** Lebanon **PT:** Samuel Nowlin Reeves Jr.; Patricia (Bond) Taylor; Paul Aaron (Stepfather) **MS:** Single **CR:** Founder, X Artists' Books (XAB); Co-Founder, Company Films; Co-Founder, Arch Motorcycle Company **CIV:** Founder, Private Cancer Foundation; Volunteer, Stand up to Cancer Telethon **CW:** Voice Actor, "Cyberpunk 2077" (2020); Cameo, "The SpongeBob Movie: Sponge on the Run" (2020); Actor, "Bill & Ted Face the Music" (2020); Actor, "John Wick: Chapter 3 - Parabellum" (2019); Appearance, "Always Be My Maybe" (2019); Voice Actor, "Toy Story 4" (2019); Executive Producer, "Already Gone" (2019); Cameo, "Between Two Ferns: The Movie" (2019); Producer, Actor, "Siberia" (2018); Actor, "Destination Wedding" (2018); Producer, Actor, "Replicas" (2018); Actor, "Swedish Dicks" (2016-2018); Actor, "To the Bone" (2017); Actor, "John Wick: Chapter 2" (2017); Cameo, "A Happening of Monumental Proportions" (2017); Cameo, "SPF-18" (2017); Producer, Actor, "Exposed" (2016); Voice Cameo, "Keanu" (2016); Actor, "The Neon Demon" (2016); Actor, "The Bad Batch" (2016); Actor, "The Whole Truth" (2016); Executive Producer, Actor, "Knock Knock" (2015); Narrator, Documentary, "Deep Web" (2015); Narrator, Documentary, "Mifune: The Last Samurai" (2015); Author, "Shadows: A Collaborative Project by Alexandra Grant and Keanu Reeves" (2014); Actor, "John Wick" (2014); Director, Actor, "Man of Tai Chi" (2013); Actor, "47 Ronin" (2013); Producer, Appearance, Documentary, "Side by Side" (2012); Actor, "Generation Um..." (2012); Author, "Ode to Happiness" (2011); Actor, "Henry's Crime" (2010); Actor, "The Private Lives of Pippa Lee" (2009); Cameo, "Bollywood Hero" (2009); Actor, "Street Kings" (2008); Actor, "The Day the Earth Stood Still" (2008); Actor, "A Scanner Darkly" (2006); Actor, "The Lake House" (2006); Narrator, Documentary, "The Great Warning" (2006); Actor, "Constantine" (2005); Actor, "Thumbsucker" (2005); Cameo, "Ellie Parker" (2005); Actor, "The Matrix Reloaded" (2003); Actor, "The Animatrix" (2003); Actor, "The Matrix Revolutions" (2003); Actor, "Something's Gotta Give" (2003); Voice Actor, Video Game, "Enter the Matrix"

(2003); Actor, "Sweet November" (2001); Actor, "Hardball" (2001); Actor, "The Replacements" (2000); Actor, "The Watcher" (2000); Actor, "The Gift" (2000); Actor, "The Matrix" (1999); Cameo, "Me and Will" (1999); Actor, "The Last Time I Committed Suicide" (1997); Actor, "The Devil's Advocate" (1997); Actor, "Chain Reaction" (1996); Actor, "Feeling Minnesota" (1996); Actor, "Johnny Mnemonic" (1995); Actor, "A Walk in the Clouds" (1995); Actor, "Speed" (1994); Actor, "Much Ado About Nothing" (1993); Actor, "Even Cowgirls Get the Blues" (1993); Cameo, "Freaked" (1993); Actor, "Little Buddha" (1993); Actor, "Bram Stoker's Dracula" (1992); Actor, "Point Break" (1991); Actor, "Bill & Ted's Bogus Journey" (1991); Actor, "My Own Private Idaho" (1991); Voice Actor, "Bill & Ted's Excellent Adventures" (1990); Actor, TV Film, "Life Under Water" (1989); Guest Appearance, "The Tracey Ullman Show" (1989); Actor, "Parenthood" (1989); Actor, "The Night Before" (1988); Actor, "Permanent Record" (1988); Actor, "The Prince of Pennsylvania" (1988); Actor, "Dangerous Liaisons" (1988); Guest Appearance, "Trying Times" (1987); Guest Appearance, "The Disney Sunday Movie" (1986); Actor, TV Film, "Babes in Toyland" (1986); Actor, TV Film, "Act of Vengeance" (1986); Actor, TV Film, "Brotherhood of Justice" (1986); Actor, TV Film, "Under the Influence" (1986); Actor, "Youngblood" (1986); Actor, "Flying" (1986); Actor, "River's Edge" (1986); Actor, Short Film, "One Step Away" (1985); Actor, TV Film, "Letting Go" (1985); Guest Appearance, "Night Heat" (1985); Appearance, "Fast Food" (1985); Appearance, "Hangin' In" (1984) **AW:** Favorite Celebrity of the Year, Golden Schmoes Awards (2019); CinemaCon Vanguard Award (2016); Best Actor - International, Bambi Awards (2008); Movies - Choice Liplock, Teen Choice Awards (2006); Star, Hollywood Walk of Fame (2005); Taurus Honorary Award, World Stunt Awards (2004); Favorite Actor - Action/Science Fiction, Blockbuster Entertainment Awards (2000); MTV Movie Awards for Best Fight and Best Male Performance (2000); MTV Movie Award for Best Performance in a Movie (2000); Best Actor in a Leading Role, Csapnivalo Awards (2000); Co-Recipient, MTV Movie Award for Best On-Screen Duo (1995); Best Actor (Schauspieler), Bravo Otto (1994); Most Desirable Male, MTV Movie Awards (1992)

REGENBOGEN, ADAM ESQ., T: Judge **I:** Law and Legal Services **DOB:** 06/12/1947 **PB:** Steyer **SC:** Austria **PT:** William Regenbogen; Pauline (Feuerstein) Regenbogen **MS:** Married **SPN:** Helen Busuttil Drwal (04/20/1996); Paula Ruth Rothenberg (06/27/1970, Divorced 10/1992) **CH:** Stacy; Candice; Jason (Stepson) **ED:** JD, Temple University (1980); MSW, University of Pennsylvania (1972); BA, Temple University (1969) **C:** Judge, Workers' Compensation Board, NY (1998-Present); Workers' Compensation Law Judge, Binghamton District and Albany District, NY (1998-Present); Judge, Assigned to World Trade Center 9/11 Cases (2002); Conciliator, Acting Judge, Workers' Compensation Board, NY (1992-1998); Private Practice, NY (1983-1998); Director of Quality Assurance, New York State Office of Mental Health, Willard, NY (1987-1991); Quality Assurance Director, Northport VA Medical Center, Northport, NY (1980-1987); Supervisor, Northport VA Medical Center, Northport, NY (1978-1980); Social Worker, Coatesville Veterans Affairs Medical Center, Coatesville, PA (1974-1978) **CIV:** Organizer/Incorporator, Ithaca Reform Temple (URJ), NY (1992); Organizer, Parents Without Partners, Ithaca, NY (1992) **AW:** Pro Bono Service Award, Suffolk County Bar Association (1986) **BAR:** New York (1983) **MH:** Albert Nelson Marquis Lifetime Achievement Award

REICH, STEVE, T: Composer **I:** Media & Entertainment **DOB:** 10/3/1936 **PB:** New York **SC:** NY/USA **PT:** Leonard Reich; June Sillman **MS:** Married **SPN:** Beryl Korot **CH:** Ezra; Michael **ED:** Honorary Doctorate, California Institute of the Arts (2000); Student, Biblical Cantillation, Israel (1976-1977); Student, Drumming, Ghana (1970); Master of Arts in Composition, Mills College, Oakland, CA (1963); Student, William Bergsma and Vincent Persichetti, Juilliard School (1958-1961); Student, Composition, Hall Overton (1957-1958); Bachelor of Arts in Philosophy, Cornell University (1957); Student, Drums, Rolnd Kohloff **C:** International Composer (1971-Present); Organizer, Ensemble, Steve Reich and Musicians (1966); Recordings with Various Companies, including, Columbia Records, Deutsche Grammophon, Nonesuch, Disques Shandar, Hungaraton, Angel, ECM, Phillips, Virgin Classics, and Argo **CR:** Regents Lecturer, University of California Berkeley (2000) **CW:** Composer, Performer, Album, "Pulse / Quartet" (2018); Composer, Performer, Album, "Runner" (2016); Composer, Performer, Album, "Pulse" (2015); Composer, Performer, Album, "Quartet" (2013); Composer, Performer, Album, "Radio Rewrite" (2012); Composer, Performer, Album, "Finishing the Hat" (2011); Composer, Performer, Album, "WTC 9/11" (2010); Composer, Performer, Album, "Mallet Quartet" (2009); Composer, Performer, Album, "2x5" (2008); Composer, Performer, Album, "Double Sextet" (2007); Composer, Performer, Album, "Daniel Variations" (2006); Composer, Performer, Album, "Variations for Vibes, Pianos and Strings" (2005); Composer, Performer, Album, "You Are" (2004); Composer, Performer, Album, "Cello Counterpoint" (2003); Composer, Performer, Album, "Drumming" (2003); Composer, Performer, Album, "Dance Patterns" (2002); Composer, Performer, Album, "Three Tales" (2002); Author, Book, "Writings on Music, 1965-2000" (2002); Author, "Writings on Music" (2002); Commissioned Composer, Lincoln Center Festival, New York, NY (1999); Composer, Performer, Album, "Triple Quartet" (1999); Composer, Performer, Album, "Proverb" (1996); Composer, Performer, Album, "City Life" (1995); Recordings, "Steve Reich Works" (1965-1995); Composer, Performer, Album, "The Cave" (1994); Commissioned Composer, Brooklyn Academy Music, Next Wave Festival (1993); Commissioned Composer, Kronos Quartet (1988); Composer, Performer, Album, "Different Trains" (1988); Composer, Performer, Album, "Electric Counterpoint" (1987); Composer, Performer, Album, "The Four Sections" (1987); Commissioned Composer, Brooklyn Academy Music (1987); Commissioned Composer, St. Louis Sympony (1987); Composer, Performer, Album, "Sextet" (1986); Composer, Performer, Album, "Six Marimbas" (1986); Commissioned Composer, Fromm Music Foundation (1985); Commissioned Composer, Richard Stoltzman (1985); Commissioned Composer, West German Radio, Cologne (1984); Composer, Performer, Album, "The Desert Music" (1984); Composer, Performer, Album, "Tehillim" (1982); Commissioned Composer, Rothko Chapel (1981); Commissioned Composer, San Francisco Symphony (1980); Composer, Performer, Album, "Octet" (1980); Composer, Performer, Album, "Music for a Large Ensemble" (1980); Commissioned Composer, Radio Frankfurt (1979); Commissioned Composer, Holland Festival (1978); Composer, Performer, Album, "Music for Eighteen Musicians" (1978); Author, "Writings About Music" (1974); Author, Book, "Writings About Music" (1974); Composer, Performer, Album, "Six Pianos" (1973); Composer, Performer, Album, "Four Organs" (1973); Composer, Performer, Album, "Music for Mallet Instruments, Voices, and Organ" (1973); Composer, Performer, Album, "Drumming" (1971); Composer, Performer, Album, "Four Organs" (1970); Composer, Performer, Album, "Phase Patterns" (1970); Composer, Performer, Album, "It's Gonna Rain" (1969); Composer, Performer, Album, "Violin Phase" (1969); Composer, Performer, Album, "Come Out" (1967); Composer, Vermont Counterpoint; Composer, Variations for Winds; Composer, Strings and Keyboards; Composer, Eight Lines for Chamber Orchestra; Composer, Piano Phase; Composer, Clapping Music; Composer, Pendulum Music; Composer, Music for Pieces of Wood; Composer, Nagoya Marimbas; Commissioned Composer, with Beryl Korot, Vienna Festival; Commissioned Composer, Holland Festival; Commissioned Composer, Festival d'Automne à Paris; Commissioned Composer, Theatre de la Monnaie, Brussels; Commissioned Composer, Hebbel Theatre, Berlin; Commissioned Composer, South Bank Centre/Serious Speakout, London, England; Commissioned Composer, Barbican Center, London, England; Commissioned Composer, SPoleto Festival; Commissioned Composer, Brooklyn Academy of Music; Commissioned Composer, Music Strassbourg, Hebbel Theater, Berlin AW: Polar Music Prize (2007); Praemium Imperiale Award, Japan Art Association (2006); Koussevitzky Foundation Award (1981, 2002); Schuman Prize, Columbia University (2000); Named, Composer of the Year, Musical America (2000); Montgomery Fellow, Dartmouth College (2000); Grammy Award, for "Music for Eighteen Musicians" (1999); Named, Commissioner dans l'Ordre des Arts et des Lettres (1999); Bayerische Akademie der Schönen Künst (1995); Elected, American Academy of Arts and Letters (1994); Grantee, National Endowment for the Arts (1974, 1976, 1991); Grantee, Rockefeller Foundation (1975, 1978, 1981, 1990); Grammy Award, for "Different Trains" (1989); Guggenheim Fellow (1978); Grantee, New York State Council Arts (1974) MEM: Fellow, American Academy of Arts & Sciences

REID, JOHN REYNOLDS JR., PHD, T: Geologist, Geomorphologist, Educator I: Education/Educational Services DOB: 01/04/1933 PB: Melrose SC: MA/USA PT: John Reynolds Reid; Elva Marguerite (Taylor) Reid MS: Married SPN: Barbara Ann Pulsford Reid (06/30/1956) CH: Valerie Reid-Collins; William Reid; Karen Spahr; Linda Rourke (Deceased) ED: PhD, University of Michigan (1961); MS, University of Michigan (1957); BS, Tufts University (1955) C: Assistant Professor to Professor, University of North Dakota, Grand Forks, ND (1961-1998); Assistant Professor, Mount Union College, Alliance, OH (1958-1959) CR: Consultant, U.S. Army Corps of Engineers (1980-1990); Visiting Professor, The University of Edinburgh, Scotland (1987); Visiting Professor, University of Bergen, Norway (1986); Director, Regional Environmental Assessment Program, North Dakota Legislative Council, Bismarck, ND (1977-1978); Associate Director, Regional Environmental Assessment Program, North Dakota Legislative Council, Bismarck, ND (1975-1977) CIV: Volunteer, Local Senior Center (2001-Present); Volunteer Ombudsman, Office on Aging, Larimer County (2001-Present); Volunteer Teacher, Local Schools (2001-2017) CW: Contributor, Numerous Peer-Reviewed Research Publications in National and International Journals AW: Arthur Gray Leonard Award (2019); Lifetime Achievement Award, Larimer County, Colorado (2017); North Dakota Professor of the Year, Carnegie Foundation for Advancement of Teaching (1996); B.C. Campbell Award for Individual Excellence in Teaching (1992); Outstanding Teacher, Amoco Foundation (1967); W. H. Hobbs Fellow, University of Michigan (1957); Olmsted Scholarship, Tufts University (1954) MEM: Fellow, The Geological Society of America, Inc.; NAGT; AMQUA; North Dakota Academy of Science; Sigma Xi, The Scientific Research Society MH: Albert Nelson Marquis Lifetime Achievement Award; Marquis Who's Who Top Professional AS: Dr. Reid attributes his success to accepting invitations to work in unusual places, sometimes for minimal pay. B/I: Dr. Reid was inspired to enter his profession by his mother's family from Canada who worked in gold mines. AV: Bicycling; Hiking; Gardening; Collecting stamps; Taking photographs PA: Independent RE: Protestant

REIF, L. RAFAEL, T: President I: Education/Educational Services CN: Massachusetts Institute of Technology (MIT) DOB: 08/21/1950 SC: Maracaibo/Venezuela MS: Married SPN: Christine Chomiuk CH: Jessica; Blake ED: Honorary Doctorate, Arizona State University (2018); Honorary Doctorate, Technion (2017); Honorary Doctorate, Tsinghua University (2016); Doctor of Law Degree, Chinese University of Hong Kong (2015); PhD in Electrical Engineering, Stanford University (1979); BS in Electrical Engineering, Universidad de Carabobo, Valencia, Venezuela (1973); IBM Faculty Fellowship, Center for Materials Science and Engineering, Massachusetts Institute of Technology (MIT) C: President, Massachusetts Institute of Technology (MIT), Cambridge, MA (2012-Present); Provost, Massachusetts Institute of Technology (MIT), Cambridge, MA (2005-2012); Department Head, Electrical Engineering and Computer Science (EECS), Massachusetts Institute of Technology (MIT), Cambridge, MA (2004-2005); Associate Department Head, Electrical Engineering, Department of Electrical Engineering and Computer Science (EECS), Massachusetts Institute of Technology (MIT), Cambridge, MA (1999-2004); Director, Microsystems Technology Laboratories, Massachusetts Institute of Technology (MIT), Cambridge, MA (1990-1999); Professor, Massachusetts Institute of Technology (MIT), Cambridge, MA (1988); Associate Professor, Massachusetts Institute of Technology (MIT), Cambridge, MA (1983-1988); Assistant Professor, Electrical Engineering, Massachusetts Institute of Technology (MIT), Cambridge, MA (1980-1983); Assistant Professor, Universidad Simon Bolivar, Caracas, Venezuela (1973-1974); Visiting Assistant Professor, Department of Electrical Engineering, Stanford University CR: Board of Directors, Schlumberger (2007-Present); Board of Directors, Arconic (2016-2017); Board of Directors, Alcoa (2015-2016); Board, Conservation International; Analog Devices Career Development Professorship, Department of Electrical Engineering and Computer Science (EECS), Massachusetts Institute of Technology (MIT), Cambridge, MA CIV: Donor, $850,000, Four Nonprofits Supporting Survivors of Sexual Abuse CW: Editor, Co-Editor, Five Books AW: Engineer of the Year, Great Minds in STEM (2018); Frank E. Taplin, Jr. Public Intellectual Award, Woodrow Wilson National Fellowship (2015); Listee, "Top 20 Most Influential, Outstanding, Creative and Talented Hispanic Professionals Working in the U.S. Technology Industry," CBS Interactive (2015); 2012 Tribeca Disruptive Innovation Award (2012); Aristotle Award, Semiconductor Research Corporation (2000); Presidential Young Investigator Award (1984) MEM: Fellow, Institute of Electrical and Electronics Engineers (IEEE); Fellow, National Academy of Inventors; American Academy of Arts and Sciences; National Academy of Engineering; Foreign Member, Chinese Academy of Engineering; Electrochemical Society; Tau Beta Pi

REINLEITNER, KATHERINE M., PHD, T: Psychologist; Foundation Administrator I: Health, Wellness and Fitness DOB: 05/10/1948 PB: Scarsdale SC: NY/USA PT: Eugene Mindlin; Sarah Mindlin MS: Married SPN: Lee A. Reinleitner, PhD (1990); Theodore B. Day (1968, Divorced 1980); CH: Eleanor Day; T. Eugene Day; Jennifer Day; David A.; Mark A.; Paul H. ED: Intern, The Astor Home for Children, Reinbeck, NY; PhD, University of Washington (1974); MA, Columbia University (1968); BA, Barnard College, with Honors (1967) CT: International College of Psychopharmacology (Now International College of Neuropsychopharmacology (CINP)) (1995); Diplomate, American Board of Advanced Practice Psychologists; American Board of Psychopharmacology and American Board of Forensic Psychology, Inc. C: Private Practice, Redmond, WA (2000-Present); Administrator, The Mindlin Foundation, Bellevue, WA (1988-Present); Private Practice, Bainbridge Island, WA (1983-2000); Private Practice, Mercer Island, Bellevue, WA (1976-2000); Psychologist, Seattle Children's Hospital, Seattle, WA (1974-1983) CR: Board of Directors, Curriculum Committee, Prescribing Psychologists Register (1996-Present); Lecturer, Assistant Professor, University of Washington (1975-1983); Governor's Council, Abuse and Neglect, State of Washington, Olympia (1978-1980); Seminars, International College of Prescribing Psychologists CW: Author, "What to Do After You've Seen the Zoo" (1983); Author, Five Children's Books AW: Training Fellowship I and IV, Veterans Administration (1970-1971, 1973-1974); National Institute of Mental Health (1969-1970) MEM: American Association for the Advancement of Science; International College of Prescribing Psychologists; American Psychological Association; Washington State Psychological Association MH: Albert Nelson Marquis Lifetime Achievement Award; Marquis Who's Who Top Professional B/I: Dr. Reinleitner was teaching history at the University of Washington, and spoke to many of her students after study hours about their issues. One of her students was suicidal; she went to the clinical psychology department at her campus to seek help, and ended up bringing the student along. Her ability to help the student impressed the faculty of the psychology department so much that they convinced her to take a PhD in clinical psychology, which she has been doing ever since. AV: Pianist; Irish harp; Gardening, Wildlife photography

REINTGEN, DOUGLAS SCOTT MD, T: Professor of Surgery I: Education/Educational Services CN: University of South Florida DOB: 07/22/1953 PB: Latrobe SC: PA/USA PT: Robert Joseph Reintgen; Patricia Lou (Cunningham) Reintgen MS: Married SPN: Ellen Verena Jorgenson, MD (11/19/1988); Margaret Ann Palmer (09/10/1978, Divorced 12/1982) CH: Christian; Michael; Eric ED: Chief Resident in Surgery, Duke University Medical Center, Durham, NC (1986-1987); Senior Assistant Resident, Duke University Medical Center, Durham, NC (1983-1986); Research Fellow in Surgical Oncology, Duke University Medical Center, Durham, NC (1981-1983); Junior Assistant Resident in Surgery, Duke University Medical Center, Durham, NC (1980-1981); Intern, Duke University Medical Center, Durham, NC (1979-1980); Doctor of Medicine, Duke University (1979); Bachelor of Arts, Duke University (1975) C: Program Leader in Cutanous Oncology, Moffitt Cancer Center, Tampa, FL (2010-Present); Professor, University of South Florida, Tampa, FL (2010-Present); With, Lakewyn Regional Cancer Center (2002-2010); Associate Professor, University of South Florida, Tampa, FL (1991-1995); Assistant Professor of Surgery, University of South Florida, Tampa, FL (1987-1991) CIV: Basketball Coach, Amateur Athletic Union CW: Editor, Cancer Screening (1996); Editorial Board, Annals of Surgical Oncology (1993); Guest Editor, Journal of Surgical Oncology (1993); Guest Editor, Annals of Plastic Surgery (1992); Designer, Lymphatic Mapping Technique for Breast Cancer and Melanoma **AW:** Named, Best Scientific Paper at the Annual Meeting (1999); James IV Traveling Fellowship Award (1995); Shipley Award, Southern Surgical Association; Named, One of the Best Cancer Specialists in the Country, Good Housekeeping Magazine; Named, One of the Best Doctors in America, Woodward/White Inc. **MEM:** President, Bassett Surgical Society (1995); American College of Surgeons; Society of Surgical Oncology; Society of Academy Surgery; Southeastern Surgical Society; Sabiston Surgical Society **MH:** Albert Nelson Marquis Lifetime Achievement Award **B/I:** Ever since high school, Dr. Reintgen thought medicine would be a useful profession to enter. He wanted to help people and was always interested in surgery, because he was not interested in chronic conditions. Dr. Reintgen was more interested in the quick fixes. If a patient had cancer, he wanted to be able to remove the cancer and cure them. **AV:** Running; Golf; Collecting art **PA:** Republican **RE:** Roman Catholic

REIS, PEGGY D., T: Township Official **I:** Government Administration/Government Relations/Government Services **DOB:** 08/03/1942 **PB:** Stearns **SC:** KY/USA **PT:** Milton; Fannie F. (Lay) Dagley **MS:** Single **SPN:** Gordon Reis III (02/29/1972); Robert L. Couch (09/16/1962, Divorced 1972) **CH:** Thea L. Reis, Morgan; Troy Couch II **ED:** Coursework, University of Cincinnati (1965) **C:** Board of Township Trustees, Anderson Township (1989-Present); President, Board of Township Trustees, Anderson Township (1992-1993); Stockbroker, Seasongood & Mayer (1966-1980, 1984-1987); Co-founder, Co-owner, Dance Centre of Cincinnati (1981-1983); Field Assistant, Community Action Commission (1964-1965) **CR:** Appointee, Ohio State and Local Government Commission (1993) **CIV:** Board of Directors Parent Association; Seven Hills Churches; With, Doherty Campus, Hyde Park Community Methodist Church; With, Hamilton County and Women's Republican Club; Founder, Anderson Trails **MEM:** Queen City Municipal Bond Club; Cincinnati Stock and Bond Club; Public Securities Association; National Association of Securities Dealers; Turpin Hills Swim and Racquet Club; Ohio Township Association; Hamilton County Township Association; Ohio Governmental Development Association **MH:** Albert Nelson Marquis Lifetime Achievement Award **B/I:** Mrs. Reis began her career as a stockbroker. She spent nearly 20 years in the profession before the birth of her firstborn child. By then she began to put her stockbroker career on hold, and became interested in opening a fitness apparel store, which she pursued along with a friend. After departing from this role, she was asked to run for public office by a friend and local attorney, after which she won a seat for the Anderson Township central committee. **AV:** Tennis; Reading; Aerobic workouts; Gardening

REMNICK, DAVID JAY, T: Editor **I:** Publishing **CN:** The New Yorker **DOB:** 10/29/1958 **PB:** Hackensack **SC:** NJ/USA **PT:** Edward C. Remnick; Barbara (Seigel) Remnick **MS:** Married **SPN:** Esther B. Fein **CH:** Alexander; Noah; Natasha **ED:** BA in Comparative Literature, Princeton University, Summa Cum Laude (1981); Diploma, Pascack Valley High School **C:** Editor-In-Chief, The New Yorker, Conde Nast Publications, New York, NY (1998-Present); Staff Writer, The New Yorker, Conde Nast Publications, New York, NY (1992-1998); Moscow Correspondent, The Washington Post (1988-1992); Reporter, The Washington Post (1982-1988) **CR:** Commencement Speaker, Syracuse University (2014); Guest Commentator, Contributor, Winter Olympics, Sochi, Russia (2014); Lecturer, Columbia University, Princeton University; Host, "The New Yorker Radio Hour" **CIV:** Board of Trustees, New York Public Library **CW:** Author, "Account Settings," The Talk of the Town, The New Yorker (2018); Author, "One Hundred Days," The Talk of the Town, The New Yorker (2017); Author, "Trump, Putin and the New Cold War," Annals of Diplomacy, The New Yorker (2017); Author, "New and Improved: Goings on About Town Gets a New Look Online," The New Yorker (2016); Author, "Unretiring," Showcase, The New Yorker (2016); Author, "The Choice," The Talk of the Town: Comment, The New Yorker (2016); Author, "Friday Night Lights Out," The Talk of the Town: Comment, The New Yorker (2016); Author, "Today's Woman," The Talk of the Town: Comment, The New Yorker (2015); Author, "The Fire This Time," The Talk of the Town: Comment, The New Yorker (2015); Author, "Aflame," The Town of the Town: Comment, The New Yorker (2014); Author, "Putin's Pique," The Talk of the Town: Comment, The New Yorker (2014); Author, "Patriot Games: Vladimir Putin Lives His Olympic Dream," Letter From Sochi, The New Yorker (2014); Author, "Glad to Be Unhappy," The Talk of the Town: In the Studio, The New Yorker (2013); Author, "The Culprits," The Talk of the Town: Homeland, The New Yorker (2013); Author, "Danse Macabre: A Scandal at the Bolshoi Ballet," Letter from Moscow, The New Yorker (2013); Author, "The Party Faithful," The New Yorker (2013); Author, "Books: The STate of the Union," The New Yorker (2012); Author, "Letter from Moscow: The Civil Archipelago," The New Yorker (2011); Author, "The Talk of the Town: Comment: No More Magical Thinking," The New Yorker (2012); Author, "Decline and Fail," The Talk of the Town: Comment, The New Yorker (2011); Author, "The Bridge: The Life and Rise of Barack Obama" (2010); Editor, "The Only Game in Town: Sports Stories from the New Yorker" (2010); Author, "Blago Speaks: Again," The Talk of the Town: The Blotter, The New Yorker (2009); Author, "Homelands," The Talk of the Town: Comment, The New Yorker (2009); Editor, "Disquiet, Please! More Humor Writing from the New Yorker" (2008); Author, Editor, "Secret Ingredients: The New Yorker Book of Food and Drink" (2007); Author, "Reporting: Writings from the New Yorker" (2006); Co-Author, "Fierce Pajamas: An Anthology of Humor Writing from the New Yorker" (2001); Co-Author, "Wonderful Town: New York Stories from the New Yorker" (2000); Author, Editor, "The New Gilded Age: The New Yorker Looks at the Culture of Affluence" (2000); Author, Editor, "Life Stories: Profiles from the New Yorker" (2000); Author, "King of the World: Muhammad Ali and the Rise of an American Hero" (1998); Author, "Resurrection: The Struggle for a New Russia" (1997); Author, "The Devil Problem and Other True Stories" (1996); Author, "Lenin's Tomb: The Last Days of the Soviet Empire" (1993); Founding Member, The Nassau Weekly **AW:** National Magazine Award for Public Interest, American Society of Magazine Editors (2011); Listee, 50 Highest-Earning Political Figures, Newsweek (2010); National Magazine Award for General Excellence (2008); Benjamin C. Bradlee Editor of the Year, National Press Foundation (2006); Editor of the Year, Advertising Age (1999-2000); Pulitzer Prize (1994); George Polk Award for Excellence in Journalism (1994); Helen Bernstein Award, New York Public Library (1994); Livingston Award (1991) **MEM:** Fellow, American Academy of Arts and Sciences; University Press Club **RE:** Jewish

REN, DINGKUN, DENG, T: Development Engineer **I:** Engineering **CN:** Lumileds **ED:** DEng in Electrical and Computer Engineering, University of California Los Angeles (2018); MSEE, University of California Los Angeles (2013); BE in Precision Instruments, Tianjin University, China (2011); Exchange Student, Electronics & Electrical Engineering, University of Glasgow (2010-2011) **C:** Developmental Engineer, Lumileds, San Francisco, CA (2019-Present); Postdoctoral Researcher, University of California Los Angeles (2018); Teaching Fellow, University of California Los Angeles (2013-2018); Graduate Student Researcher, University of California Los Angeles (2013-2018); Research Assistant, University of California Los Angeles (2011-2013); Research Assistant, University of Glasgow (2010-2011) **CR:** University of California, Los Angeles, Teaching Fellow (2016); Honeywell Fellowship (2010) **CIV:** Volunteer, University of California Los Angeles Volunteer Center; Ad-Hoc Reviewer, University of California Los Angeles School of Engineering Scholarships **CW:** Co-Author, "Feasibility of achieving high detectivity at short- and mid-wavelength infrared using nanowire photodetectors with p-n heterojunctions," Nanotechnology (2019); Author, Dissertation, "Nanowire Optoelectronics at Infrared: Modeling, Epitaxy, and Devices" (2018); Author, Thesis, "Modeling of Electronic Cell-Substrate Impedance Sensing for Single Cell" (2013); Author, "Measurement of Wafer Thickness Using Michelson Interferometer Based on White Light Interference" (2011); Reviewer, Over 20 International Journals; Ad-Hoc Reviewer, Scientific Journals Including ACS Sensors, Optics Letters, Optics Express, Optical Materials Express, Applied Optics, Journal of the Optical Society of America B, OSA Continuum, Applied Physics Letters, Journal of Applied Physics, Scientific Reports, Nanoscale Research Letters, Journal of Luminescence, Journal of Alloys and Compounds, Photonics Journal, Micro & Nano Letters, IET Optoelectronics, Electronics Letters, Materials, Coatings, Electronics, Crystals, Applied Science, Sustainability, Energies, Materials Research; Contributor, Articles, Professional Journals **AW:** Nominee, University of California, Los Angeles, Henry Samueli School of Engineering Best Teaching Assistant (2016-2018); MRS Spring Meeting & Exhibit Travel Award (2017); Best Undergraduate Thesis Award (2011); Tianjin University Scholarship (2008-2009) **MEM:** Optical Society of America; Society of Photographic Instrumentation Engineers; Program Committee, Ad-Hoc Reviewer, 17th IEEE International Conference on Nanotechnology **B/I:** Dr. Ren dreamed of becoming an engineer from the time he was in high school. During his undergraduate studies, he attended the University of Glasgow in Scotland as an exchange student. At that time, he was inspired by an advisor that introduced him to the world of electrical engineering. He always had a passion for it.

RENO, JOSEPH DAVID, T: Protective Services Official, Researcher, Writer **I:** Other **CN:** Universal Life Church **DOB:** 02/03/1949 **PB:** Bethlehem **SC:** PA/USA **PT:** Dr. Joseph Harry Reno; Maude Olivia (Mutchler) Reno, RN **MS:** Married **SPN:** Anna Elizabeth Thal (07/04/1994) **ED:** Cape Cod Conferences (2007); Boston Graduate School of Psychoanalysis (2004-2005); Postgraduate Coursework, Northeastern University (1999-2000); Postgraduate Coursework, University of Massachusetts, Boston, MA (1996-1997); MA in Communications Studies, Emerson College (1994); BS in Mass Communications, Emerson College (1973) **CT:** Certificate, Screenwriting, Emerson College (2007); Computer Applications, Northeastern University (1999-2000); Legal Studies, University of Massachusetts, Boston, MA **C:** Police Clerk, Boston Police (1983-Present); Teacher, Boston Schools (1979-1983); Computer Operator, Consultant, Museum of Fine Arts, Boston, MA (1978-1981); Library Service, Boston University (1976-1983); Investigative Reporter, New England Business Journal, Boston, MA (1975-1976); Research Assistant, New England

Historical Genealogy Society, Boston, MA (1973); Security Guard, Pinkertons, Boston, MA **CR:** Public Relations, Hackney Unit, Boston Police Headquaters (1998-Present); Lecturer, Speech-Mystery Writers of America (1995); Herbert O. Yardley Biography Research Assistant, Dr. David Kahn (1995); Steve Fox, Blood and Power (1991); Book Seller, Albion Press, St. Louis, MO (1986) **CIV:** Panelist, National Convention, National Alliance of Housing and Urban Development Tenants (1999); Panelist, National Low Income Housing Coalition (1998); Board of Directors, National Association of Housing and Urban Development Tenants (1997) **CW:** Contributor, Articles, Investigative Reporters and Editors Journal (1986-Present); Co-Author, "Secret New England" (1991); Acknowledgements in Lawrence Ferlinghetti and Nancy S Peter's Literary San Francisco; Steve Fox's Blood and Power; Dr. David Kahn's The Reader of Gentleman's Mail. Presentations at First Church of Boston's Adult Education on How to background a person using public records, investigative reporting, "Biography of a Bookie Joint," The Art of Dashiell Hammett, etc. **AW:** David Atlee Phillips New England Chapter Award (1989) **MEM:** Board of Directors, Electronic Librarian, Association of Former Intelligence Officers (1996-Present); Secretary, Electronic Librarian, Association of Former Intelligence Officers (1995-Present); Electronic Library, New England Chapter, Association of Former Intelligence Officers (1986-Present); Secretary, Negotiating Committee, Service Employees International Union (1991, 1996); American Association for the Advancement of Science; American Civil Liberties Union; National Coalition of Independent Scholars; Alliance of Independent Scholars; Investigative Reporters Editors; Society of Professional Journalists; Society of Professional Journalists; National Writers Union; Piano Craft Guild Tenants Association, Boston Chapter; Canadian Association Journalists; Boston Athenæum, Emerson College Alumni Association **MH:** Albert Nelson Marquis Lifetime Achievement Award **AS:** Mr. Reno attributes his success to two educated parents who could answer questions and encouraged reading. He was raised in a home of books and magazines. Additionally, he was inspired by the influence of F. Lee Bailey, who once described people as "learned ignoramuses"; an eclectic reading list, which included the books of Robert B. Downs, Gore Vidal, Will and Ariel Durant; investigative reporters and editors; and Professor Walter Littlefield of Emerson College, a gentleman and a scholar. He saw reading as a pool game in which one book leads to another if you read the footnotes and seek out other sources. Additionally, he has traveled to 48 of the 50 states, all presidential libraries, London, Paris, Vienna, Rome, Florence, Zürich. He also attributes his success to an inquiring mind and the ability to satisfy it, which is the goal of education. **B/I:** Mr. Reno became involved in his profession because he enjoyed learning and his parents encouraged him to educate himself. He followed the title of Theodore Roosevelt's son's book, "For Lust of Knowing." "While I have not overthrown Iran, I appreciated the title," he noted. "I have gone beyond the job. I did research at Scotland Yard, Interpol to learn their methods." **AV:** Theater; Traveling; Book collecting; Dialogues; Using the city as an educational resource **PA:** Ward 9 Democratic Committee (2004-Present); Delegate to Numerous Mass State Conventions. Elaine Noble Campaign (1975); Political Director, Gallery at the Piano Factory **RE:** First Church in Boston, Unitarian Universalist; Doctor of Divinity, Universal Life Church **THT:** Mr. Reno said, "Life is an adventure, a journey, a novel one writes. Do what you can with what you have. Prepare for the unknown which is your life. When given an opportunity, take it. Figure your tradition, learn from the past, and proceed to the future. When things don't work out, learn from your mistakes. Once you have mastered your skills use them to add value. I was influenced by an episode of The Twilight Zone, 'A Game of Pool' in which a pool shark wants to play the deceased all-time champ. While seemingly about a pool game, the dialogue speaks to life, values, and the cost of pursuing a goal."

RENUART, RONALD, "DOC" JOSEPH SR., DO, FACP, T: Osteopathic Physician **I:** Medicine & Health Care **DOB:** 01/05/1964 **PB:** Coral Gables **SC:** FL/USA **PT:** Gerald Joseph Renaurt; Maureen Roberta (Geller) Renuart **MS:** Married **SPN:** Tamara Ferrell Renuart (03/24/2012) **CH:** Jennifer Lynn; Scarlett Rose; Ronald Joseph Jr.; Christopher Young; Shannon Young; Matthew Young; Ashley Young **ED:** Resident in Internal Medicine, University of Florida, Jacksonville, FL (1991-1994); Intern in Osteopathic Medicine, Metropolitan General Hospital, Pinellas Park, FL (1990-1991); DO, Nova Southeastern University (1990); BS, University of Florida (1986); AA, University of Florida (1984) **CT:** Diplomate, American Board of Internal Medicine **C:** Internist, Baptist Primary Care, Baptist Health (1996-Present); President, Florida Osteopathic Medical Association (2017-2018); Legislator/Member, District 18/17 , Florida House of Representatives, Tallahassee, FL (2008-2015); Chief of Staff, Baptist Medical Center Beaches, Baptist Health (2004-2005); Chairman, Department of Medicine, Baptist Medical Center Beaches, Baptist Health, Jacksonville Beach, FL (1998-2001); Internist, Baptist/St. Vincent's Primary Care Network (1996-2000); Internist, Lynch, Vetere & Renuart, Jacksonville, FL (1994-1996); Emergency Medical Technician, Atlantic Ambulance Service Acquisition, Inc., Fort Lauderdale, FL (1986); Firefighter/EMT, Micanopy Fire Department, FL (1985-1986); Emergency Medical Technician, Alachua County EMS, Gainesville, FL (1985-1986); Phlebotomist, Alachua General Hospital, Gainesville, FL (1983-1986) **CR:** Vice Chairman, Health and Human Services Policy Committee, Florida Legislature (2015); Chairman, St. John's County Legislative Delegation, Florida Legislature (2009, 2011-2012, 2014-2015); Vice Chairman, North Florida Delegation, Florida Legislature (2013-2014); Chairman, Veterans and Military Affairs Subcommittee, Florida Legislature (2012-2014); Vice Chairman, K-12 Education Subcommittee, Florida Legislature (2012-2014); Vice Chairman, Healthcare Policy Quality Subcommittee, Florida Legislature (2010-2012); Florida Medicaid Pharmaceutical and Therapeutics Committee (2005-2008); Assistant Medical Director, Fleet Landing Health Center, Atlantic Beach, FL (1994-2000) **CIV:** President-elect Nominee, Member, Rotary Club of Ponte Vedra Beach, FL; The American Legion; Member, Knights of Columbus; VFW; Former County Executive Board Member, United Way of St. Johns County; Executive Board and Secretary, Professionals Resource Network, FL **MIL:** Chief Medical Officer, Florida Army National Guard (2004-2010); Colonel, Florida Army National Guard (1990-2010); Flight Surgeon, Florida Army National Guard, Operation Iraqi Freedom (2007); Field Surgeon, Florida Army National Guard, Operation Enduring Freedom (2005-2006); Field Surgeon, Florida Army National Guard, Operation Iraqi Freedom (2003) **CW:** Co-editor, Co-author, "Directory of Florida Rural Practice Sites for Health Care Professionals" (1989) **AW:** Veterans of Influence Award, Jacksonville Business Journal (2014); Named Champion for Dentistry, Florida Dental Association (2014); Champion of Economic Freedom Award, Americans for Prosperity (2014); Named to Honor Roll, Florida Chamber of Commerce (2009-2014); Certificate of Appreciation for Leadership on Public Policy Changes, United States Department of Defense (2011, 2013); Defender of Liberty Award, American Conservative Union (2013); Certificate of Appreciation, Professional Resource Network, FL (2013); Named Legislator of the Year, Florida Dental Association (2013); Friend of Free Enterprise Award, Associated Builders and Contractors (2009, 2010, 2011, 2012); Dr. Lewis Earle Legislative Service Award, Florida Dental Association (2012); Florida Legislative Award, American Cancer Society (2012); Celebration of Excellence, Distinguished Alumni Award, Nova Southeastern University (2012); Named Diabetic Master Clinician, Florida Academy of Family Physicians (2011); Named ACU Conservative, American Conservative Union (2011); Leadership Award, American Cancer Society (2011); Named Legislator of the Year, Florida Osteopathic Medical Association (2011); Guardian of Independent Higher Education Award (2010); Fellow, American College of Physicians (2010); Legislative Champion Award, American Diabetes Association (2010); Named Legislator of the Year, American Heart Association, Inc. (2010); Named Honorary Member, Miami-Dade Legislative Delegation (2010); Distinguished Alumni Award, Independent Colleges and Universities of Florida (ICUF) (2001, 2009); Faith and Family Award, Christian Coalition of Florida (2009); Hometown Hero Award, Jacksonville Young Republicans Club (2009); Named Legislator of the Year, Pinellas County Osteopathic Medical Society (2009); Paul Harris Fellow, Rotary International (2009); Named Physician of the Year, Florida Osteopathic Medical Association (2006); Celebration of Leadership Recipient, Community Connections of Jacksonville, Inc. (2004); Rose Community Service Award, Nova Southeastern University (1990); Eagle Scout Award, Boy Scouts of America (1977); Florida Cross; United States Army Meritorious Service Medal; United States Army Commendation Medal with Two Oak Leaf Clusters; United States Army Achievement Medal; United States Army Humanitarian Medal; Reserve Component Achievement Award **MEM:** Delegate, American Osteopathic Association (AOA) (2001-2008, 2015-2020); Florida Osteopathic Medical Association; Gator Boosters, Inc.; Charter Life Member, University of Florida Alumni Association; Kappa Alpha Order; Republican Executive Committee **MH:** Albert Nelson Marquis Lifetime Achievement Award; Marquis Who's Who Top Professional **AS:** Dr. Renuart has dedicated his life to continued learning to enhance his skills to serve others in the art of internal medicine. He has also extended his drive to service others to include his country as a service member in the military and his state as an elected state legislator. **B/I:** Dr. Renuart always wanted to be a physician to serve others. In addition, Dr. Renuart became involved in the osteopathic profession because while he was a student at the University of Florida during his undergraduate education he was exposed to it for the first time. He was intrigued with the philosophy that focused on the patient as a whole and not just on a medical condition or concern. Osteopathic medicine has a strong focus on preventive care, in addition to providing complete patient care. He chose internal medicine based on influences from mentors he had in medical school. **AV:** Attending college and NFL football games; Camping; Hiking; Photography; Restoration of American muscle cars; Running; Target shooting; Whitewater rafting; Kayaking **PA:** Republican **RE:** Roman Catholic **THT:** Dr. Renuart believes that it is our duty to serve and care for those who are unable to care for themselves and use our God given skills to assist others in realizing their full potential to be successful. He was blessed to be able to serve and not be served.

REPP, MICHAEL, T: Public Relations, Community Outreach, Patron Liaison **I:** Media & Entertainment **CN:** The SunTrapp **PB:** Wheat Ridge **SC:** CO/USA **PT:** Sioux Robbins; Rocky Bartels **C:** Public Relations, Community Outreach, Patron Liaison, The SunTrapp (2015-Present) **CIV:** Utah Gay Rodeo Foundation; Utah AIDS Foundation; Hospital Clinic 1-A, University of Utah **MEM:** American Board of Certified Colorists **AS:** Mr. Repp attributes his success to growing up on a farm with parents who encouraged him to do great things. He also notes his co-workers and loving community. **B/I:** Mr. Repp became involved in his profession as a favor to a close family friend who owned The SunTrapp.

RESCHENTHALER, GUY LORIN, T: U.S. Representative from Pennsylvania; Lawyer **I:** Government Administration/Government Relations/Government Services **DOB:** 04/27/1983 **PB:** Pittsburgh **SC:** PA/USA **ED:** JD, Duquesne University School of Law (2007); BA in Political Science, The Pennsylvania State University Behrend, Erie, PA (2004) **C:** Member, U.S. House of Representatives from Pennsylvania's 14th Congressional District (2019-Present); Member, District 37, Pennsylvania's Senate (2015-Present); Magisterial District Judge, Pittsburgh's South Hills, PA (2013-Present); Of Counsel, Brennan, Robins & Daley P.C. **CIV:** Member, Political Science Advisory Board, The Pennsylvania State University Behrend **MIL:** With, United States Navy Judge Advocate General's Corps (2007-2012) **CW:** Co-host, Radio Program (2013) **AW:** Michael Taylor Shelby Award for Professional, Ethics and Dedication in the Practice of Law **PA:** Republican

RESIO, DONALD T., PHD, T: Director **I:** Education/Educational Services **CN:** University of North Florida **SC:** VA/USA **MS:** Married **SPN:** Kathryn (1983) **CH:** Two Children; Two Stepchildren **ED:** PhD in Environmental Science, Fluid Dynamics, University of Virginia (1974); MA in Environmental Science, University of Virginia (1971); BA in Physical Geology, University of Virginia (1969) **C:** Professor of Ocean Engineering, University of North Florida (2011-Present); Director, Taylor Engineering Research Institute, University of North Florida (2011-Present); Senior Scientist, Coastal Hydraulics Laboratory, Corps of Engineers, U.S. Army (1994-2014); Associate Professor, Florida Institute of Technology (1990-1994); Owner, Offshore & Coastal Technologies Inc. (1983-1990); Vice President, OceanWeather Inc. (1981-1983); Research Scientist, Corps of Engineers, U.S. Army (1974-1981) **CR:** Affiliate, Interagency Performance Task Force (2005); Consultant, FEMA; Co-Leader, Post-Katrina Inter-Agency Forensics Study, FEMA; Leader, Risk Analysis Team, South Louisiana Hurricane Protection Project, FEMA; Co-Leader, Meteorological Organization Committee, United Nations **CW:** Patent; Contributor, Articles, Professional Journals; Contributor, Book Chapters **AW:** International Engineering Award, Coasts, Oceans, Ports, and Rivers Institute, American Society of Civil Engineers (2015); Certificate of Appreciation for Outstanding Service, National Research Council of the National Academies (2014); International Coastal Engineering Award, Coasts, Oceans, Ports, and Rivers Institute, American Society of Civil Engineers (2013); Professor of the Year Award, Northeast Florida's Engineers Week (2013); Distinguished Civilian Service Award, Department of the U.S. Army (2011); Engineering News Record Award of Excellence, McGraw Hill Education (2008); Researcher of the Year Award, Corps of Engineers, U.S. Army (2007); Researcher

of the Year Award, Engineer Research and Development Center, Corps of Engineers, U.S. Army (2007); Development Achievement Award, Engineer Research and Development Center, Corps of Engineers, U.S. Army (2007); Meritorious Civilian Service Award, Department of the U.S. Army (2007); Chief of Engineers Award for Leadership Role in Interagency Performance Evaluation Task force (2007); Research and Development Achievement Award, Engineer Research and Development Center, Corps of Engineers, U.S. Army (2006); Research and Teaching, Improving the State of the Art in Ocean and Atmospheric Modeling **MEM:** Academic Society, Phi Kappa Phi (2019-Present); American Society of Civil Engineers; American Meteorological Society; American Geophysical Union; Army Engineer Association; Delegate, Joint Committee for Oceanography and Marine Meteorology, United Nations; Co-Chairman, World Meteorological Association Coastal Inundation Forecast Demonstration Project, United Nations **MH:** Marquis Who's Who Top Professional **AS:** Dr. Resio attributes his success to being innovative and thinking out of the box.

RESNICK, LYNDA RAE, T: Businesswoman **I:** Health, Wellness and Fitness **CN:** The Wonderful Company LLC **PB:** Baltimore **SC:** MD/USA **PT:** Jack H. Harris; Muriel (Goodman) Harris **MS:** Married **SPN:** Stewart Resnick (1973); Hershel Sinay (Divorced) **CH:** Jason Sinay; Jonathan Sinay; Bill (Stepson); Ilene (Stepdaughter); Jeff (Stepson) **ED:** Diploma, Harriton High School **C:** Co-Owner, Roll International; Co-Owner, Vice Chairman, Franklin Mint **CR:** Chairman, Teleflora (1979-Present) **CIV:** Chairman, Marketing Committee, Conservation International; Board of Directors, CaP CURE, Association for the Cure of Cancer of the Prostate, Milken Family Foundation; Executive Committee, Trustee, Chairman of Acquisitions Committee, Los Angeles County Museum of Art; Committee on Sculpture and Decorative Arts, Metropolitan Museum of Art; Trustee, Philadelphia Museum of Art **AW:** Top 200 Collectors, ARTnews Magazine (2008); Gold Effie Award (1983); Top 50 U.S. Women Business Owners, Working Women; Top 100 U.S. Art Collectors, Art & Antiques Magazine; Number One Los Angeles Based Woman Business Owner, Los Angeles Business Journal **AV:** Collecting Old Master paintings

RESNICK, STEWART ALLEN, T: Chairperson, President **I:** Financial Services **CN:** The Wonderful Company **DOB:** 12/24/1936 **SC:** NJ/USA **MS:** Married **SPN:** Lynda Rae Harris (1973); Sandra Frazier (Divorced) **CH:** Bill; Ilene; Jeff; Jason Sinay (Stepson); Jonathan Sinay (Stepson) **ED:** Bachelor of Science, University of California Los Angeles (1959); Doctor of Jurisprudence, University of California Los Angeles School of Law **C:** President, Chairperson, The Wonderful Company (1979-Present); Chairperson, Chief Executive Officer, The Franklin Mint (1986-2006) **CR:** Owner, POM Wonderful; Owner, Fiji Water; Owner, Wonderful Halos; Owner, Wonderful Pistachios and Almonds; Owner, JUSTIN Wines; Owner, Landmark Wines; Owner, JNSQ Wines; Owner, Suterra Pest Control; Owner, Teleflora **CIV:** Donor, Caltech (2009, 2019); Donor, Hammer Museum (2018); Donor, Los Angeles County Museum of Art (2008); Donor, Children's Hospital Central California (2006); Board of Directors, LeapFrog Enterprises (2002-2005); Trustee Emeriti, J. Paul Getty Trust; Board of Visitors, UCLA Anderson School of Management; Board of Trustees, Bard College and Conservation International; Board of Advisers, University of California Davis, Lowell Milken Institute for Business Law and Policy at University of California Los Angeles; Senior Trustee, Caltech

RESTIVO, TODD, T: Attorney **I:** Law and Legal Services **CN:** Restivo & Murphy LLP **MS:** Married **SPN:** Diane **CH:** Nicholas; Scott; Michael; Madeline **ED:** JD, Touro College Jacob D. Fuchsberg Law Center, Huntington, NY (1997); BA in English Literature, State University of New York at Oswego (1991) **C:** Attorney, Restivo & Murphy, LLP (2002-Present) **AW:** Listee, Top 5% Practicing Attorneys, Super Lawyers; Recognition, New Yorker Magazine **MEM:** New York State Trial Lawyers Association; American Bar Association **BAR:** New York; U.S. District Court Eastern District of New York; U.S. District Court Southern District of New York **MH:** Albert Nelson Marquis Lifetime Achievement Award; Marquis Who's Who Top Professional **AS:** Mr. Restivo attributes his success to his desire to help others, as that is how he represents his clients. It is why he opened his own office. He wants to help others the best he can. He became interested in law by growing up and watching someone sacrifice greatly to help others. **B/I:** Mr. Restivo was the first person in his family to ever go to college. He wanted to go as far he could go with his education. In college, he became interested in pursuing a career in law. Later, he became involved in personal injury law after working with a firm in New York City.

RETZ, LINDA J., JD, ESQ., T: Proprietor **I:** Law and Legal Services **CN:** Law Offices of Linda J. Retz **DOB:** 04/15/1953 **PB:** Sacramento **SC:** CA/USA **PT:** Thomas J. Burke; June Louise Gil **MS:** Married **SPN:** Kirk J. Retz (11/27/1994) **ED:** JD, Loyola Law School (1993); BA in Paralegal Studies, University of West Los Angeles (1977) **CT:** Certified Specialist Estate Planning, Trust and Probate Law (1998); Board of Legal Specialization, State Bar of California **C:** Law Office of Linda J. Retz, Esq. (2007-Present) **CR:** Chair, Professional Responsibility Committee (2018-Present); Fellow, American College of Trust and Estate Counsel; Chair, Estate Planning, California State Bar; Trust and Probate Law Advisory Commission; Advisory Board, Estate Planning Institute, Continuing Education of the Bar, University of California Los Angeles **CIV:** Boards of Directors, Various Charitable Organizations, Rescue and Prevention of Cruelty to Animals; Estate Planning Institute; Chair, Professional Responsibility Subcommittee, American College of Trust and Estate Counsel **CW:** Co-Author, "Engagement Letters Guide for Practitioner, Third Edition" (2017); Contributor, Treatises and Syllabuses, Tax Institute, University of Southern California; Contributor, Treatises and Syllabuses, Trust and Estate Conference, Continuing Education of the Bar, University of California Los Angeles; Contributor, Treatises and Syllabuses, California CPA Education Foundation; Continuing Education Bar Journal **AW:** First Ranking in the Los Angeles Area, U.S. News & World Report; Third Tier Nationally, U.S. News & World Report; Tier One, U.S. News & World Report; Best Law Firm Award; Best Lawyer; Listee, Top Women Attorneys, Los Angeles Magazine **MEM:** Humane Society; California State Bar Association; Los Angeles State Bar Association **BAR:** California (1993) **AS:** Mrs. Retz attributes her success to great mentors and hard work. **B/I:** Mrs. Retz began her profession as a paralegal at a prestigious law firm. The lawyers encouraged Mrs. Retz to pursue a career in law, and she went on to work for a number of lawyers. While working as a paralegal, Mrs. Retz discovered that she was well-equipped to help families grieving the loss of a loved one. She found that she could help families because of her own experience of losing her husband. **AV:** Listening to music; Dancing; Traveling; Caring for animals; Cooking **THT:** Mrs. Retz believes in collaboration because she enjoys meeting other high-caliber professionals.

REVELEY, W. TAYLOR III, T: President Emeritus **I:** Education/Educational Services **CN:** William & Mary **DOB:** 01/06/1943 **PB:** Churchville **SC:** VA/USA **PT:** Walter Taylor Reveley II; Marie Eason Reveley **MS:** Married **SPN:** Helen Bond Reveley (12/18/1971) **CH:** Walter Taylor Reveley IV; George Everett Bond; Nelson Martin Eason; Helen Lanier Reveley **ED:** JD, University of Virginia (1968); AB, Princeton University (1965) **C:** President Emeritus, William & Mary (2018-Present); President, William & Mary (2008-2018); Dean, John Stewart Bryan Professor of Jurisprudence, William & Mary Law School (1998-2008); Partner, Hunton & Williams, Richmond, VA (1976-1998); Managing Partner, Hunton & Williams, Richmond, VA (1982-1991); Associate, Hunton & Williams, Richmond, VA (1970-1976); International Affairs Fellow, Council on Foreign Relations (1972-1973); Fellow, Woodrow Wilson International Center for Scholars (1972-1973); Law Clerk to Justice Brennan, Supreme Court of the United States, Washington, DC (1969-1970); Assistant Professor, University of Alabama Law School (1968-1969) **CIV:** Board Member, St. Catherine's School (2020-Present); Board Member, Medical College of Virginia Foundation (2019-Present); Chair, Oak Spring Garden Foundation (2016-Present); Board Member, Oak Spring Garden Foundation (2016-Present); Chair, Jefferson Science Associates, Jefferson National Laboratory (2016-2018); Board Member, Jefferson Science Associates, Jefferson National Laboratory (2016-2018); Board Member, Virginia Council of State University Presidents (2008-2018); Chair, Virginia Council of State University Presidents (2016-2017); Chair, Andrew W. Mellon Foundation (2012-2015); Board Member, Andrew W. Mellon Foundation (1994-2015); Chair, Virginia Historical Society (2010-2012); Board Member, Virginia Historical Society (1991-1996, 2003-2012); Board Member, Carnegie Endowment for International Peace (1999-2011); Board Member, JSTOR (1995-2008); Member, Education of Lawyers Section, Virginia State Bar (1992-2008); Board Member, Virginia Foundation for the Humanities (2001-2007); Chair, Virginia Museum of Fine Arts (2003-2005); Board Member, Virginia Museum of Fine Arts (1995-2005); Board Member, Presbyterian Outlook Foundation (1986-2003); Board Member, Princeton University (1986-1990, 1991-2001); Board Member, Union Theological Seminary (1992-2000); Board Member, Presbyterian Church Foundation (1991-1997); Chair, Education of Lawyers Section, Virginia State Bar (1992-1995); Chair, Presbyterian Outlook Foundation (1992-1995); Board Member, Virginia Museum of Fine Arts Foundation (1990-1995); Board Member, Richmond Symphony Orchestra (1980-1992); Chair, Richmond Symphony Orchestra (1988-1990); Chair, Princeton Association of Virginia (1983-1985); Chair, Fan District Association, Richmond, VA (1979-1980); Board Member, Fan District Association, Richmond, VA (1976-1980) **CW:** Author, "War Powers of the President and Congress: Who Holds the Arrows and Olive Branch?" (1981); Contributor, Articles, Professional Journals **AW:** Honorary Degree, King University; Honorary Degree, Hampden-Sydney College; Honorary Degree, College of William & Mary **MEM:** Phi Beta Kappa; Omicron Delta Kappa; Raven Society **BAR:** District of Columbia (1976); Virginia (1970) **MH:** Albert Nelson Marquis Lifetime Achievement Award **RE:** Presbyterian

REVERDIN, BERNARD J., T: Lawyer **I:** Law and Legal Services **DOB:** 06/21/1919 **PB:** Baden **SC:** Switzererland **PT:** Jean; Germaine Reverdin **MS:** Married **SPN:** Marcelle Coicou Reverdin **CH:** Caroline Flanagan; Brigitte; Nathalie **ED:** Postgraduate Coursework, Harvard Law School (1949); LLB, University of Geneva (1942) **C:** Senior Counsel Intern, Eaton & Van Winkle, New York, NY (1998-2009); Partner, Eaton & Van Winkle, New York, NY (1988-1997); Partner, Counsel, Hunton & Williams, New York, NY (1984-1988); Associate, Partner, Lovejoy, Wasson & Ashton, New York, NY (1951-1984); Foreign Attorney, Sullivan & Cromwell, New York, NY (1949-1951); Attorney, Legal Assistant, Geneva Government (1945-1948); Private Pratice **CR:** Director, Subsidiary of European Corps; Representative, Drafter Business Corps **CW:** Contributor, Articles, Professional Journals; Lecturer in Field **MEM:** Chair, Committee for International Trust and Estate, American Bar Association; New York State Bar Association (1988-1990); Former President, American Foreign Law Association; Former President, Consular Law Society; Former President, Swiss Society of New York; Bar for the City of New York **BAR:** New York (1955); Switzerland (1945) **MH:** Albert Nelson Marquis Lifetime Achievement Award; Marquis Who's Who Top Professional **B/I:** Mr. Reverdin chose to go into his profession because he wanted to be a lawyer. He was inspired by several family members who were well-respected law professionals.

REW, ROBERT, I: Medicine & Health Care **CN:** Pharmacologist **DOB:** 08/14/1943 **PB:** Pendleton **SC:** OR/USA **PT:** Ronald Royal; Patricia (Sherrard) Rew **MS:** Married **SPN:** Nora Eileen Kozan (11/01/1974) **CH:** Keenan Jay **ED:** ScD, Johns Hopkins Medical Institutes, Baltimore (1974); MS, Washington State University, Pullman (1968); BS, Whitman College, Walla Walla, WA (1966) **C:** President, Rewsearch Consulting, West Chester, Pennsylvania (2001-Present); Manager, Technical Services, Pfizer Incorporated, Exton, Pennsylvania (1996-2001); Associate Director, Product Development, Pfizer Incorporated, New York (1990-1996); Managing Parasitology Researcher, Smith Kline Beecham, West Chester, Pennsylvania (1986-1990); Visiting Scientist, CSIRO, Sydney (1985-1986); Senior Research Fellow, Merck Institute, Rahway, NJ (1982-1985); Laboratory Chief, U.S. Department of Agriculture, Beltsville, MD (1976-1982); Research Associate, Notre Dame University, South Bend, IN (1972-1976) **CR:** President, Rew Ranches, Incorporated, Pendleton, OR (1993-Present); Director, Malaria Researcher, Doctors for Life, South Africa (2003-2004); Adjunct Professor, University of Pennsylvania, Philadelphia (1987-2003); Adjunct Professor, New York Medical College (1984-1986); Adjunct Professor, University of Maryland, College Park (1980-1982); Postdoctoral Fellow, National Institute of Health, Notre Dame University (1972-1977); Research Assistant, U.S. Public Health, Johns Hopkins University (1968-1972); Teaching Assistant, U.S. Public Health Service, Washington State University (1966-1968) **CIV:** Encuentro Ministries (2005-Present); Ancient of Days (2000-2006); Board of Directors, House of His Creation, Gap, Pennsylvania (1997-2005); Religious Volunteer, Chester County Prison; Missionary, Nigeria, Kenya, South Africa **CW:** Editor, "Macrocyclic Lactones in Antiparasitic Therapy" (2003); Author, "Antimicrobial Therapy in Veterinary Medicine" (1993); Editor, "Chemotherapy of Parasite Diseases" (1986); Author, "Agriculture Chemicals of the Future" (1984) **MEM:** President, American Association of Veteran Parasitologists (1999-2000); President-Elect, American Association of Veteran Parasitologists (1998-1999); Industry Committee, American Society of Parasitologists (1994-1998); Society of Wash; World Association for Advancement of Veterinary Parasitologists; President, Rew Investment LLC; Times Square Church, New York, NY **MH:** Albert Nelson Marquis Lifetime Achievement Award **B/I:** Dr. Rew attended Whitman College; it was there that he enrolled in a course on tropical medicine. He was fascinated. In the first laboratory session, the professor took a needle and drew his own blood; he then put it on a slide for each of the students to look at. The professor said the red blood cells on the slide were infected with malaria. This professor, Donald Leahmann, is the reason that Dr. Rew became interested in tropical medicine. **AV:** Skiing; Fishing; Coaching **RE:** Christian

REYES, ARIANNE, T: Assistant Chief of Airport Operations **I:** Leisure, Travel & Tourism **CN:** The Port Authority of New York and New Jersey **ED:** BS in Airport Management/ATC, College of Aeronautics (2003) **C:** Assistant Chief of Airport Operations, John F. Kennedy International Airport, The Port Authority of New York and New Jersey (2012-Present); Landslide Operations Duty Manager, John F. Kennedy International Airport, The Port Authority of New York and New Jersey (2008-2012); Airport Operations Coordinator, AvPORTS, Teterboro, NJ (2004-2008) **AS:** Ms. Reyes attributes her success to the example her mother set by never giving up for anything. Her mother was a single mother who worked very hard to provide for the family. Ms. Reyes was trained to have drive from a very young age and it has continued to follow her throughout her entire career.

REYNOLDS, ALBERT BARNETT, T: Nuclear Engineer, Educator **I:** Engineering **DOB:** 02/01/1931 **PB:** Lebanon **SC:** TN/USA **PT:** George Lazenby Reynolds; Marion (Barnett) Reynolds **MS:** Married **SPN:** Helen Buck (09/06/1954) **CH:** Albert Jr.; Charlotte; Marion **ED:** ScD in Chemical Engineering, Massachusetts Institute of Technology (1959); MS in Nuclear Engineering, Massachusetts Institute of Technology (1955); BS in Physics, Massachusetts Institute of Technology (1953); Coursework, University of the South (1948-1951) **C:** Professor Emeritus, The University of Virginia, Charlottesville, VA (1996); Professor of Nuclear Engineering, The University of Virginia, Charlottesville, VA (1968-1996); Chairman, Department of Nuclear Engineering and Engineering Physics, The University of Virginia, Charlottesville, VA (1991-1992); Physicist-Manager, General Electric Company, San Jose, CA (1959-1968) **CR:** Consultant, U.S. Department of Energy (1987-1989); Consultant, Nuclear Regulatory Commission (1970-1984) **CIV:** Co-Founder, Blue Ridge Chapter, United Nations Foundation (2003-2018) **CW:** Author, "Bluebells and Nuclear Energy" (1996); Co-Author, "Fast Breeder Reactors" (1981); Contributor, Numerous Articles, Professional Journals **AW:** Annual Award for Public Education in Nuclear Energy, American Nuclear Society **MEM:** American Nuclear Society (1955-Present); Chair, Virginia Section, America Nuclear Society (1986-1987); Executive Committee, Division of Nuclear Reactor Safety, American Nuclear Society (1980-1983); Fellow, American Nuclear Society (1980); ASME; IEEE; ASEE; Sigma Xi, The Scientific Research Honor Society; The Tau Beta Pi Association, Inc. **MH:** Albert Nelson Marquis Lifetime Achievement Award (2019) **B/I:** Dr. Reynolds became involved in his profession because of his lifelong interest in math and science. The use of nuclear power for electricity was new when he was in college. He was in the first class that MIT offered in nuclear energy. **AV:** Playing tennis and the fiddle

REYNOLDS, GLENN FRANKLIN, T: Medicinal Research Scientist (Retired) **I:** Sciences **CN:** Merck & Co., Inc. **DOB:** 07/16/1944 **PB:** Rahway **SC:** NJ/USA **PT:** Frank Vanderbilt Reynolds; Estelle (Ohlott) Reynolds **MS:** Widower **SPN:** Marianne DelliSanti (11/25/1967, Deceased 2016) **CH:** William Matthew; David Glenn (Deceased 1995); Wendy Joy

ED: BS in Chemistry, Philadelphia College of Pharmacy and Science (1967); Coursework, Union College (1963-1965); Coursework, Rutgers University, The State University of New Jersey (1962-1963) **C:** Medicinal Research Scientist (Retired); Senior Research Associate, Merck & Co. Inc., Rahway, NJ (1991-2004); Research Chemist, Merck & Co. Inc., Rahway, NJ (1977-1986); Staff Chemist, Merck & Co., Inc., Rahway, NJ (1970-1977); Research Scientist, Merck & Co. Inc., Rahway, NJ (1967-1970) **CR:** Merck Recruiter, Rutgers University, The State University of New Jersey (1985); Merck Recruiter, University of North Carolina at Chapel Hill (1981); Merck Recruiter, Fairleigh Dickinson University (1980); Merck Recruiter, Howard University (1980) **CW:** Author, 27 Articles, Professional Journals **AW:** Inventor of the Year, Intellectual Property Owners (1993) **MEM:** Apache Junction Mounted Rangers (2018-Present); American Chemical Society; Freemason, Lafayette Lodge #27; Shriner, Salam Temple **MH:** Albert Nelson Marquis Lifetime Achievement Award; Marquis Who's Who Top Professional; Marquis Who's Who Humanitarian Award **B/I:** Mr. Reynolds got involved in organic chemistry because first there was no one in the family related that way, but his dad early on was in the medical field, and that kind of pushed him toward some sort of technical background. **AV:** Computer science; Biking; Skiing; Arabian horses **PA:** Independent

REYNOLDS, KIM KAY, T: Governor of Iowa **I:** Government Administration/Government Relations/Government Services **DOB:** 08/04/1959 **PB:** St. Charles **SC:** IA/USA **MS:** Married **SPN:** Kevin Reynolds (04/03/1982) **CH:** Nicole; Jennifer; Jessica **ED:** BA in Liberal Studies, Iowa State University (2016); Coursework, Southwestern Community College (1992-1995); Coursework, Southeastern Community College; Coursework, Northwest Missouri State University (1977-1980) **C:** Governor, State of Iowa (2017-Present); Lieutenant Governor, State of Iowa, Des Moines, Iowa (2011-2017); Member, District 48, Iowa State Senate (2008-2010); Treasurer, Clarke County, Iowa (1994-2008); Member, Iowa Public Employees Retirement System Board (1996-2001); President, Iowa State County Treasurers Association (ISCTA) (2000); Treasurer, Clarke County Treasurer's Office; Pharmacist Assistant **PA:** Republican **RE:** Methodist

REYNOLDS, RYAN, T: Actor, Producer **I:** Media & Entertainment **DOB:** 10/23/1976 **PB:** Vancouver **SC:** British Columbia/Canada **PT:** James Reynolds; Tammy Lee (Stewart) Reynolds **MS:** Married **SPN:** Blake Lively (09/09/2012); Scarlett Johansson (09/27/2008, Divorced 2011) **CH:** James; Inez; Betty **ED:** Coursework, Kwantlen Polytechnic University **C:** Actor (1991-Present) **CR:** Stakeholder, Mint Mobile (2019); Stakeholder, Aviation American Gin (2018) **CW:** Voice Actor, "The Croods 2" (2020), Actor, "Red Notice" (2020); Actor, Producer, "Free Guy" (2020); Actor, "The Hitman's Wife's Bodyguard" (2020); Appearance, "Jeopardy! The Greatest of All Time" (2020); Actor, "6 Underground" (2019); Actor, "Fast & Furious Presents: Hobbs & Shaw" (2019); Actor, Music Video, "You Need to Calm Down" by Taylor Swift (2019); Actor, "Detective Pikachu" (2019); Actor, Producer, Screenwriter, "Deadpool 2" (2018); Actor, "The Hitman's Bodyguard" (2017); Actor, "Life" (2017); Actor, Co-writer, Short Film, "No Good Deed" (2017); Voice Actor, "Family Guy" (2011, 2012, 2017); Actor, Producer, "Deadpool" (2016); Actor, "Criminal" (2016); Actor, "Self/less" (2015); Actor, "Woman in Gold" (2015); Actor, "Mississippi Grind" (2015); Actor, "A Million Ways to Die in the West" (2014); Actor, "The Captive" (2014); Actor, Voice Actor, "The Voices" (2014); Actor, "R.I.P.D."

(2013); Voice Actor, "Turbo" (2013); Voice Actor, "The Croods" (2013); Executive Producer, TV Film, "Murder in Manhattan" (2013); Actor, "Ted" (2012); Actor, "Safe House" (2012); Appearance, "Top Gear" (2012); Narrator, Executive Producer, Documentary, "The Whale" (2011); Actor, "The Change-Up" (2011); Actor, "Green Lantern" (2011); Actor, "Buried" (2010); Actor, "Paper Man" (2009); Actor, "The Proposal" (2009); Actor, "X-Men Origins: Wolverine" (2009); Actor, "Adventureland" (2009); Host, "Saturday Night Live" (2009); Actor, "Fireflies in the Garden" (2008); Actor, "Definitely, Maybe" (2008); Actor, "Chaos Theory" (2008); Actor, "The Nines" (2007); Actor, "Smokin' Aces" (2006); Actor, "Just Friends" (2005); Actor, "Waiting..." (2005); Actor, "The Amityville Horror" (2005); Actor, TV Film, "School of Life" (2005); Voice Actor, "Zeroman" (2004-2005); Actor, "Blade: Trinity" (2004); Actor, "Harold & Kumar Go to White Castle" (2004); Actor, "Foolproof" (2003); Actor, "The In-Laws" (2003); Actor, "Scrubs" (2003); Actor, "Buying the Cow" (2002); Actor, "National Lampoon's Van Wilder" (2002); Actor, "Finder's Fee" (2001); Actor, "Two Guys and a Girl" (1998-2001); Actor, "We All Fall Down" (2000); Actor, "Boltneck" (2000); Actor, "Dick" (1999); Actor, "Coming Soon" (1999) Actor, "The Outer Limits" (1998, 1997, 1995); Actor, "The Alarmist" (1997); Actor, "In Cold Blood" (1996); Actor, TV Film, "When Friendship Kills" (1996); Actor, "The John Laroquette Show" (1996); Actor, "The X-Files" (1996); Actor, TV Film, "Serving in Silence: The Margarethe Cammermeyer Story" (1995); Actor, TV Film, "My Name is Kate" (1994); Actor, "The Odyssey" (1993-1994); Actor, "Ordinary Magic" (1993); Actor, "Fifteen" (1991-1993) **AW:** Honoree, Star, Hollywood Walk of Fame (2017); Best Actor, "Deadpool," Saturn Awards (2017); Named Favorite Movie Actor, "Deadpool," People's Choice Awards (2017); Named Man of the Year, Hasty Pudding (2017); Named One of the "100 Most Influential People," TIME Magazine (2017); Entertainer of the Year Award, Entertainment Weekly (2016); Named Best Actor in a Comedy, "Deadpool," Critics' Choice Movie Awards (2016); Named Best Comedic Performance, "Deadpool," MTV Movie Awards (2016); Named Best Fight, "Deadpool," MTV Movie Awards (2016); Named Favorite Action Movie Star, "Green Lantern," People's Choice Awards (2012); Named "Sexiest Man Alive," People Magazine (2010); Favorite Movie Superhero, "Green Lantern," People's Choice Awards (2012); Young Hollywood Award, Next Generation - Male (2003); Numerous Other Awards and Accolades

RHAMES, VING, T: Actor **I:** Media & Entertainment **DOB:** 05/12/1961 **PB:** Harlem **SC:** NY/USA **MS:** Married **SPN:** Deborah Reed (12/25/2000); Valerie Scott (1994, Divorced 1999) **CH:** Tiffany; Rainbow; Freedom **ED:** BFA, Drama Division, Juilliard School (1983); Coursework, Drama, State University of New York (SUNY) at Purchase **CW:** Actor, TV Film, "Cagney and Lacey" (2018); Actor, "Mission: Impossible - Fallout" (2018); Actor, "Con Man" (2018); Actor, "Father Figures" (2017); Voice Actor, "The Star" (2017); Voice Performer, Video Game, "Call of Duty: WWII" (2017); Actor, "Guardians of the Galaxy Vol. 2" (2017); Narrator, Team Introductions, New England Patriots and Atlanta Falcons, Super Bowl LI (2017); Actor, "A Sunday Horse" (2016); Actor, TV Film, "Untitled NBA Project" (2015); Actor, "Operator" (2015); Actor, "Mission: Impossible - Rogue Nation" (2015); Actor, TV Film, "A Day Later and a Dollar Short" (2014); Actor, "Jamesy Boy" (2014); Actor, "Percentage" (2014); Actor, "Force of Execution" (2013); Actor, "Armed Response" (2013); Actor, TV Series, "Monday Mornings" (2013); Actor, "Death Race: Inferno" (2013); Actor, Short Film, "Btd" (2012);

Actor, "Mafia" (2012); Actor, "Won't Back Down" (2012); Actor, "Money Fight" (2012); Actor, "Soldiers of Fortune" (2012); Actor, "Piranha 3DD" (2012); Actor, "7 Below" (2012); Actor, TV Film, "Black Jack" (2011); Actor, "Mission: Impossible - Ghost Protocol" (2011); Actor, TV Film, "Zombie Apocalypse" (2011); Actor, "Julia X" (2011); Actor, "Pimp Bullies" (2011); Actor, "The River Murders" (2011); Guest Appearance, "Cubed" (2011); Actor, "Death Race 2" (2010); Actor, "Caged Animal" (2010); Actor, "King of the Avenue" (2010); Actor, "Piranda 3D" (2010); Actor, "Operation: Endgame" (2010); Actor, "Love Chronicles: Secrets Revealed" (2010); Actor, TV Series, "Gravity" (2010); Actor, "'Master Harold' ... And the Boys" (2010); Executive Producer, Producer, "King of the Avenue" (2010); Actor, "Evil Angel" (2009); Actor, "Surrogates" (2009); Actor, "The Tournament" (2009); Actor, "The Bridge to Nowhere" (2009); Actor, "The Goods: Live Hard, Sell Hard" (2009); Actor, "Give 'em Hell Malone" (2009); Actor, "Echelon Conspiracy" (2009); Actor, "Saving God" (2008); Actor, Producer, "Phantom Punch" (2008); Actor, "Day of the Dead" (2008); Actor, Executive Producer, "Animal 2" (2008); Actor, "A Broken Life" (2007); Actor, TV Film, "Football Wives" (2007); Actor, "I Now Pronounce You Chuck & Larry" (2007); Actor, Producer, "Ascension Day" (2007); Executive Producer, Short Film, "The Final Chapter" (2007); Actor, "Idlewild" (2006); Actor, "Aquaman" (2006); Voice Actor, "Leroy & Stitch" (2006); Actor, "Mission: Impossible III" (2006); Actor, "Shooting Gallery" (2005); Actor, Executive Producer, Writer, "Animal" (2005); Actor, Co-Executive Producer, "Back in the Day" (2005); Actor, Co-Executive Producer, TV Series, "Kojak" (2005); Voice Performer, Video Game, "Driv3r" (2004); Actor, "Dawn of the Dead" (2004); Voice Actor, TV Series Documentary, "Freedom: A History of US" (2003); Actor, TV Series, "The System" (2003); Actor, "Sin" (2003); Voice Performer, Video Game, "Mission: Impossible - Operation Surma" (2003); Voice Actor, TV Series, "The Adventures of Jimmy Neutron: Boy Genius" (2003); Voice Actor, TV Series, "Lilo & Stitch: The Series" (2003); Actor, "Dark Blue" (2002); Voice Actor, TV Series, "The Proud Family" (2002); Actor, TV Movie, "RFK" (2002); Voice Actor, "Lilo & Stitch" (2002); Actor, "Undisputed" (2002); Actor, TV Film, "Little John" (2002); Actor, TV Film, "Sins of the Father" (2002); Actor, TV Series, "UC: Undercover" (2001); Voice Actor, "Final Fantasy: The Spirits Within" (2001); Actor, "Baby Boy" (2001); Actor, TV Film, "Holiday Heart" (2000); Actor, TV Film, "American Tragedy" (2000); Actor, "Mission: Impossible II" (2000); Actor, "Bringing Out the Dead" (1999); Actor, "Entrapment" (1999); Actor, "Out of Sight" (1998); Actor, "Body Count" (1998); Actor, TV Film, "Don King: Only in America" (1997); Actor, "Con Air" (1997); Actor, "Rosewood" (1997); Actor, "Dangerous Ground" (1997); Actor, "Striptease" (1996); Actor, "Mission: Impossible" (1996); Actor, TV Film, "Deadly Whispers" (1995); Actor, TV Series, "New York Undercover" (1995); Actor, TV Film, "Ed McBain's 87th Precinct: Lightning" (1995); Actor, TV Series, "ER" (1994-1996); Actor, TV Series, "Philly Heat" (1994); Actor, "Drop Squad" (1994); Actor, "Pulp Fiction" (1994); Actor, "The Saint of Fort Washington" (1994); Actor, "The Saint of Fort Washington" (1993); Actor, "Dave" (1993); Actor, "Blood In, Blood Out" (1993); Actor, TV Film, "Terror on Track 9" (1992); Actor, "Stop! Or My Mom Will Shoot" (1992); Actor, "The People Under the Stairs" (1991); Actor, TV Film, "Iran: Days of Crisis" (1991); Actor, TV Series, "Screenplay" (1991); Actor, "Homicide" (1991); Actor, "Flight of the Intruder" (1991); Actor, "Jacob's Ladder" (1990); Actor, TV Film, "When You Remember Me" (1990); Actor, "The Long Walk Home" (1990); Actor, TV Film, "Rising Son"

(1990); Actor, TV Series, "Men" (1989); Actor, TV Series, "The Equalizer" (1989); Actor, "Casualties of War" (1989); Actor, "Patty Hearst" (1988); Actor, TV Series, "Spenser: For Hire" (1988); Actor, TV Series, "Tour of Duty" (1987); Actor, TV Series, "Miami Vice" (1987, 1985); Actor, "Native Son" (1986); Actor, TV Series, "Crime Story" (1986); Actor, TV Series, "Crime Story" (1986); Actor, TV Series, "Another World" (1986); Actor, TV Series, "American Playhouse" (1985); Actor, "Go Tell It on the Mountain" (1984); Actor, Theater, "The Winter Boys" (1984); Narrator, Ultimate Fighting Championship (UFC); Voice Actor, Numerous Commercials **AW:** Best Actor (in a DVD Premiere Movie), "Animal," DVD Exclusive Awards (2006); Special Mention, "Baby Boy," Locarno International Film Festival (2001); Best Supporting Actor, ShoWest Convention (2000); Golden Globe Award, Best Actor in Mini-Series of Motion Picture, "Don King: Only in America" (1998); OFTA Television Awrad, Best Actor in a Motion Picture or Miniseries, "Don King: Only in America," Online Film & Television Association (1998)

RHEI, ESTHER, T: Medical Director **I:** Medicine & Health Care **CN:** Brigham and Women's Hospital **ED:** Fellowship, Memorial Sloan Kettering Cancer Center (1996-1998); MD, Robert Wood Johnson Medical School, Rutgers, The State University of New Jersey (1990); Residency, SUNY Downstate Health Sciences University **CT:** Certified in Surgery (1996) **C:** Surgeon, Brigham and Women's Hospital (1998-Present); Surgeon, Dana-Farber Cancer Institute (1998-Present) **CR:** Assistant Professor, Harvard Medical School **AW:** Top Doctor, Boston Magazine (2019); America's Top Doctors, Castle Connolly (2019) **MEM:** American College of Surgeons; Society of Surgical Oncology **AS:** Dr. Rhei attributes her success to her patients. She feels we are very fortunate to be living in an era where we have the outstanding ability to diagnose diseases early and cure them with the medical technology we have available. Dr. Rhei genuinely loves her patients and the work that she does. She is told over and over how much it shows through her work and enthusiasm. She treats all of her patients as if they're her mother or sister. **B/I:** Dr. Rhei became involved in her profession because she has always been interested in women's health. She is very hands on with patients and feels that breast disease is a very multidisciplinary discipline. The collaboration with people and the ability to cure women of a common disease is a very inspiring and driving force for surgeons who want to make a difference. Being able to help women and cure them of a disease has been a driving force for Dr. Rhei. She began her career at the Dana-Faber Cancer Center in 1998 when she completed her fellowship at Memorial Sloan-Kettering Cancer Center. She originally trained as a general surgeon but eventually began specializing in breast surgeries.

RHETT, WILLIAM PATERSON JR., T: The Reverend Doctor **I:** Education/Educational Services **DOB:** 08/04/1931 **PB:** Charleston **SC:** SC/USA **PT:** William Paterson Rhett; Margaret Fishburn (Hughes) Rhett **MS:** Widowed **SPN:** Dorothy Irene Carson Rhett (07/12/1944, Deceased 2014) **ED:** EdD, Auburn University (1971); MEd, Temple University (1968); MDiv, Virginia Theological Seminary (1960); BS, College of Charleston (1953) **CT:** Ordained Priest, Episcopalian Church (1961); Licensed Psychologist, State of South Carolina **C:** Retired (1995); Professor, The Citadel (1968-1995); Professor, The Military College of South Carolina (1968-1995) **CR:** Private Practice in Psychology, Charleston, SC (1973-1995); Coordinator, Professor of Counselor Education, The Citadel, The Military College of South Carolina, Charleston, SC (1968-1995); Assistant Rector, St. Michael's Parish, Charleston, SC (1962-1963); Visar, Christ-St. Paul's Parish, Adams Run, SC (1960-1962); Priest Associate, St. Philips Church, Charleston, SC **MIL:** Retired, Colonel, United States Air Force (1995) **MEM:** American Psychological Association; The Society of First Families South Carolina 1670-1700; St. Cecelia Society, Society Colonial Wars; The Society of the Cincinnati; Reserve Officers Association of the United States; American Association Marriage and Family Therapy; Carolina Yacht Club; Charleston Men's Club **MH:** Albert Nelson Marquis Lifetime Achievement Award **AS:** Dr. Rhett attributes his success to experience and commitment. **B/I:** Dr. Rhett felt a theological call to the priesthood. He began teaching psychotherapy at the Citadel after he was asked. **AV:** Painting portraits **PA:** Republican **RE:** Anglican

RHIMES, SHONDA, T: Television Producer, Director, Writer **I:** Media & Entertainment **DOB:** 01/13/1970 **PB:** Chicago **SC:** IL/USA **PT:** Ilee Rhimes Jr.; Vera P. (Cain) Rhimes **CH:** Harper (Adopted Daughter); Emerson Peal (Adopted Daughter); Beckett Rhimes (Adopted Daughter) **ED:** Honorary Doctorate, Dartmouth College, Hanover, NH (2014); Gary Rosenberg Writing Fellowship, USC School of Cinematic Arts, Los Angeles, CA (1994); MFA, USC School of Cinematic Arts, Los Angeles, CA (1994); BA in English and Film Studies, Dartmouth College, Hanover, NH (1991) **C:** Founder, Production Company, Shondaland (2005-Present) **CIV:** Founder, Rhimes Family Foundation (2016); Appointed, Trustee, Kennedy Center For The Performing Arts (2013); Co-Founder, Time's Up; Board Member, Numerous Nonprofit Organizations, including Humanitas, American Film Institute, Beyond 12, and Planned Parenthood **CW:** Producer, "Station 19" (2018-Present); Producer, "How to Get Away with Murder" (2014-Present); Creator, Writer, Producer, "Grey's Anatomy" (2005-Present); Producer, "Bridgerton" (2020); Producer, "For the People" (2018-2019); Producer, "Still Star-Crossed" (2017); Producer, "The Catch," (2016-2017); Author, "Year of Yes: How to Dance It Out, Stand In the Sun and Be Your Own Person" (2016); Creator, Writer, Producer, "Scandal" (2012-2018); Producer, "Gilded Lilys" (2012); Producer, "Off the Map" (2011); Creator, Producer, "Seattle Grace: Message of Hope" (2009); Creator, Producer, "Seattle Grace: On Call" (2009); Producer, "Inside the Box" (2009); Creator, Writer, Producer, "Private Practice" (2007-2013); Screenwriter, "The Princess Diaries 2: Royal Engagement" (2004); Screenwriter, "Crossroads" (2002); Screenwriter, "Introducing Dorothy Dandridge" (1999); Director, Screenwriter, "Blossoms and Veils" (1998); Research Director, "Hank Aaron: Chasing the Dream" (1995) **AW:** Inductee, Television Academy of Arts & Sciences Hall of Fame (2017); Champion of Change Award, Planned Parenthood (2017); Lifetime Achievement Award in Television, PGA Awards (2016); MIPCOM 2016 Personality of the Year Award (2016); Co-Honoree, DGA Diversity Award, Directors Guild of America (2014); Showmanship Award, Television, Publicists Guild of America (2014); TV Guide Award, Fan Favorite Awards, "Scandal," TV Guide Awards (2013); WIN Award, Outstanding Film/Show Written by a Woman, "Scandal," Women's Image Network Awards (2013); Golden Gate Award, GLAAD Media Awards (2012); Image Award for Outstanding Writing in a Dramatic Series, "Did You Hear What Happened to Charlotte King?" "Private Practice," Image Awards (NAACP) (2011); Image Award for Outstanding Writing in a Dramatic Series, "What a Difference a Day Makes," "Grey's Anatomy," Image Awards (NAACP) (2010); Image Award for Outstanding Writing in a Dramatic Series, "Freedom," "Grey's Anatomy," Image Awards (NAACP) (2009); Outstanding Writing in a Dramatic Series, "A Change Is Gonna Come," Grey's Anatomy," Image Awards (NAACP) (2008); Outstanding Writing in a Dramatic Series, "It's the End of the World," "Grey's Anatomy" Image Awards (NAACP) (2007); Outstanding Producer of Episodic Television, Drama, "Grey's Anatomy," PGA Awards (2007); Lucy Award, Women in Film Lucy Awards (2007); Gold Derby TV Award, "Grey's Anatomy," Gold Derby Awards (2006); PGA Award, Television Series - Drama, "Grey's Anatomy," Producers Guild of America Awards (2006); WGA Award, New Series, "Grey's Anatomy," Writers Guild of America (2005); International Emmy Founders Award; W.E.B. Du Bois Medal, Harvard University; Sherry Lansing Leadership Award, The Hollywood Reporter; Ally for Equality Award, Human Rights Council; Eleanor Roosevelt Global Women's Rights Award, Feminist Majority Foundation; Inductee, National Association of Broadcasters Broadcasting Hall of Fame; listed, "100 Liste of the Most Influential People," Time Magazine; Listed, "50 Most Powerful Women in Business," Fortune Magazine; Numerous Other Awards and Accolades **MEM:** Television Academy Executive Committee; USC Film Council; Obama Foundation Storytelling Committee; Writers Guild Inclusion Committee

RICE, ANNE, T: Writer **I:** Writing and Editing **DOB:** 10/14/1941 **PB:** New Orleans **SC:** LA/USA **PT:** Howard O'Brien; Katherine (Allen) O'Brien **MS:** Widowed **SPN:** Stan Rice (10/14/1961, Deceased 2002) **CH:** Christopher Rice; Michele Rice (Deceased) **ED:** Master of Arts in Creative Writing, San Francisco State University (1971); Bachelor of Arts in Political Science, San Francisco State University (1964); Coursework, Texas Woman's University (1959) **C:** Writer (1965-Present) **CW:** Author, "Blood Communion: A Tale of Prince Lestat," The Vampire Chronicles Series (2018); Author, "Ramses the Damned: The Passion of Cleopatra" (2017); Author, "Prince Lestate and the Realms of Atlantis," The Vampire Chronicles Series (2016); Author, A.N. Roquelaure, "Beauty's Kingdom" (2015); Author, "Prince Lestat," The Vampire Chronicles Series (2014); Author, "The Wolves of Midwinter," The Wolf Gift Chronicles Series (2013); Author, "The Wolf Gift," The Wolf Gift Chronicles Series (2012); Author, "Interview with the Vampire: Claudia's Story," The Vampire Chronicle Series (2012); Author, "Of Love and Evil," Songs of the Seraphim Series (2010); Author, "Angel Time," Songs of the Seaphim Series (2009); Author, "Christ the Lord: The Road to Cana," Christ the Lord Series (2008); Author, "Called Out of Darkness: A Spiritual Confession" (2008); Author, "Christ the Lord: Out of Egypt," Christ the Lord Series (2003); Author, "Blood Canticle," The Vampire Chronicle Series (2003); Author, "Blackwood Farm," The Vampire Chronicle Series (2002); Author, "Blood and Gold," The Vampire Chronicle Series (2001); Author, "Merrick," The Vampire Chronicle Series (2000); Author, "Vittorio the Vampire," New Tales of the Vampires Series (1999); Author, "The Pandora," New Tales of the Vampires Series (1998); Author, "The Vampire Armand," The Vampire Chronicle Series (1998); Author, "Violin" (1997); Author, "Servant of the Bones" (1996); Author, "Memnoch the Devil," The Vampire Chronicle Series (1995); Author, "Taltos," Lives of the Mayfair Witches Series (1994); Author, "Lasher," Lives of the Mayfair Witches Series (1993); Author, "The Tale of the Body Thief," The Vampire Chronicle Series (1992); Author, "The Witching Hour," Lives of the Mayfair Witches Series (1990); Author, "The Mummy, or Ramses the Damned" (1989); Author, "The Queen of the Damned," The Vampire Chronicle Series (1988); Author, as Anne

Rampling, "Belinda" (1986); Author, "The Vampire Lestat," The Vampire Chronicle Series (1985); Author, as Anne Rampling, "Exit to Eden" (1985); Author, as A.N. Roquelaure, "Beauty's Release" (1985); Author, as A.N. Roquelaure, "Beauty's Punishment," Sleeping Beauty Series (1984); Author, Short Fiction, "The Master of Rampling Gate" (1984); Author, as A.N. Roquelaure, "The Claiming of Sleeping Beauty," Sleeping Beauty Series (1983); Author, "The Feast of All Saints" (1979); Author, "Interview with the Vampire," The Vampire Chronicle Series (1976); Author, "Short Fiction, "Nicholas and Jean" (1966); Author, Short Fiction, "October 4, 1948" (1965); Numerous Film, TV, Theater and Comic Book Adaptations Of Her Work **AW:** Best Horror, "Prince Lestat," Goodreads Choice Awards (2014); Bram Stoker Award for Lifetime Achievement (2003); World Horror Convention Grand Master Award (1994)

RICE, CONDOLEEZZA, T: Political Science Professor, Former U.S. Secretary of State **I:** Education/Educational Services **DOB:** 11/14/1954 **PB:** Birmingham **SC:** AL/USA **PT:** John Wesley Rice Jr.; Angelena Ray Rice **ED:** Honorary DCL, Sewanee: The University of the South (2018); Honorary Doctor of Public Service, William & Mary (2015); Honorary LLD, Southern Methodist University (2012); Honorary DLitt, Air University (2008); Honorary LLD, Boston College (2006); Honorary DHL, Michigan State University (2004); Honorary Doctor of Public Service, University of Louisville (2004); Honorary LLD, Mississippi College School of Law (2003); Honorary Doctor of National Security Affairs, National Defense University (2002); Doctorate, University of Notre Dame (1995); Honorary DHL, University of Alabama (1994); LLD, Morehouse College (1991); PhD in Political Science, Josef Korbel School of International Studies, University of Denver (1981); Intern, RAND Corporation, Santa Monica, CA (1978); Intern, Bureau of Educational and Cultural Affairs (ECA), U.S. Department of State (1977); MA in Political Science, University of Notre Dame (1975); BA in Political Science, University of Denver, Cum Laude (1974); Dual Expertise Fellowship in Soviet Studies and International Security, Ford Foundation **C:** Denning Professor in Global Business and the Economy, Stanford Graduate School of Business (2012-Present); Founding Partner, Rice, Hadley, Gates & Manuel LLC (2012-Present); Professor, Political Science, Senior Fellow, Hoover Institution, Stanford University (2009-Present); Member, College Football Playoff Selection Committee (2013-2016); Senior Adviser, Regions Financial Corporation, Regions Bank, Birmingham, AL (2009); U.S. Secretary of State, George W. Bush Administration (2005-2009); Senior Fellow, Hoover Institution, Stanford University, CA (1991-1993, 1999-2001); Assistant to the U.S. President for National Security Affairs, National Security Council (2000); Provost, Stanford University (1993-1999); Associate Professor, Political Science, Stanford University (1987-1993); Soviet and Eastern Europe Affairs Adviser to President George H. W. Bush, National Security Council (1989-1991); Assistant Professor, Political Science, Stanford University (1981-1987); Special Assistant to the Director, Joint Chiefs of Staff, U.S. Department of Defense (1986); Political Science Consultant, Stanford University (1980-1981) **CR:** Member, Board of Directors, KiOR, Inc. (2011-Present); Member, Board of Directors, Charles Schwab Corporation (Charles Schwab & Co.) (1999-2001); Member, Board of Directors, Transamerica Corporation (1991-2001); Member, Board of Directors, Chevron Corporation (1991-2001) **CIV:** Ex Officio Member, Board of Trustees, John F. Kennedy Center for the Performing Arts (2009-2012) **CW:** Co-author, "To Build a Better World: Choices to End the Cold War and Create a Global Commonwealth" (2019); Co-author, "Political Risk: How Businesses and Organizations Can Anticipate Global Insecurity" (2018); Author, "Democracy: Stories from the Long Road to Freedom" (2017); Author, "Inside the Mind of George W. Bush: 43rd President of the United States of America" (2013); Author, "No Higher Honor: A Memoir of My Years in Washington" (2011); Author, "Extraordinary, Ordinary People" (2010); Author, "Condoleezza Rice: A Memoir of My Extraordinary, Ordinary Family and Me" (2010); Co-author, "The Strategy of Campaigning: Lessons from Ronald Reagan and Boris Yeltsin" (2007); Co-author, "Germany Unified and Europe Transformed: A Study in Statecraft" (1995); Author, "Uncertain Allegiance: The Soviet Union and the Czechoslovak Army, 1948-1983" (1984); Author, Contributor, Numerous Published Works **AW:** Honoree, Grand Cordon of the Order of the Rising Sun (2017); Named One of the "50 Highest-Earning Political Figures," Newsweek (2010); Named One of the "Women of the Year," Glamour (2008); Named One of the "Most Influential Black Americans," Ebony Magazine (2006-2008); Named One of the "100 Most Powerful Women," Forbes Magazine (2005-2008); Named One of the "50 Most Powerful People in D.C.," GQ Magazine (2007); Named One of the "100 Most Influential People in the World," TIME Magazine (2004-2007); Named to the "10 Most Fascinating People of 2005," Barbara Walters Special (2005); President Award, NAACP Image Awards (2002); Honoree, Knight's Cross of the Order of Polonia Restituta (1998); Dean's Award for Distinguished Teaching, Stanford University School of Humanities and Sciences (1993); Walter J. Gores Award for Excellence in Teaching, Stanford University (1984) **MEM:** Fellow, Arms Control and Disarmament Program, Stanford University (1980-1981); Fellow, American Association for the Advancement of Science; Council on Foreign Relations; Augusta National Golf Club; Gamma Delta Chapter, Alpha Chi Omega; The Phi Beta Kappa Society **PA:** Republican

RICE, HUGH, "TOM" THOMPSON JR., T: U.S. Representative from South Carolina; Lawyer **I:** Government Administration/Government Relations/Government Services **DOB:** 08/04/1957 **PB:** Charleston **SC:** SC/USA **PT:** Hugh Thompson Rice; Katherine Louise (Miller) Rice **MS:** Married **SPN:** Wrenzie Lee Calhoun (08/07/1982) **CH:** Hugh Thompson III; Jacob Calhoun; James Lucas **ED:** JD, University of South Carolina School of Law (1982); MS in Accounting, University of South Carolina (1982); BS in Accounting, University of South Carolina (1979) **C:** Member, U.S. House of Representatives from South Carolina's Seventh Congressional District, United States Congress, Washington, DC (2013-Present); Member, U.S. House Committee on Transportation and Infrastructure (2013-Present); Member, U.S. House Committee on Small Business (2013-Present); Member, U.S. House Committee on the Budget (2013-Present); Chairman, Horry County Council (2010-2012); Founding Partner, Rice & MacDonald Law Firm (1997-2012); Partner, Van Osdell, Lester, Howe & Rice, P.A., Myrtle Beach, SC (1984-1997); Senior Tax Consultant, Deloitte Haskins & Sells, Charlotte, NC (1982-1984); Member, Committee on Ways and Means **CR:** Adjunct Professor, Accounting, University of South Carolina, Myrtle Beach, SC (1985-1986) **CIV:** President, YMCA, Myrtle Beach Haven, SC (1994-Present); Board of Directors, YMCA, Myrtle Beach Haven, SC (1989-Present); Probate Advisory Board, Horry County (1989-Present); Finance Chairman, Capital Building Fund (1990-1992); Treasurer, Capital Building Fund (1989-1992); Vestry Episcopal Church (1989-1992); Volunteer, Brothers and Sisters Community Action (Now Big Brothers Big Sisters of America), Columbia, SC (1978-1982) **AW:** Centurion Award, Sertoma, Inc. (1988); Gem Award, Sertoma, Inc. (1987); Outstanding Service Award, Brothers and Sisters Community Action (Now Big Brothers Big Sisters of America) (1980, 1981) **MEM:** Chairman, Board of Directors, Sertoma, Inc. (1990-1991); President, Sertoma, Inc. (1989-1990); Secretary, Sertoma, Inc. (1988-1989); South Carolina Bar Association; South Carolina Association of CPAs (SCACPA); Sertoma, Inc. **BAR:** State of South Carolina (1982); CPA, State of South Carolina; Certified Tax Specialist; Certified Specialist in Taxation and Estate Planning, South Carolina Bar Association **AV:** Fishing; Hunting; Golfing; Spending time with family and friends **PA:** Republican **RE:** Episcopalian

RICE, JERRY LEE SR., T: Former Professional Football Player **I:** Athletics **DOB:** 10/13/1962 **PB:** Starkville **SC:** MS/USA **PT:** Joe Nathan Rice; Eddie Rice **MS:** Married **SPN:** Latisha Pelayo (10/21/2019); Jacqueline Bernice Mitchell (09/08/1987, Divorced 2009) **CH:** Jacqui Bonet; Jerry Rice Jr.; Jada Symone **ED:** Coursework, Mississippi Valley State University (1981-1984) **C:** Co-host, "Sports Sunday," Station KNTV NBC-TV, NBCUniversal Media, LLC, San Francisco, CA (2006-Present); NFL Analyst, ESPN (2011-2013); Retired Professional Football Player (2006); Wide Receiver, Seattle Seahawks, NFL (2004); Wide Receiver, Oakland Raiders, NFL (2001-2004); Wide Receiver, San Francisco 49ers, NFL (1985-2000) **CIV:** Spokesperson, Foundation for Chiropractic Progress **CW:** Co-author, "America's Game: The NFL at 100" (2019); Co-author, "50 Years, 50 Moments: The Most Unforgettable Plays in Super Bowl History" (2015); Appearance, Video Game, "Jerry Rice & Nitus' Dog Football" (2011); Actor, "Without a Paddle: Nature's Calling" (2009); Guest Appearance, "Rules of Engagement" (2009); Co-author, "Go Long!: My Journey Beyond Fame and the Game" (2006); Contestant, "Dancing with the Stars" (2005-2006); Co-author, "Rice" (1996) **AW:** Inductee, Pro Football Hall of Fame (2010); Selected as "The Greatest Player in NFL History," "The Top 100: NFL's Greatest Players," NFL Networks (2010); Listed, "All-Time College All-Stars," Sports Illustrated (2008); Inductee, Mississippi Sports Hall of Fame (2007); Inductee, Bay Area Sports Hall of Fame (2007); Inductee, College Football Hall of Fame (2006); Named Pro Bowl MVP, National Football League (NFL) (1995); Named to First Team All-Pro (1986-1990, 1992-1996); Named Super Bowl XXIII MVP (1989); Named National Football League (NFL) MVP, Pro Football Writers Association (Now Pro Football Writers of America) (1987); Bert Bell Award (1987); Named Sporting News and NFL Player of the Year (1987); Named Offensive Player of the Year, The Associated Press (1987, 1993); Named Sports Illustrated Player of the Year (1986, 1990, 1993); Named NFC Offensive Rookie of the Year (1985); Named 12-Time All-Pro; Recipient, Numerous Awards and Accolades in Football

RICE, JOAN S., T: Pediatric Nurse, Author, Parent Educator **I:** Other **DOB:** 04/27/1948 **PB:** Plainfield **SC:** NJ/USA **PT:** Albert L. Schweickart; Constance (Harrison) Schweickart **MS:** Married **SPN:** Gary T. Rice (06/21/1992); Benjamin N. Cittadino (04/10/1971, Divorced 1991) **CH:** Julia; Benjamin; Marc **ED:** BSN, Duke University, Magna Cum Laude (1970) **CT:** California Teaching Credential in Parent Education (1995); School Nurse Credential, California State University, Northridge University (1995); School Nurse Credential, Trenton State College (Now University of New Jersey) (1992); Certification in Audiometry **C:** Parent Educator, Warner Brothers, Burbank, CA (1992-Present);

School Nurse, Parent Educator, Burbank Unified School District (1993-Present); Parent Educator (1978-Present); Infant-Toddler Program Director, Warner Brothers Children Center, Burbank, CA (1992-1993); Parent Education Director, Family Resource Infant Center, Princeton, NJ (1979-1992); Nursing Instructor of Pediatrics, Memorial Hospital School Nursing, South Bend, IN (1972-1974); Staff Nurse, Child Psychiatric Unit, Medical University of South Carolina, Charleston, SC (1971-1972); Staff Nurse, Children's Hospital of Los Angeles, Hollywood, CA (1970-1971) CR: College Health Nurse, Allan Hancock College, Santa Maria, CA (2002-Present); San Luis Coastal Unified School District, Adult School (1995-2017); Lucia Mar Unified School District (1995-2017); School Nurse, Santa Maria Bonita School District, Santa Maria, CA (1999-2002); School Nurse, Burbank Unified School District, Burbank, CA (1993-1999); Presenter, National Association of the Education of Young Children; Part-Time Faculty, Allan Hancock College CIV: Dining for Women; Volunteer, Monthly Delivery of Hygiene Supplies to the Homeless Coalition; Volunteer, Children's Resource Network for Needy Children of the Five Cities; Hospital Volunteer, Pre-Surgery Puppet Therapy, Princeton Medical Center CW: Author, "Parenting Solutions: Encouragement for Everyday Parenting Concerns," Paragon House Publishers (2009) AW: Inductee, Sigma Theta Tau International Honor Society of Nursing MEM: American Nurses Association; Sigma Theta Tau International Honor Society of Nursing MH: Albert Nelson Marquis Lifetime Achievement Award B/I: Ms. Rice became involved in her profession because of her love of science and her desire to help children. AV: Traveling; Reading

RICE, JOY KATHARINE, PHD, T: Psychologist, Educator I: Medicine & Health Care CN: University of Wisconsin School of Medicine and Public Health PB: Oak Park SC: IL/USA PT: Joseph Theodore Straka; Margaret Sophia (Bednarik) Straka MS: Married SPN: David Gordon Rice (09/01/1962) CH: Scott Alan; Andrew David; Grandchildren Addison Rose, Ashlyn Sophia; Alek Scott ED: PhD, University of Wisconsin (1967); MS, University of Wisconsin (1964); MS, University of Wisconsin (1962); BFA, University of Illinois, with High Honors (1960) CT: Licensed Clinical Psychologist (1967-2016) C: Clinical Professor, Psychiatry, University of Wisconsin–Madison (1995-Present); Professor, Educational Policy Studies and Women's Studies, University of Wisconsin–Madison (1974-1995); Director, Office of Continuing Education Services, University of Wisconsin–Madison (1972-1978); Private Practice, Psychology, Psychiatric Services, Madison (1967-2015); Assistant Director, Counseling Center, University of Wisconsin–Madison (1966-1974); United States Public Health Service Pre-Doctoral Fellow, Department of Psychiatry, Medical School, University of Wisconsin–Madison (1964-1965) CR: Adult Education Commission, United States Office of Career Education, Washington, DC (1978); State Wisconsin Educational Approval Board, Madison (1972-1973) CIV: Associate Vice President, Madison Symphony Orchestra League Board of Directors (2013-2018); Executive Board Family Services Dane County (2004-2014); President, Family Services, Dane County Board (2011-2012); Board of Directors, Madison Friends of International Students (2006-2011); Board of Directors, Madison Repertory Theater (2007-2010); Co-Chair, Wisconsin Lieutenant Governor's Task Force on Women and Depression (2005-2008); Board of Directors, Big Brothers Big Sisters, Dane County (1997-2007); President, Big Brothers Big Sisters, Dane County (2002) CW: Author, "Transnational Psychology of Women, Expanding International and Intersectional Approaches" (2019); Author, "Psychological Practice with Women, Guidelines, Diversity, Empowerment" (2014); Consultant Editor, "Handbook of Feminism and Women's Rights Worldwide" (2010); Author, "Transforming Leadership Diverse Visions and Women's Voices" (2007); Consultant Editor, "Handbook of Girls' and Women's Psychological Health" (2005); Consultant Editor, "Handbook of Couple Therapy" (2005); Consultant Editor, "Encyclopedia of Women and Gender" (2001); Consultant Editor, "Handbook of Adult and Continuing Education" (1989); Consultant Editor, "Psychology Women Quarterly" (1986-1988); Author, "Living Through Divorce, A Developmental Approach to Divorce Therapy" (1985); Editorial Board, "Lifelong Learning" (1979-1986); Contributor, Articles, Professional Journals AW: Elder Recognition Award for Distinguished Contributions to Counseling Psychology, American Psychological Association (2015); Denmark Reuder Award, Outstanding International Contributions to the Psychology of Women & Gender (2011); Woman of the Year Award, Section Advancement of Women in Counseling Psychology (2007); Distinguished Leadership Award, International Council of Psychologists (2004); John Fritschler Junior Award for Distinguished Achievement (2004); Distinguished Achievement Award, Educational Press Association of America (1992); Teaching Fellow, University of Wisconsin, Madison (1962-1963); Knapp Fellow (1960-1962) MEM: Rotary International (2004-Present); Executive Board, Psychology of Women's Division, American Psychological Association (1994-Present); Board of Directors, TEMPO International Foundation (2016-2018); Executive Board, International Psychology Division, American Psychological Association (1998-2018); Board Director, Secretary, International Council of Psychologists (1998-2018); Membership Board, American Psychological Association (2008-2010); Board of Directors, Secretary, President Elect, President TEMPO International (2000-2010); Board Director, Secretary, President Elect, President TEMPO International (2000-2010); President, International Psychology Division, American Psychological Association (2006); Chair, Committee on International Relations in Psychology, American Psychological Association (2003-2005); Chair, International Committee of Women, American Psychological Association (2000-2002); National Association of Women's Education (1984-1991); American Association Continuing and Adult Education (1978-1982); Fellow of 5 American Psychological Association Divisions, Psychology of Women, International Psychology, Counseling Psychology, Independent Practice and Psychotherapy MH: Albert Nelson Marquis Lifetime Achievement Award B/I: Dr. Rice became involved in her profession because she graduated with a fine arts degree, but knew she wanted to pursue a graduate degree. As a senior in college, she had the opportunity to be a freshman counselor for her sorority which was a very positive and inspiring experience. She received a full graduate fellowship to the University of Wisconsin-Madison in counseling. Once she started, she realized that clinical psychology would be the right fit for her and changed her major accordingly. A strong interest in teaching and research led her to become an academician as well as a clinician. AV: Oil painting; Gardening; Traveling

RICE, KATHLEEN MAURA, T: U.S. Representative, Former Prosecutor I: Government Administration/ Government Relations/Government Services DOB: 02/15/1965 PB: Manhattan SC: NY/USA PT: Laurence Rice; Christine Rice ED: JD, Touro College Jacob D. Fuchsberg Law Center (1991); BA, Catholic University (1987) C: U.S. Representative, New York's Fourth Congressional District, United States Congress, Washington, DC (2015-Present); District Attorney, Nassau County, NY (2005, 2009, 2013); Assistant U.S. Attorney, Eastern District of Pennsylvania, The U.S. Department of Justice, Philadelphia, PA (1999-2005); Assistant District Attorney, Kings County, NY (1992-1999); Member, Committee on Homeland Security; Member, Committee on Veterans' Affairs CR: Co-Chair, Moreland Commission to Investigate Public Corruption (2013-2014) MEM: President, District Attorneys Association of the State of New York (2013-Present) PA: Democrat RE: Roman Catholic

RICH, ROBERT F., PHD, T: Law Educator I: Education/Educational Services PT: Max F. Rich; Adele Rich MS: Married SPN: Lucy (Schauble) CH: Three Children ED: PhD in Political Sciences, University of Chicago, Chicago, IL (1975); MA in Political Sciences, University of Chicago, Chicago, IL (1973); Coursework, Free University of Berlin, Berlin, Germany (1971-1972); BA in Government, Oberlin College, Oberlin, OH, With Honors (1971) C: Retired (2012); Director, Institute of Government and Public Affairs, University of Illinois at Urbana-Champaign (2005-2012); Professor, University of Illinois at Urbana–Champaign (1986-2012); Visiting Fellow, Max Planck Institute for Foreign and International Social Awareness (2004); Mercator Professor, Humboldt University of Berlin, Berlin, Germany (2002-2003); Acting Head, Medical Humanities and Social Sciences Program, University of Illinois at Urbana-Champaign (1988-1997); Director, Institute of Government and Public Affairs, University of Illinois at Urbana-Champaign (1986-1997); Fellow, Johns Hopkins University Center for the Study of American Government, Washington, Washington, DC (1993-1995); Associate Professor, Political Science, Public Policy and Management, School of Urban and Public Affairs (SUPA), Carnegie Mellon University (1982-1986); Coordinator, Domestic and Urban Policy Field, Woodrow Wilson School of Public and International Affairs, Princeton University (1976-1982); Assistant Professor, Politics and Public Affairs, Princeton University (1976-1982); Lecturer, Department of Political Science, University of Michigan Center for Research on Utilization of Scientific Knowledge (1975-1976); Project Director, Assistant Research Scientist, Center for Research on Utilization Science Knowledge, Institute for Social Research, University of Michigan CR: Lecturer, Osher Lifelong Learning Institute (OLLI) (2012-Present); Consultant, U.S. Department of Health and Human Services (HHS), Carnegie Mellon University (1986-Present); Distinguished Lecturer, German Marshall Fund, Hamburg, Germany (1997); Consultant, American Career Society (1996-1997); Consultant, Food, Drug and Law Institute, Department of Health and Human Services (1989); Consultant, MacArthur Foundation, National Institute of Mental Health (NIMH) (1988-1989); Visiting Scholar, Hastings Center for Society, Ethics and Life Sciences (1982) CIV: Kiwanis; Various Education Programs; Young Kiwanis CW: Author, "Consumer Choice: Social Welfare and Health Policy" (2005); Co-Editor, "Health Policy, Federalism and the Role of the American States" (1996); Co-Editor, "Competitive Approaches to Health Policy Reform" (1993); Editor, "Knowledge, Creation, Diffusion, Utilization" (1979-1991); Associate Editor, Evaluation Review (1985-1989); Associate Editor, Society (1984-1988); Member, Editorial Board, Law and Human Behavior (1983-1987); Member, Editorial Board, Policy Studies Rev. Series (1980-1983); Editorial Board, Evaluation and Change (1979-1982); Author, Book, "Social Science Information and Public Policy Making: The Interaction Between Bureaucratic

Politics and the Use of Survey Data" (1981); Editor, "The Knowledge Cycle" (1981); Co-Author, "Government Information Management: A Counter-Report of the Commission on Federal Paperwork" (1980); Editor, "Translating Evaluation into Policy" (1979); Contributor, Numerous Articles, Professional Journals; Contributor, Numerous Chapters, Books **AW:** Guest Fellow, Humboldt University of Berlin (2002); Aaron Wildavsky Award, Policy Studies Association (1994); Professor Emil Limbach Teaching Award, School of Urban and Public Affairs (SUPA), Carnegie Mellon University (1985); Russel Sage Foundation Research Fellow (1974-1975); German Government Fellow (1974); National Opinion Research Center Fellow (1972-1973); Fellow, Germany Academy Exchange Program, Federal Republic of Germany (1971-1972) **MEM:** Chairman, Committee on Mental Health Needs of Victims, World Federation for Mental Health (1985-Present); Board of Directors, Society for Traumatic Stress Studies (1980-Present); President, Howard R. Davis Society for Knowledge Utilization and Planned Change (1986-1989); Task Force on Victims of Crime and Violence, American Psychological Association (1982-1984); Vice Chairman, World Federation for Mental Health (1981-1983); Political Science 400; Phi Beta Kappa; Sigma Xi; Phi Kappa Phi **MH:** Albert Nelson Marquis Lifetime Achievement Award **B/I:** Dr. Rich was inspired to become an educator by Donald T. Campbell, a prolific writer involved with empirical data. Throughout his career, Mr. Rich became involved in a number of fields, including psychology, political science, medicine, and law. As he gained experience, he took a special interest in health, mental health, and policy law. He was later inspired to teach as a result of gaining mentors at the University of Chicago. **AV:** Fishing; Learning

RICHARDS, KEITH, T: Guitarist **I:** Media & Entertainment **DOB:** 12/18/1943 **PB:** Dartford **SC:** Kent/England **PT:** Bert Richards; Doris (Dupree) Richards **MS:** Married **SPN:** Patti Hansen (12/18/1983) **CH:** Hansen; Theodora Dupree; Alexandra Nicole; Marlon; Angela (Dandelion); Tara (Deceased) **ED:** Coursework, Sidcup Art College **C:** Guitarist, Songwriter, The Rolling Stones (1962-Present) **CW:** Musician, Songwriter, Album, "Blue & Lonesome," The Rolling Stones (2016); Musician, Songwriter, Solo Album, "Crosseyed Heart" (2015); Himself, TV Film, "Keith Richards: Under the Influence" (2015); Author, "Gus & Me: The Story of My Granddad and My First Guitar" (2014); Himself, TV Film, "Rolling Stones: One More Shot" (2012); Himself, Documentary, "Tools and Maytals: Reggae Got Soul" (2011); Musician, Songwriter, Compilation Solo Album, "Vintage Vinos" (2010); Author, "Life" (2009); Performer, Documentary, "Shine a Light" (2008); Actor, "Pirates of the Caribbean: At World's End" (2007); Musician, Songwriter, Album, "A Bigger Bang," The Rolling Stones (2005); Guest Appearance, Voice Actor, "The Simpsons" (2002); Musician, Songwriter, Album, "Bridges to Babylon," The Rolling Stones (1997); Musician, Songwriter, Album, "Voodoo Lounge," The Rolling Stones (1994); Musician, Songwriter, Solo Album, "Main Offender" (1992); Musician, Songwriter, Album, "Steel Wheels," The Rolling Stones (1989); Musician, Live Solo Album, "Live at the Hollywood Palladium, December 5, 1988" (1988); Musician, Songwriter, Solo Album, "Talk Is Cheap" (1988); Musician, Songwriter, Album, "Dirty Work," the Rolling Stones (1986); Musician, Songwriter, Album, "Undercover," The Rolling Stones (1983); Musician, Songwriter, Album, "Tattoo You," The Rolling Stones (1981); Musician, Songwriter, Album, "Emotional Rescue," The Rolling Stones (1980); Musician, Songwriter, Album, "Some Girls," The Rolling Stones (1978); Musician,

Songwriter, Album, "Black and Blue," The Rolling Stones (1976); Musician, Songwriter, Album, "It's Only Rock 'n Roll" (1974); Musician, Songwriter, Album, "Goats Head Soup," The Rolling Stones (1973); Musician, Songwriter, Album, "Exile on Main St.," The Rolling Stones (1972); Musician, Songwriter, Album, "Sticky Fingers," The Rolling Stones (1971); Musician, Songwriter, Album, "Let It Bleed," The Rolling Stones (1969); Actor, "Man on Horseback" (1969); Musician, Songwriter, Album, "Beggars Banquet," The Rolling Stones (1968); Musician, Songwriter, Album, "Their Satanic Majesties Request" (1967); Musician, Songwriter, Album, "Between the Buttons," The Rolling Stones (1967); Musician, Songwriter, Album, "Aftermath," The Rolling Stones (1966); Musician, Songwriter, Album, "December's Children (And Everybody's)," The Rolling Stones (1965); Musician, Songwriter, Album, "Out of Our Heads," The Rolling Stones (1965); Musician, Songwriter, Album, "The Rolling Stones, Now!," The Rolling Stones (1965); Musician, Songwriter, Album, "12 X 5," The Rolling Stones (1964); Musician, Songwriter, Album, "The Rolling Stones (England's Newest Hit Makers)," The Rolling Stones (1964); Musician, Numerous Rolling Stones Live Albums and Performances for Film and TV; Guest Appearance, Numerous Albums, Songs, and Performances **AW:** Legend Award, Men of the Year Awards, GQ (2015); Inductee (with the Rolling Stones), The Rock and Roll Hall of Fame (1989); Co-Recipient, Greatest Touring Band of All Time, The Rolling Stones, World Music Awards (2006); Ivor Novello Award for Outstanding Contribution to British Music, The Rolling Stones (1991); Living Legend Award, International Rock Awards (1989); Co-Recipient, Recording Academy Lifetime Achievement Award, The Rolling Stones, Grammy Awards (1986); Co-Recipient, Silver Clef Award, The Rolling Stones (1982); Numerous Awards and Accolades as a Member of the Rolling Stones

RICHARDS, THOMAS EDWARD, T: Executive Chairman, President (Retired), Chief Executive Officer (Retired) **I:** Technology **CN:** CDW Corporation **MS:** Married **SPN:** Mary Beth Richards **CH:** Two Children **ED:** MS in Management, Massachusetts Institute of Technology (MIT), Cambridge, MA; BA in Business and Managerial Economics, University of Pittsburgh **C:** Executive Chairman, Board of Directors, CDW Corporation (2019-Present); Chief Executive Officer, President, Chairman, CDW Corporation (2013-2019); Chief Executive Officer, President, CDW Corporation (2011-2013); President, Chief Operating Officer, CDW Corporation (2009-2011); Executive Vice President, Chief Operating Officer, Qwest Communications International, Inc. (2008-2009); Executive Vice President, Business Markets Group, Qwest Communications International, Inc. (2005-2008); Chairman, President, Chief Executive Officer, Clear Communications Corporation (1999-2003); Executive Vice President, Communications and Information Products, Ameritech (1995-1999); Numerous Sales, Marketing and Operations Positions in Telecommunications and Computer Services, Bell Atlantic (1983-1995); Numerous Management Positions, Bell of Pennsylvania (1976-1983) **CR:** Board Member, UPMC (2019-Present); Member, Board of Trustees, University of Pittsburgh; Board Member, Junior Achievement of Chicago; Board Member, Northern Trust; Former Trustee, Rush University Medical Center **CIV:** Member, Pittsburgh Council, Boy Scouts America; Board of Directors, Greater Pittsburgh Chamber of Commerce; Board of Directors, Pennsylvania Economic Development Association; Board of Directors, Pennsylvania Economic League **AW:** Alfred P. Sloan Fellow **MEM:** Economic Club of Chicago; Executives' Club of Chicago

RICHARDSON, ERNEST RAY, T: Housing Program Supervisor (Retired) **I:** Civil Service **DOB:** 09/05/1932 **PB:** Cominto **SC:** AR/USA **PT:** Louis Richardson Jr.; Leila Mae (Purdom) Richardson **MS:** Married **SPN:** Shirley A. Richardson; Deloris Cobb (03/25/1955, Divorced 1964); Doretha L. Tolbert (04/1964, Divorced 1978) **CH:** Victor Ray; Rodney Lynn (Deceased, 2006); Regenia Ann; Kassandra D. Porter; Kimberly Ann Richardson; Janet L. Linton (Stepdaughter); Kay F. Pate (Stepdaughter); Jerome Pate (Stepson); Andre Richard (Stepson) **ED:** Graduate Coursework, Leadership Modesto (1996); Graduate Coursework, Intergovernmental Management Training (1993); Graduate Coursework, Lewis University, Romeoville, IL (1980-1983); AA in Real Estate, Parkland College (1978); BA in Business Administration, Franklin University (1975); MBA Coursework **CT:** Certified Real Estate Broker, Illinois; Certified Public Housing Manager (PHM); Master Residential Real Appraiser (MRA); Master Farm and Land Appraiser (MFLA); Master Senior Appraiser; Business Appraiser **C:** Housing Program Supervisor, Modesto, CA (1989-2003); Executive Director, Personnel Director, Aurora Housing Authority (1987-1989); Director, Neighborhood Services Division, Joliet, IL (1982-1987); Financial Specialist, Neighborhood Services Division, Joliet, IL (1979-1982); Financial Specialist, Community Development Division, Urbana, IL (1975-1979); Executive Director, Personnel Director, Champaign County Opportunities Industrialization Center CCVOC), Champaign, IL (1970-1973); Director, Education and Training, Champaign County Opportunities Industrialization Center (CCVOC), Champaign, IL (1968-1970) **CR:** Recording Secretary (1997-1998); Alternate Member, Stanislaus County Civil Grand Jury (1996-1997); Management Continuous Improvement Committee, Modesto, CA (1995-1996); Central Valley Opportunity Center, Inc., Modesto, CA (1992-1996); Vice Chairman, Management, Development Committee, Modesto, CA (1993-1994); National Funds Allocation and Review Committee, National Opportunities Industrialization Center (1971-1972) **CIV:** Local Chapter, National Association for the Advancement of Colored People (NAACP); Latino Community Roundtable **MIL:** Technical Sergeant, U.S. Air Force (1951-1967) **CW:** Featured, Central Valley Opportunity Centers Executive Directors Quarterly Newsletter (2019); Featured, Grid Alternatives Central Valleys Newsletter (2018) **AW:** Outstanding 2018 Senior Volunteer for Stanislaus, District One (2018); Outstanding Board Member of the Year (2004, 2006, 2014); Quality of Life Award (2013); Member of the Year, National Association of Real Estate Appraisers (1988); Letters of Appreciation, Internal Revenue Service (IRS), California Franchise Tax Board; Letters of Appreciation, Antioch **MEM:** President, Illinois Chapter, National Association of Real Estate Appraisers (1985-1986); American Legion; Modesto Kiwanis Club; National Association for the Advancement of Colored People (NAACP); Freemasons, King Solomon's Lodge **MH:** Albert Nelson Marquis Lifetime Achievement Award **AS:** Mr. Richardson attributes his success to advice from his mother and listening to his father, grandparents, and positive-thinking friends. **AV:** Working with income tax business; Working with environmental consulting business; Appraising real estate; Walking; Reading; Traveling; Watching television **PA:** Democrat **RE:** Protestant, Church of Christ

RICHIE, LIONEL B. JR., T: Singer, Lyricist, Theater Producer **I:** Media & Entertainment **DOB:** 06/20/1949 **PB:** Tuskegee **SC:** AL/USA **PT:** Lionel Brockman Richie Sr.; Alberta Richie **MS:** Married **SPN:** Diane Alexander (1996); Brenda

Harvey (1975, Divorced) **CH:** Miles; Sofia; Nicole (Adopted Daughter) **ED:** Honorary MusD, Boston College (1986); Honorary MusD, Tuskegee University (1985); BS in Economics, Tuskegee University (1971) **C:** President, Brockman Music, Los Angeles, CA **CIV:** Featured Performer, Soirée Bouquet, Breast Cancer Research Foundation (2003); Donor, More Than $3 Million, Breast Cancer Research Foundation **CW:** Judge, "American Idol" (2018-Present); Guest Appearance, "The Rookie" (2020); Singer, Live Album, "Hello from Las Vegas" (2019); Guest Appearance, "American Housewife" (2019); Singer, Producer, Album, "Tuskegee" (2012); Singer, Producer, Album, "Just Go" (2009); Singer, Live Album, "Symphonica in Rosso" (2008); Singer, Live Album, "Live in Paris/Live - His Greatest Hits and More" (2007); Voice Actor, "The Simpsons" (2007); Singer, Producer, Album, "Coming Home" (2006); Singer, Producer, Album, "Just for You" (2004); Singer, Live Album, "Encore" (2002); Singer, Producer, Album, "Renaissance" (2000); Singer, Producer, Album, "Time" (1998); Actor, "Gang Land" (1998); Singer, Producer, Album, "Louder Than Words" (1996); Actor, "The Preacher's Wife" (1996); Singer, Producer, Album, "Dancing on the Ceiling" (1986); Singer, Producer, Album, "Can't Slow Down" (1983); Singer, Producer, Album, "Lionel Richie" (1982); Singer, Album, "In the Pocket," The Commodores (1981); Singer, Album, "Heroes," The Commodores (1980); Singer, Album, "Midnight Magic," The Commodores (1979); Singer, Album, "Natural High," The Commodores (1978); Singer, Album, "Commodores," the Commodores (1977); Guest Appearance, "Scott Joplin" (1977); Singer, Album, "Hot on the Tracks," The Commodores (1976); Singer, Album, "Movin' On," The Commodores" (1975); Singer, Album, "Caught in the Acid," The Commodores (1975); Singer, Album, "Machine Gun," The Commodores (1974) **AW:** Honoree, Kennedy Center Honors (2017); MusiCares Person of the Year, Grammy Awards (2016); Lifetime Achievement Award, BET Awards (2014); Icon Award, TV Land Awards (2008); Goldene Kamera for Lifetime Achievement, Music International, Goldene Kamera, Germany (2007); Honoree, Star, Walk of Fame (2003); SCAP Award, Most Performed Feature Film Standards, "Endless Love," ASCAP Film and Television Music Awards (1991); Entertainer of the Year Award, Image Awards (NAACP) (1989); American Music Award for Favorite Pop/Rock Video, "Dancing on the Ceiling," American Music Awards (1987); Best Music, Original Song, "Say You, Say Me," "White Nights," Academy Awards (1986); Best Original Song - Motion Picture, "Say You, Say Me," "White Nights" (1986); Co-Recipient, Song of the Year, "We Are the World," Grammy Awards (1986); Writer of the Year, American Society of Composers (1984, 1985, 1986); Co-Recipient, Producer of the Year, Non-Classical, Grammy Awards (1985); Album of the Year, "Can't Slow Down," Grammy Awards (1985); American Music Award for Favorite Soul/R&B Video, "Hello," American Music Awards (1985); Publisher of the Year, American Society of Composers (1985); Best Pop Vocal Performance, Male, "Truly," Grammy Awards (1983) **MEM:** American Society of Composers; Kappa Kappa Psi; Alpha Phi Alpha

RICHMOND, CEDRIC LEVON, T: U.S. Representative from Louisiana **I:** Government Administration/Government Relations/Government Services **DOB:** 09/13/1973 **PB:** New Orleans **SC:** LA/USA **MS:** Married **SPN:** Raquel Greenup (2015) **CH:** One Child **ED:** JD, Tulane University Law School (1998); BA, Morehouse College (1995); Diploma, Graduate Executive Program, Harvard Kennedy School, John F. Kennedy School of Government **C:** Member, U.S. House of Representatives from Louisiana's Second Congressional District, United States Congress, Washington, DC (2011-Present); Member, U.S. House Committee on Small Business (2011-Present); Member, District 101, Louisiana House of Representatives (2000-2010) **AW:** Named, One of the Politics 40 Under 40, TIME Magazine (2010) **MEM:** Louisiana Bar Association **PA:** Democrat **RE:** Baptist

RICHMOND, ROCSAN, T: Television Producer **I:** Media & Entertainment **CN:** Richmond Cmty Rels.

RICHTER, JANELL, T: Principal, Minister **I:** Religious **DOB:** 03/20/1945 **PB:** West Point **SC:** MS/USA **PT:** Alvin Lee Johnston; Lola Marie Wheeler **MS:** Married **SPN:** James F. Richter Sr. (7/14/1965) **CH:** James Richter Jr.; Janna Faith; Joanna Felicia **ED:** BS, Columbus University, Georgia (1980); AA, Columbus College, Georgia (1965) **CT:** Ordination Certification, Pentecostal Church of God (1996) **C:** Principal, Evangel Temple Christian Academy, Morrow (1997-2013); State Director, Women's Ministries, Pentecostal Church of God (1990-2000); Assistant Pastor, Evangel Temple, Morrow (1995-1997); State Director, Christian Education, Pentecostal Church of God, Georgia (1983-1990); State Secretary-Treasurer Corporation, Pentecostal Church of God, Georgia (1974-1975); Co-Owner, Bookkeeper, Ye Olde Bible Shoppe, Royal Books, Newnan, Georgia (1972-1982) **CR:** Central Committee, Women's Ministries Pentecostal Church of God, Joplin, MO (1990-2000); Publicity Committee, MO (1985-1989); Advisory Board, Christian Education (1985-1995) **CIV:** Curriculum Committee, Clayton School Board, Clayton County, GA (1994); Campaign Assistant, Republican Party, Clayton County, Georgia (1990) **CW:** Featured, ETC Academy News (2010); Editor, Spirit (2002-2003); Contributor, Articles, Professional Journals; Editor, "From the Cotton Patch to the Pulpit" **AW:** Plaque for Service, Women's Ministry, Georgia (2000) **MEM:** Georgia Music Educators Association; Phi Beta Kappa; Multiple Churches **MH:** Albert Nelson Marquis Lifetime Achievement Award **B/I:** Ms. Richter was born Carol Janell Johnston in Mississippi to a preacher's family. They moved to Georgia when she was 3 and she was reared and educated in Columbus, Georgia. When she was 6, she began piano lessons and at the age of 12 became the pianist for her home church. After receiving her AA with honors, she interrupted her college to marry a preacher. After marriage, she attended West Georgia taking music theory, finally moving back to Columbus where she completed her degree at Columbus University, a major in education, minor in music. In the 1980's, Ms. Richter directed a youth choir at Camp Bethel, a church summer camp for youths under 20. Not only were the voices beautiful and powerful, but every musician was under 20! The local TV station invited the choir to perform, building an outdoor venue for the taping! In 1998 she founded a Christian school at Evangel Temple in Clayton County. She joined the Georgia Music Assoc. and her students competed in All–State music. Her youngest child, Joanna, a student at Evangel Christian Academy, was an All-State vocalist for six years, attending the Annual All State Productions in Savannah. Ms. Richter's ensembles, trios, and duets always won awards in the annual Student Conventions sponsored by the home school association to which their school belonged. Ms. Richter comments about her work, "It is a great joy to help youth develop their God-given talents, then show them how to use those talents to bring glory to God." **AV:** Reading; Writing; Music; Vocal and keyboard performance; Gardening **PA:** Republican **RE:** Pentecostal Church Of God, Protestant Christian

RICHTER, PETER C., T: Lawyer **I:** Law and Legal Services **CN:** Miller Nash Graham & Dunn **DOB:** 06/13/1944 **PB:** Opava **SC:** Czechoslovakia **PT:** Alzbeta (Kindlarova) Richter (Deceased 2015); Hanus Richter (Deceased 1997) **MS:** Married **SPN:** Leslie Dianne Rousseau (11/27/1967) **CH:** Timothy Jason; Lindsey Bertha **ED:** JD, University of Oregon (1971); BS, University of Oregon (1967) **C:** Partner, Lawyer, Miller Nash Graham & Dunn, Miller Nash LLP, Portland, OR (1978-Present); Associate, Miller Nashe LLP, Portland, OR (1973-1978); Associate, Veatch, Lovett & Stiner, Portland, OR (1971-1973) **CR:** Trial Advocacy College Planner, Instructor, Oregon State Bar (1998-Present); Contributor, Oregon State Bar Trial Advocacy Seminars (1988-Present); Adjunct Professor, Law Trial Advocacy Northwestern School of Law, Lewis & Clark College, Portland, OR (1986-Present); Pro Temp Ore Judge, Multnomah County Circuit Court, Portland, OR (1985-1998); California Trial Judge **CIV:** Board of Advisers, Pacific Crest Outward Bound (2000); Trustee, Board of Directors, Parry Center for Children, Portland, OR (1990-1993); Former Member, Portland, National Conference Christians and Jews, Portland, OR (1983); Former Member, Board of Directors, Boy Scouts of America; Columbia Pacific Council **MIL:** Oregon Army National Guard (1967-1975) **CW:** Author, "The Quick Step Guide to Trial Advocacy" (1997-Present); Co-Author, "Oregon State Bar Damage Manual" (1985, 1990); Editor, "Program Planner Sales: The Oregon Experience" (1989); Author, "Oregon State Bar" (1987, 1988, 1989); Contributor, Articles **AW:** Best Lawyer 25 Years (1996-Present); Certificate of Appreciation Northwestern School of Law (1990); Certificate of Appreciation, Oregon Association of Defense Counsel (1987-1989); Named One of 10 Best Litigators in Oregon, National Bar Journal; Super Lawyer Top 50 in Oregon; AV Rated Martindale Hubbell; Judicial Excellence Award, Martindale and Hubbell; Top Lawyer in Real Estate Litigation **MEM:** Fellow, American Bar Foundation; Trial Techniques Committee, American Bar Association; Oregon Chapter, Federal Bar Association; Advocate, American Board of Trial Advocates; Former Board of Directors, Multnomah Bar Association; Oregon Association of Defense Counsel; Inns of Court; Trustee, President, Multnomah Athletic Club; Board of Directors, Arlington Club; National Academy of Trial Lawyers; International Academy of Trial Lawyers; Judicial Administration Committee, Business Litigation Secretary Executive Communications; **BAR:** Supreme Court of the United States (1983); U.S. District Court for the District of Oregon (1972); Oregon (1971); U.S. Court of Appeals for the Ninth Circuit (1972) **MH:** Albert Nelson Marquis Lifetime Achievement Award; Marquis Who's Who Top Professional **B/I:** Mr. Richter became involved in his profession because he had an innate sense of justice, of what's right and what's wrong, from his father, Hanus Richter, who attempted to study law before the family immigrated to the United States in 1951. Mr. Richter's father played an integral part in his decision to become interested in law, which led him to pursue his career as one of the top lawyers in Portland, Oregon. **AV:** Playing squash; Playing tennis; Skiing; Playing golf; Reading; Motorcycling riding

RICKETTS, JOHN, "PETE" PETER, T: Governor of Nebraska **I:** Government Administration/Government Relations/Government Services **DOB:** 08/19/1964 **PB:** Nebraska City **SC:** NE/USA **PT:** Joe Ricketts; Marlene (Volkmer) Ricketts **MS:** Married **SPN:** Susanne Shore **CH:** Roscoe; Margot; Eleanor **ED:** MBA in Marketing and Finance, The University of Chicago Booth School of Business (1991); Bachelor in Biology, The University of Chicago (1986)

C: Governor, State of Nebraska (2015-Present); Senior Vice President of Strategy and Business Development, TD Ameritrade (1993-2005); Senior Vice President of Product Development, TD Ameritrade (1993-2005); Senior Vice President of Marketing, TD Ameritrade (1993-2005); Various Leadership Positions Including Chief Operating Officer, Executive Vice President, Corporate Secretary, President, Private Client Division, TD Ameritrade (1993-2005); Salesman for Chicago Environmental Consultant; With, Union Pacific Railroad, Omaha, NE; Founder, Drakon, LLC **CR:** Chair, Republican Governors Association (2018-Present); Board of Directors, TD Ameritrade (1999-2006, 2007-2016); Co-Owner, Chicago Cubs Baseball Team, World Series Champion (2016); Board Chairman, Platte Institute for Economic Research (2007); Board of Directors, Chicago Cubs Baseball Team; Board of Directors, ZNRG, Inc.; Past Vice Chairman, TD Ameritrade **CIV:** Board of Directors, Knights of Columbus; Board of Directors, Fund for Omaha Committee; Board of Directors, Community Health Charities of Nebraska; Member, Gambling with the Good Life; Board of Trustees, American Enterprise Institute; Board Adviser, Alumni Capital Network; Member, Republican Forum; Member, Nebraska Coalition for Ethical Research; The University of Chicago Booth School of Business; Chairman, Children's Scholarship Fund; Omaha President, Board of Directors, Platte Institute **AW:** Knight, Order of the Holy Sepulchre **MEM:** Knights of Columbus **PA:** Republican **RE:** Roman Catholic

RICKLEFS, KAREN LEE, T: Quality Assurance Consultant **I:** Other **DOB:** 02/12/1937 **PB:** Elmore **SC:** MN/USA **PT:** Ole Andrew Anderson; Florence Dorothy (Peterson) Anderson **MS:** Married **SPN:** Merlin John Ricklefs (09/28/1958) **CH:** Kristin Kay Ricklefs Bennett (1970); Lowell John (1961); Linda Lee Ricklefs Baudry (1960) **ED:** Postgraduate Coursework, University of Minnesota (1962, 1970, 1980); Postgraduate Coursework, Pace University (1976-1978); BS in Mathematics, Iowa State University (1957-1960); Coursework, St. Olaf College (1955-1957); Postgraduate Coursework, Manhattanville College **C:** Senior Consultant, Co-Founder, Quality Associates International, Rochester (1991-Present); Executive Assistant, University of Minnesota, Duluth, MN (1991-1992); Realtor, K & K Realty, Rochester, MN (1987-1990); Director, Founder, College and Career Resource Center, Mayo High School, Rochester, MN (1985-1990); Teacher of Mathematics, Various Schools, Minnesota, New York (1960-1969); Officer Assistant, National Academy of Sciences, Ames, IA (1959-1960) **CR:** Consultant, Minnesota Academy of Excellence Foundation, St. Paul, MN (1992); Minnesota Partners for Quality, St. Paul, MN (1992); Presenter in Field **CIV:** President, Founder, Rochester Foundation of Educational Excellence (1987-1994); Board of Directors, President, Olmsted Medical Center (1979-1985); Vice President, Founder, Governance Board, Southeast Minnesota Educational Computer Consortium (1973-1976); Commissioner, Advisory Council, Minnesota State Board of Education (1973-1976); President, Founder, Rochester Area Intergovernmental Council (1973-1976); Executive Board, Minnesota Environmental Education Council, St. Paul, MN (1972-1976); Treasurer, Vice President, President, Chairman, Board of Directors, Rochester Board of Education (1970-1976); Minnesota Representative, National Energy Conference (1974) **AW:** Friend of Education, Rochester Principals Association (1989); Outstanding School Board Member, Rochester School Board (1975); Good Citizenship Award, City of Rochester (1974); Outstanding Young Women of America (1970) **MEM:** Co-Chair, Foundation Member, Rotary (1997-Present); President, American Association

of University Women (1963); American Society for Quality Control; Minnesota Orchestral Association; Rochester Chamber of Commerce; Sons of Norway **B/I:** Mrs. Ricklefs became involved in her profession because she saw a need in the field and wanted to try and fill it. Education has always been important to her because of her fathers' influence. He left school at a young age to help take care of his family, so she was determined to go to college. **AV:** Reading; Playing piano; Boating; Traveling **PA:** Republican **RE:** Lutheran

RIDDLE, DOUGLAS S., MMUS, T: Music Educator, Choral Director **I:** Education/Educational Services **DOB:** 08/21/1951 **PB:** Vallejo **SC:** CA/USA **MS:** Widowed **SPN:** Gabrielle Karoline Hurler (6/2/1973, Deceased 2010) **ED:** Master of Music in Choral Conducting, Northern Arizona University (1991); Bachelor of Music in Music Education, University of the Pacific Conservatory of Music, Stockton, CA (1973) **CT:** Teaching Credential State of Arizona (1989); Standard Secondary Lifetime Teaching Credential, California (1974); English as a Second Language, Arizona **C:** Curry Summer Music Camp Instructor, Northern Arizona University, Flagstaff, AZ (1991-1998, 2004-2006, 2018-2019); Choral Music Educator, Coconino High School, Flagstaff, AZ (1989-2013); Choral Music Educator, Lodi High School, Lodi, CA (1977-1989); Choral Camp Chair, Pacific Summer Music Camp, University of the Pacific, Stockton, CA (1976-1982); Choral Music Educator, East Union High School, Manteca, CA (1973-1977) **CR:** Church Choir Musician, Various Times and Places (1973-2020); Choral Clinician and Adjudicator, Northwest Region High School Honor Choir Adjudicator (2014-2019); Solo Ensemble Chairperson, Arizona Music Educator's Association (2006-2011); Chairperson, Repertoire and Standards, Women's Chorus, Arizona American Choral Director's Association (2004-2006); Regional Governor, North West Region Arizona Music Educator's Association (2002-2006); Vice President, Choral Activities, Choral Directors of Arizona (1996-1998) **CIV:** Board Treasurer, Grant Writer, Flagstaff Light Opera Company (2020-Present); Board Member, Flagstaff Light Opera Company (2012-Present); Board President, Flagstaff Light Opera Company (2018-2020); Lodi Arts Commission, California (1987-1989) **AW:** Lifetime Achievement Award, Arizona Music Educators Association (2015); George C. Wilson Leadership Service Award, Arizona Music Educators Association (1998); O.M. Hartsell Excellence in Teaching Award, Arizona Music Educators Association (1995); Scholarship Paid Choir Member, Saratoga Potsdam Chorus (1985) **MH:** Albert Nelson Marquis Lifetime Achievement Award; Marquis Who's Who Top Professional **AS:** Mr. Riddle attributes his success to the guidance of numerous outstanding mentors. He was also fortunate to work closely with many outstanding choral conductors. **B/I:** Hailing from a long line of educators, Mr. Riddle was inspired to follow the same profession. As a singer and band musician in high school, he received a scholarship to attend college for music. **AV:** Sports; Community musical theater; Travel: Master chorale of Flagstaff: Mountain chorale of Flagstaff **PA:** Democrat **RE:** Catholic

RIDENHOUR, CARLTON, "CHUCK D." DOUGLAS, T: Rap Musician **I:** Media & Entertainment **DOB:** 08/01/1960 **PB:** Queens **SC:** NY/USA **ED:** Honorary Doctorate, Adelphi University (2013); BFA in Graphic Design, Adelphi University (1984) **C:** Founding Member, Rapper, Public Enemy; Member, PE 2.0, Prophets of Rage, and Confrontation Camp **CW:** Rapper, Album, "Celebration of Ignorance" (2018); Rapper with Public Enemy, Album, "Nothing Is Quick in the Desert" (2017);

Rapper with Prophets of Rage, Album, "Prophets of Rage" (2017); Rapper, Album, "If I Can't Change the People Around Me I Change the People Around Me" (2016); Rapper with Prophets of Rage, Album, "The Party's Over" (2016); Actor, "The Bet" (2016); Rapper with Public Enemy, Album, "Man Plans God Laughs" (2015); Rapper, Album, "The Black in Man" (2014); Featured, Documentary Miniseries, "Sonic Highways" (2014); Rapper with Public Enemy, Album, "The Evil Empire of Everything" (2012); Rapper with Public Enemy, Album, "Most of My Heroes Still Don't Appear on No Stamp" (2012); Rapper, Compilation Album, "Don't Rhyme for the Sake of Riddlin'" (2012); Featured, Documentary, "Something from Nothing: The Art of Rap" (2012); Rapper, Compilation Album, "Action" (2010); Featured, Documentary, "The Black Candle" (2008); Rapper, Album, "How You Sell Soul to a Soulless People Who Sold their Soul?" (2007); Narrator, Documentary, "Quilombo Country" (2006); Featured, Documentary, "The Rap Report - Part 2" (2006); Featured, Documentary, "Hip Hop: Beyond Bets and Rhymes" (2006); Rapper with Public Enemy, Album, "New Whirl Odor" (2005); Narrator, Documentary, "Harlem Globetrotters: The Team That Changed the World" (2005); Actor, "Wake Up, Ron Burgundy: The Lost Movie" (2004); Featured, Documentary, "The Blues: Godfathers and Sons" (2003); Rapper with Public Enemy, Album, "Revolverlution" (2002); Rapper, Album, "Objects in the Mirror Are Closer Than They Appear," Confrontation Camp (2000); Rapper with Public Enemy, Album, "There's a Poison Goin' On" (1999); Featured, "An Alan Smithee Film: Burn Hollywood Burn" (1998); Featured, Documentary, "Rhyme & Reason" (1997); Rapper, Album, "Autobiography of Mistachuck" (1996); Rapper with Public Enemy, Album, "He Got Game" (1994); Rapper with Public Enemy, Album, "Apocalypse 91... The Enemy Strikes Black" (1991); Rapper with Public Enemy, Album, "Fear of a Black Planet" (1990); Rapper with Public Enemy, Album, "It Takes a Nation of Millions to Hold Us Back" (1988); Rapper with Public Enemy, Album, "Yo! Bum Rush the Show" (1987); Rapper, Numerous Songs and Live Performances; Guest Appearances, Numerous Television Shows and Documentaries **AW:** Woody Guthrie Prize (2019); Ranked #12, "Top 50 Hip-Hop Lyricists of All Time," The Source

RIEGER, TERRY, CUSTOM DESIGNED JEWELRY, T: Owner, Jeweler **I:** Retail/Sales **CN:** Diamonds By Terry **DOB:** 02/25/1935 **PB:** Portland **SC:** OR/USA **YOP:** 2019 **PT:** Maria and Ernest Forrest **MS:** Married **SPN:** Frederick O. Rieger (Deceased) **CH:** David; Joseph **CT:** Gemologist **C:** Owner, Jeweler, Designer, Caster, Diamond Setter, Gemologist, Antique Jewelry Repair, Baked French Enamel, Diamonds By Terry (1972-Present) **CIV:** House of Hope; Hospice; United for Families; American Heart Association; Hibiscus Children's Center; Alzheimer's: Boys and Girls Club; Safe Space; Tykes & Teens; Woman's Club of Stuart, Mary's Shelter; Heart Association; Make-A-Wish Foundation of America; Salvation Army; Donator, 97 Charities **AS:** Ms. Rieger attributes her success to her mentor, Ken Liggett, who supported her and her designs and taught her what she knows.She always tells her clients if you can dream it, she can make it. **B/I:** Ms. Rieger became involved in her profession because the local jeweler thought that she had talent. She did not have any intention of becoming a jeweler - back then, women were not in that industry. The jeweler thought that her designs needed to be produced in gold. Ms. Rieger lived in a little town in Illinois and one year she wanted to make the crystal panoramic egg for Easter that she had as a child in Philadelphia. She researched and found the molds and how they were made. She accidentally made one extra egg, which she gave to the local jeweler and his wife. The jeweler looked at the egg, complimented Ms. Rieger for her talent and said that she should try to replicate the piece in gold. Ms. Rieger did not take him up on his advice at first, but over time he would offer to purchase tools for her or find someone to teach her, and eventually she agreed to learn. Though some of her methods were unorthodox, such as not measuring ingredients for casting, she has enjoyed great success. Ms. Rieger had one accident in the beginning; a casting blew up. That was her only accident and she has been a jeweler for 47 years. **RE:** Catholic **THT:** Ms. Rieger's motto is "What goes around comes around." She designs, creates, casts, and set diamonds, saying, "For that one of a kind design made just for that client...perhaps you want a pendant made of your pet dog or a one of a kind engagement ring. Whatever you can dream, Terry can create just for you. She casts in 14kt, 18kt, 22kt or platinum."

RIGALI, JUSTIN FRANCIS, T: Cardinal **I:** Religious **DOB:** 4/19/1935 **PB:** Los Angeles **SC:** CA/USA **PT:** Henry Alphonsus Rigali; Frances Irene (White) Rigali **ED:** Honorary Doctor of Humane Letters, Saint Louis University (1995); Licentiate in Canon Law, Pontifical Gregorian University (1964); Licentiate in Canon Law, Pontifical Gregorian University (1963); Bachelor's Degree in Sacred Theology, Catholic University America (1961) **C:** Archbishop Emeritus of Philadelphia (2011-Present); Cardinal-Priest, of Santa Prisca (2003-Present); Archbishop, of Philadelphia (2003-2011); Elevated to Cardinal (2003); Archbishop of Saint Louis (1994-2003); Secretary, College of Cardinals (1990-1994); Secretary, Congregation of Bishops (1989-1994); Numerous Vatican Posts (1985-1990); President, Pontifical Ecclesiastical Academy, Rome, Italy (1985-1989); Ordained, of Volsinium (1985); Appointed Titular Archbishop of Volsinium (1985); Magistral Chaplain, Order of the Knights of Malta (1984); Prelate of Honor of His Holiness (1980); Director, English Section, Secretariat of State (1970); English Translator, Pope Paul VI (1970); Apostolic Nunciature to, Madagascar (1966-1970); Joined, English-Language Department, Secretariat of State, Vatican City (1964-1970); Named, Papal Chamberlain to Pope Paul VI (1967); Associate Pastor, Pamona, CA (1964); Assistant, Second Vatican Council (1963-1964); Ordained Priest of Los Angeles (1961); Professor, Pontifical Ecclesiastical Academy, Rome, Italy **CR:** Member, Administration of the Patrimony of the Apostolic See, Committee Vox Clara, Congregation for Divine Worship and the Discipline of the Sacraments, Congregation for Bishops (2007-Present); Apostolic Administrator of Scranton (2009-2010); Member, Numerous Committees, U.S. Bishops' Conference **RE:** Roman Catholic

RIGGLEMAN, DENVER LEE III, T: U.S. Representative from Virginia **I:** Government Administration/Government Relations/Government Services **DOB:** 03/17/1970 **PB:** Manassas **SC:** VA/USA **MS:** Married **SPN:** Christine Blair Riggleman (1989) **CH:** Lillian; Abigail; Lauren **ED:** Diploma/Graduate Certificate, Project Management, Villanova University (2007); BA in Foreign Affairs, University of Virginia (1998); AS in Avionics Systems, Air University Community College of the Air Force (1996) **C:** Member, U.S. House of Representatives from Virginia's Fifth Congressional District (2019-Present); Founder, Owner, Silverback Distillery (2014-Present) **MIL:** With, United States Air Force **PA:** Republican

RILEY, PATRICK JAMES, T: Professional Sports Team Executive **I:** Athletics **DOB:** 03/20/1945 **PB:** Rome **SC:** NY/USA **PT:** Leon Riley **MS:** Married

SPN: Chris Rodstrom **CH:** James Patrick; Elisabeth Marie **ED:** Graduate, University of Kentucky (1967) **C:** President, Basketball Operations, Miami Heat (2003-Present); Head Coach, Miami Heat (1995-2003, 2005-2008); Head Coach, New York Knicks (1991-1995); Head Coach, Los Angeles Lakers (1981-1990); Assistant Coach, Los Angeles Lakers (1979-1981); Guard, Los Angeles Lakers (1970-1975); Guard, Phoenix Suns (1975-1976); Guard, San Diego Rockets (1967-1970) **CR:** Broadcaster, NBC Sports (1990-1991); Broadcaster, Los Angeles Lakers Games, Station KLAC and Station KHJ-TV (1977-1979) **CW:** Author, "The Winner Within: A Life Plan for Team Players" (1993); Basis, Sega Genesis Video Game, "Pat Riley Basketball" (1990); Author, "Show Time: Inside the Lakers' Breakthrough Season" (1988) **AW:** Chuck Daly Lifetime Achievement Award, National Basketball Coaches Association (2012); Co-Recipient, NBA Executive of Year Award, NBA (2011); NBA Executive of the Year, The Sporting News (2011); Inductee, Naismith Memorial Basketball Hall of Fame (2008); NBA Champion as Head Coach (1982, 1985, 1987-1988, 2006); Coach of the Year, NBA (1990, 1993, 1997); NBA Champion (1972, 1980); Top 10 Coaches in NBA History

RINGER, MERIKAY PHD, T: Professor Emeritus, Psychologist **I:** Education/Educational Services **PT:** James Boe Murphy Junior; Rosanne Mary Kennedy Murphy **MS:** Widow **SPN:** Donald Clyde Ringer (12/23/1968, Deceased 01/19/1972) **CH:** Donald Dale; Marianne Kennedy Ringer **ED:** PhD, University of Southern Mississippi (1987); Master in Education, Louisiana State University (1975); BS in Education, University of Kansas (1969) **CT:** Licensed Psychologist, Louisiana (1992); Nationally Certified School Psychologist, National Association of School Psychologists (1990) **C:** Professor, Director, Specialist, School Psychology Program, Louisiana State University Shreveport (1999-Present); Professor Emeritus/Psychologist (2006); Associate Professor, Louisiana State University Shreveport (1993-1999); Psychologist, Psychological Associates (1989-1995); Assistant Professor, Louisiana State University Shreveport (1988-1993); Behavior Management Specialist, Department of Defense Dependent Schools, Kaiserslautern, Germany (1986-1988); Teacher, Counselor, Southside Baptist School (1976-1982); Teacher, Brentwood Hospital, Shreveport, LA (1973-1976) **CR:** Caddo, Bossier Mental Health Association, Shreveport, LA (2000-2001); Board Member, Louisiana Play Therapy Associate (1996-1998); Center for Families (1996-1998) **AW:** Grantee, Louisiana State Board of Regents (2000) **MEM:** National Association of School Psychologists; American Psychological Association; President, Kappa Delta Phi Honor Education Fraternity; Phi Delta Kappa Professional Education Fraternity; Louisiana School Psychologists Association **MH:** Albert Nelson Marquis Lifetime Achievement Award **B/I:** Dr. Ringer became involved in psychology after gaining experience as a teacher. She started by working with students with behavioral problems, which led her to study the field at Louisiana State University and then the University of Mississippi. **AV:** Traveling **PA:** Independent **RE:** Lutheran

RINK, LAWRENCE D., T: Cardiologist, Director of Cardiac Rehabilitation **I:** Medicine & Health Care **CN:** Indiana University Health **DOB:** 10/14/1940 **PB:** Indianapolis **SC:** IN/USA **PT:** Joe Donald Rink; Mary Ellen (Rand) Rink **MS:** Married **SPN:** Eleanor Jane (Zimmerly) Rink (08/10/1963) **CH:** Scott; Virginia (Deceased) **ED:** Limited Cardiology Fellowship, Massachusetts General Hospital (1984); Cardiology Fellowship, Indiana Uni-

versity (1979-1981); Internal Medicine Residency, Indiana University (1971-1974); Internship, Parkland Memorial Hospital, The University of Texas Southwestern Medical Center (1967); MD, Indiana University (1966); BS, DePauw University (1962) **CT:** Diplomate, American Board of Internal Medicine; ABCM, Inc. **C:** Cardiologist, Indiana University Health (2017-Present); Clinical Professor of Medicine, School of Medicine, Indiana University (1985-Present); Cardiologist, IMA, Inc. (1974-2017); Chairman of the Board, Chief Executive Officer, Premier Health Care (2004-2014); Director of Cardiology, Bloomington Hospital (1983-2010); Chairman, Board of Directors, Chief Executive Officer, IMA Inc. (1995-2004); Director of Cardiac Rehabilitation, Human Performance Laboratory, Indiana University Bloomington (1994); Clinical Associate Professor, School of Medicine, Indiana University (1979-1985); Clinical Assistant Professor, School of Medicine, Indiana University (1973-1979); Director of Cardiac Rehabilitation, Bloomington Hospital (1976) **CR:** Former Director, Lawrence D. Rink Sports Medicine and Technology Center, Indiana University (2018-Present); Emeritus Chairman, Medical Commission, FISU (2016-Present); Physician, Basketball Team, Indiana University (1979-Present); President, Medical Commission, FISU, (2000-2016); USA Team Physician, World University Games (1991); U.S. Olympic Physician, Olympic Sports Festival (1989); Co-Director, Combined Degree Program, School of Medicine, Indiana University (1976-1988); Medical Director, Track and Field, Pan American Games (1987); USA Team Physician, Olympic Games in Spain, Korea, Japan, China and Russia **CIV:** Board of Directors, Dean's Council, School of Medicine, Indiana University (1992-2000); Founding Board Member, YMCA (1982) **MIL:** Lieutenant Commander, Flight Surgeon, U.S. Navy (1968-1972) **CW:** Board of Directors, J.O. Ritchie Society, School of Medicine, Indiana University **AW:** Inductee, Monroe County Hall of Fame (2016); Corvitae Award, American Heart Association (2003); Most Outstanding Alumnus, School of Medicine, Indiana University (1998); Quality of Life Award (1978); Most Outstanding Flight Surgeon, U.S. Navy (1968); Honorary Member, Indiana University **MEM:** Men's Association, Indiana University (2014-Present); Fellow, American College of Cardiology; American Heart Association; American Society of Critical Care; American College of Sports Medicine, American Medical Association; Medical Alumnae Association, Indiana University **MH:** Albert Nelson Marquis Lifetime Achievement Award; Marquis Who's Who Top Professional **B/I:** Dr. Rink's main goal was to help other people. He attended DePauw University in 1962 and became a cardiologist after attending Indiana University in 1966. He chose cardiology because there were many new advances in the field. **AV:** Reading; Writing; Golfing; Playing tennis

RIORDAN, RICK, T: Writer **I:** Writing and Editing **DOB:** 06/05/1946 **PB:** San Antonio **SC:** TX/USA **MS:** Married **SPN:** Becky Riordan (1985) **CH:** Haley; Patrick **ED:** Degrees in English and History, University of Texas at Austin; Coursework, North Texas State University **CT:** Teaching Certification, English and History, University of Texas at San Antonio **C:** Former Teacher, English, Social Studies, Presidio Hill School, San Francisco, CA **CW:** Curator, Author, "Rick Riordan Presents" (2018-Present); Author, "The Tower of Nero," The Trials of Apollo Series (2020); Author, "Camp Jupiter Classified" (2020); Author, "The Tyrant's Tomb," The Trials of Apollo Series (2019); Author, "The Burning Maze," The Trials of Apollo Series (2018); Author, "The Ship of the Dead," Magnus Chase and the Gods of Asgard Series (2017); Author, "Camp Half-Blood Confidential" (2017); Author, "The

Son of Neptune Graphic Novel" (2017); Author, "The Dark Prophecy," The Trials of Apollo Series (2017); Author, "The Hammer of Thor," Magnus Chase and the Gods of Asgard Series (2016); Author, "Demigods and Magicians" (2016); Author, "The Hidden Oracle," The Trials of Apollo Series (2016); Author, "Percy Jackson's Greek Heroes" (2015); Author, "Demigods of Olympus" (2015); Author, "The Sword of Summer," Magnus Chase and the Gods of Asgard Series (2015); Author, "Percy Jackson's Greek Gods" (2014); Author, "The Blood of Olympus," The Heroes of Olympus Series (2014); Author, "The Lost Hero Graphic Novel" (2014); Author, "The House of Hades," The Heroes of Olympus Series (2013); Author, "The Titan's Curse Graphic Novel" (2013); Author, "Demigods and Monsters" (2009, 2013); Author, "The Mark of Athena," The Heroes of Olympus Series (2012); Author, "The Serpent's Shadow," The Kane Chronicles (2012); Author, "The Demigod Diaries" (2012); Contributor, "The Red Pyramid Graphic Novel" (2012); Author, "The Son of Neptune," The Heroes of Olympus Series (2011); Author, "The Throne of Fire," The Kane Chronicles (2011); Author, "Vespers Rising," The 39 Clues Series (2011); Author, "The Lost Hero," The Heroes of Olympus Series (2010); Author, "The Lightning Thief Graphic Novel" (2010); Author, "The Red Pyramid," The Kane Chronicles (2010); Author, "The Demigod Files" (2009); Author, "The Last Olympian," Percy Jackson & the Olympians Series (2009); Author, Introduction, "Tales of the Greek Heroes" by Roger Lancelyn Green (2009); Author, "The Battle of the Labyrinth," Percy Jackson & the Olympians Series (2008); Author, "Rebel Island," Tres Navarre Series (2008); Author, "The Maze of Bones," The 39 Clues Series (2008); Author, "The Titan's Curse," Percy Jackson & the Olympians Series (2007); Author, "The Sea of Monsters," Percy Jackson & the Olympians Series (2006); Author, "The Lightning Thief," Percy Jackson & the Olympians (2005); Author, "Mission Road," Tres Navarre Series (2005); Author, "Southtown," Tres Navarre Series (2004); Author, "Cold Springs" (2004); Author, "The Devil Went Down to Austin," Tres Navarre Series (2002); Author, "The Last King of Texas," Tres Navarre Series (2001); Author, "The Widower's Two-Step," Tres Navarre Series (1998); Author, "Big Red Tequila," Tres Navarre Series (1997) **AW:** Stonewall Book Award for Children's Literature, "The Hammer of Thor" (2017); Best Fiction Book for Children in Bulgaria, "The Mark of Athena" (2013); Indian Paintbrush Award, "The Red Pyramid" (2012); Milner Award (2011); Wyoming Soaring Eagle Book Award, "The Last Olympian" (2011); Children's Choice Book Awards, Fifth Grade and Sixth Grade Book of the Year, "The Red Pyramid" (2011); Children's Choice Book Award, Author of the Year (2011); Rebecca Caudill Award, "The Lightning Thief" (2009); Mark Twain Award, "The Sea of Monsters" (2009); Mark Twain Award, "The Lightning Thief" (2008); Edgar Award, Best Paperback Original, "The Widower's Two-Step" (1999); Shamus Award for Best First PI Novel, "Big Red Tequila" (1998); Anthony Award for Best Paperback Original, "Big Red Tequila" (1998) **MEM:** Texas Institute of Letters (2003) **AV:** Reading; Swimming; Playing guitar; Traveling

RIPA, KELLY MARIA, T: Television Personality, Actress **I:** Media & Entertainment **CN:** Live! with Kelly and Ryan **DOB:** 10/02/1970 **PB:** Berlin **SC:** NJ/USA **PT:** Joseph Ripa; Esther Ripa **MS:** Married **SPN:** Mark Consuelos (05/01/1996) **CH:** Michael Joseph; Lola Grace; Joaquin Antonio **ED:** Coursework in Psychology, Camden Community College, New Jersey; Diploma, Eastern Regional High School, Voorhees Township, NJ **C:** Co-Host, "Live! with Kelly and Ryan"

(2017-Present); Co-Host, "Live! with Kelly and Michael" (2012-2016); Host, "Live! with Kelly" (2011-2012); Co-Host, "Live! with Regis and Kelly," New York, NY (2001-2011) **CR:** Spokesperson, Electrolux Kitchen Appliances (2008); Launched, Active Wear Line, "The Kelly Ripa Collection," Rykä (2008); Co-Founder, Milojo (2007); Former Partner, Tide, 7 Up, Pantene, TD Bank **CIV:** Host, Super Saturday, Ovarian Cancer Research Fund (2011-Present); Fundraiser, Tomorrow's Children's Fund (2001); Mothers Against Drunk Driving **CW:** Voice Actress, "Santa's Helpers" (2020); Guest Appearance, "Riverdale" (2019); Co-Host, "CNN Heroes" (2016-2019; Guest Appearance, "Nightcap" (2016); Guest Appearance, "Broad City" (2015); Guest Appearance, "Google+ Hangout" (2013); Host, TV Land Awards (2007-2012); Host, "Live From Lincoln Center" (2011); Guest Appearance, "30 Rock" (2011); Guest Appearance, "Hannah Montana" (2011); Host, Executive Producer, "Homemade Millionaire" (2010); Panelist, "The Marriage Ref" (2010); Actress, "All My Children" (1990-2002, 2010); Guest Appearance, "Brothers & Sisters" (2009); Guest Appearance, "Damages" (2009); Co-Host, Disney Parks Christmas Day Parade (2001-2009); Guest Appearance, "Ugly Betty" (2008); Featured, Song, "Kelly Ripa" (2008); Voice Actress, "Fly Me to the Moon" (2008); Voice Actress, "Delgo" (2008); Cameo, "The Great Buck Howard" (2008); Guest Appearance, "The Knights of Prosperity" (2007); Host, "50 Funniest Women Alive" (2007); Actress, "Hope & Faith" (2003-2006); Guest Appearance, "1-800-Missing" (2005); Guest Appearance, "Duck Dodgers" (2005); Cameo, "Cheaper by the Dozen" (2003); Guest Host, "Saturday Night Live" (2003); Voice Actress, "Batman: Mystery of the Batwoman" (2003); Voice Actress, "Kim Possible: A Sitch in Time" (2003); Cameo, "It's a Very Merry Muppet Christmas Movie" (2002); Guest Appearance, "Family Guy" (2002); Guest Appearance, "Ed" (2002); Actress, "Someone to Love" (2001); Appearance, "Who Wants to Be a Millionaire?" (2001); Actress, "The Stand-In" (1999); Actress, "Marvin's Room" (1996); Dancer, "Dance Party USA" (1986-1992) **AW:** Inductee, New Jersey Hall of Fame (2017); Co-Recipient, Daytime Emmy Award for Outstanding Entertainment Talk Show Host, "Live! with Regis and Kelly" (2015-2016); Star, Hollywood Walk of Fame (2015); Co-Recipient, Daytime Emmy Award for Outstanding Talk Show Entertainment, "Live! with Regis and Kelly" (2012); Co-Recipient, Daytime Emmy Award for Outstanding Talk Show Host, "Live! with Regis and Kelly" (2011-2012); Person of the Year, Inductee to Hall of Fame, Broadcast Pioneers (2010); Emmy Award for Outstanding Special Class Special, Disney Parks Christmas Day Parade (2006); Best Actress Award, "The Stand-In," New York International Independent Film and Video Festival (1999); Five Soap Opera Digest Awards; Soap Opera Digest Award for Outstanding Younger Lead Actress, Soap Opera Digest Award for Hottest Romance, "All My Children" **RE:** Catholic

RIPOLL, SHAKIRA ISABEL, T: Singer **I:** Media & Entertainment **DOB:** 02/02/1977 **PB:** Barranquilla **SC:** Colombia **PT:** William Mebarak Chadid Ripoll; Nidia Ripoll **MS:** Life Partner **SPN:** Gerard Piqué (2011); Antonio de la Rúa (2000-2010) **CH:** Milan; Sasha **CR:** Launched, Beauty Line, "S by Shakira," Puig (2010); Launched, Several Fragrances **CIV:** Global Goodwill Ambassador, UNICEF (2003-Present); Founder, Barefoot Foundation (2018); President's Advisory Commission on Educational Excellence for Hispanics (2011); Founder, Pies Descalzos (1997); Honorary Chairman, Global Campaign for Education; Founder, Three Elementary Schools, Colombia **CW:** Cameo, "Miss

Americana" (2020); Musician, "El Dorado" (2017); Voice Actress, "Zootopia" (2016); Featured, Video Games, "Angry Birds POP!," "Love Rocks" (2015); Musician, "Shakira" (2014); Coach, Mentor, "The Voice" (2013-2014); Musician, "Sale el Sol" (2010); Musician, "She Wolf" (2009); Appearance, "Saturday Night Live" (2001, 2005, 2009); Musician, "Oral Fixation, Vol. 2" (2005); Musician, "Fijación Oral, Vol. 1" (2005); Mentor Assistant, "Popstars" (2002); Musician, "Laundry Service" (2001); Musician, "Dónde Están los Ladrones?" (1998); Musician, "Pies Descalzos" (1995); Actress, "El Oasis" (1994); Musician, "Peligro" (1993); Musician, "Magia" (1991); Appearances, Numerous Documentaries, TV Shows **AW:** Top 10 Most Streamed Female Artists of the Decade, Spotify (2018); Latin Pop Album of the Year, Tropical Song of the Year, Latin Pop Artist of the Year, Solo, Top Latin Album Artist of the Year, Female, Latin Billboard Music Awards (2018); Hot Latin Songs Artist of the Year, Female, Latin Billboard Music Awards (2016-2018); Latin Album of the Year, iHeartRadio Music Awards (2018); Best Latin Pop Album, Grammy Awards (2001, 2018); 16 Winning Songs, BMI Latin Awards (2000-2018); Favorite Song Tropical, Song of the Year, Latin American Music Awards (2017); Single of the Year, Tropical Song, Lo Nuestro Awards (2017); Best Contemporary Pop Vocal Album, Latin Grammy Awards (2017); Crystal Award (2017); Video of the Year, Lo Nuestro Awards (2010, 2017); Favorite Latin Artist, American Music Awards (2005-2006, 2010, 2012, 2017); Latin Pop Song of the Year, Latin Billboard Music Awards (2016); Two 50th Anniversary Golden Music Awards, Los 40 Music Awards (2016); Social Artist of the Year, Latin Billboard Music Awards (2013-2016); Song of the Year, Record of the Year, Latin Grammy Awards (2006, 2016); Best Female Artist, Heat Latin Music Awards (2015); Pop Female Artist, Lo Nuestro Awards (1997, 1999-2000, 2003, 2015); Favorite Latin Song, Nickelodeon Kid's Choice Awards Colombia (2014); Hero Award, Radio Disney Music Awards (2014); Songs Artist of the Year, Female, Latin Billboard Music Awards (2013); Latin Pop Songs Artist of the Year, Solo, Latin Billboard Music Awards (2012-2013); Pop Song of the Year, Artist of the Year, Lo Nuestro Awards (2012); Honor for the Career, NRJ Music Awards (2012); Chevalier De L'Ordre des Arts et des Lettres (2012); Top Latin Artist, Billboard Music Awards (2011-2012); Latin Social Artist of the Year, Top Latin Albums - Female Artist of the Year, Latin Billboard Music Awards (2011-2012); Hot Latin Songs - Female Artist of the Year, Latin Billboard Music Awards (2010-2012); Best International Artist In Spanish Language, Los 40 Music Awards (2009-2012); Best Female Artist, Lo Nuestro Awards (2004, 2007, 2011-2012); Pop Album of the Year, Lo Nuestro Awards (1999, 2006, 2012); Top Latin Song, Billboard Music Awards (2011); Harvard Foundation Artist of the Year (2011); Latin Digital Album of the Year, Latin Digital Download of the Year, Latin Pop Airplay - Solo Artist of the Year, Latin Billboard Music Awards (2011); Most Influential Latin Artist in the World, Los 40 Music Awards (2011); Star, Hollywood Walk of Fame (2011); Person of the Year, Latin Grammy Special Awards (2011); Latin Recording Academy Person of the Year (2011); Best Female Pop Vocal Album, Latin Grammy Awards (2006, 2011); International Song of the Year, NRJ Music Awards (2003, 2007, 2011); International Female Artist of the Year, NRJ Music Awards (2003, 2011); Tropical Airplay - Female Artist of the Year, Latin Billboard Music Awards (2010); Online Video's Most Viral Artists (2010); UN International Labour Organization Medal (2010); Solo Female Artist of the Year, Orgullosamente Latino Awards (2010); MTV Free Your Mind Award, MTV European Music Awards (2010); International Pop Artist, Bambi

Awards (2009); Best International Song In Spanish Language, Los 40 Music Awards (2009); Agent of Change, Los Premios MTV Latinoamérica (2009); Humanitarian Award, ALMA Awards (2008); Song of the Year, Latin Ringtone of the Year, BMI Latin Awards (2007); Best Latin/Reggaeton Track, International Dance Music Awards (2007); Favorite Pop Song, People's Choice Awards (2007); Latin Tour of the Year, Latin Billboard Music Awards (2007); Most Earthshattering Collaboration, MTV Video Music Awards (2007); Hot Latin Song of the Year-Vocal Duet or Collaboration, Latin Billboard Music Awards (2006-2007); Three Winning Songs, BMI Pop Awards (2003-2007); Top Pop 100 Airplay Track, Billboard Music Awards (2006); Album of the Year, Latin Grammy Awards (2006); Song of the Year, Best Duo or Group, Lo Nuestro Awards (2006); Song of the Year, Los Premios MTV Latinoamérica (2006); Best Latin Rock/Alternative Album, Grammy Awards (2006); Best Latin Track, International Dance Music Awards (2006); BMI Urban Award - Billboard No. 1s, BMI Latin Awards (2006); Best Choreography in a Video, MTV Video Music Awards (2006); Solo Artist of the Year, Orgullosamente Latino Awards (2006); Best International Artist, Best International Song, Los 40 Music Awards (2006); Spirit of the Hope, Hot Latin Song of the Year, Latin Pop Airplay Song of the Year - Duo or Group, Latin Ringtone of the Year, Latin Billboard Music Awards (2006); Album of the Year, Outstanding Female Performer, Female, ALMA Awards (2002, 2006); Latin Album Artist of the Year, Latin Song of the Year, Latin Album of the Year, Billboard Music Awards (2005); Best Female, MTV Europe Music Awards (2005); Best Artist - Central, Best Pop Artist, Best Female Artist, Artist of the Year, Video of the Year, Los Premios MTV Latinoamérica (2005); Best International Female Artist, Echo Awards (2003); Best Selling International Female Album, MÜ-YAP Turkish Phonographic Industry Society Awards (2003); Popular Rock Artist, Lo Nuestro Awards (2003); Best Spanish Pop, Lunas del Auditorio (2003); International Album of the Year, NRJ Music Awards (2003); Video of the Year, Best Artist - North, Best Pop Artist, Best Female Artist, Artist of the Year, Los Premios MTV Latinoamérica (2002); Best Short Form Music Video, Latin Grammy Awards (2002); People Choice Pop/Rock, Lo Nuestro Awards (2002); Viewer's Choice Award, Latin Billboard Music Awards (2002); Best International Artist Video, People's Choice: Favorite International Artist, MuchMusic Video Awards (2002); International Viewer's Choice - Latin America (North), MTV Video Music Awards (2000, 2002); Best Latino Artist with the Album, Latin Billboard Music Awards (2001); Rock Album of the Year, Rock Artist of the Year, Lo Nuestro Awards (2001); Best Female Pop Vocal Performance, Best Female Rock Vocal Performance, Latin Grammy Awards (2000); New Pop Artist, Lo Nuestro Awards (1997); Best New Artist, Best Video of the Year, Best Pop Album, Latin Billboard Music Awards (1997); Several Others

RISCH, JAMES, "JIM" ELROY, T: U.S. Senator from Idaho; Lawyer **I:** Government Administration/Government Relations/Government Services **DOB:** 05/03/1943 **PB:** Milwaukee **SC:** WI/USA **PT:** Elroy A. Risch; Helen B. (Levi) Risch **MS:** Married **SPN:** Vicki L. Choborda (06/08/1968) **CH:** James E.; Jason S.; Jordan D. **ED:** JD, University of Idaho College of Law (1968); BS in Forestry, University of Idaho (1965) **C:** Chairman, Senate Committee on Foreign Relations (2019-Present); U.S. Senator, State of Idaho (2009-Present); U.S. Senate Joint Economic Committee (2009-Present); Member, U.S. Senate Select Committee on Intelligence (2009-Present); Member, U.S. Senate Select

Committee on Ethics (2009-Present); Member, U.S. Senate Committee on Energy and National Resources (2009-Present); Member, U.S. Senate Committee on Foreign Relations (2009-Present); Partner, Risch Goss & Insinger, Boise, ID (1975-Present); Chairmen, Senate Committee on Small Business (2017-2019); Lieutenant Governor, State of Idaho, Boise, ID (2003-2006, 2007-2009); Governor, State of Idaho, Boise, ID (2006-2007); Majority Leader, Idaho State Senate, Boise, ID (1997-2002); Independent Counsel to Governor, State of Idaho, Boise, ID (1996); Member, District 18, Idaho State Senate, Boise, ID (1995-2002); President Pro Tempore, Idaho State Senate, Boise, ID (1983-1988); Majority Leader, Idaho State Senate, Boise, ID (1977-1982); Member, District 18, Idaho State Senate, Boise, ID (1974-1988); Prosecuting Attorney, Ada County, ID (1971-1975); Chief Deputy Prosecuting Attorney, Ada County, ID (1969-1970); Deputy Prosecuting Attorney, Ada County, ID (1968-1969) **CR:** Professor of Law, Boise State University (1972-1975) **CIV:** Chairman, Board of Directors, American Trailer Manufacturing Company (1995-Present); Board of Directors, State Legislative Leaders Foundation (2002); Board of Directors, Idaho Co. (1992-1994); General Counsel, Idaho Republican Party (1991-2002); Chairman, George Bush Presidential Campaign (1988); President, Idaho Prosecuting Attorneys Association, Inc. (1970-1974); Board of Directors, National District Attorneys Association (1973) **MEM:** American Bar Association; Idaho Bar Association; Boise Bar Association; Ducks Unlimited; National Rifle Association of America; National Cattleman's Beef Association; Idaho Cattle Association; American Angus Association; Idaho Angus Association; American Legislative Exchange Council; Boise Valley Angus Association; Phi Delta Theta Fraternity; Xi Sigma Pi **AV:** Hunting; Fishing; Skiing **PA:** Republican **RE:** Roman Catholic

RISS, RICHARD MICHAEL, PHD, T: Associate Dean of Traditional Undergraduate Studies, Professor of History and Biblical Studies **I:** Education/Educational Services **CN:** Pillar College **DOB:** 05/22/1952 **PB:** Rochester **SC:** NY/USA **PT:** Walter Riss; Barbara Ann (Johnson) Riss **MS:** Married **SPN:** Kathryn Janet Grieser (03/03/1979) **ED:** PhD, Drew University (2007); MPhil, Drew University (2002); MA, Trinity Evangelical Divinity School, Deerfield, IL (1988); MCS, Regent College (1979); BA, University of Rochester (1974) **C:** Associate Dean, Pillar College (2020-Present); Professor of Church History, Pillar College (1990-Present); Research Associate to Chief Economist, C.J. Lawrence/Deutsche Bank Securities Corporation, New York, NY (1991-1996); Research Associate to Chief Economist, Prudential Securities, New York, NY (1988-1991); Data Base Manager, Systems and Management Information Services, First Chicago Corporation (1980-1985); Instructor of Church History, Christian Life College, Mount Prospect, IL (1980-1983) **CW:** Author, "Images of Revival" (1997); Author, "A Defense of the Revival" (1996); Author, "A History of the Worldwide Awakening, 1992-95" (1995); Author, "A Survey of Twentieth Century Revival Movements in North America" (1988); Author, "Latter Rain" (1987); Author, "The Evidence for the Resurrection of Jesus Christ" (1977); Contributor, Articles, New International Dictionary of Pentecostal and Charismatic Movements, Encyclopedia of Hanoverian England, Encyclopedia of Religious Revivals in America, and the Library of Christian Worship **MEM:** American Conference of Academic Deans; Society for Pentecostal Studies; Conference on Faith & History; The Evangelical Theological Society; Society of Christian Philosophers; American Society of Church History; Wesleyan Theological Society **MH:** Albert Nelson Marquis Lifetime

Achievement Award; Marquis Who's Who Top Professional **B/I:** Dr. Riss became involved in his profession because he attended Regent College and one of his professors, Dr. Rennie had an impact on him. He instilled in him a love and enthusiasm for church history. **AV:** Playing violin

RITCHIE, ALBERT, T: Lawyer **I:** Law and Legal Services **DOB:** 09/29/1939 **PB:** Charlottesville **SC:** VA/USA **PT:** John Ritchie; Sarah Dunlop (Wallace) Ritchie **SPN:** Jennie Wayland (04/29/1967) **CH:** John; Mary **ED:** LLB, University of Virginia (1964); BA, Yale University, Summa Cum Laude (1961) **C:** Retired, Sidley Austin LLP, Chicago, IL (1999); Partner, Sidley Austin LLP, Chicago, IL (1972-1999); Associate, Sidley Austin LLP, Chicago, IL (1964-1971) **CIV:** Trustee, University of Virginia Law School Foundation (1997-1999); Board of Directors, United Charities of Chicago (1979-1990); Board of Directors, Erie Neighborhood House, Chicago, IL (1978-1988); Nutrition Program, Church **MIL:** Captain, U.S. Army (1965-1967) **CW:** Lecturer, Professional Programs **MEM:** President, University of Virginia Law School Alumni Association (1993-1995); Vice President, University of Virginia Law School Alumni Association (1989-1993); President, Legal Club of Chicago (1986-1987); Life Member, University of Virginia Law School Alumni Association; Former Member American Bar Association; Former Member, American College Real Estate Lawyers; Former Member, Chicago Legal Aid Society; Cherokee Country Club **BAR:** Tennessee (2000); Illinois (1964) **MH:** Albert Nelson Marquis Lifetime Achievement Award **B/I:** Mr. Ritchie became involved in his profession because his father was a law school educator and the dean of law schools at the University of Wisconsin and Northwestern University. His father was a graduate of the University of Virginia School of Law, which is why Mr. Ritchie went into the legal profession and aspired to graduate from the same institution. He especially liked real estate law because it gave him the opportunity to work with various people and help them reach their different goals. He thought it was a very diverse specialty. **RE:** Methodist **THT:** Mr. Ritchie represented three or four different families at different times that were surviving members of a family that had farmed land mainly in Fox River Valley. He represented them in the sales of their family land and he found it to be interesting because he liked real estate law and also he felt good about those transaction because the fore-bearers had picked good properties and they were major sales for the surviving families.

RITCHIE, JAMES, "JIM" BOWERS III, James Bowers Ritchie III, is the natural-born male son of his mother and by her husband, his natural father. His father was born in Linn County, Iowa in 1916; and his mother, who was of Danish descent, was born in Omaha, Nebraska in 1918. Both of his parents were raised in Omaha, where they met in their late teens. They secretly and legally married in June 1938. His birth date is September 29, 1942, and his birth place is Fort Worth, Texas. For the year-and-a-half before the Japanese surprise attack of December 7, 1941, against US Naval ships in Pearl Harbor, Hawaii; his parents lived in San Diego, where his father worked as Foreman with Consolidated Aircraft Company building US military bombers. After the war started, President Franklin Roosevelt authorized military production to be moved off the Pacific coast inland to such places as Fort Worth and there his parents had recently moved when Mr. Ritchie was born. **T:** Attorney-At-Law Esquire, Preeminent Attorney, Emeritus Attorney; Protestant Army Chaplain (Captain), Army Combat Infantry Battalion Chaplain, Army Basic Training Co-Brigade Chaplain;

Levels One and Two K-12 Substitute Teacher, Levels One and Two Educational Assistant **I:** Law and Legal Services **CN:** "James B. Ritchie, Attorney, Professional Corporation" [1973-2010] **DOB:** 09/29/1942 **PB:** Fort Worth, Tarrant County, Texas, Certificate of Birth Register No. 3337 **SC:** Natural-born citizen of Texas, United States of America **PT:** Paternal Line: Father: James "Bud" Bowers Ritchie, 1916-1999 (born Linn County, IA). Grandfather: James B. Ritchie, 1879-1959 (St. Louis, MO). Grandmother: Mary Cecilia Bowers Ritchie, 1894-1929 (Assumption, IL). Great-Grandfather: Frank E. Ritchie, 1848-1923 (St. Louis, MO). Great-Great-Grandfather: James Ritchie, 1804-1885 (Scotland). Maternal Line: Mother: Helen Marion Anholm Bogh, 1918-2006 (Omaha, NE). Grandmother: Edith Jensen, 1895-1976/Bogh/Christensen/Mekkelsen. Grandfather: Mandrup Bogh, 1885-unknown (Denmark). Great-Grandmother: Eda Jensen (Silkeborg Denmark), 1872-1964. Mother's Beloved Father: Pete Christensen (Policeman Denmark Migrated Omaha). Beloved Grandfather: Walter Mekkelsen (Knebel Denmark Migrated Omaha) **MS:** Married **SPN:** Patricia Diane Jenkins McKinney Ritchie, Collin County, Texas (09/10/2010) **CH:** Brian Patrick Ritchie born May 29, 1987, in Atlanta, Fulton, Georgia [Record of Birth #110-713078] **ED:** University of Alabama, Bachelor of Arts (AB) 1964; Emory University Lamar School of Law, Bachelor of Laws (LLB) 1966, Doctor of Law (JD) 1970; Boston University School of Theology (Graduate School), Master of Arts Church History (MA-CH) 1968 **CT:** High School: "Quill & Scroll International Journalism Honor Society"; University of Alabama: Lambda Chi Alpha (Social Fraternity), "Scabbard & Blade Military Honor Society" [Air Force ROTC]; Emory University Lamar School of Law: "The International Legal Fraternity of Phi Delta Phi", and "The Case Club" [third-year honor] **C:** Youth and Early Adult Employment: Mr. Ritchie had a series of preparatory jobs from ages 14 to 23: Johnson Oil Equipment (as an early learner under a mechanic who was a WWI veteran- 1917-18); Camp Dixie for Boys (Canoe Counselor); Sky Valley Ranch for Boys (Wilderness Counselor); J.J. Finnigan Steel Co. (Southern Railroad cars refurbished); Fideli-facts of Georgia (private investigator); and the Law Firm of Shoob, McLain & Jessee (investigator then law clerk). Given the Opportunity to Become a Military Chaplain: Before being drafted, an unexpected offer reached newly admitted Attorney Ritchie in the "summer of 1966". The Church in which he had been raised invited him to Boston MA, and outlined a path for becoming a military chaplain. He accepted the commitment to take two full years of Christian seminary schooling followed by four full years as a United States Army Protestant Chaplain. At the Boston University School of Theology [BUST], he started as a second-year seminarian in a three-year track of Christian Theological Studies. By 1968, he had earned his degree of Master of Arts in Church History. During four years of the Vietnam War 1968-1972, he was an active duty U.S. Army Chaplain (Captain): During his two years at Boston University School of Theology, military draft-mandated Mr. Ritchie accumulated ministerial experiences: Boston State (Mental) Hospital, at Norfolk State Prison, at Augusta Georgia Veterans' Mental Hospital, and at Fort Gordon Military Prison Facility. Mr. Ritchie chose Army service in June 1968; he was commissioned First LT-USAR at the Army's Chaplain Training Facility at Fort Hamilton, Brooklyn, NY; he was re-commissioned Army Captain AUS during the training. His first assignment for active duty placed Chaplain (Captain) Ritchie in September 1968, at Fort Bragg, North Carolina, as Assistant Unit Chaplain of the 50th Signal Battalion (Airborne). Chap-

lain Ritchie requested and was assigned to Fort Benning's Parachute Training Course ("Jump School") of five weeks. He qualified for his Parachute Badge ("Jump Wings") in December 1968. In March 1969, he could "feel the orders to Vietnam" coming his way. Chaplain Ritchie's Vietnam Combat Tour Orders arrived. **CR:** Army Chaplain Unarmed and Without Chaplain Assistant in Combat: During Chaplain Ritchie's combat tour of duty, an entire 365-day year inclusive of travel, his first assignment was Battalion Chaplain for the Army's First Battalion 52nd Infantry [1/52], 198th Brigade, American Division [23rd Division], and he reported for duty at the remote Fire Support Base [FSB] named Landing Zone Buff, shortly renamed LZ Stinson. He went into combat unarmed and without a chaplain assistant willing to accompany him into combat [he relates that his CAs refused combat and stayed in the rear doing paperwork]. This proved to be his situation for all the coming months until the completion of his Vietnam tour in May 1970. Chaplain Ritchie chose not to locate and operate from the safer "rear areas". Rather, he chose to minister closer to combat "on and off the Hill" [FSB] six days a week, giving field worship services throughout the Battalion's Area of Operation [AO]. This AO [the size of two counties] was for his men and officers to protect and defend constantly. Gradually, he earned his men's respect, and was welcomed by most but prayed for all. He proclaimed the Bible's Truth and the Gospel Message by witnessing in combat week in and week out. On numerous occasions, he stayed [night laager] overnight with his field-combat companies sharing threats of hostile gunfire, mortar blasts, and booby-traps which far too many times maimed or killed his infantry soldiers. Then from March 10, 1970 until April 30, 1970, Chaplain Ritchie was reassigned "in-country" to be the Chaplain for the same helicopter unit which had been providing all of his "field-chaplain services" since May 1969. It was the 14th Combat Aviation Battalion. Many of his men of both battalions died during his 1969-1970 year. On LZ Stinson, he gave memorial services in honor of each man performed in Godly and Christian reverence [Jewish rabbis served their casualties]. For 365 days, Chaplain Ritchie humbly served his men: all, like him, had faced the compulsory military draft and he was witness to the fact that every man "in a foxhole" appreciated their Army Combat Chaplain. Return Stateside to Fort Dix, NJ Completing His Final Two-Years as Combat Chaplain: Chaplain Ritchie's exit Vietnam Orders sent him to Fort Dix New Jersey and assignment as Co-Brigade Chaplain for the Third Basic Combat Training Brigade from June 1970 until July 1972. After almost seven years away from Attorney Ritchie's own Georgia law practice, Marvin Shoob, Bless Him, rehired him as an Associate Attorney with the Law Firm of Shoob, McLain & Jessee in Atlanta. **CIV:** Military Draft-Obligation Concluded, He Returned to Take-Up His Legal Trial Practice: Within a few months after becoming a civilian once again, in early 1973, Mr. Ritchie visited his law-mentor Marvin Shoob, founder of the Law Firm, Shoob, McLain & Jessee, who had last seen him off to Boston in September 1966. In a brief conference, Attorney Shoob rehired Attorney Ritchie [he had almost forgotten he was still an attorney]. He labored under the memory that he had been to seminary and had been a military Christian Chaplain, and in trials, truth is fought-over by both sides. For him, a high ranking by the nationally known attorney-rating firm: Martindale-Hubbell was a goal he worked to attain. In fact, he practiced law from 1973 on into 1978 when his national ranking was elevated to the highest, "AV". By 1995, he had seen his Martindale-Hubbell rating raised to "AV Preeminent" and his high standing was

nationally published in the "Martindale-Hubbell Bar Register of Preeminent Lawyers, 1995 79th Edition". His AV Preeminent ranking has recently been reaffirmed by M-H in 2019. In addition, he holds another title of which he is grateful, that of "Emeritus Attorney"; which is his published status by The State Bar of Georgia [meaning spotless record from 1966 until 2020]-that too was recently reaffirmed by the Georgia Bar in 2019 [Georgia State Bar #606700]. **MIL:** One Family's Sacrifice for Our Nation's Freedom: His Brother's 1972 Navy Service Death: Then a truly tragic event on October 10, 1972, brought the Ritchie family and Mr. Ritchie into the thousands of families who lost a loved one to the agonies of The Vietnam War. His brother, Ronald Brian Ritchie, a Clemson University Graduate and Navy Lieutenant Junior Grade Flight Officer, died stateside in the crash-dive from two miles high into the ground, of the Douglas A-3B Skywarrior strategic aircraft carrier bomber flown out of Naval Air Station Oceana VA. The Skywarrior's flight crew were only the three Naval Flight Officers: LTjg David H. Grant, LTjg Jeffrey R. Haushalter, and LTjg Ronald Brian Ritchie; and all three died. Reference: Aviation Safety Network, Wikibase Occurrence #220620. The fatal crash site is reported as: "1.6 miles NW of Holland, VA"; and reads: "Aircraft reportedly crashed while on instrument training. Witnesses saw two parachutes and said plane was engulfed in flames as it plunged to earth". This ASN refers to Bulletin 138968. Earlier Bulletin Third Series #135774-140052 about the same Skywarrior: "converted to special electronic configuration July 1967." Looking back, Mr. Ritchie realized that his brother's active flight career was only from May 29, 1970 until his death on October 10, 1972. Mr. Ritchie returns to Headstone Site # 35/4469, Arlington National Cemetery, the Memorial of: "LTjg Ronald Brian Ritchie, Vietnam". Brian is his only sibling. **CW:** Author, Online Article, "A Chaplain's Story"; Author, Online Article, "It's Not Time That Tarnishes True Patriotism!"; Author, Online Article, "July 1969 At Fire Base Stinson"; Author, Online Article, "In Memory and Honor of Ronald Brian Ritchie, U.S. Navy (Deceased 1972); Author, Online Article, "UnScriptural Textbook" **AW:** James Bowers Ritchie III, Service Number 02337846, possesses his Department of Defense Form DD 214, and related Army documents, allowing him to list his own medals and evidences of achievement, as follow: A) 'The Bronze Star Medal' [first]; B) 'The Bronze Star Medal' [second] with First Oak Leaf Cluster; C) 'The Bronze Star Medal' [third] with Second Oak Leaf Cluster; D) 'The Air Medal' [14 "hot LZ" air-assaults] [No "Purple Heart"-never wounded]; E) 'Vietnam Service Medal' with Two Overseas Bars; F) 'Republic of Vietnam Campaign Medal'; G) 'The Army Commendation Medal' [first] 14th Combat Aviation Battalion; H) 'The Army Commendation Medal' [second] Third Basic Combat Training, Fort Dix; I) 'Letter of Appreciation' by Colonel T.J. Charney, Fort Dix; J) Captain's Insignia of Two Silver Bars (O-3); K) Army Chaplain Corps Insignia Shield; L) Protestant Christian Silver Crosses (Lapels); M) Parachutist Badge & Airborne Cap-Insignia. **BAR:** State Bar of Georgia: Admissions June 1966: (1) Superior Court of Fulton County, State of Georgia, (2) Court of Appeals of the State of Georgia, (3) Supreme Court of the State of Georgia, (4) United States District Court for the Northern District of Georgia, [Later] (5) Other Federal District Courts, (6) United States Court of Appeals for the Federal Circuit, (7) other Circuit Courts of Appeals, and (8) United States Court of Federal Claims. **AS:** Mr. Ritchie affirms: "My Divine Guide Throughout My Life Is the Living God of The Holy Bible; and without Him, I could have accomplished nothing. He placed many wonderful people in my life so that I would follow His leading in order that His Good Will for me, a saved sinner, would be expressed through them, as well as through His Living Word: The Scriptures." **B/I:** Mr. Ritchie states "this is why" in his own words: "I was a Christian by birth, and since 1999, I am a Reformed Christian, which simply means that the Protestant Reformation of the 16th century has provided the reasonable and well-reasoned grounds for my understanding and application of The Holy Bible as being entirely inerrant and infallible. The Scriptures are truly God's Word and are unchangeable throughout all Eternity; and are the sufficient daily guide for every believer whose Savior is Jesus Christ. We know that The Bible reveals on its face that God is of one substance in three persons: The Father, The Son, and The Holy Spirit. In other words, The Bible speaks for itself throughout Eternity. God is Sovereign. Christ is Prophet, Priest, and King." **THT:** Mr. Ritchie's conclusion in his own words is: "Given my ages 69 to 77, my time spent with the young people, ages 5 to 19, who have attended the K-12 Classes in the LAPS elementary, middle, and high schools, with hundreds always calling out to me: 'Hi! Mister Jim', these seven years have exceeded my expectations beyond everything I could have wished. Love for my three professions adds up to a life well-lived."

RITCHIE, ROBERT (KID ROCK), T: Singer **I:** Media & Entertainment **DOB:** 01/17/1971 **PB:** Romeo **SC:** MI/USA **PT:** William Ritchie; Susan Ritchie **SPN:** Pamela Anderson (2006, Divorced 2006) **CH:** Robert James Richie Jr. **CW:** Singer, "Sweet Southern Sugar" (2017); Singer, "First Kiss" (2015); Himself, "Silicon Valley" (2014); Narrator, "30 for 30" (2014); Himself, "Who is Vermin Supreme? An Outsider Odyssey" (2014); Himself, "$ellebrity" (2012); Himself, "A Band Called Death" (2012); Actor, "Americans" (2012); Singer, "Rebel Soul" (2012); Singer, "Born Free" (2010); Singer, "Rock n Roll Jesus" (2007); Himself, "Larry the Cable Guy: Health inspector" (2006); Himself, "CSI: NY" (2006); Actor, "Stacked" (2005); Himself, "Fat Actress" (2005); Singer, "Kid Rock" (2003); Actor, "Biker Boyz" (2003); Voice Actor, "Stripperella" (2003); Voice Actor, "King of the Hill" (2002); Singer, "Cocky" (2001); Actor, "Joe Dirt" (2001); Voice Actor, "Osmosis Jones" (2001); Voice Actor, "The Simpson" (2000); Singer, "Devil Without a Cause" (1998); Singer, "Early Mornin' Stoned Pimp" (1996); Singer, "The Polyfuze Method" (1993); Singer, "Grits Sandwiches for Breakfast" (1990) **AW:** Inductee, Music City Walk of Fame (2009); Echo Award for Song of the Year, "All Summer Long" (2009); People's Choice Award for Favorite Rock Song, "All Summer Long" (2009); World Music Award for World's Best Selling Pop Male Artist (2008); American Music Award for Favorite Male Artist (2001)

RIVERA, CHITA, T: Actress, Singer, Dancer **I:** Media & Entertainment **DOB:** 01/23/1933 **PB:** Washington, DC **SC:** USA **PT:** Pedro Julio Figuerva del Rivero; Katherine (Anderson) Rivero **MS:** Divorced **SPN:** Anthony Mordente (1957, Divorced 1966) **ED:** Honorary DFA, University of Florida (2018); Coursework, School of America Ballet, New York, NY **C:** Actress, Singer, Dancer (1952-Present) **CW:** Actress, Singer, Dancer, Theater, "The Visit" (2001, 2004, 2008, 2011, 2014, 2015); Actress, Singer, Dancer, Theater, "Chita: A Legendary Celebration" (2013); Actress, Singer, Dancer, Theater, "Ring Them Bells! A Kander & Ebb Celebration" (2013); Featured, Documentary, "Move" (2012); Featured, Documentary, "Ben Vereen: Last of the Showmen" (2012); Featured, Documentary, "Show Stopper: The Theatrical Life of Garth Drabinsky" (2012); Featured, Documen-

tary, "Carol Channing: Larger Than Life" (2012); Actress, Singer, Dancer, Theater, "The Mystery of Edwin Drood" (2012); Actress, Singer, Dancer, Theater, "Chita Rivera: The Dancer's Life" (2005, 2006); Actress, "Kalamazoo?" (2006); Voice Actress, "Dora the Explorer" (2004); Actress, Singer, Dancer, Theater, "Nine" (2003); Featured, Documentary, "Broadway: The Golden Age, by the Legends Who Were There" (2003); Actress, "Chicago" (2002); Actress, Singer, Dancer, Theater, "Casper: The Friendly Musical" (2001); Actress, Singer, Dancer, Theater, "Anything Goes" (2000, 1982); Actress, Singer, Dancer, Theater, "Chicago: The Musical" (1975, 1977, 1985, 1997, 1999); Actress, Singer, Dancer, Theater, "Dear World" (1998); Actress, Singer, Dancer, Theater, "Kiss of the Spider Woman" (1992, 1993, 1994); Actress, Singer, Dancer, Theater, "Can-Can" (1953, 1988); Actress, "Mayflower Madam" (1987); Actress, Singer, Dancer, Theater, "Jerry's Girls" (1985); Actress, Singer, Dancer, Theater, "The Rink" (1984); Actress, Singer, Dancer, Theater, "Merlin" (1983); Featured, Documentary, "He Makes Me Feel Like Dancin'" (1983); Actress, "One Life to Live" (1982); Actress, "Pippin: His Life and Times" (1981); Actress, Singer, Dancer, Theater, "Bring Back Birdie" (1981); Actress, "Sgt. Pepper's Lonely Hearts Club Band" (1978); Actress, "Once Upon a Brothers Grimm" (1977); Actress, Singer, Dancer, Theater, "Kiss Me, Kate" (1974); Actress, "The New Dick Van Dyke Show" (1973-1974); Actress, Singer, Dancer, Theater, "Sondheim: A Musical Tribute" (1973); Actress, "The Marcus-Nelson Murders" (1973); Actress, Singer, Dancer, Theater, "Born Yesterday" (1972); Actress, "The Carol Burnett Show" (1971); Actress, Singer, Dancer, Theater, "Zorba" (1969, 1970); Actress, Singer, Dancer, Theater, "1491" (1969); Actress, "Sweet Charity" (1969); Actress, Singer, Dancer, Theater, "Irma La Douce" (1968); Actress, Singer, Dancer, Theater, "Sweet Charity" (1967); Actress, Singer, Dancer, Theater, "The Threepenny Opera" (1966); Actress, Singer, Dancer, Theater, "Flower Drum Song" (1966); Actress, Singer, Dancer, Theater, "Bajour" (1964); Actress, "The Outer Limits" (1964); Actress, Singer, Dancer, Theater, "Zenda" (1963); Actress, Singer, Dancer, Theater, "Bye Bye Birdie" (1960, 1961); Actress, Singer, Dancer, Theater, "West Side Story" (1957, 1958); Actress, Singer, Dancer, Theater, "Shinbone Alley" (1957); Actress, Singer, Dancer, Theater, "Mr. Wonderful" (1956); Actress, Singer, Dancer, Theater, "The Shoestring Revue" (1955); Actress, Singer, Dancer, Theater, "Seventh Heaven" (1955); Actress, Singer, Dancer, Theater, "Guys and Dolls" (1951); Actress, Singer, Dancer, Theater, "Call Me Madam" (1951, 1952) **AW:** Life Achievement in Theatre, Tony Awards (2018); Honoree, Eight Over Eighty Gala, The New Jewish Home (2016); John Willis Award for Lifetime Achievement in the Theatre, Theatre World Analysis (2015); Distinguished Performance, Drama League Awards (2015); Presidential Medal of Freedom, President Barack Obama, The White House (2009); Rolex Dance Award, Career Transition for Dancers (2006); Ellis Island Medal of Honor (2000); Honoree, Kennedy Center Honors (2002); Outstanding Actress in a Musical, "Kiss of the Spider Woman," Drama Desk Awards (1993); Best Performance by a Leading Actress in a Musical, "Kiss of the Spider Woman," Tony Awards (1986); Outstanding Actress in a Musical, "The Rink," Drama Desk Awards (1984); Best Performance by a Leading Actress in a Musical, "The Rink," Tony Awards (1983) **MEM:** American Federation of Television and Radio Artists; SAG-AFTRA; Actors' Equity Association

RIVERA, GERALDO, T: Attorney, Reporter, Author **I:** Media & Entertainment **DOB:** 07/04/1943 **PB:** Brooklyn **SC:** NY/USA **PT:** Cruz Rivera; Lillian

(Friedman) Rivera **MS:** Married **SPN:** Erica Michelle Levy (2003); C.C. Dyer (1987, Divorced 2000); Sherryl Raymond (12/31/1976, Divorced 1984); Edie Bucket Vonnegut (12/14/1971, Divorced 1975); Linda Coblentz (1965, Divorced 1969) **CH:** Sol Liliana; Simone Cruickshank; Isabella Holmes; Gabriel Miguel; Cruz Grant Rivera **ED:** JD, Brooklyn Law School (1969); BS, University of Arizona (1965) **C:** Host, Radio Talk Show, "Geraldo Show," WABC (AM), New York, NY (2012-Present); Host, "Geraldo at Large," Fox News (2005-Present); Special Correspondent, Fox News (2001-Present); Host, "Upfront Tonight," CNBC, New Jersey (1998-2001); Reporter, NBC (1997-2001); Host, "Rivera Live," CNBC (1994-2001); Host, Talk Show, "The Geraldo Rivera Show" (1987-1998); Correspondent, Senior Producer, "20/20," ABC-TV (1978-1985); Correspondent, Host, "Good Night America," ABC-TV (1975-1977); Reporter, "Good Morning America," ABC-TV (1973-1976); Reporter, "Eyewitness News," WABC-TV, New York, NY (1970-1975); Member, Anti-Poverty Neighborhood Law Firms, Harlem Assertion Rights & Community Action Legal Services, New York, NY (1968-1970) **CW:** Author, "The Geraldo Show: A Memoir" (2018); Contestant, "Dancing with the Stars" (2016); Contestant, "Celebrity Apprentice" (2015); Author, "The Great Progression: How Hispanics Will Lead America to a New Era of Prosperity" (2009); Author, "HisPanic: Why Americans Fear Hispanics in the U.S." (2008); Author, "Exposing Myself" (1992); Author, "A Special Kind of Courage: Profiles of Young Americans" (1977); Author, "Puerto Rico: Island of Contrasts" (1973); Author, "Miguel Robles - So Far" (1973); Author, "Willowbrook: A Report on How It Is and Why It Doesn't Have to be That Way" (1972) **AW:** ALMA Award for Outstanding Host in a National Information Program (2001); ALMA Award for Outstanding Host in a National Information Program (2000); Robert F. Kennedy Journalism Award (2000); George Foster Peabody Award, "Eyewitness News" (1970); Numerous Other Awards and Accolades **MEM:** Tau Delta Phi **AV:** Sailing **PA:** Republican **RE:** Jewish

RIVERA, MARIANO, T: Professional Baseball Player (Retired) **I:** Athletics **CN:** New York Yankees **DOB:** 11/29/1969 **PB:** Panama City **SC:** Panama **PT:** Mariano Rivera Palacios; Delia (Jiron) Rivera **MS:** Married **SPN:** Clara Rivera (11/09/1991) **CH:** Mariano III; Jafet; Jaziel **ED:** Honorary Doctor of Humane Letters, New York University (2014); Student, La Escuela Secundaria Pedro Pablo Sanchez **C:** Pitcher, New York Yankees (1995-2013) **CR:** Speaker, Washington Speakers Bureau (2019); Partner, eBay (2019); Launched, Toyota and Scion Dealership, Mount Kisco, NY (2015); Investor, Siro's, New York, NY (2012); Investor, Clubhouse Grill, New Rochelle, NY (2006); Spokesperson, Nike, Canali, Acura, Skechers, Hartford Financial Services Group **CIV:** Participant, Christians United for Israel Conference (2019); Co-Host, Fundraiser Dinner, America First Action (2018); Opioid and Drug Abuse Commission (2017); Co-Chair, President's Council on Sports, Fitness, and Nutrition (2017); Founder, Refugio de Esperanza, New Rochelle, NY (2014); Donor, Giving Back Fund (2012); Mariano Rivera Foundation; White Plains Hospital; Mariano Rivera Foundation 5K & Kids Run **CW:** Co-Author, "The Closer" (2014) **AW:** Presidential Medal of Freedom (2019); Inductee, National Baseball Hall of Fame (2019); Inductee, Little League Hall of Excellence (2015); ROBIE Humanitarian Award, Jackie Robinson Foundation (2014); Jefferson Award for Public Service (2014); AL Comeback Player of the Year (2013); Sporting News Comeback Player of the Year Award (2013); Commissioner's Historic Achievement Award (2013); All-Star Game MVP Award (2013);

Man of the Year, New York Board of Rabbis (2013); Marvin Miller Man of the Year Award (2013); All-Star (1997, 1999–2002, 2004–2006, 2008–2011, 2013); American League Player of the Week (2008-2009, 2011); Clutch Performer of the Month Award (2010); Sporting News Pro Athlete of the Year Award (2009); Delivery Man of the Month Award (2008-2009); Delivery Man of the Year (2005–2006, 2009); This Year in Baseball's Closer of the Year Award (2004-2006, 2009); AL Rolaids Relief Man Award (1999, 2001, 2004–2005, 2009); Sporting News Reliever of the Year Award (1997, 1999, 2001, 2004-2005, 2009); World Series Champion (1996, 1998–2000, 2009); ALCS MVP (2003); Thurman Munson Award (2003); World Series MVP (1999); Babe Ruth Award (1999) **RE:** Christian

RIVERS, DOC, T: Professional Basketball Coach **I:** Athletics **CN:** Los Angeles Clippers **DOB:** 10/13/1961 **PB:** Chicago **SC:** IL/USA **PT:** Grady Alexander Rivers; Betty Rivers **MS:** Married **SPN:** Kristen Rivers (1987) **CH:** Austin; Callie; Jeremiah; Spencer **ED:** BA in Pre-Law and Political Science, Marquette University (1985); Coursework, Marquette University (1980-1983) **C:** Head Coach, President, Basketball Operations, Los Angeles Clippers (2014-Present); Head Coach, Senior Vice President, Basketball Operations, Los Angeles Clippers (2013-2014); Head Coach, Boston Celtics (2004-2013); Head Coach, Orlando Magic (1999-2003); Sports Analyst, ABC Sports (2003-2004); Sports Analyst, Turner Sports (1996-1999); Player, San Antonio Spurs (1994-1996); Player, New York Knicks (1992-1994); Player, Los Angeles Clippers (1991-1992); Player, Atlanta Hawks (1983-1991) **CR:** Assistant Coach, U.S.A. Men's Basketball Team Goodwill Games, Brisbane, Australia (2001) **CIV:** Member, National Advisory Board for Positive Coaching Alliance **AW:** Male Coach of Year, Rainbow Sports Awards (2000); Coach of the Year (2000); J. Walter Kennedy Basketball Citizenship Award, Pro Basketball Writers (1990); USA Basketball Male Athlete of the Year (1982); Mr. Basketball USA (1980)

ROBBIE, MARGOT, T: Actress, Producer **I:** Media & Entertainment **DOB:** 07/02/1990 **PB:** Dalby **SC:** QLD/Australia **PT:** Doug Robbie; Sarie Kessler **MS:** Married **SPN:** Tom Ackerley **ED:** Degree in Drama, Somerset College **C:** Actress, Producer (2008-Present) **CR:** Ambassador, Chanel (2018); Model, Deep Euphoria, Calvin Klein (2016) **CW:** Actress, "The Suicide Squad" (2021); Voice Actress, "Peter Rabbit 2: The Runaway" (2021); Actress, Producer, "Birds of Prey: And the Fantabulous Emancipation of One Harley Quinn" (2020); Actress, Music Video, "Diamonds," Megan Thee Stallion and Normani (2020); Producer, "Promising Young Woman" (2020); Actress, "Bombshell" (2019); Executive Producer, "Dollface" (2019); Actress, One Episode, "Dollface" (2019); Actress, "Once Upon a Time... in Hollywood" (2019); Actress, Producer, "Dreamland" (2019); Actress, "Mary Queen of Scots" (2018); Actress, "Slaughterhouse Rulez" (2018); Actress, Producer, "Terminal" (2018); Narrator, Voice Actress, "Peter Rabbit" (2018); Actress, Producer, "I, Tonya" (2017); Actress, "Goodbye Christopher Robin" (2017); Actress, "Suicide Squad" (2016); Actress, "The Legend of Tarzan" (2016); Featured, Short, "Australian Psycho" (2016); Actress, "Whiskey Tango Foxtrot" (2016); Host, "Saturday Night Live" (2016); Guest Appearance, "The Big Short" (2015); Actress, "Focus" (2015); Actress, "Z for Zachariah" (2015); Featured, "Top Gear" (2015); Actress, "Suit Française" (2014); Voice Actress, Video Game, "Family Guy: The Quest for Stuff" (2014); Actress, "The Wolf of Wall Street" (2014); Actress, "About Time" (2013); Actress, "Pan Am"

(2011-2012); Actress, "Neighbours" (2008-2011); Actress, Associate Producer, "I.C.U." (2009); Actress, "The Elephant Princess" (2009); Actress, "Vigilante" (2008); Actress, "Review with Myles Barlow" (2008); Actress, "City Homicide" (2008) **AW:** Best International Supporting Actress, Cinema, "Bombshell," Australian Academy of Cinema and Television Arts Awards (2020); Best Actress in a Foreign Film, "Once Upon a Time... in Hollywood" (2020); Best International Lead Actress, Cinema, "I, Tonya," Australian Academy of Cinema and Television Arts Awards (2018); Best Actress in a Comedy Movie, "I, Tonya," Critics Choice Awards (2018); Bravest Performance, "I, Tonya," Alliance of Women Film Journalists (2018); Hollywood Ensemble Award, "I, Tonya," Hollywood Film Awards (2017); Best Actress, "I, Tonya," Florida Film Critics Circle (2017); Best Actress, "I, Tonya," New York Film Critics Online (2017); Favorite Action Movie Actress, "Suicide Squad," People's Choice Awards (2017); Best Actress, "I, Tonya," San Francisco Bay Area Film Critics Circle (2017); 100 Most Influential, Time (2017); Best Actress in an Action Movie, "Suicide Squad," Critics Choice Awards (2016); Choice Movie Actress, "Suicide Squad," Teen Choice Awards (2016); Best Female Newcomer, "The Wolf of Wall Street," Empire Awards (2014)

ROBBINS, CHUCK, T: Chief Executive Officer **I:** Business Management/Business Services **CN:** Cisco Systems, Inc. **PB:** Grayson **SC:** GA/USA **MS:** Married **CH:** Four Children **ED:** BS in Mathematics, University of North Carolina at Chapel Hill (1987); Diploma, Rocky Mount High School **C:** Chief Executive Officer, Cisco Systems, Inc. (2015-Present); Senior Vice President, Worldwide Field Operations, Cisco Systems, Inc. (2012-2015); Senior Vice President, Americas, Cisco Systems, Inc. (2011-2012); Senior Vice President, U.S. Enterprise, Commercial & Canada, Cisco Systems, Inc. (2009-2011); Senior Vice President, U.S. Commercial, Cisco Systems, Inc. (2007-2009); Segment Vice President, U.S. Channel Sales, Cisco Systems, Inc. (2005-2007); Vice President, U.S. Channel Sales, Cisco Systems, Inc. (2002-2005); Operations Director, U.S. Channels Sales, Cisco Systems, Inc. (1999-2002); Regional Manager, Cisco Systems, Inc. (1998-1999); Accountant Manager, Cisco Systems, Inc. (1997-1998); Sales, Ascend Communications (1996-1997); Sales, Wellfleet Communications (1992-1996); Applications Developer, NCNB, North Carolina (1987-1992) **CR:** Member, Board of Directors, Cisco Systems, Inc. (2016-Present); Speaker, Annual General Meeting, World Economic Forum (2018-2019); Speaker, World Economic Forum, Davos, Switzerland (2016-2017) **CIV:** Member, Georgia Technical Advisory Board; President, Georgia Tech (Georgia Institute of Technology); Board Member, National Multiple Sclerosis Society (Northern California Chapter); Member, International Council, Belfer Center for Science and International Affairs, Harvard University; Chair, IT Governors Steering Committee, World Economic Forum; Member, International Business Council, World Economic Forum; Member, Board of Trustees, Ford Foundation; Director, BlackRock; Director, Business Roundtable; Chair, Immigration Committee, Business Roundtable **MEM:** American Academy of Arts and Sciences (2019-Present); Chair, U.S.-Japan Council

ROBBINS, FRANCES E., T: Educational Administrator **I:** Education/Educational Services **DOB:** 10/27/1928 **PB:** Prescott **SC:** MI/USA **PT:** Arlington Clifford; Anna Maria (Melrose) Osborne **MS:** Widowed **SPN:** Robert Allen Robbins (7/29/1950, Deceased 1992) **CH:** Gloria Jean; Reginald David; Eric Lynn (Deceased) **ED:** Master of Arts, North-

ern Michigan University (1974); Bachelor of Science, Northern Michigan University (1967); Coursework, Central Michigan University (1948) **CT:** Certified Elementary Teacher, Principal, Michigan **C:** Principal, Brimley Elementary School, Michigan (1970-1995); Teacher, Coordinator, Brimley Elementary School, Michigan (1969-1970); Teacher Kindergarten, Brimley Elementary School, Michigan (1966-1969); Teacher, Skandia Elementary School, Michigan (1964-1966); Teacher, Pickford Elementary School, Michigan (1962-1964); Teacher, Rudyard Elementary School, Michigan (1961-1962); Teacher, Kindergarten, Rose City Elementary School, Michigan (1948-1951) **CR:** Adjunct Professor, Michigan State University (1997-Present); Supervisor of Intern Teachers, Michigan State University and Lake Superior State University (1997-Present); Owner, Robbins Refinishing and Repair, Brimley (1985-1995); Advisory Board, Eastern Upper Peninsula Substance Abuse, Sault Ste. Marie, MI (1975-1977) **CIV:** Choir Director, Sunday School Teacher, Brimley Congregational Church (1970-Present); Volunteer, Superior Township Ambulance Corporation, Brimley, MI (1972-1991) **AW:** Eponym, Frances Robbins Library, Brimley Public School (2013); Celebrate Literacy Award, International Reading Association (1986); Woman of Distinction Award, Alpha Tau Chapter, Delta Kappa Gamma (1988) **MEM:** Chippewa-Mackinac Association of Retired Personnel (1995-Present); Alpha Tau Chapter (1970-Present); Bay Mills, Brimley Historical Society (1996); State Recording Secretary, Delta Kappa Gamma (1989-1991); Delta Kappa Gamma; Alpha Dota State; National Association of Elementary School Principals, Michigan Association of Retired School Personnel; Michigan Elementary and Middle School Principals Association; Eastern Upper Peninsula Reading Association; Chippewa Mackinaw Area Retired School Personnel; Brimley Historical Society; Brimley Bay Milles Historical Society **MH:** Albert Nelson Marquis Lifetime Achievement Award; Marquis Who's Who Top Professional **B/I:** Ms. Robbins drew inspiration from her mother in deciding to become a teacher. When Robbins served as a teacher at Brimley Elementary school, there was no principal, and so the superintendent of the schools asked if she would work as a coordinator between himself and the teachers, relaying information between the two. Eventually her responsibilities grew into becoming the principal of the school. **AV:** Knitting; Travel

ROBBINS, TIM, T: Actor, Film Director, Screenwriter **I:** Media & Entertainment **DOB:** 10/16/1958 **PB:** West Covina **SC:** CA/USA **PT:** Gil Robbins; Mary Robbins **CH:** Miles Guthrie; John Henry; Eva Maria **ED:** BA in Drama, School of Film, Theater and Television, UCLA, with Honors (1981) **C:** Founder, Artistic Director, The Actors' Gang (1981) **CW:** Actor, "Castle Rock" (2019); Actor, "Dark Waters" (2019); Actor, Executive Producer, "VHYes" (2019); Director, Documentary, "45 Seconds of Laughter" (2019); Actor, "Here and Now" (2018); Actor, "Marjorie Prime" (2017); Executive Producer, "Ultimate Ultimate" (2017); Executive Producer, Short, "Hot Winter: A Film by Dick Pierre" (2017); Actor, Producer, "The Brink" (2015); Director, One Episode, "The Brink" (2015); Actor, "The Spoils Before Dying" (2015); Actor, "A Perfect Day" (2015); Actor, "Welcome to Me" (2014); Actor, "Life of Crime" (2013); Actor, "Back to 1942" (2012); Actor, "Thanks for Sharing" (2012); Actor, "Portlandia" (2012); Co-Executive Producer, Documentary, "Elena" (2012); Executive Producer, Documentary, "The Big Fix" (2012); Director, Two Episodes, "Treme" (2012, 2011); Actor, "Green Lantern" (2011); Actor, "Cinema Verite" (2011); Musician, Album, "Tim Robbins and the Rogues

Gallery Band" (2010); Director, Screenwriter, Executive Producer, TV Film, "Possible Side Effects" (2009); Actor, "City of Ember" (2008); Actor, "The Lucky Ones" (2008); Actor, Video Short, "Behind the Director's Cut" (2007); Actor, "Noise" (2007); Actor, "Tenacious D in the Pick of Destiny" (2006); Actor, "Catch a Fire" (2006); Actor, "Zathura: A Space Adventure" (2005); Actor, "The Secret Life of Words" (2005); Voice Actor, "Jack & Bobby" (2005); Actor, Executive Producer, Video, "Embedded" (2004); Actor, "Anchorman: The Legend of Ron Burgundy" (2004); Director, Video, "Embedded" (2004); Voice Actor, "Freedom: A History of US" (2003); Actor, "Code 46" (2003); director, Episode, "Queens Supreme" (2003); Actor, "Mystic River" (2003); Actor, "The Truth About Charlie" (2002); Executive Producer, Documentary, "The Spectre of Hope" (2002); Actor, "Human Nature" (2001); Actor, "Antitrust" (2001); Actor, "High Fidelity" (2000); Actor, "Mission to Mars" (2000); Voice Actor, "The Simpsons" (1999); Actor, "Austin Powers: The Spy Who Shagged Me" (1999); Director, Screenwriter, Producer, Voice Actor, "Cradle Will Rock" (1999); Actor, "Arlington Road" (1999); Actor, "Nothing to Lose" (1997); Executive Producer, Documentary, "The Typewriter, the Rifle & the Movie Camera" (1996); Director, Co-Screenwriter, "Dead Man Walking" (1995); Actor, "I.Q." (1994); Actor, "Ready to Wear" (1994); Actor, "The Shawshank Redemption" (1994); Actor, "The Hudsucker Proxy" (1994); Actor, "Short Cuts" (1993); Director, Screenwriter, Actor, "Bob Roberts" (1992); Actor, "The Player" (1992); Actor, "Jungle Fever" (1991); Actor, "Jacob's Ladder" (1990); Actor, "Cadillac Man" (1990); Actor, "Erik the Viking" (1989); Actor, "Miss Firecracker" (1989); Actor, "Twister" (1989); Actor, "Bull Durham" (1988); Actor, "Tapeheads" (1988); Actor, "Five Corners" (1987); Guest Appearance, "Saturday Night Live" (1986); Actor, "Howard the Duck" (1986); Actor, "Top Gun" (1986); Actor, "Amazing Stories" (1986); Actor, "Malice in Wonderland" (1985); Actor, "Fraternity Vacation" (1985); Actor, "Moonlighting" (1985); Actor, "The Sure Thing" (1985); Actor, "No Small Affair" (1984); Actor, "Toy Soldiers" (1984); Actor, "Hill Street Blues" (1984); Actor, "The Love Boat" (1984); Actor, "Santa Barbara" (1984); Actor, "Legmen" (1984); Actor, "Quarterback Princess" (1983); Actor, "At Ease" (1983); Actor, "St. Elsewhere" (1982); Playwright, "Carnage, a Comedy"; Playwright, "Violence: The Misadventures of Spike Spangle, Farmer" **AW:** Berlinale Camera, Berlin International Film Festival (2016); Honoree, Star, Hollywood Walk of Fame (2008); Best Performance in a Leading Role, "The Secret Life of Woods," ADIRCAE Awards (2006); Best Actor in a Supporting Role, "Mystic River," Academy Awards (2004); Best Performance by an Actor in a Supporting Role in a Motion Picture, "Mystic River," Golden Globes (2004); Critics Choice Award, Best Supporting Actor, "Mystic River," Broadcast Film Critics Association Awards (2004); Best Supporting Actor, "Mystic River," Central Ohio Film Critics Association (2004); Outstanding Performance by a Male Actor in a Supporting Role, "Mystic River," Screen Actors Guild Awards (2004); Best Actor in a Supporting Role, "Mystic River," Awards Circuit Community Awards (2003); Tribute to Independent Vision Award, Sundance Film Festival (1997); Prize of the Ecumenical Jury, "Dead Man Walking," Berlin International Film Festival (1996); Prize of the Guild of German Art House Cinemas, "Dead Man Walking," Berlin International Film Festival (1996); Reader Jury of the "Berliner Morgenpost," Dead Man Walking," Berlin International Film Festival (1996); Crystal Iris, Brussels International Film Festival (1996); Co-Recipient, Special Award, "Short Cuts," Golden Globes (1994); Best Performance by an Actor in a Motion Picture - Comedy or Musical, "The Player," Golden Globes (1993); Best Actor, "The Player," Cannes Film Festival (1992); Numerous Other Awards and Accolades

ROBERTS, CARTER S., T: President, Chief Executive Officer **I:** Nonprofit & Philanthropy **CN:** World Wildlife Fund **MS:** Married **CH:** Three Children **ED:** MBA in Management, Harvard University (1988); AB in History, Princeton University (1982) **C:** President, Chief Executive Officer, World Wildlife Fund, Washington, DC (2005-Present); Chief Conservation Officer, Chief Operating Officer, World Wildlife Fund, Washington, DC (2004-2005); Massachusetts State Director, Nature Conservancy (1990-1996); Vice President, Director, Strategic Planning And Global Priorities, Nature Conservancy; Division Vice President, Central America, Nature Conservancy; Director, Strategic Planning, Nature Conservancy; Leader, Marketing And Management Teams, Procter & Gamble, Gillette

ROBERTS, CHARLES, "PAT" PATRICK, T: U.S. Senator **I:** Government Administration/Government Relations/Government Services **DOB:** 04/20/1936 **PB:** Topeka **SC:** KS/USA **MS:** Married **SPN:** Frankie Fann (1969) **CH:** David; Ashleigh; Anne-Wesley **ED:** BA in Journalism, Kansas State University (1958) **C:** Chairman, Senate Committee on Agriculture (2015-Present); U.S. Senator, State of Kansas, Washington, DC (1997-Present); Chairman, U.S. Senate Select Committee on Intelligence, Washington, DC (2003-2007); Chairman, U.S. Senate Select Committee on Ethics, Washington, DC (1999-2001); Chairman, U.S. House Committee on Agriculture, Washington, DC (1995-1997); U.S. Representative, Kansas' First Congressional District, United States Congress, Washington, DC (1981-1997); Administrative Assistant to Representative Keith Sebelius, U.S. House of Representatives, Washington, DC (1968-1980); Administrative Assistant to Senator Frank Carlson, U.S. Senate, Washington, DC (1967-1968); Publisher, Litchfield Park, AZ (1962-1967) **MIL:** Advanced through Grades to Captain, U.S. Marine Corps (1958-1962) **CW:** Reporter, Editor, Several Arizona Newspapers (1962-1967) **AW:** John H. Chafee Award for Public Service, Republican Main Street Partnership (2003); Public Service Award, American Chemical Society (2001); Wheat Man of the Year, National Association of Wheat Growers (1993); American Farmer Award, Future Farmers of America (1986); Distinguished Service Award, Kansas Farm Bureau, Inc.; Distinguished Leadership Award, Production Credit Association **PA:** Republican **RE:** Methodist

ROBERTS, DELMAR, "DEL" LEE, T: Managing Editor Emeritus **I:** Writing and Editing **CN:** Law Practice Management Magazine of the American Bar Association **DOB:** 04/09/1933 **PB:** Raleigh **SC:** NC/USA **PT:** James Delmer (Deceased 01/28/1971); Nellie Brocklebank (Tyson) R (Deceased 06/29/1998) **MS:** Single **ED:** MA in Journalism, University of South Carolina (1974); Postgraduate Coursework, Institute of Political Studies, University of Paris (1963); BS in Textile Management, North Carolina State University (1956); Diploma, Kings Business College, Raleigh, NC (1952) **C:** Managing Editor Emeritus, Law Practice Management Magazine of the American Bar Association, Chicago, IL (2000-Present); Managing Editor, Art Director, Law Practice Management Magazine of the American Bar Association, Chicago, IL (1990-2000); Managing Editor, Art Director, Legal Economics Magazine of the American Bar Association, Chicago, IL (1975-1989); Chief, Editorial Vice President, Sandlapper-The Magazine of South Carolina, Columbia, SC (1968-1974); Editor-in-Associate Editor, South Carolina History Illustrated Magazine, Columbia, SC (1970); Process Improvement Engineer, Allied Chemical Company, Irmo, SC (1965-1967); Product Development Engineer, United States Rubber Company (Uniroyal), Winnsboro, SC (1959-1963) **CIV:** Board of Directors, English-Speaking Union (2003-Present); Active, World Affairs Council of Columbia (1997-Present); 1st Vice President, English-Speaking Union (1996, 2013); President, English-Speaking Union (1997-2012) **MIL:** With United States Army (1956-1958) **CW:** Editor, "The Best of Legal Economics" (1979); Freelance Editor, Designer, Over 35 Books **AW:** Honorary Fellow, College of Law Practice Management, Golden, CO (1995-Present) **MEM:** Society of Professional Journalists; University of South Carolina Horseshoe Society; University of South Carolina Guardian Society; Charter Member, Capital City Club, Columbia, SC; Columbia Drama Club; Phi Kappa Tau; Kappa Tau Alpha **MH:** Albert Nelson Marquis Lifetime Achievement Award **AS:** Mr. Roberts parents, James Delmer and Nellie Brocklebank (Tyson) R, as a rule, gave him a lot of freedom to do what he wanted to do, expect he wanted to major in journalism, but his father told him that Journalist starve, and that Mr. Roberts's brother was an engineer. So, he went the route his father wanted him to go in. Then when he was able to do it on his own, he did what he wanted to do, and got his master's degree in journalism. He was very lucky, too, because not every college of journalism would permit someone to come in with a totally different bachelor's degree and start right in. So, he didn't have to take certain courses, because he had his grades to show when he was working on his bachelor's degree, where he made straight A's in courses such as literature and writing. So, they accepted that as proof that he was capable of starting right into his grad work. **B/I:** Mr. Roberts always wanted to be a journalist but his father told him, that journalists starve and that he should be an engineer like his brother who was an aeronautical engineer at the time. Mr. Roberts joined the Army and he was able to get educational benefits for his service. He was lucky after his first semester of college to get a scholarship, to eventually get his master's degree in journalism. **AV:** Travel; Turkish carpet/kilim collecting; Antiques **PA:** Independent

ROBERTS, JOHN GLOVER JR., T: Chief Justice **I:** Government Administration/Government Relations/Government Services **CN:** Supreme Court of the United States **DOB:** 01/27/1955 **PB:** Buffalo **SC:** NY/USA **PT:** John Glover Roberts; Rosemary (Podrasky) Roberts **MS:** Married **SPN:** Jane Marie (Sullivan) Roberts (07/27/1996) **CH:** John "Jack" (Adopted); Josephine "Josie" (Adopted) **ED:** JD, Harvard Law School, Magna Cum Laude (1979); BA in History, Harvard University, Summa Cum Laude (1976) **C:** Chief Justice, Supreme Court of the United States, Washington, DC (2005-Present); Judge, United States Court of Appeals District of Columbia Circuit, Washington, DC (2003-2005); Partner, Hogan & Hartson, LLP (Now Hogan Lovells), Washington, DC (1988-1989, 1993-2003); Principal Deputy Solicitor General, U.S. Department of Justice, Washington, DC (1989-1993); Associate, Hogan & Hartson, LLP (Now Hogan Lovells), Washington, DC (1986-1987); Associate Counsel to President Ronald Reagan, The White House, Washington, DC (1982-1986); Special Assistant to U.S. Attorney General William French Smith, The U.S. Department of Justice, Washington, DC (1981-1982); Law Clerk to Associate Justice William H. Rehnquist, Supreme Court of the United States, Washington, DC (1980-1981); Law Clerk to Honorable Henry Friendly, United States Court of Appeals for the Second Circuit, New York, NY (1979-1980) **CW:** Managing Editor, Harvard

Law Review; Contributor, Articles, Professional Journals **AW:** One of the World's Most Powerful People, Forbes Magazine (2009, 2012-2014); One of the 50 Most Powerful People in DC, GQ Magazine (2009); One of the 100 Most Influential People in the World, Time Magazine (2006, 2007); Bowdoin Prize for Best Dissertation in the English Language, Harvard University (1976) **MEM:** Fellow, American Academy of Arts and Sciences; The Supreme Court Historical Society; Edward Coke Appellate Inn of Court; American Academy of Appellate Lawyers; The American Law Institute; Robert Trent Jones Golf Club; Metropolitan Club; Lawyers Club; The Phi Beta Kappa Society **BAR:** United States Court of Appeals of the Third Circuit (1996); United States Court of Appeals of the Seventh Circuit (1996); United States Court of Appeals of the Tenth Circuit (1996); United States Court of Appeals of the District of Columbia Circuit (1988); United States Court of Appeals of the Fifth Circuit (1988); United States Court of Appeals of the Ninth Circuit (1988); Supreme Court of the United States (1987); United States Court of Appeals of the Federal Circuit (1982); United States Court of Claims (1982); The District of Columbia Bar (1981) **PA:** Republican **RE:** Roman Catholic

ROBERTS, JULIA, T: Actress **I:** Media & Entertainment **DOB:** 10/28/1967 **PB:** Smyrna **SC:** GA/USA **PT:** Walter Roberts; Betty Roberts **MS:** Married **SPN:** Daniel Moder (07/04/2002); Lyle Lovett (06/25/1993, Divorced 1995) **CH:** Hazel Patricia; Phinnaeus Walter; Henry Daniel **ED:** Student, Acting Classes, Click Modeling Agency, New York, NY; Coursework, Georgia State University **C:** Runner, Executive Producer, Red Om Films **CR:** Global Ambassador Lancôme (2010) **CIV:** Contributor, Patron, UNICEF; Lent Celebrity Name to Help Raise Money for Research to Develop a Cure for Rett Syndrome **CW:** Actress, Short Film, "Let's Dance" (2018); Actress, Executive Producer, "Homecoming" (2018); Actress, "Ben Is Back" (2017); Actress, "Wonder" (2017); Voice Actress, "Smurfs: The Lost Village" (2017); Actress, "Money Monster" (2016); Actress, "Mother's Day" (2016); Actress, "Secret in Their Eyes" (2015); Voice Actress, Short Film, "Nature Is Speaking," Conservation International (2014); Actress, "The Normal Heart" (2014); Herself, "Running Wild with Bear Grylls" (2014); Actress, "August: Osage County" (2013); Actress, "Mirror Mirror" (2012); Actress, "Larry Crowne" (2011); Voice Actress, "Love, Wedding, Marriage" (2011); Executive Producer, TV Movie, "Extraordinary Moms" (2011); Executive Producer, "Jesus Henry Christ" (2011); Actress, "Eat Pray Love" (2010); Actress, "Valentine's Day" (2010); Actress, "Duplicity" (2009); Actress, "Fireflies in the Garden" (2008); Executive Producer, "Kit Kittredge: An American Girl" (2008); Actress, "Charlie Wilson's War" (2007); Voice Actress, "Charlotte's Web" (2006); Executive Producer, TV movie, "An American Girl Adventure" (2005); Actress, Music Video, "Dreamgirl" by Dave Matthews Band (2005); Actress, "Ocean's Twelve" (2004); Actress, "Closer" (2004); Executive Producer, TV Movie, "An American Girl Holiday" (2004); Actress, TV Series Documentary, "Freedom: A History of US" (2003); Actress, "Mona Lisa Smile" (2003); Executive Producer, Three Episodes, "Queens Supreme" (2003); Actress, "Confessions of a Dangerous Mind" (2002); Actress, "Full Frontal" (2002); Actress, "Grand Champion" (2002); Actress, "Ocean's Eleven" (2001); Actress, "America's Sweethearts" (2001); Actress, "The Mexican" (2001); Actress, "Erin Brockovich" (2000); Narrator, Documentary, "Silent Angels" (2000); Actress, "Runaway Bride" (1999); Actress, "Notting Hill" (1999); Actress, "Law & Order" (1999); Actress, Executive Producer, "Stepmom"

(1998); Actress, "Murphy Brown" (1998); Actress, "Conspiracy Theory" (1997); Actress, "My Best Friend's Wedding" (1997); Actress, "Everyone Says I Love You" (1996); Actress, "Michael Collins" (1996); Actress, "Mary Reilly" (1996); Actress, "Friends" (1996); Actress, "Something to Talk About" (1995); Actress, "Ready to Wear" (1994); Actress, "I Love Trouble" (1994); Actress, "The Pelican Brief" (1993); Herself, "The Player" (1992); Actress, "Hook" (1991); Actress, "Dying Young" (1991); Actress, "Dying Young" (1991); Actress, "Sleeping with the Enemy" (1991); Actress, "Flatliners" (1991); Actress, "Pretty Woman" (1990); Actress, "Steel Magnolias" (1989); Actress, "Blood Red" (1989); Actress, "Mystic Pizza" (1988); Actress, "Miami Vice" (1988); Actress, TV Movie, "Baja Oklahoma" (1988); Actress, "Satisfaction" (1988); Actress, "Firehouse" (1987); Actress, "Crime Story" (1987) **AW:** Star, Hollywood Walk of Fame (2020); Best Actress in a Television Series Drama, "Homecoming," Satellite Awards (2019); Supporting Actress of the Year, "August: Osage County," Hollywood Film Festival Awards (2013); Spotlight Award, "August: Osage County," Palm Springs International Film Festival Awards (2013); Academy Award for Best Actress, "Erin Brockovich" (2000); Best Film Actress in a Leading Role, "Erin Brockovich" (2000); Best Movie Actress, "Erin Brockovich," Critics' Choice Awards (2000); Best Actress in a Motion Picture - Drama, "Erin Brockovich" (2000); Outstanding Performance by a Female Actor in a Leading Role in a Motion Picture, "Erin Brockovich," Screen Actors Guild Awards (2000); Favorite Actress - Drama, "Erin Brockovich," Blockbuster Entertainment Awards (2000); Choice Actress, "Erin Brockovich," Teen Choice Awards (2000); Actress of the Year, "Erin Brockovich," London Film Critics' Circle Awards (2000); Best Actress, "Erin Brockovich," Los Angeles Film Critics Association Awards (2000); Best Actress, "Erin Brockovich," National Board of Review Awards (2000); Best Female Performance, "Runaway Bride," MTV Movie Awards (1999); Favorite Actress - Drama, "Stepmom," Blockbuster Entertainment Awards (1998); Favorite Actress - Comedy, "My Best Friend's Wedding," Blockbuster Entertainer Awards (1997); Favorite Actress - Suspense, " Blockbuster Entertainment Awards (1997); Best Actress in a Motion Picture - Musical or Comedy, "Pretty Woman," Golden Globe Awards (1990); Best Supporting Actress - Motion Picture, "Steel Magnolias," Golden Globe Awards (1989) **RE:** Hindu

ROBERTS, MICHELE A., T: Lawyer, Union Leader **I:** Law and Legal Services **DOB:** 09/14/1956 **PB:** New York **SC:** NY/USA **ED:** JD, Boalt Hall School Law, University of California Berkeley, (Now University of California Berkeley, School of Law) (1980); BA, Wesleyan University (1977) **C:** Executive Director, National Basketball Players Association (2014-Present); Partner, Litigation Group, Skadden, Arps, Slate, Meagher & Flom LLP, Washington, DC (2011-2014); Partner, Civil/White Collar Litigation, Akin Gump Strauss Hauer & Feld LLP, Washington, DC (2004-2011); Partner, Shea & Gardner (2001-2004); Partner, Rochon & Roberts (1992-2001); Attorney, Public Defender Service, Washington, DC (1986-1992) **CR:** District of Columbia Sentencing Commission; Past Instructor, National Institute for Trial Advocacy; Former Member, Adjunct Faculty, George Washington University Law School; Adjunct Faculty, Harvard Law School **AW:** Listee, ESPNW's "Impact 25" (2014); Listee, "Top Litigation Trial Lawyers," Chambers Global (2011) Recognized, Chambers USA (2010); Listee, "The 100 Most Powerful Women in D.C.," Washingtonian Magazine (2009); Listee, "Washingtonian's Big Guns: Top 30 Lawyers in D.C." (2007); Listee,

"Washington's 10 Leading Criminal Defense Lawyers," Legal Times (2006); Listee, "Washington's Top 75 Lawyers" (2004, 2002); Listee, "America's Top Black Lawyers," Black Enterprise Magazine (2003) **MEM:** Fellow, American College of Trial Lawyers (ACTL); American Bar Association; National Association of Criminal Defense Lawyers; National Bar Association; District of Columbia Bar **BAR:** Washington, DC (1980)

ROBERTS, NORA, T: Writer **I:** Writing and Editing **DOB:** 10/10/1950 **PB:** Silver Spring **SC:** MD/USA **MS:** Married **SPN:** Bruce Wilder (1985); Ronald Aufdem-Brinke (1970, Divorced 1983) **CH:** Dan; Jason **C:** Writer (1981-Present) **CW:** Author (as J.D. Robb), "Golden in Death" (2020); Author, "Hideaway" (2020); Author, "The Rise of Magicks" (2019); Author (as J.D. Robb), "Vendetta Death" (2019); Author, "Under Currents" (2019); Author (as J.D. Robb), "Connections in Death" (2019); Author, "Of Blood and Bone: Chronicles of The One, Book 2" (2018); Author (as J.D. Robb), "Leverage in Death" (2018); Author, "Shelter in Place" (2018); Author (as J.D. Robb), "Dark in Death" (2018); Author, "Year One: Chronicles of The One, Book 1" (2017); Author (as J.D. Robb), "Secrets in Death" (2017); Author, "Come Sundown" (2017); Author (as J.D. Robb), "Echoes in Death" (2017); Author, "Island of Glass" (2016); Author (as J.D. Robb), "Apprentice in Death" (2016); Author, "Bay of Sighs" (2016); Author, "The Obsesion" (2016); Author (as J.D. Robb), "Brotherhood in Death" (2016); Author, "Stars of Fortune" (2015); Author (as J.D. Robb), "Devoted in Death" (2015); Author, "The Liar" (2015); Author (as J.D. Robb), "Obsession in Death" (2015); Author (as J.D. Robb), "Festive in Death" (2014); Author, "Blood Magick" (2014); Author, "The Collector" (2014); Author, "Shadow Spell" (2014); Author (as J.D. Robb), "Concealed in Death" (2014); Author, "Dark Witch" (2013); Author (as J.D. Robb), "Taken in Death" (2013); Author (as J.D. Robb), "Thankless in Death" (2013); Author, "Whiskey Beach" (2013); Author (as J.D. Robb), "Calculated in Death" (2013); Author, "The Perfect Hope" (2012); Author (as J.D. Robb), "Delusion in Death" (2012); Author, "The Last Boyfriend" (2012); Author, "The Witness" (2012); Author (as J.D. Robb), "Celebrity in Death" (2012); Author, "The Next Always" (2011); Author (as J.D. Robb), "Chaos in Death" (2011); Author, "New York in Dallas" (2011); Author (as J.D. Robb), "Time of Death" (2011); Author, "Chasing Fire" (2011); Author (as J.D. Robb), "Treachery in Death" (2011); Author, "Secrets and Sunsets" (2010); Author, "Happy Ever After" (2010); Author (as J.D. Robb), "Possession in Death" (2010); Author (as J.D. Robb), "Indulgence in Death" (2010); Author, "The Search" (2010); Author, "Savor the Moment" (2010); Author (as J.D. Robb), "Big Jack" (2010); Author, "Hot Rocks" (2010); Author (as J.D. Robb), "Fantasy in Death" (2010); Author, "Worth the Risk" (2009); Author, "Windfall" (2009); Author, "Vision in White" (2009); Author (as J.D. Robb), "Promises in Death" (2009); Author (as J.D. Robb), "Missing in Death" (2009); Author, "The Law of Love" (2009); Author (as J.D. Robb), "Kindred in Death" (2009); Author, "Black Hills" (2009); Author, "Bed of Roses" (2009); Author, "Tribute" (2008); Author, "Treasures" (2008); Author (as J.D. Robb), "Three in Death" (2008); Author (as J.D. Robb), "Strangers in Death" (2008); Author (as J.D. Robb), "Salvation in Death" (2008); Author (as J.D. Robb), "Ritual in Death" (2008); Author, "The Pagan Stone" (2008); Author, "the Hollow" (2008); Author, "First Impressions" (2008); Author, "The MacGregors: Robert ~ Cybil" (2007); Author, "Stars" (2007); Author, "Irish Hearts" (2007); Author, "Irish Dreams" (2007); Author, "High Noon" (2007); Author (as J.D. Robb), "Eternity in Death" (2007); Author (as J.D. Robb),

"Creation in Death" (2007); Author, "Blood Brothers" (2007); Author (as J.D. Robb), "Innocent in Death" (2006); Author, "Valley of Silence" (2006); Author, "The Quinn Legacy: Phillip & Seth" (2006); Author, "The Quinn Brothers: Cam & Ethan" (2006); Author, "Morrigan's Cross" (2006); Author (as J.D. Robb), "Memory in Death" (2006); Author, "Dream Makers" (2006); Author, "Dance of the Dogs" (2006); Author, "Cordina's Royal Family: Gabriella & Alexander" (2006); Author, "Cordina's Royal Family: Bennett & Camilla" (2006); Author (as J.D. Robb), "Born in Death" (2006); Author (as J.D. Robb), "Haunted in Death" (2006); Author, "Angels Fall" (2006); Author, "Blue Smoke" (2006); Author, "Northern Lights" (2004); Author, "Birthright" (2003); Author, "Three Fates" (2002); Author, "Midnight Bayou" (2001); Author, "Considering Kate" (2001); Author, "The Villa" (2001); Author, "Carolina Moon" (2000); Author, "River's End" (1999); Author, "The Perfect Neighbor (1999); Author, "The MacGregor Grooms" (1998); Author, "The Winning Hand" (1998); Author, "The Reef" (1998); Author, "Homeport" (1998); Author, "Waiting for Nick" (1997); Author, "Sanctuary" (1997); Author, "Finding the Dream" (1997); Author, "The MacGregor Brides" (1997); Author, "Holding the Dream" (1997); Author, "Daring to Dream" (1996); Author, "Born in Shame" (1996); Author, "Montana Sky" (1996); Author, "Born in Ice" (1995); Author, "True Betrayals" (1995); Author, "Convincing Alex" (1994); Author, "Born in Fire" (1994); Author, "All I Want for Christmas (1994); Author, "Hidden Riches" (1994); Author, "The Best Mistake" (1994); Author, "Private Scandals" (1993); Author, "Falling for Rachel" (1993); Author, "Divine Evil" (1992); Author, "Honest Illusions" (1992); Author, "Unfinished Business" (1992); Author, "Carnal Innocence" (1991); Author, "Luring a Lady" (1991); Author, "Courting Catherine" (1991); Author, "Genuine Lies" (1991); Author, "Public Secrets" (1990); Author, "Times Change" (1990); Author, "Taming Natasha" (1990); Author, "Without a Trace" (1990); Author, "In From the Cold" (1990); Author, "The Welcoming" (1989); Author, "Gabriel's Angel" (1989); Author, "Impulse" (1989); Author, "Sweet Revenge" (1988); Author, "The Name of the Game" (1988); Author, "Local Hero" (1988); Author, "Rebellion" (1988); Author, "Dance the Piper" (1988); Author, "The Last Honest Woman (1988); Author, "Skin Deep" (1988); Author, "Temptation" (1987); Author, "Hot Ice" (1987); Author, "For Now, Forever" (1987); Author, "Mind Over Matter" (1987); Author, "Home for Christmas" (1986); Author, "A Will and a Way" (1986); Author, "Risky Business" (1986); Author, "Treasures Lost, Treasures Found" (1986); Author, "The Art of Deception" (1986); Author, "Dual Image" (1985); Author, "The Right Path" (1985); Author, "Partners" (1985); Author, "Night Moves" (1985); Author, "Boundary Lines" (1985); Author, "Playing the Odds" (1985); Author, "Tempting Fate" (1985); Author, "All the Possibilities" (1985); Author, "One Man's Art" (1985); Author, "Opposites Attract" (1984); Author, "Rules of the Game" (1984); Author, "The Law is a Lady" (1984); Author, "Less of a Stranger" (1984); Author, "A Matter of Choice" (1984); Author, "First Impression" (1984); Author, "Sullivan's Woman" (1984); Author, "Promise Me Tomorrow" (1984); Author, "Storm Warning" (1984); Author, "Endings & Beginnings" (1984); Author, "The Magic Moment" (1983); Author, "Untamed" (1983); Author, "Tonight and Always" (1983); Author, "Once More With Feeling" (1983); Author, "Her Mother's Keeper" (1983); Author, "From This Day" (1983); Author, "Reflections" (1983); Author, "The Heart's Victory" (1982); Author, "Island of Flowers" (1982); Author, "Search for Love" (1982); Author, "Song of the West" (1982); Author, "Blithe Images" (1982) **AW:** The World's Most Influential People,

Time Magazine (2007); Lifetime Achievement Award, Waldenbooks (1991) **MEM:** Novelists, Inc.; Crime League America; Sisters in Crime; Mystery Writers America; Romance Writers America

ROBERTS, RICKY ELIAS, PHD, THD, T: Linguist, Educator **I:** Religious **CN:** True Light Ministries, Inc. **DOB:** 10/20/1961 **PT:** George Roberts; Dorothy V. Roberts **MS:** Single **ED:** PhD in Old Testament and New Testament, Christian Bible College (1991); ThD in Greek, Hebrew, Latin, and Aramaic **C:** Founder, President, True Light Ministries, Inc., Jacksonville, FL (1997-Present) **CR:** Counseling; Prayer Ministries; Exorcisms **CW:** Author, "Walk Through Tears"; Author, "God Through the Storms"; Author, "The Gift of Tongues Examined"; Author, "Angelic Mysteries"; Televised Sermons, TBN Daystar **MH:** Albert Nelson Marquis Lifetime Achievement Award

ROBERTS, ROBIN RENÉ, T: Co-anchor **I:** Media & Entertainment **DOB:** 11/23/1960 **PB:** Tuskegee **SC:** MS/USA **PT:** Lawrence Roberts; Lucimarian Roberts **ED:** BA in Communications, Southeastern Louisiana University, Cum Laude (1983) **C:** Co-anchor, "Good Morning America," ABC News (2005-Present); Featured Reporter, News Anchor, "Good Morning America," ABC News, New York, NY (1995-2005); Reporter, Interviewer, Anchor, "SportsCenter," ESPN, Bristol, CT (1990-2005); Host, "Wide World of Sports," ABC News (1996-1998); Sports Anchor, Reporter, WAGA-TV, Atlanta, GA (1988-1990); Sports Anchor, Reporter, WSMV-TV, Nashville, TN (1986-1988); Sports Anchor, Reporter, WLOX-TV, Biloxi, MS (1984-1986); Sports Anchor, Reporter, WDAM-TV, Hattiesburg, MS (1983-1984); Sports Director, WHMD/WFPR Radio, Hammond, LA (1980-1983) **CR:** Host, Academy Awards Pre-Show, ABC (2009, 2011); Appointed FIFA Women's World Cup Advisory Board (1999) **CIV:** Mentor, #DreamBigPrincess Campaign, Disney **CW:** Co-author, "Everybody's Got Something" (2014); Performer, Audiobook, "Everybody's Got Something" (2014); Co-author, "My Story, My Song" (2012); Author, "From the Heart: Seven Rules to Live By" (2007) **AW:** Named, Honorary Harlem Globetrotter (2015); Walter Cronkite Award for Excellence in Journalism (2014); Named One of the "10 Most Fascinating People of 2013," Barbara Walters' Special (2013); Listed, "The 50 Most Powerful Women in New York City," New York Post (2008); Named Journalist of the Year, Ebony Magazine (2002); Named a Louisiana Legend, Louisiana Public Broadcasting (2001); Mel Greenberg Media Award, Women's Basketball Coaches Association (2001); Listed, "Most Intriguing People in College Basketball," Basketball Times (1997); Inductee, Women's Institute of Sports and Education Foundation Hall of Fame (1994); Excellence in Sports Journalism Award, Center for the Study of Sport in Society, Northeastern University (1993); TV Award of Merit, Daughters of the American Revolution (Now National Society Daughter of the American Revolution) (1990); Recipient, Three Emmy Awards for Broadcasting, Television Academy

ROBERTSON, ARTHUR K. JR., T: Entrepreneur; Minister; Communications Specialist **I:** Corporate Communications & Public Relations **CN:** Effective Communication & Development, Inc. **DOB:** 05/20/1937 **PB:** Oakland **SC:** CA/USA **PT:** Arthur Kenneth Robertson; Laura Bernice Arnerich Robertson **MS:** Married **SPN:** Linda Louise Kauffman Robertson (06/15/1963) **CH:** Scott Alan **ED:** PhD in Religious Education, New York University (1975); MST, in Pastoral Psychology, New York Theological Seminary (1968); BD in Pastoral Psychology, New York Theological Seminary (1968); ThM in New

Testament, Greek, Dallas Theological Seminary (1963); BA in Economics and Pre-Law, University of California Los Angeles (1959) Postgraduate Coursework in Finance, Communication and Psychology **CT:** Pastor-at-large, The Christian and Missionary Alliance (2016-to present); Ordained to Ministry, Plymouth Brethren Christian Church (1963) **C:** Pastor-at-large, The Christian and Missionary Alliance (2016-Present); Co-founder, Director, Billing Adjustment Consultant, Ossining, NY (1991-Present); President of Book Division, Effective Communication & Development Incorporated, Ossining, NY (1991-Present); President, Effective Communication & Development, Incorporated, Ossining, NY (1981-Present); Creator, Marital Communication Enhancement Program, MarriageMirror.com (2010-2020); Senior Pastor, Ridgeway Alliance Church (1992-2010); Teacher, Biblical Communication, Venezuela, Denmark, Russia, Canada (1979-2008); Professor, The King's College, Briarcliff Manor, NY (1968-1981); Walk Thru the Bible Instructor, (1975-1978); Bible Teacher and Chapel Speaker, New York Giants' Football Team, NFL (1975, 1976); Chapel Speaker, New York Yankees Baseball Team, MLB (1975, 1976); Pastor/Teacher, Brooklyn Believers Chapel (1964-1972); Pastor, Bible Teacher, Chaplain, McAuley Water Street Mission, New York, NY (1964) **CR:** Financial Professional, Prudential Financial, Inc. (2010-2016); Communication Consultant, Various Companies Including IBM, AT&T, GM, General Foods, Brystol-Myers Squibb Company, FBI Training Academy, R.R. Donnelly & Sons Company, Coca-Cola of New York, Nestlé Co., New York Life Insurance Company and DuPont; Creator, Business Ethics Program, IBM, General Motors **CIV:** Founder, Chairman, Westchester County Leadership Prayer Breakfast, White Plains, NY (1983-Present); New York State Representative, National Prayer Breakfast (1985-Present); Senior Pastor, Ridgeway Alliance Church, White Plains, NY (1992-2010); Elder, Community Bible Church, Ossining, NY (1985-1993); Member, Advisory Board, Christian Herald SP Foundation, Chappaqua, NY (1988); Co-chairman, Fernbrook Parents' Organization (Now Ossining Union Free School District PTA), Ossining, NY (1972); Advisory Board, Christian Herald Foundation; Former Board Member, "The Christian Embassy", Ministry to Diplomats at United Nations **MIL:** Chaplain, United States Army Reserve, Brooklyn, NY (1964-1965); First Lieutenant, Chaplain, Texas Army National Guard (1963) **CW:** Author, "Work a 4-Hour Day, Achieving Business Efficiency on Your Own Terms" (1994); Author, "Listen for Success" (1994); Author, "Language of Effective Listening" (1991); Author, "Values That Pay: Business Ethics" (1986); Author, "Commentary on The Gospel of Matthew" (1975); Contributor, Articles to Professional Publications; Creator, MarriageMirror.com, Marital Communication Program That Enhances Marital Communication **AW:** Eponym, Recognition Day for Dr. Arthur K. Robertson, White Plains, NY (1991); Student Government Award for Outstanding Teaching, The King's College; Outstanding Educator Award **MEM:** Lifetime Member, Founding Member, International Listening Association; Founding Member, Westchester County Leadership Prayer Breakfast Committee **MH:** Who's Who in America, Who's Who in the World, Who's Who in the East, Who's Who in Religion, Who's Who in Business; Who's Who in Education; Albert Nelson Marquis Lifetime Achievement Award **AS:** Mr. Robertson attributes his success to hard work, a supporting family, help from numerous people at crucial times and the grace of God. **B/I:** Mr. Robertson entered his profession because while he was studying the claims of Jesus Christ as a student at the University of California Los Angeles, he became convinced that trusting His Spirit and following Him was the key to a successful life. He was a pre-law student at UCLA with a major in economics and concluded that as a future attorney he would be faced with all kinds of ethical dilemmas and he wanted to make sure he was properly oriented and had the right foundation to be able to handle the ethical decisions that would be coming his way. He investigated his professors and talked with them and other students, and came to the conclusion that Jesus Christ was probably the best leader that he could possibly find. He decided that he was going to follow Him and went to a graduate school to learn Hebrew; he spent three years learning Hebrew and four years learning Greek in order to find out what the scriptures had to say, that he might make a decision based upon what the scripture says, and not a commentator or one of the many denominations or religious groups might have to say. While he was in seminary, he was encouraged by and saw the opportunity and was very successful in working with young men and knew that he had some of the answers that everyone was looking for. He was encouraged to become a U.S. Army Chaplain; he joined the National Guards upon graduation, and transferred to the Army and went to chaplain school. He graduated and was proceeding in that direction until he was asked to teach at a college. He became a college professor for a number of years. He found that he couldn't live in Westchester county; his wife is a school teacher and she was excessed because the population where she was teaching decreased and they had to let some teachers go. He was faced with how will he support his family; he called IBM and asked them for an application to teach in summer school. He taught for a while at various schools and then he was asked to be a senior pastor at a church in White Plains. He served at that church for 19 years; coming out of there, he began developing the Marriage Mirror, as well as redoing a couple of books. **AV:** Running; Skiing; Biking; Swimming; Reading; Weight training **PA:** Independent **RE:** Committed to and follower of Jesus Christ **THT:** Mr. Robertson created "The Marriage Mirror," a computerized communication inventory to enhance marital communication and encourage positive marriages. For more information, please visit the following link: http://www.marriagemirror.com. Mr. Robertson's says, "Commit your way to the Lord; trust in Him and He shall bring it to pass." Psalm 37:5.

ROBERTSON, JULIAN HART JR., T: Hedge Fund Manager **I:** Financial Services **CN:** Tiger Management **DOB:** 06/25/1932 **PB:** Salisbury **SC:** NC/USA **PT:** Julian Hart Robertson Sr.; Blanche (Spencer) Robertson **MS:** Widowed **SPN:** Josephine Tucker Robertson (1972, Deceased 2010) **CH:** Three Children **ED:** BBA, University of North Carolina at Chapel Hill (1955); Diploma, Episcopal High School (1951) **C:** Chairman, Forstmann Little & Co., New York, NY (2011-Present); Founder, Chairman, Chief Executive Officer, Tiger Management Corp. (1980-2000); Chairman, Chief Executive Officer, Webster Management Corp., Kidder, Peabody & Co. (1974-1978); Vice President, Stockbroker, Kidder, Peabody & Co. (1966-1974); Various Sales Positions, Kidder, Peabody & Co. (1957-1966) **CR:** Co-Founder, The Robertson Foundation (1996); Board of Directors, General Alumni Association, University of North Carolina; Board of Visitors, Kenan-Flagler Business School; Owner, The Farm, Cape Kidnappers, New Zealand; Owner, Kauri Cliffs Lodge, Kerikeri, New Zealand; Owner, Matakauri Lodge, Queenstown, New Zealand **CIV:** The Giving Pledge (2010-Present); Donor, Success Academy Charter Schools (2016); Donor, Restore Our Future (2012); Donor, New York Stem Cell Foundation (2010); Donor, Auckland Art Gallery (2009); Founder, Benefactor, Robertson Scholars Program; National Board of Advisers, Children's Scholarship Fund; Founder, Robertson Scholars Progressive, Duke University/University of North Carolina; Executive Committee, Lincoln Center for the Performing Arts; Board of Trustees, Cancer Research Institute, New York, NY; Board of Trustees, Rockefeller University; Board of Trustees, Wildlife Conservation Society; Board of Trustees, Cathedral Church of St. John the Divine **MIL:** Officer, U.S. Navy (1955-1957) **AW:** Honorary Knight Companion of the New Zealand Order of Merit (2010); Named, Forbes 400: Richest Americans (2009); Inductee, Alpha's Hedge Fund Manager Hall of Fame (2008); Oliver R. Grace Award For Distinguished Service In Advancing Cancer Research, Cancer Research Institute (2006); Davie Award, University of North Carolina Board of Trustees (1992); Named, The World's Billionaires List, Forbes Magazine **MEM:** Zeta Psi **PA:** Republican

ROBERTSON, PATRICIA R., T: Language Professional, Assistant Professor of English **I:** Education/Educational Services **CN:** University Southwestern Louisiana, Lafayette **DOB:** 08/04/1935 **PB:** Black Mountain **SC:** NC/USA **PT:** Walter O'Dell Calloway; Lela Mae (Odom) Calloway **MS:** Married **SPN:** Gordon Robertson Junior (1964-2004); John Vernon Robinson (02/03/1959); Clarence Ray Smotherman (09/03/1950) **CH:** Michael O'Dell **ED:** Postgraduate Coursework, Louisiana State University (1973-1975); MA in English, University of North Carolina (1969); BA, Western Carolina College (1964) **C:** Retired (2004); Assistant Professor, English, University of Southwestern Louisiana, Lafayette, LA (1968-2004); Secretary, Louis Round Wilson Library, University of North Carolina at Chapel Hill (1966-1967); Teacher, English, Guy B. Phillips Junior High School, Chapel Hill, NC (1965-1966); Secretary, School of Public Health, University of North Carolina at Chapel Hill (1964-1965); Nurse, Aston Park Hospital, Asheville, NC (1961-1962); Nurse, St. Joseph's Hospital, Asheville, NC (1960-1962); Dental Assistant, Receptionist, Dr. C.A. Pless Junior, Asheville, NC (1959-1960); Nurse, Shipman Nursing Home, Weston, OH (1951-1959) **CR:** Member, University Southwestern Louisiana Faculty Senate (1972-Present); Member, Popular Culture Conference, San Antonio, TX (1991); Member, Conference on College Composition and Communication, Chicago, IL (1990); Session Chair, Sentence Combining Conference, Miami, OH (1983); Real Estate Salesperson, Lafayette Realty (1969-1983); Member, Louisiana National Teachers Examination Validation Panel, Baton Rouge, LA (1982) **CIV:** Alternate Pianist, Kitchens Creek Baptist Church, Ball, LA (1985-Present); Active Citizens Advisory Panel, American Institute of Cancer Research (1985-Present); Judge, Louisiana Junior Beta Club Creative Writing Contest, Lafayette, LA (1989-1994); Model, Winds of Change Benefit for Children's Shelter (1989) **CW:** Contributor, Articles, Professional Journals **MEM:** Treasurer, American Association of University Professors (1988-Present); President, University of Southwestern Louisiana Chapter, American Association of University Professors (1979); Editor, Bulletin, American Association of University Professors (1973-1978); South Central Modern Language Association; Arkansas Philological Association; Philosophy Association of Louisiana; Popular Culture Association; American Culture Association; Alpha Phi Sigma **MH:** Albert Nelson Marquis Lifetime Achievement Award; Marquis Who's Who Top Professional; Marquis Who's Who Humanitarian Award **B/I:** Mrs. Robertson became a nurse, she loved nursing and she did that for nine years until she had her own child. After, she decided to become a teacher and went back to college to teach on a higher level of education. Teaching was something she longed to do. **AV:** Gardening; Reading; Playing piano; Exercising **PA:** Democrat

ROBINOWITZ, JOE REECE, T: Media Executive **I:** Media & Entertainment **CN:** News Corporation **DOB:** 12/13/1950 **PB:** Houston **SC:** TX/USA **PT:** Milton Earl Robinowitz; June Pearl (Stone) Robinowitz **MS:** Married **SPN:** Marjorie Anne Meiman (01/22/1999) **CH:** Jay; Sarah; Lara **ED:** BS in Journalism, Northwestern University (1973) **C:** Managing Editor, New York Post (1993-2020); Editor-in-Chief, Community Newspaper Group (2006-2011); Editor, Executive Vice President, TV Guide Magazine, Radnor, PA (1989-1993); Vice President, General Manager, Station WFXT-TV, Boston, MA (1987-1989); Editor, Boston Herald (1982-1986); Assistant Managing Editor, New York Post, New York, NY (1978-1982); Makeup Editor, The Star, New York, NY (1977-1978); Reporter, Copy Editor, San Antonio Express-News (1973-1977) **MH:** Albert Nelson Marquis Lifetime Achievement Award **AS:** Mr. Robinowitz attributes his success to great mentors. **B/I:** Mr. Robinowitz became involved in his profession because at nine years old, he founded a community newspaper with a group of friends. Since then, he has remained in the industry. **AV:** Photography; Baseball; Music **RE:** Jewish

ROBINSON, ANN, T: State Representative **I:** Government Administration/Government Relations/Government Services **DOB:** 10/09/1947 **PB:** Aberdeen **SC:** WA/USA **PT:** Alfred T. "Lefty" Graham; Ada Frances Little Graham **MS:** Married **SPN:** Marvin D. Robinson **CH:** Marla; Cody **ED:** AA, Casper College (1991); ParalegalAAS, Casper College (1987); Petroleum Technology Program **CT:** Confidential Adoption Intermediary **C:** Paralegal, Confidential Adoption Intermediary (1991-2016); State Representative, House District 58, Wyoming State Legislature, Cheyenne, WY (1997-2006); Engineer, Regulatory Technician, Oil and Gas Industry (1979-1986) **CR:** Editor, Wyoming State Democratic Newspaper, The Spokesman (1979-1981); Wyoming State Legislature Member Labor, Health and Social Services Committee; Member, Education Committee; Member, Judiciary Committee; Member, Management Council **CIV:** Chairman, Rocky Mountain Regional Fiddle Championships & Music Festival (1992-2017) **CW:** Columnist, Writing Column, "Hodgepodge," Casper Journal **AW:** 2006 Wyoming Woman of Distinction (2006); 2000 Wyoming Early Childhood Education Legislator of the Year (2000); First Place, Wyoming Press Association Award & National Press Association Award for "Hodgepodge" Column in Casper Journal **MEM:** Fort Caspar Chapter, National Society Daughters of the American Revolution; Wyoming Old-Time Fiddlers Association District 4; Casper Antique & Collectors Club; Natrona County Genealogy Society; United States Bowling Congress **MH:** Albert Nelson Marquis Lifetime Achievement Award **B/I:** Ms. Robinson became involved in her profession because it was rewarding; confidential adoption intermediary work, which she did for 25 years, reunites people who were separated by adoption and got their cases through the court. **AV:** Fiddling; Bowling; Genealogy; Pinochle **PA:** Democrat **RE:** Christian

ROBINSON, DAVID, T: Drummer **I:** Media & Entertainment **CN:** The Cars **DOB:** 04/02/1949 **PB:** Malden **SC:** MA/USA **C:** Owner, Art Gallery, Rockport, MA; Drummer, Numerous Bands; Former Owner, Restaurant **CW:** Drummer, Album, "Move Like This," The Cars (2011); Extra, Film, "The Crucible" (1996); Extra, Film, "Housesitter" (1992); Drummer, Cover Designer, Album, "Door to

Door," The Cars (1987); Drummer, Cover Designer, Album, "Heartbeat City," The Cars (1984); Drummer, Cover Designer, Album, "Shake It Up," The Cars (1981); Drummer, Album, "The Original Modern Lovers," The Modern Lovers (1981); Drummer, Cover Designer, Album, "Panorama," The Cars (1980); Drummer, Cover Designer, "Candy-O," The Cars (1979); Drummer, Album, "The Cars," The Cars (1978); Drummer, Album, "Modern Lovers 'Live,'" The Modern Lovers (1977); Drummer, Album, "Rock 'n' Roll with the Modern Lovers," The Modern Lovers (1977); Drummer, Album, "The Modern Lovers," The Modern Lovers (1976); Drummer, Numerous Bands AW: Inductee, The Cars, Rock and Roll Hall of Fame (2018)

ROBINSON, DAVID MAURICE, T: Former NBA Player **I:** Athletics **DOB:** 04/06/1965 **PB:** Key West **SC:** FL/USA **MS:** Married **SPN:** Valerie Robinson **CH:** David Jr.; Corey; Justin **ED:** BS in Mathematics, U.S. Naval Academy, Annapolis, MD (1987) **C:** Center, San Antonio Spurs (1989-2003) **CR:** Member, U.S. Olympic Basketball Team (1988, 1992, 1996) **CIV:** Founder, Patron, The Carver Academy, San Antonio, TX (1997-Present); Founder, David Robinson Foundation, San Antonio, TX (1992-Present); Founder, Admiral Capital Group **MIL:** Commissioned Ensign, Lt. Junior Grade, U.S. Navy (1987-1989) **AW:** Inductee, FIBA Hall of Fame (2013, 2017); NCAA Silver Anniversary Award (2012); Children's Champion Award, Children's Hunger Fund (2011); Inductee, Naismith Basketball Hall of Fame (2009, 2010); Inductee, U.S. Olympic Hall of Fame (2008, 2009); NBA Shooting Stars Champion (2008); Coach Wooden "Keys to Life" Award (2004); Sportsman of the Year, Sports Illustrated (2003); NBA Sportsmanship Award (2001); NBA MVP (1995); NBA Defensive Player of the Year (1992); NBA Rookie of the Year (1990); Gold Medal, 1986 FIBA World Championship (1986); Two Olympic Gold Medals; Olympic Bronze Medal; William E. Simon Prize for Philanthropic Leadership; Numerous Other Awards and Accolades **RE:** Christian

ROBINSON, DUNCAN, T: Army School Instructor **I:** Military & Defense Services **CN:** Dinwiddie County Public Schools **DOB:** 07/05/1962 **PB:** Baltimore **SC:** Maryland **MS:** Married **CH:** Antonio, Scott, Laryn, Leah **ED:** MEd, Regis University (Present); BS in Criminal Justice, West Virginia State University (1984) **CT:** Level II Certification, Command and General Staff College, Fort Leavenworth, KS (2015); Certificate, Capability's Development, Defense Acquisition University (2010); Certificate, Fundamentals of System Acquisition Management, Defense Acquisition University **C:** Senior Army Instructor, U.S. Army Junior Reserve Officers' Training Corps (2018-Present); Deputy Senior Watch Officer, Pentagon Force Protection Agency Washington, DC (2015-2018); Air Security, Pentagon Force Protection Agency (2015-2017); Capability Developer Major, Department of the Army Sustainment Center of Excellence (2010-2015); Liaison Officer, Major, Department of Army CENTCOM Deployment and Distribution Operation Center, Kandahar, Afghanistan (2013-2018); Army Operations Officer Staff Analyst, Major Department of the Army, 82nd Airborne Division, BAGRAM Afghanistan, Ft. Bragg (2009-2010); Maintenance and Contracting Officer, 82nd Airborne Division, Combined Joint Task Force 82 (2009-2010); Support Group Logistics Officer, 507th Corps Support Group (2008-2010); Corps Support Group Logistics Officer, 507th Corps Support Group, Ft. Bragg, NC (2008-2009); Brigade Logistics Officer, Major, 15th Signal Brigade, Ft. Gordon, GA (2007-2008); LOGCAP Support Officer, Major, Army Material Command, LOGCAP Support Detachment, Ft.

Belvior, VA (2006-2007); Operation Analyst, Supervisor GS 12-6, Pentagon Force Protection Agency, Washington, DC (2003-2006); Territory Sales Manager, Pepsi Cola, Augusta, GA (1995-2003); Branch Chief, Fort Knox Armor School (1991-1995) **CIV:** Alpha Phi Alpha Fraternity **MIL:** Instructor, Writer, United States Armor School, Fort Knox, KY (1992-1995); Company Command, 2-66 Armor, 2nd Armored Division (FWD) Garlstedt, Germany (1989-1991); Battalion Staff Officer, 2nd Armored Division (FWD) Garlstedt, Germany (1988-1989); Armor Platoon and Executive Officer, 3-70 Armor, 5th Infantry Division Fort Polk, LA (1984-1988) **AW:** Hall of Fame, West Virginia State University; Prince Hall Mason; Alpha Phi Alpha Fraternity Distinguish Collegiate; Who's Who in College and University; Army Reserve Components Overseas Training Ribbon; Overseas Service Ribbon; Army Service Ribbon; Joint Meritorious Unit Award; Kuwait Liberation Medal, Saudi Arabia; Kuwait Liberation Medal, Kuwait; Global War on Terrorism Medal; Afghanistan Campaign Medal; Southwest Asia Campaign Medal; National Defense Service Medal; Armed Forces Reserve Medal; Joint Service Achievement Medal; Army Reserve Components Achievement Medal; Army Achievement Medal; Army Commendation Medal; Meritorious Service Medal Distinguish Meritorious Service Medal; Bronze Star Medal **MEM:** Whos Who in Colleges and Universities; The Ordnance Order of Samuel Sharpe; Prince Hall Freemasonry Alpha Phi Alpha Fraternity INC Pershing Rifles **B/I:** Mr. Robinson's became involved in his after being inspired by his father who was a chemist and served in the Navy. He had numerous uncles that also served in the Army and the Navy. His mother taught for 35 years. He later joined the U.S. Army Reserve Officers' Training Corps. **THT:** Mr. Robinson's motto is, "Don't Quit."

ROBINSON, JAMES SIDNEY, T: Public Health Service Officer **I:** Education/Educational Services **DOB:** 02/18/1947 **PB:** Lake Arthur **SC:** LA/USA **PT:** James Sidney Robinson; Vernita Robinson **MS:** Married **SPN:** Yvonne Victoria Jones **CH:** Samantha Ann; Curtis James Abernathy; Talliferro Jones; Derrick James; Tiana Nasatja Collazo **ED:** MPA in Human Resources Management, Golden Gate University, San Francisco, CA (1985) **CT:** Certified in Addiction Treatment, California Association for Drug/Alcohol Educators (CAADE) (2003) **C:** Department Head, San Bernardino County Probation Department, San Bernardino, CA (2001-2015); Supervising Officer, San Bernardino County Probation Department, San Bernardino, CA (1986-2001); Supervising Caseworker, St. John's School, Whitewater, CA (1985-1986) **CR:** Director, Student Assistant Program, San Bernardino Valley College, San Bernardino, CA (1996-2006) **MIL:** Maintenance Superintendent, United States Air Force (1965-1985) **AW:** Decorated Numerous Awards, United States Air Force; Nominated, Professor of the Year **MEM:** Chair, Grievance Representative, California Association for Drug/Alcohol Educators (CAADE) (1998-Present) **MH:** Albert Nelson Marquis Lifetime Achievement Award; Marquis Who's Who Top Professional **AV:** Fishing; Camping; Reading; Travel **PA:** Democrat **RE:** Methodist

ROBINSON, KASSIE, T: Sales and Marketing Manager **I:** Advertising & Marketing **CN:** Madden Elevator **ED:** Diploma, Clarksville High School **CT:** Skills for Success, Dale Carnegie & Associates, Inc. (2015); Attitudes for Service, Dale Carnegie & Associates, Inc. **C:** Sales and Marketing Manager, Madden Elevator (2019-Present); Project Coordinator, Madden Elevator (2017-2019); Office Manager, Madden Elevator (2015-2017); Dispatch Coordinator, Madden Elevator (2015-2016)

MEM: National Association of Elevator Contractors **AS:** Ms. Robinson attributes her success to her motivation to better herself. She also attributes her success to her colleagues; they are a constant support system and they help each other when needed.

ROBINSON, MARILYNNE, T: Writer **I:** Writing and Editing **DOB:** 11/26/1943 **PB:** Sandpoint **SC:** ID/USA **PT:** John J. Summers; Ellen (Harris) Summers **MS:** Divorced **SPN:** Fred Miller Robinson (1967, Divorced 1989) **CH:** James; Joseph **ED:** LittD (Honoris Causa), Brown University (2013); PhD in English, University of Washington (1977); BA, Brown University (1966); Honorary Degrees, College of the Holy Cross, Notre Dame, Amherst College, Skidmore College, University of Oxford, and Yale University **C:** F. Wendell Miller Professor of English and Creative Writing, Faculty Member, Iowa's Writer's Workshop, University of Iowa (1991-2016) **CR:** Dwight H. Terry Lectureship, Yale University (2009); Speaker in the Field; Writer-in-Residence, Visiting Professor, University of Kent, Amherst and University of Massachusetts Amherst's MFA Program for Poets and Writers **CW:** Author, "Jack" (2020); Author, "Which Way to the City on a Hill?," New York Review of Books (2019); Author, "What Are We Doing Here?: Essays" (2018); Author, "The Givenness of Things: Essays" (2015); Author, "Humanism, Science, and the Radical Expansion of the Possible," The Nation (2015); Author, "Fear," New York Review of Books (2015); Interviewer, Barack Obama, New York Review of Books (2015); Author, "Lila" (2014); Author, "When I Was a Child I Read Books" (2012); Author, "On 'beauty,'" Tin House (2011); Author, "Absence of Mind: The Dispelling of Inwardness from the Modern Myth of the Self" (2010); Author, "Home" (2008); Author, "Gilead" (2004); Author, "The Death of Adam: Essays on Modern Thought" (1998); Author, "Mother Country: Britain, the Welfare State, and Nuclear Pollution" (1989); Author, "Housekeeping" (1980) **AW:** Library of Congress Prize for American Fiction (2016); Dayton Literary Peace Prize (2016); Man Brooker Prize Longlist, "Lila" (2015); National Book Award Finalist, "Lila" (2014); National Book Critics Circle Award, "Lila" (2014); Park Kyong-ni Prize (2013); National Humanities Medal for "grace and intelligence in writing" (2012); National Humanities Medal, National Endowment for the Arts (2012); Orange Prize for Fiction, "Home" (2009); Los Angeles Times Book Prize for Fiction, "Home" (2008); National Book Award Finalist, "Home" (2008); University of Louisville Grawemeyer Award in Religion (2006); Ambassador Book Award, "Gilead" (2005); Pulitzer Prize for Fiction, "Gilead" (2005); National Book Critics Circle Award for Fiction, "Gilead" (2004); PEN/Diamonstein-Spielvogel Award for the Art of the Essay, "The Death of Adam: Essays on Modern Thought" (1999); Mildred & Howard Strauss Living Award (1998); National Book Award for Nonfiction Shortlist, "Mother Country: Britain, the Welfare State, and Nuclear Pollution" (1989); Hemingway Foundation/PEN Award, "Housekeeping" (1982); Richard & Hinda Rosenthal Award, American Academy of Arts and Letters **MEM:** Fellow, American Academy of Arts and Sciences (2010); Fellow, Mansfield College, Oxford **RE:** Congregationalist

ROBINSON, RICHARD GARY, T: President **I:** Financial Services **DOB:** 08/17/1931 **PB:** Oakland **SC:** CA/USA **PT:** William Albert Robinson; Inez Wilhelmina (Zetterblad) Robinson **MS:** Widowed **SPN:** Lorraine Mary Deshaies (11/13/1965, Deceased 1984); Rosemary Elsen (06/18/1955, Deceased 1963) **CH:** Elisabeth Claudine (Deceased 1970); Christopher Paul **ED:** MBA in International

Management, Thunderbird School of Global Management (1980); Graduate, Industrial College of the Armed Forces (Now Dwight D. Eisenhower School for National Security and Resource Strategy) (1972); BBA, University of Minnesota (1955); ABD in International Economics, University of Denver **CT:** Certified Public Accountant (CPA), Colorado, New Mexico; Certified Management Consultant, Chartered Global Management Accountant **C:** President, Aim High Financial, Inc. (2015-Present); Managing Partner, Santa Fe Business Solutions, LLC (1999-Present); Private Practice, Santa Fe, CA (1995-Present); President, Santa Fe Business Solutions (1980-Present); Managing Partner, A-Action Accounting & Tax Professionals, Colorado Springs, CO (1994-1996); Private Practice, Colorado Springs, CO (1976-1996); Retired (1976); Project Manager, Director, Management Information System, Department of Defense Activities, U.S. Air Force, Southeast Asia; Commander, Strategic Missile Operation and Maintenance Functions, U.S. Air Force; Director, Radar Operations, Tactical Air Warfare, U.S. Air Force **CR:** Consultant, People to People Project Assist to Baltic States Governments on Trade and Economic Legislation; Director, Chief Financial Officer, Unique Equipment Corporation; Board of Directors, United Air Freight Ltd (United Air Services Ltd); Chief Financial Officer, Board of Directors, U.S. Gaming Finance Corp. ; Advisory Board, Pegasus Learning Co., Inc.; Adjunct Faculty, Embry Riddle Aeronautical University, Luke Air Force Base, Arizona Faculty, University of Phoenix, Adjunct Professor of Economics and International Business, Regis University, Colorado Springs University, College of Santa Fe **CIV:** Director, Chief Financial Officer, Americare Clinical Technology Holdings Inc. and its Subsidiaries (Present); Business Advisory Council, Colorado Office of Economic Development and International Trade; Board of Directors, Santa Fe Family YMCA; Board of Directors, Estate Planning Council of Santa Fe **MIL:** Commissioned Officer, 2nd Lt., Advanced Through Grades to Major, U.S. Air Force (1955-1976) **AW:** Decorated Meritorious Service Medal with Oak Leaf Cluster; Air Force Commendation Medal with Two Oak Leaf Clusters **MEM:** Colorado Springs Estate Planning Council; Past President, Santa Fe Estate Planning Council, International Business Association of the Rockies; Board of Directors, Colorado Springs World Affairs Council; American Marketing Association; Armed Forces Communications and Electronics Association; American Management Association; National Association of State Boards of Accountancy; Institute of Management Consultants USA; Association for Political Risk Analysis; North American Society for Corporate Planning **MH:** Albert Nelson Marquis Lifetime Achievement Award **B/I:** Mr. Robinson became involved in his profession because it was around the time that the Korean War was going on and he elected to do his military service on his own terms, so he went to the Air Force. It turned into a career instead of a three- or four-year hitch. When he retired, he discovered that his first retirement check was quite a surprise, so he decided he had to go to work and, as a result of that, he did a one-year management contract for a company in Iran working with its military complex. When he completed that, he realized he was tired of talking computers and wanted to learn to talk business and decided the best way to do that was in the accounting and tax business. **AV:** Fitness; Gardening **RE:** Lutheran

ROBO, JAMES L., T: Chairman, Chief Executive Officer **I:** Oil & Energy **CN:** NextEra Energy, Inc. **ED:** MBA, Harvard Business School; BA, Harvard College, Summa Cum Laude **C:** Chairman, Chief Executive Officer, President, NextEra Energy, Inc.

(2013-Present); Chairman, Florida Power & Light Company (2012-Present); Chairman, Chief Executive Officer, NextEra Energy Partners, LP (2012-2013); President, Chief Operating Officer, NextEra Energy, Inc. (2006-2012); President, NextEra Energy Resources, LLC (2006); Vice President, Corporate Development and Strategy, NextEra Energy, Inc.(2002-2006); President, Chief Executive Officer, Major Division, GE Capital; Chairman, Chief Executive Officer, GE Mexico; Member, GE Corporate Development Team; Vice President, Strategic Planning Associates **CR:** Lead Independent Director, J.B. Hunt Transport Services, Inc., Lowell, AR (2012-Present); Member, Board of Directors, J.B. Hunt Transport Services, Inc., Lowell, AR (2003-Present) **AW:** Baker Scholar, Harvard Business School **MEM:** Phi Beta Kappa

ROBSON, JOHN EDWARD, T: Nursing Administrator **I:** Medicine & Health Care **DOB:** 08/04/1948 **PB:** Grove City **SC:** PA/USA **PT:** Clair Eugene Robson; Grace Louise (Winger) Robson **MS:** Married **SPN:** Shirley Ann Todd (02/07/1968) **CH:** Daniale Elaine; Chad Edward **ED:** MPA, Troy State University, Alabama (1992); BS, Park College, Parkville, MO (1982); Diploma, Alexian Brothers Hospital, Chicago, IL (1969) **C:** Retired Nursing Administrator, Executive Officer, Cherry Point Naval Hospital (1996-1999); Director, Nursing, Camp Lejeune Naval Hospital, Jacksonville, NC (1992-1996); Director, Nursing, Guantanamo Bay Naval Hospital (1991-1992); Assistant Director, Nursing, Cherry Point Naval Hospital, Havelock, NC (1987-1991); Charge Nurse, Inpatient Coordinator, Portsmouth Naval Hospital (1982-1987); Outpatient Coordinator, Flight Nurse, Naval Hospital, Corpus Christi, TX (1979-1982); Charge Nurse, Flight Nurse, Naval Hospital Whidbey Island, Oak Harbor, WA (1976-1979); Charge Nurse, Naval Officer, Naval Hospital, Yokosuka, Japan (1973-1976); Staff Nurse, Naval Hospital Memphis, Millington, TN (1969-1973) **CR:** Clinical Coordinator, Naval Base-haitian Migrant Camp, Guantanamo Bay (1991-1992); Advisor, Flight Nurse, U.S. Coast Guard Station, Corpus Christi, TX (1979-1982); Rural Nursing Instructor, Emergency Nurses Association, Washington State (1978-1979) **CIV:** Member, High School Boosters, Havelock (1987-1990); Coach, Babe Ruth Baseball Program, Havelock (1987-1990) **MIL:** Retired, U.S. Navy (1999) **AW:** Sharpshooter Award, U.S. Navy (1991); Two Decorated Meritorious Service Medals; Two Navy Commendation Medals; **MEM:** Emergency Nurses Association **MH:** Albert Nelson Marquis Lifetime Achievement Award **B/I:** In high school , Mr. John Robson volunteered at the local hospital and the director of nursing convinced him to pursue nursing. It was the way he was brought up, he worked as an orderly in the hospital through high school and in the military, he got a draft notice in 1968. **AV:** Family activities; Sports; Golf **RE:** Methodist

ROBY, MARTHA KEHRES, T: U.S. Representative, Lawyer **I:** Government Administration/Government Relations/Government Services **DOB:** 07/26/1976 **PB:** Montgomery **SC:** AL/USA **PT:** Joel Fredrick Dubina **MS:** Married **SPN:** Riley Roby **CH:** Margaret; George **ED:** JD, Cumberland School of Law, Samford University, Birmingham, AL (2001); BA in Music, New York University (1988) **C:** Member, U.S. Representative, Alabama's Second Congressional District, United States Congress, Washington, DC (2011-2021); Member, Select Committee on the Events Surrounding the 2012 Terrorist Attack in Benghazi, U.S. House of Representatives (2014-2021); Member, Committee on Armed Services, U.S. House of Representatives (2011-2021); Member, Committee on Education and the Workforce, U.S. House of Representatives

(2011-2021); Member, Committee on Agriculture, U.S. House of Representatives (2011-2021); Member, District Seven, Montgomery City Council (2003-2010); Attorney, Copeland, Franco, Screws & Gill (Now Copeland Franco), Montgomery, AL **CIV:** Board Director, Sav-A-Life of Montgomery, Inc.; Member, Executive Board, Montgomery Weed and Seed; Member, Montgomery Area Business Committee for the Arts **MEM:** Alabama Bar Association; Mississippi Bar Association; YMCA of Greater Montgomery; Britton YMCA **PA:** Republican **RE:** Presbyterian

ROBY, PAMELA ANN, PHD, T: Sociologist, Educator **I:** Education/Educational Services **PB:** Milwaukee **SC:** WI/USA **PT:** Clark Dearborn Roby; Marianna Roby **MS:** Divorced **ED:** PhD, New York University, New York, NY (1971); MA, Syracuse University, Syracuse, New York, NY (1966); BA, University of Denver, Denver, CO (1963) **C:** Professor Emerita of Sociology and Women's Studies, University of California Santa Cruz (2007-Present); Director, Sociology Doctoral Program, University of California Santa Cruz (1988-1991, 2007); Chair, Department of Sociology, University of California Santa Cruz (1998-2001); Visiting Scholar, Department of Sociology and Northwest Center for Research on Women, University of Washington (1991-1992); Director, Teaching Assistant Training Program, University of California Santa Cruz (1989-1991); Director of Sociology Doctoral Program, University of California Santa Cruz (1988-1991); Acting Chair, Department of Sociology, University of California Santa Cruz (1986); Professor of Sociology and Women's Studies, University of California Santa Cruz (1983-2007); Chair of Community Studies Board, University of California Santa Cruz (1979); Professor of Sociology and Community Studies, University of California Santa Cruz (1977-1983); Chair of Community Studies Board, University of California Santa Cruz (1974-1976); Associate Professor, Sociology and Community Studies, University of California Santa Cruz (1973-1977); Assistant Professor, Department of Sociology and the Florence Heller School for Advanced Studies in Social Welfare, Brandeis University, Waltham, MA (1971-1973); Assistant Professor, Department of Sociology, The George Washington University, Washington, DC (1970-1971); Research Assistant, Russell Sage Foundation (1966-1967); Instructor, Department of Educational Sociology, New York University, New York, NY (1966); Research Assistant, Youth Development Center, Syracuse University, Syracuse, NY (1965); Teacher, Jefferson County Public Schools (Jeffco Public Schools), Denver, CO (1964) **CR:** Faculty Member, Professor, University of California Santa Cruz Merrill College (2012); Member of Postdoctoral and Dissertation Fellowship Evaluation Panel, Ford Foundation (2005-2009); Assessor of Social Sciences and Humanities Research Council of Canada, Toronto, Canada (1993); Member of Anthropology, Linguistics and Sociology Panel, National Science Foundation, Washington, DC (1993); Member, Sociology Program Review Committee, Northeastern University, Boston, MA (1990); Consultant, The James Irvine Foundation, San Francisco, CA (1986); Vice Chair, National Commission on Working Women, Washington, DC (1977-1980); Member, Social Science Research Review Committee, National Institute of Mental Health, Washington, DC (1976-1980); Member, Commission of Women in Higher Education, American Council on Education, University of California Santa Cruz (1973-1976); Coordinator, Urban Sociology Program, The George Washington University, Washington, DC (1970-1971); Assistant Dean of Students, Syracuse University, Syracuse, NY (1964-1965); Member of Postdoctoral Fellowship Review Committee, The National Academy of

Sciences, Ford Foundation Sociology Dissertation CIV: Indian Council on Social Science Research (ICSSR) (1979); Active Member, St. Peter's United Church of Christ CW: Curator, Two Art Shows, St. Peter's United Church of Christ (2018); Associate Editor, "Contemporary Sociology" (2006-2007); Advisory Editor, "Sociological Quarterly" (1990-1993); Advisory Editor, "Gender and Society" (1986-1989); Member, Editorial Board, "Sage Studies in International Sociology" (1978-1982); Author, "Women in the Workplace" (1981); Editor, "Child Care: Who Cares? Foreign and Domestic Infant and Early Childhood Development Policies" (1973-1975); Editor, "The Poverty Establishment" (1974); Co-author with S. M. Miller, "The Future of Inequality" (1970); Contributor, Articles, Annals of the American Academy of Political and Social Science, Contemporary American Sociology, Labor Studies, The Nation, Social Problems and Other Journals; Consulting Editor, The American Journal of Sociology; Consulting Editor, The Journal of Applied Behavioral Science; Advisory Editor, "Sociological Symposium"; Contributor, American Sociological Review, American Journal of Sociology, Gender & Society, Journal of Applied Sociology, Journal of Occupational and Organizational Psychology, Social Forces, Social Problems, Social Science Quarterly, Sociological Inquiry, Sociological Forum, The Sociological Quarterly, Sociology and Social Research, Sociology of Education, Sociology of Work and Occupations: an International Journal, Teaching Sociology, and Women's Studies: An Interdisciplinary Journal AW: Alfred McClung Lee and Elizabeth Briant Lee Founders Award "in Recognition of Significant Achievements Over a Distinguished Career," The Society for the Study of Social Problems, SSSP (2016); Named, Favorite Faculty Member, University of California Santa Cruz (2002, 2009, 2011-2012); Chancellor's and Women's Studies' 25th Anniversary Award "for Courage and Vision in Founding Women's Studies," University of California Santa Cruz (2000); Academic Senate Innovations in Teaching Award, University of California Santa Cruz (1993); Visiting Scholarship, University of Washington, Seattle, WA (1991-1992); Andrew W. Mellon Senior Scholarship, Wellesley College (1978-1979); Eponym, Pamela Ann Roby Class and Gender Award Endowment, Sociology Department, University of California Santa Cruz MEM: Leader, Lifelong Learning Institute Writing Genealogical History Group, University of California Santa Cruz (2016-Present); Re-evaluation Counseling College and University Faculty Reference Person, Alpha Kappa Delta International Honor Society (1980-2014); Vice President, The Pacific Sociological Association (1996-1997); President, The Society for the Study of Social Problems, SSSP (1996-1997); Elected Member, Research Council, Member-at-Large, ISA, International Sociological Association (1978-1982); President, Sociologists for Women in Society (1978-1980); Executive Council Member-at-Large, American Sociological Association (1975-1978); Chair, Section on Sex and Gender, American Sociological Association (1974-1978); Executive Council Member-at-Large, Eastern Sociological Society (1973-1974); The Phi Beta Kappa Society; Co-chair, Vera Taylor Scholarships Committee, St. Peter's United Church of Christ; Member, Finance and Retreat Planning Committees, St. Peter's United Church of Christ; Former President, Sociologists for Women in Society; Massachusetts Sociological Society; American Association of University Professors; American Federation of Teachers, AFL-CIO; University of California Faculty Association MH: Albert Nelson Marquis Lifetime Achievement Award AS: Dr. Roby attributes her success to wonderful teachers and professors. B/I: Dr. Roby became involved in her profession because of Wis-

consin Shorewood Public High School teacher, Dr. Zelma Oole. Dr. Oole began her creative classes by telling her students that she did not intend to teach grammar. Rather, she simply wanted them to write. During her classes, her students all wrote whatever they chose and then met with Dr. Oole one at a time for 15 minutes or so each. During these sessions she read over their manuscripts, validated what she considered strong points of their manuscripts, and occasionally told them that she would be interested in reading more about one or another matter that they had mentioned. She would then ask them whether they had any more to say about it and would they be interested in writing more. AV: Camping; Hiking; Painting; Swimming; Pen and ink drawing; Nonfiction writing

ROCHELLE, LUGENIA NMN DPD, T: Assistant Professor of English, Director, QEP I: Education/Educational Services CN: Voorhees College DOB: 07/14/1943 PB: Maple Hill SC: NC/USA PT: Mr. John Edward Rochelle; Mrs. Ruby Lee Holmes Rochelle MS: Single ED: Honorary Doctor of Pedagogy, Barber-Scotia College, Salisbury, NC (1992); Coursework, The Catholic University of America, Washington, DC; Coursework, University of North Carolina at Chapel Hill; MS in English Education, North Carolina A&T State University, Greensboro, NC (1969); BA, St. Augustine's College (now University), Raleigh, NC; High School Diploma, Georgetown High School, Jacksonville, NC (1961) CT: Certificate of Leadership Development, IBM Leadership Class, Armonk, NY (1992); Certificate of Leadership Development, Atlanta University National Center, Falls Church, VA (1979); Certified in Personal Development, Patricia Stevens School of Charm, Atlanta, GA (1971); Certified in Writing Behavioral Modification Objectives, Project Upward Bound, North Carolina A & T State University, Greensboro, NC (1969-1976) C: Interim Vice President, Academic and Student Affairs, Voorhees College, Denmark, SC (2017-Present); Interim Vice President, Academic Affairs, Voorhees College, Denmark, SC (2014); Chair, Division of General Studies, Assistant Professor, English, Chair, Academic/Financial Aid Review Committee, Voorhees College, Denmark, SC (2002-2014); Director, Andrew W. Mellon Center for Excellence in the Humanities (2000-2002); Special Assistant to the President, External Affairs, Voorhees College, Denmark, SC (1999-2002); Coordinator, Title II, Voorhees College, Denmark, SC (2000-2001); Director, General Education, Voorhees College, Denmark, SC (1997-1998); Director, General Education/Freshman Year Experience, Assistant Professor of English, Voorhees College, Denmark, SC (1996-1997); Member, Dean's Council, Voorhees College, Denmark, SC (1996-1997); Associate Professor of Philosophy, St. Augustine's College, Raleigh, NC (1995-1997); Dean, Lower College, Associate Professor of English, Member, Administrative Council, St. Augustine's College, Raleigh, NC (1994-1995); Dean of the Lower College, Associate Professor of English, St. Augustine's College, Raleigh, NC (1991-1995); Member, Administrative Council, St. Augustine's College, Raleigh, NC (1986-1995); Dean, Lower College, Assistant Vice President, Academic Affairs, Associate Professor of English, Member, Administrative Council, St. Augustine's College, Raleigh, NC (1991-1993); National Teaching Fellow, North Carolina A & T State University, Greensboro, NC (1968-1970); Teacher, French and English, Butler High School, Barnwell, SC (1965-1967) CR: Presenter, Participant, Bamberg Ancestral and Genealogical Society (BAAGS) (2012); Effected the Charter, Phi Eta Sigma, Saint Augustine's College (1995); Planner, Organizer, Director, Pre-college Program for High School Graduates, St. Augustine's College, Raleigh, NC (1987); Program Par-

ticipant, National Council of Teachers of English Convention, Philadelphia, PA (1972); President, Graduate School Club (1967-1968); Received Training in Quality Education for Minorities Network (QEM); Participant, Institute for Higher Education Policy, Santa Ana Pueblo, NM; Director, Honors College Consultant, Presenter, Learning to Learn Publication, Voorhees College; Freshman Class Advisor, Voorhees Campus Coordinator, Coach of Honda All-Star Campus Challenge, Voorhees College; Designer, Composer, Vocational Education Modules in Folklore, North Carolina State Department of Public Instruction, Raleigh, NC; Attendee, Numerous Annual SACS Meetings; Attendee, UNCF Institute Faculty Development Programs; Consultant, Presenter, Learning to Learn Publication, Miami, Florida, Salisbury, NC; Designer, Composer, Vocational Education Modules on Folklore, North Carolina State Department of Public Instruction, Raleigh, NC; Literary Assistant to the Dean, Graduate School, North Carolina A&T State University, Greensboro, NC; Founder, Editor, The Courier; Studied, Academic Curricula, Colleges, Universities, Rikkyo University, Trinity College, and Christ Church College, Japan, the Philippines, England CIV: Volunteer, Apprising Young Men and Women of the Importance of Financial Management; Supporter, Community Programs aimed at Developing and Advancing the Academic Performance of High School Students; Advocate, Community Progress and Beautification CW: Author, "Survival Tips for the Freshman Year Experience," Off to College; Author, "Embracing Diversity," Off to College (1998); Author, Information Manual to Prepare Faculty, Staff and Students for the NCATE Visit, Saint Augustine's College (1992); Author, Narrative of a Film, Director, Arrangement of the Scenes for the Film and the Narrative, Music Selection for Film, Saint Augustine's College, Raleigh, NC (1983); Principal Writer, Proposals, Proofreader, Editor, Numerous Documents, Writing and Reading Across the Curriculum, Bush-Hewlett Foundation, Saint Augustine's College, Raleigh, NC (1977-1995) AW: Excellence in Teaching Award, Voorhees College (2009-2010, 2018-2019); President's Medallion, Saint Augustine's College (1983); Certificate of Appreciation for 15 years of Service at Saint Augustine's College MEM: Advisory Board, Off to College (1998-2020); Sigma Tau Delta International English Honor Society; South Carolina Women in Higher Education; Honorary Member, Phi Eta Lambda; Phi Eta Sigma Honor Society; Rome Baptist Church Scholar Foundation, Denmark, SC AS: She attributes her success to many immediate family members and other relatives and friends who encouraged and supported her in developing the maximum of her potentials. More specifically, she attributes her success to her Aunt Carrie who nurtured and taught her to believe in herself and capabilities and her father who paid for her undergraduate education and who wanted her to be primarily financially independent. She attributes her success to her mother; she watched her take her last breath of life when she was 4 years and 9 months old. Her short life has motivated her to aim for excellence because she believes her mother would have wanted her to do so. Furthermore, she attributes her success to her ethos that success is not merely for her but also for her to pass on to others the blueprint for success to the extent that she can. B/I: She became an educator because several of her aunts and cousins were educators and because her teachers from elementary school through college impressed upon her the importance of gaining as much knowledge as possible and preparing herself to share that knowledge. She is an advocate of effective oral and written communication and have devoted her career to teaching students the levels of usage appropriate for specific audiences and/or situations. **AV:** Collecting porcelain antique small birds, small perfume bottles, porcelain dolls; Reading; Listening to jazz; Promoting the good qualities and deeds of the human enterprise **PA:** Democrat **RE:** Episcopalian **THT:** To be an example of the epitome of love, compassion, understanding, equity, and goodwill.

ROCHESTER, LISA LATRELLE BLUNT, T: U.S. Representative from Delaware **I:** Government Administration/Government Relations/Government Services **DOB:** 02/10/1962 **PB:** Philadelphia **SC:** PA/USA **PT:** Ted Blunt; Alice LaTrelle **MS:** Widowed **SPN:** Charles Rochester (2006, Deceased 2014); Alex Bradley (1982, Divorced 2003) **ED:** Master's in Urban Affairs and Public Policy, University of Delaware; BA in International Relations, Fairleigh Dickinson University; Coursework, Villanova University **C:** Member, U.S. House of Representatives from Delaware's At-large Congressional District (2017-Present); Chief Executive Officer, Metropolitan Wilmington Urban League (2004-2007); State Personal Director, CA (2001-2004); Secretary, U.S. Department of Labor (1998-2001); Deputy Secretary, Department of Health and Social Services (1993-1998); Member, Committee on Agriculture; Member, Committee on Education and the Workforce **CW:** Co-author, "THRIVE: 34 Women, 18 Countries, One Goal" **PA:** Democrat

ROCK, CHRIS, T: Comedian **I:** Media & Entertainment **DOB:** 02/07/1965 **PB:** Brooklyn **SC:** NY/USA **PT:** Julius Rock; Rosalie (Tingman) Rock **MS:** Married **SPN:** Malaak Compton (11/23/1996, Divorced 2016) **CH:** Lola Simone; Zahra Savannah **C:** Actor, Comedian (1985-Present) **CW:** Director, Episode, "The Kenan Show" (2021); Actor, "Fargo" (2020); Actor, "The Witches" (2020); Actor, Executive Producer, "Spiral" (2020); Actor, "Dolemite Is My Name" (2019); Actor, Music Video, "Old Town Road" by Lil Nas Featuring Billy Ray Cyrus (2019); Actor, "Nobody's Fool" (2018); Actor, "Kevin Can Wait" (2018); Actor, "The Week Of" (2018); Comedian, Stand-Up Special, Album, "Chris Rock: Tamborine" (2018); Actor, "Sandy Wexler" (2017); Narrator, Short, "An Ode to Hannibal Buress" (2016); Host, "The Oscars" (2016); Narrator, "Dancing in the Light: The Janet Collins Story" (2015); Guest Appearance, "A Very Murray Christmas" (2015); Actor, "Empire" (2015); Guest Appearance, "The Jim Gaffigan Show" (2015); Guest Appearance, "Broad City" (2015); Director, Special, "Amy Schumer: Live at the Apollo" (2015); Actor, Director, Screenwriter, "Top Five" (2014); Actor, "Fargo" (2014); Host, "Saturday Night Live" (2014); Actor, "Grown Ups 2" (2013); Guest Appearance, "A.N.T. Farm" (2013); Guest Appearance, "Louie" (2012, 2011); Voice Actor, "Madagascar 3: Europe's Most Wanted" (2012); Actor, "What to Expect When You're Expecting" (2012); Actor, "2 Days in New York" (2012); Actor, "Grown Ups" (2010); Voice Actor, Short, "Merry Madagascar" (2009); Narrator, Producer, Documentary, "Good Hair" (2009); Narrator, Creator, "Everybody Hates Chris" (2005-2009); Voice Actor, "Madagascar: Escape 2 Africa" (2008); Actor, "You Don't Mess with the Zohan" (2008); Comedian, Stand-Up Special, "Chris Rock: Kill the Messenger" (2008); Voice Actor, "Bee Movie" (2007); Actor, "I Think I Love My Wife" (2007); Voice Actor, "Madagascar" (2005); Actor, "The Longest Yard" (2005); Comedian, Stand-Up Special, Album, "Chris Rock: Never Scared" (2004); Actor, "Paparazzi" (2004); Actor, Director, Screenwriter, "Head of State" (2003); Guest Appearance, "The Bernie Mac Show" (2003); Actor, "Pauly Shore Is Dead" (2003); Actor, "Bad Company" (2002); Actor, "Jay and Silent Bob Strike Back" (2001); Voice Actor, "Osmosis Jones" (2001); Actor, "Pootie Tang" (2001); Voice Actor,

"A.I. Artificial Intelligence" (2001); Actor, "Down to Earth" (2001); Actor, "Disappearing Acts" (2000); Guest Appearance, "DAG" (2000); Actor, "Nurse Betty" (2000); Comedian, Stand-Up Special, Album, "Chris Rock: Bigger & Blacker" (1999); Guest Appearance, "Jackie's Back!" (1999); Actor, "Dogma" (1999); Actor, "Lethal Weapon 4" (1998); Voice Actor, "Doctor Dolittle" (1998); Voice Actor, "King of the Hill" (1998); Executive Producer, "The Hughleys" (1998-2002); Comedian, Album, "Roll with the New" (1997); Voice Actor, "Happily Ever After: Fairy Tales for Every Child" (1997); Actor, "Beverly Hills Ninja" (1997); Author, "Rock This!" (1997); Host, "The Chris Rock Show" (1997-2000); Comedian, Stand-Up Special, "Chris Rock: Bring the Pain" (1996); Actor, "Homicide: Life on the Street" (1996); Actor, "Sgt. Bilko" (1996); Actor, "Martin" (1996); Voice Actor, "The Moxy & Flea Show" (1995-1997); Actor, "The Immortals" (1995); Actor, "The Fresh Prince of Bel-Air" (1995); Actor, "Panther" (1995); Comedian, Stand-Up Special, "Chris Rock: Big Ass Jokes" (1994); Performer, "In Living Color" (1994, 1993); Actor, "CB4" (1993); Actor, "Boomerang" (1992); Actor, "New Jack City" (1991); Comedian, Album, "Born Suspect" (1991); Performer, Writer, "Saturday Night Live" (1990-1993); Actor, "I'm Gonna Git You Sucka" (1988); Actor, "Miami Vice" (1987); Actor, "Beverly Hills Cop II" (1987); Actor, "Krush Groove" (1985); Himself, Numerous TV Shows and Events **AW:** Creative Impact in Comedy Award, "Top Five," Palm Springs International Film Festival (2015); Best Screenplay (Original or Adapted), "Top Five," Black Reel Awards (2015); Hollywood Comedy Film Award, "Top Five," Hollywood Film Awards (2014); Outstanding Documentary, "Good Hair," NAACP Image Awards (2010); Outstanding Writing for a Variety, Music or Comedy Program, "Chris Rock: Kill the Messenger," Emmy Awards (2009); Best Comedy Album, "Chris Rock: Never Scared," Grammy Awards (2009); Episodic Comedy, "Everybody Hates Chris," Environmental Media Awards (2008); Named One of "The 100 Most Influential People in the World," Time (2008); Top TV Program of the Year, "Everybody Hates Chris," AFI Awards (2007); Best International Comedy TV Show, "Everybody Hates Chris," British Comedy Awards (2006); Favorite Voice from an Animated Movie, "Madagascar," Nickelodeon Kids' Choice Awards (2006); Outstanding Comedy Series, "Everybody Hates Chris," NAACP Image Awards (2006); Outstanding Supporting Actor in a Theatrical Film, "The Longest Yard," BET Awards (2005); Honoree, Star, Hollywood Walk of Fame (2003); Best Comedy Album, "Chris Rock: Bigger & Blacker," Grammy Awards (2000); Funniest Male Performer in a TV Special (Leading or Supporting) Network, Cable or Syndication, "Chris Rock: Bigger & Blacker," American Comedy Awards (2000); Outstanding Writing in a Variety of Music Program, "The Chris Rock Show," Emmy Awards (1999); Favorite Supporting Actor - Action/Adventure, "Lethal Weapon 4," Blockbuster Entertainment Awards (1999); Best Comedy Album, "Chris Rock: Roll with the New," Grammy Awards (1998); Outstanding Writing for a Variety or Music Program, "Chris Rock: Bring the Pain," Emmy Awards (1997); Outstanding Variety, Music, or Comedy Special," Chris Rock: Bring the Pain," Emmy Awards (1997); Best Entertainment Host, "The Chris Rock Show," CableACE Awards (1997); Best Variety Special or Series, "The Chris Rock Show," CableACE Awards (1997); Best Stand-Up Comedy Special, "HBO Comedy Half-Hour," CableACE Awards (1995)

ROCKEFELLER, SHARON LEE, T: Former First Lady **I:** Government Administration/Government Relations/Government Services **CN:** State of West Virginia **DOB:** 12/10/1944 **PB:** Oakland **SC:** CA/USA

PT: Charles Harting Percy; Jeanne Valerie (Dickerson) Percy **MS:** Married **SPN:** John Davison Jay Rockefeller IV (1967) **CH:** John Davison V; Valerie; Charles; Justin Aldrich **ED:** Honorary LHD, Wheeling College (1984); Honorary LHD, Hamilton College (1982); Honorary LHD, West Liberty State College (1980); Honorary LLD, Beloit College (1978); Honorary LLD, University of Charleston (1977); Honorary DPS, Alderson-Broaddus College (1977); BA, Stanford University, Cum Laude (1966) **C:** President, Chief Executive Officer, Station WETA-TV-FM, Washington, DC (1989-Present); Board of Directors, Station WETA-TV-FM, Washington, DC (1987-1989); Chairman, Corporate Public Broadcasting, Washington, DC (1981-1984); Founder, Chairman, Mountain Artisans (1968-1978); Teacher's Assistant, Head Start, Head Start Program, Coal Branch Heights, WV **CR:** Trustees Council, National Gallery of Art; Board of Directors, Rockefeller Family Office, New York, NY; Rockefeller Brothers Fund; Colonial Williamsburg Foundation; Phillips Collection, George Washington University; University of Chicago; Stanford University; National Cathedral; National Gallery of Art; Smithsonian Institution; PepsiCo; Corporation for Public Broadcasting; West Virginia Education Broadcasting Authority; Public Broadcasting Service; Former Chairman, Virginia Association of Public TV Stations **CIV:** Member-at-Large, Democratic National Committee (1980-Present); Advisory Board, National Women's Political Caucus (1975-Present); Delegate, Democratic National Convention (1984); Co-Chairwoman, ERAmerica (1972-1982); Advisory Board, Board of Directors, Women's Campaign Fund (1975-1981); International Council, Museum of Modern Art, New York, NY (1973-1981); Delegate, Democratic National Convention (1980); Delegate, Democratic National Convention (1976); Board Member, Day Care and Child Development Council of America (1969-1972); Member-at-Large, Democratic National Convention; Trustee, Federal City Council; Former Chairman, Virginia Association of Public TV Stations; Board Member, Colonial Williamsburg Foundation; Board Member, Sotheby's, New York, NY; Former Member, Board Director, Sunrise Museum, West Virginia **AW:** Listee, Top 200 Collectors, ArtNews Magazine (2004-2008); Washingtonian of the Year, Washingtonian Magazine (1994); Distinguished Broadcaster Award (1994); Charles Frankel Prize, National Endowment for the Humanities (1994); CINE Lifetime Achievement Award, Woman of Vision Award, Women in Film and Video **MEM:** Fellow, American Academy of Arts & Sciences; Fellow, Board Member, Smithsonian American Art Commission; Former Chairman, Stanford-in-Washington Council **AV:** Collecting 19th-century American impressionist art

ROCKWELL, SAM, T: Actor **I:** Media & Entertainment **DOB:** 11/05/1968 **PB:** Daly City **SC:** CA/USA **PT:** Pete Rockwell; Penny Hess Rockwell **MS:** Partner **SPN:** Leslie Bibb (2007) **ED:** Coursework, Professional Actor Training Program, William Esper Studio, New York, NY **CW:** Actor, Theater, "American Buffalo" (2020); Voice Actor, "The One and Only Ivan" (2020); Voice Actor, "Trolls World Tour" (2020); Actor, "Richard Jewell" (2019); Actor, "Jojo Rabbit" (2019); Actor, "Fosse/Verdon" (2019); Actor, "The Best of Enemies" (2019); Executive Producer, Eight Episodes, "Fosse/Verdon" (2019); Actor, "Vice" (2018); Actor, Executive Producer, "Blue Iguana" (2018); Actor, "Mute" (2018); Actor, "Blaze" (2018); Voice Actor, "F Is for Family" (2015-2018); Actor, "Woman Walks Ahead" (2017); Actor, "Three Billboards Outside Ebbing, Missouri" (2017); Actor, "The Dark of Night" (2017); Executive Producer, "1 Mile to You" (2017); Voice Actor, "Dishonored 2" (2016); Actor, "Inside Amy Schumer" (2016); Actor, Theater, "Fool for Love" (2015); Actor, "Drunk History" (2015); Actor, "Mr. Right" (2015); Actor, "Poltergeist" (2015); Actor, Video Short, "Flight Facilities" (2015); Actor, Executive Producer, "Don Verdean" (2015); Actor, "Digging for Fire" (2015); Actor, Executive Producer, "Loitering with Intent" (2014); Actor, "Better Living Through Chemistry" (2014); Actor, "Laggies" (2014); Actor, "A Case of You" (2013); Actor, Executive Producer, "Trust Me" (2013); Actor, Executive Producer, "A Single Shot" (2013); Actor, "The Way Way Back" (2013); Actor, "Seven Psychopaths" (2012); Voice Actor, "Napoleon Dynamite" (2012); Actor, "The Sitter" (2011); Actor, "Cowboys & Aliens" (2011); Actor, Theater, "Behandling in Spokane" (2010); Actor, "Conviction" (2010); Actor, Short, "F–K" (2010); Actor, "Iron Man 2" (2010); Actor, "Everybody's Fine" (2009); Actor, "Gentlemen Broncos" (2009); Voice Actor, Video Game, "G-Force" (2009); Voice Actor, "G-Force" (2009); Actor, "Moon" (2009); Actor, Executive Producer, "The Winning Season" (2009); Actor, "Frost/Nixon" (2008); Actor, "Choke" (2008); Actor, "Woman in Burka" (2008); Actor, "The Assassination of Jesse James by the Coward Robert Ford" (2007); Actor, "Joshua" (2007); Actor, "Snow Angels" (2007); Actor, "Stella" (2005); Actor, "Robin's Big Date" (2005); Actor, "The F Word" (2005); Actor, "The Hitchhiker's Guide to the Galaxy" (2005); Actor, "Piccadilly Jim" (2004); Actor, "Matchstick Men" (2003); Actor, "Stella Shorts 1998-2002" (2002); Actor, "Confessions of a Dangerous Mind" (2002); Actor, "Welcome to Collinwood" (2002); Actor, Short, "Running Time" (2002); Actor, "13 Moons" (2002); Actor, Short, "D.C. Smalls" (2001); Actor, "Pretzel" (2001); Actor, "Heist" (2001); Actor, "Made" (2001); Actor, Short, "BigLove" (2001); Actor, Theater, "Dumb Waiter" (2001); Actor, Theater, "Zoo Story" (2001); Actor, "Charlie's Angels" (2000); Actor, "Prince Street" (1997, 2000); Actor, "Galaxy Quest" (1999); Actor, "The Green Mile" (1999); Actor, "A Midsummer Night's Dream" (1999); Actor, "The Call Back" (1998); Actor, "Celebrity" (1998); Actor, "Safe Men" (1998); Actor, "Louis & Frank" (1998); Actor, "Jerry and Tom" (1998); Actor, "Lawn Dogs" (1997); Actor, "SUBWAYStories: Tales from the Underground" (1997); Actor, "Arresting Gena" (1997); Actor, "Box of Moonlight" (1996); Actor, Short, "Bad Liver & Broken Heart" (1996); Actor, "NYPD Blue" (1995); Actor, "Mercy" (1995); Actor, "Glory Daze" (1995); Actor, "Drunks" (1995); Actor, "The Search for One-eye Jimmy" (1994); Actor, "Somebody to Love" (1994); Actor, "Lifestories: Families in Crisis" (1993); Actor, "Law & Order" (1992, 1993); Actor, "Jack and His Friends" (1992); Actor, "Happy Hell Night" (1992); Actor, "Light Sleeper" (1992); Actor, "In the Soup" (1992); Actor, "Strictly Business" (1991); Actor, "Teenage Mutant Ninja Turtles" (1990); Actor, "ABC Afterschool Specials" (1990); Actor, "Last Exit to Brooklyn" (1989); Actor, "Dream Street" (1989); Actor, "Clownhouse" (1989); Actor, "The Equalizer" (1988); Actor, "Joan Crawford's Children" (1979) **AW:** Screen Actors Guild Award for Outstanding Performance by a Male Actor in a Television Movie or Limited Series, "Fosse/Verdon," SAG-AFTRA (2020); Named Best Performance by an Actor in a Supporting Role, "Richard Jewell," Faro Island Film Festival (2020); Tribute Award, Gotham Awards (2019); Academy Award for Best Performance by an Actor in a Supporting Role, "Three Billboards Outside Ebbing, Missouri," Academy of Motion Picture Arts and Sciences (2018); Named Best Supporting Actor, "Three Billboards Outside Ebbing, Missouri," BAFTA Awards (2018); Named Best Supporting Actor, "Three Billboards Outside Ebbing, Missouri," AACTA International Awards (2018); Named Best Supporting Actor, "Three Billboards Outside Ebbing, Missouri," Broadcast Film Critics Association Awards (2018); Named Best Supporting Male, "Three Billboards Outside Ebbing, Missouri," Film Independent Spirit Awards (2018); Named Best Supporting Actor, "Three Billboards Outside Ebbing, Missouri," Hawaii Film Critics Society (2018); Named Best Supporting Actor, "Three Billboards Outside Ebbing, Missouri," Houston Film Critics Society Awards (2018); Named Best Actor in a Supporting Role, "Three Billboards Outside Ebbing, Missouri," Awards Circuit Community Awards (2017); Capri Supporting Actor Award, "Three Billboards Outside Ebbing, Missouri," Capri, Hollywood (2017); Named Best Supporting Actor, "Three Billboards Outside Ebbing, Missouri," Dallas-Forth Worth Film Critics Association Awards (2017); Named Best Supporting Actor, "Three Billboards Outside Ebbing, Missouri," Florida Film Critics Circle Awards (2017); Named Supporting Actor of the Year, "Three Billboards Outside Ebbing, Missouri" (2017); Named Best Actor, "Conviction," Boston Film Festival (2010); Named Best Actor of the Year, "Moon," Golden Schmoes Awards (2009); Named Best Actor, Golden Space Needle Award, "Moon," Seattle International Film Festival (2009); Named Best Actor, "Confessions of a Dangerous Mind," Berlin International Film Festival (2003); Numerous Other Awards and Accolades

ROCQUE, VINCENT, "VIN" JOSEPH, T: Attorney at Law **I:** Law and Legal Services **CN:** Vincent J. Rocque, Attorney at Law **DOB:** 11/27/1945 **PB:** Franklin **SC:** NH/USA **YOP:** 1971 **PT:** Francis Albert Rocque; Mary Helen Rocque **MS:** Married **SPN:** Emily Adams Arnold (05/31/1969) **CH:** Amanda Adams Rocque; Peter O'Connor Rocque; Caroline Quin Rocque **ED:** JD, Columbia University, New York, NY (1970); BA, Georgetown University, Washington, DC, Magna Cum Laude (1967) **C:** Private Law Practice, Washington, DC (1990-Present); Partner, Sullivan & Worcester, Washington, DC (1980-1990); Assistant Director, Bureau of Trade Regulation, U.S. Department of Commerce, Washington, DC (1977-1980); Counsel, Special Assistant, Commissioner Barbara Franklin, U.S. Consumer Product Safety Commission, Washington, DC (1973-1977); Associate, Hogan & Hartson, Washington, DC (1970-1973) **CIV:** Co-Founder and Head Janitor, Keys to the Kingdom Young Peoples Meeting of Alcoholics Anonymous, Cleveland Park Neighborhood, Washington, DC (2017-Present); Principal Volunteer Driver, Northwest Neighbors Village (2011-Present); Volunteer Coordinator, Homeless Shelters, Catholic Charities, Washington, DC, Silver Spring, MD (1984-1990); Vice President, Co-President, Janney Public Elementary School Parent Teacher Association, Washington, DC (1982-1984) **MIL:** Staff Sgt., U.S. Army Reserve (1969-1975) **MEM:** American Bar Association; District of Columbia Bar; Mid-Atlantic Literary Edification Society; Swarthmore College Book Club of Washington, DC; Alcoholics Anonymous; Phi Beta Kappa **BAR:** Supreme Court of the United States (1973); District of Columbia (1971) **MH:** Albert Nelson Marquis Lifetime Achievement Award **AS:** Mr. Rocque attributes his success to serving others and Alcoholics Anonymous. **B/I:** Mr. Rocque became involved in his profession because he saw lawyers as being of use to others in a variety of ways. **AV:** Reading; Traveling; History; Service to others **PA:** Registered Democrat **RE:** Catholic **THT:** Mr. Rocque said, "We were not born for ourselves alone..."

RODENBAUGH, MARCIA WIMER, T: Retired Elementary School Educator **I:** Education/Educational Services **DOB:** 11/11/1942 **PB:** Pittsburgh **SC:** PA/USA **PT:** E. Thomas Wimer; Lucy Indiana (Fry) Wimer **MS:** Married **SPN:** Richard Alan Rodenbaugh (08/03/1975, Divorced 1989); John Anthony Lee (03/21/1964, Divorced 1971) **CH:** Ken (Stepchild); Tiffany (Stepchild); Tricia (Stepchild) **ED:** MEd in Remedial Reading, Westminster College, New Wilmington, PA (1966); BA in Education, Westminster College, New Wilmington, PA (1964) **C:** Retired, Teacher, Central Bucks School District, Doylestown, PA (1969-2001); Teacher, North Hills School District, Pittsburgh, PA (1964-1969) **CR:** Fellow, Pennsylvania Writing Project, West Chester University (1990); Presenter in Field **CIV:** Board Directors, President, Tutor Refugee Families Myanmar (2005-Present); Secretary, Doylestown Branch Bucks County Library (2002-Present); Deacon, Doylestown Presbyterian Church (2015-2017); President, Chestnut Grove Condo Association (2004-2005); President, Wesley College Parents Association, Dover, DE (1985-1986); President, Maple Leaf Day Care Center Board, Warminster, PA (1971); Volunteer, Meals on Wheels; Inner-City Schools Board of Directors, Friends of the Library; Local Judge History Day, Ursinus College; Home Tutor Board; Volunteer, Coalition to Shelter and Support Homeless (CSSH) **CW:** Author, "Marci Books" Series (1983-1999) **AW:** Vietnamese Student Award **MEM:** President, Condominium Association (2006-2007); National Education Association; Pennsylvania Education Association; Central Bucks Education Association; Philanthropic Education Organization (PEO) **MH:** Albert Nelson Marquis Lifetime Achievement Award **AS:** Ms. Rodenbaugh attributes her success to how much she enjoys helping others and bringing joy into their lives. **B/I:** Ms. Rodenbaugh's mother was a kindergarten teacher, which is what inspired her to pursue the field. Growing up, she helped her mother with her classroom; Ms. Rodenbaugh remembers this time fondly. **AV:** Reading; Sailing; Writing; Playing piano; Singing in the church choir; Exercising **PA:** Republican **RE:** Presbyterian

RODGERS, AARON CHARLES, T: Professional Football Player **I:** Athletics **CN:** Green Bay Packers **DOB:** 12/02/1983 **PB:** Chico **SC:** CA/USA **PT:** Edward Wesley Rodgers; Darla Leigh (Pittman) Rodgers **ED:** Coursework in American Studies, University of California Berkeley (2003-2005); Coursework, Butte College, Oroville, CA (2002-2003) **C:** Quarterback, Green Bay Packers (2005-Present) **CR:** Limited Partner, Milwaukee Bucks (2018) **CIV:** Founder, Co-Creator, itsAaron; Supporter, MACC Fund; Supporter, RAISE Hope for Congo **CW:** Guest Appearance, "Key & Peele" (2015); Contestant, "Celebrity Jeopardy" (2015); Featured, Numerous State Farm Insurance Commercials; Featured, Pizza Hut Advertisements; Featured, Numerous Local Wisconsin-Based Advertisements **AW:** Two-Time Winner, Never Say Never Award (2013, 2014); Two-Time Winner, NFC Offensive Player of the Year (2011, 2014); Two-Time Winner, FedEx Air NFL Player of the Year (2010, 2014); Honorable Mention, All-American, Sports Illustrated (2004); Second-Team Academic All-Pac-10 (2004); First-Team All-Pac-10 (2004); California Golden Bears Co-Offensive MVP (2004); Insight Bowl Offensive MVP (2003); Honorable Mention, All-Pac-10 (2003) **RE:** Christian

RODGERS, WILMA LOUISE, PHD, T: Mathematics Educator (Retired) **I:** Education/Educational Services **DOB:** 11/21/1948 **PB:** Independence **SC:** MO/USA **PT:** Warren Martin Garrett; Margaret Geraldine (Faulkenberry) Garrett **MS:** Widowed **SPN:** Jerry Allen Rodgers (02/27/1970, Deceased) **CH:** David Allen Rodgers; Richard Warren Rodgers **ED:** Doctor of Philosophy in Education & Mathematics, University of Missouri, Kansas City, MO (1996); Master of Science in Mathematics, Central Missouri State University (1988); Bachelor's Degree in Secondary Education, Central Missouri State University, Magna Cum Laude (1970) **C:** Adjunct Professor, Metropolitan Community College (2008-2018); Professor of Mathematics, Delta State University, Cleveland, MS (2000-2003); Associate Professor of Mathematics, Delta State University, Cleveland, MS (1994-2000); Instructor of Mathematics, Central Missouri State University, Warrensburg, MO (1988-1994); Teacher, Math and Physics, Odessa High School, MO (1979-1988); Teacher, Math and Physics, Holden Public School, MO (1970-1975, 1978-1979) **CR:** Curriculum Committee, Department of Mathematics; Faculty Senate Press Committee; Course Coordinator; Convention Presentations; Workshop Presentations; Staff Development and Consultation, Public Schools **CW:** Author, Thesis, "Some Recent Developments in Connected and Locally Connected Spaces"; Author, Dissertation, "The Effects of Writing to Learn on Performance and Attitude Towards Mathematics" **AW:** Honorable Mention, Gradate Research Paper Competition, University of Central Missouri (1989); Academic Achievement Award, School of Education, University of Missouri, Kansas City, MO; Alpha Lambda Delta; Alpha Phi Sigma; Kappa Delta Pi; Kappa Mu Epsilon; Sigma Zeta **MEM:** Mathematics Association of America; National Council of Teachers of Mathematics; Mississippi Council of Teachers of Mathematics; Mississippi Council of Supervisors of Mathematics **MH:** Albert Nelson Marquis Lifetime Achievement Award **AS:** Dr. Rodgers attributes her success to her strong desire to see people succeed. She has the ability to break down scientific and mathematical concepts into an easy-to-understand format. Those students are then able to become better teachers for their own students. **B/I:** Dr. Rodgers became involved in her profession after discovering that explaining difficult concepts to others came naturally to her. **AV:** Gardening; Needlework

RODNEY, PAUL FREDERICK, PHD, T: Physicist **I:** Oil & Energy **DOB:** 09/14/1944 **PB:** Montclair **SC:** NJ/USA **PT:** William David Rodney; Mary Helen (Frassnacht) Rodney **MS:** Married **SPN:** Arlene Fay Davis (11/15/1969) **CH:** Ruth Ann; Karen Elizabeth **ED:** PhD in Physics, University of Wyoming (1975); MS in Physics, University of Rochester (1971); BS in Physics, Bucknell University (1966) **C:** Technology Fellow, Technology Chief, Halliburton (2010-2019); Chief Scientist Technician, Sperry-Sun Drilling Services, Inc., Technology Division, Dresser Industries, Houston, TX (1988-2010); Manager of Sensor Physics and Electronics, National Lead Baroid Research and Development, Houston, TX (1983-1988); Senior Scientist, Baroid Division, Houston, TX (1979-1983); Vice President, Terrene Technologies Inc., Rufugio, TX (1975-1979) **CIV:** Lay Preacher, Retirement Communities **CW:** Speaker, Address on FEWD, Advanced Energy Consortium (2010); Keynote Speaker, SPE/ATCE Conference, Denver, CO (2003); Contributor, Several Articles, Professional Journals **AW:** Editor's Award for a Paper on the First Electromagnetic Wave Resistivity Sensor, The Electromagnetic Wave Resistivity MWD Tool, 58th Annual Technical Conference and Exhibition, San Francisco, CA (1983); 100 Patent Award, Halliburton; 40-Year Award, Halliburton; Numerous VIP Awards, Halliburton **MEM:** IEEE; Transactions on Acoustics, Speech, and Signal Processing, IEEE; IEEE Information Theory Society; Society of Petroleum Engineers; SPWLA; Toastmasters International **MH:** Albert Nelson Marquis Lifetime Achievement Award **AS:** Dr. Rodney attributes his success to his father, a mechanical engineer who wanted to double as an electrical engineer. Growing up, his father allowed him to experiment. After witnessing Sputnik, he channeled his expertise in mathematics and sciences into his work. Additionally, he was inspired

by "1-2-3 Infinity" by George Gamov, "Engineer's Dreams" by Willey Ley and Plato's "Republic." **B/I:** Dr. Rodney became involved in his profession because there was a severe cutback in federal funding for space science and astrophysics-related research. Instead of pursuing a career in the field, he went for a postdoctoral degree and ended up pursuing a career in physics. **AV:** Studying theology, philosophy and mathematics; Listening to classical music; Playing an electric keyboard; Reading philosophical and theological classes; Canoeing; Hiking **PA:** Republican **RE:** Presbyterian

RODRIGUEZ, ALEX, T: Former Professional Baseball Player **I:** Athletics **DOB:** 07/27/1975 **PB:** New York **SC:** NY/USA **PT:** Victor Rodriguez; Lourdes Navarro Rodriguez **MS:** Engaged **SPN:** Jennifer Lopez (2019); Cynthia Scurtis (11/02/2002, Divorced 2008) **CH:** Natasha Alexander; Ella Alexander **C:** Special Adviser, New York Yankees (2016-Present); Third Baseman, New York Yankees (2004-2016); Shortstop, Texas Rangers (2001-2003); Shortstop, Seattle Mariners (1994-2000) **CR:** Broadcaster, "Sunday Night Baseball," ESPN (2018-Present); MLB Studio Analyst, Fox Sports (2017-Present); Founder, A-Rod Corp (2003-Present); Guest Analyst, American League Championship Series, World Series, Fox Sports (2015-2016); Member, Dominican Republic National Team, World Baseball Classic (2009); Member, U.S. National Team (2006) **CIV:** Co-Chair, Robin Hood Foundation Event (2017); Contributor, University of Miami (2003); Supporter, Keep A Child Alive; Supporter, Raising Malawi; Supporter, Soles4Souls; Supporter, UNICEF; Contributor, Numerous National and International Organizations **CW:** Author, "Out of the Ballpark" (2012); Co-Author, "Hit a Grand Slam!" (1998) **AW:** 14-Time American League All-Star (1996-1998, 2000-2003, 2004-2008, 2010-2011); Babe Ruth Award (2009); 10 Silver Slugger Awards (1996, 1998-2003, 2005, 2007, 2008); Three-Time American League Most Valuable Player (MVP) Award (2003, 2005, 2007); Three Babe Ruth Home Run Awards (2002, 2003, 2007); Three-Time Sporting News Player of the Year (1996, 2002, 2007); GIBBY/This Year in Baseball Awards for Outstanding Player of the Year (1996, 1998, 2001-2003, 2007); Four Hank Aaron Awards (2001-2003, 2007); GIBBY/This Year in Baseball Awards for Hitter of the Year (2007); Pepsi Clutch Performer of the Year (2007); Edward T. Foote II Alumnus of Distinction Award, University of Miami (2007); GIBBY/This Year in Baseball Awards for Individual Performance of the Year (2005); Two Rawlings Gold Glove Awards (2002, 2003); Two-Time Baseball America Major League Player of the Year (2000, 2002); Three-Time Texas Rangers Player of the Year (2001-2003); Two-Time Seattle Mariners Player of the Year (1998, 2000); Seattle Mariners Minor League Player of the Year (1994); Gatorade National Baseball Player of the Year (1993); 13 Major League Baseball Player of the Week Awards; 10 Major League Baseball Player of the Month Awards **MEM:** Honorary Alumnus, University of Miami (2004); Board of Trustees, University of Miami

RODRIGUEZ, ERNESTO A., T: Passenger Service Representative, Artist, Researcher **I:** Fine Art **DOB:** 08/19/1947 **PB:** New York **SC:** NY/USA **PT:** Pedro; Hazel Valencia Rodriguez **MS:** Single **ED:** Bachelor of Fine Arts, Parsons School of Design (1979); Independent Research, University of Innsbruck, Austria (1969); Coursework, Art Students League, New York, NY; Coursework, Brooklyn Museum of Art, Brooklyn, NY **C:** Art Instructor, St. Francis of the Assisi, New York, NY (1984-1993, 2010-2014); Passenger Service Representative, Private Company, New York, NY (2005-2006); Commissioned

Artist, Owner, E. A. Rodriguez, New York, NY (1990-2005); Teacher, Board of Education, Bronx, NY (2001-2002); Supervisor Trainer, Saks Fifth Ave, New York, NY (1990-1994); Senior Crafts Instructor, Jewish Guild for the Blind, New York, NY (1987-1988); Art Specialist, Camp Oakhurst, New Jersey (1982-1986); Substitute Teacher, Metropolitan Area Educational Services, New York, NY (1981); Artist Instructor, Studio in a School, New York, NY (1979-1981); Art Specialist, Elko Lake Camps, New York (1978-1980); Academic Instructor, Baldwin School, New York, NY (1975-1977); Art and Woodworking Instructor, Emerson School, New York, NY (1970-1972) **CR:** Teacher, Trinity Lutheran School, Bronx, NY (1983-1986) **CIV:** Counselor, Covenant House, New York, NY (1988); Rehabilitation Specialist, Project Reachout, New York, NY (1988) **CW:** Group Exhibition, Mercer Gallery, Rochester, NY (2012); Group Exhibition, Hilltop, Inc., New York, NY (2002-2004); Group Exhibition, J & R Co., New York, NY (2002-2003); Group Exhibition, Durban Art Gallery, Durban, South Africa (1999); Group Exhibition, Arts Communication International, Philadelphia, PA (1996); Group Exhibition, Madison Square Garden, New York, NY (1989); Group Exhibition, Pennsylvania Hotel, New York, NY (1989); Group Exhibition, Pine Tree Art Gallery, Troy, AL (1987); Group Exhibition, International Art Gallery, Bogota, Colombia (1986); One-Man Show, Saint Francis of Assisi, New York, NY (1984); Group Exhibition, Winners Circle Art Gallery, Van Nuys, CA (1983-1984); Juried Exhibition, Gallery II RSVP, Charlottesville, VA (1983); Juried Exhibition, Long Beach Museum of Art, Long Beach, NY (1982); Group Exhibition, Rare Discoveries Gallery, Dallas, TX (1981-1982); Group Exhibition, Zoma Art Gallery, New York, NY (1981); Juried Exhibition, Hudson River Museum, Yonkers, NY (1981); Group Exhibition, Salmagundi Club, New York, NY (1980); Group Exhibition, Keane Mason Galleries, New York, NY (1978); Group Exhibition, Lincoln Center for the Performing Arts, New York, NY (1978); Group Exhibition, Marcoleo Art Gallery, New York, NY (1973); Group Exhibition, Queens College, Flushing, NY (1973); Group Exhibition, University of Wyoming (1973); Group Exhibition, Center Art Gallery, New York, NY (1972); Group Exhibition, Spectrum Art Gallery, Bochum, Germany (1969) **AW:** Change Incorporated Grant (1975); Fellow, Max Beckmann (1968) **MEM:** Boys Harbour, New York, NY (1970-1971); New York Society Science; International Society Poets; Saks Fifth Avenue President's Executive Club; Museum of Art Educational Counselor **MH:** Albert Nelson Marquis Lifetime Achievement Award; Marquis Who's Who Top Professional; Marquis Who's Who Humanitarian Award **B/I:** While coming of age, Mr. Rodriguez suffered greatly from asthma, and was inspired to pursue a career in art due to his struggles. As he grew up, he continued to study art domestically and internationally, which eventually led him to become an educator. **AV:** Acting; Canoeing; Horseback riding; Travel; Art; Cuisine; Fashion **PA:** Independent **RE:** Episcopalian

RODRIGUEZ, GINA, T: Actress **I:** Media & Entertainment **DOB:** 07/30/1984 **PB:** Chicago **SC:** IL/USA **PT:** Magall Rodriguez; Gino Rodriguez **MS:** Married **SPN:** Joe LoCicero (05/05/2019) **ED:** BFA in Drama, Atlantic Theater Company, Experimental Theater Wing, Tisch School of the Arts, New York University (2006) **CIV:** Member, Board of Directors, Hispanic Scholarship Fund (2015-Present); Partner, Naja (2015-Present); Contributor, Numerous Charities and Philanthropic Efforts **CW:** Actress, "Awake" (2020); Voice Actress, "Carmen Sandiego: To Steal or Not to Steal" (2020); Actress, "Kajillionaire" (2020); Actress, Executive Producer, Director, "Diary of a Future President" (2020); Actress,

"Miss Bala" (2019); Actress, Producer, "Someone Great" (2019); Actress, "Andy's Song" (2019); Voice Actress, "Robot Chicken" (2019); Voice Actress, "Carmen Sandiego" (2019); Executive Producer, "Jane the Novela" (2019); Voice Actress, "Elena of Avalor" (2018, 2019); Director, Episode, "Charmed" (2019); Voice Actress, "Big Mouth" (2018-2019); Actress, "Jane the Virgin" (2014-2019); Actress, "Sharon 1.2.3." (2018); Voice Actress, "Smallfoot" (2018); Narrator, "Animals" (2018); Actress, "Brooklyn Nine-Nine" (2018); Actress, "Annihilation" (2018); Executive Producer, "Illegal" (2018); Executive Producer, Co-Executive Producer, Director, "Jane the Virgin" (2017-2019); Voice Actress, "Ferdinand" (2017); Voice Actress, "The Star" (2017); Actress, "Deepwater Horizon" (2016); Actress, "The Backup Dancer" (2016); Executive Producer, "Marie Claire Young Women's Honors" (2016); Actress, "C'est Jane" (2014); Actress, "Since I Laid Eyes" (2014); Actress, "Wild Blue" (2014); Actress, "Interstate" (2013); Actress, "Una Y Otra Y Otra Vez" (2013); Voice Actress, "The Price We Pay" (2013); Actress, "Rizzolli & Isles" (2013); Actress, "Sleeping with the Fishes" (2013); Actress, "Longmire" (2013); Actress, "Enter the Dangerous Mind" (2013); Actress, "California Winter" (2012); Actress, "No Names" (2012); Actress, "Filly Brown" (2012); Actress, "The Bold and the Beautiful" (2011-2012); Actress, "The Mentalist" (2011); Actress, "Happy Endings" (2011); Actress, "Go for It!" (2011); Actress, "My Super Sweet 16: Part 2" (2010); Actress, "Little Spoon" (2010); Actress, "Army Wives" (2010); Actress, "10 Things I Hate About You" (2010); Actress, "Our Family Wedding" (2010); Actress, "Osvaldo's" (2009); Actress, "Eleventh Hour" (2009); Actress, "Ten: Thirty One" (2008); Actress, "Calling It Quits" (2008); Actress, "Law & Order" (2008, 2004); Actress, "Jonny Zero" (2005) **AW:** Honoree, TVLine Performance of the Week, "Jane the Virgin" (2019); Honoree Award, "Jane the Virgin," ALMA Awards (2018); Honoree for Activism, Eva Longoria Foundation Awards (2018); Favorite Lead Actress in a Comedy Series, "Jane the Virgin," Tell-Tale TV Awards (2018); Choice TV Actress - Comedy, "Jane the Virgin," Teen Choice Awards (2018); Best Actress, "Jane the Virgin," Tell-Tale TV Awards (2017); Honoree, ACLU Social Rights Award, "Jane the Virgin" (2017); Honoree, "Jane the Virgin," Icon Hispanic Heritage Month (2017); Honoree, Unite 4 Humanity Awards (2016); Female Star of Tomorrow, CinemaCon Awards (2016); Best Actress - Television, Imagen Awards (2016); "SuperSoul 100" List of Visionaries and Influential Leaders, Oprah (2016); Honoree, NHMC Impact Gala Award (2015); Honoree, Girl Power Media Role Model (2015); Rising Star Award, Dorian Awards (2015); Best Actress - Television, Imagen Awards (2015); Breakthrough Performer of the Year, Gold Derby Awards (2015); Best Actress - Comedy, EWwy Award (2015); Best Actress - Television Series Musical or Comedy, Golden Globe Awards (2015); Rising Star of the Year, Young Hollywood Awards (2014); Honoree, Inaugural Lupe Special Achievement Award (2013); Co-Recipient, Alma Award, Achievement in Film, "Filly Brown" (2013); Best Actress - Feature Film, Imagen Awards (2012)

RODRIGUEZ, JAVIER J., T: Chief Executive Officer **I:** Medicine & Health Care **CN:** DaVita Inc. **ED:** MBA, Harvard University; Coursework, Executive Program, Stanford Graduate School of Business; BS in Finance and Marketing, Boston College **C:** Chief Executive Officer, DaVita Inc., Denver, CO (2019-Present); Chief Executive Officer, DaVita Kidney Care (2014-2019); President, DaVita Kidney Care (2012-2014); Senior Vice President, DaVita Kidney Care (1998-2012); Finance Specialist, Baxter International Inc. (1995-1996)

ROE, CHARLES P., T: Aeronautical Information Specialist I: Government Administration/Government Relations/Government Services **CN:** United States Department of Transportation **PB:** Bolling Air Force Base, Washington, DC **SC:** DC/USA **PT:** TSgt. Dallas Huston Roe (United States Air Force); Joan Ellinor (Carr) Roe **MS:** Married **SPN:** Major Barbara Diane (Dunker) Roe (United States Army) **ED:** MA in History, Marshall University, Huntington, WV; BA in Spanish, Norwich University, Northfield, VT; AA, New Mexico Military Institute, Roswell, NM; AAS, Donnelly College, Kansas City, KS; AS, Community College of Allegheny County, Pittsburgh, PA; AS, Jefferson Community College, Watertown, NY; AS, Mountain State University, Beckley, WV; BS, University of Maryland Global Campus, College Park, MD; Graduate, United States Army Engineering Officers Advanced Course, Command and Staff College, Marine Corps University, Quantico, VA; Coursework, United States Army Command and General Staff College, Leavenworth, KS; High School Diploma, Oxon Hill High School, Oxon Hill, MD **C:** Aeronautical Information Specialist, United States Department of Transportation (2002-Present); Aeronautical Information Specialist, Federal Aviation Administration (2002-2019); Geographer with HQ, Bureau of the Census, Field Division, Geographic Support and Address Coverage Branch, United States Department of Commerce (1996-2002) **CR:** County Executive, State of Maryland **CIV:** Volunteer, Catholic Pastoral Care Services, Walter Reed National Military Medical Center American Red Cross; Civil Air Patrol Aerospace Education Program **MIL:** Retired, Field-Grade Officer in Infantry and Aviation, with a Top Secret Clearance, Major, United States Army; Airborne/Ranger Infantry Officer with B-Rangers 1/29 Infantry and in Mechanized Infantry, United States Army; Combat Pilot, Battle Captain, Test Pilot, Aviation Commander, United States Army Aviation Branch; 10th Mountain Division Liaison Officer to 18 Airborne Corps as an Actions Officer **AW:** Governor's Citation, State of Maryland (2019); Soldier's Medal for Heroism; Army Commendation Medal for Saving 199 Infantry Soldiers; Cash Award for Superior Performance; Cash in a Flash, United States Census Bureau; Numerous Awards, United States Census Bureau; Award for 8,000 Hours, Veterans Assistance; Presidential Letter **MEM:** The American Legion; Disabled American Veterans; Veterans of Foreign Wars; Catholic War Veterans Association; Order of the Arrow, Boy Scouts of America; Fourth Degree, Knights of Columbus; National Society of the Sons of the American Revolution; Hacker's Creek Pioneer Descendants **AS:** Mr. Roe attributes his success to becoming injured in the military, which permanently limited his mobility, yet gave him the opportunity to begin working with the government. **B/I:** Mr. Roe became involved in his profession because of his patriotism. **THT:** Mr. Roe is an Aeronautical Information Specialist FG-13 step 8, located in the VP Mission Support Services, Aeronautical Information Services, En Route & Visual Charts Group, VFR Charting Team, and VFR Sub-Team A, AJV-5221, located in Silver Spring, Maryland. He works with Sectional Aeronautical VFR Navigation Charts, VFR Terminal Area Charts, and World Aeronautical Charts. He has worked with the United States airspace between Russian, Canadian, Mexican and Caribbean Islands. During national emergencies he mapped sectionals affected by Hurricanes Isabel (2003), Charles (2004), Frances (2004), Ivan (2004), Jeanne (2004), Dennis (2005), Katrina (2005), Rita (2005), Wilma (2005), Ike (2008), Sandy (2012), Harvey (2017), and Maria (2017). He also mapped sectionals affected by earthquakes Denali (2002), Gulf of Mexico (2006), Southeastern Alaska (2013 & 2014), Aleutian Islands (2014), Southern Alaska (2014), Chirikof Island (2015), Nikolski (2015), Redoubt Volcano (2015), Old Iliamna (2016), Gulf of Alaska (2016), Kaktovik (2018) and Anchorage (2018). In addition, he mapped World Aeronautical Charts affected by earthquakes in the Dominican Republic (2003), Guadeloupe, Dominica (2004), and Martinique (2007). He also did the mapping of the recovery mission Space Shuttle Columbia disaster on February 1, 2003, designated during re-entry into Earth's atmosphere. Mr. Roe received a cash award for superior performance. He saved 50 school students from a bus/forest fire and prevented a mini-mart gas station fire/explosion. He was with the United States Department of Commerce as a Bureau of the Census employee from November 1996 to March 2002. He worked as a geographer with HQ, Bureau of the Census, Field Division, Geographic Support and Address Coverage Branch, supervising all fields (United States and Territories). He used digitizing map programs such as Master Address File and Geocoding, Office Resolution, Targeted Map Update, TIGER Improvement Program, Local Update of Census Addresses, Statistical Areas, Redistricting Data Program, Boundary and Annexation Survey, American Indian Reservation Boundaries, and other geographic programs as assigned. He served as a military team liaison for geographic support for the Bureau of the Census operations Pentagon for troop enumeration. He was injured at the Pentagon on September 11, 2001 and was hospitalized to March 2002. He received several accolades, such as Cash in a Flash, performance and other Bureau of the Census awards. Mr. Roe's grandfather, Dallas H. Roe, was buried at Austin family cemetery in Point Pleasant, West Virginia.

ROE, DAVID, "PHIL" PHILLIP, MD, T: U.S. Representative from Tennessee; Physician **I:** Government Administration/Government Relations/Government Services **DOB:** 07/21/1945 **PB:** Clarksville **SC:** TN/USA **MS:** Married **SPN:** Clarinda Jeanes (2017); Pam (Alford) Roe (1995, Deceased 2015) **CH:** David; Whitney; John **ED:** MD, The University of Tennessee Health Science Center College of Medicine, Memphis, TN (1970); BS in Biology, Austin Peay State University, Clarksville, TN (1967) **C:** Chairmen, House Committee on Veterans' Affairs (2017-Present); Member, U.S. House of Representatives from Tennessee's First Congressional District, United States Congress, Washington, DC (2009-Present); Mayor, Johnson City, TN (2007-2009); Commissioner, Johnson City Board of Commissioners (2003-2008); Vice-Mayor, Johnson City, TN (2003-2007); Private Practice, Obstetrics-gynecology, Johnson City, TN (1974-2005) **CR:** Delegate, Tennessee Medical Association; Past President, Tri-County Medical Society **CIV:** Board of Directors, East Tennessee State University Foundation (2006-Present); Munsey Memorial United Methodist Church **MIL:** Major, United States Army Medical Corps (1973-1974) **AW:** Excellence in Philanthropy Award, Tennessee Board of Regents **PA:** Republican **RE:** Methodist

ROEHL, JERRALD J., T: Attorney **I:** Law and Legal Services **CN:** The Roehl Law Firm **PB:** Austin **SC:** TX/USA **CH:** RJ; Mason; Arwen; Max; Sailor **ED:** JD, Washington & Lee University, Lexington City, VA (1971); BA, University of New Mexico (1968) **CIV:** Board of Visitors, Washington and Lee University School of Law (2000-2008); Board of Advisors, American Bar Association Journal (1980-1982); Note and Comment Editor, Washington and Lee Review (1970-1971); Finalist, Burks Moot Court Competition (1969); Founder, Concours Du Soleil **CW:** "The Law of Medical Malpractice in New Mexico," New Mexico Law Review 294 (1973); "Reciprocity as a Basis for Preliminary Injunctive Relief

Denying Proposed Conglomerate Merger," Washington and Lee Law Review 311 (1970); Author, "The Wire Strike" **MEM:** Governing Council, Tort and Insurance Practice Section (1981-1983); Select Committee on Economics of Insurance Practice, Defense Research Institute (1979-1981); Executive Council, Young Lawyers Division (1978-1980); American Bar Association; Governing Council, Section on Economics of Law Practice (1977-1979); Board of Directors, Albuquerque Bar Association (1976-1979); President, Young Lawyers Section, State Bar of New Mexico (1975-1976); New Mexico Trial Lawyers Association; American Association of Justice; American Board of Trial Advocates (ABOTA); Roehl Circle of Honor for Trial Lawyers; Board of Trustees, Albuquerque Community Foundation; Board of Trustees University, New Mexico Foundation; Law Council, Washington and Lee University School of Law **MH:** Albert Nelson Marquis Lifetime Achievement Award **B/I:** Mr. Roehl was inspired to become a lawyer by his father, who was also a lawyer.

ROESSNER, KARL A., T: Chief Executive Officer (Retired) **I:** Financial Services **CN:** E*TRADE **ED:** JD, St. John's University (1992); BBA in Accounting, Siena College (1989) **C:** Senior Adviser, E*TRADE, New York, NY (2019); Chief Executive Officer, E*TRADE, New York, NY (2016-2019); Executive Vice President, General Counsel, Corporate Secretary, E*TRADE, New York, NY (2009-2016); Partner, Clifford Chance (2001-2009); Associate, Clifford Chance (2000-2001); Associate, Rogers & Wells (1992-2000) **CW:** St. John's University Law Review **MEM:** Student Bar Association, St. John's University

ROETHLISBERGER, BEN, "BIG BEN" TODD SR., T: Professional Football Player **I:** Athletics **CN:** Pittsburgh Steelers **DOB:** 03/02/1982 **PB:** Lima **SC:** OH/USA **PT:** Kenneth "Ken" Todd Roethlisberger; Ida Jane (Foust) Roethlisberger **MS:** Married **SPN:** Ashley Harlan (07/23/2011) **CH:** Benjamin Todd Jr.; Baylee Marie; Bodie **ED:** Bachelor of Education, Miami University, Ohio (2012) **C:** Quarterback, Pittsburgh Steelers (2004-Present) **CR:** Launched, Big Ben's BBQ Sauce **CIV:** Donor, Miami University (2014); Founder, Ben Roethlisberger Foundation **CW:** Cameo, "The Dark Knight Rises" (2012); Host, WWE Raw (2009); Presenter, Grammy Awards (2006); Appearance, "Late Show with David Letterman" **AW:** Pro Bowl Champion (2007, 2011, 2014–2017); Super Bowl Champion (2006, 2009); Offensive Rookie of the Year, Associated Press (2004); MAC Most Valuable Player (2003); MAC Offensive Player of the Year (2003); MAC Freshman of the Year (2001)

ROGERS, AILENE, T: Retired Secondary School Educator **I:** Education/Educational Services **DOB:** 01/17/1938 **PB:** Jamaica **SC:** NY/USA **PT:** Daniel H. Kane; Helen (Shirkey) Kane **MS:** Married **SPN:** Edward Lee Rogers (11/18/1961, Deceased 3/1998) **CH:** Ruth; John; Helen; Daniel (Deceased) **ED:** MS in Environmental Biology, George Mason University (1998); Coursework, Stony Brook University (1970, 1971); MS in Biology, American University (1963); BA, Middlebury College (1959) **C:** Assistant Director, Student Censer Water Program; Coordinator, Water Logging Program, Cornell Cooperative Extension Suffolk County (2003-2008); Educator, Marine Program, Cornell Cooperative Extension Suffolk County (2003-2008); Retired (2000); Teacher, Science, Upper School, National Cathedral School, Washington (1982-2000); Head, Science Department, National Cathedral School, Washington (1989-1995); Teacher, Science, Lower School, National Cathedral School, Washington (1979-1982); Head, Science Department, Oak

Grove Coburn School, Vassalboro, ME (1976-1979); Teacher, Science, Oak Grove Coburn School, Vassalboro, ME (1974-1975); Teacher, Science, Hauppauge Middle School, New York (1972-1973); Naturalist, National Park Service (1966-1968); Teaching Assistant, America University, Washington DC (1961-1962); Co-director, Student Conservation Association, Charlestown, NH (1960); Assistant Director, Student Conservation Association, Washington, New Hampshire (1959-1960) **CR:** Member, United Methodist Women (2009-2014); Member, Taproots Workshop, Stony Brook University (2009-2014); Teacher, Consultant, National Association of Biology Teachers (1993); Consultant, National Geographic Society Education Programs (1982-1992); Consultant, Greenhouse Crisis Foundation (1991); Co-director, Science Camp, The Potomac School, McLean, VA (1991); Lecturer, Young Association Program, Smithsonian Institute (1989, 1988); Director, Science Camp, Virginia (1986-1988); Counselor, Science Camp, Virginia (1982-1988) **CIV:** Fundraiser, Middlebury College, Vermont (2011-Present); Director, Rachel Carson Council (1990-2000); Marine Science Teacher, Oceans Program Phillips Academy, Andover, MA (1994); Consultant, Population Reference Bureau (1995); Facilitator, Committee for Mathematics and Science, Washington DC (1993-1995); Member, State Team DC, Mid-Atlantic Consortium Mathematics and Science Education, Dwight D. Eisenhower National Program on Mathematic and Science Education (1989-1994); Co-president, McLean High School Student-Parent-Teacher Association (1982-1984); Board of Directors, Student Conservation Program (1972-1982); Chairman, Pittston Conservation Commission (1975-1978); Board of Governors, Setauket Environmental Center (1970-1972); Consultant, School Wide Environmental Education Program, New York, NY (1971); Founder, Setauket Environmental Center (1970) **AW:** Named, Environmentalist of Year for Town of Huntington, Northport Times (2004); Chopinsky Fellow, Ukrainian Educational Exchange (1994); National Science Foundation Grantee, American University (1961-1962) **MEM:** Director, Maine chapter, Nature Conservancy (1976-1978); National Parks and Conservation Association; Student Conservation Association; International Star Class Yacht Racing Association **MH:** Albert Nelson Marquis Lifetime Achievement Award **B/I:** Ms. Rogers became involved in her profession because she was the oldest of four children and was always involved in tutoring neighborhood children. She became the first water front director at St. Port Yacht Club while she was in high school. She enjoyed it very much and teaching became a very natural feeling for her so that led her into the teaching profession. **RE:** Methodist

ROGERS, HAROLD, "HAL" DALLAS, T: U.S. Representative **I:** Government Administration/ Government Relations/Government Services **DOB:** 12/31/1937 **PB:** Barrier **SC:** KY/USA **MS:** Married **SPN:** Cynthia Doyle Stewart (1999); Shirley McDowell (1958, Deceased 1995) **CH:** Three children **ED:** LLB, University of Kentucky (1964); BA, University of Kentucky (1962) **C:** Chairman, House Committee on Appropriations, Washington, DC (2011-Present); U.S. Representative, Kentucky's Fifth Congressional District, United States Congress, Washington, DC (1981-Present); Commonwealth Attorney, Pulaski and Rockcastle Counties, KY (1969-1980); Private Law Practice, Somerset, KY (1967-1969); Associate, Smith & Blackburn (1964-1967) **CR:** Tennessee Valley Authority Caucus; Congressional House Caucus **CIV:** Founder, South Western Kentucky Economic Development Council **MIL:** With, Kentucky Army National Guard (1957-1964); With, North Carolina

Army National Guard (1957-1964) **MEM:** Former President, Kentucky Commonwealth's Attorneys' Association **BAR:** Louisiana State Bar Association (1964) **PA:** Republican

ROGERS, KENNETH, "KENNY" RAY, T: Country Singer **I:** Media & Entertainment **DOB:** 08/21/1938 **PB:** Houston **SC:** TX/USA **YOP:** 2020 **PT:** Edward Floyd Rogers; Lucille Lois (Hester) Rogers **MS:** Married **SPN:** Wanda Miller (06/01/1997); Marianne Gordon (10/01/1977, Divorced 1993); Margo Anderson (1964, Divorced 1976); Jean Rogers (1960, Divorced 1963); Janice Gordon (05/15/1958, Divorced 1960) **CH:** Carole Lynne; Kenny Jr.; Justin Charles; Jordan Edward; Christopher Cody **ED:** Diploma, Jefferson Davis High School (Now Northside High School) (1956); Coursework, University of Houston **C:** Co-Founder, Kenny Rogers Roasters (1991) **CR:** Co-Founder, Recording Artist, Dreamcatcher Entertainment (1998-2000); Recording Artist, Magnatone Records (1996-1997); Recording Artist, Atlantic Records (1993-1994); Recording Artist, Warner Records (1988-1993); Recording Artist, RCA Records (1983-1988); Recording Artist, Liberty Records (1976-1982) **CIV:** Honorary Captain, U.S. Gymnastics Team (1988) **CW:** Musician, "Once Again It's Christmas" (2015); Musician, "You Can't Make Old Friends" (2013); Musician, "The Love of God" (2011); Guest Narrator, "How I Met Your Mother" (2009); Musician, "Water & Bridges" (2006); Guest Appearance, "Reno 911!" (2003); Musician, "Back to the Well" (2003); Actor, "Longshot" (2001); Musician, "There You Go Again" (2000); Guest Appearance, "Touched by an Angel" (2000); Musician, "She Rides Wild Horses" (1999); Musician, "Christmas from the Heart" (1998); Musician, "Across My Heart" (1997); Actor, TV Film, "Get to the Heart: The Barbara Mandrell Story" (1997); Actor, TV Film, "Big Dreams and Broken Hearts: The Dottie West Story" (1996); Musician, "The Gift" (1996); Musician, "Vote for Love" (1996); Contributing Musician, "Timepiece" (1994); Actor, TV Film, "MacShayne: The Final Roll of the Dice" (1994); Actor, TV Film, "MacShayne: Winner Takes All" (1994); Actor, TV Film, "The Gambler V: Playing for Keeps" (1994); Guest Appearance, "Dr. Quinn, Medicine Woman" (1994); Actor, TV Film, "Rio Diablo" (1993); Musician, "If Only My Heart Had a Voice" (1993); Narrator, Documentary, "The Real West" (1992); Actor, TV Film, "The Gambler Returns: The Luck of the Draw" (1991); Musician, "Back Home Again" (1991); Musician, "Love Is Strange" (1990); Actor, TV Film, "Christmas in America" (1990); Musician, "Christmas in America" (1989); Musician, "Something Inside So Strong" (1989); Musician, "I Prefer the Moonlight" (1987); Actor, TV Film, "Kenny Rogers as the Gambler Part III: The Legend Continues" (1987); Musician, "They Don't Make Them Like They Used To" (1986); Musician, "The Heart of the Matter" (1985); Actor, TV Film, "Wild Horses" (1985); Contributing Musician, "Once Upon a Christmas" (1984); Musician, "What About Me?" (1984); Musician, "Eyes That See in the Dark" (1983); Musician, "We've Got Tonight" (1983); Actor, TV Film, "Kenny Rogers as the Gambler: The Adventure Continues" (1983); Actor, "Six Pack" (1982); Musician, "Love Will Turn You Around" (1982); Musician, "Christmas" (1981); Musician, "Share Your Love" (1981); Actor, TV Film, "Coward of the County" (1981); Actor, TV Film, "Kenny Rogers as the Gambler" (1980); Musician, "Gideon" (1980); Musician, "Kenny" (1979); Contributing Musician, "Classics" (1979); Musician, "The Gambler" (1978); Musician, "Love or Something Like It" (1978); Contributing Musician, "Every Time Two Fools Collide" (1978); Musician, "Daytime Friends" (1977); Musician, "Kenny Rogers" (1976); Musician, "Love Lifted Me" (1976);

Actor, TV Film, "The Dream Makers" (1975); Actor, TV Film, "Saga of Sonora" (1973) **AW:** Inductee, Texas Country Music Hall of Fame (2017); Willie Nelson Lifetime Achievement Award, Country Music Association Awards (2013); Inductee, Country Music Hall of Fame (2013); American Eagle Award (2010); Co-Recipient, Cliffie Stone Pioneer Award, ACM Honors (2009); ASCAP Golden Note Award (2007); Album of the Year, "Water & Bridges," CMT Music Awards (2007); Favorite All Time Country Duet, "Island in the Stream," CMT Music Awards (2005); Ranked, CMT's 100 Greatest Cheating Songs (2004); Lifetime Achievement Award, International Entertainment Buyers Association (2003); Named, CMT's 100 Greatest Country Songs (2003); Named, CMT's 40 Greatest Men of Country Music (2002); Career Achievement Award, TNN Music Awards (2000); Named, BBC's Greatest Country Singers (1999); Best Duo Country Vocal Performance, "Make No Mistake She's Mine," Grammy Awards (1988); Favorite Singer of All Time, USA Today (1986); Favorite Male Country Artist, Favorite Country Album, "Eyes That See in the Dark," American Music Awards (1985); Co-Recipient, Single of the Year for "Islands in the Stream," Top Vocal Duet, Academy of Country Music Awards (1983); Favorite Pop/Rock Country Artist, Favorite Country Single for "Love Will Turn You Around," American Music Awards (1983); Favorite Single, "Islands in the Stream," ASAP Awards (1983); Favorite Country Album, "Greatest Hits," American Music Awards (1982); Favorite Pop/Rock Male Artist, Favorite Country Album for "The Gambler," Favorite Country Single for "Coward of the County," American Music Awards (1981); Favorite Male Country Artist, Favorite Country Album for "The Gambler," American Music Awards (1980); Single of the Year, Music City News Country (1980); Favorite Male Country Artist, Favorite Country Album for "10 Years of Gold," American Music Awards (1979); Male Vocalist of the Year, Vocal Duo of the Year, Album of the Year for "The Gambler," Country Music Association Awards (1979); Male Artist of the Year, Single of the Year for "The Gambler," Music City News Country (1979); Best Male Country Vocal Performance, "The Gambler," Grammy Awards (1979); Favorite Single for "Lucille," American Music Awards (1978); Vocal Duo of the Year, Country Music Association Awards (1978); Entertainer of the Year, Top Male Vocalist, Academy of Country Music Awards (1978); Single of the Year for "Lucille," Country Music Association Awards (1977); Top Male Vocalist, Single of the Year and Song of the Year for "Lucille," Academy of Country Music Awards (1977); Best Male Country Vocal Performance, "Lucille," Grammy Awards (1977)

ROGERS, MIKE, "MIKE" DENNIS, T: U.S. Representative from Alabama **I:** Government Administration/Government Relations/Government Services **DOB:** 07/16/1958 **PB:** Hammond **SC:** IN/USA **MS:** Married **SPN:** Beth Rogers **CH:** Emily; Evan; Elliot **ED:** JD, University of Birmingham Law School (1991); MPA, Jacksonville State University (1985); BA in Political Science, Jacksonville State University (1981) **C:** Member, U.S. House of Representatives from Alabama's Third Congressional District, United States Congress, Washington, DC (2003-Present); Member, Alabama House of Representatives (1994-2002); Member, Committee on Appropriations; Associate then Partner, Rogers, Young, Wollstein and Hughes; Attorney, Bolt, Isom, Jackson and Bailey; Community Representative, Psychiatric Counselor, Northeast Alabama Regional Medical Center; Director, Dislocated Worker's Project, United Way of Etowah County **CIV:** Active Member, State Republican Executive Committee (1990-Present); Member, Calhoun County Commission (1987-1991) **AW:** Named Commander, Order of the Star of Romania (2017) **PA:** Republican **RE:** Baptist

ROJAS, CARMEN, PHD, T: Founder, Chief Executive Officer **I:** Financial Services **CN:** The Workers Lab **ED:** Doctor of Philosophy in City and Regional Planning, University of California Berkeley (2010); Bachelor of Arts in Politics, University of California Santa Cruz (2000) **C:** Founder, Chief Executive Officer, The Workers Lab, Oakland, CA (2014-Present); Associate Director of Program Strategies, Living Cities, New York, NY (2011-2014); Faculty, Department of City and Regional Planning, University of California Berkeley (2011-2012); Director of Strategic Grantmaking, Mitchell Kapor Foundation (2008-2011); African American Outmigration Task Force Coordinator, San Francisco Redevelopment Agency (2006-2007) **CR:** Fulbright Scholar (2007-2008) **CIV:** Neighborhood Funders Group **CW:** Contributor, "An Uplifting Look at Urban Food," Living Cities (2013); Contributor, "How Federal Investments Can Create Domestic Jobs," Living Cities (2013); Contributor, "How to Create Good, Local Jobs By Scaling Business Enterprises," Living Cities (2013); Contributor, "Reimagining Prosperity," Living Cities (2013); Contributor, "Equitable TOD: Meeting the Needs of People & Places," Living Cities (2012); Contributor, "Revolutionary Urbanism: The Struggle for the Streets of a City"; Contributor, "Scale Pathways," Living Cities; Contributor, "Voices of Climate Justice," Reimagine

ROKUSEK, CECILIA F., EDD, MSC, RDN, T: President, Chief Executive Officer **I:** Museums & Institutions **CN:** National Czech & Slovak Museum & Library **PB:** Yankton **SC:** SD/USA **PT:** John C. Rokusek; Alice T. Fiala Rokusek **MS:** Married **SPN:** Dr. Robert J. Petrik **ED:** Postgraduate Coursework, Bryn Mawr College, Bryn Mawr, PA (1994); EdD in Adult and Higher Education Administration, University of South Dakota, Vermillion, SD (1983); Postgraduate Coursework, University of Michigan, Ann Arbor, MI (1979); MS in Human Nutrition, University of Nebraska-Lincoln, Lincoln, NE (1976); BA in Home Economics, Dietetics, Oral Communication, Mount Marty College (Now Mount Mye, Yankton, SD (1975) **CT:** RDN (Registered Dietitian Nutritionist) **C:** President, Chief Executive Officer, National Czech & Slovak Museum & Library, Cedar Rapids, Iowa (2018-Present); Chief Executive Officer, Chief Executive Officer, and Provost, Larkin University (2018); International Education Consultant, Larkin University (2016-2017); Assistant Dean, Research and Innovation, Nova Southeastern University College of Osteopathic Medicine, Ft. Lauderdale, FL (2006-2016); Professor, Department of Family Medicine, Public Health (MPH), Medical Education, Disaster and Emergency Preparedness/Management, and Nutrition, Nova Southeastern University College of Osteopathic Medicine, Fort Lauderdale-Davie, FL (2006-2016); Dean, Winona State University College of Education, Winona, MN (2005-2006); Professor, Department of Educational Leadership and Adult and Continuing Education, Winona State University College of Education, Winona, MN (2005-2006); Research & Planning Consultant, Advising the College of Osteopathic Medicine on New Programs, Grant Opportunities, and Development of Innovative Centers and Institutes, Nova Southeastern University, Fort Lauderdale, FL (2003-2005); Dean, Florida Gulf Coast University, Fort Myers, FL (1999-2005); Professor, Department of Health Sciences, Florida Gulf Coast University College of Health Professions (1999-2005); Dean, Governors State University College of Health Professions, University Park, IL (1993-1999); Professor, Department of Health Services Administration, Governors State University College of Health Professions, University Park, IL (1993-1999); Associate Professor, Department of Family Medicine, University of South Dakota School of Medicine, Vermillion, SD (1991-1993); Adjunct Assistant Professor, Department of Psychiatry, University of South Dakota School of Medicine, Vermillion, SD (1990-1993); Adjunct Assistant Professor, Department of Nutrition and Food Service Management, South Dakota State University, Brookings, SD (1988-1993); Nutrition Curriculum Consultant, South Dakota Head Start Program, University of South Dakota School of Education, Vermillion, SD (1982-1993); Assistant Vice President, Health Affairs, University of South Dakota, Vermillion, SD (1981-1993); Instructor, Presidential Consultant, Kilian Community College, Sioux Falls, SD (1986-1992); Assistant Professor, Department of Family Medicine, University of South Dakota School of Medicine, Vermillion, SD (1984-1991); Adjunct Assistant Professor, Department of Dental Hygiene, University of South Dakota College of Arts and Sciences (1977-1991); Assistant Professor, Division of Allied Health Sciences, University of South Dakota School of Medicine (1981-1983); Assistant Professor, Department of Home Economics, Dietetics Program Chair, Mount Marty College, Yankton, SD (1976-1981); Adjunct Instructor, Food Service Management Program, University of South Dakota, Springfield, SD (1976-1979); Graduate Teaching, Research Assistant, University of Nebraska-Lincoln (1975-1976) **CR:** Appointed Member, Slovak Honorary Council, Slovak Ministry of Foreign Affairs (2008-Present); Elected Vice-chair, Faculty Council, Nova Southeastern University College of Osteopathic Medicine, Ft. Lauderdale, FL (2016); Chair, College of Osteopathic Medicine Research Committee, Health Professions and Basic Medical Sciences (2011-2016); Chair International and Medical Outreach Community of the College of Osteopathic Medicine (2010-2016); Appointed, Health and Human Services Secretary, National Advisory Committee for Interdisciplinary Community Based Linkages (2010-2013); Vice President, Czechoslovak Society of Arts and Sciences (2008-2013); Professor, College of Osteopathic Medicine (2006-2016); Co-chair, University Task Force on Emergency Preparedness (2008-2010); Institutional Research Board, Winona State University, Winona, MN (2006); President's Cabinet, Winona State University (2005-2006); Executive Board and Chair, Southwest Florida Healthy Start Program (Now The Healthy Start SWFL, Inc.) (2003-2005); Founder and Member, Board of Directors, Kleist Health Education Center, Florida Gulf Coast University (2001-2005); American Association of Schools of Allied Health Professions Substance Abuse Task Force (2004); Board of Directors, Addictions Training Center of Illinois (1994-1999); Governors State University Budget Committee (1994-1999); Chair, Physician Assistant, Curriculum Advisory Committee, Malcom X Community College (1993-1999); President, Chicago South Suburban Dietetic Association (1997-1998); Visiting Professor, Yonsei University, Ewha Women's School, Seoul, Korea (1997); Administrative Representative, IL New Faculty Union Contract and Negotiation Process (1996-1997); Chair, Chicago Southland Chamber of Commerce, Drug Free Workplace Task Force (1995-1996); Chair, Vice Chair, Deans Group of the American Association of Schools of Allied Health (1994-1996); Chair, Governor Appointed State Health Planning Council (1983-1994); State Chair, Continuing Dietetic Education (1990-1993); National Board of Directors, American Association of University Affiliated Programs (1988-1993); South Dakota Nutrition Coordinating Council (1987-1993); Chair, State Personnel Preparation Standards for Nutrition Professionals

Working with the Birth-5 Population, South Dakota Department of Education (1989-1992); State Strategic Planning Committee for Developmental Disabilities (1989-1992); Governor, Appointed State Developmental Disabilities Planning Council (1987-1992); Lecturer, School of Medicine, Budapest; Visiting Professor, Comenius University, Faculty of Medicine, Bratislava, SK; Lecturer, Faculty of Nursing, College of Nursing, Jesenice, Slovenia **CIV:** National Advisory Committee, Alzheimer's Education (2015-2018); Founder, Chair, National Fundraiser, Roma Scholarship Fund (2011-Present); Board of Directors, American Heart Association, Inc. (1995-1999); National Board of Directors, American Association on Mental Retardation (Now American Association on Intellectual and Developmental Disabilities) (1988-1991); National President, Division of Nutrition and Dietetics, American Association on Mental Retardation (Now American Association on Intellectual and Developmental Disabilities) (1988-1990); National Secretary, American Dietetic Association Section on Nutrition in Medical and Dental Education (1988-1989); State President, Business and Professional Women's Organization (1979-1980); Fundraising, Numerous Causes/Organizations **CW:** Author and Co-author, Numerous Articles, Professional Journals (1976-2016); Presenter, Frequent National and International Conferences **AW:** Woodrow Wilson Leadership Award, Slovak Embassy in Washington, DC (2018); Silver Medal of Honor, Outstanding Leadership, Slovak Government (2018); Comenius Award for Excellence in International Education, Comenius University, Bratislavia, Slovakia (2014); Five-year Outstanding Service Award, Nova Southeastern University (2012); Recognized, Miami-Dade County Health Department for Outstanding Volunteerism, Development of the Statewide Medical Reserve Corps (2008-2010); Presidential Citation, Medal of Honor, International Society for Czech-Slovak Arts and Sciences (Now Czechoslovak Society of Arts and Sciences) (2006); "Outstanding Leader" Recognition, Southwest Florida Health Start (Now The Healthy Start SWFL, Inc.) (2005); Named to "Top 10 Most Powerful and Influential Women for 1998" in Chicago, The Times (2005); Bush Foundation Leadership Midwest Regional Finalist, Minneapolis, MN (1992); Ten-year Distinguished Service Recognition, University of South Dakota (1989); SDUAP/CDD Spark Plug Award for "Outstanding Dedication and Energy to the Goals of the SDUAP and UAP Network" (1986); Mount Marty College Outstanding Alumna National Award for Professional Achievement, Yankton, SD (1985); Yankton Jaycee Outstanding Young Citizen Award, Yankton, SD (1982); State's Outstanding Young Woman, Governor of South Dakota (1981); Outstanding Young Alumna Award, Mount Marty College, Yankton, SD (1980) **MEM:** National Board Member, American Friends of Czech Republic; National Board Member, American Friends of Slovakia (Now Friends of Slovakia); Trustee, Larkin University; American Dietetic Association (Now Academy of Nutrition and Dietetics); Rotary International; Czechoslovak Society of Arts and Sciences **AV:** Music; Travel; Writing **RE:** Catholic **THT:** Dr. Rokusek's motto from her mother is, "Reach for the stars and be whatever you can be, but always leave a piece of symbolic morality behind you for others to follow and make the world a better place. Love life!"

ROLLINS, SONNY, T: Composer, Musician **I:** Media & Entertainment **DOB:** 09/07/1930 **PB:** New York **SC:** NY/USA **PT:** Walter Rollins; Valborg (Solomon) Rollins **MS:** Married **SPN:** Lucille Pearson (09/06/1959, Deceased 2004); Dawn Finney (1956, Divorced) **ED:** Honorary MusD, University of Hartford (2015); Honorary MusD, Juilliard School (2013); Honorary PhD, Rutgers, The State University of New Jersey (2009); Honorary PhD, Colby College (2007); Honorary MusD, Berklee College of Music (2003); DMus, New England Conservatory of Music (2002); Honorary DMus, Duke University (1999); ArtsD, Duke University (1999); Honorary ArtsD, Wesleyan University (1998); Honorary ArtsD, Long Island University (1998); Honorary ArtsD, Bard College (1992) **C:** Co-Founder, Doxy Records, New York, NY (2005-Present); Tenor Saxophonist (1971-Present); Leader, Max Roach-Clifford Brown Quintet (1956-1957); Member, Max Roach-Clifford Brown Quintet (1955-1957); Tenor Saxophonist (1961-1968); Tenor Saxophonist (1946-1959) **CIV:** Avid Environmentalist **CW:** Musician, Live Album, "Road Shows, Vol. 4: Holding the Stage" (2016); Musician, "Road Shows, Vol. 3" (2014); Musician, Live Album, "Road Shows, Vol. 2" (2011); Musician, Live Album, "Road Shows, Vol. 1" (2008); Musician, Album, "Sonny, Please" (2006); Musician, Live Album, "Without a Song: The 9/11 Concert" (2001); Musician, Album, "This Is What I Do" (2000); Musician, Album, "Global Warming" (1998); Musician, Album, "Sonny Rollins + 3" (1996); Musician, Album, "Old Flames" (1993); Musician, Album, "Here's to the People" (1991); Musician, Album, "Falling in Love with Jazz" (1989); Musician, Album, "Dancing in the Dark" (1987);Musician, Live Album, "G-Man" (1987); Musician, Album, "Sunny Days, Starry Nights" (1984); Musician, Album, "Reel Life" (1982); Musician, Album, "No Problem" (1981); Musician, Album, "Love at First Sight" (1980); Musician, Album, "Don't Ask" (1979); Musician, Album, "Easy Living" (1977); Musician, Album, "The Way I Feel" (1976); Musician, Album, "Nucleus" (1975); Musician, Live Album, "The Cutting Edge" (1974); Musician, Album, "Horn Culture" (1973); Musician, Live Album, "Sonny Rollins in Japan" (1973); Musician, Album, "Next Album" (1972); Musician, Album, "East Broadway Run Down" (1966); Musician, Album, "Alfie" (1966); Musician, Album, "Sonny Rollins on Impulse!" (1965); Musician, Live Album, "There Will Never Be Another You" (1965); Musician, Album, "The Standard Sonny Rollins" (1964); Musician, Album, "Sonny Meets Hawk!" (1963); Musician, Album, "What's New?" (1962); Musician, Album, "The Bridge" (1962); Musician, Live Album, "Our Man in Jazz" (1962); Musician, Live Album, "Oleo 1959" (1959); Musician, Live Album, "Sonny Rollins at Music Inn" (1959); Musician, Album, "Sonny Rollins and the Contemporary Leaders" (1958); Musician, Album, "Sonny Rollins and the Big Brass" (1958); Musician, Album, "Freedom Suite" (1958); Musician, Album, "Sonny Rollins Plays" (1957); Musician, Album, "The Sound of Sonny" (1957); Musician, Album, "Sonny Rollins, Vol. 2" (1957); Musician, Album, "Way Out West" (1957); Musician, Album, "Sonny Rollins, Vol. 1" (1957); Musician, Live Album, "A Night at the Village Vanguard" (1957); Musician, Album, "Sonny Boy" (1956); Musician, Album, "Tour de Force" (1956); Musician, Album, "Rollins Plays for Bird" (1956); Musician, Album, "Saxophone Colossus" (1956); Musician, Album, "Tenor Madness" (1956); Musician, Album, "Sonny Rollins Plus 4" (1956); Musician, Album, "Work Time" (1955); Musician, Album, "Moving Out" (1954); Musician, Album, "Sonny Rollins with the Modern Jazz Quartet" (1953); Featured Musician, Numerous Miles Davis Albums; Featured Musician, Numerous Albums, including "Tattoo You" by the Rolling Stones **AW:** Honoree, Kennedy Center Honors (2011); Edward MacDowell Medal (2010); Miles Davis Award, Montreal Jazz Festival (2010); National Medal of Arts (2010); Austrian Cross of Honour for Science and Art, 1st Class (2009); Polar Music Prize (2007); Golden Plate Award, American Academy of Achievement (2006); "Jazzman of the Year," "#1 Tenor Sax Player," "Recording of the Year," DownBeat (2006); Grammy Award, Lifetime Achievement (2004); Jazz Artist of the Year, DownBeat (1997); Honoree, "Jazz Master," National Endowment for the Arts (1983); Inductee, "DownBeat" Jazz Hall of Fame (1973) **MEM:** American Academy of Arts and Sciences (2010-Present)

ROMAN, MICHAEL F., T: Chairperson, Chief Executive Officer **I:** Consumer Goods and Services **CN:** 3M **ED:** Master of Science in Electrical Engineering, University of Southern California (1987); Bachelor of Science in Electrical Engineering, University of Minnesota Twin Cities (1982); Diploma in Engineering, University of Wisconsin-Stevens Point (1980) **C:** Chairperson of the Board, 3M, Minneapolis, MN (2019-Present); Chief Executive Officer, 3M, Minneapolis, MN (2018-Present); Chief Operating Officer, Executive Vice President, 3M, Minneapolis, MN (2017-2018); Executive Vice President, 3M Industrial Business Group (2014-2017); Senior Vice President of Business Development, Minneapolis, MN (2013-2014); Vice President, General Manager, Industrial Adhesives and Tapes Division, 3M, Minneapolis, MN (2011-2013); Vice President, General Manager, Renewable Energy Division, 3M, Minneapolis, MN (2009-2011); Asia Vice President, Optical Systems Division, 3M (2008-2009); Managing Director, 3M, Seoul, Korea (2005-2008); Six Sigma Director, 3M, Minneapolis, MN (2003-2005); European Business Unit Director, 3M, Belgium (2000-2003); Program Manager, 3M, St. Paul, MN (2000); Lab Manager, 3M, St. Paul, MN 1994-2000); Senior Design Engineer, 3M, St. Paul, MN (1988-1994); Group Head, Hughes Aircraft Company (1983-1988) **CIV:** Trustee, University of Minnesota Foundation; Supporter, Big Brothers Big Sisters of America

ROMETTY, GINNI, T: Executive Chairman **I:** Technology **CN:** IBM **DOB:** 07/29/1957 **PB:** Chicago **SC:** IL/USA **MS:** Married **SPN:** Mark Anthony Rometty (1979) **ED:** Honorary Doctoral Degree, Northwestern University (2015); Honorary Doctoral Degree, Rensselaer Polytechnic Institute (2014); BS in Computer Science and Electrical Engineering, Robert R. McCormick School of Engineering and Applied Science, Northwestern University, Evanston, IL, With High Honors (1979); Honorary Degree, North Carolina State University **C:** Executive Chairman, IBM (2020-Present); Chairman, President, Chief Executive Officer, IBM (2012-2020); Senior Vice President, Group Executive of Sales, Marketing and Strategy, IBM (2010-2012); Senior Vice President of Global Business Services, IBM (2005-2009); Senior Vice President of Enterprise Business Services and IBM Global Services, IBM (2005); Member, Consulting Group, IBM (1991); Business and Information Technology Consultant, IBM (1985-1991); Systems Analyst, Systems Engineer, IBM (1981-1985); Staff Member, Application and Systems Development, IBM (1979-1981); General Manager of Global Services for America, IBM; General Manager of Strategy, Marketing and Sales Operations, Global Services Worldwide, IBM; Numerous Positions, including General Manager, Global Insurance and Financial Services Sector, IBM **CR:** Member, Board of Directors, IBM (2012-Present); Co-Chair, World Economic Forum (2017); Member, Business Advisory Panel, White House (2017); Member, Board of Directors, American International Group, Inc.(2006-2009); Active Participant, Women in Technology Council, Women's Executive Council, Women's Leadership Council, IBM **CIV:** Member, Board of Overseers, Board of Managers, Memorial Sloan Kettering Cancer Center (2013-Present); Member, Board of Trustees, Northwestern University **AW:** 50 Most

Powerful Women in Business, Fortune (2005-Present); Edison Achievement Award, Northwestern University (2019); Ranked #6, 20 Most Important Person in Tech, Time (2018); Ranked #11, The World's 100 Most Powerful Women, Forbes (2016); Listee, World's 100 Most Powerful People, Forbes (2014); Listee, 50 Most Influential People in the World, Bloomberg (2012); Time 100, Time (2012); Alumni Merit Award, Northwestern Alumni Association (2010); Carl Sloane Award, Association of Management Consultant Firms (2006); Scholarship, General Motors; Numerous Accolades and Recognitions in the Field **MEM:** Council on Foreign Relations; Co-Chair, Cyber Group, The Aspen Institute; Kappa Kappa Gamma **AV:** Going to Broadway shows; Scuba diving

ROMNEY, WILLARD, "MITT" MITT, T: U.S. Senator from Utah **I:** Government Administration/ Government Relations/Government Services **DOB:** 03/12/1947 **PB:** Detroit **SC:** MI/USA **PT:** George Wilcken Romney; Lenore (Lafount) Romney **MS:** Married **SPN:** Ann (Davies) Romney (03/21/1969) **CH:** Taggart; Matthew; Joshua; Benjamin; Craig **ED:** Honorary Doctorate, Liberty University (2012); MBA, Harvard Business School (1975); JD, Harvard Law School (1975); BA, Brigham Young University, Provo, Utah (1971) **C:** U.S. Senator, State of Utah (2019-Present); Chairman, Executive Committee, Solamere Capital, LLC, Boston, MA (2013-Present); Governor, Commonwealth of Massachusetts (2003-2007); Chairman, Chief Executive Officer, Bain & Company, Inc., Boston, MA (1991-2001); Managing Partner, Chief Executive Officer, Bain Capital, LP, Boston, MA (1984-2001); Vice President, Bain & Company, Inc., Boston, MA (1978-1984); Consultant, Bain & Company, Inc., Boston, MA (1977-1978); Consultant, Boston Consulting Group (1975-1977) **CR:** Board of Directors, Marriott International, Inc. (2009-2011, 2012-Present); Candidate, 2012 Republican Party Presidential Nomination (2012); Candidate, 2008 Republican Party Presidential Nomination (2008); Board of Directors, Marriott International, Inc., Bethesda, MD (1992-2002); Board of Directors, Staples Inc., Framingham, MA (1986-2001) **CIV:** President, Chief Executive Officer, Salt Lake Organizing Committee, Winter Olympics, Utah (1999-2002); President, Boston Stake Latter-day Saints Church (1986-1994); Member, National Executive Board, Boy Scouts of America; Member, Visiting Committee, Harvard Business School; Member, Advisory Board, Brigham Young University Marriott School of Business **CW:** Author, "No Apology: The Case for American Greatness" (2010); Author, "Turnaround: Crisis, Leadership, and the Olympic Games" (2004) **AW:** Named One of the 100 Most Influential People in the World, TIME Magazine (2012); Baker Scholar, Harvard Business School (1975) **MEM:** Belmont Hill Club **PA:** Republican **RE:** LDS Church

RONAN, SAOIRSE, T: Actress **I:** Media & Entertainment **DOB:** 04/12/1994 **PB:** Bronx **SC:** NY/USA **PT:** Monica (née Brennan) Ronan; Paul Ronan **CR:** Model, Raf Simon's "Women," Calvin Klein (2018) **CIV:** Ambassador, Irish Society for the Prevention of Cruelty to Children; Contributor, Home Sweet Home **CW:** Actress, "Ammonite" (2020); Actress, "The French Dispatch" (2020); Actress, "Little Women" (2019); Actress, "Mary Queen of Scots" (2018); Actress, "The Seagull" (2018); Host, "Saturday Night Live" (2017); Actress, Video Short, "Great Performers: Horror Show" (2017); Actress, "On Chesil Beach" (2017); Actress, "Lady Bird" (2017); Voice Actress, "Loving Vincent" (2017); Actress, Music Video, "Galway Girl" by Ed Sheeran (2017); Actress, Theater, "The Crucible" (2016); Actress, Music Video, "Cherry Wine"

by Hozier (2016); Voice Actress, "Weepah Way for Now" (2015); Actress, "Brooklyn" (2015); Actress, "Stockholm, Pennsylvania" (2015); Voice Actress, Two Episodes, "Robot Chicken" (2014); Actress, "Lost River" (2014); Actress, "Muppets Most Wanted" (2014); Actress, "The Grand Budapest Hotel" (2014); Voice Actress, "Justin and the Knights of Valour" (2013); Actress, "How I Live Now" (2013); Actress, "The Host" (2013); Actress, Music Video, "Garden's Heart" by Bat for Lashes (2013); Actress, "Byzantium" (2012); Actress, "Violet & Daisy" (2011); Actress, "The Way Back" (2010); Voice Actress, "The Secret World of Arrietty" (2010); Actress, "The Lovely Bones" (2009); Actress, "City of Ember" (2008); Actress, "Death Defying Acts" (2007); Actress, "Atonement" (2007); Actress, "The Christmas Miracle of Jonathan Toomey" (2007); Actress, "I Could Never Be Your Woman" (2007); Actress, Four Episodes, "Proof" (2005); Actress, Four Episodes, "The Clinic" (2003, 2004) **AW:** Best Actress, "Little Women," Boston Society of Film Critics (2019); Best Actress in a Motion Picture - Musical or Comedy, "Lady Bird," Golden Globe Awards (2018); British/Irish Actress of the Year, "Lady Bird," London Film Critics' Circle (2018); Desert Palm Achievement Award, "Lady Bird," Palm Springs International Film Festival (2018); Santa Barbara Award, "Lady Bird," Santa Barbara International Film Festival (2018); Best Actress, "Lady Bird," Chicago Film Critics Association (2017); Best Actress, "Lady Bird," Chicago Indie Critics (2017); Best Actress, "Lady Bird," Denver Film Critics Society (2017); Best Actress, "Lady Bird," Gotham Independent Film Awards (2017); Best Actress, "Lady Bird," Detroit Film Critics Society (2017); Best Actress, "Lady Bird," Georgia Film Critics Association (2017); Best Actress, "Lady Bird," Indiana Film Journalists Association (2017); Best Actress, "Lady Bird," Iowa Film Critics (2017); Best Actress, "Lady Bird," New York Film Critics Circle (2017); Best Actress, "Lady Bird," Seattle Film Critics society (2017); Best Actress, "Lady Bird," Vancouver Film Critics Circle (2017); Best Lead Performance, "Lady Bird," Village Voice Film Poll (2017); International Star Award, "Brooklyn," Palm Springs International Film Festival (2016); Best Actress - Motion Picture, "Brooklyn," Satellite Awards (2016); Outstanding Performer of the Year, "Brooklyn," Santa Barbara International Film Festival (2016); Featured, "Next Generation Leaders," Time (2016); Featured, "30 Under 30" Lists (2016); New Hollywood Award, "Brooklyn," Hollywood Film Awards (2015); Best Actress, "Brooklyn," British Independent Film Awards (2015); Best Actress, "Brooklyn," Washington DC Area Film Critics Association (2015); Best Actress, "Brooklyn," North Carolina Film Critics Association (2016); Best Actress, "Brooklyn," Austin Film Critics Association (2015); Best Actress, "Brooklyn," Boston Online Film Critics Association (2015); Best Actress, "Brooklyn," New York Film Critics Circle (2015); Best Actress, "Brooklyn," San Francisco Film Critics Circle (2015); Kick Ass Award for Best Female Action Star, "Hanna," Alliance of Women Film Journalists (2012); Best Performance by a Youth in a Lead or Supporting Role - Female, "Hanna," Phoenix Film Critics Society (2011); Best Young Actor/ Actress, "The Lovely Bones," Critics' Choice Movie Awards (2010); Best Performance by a Younger Actor, "The Lovely Bones," Saturn Awards (2010); Virtuoso Award, "The Lovely Bones," Santa Barbara International Film Festival (2010); Best Performance by a Youth - Female, "The Lovely Bones," Phoenix Film Critics Society (2009); Best Performance by a Youth in a Lead or Supporting Role - Female, "Atonement" (2007); Breakthrough Award, "Atonement," Dublin

Film Critics' Circle (2007); Best Newcomer, "Atonement," Alliance of Women Film Journalists (2007); Numerous Other Awards and Accolades

RONSON, MARK DANIEL, T: Music Producer **I:** Media & Entertainment **DOB:** 09/04/1975 **SC:** Notting Hill/England **PT:** Laurence Ronson; Ann Dexter Ronson; Mick Jones (Stepfather) **MS:** Divorced **SPN:** Joséphine de La Baume (9/3/2011, Divorced 10/2018) **ED:** Coursework, Vassar College; Coursework, New York University; Diploma, Collegiate School, New York, NY **C:** Musician, Silk City (2018-Present) **CIV:** Participant, Please Don't Wear Any Fur, PETA (2009) **CW:** Co-Writer, Producer, "She is Coming" (2019); Co-Writer, "Father of the Bride" (2019); Musician, EP, "Electricity" (2019); Musician, "Late Night Feelings" (2019); Featured Musician, "Diamonds Are Invincible" (2018); Co-Writer, "A Star is Born" (2018); Producer, "(((echo chamber)))" (2018); Co-Writer, Producer, "Crazy Rich Asians" (2018); Contributing Musician, "God's Favorite Customer" (2018); Producer, Co-Writer, Programmer, Contributing Musician, "No Shame" (2018); Programmer, Contributing Musician, "Dua Lipa" (2017); Producer, "Villains" (2017); Appearance, "Gaga: Five Foot Two" (2017); Producer, Co-Writer, Contributing Musician, "Ghostbusters (Original Motion Picture Soundtrack)" (2016); Producer, Co-Writer, Contributing Musician, "Suicide Squad: The Album" (2016); Producer, Co-Writer, Contributing Musician, "Joanne" (2016); Producer, "The Jungle Book (Original Motion Picture Soundtrack)" (2016); Producer, Contributing Musician, "25" (2015); Featured Musician, "Everyday" (2015); Musician, "Uptown Special" (2015); Appearance, "Amy" (2015); Producer, Co-Writer, "Heart Blanche" (2015); Producer, Co-Writer, Contributing Musician, "At. Long. Last. ASAP" (2015); Composer, "Mortdecai (Original Motion Picture Soundtrack)" (2015); Producer, Co-Writer, Contributing Musician, "Mr. Wonderful" (2015); Producer, Co-Writer, "Paper Gods" (2015); Contributing Musician, "We Fall" (2015); Producer, Contributing Musician, "Midnight Sun" (2014); Producer, "New" (2013); Producer, Contributing Musician, "Unorthodox Jukebox" (2012); Producer, Programmer, Contributing Musician, "Out of the Game" (2012); Musician, "Anywhere in the World" (2012); Producer, Composer, "Arthur: Original Motion Picture Soundtrack" (2011); Producer, "Lioness: Hidden Treasures" (2011); Producer, "Arabia Mountain" (2011); Producer, Contributing Musician, "All You Need is Now" (2010); Producer, "Q Soul Bossa Nostra" (2010); Producer, Contributing Musician, "Record Collection" (2010); Producer, Co-Writer, "Release Me" (2010); Musician, "Record Collection" (2010); Producer, "A Son Unique" (2009); Producer, "Welcome to the Walk Alone" (2009); Producer, Engineer, "Love & War" (2009); Producer, Co-Composer, "Attention Deficit" (2009); Co-Producer, Synthesizer, Engineer, "The Atlantic Ocean" (2009); Producer, "Back to the Feature" (2009); Co-Producer, "Can't Slow Down" (2009); Co-Producer, "All in One" (2009); Producer, "See Clear Now" (2008); Producer, Engineer, Contributing Musician, "Off with Their Heads" (2008); Producer, Co-Writer, "Nas" (2008); Co-Producer, Co-Writer, "Sol-Angel and the Hadley St. Dreams" (2008); Producer, "The Mixtape About Nothing" (2008); Producer, Contributing Musician, "Shine" (2008); Producer, Contributing Musician, Programmer, "19" (2008); Producer, "Man in the Mirror" (2008); Producer, "100 Miles & Running" (2007); Musician, "Version" (2007); Musician, "Just" (2006); Producer, "More Fish" (2006); Producer, "Half Nelson: Original Motion Picture Soundtrack" (2006); Producer, Engineer, Contributing Musician, "Rudebox" (2006); Producer, Co-Writer,

Engineer, Contributing Musician, "Back to Black" (2006); Co-Producer, Engineer, Contributing Musician, "Back to Basics" (2006); Co-Producer, Co-Writer, Engineer, Contributing Musician, "Blue Collar" (2006); Co-Producer, Co-Writer, Contributing Musician, "Alright, Still" (2006); Producer, "Beef or Chicken" (2005); Contributing Musician, "TheErthMoovsAroundTheSun" (2005); Producer, Co-Writer, "Osirus" (2005); Producer, Contributing Musician, "Here Comes the Fuzz" (2003); Programmer, Contributing Musician, "The Trouble with Being Myself" (2003); Musician, "Here Comes the Fuzz" (2003); Producer, "The Best of Saigon a.k.a. The Yardfather Volume 1" (2002); Producer, Contributing Musician, "Dutty Rock" (2002); Contributing Musician, "The Bathroom Wall" (2002); Co-Producer, "Zoolander (Music From the Motion Picture)" (2001); Cameo, "Zoolander" (2001); Appearance, Music Video, "More Than a Woman" (2001); Co-Producer, Co-Writer, "Everybody Got Their Something" (2001); Programmer, "Home Field Advantage" (1999); Producer, "The Flip Squad All-Star DJs" (1998); Creator, "Circuit Breaker"; Producer, Numerous Other Songs **AW:** Best Original Song, "Shallow," Houston Film Critics Society (2019); Best Original Song, "Shallow," Academy Awards (2019); Best Song, "Shallow," Critics' Choice Movie Awards (2019); Best Original Song, "Shallow," Georgia Film Critics Association (2019); Best Original Song, "Shallow," Golden Globe Awards (2019); Best Song Written for Visual Media for "Shallow," Best Dance Recording for "Electricity," Grammy Awards (2019); Best Original Song, "Shallow," Los Angeles Online Film Critics Society (2018); BMI Champion Award (2018); International Work of the Year, "Uptown Funk," APRA Music Awards (2016); Collaboration of the Year, "Uptown Funk," iHeartRadio Music Awards (2016); Best Pop Duo/Group Performance, Record of the Year, "Uptown Funk," Grammy Awards (2016); Most Stylish Man of the Year, GQ Men of the Year Awards (2016); Best Pop Award, "Uptown Funk," MelOn Music Awards (2015); BMI Pop Song of the Year for "Uptown Funk" (2015); Video of the Year, Song of the Year, "Uptown Funk," Soul Train Music Awards (2015); Best Pop Video - UK, "Uptown Funk," UK Music Video Awards (2015); Song of the Year, "Uptown Funk," Telehit Awards (2015); Named, Top 10 Gold International Gold Songs, "Uptown Funk," RTHK International Pop Poll Awards (2015); Best Male Video, "Uptown Funk," MTV Video Music Awards (2015); British Single of the Year, "Uptown Funk," Brit Awards (2015); British Male Solo Artist, Brit Awards (2008); Record of the Year for "Rehab," Best Pop Vocal Album for "Back to Black," Producer of the Year, Non-Classical, Grammy Awards (2008); Man of the Year, Glamour Women of the Year (2008); Best Live Male, Vodafone Live Music Awards (2008) **RE:** Jewish

RONSTADT, LINDA MARIE, T: Singer **I:** Media & Entertainment **DOB:** 07/15/1946 **PB:** Tucson **SC:** AZ/USA **PT:** Gilbert Ronstadt; Ruthmary (Copeman) Ronstadt **MS:** Single **CH:** Mary Clementine (Adopted Daughter); Carlos Ronstadt (Adopted Son) **ED:** Honorary Doctorate of Music Degree, Berklee College of Music (2009) **C:** Singer, Songwriter, Performer (1967-Present) **CR:** Appointed, Artistic Director, San Jose Mariachi and Mexican Heritage Festival (2008) **CIV:** Activist, Environmental and Community Issues; Advocate, Gay Rights and Same-Sex Marriage **CW:** Singer, "Live in Hollywood" (2019); Herself, Singer, "Linda Ronstadt: The Sound of My Voice" (2019); Co-Singer, "The Complete Trio Collection" (2016); Author, "Simple Dreams: A Musical Memoir" (2013); Co-Singer, "Adieu False Heart" (2006); Author, Introduction, "Classic Ferrington Guitars" (2005); Singer, "Hummin' to Myself" (2004); Author, "The

NPR Curious Listener's Guide to American Folk Music" (2004); Singer, "A Merry Little Christmas" (2000); Co-Singer, "Western Wall: The Tucson Sessions" (1999); Co-Singer, "Trio II" (1999); Singer, Album, "We Ran" (1998); Singer, "Dedicated to the One I Love" (1996); Singer, "Feels Like Home" (1995); Singer, "Winter Light" (1993); Singer, "The Young Indiana Jones Chronicles" (1993); Singer, "Frenesí" (1992); Voice Actress, "The Simpsons" (1992); Singer, "Mas Canciones" (1991); Actress, "Great Performances" (1991); Singer, "Cry Like a Rainstorm, Howl Like the Wind" (1989); Musical Guest, "Sesame Street" (1989); Vocalist, "Canciones de Mi Padre" (1988); Singer, "Canciones de Mi Padre" (1987); Co-Singer, "Trio" (1987); Singer, "For Sentimental Reasons" (1986); Singer, "Lush Life" (1984); Actress, "La bohème" (1984); Actress, "The Pirates of Penzance" (1983); Singer, "What's New" (1982); Singer, "Get Closer" (1982); Actress, "The Pirates of Penzance" (1981-1982); Singer, "Mad Love" (1980); Herself, "The Muppet Show" (1980); Actress, "The Pirates of Penzance" (1980); Singer, "Living in the USA" (1978); Singer, "Simple Dreams" (1977); Singer, "Greatest Hits" (1976); Singer, "Hasten Down the Wind" (1976); Singer, "Prisoner in Disguise" (1975); Herself, "Cher" (1975); Singer, "Different Drum" (1974); Singer, "Heart Like a Wheel" (1974); Singer, "Don't Cry Now" (1973); Singer, "Linda Ronstadt" (1972); Singer, "Silk Purse" (1970); Herself, "The Darin Invasion" (1970); Herself, "Playboy After Dark" (1970); Herself, "Hee Haw" (1970); Herself, "The Johnny Cash Show" (1969-1971); Singer, Album, "Hand Sown ... Home Grown" (1969); Herself, "It's Happening" (1969, 1968); Musical Guest, "Saturday Night Lives" (Four Times); Singer, Numerous Compilation Albums **AW:** Honoree, Kennedy Center Honors (2019); Lifetime Achievement Award, Grammy Awards (2016); Honoree, National Medal of Arts, National Endowment for the Arts (2014); Inductee, Rock and Roll Hall of Fame (2014); Latin Recording Academy Lifetime Achievement Award, Latin Grammy Awards (2011); Trailblazer Award for Contribution to American Music, American Latino Medal Arts Awards (2008); Inductee, Arizona Music and Entertainment Hall of Fame (2007); Best Country Collaboration with Vocals, "After the Gold Rush," Grammy Awards (1999); Best Musical Album for Children, "Dedicated to the One I Love," Grammy Awards (1996); Best Mexican-American Album, "Mas Canciones," Grammy Awards (1992); Best Tropical Latin Album, "Frenesi," Grammy Awards (1992); Best Pop Vocal Performance by a Duo or Group with Vocal, "All My Life," "Cry Like a Rainstorm, Howl Like the Wind," Grammy Awards (1990); Primetime Emmy Award for Outstanding Individual Performance in a Variety or Music Program, "Canciones de Mi Padre" (1989); Co-Recipient, Vocal Event of the Year, "Trio," Country Music Association Awards (1988); Best Country Performance by a Duo or Group with Vocal, "Trio," Grammy Awards (1987); Album of the Year, "Trio," Academy of Country Music Awards (1987); Best Pop Vocal Performance, Female, "Hasten Down the Wind," Grammy Awards (1976); Best Country Vocal Performance, Female, "I Can't Help It (If I'm Still in Love with You)," "Heart Like a Wheel," Grammy Awards (1975); Best New Female Artist, Academy of Country Music Awards (1974); Recipient, Numerous Other Awards and Accolades

ROONEY, LAURENCE, "FRANCIS" FRANCIS, T: U.S. Representative from Florida; Construction Executive **I:** Government Administration/Government Relations/Government Services **DOB:** 12/04/1953 **PB:** Muskogee **SC:** OK/USA **PT:** Laurence Francis Rooney; Lucy Turner Rooney **MS:** Married **SPN:** Kathleen Collins (1976) **CH:** Three Children **ED:** Honorary Doctorate, Univer-

sity of Dallas (2010); Honorary PhD, University of Notre Dame (2006); JD, Georgetown University Law Center (1978); AB, Georgetown University (1975) **CT:** 100-Ton Master's License, United States Coast Guard **C:** Member, U.S. House of Representatives from Florida's 19th Congressional District (2017-Present); Chairman, President, Chief Executive Officer, Rooney Holdings, Inc., Naples, FL (1984-Present); U.S. Ambassador to The Holy See, U.S. Department of State (2005-2008); Member, Committee on Education and the Workforce; Member, Committee on Foreign Affairs; Member, Economic Committee **CR:** Board of Directors, Laredo Petroleum, Inc. (2010-Present); Board of Directors, Vetra Energy Group, LLC (2009-Present); Board of Directors, Helmerich & Payne, Inc. (2008-Present); Board of Directors, Florida Corporation (2008-2009); Board of Directors, Cimarex Energy Company (2002-2005); Board of Directors, BOK Financial Corporation (1995-2005); Board of Directors, BOL Financial Corporation; Member, Oklahoma Capital Investment Board; Member, New York Stock Exchange; Vice Chairman, NASDAQ; Member, Oklahoma Turnpike Authority; Member, Transition Team for Governor-elect Brad Henry, State of Oklahoma; Director, 20/20 Committee, Washington Advisory Council, Center for Strategic and International Studies **CIV:** Member, School of Architecture Council, University of Notre Dame; Board Advisor, Panama Canal Authority; Trustee, Center for the Study of the Presidency and Congress (CSPC); Member, Sovereign Military Order of Malta (Federal Association), Washington, DC **MEM:** International President, Young Presidents Organization (YPO) (1997-1998); Director, Young Presidents Organization (YPO) (1992-1998); Young Presidents Organization (YPO) **BAR:** State of Texas; The District of Columbia **PA:** Republican **RE:** Roman Catholic

RORSCHACH, RICHARD GORDON, T: Lawyer **I:** Law and Legal Services **DOB:** 08/09/1928 **PB:** Tulsa **SC:** OK/USA **PT:** Harold Emil Rorschach; Margaret (Hermes) Rorschach **MS:** Married **SPN:** Martha Kay King (12/23/1979) **CH:** Richard Helm; Reagan Cartwright; Andrew Maxwell **ED:** JD, University of Houston (1961); MS, University of Oklahoma (1952); BS, Massachusetts Institute of Technology (1950) **CT:** Licensed Professional Engineer, Texas **C:** Partner, R.G. Rorschach & Associates, Kilgore, TX (1980-Present); Partner, Ragan, Russell & Rorschach, Houston, TX (1968-1980); Partner, Broady, Kells & Rorschach, Houston, TX (1964-1968); Attorney, Marathon Oil Company (1961-1964); Petroleum Engineer, Marathon Oil Company, Houston, TX (1957-1961); Petroleum Engineer, Marathon Oil Company, Bay City, TX (1956-1957); Consultant Engineer, Freese, Nichols & Turner, Houston, TX (1955-1956); Consultant, Civil Engineer, Freese & Nichols, Fort Worth, TX (1955) **CR:** Managing Partner, Pentagon Oil Company (1988-Present); Owner, Breeder, Exhibitor, Arabian Horses, Shadowbrook Farm, Kilgore, TX (1980-Present); Vice President, General Counsel Building Innovations, LLC (2010-2017); Hilton Head Island, SC (2011); Chairman, National Association of Royalty Owners, Inc. (1996-1999); President, National Association of Royalty Owners-Texas (1993-1996); Officer, Little River Oil & Gas Company (1980-1988); Executive Committee, Colonial Royalties Co., Tulsa, OK (1970-1977) **MIL:** 1st Lieutenant, United States Army (1952-1954) **CW:** Author, "How to Protect Your Royalty Interests: Texas Perspectives, Vols. 1 & 2" (2002); Author, "The Ultimate Royalty Owner's Guide: A Manual of Procedure and Operation" **MEM:** President, Kilgore Chapter, Rotary Club (1984-1985); American Society of Civil Engineers; Society of Petroleum Engineering; Legion of Honors; Texas

Bar Association; Sigma Xi; Sigma Alpha Epsilon **BAR:** Texas (1961) **MH:** Albert Nelson Marquis Lifetime Achievement Award **AV:** Fly fishing; Fly tying; Golfing; Playing tennis **PA:** Republican **RE:** Presbyterian

RORTY, MARY VARNEY, PHD, T: Philosopher, Bioethicist **I:** Sciences **DOB:** 08/13/1939 **PB:** Potlatch **SC:** ID/USA **PT:** Richard Marvin; Vivian Pearson Varney **MS:** Widowed **SPN:** Richard McKay Rorty (11/04/1972) **CH:** Patricia; Kevin **ED:** MA in Clinical Ethics, University of Virginia (1992); PhD in Philosophy, Johns Hopkins University (1970); BA, Barnard College (1961) **C:** Clinical Associate Professor, Stanford University Medical Center (1999-Present); Director, Advanced Studies, Center of Biomedicine Ethics, University of Virginia School of Nursing (1991-1998); Research Associate, University of Virginia School of Nursing (1987-1991); Lecturer, Assistant Professor, State University of New York at Buffalo (1965-1972); Associate Professor, San Francisco State College (1970-1971) **CW:** Co-Editor, "Ethical Dilemmas in Pediatrics" (2005); Co-Author, "Organization Ethics in Healthcare" (2000); Contributor, Over 30 Articles, Professional Journals **AW:** Batten Fellow, Darden School of Business, Charlottesville, VA (2002) **MH:** Albert Nelson Marquis Lifetime Achievement Award **B/I:** Ms. Rorty became involved in her profession because of her combination of aptitude and interest as an undergraduate student. Likewise, she was inspired by her excellent teachers.

ROSA, LUCILLE MARIE, T: Supervisory Librarian (Retired) **I:** Library Management/Library Services **DOB:** 07/31/1947 **PB:** Fall River **SC:** MA/USA **PT:** Joseph T. Lavallee; Aline M. Lavallee **MS:** Widowed **SPN:** Joseph F. Rosa (Deceased) **CH:** Anne-Marie J.; Robert W.; Jennifer A. **ED:** MLS, University of Rhode Island, Kingston, RI (1980); BFA, University of Massachusetts, Dartmouth, MA (1975); BA in History, University of Massachusetts, Dartmouth, MA (1970) **C:** Cataloger, Freetown Historical Society, Assonet, MA (2015-Present); Head, Technological Services Division, U.S. Naval War College (1990-2013); Chief, Cataloging, U.S. Naval War College, Newport, RI (1989-1990); Associate Head, Cataloging, Massachusetts Institute of Technology, Cambridge, MA (1988-1989); Head, Cataloging, State Library of Massachusetts, Boston, MA (1986-1988); Catalog Librarian, Boston College, Chestnut Hill, MA (1984-1986); Rare Book Cataloger, The John Carter Brown Library, Brown University, Providence, RI (1980-1984); Cataloger, The Rhode Island Historical Society, Providence, RI (1976-1980); Teacher, St. Bernadette's Elementary School, New Haven, CT (1970-1972) **CR:** Bookseller, Assonet Books, Amazon (2013-Present) **CIV:** Chairman, Library Planning Committee, Freetown, MA (2001-Present); Web Master, Freetown Lions Club (2001-Present); Trustee, Board Library Trustees, Freetown, MA (1995-Present); President, Freetown Lions Club (2002-2003, 2013-2014, 2019-2020); Chairman, Board Library Trustees (2013-2019); Treasurer, Freetown Lions Club (2014-2017); First Vice President, Freetown Lions Club (2009-2013); Secretary, Freetown Representative, Town Committee, MA (2008-2012); Chairman, Board Library Trustees (1997-2001) **CW:** Bulletin Editor, Freetown Lions Club (2002-Present) **AW:** Round Table Distinguished Service Award, American Library Association Federal and Armed Services Libraries (Now Federal & Armed Forces Libraries Round Table (FAFLRT)) (2011); Helen Keller Award, Freetown Lions Club (2011) **MEM:** Board of Directors, Massachusetts Library Trustees Association (2012-Present); Armed Forces Director, Federal and Armed Forces, Libraries Round Table, American Library Association (2003-

2013); President, Federal and Armed Forces, Libraries Round Table, American Library Association (1997-1998); Association of College and Research Libraries, American Library Association **B/I:** Ms. Rosa worked part-time in the library while she was an undergraduate. She decided during that time that she liked it and should pursue the field as a career. She became a librarian because when she was going to college, she started working in the catalogue department and after she got her degree, she continued to work there. After she got married, her husband encouraged her to go back to college and get her master's degree in library science. Upon completion, she was able to get professional positions. **PA:** Conservative **RE:** Roman Catholic

ROSE, JOHN WILLIAMS, T: U.S. Representative from Tennessee; Farmer **I:** Government Administration/Government Relations/Government Services **DOB:** 02/23/1965 **PB:** Cookeville **SC:** TN/USA **MS:** Married **SPN:** Chelsea Rose **CH:** One Son **ED:** JD, Vanderbilt University Law School; MS in Agricultural Economics, Purdue University, Lafayette, IN; BS in Agribusiness Economics, Tennessee Technological University **C:** Member, U.S. House of Representatives from Tennessee's Sixth Congressional District (2019-Present); 33rd Agricultural Commissioner, TN (2002-2003); Owner, President, Boson Software and Technology, Boson Holdings, LLC; Founder, Transcender Corporation; Farmer **CIV:** Chairman, Tennessee State Fair Association (2010-Present) **PA:** Republican

ROSE, MAX N., T: U.S. Representative from New York **I:** Government Administration/Government Relations/Government Services **DOB:** 11/28/1986 **PB:** Brooklyn **SC:** NY/USA **MS:** Married **SPN:** Leigh Byrne (2018) **CH:** One Son (Adopted) **ED:** MS in Philosophy and Public Policy, London School of Economics; BA in History, Wesleyan University (2008); Intern, U.S. Senator Cory Booker; Coursework, University of Oxford **C:** Member, U.S. House of Representatives from New York's 11th Congressional District (2019-Present); Director, Public Engagement, Brooklyn District Attorney Kenneth P. Thompson **CIV:** Chief of Staff, Brightpoint Health **MIL:** Captain, United States Army (2010-2015); Company Commander, New York National Guard (2015-Present) **AW:** Purple Heart; Bronze Star Medal; Combat Infantryman Badge; Ranger Tab **PA:** Democrat **RE:** Jewish

ROSE, PETER EDWARD, T: Professional Baseball Player (Retired), Professional Baseball Coach (Retired) **I:** Athletics **DOB:** 04/14/1941 **PB:** Cincinnati **SC:** OH/USA **PT:** Harry Rose; LaVerne Rose **MS:** Partnered **SPN:** Kiana Kim; Carol J. Woliung (1984, Divorced 2011); Karolyn Ann Anglehardt (01/25/1964, Divorced 1980) **CH:** Fawn; Peter; Cara; Tyler **C:** Color Analyst, Fox Sports (2015-2017); Manager, Cincinnati Reds (1986); Professional Baseball Player, Manager, Cincinnati Reds (1984-1986); Professional Baseball Player, Montreal Expos (1984); Professional Baseball Player, Philadelphia Phillies (1979-1983); Professional Baseball Player, Cincinnati Reds (1963-1978) **CW:** Author, "Play Hungry: The Making of a Baseball Player" (2019); Himself, Reality Show, "Pete Rose: Hits & Mrs." (2013); Guest Host, "WWE Raw" (2010); Co-Author, "My Prison Without Bars" (2004); Himself, "WrestleMania," "WrestleMania 2000" (1998-2000); Himself, "Arli$$" (1997); Host, Weekly Radio Show, "Pete Rose on Baseball," WCKY, Cincinnati, OH (1992); Actor, "Babe Ruth" (1991); Co-Author, "Peter Rose: My Story" (1989); Co-Author, "Pete Rose on Hitting" (1985); Co-Author, "Countdown to Cobb: My Diary of the Record Breaking 1985 Season" (1985); Co-Author, "Official Pete Rose Scrapbook"

(1985); Author, "Pete Rose: MY Life in Baseball" (1979); Co-Author, "Pete Rose's Winning Baseball" (1976); Co-Author, "Charlie Hustle" (1975); Guest, Numerous Radio Shows **AW:** Inductee, Cincinnati Reds Hall of Fame (2016); 17-Time All Star (1985, 1973-1982, 1967-1971, 1965); Silver Slugger Award (1981); Roberto Clemente Award (1976); World Series MVP (1975); Three-Time National League Batting Champion (1973, 1969, 1968); National League MVP (1973); Two Gold Glove Awards (1970, 1969); National League Rookie of the Year (1963)

ROSE, RICHARD LOOMIS RICHARD, T: Attorney (Retired) **I:** Law and Legal Services **CN:** Fox Rothschild LLP **DOB:** 10/21/1936 **PB:** Long Branch **SC:** NJ/USA **PT:** Charles Frederick Perrott Rose; Jane Mary (Crotta) Rose **MS:** Married **SPN:** Marian Frances Irons (04/01/1960) **CH:** Linda; Cynthia; Bonnie **ED:** JD, Washington and Lee University (1963); BA, Cornell University (1958) **C:** Attorney (Retired), Principal, Fox Rothschild LLP (2010); Principal, Murtha Cullina LLP (2005-2009); Principal, Roberts & Bates, P.C., Professional Corporation, Stamford, CT (1995-2005); Of Counsel, Whitman Breed Abbott & Morgan LLC, Greenwich, CT (1993-1995); Partner, Kleban & Samor, P.C., Southport, CT (1991-1993); Partner, Cummings & Lockwood LLC, Stamford, CT (1965-1991) **CR:** Member, Advisory Committee, Connecticut Banking Commissioner on Connecticut Securities Laws (1982-Present); Member, Board of Directors, Connecticut World Trade Association **CIV:** Board of Directors, New Canaan Preservation Alliance, Inc. (2007-Present); Commissioner, New Canaan Historic District Commission (1995-Present); Board of Directors, German School of Connecticut, Inc. (1992-Present); Chairman, Foreign Trade Zone Committee to Mayor of City of Bridgeport, CT (1988-1990); Member, Foreign Trade Awareness Committee, Southwest Area Industry and Commerce Association, Task Force (1987-1988) **MIL:** 1st Lt., U.S. Army, Korea (1958-1960) **CW:** Editor, "Washington and Lee Law Review" **MEM:** American Bar Association; Executive Committee, Business Law Section, Connecticut Bar Association; International Bar Association; New Canaan Country Club; Gridiron Club of New Canaan; Poinsettia Club of New Canaan; Phi Delta Phi; Omicron Delta Kappa; Phi Delta Theta **BAR:** Admitted to Practice, Supreme Court of the United States (1970); Admitted to Practice, Connecticut Bar Association (1966); Admitted to Practice, U.S. District Court for the District of Connecticut (1966); Admitted to Practice, U.S. District Court for the Eastern District of New York (1965); Admitted to Practice, U.S. Court of Appeals for the Second Circuit (1965); Admitted to Practice, U.S. District Court for the South District of New York (1964); Admitted to Practice, New York State Bar Association (1963) **MH:** Albert Nelson Marquis Lifetime Achievement Award **PA:** Republican **RE:** Episcopal **THT:**

ROSEMAN, CHARLES S., T: Lawyer **I:** Law and Legal Services **DOB:** 02/26/1945 **PB:** Jersey City **SC:** NJ/USA **PT:** Leon; Edith (Neidorf) R. **MS:** Single **ED:** Doctor of Jurisprudence, University of San Diego (1971); Bachelor of Arts, California State University, Northridge (1968) **C:** Founding Partner, Roseman Dispute Resolution & Arbitration Mediation Services (2009-Present); Private Practice, San Diego, CA (1971-1978, 1992-Present); Also Arbitrator, Mediator (1977-Present); Judge Pro Tempore, San Diego County Superior Court (1975-Present); Founding Partner, I2I Resolutions (2001); Partner, Roseman And Mann (1986-1992); Partner, Frank, Roseman, Freedus & Mann, San Diego, CA (1982-1986); Partner, Roseman & Small, San Diego, CA (1978-1982); Partner, Roseman & Roseman, San Diego, CA (1973-1978); Associate,

Greer, Popko, Nickoloff & Miller, San Diego, CA (1972-1973) **CIV:** Board of Directors, San Diego County Anti-Defamation League (1985-Present); Homeys Youth Foundation (2002-2006); Board of Directors, San Diego County Legal Aid Society (1988-1989); President, Tifereth Israel Synagogue (1982-1984); Big Brothers San Diego County (1973-1981); Board of Directors, Glenn Aire Community Development Association, San Diego (1972-1973) **AW:** Recognition of Experience Award, Consumer Attorneys of California (1985) **MEM:** Arbitrator, American Arbitration Association (1985-1986); Board of Directors, Consumer Attorneys of San Diego (1982-1984); President, B'nai B'rith (1978); Board of Directors, University of San Diego School Law Alumni Association (1972-1973); San Diego Bar Association; American Bar Association; American Association for Justice; Federal Bar Association; Consumer Attorneys of California; California Bar Association **BAR:** United States Court of Claims (1990); Supreme Court of the United States (1980); United States District Court for the Central District of California (1975); United States District Court for the Southern District of California (1972); California (1972) **MH:** Albert Nelson Marquis Lifetime Achievement Award **PA:** Democrat

ROSEN, JACKLYN, "JACKY" SHERYL, T: U.S. Senator from Nevada **I:** Government Administration/Government Relations/Government Services **CN:** U.S. Senate **DOB:** 08/02/1957 **PB:** Chicago **SC:** IL/USA **PT:** Leonard Spektor; Carol Spektor **MS:** Married **SPN:** Larry Rosen (1993); Lloyd Dean Neher (Divorced) **CH:** Miranda Rosen **ED:** Bachelor of Arts in Psychology, University of Minnesota, Minneapolis (1979); Associate of Applied Science in Computing and Information Technology, Clark County Community College (1985) **C:** U.S. Senator, State of Nevada (2019-Present); Member, U.S. House of Representatives from Nevada's Third Congressional District (2017-2019); Owner, Consulting Business (1993); With, Southwest Gas (1990-1993); Member, Committee on Armed Services; Member, Committee on Science, Space, and Technology; With, Summa Corporation **PA:** Democrat

ROSEN, JEFFREY ADAM, T: United States Deputy Attorney General **I:** Law and Legal Services **CN:** U.S. Department of Justice **DOB:** 04/02/1958 **PB:** Boston **SC:** MA/USA **MS:** Married **SPN:** Kathleen Nichols Rosen, MD (05/29/1982) **CH:** Three Children **ED:** JD, Harvard Law School, Cambridge, MA, Magna Cum Laude (1982); BA in Economics, Northwestern University, With Highest Distinction (1979) **C:** United States Deputy Attorney General, U.S. Department of Justice (2019-Present); United States Deputy Secretary of Transportation, U.S. Department of Transportation (2017-2019); Senior Litigation Partner, Kirkland & Ellis LLP, Washington, DC (2009-2017); General Counsel, Senior Policy Advisor, Office of Management and Budget, Executive Office of the President, Washington, DC (2006-2009); General Counsel, U.S. Department of Transportation, Washington, DC (2003-2006); Partner, Kirkland & Ellis LLP, Washington, DC (1988-2003); Associate, Kirkland & Ellis LLP, Washington, DC (1982-1988) **CR:** Board of Directors, Amtrak (2005-2006); Adjunct Professor, Georgetown University Law Center (1998-2003) **CIV:** Board of Visitors, Northwestern University Weinberg College of Arts & Sciences (2009-2017); Arlington County Historical Affairs and Landmark Review Board (1991-1993) **CW:** Co-Author, "The Regulatory Budget Revisited" (2014) **AW:** Washington DC Super Lawyer (2012-2016) **MEM:** Chair, Section of Administrative Law and Regulatory Practice, ABA (2015-2016); Virginia Historical Society; Supreme Court Historical Society; The American Law Institute **BAR:** United States Court of Appeals for the Third

Circuit (1996); United States Court of Appeals for the Sixth Circuit (1990); United States Court of Appeals for the 11th Circuit (1988); Supreme Court of the United States (1986); United States Court of Appeals for the District of Columbia Circuit (1983); United States Court of Appeals for the Federal Circuit (1983); United States District Court for the District of Columbia (1983); The District of Columbia Bar (1982); United States Court of Appeals for the Fourth Circuit; United States District Court for the Northern District of Illinois; United States District Court for the Eastern District of Michigan **PA:** Republican

ROSEN, NATHAN AARON JD, MLS, T: Law Librarian, Lawyer, Consultant **I:** Law and Legal Services **DOB:** 09/12/1955 **PB:** Kansas City **SC:** MO/USA **PT:** Emanuel Rosen; Golda (Singer) Rosen **MS:** Married **SPN:** Priva Hannah Simon (10/27/1985) **ED:** MLS, Columbia University (1984); JD, University of Missouri (1979); BA, University of Missouri (1977) **CT:** U.S. Supreme Court (1989); U.S. District Court for the Western District of Missouri (1980); U.S. Court of Appeals for the Eighth Circuit (1980); U.S. Tax Court (1980) **C:** Associate Director, Library, Proskauer, Rose, Goetz & Mendelsohn, New York, NY (1984-Present); Associate, Charles, House & Associates, Kansas City, MO (1982-1984); Associate, Martin, Gorin & Associates, Kansas City, MO (1980-1982); Manager of Research & Knowledge Services, Herrick, Feinstein LLP LAC Group;Library Research Manager, Dechert LLP; Information Resources Manager - New York, Morrison & Foerster LLP; Vice President, Legal & Compliance Department, Credit Suisse; Director of Library & Technology Center, Association of the Bar of the City of New York **CR:** Consultant, Law Research Institute Inc., New York, NY, and Kansas City, MO (1980-Present) **CW:** Speaker, SLA, LLAGNY, AALL, NYPL, ILTA, & ALA; Contributor, Articles, Professional Journals **AW:** New Jersey State Professional Librarian Certificate; New York State Public Librarian Certificate **MEM:** American Association of Law Libraries; Law Library Association of Greater New York; Special Libraries Association **BAR:** Missouri (1980) **MH:** Albert Nelson Marquis Lifetime Achievement Award **AV:** Toastmasters International

ROSENBERG, HOWARD, T: Founder, Chief Executive Officer **I:** Other **CN:** B-Stock Solutions, LLC **MS:** Married **CH:** Two Children **ED:** MBA, Harvard Business School, Cambridge, MA (1999); BS in Economics, The Wharton School, The University of Pennsylvania, Philadelphia, PA (1989); Diploma, Hingham High School (1985) **C:** Founder, Chief Executive Officer, B-Stock Solutions, LLC (2009-Present); Advisory Board Member, The Talk Market (2008-Present); Advisory Board Member, Reverse Logistics Association (2004-2008); General Manager, Private Marketplaces, eBay Inc. (2002-2008); Chief Executive Officer, President, Always Independent Entertainment (2000-2001); President, Scott Street Ventures (1999-2000); Vice President, Senior Associate, Rosewood Capital (1992-1997); Finance Analyst, Blackstone Group (1990-1991)

ROSENSTEIN, ROBERT A., PHD, T: Scientific Consultant **I:** Consulting **DOB:** 07/12/1938 **PB:** Chicago **SC:** IL/USA **PT:** Milton W. Rosenstein; Gale (Blacher) Rosenstein **MS:** Single **CH:** Daniel Jeremy **ED:** PhD in Theoretical Physical Chemistry, Northwestern University (1970);BS in Chemistry, University of Illinois, With Honors (1961) **C:** PI Solid State Hydrogen Storage, Green Fortress Engineering (2017); Science Consultant, Chicago, IL (1982-2016); Application Programmer, Nuclear Data (1981-1982); Coatings Engineer, VRWesson (1979-1980); Senior Research Chemist, Armak Research Laboratory (Now Akzo Chemie

USA) (1977-1979); Consultant, Chicago, IL (1972-1976); Research Associate, Technical University of Munich (1970-1972); Aerospace Technologist, Lewis Research Center, NASA (1961-1964); Tutor, Community College **CR:** National Space Society (2017-Present); The Chicago Council on Science and Technology (2008-Present); Topical Group Organizer, Chicago Section, American Chemical Society (2007-2012); Member-At-Large, Prairie Section, American Physical Society (2008-2010); President, The Chemists Club (1986-1987); Consultant, Commission on Solubility Data, IUPAC (1978-1987) **CIV:** JCFS Chicago (1975-1998); Jewish Council on Urban Affairs; AARP; Founding Member, Chicago Public School Alumni Association **AW:** Predoctoral Fellow, National Institutes of Health (1967) **MEM:** Chicago Section, American Chemical Society; American Physical Society; The Chicago Council on Science and Technology; Union of Concerned Scientists; Sierra Club; Green America; National Space Society; University of Illinois Alumni Association; Northwestern Alumni Association **MH:** Albert Nelson Marquis Lifetime Achievement Award; Marquis Who's Who Top Professional **B/I:** Dr. Rosenstein became involved in his profession because he wanted to understand the forces of nature. **AV:** Studying History; Remaining up to date on current events; Listening to Wagnerian opera

ROSENSTEIN, ROD JAY, T: Former United States Deputy Attorney General; Lawyer **I:** Law and Legal Services **DOB:** 01/13/1965 **PB:** Philadelphia **SC:** PA/USA **PT:** Robert Jacob Rosenstein; Gerry M. (Stoloff) Rosenstein **MS:** Married **SPN:** Lisa (Barsoomian) Rosenstein **CH:** Two Children **ED:** JD, Harvard Law School (1989); BS in Economics, University of Pennsylvania, Philadelphia, PA (1986) **C:** Partner, Special Matters and Government, King & Spalding LLP, Washington, DC (2020-Present); United States Deputy Attorney General, Washington, DC (2017-2019); U.S. Attorney, District of Maryland, U.S. Department of Justice, Baltimore, MD (2005-2017); Principal Deputy Assistant Attorney General, Tax Division, U.S. Department of Justice, Washington, DC (2002-2005); Deputy Assistant Attorney General, Criminal Matters, U.S. Department of Justice, Washington, DC (2001-2002); Assistant U.S. Attorney, District of Maryland, U.S. Department of Justice, Washington, DC (1997-2001); Associate Counsel, Office of Independent Counsel, Washington, DC (1995-1997); Special Assistant, Criminal Division, U.S. Department of Justice, Washington, DC (1994-1995); Counsel to Deputy Attorney General, U.S. Department of Justice, Washington, DC (1993-1994); Trial Attorney, Public Integrity Section, Washington, DC (1990-1993); Law Clerk to Honorable Douglas H. Ginsburg, United States Court of Appeals for the District of Columbia Circuit, Washington, DC (1989-1990) **CR:** Adjunct Professor, University of Baltimore School of Law and University of Maryland School of Law **CIV:** Temple Sinai, Washington, DC (2008-2014); Board of Directors, United States Holocaust Memorial Museum (2001-2011) **BAR:** United States Court of Appeals for the First Circuit (2004); United States Court of Appeals for the Second Circuit (2004); United States Court of Appeals for the Tenth Circuit (2004); United States Court of Appeals for the Eleventh Circuit (2004); United States Tax Court (2003); United States Court of Appeals for the Eighth Circuit (2003); State of Maryland (2002); Supreme Court of the United States (2002); United States Court of Appeals for the Fourth Circuit (1998); United States Court of Appeals for the Ninth Circuit (1992); United States Court of Appeals for the Fifth Circuit (1991); The

District of Columbia (1992); United States Court of Appeals for the District of Columbia (1990); Pennsylvania (1989); **RE:** Jewish

ROSENZWEIG, RACHEL ZOE, T: Fashion Stylist **I:** Apparel & Fashion **DOB:** 09/01/1971 **PB:** New York **SC:** NY/USA **PT:** Ron Rosenzweig; Leslie Rosenzweig **MS:** Married **SPN:** Rodger Berman **CH:** Skyler Morrison; Kaius Jagger **ED:** Diploma in Psychology and Sociology, George Washington University (1993); Diploma, Millburn High School **C:** Collaboration, Lindex (2011); Launched, Clothing Line, Rachel Zoe Collection (2011); Launched, RZ Accessories Line (2009); Fashion Stylist, Various Celebrities Including Cameron Diaz, Jennifer Garner, Kate Hudson, Kate Beckinsale, Debra Messing, Demi Moore, Liv Tyler, Joy Bryant, Molly Sims, Beau Garett, Eva Mendes, Paula Patton, Anne Hathaway, Jennifer Lawrence, Miley Cyrus, Pauly Shore **CR:** Founder, "The Zoe Report" (2009-2019); Collaborator, Quinny and Maxi-Cosi, Dorel Juvenile Group USA (2016); Launched, Box of Style, CURATEUR (2015); Founder, Zoe Beautiful (2011); Consultant, Piperlime.com; Collaborator, Line of Bags, Judith Leiber; Spokeswoman, BlackJack Cell Phone National Ad Campaign, Samsung; Launched, Luxe Rachel Zoe, QVC; Co-founder, DreamDry; Founder, Newsletters; Founder, AccessZOEries **CW:** Host, "Fashionably Late with Rachel Zoe" (2015); Author, "Living in Style: Inspiration and Advice for Everyday Glamour" (2014); Executive Producer, "The Rachel Zoe Project" (2008-2013); Appearance, "Entourage" (2011); Appearance, "America's Next Top Model" (2006, 2011); Co-author, "Style A to Zoe: The Art of Fashion, Beauty and Everything Glamour" (2007); Appearance, "Project Runway" (2006); Appearance, "The Simple Life" (2006)

ROSS, DIANA, T: Singer; Actress; Entertainer; Fashion Designer **I:** Media & Entertainment **DOB:** 03/26/1944 **PB:** Detroit **SC:** MI/USA **PT:** Fred Ross Sr.; Ernestine Ross **MS:** Divorced **SPN:** Arne Næss Jr. (10/23/1985, Divorced 2000); Robert Ellis Silberstein (1971, Divorced 1976) **CH:** Tracee Ellis Ross; Evan Ross; Rhonda Ross Kendrick; Ross Naess; Chudney Ross **C:** Founder, Owner, President, Diana Ross Enterprises, Inc.; President, Rossville Music; President, Diana Ross Charitable Foundation; President, RTC Management Corporation; President, Chondee, Inc.; President, Rosstown, Inc.; President, Rossville, Inc. **CR:** Performer, Mini-residency, Wynn Las Vegas Hotel & Casino, Wynn Resorts Holdings, LLC (2018-Present) **CW:** Singer, Album, "I Love You" (2006); Singer, Album, "Blue" (2006); Author, "Diana Ross: Going Back" (2002); Singer, Album, "Every Day Is a New Day" (1999); Actress, "Double Platinum" (1999); Author, "When You Dream" (1995); Singer, Album, "Take Me Higher" (1995); Singer, Album, "A Very Special Season" (1994); Actress, "Out of Darkness" (1994); Author, "Secrets of a Sparrow" (1993); Singer, Live Album, "Stolen Moments: The Lady Sings... Jazz and Blues" (1993); Singer, Live Album, "Christmas in Vienna" (1993); Singer, Album, "The Force Behind the Power" (1991); Singer, Album, "Workin' Overtime" (1989); Singer, Live Album, "Greatest Hits Live" (1989); Singer, Album, "Red Hot Rhythm & Blues" (1987); Singer, Album, "Eaten Alive" (1984); Singer, Album, "Swept Away" (1984); Singer, Album, "Ross" (1983); Singer, Album, "Silk Electric" (1982); Singer, Album, "Why Do Fools Fall in Love" (1981); Singer, Soundtrack Album, "Endless Love: Original Motion Picture Soundtrack" (1981); Singer, Album, "Diana" (1980); Actress, "The Wiz" (1978); Singer, Soundtrack Album, "The Wiz" (1978); Singer, Album, "Baby It's Me" (1977); Singer, Live Album, "An Evening with Diana Ross" (1977); Singer, Album, "Diana Ross" (1976); Actress, "Mahogany" (1975); Singer, Soundtrack

Album, "Mahogany" (1975); Singer, Live Album, "Live at Caesars Palace" (1974); Singer, Album, "Last Time I Saw Him" (1973); Singer, Album, "Diana & Marvin" (1973); Singer, Album, "Touch Me in the Morning" (1973); Actress, "Lady Sings the Blues" (1972); Singer, Soundtrack Album, "Lady Sings the Blues" (1972); Singer, Album, "Surrender" (1971); Singer, Soundtrack Album, "Diana!" (1971); Singer, Album, "Everything Is Everything" (1970); Singer, Album, "Diana Ross" (1970); Singer, The Supremes, Album, "The Supremes Sing Rodgers & Hart" (1967); Singer, The Supremes, Album, "The Supremes Sing Holland-Dozier-Holland" (1967); Singer, The Supremes, Album, "The Supremes A' Go-Go" (1966); Singer, The Supremes, Album, "Merry Christmas" (1965); Singer, The Supremes, Album, "More Hits by The Supremes" (1965); Singer, The Supremes, Album, "We Remember Sam Cooke" (1965); Singer, The Supremes, Album, "The Supremes Sing Country, Western and Pop" (1965); Singer, The Supremes, Album, "A Bit of Liverpool" (1964); Singer, The Supremes, Album, "Where Did Our Love Go" (1964); Singer, The Supremes, Album, "Meet the Supremes" (1962); Singer, Member, The Primettes; Performer, Numerous Tours and Residency Shows; Appearances/Performer, Numerous Television Shows and Events **AW:** Lifetime Achievement Award, American Music Awards (2017); Honoree, Presidential Medal of Freedom (2016); YMA Awards of Excellence, Youth Media Alliance (2015); Lifetime Achievement Award, Grammy Awards, Recording Academy (2012); Honoree, Kennedy Center Honors, John F. Kennedy Center for the Performing Arts (2007); Lifetime Achievement Award, BET Music Awards (2007); Named Most Memorable TV Performance, "1983 Concert in Central Park," TV Land Awards (2006); Lifetime Achievement Award, National Association of Black Owned Broadcasters (2003); Named Legendary Female Artist, UK Capital Awards (2003); Heroes Award, National Academy of Recording Arts and Sciences (NARAS) (Now Recording Academy) (1999); Honoree, Star, BET Walk of Fame (1999); The Hitmaker Award, Songwriters Hall of Fame (1998); Inductee, Soul Train Hall of Fame (1996); Named Female Entertainer of the Century, Billboard Magazine (1996); Heritage Award, Soul Train Music Awards (1995); Honoree, Commander of the Order of Arts and Letters (1994); Lifetime Achievement Award, MIDEM (World Music Market) (1994); Recipient, (as a Member of The Supremes), Star, Hollywood Walk of Fame (1994); Named Most Successful Female Singer of All Time, Guinness Book of World Records (1993); Inductee, The Supremes, Rock and Roll Hall of Fame (1988); Named Song of the Year, "We Are the World," American Music Awards (1986); Named Favorite New Song, "We Are the World," People's Choice Awards (1986); Viewer's Choice, "We Are the World," MTV Video Music Awards (1985); Named Favorite Pop/Rock Female, "Endless Love," American Music Awards (1983); Recipient, Star, Hollywood Walk of Fame (1982); Named Favorite R&B Female, American Music Awards (1981); Named Favorite Soul/R&B Single, American Music Awards (1981); Award for General Entertainment (Music), Cable Ace Awards (1981); Special Tony Award, "An Evening with Diana Ross," Tony Awards (1977); Named Female Entertainer of the Century, "Diana Ross," Billboard Awards (1976); Favorite R&B Female, "Last Time I Saw Him," American Music Awards (1975); Named Favorite Pop/Rock Album, "Lady Sing the Blues," American Music Awards (1974); Golden Globe for Most Promising Newcomer, Female, "Diana Ross," Hollywood Foreign Press Association (1973); Named Entertainer of the Year, "Diana Ross," Cue Magazine (1973); Named Female Entertainer of the Year, "Diana Ross," NAACP Image Awards (1970)

ROSS, IVY E., T: Apparel Executive, Artist **I:** Retail/Sales **CN:** Google **PB:** Yonkers **SC:** NY/USA **ED:** Professional Management Development Program, Harvard Business School (1994); Coursework in Jewelry Design, Fashion Institute of Technology; Coursework in Industrial Design, Syracuse University School of Design; Diploma in Fine Art and Psychology, High School of Art and Design **C:** Senior Vice President, Chief Creative Officer, Disney Store North America (2007-Present); Executive Vice President, Product Design & Development, Old Navy Brand, Gap, Inc. (2004-2007); Senior Vice President, Design, Mattel, Inc.; Various Positions, Bausch & Lomb, Victoria's Secret, Swatch Watch, Calvin Klein, Liz Claiborne, Coach **CR:** Lecturer, Workshops, Rhode Island School of Design, Philadelphia College of Art, Fashion Institute of Technology, Cooper-Hewitt Museum, Montreal Visual Arts Center **CW:** Permanent Collections, Smithsonian Institute, Victoria and Albert Museum London, Cooper-Hewitt Museum; Contributor, Chapters, Books **AW:** Named, 25 Masters of Innovation, BusinessWeek; Diamond International Award, Women in Design Awards; National Endowment for the Arts Grant

ROSS, STEPHEN MICHAEL, T: Real Estate Company Executive, Professional Sports Team Owner **I:** Real Estate **DOB:** 05/10/1940 **PB:** Detroit **SC:** MI/USA **MS:** Married **SPN:** Kara Ross **ED:** LLM in Taxation, New York University (1966); JD, Wayne State University (1965); BS, University of Michigan (1962) **C:** Principal Owner, Miami Dolphins and Dolphin Stadium (Now Hard Rock Stadium) (2008-Present); Founder, Chairman, Chief Executive Officer, Related, New York, NY (1972-Present); Co-Owner, Miami Dolphins (2008-2009); Founder, Director, Charter Municipal Mortgage Acceptance Company; Director, Insignia Financial Group, Inc.; Tax Attorney, Coopers & Lybrand, Detroit, MI **CR:** Chairperson Emeritus, Real Estate Board of New York; Owner, Equinox Fitness Clubs; Co-Owner, Kangaroo Media **CIV:** Member, Board of Trustees, The Solomon R. Guggenheim Foundation; Trustee, New York Presbyterian Hospital; Trustee, Urban Land Institute; Trustee, New York Chapter, JDRF; Trustee, Levin Institute; Director, Jackie Robinson Foundation; Director, World Resources Institute; Chairman, Board of Trustees, Centerline Holding Company; Trustee, National Building Museum; Trustee, Lincoln Center **AW:** Richest Americans, Forbes 400 (2006-Present); The Harry B. Helmsley Distinguished New Yorker Award, Real Estate Board of New York (2005); Jack D. Weiler Award, United Jewish Appeal (2003); One of The 100 Most Influential Leaders in Business, Crain's New York Business (2002); Leadership in Tourism Award, New York & Company (2002); Henry Pearce Award, Jewish Association for Services for the Aged (2001); Owner & Developer of the Year, New York Construction News (2000); "What New York Needs" Award, The Dow Fund (1999); Tree of Life Award (1998); Housing Person of the Year, National Housing Conference; Numerous Honors and Accolades for Business, Civic, and Philanthropic Efforts **MEM:** Director, Real Estate Board of New York

ROSS, WILBUR LOUIS JR., T: United States Secretary of Commerce **I:** Government Administration/Government Relations/Government Services **DOB:** 11/28/1937 **PB:** Weehawken **SC:** NJ/USA **PT:** Wilbur Louis Ross; Agnes (O'Neill) Ross **MS:** Married **SPN:** Hilary Geary (10/09/2004); Betsy McCaughey (12/07/1995, Divorced 2000); Judith Nodine (05/26/1961, Divorced 1995) **CH:** Jessica; Amanda **ED:** MBA, Harvard Business School, with Distinction (1961); BA in English Literature, Yale University (1959) **C:** United States Secretary of

Commerce, U.S. Department of Commerce, Washington, DC (2017-Present); Chairman, Chief Executive Officer, W.L. Ross & Co., LLC, New York, NY (2000-2017); Chairman, Chief Investment Officer, Rothschild Recovery Fund, New York, NY (1997-2000); Senior Managing Director, Rothschild, Inc., New York, NY (1976-2000); Chief Executive Officer, News Communications Inc., New York, NY (1996-1998); President, Faulkner, Dawkins and Sullivan Securities Corp., New York, NY (1964-1976); Associate, Wood, Struthers & Winthrop, New York, NY (1963-1964) **CR:** Director, Ocluen Financial Corporation (2013-Present); Board of Directors, Talmer Bancorp, Inc. (2010-Present); Board of Directors, Sun Bancorp Inc. (2010-Present); Board of Directors, BankUnited Inc. (2009-Present); Board of Directors, International Textile Group (2005-Present); Board of Directors, Arcelor Mittal Steel Co. (2005-Present); Board of Directors, Ohizumi Manufacturing Co., Japan (2003-Present); Board of Directors, Burlington Industries (2003-Present); Board of Directors, Air Lease Corporation (2010-2013); Board of Directors, The Greenbrier Companies Inc. (2009-2013); Board of Directors, International Coal Group (2005-2011); Board of Directors, Montpelier Re Holdings, Ltd. (2006-2010); Board of Directors, Wagon, PLC (2006-2008); Board of Directors, Marquis Who's Who Inc. (2004-2006); Board of Directors, Mittal Steel Co. (Now ArcelorMittal S.A.), Japan (2004-2006); Board of Directors, Marquis Who's Who LLC (2003-2006); Board of Directors, International Steel Group, Inc., Cleveland, Ohio (2002-2004); Board of Directors, Casella Waste Systems Inc. (1999-2003) **CIV:** Chairman, Economic Studies Council, The Brookings Institution (2011-Present); Chairman, Japan Society (2010-Present); Board Advisor, Yale University School of Management (2009-Present); Board of Directors, Turnaround Management Association (2001-Present); American Art Forum, Smithsonian Institution (1987-Present); Chairman, Absolute Recovery Hedge Fund, Ltd., Hamilton, Bermuda, Taiyo Fund (2003-2013); Japan Real Estate Recovery Fund (2003-2008); Chairman, Board, Smithsonian Institute National Board (1995); The New Museum (New Museum of Contemporary Art) (1993-1995); American Federation of Arts (1993-1995); President, Parrish Art Museum (1991-1995); Vice Chairman, Brooklyn Museum (1981-1995); Chairman, National Museum of American Art (Smithsonian American Art Museum), Washington, DC (1991-1994); Trustee, Vice Chairman, National Museum of American Art (Smithsonian American Art Museum), Washington, DC (1986-1991); Trustee, Sarah Lawrence College (1986-1991); Chairman, National Academy of Design, New York, NY (1985-1989); Chairman, University Council Committee on Art, Yale University (1983-1988); Treasurer, New York State Democratic Committee (1980-1983); Trustee, Museum of American Financial History; Board Advisor, Harvard Business School; National Museum of American Financial History; Whitney Museum of American Art; Preservation Foundation of Palm Beach; Yale University School of Management; Committee on University Relations, Harvard University; Committee on Capital Markets Regulation, Harvard University; Contributor, $10 Million, Yale School of Management **MIL:** First Lieutenant, U.S. Army (1961-1963) **AW:** Listee, Forbes 400: Richest Americans (2006-Present); Medal of the Order of the Rising Sun, Gold and Silver Star, Ambassador Sumio Kusaka (2015); Listee, 50 Most Influential People in Global Finance, Bloomberg Markets (2011); Legend in Leadership Award, Yale School of Management (2005); Order of Industrial Service Merit Medal, South Korea President Kim Dae Jung **MEM:** Fellow, Jonathan Edwards College, Yale University; Chartered Member, Financial Analysts Fed-

eration; Sterling Fellow, Yale University; Business Roundtable; Bath and Tennis Club; Everglades Club; Board of Directors, Harvard Business School Club of New York; Beach Club **AV:** Collecting art

ROTCH, JAMES, T: Attorney/Shareholder **I:** Law and Legal Services **CN:** Maynard Cooper & Gale **DOB:** 03/26/1945 **PB:** Auburn **SC:** AL/USA **PT:** Elroy B. Rotch; Martha (Ellisor) Rotch **MS:** Married **SPN:** Darlene Edwards (06/26/1999) **CH:** Jamison B.; Susannah R.; Amie L. Vaughn **ED:** JD, University of Virginia School of Law (1971); Postgraduate Coursework, Auburn University (1967-1968); BS, Auburn University (1967) **C:** Attorney/Shareholder, Maynard Cooper & Gale (2018-Present); Partner, Bradley, Arant, Rose & White Llp, Birmingham, AL (1976-Present); Administrative Partner, Bradley, Arant, Rose & White Llp, Birmingham, AL (1990-1993); Associate, Bradley Arant Rose & White Llp, Birmingham, AL (1971-1976); Clerk, U.S. Judiciary System, Birmingham, AL (1971-1972); Research Assistant, Office of Institutional Research, Auburn University (1967-1968); Chairman, Board of Directors, Kaleidoscope Productions, Inc. **CR:** Advisory Committee, Bioelastics Research Ltd., Birmingham, AL (1992-Present); Governor's Task Force on Biotechnology (1993) **CIV:** Chairman, Birmingham Pledge Foundation (2000-Present); Entrepreneurial Center Inc. (1996-Present); Board of Directors, Operation New Birmingham (1990-Present); Co-Chairman, Community Affairs Committee, Coalition for Better Education, Birmingham, AL (1990-Present); Alabama Sports Foundation (1994-1998); Board of Directors, Birmingham Committee for Olympic Soccer (1994-1996); Boy Scouts of America; Administrative Board, Canterbury United Methodist Church (1991-1993); President, Advisory Committee, Birmingham Museum of Art (1989-1992); Chairman, Birmingham Area Tech Leadership Alliance **MIL:** Captain, U.S. Army Reserve (1972-1978) **CW:** Author, "The Birmingham Pledge" (1997) **AW:** Listee, The Best Lawyers in America (2016-Present); Mergers & Acquisitions Law, The Best Lawyers in America (2010-Present); Listee, Corporate Law, The Best Lawyers in America (2006-Present); AV Preeminent Rated, Martindale-Hubbell; Alabama Super Lawyers in Business/Corporate Law (2008-2010); Birmingham Civil Rights Institute Appreciation Award (2009); National Conference for Community and Justice Award (2007); Birmingham Bar Burton Barnes Award (2006); Listee, Men of Substance and Style, Birmingham Business (2004); Communicator of the Year, Birmingham Business Journal (2001); Liberty and Justice Lifetime Achievement Award (2000); Operation New Birmingham Outstanding Achievement Award (1999); Alabama State Bar, Award of Merit (1999); Exceptional Leadership Award, Kiwanis Club of Birmingham (1999) **MEM:** Board of Directors, Leadership Alabama (1998-Present); Board of Directors, Birmingham Regional Chamber of Commerce (2001-2005); Board of Directors, Birmingham Venture Club (2001); American Library Association; Auburn University Bar Association; Birmingham Bar Association; International Bar Association; Alabama State Bar Association; Leadership Birmingham; Advisory Council, Auburn College of Liberal Arts; University of Virginia Alumni Association; Newcomen Society; Auburn University Alumni Association; Country Club of Birmingham; Jockey Club; Summit Club; Kiwanis **BAR:** U.S. District Court for the Northern District of Alabama (1973); Alabama (1971) **MH:** Albert Nelson Marquis Lifetime Achievement Award **AV:** Riding horses; Bird hunting; Cattle farming; Golfing **RE:** Methodist

ROTH, GEORGIA ANN MIDDLEBROOKS, T: Accounting and Business Law Educator (Retired) **I:** Education/Educational Services **DOB:** 12/08/1937 **PB:** Henderson **SC:** TX/USA **PT:** Melvin Todd Middlebrooks; Dorothy (Baxter) Middlebrooks **MS:** Widow **SPN:** Charles Nelson Roth (Married 08/16/1958, Deceased 04/10/18) **CH:** Stuart Todd; Douglas Spicer; Charles Rankine **ED:** Master of Business Administration, University of Arkansas (1961); Bachelor of Science in Business Administration, Science of Business Administration, University of Arkansas, Cum Laude (1959) **C:** Associate Professor, Accounting, Jackson State Community College (1974-2005); Assistant Professor, Accounting, Lambuth University, Jackson (1969-1971); Teacher, Accounting, Union University, Jackson, TN (1965-1969); Teacher, Accounting, Centenary College, Shreveport (1962-1965); Staff, Hancock Mazo and Company, Savannah, GA (1959-1960) **CR:** Faculty Member Representative, Tennessee State Board Regents (1985-1986); Advisor Students, Free Enterprise, Jackson, MO (1998-1999); College Orientation Instructor (1989-1999); Certified Professional Secretaries Review Instructor (1979-1999); Chairman, Business Department, Jackson State Community College (1990-1993); Commencement Speaker (1989); Chairman, Faculty Council (1985-1986); Attendee, 16th Annual International Conference on Teaching Excellence, Austin, TX **CIV:** Debutante Ball Chair (1985); Jackson Service League (1972-1974); Jackson Symphony League (1971); Jackson Cotillion Club (1967-1969); President, Jackson Newcomers Club (1966-1968); Chairman, Symphony Ball; Jackson Symphony League **CW:** Poet, "Lives Changed Forever for 9/11" (2002) **AW:** Excellence Award, National Institute of Staff and Organizational Development (2005); JSCC Excellence Teaching Award (2005); Sam Walton Free Enterprise Fellow (1998-1999); Outstanding Faculty Award, JSCC Student Government Association (1993) **MEM:** Beta Gamma Sigma (1959); Epsilon (1956); Teachers of Accounting in 2-Year Colleges; Zeta Tau Alpha **MH:** Albert Nelson Marquis Lifetime Achievement Award **AS:** Ms. Roth enjoyed every day that she stepped into the classroom. **B/I:** Ms. Roth's parents were both accountants. She has always liked numbers and mathematics. **AV:** Playing tennis and bridge; Poetry; Growing roses; Researching genealogy; Practicing photography; Antique collecting; Caring for dogs **PA:** Republican **RE:** Methodist

ROTH, PHILIP MILTON, T: Author; Professor **I:** Writing and Editing **DOB:** 03/19/1933 **PB:** Newark **SC:** NJ/USA **PT:** Herman Roth; Bess (Finkel) Roth **MS:** Divorced **SPN:** Claire Bloom (04/29/1990, Divorced 1994); Margaret Martinson (02/22/1959, Deceased 1968) **ED:** Honorary Doctorate, Jewish Theological Seminary of America (2014); Honorary LittD, Harvard University (2003); Honorary LHD, University of Pennsylvania (2003); Honorary LittD, Brown University (2001); Honorary LHD, Rutgers, The State University of New Jersey (1987); Honorary LHD, Columbia University (1987); Honorary LittD, Bard College (1985); Honorary Doctorate, Bucknell University (1979); MA in English Literature, The University of Chicago (1955); AB in English, Bucknell University (1954); Coursework, Rutgers, The State University of New Jersey **C:** Retired, University of Pennsylvania (1991); Adjunct Professor, Comparative Literature, University of Pennsylvania (1967-1991); Writer-in-Residence, Princeton University (1962-1964); Faculty, Iowa Writers Workshop (1960-1962); English Teacher, The University of Chicago (1956-1958) **CR:** Distinguished Professor, City University of New York Hunter College (1989-1992) **CW:** Author, "Nemesis" (2010); Author, "The Humbling" (2009); Author, "Indignation" (2008);

Author, "Exit Ghost" (2007); Author, "Everyman" (2006); Author, "The Plot Against America" (2004); Author, "The Dying Animal" (2001); Author, "Shop Talk" (2001); Author, "The Human Stain" (2000); Author, "I Married a Communist" (1998); Author, "American Pastoral" (1997); Author, "Sabbath's Theater" (1995); Author, "Operation Shylock: A Confession" (1993); Author, Memoir, "Patrimony: A True Story" (1991); Author, "Deception: A Novel" (1990); Author, Memoir, "The Facts: A Novelist's Autobiography" (1988); Author, "The Counterlife" (1986); Author, "The Prague Orgy" (1985); Author, "The Anatomy Lesson" (1983); Author, "Zuckerman Unbound" (1981); Author, "A Philip Roth Reader" (1980); Author, "The Ghost Writer" (1979); Author, "The Professor of Desire" (1977); Author, "Reading Myself and Others" (1976); Author, "My Life as a Man" (1974); Author, "The Great American Novel" (1973); Author, "The Breast" (1972); Author, "Our Gang" (1971); Author, "Portnoy's Complaint" (1969); Author, "When She Was Good" (1967); Author, "Letting Go" (1962); Author, "Goodbye, Columbus" (1959); Author, Multiple Novels AW: Commander of the Legion, Republic of France (2013); Lifetime Achievement Award from PEN/ALLEN Foundation, PEN America (2013); Prince of Asturias Award for Literature (2012); Library of Congress Creative Achievement Award (2012); Man Booker International Prize (2011); Inductee, New Jersey Hall of Fame (2010); PEN/Faulkner Award for Fiction, PEN America (1994, 2001, 2007); PEN/Saul Bellow Award for Achievement in American Fiction, PEN America (2007); PEN/Nabokov Award for Lifetime Achievement, PEN America (2006); Sidewise Award for Alternate History (2005); Award for Distinguished Contribution to American Letters, National Book Foundation (2002); Prix Médicis Étranger, Republic of France (2002); Gold Medal in Fiction, American Academy of Arts and Letters (2001); WH Smith Literary Award (2001); Prix du Meilleur Livre Étranger, Republic of France (2000); National Medal of Arts, The White House (1998); Pulitzer Prize for Fiction (1997); National Book Award (1960, 1995); Karel Capek Prize, Czech Republic (1994); Literary Medal of Honor, National Arts Club (1991); National Book Critics Circle Award (1986, 1991); Grantee, Rockefeller Foundation (1966); Daroff Award, Jewish Book Council of America (1960); Grantee, Guggenheim Foundation (1959-1960); Recipient, Numerous Awards

ROTH, VERONICA, T: Author **I:** Writing and Editing **DOB:** 08/19/1988 **PB:** New York **SC:** NY/USA **MS:** Married **SPN:** Nelson Fitch (2011) **ED:** Coursework, Creative Writing Program, Northwestern University **C:** Professional Author (2011-Present) **CW:** Author, "Chosen Ones" (2020); Author, "The End and Other Beginnings" (2019); Author, "The Fates Divide" (2018); Author, "We Can Be Mended: A Divergent Story" (2017); Author, "Cave the Mark" (2017); Author, "Four: A Divergent Collection" (2014); Author, "Allegiant" (2013); Author, "The World of Divergent: The Path to Allegiant" (2013); Author, Short Story, "Hearken" (2013); Author, "Insurgent" (2012); Author, "Divergent" (2011) **AW:** Young Reader's Choice Award (2014); Sequoyah Book Award (2014); Nutmeg Book Award (2014); Grand Canyon Reader Award (2014); Evergreen Young Adult Book Award (2014); Gateway Readers Award (2013); Green Mountain Book Award (2013); Goodreads Choice Award, Young Adult Fantasy, "Allegiant" (2013); Black-Eyed Susan Award, High School, "Divergent" (2012); Georgia Peach Book Award for Teen Readers, Young Adult, "Divergent" (2012); Goodreads Choice Award, Young Adult Fantasy (2012); Goodreads Choice Award, Goodreads Author (2012); Goodreads Choice Award, Favorite Book of 2011, "Divergent" (2011); Goodreads Choice Award, Young Adult Fantasy, "Divergent" (2011); RT Reviewers Choice Award, Young Adult Protagonist, "Divergent" (2011); Numerous Awards and Accolades

ROTHBLATT, MARTINE ALIANA, T: President, Chief Executive Officer **I:** Biotechnology **CN:** United Therapeutics Corporation **PB:** Chicago **SC:** IL/USA **PT:** Hal Rothblatt; Rosa Lee Rothblatt **MS:** Married **SPN:** Bina Aspen (1982) **CH:** Sunee; Gabriel; Jenesis; Eli **ED:** Honorary LLD, University of Victoria (2019); Doctorate Honoris Causa in Commercial Science, New York University (2018); Honorary DSc, North Carolina State University (2017); Honorary Doctorate, Ben Gurion University (2010); PhD in Medical Ethics, Barts and the London School of Medicine and Dentistry (2001); Coursework, University of Maryland, College Park (1982); JD, MBA, UCLA (1981); BA, UCLA, Summa Cum Laude (1977) **C:** Founder, President, Chief Executive Officer, United Therapeutics Corporation (1996-Present); Co-Founder, Sirius XM Radio Inc. (1990-1993) **CIV:** Founder, Terasem Movement (2004); Donor, SpacePAC; Board of Trustees, Space Studies Institute **CW:** Author, "Virtually Human," St. Martin's Press (2014); Author, "From Transgender to Transhuman: A Manifesto on the Freedom of Form" (2011); Executive Producer, "The Singularity Is Near" (2010); Executive Producer, "2B" (2009); Author, "Two Stars for Peace," iUniverse (2003); Author, "Your Life or Mine," Ashgate (2003); Author, "Unzipped Genes," Temple University Press (1997); Author, "Apartheid of Sex," Crown (1995); Author, "Radiodetermination Satellite Services and Standards," Artech House (1987); Blogger, "Mindfiles, Mindware and Mindclones" **AW:** America's Self-Made Women, Forbes (2019) **MEM:** Elected Member, American Philosophical Society; International Bar Association

ROTHENBERG, ROBERT PHILIP, T: Public Relations Counselor **I:** Corporate Communications & Public Relations **CN:** Rothenberg Public Relations **DOB:** 06/05/1936 **PB:** New York **SC:** NY/USA **PT:** Robert Edward Rothenberg; Lillian Babette (Lustig) Rothenberg **MS:** Single **ED:** MS, Boston University (1958); BA, Cornell University (1956) **C:** Chairman, President, Rothenberg Public Relations Communications Counsel, New York, NY (1988-Present); Director of Public Relations, BigChange Networks, LLC, Washington, DC (1998-2004); Vice President, Medbook Publications, Inc. (1995-2004); Senior Executive Vice President, Robert Marston and Associates, New York, NY (1978-1988); Partner, President, Marston and Rothenberg Public Affairs, Inc., New York, NY (1977-1988); Partner, Executive Vice President, Robert Marston and Associates, New York, NY (1970-1988); Senior Vice President, The Rowland Company, New York, NY (1967-1970); Vice President, The Rowland Company, New York, NY (1965-1967); With, The Rowland Company, New York, NY (1963-1970); Press Secretary, Gubernatorial Candidate William R. Anderson, TN (1962); Assistant to President, Harry N. Abrams Publishing Co. (Now Abrams), New York, NY (1960-1962); Public Relations Director, Harry N. Abrams Publishing Co. (Now Abrams), New York, NY (1960-1962); With, Publicity Department, Columbia Pictures, New York, NY (1959-1960); Senior Consultant, The Lund Group, Inc. **CIV:** Fellow, The Metropolitan Museum of Art (1990-Present); Board of Directors, Amas Musical Theatre (2002-2003); President, Chairman, Board of Trustees, St. Bartholomew's Preservation Foundation (Now St. Bartholomew's Conservancy) (1992-1995); Board of Directors, Foundation to Save African Endangered Wildlife (Now African Wildlife Foundation), World Rehabilitation Fund, New York, NY (1982-1998); Trustee, Museum of Holography, New York, NY; Associate, National Park Foundation; Counselor, American Business Cancer Research Foundation, Southport, CT; Member, Blue Hill Troupe; Producer, Warner Theatre, Northwest Connecticut Association for the Arts, Inc., Torrington, CT **MIL:** With, United States Air Force Reserve (1959-1965) **MEM:** Elizabeth Hamilton Cullum Society, Memorial Sloan Kettering Cancer Center (2016); Clara Barton Society, The American National Red Cross (2015); International Society of Poets; Pride and Alarm Society; Christian Centurion Society; Harriman Society, The American National Red Cross; Trustee, Media Research Center; The English-Speaking Union of the United States; Anchor Society; The Morgan Library & Museum; DeWitt Clinton Society; Museum of the City of New York; Kent Historical Society; Kent Library Association, Inc.; Blue Hill Troupe; Players Club; The Coffee House **RE:** Unitarian Universalist

ROTHSCHILD, JEFF, T: Vice President of Infrastructure Software **I:** Internet **CN:** Facebook **DOB:** 02/28/1954 **SC:** USA **PT:** William B. Rothschild; Beverley Rothschild **MS:** Married **SPN:** Marieke **CH:** Three Children **ED:** MS, Vanderbilt University (1979); BS, Vanderbilt University (1977) **C:** Vice President of Infrastructure Software, Facebook (2005-Present); Adviser, Venture Partner, Accel (1999-Present); Co-founder, Veritas Software (1988-Present); Co-founder, Mendocino Software (2003-2008); Co-founder, Mpath Interactive (1995-2001) **CR:** Vice Chair, Board of Trust, Vanderbilt University **CIV:** Contributor, $20 Million, Vanderbilt University (2016); Endowed Two Scholarships in the School of Engineering and College of Arts and Science, Vanderbilt University (2013) **AW:** Listed, "Billionaires 2020," Forbes (2020); Listed, "Forbes 400 2019," Forbes (2019); Listed, "Richest in Tech 2017," Forbes (2017)

ROTROFF JACOBS, LINDA ROTROFF, T: Elementary School Educator **I:** Education/Educational Services **DOB:** 06/10/1942 **PB:** Peebles **SC:** OH/USA **PT:** Joseph Harold Rotroff; Mary Lucile (Peterson) Rotroff Nixon **MS:** Married **SPN:** Donald Eugene Jacobs (11/29/1968) **CH:** Donald Bret Jacobs; Stephanie Jacobs (Daughter in-law) **ED:** Postgraduate Coursework, Mount St. Joseph University (1968); Postgraduate Coursework, University of Cincinnati (1968); Postgraduate Coursework, Miami University (1968); Postgraduate Coursework, Xavier University (1968); MA in Education, University of Cincinnati (1968); BS in Education, Ohio State University (1963) **CT:** Teacher, State of Ohio **C:** Tour Director, Escort, MKL Tours (2000-2005); Teacher, Pupil Enrichment Program, Mercer Elementary School, Forest Hills, Cincinnati, Ohio (1997-2000); Teacher, Kindergarten, Mercer Elementary School, Forest Hills, Cincinnati, Ohio (1977-2000); Teacher, Reading, Adult Education, Chillicothe, Ohio (1974-1977); Teacher, Kindergarten, Board of Education, Chillicothe, Ohio (1974-1977); Teacher, K-8, Board of Education, Forest Hills, Cincinnati, Ohio (1963-1974, 1977) **CR:** Master, Teacher, Adviser, Entry Teachers, Forest Hills, Ohio (1993-Present); Cooperating Teacher, Student Teachers, Ohio University (1965-Present); Cooperating Teacher, Student Teachers, University of Cincinnati (1965-Present); Cooperating Teacher, Student Teachers, Northern Kentucky University (1965-Present); Member, Professional Development, CADRE (1999-2000); Member, Steering Committee, Accelerated Schools (1997-1998); Facilitator, Summer School, Forest Hills, Ohio (1993-1996, 1997-1999); Member, Responsive Classroom Team (1996-1997); Coordinator, Early Entrance Screening, Hamilton County, Ohio (1994, 1995); Faculty Member, Intervention Based Multifactored Evaluation Committee (1994, 1995); Member, Collaboration Team, Inclusion of Special Children (1994, 1995); Career Mentor, Ashford-McCarthy Resources, Inc. (1993-1994); Representative, Parent Teacher Association, Cincinnati, Ohio (1967, 1973, 1982, 1989); Member, Superintendent's Council, Forest Hills, Cincinnati, Ohio (1979, 1982, 1988); Coordinator, Kindergarten, Forest Hills, Hamilton County, Cincinnati, Ohio (1965-1970, 1983-1985); Teacher, Kindergarten, First Grade, Forest Hills, Cincinnati, Ohio (1978-1982); Teacher, Representative, Head Start, Chillicothe, Ohio (1975-1977); Teacher, Fourth Grade, Seventh Grade, Mathematics, Language Arts, Summer School, Cincinnati, Ohio (1964-1968); Member, Diversity, Great Aspirations Pilot Program, Dadre Accelerated Schools, Mercer Elementary School **CIV:** Consultant, Women Helping Women, Cincinnati, Ohio (1989) **CW:** Author, "Parenting Tips" (1992); Author, Intervention Assistance Team Handbook (1992); Author, "Getting Ready for Kindergarten" (1978) **AW:** Named Educator of the Year, Anderson Area Chamber of Commerce (2000); Scarlet and Gray Award, Ohio State University (1995); Named Martha Holden Jennings Scholar (1976-1977); Named Teacher of the Year, Hamilton County (1965); Named Teacher of the Year, Numerous Years **MEM:** Empower Youth, Clermont County, Ohio (2016-Present); Chaplain, National Society Daughters of the American Revolution (NSDAR) (2014-Present); Travel Liaison, Retired Staff, Forest Hills (2014-Present); Secretary, Herb Society (The Herb Society of America, Inc.) (2008-Present); Secretary, The Ohio State University Alumni Association, Clermont County, Ohio (1995-Present); Secretary, Alpha Kappa Delta International Honor Society (1975-Present); Secretary, Forest Hills Education Association (1964-1968); Delegate, Ohio Education Association (1965); National Education Association; Representative, National Parent Teacher Association (PTA); Teachers Applying Whole Language (TAWL); Southwestern Ohio Education Association; Anderson Hills Historical Society; Forest Hills Retired Staff Association; Hamilton County Retired Teachers Association; Police Officers Hall of Fame; Clermont County Herb Society **MH:** Albert Nelson Marquis Lifetime Achievement Award **B/I:** Mrs. Jacobs' mother, grandfather, and four uncles were teachers. Her grandfather told her she would make an excellent nurse, but to pursue teaching if she wanted to help young people. When Mrs. Jacobs was a teenager, she worked with children in a Bible school and found she enjoyed it. Following her grandfather's advice, she decided to teach to make a difference in children's lives, as well as to achieve personal satisfaction. **AV:** Interior decorating; Writing stories; Writing poems; Music; Landscaping; Reading **RE:** Church of Christ **THT:** Mrs. Jacobs has been a guest speaker for various organizations. Mrs. Jacobs is the coordinator and interviewer for the Ohio State University.

ROUDA, HARLEY EDWIN JR., T: U.S. Representative from California; Lawyer; Real Estate Executive **I:** Government Administration/Government Relations/Government Services **DOB:** 12/10/1961 **PB:** Columbus **SC:** OH/USA **PT:** Harley Edwin Rouda Sr. (Deceased); Marlese Rouda **MS:** Married **SPN:** Kaira (Sturdivant) Rouda **CH:** Trace; Avery; Shea; Dylan **ED:** JD, Capital University Law School; MBA, The Ohio State University; BA, University of Kentucky **C:** Member, U.S. House of Representatives from California's 48th Congressional District (2019-Present); Chief Executive Officer, General Counsel, Real Living Inc., Columbus, Ohio (2002-Present); Chief Executive Officer, HER Realtors, Columbus, Ohio (1999-2002); General Counsel, HER Realtors, Columbus, Ohio (1997-2002); President, HER Realtors (1996-1999); Attorney, Porter Wright Morris & Arthur LLP **CR:** Board of

Directors, Rocky Shoe and Boots (RockyBoots. com) (2003); Speaker in Field; Board of Directors, Real Living Mortgage; Board of Directors, The Realty Alliance **CIV:** Member, Greater Columbus Chamber of Commerce; Member, Capital University Law School; Member, The Ohio State University; Member, The Fisher College; Member, World of Children; Member, COSI; Member, Southern Theatre Restoration; Member, Upper Arlington Civic Association; Member, St. John's Church; Member, BalletMet; Member, Columbus Area Leadership Program; Member, Mid-Ohio Foodbank; Member, Prevent Blindness; Member, March of Dimes; Member, Upper Arlington Cultural Arts Commission; Member, Columbus Theatrical Association (Columbus Association for the Performing Arts) **AW:** Named One of Real Estate's 25 Most Influential Thought Leaders, Realtor Magazine (2006); Named Entrepreneur of the Year, Ernst & Young (2002)

ROUSE, LEO E., T: Professor and Dean Emeritus, ADEA Consultant **I:** Education/Educational Services **CN:** American Dental Education Association **MS:** Married **ED:** Honorary Doctorate, Western University of Health Sciences, Pomona, CA (2014); Coursework, Walson Army Hospital, Fort Dix, NJ (1976-1978); DDS, Howard University College of Dentistry (1969- 1973) **C:** Senior Scholar-in-Residence, Consultant, American Dental Education Association (ADEA) (2016-Present); Board of Regents, Uniform Services University of the Health Sciences (2015-Present); President Elect, American College of Dentists (2020); At Large Regent, American College of Dentists (2016-2019); Dean, Professor, Howard University (1997-2015); President, Board of Directors, American Dental Education Association (ADEA) (2011); Commander, United States Army Dental Command (1995-1997) **CR:** Examiner, Consultant, Member, Examination Development Committee, Northeast Regional Board of Dental Examiners; Senior Scholar in Residence, American Dental Education Association (ADEA); ADEA Consultant; Chair, ADEA Gies Foundation Board of Trustees **MIL:** Commander, Chief Operating Officer, Dental Command, U.S. Army (1995-1997); Colonel, U.S. Army (1972-1997) **AW:** American Dental Association Distinguished Service Award (2020); American Dental Education Association Distinguished Service Award (2017); Student Clinician ADA Achievement Award; Trailblazer Award; Doctor of Humane Letters; Howard University College of Dentistry Distinguished Alumni Award **MEM:** President, American Dental Education Association (2011-Present); Fellow, American College of Dentists; American Dental Association; American Association of Dental Examiners; National Dental Association; Omicron Kappa Upsilon **MH:** Albert Nelson Marquis Lifetime Achievement Award; Marquis Who's Who Top Professional

ROUZER, DAVID CHESTON, T: U.S. Representative from North Carolina **I:** Government Administration/Government Relations/Government Services **DOB:** 02/16/1972 **PB:** Landstuhl **SC:** Germany **ED:** BA in Agricultural Business Management, Agricultural Economics and Chemistry, North Carolina State University (1994) **C:** Member, U.S House of Representatives from North Carolina's Seventh Congressional District (2015-Present); Member, District 12, North Carolina State Senate (2009-2013); Associate Administrator, U.S. Department of Agriculture (2005-2006); Assistant to Dean, North Carolina State University College of Agriculture and Life Sciences (2001-2002); Legislative Aide, Senior Policy Advisor to Senator Jesse Helms, U.S. Senate (1996-2001); Owner, The Rouzer Company and the Warehouse Distribu-

tion; Member, Committee on Transportation and Infrastructure; Member, Committee on Agriculture **MEM:** Phi Delta Theta Fraternity **PA:** Republican

ROWE, DONALD EUGENE, T: Professional Director (Retired) **I:** Consulting **CN:** YMCA/American City Bureau **DOB:** 11/10/1938 **PB:** South Bend **SC:** IN/USA **PT:** Devon Dolphia Rowe; Bessie Caroline (Brown) Rowe **MS:** Married **SPN:** Barbara Ann Rowe (8/20/1960) **CH:** Michele Rene Kocsis; Sheri Lyne Rowe-Lopez **ED:** Bachelor of Science, Manchester University (1961) **CT:** Indiana Teaching Certification, Manchester University (1961); YMCA Professional Staff Certification, George Williams College; Approved Professional Staff Requirements, YMCA of the USA **C:** Retired (2001); Senior Counsel, American City Bureau, Hoffman Estates, IL (1989-2001); President, Chief Executive Officer, YMCA of Greater Michiana, South Bend, IN (1986-1989); Senior Counsel, American City Bureau, Hoffman Estates, IL (1982-1986); Executive Director, Racine YMCA, Wisconsin (1974-1982); Associate Executive Director, Racine YMCA, Wisconsin (1971-1974); Youth Director, Racine YMCA, Wisconsin (1966-1971); Youth Director, YMCA of Metropolitan, South Bend-Mishawaka, IN (1964-1966); Program Director, Mishawaka Family YMCA, Indiana (1962-1964); Assistant Youth Director, South Bend YMCA (1961-1962) **CR:** Consultant, Campaign Director, Salvation Army, Hartford, CT (1994); Consultant, Campaign Director, Diocese of Greensburg, PA (1992-1994); Consultant, Campaign Director, Kenmore Mercy Hospital, Tonawanda, NY (1991-1992); Consultant, Associate Director, Director, Archdiocese of Boston, MA (1989-1991); Campaign Consultant, Associate Director, Worcester YMCA Campaign, Massachusetts (1982); Consultant, Campaign Director, YMCA and YWCA Corporate Nonprofit Organizations, Pasadena, CA; Consultant, Campaign Director to Build a New YMCA Facility, Oakland, CA; Consultant, Campaign Director, Butte YMCA, Montana; Counsel, Campaign Director, Ball Memorial Hospital's New Cancer Center, Muncie, IN; Counsel to Restore the Paramount Theater, Lexington, KY **CIV:** Member, Nappanee Missionary Church, Nappanee, IN (2005-Present); Member of Executive Council Committee of United Way, South Bend, IN (1986-1989); Chairman, Year Round Schools Task Force, Racine, WI (1973-1974); Mentor, Big Brothers Big Sisters, Racine, WI; Soar Ministries **AW:** Paul Harris Distinguished Fellowship Award, Rotary International (1992); Distinguished Service Award, Wisconsin Cluster YMCAs, Oshkosh, WI (1982); Eponym, Day of Community (1982); Outstanding Service Award, Big Brothers Organization, Racine, WI (1980); Named, One of the Outstanding Young Men of America (1966) **MEM:** South Bend Rotary Club (1986-Present); Board of Directors, Racine Rotary Foundation (1979-1982); President, Racine Rotary Club, Racine, WI (1979-1980); Chairman, South Bend Rotary Club's Youth Exchange Committee, South Bend, IN; South Bend Rotary Club of Indiana; South Bend Alumni Association **MH:** Albert Nelson Marquis Lifetime Achievement Award; Marquis Who's Who Humanitarian Award **B/I:** Mr. Rowe became involved in his profession after graduating from Manchester College, whereupon he moved back to South Bend, Indiana, and received a job as an assistant youth director of a YMCA. **AV:** Swimming; Reading; Traveling; Watching sports; Family events; Helping groups and people achieve their dreams **PA:** Republican **RE:** Protestant

ROWE, LARRY JORDAN, T: Lawyer **I:** Law and Legal Services **DOB:** 05/24/1958 **PB:** Boston **SC:** MA/USA **PT:** Benson Rowe; Marcia Rowe **MS:** Married **SPN:** Nancy Ellen Cardinal **CH:** Jonathan B.; Elizabeth J.; David C **ED:** JD, Harvard

University (1984); MPP, Harvard University (1984); AB, Dartmouth College (1980) **C:** Co-Head, Natural Resources Group, Ropes & Gray (2014-Present);Partner, Corporate Department, Ropes & Gray (1993-Present); Co-head, Private Funds Group, Ropes & Gray (2003-2006); Co-head, Private Equity Practice Group, Ropes & Gray (2001-2006); Associate, Ropes & Gray, Boston, MA (1984-1993) **CIV:** Sudbury Finsncial Committee, Massachusetts (1998-2007); Board of Directors, Hillel Foundation of New England (1986-2005); President, Hillel Foundation of New England (1991-1994); Counsel, Physicians for Human Rights **CW:** Editor, Harvard International Law Journal **AW:** Lawyer of the Year (2018); Best Lawyers in the United States; Best Lawyers of America **MEM:** Boston Bar Association **BAR:** Commonwealth of Massachusetts (1985); United States District Court for the District of Massachusetts **MH:** Albert Nelson Marquis Lifetime Achievement Award **B/I:** Mr. Rowe always wanted to be a lawyer. When he was in junior high school, he was part of an informal group, organized by one of the teachers, which gave students the chance to see various lawyers in action in court and maybe that's what got him started.

ROWE, LARRY JORDAN, T: Partner **I:** Law and Legal Services **CN:** Ropes & Gray LLP **DOB:** 05/24/1958 **PB:** Boston **SC:** MA/USA **PT:** Benson Rowe; Marcia Rowe **MS:** Married **SPN:** Nancy Ellen Cardinal **CH:** Jonathan B.; Elizabeth J.; David C. **ED:** JD, MPP, Harvard University (1984); BA in Government, Dartmouth College (1980) **C:** Co-Chair, Natural Resources Group, Ropes & Gray, LLP (2014-Present); Partner, Corporate Department, Ropes & Gray, LLP (1993-Present); Co-Head, Private Funds Group, Ropes & Gray, LLP (2003-2006); Co-Head, Private Equity Practice Group, Ropes & Gray, LLP (2001-2006); Associate, Ropes & Gray, LLP (1984-1993) **CIV:** Sudbury Finance Committee, MA (1998-2007); Board of Directors, Hillel Foundation (1986-2005); President, Hillel Foundation (1991-1994) **CW:** Editor, Harvard International Law Journal **AW:** Lawyer of the Year (2018); Legal 500; Best Lawyers in the United States **MEM:** Boston Bar Association **BAR:** Massachusetts Bar Association (1985); United States District Court District of Massachusetts **AS:** Mr. Rowe attributes his success to the incredibly great atmosphere at Ropes & Gray and the talent and generosity of his colleagues. **B/I:** Mr. Rowe became involved in his profession because of his desire to help others.

ROWLAND, PLEASANT, T: Founder **I:** Other **CN:** American Girl **DOB:** 03/08/1941 **PB:** Chicago **SC:** IL/USA **PT:** Edward Thiele **MS:** Married **SPN:** Jerry Frautschi **ED:** Honorary LHD, Edgewood College, Madison, WI (2010); Graduate, Wells College (1962) **C:** Vice Chairman, Mattel, Inc. (1998-2000); Founder, President, Pleasant Co. (Now American Girl, Inc.) (1986-1998); Creator, American Doll Collection (1985); Publisher, Children's Magazine Guide (1981-1989); Vice President, Boston Educational Research Company (1971-1978); Television News Reporter, Anchor, KGO-TV, San Francisco, CA (1968-1971); Elementary Teacher, States of Massachusetts, California, Georgia and New Jersey (1962-1968) **CIV:** Founder, Pleasant T. Rowland Foundation (2003); Creator, Superkids (1978); Founder, Aurora Women and Girls Foundation; Founder, Beginning to Read, Write and Listen; Donor, Overture Center for the Arts **AW:** America's Top 50 Women Business Owners, Working Women Magazine (1993-1998); Best and Brightest in Marketing Award, Advertising Age (1993); 12 Outstanding Entrepreneurs, Institute of American Entrepreneurs (1990) **MEM:** International Women's Forum; Committee of 200

ROWLING, J.K., T: Writer **I:** Writing and Editing **DOB:** 07/31/1965 **PB:** Yate **SC:** Gloucestershire, England **PT:** Peter Rowling; Anne Rowling **MS:** Married **SPN:** Neil Murray (12/26/2001); Jorge Aranted (10/16/1992, Divorced 1993) **CH:** David; Mackenzie; Jessica **ED:** LittD (Honorary), Harvard University (2008); LLD (Honorary), Aberdeen University (2006); Honorary Degree, University of Edinburgh (2004); Honorary Degree, University of St. Andrews (2000); LittD (Honorary), University of Exter (2000); LittD (Honorary), Dartmouth College (2000); LittD (Honorary), Napier University (2000); Student, Teacher Training Course, Moray House School of Education, Edinburgh University (1995); BA in French and Classics, University of Exeter(1986) **C:** Professional Author (1997-Present); Former Teacher, English, Portugal; Former Teacher, Secondary Languages, Leith Academy; Former Researcher, Amnesty International **CIV:** Co-Founder, Children's High Level Group (Now Lumos) (2005-Present); Founder, Volant Charitable Trust (2000-Present); Ambassador One Parent Families (Now Gingerbread), London, England (2000-Present); Philanthropic Donations and Volunteer Work for Numerous Charities including Comic Relief, Multiple Sclerosis Society Great Britain, and One Parent Families **CW:** Producer, Television Series, "Strike" (2017-Present); Screenwriter, Producer, "Fantastic Beasts: The Crimes of Grindelwald" (2018); Author (Under a Pseudonym), "Lethal White" (2018); Screenwriter, Producer, "Fantastic Beasts and Where to Find Them" (2016); Author, e-book, "Hogwarts: An Incomplete and Unreliable Guide" (2016); Author, e-book, "Short Stories from Hogwarts of Heroism, Hardship and Dangerous Hobbies" (2016); Author, e-book, "Short Stories from Hogwarts of Power, Politics and Pesky Poltergeists" (2016); Author (Under a Pseudonym), "Career of Evil" (2015); Producer, Television Miniseries, "The Casual Vacancy" (2015); Author (Under a Pseudonym), "The Cuckoo's Calling" (2013); Author, "The Casual Vacancy" (2012); Producer, Film, "Harry Potter and the Deathly Hallows Part 2" (2011); Producer, Film, "Harry Potter and the Deathly Hallows Part 1" (2010); Author, "The Tales of Beedle the Bard" (2008); Author, "Harry Potter and the Deathly Hallows" (2007); Author, "Harry Potter and the Half-Blood Prince" (2005); Author, "Harry Potter and the Order of the Phoenix" (2003); Author, "Harry Potter and the Order of the Phoenix" (2003); Voice Actress, "The Simpsons" (2003); Author, "Fantastic Beasts and Where to Find Them" (2001); Author (Under a Pseudonym), "Quidditch Through the Ages" (2001); Author, "Harry Potter and the Goblet of Fire" (2000); Author, "Harry Potter and the Prisoner of Azkaban" (1999); Author, "Harry Potter and the Chamber of Secrets" (1998); Author, "Harry Potter and the Philosopher's Stone" (1997); Author, Articles and Op-Eds, Numerous Publications **AW:** Honoree, Order of the Companions of Honour, Birthday Honours (2017); Honoree, Freedom of the City of London (2012); Co-Recipient, Outstanding British Contribution to Cinema, "Harry Potter" Film Series, British Academy Film Awards (2011); Hans Christian Andersen Literature Award (2010); Honoree, Chevalier de la Légion d'honneur (2009); The Edinburgh Award (2008); Outstanding Achievement, British Book Awards (2008); Named, Barbara WAlter's Most Fascinating Person of the Year (2007); Blue Peter Badge, Gold (2007); British Book of the Year, "Harry Potter and the Half-Blood Prince" (2006); Bram Stoker Award for Best Work for Young Readers, "Harry Potter and the Order of the Phoenix" (2003); Premio Principe de Asturias, Concord (2003); Hugo Award for Best Novel, "Harry Potter and the Goblet of Fire" (2001); Locus Award, "Harry Potter and the Prisoner of Azkaban" (2000); Honoree, Officer of the Order of the British

Empire (2000); Author of the Year, British Book Awards (2000); Children's Book of the Year, "Harry Potter and the Prisoner of Azkaban," Whitbread Awards (1999); Children's Book of the Year, "Harry Potter and the Chamber of Secrets," National Book Awards (1999); Gold Award, "Harry Potter and the Prisoner of Azkaban," Nestlé Smarties Book Prize (1999); British Children's Book of the Year, "Harry Potter and the Philosopher's Stone" (1998); Gold Award, "Harry Potter and the Chamber of Secrets," Nestlé Smarties Book Prize (1998); Gold Award, "Harry Potter and the Philosopher's Stone," Nestlé Smarties Book Prize (1997) **MEM:** Fellow, Royal College of Physicians of Edinburgh (2011); Honorary Fellow, Royal Society of Edinburgh (2002); Fellow, Royal Society of Literature (2002)

ROWSON, RICHARD CAVANAGH, T: Foreign Affairs Publishing **I:** Other **DOB:** 04/07/1926 **PB:** Los Angeles **SC:** CA/USA **PT:** Louis Cavanagh Rowson; Mable Louise (Montney) Rowson **MS:** Married **SPN:** Elena Louisa Costabile (11/22/1952) **CH:** Peter Cavanagh; John Cummings **ED:** MIA, Columbia University (1950); BA, University of California, Berkeley (1946) **CT:** Certificate, Sorbonne (1949) **C:** President, R.R. Bowker (1980); President, Pergamon Press (1977-1980); President, Praeger Publishing Inc. (1975-1977); Director of Special Studies, Praeger Publishing., Inc., New York, NY (1969-1977); Director of Policy and Planning, Radio Free Europe (1964-1969); Radio Free Europe (1962-1969); Foreign Policy Association (1951-1962); Director, World Affairs Council of Rhode Island (1951-1952); Trainee, Foreign Policy Association (1950); Director of Finance and Development, Northeast Region, Foreign Policy Association **CR:** Chair, Council for a Community of Democracies (2014-2016); Chair, Champion of Democracy (2008); Publishing Consultant, Lecturer, President, Chief Executive Officer, Council for Community of Democracies (2003-2008); Director, Executive Service Corps of Washington (2000-2003); Vice President, National Executive Service Corps (1999-2000); Publisher, Woodrow Wilson Center Press (1992-1993); Senior Consultant, Editor (1990-1991); Director, American University Press (1989-1991); Director, Duke University Press (1981-1990) **MIL:** Lieutenant, U.S. Navy (1944-1947) **CW:** Author, "The Role of Retired Executives in Community Service"; Contributor, Articles, Professional Journals **AW:** Champion of Democracies, Council for the Community of Democracies (2008); Marquis Top Executives **MEM:** Association for Slavic, East European, and Eurasian Studies; New York Academy of Sciences; Cal Alumni Association; Alumni Association, Columbia University; Overseas Press Club, Alumni Association, Pomona College; The Washington Institute of Foreign Affairs **MH:** Albert Nelson Marquis Lifetime Achievement Award **B/I:** Mr. Rowson became involved in his profession because he had a very wonderful high school teacher of international relations at Beverly Hills High School; it was an exceptional high school and they had a special area of International Affairs as part of their history department. He was introduced to global affairs and that led him to become interested to working in that area himself and contributing something positive to the development of a peaceful world; a world united under the United Nations; a world who would have protection of its self through NATO and international alliances or international corporations. **AV:** Playing flute **PA:** Democrat

ROY, CHARLES, "CHIP" EUGENE, T: U.S. Representative from Texas; Lawyer **I:** Government Administration/Government Relations/Government Services **DOB:** 08/07/1972 **PB:** Bethesda **SC:** MD/USA **MS:** Married **SPN:** Carrah Roy **CH:** Two

Children **ED:** JD, The University of Texas at Austin School of Law (2003); MA in Management Information Systems, University of Virginia (1995); BA, University of Virginia (1994) **C:** Member, U.S. House of Representatives from Texas' 21st Congressional District (2019-Present); Senior Advisor to Senator Ted Cruz, U.S. Senate (2014-Present); First Assistant Attorney General, Texas (2015-2016); Chief of Staff to Senator Ted Cruz, U.S. Senate, Washington, DC (2012-2014); Staff Member to Senator John Cornyn, U.S. Senate, Washington, DC (2002-2009); Director, State-federal Relations, State of Texas, Austin, Texas; Special Assistant U.S. Attorney, Eastern District of Texas, U.S. Department of Justice, Beaumont, Texas; Member, Committee on Budget; Member, Committee on Oversight and Reform; Member, Committee on Veterans' Affairs; Ranking Member, Oversight Subcommittee on Civil Rights and Civil Liberties **CR:** Investment Banking Analyst, NationsBanc Capital Markets; Technology Consultant **CIV:** Vice President of Strategy, Texas Public Policy Foundation **PA:** Republican

ROYBAL-ALLARD, LUCILLE ELSA, T: U.S. Representative from California **I:** Government Administration/Government Relations/Government Services **DOB:** 06/12/1941 **PB:** Boyle Heights **SC:** CA/USA **PT:** Edward Ross Roybal; Lucille (Beserra) Roybal **MS:** Married **SPN:** Edward T. Allard III **CH:** Angela (Stepdaughter); Guy Mark (Stepson); Ricardo; Lisa Marie **ED:** BA in Speech, California State University, Los Angeles, CA (1965); Honorary LHD, National Hispanic University **C:** Member, U.S. House of Representatives from California's 40th Congressional District, U.S. Congress (2013-Present); Member, U.S. House of Representatives from California's 34th Congressional District, U.S. Congress (2003-2013); Member, U.S. House of Representatives from California's 33rd Congressional District, U.S. Congress (1993-2003); Member, District 56, California State Assembly (1986-1992); Assistant Director, East Los Angeles Alcoholism Council; Employee, United Way; Member, House Committee on Appropriations **CR:** Chair, Congressional Hispanic Caucus (1999-2000); Member, Congressional Children's Working Group; Member, Homeland Security Task Force; Member, Livable Communities Task Force **CIV:** Founder, Women's Working Group on Immigration Reform **AW:** Madre y Mujer Award, Kimberly-Clark (KCWW) (2006) **PA:** Democrat **RE:** Roman Catholic

ROYCE, EDWARD, "ED" RANDALL, T: Former U.S. Representative from California **I:** Government Administration/Government Relations/Government Services **DOB:** 10/12/1951 **PB:** Los Angeles **SC:** CA/USA **MS:** Married **SPN:** Marie Therese Porter (1985) **ED:** BA in Accounting and Finance, California State University, Fullerton, CA (1977) **C:** Member, U.S. House of Representatives from California's 39th Congressional District, United States Congress, Washington, DC (1993-2003, 2013-2019); Chairman, U.S. House Committee on Foreign Relations (2013-2019); Member, U.S. House of Representatives from California's 40th Congressional District, United States Congress, Washington, DC (2003-2013); Member, District 32, California State Senate (1983-1992); Tax Manager, Southwestern Portland Cement Company **AW:** Visionaries for Africa Award, The Africa Society of the National Summit on Africa (2004); Taxpayers Hero Award, Citizens Against Government Waste (1994); Taxpayers Friend Award, National Taxpayers Union (NTU) (1994); Named Child Advocate of the Year, California Association of Service for Children (Now California Alliance of Child and Family Services) (1987); Named Legislator of the Year, Orange County Republican Committee (1986); Medal of Commendation, Veterans of Foreign Wars

(VFW) (1985); Named to Order of Brilliant Star with Grand Cordon, Taiwan, Republic of China; Named to Order of Brilliant Star with Special Grand Cordon, Taiwan, Republic of China **MEM:** Anaheim Chamber of Commerce; Fullerton Chamber of Commerce (Now North Orange County Chamber of Commerce; Literacy Volunteers of America (LVA) **PA:** Republican **RE:** Roman Catholic

RUBENSTEIN, DAVID MARK, T: Co-Founder, Co-Executive Chairman, Private Equity Firm Executive, Lawyer, Philanthropist **I:** Financial Services **CN:** The Carlyle Group **DOB:** 08/11/1949 **PB:** Baltimore **SC:** MD/USA **MS:** Divorced **SPN:** Alice Nicole Rogoff (05/21/1983, Divorced 2017) **CH:** Alexandra; Gabrielle; Andrew **ED:** JD, The University of Chicago Law School (1973); BA, Duke University, Magna Cum Laude (1970) **C:** Co-Founder, Managing Director, Co-Chief Executive Officer, The Carlyle Group (1987-Present); Deputy Assistant to President for Domestic Policy, The White House (1977-1981); Chief Counsel, Judiciary Committee, Subcommittee on Constitutional Amendments, United States Senate, Washington, DC (1975-1976); With, Paul, Weiss, Rifkind, Wharton & Garrison LLP, New York, NY (1973-1975); With, Shaw, Pittman, Potts & Trowbridge (Now Pillsbury Winthrop Shaw Pittman LLP) **CR:** Member, National Advisory Committee, JPMorgan Chase & Co.; Member, Business Council, World Economic Forum; Member, Advisory Board, Stanford Institute for Economic Policy Research **CIV:** Trustee, The University of Chicago (2007-Present); Trustee, John F. Kennedy Center for the Performing Arts (2004-Present); Chairman, Member, Board of Trustees, Duke University (2013-2017); Council Member, National Trust for Historic Preservation; Member, James Madison Council, Library of Congress; Member, Trustees' Council, National Gallery of Art; Member, Board of Overseers, Hoover Institution; Member, Visiting Committee, Kennedy School of Government, Harvard University; Member, Board of Trustees, Memorial Sloan Kettering Cancer Center; Member, Board of Trustees, John Hopkins University; Vice Chairman, Lincoln Center of the Performing Arts; Member, Dean's Council, Woodrow Wilson School of Public and International Affairs, Princeton University; Participant, The Giving Pledge **CW:** Host, "The David Rubenstein Show: Peer to Peer Conversations" (2016-Present); Author, "The American Story: Interviews with Master Historians" (2019) **AW:** One of the Forbes 400 Richest Americans (2009-Present); One of the 50 Most Influential People in Global Finance, Bloomberg Markets (2011); One of the 50 Most Powerful People in DC, GQ Magazine (2007); Golden Plate Award, Academy Achievement (2006) **MEM:** The Phi Beta Kappa Society **RE:** Jewish

RUBIN, GRETCHEN ANNE, T: Author, Blogger **I:** Writing and Editing **DOB:** 12/15/1965 **PB:** Kansas City **SC:** MO/USA **MS:** Married **SPN:** James "Jamie" Rubin **CH:** Two Children **ED:** JD, Yale Law School, New Haven, CT; BA, Yale University, New Haven, CT; Diploma, Pembroke Hill School, Kansas City, MO **C:** Former Chief Advisor, Chairman Reed Hundt, Federal Communications Commission; Former Law Clerk, Justice Sandra Day O'Connor, Supreme Court of the United States **CR:** Lecturer, Yale School of Management, Yale Law School **CW:** Author, "Outer Order: Inner Calm" (2019); Author, "The Four Tendencies: The Indispensable Personality Profiles That Reveal How to Make Your Life Better (and Other People's Lives Better, Too)" (2017); Author, "Better than Before: What I Learned About Making and Breaking Habits - to Sleep More, Quit Sugar, Procrastinate Less, and Generally Build a Happier Life" (2015); Author, "Happier at Home: Kiss More, Jump More, Abandon a Project, Read

Samuel Johnson, and My Other Experiments in the Practice of Everyday Life" (2012); Author, "The Happiness Project" (2009); Author, "Profane Waste" (2006); Author, "Forty Ways to Look at JFK" (2005); Author, "Forty Ways to Look at Winston Churchill: A Brief Account of a Long Life" (2003); Author, "Power Money Fame Sex: A User's Guide" (2000); Contributor, "The Persistence of Dread in Law and Literature," The Yale Law Journal (1992); Founder, "The Happiness Project"; Speaker, Various Radio Talk Shows **AW:** Listee, New York Times Bestseller List; Listee, Publishers Weekly Bestseller List

RUBINO, MICHAEL C., T: Of Counsel **I:** Law and Legal Services **CN:** Fenton Grant Mayfield Kaneda & Litt **ED:** JD, McKinney School of Law, Indianapolis, IN (1983); BS in Psychology and Communication Arts and Sciences, DePauw University, Greencastle, IN, Cum Laude (1980) **C:** Of Counsel, Fenton Grant Mayfield Kaneda & Litt, LLP (2014-Present); Partner, Canepa, Riedy & Rubino, Las Vegas, NV (1997-2014); Judicial Law Clerk to the Honorable Dixon W. Prentice, Indiana Supreme Court **CR:** Defended Developers, Contractors, and Subcontractors, Over 100 Construction Defect Lawsuits, San Diego, CA **CW:** Associate Editor, Indiana Law Review **AW:** AV Rating, Martindale-Hubbell; Listee, Top 100 Trial Lawyers, The National Trial Lawyers **MEM:** American Bar Association; Nevada Bar Association; California Bar Association; Clark County Bar Association; American Justice Association; Nevada Justice Association; Moot Court Society **BAR:** California; Nevada; U.S. District Court for the Southern District of California; U.S. Court of Appeals for the Ninth Circuit; U.S. District Court for the District of Nevada; Indiana (Inactive) **MH:** Albert Nelson Marquis Lifetime Achievement Award; Marquis Who's Who Top Professional **AS:** Mr. Rubino attributes his success to attention to detail and working long hours. **B/I:** Mr. Rubino became involved in his profession because he was inspired by the television show, "Perry Mason." Though he considered pursuing politics, he slowly but surely became involved in the legal field. For 12 years, Mr. Rubino defended subcontractors to developers, which gave him enough experience to become a partner at a Las Vegas law firm.

RUBIO, MARCO ANTONIO, T: U.S. Senator from Florida **I:** Government Administration/Government Relations/Government Services **DOB:** 05/28/1971 **PB:** Miami **SC:** FL/USA **PT:** Mario Rubio Reina; Oriales (Garcia) Rubio **MS:** Married **SPN:** Jeanette Dousdebes (1998) **CH:** Amanda; Daniella; Anthony; Dominic **ED:** JD, University of Miami School of Law (1996); BS in Political Science, University of Florida (1993); Coursework, Tarkio College (1989-1990) **C:** Chairman, Senate Committee on Small Business (2019-Present); U.S. Senator, State of Florida, Washington, DC (2011-Present); Member, U.S. Senate Committee on Foreign Relations, Washington, DC (2011-Present); Member, U.S. Senate Committee on Small Business and Entrepreneurship, Washington, DC (2011-Present); Member, U.S. Senate Select Committee on Intelligence, Washington, DC (2011-Present); Member, U.S. Senate Committee on Commerce, Science and Transportation, Washington, DC (2011-Present); Visiting Professor, Florida International University Jorge M. Pérez Metropolitan Center (2008); Speaker, Florida House of Representatives (2006-2008); Member, District 111, Florida House of Representatives (2000-2008); Majority Leader, Florida House of Representatives (2003-2006); City Commissioner, West Miami, FL (1998-2000) **CR:** Candidate, 2016 Republican Party Presidential Nomination (2016); Political Analyst, Univision (2008) **CW:** Author, "American Dreams:

Restoring Economic Opportunity for Everyone" (2015); Author, "An American Son: A Memoir" (2012); Author, "100 Innovative Ideas for Florida's Future: A Plan of Action" (2006) **AW:** Named One of the 100 Most Influential People in the World, TIME Magazine (2012); Named Freshman Legislator of the Year, Florida Petroleum Marketers Association, Inc. **PA:** Republican **RE:** Roman Catholic

RUDDY, CHRISTOPHER, T: News Media Executive **I:** Media & Entertainment **DOB:** 01/28/1965 **PB:** Mineola **SC:** NY/USA **PT:** Francis Ruddy; Marie (Lynch) Ruddy **ED:** MS in Economics, London School of Economics (LSE) (1988); BA in History, St. John's University, Jamaica, NY (1987) **C:** Chief Executive Officer, Founder, Newsmax Media (1998-Present); National Correspondent, Pittsburgh Tribune-Review (1995-1998); Investigative Reporter, New York Post (1993-1994); Editor in Chief, New York Guardian (1990-1993); Teacher, Social Studies, High School, Bronx, NY **CR:** Media Fellow, Hoover Institution on War, Revolution, and Peace; Founding Board Member, Financial Publishers Association; Former Representative, U.S. Delegation, NATO 44th Munich Security Conference **CIV:** Patron, Sustaining Donor, Wikimedia Foundation **CW:** Author, "Bitter Legacy: NewsMax Reveals the Untold Story of the Clinton-Gore Years" (2002); Co-Editor, "Catastrophe: Clinton's Role in America's Worst Disaster" (2002); Author, "The Strange Death of Vincent Foster: An Investigation" (1997); Author, "Vincent Foster: The Ruddy Investigation" (1996) **AW:** Media Fellow, Stanford University (1996); Courage in Journalism Award, Western Journalism Center (1994) **MEM:** New York Press Club; International Council; Alumnus, American Swiss Foundation

RUGGERA, PAUL S., MS, T: Special Product Engineer **I:** Engineering **DOB:** 08/30/1944 **PB:** Rock Springs **SC:** WY/USA **PT:** David Joe Ruggera; Anna Eva (Ribovich) Ruggera **MS:** Married **SPN:** Doris Ann Hankins (07/10/1971) **ED:** MS in Bioengineering, University of Wyoming (1968); BSEE, University of Wyoming (1966) **CT:** Registered Professional Engineer, Virginia **C:** Independent Consultant, Electromagnetic Compatibility of Medical Devices (2014-Present); Special Product Engineer, Center for Devices and Radiological Health, Rockville, MD (1982-Present); Civil Servant, Center for Devices and Radiological Health, FDA (1998-2006); Consultant to FDA (2007-2013); Special Medical Products Engineer, Bureau Radiological Health, Rockville, MD (1972-1982); Staff Engineer, National Center for Radiological Health, Rockville, MD (1968-1972) **CR:** Life Member, The Institute of Electrical and Electronics Engineers (IEEE)(1963-Present); Member, IEEE EMC Society **MIL:** Commissioned Officer, U.S. Public Health Service (1968-1998); Advanced to Captain, U.S. Public Health Service (1986) **CW:** Contributor, Articles, IEEE EMC Society Proceedings, IEEE Transactions on Biomedical Engineering, International Journal Hyperthermia, Cryobiology, Biomedical Instrumentation and Technology, Pace, Physics in Medicine and Biology, Magnetic Resonance Imaging, Surgical Rounds for Orthopedics **AW:** U.S. Food and Drug Administration Group Award (1996, 2001, 2003, 2004); Unit Citation, U.S. Public Health Service (1995, 1997); PHS Citation (1991, 1992); Outstanding Unit Citation (1991); Commendation Medal, U.S. Public Health Service (1980, 1991) **MEM:** Electromagnetic Compatibility Committee, Association for Advancement Medical Instrumentation (1995-2000); Pacemaker Subcommittee on Electro-magnetic Compatibility, Association for Advancement Medical Instrumentation (1998); AE-4 committee on Electromagnetic Compatibility, Society Automotive Engineers (1972-1998); Senior

Life Member, IEEE; Eagles **MH:** Albert Nelson Marquis Lifetime Achievement Award **B/I:** Mr. Ruggera is especially proud of obtaining a patent, along with co-inventor, Gideon Kantor, PhD, Helical Coil for Diathermy Apparatus. He later obtained another patent for a diathermy coil. **AV:** Photography **PA:** Democrat **RE:** Roman Catholic

RUHLE, STEPHANIE LEIGH, T: Anchor, Senior Business Correspondent **I:** Media & Entertainment **CN:** MSNBC Live **DOB:** 12/24/1975 **PB:** Park Ridge **SC:** NJ/USA **PT:** Frank Ruhle; Louise Ruhle **MS:** Married **SPN:** Andy Hubbard **CH:** Three Children **ED:** BA in International Business, Lehigh University (1997) **C:** Senior Business Correspondent, NBC News (2020-Present); Anchor of "MSNBC Live with Stephanie Ruhle," Co-Anchor of "Velshi and Ruhle," NBC News (2016-Present); Contributor, New Baby New Body Column, Shape Magazine, New York, NY (2013-Present); TV Anchor, Managing Editor, Bloomberg News Editor-at-Large, Bloomberg, New York, NY (2011-2016); Managing Director, Deutsche Bank (2003-2011); Vice President, Credit Suisse (1997-2003) **CIV:** Board Member, Girls Inc. NYC (2011-Present); Board Member, React to Film (2010-Present); Board of Directors, Deutsche Bank; MBA Fellows Program, Steering Committee, Women on Wall St. Network **AW:** Named, Banks Leaders in Diversity (2008) **MEM:** 100 Women in Hedge Funds (2011-Present); Womens Bond Club (2010-Present); Corporate Advisory Board, I-Mentor (2011-2012); Corporate Council, White House Project (2009-2012) **RE:** Catholic

RUIZ, RAUL, MD, T: U.S. Representative from California; Physician **I:** Government Administration/Government Relations/Government Services **DOB:** 08/25/1972 **PB:** Zacatecas City **SC:** Mexico **MS:** Married **SPN:** Monica Rivers (2014) **CH:** Two Daughters **ED:** Residency in Emergency Medicine, University of Pittsburgh; Fellowship in International Emergency Medicine, Brigham and Women's Hospital; MS in Public Health, Harvard T.H. Chan School of Public Health (2007); Masters of Public Policy, Harvard Kennedy School, John F. Kennedy School of Government (2001); MD, Harvard Medical School (2001); BS, University of California Los Angeles (1994) **C:** Member, U.S. House Committee on Veterans' Affairs (2013-Present); Member, U.S. House of Representatives from California's 36th Congressional District, Washington, DC (2013-Present); Member, U.S. House Committee on Natural Resources (2013-Present); Senior Associate Dean, University of California Riverside School of Medicine (2011-2012); Emergency Physician, Eisenhower Medical Center (Eisenhower Health); Consultant, El Salvadoran Ministry Health; Consultant, Serbian Ministry of Health **CR:** Medical Director, J/P Haitian Relief Organization (2010); Founder, Coachella Valley Healthcare Initiative (2010) **CIV:** Member, Seventh-day Adventist Church **AW:** Commander's Award for Public Service, 82nd Airborne Division, United States Army (2011) **PA:** Democrat **RE:** Seventh-day Adventist

RUMMEL, RAYMOND, "BUTCH" HOWARD, EDS, MED, T: Mathematics Educator (Retired) **I:** Education/Educational Services **CN:** School Board of Alachua County **DOB:** 04/15/1956 **PB:** Pittsburgh **SC:** PA/USA **PT:** Raymond Alfred Rummel; Evelyn Louis Getchell **MS:** Married **SPN:** Eva Rummel, RN **CH:** Britta Gruenwald; Raymond Ryan Rummel; Christa Rummel **ED:** EdS in Educational Leadership, University of Florida (1991); MEd in Mathematics Education, University of Florida(1983); BS in Business Administration with Honors, University of Florida, with Honors (1981); AA University of Florida (1979); High School Diploma, PK Yonge Laboratory School, Gainesville, FL (1974) **CT:** Cer-

tified, Educational Leadership (All Areas), Secondary Education (Grades 9-12), Mathematics, Middle School Education (Grades 5-8) and Mathematics **C:** Retired (2018); Teacher, Howard Bishop Middle School, Academy of Technology, Science and Gifted Studies, Grade 8, Gainesville, FL (14 Years); Teacher, Newberry High School, Grades 9-12, Newberry, FL (10 Years); Teacher, Oak View Middle School (Opened New School), Grade 8, Newberry, FL (1/2 Year); Teacher, Newberry Jr. High School (Now Oak View Middle School), Grade 8, Newberry, FL (3 1/2 Years); Teacher, Spring Hill Middle School (Open Space Concept), Grades 5-8, High Springs, FL (8 Years) **CR:** Mathematics Teacher, Reach Out Program, Santa Fe College; Summer School Mathematics Teacher, Adult Education, GED Mathematics Teacher, Mathematics Instructor, Sylvan Learning, LLC; Exceptional Student Education Teacher; Coach, Competitive Mathematics, MATHCOUNTS Foundation; NEWMAST (NASA Workshop for Math and Science Teachers) **AW:** STAR Teacher Award (2007); Named Teacher of the Year, Howard Bishop Middle School (2006-2007); Runner Up, Teacher of the Year, Huntington Learning Center Student's Choice Teacher Award (2005-2006); Named Sigma Xi Math/Science Teacher of the Year (1995); Inductee, Pi Lamdba Theta/Alpha Phi Chapter Honor Society (1989); Inductee, Kappa Delta Pi (Now Kappa Delta Pi, International Honor Society in Education), Upsilon Chapter (1982); Coach of Second Place Team in State; Selected One of 25 Teachers, FL, GA and Puerto Rico **MH:** Listee, Marquis Who's Who for the American Educator Award (2020); Listee, Who for American Teachers Award (1994, 1996, 1998, 2002-2005); Listee, Who's Who for the American Education Award (1990) **AS:** Mr. Rummel was always student-centered. He believes that every one of his students has a gift to do something better than he can do and his job as a teacher is to help them find that gift and enhance it. **B/I:** Mr. Rummel wanted to help young people and make a contribution to the betterment of society. He thought mathematics was sequentially taught. He believes math is a subject that a lot of people cannot understand right away and students need someone who is capable of breaking it down to their level so that they can understand. When Mr. Rummel was in college, he was a business major. Due to working full time to support his young family, he did not have much time where he was able to go to the library (card catalog) and write papers. That being said, all of his elective courses were math-related so that he didn't have to write papers. He is self taught. After graduating in business administration, he went into the teaching profession for family reasons. **AV:** Volunteering and helping people **THT:** Mr. Rummel has had several teaching mentors, including Dr. Don Bernard, University of Florida, Professor for Math Education and Raymond A. Rummel, his father, University of Florida Professor in Material Science and winner of the UF Presidential Award for best teacher. Mr. Rummel's children are Britta Gruenwald, Radiology, Ryan Rummel (Philosophy) and Christa Rummel, in Business Administration; Mr. Rummel has three grandchildren, Madeline Gruenwald, Dalton Gruenwald and Charlie Rummel. Mr. Rummel's motto is, "To teach, is to learn twice" quoted by Joseph Joubert.

RUMSFELD, DONALD HENRY, T: Former U.S. Secretary of Defense **I:** Government Administration/Government Relations/Government Services **DOB:** 07/09/1932 **PB:** Chicago **SC:** IL/USA **PT:** George Donald Rumsfeld; Jeannette Kearsley (Husted) Rumsfeld **MS:** Married **SPN:** Joyce Pierson (1954) **CH:** Three Children **ED:** Honorary PhD, Pardee RAND Graduate School (1993); Honorary

LLD, Lake Forest College (1975); AB, Princeton University (1954); Honorary PhD, Hampden-Sydney College; Honorary PhD, Illinois Wesleyan University; Honorary PhD, Claremont Graduate University, CA; Honorary PhD, Bryant College (Now Bryant University); Honorary PhD, National College of Education, National Louis University; Honorary PhD, Tuskegee Institute; Honorary PhD, Park College (Now Park University); Honorary PhD, Illinois College; Honorary PhD, DePaul University College of Commerce (Now Driehaus College of Business) C: Distinguished Visiting Fellow, Hoover Institution, Stanford University (2007-Present); U.S. Secretary, U.S. Department of Defense, Washington, DC (1975-1977, 2001-2006); Chairman, Gilead Sciences, Inc., Foster City, CA (1997-2001); Chairman, Chief Executive Officer, General Instrument Corp., Chicago, IL (1990-1993); Senior Adviser, William Blair & Company, L.L.C., Chicago, IL (1985-1990); Chairman, Chief Executive Officer, G.D. Searle & Co., Skokie, IL (1985); Special Presidential Ambassador to Middle East, The White House, Washington, DC (1983-1984); President, Chief Executive Officer, G.D. Searle & Co., Skokie, IL (1977-1985); Chief of Staff to President, The White House, Washington, DC (1974-1975); Chair Transition to Presidency of Gerald R. Ford, The White House, Washington, DC (1974); U.S. Ambassador and Permanent Representative to NATO, U.S. Department of State, Brussels, Belgium (1973-1974); Director, Cost of Living Council, The White House, Washington, DC (1971-1973); Counselor to the President, The White House, Washington, DC (1970-1973); Director, Office of Economic Opportunity, The White House, Washington, DC (1969-1970); Assistant to the President, The White House, Washington, DC (1969-1970); Member, U.S. House of Representatives from Illinois' 13th Congressional District, United States Congress, Washington, DC (1963-1969); Investment Broker, A.G. Becker & Co., Chicago, IL (1960-1962); Member, Staff to Representative Robert Griffin, U.S. House of Representatives (1959); Administrative Assistant to Representative David Dennison, U.S. House of Representatives (1957-1959) CR: Member, U.S. Commission to Assess National Security Space Management and Organization (2000); Commissioner, U.S. Federal Trade Deficit Review Commission (1999-2000); Chairman, U.S. Commission to Assess the Ballistic Missile Threat to the U.S. (1998); Member, Commission on U.S./Japan Relations (1989-1991); Board of Visitors, National Defense University (1988-1992); Member, National Economic Commission (1988-1989); Member, National Commission on Public Service (1987-1990); Senior Adviser to the President, Panel on Strategic Systems (1983-1984); Member, General Advisory Committee on Arms Control (1983-1984); Adviser to the Government on National Security Affairs (1983-1984); Member, U.S. Joint Advisory Commission on U.S./Japan Relations (1983-1984); Member, Special Presidential Envoy on the Law of the Sea Treaty (1982-1983) CIV: Founder, The Rumsfeld Foundation (2007-Present) MIL: Captain, United States Navy (1975-1989); With, U.S. Navy Reserve (1957-1975); Aviator, U.S. Navy (1954-1957) CW: Appearance, Documentary, "The Unknown Known" (2014); Appearance, Documentary, "The World According to Dick Cheney" (2013); Author, "Rumsfeld's Rules: Leadership Lessons in Business, Politics, War, and Life" (2013); Author, "Known and Unknown: A Memoir" (2011); Author, "Strategic Imperatives in East Asia" (1988) AW: Named Grand Cordon, Order of the Rising Sun (2015); National Flag Award, Albania's President Bujar Nishani (2013); Defender of the Constitution Award, Conservative Political Action Conference (2011); Named Special Grand Cordon, Order of Brilliant Star, China (2011); Victory of Freedom Award, Richard Nixon Foundation (2010); Claremont Institute Statesmanship Award (2007); Gold Medal for Citizenship, Union League of Philadelphia (2006); Named Grand Cross, Order of Merit of the Republic of Poland (2005); Gerald R. Ford Medal, Ford Foundation (2004); Ronald Reagan Freedom Award (2003); James H. Doolittle Award, Hudson Institute (2003); Statesmanship Award, United States Association of Former Members of Congress (2003); Lone Sailor Award, United States Navy Memorial Foundation (2002); Dwight David Eisenhower Medal (1993); Woodrow Wilson Award, Princeton University (1985); George Catlett Marshall Award (1984); George C. Marshall Medal, Association of the United States Army (1984); Outstanding Chief Executive Officer in the Pharmaceutical Industry Award, Wall Street Transcript and Financial World (1980); Presidential Medal of Freedom with Distinction, The White House (1977); Distinguished Eagle Scout Award (1975); Named to Order of Anthony Wayne, Valley Forge Military Academy; Distinguished Eagle Scout Award by the Boy Scouts of America PA: Republican

RUNYON, CHUCK, T: Chief Executive Officer I: Business Management/Business Services CN: Self Esteem Brands C: Chief Executive Officer, Co-Founder, Self Esteem Brands, LLC, Minneapolis, MN (2002-Present) CW: Contributor, "5 Essential Leadership Traits For The New Transparency Era," Huffington Post (2013); Contributor, "Are You A Level 5 Company?," Fast Company (2012); Contributor, "4 Rules For Tattoo-Level Brand Loyalty," Fast Company (2012); Contributor, "Working Out Sucks," Da Capo Lifelong Books (2012) AW: Listee, Top Global Franchise, Entrepreneur Magazine (2016); Listee, Best Franchises in America, Forbes (2016); Listee, Fastest-Growing Fitness Club in the World, Entrepreneur Magazine (2016); Listee, Franchise 500, Fitness Business Category, Entrepreneur Magazine (2016); Listee, #1 Franchise for Veterans, Top Global Franchise, Entrepreneur Magazine (2015); Listee, Best Franchises to Buy, Forbes (2015); Listee, Franchise 500, Entrepreneur Magazine (2013); Best Company to Work For in Minnesota, Minnesota Business Magazine (2013); Fastest-Growing Fitness Club in the World, Club Business International (2013); Listee, America's Most Promising Companies, Forbes (2013); #1 Fitness Business, Entrepreneur Magazine (2013); Top Military Friendly Franchise, GI Jobs (2013); Best Franchise Business Model, FranchiseChattter. com (2011); Listee, 10 Great Franchise Bets, CNN Money (2011); John McCarthy Industry Visionary Award, IHRSA (2009)

RUPPERSBERGER, CHARLES, "DUTCH" ALBERT III, T: U.S. Representative from Maryland I: Government Administration/Government Relations/Government Services CN: U.S. House of Representatives DOB: 01/31/1946 PB: Baltimore SC: MD/USA PT: Charles Albert Ruppersberger; Margaret (Wilson) Ruppersberger MS: Married SPN: Kay Murphy (12/28/1968) CH: Charles Albert; Jill Ann ED: Doctor of Jurisprudence, University of Baltimore School of Law (1970); Bachelor of Arts, University of Maryland (1967) C: Member, U.S. House of Representatives from Maryland's Second Congressional District, United States Congress (2003-Present); Ranking Member, U.S. House Permanent Select Committee on Intelligence (2011-2015); Member, U.S. House Permanent Select Committee on Intelligence (2003-2015); Partner, Mister, Winter & Bartlett LLC, Timonium, MD (1980-1994); Assistant State Attorney, Baltimore County State Attorney, Towson, MD (1972-1980); Law Clerk to Presiding Justice, Baltimore County Circuit Court, Towson, MD (1970-1972); Claims Adjuster, U.S. Fidelity & Guaranty Company, Baltimore, MD (1969-1970); Social Worker, Baltimore City Schools (1967-1969) CR: Liaison, Baltimore County Police Department/Maryland State Police (1973-1980); Chief Investigation, Division of State Attorney's Office, Towson, MD (1972-1980) CIV: Board of Directors, Timonium United Methodist Church (1984-Present); President, Greater Timonium Community Council, MD (1980-Present); Coach, Vice President, Cockeysville Recreation Council (1978-Present); Councilman, Baltimore County Council (1985-1994); Campaign Manager, Senator Francis X. Kelly, Annapolis, MD (1980-1985); President, Topfield Condominium Association, Cockeysville, MD (1975-1978); Member, Legal Council, Baltimore County Athletic League AW: Named, One of the Outstanding Young Marylanders, Jaycees (1979); Appreciation Award, Baltimore County Fraternal Order of Police (1977, 1979) MEM: Advisor, National College of District Attorneys (1974-1980); Vice President, University of Maryland Alumni Association; Chairperson, Bench-bar Committee, Baltimore County Bar Association; Grievance Committee, Maryland Bar Association; National College of District Attorneys; University of Maryland Alumni Association; Baltimore County Bar Association; Maryland Bar Association; Masons BAR: Supreme Court of the United States (1977); State of Maryland (1972) PA: Democrat RE: Methodist

RUSH, BOBBY LEE, T: U.S. Representative I: Government Administration/Government Relations/Government Services DOB: 11/23/1946 PB: Albany SC: GA/USA MS: Married SPN: Carolyn Ryan CH: Five Children ED: Honorary HHD, Illinois Institute of Technology (2017); MA in Theological Studies, McCormick Theological Seminary (1978); MA in Political Science, The University of Illinois at Chicago (1974); BA in General Studies, Roosevelt University, with Honors, Chicago, IL (1973) C: U.S. Representative, Illinois' First Congressional District, United States Congress (1993-Present); Deputy Chairman, Illinois Democratic Party (1990); Democratic Committeeman, Central Illinois (1990); City Alderman, Chicago, IL (1984-1993); Democratic Committeeman, Chicago Second Ward, IL (1984, 1988); Member, Committee on Energy; Member, Committee on Commerce; Chairman, Capitol Development Committee; Chairman, Historic Landmark Preservation Committee; Chairman, Committee on Budget; Chairman, Committee on Government Operations; Chairman, Environmental Protection, Energy and Public Utilities Committee; Insurance Agent, Prudential Insurance Company (Prudential Financial, Inc.); Associate Dean, Daniel Hale Williams University; Financial Planner, Sanmar Financial Planning Corporation CIV: Founder, Illinois Black Panther Party; Former Coordinator, Free Medical Clinic; Former Coordinator, Free Breakfast for Children AW: One of the Power 150, Ebony Magazine (2008); One of the Most Influential Black Americans (2006); Distinguished Political Leadership Award, Chicago Black United Communities; Outstanding Business and Professional Achievement Award, South End Jaycees; Outstanding Community Service Award, Henry Booth House; Outstanding Young Man Award, Operation PUSH; Enterprise Zone Award, Illinois Department of Commerce and Community PA: Democrat

RUSHDIE, SALMAN, T: Writer I: Writing and Editing DOB: 06/19/1947 PB: Mumbai SC: India PT: Anis Ahmed Rushdie; Negin (Butt) Rushdie SPN: Padma Lakshmi (2004, Divorced 2007); Elizabeth West (1997, Divorced 2004); Marianne Wiggins (1988, Divorced 1993); Clarissa Luard (1976, Divorced 1987) CH: Zafar; Milan ED: DHL (Honorary), Chapman University, Orange, CA (2008); MA in History, King's College, Cambridge University, England, With Honors (1968) **C:** Distinguished Writer in Residence, English Department, Emory University, Atlanta, GA (2007-Present); Freelance Advertising Copywriter, Ayer Barker; Freelance Advertising Copywriter, Ogilvy & Mather **CR:** Honorary Visiting Professor of the Humanities, Massachusetts Institute of Technology (MIT) (1993-Present); President, PEN American Center (2004-2006); Founder, PEN World Voices Festival **CW:** Author, "Quichotte" (2019); Author, "The Golden House" (2017); Author, "Two Years Eight Months and Twenty-Eight Nights" (2015); Author, "Joseph Anton: A Memoir" (2012); Author, "In the South," Booktrack (2012); Author, "Luka and the Fire of Life" (2010); Author, "A fine pickle," The Guardian (2009); Author, "The Enchantress of Florence" (2008); Author, "Shalimar the Clown" (2005); Author, "The East Is Blue" (2004); Author, "Step Across This Line: Collected Nonfiction 1992-2002" (2002); Author, "Fury" (2001); Author, "The Ground Beneath Her Feet" (1999); Author, "Imagine There Is No Heaven," Letters to the Six Billionth World Citizen, The Guardian (1999); Author, "The Moor's Last Sigh" (1995); Author, "Haroun and the Sea of Stories" (1990); Author, "The Satanic Verses" (1988); Author, "The Jaguar Smile: A Nicaraguan Journey" (1987); Author, "Shame" (1983); Author, "Midnight's Children" (1981); Author, "Grimus" (1975) **AW:** Swiss Freethinkers Award (2019); Hans Christian Andersen Literature Award (2014); St. Louis Literary Award, Saint Louis University Library Associates (2009); The Best of the Booker, "Midnight's Children" (2008); Honoree, Knight Bachelor, Queen Elizabeth II (2007); Aristeion Prize for European Literary (1996); Costa Novel Award, "The Moor's Last Sigh" (1995); Mythopoeic Fantasy Award for Children's Literature (1992); James Tait Black Memorial Prize - Fiction, "Midnight's Children" (1981); Booker Prize, "Midnight's Children" (1981); Golden PEN Award; Outstanding Lifetime Achievement in Cultural Humanism, Harvard University; PEN Pinter Prize; State Prize for Literature; Writers' Guild Award; Two Whitbread Prizes for Best Novel; Numerous Other Awards and Accolades **MEM:** Fellow, Royal Society of Literature; Honorary Member, American Academy of Arts and Letters

RUSSELL, STEVEN, "STEVE" DANE, T: Former U.S. Representative from Oklahoma **I:** Government Administration/Government Relations/Government Services **DOB:** 05/25/1963 **PB:** Oklahoma City **SC:** OK/USA **PT:** Clyde E. "Gene" Russell; Donna J. Porter Russell **MS:** Married **SPN:** Cindy (Myers) Russell (1985) **CH:** Five Children **ED:** Master of Military Arts and Sciences in Military History, Command and General Staff College (1998); BS in Public Speaking, Ouachita Baptist University (1985) **C:** Member, U.S. House of Representatives from Oklahoma's Fifth Congressional District, United States Congress, Washington, DC (2015-2019); Member, District 45, Oklahoma State Senate (2008-2013); Member, Committee on Armed Services, United States Congress; Member, Committee on Oversight and Government Reform, United States Congress; Member, House Republican Steering Committee **CR:** Featured Speaker, Premiere Speakers Bureau (2007-Present); Founder, Owner, Two Rivers Arms **CIV:** Member, First Southern Baptist Church, Del City, OK **MIL:** Advanced through Grades to Lieutenant Colonel, United States Army, Kosovo, Kuwait, Afghanistan and Operation Iraqi Freedom (1985-2006) **CW:** Author, "We Got Him! A Memoir of the Hunt and Capture of Saddam Hussein" (2011); Featured, Documentary, "Sacred Honor"; Military and Foreign Affairs Commentator, National Television and Radio Shows; Contributor, Articles, Professional Journals

AW: Inductee, Del City Hall of Fame; Decorated Valorous Unit Award; Combat Infantryman Badge, United States Army; Bronze Star with Valor Device and Oak Leaf Cluster; Legion of Merit; Six Meritorious Service Medals; Joint Service Commendation Medal; Three Army Commendation Medals; Four Army Achievement Medals; Two National Defense Service Medals; Armed Forces Expeditionary Medal; Kosovo Campaign Medal; Afghanistan Campaign Medal; Iraq Campaign Medal; Global War on Terrorism Expeditionary Medal; Global War on Terrorism Service Medal; Military Outstanding Volunteer Service Medal; NATO Medal for Kosovo; Ranger Tab; United States Army and Korean Parachutists Badge **MEM:** Military Order of the Loyal Legion of the United States **AV:** Teaching Sunday school; Reading and studying history; Playing guitar; Singing; Collecting military antiques and firearms **PA:** Republican **RE:** Baptist

RUSSIN, JONATHAN, T: Lawyer, Consultant **I:** Law and Legal Services **CN:** Russin & Vecchi PC **DOB:** 10/30/1937 **PB:** Kingston SC: PA/USA **PT:** Jacob S. Russin; Anne (Wartella) Russin **MS:** Married **SPN:** Antoinette Stackpole (10/06/1962) **CH:** Alexander; Andrew; Benjamin; Jacob **ED:** LLB, Yale Law School (1963); BA, Yale University (1959); Coursework in Spanish Language Training, Foreign Service Institute **C:** Partner, Director, Russin & Vecchi PC, Washington, DC (2014-Present); Partner, Director, Russian Practice Group, Russin & Vecchi, Moscow, Russia (1992-2013); Partner, Kaplan Russin & Vecchi, Washington, DC (1981-1992); Partner, Kaplan Russin & Vecchi, Madrid, Spain (1978-1981); Partner, Kirkwood, Kaplan, Russin & Vecchi, Washington, DC (1974-1978); Partner, Kirkwood, Kaplan, Russin & Vecchi, Santo Domingo, Dominican Republic (1969-1974); Regional Legal Adviser for Caribbean, Agency for International Development (1967-1969); General Counsel's Office, Agency for International Development, Ankara, Turkey (1963); Research Assistant, Law Faculty, University of East Africa, Dar es Salaam, Tanganyika, United Republic of Tanzania (1961-1962); Guide Interpreter, American National Exhibit, Moscow, Russia (1959) **CR:** Team Leader, Russian Law Advice for ExxonMobil, Shell, and BP Amoco, Russin & Vecchi PC (2001-Present); Legal Adviser, Orthodox Church in America (1985-2006); Convener, Advisory Council, Institute of European, Russian and Eurasian Studies, The George Washington University (1990-1996); Washington Representative, Moscow Patriarchate, Russian Orthodox Church (1992-1995); Trustee, Saint Vladimir's Orthodox Theological Seminary, Crestwood, NY (1985-1993); Trustee, St. Nicholas Orthodox Cathedral, Washington, DC (1982-1993); Member, Advisory Board, Caribbean American Directory (1985-1992); Consultant on Russian Business Issues and Supervision of Moscow Office Work, Banking Clients Including Commercial Bank of India, Credit Agricole Indosuez, European Bank for Reconstruction and Development (EBRD), HSH Nordbank AG, Moscow Narodny Bank, UPS Capital Business Credit; Coordinated and Supervised Advice Provided to Contractors of Energy Projects Including Aker Marine Contractors, The Armor Group, Crowley Marine Services (Crowley Maritime Corporation), Ecology and Environment, Inc., Foss Maritime, General Dynamics Corporation, Mitsui & Co. (U.S.A.), Posco Engineering & Construction, LTD., Raytheon Technical Services, Stolt Offshore Services (Now Stolt-Nielsen), Velosi America, and WorleyParsons; Organizer, Leader, Workshops on Issues Related to Contractors and Subcontractors, Annual Sakhalin Oil and Gas Conferences, London, England, United Kingdom, and Yuzhno-Sakhalinsk, Russia; Lecturer, Russian Legal Matters, Australian Embassy, Annual

Economic Conference, Moscow, Russia; Lecturer, Russian Oil and Gas Review, Moscow, Russia; Lecturer, Off-shore Technology Conference, Houston, Texas; Lecturer, Conference on Business in Russia, Chicago, IL; Founder, Supervisor, Russian Practice Group, Vladivostok, Russia and Yuzhno-Sakhalinsk, Russia **CIV:** Board of Directors, Fund for Democracy and Development, Washington, DC (1993-2001); Board of Directors, MUCIA Global Education Group, Inc. (1996-2000); Board of Directors, Delphi International, Inc., Washington, DC (1988-2000); Board of Directors, National Council for International Visitors (Global Ties), Washington, DC (1987-1993); Board of Directors, Dominican-American Cultural Institute, Santo Domingo, Dominican Republican (1988-1992); Advisor, U.S. Personnel on Cross-cultural Issues Affecting Policy and Strategy for ABA CEELI, Catholic Relief Services, Eurasia Foundation, Foundation for Russian American Economic Cooperation (FRAEC), International Orthodox Christian Charities, Orthodox Church in America, St. Seraphim Foundation, Rostropovich Vishnevskaya Foundation **CW:** Author, "Russia Chapter: International Encyclopedia of Agency and Distribution Agreements," Kluwer Law International (2012); Co-author, Chapter, "Labour Law: A Practical Global Guide," Globe Law and Business (2010); Co-author, Chapter, "Mergers & Acquisitions: A Practical Global Guide," Globe Business Publishing Ltd. (2007); Co-author, Chapter, "Company Formation: A Practical Global Guide," Globe Business Publishing Ltd. (2006); Author, "Business in Russia Today," Pacific Russia Oil & Gas Report (2002); Author, "The Powers That Be, The Constitutional Court of the Russian Federation," American Chamber of Commerce in Russia (2000); Author, "Forming a Russian Company," Sponsored by the Embassy of the Russian Federation in Washington, DC (1995); Author, "Forming a Dominican Company, 12th Edition," American Chamber of Commerce, Dominican Republic (1994); Contributor, Articles to Professional Journals **AW:** Named to Order of St. Vladimir, Moscow Patriarchate, Russian Orthodox Church (1991); Grantee, Ford Foundation (1961-1962); Research Grant, Royal Agricultural Society of England **MEM:** Board of Directors, Rostropovich Vishnevskaya Foundation (2019); Board of Directors, International Orthodox Christian Charities (IOCC) (2016); The District of Columbia Bar; The Yale Club of Washington, D.C.; The Yale Club of New York; ABA; Cosmos Club, Washington, DC **BAR:** The District of Columbia Bar (1964) **MH:** Albert Nelson Marquis Lifetime Achievement Award **B/I:** Mr. Russin became involved in his profession because since college, he has been interested in the problems of third world economic and political development. He spent a year in Africa assisting in the establishment of the first law school in East Africa. He worked for the Agency for International Development, where he was first a resident in Ankara, Turkey, and subsequently became the regional legal adviser resident in Santo Domingo, Dominican Republic. Mr. Russin then became a founding partner of Kirkwood, Kaplan, Russin & Vecchi, with law offices in Bangkok, Thailand, Saigon, Vietnam, Washington, DC and Santo Domingo, Dominican Republic. All of the projects he worked on shared the objective of promoting the economic and political development of local populations.

RUTHERFORD, JOHN HENRY, T: U.S. Representative from Florida; Former Sheriff **I:** Government Administration/Government Relations/Government Services **DOB:** 09/02/1952 **PB:** Omaha **SC:** NE/USA **MS:** Married **SPN:** Patricia Rutherford **CH:** Michelle; Lee **ED:** BS in Criminology, Florida State University (1974); AS in Criminology, Florida State College at Jacksonville (1972);

Diploma, National Executive Institute; Diploma, Florida National Academy **C:** Member, U.S. House of Representatives from Florida's Fourth Congressional District (2017-Present); Sheriff, City of Jacksonville, FL (2003-2015); Director of Corrections, City of Jacksonville, FL (1995-2003); Chief Patrol, City of Jacksonville, FL; Chief, Traffic and Special Operations, City of Jacksonville, FL; Chief of Services, City of Jacksonville, FL; Captain, City of Jacksonville, FL; Director, Region Five Criminal Justice Training Center, City of Jacksonville, FL; Lieutenant, Patrol and Detective Division, City of Jacksonville, FL; Sergeant, City of Jacksonville, FL; Uniformed Patrolman, City of Jacksonville, FL; Member, Committee on Homeland Security; Member, Committee on Veterans' Affairs **CIV:** Member, Assumption Catholic Church, Jacksonville, FL **RE:** Catholic

RUTHERFORD, WILLIAM D., T: Investment Executive **I:** Financial Services **CN:** Rutherford Investment Management **DOB:** 01/14/1939 **PB:** Marshalltown **SC:** IA/USA **PT:** William Donald Rutherford; Lois Esther (Drake) Rutherford **MS:** Widowed **SPN:** Joan Lamb; Karen Anderegg (01/02/1994, Deceased 2010); Janice W. Rutherford (02/04/1965, Divorced 03/1982) **CH:** Wayne Donald; Mel Drake **ED:** LLB, Harvard University (1964); BS, University of Oregon (1961) **C:** Principal, Rutherford Investment Management (1994-Present); Chief Executive Officer, Fiberboard Asbestos Compensation Trust, Portland, OR (1997); Managing Director, Macadam Capital Partners (1995-1996); Director of Special Projects, Metallgesellschaft AG (1994-1995); Board of Directors, President, Société Générale (1990-1993); President, Chief Executive Officer, ABD International, LLC (1988-1989); Executive Vice President, Director for U.S. and Australian Operations, ABD International, LLC (1987-1988); Chairman, Oregon Investment Council (1986-1987); Treasurer, State of Oregon (1984-1987); Member, Oregon House of Representatives (1977-1984); Private Practice, McMinnville, OR (1971-1984); House Counsel, May & Company (1969-1970); Associate, Cosgrave Vergeer Kester LLP (1966-1969) **CR:** Former Chairman, Board of Directors, Metro One Telecommunications **CIV:** Member, Investment Board, Oregon Community Foundation (2006-Present); Trustee, The Nature Conservancy (2005-2013); Board of Directors, Portland Opera (1995-1999) **MIL:** First Lieutenant, U.S. Army Reserves **CW:** Author, "Who Shot Goldilocks?: How Alan Greenspan Did in Our Jobs, Savings, and Retirement Plans Revised Edition" (2006) **AW:** Individual Freedom Award, American Civil Liberties Union (1981) **MEM:** Executive Committee, National Association of State Auditors, Comptrollers and Treasurers (1987); Executive Vice President, National Association of State Treasurers (1985-1986) **BAR:** U.S. District Court District of Oregon (1966); Oregon State Bar (1964) **MH:** Albert Nelson Marquis Lifetime Achievement Award; Marquis Who's Who Top Professional **B/I:** Mr. Rutherford became involved in his profession because he started working in his family business when he was 7 years old. He took on more and more responsibilities in the family business and by the time he was 10 he was handling the cash receipts, making out the bank statements and going to the bank and making deposits.

RUTLEDGE, THOMAS M., T: Chairman, Chief Executive Officer **I:** Corporate Communications & Public Relations **CN:** Charter Communications, Inc. **ED:** Graduate, Advanced Management Program, Harvard Business School, Harvard University (1995); BA in Economics, California University, California, PA (1977) **C:** Chairman, Chief Executive Officer, Charter Communications, Inc.

(2016-Present); President, Director, Chief Executive Officer, Charter Communications, Inc. (2012-2016); Chief Operating Officer, Cablevision Systems Corporation (2004-2011); President, Cable and Communications, Rainbow Media Holdings, LLC (2002-2004); President, Time Warner Cable (2001); Senior Executive Vice President, Time Warner Cable (1991-2001); Manager Trainee, Division President, Numerous Positions American Television and Communications (ATC) **CR:** Chairman, National Cable and Telecommunications Association (NCTA); Member, Board, CableLabs; Member, Board, C-SPAN **CIV:** Member, Board of Directors, CTAM Educational Foundation **AW:** Vanguard Award for Distinguished Leadership, National Cable and Telecommunications Association (NCTA); Inductee, Broadcasting and Cable Hall of Fame; Inductee, Cable Hall of Fame

RUTNER, STEPHEN M., PHD, T: 1) Brigadier General 2) Professor **I:** Military & Defense Services **CN:** 1) U.S. Army 2) Texas Technical University **PT:** Stephen J. Rutner; Patricia Rutner **MS:** Married **SPN:** Paige Springer **ED:** PhD in Business, Logistics, and Transportation, University of Tennessee, Knoxville (1995); MBA in Logistics and Marketing, University of Alabama (1992); BA in History, Millersville University, Millersville, PA (1987); MS in Strategic Studies, Military Strategic Studies, General, The U.S. Army War College **C:** Supply Chain Professor, Texas Technical University (2016-Present); Brigadier General, U.S. Army Reserve (1987-Present); Professor of Logistics and Transportation, Georgia Southern University (1996-2015); Visiting Associate Professor, University of Arkansas (2000-2002); Associate Professor, Georgia Southern University (1996-2001); Adjunct Professor, University of Tennessee (1992-1995); Strategic Analyst, International Business Machines, Charlotte, NC (1991) **CR:** Faculty Senate, Alternate (2012-Present); University Information Technology Advisory Panel (2004-2007); American Democracy Project Committee (2004-2006); Conference Co-Chairman, Logistics Educators' Conference, Council of Logistics Management, Philadelphia, PA (2005); Program Review Coordinator of Logistics and Intermodal Transportation (2000-2001); Reviewer, Council of Logistics Management Academic Conference (2000-2001); Faculty Senate, Alternate (1999-2001); Editor, American Society of Transportation and Logistics Annual Conference (2000); Reviewer, Academy for Marketing Science (2000); Reviewer, Intermodal Distribution Educational Academy (1997-2000); Reviewer, Alabama State University Transportation Center (1999); Track Chair, Reviewer, Academy of Marketing Theory and Practice (1998-1999) **CIV:** Angel Flight **MIL:** Deputy Commander, 84th Training Command, Fort Knox, KY (2018-Present); Captain, Army National Guard (1990-1996); Regular Army Second Lieutenant, U.S. Army (1987-1990) **CW:** Author, More Than 20 Civilian Publications, Articles, Defense Transportation Journal, Army Logistician **AW:** Bronze Star Medal; Defense Meritorious Service Medal; Meritorious Service Medal, 2 Oak Leaf Clusters; Army Commendation Medal, 5 Oak Leaf Clusters; U.S. Navy and Marine Corps Commendation Medal; Army Achievement Medal, Oak Leaf Cluster; Army Reserve Component Achievement Medal, 4 Oak Leaf Clusters; National Defense Service Medal, Bronze Star Device; Armed Forces Reserve Medal, M device and Bronze Hourglass; Iraq Campaign Medal; Global War on Terrorism Expeditionary and Service Medals; Army Service Ribbon; Army Overseas Ribbon; Army Reserve Overseas Training Ribbon; Joint Meritorious Unit Award; Army Meritorious Unit Commendation Award **MEM:** Academy of Marketing Science; American Marketing Association;

American Society of Transportation and Logistics, Incorporated; Association of Transportation, Law, Logistics, & Policy; Council of Logistics Management; Delta Nu Alpha Transportation Society; Warehouse Education and Research Council; National Defense Transportation Association; Transportation Corps Regimental Association; Army Reserve Association **AS:** Dr. Rutner attributes his success to academic and military mentors that have encouraged him to do the right thing and helped guide him in the right direction. **B/I:** Dr. Rutner became involved in his profession because as a young Army officer, he had many responsibilities. One of the secondary duties was to keep the tanks working, working with the maintenance and parts, and feeding the soldiers. After he got out of the military, he tried to figure out what he was going to do for the rest of his life. Back in the 1990s, companies were "dying" to get people with PhDs in the field of transportation. He thought it was a good opportunity and found out he really enjoyed the academic side. Thirty years later, he helps men and women find what they want to do with logistics. Jay Sterling, one of his mentors, said he would be really good as a professor, to which he thought, "Yeah, maybe," but in those days, he noted, "you could move back and forth between academia industry pretty easily with a degree in logistics and transportation...the PhD was a golden opportunity to either help the industry side and keep open the academic side." Once he got into the academic side, he realized his passion for it and that it was a right fit and that he will still be able to make a difference in people's lives. **THT:** Brigadier General Stephen M. Rutner is currently serving as the Deputy Commanding General for the 84th Training Command in Fort Knox, Kentucky as of July 2018. BG Rutner was commissioned as a Regular Army Second Lieutenant upon graduation from Millersville University in 1987. BG Rutner served on active duty in 4-64 Armor in the 24th Infantry Div (Mech) at Fort Stewart, GA. His assignments included armor platoon leader, company executive officer and battalion S3 Air. After serving on active duty, BG Rutner moved to the Alabama National Guard. He served in the 31st Separate Armor Bde as the Brigade Liaison Officer. Later he moved to the 1-152nd Armor Battalion as the S2 Intelligence Officer. In 1997, BG Rutner moved to the US Army Reserve and joined the 1189th Transportation Terminal Bde in Charleston, SC. Over the next 10 years, he served in a number of Positions to include Asst. S3, Vessel Officer, Terminal Officer, Vessel Chief and Pre-Stow Chief. His last position in the 1189th was as the Bde S3 Operations Officer while assigned in SW Asia operating multiple ports in support of both Operation Iraqi Freedom and Operation Enduring Freedom. BG Rutner assumed command of the 1181st Transportation Terminal Battalion in Oct of 2008. He mobilized the battalion back to SW Asia in 2009 where it earned the Meritorious Unit Commendation. He was then the G3 (Chief of Operations) of the Deployment Support Command, Birmingham, Alabama. BG Rutner then served as the Commander, Army Reserve Element, Defense Logistics Agency, Ft. Belvoir, Virginia. In 2014, BG Rutner took command of the 1189th Transportation Bde, in Charleston, SC before serving in his current position. BG Rutner is an honor graduate of the Armor Officer Basic and Advanced Courses, the Transportation Corps Officer Advance Course, the NBC Officer Course, the Junior Officer Maintenance Course, the US Army Airborne School, the Combined Arms and Services Staff School, the U.S. Army Command and General Staff College and the U.S. Army War College.

RYAN, CLAYTON, T: Manager **I:** Nonprofit & Philanthropy **CN:** Everyday Heroes, Inc **ED:** Coursework, University **C:** Manager, Everyday Heroes, Inc. (2012-Present) **AW:** Recipient, Several National Guard Awards **MEM:** Lions Club; Elk's Lodge **MH:** Marquis Who's Who Top Professional; Distinguished Humanitarian **AS:** Mr. Ryan attributes his success to the cause of his charity. 100% of all proceeds raised from his business go directly to veterans. **B/I:** Mr. Ryan was unable to serve in the military. His hometown has a high population of military veterans that need help doing tasks. Mr. Ryan felt compelled to help, and so he began Everyday Heroes, Inc. The company was started by his father and another veteran in 2006.

RYAN, EARL MARTIN, T: Public Affairs Analyst **I:** Government Administration/Government Relations/Government Services **DOB:** 10/23/1942 **PB:** Detroit **SC:** MI/USA **PT:** Thomas M. Ryan: Margaret L. (Halsey) Ryan **MS:** Married **SPN:** Jo Ellen Junod (07/03/1965) **CH:** Andrew M.; Jeffrey A. **ED:** MA in Political Science, Wayne State University (1968); BA in Political Science, University of Michigan (1964) **C:** President, Citizens Research Council of Michigan (1994-2009); President, Indian Fiscal Policy Institute (1987-1994); President, Public Affairs Research Council of Louisiana, Baton Rouge, LA (1984-1987); Director, Research, Citizens Research Council of Michigan, Detroit, MI (1977-1984); Director, Research, Legislature Program Effectiveness Review, Lansing, MI (1974-1977); Director, Research, Office of Program Effectiveness Review, Lansing, MI (1971-1974); Director, Research, Health Impact Project, Lansing, MI (1971); Budget Analyst, Department of Social Services, Lansing, MI (1970-1971); Research Associate, Citizens Research Council of Michigan, Lansing, MI (1967-1970); Director, Research, Detroit Urban League (1965-1967) **CR:** Adjunct Professor, Political Science, Wayne State University, Detroit, MI (2009-2016); Blue Ribbon Panel, Indianapolis Business Journal (1992-1994); Political Analyst, Station WWL-TV, New Orleans, LA (1986) **CIV:** Advisor, Transparency Project, Tunis, Tunisia (2014); Financial Services Volunteer Corporation **CW:** "Making Democracy Work: 100 Year history of the Citizens Research Council" (2016); Reporter, "Improving Financial Government in Tunisia, Financial Volunteer Services Corp." (2014) **AW:** Frederick Gruenberg Award, Governmental Research Association (2011); Distinguished Alumni Award (2000); Distinguished Achievement Award, Graduate Program of Public Administration Wayne State University, Detroit, MI (1991) **MEM:** President, Governmental Research Association (1985-1986); Governmental Financial Officers Association **MH:** Albert Nelson Marquis Lifetime Achievement Award **B/I:** When Mr. Ryan was at the University of Michigan, he declared his major as political science. In graduate school, he became interested in public administration. He later began working with the Citizens Research Council, which was associated with Wayne State University, where he got a master's degree. **AV:** Practicing photography **PA:** Independent **THT:** The organizations that Mr. Ryan ran were fact-based organizations; they spent a lot of time to make sure that the statements and conclusions they made were factual. In this environment, when the truth is up for grabs, his organizations were critical. He is proud to be a part of it.

RYAN, ELIZABETH ELLEN, T: Chief Executive Director, Film Director **I:** Media & Entertainment **CN:** Ryanworks **DOB:** 02/18/1959 **PB:** Oneida **SC:** NY/USA **PT:** Eric James Ryan, Jr.; Cynthia (Deitz) Ryan **ED:** AB, Harvard University (1981) **C:** Director, Producer, Assistant Director, Features and Television, Universal Pictures (1992-Present); Director, Producer, Assistant Director, Features and Television, Twentieth Century Fox (1992-Present); Director, Producer, Assistant Director, Features and Television, Walt Disney Studios (1992-Present); Director, Producer, Assistant Director, Features and Television, Paramount Pictures (1992-Present); Director, Producer, Assistant Director, Features and Television, Indie Studios (1992-Present); Chief Executive Officer, Ryanworks, Inc. (1986-Present); Trainee, Member, Directors Guild of America (1983-1985); Finance Analyst, Morgan Stanley, New York, NY (1981-1983); Reporter, Time Inc. (Now Meredith) (1977-1981); Stringer, Time Inc. (Now Meredith) (1977-1981); Reporter, Stringer, The New York Times Company (1977-1981) **CR:** Freelance Writer, Premier Magazine, New York, NY (1986-Present); Freelance Writer, Premier Magazine, Los Angeles, CA (1986-Present); Freelance Writer, Time Inc. (Now Meredith) (1986-Present); Script Doctor (1986-Present); Career Advisor, Harvard University (1981-Present) **CIV:** Board Member, Friends of the Levitt Pavilion Mac Arthur Park (2009-2015) **CW:** Unit Production Manager, "Rosewood" (2015-2016); Assistant Director, "Leave It to Beaver" (1997); Assistant Director, "Waiting for Guffman" (1997); Assistant Director, "Alien 3" (1992); Assistant Director, "For the Boys" (1991); Assistant Director, "Another You" (1991); Assistant Director, "Green Card" (1991); Assistant Director, "Betsy's Wedding" (1990); Assistant Director, "State of Grace" (1990); Associate Producer, "Pepito's Dream" (1990); Assistant Director, "Jacknife" (1989); Assistant Director, "Shakedown" (1988); Assistant Director, "Black Widow" (1987); Assistant Director, "Punchline"; Assistant Director, "NYPD Blue" **AW:** Frank Capra Award, Directors Guild of America (2008) **MEM:** National Board Associate, DGA (2011-Present); Producers Guild of America (2008-Present); Board of Trustees, Producers Training Program, DGA (2007-Present); Council Member, DGA (1986-Present); Elected Director, Harvard Alumni Association (2009-2013); Screen Actors Guild; New York Women in Film & Television; Women in Film Los Angeles **MH:** Albert Nelson Marquis Lifetime Achievement Award **AS:** Ms. Ryan attributes her success to having enthusiasm, optimism, and determination. **B/I:** Ms. Ryan became involved in her profession because she grew up in a community where people did not read books, and, instead, got their entire view of the world from television and movies. It bothered her that no one she saw in those productions reflected her life experiences, so she decided to get involved in television and movies to change the content to better reflect the various challenges that people experience in real life.

RYAN, HARRIET, T: Reporter **I:** Writing and Editing **CN:** The Los Angeles Times **ED:** BA in English, Columbia University (1996) **C:** Writer, Reporter, The Los Angeles Times (2008-Present); Senior Correspondent, Court TV Online (1999-2007); Reporter, Asbury Park Press (1996-1999) **AW:** Co-Recipient, Pulitzer Prize (2019)

RYAN, MATT THOMAS, T: Professional Football Player **I:** Athletics **CN:** Atlanta Falcons **DOB:** 05/17/1985 **PB:** Exton **SC:** PA/USA **PT:** Michael Ryan; Bernice (Loughery) Ryan **MS:** Married **SPN:** Sarah Ryan **CH:** Marshall; Johnny **ED:** BS in Management, Boston College (2007); Diploma, William Penn Charter School **C:** Offensive Captain, Atlanta Falcons (2009-Present); Quarterback, Atlanta Falcons (2008-Present) **CR:** Active Participant, American Century Celebrity Golf Classic **CIV:** Participant, Online Reading Program, "Read with a Falcon" **CW:** Featured, "Schooled" (2019) **AW:** NFL Most Valuable Player (2016); NFL Offensive Player of the Year (2016); Bert Bell Award (2016); Four-Time Winner, Pro Bowl Champion (2010, 2012, 2014, 2016); NFC Offensive Player of the Month (2010, 2012, 2016); NFC Player of the Month (2010); ESPY Award for Best Breakthrough Athlete (2009); NEXT Athlete Award, ESPN The Magazine (2009); Pepsi NFL Rookie of the Week (2008); NFL Offensive Rookie of the Year (2008); ACC Player of the Year (2007); Manning Award (2007); Johnny Unitas Golden Arm Award (2007); MTV, MPC Computers Bowl (2005) **AV:** Playing golf **RE:** Roman Catholic

RYAN, NOLAN, T: Professional Baseball Team Executive, Former Professional Baseball Player **I:** Athletics **DOB:** 01/31/1947 **PB:** Refugio **SC:** TX/USA **PT:** Lynn Nolan Ryan; Martha (Hancock) Ryan **MS:** Married **SPN:** Ruth Elsie Holdruff (06/26/1967) **CH:** Reid; Reese; Wendy **ED:** Coursework, Alvin Junior College (Now Alvin Community College), Texas (1966-1969) **C:** Executive Adviser, Houston Astros (2014-2019); Chief Executive Officer, Texas Rangers (2011-2013); President, Texas Rangers (2008-2011); Pitcher, Texas Rangers (1989-1993); Pitcher, Houston Astros (1980-1988); Pitcher, California Angels (Now Los Angeles Angels) (1972-1979); Pitcher, New York Mets (1968-1971, 1966) **CR:** Majority Owner, Chairman, Express Bank of Alvin (2005); Owner, Corpus Christi Hooks; Principal Owner, Ryan Sanders Sports and Entertainment; Owner, Nolan Ryan's Waterfront Steakhouse & Grill, Three Rivers, TX **CIV:** Commissioner, Texas Parks and Wildlife Commission (1995-2001); Vice Chairman, Texas Parks and Wildlife Commission (1995-1997); Founder, Nolan Ryan Foundation; Member, Board of Directors, Nolan Ryan Foundation; Member, Board of Directors, Natural Resources Foundation, Texas; Member, Board of Directors, Texas Water Foundation; Member, Board of Directors, Justin Cowboy Crisis Fund **CW:** Co-Author, "The Road to Cooperstown" (1999); Co-Author, "Kings of the Hill" (1992); Co-Author, "Miracle Man" (1992); Co-Author, "Nolan Ryan's Pitcher's Bible" (1991); Co-Author, "Throwing Heat" (1988); Co-Author, "Pitching and Hitting" (1977); Co-Author, "Nolan Ryan: Strike-Out King" (1975); TV Spokesman, Advil **AW:** Inductee, Texas Cowboy Hall of Fame (2010); Inductee, Baseball Hall of Fame (1999); Member, National League All-Star Team (1989, 1985, 1981); Member, American League All-Star Team (1979, 1977, 1975, 1972-1973); Named, American League Pitcher of the Year, Sporting News (1977); Inductee, Angels Hall of Fame; Inductee, Houston Astros Hall of Fame; Inductee, Texas Rangers Hall of Fame

RYAN, PAUL DAVIS, T: Former Speaker of the House **I:** Government Administration/Government Relations/Government Services **CN:** U.S. House of Representatives **DOB:** 01/29/1970 **PB:** Janesville **SC:** WI/USA **PT:** Paul Murray Ryan; Elizabeth A. (Hutter) Ryan **MS:** Married **SPN:** Janna Christine (Little) Ryan (2000) **CH:** Elizabeth Ann; Charles Wilson; Samuel Lowery **ED:** Honorary Doctorate, Miami University, Ohio (2009); BS in Economics and Political Science, Miami University, Ohio (1992) **C:** Speaker, U.S. House of Representatives, U.S. Congress (2015-2019); U.S. House of Representatives from Wisconsin's First Congressional District, U.S. Congress, Washington, DC (1999-2019); Chairman, U.S. House Committee on Ways and Means (2015-2017); Chairman, U.S. House Committee on Budget (2011-2015); Marketing Consultant, Ryan Inc. Central, Janesville, WI (1997-1998); Legislative Director to Rep. Sam Brownback, U.S. House of Representatives, Washington, DC (1995-1997); Economic Advisor, Speechwriter to Bill Bennett and Jack Kemp, Empower America Project, Washington, DC (1993-1995); Aide to Sen. Bob Kasten, U.S. Senate, Washington, DC (1992) **CR:** Board of

Directors, Fox Corporation (2019-Present); Faculty, University of Notre Dame (2019-Present); Republican Candidate for Vice President, U.S. Presidential Election (2012) **CW:** Author, "The Way Forward: Renewing the American Idea" (2014); Co-Author, "Young Guns: A New Generation of Conservative Leaders" (2010) **AW:** Named, 100 Most Influential People in the World, TIME Magazine (2011, 2016); Named, 50 Most Influential People in Global Finance, Bloomberg Markets (2012); Freedom and Prosperity Award, Mason Contractors Association of America (2011); Leadership Award, Jack Kemp Foundation (2011); Named, 50 Politicos to Watch, Politico (2010); Guardian of Small Business Award, National Federation of Independent Business (2010); Award for Manufacturing Legislative Excellence, National Association of Manufacturers (2009) **MEM:** Janesville YMCA (Now YMCA of Northern Rock County); Janesville Bowmen Inc. **PA:** Republican **RE:** Roman Catholic

RYAN, TIMOTHY, "TIM" JOHN, T: U.S. Representative from Ohio **I:** Government Administration/Government Relations/Government Services **DOB:** 07/16/1973 **PB:** Niles **SC:** OH/USA **PT:** Allen Leroy Ryan; Rochelle Maria (Rizzi) Ryan **MS:** Married **SPN:** Andrea Zetts (2013) **CH:** Brady **ED:** JD, University of New Hampshire Franklin Pierce School of Law, Concord, NH (2000); BA in Political Science, Bowling Green State University (1995); Coursework, Youngstown State University; Intern, Trumbull County Prosecutor's Office **C:** Member, U.S. House of Representatives from Ohio's 13th Congressional District, U.S. Congress (2013-Present); Candidate, Democratic Nominee, 2020 Presidential Election (2019); Member, U.S. House of Representatives from Ohio's 17th Congressional District, U.S. Congress (2003-2013); Member, District 32, Ohio State Senate, Columbus, Ohio (2001-2002); Congressional Aide to Representative James A. Traficant, U.S. House of Representatives (1995-1997); Member, Committee on Appropriations; Member, Committee on the Budget **AW:** Friend of National Parks Award, National Parks Conservation Association (2005); Legislative Leadership Award for Domestic Manufacturing, U.S. Business and Industry Council (2004) **MEM:** International Narcotic Enforcement Officers Association; Ancient Order Hibernians; Sons of Italy (Now Order Sons and Daughters of Italy in America); Elks **PA:** Democrat

RYANS, LISA, T: Director of Communications **I:** Corporate Communications & Public Relations **CN:** AutoNation, Inc. **CH:** One Daughter **ED:** MACC, Nova Southeastern University (2008); BACC, St. Thomas University, Miami, FL (2007) **C:** Director of Corporate Communications, AutoNation, Inc. (2018-Present); Senior Management, Corporate Communications, AutoNation, Inc. (2017-2018); Manager, Corporate Communications, AutoNation, Inc. (2015-2017); Manager, Investor Relations, AutoNation, Inc. (2015); Senior Analyst, Investor Relations, AutoNation, Inc. (2013-2015); Senior Analyst, Treasury, AutoNation, Inc. (2011-2013); Staff Accountant, AutoNation, Inc. (2008-2011); Account, Southern Wine and Spirits (2006-2008) **CR:** Adjunct Professor, Broward College (2014-2015) **CIV:** Vice-Chair, Kingdom Resource Center **AW:** Overdrive Award, AutoNation (2014, 2017) **AS:** Ms. Ryans attributes her success to self-confidence. She is always open to new opportunities and meeting great mentors. One of her greatest mentors was Sheryl Miller, the CEO of AutoNation. **B/I:** Ms. Ryans always wanted to be an attorney. However, she quickly discovered that she was better suited for the business industry. After exploring accounting, she once again discovered that she longed to be elsewhere. Building off her experience as an

accountant for AutoNation, she took on a job in the treasury department when it opened up. From there, she grew within the company.

SABAN, NICK, T: College Football Coach, Former Professional Football Coach **I:** Athletics **DOB:** 10/31/1951 **PB:** Fairmont **SC:** WV/USA **PT:** Nicholas Lou Saban; Mary Saban **MS:** Married **SPN:** Terry Constable (12/18/1971) **CH:** Nicholas; Kristen **ED:** MA in Sports Administration, Kent State University (1975); BS in Business, Kent State University (1973) **C:** Head Coach, University of Alabama Crimson Tide, Tuscaloosa, AL (2007-Present); Head Coach, Miami Dolphins (2005-2007); Head Coach, Louisiana State University Fighting Tigers, Baton Rouge, LA (2000-2005); Defensive Coordinator, Cleveland Browns (1991-1994); Head Coach, Toledo University Rockets (1990); Secondary Coach, Houston Oilers (1988-1989); Head Coach, Michigan State University Spartans (1995-2000); Secondary Coach, Defensive Coordinator, Michigan State University Spartans, East Lansing, MI (1983-1987); Secondary Coach, U.S. Naval Academy Midshipmen, Annapolis, MD (1981); Secondary Coach, Ohio State University Buckeyes, Columbus, OH (1980-1981); Secondary Coach, West Virginia University Mountaineers, Morgantown, WV (1978-1979); Outside Linebackers Coach, Syracuse University Orangemen (1977); Linebackers Coach, Kent State University Golden Flashes (1975-1976); Graduate Assistant, Kent State University Golden Flashes (1973-1974) **CIV:** Active Contributor, Children's Miracle Network; Co-Founder, Nick's Kids **CW:** Co-Author, "How Good Do You Want to Be?: A Champion's Tips on How to Lead and Succeed at Work and in Life" (2007); Co-Author, "Tiger Turnaround: LSU'S Return to Football Glory" (2002) **AW:** Two-Time Walter Camp Coach of the Year, National Collegiate Athletic Association (NCAA) Division I Football Bowl Subdivision (FBS) (2008, 2018); Named Coach of Year, Southeastern Conference (2003, 2008, 2009, 2016); George Munger Award (2016); Inductee, Alabama Hall of Fame (2013); Bobby Dodd Coach of the Year (2013); Home Depot Coach of the Year (2008); Sporting News Coach of the Year (2008); Two-Time Associated Press College Football Coach of the Year (2003, 2008); Two-Time Eddie Robinson Coach of the Year (2003, 2008); Paul "Bear" Bryant Award (2003); Numerous Coach of the Year Awards **AV:** Playing golf

SABLAN, GREGORIO KILILI CAMACHO, T: Delegate to the U.S. House of Representatives from the Northern Mariana Islands **I:** Government Administration/Government Relations/Government Services **DOB:** 01/19/1955 **PB:** Saipan **SC:** Commonwealth of the Northern Marian Islands **MS:** Married **SPN:** Andrea Sablan **CH:** Six Children **ED:** Coursework, University of Hawai'i at Manoa (1989-1990); Coursework, University of California Berkeley; Coursework, University of Guam **C:** Delegate, U.S. House of Representatives from the Northern Mariana Islands' At-large Congressional District, Washington, DC (2009-Present); Executive Director of the Commonwealth Election Commission (2002-2009); Special Assistant to Governor Pedro P. Tenorio (1998-2002); Special Assistant for Management and Budget, Governor Froilan Tenorio (1994-1998); Member, Northern Mariana Islands Commonwealth Legislature (1982-1986); Special Assistant to U.S. Senator Daniel Inouye; Member, Committee on Education and the Workforce; Member, Committee on Natural Resources; Member, Committee on Veterans' Affairs **PA:** Independent **RE:** Roman Catholic

SABOL, STEVE DOUGLAS, T: Filmmaker **I:** Media & Entertainment **CN:** NFL Films **DOB:** 10/2/1942 **PB:** Moorestown **SC:** NJ/USA **PT:** Ed Sabol **MS:** Married **SPN:** Penny Sabol; Lisa Sabol (Divorced) **CH:** Casey **C:** Filmmaker, NFL Films **CW:** Executive Producer, Documentary, "2012 Baltimore Ravens: Super Bowl XLVII Champions" (2013); Producer, Documentary, "NFL Characters Unite" (2012); Executive Producer, Documentary, "The San Francisco 49ers Team of the '80s" (2012); Executive Producer, Documentary, "Truth in 24 II: Every Second Counts" (2012); Executive Producer, TV Documentary, "Namath" (2012); Executive Producer, TV Documentary, "Greatest Super Bowl Moments" (2011); Executive Producer, TV Documentary, "Lombardi" (2010); Executive Producer, TV Series, "NFL Full Contact" (2010); Executive Producer, TV Documentary, "NFL Films Presents: Love, Hate and Grief in the NFL" (2009); Executive Producer, TV Series, "Hard Knocks" (2001-2009); Executive Producer, "Dallas Cowboys 10 Greatest Games" (2008); Executive Producer, Documentary, "Truth in 24" (2008); Executive Producer, "Packers Team Marketing NFL Greatest Games Series" (2008); Executive Producer, "In Just One Play: The Big-Play Men of the NFL" (2008); Executive Producer, "Manning, Brady and Favre: The Quarterbacks" (2008); Executive Producer, TV Documentary, "Hard Knocks: Training Camp with the Kansas City Chiefs" (2007); Executive Documentary, "Kansas City Chiefs: The Complete History" (2007); Director, "NFL Top 10" (2007); Executive Producer, Writer, "NFL: Favre 4 Ever" (2006); Executive Producer, TV Documentary, "The Complete History of the Philadelphia Eagles" (2004); Executive Producer, TV Documentary, "2003 New England Patriots: Super Bowl XXXVIII Champions" (2004); Executive Producer, TV Documentary, "The Wild Ride to Super Bowl I" (2004); Executive Producer, TV Documentary, "2002 Tampa Bay Buccaneers Super Bowl XXXVII Champions" (2003); Co-Executive Producer, TV Series, "Sounds of the Game" (2003); Executive Producer, TV Documentary, "The Bravest Team: The Rebuilding of the FDNY Football Club" (2002); Executive Producer, TV Documentary, "The Game of Their Lives: Pro Football's Wonder Years" (2001); Director, Executive Producer, Short Documentary, "The NFL's Hard-Hitting Grooves" (2001); Executive Producer, TV Documentary, "The NFL's Greatest Games: '58 Championship" (1998); Executive Producer, TV Film, "Football America" (1996); Executive Producer, TV Documentary, "NFL's 100 Greatest Follies" (1994); Executive Producer, TV Documentary, "75 Seasons: The Story of the NFL" (1994); Executive Producer, "NFL Rocks" (1992); Producer, "NFL: Foul-ups, Fumbles, & Follies" (1991); Producer, TV Documentary, "Sports Illustrated Greatest Highlights of the Super Bowl" (1991); Producer, TV Documentary, "Football Follies on Parade" (1990); Producer, TV Film, "The Super Duper Football Follies" (1989); Producer, "NFL's Greatest Hits" (1988); Producer, Writer, Editor, "The Very Best of the Football Follies" (1988); Producer, TV Documentary, "Follies, Crunches and Highlights" (1988); Producer, TV Film, "The NFL TV Follies" (1987); Producer, TV Documentary, "Strange But True Football Stories" (1987); Producer, TV Series, "NFL Game of the Week" (1973-1986); Producer, Writer, Editor, "Best of the Football Follies" (1985); Producer, TV Documentary, "NFL Crunch Course" (1985); Senior Producer, TV Series, "NFL Monday Night Matchup" (1985); Producer, "Dio: Special from the Spectrum" (1984); Editor, "The Greatest Adventure–The Story of Man's Voyage to the Moon" (1983); Producer, "NFL Follies Go Hollywood" (1983); Producer, TV Documentary, "The History of Pro Football" (1983); Producer, "Stripes: The Story of the 1981 AFC Championship" (1982);

Producer, TV Documentary, "Wake Up the Echoes: The History of Notre Dame Football" (1982); Producer, TV Film, "Sports Illustrated: The First 25 Years" (1981); Producer, "The NFL Symfunny" (1980); Producer, TV Film, "The Son of the Football Follies" (1976); Producer, "The Football Follies" (1968); Producer, Writer, Short Documentary, "They Call It Pro Football" (1966); Author, Poem, "The Autumn Wind" **AW:** Inductee, Pro Football Hall of Fame (2020); Champions – Pioneers & Innovators in Sports Business Award, Sports Business Journal (2012); Inductee, Sports Broadcasting Hall of Fame (2011); Inductee, Philadelphia Sports Hall of Fame (2011); Lamar Hunt Award for Professional Football (2011); Sports Leadership Award, March of Dimes 27th Annual Sports Luncheon (2010); Dan Reeves Pioneer Award, Pro Football Hall of Fame (2007); Lifetime Achievement Emmy, National Academy of Television Arts and Sciences (2003); Sports Executive of the Year, Sporting News (2002); Hall of Fame, Broadcast Pioneers of Philadelphia (1996); Pete Rozelle Award

SABRINA, DANIELLE, T: Founder, Chief Executive Officer **I:** Business Management/Business Services **CN:** Tribe Builder Media **ED:** Coursework in Business, Management, Marketing, and Related Supported Services, Southern New Hampshire University (2000-2003) **C:** Expert Public Relaions Writer, Entrepreneur Media (2018-Present); Member, Forbes Agency Council (2018-Present); Founder, Chief Executive Officer, Tribe Builder Media (2008-Present); Contributor, The Huffington Post (2015-2018); Director of Financial Planning, NPA Financial Planning Associates (2003-2008); Broker Relations, Brokerage Services, Jefferson Pilot Financial (2002-2003); Stock Trader, Fidelity Investments (2000-2002) **AW:** Listee, 2018 Top Female Entrepreneur, CIO (2018); Recognized, Inc. 500; Recognized, "Next Billion-Dollar Startup," Forbes; Recognized, Entrepreneur 360

SAKALL, DAN, MPA, BTH, T: Educator, Chaplain, Cognitive Behavioral Therapist, Author **I:** Education/Educational Services **DOB:** 11/26/1925 **PB:** Mount Clemons **SC:** MI/USA **PT:** Basil Sakall; Juliana Bese Sakall **MS:** Married **SPN:** Melanie Lee Hollifeld (07/17/1971); Mildred Louise Wells (03/18/1952, Divorced 1962) **CH:** William Jeffrey Lueck; Theodore Lee Lueck; Daniel Gregory Sakall **ED:** MPA, University of Arizona (1962); BTh, William Tyndale College (1959); BA, Alma College (1959) **CT:** Certified, Chaplin in Terrorism (2013-Present); Ordained Ruling Elder, Presbyterian Church in America (1958); Ordained Minister, South Field Community Church (1955) **C:** Active Volunteer, Alzheimer's and Dementia Patients (1982-Present); Historic Home Restorations, Family Co., Prescott, AZ (1978-1986); Professor, Yavapai College, Prescott, AZ (1980-1985); Lecturer, The University of Arizona (1963-1980); Professor, Cochise College, Douglas, AZ (1965-1976); Senior Probation Officer, Superior Court, Tucson, AZ (1962-1976); Supply Pastor, Three Presbyterians Churches, Michigan, Indiana (1952-1961); Member, Credentials Committee, Presbyterian Church in America; Senior Chaplain, Love Thy Neighbor Ministry **CR:** Teacher of 18 Different Graduate and Undergraduate Subjects, University of Arizona; Senior Probation Officer, Superior Court of Arizona **CIV:** Association for Psychiatric Offenders International (1969-1977); Treasurer, Southern Arizona Mental Health Association (1970-1976); President, ADD Public Administration Association, Tucson, AZ (1964-1976) **MIL:** U.S. Navy Special Assignment (1942-1946) **CW:** Author, "You're Just Smart Enough for Hell" (2008); Co-Author, with Carol Gulley, "100 Words in Dialogue with Christ" (2006); Author, "100 Words in Dialogue with Holy Spirit" (2003); Author, "100

Words to God from Genesis" (2000); Co-Author, with Alan Harrington, "Love and Evil: From a Probation Officer's Casebook" (1974); Contributor, 105 In-Service Articles **AW:** Most Articulate Speaker Award, Western Interstate Conference on Higher Education (1975); Presidential Commission Citation Award (1975) **MEM:** Verbi Domini Ministero, Ministers for Competency in Bible (2001); Charter Member, American Association of Christian Counselors **MH:** Albert Nelson Marquis Lifetime Achievement Award **B/I:** Mr. Sakall became involved in his profession because he has always had a compassionate feeling for others and that compassion gives him a complete joy in helping others. **AV:** Writing; Christian counselling **PA:** Republican **RE:** Presbyterian, Reformed Christian

SALAMANCA, MARIA, T: Investor **I:** Financial Services **CN:** Unshackled Ventures **ED:** Bachelor of Arts in Government and Legal Studies, University of California Berkeley (2015); Coursework, Public Policy Analysis, Goldman School of Public Policy (2011-2015); Coursework, Summer Venture in Management Program, Harvard Business School (2014); Coursework, Kings-Pembroke College, University of Cambridge (2014); Diploma, Timber Creek High School (2011) **C:** Principal, Unshackled Ventures, San Francisco, CA (2015-Present); Senior Advisor, Operations and Strategy, Swing Left, San Francisco, CA (2017-2018); Venture Research Fellow, Higher Ground Labs, Chicago, IL (2017-2018); Founder, College Access and Success Initiative, Orange County Public Schools, Orlando, FL (2015-2018); Chief Operating Officer, Swing Left, San Francisco, CA (2017); Finance Team, Silicon Valley, Hillary for America, San Francisco, CA (2015-2016); Executive Associate, FWD.us, San Francisco, CA (2014-2015); Undergraduate Course Instructor, "Public Policy 198: The Politics, Law and Policy of Education Reform," Berkeley, CA (2014-2015); Co-Founder, Encire, San Francisco, CA (2014-2015); National Programs Data Analyst, Education Pioneers (2013); Organizing Fellow, Obama Campaign, Organizing for Action (2012) **CR:** Education Fellow, Clinton Global Initiative University (2015-2016) **CIV:** Advisor, IDEO (2017-Present); Board of Advisors, Manny's (2017-Present); Advisor, Stanford Latino Entrepreneurship Initiative (2016-Present); Fellows Selection Committee, Code2040 (2017); Mentor, Nasdaq Entrepreneurial Center (2016); Board of Directors, Nuestra Casa (2016); Mentor, Year Up (2015-2016); Mentor, BUILDUP Fund Inc. (2015); JusticeCorps Legal Fellow, AmeriCorps (2013-2014) **AW:** Hispanic Shark of the Year, California Hispanic Chamber of Commerce (2017); Berkeley Leadership Scholar, University of California Berkeley (2014); Segal Education Award, AmeriCorps (2014)

SALAS, ANGELA M., T: Small Business Management; Tax Consultant **I:** Business Management/Business Services **DOB:** 03/14/1942 **PB:** Laredo **SC:** TX/USA **PT:** Hipolito Lucio Salas; Encarnacion (Sanchez) Salas **MS:** Single **ED:** PhD, University of Wisconsin - Madison (1985); MSW, Our Lady of the Lake University (1973); BS, Marillac College (1969) **C:** Instructor, San Antonio College (1985-Present); President, Southwest Urban Management, San Antonio, Texas (1985-Present); Consultant, Technology, Training, National Association of Government Employees, San Antonio, Texas (1986-1989); Coordinator, Vocational Training, San Antonio College (1986-1988); Program Specialist, Administration on Aging, U.S. Department of Health & Human Services, Chicago, IL (1975-1978) **CR:** Coordinator, Cuban Entrants, Madison Area Technical College, Madison, WI (1981-1982); Trainer, Wisconsin Department of Corrections (1981); Lecturer, School of Social Work, University of Wisconsin

- Madison **CIV:** Chairperson, Equal Employment Opportunity Commission, San Antonio, Texas (1984-Present); Education Specialist, San Antonio College (1989); President, Chairperson, Board, South San Antonio Independent School District (1985-1988); Chairperson, Organizer, Governor's Office, State of Wisconsin, Madison, WI (1980-1982); Organizer, Coordinator, Hispanic Elderly, Bureau of Aging and Disability Resources, Wisconsin Department of Health Services, Madison, WI (1982); Administrator, Consultant, Project Job Match, City of San Antonio, Texas **MEM:** Council on Social Work Education; US-Mexican Chamber of Commerce (USMCOC); Democratic National Committee **MH:** Albert Nelson Marquis Lifetime Achievement Award **B/I:** Ms. Salas has always had an interest in math and statistics, and this laid the groundwork for her career path. After earning her Master's in Social Work, she worked as a program specialist for the Aging division of the Department of Health & Human Services in Chicago. Later, she was a coordinator for a vocational training program at San Antonio College. **PA:** Democrat **RE:** Roman Catholic

SALAZAR, EDWARD J., T: 1) Respiratory Therapist 2) Vice President **I:** Medicine & Health Care **CN:** 1) All County Health Care 2) American Telemedicine Inc. **PB:** Adrian **SC:** MI/USA **PT:** Ruth Ann McGee; Sebastian John Salazar **MS:** Widower **SPN:** Carol Ann Salazar (Deceased, 2016) **CH:** Christopher; Brian; Jeniffer; Shawn; Nine grandchildren **ED:** Associate of Science in Respiratory Therapy Technology, Broward College Community College (1974) **CT:** Registered Respiratory Therapist; Certified Pulmonary Function Technologist; Registered Polysomnographic Technologist **C:** Vice President, American Tele-Medicine Inc. (2020-Present); Clinical Specialist, Sovereign Medical Inc. (2019-Present); President, Advanced Diagnostic Sleep Center, CDE Inc. (2008-Present); Respiratory Therapy Consultant, All County Health Care Inc. (2003-Present); President, EJ Salazar & Associates (2002-Present); Agency Staffing and Medical Equipment Sales (1982-2002); Technical Director of Cardiopulmonary Services, North Ridge General Hospital, Ft. Lauderdale, FL (1975-1981) **CR:** With, Advisory Board, All County Health Care Inc.; With, Advisory Board, Nova Southern University School of Cardiopulmonary Sciences; Patient Advocate, Patient Safety Movement **CIV:** Patient Advocate, The Patient Safety Movement (2014-Present); Speaker, Respiratory Care Congress, American Association for Respiratory Care; Advisory Board, All County Health Care; Committee, Patient Safety and Quality Control, Broward Health Coral Springs Hospital **CW:** Author, Non-Fiction Book, "A Free Kill"; Guest Speaker, South Florida Radio and Television **MEM:** Florida Society for Respiratory Care; American Association of Respiratory Care **MH:** Albert Nelson Marquis Lifetime Achievement Award; Marquis Who's Who Top Professional **AS:** Mr. Salazar credits his success on his parents, who instilled within him a strong work ethic. He also attributes the influence of his past and present wives, whom he believes had a major role in his passion for his career. **B/I:** Mr. Salazar originally wanted to be a physical therapist, having initially worked at a local hospital. He found the profession to be very appealing and stuck with it. He found a school in Fort Lauderdale for respiratory therapy, enrolled and fell in love with the profession. **PA:** Republican **RE:** Roman Catholic

SALERNO, ALEXANDRA, MS, NCC, LPC, T: Behavioral Health Therapist **I:** Social Work **CN:** Western Psychiatric Hospital **PT:** Philip Salerno Sr.; Dawn Salerno **ED:** Master of Science in Rehabilitation and Mental Health Counseling, University of Pittsburgh, Pittsburgh, PA (2017); Bachelor of Science in Psychology, Concentration in Sport, Robert Morris University, Moon Township, PA, Cum Laude with Dean's List Honors (2013) **CT:** CPR Certification; Certified, National Board of Certified Counselors; Pursuing, Licensed Professional Counselor in the State of Pennsylvania **C:** Behavioral Health Therapist, UPMC Center for Eating Disorders at Western Psychiatric Institute, Pine Township and Pittsburgh, PA (2018-Present); Mental Training Consultant, KPEX Consulting, Pittsburgh, PA (2016-Present); Professional Dancer, Gia T. Presents (2014-Present); Standardized Patient, Nursing Department, Robert Morris University, Moon Township, PA (2010-Present); Professional Dancer, Instructor, Gia T. Presents, Bodiography Contemporary Ballet Company, Pittsburgh Musical Theater, RWS & Associates, Holland America Cruiselines, Bodiography Contemporary Ballet Company, Keystone State Musical Theater, Pittsburgh, PA (2009-Present); Rehabilitation Specialist, Hiram G. Andrews Center, Johnstown, PA (2015-2017); Key Leader, Lululemon Athletica, Pittsburgh, PA (2014-2017); Practicum Student, Pittsburgh Public Schools, Pittsburgh, PA (2016) **CR:** Intern, UPMC Center for Eating Disorders at Western Psychiatric Institute, Pine Township, PA **CIV:** Volunteer Coordinator, Pittsburgh Counseling Student Organization, University of Pittsburgh, Pittsburgh, PA (2016-2017); Volunteer, Ballroom Dance Sessions, Individuals of all Ages with Multiple Sclerosis, Yes You Can Dance! (2015-2017); Volunteer, Genesis of Pittsburgh (2015) **CW:** Career Discussion Panelist, Robert Morris University (2018); Guest Speaker, Chatham University (2016-2018) **AW:** Making A Difference Award, Western Psychiatric Institute (2018); Virginia Kauffman Scholarship Award, University of Pittsburgh (2017) **MEM:** American Counseling Association; National Board for Certified Counselors **AS:** Ms. Salerno attributes her success to her mentors. They were open and willing to teach everything that they have learned. She also credits her success on her passion for learning. She is very patient and does her best to collaborate with her team. **B/I:** Ms. Salerno became involved in her profession due to her fascination with psychology, as well as her desire to become a professional dancer. Naturally, she sought a career that could leverage both professions. **AV:** Hot yoga; Traveling abroad; Spending time with friends and family

SALKE, JENNIFER, T: Head **I:** Media & Entertainment **CN:** Amazon Studios **C:** Head, Amazon Studios (2018-Present); President, NBC Entertainment **AW:** Named to Power Women, Forbes (2019)

SALL, JOHN, T: Co-Founder **I:** Business Management/Business Services **CN:** SAS Institute **PB:** Rockford **SC:** IL/USA **MS:** Married **CH:** Four Children **ED:** Honorary Doctorate in Statistics, North Carolina State University (2003); MS in Economics, Northern Illinois University; BS in History, Beloit College **C:** Developer, Head, JMP Business Division, SAS Institute (1989-Present); Co-Founder, Executive Vice President, SAS Institute (1976-Present) **CR:** Chairman, Interface Foundation of North America (1994) **CIV:** Board Member, The Nature Conservancy (2002-2011); Contributor, World Wide Fund for Nature; Contributor, CARE; Contributor, Numerous Nonprofits; Advisory Board, Smithsonian National Museum of Natural History; Board Member, World Wildlife Fund; Former Member, North Carolina State University Board of Trustees **CW:** Co-Author, "JMP Start Statistics: A Guide to Statistics and Data Analysis Using JMP" **AW:** Listee, "Forbes 400: Richest Americans"

(2006-Present) **MEM:** Fellow, American Statistical Association; Fellow, American Association for the Advancement of Science

SALMOIRAGHI, GIAN CARLO, T: Physiologist, Educator **I:** Education/Educational Services **DOB:** 09/19/1924 **PB:** Gorla Minore **SC:** Italy **PT:** Giuseppe Carlo Salmoiraghi; Dina (Rinetti) Salmoiraghi **MS:** Married **SPN:** Eva Tchoukourlieva (12/5/1970) **CH:** George Charles **ED:** Honorary DSc, Hahnemann University (1995); PhD, McGill University (1959); MD, University of Rome (1948) **C:** Chairman, Department of Physiology, Assistant Vice President, Science Affairs, Hahnemann University, Philadelphia, PA (1986-1994); Professor, Neurology and Physiology, Hahnemann University, Philadelphia, PA (1984-1994); Vice Provost for Research Affairs, Hahnemann University, Philadelphia, PA (1984-1985); Associate Director for Research, National Institute of Alcohol Abuse, Department of Health and Human Services, Bethesda, MD (1977-1984); Associate Commissioner of Research, New York State Department of Mental Hygiene, Albany, NY (1973-1977); Clinical Professor of Psychiatry, George Washington University (1966-1973); Neurophysiologist, Director, Division of Special Mental Health Research, National Institute of Mental Health, Washington, DC (1959-1973); Lecturer, Department of Physiology, McGill University, Montreal, Canada (1956-1958); Research Fellow, Cleveland Clinic Foundation (1952-1955); Senior Medical Officer, International Refugee Organization, Naples, Italy (1949-1952) **CW:** Contributor, Articles, Professional Journals **AW:** Superior Service Award, Department of Health (1970) **MEM:** Fellow, American College of Neuropsychopharmacology; American Association for the Advancement of Science; American Physiological Society; American Society of Pharmacology and Experimental Therapeutics; International Brain Research Organization; International Society of Psychoneuroendocrinology; American Psychiatric Association; Society of Neuroscience; Royal Society of Medicine; Society of Biological Psychiatric; Association of Research of Neurological and Mental Disease; Research Society Alcoholism; Association Chairman, Department of Physiology; Science Research Society; Sigma Xi; Cosmos **MH:** Albert Nelson Marquis Lifetime Achievement **AS:** Dr. Salmoiraghi attributes his success to the influence of his hard-working parents. His mother, Dina Rinetti, was one of the first women to graduate from college in Italy. **B/I:** Dr. Salmoiraghi was influenced by a book that he read on public health by a famous author, Cronin. The book detailed an outbreak of typhoid fever in a civilization. Determined to succeed, Dr. Salmoiraghi skipped years of high school and accelerated through his medical school program. **AV:** Reading; Researching history; Practicing art; Listening to music; Playing soccer **THT:** Mr. Salmoiraghi's life goal was to find the pill to cure humanity.

SAMPRAS, PETE, T: Professional Tennis Player (Retired) **I:** Athletics **DOB:** 08/12/1971 **PB:** Washington, DC **SC:** USA **PT:** Sam Sampras; Georgia Sampras **MS:** Married **SPN:** Bridgette Wilson (09/30/2000) **CH:** Christian Charles; Ryan Nikolaos **C:** Tennis Player, ATP (1988-2002, Retired) **CR:** Olympic Team, Atlanta, GA (1996); Member, U.S. Davis Cup Team (1995, 1992) **CIV:** Chairman, Charities Program, ATP Tour, Inc. (1992) **CW:** Co-Author, "A Champion's Mind: Lessons from a Life in Tennis" (2008) **AW:** Inductee, International Tennis Hall of Fame (2007); The Top Tennis Player of the Last 40 Years, Tennis Magazine (2006); ESPY Tennis Player of the Year (2001); Man of the Year, Individual Athlete Category, GQ (2000); Sportsman of the Year, U.S. Olympic Committee (1997);

Player of the Year, ATP Tour, Inc. (1993-1998); Jim Thorpe Tennis Player (1993); Winner, Numerous Tournaments, including Philadelphia, Manchester, the U.S. Open, Grand Slam Club, Los Angeles, Indianapolis, Lyon, IBM/ATP Tour World Championship-Frankfurt, U.S. Pro Indoor, Lipton International, Wimbledon, Australian Open, Italian Open, U.S. Open, San Jose Open, Memphis Open, ATP Your World Championship/Hanover, Germany, Australian Open Wimbledon and Advanta Championships (1990-2002); Number Two Player of the Century, Associated Press Men; Ranked Number 48, Top 50 Greatest North American Athletes of ESPN's Sports Century

SAMUELI, HENRY, T: Chief Technology Officer **I:** Technology **DOB:** 09/20/1954 **PB:** Buffalo **SC:** NY/USA **PT:** Aron Samueli; Sala (Traubman) Samueli **MS:** Married **SPN:** Susan Faye Eisenberg (08/22/1982) **CH:** Leslie Pamela; Jillian Meryl; Erin Sydney **ED:** PhD in Electrical Engineering, University of California Los Angeles (UCLA) (1980); MSEE, University of California Los Angeles (UCLA) (1976); BSEE, University of California Los Angeles (UCLA) (1975) **C:** Chief Technical Officer, Broadcom Inc. (2018-Present); Chief Technical Officer, Broadcom Ltd. (2016-Present); Chairman, Broadcom Corporation, Irvine, CA (2012-Present); Distinguished Adjunct Professor, Electrical Engineering and Computer Science, University of California Los Angeles (UCLA) (2003-Present); Co-Founder, Chief Technology Officer, Broadcom Corporation, Irvine, CA (1991-Present); Chief Technical Officer, Co-Founder, Broadcom Corporation (2009-2016); Technology Adviser, Co-Founder, Broadcom Corporation (2008-2009); Chairman, Chief Technology Officer, Co-Founder, Broadcom Corporation (2003-2008); Professor, University of California Los Angeles (UCLA) (1994-1995); Associate Professor, University of California Los Angeles (UCLA) (1990-1994); Assistant Professor, University of California Los Angeles (UCLA) (1985-1990); Vice President, Research & Development, Co-Chairman, Broadcom Corporation, Irvine, CA (1991-2003); Co-Founder, Chief Scientist, PairGain Techs., Inc., Tustin, CA (1988-1994); Consultant, TRW Inc., Redondo Beach, CA (1985-1989); Section Manager, TRW Inc., Redondo Beach, CA (1983-1985); Staff Engineer, TRW Inc., Redondo Beach, CA(1980-1983) **CR:** Co-Owner, Anaheim Ducks (Formerly Mighty Ducks of Anaheim), National Hockey League (2005-Present) **CIV:** Member, Giving Pledge (2012-Present); Founding Director, Broadcom Foundation (2009-Present); Founder, Samueli Foundation (1998-Present); Major Contributor, UCLA School of Engineering and Applied Science, UC Irvine School of Engineering (1999) **AW:** Prize for "global contribution to innovation," Israeli Government (2015); Marconi Prize (2012); Golden Plate Award, Academy Achievement (2006); Presidential Award, University of California (2000); Irvine Medal, University of California (2000); Alumnus of the Year Award, UCLA School of Engineering and Applied Science (2000); Listee, "Top 20 Entrepreneurs of 1997," The Red Herring Magazine (1997); Listee, "Top 50 Cyber Elite," Time Digital Magazine (1997) **MEM:** Fellow, National Academy of Inventors (2017-Present); Fellow, Institute of Electrical and Electronics Engineers (IEEE); Fellow, American Academy of Arts and Sciences (AAAS); National Academy of Engineers (NAE) **PA:** Republican **RE:** Jewish

SAN NICOLAS, MICHAEL FRANKLIN QUITUGUA, T: Delegate to the U.S. House of Representatives from Guam **I:** Government Administration/Government Relations/Government Services **CN:** U.S. House of Representatives **DOB:** 1/30/1981 **PB:** Talofofo **SC:** Guam **PT:** Miguel Borja San

Nicolas; Eva Quitugua San Nicolas **MS:** Married **SPN:** Kathryn Santos Ko (2005) **CH:** Two Children **ED:** Bachelor of Arts in History, University of Guam (2004) **C:** Delegate, U.S. House of Representatives from Guam's At-Large Congressional District, Washington, DC (2019-Present); Assistant Majority Whip, Guam Legislature (2015-2019); Member, Guam Legislature (2013-2019); Vice Chair, Committee on Financial Services; Member, Committee on Natural Resources; Assistant Vice President and Financial Adviser, Bank of Guam; Chief of Staff, Senator Carmen Fernandez, 27th Guam Legislature **MEM:** President, Student Government Association, University of Guam (2002-2003); Speaker, 22nd Guam Youth Congress, University of Guam (1998-2000) **PA:** Democrat

SANCHEZ, NICOLE, T: Founder, Managing Partner **I:** Business Management/Business Services **CN:** Vaya Consulting, LLC **ED:** MBA, Haas School of Business, University of California Berkeley (2012); BA in American Studies, Stanford University (1994) **C:** Founder, Managing Partner, Vaya Consulting, LLC, San Francisco, CA (2014-Present); Lecturer, Haas School of Business, University of California Berkeley (2017-2019); Vice President, Social Impact, GitHub, San Francisco, CA (2015-2017); Managing Partner, Chief Operating Officer, Kapor Center for Social Impact, Oakland, CA (2010-2014); Executive Director, Berkeley Alliance (2009-2010); Co-Founder, Executive Director, New Global Citizens (2003-2008); Associate Director, Program in Ethics in Society, Stanford University (2000-2003); Business Analyst, Public Consulting Group (1998-1999); National Program Director, City Year (1994-1998)

SÁNCHEZ, LINDA TERESA, T: U.S. Representative from California **I:** Government Administration/Government Relations/Government Services **DOB:** 01/28/1969 **PB:** Orange **SC:** CA/USA **PT:** Ignacio Sánchez; Maria (Macias) Sánchez **MS:** Married **SPN:** Jim Sullivan (04/13/2009); Mark Valentine (Divorced) **CH:** Joaquin Sánchez; Brendan (Stepson); Jack (Stepson); Seamus (Stepson) **ED:** JD, University of California Los Angeles School of Law (1995); BA in Spanish Literature, University of California Berkeley (1991) **C:** Chair, Congressional Hispanic Caucus (2015-Present); Member, U.S. House Select Committee on the Events Surrounding the 2012 Terrorist Attack in Benghazi (2014-Present); Ranking Member, U.S. House Ethics Committee (2011-Present); Member, U.S. House of Representatives from California's 38th Congressional District, United States Congress, Washington, DC (2013-Present); Vice-Chair, House Democratic Caucus (2017-2019); Member, U.S. House of Representatives from California's 39th Congressional District, United States Congress, Washington, DC (2003-2013); Compliance Officer, International Brotherhood of Electrical Workers (IBEW), National Electrical Contractors Association (1998-2002); Law Clerk to Chief Justice Terry Hatter Jr., United States District Court for the Central District of California **CR:** Lecturer, National Association of Latino Elected and Appointed Officials (NALEO) (1998-Present); Campaign Aide, Loretta Sanchez for United States Congress (1996, 1998) **CW:** Co-Author, "Dream in Color: How the Sanchez Sisters are Making History in Congress" (2008) **MEM:** International Brotherhood of Electrical Workers (IBEW) (Local 441) **BAR:** State of California (1995) **PA:** Democrat **RE:** Roman Catholic

SAND, SHARA, PSY.D., T: Psychologist **I:** Medicine & Health Care **CN:** Shara Sand, Psy.D. **DOB:** 09/09/1962 **PB:** Brooklyn, NY **SC:** NY/USA **YOP:** N/A **PT:** Adolf Sand; Jessica Sand **MS:** Domestic Partnership **SPN:** Sharon Gordon, LCSW., MS.Ed.

CH: Spencer Gordon-Sand **ED:** Doctor of Psychology in Clinical Psychology, Yeshiva University, Bronx, NY (1993); MA in Psychology, Yeshiva University Ferkauf Graduate School of Psychology (1990); MA in Trombone Performance, Brooklyn Conservatory of Music, Brooklyn, NY (1985); MusB in Trombone, Manhattan School of Music, New York, NY (1983) **CT:** Licensed Psychologist, NYS 012174-1 **C:** Director, Counseling Services, Manhattan School of Music, New York, NY (2012-Present); Co-chair, Committee on Sexualities and Gender Identities, APA Div. 39: Society for Psychoanalysis and Psychoanalytic Psychology, American Psychological Association (2011-Present); Associate Professor, Psychology, LaGuardia Community College, Long Island City, NY (2008-Present); Psychologist, Shara Sand, Psy.D., New York, NY (1995-Present); Assistant Director, Clinical Training, Yeshiva University Ferkauf Graduate School of Psychology, Bronx, NY (1994-Present); Former Faculty, Yeshiva University, New York, NY (1988-2008); Adjunct Clinical Supervisor, Counseling Center, Pace University, New York, NY (2005-2008) **CIV:** Committee on Sexualities and Gender Identities, APA Div. 39: Society for Psychoanalysis and Psychoanalytic Psychology, American Psychological Association (2016); President, Division of Social Issues, New York State Psychological Association (2010-2011); Pro Bono, Asylum Evaluations, HealthRight International **CW:** Freelance Trombonist; Performer, Carnegie Hall, Carnegie Recital Hall (Now Weill Recital Hall), Avery Fisher Hall, Town Hall of Music, Radio City Music Hall, 92nd Street Y, Goodman House of Music (Now Kaufman Music Center), Garden State Arts Center (Now PNC Bank Arts Center), Jones Beach Music Center (Now Northwell Health at Jones Beach Theater), Spoleto Festival USA, Italy Music Festival, Spain Choral Festival, World Tours with the Kit McClure All Women's Big Band **AW:** Diversity Award, APA Div. 39: Society for Psychoanalysis and Psychoanalytic Psychology, American Psychological Association (2019); Forensic Division, New York State Psychological Association (2018); Certificate of Appreciation, APA Div. 44: Society for the Psychology of Sexual Orientation and Gender Diversity, American Psychological Association (2014) **MEM:** American Psychological Association, Divisions 10, 35, 39 and 44; New York State Psychological Association; Local 802, Associated Musicians of Greater New York, American Federation of Musicians; Performing Arts Medicine Association **AS:** Dr. Sand attributes her success to flexible thinking and openness to others' experiences. She only worries about the things she has the capacity to change, as opposed to those she has no power over. **B/I:** While trying to make a living as a musician, Dr. Sand supported herself by working for a psychotherapy institute. She became increasingly interested in psychology and frustrated with her music career, and decided to make a change. She returned to school as a psychology major, where she studied human behavior and decision-making. Her parents believed that she should be exposed to a variety of things, music lessons, dance lessons, art, and she loved music. They were supportive, but not happy with her career choice, fearing her ability to earn a living. She continues to enjoy music, but is also happy that she can now pay her rent. **AV:** Photography; Attending concerts and theater **RE:** Spiritual, Secular Jewish **THT:** Life is a convoluted maze. It is a path that often makes much sense, but sometimes makes no sense. Dr. Sand believes listening to ones gut and intuition

SANDERS, SARAH ELIZABETH, T: Former White House Press Secretary **I:** Government Administration/Government Relations/Government Services **DOB:** 08/13/1982 **PB:** Hope **SC:** AK/USA **PT:** Mike

Huckabee; Janet (McCain) Huckabee **MS:** Married **SPN:** Bryan Sanders (05/25/2010) **ED:** BA, Ouachita Baptist University **C:** Contributor, Fox News (2019-Present); White House Press Secretary, Washington, DC (2017-Present); Principal, White House Deputy Press Secretary, Washington, DC (2017); Senior Adviser, Donald Trump's Presidential Campaign (2016); Manager, Mike Huckabee's Presidential Campaign (2016); Campaign Manager, John Boozman for U.S. Senate (2010); With, U.S. Department of Education, Washington, DC (2004); Executive Director, Huck PAC; Founding Partner, Second Street Strategies, Little Rock, AR **CIV:** National Campaign Manager, ONE Campaign **AW:** Named One of the Politics 40 Under 40, TIME Magazine (2010) **PA:** Republican

SANFORD, THOMAS DENNY, T: Founder, Chief Executive Officer, Philanthropist **I:** Financial Services **CN:** First Premier Bank **DOB:** 12/23/1935 **PB:** Saint Paul **SC:** MN/USA **PT:** William B. Sanford; Edith Sanford **MS:** Divorced **SPN:** Colleen Anderson (1995, Divorced 2005); Anne Sanford (1960, Divorced 1982) **CH:** Scott; Bill **ED:** Bachelor's Degree in Psychology, University of Minnesota (1958) **C:** Founder, First Premier Bank (1986-Present); Chief Executive Officer, United National Corporation; Founder, Contech Inc., Minneapolis, MN; Salesman, Armstrong Cork Company, Pittsburgh, PA **CIV:** Participant, The Giving Pledge (2010); Benefactor, Sanford Health (2007); Founder, Sanford Institute of Philanthropy **AW:** Listee, World's Billionaires List, Forbes (2018-2020); Named, One of the Forbes 400 (2007-2009, 2019); Named, One of the Philanthropy 50: Americans Who Gave the Most in 2007, The Chronicle of Philanthropy (2007); Named, One of the 50 Most Generous Philanthropists, Bloomberg Businessweek (2006)

SANTANA, CARLOS, T: Guitarist, Musician **I:** Media & Entertainment **DOB:** 7/20/1947 **PB:** Autlán de Navarro **SC:** Mexico **PT:** José Santana; Josefina Barragan de Santana **MS:** Married **SPN:** Cindy Blackman (12/2010); Deborah King (1973, Divorced) **CH:** Salvador; Angelica; Stella **ED:** Diploma, Mission High School (1965) **CW:** Musician, "In Search of Mona Lisa" (2019); Musician, "Africa Speaks" (2019); Musician, "Santana IV" (2016); Author, "The Universal Tone: Bringing My Story to Light" (2014); Musician, "Corazón" (2014); Musician, "Shape Shifter" (2012); Musician, "Guitar Heaven" (2010); Musician, "All That I Am" (2005); Musician, "Shaman" (2002); Musician, "Supernatural" (1999); Musician, "Santana Brothers" (1994); Musician, "Milagro" (1992); Musician, "Spirits Dancing in the Flesh" (1990); Musician, "Freedom" (1987); Musician, "Blues for Salvador" (1987); Musician, "Beyond Appearances" (1985); Musician, "Havana Moon" (1983); Musician, "Shangó" (1982); Musician, "Zebop!" (1981); Musician, "The Swing of Delight" (1980); Musician, "Oneness - Silver Dreams Golden Reality" (1979); Musician, "Marathon" (1979); Musician, "Inner Secrets" (1978); Musician, "Moonflower" (1977); Musician, "Festival" (1977); Musician, "Amigos" (1976); Musician, "Borboletta" (1974); Musician, "Illuminations" (1974); Musician, "Love Devotion Surrender" (1973); Musician, "Welcome" (1973); Musician, "Caravanserai" (1972); Musician, "Santana III" (1971); Musician, "Abraxas" (1970); Musician, "Santana" (1969); Musician, Several Live Albums, Compilation Albums, Collaboration Albums, Featured Songs **AW:** Honoree, Kennedy Center Honors (2013); Hall of Fame Award, NAACP Image Awards (2006); Best International Rock/Pop Male Artist, Echo Music Prize (2001); Patrick Lippert Award (2001); Award for Social Engagement, UCLA Cesar E. Chavez Spirit Awards (2001); Man of the Year, VH1 Awards (2000); Medallion of

Excellence for Community Service, CHCI Medallions of Excellence (1999); Latino Music Legend of the Year, Chicano Music Awards (1997); Star, Hollywood Walk of Fame (1997); Billboard Century Award (1996); Best Rock Instrumental Performance (Orchestra, Group Or Soloist), Grammy Awards (1988)

SANTER, RICHARD ARTHUR, T: Geography Educator (Retired) **I:** Education/Educational Services **CN:** Ferris State University **DOB:** 09/26/1937 **PB:** Detroit **SC:** MI/USA **PT:** Arthur James Santer; Hazel Luella (Houghten) Santer **MS:** Married **SPN:** Ruth Margaret Boyce (08/29/1959) **CH:** Carolyn M.; Catherine R. **ED:** PhD, Michigan State University (1970); MS, Eastern Michigan University (1965); BS, Eastern Michigan University (1959) **CT:** Certified Secondary Teacher, State of Michigan **C:** Retired, Ferris State University, Big Rapids, MI (1996); Professor of Geography, Ferris State University, Big Rapids, MI (1969-1996); Teacher of Geography, Wyandotte Public Schools, MI (1963-1966) **CR:** Michigan Consultant Graphic Learning Corp., Tallahassee, FL (1983); Coordinator, Governors Conference, Upper Great Lakes Commission, Big Rapids, MI (1980) **CIV:** Member, Board of Trustees, Historical Society of Michigan (1993-1996); Chairman, Michigan Conference, United Church of Christ, Commission of Church and Pastoral Ministries (1993); Commission, Ferris State University (1990-1993); Member, Michigan Conference, United Church of Christ, Commission of Church and Pastoral Ministries (1988-1991); Chair, Ferris State University Centennial Task Force (1980-1984); Member, Mecosta County Zoning Commission, Big Rapids, MI (1978-1981); Board of Directors, Elder, The United Church of Big Rapids (1970-1981); Co-chairman, Mecosta County Bicentennial Commission, Big Rapids, MI (1974-1975); Member, Mapper ,Green Township Plan Commission, Paris, MI (1973-1974) **MIL:** First Lieutenant, United States Army (1959-1962) **CW:** Co-author, "Michigan Geography and Geology" (2009); Co-editor, Team Leader, "The Autobiography of Woodbridge N. Ferris" (1995); Author, "Geography of Michigan and the Great Lakes Basin" (1993); Contributing Author, "Michigan Visions of Our Past" (1989); Published, "Authority on Michigan Boundaries Islands" Booklet, Saying of WN Ferris, Ferris State University (1983); Author, "Michigan: Heart of Great Lakes" (1977); Author, "Green Township Atlas" (1974); Author, Chapter One, "Defining State of Michigan"; Published, W/2 Reprints, Booklet, "Ferris Christmas Greetings (1908-1927)" **AW:** State Government Recognition for Contributions to Michigan Education (2018); Historical Society of Michigan "History Hero" Award (2018); Certificates of Appreciation, National Geography Bee, National Geographic Society (1989-1996); Certificates of Appreciation, Michigan Sesquicentennial Commission (1987); Certificates of Appreciation, Population Institute (1987); Recognition Award, Population Action Council (1983); Named Distinguished Faculty Member, MI Associates Governing Board (1982) **MEM:** Michigan Association of Retired School Personnel (1998-2019); Section Chairman, Michigan Academy of Science, Arts, and Letters (1974-1975, 1994-1995); Chapter Chairman, Phi Delta Kappa (PDK International) (1990-1991); Institution Representative, Michigan Academy of Science, Arts, and Letters (1988-1989); Michigan Coordinator, National Council for Geographic Education (1970-1974); American Association of Geographers (AAG); National Council for Geographic Education; Michigan Academy of Science, Arts, and Letters; Phi Delta Kappa (PDK International) **MH:** Albert Nelson Marquis Lifetime Achievement Award **B/I:** Dr. Santer grew up in the city of Detroit and for his senior English class they all had to turn in a term paper. His teacher directed that he go to the library of Detroit and do research on Isle Royale, which sparked his interest. **AV:** Outdoor nature recreation; Reading **RE:** Presbyterian

SANTI, ERNEST SCOTT, T: Chief Executive Officer, Chairperson **I:** Manufacturing **CN:** Illinois Tool Works **ED:** Master of Business Administration, Northwestern University Kellogg School of Management (1992); Bachelor's Degree in Accounting, University of Illinois (1983) **C:** Chief Executive Officer, Chairman, Illinois Tool Works (2015-Present); President, Chief Executive Officer, Illinois Tool Works (2012-2015); Vice Chairperson, Illinois Tool Works (2008-2012); Executive Vice President, Illinois Tool Works (2004-2008) **CR:** Board of Directors, W.W. Grainger

SANTILLI, ARTHUR ATTILIO, PH.D., T: Senior Research Fellow, Chemist (Retired) **I:** Pharmaceuticals **CN:** Wyeth Pharmaceuticals (now Pfizer) **DOB:** 07/25/1929 **PB:** Everett **SC:** MA/USA **PT:** Harry Santilli; Minnie DeMasi Santilli **MS:** Married **SPN:** Kathryn Madenford (06/13/1964) **CH:** David Arthur Santilli; Pamela (Hinton) Santilli (Daughter-in-Law); Andrew Paul Santilli (Grandson); Cara Elizabeth Santilli (Granddaughter) **ED:** Postdoctoral Fellow, Tufts University, Medford, MA (1958-1960); PhD in Chemistry, University of Massachusetts, Amherst, MA (1958); Postdoctoral Fellow, University of Massachusetts, Amherst, MA (1957); MS in Chemistry, Tufts University, Medford, MA (1952); AB in Chemistry, Boston University (1951) **C:** Medicinal Chemist to Senior Research Fellow, Wyeth Pharmaceuticals Company (now Pfizer) (1960-2004) **CIV:** Church Choir Member, (1985-Present); Vice President then President, Holy Name Society, St. Pius X Church, Broomall, PA (1970-Present) **MIL:** Sergeant, U.S. Army Chemical Corps., Korean War (1952-1954) **CW:** Co-author, Over 50 Articles, Professional Journals; Co-inventor, 137 U.S.A. Patents dealing in Experimental Medicinal Agents Field some with Foreign Equivalents; Reviewer, Journal of Medicinal Chemistry; Reviewer, Journal of Heterocyclic Chemistry; Reviewer, Journal of Organic Chemistry **AW:** Co-recipient of Thomas Alva Edison Patent Award, Research and Development Council of New Jersey (2006); Named Man of Year, Holy Name Society (1978); Emeritus Status, American Chemical Society **MEM:** American Chemical Society; Philadelphia Organic Chemist's Club; Member, The Society of the Sigma Xi Devoted to the Promotion of Research in Science **MH:** Albert Nelson Marquis Lifetime Achievement Award **AS:** He attributes the successful outcome of the work which is presented in this biography to the hard work and perseverance of his capable assistants, along with his own efforts, guidance and encouragement. **B/I:** His interest in chemistry began in high school, when he was awarded with a Lange's Handbook of Chemistry at the end of a chemistry course for receiving the highest grade. Upon graduating, his interest increased when he majored in chemistry at Boston University, after which he enrolled at Tufts University in the same field. After receiving his master's degree from Tufts, he decided to study for a PhD after serving in the army. **RE:** Roman Catholic **THT:** Dr. Santilli has learned it is important in life to respect one's self as well as the rights of others. Providing for the needs of one's family and, if possible, offering assistance to others in need, are noble objectives to be pursued.

SARANDON, SUSAN, T: Actress **I:** Media & Entertainment **DOB:** 10/04/1946 **PB:** New York **SC:** NY/USA **PT:** Phillip Leslie Tomalin; Lenora Marie (Criscione) Tomalin **MS:** Married **SPN:** Chris Sarandon (09/67/1967, Divorced 1979) **CH:** Eva Maria Livia Amurri; Jack Henry Robbins; Miles Guthrie Robbins **ED:** BA in Drama and English, Catholic University of America (1968) **C:** Member, Social Impact Advisory Board, San Diego International Film Festival (2018-Present) **CIV:** Appointed as FAO Goodwill Ambassador (2010); Member, Advisory Committee, 2004 Racism Watch (2004); Speaker, Advocate, Activist, Numerous Civil Rights and Current Issues; Anti-War Activist; Advocate, Donor, EMILY's List **CW:** Actress, "Tunnels" (2020); Narrator, "Revolution of the Heart: The Dorothy Day Story" (2020); Actress, "Love" (2019); Actress, "The Jesus Rolls" (2019); Voice Actress, "Robot Chicken" (2019); Actress, Executive Producer, "VHYes" (2019); Actress, "Blackbird" (2019); Actress, "Roger Viver's Jewels to Shoes" (2019); Herself, "At Home with Amy Sedaris" (2019); Actress, "The Death and Life of John F. Donovan" (2018); Actress, "Ray Donovan" (2017-2019); Actress, "Neo Yokio" (2017-2018); Actress, "Viper Club" (2018); Producer, Documentary, "Survivors Guide to Prison" (2018); Actress, "Jay-Z: Legacy" (2017); Actress, "A Bad Moms Christmas" (2017); Voice Actress, "Rick and Morty" (2017); Actress, Producer, "Feud: Better and Joan" (2017); Executive Producer, Documentary, "Soufra" (2017); Executive Producer, Documentary, "Bombshell: The Hedy Lamarr Story" (2017); Voice Actress, "Cassius Clay" (2016); Voice Actress, "American Dad!" (2016); Voice Actress, "My Entire High School Sinking Into the Sea" (2016); Actress, "Ace the Case" (2016); Actress, "Mothers and Daughters" (2016); Voice Actress, "Spark: A Space Tail" (2016); Actress, "Zoolander 2" (2016); Actress, "Skylanders Academy" (2016-2017); Actress, "The Crossing" (2015); Herself, "The Other Side of the Lake the Purple Girl: Episode IV - The New Visitor" (2015); Voice Actress, "Hell and Back" (2015); Actress, Executive Producer, "The Meddler" (2015); Actress, "3 Generations" (2015); Voice Actress, "April and the Extraordinary World" (2015); Actress, "The Secret Life of Marilyn Monroe" (2015); Executive Producer, Documentary, "Deep Run" (2015); Executive Producer, Documentary, "Radical Grace (2015); Executive Producer, Documentary, "Silenced" (2014); Actress, "The Calling" (2014); Actress, "Tammy" (2014); Actress, "Mike & Molly" (2014, 2013); Actress, "Ping Pong Summer" (2014); Herself, "Doll & Em" (2013); Actress, "The Last of Robin Hood" (2013); Actress, "The Big Wedding" (2013); Executive Producer, Documentary Short, "Waiting for Mamu" (2013); Actress, "Snitch" (2013); Voice Actress, Video Game, "Dishonored" (2012); Actress, "Cloud Atlas" (2012); Actress, "The Company You Keep" (2012); Actress, "That's My Boy" (2012); Actress, "The Big C" (2012); Actress, "30 Rock" (2012, 2011); Actress, "Arbitrage" (2012); Actress, "Robot & Frank" (2012); Actress, "The Miraculous Year" (2011); Actress, "Jeff, Who Lives at Home" (2011); Actress, "Saturday Night Live" (2011, 2009); Actress, Music Video, "3-Way" by The Lonely Island Feat. Lady Gaga and Justin Timberlake (2011) Narrator, "La Mama: An American Nun's Life in a Mexican Prison" (2010); Actress, "Wall Street: Money Never Sleeps" (2010); Actress, "Peacock" (2010); Actress, "You Don't Know Jack" (2010); Actress, "The Lovely Bones" (2009); Voice Actress, "One Million Strong" (2009); Actress, "Solitary Man" (2009); Actress, Music Video, "Motherlover" by The Lonely Island Feat. Justin Timberlake (2009); Actress, "ER" (2009); Actress, "The Greatest" (2009); Actress, "Middle of Nowhere" (2009); Actress, Theater, "Exit the King" (2009); Actress, "Speed Racer" (2008); Actress, "Enchanted" (2007); Actress, "Emotional Arithmetic" (2007); Actress, "Mr. Woodcock" (2007); Actress, "In the Valley of Elah" (2007); Actress, "Rescue Men" (2006-2007); Actress, "Bernard and

Doris" (2006); Actress, "Irresistible" (2006); Narrator, "Sonnet 22" (2005); Actress, "Romance & Cigarettes" (2005); Actress, "Elizabethtown" (2005); Actress, "Alfie" (2004); Actress, "Shall We Dance" (2004); Herself, "Jiminy Glick in Lalawood" (2004); Actress, "Noel" (2004); Actress, Documentary, "Freedom: A History of US" (2003); Actress, "Ice Bound" (2003); Actress, "Children of Dune" (2003); Narrator, "Little Miss Spider" (2002); Actress, "Moonlight Mile" (2002); Actress, "The Banger Sisters" (2002); Executive Producer, "Moonlight Mile" (2002); Actress, "Igby goes Down" (2002); Actress, "Malcolm in the Middle" (2002); Voice Actress, "Cats & Dogs" (2001); Actress, "Friends" (2001); Voice Actress, "Rugrats in Paris: The Movie" (2000); Actress, "Joe Gould's Secret" (2000); Voice Actress, "Goodnight Moon & Other Sleepytime Tales" (1999); Actress, "Anywhere But Here" (1999); Actress, "Cradle Will Rock" (1999); Actress, "Earthly Possessions" (1999); Voice Actress, "Our Friend, Martin" (1999); Actress, Executive Producer, "Stepmom" (1998); Narrator, "For Love of Julian" (1998); Actress, "Illuminata" (1998); Actress, "Twilight" (1998); Narrator, "The Need to Know" (1997); Voice Actress, "James and the Giant Peach" (1996); Actress, "Dead Man Walking" (1995); Voice Actress, "The Simpsons" (1995); Narrator, "American Experience" (1995); Narrator, "School of the Americas Assassins" (1994); Actress, "Safe Passage" (1994); Actress, "Little Women" (1994); Actress, "The client" (1994); Actress, "Lorenzo's Oil" (1992); Herself, "The Player" (1992); Actress, "Light Sleeper" (1992); Actress, "Thelma & Louise" (1991); Actress, "White Palace" (1990); Actress, "A Dry White Season" (1989); Actress, "The January Man" (1989); Actress, "Sweet Hearts Dance" (1988); Actress, "Bull Durham" (1988); Actress, "The Witches of Eastwick" (1987); Actress, "Women of Valor" (1986); Actress, "Mussolini and I" (1985); Actress, "Compromising Positions" (1985); Actress, "A.D." (1985); Actress, "Oxbridge Blues" (1984); Actress, "Faerie Tale Theatre" (1984); Actress, "The Buddy System" (1984); Actress, "The Hunger" (1983); Actress, "Tempest" (1982); Actress, "American Playhouse" (1982); Actress, "Loving Couples" (1980); Actress, "Atlantic City" (1980); Actress, Theater, "A Coupla White Chicks Sitting Around Talking" (1980-1981); Actress, "Something Short of Paradise" (1979); Actress, "King of the Gypsies" (1978); Actress, "Pretty Baby" (1978); Actress, "The Other Side of Midnight" (1977); Actress, Co-Producer, "The Great Smokey Roadblock" (1977); Actress, "Checkered Flag or Crash" (1977); Actress, "Dragonfly" (1976); Actress, "The Rocky Horror Picture Show" (1975); Actress, "The Great Waldo Pepper" (1975); Actress, "The Front Page" (1974); Actress, "The Lives of Benjamin Franklin" (1974); Actress, "Lovin' Molly" (1974); Actress, "F. Scott Fitzgerald and 'The Last of the Belles'" (1974); Actress, "The Wide World of Mystery" (1974, 1973); Actress, "Great Performances" (1974, 1972); Actress, "Calucci's Department" (1973); Actress, "Search for Tomorrow" (1972); Actress, Theater, "An Evening with Richard Nixon and..." (1972); Actress, "Lady Liberty" (1971); Actress, "Owen Marshall, Counselor at Law" (1971); Actress, "Fleur bleue" (1971); Actress, "A World Apart" (1970-1971); Actress, "Joe" (1970); Actress, Numerous Plays; Herself, Narrator, Numerous Documentaries **AW:** International Lifetime Achievement Award, Golden Kamera (2015); Outstanding Artistic Life Award for her Outstanding Contribution to World Cinema, Shanghai International Film Festival (2011); Inductee, New Jersey Hall of Fame (2010); Lifetime Achievement Award, Stockholm International Film Festival (2009); Bette Davis Lifetime Achievement Award, Bette Davis Centenary Tribute, Boston Uni-

versity (2008); Action Against Hunger Humanitarian Award (2006); Best Supporting Actress, "Igby Goes Down," "Moonlight Mile," Las Vegas Film Critics (2002); Academy Award for Best Actress, "Dead Man Walking" (1995); Screen Actors Guild Award for Outstanding Performance by a Female Actor in a Leading Role, "Dead Man Walking" (1995); Best Actress, "Dead Man Walking," Kansas City Film Critics Circle (1995); BAFTA Award for Best Actress in a Leading Role, "The Client" (1994); Actress of the Year, "Thelma & Louise," London Film Critics Circle (1991); Co-Recipient (with Geena Davis), Best Actress, "Thelma & Louise," National Board of Review (1991); Best Actress, "Atlantic City," Kansas City Film Critics Circle (1981) **MEM:** American Federation of Television and Radio Artists; Screen Actors Guild; Actors' Equity Association; Academy of Motion Picture Arts and Sciences; National Organization for Women; MADRE; Amnesty International, American Civil Liberties Union (ACLU)

SARBANES, JOHN PETER SPYROS, T: U.S. Representative, Lawyer **I:** Government Administration/Government Relations/Government Services **DOB:** 05/22/1962 **PB:** Baltimore **SC:** MD/USA **PT:** Paul Sarbanes; Christine (Dunbar) Sarbanes **MS:** Married **SPN:** Dina Eve Caplin (1988) **CH:** Three children **ED:** JD, Harvard Law School (1988); BA, Woodrow Wilson School of Public and International Affairs, Princeton University, Cum Laude (1984) **C:** U.S. Representative, Maryland's Third Congressional District United States Congress, Washington, DC (2007-Present); Chairman, Health Care Practice, Venable LLP (2000-2006); Associate to Partner, Venable LLP, Baltimore, MD (1989-2006); Member, Hiring Committee, Venable LLP (1992-1996); Law Clerk to Honorable J. Frederick Motz, United States District Court District of Maryland (1988-1989); Member, Committee on Energy and Commerce, Maryland's Third Congressional District United States Congress; Member, Committee on Education and the Workforce, Maryland's Third Congressional District United States Congress; Member, Committee on Resources, Maryland's Third Congressional District United States Congress; Member, Committee on Government Oversight, Maryland's Third Congressional District United States Congress **CR:** President, Public Justice Center, Baltimore, MD (1994-1997); Special Assistant to Superintendent of Schools, State of Maryland **CIV:** Co-Chair, Law School Democrats of America (1988); Board Member, Institute for Christian & Jewish Studies (Now ICJS) **AW:** Fulbright Scholar (1985) **MEM:** ABA; Maryland State Bar Association; the District of Columbia Bar **BAR:** The District of Columbia Bar (1988); Maryland State Bar Association (1988) **PA:** Democrat **RE:** Greek Orthodox

SARGENT, WALTER HARRIMAN II, T: Lawyer, President of Law Firm Handling State and Federal Civil Appeals **I:** Law and Legal Services **CN:** Walter H. Sargent, A Professional Corporation **DOB:** 08/26/1958 **PB:** Norfolk **SC:** VA/USA **PT:** Richard E. Sargent; Martha F. (Bassett) Sargent **MS:** Single **ED:** JD, Harvard University (1987); BS in Computer Science and Engineering, Massachusetts Institute of Technology (1980); BS in Philosophy, Massachusetts Institute of Technology (1980) **C:** Private Practice, Walter H. Sargent, a Professional Corporation, Colorado Springs, CO (1996-2018); Associate, Holme Roberts & Owen, Colorado Springs, CO (1987-1995) **CR:** Civil Appeals Practitioner, State and Federal Appellate Courts **CIV:** Board of Trustees, Colorado Legal Aid Foundation (1998-2004); Board of Directors, Pikes Pikes Legal Aid Services; Board of Directors, ARC of the Pikes Peak Region; Board of Directors, Pikes Peak Adult Literacy Coa-

lition **MIL:** U.S. Air Force Officer, Air Force Data Services Center, The Pentagon, Washington, DC (1980-1984) **CW:** Contributing Author, "Colorado Appellate Handbook," CLE in Colorado, Inc. (2000-2018); Author, "The Insider's Guide to the Colorado Appellate Courts," in "Appellate Practice Compendium," ABA Publishing (2012); Author, "Appellate Standards of Review, in Appellate Practice in State and Federal Courts," Law Journal Press (2011); Tenth Circuit Editor, "Superseding and Staying Judgments: A National Compendium," ABA Publishing (2007); Articles Editor, "Harvard Journal of Law & Public Policy" (1987) **AW:** Best Lawyers in America (2006-Present); Colorado Super Lawyers (2006-Present); Fellow, American Academy of Appellate Lawyers (2004-Present); AA Rating, Martindale-Hubbell (1997-Present); John M. Olin Commencement Prize for Outstanding Writing in Law and Economics, Harvard Law School (1987); John M. Olin Fellow of Law and Economics, Harvard Law School (1987); Sigma Xi, Honor Society for Scientific Researchers, M.I.T. (1981-Present); Eagle Scout (1973) **MEM:** Fellow, American Academy of Appellate Lawyers (2004-Present); Chair, Appellate Practice Committee of Litigation Section, American Bar Association; Co-Founder, Appellate Practice Subcommittee of Litigation Section, Colorado Bar Association; Chair, Solo and Small Firm Practice Section, Colorado Bar Association **BAR:** Supreme Court of the United States (1992); U.S. District Court for the District of Colorado (1988); Colorado (1987); U.S. Court of Appeals for the Third, Sixth, Ninth, Tenth, and Federal Circuits **MH:** Albert Nelson Marquis Lifetime Achievement Award **AS:** Mr. Sargent attributes his success to, in his own words, "just try[ing] to be honest, and I try not to screw up." **B/I:** Mr. Sargent became involved in his profession because he was interested in the philosophy of law, or jurisprudence, and regarded the profession of law as a kind of "secular priesthood" that helped to order society and act as guardians of that order. **AV:** Running - Qualifier, U.S. Olympics Marathon Trials (1992); 50 Fastest U.S. Marathoners of the Year (1988, 1990); First American Finisher, San Diego International Marathon (1988); Fourth American Finisher, Chicago Marathon (1988); Three-Time Runner Up, Pikes Peak Ascent (1986, 1988, 1991); Chess - Rated Chess Expert (1980-Present); Third Place, U.S. Air Force Chess Championships and member U.S. Air Force National Chess Team (1981); Member, M.I.T. Chess Team (1976-2000); Top 50 Finishers, National High School Chess Championships (1975), Mr. Sargent remains involved in running and chess; his other interests include classic films. **THT:** Mr. Sargent said, "Although I've made my living in litigation, I also believe that few things are really worth fighting about," "Be kind and be honest," "Don't judge people too quickly," and, as Katharine Hepburn said in "The Philadelphia Story," "The time to make up your mind about people is never."https://www.attorneyatwork.com/enterprising-lawyer-walter-h-sargent/ https://www.superlawyers.com/colorado/article/marathon-man/c35986a1-1902-4e59-a7c8-6341c85a4b5f.html

SARRATT, JANET PLATT, T: Librarian **I:** Library Management/Library Services **CN:** John E. Ewing Middle School **DOB:** 10/03/1949 **PB:** Philadelphia **SC:** PA/USA **PT:** James Mellor Platt; Dorothy (Young) Platt **MS:** Divorced **SPN:** David Glenn Serratt (05/28/1971, Divorced 03/1978) **ED:** MLS, University of South Carolina (1980); MA in Education, Winthrop University (1974);BLS, Mansfield University of Pennsylvania (1971) **CT:** Certified Librarian Media Specialist, SC **C:** Volunteer Librarian, The Village School of Gaffney, SC (2012-Present); School Library Media Specialist, John E. Ewing Middle School, Gaffney, SC (1971-2006); Girl Scouts of the

United States of America, National Center West, Summer (1971) **CR:** School Advisor Council, John E. Ewing Middle School (1997-2000); Advisory Committee, Gale Publishing Group (Now Gale, A Cengage Company), Detroit, MI (1994-1999); South Carolina Instructional Television, Columbia, SC (1980) **CIV:** The Garden Club of North Carolina, Blowing Rock, NC (2017-Present); Volunteer Usher, Blumenthal Performing Arts Center, Charlotte, NC (1996-Present); Membership Chair, Blowing Rock Community Library Association (2017-2018); Blowing Rock Community Library Association, Blowing Rock, NC (2017); Michael Printz Award Committee, Young Adult Library Service Association (2011); Board Director, Girl Scouts Piedmont Area, Girl Scouts of the United States of America, Spartanburg, SC (1999-2003); Andrew Carnegie Award Committee, Association Library Service to Children (2000); Margaret Edwards Award Committee, Young Adult Library Service Association (1993); Leader, Trainer, Board, Girl Scouts Piedmont Area, Girl Scouts of the United States of America, Spartanburg, SC (1971-1992); Donor, Toys for Tots Foundation; Agusta (Baker Dozen) Festival, SC; Founding Chairman, Junior Book Award, South Carolina Association of School Librarians **MEM:** Program Vice President, American Association of University Women (AAUW) (2019-Present); Secretary, American Association of University Women (AAUW) (1981-1987, 2015-2019); President, Cherokee County Education Association (2015-2016); President, American Association of University Women (AAUW) (2011-2015); Retired, Cherokee County Education Association (2006); Co-building Representative, The South Carolina Education Association (SCEA) (2000-2006); Cherokee County Education Association (1971-2006); Chairman, American Association of School Librarians (1993); Board of Directors, South Carolina Association of School Librarians (1990-1992); Vice President, American Association of University Women (AAUW) (1981-1983); National Education Association; American Association of University Women (AAUW); Membership Chair, American Association of University Women (AAUW); The South Carolina Education Association (SCEA); Cherokee County School Librarians President, Cherokee County School Librarians; Cherokee County Reading Association (Now Cherokee County Literacy Association); American Association of School Librarians; Liaison Committee, American Association of School Librarians; Life Member, American Librarians Association; Association for Library Service to Children; Young Adult Library Service Association; South Carolina Association of School Librarians **MH:** Marquis Lifetime Achievement Award **B/I:** Mrs. Sarratt became involved in her profession since she went to junior high, where she liked to read and joined the library club. She found the great things about the library and her junior high librarian inspired her. Her high school librarian would inspire her as well and she worked as a student assistant. **AV:** Horseback riding (owns two horses); Reading; Sewing; Crafts; Camping; Gardening; Traveling **THT:** Ms. Sarratt really enjoys her horses as she can't imagine life without it. She bought her first horse with her first paycheck from her junior high work. She was also an attendee at the Jones Sparrow Story Telling Festival, which she hasn't missed since her retirement she began volunteering as a tent monitor since 2006 and hasn't missed a year since.

SARSOUR, LINDA, T: Political Activist; Former Executive Director **I:** Civil Service **PB:** Brooklyn **SC:** NY/USA **MS:** Married **SPN:** Maher Judeh **CH:** Three Children **ED:** Coursework, Kingsborough Community College; Coursework, Brooklyn College **C:** Co-chair, Women's March (2017);

Co-chair, Day Without a Woman (2017); Executive Director, Arab American Association of New York (2005-2017); Co-founder, MPower Change **CR:** Speaker in the Field **CIV:** Co-launcher, Crowdfunding Campaign to Repair and Restore a Jewish Cemetery in St. Louis, MO; Fundraiser, Hurricane Harvey Relief and Numerous Other Causes; Political Activist, Muslim Rights, Women's March, Black Lives Matter, Immigration, Stop-and-frisk, Jewish-American Advocacy Groups, and Numerous Other Issues **CW:** Author, "We Are Not Here to Be Bystanders: A Memoir of Love and Resistance" (2020); Media Commentator, Numerous Outlets **AW:** Listed, "Time 100 Most Influential People" (2017); Eleanor Roosevelt Human Rights Award, Unitarian Universalist Service Committee (2017); Recognized, One of the "50 Greatest Leaders," Time Magazine **MEM:** Democratic Socialists of America **RE:** Church of Jesus Christ of Latter-day Saints

SASAHARA, ARTHUR ASAO, MD, T: Senior Physician **I:** Medicine & Health Care **CN:** Brigham and Women's Hospital **DOB:** 05/11/1927 **PB:** Del Rey **SC:** CA/USA **PT:** Harold Hango Sasahara; Blanche (Takayama) Sasahara **MS:** Married **SPN:** Alice Ann Guenther (04/02/1955) **CH:** Ann Mariko; Claire Michiko; Ellen Reiko; Karen Hideko; Mark Tadao **ED:** Honorary AM, Harvard University (1987); Senior Resident in Medicine, Yale New Haven Hospital, Yale New Haven Health (1959-1960); Fellow in Pediatrics Cardiology, Children's Hospital Medical Center (Now Boston Children's Hospital), Boston, MA (1958-1959); Fellow in Cardiology, VA Hospital, VA Boston Healthcare System, West Roxbury, MA (1957-1958); Junior Assistant Medical Resident, Massachusetts General Hospital, Boston, MA (1956-1957); Intern, Boston City Hospital (Now Boston Medical Center) (1955-1956); MD, Case Western Reserve University (1955); AB, Oberlin College and Conservatory (1951) **CT:** Diplomate, American Board of Internal Medicine (1962) **C:** Professor Emeritus, Harvard Medical School (1993-Present); Senior Physician, Brigham and Women's Hospital, Boston, MA (1982-2018); Professor of Medicine, Harvard Medical School, Boston, MA (1974-1993); Chief Medical Service, VA Hospital, VA Boston Healthcare System, West Roxbury-Brockton, MA (1982-1987); Consultant, Cardiovascular-Pulmonary Diseases, Boston, MA (1965-1987); Consultant, Pediatric Cardiology, Children's Hospital Medical Center (Now Boston Children's Hospital), Boston, MA (1976-1986); Physician, Brigham and Women's Hospital, Boston, MA (1979-1982); Chief Medical Service, VA Hospital, VA Boston Healthcare System, West Roxbury, MA (1974-1982); Associate Chief of Staff for Research and Education, VA Hospital, VA Boston Healthcare System, West Roxbury, MA (1970-1976); Chief Cardiopulmonary Section, VA Hospital, VA Boston Healthcare System, West Roxbury, MA (1971-1974); Assistant Chief of Medical Service, VA Hospital, VA Boston Healthcare System, West Roxbury, MA (1960-1970); Director, Cardiopulmonary Laboratory, VA Hospital, VA Boston Healthcare System, West Roxbury, MA (1960-1970); Deputy Chairman, Research and Education Committee, VA Hospital, VA Boston Healthcare System, West Roxbury, MA (1960-1970) **CR:** Arthur A. Sasahara Lectureship (2012-Present); Senior Physician, Venous Thromboembolism Research Group, Brigham and Women's Hospital, Boston, MA (2000-Present); Senior Physician, Cardiovascular Division, Brigham and Women's Hospital, Boston, MA (1998-Present); Senior Medical Director, Abbott Laboratories, Abbott (1995-1997); Director, Thrombolytics Research, Pharmaceutical Products Division, IL (1987-1995); Fellow, American College of Physicians **MIL:** U.S. Army (1945-1947) **CW:** Author/Editor, "New Therapeutic

Agents in Thrombosis and Thrombolysis, Second Edition" (2002); Author/Editor, "New Therapeutic Agents in Thrombosis and Thrombolysis" (1997); Editorial Board, Primary Cardiology (1986-1989); Editorial Board, Journal of Cardiovascular Medicine (1980-1986); Editorial Board, VASA (1978-1985); Editorial Board, The Journal of Nuclear Medicine (1981-1983); Editorial Board, Circulation (1973-1978); Author/Editor, "Pulmonary Emboli" (1975); Designer, Constant Infusion Medical Pump, Harvard Apparatus (1973); Editorial Board, New England Journal of Medicine (1971-1973); Editorial Board, The American Journal of Medicine (1971-1972); Author/Editor, "Pulmonary Embolic Disease" (1965); Contributor, Articles to Professional Journals; Contributor, Approximately 325 Articles and Scientific Papers to Professional Publications **AW:** VA Grantee (1961-1987); Grantee, National Institutes of Health (1963-1982) **MEM:** Co-Founding Director, North American Thrombosis Forum (2006-Present); American College of Chest Physicians; American College of Cardiology Foundation; American Association for the Advancement of Science; International Society for Fibrinolysis and Thrombolysis; American Federation for Clinical Research (Now American Federation for Medical Research); International Society on Thrombosis and Haemostasis, Inc.; American Heart Association, Inc.; Alpha Omega Alpha Honor Medical Society **MH:** Albert Nelson Marquis Lifetime Achievement Award **B/I:** Dr. Sasahara became involved in his profession because he always wanted to be a physician to help people, especially veterans. Therefore, he became assistant chief of medicine, chief of cardiology and chief of medicine during his 30 years at the West Roxbury VA Hospital, now the Boston Healthcare System. After retiring, he moved over to the Brigham and Women's Hospital. **PA:** Democrat **RE:** Episcopalian

SASSE, BENJAMIN, "BEN" ERIC, PHD, T: U.S. Senator from Nebraska **I:** Government Administration/Government Relations/Government Services **DOB:** 02/22/1972 **PB:** Plainview **SC:** NE/USA **PT:** Gary Lynn Sasse; Linda K. (Dunklau) Sasse **MS:** Married **SPN:** Melissa (McLeod) Sasse **CH:** Elizabeth; Alexandra; Breck **ED:** PhD in American History, Yale University, New Haven, CT; MA in Liberal Arts, St. John's College Graduate Institute (1998); AB in Government, Harvard University, Cambridge, MA (1994); Coursework, University of Oxford (1992) **C:** U.S. Senator, State of Nebraska (2015-Present); Member, Committee on Armed Services (2015-Present); Member, Committee on Banking, Housing, and Urban Affairs (2015-Present); Member, Joint Economic Committee (2015-Present); Member, Committee of the Judiciary (2015-Present); President, Professor of History, Midland University, Freemont, NE (2010-2014); Assistant Professor of Public Affairs, The University of Texas at Austin Lyndon B. Johnson School of Public Affairs, Austin, Texas (2009-2010); Assistant Secretary for Planning and Evaluation, U.S. Department Health and Human Services (2007-2009); Counselor to Secretary, U.S. Department of Health and Human Services (2006-2007); Chief of Staff to Representative Jeff Fortenberry, U.S. House of Representatives, Washington, DC (2005); Chief of Staff, Office Legal Policy, U.S. Department of Justice (2003-2005); Associate Consultant, Boston Consulting Group (1994-1995) **CIV:** Member, Board of Trustees, Westminster Seminary California; Member, Grace Church Fremont, CA; Director, Alliance of Confessing Evangelicals, Inc. **CW:** Author, "Them: Why We Hate Each Other - and How to Heal" (2018); Author, "The Vanishing American Adult" (2017); Co-editor, "Here We Stand!: A Call from Confessing Evangelicals for a

Modern Reformation" (1996) **AW:** George Washington Egleston Historical Prize; Theron Rockwell Field Prize **PA:** Republican **RE:** Lutheran

SATRIANO, PIETRO, T: Chairperson, President, Chief Executive Officer **I:** Food & Restaurant Services **CN:** US Foods Holding Corp. **ED:** Master of Business Administration, Harvard Business School, Harvard University (1992); Bachelor of Arts in Economics, Harvard University (1982-1985) **C:** Chairperson, President, Chief Executive Officer, US Foods Holding Corp. (2017-Present); Chief Executive Officer, President, US Foods Inc. (2015-Present); Chief Merchandising Officer, US Foods Holding Corp. (2011-2015); President, LoyaltyOne Canada (2009-2011); Executive Vice President, Food Segment, Loblaw Companies (2007-2008); Executive Vice President, Loblaw Brands, Loblaw Companies (2002-2006); Senior Vice President, US Loyalty, The Loyalty Group (2000-2002); Vice President, General Manager, Direct Sales, The Loyalty Group (1998-2000); Senior Director, Rewards Services, The Loyalty Group (1996-1998); Director, Procurement, Delray Farms (1994-1995); Director, Deli-Seafood, Merchandising and Operations, Loblaw Companies (1992-1994); Consultant, The Monitor Group (1987-1990); Associate, The Boston Consulting Group, Inc. (1985-1987) **CR:** Member, Board, Canadian Springs Water Co., Ltd.

SAUNDERS, MARTHA A., T: Professor of English Emerita **I:** Education/Educational Services **DOB:** 07/20/1930 **PB:** Springfield **SC:** OH/USA **PT:** Dewey Saunders; Ruth Harriet (Swanson) Saunders **MS:** Widow **SPN:** C. Vann Saunders (08/06/1955, Deceased) **CH:** Pamela; C. Vann III (Deceased); Hunter **ED:** PhD, Georgia State University (1983); MA, Auburn University (1954); AB, DePauw University (1952) **CT:** Trainer of Trainers, Girl Scouts of the USA **C:** Professor, West Georgia College (1993-1995); Associate Professor, West Georgia College (1985-1993); Assistant Professor, West Georgia College (1974-1985); Instructor, West Georgia College (1965-1974); Teacher, Talbot County High School, Talbotton, GA (1956-1957); Teacher, Fort Hawkins School, Macon, GA (1955-1956); Instructor, Ohio Northern University (1954-1955); Graduate Teaching Assistant, Auburn University (1952-1954) **CIV:** President, Georgia Federation of Women's Clubs 6th District (2014-2016); President, Carrollton Literary Music Club (2013-2015); Vice President, President, Carrollton Civic Woman's Club (2000-2006); Vice President, President, Pine Valley Council Girl Scouts of the USA (1993-1997); Vice President, Georgia League of Women Voters (1991-1993); President, Carrollton/Carroll County League of Women Voters (1998-1990) **CW:** Contributor, Articles, Professional Journals **AW:** Citizen of the Year Award, Carrollton Civic Woman's Club (1998, 2007, 2017); Eleanor Raoul Greene Award for Lifetime Achievement, Georgia League Of Women Voters (2013); Clubwoman of the Year Award, Georgia Federation Of Women's Clubs 6th District (2013); Clubwoman of the Year Award, Carrollton Civic Woman's Club (2005, 2013); Oxford Award, Atlanta Delta Gamma Alumnae (2008); Listee, "Georgia's Legacy: Older Women: Active And Alive: Well Past 65"; Inductee, Georgia Commission on Women (2005); Humanitarian Award, Carrollton Sertoma Club (1993); Citizenship Award Carrollton/Carroll County League of Women Voters (1991); Woman of Achievement Award, Business and Professional Women of Carroll County (1989); Women Making History In Education Award, West Georgia National Organization Of Women (1988); Thanks Badge, Pine Valley Girls Scouts of the USA (1973); J. Owen Moore Faculty Award, University of West Georgia National Alumni Association **MEM:** President, Georgia-South Carolina College English Association (1988-1990); President, Phi Kappa Phi (1976-1977); President, Gamma Iota Chapter, Delta Gamma (1951-1952); National Council of Teachers of English; South Atlantic Modern Language Association; Southeastern English in Two-Year Colleges Association; Conference on College Composition and Communication **MH:** Albert Nelson Marquis Lifetime Achievement Award; Marquis Who's Who Top Professional **B/I:** Dr. Saunders was inspired to be a teacher because her parents, Dewey and Ruth Harriet, were both teachers. Her father was a math professor and her mother was an elementary school teacher. Further, she loved to learn, which motivated her to earn a PhD. **AV:** Aerobic exercising; Volunteering; Dancing **RE:** Methodist

SAVAGE, ROBERT CHARLES, T: Insurance and Finance Company Executive **I:** Insurance **DOB:** 12/25/1937 **PB:** Toledo **SC:** OH/USA **PT:** John Michal Savage; Katheryn Marie (Fox) Savage **MS:** Married **SPN:** Susan M. Savage (05/21/1966) **CH:** Robert J.; Lisa M.; Eric G.; Michelle K.; Mark J.; Matthew C. **ED:** Honorary Doctoral Degree, University of Toledo, Toledo, OH (2013); Bachelor of Business Administration, University of Toledo, Toledo, OH (1959) **CT:** Chartered Life Underwriter (CLU); Chartered Financial Consultant (ChFC) **C:** Chairman Emeritus, Savage & Associates Inc., Toledo, OH (2002-Present); President, Savage & Associates Inc., Toledo, OH (1961-2002); Vice President, Savage & Associates Inc., Toledo, OH (1959-1961) **CR:** Former Member, Board of Directors, Cedar Fair; Former Member, Board of Directors, Solar Cells Inc.; Former Member, Board of Directors, Centerior Energy **CIV:** Board of Trustees, Committee of 100, City of Toledo (1988); Board of Directors, University of Toledo, Toledo, OH (1988); President, Board of Directors, St. Vincent Hospital, Toledo, OH (1972); Vice Mayor, Toledo City Council (1966); Member, Toledo City Council (1962) **AW:** Outstanding Philanthropists Award, Northwest Ohio Chapter, Association of Fundraising Professionals (2017); The College of Business Administration and Innovation Pacemaker Award (2010); Gold T Award, University of Toledo, Toledo, OH (2003); Hospital Planning Distinguished Service Award, St. Vincent Hospital, Toledo, OH (1972); University Toledo Pacemaker (1966); Named Outstanding Young Man of the Year, Toledo, OH (1965) **MEM:** Million Dollar Round Table **MH:** Albert Nelson Marquis Lifetime Achievement Award; Marquis Who's Who Top Professional **B/I:** Mr. Savage became involved in his profession due to the influence of his parents, who graduated from college in Upstate New York. He decided to major in finance while attending local university. **RE:** Roman Catholic

SAVOY, CHYRL LENORE, T: Artist, Educator **I:** Education/Educational Services **DOB:** 05/23/1944 **PB:** New Orleans **SC:** LA/USA **PT:** Frank Peter Savoy Jr.; Bobby Adrienne (Rawls) Savoy **CH:** Bobby Frances Savoy **ED:** MFA, Wayne State University (1970); BA, Louisiana State University (1966); Diploma in Language, Università degli Studi di Firenze **C:** Professor, University of Louisiana at Lafayette (1978-2015); Assistant Professor of Fine Arts, Louisiana State University (1973-1977); Graduate Assistant, Wayne State University, Detroit, MI (1970); Art Teacher, Saint Martin de Porres High School (1969) **CR:** Coordinator, Sculpture (1989-Present); Faculty Senator (1992-1996); Curriculum Committee, Visual Arts Department (1991); Director, School of Art and Architecture Search Committee (1989); Director, Coordinator Models Program (1989); Studio Position Search Committee (1988-1989); Co-Chair, Sculpture Position Search Committee (1988-1989); Sculpture Committee (1986-1987); Drawing Committee (1986-1987); Academy Student Adviser, Department of Visual Arts (1986); Library Representative (1986); Drawing Committee, University of South Louisiana (Now University of Louisiana at Lafayette) (1985); Adviser of Art and Architecture, Student Association (1985); Ways and Means Committee **CIV:** Chair, Art Committee (1976-1977); Art Committee, R.S. Barnwell Garden and Art Center (1975-1976) **CW:** Featured, Beginning Sculpture (2004); Featured, The Sculptural Reference (2004); Solo Exhibition, Universidad de las Américas Puebla (2003); Solo Exhibition, Northeastern State University (2001); Solo Exhibition, School of Humanities, University of Amsterdam (1996); Solo Exhibition, Clark Hall Gallery, Southeastern Louisiana University (1995); Featured Artist, Group Show, 28th Annual National Drawing and Small Sculpture Show, Corpus Christi, TX (1994); Featured Artist, Group Show, 15th Annual Art Exhibition, Columbia, MO (1994); Featured Artist, Group Show, Alexandria Museum of Art (1993); Solo Exhibition, Artists Alliance, Lafayette, LA (1992); Featured Artist, Group Show, Premier National Annual Exhibition World Trade Center, New Orleans, LA (1991); Solo Exhibition, Academia Nacional de Artes Plásticas, Monterrey, Mexico (1987); Solo Exhibition, University Art Center, University of Southwest Louisiana (1983); Solo Exhibition, Maison du Quebec, Lafayette, LA (1983); Solo Exhibition, New Orleans Museum of Art (1972); Solo Exhibition, University Art Gallery, Wayne State University (1970); Featured Artist, Group Show, Louisiana Arts and Sciences Center and New Orleans Contemporary Art Center; Permanent Collection, Hillard Art Museum, University of Louisiana at Lafayette; Permanent Collection, New Orleans Museum of Art; Permanent Collection, Alexandria Museum of Art; Presenter, Works by Women, National Sculpture Conference, Cincinnati, OH **AW:** Grant, BORSF (2004); Teacher of the Year, Beacon Club, University of Louisiana at Lafayette (2000); Instruction and Improvement Grantee (1985, 1986) **MEM:** Artists Alliance; The Phi Beta Kappa Society **MH:** Albert Nelson Marquis Lifetime Achievement Award; Marquis Who's Who Top Professional **B/I:** Ms. Savoy became involved in her profession because she was inspired by the 1952 film, "Moulin Rouge." **AV:** Listening to music; Reading poetry

SAWARDEKER, JAWAHAR SAZRO, PHD, T: Group Quality Worldwide (Retired) **I:** Pharmaceuticals **CN:** Glaxo Holdings **DOB:** 11/22/1937 **PB:** Goa **SC:** India **PT:** Sazro K. Sawardeker; Nirabai S. (Singbal) Sawardeker **MS:** Married **SPN:** Prabha J. (12/14/1966) **CH:** Shubhra; Priscilla; Prasad **ED:** PhD, The University of Iowa (1964); MS, The University of Iowa (1961); BS, Wilson College, Bombay, India (1957) **C:** Corporate Vice President, Director of Group Quality Worldwide, Glaxo Holdings, London, England (1991-1994); Vice President of Technical Affairs for Latin America and the Far East, Glaxo Holdings, Member, Glaxo International Board, Research Triangle Park, NC (1988-1991); Vice President of Quality, Glaxo Inc. Operating Committee Member, Research Triangle Park, NC (1987-1988); Vice President of Quality, Operating Committee, Glaxo, Inc., Research Triangle Park, NC (1981-1987); Director of Quality, American Home Products, NY (1977-1981); Group Manager of Quality, Johnson & Johnson, NJ (1970-1977); Group Leader, Ortho Pharmaceuticals (1970); Senior Scientist, Ortho Pharmaceuticals (1968); Scientist, Ortho Pharmaceuticals (1967); Chemist, U.S. Department of Agriculture, Peoria, IL (1964-1966) **CW:** Author, Numerous Papers, Journal of Analytical Chemistry **AW:** Order of Long Leaf Pine Award, Governor of North Carolina James Hunt (1983); Notable Americans of the Bicentennial Era (1976) **MEM:** Local Chapter, Jaycees **MH:** Albert

Nelson Marquis Lifetime Achievement Award **B/I:** Dr. Sawardeker became involved in his profession because he had always been interested in pharmaceuticals. With additional encouragement from his parents, he knew that was the field for him. They provided endless support and were a great source of inspiration. **THT:** Dr. Sawardeker said, "You may be smart but one smart person is not as effective as hundreds. Hire the best minds, create a vision, promote it, and walk the talk."

SAWYER, HUGH, DOB: 04/30/1952 **PB:** Norfolk **SC:** VA/USA **PT:** John Wilkins Sawyer; Vallie (Lucas) Sawyer **ED:** BBA, Roanoke College, Summa Cum Laude (1974) **CT:** CPA, State of Virginia; Certified Financial Planner **C:** Owner, Sawyer & Co., C.P.A.'s (1984-Present); President, Financial Planning of Virginia, Roanoke, VA (1984-Present); Tax Manager, Ernst & Whinney, C.P.A.'s, Roanoke, VA (1978-1984); Supervisor, Brown Edward & Co., C.P.A.'s, Roanoke, VA (1974-1978) **CW:** Contributor, Articles, Professional Journals **AW:** Wall Street Journal Award (1974) **MEM:** Fellow, Virginia Society of C.P.A.'s; Roanoke Chamber of Commerce; International Association of Financial Planning; National Association of Accountants; American Institute of C.P.A.'s; Boardroom Club; Phi Beta Kappa **AV:** Playing tennis and racquetball **PA:** Republican **RE:** Baptist

SAYEGH, MONET NASSER, MD, T: General Surgery/Medical Senior Consultant **I:** Medicine & Health Care **CN:** University of Southern California; Siemens Healthcare (Siemens Medical Solutions USA, Inc.) **DOB:** 03/30/1956 **PB:** Nazareth **SC:** Israel **PT:** Nasser Sayegh Sr.; Nadia Sayegh **MS:** Married **SPN:** INAM **CH:** Nadine; Natalie; Nadia Jr.; Nasser Jr. **ED:** Postgraduate General Surgery Residency, University of Southern California (1999-2004); MD, American University of the Caribbean School of Medicine (1999); MS in Health Sciences, Hematology/Oncology, American University, Washington, DC (1995); BS in Medical Technology, Anderson Memorial Hospital School of Medical Technology (1985); BS in Medical Technology, Health Sciences, University of South Alabama (1983); BS in Chemistry, Biology, University of Mobile (1982) **CT:** California Clinical Scientist; Florida Clinical Laboratory Supervisor; Board Certified, Clinical Immunology; Board Certified, Hematology Specialist; Board Certified, Certificate of Membership, American Society for Clinical Pathologists; Certificate of Professional Member, American Academy of Anti-Aging Medicine (A4M); American Diabetes Association; Board Eligible, General Surgery **C:** Senior Medical Consultant, Siemens Healthcare (Now Siemens Medical Solutions USA, Inc.), Los Angeles, CA (2007-Present); General Surgeon, University of Southern California (1999-2007); Physician in Training, City of Hope National Medical Center, Duarte, CA (1998-1999); Clinical Consultant, Quest Diagnostics, Van Nuys, CA (1997-1998); Senior Clinical Scientist, Columbia/JFK Medical Center, Atlantis, FL (1995-1997); Clinical Laboratory Director, Premier Medical Group (1993-1995); Nationwide Laboratory Consultant, Star Medical Staffing Corporation, Tampa, FL (1989-1993); Senior Medical Technologist, Hudson Regional Medical Center (Now Regional Medical Center Bayonet Point), C-HCA, Inc., Hudson, FL (1987-1989); General Laboratory Supervisor, Laurens District Hospital (Now Laurens County Hospital), Prisma Health, Laurens, SC (1983-1987); Phlebotomist, Infirmary Health, Mobile, AL (1981-1982) **CW:** Multinational Musician, Professional Singer, Guitar and Lute Professional Player **AW:** Top Doctor Award for Minimally Invasive Laparoscopic Abdominal Surgery (2016-2017); Named to Who's Who Among Students In American Universities

and Colleges (1980-1981); Award of Achievement, Medical Staff, Premier Medical Center; Certificate of Excellence Award, St. Mary's Hospital; Medical Microbiology Certificate of Excellence Award, Graduate School; Lorraine O'Hare Award for Dedication, Palladia Incorporated; Lifetime Member, Cambridge Who's Who **MEM:** State of California Hematopathology/Flowcytometry Association; American Immunology Association (Now The American Association of Immunologists, Inc.); American Academy of Anti-Aging Medicine (A4M); American Medical Association; American Diabetes Association; Doctors Without Borders; American Association for Clinical Chemistry; Clinical Laboratory Management Association; State of Florida Clinical Laboratory Business and Professional Association **AS:** Dr. Sayegh attributes his success to his wife. She was the one that was there through everything and loves him no matter what. **B/I:** When Dr. Sayegh was growing up. He thought he was going to be an actor or a singer. His family thought he had a good voice. However, when he was completing his undergraduate coursework, he did volunteer work at the hospital. He was a phlebotomist. This was his first exposure to patients with various conditions. **THT:** Dr. Sayegh's motto is, "Go for your dreams, it does not matter how long your path is." Dr. Sayegh received his Bachelor of Science in biology and chemistry from the University of Mobile in Mobile, AL, Medical Technology from Anderson Memorial Hospital School of Medical Technology in Anderson, SC, Master of Science in Health Sciences with emphasis on Hematology/Oncology from the American University School of Graduate Studies in Coral Gables, FL and awarded a Doctor of Medicine Degree from the American University School of Medicine in Coral Gables, FL. His postgraduate training is in general surgery with emphasis on emergency non-trauma minimally invasive laparoscopic surgery from the University of Southern California in Los Angeles, CA. Dr. Sayegh has over 30 years of experience in the fields of medicine, research, abdominal laparoscopic surgery and clinical laboratory science. His background includes extensive research in immunology/allergy, hematology/oncology, endocrinology, special chemistry, HLA histocompatiblity and maternal screen. He held key consulting positions focused on multiple disciplines in medicine, surgery and laboratory science, both hospital and reference laboratories. Dr. Sayegh identifies key disease areas in the market and collaborates with external and internal scientists to have the highest potential for generating innovative products. He provides long term scientific and clinical input into the strategic planning process for disease panels and participates in major IVD and medical annual meetings/expositions. He also provides technical support for field personnel, internal and external clients. Dr. Sayegh frequently provides seminars (CEU and CME-accredited) to key opinion leaders, academic institutes, laboratory personnel and medical doctors, and writes publications and white papers. Dr. Sayegh is Physician/Surgeon/Senior Medical Consultant and a member of the Disease State Education group at Siemens Healthcare, with a focus on cardiovascular, oncology and infectious diseases.

SCAFFIDI, ROY F., T: Senior Member **I:** Law and Legal Services **CN:** Scaffidi & Associates **MS:** Married **ED:** JD, Fordham University School of Law (1978) **C:** Senior Partner, Scaffidi & Associates, NY (1985-Present) **AW:** AV Rating in Skill and Ethics, Martindale-Hubbell; Named, The Best Lawyers in America; Named, New York Area's Best Lawyers; Named, Super Lawyers Publications **MEM:** American Board of Trail Attorneys; Litigation Counsel of America **AS:** Mr. Scaffidi attributes his success to

his hard work. He believes that everyone is entitled to justice. **B/I:** Mr. Scaffidi became inspired to pursue a career in law because he wanted to "level the playing field" for those who don't have the money to hire expensive litigation lawyers. When he first graduated law school, he got a job doing defense work for doctors and hospitals. He eventually left that specialty for the personal injury medical malpractice

SCALES, JAMES L. JR., MS, MD, T: Physician **I:** Medicine & Health Care **CN:** Premier Health Associates **DOB:** 05/15/1952 **PB:** Sacramento **SC:** CA/USA **PT:** Dr. James Leonard Scales; Ruth Marie Scales **MS:** Married **SPN:** Dr. Donna M. Coppola **CH:** Chris Scales; Steven Scales; Kevin Scales **ED:** Resident in Orthopedic Surgery, University of Medicine and Dentistry of New Jersey (UMDNJ), (Now Rutgers New Jersey Medical School), Newark, NY (1982-1986); Resident in General Surgery, University of Medicine and Dentistry of New Jersey (UMDNJ), (Now Rutgers New Jersey Medical School), Piscataway, NJ (1979-1980); Graduate Coursework, Joint MD-PhD Curriculum, University of Medicine and Dentistry of New Jersey (UMDNJ), (Now Rutgers New Jersey Medical School) and Rutgers, The States University of New Jersey (1980-1982); MD, University of Medicine and Dentistry of New Jersey (UMDNJ), (Now Rutgers New Jersey Medical School), Piscataway, NJ (1979); MS in Physiology, Rutgers, The State University of New Jersey (1978); AB in Psychology, Harvard University, Cambridge, MA, Cum Laude (1974) **CT:** Recertified, American Board of Orthopaedic Surgery, Inc. (2018); Diplomate, American Board of Orthopaedic Surgery, Inc. (1988) **C:** Clinical Peer Reviewer, Genex Services, Inc./CID Management, Inc., Westlake Village, CA (2011-2020); Partner, Premier Health Associates, Newton, NJ (2016-Present); Physician Consultant, Livanta LLC (2018-2019); President, Andover Orthopedic Surgery & Sports Medicine Group, Newton, NJ (1988-2016); Independent Medical Examiner, Chief Financial Officer, Medical Services, Roseland, NJ (2006-2008); Orthopedic Surgeon, D'Ascoli Orthopedic Surgery, Sparta, NJ (1986-1988); Staff Physician, Medical Unit, Meadowlands Sports Complex, New Jersey Sports and Exposition Authority, East Rutherford, NJ (1980-1988); General Practitioner, Catholine A. Gibbs Memorial Health Center (1982-1986) **CR:** Chairman, Quality Performance Committee, Volunteer Physician, Medical Director, New Jersey Surgery Center, Newton, NJ (2002-2005); Vice Chief, Medical Staff, Newton Memorial Hospital (Now Newton Medical Center), Atlantic Health System, Newton, NJ (1998); Orthopedic Consultant, Professional Baseball Team, New Jersey Cardinals, Augusta, NJ (1997-2005); With, Garden State Orthopedic Network, IPA (1996-2000); Executive Board of Directors, Medical Management Committee, Wes-Com Health Care Inc., PHO (1996-1998); Medical Staff Representative, Newton Memorial Hospital Foundation (Now Newton Medical Center Foundation) (1996-1998); Chief of Surgery, Newton Memorial Hospital (Now Newton Medical Center), Atlantic Health System (1994-1996) **CIV:** Interviewer, Schools Committee, Harvard Club of New Jersey (1975-2016); Volunteer Sideline Physician, High School Football Games, Four High Schools, Sussex County, NJ and Pike County, PA (1991-2015); Physician, Sports Medicine Clinic, United States Olympic & Paralympic Committee, Volunteer Medical Program, U.S. Olympic & Paralympic Training Centers, Lake Placid, NY (1997) **CW:** Author, Interviewed for More Than 30 Articles, "Ask the Expert" Columns, Health Connections Magazine and New Jersey Herald Newspaper (2012-2015) **AW:** Harvard Club of New Jersey Scholar (1971) **MEM:** Fellow, American Academy of Orthopedic

Surgeons; American Medical Association; U.S. Olympic Sports Medicine Society; Sussex County Medical Society; Medical Society of New Jersey; Pennsylvania Orthopedic Society; New Jersey Orthopedic Society **MH:** Albert Nelson Marquis Lifetime Achievement Award, Marquis Who's Who Publications Board, May 2017 **AV:** Music; Exercise

SCALIA, EUGENE, T: United States Secretary of Labor **I:** Government Administration/Government Relations/Government Services **CN:** United States Department of Labor **DOB:** 08/14/1963 **PB:** Columbus **SC:** OH/USA **PT:** Antonin Scalia; Maureen (McCarthy) Scalia **MS:** Married **SPN:** Patricia Larsen (10/16/1993) **CH:** Antonin; Megan McCarthy; John Christie; Bridget Ann; Luke Francis; Erin Larsen; Isabella **ED:** Doctor of Jurisprudence, The University of Chicago The Law School, Cum Laude (1990); Bachelor of Arts, University of Virginia, with Distinction (1985) **C:** United States Secretary of Labor, Washington, DC (2019-Present); Partner, Gibson, Dunn & Crutcher LLP (2003-2019); Solicitor, United States Department of Labor, Washington, DC (2002-2003); Associate Partner, Gibson, Dunn & Crutcher LLP, Washington, DC (1993-2001); Assistant to Attorney General, United States Department of Justice, Washington, DC (1992-1993); Associate, Gibson, Dunn & Crutcher LLP, Los Angeles, CA (1990-1992); Assistant to Chief of Staff, United States Department of Education, Washington, DC (1985-1987); Member, Executive Committee, Gibson, Dunn & Crutcher LLP **CR:** Member, Visiting Committee, The University of Chicago The Law School (1998-2001) **CW:** Member, Advisory Board, The University of Chicago Law Review (1996); Editor-in-Chief, The University of Chicago Law Review (1989-1990) **AW:** Named, One of Litigation's Rising Stars, The American Lawyer (2007); Named, Lawyer of the Year, Compliance Reporter Magazine (2006); Named, Top Washington, D.C. Lawyer in Employment Litigation, Washington Business Journal (2006) **BAR:** The District of Columbia Bar (1995); Virginia State Bar (1993); State Bar of California (1990) **RE:** Roman Catholic

SCALING, SAM, "CHIPPER , CHIP" TILDEN MD, FOUNDER, PRESIDENT (RETIRED), T: Obstetrician, Gynecologist **I:** Medicine & Health Care **CN:** Womens Health Associates of Wyoming **DOB:** 08/16/1945 **PB:** Fort Monmouth **SC:** NJ/USA **PT:** Sam T. Scaling; Helen Louise Scaling **MS:** Married **SPN:** Lisa Janine Peck (08/06/1988) **CH:** Micah; Traci; Craig; Chad; Chris; Cory; Tiffany **ED:** Chief Resident of Obstetrics and Gynecology, Baylor College of Medicine, Houston, TX (1977-1978); Resident in Obstetrics-Gynecology, Baylor College of Medicine, Houston, TX (1975-1978); OB-GYN Residency, Baylor College of Medicine Medical Center, Houston, TX (1975-1978); MD, University of Tennessee, Memphis, TN (1971); Intern, Confederate Memorial Medical Center, Shreveport, LA (1971); BS, University of New Mexico, Albuquerque, NM (1967) **CT:** Diplomate, American Board of Obstetrics and Gynecology **C:** Private Practice, Obstetrics, Gynecology and Infertility Casper, WY (1978-Present); Medical Staff, Wyoming Medical Center (1978-Present); Retired (2019); Founder, President, Women's Health Associates Wyoming, Casper, WY (2001-2019); Chairman, Department of Obstetrics and Gynecology, Wyoming Medical Center, Memorial Hospital, Natrona County, Wyoming (2002-2005); Chairman, Department of Obstetrics and Gynecology, Wyoming Medical Center, Memorial Hospital, Natrona County, Wyoming (2001); Chief of Staff, Wyoming Medical Center, Memorial Hospital, Natrona County, Wyoming (1993-1995); Vice Chief of Staff, Wyoming Medical Center, Memorial

Hospital, Natrona County, Wyoming (1991-1993); Secretary, Medical Staff, Wyoming Medical Center, Memorial Hospital, Natrona County, Wyoming (1989-1991); Chairman, Department of Obstetrics and Gynecology, Wyoming Medical Center, Memorial Hospital, Natrona County, Wyoming (1986-1988); Chairman, Department of Obstetrics and Gynecology, Wyoming Medical Center, Memorial Hospital, Natrona County, Wyoming (1981-1983) **CR:** Clinical Assistant Professor, Instructor, Obstetrics and Gynecology, Wyoming Family Practice Program, Casper, NY (1978-Present); President, Wyoming State Board of Medical Examiners (1990-1992); Vice President, Wyoming State Board of Medical Examiners (1984-1992); Vice President, Wyoming State Board of Medical Examiners (1989-1990); Medical Director, Wyoming Medical Center, PMS Clinic (1987-1990); Medical Director, Caring Center, Casper, WY (1986-1990); Medical Director, Christ-Centered Childbirth (1984-1987); Medical Director, Casper Family-Centered League Lamaze Prepared Childbirth (1980-1984); Presenter in Field **CIV:** Member, Advisory Board, Caring Center (2001-Present); Board of Directors, Wyoming Community Health Care Alliance (1997-Present); Board of Directors, Christian Solidarity Worldwide-USA (1997-2000); Member, Little Dilly Golf Tournament Committee, Casper Country Club (1994-1996); Advisory Board, Highland Park Community Church (1994-1995); Vice President, Board of Directors, Casper Children's Chorale (1981-1982); Member, Healing Place Counseling Center **MIL:** U.S. Air Force Reserves (1975-1977); Major, U.S. Air Force (1972-1975) **CW:** Author, Nine Children's Books **AW:** Named, America's Top Obstetricians and Gynecologists, Consumers Research Council of America (2007-2014); Dr. Paul Johnson Driving Passion Award (2007); Named, America's Top Obstetricians and Gynecologists, Consumers Research Council of America (2002-2003); Summer Scholar, National Science Foundation, New Mexico Highlands University (1962); Alpha Omega Alpha Honor Medical Society **MEM:** National Advisory Council, American Society for Reproductive Medicine (1997); Natrona County Medical Society; American Association of Pro-Life Obstetricians and Gynecologists; American College of Physician Executives; Society of Reproductive Surgeons; American Association of Gynecologic Laparoscopists; Wyoming State Medical Society; Central Association of Obstetricians and Gynecologists; Lifetime Member, Foundation of North America Wild Sheep; Alaska Professional Hunters Association; Lifetime Member, Bass Anglers Sportsman Society; Lifetime Member, North America Hunting Club; Lifetime Member, Boone and Crockett Club; Lifetime Member, Safari Club International; Rocky Mountain Elk Foundation; Alpha Omega Alpha; Fellow, American College of Surgeons; American College of Obstetrics and Gynecology; American Fertility Society **MH:** Albert Nelson Marquis Lifetime Achievement Award; Marquis Who's Who Top Professional **AS:** Dr. Scaling attributes his success to The Lord. His mentor was Dr. Alan Kaplan, a gynecologic cancer professor and instructor at Baylor College of Medicine and he was fantastic. **B/I:** Dr. Scaling knew from when he was young that he wanted to be a doctor. While he was in medical school, he rotated through all the different areas and specialties and just loved being around ladies having babies and delivering babies and that's how he wound up as an obstetrician in women's health care. **AV:** Former Hunter; Fishing; Camper; Hiking; Gun collecting; Coin collecting/numismatics **PA:** Republican **RE:** Pentecostal Christian **THT:** Not so much the path you take as the trail you leave behind. Follow the Lord and all his goodness!

SCALISE, STEPHEN, "STEVE" JOSEPH, T: U.S. Representative from Louisiana **CN:** U.S. House of Representatives **DOB:** 10/06/1965 **PB:** New Orleans **SC:** LA/USA **PT:** Alfred Joseph Scalise; Carol Schilleci **MS:** Married **SPN:** Jennifer Ann Letulle (04/09/2005) **CH:** Madison Carol; Harrison Joseph **ED:** Bachelor of Science in Computer Science, Minor in Political Science, Louisiana State University (1989) **C:** Minority Whip, U.S. House of Representatives (2019-Present); Dean, Louisiana Congressional Delegation (2017-Present); Member, U.S. House of Representatives from Louisiana's First Congressional District, U.S. Congress, Washington, DC (2008-Present); Assistant Majority Leader (Majority Whip), U.S. House of Representatives (2014-2019); Chairperson, Republican Study Committee (2013-2014); Member, District Nine, Louisiana State Senate (2008); Member, District 82, Louisiana House of Representatives (1996-2007); Software Engineer, Computer Programmer, Technology Company Marketing Executive, Louisiana **CR:** Member, Committee on Energy and Commerce, U.S. House of Representatives (2017-2018, 2019-2020); Member, Subcommittee on Communications and Technology, Energy and Commerce Committee, U.S. House of Representatives (2015-2016); Member, Subcommittee on Communications and Technology, Subcommittee on Energy and Power, Subcommittee on Oversight and Investigations, Energy and Commerce Committee, U.S. House of Representatives (2011-2012, 2013-2014) **CIV:** Board Member, Jefferson Senior Center; Board Member, American Italian Renaissance Foundation, American Italian Cultural Center; Board Member, Teach for America Inc., New Orleans, LA **AW:** Named, One of the 50 Politicos to Watch, Politico (2010); Named, Legislator of the Year, Citizens Against Lawsuit Abuse (1999); Named, Man of the Year, Associated Builders and Contractors Inc. (2001); Named, Legislator of the Year, New Orleans Chamber of Commerce (2001); Named, Man of the Year, AARP, Central Metairie Chapter (1998); Named, Legislator of the Year, Alliance for Good Government, Jefferson/New Orleans Chapter; Outstanding Legislator Award, Victims and Citizens Against Crime; Business Champion Award, New Orleans Chamber of Commerce; Patrick F. Taylor Republican Leadership Award; Distinguished Service Award, Louisiana Restaurant Association; Letter of Commendation, United States Navy Reserve **MEM:** Young Leadership Council; Louisiana Young Republicans; Acacia Fraternity **PA:** Republican **RE:** Roman Catholic

SCAPPLE, SHARON, "SHARI" M., PHD, T: Professor Emeritus **I:** Education/Educational Services **DOB:** 09/17/1947 **PB:** Menomonie **SC:** WI/USA **PT:** Myron; Regina Scapple **MS:** Single **ED:** Doctor of Philosophy in Children's and Adolescent Literature, University of Minnesota, Minneapolis, MN (1983); Master of Science in English, Winona State University, Minnesota, MN (1974); Bachelor of Arts in English, University of Wisconsin, Eau Claire, WI (1969) **C:** Professor Emeritus, Minnesota State University (2019-Present); Coordinator, English Education, Minnesota State University (2001-2019); Professor, English, Minnesota State University, Moorhead, MN (2001-2019); Owner, Black Bear Studio (2018); Founder, Great Plains Reading Revisor, Minnesota State University (2002); College Teacher, University of Wisconsin-River Falls (2000-2001); College Teacher, University of Minnesota, Minneapolis, MN (1994-2001); College Teacher, Department English, Metropolitan State University, St. Paul, MN (1987-2001); College Teacher, University of St. Thomas, St. Paul, MN (1990-1992); College Teacher, Normandale Community College, Bloomington, MN (1986-1990); English Teacher, Shawano High School, Shawano, WI (1970-1972);

Teacher, Marshfield High School, Marshfield, WI (1969-1970) **CR:** Freelance Editor, Children's Literature **CIV:** Prairie Public TV, Fargo, ND (2002); Juror, Reading Rainbow; Juror, Writing Competition, Red Cross, Fargo, ND **CW:** Founder and Chief Editor, Great Plains Reading Review (2005-Present); One-Woman Exhibition, Hawley Art Show, Honorable Mention (2016, 2017, 2018); Juried Art Exhibition, Auction to Support the Educational Unit of the Museum (2014, 2015, 2016, 2017, 2018); One-Woman Exhibition, Rourke Museum, Midwest Show, Moorhead, MN (2016); One-Woman Exhibition, Plains School of Abstract Painting, Plains Art Museum (2015); One-Woman Exhibition, Rural Art Show, "On the Farm", Abstract Art, Wahpeton, ND (2015); Book Reviewer, "The Real Thing" (2005); Author, Essay, "Moving Beyond the Notion of Universal Voice," (2003, 2004); Co-Editor and Contributor, "An Exciting and Exacting Wisdom" (2002); Author, Essay, "Facing Intolerance: All-American Boys, Frank Mosca" (2002); Contributor, "The Oxford Companion to Fairy Tales" (2000); Book Reviews, Books for Young Readers, College of Education, University of Minnesota (1985, 1988, 2000); Book Review, "The Lion and Unicorn" (1998); Book Review, "History of Children's Books Revisited, The Lion and Unicorn" (1997); Author, Critical Essay, "The Phoenix Award of the Children's Literature Association" (1996); Book Review, "Five Owls" (1989-1990); One-Woman Exhibition, Plains Art Museum, Spring Gala, Fargo, ND; Author, Essay, "Transformation of Myth in Tale of Time City"; Author, Three Poems **AW:** Faculty Development Grants (2002, 2005-2006); Nominee, Outstanding Advising, Minnesota State University (2005); Academy Affairs Teaching Excellence Award, Minnesota State University (2005); Named, Teacher of the Month (2004); Outstanding Teacher of the Year, Metropolitan State University (1991) **MEM:** Children Literature Association (1999-2002, 1978-Present); Phoenix Award Committee, Children's Literature Association (1991-1995); Society of Children's Book Writers & Illustrators; American Library Association **MH:** Marquis Lifetime Achievement Award **B/I:** Ms. Scapple became involved in her profession of art because her undergraduate professor understood her desire to teach teaching. She also enjoys working with young people, and pursued her doctorate in children's literature. **AV:** Organic gardening; Wood refinishing

SCARAMUCCI, ANTHONY, "THE MOOCH", T: Former White House Director of Communication; Finance Executive **I:** Financial Services **DOB:** 01/06/1964 **PB:** Long Island **SC:** NY/USA **PT:** Alexander Scaramucci; Maria DeFeo Scarmucci **MS:** Married **SPN:** Deidre Ball (2014); Lisa Miranda (1988, Divorced 2014) **ED:** JD, Harvard Law School (1989); BA in Economics, Tufts University, Summa Cum Laude, Medford, MA (1986) **C:** Co-founder, Managing Partner, SkyBridge Capital, LLC (2005-Present); Director of Communication, White House, Washington, DC (2017); Managing Director, Investment Management Division, Neuberger Berman Group LLC (2003-2005); Managing Director, Private Asset Management Group, Neuberger Berman Group LLC (2001-2003); Co-founder, Senior Partner, Oscar Capital Management LLC (1996-2001); Vice President, Private Wealth Management, Goldman Sachs & Co. (1993-1996); Various Positions, Goldman Sachs & Co. (1989-1993) **CR:** Member, Advisory Committee, New York City Financial Services **CIV:** Member, Board of Overseers, Tufts University School of Arts and Sciences; Board of Directors, Brain Tumor Foundation; Board of Directors, Lymphoma Foundation of America **CW:** Author, "Trump, the Blue-Collar President" (2018); Guest Appearance, Podcast, "Right on Point" (2018); Guest Appearance, Pod-

cast, "Pardon My Take" (2017); Author, "Hopping Over the Rabbit Hole: How Entrepreneurs Turn Failure into Success" (2016); Author, "The Little Book of Hedge Funds: What You Need to Know About Hedge Funds but the Managers Won't Tell You" (2012); Author, "Goodbye Gordon Gekko: How to Find Your Fortune Without Losing Your Soul" (2010) **MEM:** The Phi Beta Kappa Society **PA:** Republican

SCARBOROUGH, JOE, T: Talk Show Host **I:** Media & Entertainment **DOB:** 04/09/1963 **PB:** Atlanta **SC:** GA/USA **PT:** George Francis Scarborough; Mary Joanna (Clark) Scarborough **MS:** Married **SPN:** Mika Brzezinski (11/24/2018); Susan Warren (10/20/2001, Divorced 2013); Melanie Ann Hinston (07/19/1986, Divorced 1999) **CH:** Joey; Andrew; Kate (Stepdaughter) **ED:** JD, University of Florida Fredric G. Levin College of Law (1990); BA in History, The University of Alabama (1985) **C:** Co-host, "Morning Joe," MSNBC (2007-Present); Host, "Scarborough Country," MSNBC (2003-2007); Appointed Member, President's Council on the 21st Century Workforce (2002); Member, U.S. House of Representatives, Florida's First District (1995-2001); Attorney, PA (1990); Member, Government Reform Committee, Judiciary Committee, Armed Service Committee, United States Congress; Partner, Beggs & Lane, FL **CR:** Member, Board of Directors, Emerald Coast Pediatrics Primary Care, Inc.; Co-chairman, New Federalists **CW:** Musician, Extended Play, "Mystified" (2017); Author, "The Right Path: From Ike to Reagan, How Republicans Once Mastered Politics-and Can Again" (2013); Co-host, Radio Show, WABC (2008-2010); Author, "The Last Best Hope" (2009); Author, "Rome Wasn't Burnt in a Day: The Real Deal on How Politicians, Bureaucrats, and Other Washington Barbarians Are Bankrupting America" (2005) **AW:** Named One of the "100 Most Influential People in the World," TIME Magazine (2011); Listed, "The 50 Highest-Earning Political Figures," Newsweek (2010); Guardian of Seniors' Rights Award, 60 Plus Association; Taxpayer's Hero Award, Citizen Against Government Waste; Spirit of Enterprise Award, U.S. Chamber of Commerce; Guardian of Small Business Award, National Federation of Independent Business; Friend of the Taxpayer Award, Americans for Tax Reform **MEM:** Former Member, Gulf Coast Economics **BAR:** The Florida Bar (1991) **PA:** Republican **RE:** Baptist

SCARBROUGH, GLENDA JUDITH, T: Elementary School Educator **I:** Education/Educational Services **DOB:** 07/17/1940 **PB:** Hill County **SC:** TX/USA **PT:** Roland Leon; Bessie Bell (Ferguson) Blocker **MS:** Married **SPN:** Johnny Ray Scarbrough (02/20/1959) **CH:** Deborah Lynn Randolph **ED:** MEd, Sul Ross State University (1985); BS, University of the Southwest (1969) **CT:** Reading Specialist **C:** Retired (2003); Reading Specialist, Andrews Indiana School District (1986-2003); Elementary Teacher, Andrews Indiana School District (1969-1986) **CR:** Teacher's Professional Practices Commission, Texas Governor (1991-1993); Texas State Textbook Selection Committee (1993) **AW:** Two-Time Winner, "Teacher of the Year," San Andres Elementary **MEM:** State Board of Directors, ATPE (1986-1990); Regional Committee for Dyslexia Guidelines, ATPE (1987); President, ATPE (1984-1986); Regional Vice President, ATPE (1983-1984); Campus Representative, Chapter President, ATPE (1982-1984); DKGSI **MH:** Albert Nelson Marquis Lifetime Achievement Award **B/I:** Ms. Scarbrough became involved in her profession because she was inspired by her mother, Bessie Belle Blocker, who was a teacher. **PA:** Republican

SCHAFFNER, J., "SKIP" LURAY, ARTIST, T: Vice President **I:** Fine Art **CN:** Designers Two **DOB:** 04/14/1939 **PB:** Columbus **SC:** OH/USA **PT:** John Ralph Schirtzinger; Vera Schirtzinger **MS:** Married **SPN:** John Albert Schaffner **CH:** Shawn Michael Schaffner; Jorn Michael Schaffner **ED:** Coursework, Ohio State University; BFA in Advertising Design, Columbus College of Art & Design, Columbus, OH **C:** Advertising Designer, Paul L. Devaney Art Studio, Columbus, OH; Warner P. Advertising Agency, Upper Arlington, OH; Vice President, Designers Two **CIV:** Long Beach Civic Association, Long Beach, MD **CW:** Artist, Numerous Watercolor, Collage, Mixed Media Paintings; Artist, Juried Exhibition, Annual James River Exhibition, Newport News, VA; Artist, Juried Exhibition, Athenaeum Juried Shows, Alexandria, VA; Artist, Juried Exhibition, Annual Paper Works Show, Charlottesville, VA; Artist, Juried Exhibition, International Exhibit of Monoprints, Atlanta, GA; Artist, Juried Exhibition, 19th Area Exhibition of the Corcoran Gallery of Art, Washington, DC; Artist, Juried Exhibition, Contemporary Women Artists of St. Louis Exhibit, St. Louis, MO; Artist, Juried Exhibition, Society Annual Exhibition; Artist, Juried Exhibition, Kansas Watercolor Society, Wichita, KS; Artist, Juried Exhibition, International Pastel Society Exhibit, Wichita, KS; Artist, Juried Exhibition, National Watercolor Society, Houston, TX; Artist, Juried Exhibition, Annual National Watercolor, Oklahoma City, OK; Artist, Juried Exhibition, National Western Colorado Watercolor Society, Junction, CO; Artist, Juried Exhibition, Society of Artists-Grand Exhibition, Akron, OH; Artist, Juried Exhibition, North Coast Collage Society, Spokane, WA; Artist, Juried Exhibition, New Mexico Annual Small Paining Annual, Taos, NM; Artist, Juried Exhibition, Annual Quad State Juried Exhibition, Quincy, IL; Artist, Juried Exhibition, Annual Salmagundi Art Exhibition, New York, NY; Artist, Juried Exhibition, Northwest Watercolor Society Annual, Kirkland, WA; Artist, Juried Exhibition, Allied Artists of America, New York, NY; Artist, Juried Exhibition, Watercolor Society of Alabama National, Florence, AL; Artist, Juried Exhibition, Southern Watercolor Society Annual Meeting; Artist, Juried Exhibition, MOAK-Four State Regional Exhibit, Springfield, MO; Artist, Juried Exhibition, Adirondacks National Exhibition of American Watercolors, New York, NY; Artist, Juried Exhibition, Society of Experimental Artists Annual Meeting; Artist, Juried Exhibition, Aqueous Annual National, Frankfort, KY; Artist, Juried Exhibition, National Watercolor Society Member Exhibit, Fullerton, CA; Artist, Juried Exhibition, Texas Watercolor Society Annual Exhibit, San Antonio, TX; Artist, Juried Exhibition, Louisiana Watercolor Society Annual Exhibit, San Antonio, TX; Artist, Juried Exhibition, Louisiana Watercolor Society Annual International, New Orleans, LA; Artist, Juried Exhibition, New England Watercolor Society, Boston, MA; Artist, Juried Exhibition, Catherine Lorillard Wolfe Art Club Annual, New York, NY; Artist, Juried Exhibition, Baker's Dozen Collage Society Exchange, New Zealand; Artist, Juried Exhibition, Touch Exhibition, Annmarie Sculpture Gardens, Dowell, MD; Artist, Juried Exhibition, Proximity Exhibition, Annmarie Sculpture Gardens, Dowell, MD; Artist, Juried Exhibition, HearSee Exhibition, Torpedo Factory Art Center, Alexandria, VA; Artist, Juried Exhibition, Treasured Exhibit, Annmarie Sculpture Garden, Dowell, MD; Artist, Juried Exhibition, Glitz Exhibition, Annmarie Sculpture Garden, Dowell, MD; Artist, Juried Exhibition, Touchstone Mini Solo Exhibit '13, Touchstone Gallery, Washington, DC; Artist, Juried Exhibition, NorthEnd Gallery Invitational, Leonardtown, MD; Artist, Juried Exhibition, Beachcomber Exhibit, Annmarie Sculpture Garden, Dowell, MD; Artist, Juried Exhibition,

Touchstone Mini Solo Exhibit '14, Touchstone Gallery, Washington, DC; Artist, Collection, National Education Association, Cleveland, OH; Artist, Collection, Communications Satellite Corporation, Washington, DC; Artist, Collection, Prather, Seegar, Farmer & Doolittle, Washington, DC; Artist, Collection, Hilco Industries, St. Louis, MO; Artist, Collection, Rollins College, Winter Park, FL; Artist, Collection, American Fuel and Petrochemical Manufacturers, Washington, DC; Artist, Collection, Macy's Department Stores, Washington, DC; Artist, Collection, KPMG Peat Marwick, Cleveland, OH; Artist, Numerous Collections **AW:** Recipient, Numerous Awards, National and International Juried Shows **MEM:** Kansas Watercolor Society; National Watercolor Society; Watercolor Society of Alabama; Allied Artists of America; Society of Experimental Artists; Torpedo Factory Art Center, Alexandria, VA; National Association of Independent Artists **MH:** Albert Nelson Marquis Lifetime Achievement Award **AS:** Ms. Schaffner attributes her success to her determination and the encouragement she received from those around her. **B/I:** Ms. Schaffner believes she was born to be an artist. She has been drawing since she was a small child.

SCHAFFNER, JOHN ALBERT, T: Retail Merchandising Executive, Designer **I:** Retail/Sales **DOB:** 12/24/1937 **PB:** Basil **SC:** OH/USA **PT:** Samuel Stanley Schaffner; Pauline E. (Stalter) Schaffner **MS:** Married **SPN:** Luray Schirtzinger (07/06/1962) **CH:** Shawn Michael; Jorn Michael **ED:** BS in Industrial Design, Columbus College of Art & Design (1960); Certification Outstanding Senior Award (1960) **C:** Retired (1997); Vice President, Store Planning, Merchandising, May Design & Constitution Inc. Division of May Department Stores, St. Louis, MO (1987-1997); Vice President, Director, Store Planning, Hecht's, Division of May Department Stores, Washington, DC (1985-1987); Vice President, Design and Planning, May Design & Constitution Inc. (Division of May Department Stores), St. Louis, MO (1981-1985); Director, Store Planning, Hecht's, Division of May Department Stores, Washington, DC (1969-1981);Director of Design, F.R. Lazarus (Federal Department Stores), Columbus, OH (1964-1969);Designer, Schwartz Showell Inc., Columbus, OH (1962-1964); Designer, Dave Ellis Industries Design Inc., Columbus, OH (1960-1962) **MIL:** U.S. Army **CW:** Group Exhibitions, Evansville Art Museum (1989, 1992); Group Exhibitions, Missouri State College (1989); Represented in Public Collections **AW:** Golden Dragon Sadler Award, Best in Sculpture Award, Midwest Salute to the Masters (1996, 1997); Annual Centennial Sculpture Award, St. Louis Artists Guild (1991); Boeschenstein Memorial Award, St. Louis Artists Guild (1988); Gardner Award, Virginia Beach Artist Association (1973) **MEM:** Board of Governors, St. Louis Artists Guild (1991-1993); Ways and Means Committee, Institute of Store Planners (1981-1987); St. Louis Artist Coalition; Northern Virginia Art League; Art and Education Council; Washington Sculptors Group; Annmarie Sculpture Garden & Art Center **MH:** Albert Nelson Marquis Lifetime Achievement Award **B/I:** Mr. Schaffner became involved in his profession because he always wanted to be in the arts since he was very young.

SCHAKOWSKY, JANICE, "JAN", T: U.S. Representative from Illinois **I:** Government Administration/Government Relations/Government Services **DOB:** 05/26/1944 **PB:** Chicago **SC:** IL/USA **PT:** Irwin Danoff; Tillie (Cosnow) Danoff **MS:** Married **SPN:** Robert B. Creamer (12/06/1980); Harvey E. Schakowsky (02/17/1965, Divorced 1980) **CH:** Ian; Mary; Lauren (Stepchild) **ED:** BS in Elementary Education, The University of Illinois (1965) **CT:** Certified Elementary Teacher, State of Illinois **C:** Member, U.S. House of Representatives from Illinois' Ninth Congressional District, U.S. Congress, Washington, DC (1999-Present); Member, U.S. House Committee on Government Reform (1999-2000); Member, U.S. House Committee on Banking and Financial Services (1999-2000); Member, Illinois House of Representatives (1990-1998); Executive Director, Illinois State Council of Senior Citizens, Chicago, IL (1985-1990); Organizer, Illinois Public Action Council, Chicago, IL (1976-1985); Teacher, Chicago Board of Education (1965-1967); Member, Committee on Energy and Commerce, United States Congress; Member, Permanent Select Committee on Intelligence, U.S. Congress **CIV:** Member, Governing Council, American Jewish Congress (1990-Present); Delegate, National Democratic Convention (1988); Member, Steering Committee, Cook County Democratic Women (1986-1990); Board of Directors, 4 C's Daycare Council, Evanston, IL; Board of Directors, Illinois Public Action **AW:** Named Legislator of the Year, Association of Community Mental Health Authorities of Illinois (ACMHAI) (1994); Award, Coalition for Citizens with Disabilities/Illinois State Council of Senior Citizens (1993); Named an Outstanding Legislator, Interfaith Council for the Homeless (1993); Award, Illinois Nurses Association (1992); Award, Champaign County Health Care Association (1992); Award, Community Action Association (1991); Rookie of the Year, Illinois Environmental Council (1991) **MEM:** National Organization for Women; American Civil Liberties Union; Rogers Park/West Ridge Historical Society; Evanston Friends of the Public Library; Evanston Historical Society; Evanston Mental Health Association; Illinois Pro-Choice Alliance; National Council of Jewish Women; Delta Phi Epsilon International Sorority **AV:** Traveling; Horseback riding; Reading **PA:** Democrat **RE:** Jewish

SCHARF, CHARLES W., T: Chief Executive Officer, President **I:** Business Management/Business Services **CN:** Wells Fargo & Company **MS:** Married **SPN:** Amy E. Scharf **CH:** Two Children **ED:** MBA, New York University; BA, Johns Hopkins University **C:** Chief Executive Officer, President, Wells Fargo & Company (2019-Present); Chief Executive Officer, Bank of New York Mellon Corporation (2017-2019); Chairman of the Board, Bank of New York Mellon Corporation (2018); Chief Executive Officer, Director, Visa Inc. (2012-2016); Managing Director, One Equity Partners, JPMorgan Chase & Company (2011-2012); Chief Executive Officer, Retail Financial Services, JPMorgan Chase & Company (2004-2012); Chief Executive Officer, Chief Financial Officer, Bank One Corporation (2000-2002); Chief Financial Officer, Global Corporate and Investment Bank Division, Citigroup, Inc. (1999-2000); Chief Financial Officer, Salomon Smith Barney (1995-1999); Commercial Credit Corporation (1987-1995) **CR:** Board of Directors, Microsoft Corp (2014-Present); Board of Directors, Visa U.S.A., Inc. (2012-Present); Board of Directors, Visa Inc. (2007-Present); Board of Directors, Travelers Property Casualty Corporation (2002-2005) **CIV:** Board of Trustees, Johns Hopkins University; Board of Directors, Financial Services Roundtable; Chairman, New York City Ballet **MEM:** The Business Council

SCHARFF, ANDREA, T: Owner **I:** Business Management/Business Services **CN:** Andrea Scharff Landscape Design **MS:** Married **CH:** Two Children **ED:** BA in Art History, The Colorado College (1989) **CT:** Certificate of Landscape Design, New York Botanical Garden (2001) **C:** Principal/Owner, Andrea Scharff Landscape Design (2000-Present); Manager, Data Mining and Direct Marketing Services, Ingram Micro (1997-1999) **AW:** Luxe Magazine Gold List Honoree in Landscape Architecture (2019) **MEM:** Board Member, Bel-Air Garden Club **AS:** Ms. Scharff attributes her success to pursuing her passion. She is excited to see the gardens she has planted live into the future. This way, there are many little pieces of her around the world. **B/I:** Though Ms. Scharff started her career in technology, she quickly found a passion for landscaping. She promptly decided to pursue a career in the field. **THT:** Ms. Scharff's motto is, "Lead with your ears and with your heart."

SCHATZ, BRIAN EMANUEL, T: U.S. Senator from Hawaii **I:** Government Administration/Government Relations/Government Services **DOB:** 10/20/1972 **PB:** Ann Arbor **SC:** MI/USA **PT:** Irwin Jacob Schatz; Barbara Jane (Binder) Schatz **MS:** Married **SPN:** Linda Kwok Kai Yun **CH:** Tyler; Mia **ED:** BA in Philosophy, Pomona College, Claremont, CA (1994) **C:** Member, U.S. Senate Committee on Commerce, Science and Transportation (2013-Present); Member, U.S. Senate Committee on Indian Affairs (2013-Present); Member, U.S. Senate Committee on Energy and Natural Resources (2013-Present); U.S. Senator, State of Hawaii (2012-Present); Lieutenant Governor, State of Hawaii, Honolulu, Hawaii (2010-2012); Chairman, Democratic Party of Hawaii (2008-2010); Chief Executive Officer, Helping Hands Hawaii (2002-2010); Member, District 25, Hawaii House of Representatives (2002-2006); Member, District 24, Hawaii House of Representatives (1998-2002); Teacher, Punahou School **CR:** Member, Democratic Party State Central Committee (1997-1998) **CIV:** Candidate, Lieutenant Governor, State of Hawaii (2010); Director, Makiki Community Library; Director, Center for a Sustainable Future **AW:** Named Community Leader of the Year, Bank of Hawaii, Inc. (2004); Environmental Hero Award, National Oceanic and Atmospheric Administration (NOAA); President's Award, Hawaii Audubon Society **PA:** Democrat **RE:** Jewish

SCHEIER, MINDY, T: President, Founder **I:** Nonprofit & Philanthropy **CN:** Runway of Dreams Foundation **CH:** Oliver; Stella; Beau **ED:** Bachelor of Arts in Fashion and Apparel Design, Fashion Institute of Technology (1993); Bachelor of Arts in Fashion and Apparel Design, University of Vermont **C:** Founder, President, Runway of Dreams, Livingston, NJ (2013-Present); Owner, Future Fasionistas (2009-2013); Key Member, Design Team, INC Collection; Stylist, Saks Fifth Avenue, New York, NY **CR:** Consultant, Tommy Adaptive; Advisory Council, Zappos Adaptive **AW:** Named, "The Creative Class of 2019: Innovators," Newsweek (2019); Named, "Heroes Among Us," People; Named, "Changemaker: Making the Fashion Industry More Inclusive," Pix 11; Catalyst Award for Marketing Influencer of the Year; Women at the Wheel Leadership Excellence Award; Association of Image Consultants International Bravo Award; Michael Graves Award for Creativity and Persistence, Enable Inc. **AS:** Ms. Scheier credits her success on finding the balance between living out her dreams and supporting her family. **B/I:** Having found success in the fashion industry, Ms. Scheier entered the nonprofit profession due to her children, one of whom was afflicted with a rare form of muscular dystrophy. When he told her that he wanted to wear clothes like most other children, instead of sweatpants, she decided to leverage her background in apparel in designing an adaptive line of clothing for people with disabilities. **AV:** Family

SCHELLING, THOMAS CROMBIE, PHD, T: Distinguished Professor Emeritus; Economist **I:** Education/Educational Services **CN:** University of Maryland **DOB:** 04/14/1921 **PB:** Oakland **SC:** CA/USA **PT:** John Schelling; Zelda (Ayres) Schelling

MS: Married **SPN:** Alice M. Coleman (11/08/1991); Corinne Tigay Saposs (09/13/1947, Divorced) **CH:** Andrew; Thomas; Daniel; Robert; Two Stepsons **ED:** Honorary Doctorate, University of Manchester (2010); Honorary Doctorate, Yale University (2009); Honorary Degree, RAND Graduate School of Public Analysis (2009); Honorary Doctorate, Erasmus University (2003); PhD in Economics, Harvard University (1951); AB in Economics, University of California Berkeley (1944) **C:** Distinguished Professor Emeritus, Economics, University of Maryland, College Park, MD (2003-2016); Professor, Economics and Public Affairs, University of Maryland, College Park, MD (1990-2003); Lucius N. Littauer Professor, Political Economy, Harvard University, Cambridge, MA (1969-1990); Professor, Economics, Harvard University, Cambridge, MA (1958-1990); Associate Professor, Then Professor, Economics, Yale University, New Haven, CT (1953-1958); Economist, Executive Office of President, The White House, Washington, DC (1951-1953); Economist, The Marshall Plan, Paris, France and Copenhagen, Denmark (1948-1950); Economist, Bureau of Budget and Planning, U.S. Department of State, Washington, DC (1945-1946) **CR:** Director, Institute Study of Smoking Behavior & Policy, Harvard University (1984-1990); Chairman, Research Advisory Board, Committee of Economic Development, Washington, DC (1978-1981, 1984-1985); Member, Military Economic Advisory Panel, CIA (1980-1985); Senior Staff Member, RAND Corporation, Santa Monica, CA (1958-1959); Co-Faculty Member, New England Complex Systems Institute **CW:** Author, "Strategies of Commitment" (2006); Author, "Choice and Consequence" (1984); Author, "Thinking Through the Energy Problem" (1979); Author, "Micromotives and Macrobehavior" (1978); Author, "Arms and Influence" (1966); Co-Author (with Morton H. Halperin), "Strategy and Arms Control" (1961); Author, "The Strategy of Conflict" (1960); Author, "International Economics" (1958); Author, "National Income Behavior" (1951) **AW:** Co-Recipient, Nobel Prize in Economic Science (2005); Award for Behavior Research Relevant to the Prevention of Nuclear War, National Academy of Sciences (1993); Frank E. Seidman Distinguished Award in Political Economy (1977); Distinguished Fellow Award, American Economic Association **MEM:** President, Eastern Economic Association (1996); President, American Economic Association (1991); Fellow, American Association for the Advancement of Science; Fellow, Association for Public Policy Analysis and Management; Fellow, American Economic Association; National Academy of Sciences; Institute of Medicine; Eastern Economic Association

SCHIFF, ADAM BENNETT, T: U.S. Representative from California; Lawyer **I:** Government Administration/Government Relations/Government Services **DOB:** 06/22/1960 **PB:** Framingham **SC:** MA/USA **PT:** Edward Maurice Schiff; Sherrill Ann (Glovsky) Schiff **MS:** Married **SPN:** Eve (Sanderson) Schiff (1995) **CH:** Alexa Marion; Elijah Harris **ED:** JD, Harvard Law School, Cum Laude (1985); BA, Stanford University (1982) **C:** Chairman, House Intelligence Committee (2019-Present); Ranking Member, U.S. House Permanent Select Committee on Intelligence (2015-Present); Member, U.S. House Select Committee on the Events Surrounding the 2012 Terrorist Attack in Benghazi (2014-Present); Member, U.S. House of Representatives from California's 28th Congressional District, United States Congress, Washington, DC (2013-Present); Member, U.S. House Appropriations Committee (2013-Present); Member, U.S. House Permanent Select Committee on Intelligence (2013-2015); Member, U.S. House of Representatives from California's 29th Congressional District, United States Congress, Washington, DC (2003-2013); Member, U.S. House of Representatives from California's 27th Congressional District, United States Congress, Washington, DC (2001-2003); Member, California State Senate (1996-2000); Prosecutor, U.S. Attorney's Office, Central District of California, U.S. Department of Justice (1987-1993); Associate, Gibson, Dunn & Crutcher LLP, Los Angeles, CA (1986); Member, Committee on Transportation and Infrastructure, United States Congress; Member, Committee on Veterans' Affairs, United States Congress **CR:** Special Assignment to Czechoslovakia, U.S. Department of Justice, Bratislava, Slovakia (1992) **CIV:** Mock Trial Coach, Burbank High School, Burbank Unified School District; National Board Member, Big Brothers Big Sisters of America **MEM:** Glendale Chamber of Commerce; Burbank Chamber of Commerce **BAR:** State of California (1986) **AV:** Creative writing **PA:** Democrat **RE:** Jewish

SCHIFF, CRAIG M., T: President, Chief Executive Officer **I:** Consulting **CN:** BPM Partners, Inc. **DOB:** 06/11/1955 **PB:** New York **SC:** NY/USA **MS:** Divorced **ED:** MBA in Finance, Fordham University (1987); BS in Biology, State University of New York, New Paltz (1977) **C:** Chief Executive Officer, Founder, BPM Partners, Inc., Stamford, CT (2002-Present); Chief Executive Officer, Co-founder, OutlookSoft (now part of SAP), Stamford, CT (1999-2002); Senior Vice President, Hyperion Solutions (formerly IMRS, Incorporated and now part of Oracle), Stamford, CT (1983-1998); Project Manager, GE, New York, NY (1980-1983); Financial Programmer, Gulf & Western, New York, NY (1979-1980); Programmer, NPD Research, Floral Park, NY (1977-1979) **CIV:** Treasurer, Victoria Community, Incorporated (2013-Present); President, Majestic Tenants Corporation, Forest Hills, NY (1982-1996) **AW:** Ernst & Young Entrepreneur of the Year; Small Jewels of Consulting **MH:** Albert Nelson Marquis Lifetime Achievement Award **B/I:** Mr. Schiff took a class in computer science while in college. He was a biology major on a pre-med path and one of the requirements was to either take a math course or a computer science course. He chose the computer science course, and it changed the trajectory of his career. He decided to focus on computers and software as his future career. He still graduated with a degree in biology because it was so late in his studies that he could not change but his exposure to computers began there. **AV:** Travel; Photography; Reading **PA:** Independent

SCHILLER, JUSTIN GALLAND, T: Antiquarian Bookseller, Researcher, Editor **I:** Fine Art **CN:** Battledore Ltd **DOB:** 09/10/1943 **PB:** Brooklyn **SC:** NY/USA **PT:** Gary Schiller; Constance Audrey (Galland) Schiller **MS:** Married **SPN:** Dennis M. V. David **ED:** Graduate Coursework, Harpur College of Arts and Sciences, State University of New York at Binghamton (1966); Postgraduate Coursework, Binghamton University, State University of New York (1965-1966); Bachelor of Arts in English Renaissance Literature, Ithaca College (1965) **C:** President, Battledore Limited, Kingston, NY (1988-Present); President, Justin G. Schiller, Limited, New York (1969-2020); Associate Professor, Columbia University, University of Virginia (1984-1996); Principal, Justin G. Schiller, Brooklyn (1960-1969) **CR:** University of Virginia, Charlottesville, NC (1996-Present); Instructor, History, Children's Literature Rare Books School, Columbia University (1984-1989); Lecturer in Field **CIV:** Fellowship Committee, Bibliographical Society America (2003-2008); Council, Bibliographical Society America (2001-2007) **CW:** Curator, Exhibition, Little Red Book, Grolier Club (2014-2015); Co-curator, "Maurice Sendak, a Celebration of The Artist and His Work" (2013); Co-Editor, Garland's Classics in Children's Literature, 73 Volumes; Contributor, Articles, Professional Magazines **AW:** Featured in D. W. Young's Documentary Film, "The Booksellers" (2019) **MEM:** Lenox Society Steering Committee, New York Public Library (1986-Present); American Antiquarian Society (1984-Present); The Grolier Club (1982-Present); Bibliographical Society of America (1969-Present); Antiquarian, Booksellers Association of America (1967-Present); Association Internationale de Bibliophilie (1983-2012); Council, Bibliographical Society of America (2001-2007); Board of Directors, Lewis Carroll Foundation (1988-1995); Antiquarian Booksellers Association of Britain (1969-1989); Board of Governors, Booksellers Association of America (1976); Chairperson, Board of Directors, Antiquarian Booksellers Center (1973-1976); Council, International Wizard of Oz Club (1957-1975); Founder, International Wizard of Oz Club (1957) **MH:** Albert Nelson Marquis Lifetime Achievement Award; Marquis Who's Who Top Professional **AS:** Mr. Schiller attributes his success on the principles of honesty, sincerity and a commitment to his profession. **B/I:** Mr. Schiller became involved in his profession due to his early childhood experiences as a book collector. **PA:** Democrat **RE:** Jewish

SCHILLING, BRITTANY, T: Biology Teacher **I:** Education/Educational Services **MS:** Married **ED:** MA, University of Saint Joseph, West Hartford, CT (2019); BA, William Paterson University, Wayne, NJ (2014) **C:** Teacher, Biology, Anatomy and Physiology **MEM:** New Jersey Education Association; National Science Teaching Association (NSTA) **AS:** Mrs. Schilling attributes her success to passion and drive, as well as the support system afforded to her by her husband and family, who have stuck by her side through everything. **B/I:** Mrs. Schilling wanted to pursue teaching from a young age; she had considered entering the medical field, but realized that she enjoyed helping students learn and discover their passions. She adores watching students begin to understand concepts that had given them trouble over a period of time. **THT:** Mrs. Schilling enjoys participating in charitable walks and fundraising drives through her school. Most recently, she has worked to assist those who could not afford food during the holidays.

SCHILLING-NORDAL, GERALDINE A., T: Secondary School Educator (Retired) **I:** Education/Educational Services **DOB:** 02/04/1935 **PB:** Springfield **SC:** MA/USA **PT:** Robert Schilling; Helen Schilling **MS:** Married **SPN:** Reidar Nordal **ED:** MEd, Boston University (1957); BS, Boston University (1956); Postgraduate Coursework, Anna Maria College; Postgraduate Coursework, Springfield College **C:** Teacher of Art, Agawam High School (1958-2003); K-12 Art Academy Coordinator, Agawam High School (1995-1996); Head of Art Department, Agawam High School (1970-1995); Teacher of Art, Agawam Junior High School, MA (1957-1958) **CR:** Instructor of Creative Arts, Agawam Evening School (1973-1980); Instructor of Oil Painting, University Extension Course, Agawam Night School (1957-1958) **CIV:** Member, Agawam Catholic Women's Club (1995-Present); Co-chairman, Chairman, Agawam Catholic Women's Club (2007-2011, 2002-2004, 2018); Historian, Agawam Catholic Women's Club (2014-2015); Mr. and Mrs. Club, Agawam Baptist Church (2007-2014); Art Judge, Hampden County 4H (1998-2002); Appeal Volunteer, Catholic Charity (1995-2002); Banquet Committee, Agawam Catholic Women's Club (1997, 1999); Agawam Cultural Council (1994-1997); Co-chairman, 50th Anniversary Committee, St. John the Evangelist Church, Agawam, MA (1996); Decoration Chairman, Town-wide Halloween Parties (1971-1994); Agawam Minerva Davis Library Study Committee (1987-1988); Agawam Historical Commission (1979-1987); Secretary, Agawam Town Beautification Committee (1974-1987); Chairman, 40th Anniversary, St. John the Evangelist Church, Agawam, MA (1986); Agawam Arts and Humanities Committee (1979-1985); Member, Renovation Committee, St. John the Evangelist Church, Agawam, MA (1983); Member, Town Teachers Representative, Agawam Bicentennial Committee (1975-1977); Active, Agawam Town Report Committee (1967-1977); Past Recruiter, Miss Agawam Pageant (1972-1976); Chairman, Various High School and College Reunions CW: Artist, Five Photo Exhibits, Agawam Public Library (2009-2012, 2015-2018); Award for 45-Years Service, Agawam Teachers Wall of Fame (2002) MEM: Board Member, Friends of Agawam Senior Center (2012-Present); Secretary, Hampden West Chapter, Retired Educators Association of Massachusetts (REAM) (2009-Present); Class Agent, Boston University Alumni Club, Springfield Area (1985-Present); Alpha Chapter, Delta Kappa Gamma (DKGSI) (1965-Present); Chairman, Spring Banquet, St. John's Over 60 Club (2008-2015); Scholarship Committee, St. Ann's Society (2009-2014); Area Scholarship Committee , Boston University Alumni Club, Springfield Area (1995-2014); Co-chair, Bakeless Bake Sale Fund Raiser, St. Ann's Society (2012); Life Member, National Education Association; AARP; AHS Addition Dedication Committee (1998-1999); Scholarship Committee (1997); Secretary, Agawam Educators Association (1970-1974, 1976-1977); President, West Springfield Neighborhood House Alumni Association (1966, 1972-1974); First Vice President, West Springfield High School Alumni Association (1970-1971); Third Vice President, West Springfield High School Alumni Association (1968-1970); Advisor, West Springfield Neighborhood House Alumni Association (1968); Organizer, Area Giving Campaigns, Boston University Alumni Club, Springfield Area (1957-1962); President, Zeta Chi Delta (1955-1956); Hampden County Teachers Association; Life Member, Massachusetts Teachers Association; Massachusetts Art Education Association; National Art Education Association; New England Art Education Association; Massachusetts Catholic Order of Foresters; West Springfield Neighborhood House Alumni Association; West Springfield High School Alumni Association; Boston University Alumni Club, Springfield Area; Retired Educators Association of Massachusetts (REAM); Retired State, County and Municipal Employees Association of Massachusetts; Agawam Retired Employees Association; St. Ann's Society; Life Member, Ramapogue Historical Society; Auxiliary Life Member, The American Legion; St. John's Over 60 Club; Zeta Chi Delta; Delta Kappa Gamma (DKGSI); Art Chair, Delta Kappa Gamma (DKGSI); Reservation Chairman, Delta Kappa Gamma (DKGSI); Art Work and History Archives, Delta Kappa Gamma (DKGSI); Hospitality 50th and 60th Annual Committee, Delta Kappa Gamma (DKGSI); Scholarship Committee, Delta Kappa Gamma (DKGSI); Springfield Museum; Friends of Agawam Public Library MH: Albert Nelson Marquis Lifetime Achievement Award AV: Photography

SCHIMKE, CLYDE V., T: Owner, Inventor **I:** Other **CN:** Schimke Design **DOB:** 03/18/1949 **PB:** Kowloon, Hong Kong **SC:** China **MS:** Single **ED:** Coursework in Architectural Design **MH:** Albert Nelson Marquis Lifetime Achievement Award **B/I:** Mr. Schimke became involved in this profession because, in the past, he had a patient come in the hospital who wanted to know if they had any way they could move his bed so he didn't have to call the nurse all the time. They had puff tubes to change channel on the television, and a puff tube to call a nurse, but nothing like this. He looked

through all of their suppliers, and no one had anything for beds. He had experience repairing beds throughout his 20-year career with Fawcett Hospital, so he invented the product himself. **AV:** Gardening **RE:** Seventh-Day Adventist

SCHIMMELFENNIG, LADONA BETH, T: Special Education Educator, Management Consultant, School System Administrator **I:** Education/Educational Services **DOB:** 04/29/1948 **PB:** Tulsa **SC:** OK/USA **PT:** James Wyatt Holder; Ladona Babe (Robertson) Holder **MS:** Married **SPN:** W. Bryan Anapuni Schimmelfennig (07/04/1988) **CH:** Malia M. **ED:** MEd, Pepperdine University (1976); BS in Special Education, University of Tulsa (1969) **CT:** Certificate of Completion, Compliance With Federal Civil Rights Laws in Education Programs and Activities (2015); Certificate of Completion, Harassment and Hostile Environment: An Overview of Policies and Preventive Measures (2015); Certificate of Completion, Discrimination Complaint Investigations: Proper Process and Technique (2015); Diplomate, Council on Education in Management, George Washington University (2003); Diplomate, Faculty Training, University of Phoenix (1999) **C:** Acting Director of Civil Rights Compliance, Office of the Superintendent, Hawaii State Department of Education (2014-Present); Adjunct Instructor, Hawaii Pacific University (2011-Present); Civil Rights Compliance Specialist III, Office of the Superintendent, Hawaii State Department of Education (2004-Present); Acting Director of Civil Rights Compliance, Superintendent Office, Hawaii State Department of Education (2004-2017); Acting Director of Civil Rights Compliance, Superintendent Office, Hawaii State Department of Education (2005); Management Analysis and Civil Rights Compliance Specialist, Hawaii State Department of Education (2002-2004); District Education Specialist II in Special Education, Windward Oahu District Office, Hawaii State Department of Education (1979-2002); Special Education Specialist for the Emotionally Handicapped, Office of Instructional Services, Hawaii State Department of Education (1984); Director of Special Education, Department of Education, Government of American Samoa (1977-1979); Director, Special Olympics, Government of American Samoa (1977-1979); Assistant Director of Special Education, Department of Education, Government of American Samoa (1976-1977); Special Education Coordinator, Oahu Head Start, Honolulu Community Action Program (1976-1977); Special Education Teacher, Kaewai Elementary School, Oahu Head Start, Honolulu Community Action Program (1973-1976); Special Education Teacher, Makaha Elementary School, Oahu Head Start, Honolulu Community Action Program (1973-1974); Volunteer, Suicide Prevention Hotline, Mental Health Association in Tulsa, Inc. (1971-1973); Special Education Teacher, Monroe Demonstration School, Tulsa Public Schools (1970-1973); Special Education Teacher, SECOH (1969-1970); Educational Assistant, Sarasota Head Start (Now Children First) (1968) **CR:** Director, First American Samoa Special Olympics (1978-1979) **CIV:** Board of Directors, Hawaii Special Olympics (1980-1984); Public Relations Chairman, Hawaii Special Olympics (1980-1984); Secretary-Treasurer, The Pacific Basin Consortium for Environment and Health (1977-1979); Advisory Panel on Education for Handicapped Children, Southwestern Region, Deaf-Blind Center (1977-1979); Board of Directors, Special Parent Information Network, Wai Nani Way Hoeke; President, Queen Emma Preschool; President, Parent's Group, St. Clements' Preschool; President's Advisory Panel on the Education of Handicapped Children **CW:** Contributor, Articles, Professional Journals **MEM:** State Office Leadership Academy (2016); Chapter President,

Council for Exceptional Children (1969); National Association of State Directors of Special Education; National Information for Special Education Management; Southwest Deaf/Blind Association; Association of American Educators; Pacific Equity Academy; National Association for the Education of Young Children; National Information Network for Special Education; Special Parent Information Network; Northwest Regional Education Lab (Now Education Northwest); Pacific Basin Consortium for Environment and Health; Wai Nani Way Hoike **MH:** Albert Nelson Marquis Lifetime Achievement Award; Marquis Who's Who Top Professional **B/I:** Ms. Schimmelfennig became involved in her profession because her father was in an iron lung after he contracted polio during the Korean conflict. Not only did he live, but he walked. Her younger brother was disabled and she saw firsthand how this impacts everyone. Her family gave her values. **AV:** Travel; Exercise; Hiking

SCHIPPERS, DAVE A., SCD, CISSP, T: Assistant Professor; Professional Cyber Investigator **I:** Technology **CN:** Walsh College; Iron Dog LLC **DOB:** 12/05/1970 **MS:** Married **SPN:** Leslie (Fase) Schippers (2003) **CH:** Hannah **ED:** DSc in Cybersecurity, Capitol Technology University (2018); MS in Information Systems Management, Ferris State University (2013); BS in Information Security and Intelligence, Ferris State University, (2010); AS in Computer Information Systems, Network Administration, Grand Rapids Community College (2009) **CT:** Network, CompTIA (2017); Certified, AccessData Examiner, Guidance Software (2015); Licensed Investigator, Professional Investigation Agency (2014); Certified, Information Systems Security Professional (2013); Certified, EnCase Examiner, Guidance Software (2012); A+, CompTIA (2000) **C:** Chair, Information Technology Decision Sciences, Walsh College (2018-Present); Assistant Professor, Walsh College (2018-Present); Professional Cyber Investigator, Iron Dog LLC (2014-Present); Instructor, Walsh College (2016-2018); Technology Director, Hudsonville Public Schools (2004-2016); Adjunct Instructor, Ferris State University (2013-2015); Network Operations, Security Intern, Ottawa Area Intermediate School District (Ottawa Area ISD) (2010); Business Analyst, Developer, Meijer, Inc. (2001-2004); Development Specialist, Vendor, Electronic Commerce, Meijer, Inc. (2000-2001); Regional Systems Specialist, Meijer, Inc. (2000); Receiving Systems Specialist (1995-2000); Receiving Area Team Leader, Meijer 128 (1993-1994) **CIV:** Volunteer, Conference Technical Support **CW:** Author, "Cybersecurity Military Vehicle Industry Collaborative (MVIC): Integrating Cyber Resiliency for Military Platforms," NDIA (2019); Lecture, "Cyber Training and Research Panel," Auto-ISAC Global Conference (2018); Lecture, "Cybersecurity: Certainty in Uncertain Times," MICPA Regional Conference (2018); Lecture, "Equifax, WannaCry, Uber: Certainty in Uncertain Times," MICPA Regional Conference (2018); Author, "Cybersecurity, Industry 4.0: From Vision to Implementation" (2017); Lecture, "The Game Has Changed," Rochester Hills Community Presentation (2017); Lecture, "GeoLocation Accuracy and Investigations," HCTIA Monthly Meeting (2017); Lecture, "Location Accuracy," Enfuse Global Conference (2016); Lecture, "GPS Location Accuracy (Integrating GPS Data into Digital Investigations," Guidance Software Webinar Series (2015); Lecture, "Digital Forensics - Internal and Formal Investigations," Ottowa Area Technical Directors, Ottowa Area ISD (2010); Lecture, "Digital Forensics - Internal and Formal Investigations," Michigan Association for Educational Data Systems (2009); Lecture, "Moodle: Installing the Application," Michigan Association for Computers in Learning (2009)

AW: Student Excellence Award, Ferris State University (2013) MEM: Association of Information Technology Professionals (2012-Present); Information Systems Security Association (ISSA) (2012-Present); Workforce Advisory Committee, Grand Rapids Community College (2010-Present); UCCnet Guidelines Committee, Global E-Commerce Body, Universal Price Code and Global Trade Identification Number (2000-2001) MH: Marquis Who's Who Top Professional AS: Dr. Schippers attributes his success to challenging his fears. He is always looking to push his boundaries of knowledge as technology is constantly changing. B/I: In the 1990s, Dr. Schippers was given a technology job opportunity. He had always been interested in technology and additionally held some useful background knowledge of mechanics. AV: Electronics; 3D-Printing THT: Dr. Schippers' motto is by Miyamoto Musashi: "Truth is not what you want it to be; it is what it is, and you must bend to its power or live a lie."

SCHIZER, DAVID MICHAEL, T: Dean, Law Educator, Economics Professor I: Education/Educational Services DOB: 12/05/1968 PB: Brooklyn SC: NY/USA PT: Zevie Baruch Schizer; Hazel Gerber Schizer MS: Married SPN: Meredith Wolf CH: Three Children ED: Doctor of Jurisprudence, Yale University (1993); Master of Arts in History, Yale University (1990); Bachelor of Arts in History, Yale University, Summa Cum Laude (1990) C: Professor, Columbia University Law School, New York, NY (1998-Present); Dean, Lucy G. Moses Professor of Law, Columbia University Law School (2004-2014); Chair, Columbia Appointment Committee, Columbia University Law School, New York, NY (2002-2004); Wilbur H. Friedman Professor of Tax Law, Columbia University Law School, New York, NY (1998-2004); Tax Law Attorney, Davis Polk & Wardwell, New York, NY (1995-1998); Law Clerk, Justice Ruth Bader Ginsburg, Supreme Court of the United States (1994-1995); Law Clerk for Judge Alex Kozinski, U.S. Court of Appeals (1993-1994) CR: Chair, Columbia University Clerkship Committee (2000-2002) CW: Executive Editor, Yale Law Journal; Contributor, Articles, Law Journals AW: Named, 40 Under 40, Crain's New York Business (2006); Named, Top 40 Lawyers Under 40, National Law Journal (2005); Willis L.M. Reese Prize for Excellence in Teaching (2002) MEM: Tax Forum; Tax Club; Executive Committee, Co-Chair of Committee on Finance Institutes, New York State Bar Association; Chief Executive Officer, American Jewish Joint Distribution Committee; Federalist Society RE: Jewish

SCHLESINGER, TIM, T: Attorney I: Law and Legal Services CN: Paule, Camazine & Blumenthal, P.C. MS: Married CH: Two children ED: JD, University of Missouri, Columbia, MO (1983); BA in Journalism, University of Missouri, Columbia, MO (1979) CT: Licensed to Practice Law, State of Oklahoma (2019) C: Attorney, Paule, Camazine & Blumenthal, P.C. (2002-Present); Shareholder, Paule, Camazine & Blumenthal, P.C. (2002-Present); Adjunct Instructor, School of Law, Washington University in St. Louis (2008-2009); Partner, Campbell & Coyne, P.C. (1995-2002); Attorney, Campbell & Coyne, P.C. (1994-2002); Managing Partner, Campbell & Coyne, P.C. (1998-2001); Attorney, Susman, Schermer, Rimmel & Shifrin, LLC (1988-1994); Attorney, Spalding, Westhus & Meyer, P.C. (1986-1988); Attorney, Law Offices of Tim Schlesinger (1984-1986); Attorney, Padberg, McSweeney, Slater & Merz, P.C. (1983-1984) CR: Adviser, Uniform Law Commission, Study Committee on the Disposition of Embryos, Family Law Section, American Bar Association CIV: Pro Bono, Safe Connections (2018-Present); Pro Bono, St. Louis City Public

Schools (2016-Present); Board of Directors, The Women's Safe House (2006-2015); Pro Bono, Fee Dispute Resolution Committee, Bar Association of Metropolitan St. Louis (1994-2002); Pro Bono, Volunteer Lawyers and Accountant for the Arts (1985-1994) CW: Lecturer, Presenter, "Can Art Survive Death and Divorce?" American Bar Association Webinar (2019); Lecturer, Presenter, "Art and The Constitution," Family Law Conference, American Bar Association, Dominican Republic (2019); Lecturer, Presenter, "Use of Forensic Accounting in Divorce Proceedings," Family Law Conference, The Missouri Bar, Branson, MO (2019); Lecturer, Presenter, "Surrogacy, IVF, Embryo Disputes & More," Bar Association of Metropolitan St. Louis (2019); Lecturer, Presenter, "How To Counsel Third-Party Patients-An Attorney's Perspective," Society for Reproductive Endocrinology and Infertility, Denver, CO (2018); Lecturer, Presenter, "Conflicts of Interest in the Surrogacy Chain," Society for Ethics in Egg Donation and Surrogacy Annual Conference, Los Angeles, CA (2018); Author, "Disposition of Frozen Embryos in Family Law Cases," American Journal of Family Law (2018); Lecturer, Presenter, "The Trials of an Art Case, Anatomy of a Lawsuit," Annual Congress, American Society for Reproductive Medicine, San Antonio, TX (2017); Lecturer, Presenter, "Disposition of Frozen Embryos," Family Law Conference, American Bar Association, Beaver Creek, CO (2017); Lecturer, Presenter, "What Do We Do with the Embryos? Disposition of Frozen Embryos Upon Dissolution of Marriage," Family Law Conference, The Missouri Bar, Branson, MO (2017); Lecturer, Presenter, "The Mechanics of Valuing and Dividing Marital Property," National Business Institute, St. Louis, MO (2017); Lecturer, Presenter, "Surrogacy For the Family Law Attorney," Family Law Conference, The Missouri Bar, Branson, MO (2016); Author, "Reproductive Surrogacy in Missouri," Cambridge University Press (2016); Author, "What Do We Do With the Embryos? - Disposition of Frozen Embryos Upon Separation or Divorce," St. Louis Bar Journal (2016); Author, "Embryo Disposition Upon Separation or Divorce," The Sci-Tech Lawyer (2016); Lecturer, Presenter, "It May Not BE Over When It's Over: A Discussion of the Disposition of Embryos and Genetic Material Upon Divorce, Separation and Death," Family Law Section, American Bar Association (2015); Author, "Third Party Assisted Reproduction: Assisting Couples Amidst the Changing Legal Landscape," Aspatore Publishing (2014); Author, "Surrogacy and Egg Donation Agreements - The Search for Certainty in an Uncertain Field," St. Louis Bar Journal (2013); Lecturer, Presenter, "Navigating Complex Asset Cases," National Business Institute, St. Louis, MO (2013); Author, "Alternative Means of Reproduction," Family Law Deskbook" The Missouri Bar (2012); Lecturer, Presenter, "Litigating Alimony Issues," National Business Institute National Teleconference (2012); Lecturer, Presenter, "Navigating Complex Asset Cases," National Business Institute, St. Louis, MO (2011); Author, "Surrogacy and Donation: The Evolving Law of Assisted Reproductive Technologies," The Briefcase (2011); Lecturer, Presenter, "A Roadmap Through Divorce Proceedings," National Business Institute, St. Louis, MO (2009); Author, "Forensic Accountants as Experts in Missouri Divorce Proceedings," St. Louis Bar Journal (2009); Author, "Assisted Human Reproduction: Unresolved Issues in Parentage, Child Custody and Support," Journal of the Missouri Bar (2005); Author, "Alternative Means of Reproduction," Family Law Deskbook, The Missouri Bar (2005); Lecturer, Presenter, "Critical Financial Mistakes in Divorce Proceedings," St. Louis, MO (2004); Lecturer, Presenter, "Child Custody and Visitation," National Business Institute, St. Louis, MO (2001);

Lecturer, Presenter, "Spousal Support in Missouri Divorce Proceedings," National Business Institute, St. Louis, MO (2001); Lecturer, Presenter, "Gathering, Organizing and Using Financial Information in Divorce Cases," Half Moon Seminars, St. Louis, MO (2000); Lecturer, Presenter, "Child Custody and Visitation," National Business Institute, St. Louis, MO (1999); Lecturer, Presenter, "Important Developments in Family Law," University of Missouri, Columbia, MO (1997); Lecturer, Presenter, "Abuse Issues in Child Custody Cases," Lorman Business Centers, St. Louis, MO (1996); Author, "Sex Abuse Allegations in Child Custody Cases - Defending a Parent's Worst Nightmare," St. Louis Bar Journal (1995); Author, "A Brief Look at the Defense of Child Sexual Assault Cases," St. Louis Bar Journal (1995) MEM: Fellow, Academy of Adoption and Assisted Reproduction Attorneys; American Society for Reproductive Medicine; Family Law Section, The Missouri Bar; Family Law Section, American Bar Association; Society for Ethics for Egg Donation and Surrogacy BAR: Tennessee Bar Association (2015); United States Court of Appeals District of Columbia Circuit (1991); Supreme Court of the United States (1990); Illinois State Bar Association (1985); United States Court of Appeals for the Eighth Circuit (1984); The Missouri Bar (1983) MH: Marquis Who's Who Top Professional AS: Mr. Schlesinger attributes his success to his passion for what he does. B/I: Mr. Schlesinger became involved in his profession because he wanted to do something that gave him the power and ability to help others as well as find something intellectually stimulating enough to keep him interested for years to come. He chose the specialty of reproductive assistance because he wanted to aid people in growing their families in a nontraditional way. It was a search to do something rewarding and help and grow families.

SCHLIFSKE, JOHN E., T: Chairman, Chief Executive Officer I: Financial Services CN: Northwestern Mutual PB: Milwaukee SC: WI/USA MS: Married SPN: Kim CH: Six Children ED: Master's in Finance and Accounting, Northwestern University Kellogg Graduate School of Management, Evanston, IL (1983); BA in Economics, Carleton College, Northfield, MN (1981) C: Chairman, Chief Executive Officer, Northwestern Mutual (2010-Present); President, Northwestern Mutual (2009-2010); President, Chief Executive Officer, Russell Investment Subsidiary, Northwestern Mutual (2008-2009); Executive Vice President, Investment Products, Services & Affiliates, Northwestern Mutual (2004-2008); Investment Specialist, Numerous Investment and Real Estate Management Positions, Northwestern Mutual (1987-2004) CR: Board Director, Kohl's Corporation (2011-Present); Member, Board of Trustees, Northwestern Mutual CIV: Member, Greater Milwaukee Committee (2011-Present); Board Member, Froedtert Health (Now Froedtert & the Medical College of Wisconsin) (2010-Present); Board Member, Metropolitan Milwaukee Association of Commerce (2010-Present); Board Member, Children's Hospital of Wisconsin (Children's Wisconsin)

SCHLOSSBERG, DAN, T: Writer, Author, Broadcaster I: Writing and Editing DOB: 05/06/1948 PB: New York SC: NY/USA PT: Ezra Schlossberg; Miriam Schlossberg MS: Married SPN: Phyllis Linda Geiger (07/30/1989); Karen Sue Spindel (06/12/1969, Divorced 1976) CH: Samantha ED: BA in Political Science, Syracuse University (1969); BA in Newspaper Journalism, Syracuse University (1969) C: Freelance Writer (1986-Present); Editor-In-Chief, Bergen Jewish News, Paramus, NJ (1986); Editor, Healthgrad, University of Medicine and Dentistry, Newark, NJ (1984); Travel Account

Executive, M. Silver Associates, New York, NY (1976-1977); Editor-In-Chief, Motor Club of America, Newark, NJ (1971-1975); Sports Editor, Associated Press, Newark, NJ (1969-1971) **CR:** President, North American Travel Journalists Association (1994-2016); President, Working Press Association of New Jersey (2002-2003) **CIV:** Guest Speaker on Baseball, Local Libraries, Civic and Religious Groups **MIL:** Specialist, U.S. Army Reserve (1969-1974) **CW:** Author, "The New Baseball Bible" (2020); Co-Author, "Designated Hebrew: The Ron Blomberg Story" (2006, 2020); Author, "When the Braves Ruled the Diamond: Fourteen Flags Over Atlanta' (2019); Co-Author, "Called Out But Safe: a Baseball Umpire's Journey" (2014); Author, 'The 300 Club: Have We Seen The Last of Author, "Baseball Bits" (2008); Author, "Baseball Gold" (2007); Co-Author, "Making Airwaves: Sixty Years at Milo's Microphone" (2006); Co-Author, "Total Braves" (1996); Author, "The Baseball Catalog" (1980); Author, "BaseballLaffs" (1976); Author, "Barons of the Bullpen" (1975); Author, "Hammerin' Hank: the Henry Aaron Story" (1974); Author, Numerous Books **AW:** Garden State Journalists Association Awards (2017-2019); Journalist of the Year, Historic Hotels of America (2015); North American Travel Journalists Association Awards (1991-2006) **MEM:** Group Against Smoking Pollution; Garden State Journalists Association; American Society of Journalists and Authors; Society for American Baseball Research; North American Travel Journalists Association; Internet Baseball Writers Association of America **MH:** Albert Nelson Marquis Lifetime Achievement Award **AS:** At the Newhouse School of Public Communication at Syracuse University, Mr. Schlossberg learned how to write tight and fast, as well as to never to call a living person dead or spell someone's name wrong. He also learned never to sacrifice accuracy for speed, never to duplicate the work of someone else, always to present both sides of a story, and always to serve the needs of his readers, listeners, and viewers. A lifelong fan of Superman, he always considered Clark Kent a role model as a paragon of truth, justice, and the American way. **B/I:** Mr. Schlossberg became involved in his profession because he always enjoyed writing as a kid. Growing up, he made his own magazines and comic strips, designing them based upon people he knew from school. He also designed baseball magazines and was first published professionally at age 12. **AV:** Playing baseball; Traveling; Playing Scrabble; Playing tennis; Watching movies **PA:** Democrat **RE:** Jewish

SCHMALTZ, LAWRENCE, "LARRY" G., T: Engineer, Consultant, General Contractor **I:** Engineering **CN:** NOVA Engineering **DOB:** 02/11/1957 **PB:** Belle Fourches **SC:** SD/USA **PT:** Tony J.; Evalyne Marie (Kouf) S. **MS:** Married **SPN:** Patricia Schmaltz **ED:** BSCE, South Dakota School of Mines & Technology (1979); Postgraduate in Remediation Engineering, Wright State University; Postgraduate Coursework, University of Phoenix **CT:** Registered Professional Engineer, Florida, Georgia, North Carolina, Alabama, South Dakota, North Dakota; Licensed General Contractor, Florida **C:** Senior Vice President, NOVA Engineering and Environmental (2016-Present); Vice President, Adamo Properties (1998-Present); President, CEO, A2L Techs. Inc. (1992-Present); Managing Principal, E-Net Ventures, LLC (2000-2002); President, CE Systems, Inc., (1989-1995); Adjunct Faculty, University of North Florida, (1989-1992)Vice president, Atcon, Inc. (1989-1991); Regional Manager, Burdco Environmental, Inc., Longwood, FL (1988); Project Engineer, Canonie Environmental Services, Denver, CO (1988); Regional Manager, Waste Environmental Tech., Denver, CO (1986-1987); Project Manager, U.S. Department of Defense,

Rapid City, SD (1982-1984); Engineer, Skidmore, Owings & Merrill, Denver, CO (1979-1982) **CR:** Florida Licensed Mold Assessor; USEPA Licensed Lead Inspector, Risk Assessor; ASTM Standards Committee Member; SDSM&T Foundation Trustee; SDSM&T Professional Advisory Board; SDSM&T Guest Lecturer; **CIV:** Trustee, South Dakota School of Mines and Technology Foundation (2014-Present); Board of Directors, Cherry Creek Special Education Advisory Board, Englewood, CO (1985); Board Member; Professional Advisory Board, South Dakota School of Mines and Technology **AW:** Distinguished Alumni, South Dakota School of Mines and Technology; Letter of Commendation, B1 Bomber Program, United States Air Force (1984); Distinguished Alumni, South Dakota School of Mines and Technology **MEM:** American Society for Testing and Materials; National Registry of Environmental Professionals; American Society of Civil Engineers; American Industrial Hygiene Association **MH:** Who's Who Lifetime Achievement Award **B/I:** Mr. Schmaltz became involved in his profession because he grew observing his father's construction business and developed a natural affinity for engineering. **AV:** Running; Reading; Scuba Diving; Boxing; Weightlifting; Playing the Piano

SCHMIDT, ERIC EMERSON, T: Chairman **I:** Military & Defense Services **CN:** U.S. Department of Defense **DOB:** 04/27/1955 **PB:** Falls Church **SC:** VA/USA **PT:** Wilson Emerson Schmidt; Eleanor Schmidt **MS:** Married **SPN:** Wendy Susan Boyle (1980) **CH:** Sophie; Alison (Deceased) **ED:** PhD in Computer Science, University of California Berkeley (1982); MS in Computer Science, University of California Berkeley (1979); BSEE, Princeton University, New Jersey (1976) **C:** Chairman, Alphabet Inc. (2015-2017); Executive Chairman, Google, Inc., Mountain View, CA (2011-2017); Chairman, Chief Executive Officer, Google, Inc., Mountain View, CA (2001-2011); Chairman, Chief Executive Officer, Novell, Inc., Provo, UT (1997-2001); Chief Technology Officer, Sun Microsystems, Mountain View, CA (1994-1997); President, Sun Technology Enterprises, Inc., Mountain View, CA (1991-1994); Vice President, General Systems Group, Sun Microsystems, Mountain View, CA (1988-1991); Vice President, General Manager, Software Products Division, Sun Microsystems, Mountain View, CA (1985-1988); Software Director, Sun Microsystems, Mountain View, CA (1984-1985); Software Manager, Sun Microsystems, Mountain View, CA (1983-1984); Research Staff, Xerox Parc, Palo Alto, CA (1980-1983); Research Intern, Xerox Parc, Palo Alto, CA (1979-1980); Zilog; Bell Laboratories **CR:** Member, President's Council of Advisers on Science & Technology (2009-Present); Chairman, New America Foundation (2008-Present); Member, Board of Directors, Google, Inc. (2001-Present); Member, Board of Directors, Apple Inc. (2006-2009) **CIV:** Co-Founder, Schmidt Transformative Technology Fund, Princeton University (2009); Co-Founder, Schmidt Family Foundation (2006); Co-Founder, Schmidt Science Fellows Program; Trustee, Princeton University; Frequent Donor, Numerous Institutions and Causes **CW:** Co-Author, "Trillion Dollar Coach: The Leadership Playbook of Silicon Valley's Bill Campbell" (2019); Co-Author, "How Google Works" (2014); Featured, "Dumb and Dumber To" (2014); Co-Author, "The New Digital Age: Transforming Nations, Businesses, and Our Lives" (2013); Featured, "Silicon Valley" **AW:** Top 200 Art Collectors, ArtNews (2007-Present); World's Richest People, Forbes Magazine (2006-Present); Richest Americans, Forbes 400 (2004-Present); Business People of the Year, Fortune Magazine (2010); Top 25 Market Movers, U.S. News & World Report (2009); 50 Most Influential

People In Sports Business, Street & Smith's Sports-Business Journal (2008); Global Elite, Newsweek Magazine (2008); Listed, "200 Top Art Collectors in 2008," ARTnews (2008); 25 Most Powerful People In Business, Fortune Magazine (2007); 50 Most Important People On The Web, PC World (2007); 50 Who Matter Now, Business 2.0 (2007) **MEM:** Fellow, American Academy of Arts & Sciences; IEEE; Association of Computing Machinery; 21st Century Council, Berggruen Institute; Board of Directors, Berggruen Institute; Bilderberg Group; Trilateral Commission; International Advisory Board, Blavatnik School of Government, University of Oxford; Sigma Xi, The Scientific Research Honor Society

SCHMIDT, JAMES ROBERT, T: Facilities Engineer **I:** Engineering **DOB:** 09/22/1932 **SC:** Rome/Italy **PT:** Floyd Vincent Schmidt; Sophia Louise (Halupka) Schmidt **SPN:** Suzanne Mae Thrasher (03/27/1965) **CH:** Mark Adrian; Tara Lee **ED:** MBA, Syracuse University (1967); BS, Utica College (1962); AAS, Mohawk Valley Community College (1951) **CT:** Registered Professional Engineer, New York; Registered Professional Engineer, Massachusetts **C:** Senior Facilities Engineer, Horizons Tech., Billerica, MA (1984-Present); Construction Surveillance, Horizons Tech./Usaf, Thule, Greenland (1983-1984); Manager, Plant Engineering, Savin Corp., Binghamton, NY (1982-1983); Senior Project Engineer, Xerox Corp., Webster, NY (1970-1981); Project Coordinator, Rome Cable Corp. (1968-1969); Designer, Rome Cable Corp. (1956-1967); Draftsman, Rome Cable Corp. (1951-1955); Facilities Engineer, Horizons Tech Inc., Billerica, MA **CIV:** Church Official Board, Methodist Church, Shortsville, NY (1979); Chairman, Community Action Steering Committee, Lee Center (1968) **MIL:** U.S. Army (1951-1954) **MEM:** American Institute of Plant Engineers; American Military Engineers; Charter Member, Cogeneration Institute; Association of Energy Engineers; National Society of Professional Engineers **MH:** Albert Nelson Marquis Lifetime Achievement Award; Marquis Who's Who Top Professional **PA:** Independent **RE:** Methodist

SCHMIDT, VALERIE A., T: Marketing Director **I:** Consumer Goods and Services **DOB:** 01/16/1956 **PB:** Cincinnati **SC:** OH/USA **ED:** MBA, University of Cincinnati, Cincinnati, OH (1978); BBA, University of Cincinnati, Cincinnati, OH, Magna Cum Laude (1977) **C:** Director, Marketing & Communications, Cincinnati Bell (2001-2008); Senior Product Manager, Cincinnati Bell (1996-2001); Product Manager, Cincinnati Bell Inc. (1993-1996); Consumer Promotions Manager, Drackett, Cincinnati, OH (1991-1993); Manager, Coupon Administration, Drackett, Cincinnati, OH (1990-1991); Sales Promotions Manager, Drackett, Cincinnati, OH (1981-1991); Assistant Brand Manager, Drackett, Cincinnati, OH (1989-1990); Associate Promotions Manager, Drackett, Cincinnati, OH (1978-1981) **CR:** Marketing Course Instructor, Thomas More College; Management Course Instructor, University of Cincinnati **CIV:** Volunteer Math Tutor, Covedale School (2011-Present); Volunteer Middle School Volleyball Coach (2003-Present); Freshman Volleyball Coach, Mother of Mercy High School (2009-2015); SPCA Volunteer and Education Presenter (2008-2011); Club Volleyball Coach (1999-2010); Volunteer Career Counselor, University of Cincinnati Career Center (2001-2009); Junior Achievement Instructor (1994-2001); Volunteer Reading Tutor, Midway School (1996-2000); Volunteer Speaker, Trainer, Hamilton County Criminal Justice Task Force (1988-2000); Volunteer, Math/English GED Tutor (1985-1995); Delta Queen Celebration (1980-1992); Downtown Council Committee Member, Oktoberfest, Taste of Cincinnati, Fork in the Road Race; American Heart Association Mini-Marathon; Chairperson, Children's Riverfront Easter Egg Event; Flying Pig Marathon; Chairperson, Chilifest; Holiday on the Square **AW:** Encore Award as One of the Top Employees, Cincinnati Bell (2000); Recognized, Top 1% Employees, Cincinnati Bell (1999); Recipient, Four Gold National Industry Awards; Two-Time Winner, Bronze Awards; Gold Industry Award, "Best Original Score in a Radio Ad," Advertising Club; Achiever's Award; Recipient, National Industry Hall of Fame Award for Children's Education Program **MEM:** American Marketing Association; Beta Gamma Sigma; Pi Chi Epsilon; Delta Sigma Pi **MH:** Albert Nelson Marquis Lifetime Achievement Award

SCHMIDTMAN, ANDREW A. JR., CPA, T: Accountant **I:** Financial Services **DOB:** 09/07/1937 **PB:** Benton Harbor **SC:** MI/USA **PT:** Andrew A. Schmidtman; Ruth H. (Ferrier) Schmidtman **MS:** Married **SPN:** Cathy A. Schmidtman (08/18/1986); Katherine A. Rector (08/12/1960, Divorced 06/1986) **CH:** Cory **ED:** BA, Michigan State University (1960) **C:** Owner, Andrew Schmidtman, CPA, Saint Joseph, MI (1987-Present); Partner, Rendel & Schmidtman, CPAs, Saint Joseph, MI (1975-1987); Principal, Siedman & Seidman, CPAs, Saint Joseph, MI (1972-1975); Principal, Harris Reames & Ambrose, CPAs, Saint Joseph, MI (1966-1972); Accountant, Palladium Publishing Co., Benton Harbor, MI (1963-1966); Field Representative, General Motors Acceptance Corporation (GMAC), South Bend, IN (1960-1963) **CIV:** Treasurer, The American National Red Cross, Gateway, Inc., Berrien County, MI (1972-2017); Board of Directors, Watervliet Municipal Airport Board (1989-1992); Chairman, Saint Joseph Library Board, Benton Harbor, MI (1972-1976); Clerk, Saint Joseph Township, Benton Harbor, MI (1969-1972); Board of Directors, Treasurer, Blossomtime Inc. **MIL:** With, United States Naval Reserves (1955-1961) **AW:** Named Kiwanian of the Year, Kiwanis Club of Saint Joseph, Benton Harbor, MI **MEM:** American Institute of Certified Public Accountants (AICPA); Michigan Association CPAs (MICPA); Board of Directors, Berrien Hills Country Club; Treasurer, Twin City Camera Club **MH:** Albert Nelson Marquis Lifetime Achievement Award **B/I:** Mr. Schmidtman became involved in his profession because when he was in the ninth grade civic class he wrote a paper on the CPA. It was in the ninth grade he decided what he was going to do. **AV:** Photography

SCHMITT, GEORGE FREDERICK JR., FSAMPE, MBA, T: Director of International Programs **I:** Civil Service **CN:** Air Force Research Laboratory Materials and Manufacturing Directorate **DOB:** 11/03/1939 **PB:** Louisville **SC:** KY/USA **PT:** George Frederick Schmitt; Jane Limbird (Hurst) Schmitt **MS:** Married **SPN:** Ann Cheatham (07/31/1965) **CH:** Galen; Brandon **ED:** Diploma, Extended Training Program, Air War College (1970); MBA, The Ohio State University (1966); MS, University of Louisville (1963); BS, University of Louisville (1962) **CT:** Certified Level 3 in Acquisitions, United States Air Force **C:** Director, International Programs, Air Force Research Laboratory (2005-Present); Chief of Integration and Operations Division, U.S. Air Force Materiels Laboratory, Wright Patterson Air Force Base, Ohio (1997-2005); Assistant Chief, Nonmetallic Materials Division, U.S. Air Force Materiels Laboratory, Wright Patterson Air Force Base, Ohio (1991-1996); Chief, Plans and Programs Branch, U.S. Air Force Materiels Laboratory, Wright Patterson Air Force Base, Ohio (1989-1990); Advanced Engineering Development Manager, U.S. Air Force Materiels Laboratory, Wright Patterson Air Force Base, Ohio (1986-1990); Director, International Programs, U.S. Air Force Materiels Directorate, Wright Patterson Air Force Base, Ohio **CR:** Guest Lecturer, University of Dayton (1995); Guest Lecturer, University of Michigan (1975); Guest Lecturer, The Catholic University of America (1973); Guest Lecturer, University of Dayton (1970) **CIV:** Windjammers Circus Music Preservation Society, Windjammers Unlimited, Inc. (2001-Present); Dayton Philharmonic Chorus (1999-Present); Society for the Advancement of Material and Process Engineering (SAMPE) (1968-Present); The Kettering Civic Band (1965-Present); Dayton Letter Carriers Band (2000-2017); Global Board of Directors, Society for the Advancement of Material and Process Engineering (SAMPE) (2013-2015); Affiliate, Societies Council of Dayton (1972-1981) **MIL:** First Lieutenant, United States Air Force (1963-1966) **CW:** Contributor, Articles to Professional Journals; Contributor, Chapters to Books **AW:** Mort Kushner Lifetime Achievement Award, SAMPE North America (2014); International Program Award, United States Air Force (2007); International Award, United States Air Force Materiel Command (2006); International Program Supervisor Award (2002); Technology Transfer Award, Federal Laboratory Consortium for Technology Transfer (2001); Burton Award, Playhouse South Community Theater (1998); Meritorious Civilian Service Award, United States Air Force (1994); Award of Merit, American Society for Testing and Materials (ASTM) (1981); Named One of the Ten Outstanding Engineers, Engineers Week (1975); Named Federal Professional Employee of the Year, Dayton, Ohio (1972) **MEM:** Trustee, Society for Advancement Materials and Process Engineers (SAMPE) (1991-Present); Secretary, Board of Trustees, Society for the Advancement of Material and Process Engineering (SAMPE) Foundation (2005-2018); Chairman, International Society for the Advancement of Material and Process Engineering (SAMPE) Symposium (2013); Global Oversight Board Member, Society for Advancement Materials and Process Engineers (SAMPE) (2011-2013); Associate Fellow, Materials Technical Committee, American Institute of Aeronautics and Astronautics (1993-1996); Chairman, Long-range Planning Committee, Society for Advancement Materials and Process Engineers (SAMPE) (1983-1987); Chairman, Liaison Subcommittee, American Society for Testing and Materials (ASTM) (1979-1983); National President, Society for Advancement Materials and Process Engineers (SAMPE) (1981-1982); National Vice President, Society for Advancement Materials and Process Engineers (SAMPE) (1979-1981); Chairman, Committee on Erosion and Wear, American Society for Testing and Materials (ASTM) (1976-1979); Recording Secretary, Committee G-2, American Society for Testing and Materials (ASTM) (1972-1975); Fellow, Society for the Advancement of Material and Process Engineers (SAMPE); American Institute of Aeronautics and Astronautics; American Society for Testing and Materials (ASTM); American Chemical Society; ASM International **MH:** Albert Nelson Marquis Lifetime Achievement Award **AS:** Mr. Schmitt attributes his success to his upbringing and work ethic, as well as the satisfaction and fulfillment he feels in job challenges and the superb organization in which he has worked. **B/I:** Mr. Schmitt entered his profession because his father was an engineer and worked for a telephone company. He developed a fascination with the subject in high school, and then studied chemical engineering while pursuing his undergraduate degree. Early in his career, Mr. Schmitt did research on rain erosion associated with aircraft and missiles. A part of that was the development of protective coatings. **AV:** Vocal and instrumental music **PA:** Republican **RE:** Lutheran

SCHMITTLEIN, DAVID C., T: Dean **I:** Education/Educational Services **ED:** Summer Research Fellowship, University of Pennsylvania (1982); Columbia University Graduate School of Business Fellowships (1980-1982); PhD in Marketing, Columbia Business School, Columbia University (1980); MPhil in Business, Columbia Business School, Columbia University (1979); BA in Mathematics, Brown University, Magna Cum Laude (1977) **C:** John C. Head III Dean, MIT Sloan School of Management (2007-Present); Interim Dean, The Wharton School, University of Pennsylvania (2007); Deputy Dean, The Wharton School, University of Pennsylvania (2000-2007); Faculty Member, The Wharton School, University of Pennsylvania (1980-2007); Ira A. Lipman Professor, The Wharton School, University of Pennsylvania (1996-2007); Professor of Marketing, The Wharton School, University of Pennsylvania (1990-2007); Vice Dean, Director, Wharton Doctoral Programs, The Wharton School, University of Pennsylvania (1993-1995); Associate Professor of Marketing, The Wharton School, University of Pennsylvania (1983-1990); Assistant Professor of Marketing, The Wharton School, University of Pennsylvania (1980-1983) **CR:** August A. Busch, Jr. Distinguished Scholar in Residence, John M. Olin School of Business, Washington University (1992-1993); Visiting Professor, Faculty of Economics, University of Tokyo (1992); Member, Board, CIGNEX Datamatics; Member, Global Agenda Council for Marketing and Branding, World Economic Forum; Member, Advisory Board, Tsinghua University School of Economics and Management; Member, International Advisory Council, Guanghua School of Management, Peking University; Member, Academic Advisory Board, China Europe International Business School (CEIBS); Member, International Advisory Council, Groupe HEC **CW:** Contributor, Numerous Articles, Professional Journals; Member, Numerous Editorial Boards; Reviewer, Numerous Publications; Quoted and Cited in Numerous Publications **AW:** John D.C. Little Award for Best Marketing Paper in an INFORMS Journal (1995); Best Paper Award, American Marketing Association Advanced Research Techniques Forum (1994); Wharton Undergraduate Teaching Award (1993); Outstanding Reviewer, Editorial Review Board, Journal of Marketing Research (1991-1992) **MEM:** Institute for Operations Research and the Management Sciences; American Statistical Association; American Marketing Association

SCHMITZ, JOHN, T: Writer, Educator **I:** Education/Educational Services **DOB:** 03/09/1937 **PB:** Fond du Lac **SC:** WI/USA **PT:** John L. Schmitz; Josephine Knaus **MS:** Widower **CH:** David Schmitz; Dr. Rebecca Williamson **ED:** BA, St. Francis Seminary (1963) **CT:** Chartered Life Underwriter, American College Life Underwriters (1975) **C:** President, Food for Hungry Incorporated, Wisconsin (2002-Present); Instructor, Hondros College, Columbus, OH (1994-2003); President, John Schmitz Agency, Brookfield, Wisconsin (1992) **CR:** Consultant, Bryant and Stratton College, Milwaukee, WI (2003-2004) **CIV:** Board Member, Officer, Elmbrook School Board, Brookfield, WI (1988-1992); President, Founder, Food for the Hungry, Wisconsin; Board Member, Knights of Columbus, West Dallas; Board Member, My Good Morning Place; Board of Directors, Retirees Group, My Good Morning Place; Board Member for the School District; The Milhauwkee Homeless Veterans Services **CW:** Author, "A Funny Thing Happened On My Way Out of Church"; Author, "JoAnn: In Search of N.E.D."; Author, "You're Not The One Who Died" **AW:** Medallion Award for Community Service, Knights of Columbus **MEM:** President, Columbus Club (2008-Present); Association Grand Knight,

Knights of Columbus, West Dallas (1996-1997) **MH:** Albert Nelson Marquis Lifetime Achievement Award; Marquis Who's Who Top Professional **B/I:** Mr. Schmitz had always tried to make the world a better place while he is here. **AV:** Writing; Photography; Travel **RE:** Catholic

SCHMITZ, MATTHEW, T: Physician **I:** Medicine & Health Care **MS:** Married **SPN:** Dr. Gillian Schmitz **CH:** Kaylie; Austyn Grace **ED:** Doctor of Medicine, Stritch School of Medicine, Loyola University Chicago, Maywood, IL (2004); Bachelor of Science in Biology, U.S. Air Force Academy, Colorado Springs, CO (2000) **CT:** Certificate in Pediatric Orthopaedic Surgery (2012); Board Certified, American Board of Orthopaedic Surgery (2011); Unrestricted Texas Medical License; Unrestricted Colorado Medical License **C:** Associate Professor of Surgery, Department of Surgery, Uniformed Services University of Health Sciences, F. Edward Herbert School of Medicine, Bethesda, MD (2018-Present); Associate Professor of Clinical Orthopaedics, Baylor University, Waco, TX (2017-Present); Chair, Department of Orthopaedics, San Antonio Military Medical Center, Houston, TX (2017-Present); Chief of Pediatric Orthopaedic Surgery Service, Chief of Young Adult Hip Preservation Service, Department of Orthopaedic Surgery, San Antonio Military Medical Center, Houston, TX (2012-Present); Assistant Professor Surgery, Department of Surgery, Uniformed Services University of Health Sciences, F. Edward Herbert School of Medicine, Bethesda, MD (2012-2018); Chief, Orthopaedic Surgery, Craig Joint Theater Hospital, Bargram Air Field, Afghanistan (2017); Chief of In-Patient Division, Department of Orthopaedic Surgery, San Antonio Military Medical Center, Houston, TX (2016-2017); Assistant Professor, Clinical Orthopaedics, Baylor University, Waco, TX (2015-2017); Staff Orthopaedic Surgeon, Malcolm Grow Medical Center, Department of Orthopaedic Surgery, Andrews Air Force Base, Maryland (2009-2011) **CR:** Staff Physician, Credentialed at Methodist Hospital, Pediatric Orthopedic Associates of San Antonio (2013-Present); Invited Faculty, Miller Orthopaedic Review Course (2010-Present); Board of Directors, U.S. Air Force Academy Rugby Affinity Group (2012-2018); Associate Program Director, Orthopedic Surgery Residency, SAUSCHEC/San Antonio Military Medical Center (2013-2017) **CIV:** Medical Mission Trip, Ecuador (2013-2017) **MIL:** Lieutenant Colonel, Medical Corps, U.S. Air Force (2016-Present); Major, Medical Corps, U.S. Air Force (2010-2016); Captain, Medical Corps, U.S. Air Force (2004-2010) **CW:** Reviewer, Journal of American Academy of Orthopaedic Surgeons (2018-Present); Reviewer, Clinical Orthopaedics and Related Research (2018-Present); Associate Editor Panel, Journal of Bone and Joint Surgery (2016-Present); Reviewer, American Journal of Sports Medicine (2015-Present); Reviewer, Journal of Bone and Joint Surgery American (2014-Present); Editorial Board, World Journal of Orthopaedics (2015-2017); Co-Editor, Stryker Disaster Preparedness Blog (2012-2014); Editorial Board, Pocket Orthopaedica (2010); Contributor, Numerous Oral Presentations, Invited Lectures, National/International Meetings, Posters/Scientific Exhibits, and Local/Regional Meetings; Contributor, Numerous Publications and Book Chapters **AW:** American Academy of Orthopaedic Surgeons Leadership Fellows Program (2019-Present); American Orthopaedic Association Emerging Leaders Program (2013-Present); U.S. Army Order of Military Medical Merit (2019); Texas Monthly Super Doctor's Rising Stars (2018); Air Force Achievement Medal (2018); San Antonio Scene Best Doctors for Pediatric Orthopaedics (2018); San Antonio Military Medical Center Department of Orthopaedics Warren Kadrmas

Memorial Resident Teaching Award (2017); Texas Monthly Super Doctor's Rising Stars (2017); American Academy of Orthopaedic Surgeons Achievement Award (2016); Air Force Meritorious Service Medal (2015); 2015 San Antonio Business Journal's "40 Under 40" (2015); Best e-Poster, Pediatric Orthopedic Society of North American Annual Meeting in Toronto, Canada (2013); Sponsorship, Pediatric Orthopedic Society of North America to 2012 AAOS/Orthopedic Research Society/ Orthopedic Research Education Fund Clinician Scholar Development Program (2012); Lena Sefton Clark Pediatric Fellowship Award, Rady Children's Hospital San Diego (2012); Early Career Achievement Award from Loyola University Chicago Stritch School of Medicine (2010); Air Force District of Washington Surgical Excellence Award as Outstanding Surgeon in Major Command (2010); Annual Roy Davis Award for Outstanding Resident Research, San Antonio Orthopedic Society (2009); Second Place for Resident Research, Annual Texas Orthopedic Association Annual Meeting, Austin, TX (2009); Outstanding Orthopedic Resident Paper, 55th Annual Society of Air Force Clinical Surgeons Meeting, Denver, CO (2009); Dr. Fred Miller Memorial Scholarship in Orthopedics from Loyola Chicago (2003) **MEM:** International Society of Dip Arthroscopy (2017-Present); Fellow, American Orthopaedic Association (2017-Present); Associate Member, Arthroscopy Association of North America (2014-Present); Founding Member, Pediatric Research in Sports Medicine (2014-Present); Texas Orthopaedic Association (2013-Present); Specialty Fellow, American Academy of Pediatrics (2013-Present); Orthopaedic Research Society (2013-Present); International Rugby Board Science Network (2012-Present); Texas Medical Association (2012-Present); San Antonio Orthopaedic Society (2006-2009, 2012-Present); Pediatric Orthopedic Society of North America (2011-Present); Society of Military Orthopaedic Surgeons (2007-Present); Fellow, American Academy of Orthopaedic Surgeons (2005-Present); American Orthopaedic Association Emerging Leaders Program (2013-2017) **AS:** Dr. Schmitz attributes his success to his network of mentors, including Dr. John Tokish and Dr. Warren Kadrams. **B/I:** Dr. Schmitz became involved in his profession due to the influence of his grandfather, who had succeeded as a surgeon in his own right. **PA:** Fellow, American Academy of Orthopaedic Surgeons; Fellow, American Orthopaedic Association; Specialty Fellow, American Academy of Pediatrics

SCHNEIDER, BRADLEY, "BRAD" SCOTT, T: U.S. Representative from Illinois **I:** Government Administration/Government Relations/Government Services **DOB:** 08/20/1961 **PB:** Denver **SC:** CO/USA **MS:** Married **SPN:** Julie (Dann) Schneider (1989) **CH:** Daniel; Adam **ED:** MBA, Northwestern University Kellogg School of Management (1988); BS in Industrial Engineering, Northwestern University (1983) **C:** Member, U.S. House of Representatives from Illinois' 10th Congressional District United States Congress, Washington, DC (2013-2015, 2013-Present); Member, U.S. House Committee on Small Business (2013-Present); Member, U.S. House Committee on Foreign Affairs (2013-Present); Founder, Cadence Consulting Group, LLC (2008-Present); Director, Strategic Services Group, Blackman Kallick (2003-2008); Managing Principal, Davis Dann Adler Schneider, LLC (1997-2003); Founder, Managing Principal, Schneider Consulting Group (1994-1997); Head of Strategy, Mergers and Acquisitions, Commerce Clearing House (1993-1994); Senior Consultant, PriceWaterhouseCoopers (PwC) (1983) **PA:** Democrat **RE:** Jewish

SCHNITZER, ALAN D., T: Chief Executive Officer and Chairman **CN:** The Travelers Companies Inc. **DOB:** 12/6/1965 **PB:** Dallas **SC:** TX/USA **ED:** JD, Columbia Law School (1991); BSE, The Wharton School of the University of Pennsylvania, Magna Cum Laude (1988) **C:** Chairman, The Travelers Companies, Inc. (2017-Present); Chief Executive Officer, Vice Chairman, Business and International Insurance, The Travelers Companies, Inc. (2015-Present); Vice Chairman, Chief Legal Officer, The Travelers Companies, Inc. (2007-2015); Partner, Simpson Thacher & Bartlett LLP (1999-2007); Associate, Simpson Thacher & Bartlett LLP (1991-1999) **CR:** Member, Investor Advisory Committee, U.S. Securities and Exchange Commission; Member, Board of Directors, American Property Casualty Insurance Association; Member, Board of Directors, Partnership for New York City **CIV:** Vice Chair, Advisory Board, Penn Institute for Urban Research; Vice Chair, Corporate Fund Board, Kennedy Center; Member, Board of Trustees, University of Pennsylvania; Member, Board of Directors, Connecticut Council for Education Reform; Member, Board of Directors, New York City Balley; Member, Board of Directors, Memorial Sloan Kettering Cancer Center; Member, Business Committee, Metropolitan Museum of Art; Board Director, Member, Audit Committee, Legal Aid Society **CW:** Member, Columbia Law Review **AW:** Business Committee Civic Leadership Award, Metropolitan Museum of Art (2015); Harlan Fiske Stone Scholar, Columbia Law School **MEM:** American Bar Association; New York State Bar Association; New York Bar Association; Council on Foreign Relations; The Economic Club of New York; The Business Council; Business Roundtable **BAR:** New York (1992)

SCHOPPER, SUE, T: Maternal, Women's Health and Medical/Surgical Nurse **I:** Medicine & Health Care **DOB:** 03/25/1938 **PB:** Stigler **SC:** OK/USA **PT:** Everett Franks; Ruby (McCaslin) Franks **MS:** Widowed **SPN:** Jared B. Schopper (01/27/1978, Deceased) **CH:** Robert; Jenny; Melody **ED:** BSN, Northeastern State University, Tahlequah, OK (1991); Associate Diploma in Nursing, Bacone College, Muskogee, OK (1973) **CT:** Registered Nurse, State of Oklahoma **C:** Pediatric Nurse, Pediatric Clinic, Tahlequah, OK (1990-Present); Charge Nurse, Surgical Floor, Tahlequah City Hospital (Now Northeastern Health System), OK (1983-1990); Charge Nurse, Obstetrics-labor-delivery Room, Newborn Nursery, Hastings Hospital (Now Cherokee Nation W.W. Hastings Indian Hospital), Tahlequah, OK (1979); Supervisor, VA Medical Center (Now Eastern Oklahoma VA Health Care System), Muskogee, OK (1973-1978) **CR:** RN Consultant, Green Acres Retirement Center, Tahlequah, OK (1989-Present) **CIV:** Member, Baptist, Church **AW:** Nightingale Award for Excellence in Nursing **MEM:** Attendant, Numerous Seminars in Legal, Medicine, and Church Activities **MH:** Albert Nelson Marquis Lifetime Achievement Award **AV:** Reading; Writing; Learning; Helping children; Grandchildren; Investing in tomorrow by helping others today **PA:** Democrat **RE:** Baptist

SCHRADER, WALTER, "KURT" KURT, DVM, T: U.S. Representative from Oregon; Veterinarian **I:** Government Administration/Government Relations/Government Services **DOB:** 10/19/1951 **PB:** Bridgeport **SC:** CT/USA **MS:** Married **SPN:** Susan Mora (2016); Martha (Northam) Schrader (1975, Divorced) **CH:** Five Children **ED:** DVM, University of Illinois College of Veterinary Medicine (1977); BS, University of Illinois Urbana-Champaign (1975); BA in Government, Cornell University, Ithaca, NY (1973) **C:** Member, U.S. House of Representatives from Oregon's Fifth Congressional District U.S. Congress, Washington, DC

(2009-Present); Member, District 20, Oregon State Senate (2003-2008); Member, District 23, Oregon House of Representatives (1997-2003); Member, Committee on Energy and Commerce, U.S. Congress; Veterinarian, Owner, Manager, Clackamas County Veterinary Clinic, Oregon City, OR **CR:** Member, Canby Planning Commission (1981-1996) **AW:** Distinguished Leadership by Community Planner Award, American Planning Association **MEM:** American Association of Equine Practitioners; Oregon Veterinary Medical Association; American Veterinary Medical Association; Canby Area Chamber of Commerce; Oregon City Chamber of Commerce; Oregon Farm Bureau; National Federation of Independent Business **PA:** Democrat

SCHRAM, GERALDINE PHYLLIS, T: Security Administrator **I:** Business Management/Business Services **DOB:** 01/01/1935 **PB:** Kinde **SC:** MI/USA **PT:** Charles Harold; Stella Mary (Horetski) Moore **CH:** Robert Charles; Kelly Jo **ED:** BS in Management/Marketing, Northwood Institute, Midland, MI (1988); BAA in Business, Delta College, University Center, MI (1983); Accounting Degree, Cleary College (1954) **CT:** Certification in Business, Cleary College (1954) **C:** Consultant/Lecturer, Janus Associates (1977-2000); Government Security Administrator, Dow Corning Corp., Midland, MI (1980-1996); Public Relations Staff, Dow Chemical Company, Midland, MI (1980-1996); Account Manager, Bloom Associates, Detroit, MI (1960-1962); Registered Medical Secretary, Hubbard Memorial Hospital, University of Michigan, Ann Arbor, MI (1955-1958) **CR:** Facilitator, World Association Document Examiners, Chicago, IL (1989-Present); Lecturer, Presenter in Field **CW:** Author, "Personalities at Risk" (1993); Author, "Survival Skills for the Information Age"; Author, "Disabled Personalities"; Contributor, Articles, Professional Journals **AW:** International Grapho-Analyst of the Year (1994) **MEM:** Instructor, International Graphoanalysis Society (1976-Present); American Defense Preparedness Association; World Association of Document Examiners; Chamber of Commerce; American Society Industrial Security **MH:** Albert Nelson Marquis Lifetime Achievement Award **B/I:** Ms. Schram had always been interested in studying people. She comes from a background where she had to work to pay for her education. She always had the desire to become a grapho-anaylst but there were not many opportunities considering she was married with children. Eventually, an opportunity presented itself where she would be able to continue her family life alongside funding her education and pursuing the career path. **AV:** Painting; Playing music; Writing **PA:** Republican **RE:** Roman Catholic **THT:** Ms. Schram is the oldest of seven children. She grew up on a farm. Her parents instilled a strict work ethic in her. She was the only master grapho-analyst that did an analysis of 75 years of Sigmund Freud's writings.

SCHRANK, SHIRLEY ANN, T: Artist **I:** Fine Art **DOB:** 01/30/1933 **PB:** Nunda **SC:** NY/USA **PT:** Ward Donald Crane; Norma Mae (Kelley) Crane **MS:** Widow **SPN:** William Thomas Schrank (Deceased); John Roberts McKalip Junior (10/08/1966, Deceased 1974) **CH:** Catherine "Cathy" McKalip; William "Billy" Ward McKalip **ED:** MS in Nursing Education, University of Rochester (1961); BSN, University of Rochester (1960); Degree in Nursing, University of Rochester (1954) **C:** Samuel Merritt Hospital School of Nursing, Oakland, CA (1967); Instructor of Medicine, Surgical And ICU Nursing, Samuel Merritt Hospital School of Nursing, Oakland, CA (1963-1967); Nurse, Private Duty Surgical Patients, Presbyterian Medical Center Hospitals, San Francisco, CA (1962); Staff Nurse, Eye Surgery, Children's Hospital, San Francisco, CA (1961); Instructor, Pediatric Nursing, Genesee Hospital, Rochester, NY (1960-1961); Team Leader, Department of Medicine, University of Rochester (1956-1960); Staff Nurse, Department of Psychiatry, University of Rochester (1954-1956) **CR:** The Blackhawk Gallery, Danville, CA (1995-2006); California Watercolor Association (2005); La Junta Artists Association (1974-1976, 2005); East Bay Women Artists, Oakland, CA (1989-1999); San Francisco Women Artists (1989-1992) **CIV:** Stephen Minister, Stephen Teaching Leader, Choir; Nursing Students Association of New York State (NSANYS) **CW:** Sculptor, Numerous Figure Sculptures in Ceramic and Bronze; Painter, Landscape Paintings **MH:** Albert Nelson Marquis Lifetime Achievement Award; Marquis Who's Who Top Professional **B/I:** In the 1960s, the federal government needed more nurses due to a shortage following World War II. They began a training program with a $240 a month living stipend plus full tuition. Ms. Schrank was lucky enough to be offered the opportunity and was only required to work 4 1/2 years as a teacher, which she did and more. Regarding her art, Ms. Schrank had been interested in the field her entire life. After retiring from nursing, she began to take art more seriously. She took classes while still living in Rochester, New York. She never stopped creating art although she has taken breaks from much of her art activities to take care of family responsibilities. **AV:** Camping; Traveling; Singing; Practicing needlepoint; Gardening; Painting; Sketching; Skiing **PA:** Republican **RE:** Presbyterian

SCHRIER, KIMBERLY, "KIM" MERLE, MD, T: U.S. Representative from Washington; Physician **I:** Government Administration/Government Relations/Government Services **DOB:** 08/23/1968 **PB:** Los Angeles **SC:** CA/USA **MS:** Married **SPN:** David Gowing **CH:** One Son **ED:** Resident, Stanford University School of Medicine, Stanford Medicine; MD, University of California Davis School of Medicine; BS, University of California Berkeley **C:** Member, U.S. House of Representatives from Washington's Eighth Congressional District (2019-Present); Physician, Virginia Mason Medical Center, Issaquah, WA (2001-Present); Pediatrician, Ashland, OR **MEM:** The Phi Beta Kappa Society **PA:** Democrat

SCHROEDER, DONNA, OSB, PHD, T: Professor Emeritus of Biology **I:** Education/Educational Services **CN:** College of St. Scholastica **DOB:** 09/15/1938 **PB:** Lakota **SC:** ND/USA **PT:** John Harold Schroeder; Grace Jeannette Davidson-Schroeder **ED:** Doctor of Philosophy, University of North Carolina at Chapel Hill (1981); Master of Science, Saint Mary's University of Minnesota (1971); Bachelor of Arts, College of St. Scholastica (1961) **CT:** Certified in Monastic Studies, St. John's University, Collegeville, MN (2008) **C:** Associate Professor, College of St. Scholastica (1969-2013); Biology Teacher, Gerard High School, Phoenix, AZ (1963-1969) **CR:** Director, Sisters in First Profession (2008-2019); Chairperson, Biology Department, College of St. Scholastica (1977-1997) **CIV:** Board of Trustees, College of St. Scholastica, Duluth, MN (2018-Present) **AW:** Teaching Award, College of St. Scholastica (1992) **MH:** Albert Nelson Marquis Lifetime Achievement Award **AS:** Ms. Schroeder attributes her success to curiosity and an innate love for learning. She also enjoyed problem solving. **B/I:** Ms. Schroeder became involved in her profession because she found the content both fascinating and practical. **AV:** Reading; Writing **RE:** Roman Catholic

SCHROEDER, MARSHA, MA, LPC, PLLC, T: Therapist, Licensed Professional Counselor **I:** Health, Wellness and Fitness **DOB:** 08/01/1944 **PB:** Tawas City **SC:** MI/USA **PT:** Francis Cardinal; Marcella Cardinal **MS:** Married **SPN:** Tim Edwin Schroeder (08/29/1964) **CH:** Tim E. II; Steven M. **ED:** MS in Counseling, Central Michigan University (1992); BA in Psychology, Saginaw Valley State University (1985) **CT:** Licensed Professional Counselor, Central Michigan University (1993) **C:** Private Practice, Marsha Schroeder, MA, LPC, PLLC, East Tawas, MI (2003-Present); Therapist, Catholic Family Service, Saginaw, MI (1992-2010); Adjunct Faculty, Delta College, University Center, MI (1990-2005); Therapist, Catholic Family Service, Midland, MI (1999-2003); Staff, St. Stephen Catholic School, Saginaw, MI (1997-2000); Staff, Saints Peter and Paul Catholic School (1994-1999); Staff, St. Helen Catholic School (1993-1994) **MEM:** American Counseling Association **MH:** Albert Nelson Marquis Lifetime Achievement Award; Marquis Who's Who Top Professional; Marquis Who's Who Humanitarian Award **B/I:** Mrs. Schroeder became involved in her profession because she has always had a natural way to relate to people and to help them. She believes that it came from God. She feels very comfortable in her job; she loves it. She believes that she is just the messenger and that God gave her the ability to do her work. She is also the first to graduate from college in her family. She looks at her career not as a job, but a vocation. **AV:** Swimming; Tennis; Travel; Writing; Car shows and racing; Gardening; Spending time with family; Traveling; Horseback riding **RE:** Roman Catholic **THT:** Mrs. Schroeder's motto is, "Life is a gift from God! It is each person's responsibility to make it the best life it can be!"

SCHROER-LAMONT, ANNE CHRISTINE, PHD, T: University Administrator; Psychologist **I:** Education/Educational Services **DOB:** 12/13/1944 **PB:** Kane **SC:** PA/USA **PT:** Charles Howard Schroer; Lucille Grace Partchey Schroer **MS:** Married **SPN:** Lawrence M. Lamont (11/28/1987); Nathan A. Schroer (07/23/1966, Divorced 1987) **CH:** Jonathan P.; Matthew C. **ED:** Coursework, Theological Education by Extension, School of Theology, The University of the South (2005-2009); PhD in Administration and Counseling, University of Northern Colorado (1977); MA in Foreign Languages, Washington State University (1972); BA in French and Spanish, Defiance College, Ohio (1967); Diplôme des Etudes Francaises Modernes, University of Strasbourg, France (1966) **CT:** Diplomate, National Board of Certified Counselors (NBCC) (1981-Present); Diplomate, National Board of Certified Career Counselors, National Board of Certified Counselors (NBCC) (1981-Present); Diplomate, National Academy of Clinical Mental Health Counselors (1981-Present) **C:** Associate Dean, Psychologist, Washington and Lee University, Lexington, VA (1985-2004); University Counseling Psychologist, Texas A&M University, College Station, Texas (1981-1985); Director, Career Development and Counseling, Houghton College, New York, NY (1974-1981); Graduate Teaching Assistant, French, Washington State University (1968-1971); Foreign Language Teacher, Washington Irving High School, Clarksburg, WV (1967-1968) **CR:** Delegate, International Women's Leadership Association (2013-Present); Executive Committee Member, Virginia Network for Women Leaders, Richmond, VA (1997-Present); Executive Board, Central Virginia Chapter, Fulbright Association (2007-2009); With, Snowmass Institute (2003); Executive Board, American Council on Education, The Virginia Network (1996-2004); Scholar-in-residence, Center for Women's Research (Now Center for Gender Research), University of Oslo, Norway (1996); Governor's Task Force, Campus Sexual Assault, State of Virginia (1989-1994); Faculty Member, Family Business Institute, Washington and Lee University (1986-1990); International Presentations on Women's Issues, Norway, China, Scotland, United Kingdom, France, Spain, Sweden, and Germany CIV: Anti-Violence Coordinating Committee, Lexington, KY (1996-Present); Founding Member, Rockbridge Area Coalition Against Sexual Assault (1990-1997); Altar Guild Episcopal Church, Lexington, KY (1988-1990); Board of Directors, Fine Arts, Rockbridge, Lexington, KY (1987-1990) CW: Musical Performance, Taizé Musical Group, Clarinet (2010-Present); Musical Performance, Washington and Lee University Wind Ensemble (2006-Present); Contributor, Articles, Professional Journals; Musical Performance, Egypt; Musical Performance, Costa Rica; Musical Performances, Grace Episcopal Church Choir, Lexington, VA AW: Scholarship Award, International Leadership Program, University of Oxford (2002); Outstanding Alumnae Award, Defiance College, Ohio (2001); Outstanding Service Award, WACRA - The World Association for Case Method Research & Application (1999); Leadership Award, State Council of Higher Education in Virginia: Program Development on Campus Sexual Assault in Virginia (1994); Recipient, Grant to Study at Harvard, Lifespan Clinical-Developmental Psychology Institute (1984) MEM: Lifetime Member, American Psychological Association; National Association for Women in Education; National Associate, The America-Scandinavian Foundation; American Mental Health Counselors Association; American Association of University Women (AAUW) MH: Albert Nelson Marquis Lifetime Achievement Award; Marquis Who's Who Top Professional; Marquis Who's Who Humanitarian Award B/I: Dr. Schroer-Lamont was inspired to become a foreign language French teacher because of her high school language teachers. They were very inspirational, and she knew she wanted to teach. In those days, a women could become a nurse, teacher, or secretary. She loved teaching, and she loved the kids; her students would come talk to her before or after school and she couldn't believe the problems they were having at home. That is what lead her into counseling. AV: Photography; Hiking; Fly fishing; Travel; Gardening; Education for ministry; Skiing; Tennis; Biking; Reading; Swimming PA: Independent RE: Episcopalian THT: Dr. Shroer-Lamont has always loved music. Her father was a conductor, which made it easy for her to stay with music as her life long hobby. When Dr. Shroer-Lamont's father accepted a position at Defiance College, she eagerly attended and continued working on music with him. She has been in academia since she was 18. She is proud of the fact that she never left. Additionally, her faith has been an ongoing inspiration which brings her endless joy and guides her when needed.

SCHUCKMAN, NANCY LEE, T: Principal (Retired) **I:** Education/Educational Services **DOB:** 06/03/1939 **PB:** Brooklyn **SC:** NY/USA **PT:** Abraham Benjamin Schuckman; Sophie (Kalefsky) Schuckman **ED:** Postgraduate Studies, Columbia University (1979-1980); Postgraduate Studies, Hofstra University (1970-1972); Postgraduate Studies, Brooklyn College (1965-1969); MS, Brooklyn College (1964); BA, Brooklyn College (1961) **C:** Co-Owner, Lanah Educational Toys, Brooklyn, NY (1975-1976); Educational Journalist, Starrett City Sun, Brooklyn, NY (1975-1976); Educational Journalist, East New Yorker, East New York Development Corporation, Brooklyn, NY (1974-1976); Principal, New York City Board of Education, Brooklyn, NY (1977-1997); Administrator, New York City Board of Education, Brooklyn, NY (1969-1977); Teacher, New York City Board of Education (1961-1969) **CR:** Photographer **CIV:** Member, Thomas Jefferson Democratic Club, Brooklyn, NY (1978-Present); Member, Kings County Democratic Committee (1981-1997); Member, Advisory Board, Principal's Center, Brooklyn College (1989-1995); Political Campaign Coordinator John F. Kennedy Democratic Club, Brooklyn, NY (1974-1976) **AW:** Educational Leadership Recognition Award, New York City District 19, Council of School Supervisors and Administrators (1997); Service Appreciation Award, New York City Elementary School Principals Association (1997); Legislative Resolution, New York State Assembly/Senate (1997); Congressional Record Recognition, U.S. Congress (1997); City Council Proclamation New York City Council (1987) **MEM:** Excel Board, New York City Elementary School Principals Association (1984-1997); Convention Registration Chairman, Council of School Supervisors and Administrators (1985-1988); Association for Supervision and Curriculum Development; National Association of Elementary School Principals; Council of School Supervisors and Administrators; Administrative Women in Education; AASA; National Association of Elementary School Principals; New York City Elementary School Principals Association; New York State Reading Council; Brooklyn Reading Council **MH:** Albert Nelson Marquis Lifetime Achievement Award **B/I:** Ms. Schuckman became involved in her profession because she had special teachers in the fifth and sixth grade who inspired her. They told her mom that she would succeed in the three-years honor program, which she did, becoming one of the first groups on television. She wanted to go into law and sports journalism but felt she could make more of an impact as an educator. She traveled a lot all over the world and would take pictures, which is how she got involved in photography. **AV:** Education law; Journalism; Painting; Traveling; Sports **PA:** Democrat **RE:** Jewish

SCHULER, JOHN, T: Chief Executive Officer **I:** Apparel & Fashion **CN:** Schuler Shoes **MS:** Married **CH:** Four Children **C:** Store Owner, Chief Executive Officer, Schuler Shoes (1972-Present); Retailer, Schuler Shoes (1967) **CIV:** Shoe Away Hunger **AW:** Award for One of the Top 100 Companies to Work for in Minnesota, Twin Cities Business Magazine (2017); Retailer of the Year, National Shoe Retailers Association (2009); Retailer of the Year, Northwest Shoe Travelers Association; The Chairman's Award, New Balance **MEM:** National Shoe Retailers Association **AS:** Mr. Schuler attributes his success to his father teaching him the responsibilities of being an entrepreneur and a retail owner. He also attributes his success to the grace of God. He has always had strong faith and strived to do the right thing. **B/I:** Mr. Schuler became involved in his profession because he inherited the family business, which his father originally owned. He worked numerous jobs within Schuler Shoes until his father passed it down to him. His father told him if he worked hard, this could be a very successful business for him. Mr. Schuler took that to heart and started opening and closing and remodeling multiple locations. **AV:** Being an outdoorsman **THT:** Mr. Schuler's motto is "TOP (trust, obey, patient). Trust relationships [and] obey the rules and be patient." His youngest son is the vice president of Schuler Shoes. Shoe Away Hunger offers affordable quality footwear for those in need. In addition, it helps them to raise the money they need to continue feeding more than 4,000 people each month through Feeding The Future programs and services.

SCHULMAN, DANIEL H., T: President, Chief Executive Officer **I:** Financial Services **CN:** PayPal **DOB:** 01/19/1958 **PB:** Newark **SC:** NJ/USA **PT:** Melvin Schulman; S. Ruth Schulman **MS:** Married **SPN:** Jennie Ann Kassanoff **CH:** One Son; One Daughter **ED:** Honorary Doctorate, Rutgers, the State University of New Jersey (2018); MBA in Finance, New York University (1986); BS in Economics and Geography, Middlebury College (1980); Diploma, Princeton High School **C:** President, Paypal, Inc., San Jose, CA (2014-Present); Non-Executive Chairman, Symantec (2013-Present); Group President, Enterprise Growth, American Express Co., New York, NY (2010-2014); President, Sprint Prepaid, Sprint Nextel, Overland Park, KS (2009-2010); Chief Executive Officer, Virgin Mobile USA (Now Sprint Nextel), Warren, NJ (2001-2010); President, Chief Executive Officer, Priceline.com (2000-2001); President, Chief Operating Officer, Priceline.com (1999-2000); President, Worldnet Service, AT&T Corp. (1997-1998); Small Business Marketing Vice President, Business Markets Division, AT&T Corp. (1994-1995); Senior Executive, Operations Group, AT&T Corp.; President, AT&T Consumer Markets Division, AT&T Corp.; Vice President, Business Services Marketing, Business Markets Division, AT&T Corp. **CR:** Chairman, Symantec (2013-Present); Board of Directors, Flextronics International Ltd. (2009-Present); Board of Directors, Symantec (2000-Present); Board of Directors, Net2Phone (1999-2004); Advisory Committee, Greycroft Partners; Board of Directors, Verizon, Autism Speaks **CIV:** Board Trustee, Rutgers, the State University of New Jersey; Partner, StandUp for Kids **AW:** CFSI Financial Health Visionary Award, Center for Financial Services Innovation (2018); Businessperson of the Year, Fortune (2017-2018); Brennan Legacy Award, Brennan Center for Justice (2017); Visionary Award, Council for Economic Education (2017); Entrepreneur of the Year, Ernst & Young (2009); Named, Top 20 People to Watch in Media, Business Week **AV:** Hiking

SCHUMER, AMY, T: Comedienne, Actress **I:** Media & Entertainment **DOB:** 06/01/1981 **PB:** New York **SC:** NY/USA **PT:** Gordon Schumer; Sandra (Jones) Schumer **MS:** Married **SPN:** Chris Fischer (02/13/2018) **CH:** Gene **ED:** Postgraduate Coursework, William Esper Studio (2003-2005); BA in Theatre, Towson University (2003) **C:** Actress, Comedian (2003-Present) **CW:** Host, Podcast, "Amy Schumer Presents: 3 Girls, 1 Keith" (2018-Present); Performer, Stand-Up Special, "Amy Schumer: Growing" (2019); Host, "Saturday Night Live" (2018, 2015); Actress, "I Feel Pretty" (2018); Performer, Stand-Up Special, "Amy Schumer: The Leather Special" (2017); Performer, Stand-Up Album, "Amy Schumer: The Leather Special" (2017); Actor, Theater, "Meteor Shower" (2017); Actress, "Thank You for Your Service" (2017); Actress, "Snatched" (2017); Herself, "Family Feud" (2017); Author, "The Girl with the Lower Back Tattoo" (2016); Voice Actress, Audiobook, "The Girl with the Lower Back Tattoo" (2016); Voice Actress, "Bob's Burgers" (2016); Voice Actress, "Family Guy" (2016); Voice Actress, "The Simpsons" (2016); Performer, Stand-Up Album, "Amy Schumer: Live at the Apollo" (2016); Performer, Stand-Up Special, "Amy Schumer: Live at the Apollo" (2015); Actress, Screenwriter, "Trainwreck" (2015); Voice Actress, "BoJack Horseman" (2015); Host, "2015 MTV Movie Awards" (2015); Actress, "Girls" (2014, 2013); Actress, Creator, Writer, Executive Producer, Director, "Inside Amy Schumer" (2013-2016); Co-Performer, Stand-Up Special, "Women Who Kill" (2013); Actress, "Seeking a Friend for the End of the World" (2012); Actress, "Price Check" (2012); Actress, "Sleepwalk with Me" (2012); Herself, "Dave's Old Porn" (2012); Performer, Stand-Up Special, "Amy Schumer: Mostly Sex Stuff" (2012); Performer, "Comedy Central Roast of Roseanne Barr" (2012); Voice Actress, "Louie" (2012); Actress, "Delocated" (2012); Performer, "Comedy Central Roast of Charlie Sheen" (2011); Actress, "Curb Your Enthusiasm" (2011); Featured Performer, Stand-Up Album, "Cutting" (2011); Performer, "Comedy Central Presents" (2010); Performer, "John Oliver's New York Stand-Up Show" (2010); Actress, "30 Rock" (2009); Actress, "Cupid" (2009); Actress, "Reality Bites Back" (2008); Contestant, "Last Comic Standing" (2007); Performer, "Live at Gotham" (2007); Actress, "Sense Memory" (2006); Actress, Theater, "Keeping Abreast" (2003) **AW:** Wilde Wit of the Year, Dorian Awards, GALECA (2016); Writers Guild of America Award for Best Comedy/Variety - Sketch Series, "Inside Amy Schumer" (2016); MVP Award, Critics' Choice Movie Awards (2016); Best Actress in a Comedy, Critics' Choice Movie Awards (2016); Kerrang! Award for Best Comedian (2016); Satellite Special Award for Breakthrough Comedian, "Trainwreck" (2016); Young Hollywood Award for Comedian of the Year (2014); Primetime Emmy Award for Outstanding Variety Sketch Series, "Inside Amy Schumer" (2015); Television Critics Association Award for Best Actress in a Comedy Series, "Inside Amy Schumer" (2015); Television Critics Association Award for Outstanding Achievement in Comedy, "Inside Amy Schumer" (2015); Charlie Chaplin Britannia Award for Excellence in Comedy (2015); Named One of "The Top 10 Most Fascinating People of 2015," Barbara Walters Special (2015); Television Critics Association Award for Individual Achievement in Comedy, "Inside Amy Schumer" (2015); Peabody Award (2014) **RE:** Jewish

SCHWARTZ, BART M., T: Chairman **I:** Consulting **CN:** Guidepost Solutions **MS:** Married **CH:** Three Children **ED:** Doctor of Jurisprudence, New York University School of Law (1971); Bachelor of Science in Biology, Minor in Chemistry, University of Pittsburgh (1968) **C:** Chairperson, Board of Directors, Chairperson, Compliance Committee, Kadmon Holdings Incorporated (2016-Present); Chairperson, Board of Directors, Guidepost Solutions LLC (2010-Present); Chairperson, Chief Executive Officer, SolutionPoint International, New York, NY (2010-Present); Public Company Board, HMS (2010-Present); Founder, Chief Executive Officer, Decision Strategies LLC (1991-2003); Chief, Criminal Division, United States Attorney's Office, Southern District of New York, NY (1983-1985) **CIV:** National Board, All Stars Project; Board, New York Police Athletic League; Stuyvesant High School Alumni Association; Board Member, Audit Committee; Compliance Committee, HMS **CW:** Contributor, Articles to Professional Journals **AW:** Number 12, Top 50 Most Powerful Lawyers, New York, CSNY - City & State (2019); Number 11, Law-Power List of 50 Power Players, New York City **AS:** Mr. Schwartz attributes his success to a lot of hard work. **B/I:** Mr. Schwartz became interested in law because he thought that it would be the best training for life in terms of learning how to approach problems and thinking quickly. He received a summer internship working at the U.S. attorney's office; that is where he decided that he wanted to be a trial lawyer. **AV:** Fly fishing

SCHWARTZ, DONALD RAY, T: Communications Educator, College Official, Associate Professor **I:** Education/Educational Services **DOB:** 02/19/1943 **PB:** Louisville **SC:** KY/USA **PT:** Herman Schwartz; Selma (Pearson) Schwartz **MS:** Married **SPN:** Ann Sandra Kibel (08/03/1969) **CH:** Rabbi Doctor Marcus Mordecai Schwartz **ED:** Postgraduate Studies, University of Nebraska, Lincoln, NE (1984-1985); Postgraduate Studies (Toward PhD in Theater), The Ohio State University, Columbus, OH (1974-1978); MA in Speech and Theater, University of Louisville, Louisville, KY (1974); Apprenticeship, Videotone Film Productions (1967-1970);

BA, University of Kentucky, Lexington, KY (1965) **C:** Associate Professor in Speech, Theater and Mass Communication, Community College of Baltimore County (CCBC) (Retired); Speech, Theater and Mass Communication Instructor, Coordinator, Cooperative Vocational Education Internship, Peru State College, Nebraska (1984-1998); Freelance Writer, Omaha, NE (1982-1984); Director, Teacher, Ashland College, Ohio (1980-1982); Communications **CR:** Presenter, Writing Seminars, Metropolitan Community College, Omaha, NE (1987-Present); Editor, Drama Network Newsletter, Conference on Alternatives in Jewish Education (1990-1994) **MIL:** Major, Missile Launch Officer, Missile Launch Training Officer, Intelligence Officer, U.S. Air Force Reserves **CW:** Author, "Hearts" (2018); Co-Author, "Deeptide Vents...of Fire" (2017); Author, "Noah's Ark: An Annotated Encyclopedia of Every Animal Species in the Hebrew Bible" (2000); Co-Author, "Lillian Russell: A Bio-Bibliography" (1997); Author, Novella, "The Curse of the Days" (1984); Writer, Producer, Director, Numerous Plays; Contributor, More Than 200 Stories, Articles, Essays, Reviews, and Encyclopedia Entries **AW:** First Place Award for "The Cross-Country Journey of Jennifer X. Dreifus," National Epic Poetry Contest, Mellen Poetry Press (1993); Ohio Humanities Council Grantee (1981); Samuel Luchs Visiting Artist Grantee (1978); Kennedy Center Award for Ensemble for "Taming of the Shrew," Essex Academic Theater (CCBC); Jewish Book Selection of the Year, "Noah's Ark: An Annotated Encyclopedia of Every Animal Species In The Hebrew Bible" **MEM:** Speech Communications Association; Cooperative Education Association; B'nai Brith **MH:** Albert Nelson Marquis Lifetime Achievement Award; Marquis Who's Who Top Professional **B/I:** Professor Schwartz became involved in his profession because he was writing as early as elementary school, then found acting in academy theater and summer stock, which led him to producing and directing. **AV:** Biblical scholarship; Teaching synagogue-level Bible Midrash

SCHWARZ, MICHAEL, T: Lawyer **I:** Law and Legal Services **DOB:** 10/19/1952 **PB:** Brookline **SC:** MA/USA **PT:** Jules Lewis Schwarz; Estelle (Kosberg) Schwarz **MS:** Married **SPN:** Rebecca Handy **CH:** Patrick Joshua Charles **ED:** Diploma in Legal Studies, University of Cambridge (1981); Degree in Negligence Law, University of Oxford (1978); JD, University of New Mexico (1980); BA, University of Northern Colorado, Magna Cum Laude, (1975) **C:** Private Practice (1982-Present); Law Clerk to Chief Justice, New Mexico Supreme Court (1981-1982); Law Supervisor, University of Cambridge (1980-1981); Research Fellow, New Mexico Legal Aid, Inc. (1978-1979); Volunteer, AmeriCorps (1975-1977) **CR:** Chairman, Legal Specialization Committee, Employment and Labor Law Section, New Mexico Supreme Court (2005, 2008); Chairman, Committee for Professional Responsibility, New Mexico Supreme Court (1998-2007); Committee for Professional Responsibility, New Mexico Supreme Court (1990-2007); Domestic Relations Task Force Committee, New Mexico Supreme Court (2004-2006); West Editorial Advisory Committee, Social Security Reporting Service (1983-1995); Special Assistant Attorney General (1986-1988); Special Prosecutor, City of Santa Fe (1985) **CIV:** Director of New Mexico Coaching Education, U.S.A. Hockey Association (2004-2005); New Mexico Acupuncture Licensing Board (1983); Scoutmaster, Great Southwest Area Council, Boy Scouts of American (1977-1979); Vice Director, Colorado Public Interest Research Group (1974) **CW:** Author, "New Mexico Appellate Manual, Second Edition" (1996); Author, "New Mexico Appellate Manual" (1990); Contributor, Articles, Professional Journals

AW: Southwest Super Lawyer in Law and Politics (2007-2014, 2017-Present); Best Lawyers in America (2009-Present); Justice Pamela B. Minzner Professionalism Award, State Bar of New Mexico (2008); Certification for Outstanding Service to the Legal System, New Mexico Supreme Court (2001); Certificate of Recognition for Maintaining High Ethical Standards, New Mexico Supreme Court (1992-1993, 1995); Certificate of Appreciation, Cambridge University (1981); Nathan Burke Memorial Award (1980) **MEM:** Associate Coach-in-Chief, Rocky Mountain District (2004-2010); Board of Directors, Santa Fe Hockey Association (2001-2002); Board Member, Family Law Section, State Bar of New Mexico (1999-2001); Board of Directors, Employment Law Section, State Bar of New Mexico (1990-1996); First Judicial District Bar Associate President, Chairman, State Bar of New Mexico (1990-1991); Litigation Committee, American Bar Association; Restatement Employment Law and Principles of Government Ethics Committee, The American Law Institute **BAR:** Supreme Court of the United States (1983); United States Tax Court (1982); United States Court of International Trade (1982); The United States Court of Appeals for the Tenth Circuit (1982); United State Court of Appeals District of Columbia Circuit (1982); United States Court of Appeals for the Federal Circuit (1982); State Bar of New Mexico (1980); United States District Court District of New Mexico (1980) **MH:** Albert Nelson Marquis Lifetime Achievement Award **AV:** Hiking; Woodworking; Reading **PA:** Democrat

SCHWARZE, MARTIN W., DO, T: Cardiologist **I:** Medicine & Health Care **DOB:** 11/14/1946 **PB:** St. Louis **SC:** MO/USA **PT:** William C Schwarze; Mary Constance (Glaser) Schwarzwe **MS:** Married **SPN:** Janet Louise Musial (06/09/1973) **CH:** Julie; Brian **ED:** DO, A.T. Still University Kirksville College of Osteopathic Medicine, Kirksville, MO (1973); BS in Chemistry, Saint Louis University, St. Louis, MO (1968) **CT:** Diplomate, Subspecialty of Cardiovascular Disease (1982); American Osteopathic Board of Internal Medicine (AOA) (1981); Missouri (1974) **C:** Clinical Professor of Medicine, Division of Cardiology, Saint Louis University Hospitals, SSM Health (1999-Present); Clinical Professor, Department of Medicine, A.T. Still University Kirksville College of Osteopathic Medicine (1988-Present); Clinical Instructor, Department of Medicine, New England College of Osteopathic Medicine (1985-Present); Chief of Cardiology, St. Luke's Des Peres Hospital (1994-2010); Director of Cardiac Rehabilitation, Barnes-Jewish St. Peters Hospital, BJC HealthCare (1995-2005); Director, Non-Invasive Cardiology Department, Barnes-Jewish St. Peters Hospital, BJC HealthCare (1987-2000); Assistant Clinical Professor of Medicine, Division of Cardiology, Saint Louis University Hospitals (1981-1999) **CR:** Treasurer, Department of Internal Medicine, Normandy Osteopathic Hospitals (1985-1987); Chairman, Department of Internal Medicine, Normandy Osteopathic Hospitals (1984-1985); Director, Medical Intensive Care Unit, St. Peters Community Hospital (Now Barnes-Jewish St. Peters Hospital, BJC HealthCare) (1982-1983); Director, Cardiac Rehabilitation Program, Normandy Osteopathic Hospital-South (1978-1982) **CW:** Author, Publication, "Statins in the Elderly," Clinical Geriatrics (2004); Author, Publication, "Coronary Risk Stratification Using High-Sensitivity C-Reactive Protein (HSCRP), A Coronary Inflammatory Risk Marker," A Monograph Based on an Expert Panel Discussion (2001); Author, Publication, "Selecting Therapy for Elderly at Risk for Coronary Heart Disease or Stroke," Clinical Geriatrics (2000); Co-author, Publication, "Myocarditis," Journal of the American Osteopathic Association (1990); Author,

Publication, "Practical Considerations in the Treatment of Congestive Heart Failure," Osteopathic Annals (1987); Co-author, Publication, "Treatment of Chronic Acute Myocarditis with Immunosuppression Therapy," Presented at the American College of Cardiology Scientific Sessions (1984); Author, Publication, "ACE Inhibitors in CHF-Comparative Evaluation and Practical Considerations," Osteopathic Annals, Vol. 15 (1988); Author, Publication, "Management of CHF in the 1990s," JAOA; Contributor, Numerous Lectures; Researcher, Numerous Studies AW: Named to Best Doctors, St. Louis, MO (2008-Present); Master Fellow, American College of Osteopathic Internists (MACOI) (2017); Barnes-Jewish St. Peters/Progress Hospital Foundation "Super Hero" Award Honoree (2015); American Heart Association's Hugh D. McCulloch Medical Honoree Award (2008); Educator of the Year (2006, 2000, 1999); Arthur E. Strauss Lifetime Achievement Award, American Heart Association, Inc. (2003); Named One of the Cardiology Diagnostics-Educators of the Year, Deaconess West Campus (Beth Israel Deaconess Medical Center) (1993); Educator of the Year, Normandy Osteopathic Hospitals (1987) MEM: Board of Governors, Missouri Chapter, American College of Cardiology (1997-2002); Physician Advisory Board, Blue Cross Blue Shield Association (1995-2010); Assistant Secretary, St. Louis Chapter, American Heart Association, Inc. (1988-2008); President, St. Louis Chapter, American Heart Association, Inc. (1992-1994); Board of Directors, Visiting Nurse Association of America (VNAA) (1989-1993); Chairman, Nominating Committee, Metropolitan Medical Center, Deaconess West (1988-1993); Vice President, Board of Directors, American Heart Association, Inc. (1990-1992); President, St. Louis Cardiac Club (1990-1991); Medical Executive Committee, Quality Assurance Committee, Barnes-Jewish St. Peters Hospital, BJC HealthCare (1989-1991); Vice President, St. Louis Cardiac Club (1989-1990); Future Planning Committee, Normandy Osteopathic Hospitals (1978-1990); Secretary-Treasurer, St. Louis Cardiac Club (1988-1989); Quality Assurance Committee, St. Peter's Community Hospital (Now Barnes-Jewish St. Peters Hospital), BJC HealthCare (1987-1988); Institutional Review Board, Saint Louis University Hospitals (1983-1987); Chairman, Patient Care Committee, St. Peter's Community Hospital (Now Barnes-Jewish St. Peters Hospital, BJC HealthCare) (1985-1986); Utilization Review Committee, Saint Louis University Hospitals (1981-1984); Patient Care Committee, St. Peter's Community Hospital (1981-1983); Medical Audit Committee, Saint Louis University Hospitals (1979-1980); Intensive Care Committee, Normandy Osteopathic Hospitals (1978-1989); American Osteopathic Association (AOA); American College Osteopathic Internists (ACOI); Board of Directors, St. Louis Chapter, American Heart Association, Inc.; St. Louis Metropolitan Medical Society; St. Louis Cardiac Club; Missouri Association of Osteopathic Physicians and Surgeons (MAOPS); Society of Critical Care Medicine; American Society of Echocardiography MH: Albert Nelson Marquis Lifetime Achievement Award; Marquis Who's Who Top Professional B/I: Dr. Schwarze became involved in his profession because he grew up in a medical family and he was named after his grandfather, who was a physician and surgeon and attended the Washington School of Medicine at the turn of the last century. He was the first grandson that was named after him so he used to go with him to the hospital when he was old enough and go to the office and hang out with him. He was around his grandfather a lot growing up, and so by the time he was in the eighth grade, he was sure he wanted to be a physician. Dr. Schwarze also had an uncle who was

an orthopedic surgeon. AV: Antique convertible automobiles; Model trains; Horticulture THT: Dr. Schwawrze is still teaching.

SCHWARZNEGGER, ARNOLD ALOIS, T: Actor, Former Politician **I:** Media & Entertainment **DOB:** 07/30/1947 **PB:** Thal **SC:** Austria **PT:** Gustav Schwarzenegger; Aurelia (Jadrny) Schwarzenegger **MS:** Divorced **SPN:** Maria Shriver (04/26/1986, Divorced 2017) **CH:** Katherine Eunice; Christina Maria Aurelia; Patrick Arnold Shriver; Christopher Sargent Shriver; Joseph Baena **ED:** Honorary DHL, University of Houston (2017); Honorary LLD, Emory University (2010); Honorary LHD, University of Southern California (2006); Honorary LHD, University of Wisconsin - Superior (1996); BA, University of Wisconsin - Superior; Coursework, Santa Monica College **C:** Actor (1969-Present); 38th Governor of California (2003-2011); Professional Bodybuilder (1968-1980) **CR:** Owner, Schatzi on Main (1992-1998) **CIV:** Chairman, President's Council on Physical Fitness and Sports (1990-1993) **MIL:** Austrian Army (1965) **CW:** Guest Appearance, "Chad Goes Deep" (2019); Actor, Producer, "Viy 2: Journey to China" (2019); Actor, "Terminator: Dark Fate" (2019); Producer, Documentary, "The Game Changers" (2018); Actor, Producer, "Aftermath" (2017); Host, "The New Celebrity Apprentice" (2017); Actor, Producer, "Killing Gunther" (2017); Producer, Narrator, Documentary, "Wonders of the Sea 3D" (2017); Producer, "Years of Living Dangerously" (2014-2016); Actor, Producer, "Maggie" (2015); Actor, "Terminator Genisys" (2015); Guest Appearance, "Two and a Half Men" (2015); Actor, "Sabotage" (2014); Actor, "The Expendables 3" (2014); Actor, "The Last Stand" (2013); Actor, "Escape Plan" (2013); Author, "Total Recall" (2012); Actor, "The Expendables 2" (2012); Actor, "The Expendables" (2010); Appearance, "Terminator Salvation" (2009); Cameo, "The Kid & I" (2005); Cameo, "Around the World in 80 Days" (2004); Actor, "Terminator 3: Rise of the Machines" (2003); Cameo, "The Rundown" (2003); Guest Appearance, "Liberty's Kids" (2002-2003); Actor, "Collateral Damage" (2002); Actor, Producer, "The 6th Day" (2000); Actor, "End of Days" (1999); Co-Author, "The New Encyclopedia of Modern Bodybuilding" (1998); Actor, "Batman & Robin" (1997); Actor, "Eraser" (1996); Actor, "Jingle All the Way" (1996); Actor, "True Lies" (1994); Actor, "Junior" (1994); Cameo, "Dave" (1993); Actor, Producer, "Last Action Hero" (1993); Cameo, TV Film, "Beretta's Island" (1993); Cameo, Director, TV Film, "Christmas in Connecticut" (1992); Voice Actor, TV Film, "Lincoln" (1992); Actor, "Terminator 2: Judgment Day" (1991); Actor, "Total Recall" (1990); Guest Appearance, Director, "Tales from the Crypt" (1990); Actor, "Kindergarten Cop" (1990); Actor, "Red Heat" (1988); Actor, "Twins" (1988); Actor, "Predator" (1987); Actor, "The Running Man" (1987); Actor, "Raw Deal" (1986); Actor, "Red Sonja" (1985); Actor, "Commando" (1985); Actor, "Conan the Destroyer" (1984); Actor, "The Terminator" (1984); Actor, "Conan the Barbarian" (1982); Co-Author, "Arnold's Bodybuilding for Men" (1981); Appearance, Documentary, "The Comeback" (1980); Actor, TV Film, "The Jayne Mansfield Story" (1980); Actor, "The Villain" (1979); Co-Author, "Arnold's Bodyshaping for Women" (1979); Cameo, "Scavenger Hunt" (1979); Appearance, Documentary, "Pumping Iron" (1977); Guest Appearance, "The Streets of San Francisco" (1977); Co-Author, "Arnold: The Education of a Bodybuilder" (1977); Author, "Arnold: Developing a Mr. Universe Physique" (1977); Guest Appearance, "The San Pedro Beach Bums" (1977); Actor, "Stay Hungry" (1976); Cameo, TV Film, "Happy Anniversary and Goodbye" (1974); Cameo, "The Long Goodbye" (1973); Actor, "Hercules in New York"

(1969); Voice Actor, Producer, "Superhero Kindergarten"; Voice Actor, Numerous Video Games; Appearances, Music Videos **AW:** Honorary Ring of the Federal State of Styria (2017); Commander of the French Legion of Honor (2017); Legend of the Century, GQ Men of the Year Awards (2017); International Lifetime Achievement Award, Goldene Kamera (2015); Inductee, WWE Hall of Fame (2015); Action Hero of Our Lifetime Award, Empire Awards (2014); Inductee, International Sports Hall of Fame (2012); Cavalier of the French Legion of Honor (2011); Medal for Humanity Merit, Austrian Albert Schweitzer Society (2011); Maverick Tribute Award, Cinequest Film Festival (2004); Taurus Honorary Award, Taurus World Stunt Awards (2001); World Artist Award, Blockbuster Entertainment Awards (1998); American Cinematheque Award, American Cinematheque Gala Tribute (1998); Best International Actor, Caméra d'Or (1997); Humanitarian Award, ShoWest Convention (1997); Male Star of the Year, Golden Apple Awards (1996); Film – International Award, Bambi Awards (1996); Special Award – International Star of the Decade, ShoWest Convention (1993); Grand Decoration of Honour for Services to the Republic of Austria in Gold (1993); Inductee, Hall of Fame, Nickelodeon Kids' Choice Awards (1992); Life Career Award, Saturn Awards (1992); Best Male Performance, MTV Movie Awards (1992); Favorite Movie Actor, Nickelodeon Kids' Choice Awards (1989, 1991); Star, Hollywood Walk of Fame (1987); Special Award – International Star of the Year, ShoWest Convention (1985); Mr. Olympia, Bodybuilding (1970-1975, 1980); Best Acting Debut in a Motion Picture – Male, Golden Globe Awards (1977); AAU Mr. World (1970); Professional Mr. Universe, Bodybuilding (1968-1970); World Amateur Bodybuilding Champion (1969); Winner, German Powerlifting Championships (1968); Amateur Mr. Universe, Bodybuilding (1967); Winner, International Powerlifting Championships (1966); Best Built Man of Europe (1966); Winner, German Austrian Weightlifting Championships (1965); Winner, Styrian Junior Weightlifting Championships (1964) **PA:** Republican

SCHWEIGHARDT, FRANK K., PHD, T: Chemist **I:** Education/Educational Services **DOB:** 05/12/1944 **PB:** Passaic **SC:** NJ/USA **PT:** Frank Schweighardt; Anne (Mester) Schweighardt **MS:** Married **SPN:** Yvonne **CH:** Brian; Jennine **ED:** Certificate, Management of Technology, Massachusetts Institute of Technology, Sloan School of Management (1990); PhD in Molecular Bio-Physics, Duquesne University (1970); BS in Chemistry, Seton Hall University (1966) **C:** Chief Executive Officer, Executive Director, Chairman, Da Vinci Science Center (2007-2014); Consultant, Process Analytical, AM International (2006-2014); Lead Chemist, Coal Liquefaction, United States Department of Energy, Bureau of Mines (1972-1979); National Research Council Fellow, Pittsburgh Energy Technology Center (1972-1973); Chemist, Drug Analysis, Allegheny County Morgue (1971-1972); Global Manager, Process Analytical, Air Products and Chemicals, Inc. (1970-2006); Assistant Dean, Graduate Research, Duquesne University School of Pharmacy (1970-1972); Lecturer, Speaker Bureau, Air Products and Chemists, Inc., Allentown, PA **CR:** Consultant in Field, Pittsburgh, PA (1975-1979); Consultant, Special Gas, Mexico, Throughout South America **CIV:** Chairman, Health Professional Committee (1990-Present); Board of Directors, Lehigh Valley March of Dimes, Allentown, PA (1987-Present); Board of Trustee Chairman, Da Vinci Science Center; Chief Executive Officer, Mentor, Allentown Schools **CW:** Patentee, 29 United States Patents; Contributor, 120 Published Articles, Three Books **AW:** United States Department Energy Grant

(1979-1982) **MEM:** Editor Journal, Pennsylvania Academy of Science (1987-Present); Pittsburgh Con Committee, Analytical Chemistry Society (1970-Present); Board of Directors, Fuel Division, Director of Advertising, American Chemical Society (1973-1984); American Association for the Advancement of Science; American Society for Testing and Materials; Spectroscopy Society; Chairman, International Foundation Process Analytical Chemistry **MH:** Albert Nelson Marquis Lifetime Achievement Award; Marquis Who's Who Top Professional **AS:** Dr. Schweighardt attributes his success to listening to others and understanding their needs. He always goes out of his way to get things done and this has helped contribute to his success. He enjoys mentoring middle school kids with their science fairs. **B/I:** After Dr. Schweighardt received his PhD at Duquesne University, he was asked to join the school of pharmacy and become the Assistant Dean of Research and had their very first PhD student. It all started during the Sputnik era. Dr. Schweighardt was in 7th grade and became very interested in rockets and science programs. He was the president of the Fair Lawn NJ rocket club in high school. **AV:** Fishing; Music; Gardening; Traveling **RE:** Roman Catholic **THT:** https://www.davincisciencecenter.org/; https://www.davincisciencecenter.org/public-service/wise-network/; https://www.davincisciencecenter.org/about/leadership/board-of-trustees/frank-k-schweighardt-ph-d/

SCHWEIKERT, DAVID S., T: U.S. Representative from Arizona; Real Estate Executive **I:** Government Administration/Government Relations/Government Services **DOB:** 03/03/1962 **PB:** Los Angeles **SC:** CA/USA **MS:** Married **SPN:** Joyce Schweikert (2006) **ED:** MBA, Arizona State University W.P. Carey School of Business (2005); BA in Finance and Real Estate, Arizona State University (1985) **C:** Member, U.S. House of Representatives from Arizona's Sixth Congressional District United States Congress, Washington, DC (2013-Present); United States Congress Joint Economic Committee (2013-Present); Member, U.S. House Committee on Space, Science and Technology (2013-Present); Member, U.S. House Small Business Committee (2013-Present); Member, U.S. House of Representatives from Arizona's Fifth Congressional District United States Congress, Washington, DC (2011-2013); Member, U.S. House Financial Services Committee (2011-2012); Treasurer, Maricopa County, AZ (2004-2007); Chief Deputy Treasurer, Maricopa County, AZ (2004); Majority Whip, Arizona House of Representatives (1993-1994); Member, District 28, Arizona House of Representatives (1991-1995); Real Estate Agent, Fountain Hills, AZ **CR:** Chair, Arizona State Board of Equalization (1995-2004) **PA:** Republican **RE:** Roman Catholic

SCHWERY, LUETTA, RN, BSN, T: Community Health Nurse **I:** Medicine & Health Care **DOB:** 11/23/1932 **PB:** Shelby County **SC:** IA/USA **PT:** Anthony J. Klein; Anna M. (Kloewer) Klein **MS:** Widowed **SPN:** Michael A. Schwery (01/26/1955, Deceased) **CH:** Mark; Laura; Neil; Diane; David; Denise; Lisa; Kathy; Karen; Paul **ED:** BS in Nursing, Clarkson College (1989); Coursework, Bellevue College (1986-1987); Coursework, Iowa Western Community College (1985); Diploma, Mercy Hospital School of Nursing, Council Bluffs, Iowa (1953) **CT:** Registered Nurse **C:** Retired (1997); Community Health Nurse, Shelby County Public Health Services (Myrtue Medical Center), Harlan, Iowa (1987-1997); CHI Health Mercy Council Bluffs, Iowa (1953); Community Health Nurse, Crawford County Home Health Agency, Denison, Iowa; Surgical Nurse, Myrtue Memorial Hospital (Myrtue Medical Center), Harlan, Iowa; Staff

Nurse, Little Flower Haven, Earling, Iowa **AW:** Mr. & Mrs. Frank Fredrick Lahr Scholar; Ambrose & Timothy Pfeifer Scholar; Thomas A. Magruder Junior Memorial Scholar; Bishop Clarkson Memorial Hospital Medical-Dental Staff Scholarship **MH:** Albert Nelson Marquis Lifetime Achievement Award; Marquis Who's Who Top Professional **B/I:** Mrs. Schwery was the first in her family to go to college. She wanted to be involved in peoples' lives and take care of them. In addition, when Mrs. Schwery became involved in her profession, it was not something that she chose, it was something that worked in her life situation. She thinks surgery was her first love in nursing; she worked in surgery for two years. All the years that she worked at the nursing home, she enjoyed her work there, the patients, and the people she worked with; it was close to home so she could be near her children. Then she always wanted to be in home health, so when the situation changed, she went into home health for about 10 years. She retired at the age of 65. **AV:** Quilting; Cards; Reading

SCOTT, BARBARA ANN, PHD, T: Sociology Professor, Peace Activist **I:** Education/Educational Services **DOB:** 01/03/1937 **PB:** New York **SC:** NY/USA **PT:** Richard W.; Lia (Varell) Scott **MS:** Divorced **SPN:** Josiah Bartlett Page (06/08/1958, Divorced 1975) **CH:** Evan Bartlett; Eric Scott **ED:** PhD in Sociology, The New School (1979); MA in Sociology, The New School (1972); BA, Pembroke College, Brown University, Magna Cum Laude (1958) **C:** Professor Emeritus, State University of New York, New Paltz (2002-Present); Associate Professor, State University of New York, New Paltz (1984-2002); Assistant Professor, State University of New York, New Paltz (1979-1984); Instructor of Sociology, State University of New York, New Paltz (1973-1979); Elementary Teacher, Poughkeepsie Day School (1968);Elementary Teacher, The Harley School (1958-1961) **CR:** Member, Advisory Board, Consultant Speaker, Flasco Cuba, University of Havana (1993); Visiting Scholar, Center for Defense Information (1986-1987); Co-Organizer, Co-Chairman, Intercollegiate Conference, Liberal Arts in a Time of Crisis (1981) **CIV:** Trustee, Shoreline Foundation for Folk Literature and Art (1983-Present); Delegate Conferences on Media in Wartime (1997); Delegate Conference on Women Refugees in a Time of War (1994); Delegate Conference on Women and Peace in Crete (1992); Expert Group, United Nations Division of Advancement of Women (1991); Delegate Conference on Media in a Time of Crisis, Sweden (1989); Founder, Coordinator, Mid-Hudson Chapter, Educators for Social Responsibility (1983-1987); Alumni Speaker, The New School (1977) **MIL:** Active Associate Member, Veterans for Peace (2005-Present) **CW:** Editor, "The Liberal Arts in a Time of Crisis" (1991); Author, "Crisis Management in American Higher Education" (1983); Contributor, Articles, Professional Journals **AW:** Research Grant, The Research Foundation for the State University of New York (1984, 1986-1987, 1989-1991, 1996, 2000); Research Grant, American Council of Learned Societies (1999); Second Prize, Quest for Peace Essay Contest, Citizen Education, Peace Project Inc. (1988) **MEM:** Speaker, Annual Meeting, Association for Humanist Sociology (2001); Delegate, 25th Annual Conference Netherlands, International Peace Research Association (1990); Member, Issue Focus Grant, AAUW (1988-1989); Peace & Justice Studies Association; International Advisory Board, Radio for Peace International; International Action Center; WILPF; American Sociological Association; War Resisters League; The Phi Beta Kappa Society **MH:** Albert Nelson Marquis Lifetime Achievement Award **B/I:** Ms. Scott became involved in her profession after being a housewife and mother for

many years; she wanted to stretch her capabilities. **AV:** Gardening; Reading magazines and books **PA:** Progressive populist socialist

SCOTT, DAVID ALBERT, T: U.S. Representative from Georgia; Advertising Company Executive **I:** Government Administration/Government Relations/Government Services **DOB:** 07/27/1945 **PB:** Aynor **SC:** SC/USA **PT:** Albert Scott; Mamie (Polite) Scott **MS:** Married **SPN:** Alfredia (Aaron) Scott (10/26/1969) **CH:** Dayna Dorienda; Marcye Michelle **ED:** MBA, The Wharton School, The University of Pennsylvania (1969); BA in Finance, Florida A&M University (1967) **C:** Member, U.S. House of Representatives from Georgia's 13th Congressional District, United States Congress, Washington, DC (2003-Present); Chairman, Rules Committee, Georgia Senate, Atlanta, GA (1994-2002); Member, Georgia Senate, Atlanta, GA (1983-2002); Chairman, Education Committee, Georgia Senate, Atlanta, GA (1993); Member, Georgia House of Representatives, Atlanta, GA (1975-1982); President, Owner, Dayn-Mark Advertising, Atlanta, GA; Member, Committee on Agriculture, United States Congress; Member, Committee on Financial Services, United States Congress **CR:** Chairman, Fulton County Senate Delegation, Atlanta, GA (1992-1994) **CIV:** Executive Board of Directors, The Wharton School, The University of Pennsylvania; Board of Directors, Georgia Chamber of Commerce **CW:** Creator, Producer, Director, Film, "Langston!"; Creator, Producer, Director, National Radio Program, "Inside Black America" **AW:** Listee, Power 150 (2008); Listee, Most Influential Black Americans, Ebony Magazine (2006); Telly Award (1994); Silver Microphone Award (1986, 1992, 1993, 1994); Four-Time Winner, Emmy Awards; Best Cultural Affairs Program Award, The National Academy of Television Arts & Sciences; Special Recognition, Congressional Black Caucus; Bronze Jubilee Award; Special Community Service Award, Mayor of Chicago; James Weldon Johnson Journalism Award, National Association for the Advancement of Colored People (NAACP); Special Citation, City of Highland Park, MI; Special Broadcasting Community Service Award, Detroit City Council; Special Tribute, Michigan House of Representatives **MEM:** National Association for the Advancement of Colored People (NAACP); Congressional Black Caucus; National Association of Black Elected Officials; Georgia Chamber of Commerce; America Georgia Business Council; Alpha Phi Alpha Fraternity, Inc. **AV:** Reading; Writing; Watching movies; Appreciating theater **PA:** Democrat **RE:** Baptist

SCOTT, JAMES, "AUSTIN" AUSTIN, T: U.S. Representative from Georgia; Insurance Company Executive **I:** Government Administration/Government Relations/Government Services **DOB:** 12/10/1969 **PB:** Augusta **SC:** GA/USA **PT:** Jim Scott, MD; Becky Scott **MS:** Married **SPN:** Vivien **CH:** Wells; Gabriela; John Philip **ED:** BBA in Risk Management and Insurance, University of Georgia, Athens, GA (1993) **CT:** RHU The American College of Financial Services (2000); Chartered Financial Consultant (ChFC), The American College of Financial Services (1995); Chartered Life Underwriter, The American College of Financial Services (1995); Completed, Series 7 Exam **C:** Member, U.S. House of Representatives from Georgia's Eighth Congressional District, U.S. Congress, Washington, DC (2011-Present); Member, U.S. House Armed Services Committee, Washington, DC (2011-Present); Member, U.S. House Committee on Agriculture, Washington, DC (2011-Present); Owner, Insurance Agent and Investment Salesman, The Southern Group, LLC (1998-Present); Member, District 153, Georgia State House of Representatives, GA (2004-2010); Member, District 138, Georgia State House of Representatives, GA (2003-2004); Member, District 165, Georgia State House of Representatives, GA (1997-2003); Senior Agent, The Principal Financial Group, Inc. (1993-1998); Agent, Life of South Agency (1992-1993) **CR:** Member, American Legislative Exchange Council (2004); Partner, Lockett Station Group, LLC **CIV:** Member, First Baptist Church, Tifton, GA **MEM:** Life Member, National Rifle Association of America; National Association of Insurance and Financial Advisors (NAIFA) **PA:** Republican **RE:** Baptist

SCOTT, JANE, T: Artist **I:** Fine Art **PB:** Philadelphia **SC:** PA/USA **PT:** Martin J. Wurster; Irella Jacobs **SPN:** Vernon Scott (Divorced 1990) **CH:** Vernon IV; Ashley **ED:** Bachelor's Degree, Harcum College **CR:** Hostess, "Hollywood Diary" **CW:** One-person Show, Gallery Vendome, Beverly Hills, CA (2002); One-person Show, Wentworth Gallery (1990-1995); Featured Works, "An America Jubilee: The Art of Jane Wooster Scott," Cross River Press (1994); Featured Artist, Petersen Galleries, Beverly Hills, CA (1980-1986); Featured Artist, Grand Central Art Galleries, NY (1977-1979); Featured Artist, De Ville Galleries, Beverly Hills, CA (1976-1978); Featured Artist, Ankrum Gallery, Beverly Hills, CA (1972-1975) **AW:** Distinguished Alumnae Award, Friends of Central School, PA (1987); Named One of LA's Most Influential Women, "Insider Exclusive"; Named Most Reproduced Artist in America, "Guinness Book of World Records" **MH:** Albert Nelson Marquis Lifetime Achievement Award **B/I:** Mrs. Scott came out to California when she was 18 and under contract with 20th Century Fox. Her girlfriend was moving into an Early American House in California, and mentioned that she needed a picture of Grandma Moses over the fireplace. Although Mrs. Scott never painted before, she thought it would be amusing as a gift. She painted a copy of Grandma Moses and called it Grandma Wooster. Mrs. Scott realized that she enjoyed painting and started painting her own creations.

SCOTT, LISA, T: Owner, Founder **I:** Law and Legal Services **CN:** Scott Global Migration Law Group **CH:** One Daughter **ED:** JD, School of Law, Case Western Reserve University (1986); BA in Psychology, Vassar College (1981) **C:** Adjunct Professor of Immigration Law, Case Western Reserve University School of Law (2017-Present); Lawyer, Owner, Founder, Scott Global Migration Law Group (1986-Present) **CR:** Montessori School Teacher **CIV:** Co-Regional Leader, Chicago Connects, National Association of Women Business Owners (2017-Present); Admissions Volunteer, Chicago Vassar Club, 1 Trainer/CEP Dean, Pathways for Permanent Residence, NAFSA (2016-Present); Volunteer, Various Community Organizations, Scott Immigration Law Group (1986-Present); Pro Bono Legal Representation, Barrington Hills Polo Club (2013-2014) **AW:** Recognized Practitioner, Chambers and Partners (2017); Who's Who Legal in Corporate Immigration (2016); Best of Conference, NAFSA (2016); Client's Choice Award, AVVO (2016); Top 20 Immigration Lawyers in Chicago, Expertise (2016); Bar Register of Preeminent Women Lawyers, Martindale-Hubbell (2011); AV-Rated, Martindale Hubbell (1999); Certified Women Owned Business **MEM:** NAFSA; International Bar Association; American Immigration Lawyers Association; Illinois State Bar Association **BAR:** Illinois State Bar Association **AS:** Ms. Scott attributes her success to her passion and her perseverance. **B/I:** Ms. Scott became involved in her profession because she started as a paralegal at an immigration law office after college and grew within the field.

SCOTT, PHILIP, "PHIL" BRIAN, T: Governor of Vermont **I:** Government Administration/Government Relations/Government Services **DOB:** 09/04/1958 **PB:** Barre City **SC:** VT/USA **MS:** Married **SPN:** Diana McTeague **CH:** Erica; Rachel **ED:** BS, University of Vermont (1980) **C:** Governor, State of Vermont (2017-Present); Lieutenant Governor, State of Vermont (2011-2017); Co-Owner, Dubois Construction, Inc., Middlesex, VT (1986-2016); Member, Washington District, Vermont State Senate, VT (2001-2011); Co-Owner, Shoney's Restaurant, Shoney's North America, LLC, Berlin, VT **CIV:** Founder, Wheels for Warmth (2004-Present); President, Associated General Contractors of America (AGC) (1997-1998) **AW:** Winner, Thunder Road Late Model Series Feature Race (2017); Thunder Road Champion (2002); Airborne Late Model Series Track Champion (2002); American Canadian Tour Champion (2002); Winner, Thunder Road Milk Bowl (1997, 1999); Thunder Road Late Model Series (LMS) Championship, (1996, 1998) **MEM:** Associated General Contractors of America (AGC) **AV:** Stock car racing **PA:** Republican

SCOTT, RICHARD, "RICK" LYNN, T: U.S. Senator from Florida; Healthcare Executive **I:** Government Administration/Government Relations/Government Services **DOB:** 12/01/1952 **PB:** Bloomington **SC:** IL/USA **PT:** Orba Scott; Esther Scott **MS:** Married **SPN:** Frances Annette Holland (04/20/1972) **CH:** Allison; Jordan **ED:** JD, Southern Methodist University Dedman School of Law (1978); BBA, University of Missouri (1975) **C:** U.S. Senator, State of Florida (2019-Present); Governor, State of Florida (2011-2019); Founder, Conservatives for Patients' Rights (CPR) (2009-2019); Co-founder, Chairman, Solantic Corp., Jacksonville, FL (2001-2011); President, Chief Executive Officer, Richard L. Scott Investments, LLC (Now G. Scott Capital Partners, LLC), Naples, FL (1997-2001); Chairman, Chief Executive Officer, Columbia/HCA Healthcare Corp., Nashville, TN (1987-1997) **CR:** Board of Directors, Secure Computing Corporation (2006-2008); Board of Directors, Solantic Corp. (2001-2011); Board of Directors, CyberGuard (2001-2003) **CIV:** Member, National Board, United Way (1997-2003) **MIL:** With, United States Navy (1971-1974) **AW:** Entrepreneurship Award, The George Washington University (2007); Named One of America's 25 Most Influential People, TIME Magazine (1996); Named CEO of the Year, Financial World Magazine (1995); Named One of the Top 25 Performers, U.S. News & World Report L.P. (1995); Second Century Award for Excellence in Health Care, Columbia University School of Nursing (1995) **MEM:** The Business Council; Business Roundtable; Healthcare Leadership Council **BAR:** State of Texas **PA:** Republican **RE:** Christian

SCOTT, ROBERT, "BOBBY" CORTEZ, T: U.S. Representative, Lawyer **I:** Government Administration/Government Relations/Government Services **DOB:** 04/30/1947 **PB:** Washington, DC **SC:** USA **PT:** Charles Waldo Scott, MD; Mae Hamlin-Scott **ED:** Honorary DHL, Virginia Commonwealth University (2008); Honorary LLD, Commonwealth College (Now Virginia Commonwealth University), Hampton, VA (1988); JD, Boston College Law School (1973); BA in Government, Harvard University, Cambridge, MA (1969) **C:** U.S. Representative, Virginia's Third Congressional District, United States Congress, Washington, DC (1993-Present); Chairman, Education and Labor Committee, U.S. House of Representatives (1993-Present); Member, Virginia State Senate (1983-1993); Lawyer, Private Practice, Newport News, VA (1973-1991); Member, Virginia House of Delegates (1978-1983) **CIV:** Chairman, First District, Virginia Democratic Party (1980-1985); President, Board of Directors,

Peninsula Legal Aid Center, Hampton, VA (1977-1981); Member, Advisory Committee, Peninsula Boy Scouts of America; Board President, NAACP, Newport News, VA; Board of Directors, Hampton Roads March of Dimes **MIL:** U.S. Army Reserve (1974-1976); Massachusetts National Guard (1970-1973) **AW:** One of 100 Most Influential Black Americans, Ebony Magazine (2006); Outstanding Legislator, Southern Health Association (1989); Distinguished Service Award, State Fraternal Order of Police, Commonwealth of Virginia (1987); Child Advocate Award, Virginia Chapter, American Academy of Pediatrics (1987); Brotherhood Citation Award, National Conference for Christians and Jews (1985) **MEM:** Virginia Peninsula Chamber of Commerce; Sigma Pi Phi; Alpha Phi Alpha **PA:** Democrat **RE:** Episcopalian

SCOTT, TIMOTHY, "TIM" EUGENE, T: Junior U.S. Senator from South Carolina; Insurance Company Executive **I:** Government Administration/Government Relations/Government Services **DOB:** 09/19/1965 **PB:** Charleston **SC:** SC/USA **PT:** Ben Scott Sr.; Frances Scott **ED:** BS in Political Science, Charleston Southern University (1988); Coursework, Presbyterian College (1983-1984) **C:** Junior U.S. Senator, State of South Carolina (2013-Present); Member, U.S. Senate Special Committee on Aging (2013-Present); Member, U.S. Senate Committee on Small Business and Entrepreneurship (2013-Present); Member, U.S. Senate Health, Committee on Education, Labor & Pensions (2013-Present); Member, U.S. Senate Committee on Energy and Natural Resources (2013-Present); Member, U.S. Senate Committee on Commerce, Science and Transportation (2013-Present); Member, U.S. House Rules Committee, Washington, DC (2011-2013); Member, U.S. House of Representatives from South Carolina's First Congressional District, United States Congress, Washington, DC (2011-2013); Member, District 117, South Carolina House of Representatives (2009-2011); Chairman, Charleston County Council (2007-2008); Councilman, Charleston County Council (1995-2008); Partner, Pathway Real Estate Group, LLC, Charleston, SC; Owner, Tim Scott Allstate, Charleston, SC **CR:** Co-chairman, Financial Services Committee, Allstate National Advisory Board (2004-2008) **CIV:** Member, Seacoast Church, Charleston, SC **AW:** Named One of the 50 Politicos to Watch, Politico (2010); South Carolina Agency Owner of the Year Award **PA:** Republican **RE:** Evangelical Christian

SCOULAR, ROBERT F., T: Lawyer **I:** Law and Legal Services **DOB:** 07/09/1942 **PB:** Del Norte **SC:** CO/USA **PT:** Duane William Scoular; Marie Josephing (Moloney) Scoular **MS:** Married **SPN:** Donna V. Scoular (06/03/1967) **CH:** Bryan T; Sean D; Bradley R **ED:** JD, St. Louis University (1968); BS in Aeronautical Engineering, St. Louis University (1964) **C:** Partner, Dentons (Formerly SNR Denton, Sonnenschein Nath, Rosenthal), Los Angeles, CA (1990-Present); Managing Partner, Sonnenschein, Nath, & Rosenthal LLP, Los Angeles, CA (1990-2005); Section Leader Technician, Computer and Intellectual Property Law, Bryan, Cave, McPheeters & McRoberts, Los Angeles, CA (1985-1989); Executive Committee, Bryan, Cave, McPheeters & McRoberts, Los Angeles, CA (1984-1985); Managing Partner, Bryan, Cave, McPheeters & McRoberts, Los Angeles, CA (1979-1985); Partner, Bryan, Cave, McPheeters & McRoberts, St. Louis, MO (1969-1989); Law Clerk, Chief Judge, United States Court of Appeals for the Eighth Circuit (1968-1969) **CR:** Chairman, Public Counsel, Missouri Lawyers Credit Union (2012-2013); Co-leader, Intellectual Property Practice (1990-1998); Director, Missouri Lawyers Credit Union

(1978-1979) **CIV:** Board of Directors, St. Louis Bar Foundation (2004-Present); Executive Committee, St. Louis Bar Foundation (2004-Present); Public Counsel, St. Louis Bar Foundation (2004-Present); Honorary Dean, Dubourg Society, Dean's Council, School of Law, St. Louis University (2000-Present); Board of Directors, St. Louis Bar Foundation (1979, 1975-1976); League Commissioner, American Youth Soccer Organization; Board of Directors, Boy Scouts of America Greater Los Angeles Area Council; General Counsel, Boy Scouts of America Greater Los Angeles Area Council; President, Boy Scouts of America Greater Los Angeles Area Council; Chairman, Boy Scouts of America Greater Los Angeles Area Council **CW:** Contributor, Articles, Professional Journals **AW:** National Distinguished Eagle Scout Award; Distinguished Service Award **MEM:** Board of Directors; Association of Business Trial Lawyers (2004-2008); Alumni Council, St. Louis University (1979-1982); National Director, American Bar Association, Young Lawyers Division (1977-1978); Chairman, Federal Bar Association, Young Lawyers Section (1976-1977); Chairman, Missouri Bar Association, Young Lawyers Section (1976-1977); Chairman, Bar Association of Metropolitan St. Louis, Young Lawyers Section (1975-1976); California Club; Chancery Club; Ferrari Club of California; California Bar Association; Los Angeles County Bar Association **BAR:** California (1979); Supreme Court of the United States (1972); North Dakota (1968); Colorado (1968); Missouri (1968) **MH:** Albert Nelson Marquis Lifetime Achievement Award; Marquis Who's Who Top Professional **B/I:** Mr. Scoular initially went to engineering school, but eventually gained interest in law classes and added them to his curriculum. **AV:** Driving a Ferrari

SCREMIN, ANTHONY JAMES, T: Lawyer, Head Trial Attorney **I:** Law and Legal Services **CN:** Scremin Law **DOB:** 06/21/1941 **PB:** Miami **SC:** FL/USA **PT:** Anthony Scremin; Rose Marie (Zullo) Scremin **MS:** Married **SPN:** Iliana Rodriguez Scremin; Barbara Jean Thompson (10/22/1960, Divorced 07/1977) **CH:** Anthony J. Scremin III; Julie Beth; Ann Marie; Sylvia Ann **ED:** JD, University of Miami (1968); BBA, University of Miami (1966) **C:** Principal, Lawyer, Head Trial Attorney, Anthony J. Scremin P.A., Miami, FL (1978-Present); Partner, Trial Attorney, Abramson, Scremin et al, Miami, FL (1971-1978); Head Trial Attorney, Metro Transit Authority, Miami, FL (1970-1971); Associate, Trial Assistant, Welch & Carroll, Miami, FL (1969-1970); Associate, Trial Assistant, Steven, Demos, et al, Miami, FL (1969-1970); Associate, Hawkesworth & Kay, Miami, FL (1968-1969) **MIL:** Coast Guard (1959-1960) **AW:** Certificate of Merit, Bar and Gavel Legal Society, University of Miami (1968); Outstanding Service Award, Labor Law Society, University of Miami (1968) **MEM:** American Arbitration Association; Academy of Trial Lawyers of America; New York State Trial Lawyers Association; Florida Bar Association; Association of Florida Trial Lawyers; National Association of Criminal Defense Lawyers; National Italian-American Bar Association; Phi Delta Phi **BAR:** United States Court of Appeals for the Eleventh Circuit (1987); United States Court of Appeals for the Ninth Circuit (1986); United States Court of Appeals for the Third Circuit (1985); United States District Court for the Southern District of Florida (1969); Florida (1968) **MH:** Albert Nelson Marquis Lifetime Achievement Award; Marquis Who's Who Top Professional **B/I:** Mr. Scremin became involved in his profession because of his upbringing and family history. His dad Anthony Scremin told him to get a college education and law would be good. His son

Anthony J. Scremin III is also a lawyer. **AV:** Karate; Weight-lifting; Construction **PA:** Republican **RE:** Roman Catholic

SCROGGS, LARRY K., T: Lawyer, State Legislator **I:** Law and Legal Services **DOB:** 10/08/1941 **PB:** Beebe **SC:** AR/USA **PT:** Kenneth Chalmers; Mildred Lorene (McDonald) S **MS:** Married **SPN:** Mary Patricia Rushing (08/25/1967) **CH:** Larry Kenneth Junior; James Kevin; Michael Kyle **ED:** Doctor of Jurisprudence, Vanderbilt University (1971); Bachelor of Arts, Harding University (1963) **C:** Senior Counsel, Tennessee Treasury Department (2016-Present); Chief Administrative Officer, Chief Counsel, Juvenile Court of Memphis and Shelby County (2006-2016); Partner, Burch, Porter & Johnson, Memphis, TN (2003-2006); Partner, Scroggs & Rogers, Collierville, TN (1997-2003); Private Practice, Germantown, TN (1992-1996); Partner, Less & Scroggs, Memphis, TN (1980-1992); Partner, Holt, Batchelor, Spicer, Memphis, TN (1976-1980); Associate, Holt, Batchelor, Spicer, Memphis, TN (1972-1976); Associate, Law Firm of Leo Bearman, Memphis, TN (1971-1972) **CR:** Attorney for County Trustee, Shelby County, Memphis, TN (1990-2006); Municipal Court Judge, City of Germantown, TN (1980-1986) **CIV:** Tennessee House Representatives, Nashville, TN (1996-2002) **MIL:** Lieutenant, United States Navy (1964-1967) **CW:** Contributor, Six Columns in The Commercial Appeals, Memphis, TN (2003-2016) **AW:** Legislator of the Year, Tennessee District Attorneys General Conference (1999); Fellow, Memphis Bar Foundation **MEM:** Board of Directors, Memphis Bar Association (1990-1991); Tennessee Bar Association **BAR:** Tennessee (1971) **MH:** Albert Nelson Marquis Lifetime Achievement Award; Marquis Who's Who Top Professional **AS:** Mr. Scroggs attributes much of his success to the influence of his father, as well as his three uncles, whose military service inspired him. Likewise, his mother had a tremendous work ethic, and encouraged him to become more well-read. **B/I:** Mr. Scroggs first became involved in legal service due to his early career in journalism and social science, as well as his tour of duty in Vietnam. During his service overseas, he met several people who were interested in the law, and he became convinced of the positive impact he could have on others through such a profession. **AV:** Photography; Boating; Golf; Family time; Coaching **PA:** Republican **RE:** Church of Christ

SCUDDER, THAYER, T: Anthropologist **I:** Sciences **DOB:** 08/04/1930 **PB:** New Haven **SC:** CT/USA **PT:** Townsend Scudder III; Virginia (Boody) Scudder **MS:** Married **SPN:** Mary Eliza Drinker (08/26/1950) **CH:** Mary Eliza; Alice Thayer **ED:** Postgraduate Studies, London School of Economics (1960-1961); Postgraduate Studies, Yale University (1953-1954); PhD, Harvard University (1960); AB, Harvard University (1952); Graduate, Phillips Exeter Academy (1948) **C:** Professor Emeritus, California Institute of Technology, Pasadena, CA (2000-Present); Commissioner, World Commission on Dams (1998-2000); Director, Institute for Development Anthropology, Binghamton, NY (1976-2002); Professor, Anthropology, California Institute of Technology, Pasadena, CA (1969-2000);Associate Professor, California Institute of Technology, Pasadena, CA (1966-1969); Assistant Professor, California Institute of Technology, Pasadena, CA (1964-1966);Research Fellow, Center for Middle Eastern Studies, Harvard University (1963-1964); Assistant Professor, American University in Cairo (1961-1962); Senior Research Officer, Rhodes-Livingstone Institute (1962-1963); Research Officer, Rhodes-Livingstone Institute (1956-1957) **CR:** Consultant, United Nations Devel-

opment Programme; Consultant, Food and Agriculture Organization; Consultant, International Bank for Reconstruction and Development; Consultant, World Health Organization; Consultant, Ford Foundation; Consultant, Navajo Tribal Council; Consultant, Agency for International Development; Consultant, World Conservation Union; Consultant, Lesotho Highlands Development Authority; Consultant, South China Electric Power Joint Venture Corporation; Consultant, U.S. National Research Council; Consultant, Hydro-Québec; Consultant, Environmental Defense Fund; Consultant, Ministry of Energy & Mines; Consultant, Lao People's Democratic Republic, Nature Conservancy; Visiting Scholar **CW:** Author, "A Retrospective Analysis of Lao's Nam Theun Dam, International Journal of Water Resources Development" (2019); Author, "Aswan Resettlement of Egyptian Nubbins" (2016); Author, "Global Threats, Global Futures Living With Declining Living Standards" (2010); Author, "The Future of Large Dams: Dealing with Social, Environmental, Institutional and Political Costs" (2005); Co-Author, "The IUCN Review of the Southern Okavango Integrated Water Development Project"(1993); Author, "For Prayer and Profit: The Ritual, Economic and Social Importance of Beer in Gwembe District, Zambia" (1950-1982, 1988); Co-Author, "No Place to Go: The Impacts of Forced Relocation on Navajos" (1982); Author, "Secondary Education and the Formation of an Elite: The Impact of Education on Gwembe District, Zambia" (1980); Co-Author, "Long-Term Field Research in Social Anthropology" (1979); Author, "The Ecology of the Gwembe Tonga" (1962) **AW:** John Phillips Award, Phillips Exeter Academy (2005); Bronislaw Malinowski Award, Society for Applied Anthropology (1999); (1ˢᵗ) Lucy Mair Medal for Applied Anthropology, Royal Anthropological Institute (1998); Edward J. Lehman Award, American Anthropological Association (1991); Solon T. Kimball Award for Published and Applied Anthropology, American Anthropological Association (1984); Fellow, John Simon Guggenheim Memorial Foundation (1975) **MEM:** Phi Beta Kappa (2011-2013); American Anthropological Association; Society for Applied Anthropology **B/I:** Dr. Scudder became involved in his profession because coincidences have played a major role in his life; he initially wanted to be a mountaineer. He was hired by the Arctic Institute of North America to be the mountaineer in charge of a group of scientists who were doing glaciological work on the boarder of Alaska and the Yukon. Just as he and his family were leaving to be based in Montreal, his boss, Colonel Waldre Wood, had decided to end that particular project so he had no job. The project ended because the Colonel's wife and daughter were on the glacier with him and when his wife wanted to come back to New York unfortunately, their plane has never been recovered to this day. His wife encouraged him to go to graduate school to obtain his PHD, which he did. When he was a graduate student at Harvard, he was invited by an anthropologist at Berkley, Elizabeth Colson, who was the leading anthropologist at the time. She had been asked by the research institute in Zambi to do a study of the Cariba Dam and needed a colleague. She asked him to join her as a junior colleague.

SCULLY, VINCENT EDWARD, T: Sports Broadcaster **I:** Media & Entertainment **DOB:** 11/29/1927 **PB:** Bronx **SC:** NY/USA **PT:** Vincent Aloysius Scully; Bridget (Freehill) Scully **MS:** Married **SPN:** Sandra Hunt (11/11/1973) **CH:** Michael; Kevin; Todd; Erin; Kelly; Catherine Anne **ED:** Honorary Doctorate Degree, Pepperdine University, Malibu, CA (2008); DHL (Honorary), Fordham University (2000); BA in English, Fordham University,

Bronx, NY (1949) **C:** Sports Announcer, NBC-TV (1982-1989); Sports Announcer, CBS-TV (1975-1982); Sports Announcer, Los Angeles Dodgers (1958-2016); Sports Announcer, Brooklyn Dodgers (1950-1957); Founder, WFUV, Fordham University **CR:** Co-Host, Tournament of Roses Parade, ABC (1967) **CIV:** U.S. Navy (1944-1945) **CW:** Himself, "For Love of the Game" (1999); Host, "Challenge of the Sexes," CBS (1977); Host, "The Vin Scully Show" (1973); Host, "It Takes Two," NBC (1969-1970); Announcer, "Occasional Wife" (1966-1967); Narrator, "Fireball 500" (1966); Himself, "Bachelor in Paradise" (1961); Actor, "Wake Me When It's Over" (1960); Featured, Numerous Films and TV Series; Announcer, Numerous "MLB" Video Games, Sony PlayStation **AW:** Icon Award, ESPY Awards (2017); Inductee, Shrine of the Eternals, The Baseball Reliquary (2017); National Sportscaster of the Year, National Sports Media Association (1965, 1978, 1982, 2016); Presidential Medal of Freedom (2016); Friends of the Family Award, Boone Center for the Family, Pepperdine University (2016); Commissioner's Historic Achievement Award (2014); Named, Grand Marshal, Rose Parade (2014); Ambassador Award of Excellence, LA Sports & Entertainment Commission (2009); Top Sportscaster of all Time, Top 50 List, American Sportscasters Association (2009); Inductee, NAB Broadcasting Hall of Fame (2009); Vin Scully Lifetime Achievement Award, WFUV (2008); Inductee, California Sports Hall of Fame (2008); Sportscaster of the Century, American Sportscasters Association (2000); Inductee, National Radio Hall of Fame (1995); Lifetime Achievement Emmy Award (1995); Inductee, American Sportscasters Association Hall of Fame (1992); Inductee, National Sports Media Association Hall of Fame (1991); Ford Frick Award, National Baseball Hall of Fame (1982); 33-Time California Sportscaster of the Year, National Sports Media Association; Honoree, Star, Hollywood Walk of Fame; Numerous Other Awards and Accolades **MEM:** American Federation of Television and Radio Artists (AFTRA); Screen Actors Guild; Academy of Television Arts & Sciences; Catholic Actors' Guild of America; The Lambs Club; Bel-Air Country Club **RE:** Roman Catholic

SEACREST, RYAN JOHN, T: Television and Radio Personality, Entrepreneur **I:** Media & Entertainment **DOB:** 12/24/1974 **PB:** Atlanta **SC:** GA/USA **PT:** Gary Lee Seacrest; Constance Marie (Zullinger) Seacrest **MS:** Single **ED:** Honorary LHD, University of Georgia (2016); Coursework in Journalism, University of Georgia (1992-1993); Diploma, Dunwoody High School (1992) **C:** Host, Executive Producer, On-Air with Ryan Seacrest (2004, 2008-Present); Co-Host, DJ, 102.7 KIIS-FM Los Angeles (2004-Present); Host, American Top 40 (2004-Present); DJ, 98.7 FM (1995-2003); On-Air Personality, KYSR, WSTR **CR:** Partner, "Polished," Harold Lancer (2017); Launched, Fashion Line, R Line (2005); Part Owner, Katana, Sushi Roku, Boa **CIV:** Founder, Ryan Seacrest Foundation (2010-Present); Board of Trustees, Los Angeles County Museum of Art; Honorary Co-Chair, Grammy Foundation Board (Now Grammy Museum Foundation) **CW:** Co-Host, Executive Producer, "Live With Kelly and Ryan" (2017-Present); Producer, "Bank of Hollywood" (2009-Present); Executive Producer, "E! Live from the Red Carpet" (2006-Present); Host, "Walt Disney World Christmas Day Parade" (2005-Present); Executive Producer, Host, "Dick Clark's New Year's Rockin' Eve" (2005-Present); Co-Host, Host, "American Idol" (2002-Present); Appearance, "The Real Housewives of Beverly Hills" (2018); Executive Producer, "Insatiable" (2018); Executive Producer, "Life of Kylie" (2017); Executive Producer, "Shades of Blue" (2016-2017); Executive Producer, Creator, "Keeping Up With the Kardashians" (2007-

2017); Executive Producer, "Sugar & Sparks" (2016); Executive Producer, "Rob & Chyna" (2016); Executive Producer, Host, "Knock Knock Live" (2015); Co-Host, "E! News" (2006-2015); Executive Producer, "Preaching Alabama" (2014); Executive Producer, Host, "Fashion Rocks" (2014); Executive Producer, "Webheads" (2014); Creator, Producer, "I Wanna Marry 'Harry'" (2014); Executive Producer, "Mixology" (2014); Executive Producer, "Montecito" (2014); Executive Producer, "How I Rock It" (2013); Executive Producer, Host, "The Million Second Quiz" (2013); Executive Producer, Host, TV Documentary, "Ryan Seacrest with Selena Gomez" (2013); Executive Producer, "The Wanted Life" (2013); Executive Producer, "Kourtney and Kim Take Miami" (2009-2013); Executive Producer, "Married to Jonas" (2012); Executive Producer, "Melissa & Tye" (2012); Executive Producer, "Shahs of Sunset" (2012); Executive Producer, "I Kid with Brad Garrett" (2011); Executive Producer, "Host, Dick Clark's New Year's Rockin' Eve (2011); Executive Producer, "Khloe & Lamar" (2011); Executive Producer, "The Dance Scene" (2011); Executive Producer, "Kourtney and Kim Take New York" (2011); Executive Producer, "Jamie Oliver's Food Revolution" (2010-2011); Voice Actor, "Shrek Forever After" (2010); Guest Appearance, "The Simpsons" (2010); Executive Producer, "Bank of Hollywood" (2009-2010); Guest Host, "Larry King Live" (2003-2010); Host, Academy Awards (2009); Executive Producer, Creator, "Denise Richards: It's Complicated" (2008-2009); Executive Producer, Creator, "Bromance" (2008-2009); Executive Producer, Creator, "Momma's Boys" (2008-2009); Executive Producer, TV Film, "Victoria's Secret: What is Sexy?" (2008); Cameo, "Get Smart" (2008); Co-Host, 60th Primetime Emmy Awards (2008); Host, Pregame and Halftime Shows, Super Bowl XLII (2008); Host, "American Idol Rewind" (2007-2008); Executive Producer, "Crash My School" (2007); Cameo, "Knocked Up" (2007); Executive Producer, "Paradise City" (2007); Host, 59th Primetime Emmy Awards (2007); Guest Appearance, "Punk'd" (2005); Guest Appearance, "Mind of Mencia" (2005); Guest Appearance, "Robot Chicken" (2005); Executive Producer, "On-Air with Ryan Seacrest" (2004); Executive Producer, "New Year's Eve Live from Times Square with Ryan Seacrest" (2004); Guest Host, "Good Day Live" (2003); Host, "America's Party: Live from Las Vegas" (2003); Host, "American Juniors" (2003); Co-Host, Radio Music Awards (2003); Host, "Ultimate Revenge" (2002); Host, "Disneyland 2000: 45 Years of Magic" (2000); Guest Host, "Beverly Hills, 90210" (2000); Host, "The NBC Saturday Night Movie" (2000); Guest Appearance, "Hey Arnold!" (1999); Host, "Click" (1997); Co-Host, "CNET Central" (1996); Host, "The New Edge" (1996); Actor, "Reality Check" (1995); Host, "Wild Animal Games" (1995); Co-Host, "Gladiators 2000" (1995) **AW:** Co-Recipient, Daytime Emmy Award for Outstanding Entertainment Talk Show Host (2019); Listee, 40 Under 40, Fortune Magazine (2011); Marconi Radio Award for Personality of the Year, National Association of Broadcasters (2008, 2011); Choice TV: Personality, Teen Choice Awards (2010); Listee, 100 Most Powerful Celebrities, Forbes.com (2007-2008); Teen Choice Award for Choice Hissy Fit (2007); Maverick, Details Magazine (2007); Star, Hollywood Walk of Fame (2005); Listee, 50 Most Beautiful People, People Magazine (2003)

SEAGLE, EDGAR FRANKLIN, DR. P.H., P.E., T: Environmental Engineer, Consultant **I:** Engineering **DOB:** 06/27/1924 **PB:** Lincolnton **SC:** NC/USA **PT:** Franklin Craig Seagle; Lillie Mae (James) Seagle **MS:** Married **SPN:** Doris Elaine Long (03/23/1958) **CH:** Rebecca Jan; Mary Elaine; James Craig; William Franklin **ED:** DrPH, University of Texas (1974);

BCE, University of Florida (1961); MS in Public Health, University of North Carolina (1954); BA in Chemistry, University of North Carolina (1949) **CT:** Registered Professional Engineer, Alabama **C:** Independent Engineering Consultant, Rockville, MD (1988-2005, 1984-1985); Public Health Engineer, Maryland Department of the Environment, Baltimore, MD (1985-1988); Assistant Director, Fellowship Office, National Academy Sciences, Washington, DC (1978-1983); Engineer Director, U.S. Public Health Service (USPHS), Rockville, MD (1961-1978); Chief, Industrial Hygiene Section, Health Department, Charlotte, NC (1956-1959); Sanitation Consultant, North Carolina State Board of Health (1954-1956); Senior Sanitarian, Health Department, City of Charlotte, NC (1950-1952) **CR:** Engineer, Atomic Energy Commission, Nuclear Test Site, Nevada **MIL:** U.S. Navy, World War II (1943-1946, Honorably Discharged) **CW:** Contributor, Numerous Articles, Professional Publications in the Field **AW:** Commendation Medal, U.S. Public Health Service (USPHS) (1968) **MEM:** American Society of Civil Engineers; American Public Health Association; Diplomate, American Academy of Environmental Engineers and Scientists (AAEES) **MH:** Albert Nelson Marquis Lifetime Achievement Award; Marquis Who's Who Top Professional **B/I:** Mr. Seagle became involved in his profession because when he returned from the service he went back to college and finished his first degree. He worked for general motors and retail credit company although his degree was in chemistry but the jobs were available there. He then worked for the Charlotte City Health Department and was so impressed by the health officer and the way he managed things. It impressed him enough to stay in the public health area. **AV:** Former big band drummer in the 1940s **PA:** Democratic **RE:** Methodist

SEAGO, JAMES L., T: Biologist, Educator **I:** Education/Educational Services **DOB:** 06/02/1941 **PB:** Alton **SC:** Illinois **PT:** James Lynn Seago; Dorothy Florence (Watkins) Seago **MS:** Married **SPN:** Marilyn Ann Meiss (11/25/1982); Jill Penton Dabbs (12/24/1969, Divorced 1977) **CH:** Kirstjan Erika; Robert Maclean **ED:** Doctor of Philosophy, University of Illinois (1969); Master of Arts, Miami University, Oxford, OH (1966); Bachelor of Arts, Knox College (1963) **C:** Professor Emeritus of Biology, State University of New York, Oswego, NY (1991-2014); Assistant Professor to Associate Professor, State University of New York, Oswego, NY (1968-1991) **CR:** Consultant, Various Published Books (1978-Present); Consultant, Various Botanical Journals **CW:** Editorial Board, Environmental and Experimental Botany (1992-2007); Reviewer, American Journal of Botany; Reviewer, Canadian Journal of Botany; Reviewer, International Journal of Plant Science; Reviewer, Bulletin Torrey Botanist Club; Contributor, Articles to American Biology Teacher, American Journal of Botany, Canadian Journal of Botany, Annals of Botany and the Flora Journal of Botany **AW:** President's Award for Scholarly and Creative Activity, State University of New York at Oswego (2010); Centennial Award, Botanist Society of America (2006); Distinguished Fellow, Botanical Society of America (2004); Grantee, National Science Foundation (1981, 1992) **MEM:** Botanist Society of America; Torrey Botanist Club; Nature Conservancy; Society for Economic Botany **MH:** Albert Nelson Marquis Lifetime Achievement Award **B/I:** Dr. Seago first became involved in his profession while studying pre-medicine in college. After deciding against following his career aspirations along that path, he decided to conduct extensive independent research on the subject of plant life.

SEALE, JAMES LAWRENCE JR., PHD, T: Agricultural Studies Educator **I:** Education/Educational Services **CN:** University of Florida **DOB:** 04/12/1949 **PB:** Memphis **SC:** TN/USA **PT:** James Lawrence Seale; Mary Helen (Keefe) Seale **MS:** Married **SPN:** Zoe Haynes Seale **ED:** PhD, Michigan State University (1985); Postgraduate Coursework, University of Chicago (1978-1979); BA, University of Mississippi (1972) **C:** Professor of Agricultural Economics, University of Florida, Gainesville, FL (1995-Present); Associate Professor of Agricultural Economics, University of Florida, Gainesville, FL (1990-1995); Assistant Professor of Agricultural Economics, University of Florida, Gainesville, FL (1985-1990); Specialist, Michigan State University, Fayoum, Arab Republic of Egypt (1980-1983); Agricultural Advisor, Harvard Institute for International Development, Abyei, Sudan (1978); Agricultural Volunteer, Peace Corps, Tondo, Zaire (1973-1975) **CR:** Honorary Visiting Professor, University of Leicester, England (1995); Honorary Fellow, University of Leicester (1995); Visiting Professor, University of Leicester, England (1992, 1994); Senior Research Fellow, McKethan-Matherly (1991-1994); Research Fellow, McKethan-Matherly (1986-1988); Research Fellow, Cairo University (1980-1983) **CIV:** Volunteer, Agricultural Business Services, Wenrock International, Russia (1998); Volunteer, Farmer to Farmer, Wenrock International (1994); Volunteer, Farmer to Farmer, UOCA, Namibia (1994) **CW:** Editor, Special Edition, Journal of Agricultural and Applied Economics (2002-2003); Editor, Journal of Agricultural and Applied Economics (1998-2001); Co-Author, "Advances in Econometrics, a Research Annual: International Evidence on Consumption Patterns," Jai Press (1989); Contributor, Articles, Professional Journals **AW:** Honoree, Research of the Year, University of Florida (2006-2007); Traveling Scholar, University of Michigan (1979); Scholar, National Institute of Mental Health, University of Chicago (1978-1979) **MEM:** American Economic Association; Agricultural & Applied Economics Association; International Association of Agricultural Economists; International Agricultural Trade Research Consortium; Gamma Sigma Delta **MH:** Albert Nelson Marquis Lifetime Achievement Award **B/I:** Dr. Seale was inspired by his experience as an agricultural volunteer for the Peace Corps in Tondo, Zaire, between 1973 and 1975. **AV:** Scuba diving; Karate **RE:** Episcopalian **THT:** Dr. Seale dedicates this award to Henri Theil, his mentor.

SEARLE, ROBERT FERGUSON, BS, MDIV, DMIN, MA, T: Minister **I:** Religious **DOB:** 07/13/1951 **PB:** Auburn **SC:** NY/US **PT:** Loren Rawson Searle; Esther Lucille (Ferguson) Searle **MS:** Married **SPN:** Elizabeth Jane Anderson (1981) **CH:** Joshua Michael Anderson; Nathanael Jeremiah Ferguson **ED:** MA, St. John's College (2005); Doctor of Ministry, Asbury Theological Seminary (1997); MDiv, Princeton Theological Seminary (1977); BS, Cornell University (1973) **CT:** Board Certified Chaplain, NAVAC (2004); Certified in Pastoral Care (1981); Ordained Elder, United Methodist Church (1980); Ordained Deacon, United Methodist Church (1978); Board Certified Chaplain, Association of Professional Chaplains **C:** Chaplain, 98th Training Division, IET (2007-Present); Pastor, Red Creek Westbury United Methodist Church (2004-Present); Pastor, Sterling United Methodist Church (2004-Present); Contract Chaplain, Canandaigua VA Medical Center (2000-Present); Contract Chaplain, Syracuse VA Medical Center (2000-Present); Adjunct Professor, Spiritual Formation, Northeastern Seminary, Rochester, NY (2000-Present); Chaplain, United States Army Reserve (1991-Present); Mobilized as Chaplain, Operation Enduring Freedom (2003); Pastor, Clyde United Methodist Church (1999-2003); Chaplain Resident, Duke University Medical Center (1998-1999); Pastor, Pennsylvania Avenue United Methodist Church, Pine City, NY (1984-1998); Pastor of Blodgett Mills United Methodist Church, NY (1978-1984); Pastor of Freetown Methodist Church, NY (1978-1984); Pastor of Blodgett Mills, Freetown and McGraw United Methodist Church, NY (1978-1984) **CR:** District Youth Director, Syracuse, NY (1981-1984); Member, Conference Board (1980-1985); Member, District Board, Ordained Ministry, Syracuse, NY (1980-1984); Member, Hospital Committee, Cortland County Council of Churches (1980-1984); Member, Cortland County Youth Bureau (1980-1981) **CIV:** Member, Design Team, Central Lakes District Academy of Spiritual Development (1999-2003); Spiritual Director, Spiritual Exercises, High Acres, Geneva, NY (1999-2003); Member, Education and Research Institutional Review Board, Arnot Ogden Medical Center, Arnot Health, Elmira, NY (1995-1998); Spiritual Director, Walk to Emmaus, Rome, NY (1993); Member, Community Board, Southport Correctional Facility (1987-1998); Spiritual Director, Spiritual Exercises, High Acres, Geneva, NY (1986-1998); CPC, Elmira, NY (1985-1993); Board of Directors, Meals on Wheels America, Elmira, NY (1985-1988); Member, McGraw Board of Education (1981-1984) **MEM:** Charles Wesley Society; Masons; Knight Templar **MH:** Albert Nelson Marquis Lifetime Achievement Award; Marquis Who's Who Humanitarian Award **AV:** Reading; Traveling; Music; Exercising **PA:** Republican

SEATON, DAVID T., T: Chairman, Chief Executive Officer **I:** Business Management/Business Services **CN:** Fluor Corporation **ED:** Bachelor of Science, University of South Carolina **CT:** Postgraduate Certificate, Thunderbird School of Global Management **C:** Chairman, Chief Executive Officer, Fluor Corporation (2012-Present); Chief Executive Officer, Fluor Corporation (2011-2012); Chief Operating Officer, Fluor Corporation (2009-2011); Senior President of Energy, Fluor Corporation (2009); President of Energy and Chemicals, Fluor Corporation (2007-2009); Senior Vice President of the Corporate Sales Board, Fluor Corporation (2005-2007); Senior Vice President of Chemical Business, Fluor Corporation (2004-2005); Senior Vice President of Oil and Gas Sales, Fluor Corporation (2002-2004)

SEAVER, TOM, T: Professional Baseball Player (Retired) **I:** Athletics **DOB:** 11/17/1944 **PB:** Fresno **SC:** CA/USA **YOP:** 2020 **PT:** Charles H. Seaver; Betty Lee (Cline) Seaver **MS:** Married **SPN:** Nancy Lynn McIntyre (06/09/1966) **CH:** Sarah; Anne Elizabeth **ED:** Coursework, University of Southern California (1965-1968); Coursework, Fresno City College (1964) **C:** Analyst, New York Mets (1995-2005); Owner, Seaver Family Vineyards (2002); Analyst, New York Yankees (1989-1993); Pitcher, New York Mets (1967-1977, 1983-1984, 1987); Pitcher, Boston Red Sox (1986); Pitcher, Chicago White Sox (1984-1986); Pitcher, Cincinnati Reds (1977-1982); Pitcher, Jacksonville Suns (1966) **CR:** Color Commentator, New York Mets, New York Yankees (1989) **MIL:** Served, Marine Corps Air Ground Combat Center (MCAGCC), U.S. Marine Corps Reserves (1962-1963) **CW:** Author, "Great Moments in Baseball" (1994); Author, "Baseball: Murder at the World Series" (1991); Co-Author, "Beanball" (1989); Co-Author, "Tom Seaver's Basball Card Book" (1985); Co-Author, "The Art of Pitching" (1984); Author, "Pitching with Tom Seaver" (1973) **AW:** Inductee, Cincinnati Reds Hall of Fame (2006); Selected as "Hometown Hero," Mets Franchise, ESPN (2006); Inductee, Marine Corps Sports Hall of Fame (2003); Ranked #32, 100 Greatest Baseball Players, The Sporting News (1999); Inductee, Baseball Hall of Fame (1992); Inductee, New York Mets Hall of Fame (1988); Sportsman of the Year, Sports Illustrated (1969); Cy Young Awards (1969, 1973, 1975); Rookie of the Year, National League (1967)

SEBERT, KESHA ROSE, T: Singer **I:** Media & Entertainment **DOB:** 03/01/1987 **PB:** Los Angeles **SC:** CA/USA **PT:** Rosemary Patricia "Pebe" Seber **ED:** Coursework, Barnard College **C:** Singer, Songwriter, Rapper **CW:** Singer, Songwriter, Album, "High Road" (2020); Appearance, "Carpool Karaoke: The Series" (2020); Appearance, "Rainbow: The Film" (2018); Singer, Songwriter, Album, "Rainbow" (2017); Actress, "A Ghost Story" (2017); Guest Judge, "RuPaul's Drag Race" (2017); Appearance "Nashville" (2016); Appearance, "Hollywood Game Night" (2016); Actress, "Jem and the Holograms" (2015); Guest Judge, "Project Runway: All Stars" (2015); Actress, "Jane the Virgin" (2015); Judge, "Rising Star" (2014); Featured, Music Video, "My Song 5" by HAIM (2014); Appearance, "Kesha: My Crazy Beautiful Life" (2013); Appearance, "The Show with Vinny" (2013); Voice Actress, "Robot Chicken" (2013); Singer, Songwriter, Album, "Warrior" (2012); Singer, Songwriter, Extended Play, "Deconstructed" (2012); Appearance, "Katy Perry: Part of Me" (2012); Guest Mentor, "The X Factor" (2012); Producer, Remix Album, "I Am the Dance Commander + I Command You to Dance: The Remix Album" (2011); Actress, "Walt Disney's Princess Ke$ha" (2011); Herself, "Victorious" (2011); Musical Guest, "Saturday Night Live" (2010); Singer, Songwriter, Album, "Animal" (2010); Singer, Songwriter, Extended Play, "Cannibal" (2010); Herself, "The City" (2010); Actress, "Final Flesh" (2009); Featured, Music Video, "I Kissed a Girl" by Katy Perry (2008); Appearance, "Bravo Supershow" (2007); Appearance, "The Simple Life" (2005); Featured Artist, Songwriter, Numerous Songs, Other Artists; Numerous Live Appearances, TV Shows and Events; Singer, Numerous Tours **AW:** Named Most Performed Song, "Good Old Days," ASCAP Pop Music Awards (2019); Named Voice for the Animals, Humane Society of the United States' 2019 To the Rescue! Los Angeles Gala (2019); Named Best Online Music Film, "Rainbow: The Film," Webby Awards (2019); Numerous BMI Pop Awards for Songs (2011, 2012, 2019); Named One of the "100 Most Influential," TIME Magazine (2018); Trailblazer Award, Billboard Women in Music (2016); Visibility Award, Human Rights Campaign Equality Gala (2016); Choice Style: Female, Teen Choice Awards (2016); Award for Best Collaboration, "Timber" with Pitbull, iHeart Radio Music Awards (2014); Gretchen Wyler Award, Genesis Awards (2013); Most Animal Friendly Pop/Hip-Hop Artist, PETA Libby Awards (2012); Most Performed Song, "Tik Tok," ASCAP Pop Music Awards (2011); Best International Artist, ARIA Music Awards (2011); Best New Act, MTV Europe Music Awards (2010); Award for Best Female Singer, Bravo Otto (2010); Named Best New Artist, Eska Music Awards (2010)

SECCHIAROLI, LAWRENCE NAZZARETH, T: Mechanical Design Engineer (Retired) **I:** Engineering **DOB:** 05/28/1955 **PB:** Bridgeport **SC:** CT/USA **PT:** Nazarino Louis Secchiaroli; Patricia Jean (Bizak) Secchiaroli **MS:** Single **ED:** Master in Engineering, University of Bridgeport (1982); Bachelor in Engineering, University of Bridgeport (1978); Associate in Engineering, Norwalk State Technical College (Now Norwalk Community College), CT (1976) **C:** Propulsion Design Engineer, Sikorsky Aircraft Division, United Technologies Corporation, Stratford, CT (1995-2014); Production Engineering Representative, Sikorsky Aircraft Division, United Technical Corporation, Stratford, CT (1993-1995); Design Engineer Leader, Sikorsky

Aircraft Division, United Technical Corporation, Trumbull, CT (1991-1993); Design Engineer Manager, Sikorsky Aircraft Division, United Technical Corporation, Stratford, CT (1990-1991); Propulsion Representative, Sikorsky Aircraft Division, United Technical Corporation, Nagoya, Japan (1990); Production Engineering Representative, Sikorsky Aircraft Division, United Technical Corporation, Stratford, CT (1987-1990); Design Engineering Manager, Sikorsky Aircraft Division, United Technical Corporation, Stratford, CT (1985-1987); Design Engineer, Sikorsky Aircraft Division, United Technical Corporation, Stratford, CT (1980-1985); Junior Engineer, Propulsion Engineering, Stratford, CT (1978-1979) **CW:** Patent, Computerized Fuel System, Valves and Pumps; Patent, Aluminum Body Valve with a Stainless Steel Innards for High Temperature Application **MEM:** The American Society of Mechanical Engineers **MH:** Albert Nelson Marquis Lifetime Achievement Award **B/I:** Mr. Secchiaroli was in his early teens when the space race was going on to the moon and that inspired him. He wanted to be an aerospace engineer, also he liked working with mathematics and sciences. Mr. Secchiaroli was also the first generation college graduate in his family. **PA:** Republican **RE:** Roman Catholic

SECUNDA, THOMAS, "TOM", T: Financial Services Executive **I:** Financial Services **CN:** Bloomberg LP **PB:** Bethpage **SC:** NY/USA **MS:** Married **SPN:** Cynthia "Cindy" Cohen **CH:** Two Daughters **ED:** Master of Science in Mathematics, State University of New York at Binghamton; Bachelor of Science in Mathematics, State University of New York at Binghamton **C:** Co-Founder & Global Head, Financial Products & Services, Bloomberg LP (1982-Present); Systems Analyst, Salomon Brothers **CIV:** Chairperson, Board of Directors, National Parks Conservation Association (2011); Signatory, Giving Pledge; Board of Trustees, Intrepid Museum Foundation; Board of Directors, Manhattan Theater Club **AW:** Award, Simon Wiesenthal Center (2012); Named, Forbes 400: Richest Americans (2009) **RE:** Jewish

SEEMAN, LINDA, T: Counselor **DOB:** 04/19/1950 **PB:** Richmond **SC:** VA/USA **PT:** David Kamsky; Margaret (Rosenberg) Kamsky **MS:** Married **SPN:** Irvin Jay Seeman (07/25/1971) **CH:** Benjamin Gary; Paul Lawrence **ED:** PhD, Virginia Commonwealth University (1987); MS, The University of Texas (1977); BS in Education, University of Georgia (1971) **CT:** Licensed Professional Counselor; Certified Rehabilitation Counselor; Certified Clinical Mental Health Counselor **C:** Private Practice, Richmond, VA (1984-Present); Mental Health Counselor, Richmond Rehabilitation Services (1981-1984); Vocational Rehabilitation Program Director, Rehabilitation Commission, El Centro College (Now Dallas College), Dallas, Texas (1978-1980); Spanish and English Teacher, Glenn Hills High School, Augusta, GA (1971-1974) **CR:** Secretary, Jewish Family Services (1994-Present); Chairman, Adoption Committee, Jewish Family Services (1993-Present); Board of Directors, Jewish Family Services (1987-Present); Women's Resource Center, University of Richmond (1986-1992); Virginia Rehabilitation Counselors Association (1980-1992); Board of Directors, Dallas Epilepsy Association (1978-1980) **CIV:** Committee Member, Virginia Women's Conference (1990-Present); Active, Policy Board for Society Resettlement (1990-1993); Chair, Volunteer Recognition for Soviet Resettlement (1991); Developer, Chair, Annual Leadership Symposium, Women's Resource Center, University of Richmond (1986, 1988) **MEM:** AACD; Virginia Counselors Association; Virginia Mental Health Counselors Association; The Honor Society of Phi Kappa Phi; Phi Delta Kappa (PDK International) **MH:** Albert Nelson Marquis Lifetime Achievement Award **RE:** Jewish

SEGER, BOB, T: Musician **I:** Media & Entertainment **DOB:** 05/06/1945 **PB:** Ann Arbor **SC:** MI/USA **PT:** Stewart Seger; Charlotte Seger **MS:** Married **SPN:** Juanita Dorricott (1993); Annette Sinclair (1987, Divorced 1988); Renee Andrietti (1968, Divorced) **CH:** Christopher Cole Seger; Samantha Char Seger **C:** Musician **CW:** Musician, Singer, Songwriter, "I Knew You When" (2017); Musician, Singer, Songwriter, "Ride Out" (2014); Musician, Singer, Songwriter, "Face the Promise" (2006); Musician, Singer, Songwriter, "It's a Mystery" (1995); Musician, Singer, Songwriter, "Like a Rock" (1986); Musician, Singer, Songwriter, "The Distance" (1982); Musician, Singer, Songwriter, "Nine Tonight" (1981); Musician, Singer, Songwriter, "Against the Wind" (1980); Musician, Singer, Songwriter, "Stranger in Town" (1978); Musician, Singer, Songwriter, "Night Moves" (1976); Musician, Singer, Songwriter, "Live Bullet" (1976); Musician, Singer, Songwriter, "Beautiful Loser" (1975); Musician, Singer, Songwriter, "Seven" (1974); Musician, Singer, Songwriter, "Back in'72" (1973); Musician, Singer, Songwriter, "Smokin' O.P.'s" (1972); Musician, Singer, Songwriter, "Brand New Morning" (1971); Musician, Singer, Songwriter, "Mongrel" (1970); Musician, Singer, Songwriter, "Noah" (1969); Musician, Singer, Songwriter, "Ramblin' Gamblin' Man" (1969); Featured Artist, Numerous Film Soundtracks **AW:** Honoree, Legend of Live, Billboard, Billboard Touring Conference & Awards (2015); Inductee, Songwriters Hall of Fame (2012); Inductee, Rock and Roll Hall of Fame (2004); ASCAP Award for Most Performed Songs from Motion Pictures, "Shakedown" from "Beverly Hills Cop II," ASCAP Film and Television Music Awards (1988); Honoree, Star, Hollywood Walk of Fame (1987)

SEINFELD, JERRY, T: Comedian, Actor, Television Producer, Writer **I:** Media & Entertainment **DOB:** 04/29/1954 **PB:** Brooklyn **SC:** NY/USA **PT:** Kálmán Seinfeld; Betty S. Seinfeld **MS:** Married **SPN:** Jessica Sklar (12/25/1999) **CH:** Sascha; Julian Kal; Shepard Kellen **ED:** Degree in Communications and Theater, Queens College, CUNY (1976); Coursework, State University of New York at Oswego **C:** Stand-Up Comedian (1976-Present) **CW:** Host, Creator, Producer, "Comedians in Cars Getting Coffee" (2012-Present); Himself, Music Video, "Sunflower" by Vampire Weekend Feat. Steve Lacy (2019); Executive Producer, "Standup and Away! with Brian Regan" (2018); Stand-Up Comedian, Album, "Jerry Before Seinfeld" (2017); Stand-Up Comedian, Executive Producer, TV Special, "Jerry Before Seinfeld" (2017); Actor, "Mystery Science Theater 3000: The Return" (2017); Director, "Colin Quinn: The New York Story" (2016); Himself, "The Jim Gaffigan Show" (2016); Himself, "Inside Amy Schumer" (2015); Executive Producer, "Colin Quinn: Unconstitutional" (2015); Himself, "Top Five" (2014); Himself, "Louie" (2012-2014); Director, Executive Producer, "Colin Quinn: Long Story Short" (2011); Creator, Executive Producer, "The Marriage Ref" (2010-2011); Actor, "Curb Your Enthusiasm" (2009); Creator, "Sincerely, Ted L. Nancy" (2008); Himself, "New Family" (2008); Voice Actor, Video Game, "Bee Movie" (2007); Voice Actor, Screenwriter, Producer, "Bee Movie" (2007); Himself, "30 Rock" (2007); Actor, "The Thing About My Folks" (2005); Actor, Writer, "Hindsight is 20/20..." (2004); Actor, Writer, "A Uniform Used to Mean Something..." (2004); Himself, Executive Producer, "Comedian" (2002); Voice Actor, "Dilbert" (2000); Actor, "Pros & Cons" (1999); Actor, "Larry David: Curb Your Enthusiasm" (1999); Stand-Up Comedian, Album, "Jerry Seinfeld: I'm Telling You for the Last Time" (1998); Stand-Up Comedian, TV Special, "Jerry Seinfeld: I'm Telling You for the Last Time" (1998); Himself, "Mad About You" (1998); Himself, "The Larry Sanders Show" (1993, 1998); Actor, Creator, Writer, Producer, Executive Producer, "Seinfeld" (1989-1998); Himself, "Eddie" (1996); Himself, "Love & War" (1993); Himself, "Carol Leifer: Gaudy, Bawdy & Blue" (1992); Stand-Up Comedian, TV Special, "Jerry Seinfeld: Stand-Up Confidential" (1987); Executive Producer, "Hearts and Diamonds" (1985); Actor, "The Ratings Game" (1984); Stand-Up Comedian, "An Evening at the Improv" (1982); Actor, "Square Pegs" (1982); Actor, "Benson" (1980); Stand-Up Comedian, Numerous TV Shows; Host, Numerous TV Specials and Events **AW:** Webby Award, Online Film & Video: Best Web Personality/Host, "Comedians in Cars Getting Coffee" (2016); Webby Award, Online Film & Video: Best Web Personality/Host, "Comedians in Cars Getting Coffee" (2014); Clio Honorary Award, Clio Awards (2014); Webby Award, Online Film & Video: Best Web Personality/Host, "Comedians in Cars Getting Coffee" (2013); Named One of "The 100 Most Powerful Celebrities," Forbes.com (2008); AFI Star Award, U.S. Comedy Arts Festival (1999); Guinness World Record Winner, Highest Annual Earnings for a Television Actor, "Seinfeld" (1998); Co-Recipient, Screen Actors Guild Award for Ensemble in a Comedy Series, "Seinfeld" (1997); Co-Recipient, Screen Actors Guild Award for Ensemble in a Comedy Series, "Seinfeld" (1996); Co-Recipient, Screen Actors Guild Award for Ensemble in a comedy Series, "Seinfeld" (1994); Golden Globe Award for Best Comedy Actor - TV, "Seinfeld" (1994); Co-Recipient, Nova Award for Most Promising Producer in Television, "Seinfeld," PGA Awards (1994); Primetime Emmy Award for Outstanding Comedy Series, "Seinfeld" (1993); American Television Award for Best Actor in a Situation Comedy, "Seinfeld" (1993); American Comedy Award for Funniest Male Performer in a TV Series, "Seinfeld" (1993); Q Award, Best Actor in a Quality Comedy Series, "Seinfeld" (1993); American Comedy Award for Funniest Male Performer in a TV Series, "Seinfeld" (1992); American Comedy Award for Comedy Club Stand-Up Comic - Male (1988) **RE:** Jewish

SEITZ, CAROLE J., BME, MME, T: Associate Professor Emerita, Coordinator of Music Division **I:** Education/Educational Services **CN:** Creighton University **PT:** Charles N. Hicks; Ermagene Virginia (Riley) Hicks **MS:** Married **SPN:** Richard John Seitz, MD, FACP (08/10/1991) **CH:** Kimberly Ann Santora; Jeffrey Ward Bean **ED:** Master of Music Education in Conducting, Wichita State University, Wichita, KS (1961); Bachelor of Music Education in Violin, Wichita State University, Wichita, KS, Cum Laude (1960) **CT:** Teaching Certificate, K-12, States of Iowa and Nebraska **C:** Associate Professor Emerita, Coordinator of Music Division, Creighton University, Omaha, NE (2015); Associate Chair of Performing Arts, Creighton University, Omaha, NE (2001); Associate Professor and Tenure, Creighton University, Omaha, NE (1985); Coordinator of Music, Creighton University, Omaha, NE (1980); Assistant Professor, Creighton University, Omaha, NE (1979); Adjunct Professor, Creighton University, Omaha, NE (1976); Ballet Accompanist, Creighton University, Omaha, NE (1975-1979); Director of Choral Activities, Thomas Jefferson High School, Council Bluffs, Iowa (1963); Vocal Music Instructor, Omaha Public Schools (1961); Acting Chair, Department of Fine Arts, Iowa Western Community College, Council Bluffs, Iowa; Violin Instructor, Conductor, Junior Symphony, Westside Public Schools (Now Westside Community Schools), Omaha, NE **CR:** Junior Choir Director, Soprano Soloist, St. Andrew's Episcopalian

Church, Omaha, NE (1980-1989); Assistant Conductor, Chorus Master, Opera Omaha (1976-1989); Violinist, Des Moines Symphony (1972-1979); Violinist, Lincoln Symphony Orchestra, NE (1972-1979); Council Bluffs Community Chorus, Council Bluffs, Iowa (1969-1973); Violinist, Omaha Symphony (1961-1975); Violinist, Wichita Symphony Orchestra (1958-1960); Director of Music, Saint John Lutheran Church, Council Bluffs, Iowa; Director, Canterbury Choir, St. Augustine of Canterbury Episcopal Church, Elkhorn, NE; Musical Director, Chanticleer Community Theatre, Council Bluffs, Iowa CIV: Delegate, Nebraska Diocesan Council (2007-2008); Senior Warden, Head of the Vestry, St. James Episcopal Church (2007); Founder and President, Council Bluffs Arts Council (1970-1973); Vestry Member, St. James Episcopal Church, Fremont, NE; Board Member, Omaha Academy of Ballet, Omaha, NE; Board Member, Metropolitan Arts Council, Omaha, NE; Iowa Board Member, Mid-America Arts Alliance; Committee Member, Iowa Arts Council; Committee Member, Organizing the First Art Festival, Omaha Fine Arts Festival; Board of Governors, Omaha Symphony; Member, Several Different Committees, Nebraska Arts Council CW: Composer, Play, "The Devils"; Choral Compositions, "Midwinter Carol Two Wee Girls," "Christmas Eve Prayer," "Alleluia," and "He is Risen"; Composer, 35 Dance Compositions, Music for Individual Ballet Practice; Dance Composition, "Dances for the Young Ballerina"; Dance Competition, "Music for Individual Practice"; String Orchestra, "Little Fugue"; String Quartet, "Requiem" Inspired by Poem by Desmond Egan for Violin and Piano; Composer, "Dance" for Two Violins and Piano AW: Citizenship Award, American Association of University Women (AAUW) (1960); Two-time Recipient, Dean's Special Service Award for Planning and Performance, Creighton University, Omaha, NE; Named to "Outstanding Young Women of America" MEM: Assistant to the President, American String Teachers Association (2000); The Film Music Institute; The College Music Society; American Choral Directors Association; Iowa Board Member, American Choral Directors Association; Nebraska Choral Directors Association; Music Educator's National Conference (Now National Association for Music Education (NAfME)); Omaha Musician's Association (Now Omaha Music); Wichita Musicians' Association, American Federation of Musicians; Mortar Board; Mu Phi Epsilon MH: Albert Nelson Marquis Lifetime Achievement Award; Marquis Who's Who Top Professional B/I: Mrs. Seitz became involved in her profession because her mother was a pianist. She and her sister took piano lessons since she was 4 years old and in Wichita, where she grew up, they had a wonderful string program. She started violin in the fourth grade and they were free lessons that were given by the public schools. In addition, she started in her profession because she had outside teachers, she loved violin, and one of the rare things about America, is that they will come around the public school and asked who wants to play the violin, and she said she did; she started playing the violin when she was 10 years old. AV: Horseback riding; Travel; Reading; Knitting PA: Independent RE: Episcopalian

SEIZER, FERN VICTOR, T: Health Services Administrator **I:** Nonprofit & Philanthropy **DOB:** 10/29/1934 **PB:** New York **SC:** NY/USA **PT:** David L. Seizer; Florence Maisel Victor Seizer **MS:** Married **SPN:** Robert J. Seizer (08/28/1955) **CH:** Steven Seizer, MD; Susan Seizer, PhD **ED:** BA, University of California Los Angeles (1956) **C:** Director, Community Relations, Didi Hirsch Community Mental Health Center, Culver City, CA (1994-2000); Executive Director, Venice Family

Clinic, Los Angeles, CA (1982-1994); Executive Director, Fair Housing Council of San Fernando Valley, Los Angeles, CA (1980-1982); Director, Public Affairs and Education, National Council of Jewish Women, Los Angeles, CA (1968-1980) **CR:** Corporate Council, Executives United Way of Greater Los Angeles (1991-1993); Administrators Forum and Community Outreach Task Force, David Geffen School of Medicine at UCLA (1990-1993); Managing Editor, City Editor, Daily Bruin, University of California Los Angeles (1953-1954) **CIV:** Board of Directors, Venice Family Clinic (1996-Present); Board of Directors, National Multiple Sclerosis Society, Los Angeles, CA (1995-Present); Board of Directors, St. John's Hospital and Health Center, Santa Monica, CA (1994-2000); Social Services Commission, City of Santa Monica (1998-1999); Advisory Committee on Primary Care, California State Department of Health Services, Sacramento, CA (1990-1993); Managed Care Planning Council, Los Angeles County (1989-1990) **AW:** Outstanding Contribution to the Community Award, Los Angeles City and County, Los Angeles, CA (2000); Unsung Hero Award, California Community Foundation (2000); Most Valuable Trustee Award, National Multiple Sclerosis Society (1999); Alumni Award for Excellence in Professional Achievement, University of California, Los Angeles (1995) **MEM:** Phi Beta Kappa **MH:** Albert Nelson Marquis Lifetime Achievement Award **B/I:** Mrs. Seizer always felt that nonprofit organizations were important to the community. When she re-entered the workforce after having children, she went into the nonprofit field. **AV:** Attending movies and theater; Traveling; Playing bridge

SELDEN, LYNDE, T: General Counsel **I:** Law and Legal Services **CN:** Plaza Home Mortgage, Inc. **ED:** JD, USC Gould School of Law (1976); BS in Economics, New York University **C:** In-house Counsel, General Counsel, Plaza Home Mortgage, Inc., San Diego, CA (2008-Present) **CIV:** USO, League of Warriors **MIL:** U.S. Navy (1967-1971) **MEM:** William Todd; Legion NXT; Mortgage Bankers Association

SELES, MONICA, T: Professional Tennis Player (Retired) **I:** Athletics **DOB:** 12/02/1973 **PB:** Novi Sad **SC:** Serbia/Yugoslavia **PT:** Karolj Seles; Esther Seles **MS:** Married **SPN:** Tom Golisano **C:** Professional Tennis Player (1989-2008) **CR:** Paid Spokesperson, Shire Pharmaceuticals (2015); Member, U.S. Fed Cup Team (1996, 1999, 2000); Member, Players' Council, Women's Tennis Association (1998-1999) **CIV:** Active Participant, Special Olympics **CW:** Author, "The Academy: Love Match" (2014); Author, "The Academy of Game On" (2013); Author, "Getting a Grip On My Body, My Mind, My Self" (2009); Contestant, "Dancing with the Stars" (2008); Co-Author, "Monica: From Fear to Victory" (1996); Guest Appearance, "The Nanny" (1996) **AW:** Inductee, International Tennis Hall of Fame (2009); Sanex Hero of Year Award, WTA Tour (2002); Flo Hyman Memorial Award, Women's Sports Foundation (2000); Named "Player Who Makes a Difference," Family Circle Cup (1999); Commitment to Community Award, Florida Times-Union (1999); Comeback Player of Year Award, WTA Tour (1995, 1998); Female Pro Athlete of Year, Florida Sports Hall of Fame (1998); Comeback Player of Year, TENNIS Magazine (1995); Female Athlete of Year, Associated Press (1991, 1992); Player of the Year, WTA Tour (1991); Ted Tinling Diamond Award (1990); Most Improved Player (1990); Rado Topspin Award (1990); Female Rookie of the Year, TENNIS Magazine/Rolex Watch (1989); Sportswoman of the Year, Yugoslavia (1985); Named Among the "30 Legends of Women's Tennis: Past, Present and Future," Time Magazine

SELF, BILL, T: College Basketball Coach **I:** Athletics **DOB:** 12/27/1962 **PB:** Okmulgee **SC:** OK/USA **MS:** Married **SPN:** Cindy Self **CH:** Lauren; Taylor **ED:** MS in Athletic Administration, Oklahoma State University (1989); BSBA, Oklahoma State University (1985) **C:** Head Coach, Basketball, University of Kansas (2003-Present); Head Coach, Basketball, University Illinois at Urbana-Champaign (2000-2003); Head Coach, Basketball, University of Tulsa (1997-2000); Head Coach, Basketball, Oral Roberts University (1993-1997); Assistant Coach, Basketball, Oklahoma State University (1986-1993); Assistant Coach, Basketball, University of Kansas (1985-1986) **CR:** Member, Competition Committee, USA Men's Basketball (2005-Present); Board Member, National Association of Basketball Coaches **CIV:** Co-Founder, Assists Foundation **AW:** Six-Time Big 12 Coach of the Year (2006, 2009, 2011, 2012, 2017, 2018); Five-Time AP Big 12 Coach of the Year (2006, 2009, 2011, 2015, 2016); Two-Time AP College Coach of the Year (2009, 2016); NABC Coach of the Year (2016); National Coach of the Year, USA Today (2016); Inductee, Oklahoma Sports Hall of Fame (2013); John R. Wooden Legends of Coaching Award (2013); National Coach of the Year, The Sporting News (2000, 2009, 2012); Naismith College Coach of the Year (2012); Adolph Rupp Cup (2012); District VI Coach of the Year, U.S. Basketball Writers Association (2011); Guardians of the Game Pillar Award (2011); Henry Iba Award (2009); WAC Coach of the Year (2000); Don Haskins Coach of the Year, Western Athletic Conference (2000); John and Nellie Wooden Coach of the Year, Utah Tipoff Club (2000); Holder, Numerous Medal Records; Numerous Other Coaching Accolades

SELLECK, TOM, T: Actor **I:** Media & Entertainment **DOB:** 01/29/1945 **PB:** Detroit **SC:** MI/USA **PT:** Robert Dean Selleck; Martha Selleck **MS:** Married **SPN:** Jillie Joan Mack (08/07/1987); Jacquelyn Ray (05/15/1971, Divorced 1982) **CH:** Hannah Margaret; Kevin (Stepson) **ED:** Honorary PhD, Pepperdine University (2000); Coursework in Acting, Beverly Hills Playhouse; Coursework, University of Southern California; Coursework, Los Angeles Valley College **CIV:** Board Member, Michael Josephson Institute of Ethics (Now Josephson Institute) **MIL:** Served, 160th Infantry Regiment, California Army National Guard (1967-1973) **CW:** Actor, "Blue Bloods" (2010-Present); Actor, Executive Producer, "Jesse Stone: Lost in Paradise" (2015); Actor, Executive Producer, "Jesse Stone: Benefit of the Doubt" (2012); Actor, Executive Producer, "Jesse Stone: Innocents Lost" (2011); Actor, Executive Producer, "Killers" (2010); Actor, Executive Producer, "Jesse Stone: No Remorse" (2010); Actor, Executive Producer, "Jesse Stone: Thin Ice" (2009); Actor, "Las Vegas" (2007-2008); Actor, Executive Producer, "Jesse Stone: Sea Change" (2007); Voice Actor, Video Game, "Meet the Robinsons" (2007); Voice Actor, "Meet the Robinsons" (2007); Actor, "Boston Legal" (2006); Actor, Executive Producer, "Jesse Stone: Death in Paradise" (2006); Actor, Executive Producer, "Jesse Stone: Night Passage" (2006); Actor, Executive Producer, "Jesse Stone: Stone Cold" (2005); Actor, "The Young and the Restless" (1974-1975, 2005); Narrator, "Dwight D. Eisenhower: Supreme Commander-in-Chief," "Biography" (2004); Actor, "Ike: Countdown to D-Day" (2004); Actor, "Reversible Errors" (2004); Actor, "Touch 'Em All McCall" (2003); Actor, "Twelve Mile Road" (2003); Actor, "Monte Walsh" (2003); Actor, Executive Producer, "Crossfire Trail" (2001); Actor, "Running Mates" (2000); Actor, "Friends" (2000, 1996); Actor, "The Love Letter" (1999); Actor, Executive Producer, "The Closer" (1998); Actor, "In & Out" (1997); Actor, Executive Producer, "Last Stand at Saber River" (1997); Actor, Executive Producer, "Ruby

Jean and Joe" (1996); Actor, "Broken Trust" (1995); Actor, "Open Season" (1995); Actor, "Mr. Baseball" (1992); Actor, "Christopher Columbus: The Discovery" (1992); Actor, "Folks!" (1992); Executive Producer, "Silverfox" (1991); Actor, "Three Men and a Little Lady" (1990); Executive Producer, "B.L. Stryker" (1989-1990); Actor, "Quigley Down Under" (1990); Actor, "An Innocent Man" (1989); Actor, "Her Alibi" (1989); Actor, "Three Men and a Baby" (1987); Actor, "Murder, She Wrote" (1986); Actor, "Runaway" (1984); Actor, "Lassiter" (1984); Actor, "High Road to China" (1983); Actor, "Simon & Simon" (1982); Actor, "The Shadow Riders" (1982); Actor, "Divorce Wars: A Love Story" (1982); Actor, "The Fall Guy" (1982); Actor, Executive Producer, "Magnum, P.I." (1980-1988); Actor, "The Rockford Files" (1979, 1978); Actor, "Concrete Cowboys" (1979); Actor, "Stockard Channing in Just Friends" (1979); Actor, "The Sacketts" (1979); Actor, "The Chinese Typewriter" (1979); Actor, "Taxi" (1978); Actor, "The Gypsy Warriors" (1978); Actor, "Superdome" (1978); Actor, "Coma" (1978); Actor, "Bunco" (1977); Actor, "The Washington Affair" (1977); Actor, "Charlie's Angels" (1976); Actor, "Midway" (1976); Actor, "Most Wanted" (1976); Actor, "Doctors' Hospital" (1976); Actor, "The Streets of San Francisco" (1975); Actor, "Returning Home" (1975); Actor, "Mannix" (1975); Actor, "Lucas Tanner" (1975); Actor, "Marcus Welby, M.D." (1974, 1975); Actor, "A Case of Rape" (1974); Actor, "The Wide World of Mystery" (1974); Actor, "Owen Marshall, Counselor at Law" (1973); Actor, "The F.B.I." (1973); Actor, "Terminal Island" (1973); Actor, "Daughters of Satan" (1972); Actor, "Sarge" (1971); Actor, "Myra Breckenridge" (1970); Actor, "The Movie Murderer" (1970); Actor, "Bracken's World" (1969, 1970); Actor, "Judd for the Defense" (1969); Actor, "Lancer" (1969) **AW:** Inductee, Online Film & Television Association Hall of Fame (2017); Co-recipient, Hero Award, "Magnum, P.I.," TV Land Awards (2009); Bronze Wrangler, Television Feature Film, "Monte Walsh," Western Heritage Awards (2004); Bronze Wrangler, Television Feature Film, "Crossfire Trail" (2002); Film in Hawaii Award, Hawaii International Film Festival (2000); Bronze Wrangler, Television Feature Film, "Last Stand at Saber River" (1998); Horizon Award, U.S. Congress (1997); Golden Boot Award (1992); Honoree, Star, Hollywood Walk of Fame (1986); Golden Globe for Best Performance by an Actor in a Television Series - Drama, "Magnum, P.I.," Hollywood Foreign Press Association (1985); Co-recipient, Favorite All-Around Male Entertainer, People's Choice Awards (1985); Named Favorite Male TV Performer, People's Choice Awards (1983-1985); Primetime Emmy, Outstanding Lead Actor in a Drama Series, "Magnum, P.I.," Television Academy (1984); Named Best Male TV Star, Bravo Otto (1984); Named Male Star of the Year, Golden Apple Awards (1982, 1983); Named Favorite Male Performer in a New TV Program, People's Choice Awards (1981); Federal Service Ribbon, California Army National Guard; California State Service Ribbon; California Drill Attendance Ribbon **MEM:** National Rifle Association of America (NRA); Sigma Chi

SENSENBRENNER, FRANK, "JIM" JAMES JR., T: U.S. Representative **I:** Government Administration/Government Relations/Government Services **DOB:** 06/14/1943 **PB:** Chicago **SC:** IL/USA **PT:** James Sensenbrenner; Margaret Sensenbrenner **MS:** Married **SPN:** Cheryl (Warren) Sensenbrenner (03/26/1977) **CH:** James Frank III; Robert Alan **ED:** JD, University of Wisconsin-Madison Law School (1968); BA in Political Science, Stanford University, CA (1965) **C:** U.S. Representative, Wisconsin's Fifth Congressional District, United States Congress, Washington, DC (2003-Present);

Chairman, Judiciary Committee, District Five, United States Congress, WI (2001-2007); Chairman, Science Committee, District Five, United States Congress, WI (1997-2001); U.S. Representative, Wisconsin's Ninth Congressional District, United States Congress, Washington, DC (1979-2003); Assistant Minority Leader, Wisconsin State Senate (1977-1979); Member, Wisconsin State Senate (1975-1979); Member, Wisconsin State Assembly (1969-1975); Member, Committee on the Judiciary, United States Congress; Member, Committee on Foreign Affairs, United States Congress **MEM:** American Philatelic Society; Chenequa Country Club; Capitol Hill Club **BAR:** Supreme Court of the United States (1972); State Bar of Wisconsin (1968) **PA:** Republican **RE:** Catholic

SERKIS, ANDY CLEMENT, T: Actor **I:** Media & Entertainment **DOB:** 04/20/1964 **PB:** London **SC:** United Kingdom **PT:** Clement Serkis; Lylie (Weech) Serkis **MS:** Married **SPN:** Lorraine Ashbourne (07/22/2002) **CH:** Ruby; Sonny; Louis George **ED:** Diploma, Lancaster University (1985) **C:** Co-founder, The Imaginarium Studios (2011); With, Royal Exchange Theater, Manchester, England, United Kingdom (1989); With, Duke's Playhouse, Lancaster, England, United Kingdom (1985); With, Touring Companies **CW:** Voice Actor, "A Christmas Carol" (2020); Voice Actor, "Star Wars: The Rise of Skywalker" (2019); Actor, "Long Shot" (2019); Director, Voice Actor, "Mowgli: Legend of the Jungle" (2018); Actor, "Black Panther" (2018); Voice Actor, "Star Wars: The Last Jedi" (2017); Producer, "The Ritual" (2017); Director, "Breathe" (2017); Voice Actor, "War for the Planet of the Apes" (2017); Actor, "Avengers: Age of Ultron" (2015); Actor, "Star Wars: The Force Awakens" (2015); Actor, "Fungus the Bogeyman" (2015); Actor, "Dawn of the Planet of the Apes" (2014); Actor, "The Hobbit: An Unexpected Journey" (2012); Voice Actor, "The Adventures of Tintin" (2011); Voice Actor, "Arthur Christmas" (2011); Actor, "Death of a Superhero" (2011); Actor, "Rise of the Planet of the Apes" (2011); Actor, "Wild Bill" (2011); Actor, Executive Producer, "Sex & Drugs & Rock & Roll" (2010); Actor, "Brighton Rock" (2010); Voice Actor, "Animals United (2010); Actor, "Burke and Hare" (2010); Actor, "Little Dorrit" (2008); Actor, "Einstein and Eddington" (2008); Actor, "The Cottage" (2008); Actor, "Inkheart" (2008); Actor, "Extraordinary Rendition" (2007); Actor, "Longford" (2006); Actor, "Stories of Lost Souls" (2006); Voice Actor, "Stingray" (2006); Actor, "Stormbreaker" (2006); Actor, "The Prestige" (2006); Voice Actor, "Flushed Away" (2006); Actor, "King Kong" (2005); Actor, "Blessed" (2004); Actor, "13 Going on 30" (2004); Actor, "Standing Room Only" (2004); Author, "Gollum: How We Made Movie Magic" (2004); Actor, "The Lord of the Rings: The Return of the King" (2003); Director, "The Double Bass" (2003); Actor, "24 Hour Party People" (2002); Actor, "Deathwatch" (2002); Actor, "The Lord of the Rings: The Two Towers" (2002); Actor, "Othello" (2002); Actor, "The Lord of the Rings: The Fellowship of the Ring" (2001); Actor, "The Escapist" (2001); Actor, "A Lie of the Mind" (2001); Actor, "Shiner" (2000); Actor, "Pandaemonium" (2000); Actor, "The Jolly Boys' Last Stand" (2000); Actor, "Arabian Nights" (2000); Actor, "Five Seconds to Spare" (1999); Actor, "Topsy-Turvy" (1999); Actor, "Oliver Twist" (1999); Actor, "Touching Evil III" (1999); Actor, "Shooting the Past" (1999); Actor, "Insomnia" (1998); Actor, "Clueless" (1998); Actor, "Among Giants" (1998); Actor, "The Tale of Sweety Barrett" (1998); Actor, "Jump" (1998); Actor, "Hurlyburly" (1997); Actor, "Loop" (1997); Actor, "Career Girls" (1997); Actor, "Mojo" (1997); Actor, "The Pale Horse" (1997); Actor, "Stella Does Tricks" (1996); Actor, "The Near

Room" (1995); Actor, "Mojo" (1995); Actor, "Prince of Jutland" (1994); Actor, "Grushko" (1994); Actor, "Cabaret" (1993); Actor, "The Queen and I" (1993); Actor, "Punchbag" (1993); Actor, "King Lear" (1993); Actor, "Hush" (1992) **AW:** British Academy Film Award for Outstanding British Contribution to Cinema (2020); SAG Award for Outstanding Performance by a Cast in a Motion Picture, SAG-AFTRA (2013, 2018); Inspiration Award, Empire Awards (2010); Empire Award for Best British Actor (2004); Numerous Awards

SERRANO, JOSÉ ENRIQUE, T: U.S. Representative from New York **I:** Government Administration/Government Relations/Government Services **DOB:** 10/24/1943 **PB:** Mayagüez **SC:** Puerto Rico **PT:** José E. Serrano; Hipolita (Soto) Serrano **MS:** Married **SPN:** Mary (Staucet) Serrano **CH:** Lisa Marie; José Marco; Justine; Benjamin; Jonathan **ED:** Coursework, The City University of New York Lehman College (1961) **C:** Member, U.S. House of Representatives from New York's 15th Congressional District, United States Congress, Washington, DC (2013-2020); Member, U.S. House Appropriations Committee (1993-1995, 1996-2020); Member, U.S. House of Representatives from New York's 16th Congressional District, United States Congress, Washington, DC (1993-2013); Member, U.S. House of Representatives from New York's 18th Congressional District, United States Congress, Washington, DC (1990-1993); Member, District 73, New York State Assembly (1983-1990); Member, District 75, New York State Assembly (1975-1983); Member, New York City Board of Education, NY (1969-1974); With, Manufacturers Hanover Trust Co. (1961-1969) **CR:** Delegate, Democratic National Convention (1976); Chairman, South Bronx Community Corporation **MIL:** With, 172nd Support Battalion Medical Corps, United States Army (1964-1966) **AW:** Friend of the National Parks Award, National Parks Conservation Association (2005); Man of the Year Award, Bronx Puerto Rican Day Parade (2003); Evelina Lopez Antonetty Award, Distinguished Public and Community Service, The City of New York Hunter College Center for Puerto Rican Studies (2003); Congressional Recognition Award, National Council of La Raza (Now UnidosUS) (1993) **PA:** Democrat **RE:** Roman Catholic

SEVENICH, DAVID MARK PHD, T: Senior Scientist **I:** Research **CN:** Bayer Crop Science **DOB:** 07/15/1961 **PB:** Stevens Point **SC:** WI/USA **PT:** James R. Sevenich; Bernice E. Sevenich **MS:** Married **SPN:** Donna M. Schulist **CH:** James M. Sevenich; Claire M. Sevenich **ED:** Doctor of Philosophy in Analytical Chemistry, University of Iowa (1990); Bachelor of Science in Chemistry, University of Wisconsin, Stevens Point (1984); High School Diploma, Pacelli High School, Stevens Point, WI (1979) **C:** Senior Scientist, North American Crop Breeding Analytical Lead, Bayer Crop Science, Ankeny, IA (2018-Present); North American Crop Breeding Analytical Lead, Monsanto, Ankeny, IA (2018); Cellulosic Ethanol Laboratory Manager, DuPont Industrial Biosciences, Nevada, IA (2017-2018); Senior Research Scientist, DuPont Pioneer, Johnston, IA (2002-2016); Global Process Analyzer Engineer, E.I. du Pont de Nemours Inc., La Porte, TX (1999-2002); Senior Process Analytical Chemist, E.I. du Pont de Nemours Inc., La Porte, TX (1997-1999); Section Chemist, E.I. du Pont de Nemours Inc., La Porte, TX (1994-1997); Area Chemist, E.I. Dupont de Nemours Inc., La Porte, TX (1990-1994); Research Assistant, University of Iowa, Iowa City, IA (1988-1990); Teaching Assistant, University of Iowa, Iowa City, IA (1984-1988); Lab Assistant, University of Wisconsin, Stevens Point, WI (1981-1984); Undergraduate Summer Research Intern, US Department of Energy (US DOE), Ames Laboratory, Ames, IA **CR:** Technical Monitor, Center for Process Analytical Chemistry, University of Washington, Seattle, WA (1990-2002); Researcher, University of Wisconsin, Stevens Point, WI (1983-1984); Tutor, University of Wisconsin, Stevens Point, WI (1982-1983) **CIV:** Board of Directors, NIRS Consortium, University of Wisconsin-Madison, Wisconsin; Board of Directors, Johnston Community Schools Foundation, Johnston, IA; USDA-GIPSA Grain Inspection Advisory Board **CW:** Contributor, Articles to Various Professional Journals, Including the International Sugar Journal, the Journal of Animal Science, Studies in Organic Chemistry, Journal of Catalysis, Chemical Abstracts Journal and Analytica Chimica Acta **AW:** Nominee, Pioneer Hi-Bred Crop Genetics R&D "Gene Dalton Evolutionary Impact Award"; DuPont Agricultural Products - Product Delivery Systems Quality Award; EPA 33/50 Success Story, "Reducing Toluene Emissions from Fungicide Production"; DuPont Safety, Health and Environmental Excellence Award; DuPont Agricultural Products Environmental Excellence Award; Order of the Arrow Vigil Honor, Boy Scouts of America **MEM:** American Chemical Society; Sigma Xi; Alpha Chi Sigma **AS:** Dr. Sevenich attributes his success to his strong values, morals, discipline and work ethic. Likewise, he benefited greatly from the influence of his family, as well as the professional mentorship of Dr. Syd Fleming and Dr. John Steichen. **B/I:** Dr. Sevenich became involved in his profession due to his intense interest and curiosity for the subject of physical sciences, as well as the inspiration of his older brothers, Stephen and Gregory. **AV:** Genealogy; Model railroading; Alpine skiing; Bicycling; Building personal computers **RE:** Roman Catholic

SEWELL, TERRYCINA, "TERRI" ANDREA, T: U.S. Representative, Lawyer **I:** Government Administration/Government Relations/Government Services **DOB:** 01/01/1965 **PB:** Huntsville **SC:** AL/USA **PT:** Andrew A. Sewell; Nancy (Gardner) Sewell **MS:** Divorced **SPN:** Theodore Dixie (1998, Divorced) **ED:** JD, Harvard Law School (1992); MA, University of Oxford, with Honors; BA, Princeton University (1986) **C:** U.S. Representative, Alabama's Seventh Congressional District, United States Congress, Washington, DC (2011-Present); Member, U.S. House of Representatives Committee on Space, Science and Technology (2011-Present); Member, Committee on Agriculture, U.S. House of Representatives (2011-Present); Partner, Maynard Cooper & Gale, Birmingham, AL (2004-2010); Chair, The House Committee on Transportation and Infrastructure (2001-2007); Associate, Davis, Polk & Wardwell LLP (1994-2004); Staff Member to Senator Howell Heflin, Alabama State Senate; Law Clerk to Chief Judge U.W. Clemon, United States District Court for the Northern District of Alabama; Staff Member to Representative Richard Shelby, U.S. House of Representatives, Washington, DC; Member, Committee on Natural Resources, United States Congress **CIV:** Community Advisory Board Member, Minority Health & Health Disparities Research Center, The University of Alabama at Birmingham; Board Treasurer, Chair, Finance Committee, St. Vincent's Foundation; Board Member, Girl Scouts of North-Central Alabama; Member, Corporate Partners Council, Birmingham Museum of Art; Member, Governor Board, Alabama Council on Economic Education; Member, Brown Chapel AME Church, Selma, AL **AW:** Alabama Super Lawyer (2008, 2009); Minority Business Rising Star Award, Birmingham Business Journal (2007); One of the Top Birmingham Women, Birmingham Business Journal (2005) **MEM:** Leadership Alabama (2008-2009); Women Leadership Momentum Class, YMCA (2007-2008); Leadership Birmingham (2006-2007); Alpha Kappa Alpha Sorority, Inc. **PA:** Democrat **RE:** Baptist

SEYMOUR, LESLEY JANE, T: Editor, Author, Entrepreneur **I:** Writing and Editing **CN:** CoveyClub **DOB:** 01/04/1957 **PB:** San Juan **SC:** Puerto Rico **MS:** Married **SPN:** Jeffrey Seymour **CH:** Two Children **ED:** BA, Duke University (1978); Diploma, Dana Hall School, Wellesley, MA (1974) **C:** Chief Executive Officer, Event Producer for CoveyClub Salons, CoveyClub (2017-Present); Editor-in-chief, More Magazine (2008-Present); Editor-in-chief, Marie Claire Magazine, New York, NY (2001-2006); Editor-in-chief, Redbook, New York, NY (1998-2001); Editor-in-chief, YM/Young & Modern, New York, NY (1997-1998); Beauty Director, Glamour (1994-1997); Writer, Senior Editor, Vogue (1982-1992); Reporter, New York Daily News Tonight (1981-1982); Reporter, Women's Wear Daily (1978) **CR:** Influencer, LinkedIn (2010-Present); Motivational Speaker, Keynote Speaker, MC Host, Panelist, Lesley Jane Seymour, LLC (2006-Present); Executive Director, Meredith's Beauty Center of Excellence (2012); Speaker, Matrix Awards (2011); Adjunct Professor, New York University Center for Publishing (2007-2009); Freelance Writer (1992-1993) **CIV:** Global Ambassador, Vital Voices (2013-2016); Former Trustee, Dana Hall School; Creator, One World/One Wish Campaign; Time to Talk Day **CW:** Chair, Editorial Advisory Board, Duke Magazine (2013-2016); Author, "On the Edge; Images from 100 Years of VOGUE" (1992); Author, "I Wish My Parents Understood: A Report on the Teenage Female" (1985); Contributor, The Huffington Post; Appearances, "Today," "Good Morning America," "MSNBC," "Hardball," CNN **AW:** Named Hot List, Mediaweek (2010); Meredith Creative Excellence Award (2008-2010); Named Most Powerful Fashion Editors List, Forbes (2009); Exceptional Merit in Media Award (2003-2004)

SHABAKER, LIZ, T: Chief Executive Officer **I:** Financial Services **CN:** Versant Capital Management, Inc. **CH:** One Child **ED:** BA in Business Management, University of Phoenix (2005) **CT:** Certified Financial Planner **C:** Chief Executive Officer, Versant Capital Management, Inc. (2018-Present); Chief Operating Officer, Versant Capital Management, Inc. (2012-Present); Senior Investment Counselor, Versant Capital Management, Inc. (2010- Present); Director of Operations and Relationship Manager, GenSpring Family Offices (2003-2010); Senior Associate, KPMG, LLP, Phoenix, AZ (2000-2003); Associate, Petersen Financial (Petersen Advisors) (1996-1993) **CR:** Adjunct Faculty Member, Institute for Preparing Heirs **CIV:** Advisory Board, Schwab Advisor Services (Charles Schwab & Co., Inc. ("Schwab")) (2017-2019) **AW:** Named One of the Most Influential Women, State of Arizona (2018); Named One of the Most Admired Leaders, Phoenix Business Journal (2018) **MEM:** Financial Planning Association; Free Arts for Abused Children of Arizona (Free Arts); National Charity League, Inc., East Valley Chapter, AZ; Planned Giving Committee, Phoenix Art Museum; Gen Next; UMOM **AS:** Ms. Shabaker attributes her success to the great mentors she's had around her, as well as the great team she has been surrounded with. She also never forgets to put her clients first. **B/I:** Ms. Shabaker's grandfather, John Bartowick, had an accounting firm in Carmel, California, where she grew up. She began in business in accounting and tax. She began to get used to how things worked in the field and decided she wanted to pursue a career in wealth management because of all the places she witnessed people needed help when it came to managing their money.

SHAEFFER, CHARLIE WILLARD, MD, T: Cardiologist, Lipidologist **I:** Medicine & Health Care **DOB:** 02/08/1938 **PB:** Philadelphia **SC:** PA/USA **PT:** Charlie Willard Shaeffer; Lucy Virginia (Chambliss) Shaeffer **MS:** Married **SPN:** Claire Brightwell (02/24/1959) **CH:** Charlie Willard III; James Robert **ED:** MD, Washington University, St. Louis, MO (1964); BS, Florida State University (1960) **CT:** Board Certified, American Board of Clinical Lipidology (2007-Present); Diplomate, American Board of Internal Medicine; American Board of Cardiovascular Disease **C:** Lipidologist, Eisenhower Medical Center, Rancho Mirage, CA (2015-2017); Retired, Cardiologist, Desert Cardiology Consultant, Inc., Rancho Mirage, CA (1974-2014); Chief, Cardiology, Naval Hospital, Portsmouth, VA (1971-1974); Staff, Cardiology, Naval Hospital, Portsmouth, VA (1970-1971); Fellow, Cardiology, Naval Hospital, Bethesda, MD (1968-1970); Resident, Internal Medicine, Naval Hospital, Oakland, CA (1965-1968); Rotating Intern, Naval Hospital, Bethesda, MD (1964-1965) **CR:** Board of Directors, Instructor, Advanced Cardiopulmonary Life Support, American Heart Association, Dallas, TX (1983-Present); American Board of Lipidology (2007); Chief of Cardiology, Eisenhower Medical Center, Rancho Mirage, CA (1976-1978); Consultant, Naval Hospital, San Diego, CA (1974-1975) **CIV:** Chair, Tobacco Issues Subcommittee, American Heart Association (1998-Present); Board of Directors, Eisenhower Medical Center, Rancho Mirage, CA (2002-2009); Volunteer Advocate, American Heart Association (2006); Chairman, Public Policy Subcommittee, American Heart Association (1996-1999); Chairman, Southwest Region, American Heart Association (1992-1993); Board of Directors, Eisenhower Memorial Hospital, Rancho Mirage, CA (1990-1993); Board of Directors, Eisenhower Medical Center, Rancho Mirage, CA (1990-1993); Chairman, Southwest Region, American Heart Association (1989-1990); Desert Division, American Heart Association, Palm Desert, CA (1989-1990); California Affiliate, American Heart Association, Burlingame, CA (1984-1985); President, Riverside County Heart Association (1978-1979) **MIL:** U.S. Navy Medical Corps (1964-1974) **CW:** Chapter, Author, Textbook (2008); Contributor, Articles, Professional Journals **AW:** Jefferson Award (2013); Gold Heart Award, American Heart Association (2010); Advocacy Award, American Heart Association (2004); Community Service Award, Riverside County Medical Association (2002); Sol Azteca Award, La Prensa Hispansa (2000); Honoree, Eisenhower Medical Center Auxiliary (1999); Physician of the Year, American Heart Association (1996); Gold Service Award (1988); Silver Service Award (1983, 1985, 1987); Bronze Service Award, California Affiliates, American Heart Association (1982) **MEM:** Fellow, American College of Physicians; Council on Clinical Cardiology, American Heart Association; American College of Cardiology; American College of Chest Physicians **MH:** Albert Nelson Marquis Lifetime Achievement Award **AS:** Dr. Shaeffer attributes his success to finding a career that was truly rewarding and stimulating. **B/I:** Dr. Shaeffer was always attracted to medicine. He chose to specialize in cardiology because of the opportunity to diagnose and treat from both his head and his hands. **AV:** Jogging; Listening to music; Reading; Traveling; Volunteering **THT:** Dr. Shaeffer makes the most of his life.

SHAEVSKY, MARK, T: Lawyer **I:** Law and Legal Services **CN:** Mark Shaevsky & Associates LLC **DOB:** 12/02/1935 **PB:** Harbin **SC:** China **PT:** Tolio Shaevsky; Rae (Weinstein) Shaevsky **MS:** Married **SPN:** Lois Levi Shaevsky **CH:** Thomas Lyle Shaevsky; Lawrence Keith Shaevsky **ED:** Doctor of Jurisprudence, University of Michigan Law School,

Highest Distinction (1959); Bachelor of Arts, University of Michigan, Highest Distinction (1956); Coursework, Wayne State University, Detroit, MI (1952-1953) **C:** Principal, Owner, Mark Shaevsky & Associates LLC, Farmington Hills, MI (2006-Present); Partner, Honigman, Miller, Schwartz & Cohn (1965-2005); Associate, Honigman, Miller, Schwartz & Cohn, Detroit, MI (1961-1964); Law Clerk, Presiding Judge, United States District Court, Detroit MI (1960-1961) **CR:** Director, H.W. Kaufman Financial Group Inc. (2006-Present); Director, Atain Specialty Insurance Company (2006-Present); Director, 1911 Trust Co. (2006-2016); Director, Freya Fanning Management, LLC (2006-2016); Director, Charter One Financial Inc. (1995-2004); Director, Charter One Bank (1995-2004); Director, First Federal Michigan (1986-1995); Instructor, Law, Wayne State University Law School, Detroit, MI (1961-1964); Commercial Arbitrator, American Arbitration Association, Detroit, MI **CIV:** Board Director, Shaevsky Family Foundation (2000-Present); Board Director, Beaumont Indemnity Company (2007-2013); Board Director, Vice Chairman, Chair of Finance and Audit Committees, William Beaumont Hospital (2002-2013); Trustee, William Beaumont Hospital (1997-2013); Trustee, Beaumont Foundation (1997-2005); Capital Needs Committee, Jewish Welfare Federation (1986-1997); Secretary, Director, American Friends of the Hebrew University (1976-1984); Director, Detroit Mens Organization of Rehabilitation through Training (1969-1979); Trustee, Jewish Vocational Services (1973-1976); Executive Board, American Jewish Committee (1965-1974) **MIL:** U.S. Army (1959-1960) **CW:** Editor, University of Michigan Law Review (1957-1959); Contributor, Editor, Articles to Professional Journals **AW:** Burton Abstract Fellow (1959) **MEM:** American Bar Association; Michigan Bar Association; Franklin Hills Country Club; Detroit Athletic Club; Order of the Coif; Phi Beta Kappa **BAR:** Michigan (1959) **MH:** Albert Nelson Marquis Lifetime Achievement Award **B/I:** Mr. Shaevsky became involved in law because he wanted to use ethics to help solve people's personal and business problems.

SHAH, GULZAR H., T: Professor & Department Chair of Health Policy and Management **I:** Education/Educational Services **CN:** Georgia Southern University **PB:** Faisalabad, Pakistan **SC:** Pakistan **PT:** Syed Nazir Shah; Razia Bano **MS:** Married **SPN:** Bushra Shah **ED:** PhD in Sociology, Demography, Sociology of Health, Utah State University, Logan, UT (1995); MS in Sociology, Anthropology, Statistics, Utah State University, Logan, UT (1989); MS in Statistics, University of Punjab, Lahore, Pakistan (1987); BA in Applied Mathematics & Statistics, University of Punjab, Lahore, Pakistan (1984); BA in Anthropology, Statistics, Sociology, Utah State University, Logan, UT **C:** Professor, Department Chairman, Health Policy & Behavior, Jiann-Ping Hsu College of Public Health, Georgia Southern University (2018-Present); Department Chairman, Health Policy & Community Health, Jiann-Ping Hsu College of Public Health, Georgia Southern University (2017-Present); Associate Dean, Associate Professor, Health Policy & Management, Jiann-Ping Hsu College of Public Health, Georgia Southern University (2012-Present); Associate Dean, Associate Professor, Department of Health Policy and Management, Georgia Southern University (2012-Present); Lead Research Scientist, National Association of County & Health Officials (2008-2011); Adjunct Professional Lecturer, George Washington University, Washington, DC (2008-2011); Director of Research, National Association of Health Data Organizations, Salt Lake City, UT (2005-2007); Associate Professor, Lahore University of Management Sciences (LUMS) (2003-2005); Senior Programmer Analyst, Utah Department of Health (1996-2002); Consultant, National Institute of Population Studies (1987-1988) **CR:** Member, Academy Health: Health Information Technology IG Advisory Committee (2019-Present); President, Gamma Theta Chapter of Delta Omega Honor Society (2017-2018); Co-Chair, Planning Committee for the Research Section, Association of School & Programs of Public Health (2017-2018); Member, National Advisory Committee, National Association of Quality & City Health Officials, National Profile of Local Health Departments **CIV:** Public Health Volunteer; Chairman, Planning Committee, Research Section Association of School & Programs of Public Health; National Advisory Committee, National Association of Quality & City Health Officials, National Profile of Local Health Departments **CW:** Editorial Board, American Journal of Public Health (2019-2022); Consulting Editor, Journal of Public Health Management and Practice; Poet, "Chocolate Aur Phool"; Author, 140 Peer-Reviewed Articles; Associate Editor, BMC Public Health Journal; Editor, Journal of Public Health Management and Practice; Editorial Board, Ellion Journal **AW:** Award for Research and Scholarly Activity, Georgia Southern University (2016); Karl E. Peace Leadership Award, Delta Omega Honor Society (2016); Mentor of the Year Award, Jiann-Ping Hsu College of Public Health (2016); Nancy Rawding National Association of County and City Health Officials' Employee of the Year Award (2009) **MEM:** American Public Health Association; Association of Schools & Programs of Public Health; National Association of County and City Health Officials **AS:** Dr. Shah attributes his success to dedication, hard work and sincerity in his duties of service. **B/I:** Dr. Shah became involved in his profession after receiving his PhD in 1995. He began his career in the State of Utah Department of Health. Pursuing public health practice, rather than more lucrative career in private sector was sparked by his desire to make a meaningful contribution to the society through participation in public health practice and science. He believed there is unparalleled satisfaction in seeing his public health work resulting in disease prevention and health promotion towards healthy prolonged lives. To Dr. Shah, the public health field is a noble profession and a great fit for his career goals. As his career progressed, he began to have the desire to pass his knowledge to others. He then began a teaching career and moved full-time into academia. **THT:** "Creating evidence that can improve public health is the best and most purposeful research to be done."

SHAH, RISHI U., T: Co-Founder **I:** Medicine & Health Care **CN:** Outcome Health **PB:** Oak Brook **SC:** IL/USA **PT:** Dr. Upendra Shah; Sonal Shah **ED:** Coursework, Northwestern University (2005-2008); Coursework, Harvard University (2005) **C:** Co-Founder, Managing Director, JumpStart Ventures (2011-Present); Chief Executive Officer, Chairman, Outcome Health (2006-2018); Co-Founder, Outcome Health (2006) **CIV:** Past Chairperson, Institute for Student Business Education **CW:** Member, Board of Advisers, Northwestern Business Review **AW:** Listed, "Forbes 400," Forbes (2017); Named, Among the "40 Under 40," Crain's Chicago Business (2009)

SHAH, VINOD P. PHD, PRESIDENT, T: Pharmaceutical Consultant **I:** Consulting **CN:** VPS Consulting LLC **DOB:** 09/02/1939 **PB:** Baroda **SC:** Gujarat, India **PT:** Purushottam; Taraben Shah **MS:** Married **SPN:** Manjula Shah (02/18/1965) **CH:** Manish; Sujata **ED:** Doctor of Philosophy in Pharmaceutical Chemistry, University of California San Francisco (1964); Bachelor's Degree in Pharmacy, University of Madras (1959) **C:** President, VPS Consulting, Potomac, MD (2005-Present); Pharmaceutical Chemist, Expert Consultant, NDA Partners LLC (Present); Research Coordinator, Topical Drug Products, Romania, (Present); Senior Research Scientist, Food and Drug Administration, Rockville, MD (1994-2005); Associate Director, Food and Drug Administration, Rockville, MD (1990-1994); Assistant Director, Food and Drug Administration, Rockville, MD (1988-1990); Branch Chief, Food and Drug Administration, Rockville, MD (1984-1988); Pharmaconkinetics Reviewer, Food and Drug Administration, Rockville, MD (1981-1984); Senior Research Chemist, Technical Coordinator, Food and Drug Administration, Washington, DC (1975-1981); Postdoctoral Research Fellow, University of California San Francisco, California (1969-1975); Pharmaceutical Research and Development Chemist, Sarabhai Chemical, Baroda, India (1964-1969) **CR:** Chairman, International Scientific Committee, Society for Pharmaceutical Development Science (2013-Present); Biopharmaceutics Expert Consultant, United States Pharmacopeia (2005-2014); Science Secretary, Board of Pharmaceutical Sciences, Food and Drug Administration (1975-2005); Expert Member, International Pharmaceutical Federation **CW:** Editor, "Desk Book of Pharmaceutical Dissolution Science and Applications" (2015); Editor, "Topical Drug Bioavailability, Bioequivalence and Penetration" (1993, 2014); Editor, "Integration of Pharmocokinetics, Pharmacodynamics and Toxicokinetics in Rational Drug Development" (1993); Advisory Board, Skin Pharmacology Journal (1987-1992); Contributor, Articles to Professional Journals **AW:** Honor of Merit, Hungary Pro Universidad (2019); Global Leader Award, American Association of Pharmaceutical Scientists (2018); Distinguished Pharmaceutical Scientist Award, American Association of Pharmaceutical Scientists (2017); Doctor Honoris Causa, University of Medicine and Pharmacy Carol Davila, Bucharest, Romania (2016); Doctor Honoris Causa, Semmelweis University, Budapest, Hungary (2012); Lifetime Achievement Award in Pharmaceutical Sciences, International Pharmaceutical Federation (2012); Fellow, International Pharmaceutical Federation (2006); Fellow, American Association of Pharmaceutical Scientists (1990); Gold Medal, University of Madras (1959) **MEM:** Co-Chairman, Science Workshops, American Association of Pharmaceutical Scientists (1986-Present); Regulatory Science Chairman, International Pharmaceutical Federal (2011-2016); Science Secretary, International Pharmaceutical Federal (2003-2011); President, American Association of Pharmaceutical Scientists (2003) **MH:** Albert Nelson Marquis Lifetime Achievement Award; Marquis Who's Who Top Professional **B/I:** Dr. Shah became involved in his profession because he was interested in getting a better education and an interest in increasing the quality of drug products. At the encouragement of his parents, he traveled to California after graduating as a pharmacist.

SHAHEEN, CYNTHIA, "JEANNE" JEANNE, T: U.S. Senator **I:** Government Administration/Government Relations/Government Services **DOB:** 01/28/1947 **PB:** St. Charles **SC:** MO/USA **PT:** Ivan E. Bowers; Belle E. Bowers **MS:** Married **SPN:** William H. Shaheen (1972) **CH:** Stefany; Stacey; Molly **ED:** Master of Social Science in Political Science, The University of Mississippi (1973); BA in English, Shippensburg University (1969) **C:** U.S. Senator, State of New Hampshire (2009-Present); Ranking Member, Small Business Committee, United States Senate (2015-2018); Chair, Committee on Foreign Relations, Subcommittee on European Affairs, United States Senate (2009-2013); Director, Institute of Politics, Harvard University, Cambridge,

MA (2005-2007); National Chair, John Kerry's Presidential Campaign (2004); Vice Chair, Democratic National Convention Committee (2004); Governor, State of New Hampshire, Concord, NH (1997-2003); Member, District 21, New Hampshire State Senate (1991-1996); Campaign Manager, Governor Paul McEachon (1988); Campaign Manager, Governor Paul McEachon (1986); Campaign Manager, Gary Hart's Presidential Campaign (1984); Campaign Manager, President Jimmy Carter's Presidential Campaign, NH (1980); Teacher, NH (1973); Teacher, High School, MS **CR:** Chair, Education Commission of the States (2000-2001) **PA:** Democrat **RE:** Protestant

SHAHIDI, FREYDOON, PHD, T: Mathematician, Mathematics Educator, Distinguished Professor of Mathematics **I:** Education/Educational Services **CN:** Purdue University **DOB:** 06/19/1947 **PB:** Tehran **SC:** Iran **PT:** Manoochehr Shahidi; Aghdas Shahidi **MS:** Married **SPN:** Guity Ravai (09/21/1977) **CH:** Alireza; Amir **ED:** PhD, Johns Hopkins University (1975); BS, University of Tehran (1969) **C:** Professor of Mathematics, Purdue University (1986-Present); Distinguished Professor of Mathematics, Purdue University (2001); Visiting Member, Institute for Advanced Study (1975-1976, 1983-1984, 1990-1991); Associate Professor of Mathematics, Purdue University (1982-1986); Assistant Professor, Purdue University (1977-1982); Visiting Assistant Professor, Indiana University Bloomington (1976-1977) **CR:** Visiting Assistant Professor, University of Toronto, University Paris VII, University of Chicago, California Institute of Technology, Morningside Institute, Tsinghua University, Brown University, University of Minnesota **MIL:** Second Lieutenant, Iran (1969-1971) **CW:** Co-Author, "Analytic Properties of Automorphic L-Functions"; Editor, American Journal of Mathematics; Editor, Canadian Journal of Mathematics; Editor, International Mathematics Research Notices; Editor, Journal of Representation Theory **AW:** Grant, National Science Foundation (1977-Present); Sigma Xi, The Scientific Research Honor Society (2020); Ruth and Joel Spira Faculty Teaching Award (2019); Fellow, American Mathematical Society (2012); Fellow, American Academy of Arts and Sciences (2010); Fellowship, Guggenheim Museum (2001); Fellow, Kyoto University (1993, 1996) **MEM:** Honorary Member, Iranian Mathematical Society; American Mathematical Society **MH:** Albert Nelson Marquis Lifetime Achievement Award **AS:** Dr. Shahidi became involved in his profession because of his passion for his work and support from his family. **B/I:** Dr. Shahidi became involved in his profession because of his experiences in the military and his passion for mathematics. **AV:** Listening to music **RE:** Muslim

SHAINMAN, JACK, T: Co-Founder **I:** Fine Art **CN:** Jack Shainman Gallery **DOB:** 07/21/1957 **PB:** Pittsfield **SC:** MA/USA **PT:** Irwin Shainman; Bernice (Cohen) Shainman **ED:** Bachelor of Science, American University (1980) **C:** Owner, Director, Jack Shainman Gallery, New York, NY (1986-Present); Owner, Director, Jack Shainman Gallery, Washington, DC (1984-1988); Director, Massimo, Provincetown, MA (1983-1984); Assistant Director, Osuna Gallery, Washington, DC (1981-1983)

SHALALA, DONNA EDNA, PHD, T: U.S. Representative from Florida; Educator **I:** Education/Educational Services **DOB:** 02/14/1941 **PB:** Cleveland **SC:** OH/USA **PT:** James Abraham Shalala; Edna (Smith) Shalala **ED:** PhD, Syracuse University Maxwell School of Citizenship and Public Affairs (1970); MSSC, Syracuse University (1968); AB, Western College (1962) **C:** Member, U.S. House of Representatives from Florida's 27th Congressional

District (2019-Present); President, Clinton Foundation (2015-2017); Secondary Faculty, Department of Epidemiology, University of Miami (2002-2015); Professor, Political Science, University of Miami (2001-2015); President, University of Miami (2001-2015); Secretary, U.S. Department of Health and Human Services, Washington, DC (1993-2001); Professor, Political Science and Educational Policy Studies, University of Wisconsin-Madison (1987-1993); Chancellor, University of Wisconsin-Madison (1987-1993); Professor, Political Science, Hunter College, City University of New York (1980-1987); President, Hunter College, City University of New York (1980-1987); Assistant Secretary for Policy Development and Research, U.S. Department of Housing and Urban Development (HUD), Washington, DC (1977-1980); Associate Professor, Chair, Program in Politics and Education, Teachers College, Columbia University (1972-1979); Assistant Professor, Political Science, Baruch College, City University of New York (1970-1972) **CR:** Board of Directors, MEDNAX Services, Inc. (2010-Present); Co-Chair, President's Commission on Care for America's Returning Wounded Warriors (2007-Present); Board of Directors, Gannett Co., Inc., McLeon, VA (2001-Present); Board of Directors, Lennar Corporation (2001-Present); Director, Treasurer, Municipal Assistance Corporation, New York, NY (1975-1977); Visiting Professor, Yale Law School (1976) **CIV:** Co-Chair, Mother's Day Every Day (2009-Present); Board of Directors, U.S. Soccer Federation (2008-Present); Board of Directors, Institute for International Economics (Now Peterson Institute for International Economics) (1981-Present); Trustee, Henry J. Kaiser Family Foundation (2001-2011); Member, Homes for Working Families (HWF) (2004-2008); Board of Directors, The Michael J. Fox Foundation for Parkinson's Research (2001-2008); Board of Directors, UnitedHealth Group, Inc., Minneapolis, MN (2001-2007); Trustee, John F. Kennedy Center for the Performing Arts, Washington, DC (1993-2001); Board of Directors, The American Ditchley Foundation (1981-1993); Board of Directors, Children's Defense Fund (1980-1993); Board of Directors, M&I Bank of Madison (Now BMO) (1991-1992); Trustee, Brookings Institution (1989-1992); The Trilateral Commission (1988-1992); Board of Directors, The Spencer Foundation (1988-1992); Trustee, Committee on Economic Development (1982-1992); Board of Directors, NCAA Foundation (1991); Knight Commission on Intercollegiate Athletics (1989-1991); Trustee, TIAA (1985-1989); Board of Governors, American Stock Exchange (1981-1987); Volunteer, United States Peace Corps (1962-1964) **CW:** Author, "The Decentralization Approach" (1974); Author, "The Property Tax and the Voters" (1973); Author, "The City and the Constitution" (1972); Author, "Neighborhood Governance" (1971) **AW:** Presidential Medal of Freedom, The White House (2008); Radcliffe Medal, Radcliffe Institute for Advanced Study, Harvard University (2008); Listee, 25 Great Public Servants, Council for Excellence (2008); Ellis Island Family Heritage Award in Education, The Statue of Liberty-Ellis Island Foundation, Inc. (2008); Urban Leadership Award, Penn Institute from Urban Research, The University of Pennsylvania (2008); Images in Excellence Award, Black Coaches Association (2007); Silver Medallion Award for Service to Humanity, National Conference for Community and Justice (2005); Listee, America's Best Leaders, U.S. News & World Report and Center for Public Leadership, Harvard Kennedy School, John F. Kennedy School of Government (2005); John P. McGovern Award, American Association of Colleges of Nursing (AACN) (2003); Medal, University of California San Francisco (2002); Distinguished Leader Award for a Lifetime of Public Service, League

of Women Voters (2000); Margaret E. Mahoney Award for Outstanding Contributions to Health Policy, New York Academy of Medicine (1997); Ryan White Youth Service Award for Outstanding Contributions to the Fight Against Teen HIV/AIDS (1997); Listee, Women of the Year, Glamour Magazine (1994); Hubert Humphrey Award, APSA (1994); Annual Career Achievement Award for Distinguished Scholarships in Urban Politics, APSA (1992); National Public Service Award, The American Society for Public Administration (1992); Distinguished Service Medal, Teachers College, Columbia University (1989); Elizabeth Morrow Cutter Award, YWCA of Greater New York (1982); Donald C. Stone Award, The American Society for Public Administration (1981); Guggenheim Fellow (1975-1976); Spencer Fellow, National Academy of Education (1972-1973); Carnegie Fellow (1966-1968); Trustee Scholar, Western College (1958-1962); Ohio Newspaper Women's Scholar (1958) **MEM:** Leadership Fellow, Japan Society (1987); Vice President, APSA (1984-1985); Fellow, American Academy of Political and Social Science; Council Member, Institute of Medicine (National Academy of Medicine); National Academy of Public Administration; The American Society for Public Administration; National Academy of Social Insurance; American Academy Arts & Sciences; Council of Foreign Relations; The American Philosophical Society; SWHR; National Academy of Education; Japan Society; American Academy of Political and Social Science **PA:** Democrat

SHANAHAN, PATRICK MICHAEL, T: Former Acting United States Secretary of Defense **I:** Government Administration/Government Relations/Government Services **DOB:** 06/27/1962 **PB:** Palo Alto **SC:** CA/USA **PT:** Michael George Shanahan; Jo-Anne Genevieve (David) Shanahan **CH:** Three Children **ED:** MBA, Massachusetts Institute of Technology Sloan School of Management; MS in Mechanical Engineering, Massachusetts Institute of Technology; BS in Mechanical Engineering, University of Washington **C:** Acting United States Secretary of Defense, Washington, DC (2019); Deputy United States Secretary of Defense, Washington, DC (2017-2019); Senior Vice President, Supply Chain and Operations Worldwide, Boeing Company (2016-2017); Vice President, General Manager, Airplane Programs, Boeing Commercial Airplanes, Boeing Company (2008-2016); Vice President, General Manager, 787 Dreamline Program, Boeing Company (2004); Vice President, General Manager, Boeing Missile Defense System, Boeing Company, Washington, DC (2004); With, Boeing Company (1986); Vice President, General Manager, Rotorcraft System, Boeing Company, Philadelphia, PA; Vice President, General Manager, Boeing Commercial Airplanes, Boeing Company; Director, 767 Manufacturing Business Unit, Director, Tooling Business Unit, Fabrications Division, Boeing Company; Program Manager, Boeing 767-400ER, Boeing Company **CIV:** Board of Directors, American Parkinson Disease Association (2004); Secretary, Treasurer, American Helicopter Society (Now The Vertical Flight Society); Fellow, SME; Fellow, Royal Aeronautical Society **AW:** Distinguished Service, University of Washington College of Engineering (2019)

SHARFMAN, WILLIAM L., T: Author, Writer, Interviewer, Consulting Strategist **I:** Writing and Editing **DOB:** 10/11/1942 **SC:** WA/USA **PT:** Warren Leonard Sharfman; Amalie (Schenthal) Sharfman **MS:** Single **SPN:** Caroline Sharp (09/05/1964, Divorced 1985) **ED:** PhD in English and Comparative Literature, Columbia University (1969); MA in English, Columbia University (1965); BA in English, Minor in Psychology and Art History, University of

Michigan (1964) CT: Dr. W. Edwards Deming, Quality, Productivity, and Competitive Position (1991); Graduate Certificate, The School of Jazz, Lenox (1958-1959) C: Principal, Sharfman & Company, New York, NY (1985-Present); Director of Judging, Automotive News PACE Awards for Innovation, NY (1994-2009); Senior Vice President, Strategic Planning, J. Walter Thompson U.S.A., New York, NY (1982-1985); Senior Vice President, Strategic Planning, Corporate Communications, J. Walter Thompson Company, New York, NY (1978-1982); Vice President, Marketing, Metagraphic Systems, New York, NY (1973-1976); President, Time-Sharing Information Services, Philadelphia, PA (1972-1973); Vice Chairman, English Department, Idaho State University (1970-1972); Founder, Courses for College Credit, Sun Valley, ID (1971); Lecturer, Preceptor, Columbia University, New York, NY (1966-1970) CR: Judge, Greenwich Concours (1998-2015); Authors Guild; National Writers Union CIV: Volunteer, Conservation, Environmental, Political Causes CW: Studio Regular, The Auto Lab Radio Broadcast, New York, NY (2006-Present); Contributing Writer, Las Vegas Life (2001-2003); Contributing Writer, Automobile Magazine (1986-2001); Author, "A Time to Stir: Columbia 1968"; Contributor, Articles, Professional Journals; Writer, Journalist, Interviewer, Literary Criticism AW: Recognition of Excellence in International Automotive Media (1999) MEM: Life Member, University of Michigan Alumni Association; Life Member, Columbia University Graduate Faculties Alumni Association; The Authors Guild; The National Writers Union; Board Member, International Motor Press Association MH: Albert Nelson Marquis Lifetime Achievement Award; Marquis Who's Who Top Professional B/I: Mr. Sharfman became involved in his profession because he was in charge of John F. Kennedy's luggage during his freshman year of college. It was the night President Kennedy stayed in Ann Arbor, Michigan, announcing his concept of the Peace Corps. The commencement speaker was Lyndon Johnson. Mr. Sharfman was privy to and part of more than the average person at the time. His family and surroundings had an enormous impact on his upbringing.

SHARMA, PANKAJ, MD, PHD, FRCP, T: Neurologist, Researcher, Scientist **I:** Medicine & Health Care **CN:** University of London **PB:** New Delhi **SC:** India **PT:** Kewal Krishan Sharma; Janak Sharma **MS:** Married **SPN:** Sapna Devi Sharma, MD, DRCOG, MRCGP, MBChB **CH:** Aarti Rani; Shyam Sunder **ED:** Fellow, Royal College of Physicians (FRCP); PhD, University of Cambridge; MD, University of London; MB, BS, University of London; Diploma, History of Medicine, Society of Apothecaries (DHMSA), Worshipful Society of Apothecaries of London **CT:** Medical License, London, England (1988) **C:** Director, Institute of Cardiovascular Research, Royal Holloway, University of London (2014-Present); Professor, Neurology, Royal Holloway, University of London (2014-Present); Consultant Neurologist, Hammersmith Hospital & Imperial College NHS Hospital (Now Imperial College Healthcare NHS Trust), London, England (2003-Present); British Heart Foundation Clinician Scientist, University of Cambridge (1994-2000); Senior Fellow, Department of Health, United Kingdom (1994-1999) **CR:** External Advisor, Parliamentary and Health Service Ombudsman, United Kingdom (2019-Present); President, London Cardiovascular Society (2006-Present); Medical Director, Different Strokes, London, England (2004-Present) **CIV:** Court of Benefactors, Gonville & Caius College, University of Cambridge (2019-Present); Chair, Lotus Partners Foundation (2017-Present); Co-Founder, Treasurer, Board Trustee, South Asian Health Foundation, London, England (1997-2016)

CW: International Editorial Board, Journal of the Royal Society of Medicine in Cardiovascular Disease (2019-Present); Founding Editor-in-Chief, Journal of the Royal Society of Medicine in Cardiovascular Disease (2012-2018); Media Commentator, BBC TV and Radio, CNN International; Contributor, Articles, Professional Journals **AW:** Named, UK Top Asian Doctor, British Indian Awards (2015); British Heart Foundation Clinician Scientist Award (1994-2000); Fulbright Scholar, Harvard Medical School and Massachusetts General Hospital, Boston, MA (1998-1999); Fulbright Scholar, Gonville & Caius College, University of Cambridge (1994-1997); Fulbright Scholar, London Hospital Medical College, University of London (Now Barts and the London School of Medicine and Dentistry, Queen Mary University of London) (1983-1988) **MEM:** President, British Fulbright Scholars Association, London, England (2004-2006); President, Gonville Hall Debating Society, University of Cambridge (1995-1997); Fellow, Royal College of Physicians, London, England; Fellow, Medical Society of London; Hurlingham Polo Association **MH:** Albert Nelson Marquis Lifetime Achievement Award **AV:** Collecting antiquarian inscribed books; Theater; Tennis; Fencing; Debating; Polo **RE:** Hindu **THT:** Prof. Sharma is the son of Kewal Krishan Sharma, a member of the Indian Foreign Diplomatic Corps who served under three prime ministers, Nehru, Shastri & Indira Gandhi; his mother is Janak Sharma, who worked for the Bank of England. His family is noted for holding the national license for Kodak in India prior to Partition of India.

SHARP, DAVID H., PHD, T: Physicist **I:** Sciences **DOB:** 10/14/1938 **PB:** Buffalo **SC:** NY/USA **PT:** Russel Howland Sharp; Margaret E. (Dorries) Sharp **MS:** Married **SPN:** Gloria Evanitsky (01/09/1982) **CH:** Lisa E.; Michele L. **ED:** PhD in Theoretical Physics, California Institute of Technology (1964); BA in Physics, Princeton University (1960) **C:** Consultant, Department of Mechanical Engineering, Stanford University (2014-Present); Guest Scientist, Los Alamos National Laboratory (2012-Present); Lifetime Appointment, Laboratory Fellow, Los Alamos National Laboratory(1984-Present); Chief Scientist, Science Technology and Engineering Directorate, Los Alamos National Laboratory (2006-2008); Deputy Chief Science Officer, Los Alamos National Laboratory (2004-2005); Senior Science Adviser, Applied Physics Division, Los Alamos National Laboratory (2002-2004); Group Leader, Complex Systems Group, Theoretical Division, Los Alamos National Laboratory (2002-2004); Staff Member, Los Alamos National Laboratory (1974-2012); Assistant Professor, University of Pennsylvania (1967-1974) **CR:** Consultant, Department of Ecology and Evolution, The University of Chicago (2012-Present); Member, Industrial Advisory Board, IMA (2002-Present); Adjunct Professor of Applied Mathematics and Statistics, Stony Brook University (1990-Present); Research Fellow, California Institute of Technology (1966-Present); Member, National Laboratory Research Advisory Board, University of California, Davis (2007-2011); Member, Board of Governors, Institute for Mathematics and its Applications (2007-2011); Member, Office of the Vice Chancellor for Research, University of California (2006-2012); Member, New Mexico Research Council (2005-2006); Visiting Fellow, Center for Theoretical Neuroscience, Salk Institute for Biological Studies (1995-1998); Member, Editorial Board, Journal of Mathematical Physics (1985-1987); Instructor, Princeton University (1966-1967); Research Fellow, Technische University of Munich (1965-1966) **CIV:** Chairman, J. Robert Oppenheimer Memorial Committee (1978); Vice Chairman, J. Robert Oppenheimer Memorial Committee (1977); Active, J. Robert Oppenheimer

Memorial Committee (1976-1996) **CW:** Contributor, More Than 250 Articles, Professional Journals **AW:** Defense Programs Award Of Excellence, U.S. Department of Energy (2001); Postdoctoral Fellow, National Science Foundation (1963-1964) **MEM:** Editorial Board, Journal Proceedings, American Mathematical Society (1992-2003); Fellow, American Association for the Advancement of Science; Fellow, American Physical Society; Fellow, Society for Industrial and Applied Mathematics; International Association of Mathematical Physics; International Society on General Relativity and Gravitation; New York Academy of Sciences; Former Member, Society of Petroleum Engineers; New Mexico Academy of Science; International Neural Network Society **MH:** Albert Nelson Marquis Lifetime Achievement Award **AS:** Dr. Sharp attributes his success to hard work and good luck. **B/I:** Dr. Sharp became involved in his profession because he was very interested in science as a young boy.

SHARP, GARY DUANE, PHD, T: Marine Biologist **I:** Sciences **CN:** Center for Climate and Ocean Resources Study **DOB:** 02/22/1944 **PB:** Lubbock **SC:** TX/USA **PT:** J.E. Sharp; Dorothy Lillian (Christian) Sharp **MS:** Married **SPN:** Kathleen Teresa Dorsey (10/31/1981) **ED:** PhD in Marine Biology, UC San Diego (1972); MS in Biology, San Diego State University (1968); BS in Zoology, San Diego State University (1967) **C:** Consulting, Center for Climate and Ocean Resources Study (1991-Present); Independent Consultant, Ocean Resources-Related Climate (1983-Present); Scientific Director, The Cooperative Institute for Ocean Exploration, Research & Technology (1991); Consulting Science Adviser, Undersecretary of Oceans and Atmosphere (1990-1991); Contract Worker, Science Adviser, Administrator, Center for Ocean Analysis and Prediction, National Oceanographic and Atmospheric Administration, Monterey, CA (1988-1991); Consultant, Center for Climate and Ocean Resources Study, Gainesville, FL (1983-1988); Fisheries Resources Officer, Fisheries Resources and Environment Division, Food and Agriculture Organization of the United Nations, Rome, Italy (1978-1983); Senior Scientist, Inter-American Tropical Tuna Commission, La Jolla, CA (1969-1978); Biologist, Bureau of Commercial Fisheries, La Jolla, CA (1968-1969); Laboratory Assistant, Biochemical Genetics, San Diego State University (1966-1968); Gear Development Group, La Jolla Bureau of Commercial Lab, La Jolla, CA (1967) **CR:** Special Science and Policy Adviser, Monterey Bay National Marine Sanctuary Advisory Council (1993-2010); Adjunct Professor, Fisheries Centre, The University of British Columbia (1993-2004); Technology and Curriculum Integration Planner, California State University, Monterey Bay (1995-1997); Cooperative Institute for Research in the Integrated Ocean Sciences (1991-1997); Contracted by Provost Steve Arvizu, Development of the Initial Science Curriculum and Planning, Staff Selection Activities, California State University, Monterey Bay (1993) **MIL:** Principal Horn, The U.S. Air Force Band of The Rockies, U.S. Air Force, Denver, CO (1961-1965) **CW:** Co-Author, "Climate and Fisheries: Forecasting Contextual Changes,Instead of Hindcasting from Meaningless Means," Symposium 49, American Fisheries Society (2008); Co-Author, "Out of Fishermen's Hands...Fishermen's Role In Society and Natural Systems" (2004); Co-Author, "Climate and Fisheries: Forecasting Contextual Changes, Instead of Hindcasting from Meaningless Means," Proceedings of the Fourth World Fisheries Congress, Vancouver, Canada, British Columbia (2004); Co-Author, "Ocean Fisheries, and Aquatic Ecosystems-in Response to Daily, Seasonal and Climate Scale Forcing," The Association for the Sciences of Limnology and Oceanography (2004); Contributor,

"Future Climate Change and Regional Fisheries:A Collaborative Analysis," Fisheries Department, Food and Agriculture Organization, Rome, Italy (2003); Contributor, "The Past Present and Future of Fisheries Science; Refashioning a Responsible Fisheries Science" (2000); Contributor, "Climate and Fisheries: Cause and Effect-A System Review" (1991); Contributor, "Climate and Fisheries: Cause and Effect or Managing the Long and Short of it All," South African Journal of Marine Science (1987); Contributor, "Climate and Fisheries: Cause and Effect and the Quest for Elusive Time Series," The Human Consequences of 1985s Climate Conference, American Meteorological Society (1986); Co-editor, "Reports of the Expert Consultation to Examine Changes in Abundance and Species Composition of Neritic Fish Resources (1983); Senior Editor, "FAO Atlas of Living Resources of the Seas" (1980); Author, Editor, "The Physiological Ecology of Tunas" (1978); Contributor, Articles, Professional Journals **MEM:** The Association for the Sciences of Limnology and Oceanography; American Geophysical Union; American Society for the Advancement of Science; The Oceanography Society **MH:** Albert Nelson Marquis Lifetime Achievement Award **B/I:** Dr. Sharp became involved in his profession because his stepfather was a chief engineer in the San Diego tuna fishing industry; he followed in his father's footsteps. **AV:** Playing the French horn

SHARP, GEORGE RICHARD, T: Aerospace Engineer **I:** Engineering **DOB:** 05/01/1934 **PB:** Newark **SC:** NJ/USA **PT:** Joseph Feinour Sharp; Mildred (Cascaden) Sharp **MS:** Married **SPN:** Evelyn Alice Gadd (11/02/1957) **CH:** Lynda Ann; Gary Richard **ED:** MS in Engineering Mechanics, Case Western Reserve University, Cleveland, OH (1967); BS in Industrial Engineering, New York University (1956) **CT:** Registered Professional Engineer, Ohio **C:** Chief Engineer, Space Experiments Division, NASA/Lewis Research Center, Cleveland, OH (1991-1993); Senior Project Engineer, NASA/Lewis Research Center, Cleveland, OH (1963-1991); Designer, Goodyear Aerospace Corp., Akron, OH (1958-1963); Project Engineer, Goodyear Tire & Rubber Company, Akron, OH (1956-1958) **CW:** Thermal and Electrically Isolating Support Structure for Traveling Wave Tube for NASA/Canada CTS Communications Satellite; Satellite Preceded and Provided Technology for Both Dish and Direct TV Satellite Systems **AW:** Numerous NASA Awards **MEM:** American Institute of Aeronautics and Astronautics **MH:** Albert Nelson Marquis Lifetime Achievement Award **B/I:** Mr. Sharp became involved in his profession because he always had an interest in aircraft. He attended an air show when he was about 10 years old, and to this day, he can still picture watching the performance of the military planes. While a freshman in high school, he wrote a paper about his aspiration to become an aircraft designer. He wanted to be an engineer and had registered to become an aerodynamic engineer, and when he got there, he found out that for aircraft design, only a few people and the others contribute to it. He did some soul-searching and decided to study industrial engineering. When he was at the Goodyear Tire & Rubber Company, he worked on air springs. The department was reduced at some point, and so he went to work for Goodyear Aerospace and that is how he got started in aerospace business. From there, NASA got started and that is when he applied and got a job there. **AV:** Sailing; Hiking **RE:** Unitarian Universalist

SHARP, JAMES FRANKLIN, PHD, T: Finance Educator, Portfolio Manager **I:** Financial Services **DOB:** 09/29/1936 **PB:** Johnson County **SC:** IL/USA **PT:** James Albert Sharp; Edna Mae Sharp **ED:** PhD,

Purdue University (1966); MS, Purdue University (1961); BS in Industrial Engineering, University of Illinois (1959) **CT:** Investment Performance Measurement (2011); Faculty Manager (1997); Chartered Financial Analyst (1980); Management Accountant (1979) **C:** Chairman, Sharp Seminars (1986-Present); Professor, Finance, Graduate School of Business, Pace University, New York, NY (1975-1991); Assistant Finance Chairman, Graduate School of Business, Pace University, New York, NY (1975-1991); Management, Internal Consulting, Financial Planning, AT&T, New York, NY (1974-1985); Associate Professor, New York University Graduate School of Business (1967-1974); Assistant Professor, Engineering, Economics, Rutgers University, The State University of New Jersey, New Brunswick, NJ (1964-1967) **CR:** Consultant, Sharp Investment Management (1967-Present); Speaker, Moderator, Local, National, International Meetings (1965-Present); Speaker in Fields **CW:** Author, 36 Books; Contributor, Articles, Numerous Professional Journals **AW:** Distinguished Alumnus Award, University of Illinois (2016); Masters Outstanding Alumnus Award (2010); Outstanding Alumnus Award, Purdue University (2010) **MEM:** Vice President, American Association of University Professors, Pace University (1988-1990); Chartered Financial Analyst, New York Society of Security Analysts (1985-1987); Council, International Affiliation of Planning Societies (1978-1984); President, Planning Ground, Operations Research Society (1976-1982); Board of Directors at Large, North America Society Corporation (1977-1978); Treasurer, North America Society Corporation Planning (1976-1977); Chapter President, Institute of Management Science (1976-1977); Vice President, Membership, Institute of Management Science (1975-1976); Vice President, Program, Institute of Management Science (1974-1975); Chapter Academic Vice President, Institute of Management Science (1972-1974); Theta Xi; Mensa **MH:** Albert Nelson Marquis Lifetime Achievement Award **AV:** Writing **PA:** Republican

SHARPLES, EDWARD, PHD, T: Academic Administrator, English Professor **I:** Education/Educational Services **DOB:** 04/09/1933 **PB:** Westport **SC:** MA/USA **PT:** Edward Sharples; Winifred Kirby (Gifford) Sharples **MS:** Widowed **SPN:** Mona Diane Erickson (07/07/1956) **CH:** Edward Eric; Matthew Ward **ED:** PhD, University of Rochester (1964); BA, University of Massachusetts (1955) **C:** Interim Dean, College of Lifelong Learning, Wayne State University (1998-1996); Assistant Vice President, Associate Provost, Wayne State University, Detroit, MI (1988-1994); Assistant Vice President, Wayne State University, Detroit, MI (1985-1988); Ombudsman, Wayne State University, Detroit, MI (1981-1985); Chair, English Department, Wayne State University, Detroit, MI (1975-1979); Associate Chair, English Department, Wayne State University, Detroit, MI (1965-1975); Instructor, English Department, Wayne State University, Detroit, MI (1961-1965) **CR:** President, National Ombudsman's Association (1984-1985) **CIV:** President, Ferndale Board of Education (1981-1995); President, Birmingham Unitarian Church **MIL:** United States Army Reserves (1958-1965); United States Army (1958) **CW:** Contributor, Articles, Professional Journals **AW:** Special Recognition, Ombudsman's Association (1991); Emeritus Professor, Wayne State University **MEM:** Chair, By-Laws Commission, American Management Services Users' Group (1991-1992); Modern Language Association; Michigan Association of Collegiate Registrars and Admissions Officers; American Association of Collegiate Registrars and Admissions Officers **MH:** Albert Nelson Marquis Lifetime Achievement Award **AS:** Dr. Sharples grew up on a

farm where he was taught the values of hard work and family. His love of literature and the support of his family allowed him the freedom to choose his own path in life. **B/I:** Dr. Sharples grew up on a farm, where it was originally expected of him to take over the farm one day, but he had other plans. Building on his love for literature, he studied Victorian literature to earn a PhD. He figured teaching would be the perfect way to pass and share his love of literature. **AV:** Playing piano; Listening to symphonic music; Reading; Worshipping at Birmingham Unitarian Church **PA:** Independent Democrat **RE:** Unitarian Universalist **THT:** "When it all comes down to it, I am just a fellow human being doing what I can..." said Dr. Sharples.

SHARPLESS, KARL, T: Chemist, Educator **I:** Sciences **DOB:** 04/28/1941 **PB:** Philadelphia **SC:** PA/USA **MS:** Married **SPN:** Jan Deuser (04/28/1965) **CH:** Hannah; William; Isaac **ED:** Honorary Doctorate, Wesleyan University (1999); Honorary Doctorate, Catholic University of Louvain (1996); Honorary Doctorate, Technical University of Munich (1995); Honorary Doctorate, KTH Royal Institute of Technology (1995); Postdoctoral Studies, Harvard University, Cambridge, MA (1969-1970); Postdoctoral Studies, Stanford University, Stanford, CA (1968-1969); PhD, Stanford University, Stanford, CA (1968); BA, Dartmouth College, Hanover, NH (1963) **C:** Professor, Skaggs Institute for Chemical Biology, Scripps Research (1996-Present); W. M. Keck Professor of Chemistry, Scripps Research (1990-Present); Professor, Arthur C. Cope Professor, Massachusetts Institute of Technology (MIT) Cambridge, MA (1970-1977, 1980-1990); Professor, Department of Chemistry, Stanford University (1977-1980); Postdoctoral Associate, Harvard University, Cambridge, MA (1969-1970); Postdoctoral Associate, Stanford University (1968-1969) **CR:** Visiting Professor, Kitasato University, Japan (2002-Present); Honorary Distinguished Professor, Hong Kong Polytechnic University (2002) **AW:** Prestley Medal, American Chemical Society (2019); Half-Share, Nobel Prize in Chemistry (2001); Wolf Prize (2001); Benjamin Franklin Medal (2001); Rylander Award (2000); Chemical Sciences Award (2000); Chirality Medal (2000); Rhone Poulenc Medal (2000); Harvey Prize (1998); Listee, "Top 75 Contributors to the Chemical Enterprise," American Chemical Society (1998); Richards Medal, American Chemical Society (1998); Microbial Chemistry Medal (1997); Roger Adams Award, American Chemical Society (1997); Cliff Hamilton Award (1995); King Faisal International Prize (1995); Tetrahedron Prize (1993); Centenary Lectureship Medal (1993); Arthur C. Cope Award, American Chemical Society (1992); Scheele Award (1991); Remsen Award, American Chemical Society (1989); Chemical Pioneer Award (1988); Harrison Howe Award, American Chemical Society (1987); Dr. Paul Janssen Prize (1986); Allan Day Award (1985); Creative Work in Synthetic Organic Chemistry Award, American Chemical Society (1983) **MEM:** Fellow, American Association for the Advancement of Science; Fellow, American Academy of Arts and Sciences; Fellow, Royal Society of Chemistry; Honorary Member, National Academy of Sciences; Honorary Member, American Chemical Society

SHATNER, WILLIAM, T: Actor **I:** Media & Entertainment **DOB:** 03/22/1931 **PB:** Montreal **SC:** Quebec/Canada **PT:** Joseph Shatner; Anne Shatner **MS:** Married **SPN:** Elizabeth Shatner (2001); Nerine Kidd (11/15/1997, Divorced 1999); Marcy Lafferty (10/20/1973, Divorced 1996); Gloria Rosenberg (08/12/1956, Divorced 1969) **CH:** Melanie Shatner; Lisabeth Shatner; Leslie Carol Shatner **ED:** DLitt (Honorary), New England Institute of

Technology (2018); DLitt (Honorary), McGill University (2011); Bachelor of Commerce, McGill University (1952) **CW:** Actor, "Creators: The Past" (2020); Actor, "Devil's Revenge" (2019); Voice Actor, "To Your Last Death" (2019); Actor, "The Big Bang Theory" (2019); Actor, "Private Eyes" (2017, 2019); Co-Author, "Live Long And...: What I Might Have Learned Along the Way" (2018); Singer, Album, "Shatner Claus" (2018); Singer, Album, "Why Not Me" (2018); Voice Actor, "The Steam Engines of Oz" (2018); Voice Actor, "Aliens Ate My Homework" (2018); Co-Author, "Spirit of the Horse: A celebration in Fact and Fable" (2017); Actor, "The Indian Detective" (2017); Voice Actor, "Batman vs. Two-Face" (2017); Voice Actor, "My Little Pony: Friendship Is Magic" (2017); Co-Author, "Leonard: My Fifty-Year Friendship with a Remarkable Man" (2016); Actor, "A Sunday Horse" (2016); Actor, "Range 15" (2016); Actor, "Hashtaggers" (2016); Narrator, "Breaking Ground" (2015); Narrator, "William Shatner War Chronicles: German" (2015); Actor, "Haven" (2015); Actor, "Just in Time for Christmas" (2015); Narrator, Director, "William Shatner War Chronicles" (2015); Actor, "Baby, Baby, Baby" (2015); Actor, "Murdoch Mysteries" (2015); Actor, "A Christmas Horror Story" (2015); Director, Documentary, "Chaos on the Bridge" (2014); Voice Actor, Video Game, "Elite: Dangerous" (2014); Voice Actor, Video Game, "Family Guy: The Quest for Stuff" (2014); Actor, "Hot in Cleveland" (2013); Singer, Album, "Ponder the Mystery" (2013); Director, "The Captains Close Up: Patrick Stewart" (2013); Director, Documentary, "Still Kicking" (2013); Narrator, "The All Glory Project" (2013); Actor, "Brian Evans: At Fenway" (2013); Voice Actor, "Escape from Planet Earth" (2013); Director, Documentary, "Get a Life!" (2012); Actor, "Rookie Blue" (2012); Actor, "Psych" (2012, 2011); Co-Author, "Shatner Rules" (2011); Director, Documentary, "The Captains" (2011); Actor, "Horrorween" (2011); Actor, "$#*! My Dad Says" (2010-2011); Voice Actor, "Quantum Quest: A Cassini Space Odyssey" (2010); Voice Actor, "The True Story of Puss'N Boots" (2009); Co-Author, "Up Till Now: The Autobiography" (2008); Actor, "Fanboys" (2009); Voice Actor, "Gotta Catch Santa Claus" (2008); Actor, "Everest" (2007); Voice Actor, "The Tuttles: Macap Misadventures" (2007); Narrator, "Live Life" (2007); Voice Actor, "Over the Hedge" (2006); Voice Actor, "The Wild" (2006); Narrator, "Stalking Santa" (2006); Actor, "Last Laugh '05" (2005); Voice Actor, "Atomic Betty" (2005); Actor, "Invasion Iowa" (2005); Actor, "Miss Congeniality 2: Armed & Fabulous" (2005); Actor, "Boston Legal" (2004-2008); Singer, Album, "Has Been" (2004); Actor, "Dodgeball: A True Underdog Story" (2004); Actor, "Chilly Beach" (2004); Actor, "The Practice" (2004); Actor, "A Carol Christmas" (2003); Co-Author, "Star Trek: I'm Working on That: A Trek from Science Fiction to Science Fact" (2002); Actor, Director, "Groom Lake" (2002); Actor, "American Psycho II: All American Girl" (2002); Voice Actor, "Futurama" (2002); Actor, "Showtime" (2002); Actor, "Shoot or Be Shot" (2002); Voice Actor, "The Kid" (2001); Actor, "Bob Patterson" (2001); Voice Actor, "Osmosis Jones" (2001); Actor, "Falcon Down" (2001); Actor, "Miss Congeniality" (2000); Actor, "3rd Rock from the Sun" (2000, 1999); Co-Author, "Get a Life!" (1999); Actor, "A Twist in the Tale" (1999); Voice Actor, "Hercules" (1998); Actor, "Free Enterprise" (1998); Actor, "Land of the Free" (1998); Actor, "Cosby" (1997); Actor, "The First Men in the Moon" (1997); Actor, Director, "Perversions of Science" (1997); Actor, "The Prisoner of Zenda, Inc. (1996); Actor, "The Fresh Prince of Bel-Air" (1996); Actor, "Dead Man's Island" (1996); Actor, Director, "TekWar" (1994-1996); Co-Author, "Star Trek Movie Memories" (1994); Actor, "Janek: The Silent Betrayal"

(1994); Actor, "Stark Trek: Generations" (1994); Actor, "TekWar: TekJustice" (1994); Actor, "SeaQuest 2032" (1994); Actor, "TekWar: TekLab" (1994); Actor, "TekWar: TekLords" (1994); Actor, "TekWar" (1994); Actor, "Columbo" (1994, 1976); Actor, "Eek!stravaganza" (1993-1995); Co-Author, "Star Trek Memories" (1993); Actor, "Family of Strangers" (1993); Actor, "Loaded Weapon 1" (1993); Actor, "The Larry Sanders Show" (1992); Actor, "Star Trek VI: The Undiscovered Country" (1991); Actor, Director, "Star Trek V: The Final Frontier" (1989); Co-Author, "Captain's Log: William Shatner's Personal Account of the Making of 'Star Trek V: The Final Frontier'" (1989); Voice Actor, "The Trial of Standing Bear" (1988); Actor, "Broken Angel" (1988); Actor, "North Beach and Rawhide" (1985); Actor, "The Ray Bradbury Theatre" (1985); Actor, "Secrets of a Married Man" (1984); Actor, "Star Trek III: The Search for Spock" (1984); Actor, Director, "T.J. Hooker" (1982-1986); Actor, "Airplane II: The Sequel" (1982); Actor, "Star Trek II: The Wrath of Khan" (1982); Actor, "Visiting Hours" (1982); Actor, "Police Squad!" (1982); Actor, "The Babysitter" (1980); Actor, "The kidnapping of the President" (1980); Actor, "Star Trek" (1979); Actor, "Disaster on the Coastliner" (1979); Actor, "Riel" (1979); Actor, "Crash" (1978); Actor, "Little Women" (1978); Actor, "The Third Walker" (1978); Actor, "Land of No Return" (1978); Actor, "The Bastard" (1978); Actor, "How the West Was Won" (1978); Actor, "The Oregon Trail" (1977); Actor, "Kingdom of the Spiders" (1977); Actor, "Testimony of Two Men" (1977); Actor, "A Whale of a Tale" (1976); Actor, "The Tenth Level" (1976); Actor, "Perilous Voyage" (1976); Actor, "Barbary Coast" (1975-1976); Actor "The Devil's Rain" (1975); Actor, "The Rookies" (1975); Actor, "Police Woman" (1974); Actor, "Amy Prentiss" (1974); Actor, "Police Story" (1974); Actor, "Kodiak" (1974); Actor, "Petrocelli" (1974); Actor, "The Collaborators" (1974); Actor, "Kung Fu" (1974); Actor, "Big Bag Mama" (1974); Actor, "The Six Million Dollar Man" (1974); Actor, "The Magician" (1974); Actor, "Impulse" (1974); Actor, "Police Surgeon" (1974, 1973); Voice Actor, "Star Trek: The Animated Series" (1973-1974); Actor, "Pioneer Woman" (1974); Actor, "Mannix" (1973); Actor, "The Horror at 37,000 Feet" (1973); Actor, "Barnaby Jones" (1973); Actor, "Go Ask Alice" (1973); Actor, "Incident on a Dark Street" (1973); Actor, "The Bold Ones: The New Doctors" (1973); Actor, "Norman Corwin Presents" (1972); Actor, "Marcus Welby, M.D." (1972); Actor, "Owen Marshall, Counselor at Law" (1972, 1971); Actor, "Mission: Impossible" (1972, 1971); Actor, "Hawaii Five-O" (1972); Actor, "The Sixth Sense" (1972); Actor, "The Hound of the Baskerville" (1972); Actor, "The People" (1972); Actor, "Cade's County" (1971); Actor, "Men at Law" (1971); Actor, "Vanished" (1971); Actor, "Ironside" (1970-1974); Actor, "The Name of the Game" (1970); Actor, "Swing Out, Sweet Land" (1970); Actor, "The F.B.I." (1970); Actor, "The Andersonville Trial" (1970); Actor, "Medical Center" (1970); Actor, "Paris 7000" (1970); Actor, "Sole Survivor" (1970); Actor, "The Virginian" (1969, 1965); Actor, "The Skirts of Happy Chance" (1969); Actor, "CBS Playhouse" (1969); Actor, "White Comanche" (1968); Actor, "Off to See the Wizard" (1968); Actor, "Insight" (1967); Actor, "Star Trek" (1966-1969); Actor, "Bob Hope Presents the Chrysler Theatre" (1966, 1964); Actor, "Gunsmoke" (1966); Actor, "Incubus" (1966); Actor, "The Big Valley" (1966); Actor, "The Fugitive" (1965); Actor, "12 O'Clock High" (1965); Actor, "For the People" (1965); Actor, "Dr. Kildare" (1961-1966); Actor, "The Defenders" (1961-1965); Actor, "The Man from U.N.C.L.E." (1964); Actor, "The Reporter" (1964); Actor, "Outrage" (1964); Actor, "The Outer Limits" (1964); Actor, "Burke's Law" (1964); Actor,

"Arrest and Trial" (1964); Actor, "Alexander the Great" (1963); Actor, "Route 66" (1963); Actor, Numerous Plays; Himself, Numerous Documentaries; Author, Co-Author, Numerous Books; Singer, Nine Albums **AW:** Appointed, Officer of the Order of Canada, Canadian Governor General Julie Payette (2019); Voice Arts Icon Award (2015); NASA Distinguished Public Service Medal (2014); Governor General's Performing Arts Award (2011); Streamy Award, Best Reality Web Series (2009); Prism Award (2009); Inductee, Television Academy Hall of Fame (2006); Golden Globe Award (2005); Emmy Award, Best Supporting Actor in a Drama Series, "Boston Legal" (2005); Emmy Award for Outstanding Guest Actor in a Drama Series (2004); Honoree, Star, Canada's Walk of Fame (2000); Honoree, Star, Hollywood Walk of Fame (1983); Saturn Awards (1980, 1983); Theatre World Award (1958); Tyrone Guthrie Award (1956); Numerous Other Awards and Accolades **MEM:** American Federation of Television and Radio Artists; Screen Actors Guild (SAG); Directors Guild of America; Actors Equity Association

SHAW, RODERICK, DDS, T: General Dentistry **I:** Medicine & Health Care **CN:** Shaw Dental **DOB:** 12/15/1956 **PB:** Tallahassee **SC:** FL/USA **PT:** Roderick Kirkpatrick Shaw Jr.; Floride Wilkinson Shaw **MS:** Married **SPN:** Kathleen **CH:** Roderick; Carolyn **ED:** Doctor of Dental Medicine, University of Florida College of Dentistry (1986); BS in Chemistry and Biochemistry, Auburn University; Coursework, Comprehensive Dental Master Track Program 22, University of Florida College of Dentistry (2002-2004); **C:** Private Practice, Shaw Dental, Madison, FL (1997) **CIV:** Chairman, Madison Campaign, Davis for Governor (2006); Finance Chairman, First United Methodist Church, Madison, FL (2003); Treasurer, Madison Avenue Presbyterian Church, FL (1998-2000); Elder, Madison Presbyterian Church, FL (1996-2000) **CW:** Contributor, Articles to Professional Journals Including AGD Focus and Local Madison Newspaper **AW:** Lifetime Learning & Service Recognition (LLSR) (2018); Recognition Award, American College of Dentists (2010); Mastership Award, Academy of General Dentistry (2005); Fellowship, Academy of General Dentistry (2001) **MEM:** Comprehensive Dental Master Track Program 22, American Dental Association (2002-2004); Academy General Dentistry; Northeast District Dental Association; Florida Dental Association; Charter Member, Florida Academy of Cosmetic Dentistry; Academy of Operative Dentistry; Chemical Honor Society (Phi Lambda Upsilon) **MH:** Albert Nelson Marquis Lifetime Achievement Award **AV:** Boating; Running **PA:** Conservative **RE:** Presbyterian

SHEA, JAMES L., T: Chairman Emeritus, Attorney **I:** Law and Legal Services **CN:** Venable LLP **DOB:** 06/19/1952 **PB:** Baltimore **SC:** MD/USA **MS:** Married **SPN:** Barbara **CH:** Four Children **ED:** JD, University of Virginia School of Law (1977); AB in History, Princeton University, Cum Laude (1974) **C:** Chairman Emeritus (2017-Present); Attorney, Venable LLP (1983-Present); Chairman, Venable LLP (2006-2017); Managing Partner, Venable LLP (1994-2006) **CR:** Assistant Attorney General, Maryland (1981-1983); Hon. Joseph H. Young, U.S. District Court for the District of Maryland (1977-1978) **CIV:** Chair, Board of Regents, University System of Maryland; Chair, Central Maryland Transportation Alliance; Chair, Empower Baltimore Management Corporation; Chair, Downtown Partnership of Baltimore; Board Member, Greater Baltimore Committee; Board Member, Mercantile Bank Shares and Mercantile Bank & Trust; Board Member, Equal Justice Council; Trustee, Hippodrome Foundation; Trustee, Calvert School; Cornerstone Partner,

Legal Aid Bureau **AW:** Eminent Practitioner, Litigation: General Commercial, Maryland, Chambers USA (2019); Listee, Benchmark Litigation, "Local Litigation Stars" for Maryland (2019); Listee, Washington, DC Super Lawyers (2014-2019); Eminent Practitioner, Litigation: General Commercial, Maryland, Chambers USA (2017); Listee, Maryland Super Lawyers (2008-2017); Recognition for Leadership and Commitment, House of Ruth (2016); Litigation: General Commercial, Maryland, Chambers USA (2013-2016); Whitney M. Young Jr. Memorial Award, Greater Baltimore Urban League (2014); Listee, Super Lawyers Business Edition, Business Litigation, Baltimore, MD (2013); Listee, Benchmark Litigation, "Local Litigation Stars" for Maryland (2013); Listee, "Power 50: The Men And Women Who Rule," Baltimore Magazine (2007); Listee, "Power 50: The Men And Women Who Rule", Baltimore Magazine (2003); Leadership in Law Award, The Daily Record; Listed, Best Lawyers in America, Woodward/White, Inc.; AV Peer-Review Rated, Martindale-Hubbell **MEM:** Fellow, American College of Trial Lawyers; Order of the Coif **BAR:** Maryland (1977); District of Columbia **MH:** Marquis Who's Who Top Professional **AS:** Mr. Shea attribute his success to his hard work. **B/I:** Mr. Shea's maternal grandfather was a lawyer and a judge, and he was inspired by his example. **AV:** Golfing **THT:** Mr. Shea pursues his clients' interests with integrity and effectiveness. Two of his children are attorneys, and one child is studying law.

SHEA-STONUM, MARILYN, T: Federal Bankruptcy Judge (Retired) **I:** Law and Legal Services **CN:** www.neostarinc.org/ **MS:** Married **SPN:** Gary Lee Stonum **CH:** Lee Stonum **ED:** JD, Case Western Reserve University (1975); AB, University of California Santa Cruz (1969) **C:** Retired (2014); Federal Bankruptcy Judge, United States District Court for the North District of Ohio, Akron, Ohio (1994-2014); Partner, Jones, Day, Reavis & Pogue (Now Jones Day), Cleveland, Ohio (1984-1994); Law Clerk to Honorable Frank J. Battisti, Cleveland, Ohio (1975-1976) **CR:** Working with Undergraduate School to Increase Endowment at Crown College; Founder, Working Locally, NEO Faith Trails and Routes Inc. (Neo Star); Community Advisory, Local Public Radio Station WKSU **CW:** Editor-in-chief, American Bankruptcy Law Journal, National Conference of Bankruptcy Judges **AW:** Liberty Bell Award, Akron Bar Association (2014); Inductee, Society of Benchers, Case Western Reserve University; Centennial Medal, Case Western Reserve University School of Law **MEM:** Order of the Coif **MH:** Albert Nelson Marquis Lifetime Achievement Award; Marquis Who's Who Top Professional **B/I:** When Mrs. Shea-Stonum was growing up, she thought she would be a journalist. When she graduated from college, she wound up working with Eugene Feinblatt, who was the one man kitchen cabinet to the mayors of Baltimore. She was his research assistant, and since Mr. Feinblatt was a great problem solver she decided that is what she wanted to do. She was attending law school while she was working with Mr. Feinblatt. Her husband finished his PhD and they moved to and she finished her Law degree in Ohio. One she started practicing, she went more toward problem solving and in bankruptcy law you are solving problems.

SHEEN, MARTIN, T: Actor **I:** Media & Entertainment **DOB:** 08/03/1940 **PB:** Dayton **SC:** OH/USA **PT:** Francisco Estevez; Mary Ann (Phelan) Estevez **MS:** Married **SPN:** Janet Sheen (12/23/1961) **CH:** Emilio; Carlos; Ramon; Renee **ED:** Honorary DHL, University of Dayton (2015); Honorary DLitt, Marquette University (2003); Coursework, Stella Adler Studio of Acting **CIV:** Honorary Mayor, Malibu, CA (1989); Activist, Human Rights, Environmental Issues; Advocate, Sea Shepherd Conservation Society (SSCS) **CW:** Actor, "Untitled Fred Hampton Project" (2020); Narrator, "The Adventures of Theor's Star" (2019); Actor, "The Devil Has a Name" (2019); Actor, "Princess of the Row" (2019); Voice Actor, "The Boxcar Children - Surprise Island" (2018); Actor, "Come Sunday" (2018); Actor, "Lt. Montgomery's Anne of Green Gables: Fire & Dew" (2017); Actor, "Lt. Montgomery's Anne of Green Gable: The Good Stars" (2017); Actor, "Rules Don't Apply" (2016); Actor, "The Vessel" (2016); Actor, "Popstar: Never Stop Never Stopping" (2016); Actor, "Anne of Green Gables" (2016); Actor, "Grace and Frankie" (2015-2021); Voice Actor, "All Creatures Big and Small" (2015); Actor, "Badge of Honor" (2015); Actor, "Selma" (2014); Actor, "Bhopal: A Prayer for Rain" (2014); Actor, "Trash" (2014); Actor, "Ask Me Anything" (2014); Actor, "The Amazing Spider-Man 2" (2014); Voice Actor, "The Boxcar Children" (2014); Actor, "The Whale" (2013); Narrator, "Amazonia" (2013); Actor, "Anger Management" (2012-2014); Actor, "Seeking a Friend for the End of the World" (2012); Actor, "The Amazing Spider-Man" (2012); Voice Actor, Video Game, "Mass Effect 3" (2012); Actor, "8" (2012); Co-Author, "Along the Way: The Journey of a Father and Son" (2012); Actor, "The Double" (2011); Actor, "Stella Days" (2011); Voice Actor, "Wrinkles" (2011); Actor, "The Way" (2010); Voice Actor, Video Game, "Mass Effect 2" (2010); Actor, "Gloves of Stone" (2009); Narrator, "The Bell" (2009); Actor, "Love Happens" (2009); Actor, "Imagine That" (2009); Actor, "Echelon Conspiracy" (2009); Actor, "Man in the Mirror" (2008); Narrator, "Hope Not Lost" (2008); Voice Actor, "Flatland: The Movie" (2007); Voice Actor, "Studio 60 on the Sunset Strip" (2007); Actor, "Talk to Me" (2007); Actor, "Bordertown" (2007); Actor, "The Departed" (2006); Actor, "Bobby" (2006); Actor, "Two and a Half Men" (2005); Actor, "Jerusalemski sindrom" (2004); Voice Actor, "Freedom: A History of US" (2003); Voice Actor, "The 3 Wise Men" (2003); Actor, "The Commission" (2003); Actor, "Mercy of the Sea" (2003); Actor, "Catch Me If You Can" (2002); Actor, "Spin City" (2002); Actor, "We the People" (2002); Actor, "O" (2001); Actor, "The West Wing" (1999-2006); Actor, "A Stranger in the Kingdom" (1999); Actor, "Thrill Seekers" (1999); Actor, "Forget Me Never" (1999); Actor, "D.R.E.A.M. Team" (1999); Actor, "A Texas Funeral" (1999); Actor, "Chicken Soup for the Soul" (1999); Actor, "Total Recall 2070" (1999); Actor, "Lost & Found" (1999); Actor, "Gunfighter" (1999); Actor, "The Darklings" (1999); Actor, "Ninth Street" (1999); Actor, "Family Attraction" (1998); Voice Actor, "Stories from My Childhood" (1998); Actor, "Free Money" (1998); Actor, "A Letter from Death Row" (1998); Actor, "Babylon 5: The River of Souls" (1998); Actor, "No Code of Conduct" (1998); Actor, "Voyage of Terror" (1998); Narrator, "Shadrach" (1998); Actor, "Monument Ave." (1998); Actor, "Medusa's Child" (1997); Voice Actor, "The Simpsons" (1997); Actor, "Spawn" (1997); Actor, "Screen One" (1997); Actor, "Truth or Consequences, N.M." (1997); Actor, "Gun" (1997); Voice Actor, Documentary, "1914-1918" (1996); Actor, "Alchemy" (1996); Actor, "Crystal Cave" (1996); Actor, "The Elevator" (1996); Actor, "Entertaining Angels: The Dorothy Day Story" (1996); Actor, "The War at Home" (1996); Actor, "Project: ALF" (1996); Actor, "Captain Nuke and the Bomber Boys" (1995); Actor, "Present Tense, Past Perfect" (1995); Actor, "Sacred Congo" (1995); Actor, "The American President" (1995); Actor, "Dead Presidents" (1995); Actor, "The Break" (1995); Actor, "Dillinger and Capone" (1995); Actor, "Gospa" (1995); Actor, "Running Wild" (1995); Actor, "One Hundred and One Nights" (1995); Narrator, Actor, Live Performance, "Bah Humbug!: The Story of Charles Dickens' 'A Christmas Carol'" (1994); Actor, "Hits!" (1994); Actor, "Guns of Honor" (1994); Actor, "Boca" (1994); Actor, "Roswell" (1994); Actor, "Trigger Fast" (1994); Actor, "One of Her Own" (1994); Actor, "When the Bough Breaks" (1994); Actor, "Fortunes of War" (1994); Narrator, Documentary, "My Home, My Prison" (1993); Actor, "A Matter of Justice" (1993); Actor, "Tales from the Crypt" (1993); Actor, "Gettysburg" (1993); Actor, "Murphy Brown" (1993); Actor, "Hot Shots! Part Deux" (1993); Actor, "Hear No Evil" (1993); Actor, "Grey Knight" (1993); Actor, "Queen" (1993); Actor, "Another Time, Another Place" (1992); Voice Actor, "Captain Planet and the Planeteers" (1990-1992); Voice Actor, "The Water Engine" (1992); Actor, "Original Intent" (1992); Actor, "Touch and Die" (1992); Actor, "The Last P.O.W.? The Bobby Garwood Story" (1992); Narrator, "A Legacy of Genocide: The Serbian Death Squads" (1991); Narrator, "Help Croatia" (1991); Narrator, "The Yugoslav Army Is Helping Serbian Terrorism" (1991); Narrator, "JFK" (1991); Actor, "Guilty Until Proven Innocent" (1991); Actor, "The Maid" (1990); Actor, "Cadence" (1990); Actor, "Marked for Murder" (1990); Actor, "Beverly Hills Brats" (1989); Actor, "Cold Front" (1989); Actor, "Beyond the Stars" (1989); Actor, "Nightbreaker" (1989); Actor, "Judgment in Berlin" (1988); Actor, "Da" (1988); Actor, "Wall Street" (1987); Actor, "Siesta" (1987); Voice Actor, Documentary, "Dear America: Letters Home from Vietnam" (1987); Actor, "The Believers" (1987); Actor, Documentary, "Conspiracy: The Trial of the Chicago 8" (1987); Actor, "CBS Schoolbreak Special" (1987); Narrator, "A Life in the Day" (1986); Actor, "A State of Emergency" (1986); Actor, "Samaritan" (1986); Actor, "News at Eleven" (1986); Actor, "Shattered Spirits" (1986); Actor, "Alfred Hitchcock Presents" (1985); Actor, "Out of the Darkness" (1985); Actor, "The Fourth Wise Man" (1985); Actor, "The Atlanta Child Murders" (1985); Actor, "Consenting Adult" (1985); Actor, "The Guardian" (1984); Actor, "Firestarter" (1984); Actor, "Nobody's Heroes" (1983); Actor, "Choices of the Heart" (1983); Actor, "Kennedy" (1983); Actor, "The Dead Zone" (1983); Actor, "Man, Woman and Child" (1983); Actor, "In the King of Prussia" (1983); Narrator, "No Place to Hide" (1983); Actor, "That Championship Season" (1982); Actor, "Gandhi" (1982); Actor, "Enigma" (1982); Actor, "In the Custody of Strangers" (1982); Actor, "Loophole" (1981); Actor, "The Final Countdown" (1980); Narrator, Numerous Documentaries; Actor, Numerous Plays **AW:** Co-Recipient, Best Vocal Ensemble in a Video Game, "Mass Effect 3," Behind the Voice Actors Awards (2013); Career Achievement Award, Chicago International Film Festival (2011); Laetare Medal, University of Notre Dame (2008); COFCA Award, Best Ensemble, "The Departed," Central Ohio Film Critics Association (2007); Co-Recipient, Gotham Independent Film Award, Best Ensemble Performance, "Talk to Me," Gotham Awards (2007); Screen Actors Guild Award, Outstanding Performance by a Male Actor in a Drama Series, "The West Wing" (2001); Golden Globe Award, Best Performance by an Actor in a TV Series - Drama (2001); ALMA Award, Outstanding Actor in a Television Series, "The West Wing" (2001); Lifetime Achievement Award, Imagen Foundation (1998); Emmy Award, Outstanding Guest Actor in a Comedy Series, "Murphy Brown" (1994); Star, Hollywood Walk of Fame (1989); Daytime Emmy, Outstanding Individual Achievement in Children's Programming - Directing, "CBS Schoolbreak Special" (1986); Daytime Emmy, Outstanding Individual Achievement in Religious Programming - Performers, "Insight" (1981); Best Foreign Movie Performer, "Apocalypse Now," Fotogramas de Plata (1980); Recipient, Numerous Other Awards and Accolades; Favorite Actor in a New Series, TV Guide Awards **RE:** Roman Catholic

SHEERAN, ED, T: Musician **I:** Media & Entertainment **DOB:** 02/17/1991 **PB:** Halifax **SC:** England **PT:** John Sheeran; Imogen Lock Sheeran **MS:** Married **SPN:** Cherry Seaborn (2018) **ED:** Honorary Doctorate, University of Suffolk, England (2015); Coursework in Artist Development and Access to Music **CW:** Musician, Album, "No. 6 Collaborations Project" (2019); Actor, "Star Wars: The Rise of Skywalker" (2019); Actor, "Modern Love" (2019); Actor, "Yesterday" (2019); Himself, Documentary, "Songwriter" (2018); Voice Actor, "The Simpsons" (2018); Musician, Album, "÷" (2017); Actor, "Game of Thrones" (2017); Featured, "Popstar: Never Stop Never Stopping" (2016); Featured, "Bridget Jones's Baby" (2016); Featured, Documentary, "Jumpers for Goalposts: Live at Wembley Stadium" (2015); Actor, "The Bastard Executioner" (2015); Actor, "Home and Away" (2015); Featured, "Undateable" (2015); Musician, Album, "×" (2014); Featured, "Shortland Street" (2014); Musician, Album, "+" (2011); Songwriter, Numerous Artists **AW:** Global Success Award, Brit Awards (2019); Top Touring Artist, Billboard Music Awards (2019); Best International Rock/Pop Male Artist, Best International Rock/Pop Male Artist, Echo (2015, 2016, 2018); Best Pop Vocal Album, "÷," Grammy Awards (2018); Best Pop Solo Performance, "Shape of You," Grammy Awards (2018); Top Radio Song, "Shape of You," Billboard Music Awards (2018); Top Hot 100 Artist, Top Song Sales Artist, Top Radio Songs Artist, Top Male Artist, Top Artist, Billboard Music Awards (2018); International Work of the Year, "Shape of You," APRA Awards (2018); Numerous Awards, BMI London Awards (2013-2014, 2016-2017); Best British Solo Act, BBC Radio 1's Teen Awards (2014, 2015, 2017); Artist of the Year, MTV Video Music Awards (2017); Song of the Year, Best Pop Solo Performance, "Thinking Out Loud," Grammy Awards (2016); Favorite Male Artist, People's Choice Awards (2016); Favorite Male Artist, Favorite Album, "×," People's Choice Awards (2015); Favorite Male Artist - Pop/Rock, American Music Awards (2015); British Artist of the Year, BBC Music Awards (2014); Best Male Video, "Sing," MTV Video Music Awards (2014); Numerous Other Awards and Accolades

SHEFFIELD, DEWEY, T: Retired **I:** Insurance **ED:** Coursework, University of North Carolina at Chapel Hill (1956-1960); Coursework, Oak Ridge Military Institute **CT:** Real Estate License (1973); Insurance License (1965) **C:** Retired, Insurance and Real Estate Brokerage and Sales (2011); Regional Director and Regional Director of Sales Training; Judicial Branch of Government (Six Years); Town Clerk, Sims, NC (Four Years) **CR:** Member, North Carolina Business Advisory Council; Co-founder, State Insurance Services, Inc.; Member, Board of Directors, State Insurance Services, Inc.; Lecturer on Motivational Psychology, Two-week Course **CIV:** Senior Member, Executive Committee, North Carolina State Democratic Party (1986-Present); Delegate, North Carolina State Democratic Conventions (1956-2006); Board Member, For the Love of Dogs; Past Chairman, Advisory Board, W.C.T.C. Insurance; Habitat for Humanity International; Friends of the Library; Past Member, Mayor's Committee on the Handicapped (Now The Mayor's Committee on the Handicapped); Past President, Wilson County Society for Crippled Children and Adults; Past President, Wilson County Hemophilia; Past President, Wilson County March of Dimes; Past President, Wilson County Arthritis Association; Past Chairman, Past Member, Board of Directors, North Carolina Chiropractic Politi-

cal Action Committee (NCC-PAC); Past President, Wilson County Young Democrats; Past Chairman, Second Congressional District Young Democrats; Executive Committee, Wilson County Democratic Party; Precinct Chairman, Wilson County Democratic Party; Contributing Member, Democratic National Committee; Past Member, President's Club, National Democratic Party; Member, Democratic Leadership Council; Member, State Executive Committee, North Carolina Democratic Party **CW:** Author, Numerous Published Articles **AW:** Named to The Order of the Long Leaf Pine Society **MEM:** Honorable Order of Kentucky Colonels; Honorary Member, North Carolina Sheriff's Association; Travelers Protection Association; State Capitol Society; Wilson Humane Society; UNC General Alumni Association; Wilson County Pomona Grange; North Carolina State Grange (Now NC Grange); Seventh Degree, National Grange

SHELBY, RICHARD CRAIG, T: U.S. Senator from Alabama; Lawyer **I:** Government Administration/Government Relations/Government Services **DOB:** 05/06/1934 **PB:** Birmingham **SC:** AL/USA **PT:** Ozie Houston Shelby; Alice L. (Skinner) Shelby **MS:** Married **SPN:** Annette (Nevin) Shelby (06/11/1960) **CH:** Richard Craig; Claude Nevin **ED:** LLB, The University of Alabama (1963); AB, The University of Alabama (1957) **C:** Chairman, Senate Appropriations Committee (2018-Present); Chairman, Senate Rules Committee (2017-Present); U.S. Senator, State of Alabama (1987-Present); Chairman, Senate Banking Committee (2015-2017); Chairman, U.S. Senate Committee on Banking, Housing and Urban Affairs (2003-2007); Chairman, Senate Intelligence Committee (2001); Member, U.S. House of Representatives from Alabama's Seventh Congressional District, United States Congress, Washington, DC (1979-1987); Member, District 16, Alabama State Senate (1971-1978); Law Practice, Tuscaloosa, AL (1963-1978); Special Assistant Attorney General, State of Alabama (1968-1971); Prosecutor, City of Tuscaloosa, AL (1963-1971); Magistrate Judge, United States District Court for the Northern District of Alabama (1966-1970); Law Clerk, Supreme Court of Alabama (1961-1962) **CIV:** Board of Governors, National Legislative Conference (1975-1978); President, Mental Health Association in Tuscaloosa County (1969-1970); Active Member, Boy Scouts of America **AW:** Congressional Leadership Award, Airports Council International-North America (2003); Taxpayer's Friend Award, National Taxpayers Union (NTU) (1998) **MEM:** Former President, Mental Health Association in Tuscaloosa County; American Bar Association; Alabama Bar Association; Tuscaloosa County Bar Association; The Bar Association of DC; American Judicature Society; National Exchange Club; Mental Health Association in Tuscaloosa County **BAR:** The District of Columbia (1979); The State of Alabama (1961) **PA:** Republican **RE:** Presbyterian

SHELLENBERGER, JEFFREY, T: President, Chief Executive Officer **I:** Automotive **CN:** Shelly Truck Driving School LLC **DOB:** 05/26/1960 **PB:** York **SC:** PA/USA **MS:** Single **CH:** Jeffrey Jr.; Nicole **ED:** Coursework in Psychology, The Pennsylvania State University **C:** President, Owner, Shelly Truck Driving School LLC (2015-Present); Board of Directors, S&H Express **CIV:** Christian School, India **MEM:** American Trucking Association; Traffic Insurance LTD **AS:** Mr. Shellenberger attributes his success to the influence of his parents, whom he loves very much. **B/I:** Mr. Shellenberger first became involved in his profession after serving as a plant manager at a large printing company until the advent of the internet, which made the business obsolete. Following the example of his father, who worked in transportation and purchased a small trucking

company in 1994, he elected to join the family business in 1996. **AV:** Go-fast boats **THT:** "A bad day of fishing is better than a good day at work."

SHELTON, BLAKE TOLISON, T: Musician **I:** Media & Entertainment **DOB:** 06/18/1976 **PB:** Ada **SC:** OK/USA **PT:** Richard Shelton; Dorothy Shelton **MS:** Divorced **SPN:** Miranda Meigh Lambert (05/14/2011, Divorced 2015); Kaynette Williams (11/17/2003, Divorced 2006) **C:** Owner, Ole Red (2017-Present) **CW:** Coach, "The Voice" (2011-Present); Voice Actor, "UglyDolls" (2019); Musician, Compilation Album, "Fully Loaded: God's Country" (2019); Musician, Album, "Texoma Shore" (2017); Musician, Album, "If I'm Honest" (2016); Voice Actor, "The Angry Birds Movie" (2016); Musician, Compilation Album, "Reloaded: 20 #1 Hits" (2015); Actor, "Pitch Perfect 2" (2015); Actor, "The Ridiculous 6" (2015); Musician, Album, Bringing Back the Sunshine" (2014); Featured, Documentary, "Glen Campbell: I'll Be Me" (2014); Musician, Album, "Based on a True Story..." (2013); Musician, Album, "Cheers, It's Christmas" (2012); Musician, Compilation Album, "Original Album Series" (2012); Musician, Album, "Red River Blue" (2011); Musician, Compilation Album, "Loaded: The Best of Blake Shelton" (2010); Musician, Compilation Album, "Blake Shelton - The Essentials" (2009); Musician, Album, "Startin' Fires" (2008); Featured, Documentary, "Hitman: David Foster & Friends" (2008); Musician, Album, "Pure BS" (2007); Himself, "The Christmas Blessing" (2005); Musician, Album, "Blake Shelton's Barn & Grill" (2004); Musician, Album, "The Dreamer" (2003); Musician, Album, "Blake Shelton" (2001); Featured, Numerous Appearances, Television Shows and Specials **AW:** Numerous Awards, American Society of Composers, Authors and Publishers (2002-2003, 2005, 2008-2019); Artist Humanitarian Award, Country Radio Seminar (2019); Favorite Country Song, "God's Country," American Music Awards (2019); Video of the Year, "Forever Country," Academy of Country Music Awards (2017); Top Country Artist, Billboard Music Awards (2017); Social Superstar of the Year, CMT Music Awards (2016); Favorite Male Country Artist, People's Choice Awards (2016); Favorite Country Male Artist, American Music Awards (2016, 2013); Inductee, Oklahoma Hall of Fame (2014); Gene Weed Special Achievement Award, Academy of Country Music Awards (2013); Song of the Year, "Over You," Academy of Country Music Awards (2013); Music Video by a Male Artist, "Sure Be cool If You Did," American Country Awards (2013); Great American County-Music Video of the Year, "Sure Be Cool If You Did," American Country Awards (2013); Male Vocalist of the Year, Academy of Country Music Awards (2012); Entertainer of the Year, Country Music Association Awards (2012); Favorite Country Male Artist, American Music Awards (2011); Vocal Event of the Year, "Hillbilly Bone," Academy of Country Music Awards (2010); Numerous Awards, American Country Awards; Numerous Other Awards and Accolades **MEM:** Grande Ole Opry (2010-Present)

SHENEFELT, PHILIP D, T: Dermatologist **I:** Medicine & Health Care **CN:** University of South Florida **C:** Dermatologist, University of South Florida (49 Years)

SHEPHERD, DEBORAH GULICK, T: Elementary School Educator (Retired) **I:** Education/Educational Services **CN:** Chester M. Stephens Elementary **DOB:** 10/21/1953 **PB:** Edenton **SC:** NC/USA **PT:** Lyman Mark; Rena (Bakker) Gulick **MS:** Married **SPN:** Ronald W. Shepherd (2003) **ED:** Master of Arts, Fairleigh Dickinson University (1981); Bachelor of Arts, Oral Roberts University (1976); Associate of Arts, Centenary College, Hackettstown, NJ (1974) CT: Elementary and Middle School Teacher, K-12 Supervisor, New Jersey C: Financial Secretary, First Presbyterian Church, Hackettstown, NJ (2014-Present); Teacher, CMS Elementary (2001-2009); Teacher, Mount Olive Township, Board of Education, Budd Lake, NJ (1976-2009); Teacher, Chester M. Stephens Elementary (2001); Teacher, Mountainview Elementary (1988-2001); Teacher, Sandshore Elementary (1976-1988) CIV: Sussex County Oratorio Society (2013-Present); Sunday School Teacher, First Presbyterian Church, Hackettstown, NJ (2010-Present); Church Historian, First Presbyterian Church, Hackettstown, NJ (2010-Present); Organizer of Yarn Girls, First Presbyterian Church, Hackettstown, NJ (2010-Present); Senior Choir, First Presbyterian Church, Hackettstown, NJ (1993-Present); Sunday School Treasurer, First Presbyterian Church, Hackettstown, NJ (1996-2000); Board of Directors, Heaven Sent Nursery School (1997-1999); Chancel Choir, United Presbyterian Church, Flanders, NJ (1988-1992) CW: Editor, Church Newsletter, Light from the Steeple (1998-2010); Editor, Newsletter, Mountain View News (1986-1997) AW: Governor's Teacher Recognition Award, State of New Jersey (19910 MEM: New Jersey Retired Educators Association; Morris County Council Retired Educators Association; National Education Association; Building Representative & Officer, Education Association of Mount Olive MH: Marquis Lifetime Achievement Award AS: Ms. Shepherd attributes her success to perseverance, which has served her well. B/I: Ms. Shepherd became involved in her profession because she always enjoyed school and was interested in all subjects. As an elementary school teacher, she discovered she could work in all these subjects and help children. AV: Sewing; Knitting; Reading; Singing; Cross stitch; Book club RE: Presbyterian

SHEPPARD, NAOMI KATE, T: Nursing Educator (Retired) I: Education/Educational Services CN: University of Mary Hardin-Baylor DOB: 08/12/1929 PB: Portsmouth SC: OH/USA PT: Harold Wolf Taylor; Thelma Marie (Copas) Taylor MS: Widowed SPN: William Hill Sheppard (09/04/1947, Deceased 1/2011) CH: Molly Renee Sheppard Mikes; Julie Kay Sheppard Maxfield; Amy Lou Sheppard Mikes ED: MSN, The University of Texas at Austin (1973); BA in Sociology and Biology, University of Mary Hardin-Baylor, Belton, TX (1966); AA, Temple Junior College (1955); Diploma, Scott and White Hospital School of Nursing (1955) CT: Certification in Psychiatric Nursing, American Nursing Association (1975) C: Associate Professor, University of Mary Hardin-Baylor, Belton, TX (1972-1992); In-Service Education Coordinator, Scott & White Hospital, Temple, TX (1966-1971); Head Nurse of Medical, Scott & White Hospital, Temple, TX (1963-1964); Staff Nurse, Scott & White Hospital, Temple, TX (1955-1963) MEM: American Nurses Association (Past President); American Psychiatric Nurses Association; Vashti Chapter, Texas Nurses Association; Eastern Star EIKS Auxiliary; National Association of Retired and Veteran Railway Employees MH: Albert Nelson Marquis Lifetime Achievement Award B/I: Ms. Sheppard entered her profession because her mother wanted her to be a school teacher or a nurse. She chose nursing. AV: Sewing; Gardening

SHERMAN, BRADLEY JAMES, T: U.S. Representative from California I: Government Administration/Government Relations/Government Services DOB: 10/24/1954 PB: Los Angeles SC: CA/USA PT: Maurice H. Sherman; Lane (Moss) Sherman MS: Married SPN: Lisa Nicola (Kaplan) Sherman (12/03/2006) CH: Lucy Rayna; Naomi Claire; Molly

Hannah ED: JD, Harvard Law School, Magna Cum Laude (1979); BA, University of California Los Angeles, Summa Cum Laude (1974) CT: Certified Public Accountant, State of California C: Member, U.S. House of Representatives from California's 30th Congressional District, United States Congress, Washington, DC (2013-Present); Member, U.S. House of Representatives from California's 27th Congressional District, United States Congress, Washington, DC (2003-2013); Member, U.S. House of Representatives from California's 24th Congressional District, United States Congress, Washington, DC (1997-2003); Member, California Franchise Tax Board (1991-1995); Member, District Four (1990-1997); Private Practice, Los Angeles, CA (1980-1991) CR: Chairman, District Four, California State Board of Equalization (1991-1995) CIV: Board of Directors, Representative Tax Issues, California Common Cause (1985-1989) CW: Contributor, Articles, Professional Journals; Lecturer in Field (tax law and policy) MEM: California Bar Association BAR: State of California (1979) PA: Democrat RE: Jewish

SHERMAN, CINDY, T: Artist, Photographer I: Fine Art DOB: 01/19/1954 PB: Glen Ridge SC: NJ/USA MS: Divorced SPN: Michel Auder (1984, Divorced 1999) ED: Honorary Doctorate Degree, Royal College of Art, London, England (2013); MacArthur Fellowship (1995); Bachelor of Arts, State University College at Buffalo (1976) C: Co-Founder, Artists Against Fracking (2012-Present); Photographer (1976-Present); Co-Founder, Hallwalls (1974-Present) CW: Photographer, Photo Gallery, "The Imitation of Life" (2016); Photographer, Retrospective Exhibition, "Cindy Sherman," Museum of Modern Art, New York, NY (2012); Subject, Book, "Cindy Sherman: The Early Works 1975-1977" (2012); Photographer, Exhibition, Museum of Art (2009); Photographer, Exhibition, Jeu De Paume (2006-2007); Photographer, Exhibition, Martin Gropius Bau (2006); Subject, Book, "Cindy Sherman: The Complete Untitled Film Stills" (2003); Photographer, Exhibition, Serpentine Gallery (2003); Subject, Book, "Cindy Sherman: Retrospective" (1997); Subject, Book, "Cindy Sherman 1975-1993"; Photographer, One-Woman Exhibition, Museo de Monterrey, Mexico (1992); Photographer, One-Woman Exhibition, Linda Cathcart Gallery, Santa Monica, CA (1992); Photographer, Group Exhibition, Whitney Museum of American Art, New York (1983, 1985, 1991); Photographer, One-Woman Exhibition, Akron Art Museum (1984); Photographer, One-Woman Exhibition, Seibu Gallery Contemporary Art, Tokyo, Japan (1984); Photographer, One-Woman Exhibition, Douglas Drake Gallery, MO (1983, 1984); Photographer, One-Woman Exhibition, Metro Pictures, New York (1980, 1983); Kansas City, Photographer, One-Woman Exhibition, Rhona Hoffman Gallery, Chicago, IL (1983); Photographer, One-Woman Exhibition, Fine Arts Center Gallery, Stony Brook University (1983); Photographer, One-Woman Exhibition, St. Louis Art Museum (1983); Photographer, Group Exhibition, Hirshhorn Gallery, Washington, DC (1983); Photographer, Group Exhibition, Young Hoffman Gallery, Chicago, IL (1983); Photographer, Group Exhibition, Institute of Contemporary Arts, Philadelphia, PA (1982); Photographer, Group Exhibition, Grey Art Gallery, New York (1982); Photographer, Group Exhibition, Institute of Contemporary Arts, London, England (1982); Photographer, Group Exhibition, San Francisco Museum of Modern Art (1982); Photographer, Group Exhibition, Chantall Crousel Gallery, Paris, France (1982); Photographer, Group Exhibition, Document 7, Kassel, West Germany (1982); Photographer, Group Exhibition, La Ciennale de Venezia, Venice, Italy (1982); Photographer, Group Exhibition, Retro Pictures, New York (1982); Pho-

tographer, Group Exhibition, Renaissance Society, University of Chicago (1982); Photographer, One-Woman Exhibition, Stedelijk Museum, Amsterdam (1982); Photographer, One-Woman Exhibition, Chantal Crousel Gallery, Paris, France (1982); Photographer, One-Woman Exhibition, Young/Hoffman Gallery, Chicago, IL (1981); Photographer, One-Woman Exhibition, Saman Gallery, Genoa, Italy (1981); Photographer, Group Exhibition, NIT (1981); Photographer, Group Exhibition, Centre Pompidou, Paris, France (1981); Photographer, One-Woman Exhibition, The Kitchen, New York (1980); Photographer, One-Woman Exhibition, Contemporary Arts Museum, Houston, TX (1980); Photographer, Group Exhibition, Castelli Graphics, New York (1980); Photographer, Group Exhibition, Lisson Gallery, London, England (1980); Photographer, Group Exhibition, Max Protetch Gallery, New York (1979); Photographer, Group Exhibition, Artists Space, New York (1978); Photographer, One-Woman Exhibition, Hallwalls Gallery, Buffalo, NY (1976, 1977); Photographer, Group Exhibition, Albright-Knox Art Gallery, Buffalo, NY (1975); Photographer, Represented in Permanent Collections, Numerous Museums and Venues; Subject, Contributor, Numerous Books AW: Time Magazine's 100 Most Influential People (2017); Roswitha Haftmann Prize, Roswitha Haftmann Foundation (2012); Inductee, Royal Academy of Arts (2010) MEM: American Academy of Arts and Letters

SHERMAN, DANYA, T: Chief Executive Officer, Founder I: Other CN: KnoNap, LLC ED: MBA, Georgetown University; BA in International Relations, Affairs and Security Policy, George Washington University (2019) C: Founder, Chief Executive Officer, KnoNap, LLC, Washington, DC (2017-Present); Legislative Intern, Congressman Paul Gosar, Arizona House of Representatives, Washington, DC (2017); Finance Intern, Republican National Committee, Washington, DC (2016); Development Intern, Free the Slaves (2016); Assistant Figure Skating Coach, Ice Den, Arizona (2014-2015); Party Coordinator, Ice Den, Arizona (2012-2015) CR: Fellow, Future Founders, Washington, DC (2018-Present); Fellow, Kairos, Washington, DC (2017-Present); Incubator Fellow, Target, Minneapolis, MN (2019); Graduate Teaching Assistant, Conflict Management and Negotiation, George Washington University (2018); Incubator Fellow, Halcyon, Washington, DC (2017-2018); Undergraduate Teaching Assistant in Ecology, George Washington University (2017) CIV: Representative, Entrepreneurs' Organization Global Student Entrepreneur Award USA (2018); Representative, G20 Young Entrepreneur's Alliance USA (2018); Representative, Entrepreneurs' Organization Global Student Entrepreneur Award DC (2017); Student Ambassador, George Washington University Ballroom (2017); Youth Ambassador, Miracle League of Arizona (2010-2015) AW: 30 Under 30 Social Entrepreneurs, Forbes (2020); Winner, eMerge America's Pitch Competition (2019); Winner, Draper Competition Product Track (2019); Business Model Competition Finalist, Tulane University (2019); First Place, HERimpactDC (2019); Inductee, Technology Hall of Fame, Washington Life (2019); Young Social Innovation Award, Booz Allen Hamilton (2018); Winner, WBENC Student Entrepreneur Program Pitch Competition (2018); Cafe 100 Change-Makers (2018); Named, Top 7 Ventures, Entrepreneurs' Organization Global Student Entrepreneur Awards (2018); Finalist, Vinetta Showcase (2018); Mother of Invention Award, Toyota (2018); Finalist, Female Entrepreneur of the Year USA, Impact Awards (2018); Audience's Choice Award, AlphaLab Gear Hardware Cup (2018); Tech 25 Innovators and Disruptors, Washington Life (2017); New Venture Competition

Audience's Choice Award, George Washington University (2017); Pitch George First Place Undergraduate Award + Audience's Choice Award (2017) **MEM:** Phi Sigma Pi National Honor Fraternity

SHERRILL, REBECCA, "MIKIE" MICHELLE, T: U.S. Representative from New Jersey; Lawyer **I:** Government Administration/Government Relations/Government Services **DOB:** 01/19/1972 **PB:** Alexandria **SC:** VA/USA **MS:** Married **SPN:** Jason Hedberg **CH:** Four Children **ED:** JD, Georgetown University Law Center (2007); MS in Economic History, London School of Economics (2003); BS, United States Naval Academy (1994) **CT:** Certificate, Arabic Language, The American University in Cairo **C:** Member, U.S. House of Representatives from New Jersey's 11th Congressional District (2019-Present); Assistant United States Attorney, District of New Jersey (2015); Associate, Litigation Department, Kirkland & Ellis LLP (2008-2011); Summer Associate, Kirkland & Ellis LLP (2007) **MIL:** Advanced through Grades to Lieutenant Commander, United States Navy (1994-2003) **PA:** Democrat

SHEWARD, CLARENCE W., T: Gaseous Diffusion Company Executive **I:** Oil & Energy **DOB:** 02/06/1942 **PB:** Jackson County **SC:** OH/USA **PT:** Delmar Jay Sheward; Mildred Alice (Rapp) Sheward **MS:** Married **SPN:** Ann Carlisle Sheward **CH:** Heather Lynn Dratwa; Bethany Dawn Newsome **ED:** MBA, Capital University (1980); BS, United States Air Force Academy (1964) **CT:** Certified Senior Pilot, United States Air Force; Certified Project Manager **C:** Vice President of Engineering Services (2010-2014); President, TPMC, PGDP Infrastructure Operations (2005-2010); Manager PGDP Standby Operations, Bechtel-Jacobs Inc. (2001-2004); Independent Contractor, Gaseous Diffusion Operations (1998-2000); Division Manager, Operations, PGDP (1995-1998); Manager, Process Maintenance, PGDP (1993-1995); Division Manager, Waste Management Division, PGDP (1991-1993); Manager, Process Maintenance, PGDP (1989-1991); Superintendent of Security, Goodyear Atomic Corp. (1985-1989); Superintendent of Uranium Operations, Goodyear Atomic Corp. (1983-1985); Supervisor of Maintenance Services, Goodyear Atomic Corp. (1979-1983); Division Safety Coordinator, Goodyear Atomic Corp., Piketon, Ohio (1976-1978); Plant Engineer, Jackson Corp., Ohio (1972-1976); Division Manager, Environment Safety & Health, Portsmouth Gaseous Diffusion Plant **CR:** Teacher, Rio Grande Community College (Now University of Rio Grande & Rio Grande Community College), Ohio (1980-Present); Member, Advisory Board, Buckeye Hills Vocational Center (Now Buckeye Hills Career Center) (1976-1978) **CIV:** Deacon, Elder, Local Presbyterian Church, Jackson, Ohio; Elder, Frankfort Presbyterian Church, Ohio; Former Member, Ohio Rotary **MIL:** Captain, United States Air Force (1972); Commissioned Second Lieutenant, United States Air Force (1964); Cadet, United States Air Force Academy (1964) **AW:** Inductee, High Military Hall of Fame (2010); Decorated, Air Medal with Nine Oak Leaf Clusters; Decorated, Three Distinguished Flying Cross with Two Oak Leaf Clusters **MEM:** Association of Graduates of the United States Air Force Academy; American Association of MBA Executives (AMBA); Institute for Healthcare Improvement; Lions Clubs International **MH:** Albert Nelson Marquis Lifetime Achievement Award; Marquis Who's Who Top Professional **B/I:** When Mr. Sheward was young, there was an energy plant built in his town. He had always been interested in how it worked, which is why he became the foreman on staff in 1976. He

stayed there until he retired from the position of division manager. **AV:** Family; Grandchildren; Reading **PA:** Republican **RE:** Presbyterian

SHIH, SHENG YUN, T: Church Deacon **I:** Religious **CN:** San Francisco True Light Baptist Church **DOB:** 01/03/1935 **PB:** Beijing **SC:** China **MS:** Married **SPN:** Guo Hua Wang **CH:** Three Children **ED:** Degree, America Chinese Evangelical Seminary (2007); Degree, Beijing Normal University (1984); Degree, People's University of China (1983) **CT:** Extension Certificate, America Chinese Evangelical Seminary (2007); Certificate for Qualification of Single-subject, Chinese Language, Beijing Normal University, Beijing Examination Committee of Higher Education to Self-taught Students (1984); Certificate for Qualification of Single-subject, Logic, People's University of China, Beijing Examination committee of Higher Education to Self-taught Students (1983) **C:** Deacon, San Francisco True Light Baptist Church (2010-2015, 2019-Present); Church Secretary, San Francisco Mandarin Baptist Church, CA (2003-2007); AT&T Bilingual Customer Service Representative (1997-2003) **CR:** Violin Instructor (1958-Present); Professional Violinist (1951-Present) **MEM:** Chinese Musician's Association; Valley United Presbyterian Church, Waverly, NY (Formerly First Presbyterian Church Athens, Pennsylvania); San Francisco True Light Baptist Church, San Francisco, CA **B/I:** Mr. Shih started playing the violin at the age of 12 while living in Beijing, China. By age 16, he began performing professionally. He took lessons from a foreign teacher named Mr. Otto Praflovski who was only 1 of 2 instructors in the region. From there, that is where his love for the instrument. Mr. Shih was able to receive his greencard because of an executive order set by President George H.W. Bush, due to the incident in Tiananmen Square, China. When he came to America, converted to Christianity and was baptized at First Presbyterian Church Anthens, Pennsylvania. He had difficulty finding a job. Eventually in 1990, he moved to San Francisco, and joined San Francisco Mandarin Baptist Church. By 1997, he received a job with AT&T as a bilingual customer service representative until 2003, where he joined San Francisco True Light Baptist Church and pursued his education to become a deacon. **RE:** Christianity

SHILLADY, DONALD, "DON" DOUGLAS, PHD, T: Professor Emeritus of Chemistry **I:** Education/Educational Services **CN:** Virginia Commonwealth University **DOB:** 08/27/1937 **PB:** Norristown **SC:** PA/USA **PT:** John Nelson Shillady Jr.; Orpha (Schaefer) Shillady **MS:** Married **SPN:** Nancy Lee Knopf **CH:** Lucinda Teachey; Douglas Shillady; Amy Frye **ED:** PhD in Chemistry, The University of Virginia (1970); MS in Physical Chemistry, Princeton University (1964); BS in Chemistry, Drexel Institute Technology (Now Drexel University) (1962); Intern, NASA-Langley, VA **C:** Professor Emeritus, Virginia Commonwealth University, Richmond, VA (2003-Present); Adjunct Assistant Professor, Randolph-Macon College, Ashland, VA (2003-2004); Professor of Chemistry, Virginia Commonwealth University (1986-2003); Associate Professor, Virginia Commonwealth University (1975-1986); Postdoctoral Associate, The University of Virginia, Charlottesville, VA (1969-1970) **CR:** President, Quantum Mechanics LLC, Ashland, VA (2000-Present); Adjunct Assistant Professor, Randolph Macon College (2009); Adjunct Assistant Professor, Randolph Macon College (2003-2004) **CIV:** Elder, Brandermill Church, Brandermill Planned Community (1996-1999) **CW:** Co-author with J.U. Reveles and C. Trindle, "Mn5: High Spin Structures and Energetics," SPIE (2016); Co-author with R. Michelson and R. Walker), "Cluster Models

of Aqueous Na+ and Cl- in Sea Water/Ice," Journal of Nanoparticle Research (2014); Author, "Essentials of Physical Chemistry," CRC Press, Boca Raton, FL (2012); Author, "Essentials of Physical Chemistry", Indonesian Translation as "Dasar-Dasar Kimia Fisika" (2012); Author, "Essentials of Physical Chemistry," CRC Press (2011); Co-author with C. Trindle, "Electronic Structure Modeling, Connections Between Theory and Software," CRC Press (2008); Co-author with R. Sasin, "Chemistry in the News" (1998); Co-editor with M. Allen, S. Cleary and A. Sowers, "Charge and Field Effects in Biosystems" (1991, 1994); Author, Thesis "Some Electronic Effects of Covalency," The University of Virginia (1970); Contributor, Numerous Articles, Refereed Publications in Quantum Chemistry and Physical Chemistry **AW:** Distinguished Service Award, Virginia Section, American Chemical Society (1992); Award, Fifty-Year Member, American Chemical Society **MEM:** Chairman, Virginia Section, American Chemical Society (1986-1987) **MH:** Albert Nelson Marquis Lifetime Achievement Award; Marquis Who's Who Top Professional **AS:** Dr. Shillady attributes his success to his father's industrial chemistry experience and his mother's precise numerical bookkeeping. He also credits his friendship and competition with classmate James Harrison, who was later a professor at Michigan State University, and was a longtime positive stimulus to study thermodynamics and quantum chemistry. Later collaboration with the polished style of Prof. Carl Trindle was very constructive. Dr. Shillady also credits the support and patience of his wife. **B/I:** Dr. Shillady entered his profession because he possessed a good aptitude for mathematics. His childhood memories of the cultural effect of the 1945 Atomic Age led him to physical chemistry and later to quantum chemistry. **AV:** Sailing; Constructing replicas of Model A Ford **PA:** Republican **RE:** Lutheran **THT:** While religious faith provides comfort in times of crisis, experiencing connections between mathematics and experimental facts has been a stabilizing influence in Dr. Shillady's life. The importance of a supportive wife cannot be underestimated.

SHIMKUS, JOHN MONDY, T: U.S. Representative from Illinois **I:** Government Administration/Government Relations/Government Services **DOB:** 02/21/1958 **PB:** Collinsville **SC:** IL/USA **PT:** Gene Louis Shimkus; Kathleen (Mondy) Shimkus **MS:** Married **SPN:** Karen Kay (Muth) Shimkus (1987) **CH:** David; Joshua; Daniel **ED:** MBA, Southern Illinois University Edwardsville School of Business (1997); BS, United States Military Academy (1980) **C:** Member, U.S. House of Representatives from Illinois' 15th Congressional District, United States Congress, Washington, DC (2013-Present); Member, U.S. House of Representatives from Illinois' 19th Congressional District, United States Congress, Washington, DC (1997-2013); Treasurer, Madison County, Edwardsville, IL (1990-1996); Teacher, Metro-East Lutheran High School, Edwardsville, IL (1986-1990); Member, Committee on Energy and Commerce, United States Congress; Member, Republican Study Committee, United States Congress **CR:** Treasurer, Southern Illinois Law Enforcement Commission (SILEC) (1990-1996); Liaison Officer, United States Military Academy (1987-1996) **CIV:** Representative Precinct Committeeman, Collinsville, IL (1988-Present); Trustee, Collinsville Township, IL (1989-1993); Board of Directors, Senior Citizen Companion Progressive, Belleville, IL (1991); Holy Cross Lutheran Church, Collinsville, IL **MIL:** Lieutenant Colonel, United States Army Reserve (1986-Present); United States Army, Monterey, CA (1985-1986); United States Army, Columbus, GA (1980-1981, 1985); United States Army, Bamberg, Germany

(1981-1984); Advanced through Grades to Captain, United States Army (1980-1986) **AW:** Expert Infantry Badge; Ranger Tab; Parachutist Badge **MEM:** Illinois County Treasurers' Association; Board of Directors, National Association of County Collectors, Treasurers & Finance Officers (NACCTFO); American Legion Post 365 **PA:** Republican **RE:** Lutheran

SHINE, WILLIAM, "BILL", T: Senior Adviser, White House Director of Communications (Retired) **I:** Government Administration/Government Relations/Government Services **DOB:** 07/04/1963 **PB:** Farmingville **SC:** NY/USA **MS:** Married **SPN:** Darla (Seneck) Shine **ED:** BA in Communications, State University of New York at Oswego **C:** Senior Adviser, 2020 Presidential Re-Election Campaign (2019-Present); Director of Communications, The White House, Washington, DC (2018-2019); Deputy White House Chief of Staff for Communications, Washington, DC (2018-2019); Co-President, News and Business, Fox News Channel (2016-2017); Senior Executive Vice President of Programming, Fox News Channel (2014-2016); Vice President, Fox News Channel (2004-2014); Executive Producer, Prime Time Programming, Fox News (2000-2004); Senior Prime Time Producer, Fox News (1999-2000); Producer, Local Television Stations Including WLIG-TV (Now WLNY-TV) (1985) **PA:** Republican

SHIRLEY, FRANK CONNARD, T: Forester, Consultant **I:** Consulting **DOB:** 12/18/1933 **PB:** Minneapolis **SC:** MN/USA **CH:** Crawford; Timothy; David; Spencer **ED:** AM, PhD, University of Michigan, Ann Arbor, MI (1969); MF, State University of New York College of Environmental Science and Forestry, Syracuse, NY (1960); AB, Cornell University, Ithaca, NY (1955) **CT:** Certified Forester **C:** President, Aspen Forest Conservation Systems, Vaughn, WA (1985-Present); President, Shirley Forests, Inc., Elizabethtown, NY (1981-Present); Operators Research Analyst, St. Regis/Champion International, Tacoma, WA (1974-1985); Associate, Wesley Rickard, Inc., Gig Harbor, WA (1973-1974); Assistant Professor, Colorado State University, Fort Collins, CO (1969-1972); Forester, U.S. Forest Service, Vancouver, WA (1960-1964) **CR:** Washington State Forest Stewardship Coordinator Committee, Olympia, WA (1992-2012) **MIL:** U.S. Army (1955-1957) **CW:** Co-Author, "The Western United States Millwork Industry" (1972); Co-Author, "Colorado's Softwood Millwork Industry: Characteristics, Trends, and Future Outlook" (1971) **AW:** Washington State Forester of the Year, Society of American Foresters (1985) **MEM:** Chair, Northwest Chapter, Association of Consulting Foresters of American (1990-1991); Club President, Toastmasters (1979); Fellow, Society of American Foresters; Sigma Xi **MH:** Albert Nelson Marquis Lifetime Achievement Award **AS:** Dr. Shirley attributes his success to his happiness. He is quiet and patient, and he finds joy in listening to others. **B/I:** Dr. Shirley became involved in his profession because his father was a forester and the dean of the State University of New York College of Environmental Science and Forestry in Syracuse. He chose this career to follow in his father's footsteps. **AV:** Sail boating; Square dancing; Assisting in rebuilding the local historical society

SHIRLEY, OTIS ALLEN, T: Criminal Justice Educator; Management Consultant **I:** Military & Defense Services **CN:** United States Army **PB:** Birmingham **SC:** AL/USA **PT:** Otis Allen Shirley; Sybil Kathryn (Dial) Shirley **MS:** Married **SPN:** Frances Walls (11/13/1959) **CH:** Susan Lynn **ED:** MA, Beacon College (1983); BS, University at Albany, State University of New York (1981); Diploma, Command and Staff College, Marine Corps University, Leav-

enworth, KS (1978); Coursework, Air Command and Staff College, Air University, Maxwell Air Force Base, AL (1976); Diploma, Georgia Military Institute (1965); JD, Atlanta Law School (1964); LLB, Atlanta Law School (1964) **CT:** Certified Criminal Justice Administrator; Security Systems Engineer **C:** Director, Ivanhoe International Ltd., Kansas City, KS (1976-Present); President, Ivanhoe International Ltd., Kansas City, KS (1991-1993); Consultant, Electro Signal Laboratory, Boston, MA (1988-1993); Provost Marshal, Department of the Army, Independence, MO (1987-1990); Field Faculty Advisor and Professor, Norwich University, Plainfield, VT (1987-1989); Staff Counsel, Electro Signal Lab, Inc., Boston, MA (1987-1988); Consultant, Koenig & Associates, LLC, Montgomery, AL (1977-1987); Director, Department of Justice Administration, Beacon College, Washington, DC (1982-1986); Chairman, Academic Commission, Criminal Justice Commission, Montgomery, AL (1981-1986); Consultant, Brookdale Community College, Lincroft, NJ (1981-1984); Director, Academy Development, Eastern Region Criminal Justice Commission (1980-1982); Director of Procurement, Passport International, Kansas City, MO (1976-1979); Consultant, Ivanhoe Enterprises, Inc., Atlanta, GA (1968-1975); Director, Pan American Operations International Leasing Corp., Detroit, MI (1965-1967); Claim Manager, USF & G Insurance Co., Savannah, GA **CR:** Lecturer to Law Enforcement, Civic Organizations Aide to Governor Office, Atlanta, GA (1964); President, Law Enforcement Guild (6 Years) **MIL:** Retired Lieutenant Colonel, United States Army (1986); Lieutenant Colonel, United States Army, Vietnam (1967-1968) **AW:** Academic Program Design Grant (1984); Research Grant, Criminal Justice Commission (1983); Leadership Award, Sigma Delta Kappa (1965); Meritorious Service Medal with Four Oak Leaf Clusters; Vietnam Campaign Medal with Three Campaign Stars; Army Commendation Medal with Two Oak Leaf Clusters; National Defense Service Medal; Army Service Medal; Army Overseas Service Medal; Good Conduct Medal; Presidential Unit Citation; Parachutist Badge; Vietnam Parachutist Badge; Aerial Observer Badge; Combat Infantry Badge; Recondo Badge; Decorated Purple Heart; Cross of Gallantry; Air Medal with Oak Leaf Cluster; Meritorious Service Medal with Oak Leaf Cluster; Legion of Merit; Meritorious Unit Citation **MEM:** Alumni Member, President, Alpha Lambda Epsilon (1983-1984); President, Law Enforcement Guild (1981-1985); Secretary, International, Frankfurt, Germany (1969-1970); Alumni Member, Sigma Delta Kappa; Atlanta Claims Association; American Criminal Justice Association; Law Enforcement Guild; Master, Masons **MH:** Albert Nelson Marquis Lifetime Achievement Award **B/I:** Mr. Shirley had an interest in a new kind of law enforcement where you looked at it on all aspects rather then just throwing someone in jail. **PA:** Republican **RE:** Baptist

SHOAF, BRUCE ALLEN, T: Instrument Engineer (Retired) **I:** Engineering **DOB:** 04/08/1950 **PB:** Meadville **SC:** PA/USA **PT:** Nevin Gray Shoaf; Nellie Adrienne (Rickard) S. **MS:** Married **SPN:** Jane **ED:** Associate in Engineering Science, Erie Institute of Technology, Erie, PA (1968-1970) **CT:** Radiation Safety **C:** Retired (2004); Instrument Engineer, Reliability Engineer, Radiation Safety Officer, Eramet Marietta Inc., Marietta, OH (1999-2004); Instrument Engineer, Elkem Metals Co., Marietta, OH (1994-1999); Engineering Technician, Cleveland Electric Illuminating Co., Ashtabula, OH (1994); Senior Instrument Technician, Elkem Metals Co., Ashtabula, OH (1973-1994); Welder, General Electric, Erie, PA (1972-1973); Machine Tool Operator, Teledyne Penn Union Electric, Edinboro, PA (1972)

AW: Certificate of Merit, Western Pennsylvania Physics Teachers Association; Inductee, Elkem Metals Co. Quality Club **MEM:** Senior Member, Instrument Society of America; Founding Member, Industrial Computing Society; Institute of Electrical and Electronics Engineers Computer Society; Institute of Electrical and Electronics Engineers Nuclear & Plasma Sciences Society; Institute of Electrical and Electronics Engineers Aerospace & Electronic Systems Society **MH:** Albert Nelson Marquis Lifetime Achievement Award **AS:** Mr. Shoaf attributes his success on his propensity for always doing the best he could, as well as his inability to quit. **B/I:** Mr. Shoaf first became interested in engineering after watching the Mr. Wizard television program, and due to the influence of his uncle, Zane, who encouraged his fascination in physics and electronics. **AV:** Running; Science; Reading; Electronics; Flying

SHOEMAKER, FRANCES, T: Sculptor **I:** Fine Art **DOB:** 11/11/1942 **PB:** Oregon City **SC:** Oregon/USA **PT:** Fred Denham; Melba Verna (Hinshaw) Patton **MS:** Married **SPN:** Ronald Dale Shoemaker (08/09/1968) **CH:** Shanti Kirstin Adrienne **ED:** Teacher Intern, Teacher Corps, Corvallis, OR (1967-1968); BA, Linfield College (Now Linfield University) (1964); Coursework, State University of New York (1973-1974); Coursework, Oregon State University (1967-1968); Coursework, Portland State University (1966-1967) **CT:** Certified Art Teacher, K-12, Elementary Education, K-6, State of New York **C:** Sculptor, Adams Center, NY (1976-Present); Owner, Craft Business, Adams Center, NY (1985-1996); Data Collector, Real Estate Tax Department, Watertown, NY (1975-1976); Substitute Teacher, Meade Elementary School, Watertown City School District, Watertown, NY (1976); Clerk Librarian, Multnomah County Library, Portland, OR (1964-1965) **CR:** Retired Librarian **CIV:** Librarian, Adams Center Free Library, NY (2003-Present); Founder, President, Friends of Adams Center Free Library, NY (2002) **CW:** Sculptor, Toothpick Animals; Artist, Craftwork, Christmas Cards (60) Every Year **MEM:** ACLU **MH:** Albert Nelson Marquis Lifetime Achievement Award **AS:** Mrs. Shoemaker's parents encouraged her to read from an early age. She is interested in many things: people, history, science, different religions.She loved working in the library, buying books with the patron's interests in mind. **B/I:** Mrs. Shoemaker became involved in her profession because she loved books. She loved reading and talking to people about books and helping them find the books they liked or needed. Art was always embedded in her and she always drew in watercolor and oil but she liked watercolor best. **AV:** Craftwork; Reading; Collecting books; Listening to music **PA:** Democrat **THT:** Mrs. Shoemaker says, "Life is fascinating. I wonder how our brains began to work. How does it know what we should or should not do? How do we learn to talk with people who are so different from each other? Why are some people criminals? I've been thinking a lot about that lately because of what is going on with the aftermath of the policeman killing George Floyd. I was taught that the police were there to not only catch criminals but help people who are in trouble. I think about nature - how do the birds know what is right for them to eat and why are they so different from lions and tigers. ('Oh, my!')"

SHORE, KIRK, T: Senior Vice President of Integrated Product Team **I:** Business Management/Business Services **CN:** Clever Devices **MS:** Married **CH:** Three Children **ED:** BA in Psychology, Covenant College (1999) **C:** Senior Vice President, Integrated Product Group, Clever Devices (2018-Present); Vice President of Product Management, Clever Devices (2017-Present); Director of

Product Management, Clever Devices (2013-2017); AVM Product Line Manager, Clever Devices (2009-2013) **CIV:** Volunteer, Vocational Bible School **CW:** Patentee, United States Patent for Risk Mitigation Algorithm Fault IQ (2017) **AW:** Listee, Top 40 Under 40, Mass Transit Magazine (2015); Top Software Product AVM, Long Island Software Awards (2013); O-Line Coach Award Youth League, Rock Spring Georgia (2011); Technician of the Year, Engineering Week Magazine (2009); Early Innovator Finalist (2007); Player of the Week, Right Guard/Nose Guard Line (2005); Volunteer of the Year, Chattanooga Boys Club (1999) **AS:** Mr. Shore attributes his success to hard work, mentorship, and the Lord's blessing. **B/I:** Mr. Shore grew up on a dairy farm. His family worked incredibly hard. When he got older, he worked three jobs to get through college. Later, the president of the Electric Company in Chattanooga and asked if there were graduates he could rely on to hire. Mr. Shore's name came up, which is how he got on the path of technology and transportation. **THT:** Mr. Shore's motto is, "Commitment to excellence, and serving leadership."

SHORT, MARTIN, T: Actor **I:** Media & Entertainment **DOB:** 03/26/1950 **PB:** Ontario **SC:** Canada **PT:** Charles Patrick Short; Olive Short **MS:** Widowed **SPN:** Nancy Dolman (1980, Deceased 2010) **CH:** Henry; Katherine Elizabeth; Oliver Patrick **ED:** BA in Social Work, McMaster University (1971) **C:** Actor, Film, Television, Theater (1972-Present) **CIV:** Active Campaigner, Women's Research Cancer Fund **CW:** Voice Actor, "The Willoughbys" (2020); Actor, "Good People" (2020); Actor, "The Morning Show" (2019); Voice Actor, "The Addams Family" (2019); Voice Actor, "Big Mouth" (2019); Performer, Executive Producer, Writer, Netflix Special, "Steve Martin and Martin Short: An Evening You Will Forget for the Rest of Your Life" (2018); Voice Actor, "Elliot the Littlest Reindeer" (2018); Voice Actor, "The Magic School Bus Rides Again" (2018); Actor, "The Last Man on Earth" (2018); Voice Actor, "The Cat in the Hat Knows a Lot About That!" (2010-2018); Voice Actor, "The Simpsons" (2017); Voice Actor, "BoJack Horseman" (2017); Appearance, "Jimmy Kimmel Live!" (2017); Voice Actor, "The Cat in the Hat Knows a Lot About Space!" (2017); Actor, "Hairspray Live!" (2016); Voice Actor, "The Cat in the Hat Knows a Lot About Halloween!" (2016); Actor, "Modern Family" (2016); Actor, Producer, Writer, "Maya & Marty" (2016); Voice Actor, "The Cat in the Hat Knows a Lot About Camping!" (2016); Actor, Theater, "It's Only a Play" (2015); Actor, "Difficult People" (2015); Actor, "Unbreakable Kimmy Schmidt" (2015); Actor, "Mulaney" (2014-2015); Actor, "Inherent Vice" (2014); Actor, "Working the Engels" (2014); Voice Actor, "Legends of Oz: Dorothy's Return" (2014); Voice Actor, "The Wing Rises" (2013); Host, "Saturday Night Live" (2012, 1996, 1986); Voice Actor, "The Cat in the Hat Knows a Lot About Christmas!" (2012); Voice Actor, "Frankenweenie" (2012); Voice Actor, "Madagascar 3: Europe's Most Wanted" (2012); Actor, "I, Martin Short, Goes Home" (2012); Voice Actor, "BuzzKill" (2012); Actor, "How I Met Your Mother" (2011, 2012); Actor, "Weeds" (2011); Voice Actor, "Hoodwinked Too! Hood vs. Evil" (2011); Actor, "Tax Man" (2010); Actor, "Damages" (2010); Voice Actor, "The Spiderwick Chronicles" (2008); Performer, Theater, "Martin Short: Fame Becomes Me" (2006-2007); Actor, "The Santa Clause 3: The Escape Clause" (2006); Voice Actor, "The Blue Elephant" (2006); Actor, "Law & Order: Special Victims Unit" (2005); Actor, "Arrested Development" (2005); Voice Actor, "Barbie as The Princess and the Pauper" (2004); Actor, Producer, Writer, "Jiminy Glick in Lalawood" (2004); Actor, Theater, "The Producers" (2003); Actor, "CinéMagique" (2002); Voice Actor, "101 Dalmatians 2: Patch's London Adventure" (2002); Actor, "Curb Your Enthusiasm" (2002); Voice Actor, "Treasure Planet" (2002); Actor, Executive Producer, Writer, "Primetime Glick" (2001-2003); Voice Actor, "Jimmy Neutron: Boy Genius" (2001); Actor, "Prince Charming" (2001); Actor, "Get Over It" (2001); Performer, Executive Producer, "The Martin Short Show" (1999-2000); Actor, "Mumford" (1999); Actor, "Alice in Wonderland" (1999); Actor, Theater, "Little Me" (1998-1999); Actor, "Akbar's Adventure Tours" (1998); Voice Actor, "The Prince of Egypt" (1998); Actor, "Merlin" (1998); Actor, "A Simple Wish" (1997); Actor, "Jungle 2 Jungle" (1997); Actor, "Mars Attacks!" (1996); Actor, "Father of the Bride Part II" (1995); Voice Actor, "The Pebble and the Penguin" (1995); Actor, Executive Producer, "The Martin Short Show" (1994); Actor, "Clifford" (1994); Actor, Theater, "The Goodbye Girl" (1993); Voice Actor, "We're Back! A Dinosaur's Story" (1993); Actor, "Screen One" (1993); Actor, "Captain Ron" (1992); Narrator, "Shelley Duvall's Bedtime Stories" (1992); Actor, "Father of the Bride" (1991); Actor, "Maniac Mansion" (1991); Actor, "Pure Luck" (1991); Actor, "The Earth Day Special" (1990); Actor, "The Tracey Ullman Show" (1990, 1989); Actor, "I, Martin Short, Goes Hollywood" (1989); Actor, "The Big Picture" (1989); Actor, "Three Fugitives" (1989); Actor, Writer, "The Completely Mental Misadventures of Ed Grimley" (1988); Actor, "Cross My Heart" (1987); Actor, "Innerspace" (1987); Actor, "Really Weird Tales" (1987); Actor, "Three Amigos" (1986); Actor, "Tall Tales & Legends" (1986); Actor, "Dave Thomas: The Incredible Time Travels of Henry Osgood" (1986); Performer, Writer, "Saturday Night Live" (1984-1985); Performer, Writer, "SCTV" (1982-1983); Actor, "Sunset Limousine" (1983); Actor, "SCTV Network" (1982-1983); Voice Actor, "Miss Peach of the Kelly School" (1982); Actor, "Taxi" (1981); Actor, "I'm a Big Girl Now" (1980-1981); Voice Actor, "SCTV" (1981); Actor, "The Love Boat" (1980); Actor, "The Associates" (1979-1980); Actor, "The Family Man" (1979); Actor, "Lost and Found" (1979); Actor, "For the Record" (1979); Actor, "The David Steinberg Show" (1976-1977); Actor, "Peep Show" (1975); Actor, "Cucumber" (1972); Actor, "Right On" (1972); Appearances, Numerous Television Shows and Specials **AW:** Canadian Screen Award, Best Performance, Animation, "The Cat in the Hat Knows a Lot About That!," Academy of Canadian Cinema and Television (2017, 2018, 2019); Lifetime Achievement Award, Canadian Screen Awards, Academy of Canadian Cinema and Television (2016); Robert Altman Award, "Inherent Vice," Film Independent Spirit Awards (2015); Primetime Emmy, Outstanding Variety Special, "AFI Life Achievement Award: A Tribute to Mel Brooks," Television Academy (2013); Courage Award, Women's Research Cancer Fund (2011); DVDX Award, Best Animated Character Performance in a DVD Premiere Movie, "101 Dalmatians II: Patch's London Adventure," DVD Exclusive Awards (2003); OFTA Television Award, Best Host or Performer in a Variety, Musical, or Comedy Series, "Primetime Glick," Online Film & Television Association (2002); Sir Peter Ustinov Award, Banff Television Festival (1999); OFTA Television Award, Best Supporting Actor in a Motion Picture or Miniseries, "Alice in Wonderland" (1999); Earle Grey Award, Gemini Awards (1995); Primetime Emmy, Outstanding Writing in a Variety or Music Program, "SCTV Network 90," Television Academy (1981) **MEM:** Artists Against Racism

SHOTWELL, GWYNNE, T: President, Chief Operating Officer **I:** Sciences **CN:** SpaceX **DOB:** 11/23/1963 **PB:** Evanston **SC:** IL/USA **PT:** Wilbur Rowley **MS:** Married **SPN:** Robert Shotwell **CH:** Two Children **ED:** MME in Applied Mathematics, Northwestern University, With Honors (1988); BS in Mechanical Engineering, Northwestern University, With Honors (1986) **C:** President, Chief Operating Officer, SpaceX (Space Explorations Technologies Corp.), Hawthorne, CA (2008-Present); Vice President, Business Development, SpaceX (Space Explorations Technologies Corp.), Hawthorne, CA (2002-2008); Director, Space Systems Division, Microcosm Inc. (1998-2002); Chief Engineer, MLV Class Satellite Program, Aerospace Corp., El Segundo, CA (1988-1998); Management Training Program, Chrysler Corp. (1988) **CR:** Board of Directors, California Space Authority (2004-Present) **AW:** Listee, 100 Most Powerful Women, Forbes Magazine (2014); Inductee, Women in Technology International Hall of Fame (2012); World Technology Award for Individual Achievement in Space (2011)

SHPILBERG, VICTOR J., T: Physician **I:** Medicine & Health Care **CN:** Norton Healthcare **PT:** George Shpilberg **MS:** Married **SPN:** Karen **CH:** Jacob; Andrea **ED:** Doctor of Medicine, University of Louisville School of Medicine, Louisville, KY (1988); Bachelor of Arts in Art History, University of Louisville, Louisville, KY (1983) **CT:** Level 3 Certification, Patient Centered Medical Home (2017-2018); Board Certified in the Specialty of Family Practice (1996, 2006, 2014); Board Certified in the Specialty of Ambulatory Medicine (2003, 2010); American Board of Family Practice; American Board of Urgent Care; Kentucky Medical License; Arizona Medical License; DEA License **C:** Director, Principal Investigator, Diabetes Research Norton Community Medical Associates (2019-Present); Physician, Norton Community Medical Associates, Pleasure Ridge Park, KY (2010-Present); Managing Partner, Dixie Primary Care (2008-2010); Clinical Director, Laboratory Services, Pleasure Ridge Primary Care (1992-2008); Managing Partner, Pleasure Ridge Primary Care (1990-2008); Residency, Internal Medicine, Tucson Hospitals Medical Education Center (1990); Internship, Internal Medicine, Tucson Hospitals Medical Education Center (1989) **CR:** Voluntary Faculty Status, Indiana Wesleyan University, Mayfield Heights, OH (2015-Present); Voluntary Faculty Status, Allied Health Professionals in Clinical Sciences, University of Kentucky, Lexington, KY (2003-Present); Medical Director, Kings Daughters and Sons Nursing Home (2004-2008); Member, Active or Courtesy Staff, Department of Family Practice, Norton Hospital, Jewish Hospital, Caritas Hospital, Norton Audubon Hospital, Norton Women's and Children's Hospital, Alliant Medical Pabilion/Norton Children's Hospital, Baptist East Hospital, and Kindred Hospital **CIV:** Volunteer, Food Banks; Volunteer, Chabad House; Volunteer, Melton Program; Volunteer, Diabetes Task Force, Norton Healthcare; Research Arms of Clinical Healthcare; Member, Diabetes Care Committee **CW:** Lecturer, Alfred Dietz Lecture, "Integration of House Bill 1 and Controlled Substance Regulations into the EPIC Electronic Medical Record; Tips & Tricks," Norton Hospitals CME Programs (2014); Guest Speaker, "Use of Newer Agents for Treatment of Major Depression Disorder," Kentucky Association of Nurse Practitioners, Forest Pharmaceuticals (2013, 2014); Guest Speaker, "Use of Angiotensin Receptor Blockers and Hypertension" (2002); Guest Speaker, PRIME MD Lecture Series (1998); Lecturer, Periodic Lecture to the Lay Public Through the Jewish Hospital Health and Information Centers; Lecturer, Grand Rounds Lecture Series, University of Louisville Department of Family and Community Medicine **AW:** Most Compassionate Physician Award, Healthgrades (2012, 2013, 2014); Physician Recognition Award, American Medical Association (1995-1997, 1998-2001, 2002-2005, 2006-2009, 2010-2012, 2013-2015); Who's Who in Medicine **MEM:** Clinical Advisory

Board, Health Care Excel of Kentucky (2003-Present); Clinical Advisory Board, Forest Pharmaceuticals (2000-Present); Clinical Advisory Board, Novo Nordisk (2019-2020); Clinical Advisory Board, Sanofi Pharmaceuticals (2004-2010); Clinical Advisory Board, Wyeth Pharmaceuticals (2004-2010); Clinical Advisory Board, KOS Pharmaceuticals (2004-2010); Clinical Advisory Board, Blovail Pharmaceuticals (2004-2008); Clinical Advisory Board, Novartis Pharmaceuticals (2002-2008); Clinical Advisory Board, Janssen Pharmaceuticals (2001-2006); Physician Coordinator, Jewish Hospital Executive Health Program (2000); Faculty Member, Healthstart Aggrenox S.M.A.R.T. (2000); American Association of Physician Specialists; American Board of Physician Specialties; Jefferson County Medical Society; Kentucky Medical Association; Kentucky Association of Family Practitioners; American Association of Family Practitioners; American Association of Physician Specialists; American Medical Association; Southern Association of Family Practitioners; American Society of Contemporary Medicine and Surgery; American Academy of Urgent Care Medicine; American College of Physicians **MH:** Marquis Who's Who Top Professional **AS:** Dr. Spilberg attributes his success to his dedication and continued involvement within different fields of medicine, particularly in the realms of the science and business of it. **B/I:** Dr. Shpilberg became involved in his profession because he is empathetic and likes to communicate with others. Being a people person, combined with his love for medical science, he thought being a physician would be a great fit for himself. He was also fascinated by human physiology. **AV:** Hiking; Traveling; Stamp collecting; Cycling **RE:** Jewish **THT:** "Practice grace."

SHURTLEFF, WILLIAM ROY, AUTHOR, FOUNDER, SOYINFO CENTER, T: Author, Publishing Executive **I:** Publishing **DOB:** 04/28/1941 **PB:** Oakland **SC:** CA/USA **PT:** Lawton Lothrop Shurtleff; Barbara Anne (Reinhardt) Shurtleff **MS:** Divorced **SPN:** Akiko Aoyagi (03/10/1977, Divorced 1995) **CH:** Joseph Aoyagi Shurtleff (02/1987) **ED:** MEd, Stanford University, Stanford, CA (1966); Coursework, Alliance Francaise, Paris, France (1966); BA, Stanford University, Stanford, CA, With Distinction, Honors (1963); BS in Industrial Engineering and Physics, Stanford University, Stanford, CA (1962); Coursework, Stanford University, Germany (1961-1962); Coursework, Goethe Institute, Munich, Germany (1961) **C:** Founder, Director, Soyfoods Center, Lafayette, California (1976-Present); Co-Founder, Director, Esalen Program in Human Awareness, Stanford University (1967-1968); Industrial Engineer, United States Steel Corporation, Pittsburg, PA (1963) **CR:** Speaker in Field **CIV:** Volunteer Physics and Mathematics Teacher, Peace Corps, Nigeria (1963-1965); Eagle Scout (1956) **CW:** Author, Numerous Books (1976-Present); Author, "Thesaurus for SoyaScan" (1999); Author, "Tempeh Production" (1986); Author, "History of Tempeh" (1985); Author, "Tofutti and Other Soy Ice Creams: Non-Dairy Frozen Dessert Industry and Market" (1985); Author, "Soymilk, Industry and Market: Worldwide and Country-by-Country Analysis" (1984); Author, "Soyfoods, Industry and Market: Directory and Databook" (1984); Author, "Miso Production" (1981); Author, "The Book of Tempeh" (1979); Author, "Tofu and Soymilk Production" (1979); Author, "The Book of Miso" (1976); Author, "The Book of Tofu" (1975); Producer, Computerized Bibliographic Database, "SoyaScan"; Compiler, Over 86 Bibliographies **AW:** Award, American Library Association (2009); Plaque for Outstanding Contributions to Increasing Understanding and Awareness of the Health Effects of Soy Foods and Soybean Constituents,

Fifth International Symposium on the Role of Soy in Preventing and Treating Chronic Disease (2003); Winner, Oberley Award **MEM:** Co-Chair, Tofu Standards Committee (1984-1986); Board of Directors, Soyfoods Association of America; Board of Directors, Earthsave Foundation; Tau Beta Pi, Stanford University **MH:** Albert Nelson Marquis Lifetime Achievement Award **B/I:** Mr. Shurtleff became involved in his profession after living in Japan for seven years. During that time, he had relatively little money. He had just graduated from Stanford University and he found that he was using tofu as his main protein source. Mr. Shurtleff was aware of the nutritional needs of the human body, including the need for protein every day. He wondered why no one knew of this in America; he had never heard of tofu in the states, as it was not well known. Mr. Shurtleff decided to write a book about the wonders of tofu. That was the first book he and his wife wrote together, which led him to see there was a real interest in the subject. As a result of that book, hundreds of companies starting making tofu in America. After it was published, he and his wife did a nationwide tour, informing every attendee about tofu's numerous nutritional benefits. **AV:** Swimming

SIARNY, WILLIAM D., T: Librarian, Archivist **I:** Library Management/Library Services **DOB:** 04/11/1945 **PB:** Chicago **SC:** IL/USA **PT:** William D. Siarny; Ann E (Walczyk) Siarny **MS:** Widower **SPN:** Cynthia A. Skarbek (10/06/1973, Deceased 2011) **CH:** Gerard B; David B; Matthew A. Goto; Monica R. (Deceased); Elizabeth M. **ED:** MA in Library Science, Rosary College, River Forest, IL (1974);BA, DePaul University, Chicago, IL (1971) **CT:** Certificate in Organization Management, North-Western University; Certificate of Library Automation, Wisconsin **C:** Librarian, Archivist, American Meat Science Association, Chicago, IL (1980); Library Director, National Livestock & Meat Board (Now National Cattlemen's Beef Association), Chicago, IL (1979-1980); Assistant Librarian, National Dairy Council, Rosemont, IL (1974-1979); Northwestern Medical Library (1960-1970) **CR:** Archivist, American Meat Science Association, Chicago, IL (1980-Present); Coordinator, Illinois Health Libraries, Consortium, Chicago, IL (1975-Present); Chairman, Map Workshop Committee, Illinois Documents Libraries, Chicago, IL (1973) **CIV:** Chairman, Pack Committee, Oak Park, IL (1978-2000); Religious Education Teacher, Ascension Parish, Oak Park, IL (1978-1994); Chairman, Troop Committee, Boy Scouts of America, River Forest, IL (1990-1993) **MIL:** U.S. Army Reserve (1965-1974) **CW:** Editor, American Meat Science Association Production (Microfilm Edition) (1983) **AW:** Grade One Librarian **MEM:** Bylaws Committee, Medical Library Association (1977-1979); American Library Association; Special Libraries Association; Academy of Health Information Profiles; Special Libraries Association; Society of American Archivists; Association for Information Science and Technology; Association Records Management Administration (ARMA) International **MH:** Albert Nelson Marquis Lifetime Achievement Award **B/I:** Mr. Siarny became involved in his profession because he believes in knowledge. He found that libraries are one way he could learn indefinitely and that he could help others by not being tied down by educational rules. In addition, Mr. Siarny became involved at Northwestern because he was looking for a part-time job. Though he fell into library sciences by accident, he found a true passion for the work. **AV:** Practicing photography **PA:** Independent **RE:** Roman Catholic

SIBILLO, AGOSTINO, "AGO", PHD, T: Chief Executive Officer, Computer Scientist **I:** Sciences **CN:** Spychatter inc. **MS:** Married **SPN:** Emanuela **CH:** Elizabeth; Ethan **ED:** PhD in Computer Software Engineering, Italy; PhD in Criminal Law, Sciences of Finance, Italy **C:** President, Chief Executive Officer, SpyChatter, Inc., Los Angeles, CA (2015-Present); Chief Executive Officer, SpaceNet (2005-Present) **CR:** Lecturer, Various Universities **AW:** Award, Harvard University **AS:** Dr. Sibillo attributes his success to never giving up on his dreams. Likewise, he never lets obstacles deter him from achieving his goals. He said, "We must destroy the obstacles inside before we set out in the world." **B/I:** Dr. Sibillo became involved in his profession to help solve problems, push the field forward, and make the world better. He believes that there are things in life that cannot be part of society's desire to get rich, including scientific research. He believes science's only purpose should be to help humanity evolve, live longer, and be better.

SIBLEY, CHARLOTTE ELAINE, T: Independent Director **I:** Pharmaceuticals **CN:** Advicenne, S.A. **DOB:** 06/11/1946 **PB:** Holliston **SC:** MA/USA **PT:** C. Edward Sibley; Jane Forbes (Kelly) Sibley **MS:** Widowed **SPN:** Leif Magnusson (10/01/1988; Deceased 2019) **ED:** MBA, The University of Chicago Booth School of Business, Chicago, IL (1970); AB, Middlebury College, Middlebury, VT (1968) **CT:** Leadership Fellow, National Association of Corporate Directors (NACD) **C:** Independent Board Director, Advicenne, S.A. (EURONEXT: ADV), (2018-Present); Chair, Board of Directors, Fort Hill Company, Inc. (2015-Present); Chair, Compensation Committee, Fort Hill Company, Inc. (2017-Present); Leader, Management Transaction Plan, Member, CEO Search Committee, Chair, Nominating/Governance Committee, Taconic Biosciences, Inc. (2013-2019); Board Member, American Pacific Corporation (AMPAC) (2010-2014); Senior Vice President, Business Management, Shire plc. (Now Takeda Pharmaceutical Company Limited) (2005-2010); Vice President, Millennium Pharmaceuticals, Inc. (Now Takeda Pharmaceutical Company Limited) (2003-2004); Vice President, Pharmacia (Now Pfizer, Inc.) (1999-2003); President, Isis Research, Ltd. (1998-1999); Senior Director, Bristol-Myers Squibb Company (1987-1988) **CR:** Advisory Board Member, ValuedSolutions (2017-Present); Board Member, MindField Solutions (2011-Present); Advisory Board Member, Galileo Analytics (2011-Present); Member, Market Research Institute International (2009-Present); Member, St. Joseph's University Healthcare Executive MBA Advisory Board (2011-Present); Board Director, Taconic Biosciences, Inc. (2013-2019); Board Director, American Pacific Corp. (AMPAC) (2010-2014); President, Market Research Institute International (2010); President, Isis Research Inc., Princeton, NJ (1998); Senior Director, Business Information and Analysis (1995-1997); President, Healthcare Businesswomen's Association (HBA), New York, NY (1994-1995); Vice President, Research, Healthcare Businesswomen's Association (HBA), New York, NY (1991-1994); President, International Pharmaceutical Marketing Research Group, NJ (1990-1991); Director, Worldwide Marketing Research, Bristol-Myers Squibb Company, Princeton, NJ (1987-1995); Research Director, Medical Economics Company, Inc., Oradell, NJ (1984-1987); Market Research Manager, Johnson & Johnson Services, Inc., New Brunswick, NJ (1980-1984); Marketing Research Manager, Lipton Co., Englewood Cliffs, NJ (1978-1980); Consultant, New York, NY (1976-1978); Security Analyst, Donaldson, Lufkin & Jenrette, New York, NY (1973-1976); Market Research Manager, Pfizer Inc., New York, NY (1970-1973) **CIV:** Chair, Board of Directors, Mendelssohn Chorus of Philadelphia (2007-Present); Vice President, Treasurer, The Cecilia Chorus of New York, NY (1970-1988); Consultant, Volunteer, Urban Consulting Group, LLC, New York, NY (1974-1978) **CW:** Editorial Advisory Board, Pharmaceutical Executive (2008-2013) **AW:** Alumni Achievement Award, Middlebury College (2018); Inductee, Natick High School Wall of Achievement (2015); Named Woman of the Year, Healthcare Businesswomen's Association (HBA) (2008); Listee, 100 Most Inspiring People in Life Sciences, PharmaVoice (2006); Lifetime Achievement Award, Pharmaceutical Business Intelligence and Research Group (PBIRG) (2003) **MEM:** Market Research Institute international (MRII) (2009-Present); Treasurer, Product Development and Management Association (PDMA) (1990-1993) **MH:** Albert Nelson Marquis Lifetime Achievement Award **AS:** Mrs. Sibley attributes her success to P.R.I.D.E.: Persistence, Resilience, Integrity, Do good work, and Energy. She also credits innocence and competence, and treats everyone with respect and dignity. **B/I:** Mrs. Sibley was always interested in science and math, but loved languages more. She intended to go to Yale for a doctorate in French literature when she worked one summer on Wall Street. The business world was more interesting than she thought, so she decided to pursue an MBA. She was one of 10 women in a class of over 300 men. The pharmaceutical industry always interested her more than consumer products, and she was fortunate to be able to spend her career in the pharma/biotechnology industry, building analytics and insights groups and heading up Leadership Development. **AV:** Theater; Opera; Orchestra; Reading; Travel **PA:** Democrat **RE:** Episcopalian **THT:** Mrs. Sibley's motto is, "Life is short, so tell that person you love him/her, take that trip, buy that thing. Be grateful, live one day at a time, take the action, and don't project the outcome."

SICKAFOOSE, TODD, T: Jazz Musician, Composer, Producer **I:** Media & Entertainment **PB:** San Francisco **SC:** CA/USA **ED:** Coursework, California Institute of the Arts **C:** Acoustic Bassist, Keyboardist, Ani DiFranco (2004-Present) **CR:** Founder, Todd Sickafoose's Tiny Resistors; Band Member, Jenny Scheinman, Scott Amendola, Adam Levy, Allison Miller, Noe Venable; Performer, Don Byron, Trey Anastasio, Nels Cline, Ron Miles, Myra Melford, Skerik, Stanton Moore, Bobby Previte, Will Bernard, Steven Bernstein, Jessica Lurie, Erin McKeown, Sean Hayes, Carla Bozulich, Etienne de Rocher, Shane Endsley, Tony Furtado, Darol Anger, Andrew Bird, Art Hirahara, John Zorn **CW:** Producer, "Hadestown Live Original Cast Recording" (2017); Producer, "Young Man in America" (2012); Producer, Arranger, Composer, "Hadestown" (2010); Musician, "Tiny Resistors" (2008); Musician, "Blood Orange" (2006); Musician, "Dogs Outside" (2000); Producer, Rupa & the April Fishes, Nels Andrews, Mipso **AW:** Best Musical Theater Album, Grammy Awards (2019); Co-Recipient, Tony Award for Best Orchestrations (2019)

SIDEBOTTOM, CHARLES B., T: Engineering Executive (Retired) **I:** Consulting **CN:** PPO Standards LLC **PT:** Oscar H. Sidebottom; Goldia B. Sidebottom **MS:** Married **SPN:** Carolyn Sue Padley (5/25/1969) **ED:** MSEE, University of Missouri, Columbia, MO (1979); BSEE, Iowa State University of Science and Technology, Ames, IA (1968) **CT:** Registered Professional Engineer, State of Missouri **C:** Retired (2020); Managing Partner, PPO Standards LLC (2014-2019); Director, Corporation Standards, Medtronic (2000-2014); Manager of Standards, Medtronic (1992-2000); Manager, Engineering Department, Medtronic (1989-1992); Product Planner, Medtronic (1987-1989); Engineering

Project Manager, Medtronic (1985-1987); Manager of Software Systems, Medtronic, Minneapolis, MO (1984-1985); Manager, Technical Services, KCP&L (1974-1980); Systems Planning Engineer, KCP&L (1973-1974); Industrial Engineer, KCP&L (1968-1969); Engineering Executive **CR:** Consultant (2019); Secretary, International Standards Organization Committee (2007-2019); Secretary, Committee 62A, International Electrotechnical Commission, Geneva, Switzerland (1996-2018) **CIV:** Spirit of Hope United Methodist Church, Golden Valley, MN (1984-Present); Capitol Society, Colonial Williamsburg, Williamsburg, VA (1987) Co-Chairman, Planning Board, USE, Inc., Washington DC (1983-1984); Chairman, USE, Inc., Minneapolis, MN (1982-1984) **MIL:** U.S. Navy (1969-1973) **CW:** Author, "International Labeling Requirements for Medical Devices, Medical Equipment, and Diagnostic Products"; Contributor, Reference Book; Contributor, Articles, Professional Journals **AW:** Leadership Award, Association for the Advancement of Medical Instrumentation (2015); Merit Award, ASTM International (2015); Honoree, Order of the Knoll, Iowa State University of Science and Technology (2012); Medtronic Technical Fellowship (2011); Patrick Laing Award, ASTM (2009); Standards Developer Award, Association for the Advancement of Medical Instrumentation (2007); Robert Fairer Award, ASTM (2005); Ronald H. Brown Standards Leadership Award, American National Standards Institute and National Institute of Science and Technology **MEM:** Producer, Vice Chairman, ASTM International (2014-Present); Fellow, Association Advancement Medical Instrumentation (2019); Emeritus Member, Association for the Advancement of Medical Instrumentation (2016); Board Member, ASTM International (2012-2014); Recording Secretary Committee, ASTM International (2008-2013); Past Board Chairman, Association for the Advancement of Medical Instrumentation (2010-2012); Director, Association for the Advancement of Medical Instrumentation (2000-2012); Board Chairman, Association for the Advancement of Medical Instrumentation (2008-2010); Nominating Committee, Association for the Advancement of Medical Instrumentation (2006-2010); Chair Elect, Association for the Advancement of Medical Instrumentation (2006-2008); Co-Chairman, Standards Board, Association for the Advancement of Medical Instrumentation (2005-2008); Secretary Committee, ASTM International (2002-2007); Industry Vice Chairman, Association for the Advancement of Medical Instrumentation (2004-2006); Chair, Pacemaker Committee, Association for the Advancement of Medical Instrumentation (1993-2003); Fellow, ASTM; Standards Engineering Society; Lifetime Member, Institute of Electrical and Electronics Engineers (IEEE); Fellow, Association for the Advancement of Medical Instrumentation **MH:** Albert Nelson Marquis Lifetime Achievement Award **B/I:** Mr. Sidebottom had a mentor who helped in the early years, which is how he became involved in his field. **AV:** Woodworking; Volunteering

SIDER, E. MORRIS, T: Professor Emeritus of History and English Literature **I:** Education/Educational Services **CN:** Messiah University **DOB:** 11/20/1928 **PB:** Cheapside, Ontario **SC:** Canada **PT:** Earl Morris Sider; Elsie (Sheffer) Sider **MS:** Married **SPN:** Leone Dearing (08/11/1951) **CH:** Karen Redfern; Donna Gable **ED:** PhD, State University of New York (University at Buffalo), Buffalo, NY (1966); MA, Western University, London, Ontario, Canada (1955); ThB, Upland College, CA (1953); AB, Upland College, CA (1952) **CT:** Ordained to Ministry, Brethren in Christ U.S. (1954) **C:** Professor Emeritus of History and English Literature, Messiah University, Grantham, PA (2000-Present);

Professor of History and English Literature, Messiah University, Grantham, PA (1963-2000); Principal, Niagara Christian Collegiate, Fort Erie, Ontario, Canada (1956-1958) **CR:** Director, Center for Brethren in Christ Studies (1994-2000); Archivist, Brethren in Christ U.S. (1979-2000); Executive Director, Brethren in Christ Historical Society (1994-1998); Committee Member, Eastern Mennonite College (Now Eastern Mennonite University) and Eastern Mennonite Seminary, Harrisonburg, VA (1990-1994); Board of Administration, Brethren in Christ U.S. (1984-1990); Board for Ministry and Doctrine, Brethren in Christ U.S. (1984-1990); Assistant Moderator, Brethren in Christ U.S. (1986-1988); Member, Publisher Board, Brethren in Christ U.S. (1958-1961); Executive Board Member, Conference on Faith & History **CW:** Member, Advisory Council, Pietism Studies Group (2000-Present); Consultant Editor, Mennonite Quarterly Review, Goshen, IN (1986-Present); Editor, Brethren in Church History and Life Journal, Grantham, PA (1978-Present); Member, Editorial Board, Pennsylvania Mennonite Heritage (1965-1998); Author, "The Brethren in Christ in Canada" (1988); Author, "Messiah College: A History" (1984); Author, "Nine Portraits" (1978); Author, "A Vision for Service" (1976); Author, Books; Contributor, Articles to Professional Journals **AW:** Fellow, Elizabethtown College (2000); Eponym, Sider Institute for Anabaptist, Pietist, and Wesleyan Studies Center, Messiah College (2000); Distinguished Alumnus Award, Messiah College/Upland College Alumni Association (1997); Teaching Excellence and Campus Leadership Award, Sears-Roebuck (1991); Excellence in Teaching Award, Messiah College (1987); Named Alumnus of the Year, Niagara Christian Collegiate (1983); Canadian Council Fellow (1958-1959) **MEM:** Canadian Historical Association; American Historical Association **MH:** Albert Nelson Marquis Lifetime Achievement Award **B/I:** Dr. Sider grew up in rural Ontario, Canada on a farm and he wanted to be a farmer, but his parents thought that he could do better than farming. He dreamt that his parents sold the farm and he could not be a farmer, which eventually came true. And the only other option in that area was education, so he started out as an elementary school teacher. He started teaching at the age of 18 in a one room schoolhouse. He got hooked on teaching and he followed through on teaching. After the war, teachers in rural Ontario, Canada, were very scarce. Children with decent records in high school started teaching out of grade 12, and he had to take summer courses for certification; it was primarily for the teachers shortage. In addition, it was a great place for him to begin his teaching because that is where he really learned to love it. **AV:** Reading a book per week; Reading poetry; Attending concerts

SIDERIS, RHONDA CANNADA, T: President, Founder **I:** Business Management/Business Services **CN:** Park City Lodging **C:** President, Founder, Park City Lodging (1984-Present) **CIV:** Historic Park City Association; Recycled Utah Green Business; Women's Giving Fund **AW:** Best of State (2018-2019); Recycler of the Year, State Organization; Green Business of the Year; Affiliate of the Year; Conservationist of the Year **MEM:** Citizens' Open Space Advisory Committee (2013); Vacation Rental Manager's Association; Park City Area Lodging Association **AS:** Ms. Sideris attributes her success to her employees, her staff, and her team. **B/I:** Ms. Sideris became involved in her profession because she saw a need for professional management, which was from an owner's point of view, as well as the guest's point of view.

SIDWELL, ROBERT WILLIAM, PHD, T: Virologist, Educator (Retired) **I:** Pharmaceuticals **DOB:** 03/17/1937 **PB:** Huntington Park **SC:** CA/USA **PT:** Robert Glen Sidwell; Eva Amalie (Gordy) Sidwell **MS:** Married **SPN:** Rhea Julander (05/31/1957) **CH:** Richard Dale; Jeanette Kathleen; David Eugene; Cynthia Diane; Michael Jason; Robert Odell **ED:** PhD, The University of Utah (1963); MS, The University of Utah (1961); BS, Brigham Young University (1958) **C:** Retired Virologist, Educator (2012); Consulting, Drugs that Treat Virus Diseases (2007-2012); Director of Institute of Antiviral Research, Utah State University, Logan, Utah (1992-2007); Retired, Trustee Professor of Animal, Dairy and Veterinary Science, Utah State University, Logan, Utah (2007); Trustee Professor of Animal, Dairy and Veterinary Science, Utah State University, Logan, Utah (1977-2007); Director of Institute, ICN Nucleic Acid Research Institute (1975-1977); Head of Chemotherapy Division, ICN Nucleic Acid Research Institute (1972-1975); Head of Department of Virology, ICN Nucleic Acid Research Institute, Irvine, CA (1969-1972); Member of Faculty, The University of Alabama School of Medicine (1968-1969); Head of Virus Division, Southern Research Institute, Birmingham, AL (1963-1969); Head of Serology, Rickettsiology and Virus Research, Epizoology Laboratory, The University of Utah (1958-1963) **CR:** Researcher and Lecturer in Field **CIV:** Chairman, Basic Research Subcommittee, Division of AIDS, National Institute of Allergy and Infectious Diseases, National Institutes of Health (1990); Member, Nibley City Planning and Zoning Commission, Utah (1978-1980); Chairman, Health Education Awareness Forum (1975); Member, Steering Committee, Irvine School Board (1972) **MIL:** With, United States Naval Reserve (1953-1960) **CW:** Editorial Board, International Antiviral News (1992-2007); Editor, ISAR News (1992-2007); Editorial Board, Antiviral Research (1980-2007); Editorial Board, Chemotherapy (1974-2007); Editorial Board, Antimicrobial Agents and Chemotherapy (1972-2007); Editor, "The Sawmill," Publication of the Temple Fork Chapter of the Sons of Utah Pioneers; Contributor, Articles and Antiviral Reviews to Professional Journals **AW:** Named, College of Agriculture Professor of the Year (1989); Governor's Medal for Science and Technology, Utah State University (1988); E. Wynne Thorne Research Award, Utah State University (1987); Silver Beaver Award, Boy Scouts of America (1987); Scholarship, Order of Eagles (1954); Scholarship, U.S. Department of the Interior (1954) **MEM:** Executive Committee, International Society of Chemotherapy (1991-2007); Fellow, Infectious Disease Society of America (IDSA); American Association for the Advancement of Sciences; The American Association of Immunologists, Inc.; Society for Experimental Biology and Medicine; Pan American Medical Association; Inter-American Society of Chemotherapy; The America Society for Microbiology; American Society for Virology; National Association of Colleges and Teachers in Agriculture; American Association of University Professors (AAUP); International Society for Antiviral Research; Sigma Xi, The Scientific Research Honor Society **MH:** Albert Nelson Marquis Lifetime Achievement Award; Marquis Who's Who Top Professional **AS:** Dr. Sidwell attributes his success to the love and support of his wife and family. **B/I:** Dr. Sidwell had a sister who had severe polio and that stimulated him to go into the virus field so he could seek to find drugs to treat virus diseases. **AV:** Genealogical research; Gardening; Watercolor painting **PA:** Republican **RE:** The Church of Jesus Christ of Latter-day Saints **THT:** Dr. Sidwell has a continuing love of God, a strong belief in prayer, and is constantly trying to understand the scriptures. He hopes he has left his family, whom he loves dearly, with those same directions in life.

SIEBEL, THOMAS M., T: Chief Executive Officer **I:** Technology **DOB:** 11/20/1952 **PB:** Chicago **SC:** IL/USA **PT:** Arthur Francis Siebel; Ruth A. (Schmid) Siebel **MS:** Married **SPN:** Stacey Siebel **ED:** Honorary Doctorate of Engineering, University of Illinois-Urbana-Champaign; MBA, University of Illinois-Urbana-Champaign; MS in Computer Science, University of Illinois-Urbana-Champaign; BA, University of Illinois-Urbana-Champaign **C:** Founder, Chairman, Chief Executive Officer, C3.ai (2009-Present); Co-Founder, Chairman, Chief Executive Officer, Siebel CRM Systems, Inc. (1993-2006); Chief Executive Officer, Gain Technology (1990-1992); Executive, Numerous Management Positions, Oracle Corporation (1984-1990) **CR:** Chairman of the Board, American Agora Foundation; Chairman, First Visual Group; Director, Hoover Institution, Stanford University **CIV:** Founder, Chairman, Thomas and Stacy Siebel Foundation; Founder, Montana Meth Project; Member, Board of Advisers, Stanford University College of Engineering, University of Illinois College of Engineering, and UC Berkeley College of Engineering; Donor, $25 Million, Construction of the Siebel Center for Design, University of Illinois Urbana-Champaign; Donor, $32 Million, Construction of the Siebel Center for Computer Science, Department of Computer Science, University of Illinois Urbana-Champaign **CW:** Author, "Digital Transformation: Survive and Thrive in an Era of Mass Extinction" (2019); Author, "Taking Care of eBusiness" (2001); Author, "Cyber Rules" (1999); Author, "Virtual Selling" (1996); Author, Numerous Articles, Professional Publications **AW:** Most Intriguing Entrepreneur, Goldman Sachs (2018); Top CEO, Glassdoor (2018); Entrepreneur of the Year, EY (2017, 2018); Most Admired CEO Achievement Award, San Francisco Business Times (2016); Chancellor's Citation, University of California Berkeley (2014); Named, One of the World's Top 250 Eco-Innovators, Fortune (2014); Woodrow Wilson Award for Corporate Citizenship, Woodrow Wilson International Center for Scholars, Smithsonian Institution (2010); Inductee, Engineering at Illinois Hall of Fame, University of Illinois Urbana-Champaign (2010); Lewis & Clark Pioneers in Industry Award, University of Montana (2006); Master Entrepreneur of the Year, Ernst & Young (2003); Inductee, CRM Hall of Fame (2003); David Packard Award, Business Executives for National Security (2002); University of Illinois Presidential Award and Medallion (2001); Named One of the "Top 25 Managers in the World," BusinessWeek (2000, 2001); Named One of the Top 25 Managers in Global Business, Businessweek (1999-2001); Inductee, Call Center Magazine Hall of Fame (2000); Top 10 CEOs, Investor's Business Daily (2000) **MEM:** American Academy of Arts and Sciences (2013-Present); Trustees of Princeton University (2008-2011)

SIEGEL, STUART, "STU" E., MD, T: Pediatric Hematologist-Oncologist; Educator (Retired) **I:** Medicine & Health Care **CN:** Children's Hospital Los Angeles, Keck School of Medicine of USC **DOB:** 07/16/1943 **PB:** Plainfield **SC:** NJ/USA **PT:** Hyman Siegel; Charlotte Pearl (Freinberg) Siegel **MS:** Married **SPN:** Barbara Frankel (05/29/2005); Linda Wertkin (01/20/1968, Deceased 2003) **CH:** Joshua **ED:** Fellow, Leukemia Service, Medicine Branch, National Cancer Institute, National Institutes of Health (1969-1972); Resident, Department of Pediatrics, University of Minnesota Hospital (University of Minnesota Medical Center) (1968-1969); Intern, Department of Pediatrics, University of Minnesota Hospital (University of Minnesota Medical Center) (1967-1968) MD, Boston University, Magna Cum Laude (1967); BA, Boston University, Summa Cum Laude (1967); Diploma, North Plainfield High School (1961) **CT:** Diplomate, The American Board of Pediatrics; Diplomate, Pediatric Hematology-Oncology, The American Board of Pediatrics; Medical License, California **C:** Director, Center for Global Health, Children's Hospital Los Angeles (2013-2015); Co- director, Adolescent and Young Adult Oncology Program, Keck School of Medicine of USC (2013-2015); Professor, Keck School of Medicine of USC (1981-2015); Director, Children's Center for Cancer and Blood Diseases (1996-2013); Head, Division of Hematology-Oncology, Children's Hospital Los Angeles (1976-2013); Vice Chairman, Department of Pediatrics, Keck School of Medicine of USC (1994-2010); Deputy Physician-in-chief, Children's Hospital Los Angeles (1987-1991); Associate Professor, Keck School of Medicine of USC (1976-1981); Assistant Professor, Pediatrics, Keck School of Medicine of USC (1972-1976); Clinical Associate, National Institutes of Health (1969-1972) **CR:** President, Southern California Children's Cancer Services (1977-1995); Member, Clinical Cancer Program Project Committee, National Cancer Institute, National Institutes of Health, U.S. Department of Health and Human Services (HHS) (1978-1982) **CIV:** Chair, Board of Directors, DNA SEQ Alliance (2019-Present); Advisory Committee, Dissolve, Inc. (2018-Present); President, Health Care Foundation for Ventura County (2017-Present); Member, Scientific Advisory Committee DNA-SEQ Inc. (Now DNA SEQ Alliance) (2014-Present); Member, Education Committee, American Association for Cancer Research (AACR) (2013-Present); Board of Directors, CureSearch for Children's Cancer (2005-Present); Board of Directors, Global Board, Ronald McDonald House Charities (RMHC) (1995-Present); Chair, Grants Committee, Children's Cancer Research Fund (1990-Present); Chair of Board, CureSearch for Children's Cancer (2011-2020); Secretary, Critical Mass: The Young Adult Cancer Alliance (2011-2018); Vice President, Health Care Foundation for Ventura County (2014-2016); Board of Trustees, Children's Hospital Los Angeles (2000-2015); Member, Pediatrics Research Cancer Development Committee, American Association for Cancer Research (AACR) (2014); Vice President, Board of Directors, ThinkCure (2008-2014); Grants Committee, Alex's Lemonade Stand Foundation (2010, 2013-2014); Grant Review Committee, St. Baldrick's Foundation (2010-2014); Grant Review Committee, Hyundai Hope on Wheels (2010-2013); President, Board of Directors, Children's Specialty Care Coalition, CA (2010-2012); Secretary, Member, Board of Directors, Children's Specialty Care Coalition, CA (2009-2012); Member, Steering Committee, Live Strong Young Adult Alliance (2005-2011); Board of Directors, National Leukemia Broadcast Council (1987-2010); President Emeritus, Ronald McDonald House Charities (RMHC), Southern California (2008); President, Ronald McDonald House Charities (RHMC), Southern California (1996-2008); Vice President, Treasurer, Padres Contra El Cancer (2003-2004); Board of Directors, Children's Hospital Los Angeles Foundation (1994-2000); President, Southern California Children's Cancer Services (1978-1996); Board of Directors, Ronald McDonald Children's Charities (RMCC) (1988-1995); Board of Directors, Make-A-Wish Foundation of America (1987-1995); Member, Science Review Committee, American Association for Cancer Research (AACR) **MIL:** Surgeon, U.S. Public Health Service (1969-1972) **CW:** Associate Editor, World Journal of Pediatric Surgery, China (2020-Present); Associate Editor, Pediatric Investigation, China (2017-Present); Co-editor, "Cancer in Adolescent and Young Adults" (2007); Co-editor, "Pediatrics 1: Hematology and Oncology"; Author, 238 Peer-reviewed Medical/Scientific Journal Articles, 213 Abstracts, 31 Book Chapters, Eight Books; Presenter, Over 400 Invited Lectures **AW:** Archie Bleyer AYA Trailblazer Award, Critical Mass (2016); Named Honorary Professor, National Center for Maternal and Child Health, Mongolia (2015); Silk Road Award, Mongolian National Chamber of Commerce and Industry (2008); Gold Medal, N.N. Blokhin Russian Cancer Research Center (2004); Distinguished Alumnus Award, Boston University (2003); Inductee, National Caring Hall of Fame (2001); Named, Outstanding Intellectuals of the 20th Century, International Biographical Centre, Cambridge, United Kingdom (2001); National Caring Award, Caring Institute (2001); Commendation, Governor Grey Davis, CA (2000); Named International Man of the Year, Warrant of the Proclamation, International Biographical Centre of Cambridge (1999-2000); Named Best Hematologist in Los Angeles, Los Angeles Business Journal (1999); Distinguished Alumnus Award, Boston University School of Medicine Alumni Association (1997); Named, Honorary Professor of Pediatrics, Postgraduate Medical School of the People's Liberation Army (PLA), China (1997); Commendation, Governor Pete Wilson, CA (1997); Listee, International Who's Who of Professionals (1995); Stuart E. Siegel, MD Endowed Chair in Pediatric Oncology, Keck School of Medicine of USC (1995); Honoree, Israel Cancer Research Fund (ICRF) (1994); Commendation, President Bill Clinton (1994); Commendation, President George H.W. Bush (1991); Commendations, State of California Senate Rules Committee, State of California Assembly Resolution, City of Los Angeles, City of Beverly Hills, Mayor of Los Angeles, and County of Los Angeles, CA (1991); Named, Outstanding Professional, National Philanthropy Day (1991); Alpha Omega Alpha Honor Medical Society (1967); The Phi Beta Kappa Society (1966); Named One of the Best Doctors in America, Pacific Region; Kim Hill Award, Los Angeles Ronald McDonald House **MEM:** Fellow, American Academy of Pediatrics; The American Society of Pediatric Hematology/Oncology; American Society of Clinical Oncology (ASCO); American Association for Cancer Research (AACR); American Medical Association **MH:** Albert Nelson Marquis Lifetime Achievement Award; Marquis Who's Who Humanitarian Award; Marquis Who's Who in America **AS:** Dr. Siegel attributes his success to enthusiasm, commitment, and willingness to take risks when presented with opportunities. **B/I:** Dr. Siegel very much enjoyed caring for and being involved with young people as he was working his way through college and has always had an interest in pediatric medicine. He wanted to be involved in an area for which there were not a lot of answers and could be a part of the effort to find answers for the diseases he treated. As a result, Dr. Siegal had an opportunity to do his military training at the National Institutes of Health in the U.S. Public Health Service. He became interested in pediatric hematology-oncology because it met those criteria and it was an area where, at that time, survival was poor, and he had an opportunity to not just be involved in the care of these children, but in the research as well. He has always enjoyed mentoring and teaching young students, so academic medicine was a natural logical interest. **AV:** Traveling; Being a fan of ice hockey; Museums; Opera; Movies; Historical novels and places **PA:** Independent **RE:** Jewish **THT:** Dr. Siegel is on the advisory committee of Dissolve, Inc., a startup company seeking to develop a no or low-cost technology solution to help families fill out the myriad of forms for medical/government services, particularly for health-related programs. Dr. Siegel is also the Chairman of the Board of DNA SEQ Alliance, a startup biotech company that is using a novel machine-learning algorithm to design new drugs for patients resistant to kinase inhibitor drugs for cancer and autoimmune diseases. He says, "I feel very lucky to have had a career doing both things that I enjoy and providing me unique rewards, especially the ability to help others."

SIEKIERSKI, KAMILLA MALGORZATA CDT, T: Dental Laboratory Technologist **I:** Medicine & Health Care **DOB:** 08/04/1938 **PB:** Warsaw **PT:** Tomasz Piotrowski; Janina W. (Sendzimir) Piotrowski **MS:** Married **SPN:** Kazimierz Siekierski (11/25/1959) **CH:** Marzanna; Eva **CT:** Certified Dental Technician, School Dental Technicians, Krakow, Poland (1957) **C:** President, Dentek, Inc., Milford, CT (1970-2004); Dental Technician, Wilcox Dental Laboratory, Wethersfield, CT (1965-1968); Dental Technician, Dan's Dental Laboratory, Waterbury, CT (1963-1965); Owner and Operator, Kama's Dental Laboratory, Krakow, Poland (1963) **CR:** Lecturer, Smile Seminars (1990-Present); Consultant, Dental Laboratories to Bring Dentistry Standards Worldwide; Lecturer in Field of Dental Prosthetic **MEM:** President, Connecticut Dental Laboratory Association (1977-1979); Conference Dental Laboratories; National Association of Dental Laboratories **MH:** Albert Nelson Marquis Lifetime Achievement Award **B/I:** Ms. Siekierski became involved in her profession because she was in classical ballet and, at that time, she was also in an art school, painting and sculpturing. Her father said she was "not Michelangelo" and that when she's 35, some young ballerinas are going to replace her, and she should be a teacher. He was an economist and told her she had to go and do something through which she could make a living anywhere in the world and pushed her to go to dental technology school. She could not, in those days, say "no" to her parents and just had to do what they told her to do. And, in her case, she was grateful to him for how he helped shape her life. She did fight it first by flunking exams as much as she could. However, she ultimately succeeded 100 percent and people saw she was a top student; she knew every answer and was accepted. Shortly afterward, she got interested in science medicine, which she liked very much, and creating artistry. Before she knew it, she became good at that. She was always extremely grateful to her father, who redirected her career.

SIGNORILE, VINCENT, T: Lawyer **I:** Law and Legal Services **DOB:** 03/22/1959 **PB:** Jersey City **SC:** NJ/USA **PT:** Ralph; Rita **MS:** Married **SPN:** Dana **ED:** MPA, Fairleigh Dickinson University (2010); JD, Seton Hall University (1985); BS, St. Peter's College (Now Saint Peter's University), Jersey City, NJ (1981) **C:** Assistant Hudson County Counsel (2016-Present); Senior Supervisor Attorney, Jersey City Law Department (2007-2016); Judge, Jersey City Municipal Court (1996-2007); Chief Judge, Jersey City Municipal Court (1999-2003); Attorney, Bayonne City Ethics Board (1995-1997); Attorney, Jersey City Zoning Board Adjustment (1994-1997); Partner, Signorile & Saminski, Jersey City, NJ (1989-1997); Associate Attorney, Jersey City, NJ (1986-1989); Law Secretary, Superior Court of New Jersey for Hudson County, Jersey City, NJ (1985-1986); Law Clerk, Corporate Counsel, Jersey City, NJ (1981-1985); Aide, Office of Mayor, City of Jersey City, NJ (1981); Aide, Jersey City Municipal Council (1980-1981) **CIV:** Trustee, Lincoln Association of Hudson County (Now Lincoln Association of Jersey City) (2019-Present); Trustee, Dante Alighieri Society (2010-Present); Jersey City Planning Board Committee (1991-1993); Jersey City Insurance Fund Committee (1989-1993); Elected to Municipal Council, Jersey City, NJ (1989-1993); Jersey City Environmental Committee (1989-1993); Co-chairman, Hudson County Columbus Parade (1984-1985); President, Elected Member, Hudson County Democratic Committee (1977-1981); University Club of Hudson County **AW:** Named Man of the Year, Dante Alighieri Society (2019) **MEM:** Lincoln Association of Hudson County; Dante Alighieri Society; President, University Club of Hudson County (2003-2004, 2012-2013) **BAR:** New Jersey (1985); Pennsylvania (1985) **MH:** Albert Nelson Marquis Lifetime Achievement Award **B/I:** Mr. Signorile wanted to be of service to the community. He was highly involved in civic and community activities while growing up. **RE:** Roman Catholic

SILBERMANN, BEN, T: Co-Founder, Chief Executive Officer **I:** Information Technology and Services **CN:** Pinterest, Inc. **DOB:** 7/14/1982 **PB:** Des Moines **SC:** IA/USA **PT:** Neil Silbermann; Jane (Wang) Silberman **MS:** Married **SPN:** Divya Bhaskaran **CH:** Two Children **ED:** BA in Political Science, Yale College (2003); Attended, Research Science Institute, Massachusetts Institute of Technology (MIT) **C:** Co-Founder, Chief Executive Officer, Pinterest, Inc., San Francisco, CA (2009-Present); Product Specialist, Google (2006-2008); Consultant, Gartner (2003-2006) **AW:** Named One of "The 35 Under 35," MIT Technology Review (2013); Named One of "The 40 Under 40," Fortune (2012-2014); Webby Award for Best Social Media App; People's Voice Award for Best Functioning Visual Design; Tenyck Award; Crunchie Award; Winner, Yale 50K Business Plan Competition

SILLIMAN, THOMAS BOUGHTON, PE, T: Electrical Engineer **I:** Engineering **DOB:** 03/15/1945 **PB:** Washington, DC **SC:** DC/USA **PT:** Robert Mitchel Silliman; Elizabeth (Peterson) Silliman **MS:** Married **SPN:** Sally Silliman; Jeanne Carol Thrall (06/08/1994, Divorced) **CH:** Rebecca; June; Rachel Elizabeth **ED:** MEE., Cornell University (1970); BEE, Cornell University (1969) **CT:** Registered Professional Engineer, States of Indiana, Maryland, and Minnesota **C:** President, Electronics Research, Inc., Chandler, IN (1962-Present) **CIV:** Volunteer, Troop 175, Boy Scouts of America, Linville IN **CW:** Author, Numerous Papers, IEEE; Host, One Hour Webinar **AW:** Broadcast Technology Society Special Service Award, IEEE (2018); Jules E Cohen Outstanding Engineering Achievement Award, IEEE (2015); Lifetime Engineering Award, National Association of Broadcasters (NAB) (2008) **MEM:** Association of Federal Communications Consulting Engineers (AFCCE) **MH:** Albert Nelson Marquis Lifetime Achievement Award; Marquis Who's Who Top Professional **B/I:** Mr. Silliman always wanted to be an engineer. When he was in the 7th grade, his father took him out of regular school and put him in a preparatory school that leaned toward engineering. Mr. Silliman started working for his father's consulting firm, Silliman, Moffett, and Kowalski. at the age of 14 years of age, as an office boy. The company was formed during World War II and during the war, his father and a man named Mr. Caraway were engineers working on a radio research lab project in Boston. After the war, his father moved to Washington, DC, to be a consultant engineer for the FCC for radio stations and TV stations; Mr. Caraway continued running Electronics Research in Evansville. Mr. Caraway hired his father as a consultant. At 16, Mr. Caraway passed away from a massive heart attack and his father bought the company. They converted the basement into an R & D Laboratory and he assisted his father in making and designing components, and he was able learn about measurements and welding. Some of the products that Mr. Silliman designed in college are still being made today. **AV:** White water kayaking; Riding horses; Roping cattle (Western horseman); Snow skiing; Climbing; Gym;

SILLIN JOHNSON, JULIE E., T: Educator (Retired) **I:** Education/Educational Services **DOB:** 03/30/1963 **PB:** Lima **SC:** OH/USA **PT:** David Andrew Sillin; Judith Ann Sillin **MS:** Married **SPN:** Robert Paul Johnson II (05/1996) **ED:** Various Coursework, University of Cincinnati (2000-2010); MA, Miami University, Oxford, OH (1995); Coursework, Paideia Instructional Training, Xavier University (1990); BS, Ohio State University (1986) **C:** Education Coordinator, Workshop Developer, Kids Voting (2002); Evaluator, Data Recognition Inc., Mason, OH (1998-2002); Presenter, Englefield & Arnold, Inc., Columbus, OH (1997-2001); Social Studies Teacher, Laboratory Coach, Hughes Alternative Center (1990-1994); Educator, Cincinnati Public Schools (1988-1994) **CR:** Social Committee Chair, Hughes High School; Academic Advisor, Ohio Mock Trial Program; Voter Registration Facilitator; Scholarship Committee Chair, OSU Alumni Club of Greater Cincinnati **CIV:** Greyhound Adoption of Greater Cincinnati (2002-Present) **AW:** Graduate Fellowship, National Endowment for the Humanities (1992) **MEM:** OSU Alumni Club of Greater Cincinnati **MH:** Albert Nelson Marquis Lifetime Achievement Award **AS:** Ms. Johnson attributes her success to determination. **B/I:** Ever since she was a child, Ms. Johnson wanted to become an educator. She felt that being a teacher would give her an opportunity to help young students in need. **AV:** Gardening; Sewing; Cooking **RE:** Christian **THT:** Ms. Johnson believes in forgiving everyone, as it frees society to live free with joy.

SILVER, LEON THEODORE, PHD, T: W.M. Keck Foundation Professor for Resource Geology, Emeritus **I:** Sciences **CN:** California Institute of Technology **DOB:** 04/09/1925 **PB:** Monticello **SC:** NY/USA **PT:** Jacob Silver; Bessie Kramer Silver **MS:** Married **SPN:** Arlana Marlane Bostrom (11/12/1998); Betty Lynds (04/04/1947, Divorced 1973) **CH:** Victoria Silver; Stuart Silver (Deceased); Lauren Connolly (Stepdaughter); Todd Bostrom (Stepson) **ED:** PhD in Geology and Geochemistry, California Institute of Technology (1955); MS in Geology, University of New Mexico (1948); BS in Civil Engineering, University of Colorado (1945) **C:** W.M. Keck Foundation Professor for Resource Geology, Emeritus, California Institute of Technology, Pasadena, CA (1996-Present); W.M. Keck Foundation Professor for Resource Geology, California Institute of Technology (1983-1996); Professor of Geology, California Institute of Technology (1965-1983); Senior Geologist, United States Geological Survey (USGS) (1969-1974); Associate Professor of Geology, California Institute of Technology (1962-1965); Assistant Professor of Geology, California Institute of Technology (1955-1962); Research Geologist in Geochemistry of Uranium, Division of Geological Sciences, Atomic Energy Commission (AEC) Contract Research (1952-1955); Junior Geologist, United States Geological Survey (USGS) (1948-1955) **CR:** Board of Directors, University of New Mexico Caswell Silver Foundation (1981-Present); Consultant, U.S. Department of Energy (1995-2001); Vice Chairman, Member, Environmental and Energy Advisory Board (1995-2001); Presidential Advisory Committee on the Redesign of the Space Station (1993-1994); Counselor, National Academy of Sciences (1989-1992); Member, Governing Board, National Research Council (1989-1992); Member, Advisory Committee, United States Geological Survey (USGS) (1975-1985); Ad Hoc Subcommittee on Scientist-Astronauts, Space Program Advisory Council (1974-1975); Lunar Sample Analysis Planning Team, Manned Spacecraft Center, NASA, Houston, Texas (1972-1974); Lunar Surface Geology Experiment Team (Apollo Missions 13-17), Lunar Sample Preliminary Examination Team (Apollo 15-17), Lunar Surface Traverse Planning Team (Apollo 15-17), and Lunar Science Working Panel (Apollo 15-17), NASA (1969-1974) **CIV:** Member, President's Advisory Committee, Redesign of the Space Station (1993); Chairman, Advisory Committee, Office of Basic Energy Sciences, U.S. Department of Energy (1990-1991, 1991-1992); Member, Steering Committee, NASA Synthesis Group, President's Space Exploration Initiative (1990-1991) **MIL:** Ensign, United States Naval Reserve (1943-1946) **CW:** Author, "Observations on the Extended Tectonic History of the Southern Sierra Nevada," Geological Society of America Joint Cordilleran and Rocky Mountain Section Meeting, The Geological Society of America, Inc., Reno, NV (1993); Co-author, "Earthquake and Seismicity Research Using SCARLET and CEDAR: Final Technical Report," Seismological Laboratory, California Institute of Technology, Pasadena, CA (1990-1992, 1993); Co-author, "Geochemical Logging in the Cajon Pass Drillhole and its Application to a New Oxide, Igneous Rock Classification Scheme," Journal of Geological Research (1992); Co-author, "87Sr/86Sr and 18O/16O Isotopic Systematics and Geochemistry of Granitoid Plutons Across a Steeply Dipping Boundary Between Contrasting Lithologic Blocks in Western Idaho," Contributions in Mineralogical Petrology (1992); Co-author, "Aspects of the Crustal Structure of the Western Mojave Desert, California, from Seismic Reflection and Gravity Data," Journal of Geologic Research (1992); Author, "Daughter-parent Isotope Systematics in U-Th-bearing Igneous Accessory Mineral Assemblages as Potential Indices of Metamorphic History: A Discussion of the Concept," The Geochemical Society, Special Publication (1991); Co-author, "The Metamictization of Zircon: Radiation Dose-Dependent Structural Characteristics," Mineralogical Society of America (1991); Co-author, "The Peninsular Ranges Batholith: An Insight into the Evolution of the Cordilleran Batholiths of Southwestern North America." Transnational Royal Society of Edinburgh (1988); Co-editor, "Uranium in Granites from the Southwestern United States: Actinide Parent-Daughter Systems, Sites and Mobilization: Second Year Report," US Department of Energy, Assistant Secretary for Resource Applications, Grand Junction Office, Grand Junction, CO (1984); Co-editor, "Geological Implications of Impacts of Large Asteroids and Comets on the Earth: Conference on Large Body Impacts and Terrestrial Evolution: Geological, Climatological, and Biological Implications," The Geological Society of America, Inc., Boulder, CO (1982); Co-author, "Geology and Ore Deposits of the Dragoon Quadrangle, Cochise County, Arizona," U.S. Government Printing Office, Washington, DC (1964); Co-author, "Agua Blanca Fault: A Major Transverse Structure of Northern Baja California, Mexico," The Society, NY (1960); Contributor, Numerous Articles to Professional Journals **AW:** Centennial Distinguished Alumnus Award, University of New Mexico (1989); NASA Group Achievement Award, Earth Resources Experiment Team (1974); NASA Group Achievement Award, Lyndon B. Johnson Space Center (1974); NASA Group Achievement Award, Lunar Landing Team (1973); Award for Professional Excellence, American Institute of Professional Geologists (1972); NASA Group Achievement Award, Crew Training and Simulation Team (1971); NASA Group Achievement Award, Lunar Traverse Planning Team (1971); NASA Exceptional Scientific Achievement Medal (1971); Guggenheim Fellowship (1964) **MEM:** President, The Geological Society of America, Inc. (1979); American Academy of Arts & Sciences (1979); Vice President, The Geological Society of America, Inc. (1978); Councilor, The Geological Society of America, Inc. (1974-1976); National Academy of Sciences (1974); Fellow, The Geological Society of America, Inc.; Senior Fellow, Mineralogical Society of America; Fellow, American Association for the Advancement of Science; American Geophysical Union; The Geochemical Society; The Meteoritical Society; Society of Economic Geologists, Inc.; Society of Economic Mineralogists and Paleontologists; Sigma Xi, The Scientific Research Honor Society; The Tau Beta Pi Association, Inc.; The Honor Society of Phi Kappa Phi; Sigma Tau; Chi Epsilon, Inc. **MH:** Albert Nelson Marquis Lifetime Achievement Award **B/I:** Dr. Silver was inspired to become a geologist by his older brother, Caswell Silver, who was a geologist as well.

SILVERIO, NICK E., T: Founder **I:** Nonprofit & Philanthropy **CN:** Gloria M. Silverio Foundation -A safe haven for Newborns **PB:** Wisconsin **SC:** FL/USA **MS:** Widower **ED:** College Courses **C:** Founder, Gloria M. Silverio Foundation, Not for Profit 501(c)-A Safe Haven for Newborns (2001-Present); Nick E. Silverio and Associates, Inc. (1983-2003) **MIL:** Florida National Guard **AW:** Points of Light; Hall of Fame, Archbishop Curley High School; CNN Heroes Among Us, People Magazine; Impacting Your World, featured in the book Unselfish **MEM:** AFP (Association of Fundraising Professionals); Knights of Columbus; St. Lazarus of Jerusalem **AS:** Mr. Silverio attributes his success to being 100 percent committed to his nonprofit's mission and stated goals and understanding the societal issues relating to infant abandonment and the demographics. Additionally, he attributes the success of his organization to building a team and network of committed volunteers, use of technology, establishing a 24/7 multilingual helpline, collaboration and networking and building relationships, and creating realistic fundraising campaigns (5K Run/Walk; Tee off for a cause golf tournament; Gala, celebrating the lives of the children saved from abandonment. and relying on the generosity of donors and corporations), their door retention rate is in the high 90s. In addition, it is "faith" in believing that he could make it happen. Faith in God that he would pull him through those times. **B/I:** Mr. Silverio became involved in his profession because he wanted to turn a personal tragedy into joy. The Gloria M. Silverio Foundation, a nonprofit 'Safe Haven for Newborns,' was created in 2001 to honor his wife Gloria, who was killed in a car accident caused by a speeding driver. They were married for 32 years and, although they had no children, they had a deep love for children and served as godparents to 14. His new purpose in life was to speak up for the voiceless, innocent, and helpless newborns. **AV:** Saving innocent newborn lives giving them a chance for a future **RE:** Catholic **THT:** God gave all of us special talents and so many minutes, hours, days to live a meaning, purposeful life. So, find your purpose in life. It is never too late. Leave a footprint, live a life of meaning, "Make a Difference" whether large or small, behind the scenes, only those you helped need to know. Remember, the gift of giving is a sense of gratitude. To quote Mark Twain "The most important days in your life are the day you were born and the day you find out why".

SILVERMAN, SARAH, T: Comedian, Actress **I:** Media & Entertainment **DOB:** 12/01/1970 **PB:** Bedford **SC:** NH/USA **PT:** Donald Silverman; Beth Ann Silverman **ED:** Student, New York University **CIV:** Advocate, Endorser, Bernie Sanders for President of the United States (2016); Contributor,

Open Letter for Women Rights for the ONE Campaign (2015); Primary Investor, Lowell Herb Co **CW:** Actress, "Marry Me" (2020); Voice Actress, "Bob's Burgers" (2011-2020); Actress, "The Jim Jefferies Show" (2018); Voice Actress, "Ralph Breaks the Internet" (2018); Voice Actress, "Last Week Tonight with John Oliver" (2018); Narrator, Executive Producer, "Please Understand Me" (2018); Herself, Music Video, "Girls Like You," Maroon 5 feat. Cardi B (2018); Host, Writer, Executive Producer, "I Love You, America with Sarah Silverman" (2017-2018); Comedian, Stand-up Special, Album, "Sarah Silverman: A Speck of Dust" (2017); Actress, "Battle of the Sexes" (2017); Actress, "The Book of Henry" (2017); Actress, "Bajillion Dollar Propertie\$" (2017); Actress, "Michael Bolton's Big, Sexy Valentine's Day Special" (2017); Actress, "Untitled Sarah Silverman Project" (2016); Actress, Music Video, "Don't Wanna Know," Maroon 5 (2016); Actress, "Popstar: Never Stop Never Stopping" (2016); Actress, "Lady Dynamite" (2016); Actress, "Great Minds with Dan Harmon" (2016); Actress, "You Can Never Really Know Someone" (2016); Actress, "Punching Henry" (2016); Actress, "Conan" (2016); Voice Actress, "The Simpsons" (2010, 2012, 2014, 2016); Actress, "Masters of Sex" (2014-2016); Actress, "Gravy" (2015); Voice Actress, "Disney Infinity 3.0" (2015); Actress, "Ashby" (2015); Voice Actress, "Man Seeking Woman" (2015); Actress, "I Smile Back" (2015); Comedian, Album, "Sarah Silverman: We Are Miracles" (2014); Voice Actress, "Disney Infinity: Marvel Super Heroes" (2014); Actress, "A Million Ways to Die in the West" (2014); Actress, "Maron" (2014); Actress, "Louie" (2012, 2014); Comedian, Stand-up Special, "Sarah Silverman: We Are Miracles" (2013); Actress, "People in New Jersey" (2013); Actress, "We Do Not Belong" (2013); Voice Actress, "Disney Infinity" (2013); Actress, "Fête des Pets" (2013); Actress, "Out There" (2013); Actress, "The League" (2011-2013); Voice Actress, "Futurama" (2000, 2013); Actress, "Susan 313" (2012); Voice Actress, "Wreck-It Ralph" (2012); Actress, "Bored to Death" (2011); Actress, "The Muppets" (2011); Actress, "Take This Waltz" (2011); Actress, "Childrens Hospital" (2011); Actress, "The Good Wife" (2011); Performer, Album, "Songs of the Sarah Silverman Program: From Our Rears to Your Ears!" (2010); Actress, "Peep World" (2010); Actress, "Darker Side of Green" (2010); Herself, "Funny People" (2009); Actress, "Saint John of Las Vegas" (2009); Actress, "Monk" (2008, 2007, 2004); Actress, "A Bad Situationist" (2008); Performer, Creator, Executive Producer, "The Sarah Silverman Program" (2007-2010); Voice Actress, "Crank Yankers" (2007, 2003, 2002); Voice Actress, "Futurama: Bender's Big Score" (2007); Comedian, Album, "Jesus Is Magic" (2006); Voice Actress, "Robot Chicken" (2006); Actress, "School for Scoundrels" (2006); Actress, "I Want Someone to Eat Cheese With" (2006); Comedian, Stand-up Special, "Sarah Silverman: Jesus Is Magic" (2005); Herself, "Now That's Funny" (2005); Actress, "Rent" (2005); Actress, "The Most Extraordinary Space Investigations" (2005); Voice Actress, "Tom Goes to the Mayor" (2005); Voice Actress, "American Dad!" (2005); Voice Actress, "Untitled Phil Hendrie Project" (2004); Voice Actress, "Drawn Together" (2004); Actress, "Greg the Bunny" (2004, 2002); Voice Actress, "Aqua Teen Hunger Force" (2004); Actress, "Pilot Season" (2004); Herself, "Entourage" (2004); Voice Actress, "Hair High" (2004); Actress, "Nobody's Perfect" (2004); Actress, "Frasier" (2003); Actress, "School of Rock" (2002); Actress, "Strippers Pole" (2002); Voice Actress, "Saddle Rash" (2002); Actress, "V.I.P." (2002); Actress, "Run Ronnie Run" (2002); Actress, "Evolution" (2001); Actress, "Heartbreakers" (2001); Actress, "Say It Isn't So" (2001); Actress, "Black

Days" (2001); Actress, "Rocky Times" (2000); Actress, "Super Nerds" (2000); Actress, "The Way of the Gun" (2000); Actress, "Manhattan, AZ" (2000); Actress, "Screwed" (2000); Actress, "Smog" (1999); Actress, "The Bachelor" (1999); Actress, "Work with Me" (1999); Actress, "Late Last Night" (1999); Actress, "Mr. Show and the Incredible, Fantastical News Report" (1998); Actress, "There's Something About Mary" (1998); Actress, "Bulworth" (1998); Actress, "The Larry Sanders Show" (1998, 1996); Actress, "Overnight Delivery" (1998); Actress, "Under the Big Muu-Muu" (1997); Actress, "The Naked Truth" (1997); Actress, "JAG" (1997); Actress, "Who's the Caboose?" (1997); Actress, "Brotherly Love" (1997); Actress, "Mr. Show with Bob and David" (1995-1997); Actress, "Star Trek: Voyager" (1996); Performer, Writer, "Saturday Night Live" (1993-1994); Herself, Numerous TV Specials **AW:** Honoree, Star, Hollywood Walk of Fame (2018); Seymour Cassel Award, Outstanding Performance by an Actress, "I Smile Back," Oldenburg Film Festival (2015); Primetime Emmy, Outstanding Writing for a Variety Special, "Sarah Silverman: We Are Miracles," Primetime Emmy Awards (2014); Co-Recipient, BTVA Feature Film Voice Acting Award, Best Vocal Ensemble in a Feature Film, "Wreck-It Ralph," Behind the Voice Actor Awards (2013); Webby Award, Best Actress, The Webby Awards (2009); Primetime Emmy, Outstanding Original Music and Lyrics, "I'm F**king Matt Damon," "Jimmy Kimmel Live!" (2008)

SILVERSHEIN, JOEL MICHAEL, ESQ., T: Assistant State Attorney **I:** Law and Legal Services **DOB:** 08/03/1961 **PB:** Brooklyn **SC:** NY/USA **PT:** Milton Silvershein; Joyce (Pullman) Silvershein **MS:** Married **SPN:** Marcia Gelman **ED:** JD, Nova University (1986); BA in History, Tulane University (1983) **C:** Assistant State Attorney, Broward County, Fort Lauderdale, FL (1986-Present) **CW:** Co-author, "Florida Juvenile Law and Practice, 15th Edition" (2018); Co-author, "Florida Juvenile Law and Practice, 14th Edition" (2016); Co-author, "Florida Juvenile Law and Practice, 13th Edition" (2013); Co-author, "Florida Juvenile Law and Practice, 12th Edition" (2011); Co-author, "Florida Juvenile Law and Practice, 11th Edition" (2009); Co-author, "Florida Juvenile Law and Practice, 10th Edition" (2007); Co-author, "Florida Juvenile Law and Practice, Ninth Edition" (2005); Co-author, "Florida Juvenile Law and Practice, Eighth Edition" (2003); Co-author, "Florida Juvenile Law and Practice, Seventh Edition" (2001); Co-author, "Florida Juvenile Law and Practice, Sixth Edition" (1999); Co-author, "Florida Juvenile Law and Practice, Fifth Edition" (1997); Co-author, "Florida Juvenile Law and Practice, Fourth Edition" (1995); Co-author, "Florida Juvenile Law and Practice, Third Edition" (1992); Researcher, "The Law of Life and Health Insurance" (1988) **MEM:** Juvenile Rules Committee, Florida Bar Association (The Florida Bar) (1987-2002, 2008-2014, 2017-Present); Criminal Law Section Executive Council, Florida Bar Association (The Florida Bar) (2008-Present); Criminal Rules Committee, Florida Bar Association (The Florida Bar) (2002-2008); Florida Bar Association (The Florida Bar) **BAR:** United States District Court for the Southern District of Florida (2012); United States Claims Court (1987); United State Court of Appeals for the Eleventh Circuit (1987); United States Tax Court (1987); Florida (1986) **MH:** Albert Nelson Marquis Lifetime Achievement Award; Marquis Who's Who Top Professional **B/I:** Mr. Silvershein became involved in his profession because he decided when he was a junior that he wanted to go to law school. At that time, Florida was a state that was blooming so he wanted to move to Florida and go into law school. In his last year, he went into an internship program at Palm Beach County.

He started to enjoy being a trial lawyer because of the ability to have a job that would help people and enjoyed government service as well. So it was combining the best of both worlds.

SILVERSTEIN, HERBERT, MSC, MD, FACS, T: President **I:** Medicine & Health Care **CN:** Silverstein Institute and Ear Research Foundation **DOB:** 08/06/1935 **PB:** Philadelphia **SC:** PA/USA **MS:** Married **CH:** Gary Robert; David Neal **ED:** MSc in Physiology, Temple University Medical School (1957-1963); MD, Temple University Medical School (1957-1961); BSc, Dickenson College Cum Laude (1953-1957); BA, Central High School, Philadelphia, PA (1949-1953) **CT:** Board Certified, American Board of Otolaryngology **C:** President, Silverstein Institute **CR:** Clinical Instructor, Otolaryngology, Department of Otolaryngology, Harvard Medical School, Massachusetts Eye & Ear Infirmary, Boston, MA (1968-1971); Teaching Fellow, Department of Otolaryngology, Harvard Medical School, Massachusetts Eye & Ear Infirmary, Boston, MA (1965-1966) **CIV:** President, Ear Research Foundation **MIL:** Staff Otolaryngologist, Tripler General Hospital, Honolulu, HI (1966-1968); Captain, U.S. Army Medical Corps **AW:** Honor Award, Foundation for Innovation, Education, and Research in Otolaryngology (2017); Vice Presidential Citation, Triological Society (2013); City of Sarasota Proclamation, Dr. Herbert Silverstein Day (2012); Board of Governor's Award, American Academy of Otolaryngology (2011); Award of Merit, American Otological Society (2006); Guest of Honor, Otosclerosis Study Group (2004); Presidential Citation, American Academy of Otolaryngology (2002); Guest of Honor, Triological Society Southern Section (2002); Guest of Honor, Canadian ENT Society (1999); Listee, Best Doctors in America, Woodward & White (1998); Distinguished Service Award, American Academy of Otolaryngology (1997); Gold Medal Honor Award, Guest of Honor, Prosper Meniere Society (1996); Guest Speaker, XXX Graduation of Department of OTO-HNS, University of Puerto Rico School of Medicine (1995); Guest of Honor, Intituto Otorrinolaringologico Antolicandela (1995); Listee, Best Doctors in America, Woodward & White (1992-1993); Howard P. House Award, Ear Foundation, Nashville, TN (1992); Best Medical Specialist in the US, Town and Country (1984); Tracoustics Outstanding Faculty Award, XVII Colorado Otology-Audiology (1983); Best Doctors in the USA, John Pekkanen, Simon and Shuster (1979); First Prize Research Award, American Academy of Otolaryngology (1966); Charles Burr Award for Research, Philadelphia General Hospital (1962); Honorable Mention, Scientific Forum, SAMA (1961); Alpha Omega Alpha, Temple University (1960) **MEM:** Sarasota Memorial Hospital (1975); Diplomat, American Board of Otolaryngology (1967) **MH:** Marquis Who's Who Top Professional **B/I:** When Dr. Silverstein was young, his father decided to enroll him in a program that would introduce him to neuropsychiatry. Follow his father's wishes, Dr. Silverstein completed the program and began practicing music as a hobby.

SIMMONS, BETTY JO, T: Civil Engineer, Draftsman **I:** Engineering **DOB:** 12/13/1936 **PB:** Caddo **SC:** OK/USA **PT:** Robert Lee; Beatrice (Alexander) Lee **MS:** Divorced **ED:** Coursework, City College, University of California Santa Barbara; Coursework, University of California Los Angeles; Coursework, University of California Riverside; Coursework, University of California, Fresno, CA **CT:** Ordained Minister (1978) **C:** Customer Services Coordinator, Caltran, Los Angeles, CA (1997-2000); State Department of Transportation (1959-2000); District Materiel Manager, Caltran, Los Angeles, CA (1994-1997); District Claims Officer, Caltran,

Los Angeles, CA (1993-1994); Chief Facilities Operations, Caltran, Los Angeles, CA (1989-1993); Coordinator, Governmental Affairs, Caltran, Los Angeles, CA (1989); Project Manager Pre-Apprenticeship Training Program, Caltrans, Compton, CA (1987-1989); Liaison Consultant, Civil Rights, Caltrans (1983-1987); Supervisor, Civil Engineer Draftsperson, Caltrans (1977-1982); Equal Employment Opportunity Counselor, Caltrans (1973-1977); Supervisor, Civil Engineering Draftsperson, Caltrans (1962-1973); Junior Civil Engineering Draftsperson, Caltrans (1959-1962); Drafting Clerk, PacBell (1956-1959) **CR:** Facilitator, Governors Commission on the Status of Women, Fresno, CA (1980) **CIV:** Fundraiser, Hunger Project, Los Angeles, Fresno, CA (1980-Present); Youth at Risk, Los Angeles, CA (1986-Present); Board of Directors, Morgan Canyon Institute of Higher Learning, Fresno, CA (1978-1982) **MIL:** Navy Wave Reserves (1957-1959) **CW:** Producer, "Building a Future" (1988) **AW:** Excellence in Transportation Facilities Award (1993); Employee of the Year (1992) **MEM:** Wisdom Community; Landmark Worldwide, Inc. **MH:** Albert Nelson Marquis Lifetime Achievement Award **AV:** Painting; Flying; Scuba diving; Traveling; Whitewater rafting; Studying metaphysics

SIMONDS, JOHN E., T: Newspaper Editor (Retired) **I:** Writing and Editing **DOB:** 07/04/1935 **PB:** Boston **SC:** MA/USA **PT:** Alvin E. Simonds; Ruth Angeline (Rankin) Simonds **MS:** Married **SPN:** Rose B. "Kitty" Muller (11/16/1968) **CH:** Maximillian P.; Malia G.; Rachel K. Olson; Dr. John B. Simonds (Deceased) **ED:** Bachelor of Arts, Bowdoin College, Brunswick, ME (1957) **C:** Retired (2002); Consultant, The Honolulu Advertiser and Gannett Foundation (2002-2004); Reader Representative, The Honolulu Advertiser, Honolulu, HI (1999-2002); Market Development Editor, Hawaii Newspaper Agency, Honolulu, HI (1993-1999); Senior Editor, Editorial Page Editor, Honolulu Star Bulletin (1987-1993); Executive Editor, Honolulu Star Bulletin (1980-1987); Managing Editor, Honolulu Star Bulletin (1975-1980); Correspondent, Gannett News Service, Washington, DC (1966-1975); Reporter, Assistant City Editor, Washington Evening Star (1965-1966); Reporter, Assistant City Editor, Providence Journal Bulletin (1960-1965); Reporter, United Press International, Columbus, OH (1958-1960); Reporter, Daily Tribune, Seymour, IN (1957-1958) **MIL:** U.S. Army Reserve (1958-1965); U.S. Army (1958) **CW:** Author, Poetry, "Footnotes to the Sun" (2015); Author, Poetry, "Waves From a Timed-Zoned Brain" (2009) **MEM:** News Leaders Association; Society of Professional Journalists; Association of Opinion Journalists; Organization of News Ombudsmen; Association of Writers and Writing Programs; Hawaii Literary Arts Council; Friends of the East-West Center; Mid-Pacific Road Runners Club **MH:** Albert Nelson Marquis Lifetime Achievement Award **AS:** Mr. Simonds attributes his success to his family in Hawaii, including his busy wife, "Kitty" (Rose), and a diverse local network of many in-laws and friends whose support has been crucial to his career. Additionally, he credits early newspaper mentors, understanding readers, encouraging colleagues and patient employers. **B/I:** Mr. Simonds became involved in his profession after receiving a Bachelor of Arts from Bowdoin College in 1957, whereupon he began newspaper work in Indiana. He sought a career that offered adventure and chances to explore communities, and write about people and events on a daily basis. **AV:** Distance running; Poetry **PA:** Independent **RE:** Shared Faiths

SIMONS, NATHANIEL, "NAT", T: Co-Founder **I:** Business Management/Business Services **CN:** Sea Change Foundation **PT:** James Harris

Simons; Barbara Simons **MS:** Married **SPN:** Laura Baxter-Simons **CH:** Two Children **ED:** MS in Mathematics, University of California Berkeley (1994); BS in Economics, University of California Berkeley (1989) **C:** Co-Founder, Prelude Ventures (2009); Principal, Renaissance Technologies, East Setauket, NY (1994-2011); Cylink Corp, Sunnyvale, CA (1989) **CR:** Co-Founder, Prelude Ventures (2009); Co-Founder, Prelude Ventures (2009); Speaker, National Clean Energy Project Roundtable (2009) **CIV:** Breakthrough Energy Coalition (2015-Present); Co-Founder, Sea Change Foundation (2006-Present); The Giving Pledge (2017); SERC; Berkeley Tsinghua Joint Research Center on Energy and Climate Change **AW:** Listee, Fortune's World's Top 25 Eco-Innovators (2009) **MEM:** Board Member, Renaissance Technologies; Vice-Chairman, Renaissance Technologies; Senior Managing Director, Meritage Group; Chairman, Meritage Group

SIMPKINS, LUCILLE ANGELIQUE, T: Personnel Administrator, Ecumenical Minister **I:** Religious **DOB:** 05/26/1944 **PB:** New Orleans **SC:** LA/USA **PT:** Robert Aunding; Addie Grace (Frazier) Elmore **MS:** Widow **SPN:** Leonard W. Simpkins Junior (11/22/1960, Deceased 2012) **CH:** Terri; Leonard W. **ED:** Master of Education, Temple University (1982); Bachelor of Arts, Coppin State College (1979) **CT:** Certified Personnel Administrator **C:** Retired (2014); Office Manager, Personnel Administrator, Opportunities Academy Management Training Inc./Opportunities Industrialization Center of America, Philadelphia, PA (1975-2014); Secretary, Fiscal Department, National Progress Association for Economic Development, Philadelphia, PA (1970-1972); Administrative Assistant to President of External Affairs, University of Pennsylvania, Philadelphia, PA (1969-1970); Secretary to Branch Manager, West Branch Opportunities Industrialization Center, Philadelphia, PA (1967-1969); Clerk Stenographer, Unemployment Compensation Board Review, Philadelphia, PA (1964-1966) **CIV:** Board Member, North Central Branch, YWCA (1984-Present); Vice President, St. Barbara's Parish Council (1989) **MEM:** Board Member, Industrial Human Services Council (1985-1989); Co-Editor, Educators' Roundtable Inc. (1985-1988); American Society for Training and Development; Society of Human Resource Management **MH:** Albert Nelson Marquis Lifetime Achievement Award **AV:** Fishing; Reading; Skiing; Writing; Listening to music; Gardening; Church **RE:** Roman Catholic

SIMPSON, MICHAEL, "MIKE" KEITH, DDS, T: U.S. Representative from Idaho **I:** Government Administration/Government Relations/Government Services **CN:** U.S. House of Representatives **DOB:** 09/08/1950 **PB:** Burley **SC:** ID/USA **MS:** Married **SPN:** Kathy (Johnson) Simpson (1977) **ED:** Doctor of Dental Surgery, Washington University School of Dental Medicine, St. Louis, MO (1978); Bachelor of Science, Utah State University (1972) **C:** Member, U.S. House of Representatives from Idaho's Second Congressional District, United States Congress, Washington, DC (1999-Present); Dentist, Blackfoot, ID (1978-Present); Speaker, Idaho House of Representatives (1991-1999); Assistant Majority Leader, Idaho House of Representatives (1989); Member, Idaho House of Representatives (1985-1999); Member, Blackfoot City Council (1980-1984); Member, House Appropriations Committee, United States Congress; Member, Committee on Agriculture, United States Congress; Member, Committee on Resources, Transportation and Infrastructure, United States Congress; Member, Committee on Veteran Affairs, United States Congress **CR:** Former Speaker, Majority Caucus; Chairperson, Assistant Majority Leader, Idaho House

of Representatives **AW:** President's Award, Idaho State Dental Association (1998); Citizen of the Year Award, Idaho Family Forum (1996); Friend of Education Award (1994); Jefferson Award, American Legislative Exchange Council (1994); Inductee, Idaho's Republican Party Hall of Fame; Boyd A. Martin Award, Association of Idaho Cities **MEM:** State Chairperson, American Legislative Exchange Council; National Board of Directors, American Legislative Exchange Council; Idaho State Dental Association **AV:** Golf; Chess; Reading; Painting **PA:** Republican

SIMPSON, RAYMOND W., PHD, T: Electronics Engineer **I:** Engineering **DOB:** 08/04/1944 **PB:** Merrick **SC:** NY/USA **PT:** Raymond G. Simpson; Lucy (Scheier) Simpson **MS:** Widowed **SPN:** Carole Irene Hyams (5/23/1971, Deceased 2004) **CH:** Raymond M.; David W.M. **ED:** PhD, University of Pennsylvania (1976); MSEE, Polytechnic Institute of Brooklyn (1966); BSEE, Polytechnic Institute of Brooklyn (1966) **C:** Technical Advisor, Teledyne Princeton Instruments (2019 -Present); Chief Engineer, Princeton Instruments (2003-2019); Distinguished Member of Technical Staff, Princeton Optronics (1999-2003); Engineering Manager, Princeton Instruments, Inc., Trenton, NJ (1991-1999); Vice President, Engineering, O'neill Communications Inc., Princeton, NJ (1988-1991); Consultant, PA Consultant Group, Princeton, NJ (1981-1988); Senior Engineer, Bactomatic, Inc., Princeton, NJ (1980-1981); Technical Staff, RCA Astro-Space, Princeton, NJ (1979-1980); Senior Engineer, EG&G Princeton Applied Research, Inc. (1974-1979); Detection Engineer, Grumman Aerospace, Bethpage, NY (1968-1970) **MIL:** 1st Lieutenant, United States Army (1966-1968) **CW:** Contributor, Articles, Professional Journals **MEM:** Panelist, Institute of Electrical and Electronics Engineers (IEEE); Life Member, American Radio Relay League **MH:** Albert Nelson Marquis Lifetime Achievement Award **B/I:** Dr. Boris Beizer was Dr. Simpson's cousin who worked on the F-105 project. At age 12, he brought Dr. Simpson to a Republic Aviation open house, which is where Dr. Simpson saw the F-105. This experience essentially sparked his interest in engineering. **AV:** Exploring amateur radio; Restoring cars

SIMS, LOWERY STOKES, T: Curator, Art Historian; Writer; Educator **I:** Museums & Institutions **DOB:** 02/13/1949 **PB:** Washington **SC:** WA/USA **PT:** John Jacob Sims; Bernice Marion (Banks) Sims **MS:** Single **ED:** ArtsD, Brown University, Providence, RI (2003); PhD in Art History, City University of New York (1995); Honorary ArtsD, Moore College of Art & Design, Philadelphia, PA (1990); MPhil, The Graduate Center, The City University of New York (1989); Honorary LHD, Maryland Institute College of Art, Baltimore, MD (1988); MA in Art History, Johns Hopkins University, Baltimore, MD (1972); BA in Art History, Queens College (1970) **C:** Retired (2015); Chief Curator, Museum of Arts and Design (2007-2015); Adjunct Curator, The Studio Museum Harlem, New York, NY (2006-2007); President, The Studio Museum Harlem, New York, NY (2005-2006); Executive Director, The Studio Museum Harlem, New York, NY (1999-2005); Curator, The Metropolitan Museum of Art, New York, NY (1995-1999); Associate Curator, The Metropolitan Museum of Art, New York, NY (1979-1995); Assistant Curator, The Metropolitan Museum of Art, New York, NY (1975-1979); Museum Education Associate, The Metropolitan Museum of Art, New York, NY (1972-1975) **CR:** Kirk Varnedoe Distinguished Professor, The Institute of Fine Arts, New York University (2018); Lecturer, Curatorial and Museum Training Internship Courses, The Institute of Fine Arts, New York

University; Visiting Critic and Lecturer, University of Pennsylvania; Visiting Critic and Lecturer, Maryland Institute College of Art; Visiting Critic and Lecturer, The University of Texas at Austin; Visiting Critic and Lecturer, University of Hawai'i **CIV:** Board of Directors, Tiffany Foundation, New York, NY (2005-2018); Board of Directors, Art Matters Foundation (1990-2017); Board of Directors, Art 21 (2006-2007); Board of Directors, The Metropolitan Museum of Art (2005-2007) **CW:** Author, "US/Mexico Border: Place, Imagination and Possibility" (2017); Author, "Harriet Tubman and Other Truths" (2017); Author, "New Territories, Laboratories for Design, Craft and Art" (2014); Co-curator, Exhibition, "Dead or Alive" (2010); Co-curator, Exhibition, "The Global Africa Project" (2010); Co-curator, Exhibition, "Second Lives: Remixing the Ordinary" (2008); Editor, Essayist, Catalogue of the National Museum of the American Indian's Retrospective of Fritz Scholder (2008); Curator, "Persistence of Geometry, Cleveland Museum of Art" (2006); Coordinator, Exhibition, "Challenge of the Modern: African-American Arts, 1925-1945" (2002-2003); Co-author, Book, "Wifredo Lam and the International Avant-Garde, 1923-1982" (2002); Organizer, Exhibition, "Stuart Davis, American Painter" (1991) **AW:** Distinguished Feminist Award (2018); Distinguished Service in the Visual Arts, Art Table (2017); Trailblazers, Brooklyn Museum (2016); Mather Award for Art Criticism, College Art Association of America, Inc. (1991) **MEM:** Board of Directors, College Art Association of America, Inc. (1993-1997); New York City Commission on the Status of Women (1981); Board, Art Matters **MH:** Albert Nelson Marquis Lifetime Achievement Award **B/I:** Dr. Sims became involved in her profession because she was very interested in studio art as a child. She was always drawing. When she was a freshman in high school, she won the Catholic Youth Organization First Prize for her drawing of Madonna, a religious figure. One of her high school teachers, Sister Mary Vincent, conducted a very comprehensive survey of art history; when Dr. Sims went into college, she majored in art history because it combined her love of the visual arts, history, and writing. Initially, she thought she would get her doctorate and teach, but as she was graduating, she was recruited by the Brooklyn Museum to work in their education department on a special project, taking donated art from the late great Merton D. Simpson. This led to an interest in museum education and that is how she started her career. In 1970, she received a position to work at the Metropolitan Museum of Art. After a few years of working there, she realized that she could make an impact by helping build various collections, so she started campaigning to receive a curatorial position. She found a supporter in Henry Geldzahler, who was a legendary curator. He hired Dr. Sims and she was the first African American curator at the Metropolitan Museum of Art. In addition, Dr. Sims' family and upbringing had an influence on her career because she grew up in New York and her mother, Bernice Marion (Banks) Sims, brought her to museums, symphonies, plays, and prominent buildings. Her father, John Jacob Sims, was an architect, which piqued her interest in that field. **AV:** Needlepoint; Collecting Black memorabilia **PA:** Democrat

SIMS, MARSHA LOIS, T: Archaeologist (Retired) **I:** Other **DOB:** 11/13/1950 **PB:** Connersville **SC:** IN/USA **PT:** Theodore Edward Sims; Marjorie Anna (Martin) Sims **MS:** Divorced **SPN:** Peter Stephen Baenziger (03/13/1976, Divorced) **CH:** Two Children, Two Grandchildren **ED:** Student, Numerous Courses in Editing and Cultural Resources Management, Numerous Locations, United States (1974-2015); Postgraduate Coursework, University of Missouri (1990-1992); MA in Anthropology, University of Nebraska (1990); BA in Anthropology and Design, Purdue University (1974) **CT:** Registered Professional Archaeologist, Register of Professional Archaeologists (RPA) **C:** Editor, Soil Conservation Service, U.S. Department of Agriculture, Lincoln, NE (1989-1995); Research Assistant for Dr. Deborah Pearsall, University of Missouri, Columbia, MO (1990-1992); Research Assistant for Dr. Tom Dillehay, University of Illinois, Champaign, IL and University of Missouri, Columbia, MO (1992); Teaching Assistant for Dr. Raymond Wood, University of Missouri, Columbia, MO (1991); Teaching Assistant for Dr. Robert Hitchcock, University of Nebraska, Lincoln, NE (1990); Editor, Soil Conservation Service, United States Department of Agriculture, Lanham, MD (1978-1980); Editorial Assistant, Soil Conservation Service, United States Department of Agriculture, Hyattsville, MD (1977-1978); Clerk-Typist for Dr. Sturtevant, Dr. Gibson, and Dr. Crocker, Anthropology Department, Smithsonian Institution, Washington, DC (1976-1977); Lab and Field Assistant for Dr. Kort Lessman, Purdue University, Lafayette, IN (1972-1975) **CR:** Hispanic Emphasis Program Manager (1996-2015); Sociology Coordinator (1996-2015); Lead Archaeologist, Natural Resources Conservation Service, U.S. Department of Agriculture, Denver, Colorado (1995-2015); Chosen Lead Archaeologist for the Burn Area Rehabilitation Team (BAER), Natural Resources Conservation Service and National Forest Service, U.S. Department of Agriculture, Denver, CO (2000); Visiting Professor, Regis University, Grand Junction, Colorado (1997); Consultant, State Museum, University of Nebraska (1994-1995); Visiting Research Technician, Department of Agronomy, University of Nebraska (1992-1995) **CW:** Invited Presenter, Purdue University Campus (2013); Author, Several Reports, Submitted to the Historic Preservation Officer; Contributor, Published Numerous Abstracts, Three Papers **AW:** Numerous Awards, U.S. Department of Agriculture; Graduate Award, University of Nebraska **MEM:** Society for American Archaeology; Plains Anthropological Society; Colorado Council of Professional Archaeologists (CCPA); Honorary Member, Alpha Kappa Delta, Purdue University **MH:** Albert Nelson Marquis Lifetime Achievement Award; Marquis Who's Who Top Professional **B/I:** Ms. Sims became involved in her profession because archaeology was an area where she could work on unearthing information, which would help today's society understand both the past and the future. **AV:** Horses; Skiing; Gardening; Home remodeling

SINCLAIR-SMITH, SUSANNE, "SUSIE", T: Chief Executive Officer **I:** Nonprofit & Philanthropy **CN:** Montgomery County Coalition for the Homeless **ED:** MPA, Public Policy and Administration, Management, Negotiation, Harvard Kennedy School (1993); JD, Poverty and Clinical Practice, Antioch School of Law (1985); BA, Public Policy and Photography, Hampshire College (1978) **C:** Chief Executive Officer, Executive Director, Montgomery County Coalition for the Homeless (2011-Present); Expert Consultant on Homeless Initiatives, US Department of Health and Human Services (2010-2011); Consulting/Technical Assistance, THC Housing Families Transforming Lives, Open Arms Housing, Pathways to Housing, LISC (2006-2011); Strategic Initiative on Homelessness Consultant, William S. Abell Foundation (2006-2010); Director, Policy and Leadership Development, Fannie Mae Foundation (2003-2006); Senior Policy Officer, Program Officer, National Policy & Local WDC Program Offices, Local Initiatives Support Corporation (LISC) (1993-2003); Founding Executive Director, Washington Legal Clinic for the Homeless (1986-1991) **CIV:** Commissioner, Chair, Strategic Planning Committee, Montgomery County Interagency Commission on Homeless; Former Vice Chair, Nonprofit Montgomery **AW:** Nonprofit of the Year Award, Nonprofit Village (2018); Moxie Award for Excellence **MH:** Marquis Who's Who Top Professional **AS:** Mrs. Sinclair-Smith attributes her success to her connection to her clients. They are the largest nonprofit in Montgomery County that is exclusively dedicated to ending homelessness. Also being able to work with the county to create changes, it is very rewarding. **B/I:** Mrs. Sinclair-Smith was inspired by her parents; her father was a physician from Australia and the national healthcare system was very important to him. Her mother was a Quaker and talked about the Quakers roles in the underground railroad and helping to create equality. So she has been very concerned about people who are truly vulnerable in our society. A country like the United States that is so well off that no one should experience homelessness here. She thinks if people understand that there are tools to help end homelessness that it gives you energy and commitment to do the work.

SINEMA, KYRSTEN LEA, PHD, T: 1) U.S. Senator from Arizona 2) Lawyer **I:** Government Administration/Government Relations/Government Services **CN:** 1) U.S. House of Representatives 2) Private Law Practice **DOB:** 07/12/1976 **PB:** Tucson **SC:** AZ/USA **PT:** Dan Sinema; Marilyn Sinema **MS:** Divorced **SPN:** Blake Dain (Divorced) **ED:** Doctor of Philosophy in Justice Studies, Arizona State University (2012); Doctor of Jurisprudence, Arizona State University Sandra Day O'Connor College of Law (2004); Master of Science in Social Work, Arizona State University (1999); Bachelor of Arts, Brigham Young University (1995) **C:** U.S. Senator, State of Arizona (2019-Present); Attorney, Private Practice (2005-Present); Member, U.S. House Committee on Financial Services (2013-2019); Member, U.S. House of Representatives from Arizona's Ninth Congressional District, United States Congress, Washington, DC (2013-2019); Member, District 15, Arizona State Senate (2011-2012); Member, District 15, Arizona House of Representatives (2005-2011); Social Worker, Washington Elementary School District, Phoenix, AZ (1995-2002); Assistant Minority Leader, Arizona House of Representatives **CR:** Member, Commission Prevent Violence Against Women (2006-Present); Adjunct Professor, Arizona State University School of Social Work (2003-Present); Adjunct Professor, Business Law, Arizona Summit Law School **CIV:** Board of Directors, Arizona Center Progressive Leadership (2006-Present); President, Board of Directors, Community Outreach & Advocacy for Refugees (2005-Present); Board of Directors, Girls for a Change (2005-Present); Board of Directors, Arizona Death Penalty Forum (2003-Present) **CW:** Author, "Who Must Die in Rwanda's Genocide?: The State of Exception Realized" (2015); Author, "Unite and Conquer: How to Build Coalitions That Win and Last" (2009) **AW:** Named, One of the Politics 40 Under 40, TIME Magazine (2010); Legislator of the Year, National Association of Social Workers (2006); Named, Legislative Hero, League Conservation Voters, AZ (2006); Named, Legislator of the Year, Arizona Public Health Association (2006); CHOICE Award, Planned Parenthood Federation of America Inc. (2006); Most Valuable Player, Sierra Club (2005, 2006); Legislator of the Year Award, Stonewall Democrats (2005) **MEM:** National Board of Directors, Progressive Democrats of America (2005-Present); National Organization for Women; Progressive Democrats of America; National Association of Social Workers; League of Women Voters; Arizona Education

Association; Arizona Attorneys for Criminal Justice; Arizona Advocacy Network; Blue Dog Coalition; Sierra Club **PA:** Democrat

SINGH, BHAWANDEEP, T: Researcher, Lecturer, Independent Consultant **I:** Education/Educational Services **CN:** San Jose State University **PT:** Satkar Singh; Inderjit Kaur **ED:** Doctor of Philosophy in Computer Science and Engineering, Santa Clara University (2022); Master of Science in Electrical Engineering, Computer Architecture and Digital Systems Design, San Jose State University; Bachelor of Engineering in Electronics and Communications Engineering, Ramaiah Institute of Technology **C:** Lecturer, San Jose University (2018-Present); FPGA Design Engineer, SAI Technology (2018-2019); Solar Consultant, Infinity Energy Inc (2016, 2018); Lab Manager, Vapor Maven (2016); Component Design Engineer, Intel Corporation (2012-2014); Intern, Intel Corporation (2011-2012); Teaching Assistant, San Jose University (2011); Embedded Systems Engineer, BOSCH India Ltd (2007-2009); Intern/Trainee, Indian Institute of Science (2008); Project Intern, Indian Space Research Organisation (2007); Professor of Electrical Engineering, San Jose State University **AS:** Mr. Singh attributes his success to the support of his family. **B/I:** Mr. Singh became involved in his profession due to his passion for mathematics.

SINGH, LILLY, T: YouTuber, Comedian, Talk Show Host **I:** Media & Entertainment **CN:** A Little Late with Lilly Singh **DOB:** 09/26/1988 **PB:** Scarborough **SC:** ON/Canada **PT:** Sukhwinder Singh; Malwinder Kaur **MS:** Single **ED:** BA in Psychology, York University, Toronto, ON, Canada (2010); Diploma, Lester B. Pearson Collegiate Institute, Toronto, ON, Canada (2006) **CR:** Partner, Calvin Klein (2017); Ambassador, Pantene (2017) **CIV:** UNICEF Goodwill Ambassador (2017-Present); Girl Guides of Canada **CW:** Host, "A Little Late with Lilly Singh" (2019-Present); Creator, "Lilly Singh Vlogs" (2011-Present); Creator, "IISuperwomanII" (2010-Present); Guest Appearance, "Medical Police" (2020); Appearance, Music Video, "Girls Like You" (2018); Actress, TV Film, "Fahrenheit 451" (2018); Guest Appearance, "Bizaardvark" (2017); Author, "How to Be a Bawse: A Guide to Conquering Life" (2017); Appearance, Music Video, "H.A.I.R." (2017); Appearance, Music Video, "Hold My Heart" (2017); Cameo, "F the Prom" (2017); Executive Producer, Appearance, Documentary, "A Trip to Unicorn Island" (2016); Creator, "Voices" (2016); Cameo, "Bad Moms" (2016); Voice Actress, "Ice Age: Collision Course" (2016); Guest Appearance, "Epic Rap Battles of History" (2016); Guest Appearance, "Terminator Genisys: The YouTube Chronicles" (2015); Musician, "#IVIVI" (2015); Musician, "The Clean Up Anthem" (2015); Actress, Web Series, "Lana Steele: Makeup Spy" (2015); Guest Appearance, "Brooklyn Nine-Nine" (2014); Cameo, "Dr. Cabbie" (2014); Musician, "#LEH" (2014); Featured Musician, "Mauj Ki Malharein" (2014); Featured Musician, "Hipshaker" (2013); Background Dancer, "Speedy Singhs" (2011); Background Dancer, "Thank You" (2011) **AW:** Named, Time's 100 Next (2019); Favorite YouTube Star, People's Choice Awards (2017); First Person, Purpose Awards Honoree - Creator, Streamy Awards (2017); Social Good Campaign, Feature, Streamy Awards (2016); Choice Web Star: Female, Choice Web Star: Comedy, Teen Choice Awards (2016); Honoree, Just For Laughs Film Festival, Montreal, QC, Canada (2016); Named, 10 Comics to Watch, Variety (2016); Named, 100 Most Creative People in Business, Fast Company (2015); Named, World's Top-Earning YouTube Stars, Forbes (2015); Named, Ones to Watch, People Magazine (2015); First Person, Streamy Awards (2015); Social Superstar of the Year, MTV Fandom Awards (2015); Named, New Media Rockstars Top 100 Channels (2014)

SINGH, NITIN KUMAR, T: Scientist **I:** Sciences **CN:** NASA Jet Propulsion Laboratory (JPL) **ED:** Postdoctoral Fellow, NASA, Jet Propulsion Laboratory (2016-2017); Research Fellow, SCELSE, NTU, Singapore (2015); PhD in Life Science (Microbiology), Institute of Microbial Technology, Chandigarh, India (2015); MSc in Biotechnology, MNIAS, University of Bikaner, Bikaner, India (2009); BS in Biotechnology, MNIAS, University of Bikaner, Bikaner, India (2007) **C:** Planetary Protection Engineer II, NASA-JPL (2017-Present) **CW:** Contributor, Author, Co-Author, Numerous Publications; Contributor, Numerous Manuscripts Under Review/Writing; Contributor, Manuscript, International Journal of Systematic and Evolutionary Microbiology; Contributor, Manuscript, International Journal of Astrobiology; Contributor, Manuscript, Microbiome; Contributor, Manuscript, Applied Microbiology and Biotechnology; Contributor, Manuscript, Food Chemistry Nanotechnology; Contributor, Manuscript, Journal Life; Contributor, Numerous Manuscripts; Speaker, Contributor, Work Presentations **AW:** NASA Research Award (2018); Gold Medalist, Biotechnology, MGS University (2009); Most Disciplined Student Award, MNIAS (2007); PI on GeneLab Innovation Award for "MANGO: An interactive tool for microbiome data analysis and visualization," NASA Space Biology Research **MEM:** Editorial Board, Journal of Veterinary Medicine and Animal Sciences; Editorial Board, Laboratory Cell Biological Technic; Editorial Board, Microbiome in Health and Disease **MH:** Marquis Who's Who Top Professional **AS:** Dr. Singh attributes his success to his brother, who was always there to support him. He comes from a very conservative family but his brother always saw potential in him, never questioned his intentions, and always supported what he was doing. Dr. Singh is the first in his family to obtain a PhD. **B/I:** Dr. Singh became involved in his profession because while he was in his PhD program, he got infected with the organism he was studying, which sent him to the ICU for a month. When he became infected with this organism, that is when he decided to revolve his PhD around it.

SINGH, YESH P., PHD, T: Professor Emeritus **I:** Education/Educational Services **DOB:** 01/01/1940 **PB:** Muzaffarnagar **SC:** India **PT:** Gyandevi Singh; Chhatar Singh **MS:** Married **SPN:** Veera Singh (02/27/1963) **CH:** Sveta Singh; Vinay K. Singh **ED:** PhD in Mechanical Engineering, University of Wisconsin-Milwaukee (1984); Graduate Coursework, University at Buffalo (1974-1975); MSME, Youngstown State University (1974); BSME, Indian Institute of Technology Roorkee (1962); Diploma in Civil Engineering, Indian Institute of Technology Roorkee (1959) **CT:** Professional Engineer, State of Texas (1986); Professional Engineer, State of Wisconsin (1976) **C:** Professor Emeritus, Professor, Chairman, Associate Professor, Mechanical Engineering, The University of Texas at San Antonio (1985-2019); Associated Faculty of Biomedical Engineering, Joint Program The University of Texas at San Antonio (2003-2016); Senior Engineer II, Senior Engineer I, Engineer, Allis-Chalmers Corporation, Milwaukee, WI (1975-1985); Design Engineer, Birdsboro Steel (1971-1973); Mechanical Engineer, Desengcon Corporation, Reading, PA (1971-1972); Design Engineer, Assistant Engineer, Heavy Engineering Corporation Limited (HEC Ltd), Ranchi, India (1962-1970); Design Engineer, Youjuralmashzvod (1964-1965) **CR:** Chairman, Adviser of Records, Mechanical Engineering Graduate Program, The University of Texas at San Antonio (1998-2001); Chair, Mechanical Design Group (1985-2000); Chairman, Mechanical Engineering, The University of Texas at San Antonio (1993-1996) **CW:** Contributor, Articles, National and International Journals **AW:** Paul Lewis Award (2019); Charles E. Balleisen Award (1999); Clifford H. Schumaker Award (1998); Outstanding Alumni Award, Mechanical Engineering Department, University of Wisconsin-Milwaukee (1996); Mechanical Design Award, Youzuralmashzvod, Orsk, USSR (1965); Mathematics Medal, Indian Institute of Technology Roorkee (1959) **MEM:** Life Fellow, The American Society of Mechanical Engineers (2008); Chairman of Professional Development, San Antonio Section, The American Society of Mechanical (1998-1999); Chairman of Professional Practice, San Antonio Section, The American Society of Mechanical (1997-1998); Chairman, San Antonio Section, The American Society of Mechanical Engineers (1994-1995); Vice Chairman, San Antonio Section, The American Society of Mechanical (1993-1994); Secretary, San Antonio Section, The American Society of Mechanical (1992-1993); Fellow, The American Society of Mechanical Engineers (1992); Treasurer, San Antonio Section, The American Society of Mechanical (1991-1992); SME; ASEE; Association for Iron & Steel Technology; American Contract Bridge League **MH:** Albert Nelson Marquis Lifetime Achievement (2019) **AV:** Playing tennis, chess and soccer

SINNING, ALLAN, T: Interim Chair/Professor **I:** Education/Educational Services **CN:** University of Mississippi Medical Center **DOB:** 01/19/1957 **PB:** Miller **SC:** SD/USA **PT:** Elvin Lee Sinning; Fern Harriet (Drake) Sinning **MS:** Married **SPN:** Christina Rita Litzlbeck (08/13/1983) **CH:** Gregory Charles; Geoffrey Allan **ED:** PhD in Anatomy, University of North Dakota (1985); MS in Anatomy, University of North Dakota (1983); BS in Zoology/Animal Biology, University of Wisconsin-Platteville, WI (1979) **C:** Interim Chair, University of Mississippi Medical Center; Professor, Director of Clinical Anatomy, University of Mississippi Medical Center (2014-Present); Professor, Director of Medical Gross Anatomy, University of Mississippi Medical Center (2009-Present); Professor, Director of Body Donation Program, University of Mississippi Medical Center (2009-2019); Associate Professor, University of Mississippi Medical Center, Jackson, MS (1997-2009); Assistant Professor, University of Mississippi Medical Center, Jackson, MS (1990-1996); Postdoctoral Fellow, Medical College of Wisconsin (1985-1990) **CW:** Author, "Molecular Biology of the Cardiovascular System" (1990); Contributor, Articles, Professional Journals **AW:** Grant-in-Aid (1991, 1994); Postdoctoral Fellowship, American Heart Association (1986); Hamre Fellowship, Department of Anatomy (1984) **MEM:** American Association of Anatomy **MH:** Marquis Who's Who Top Professional **AS:** Dr. Sinning attributes his success to an innate curiosity in his work, as well as his eagerness to figure out the intricacies of biology. **B/I:** Dr. Sinning had always been intrigued by human development from single-cell organisms to complex multi-cellular beings. When he began his research, that was his area of focus. He always loved biology, but he became even more intrigued by the subject when he enrolled in a comparative anatomy class in college. **AV:** Golfing; Spending time with family and friends

SIRES, ALBIO B., T: U.S. Representative from New Jersey **I:** Government Administration/Government Relations/Government Services **DOB:** 01/26/1951 **PB:** Bejucal **SC:** Cuba **MS:** Married **SPN:** Adrienne Sires **CH:** Tara Kole (Stepchild) **ED:** MA in Spanish, Middlebury College, VT (1985); BA in Spanish and Marketing, Saint Peter's College, Englewood Cliffs, NJ (1974) **C:** Member, U.S. House of Representatives from New Jersey's Eighth Congressional District, United State Congress, Washington, DC (2013-Present); Vice Chairman, Democratic Congressional Campaign Committee (2009-Present); Member, U.S. House of Representatives from New Jersey's 13th Congressional District, United State Congress, Washington, DC (2006-2013); Speaker, New Jersey General Assembly (2002-2006); Acting Governor, State of New Jersey (2002, 2005); Member, District 33, New Jersey General Assembly (2000-2006); Mayor, Town of West New York, NJ (1995-2006); Director, Hispanic Outreach, Department of Community Affairs, State of New Jersey (1987-1988); Owner, A.M. Title Agency, Inc.; Member, Committee on Foreign Affairs, United States Congress; Member, Committee on Transportation, United States Congress **AW:** William J. Brennan Citation for Justice, New Jersey Bar Association (2005); Named Mayor of the Year, New Jersey Conference of Mayors (2004); Community that Works Award, State of New Jersey **MEM:** Legislative Services Commission **PA:** Democrat **RE:** Roman Catholic

SIRIANNI, JOYCE ELAINE, PHD, T: Anthropologist, Educator **I:** Education/Educational Services **DOB:** 04/27/1942 **PB:** Niagara Falls **SC:** NY/USA **PT:** Josef W. Sirianni; Ruth P. (Blackburn) Sirianni **MS:** Married **SPN:** John W. Owen Jr. (01/13/1978) **ED:** MDiv, Colgate Rochester Crozer Divinity School (1998); PhD, University of Washington (1974); MA, State University of New York (1967); BA, State University of New York at Buffalo (1965) **CT:** Ordained, Presbyterian Minister (1999) **C:** SUNY Distinguished Teaching Professor, Department of Anthropology, University at Buffalo (1992-Present); Professor, Chair, State University of New York (1986-1992); Professor, Department of Anthropology, State University of New York (1986-1992); Associate Professor, State University of New York (1978-1986); Visiting Scientist, Regional Primate Research Center, University of Washington (1975-1979); Assistant Professor, Anthropology, State University of New York (1972-1978); Instructor, Anthropology, Shoreline Community College, Seattle, WA (1970-1971); Research Assistant in Anthropology, University of Washington, Seattle, WA (1968-1969); Research Assistant in Anthropology, State University of New York (1965-1966); Vice Provost of Graduate Education, Dean of Graduate School, State University of New York at Buffalo **CR:** Minister, Faith United Presbyterian Church **CIV:** Chaplain, Consultant, Town of Amherst Police Department (2009-Present); Specialized Medical Assistance Response Team, Erie County, NY **CW:** Author, "Comparative Primate Anatomy: Laboratory and Atlas" (2010); Author, "Forgotten People, Forgotten Places"; Author, "Longitudinal Growth and Development of the Pigtailed Macaque"; Contributor, Articles, Professional Journals **AW:** Chancellor's Award, State University of New York at Buffalo (1978) **MEM:** Chair, Numerous Committees, American Society of Primatologists (1978-Present); Chair, Numerous Committees, American Association of Primatologists (1978-1992); President, Co-Chairman, Undergraduate Teaching Committee, American Association of Physical Anthropologists (1980-1991); Teacher, Sigma Xi (1976-1978); New York Academy of Science; International Primatology Society; American Association of Anatomists; American Association of Dental Research **MH:** Albert Nelson Marquis Lifetime Achievement Award; Marquis Who's Who Top Professional **B/I:** Dr. Sirianni became interested in anthropology in college. After earning a Master's degree, she became a teaching assistant, which introduced her to the field of education. She

has since pursued both of her passions in professional aspects. She is passionate about excavating preserved sites and educating others on the wonders of her field. **AV:** Golfing; Serving as minister at local church; Gardening **PA:** Democrat **RE:** Presbyterian

SIRIANO, CHRISTIAN, T: Fashion Designer **I:** Apparel & Fashion **DOB:** 11/18/1985 **PB:** Annapolis **SC:** MD/USA **PT:** Peter Siriano; Joye Siriano **MS:** Married **SPN:** Brad Walsh (08/09/2016) **ED:** Intern, Vivienne Westwood, London, England; Intern, Alexander McQueen, London, England; Graduate, American InterContinental University, London, England **C:** Designer, Shoes and Handbags, Payless ShoeSource (2009-Present); Designer, Christian Siriano (2008-Present); Curator, Boutique, The Curated NYC, New York, NY (2018); Launched Fragrance Line (2014); Launched, Clothing Line for HSN, Striking by Christian Siriano (2013); Owner, Christian Siriano Ltd. (2012); Launched, Limited Edition Collection, Christian Siriano for Spiegel (2011); Launched, Makeup Line for Victoria's Secret, Christian Siriano for VS Makeup (2009); Collaborator, Starbucks, Limited Edition Gift Card (2009); Designer, Maternity Line, Fierce Mamas (2008); Designer, Puma (2008); Co-Founder, Send the Trend, Inc.; Freelance Make-up Artist, New York, NY **CIV:** Volunteer, Sewing Face Masks for Medical Professionals (2020) **CW:** Executive Producer, Producer, "Project Runway" (2019); Judge, "Project Runway: Junior" (2015-2016); Costume Designer, "The Pirate Fairy" (2014); Himself, "The Tents" (2012); Himself, "Making the Boys" (2011); Subject, Bravo Special, "Christian Siriano: Having a Moment" (2010); Co-Author, "Fierce Style: How To Be Your Most Fabulous Self" (2009); Himself, "Ugly Betty" (2008); Himself, Music Video, "No Substitute Love," Estelle (2008); Contestant, "Project Runway" (2007-2008) **AW:** Named, Time 100 Most Influential (2018); Couture for a Cause Designer of the Decade Award (2016); Designer of the Year, AAFA American Image Awards (2016); Named, "30 Under 30," Forbes (2015); Named to Council Fashion Designers of America (2013); Named, "40 Under 40," Crain's New York Business (2010); Named "The New King of Old-School Glamour," Elle **MEM:** Council of Fashion Designers of America (CFDA) (2013-Present)

SISOLAK, STEPHEN, "STEVE" F., T: Governor of Nevada **I:** Government Administration/Government Relations/Government Services **DOB:** 12/26/1953 **PB:** Milwaukee **SC:** WI/USA **PT:** Edward F. Sisolak; Mary Sisolak **MS:** Married **SPN:** Kathy Ong (2018); Lori "Dallas" Garland (1987, Divorced 2000) **CH:** Two Daughters **ED:** MBA, Lee Business School, University of Nevada, Las Vegas (1978); BS in Business, University of Wisconsin-Milwaukee (1974) **C:** Governor, State of Nevada (2019-Present); Chair, Clark County Commission (2013-2019); Vice Chair, Clark County Commission (2011-2013); Member, Clark County Commission District A (2009-2019); Member, Nevada Board of Regents Second District (1999-2008) **CR:** Partner, American Distributing Company; Partner, Associated Industries **CIV:** Supporter, Numerous Civic, Charitable and Business Organizations Including Henderson Chamber of Commerce, The American National Red Cross-Clark County Chapter (Southern Nevada Chapter), University of Nevada Las Vegas Alumni Association; Seniors United, The American National Red Cross Leadership Council, Las Vegas Chamber of Commerce, Better Business Bureau, Las Vegas, Boys & Girls Clubs of America, Hispanics in Politics, Saint Joseph, Husband of Mary Roman Catholic Church, and Nevada Partnership for Homeless Youth **PA:** Democrat

SKARSGÅRD, ALEXANDER, T: Actor **I:** Media & Entertainment **DOB:** 08/25/1976 **PB:** Stockholm **SC:** Sweden **PT:** Stellan Skarsgård; My Skarsgård **ED:** Honorary Degree, Leeds Metropolitan University (Now Leeds Beckett University) (2011); Coursework, Theater Course, Marymount Manhattan College; Coursework, Leeds Metropolitan University **CIV:** Ambassador, American Team, Fundraising Event, Walking with the Wounded **CW:** Actor, Executive Producer, "The Northman" (2021); Actor, "Passing" (2020); Actor, "Godzilla vs. Kong" (2020); Actor, "The Stand" (2020); Actor, "On Becoming a God in Central Florida" (2019); Actor, "The Kill Team" (2019); Actor, "Long Shot" (2019); Actor, "The Aftermath" (2019); Actor, "Big Little Lies" (2017-2019); Actor, "The Little Drummer Girl" (2018); Actor, "Hold the Dark" (2018); Actor, "The Hummingbird Project" (2018); Actor, "Mute" (2018); Actor, "Drunk History" (2018); Co-producer, "It's Supposed to be Easy" (2017); Actor, "The Legend of Tarzan" (2016); Actor, "War on Everyone" (2016); Actor, "Zoolander 2" (2016); Actor, "Hidden" (2015); Actor, "The Diary of a Teenage Girl" (2015); Actor, "The Giver" (2014); Actor, "True Blood" (2008-2014); Actor, "Eastbound & Down" (2013); Actor, "The East" (2013); Actor, "Disconnect" (2012); Actor, "What Maisie Knew" (2012); Actor, "Battleship" (2012); Actor, "Straw Dogs" (2011); Actor, "Melancholia" (2011); Actor, "Trust Me" (2010); Voice Actor, "Moomins and the Comet Chase" (2010); Actor, "13" (2010); Actor, "Beyond the Pole" (2009); Voice Actor, "Metropia" (2009); Actor, Music Video, "Paparazzi," Lady Gaga (2009); Actor, "Generation Kill" (2008); Actor, "Järnets Anglar" (2007); Actor, "Golden Brown Eyes" (2007); Actor, "Exit" (2006); Actor, "Cuppen" (2006); Actor, "The Last Drop" (2006); Actor, "Kill Your Darlings" (2006); Actor, "Never Be Mine" (2006); Actor, "Om Sara" (2005); Actor, "Revelations" (2005); Actor, "Double Shift" (2005); Actor, "Hearbeat" (2004); Director, Writer, "Att Döda ett Barn" (2003); Actor, "The Dog Trick" (2002); Actor, "D-dag - Den Færdige Film" (2001); Actor, "Zoolander" (2001); Actor, "Kites Over Helsinki" (2001); Actor, "Hundtricket" (2000); Actor, "Wings of Glass" (2000); Actor, "White Water Fury" (2000); Actor, "Judith" (2000); Actor, "The Diver" (2000); Actor, "D-dag" (2000); Actor, "D-dag - Lise" (2000); Actor, "Happy End" (1999); Actor, "Vita lögner" (1999); Actor, "The Dog That Smiled" (1989); Actor, "Idag Röd" (1987); Actor, "Åke och Hans Värld" (1984) **AW:** STARmeter Award, Fan Favorite, IMDb Awards (2019); Golden Globe for Best Performance by an Actor in a Supporting Role in a Series, Limited Series of Motion Picture Made for Television, "Big Little Lies," Hollywood Foreign Press Association (2018); Critics Choice Award for Best Supporting Actor in a Movie or Limited Series, "Big Little Lies," Broadcast Film Critics Association Awards (2018); Screen Actors Guild Award, Outstanding Performance by a Male Actor in a Television Movie or Limited Series, "Big Little Lies," SAG-AFTRA (2018); Primetime Emmy Award for Outstanding Supporting Actor in a Limited Series of Movie, "Big Little Lies," The Television Academy (2017); Gold Derby TV Award for TV Movie/Mini Supporting Actor, "Big Little Lies," Gold Derby Awards (2017); Named Breakthrough Performer, "Melancholia," Hamptons International Film Festival (2011); Scream Award, Best Horror Actor, "True Blood," Scream Awards (2010, 2011); Scream Award, Best Villain, "True Blood," Scream Awards (2009); Grand Prix, "Att Döda ett Barn," Odense International Film Festival (2003); Press Award, "Att Döda ett Barn," Odense International Film Festival (2003)

SKERRITT, ELIZABETH, T: Prof. Librarian, Information Scientist **I:** Library Management/Library Services **PB:** New York **SC:** NY/USA **PT:** James Lewis Skerritt; Grace M. Skerritt **ED:** MS, Columbia University (1973); MA in Art History, Columbia University (1965); BA in Government, Smith College (1954) **CT:** New York State Professional Library Certificate (1972) **C:** Assistant Librarian, Bolling Library, St. Luke's Hospital, New York (1986-1990); Consultant, Researcher, New York, NY (1985-1986); Corporate Librarian, Corporate Information Center, International Paper Company, New York, NY (1977-1985); Head Librarian, American Banker Newspaper, New York, NY (1973-1975); E.V. Thaw Old Masters Gallery, New York, NY (1972-1973); Slide Curator, School of Visual Arts, NY (1969-1971); Art Coordinator/Curator, Chase Manhattan Bank Headquarters Art Program (1960-1962) **CR:** Vice-Chairman, Chairman, Librarians' Information Management Committee (1980-1985); Editor, AB Annual Index (1974); Instructor, Art History, Douglass College (1968-1969); Joint Canadian-United States Special Libraries Convention, Winnipeg, Ontario, Canada; Special Libraries Assistant, New York, NY; Sales and Marketing Manager, AB Annual Index; Technical Association of the Pulp and Paper Industry (TAPPI), Atlanta, GA **CW:** Vice-Chairman of the Librarians' Committee, "Bibliography of Papermaking Terminology" (1982); Editor, Compiler, Technical Association of Pulp and Paper Industry (TAPPI) **MEM:** Chairman, Vice-Chairman, Librarians' Information Management Committee, (1983-1985); Canadian-United States Special Libraries Association Convention, Winnipeg, Ontario (1984); Conference Chairman, Advertising and Marketing Division (1984); Chair, Advertising & Marketing Group (1983-1984); Chair, Music, Arts & Humanities Group (1977-1978); Board of Directors, College University Graduate Faculties Alumnae Association (1976-1978); Chair, Bicentennial Group (1976); Chair, Newspaper Group (1974-1975); Technical Association of the Pulp and Paper Industry (TAPPI) **MH:** Albert Nelson Marquis Lifetime Achievement Award **B/I:** Ms. Skerritt became involved in her field as a result of her lifelong interest in information-print, audio-visual, and computer technology. She additionally always had a desire to provide service to others.

SKIDMORE WILSON, JOYCE FOX THORUM JACOBSEN, T: Public Relations and Communication Executive **I:** Media & Entertainment **DOB:** 12/30/1926 **PT:** Rolla Arden Thorum; Alice Luetta (Fox) Thorum **MS:** Married **SPN:** Thomas C. Wilson (01/25/2014); Clarence E. Skidmore, Jr. (08/09/1969, Deceased); E. Douglas Jacobsen (03/20/1956, Deceased) **CH:** Kelly Douglas Jacobsen **ED:** Postgraduate Coursework, University of Cambridge, England (1992); Postgraduate Coursework, University of California Irvine, Irvine, CA (1973-1974); Postgraduate Coursework, University of Southern California, Los Angeles, CA (1964); Postgraduate Coursework, University of Utah, Salt Lake City, UT (1953-1955); BS, University of Utah, Salt Lake City, UT (1950) **CR:** Brigham Young University, Provo, UT (1978-Present); Director, Public Relations Executive, Sandy City Museum (2006-2009); Adjunct Professor, Salt Lake Community College (2002-2012); Adjunct Professor, Westminster College, Salt Lake City, UT (1992-1993, 1978-1979); Adjunct Professor, Marketing and Communications Department, Colorado Mountain College, Glenwood Springs, CO (1985-1986); Adjunct Professor, Theater/Film Department, Colorado Mountain College, Glenwood Springs, CO (1985-1986); Writer, Public Service Announcements (1980); Developer, Human Resources, Oran, Algeria (1975); Guest Director, Writer, Cablevision, Newport Beach, CA (1975); Adjunct Professor of

Communications, Pepperdine University (1974); Promotions Coordinator, Utah Bicentennial Project, Salt Lake City, UT (1976); Administrative Assistant, World Headquarters, Toastmasters International, Santa Ana, CA (1973); Consultant, Public Relations, Health Costs and Tourism, Salt Lake Area Chamber of Commerce; Business Consultant, Professor of Marketing and Communications, Mountainwest College of Business, Salt Lake City, UT; Business Consultant, Professor of Marketing and Communications, Brigham Young University; Consultant, Hema USA; Consultant, Westline and Bunell Inc.; Playwright, Director, Commissioned, Various Organizations; Storyteller, Salt Lake County Aging Services **CIV:** Taylorsville Tombstone Days (2004); Dresden Storyteller, August Culture Arts Festival (2004); Actress, Taylorsville Arts Council (2003); Babcock Theatre, University of Utah (2003); Chair Playwright's Cir. Competition (2004); International First Night Festival, Salt Lake City, UT (1993-2001); Co-chair, Advertising, Utah Symphony Guild, Winter-Summer Fundraisers, Carousel Ball, Taste of the Town (1988-1989); Guest Director, Historian, MMB Reading Arts Society (1988-1989); Local Economic Development Council, Political District Development (1986); Organizer, Stavanger Theatre, Guild and Workshops (1977); Bookcliffs Arts and Humanities Council (1984-1986); Campaign Manager, Mayor, Lake Valley City, UT (1982); Consultant, Cottonwood Heights Council, Utah (1982-1983); Utah Director, National Health Screening Council for Vol. Organizations, Bethesda, MD (1982-1983); Play Writing Conference, Sundance Film Festival (1979-1980); Guest Director, Westminster Theater (1974); Originator, Organizer, Hurlburt Days, Grand Valley, CO; Originator, Organizer, Hurlburt Days Parachute, CO; Initiator, Director, Reader's Theater, Community Christmas Festival; Director, Storytelling Festival; Promoter, Neil Simon Night, Salt Lake Arts Festival; American Genealogical Lending Library, World Headquarters; Appearance Japanese Conductor, Salt Lake City Sister-City Exchange, Salt Lake City, UT; Japanese Conductor, Salt Lake City Sister-City Exchange, Japan; Fundraiser, Utah Symphony, Guild Director, Theater Art Barn; First National Competition Utah, Salt Lake City Steering Committee; Consultant, President, Instrumentation Society of America; Promoter, Utah Arts Organizations; Missionary Leader, Church of Jesus Christ of Latter-day Saints; Board of Directors, Utah Centennial Commission; The Foundation for Fighting Blindness; Vice President, Public Awareness, RP Foundation; Director, Fighting Blindness **CW:** Author, Book, "Playmates: Another View" (2016); Contributor, "Utah Sings: Poetry Collection" (2005); Utah Health Fairs (1982-1983); Author, Poems; Associate Editor, Utah Symphony Newsletter; Editor, Newsletter, National Auditor's Association (1979-1981); State Auditor's Association (1979-1981); Editor, Saga Weekly Post, Children's Page, Stavanger and Bergen, Norway (1976-1978); Author, "Happy Holidays" (1968); Journalist, The Butler Banner; Playwright, Director, Author, Book, Lyrics "They Came to Union Fort"; Playwright, Director, "Historical Musicals Shadows"; Playwright, Director, "Danish Dreams"; Playwright, Director, "A Perfect Picture"; Articles, Newspapers, California, Colorado, Norway, Utah; Poetry, International Library of Poetry, Utah Sinas VIII Anthology; Author, National Business Newsletters; Author, Family History Newsletters; Owner, Performer, "Tell Me a Story"; Contributor, Weekly Columns, The Rifle Telegram; Writer, Melodrama, "The Saga of Pepper's Hill"; Playwright, One-Act Play, "Best Laid Plans"; Playwright, One-Act Play, "Over or Under"; Playwright, One-Act Play, "Pumpkin Shell"; Author, Book, "Happy Holidays"; Contributor, Various Plays, Radio, and TV

Scripts in California, Colorado, Utah, and Norway **AW:** One-Act Play Award (2002); International Year of Child Award, Family Academy, San Francisco and Stavanger (1979); Best Director, Statue, Colorado; Top Editor's Awards, California Press Women (1977); Four Writing Awards (1977-1978); Colorado Oscar Award for Best Director (1986); National Zeta Phi Eta Scholar (1948); Southern California Credit Association Scholar (1964); Fellow, University of Utah (1953-1955) Conglomerate Cup, Utah Polo Club; Numerous Awards and Recognitions, National Press Women, Washington, D.C., California Press Women, Utah Press Women **MEM:** Captain, Daughters of Utah Pioneers, Union Fort Camp (1998-2000); President, Babcock Performing Readers (1996-2000); Board of Directors, Public Affairs, Japan-America Society (1993-2000); Vice President, Utah Press Women (1981-1982); Public Relations Society of America (1980-82); District President, League of Women Voters (1976); Instrument Society of America; Friendship Force Utah; MMB; Vice President, Reading Arts Society; International Platform Association; Board of Directors, Utah Polo Club; Utah Storytelling Guild; UN Association of Utah; Public Affairs Director, Soroptomist International; Fima Voyagers France **MH:** Albert Nelson Marquis Lifetime Achievement Award **B/I:** Ms. Wilson became involved in her profession at three years old. Her mother encouraged her to write and perform poetry. Since then, she has been involved in every aspect of communications, including writing, theater, radio, television, and teaching. **AV:** Historian; Genealogical research; Global business and education research programs; Screenwriting, film, TV

SKIRNICK, ROBERT, "BOB" ANDREW ESQ., T: Lawyer **I:** Law and Legal Services **CN:** Skirnick Partners **DOB:** 04/23/1938 **PB:** Chicago **SC:** IL/USA **PT:** Andrew Skirnick; Stella (Sanders) Skirnick **MS:** Married **SPN:** Maria Ann Castellano (03/16/1944) **CH:** Gabriella; Rebecca; David **ED:** Doctor of Law, The University of Chicago (1966); BA, Roosevelt University (1961) **C:** Partner, Skirnick Partners (2013-Present); Partner, Meredith Cohen Greenfogel & Skirnick, Professional Corporation, New York, NY and Philadelphia, PA (1997-2013); Partner, Lovell & Skirnick, LLP, New York, NY (1995-1997); Partner, Wechsler, Skirnick, Harwood, Halebian & Feffer, New York, NY (1989-1995); Partner, Kaplan, Kilsheimer & Foley (Now Kaplan Fox & Kilsheimer LLP), New York, NY (1988-1989); Partner, Wolf, Popper, Ross, Wolf & Jones (Now Wolf Popper LLP), New York, NY (1979-1987); Partner, Much, Shelist, Freed (Now Much, Shelist, P.C.), Chicago, IL (1977-1979); Partner, Fortes, Eiger, Epstein & Skirnick, Chicago (1975-1977); Associate, Torshen, Fortes & Eiger, Chicago, IL (1972-1975); Assistant Attorney General, Antitrust, Illinois Attorney General Office, Chicago, IL (1969-1972); Attorney, General Counsel Honors Program, Department of Health, Education & Welfare, Washington, DC (1966-1968) **CR:** Emeritus, American Antitrust Institute, Washington, DC (2017-Present); Founder, Skirnick Fellowships for Public Interest Law, Harvard Law School (2005-Present); Advisory Board, American Antitrust Institute, Washington, DC (2000-2017); Delegate, La Primera Conferencia de Justicia, Otavalo, Ecuador (2005); Republic of Ecuador and Petroecuador Litigation Counsel (2004-2005); Court Appointed Local Counsel for Institutional Plaintiff, AOL Time Warner Securities Litigation (2002-2005); Court Appointed Co-lead Counsel, NASDAQ Market-Makers Antitrust Litigation (1994-1999); Court Appointed Special Master, Ocean Shipping Antitrust Litigation, Hearings in Europe and United States (1983-1991); Advisory Board, Small Business Legal Defense Commission, San Francisco, CA (1982-1988); Congressional Testimony Opposing RICO Act Amendments (1987); Lecturer, Practicing Law Institute, New York, NY (1986-1987); Instructor, New York University (1979-1980); Antitrust Litigation Counsel, State of Connecticut (1976-1977); Special Antitrust Assistant Attorney General, Illinois Attorney General Office, Chicago (1972-1973); Consultant, National Legal Aid & Defender Association, Chicago, IL (1968-1969); Court Appointed Co-lead Counsel, Industrial Diamonds Antitrust Litigation, Shopping Carts Antitrust Litigation, Alcoholic Beverages Antitrust Litigation, Bread Antitrust Litigation, Bagel Inn Inc. v. All Star Dairies, First Capital Holdings Corporation Financial Products Securities Litigation, Nelson v. Compagnie de Saint-Gobain, Digital Equipment Corporation Securities Litigation, Gulf Oil/Cities Service Tender Offer Litigation, Anco Industrial Diamond Corp. v. DB Investments, Gemstone Diamonds, and Soybean Futures Litigation; Court Appointed Liaison Counsel, Ocean Shipping Antitrust Litigation, Magnetic Audiotape Antitrust Litigation; Court Appointed Plaintiffs' Executive Committee Member, Publication Paper Antitrust Litigation, Microsoft Corporation Antitrust Litigation, Vitamins Antitrust Litigation, Brand Name Prescription Drugs Antitrust Litigation, Screws Antitrust Litigation, Corn Derivatives Antitrust Litigation, Wiring Devices Antitrust Litigation; Court Appointed Interim Co-lead Counsel, Auction Houses Antitrust Litigation; Co-founder, Equal Justice Works Public Interest Law Fellowships Program **CIV:** Antitrust Litigation Counsel, State of Connecticut (1976-1977); Special Assistant, Illinois Attorney General, Antitrust (1972-1973); Assistant Illinois Attorney General, Antitrust (1968-1972); Chairman, Illinois Legislative Committee, Antitrust Section, Illinois State Bar Association (1970-1971); Attorney, Office of General Counsel Honors Program, United States Department of Health, Education and Welfare (1966-1968) **CW:** Author, "2001 ABA Survey of Securities Class Actions and Derivative Suits" (2001); Author, "Multiparty Bargaining in Class Actions," in "Attorneys' Practice Guide to Negotiations, Second Edition" (1996); Author, "Antitrust Class Actions-Twenty Years Under Rule 23" (1986); Author, "Proving Damages in Non-Class Securities Cases," Association of Trial Lawyers of America (1986); Topic and Articles Editor, Journal Forum Committee on Franchising (1981-1986); Co-author, "The State Court Class Action - A Potpourri of Differences" in "American Bar Association Forum" (1985); Author, "Subject Matter Jurisdiction of U.S. District Courts" in "Federal Civil Practice" (1974); Board of Editors, Illinois Bar Antitrust Newsletter (1969-1973) **AW:** Highest Peer and Judicial Rating for Legal Ability and Ethical Standards (1980-Present); AV Preeminent Rating, Martindale-Hubbell **MEM:** Board of Directors, Corporate Secretary, Bang on a Can, Inc. (2007-Present); Member, Committee on University Resources, Harvard University (2004-Present); Director, Maria and Robert A. Skirnick Fund For New Works at Carnegie Hall (2004-Present); Antitrust and Trade Regulation Committee, Association of the Bar of the City of New York (2004-2007); Board of Directors, Handel House Foundation of America (2002-2007); Orchestra of St. Luke's, Board of Directors (2002-2007); Advisory Board, American Antitrust Institute (2000-2017), Emeritus (2017-Present); Board of Directors, National Association of Public Interest Law (now Equal Justice Works) (1997-2008); Life Member, United States Navy League (1994-Present); Co-Chair, Securities Law Subcommittee, Litigation Section, American Bar Association (1987); Class Action Committee, New York State Bar Association; Committee on Second Circuit Courts, Federal Bar Council (1983-1986); Association of Trial Lawyers of America; Chairman, Antitrust Section, Illinois State Bar

Association (1970-1971); Member, Committee on Regulation of Futures and Derivative Instruments, American Bar Association; Member, Forum Committee on Franchising, American Bar Association; Member, Committee on Class Actions and Derivative Suits, American Bar Association; Member, Forum Committee on International Antitrust and Foreign Competition Laws, American Bar Association; New York State Trial Lawyers Association. **BAR:** United States Court of Appeals for the Fourth Circuit (2002); United States Court of Appeals for the Sixth Circuit (2002); United States Court of Appeals for the Eighth Circuit (2002); United States Court of Appeals for the Eleventh Circuit (1995); United States Court of Appeals for the Fifth Circuit (1994); United States District Court for the Northern District of California (1994); United States District Court for the Northern District of Arizona (1993); United States Court of Appeals for the Tenth Circuit (1993); United States Court of Appeals for the Second Circuit (1990); United States District Court for the Southern District of New York (1990); United States District Court for the Eastern District of New York (1990); United States District Court for the Eastern District of Michigan (1988); United States Court of Appeals for the Third Circuit (1984); New York State Bar Association (1982); United States Court of Appeals for the Ninth Circuit (1977); Supreme Court of the United States (1970); United States Court of Appeals for the Seventh Circuit (1968); United States District Court for the Northern District of Illinois (1967); Illinois State Bar Association (1967) **MH:** Albert Nelson Marquis Lifetime Achievement Award **AV:** International travel; Commissioning composers; Supporting public interest law

SKOLNICK, LAWRENCE, MD, MPH, T: Director of Neonatology (Retired) **I:** Medicine & Health Care **CN:** MidAtlantic Neonatology Associates **DOB:** 07/29/1947 **PB:** New York **SC:** NY/USA **PT:** Harry Skolnick; Sylvia Skolnick **MS:** Married **SPN:** Tamar Tumarkin (04/07/1970) **CH:** Daniel; Michael; Rachel **ED:** Neonatology Fellowship, Duke University, NC; Pediatric Residency, Jack D. Weiler Hospital of Albert Einstein College of Medicine, Bronx, NY; MPH, University of North Carolina (1980); MD, New York University School of Medicine (1972); BS, City University of New York (1968) **C:** Retired, Private Practice (2019); Private Practice, MidAtlantic Neonatology Associates (2004-2019); Retired, Co-director of Neonatology (2005); Co-director of Neonatology, Atlantic Health System (1999-2005); Director of Neonatology, Overlook Hospital (Now Overlook Medical Center), Atlantic Health System, Summit, NJ (1999); Director of Neonatology, Morristown, NJ (1980-1999); Director of Newborn Medicine, Jack D. Weiler Hospital of Albert Einstein College of Medicine, Bronx, NY (1977-1980) **CR:** Associate Professor of Medical Pediatrics, University of Medicine and Dentistry of New Jersey (UMDNJ)-Rutgers New Jersey Medical School (2001) **AW:** Named Top Doctor, Castle Connolly **MEM:** American Academy of Pediatrics **MH:** Marquis Who's Who Top Professional **B/I:** Dr. Skolnick went into medicine because he wanted to figure out he best way to help people. He picked neonatology because he liked the idea of working with families, and parents to help babies. That is why he ended up at Duke University, because back in the mid 70s, that was one of the few medical centers in the United States that connected obstetrics with pediatrics. That is way he selected that specific place for his fellowship. As a neonatology fellowship and neonatologist in that institution they were highly connected with obstetricians and perinatologist looking to improve outcomes for women with complicated pregnancies. That is

what attracted him, how to make a better outcome with a complicated pregnancy. **AV:** Family; Travel; Spending time with grandchildren

SLADE, MICHAEL, T: Playwright, Librettist, Author, Writer **I:** Writing and Editing **CW:** Writer, "After Forever" (2019); Interviewee, "Soap Central" (2019); Writer, "One Life to Live," ABC (1986-2002, 2013); Writer, "Days of Our Lives," NBC (2006); Writer, "Passions," NBC (2005); Writer, "Another World," NBC (1997); Playwright, "And a Child Shall Lead," "And the Curtain Rises," "Bye, Bye Big Guy," "Change," "Family Shots," "Garden Politics," "Gingerbread Children," "Home for the Holidays: Four One-Act Plays," "Under a Red Moon," "Unheard Voices: Haunted Files"; Author, "Becoming Christopher"; Author, "Diabetes: Close to the Heart"; Author, "The Horses of Central Park" **AW:** Daytime Emmy Award for Outstanding Digital Daytime Drama Series, "After Forever," The National Academy of Television Arts & Sciences (2019); Excellence in Web Series, "After Forever," Out on Film, Atlanta, GA (2018); Best Drama Web Series, "After Forever," Tuscany Web Fest (2018); CLIO Healthcare Award; Big Apple Award; PR Week Award

SLATER, CHRISTIAN, T: Actor **I:** Media & Entertainment **DOB:** 08/18/1969 **PB:** New York **SC:** NY/USA **PT:** Michael Hawkins Slater; Mary Jo Slater **MS:** Married **SPN:** Brittany Lopez (12/02/2013); Ryan Haddon (02/12/2000, Divorced 2006) **CH:** Jaden Christopher Haddon-Slater; Eliana Sophia Haddon-Slater; Lena **CIV:** Supporter, Numerous Charities, Including 21st Century Leaders, Global Green, Whatever It Takes; Advocate, Humanitarian Work in South Africa **CW:** Actor, "Dr. Death" (2020); Actor, "Dirty John" (2020); Voice Actor, "Milo Murphy's Law" (2016-2019); Actor, "The Lion Guard" (2016-2019); Actor, Producer, "Mr. Robot" (2015-2019); Actor, "The Public" (2018); Actor, Theater, "Glengarry Glenn Ross" (2017-2018); Actor, "The Wife" (2017); Voice Actor, "Rick and Morty" (2017); Voice Actor, "Justice League Action Shorts" (2017); Actor, "The Summit" (2017); Voice Actor, "Jeff & Some Aliens" (2017); Actor, "Dawn of the Croods" (2016); Actor, "King Cobra" (2016); Voice Actor, "Archer" (2014-2016); Actor, "Jake and the Never Land Pirates" (2015); Actor, "The Adderall Diaries" (2015); Actor, "Hot Tub Time Machine 2" (2015); Actor, Theater, "Spamalot" (2015); Appearance, "Two and a Half Men" (2014); Actor, "Mind Games" (2014); Actor, "Way of the Wicked" (2014); Actor, "Ask Me Anything" (2014); Voice Actor, "Stan Lee's Mighty 7" (2014); Actor, "Nymphomaniac: Vol. II" (2013); Actor, "Nymphomaniac: Vol. I" (2013); Actor, "Stranded" (2013); Actor, "Assassins Run" (2013); Actor, "Out There" (2013); Actor, "The Power of Few" (2013); Actor, "Bullet to the Head" (2012); Actor, "Guns, Girls and Gambling" (2012); Actor, "Soldiers of Fortune" (2012); Actor, "Hatfields and McCoys: Bad Blood" (2012); Actor, "Dawn Rider" (2012); Actor, "Freaky Deaky" (2012); Actor, "Assassin's Bullet" (2012); Voice Actor, "Phineas and Ferb" (2012); Actor, "Playback" (2012); Actor, "Rites of Passage" (2012); Voice Actor, "Back to the Sea" (2012); Actor, Producer, "Breaking In" (2011-2012); Voice Actor, "Robot Chicken" (2005-2012); Appearance, "Entourage" (2011); Actor, "The River Murders" (2011); Actor, "Sacrifice" (2011); Actor, "The Forgotten" (2009-2010); Appearance, "Curb Your Enthusiasm" (2009); Actor, "Lies & Illusions" (2009); Actor, "Dolan's Cadillac" (2009); Actor, "My Own Worst Enemy" (2008); Voice Actor, "Igot" (2008); Actor, "Love Lies Bleeding" (2008); Actor, Theater, "Swimming with Sharks" (2007-2008); Voice Actor, "The Ten Commandments" (2007); Actor, "Slipstream" (2007); Actor, "He Was a Quiet Man" (2007); Actor, "My Name Is Earl" (2006); Actor, "Bobby" (2006); Actor, "Hollow Man II"

(2006); Actor, Theater, "One Flew Over the Cuckoo's Nest" (2006); Actor, "Odd Job Jack" (2005); Actor, Executive Producer, "The Deal" (2005); Actor, "Alone in the Dark" (2005); Actor, Theater, "The Glass Menagerie" (2005); Voice Actor, "The Adventures of Jimmy Neutron: Boy Genius" (2003, 2005); Actor, Theater, "One Flew Over the Cuckoo's Nest" (2004-2005); Actor, "Churchill: The Hollywood Years" (2004); Actor, "Pursued" (2004); Actor, "Alias" (2003); Actor, "Masked and Anonymous" (2003); Actor, "The West Wing" (2002); Actor, "Windtalkers" (2002); Actor, "Hard Cash" (2002); Appearance, "Zoolander" (2001); Actor, "Who Is Cletis Tout?" (2001); Actor, "3000 Miles to Graceland" (2001); Actor, "The Contender" (2000); Actor, Theater, "Side Man" (1999); Actor, Executive Producer, "Very Bad Things" (1998); Actor, Co-producer, "Basil" (1998); Actor, Co-producer, "Hard Rain" (1998); Actor, "Merry Christmas, George Bailey" (1997); Actor, "Julian Po" (1997); Actor, "Austin Powers: International Man of Mystery" (1997); Actor, "Broken Arrow" (1996); Actor, "Bed of Roses" (1996); Actor, "Murder in the First" (1995); Actor, "Interview with the Vampire: The Vampire Chronicles" (1994); Actor, "Jimmy Hollywood" (1994); Actor, "True Romance" (1993); Actor, "Untamed Heart" (1993); Narrator, "Shelley Duvall's Bedtime Stories" (1992); Voice Actor, "FernGully: The Last Rainforest" (1992); Actor, "Where the Day Takes You" (1992); Actor, "Kuffs" (1992); Actor, "Star Trek VI: The Undiscovered Country" (1991); Actor, "Mobsters" (1991); Actor, "Robin Hood: Prince of Thieves" (1991); Actor, "Pump Up the Volume" (1990); Actor, "Young Guns II" (1990); Actor, "Tales from the Darkside: The Movie" (1990); Actor, "The Wizard" (1989); Actor, "The Edge" (1989); Actor, "Beyond the Stars" (1989); Actor, "Heathers" (1989); Actor, "Desperate for Love" (1989); Actor, "Gleaming the Cube" (1989); Actor, "Tucker: The Man and His Dream" (1988); Actor, "L.A. Law" (1988); Actor, "Secrets" (1986); Actor, "Crime Story" (1986); Actor, "The Equalizer" (1986); Actor, "Twisted" (1986); Actor, "The Name of the Rose" (1986); Actor, "Ryan's Hope" (1985); Actor, "The Legend of Billie Jean" (1985); Actor, "Tales from the Darkside" (1984); Actor, "All My Children" (1984); Actor, Theater, "Landscape of the Body" (1984); Actor, "Living Proof: The Hank Williams, Jr. Story" (1983); Actor, "ABC Weekend Specials" (1983); Actor, Theater, "Merlin" (1983); Actor, "Pardon Me for Living" (1982); Actor, "CBS Library" (1982); Actor, Theater, "Macbeth" (1982); Actor, "Standing Room Only" (1981); Actor, Theater, "Copperfield" (1981); Actor, "Search for Tomorrow" (1980); Actor, Theater, "The Music Man" (1980) **AW:** Named Best Supporting Actor in a Drama Series, "Mr. Robot," Satellite Awards (2016); Golden Globe for Best Supporting Actor - Series, Miniseries or Television Film, "Mr. Robot," Hollywood Foreign Press Association (2016); Named Best Supporting Actor in a Drama Series, "Mr. Robot," Critics' Choice Television Awards (2016); Named Ensemble of the Year, "Bobby," Hollywood Film Awards (2006); Alan J. Pakula Award, "The Contender," Critics' Choice Awards (2001); Named Best Male Performance, "Very Bad Things," Slate Awards (2000)

SLATKIN, LEONARD EDWARD, T: Composer **I:** Media & Entertainment **DOB:** 09/01/1944 **PB:** Los Angeles **SC:** CA/USA **PT:** Felix Slatkin; Eleanor (Aller) Slatkin **MS:** Married **SPN:** Cindy McTee (2011); Linda Hohenfeld (03/29/1986, Divorced); Beth Gootee (Divorced); Jerilyn Cohen (Divorced) **CH:** Daniel **ED:** Numerous Honorary Doctorates, The Juilliard School, New England Conservatory, Michigan State University, Indiana University, University of Rochester, University of Maryland, College Park, The George Washington University,

University of Missouri-St. Louis, Washington University; Coursework, Los Angeles City College; Coursework, Indiana University; Coursework, Conducting with Jean Paul Morel, The Juilliard School; Coursework with Walter Susskind, Aspen Music Festival and School; Coursework in Piano with Victor Aller and Selma Cramer; Coursework in Viola with Sol Schoenbach; Coursework in Conducting with Felix Slatkin, Amerigo Marino, and Ingolf Dahl **C:** Music Director Laureate, Detroit Symphony Orchestra (2018-Present); Directeur Musical Honoraire, Orchestre National de Lyon (2011-Present); Music Director, Detroit Symphony Orchestra (2008-2018); Part-time Instructor, Conducting and Composition, Jacobs School of Music, Indiana University, Bloomington, IN (2006); Chief Conductor, BBC Symphony Orchestra (2000-2004); Music Director, National Symphony Orchestra (1996-2008); Director, Blossom Festival, The Cleveland Orchestra and Musical Arts Association (1990-1999); Music Director, St. Louis Symphony Orchestra (1979-1996); Music Director, New Orleans Symphony (1977-1979); Assistant Conductor, St. Louis Symphony Orchestra (1968-1977); Founder, Artistic Director, Conductor, New York Youth Symphony (1966); Principal Guest Conductor, Royal Philharmonic Orchestra, Philharmonia Orchestra, Pittsburgh Symphony Orchestra, Los Angeles Philharmonic Association, Minnesota Orchestral Association, National Symphony Orchestra, and Numerous Others **CR:** Music Adviser, Nashville Symphony Orchestra (2006-2009); Distinguished Artist in Residence, American University (2007-2008); Founder, Former Director, National Conducting Institute (2000) **CW:** Principal Guest Conductor, Minnesota Orchestral Association (1974-Present); Artistic Administrator, Blossom Music Center, The Cleveland Orchestra and Musical Arts Association (1991); Guest Conductor, The Metropolitan Opera (1991); Artistic Director, Great Woods Symphony Orchestra (1990); Summer Artistic Director, Minnesota Orchestral Association (1979-1989); Music Director, New Orleans Philharmonic Symphony Orchestra (1977-1978); Guest Conductor, USSR Orchestras (1976-1977); Guest Conductor, Vienna State Opera (Wiener Staatsoper), Lyric Opera of Chicago, IL, Staatsoper Stuttgart, Stockholm and Goteborg, Sweden, Oslo, Norway, Israel, Berlin, Germany (1974); Guest Conductor, Debut, Chicago Symphony Orchestra (1974); Guest Conductor, New York Philharmonic (1974); Guest Conductor, The Philadelphia Orchestra (1974); Guest Conductor, Orchestre de Paris, France, Royal Scottish National Orchestra, Scotland, United Kingdom, NHK Tokyo (NHK (Japan Broadcasting Corporation)), Japan (1986); Guest Conductor, Concertgebouw, Royal Danish Orchestra, Tivoli, English Chamber Orchestra, BBC Manchester, London Philharmonic Orchestra, London Symphony Orchestra, Royal Philharmonic Orchestra (1974); Associate Conductor, St. Louis Symphony Orchestra (1971-1974); Assistant Conductor, St. Louis Symphony Orchestra (1968-1971); Assistant Conductor, Juilliard Opera Theater and Dance Department, The Juilliard School (1967); Conducting Debut as Assistant Conductor, New York Youth Symphony, Carnegie Hall (1966); Composer, "The Raven," "Dialogue for Two Cellos and Orchestra," and "Extension 1, 2, 3, 4"; Recording Artist, RCA (Now Sony Music Entertainment), Angel EMI (Now Warner Music Inc.), Vox, Telarc (Now Concord), Philips, and Warner Brothers (Now Warner Records); Conductor, Arthur R. Metz Foundation, Indiana University **AW:** ASCAP Foundation Deems Taylor Special Recognition Award (2013); Grammy Awards for Best Classical Album and Best Orchestral Performance, "Made in America," Recording Academy (2007); Grammy Awards for Best Classi-

cal Album and Best Choral Performance, "Songs of Innocence and Experience," Recording Academy (2005); Gold Baton Award, League of American Orchestras (2005); Appointed, Chevalier, French National Order of the Legion of Honor (2004); National Medal of Arts (2003); Charles E. Lutton Man of Music Award, Phi Mu Alpha Sinfonia (1997); Grammy Award for Best Classical Album, "Of Rage and Remembrance," Recording Academy (1996); Grammy Award for Best Instrumental Soloist with Orchestra, Recording Academy (1991); Inductee, St. Louis Walk of Fame (1990); Decoration of Honor in Silver (1986); Grammy Award for Best Classical Orchestral Recording, St. Louis Symphony Orchestra, Recording Academy (1984); 34 Grammy Award Nominations, Recording Academy **MEM:** Member, Board of Governors, Chicago Chapter, National Academy of Recording Arts and Sciences (Now The Recording Academy)

SLAVITT, BEN, JD, T: Lawyer **I:** Law and Legal Services **DOB:** 12/31/1934 **PB:** Newark **SC:** NJ/USA **PT:** Arthur Slavitt; Berdie (Goodman) Slavitt **MS:** Married **SPN:** Laraine **CH:** Lauri; Julie; Donna; John **ED:** JD, University of Virginia (1959); BA, Bucknell University (1956) **C:** Partner, Slavitt & Cowen, PA and Predecessors, Newark, NJ (1959-2019) **MIL:** Served., United States Army (1959-1960) **MEM:** New Jersey State Bar Association **BAR:** Supreme Court of the United States (1973); United States District Court for the District of New Jersey (1959); New Jersey (1959) **MH:** Albert Nelson Marquis Lifetime Achievement Award **PA:** Democrat **RE:** Jewish

SLAYTON, THOMAS KENNEDY, T: Editor, Writer **I:** Writing and Editing **DOB:** 07/29/1941 **PB:** Burlington **SC:** VT/USA **PT:** Ronald Alfred Slayton; Dorothy (Kennedy) Slayton **MS:** Married **SPN:** Elizabeth Craig (Wilson) Slayton (1964) **CH:** Ethan Augustus **ED:** BA in English, Minor in History, University of Vermont (1963) **C:** Editor-in-Chief, Vermont Life Magazine (1985-2007); Assistant Editor, Editor, Times-Argus Newspaper (1979-1985); Reporter, Bureau Chief, Vermont Press Bureau (1972-1979); Reporter, Rutland Herald Newspaper (1964-1972) **CR:** Adjunct Professor, Journalism Department, St. Michael's College, Winooski, VT (1988-Present); Adviser, Conference Board, Windham Foundation, Grafton, VT (1986-1989) **MIL:** Vermont Air National Guard (1968-1974); Reserve Duty, U.S. Army Reserve (1964-1968); Active Duty, U.S. Army Reserve 1963-1964 **CW:** Author, "Searching for Thoreau: On the Trails and Shores of Wild New England" (2007); Author, "Sabra Field, The Art of Place" (1993); Author, Introduction, "The Vermont Experience (1987); Author, "Finding Vermont" (1986) **AW:** Honorary DLitt, University of Vermont (2008); Honorary DLitt, Southern Vermont College (2000); Franklin Fairbanks Award (1997); Bicentennial Fellow, University of Vermont, Burlington, VT (1988-1991); Honorary DLitt, Sterling College **MEM:** Zen Buddhist Society of Mountains and Rivers (1992-2019); Fellow, Vermont Academy of Arts & Sciences (2008); President, International Regional Magazine Association (2008); President, Board of Directors, International Regional Magazine Association (1993-1994); Vermont Press Association; Board Member, Friends of the Vermont State House; Board Member, Vermont Natural Resources Council; Board Member, Vermont Conservation Voters **MH:** Albert Nelson Marquis Lifetime Achievement Award **B/I:** Mr. Slayton became involved in his profession at the Rutland Herald, a newspaper in Vermont. After coming back from active duty in the Army in 1963, he worked there as a reporter, where he socialized with newspaper people and where he covered a variety of events. He had an ability to write, so he was able to work for Rutland Herald and subsequently reported for the Vermont Press Bureau, the Rutland Herald and Times-Argus Sunday Edition, and as Vermont correspondent for the Boston Globe. **RE:** Buddhist

SLEDGE, WILLIAM HURT, MD, T: Deputy Chair of Psychiatry for Clinical Services (Retired) **I:** Education/Educational Services **CN:** Department of Psychiatry, Yale University School of Medicine **DOB:** 01/26/1945 **PB:** Greensboro **SC:** AL/USA **MS:** Married **SPN:** Elizabeth Rose Sledge **CH:** Ann Elizabeth Jones; Margaret Rose Sledge; Katherine Sledge Moore **ED:** Postdoctoral Fellow, Resident, Department of Psychiatry, Yale School of Medicine, New Haven, CT (1972-1975); Intern, Medicine-Psychiatry, University of Pennsylvania Service, Philadelphia General Hospital, Philadelphia, PA (1971-1972); MD, Baylor College of Medicine, Houston, Texas (1971); AB, Washington and Lee University, Lexington, VA, Cum Laude (1967) **C:** Lecturer, Humanities Department, Yale College, Yale University (2007-2019); George D. and Esther S. Gross Professor of Psychiatry, Yale College, Yale University (2004-2019); Professor of Psychiatry, Yale School of Medicine (1992-2019); Retired Deputy Chair for Clinical Affairs and Program Development, Department of Psychiatry, Yale School of Medicine (2015); Deputy Chair for Clinical Affairs and Program Development, Department of Psychiatry, Yale School of Medicine (2009-2015); Assistant Chief of Psychiatry, Yale New Haven Hospital, Yale New Haven Health (1996-2015); Master, Calhoun College, Yale University (1995-2015); Interim Chair, Department of Psychiatry, Yale School of Medicine and Acting Chief of Psychiatry, Yale New Haven Hospital, Yale New Haven Health (2007-2009); Medical Director, Mental Health Service Line Co-leader, Yale New Haven Psychiatric Hospital, Yale New Haven Health (2000-2003); Associate Chair for Education, Department of Psychiatry, Yale School of Medicine (1990-1996); Clinical Director, Connecticut Mental Health Center (CMHC), Yale School of Medicine (1989-1996); Associate Professor of Psychiatry, Yale School of Medicine (1983-1992); Director, Outpatient Division, Connecticut Mental Health Center (CMHC), Yale School of Medicine (1987-1989); Chief, Individual Psychotherapy Unit, Outpatient Division, Connecticut Mental Health Center (CMHC), Yale School of Medicine (1982-1988); Director of Graduate Education, Department of Psychiatry, Yale School of Medicine (1980-1986); Training Coordinator for PGY-3 Outpatient Residents, Connecticut Mental Health Center (CMHC), Yale School of Medicine (1980-1982); Associate Director of Graduate Education, Department of Psychiatry, Training Coordinator for PGY-2 Outpatient Residents, Connecticut Mental Health Center (CMHC), Yale School of Medicine (1979-1980); Associate Clinical Director; Ward Chief of Adolescent Unit, Yale Psychiatric Institute, Yale New Haven Health (1978-1979); Assistant Clinical Director, Director of Admissions, Yale Psychiatric Institute, Yale New Haven Health (1977-1978); Assistant Professor of Psychiatry, Yale School of Medicine (1977-1983); Clinical Assistant Professor of Psychiatry, UT Health Sciences San Antonio, Texas (1975-1977); Staff Psychiatrist, USAF School of Aerospace Medicine, Brooks AFB, San Antonio, Texas (1975-1977) **CR:** Speaker, "Treatments of the Schizophrenias and Other Psychoses," London, United Kingdom (1997); Visiting Professor of Community Psychiatry, United Medical and Dental Schools of Guy's and St. Thomas' Hospitals, University of London (1993); Roerig Visiting Professor, Eastern Tennessee State University, Johnson City, TN (1991) **CIV:** Search Committee for Chair, Child Study Center, Yale University (2013-Present); Lecturer, Whitney Humanities Center, Yale University (2007-Present);

Search Committee, Director of Psycho-oncology Program, Yale University (2013-2019); Department of Psychiatry Graduate Education Committee and Departmental Executive Committee, Yale School of Medicine (1979-1986, 1996-2019); Chair, Search Committee, Director of Psychosomatic Program, Yale New Haven Psychiatric Service, Yale New Haven Health (2011-2012); Executive Committee, Whitney Humanities Center, Yale University (2009-2012); Chief of Psychology, Connecticut Mental Health Center (CMHC) (2010-2011); VACT Search Committees for Mental Health Service Director, Connecticut Mental Health Center (CMHC) (2009-2010); Fellow, Whitney Humanities Center, Yale University (2005-2010); Chair, Search Committee for Director, Connecticut Mental Health Center (CMHC) (2008-2009); Chair of Student Life Planning Committee, Presidential Advisory Group for the Planning of New Residential Colleges, Yale College, Yale University (2007-2008); Building Committee for Cross Campus Library, Yale School of Medicine (2004-2006); Provostial Appointment to University Health Services Advisory Committee, Yale School of Medicine (2002-2005); Council of Masters, Calhoun College, Yale University (1995-2005); Presidential Committee for Phase II Plans for University Library, Yale School of Medicine (2002-2004); Kiphuth Medal Award Committee, Yale School of Medicine (2001-2003); Chair, Council of Masters, Calhoun College, Yale University (2000-2003); Search Committee, Chief of Psychiatry, Waterbury Hospital (1987-1988, 2001); Provostial Committee for Phase II Plans for University Library, Yale School of Medicine (1999); Chair, Provostial Ad Hoc Committee on Consensual Sexual Relations between Faculty and Students, Yale School of Medicine (1997); Search Committee for Dean, Yale School of Medicine (1996-1997); Search Committee for Director of University Health, Yale School of Medicine (1995-1996); Appointment and Promotions Committee for the Clinical Sciences, Yale School of Medicine (1993-1995); Fellow, Silliman College, Yale University (1984-1995); Member, Non-tenured Faculty Representative, Medical School Council, Yale School of Medicine (1984-1986); Ad Hoc Sexual Harassment Review Committee, Yale School of Medicine (1985); Fellow for Life, Calhoun College, Yale University; Board of Directors, Continuum of Care and Fellowship Place, New Haven, CT; Board of Directors, Auburn University Rural Studio of Architecture; Board of Directors, Connecticut State Pistol Permit **MIL:** Flight Surgeon, United States Air Force (1975-1977) **CW:** Author, Book Chapters, Numerous Articles **AW:** Named to Best Doctors in America (2000-Present); John P. McGovern Award and Lecture, Program in Humanities, Yale School of Medicine (2015); Best Paper Award in Psychosomatics, American Academy of Psychosomatic Medicine (2011); Innovations in Psychiatry Award, First Place for Behavioral Intervention Team, Department of Psychiatry, Yale School of Medicine (2011); Excellence in Quality of Care, First Place Winner for the Behavioral Intervention Team, Yale New Haven Health System (2010); Innovations in Psychiatry Award, Third Place for Peer Mentor Program for Recurrently Readmitted Patients, Department of Psychiatry, Yale School of Medicine (2010); Inaugural John F. Borus Lecture, Brigham and Women's Hospital, Harvard University (2009); Appreciation Award, Afro-American Cultural Center, Yale University (2005); Fellow, The American College of Psychiatrists (2003); Stephen Fleck Humanitarian Award, Department of Psychiatry, Yale School of Medicine (1999); Guest of Honor Speaker, American Association of Directors of Psychiatric Residency Training (AADPRT) Midwinter Meeting (1995); Excellence in Residency Education, Teaching Award, Yale Psychiatric Residents'

Association (1989); Named to The Phi Beta Kappa Society, Gamma of Virginia Chapter, Washington and Lee University (1989); APA Institutional Distinguished Service Award, Presented to the American Association of Directors of Psychiatric Residency Training (AADPRT) (1987); Fellow, American Psychiatric Association (1984); Named to Jane's Who's Who in Aviation and Aerospace, U.S. Edition (1983); Air Force Commendation Medal (1977); Second Place, Lustman Award for Postdoctoral Fellow Research, Department of Psychiatry, Yale School of Medicine (1975); Best Intern of the Year Award, Philadelphia General Hospital (1972); Excellence in Psychiatry, Graduation Award, Baylor College of Medicine (1971) **MEM:** Benjamin Rush Society (2015-Present); Committee on Psychotherapy, Group for the Advancement of Psychiatry (1998-Present); Fellow, American College of Psychoanalysts (1996-Present); Corresponding Member, Committee on Graduate Education (1985-1986, 1988-Present); Chair, Group for the Advancement of Psychiatry (2005-2013); Faculty, The Western New England Psychoanalytic Institute and Society (1990-2010); Board of Trustees, Group for the Advancement of Psychiatry (2005-2008); Fellow, The American College of Psychiatrists (2003); Ginsberg Fellowship Committee, Group for the Advancement of Psychiatry (1999-2001); Consultant, Commission on the Practice of Psychotherapy by Psychiatrists (1997-2001); Education Committee, The American College of Psychiatrists (1997-2000); Committee on University and Medical Education (1993-2000); Committee on Research, Group for the Advancement of Psychiatry (1993-1998); Chair, Committee on Practice of Psychotherapy (1992-1996); Committee on Psychoanalytic Education Study Group on the Interface of Psychotherapy and Psychoanalytic Training (1988-1996); The American College of Psychiatrists (1994); Subcommittee, Psychoanalytic Directors of Psychiatric Residency Training Programs (1992-1994); General Member, Association of Academic Psychiatry (1989-1992); Symposium Committee, The Western New England Psychoanalytic Institute and Society (1988-1992); Consultant, Committee on Practice of Psychotherapy (1991); Member, Numerous Organizations **MH:** Marquis Who's Who Top Professional **AV:** Flying; SCUBA diving

SLOAN, FRANK, T: Economist, Educator Emeritus **I:** Education/Educational Services **DOB:** 08/15/1942 **PB:** Greensboro **SC:** NC/USA **PT:** Harry Benjamin Sloan; Edith (Vortrefflich) Sloan **MS:** Married **SPN:** Paula Jane Rackoff (06/22/1969) **CH:** Elyse Valerie; Richard Matthew (Deceased) **ED:** PhD in Labor Economics and Public Economics, Harvard University (1969); AB in Economics, Oberlin College (1964) **C:** Emeritus Professor (2018-Present); J. Alexander McMahon Health Policy and Management Professor, Economics, Duke University, Durham, NC (1993-2018); Director, Center for Health Policy, Law and Management, Duke University, Durham, NC (1998-2003); Chairman, Department of Economics, Vanderbilt University, Nashville, TN (1986-1989); Centennial Professor, Economics, Vanderbilt University, Nashville, TN (1984-1993); Professor, Economics, Vanderbilt University, Nashville, TN (1976-1984); Associate Professor, University of Florida, Gainesville, FL (1973-1976); Assistant Professor, Economics, University of Florida, Gainesville, FL (1971-1973); Research Economist, Rand Corp., Santa Monica, CA (1968-1971) **CR:** Member, Institute of Medicine, Washington DC (1996-Present); President, American Society of Health Economists (2012-2014); Director, Health Policy Center, Vanderbilt University Institute of Public Policy Studies (1976-1993); Consultant, Advisory Council, Social Security, Washington DC (1983); Member, National

Council Health Care Technology, Washington DC (1979-1981); Member, National Allergy and Infectious Disease Council, Washington DC (1971-1974); Member, Prospective Payment Reviews Commissions **CW:** Co-author, "Insuring Medical Malpractice" (1991); Co-author, "Uncompensated Hospital Care: Rights and Responsibilities" (1986); Co-author, "Hospital Labor Markets" (1980); Co-author, "Insurance, Regulation and Hospital Costs" (1980); Co-author, "Private Physicians and Public Programs" (1978) **AW:** Victor R. Fuchs Award for Lifetime Contributions to Health Economics (2016); Graduate School Mentoring Award, Duke University (2013) **MEM:** National Academy of Medicine (1982-Present); American Economic Association; National Bureau of Economic Research **MH:** Albert Nelson Marquis Lifetime Achievement Award **B/I:** Dr. Frank Sloan always wanted to be an educator and he was inspired in economics from an introductory course he took in economics, however being a college professor and having the ability to research was his primary goal.

SLOAN, MARY, "MARY LOVE" STRINGFIELD, T: Hospital Interior Designer **I:** Architecture & Construction **DOB:** 08/07/1947 **PB:** Waynesville **SC:** NC/USA **PT:** Dr. Thomas Stringfield; Harriet Cutler Coburn Stringfield, RN **MS:** Married **SPN:** Hugh Johnston Sloan III, PhD (02/12/1982, Deceased 04/19/2020) **CH:** Hugh Johnston Sloan IV, JD; Susan Kathleen Sloan Harper (Stepdaughter) **ED:** Coursework, Graduate Studies in Industrial Design, Historic Preservation and Hospital Administration, Ohio State University Medical Center (1986-1991); Bachelor of Science, University of Tennessee, Knoxville, TN (1973) **CT:** Mississippi Certified Interior Designer (2013); NCIDQ (1981) **C:** Signage Coordinator, University of Memphis, Memphis, TN (2000-2002); Faculty, Interior Design, University of Mississippi, Oxford, MS (1995-1999); Coordinator of Interior Design, Ohio State University Medical Center, Columbus, OH (1981-1991); Director of Planning and Design, Counterpoint Inc., Knoxville, TN (1979-1981); Staff Designer, Omnia Design Inc., Charlotte, NC (1973-1979) **CR:** Member, Board of Visitors, Foundation for Interior Design Education and Research (1988-1993); Trustee, Coalition for Interior Design Licensing, Ohio (1987-1991); Vice President, Association of University Interior Designers (1988-1989); Education Chair, Ohio Regional Chapter, International Interior Design Association (1985-1986); Vice President, Tennessee Chapter, IBD (1980-1981); Instructor, University of Tennessee, Knoxville, TN (1980); National Trustee, Carolinas Chapter, Institute of Business Designers (1978-1979); Instructor, Central Piedmont Community College, Charlotte, NC (1978); Chairperson, Student Design Rally Speakers, Carolinas Chapter, Institute of Business Designers (1977); Chairperson, Student Design Rally Tours, Carolinas Chapter, Institute of Business Designers (1976) **CIV:** Women's Political Caucus, Oxford, MS (2018-Present); Republican Women's Club, Oxford, MS (2015-Present); Historian, David Reese DAR (2019-2021); Founder, General Lafayette C.A.R., Oxford, MS (2020); Regent, David Reese DAR, Oxford, MS (2017-2019); The Heritage Club, Daughters of the American Revolution (2018); Legislative Vice President, Mississippi PTA (2008-2010); Board of Directors, Mississippi PTA (2000-2010); Education Vice President, Mississippi PTA (2006-2008); President, North Central Mississippi PTA Council (1998-2000); President, Oxford Elementary PTA (1998); Volunteer, Columbus Committee for UNICEF (1982-1988); Member, Centennial Committee, King Avenue United Methodist Church, Columbus, OH (1985); Representative to State Board, Women's Political Caucus, Knoxville, TN (1980); Secretary, Young Democrats Club, Char-

lotte, NC (1978); President, ECO Inc., Charlotte, NC (1977); Board of Directors, ECO, Inc., Charlotte, NC (1975-1977); Co-Founder, Yocona International Folk Festival; Board of Directors, Yoknapatawpha Arts Council; President, United Methodist Women, Cambridge United Methodist Church **CW:** Author, "Tomorrow Today: New technologies in Interior Design Practice," IIDA Journal (1990) **AW:** Research Fellowship in Steelcase Design Partnership, IIDA (1989, 1990, 1991); Award, Association of University Interior Designers (1990); Appreciation Award, Tennessee Chapter, International Interior Design Association (1980); Outstanding Young Women of America (1979) **MEM:** Secretary, Columbus, Ohio Chapter, University of Tennessee Alumni Association (1984-1986); Ohio Preservation Alliance; National Trust for Historic Preservation; Sierra Club; World Future Society; Women's Guild for Opera, Columbus; Republican Women's Club; United Methodist Women; Woodson Ridge Homemakers Club; Oxford Ole Miss Rotary Club; Stephen Launius Civil Air Patrol; Mississippi Preservation Alliance; Cameo Society, Mississippi State, Daughters of the American Revolution; Metropolitan Opera Guild; Lifetime Member, Ohio State University Alumni Association **MH:** Albert Nelson Marquis Lifetime Achievement Award **AS:** Ms. Sloan attributes her success to good public education, parental and spousal discipline, modeling and encouragement, and her Christian faith. Likewise, she drew inspiration from her first boss, Stacy Simmons. **B/I:** Ms. Sloan became involved in her profession due to the influence of her parents, who were dedicated health care professionals. Her early ethical training guided her similarly, and her artistic focus led her towards interior design, with a particular specialization in medical environments. **AV:** Travel; Reading; Landscape design; Opera; Theater; Poetry; Stamp collecting; Collecting folk art; International folk festivals; Genealogy; Historic preservation; Sewing **PA:** Republican **RE:** United Methodist Church

SLOAN, PHILLIP REID, PHD, T: Liberal Studies Educator, Historian of Science, Philosopher of Life Science **I:** Education/Educational Services **CN:** University of Notre Dame **DOB:** 01/28/1938 **PB:** Salt Lake City **SC:** UT/USA **PT:** Reid John Sloan; Celia MaRee Sloan **MS:** Married **SPN:** Mary Katherine Tillman (07/3/2010); Sharon Lee Borg (09/02/1958, Deceased 01/28/2009) **CH:** Laura; Mary (Deceased 2019); Kathleen; Sheila **ED:** PhD in Philosophy, University of California San Diego (1970); MA in Philosophy, University of California San Diego (1967); MS in Marine Oceanography, Scripps Institution of Oceanography, La Jolla, CA (1964); BS in Zoology and Chemistry, University of Utah, Salt Lake City, Utah (1960) **C:** Professor Emeritus, University of Notre Dame, Notre Dame, IL (2010-Present); Faculty Member, Moreau College Initiative, Westville Prison, Holy Cross College Notre Dame, IN (2013-Present); Elevated to Full Professor, Program of Liberal Studies/Program in History and Philosophy of Science, University of Notre Dame, Notre Dame, IN (1991-2010); Chair, Program of Liberal Studies, University of Notre Dame, Notre Dame, IL (2002-2004); Director, Program in Science, Technology, and Values, University of Notre Dame, Notre Dame, IL (1999-2002); Director, Reilly Center for Science, Technology and Values, Acting Director, Science, Technology and Values, University of Notre Dame, Notre Dame, IN (1997-1999); Chair, Program of Liberal Studies, University of Notre Dame, Notre Dame, IN (1985-1992); Associate Professor, Program of Liberal Studies/Program in History and Philosophy of Science, University of Notre Dame, Notre Dame, IL (1979-1991); Assistant Professor, Program of Liberal Studies/Program in History and Philosophy of Sci-

ence, University of Notre Dame (1974-1979); Assistant Professor, Department of Biomedical History, University of Washington School of Medicine, Seattle, WA (1972-1974); Instructor, Department of Biomedical History, University of Washington School of Medicine, Seattle, WA (1969-1972); Teaching Assistant, Muir College History and Philosophy of Science Course (1968-1969); Advanced Research Technician, Deep Sea Biology, U.S. Naval Undersea Laboratory, San Diego, CA (1966-1968); Teaching Assistant, Humanities at Revelle College, University of California San Diego(1966-1967); Advanced Research Technician, Plant Physiology, Institute of Marine Resources, Scripps Institution of Oceanography, La Jolla, CA (1964-1965); Graduate Research Assistant, Deep Sea Biology, Scripps Institution of Oceanography (1960-1964); Expedition Biologist, Lusiad Expedition (International Indian Ocean Expedition) (1963) **CR:** Regular Faculty Member, Moreau College Initiative, Westville Prison, Holy Cross College Notre Dame, IN (2013-Present); Member, Participant, Vatican Pontifical Council Science Theology & Ontological Quest Project (2008-2013); President, International Association of Core Texts and Courses (2002-2008) **MIL:** With, United States Naval Reserve (1955-1963) **CW:** Essay Review, "Life Science and Naturphilosophie: Rethinking the Relationship," Studies in History and Philosophy of Science (2019); Author, Contributor, "Locating the Human in the Biological World: A Way into the Species Problem," Philosophie, Histoire, et Biologie (2018); Co-author and Contributor, "Darwin in the Twenty-First Century: Nature, Humanity, God," Notre Dame (2015); Editorial Board, Isis (2010-2013); Editor and Contributor, "Creating a Physical Biology: the Three-Man Paper and the Origins of Molecular Biology," Chicago (2011); Editorial Board, Journal of the History of Biology (2009-2013); Contributor, "Kant and British Bioscience, Understanding Purpose: Kant and the Philosophy of Biology," North American Kant Studies (2007); Author and Contributor, "Controlling Our Destinies: Philosophical, Historical and Theological Perspectives on the Human Genome Project," Notre Dame (2000); Author, Richard Owen's Hunterian Lectures at the Royal College of Surgeons, May-June 1837 (1992); Co-author, "From Natural History to the History of Nature: Readings from Buffon and his Critics," Notre Dame (1981); Editorial Board, Nineteenth Century Contexts; Editorial Board, Omega: Indian Journal for the Association for Science and Religion; Author, Contributor, Numerous Refereed Research Articles; Numerous Articles in Reference Works; Numerous Conference Presentations **AW:** Phillip R. Sloan Annual Award, Notre Dame Reilly Center for Science, Technology and Values for Graduate Student Outstanding Work in History and Philosophy of Science (2010-Present); University of Notre Dame Joyce Teaching Award (2010); Presidential Award of the University of Notre Dame for Service (2004); Elected Fellow, Section L, American Association for the Advancement of Science (1995); Medal of Merit, Museum National d'Histoire Naturelle, Paris, France (1994) **MEM:** American Association for the Advancement of Science; History of Science Society; International Society for the History, Philosophy and Social Studies of Biology (ISHPSSB); Association for Core Texts and Courses (ACTC) **MH:** Albert Nelson Marquis Lifetime Achievement Award; Marquis Who's Who Top Professional; Marquis Who's Who Humanitarian Award **AS:** Dr. Sloan attributes his success to a loving family, which includes a father who stimulated his intellectual interests, to inspirational teachers and mentors at crucial moments among whom he particularly notes a modest German tailor, Manfred Koesling, who introduced him to philosophy and to the world of

Beethoven and Bach. He also credits inspirational undergraduate teachers Stephen Durant (Zoology), James Sugihara (Chemistry), Jack Adamson (English) and inspiring graduate teachers Edward Fager (Biological Oceanography) and Richard Popkin (Philosophy). Beyond this, it has been the faculty and students in the Program of Liberal Studies at Notre Dame, especially Stephen Rogers and Mary Katherine Tillman. And behind his complex career was his loving wife of over 50 years, Sharon Lee Borg Sloan, and his family, whose support made this possible. **B/I:** Dr. Sloan became involved in his profession from an early love of books and science, through education in both science and later in the humanities, with encounters at crucial moments with inspiring teachers and mentors. **AV:** Piano playing; Birdwatching; Reading and re-reading the "Great Books"; Enjoying the delights of a large and loving family **PA:** Democrat **RE:** Roman Catholic **THT:** Dr. Sloan has 10 grandchildren, Angela Liskey, Dante Knapp, Sean Mabry, Derek Mabry, Alanna Mabry, Siovhan Sloan-Evans, Pauline Sloan-Evans Holly Malerba, Gabriele Malerba, and Cole Malerba. He has seven great-grandchildren, Owen Liskey, Ella Liskey, Rosalie Liskey, Violet Liskey, Adrian Mabry, Lyra Mabry, and Jade Mabry. He was raised in the Church of Jesus Christ of Latter Day Saints, but converted in 1960 to Roman Catholicism. He says, "My career following undergraduate education included active scientific research in deep-sea biology and plant physiology, followed by a long vocation as a professor of history and philosophy of science and humanistic studies. I have been inspired by the delight of teaching in an integrated liberal studies program at Notre Dame (the Program of Liberal Studies) and my work more broadly as an educator in integrated liberal arts education. I consider myself indeed blessed by good fortune by the love of family and friends. I am closing my career both with major research projects, and with teaching students from deeply disadvantaged circumstances. Key events in my life have often produced great changes in direction, but always with a deeper integration eventually emerging. I have been able to spend my professional life studying the great minds of history, especially Aristotle, Plato, Augustine, Descartes, Pascal, Newton, Kant and Darwin, and I have been greatly enriched by my study of more recent authors- especially Dostoyevsky, Edmund Husserl, Viktor Frankl, and Michael Polanyi, and by the writings of such profound voices as Eva Brann, of St. John's College, Annapolis and Leon Kass, of the University of Chicago. From these diverse and sometimes conflicting voices, I have been able to see the richness of the human person in all its dimensions, a vision I would like to transmit to others as a way of dealing with the complexities of the twenty-first century. My recent teaching in a local prison has made me appreciate even more the privileged life I have had. So much of what my life has been has been through the assistance and encouragement of others in ways they may not realize, especially the two wonderful women who have been with me on this journey, Sharon Sloan and Mary Katherine Tillman, and my supportive family. Through these people, and from my own researches, I have been able to come to what for me has been a resolution of some of the great questions of life. Much of my career has been a search for a deeper integration of issues of my Catholic faith and my work in science and philosophy."

SLOAN, TIMOTHY J., T: Chief Executive Officer **I:** Financial Services **CN:** Wells Fargo & Company **ED:** MBA in Finance and Accounting, University of Michigan, Ann Arbor, MI; BA in Economics and History, University of Michigan, Ann Arbor, MI

C: Chief Executive Officer, Wells Fargo & Company (2016-Present); President, Well Fargo & Company (2015-Present); Chief Operating Officer, Wells Fargo & Company (2015-2016); Senior Executive Vice President, Chief Financial Officer, Wells Fargo & Company, San Francisco, CA (2011-2014); Senior Vice President, Chief Administrative Officer, Corporate Communications, Social Responsibility and Human Resources, Enterprise Marketing, Government Relations and Strategic Planning, Wells Fargo & Company, San Francisco, CA (2010-2011); Head, Commercial Bank, Real Estate and Specialized Finance Services, Wells Fargo & Company, San Francisco, CA (2006-2010); Manager, Real Estate Merchant Banking Division, Wells Fargo & Company, San Francisco, CA (1994-1997); Senior Credit Officer, Group Head Real Estate Managed Assets Group, Wells Fargo & Company, San Francisco, CA (1991-1994); Vice President, Loan Adjustment Group, Wells Fargo & Company, San Francisco, CA (1987-1991); Banker, Continental Illinois Bank, Chicago, IL (1984-1987); Group Head, Specialized Finance Services, Wells Fargo & Company, San Francisco, CA **CIV:** Board of Overseers, Huntington Library; Board Member, Jardin de la Infancia Charter School; Associate Trustee, San Marino Schools Foundation; Member, Corporate Advisory Board, University of Michigan Ross School of Business

SLOANE ROEMER, ELAINE, T: Real Estate Broker **I:** Real Estate **DOB:** 04/23/1938 **PB:** New York **SC:** NY/USA **PT:** David Sloane; Marion (Frauenthal) Sloane **MS:** Married **SPN:** David Frank Roemer (06/21/1959) **CH:** Michelle Sloane Wolf; Alan Sloane Roemer **ED:** MEd, University of Miami, Coral Gables, FL (1963); BBA, University of Florida, Gainesville, FL (1959); BBA in Marketing, Educational Administration & Supervision **CT:** Licensed Real Estate Broker (1981-Present); Certified Financial Planner; Previously Licensed Mortgage Broker; Certified Teacher in Elementary School Education, Math Administration and Supervision; Certified Teacher in Business Education, Vocation Technical Education, and Economics **C:** Real Estate Broker, Miami, FL (1978-Present); Teacher, Mathematics, Saint Leo College, Miami, FL (1991-1992); Teacher, Education, Florida International University, Miami, FL (1977-1980); Teacher, Mathematics and Business, Miami Dade Community College (Miami Dade College), Miami, FL (1968-1980); Teacher, Mathematics and Business, Miami-Dade County Public Schools, Miami, FL (1959-1980); Teacher, Mathematics, Southwood Junior High School (Southwood Middle School) (1978-1979); Teacher, Mathematics, Palmetto Junior High School (Palmetto Middle School) (1975-1976); Teacher, Business Education and Mathematics, Miami Palmetto Senior High School (1970-1974); Curriculum Specialist, Cutler Ridge Elementary School (1968-1969); Acting Assistant Principal of Curriculum, Classroom Teacher, Science, Social Studies, and Mathematics, Glades Junior High School (Glades Middle School) (1964-1965); Instructor, Teacher, Numerous Schools **CR:** Instructor, Introduction to Algebra, Saint Leo College (1992); Mortgage Broker, Miami, FL (1986); Instructor, Mathematics for Elementary School Teachers, Florida International University (1982); Speaker in the Field **CW:** Contributor, Articles to Professional Journals **MEM:** President, Kendall-Perrine Association of Realtors (1995); Honor Society, Florida Association of Realtors (1995); Representative, District 4, Florida Association of Realtors (1992-1995); Secretary, Treasurer, Kendall-Perrine Association of Realtors (1992-1993); Board of Directors, Kendall-Perrine Association of Realtors (1991-1992); Arbitration Committee, Kendall-Perrine Association of Realtors (1991); Grievance Committee, Kendall-Perrine Associa-

tion of Realtors (1990); National Association of Realtors; National Education Association; Florida Education Commission; Classroom Teachers Association; Dade County Education Association; Florida Council of Teachers of Mathematics; Florida Business Education Association; Association of Classroom Educators; Dade County Association of School Administrators; Association for Supervision and Curriculum Development (ASCD); Alpha Delta Kappa **MH:** Albert Nelson Marquis Lifetime Achievement Award **B/I:** Mrs. Roemer became involved in her profession because she was living in a small town in Florida, went to college at the university and had family in NY. Her mother's side of the family was prominent financially and in business, and she was going to present herself in NY, as one of the relatives was head of federated stores. She had never met him but she was going to present herself and he would make her vice president. She went to the University of Florida and majored in business and marketing. She would go in summers to Miami and worked to gain experience; she ended up finishing college. She was completely against going into education but tried nonetheless and was hired to work in a rural area teaching first and second grade combination. She was later relocated and continued teaching. She started investing when she was teaching and her first property was her condo.

SLOTKIN, ELISSA BLAIR, T: U.S. Representative from Michigan **I:** Government Administration/ Government Relations/Government Services **CN:** U.S. House of Representatives **DOB:** 07/10/1976 **PB:** New York **SC:** NY/USA **PT:** Judith (Spitz) Slotkin **MS:** Married **SPN:** David Moore **CH:** Two Stepdaughters **ED:** Master of Arts, Columbia University School of International and Public Affairs (2003); Intern, U.S. Department of State (2002); Bachelor of Arts, Cornell University (1988) **CT:** Completed, Arabic Language, American University in Cairo (2001) **C:** Member, U.S. House of Representatives from Michigan's Eighth Congressional District, United States Congress, Washington, DC (2019-Present); Owner, Pinpoint Consulting (2017); Assistant Secretary of Defense, International Affairs (2014-2017); Assistant Secretary of Defense, International Security Affairs (2015-2017); Principal Deputy Assistant Secretary of Defense, International Security Affairs (2014-2015); Principal Deputy Under Secretary of Defense for Policy (2013-2014); Principal Deputy Assistant Secretary of Defense for Policy (2012-2013); Chief of Staff for the Assistant Secretary of Defense for Policy (2012); Adviser, Middle East Policy, Under Secretary of Defense for Policy (2011-2012); Senior Advisor, Iraq Policy, U.S. State Department (2009-2011); Staff Director, Iraq Policy, National Security Council (2007-2009); Leader, Assessment Team, Central Intelligence Agency, Iraq (2006-2007); Senior Assistant, Staff of Director of National Intelligence (2005-2006); Intelligence Briefer, Central Intelligence Agency (2004-2005); Political Analyst, Central Intelligence Agency (2003-2004) **CR:** Grant Writer, Isha L'Isha (2000-2001); Swahili Language Translator, Harbor Area Early Childhood, MA (1999-2000); Community Organizer, Roca Incorporated, MA (1998-2000)

SMALL, JAMES WILLIAM, T: Occupational and Public Health Physician (Retired) **I:** Medicine & Health Care **DOB:** 01/23/1951 **PB:** Lincoln **SC:** NE/USA **PT:** LaVerne D. Small; Nora C. Small **MS:** Married **SPN:** Susan E. Small **CH:** James J.; Nicole E. **ED:** MBA, Chadwick University (2004); Master of Medical Management, Tulane University (1999); Resident in Preventive Medicine, Walter Reed Army Institute of Research, Washington, DC (1984-1985); MPH, Johns Hopkins University (1984);

Intern in Neurology, Walter Reed National Military Medical Center, Washington, DC (1982-1983); MD, University of Nebraska Omaha (1982); BA, University of Nebraska Lincoln, with Distinction (1973) **CT:** Certified in General Preventive Medicine/Public Health and in Occupational Medicine, American Board of Preventive Medicine; Certified Physician Executive, Certifying Commission of the American College of Physician Executives; Formerly Certified in Health Care Quality and Management, American Board of Quality Assurance and Utilization Review Physicians (ABQAURP) **C:** Retired (2017); Chief Medical Officer, Texas Medicaid, Aetna (Aetna Better Health of Texas), Dallas, Texas (2013-2017); Senior Medical Director, Amerigroup Corporation, Grand Prairie, Texas (2007-2013); Senior Medical Director, Intracorp (Subsidiary of Cigna), Carrollton, Texas (2003-2007); Vice President of Medical Operations for the Southeast Region, Concentra Health Services, Atlanta, GA (1999-2003); Regional Medical Director, Concentra Health Services, Houston, Texas (1997-1999); Executive Medical Director, WorkMed Occupational Health Network, Tulsa, OK (1989-1997); Resident in Occupational Medicine, The University of Oklahoma (1989-1991); Chief Preventive Medicine III Corps, United States Army, Fort Hood, Texas (1986-1989); Epidemiologist, United States Army, Washington, DC (1985-1986) **CR:** Leader, Dallas - Fort Worth Physician Executive Network, Affiliated with the American College of Physician Executives (2007-2009); President, Oklahoma College of Occupational and Environmental Physicians, Chapter of the American College of Occupational and Environmental Physicians (Now American College of Occupational and Environmental Medicine (ACOEM)) (1996-1997); Adjunct Faculty, Occupational Medicine Instructor, Department of Family Practice, The University of Oklahoma Health Science Center, Tulsa, OK (1990-1997) **CIV:** Volunteer Veteran Mentor for Veterans being Treated in North Texas Veterans Treatment Court **MIL:** Retired Lieutenant Colonel, Oklahoma Army National Guard (1997); With, Oklahoma Army National Guard (1990-1997); Medical Battalion Commander, 120th Medical Battalion, Oklahoma Army National Guard (1994-1996); Medical Company Commander, 145th Medical Company, Oklahoma Army National Guard (1991-1994); With, United States Army Reserve (1989-1990); Resigned, Active United States Army (1989); Advanced Through Grades to Major, United States Army (1986); Personnel Officer, 101st Airborne Division, Oklahoma Army National Guard (1975-1976); Served, Infantry and Adjutant General, United States Army, Fort Campbell, KY (1973-1976); Infantry Platoon Leader, 101st Airborne Division, Oklahoma Army National Guard (1974-1975); Commissioned Second Lieutenant, United States Army (1973) **AW:** Named to America's Top Physicians, Consumers Research Council of America (2010, 2011, 2012, 2014); Meritorious Medals (1989, 1996); Army Commendation Medal, Gulf War (1991, 1995); Citation, Who's Who Among Rising Young Americans, American Society and Business (1992); Army Commendation Medal (1976, 1986) **MEM:** Fellow, American College of Occupational and Environmental Medicine (ACOEM); Fellow, American College of Preventive Medicine; Fellow, American College of Physician Executives (Now American Association for Physician Leadership (AAPL)); Life Member, Military Officers Association of America; Military Order of the World Wars; Veterans of Foreign Wars (VFW); The American Legion; American College of Physician Executives (Now American Association for Physician Leadership (AAPL)); National Rifle Association of America; Former Fellow, American Board of Quality Assurance and Utilization Review Physicians (ABQAURP); Stonebriar Com-

munity Church **MH:** Albert Nelson Marquis Lifetime Achievement Award **AS:** Dr. Small attributes his success to his faith and trust in Christ. He also credits his parents, wife, family and friends. **B/I:** Dr. Small became interested in psychology and ended up in military. He also wanted to help people. **AV:** Martial arts: Judo and Karate; Pistol shooting; Piano; Reading; Gardening; Swimming **PA:** Republican **RE:** Christian **THT:** Dr. Small's motto is, "Seek wisdom, trust God, and do your best. Think beyond yourself."

SMITH, ADRIAN MICHAEL, T: U.S. Representative from Nebraska; Real Estate Agent **I:** Government Administration/Government Relations/Government Services **DOB:** 12/19/1970 **PB:** Scottsbluff **SC:** NE/USA **MS:** Married **SPN:** Andrea McDaniel (2014) **CH:** One Child **ED:** BS in Marketing Education, University of Nebraska-Lincoln (1993); Coursework, Liberty University, Lynchburg, VA **C:** Member, U.S. House of Representatives from Nebraska's Third Congressional District, United States Congress, Washington, DC (2007-Present); Assistant Whip, United States Congress (2007-Present); Member, District 48, Nebraska Legislature, Lincoln, NE (1998-Present); Real Estate Agent, Marketing Specialist, Buyers Realty (1997-Present); Educator, Staff Development Project Manager, Educational Service Unit 13 (1994-1997); Research Assistant, University of Nebraska Foundation (1992-1993); Staff International, Marketing Specialist, Governor's Office, NE (1992); Legislative Page, Nebraska Legislature (1992); Member, Committee on Ways and Means, United States Congress **CIV:** Member, Gering City Council, NE (1994-1998); Member, Scotts Bluff County Visitors Advisory Committee (1995-1996); Board of Directors, Twin Cities Development; Chairman, Land Use Task Force, Vision 2020; Member, WyoBraska Natural History Museum; Member, Western Nebraska Regional Airport Operations Board; Member, Calvary Memorial Evangelical Free Church **MEM:** Board of Directors, Camp Kiwanis, Scottsbluff Kiwanis Club; Farm & Ranch Museum Association (Now Legacy of the Plains Museum); Riverside Zoological Society (Now Riverside Discovery Center); North Platte Valley Historical Society; Western Nebraska Board of Realtors, Scottsbluff, NE; Scottsbluff Kiwanis Club **PA:** Republican

SMITH, BARRY H., MD, PHD, T: President, Chief Executive Officer **I:** Medicine & Health Care **CN:** Rogosin Institute **DOB:** 10/06/1943 **PB:** Orange **SC:** NJ/USA **PT:** Kenneth Wright Smith; Harriet (Barr) Smith **MS:** Married **SPN:** Carley Eldredge Smith (12/13/1969) **CH:** Christopher; Sara **ED:** Resident, Massachusetts General Hospital, Boston, MA (1975-1978); Intern, Resident, New York Hospital, New York, NY (1971-1975); MD, Cornell University (1972); PhD in Neuroscience, Massachusetts Institute of Technology (1968); BA in Psychology, Harvard University (1965) **C:** President, Chief Executive Officer, Rogosin Institute (2008-Present); Director, Dreyfus Health Foundation, New York, NY (1988-Present); Director, Science and Medical, Dreyfus Medical Foundation, New York, NY (1983-1988); Deputy Director, Surgical Neurology Branch, National Institutes of Health, Bethesda, MD (1978-1983); Program Director, Neurosciences Research Program, Massachusetts Institute of Technology (1975-1978); Practicing Physician **CR:** Member, Dreyfus Charitable Foundation (2008-Present); President, Chief Executive Officer, Rogosin Institute (2008); Professor of Surgery, Cornell University, Peking University Medical College with Public Health System Research Panel, U.S. Department of Health and Human Services (2007-2008); Senior Vice President, Rogosin Institute (1998-2008); Active, CMS/CMMI Panels Related to

Kidney Care Models (Present and Ongoing); Chair, Board of Directors, Rogosin-Methodist Home for Nursing and Rehabilitation Dialysis Joint Venture; Reviewer, Numerous Journals, Including Journal of Neuro-Oncology **CIV:** Board Chair, Global Health Action (2006-2018); Board of Directors, Treasurer, Desmond Tutu Peace Foundation; Secretary, Kornfeld Foundation; Chair, Numerous Other Positions, New York City Rescue Mission **MIL:** Cmdr., Commissioned Corps of the U.S. Public Health Service (1978-1983) **CW:** Co-Editor, "Problem Solving for Better Health: A Global Perspective" (2011); Editor, Encyclopedia of the Neuroscience (1995-2005); Contributor, "Problem Solving for Better Health: A Manual (in Chinese)"; Contributor, Articles, Professional Journals **AW:** National Organization for the Advancement of Haitians (NOAH) Achievement Award (2018); Humanitarian Awards, Methodist Home for Nursing and Rehabilitation (2017); Equal Employment Opportunity Award (1983); Commendation Medal Award, U.S. Public Health Service (1982); Numerous Awards, Different Countries Around the World (1980s) **MEM:** American Medical Association; American Association for the Advancement of Science; American Public Health Association; American Association for Cancer Research (AACR); American Society of Nephrology; Society of Critical Care Medicine (SCCM); American Society of Clinical Oncology (ASCO); Phi Beta Kappa; Sigma Xi; Alpha Omega Alpha; Numerous Others **MH:** Albert Nelson Marquis Lifetime Achievement Award; Marquis Who's Who Top Professional **AS:** Mr. Smith attributes his success to Professor F. Francis Schmidt at MIT, Dr. Albert L. Rubin, the founder of Rogosin Institute, and Jack J. Dreyfus, a good friend who helped with the work they did internationally in 32 countries over the course of 20 years and the man who founded the Dreyfus & Co. and the Dreyfus Fund. **AV:** Sailing; Writing **PA:** Independent **RE:** Christian

SMITH, BILL, "DEACON BILL" RICHARD, T: Deacon **I:** Religious **CN:** Jesuit Restorative Justice Initiative (JRJI) **DOB:** 06/24/1940 **PB:** New York **SC:** NY/USA **YOP:** 80 **PT:** Harry John Smith; Catharine Marie (Wheeler) Smith **MS:** Married **SPN:** Judith Ann Smith (03/18/1961) **CH:** Shawn; Kevin; Susan; Kurt; Eric **ED:** Doctor of Ministry, Aquinas Institute of Theology (2015); ThM in Theology, Catholic Distance University, Summa Cum Laude (2008); MPA, Golden Gate University (1982); MS, United States Naval Postgraduate School (1971); BA, Iona College (1962) **CT:** Certified City Manager; Certified California Special District Manager; Ordained Catholic Deacon **C:** Chief of Staff, Jesuit Restorative Justice Initiative (JRJI) (2013-Present); Regional Assistant to Catholic Bishop, Santa Barbara Pastoral Region, CA (2005-2013); General Manager, Ventura Regional Sanitation District (VRSD) (1997-2005); City Manager, City of Westminster, CA (1994-1997); City Manager, City of Manhattan Beach, CA (1990-1994); Assistant City Manager, City of Monterey, CA (1986-1990); City Administrator, City of Sonora, CA (1984-1986); Administrative Analyst, City of Monterey, CA (1982-1984) **CR:** Adjunct Professor Golden Gate University, San Francisco, CA (1984-1990); Instructor, United States Naval Postgraduate School, Monterey, CA (1979-1982) **CIV:** Board of Directors, Monterey County AIDS Project (1987-1990) **MIL:** Lieutenant Colonel, United States Marine Corps (1962-1982) **CW:** Author, "Proclaiming the Gospel to the Troops: Toward a Resource in Social Research"; Contributor, Articles to Professional Journals **AW:** Decorated Silver Star; Bronze Star; Purple Heart w/Gold Star; Defense Meritorious Service Medal; Joint Service Commendation Medal with Gold Star; Navy Commendation Medal; Army Commendation Medal; Vietnamese Medal of Honor; Vietnamese Cross of Gallantry **MEM:** Chapter President, American Society for Public Administration (1983-1984); International City Managers Association (Now ICMA); Retired Officers Association (Now Military Officers Association of America); Disabled American Veterans (DAV); VFW; The American Legion **MH:** Albert Nelson Marquis Lifetime Achievement Award; Marquis Who's Who Top Professional; Marquis Who's Who Humanitarian Award **AS:** Dr. Smith attributes his success to perseverance and family. **B/I:** Dr. Smith has had a number of professions. His religious involvement came as a calling from God that he felt compelled to answer. He felt the calling for many years until eventually he could no longer avoid it. **THT:** Dr. Smith is the Chaplin of the Second Battalion, Third Marines Vietnam Veterans Association.

SMITH, CHARLES W., MD, T: Professor, Family Medicine **I:** Medicine & Health Care **CN:** Dr. Smith Direct Care **DOB:** 04/15/1949 **PB:** Fort Lauderdale **SC:** FL/USA **PT:** Charles Wilson Smith; Ida Meadow Smith **MS:** Married **SPN:** Constance K. Smith **CH:** Thaddeus; Cameron; Amber; Isaac; Jordan; Rachael **ED:** Bachelor of Science, University of North Carolina (1979); Doctor of Medicine, University of North Carolina (1974) **CT:** Diplomate, American Board of Family Practice **C:** Founder, Dr. Smith Direct Care (2019-Present); Professor of Family and Community Medicine, University of Arkansas for Medical Sciences, Little Rock, AR (1989-Present); Executive Associate Dean for Clinical Affairs, University of Arkansas for Medical Sciences, Little Rock, AR (1989-2015); Executive Director, Faculty Practice Plan, University of Arkansas for Medical Sciences College of Medicine, Little Rock, AR (1991-1997); Associate Dean, University of Arkansas for Medical Sciences College of Medicine, Huntsville, AL (1986-1989); Associate Dean of Clinical Affairs, University of Alabama, Huntsville, AL (1986-1987); Chief of Family Medicine, University of Alabama School of Primary Medical Care, Huntsville, AL (1986-1987); Acting Dean, University of Alabama, Huntsville, AL (1986); Associate Professor, Wright State University (1983-1986); Assistant Professor, Wright State University (1979-1983); Private Practice, Muscatine, LA (1978-1979); Resident in Family Practice, University of North Carolina Memorial Hospital (1975-1978); Resident in Psychiatry, University of North Carolina Memorial Hospital (1974-1975); Founder, Principal Owner, Medical Director, DocAmerica LLC **CR:** Director, Family Practice Residency Program, Miami Valley Hospital, Dayton, OH (1979-1986) **CIV:** Board of Directors, Nicholas J. Pisacano Foundation (1990-1994) **CW:** Deputy Editor, American Family Physician (1987-2004); Editor, Primary Care Currents (1985-1997); Co-author, "Family Practice Desk Reference," Second Edition (1995); Contributor, Numerous Articles to Professional Journals **AW:** Leadership in Family Medicine Award (2019); Small Business of the Year, eDocAmerica (2010) **MEM:** Board of Directors, Committee Member, Treasurer, President, American Board of Family Practice (1991-1992); American Medical Association; Magazine Editor, American Academy of Family Physicians; Arkansas Academy of Family Physicians; Arkansas Medical Association; Pulaski County Medical Society; Society of Teachers of Family Medicine **MH:** Albert Nelson Marquis Lifetime Achievement Award **B/I:** Dr. Smith became involved in his profession because his mother and sisters were in the teaching profession and his dad was a minister. He was inspired to help others through them and it led him to the medical vocation. **AV:** Biking; Fishing; Reading; Writing

SMITH, CHRISTINE, "TINA" ELIZABETH, T: U.S. Senator **I:** Government Administration/Government Relations/Government Services **DOB:** 03/04/1958 **PB:** Albuquerque **SC:** NM/USA **PT:** F. Harlan Flint; Christine Flint **MS:** Married **SPN:** Archie Smith **CH:** Sam; Mason **ED:** MBA, Tuck School of Business, Dartmouth College; Bachelor's Degree in Political Science, Stanford University **C:** U.S. Senator, State of Minnesota (2018-Present); Lieutenant Governor, State of Minnesota (2015-2019); Chief of Staff to Mark Dayton, State of Minnesota (2011-2015); Chief of Staff to R.T. Ryback, State of Minnesota; Founder, Marketing and Communications Firm; Vice President, External Affairs, Planned Parenthood of Minnesota, North Dakota and South Dakota; With, Trans-Alaska Pipeline, Prudhoe Bay, AK **AW:** One of America's Top 25 Most Influential Women in State Politics, Roll Call (2016) **PA:** Democrat

SMITH, CHRISTOPHER, "CHRIS", T: U.S. Representative **I:** Government Administration/Government Relations/Government Services **DOB:** 03/04/1953 **PB:** Rahway **SC:** NJ/USA **PT:** Bernard Henry Smith; Katherine Joan (Hall) Smith **MS:** Married **SPN:** Marie Hahn (07/02/1977) **CH:** Melissa; Christopher; Michael; Elyse **ED:** BA in Business Administration, Trenton State College (Now The College of New Jersey), NJ (1975); Coursework, Worcester College, England (1973-1974) **C:** U.S. Representative, New Jersey's Fourth Congressional District, United States Congress, Washington, DC (1981-Present); Legislative Agent, New Jersey General Assembly (1979); Director, Institutional Sales, Leisure Unlimited Inc., Woodbridge, NJ (1978-1980); Executive Director, New Jersey Right to Life Committee, Inc. (1976-1978); Member, Congressional-Executive Commission on China; Co-Chair, Pro-Life Caucus, United States Congress; Ranking Member, Commission on Security and Cooperation in Europe, United States Congress; Member, Committee on Foreign Affairs and International Relations, United States Congress **CR:** U.S. Representative, International Conference on Immunizing World's Children, United Nations **CIV:** Co-Chair, Coalition for Autism Research and Education; Former Chair, Commission on Security and Cooperation in Europe; Active Member, Human Rights Movements, Romania, China, Vietnam, Former Soviet Union **AW:** George "Buck" Gillispie Award for Meritorious Service, Blinded American Veterans Foundation (2003); William Wilberforce Award (2002); Leader of the Year, New Jersey State Postal Workers Union (2002); Legislator of the Year, Jewish War Veterans of the United States of America (1996); Legislator of the Year, International Chiropractors Association; Leader for Peace Award, Peace Corps; Eagle Scout Award **MEM:** National Federation of Independent Business **PA:** Republican **RE:** Roman Catholic

SMITH, DAISY MULLETT, T: Publisher **I:** Publishing **CN:** Mullett-Smith Press **DOB:** 08/17/1948 **PB:** Washington **SC:** DC/USA **PT:** Gordon Hunt Smith; Suzanne Myrick (Mullett) Smith **MS:** Single **ED:** BA, American University (1970) **CT:** Certification in Records Management, ARMA International (1987); Certification in Computer Programming, University of Southern California (1986) **C:** Typesetting Publisher, Mullett-Smith Press (2004-Present); Owner, Mullett-Smith Press (1989-Present); Web Weaver, Mullett-Smith Press (1996-Present); Music Copyist, Publisher, Mullett-Smith Press (1990-2018); Editor, Computer Specialist, Desktop Publisher, Mullett-Smith Press (1984-1989); Christian Science Practitioner, The First Church of Christ 1970-1986); Counselor, Christian Science Campus, American University (1976-1981); Clerk, Fifth Church of Christ (1971-1974) **CR:** Consultant; Speaker in Field **CIV:** Active Member, Save the Pioneer Post Office, Portland, OR (1996-Present); Historical Townhouse Wheat Row (2003-2010); Commissioner, Jefferson County, WV (2003); Christian Science Reading Room (1999-2002); Fundraising Committee, Bill Restoration Fund, U.S. Treasury (1998-2000); Participant, White House Conference on Children (1970); Interviewer, PBS Radio **CW:** Author, Editor, "A.B. Mullett: His Relevance in American Architecture and Historic Preservation" (1990); Editor, "A.B. Mullett, Architect Engineer 1862-1890"; Contributor, Articles, Professional Journals **AW:** Key to the City, Mayor of Lincoln, NE (1989) **MEM:** Web Host, National Society of Arts and Letters (2006-2010); Web Weaver, National Society of Arts and Letters (1996-2010); Treasurer, National Society of Arts and Letters (1988-1990); Editor, Publishing Directory, National Society of Arts and Letters (1971-2006); National Trust for Historic Preservation; ARMA International; AIIM; Treasury Historical Association; United States Capitol Historical Society **MH:** Albert Nelson Marquis Lifetime Achievement Award; Marquis Who's Who Top Professional **B/I:** Ms. Smith became involved in her profession because she found the diaries of A.B. Mullett, her mother's grandfather, in her home. She decided to publish the work she found and has never looked back. **AV:** Windsurfing; Enjoying art; Playing guitar

SMITH, DAVID, "ADAM" ADAM, T: U.S. Representative from Washington **I:** Government Administration/Government Relations/Government Services **DOB:** 06/15/1965 **PB:** Washington **SC:** DC/USA **PT:** Ben Smith; Leila Smith **SPN:** Sara (Bickle-Elderidge) Smith (08/1993) **CH:** Kendall; Jack **ED:** JD, University of Washington School of Law (1990); BA in Political Science, Fordham University, Bronx, NY (1987); Coursework, Western Washington University **C:** Chair, House Armed Services Committee (2019-Present); Member, U.S. House Select Committee on the Events Surrounding the 2012 Terrorist Attack in Benghazi (2014-Present); Member, U.S. House of Representatives from Washington's Ninth Congressional District, United States Congress, Washington, DC (1997-Present); Ranking Member, U.S. House Armed Services Committee, Washington, DC (2011-2019); Judge Pro Tempore, Seattle City Attorney's Office, Seattle, WA (1996); Prosecutor, Seattle City Attorney's Office, Seattle, WA (1993-1995); Attorney, Cromwell, Mendoza and Belur, Kent, WA (1991-1992); Chair, Law and Justice Committee, Washington State Senate (1993-1997); Member, District 33, Washington State Senate (1990-1996); Driver, United Parcel Service of America, Inc. (1985-1987) **CIV:** Member, Kent Drinking Driver Task Force; Member, Highline Citizens for Schools; Member, Kent-Meridian HS Site-Based Council; Board of Directors, Judson Park Retirement Home **MEM:** Kiwanis International **PA:** Democrat

SMITH, DAVID, "D. BROOKS SMITH" BROOKMAN, T: Chief Judge **I:** Law and Legal Services **CN:** United States Court of Appeals for the Third Circuit **DOB:** 12/04/1951 **PB:** Altoona **SC:** PA/USA **ED:** JD, The Pennsylvania State University Dickinson Law (1976); BA, Franklin & Marshall College (1973) **C:** Chief Judge, United States Court of Appeals for the Third Circuit (2016-Present); Judge, United States Court of Appeals for the Third Circuit (2002-2016); Chief Judge, United States District Court for the Western District of Pennsylvania (2001-2002); Judge, United States District Court for the Western District of Pennsylvania (1988-2002); Judge, Court Common Pleas of Blair County, PA (1984-1988); Managing Partner, Jubelirer, Carothers, Krier, Halpern & Smith, Altoona, PA (1981-1983); Private Practice, Jubelirer, Carothers, Krier, Halpern & Smith, Altoona, PA (1976-1984) **CR:** Committee on Space and Facilities, U.S. Judicial Conference (2006-Present); Advisory Committee on Criminal

Rules, U.S. Judicial Conference (1993-1999); Part-time District Attorney, Blair County, PA (1983-1984); Special Prosecutor, Blair County, PA (1981-1983); Part-time Assistant District Attorney, Blair County, PA (1977-1979) **CIV:** Trustee, Mount Aloysius College (2006-Present); Trustee, Philadelphia University (Now Thomas Jefferson University) (2005-2006); Trustee, St. Francis College (1992-2004) **MEM:** Board of Directors, Federal Judges Association (1993-1997, 2002); The American Law Institute; Pennsylvania Bar Association; American Judicature Society; The Pennsylvania Society; Amen Corner; Blair County Game, Fish and Forestry Association; Federal Judges Association; Inns of Court; Allegheny County Bar Association; Pi Gamma Mu Honor Society

SMITH, DAVID W., T: Reverend Doctor **I:** Religious **CN:** Wilton Maine First Congregational Church **DOB:** 03/27/1935 **PB:** Wakefield **SC:** MA/USA **PT:** Harold Smith; Eleanor Smith **MS:** Married **SPN:** Sally; Sarah (Deceased) **CH:** Derek; Matthew **ED:** Master's, Bangor Theological Seminary; Doctorate, Drew University, Madison, NJ; BS, University of Maine **C:** Reverend, First Congregational Church **CR:** Church Ad-Ministry Committee, Conference United Church, Maine **CIV:** Lions Club; Wilton Downtown Association; Wilton Ecumenical Church Organization; Farmington Area Ecumenical Ministry **MEM:** Historical Society of Wilton, ME; Historical Society of Farmington, ME **MH:** Marquis Who's Who Humanitarian Award **AS:** Reverend Smith attributes his success to family, education, a positive attitude towards life, and steadfast dedication to his profession. **B/I:** Reverend Smith became involved in his profession because although his father wanted him to go into engineering it was not working out for him. While he was sitting at a drafting board at North Eastern University he believed that God called him to be a minister. He had wonderful support from his family. **AV:** Model Trains; Painting Pictures; Reading **PA:** Independent **RE:** Protestant

SMITH, FRED, T: Chairman, President, Chief Executive Officer **I:** Consumer Goods and Services **CN:** FedEx Corporation **DOB:** 08/11/1944 **PB:** Marks **SC:** MS/USA **PT:** Frederick Smith; Sally (Wallace) Smith **MS:** Married **SPN:** Diane Avis; Linda Black Grisham (1969, Divorced 1977) **CH:** 10 Children **ED:** BS in Economics, Yale University (1966) **CT:** Certified Commercial Pilot **C:** Chairman, President, Chief Executive Officer, FedEx Corporation, Memphis, TN (1998-Present); Chairman, FedEx Corporation, Memphis, TN (1975-1998); Chief Executive Officer, FedEx Corporation, Memphis, TN (1977-1998); President, FedEx Corporation, Memphis, TN (1971-1975); Founder, FedEx Corporation, Memphis, TN (1971); Owner, Ark Aviation Sales (1970-1971) **CR:** Co-owner, Washington Redskins, NFL; Co-owner, Alcon Entertainment; Co-chairman, Energy Security Leadership Council (ESLC); Trustee, Center for Strategic and International Studies; Co-chairman, French-American Business Council; Former Chairman, US-China Business Council; Former Chairman, Board of Governors, International Air Transport Association, U.S. Air Transport Association **CIV:** Board Member, St. Jude Children's Research Hospital; Board Member, Mayo Foundation (Now Mayo Foundation for Medical Education and Research (MFMER); Co-chairman, National WWII Memorial Project; Co-chairman, Campaign, National Museum of the Marine Corps **MIL:** Honorably Discharged, United States Marine Corps (1969); Platoon Leader, Forward Air Controller, Captain, United States Marine Corps (1966-1969) **CW:** Appearance, "Cast Away" (2000) **AW:** Listed, Forbes 400: Richest Americans (2006-Present); Tony Jannus Award (2011); Bower Award for Business Leadership, The Franklin Institute (2008); Kellogg Award for Distinguished Leadership, Northwestern University Kellogg School of Management (2008); CEO of the Year, Chief Executive Magazine (2004); Champion of Workplace Learning and Performance Award, American Society for Training & Development (ASTD) (2002); Eagle of Aviation Award, Embry-Riddle Aeronautical Award (2001); Inductee, SMEI Sales & Marketing Hall of Fame (2000); Peter F. Drucker Strategic Leadership Award (1997); Inductee, Junior Achievement U.S. Business Hall of Fame (1998); Global Leadership Award, U.S.-India Business Council; George C. Marshall Foundation Award; Distinguished Business Leadership Award, Atlantic Council; Circle of Honor Award, Congressional Medal of Honor Foundation; Inductee, Aviation Hall of Fame; Two Purple Hearts; Bronze Star; Silver Star **MEM:** Business Roundtable; The Business Council; Former President, Delta Kappa Epsilon

SMITH, HARRIET G., EDUCATOR, T: Secondary School Educator, Writer **I:** Education/Educational Services **DOB:** 11/14/1927 **PB:** Goldsboro **SC:** NC/USA **PT:** Charles Harvey; Sadye Reid (Morris) Gurley **MS:** Widowed **SPN:** Albert Goodin Smith (08/29/1953, Deceased) **CH:** Susan Reid Smith Erba; Alan English Smith **ED:** Master of Education, Louisiana State University, Shreveport, LA (1982); Graduate, St. Mary's College, Raleigh, NC (1946); Bachelor of Arts, University of North Carolina (1948) **CT:** Certified Teacher, States of North Carolina, Louisiana **CIV:** Chairman, Various Committees (1970-Present); President, Faculty Women's Club, Louisiana State University Medical Center (1990); President, Shreveport Medical Society Auxiliary (1985-1986); Member, Women's Board of Directors, Centenary College; With, United Methodist Women; With, Symphony Guild; With, Opera Guild **MEM:** Teacher, Delegate to Russia, American Bridge Teachers Association (1994); Secretary, Bull and Bear Stock Club (1973-1974, 1975-1976); Life Master, Certified Teacher, American Contract Bridge League; Louisiana Real Estate Commission; Kappa Delta Pi **MH:** Albert Nelson Marquis Lifetime Achievement Award; Marquis Who's Who Top Professional **B/I:** Ms. Smith became involved in her profession due to a family tradition of entering the teaching vocation.

SMITH, JAMES EDWARD II, T: Microbiologist, Chemist **I:** Sciences **DOB:** 09/25/1950 **PB:** Salisbury **SC:** NC/USA **PT:** James Edward Smith; Mary Eugenia (Brown) Smith **MS:** Married **SPN:** Robin Elisabeth Zink (12/10/1977) **CH:** Susan Elizabeth; Jessica Katherine; Nathan Edward; Sarah Jedidah **ED:** MS, University of North Carolina (1982); BA, Catawba College (1972) **CT:** Certified Water Pollution Control Operator **C:** President, Aqua Pure Technologies Inc., Charlotte, NC (1990-Present); General Manager, Hydro Systems, Inc., Gastonia, NC (1985-1990); Manager, Water and Wastewater Division, The Perkinson Company, Inc., Charlotte, NC (1984-1985); Environmental/Analytical Chemist, City of Charlotte, NC (1974-1984) **CR:** Environmental Consultant, Smith Associates, Charlotte, NC (1985-1990); Adjunct Research Associate, University of North Carolina Charlotte, NC (1982-1985) **CW:** Patentee in Field **MEM:** The American Society for Microbiology; Technology Association Pulp & Paper Industry; American Radio Relay League, Sigma Xi, The Scientific Research Honor Society **MH:** Albert Nelson Marquis Lifetime Achievement Award **PA:** Republican **RE:** Baptist

SMITH, JAMES HOWELL, PHD, T: Historian, Educator (Retired) **I:** Education/Educational Services **CN:** Wake Forest University **DOB:** 07/17/1936 **PB:** Farmersville **SC:** TX/USA **PT:** Henry Howell Smith; Rosa Linda (Gladden) Smith **MS:** Married **SPN:** Jeanette Marie Chapman (09/02/1958) **CH:** Hilton Howell Smith; Susan Marie Dotson-Smith **ED:** Postdoctoral Coursework, Howard University (1969); PhD, University of Wisconsin (1968); MA, Tulane University (1961); BA, Baylor University (1958) **C:** Professor Emeritus, Wake Forest University (2007); Faculty, Wake Forest University, Winston-Salem, NC (1965-2007) **CR:** Visiting Faculty, Texas Christian University (1997-1998); Presenter, White House Conference on 25th Amendment (1996); Steering Committee, Work Group on the Disability of the President (25th Amendment) for the Carter Center Symposium and the Wake Forest University Symposium (1995); With, Wake Forest University London Program (1992); Founding Years, North Carolina School of the Arts, Winston-Salem, NC; Gardner-Webb University Extension Program **CIV:** Founder, President, Big Brothers/Sisters of Forsyth County, NC; Past North Carolina Coordinator, National Board, History Day Program, NC; Deacon Chair, Various Churches; Past President, Winston-Salem Torch Club; Former State Director, History Day Program, NC; Former Pre-Law Advisor, Past President, Southern Association of Pre-Law Advisors; Former Member, Visiting Committees, Southern Association of Colleges and Schools (SACS); The James W. Denmark Loan Committee, Wake Forest University **CW:** Contributor, Co-editor with Arthur S. Link & James Tool, "Presidential Disability: Papers, Discussions, and Recommendations on the Twenty-Fifth Amendment and Issues of Inability and Disability in Presidents of the United States by the Working Group, " Winston-Salem, NC (1997); Author, "History of Manufacturing in Winston Salem" (1977); Contributor, Articles and Book Reviews to Professional Journals; Contributor, Encyclopedias; Contributor, Conferences, Carter Center, Wake Forest University, The White House; Contributor, Oral History Project: Oral Histories of the Experiences of the Teachers Who Led Ins the Integration of the Winston-Salem/Forsyth County Schools, Now in the Wake Forest University Archives **AW:** Leadership Winston-Salem (1998-1999); Reynolds Research Leave (1997-1998); Schoonmaker Faculty Prize for Community Service, Wake Forest University (1997); Omicron Delta Kappa Award for Contribution to Student Lives (1979); Reynolds Research Leave, Spring (1978); Lilly Foundation Scholarship from Duke University, Lilly Endowment Inc. (1977-1978); North Carolina Faculty Intern Fellowship, North Carolina Committee for Continuing Education in the Humanities, Summer (1974); Summer Fellow, National Humanities Foundations (Now National Endowment for the Humanities) (1969); College Teaching Fellowship, Southern Fellowship Fund (1958-1961); Miscellaneous Travel and Research Grantee, University of Wisconsin, Wake Forest University; Grantee, Pew Charitable Trusts **MEM:** American Historical Association; Southern Historical Association; Southwestern Social Sciences Association; Omicron Delta Kappa; National Board, Phi Alpha Beta; Organization of American Historians; Alpha Chi Honor Society; Pi Gamma Mu Honor Society; Southern Association of Pre-Law Advisors; American Association of University Professors **MH:** Marquis Lifetime Achievement Award **AS:** Dr. Smith's strong influences on the direction of his life was that both parents were teachers and had great faith in the value of education. He had the rare privilege of attending a two-teacher, rural school, in which his mother taught the lower grades, and his father, who was principal, taught the upper grades. Another strong influence was the religious teaching that finding what is true is the most valuable goal. Dr. Smith found the teaching of history an excellent venue for seeking truth. **B/I:** At Baylor University, Dr.

Smith's history professor, Ralph Lynn, encouraged his interest in history. He was further inspired and encouraged by Tulane professor, Nels Bailkey. His professors from the University of Wisconsin, Merle Curtie and Irvin Wyllie, and their interests in studying new fields in history were strongly influential. **PA:** Democrat **RE:** Baptist **THT:** One of Dr. Smith's last projects was with Professor Suzanne Warren from Winston-Salem State University to create an oral history of the experiences of the first teachers who volunteered to lead in the integration of Winston-Salem/Forsyth County Schools. Results of this combined oral history project are now in the Wake Forest University Archives. As to thoughts on life, Dr. Smith believes the pursuit of truth is still the most valuable goal.

SMITH, JAMES RANDOLPH JR., T: Attorney **I:** Law and Legal Services **DOB:** 03/07/1945 **PB:** Martinsville **SC:** VA/USA **PT:** James Randolph Smith; Ruth (Boykin) Smith **ED:** LLB, The University of Virginia (1970); BA, Randolph-Macon College (1967) **C:** Retired (2015); Assistant Commonwealth Attorney, County of Henry, VA (2002-2015); Deputy Director, Virginia Department of Rail & Public Transportation, Richmond, VA (2000-2002); Executive Secretary, Virginia Charitable Gaming Commission, Richmond, VA (1999-2000);Private Practice, Martinsville, VA (1998-1999); Commonwealth Attorney, City of Martinsville, VA (1981-1998); Partner, Smith & Penn, Professional Corporation, Martinsville, VA (1981-1986); Assistant Commonwealth Attorney, City of Martinsville, VA (1971-1981); Law Clerk to Judge, United States District Court for the District of Delaware, Wilmington, DE (1970-1971) **CR:** Instructor Piedmont Criminal Justice Academy (Now Piedmont Regional Criminal Justice Training Academy) (1980-1997, 2002-2005) **CIV:** Treasurer, Martinsville Republican Committee (2010-Present); Deacon, Broad Street Christian Church (2019-Present); Chairman, Board of Directors Broad Street Christian Church (1996-Present); Chairman, Martinsville Republican Committee (1990-1994); Vice Chairman, Martinsville Republican Committee (1986-1990); Member, Christian Church (Disciples Of Christ) **MEM:** President, Rotary International (1993-1994); President, Martinsville-Henry County Bar Association (1984-1985); Vice President, Martinsville-Henry County Bar Association (1983-1984); The International Legal Honor Society of Phi Delta Phi; The Phi Beta Kappa Society **BAR:** United States Court of Appeals for the Fourth Circuit (1976); Supreme Court of the United States (1973); United States District Court for the Western District of Virginia (1972); Virginia (1970) **MH:** Albert Nelson Marquis Lifetime Achievement Award; Marquis Who's Who Top Professional **B/I:** Mr. Smith decided in the eighth grade that he wanted to be a lawyer. There had never been a lawyer in the family and he is still the only lawyer in the family. A high school teacher he had was teaching while saving money to go to law school, and she shared this with the class, and this is something they would talk about. She did become a lawyer, but passed away a few years ago. **AV:** Traveling to his home in North Carolina; Pro bono work **RE:** Christian **THT:** After his 2015 retirement, Mr. Smith worked as Assistant Commonwealth Attorney of Patrick County, Assistant Commonwealth Attorney of Henry County and Assistant Commonwealth Attorney of Martinsville

SMITH, JAMES (LL COOL J), T: Rap Artist, Actor **I:** Media & Entertainment **DOB:** 01/14/1968 **PB:** Bay Shore **SC:** NY/USA **PT:** James Louis Smith Jr.; Ondrea Smith **MS:** Married **SPN:** Simone I. Johnson (08/09/1995) **CH:** Najee Laurent Todd Eugene Smith; Nina Simone Smith; Samaria Leah Wisdom Smith; Italia Anita Maria Smith **ED:** Honorary DA, Northeastern University (2014); Coursework, Business of Entertainment, Media, and Sports Program, Harvard Business School, Harvard University **C:** Founder, Clothing Line, "Todd Smith" **CW:** Host, Producer, "Lip Sync Battle" (2015-Present); Actor, "NCIS: Los Angeles" (2009-Present); Voice Actor, "American Dad!" (2017); Actor, "Drudge Match" (2013); Rapper, Album, "Authentic" (2013); Host, Grammy Awards (2012-2016); Actor, "Hawaii Five-0" (2012); Co-Author, "LL Cool J's Platinum 360 Diet and Lifestyle: A Full-Circle Guide to Developing Your Mind, Body, and Soul" (2011); Actor, "NCIS" (2009); Rapper, "Exit 13" (2008); Rapper, "Exit 13" (2008); Actor, "The Deal" (2008); Actor, Producer, "The Man" (2007); Actor, "30 Rock" (2007); Rapper, "Todd Smith" (2006); Actor, "Last Holiday" (2006); Co-Author, "LL Cool J's Platinum Workout: Sculpt Your Best Body Ever with Hollywood's Fittest Star" (2006); Actor, "House" (2005); Actor, "Slow Burn" (2005); Actor, "Edison" (2005); Rapper, "The DEFinition" (2004); Actor, "Mindhunters" (2004); Actor, "S.W.A.T." (2003); Actor, "Deliver Us from Eva" (2003); Actor, "Rollerball" (2002); Rapper, "10" (2002); Author, "And the Winner Is–" (2002); Actor, "Kingdom Come" (2001); Actor, "Charlie's Angels" (2000); Rapper, "G.O.A.T." (2000); Actor, "Any Given Sunday" (1999); Actor, "Deep Blue Sea" (1999); Actor, "Halloween H20: 20 Years Later" (1998); Actor, "Woo" (1998); Co-Author, "I Make My Own Rules" (1998); Rapper, "Phenomenon" (1997); Himself, "B*A*P*S" (1997); Actor, "Touch" (1997); Actor, "In the House" (1995-1999); Rapper, "Mr. Smith" (1995); Actor, "Out-of-Sync" (1995); Actor, "The Adventures of Pete & Pete" (1994); Rapper, "14 Shots to the Dome" (1993); Actor, "Toys" (1992); Actor, "The Hard Way" (1991); Rapper, "Mama Said Knock You Out" (1990); Rapper, "Walking with a Panther" (1989); Rapper, "Bigger and Deffer" (1987); Rapper, "Radio" (1985); Featured, Numerous Music Videos **AW:** Honoree, Kennedy Center Honors (2017); Star, Hollywood Walk of Fame (2016); Outstanding Actor in a Drama Series, "NCIS: Los Angeles," NAACP Image Awards (2011-2014); Choice TV Actor: Action, "NCIS: Los Angeles," Teen Choice Awards (2013); Outstanding Male Artist, "10," NAACP Image Awards (2003); Quincy Jones Award, Outstanding Career Achievements in the Field of Entertainment, Soul Train Music Awards (2003); Source Foundation Image Award (2003); Outstanding Hip-Hop/Rap Artist, "G.O.A.T.," NAACP Image Awards (2001); Favorite Supporting Actor - Action, "Deep Blue Sea," Blockbuster Entertainment Awards (2000); Best Rap Artist, "Phenomenon," NAACP Image Awards (1997); Best Rap Solo Performance, "Hey Lover," Grammy Awards (1997); Michael Jackson Video Vanguard Award, MTV Video Music Awards (1997); Best Rap Artist, "Mr. Smith," NAACP Image Awards (1996); Best Rap Solo Performance, "Mama Said Knock You Out," Grammy Awards (1992); Best Rap Video, "Mama Said Knock You Out," MTV Video Music Awards (1991); Numerous Other Awards and Accolades

SMITH, JASON THOMAS, T: U.S. Representative **I:** Government Administration/Government Relations/Government Services **DOB:** 06/16/1980 **PB:** St. Louis **SC:** MO/USA **PT:** Bill Smith; Mary Smith **ED:** JD, School of Law, Oklahoma City University (2004); BSBA, University of Missouri (2001); BS in Agricultural Economics, University of Missouri (2001); Coursework in International Law, Trinity College, University of Cambridge, England **C:** U.S. Representative, Missouri's Eighth Congressional District, United States Congress, Washington, DC (2013-Present); Member, U.S. House of Natural Resources Committee (2013-Present); Member, District 120, Missouri House of Representatives (2013); Member, District 150, Missouri House of Representatives (2005-2013); Secretary, House Republican Conference; Member, Committee on Ways and Means; Member, Republican Study Committee; Attorney; Real Estate Agent; Small Business Owner; Farm Manager **CIV:** Member, Sunday School Teacher, Grace Community Church, Salem, MO **MEM:** NRA; American Legislative Exchange Council; Missouri Farm Bureau; The Missouri Bar; Cuba Area Chamber of Commerce; Steelville Chamber of Commerce; Salem Area Chamber of Commerce **BAR:** The Missouri Bar (2004) **PA:** Republican **RE:** Assemblies of God

SMITH, JOAN, T: Elementary Education Educator, Principal **I:** Education/Educational Services **DOB:** 09/04/1948 **PB:** Dubach **SC:** LA/USA **ED:** MEd, Stephen F. Austin State University (1991); MEd, Stephen F. Austin State University (1976);BA, Northeast Louisiana University (1971) **CT:** Teacher, Louisiana, Texas; Middle Management, Texas **C:** Retired (2014); Principal, Huntington Elementary School (1993-2014); Teacher, Huntington Independent School District (1982-1993); Teacher, Hudson Independent School District, Lufkin, TX (1976-1982); Teacher, Iberia Parish Schools, New Iberia, LA (1971-1974) **CR:** Principals Advocacy Council, Huntington Independent School District (1991-1992); District Educational Improvement Committee (1990-1992); Member, Superintendent Advocacy Council, Huntington, TX (1989-1990) **CIV:** Secretary, PTA, Huntington, TX (1992-1993); Member, Ladies Auxiliary to Veterans of Foreign Wars, Clute, TX (1989-1993) **AW:** Honoree, Angelina County Chamber of Commerce (1999-2000); Honoree, Angelina County Chamber of Commerce (1989-1990); Named Teacher of the Year, Huntington Elementary School; Named Teacher of the Year, Huntington Elementary School **MEM:** National Association of Elementary School Principals; Association for Supervision and Curriculum Development; Texas Classroom Teachers Association; Association of Texas Professional Educators; Angelina County Genealogical Society; Deep East Texas Archeological Society; Vernon Parish Historical and Genealogical Society; Texas Retired Teachers Association; Angelina County Retired Teachers Association (Now Angelina Retired Teachers and School Personnel Association) **MH:** Albert Nelson Marquis Lifetime Achievement Award **AV:** Photography; Traveling; Crafting; Collecting old school memorabilia **PA:** Republican **RE:** Baptist

SMITH, JOSEPH LEE, T: Diplomat, Academic Administrator **I:** Education/Educational Services **DOB:** 11/27/1929 **PB:** Shelbyville **SC:** IN/USA **PT:** Omer Joseph Smith; Velda May (Toon) Smith **MS:** Married **SPN:** Regina Elizabeth Derda (12/06/1969); Janet McGowan (09/09/1953, Divorced 1969) **CH:** James Lee Thompson Smith; Nicole Allyson Smith-Bowman; Elizabeth Joan Smith-Roberts; Jessica Ann Smith-Karbowski **ED:** Postgraduate Coursework, University of California Berkeley (1966-1967); JD, Indiana University (1954); Postgraduate Coursework, Yale University (1951-1952); AB, Wabash College, Crawfordsville, IN (1951) **C:** Lecturer, Eckerd College, St. Petersburg, FL (2005-2019); Director of Alumni Relations, Wabash College, Crawfordsville, IN (1980-1987); Consulting General, American Consulate, Medellin, Colombia (1977-1980); Commercial Attache, American Embassy, Bogota, Colombia (1976-1977); Economic Counselor, American Embassy, Asuncion, Paraguay (1973-1976); Consulting/Principal Officer, American Consulate, Bilbao, Spain (1970-1973); Consulting/Principal Officer, American Consulate, Valencia, Spain (1969-1970); Desk Officer for Spain, Department of State, Washington, DC (1967-1969); Second Secretary, American Embassy, Madrid, Spain (1960-1966); Vice Consulate, American Consulate General, Algiers, Algeria (1957-1960) **CR:** Board of Directors, H-C Industries (1983-1986) **MIL:** U.S. Army (1954-1956) **CW:** Editor, Legal Articles, Indiana Law Journal (1953-1954) **AW:** Meritorious Honor Award, Department of State (1974) **MEM:** American Foreign Service Association; Ouiatenon Society; Phi Beta Kappa; Kappa Sigma; Masons **BAR:** Indiana (1954) **MH:** Albert Nelson Marquis Lifetime Achievement Award **B/I:** In high school, Mr. Smith came upon a brochure detailing diplomacy. He was fascinated. He proceeded to study law and spend some time in the military prior to excelling in foreign service. **AV:** Collecting medieval coins; Researching history; Traveling **PA:** Repubican **RE:** Episcopalian

SMITH, LAURIE, T: Professor of Sociology, Dean **I:** Education/Educational Services **CN:** East Texas Baptist University **ED:** Doctor of Philosophy, The University of Texas at Austin, Austin, TX (1992); Master of Arts in Sociology, Baylor University, Waco, TX; Bachelor of Arts in English and Sociology, University of Mary Hardin-Baylor, Belton, TX **C:** Dean, School of Natural and Social Sciences, East Texas Baptist University, Marshall, TX (2017-Present); Professor of Sociology, East Texas Baptist University, Marshall, TX (1991-Present) **AW:** Professor with Distinction, East Texas Baptist University (2018); Who's Who Among America's Teachers (2002, 2005, 2006); Outstanding Young Women of America (1985, 1997); The Honor Society of Phi Kappa Phi, The University of Texas at Austin (1990); Graduate Student Fellowship, Baylor University (1988); Alpha Chi Award, University of Mary Hardin-Baylor (1986); The Mary Hardin-Baylor Loyalty Cup, University of Mary Hardin-Baylor (1986); Who's Who Among Students (1986); Inductee, Alpha Chi Honor Society, University of Mary Hardin-Baylor (1984) **MEM:** Southwestern Social Science Association; American Sociological Association **AS:** Dr. Smith attributes her success to the people she has been surrounded with, who have encouraged and supported her to do whatever task is set before her well. Likewise, she is grateful for the guiding influence of her Christian faith. **B/I:** Dr. Smith became involved in her profession because of her profound interest in the studies of people, human interactions and patterns of behavior.

SMITH, LAVENSKI, "VENCE" ROY, T: Chief Judge **I:** Government Administration/Government Relations/Government Services **CN:** United States Court of Appeals for the Eighth Circuit **DOB:** 10/31/1958 **PB:** Hope **SC:** AR/USA **MS:** Married **SPN:** Trendle **CH:** Two Children **ED:** JD, University of Arkansas School of Law (1987); BA, University of Arkansas (1981) **C:** Chief Judge, United States Court of Appeals for the Eighth Circuit (2017-Present); Judge, United States Court of Appeals for the Eighth Circuit (2002-2017); Commissioner, Arkansas Public Service Commission (2001-2002); Interim Associate Justice, Arkansas State Supreme Court (1999-2000); Chairman, Arkansas Public Service Commission (1997-1999); Regulatory Liaison to Governor, State of Arkansas, Little Rock, AR (1996-1997); Assistant Professor, John Brown University (1994-1996); Private Practice, Springdale, AR (1991-1994); Staff Lawyer, Ozark Legal Services (1987-1991); Law Clerk, Hall, Wright & Morris (1985-1987) **CIV:** Chairman, Arkansas Public Service Commission (1996-1998); Trainer, Partners for Family Training (1993-1996); Board of Directors, Northwest Arkansas Christian Justice Center **PA:** Republican

SMITH, MAGGIE, T: Actress **I:** Media & Entertainment **DOB:** 12/28/1934 **PB:** Ilford **SC:** Essex/England **PT:** Nathaniel Smith; Margaret Hutton (Little) Smith **MS:** Married **SPN:** Beverley Cross

(08/23/1975, Deceased 1998); Robert Stephens (06/29/1967, Divorced 1974) **CH:** Chris Larkin; Toby Stephens **ED:** Honorary Fellowship, Mansfield College, Oxford (2017); Honorary Doctor of Letters, University of Cambridge (1994); Honorary Doctor of Letters, University of Bath (1986); Honorary Doctor of Letters, University of St. Andrews (1971) **C:** Assistant Stage Manager, Actor, Oxford Playhouse (1951-1953) **CIV:** Contributor, 2012 Celebrity Paw Auction, Cats Protection (2012); Patron, International Glaucoma Association **CW:** Actress, "A Boy Called Christmas" (2020); Actress, "Downton Abbey" (2019); Actress, Theater, "A German Life" (2019); Voice Actress, "Sherlock Gnomes" (2018); Actress, "The Lady in the Van" (2015); Actress, "The Second Best Exotic Marigold Hotel" (2015); Actress, "Downton Abbey" (2010-2015); Actress, "My Old Lady" (2014); Actress, "Quartet" (2012); Actress, "The Best Exotic Marigold Hotel" (2011); Actress, "Harry Potter and the Deathly Hallows: Part 2" (2011); Voice Actress, "Gnomeo & Juliet" (2011); Actress, "Nanny McPhee Returns" (2010); Actress, "From Time to Time" (2009); Actress, "Harry Potter and the Half-Blood Prince" (2009); Actress, "Capturing Mary" (2007); Actress, "Harry Potter and the Order of the Phoenix" (2007); Actress, "Becoming Jane" (2007); Actress, Theater, "The Lady from Dubuque" (2007); Actress, "Keeping Mum" (2005); Actress, "Harry Potter and the Goblet of Fire" (2005); Actress, "Ladies in Lavender" (2004); Actress, "Ladies in Lavender" (2004); Actress, Theater, "Talking Heads" (2004); Actress, "Harry Potter and the Prisoner of Azkaban" (2004); Actress, "My House in Umbrella" (2003); Actress, "Harry Potter and the Chamber of Secrets" (2002); Actress, "Divine Secrets of the Ya-Ya Sisterhood" (2002); Actress, "Harry Potter and the Chamber of Secrets" (2002); Actress, Theater, "The Breath of Life" (2002); Actress, "Divine Secrets of the Ya-Ya Sisterhood" (2002); Actress, "Godford Park" (2001); Actress, "Harry Potter and the Sorcerer's Stone" (2001); Actress, "David Copperfield" (1999); Actress, "All the King's Men" (1999); Actress, "The Last September" (1999); Actress, "Tea with Mussolini" (1999); Actress, Theater, "The Lady in the Van" (1999); Actress, "It All Came True" (1998); Actress, "Washington Square" (1997); Actress, Theater, "A Delicate Balance" (1997); Actress, "The First Wives Club" (1996); Actress, "Richard III" (1995); Actress, Theater, "Three Tall Women" (1994); Actress, "Sister Act 2: Back in the Habit" (1993); Actress, "The Secret Garden" (1993); Actress, "Great Performances" (1993); Actress, Theater, "The Importance of Being Earnest" (1993); Actress, "Sister Act" (1992); Actress, "Screen Two" (1992); Actress, "Wendy" (1991); Voice Actress, "Romeo.Juliet" (1990); Actress, "Talking Heads" (1988); Actress, "The Lonely Passion of Judith Hearne" (1987); Actress, Theater, "Lettice and Lovage" (1987); Actress, Theater, "Coming Into Land" (1987); Actress, Theater, "The Infernal Machine" (1986); Actress, "A Room with a View" (1985); Actress, "A Private Function" (1984); Actress, "Lily in Love" (1984); Actress, Theater, "The Way of the World" (1984); Actress, "All for Love" (1983); Actress, "Better Late Than Never" (1983); Actress, "The Missionary" (1982); Actress, "Evil Under the Sun" (1982); Actress, "Clash of the Titans" (1981); Actress, "Quartet" (1981); Actress, Theater, "Virginia" (1980); Actress, Theater, "The Seagull" (1980); Actress, Theater, "Much Ado About Nothing" (1980); Actress, Theater, "Night and Day" (1979); Actress, "California Suite" (1978); Actress, "Death on the Nile" (1978); Actress, Theater, "Private Lives" (1978); Actress, Theater, "Macbeth" (1978); Actress, "As You Like It" (1977); Actress, Theater, "Richard III" (1977); Actress, Theater, "A Midsummer Night's Dream" (1977);

Actress, "Murder by Death" (1976); Actress, Theater, "The Guardsman" (1976); Actress, Theater, "Three Sisters" (1976); Actress, Theater, "Antony and Cleopatra" (1976); Actress, Theater, "The Way of the World" (1976); Actress, Theater, "Private Lives" (1975); Actress, Theater, "Snap" (1974); Actress, "Love and Pain and the Whole Damn Thing" (1973); Actress, Theater, "Peter Pan" (1973); Actress, "Travels with My Aunt" (1972); Actress, Theater, "Private Lives" (1972); Actress, Three Episodes, "BBC Play of the Month" (1968, 1972); Actress, Theater, "Three Sisters" (1970); Actress, Theater, "Hedda Gabler" (1970); Actress, Theater, "The Beaux' Stratagem" (1970); Actress, "Oh! What a Lovely War" (1969); Actress, "The Prime of Miss Jean Brodie" (1969); Actress, Theater, "The Country Wife" (1969); Actress, "Hot Millions" (1968); Actress, "ITV Playhouse" (1968); Actress, "Much Ado About Nothing" (1967); Actress, "The Honey Pot" (1967); Actress, Six Episodes, "ITV Play of the Week" (1957-1958, 1960, 1966); Actress, Theater, "A Bond Honoured" (1966); Actress, Theater, "Black Comedy" (1966); Actress, Theater, "Miss Julie" (1966); Actress, "Othello" (1965); Actress, "Young Cassidy" (1965); Actress, Theater, "Trelawny of the 'Wells'" (1965); Actress, Theater, "Much Ado About Nothing" (1965); Actress, "The Pumpkin Eater" (1964); Actress, Theater, "Hay Fever" (1964); Actress, Theater, "Othello" (1964); Actress, "The V.I.P.s" (1963); Actress, Theater, "The Recruiting Officer" (1963); Actress, "Do to Blazes" (1962); Actress, Theater, "The Private Ear and The Public Eye" (1962); Actress, Four Episodes, "ITV Television Playhouse" (1959-1960, 1961); Actress, Theater, "The Rehearsal" (1961); Actress, Theater, "Strip the Willow" (1960); Actress, Theater, "Rhinoceros" (1960); Actress, Theater, "What Every Woman Knows" (1960); Actress, Theater, "The Merry Wives of Windsor" (1959); Actress, Theater, "Richard II" (1959); Actress, Theater, "As You Like It" (1959); Actress, Theater, "The Double Dealer" (1959); Actress, Three Episodes, "Armchair Theatre" (1958-1960); Actress, "Nowhere to Go" (1958); Actress, Theater, "The Stepmother" (1958); Actress, "On Stage - London" (1957); Actress, "Sing for Your Support" (1957); Actress, "Kraft Theatre" (1957); Actress, Theater, "Share My Lettuce" (1957); Actress, "Aggie" (1956); Actress, "Child in the House" (1956); Actress, "Theatre Royal" (1956); Actress, Theater, "New Faces of '56" (1956); Actress, "BBC Sunday-Night Theatre" (1955); Actress, Theater, "The School for Scandal" (1955); Actress, Theater, "The Magistrate" (1955); Actress, Theater, "Listen to the Wind" (1954); Actress, Theater, "Theatre 1900" (1954); Actress, Theater, "Oxford Accents" (1954); Actress, Theater, "A Man About The House" (1954); Actress, Theater, "The Letter" (1954); Actress, Theater, "The Government Inspector" (1954); Actress, Theater, "Don't Listen Ladies" (1954); Actress, Theater, "The Ortolan" (1954); Actress, Theater, "The Love of Four Colonels" (1953); Actress, Theater, "Cakes and Ale" (1953); Actress, Theater, "Housemaster" (1953); Actress, Theater, "Rookery Nook" (1953); Actress, Theater, "Cinderella" (1952); Actress, Theater, "He Who Gets Slapped" (1952); Actress, Theater, "Twelfth Night" (1952) **AW:** Bodley Medal, Bodleian Libraries, University of Oxford (2016); Critics' Circle Award for Distinguished Service to the Arts (2016); Emmy Award for Outstanding Supporting Actress in a Drama Series, "Downton Abbey" (2016); Inductee, Actors Hall of Fame (2014); Appointed Member, Order of the Companions of Honour, Queen's Birthday Honours (2014); Evening Standard Icon Award (2013); Legacy Award, Stratford Shakespeare Festival (2012); Emmy Award for Outstanding Supporting Actress in a Miniseries or Movie, "Downton Abbey" (2011,

2012); Society of London Theatre Special Award, Laurience Olivier Awards (2010); Honoree, Star, London Avenue of Stars (2006); Emmy Award for Outstanding Lead Actress in a Miniseries or Special, "My House in Umbria" (2003); William Shakespeare Award for Classical Theatre, Shakespeare Theatre Company (1999); Inductee, American Theatre Hall of Fame (1994); Special Award, British Academy of Film and Television Arts (1993); Shakespeare Prize, Hamburg Toepfer Foundation (1991); Appointed, Dame Commander of the Order of the British Empire, Queen's New Year Honours (1990); Tony Award for Best Actress in a Play, "Lettice and Lovage" (1990); Academy Award for Best Supporting Actress, "California Suite" (1979); Appointed, Commander of the Order of the British Empire, Queen's New Year Honours (1970); Academy Award for Best Actress, "The Prime of Miss Jean Brodie" (1970); Numerous Acting Awards and Accolades **MEM:** Fellow, British Film Institute; British Academy of Film and Television Arts

SMITH, PATRICIA J. (GOERING), T: Photographer, Writer, Political Scientist **I:** Research **CN:** Patricia Smith Photography **DOB:** 04/13/1945 **SC:** KS/USA **ED:** PhD, University of Washington (1995); Coursework, Humboldt University, Berlin, Germany (1991-1992); MA, Indiana University (1969); BA, University of Kansas (1967) **CT:** Certified Public Housing Manager **C:** Photographer, Patricia Smith Photography (2009-Present); Political Scientist, Professor, Independent Scholar, University of Washington, Romanian Universities (1995-Present); Freelance Writer (1970-Present); City Planner (2000-2006); Urban Planner, Housing and Community Development Planner, Program Manager (1975-1988) **CIV:** President, International Relations Chair, Housing Chair, Organizer, Women in Politics Workshops; League of Women Voters; Emily's List; Women in International Studies; Founding Member, The Gallery of Ocean Shores; Founding Member, North Beach Singers; Civic Education Project, Romania; Co-Founder, Partnership Initiatives, Video-Conferencing Program; Organizer, Green Lake Community Council; Organizer, North End Housing Rehabilitation Cooperative; Founder, Daycare Center for Children of Inmates' Families and Friends; Founder, Tutoring Program for Inmates, Washington State Reformatory **CW:** Author, "Revolution Revisited: Behind the Scenes in East Germany, 1989" (2014); Author, "After The Wall: Eastern Germany Since 1989 (1998); Author, "Democratizing East Germany: Ideas, Emerging Political Groups, and the Dynamics of Change" (1995); Author, "See How She Runs: Effective Political Techniques (1975); Author, Numerous Articles, Publications; Author, Chapters, Books **AW:** Inductee, International Research and Exchanges Board; Dissertation Fellowship, Study in Eastern Europe;Fellowship, Latin American Studies; Listee, Outstanding Woman in Political Science; Inductee, Pi Sigma Alpha **AS:** Dr. Smith attributes her success to her curiosity and her abilities to tie together diverse ideas, groups, and other elements, as well as to her persistence. In addition, she feels that combining writing and photography is an especially powerful way to document historical and political events. **B/I:** Dr. Smith grew up in a small Swiss/German-speaking Mennonite farming community in central Kansas. Raised in this homogeneous community, she was interested in different things from a young age. This led to her interest in traveling within the United States and abroad, as well as to her interest in foreign languages. In high school, Dr. Smith had the opportunity to debate on an award-winning team, which triggered interests in research, political affairs, and foreign countries, and politics. In college, a political science professor stimulated her interests in activism, political

change, and original research. Finally, Dr. Smith was inspired to achieve a PhD after returning from a trip to the Soviet Union and Eastern Europe. **AV:** Researching genealogy and family history; Traveling in the United States and abroad; Learning foreign languages

SMITH, ROBERT, "BOB" BRUCE, PHD, I: Education/Educational Services **DOB:** 07/08/1937 **PB:** Philadelphia **SC:** PA/USA **PT:** Graeme Conlee Smith; Margaret Edith (Moote) Smith **MS:** Married **SPN:** Eileen Adele (Petznick) Smith **CH:** Monica Smith; Sara Nelson; Douglas Smith **ED:** Honorary PhD, Weber State University (2011); PhD, University of California, Berkeley (1962); BS, Wheaton College (1958) **C:** Local Historian, Idyllwild, CA (2008-Present); Provost Emeritus, Weber State University, Ogden, UT (1998-Present); Newspaper Columnist, Town Crier, Idyllwild, CA (2010-2016); Independent Consultant (1995-2003); Newspaper Columnist, Standard-Examiner, Ogden UT (1996-2001); Assistant to President, Weber State University, Ogden, UT (1996-1998); Provost, Weber State University, Ogden, UT (1993-1996); Vice President for Academic Affairs, Weber State University, Ogden, UT (1981-1993); Professor, Dean of College Science, Engineering and Mathematics, University of Nevada, Las Vegas (1968-1981); Associate Professor, Chairman of Department, University of Nevada, Las Vegas (1966-1968); Assistant Professor of Chemistry, University of Nevada, Las Vegas (1961-1966) **CR:** Director, American Academic Leadership Institute (1986-1996); Chairman, Commission on Colleges, NWCCU (1989-1994); Member, Commission on Colleges, NWCCU (1985-1994); Nevada State Board of Pharmacy (1972-1977); Nevada Board of Examiners in the Basic Science (1970-1975) **CIV:** Idyllwild Area Historical Society; Fuller Mill Creek Association; Ogden Canyon Club; Ogden Nature Center; Planned Parenthood Association of Utah; Egyptian Theatre Foundation; Treehouse Children's Museum; Rotary Club of Ogden; Nevada Public Radio; Preservation Association of Clark County; Gilbert Academy of Creative Arts **AW:** First Place, Utah Original Writing Competition (1992); Fellowship, National Science Foundation (1956-1961) **MEM:** American Association for the Advancement of Science; Honorary Life Member, Sigma Xi, The Scientific Research Society; The Honor Society of Phi Kappa Phi **MH:** Albert Nelson Marquis Lifetime Achievement Award; Marquis Who's Who Top Professional **AS:** Dr. Smith attributes his success to his strong sense of responsibility, clear set of guiding principles about human behavior, the ability to work productively with all types of people and his writing ability. **B/I:** Dr. Smith became involved in his profession because of his fascination with chemistry. **AV:** Mountain hiking; Writing nonfiction; Studying local history

SMITH, ROBERT JOHN, T: Chair **I:** Law and Legal Services **CN:** RJSmith Legal Counselors PLLC **DOB:** 06/27/1943 **PB:** Springfield Gardens **SC:** NY/USA **PT:** Robert A. Smith; Regina B. Smith **MS:** Married **SPN:** Lauren Philips Smith **CH:** Robert J. Smith Jr.; Christopher R. Smith; Thomas P. Smith **ED:** Honorary Doctor of Human Letters, Mount St. Mary's University (2018); Doctor of Jurisprudence, Georgetown University Law Center (1972); Master of Science in Labor Law and Industrial Relations, Cornell University, 1966); Bachelor of Science in History and Political Science, Mount St. Mary's University (1964) **C:** Chairman, RJSmith Legal Counselors PLLC (2014-Present); Senior Partner, Morgan Lewis (1972-2014); Site Industrial Relations Manager Houston, TX (1971); Director, Equal Employment Opportunity, Texas Instruments Inc., Dallas, TX (1968-1969); Corporate Industrial Relations Manager, Texas Instruments, Dallas, TX

(1966-1969); Human Resources Manager, Texas Instruments Inc., Attleboro, MA (1966-1968) **CR:** Board of Trustees, Mount St. Mary's Seminary (2018-Present); Board of Trustees, Governance Committee, Mount St. Mary's (2018-Present); Board of Trustees, Catholic Distance University (2013-Present); Board of Managers, Virginia Catholic Conference (2006-Present); Human Resource Committee, Order of Malta (2000-Present); Board of Directors, Catholic Charities Diocese of Arlington (1990-Present); Board Member, Paul VI High School (2015-2020); Member, Executive Committee member, Mount St. Mary's Seminary Rector's Council (2015-2018); Board Director, Mount St. Mary's University (2008-2018); Adjunct Professor, University of Virginia Law School **CIV:** Board of Trustees, Marymount University; Board of Trustees, Friends of the National Zoo; Board of Trustees, National Chamber Orchestra; Board of Trustees, St. Coletta School in Virginia and Washington, DC **AW:** Best Lawyers in America (2001-Present); Fellow, College of Labor and Employment Lawyers (1998-Present); Super Lawyers, Washington DC Area (2007-2015); AV Rating, Martindale-Hubbell; Listee, Who's Who International Labor and Employment Law; Listee, The Guide to the World's Leading Labor and Employment Lawyers; Listee, Chambers USA **MEM:** Knight of Order of Malta (2000-Present); Fellow, College of Labor and Employment Lawyers (1998-Present) **BAR:** Virginia; Washington, DC **MH:** Marquis Who's Who Top Professional **AS:** Mr. Smith attributes his success on his propensity for contributing to the community, as well as the generosity and kindness of professional and personal mentors. **B/I:** Mr. Smith became involved in his profession due to the influence of his father. His education in labor and employment law, as well as his success at Cornell University, demonstrated that he could handle the rigors of law school. **PA:** Independent **RE:** Roman Catholic

SMITH, SALLY J., T: President, Former Chief Executive Officer **I:** Food & Restaurant Services **CN:** Buffalo Wild Wings, Inc. **PB:** Sioux Falls **SC:** SD/USA **PT:** Dick Wold **ED:** BSBA in Accounting and Finance, University of North Dakota (1980) **C:** President, Chief Executive Officer, Buffalo Wild Wings, Inc. (1996-Present); Chief Financial Officer, Buffalo Wild Wings, Inc. (1994-1996) **CR:** Chief Financial Officer, Miracle Ear (1983-1994); Manager, KPMG Peat Marwick (1980-1983); Chief Financial Officer, Dahlberg, Inc. **AW:** TDn2K Workplace Legacy Award (2016) **MEM:** Gamma Phi Beta; President, Treasurer, Beta Alpha Psi; Chair, National Restaurant Association

SMITH, SHEPARD, T: Journalist **I:** Media & Entertainment **DOB:** 01/14/1964 **PB:** Holly Springs **SC:** MS/USA **PT:** David Shepard Smith; Dora Ellen (Anderson) Smith **MS:** Divorced **SPN:** Virginia Donald (1987, Divorced 1993) **ED:** Coursework in Journalism, University of Mississippi **C:** Host, "Shepard Smith Reporting," Fox News Channel (2013-2019); General Assignment, Senior Correspondent, Managing Editor, Breaking News Division, Fox News Channel (1996-2019); Host, Studio B with Shepard Smith," Fox News Channel (2002-2013); Anchor, "Fox Report," Fox News Channel (1999-2013); Correspondent, "A Current Affair" (1995); Reporter, Anchor, WSVN Channel 7, Miami, FL; Reporter, WCPX-TV, Orlando, FL; Reporter, WBBH-TV, Fort Myers, FL; Reporter, WCJB-TV, Gainesville, FL; Reporter, WJHG-TV, Panama City Beach, FL **CIV:** Contributor, $500,000, Committee to Protect Journalists **CW:** Himself, "Fahrenheit 9/11" (2004); Himself, "Volcano" (1997)

SMITH, TRACY K., T: Poet, Educator **I:** Education/Educational Services **DOB:** 04/16/1972 **PB:** Falmouth **SC:** MA/USA **MS:** Married **SPN:** Raphael Allison **CH:** Naomi; Sterling; Atticus **ED:** Stegner Fellowship in Poetry, Stanford University (1997-1999); MFA in Creative Writing, Columbia University (1997); BA, Harvard University **C:** Chair, Lewis Center for the Arts, Princeton University (2019-Present); U.S. Poet Laureate (2017-Present); Faculty, Princeton University (2006-Present); 2014 Robert Frost Chair of Literature, Bread Loaf School of English, Middlebury College (2014); Instructor, Summer Sessions, Bread Loaf School of English, Middlebury College (2011, 2012, 2014); Richard Stockton Bicentennial Preceptorship, Princeton University (2009-2012); Director, Creative Writing Program, Lewis Center for the Arts, Princeton University; Roger S. Berlind '52 Professor in the Humanities, Princeton University; Instructor, Medgar Evers College; Instructor, University of Pittsburgh; Instructor, Columbia University **CR:** Judge, Griffin Poetry Prize (2016) **CW:** Host, "The Slowdown" (2018-Present); Author, "Wade in the Water" (2018); Author, "Ordinary Light" (2015); Author, "Life on Mars (2011); Author, "Duende" (2007); Author, "The Body's Question" (2003) **AW:** American Ingenuity Award for Education (2018); Robert Creeley Award (2016); Academy of American Poets Fellowship (2014); Pulitzer Prize for Poetry, "Life on Mars" (2012); Literary Award, "Duende," Essence (2008); NAACP Image Award, Literary Work, "Duende," NAACP Image Awards (2008); James Laughlin Award, "Duende," Academy of American Poets (2006); Whiting Award (2005); Cave Canem Prize, "The Body's Question" (2002); Rona Jaffe Foundation Writers' Award; Fellowship, Bread Loaf Writers' Conference; Grantee, Ludwig Vogelstein Foundation

SMITH, WAYNE THOMAS, T: Chairman, President, Chief Executive Officer **I:** Medicine & Health Care **CN:** Community Health Systems **DOB:** 01/29/1946 **PB:** Birmingham **SC:** AL/USA **MS:** Married **SPN:** Cheryl Glass Smith **CH:** Daughter **ED:** Master's Degree in Healthcare Administration, Trinity University (1972); MS in Educational Administration, Auburn University (1969); BS in Education, Auburn University (1968); Postgraduate Studies, King's Fund College Hospital Administration **C:** Chairman of the Board, Community Health Systems (2001-Present); President, Chief Executive Officer, Community Health Systems (1997-Present); President, Chief Operating Officer, Humana, Inc. (1993-1996); With, Humana, Inc. (1973-1996); Numerous Administrative Roles, Humana, Inc.; Member, Board of Directors, Humana, Inc. **CR:** Executive Vice President, Health Plan Operations; Board of Directors, Humana Health Plan, Inc.; Louisville President, Humana Health Insurance Nevada, Inc., Humana Health Plan Florida, Inc., Humana Health Plan Ohio, Inc., Humana Health Chicago Insurance Co., Humana Kansas City, Inc.; President, Chief Operating Officer, Humana Health Plan Texas, Prime Health Management Services; President, Board of Directors, HMPK, Inc.; Board of Directors, Praxair, Inc.; Chairman of the Board, Federation of American Hospitals **CIV:** Member, Board of Directors, Kentucky Governor's Scholars Program; Member, Board of Directors, Actors Theatre of Louisville; Member, Board of Directors, Kentucky Center for the Arts; Member, Executive Committee, Greater Louisville fund for the Arts; Past Chair, Board of Directors, Louisville Collegiate School **MIL:** Captain, Medical Service Corps, U.S. Army (1973); With, U.S. Army (1969-1973) **AW:** Ranked #87, 100 Most Influential People in Healthcare, Modern Healthcares (2019); Williamson County Impact Award (2015); Voted One of the "Top CEOS," Institutional Investor (2015);

Named Among the "50 Most Powerful People in Healthcare," Becker's Hospital Review (2014); 2013 Leadership Awards, Becker's Healthcare (2013); Finalist, Most Admired CEOs Award, Nashville Business Journal (2012); Lifetime Achievement Award, Auburn University (2011); Honoree, Health Care Hero (2011); Named "A Decision Maker to Watch," Nashville Business Journal (2011); Named "America's Top Healthcare CEO," Institutional Investor (2010); Ernst and Young Entrepreneur of the Year Award, Alabama, Georgia, Tennessee (2008); Named "Top Performing CEO in the Healthcare Facilities Sector," Institutional Investor (2007); Numerous Awards for His Work in Business and the Healthcare Industry **MEM:** Board of Directors, Group Health Association of America (GHAA); Board of Directors, Health Insurance Association of America (HIAA)

SMITHIES, OLIVER, T: Geneticist; Professor **I:** Education/Educational Services **CN:** University of North Carolina at Chapel Hill **DOB:** 06/23/1975 **SC:** Halifax/England **PT:** William Smithies; Doris (Sykes) Smithies **MS:** Married **SPN:** Nobuyo Maeda; Lois Kitze (Divorced) **ED:** Honorary Doctorate, University of Oxford (2011); Honorary DSc, University of São Paulo (2008); Honorary DSc, Duke University, Durham, NC (2004); Honorary DSc, The University of Chicago (1991); PhD in Biochemistry, Balliol College, University of Oxford, England, United Kingdom (1951); MA in Biochemistry, Balliol College, University of Oxford, England, United Kingdom (1951); BA in Animal Physiology, Balliol College, University of Oxford (1946) **C:** Excellence Professor of Pathology and Laboratory Medicine, University of North Carolina School of Medicine, Chapel Hill, NC (1988-2017); Hilldale Professor of Genetics and Medical Genetics, University of Wisconsin-Madison (1980-1988); Leon J. Cole Professor of Genetics and Medical Genetics, University of Wisconsin-Madison (1971-1980); Professor, University of Wisconsin-Madison (1963-1971); Associate Professor, University of Wisconsin-Madison (1961-1963); Assistant Professor of Genetics, University of Wisconsin-Madison (1960-1961); Postdoctoral Fellow in Physical Chemistry, University of Wisconsin-Madison (1951-1953) **CR:** National Advisory of Medical Sciences Council, National Institutes of Health (1985-1990); Research Assistant, Associate, Connaught Medical Research Laboratory, Toronto, Canada (1953-1960) **CW:** Contributor, Articles, Professional Journals **AW:** Co-Recipient, Nobel Prize in Physiology/Medicine (2007); Wolf Prize in Medicine, Israel (2003); Massry Prize (2002); Oliver Max Gardner Award, University of North Carolina (2002); Albert Lasker Award for Basic Medical Research (2001); International Okamoto Award, Japan Vascular Disease Research Foundation (2000); Bristol-Meyers Squibb Award for Distinguished Achievement in Cardiovascular/Metabolic Disease Research (1997); CIBA Award, American Heart Association, Inc. (1996); Alfred P. Sloan Award, GM Cancer Research Foundation (1994); North Carolina Award for Science (1993); Gairdner Foundation International Award (1990, 1993); Karl Landsteiner Memorial Award, American Association of Blood Banks (AABB) (1984); William Allen Memorial Award, American Society of Human Genetics, Incorporated (1964) **MEM:** President, Genetics Society of America (1975); Vice President, Genetics Society of America (1974); Fellow, American Association for the Advancement of Science; National Academy of Sciences; Foreign Member, Royal Society of London; Institute of Medicine; Genetics Society of America; American Academy of Arts & Sciences

SMOOT, GEORGE FITZGERALD III, T: Astrophysicist **I:** Sciences **DOB:** 02/20/1945 **PB:** Yukon **SC:** FL/USA **ED:** PhD in Particle Physics, Massachusetts Institute of Technology (1970); BS in Mathematics and Physics, Massachusetts Institute of Technology (1966) **C:** Professor of Physics, University of California Berkeley (2010-Present); Professor of Physics, Paris Diderot University (2010-Present); Anne Pao Sohmen Professor at Large, IAS Hong Kong University of Science and Technology (2016-Present); Research Physicist, Lawrence Berkeley National Laboratory (1974-Present); Professor, Physics, University of California Berkeley (1994-Present); Research Physicist, Space Sciences Laboratory, University of California, Berkeley (1971-Present); Research Physicist, Massachusetts Institute of Technology (1970) **CR:** Member, Advisory Committee, Radio Astronomy Laboratory (1990); Member, Center for Particle Astrophysics, University of California Berkeley (1988); Member, Superconducting Magnet Facility for the Space Station Study Team (1985); Member, Advisory Committee, White Mountain Research Station (1982); Member, Management and Operations Working Group for Shuttle Astronomy (1976-1980) **CW:** Featured, Commercial, Intuit TurboTax (2016); Lecturer, TEDx (2014); Game Show Contestant, "Are You Smarter Than a Fifth Grader?" (2009); Co-Author, "Wrinkles in Time" (1993); Contributor, Articles to Professional Journals; Featured, "The Big Bang Theory" **AW:** Oersted Medal (2009); $1 Million Grand Prize Winner, "Are You Smarter Than a Fifth Grader?" (2009); Nobel Prize in Physics (2006); Chalonge Medal (2006); Gruber Prize (2006); Albert Einstein Medal (2003); E.O. Lawrence Award (1994); American Academy of Achievement Golden Plate Award (1994); Kilby Award (1993); Medal for Exceptional Scientific Achievement, NASA (1992) **MEM:** International Astronomical Union; American Physical Society; American Astronomical Society; American Association for the Advancement of Science; Sigma Xi, The Scientific Research Honor Society

SMOTHERMAN, KENNETH, T: Owner, Operator **I:** Business Management/Business Services **CN:** Smotherman Farms Ltd. **MS:** Married **SPN:** Dana **ED:** Engineering, McLennan Community College, Waco, TX (1982) **CT:** Certified Hotel Administrator, American Hotel and Motel Association (Now American Hotel and Lodging Association) (1993-Present) **C:** Business Owner, Smotherman Farms Ltd, West, TX (2002-Present); Contract Analyst, Matrix (2000-2001); Senior Product Manager, Manager of System Development, Lynx-PMS, INSI Corporation/Hotel Management Systems, Anasazi Hotel Systems (1997-2000); Software Engineer, International Headquarters Operations Center, Best Western Hotels & Resorts (1994-1997); Systems Operations Lead Specialist, Instructor, Headquarters Operations Center, Best Western Hotels & Resorts (1988-1994); General Manager, Best Western Columbus, Columbus, MS (1986-1988); Financial Controller, Quality Inn-Midtown, Denver, CO (1985-1986); Offshore Drilling: Roughneck & Logging Analyst, Dixie-Lynn Drilling/Union 76/Shlumberger (1980-1983) **CIV:** Secretary, West Lodge #475 AF&AM (2007-Present); Master, West Lodge #475 AF&AM (2012-2013) **MH:** Marquis Who's Who Top Professional **B/I:** Mr. Smotherman became involved in his profession because he and his wife had two high school daughters who would leave and be back only on the weekends, so the pace of life became a lot slower and it felt like the right move to make. **THT:** Mr. Smotherman's motto is, "Never give up."

SMUCKER, LLOYD KENNETH, T: U.S. Representative from California **I:** Government Administration/Government Relations/Government Services **DOB:** 01/23/1964 **PB:** Lancaster **SC:** PA/USA **PT:** Daniel S. Smucker; Arie Smucker **MS:** Married **SPN:** Cynthia Smucker **CH:** Paige; Regan; Nicholas **ED:** Coursework, Lebanon Valley College, Annville, PA; Coursework, Franklin & Marshall College, Lancaster, PA **C:** Member, U.S. House of Representatives from Pennsylvania's 16th Congressional District, United States Congress, Washington, DC (2017-Present); Member, District 13, Pennsylvania State Senate (2009-2016); Member, West Lampeter Township Planning Commission, PA; Former Township Supervisor, West Lampeter Township, PA; President, Smucker Company, Smoketown, PA; Commercial Construction Business Owner; Former Consultant, Start-up Company **PA:** Republican **RE:** Lutheran

SNELLING, DIANE B., T: Chair **I:** Government Administration/Government Relations/Government Services **CN:** Natural Resources Board **DOB:** 03/18/1952 **PB:** Philadelphia **SC:** PA/USA **ED:** MA in Studio Art, New York University (1994); AB in Visual and Environmental Studies, Harvard Radcliffe (1974) **C:** Chair, Natural Resources Board (2016-Present); Artist, Self-Employed (1974-Present); Senator, State of Vermont (2002-2016); Board Adviser, Horticulture Farm, The University of Vermont (2001-2002); Lecturer of Art and Communications, Trinity College (1994-1997); Selectman, Hinesburg, VT (1985-1991); Consultant, Muse Creative Management LLC (1983-1992); Art Director, Designer, Creative Manager, Account Executive, Comart Aniforms (1976-1982) **CIV:** Member, Mental Health Oversight Committee (2004-Present); Member, Elder Care Community Council (2003-2004); Board Member, Vermont Arts Council (2003-2004); Member, No Child Left Behind Oversight Committee (2002-2004); Member, Advisory Board, Robert Hull Fleming Museum (1994-2001); Board Member, King Street Center (1992-1995); Trustee, Board, Snelling Center for Government (1991-2002); Board Member, Greater Burlington Industrial Corporation (1985-1991); Planner, Hinesburg Planning Commission (1984-1985) **CW:** Artist, Exhibitions, Boston, MA, New York, NY, and Venice, Italy **AS:** Ms. Snelling attributes her success to hard work, creativity and excellent parental role models. **B/I:** Ms. Snelling became involved in her profession because in January of 2002, Governor Howard Dean appointed her to the Vermont State Senate to serve for the remainder of her mother's term when she resigned due to health issues. In November of 2002, she was elected to the State Senate and re-elected six more times, serving a total of 15 years.

SNETSINGER, KENNETH, "KEN" G. PHD, T: Retired Mineralogist **I:** Research **CN:** Ames Research Center **DOB:** 02/21/1939 **PB:** San Francisco **SC:** CA/USA **PT:** Ercell Aneas Snetsinger; Coral Binning **MS:** Married **SPN:** Judith Cady Briggs Etheridge **ED:** PhD, Stanford University (1966); MS, Stanford University (1962); BS, Stanford University (1961) **C:** Retired Mineralogist, Research Scientist, NASA/Ames Research Center (1969-1993); Postdoctoral Research Associate, NASA/Ames Research Center, Moffett Field, CA (1966-1969); Instructor, Stanford University, Palo Alto, CA (1963-1966); Research Assistant, U.S. Geological Survey, Menlo Park, CA (1958-1962) **CR:** Chairman, NASA/Ames Research Center Source Evaluation Board (1990-1993) **CW:** Contributor, Articles, Professional Journals (1966-1993) **AW:** Grantee, Sigma Xi (1970); Postdoctoral Research Associate, National Academy of Sciences (1966-1969) **MEM:** Sigma Xi Society **MH:** Albert Nelson Marquis Lifetime Achievement Award; Marquis Who's Who Top Professional **AS:** Dr. Snetsinger attributes his success to his PhD advisor, C.O. Hutton, who was an incredible mentor. **B/I:** In Dr. Snetsinger's youth, there was a mineralogist living close to his home. Dr. Snetsinger enjoyed looking over the scientist's mineral collection, which sparked his interest in the field. **THT:** Dr. Snetsinger uses a scientific approach to solve his problems.

SNIPES, WESLEY, T: Actor, Producer **I:** Media & Entertainment **DOB:** 07/31/1962 **PB:** Orlando **SC:** FL/USA **PT:** Wesley Rudolph Snipes; Marian Snipes **MS:** Married **SPN:** Nikki Park (03/17/2003); April DuBois (1985, Divorced 1990) **CH:** Alimayu Moa-Ton; Iset Jua-T; Alaafia Jehu-T; Akhenaten Kihwa-T; Jelani Asar **ED:** Bachelor of Fine Arts, State University of New York at Purchase (1985); Honorary Doctorate in Humanities and Fine Arts, State University of New York at Purchase; Coursework, Southwest College **CR:** Co-Founder, Royal Guard of Amen-Ra; Martial Artist **CW:** Actor, "Coming 2 America" (2020); Actor, "Paper Empire" (2020); Actor, "Dolemite Is My Name" (2019); Actor, "What We Do in the Shaodws" (2019); Co-Author, "Talon of God" (2018); Actor, Producer, "Armed Response" (2017); Actor, Producer, "The Recall" (2017); Actor, "Chi-Raq" (2015); Actor, "The Player" (2015); Actor, "The Expendables 3" (2014); Actor, "Gallowwalkers" (2012); Executive Producer, "Revelations of the Mayans: 2012 and Beyond" (2012); Voice Actor, "Julies Styles: The International" (2011); Actor, "Game of Death" (2011); Actor, "Brooklyn's Finest" (2009); Actor, "The Art of War II: Betrayal" (2008); Actor, "The Contractor" (2007); Actor, "Hard Luck" (2006); Actor, "The Detonator" (2006); Actor, "Chaos" (2005); Actor, "The Marksman" (2005); Actor, "7 Seconds" (2005); Actor, Producer, "Blade: Trinity" (2004); Actor, "Unstoppable" (2004); Actor, "The Bernie Mac Show" (2003); Actor, Executive Producer, "Undisputed" (2002); Actor, Producer, "Blade II" (2002); Actor, "Zig Zag" (2002); Actor, "Liberty Stands Still" (2002); Executive Producer, "Dr. Ben" (2001); Actor, Executive Producer, "Disappearing Acts" (2000); Actor, "The Art of War" (2000); Actor, "Play It to the Bone" (1999); Actor, "Futuresport" (1998); Actor, Producer, "Blade" (1998); Actor, "Down in the Delta" (1998); Actor, "U.S. Marshals" (1998); Executive Producer, "Masters of the Martial Arts Presented by Wesley Snipes" (1998); Producer, "Down in the Delta" (1998); Producer, "The Big Hit" (1998); Actor, "One Night Stand" (1997); Voice Actor, "Happily Ever After: Fairy Tales for Every Child" (1997); Actor, "Murder at 1600" (1997); Actor, "The Fan" (1996); Actor, "America's Dream" (1996); Actor, "Waiting to Exhale" (1995); Actor, "Money Train" (1995); Actor, "To Wong Foo Thanks for Everything, Julie Newmar" (1995); Actor, "Drop Zone" (1994); Actor, "Sugar Hill" (1993); Actor, "Demolition Man" (1993); Actor, "Rising Sun" (1993); Actor, "Boiling Point" (1993); Actor, "Passenger 57" (1992); Actor, "White Men Can't Jump" (1992); Actor, "The Waterdance" (1992); Actor, "Jungle Fever" (1991); Actor, "New Jack City" (1991); Actor, "Mo' Better Blues" (1990); Actor, "King of New York" (1990); Actor, "H.E.L.P." (1990); Actor, "The Days and Nights of Molly Dodd" (1989); Actor, "Major League" (1989); Actor, "A Man Called Hawk" (1989); Actor, "Vietnam War Story" (1988); Actor, Music Video, "Bad" by Michael Jackson (1987); Actor, "Critical Condition" (1987); Actor, "Miami Vice" (1986); Actor, "Streets of Gold" (1986); Actor, Stage, "Execution of Justice" (1986); Actor, "Wildcats" (1986); Actor, "All My Children" (1984) **AW:** Outstanding Supporting Actor, Motion Picture, "Dolemite Is My Name," Black Reel Awards (2020); Best Comedic Performance, "Dolemite Is My Name," San Diego Film Critics Society Awards (2019); Outstanding Contribution to Film and TV Award, Screen Nation Awards (2016); Best Supporting Actor, "Brooklyn's Finest," Black Reel Awards (2009); Favorite Actor - Horror, "Blade," Blockbuster Entertainment Awards (1999); Honoree, Star, Hollywood Walk of Fame (1998); Volpi Cup, Best Actor, "One Night Stand," Venice Film Festival (1997); Outstanding Lead Actor in a Television Movie or Mini-Series, "America's Dream," NAACP Image Awards (1997); Outstanding Lead Actor in a Motion Picture, "New Jack City," NAACP Image Awards (1993); Gold Special Jury Award, Best Actor, "The Waterdance," WorldFest Houston (1992); Actor in a Dramatic Series, "Vietnam War Story," CableACE Awards (1989)

SNYDER, JOHN G., T: Managing Director, General Counsel **I:** Law and Legal Services **MH:** Albert Nelson Marquis Lifetime Achievement Award

SNYDER, TRAVIS, T: Owner **I:** Architecture & Construction **CN:** Advantage Backhoes LLC **DOB:** 03/24/1984 **PB:** San Bernardino **SC:** CA/USA **PT:** Dave Snyder; Marianne Dourley Snyder **MS:** Married **SPN:** Krystin **CH:** Audrey; Paige **ED:** Diploma, Rim of the World High School, Lake Arrowhead, CA **CT:** Certified, Safety Trained Supervisor Construction (STSC); Small Business Enterprise (SBE); OSHA 10-Hour Construction Course; OSHA 30-Hour Construction Course; EM 385-1-1 Training, OSHA; First Aid; CPR **C:** Owner, Advantage Backhoes LLC (2007-Present); Operating Engineer, A.S.R. Constructors (2002-2007) **CIV:** Donor, Local High School and Sport Youth Programs; Donor, Local Veterinarian Clinics **AW:** Named to 40 Under 40, Construction Equipment Magazine (2018); Subcontractor of the Month Award for $150 Million VA Hospital Addition; Named Subcontractor, EQ Quality of Life, 29 Palms Marine Court Air Ground Combat Center; Named Subcontractor of the Month, Hemet Elementary School, CA **MEM:** Board of Certified Safety Professionals **B/I:** Mr. Snyder received a position as a laborer right after high school. He quickly accelerated in his apprenticeship and journeyed out as an operating engineer in just two years. He refinanced his house at 21 years old and bought a used backhoe, starting his own firm that same year with one used backhoe. **PA:** Conservative **THT:** Mr. Snyder's company has doubled gross revenue by at least 50% year after year for all 12 years. When he started the business, he didn't know much about contracts or the legality; they just kept their word and worked really hard. They took everything that came their way and never turned down work.

SNYDER-ELLINGSON, LYNSI LAVELLE, T: President **I:** Food & Restaurant Services **CN:** In-N-Out Burgers **DOB:** 05/05/1982 **PB:** Glendora **SC:** CA/USA **PT:** Harry Guy Snyder; Lynda Lou (Wilson) Snyder **MS:** Married **SPN:** Sean Ellingson (2014); Val Torres Jr. (2011, Divorced 2014); Richard Martinez (2004, Divorced 2011); Jeremiah Seawell (2000, Divorced 2003) **CH:** Four children **C:** President, In-N-Out Burgers (2010-Present) **CIV:** Fundraiser, Healing Hearts & Nations; In-N-Out Burger Foundation **CW:** Featured, "I Am Second" (2015); Guest Appearance, "Jay Leno's Garage" (2015); Featured, "In-N-Out Burger: A Behind-the-Counter Look at the Fast-Food Chain That Breaks All the Rules" (2009) **AW:** Ranked, Bloomberg Billionaires Index (2013); Hot 100, Maxim (2013) **MEM:** National Hot Rod Association **AV:** Drag racing **RE:** Evangelical Christian

SOBIESKI, JAROSLAW, T: Aerospace Engineer **I:** Engineering **CN:** Langley Research Center, NASA **DOB:** 03/11/1934 **PB:** Wilno **SC:** Poland **PT:** Stanislaw; Sabina Sobieszczanski **MS:** Married **SPN:** Wanda Dlugosz (1958-2008, Deceased) **CH:** Margaret Ann; Ian Patrick **ED:** Doctor of Engineering, Warsaw University of Technology (1964); MS in Aerospace, Warsaw University of Technology (1957); BS in Aerospace., Warsaw University of Technology (1955) **CT:** Certified Chartered Engineer, Royal Aeronautical Society (1968) **C:** Distinguished Research Associate, Langley Research Center, NASA, Hampton, VA (2006-Present); Senior Research Scientist, Langley Research Center, NASA, Hampton, VA (2001-2006); Manager, Computational AeroScience Team, Langley Research Center, NASA, Hampton, VA (1996-2001); Multidisciplinary Research Coordinator, Langley Research Center, NASA, Hampton, VA (1994-2001); Chief Scientist, Langley Research Center, NASA, Hampton, VA (1993-1996); Head Research Office, Langley Research Center, NASA, Hampton, VA (1979-1993); Aerospace Engineer, Langley Research Center, NASA, Hampton, VA (1971-1989); Associate Professor, St. Louis University (1966-1971); Research Associate, Norwegian University of Science and Technology, Trondheim, Norway (1964-1966); Consultant, Polish Aircraft Industries, Warsaw, Poland (1957-1964); Assistant and Adjunct Professor, Warsaw University of Technology, Warsaw, Poland (1955-1964) **CR:** Delft University of Technology, Netherlands (2010-Present); PhD Committee Member, Massachusetts Institute of Technology (2009-Present); Virginia Polytechnic Institute (2004-Present); Faculty Member, George Washington University (1971-2003); Faculty Member, University of Virginia (1992-1999); President, Consultant Engineer, Technical Analysis Optimization, Inc., Hampton, VA (1982-1992); Presentation Lecturer, USA, UK, Australia, China, Japan, Brazil, Germany, Norway, Denmark, France, Portugal, Belgium, Israel and Holland **CIV:** President, Civic Association, Hampton, VA (1987-1988) **MIL:** Lt., Polish Air Force (1955) **CW:** Co-Author, "Multidisciplinary Design Optimization" (2015); Co-Editor, Structural Optimization Journal (1989-2005); Contributor, Articles, Professional Journals, Book Chapters; Lecturer in the Field **AW:** Exceptional Service Medal, NASA (2005); Wright Brothers Medal, SAE International (2005); Exceptional Engineering Achievement, NASA (1988); National Award for Multidisciplinary Design Optimization, American Institute of Aeronautics and Astronautics (1986) **MEM:** Executive Board, International Society Structural and Multidisciplinary Optimization (1992-2003); Founding Chairman, Technical Committee, Multidisciplinary Design Optimization, American Institute of Aeronautics and Astronautics; Fellow, American Institute of Aeronautics and Astronautics; Co-Founder, International Society Structural and Multidisciplinary Optimization; Soaring Society of America; The National Institute of Aerospace **AV:** Skiing; Sailing; Soaring; Boating

SODERBERGH, STEVEN ANDREW, T: Film Producer, Director, Screenwriter **I:** Media & Entertainment **DOB:** 01/14/1963 **PB:** Atlanta **SC:** GA/USA **PT:** Peter Andrew Soderbergh; Marry Ann (Bernard) Soderbergh **MS:** Married **SPN:** Jules Asner (05/10/2003); Elizabeth Jeanne Brantley (12/01/1989, Divorced 1994) **CH:** Sarah **C:** Bolivian Grape Spirit, "Singani 63" (2018); Sole Exporter, Bolivian Grape Spirit (2014) **CW:** Director, "Let Them All Talk" (2020); Executive Producer, "Wireless" (2020); Executive Producer, "Bill & Ted Face the Music" (2020); Director, Producer, "The Laundromat" (2019); Director, "High Flying Bird" (2019); Executive Producer, "Leavenworth" (2019); Executive Producer, "Now Apocalypse" (2019); Producer, "The Report" (2019); Executive Producer, "Beats" (2019); Director, "Unsane" (2018); Producer, "Ocean's Eight" (2018); Executive Producer, "Perfect" (2018); Executive Producer, "Mosaic" (2018); Director, "Logan Lucky" (2017); Executive Producer, "Godless" (2017); Executive Producer, "The King" (2017); Executive Producer, "The Girlfriend Experience" (2016-2017); Executive Producer, "Red Oaks" (2014-2017); Executive Producer, "Magic Mike XXL" (2015); Executive Producer, "The Knick" (2014-2015); Executive Producer, "Citizenfour" (2014); Associate Producer, "Da Sweet Blood of Jesus" (2014); Director, "Side Effects" (2013); Director, "Behind the Candelabra" (2013); Director, "Magic Mike" (2012); Director, "Haywire" (2012); Executive Producer, "Roman Polanski: Off Man Out" (2012); Director, "Contagion" (2011); Executive Producer, "We Need to Talk About Kevin" (2011); Executive Producer, "His Way" (2011); Director, "And Everything Is Going Fine" (2010); Executive Producer, "Rebecca H. (Return to the Dogs)" (2010); Director, "The Informant!" (2009); Director, "The Girlfriend Experience" (2009); Producer, "Solitary Man" (2009); Executive Producer, "Playground" (2009); Director, "Che" (2008); Executive Producer, "Roman Polanski: Wanted and Desired"(2008); Director, "Ocean's Thirteen" (2007); Executive Producer, "I'm Not There" (2007); Executive Producer, "Micheal Clayton" (2007); Executive Producer, "Wind Chill" (2007); Director, Screenwriter, "Building No. 7" (2006); Director, "The Good German" (2006); Executive Producer, "A Scanner Darkly" (2006); Director, "Bubble" (2005); Executive Producer, "Rumor Has It..." (2005); Executive Producer, "Syriana" (2005); Executive Producer, "The Big Empty" (2005); Executive Producer, "Good Night, and Good Luck" (2005); Executive Producer, "Unscripted" (2005); Executive Producer, Symbiopsychotaxiplasm: Take 2 1/2" (2005); Director, "Ocean's Twelve" (2004); Director, Screenwriter, "Eros" (2004); Screenwriter, Producer, "Criminal" (2004); Executive Producer, "Keane" (2004); Executive Producer, "K Street" (2003); Director, Screenwriter, "Solaris" (2002); Director, "Full Frontal" (2002); Executive Producer, "Confessions of a Dangerous Mind" (2002); Executive Producer, "Far from Heaven" (2002); Executive Producer, "Naqoyqatsi" (2002); Executive Producer, "Welcome to Collinwood" (2002); Executive Producer, "Insomnia" (2002); Director, "Ocean's Eleven" (2001); Executive Producer, "Tribute" (2001); Executive Producer, "Who Is Bernard Tapie?" (2001); Director, "Traffic" (2000); Director, "Erin Brockovich" (2000); Director, "The Limey" (1999); Director, "Out of Sight" (1998); Executive Producer, "Pleasantville" (1998); Screenwriter, "Nightwatch" (1997); Director, "Gray's Anatomy" (1996); Director, Screenwriter, "Schizopolis" (1996); Executive Producer, "The Daytrippers" (1996); Director, Screenwriter, "The Underneath" (1995); Director, Screenwriter, "King of the Hill" (1993); Executive Producer, "Suture" (1993); Director, "Kafka" (1991); Director, Screenwriter, "Sex, Lies, and Videotape" (1989) **AW:** Outstanding Directorial Achievement in Movies for Television and Mini-Series, "Behind the Candelabra," Directors Guild of America (2014); Primetime Emmy for Outstanding Single-Camera Picture Editing for a Miniseries or a Movie, "Behind the Candelabra" (2013); WIRED Renegade, WIRED Rave Awards (2006); Kinema Junpo Award, Best Foreign Language Film, Best Foreign Language Film Director, "Traffic," Kinema Junpo Awards (2002); Best Director, "Traffic, " Academy Awards (2001); Best Director, "Traffic," "Erin Brockovich," Broadcast Film Critics Association Awards (2001); Best Director, "Traffic," Chicago Film Critics Association Awards (2001); Best Director, "Traffic," Dallas-Fort Worth Film Critics Association Awards (2001); Best Director, "Erin Brockovich," "Traffic," Florida Film Critics Circle Awards (2001); Golden Moon Award, Best Film, "Traffic," Faro Island Film Festival (2000); Best Director, "Traffic," Kansas City Film Critics Circle Awards (2000); Sierra Award, Best Director, "Erin Brockovich," "Traffic," Las Vegas Film Critics Society Awards (2000); Golden Moon Award, Best Film, "Kafka," Faro Island Film Festival (1991); Independent Spirit Award for Best Director, "Sex, Lies, and Videotape" Film Independent Spirit Awards (1990); Palme d'Or, "Sex, Lies, and Videotape," Cannes Film Festival (1989); Recipient, Numerous Other Awards and Accolades **MEM:** Vice President, Directors Guild of America (2004-2013); Academy of Motion Picture Arts and Sciences; Founding Member, Independent Directors Committee, Directors Guild of America **PA:** Democrat

SOENNICHSEN, JEAN, "BETTY" ELIZABETH, MA, T: Senior Advocate **I:** Other **DOB:** 11/03/1926 **PB:** Denver **SC:** CO/USA **PT:** George Nicodemus; Lillian May (Bitler) Nicodemus **MS:** Widowed **SPN:** John Melchior Soennichsen (08/10/1948) **CH:** Richard Henry; Jeanne Eileen Serrano **ED:** MA, San Jose State University (1968); BA, University of Nebraska-Lincoln (1949) **CT:** Certified Elementary Teacher, State of California; Certified Reading Specialist, State of California **C:** Senior Senator, California Senior Legislature (1988-1998); Consultant, Moreland School District (1983-1988); Teacher, Moreland School District (1963-1983) **CR:** Founder, Moreland Retired Teachers Association (1985-Present); State President, California Retired Teachers Association (2007-2009); Board of Directors, California Retired Teachers Association (1987); President, Moreland Teachers Association (1973-1974) **CW:** Editor, CalRTA Monitor (1987-1994); Author, "Moreland Spelling Program" (1986) **AW:** Teacher of the Year, San Jose Jaycees (1973) **MEM:** California Retired Teachers Association; Moreland Retired Teachers Association; National Retired Teachers Association **MH:** Albert Nelson Marquis Lifetime Achievement Award **B/I:** Ms. Soennichsen became involved in her profession because her children had grown up and she decided to wanted to become a teacher. She went back to San Jose State University to get her teaching credentials and obtained a job in the local school district. **AV:** Cross country skiing; Gardening; Sailing; Hiking; Reading **PA:** Democrat **RE:** Presbyterian

SOLAK, MAREK KRZYSZTOF, PHD, T: Senior Manager **I:** Pharmaceuticals **CN:** Pacira BioSciences Inc. **DOB:** 11/14/1953 **PB:** Warsaw **SC:** Poland **PT:** Tadeusz Solak; Maria (Z.) Solak **MS:** Married **SPN:** Grazyna **CH:** Anna; Grzegorz **ED:** PhD, Warsaw University of Technology (1981); MSc, Warsaw University of Technology (1977) **CT:** Professional Engineer, Republic of South Africa (1993) **C:** Senior Manager, Statistical Programming, Pacira Pharmaceuticals, Parsippany, NJ (2017-Present); Manager, Statistical Programming, Sandoz, Novartis, AG, Princeton, NJ (2016-2017); Principal Statistical Programmer, Vertex, Boston, MA (2011-2016); SAS Programmer III, Johnson & Johnson, Chesterbrook, PA (2010-2011); Associate Principal Scientist, Project Leader, Senior SAS Programmer, Schering Plough Research Institute (now Merck & Co.), Summit, NJ (2005-2010); SAS Programmer, Analyst, Bristol-Myers Squibb, Hopewell NJ (2003-2005); Senior SAS Programmer, Analyst, Adolor Corp., Exton, PA (2002-2003); SAS Programmer, Analyst, Merck & Co., Blue Bell, PA (2001-2002); SAS Programmer, Bristol Myers-Squibb, Cranbury, NJ (2001); Consultant, PwC, Morristown, NJ (2000-2001); Consultant, AT&T, Piscataway, NJ (1998-1999); Assistant Professor, Institute Electrical Engineering, Warsaw, Poland (1993-1997); Senior Lecturer, University Durban-Westville, Durban, South Africa (1990-1993); Visiting Assistant Professor, Cleveland State University, Cleveland, OH (1988-1990); Fulbright Scholar, Texas A&M University, College Station, TX (1986-1987); Assistant Professor, Institute of Electrical Engineering, Warsaw, Poland (1980-1986) **CW:** Publisher, IEEE Trans Automatic Control, IEEE Transactions Neural Networks, International Journal of Control and Multidimensional Systems and Signal Processing; Presenter, American Control Conferences, IEEE Control and Decision Conferences, PharmaSug; Contributor, Linear System Theory, Robust Stability, Neural Networks, Outlier Detection and Evaluation, SAS Programming **AW:** Foundation for Research Development Research Award, University of Durban-Westville, South Africa (1992); Best Paper of the Session Award, "Robust Adaptive Control: Parallel Complementary Approaches," American Control Conference (1990); Fulbright Scholar, Texas A&M University, College Station, TX (1986-1987) **MH:** Albert Nelson Marquis Lifetime Achievement Award; Marquis Who's Who Top Professional **B/I:** Mr. Solak became involved in his profession because when he was in Poland he attended a high school that had a strong mathematics program. He was trained in mathematics and it was very competitive. He became more interested in doing mathematics and he went to Warsaw University and did applied mathematics and technical physics. Mr. Solak chose to teach and do research because he wanted to be practical. **AV:** Swimming; Bridge; Tennis; Travel

SOMERS, WILLARD C., T: Chief Executive Officer/Manufacturing Executive **I:** Business Management/Business Services **CN:** Computer Power Plus **DOB:** 08/07/1939 **PB:** Jersey City **SC:** NJ/USA **PT:** Dr. Willard H. Somers; Marjorie (McDonald Campbell) Somers **MS:** Widowed **SPN:** Marilyn M. **CH:** Willard C. Jr.; Thomas M. **ED:** MBA, Harvard University, with Distinction (1966); BSE, Princeton University (1961) **CT:** IBM Certified Professional; Distinguished Architect, The Open Group **C:** Chairman, President, Somers Corporation, Navesink, NJ (1977-Present); Vice President, General Manager Family of Furnishings, Congoleum Corp., Milwaukee, WI (1971-1977); Vice President, General Interiors International, New York, NY (1966-1970) **CR:** Founder, Narragansett Surf Shops, Narragansett, RI (1964-1966) **CIV:** Board Chair, Surfers Environmental Alliance (1997-2016) **CW:** "Make Yourself Comfortable" (1994, 2008); Patentee, Patents; Contributor, Writings **AW:** Speaker/Executor of the Year, National Wholesale Furniture Association (1988) **MEM:** Board of Directors, American Association of Furniture Manufacturers (1979-Present); Sea Bright Beach Club; Princeton Club of New York **MH:** Albert Nelson Marquis Lifetime Achievement Award **AS:** Mr. Somers attributes his success to his values, family background, and fundamental education.

SONG, MOON K., PHD, T: Biomedical Research Scientist **I:** Sciences **DOB:** 05/24/1931 **PB:** Taejon **SC:** Korea **PT:** Yong Kuk Song; Kuy Nam (Min) Song **MS:** Married **SPN:** Jong Soon Lee (02/26/1966) **CH:** Julie M. Song; Albert M. Song **ED:** Postdoctoral Fellow, Indiana University School of Medicine (1974); PhD, University of Hawai'i John A. Burns School of Medicine (1972); MS, University of Hawai'i (1966); BA, University of Hawai'i (1964) **C:** Sponsor and Mentor, VA Greater Los Angeles Healthcare System, Los Angeles, CA (1998-Present); Research Professor, UCLA David Geffen School of Medicine (1993-Present); Associate Research Professor, UCLA David Geffen School of Medicine (1987-1993); Chief Research Laboratory, Department of Veterans Affairs Medical Center, Sepulveda, CA (1983-1998); Assistant Research Professor, UCLA David Geffen School of Medicine

(1980-1987); Postdoctoral Fellow, Indiana University, Indianapolis, IN (1974); Research Chemist, Department of Veterans Affairs Medical Center, North Hills, CA (1974-1983); Junior Researcher, University of Hawaii, Honolulu, Hawaii (1965-1969); Research Assistant, University of Hawai'i, Honolulu, Hawaii (1962-1965) **CR:** Manuscript Reviewer, 10 Scientific Journals (1980-Present); Ad Hoc Research Application Reviewer, National Institutes of Health, Department of Veterans Affairs Research Services, American Diabetic Association, U.S. Department of Agriculture Research Services (1980-Present) **CIV:** Member, Two Committees, Northridge United Methodist Church, CA (1988-Present); Board Member, American College of Nutrition, American Nutrition Association **CW:** Contributor, About 80 Peer-reviewed Academic Journals; Patentee, New Drug Development with Pro-Z for the Treatment and Prevention of Diabetes and Cancer Treatment and Cyclo-Z for the Prevention and Treatment of Diabetes, Obesity, Alzheimer's Disease, Immune Disorder, Atherosclerosis and Cancer Treatment (Preparation) **AW:** Grantee, National Institutes of Health (1998); DVA Medical Research Service Grantee (1982, 1985); Cancer Research Grantee, Indiana University Cancer Research Institute (1974) **MEM:** Fellow, American College of Nutrition, American Nutrition Association; American Institute of Nutrition; American Society for Clinical Nutrition; American Diabetes Association **MH:** Albert Nelson Marquis Lifetime Achievement Award; Marquis Who's Who Top Professional **B/I:** Dr. Song became involved in his profession because he was from Korea and came to the university of Hawaii. Someone suggested to him that with chemistry he could make good money, so, he started doing chemistry. Then he found out it was not for him and so he changed it to biological science. **AV:** Traveling **PA:** Democrat **RE:** United Methodist

SONNEK, BONNIE, PHD, T: Education Educator **I:** Education/Educational Services **DOB:** 10/15/1953 **PB:** Wells **SC:** MN/USA **PT:** Albert Peter; Mary Jane Sonnek **MS:** Single **SPN:** Steven Walter Nelson (11/22/1949) **ED:** Doctor of Philosophy in Language, Literacy and Culture, University of Iowa, Iowa City, IA (2003); Master of Arts in Developmental Adult Education, Texas State University, San Marcos, TX (1995); Bachelor of Science in English and Speech, Winona State University, Minnesota (1976) **C:** Retired (2018); Associate Professor, Western Illinois University, Macomb, IL (2003-2018); English Education Coordinator, Western Illinois University, Macomb, IL (2004-2012); Assistant Professor, Western Illinois University, Macomb, IL (2003-2006); Student, Teaching Supervisor, University of Iowa, Iowa City, IA (2000-2003); Professor, University of Texas, Austin, TX (1995-1998); Coordinator, Student Learning Center, Texas State University, San Marcos, TX (1993-1995); Reporter, Editor, Research & Planning Consultants Inc. (1982-1990); High School Teacher, Department Defense, Hanan, Germany (1979-1982); Teacher, NATO Base, Keflavik, Iceland (1978-1979); High School Teacher, Alexandria Senior High School, Minnesota (1976-1978) **CR:** Coordinator, Director, English Education Program (2005-2016); Educational Director, Operation Springboard, Canyon Lake, TX (1990-1992); Presenter in Field; Organizer, Project on Rhetoric of Inquiry, Student Learning Assistance Center Workshops **CIV:** Board Member, San Marcos Youth Services (1994-1996); Member, Friends of the Public Library **CW:** Author, "Remediation in the Writing Classroom"; Author, "Critical Literacy in the Classroom"; Author, "My Grandmother's Chair"; Contributor, 29 Articles, Texas National Resources Reporter; Contributor, 19 Articles, Texas Public Utility Needs **AW:** Outstanding

Advisor, National Council of Teachers of English (2004); Named, Development Education Graduate Student of the Year, Texas State University (1995) **MEM:** Illinois Literacy Association (2011-Present); Representer, Teacher Education (2009-2011); Illinois Association of Teacher Educators; National Council of Teachers of English **MH:** Albert Nelson Marquis Lifetime Achievement Award **B/I:** Ms. Sonnek became involved in her profession due to the influence of her English teachers in school, who inspired her to follow the same path. **AV:** Gardening; Reading; Quilting

SORA, SEBASTIAN ANTONY, DPS, PMC, T: Business Machines Manufacturing Executive, Educator **I:** Machinery **DOB:** 06/29/1943 **PB:** New York **SC:** NY/USA **PT:** Joseph Louis Sora; Angelina Maria (Maletta) Sora **MS:** Married **SPN:** Mary Frances Elizabeth Boscketti (10/12/1974); Janet Lee Dietz, (04/11/1970, Deceased 07/1972) **CH:** Joseph Walter; Sebastian Nicholas; Francis Anne; Jenny Concetta **ED:** DPS, Pace University (1989); PMC, Iona College (1976); MBA, Iona College (1974); BS, Brooklyn College (1964) **C:** President, Business Education Systems Tech. (1992-1995); Associate Professor, MIS, Montclair State College, Upper Montclair, NJ (1992-1995); Manager, Promotional-artificial Intelligence Systems, IBM, White Plains, NY (1990-2015); Manager, Education Program, World Trade Corp. IBM, North Tarrytown, NY (1989-1990); Program Director, Systems Research Institute, IBM, New York, NY (1984-1987); Manager, Research Staff, 1st Josephson System, IBM, Yorktown, NY (1982-1984); Senior Programmer, IBM, Boeblingen, Federal Republic of Germany (1981-1982); Analyst on Market Models, IBM, Harrison, NY (1977-1981); Manager, Program System and Design, IBM, Fishkill, NY (1971-1977); Programmer, Modeller, IBM, Yorktown, NY (1970-1972); With, U.S. Coast and Geodetic Survey, Washington (1967-1970); Manager, Programming, IBM, Yorktown, NY (1966-1967, 1970-1975); Mathematics Modeller, Associate Universities Inc. (1964-1966) **CR:** Independent Research in Artificial Intelligence (2017-Present); Management and Info System, Adelphi University (2002-2017); Associate Professor, Computer Science, Marymount College, Tarrytown, NY (1999); Visiting Professor, Long Island University (1997); Associate Professor, Information Science, Pace University, White Plains, NY (1977-1996); Consultant, Agency for International Development, Washington (1989); Assistant Professor, Management, Manhattan College, Bronx, NY (1988); Assistant Professor, Telecommunications, Iona College, New Rochelle, NY (1986); Speaker in Field **MIL:** U.S. Navy (1967-1971) **CW:** Editor, Journal of Value Based Management (1987-Present); Publisher, Paradegon Shifts in Education: Paradise Lost or Regained, University Press of America, Information Systems Ethics, Northeast Decision Science Institute (2004); Editor, Journal of Cross Cultural Management, Journal of American Management (1994-1999); Contributor, Articles, Professional Journals **MEM:** Technological Leadership Committee, IEEE (1986-Present); Information Policy Committee, IEEE (1986-1995); Data Processing Management Association; Association of Computing Machinery **MH:** Albert Nelson Marquis Lifetime Achievement Award **B/I:** Mr. Sora became involved in his profession because he had a degree in physics and mathematics as an undergraduate. He then went into Brookhaven laboratory to do research in atomic subatomic particles. **AV:** Working with flowers; Gardening **RE:** Roman Catholic

SORENSON, ARNE, T: Chief Executive Officer, President **I:** Leisure, Travel & Tourism **CN:** Marriott International **PB:** Tokyo **SC:** Japan **MS:** Married

CH: Four Children **ED:** Doctor of Jurisprudence, University of Minnesota Law School (1983); Bachelor of Arts, Luther College (1980) **C:** President, Chief Executive Officer, Marriott International, Inc. (2012-Present); President, Chief Operating Officer, Marriott International Inc. (2009-2012); Vice President, President of Lodging, Chief Financial Officer, Marriott International Inc. (2003-2009); Executive Vice President, Chief Financial Officer, Marriott International Inc. (1998-2003); Senior Vice President, Business Development, Marriott International Inc. (1996-1998); Vice President, Associate General Counsel, Marriott International Inc. (1996); Partner, Latham & Watkins (1984-1996) **CR:** Member, Board of Directors, Walmart Inc. (2008-2013) **CIV:** Advocate, LGBT Rights **AW:** CEO For All Leadership Award, Great Place to Work (2020); Named "CEO of the Year," Chief Executive Magazine (2019); 2017 Deming Cup for Operational Excellence, W. Edwards Deming Center, Columbia Business School (2017); Honoree, U.S. Travel Hall of Leaders (2017); International Hotel Investment Forum (IHIF) Lifetime Achievement Award (2016) **MEM:** Board Member, Microsoft Corporation (2017-Present); Board Member, Luther College **PA:** Democrat

SORKIN, AARON, T: Writer **I:** Media & Entertainment **DOB:** 06/09/1961 **PB:** New York **SC:** NY/USA **MS:** Divorced **SPN:** Julia Bingham (04/13/1996, Divorced 2005) **CH:** Roxy **ED:** Honorary Degree, Purchase College, State University of New York (2012); BFA in Musical Theatre, Syracuse University (1983) **CW:** Director, Screenwriter, "The Trial of Chicago 7" (2020); Playwright, "To Kill a Mockingbird" (2018); Director, Screenwriter, "Molly's Game" (2017); Screenwriter, "Steve Jobs" (2015); Creator, Writer, Executive Producer, "The Newsroom" (2012-2014); Screenwriter, "Moneyball" (2011); Himself, "30 Rock" (2011); Screenwriter, Actor, "The Social Network" (2010); Appearance, "Entourage" (2009, 2010); Screenwriter, "Charlie Wilson's War" (2007); Playwright, "The Farnsworth Invention" (2007); Creator, Writer, Executive Producer, "Studio 60 on the Sunset Strip" (2006-2007); Creator, Writer, Executive Producer, "The West Wing" (1999-2006); Creator, Writer, Executive Producer, "Sports Night" (1998-2000); Screenwriter, "The American President" (1995); Screenwriter, "Malice" (1993); Screenwriter, "A Few Good Men" (1992); Playwright, "Making Movies" (1990); Playwright, "A Few Good Men" (1989); Playwright, "Hidden in This Picture" (1988) **AW:** Golden Globe for Best Screenplay - Motion Picture, "Steve Jobs," Hollywood Foreign Press Association (2015); Named Best Adapted Screenplay, "Steve Jobs," Awards Circuit Community Awards (2015); Named Best Screenplay - Adapted, "Steve Jobs," Satellite Awards (2015); EDA Award for Best Writing, Adapted Screenplay, "Moneyball," Alliance of Women Film Journalists (2012); Academy Award for Best Writing, Adapted Screenplay, "The Social Network," Academy of Motion Picture Arts and Sciences (2011); Golden Globe for Best Screenplay - Motion Picture, "The Social Network," Hollywood Foreign Press Association (2011); BAFTA Film Award, Best Screenplay (Adapted), "The Social Network" (2011); EDA Award for Best Writing, Adapted Screenplay, "The Social Network," Alliance of Women Film Journalists (2011); Named Best Adapted Screenplay, "Moneyball," Critics' Choice Movie Awards (2011); AFCA Award for Best Adapted Screenplay, "The Social Network," Austin Film Critics Association (2010); Named Best Adapted Screenplay, "The Social Network," Awards Circuit Community Awards (2010); Davis Award, Best Adapted Screenplay, "The Social Network," Awards Circuit Community Awards (2010); Named Best Adapted Screenplay, "The Social Network,"

Critics' Choice Movie Awards (2010); Named Best Screenplay - Adapted, "The Social Network," Satellite Awards (2010); Named Best Adapted Screenplay, "The Social Network," Writers Guild of America Awards (2010); Primetime Emmy for Outstanding Drama Series, "The West Wing," Television Academy (1999, 2000, 2002, 2003); Primetime Emmy for Outstanding Special Class Program, "The West Wing Documentary Special," Television Academy (2002); Phoenix Rising Award (2001); Awards for Episodic Drama, "In Excelsis Deo," "The West Wing," Writers Guild of America Awards (2000); Numerous Other Awards and Accolades

SOROS, GEORGE, T: Hedge Fund Manager; Entrepreneur; Philanthropist **I:** Nonprofit & Philanthropy **DOB:** 08/12/1930 **PB:** Budapest **SC:** Hungary **PT:** Tivadar Soros; Elizabeth (Szucs) Soros **MS:** Married **SPN:** Tamiko Bolton (09/21/2013); Susan Weber (06/19/1983, Divorced 2005); Annaliese Witschak (09/17/1960, Divorced 1983) **CH:** Robert Daniel Soros; Andrea Soros Colombel; Jonathan Tivadar Soros; Alexander Soros; Gregory James Soros **ED:** Honorary Doctorate in Economics, University of Bologna (1995); Honorary Doctorate, Yale University (1991); Honorary Doctorate, Corvinus University of Budapest (1991); Honorary Doctorate, University of Oxford (1980); Honorary LLD, The New School for Social Research (1980); MS in Philosophy, London School of Economics (1954); BS in Philosophy, London School of Economics (1951) **C:** Chairman, Soros Fund Management, LLC, New York, NY (1996-Present); Founder, Soros Fund Management, LLC, New York, NY (1969-Present); Co-founder, Principal Adviser, Quantum Fund, Soros Fund Management, LLC (1970-Present); Vice President, Arnhold & S. Bleichroeder, New York, NY (1963-1973); Analyst, Wertheim & Co., New York, NY (1959-1963); Arbitrage Trader, F.M. Mayer, New York, NY (1956-1959); Clerk, Employee in the Arbitrage Department, Singer & Friedlander (1954-1956) **CIV:** Founder, Chairman, Open Society Institute (Now Open Society Foundations) (1993-Present); Chairman, Founding President, Central European University, Budapest, Hungary (1991); Member, Board of Directors, Center for American Progress (CAP) (2003) **CW:** Author, "In Defense of Open Society" (2019); Co-author, "The Tragedy of the European Union: Disintegration or Revival?" (2014); Author, "Financial Turmoil in Europe and the United States" (2012); Author, "The Soros Lectures at the Central European University" (2010); Appearance, Documentary, "Inside Job" (2010); Author, "The Crash of 2008 and What it Means: The New Paradigm for Financial Markets" (2009); Author, "Underwriting Democracy: Encouraging Free Enterprise and Democratic Reform Among the Soviets in Eastern Europe" (2008); Author, "The New Paradigm for Financial Markets: The Credit Crisis of 2008 and What It Means" (2008); Author, "Soros on Soros: Staying Ahead of the Curve" (2008); Author, "The Age of Fallibility: Consequences of the War on Terror" (2007); Author, "George Soros on Globalization" (2005); Author, "The Bubble of American Supremacy: Correcting the Misuse of American Power" (2004); Author, "The Bubble of American Supremacy" (2003); Author, "The Alchemy of Finance" (2001); Author, "Open Society: Reforming Global Capitalism" (2000); Author, "The Crisis of Global Capitalism: Open Society Endangered" (1998); Author, "Soros on Soros: Staying Ahead of the Curve" (1995); Author, "Opening the Soviet System" (1990); Author, "The Alchemy of Finance: Reading the Mind of the Market" (1987) **AW:** Named One of World's Richest People, Forbes (1999-Present); Named to the Forbes 400: Richest Americans (1999-Present); Ridenhour Prize for Courage (2019); Named Person of the Year, Financial Times (2018); Named One of

the 50 Most Influential People in Global Finance, Bloomberg Markets (2011); Inductee, Hedge Fund Manager Hall of Fame, Institutional Investors Alpha (2008); Named One of New York's Influentials, New York Magazine (2006); International Center Finance Award, Yale School of Management (2000) **MEM:** Honorary Fellow, The British Academy; Royal Institute of International Affairs, Council on Foreign Relations **AV:** Tennis; Skiing; Chess; Backgammon **PA:** Democrat

SOSSAMAN, SCOTT, T: Lieutenant Colonel (R), United States Army **I:** Military & Defense Services **CN:** Department of Defense **MS:** Married **ED:** MA, Human Resources Development, Webster University (2001); BS in History, Arizona State University (1989); Degree, United States Army Staff College **CT:** Certified, Arizona Department of Education Teacher **C:** Substitute Teacher, Arizona State University Preparatory Academy (2014-2015); Training Consultant, Joint Staff J7, Suffolk, VA (2009-2012); Advisor, United States Army, Iraqi Assistance Group, Baghdad, Iraq (2008-2009); Training Consultant, United States Joint Forces Command, J7, Suffolk, VA (2004-2008) **CIV:** Horse Handler, Boulder Mountain Therapy (2015); Education, Kennel Buddy, & Maintenance, Friends For Life Animal Rescue (2014); Canine Caregiver, Friends For life Animal Rescue & Adoption Organization (2014); Volunteer, Friends 4 Life Animal Shelter; Education & Shelter Tours, Plus Shelter Maintenance, Friends For Life Animal Rescue & Adoption Organization; Founding Sponsor, Museum of the United States Army **MIL:** Operations Officer, 2nd Battalion, 3rd Field Artillery Regiment, 1st Brigade, 1st Armored Division, Iraq, Giessen, Germany (2003-2004); Army Officer, U.S. Army (1989-2003) **AW:** 4 Bronze Star Medals, United States Army; 2 Defense Meritorious Service Medals; Two Presidential Unit Citations **AS:** Mr. Sossaman attributes his success to his good parenting and the values that were imputed on him from both of his grandparents who showed him that hard work pays off.

SOTO, DARREN MICHAEL, T: U.S. Representative from Florida **I:** Government Administration/Government Relations/Government Services **DOB:** 02/25/1978 **PB:** Ringwood **SC:** NJ/USA **PT:** O. Lou Soto; Jean Soto **MS:** Married **SPN:** Amanda Soto (2013) **ED:** JD, The George Washington University Law School (2004); BA in Economic, Rutgers, The State University of New Jersey (2000) **C:** Member, U.S House of Representatives from Florida's Ninth Congressional District, United States Congress, Washington, DC (2017-Present); President, D. Soto Law Offices (2005-Present); Member, District 49, Florida House of Representatives (2007-2017); Summer Associate, Luis A. Gonzalez Law Offices (2002-2004); Financial Analyst, Prudential Insurance (1998-2001); Member, Committee on Agriculture, United States Congress; Member, Committee on Natural Resources, United States Congress; Member, Criminal and Civil Justice Appropriations Committee, Florida House of Representatives; Member, Energy and Utilities Policy Committee, Florida House of Representatives; Ranking Member, Civil Justice and Courts Policy Committee, Florida House of Representatives **CIV:** Member, Civil Service Board, City of Orlando, FL (2006-Present); Member, Hispanic Chamber of Commerce of Metro Orlando, FL (2006-Present) **MEM:** Treasurer, Orange County Democrats (2007); Vice President, Communications, Orange County Young Democrats (2007); Orange County Democrats; Orange County Young Democrats **PA:** Democrat

SOUTER, DAVID HACKETT, T: Associate Justice (Retired) **I:** Government Administration/Government Relations/Government Services **CN:** Supreme Court of the United States **DOB:** 09/17/1939 **PB:** Melrose **SC:** MA/USA **PT:** Joseph Alexander Souter; Helen Adams (Hackett) Souter **ED:** Honorary LLD, Harvard University (2010); LLB, Harvard Law School (1966); BA, University of Oxford (1963); MA in Jurisprudence, University of Oxford (1963); AB in Philosophy, Harvard University, Magna Cum Laude (1961) **C:** Associate Justice, Supreme Court of the United States, Washington, DC (1990-2009); Judge, U.S. Court of Appeals for the First Circuit, NH (1990); Associate Justice, New Hampshire Supreme Court (1983-1990); Associate Justice, New Hampshire Superior Court (1978-1983); Attorney General, State of New Hampshire (1976-1978); Deputy Attorney General, State of New Hampshire (1971-1976); Assistant Attorney General, State of New Hampshire (1968-1971); Associate, Orr & Reno, Concord, NH (1966-1968) **CR:** Member, New Hampshire Governor's Commission Crime and Delinquency (1976-1978, 1979-1983); Member, New Hampshire Judicial Council (1976-1978); Member, New Hampshire Police Standards and Training Council (1976-1978); Member, Maine-NH Interstate Boundary Commission (1971) **CIV:** Trustee, New Hampshire Historical Society (2009-Present); Overseer, Dartmouth Giesel School of Medicine (1981-1987); Vice President, New Hampshire Historical Society (1980-1985); Trustee, New Hampshire Historical Society (1976-1985); Trustee, Concord Hospital (1972-1985); President, Concord Hospital (1978-1984) **AW:** Rhodes Scholar (1963); Honorary Fellow, Magdalen College, University of Oxford **MEM:** Honorary Master, Gray's Inn, London, England; Fellow, American Academy of Arts & Sciences; Fellow, Massachusetts Historical Society; Honorary Member, American College of Trial Lawyers; Honorary Member, American Bar Foundation; American Antiquarian Society; The American Philosophical Society; Honorary Member, New England Historical and Genealogical Society; Honorary Member, Pilgrim Society; Merrimack County Bar Association; New Hampshire Bar Association; Phi Beta Kappa Society **BAR:** State of New Hampshire (1967) **PA:** Republican **RE:** Episcopalian

SOUTHREY, MELISSA ANNE, T: Registered Dietitian, Certified Diabertes Educator, Aqua Instructor **I:** Health, Wellness and Fitness **CN:** Atlanticare **DOB:** 11/20/1961 **PB:** Fairhaven **SC:** MA/USA **YOP:** 1999 and 2009 **PT:** Walter Louis Slowik; Pauline Mary Slowik **MS:** Married **SPN:** Brian Douglas Southrey **CH:** Brian William Southrey; Amber Brooke Southrey **ED:** Bachelor of Science in Dietitian, University of Medicine and Dentistry of New Jersey, Newark, NJ (2008); Associate of Applied Science in Dietetic Technician, Camden Community College, Camden, NJ (1999); Coursework in General Studies, Atlantic Cape Community College, Hamilton, NJ (1997) **CT:** Certified Pound Instructor (2018-Present); Certificate of Training in Adult Weight Management (2009, 2018); Certified Cize Instructor (2016); Certified Diabetes Educator (2013); Certified, Transformational Coach, Optavia **C:** Optavia Transformational Coach (2018-Present); Instructor, Certified Pound (2018-Present); Aqua Instructor (2014-Present); Atlanticare, Registered Dietician, Certified Diabetes Educator (2013-Present); Instructor, Certified Cize (2016); Ornish Program Dietitian (2016-2017); Instructor, Water Aerobics (2014); Registered Dietician, Shore Memorial Hospital (2009-2013); Adjunct Professor, Atlantic Cape Community College (2009-2010); Dietitian, Shore Memorial Hospital (2008-2009); Registered Dietetic Technician (2000-2008); Registered, Dietetic Technician, Absecon Manor Nursing Home (1999-2000); Fore Caddy, Seaview Marriot Restaurant and Golf Course (1998) **CIV:** Mission Trips, Local Church **CW:** Founder, 20/20 What's Your Vision? **AW:** Partners in Caring Excellence Award, Clinical (2019); Listee, Marquis Who's Who (2019); Icare Award (2019); Academic Excellence Award, Camden College, Dietetic Program (1999); Employee of the Month, Shore Memorial Hospital; Pat on the Back Award **MEM:** Academy of Nutrition and Dietetics; American Association of Diabetes Educators **AS:** Ms. Southrey attributes her success to her strong support system, which consists of her husband and her late mother-in-law. Her Christian faith has also served to point her in the right direction. She has always had a desire to help people and is not afraid to try new things. **B/I:** Ms. Southrey made a lifestyle change by quitting smoking years ago. After gaining a significant amount of weight, she decided to search for a healthy meal plan, which led her to obtain a degree in nutrition three years later. After serving in the field for less than a year, she returned to school for further education and became a certified diabetes educator. In 2018, she became a certified Optavia health coach to provide lifelong transformation - one healthy habit at a time. **AV:** Golf; Softball; Swimming; Exercise; Gardening; Cooking; Knitting; Violin; Mission trips **PA:** Republican **RE:** Christian **THT:** When you smile, the whole world smiles, but when you cry, you cry alone!'

SOVERN, DOUGLAS, T: Author, Journalist; Musician **I:** Media & Entertainment **CN:** KCBS Radio **DOB:** 02/01/1961 **PB:** New York **SC:** NY/USA **PT:** Lenni Sanders; Michael I. Sovern **MS:** Married **SPN:** Dr. Sara Neumann **CH:** Mya; Jacob **ED:** Coursework, Fiction Writing Master Class, The Writers Studio, San Francisco, CA (2012-2017); Coursework, Training Program, Professional Screenwriters, Writers Boot Camp Inc., Los Angeles, CA (2000-2001); BA in History, Brown University (1984); **C:** Fiction Writer (2011-Present); Political, Investigative Reporter, KCBS Radio, San Francisco, CA (2006-Present); General Assignment Reporter, Anchor, KCBS Radio, San Francisco, CA (1997-2006); Reporter, Anchor, Editor, Writer, KCBS Radio, San Francisco, CA (1990-1997); Producer, KGO Radio, San Francisco, CA (1990); Reporter, Anchor, Assistant News Director, K101 Radio, San Francisco, CA (1985-1990); Northern California Correspondent, Associated Press Radio Network (1986-1991); Copy Clerk, The New York Times (1979); Songwriter; Composer; Vocalist **CR:** Host, Monthly Reading Series, "There," Oakland, CA (2015); Professional Bass Player, More Than 15 Bands; Vocalist, Songwriter, Radio Troupe, "Not Ready for Drive Time Players" **CW:** Author, Short Story, "Grace Notes," Catamaran (2019); Author, Short Story, "Skin," The Madison Review (2016); Author, Short Story, "Fully Committed," Alimentum (2015); Author, Short Story, "Who Knows How It Will Come Out?" EDGE Literary Journal (2015); Author, Short Story, "Where We'll Hide When the Nazis Come," Mulberry Fork Review (2015); Author, Short Story, "Morning Rush," Black and White (2014); Author, Short Story, "Indira," Narrative (2014); Author, Short Story, "Co-Anchors," Crack the Spine (2014); Author, Short Story, "Abe Vigoda Is Still Alive," Hobo Pancakes (2014); Author, Short Story, "Almost Every One of Us," Sand Hill Review (2014); Author, Short Story, "The Blogger Wolf," Green Hills Literary Lantern, Gemini (2014); Author, Twitter Novel, "Tweet-Heart" (2011); Author, 11 Published Stories, 17 Magazines, Journals **AW:** First Place, Short Story Contest, "Skin," Mendocino Coast Writers' Conference (2018); Inductee, Bay Area Radio Hall of Fame (2017); Selected for Writers Studio@80 Anthology, "Skin," Epiphany Editions (2017); duPont-Colum-bia Award, Special Citation, Columbia University (2016); Named Top Ten Finalist, "Skin," Zoetrope: All-Story, Short Story Context (2015); Named Top Ten Finalist, "Skin," Narrative, Winter Story Contest (2015); John Swett Award, California Teachers Association (2014); Named Top Five Stories of the Year, "Indira," Narrative Magazine (2014); California Journalism Award, Sacramento State University (2013); Edward R. Murrow Award (2002-2018); Best Reporter, Associated Press Television and Radio Association (1999-2018); Twice-Named, One of the Best Political Reporters in the Country, Washington Post; Eight-Time Winner, Sigma Delta Chi Award, Society of Professional Journalists; 13-Time Winner, National Headliners Award, Press Club of Atlantic City; Winner, More Than 200 Journalism Awards **MEM:** Society of Professional Journalists; Radio Television Digital News Association; Associated Press Television and Radio Association **MH:** Marquis Who's Who Top Professional **AS:** Mr. Sovern attributes his success to hard work, good luck and being raised well by his parents. **B/I:** Mr. Sovern had always been a great storyteller. He knew at a young age that he wanted to be a novelist when he grew up. He started his own newspaper by the time he was in fourth grade. He always enjoyed finding out about things and telling people about them. Mr. Sovern also enjoyed writing songs because to him, it is also a form of storytelling.

SOWERS, KATIE, T: Offensive Assistant Coach **I:** Athletics **CN:** San Francisco 49ers **DOB:** 08/01/1986 **PB:** Hesston **SC:** KS/USA **ED:** MA in Kinesiology, University of Central Missouri, Warrensburg, MO (2012); Coursework, Hesston College, Hesston, KS; Coursework, Goshen College, Goshen, IN **C:** Offensive Assistant, San Francisco 49ers, National Football League (2019-Present); Seasonal Offensive Assistant, San Francisco 49ers, National Football League (2017-2019); Training Camp Assistant, Atlanta Falcons, National Football League (2016); Football Player, West Michigan Mayhem, Women's Football Alliance; Football Player, Kansas City Titans, Women's Football Alliance **CR:** U.S. Women's National American Football Team **AW:** IFAF Women's World Champion (2013)

SOX, HAROLD, "HAL" CARLETON, T: Director of Peer Review **I:** Research **CN:** Patient-Centered Outcomes Research Institute **DOB:** 08/18/1939 **PB:** Palo Alto **SC:** CA/USA **PT:** Harold Carleton Sox; Mary (Griffiths) Sox **MS:** Married **SPN:** Carol Helen Hill (08/26/1962) **CH:** Colin Montgomery; Lara Katherine **ED:** Internship, Residency, Massachusetts General Hospital (1966-1968); MD, Harvard University, Cum Laude (1966); BS, Stanford University (1961) **CT:** Diplomate, American Board of Internal Medicine **C:** Program Director of Peer Review, Patient-Centered Outcomes Research Institute (2014-Present); Emeritus Professor of Medicine, Geisel School of Medicine, Dartmouth University (2009-Present); Editor-in-Chief, Annals of Internal Medicine, American College of Physicians, Philadelphia (2001-2009); Joseph Huber Professor, Chair, Department of Medicine, Geisel School of Medicine, Dartmouth University (1988-2001); Assistant Professor of Medicine, Professor of Clinical Medicine, Stanford Medicine (1973-1988); Instructor, Geisel School of Medicine, Dartmouth University (1970-1973); Clinical Associate, National Cancer Institute, Bethesda, MD (1968-1970) **CR:** Physician, Leaders National Drug Policy (1997-Present); Chair, Scientific Advisory Committee, The Discharge Project (2014-2019); External Advisory Board Member, University of Washington Cancer Consortium (2011-2014); Chairman, National Advisory Committee of Physicians, Faculty Scholar Program, Robert Wood Johnson

Foundation (2005-2012); Committee for Evidence Framework for Obesity Prevention, Institute of Medicine (2008-2010); Committee Standards for Systematic Reviews, Institute of Medicine (2009); Co-Chair, Committee for Priority-Setting for Comparative Effectiveness Research, Institute of Medicine (2009); Vice Chair, Committee on High Value Health Services, Institute of Medicine (2006-2007); Report Review Committee, National Research Council (2000-2005); Complementary and Alternative Medicine Committee, Institute of Medicine (2003-2004); Founding Chair, Medicare Coverage Advisory Committee (1999-2003); Chair, Committee on Health Effects of Persian Gulf War Service, Institute of Medicine (1998-2000); Chair, Task Force to Revise Internal Medicine Residency Curriculum, Federated Council of Internal Medicine (1993-1997); Chair, Committee on HIV & US Blood Supply, Institute of Medicine (1994-1995); Pretest Writing Committee, American Board of Internal Medicine (1992-1994); Chair, Committee on Priority-Setting for Health Technology Assessment, Institute of Medicine (1990-1991); Panel Member, National Board of Medical Examiners (1973-1976) **CIV:** Board of Directors, The Institute For Innovative Technology in Medical Education (2011-2014); Board of Directors, Foundation for Informed Medical Decision Making (2002-2012) **CW:** Author, "Medical Decision Making Second Edition" (2013); Associate Editor, "Scientific American Medicine (1995-2001); Editorial Board Member, New England Journal of Medicine (1990-1997); Consulting Associate Editor, American Journal of Medicine (1988-1995); Editor, "Common Diagnostic Tests Second Edition (1990); Editor, "Common Diagnostic Tests" (1987); Editor Board Member, Journal of General Internal Medicine (1985-1987); Editorial Board Member, Medical Decision Making (1980-1987); Author, Co-Author, 250 Articles, Professional Journals **AW:** Fellow, Royal College of Physicians (2018); John M. Eisenberg Award, Society for Medical Decision Making (2007); Fellow, American Association for the Advancement of Science (2002); Robert J. Glaser Award for Career Achievement, Society for General Internal Medicine (2000); Mastership, American College of Physicians (1999); Honorary Fellow, Royal Australasian College of Medicine (1999); Career Achievement Award, Society for Medical Decision Making (1998); Elected Member, Institute of Medicine (1993); Elected Member, Association of American Physicians (1990); Alpha Omega Alpha Honor Medical Society (1966) **MEM:** National Academy of Medicine (1993-Present); Association of American Physicians (1990-Present); Editorial Board Member, JAMA (2011-2019); Board of Trustees, The College of Physicians of Philadelphia (2006-2009); International Committee of Medical Journal Editors (2001-2009); Association of Professors of Medicine (1988-2001); Board of Regents, American College of Physicians (1991-2000); President, American College of Physicians (1998-1999); Chairman, Educational Policy Committee, American College of Physicians (1994-1997); Clinical Efficacy Assessment Subcommittee (1985-1992); President, Society for Medical Decision Making (1983-1984); Trustee, Society for Medical Decision Making (1989-1983); Council Member, Society for General Internal Medicine (1980-1983); Alpha Omega Alpha Medical Honor Society; Royal Australasian College of Physicians; American Association for the Advancement of Science **AS:** Mr. Sox attributes his success to his trustworthiness. **AV:** Backpacking; Mountaineering; Taking photographs; Maintaining an interest in architecture

SPACEK, SISSY, T: Actress **I:** Media & Entertainment **DOB:** 12/25/1949 **PB:** Quitman **SC:** TX/USA **PT:** Edwin Spacek; Virginia Spacek **MS:** Married **SPN:** Jack Fisk (04/21/1974) **CH:** Schuyler Fisk; Madison Fisk **ED:** Coursework, Lee Strasberg Theatrre and Film Institute **CW:** Actress, "Homecoming" (2018); Actress, Music Video, "Oh Baby," LCD Soundsystem (2018); Actress, "Castle Rock" (2018); Actress, "The Old Man & the Gun" (2018); Actress, Bloodline" (2015-2017); Actress, "Dedafall" (2012); Actress, "The Help" (2011); Actress, "Gimme Shelter" (2010); Actress, "Big Love" (2010); Actress, "Get Low" (2009); Actress, "Four Christmases" (2008); Actress, "Lake City" (2008); Actress, "Pictures of Hollis Woods" (2007); Actress, "Hot Rod" (2007); Actress, "Gray Matters" (2006); Actress, "Summer Running: The Race to Cure Breast Cancer" (2006); Actress, "An American Haunting" (2005); Actress, "North Country" (2005); Actress, "The Ring Two" (2005); Actress, "Nine Lives" (2005); Actress, "A Home at the End of the World" (2004); Actress, "Tuck Everlasting" (2002); Actress, "Last Call" (2002); Actress, "Midwives" (2001); Actress, "In the Bedroom" (2001); Actress, "Songs in Ordinary Time" (2000); Actress, "The Straight Story" (1999); Actress, "Blast from the Past" (1999); Actress, "Affliction" (1997); Actress, "If These Walls Could Talk" (1996); Actress, "Beyond the Call" (1996); Actress, "Streets of Laredo" (1995); Actress, "The Grass Harp" (1995); Actress, "The Good Old Boys" (1995); Actress, "A Place for Annie" (1994); Actress, "Trading Mom" (1994); Actress, "A Private Matter" (1992); Narrator, Segment,"Shelley Duvall's Bedtime Stories" (1992); Actress, "JFK" (1991); Actress, "Hard Promises" (1991); Actress, "The Long Walk Home" (1990); Actress, "Crimes of the Heart" (1986); Actress, "'night, Mother" (1986); Actress, "Violets Are Blue..." (1986); Actress, "Marie" (1985); Actress, "The River" (1984); Actress, "The Man with Two Brains" (1983); Actress, "Missing" (1982); Actress, "Raggedy Man" (1981); Actress, "Heart Beat" (1980); Actress, "Coal Miner's Daughter" (1980); Actress, "Great Performances" (1978); Actress, "3 Women" (1977); Actress, "Welcome to L.A." (1976); Actress, "Carrie" (1976); Actress, "Katherine" (1975); Actress, "Ginger in the Morning" (1974); Actress, "The Migrants" (1974); Actress, "The Rookies" (1973); Actress, "Badlands" (1973); Actress, "Waltons" (1973); Actress, "The Girls of Huntington House" (1973); Actress, "Love, American Style" (1973); Actress, "Prime Cut" (1972) **AW:** Inductee, Online Film & Television Association (OFTA) Film Hall of Fame (2016); Honoree, Star, Hollywood Walk of Fame (2011); Lifetime Achievement Award, Houston Film Critics Society Awards (2010); Best Performance by an Actress in a Motion Picture - Drama, "In the Bedroom," Golden Globes (2002); Best Actress, "In the Bedroom," Broadcast Film Critics Association Awards (2002); Best Actress, "In the Bedroom," Dallas-Fort Worth Film Critics Association Awards (2002); Best Female Lead, "In the Bedroom," Film Independent Spirit Awards (2002); Best Actress, "In the Bedroom," Florida Film Critics Circle Awards (2002); Best Actress, "In the Bedroom," Online Film & Television Association (OFTA) (2002); Golden Satellite Award, "In the Bedroom," Satellite Awards (2002); Film Excellence Award, Boston Film Festival (2001); Best Actress, "In the Bedroom," Los Angeles Film Critics Association Awards (2001); Best Actress, "In the Bedroom," New York Film Critics Circle Awards (2001); Best Actress, "In the Bedroom," Southeastern Film Critics Association Awards (2001); Special Jury Prize, "In the Bedroom," Sundance Film Festival (2001); Inductee, Texas Hall of Fame (2001); Best Performance by an Actress in a Motion Picture - Comedy or Musical, "Crimes of the Heart," Golden Globes (1987); Best Actress, "Crimes of the Heart," Kansas City Film Critics Circle Awards (1986); Best Actress, "Crimes of the Heart," New York Film Critics Circle Awards (1986); Best Actress in a Leading Role, "Coal Miner's Daughter," Academy Awards (1981); Best Actress in a Motion Picture - Comedy or Musical, "Coal Miner's Daughter," Golden Globes (1981); Best Actress, "Coal Miner's Daughter," Kansas City Film Critics Circle Awards (1980); Best Actress, "Coal Miner's Daughter," Los Angeles Film Critics Association Awards (1980); Best Actress, "Coal Miner's Daughter," National Board of Review (1980); Bets Actress, "Coal Miner's Daughter," New York Film Critics Circle Awards (1980); Best Supporting Actress, "3 Women," New York Film Critics Circle Awards (1977); Best Actress, "Carrie," National Society of Film Critics Awards (1977); Special Mention, "Carrie," Avoriaz Fantastic Film Festival (1977)

SPADA, JESSICA MARIE, T: Director/Owner **I:** Education/Educational Services **CN:** Magical Journey Learning Center **DOB:** 10/20/1976 **PB:** New York **SC:** NY/USA **ED:** Master of Arts in Early Childhood Education, College of New Rochelle (2012); Bachelor of Arts in American Studies and Early Childhood Education, Queens College (2008) **C:** Owner, Director, Magical Journey Learning Center **CIV:** Member, Ahwatukee Chamber of Commerce; Donator, Love Society; Donates Snacks to Kyrene School District; Collected Sports Equipment for Disadvantaged Children, Winter Wonderland Event; Donator, Baby Shower Drive for Teenage Moms; Volunteer, Big Heart Challenge, American Heart Association **AW:** Named, One of the Best Preschools (2017-Present); Best of Ahwatukee **MEM:** The Voice of Small Business; Ahwatukee Chamber of Commerce, National Association for the Education of Young Children **AS:** Ms. Spada attributes her success to hard work and caring for the individual needs to the children, families and teachers. She is also passionate about creating school environments that focus on developing thoughtful, caring and empathetic children who care about the world around them while excelling in their academic studies. She is known for being a hands-on director who makes frequent appearances in classrooms and helps both teachers and students when needed. **B/I:** Ms. Spada became involved in her profession due to her childhood fascination with the field of teaching. Working with children is the only job she has ever had. **THT:** It is important to think "outside of the box" when working with children.

SPADER, JAMES, T: Actor **I:** Media & Entertainment **DOB:** 02/07/1960 **PB:** Boston **SC:** MA/USA **PT:** Todd Spader; Jean Spader **MS:** Married **SPN:** Victoria Kheel (1987, Divorced 2004) **CH:** Sebastian; Elijah; Nathaneal **ED:** Coursework, Michael Chekhov Acting Studio; Coursework, Phillips Academy **CW:** Actor, "The Blacklist" (2013-Present); Executive Producer, "The Blacklist" (2015-2020); Actor, "Avengers: Age of Ultron" (2015); Co-executive Producer, 18 Episodes, "The Blacklist" (2014-2015); Actor, "The Homesman" (2014); Actor, "Lincoln" (2012); Actor, "The Office" (2011-2012); Actor, "Shorts" (2009); Actor, "Boston Legal" (2004-2008); Actor, "Shadow of Fear" (2004); Actor, "The Practice" (2003-2004); Actor, "Alien Hunter" (2003); Actor, "I Witness" (2003); Actor, "The Pentagon Papers" (2003); Actor, "The Stickup" (2002); Actor, "Secretary" (2002); Actor, "Speaking of Sex" (2001); Actor, "Slow Burn" (2000); Actor, "The Watcher" (2000); Actor, "It All Came True" (1998); Actor, "Seinfeld" (1997); Actor, "Critical Care" (1997); Actor, "Keys to Tulsa" (1997); Actor, "Driftwood" (1997); Actor, "2 Days in the Valley" (1996); Actor, "Crash" (1996); Actor, "Stargate" (1994); Actor, "Frasier" (1994); Actor, "Wolf" (1994); Actor, "Dream Lover" (1993); Actor, "The Music of Chance" (1993); Actor, "Storyville" (1992); Actor,

"Bob Roberts" (1992); Actor, "True Colors" (1991); Actor, "White Palace" (1990); Actor, "Bad Influence" (1990); Actor, "The Rachel Papers" (1989); Actor, "Sex, Lies, and Videotape" (1989); Actor, "Greasy Lake" (1988); Actor, "Jack's Back" (1988); Actor, "Wall Street" (1987); Actor, "Less Than Zero" (1987); Actor, "Baby Boom" (1987); Actor, "Mannequin" (1987); Actor, "Pretty in Pink" (1986); Actor, "Starcrossed" (1985); Actor, "The New Kids" (1985); Actor, "Tuff Turf" (1985); Actor, "Family Secrets" (1984); Actor, "A Killer in the Family" (1983); Actor, "Diner" (1983); Actor, "Cocaine: One Man's Seduction" (1983); Actor, "The Family Tree" (1983); Actor, "Endless Love" (1981); Actor, "Team-Mates" (1978) **AW:** Best Male Lead Vocal Performance in a Feature Film, "Avengers: Age of Ultron," Behind the Voice Actors Awards (2016); Primetime Emmy for Outstanding Lead Actor in a Drama Series, "Boston Legal," Television Academy (2005, 2007, 2008); Best Actor in a Series, Comedy or Musical, "Boston Legal," Satellite Awards (2006); Primetime Emmy for Outstanding Lead Actor in a Drama Series, "The Practice," Television Academy (2004); Best Actor, "Sex, Lies, and Videotape," Cannes Film Festival (1989)

SPAIN, JACK HOLLAND JR., T: Senior Counsel **I:** Law and Legal Services **CN:** Hunton Andrews Kurth **DOB:** 01/24/1939 **PB:** Greenville **SC:** NC/USA **PT:** Jack Holland Spain; Lucy Marie (Hardee) Spain **MS:** Married **SPN:** Mary Elizabeth Rhamstine (05/09/1964) **CH:** John Hardee; Sidney Holland **ED:** JD, Harvard University (1963); AB, The University of North Carolina at Chapel Hill (1960) **C:** Partner, Hunton & Williams (Now Hunton Andrews Kurth), Richmond, VA (1971-Present); Associate, Hunton & Williams (Now Hunton Andrews Kurth), Richmond, VA (1964-1971); Senior Counsel, Hunton Williams Andrews Kurth (Now Hunton Andrews Kurth), Richmond, VA **CR:** Virginia Chairman, Section of Urban, State and Local Government Law, ABA; State Chairman, State and Local Government Obligations Committee, ABA; Fellow, American College of Bond Counsel, Inc. **CIV:** Board of Directors, Maymont Foundation, Richmond, VA (1975-Present); President, Maymont Foundation, Richmond, VA (1980-1982); Special Counsel, Local Government Committee, Virginia Constitutional Revision Commission (1971); Member, Board of Elders, Second Presbyterian Church, Richmond, VA; City Democratic Committee, Richmond, VA; President, King and Queen County Historical Society, King & Queen Courthouse Tavern Museum **MIL:** Lieutenant Commander, United States Navy Judge Advocate General's Corps **CW:** Author, "Retracing Marco Polo" (2003) **AW:** The Phi Beta Kappa Society; Phi Eta Sigma National Honor Society, Inc.; Phi Alpha Theta National History Honor Society; Named to Highest Honorary, Order of Golden Fleece, University of North Carolina at Chapel Hill; Fellow, American College of Bond Counsel, Inc. **MEM:** American Bar Association (ABA); Chairman, Taxation Committee, Local Government Section, American Bar Association (ABA); The Virginia Bar Association; Richmond Bar Association (Now The Bar Association of the City of Richmond); American College of Bond Counsel, Inc.; President, Harvard Law School Association, VA; Downtown Club, Richmond, VA; Harvard Club of New York **BAR:** Virginia (1964); United States District Court for the Eastern District of Virginia (1964) **B/I:** Mr. Spain became involved in his profession because of his dad. He majored in history not knowing what he would do with a history degree, but his dad, who also was an attorney, told him that a legal background would give him a good background for business or anything else. **AV:** Spectator sports; Antiques; Chinese art; Farming; Writing **PA:** Democrat **RE:** Presbyterian

SPANBERGER, ABIGAIL ANNE, T: U.S. Representative from Virginia **I:** Government Administration/Government Relations/Government Services **DOB:** 08/07/1979 **PB:** Red Bank **SC:** NJ/USA **MS:** Married **SPN:** Adam Spanberger **CH:** Three Daughters **ED:** MBA, Purdue University Krannert School of Management; BA, University of Virginia **C:** Member, U.S. House of Representative from Virginia's Seventh Congressional District (2019-Present); Operations Officer, Central Intelligence Agency (2006-Present) **CR:** Substitute Teacher, English Literature, Islamic Saudi Academy of Washington (2002-2003); Federal Postal Inspector, Money Laundering Cases, Interception of Illegal Drug Shipments **CIV:** Member, Virginia Governor's Fair Housing Board

SPANO, VINCENT, "ROSS" ROSS, T: U.S. Representative from Florida **I:** Government Administration/Government Relations/Government Services **CN:** U.S. House of Representatives **DOB:** 07/16/1966 **PB:** Tampa **SC:** FL/USA **MS:** Married **SPN:** Amie Spano **CH:** Kali; Vincent; Caleb; Isaiah **ED:** Doctor of Jurisprudence, Florida State University College of Law, Cum Laude (1998); Bachelor of Arts in History, University of South Florida, Tampa, FL (1994) **C:** Member, U.S. House of Representatives from Florida's 15th Congressional District (2019-Present); Member, District 59, Florida House of Representatives (2012-2018); Shareholder, Law Practice **PA:** Republican

SPEARS, BRITNEY, T: Singer **I:** Media & Entertainment **DOB:** 12/02/1981 **PB:** McComb **SC:** MS/USA **PT:** James Spears; Lynne Spears **SPN:** Kevin Federline (2004, Divorced 2007); Jason Allen Alexander (2004, Annulled 2004) **CH:** Sean Federline; Jayden James Federline; Kori (Stepchild); Kaleb (Stepchild) **C:** Entertainer, Recording Artist (1992-Present) **CR:** Designer, Limited Edition Collection for Candie's Clothing Brand (2010); Signature Fragrance, Radiance (2010); Signature Fragrance, Circus Fantasy (2009); Signature Fragrance, Hidden Fantasy (2009); Signature Fragrance, Curious Heart (2008); Signature Fragrance, Midnight Fantasy (2007); Signature Fragrance, Curious In Control (2006); Signature Fragrance, Britney Spears: Fantasy (2005); Signature Fragrance, Curious (2004) **CIV:** Founder, Supporter, Britney Spears Foundation (1999-Present); Supporter, Donor, Nevada Childhood Cancer Foundation (2015); Supporter, Donor, "An Evening of Southern Style," St. Bernard Project (2011); Singer, "Artists Against AIDS Worldwide" (2001); Advocate, LGBTQ Rights; Supporter, Numerous Charities **CW:** Herself, "Corporate Animals" (2019); Singer, "Glory" (2016); Performer, "Britney: Piece of Me" (2013-2017); Singer, "Britney Jean" (2013); Judge, "The X-Factor" (2012-2013); Singer, Album, "Femme Fatale" (2011); Singer, "Circus" (2008); Singer, "Blackout" (2007); Herself, "Fahrenheit 9/11" (2004); Singer, "In the Zone" (2003); Herself, "Pauly Shore Is Dead" (2003); Herself, "Austin Powers in Goldmember" (2002); Actress, "Crossroads" (2002); Singer, "Britney" (2001); Actress, "Longshot" (2001); Singer, "Oops!... I Did It Again" (2000); Singer, "...Baby One More Time" (1999); Performer, Numerous Music Videos; Herself, Numerous TV Shows **AW:** Billboard Millennium Award, Billboard Music Awards (2016); Favorite Social Media Celebrity, People's Choice Awards (2016); Candie's Style Icon Award, Teen Choice Awards (2015); Favorite Pop Artist, People's Choice Awards (2014); Michael Jackson Video Vanguard Award, MTV Video Music Awards (2011); Best Dance Recording, "Womanizer," Grammy Awards (2010); Listee, "The World's Most Powerful Celebrities," Forbes (2010); Best Solo Female Artist, Virgin Media Music Awards (2009); Named

"Sexiest Woman in the World," FHM (2004, 2008, 2009); MTV Video Music Award for Video of the Year, "Pieces of Me" (2008); Best Dance Recording, "Toxic," Grammy Awards (2005); Star, Hollywood Walk of Fame (2003); Fun Fearless Female Award, Cosmopolitan (2002); Artist of the Year, Rolling Stone (2001); Best Selling Female Dance Artist, World Music Awards (2001); Best Selling Female Pop Artist (2001, 2000); Best Female Artist, Kids' Choice Awards (2001, 2000); Best International Artist, Mnet Asian Music Awards (2000); Favorite Pop/Rock New Artist, American Music Awards (2000); Album Artist of the Year, Billboard Music Awards (2000); Female Artist of the Year (1999); Best New Artist (1999); Best Female Artist, Hollywood Reporter (1999); Best New Artist (1999); Numerous Awards and Accolades

SPEIER, KAREN, "JACKIE" LORRAINE JACQUELINE, T: U.S. Representative from California **I:** Government Administration/Government Relations/Government Services **CN:** U.S. House of Representatives **DOB:** 05/14/1950 **PB:** San Francisco **SC:** CA/USA **PT:** Manfred Speier; Nancy (Kanchelian) Speier **MS:** Married **SPN:** Barry Dennis (2001); Steven K. Sierra, MD (1987, Deceased 1994) **CH:** Stephanie Katelin; Jackson Kent **ED:** Doctor of Jurisprudence, University of California Hastings College of the Law (1976); Bachelor of Arts, University of California Davis (1972) **C:** Member, U.S. House of Representatives from California's 14th Congressional District, United States Congress, Washington, DC (2013-Present); Member, U.S. House Committee on Homeland Security (2011-Present); Member, U.S. House Committee on Oversight and Government Reform (2008-Present); Member, U.S. House of Representatives from California's 12th Congressional District, United States Congress, Washington, DC (2008-2013); Member, U.S. House Special Committee on Energy Independence and Global Warming (2008-2010); Member, U.S. House Financial Services Committee (2008-2010); Of Counsel, Hanson Bridgett LLP, San Francisco, CA (2007-2008); Member, District Eight, California State Senate (1998-2006); Director, Governmental and Corporate Affairs, Poplar ReCare (1996-1998); Vice President, Governmental and Community Affairs, Electronic Arts Inc. (1996-1998); Member, District 19, California State Assembly (1986-1996); Chair, Consumer Protection Committee, California State Assembly (1991-1995); Majority Whip, California State Assembly (1988-1992); Chair, San Mateo County Board of Supervisors, CA (1980-1984, 1985-1986); Legal Council to Representative Leo J. Ryan, United States Congress (1973-1978); Member, Committee on Education and Workforce; Member, Committee on Transportation and Infrastructure **CW:** Author, "Undaunted: Surviving Jonestown, Summoning Courage, and Fighting Back" (2018); Co-author, "This is Not the Life I Ordered: 50 Ways to Keep Your Head Above Water When Life Keeps Dragging You Down" (2007) **AW:** Named, Legislator of the Year, Metropolitan Transportation Commission (2004) **BAR:** State of California **PA:** Democrat **RE:** Roman Catholic

SPEIGHT, JOSEPH B. SR., T: Chief Executive Officer, Agent **I:** Insurance **CN:** Joe Speight Insurance **DOB:** 04/08/1951 **PB:** Albemarle **SC:** NC/USA **PT:** Joseph Gad Speight; Ramona Holt Speight **MS:** Divorced **CH:** Joseph II (Jay); Christopher (Chris) **ED:** MA, University of Virginia (2006); BS, Gardner-Webb University (1974) **CT:** Life Underwriter Training Council Fellow (LUTCF) Designation **C:** Owner, Chief Executive Officer, Agent, Joe Speight Insurance, Albemarle, NC, State Farm Insurance (1987-Present) **CIV:** Volunteer, EMS/Fire Rescue, 10 Years; Coach (Five Years)

AW: Bronze Tablet, State Farm; Crystal of Excellence, State Farm; Golden Triangle, State Farm MH: Marquis Who's Who Top Professional B/I: Mr. Speight became involved in his profession because his father was in the insurance business for 30 years prior to his passing. He had an opportunity in insurance with the mindset that he would be helping others. He noted, "Education is the best way to save somebody's life."His father read a book called "This I Believe" that taught him that "you have to believe in what you're doing regardless [of anything]." He inherited that belief from his father. AV: Horses; Cars THT: Mr. Speight's one son is a professional musician while the other is vice president of a marketing firm.

SPENCE, GERRY, T: Lawyer, Writer I: Law and Legal Services DOB: 01/08/1929 PB: Laramie SC: WY/USA PT: Gerald M. Spence; Esther Sophie (Pfleeger) Spence MS: Married SPN: LaNelle Hampton Peterson (11/18/1969); Anna Wilson (06/20/1947) CH: Kip; Kerry; Katy ED: Honorary Doctor of Law, University of Wyoming (1990); Bachelor of Laws, University of Wyoming (1952); Bachelor of Science in Law, University of Wyoming (1949) C: Senior Partner, Spence Law Firm (2004-Present); Senior Partner, Spence, Moriarity & Shockey (2002-2003); Senior Partner, Spence, Moriarity & Schuster, Jackson, WY (1978-2002); Partner, Numerous Law Firms, Riverton and Casper, WY (1962-1978); County and Prosecuting Attorney, Fremont County, WY (1954-1962); Sole Practice, Riverton, WY (1952-1954) CR: Lecturer, Legal Organizations and Law Schools; Founder, Trial Lawyers College CW: Author, "Court of Lies" (2019); Author, "Police State: How America's Cops Get Away with Murder" (2015); Author, "How to Argue and Win Every Time" (2015); Author, "Bloodthirsty Bitches and Pious Pimps of Power: The Rise and Risks of the New Conservative Hate Culture" (2006); Author, "Win Your Case: How to Present, Persuade and Prevail - Every Place, Every Time" (2006); Author, "The Smoking Gun: Day by Day Through a Shocking Murder" (2003); Author, "Seven Simple Steps to Personal Freedom: An Owner's Manual for Life" (2002); Author, "Half Moon and Empty Stars" (2001); Author, "Gerry Spence's Wyoming: The Landscape" (2000); Author, "A Boy's Summer: Fathers and Sons Together" (2000); Author, "O.J.: The Last Word" (1997); Author, "The Making of a Country Lawyer" (1996); Author, "How to Argue & Win Every Time: At Home, at Work, In Court, Everywhere, Everyday" (1995); Author, "From Freedom to Slavery: The Rebirth of Tyranny in America" (1993); Author, "With Justice for None: Destroying an American Myth" (1989); Author, "Trial by Fire: The True Story of a Woman's Ordeal at the Hands of the Law" (1986); Author, "Of Murder and Madness: A True Story of Insanity and the Law" (1983); Author, "Gunning for Justice - My Life and Trials" (1982); Guest, "The Oprah Winfrey Show," "Larry King Live," "Geraldo"; Legal Consultant, O.J. Simpson Trial, NBC AW: Lifetime Achievement Award, American Association for Justice (2013); Inductee, American Trial Lawyers Hall of Fame (2009); Lifetime Achievement Award, Consumer Attorneys of California (2008) MEM: American Bar Association; Wyoming Bar Association; Wyoming Trial Lawyers Association; American Association for Justice; National Association of Criminal Defense Lawyers BAR: Supreme Court of the United States (1982); Wyoming (1952); U.S. Court of Claims (1952)

SPENCER, OCTAVIA, T: Actress, Producer, Author I: Media & Entertainment DOB: 05/25/1972 PB: Montgomery SC: AL/USA PT: Dellsena Spencer ED: BS in Liberal Arts, Auburn University (1994) CW: Actress, "The Witches" (2020); Actress,

Executive Producer, "Self Made: Inspired by the Life of Madam C.J. Walker" (2020); Voice Actress, "Onward" (2020); Voice Actress, "Dolittle" (2020); Actress, Executive Producer, "Truth Be Told" (2019-2020); Actress, Executive Producer, "Ma" (2019); Actress, "Instant Family" (2018); Narrator, "The Goldbergs: 1990-Something" (2018); Actress, "A Kid Like Jake" (2018); Executive Producer, "Green Book" (2018); Actress, "The Shape of Water" (2017); Actress, "Gifted" (2017); Actress, "Small Town Crime" (2017); Actress, "The Shack" (2017); Executive Producer, "Small Town Crime" (2017); Executive Producer, "Candid" (2017); Actress, "Hidden Figures" (2016); Actress, "Bad Santa 2" (2016); Actress, "Car Dogs" (2016); Actress, "Allegiant" (2016); Voice Actress, "Zootopia" (2016); Actress, "The Free World" (2016); Actress, "The Great Gilly Hopkins" (2015); Actress, "Fathers & Daughters" (2015); Actress, "Drunk History" (2015); Actress, "Break a Hip" (2015); Actress, "Insurgent" (2015); Actress, "Red Band Society" (2014-2015); Author, "The Sweetest Heist in History" (2015); Actress, "Black or White" (2014); Actress, "Get on Up" (2014); Actress, "Mom" (2013-2015); Actress, "Paradise" (2013); Voice Actress, "Percy Jackson: Sea of Monsters" (2013); Actress, "Snowpiercer" (2013); Actress, "Call Me Crazy: A Five Film" (2013); Voice Actress, "American Dad!" (2013); Actress, "Lost on Purpose" (2013); Actress, Co-Executive Producer, "Fruitvale Station" (2013); Herself, "30 Rock" (2013); Author, "The Case of the Time-Capsule Bandit" (2013); Actress, "Blues for Willadean" (2012); Actress, "The Perfect Fit" (2012); Actress, "The Help" (2011); Actress, "Flypaper" (2011); Actress, "Peep World" (2010); Actress, "Love & Distrust" (2010); Actress, "Dinner for Schmucks" (2010); Actress, "Hawthorne" (2010); Actress, "Small Town Saturday Night" (2010); Actress, "Raising the Bar" (2009); Actress, "Herpes Boy" (2009); Actress, "Love at First Hiccup" (2009); Actress, "Halloween II" (2009); Actress, "Just Peck" (2009); Actress, "Jesus People: The Movie" (2009); Actress, "The Soloist" (2009); Actress, "Dollhouse" (2009); Actress, "Drag Me to Hell" (2009); Actress, "Worst Week" (2009); Actress, "Next to Kin" (2008); Actress, "Seven Pounds" (2008); Actress, "Faux Baby" (2008); Actress, "The Big Bang Theory" (2008); Actress, "The Speenectomy" (2008); Actress, "CSI: Crime Scene Investigation" (2008); Actress, "Pretty Ugly People" (2008); Actress, "Wizards of Waverly Place" (2008); Producer, "The Captain" (2008); Actress, "Halfway Homes" (2007); Actress, "Ugly Betty" (2007); Actress, "The Nines" (2007); Actress, "The minor Accomplishments of Jackie Woodman" (2006-2007); Actress, "Standoff" (2006); Actress, "Pulse" (2006); Actress, "Huff" (2006); Actress, "Medium" (2005); Actress, "Wannabe" (2005); Actress, "CSI: NY" (2005); Actress, "Beauty Shop" (2005); Actress, "Miss Congeniality 2: Armed & Fabulous" (2005); Actress, "Marilyn Hotchkiss' Ballroom Dancing & Charm School" (2005); Actress, "Pretty Persuasion" (2005); Actress, "Coach Carter" (2005); Actress, "LAX" (2004-2005); Actress, "Breakin' All the Rules" (2004); Actress, "Win a Date with Tad Hamilton!" (2004); Actress, "Bad Santa" (2003); Actress, "Chicken Party" (2003); Actress, "S.W.A.T." (2003); Actress, "Legally Blonde 2: Red, White & Blonde" (2003); Actress, "Sol Goode" (2003); Actress, "NYPD Blue" (2002-2005); Actress, "Presidio Med" (2002); Actress, "Little John" (2002); Actress, "Spider-Man" (2002); Actress, "Titus" (2001-2002); Actress, "The Chronicle" (2001-2002); Actress, "Dharma & Greg" (2001); Actress, "Follow the Stars Home" (2001); Actress, "Grounded for Life" (2001); Actress, "The Journeyman" (2001); Actress, "City of Angels" (2000); Actress, "Becker" (2000); Actress, "Four Dogs Playing Poker" (2000); Actress, "Just Shoot Me!" (2000); Actress, "Auto Motives" (2000); Actress, "What

Planet Are You From?" (2000); Actress, "Missing Pieces" (2000); Actress, "Chicken Soup for the Soul" (2000); Actress, "Everything Put Together" (2000); Actress, "The Sky Is Falling" (1999); Actress, "The X-Files" (1999); Actress, "Roswell" (1999); Actress, "Chicago Hope" (1999); Actress, "Blue Streak" (1999); Actress, "Being John Malkovich" (1999); Actress, "Live Virgin" (1999); Actress, "L.A. Doctors" (1999); Actress, "Never Been Kissed" (1999); Actress, "Lansky" (1999); Actress, "Brimstone" (1999); Actress, "ER" (1998); Actress, "To Have & to Hold" (1998); Actress, "Moesha" (1998); Actress, "Sparkler" (1997); Actress, "413 Hope St." (1997); Actress, "The Sixth Man" (1997); Actress, "A Time to Kill" (1996) AW: Best Supporting Actress, "Black or White," African American Film Critics (2014); Best Supporting Actress, "Fruitvale Station," National Board of Review Awards (2013); Best Supporting Actress: Television Movie/Cable, "Call Me Crazy: A Five Film," Black Reel Awards (2013); Best Supporting Actress, "The Help," Academy Awards (2012); Best Film Actress in a Supporting Role, "The Help," British Academy of Film and Television Arts (BAFTA) Awards (2012); Best Supporting Actress - Motion Picture, "The Help," Golden Globe Awards (2012); Outstanding Performance by a Female Actor in a Supporting Role in a Motion Picture, "The Help," Screen Actors Guild Awards (2012); Best Supporting Actress, "The Help," Black Reel Awards (2012); Best Supporting Actress, "The Help," Critics Film Awards, "The Help," Critics Choice Film Awards (2012); Outstanding Supporting Actress in a Motion Picture, "The Help," NAACP Awards (2012); Best Supporting Actress, "The Help," African American Film Critics (2011); Best Supporting Actress, "The Help," Alliance of Women Film Journalists (2011); Best Supporting Actress, "The Help," Black Film Critics Circle (2011); Best Supporting Actress, "Hidden Figures," Gold Derby Film Awards (2011); Best Supporting Actress, "The Help," North Texas Film Critics Association Awards (2011); Best Supporting Actress, "The Help," Oklahoma Film Critics Circle Awards (2011); Breakthrough Performance, "The Help" (2011); Best Supporting Actress, "The Help," Washington D.C. Area Film Critics Association Awards (2011)

SPIEGEL, EVAN THOMAS, T: Entrepreneur, Application Developer I: Technology DOB: 06/04/1990 PB: Los Angeles SC: CA/USA PT: John W. Spiegel; Melissa Ann (Thomas) Spiegel MS: Married SPN: Miranda Kerr (05/27/2017) CH: Hart Kerr Spiegel; Myles Spiegel ED: BS in Product Design, Stanford University (2018); Coursework, Art Center of College Design (2007-2008); Coursework, Otis College of Art and Design C: Co-Founder, Chief Executive Officer, Snap Inc., Venice, CA (2011-Present); Software Developer, Intuit (2010); Intern, Abraxis Bioscience (2009) CIV: Co-Founder, Snap Foundation (2017) AW: Listee, "The Forbes 400," Forbes (2019); Listee, "Richest In Tech," Forbes (2017); Listee, "America's Richest Entrepreneurs Under 40," Forbes (2016); Listee, "The 100 Most Influential People in the World," Time (2014); Listee, "The 40 Under 40," Fortune (2014); Listee, "The 30 Under 30: Technology," Forbes (2014); Listee, "100 Most Influential People in the World," Time (2014); Listee, "The 30 Under 30 Changing the World," Time (2013); First Place Award for Newspaper Infographics, Columbia Scholastic Press Association (2008) MEM: 21st Century Council, Berggruen Institute; Kappa Sigma

SPIETH, JORDAN ALEXANDER, T: Professional Golfer I: Athletics DOB: 07/27/1933 PB: Dallas SC: TX/USA PT: Shawn Spieth; Mary Christine (Julius) Spieth MS: Married SPN: Annie Verret (11/2018) ED: Coursework, University of Texas (2011-2012); Diploma, Jesuit College Preparatory School (2011)

C: Professional Golfer (2012-Present) CIV: Founder, Jordan Spieth Family Foundation (2013-Present); PGA Bible Study AW: Winner, The Open Championship, Travelers Championship, AT&T Pebble Beach Pro-Am (2017); Byron Nelson Award (2015, 2017); Vardon Trophy (2015, 2017); Winner, Presidents Cup (2013, 2015, 2017); Winner, Dean & DeLuca Invitational, Hyundai Tournament of Champions, Emirates Australian Open, Ryder Cup (2016); Winner, Tour Championship, John Deere Classic, U.S. Open, Masters Tournament, Valspar Championship (2015); FedEx Cup Champion (2015); PGA Tour Player of the Year (2015); PGA Player of the Year (2015); Winner, Emirates Australian Open, Hero World Challenge (2014); Winner, John Deere Classic (2013); PGA Tour Rookie of the Year (2013); Winner, Junior Ryder Cup (2008, 2010); Rolex Junior Player of the Year, American Junior Golf Association (2009) RE: Christian

SPILKER, JAMES JULIUS JR., DENG, T: Engineer; Consulting Professor I: Engineering CN: Stanford University MS: Married SPN: Anna Marie Spilker ED: Diploma, Senior Management Program, University of California Los Angeles (1985); DEng in Electrical Engineering, Stanford University (1958); MSEE, Stanford University (1956); BSEE, Stanford University (1955) C: Consulting Professor, Electrical Engineering and Aeronautics and Astronautics Department, Stanford University (2001-2019); Co-founder, Executive Chairman, President, Chief Executive Officer, Stanford Telecommunications Inc., Sunnyvale, CA (1973-1999); Manager, Communications Sciences Department, Ford Aerospace Corporation (1963-1973); Manager, Lockheed Corporation (Now Lockheed Martin Corporation) (1958-1963) CR: Invited Lecturer, Munich and Berlin, Germany (2011); Invited Lecturer, Tsinghua University, Beijing, China (2010); Co-founder, Stanford University Research Center for Position, Navigation and Time (2005); Co-founder, Executive Chairman, AOSense Inc. (2005); Invited Lecturer, Samsung Corporation, Republic of Korea (2003); Co-founder, Chairman, Rosum; Invited Lecturer, Marconi Lab, Bologna, Italy CIV: Donor, James and Anna Marie Spilker Engineering and Applied Sciences Building, Stanford University (2012); Engineering Advisory Board, Stanford University; Communication Sciences Institute, University of Southern California; GPS Task Force, U.S. Defense Science Board; GPS Independent Review Team, Air Force Space Command CW: Co-author, "Position, Navigation, and Timing Technologies in the 21st Century: Integrated Satellite Navigation, Sensor Systems, and Civil Applications" (2019); Co-author, "Evolution of Modern Digital Communications Security Technologies," Science, Technology and National Security (2002); Co-editor, Co-author, "GPS Global Positioning System: Theory and Applications" (1996); Author, "Digital Communications by Satellite" (1977); Author, Over 100 Technical Papers, IEEE and ION AW: AIAA Sommerfield Best Book Medal, American Institute of Aeronautics and Astronautics (1996) MEM: Life Fellow, IEEE; Peer Review Committee, NAE for Electronics, National Academy of Engineering; Chairman, Technical Advisory Committee, IEEE

SPINA, ANTHONY FERDINAND, ESQ., T: Lawyer I: Law and Legal Services CN: Spina McGuire & Okal, P.C. DOB: 08/15/1937 PB: Chicago SC: IL/USA PT: John Dominic Spina; Nancy Maria (Ponzio) Spina MS: Married SPN: Anita Phyllis De Orio (01/28/1961) CH: Nancy M. Spina-Okal; John D.; Catherine M. Spina-Samatas; Maria J. Spina-Samatas; Felicia M. Spina DiGiovani ED: JD, DePaul University, Chicago, IL (1962); BS in Social Sciences, Loyola University, Chicago, IL (1959) C: Arbitrator, Circuit Court of Cook County (1990-

1998); President, Senior Counsel, Spina McGuire & Okal, P.C., Elmwood Park, IL (1985-2011); Director, Spina McGuire & Okal, P.C. (1971-1999); President, Anthony & Spina, P.C. (Now Spina McGuire & Okal, P.C. (1971-1984); Private Practice, Elmwood Park, IL (1964-1971); Associate, Epton, Scott, McCarthy & Bohling, Chicago, IL (1962-1964) CIV: Board of Directors, Sheridan Carroll Charitable Works Fund (1994-Present); Counsel, Norwood Park Street Lighting District (1988-Present); Counsel, Norwood Park, IL (1982-Present); Counsel, Cook County Highway Commissioners Traffic Fine Litigation (1999-2001); Counsel, Berwyn Township Community Mental Health Board (1997-2002); Counsel, Berwyn Township, IL (1997-1999); Counsel, Hanover Township, IL (1997); Counsel, Glen Eden Homeowners Association (1994-1999); Counsel, Hanover Township Mental Health Board (1991-2002); Counsel, Wayne, IL (1982-1984); Counsel, Maine, IL (1981-1997); Counsel, Various Cook County Townships (DuPage) (1980-1982); Counsel for Executive Director, Illinois State Association Township Officials (1975-1996); Counsel for President and Director, Cook County Township Officials, IL (1975-1996); Counsel, Cook County Highway Commissioners Traffic Fine Litigation (1974-1996); Attorney, Rosemont, IL (1971); Attorney, Leyden Township, IL (1969-1989); Counsel, Village of Elmwood Park Board (1967-1989); Board of Appeals, Elmwood Park Building Code Planning Commission CW: Contributor, Leyden Township Codified Ordinances (1987); Contributor, Elmwood Park Building Code (1975); Codifier, Rosemont Villages Ordinances (1971); Founder, Board Member, Fra Noi Magazine AW: National Attorney A/V Rating, Martindale-Hubbell (1982-Present); B. Scidmore Award, Illinois Township Attorneys Association (2002); Lacodaire Medal, Dean's Key, Housing Awards, Loyola University (1965, 1971, 1976); Appreciation Award, Township Officials of Cook County MEM: Director Emeritus, Illinois Township Attorneys Association (1999-Present); Director, Fra Noi Ethnic Publication (1995-Present); Director, Charitable Words Fund, Knights of Columbus (1991-Present); Board of Directors, Calabresi in America Organization (1991-Present); Director, Illinois Township Attorneys Association (1996-1999); Director, World Bocce League (1994-2002); President, Past Vice President, National Institute of Town and Township Attorneys (1993-1995); President, Past Vice President, Illinois Township Attorneys Association (1982-1986); Scribe, Trustee, Past Grand Knight, Building Corporate Director, Knights of Columbus (1967-1991); American Bar Association (ABA); Illinois State Bar Association; The Chicago Bar Association; Past Chairman, Unauthorized Practice Law Section, West Suburban Bar Association, Cook County, IL; American Judicature Society; Justinian Society of Lawyers; Illinois Delegate, National Institute of Town and Township Attorneys; Montclare/Leyden Chamber of Commerce; Past Board of Directors, Edgebrook Sauganash Chamber of Commerce; National Association of Italian American Lawyers; National Italian American Bar Association; Executive Committee, Joint Civic Committee of Chicago; Society of San Rocco di Simbario; Blue Key Honor Society; Delta Theta Phi; Tau Kappa Epsilon; Pi Gamma Mu Honor Society BAR: Supreme Court of the United States (2005); State of Illinois (1962) MH: Marquis Who's Who Top Professional AV: Lawn, garden, and fish pond landscaping RE: Roman Catholic THT: Mr. Spina has made a huge impact and is active within his Italian community. He founded and sits on the board of Fra Noi Magazine. He has worked together with both Republican and Democratic congressmen to assist in the recognition of the Columbus Day holiday in Chicago, Illinois.

SPIVEY, BRUCE E., MD, MS, MED, T: Ophthalmologist; Educator; Organizational Creator & Leader I: Medicine & Health Care DOB: 08/29/1934 PB: Cedar Rapids SC: IA/USA PT: William Loranzy Spivey; Grace Loretta (Barber) Spivey MS: Married SPN: Patti Amanda Birge Tyson (12/20/1987) CH: Lisa; Eric ED: Honorary DSc, Coe College (1978); MEd, University of Illinois (1969); MS, The University of Iowa (1964); MD, The University of Iowa Roy J. and Lucille A. Carver College of Medicine, Iowa City, Iowa (1959); BA, Coe College, Cum Laude (1956) CT: Diplomate, American Board of Ophthalmology C: Chief Executive Officer, Columbia-Cornell Care, Network Physicians, New York, NY (1998-2001); Chief Executive Officer, Columbia-Cornell Care, New York, NY (1997-2000); Chief Executive Officer, Northwestern Healthcare Network (Now Northwestern Memorial HealthCare), Chicago, IL (1992-1997); Founding Chief Executive Officer and Executive Vice President, American Academy of Ophthalmology, San Francisco, CA (1977-1993); President, Chief Executive Officer, California Healthcare Systems, Bay Area, CA (1986-1992); President and Chief Executive Officer, California Pacific Medical Center, San Francisco, CA (1976-1991); Director, California Pacific Medical Center (1976-1991); Professor, Department of Ophthalmology, California Pacific Medical Center (1971-1987); Chairman, Department of Ophthalmology, California Pacific Medical Center (1971-1987); Dean, University of the Pacific School of Medical Sciences (Now School of Health Sciences), San Francisco, CA (1971-1976); Associate Professor, The University of Iowa Roy J. and Lucille A. Carver College of Medicine (1968-1971); Assistant Professor, Roy J. and Lucille A. Carver College of Medicine (1966) CR: Trustee, MEDEX (Now United Healthcare Global), Baltimore, MD (1999-2010); Board of Directors, MEDEX (Now United Healthcare Global) (1999-2010); Board Secretary, MEDEX (Now United Healthcare Global) (1999-2010); Deputy Executive Vice President, Council of Medical Specialty Societies, AmericanEHR (2002-2008); Trustee, PrimeSight, San Francisco, CA (1996-1999); Board Secretary, PrimeSight (1996-1999); National Board of Directors, Volunteer Hospitals of America (Now Vizient Inc.), Northern California (1991-1996); Trustee, Ophthalmic Mutual Insurance Company (1988-2007); Board of Directors, Ophthalmic Mutual Insurance Company (1988-2007); Board Secretary, Ophthalmic Mutual Insurance Company (1988-2007); Special Medical Advisory Group, United States Department of Veteran Affairs (1987-1993); National Advisory Council, National Eye Institute, National Institutes of Health (1987-1992); Chairman, Board of Directors, Volunteer Hospitals of America (Now Vizient Inc.), Northern California (1985-1987); President, American Board of Medical Specialties (ABMS) (1980-1982); Vice President, American Board of Medical Specialties (ABMS) (1978-1980); With, American EHR (1975-2008); Board of Directors, Reliance Group Holdings Inc., New York, NY; President, Council of Medical Specialty Societies (CMSS); Multiple Lectures in Field CIV: Life Trustee, Coe College (2013-Present); Founder, International Council of Ophthalmology Foundation (2001-Present); Board Member, International Eye Foundation (2000-Present); Helen Keller International (1999-Present); Board of Directors, United States-China Educational Exchange, Institute of International Education, Inc. (1979-Present); Founder, Pacific Vision Foundation (1977-Present); Chair, Pacific Vision Foundation (2001-2019); International Council of Ophthalmology (1985-2018); Trustee, Coe College (1985-2013); American Academy of Ophthalmology Foundation (1977-2011); Chairman, MedBiquitous Consortium (2001-2007); Trustee, MedBiquitous Consortium (2000-2007)

MIL: With, 85th Evacuation Hospital, United States Army, Vietnam (1965-1966); Captain, United States Army (1964-1966) **CW:** Contributor, More than 144 Articles, Professional Journals; Member, 11 Editorial Boards **AW:** Laureate Recognition Award, American Academy of Ophthalmology (2015); Marshall M. Parks Silver Medal, Children's Eye Foundation, American Association for Pediatric Ophthalmology and Strabismus (AAPOS) (2015); Kitty Carlisle Hart Award, NY Glaucoma Research Institute (2014); Bruce E. Spivey, MD, Fund for Risk Management Studies, Ophthalmic Mutual Insurance Company (2012); Honorary Award in Ophthalmology, Societa Oftalmologica Italiana (2012); Guest of Honor, American Academy of Ophthalmology (2011); Scroll of Appreciation, American Academy of Ophthalmology Foundation (2010); EnergEYES Award, AAO Young Ophthalmologists, American Academy of Ophthalmology (2010); Secretariat Award, American Academy of Ophthalmology (2010); Jose Rizal International Gold Medal, Asia-Pacific Academy of Ophthalmology (2009); Regional Achievement Award, The International Agency for the Prevention of Blindness (IAPB) (2008); Congress of Moroccan Ophthalmological Society Recognition, Afro-Asian Congress of Ophthalmology (2007); International Blindness Prevention Award, American Academy of Ophthalmology (2007); Prince Abdulaziz bin Ahmed bin Al Saud Prevention of Blindness Shield Award, Saudi Ophthalmological Society (2007); Secretariat Award, American Academy of Ophthalmology (2007); Sir John Wilson Award, Asia-Pacific Academy of Ophthalmology (2007); Jules Francois Gold Medal, International Council of Ophthalmology (2006); Special Recognition Award, Ophthalmological Society of Nigeria (2005); El-Maghraby Award, Pan-Arab African Council of Ophthalmology (Now Middle East African Council of Ophthalmology (MEACO)) (2005); France Maitland PACME Award, Alliance for Continuing Medical Education in the Health Professions (2005); Distinguished Alumnus Award for Service, The University of Iowa Roy J. and Lucille A. Carver College of Medicine (2003); Life Achievement Honor Award, American Academy of Ophthalmology (2002); Steiff Gold Medal, Academia Ophthalmologica Internationalis (2002); ICLSO Gold Medal, International Medical Contact Lens Symposium, The International Contact Lens Society of Ophthalmologists (1998); Special Guest, Centennial Annual Meeting, American Academy of Ophthalmology (1996); George L. Tabor, M.D. Award, San Diego, CA (1994); Howe Medal, The American Ophthalmological Society (1993); Distinguished Service Award, American Academy of Ophthalmology (1992); Inaugural Harvard Lecturer in Ophthalmology (1989); Lee Allen Award, American Society of Ocularists (1987); Senior Honor Award, American Academy of Ophthalmology (1986); ABMS Distinguished Service Award, American Board of Medical Specialties (ABMS) (1986); Jackson Lecture, American Academy of Ophthalmology (1985); Harry S. Gradle Teaching Medal, PAAO - Pan-American Association of Ophthalmology (1985); Statesmanship Award, Joint Commission on Allied Health Professionals in Ophthalmology (JCAHPO) (1982); Emile Javal Gold Medal, International Contact Lens Council of Ophthalmology (1982); Award for Outstanding Application of Human Performance Technology to an Instructional Situation, National Society for Performance and Instruction (Now International Society for Performance Improvement) (1975); Distinguished Service Award, American Academy of Ophthalmology (1972); Bronze Star Medal, United States Army (1966) **MEM:** European Academy of Arts and Sciences (2011-Present); Most Venerable of the Hospital of St. John of Jerusalem (Now Order of St. John) (1999-Present); Trustee, Interna-

tional Council of Ophthalmology (1985-Present); Academia Ophthalmologica Internationalis (1981-Present); Honorary Member, Association of University Professors of Ophthalmology (AUPO) (1980-Present); Board of Directors, Pacific Vision Foundation (1978-Present); The American Ophthalmological Society (1976-Present); Knight of Justice, Order of St. John (2015); Past President, International Council of Ophthalmology (2014-2018); President, International Council of Ophthalmology (2006-2014); President, Society of Medical Administrators (1999-2001); Secretary General, International Council of Ophthalmology (1994-2006); President, The American Ophthalmological Society (1994-1995); Board of Directors, American Academy of Ophthalmology (1986-1991); Board of Directors, American Board of Ophthalmology (1975-1983); Secretary General, International Congress of Ophthalmology (Now World Ophthalmology Congress, International Council of Ophthalmology) (1978-1982); Chairman, Oral Exam, American Board of Ophthalmology (1976-1981); American Medical Association; Asia-Pacific Academy of Ophthalmology; PAAO - Pan-American Association of Ophthalmology; Pacific-Union Club; Chevy Chase Club; Knickerbocker Club; Cosmos Club; Board Member, Africa Eye Foundation, IAPB; Secretary General, African Eye Foundation, IAPB; Fellow, American College of Surgeons; Fellow, American Board of Ophthalmology **MH:** Albert Nelson Marquis Lifetime Achievement Award; Marquis Who's Who Top Professional **AS:** Dr. Spivey attributes his success to luck and hard work. **B/I:** Dr. Spivey became involved in his profession because he had friends who were pre-med in college. **AV:** Travel; Organizational development; Family **RE:** Presbyterian **THT:** Dr. Spivey's motto on life is to "Keep living it."

SPOLTER, PARI DOKHT, PHD, T: Science Writer **I:** Writing and Editing **DOB:** 01/30/1930 **PB:** Tehran **SC:** Iran **MS:** Widowed **SPN:** Herbert Spolter, MD (08/16/1958, Deceased) **CH:** David; Deborah **ED:** PhD in Biochemistry, University of Wisconsin (1961); Diploma/Licence, Chimie Biologique, University of Geneva (1952) **C:** Writer, Orb Publishing Co., Granada Hills, CA (1988-Present); Research Biochemist, U.S. Public Health Service Hospital, San Francisco, CA (1965-1968); Research Associate, Instructor, Temple University, Philadelphia, PA (1961-1965) **CW:** Author, "Gravitational Force of the Sun"; Author, "The Dance of the Moon" **MEM:** American Association for the Advancement of Science; American Mathematical Society; The New York Academy of Sciences **MH:** Albert Nelson Marquis Lifetime Achievement Award **AS:** Dr. Spolter attributes her success to her first professor, Dr. Alfred E. Harper. **B/I:** Dr. Spolter became involved in her profession because she was always good in school. She really loves and enjoys her work.

SPRENKLE, CASE PHD, T: Economist, Educator **I:** Education/Educational Services **DOB:** 08/18/1934 **PB:** Cleveland **SC:** OH/USA **PT:** Raymond E.; Helen K. (Middleton) Sprenkle **MS:** Married **SPN:** Elaine Elizabeth Jensen (06/22/1957) **CH:** David; Peter; Amy **ED:** Doctor of Philosophy, Yale University (1960); Master of Arts, Yale University (1957); Bachelor of Science, University of Colorado (1956) **C:** Professor Emeritus, University of Illinois at Urbana-Champaign (1997-Present); Director, Warsaw-Illinois Executive MBA Program, University of Illinois at Urbana-Champaign (1991-2003); Professor, University of Illinois at Urbana-Champaign (1970-1997); Faculty Staff Member, University of Illinois at Urbana-Champaign (1960-1997); Acting Head, Department of Economics, University of Illinois at Urbana-Champaign (1995-1996); Chairman, Department of Economics, University of Illi-

nois at Urbana-Champaign (1976-1980); Assistant Dean, College of Commerce, University of Illinois at Urbana-Champaign (1962-1965); Instructor of Economics, Yale University, New Haven, CT (1959-1960) **CR:** Visiting Scholar, London School of Economics (1967, 1974, 1981, 1988); Visiting Lecturer, City of London University (1981); Faculty Member, Economic Institute Boulder (1965, 1972, 1981); Consultant, Illinois Revenue Commission (1962); Board of Directors, Aggregate Equipment Company **CIV:** Board of Directors, Champaign-Urbana Mass Transit District (1983-1996); Vice Chairman, Champaign-Urbana Mass Transit District (1993-1994); Vice Chairman, Champaign-Urbana Mass Transit District (1985); Board of Directors, Champaign County Arts and Humanities Council (1977-1979); President, Champaign-Urbana Symphony (1976-1978); Treasurer, Champaign-Urbana Symphony (1972-1974) **CW:** Developer, First Model of Option Pricing; Contributor, Articles, Professional Journals; Author, Booklet, American Bankers Association **AW:** Grantee, American Bankers Association (1970-1971) **MEM:** American Finance Association; American Economics Association; Omicron Delta Epsilon **MH:** Albert Nelson Marquis Lifetime Achievement Award **RE:** Presbyterian

SPRINGMAN, CLARK ALTON BS, T: Marketing Professional **I:** Advertising & Marketing **CN:** Symons Corp. **DOB:** 09/26/1934 **PB:** Lincoln **SC:** NE/USA **PT:** Alton Clayton Springman; Mona Margaret (Peterson) Springman **MS:** Married **SPN:** Karen Louise Schug (05/21/1983); Karen Elizabeth Bahr (08/27/1954, Divorced 05/1973) **CH:** Jeffrey Clark; Jennifer Lynn (Deceased); Gregory Andrew (Deceased); David Stuart **ED:** BS in Architectural Engineering, University of Nebraska (1957) **C:** Retired (1990); Manager of Advertising, Symons Corporation, Des Plaines, IL (1979-1990); Advertising Manager, G&W Energy Products Group, Oak Brook, IL (1976-1979); Technical Writer, United States Gypsum Company, Chicago, IL (1967-1976); Supervisor, Service Literature, Cushman Motors, Lincoln, NE (1956-1967) **CIV:** Active Member, Local Council, Boy Scouts of America (1970-1973); Board of Directors, President, Willow Creek 1 Association **CW:** Author, "Construction Photography, Trade Show Selling is Different" (1990); Author, "Sound Control in Construction" (1971); Contributor, Articles, Professional Journals **AW:** Many Photography Awards, Lincoln Camera Club and Nebraska State Fair **MEM:** American Management Association; Board of Directors, American Society for Concrete Construction; Associate Council, Concrete Foundation Association; President, Lincoln Camera Club **MH:** Albert Nelson Marquis Lifetime Achievement Award **AS:** Mr. Springman attributes his success to hard work and creativity. **B/I:** Mr. Springman's mother pointed him in the direction of pursuing architecture as a career. At a young age she introduced him to the writings about Frank Lloyd Wright and other famous architects. He went on to receive a degree in Architecture. Although he never worked as an architect, while working for Cushman Motors he was a technical writer, dealing with mainly architectural writings. Eventually after discovering his gift for writing he translated his skills to advertising, marketing but never shied far from his first love of architecture. **AV:** Photography **PA:** Democrat **RE:** Presbyterian

SQUERI, STEPHEN J., T: Chief Executive Officer **I:** Business Management/Business Services **CN:** American Express Company **MS:** Married **SPN:** Ann Squeri **CH:** Marissa; Monica **ED:** MBA, Manhattan College (1986); BS, Manhattan College (1981) **C:** Chairman, Chief Executive Officer, American Express Company, New York, NY (2018-Present); Vice-Chairman, American Express Company, New York, NY (2015-2018); Group President, Global Services, American Express Company, New York (2009-2015); Executive Vice President, Chief Information Officer, American Express Company (2005-2009); President, Global Commercial Card Group, American Express Company (2002-2005); President, Establishment Services, U.S. & Canada, American Express Company (2000-2001); Management Positions, American Express Company (1985-2000); Management Consultant, Arthur Andersen LLP (1981-1985) **CR:** Board of Directors, J. Crew Group, Inc. (2010-Present); Board of Directors, The Guardian Life Insurance Company of America (2009-Present) **CIV:** Chairperson, The Valerie Fund Golf Tournament; Board of Trustees, Valerie Fund; Board of Trustees, Manhattan College; Board of Directors, Ratcliff Acquisition Corp.; Board of Trustees, Harlem Children's Zone; Board of Trustees, New York Downtown Hospital; Manhattan College School Business Advisory Council; Board of Governors, Monsignor McClancy Memorial High School

ST. ANTOINE, THEODORE, "TED" JOSEPH, T: Law Educator, Arbitrator (Retired) **I:** Law and Legal Services **DOB:** 05/29/1929 **PB:** St. Albans **SC:** VT/USA **PT:** Arthur Joseph S; Mary Beatrice (Callery) S. **MS:** Widower **SPN:** Elizabeth Lloyd (Frier) (01/02/1960) **CH:** Arthur; Claire; Paul; Sara **ED:** Postgraduate, University of London (1957-1958); Doctor of Jurisprudence, University of Michigan (1954); Bachelor of Arts, Fordham College (1951) **C:** Degan Professor Emeritus, University of Michigan Law School (1998-Present); Degan Professor, University of Michigan Law School (1981-1998); Professor, University of Michigan Law School (1969-1981); Dean, University of Michigan Law School (1971-1978); Associate Professor of Law, University of Michigan Law School, Ann Arbor, MI (1965-1969); Associate, Partner, Woll, Mayer & St. Antoine, Washington, DC (1958-1965); Associate, Squire, Sanders & Dempsey, Cleveland, OH (1954) **CR:** Chairman, United Auto Workers Public Review Board (2000-2008); Member, United Auto Workers Public Review Board (1973-2008); Chairman, Michigan Attorney Discipline Board (2002-2005); Member, Michigan Attorney Discipline Board (1995-2005); Vice Chairman, Michigan Attorney Discipline Board (2000-2002); Chairman, UAW-GM Legal Services Plan (1983-1995); Reporter, Uniform Law Commissioners (1987-1992); Special Counselor on Workers' Compensation, Governor of Michigan (1983-1985); President, National Resource Center for Consumers of Legal Services (1974-1978); Lifetime Member, Clare Hall, Cambridge University, England **MIL:** 1st Lieutenant, Judge Advocate General Corps, U.S. Army (1955-1957) **CW:** Co-author, "Labor Relations Law: Cases and Materials (1968, 2011); Editor, "The Common Law of the Workplace: The Views of Arbitrators" (2005); Contributor, Articles to Professional Journals **AW:** Distinguished Alumnus Award, University of Michigan Law School (2013); George W. Taylor Award, American Arbitration Association (2010); Champion of Justice Award, State Bar of Michigan (2002); Fulbright Grantee, University of London (1957-1958); Army Commendation Medal (1957) **MEM:** Advisory Council, National Workrights Institute (2004-Present); Executive Committee, American Arbitration Association (2008-2012); Board Director, American Arbitration Association (2000-2012); U.S. Branch Executive Board, International Society of Labor and Social Security Law (1983-2009); President, National Academy of Arbitrators (1999-2000); Vice President, National Academy of Arbitrators (1994-1996); Vice Chairman, International Society of Labor and Social Security Law (1989-1995); Past Secretary, Labor Law Section,

American Bar Association (1984-1992); Board of Governors, National Academy of Arbitrators (1985-1988); Chairman, Labor Relations Law Section, State Bar of Michigan (1979-1980); American Bar Foundation; Labor and Employment Relations Association; College of Labor and Employment Lawyers; Order of the Coif **BAR:** District of Columbia (1959); Ohio (1954); Michigan (1954) **MH:** Albert Nelson Marquis Lifetime Achievement Award **B/I:** Mr. St. Antoine became involved in his profession due to his interest in social justice, as well as his advocacy for labor rights. **AV:** Theatre; Classical music; Travel **PA:** Democrat **RE:** Roman Catholic

STABENOW, ANN, "DEBBIE", T: U.S. Senator from Michigan **I:** Government Administration/Government Relations/Government Services **CN:** U.S. Senate **DOB:** 04/29/1950 **PB:** Gladwin **SC:** MI/USA **PT:** Robert Lee Greer; Anna Merle (Hallmark) Greer **MS:** Divorced **SPN:** Tom Athans (2003, Divorced 2010); Dennis Stabenow (Divorced 1990) **CH:** Michelle Deborah; Todd Dennis; Gina (Stepdaughter) **ED:** Master of Social Work, Michigan State University, Magna Cum Laude (1975); Bachelor of Science, Michigan State University, Magna Cum Laude (1972) **C:** Chair, Senate Democratic Policy Committee (2017-Present); Ranking Member, Senate Agriculture Committee (2015-Present); Chair, U.S. Senate Democratic Steering and Outreach Committee (2007-Present); U.S. Senator, State of Michigan (2001-Present); Chair, U.S. Senate Committee on Agriculture, Nutrition and Forestry (2011-2015); Member, U.S. House of Representatives from Michigan's Eighth Congressional District, United States Congress, Washington, DC (1997-2001); Member, Michigan State Senate, Lansing, MI (1991-1994); Member, Michigan House of Representatives, Lansing, MI (1979-1990); County Commissioner, Ingham County, Mason, MI (1975-1978); With Special Services, Lansing School District, MI (1972-1973) **CIV:** Founder, Ingham County Women's Commission; Co-founder, Council Against Domestic Assault; Member, Grace United Methodist, Lansing, MI **CW:** Appearance, Film, "Batman v. Superman: Dawn of Justice" (2016) **AW:** Community Health Defender Award, National Association of Community Health Centers (2005); Public Elected Official Award, National Association of Social Workers (2004); Congressional Support for Science Award, Institute of Food Technologists (2004); Boxing Glove Award, National Committee to Preserve Social Security and Medicare (1999); Named, Home Health Hero, National Association for Home Care & Hospice (1999); Named, Friend of Farm Bureau, Michigan Farm Bureau (1999); Leadership Award, National Council of NASA Space Grant Directors (1998); Outstanding Achievement Award, National Farmers Union (1998); Legislator of the Year Award, National Multiple Sclerosis Society (1992); Legislator of the Year Award, Association for Children's Mental Health (1991); Recognition Award, State 4-H Alumni (1991); Legislator of the Year Award, Michigan Association of Volunteer Administrators (1989); Legislator of the Year Award, Citizens Alliance to Uphold Special Education (1989); Community Award, Michigan Mental Health (1988); Named, One of 10 Outstanding Young Americans, Jaycees (1986); Distinguished Service in Government Award, Arc of the United States (1986); Lawmaker of the Year Award, National Child Support Enforcement Association (1985); Distinguished Service Award, Lansing Jaycees, MI (1985); Snyder-Kok Award, Mental Health Association of Michigan (1984); Awareness Leader of the Year Award, Awareness Communications Team of the Developmentally Disabled (1984); Communicator of the Year Award, Women in Communications (1984); Service to Children

Award, Council for Prevention of Child Abuse and Neglect (1983); Distinguished Service to Michigan Families Award, Michigan Council of Family Relations (1983); Outstanding Leadership Award, National Council of Community Mental Health Centers (1983) **MEM:** National Association for the Advancement of Colored People; National Association of Social Workers; Lansing Regional Chamber of Commerce; Delta Kappa Gamma Society International **PA:** Democrat **RE:** Methodist

STAEHLE, ALAN W., T: Retired County Police and Public Safety Official, Elected Official, Emergency Manager **I:** Civil Service **CN:** Boulder County, Ouray County, Colorado **DOB:** 03/13/1941 **PB:** Rochester **SC:** NY/USA **PT:** Henry C. Staehle; Isabel M. Staehle **MS:** Married **SPN:** Mary Ann Jordan **ED:** Graduate Coursework, FBI National Academy (1989); University of Virginia (1989); Coursework, University of Colorado (1973-1974); Coursework, University of Colorado (1959-1960) **CT:** Certified Peace Officer, Colorado; Peace Officer Training Instructor, Colorado; EMT, Colorado; Wilderness EMT, FEMA Emergency Management ICS Instructor; Motorcycle Safety Instructor, MSF, MOST **C:** Ouray County Emergency Manager (2003-2013); Ouray County Commissioner (1995-2003); Undersheriff, Boulder County Sheriff's Department (1983-1991); Division Captain, Undersheriff, Boulder Sheriffs Office (1971-1991); Captain, Detectives, Boulder County Sheriff's Department (1977-1982); Captain, Patrol, Boulder County Sheriff's Department (1972, 1974-1976); Business Partner, Rocky Mountain Motorcycles Incorporated, Boulder, CO (1962-1976); Captain, Communications, Boulder County Sheriff's Department (1973); Supervisor, Boulder Police Department (1971); Police Officer, Boulder, CO (1968-1971); Patrolman, Boulder Police Department (1968-1970) **CR:** Founding Member, 6 County West Region Wildfire Council (1998-Present); Co-Chair, Montrose Emergency Telephone Service Authority (2007-2010); Chairman, Ouray County 911 Authority (2003-2010); Co-Chair, Ouray, Montrose, Delta Public Lands Partnership (1998-2003); Chairman, Ouray County Commission (1995-2003); Chairman, Automation Taskforce, Boulder County, CO (1983) **CIV:** Chairman, Ouray Fire Protection District (2014-Present); Safety Committee, Local Church, Santa Barbara, CA **MIL:** United States Army Reserve (1973-1970) **AW:** Dedication and Service Award, Montrose 911 Service Authority (2013); Emergency Manager of the Year, Colorado Emergency Management Association (2008, 2012); Outstanding Volunteer Award, Uncompahgre Plateau Project (2010); Dedication to Public Land Management Award, Department of the Interior Bureau of Land Management (1997-2010); Outstanding Citizen Award, Ridgway Ouray Community Council (2008); Group Honor for Excellence, USDA Forest Service (2007); Red Mountain Project Award (2002); John P. Murphy Public Service Award (1989); Distinguished Service Award, Boulder Optimists (1981); Officer of Month, Boulder Jaycees (1968) **MEM:** American Medical Association; International Association of Chiefs of Police; Founding Member, World Space Foundation; Planetary Society; Smithsonian Institution; American Museum of Natural History; National Sheriffs Association; FBI National Academy Associates; Cousteau Society; Colorado Historical Society; Ouray County Historical Society, Denver Museum Natural History; Trout Unlimited; American Motorcyclist Association; Charter Member, Air and Space Smithsonian; World War II Museum; American Air Museum in Britain; Commemorative Air Force **MH:** Albert Nelson Marquis Lifetime Achievement Award **AS:** Mr. Staehle attributes his success to good fortune and working with good people. **B/I:** After graduating high school, Mr.

Staehle described himself as a "goof-off". Upon entering college, he started out as a chemistry major but never finished. Eventually, he joined the Army reserves for some time, but after getting out he spent more time finding a career until becoming a police officer in 1968. That led him to acquire a more formal education, courtesy of federal grants, and his public safety career took off with some later related branches. Other areas of interest provided Mr. Staehle with many volunteer opportunities in several areas. **AV:** Practicing photography; Motorcycling; Hiking; Hunting; Fishing **PA:** Independant **RE:** Unitarian Universalist **THT:** Mr. Staehle believes the energy one puts into the universe is forever. He works hard to make sure it is positive.

STALEY, JAMES, "JES" EDWARD, T: Bank Executive **I:** Financial Services **CN:** Barclays **DOB:** 12/27/1956 **PB:** Boston **SC:** MA/USA **PT:** Paul R. Staley **MS:** Married **SPN:** Debora Nitzan Staley **CH:** Two Daughters **ED:** Bachelor of Arts in Economics, Bowdoin College, Cum Laude **C:** Group Chief Executive, Barclays (2015-Present); Managing Partner, BlueMountain Capital (2013-2015); Chief Executive, Investment Bank, J.P. Morgan (2009-2013); Chief Executive Officer, J.P. Morgan Asset Management (2001-2009); Head, Private Banking Division, J.P. Morgan (1999-2001); Head of Corporate Finance, General Manager, Latin American Division, Morgan Guaranty Trust Co. (1980-1989); Morgan Guaranty Trust Co. (1979-1980); Founding Member, Equities Business, Equity Capital Market and Syndicate, J.P. Morgan **CIV:** Elected Board Member, Human Resources and Compensation Committee and Risk Committee, UBS (2015); Board Member, Bank Policy Institute, Institute of International Finance, U.S.-China Business Council; Trustee, Bowdoin College; Advisory Board, American Museum of Natural History; Donor, Democratic Senatorial Committee **PA:** Democrat

STALLONE, SYLVESTER GARDENZIO, T: Actor, Film Director, Screenwriter, Producer **I:** Media & Entertainment **DOB:** 07/06/1946) **PB:** New York **SC:** NY/USA **PT:** Francesco "Frank" Stallone Sr.; Jacqueline (Labofish) Stallone **SPN:** Jennifer Flavin (1997); Brigitte Nielsen (12/15/1985, Divorced 1987); Sasha Czack (12/28/1974, Divorced 1985) **CH:** Sage Moonblood Stallone (Deceased); Seargeoh; Sophia; Sistine; Scarlet **ED:** BFA (Honorary), University of Miami (1999); Student, University of Miami (1967-1969); Student, American College of Switzerland (1965-1967) **C:** Co-investor, Planet Hollywood; Co-Founder, Sly Water; Founder, Tiger Eye Productions **CW:** Executive Producer, "Samaritan" (2020); Executive Producer, Director, Episode, "The International" (2020); Actor, Screenwriter, "Rambo: Last Blood" (2019); Actor, "Escape Plan: The Extractors" (2019); Producer, "The Gangster, the Cop, the Devil" (2019); Actor, "Backtrace" (2018); Actor, Screenwriter, "Creed II" (2018); Actor, "Escape Plan 2: Hades" (2018); Executive Producer, "S.T.R.O.N.G." (2018); Himself, "This Is Us" (2017); Voice Actor, "Animal Crackers" (2017); Actor, "Guardians of the Galaxy Vol. 2" (2017); Producer, Executive Producer, "Ultimate Beastmaster" (2017); Voice Actor, "Ratchet & Clank" (2016); Actor, Producer, "Creed" (2015); Actor, "Reach Me" (2014); Actor, Screenwriter, "The Expendables 3" (2014); Actor, "Grudge Match" (2013); Guest Performer, "Saturday Night Live" (2013); Actor, "Escape Plan" (2013); Screenwriter, "Homefront" (2013); Actor, "Bullet to the Head" (2012); Actor, Screenwriter, "The Expendables 2" (2012); Voice Actor, "Zookeeper" (2011); Actor, Screenwriter, Director, "The Expendables" (2010); Himself, "Incredible Love" (2009); Actor, Screenwriter, Director, "Rambo" (2008); Executive Producer,

"The Contender" (2006-2009); Actor, Director, "Rocky Balboa" (2006); Actor, "Las Vegas" (2005); Actor, "Spy Kids 3-D: Game Over" (2003); Actor, "Shade" (2003); Actor, "Taxi 3" (2003); Voice Actor, "Liberty's Kids: Est. 1776" (2002); Actor, "Avenging Angelo" (2002); Actor, "Eye See You" (2002); Actor, Screenwriter, Producer, "Driven" (2001); Actor, "Get Carter" (2000); Voice Actor, "Antz" (1998); Actor, "The Good Life" (1997); Himself, "An Alan Smithee Film: Burn Hollywood Burn" (1997); Actor, "Cop Land" (1997); Actor, "Daylight" (1996); Actor, "Assassins" (1995); Actor, "Judge Dredd" (1995); Actor, "The Specialist" (1994); Actor, "Demolition Man" (1993); Actor, Screenwriter, "Cliffhanger" (1993); Actor, "Stop! Or My Mom Will Shoot" (1992); Himself, "Dream On" (1991); Actor, "Oscar" (1991); Actor, Screenwriter, "Rocky V" (1990); Actor, "Tango & Cash" (1989); Actor, "Lock Up" (1989); Actor, Screenwriter, "Rambo III" (1988); Actor, Music Video, "Winner Takes It All," Sammy Hagar (1987); Actor, "Over the Top" (1987); Actor, Screenwriter, "Cobra" (1986); Actor, Screenwriter, Director, "Rocky IV" (1985); Actor, Screenwriter, "Rambo: First Blood Part II" (1985); Executive Producer,"Heart of a Champion: The Ray Mancini Story" (1985); Actor, Screenwriter, "Rhinestone" (1984); Actor, Screenwriter, Director, Producer, "Staying Alive" (1983); Actor, "First Blood" (1982); Actor, Director, "Rocky III" (1982); Actor, "Victory" (1981); Actor, "Nighthawks" (1981); Actor, Director, "Rocky II" (1979); Guest Star, "The Muppet Show" (1979); Actor, Director, "Paradise Alley" (1978); Actor, Screenwriter, "F.I.S.T." (1978); Actor, Screenwriter, "Rocky" (1976); Actor, "Cannonball!" (1976); Actor, "Kojak" (1975); Actor, "Police Story" (1975); Actor, "Farewell, My Lovely" (1975); Actor, "Death Race 2000" (1975); Actor, "Capone" (1975); Actor, "The Prisoner of Second Avenue" (1975); Actor, "The Lords of Flatbush" (1974); Actor, "No Place to Hide" (1973); Actor, "Bananas" (1971); Actor, "The Sidelong Glances of a Pigeon Kicker" (1970); Actor, "The Party at Kitty and Stud's" (1970); Actor, "The Square Root" (1969) **AW:** Golden Globe Award for Best Supporting Actor - Motion Picture, "Creed" (2015); Best Supporting Actor, "Creed," Critics' Choice Movie Awards (2015); Best Supporting Actor, "Creed," Austin Film Critics Association (2015); Best Supporting Actor, "Creed," National Board of Review (2015); Lifetime Achievement Award, Hollywood Film Festival (2010); Best International Actor, Golden Camera (2004); Inductee, International Boxing Hall of Fame (2010); Jaeger-LeCoultre Glory to the Filmmaker Award, Venice Film Festival (2009); Golden Icon Award, Zurich Film Festival (2008); Taurus Honorary Award, Taurus World Stunt Awards (2005); Best Actor, "Cop Land," Stockholn International Film Festival (1997); Desert Palm Achievement Award, Palm Springs International Film Festival (1998); Honorary Cesar, Cesar Awards (1992); Ordre des Arts et des Lettres (Order of Arts and Letters) (1992); Artistic Achievement Award, National Italian American Foundation (1991); Man of the Year, Hasty Pudding Theatricals (1986); Favorite Movie Actor, "Rambo: First Blood Part II," "Rocky IV," People's Choice Awards (1985); Honoree, Star, Hollywood Walk of Fame (1984); Best International Actor, "First Blood," "Rocky III," Jupiter Awards (1982); Best Foreign Actor, "Rocky," David di Donatello Awards (1976) **MEM:** Screen Actors Guild; DGA; Writers Guild of America; Honorary Member, Stuntmen's Association of Motion Pictures

STALLWORTH, TERRESA, MD, T: Clinical Director **I:** Medicine & Health Care **CN:** San Antonio State Hospital **PB:** Tuscaloosa **SC:** AL/USA **PT:** William Wesley Stallworth; Louise Catherine (Goodrich) Stallworth **MS:** Widow **ED:** MD, University of Tennessee (1963); MusB, University Tennessee (1959); Coursework, Virginia Intermont College (1954-1955) **C:** Clinical Director, San Antonio State Hospital (1997-Present); Director, Community Programs And Specialty Units, San Antonio State Hospital (1974-Present); Clinical Director, Assistant Superintendent, Acting Superintendent, Lakeshore Mental Health Institute, Knoxville, TN (1969-1974); Chief Resident, University of Missouri (1968); Resident in Psychiatry, University of Missouri (1966-1968); Resident in Neurology, City of Memphis Hospital (1964-1965); Intern, University of Tennessee Memorial Hospital and Research Center (1963-1964) **CR:** Clinical Professor, Psychiatry (1995-Present); Associate Professor, Psychiatry, University of Texas Health Sciences Center, San Antonio, TX (1974-Present); Executive Director, Camino Real Community MH/MR Services (1995-1997); Director, Camino Real State-Operated Community Mental Health Center (1993-1995); Chairman, Professional Advisory Board, Bexar County Mental Health/Mental Retardation Center (1979-1981); Medical Council, Texas Department State Health Services **CIV:** San Antonio International Piano Board (2002-2018) **CW:** Concert Pianist, Trinity University, St. Mary's University, Incarnate Word College (1975-Present) Commissioned, Yellow Rose of Texas (1997); San Antonio Symphony, San Antonio State Hospital, University of Tennessee (1989); Austrian Embassy, Washington, DC (1996); Performer, Piano Sonata (1980) **AW:** Special Service Award, Texas Society Psychiatric Physicians (2004); Special Service Award, Society of Psychiatric Physicians (2004); Bob Polunski Award (2002); Distinguished Service Award, University of Texas Health Science Center, San Antonio, TX (1997); 1st Prize, Memphis and Mid-South Piano Contest (1958) **MEM:** Fellow, American Psychiatric Association; American Medical Association; National Organization of Women; Texas Psychiatric Association; Bexar County Psychiatric Society; Texas Medical Association; Bexar County Medical Society; Chopin Foundation U.S.A.; Tuesday Music Club; Alpha Omega Alpha; Sigma Kappa Alumnae **MH:** Albert Nelson Marquis Lifetime Achievement Award **B/I:** Dr. Stallworth always had an interest in psychiatry. However, she received a scholarship to study piano in New York City. While in school, she became very homesick and had a discussion with her father about what she should do. Her father suggested she attend medical school, which turned out to be the best decision she ever made.

STANDLEY, JOHN T., T: Chairperson, Chief Executive Officer **I:** Medicine & Health Care **CN:** Rite Aid Corporation **ED:** Bachelor of Science in Accounting, Pepperdine University (1985) **C:** Chief Financial Officer, Rite Aid Corp., Camp Hill, PA (2003-2005); Senior Executive Vice President, Chief Administrative Officer, Rite Aid Corp., Camp Hill, PA (2002); Executive Vice President, Chief Financial Officer, Rite Aid Corp., Camp Hill, PA (1999-2002); Executive Vice President, Chief Financial Officer, Fleming Co. Inc., Oklahoma City, OK (1999); Senior Vice President, Chief Financial Officer, Fred Meyer, Inc., Portland, OR (1998-1999); Senior Vice President, Chief Financial Officer, Ralphs Grocery Co. (1997-1998); Senior Vice President of Administration, Smith's Food & Drug Stores, Inc., Salt Lake City, UT (1996-1997); Chief Financial Officer, Smitty's Supervalu Inc., Phoenix, AZ (1994-1996); Vice President of Finance, Food 4 Less Supermarkets Inc., Compton, CA (1991-1994); Audit Manager, Retail and Finance Industry Groups, Arthur Andersen LLP, Los Angeles, CA **CR:** Board of Directors, Rite Aid Corp. (2009-Present); Pathmark Stores Inc. (2005-2007)

STANKEY, JOHN T., T: Chief Executive Officer **I:** Business Management/Business Services **CN:** WarnerMedia, LLC **SC:** CA/USA **MS:** Married **SPN:** Shari Stankey **CH:** Three Children **ED:** MBA, University of California Los Angeles (1991); BA in Finance, Loyola Marymount University, Los Angeles, CA (1985) **C:** Chief Executive Officer, WarnerMedia LLC (2018-Present); Chief Executive Officer, Media Business, AT&T Inc. (2018); Chief Executive Officer, Time Warner Inc. (2018); Group President, Chief Strategy Officer, AT&T Inc. (2012-2018); Chief Executive Officer, AT&T Entertainment, AT&T Inc. (2015-2017); President and Chief Executive Officer, Business Solutions, AT&T Inc. (2008-2012); Group President, Telecommunication Operations, AT&T Inc. (2007-2012); Group President, Operations Support, AT&T Inc. (2007); Senior Executive Vice President, Chief Technology Officer, AT&T Inc. (2006-2007); Senior Executive Vice President, Chief Technology Officer, SBC Communications Inc. (2003-2006); President, Chief Executive Officer, SBC Southwestern Bell, SBC Communications Inc. (2002-2003); President Industry Markets, SBC Communications Inc. (2000-2002); Vice President, Industry Markets, SBC Communications Inc. (1998-2000); Executive Director, Advanced Communications Network, Local Wholesale Operations, Pacific Bell (1985-1998) **CIV:** Board Member, United Parcel Service of America, Inc. **AW:** Listee, Top 25 Chief Technology Officers, InfoWorld Magazine (2006); Listee, Premier 100 IT Leaders, Computerworld (2006)

STANLEY, RONALD ALWIN, PHD, T: Environmental Scientist **I:** Environmental Services **PB:** Edinburg **SC:** TX/USA **PT:** Hamlet Alwin Stanley; Gloria Goldie (Rinkel) Stanley **MS:** Married **SPN:** Mary Aldridge (12/26/1992); Susan Absher (Divorced 1985); Dorothy Thibault (08/29/1963, Divorced 1982) **CH:** Ronald Alwin Jr.; David A.; Catherine A. Brookes; Stanley Absher **ED:** AS, Allegany College of Maryland (2018); MPA, University of Southern California (1982); PhD, Duke University (1970); MS, University of Arkansas (1963); BS, University of Arkansas (1961); AS, College of the Ozarks (1959) **CT:** SCUBA Diving, Aqua Space SCUBA School; Wetland Identification, Rutgers the State University of New Jersey **C:** Southern Allegany Conservancy (2007-2008); Teacher, Harrisburg Area Community College (2002-2007); PA State Government (1999-2007); US Census Bureau (1998); Teacher, Frostburg State University (1996-1997); Program Manager, U.S. Agency for International Development (1989-1990); Program Manager, Multimedia Assessment, U.S. Environmental Protection Agency (EPA) (1995-1996); Coordinator, Trade and Environment Policy, U.S. Environmental Protection Agency (EPA) (1994-1995); director, Contracts Managing Group, U.S. Environmental Protection Agency (EPA) (1992-1994); Greek Environmental Assessment, World Health Organization (1987); Scientist, Manager, U.S. Environmental Protection Agency (EPA) (1976-1996); Assistant Professor, Biology, University of South Dakota (1975); Assistant Professor, Biology, Memphis State University (1975); Scientist, Tennessee Valley Authority (TVA) (1964-1975); Intern, Oak Ridge National Laboratory (1963) **CR:** Co-manager, Blackberry Hills Farm, Clearville, PA (1992) **CIV:** One-Plus-One Social Service Society (1992-Present); Reporter, Daily Weather, Community Collaborative for Rain, Hail, and Snow (2014-2020); Editor, Newsletter, Habitat for Humanity of Bedford County (1998); Duke Club of Washington International Interest Group (1995); Mentor, Environmentors (1994-1995); Trail Overseer, Potomac Appalachian Trail Club (1990-1992) **CW:** Publisher, "Holding to the Light" (1991); Author, Publisher, "Fragments of the Journey" (1991); Author, "Dark Vision" (1990); Author, Publisher, "My Mother, The Earth" (1990); Author, Publisher, "With All My Heart" (1990); Co-Author, "Environmental Management of Water Projects" (1987); Contributor, Articles to Professional Journals **AW:** Phi Beta Kappa; Sigma Xi **MEM:** Bedford County Conservation District (2007-2020); Director, Land Management, Southern Alleghenies Conservancy (1998-2020); Commissioner to Potomac River Basin Commission (2007-2019); Director, Land Management Membership Chairman, Pennsylvania Chapter, American Chestnut Foundation (1997-1999); Board of Directors, American Chestnut Foundation (1996-1997); Founding Member, Fairfax Audubon Society; Keystone Trails Association; Bedford County Bird and Nature Club; Pennsylvania Nut Growers Association; Phi Beta Kappa; Sigma Xi **MH:** Albert Nelson Marquis Lifetime Achievement Award; Marquis Who's Who Top Professional **AS:** Dr. Stanley attributes his success to long hours of hard work. **B/I:** Dr. Stanley became involved in his profession because he grew up on a farm and under the influence of his brother Jon, who loved to fish and often took him down to the local creek, he found he was not very good at fishing. So instead, he would walk along the creek and explore the nature around him and that is where his interest in the environment and the sciences began. His father was a high school dropout but he never let it get into the way of him learning things. H.A. Stanley was very self-educated. **AV:** Hiking & trail maintenance; Planting trees; Stamp collecting

STANTON, GIANCARLO CRUZ MICHAEL, T: Professional Baseball Player **I:** Athletics **CN:** New York Yankees **DOB:** 11/08/1989 **PB:** Panorama City **SC:** CA/USA **PT:** Michael Stanton; Jacinta Garay **MS:** Single **ED:** Diploma, Notre Dame High School, Sherman Oaks, CA **C:** Right Fielder, New York Yankees (2018-Present); Right Fielder, Florida / Miami Marlins (2010-2017) **AW:** Gold Medal, U.S. Baseball Team, World Baseball Classic, Los Angeles, CA (2017); National League MVP (2017); Four-Time All-Star (2012, 2014-2015, 2017); Two Silver Slugger Awards (2014, 2017); Two-Time National League Hank Aaron Award (2014, 2017); Wilson Defensive Player of the Year Award (2012)

STANTON, GREGORY, "GREG" JOHN, T: U.S. Representative from Arizona **I:** Government Administration/Government Relations/Government Services **CN:** U.S. House of Representatives **DOB:** 03/08/1970 **PB:** Phoenix **SC:** AZ/USA **MS:** Married **SPN:** Nicole Stanton (2005) **CH:** Violet; Trevor **ED:** Doctor of Jurisprudence, University of Michigan Law School; Bachelor of Arts, Marquette University **C:** Member, U.S. House of Representatives from Arizona's Ninth Congressional District (2019-Present); Mayor, Phoenix, AZ (2012-2018); Member, Phoenix City Council (2000-2001, 2005-2009) **PA:** Democrat

STAPLES, BRENT, PHD, T: Writer, Reporter **I:** Writing and Editing **CN:** The New York Times **PB:** Chester **SC:** PA/USA **ED:** PhD in Behavioral Sciences, The University of Chicago (1982); MS in Behavioral Sciences, The University of Chicago (1976); BA, Widener University (1973) **C:** Editor, The New York Times Book Review (1985-Present); Contributor, Essay, "Just Walk on By: Black Men and Public Space," Ms. Magazine (1986); Assistant Editor, Metropolitan News, The New York Times Company; Reporter, The New York Times Company; Reporter, Chicago Sun-Times; Teacher Psychology; Author, "An American Love Story," "Parallel Time: Growing up In Black and White"; Contributor, "How Hip Hop Lost Its Way and Betrayed Its Fans," Read, Reason and Write **CIV:** Editorial Board Member, The New York Times Company (1990-Present) **CW:** Author, Memoir, "Parallel Time: Growing Up in Black and White" (1994); Author, Essay, "Just Walk On By: A Black Man Ponders His Power to Alter Public Space" (1986) **AW:** Pulitzer Prize for Editorial Writing (2019); Anisfield-Wolf Book Awards (1995); Grantee, Danfort Fellowship; Finalist, Los Angeles Times Book Prize

STARKEBAUM, GORDON ALAN, MD, MACR, T: Emeritus Professor, Staff Rheumatologist **I:** Education/Educational Services **CN:** University of Washington School of Medicine **DOB:** 08/17/1944 **PB:** Borger **SC:** TX/USA **PT:** Norman Victor Starkebaum; Florence (Wishire) Starkebaum **MS:** Married **SPN:** Mary Kathyrn Hiltner (06/10/1967) **CH:** Elaine Margaret; Paul Michael; David Alan **ED:** Senior Fellow in Medicine, Division of Rheumatology, University of Washington, Seattle, WA (1975-1978); Residency in Medicine, University of Washington Affiliated Hospitals, Seattle, WA (1973-1975); Intern, Harborview Medical Center, Seattle, WA (1970-1971); MD, College of Physicians and Surgeons, Columbia University, New York, NY (1970); BS, University of Washington, Cum Laude, With College Honors in Chemistry, Seattle, WA (1966) **CT:** American Board of Internal Medicine, Sub-Specialty of Rheumatology (1978); American Board of Internal Medicine (1975); Licensure to Practice, State of Washington (1970); License, Washington State **C:** Professor Emeritus, Department of Medicine, University of Washington (2013-Present); Professor, Department of Medicine, University of Washington (1993-2013); Associate Dean, University of Washington School of Medicine (2000-2009); Acting Vice Chairman, Department of Medicine, University of Washington (1999-2000); Associate Professor, Department of Medicine, University of Washington (1985-1993); Assistant Professor, Department of Medicine, University of Washington (1980-1985); Acting Assistant Professor, Department of Medicine, University of Washington (1979-1980); Acting Instructor, Department of Medicine, University of Washington (1978-1979) **CR:** Staff Rheumatologist, University of Washington School of Medicine (2013-Present); Chief, Arthritis Section, Veterans Affairs Puget Sound Health Care System (2009-2013); Chief of Staff, Veterans Affairs Puget Sound Health Care System (2000-2009); Acting Director, Primary and Specialty Medical Care, Veterans Affairs Puget Sound Health Care System (1999-2000); Chief, Arthritis Section, Seattle Veterans Administration Medical Center (1981-2000); Acting Chief, Arthritis Section, Seattle Veterans Administration Medical Center (1980-1981); Staff Physician, Boise Veterans Administration Medical Center (1979-1980); Associate Investigator, Seattle Veterans Administration Medical Center (1977-1979) **CIV:** President, Board of Directors, Seattle Institute for Biomedical and Clinical Research (SIBCR) (2012-Present); Veterans Health Administration Health Systems Committee (2007-2009); UW Graduate Medical Education Committee (2006-2009); Veterans Health Administration Advisory Committee on Medical School Affiliations (2006-2007); Professional Meetings Committee, American College of Rheumatology (1990-1993, 1998-2001); Program Chair, American College of Rheumatology Spring Clinical Meeting, Seattle, WA (1999-2000); Program Co-Chair, American College of Rheumatology Spring Clinical Meeting, Cleveland, OH (1998-1999); Chairman, Pharmacy and Therapeutics Committee, Seattle VA Medical Center (1987-1999); VA Merit Review Board in Immunology (1990); Chairman, Research and Development Committee, Seattle VA Medical Center (1988-1989); Fellowship Review Committee, Arthritis Foundation (1986-1989); Board of Directors, ALDEA **MIL:** General Medical Officer, U.S. Army (1971-1973) **CW:** Co-Author, "Macrophage

Activation Syndrome in a Patient with Axial Spondyloarthritis on Adalimumab," Clinical Rheumatology (2019); Co-Author, "Erdheim-Chester Disease Bone Lesions After Cobimetinib Initiation," Arthritis & Rheumatology (2019); Co-Author, "Veterans Using and Uninsured Veterans Not Using Veterans Affairs (VA) Health Care," Public Health Reports (2007); Co-Author, "Prevalence of Rheumatoid Arthritis and Hepatitis C in Those Age 60 and Older in a U.S. Population Based Study," Journal of Rheumatology (2003); Co-Author, "The Development of a Telemedical Cancer Center Within the Veterans Affairs Health Care System: A Report of Preliminary Clinical Results," Telemedicine Journal and e-Health (2002); Co-Author, "Epstein-Barr Virus, Methotrexate and Lymphoma in Patients with Rheumatoid Arthritis and Primary Sjögren's Syndrome – A Case Series," Journal of Rheumatology (2001); Co-Author, "Chronic Neutropenia Mediated by Fas Ligand," Blood (2000); Co-Author, "Isolated Central Nervous System Vasculitis Associated with Hepatitis C Infection," Journal of Rheumatology (1999); Co-Author, "Colchicine-induced Rhabdomyolysis," Journal of Rheumatology (1997); Co-Author, "Immunogenetic Similarities between Patients with Felty's Syndrome and Those with Clonal Expansions of Large Granular Lymphocytes in Rheumatoid Arthritis," Arthritis & Rheumatology (1997); Co-Author, "The Lymphoproliferative Disease of Granular Lymphocytes: Updated Criteria for Diagnosis," Blood (1997); Co-Author, "Peripheral Blood Mononuclear Cells of IDDM Patients Respond to Multiple Islet Cell Proteins," Journal of Immunology (1996); Contributor, Articles, Professional Journals; Contributor, Invited Editorials and Reviews, Books, Chapters to Books, Other Publications **AW:** Masters, American College of Rheumatology (2014); Paul Beeson Award for Teaching, University of Washington Medicine House Staff (2012); Veterans Administration Associate Investigator (1977-1979) **MEM:** President, National Association of VA Physician Executives (2007-2008); President-Elect, National Association of VA Physician Executives (2006-2007); President, American College of Rheumatology, Western Region (1995-1996); First Vice President, Program Chair, American College of Rheumatology, Western Region (1994-1995); Second Vice President, American College of Rheumatology, Western Region (1993-1994); Western Association of Physicians (1993); Secretary-Treasurer, American College of Rheumatology, Western Region (1990-1993); President, Northwest Rheumatism Society (1990); President-Elect, Program Chair, Northwest Rheumatism Society (1989); Council Member, American College of Rheumatology, Western Region (1987-1990); Secretary-Treasurer, Northwest Rheumatism Society (1985-1988); Western Society for Clinical Investigation (1985); American College of Rheumatology; Northwest Rheumatism Society; National Association of VA Physician Executives **B/I:** Dr. Starkebaum became involved in his profession because his father grew up on a farm in eastern Colorado and wanted to go into medical school but couldn't afford it. He always told his son about his medical industry dreams, which inspired Dr. Starkebaum to cultivate the same dreams.

STARR, RINGO, T: Drummer **I:** Media & Entertainment **DOB:** 07/07/1940 **PB:** Liverpool **SC:** England **PT:** Richard Starkey; Elsie (Gleave) Starkey **MS:** Married **SPN:** Barbara Bach (04/27/1981); Maureen Cox (02/11/1965, Divorced 1975) **CH:** Zak; Jason; Lee **C:** Solo Performer (1970-Present); Drummer, Singer, The Beatles (1962-1969); Drummer, Singer, Rory Storm and the Hurricanes (1959-1962); Drummer, Eddie Clayton Skiffle Group (1959) **CR:** Co-Founder, Pumpkinhead Records (2003) **CW:** Musician, Songwriter, "What's My Name" (2019); Musician, Songwriter, "Give More Love" (2017); Himself, "Popstar: Never Stop Never Stopping" (2016); Musician, Songwriter, "Postcards from Paradise" (2015); Author, "Photograph" (2015); Author, "Octopus's Garden" (2014); Voice Actor, "The Powerpuff Girls: Dance Pantsed" (2014); Musician, Songwriter, "Ringo 2012" (2012); Himself, "George Harrison: Living in the Material World" (2011); Musician, Songwriter, "Y Not" (2010); Himself, "Oh My God" (2009); Musician, Songwriter, "Liverpool 8" (2008); Musician, "Ringo Starr: Live at Soundstage" (2007); Musician, Songwriter, "Choose Love" (2005); Author, "Postcards From the Boys" (2004); Musician, Songwriter, "Ringo Rama" (2003); Performer, "Concert for George" (2009); Musician, Songwriter, "I Wanna Be Santa Claus" (1999); Musician, Songwriter, "Vertical Man" (1998); Actor, "Sabrina the Teenage Witch" (1998); Himself, "The Beatles Anthology" (1995); Musician, Songwriter, "Time Takes Time" (1992); Narrator, Segment, "Shelley Duvall's Bedtime Stories" (1992); Voice Actor, "The Simpsons" (1991); Voice Actor, Narrator, "Shining Time Station" (1989-1990); Himself, "The Return of Bruno" (1988); Himself, "Walking After Midnight" (1988); Himself, "Queen: The Magic Years" (1987); Actor, "To the North of Katmandu" (1986); Actor, "Alice in Wonderland" (1985); Narrator, "Thomas the Tank Engine & Friends" (1984-1986); Actor, "Give My Regards to Broad Street" (1984); Musician, Songwriter, "Old Wave" (1983); Actor, "Princess Daisy" (1983); Actor, "The Cooler" (1982); Actor, "Caveman" (1981); Musician, Songwriter, "Stop and Smell the Roses" (1981); Musician, Songwriter, "Bad Boy" (1978); Actor, "Ringo" (1978); Musician, Songwriter, "Ringo the 4th" (1977); Actor, "Sextette" (1977); Musician, Songwriter, "Ringo's Rotogravure" (1976); Actor, "Lisztomania" (1975); Musician, Songwriter, "Goodnight Vienna" (1974); Musician, Songwriter, "Ringo" (1973); Actor, "Son of Dracula" (1973); Actor, "That'll Be the Day" (1973); Actor, "Blindman" (1971); Actor, "200 Motels" (1971); Narrator, "The Point" (1971); Musician, "Beaucoups of Blues" (1970); Musician, "Sentimental Journey" (1970); Musician, "Let It Be," The Beatles (1970); Himself, "Let It Be" (1970); Musician, Songwriter, "Abbey Road," The Beatles (1969); Musician, "Yellow Submarine," The Beatles (1969); Actor, "The Magic Christian" (1969); Musician, "The Beatles (The White Album)," The Beatles (1968); Actor, "Candy" (1968); Himself, "Yellow Submarine" (1968); Musician, "Magical Mystery Tour," The Beatles (1967); Actor, "Magical Mystery Tour" (1967); Musician, "Sgt. Pepper's Lonely Hearts Club Band," The Beatles (1967); Musician, "Revolver," The Beatles (1966); Musician, "Yesterday and Today," The Beatles (1966); Musician, "Rubber Soul," The Beatles (1965); Musician, "Help!," The Beatles (1965); Actor, "Help!" (1965); Musician, "Beatles IV," The Beatles (1965); Musician, "Beatles '65," The Beatles (1964); Musician, "Beatles for Sale," The Beatles (1964); Musician, "Something New," The Beatles (1964); Musician, "A Hard Day's Night" (1964); Actor, "A Hard Day's Night" (1964); Musician, "The Beatles' Long Tall Sally," The Beatles (1964); Musician, "The Beatles' Second Album," The Beatles (1964); Musician, "Twist and Shout," The Beatles (1964); Musician, "Meet the Beatles!," The Beatles (1964); Musician, "Introducing... The Beatles," The Beatles (1964); Musician, "With the Beatles," The Beatles (1963); Musician, "Please Please Me," The Beatles (1963) **AW:** Knight Bachelor, 2018 New Year Honours (2018); Knighted, Buckingham Palace (2018); Inductee, Solo Artist, Rock and Roll Hall of Fame (2015); Honoree, Star, Hollywood Walk of Fame (2010); Inductee, The Beatles, Rock and Roll Hall of Fame (1993); Appointed, Member of the Order of the British Empire, the Queen's Birthday Honours (1965)

STASACK, EDWARD, T: Artist, Professor Emeritus **I:** Education/Educational Services **CN:** University of Hawaii **DOB:** 10/01/1929 **PB:** Chicago **SC:** IL/USA **PT:** Clifford Clement Stasack; Elizabeth Frances (Mallek) Stasack **MS:** Married **SPN:** Diane Stasack, PhD (1993); Mary Louise Walters (6/20/1953, Divorced 1972) **CH:** Caren Marie; Jennifer Elizabeth; John Armen; Michael Clifford; David Hirsch **ED:** MFA, University of Illinois at Urbana-Champaign (1956); BFA, University of Illinois at Urbana-Champaign, With High Honors (1955) **C:** Professor Emeritus, University of Hawaii (1988-Present); Program Chairman in Printmaking, University of Hawaii (1975-1983); Affiliate, Downtown Gallery, New York, NY (1960-1980); Professor of Art, Chairman, Department of Art, University of Hawaii (1969-1972); Instructor in Art, University of Hawaii (1956-1961) **CR:** MacDowell Colony Fellow (1975); Hawaii State and U.S. Bicentennial Communications Fellow (1975); MacDowell Colony Fellow (1971); Tiffany Foundation Fellow (1962); Tiffany Foundation Fellow (1958) **MIL:** U.S. Army (1952-1954) **CW:** Co-Author, "Rock Art of Pu'uhonuao Honaunau National Park, One Report" (2004); Co-Author, "Ka'uplehu East II Petroglyphs" (2003); Co-Author, "Rock Art of Hawaii Volcanoes National Park, Nine Reports" (1995-2001); Co-Author, "Spirit of Place, Petroglyphs of Hawaii" (1999); Solo Show, Commons Gallery, University of Hawaii (1996); Solo Show, Hawaii Volcano National Park Art Center (1996); Author, "Ka'upulehu Petroglyphs" (1994); Co-Author, "Petroglyphs of Kaho'olawe" (1993); Group Show, Yuma Art Center (1990); Solo Show, Honolulu Academy of the Arts (1987); Group Show, Second International Biennial Print Exhibit, Republic of China (1986); Solo Show, Art Loft, Honolulu, HI (1983); Group Show, Art Museum of Manila, Philippines (1982); Solo Show, Ryan Gallery (1981); Solo Show, Amfac Plaza Gallery (1978); Solo Show, U.S. Embassies, Istanbul and Izmir, Turkey (1976); Solo Show, American Cultural Center, Bucharest, Romania (1976); Solo Show, Cleveland Institute of Art (1976); Solo Show, Hilo College Gallery (1976); Solo Show, Honolulu Academy of the Arts (1976); Co-Author, "Hawaiian Petroglyphs" (1970); Solo Show, Honolulu Academy of the Arts (1969); Group Show, Mexico City Museum of Modern Art (1968); Group Show, Krakow "Biennial" (1968); Group Show, Smithsonian Institution, Washington, DC (1967); Solo Show, Honolulu Academy of the Arts (1966); Group Show, Krakow "Biennial" (1966); Group Show, Leicester Gallery, London, England (1965); Group Show, Carnegie Institute, Pittsburgh, PA (1964); Solo Show, Honolulu Academy of the Arts (1961); Co-Author, "Rock Art of Kaloko-Honokohou National Historical Park, Three Reports"; Permanent Collections, Numerous Museums and Public Institutions **AW:** Grantee, McInerny Foundation (2003); Hawaii Community Foundation Grantee (1997-2001); Society of American Graphic Artists Prizes (1991); Juror's Awards, Honolulu Printmakers (1987); Society of American Graphic Artists Prizes (1978-1980); Juror's Awards, Honolulu Printmakers (1977); Juror's Awards, Honolulu Printmakers (1974); Society of American Graphic Artists Prizes (1973); Society of American Graphic Artists Prizes (1968); Juror's Awards, Honolulu Printmakers (1966-1968); Boston Printmakers Members Prize (1967); Juror's Awards, Honolulu Printmakers (1962-1963); Society of American Graphic Artists Prizes (1961-1963); Rockefeller Foundation Grantee (1959); Juror's Awards, Honolulu Printmakers (1957-1959); Society of American Graphic Artists Prizes (1956-1957); Crabtree

Award, Society of American Archaeology **MEM:** Society of American Graphic Artists; Australian Rock Art Research Association; Emeritus President, Rock Art Association of Hawaii; American Rock Art Research Association; Society of Hawaiian Archaeology; Sharlot Hall Museum **MH:** Albert Nelson Marquis Lifetime Achievement Award; Marquis Who's Who Top Professional **B/I:** Mr. Stasack became involved in his profession because, when he was about 10 years old living on the northwest side of Chicago, he decided to skip school. He took a streetcar ride to the end of the line, and it brought him to the cultural center of Chicago, where there was the museum, planetarium, and aquarium, as well as the Chicago Art Institute. He went into the Chicago Art Institute and, for the first time in his life, he saw real art. He was moved by three paintings, a painting by Seurat titled "Sunday Afternoon in the Park," Edward Hopper's "Nighthawks," and Rembrandt's "Young Woman at a Half Opened Door." All those paintings turned out to be sufficient masterpieces. Mr. Stacack was fortunate to see great art at such a young age. It thoroughly inspired him to pursue a career in the field.

STAUBER, PETER, "PETE" ALLEN, T: U.S. Representative from Minnesota **I:** Government Administration/Government Relations/Government Services **CN:** U.S. House of Representatives **DOB:** 05/10/1966 **PB:** Duluth **SC:** MN/USA **MS:** Married **SPN:** Jodi Stauber **CH:** Four Children **ED:** Bachelor of Arts in Criminology, Lake Superior State University **C:** Member, U.S. House of Representatives from Minnesota's Eighth Congressional District (2019-Present); Member, St. Louis County Commission, Fifth District (2013-Present); Professional Hockey Player, Florida Panthers (1993); Professional Hockey Player, Detroit Red Wings (1990-1993); Co-owner, Duluth Hockey Company **CIV:** Member, St. Lawrence Catholic Church; Co-founder, Stauber Brothers Military Heroes Hockey Camp **AW:** National Championship, NCAA Division I, Men's Hockey Team, Lake Superior State University (1988) **PA:** Republican **RE:** Catholic

STAUFFER, SHARON T., T: Executive Director **I:** Medicine & Health Care **DOB:** 12/05/1951 **PB:** Birmingham **SC:** AL/USA **PT:** John E. Tanner; Nellie P. Tanner **MS:** Widowed **SPN:** Lee W. Stauffer (Deceased) **CH:** Savannah Fowler **ED:** BS in Business Administration, Faulkner University, Montgomery, AL (1997) **C:** Executive Director, Positive Choices Pregnancy Resource Center (2019-Present); Office Manager, Positive Choices Pregnancy Center (2016-2018); Financial Position, School of Medicine and Medical Research Departments, The University of Alabama at Birmingham (1984-2014); State of Alabama Career Center- WIA Program (2002-2005); Teacher, Middle School **CIV:** Volunteer, Mission Outreach, Local Church **AW:** Recipient, Math Award **MEM:** Rotary Noon Club, Business Networking International Momentum (Now BNI Global LLC) Chapter; National Institute of Family and Life Advocates (NIFLA); Alumni, The University of Alabama at Birmingham **AS:** Mrs. Stauffer attributes her success to being driven to be the best at what she does and working with people she can learn from. **B/I:** Mrs. Stauffer became involved in a second profession because she retired from her financial officer position at the University of Alabama in 2014. She retired due to her husband's illness; he passed in 2015. As an adoptive parent, her heart and compassion has always been with women who are facing an unplanned pregnancy because that was the origin of her daughter's biological mother's journey. She was drawn to the organization, which serves the community, not only women, but men and families as well. They offer them choices for their particular situation. They work with outside community partners for education, medical services, and transportation. Her heart has a compassion for the community and the people who have a need for their type of services; it is personal and she feels it is a calling. It has been a very worth while journey for her. They are seeing positive changes in the community and the clients they serve. **AV:** Cooking; Outdoor activities; Exercise **RE:** Baptist **THT:** Mrs. Stauffer's follows the words of Ernerst Hemingway, "In order to write about life. first you must live it."

STECKBAUER, JAMES, "JIM" J., T: Quality Assurance Specialist (Retired) **I:** Civil Service **DOB:** 01/23/1947 **PB:** Oshkosh **SC:** WI/USA **PT:** William Jacob Steckbauer; Mary Catherine Binder Steckbauer **MS:** Single **ED:** BSBA in Management, University of Nevada, Las Vegas, NV (1986); AA in Quality Assurance, Coastline College, Fountain Valley, CA (1980) **CT:** Certified Quality Auditor, American Society for Quality Control (Now American Society for Quality) **C:** Internal Assessment Program-Quality Assurance/Technical, Defense Contract Management Command, Phoenix, AZ (1996-2002); Software Quality Assurance/Internal Assessment, U.S. Defense Plant Representative Office, Mesa, AZ (1990-1996); Software Quality Assurance, U.S. Army Plant Representative Office, Mesa, AZ (1988-1990); Electronics Instructor, Training Specialist, University of Nevada Systems, Clark County Community College, North Las Vegas, NV (1987); Quality Assurance Specialist, U.S. Department of Energy, Nevada Test Site, Mercury, NV (1983-1986); Quality Assurance Specialist, U.S. Air Force Western Space and Missile Center, Vandenberg Air Force Base, California (1982-1983); Quality Assurance Specialist, U.S. Air Force Plant Representative Office at Hughes Aircraft Corp., Fullerton, CA (1980-1982); Quality Assurance Specialist, U.S. Air Force Plant Representative Office at TRW, Redondo Beach, California (1979-1980); Electrical Mechanic, Test Technician, U.S. Naval Shipyard, Long Beach, CA (1978-1979); Avionics Supervisor, HMM-161, U.S. Marine Corps Air Station, Santa Ana, CA (1976-1977);U.S. Marine Corps Recruiter, Recruiting Station, Milwaukee, WI (1972-1976); Avionics Instructor, Naval Air Technical Training Center, Millington, TN (1970-1972); Avionics Technician-COM/NAV, HMM-161 (MCAF New River, NC & Quang Tri, RVN), HMM-263 (Marble Mountain, RVN), & MARTD (NAS Norfolk, VA), U.S. Marine Corps (1966-1970); Recruit, MCRD San Diego & Camp Pendleton, California (1966); Mechanic, Oshkosh, WI (1965-1966) **CIV:** Run Coordinator, Member, Chapter 86, Arizona American Legion Riders, Overgaard, AZ (2007-2019); Director, Chapter 86, Arizona American Legion Riders, Overgaard, AZ (2007-2012, 2017); Judge Advocate, Arizona American Legion District 6 (2010-2014); Member, E-Board, Arizona American Legion Post 86, Overgaard, AZ (2008-2012); Sergeant at Arms, Arizona American Legion Post 86, Overgaard, AZ (2008-2010); ALR Coordinator, Arizona American Legion District 6 (2007-2010); Chaplain, Sons of the American Legion, Squadron 86, Overgaard, AZ (2007-2009) **MIL:** Staff Sgt., U.S. Marine Corps (1966-1977) **MEM:** Arizona Loyal Order of the Moose Lodge #2039 (1998-Present); Arizona Fraternal Order of Eagles Aerie #3850 & #4437 (1994-Present); American Society for Quality Control (Now American Society for Quality) (1983-2003); National Contract Management Association (1988-2002); Life Member, University of Nevada Las Vegas Alumni Association; Life Member, Arizona American Legion Post 27 and 86; Life Member, USMC Combat Helicopter & Tilt-Rotor Association (POPASMOKE); Arizona Veterans of Foreign Wars Post 9399 Life Member; American Veterans (AMVETS) Life Member; Life Member, Harley Owners Group (HOG); Life Member, ABATE of Arizona Motorcycle Rights Organization; Motorcycle Riders Foundation; American Motorcycle Association; National Rifle Association (NRA) **MH:** Albert Nelson Marquis Lifetime Achievement Award **AV:** Rebuilding old sportsters **RE:** Roman Catholic

STECKLER, JESSICA A., T: Owner/Consultant **I:** Consulting **CN:** The Firm of Jessica A. Steckler **DOB:** 06/26/1941 **PB:** York **SC:** PA/USA **PT:** Edward A. Debes; Mary Elizabeth (Hoffman) Debes **MS:** Divorced **CH:** Scott Edward **ED:** Doctoral Candidate in Education, Pennsylvania State University (1992); MEd, Gannon University, Erie, PA (1979); BS in Nursing, Millersville State College (1971); Diploma in Nursing, Bryn Mawr Hospital (1963) **CT:** Certification in Staff Development, American Nurses Association; Certification in Medical Ethics Consultation, University of West Virginia **C:** Appraiser, Pathway to Excellence (2011-Present); Chairperson, Medical Ethics Team, Erie VA Medical Center (1988-Present); Associate Director, Erie VA Medical Center (1981-Present); Instructional System Specialist (2006-2010); Acting CHEP Director, Educational Specialist Employee Education Systems, Veterans Affairs (1997-2006); Instructor of Nursing, Behrend College, Pennsylvania State University, Erie, PA (1989-1992);Instructor, School of Nursing, Hamot Medical Center, Erie, PA (1973-1975); Instructor, Practical Nursing, York County Vocational-Tech (1966-1973) **CW:** Contributing Author, "Transcultural Health Care: A Culturally Competent Approach" (1997); Contributor, Articles, Professional Journals **AW:** Elected, Erie Hall of Fame, William A. Nelson Award For Excellence In Health Care (2008); William B. Nelson Excellence in Medical Ethics Award (2007); Special Contribution Award, Veterans Health Administration (2002, 2003); Customer Service Star Award, Erie VA Medical Center (2000); Recognition Award for Promoting Excellence in Evaluation in Education, National Nursing Staff Development Organization (1994) **MEM:** Pennsylvania Nurses Association **MH:** Albert Nelson Marquis Lifetime Achievement Award **B/I:** Ms. Steckler became involved in her profession because, when she was 4 years old, her mother gave birth to her sister at home. There was a wonderful nurse, Ms. Apple, who came to take care of her mother and her sister. She was the most wonderful person Ms. Steckler ever met. When she graduated, she went to the hospital and interviewed, inspired by Ms. Apple and her kindness. **AV:** Bird watching; Crafting

STEEL, DANIELLE, T: Author **I:** Writing and Editing **DOB:** 08/14/1947 **PB:** New York **SC:** NY/USA **PT:** John Schuelein-Steel; Norma Schuelein-Steel **MS:** Divorced **SPN:** Thomas Perkins (1998, Divorced 2002); John Traina (1981, Divorced 1998); William George Toth (1978, Divorced 03/1981); Danny Zugelder (1975, Divorced 1978); Claude-Eric Lazard (1965, Divorced 1974) **CH:** Trevor; Todd; Beatrix; Zara; Maxx; Vanessa; Victoria; Samantha; Nick **ED:** Coursework, New York University; Coursework, Parsons School of Design, New York, NY **C:** Blog Host, Daniellesteel.net (2018-Present); Owner, Steel Gallery of Contemporary Art, San Francisco, CA (2003-2007); Copywriter, Grey Advertising, San Francisco, CA (1973-1974); Vice President, Public Relations and New Business, Supergirls Ltd., New York, NY (1968-1971) **CW:** Author, "Moral Compass" (2020); Author, "The Numbers Game" (2020); Author, "The Wedding Dress" (2020); Author, "Daddy's Girls" (2020); Author, "Royal" (2020); Author, "All That Glitters" (2020); Author, "Turning Point" (2019); Author, "Silent Night" (2019); Author, "Blessing in

Disguise" (2019); Author, "Lost and Found" (2019); Author, "The Dark Side" (2019); Author, "Child's Play" (2019); Author, "Spy" (2019); Author, "Fall from Grace" (2018); Author, "Accidental Heroes" (2018); Author, "The Cast" (2018); Author, "The Good Fight" (2018); Author, "The Mistress" (2017); Author, "Dangerous Games" (2017); Author, "Against All Odds" (2017); Author, "The Duchess" (2017); Author, Television Film, "The Right Time" (2017); Author, "Fairytale" (2017); Author, "Past Perfect" (2017); Author, "The Apartment" (2016); Author, "Magic" (2016); Author, "Rushing Waters" (2016); Author, "The Award" (2016); Author, "Blue" (2016); Author, "Property of a Noblewoman" (2016); Author, "Prodigal Son" (2015); Author, "Country" (2015); Author, "Undercover" (2015); Author, "Power Play" (2014); Author, "A Perfect Life" (2014); Author, "Pegasus" (2014); Author, "Pretty Minnie in Paris" (2014); Author, "Until the End of Time" (2013); Author, "First Sight" (2013); Author, "Winners" (2013); Author, "Pure Joy" (2013); Author, "Betrayal" (2012); Author, "Friends Forever" (2012); Author, "The Sins of the Mother" (2012); Author, "A Gift of Hope: Helping the Homeless" (2012); Author, "44 Charles Street" (2011); Author, "Happy Birthday" (2011); Author, "Hotel Vendome" (2011); Author, "Big Girl" (2010); Author, "Family Ties," (2010); Author, "Legacy" (2010); Author, "One Day at a Time" (2009); Author, "Matters of the Heart" (2009); Author, "Southern Lights" (2009); Author, "Honor Thyself" (2008); Author, "Rogue" (2008); Author, "A Good Woman" (2008); Author, "Sisters" (2007); Author, "Bungalow 2" (2007); Author, "Amazing Grace" (2007); Author, "The House" (2006); Author, "Coming Out" (2006); Author, "H.R.H" (2006); Author, "Miracle" (2005); Author, "Toxic Bachelors" (2005); Author, "Impossible" (2005); Author, "Ransom" (2004); Author, "Second Chance" (2004); Author, "Echoes" (2004); Author, "Dating Game" (2003); Author, "Johnny Angel" (2003); Author, "Safe Harbour" (2003); Author, "The Cottage" (2002); Author, "Sunset in St. Tropez" (2002); Author, "Answered Prayers" (2002); Author, "Lone Eagle" (2001); Author, "Leap of Faith" (2001); Author, "The Kiss" (2001); Author, "The House on Hope Street" (2000); Author, "Journey" (2000); Author, "The Wedding" (2000); Author, "Bittersweet" (1999); Author, "Granny Dan" (1999); Author, "Irresistible Forces" (1999); Author, "The Long Road Home" (1998); Author, "The Klone and I" (1998); Author, "His Bright Light" (1998); Author, "Mirror Image" (1998); Author, "The Ranch" (1997); Author, "Special Delivery" (1997); Author, "The Ghost" (1997); Author, "Malice" (1996); Author, "Silent Honor" (1996); Author, "Lightning" (1995); Author, "Five Days in Paris" (1995); Author, "Accident" (1994); Author, "The Gift" (1994); Author, "Wings" (1994); Author, "Vanished" (1993); Author, "Freddie's Trip" (1992); Author, "Freddie's First Night Away" (1992); Author, "Freddie and the Doctor" (1992); Author, "Freddie's Accident" (1992); Author, "Jewels" (1992); Author, "Mixed Blessings" (1992); Author, "Heartbeat" (1991); Author, "No Greater Love" (1991); Author, "Max and Grandma and Grampa Winky" (1991); Author, "Martha and Hilary and the Stranger" (1991); Author, "Max Runs Away" (1990); Author, "Martha's New Puppy" (1990); Author, "Message from Nam" (1990); Author, "Star" (1989); Author, "Martha's New Daddy" (1989); Author, "Max and the Babysitter" (1989); Author, "Martha's Best Friend" (1989); Author, "Max's Daddy Goes to the Hospital" (1989); Author, "Max's New Baby" (1989); Author, "Martha's New School" (1989); Author, "Daddy" (1989); Author, "Zoya" (1988); Author, "Fine Things" (1987); Author, "Kaleidoscope" (1987); Author, "Wanderlust" (1986); Author, "Secrets" (1985); Author, "Family Album" (1985); Author, "Love: Poems" (1984);

Author, "Full Circle" (1984); Author, "A Perfect Stranger" (1983); Author, "Thurston House" (1983); Author, "Changes" (1983); Author, "Once in a Lifetime" (1982); Author, "Crossings" (1982); Author, "Loving" (1981); Author, "Remembrance" (1981); Author, "To Love Again" (1981); Author, "Palomino" (1981); Author, "The Ring" (1980); Author, "Summer's End" (1980); Author, "Season of Passion" (1980); Author, "Golden Moments" (1979); Author, "The Promise" (1978); Author, "Now and Forever" (1978); Author, "Passion's Promise" (1977); Author, "Going Home" (1973) **AW:** Inductee, California Hall of Fame (2009); Distinguished Service in Mental Health Award, New York Presbyterian-Columbia University Medical Center and Cornell Medical College (2009); Named to California Hall of Fame (2009); Outstanding Achievement Award, Larkin St. Youth Services, San Francisco, CA (2003); Decorated Officier, Order of Arts and Letters, France (2002); Service to Youth Award, University of San Francisco Catholic Youth Organization/St. Mary's Medical Center (1999); Outstanding Achievement Award in Mental Health, California Psychiatric Association; Distinguished Service Award, American Psychiatric Association

STEFANI, GWEN RENÉE, T: Singer I: Media & Entertainment **DOB:** 10/03/1969 **PB:** Fullerton **SC:** CA/USA **PT:** Dennis Stefani; Patti (Flynn) Stefani **MS:** Divorced **SPN:** Gavin McGregor Rossdale (9/14/2002, Divorced 4/8/2016) **CH:** Kingston James McGregor; Zuma Nesta Rock; Apollo Bowie Flynn **ED:** Coursework, California State University, Fullerton **C:** Solo Musician (2003-Present); Singer, No Doubt (1986-Present) **CR:** Launched, Shoe and Handbag Line, "Gx by Gwen Stefani," ShoeDazzle (2014-Present); Spokesperson, L'Oréal Paris (2011-Present); Designer, Creator, Fashion Line, "L.A.M.B." (2004-Present); Collaborator, Urban Decay (2016); Launched, Fragrances, "Love," "Lil' Angel," "Music," "Baby," "G (Gwen)" (2008); Launched, Fragrance, "L" (2007); Launched, Toy Doll Line, "Love. Angel. Music. Baby. Fashion Dolls" (2006) **CIV:** Donor, Japan Earthquake - Tsunami Children in Emergency Fund, Save the Children (2011) **CW:** Producer, "Kuu Kuu Harajuku" (2015-Present); Voice Actress, "Trolls World Tour" (2020); Featured Musician, "Nobody but You" (2020); Coach, Adviser, "The Voice" (2014-2015, 2017, 2019); Musician, "You Make It Feel Like Christmas" (2017); Musician, "This Is What the Truth Feels Like" (2016); Featured Musician, "Hands" (2016); Voice Actress, "Trolls" (2016); Musical Guest, "Saturday Night Live" (1996-2016); Appearance, Documentary, "Through the Eyes of Faith" (2015); Featured Musician, "Kings Never Die" (2015); Featured Musician, "Shine" (2015); Guest Appearance, "Portlandia" (2013); Musician, "Push and Shove" (2012); Featured Musician, "Glycerine (Live)" (2012); Appearance, Documentary, "Everyday Sunshine: The Story of Fishbone" (2011); Musician, "Icon" (2010); Guest Appearance, "Gossip Girl" (2009); Musician, "The Sweet Escape" (2006); Musician, "Harajuku Lovers Live" (2006); Musician, "Love. Angel. Music. Baby. (The Remixes)" (2005); Featured Musician, "Can I Have It Like That" (2005); Appearance, Documentary, "Fashion Rocks" (2005); Appearance, Documentary, "Brain Fart" (2005); Voice Actress, Video Game, "Malice" (2004); Actress, "The Aviator" (2004); Musician, "Everything in Time" (2004); Musician, "Love. Angel. Music. Baby." (2004); Musician, "The Singles 1992-2003" (2003); Musician, "Boom Box" (2003); Guest Appearance, "Dawson's Creek" (2002); Guest Appearance, "King of the Hill" (2001); Cameo, "Zoolander" (2001); Musician, "Rock Steady" (2001); Featured Musician, "What's Going On" (2001); Featured Musician, "Let Me Blow Ya Mind" (2001); Featured Musician, "South

Side" (2000); Musician, "Return of Saturn" (2000); Musician, "Collector's Orange Crate" (1997); Musician, "Tragic Kingdom" (1995); Musician, "The Beacon Street Collection" (1995); Musician, "No Doubt" (1992); Musician, Numerous Other Songs **AW:** Icon Award, Glamour Women of the Year Awards (2016); Best Hair & Make Up, Ibiza Music Video Festival (2016); Hero Award, Radio Disney Music Awards (2016); Style Icon of the Year, People Magazine Awards (2014); Celebrity Designer, Style Female, Bravo A-List Awards (2009); Song of the Year, Most Performed Song, "The Sweet Escape," ASCAP Pop Music Awards (2008); Favorite Female Singer, People Choice Awards (2008); Four Pop Song Awards, BMI Music Awards (2006-2008); Most Performed Song, ASCAP Pop Music Awards (2007); Most Performed Songs, "Rich Girl," "Hollaback Girl," ASCAP Pop Music Awards (2006); Wood Pencil, Cinematography, D&AD Awards (2006); Best International Female, Meteor Ireland Music Awards (2006); 400,000 Spins, BDSCertified Spins Awards (2006); Favorite Pop/Rock Female Artist, American Music Awards (2005); New Artist of the Year, Digital Song of the Year for "Hollaback Girl," Billboard Music Awards (2005); Album Title Award, IFPI Platinum Europe Awards (2005); Best Solo Artist, Glamour Women of the Year Awards (2005); Sh! Style Icon, Smash Hits Poll Awards (2005); International Newcomer, Premios OYE! Awards (2005); Best Alternative/Rock Dance Artist, "What You Waiting For?," International Dance Music Awards (2005); Best Pop International Artist, MTV Video Music Latino America Awards (2005); Best Dressed, MTV Australia Music Awards (2005); Best Art Direction, Best Choreography, MTV Video Music Awards (2005); Bestselling New Female Artist, World Music Awards (2005); Choice Collaboration, Visionary Award, Choice Breakout, Teen Choice Awards (2005); International Female Solo Artist, Brit Awards (2005); Sexiest Female, NME Awards (2005); People's Choice: Favorite International Artist, Much Music Video Awards (2005); Best Pop Performance by a Duo or Group with Vocals, Grammy Awards (2004); Choice Music: Tour, Teen Choice Awards (2004); Best Pop Performance by a Duo or Group with Vocals, Grammy Awards (2003-2004); Best Pop Video, Best Group Video, MTV Video Music Awards (2002, 2004); Most Performed Songs, ASCAP Pop Music Awards (1999, 2004); Outstanding Female Vocalist, California Music Awards (1998, 2003-2004); Best Pop Performance by a Duo or Group with Vocals, Grammy Awards (2003); Favorite Band, Nickelodeon Kids' Choice Awards (2003); 200,000 Spins, BDSCertified Spins Awards (2002); Best Rap/Sung Collaboration, Grammy Awards (2002); Best Female Video, Best Male Video, MTV Video Music Awards (2001); Female Singer Award, There's No "I" in Team (Best Collaboration), My VH1 Music Awards (2001); Choice R&B/Hip Hop Track, Teen Choice Awards (2001); Rock Style Award, Visionary Video, VH1 Vogue Fashion Awards (2001); FANtastic Video, Billboard Music Video Awards (2000); Most Styling Video, VH1/Vogue Fashion Awards (1999-2000); Longform Video of the Year, MVPA Awards (1998); Best International Hit, Danish Music Awards (1998); Best International Group, Brit Awards (1998); Best Group Video, MTV Video Music Awards (1997); Two Award-Winning Songs, BMI Pop Awards (1996) **RE:** Roman Catholic

STEFANIK, ELISE MARIE, T: U.S. Representative from New York **I:** Government Administration/ Government Relations/Government Services **DOB:** 07/02/1982 **PB:** Albany **SC:** NY/USA **PT:** Ken Stefanik; Melanie Stefanik **MS:** Married **SPN:** Matthew Manda **ED:** BA, Harvard University (2006) **C:** Member, U.S. House of Representative from New York's 21st Congressional District, United

Sates Congress, Washington, DC (2015-Present); Member, Committee on Armed Services (2015-Present); Marketing Management, Premium Plywood Products, Inc., Guilderland Center, NY (2012-2014); Director, Vice Presidential Debate Preparation to Representative Paul Ryan, U.S. Presidential Election (2012); Communications Director, Foreign Policy Initiative, Policy Director, Tim Pawlenty's Presidential Campaign (2012); Staff Member, Domestic Policy Council, The White House (2006-2009); Committee on Education and the Workforce; Policy Director, Foreign Policy Initiative **AW:** Women's Leadership Award, Harvard University **PA:** Republican **RE:** Roman Catholic

STEHR, JUSTIN, T: Estimating and Business Development Manager **I:** Business Management/ Business Services **CN:** Entech Innovative **MS:** Married **ED:** BS in Mechanical Engineering Technology, University of Pittsburgh at Johnstown, Johnstown, PA (2012) **C:** Estimating and Business Development Manager, Entech Creative Industries (2019-Present); Estimating and Business Development Manager, Technical Design and Engineering Manager, Mechanical Design Engineer, Entech Innovative Engineering, Rockledge, FL (2015-Present); Design Manager, Entech Creative Industries (2015-2019); Associate Engineer, Project Engineer, Back Stage Technologies, Winter Garden, FL (2014-2015); Mechanical Design Engineer, Cinnabar Florida, Inc., Orlando, FL (2012-2014) **CW:** Engineer, Numerous Show Action Equipment Pieces, Diagon Alley, Universal Studios; Contributing Designer, Water Features, Voyage to the Crystal Grotto, Shanghai Disney; Engineer, Restoration of the Empress Lily and its Conversion into the Paddlefish Restaurant, Disney Springs **AW:** Project of the Year Award, Associated Builders and Contractors **MEM:** Themed Entertainment Association (TEA); Associated Builders and Contractors; American Society of Mechanical Engineers **AS:** Mr. Stehr attributes his success to his networking abilities. The reason is, when he was in school, he was trying to find a way into the industry. He was almost about to graduate before what he attributes to dumb luck, he found his way into the industry. A presenter came to his school, talking about going out and gaining experience. After the speaker finished his presentation, he approached him and told him about the type of career he wanted. By his surprise, the man connected him to someone that he knew in that industry. By his courage to ask questions, Mr. Stehr was presented with an opportunity that eventually would change the course of his life. **B/I:** Mr. Stehr became involved in his profession because, at 13 years old, he got involved in playing a popular video game called "RollerCoaster Tycoon." He decided then that he wanted to design roller coasters for a living. After realizing that it was a very niche profession, he began to explore the possibilities of the amusement entertainment industry. He began working with companies like Disney, Universal Studios, and Sea World, as well as other amusement parks around the world. Being able to accomplish those things has become his dream and he cannot wait to continue to accomplish more.

STEIL, BRYAN GEORGE, T: U.S. Representative from Wisconsin; Lawyer **I:** Government Administration/Government Relations/Government Services **DOB:** 03/03/1981 **PB:** Janesville **SC:** WI/USA **ED:** JD, University of Wisconsin Law School, Madison, WI; BSBA, Georgetown University **C:** Member, U.S. House of Representatives from Wisconsin's First Congressional District (2019-Present); Aide, U.S. Representative Paul Ryan (2003); Legal Counsel, Regal Beloit Corporation; Attorney, McDer-

mott Will & Emery; Executive, Charter NEX Film, Milton, WI **CIV:** Board of Regents, University of Wisconsin-Madison (2016) **PA:** Republican

STEIN, ELLEN G., T: Information Technology Executive (Retired) **I:** Government Administration/Government Relations/Government Services **DOB:** 05/19/1951 **PB:** New York **SC:** NY/USA **PT:** Manuel W. Stein; Bella (Skutel) Stein **ED:** Certificate, Program for Executives in State/Local Government, Harvard University (1985); Master of Urban Planning, Hunter College, City University of New York (1976); BA, State University of New York at Stony Brook, NY (1972) **C:** Retired (2016); Associate Commissioner, Office of the Commissioner, New York City Department of Information Technology and Telecommunications (1999-2016); President, Chief Executive Officer, FEDVentures Inc. (1994-1999); Management Consultant, Project Provide Hope, USAID, Russia, Citizen's Budget Commission (1990-1994); Administrator Bureau Supplied, New York City Board of Education, New York, NY (1984-1990); Director, Citywide Audit Implementation, Mayor's Office of Operations, New York, NY (1981-1984); Deputy Assistant Director, Citywide Special Projects, Mayor's Office of Operations (1981); Group Leader, Criminal Justice, Mayor's Office of Operations (1979-1981); Senior Planner, New York City Department of Corrections (1977-1979); Senior Research Associate, Nassau Suffolk Regional Medical Program, NY (1976-1977) **MEM:** National Association Purchasing Management; American Women Economic Development; Central Women's Focus; Governor's Procurement Council, State of New York; Contracting Committee, Human Services Council **MH:** Albert Nelson Marquis Lifetime Achievement Award **B/I:** Ms. Stein graduated from college as an 18th century English literature major and, during her two-year break, she was trying to decide what she wanted to do next. She discovered urban planning, which was a new field that combined economics architecture, engineering, and sociology. She lived in New York City and loved the environment around her, so she thought it would be interesting to make a career out of making the city better and examining its future potential. She explored this field as her major, which lead to her working with city government. Her first job was on Wall Street, but she wanted something more engaging. Before she graduated with a master's degree, she was hired by a health group on Long Island. They were trying to determine the best and most cost-effective way to treat common diseases. Ms. Stein developed a cost-benefit analysis to determine the answer, which was ground-breaking back then. She stayed with the company and continued to work in criminal justice, operations, and education; her career within the government varied enormously. Ms. Stein left while doing consulting when she received the opportunity to do a project in Russia. She was in Red Square the first day that communism fell. There was a famine in Russia, and they were there to deliver 62 tons of food, creating distribution lines in order to reach the needy. It became too dangerous to remain in Russia, and she departed for a position with the UJA Federation of New York, who offered her a job to create a subsidiary corporation. She became involved with the not-for-profit world, and an opportunity came up to blend her not-for-profit and government work together, in addition to incorporating information technology.

STEIN, ROBERT, "ROBIN" M. JR., MCP, T: Special Assistant to the Mayor **I:** Government Administration/Government Relations/Government Services **CN:** City of Stamford **DOB:** 01/20/1942 **PB:** New York **SC:** NY/USA **PT:** Anita Stein; Robert Stein **MS:** Married **SPN:** Silvia Fernandez-Stein **CH:** Silvia

Stein; Guido Stein; David Stein **ED:** MCP, University of Pennsylvania (1966); BA in History, University of Michigan (1964) **CT:** American Institute of Certified Planners; Greening the Economy, Lund University; Sustainable Cities, Finding Purpose and Meaning in Life, University of Michigan **C:** Special Assistant to the Mayor, City of Stamford, CT (2014-Present); Chairman, Connecticut Siting Council (2011-2018); Chief, Land Use Bureau, City of Stamford, CT (1993-2011) **CIV:** Expert Volunteer, Land Use Planning Reform Specialist, Tanzania (2017); Board Member, Mill River Park Collaborative (2002-2016); Board Member, Norwalk Nagarote Sister City Project (2013); Chile Coordination Group, Amnesty International (1973-1980); Volunteer, Peace Corps, Chile (1966-1968) **AW:** Connecticut Chapter Award, American Planning Association (2000); Award for Census Work, City of Stamford (1990) **MEM:** American Planning Association **MH:** Marquis Who's Who Top Professional **AS:** Mr. Stein attributes his success to his ability to work with people, as well as his ability to listen and use his education and job experience to move projects and programs forward. Likewise, he is always thinking with a mind for creating a pathway to a better future for all. **B/I:** The highlight of Mr. Stein's early career occurred when he was a liberal arts history major at the University of Michigan and began to take up what he wanted to do as a career. He was fascinated by environmental planning and the Tennessee Valley Authority. Since he was raised just outside of New York City, he and his parents were involved in community work and often did everything in their power to help those in need. Mr. Stein saw urban planning as a way to combine his environmental and community interests, which is why he decided to pursue the field as a career. **AV:** Fishing; Gardening; Traveling; Practicing Tai Chi **PA:** Progressive Democrat **RE:** Jewish

STEINBERG, NEVIN, T: Sound Designer **I:** Other **MS:** Married **SPN:** Paige Price **C:** Acme Sound Partners (2001-2012) **CW:** Sound Designer, "Tina: The Tina Turner Musical" (2019); Sound Designer, "Freestyle Love Supreme" (2019); Sound Designer, "Frankie and Johnny in the Clair de Lune" (2019); Sound Designer, "Hadestown" (2019); Sound Designer, "The Cher Show" (2018); Sound Designer, "Bandstand" (2017); Sound Designer, "Dear Evan Hansen" (2016); Sound Designer, "Bright Star" (2016); Sound Designer, "Hamilton" (2015) **AW:** Best Sound Design of a Musical, "Hadestown," Tony Awards (2019); Outstanding Sound Design in a Musical, "Hadestown," Drama Desk Awards (2019); Outstanding Sound Design in a Musical, "Hamilton," Drama Desk Awards (2015); Outstanding Sound Design in a Musical, "Porgy and Bess," Drama Desk Awards (2012); Outstanding Sound Design in a Play, "Bengal Tiger at the Baghdad Zoo," Drama Desk Awards (2011); Outstanding Sound Design in a Musical, "Ragtime," Drama Desk Awards (2010); Outstanding Sound Design, "La Bohème," Drama Desk Awards (2003)

STEINFELD, HAILEE, T: Actress, Singer **I:** Media & Entertainment **DOB:** 12/11/1996 **PB:** Tarzana **SC:** CA/USA **PT:** Peter Steinfeld; Cheri (Domasin) Steinfeld **MS:** Single **C:** Spokesmodel, Miu Miu (2011) **CIV:** Appearance, Hot Pink Party, Breast Cancer Foundation (2014); What's Your Mission?; No Kid Hungry; WE Movement; Ryan Seacrest Foundation; Make-a-Wish Foundation; Robin Hood **CW:** Musician, "Wrong Direction" (2020); Musician, "Afterlife" (2019); Actress, "Between Two Ferns: The Movie" (2019); Cameo, "Charlie's Angels" (2019); Executive Producer, Actress, "Dickinson" (2019); Featured Musician, "Woke Up Late" (2019); Featured Musician, "Colour" (2018); Host,

Performer, MTV Europe Music Awards (2018); Voice Actress, "Spider-Man: Into the Spider-Verse" (2018); Actress, "Bumblebee" (2018); Featured Musician, "Ordinary Day" (2018); Advisor, Guest Appearance, "The Voice" (2015, 2017-2018); Musician, "Back to Life" (2018); Featured Musician, "Capital Letters" (2018); Featured Musician, "Let Me Go" (2017); Musician, "Most Girls" (2017); Appearance, Macy's 4th of July Fireworks Spectacular (2017); Actress, "Pitch Perfect 3" (2017); Featured Musician, "At My Best" (2017); Featured Musician, "Show You Love" (2017); Featured Musician, "Digital Love" (2017); Featured Musician, "Fragile" (2016); Actress, "Term Life" (2016); Featured Musician, "Santa Claus Is Coming to Town" (2016); Actress, "The Edge of Seventeen" (2016); Actress, "Ten Thousand Saints" (2015); Musician, EP, "Haiz" (2015); Featured Musician, "How I Want Ya" (2015); Actress, "Pitch Perfect 2" (2015); Narrator, Documentary, "Unity" (2015); Voice Actress, "When Marnie Was There" (2015); Actress, "Barely Lethal" (2015); Actress, "3 Days to Kill" (2014); Actress, "The Homesman" (2014); Actress, "The Keeping Room" (2014); Actress, "Hateship, Loveship" (2013); Actress, "Begin Again" (2013); Actress, Short Film, "The Magic Bracelet" (2013); Actress, "Romeo & Juliet" (2013); Actress, "Ender's Game" (2013); Actress, Short Film, "Without Wings" (2010); Actress, Short Film, "Grand Cru" (2010); Actress, "True Grit" (2010); Guest Appearance, "Sons of Tucson" (2010); Actress, TV Film, "Summer Camp" (2010); Actress, Short Film, "She's a Fox" (2009); Actress, Short Film, "Heather: A Fairytale" (2008); Guest Appearance, "Back to You" (2007) AW: Top Covered Artist, Billboard Music Awards (2017); Best Push Act, MTV Europe Music Awards (2017); Best Young Actress, "The Edge of Seventeen," Women Film Critics Circle (2016); Best Ensemble, "The Homesman," Women Film Critics Circle (2014); Face of the Future, MaxMara (2013); Best Supporting Actress, "True Grit," Austin Film Critics Association, Central Ohio Film Critics Association, Chicago Film Critics Association, Houston Film Critics Society, Indiana Film Journalists Association, Kansas City Film Critics Circle, Online Film Critics Society, Southeastern Film Critics Association, Toronto Film Critics Association, Vancouver Film Critics Circle (2010); Best Young Performer, "True Grit," Critics' Choice Movie Awards (2010); Youth in Film Award, "True Grit," Las Vegas Film Critics Society (2010); Best Young Female Performance, "True Grit," Phoenix Film Critics Society (2010); Best Young Actress - Feature Film, "True Grit," Young Artist Awards (2010)

STEINHORN, IRWIN HARRY, JD, T: Lawyer, Corporate Financial Executive; Educator **I:** Law and Legal Services **DOB:** 08/13/1940 **PB:** Dallas **SC:** TX/USA **PT:** Raymond Steinhorn; Libby L. (Miller) Steinhorn **MS:** Married **SPN:** Deborah Kelley Steinhorn (04/07/2002) **CH:** Leslie Robin **ED:** LLB, The University of Texas (1964); BBA, The University of Texas (1961) **C:** Senior Partner, Director, Conner & Winters, Oklahoma City, OK (1995-Present); Partner, Hastie & Steinhorn, Oklahoma City, OK (1988-1995); Vice President, General Counsel, USPCI, Incorporated Oklahoma City, OK (1987-1988); Senior Vice President, General Counsel, LSB Industries, Incorporated, Oklahoma City, OK (1970-1987); Partner, Parness, McQuire & Lewis, Dallas, Texas (1967-1970); Associate, Oster & Kaufman, Dallas, Texas (1964-1967) **CR:** Adjunct Professor, Law, Oklahoma City University School of Law (1979); Lecturer in Field **CIV:** Member, Executive Advisory Board, Oklahoma City University School of Law (2000-Present); Board of Directors, Oklahoma Venture Forum (2000-Present); Member, Advisory Committee, Oklahoma Securities Commission (1986-Present) **MIL:** Served to

Captain, United States Army Reserve (1964-1970) **AW:** Law Award (2009) **MEM:** Chairman, Oklahoma Bar Association (1988-1989); Secretary, Treasurer, Oklahoma Bar Association (1986-1989); American Bar Association (ABA); Director, Treasurer, Jewish Federation of Greater Oklahoma City; Committee to Revise Oklahoma Business Corporation Act; Business Section, Oklahoma Bar Association; State Bar of Texas; Rotary International; Phi Alpha Delta Law Fraternity, International **BAR:** United States District Court for the Western District of Oklahoma (1972); Oklahoma (1970); United States District Court for the Northern District of Texas (1965); Texas (1964) **MH:** Albert Nelson Marquis Lifetime Achievement Award **PA:** Republican **RE:** Jewish

STEININGER, JEFFREY LYNN JR., T: Makeup Artist **I:** Cosmetics **CN:** Jeffree Star Cosmetics **DOB:** 11/15/1985 **PB:** Los Angeles **SC:** CA/USA **PT:** Jeffrey L. Steininger Sr.; Marra Shubyann (Lindstrom) Steininger **MS:** Single **C:** Founder, Makeup Artist, Jeffree Star Cosmetics (2014-Present) **CW:** Featured, "The Beautiful World of Jeffree Star" (2019); Featured, "The Secret World of Jeffree Star" (2018); Musician, "Love to My Cobain" (2013); Musician, "Prom Night" (2012); Musician, "Mr. Diva" (2012); Musician, "Concealer" (2012); Musician, "Virginity" (2012); Musician, "Beauty Killer" (2009); Musician, "Cupcakes Taste Like Violence" (2008); Musician, "Plastic Surgery Slumber Party" (2007); Featured Musician, Numerous Songs; Appearances, Numerous Music Videos

STEITZ, THOMAS ARTHUR, PHD, T: Biophysicist, Professor **I:** Education/Educational Services **CN:** Yale University **DOB:** 08/23/1940 **PB:** Milwaukee **SC:** WI/USA **MS:** Married **SPN:** Joan (Argetsinger) Steitz **CH:** Jon **ED:** Honorary Doctor of Science, Lawrence University, Appleton, WI (1981); Doctor of Philosophy, Harvard University (1966); Bachelor of Arts, Lawrence University, Appleton, WI (1962) **C:** Sterling Professor, Molecular Biophysics and Biochemistry, Yale University, New Haven, CT (2001-2018); Faculty, Yale University, New Haven, CT (1970-2018); Jane Coffin Childs Postdoctoral Fellow, MRC Laboratory of Molecular Biology, University of Cambridge, England, United Kingdom (1967-1970); Postdoctoral Fellow, Harvard University (1966-1967) **CR:** Investigator, Howard Hughes Medical Institute, Chevy Chase, MD (1986-Present); Visiting Professor, University of Colorado Boulder (1992-1993) **CW:** Contributor, Articles to Professional Journals **AW:** Fellow, Royal Society (2011); Nobel Prize in Chemistry (2009); Lucia R. Briggs Distinguished Achievement Award, Lawrence University (2009); Gairdner Foundation International Award (2007); Keio Medical Science Prize (2006); Rosenstiel Award for Distinguished Work in Basic Medical Research (2001); Newcomb Cleveland Prize, American Academy of Arts & Sciences (2001); Fairchild Scholar, California Institute of Technology (1984-1985); Pfizer Award in Enzyme Chemistry, American Chemical Society (1980); Macy Fellow, Göttingen, Germany (1976-1977) **MEM:** Fellow, American Academy of Arts & Sciences; National Academy of Sciences; Delta Tau Delta

STEPHENS, DEBORAH LYNN, T: Founder, Chairman, Chief Executive Officer **I:** Health, Wellness and Fitness **CN:** Behavioral Health Systems, Inc. **DOB:** 05/30/1952 **PB:** Newton **SC:** IA/USA **PT:** Clarence Harry Wright; Nancy Elizabeth (Gass) Wright **MS:** Married **SPN:** Michael E. Stephens (05/21/1988, Divorced); David K. Brender (12/18/1971, Divorced) **ED:** BS, University of Iowa (1974); Postgraduate Coursework, University of Wisconsin-Milwaukee; Postgraduate Coursework,

University of California Berkeley **C:** Principal Shareholder, Behavior Health Systems, Inc., Birmingham, AL (2015-Present); Founder, Chairman, Chief Executive Officer, Behavioral Health Systems, Inc., Birmingham, AL (1989-Present); Executive Vice President, Chief Operating Officer, Sacred Heart Rehabilitation Hospital, Medical Rehabilitation Institute, Milwaukee, WI (1984-1988); Vice President of Finance, Chief Finance Officer, Medical Rehabilitation Institute, Milwaukee, WI (1981-1984); Assistant Controller, Unicare Health Facilities, Milwaukee, WI (1979-1981); Contract Audit Accountant, Miller Brewing Company, Milwaukee, WI (1977-1979); Assistant to the Dean of Finance, Carver College of Medicine, University of Iowa (1975-1977) **CR:** Founding Member, American Rehabilitation Network, Inc.; Prospective Payment Advisory Committee, U.S. Department of Health & Human Services; Member, Oral Examining Boards, City of Milwaukee; Consultant on Rehabilitation, Hospital Administration, Finance, Multi-Corporation Planning and Zero-Based Budgeting **CIV:** Chairman, Applecross Homeowner's Association **CW:** Contributor, Articles, Professional Journals **AW:** Top 78 National Entrepreneurs, Entrepreneur Magazine (1996); Top 5 Thriving Business Women in Birmingham, Business to Business Magazine (1995) **MEM:** Board Member, Rotary Club of Birmingham (2009-Present); Trustee, Birmingham Business Alliance (2005-Present); Rotary Club of Birmingham; Governing Board, Hospital of Finance Management Association; Prospective Payment Advisory Board, Medical-Oriented Facilities Committee, The National Association of Rehabilitation Providers and Agencies; Health Care Cost Containment Committee, Business Council of Alabama; Venture Club; Midwest Business Group on Health **MH:** Albert Nelson Marquis Lifetime Achievement Award **AV:** Skiing; Jogging; Traveling; Reading; Weight training **PA:** Democrat **RE:** Christian

STEPHENS, H. JEANNETTE JEANNETTE, BS, MS, PHD, T: Mathematics Educator **I:** Education/Educational Services **DOB:** 02/22/1944 **PB:** Waukegan **SC:** IL/USA **PT:** Clarence Francis Stephens Sr.; Harriette Josephine Stephens **MS:** Single **ED:** PhD in Math Education, University of Iowa, Iowa City, IA (1979); MS, SUNY Geneseo (1969); BS, SUNY Geneseo (1965) **CT:** Certified Teacher, New York, Iowa **C:** Teacher, Mathematics, Mathematics Education, Whatcom Community College, Bellingham, WA (1986-2016); Teacher, Mathematics, Mathematics Education, Western Washington University, Bellingham, WA (1987-1990); Teacher, Mathematics, Mathematics Education, University of Oregon, Eugene, OR (1980-1984); Teacher, Mathematics, Lane Community College, Eugene, OR (1980-1984); Teacher, Mathematics, West High School, Iowa City, IA (1975-1980); Graduate Assistant, Mathematics Education, Mathematics Teacher, Campus School, University of Iowa, Iowa City, IA (1970-1973); Teacher, Mathematics, West Junior High School, Binghamton, NY (1966-1969) **MH:** Albert Nelson Marquis Lifetime Achievement Award **AS:** Dr. Stephens attributes her success to her parents, both of whom were both math teachers. Her father, in particular, had creative teaching techniques. Both she and her mother would call him "The Mozart of Math Teaching," therefore greatly inspiring her. **AV:** Sewing; Music; Puzzles **RE:** Jewish

STEPHENSON, RANDALL L., T: Chairman, Chief Executive Officer, President **I:** Telecommunications **CN:** AT&T Inc. **DOB:** 04/22/1960 **PB:** Oklahoma City **SC:** OK/USA **MS:** Married **SPN:** Lenise H. Stephenson **CH:** Two Children **ED:** MA in Accounting, University of Oklahoma; BS in Accounting, University of Central Oklahoma **CT:** Certified

Public Accountant (CPA) **C:** Chairman, Chief Executive Officer, AT&T Inc. (2007-Present); President, Boy Scouts of America (2016-2018); Chief Operating Officer, Southwestern Bell (Now AT&T Inc.) (2004-2007); Telephone Senior Executive Vice President, Chief Financial Officer, Southwestern Bell Telephone (Now AT&T Inc.) (2001-2004); Vice President, Controller, SBC Communications, Inc. (1997); Controller, SBC Communications, Inc. (1996-1997); Director, Finance, SBC International, SBC Communications, Inc., Mexico City (1992-1996); District Manager, Finance Analysis, Southwest Bell Telephone (Now AT&T Inc.) (1991-1992); Area Manager, Southwest Bell Telephone (Now AT&T Inc.) (1986-1991); With, Southwest Bell Telephone (Now AT&T Inc.) (1982) **CR:** Member, Board of Directors, Emerson Electric Co. (2006-Present); Member, Board of Directors, AT&T Inc. (2005-Present); Chairman, Business Roundtable (2014-2016); Member, National Security Telecommunications Advisory Committee, President George W. Bush (2004); Chairman, Board of Directors, Cingular Wireless (Now AT&T Inc.) (2003-2004); Member, Audit Committee, H-E-B, C.C. Butt Grocery Company, H-E-B, LP **CIV:** Member, National Executive Board, Boy Scouts of America; Board Member, San Antonio Metropolitan Missions (SAMMinistries) Board; Member, Executive Committee, Audit Committee, United Way San Antonio **AW:** Named One of the "50 Who Matter Now," Business 2.0 (2007) **MEM:** Oklahoma Society of CPAs; Council on Foreign Relations

STERN, MATTHEW B., MD, T: Professor Emeritus of Neurology **I:** Education/Educational Services **CN:** Penn Medicine **DOB:** 06/22/1952 **PB:** Boston **SC:** MA/USA **MS:** Married **SPN:** Janet L. Ries, Esq. (1977) **CH:** Margot; Jeffrey; Jenna **ED:** Resident in Neurology, Hospital of the University of Pennsylvania (1979-1982); Intern in Internal Medicine, Hospital of the University of Pennsylvania (1978-1979); MD, Duke University (1978); BA, Harvard University (1974) **CT:** Certified, American Board of Psychiatry and Neurology (1983); Medical License, State of Pennsylvania **C:** Parker Family Professor Emeritus of Neurology, University of Pennsylvania (2017-Present); Parker Family Professor of Neurology, University of Pennsylvania (2003-2017); Professor of Neurology, University of Pennsylvania (1998-2017); Associate Professor of Neurology, University of Pennsylvania (1997-1998); Clinical Professor of Neurology, Temple University (1996-1997); Clinical Associate Professor of Neurology, Temple University (1995-1996); Associate Professor of Neurology, University of Pennsylvania (1992-1995); Assistant Professor of Neurology, University of Pennsylvania (1984-1991); Lecturer in Neurology, University of Pennsylvania (1982-1983) **CR:** Director Emeritus, Parkinson's Disease and Movement Disorders Center, Perelman School of Medicine, University of Pennsylvania (2017-Present); Vice-Chairman of Development, Department of Neurology, Perelman School of Medicine, University of Pennsylvania (2012-Present); Director, Parkinson's Disease and Movement Disorders Center, University of Pennsylvania Health System, Pennsylvania Hospital, Parkinson's Foundation Center of Excellence (1997-2017); Co-Director, Parkinson's Disease Research, Education and Clinical Center, Philadelphia Veteran's Administration Hospital (2008-2010); Director, Parkinson's Disease Research, Education and Clinical Center, Philadelphia Veteran's Administration Hospital (2001-2008); Review Committee, Department of Pharmacology, University of Pennsylvania (2002-2003); Committee on Appointments and Promotions-Subcommittee on Teaching Evaluation (2000-2002); Chair, Department of Neurology CME Committee (1999-2002); Co-Founder, SquashSmarts, Athletic and Academic Enrichment Program (2000); Chair, Department of Neurology CME Committee (1998-2000); Director, Graduate Hospital Parkinson's Disease and Movement Disorders Center, National Parkinson Foundation Center of Excellence (1991-1997); Attending Neurologist, The Graduate Hospital (1982-1997); Visiting Professor, Department of Neurology, University of Colorado School of Medicine, Denver, CO (1994); Visiting Professor, University of Tennessee, Memphis, TN (1994); Acting Chairman, Department of Neurology, The Graduate Hospital (1991); Co-Director, Graduate Hospital Parkinson's Disease and Movement Disorders Center (1983-1991); Consultant in Field; Principal Investigator in Field; Speaker in Field **CIV:** Co-Founder, Panorama Patient Network (2016-Present); Clinical Scientific Advisory Board, National Parkinson Foundation (2008-Present); Executive Scientific Advisory Board, Michael J. Fox Foundation (2016-2018); Selected Lectures by Invitation and Several Educational Programs **CW:** Reviewer, Journal of the Neurological Sciences (1998-Present); Reviewer, Movement Disorders (1990-Present); Reviewer, Neurology (1989-Present); Reviewer, Annals of Neurology (1987-Present); Reviewer, Brain (2008-2010); Reviewer, Lancet Neurology (2007-2008); Co-Presenter, "Meta-analysis of olfactory dysfunction in Alzheimer's, Parkinson's and Huntington's diseases," International Neuropsychological Society 31st Annual Meeting, Honolulu, HI (2003); Co-Presenter, "Relationship of infrared light beam finger and foot tapping to unilateral UPDRS motor scores in idiopathic Parkinson's disease," International Neuropsychological Society 31st Annual Meeting, Honolulu, HI (2003); Executive Editor, Conversations in Neurology, Embryon, Inc. Somerville, NJ (2002-2003); Co-Author, "Dopamine agonists and sleep in Parkinson's disease," Neurology (2002); Co-Author, "Subthalamic AD gene transfer in Parkinson's disease patients who are candidates for deep brain stimulation," Human Gene Therapy (2002); Co-Author, "Assessing resource demands during sentence processing in Parkinson's disease," Brain and Language (2002); Co-Author, "Information processing speed and sentence comprehension in Parkinson's disease," Neuropsychology (2002); Co-Author, "Sentence comprehension and information processing speed in Parkinson's disease," Journal of the International Neuropsychological Society (2002); Co-Author, "Bilateral stimulation of the subthalamic nucleus in Parkinson's disease: a study of efficacy and safety," Journal of Neurosurgery (2002); Co-Author, "Pergolide monotherapy titration in Parkinson's disease," Movement Disorders (2002); Co-Author, "Infrared light beam finger and foot tapping in ideopathic Parkinson's disease," Movement Disorders (2002); Chairman, Editorial Board, Clinical Seminars in Movement Disorders, NCM Publishers, Inc., New York (1991-1993); Reviewer, Journal of Neural Transmission (1991); Reviewer, Journal of Gerontology, Biological Sciences (1990); Editor-in-Chief, Electronic Journal of Neurology (1987-1988); Associate Editor, Neurology, American Medical Network E-Journal (1985-1986); Contributor, Articles, Professional Journals; Contributor, Chapters, Books; Reviewer in Field; Editor, Numerous Books **AW:** President's Distinguished Service Award, International Parkinson and Movement Disorder Society (2016); Listed, Best Doctors in America (2005-2016); Listed, Philadelphia Magazine's Top Docs (2004-2016); Named, Top Doctor, U.S. News and World Report (2007-2014); Commonwealth of Pennsylvania Citation (1991); Philadelphia City Council Resolution Honoring Work in Parkinson's Disease (1990) **MEM:** Chair, International Congress Oversight Committee, International Parkinson and Movement Disorder Society (2017-Present); Fellow, American Neurologic Association (1999-Present); Fellow, Philadelphia College of Physicians (1997-Present); Fellow, American Academy of Neurology (1996-Present); Honorary Member, International Parkinson and Movement Disorder Society (2018); President, International Parkinson and Movement Disorder Society (2013-2015); Secretary, Chairman of Website Oversight Committee, International Parkinson and Movement Disorder Society (2009-2011); Chair, Task Force on UPDRS Revision, International Parkinson and Movement Disorder Society (2004-2008); Chair, Industrial Relations Committee, International Parkinson and Movement Disorder Society (2004-2006); Chair, Liaison and Public Relations Committee, International Parkinson and Movement Disorder Society (2002-2004); TVP 1012 and TV 1203 Steering Committees, Parkinson Study Group (1996-2003); Movement Disorders Research Award Subcommittee, American Academy of Neurology (1996-1998); Executive Committee, Movement Disorders Section, American Academy of Neurology (1994-1996); Fellow, American Academy of Neurology (1993); Alpha Omega Alpha (1977); Inaugural Member, Penn's Academy of Master Clinicians; Past President, International Parkinson's and Movement Disorder Society **THT:** Matthew B. Stern, MD, is the Parker Family Professor Emeritus of Neurology at the Perelman School of Medicine at the University of Pennsylvania and Director Emeritus of the Parkinson's Disease and Movement Disorders Center.Dr Stern received his B.A. from Harvard University and medical degree from Duke University in Durham, North Carolina. He completed his training in neurology at the University of Pennsylvania. Dr. Stern co-founded Penn's Parkinson's Disease and Movement Disorders Center, which he helped build into one of the premier centers of its kind in the world. Dr Stern has authored or co-authored numerous papers on Parkinson's disease (PD) and related disorders and edited and/or co-edited 8 books. Dr. Stern has been principal investigator or co-prineipal investigator of many studies related to PD and movement disorders. He was also co-chair of VA Cooperative Study 468 investigating Deep Brain Stimulation in Parkinson's disease and founding director of the Philadelphia VA Parkinson's Disease Research, Education and Clinical Center. He serves on numerous consulting boards and has lectured throughout the world. He is an inaugural member of Penn's Academy of Master Clinicians and is a Past President of the International Parkinson and Movement Disorder Society which has awarded him its President's Distinguished Service Award and Honorary Membership. The University of Pennsylvania recently established the Howard Hurtig-Matthew Stern Professorship in Neurology to commemorate his contributions to Penn Medicine.

STERN, MICHAEL D., DDS, T: Dentist **I:** Medicine & Health Care **DOB:** 02/26/1946 **PB:** Cleveland **SC:** OH/USA **PT:** Milton B. Stern; Harriette (Hoffman) Stern **MS:** Single **SPN:** Ellen Weiner (06/09/1968) **CH:** Gregory; Jeffrey Stern; Stephanie S. Fink **ED:** Accelerated Dental Assistant, Training Program, Willoughby Hills, OH (2011); Miniresidency, Craniofacial Pain, Shands Medical Center, University of Florida, Gainesville, FL (1989); Temporomandibular Joint Certificate, Long Island University, New York, NY (1981); DDS, Ohio State University (1972); BS, Ohio State University (1968) **CT:** Board Certified, Pain Management, American Academy of Pain Management **C:** Dentistry, Craniofacial Pain, Life Extension Dentistry, Sleep Disordered Breathing, Willoughby Hills, OH (1993-Present); Dentistry, Temporomandibular Joint Disorders, Wickliffe, OH (1975-1993); Associate Dentist, Office of William Rothkopf, DDS, Cleveland, OH (1973-1975); Staff

Dentist, Rhodes and Rinaldi, Cleveland, OH (1972-1973) **CR:** Media Spokesperson, Dentistry, WJW-TV (1996-Present); Team Dentist, Cleveland Browns (2006-2009); Staff, Pain Center, South Pointe Hospital, Cleveland Clinic Health Systems, Cleveland, OH (1991-2004); Temporomandibular Joint Dysfunction and Facial Pain Consultant, Bio-Acoustics, Athens, OH (1996-1999); Preceptorship, Lecturer, Case Western Reserve University, Cleveland, OH (1986-1995); Media Spokesperson, Dentistry, Morning Exchange WEWS-TV, Cleveland, OH (1981-1985); Adjunct Graduate, Lecturer, Cleveland State University (1983-1984); Consultant, Richmond Heights Hospital (1983); Sound Health Alternatives, Inc.; Former Chair, Board of Trustees, North Coast Spring Dental Meeting **MEM:** President, Academy of Laser Dentistry (2000); State Delegate, American Dental Association, Ohio Dental Association (2000); Vice President, Academy of Laser Dentistry (1999); Secretary, Academy of Laser Dentistry (1996-1998); Public Relations Chairman, Northeast Ohio Dental Society (1979-1983); Fellow, American Endodontic Society; Academy of General Dentistry; International College of Craniomandibular Orthopedics; American Academy of Dental Sleep Medicine; American Sleep and Breathing Academy **MH:** Albert Nelson Marquis Lifetime Achievement Award; Marquis Who's Who Top Professional **B/I:** Mr. Stern became involved in his profession because he wanted to combine his interests in science and helping people. **AV:** Automobiles; Music; Gardening; Traveling

STEUBE, WILLIAM, "GREG" GREGORY, T: U.S. Representative from Florida; Lawyer **I:** Government Administration/Government Relations/Government Services **DOB:** 05/19/1978 **PB:** Bradenton **SC:** FL/USA **PT:** Brad Steube **MS:** Married **SPN:** Jennifer Steube **CH:** Ethan Gregory **ED:** JD, University of Florida Levin College of Law, Gainesville, FL (2003); Intern, U.S. House of Representatives (2000); BS in Beef Cattle Sciences, University of Florida, Gainesville, FL (2000) **C:** Member, U.S. House of Representatives from Florida's 17th Congressional District (2019-Present); Member, District 23, Florida Senate (2016-2018); Member, District 73, Florida House of Representatives (2012-2016); Member, District 67, Florida House of Representatives (2010-2012); Attorney **MIL:** Airborne Infantry Officer to Captain, Judge Advocate General's Corps, United States Army, Operation Iraqi Freedom (2004-2008) **MEM:** Alpha Gamma Rho **PA:** Republican **RE:** Methodist

STEUCKE, PAUL THEODORE SR., T: Professional Association Administrator; Artist **I:** Corporate Communications & Public Relations **DOB:** 03/03/1939 **PB:** Oneida **SC:** NY/USA **PT:** Erwin Wallace Steucke; Alice (Voodre) Steucke **MS:** Widowed **SPN:** Annette Jo Hagaman (11/04/1960, Deceased 01/17/2018) **CH:** Catherine; Stacia; Susan; Paul Jr. **ED:** BFA, Virginia Commonwealth University, (Formerly Richmond Professional Institute (RPI) AKA College of William and Mary) (1962) **C:** Retired (1994); Manager, Communications Division, 7AA, Washington, DC (1989-1994); Public Affairs Officer, Alaska Region, FAA, Anchorage, Alaska (1983-1989); Public Affairs Specialist, Alaska Natural Gas Pipeline Inspector, Anchorage, Alaska (1979-1983); Public Affairs Officer, Alaska Land Use Commission, Anchorage, Alaska (1974-1979); Executive Secretary, US Water Resources Council, Washington, DC (1971-1974); Assistant Branch Chief of Audio-visuals, U.S. Department of Agriculture Forest Service (U.S. Forest Service), Washington, DC (1968-1971); Public Information officer, U.S. Department of Agriculture Forest Service (U.S. Forest Service), Milwaukee, WI (1965-1968); Visual Information Specialist, U.S.

Department of Agriculture, Agricultural Research Service, Washington, DC (1963-1965); Director of Art, Virginia Extension Service, Blacksburg, VA (1962-1963) **CIV:** President, Vice President, Numerous Organizations **MIL:** With, Virginia Army National Guard (1958-1964) **CW:** One-man Art Shows include Anchorage and Fairbanks, Alaska, Washington DC, and Richmond, VA (1980-Present); Author, "Burbia Boy," "Burbia Man," "The Art Work of Paul Steucke," (Hard Cover) **AW:** Named Federal Employee of the Year (1986); Several Merit Awards, Public Relations Society of America, Inc. (1983); Fellow, Virginia Museum of Fine Arts (1960, 1962) **MEM:** President, Society of Federal Artists and Designers (1970); Public Relations Society of America, Inc.; Past President, Alaska Chapter, Public Relations Society of America, Inc.; Society of Federal Artists and Designers **MH:** Albert Nelson Marquis Lifetime Achievement Award **B/I:** At the age of 14, Mr. Steucke asked his father for a set of oil paints for Christmas. Initially, his mother was not a fan of the idea, but his father provided him with paints and canvases anyway. Mr. Steucke recalls taking his paintings to his 7th grade class where he received a great deal of praise from his teachers and classmates. The gratifying feeling for an artist encourages them to keep it up and so he did. While in high school, Mr. Steucke took an art class, and a teacher saw him drawing, and moved him to a table with six senior girls while he was still only a freshman. Mr. Steucke says this experience gave him great incentive to be at his best. Throughout the year, he became good friends with the girls. The following year in his art class, his teacher noticed his ability and made him focus strictly on painting for the duration of their time together. Down the line, he received a job as a surveyor. He realized that all he would ever be working that job was an errand boy. He decided that wasn't what he wanted for his life and decided to enroll in Commonwealth University to receive his Bachelor's in Fine Arts. **THT:** Mr. Steucke fell in love at the age of 19 with a woman that had been previously married and had three infant children at the time. Fast-forward, that woman became his wife Annette, of 58 years.

STEVENS, HALEY MARIA, T: U.S. Representative from Michigan **I:** Government Administration/Government Relations/Government Services **CN:** U.S. House of Representatives **DOB:** 6/24/1983 **PB:** Rochester Hills **SC:** MI/USA **ED:** Master of Arts in Social Policy and Philosophy, American University; Bachelor of Arts in Political Science and Philosophy, American University **C:** Member, U.S. House of Representatives from Michigan's 11th Congressional District (2019-Present); Chief of Staff, Presidential Task Force on the Auto Industry (2009); With, Digital Manufacturing and Design Innovation Institute, Chicago, IL; Member, House Committee on Education and Labor; Member, House Committee on Science, Space and Technology; Chairperson, Research and Technology Subcommittee, United States Congress **CIV:** Volunteer, Barack Obama Presidential Campaign (2008); Volunteer, Hillary Clinton Presidential Campaign (2008); Volunteer Organizer, Michigan Democratic Party (2006); Member, Kensington Church

STEVENS, JOHN PAUL, T: Associate Justice (Retired) **I:** Law and Legal Services **CN:** Supreme Court of the United States **DOB:** 04/20/1920 **PB:** Chicago **SC:** IL/USA **PT:** Ernest James Stevens; Elizabeth (Street) Stevens **MS:** Widowed **SPN:** Maryan Mulh (1979, Deceased 2015); Elizabeth Jane Sheeren (1942, Divorced 1979) **CH:** John Joseph Stevens (Deceased); Kathryn Stevens Jedlicka (Deceased); Elizabeth Jane Stevens Sesemann; Susan Roberta Stevens Mullen **ED:** Honor-

ary LLD, Princeton University (2015); JD, Northwestern University Pritzker School of Law, Magna Cum Laude (1947); AB, The University of Chicago (1941) **C:** Associate Justice, Supreme Court of the United States, Washington, DC (1975-2010); Judge, United States Court of Appeals for the Seventh Circuit, Chicago, IL (1970-1975); Partner, Rothschild, Stevens, Barry & Myers (Now Rothschild, Barry & Meyers LLP) (1952-1970); Associate Counsel, Subcommittee to Study Monopoly Power, United States House Judiciary Committee, Washington, DC (1951-1952); Associate, Poppenhusen, Johnston, Thompson & Raymond (1949-1952); Law Clerk, Justice Wiley B. Rutledge, Supreme Court of the United States, Washington, DC (1947-1948); Legal Work, Chicago, IL **CR:** Appellate Judge, Seminar, New York University School of Law (1972); Chief Counsel, Commission Investigating the Judgment of People v. Isaacs, Illinois Supreme Court (1969); Lecturer, Anti-trust Law, The University of Chicago Law School (1955-1958); Member, Attorney General's National Committee to Study Anti-trust Laws (1953-1955); Lecturer, Anti-trust Law, Northwestern University Pritzker School of Law (1953-1954) **MIL:** Intelligence Officer, United States Navy, Word War II (1941-1945) **CW:** Author, "The Making of a Justice: Reflections on My First 94 Years" (2019); Author, "Six Amendments: How and Why We Should Change the Constitution" (2014); Author, "Five Chiefs: A Supreme Court Memoir" (2011); Contributor, Articles to Professional Journals **AW:** Presidential Medal of Freedom, The White House (2012); Decorated Bronze Star; World War II Victory Medal **MEM:** Second Vice President, Chicago Bar Association (1970); Fellow, American Academy Arts & Sciences; The American Law Institute; Federal Bar Association; Illinois State Bar Association; ABA; Order of the Coif; The International Legal Honor Society of Phi Delta Phi; Psi Upsilon Fraternity; The Phi Beta Kappa Society **BAR:** State of Illinois (1949) **PA:** Republican **RE:** Protestant

STEVENS, LEONARD, T: Education Consultant **I:** Education/Educational Services **DOB:** 09/19/1938 **PB:** Fall River **SC:** MA/USA **PT:** Henry Bennett; Manetta (Berry) S. **MS:** Married **SPN:** Elizabeth Stevens (08/17/1963) **CH:** Lisa M.; Christopher M.; Andrew B.; Rosa B. A. **ED:** Doctor of Education, University of Massachusetts (1978); Bachelor of Science, Boston University (1960); Associate of Arts, Boston University (1958) **CT:** Certified Superintendent, Massachusetts **C:** Race-related School Planning Consultant, Sarasota, FL (1990-Present); Director, Compact for Educational Opportunity, Milwaukee, WI (1988-1990); Director, Office on School Monitoring and Community Relations, U.S. District Court for the Northern District of Ohio (1978-1988); Director, Greater Cleveland Project (1976-1978); Research Assistant, University of Massachusetts, Amherst, MA (1973-1976); Special Assistant to the Chancellor, New York City Board of Education, New York (1970-1973); Executive Editor, Change in Higher Education Magazine, New York, NY (1968-1970); Senior Editor, Cowles Communications Inc., New York, NY (1967-1968); Education Writer, Providence (1963-1967) **CR:** Consultant, Racial and Cultural Diversity and School Desegregation Planning Expert **CIV:** Board of Directors, Commission on Catholic Community Action, Cleveland, OH (1981-1988); Trustee, Institute for Child Advocacy, Cleveland, OH **MIL:** Lieutenant, Junior Grade, U.S. Navy (1960-1963) **CW:** Co-author, "Make Your Schools Work" (1975); Contributor, Articles to Professional Journals and Mass Media Publications **MH:** Albert Nelson Marquis Lifetime Achievement Award **B/I:** Mr. Stevens became involved in his profession out of a desire to become a newspaper reporter.

After working on assignments centered around education in both Rhode Island and New York, he was able to observe decentralization procedures, and was asked by a newly appointed school chancellor to join the staff, which set him on the course of working in education full-time.

STEWART, CARL E., T: Former Chief Judge **I:** Law and Legal Services **CN:** United States Court of Appeals for the Fifth Circuit **DOB:** 01/02/1950 **PB:** Shreveport **SC:** LA/USA **PT:** Corine Stewart; Richard Stewart **MS:** Married **SPN:** Jo Ann Southall **CH:** Three Children **ED:** JD, Loyola University Chicago School of Law, New Orleans, LA (1974); BA, Dillard University, Magna Cum Laude (1971) **C:** Chief Judge, United States Court of Appeals for the Fifth Circuit (2012-2019); Judge, United States Court of Appeals for the Fifth Circuit (1994-2012); Judge, Louisiana Court Appeals for the Second Circuit (1991-1994); Judge, Louisiana District Court (1985-1991); Special Assistant District Attorney, Assistant Prosecutor, City of Shreveport, LA (1983-1985); Principal, Stewart & Dixon, Shreveport, LA (1983-1985); Assistant U.S. Attorney, Western District of Louisiana, U.S. Department of Justice, Shreveport, LA (1979-1983); Staff Attorney, Louisiana Attorney General's Office, Shreveport, LA (1978-1979); Attorney, Piper & Brown, Shreveport, LA (1977-1978); Adjunct Professor, Louisiana State University, Shreveport, LA **CIV:** Chairman, National Search Committee, Boy Scouts of America; Board of Trustees, American Inns of Court Foundation; Board of Trustees, Community Foundation of Shreveport-Bossier (Now Community Foundation of North Louisiana), Shreveport, LA (1994-2004) **MIL:** Captain, Judge Advocate General's Corps, United States Army, Fort Sam Houston, Texas (1974-1977) **AW:** Times Leadership Award, Shreveport Times and Alliance for Education (2008); A.P. Tureaud Achievement Award, Black Law Students Association (BLSA), Loyola University Chicago School of Law (2008); American Silver Buffalo Award, Boy Scouts of America (2002); Silver Antelope Award, Boy Scouts of America; Silver Beaver Award, Boy Scouts of America; Liberty Bell Award, The Shreveport Bar Association; Named Distinguished Alumnus of the Year, Dillard University; Raymond Pace Alexander Award, National Bar Association Judicial Council (Now The Judicial Council of the National Bar Association); Judge William H. Hastie Award, National Bar Association Judicial Council (Now The Judicial Council of the National Bar Association); Clyde E. Fant Memorial Award for Outstanding Community Service; Named Louisiana Outstanding Young Man of the Year, U.S. Jaycees, Louisiana Chapter; Black Leader of the Year Award, Afro-American Society, Southern University at Shreveport, LA **MEM:** Louisiana State Bar Association; Bench/Bar Liaison Committee, Louisiana State Bar Association; Louisiana Conference of Court of Appeal Judges; Black Lawyers Association of Shreveport-Bossier; American Inns of Court, Harry V. Booth-Judge Henry A. Politz Chapter, Shreveport, LA; National Bar Association; Omega Psi Phi Fraternity, Inc., Rho Omega Chapter, LA

STEWART, CHRISTOPHER, "CHRIS" DOUGLAS, T: United States Representative; Author **I:** Government Administration/Government Relations/Government Services **DOB:** 07/15/1960 **PB:** Logan **SC:** UT/USA **PT:** Sybil S. Stewart **MS:** Married **SPN:** Evie Stewart **CH:** Sean; Dane; Lance; Kayla; Bryce; Megan **ED:** BS in Economics, Utah State University (1984) **C:** Member, U.S. House of Representatives, Utah's Second Congressional District, United States Congress, Washington, DC (2013-Present); Member, U.S. House Committee on Science, Space and Technology (2013-Present);

Member, U.S. House Committee on Homeland Security (2013-Present); Member, U.S. House Committee on Natural Resources (2013); President, Chief Executive Officer, Shipley Group (1998-2012); Member, U.S. House Permanent Select Committee on Intelligence; Member, Republican Study Committee; Member, Committee on Appropriations; Chairman, House Sub-Committee on the Environment **CIV:** Missionary, The Church of Jesus Christ of Latter-day Saints, TX **MIL:** Advanced through Grades to Major, United States Air Force (1984-1998) **CW:** Co-author, "The Miracle of Freedom: Seven Tipping Points That Saved the World" (2011); Author, "The Great and Terrible: Clear as the Moon" (2010); Co-author with Ted Stewart, "Seven Miracles That Saved America" (2009); Author, "Redefining Joy in the Last Days" (2009); Author, "The God of War" (2008); Author, "The Great and Terrible: From the End of Heaven" (2008); Author, "The Great and Terrible: Fury & Light" (2007); Author, "The Great and Terrible: The Second Sun" (2005); Author, "The Fourth War" (2005); Co-author with Evie Stewart, "A Christmas Bell for Anya" (2005); Author, "The Great and Terrible: Where Angels Fall" (2004); Author, "The Great and Terrible: The Brothers" (2003); Author, "The Third Consequence" (2000); Author, "The Kill Box: A Technothriller" (2000); Author, "Shattered Bone" (1997) **AW:** National Communications Award, Freedom Foundation (2009); Mackay Trophy for Significant Aerial Achievement (1995) **AV:** Rock Climbing; Hiking **PA:** Republican **RE:** Church of Jesus Christ of Latter-day Saints

STEWART, JON, T: Television Personality, Comedian **I:** Media & Entertainment **DOB:** 11/28/1962 **PB:** New York **SC:** NY/USA **PT:** Donald Leibowitz; Marian (Laskin) Leibowitz **MS:** Married **SPN:** Tracey Lynn McShane (2000) **CH:** Nathan Thomas; Maggie Rose **ED:** BS in Psychology, College of William & Mary (1984) **CIV:** Board Member, National September 11 Memorial & Museum (2011-Present); Advocate, 9/11 First Responders Bill **CW:** Director, Producer, Screenwriter, "Irresistible" (2020); Featured, "Batman v Superman: Dawn of Justice" (2016); Creator, Executive Producer, "The Nightly Show with Larry Wilmore" (2015-2016); Voice Actor, "Gravity Falls" (2015); Director, Screenwriter, "Rosewater" (2014); Voice Actor, "Phineas and Ferb" (2014); Featured "Big Time Rush" (2013); Voice Actor, "Robot Chicken" (2012); Featured, "The Beaver" (2011); Featured, "The Adjustment Bureau" (2011); Author, "Earth (The Book): A Visitor's Guide to the Human Race" (2010); Executive Producer, "Important Things with Demetri Martin" (2009-2010); Featured, "The Great Buck Howard" (2008); Voice Actor, "The Simpsons" (2008); Featured, "Evan Almighty" (2007); Actor, "Jack's Big Music Show" (2007); Voice Actor, "American Dad!" (2006); Voice Actor, "Doogal" (2006); Executive Producer, "The Colbert Report" (2005-2012); Author, "America (The Book): A Citizen's Guide to Democracy Inaction" (2004); Executive Producer, "Night of Too Many Stars: An Overbooked Event for Autism Education" (2004); Voice Actor, "The Adventures of Tom Thumb & Thumbelina" (2002); Actor, "Death to Smoochy" (2002); Actor, "Jay and Silent Bob Strike Back" (2001); Actor, "The Office Party" (2000); Actor, "Committed" (2000); Featured, Executive Producer, Writer, "The Daily Show with Jon Stewart" (1999-2015); Voice Actor, "Dr. Katz, Professional Therapist" (1997-1999); Actor, "Big Daddy" (1999); Actor, "Spin City" (1999); Actor, "Plying by Heart" (1998); Actor, "Since You've Been Gone" (1998); Actor, "Half Baked" (1998); Author, "Naked Pictures of Famous People" (1998); Actor, "The Faculty" (1998); Actor, "Wishful Thinking" (1997); Featured, "Mr. Show with Bob and David" (1997); Featured, "Space Ghost

Coast to Coast" (1997); Actor, "NewsRadio" (1997); Actor, "The Nanny" (1997); Featured, "The Larry Sanders Show" (1996-1998); Actor, "The State" (1994); Actor, "Mixed Nuts" (1994); Featured, Creator, Executive Producer, Writer, "The Jon Stewart Show" (1993-1995); Writer, Producer, Numerous Shows **AW:** Inductee, New Jersey Hall of Fame (2015); Primetime Emmy Awards for Outstanding Writing for a Variety, Music, or Comedy Program (2001, 2003-2006, 2009, 2011-2012, 2015); Freedom of Expression Award, "Rosewater," National Board of Review (2014); One of "The 50 Highest-Earning Political Figures," Newsweek (2010); Grammy Award for Best Spoken Word Album, "Earth (The Book): A Visitor's Guide to the Human Race" (2011); One of The 100 Agents of Change, Rolling Stone (2009); One of The 100 Most Powerful Celebrities, Forbes.com (2008); Honorary All-America Award, National Soccer Coaches Association of America (2006); George Orwell Award for Distinguished Contribution to Honesty and Clarity in Public Language, National Council of English (2005); Peabody Award, "The Daily Show with Jon Stewart" (2000, 2005); Thurber Prize for American Humor, "America (The Book): A Citizen's Guide to Democracy Inaction" (2005); Grammy Award for Best Comedy Album, "America (The Book): A Citizen's Guide to Democracy Inaction" (2005); One of "The 100 Most Influential People," Time (2005); Numerous Other Awards **MEM:** The Pi Kappa Alpha Fraternity

STEWART, PATRICK, T: Actor, Producer **I:** Media & Entertainment **DOB:** 07/13/1940 **PB:** Mirfield **SC:** Yorkshire/England **PT:** Alfred Stewart; Gladys (Barraclough) Stewart **MS:** Married **SPN:** Sunny Ozell (2013); Wendy Neuss (08/25/2000, Divorced 2003); Sheila Falconer (03/22/1966, Divorced 1990) **CH:** Daniel; Sophia **ED:** Honorary Degree, Vrije Universiteit Brussel (2015); Doctor of Letters, University of Leeds (2014); Doctor of Letters, University of East Anglia (2011); Honorary Fellowship, University of Wales, Cardiff (2001); Emeritus Fellow, St. Catherine's College, Oxford **CIV:** President, Huddersfield Town Academy (2010); Supporter, Huddersfield Town A.F.C. **CW:** Actor, "Star Trek: Picard" (2020-2021); Executive Producer, "Star Trek: Picard" (2020-2021); Voice Actor, "Dragon Rider" (2020); Actor, "Coda" (2019); Actor, "Charlie's Angels" (2019); Voice Actor, "American Dad!" (2005-2019); Actor, "The Kid Who Would Be King" (2019); Voice Actor, "My Memory of Us" (2018); Voice Actor, "Family Guy" (2005-2018); Narrator, "Dear Satan" (2017); Actor, "The Wilde Wedding" (2017); Voice Actor, "The Emoji Movie" (2017); Voice Actor, "Dragonheart: Battle for the Heartfire" (2017); Actor, "Logan" (2017); Actor, "National Theatre Live: No Man's Land" (2016); Actor, "What Has the ECHR Ever Done for Us?" (2016); Voice Actor, "Spark: A Space Tail" (2016); Voice Actor, "Unbreakable Kimmy Schmidt" (2016); Actor, "Blunt Talk" (2015-2016); Producer, "Blunt Talk" (2015-2016); Actor, "Christmas Eve" (2015); Voice Actor, "Oscar's Hotel for Fantastical Creatures" (2015); Narrator, "Ted 2" (2015); Actor, "Green Room" (2015); Voice Actor, "Robot Chicken" (2012-2015); Actor, "A Million Ways to Die in the West" (2014); Actor, "X-Men: Days of Future Past" (2014); Voice Actor, "Legends of Oz: Dorothy's Return" (2014); Actor, "Match" (2014); Voice Actor, "Family Guy: The Quest for Stuff" (2014); Voice Actor, "Cosmos: A Spacetime Odyssey" (2014); Actor, "The Colbert Report" (2014); Voice Actor, "Castlevania: Lords of Shadows 2" (2014); Narrator, "Sinbad: The Fifth Voyage" (2014); Actor, "The Daily Show" (2014); Voice ctor, "The Simpsons" (1995, 2013); Actor, "No Man's Land," "Waiting for Godot," "Theater Talk" (2013); Actor, "The Wolverine" (2013); Actor, "Hunting Elephants"

(2013); Voice Actor, "Futurama" (2012); Actor, "The Olympic Ticket Scalper" (2012); Actor, "The Hollow Crown" (2012); Narrator, "Ted" (2012); Voice Actor, "Ice Age: Continental Drift" (2012); Actor, "Epithet" (2012); Voice Actor, "Gnomeo & Juliet" (2011); Actor, Theater, "The Merchant of Venice" (2011); Narrator, "Lego Universe" (2010); Actor, "Great Performances" (2010); Voice Actor, "Castlevania: Lords of Shadow" (2010); Actor, Theater, "Bingo: Scenes of Money and Death" (2010); Actor, "Hamlet" (2009); Actor, "X-Men Origins: Wolverine" (2009); Actor, Theater, "Waiting for Godot" (2009); Actor, Theater, "Hamlet" (2008); Actor, Theater, "MacBeth" (2007-2008); Actor, Theater, "Twelfth Night" (2007); Actor, Theater, "A Christmas Carol" (2007); Voice Actor, "TMNT" (2007); Actor, Theater, "Antony and Cleopatra" (2006); Actor, Theater, "The Tempest" (2006); Voice Actor, "Star Trek: Legacy" (2006); Voice Actor, "The Audition" (2006); Voice Actor, "Borg War" (2006); Actor, "X-Men: The Last Stand" (2006); Voice Actor, "X-Men: The Official Game" (2006); Voice Actor, "The Elder Scrolls IV: Oblivion" (2006); Actor, "Eleventh Hour" (2006); Voice Actor, "Bambi and the Great Prince of the Forest" (2006); Voice Actor, "Bambi and the Great Prince of the Forest" (2006); Voice Actor, "The Snow Queen" (2005); Voice Actor, "Chicken Little" (2005); Voice Actor, "X-Men Legends II: Rise of Apocalypse" (2005); Actor, "Mysterious Island" (2005); Himself, "Extras" (2005); Actor, "The Game of Their Lives" (2005); Narrator, "High Spirits with Shirley Ghostman" (2005); Narrator, "Dragons: A Fantasy Made Real" (2004); Voice Actor, "X-Men Legends" (2004); Voice Actor, "Forgotten Realms: Demon Stone" (2004); Voice Actor, "Steamboy" (2004); Voice Actor, "Boo, Zino & the Snurks" (2004); Actor, "The Lion in Winter" (2003); Executive Producer, "The Lion in Winter" (2003); Actor, "Frasier" (2003); Narrator, "Water for Tea" (2003); Voice Actor, "Star Trek: Elite Force II" (2003); Actor, "X2: X-Men United" (2003); Actor, Theater, "The Caretaker" (2003); Actor, Theater, "The Master Builder" (2003); Actor, "Star Trek: Nemesis" (2002); Actor, "King of Texas" (2002); Executive Producer, "King of Texas" (2002); Voice Actor, "Jimmy Neutron: Boy Genius" (2001); Actor, Theater, "Johnson Over Jordan" (2001); Actor, Theater, "Who's Afraid of Virginia Woolf?" (2001); Actor, "X-Men" (2000); Actor, Theater, "The Ride Down Mt. Morgan" (2000); Actor, "A Christmas Carol" (1999); Executive Producer, "A Christmas Carol" (1999); Voice Actor, "Animal Farm" (1999); Voice Actor, "The Prince of Egypt" (1998); Actor, "Star Trek: Insurrection" (1998); Associate Producer, "Star Trek: Insurrection" (1998); Actor, "Wayfinders" (1998); Actor, "Safe House" (1998); Actor, "Dad Savage" (1998); Actor, "Moby Dick" (1998); Actor, "Masterminds" (1997); Actor, "Conspiracy Theory" (1997); Actor, Theater, "Othello" (1997); Actor, "Star Trek: First Contact" (1996); Actor, "The Canterville Ghost" (1996); Co-Producer, "The Canterville Ghost" (1996); Actor, "Let It Be Me" (1995); Actor, "Jeffrey" (1995); Voice Actor, "500 Nations" (1995); Actor, Theater, "The Tempest" (1995); Director, Five Episodes, "Star Trek: The Next Generation" (1991, 1992, 1993, 1994); Voice Actor, "Lands of Lore: The Throne of Chaos" (1994); Voice Actor, "The Pagemaster" (1994); Actor, "Star Trek: Generations" (1994); Actor, "In Search of Dr. Seuss" (1994); Actor, "Star Trek: The Next Generation" (1987-1994); Actor, "Robin Hood: Men in Tights" (1993); Actor, "Gunmen" (1993); Actor, "Detonator" (1993); Actor, "Star Trek: Deep Space Nine" (1993); Actor, "L.A. Story" (1991); Narrator, "Liftoff! An Astronaut's Journey" (1990); Actor, "Theatre Night" (1987); Actor, "Screenplay" (1986); Actor, "Lady Jane" (1986); Actor, "The Doctor and the Devils" (1985); Actor, "Code Name: Emerald" (1985); Actor, "Life-

force" (1985); Actor, "Wild Geese II" (1985); Actor, "Dune" (1984); Actor, "Uindii" (1984); Actor, "Pope John Paul II" (1984); Voice Actor, "Nausicaa of the Valley of the Wind" (1984); Actor, "Maybury" (1981-1983); Actor, "Smiley's People" (1982); Voice Actor, "The Plague Dogs" (1982); Actor, "Excalibur" (1981); Actor, "Little Lord Fauntleroy" (1980); Actor, "The Anatomist by James Bridie" (1980); Actor, "Hamlet, Prince of Denmark" (1980); Actor, "Tinker Tailor Soldier Spy" (1979); Actor, "BBC2 Play of the Week" (1978); Actor, "Jackanory" (1977); Actor, "Drama" (1977); Actor, "I, Claudius" (1976); Actor, "The Madness" (1976); Actor, "North & South" (1975); Actor, "Hedda" (1975); Actor, "Hennessy" (1975); Actor, "Churchill's People" (1975); Actor, "Joby" (1975); Actor, "The Gathering Storm" (1974); Actor, "Omnibus" (1970-1974); Actor, "Antony and Cleopatra" (1974); Actor, "Fall of Eagles" (1974); Actor, "2nd House" (1974); Actor, "Play for Today" (1973); Actor, "BBC Play of the Month" (1973); Actor, "Coronation Street" (1967); Actor, "Theatre 625" (1966); Actor, "Story Parade" (1964) **AW:** Saturn Award for Best Supporting Actor, "Logan" (2018); Legends of Cinema Award, Savannah Film Festival (2017); Gregory Peck Award, San Diego International Film Festival (2017); Laurence Olivier Award for Best Performance in a Supporting Role, "Hamlet" (2009); Named a Honorary Knight Commander of the Most Excellent Order of the British Empire, Her Majesty Queen Elizabeth II (2009); Sir John Gielgud Award, National Arts Club (2008); Evening Standard Theatre Award for Best Actor, "Macbeth" (2007); Grammy Award for Best Spoken Word Album for Children, "Peter and the Wolf" (1996); Computer Gaming World PREMIER Award for Best Male Voice-Over Acting in a Multimedia Game, "Lands of Lore: The Throne of Chaos" (1994); Drama Desk Award for Outstanding Solo Performance, "A Christmas Carol" (1992); Laurence Olivier Award for Best Actor in a Supporting Role, "Antony and Cleopatra" (1979)

STIGLITZ, JOSEPH, T: Economist **I:** Education/ Educational Services **DOB:** 2/9/1943 **PB:** Gary **SC:** IN/USA **PT:** Nathaniel David Stiglitz; Charlotte (Fishman) Stiglitz **MS:** Married **SPN:** Anya Schiffrin (10/29/2004) **CH:** Siobhan; Michael; Edward; Julia **ED:** Honorary Doctorate, Sciences Po, Paris (2019); Honorary Doctorate, Politecnico di Torino, Turin (2019); Honorary Doctorate, Ecole Normale Superieure de Lyon, Lyon (2019); Honorary Doctorate, BI Norwegian Business School (2018); Honorary Doctorate, University of Costa Rica (2018); Honorary Doctorate, Universita Politecnica delle Marche, Ancona, Italy (2017); Honorary Doctorate, Sant'Anna School of Advanced Studies, University in Pisa, Italy (2017); Honorary Doctorate, Chinese University of Hong Kong (2016); Honorary Doctorate, University of the Republic of Uruguay (2015); Honorary Doctorate, University of Split (2015); Honorary Doctorate, HEC Paris (2015); Honorary Doctorate, Arizona State University (2014); Honorary Doctorate, Harvard University (2014); Honorary Doctorate, Universite Paris-Dauphine (2013); Honorary Doctorate, Cambridge University (2013); Honorary Doctorate, University of Hyderabad (2013); Honorary Doctorate, University of Cordoba (2012); Honorary Doctorate, Luiss Guido Carli University (2010); Honorary Doctorate, University of Manchester (2008); Honorary Doctorate, University of Liege (2008); Honorary Doctorate, University of Venice (2008); Honorary Doctorate, Renmin university (2007); Honorary Doctorate, Universidad Mayor de San Andreas (2006); Honorary Doctorate, Universita degli Studi di Genova (2006); Honorary Doctorate, University of the Basque Country (2006); Honorary Doctorate, Lingnam University (2005); Honorary Doctorate, Durham Uni-

versity (2005); Honorary Doctorate, Universidad de La Plata (2005); Honorary Doctorate, Drexel University (2005); Honorary Doctorate, Universite d'Antananarivo (2004); Honorary Doctorate, University of Bergamo (2004); Honorary Doctorate, University of Oxford (2004); Honorary Doctorate, Pace University (2004); Honorary Doctorate, Indiana University (2004); Honorary Doctorate, Georgetown University (2004); Honorary Doctorate, Azerbaijan State Economic University (2003); Honorary Doctorate, University of Barcelona (2003); Honorary Doctorate, Doshisha University (2003); Honorary Doctorate, Universite Catholique de Louvain la Neuve Belgium (2003); Honorary Doctorate, Pomona College (2002); Honorary Doctorate, University of Macau (2002); Honorary Doctorate, Wirtschfts Universitat (2002); Honorary Doctorate, Sofia State University "Saint Clement Ohridski" (2002); Honorary Doctorate, University of Andes (2001); Honorary Doctorate, University of Beunos Aires (2001); Honorary Doctorate, Glasgow University (2001); Honorary Doctorate, University of Toronto (2001); Honorary Doctorate, Bard College (2001); Honorary Doctorate, New School University (2001); Honorary Doctorate, Northwestern University (2000); Honorary Doctorate, Technical University, Lisbon (2000); Honorary Doctorate, University of Namur (2000); Honorary Doctorate, Academia de Studii Economics, Bucharest (1999); Honorary Doctorate, Ben Gurion University (1997); Honorary Doctorate, University of Leuven (1996); DHL (Honorary), Amherst College (1974); Doctor of Philosophy in Economics, Massachusetts Institute of Technology (1966-1967); Bachelor of Arts, Amherst College (1964) **C:** Professor, Economics and Finance, Columbia Business School, Graduate School of Arts and Sciences, School of International and Public Affairs, Columbia University (2001-Present); Professor, Economics, Senior Fellow, Hoover Institution, Stanford University (1988-2001); Co-Founder, Co-President, Initiative Policy Dialogue, Columbia University, Stern Visiting Professor, Columbia University, New York, NY (2000); Professor, Economics, Princeton University, New Jersey (1979-1988); Drummond Professor, Political Economy, Oxford University, England (1976-1979); Joan Kenney Professor, Economics, Stanford University, California (1974-1976); Professor, Economics, Cowles Foundation, Yale University, New Haven, CT (1970-1974); Associate Professor, Cowles Foundation, Yale University, New Haven, CT (1968-1970); Assistant Professor, Cowles Foundation, Yale University, New Haven, CT (1967-1968); Assistant Professor, Economics, Massachusetts Institute of Technology (1966-1967) **CR:** Chairperson, Brooks World Poverty Institute, University of Manchester, England (2005-Present); Professor, Economics, Senior Fellow, Hoover Institution, Stanford University (1988-2001); Senior Fellow, Brookings Institution (2000); Senior Vice President, Chief Economist, World Bank (1997-2000); Member, Council of Economic Advisers, The White House (1993-1995); Chairperson, Economic Policy Committee, Organization of European Cooperation and Development (1993-1995); Oskar Morgenstern Distinguished Fellow, Visiting Professor, Institute for Advanced Study, Princeton University (1978-1979); Visiting fellow, St. Catherine's College (1973-1974); Research Fellow, Institute of Development Studies, University of Nairobi (1969-1971)l Visiting Professor, Department of Economics, University of Canterbury, Christchurch, New Zealand (1967); Tapp Research Fellow, Gonville & Caius College, Cambridge, England (1966-1970); Co-Chair, Committee on Global Thought, Columbia University; Chair, Management Board, Brooks World Poverty Institute, University of Manchester **CIV:** Board Member, Alliance for Climate Protection (2011-Present);

Trustee, Folger Library, Washington (2000-2005) **CW:** Author, "The Euro: How a Common Currency Threatens the Future of Europe" (2016); Author, "The Great Divide: Unequal Societies and What We Can Do About Them" (2015); Creating A Learning Society: A New Approach to Growth, Development, and Social Progress" (2014); Author, "The Price of Inequality: How Today's Divided Society Endangers Our Future" (2012); Author, "Freefall: America, Free Markets and the Sinking of the World Economy" (2010); Co-author, with Linda J. Bilmes, "The Three Trillion Dollar War: The True Cost of the Iraq Conflict" (2008); Co-author, with Andrew Charlton, "Fair Trade For All: How Trade Can Promote Development" (2006); Co-author, with B. Greenwald, "Towards a New Paradigm in Monetary Economics" (2003); Author, "The Roaring Nineties: A New History of the World's Most Prosperous Decade" (2003); Co-author, with C.E. Walsh, "Principles of Macroeconomics" (2002); Author, "The Rebel Within: Joseph Stiglitz and the World Bank" (2002); Co-author, with R. K. Sah, "Peasants Versus City-Dwellers: Taxation and the Burden of Economic Development" (2002); Author, "Globalization and Its Discontents" (2002); Author, "New Ideas About Old Age Security: Toward Sustainable Pension Systems in the 21st Century" (2001); Author, "Frontiers of Development Economics: The Future in Perspective" (2000); Author, "Whither Socialism?" (1996); Editor, Journal of Economic Perspectives (1986-1993); Associate Editor, American Economic Review (1968-1976); American Editor, Review of Economic Studies (1968-1976); Editorial Board, World Bank Economic Review **AW:** Legion of Honor (2012); Named, One of The 50 Most Influential People in Global Finance, Bloomberg Markets (2011-2012); Named, One of The 100 Most Influential People in the World, TIME Magazine (2011); Named, One of The 100 Agents of Change, Rolling Stone Magazine (2009); Foreign Member of the Royal Society (2009); Benefit Award, National Center Law & Economic Justice (2006); John Kenneth Galbraith Award, American Agricultural Economics Association (2004); Distinguished Leadership in Government Award, Columbia Business School (2002); Nobel Prize in Economics, Royal Swedish Academy of Science (2001); Rechtenwald Prize, Germany (1998); UAP Science Prize, Paris, France (1989); International Prize of Academia Lincei (1988); John Bates Clark Medal, American Economic Association (1979); Fellow, John Simon Guggenheim Memorial Foundation (1969-1970); Grantee, Fulbright Fellowship (1965-1966) **MEM:** Vice President, American Economic Association (1985); Executive Committee, American Economic Association (1982-1984); Fellow, National Academy of Sciences; Fellow, American Philosophical Society; Fellow, Econometric Society; Fellow, British Academy; Fellow, American Academy of Arts and Sciences; Pontifical Academy of Social Sciences; Serbian Scientific Society; Honorary Member, Board of Directors, Center for Global Development

STINGILY, DIAMOND, T: Artist, Poet **I:** Writing and Editing **PB:** Chicago **SC:** IL/USA **PT:** Byron Stingily **ED:** Coursework in Creative Writing, Columbia College **CW:** Solo Show, Institute of Contemporary Art, Miami, FL (2018); Exhibited, "Songs for Sabotage," New Museum Triennial (2018); Solo Show, "For The People of [_]," Freedman Fitzpatrick, Paris, France (2018); Solo Show, "Surveillance," Ramiken Crucible, Los Angeles, CA (2017); Invited Speaker, Artists Space (2017); Group Show, "Trigger: Gender as a Weapon and a Tool," New Museum, New York, NY (2017); Solo Show, "Elephant Memory," Ramiken Crucible, New York, NY (2016); Solo Show, "Kaas," Queer Thoughts, New

York, NY (2016); Group Show, "Where Did She Go?," Holiday Forever, Jackson Hole, WY (2016); Group Show, "Object Anthology," Publishing House, Gstaad, Switzerland (2016); Group Show, "Round 43: Small Business/Big Change: Economic Perspectives from Artists and Artrepreneurs," Project Row Houses, Houston, TX (2016); Group Show, "Denude," Ramiken Crucible, New York, NY (2015); Collaborator, "Notes on Gestures" (2015); Group Show, "The End of Violent Crime," Queer Thoughts, New York, NY (2015); Group Show, "Small Pillow," Queer Thoughts at Arcadia Missa, London, England (2015); Group Show, "Rainbow," Queer Thoughts, Nicaragua (2015); Group Show, "Forever in our Hearts," EGG, Chicago, IL (2014); Exhibited, The Foire Internationale d'Art Contemporain at the Grand Palais, MOCAD Detroit; Host, Podcast, "The Diamond Stingily Show"; Author, "Love, Diamond" **AW:** 30 Under 30 in Arts and Culture, Forbes (2017)

STITT, JOHN, "KEVIN" KEVIN, T: Governor of Oklahoma **I:** Government Administration/Government Relations/Government Services **DOB:** 12/28/1972 **PB:** Milton **SC:** FL/USA **MS:** Married **SPN:** Sarah Hazen (1998) **CH:** Six Children **ED:** Bachelor of Science in Accounting, Oklahoma State University, Stillwater, OK **C:** Governor, State of Oklahoma (2019-Present); Chairperson, Gateway (2018-Present); Founder, Gateway (2000-Present); Chairperson, Chief Executive Officer, Gateway (2014-2018); President, Chief Executive Officer, Gateway (2000-2014) **MEM:** Beta Theta Pi **PA:** Republican

STIVERS, STEVEN, "STEVE" ERNST, T: U.S. Representative **I:** Government Administration/Government Relations/Government Services **DOB:** 03/24/1965 **PB:** Cincinnati **SC:** OH/USA **PT:** Ernst Bambach Stivers; Carol Sue (Pullliam) Stivers **MS:** Married **SPN:** Karen Stivers **CH:** One child **ED:** MBA, Fisher College of Business, The Ohio State University, Columbus, OH (1996); BA in Economics and International Relations, The Ohio State University, Columbus, OH (1989) **C:** U.S. Representative, Ohio's 15th Congressional District, United States Congress, Washington, DC (2011-Present); Member, U.S. House Committee on Financial Services, Washington, DC (2011-Present); Chair, National Republican Congressional Committee (2017-2019); Member, District 16, Ohio State Senate (2003-2009); Licensed Securities Trader, Ohio Company; Vice President of Government Relations, Bank One Corporation; Member, Republican Study Committee **CR:** Member, Ohio Public Expenditures Council (2001-2003); Member, Ohio Public Works Commission (2000-2003) **CIV:** Board of Directors, Prevent Blindness Ohio (2004-Present); Volunteer, Big Brothers Big Sisters of America (2000-Present); Board of Directors, Trustee, Alvis House, Columbus, OH (1997-Present); Board of Directors, Contemporary American Theater Company, Columbus, OH (1997-Present); Member, Columbus Urban League (2001-2003) **MIL:** Advanced through Grades from Lieutenant Colonel to Brigadier General, Logistics Branch, Ohio National Guard (1985-Present); Active Duty Battalion Commander, Ohio National Guard, Operation Iraqi Freedom, Iraq, Kuwait, Qatar and Djibouti (2004-2005) **AW:** Legislator of the Year Award, Ohio Advocates Mental Health (2006); Watchdog the Treasury Award, United Conservatives of Ohio (2005); Decorated Bronze Star; Meritorious Service Medal; Army Commendation Medal; Reserve Good Conduct Medal; National Defense Service Medal **MEM:** Ohio National Guard Association; Athletic Club of Columbus **PA:** Republican **RE:** United Methodist

STOCKTON, BEVERLY ANN, T: Physiology and Pharmacology Educator **I:** Education/Educational Services **DOB:** 06/06/1939 **PB:** Indianola **SC:** IA/USA **PT:** Franklin Ray Stockton; Freda Ann (Courtney) Stockton **ED:** MS in Adult Education, Drake University (1987); PhD in Physiology (1972); MA in Biology, University of Oregon (1965-1972); BA in Biology, Simpson College (1963); RN, Iowa Methodist School of Nuring, Des Moines, IA (1960) **C:** Retired (1996); Professor, Physiology, Pharmacology, University of Osteopathic Medicine and Health Sciences, Des Moines, IA (1976-1996); Assistant Professor, Biology, Simpson College, Indianola, IA (1966-1969, 1975-1976); Assistant Professor, Biology, Tabor College, Hillsboro, KS (1972-1975); Instructor, Medical/Surgical, Borgess School Nursing, Kalamazoo, MI (1965-1966); Instructor, Medical/Surgical, Iowa Methodist School Nursing (1963, 1967); Emergency Room Nurse, Sacred Heart Hospital, Eugene, OR (1964-1966); RN, Iowa Methodist Medical Center, Des Moines, IA (1960-1963) **CIV:** Blank Children's Hospital, Des Moines, IA (1988-Present); Alumni Advisory Board, Biology, Simpson College, Indianola, IA (1983-2005); Displaced Homemakers Career Counseling, Drake University, Des Moines, IA (1985-1988); Trustee, Utility Board, Indianola, IA (1984-1985); Board of Directors, United Way, Indianola, IA (1983-1985) **CW:** Contributor, Articles, Professional Journals **AW:** Listee, Outstanding Young Women in America (1971) **MEM:** President, Board of Directors, American Diabetes Association (1992-1996); State Delegate, Iowa Nurses Association (1989); Secretary, American Business Women's Association (1972-1988); American Nurses Association; Institute Society Ethics; Life Sciences **MH:** Albert Nelson Marquis Lifetime Achievement Award; Marquis Who's Who Top Professional **B/I:** Ms. Stockton had her tonsils removed at age 7. The nurse who treated her inspired her so much with her kindness. Ms. Stockton decided then to pursue a career in healthcare. **AV:** Crafts **PA:** Democrat **RE:** Baptist

STONE, CHRIS, PE, FNSPE, FASCE, LEED AP, T: Chief Executive Officer, Senior Principal, Engineer **I:** Architecture & Construction **CN:** Clark Nexsen **MS:** Married **ED:** MS in Civil Engineering, University of Virginia (1980); BS in Civil Engineering, Virginia Military Institute (1978) **CT:** Certified, LEED AP **C:** Chief Executive Officer, Clark Nexsen (1993-Present); Structural Engineer, Glenn & Sadler (1980-1993) **AW:** One of the Top 300 Architecture Firms, Architectural Record (2019) **MEM:** PE Board Chair, Department of Professional and Occupational Regulations, Architects, Professional Engineers, Land Surveyors, Certified Interior Designers and Landscape Architects (2015-Present); Board of Directors, MATHCOUNTS (2015-Present); Board Member, Industry Leaders Council, American Society of Civil Engineers (2015-Present); Former National President, National Society of Professional Engineers (2011-2012); Fellow, American Society of Civil Engineers; Fellow, National Society of Professional Engineers; Former President, Virginia Society of Professional Engineers; Society of American Military Engineers

STONE, DAVID, T: Theatre Producer **I:** Fine Art **DOB:** 08/14/1966 **PB:** Marlboro Township **SC:** NJ/USA **ED:** Coursework, University of Pennsylvania **C:** Intern, Jujamcyn Theaters **CR:** Lecturer, The Juilliard School, New York University, Yale University, Columbia University, University of Pennsylvania **CIV:** Board of Governors, The Broadway League; Board of Trustees, Broadway Cares/Equity Fights AIDS **CW:** Producer, "Wicked" (2003-Present); Producer, "The Boys in the Band" (2018); Producer, "War Paint" (2017); Producer, "If/Then"

(2014); Producer, "Next to Normal" (2009-2011); Producer, "Three Days of Rain" (2006); Producer, "The 25th Annual Putnam County Spelling Bee" (2005); Producer, "The Graduate" (2002-2003); Producer, "Man of La Mancha" (2002-2003); Producer, "The Search for Signs of Intelligent Life in the Universe" (2000-2001); Producer, "Lifegame" (2000); Producer, "Taller Than a Dwarf" (2000); Producer, "Fully Committed" (1999); Producer, "The Vagina Monologues" (1999); Producer, "James Naughton: Street of Dreams" (1999); Producer, "The Diary of Anne Frank" (1997-1998); Producer, "The Santaland Diaries" (1996); Producer, "Full Gallop" (1996); Producer, "What's Wrong With This Picture?" (1994); Producer, "Family Secrets" (1993) **AW:** Tony Award for Best Revival of a Play, "The Boys in the Band" (2019)

STONE, DONALD G., T: Attorney **I:** Law and Legal Services **DOB:** 08/18/1947 **PB:** Berkeley **SC:** CA/USA **PT:** James Sherman Stone; Rachel M. (Loomis) Stone **MS:** Widowed **SPN:** Carole Jean Barrett (08/23/1969, Deceased 10/10/2012) **CH:** Nathan Stone; Suzanne Grandinetti **ED:** JD, University of Idaho (1972); BA, University of Idaho (1969) **C:** Partner, Paine, Hamblen, Coffin, Brooke & Miller LLP (Now Paine Hamblen), Spokane, WA (1979-Present); Associate, Paine, Hamblen, Coffin, Brooke & Miller LLP (Now Paine Hamblen), Spokane, WA (1976-1979) **CR:** Local Counsel, Associate Electric Gas Insurance Services (AEGIS), Federated Rural Electric Insurance Exchange, Energy Insurance Mutual Limited, Avista Corporation, Others **CIV:** President, Fire Safe Spokane **MIL:** Captain, United States Air Force, Judge Advocate General (JAG) (1972-1976) **CW:** Member, Editorial Board, Idaho Law Review (1971-1972) **AW:** General Dynamics AFROTC Award, University of Idaho (1969); McLean Scholarship Award (1969); Decorated Air Force Commendation Medal **MEM:** American Bar Association (ABA); Idaho Association of Defense Trial Lawyers (Now Idaho Association of Criminal Defense Trial Lawyers); Washington Defense Trial Lawyers Association; Defense Research Institute; Idaho State Bar Association; Washington State Bar Association; Spokane County Bar Association; The Order of Barristers; Spokane Club; Phi Beta Kappa; Blue Key Honor Society; The Honor Society of Phi Kappa Phi; Utility Arborists Association; Arbor Day Foundation **BAR:** United States District Court for the Eastern District of Washington (1976); United States Court of Military Appeals (1973); United States District Court of Idaho (1972); Washington (1972); Idaho (1972) **MH:** Albert Nelson Marquis Lifetime Achievement Award **B/I:** Mr. Stone became involved in his profession because he came from a family of engineers and his father told him if he could not do anything else that he should be a lawyer. Through geology, he found he had a long lineage of lawyers and judges in the family background more than engineers. **AV:** Golf; Cooking; Baseball; Travel **PA:** Republican **RE:** Roman Catholic

STONE, EMMA, T: Actress **I:** Media & Entertainment **DOB:** 11/06/1988 **PB:** Scottsdale **SC:** AZ/USA **PT:** Jeff Stone; Krista Stone **MS:** Engaged **SPN:** Dave McCary **CW:** Actress, "Babylon" (2021); Actress, "Cruella" (2021); Voice Actress, "The Croods 2" (2020); Actress, "Zombieland: Double Tap" (2019); Voice Actress, "My Favorite Shapes by Julio Torres" (2019); Actress, Music Video, "Who Cares," Paul McCartney (2018); Actress, "Let's Dance" (2018); Actress, "Maniac" (2018); Executive Producer, "Maniac" (2018); Actress, "The Favourite" (2018); Host, "Saturday Night Live" (2010, 2011, 2016, 2018); Actress, "Battle of the Sexes" (2017); Actress, "La La Land" (2016); Actress, "Maya & Marty" (2016); Actress, "Pop-

star: Never Stop Never Stopping" (2016); Actress, Music Video, "Anna," Will Butler (2015); Actress, "Aloha" (2015); Actress, "Irrational Man" (2015); Guest Performer, "Saturday Night Live" (2014, 2015); Actress, "Cabaret" (2014-2015); Herself, "The Interview" (2014); Actress, "Birdman or (The Unexpected Virtue of Ignorance)" (2014); Actress, "Magic in the Moonlight" (2014); Actress, "The Amazing Spider-Man 2" (2014); Voice Actress, "The Croods" (2013); Actress, "Gangster Squad" (2013); Actress, "Movie 43" (2013); Actress, "iCarly" (2012); Voice Actress, "Sleeping Dogs" (2012); Actress, "The Amazing Spider-Man" (2012); Herself, "30 Rock" (2012); Actress, "The Help" (2011); Actress, "Crazy, Stupid, Love." (2011); Actress, "Friends with Benefits" (2011); Voice Actress, "Robot Chicken" (2011); Actress, "Easy A" (2010); Voice Actress, "Marmaduke" (2010); Actress, "Zombieland" (2009); Actress, "Paper Man" (2009); Actress, "Ghosts of Girlfriends Past" (2009); Actress, "The House Bunny" (2008) Actress, "The Rocker" (2008); Actress, "Drive" (2007); Actress, "SuperBad" (2007); Actress, "Lucky Louie" (2006); Actress, "Malcolm in the Middle" (2006); Actress, "The Suite Life of Zack & Cody" (2006); Actress, "Medium" (2005); Actress, "The New Partridge Family" (2005) **AW:** Special Jury Award for Best Ensemble Performance, "The Favourite," Gotham Awards (2018); Best Actress, "La La Land," Academy Awards (2017); Best Actress in a Motion Picture - Musical or Comedy, "La La Land," Golden Globe Awards (2017); Best International Lead Actress, "La La Land," Australian Academy of Cinema and Television Arts Awards (2017); Outstanding Performance by a Female Actor in a Leading Role, "La La Land," Screen Actors Guild Awards (2017); Outstanding Performer of the Year Award, "La La Land," Santa Barbara International Film Festival (2017); Outstanding Performance by a Female Actor in a Leading Role, "La La Land," Screen Actors Guild Awards (2017); Best Actress in a Leading Role, "La La Land," British Academy of Film and Television Arts (BAFTA) Awards (2016); Volpi Cup for Best Actress, "La La Land," Venice Film Festival (2016); Best Actress, "La La Land," Detroit Film Critics Society (2016); Favorite Movie Actress, "The Amazing Spider-Man 2," Nickelodeon Kids' Choice Awards (2015); Best Supporting Actress, "Birdman," Boston Society of Film Critics (2014); Trailblazer Award, MTV Movie & TV Awards (2012); Choice Movie Actress: Drama, "The Help," Teen Choice Awards (2012); Choice Movie Actress: Comedy, "Crazy, Stupid, Love.," Teen Choice Awards (2012); Favorite Movie Actress, "The Help," People's Choice Awards (2012); Hollywood Ensemble of the Year Award, "The Help," Hollywood Film Awards (2011); Best Comedic Performance, "Easy A," MTV Movie & TV Awards (2011); Choice Movie Actress: Romantic Comedy, "Easy A," Teen Choice Awards (2011); Exciting New Face," SuperBad," Young Hollywood Awards (2008)

STONE, KIPP FRANKLIN, T: Investment Professional **I:** Financial Services **DOB:** 01/07/1943 **PB:** Brooklyn **SC:** MI/USA **PT:** Robert Charles Franklin; Barbara Boardman Franklin **MS:** Widowed **SPN:** Peter G. Stone **ED:** Bachelor Business Administration, University of Michigan, Ann Arbor, MI (1967) **CT:** Chartered Financial Analyst; Certified Financial Planner; Registered Investment Advisor; Series 7 and 65 Securities Licenses **C:** Owner, Stoney's British Public House, Wilmington, DE (2000-2009); Investment Manager, Vanguard, Valley Forge, PA (2001-2003); Corp. Secretary, Director, Flavour of Britain Co., Wilmington, DE (1994-1999); Registered Investment Adviser, Pennsylvania (1992-1994); Trust Portfolio Manager, Vice President, PNC Bank, Philadelphia, PA (1984-1991); Trust

Portfolio Manager, Fidelity Bank, Philadelphia, PA (1981-1984); Trust Administrator, Union Bank, Los Angeles, CA (1980-1981); Trust Representative, First Interstate Bank, Los Angeles, CA (1978-1979); Accountant Executive, Dean Witter Reynolds, Los Angeles, CA (1975-1977); Public Relations Representative, Bayerische Motoren Werke, Munich, Germany (1969-1971); Freelance Journalist, Various Michigan and Ohio Newspapers (1968-1971) **CR:** Britannia.com, Partner (1996-2019); Certified Financial Planner (1990-2015); International Association for Financial Planning (1992-2015); Chartered Financial Analyst (1987-2015); Flavour of Britain Catalog Co. Ltd., Partner (1994-1999) **CIV:** Veterans Administration Volunteer Services (2015-present); West Goshen Democrats, Treasurer (2015-2020); West Goshen Democrats, Zone Leader (2003-2006); Board of Directors, Executive Committee, Treasurer, Children's Country Week Association, Chester County, PA (1988-2003) **AW:** Co-Holder, World's Long Distance Motorcycling Record (1971) **MEM:** Daughters of the American Revolution (1979-2020); Association for Investment Management and Research (1987-2015); Chartered Financial Analysts (CFA) Institute (1987-2015); Certified Financial Planner (1990-2015); Secretary, Delaware Valley Certified Financial Planners (1993-1996); Philadelphia Securities Association(1984-1994); Financial Analysts of Philadelphia (1984-1994); Delaware Valley Certified Financial Planners (1991-1993) **MH:** Albert Nelson Marquis Lifetime Achievement Award; Marquis Who's Who Top Professional **AS:** Ms. Stone attributes her success to persistence, determination, intelligent and creative thinking. **B/I:** Ms. Stone found investment management fascinating because it provides financial security for families, and is impacted by everything, everywhere. It involves climate change, precious metal discoveries, vaccine development, technology, fashion, social movements; everything that is and everything that happens. What could be more interesting? **AV:** Writing; Horseback and motorcycle riding; Needle crafts; Swimming; Politics; Travel; Hospice volunteer **PA:** Democrat

STONEMARK, RAY, T: Operating Partner **I:** Food & Restaurant Services **CN:** Don's Seafood **MS:** Married **CH:** Three Children **C:** Operating Partner, Don's Seafood (2001-Present); Waiter, Landry Group; Subcontractor, PricewaterhouseCoopers **CIV:** Ascension Leadership; Dale Carnegie Student Teacher; Volunteer, Special Needs Playground **MIL:** U.S. Navy **AS:** Mr. Stonemark attributes his success to hard work and marketing. He is genuinely sincere in all conversations that he has, which yields his positive relationships with everyone with whom he works. **B/I:** Mr. Stonemark started cooking at an early age. He didn't foresee himself doing it as his career but after he left the military, he began working at a restaurant. In this role, he found a passion for the industry. From there, his career naturally progressed. **THT:** Mr. Stonemark's motto is, "Don't criticize, condemn, or complain."

STOREY, JEFFREY K., T: Chief Executive Officer **I:** Telecommunications **CN:** CenturyLink **MS:** Married **CH:** Six Children **ED:** MS in Telecommunications Systems, Southern Methodist University; Bachelor's Degree in Engineering, Physics and Mathematics, Northeastern State University **C:** Chief Executive Officer, CenturyLink (2018-Present); Chief Operating Officer, President, CenturyLink (2017-2018); Chief Executive Officer, President, Level 3 Communications (2013-2017); Chief Operating Officer, President, Level 3 Communications (2008-2013); Chief Executive Officer, President, WilTel Communications (2002-2005); Vice President, Commercial Sales, Cox Communications, Inc.; Vice President, General Manager, Cox Fibernet, Cox Communications, Inc.; Founder, Cox Business Services, Cox Communications **CR:** Board Member, CenturyLink (2017-Present); Member, National Security Telecommunications Advisory Committee (2016-Present); Board Member, Level 3 Communications (2013-2017)

STOSS, FREDERICK W. MLS, T: Librarian, Educator **I:** Library Management/Library Services **CN:** State University of New York at Buffalo **DOB:** 08/12/1950 **PB:** Gloversville **SC:** NY/USA **PT:** Dayton Robert Stoss; Katherine Gretchen (Ruzicka) Stoss **MS:** Married **SPN:** Dorothy Katherine Stoss (Holderle) (08/24/1974) **CH:** Kaeti Elizabeth **ED:** MLS, Syracuse University (1982); MS in Zoology, College at Brockport, State University of New York (1974); BA in Biology, Hartwick College (1972) **C:** Librarian, Educator, State University of New York at Buffalo (1996-Present); Research Associate, University of Tennessee, Knoxville, TN (1990-1996); Library Director, Center for Environmental Information, Rochester, NY (1982-1990); Research Associate, Syracuse Research Corporation (1978-1982); Technology Research Associate, University of Rochester Medical Center, New York (1974-1978) **CR:** Adjunct Faculty, Department of Library Information Studies, University of Buffalo (2006-Present); Member, Editorial Advisory Board, Electronic Green Journal (1990-Present); Member, Editorial Advisory Board, Environmental Abstracts (1988-Present); Member, Editorial Advisory Board, Counterpoise (1999-2005); Visiting Lecturer (1997-2002); Adjunct Lecturer, Syracuse University (1983-1985); Laboratory Instructor, University of Rochester (1975-1978) **CIV:** Member, Lutheran Campus Ministry Board, Rochester Institute of Technology (2006-Present); Member, Speakers Bureau, Susquahanna River Basin Commission (2005-Present); Member, Panel on the Environment, Rochester Democrat and Chronicle Readers (2005-2007); President, Seth Green Chapter, Trout Unlimited, Rochester, NY (1989-1990) **CW:** Associate Editor, Information Resources in Toxicology (2001) **AW:** Staff Award for Sustainability Excellence, 2020 SLICE (Sustainability Leadership Innovation and Collaborative Engagement) Award (2020); Outstanding Division Member Award, Environmental Resource Management Division, Environment and Resource Management Division (1994); Outstanding Graduate Research Award, Sigma Xi (1974) **MEM:** Past Chair, Member, Atmospheric of Science Librarians International (2010-Present); American Library Association; National Eagle Scout Association (NESA); Society Fraternity Huntwick College; North American Association for Environmental Education (NAAEE); New York State Outdoor Education Association; Special Libraries Association; National Science Teachers Association; New York Libraries Association; State University of New York Libraries Association; Sierra Club; Alpha Delta Omega; Beta Beta Beta; Sigma Xi **MH:** Albert Nelson Marquis Lifetime Achievement Award **AV:** Fly fishing; Nature photography **PA:** Democrat **RE:** Lutheran

STOUT, KRISTA, T: Digital Sales Manager **I:** Advertising & Marketing **CN:** Beasley Media Group **MS:** Married **SPN:** DJ Stout **CH:** Colson; Connor; Dillon **ED:** Bachelor's Degree in Biology, University of North Carolina at Charlotte (2006) **C:** Director of Digital Sales, Beasley Media Group (formerly CBS) (2018-Present); Integrated Marketing Group, Beasley Media Group (formerly CBS) (2014-Present); Marketing Consultant, CBS Radio (2010-2014); Managing Partner, Upward Mobility, LLC (2006-2010); Marketing and Event Coordinator, Catering Creations (2002-2006) **AW:** Gracie Allan Award Winner, PSA'S for Local Radio, The Gracies (2018,

2019); Radio Wayne Finalist, Radio Ink Magazine (2018) **MH:** Marquis Who's Who Top Professional **AS:** Mrs. Stout attributes her success to her parents who were very hard working, and she would always learn new things from them. She learned to never be completely satisfied and always continues to strive to do better for her and her family. **B/I:** Mrs. Stout loved the whole radio industry, entertainment, and being able to be creative and work with clients. What really drove her were her kids, to be successful and be a great example for them. When Mrs. Stout started in radio she was not your traditional radio seller, she was very "think outside the box" at customizing campaigns. She really believed that every successful marketing campaign was a 360 degree approach. She was very successful in the digital side and understood and saw that that was where things would grow and evolve quickly and was just a very easy and natural transition. **AV:** Running; Working out; Yoga; Palates; Rescued four dogs

STRAIT, GEORGE, T: Musician **I:** Media & Entertainment **DOB:** 05/18/1952 **PB:** Poteet **SC:** TX/USA **PT:** John Byron Strait Sr.; Doris Couser **MS:** Married **SPN:** Norma Voss (02/23/1972) **CH:** George "Bubba" Strait Jr.; Jennifer (Deceased) **ED:** Honorary Doctoral Degree, Texas State University (2006); University Degree in Agriculture, Southwest Texas State University (Now Texas State University) **C:** Co-Founder, Vaqueros Del Mar Invitational Golf Tournament and Concert **CR:** Spokesman, Wrangler National Patriot Program (2010-Present) **CIV:** Founder, Jennifer Lynn Strait Foundation **MIL:** U.S. Army (1971-1975) **CW:** Musician, "Honky Tonk Time Machine" (2019); Musician, "Cold Beer Conversation" (2015); Musician, "Love Is Everything" (2013); Musician, "Here for a Good Time" (2011); Himself, "Pure Country 2: The Gift" (2010); Musician, "Twang" (2009); Musician, "Troubadour" (2008); Musician, "It Just Comes Natural" (2006); Musician, "Somewhere Down in Texas" (2005); Musician, "Honkytonkville" (2003); Voice Actor, "King of the Hill" (2003); Himself, "Grand Champion" (2002); Musician, "The Road Less Traveled" (2001); Musician, "George Strait" (2000); Musician, "Always Never the Same" (1999); Musician, "One Step at a Time" (1998); Musician, "Carrying Your Love with Me" (1997); Musician, "Blue Clear Sky" (1996); Musician, "Lead On" (1994); Musician, "Easy Come, Easy Go" (1993); Musician, "Holding My Own (1992); Actor, "Pure Country" (1992); Musician, "Chill of an Early Fall" (1991); Musician, "Livin' It Up" (1990); Musician, "Beyond the Blue Neon" (1989); Musician, "If You Ain't Lovin' You Ain't Livin'" (1988); Musician, "Ocean Front Property" (1987); Musician, "#7" (1986); Musician, "Something Special" (1985); Musician, "Does Fort Worth Ever Cross Your Mind" (1984); Musician, "Strait from the Heart" (1982); Himself, "The Soldier" (1982); Musician, "Strait Country" (1981) **AW:** 2018 Texan of the Year, Texas Legislative Conference (2018); Cliffie Stone Icon Award, Academy of Country Music (2017); 50th Anniversary Milestone, Academy of Country Music (2015); Entertainer of the Year, Academy of Country Music (2014); Entertainer of the Year, Country Music Association (2013); Legend of Live Award, Billboard Touring Awards (2013); ASCAP Founders Award, ASCAP (2013); Country Radio Broadcasters Career Achievement Award, Country Radio Broadcasters Inc. (2013); Top Country Artist of the Past 25 Years, Billboard.com (2010); Artist of the Decade, Academy of Country Music (2009); Best Country Award, Grammy Awards (2009); Album of the Year, Country Music Association (2008); Single of the Year, Country Music Association (2008); Album of the Year, Country Music Association (2007); Song of the Year, Country Music

Association (2007); Song of the Year, Academy of Country Music (2006); Single Record of the Year (Artist), Academy of Country Music (2006); Single Record of the Year (Producer), Academy of Country Music (2006); Inductee, Country Music Hall of Fame (2006); Musical Event of the Year, Country Music Association (2005); National Medal of Arts (2003); Special Achievement Award "in recognition of 50 Number 1 songs"), Academy of Country Music (2003); Ranked #9, CMT 40 Greatest Men of Country Music (2003); Favorite Collaborative Song, Country Weekly (2002); Song of the Year, Country Music Association (2001); Vocal Event of the Year, Country Music Association (2000); Album of the Year, TNN/CMT Country Weekly Music Awards (2000); Entertainer of the Year, TNN/CMT Country Weekly Music Awards (2000); Male Artist of the Year, TNN/CMT Country Weekly Music Awards (2000); Single of the Year, TNN/CMT Country Weekly Music Awards (2000); Impact Artist of the Year, TNN/CMT Country Weekly Music Awards (2000); Album of the Year, TNN/CMT Country Weekly Music Awards (1999); Favorite Entertainer, Country Weekly Golden Pick Awards (1999); Favorite Male Artist, Country Weekly Golden Pick Awards (1999); Favorite Video Entertainer, Country Weekly Golden Pick Awards (1999); Favorite Line Dance Song, Country Weekly Golden Pick Awards (1999); Favorite Song, Country Weekly Golden Pick Awards (1999); Best Male Vocalist, Radio & Records (1998); Favorite Country Album, American Music Awards (1998); Favorite Country Male Artist, American Music Awards (1998); Male Vocalist of the Year, Country Music Association (1998); Best Male Vocalist, Radio & Records (1997); Best Album, Radio & Records (1997); Top Male Vocalist, Academy of Country Music (1997); Favorite Country Album, American Music Awards (1997); Album of the Year, Country Music Association (1997); Most Valuable Performer, Radio & Records (1996); Best Single, Radio & Records (1996); Album of the Year, Academy of Country Music (1996); Top Male Vocalist, Academy of Country Music (1996); Single of the Year, Music City News Country (1996); Voice of Music Award, ASCAP (1995); Single of the Year, Academy of Country Music (1995); Tex Ritter Movie of the Year, Academy of Country Music (1993); Favorite Country Male Artist, American Music Awards (1991); Entertainer of the Year, Country Music Association (1990); Presidential American Success Award (1989); Connie B. Gay Award (1989); Entertainer of the Year, Country Music Association (1989); Top Male Vocalist, Academy of Country Music (1988); Top Country Artist, Billboard Year-End Awards (1987); Top Country Artist, Billboard Year-End Awards (1986); Male Vocalist of the Year, Country Music Association (1986); Album of the Year, Academy of Country Music (1986); Top Male Vocalist, Academy of Country Music (1986); Album of the Year, Country Music Association (1985); Male Vocalist of the Year, Country Music Association (1985); Top Male Vocalist, Academy of Country Music (1985)

STRANGFELD, JOHN R. JR., T: Chairman, President, Chief Executive Officer **I:** Financial Services **CN:** Prudential Financial, Inc. **DOB:** 12/27/1953 **MS:** Married **SPN:** Mary Kay Strangfeld **ED:** LHD (Honorary) Susquehanna University (2017); MBA, Darden School of Business, University of Virginia; BSBA, Susquehanna University **CT:** Chartered Financial Analyst (CFA), CFA Institute **C:** Chairman, Prudential Financial, Inc. (2008-2019); Chief Executive Officer, President, Prudential Financial, Inc. (2008-2018); Vice Chairman, Investments & Insurance Division, Prudential Financial, Inc. (2002-2007); Executive Vice President, Prudential Financial, Inc. (2001-2002); Chairman, Chief Executive Officer, Prudential Securities, Inc. (2000-2001); Chief Executive Officer, Prudential Investment Management, Prudential Insurance Company of America (1998-2002); Senior Managing Director, The Private Asset Management Group, Prudential Financial, Inc. (1995-1998); Chairman, PRICOA Capital Group Europe, Prudential Financial, Inc., London, England (1989-1995); Numerous Management Positions, Prudential Financial, Inc. (1977-1989) **CR:** Emeritus Member, Board of Trustees, Susquehanna University (2017-Present); Member, Board of Managers, Wachovia Securities Financial Holdings LLC (2003-Present); Member, Board of Directors, Prudential Financial, Inc. (2008-2019); Member, Board of Trustees, Susquehanna University (1999-2017) **CIV:** Founder, Sponsor, MBA Scholarship Program, Darden School of Business, University of Virginia (2005-Present); Member, Board of Trustees, Darden School Foundation; Chair, Board of Directors, New Jersey Performing Arts Center **MEM:** Vice Chairman, Geneva Association; Executive Committee, Board, Memorial Sloan Kettering Cancer Center; Raven Society, University of Virginia

STRASBURG, STEPHEN JAMES, T: Professional Baseball Player **I:** Athletics **CN:** Washington Nationals **DOB:** 07/20/1988 **PB:** San Diego **SC:** CA/USA **PT:** Jim Strasburg; Kathleen (Swett) Strasburg **MS:** Married **SPN:** Rachel Lackey (01/09/2010) **CH:** Two Daughters **ED:** Diploma, West Hills High School, Santee, CA (2006); Coursework, San Diego State University **C:** Professional Baseball Player, Washington Nationals (2010-Present) **CR:** U.S. National Team, Olympic Games, Beijing, China (2008) **AW:** World Series Champion (2019); World Series MVP (2019); Three-Time All-Star (2012, 2016-2017); Silver Slugger Award (2012); Golden Spikes Award (2009); Dick Howser Trophy (2009); Bronze Medal, Olympic Games, Beijing, China (2008)

STREEP, MERYL, T: Actress **I:** Media & Entertainment **DOB:** 06/22/1949 **PB:** Summit **SC:** NJ/USA **PT:** Harry Jr; Mary W. Streep **MS:** Married **SPN:** Donald J. Grummer (09/15/1978) **CH:** Henry; Mary Willa; Grace; Louisa **ED:** Honorary Doctor of Arts, Harvard University (2010); Honorary Doctor of Fine Arts, Yale University (1983); Honorary Doctor of Fine Arts, Dartmouth College (1981); Master of Fine Arts, Yale University (1975); Bachelor of Arts in Drama, Vassar College (1971) **C:** Co-founder, Mothers & Others for a Livable Planet **CW:** Actress, Film, "Mamma Mia! Here We Go Again" (2018); Actress, Film, "Mary Poppins Returns" (2018); Actress, Film, "We Rise" (2017); Actress, Film, "The Post" (2017); Actress, TV Miniseries, "Five Came Back" (2017); Actress, Film, "Florence Foster Jenkins" (2016); Voice Actress, Film, "The Guardian Brothers" (2016); Actress, Film, "Ricki and the Flash" (2015); Actress, Film, "Suffragette" (2015); Actress, TV Miniseries, "The Roosevelts" (2014); Actress, Film, "The Homesman" (2014); Actress, Film, "The Giver" (2014); Actress, Film, "Into the Woods" (2014); Actress, TV Miniseries, "Makers: Woman Who Maker America" (2013); Actress, Film, "August: Osage County" (2013); Narrator, Documentary, "To the Arctic 3D" (2012); Actress, Film, "Hope Springs" (2012); Actress, Film, "The Iron Lady" (2011); Actress, TV Miniseries, "Web Therapy" (2010); Appeared in Documentary, "I Knew It Was You: Rediscovering John Cazale" (2010); Actress, Film, "Julie & Julia" (2009); Actress, Film, "It's Complicated" (2009); Voice Actress, Film, "Fantastic Mr. Fox" (2009); Actress, Film, "Mamma Mia!" (2008); Actress, Film, "Doubt" (2008); Actress, Film, "Dark Matter" (2007); Actress, Film, "Evening" (2007); Actress, Film, "Rendition" (2007); Actress, Film, "Lions for

Lambs" (2007); Actress, TV Miniseries, "Ocean Voyagers" (2007); Actress, Film, "A Prairie Home Companion" (2006); Actress, Film, "The Devil Wears Prada" (2006); Voice Actress, Film, "The Ant Bully" (2006); Actress, Play, "Mother Courage" (2006); Actress, Film, "Prime" (2005); Actress, Film, "Lemony Snicket's A Series of Unfortunate Events" (2004); Actress, Film, "The Manchurian Candidate" (2004); Actress, TV Miniseries, "Angels in America" (2003); Actress, TV Miniseries, "Freedom: A History of U.S." (2003); Actress, Film, "The Hours" (2002); Actress, Film, "Adaptation" (2002); Voice Actress, Film, "Artificial Intelligence: AI" (2001); Actress, Film, "Music of the Heart" (1999); Voice Actress, Film, "Chrysanthemum" (1999); Actress, Film, "Dancing at Lugnasa" (1998); Actress, Film, "One True Thing" (1998); Actress, Executive Producer, TV Films, "First Do No Harm" (1997); Actress, Film, "Before and After" (1996); Actress, Film, "Marvin's Room" (1996); Actress, Film, "The Bridges of Madison County" (1995); Actress, Film, "The River Wild" (1994); Actress, Film, "The House of Spirits" (1993); Actress, Film, "Death Becomes Her" (1992); Actress, Film, "Defending Your Life" (1991); Actress, Film, "Postcards From the Edge" (1990); Narrator, "A Vanishing Wilderness" (1990); Voice Actress, Film, "Rabbit Ears: The Fisherman and His Wife" (1989); Actress, Film, "She-Devil" (1989); Voice Actress, Film, "The Tailor of Gloucester" (1988); Actress, Film, "A Cry in the Dark" (1988); Voice Actress, Film, "Rabbit Ears: The Tale of Peter Rabbit" (1987); Voice Actress, Film, "Rabbit Ears: The Tale of Jeremy Fisher" (1987); Actress, Film, "Ironweed" (1987); Actress, Film, "Heartburn" (1986); Actress, Film, "Out of Africa" (1985); Actress, Film, "Plenty" (1985); Actress, Film, "Falling in Love" (1984); Narrator, "The Velveteen Rabbit" (1984); Actress, Film, "Silkwood" (1983); Actress, Film, "Sophie's Choice" (1982); Actress, TV Film, "Alice at the Palace" (1982); Actress, Film, "Still of the Night" (1982); Actress, Film, "The French Lieutenant's Woman" (1981); Actress, Film, "Manhattan" (1979); Actress, Film, "The Seduction of Joe Tynan" (1979); Actress, Film, "Kramer vs. Kramer" (1979); Actress, TV Film, "Uncommon Women and Others" (1979); Actress, TV Miniseries, "Holocaust" (1978); Actress, Film, "The Deer Hunter" (1978); Actress, TV Film, "Secret Service" (1977); Actress, TV Film, "The Deadliest Season" (1977); Actress, Film, "Julia" (1977); Actress, Broadway Plays, "Trelawny of the Wells" (1975); Appearance, "Green Mountain Guild"; Actress, Play, "27 Wagons Full of Cotton"; Actress, Play, "A Memory of Two Mondays"; Actress, Play, "Henry V"; Actress, Play, "Secret Service"; Actress, Play, "The Taming of the Shrew"; Actress, Play, "Measure for Measure"; Actress, Play, "The Cherry Orchard"; Actress, Play, "Happy End"; Actress, Play, "Wonderland"; Actress, Play, "Taken in Marriage"; Actress, Play, "Alice in Concert" **AW:** Presidential Medal of Freedom, The White House (2014); Named, Favorite Movie Icon, People's Choice Awards (2013); Lifetime Achievement Award, Honorary Golden Bear, Berlin Film Festival (2012); Golden Globe Award for Best Performance by an Actress in a Motion Picture-Drama, "The Iron Lady" (2012); BAFTA Award for Best Leading Actress, "The Iron Lady" (2012); Academy Award for Best Actress, "The Iron Lady" (2012); Named, One of The 100 Most Powerful Women in Entertainment, Hollywood Reporter (2009, 2012); New York Film Critics Circle Award for Best Actress, "The Iron Lady" (2011); Kennedy Center Honors, John F. Kennedy Center for the Performing Arts (2011); Golden Globe Award for Best Performance by an Actress in a Motion Picture-Comedy or Musical, "Julie & Julia" (2010); National Medal of Arts, National Endowment for the Arts (2010); Critics' Choice Award for Best

Actress, Broadcast Film Critics Association, "Julie & Julia" (2010); Critics' Choice Award for 2008 Best Actress in "Doubt," Broadcast Film Critics Association (2009); Screen Actors Guild Award for Outstanding Performance by a Female Actor in a Leading Role, "Doubt," (2009); Boston Society Film Critics Award for Best Actress, "Julie & Julia" (2009); New York Film Critics Circle Award for Best Actress, "Julie & Julia" (2009); Marcus Aurelius Lifetime Achievement Award, Rome Film Festival (2009); Inductee, The New Jersey Hall of Fame (2008); National Society Film Critics Award for Best Supporting Actress, "A Prairie Home Companion" (2007); Dana Reeve HOPE Award, Christopher and Dana Reeve Foundation (2007); Named, The 50 Smartest People in Hollywood, Entertainment Weekly (2007); National Society Film Critics Award for Best Supporting Actress, "The Devil Wears Prada" (2007); Golden Globe Award for Best Performance by an Actress in a Motion Picture-Musical or Comedy, "The Devil Wears Prada" (2007); Named, The 100 Most Influential People in the World, TIME Magazine (2006); Emmy Award for Outstanding Lead Actress in a Mini-series or a Movie, "Angels in America" (2004); Lifetime Achievement Award, American Film Institute (2004); Golden Globe Award for Best Supporting Actress, "Adaptation" (2003); Officer, French Ordre des Arts et des Lettres (2000); Bette Davis Lifetime Achievement Award (1999); Gotham Award for Lifetime Achievement (1999); Women in Film Crystal Award (1998); People's Choice Award (1983, 1985, 1986, 1987, 1990); New York Film Critics' Circle Award for Best Actress, "A Cry in the Dark" (1989); Star of Year Award, National Association Theater Owners (1983); Golden Globe Award for Best Actress, Sophie's Choice" (1983); Best Actress Award, National Board Review (1982); Golden Globe Award for Best Actress, "The French Lieutenant's Woman" (1982); Obie Award, "Alice in Concert" (1981); Academy Award for Best Supporting Actress, "Kramer vs Kramer" (1980); Woman of the Year Award, Hasty Pudding Society, Harvard University (1980); Best Supporting Actress Award (1979); B'nai Brith (1979); Emmy Award for Outstanding Lead Actress in a Mini-series, "Holocaust" (1978); National Society Film Critics Award for Best Supporting Actress, "The Deer Hunter" (1978); Mademoiselle Award (1976); Screen Actors Guild Award for Best Actress, "Angels in America"; Golden Globe Award for Best Actress, "Angels in America"; Emmy Award for Best Children's Recording, "The Velveteen Rabbit"; New York Film Critics' Award for Best Actress, "Kramer vs Kramer"; Golden Globe Award, "Kramer vs Kramer"; Academy Award for Best Actress, "Sophie's Choice"; Theatre World Award, "27 Wagons Full of Cotton"

STREET, ROBERT ANDERSON JR., T: Professor of Computer Information Systems **I:** Education/Educational Services **DOB:** 04/28/1944 **PB:** Memphis **SC:** TN/USA **PT:** Robert Anderson Street; Mary Carolyn (Myer) Street **MS:** Married **SPN:** Mary Esther Ray (02/18/1966) **CH:** James Robert; Cole Anderson **ED:** MS, University of Evansville (1988); PhD, Southern Seminary (1973); MDiv, Southern Seminary (1970); BA, Union University (1966); Postgraduate Coursework, University of Memphis; Postgraduate Coursework, University of Kentucky; Postgraduate Coursework, University of Pennsylvania **CT:** Microsoft Mentor **C:** Professor, Christian Studies and Computer Science, Campbellsville College (1990-Present); Assistant Professor, Professor, Christian Studies, Campbellsville College (1976-1990); Pastor, Uniontown Baptist Church (1974-1976); Instructor, Seminary Extension, Southern Baptist Convention (1974 -1976); Instructor, Hebrew, Southern Baptist

Seminary, Louisville, KY (1972-1974) **CR:** President, Kentucky Academic Computer Users Group (1991-1992); Vice President, Kentucky Academic Computer Users Group (1990) **CIV:** Scoutmaster, Troop 616, Boy Scouts of America (1977-2002); Staff Member, Camp Kia Kima (1960-1966); Staff Member, Wood Badge **CW:** Contributor, "Holman Bible Dictionary" (1991); Contributor, "Mercer Dictionary of Bible" (1990); Contributor, Articles, Professional Journals; Contributor, Over 40 Articles, Biblical Illustrator **AW:** Grantee, Appalachian College Program (1994); Grantee, Professional Development (1994); Grantee, National Endowment of Humanities (1987); Silver Beaver, Good Shepherd (BSA); Eagle Scout Certificate Signed by John F. Kennedy **MEM:** National Association Baptist Professors of Religion; Society Bible Literature; American Academy of Religion; Consortium for Computing in Small Colleges; Kentucky Academy Computer Users Group; Association to Advance Collegiate Schools of Business; Association for Computing Machinery **MH:** Albert Nelson Marquis Lifetime Achievement Award **B/I:** When Dr. Street began his career, he planned on going into the ministry. He had no intentions of pursuing a PhD until one professor offered to be his supervisor if he decided to do so. Dr. Street took him up on his offer. After he had completed his studies, he was interviewed by a small church in Kentucky. He began working with them, finding it to be a wonderful experience. Dr. Street later returned to Campbellsville to work at Southern Baptist Seminary. **AV:** Scouting; Gardening; Researching computers

STRESEN-REUTER, JARED JAMES, T: Chief Executive Officer **I:** Technology **CN:** Divine Digital Agency, LLC **DOB:** 04/12/1990 **PB:** Naples **SC:** FL/USA **PT:** Steve Stresen-Reuter; Lori Stresen-Reuter **MS:** Married **SPN:** Jennifer **CH:** Vincent; Noah **ED:** BS in Business Marketing, Palm Beach Atlantic University, West Palm Beach, FL (2012) **C:** Founder, Divine Digital Agency, LLC, Naples, FL (2016-Present); Brand Leader, Venture X, FL (2015-2016); Brand Development Manager, Plan Ahead Events (2012-2016); Director of Technical Services, United Franchise Group, West Palm Beach, FL (2012-2015); Founder, Toodol.com (2012-2015); Operations Assistant, ESPN Enterprises, Inc. (2011); Assistant Coach, Women's Basketball, Palm Beach Atlantic University, West Palm Beach, FL (2009-2010) **CIV:** Songwriter for Veterans; Sponsor, Compassion International; Night to Shine Event, Tim Tebow Foundation; Special Needs Prom, Tim Tebow Foundation **AW:** Best of Naples (2019); Davey Awards (2018, 2019); 50 Notable Alumni, Palm Beach Atlantic University (2018); Winner, JJ's Entrepreneur Contest, United Franchise Group (2012) **AS:** Mr. Stresen-Reuter attributes his success to his mentor and the founder of J.J.'s Entrepreneurs Business Plan Competition, the late J.J. Prendamano. Mr. Prendamano spent the last year of his life helping Mr. Stresen-Reuter establish his entrepreneurial foundation and develop as a businessman. **B/I:** Mr. Stresen-Reuter became involved in his profession because he wanted to be an entrepreneur from an early age. While a senior at Palm Beach Atlantic University, he won a prestigious entrepreneurial contest, which opened many opportunities for him. **PA:** Republican **RE:** Christian

STRODE, JOSEPH ARLIN, T: Lawyer **I:** Law and Legal Services **CN:** Bridges, Young, Matthews, Drake Law Firm **DOB:** 03/05/1946 **PB:** DeWitt **SC:** AR/USA **PT:** Thomas Joseph Strode; Nora (Richardson) Strode **MS:** Married **SPN:** Carolyn Taylor (02/09/1969) **CH:** Tanya Briana; William Joseph **ED:** JD, Southern Methodist University (1972); BSEE, University of Arkansas, With Honors (1969)

C: Partner, Bridges, Young, Matthews, Drake, Pine Bluff, AR (1975-Present); Associate, Bridges, Young, Matthews, Drake, Pine Bluff, AR (1972-1974); Patent Agent, Texas Instruments, Dallas, TX (1970-1972); Design Engineer, Texas Instruments Inc., Dallas, TX (1969-1970) **CIV:** Chairman, Pine Bluff Airport Commission (1993); Executive Committee, United Way of Jefferson County, Pine Bluff, AR (1983-1987); President, United Way of Jefferson County, Pine Bluff, AR (1986); Board of Directors, Leadership Pine Bluff (1983-1985); Campaign Chairman, United Way of Jefferson County, Pine Bluff, AR (1983); Board of Directors, United Way of Jefferson County, Pine Bluff, AR (1975-1977) **MEM:** Director, Pine Bluff Regional Chamber of Commerce (1981, 1984, 1994, 1997); President, Jefferson County Bar Association (1995); Lieutenant Governor, Missouri-Arkansas Division, Kiwanis International (1983-1984); Director, Arkansas Wildlife Federation (1979-1981); Director, Jefferson County Wildlife Association (1973-1980); President, Jefferson County Wildlife Association (1974-1976); Arkansas Bar Association; Order of the Coif; Tau Beta Pi; Eta Kappa Nu **BAR:** Arkansas (1972) **MH:** Marquis Who's Who Top Professional **B/I:** Mr. Strode became involved his profession because his father was a surveyor and worked a lot with a lawyer who handled boundary disputes and real estate issues and surveying issues. He came to have a great deal of respect for that lawyer and that's one of the things that led him to law. In addition, what attracted him to pursue his profession was an individual choice. His undergraduate degree was in electrical engineering, which is a technical field, but he felt he wanted to do something with more human involvement. **AV:** Hunting; Fishing

STRODE, SCOTT KREIDER, T: Communications Educator (Retired) **I:** Education/Educational Services **DOB:** 11/03/1936 **PB:** Avon **SC:** IL/USA **PT:** Everette L. Strode; Susanna K. Strode **MS:** Widower **SPN:** Joanna Melyn Ward (05/05/1963, Deceased) **CH:** Kyle; Susanna; Paul **ED:** PhD, Indiana University Bloomington, Bloomington, IN (1974); MA, University of Washington, Seattle, WA (1966); BA, University of Puget Sound, Tacoma, WA (1959) **C:** Professor Emeritus, Manchester University, North Manchester, IN (2008-Present); Professor, Manchester University, North Manchester, IN (1974-2008); Assistant Professor, Rutgers University, Newark, NJ (1971-1974); Assistant Professor, Creighton University, Omaha, NE (1963-1967) **CR:** Creative Director; Actor **MIL:** U.S. Army **CW:** One-Act Play, "Take Me With You"; Children's Play, "The Greatest Show on Earth: A Children's Play" **AW:** Lilly Endowment (2003-2004); Grantee (2001) **MEM:** Association for Asian Performance; American Theatre in Higher Education **MH:** Albert Nelson Marquis Lifetime Achievement Award; Marquis Who's Who Top Professional **B/I:** Dr. Strode became involved in his profession because his involvement in music and theater in South Kitsap high school led him to involve himself in the field in his adult career. He later became a theater instructor. **AV:** Appreciating music and theater **PA:** Democrat **THT:** Dr. Stode believes that working in, and attending, live theater replicates the beauty and vagaries of life itself.

STROH, GUY WESTON, PHD, T: Philosophy Educator **I:** Education/Educational Services **DOB:** 03/28/1931 **PB:** Elizabeth **SC:** NJ/USA **PT:** Galusha Amos; Hanna Isabel Stroh **MS:** Married **SPN:** Marrion Lorraine Kopec **ED:** Doctor of Philosophy, Princeton University (1957); Master of Arts, Princeton University (1955); Bachelor of Arts, Princeton University (1953) **C:** Emeritus Professor, Rider University (2002-2013); Professor of Philosophy, Rider

University, Lawrenceville, NJ (1966-2002); Associate Professor of Philosophy, Rider University, Lawrenceville, NJ (1963-1966); Assistant Professor of Philosophy, Rider University, Lawrenceville, NJ (1956-1963) **CW:** Editorial Board, "Dictionary of Modern American Philosophers: 1860-1960" (2005); Author, "American Ethics: A Source Book" (2000); Author, "American Ethical Thought" (1979); Author, "American Philosophy Edwards to Dewey" (1968); Author, "Plato and Aristotle" (1964); Editorial Board, "Ethics" **AW:** Distinguished Teaching Award, Lindback Foundation (1966) **MEM:** President, New Jersey State Conference, American Association of University Professors (1969-1971) **MH:** Albert Nelson Marquis Lifetime Achievement Award **AV:** Tennis

STROKER, ALI, T: Actress, Singer **I:** Media & Entertainment **DOB:** 06/16/1987 **PB:** Ridgewood **SC:** NJ/USA **PT:** Jim Stroker; Jody Schleicher **MS:** Single **ED:** Degree in Fine Arts, Drama, Tisch School of the Arts, New York University (2009); Coursework, Summer Musical Theater Conservatory, Paper Mill Playhouse, Millburn, NJ; Diploma, Ridgewood High School **CR:** Co-Founding Director, ATTENTIONTheatre **CIV:** Co-Chair, Women Who Care; Founding Member, Be More Heroic; Instructor, Workshops, ARTS InsideOut, South Africa **CW:** Guest Appearance, "Charmed" (2019); Actress, "Oklahoma!," Circle in the Square Theatre (2019); Actress, "Oklahoma!," St. Ann's Warehouse (2018); Actress, "Annie," Hollywood Bowl (2018); Actress, "The 25th Annual Putnam County Spelling Bee," Cleveland Play House (2018); Guest Appearance, "Instinct" (2018); Guest Appearance, "Drunk History" (2018); Guest Appearance, "Lethal Weapon" (2018); Guest Appearance, "Ten Day in the Valley" (2017); Actress, "Spring Awakening," Brooks Atkinson Theatre (2015-2016); Actress, "Spring Awakening," Wallis Annenberg Center (2015); Guest Appearance, "Faking It" (2014-2015); Actress, "Cotton" (2014); Guest Appearance, "Glee" (2013); Actress, "The Glee Project" (2012); Guest Appearance, "I Was a Mermaid and Now I'm a Pop Star" (2011); Actress, "The 25th Annual Putnam County Spelling Bee," Paper Mill Playhouse (2011); Solo Performer, Kennedy Center, New York Town Hall, Lincoln Center **AW:** Drama Desk Award for Outstanding Featured Actress in a Musical (2019); Tony Award for Best Featured Actress in a Musical (2019)

STRONG, CHRISTINA CORDAIRE, T: Writer, Artist **I:** Writing and Editing **DOB:** 08/21/1932 **PB:** Norfolk **SC:** VA/USA **PT:** Cordary Baker; Christina (Swann) Heiberger **MS:** Widow **SPN:** Henry Hooker Strong (07/27/1957, Deceased 1972) **CH:** Jonathan Hooker; Johanna Harrison **ED:** Master's Degree, California State University, Fresno, CA (1979); Postgraduate Coursework, California State University, Fresno, CA (1976-1979); BA in French and Art, Woman's College, University of North Carolina, Greensboro, NC (1955) **CT:** Certified Teacher, Virginia **C:** Writer (1991-Present); Salesperson, The Booke Shoppe, Elizabeth City, NC (1991-1993); Vice President, Computron, Virginia Beach, VA (1990); Teacher, Norfolk Public Schools (1955-1957); Associate Professor, College of William and Mary, Norfolk, VA (1956); Designer, Custom Kitchens, Eastern Electric, Norfolk, VA (1950-1951) **CW:** Author, "Murder Makes it Mine" (2018); Author, "Married in Black" (2008); Author, "Ride the Wind Home" (2003); Author, "Ride the Winter Wind" (2002); Author, "The Night the Stars Fell" (2001); Author, "Ride for the Roses" (2000); Author, "Loving a Lowly Stranger" (1997); Author, "Spring Enchantment" (1996); Author, "Ring for Remembrance" (1996); Author, "Loving Honor" (1995); Author, "Beloved Stranger" (1995); Author,

"Daring Illusion" (1994); Author, "Winter Longing" (1995); Author, "Forgiving Hearts" (1994); Author, "Love's Triumph" (1993); Author, "Pride's Folly" (1993); Author, "Heart's Deception" (1992) **AW:** Holt Medallion for Best Regency (1994) **MEM:** Secretary, Strawberry River Art Association (1997-Present); Secretary, Romance Writers America (1990-Present); Historian, Vice President, Daughters of the Confederacy (1987-Present); Preceptor, Vice President, Corresponding Secretary, Alpha Gamma Chapter, Beta Sigma Phi (2008-2017); Treasurer, Chesapeake Romance Writers (1995); Treasurer, President, Theta Kappa Sigma (1949-1951); River City Romance Writers; Tau Psi Omega; National Society of Daughters of the American Revolution **MH:** Albert Nelson Marquis Lifetime Achievement Award **B/I:** Ms. Strong has always been a writer. She was inspired by her uncle, who was a prolific writer, despite the fact that his work was never published. **AV:** Trail riding; Swimming; Golfing; Target shooting **PA:** Republican **RE:** Southern Baptist **THT:** Ms. Strong is a published author under several pseudonyms.

STROUCE, RICHARD ARNOLD, T: Management Consultant **I:** Consulting **DOB:** 10/13/1933 **PB:** Bethlehem **SC:** PA/USA **PT:** Frank Arnold Strouce; Anne Marie Strouce **MS:** Married **SPN:** Sallie Hummel (07/11/1964) **CH:** Lindsey Victoria; Courtney Elizabeth **ED:** MBA, Cornell University (1957); B.C.E., Cornell University (1956) **C:** Management Consultant (1993-2010); Owner, Lehigh Valley Laboratories, Allentown, PA (1985-1993); President, A&B Inc (1982-1985); President, Reading Industries Inc., Pennsylvania (1979-1982); President, American Delivery Systems, Detroit, MI (1977-1979); President, PIE Transport IU International, Philadelphia, PA (1972-1977); Vice President, North and South America, ICS, New York, NY (1969-1972); Principal, McKinsey & Company, New York, NY (1961-1969) **MIL:** Served to 1st Lieutenant, U.S. Army (1958-1960) **MEM:** Saucon Valley Country Club **MH:** Albert Nelson Marquis Lifetime Achievement Award **AS:** Mr. Strouce attributes his success to always having a general interest in business and teaching in Switzerland for a year before he went into the military, which led him to business consulting. He was one of the youngest consultants at McKinsey & Company in New York City. **B/I:** Mr. Strouce became involved in his profession because he went to business school at Cornell University, where it was suggested that he consider consulting as a career.

STRUCK, NORMA, T: Artist **I:** Fine Art **DOB:** 02/17/1929 **PB:** West Engelwood **SC:** NJ/USA **PT:** Hans Christian Johansen; Amanda (Solberg) Johansen **MS:** Married **SPN:** H. Walter Struck (08/21/1955) **CH:** Steven; Laurie **ED:** Art Students' League, New York, NY (1976-1977) **C:** Artist, Portraits, Paintings, U.S. Navy, U.S. Coast Guard, Washington (1976-Present); Artist, Portraits, Prints, Scafa-Tornabene, Nyack, NY (1976-Present); Freelance Artist, Norcross, Incorporated, New York, NY (1967-1975); Staff Artist, Norcross, Incorporated, New York, NY (1950-1960) **CR:** Coast Guard Art Program, New York, NY (1980-Present); Committee Board Member, Navy Art Cooperative Liaison, New York, NY (1976-1980); Navy Historical Museum, Washington **CW:** Exhibited, Group Show, Federal, New York, NY (1994-1997, 1986); Exhibited, Group Show, U.S. Coast Guard, New England Air Museum, Windsor Locks, Connecticut (1984); Navy Combat Art Gallery, World Trade Center, Washington (1979); Exhibited, Group Show, Navy Historical Museum, Washington (1976); One-Woman shows include Valley Cottage Gallery, New York, Bergen Community Playhouse, Oradell, New Jersey, New York Yacht Club, Nabisco Company, Fairlawn, New Jersey; Exhibited, Group, Shows, Salmagundi Club, New York, Officers Club, Governor's Island, Hudson Valley Show, White Plains, New York, Intrepid Museum, New York, Alexander Hamilton United States Custom House, Newington-Cropsey Museum, New York, Bergen County Museum Art & Science, New Jersey; Represented in Permanent Collections, United States Pentagon, Washington, Henie-Onstad Museum, Oslo, World Figure Skating Hall of Fame and Museum, Colorado Springs, Alexander Hamilton Custom House, New York, World Trade Center, New York **AW:** George Gray Award Coast Guard Art Program, Governors Island, New York (1989, 1983); Louis E. Seley Award, Navy Art Program (1979); President's Award, American Artists Professional League (1979); Grumbacher Award, Catherine Lorillard Wolfe, National Arts Club, New York, NY (1978); Exhbited Ano Award Winner, Belskie Museum Art And Science Closter, New Jersey **MEM:** Board of Directors, Art Students League (Life), Hudson Valley Association (1985-1988); Fellow, American Artists Professional League; Portrait Society of America; Society of Illustrators; Salmagundi Club; Portrait Society of America; Charter Member, Museum of Women in the Arts **MH:** Albert Nelson Marquis Lifetime Achievement Award; Marquis Who's Who Top Professional **B/I:** Ms. Struck became involved in her profession because she started drawing as a small child. She loves being in the art world and misses it now that she is retired. **AV:** Antiques; Gourmet cooking

STRUMPF, DAVID, T: Vice President of Research and Development **I:** Research **CN:** Windgo.com **CH:** One Son **ED:** Technical Training, Microchip Masters Program **C:** Vice President of Research and Development, Windgo, Inc (2016-Present); Regional Partner, Eastern Missouri, Microchip Technology (1993); Director of Research and Develop, Senior Developer, ABC (Analytical Biochemistry) Laboratories, Inc (1991-1993) **CIV:** Advisory Board, ParentLink; Founder, Eqiteach.com **AW:** Engineers Choice Award, Electronic Design Magazine (2015); Top 10 Appliances no body actually needs, Design Smart Appliances, Westinghouse, Wired Magazine (2004); Shot Out Award **B/I:** Mr. Strumpf has an adult son with Asperger's Syndrome. He is 27 years old and 22 years old is when he was diagnosed. It was in that moment that Mr. Strumpf realized that everyone has a need and what we think is going on with ourselves and others is never what you think. **THT:** Surround yourself with excellence. Don't let the average things bring you down.

STRUNK, HAROLD KENNETH, T: Insurance Company Executive, Naval Officer (Retired) **I:** Insurance **DOB:** 06/23/1933 **PB:** McCreary **SC:** KY/USA **PT:** Obal Edmund Strunk; Matilda L. (New) Strunk **MS:** Widowed **SPN:** Nancy Lou Patton (06/12/1954, Deceased 2010) **CH:** Nancy Karen; Melanie Ann; Kenneth Wayne **ED:** DrPH, UCLA (1972); MPH, UCLA (1970); MA in Social Welfare, UCLA (1969); BA in Psychology, California State University, Fullerton (1967); Student, Georgia Institute of Technology (1951-1954) **C:** Regional Manager, Hospital Relations, Blue Shield of California, San Francisco, CA (1987-1995); Physician Recruiter, Hospital Staffing Systems, Pleasanton, CA (1986-1987); Hospital Administrator, National Medical Enterprises, Taif, Saudi Arabia (1984-1985); Hospital Administrator, Saudi Arabian Ministry of Defense, Dhahran, Saudi Arabia (1982-1984); Senior Health Planner, Arabian Bechtel Corporation, Ltd., Jubail, Saudi Arabia (1980-1982); Executive Director, Take Care Health Maintenance Organization Division, Blue Cross, Oakland, CA (1978-1980); Project Director, Professional Services Review Organizations Support Center for California, San Francisco, CA (1974-1978); Executive Director, United Foundation Medical Care, San Francisco, CA (1974-1978); Assistant Chief, Adult and Child Health, Alameda County Health Department, Oakdale, CA (1972-1974) **MIL:** Captain, U.S. Naval Reserve (1977-1995); Gulf War (1990-1991); U.S. Army (1954-1956); Army National Guard, 441st Field Artillery Battalion **CW:** Co-Author, "Medical Aspects of Persian Gulf Operations: Serious Infectious and Communicable Diseases of the Persian Gulf and Saudi Arabian Peninsula," Military Medicine (1991); Author, "Basic Arabic-Getting Around"; Contributor, Numerous Articles to Professional Journals; Published Short Stories on Amazon/Kindle **AW:** Numerous Military Medals **MEM:** California Association of Healthcare Leaders; Association Military Surgeons United States; American Public Health Association; Naval Reserve Association; World Affairs Council; Middle East Institute; Sigma Phi Epsilon; Sons of The American Revolution; Association of Former Intelligence Officers; Veterans of Foreign Wars; The American Legion; Sigma Phi Epsilon Fraternity **MH:** Albert Nelson Marquis Lifetime Achievement Award **B/I:** Dr. Strunk became involved in his profession during his studies for a degree in social work. He ran the 18-year-old boys' unit at Orange County Juvenile Hall in California and in the process, he changed his major to experimental psychology. Upon completion, an adviser suggested he should go get his master's degree in psychiatric social work. To him, it seemed like a sensible career path. After a period of time, he realized the career path he had chosen wasn't for him. He went to go speak to a mentor, Dr. Al Katz, and told him his frustrations with his current path. Dr. Al Katz suggested that he should come and attend some public health courses. Dr. Strunk followed his advice and immediately fell in love with the subject of public health. **AV:** Scuba diving; Competing in rifle and pistol shooting competitions; Taking photographs underwater **PA:** Republican **RE:** Presbyterian

STRUYK, JACK, T: President, Partner **I:** Insurance **CN:** Lockton Companies **MS:** Married **CH:** Five Children **ED:** BS in Education, University of Nebraska Omaha (1979) **CT:** Associate in Risk Management (ARM) **C:** President, Lockton Companies (2011-Present); President, Shareholder, Holmes Murphy & Associates (2000-2011); Senior Vice President, Aon Risk Services (1990-2000); Underwriting Trainee, Aetna Inc. (1980) **CIV:** Board Member, Child Saving Institute; Former Board member, National Safety Council, Greater Omaha Chapter; Board Member, Heartland Family Service; Former Chairman of the Board, KWAA; Board Member, Kids' Chance of Nebraska; Founder, Chairman, Millard West High School-5th Quarter Program; Board Member, Nebraskans for Workers' Compensation Equity and Fairness (NWCEF); Former Board Member, Omaha Hearing School; Former Board Member, Special Olympics; Member, Executive Committee, 2010 Special Olympics USA National Games **AS:** Mr. Struyk attributes his success to luck and hard work. He worked hard to become a coverage expert. He had some great mentors along the way, including Kent Preslow, the Hartford underwriting manager. He took him under his wing and taught him a lot. He helped him form his career and values in business. **B/I:** Mr. Struyk became involved in his profession because he went to college with the intention of becoming a teacher. He graduated college in December and there were no teaching jobs in the middle of the school year, so he took a job with Aetna and never went back to teaching.

THT: Mr. Struyk lives by the thought that "the best part about America is hard work still wins. You have to be honest all day every day."

STUART, ROSE, T: Owner **I:** Business Management/Business Services **CN:** The Rose Boutique Etc. **CH:** Two Daughters; One Son **CT:** Berkeley Psychic Institute **C:** Owner, Metaphysical Shops, The Rose Boutique Etc (2009-Present); Psychic, Coach (1989-Present) **CIV:** Chamber of Commerce; Donor, Various Animal Societies **AW:** Top 10 Physics and Spiritual Healers, Hollywood Sentinels **AS:** Ms. Stuart attributes her success to her passion to help people, love, and wanting the make thing world a better place and allowing others to open up and become forgiving. **B/I:** Ms. Stuart is 9th generation psychic. Her family is Celtic. Her parents were running the renaissance festivals. Her dad was an astrologer/ordained minister and her mother was a psychic adviser. Her parents told her that she was reading people as early as 3 or 4 years old. When she was 7 years old, she remembers going on to a women she did not know and shaking her skirt to get her attention. She told the woman that her family was going to be back together soon and stay strong. This woman ended up crying because Ms. Stuart's words were true, the women did not understand how she had such abilities.

STUEMPFLE, ARTHUR, "ART" KARL, T: Research Scientist **I:** Research **DOB:** 01/05/1940 **PB:** Williamsport **SC:** PA/USA **PT:** Arthur Carl Stuempfle; Jeanette Esther (Jacobs) Stuempfle **MS:** Married **SPN:** Linda Jean Campbell (03/30/1961) **CH:** Jeffrey; Karl **ED:** MS in Physics, Johns Hopkins University (1971); BS in Physics, Drexel University (1962) **C:** Senior Scientist, Optimetrics, Abingdon, MD (1996-2013); Director of Operations Research and Simulation, Edgewood Research, Development and Engineering Center, Aberdeen Proving Ground (1994-1995); Chief of Test Methodology and Program Integration, Edgewood Research, Development and Engineering Center, Aberdeen Proving Ground (1992-1994); Chief, Physics Division, Research Directorate, Chemical Research, Development and Engineering Center, Aberdeen Proving Ground (1985-1992); Chief, Operational Sciences Branch, Research Directorate, Chemical Research, Development and Engineering Center, Aberdeen Proving Ground (1978-1985); Research Physicist, Chemical Systems Laboratory, Aberdeen Proving Ground (1971-1978); Physicist, Edgewood Arsenal, Aberdeen Proving Ground (1964-1971); Chief, Test Measurement Branch, United States Army Chemical School, Fort McClellan, AL (1962-1964); Student Trainee, U.S. Army Edgewood Chemical Biological Center (1958-1962) **CR:** United States Chairman, Industrial Chemicals Task Force, Technical Cooperation Program, Canada, United States, United Kingdom, Washington, DC (1994-1995); Consultant, Physical Properties Subcommittee, National Spray Drift Task Force, Wilmington, DE (1990); Tri-National Chairman, Task Force for Chem-Bio Stimulants, Canada, United States, United Kingdom (1987-1988); United States Representative for Aerosol Technology, Technical Cooperation Program, United States, United Kingdom, Canada, Australia, Washington, DC (1982-1995) **CIV:** Lay Assistant, Cantor, Committee Chair, Newsletter Editor, Building Committee Chairman, Lord of Life Lutheran Church, Edgewood (1979-2019); Founder, Editor, Edgewood Community Newsletter (2008-2010); Organizing Member, The Edgewood Civic Association DC (1990); Business Manager, LC Sewing School (1971-1975) **MIL:** First Lieutenant, United States Army Chemical Corps (1962-1968) **CW:** Author, "The Edgewood Scrapbook" (2019); Author, "Images of Edgewood" (2012); Author,

"Aerosol Wars Short History" (2011); Columnist "Pulaski Corridor News" (2009-2010); Author, "Automated Decision Aid System" (2003); Author, "Coaches: Teach, Guide, Develop" (1989); Author, "Operational Sciences" (1987); Contributor, Articles, Professional Journals **AW:** Excellence in Technology Transfer Award, Federal Laboratory Consortium for Technology Transfer (2005); Oak Leaf Cluster Award, Meritorious Civilian Service, Department of the Army, Washington, DC (1996); International Technology Development Award, U.S. Department of Defense (1990); Special Features Award, U.S. Army Materiel Command (1989); W. H. Walker Technology Leadership Award, Chemical Research, Development, and Engineering Center (1987); Meritorious Civilian Service Award (1986); Research and Development Achievement Award, U.S. Army, Washington, DC (1977); Decorated Ancient Order of the Dragon, The Chemical Corps Regimental Association (2009); Army Commendation Medal, U.S. Department of Defense (1964) **MH:** Albert Nelson Marquis Lifetime Achievement Award **AS:** Mr. Stuempfle attributes his success to perseverance, self-confidence, optimism, hard work and respect for all persons. **B/I:** Mr. Stuempfle became involved in his profession because he was always interested in science. He was the first member of his family to attend college, and his mother and father taught him to work hard. **AV:** Ballroom dancing; Practicing Tai Chi; Writing; Cooking; Traveling **PA:** Republican **RE:** Lutheran

STYCOS, MARIA NOWAKOWSKA, PHD, T: Senior Lecturer (Retired) **I:** Education/Educational Services **CN:** Cornell University **DOB:** 06/04/1937 **PB:** Lwow **SC:** Poland **PT:** Marian Zygmunt Nowakowski; Julia Demska Nowakowska **MS:** Widowed **SPN:** Joseph Mayone Stycos (Deceased 2016) **CH:** Marek Stycos **ED:** PhD in Spanish Literature, Cornell University (1977); MA in Spanish Literature, Cornell University (1967); BA in English, French and Spanish, King's College London (1958) **C:** Retired (2006); Senior Lecturer, Romance Studies, Cornell University (1986-2006); Part-Time Assistant Professor, SUNY Cortland (1982-1986); Full-Time Assistant Professor, SUNY Cortland (1983-1984); Part-Time Instructor, Romance Studies, Cornell University (1982); Director, Handwerker Art Gallery, Ithaca, NY (1981-1982); Lecturer, Division of Modern Languages, Cornell University (1979); Part-Time Assistant Professor, Ithaca College, NY (1975-1981); Lecturer in Polish, Division of Modern Languages, Cornell University (1974); Lecturer in Spanish Language and Literature, Wells College (1972); Instructor in Spanish, Ithaca College (1970); Instructor in Spanish Literature, Romance Studies, Cornell University (1968-1970); Head, Summer Spanish Program, Teacher of Advanced Placement Students, Division of Modern Languages, Cornell University (1968); Instructor in Spanish, Ithaca College (1968); Graduate Student Teacher, Cornell University (1964) **CR:** Consultant, IDESPO Project, Cornell University (1986-1987); Faculty Advisory Committee, Johnson Museum of Art, Cornell University; Guided Undergraduate Theses and Independent Studies; Member, Latin American Studies Program, Cornell University; Member, Women's Studies Program, Cornell University **CIV:** Planning Board Member, Village of Lansing, NY (2002-2015); Mentor, Middle School; Volunteer, Hospice; Planning Board Member, Ithaca City of Asylum **CW:** Co-Author, "Voces Hispanas Siglo XXI," Entrevistas con Autores en DVD, Yale University Press (2005); Contributor, Chapters in Books; Contributor, Articles on Modern Spanish, Latin America and Polish Poetry, Professional Journals **AW:** Grantee, Program for Cultural Cooperation, Spanish Ministry of Education, Culture and Sports and United States Universities (2003); Grantee, Consortium

for Language Teaching and Learning to Participate in a Workshop, Teachers of Advanced Spanish, Massachusetts Institute of Technology (2000); Grantee, Consortium for Language Teaching and Learning for a Special Audio Project (1990); Faculty Research Grant, SUC, Cortland (1983-1984); Teaching Fellow, Romance Studies, Cornell University (1982-1984); Winner, Modern Spanish Poetry, "Methods of Poetic Criticism and Twentieth-Century Hispanic Poetry," NEH Competition Summer Seminar in Theory and Practice, The University of Kansas (1978); Graduate Assistantship, Romance Studies, Cornell University (1971-1972); Graduate Assistantship, Division of Modern Languages, and Romance Studies, Cornell University (1964-1967); State Scholarship, United Kingdom (1955-1958); Grantee, King's College London, Universidad Internacional Menendez Pelayo (1957); Grantee, Department of Romance Studies, Cornell University **MEM:** Modern Language Association; Asociación Internacional de Literatura y Cultura Femenina Hispánica; Asociación Internacional de Hispanistas; International Congress of Americanists **MH:** Albert Nelson Marquis Lifetime Achievement Award; Marquis Who's Who Top Professional **B/I:** Dr. Stycos became involved in her profession because she wanted to bring American students an insight into other cultures. **AV:** Listening to music and opera; Gardening; Reading poetry; Traveling

SUAREZ ELLER, ALICIA, T: Retired Educator and Children's Music Director **I:** Education/Educational Services **DOB:** 01/16/1943 **PB:** Angol **SC:** Malleco Province/Chile **PT:** Arnaldo Suarez; Rosa Jones de Suarez **MS:** Married **SPN:** James Craig Eller (07/16/1988); Robert Albert Butler (Divorced) **CH:** Martha Butler Murray; Tony Butler; Jamie Eller **ED:** BA in Spanish Teaching, Meredith College, Cum Laude (1970); AA, Louisburg College (1965) **C:** Translator, Consultant, English as a Second Language (2001-2016); Reporter, Franklin Times, Louisburg, NC (2001-2016); Teacher, Spanish, Louisburg High School (1975-2001); Teacher, Fourth Grade, Gold Sand Elementary School, Louisburg, NC (1970-1974) **CR:** Instructor, Spanish, Tar River Baptist Association, Louisburg, NC (2002); Teacher, Counselor, ECU Legislators School for Leadership Development (1986); Founder, Ritchie Valens Spanish Honor Society, Louisburg High School (1985); Guitar Teacher; Instructor, Vance-Granville Community College Guitar; Instructor, Franklin County Arts Council Summer Music Camp; FLANC Workshops, State Department of Public Instruction; Counselor, North Carolina Conference for Junior and Senior Workshops; Delegate, National Conference, United Methodist Musicians **CIV:** Board of Directors, Franklin County Arts Council, Louisburg, NC; Council Member, Interchurch Council; Bell Choir; Chancel Choir, Louisburg Methodist Church; Children's Choir Director, Louisburg Methodist Church; Musician, Southside Emmaus Walks Weekends, Blackstone, VA **CW:** Painting; Crafting; Knitting; Practicing photography **AW:** Public Service Award, Louisburg College Alumni Association (2019); Layperson of the Year, Louisburg United Methodist Church (2002); 1st Place Winner, The Clogging Adult Co., Louisburg School of Dance, Norfolk, VA (2000); Franklin County Artist of the Year (1999-2000); Talent State Winner, Senior Olympics (1998); Louisburg High School Teacher of the Year (1981-1982); Outstanding Young Women of America (1972); Best Secondary School Practice Teacher, Meredith College (1970); May Queen, Louisburg College (1964); Inductee, Sigma Pi Alpha (1964) **MEM:** National Education Association; NCAE-NC Association of Educators; Seed Book Club; Delta Kappa Gamma; ACT; The Association of Transcribers and Speech-to-text Providers; Foreign Language Association of North Carolina **MH:** Albert Nelson Marquis Lifetime Achievement Award; Marquis Who's Who Top Professional **AS:** Ms. Ellers attributes her success to her faith in the Lord, as well as her hard-working nature. **B/I:** Ms. Ellers' father taught music and agriculture at the Normal School in Angol, Chile, where her mother was also a teacher. From the time she was a child, Ms. Ellers wanted to follow in her parents' footsteps and become a teacher. **AV:** Playing guitar, accordion, banjo, and ukelele; Dancing; Making pottery; Practicing art; Line dancing; Latin dancing **RE:** Methodist

SUBRAMANIAN, MANI, ADJUNCT PROFESSOR, I: Education/Educational Services **CN:** Georgia Institute of Technology **DOB:** 01/11/1934 **PB:** Chennai **SC:** India **PT:** Pavur R.; Kalyani Mahadevan **MS:** Married **SPN:** Ruth Pressler (06/06/1964) **CH:** Ravi; Meera **ED:** PhD, Purdue University (1964); MSEE, Purdue University (1961); Diplomate, Madras Institute of Technology (1956); BS, University of Madras (1953) **C:** Board Director, Board, NMSWorks Software, Chennai, India (2018-Present); Adjunct Research Professor, Georgia Institute of Technology, Atlanta, GA (2001-Present); Chairman of the Board, NMSWorks Software, Chennai, India (2006-2018); Chief Executive Officer, NMSWorks Software, Chennai, India (2006-2009); Professor, Indian Institute of Technology, Chennai, India (2005-2009); Founder, Chief Executive Officer, ChanneLogics, Atlanta, GA (2000-2002); Professor, Georgia Institute of Technology, Established Network Management Program (1996-2001); Chief Technology Officer, Cadnet Corp, Atlanta, GA (1994-1996); Vice President, Engineering and Operations, Melita International, Atlanta, GA (1992-1993); Vice President, Advanced Product Development, Verilink Corp, San Jose, CA (1991-1992); Vice President, Engineering, Racal Milgo Information Systems, Atlanta, GA (1987-1991); District Manager, Bell Labs, Bellcore, Piscataway, NJ (1966-1987); Assistant Professor, Purdue University, West Lafayette, IN (1964-1966) **CR:** Technology Director, Board Trustee, OSI Network Management Forum, Holmdel, NJ (1989-1990) **CIV:** Board Member, Mountain Learning and Research Center, Highlands, NC (2011-2015) **CW:** Author, "CRC Handbook on Practical Internet Computing" (2003); Contributor, Articles, Lasers, Optics, Network Management; Author, "Network Management: Principles and Practice"; Contributor, Professional Articles, Professional Journals **AW:** Bellcore's Best, Bellcore (Now Telcordia Technologies) (1985) **MEM:** IEEE **MH:** Albert Nelson Marquis Lifetime Achievement Award **B/I:** Dr. Subramanian has always had a curious and scientific mind. He came to the U.S. because he wanted to further his education. **AV:** Walking; Gym; Yoga; Music **PA:** Democrat **RE:** Unitarian Universalist **THT:** Future of life and mankind is based on the change of neurotechnology and climate change.

SUHR, JOHN NICHOLAS JR., T: Partner **I:** Law and Legal Services **CN:** Nelson Mullins Riley & Scarborough LLP **MS:** Married **SPN:** Robin P. Suhr (03/2018) **CH:** Six Children **ED:** JD, Washington College of Law, American University, Magna Cum Laude (1992); BA, University of Virginia (1988) **C:** Partner, Nelson Mullins Riley & Scarborough LLP, Charlotte, NC (2009-Present) **CIV:** Board of Directors, Mecklenburg Bar Foundation (2009-2012); Habitat for Humanity, Charlotte, NC **CW:** Contributor, Articles, Professional Journals **AW:** AV Preeminent Peer Review Rating, Martindale-Hubbell (2013); Listee, Legal Elite, Business North Carolina (2010); Best Lawyers in America, Securitization and Structured Finance (2009-2018); Rising Stars in Banking, North Carolina Super Lawyers (2009);

Listee, 40 Under 40, Charlotte Business Journal (2004) **MEM:** North Carolina Bar Association; New York Bar Association; American Bar Association; Mecklenburg Bar Association **BAR:** New York; North Carolina; United States District Court for the Eastern District of North Carolina; United States District Court for the Western District of North Carolina **MH:** Marquis Who's Who Top Professional **AS:** Mr. Suhr attributes his success to perseverance and hard work. **B/I:** Mr. Suhr comes from a long generation of lawyers, all of whom inspired him to pursue the field. **AV:** Traveling; Fishing

SUHRE, WALTER ANTHONY, T: Lawyer, Brewery Executive (Retired) **I:** Law and Legal Services **DOB:** 01/17/1933 **PB:** Cincinnati **SC:** OH/USA **PT:** Walter A.; Elizabeth V. (Heimbuch) S. **MS:** Divorced **ED:** Bachelor of Laws, University of Cincinnati, with Honors (1962); Bachelor of Science in Business Administration, Northwestern University (1956) **C:** Vice President, General Counsel, Anheuser-Busch Companies LLC, St. Louis, MO (1982-1993); Vice President, General Counsel, EaglePicher Industries Inc. Cincinnati, OH (1970-1982); With, EaglePicher Industries Inc., Cincinnati, OH (1965-1982); Associate, Taft, Stettinius & Hollister, Cincinnati, OH (1962-1965) **CIV:** Chairperson, Board of Directors, FOCUS Marines Foundation, St. Louis, MO (2009-Present); Volunteer, St. Louis Zoo (2000-Present); Patriot Guard Riders, Missouri Chapter (2015-2019); President, FOCUS Marines Foundation, St. Louis, MO (2009-2018); Board of Directors, St. Louis Zoo (2000-2015); Co-founder, FOCUS Marines Foundation, St. Louis, MO (2009); Volunteer, St Louis Cardinal Glennon Children's Hospital (1993-2000); Volunteer, St Louis Children's Hospital (1993-2000); Chairperson, Board of Directors, Operation Food Search, St. Louis, MO **MIL:** Captain, U.S. Marine Corps Reserve (1959-1962); Active Duty, U.S. Marine Corps (1956-1959) **BAR:** Missouri (1982); Ohio (1962) **MH:** Albert Nelson Marquis Lifetime Achievement Award **B/I:** Mr. Suhre became involved in his profession after having served in active duty in the U.S. military. Having previously obtained an undergraduate degree in business administration, he found himself fascinated by the law and resolved to pursue a viable career path in that field. **PA:** Republican **RE:** Presbyterian

SULLIVAN, DANIEL, "DAN" SCOTT, T: U.S. Senator from Alaska; Lawyer **I:** Government Administration/Government Relations/Government Services **DOB:** 11/13/1964 **PB:** Fairview Park **SC:** OH/USA **PT:** Thomas C. Sullivan; Sandra (Simmons) Sullivan **MS:** Married **SPN:** Julie Fate **CH:** Isabel; Laurel; Meghan **ED:** JD, Georgetown Law (1993); MS in Foreign Service, Georgetown University, Cum Laude (1993); MA in International Relations, University of Birmingham (1988); BA in Economics, Harvard University, Magna Cum Laude (1987); Intern, United States Court of Appeals for the District of Columbia Circuit **C:** U.S. Senator, State of Alaska (2015-Present); Commissioner, Alaska Department of Natural Resources (2010-2013); Attorney General, State of Alaska, Juneau, Alaska (2009-2010); Assistant Secretary for Economic, Energy and Business Affairs, U.S. Department of State, Washington, DC (2006-2009); Director, Acting Senior Director, International Economic Directorate, The White House, Washington, DC (2002-2004); Associate, Perkins Coie LLP, Anchorage, Alaska (2000-2002); Law Clerk to Chief Justice Warren Matthews, Alaska Supreme Court (1998-1999); Law Clerk to Honorable Andrew Kleinfeld, United States Court of Appeals for the Ninth Circuit, Fairbanks, Alaska (1997-1998) **CIV:** Active, Alaska's Toys for Tots Foundation (1994-Present) **MIL:** Lieutenant Colonel, United States Marine

Corps Reserve (1997-Present); Strategic Advisor, Special Assistant to Commander U.S. Central Command (CENTCOM), United States Marine Corps (2004-2006, 2009, 2013); With, United States Marine Corps (1993-1997) **CW:** Co-author, "Chosun's Tears" (1999); Contributor, Georgetown Law Journal **AW:** Decorated Defense Meritorious Service Medal; Named One of the 10 Outstanding Young Americans, U.S. Junior Chamber of Commerce; Outstanding Service Award, National Security Council **MEM:** Alaska Bar Association **PA:** Republican

SULLIVAN, JOHN JOSEPH, T: United States Deputy Secretary of State **I:** Government Administration/Government Relations/Government Services **DOB:** 11/20/1959 **PB:** Boston **SC:** MA/USA **MS:** Married **SPN:** Grace Rodriguez **CH:** Three Children **ED:** JD, Columbia Law School (1985); BA in History & Political Science, Brown University (1981) **C:** United States Deputy Secretary of State (2017-Present); Deputy Secretary, State for Management and Resources (2017-Present); Partner, Gibson, Dunn & Crutcher LLP, Washington, DC (2009-Present); Deputy Secretary, United States Department of Commerce, Washington, DC (2008-2009); General Counsel, United States Department of Commerce, Washington, DC (2005-2008); Legal Counsel, Deputy General Counsel, United States Department of Defense, Washington, DC (2004-2005); Partner, Mayer, Brown, Rowe & Maw, LLP (Now Mayer Brown) (1993-2004); Deputy General Counsel, George H.W. Bush Re-Election Campaign (1992); Counselor to Assistant Attorney General, Office of Legal Counsel, United States Department of Justice (1991); Law Clerk to Justice David H. Souter, Supreme Court of the United States; Law Clerk to Honorable John Minor Wisdom, United States Court Appeals for the Fifth Circuit **CW:** Book Reviews Editor, Columbia Law Review **AW:** Harlan Fiske Stone Scholar, Columbia Law School **PA:** Republican

SULLIVAN, NEIL SAMUEL, PHD, T: Physicist, Researcher, Educator, Former Dean **I:** Education/Educational Services **DOB:** 01/18/1942 **PB:** Whanganui **SC:** New Zealand **PT:** Reynold Richard Sullivan; Edna Mary (Alger) Sullivan **MS:** Widowed **SPN:** Robyn Annette Dawson (08/28/1965) **CH:** Raoul Samuel; Robert Alexander; David Charles **ED:** Postdoctoral Research, Centre d'Etudes Nucleaires (Now CEA), Saclay, France (1972-1974); PhD in Physics, Harvard University (1972); MSc in Physics, University of Otago, New Zealand (1965); BSc, University of Otago, New Zealand, with First Class Honors (1964) **C:** Professor of Physics, University of Florida, Gainesville, FL (1983-Present); Dean, College Liberal Arts and Sciences, University of Florida (2000-2006); Associate Dean of Research, College of Liberal Arts and Sciences, University of Florida (2000-2001); Chair, Department of Physics, University of Florida, Gainesville, FL (1989-1999); Research Physicist, Centre d'Etudes Nucleaires (Now CEA), Saclay, France (1974-1982) **CR:** Co-Principal Investigator, National MagLab, Tallahassee, FL (1990-2017); Co-Founder, Microkelvin Research Laboratory, University of Florida, Gainesville, FL **CW:** Editor-in-Chief, "Journal of Low Temperature Physics"; Contributor, Articles on Quantum Solids and Nuclear Magnetism, Professional Journals **AW:** Teacher of the Year (1988); Prix La Caze, Physics, Académie des Sciences, Paris, France (1982); Prix Saintour, Collège de France, Paris, France (1978); Frank Knox Memorial Fellowship, Harvard University, Cambridge, MA (1965-1967); Fulbright Scholar (1965) **MEM:** Fellow, American Physical Society; Institute of Physics; Société Française de Physique; European Physical Society **MH:** Albert Nelson Marquis Lifetime Achievement Award

B/I: Mr. Sullivan became involved in his profession when he attended high school in New Zealand; his biology and math teachers were especially influential and encouraging. He found that he enjoyed making things, and saw that taking technology just one step further is fundamental to valuable research. When Mr. Sullivan attended Harvard, he was lucky enough to work with renowned physicist Professor Robert Pound, another influential mentor with whom Mr. Sullivan shared research interests.

SULLIVAN, WARREN GERALD, T: Lawyer, Consultant **I:** Law and Legal Services **DOB:** 09/08/1923 **PB:** Chicago **SC:** IL/USA **PT:** Gerald Joseph Sullivan; Marie (Fairrington) Sullivan **MS:** Married **SPN:** Helen Louise Curtis (07/27/1974); Helen Ruth Young (08/21/1948, Divorced) **CH:** Janet M.; Douglas W.; William C. **ED:** Doctor of Jurisprudence, Northwestern University (1950); Bachelor of Arts, University of Illinois at Urbana-Champaign (1947) **C:** Retired (1993); Management Consultant (1984-1993); Vice President of Industrial Relations, Administration and Labor Law, General Dynamics Corporation, St. Louis, MO (1975-1984); Vice President of Personnel and Administration, Avco Corporation, Greenwich, CT (1969-1975); Associate to Partner, Naphin, Sullivan & Banta and Predecessors (1952-1969); Attorney, Illinois Department of Revenue, Chicago, IL (1950-1952) **CR:** Fellow Emeritus, College of Labor & Employment Lawyers **CIV:** Board of Directors, YMCA; Board of Directors, Greater St. Louis Zoo **MIL:** Corporal to First Lieutenant, Military Intelligence Service, U.S. Army Reserve (1942-1945); Military Government (1949-1954) **CW:** Contributor, Articles to Professional Journals **MEM:** Fellow, College of Labor and Employment Lawyers; American Bar Association; Connecticut Bar Association; Missouri Bar Association; Bellerive Country Club, Creve Coeur, MO; Delta Tau Delta; Phi Delta Phi **BAR:** Missouri (1981); United States Court of Appeals for the Second Circuit (1974); Connecticut (1971); Supreme Court of the United States (1968); United States Court of Appeals for the Sixth Circuit (1966); United States Court of Appeals for the District of Columbia Circuit (1964); United States Court of Appeals for the Seventh Circuit (1955); Illinois (1950) **MH:** Albert Nelson Marquis Lifetime Achievement Award **B/I:** Mr. Sullivan became involved in his profession due to the influence of his father, who had wanted to become a lawyer but never managed to do so.

SUMMERS, CHARLES PHD, T: Entomologist, Educator **I:** Education/Educational Services **DOB:** 12/24/1941 **PB:** Ogden **SC:** UT/USA **PT:** Charles R. Summers; Selma Geddes Summers **MS:** Widower **SPN:** Beverly Hill (02/11/1977, Deceased 2009) **ED:** PhD, Cornell University (1970); MS, Utah State University (1966); BS, Utah State University (1964) **C:** Professor, University of California, Davis (1992-2012); Associate Professor, University of California, Berkeley, (1976-1992); Assistant Professor, University of California, Berkeley (1970-1976) **CR:** Director, Kearney Agricultural Center, Parlier, CA (1983-1985) **CW:** Contributor, More than 200 Articles, Numerous Science Journals **AW:** C. W. Woodworth Award, Pacific Branch, Entomology Society, (2009); Grant, United States Department of Agriculture (1982-1985); Grant, United States Environmental Protection Agency (1979-1981); Grant, National Science Foundation (1974-1976) **MEM:** American Phytopathological Society; Entomological Society of Canada; Entomological Society of America **MH:** Albert Nelson Marquis Lifetime Achievement Award **B/I:** Mr. Summers became involved in his profession because when he was an undergraduate in college, he took his first entomology class and fell in love with bugs. He continues to enjoy his career to this day. **PA:** Liberal **RE:** Church of Jesus Christ of Latter-day Saints

SUMNER, GORDON, "STING" MATTHEW THOMAS, T: Musician **I:** Media & Entertainment **DOB:** 10/2/1951 **PB:** Wallsend **SC:** England **PT:** Ernest Matthew Sumner; Audrey (Cowell) Sumner **MS:** Married **SPN:** Trudie Styler (08/20/1992); Frances Tomelty (05/01/1976, Divorced 1984) **CH:** Joseph; Fuchsia Katherine; Brigitte Michael; Jake: Eliot Pauline; Giacomo Luke **ED:** Coursework, Northumbria University (1971-1974); Coursework, University of Warwick **C:** Solo Musician (1985-Present); Lead Singer, Bassist, Songwriter, The Police (1977-1984) **CR:** Musician, Phoenix Jazzmen, Newcastle Big Band and Last Exit; Teacher, St. Paul's First School, Cramington, United Kingdom; Tax Officer; Building Laborer; Bus Conductor **CIV:** Supporter, Rainforest Fund, Amnesty International and Live Aid **CW:** Solo Musician, "2 in a Million" (2019); Solo Musician, "Silent Night (Christmas is Coming)" (2019); Solo Musician, "Just One Lifetime" (2019); Solo Musician, "My Songs" (2019); Solo Musician, "Gotta Get Back My Baby" (2018); Solo Musician, "Don't Make Me Wait" (2018); Solo Musician, "I Can't Stop Thinking About You" (2016); Solo Musician, "57th & 9th" (2016); Composer, "The Last Ship" (2014-2015); Solo Musician, "The Last Ship" (2013); Solo Musician, "And Yet" (2013); Practical Arrangement" (2013); Solo Musician, "Deep in the Meadow (Lullaby)" (2012); Solo Musician, "Symphonicities" (2010); Solo Musician, "If on a Winter's Night..." (2009); Solo Musician, "Soul Cake" (2009); Solo Musician, "Songs from the Labrynith" (2006); Solo Musician, "Stolen Car (Take Me Dancing)" (2004); Solo Musician, "Whenever I Say Your Name" (2003); Author, "Broken Music" (2003); Solo Musician, "Sacred Love" (2003); Solo Musician, "Send Your Love" (2003); Solo Musician, "Fragile 2001" (2001); Solo Musician, "My Funny Friend and Me" (2000); Solo Musician, "After the Rain Has Fallen" (2000); Solo Musician, "Dessert Rose" (2000); Solo Musician, "Brand New Day" (1999); Solo Musician, "I'm So Happy I Can't Stop Crying" (1996); Solo Musician, "I Was Brought to My Senses" (1996); Solo Musician, "You Still Touch Me" (1996); Solo Musician, "Let Your Soul Be Your Pilot" (1996); Solo Musician, "Mercury Falling" (1996); Solo Musician, "This Cowboy Song" (1995); Solo Musician, "When We Dance" (1994); Solo Musician, "If I Ever Lose My Faith in You" (1993); Solo Musician, "Seven Days" (1993); Solo Musician, "She's Too Good for Me" (1993); Solo Musician, "Fields of Gold" (1993); Solo Musician, "Nothing 'Bout Me" (1993); Solo Musician, "Shape of My Heart" (1993); Solo Musician, "Love is Stronger Than Justice (Munificent Seven)" (1993); Solo Musician, "All for Love" (1993); Solo Musician, "Ten Summoner's Tales" (1993); Solo Musician, "It's Probably Me" (1992); Solo Musician, "The Soul Cages" (1991); Solo Musician, "They Dance Alone" (1988); Solo Musician, "Fragile" (1988); Solo Musician, "Englishman in New York" (1988); Solo Musician, "Be Still My Beating Heart" (1988); Solo Musician, "We'll Be Together" (1987); Solo Musician, "...Nothing Like the Sun" (1987); Solo Musician, "We Work the Black Seam" (1986); Solo Musician, "Moon Over Bourbon Street" (1986); Solo Musician, "Russians" (1985); Solo Musician, "Fortress Around Your Heart" (1985); Solo Musician, "Love is the Seventh Wave" (1985); Solo Musician, "If You Love Somebody Set Them Free" (1985); Solo Musician, "The Dream of the Blue Turtles" (1985); Musician, The Police, "Synchroncity" (1983); Narrator, "Yanomamo" (1983); Musician, The Police, "Every Breath You Take" (1983); Musician, The Police, "Wrapped Around Your Finger" (1983); Musician, The Police, "Synchronicity II" (1983); Musician, The Police, "King of Pain" (1983); Musician, The Police, "Secret Journey" (1982); Solo Musician, "Spread a Little Happiness" (1982); Musician, The Police, "Ghost in the Machine" (1981); Musician, The Police, "Invisible Sun" (1981); Musician, The Police, "Every Little Thing She Does is Magic" (1981); Musician, The Police, "Spirits in the Material World" (1981); Musician, The Police, "Zenyatta Mondatta" (1980); Musician, The Police, "The Bed's Too Big Without You" (1980); Musician, The Police, "Don't Stand So Close to Me" (1980); Musician, The Police, "De Do Do Do, De Da Da Da" (1980); Musician, The Police, "Reggatta de Blanc" (1979); Musician, The Police, "Message in a Bottle" (1979); Musician, The Police, "Walking on the Moon" (1979); Musician, The Police, "Bring on the Night" (1979); Musician, The Police, "Outlandos d'Amour" (1978); Musician, The Police, "Roxanne" (1978); Musician, The Police, "Can't Stand Losing You" (1978); Musician, The Police, "So Lonely" (1978); Musician, The Police, "Fall Out" (1977); Author, "Lyrics by - Sting"; Numerous Appearance, Various Television Shows and Movies Including "The Simpsons," "Ally McBeal," "Bee Movie," "Bruno," and "Zoolander 2" **AW:** Grammy Award for Best Reggae Album, The Recording Academy (2019); Polar Music Prize (2017); Award of Merit, American Music Awards (2016); Lifetime Contribution, Kennedy Center Honors (2014); David Angell Humanitarian Award, American Screenwriters Association (2004); Grammy Award for Best Pop Collaboration with Vocals, The Recording Academy (2004); Century Award, Billboard Music Awards (2003); Inductee with The Police, Rock and Roll Hall of Fame (2003); Outstanding Contribution to Music, BRIT Awards (2002); Inductee, Songwriters Hall of Fame (2002); Primetime Emmy Award for Outstanding Individual Performance in a Variety or Music Program, Television Academy (2002); Golden Globe Award for Best Original Song, Hollywood Foreign Press Association (2002); Grammy Award for Best Male Pop Vocal Performance, The Recording Academy (1988, 1994, 2000, 2001); Grammy Award for Best Pop Vocal Album, The Recording Academy (2000); Best British Male Solo Artist, BRIT Awards (1994); Grammy Award for Best Engineered Album, Non-Classical, The Recording Academy (1994); Grammy Award for Best Music Video, Long Form, The Recording Academy (1987, 1994); Grammy Award for Best Rock Song, The Recording Academy (1992); Best British Album, BRIT Awards (1988); Grammy Award for Song of the Year, The Recording Academy (1984); Grammy Award for Best Rock Performance by a Duo or Group with Vocal, The Recording Academy (1981, 1984); Grammy Award for Best Rock Instrumental Performance, The Recording Academy (1980, 1981, 1984); Numerous Awards

SUNUNU, CHRISTOPHER, "CHRIS" T., T: Governor of New Hampshire **I:** Government Administration/Government Relations/Government Services **DOB:** 11/05/1974 **PB:** Salem **SC:** NH/USA **PT:** John H. Sununu; Nancy (Hayes) Sununu **MS:** Married **SPN:** Valerie Sununu **CH:** Calvin; Edie; Leo **ED:** BS in Civil and Environmental Engineering, Massachusetts Institute of Technology (1998) **C:** Governor, State of New Hampshire (2017-Present); Member, New Hampshire Executive Council, Third District (2011-2017); Chief Executive Officer, Waterville Valley Resort (2010); Owner, Director, Sununu Enterprises, Exeter, NH (2006-2010); Environmental Engineer (1998-2006) **AV:** Skiing; Playing rugby

SUOZZI, THOMAS, "TOM" RICHARD, T: U.S. Representative from New York **I:** Government Administration/Government Relations/Government Services **CN:** U.S. House of Representatives **DOB:** 08/31/1962 **PB:** Glen Cove **SC:** NY/USA **PT:** Joseph A. Suozzi; Marguerite Suozzi **MS:** Married **SPN:** Helene Suozzi **CH:** Caroline Helene; Joseph Anthony; Michael Anthony **ED:** Doctor of Jurisprudence, Fordham University School of Law (1989); Bachelor of Arts, Boston College (1984) **CT:** CPA **C:** Member, U.S. Representative from New York's Third Congressional District, United States Congress, Washington, DC (2017-Present); Senior Advisor, Lazard (2010-2012); Executive, Nassau County, NY (2002-2009); Mayor, City of Glen Cove, NY (1994-2001); Member, House Committee on Foreign Affairs, United States Congress; Member, House Committee on Armed Services, United States Congress; Of Counsel, Harris Beach PLLC; Litigator, Shearman & Sterling; Law Clerk to the Chief Judge of the Eastern District; Auditor, Arthur Anderson & Co.; Vice Chair, Bipartisan Problem Solvers Caucus; Co-chair, Long Island Sound Caucus; Co-chair, Quiet Skies Caucus **AW:** Named, Environmentalist of the Year, New York State League of Conservation Voters (2008); Named, Public Official of the Year, Governing Magazine (2005)

SUTHERLAND, ALEXANDER, "ALEC" CHARLES, T: Professor Emeritus of English (Retired) **I:** Education/Educational Services **CN:** Nazareth College of Rochester **DOB:** 09/12/1938 **PB:** Manilla **SC:** Phillippines **PT:** Edwin Van Valkenburg Sutherland; Eleanor Austin Sutherland **MS:** Married **SPN:** Mindy Fay Ward (12/18/1998); Barbara Joan Drysdale (06/30/1979, Deceased 03/1985) **ED:** PhD in English, New York University (1978); MA in English, New York University (1968); AB in English, Princeton University (1962) **C:** Professor Emeritus, English Nazareth College of Rochester (2006-2016); Visiting Faculty, American University Of Kosovo, Pristina, Kosovo (2006); Rotary International Professorship, Peradeniya, Sir Lanka (1999-2000); Professor Emeritus (1998); Professor of English, Nazareth College of Rochester, New York (1973-1998); Fulbright Professor, Kelaniya University, Sri Lanka (1990-1991); Fulbright Professor, Sana'a University (1984-1985) **CIV:** Christ Episcopal Church, Pittsford, NY **MIL:** First Lieutenant, U.S. Army (1963-1966) **CW:** "The Pictures of Adelaide Douglas Austin with Additional Pictures and Notes By Her Grandson, Alec Sutherland" (2016) **AW:** Nazareth College Senior Excellence in Teaching Award (1992-1993); Outstanding Campus Service Award, Nazareth College (1989-1990); Distinguished Colleague Award, Nazareth College (1989); CASE Professor of the Year Award, Nazareth College Nominee (1987); Award of Merit, Society for Technical Communications (1984); Outstanding Achievement in the Teaching of English, New York State English Council (1982) **MH:** Albert Nelson Marquis Lifetime Achievement Award **B/I:** Dr. Sutherland has always loved to read. His father was the chairman of the English department at West Point; he was his inspiration to teach. **AV:** Researching family history **RE:** Episcopalian

SUTHERLAND, KIEFER, T: Actor **I:** Media & Entertainment **DOB:** 12/21/1996 **SC:** London/England **PT:** Donald Sutherland; Shirley Douglas Sutherland **MS:** Divorced **SPN:** Kelly Winn (07/29/1996, Divorced 2004); Camelia Kath (09/12/1987, Divorced 1990 **CH:** Sarah Jude Sutherland **C:** Co-Owner, Ironworks Record Label **CIV:** Artists Against Racism **CW:** Actor, "The Fugitive" (2020); Musician, "Reckless & Me" (2019); Actor, "Black Ops 4: Dead of the Night" (2018); Actor, "Flatliners" (2017); Actor, "Where Is Kyra?" (2017); Actor, "Designated Survivor" (2016-2019); Executive Pro-

ducer, "Designated Survivor" (2016-2019); Executive Producer, "24: Legacy" (2016-2017); Musician, "Down in a Hole" (2016); Himself, "Zoolander 2" (2016); Actor, "Forsaken" (2015); Actor, "Metal Gear Solid V: The Phantom Plain" (2015); Himself, "Rammstein in Amerika" (2015); Actor, "Marked" (2014); Actor, "Twin Peaks: The Missing Pieces" (2014); Actor, "24: Live Another Day" (2014); Executive Producer, "24: Live Another Day" (2014); Guest Appearance, "Saturday Night Live" (2014); Actor, "Metal Gear Solid V: Ground Zeroes" (2014); Actor, "Pompeii" (2014); Actor, "Touch" (2012-2013); Executive Producer, "Touch" (2012-2013); Actor, "The Reluctant Fundamentalist" (2012); Voice Actor, "Night of the Living Carrots" (2011); Actor, "Melancholia" (2011); Actor, "The Confession" (2011); Executive Producer, "The Confession" (2011); Voice Actor, "The Simpsons" (2006, 2007, 2011); Voice Actor, "Marmaduke" (2010); Narrator, "Twelve" (2010); Executive Producer, "24" (2006-2010); Actor, "24" (2001-2010); Voice Actor, "Monsters vs Aliens: Mutant Pumpkins from Outer Space" (2009); Voice Actor, "B.O.B.'s Big Break" (2009); Voice Actor, "Monsters vs. Aliens" (2009); Executive Producer, "Stalking Rocco Deluca" (2009); Actor, "24: Redemption" (2008); Executive Producer, "24: Redemption" (2008); Voice Actor, "Call of Duty: World at War" (2008); Voice Actor, "Call of Duty: World at War - Final Fronts" (2008); Actor, "Mirrors" (2008); Executive Producer, "Mirrors" (2008); Himself, "Corner Gas" (2008); Voice Actor, "Dragonlance: Dragons of Autumn Twilight" (2008); Actor, "24: Day Six - Debrief" (2007); Executive Producer, "24: Day Six - Debrief" (2007); Voice Actor, "Family Guy" (2006); Actor, "The Sentinel" (2006); Voice Actor, "The Wild" (2006); Voice Actor, "24: The Game" (2006); Co-Executive Producer, "24" (2003-2006); Actor, "River Queens" (2005); Narrator, "Flight 93: The Flight That Fought Back" (2005); Himself, "Jiminy Glick in Lalawood" (2004); Actor, "Taking Lives" (2004); Narrator, "NASCAR: The IMAX Experience" (2004); Voice Actor, "The Land Before Time X: The Great Longneck Migration" (2003); Actor, "L.A. Confidential" (2003); Actor, "Paradise Found" (2003); Actor, "Behind the Red Door" (2003); Producer, "24" (2002-2003); Actor, "Phone Booth" (2002); Actor, "Dead Heat" (2002); Actor, "Desert Saints" (2002); Actor, "To End All Wars" (2001); Actor, "Cowboy Up" (2001); Actor, "The Right Temptation" (2000); Actor, "Picking Up the Pieces" (2000); Actor, "After Alice" (2000); Actor, "Beat" (2000); Himself, "The Industry" (1999); Actor, "Woman Wanted" (1999); Director, "Woman Wanted" (1999); Actor, "Ground Control" (1998); Actor, "Break Up" (1998); Actor, "A Soldier's Sweetheart" (1998); Actor, "Dark City" (1998); Actor, "Truth or Consequences, N.M." (1997); Director, "Truth or Consequences, N.M." (1997); Actor, "Four Tales of Two Cities" (1996); Actor, "The Last Days of Frankie the Fly" (1996); Actor, "A Time to Kill" (1996); Voice Actor, "Armitage III: Polymatrix" (1996); Actor, "Duke of Groove" (1996); Actor, "Freeway" (1996); Actor, "Eye for an Eye" (1996); Actor, "Hourglass" (1995); Actor, "Fallen Angels" (1995); Actor, "The Cowboy Way" (1994); Actor, "Teresa's Tattoo" (1994); Executive Producer, "Natural Selection" (1994); Actor, "The Three Musketeers" (1993); Actor, "Last Light" (1993); Director, "Last Light" (1993); Actor, "The Vanishing" (1993); Actor, "A Few Good Men" (1992); Actor, "Twin Peaks: Fire Walk with Me" (1992); Actor, "Article 99" (1992); Voice Actor, "The Nutcracker Prince" (1990); Actor, "Flatliners" (1990); Actor, "Young Guns II" (1990); Actor, "Chicago Joe and the Showgirl" (1990); Actor, "Flashback" (1990); Actor, "Renegades" (1989); Actor, "1969" (1988); Actor, "Young Guns" (1988); Actor, "Bright Lights, Big City" (1988); Actor, "Crazy Moon" (1987); Actor, "The Killing Time"

(1987); Actor, "Promised Land" (1987); Actor, "The Lost Boys" (1987); Actor, "Stand By Me" (1986); Actor, "Amazing Stories" (1986); Actor, "The Brotherhood of Justice" (1986); Actor, "Trapped in Silence" (1986); Actor, "At Close Range" (1986); Actor, "Amazing Stories" (1985); Actor, "The Bay Boy" (1984); Actor, "Max Dugan Returns" (1983) **AW:** GoldenEye Award for Lifetime Achievement, Zurich Film Festival (2015); Man of the Year, Hasty Pudding Theatricals (2013); Star, Hollywood Walk of Fame (2008); Outstanding Performance by a Male Actor in a Drama Series, "24," Screen Actors Guild Awards (2006); Inductee, Canada's Walk of Fame (2005); Best Foreign TV Personality - Male, Aftonbladet TV Prize, Sweden (2003)

SUTTON, MARK STEPHAN, T: Chairman, Chief Executive Officer **I:** Manufacturing **CN:** International Paper **MS:** Married **SPN:** Laurie Sutton **CH:** Two Children **ED:** BSEE, Louisiana State University (1983) **C:** Chairman, Board of Directors, International Paper (2015-Present); Chief Executive Officer, International Paper (2014-Present); President, Chief Operating Officer, International Paper (2014); Senior Vice President, Industrial Packaging, International Paper (2011-2014); Senior Vice President of Printing and Commercial Papers for the Americas, International Paper (2009-2011); Senior Vice President, Global Supply Chain, International Paper (2007-2009); Vice President of Corporate Strategic Planning, International Paper (2005-2007); Vice President, General Manager of Corrugated Packaging Operations for Europe, the Middle East and Africa, International Paper (2002-2005); Director, European Corrugated Packaging Operations, International Paper (2000-2002); General Manager, Pressure Sensitive Products, International Paper (1998-2000); Mill Manager, Thilmany Mill, Wisconsin, International Paper (1994-1998); Engineering Manager, Production Manager, International Paper (1991-1993); Engineer, Pineville Mill, Louisiana, International Paper (1984) **CR:** Member, Board of Directors, The Kroger Company; Member, Board of Directors, American Forest & Paper Association; Member, Board of Directors, Business Roundtable; Member, International Advisory Board, Moscow School of Management; Chairman, U.S.–Russia Business Council; Member, Board of Directors, Memphis Tomorrow; Member, Board of Governors, New Memphis Institute **CIV:** Member, Advisory Board, Wang Center for International Business Education; Trustee, New Mexico Institute; Board of Directors, RISE **MEM:** The Business Council; Business Roundtable

SUWANAKUL, SONTACHAI, T: Economist, Educator **I:** Education/Educational Services **DOB:** 07/18/1950 **PB:** Songkhla **SC:** Thailand **ED:** Doctor of Philosophy in Economics, University of Arkansas (1986); Master of Arts in Economics, Middle Tennessee State University (1974); Bachelor of Arts in Business Administration, Chiengmai University, Thailand (1971) **CT:** The U.S. Business System, University of Dallas, Irving, TX **C:** Associate Professor, Alabama State University, Montgomery, AL (1994-Present); Professor of Economics, Alabama State University (2004); Assistant Professor of Economics, Alabama State University, Montgomery, AL (1989-1993); Visiting Assistant Professor of Economics, Mississippi State University, Starkville, MS (1987) **CW:** Contributor, Articles to Professional Journals, Including the American Journal of Agricultural Economics, Regional Science and Urban Economics, the Journal of Original Science, Public Finance Quarterly and More **AW:** Faculty Leadership Award in Research and Publications, College Of Business Administration, Alabama State University (2004, 2005); Promoted to Personal Growth Involvement Level II, Optimist Club (1997);

List in Directory Research Scholar, Harvard University (1995) **MEM:** Chapter Advisor, Gamma Epsilon (1996-Present); Advisor, Delta Mu Delta (1995-Present); Community Service Committee, Optimist Club (1993-Present); American Economic Association; Southwestern Economics Society **MH:** Albert Nelson Marquis Lifetime Achievement Award; Marquis Who's Who Top Professional **AV:** Camera collector; Reading **RE:** Buddhist

SVOBODA, JANICE J., RN, BSN, HNB-BC, T: Nurse **I:** Medicine & Health Care **DOB:** 06/13/1933 **SC:** WI/USA **MS:** Widowed **SPN:** Glenn R. Svoboda (07/20/1957, Deceased 2015) **CH:** Melora; Kevin; Craig **ED:** Coursework, Alverno College, Milwaukee, WI (1991-1992); BS in Health Education, University of Wisconsin-Milwaukee, Cum Laude (1980); Coursework, University of Wisconsin-Madison (1955-1957); Diploma, Luther Hospital, Eau Claire, WI (1954) **CT:** Certified and Recertified, American Holistic Nurses Association (2010); Certified Head Nurse, Wisconsin (1955) **C:** Nutritional Counselor, Nutrisystem, Grafton, WI (1987-1990); Instructor, Seminar, Cardinal Stritch College (Now Cardinal Stritch University), Milwaukee, WI (1985-1987); Public Health Nurse, Ozaukee County, WI (1986); Assistant Instructor, Nursing, Milwaukee Area Technical College, (1979-1983); Public Health Nurse, Ozaukee County, WI (1979) **CR:** Nutrition and Herbal Therapy (1997-Present); Apple Orchard Conservation Restoration Program, Beechwood Orchard (1970-Present); Designed, Implemented, Alternative Health and Healing Seminar (1994-1997); Health Seminars, Alverno College, Milwaukee, WI (1991-1995); Coping with Stress Course (1985-1986); Assertiveness Training Course (1985); Instructor, Seminar, Milwaukee Area Technical College (1983-1990); Holistic Nurse Consultant, Private Practice **CIV:** Public Lecturer, Nutrition and Anti-Aging, Senior Centers, Churches; Volunteer, Pilgrim United Church; Active Member, YMCA; Past Board Member, YMCA; Member, Church **AW:** Listee, Cambridge Who's Who (2011-2012); Listee, Global Directory Who's Who (2011) **MEM:** American Holistic Nurses Association; Center for Science in the Public Interest; Port Washington Woman's Club **MH:** Albert Nelson Marquis Lifetime Achievement Award; Marquis Who's Who Top Professional **B/I:** Mrs. Svodoba has been health conscious all of her life. She additionally was always fascinated by what makes people angry. These two qualities encouraged her desire to ensure her knowledge of caregiving was passed to others. As a holistic nurse, Mrs. Svodoba was taught some practices that she didn't agree with. She thought certain practices could serve a more preventative role in illnesses, as well as being cheaper. **AV:** Reading; Cross-country skiing; Investing; Gardening

SWAGEL, PHILLIP, "PHIL" LEE, PHD, T: Director; Professor of Economics **I:** Education/Educational Services **CN:** Congressional Budget Office **DOB:** 06/08/1966 **PB:** New York **SC:** NY/USA **MS:** Married **SPN:** Judith K. (Hellerstein) Swagel **CH:** Gabriel; Ethan; Oren **ED:** PhD in Economics, Harvard University (1993); MS in Economics, Harvard University (1990); AB in Economics, Princeton University (1987) **C:** Director, Congressional Budget Office (2019-Present); Professor, International Economics, University of Maryland School of Public Policy, College Park, MD (2011-Present); Senior Fellow, Milken Institute, Washington, DC (2011-Present); Visiting Professor, Director, Center for Financial Institutions, Policy & Governance, Georgetown University McDonough School of Business (2009-2011); Assistant Secretary for Economic Policy, U.S. Department of the Treasury, Washington, DC (2006-2009); Resident Scholar, American Enterprise Institute (2005-2006); Chief of Staff, Council of Economic Advisers, Executive Office of the President (2002-2005); Senior Economist, Council of Economic Advisers, Executive Office of the President (2000-2001); Economist, International Monetary Fund (1996-2002); Economist, Federal Reserve Board (1992-1994) **CR:** Adjunct Professor, Economics, The University of Chicago Booth School of Business (2006, 2009, 2005-Present); Visiting Assistant Professor, Northwestern University (1994-1996); Visiting Scholar, American Enterprise Institute **PA:** Democrat **RE:** Jewish

SWAIM, JOHN, "FRANK" FRANKLIN, MD, ABFP, AAFP, T: Physician, Healthcare Executive **I:** Medicine & Health Care **CN:** Parke Clinic, PC **DOB:** 12/24/1935 **PB:** Bloomingdale **SC:** IN/USA **PT:** Max DeBaun Swaim; Edna Marie (Whitley) Swaim **MS:** Married **SPN:** Peggy Lou Sankey (05/30/1979); Joan Dooley (09/19/1957, Divorced 04/1979) **CH:** John Franklin; Parke Allen; Pamela Ann; Anne-Marie Swaim; Heather Norman **ED:** MD, Indiana University–Purdue University Indianapolis (IUPUI) (1963); BS, Indiana State University, Cum Laude (1959) **CT:** Diplomate, America Board of Family Practice (American Board of Family Medicine, Inc.) with Added Certificate in Geriatrics; Former Licensed Health Facility Administrator **C:** President, Parke County Health Officer (1999-Present); Medical Director, Parke Clinic, Rockville, IN (1969-Present); Medical Director, Newport Chemical Depot, IN (1968-2010); President, Vermillion Health Care Corp., Clinton, IN (1977-2003); President, Swaim Investment Corp. (2001); President, Swaim Farm Corporation (1998); Medical Director, Rockville Correctional Facility (1970-1998); President, Parke County Coroner (1980); President, Parke Investment Company, LLC, Rockville, IN (1972) **CR:** Medical Director, Lee Alan Bryant Healthcare Facility (1980-2010); With, Parke County Jail and Vermillion County Jail (1990-2000) **CIV:** Coroner, Parke County, IN (1972-1982) **MIL:** Captain, United States Air Force, Vietnam (1963-1967); Commanding Officer, 559th Medical Service Flight **CW:** Author, "One Year and Eternity" (1978); Contributor, Articles to Professional Journals **AW:** Inductee, Hall of Fame Rockville High School (2013); Doc Hollywood Award (2011); Weinbaum Award, Union Hospital, Union Health Foundation (2010); Decorated Bronze Star **MEM:** District President, Indiana Medical Association (Now Indiana State Medical Association (ISMA))American Academy of Family Physicians; American Medical Association; Indiana Medical Association (Now Indiana State Medical Association (ISMA)); Hoosiers Associates Club; Elks; Masons; Shriners International **MH:** Albert Nelson Marquis Lifetime Achievement Award **AS:** Dr. Swaim attributes his success to hard work, and the ability to care for oneself and create opportunities and help other people. **B/I:** Dr. Swaim came from a farming family; he farmed for two years and then decided he wanted to go to college. He always liked to read and he started to become a teacher but he got interested in medicine along the way, and then he decided to be a doctor. Dr. Swaim is the first doctor in his family. **AV:** Reading; Investing **PA:** Republican **RE:** Friends Church **THT:** Dr. Swaim's motto is, "Work conquers all," "Life is for living, not existing," and "The only meaning to life is what you put into it."

SWALWELL, ERIC MICHAEL JR., T: U.S. Representative from California **I:** Government Administration/Government Relations/Government Services **DOB:** 11/16/1980 **PB:** Sac City **SC:** IA/USA **PT:** Eric Nelson Swalwell; Vicky Joe Swalwell **MS:** Married **SPN:** Brittany (Watts) Swalwell (2016) **CH:** Nelson; Cricket **ED:** JD, University of Maryland School of Law (2006); BA in Government and Politics, University of Maryland (2003); Intern for Representative Ellen Tauscher, U.S. House of Representatives (2001-2002) **C:** Member, U.S. House of Representatives from California's 15th Congressional District, United States Congress, Washington, DC (2013-Present); Member, U.S. House Committee on Space, Science and Technology (2013-Present); Member, U.S. House Committee on Homeland Security (2013-Present); Candidate, Democratic Nominee, 2020 Presidential Election (2019); Deputy District Attorney, Alameda County, CA (2006-2012) **CR:** Member, Dublin City Council, CA (2010-2012); Member, Dublin Planning Commission, CA (2008-2010); Chairperson, Dublin Heritage and Cultural Arts Commission (2006) **CIV:** Director, San Ramon Soccer Club (San Ramon FC) (2006-2009) **MEM:** Alpha Sigma Phi Fraternity, Inc. **PA:** Democrat

SWAN, ANNA ROSE, RN, BSN, T: School Nurse **I:** Medicine & Health Care **DOB:** 03/14/1953 **PB:** Albuquerque **SC:** NM/USA **PT:** Robert Stutz; Lupita (Lujan) Swan **ED:** BSN, The University of New Mexico (1985) **C:** Nurse, Albuquerque Public Schools, NM (2016-Present); School Nurse, Albuquerque Public Schools (1997-Present); Clinical Instructor, Albuquerque Technical Vocational Institute (1993-1996); Research Nurse, Department of Psychiatry, The University of New Mexico, Albuquerque, NM; School Nurse, Los Lunas Public Schools, NM; Life's Masters, (Acquired by Staywell Company); Nurse, President, Hospital, Albuquerque, NM; Clinical Skills as a Psychiatric Nurse, Presbyterian Hospital; Nurse, Children's Psychiatric Hospital/Heights Psychiatric Hospital, Albuquerque, NM **CR:** Member, Nursing Practice Advisory Committee, New Mexico Board of Nursing, NM (1993-1995); Public Health Nurse, Albuquerque, NM; Director, Health Unit/Coordinator Program, Albuquerque Technical Vocational Institute **CIV:** Camp Nurse, Girl Scouts of the United States of America, Albuquerque, NM; Eucharistic Minister **AW:** Breakthrough to Nursing Award for Minority Students (1985) **MEM:** Committee/Council, Albuquerque Public Schools (2019-Present); National School Nurses Association (Now National Association of School Nurses); School Nurse Leadership **MH:** Albert Nelson Marquis Lifetime Achievement Award; Marquis Who's Who Top Professional **AS:** Ms. Swan attributes her success to God, prayer, and the kindness of many people along the way. **B/I:** Ms. Swan saw it as a stepping stone to becoming an attorney, which she thought was a way she could help the most people. **AV:** Travel **PA:** Republican **RE:** Roman Catholic

SWAN, ROBERT HOLMES, T: Chief Executive Officer **I:** Technology **CN:** Intel Corporation **PB:** Syracuse **SC:** NY/USA **MS:** Married **CH:** Two Children **ED:** MBA, Binghamton University, State University of New York (1985); BS in Business Administration, University at Buffalo (1983) **C:** Chief Executive Officer, Intel Corporation (2019-Present); Interim Chief Executive Officer, Chief Financial Officer, Intel Corporation (2018); Executive Vice President, Chief Financial Officer, Intel Corporation (2016-2018); Operating Partner, General Atlantic LLC (2015-2016); Senior Vice President of Finance, Chief Financial Officer, eBay Inc., San Jose, CA (2006-2015); Executive Vice President, Chief Financial Officer, Electronic Data Systems, Plano, Texas (2003-2006); Executive Vice President, Chief Financial Officer, TRW Inc. (2001-2002); Chief Financial Officer, Northrop Grumman Corporation (2001); Chief Executive Officer, Webvan Group, Inc. (2001); Chief Operating Officer, Webvan Group, Inc. (2000-2001); Vice President of Finance, Chief Financial Officer, Webvan Group, Inc. (1999-2001); Vice

President of Finance, Chief Financial Officer, GE Lighting, General Electric Company (1998-1999); Vice President of Finance, GE Healthcare, General Electric Company (1997-1998); Chief Financial Officer, GE Transportation, General Electric Company (1994-1997); Auditor, GE Corporate Audit Staff, General Electric Company (1988-1994) **CR:** Board of Directors, eBay Inc. (2011-Present); Board of Directors, Skype Global, Microsoft (2009-Present); Board of Directors, Applied Materials, Inc. (2009-Present)

SWANK, HILARY, T: Actress, Producer **I:** Media & Entertainment **DOB:** 07/30/1974 **PB:** Lincoln **SC:** NE/USA **PT:** Stephen Swank; Judy Swank **MS:** Married **SPN:** Philip Schneider (08/18/2018); Chad Lowe (09/28/1997, Divorced 2006) **ED:** Coursework, Santa Monica College **C:** Co-founder, 2S Films (2008) **CW:** Actress, "Fatale" (2020); Actress, "The Hunt" (2020); Voice Actress, "BoJack Horseman" (2019-2020); Actress, "I Am Mother" (2019); Actress, "Trust" (2018); Actress, "What They Had" (2018); Executive Producer, "What They Had" (2018); Actress, Executive Producer, "55 Steps" (2017); Actress, "Logan Lucky" (2017); Voice Actress, "Spark: A Space Tail" (2016); Actress, Music Video, Fergie Featuring YG, "L.A. Love (La La)" (2014); Actress, "You're Not You" (2014); Actress, "The Homesman" (2014); Executive Producer, "Fox's Cause for Paws: An All-Star Dog Spectacular" (2014); Actress, "Mary and Martha" (2013); Actress, "New Year's Eve" (2011); Actress, Executive Producer, "The Resident" (2011); Executive Producer, Video Documentary, "Choose You" (2011); Producer, "Something Borrowed" (2011); Actress, Executive Producer, "Conviction" (2010); Actress, Executive Producer, "Amelia" (2009); Actress, "Birds of America" (2008); Actress, "P.S. I Love You" (2007); Actress, "The Reaping" (2007); Actress, "Freedom Writers" (2007); Executive Producer, "Freedom Writers" (2007); Actress, "The Black Dahlia" (2006); Producer, "Beautiful Ohio" (2006); Actress, "Million Dollar Baby" (2004); Actress, "Red Dust" (2004); Actress, "Iron Jawed Angels" (2004); Actress, Executive Producer, "11:14" (2003); Actress, "The Core" (2003); Actress, "The Space Between" (2002); Actress, "Insomnia" (2002); Actress, "The Affair of the Necklace" (2001); Actress, "The Gift" (2000); Actress, "The Audition" (2000); Actress, "Heartwood" (2000); Actress, "Boys Don't Cry" (1999); Actress, "Heartwood" (1998); Actress, "Beverly Hills, 90210" (1997-1998); Actress, "Quiet Days in Hollywood" (1997); Actress, "Leaving L.A." (1997); Actress, "The Sleepwalker Killing" (1997); Actress, "Dying to Belong" (1997); Actress, "Kounterfeit" (1996); Actress, "Sometimes They Come Back... Again" (1996); Actress, "The Next Karate Kid" (1994); Actress, "Cries Unheard: The Donna Yaklich Story" (1994); Actress, "Camp Wilder" (1992-1993); Actress, "Camp Bicknell" (1992); Actress, "Buffy the Vampire Slayer" (1992); Actress, "Growing Pains" (1991, 1992); Actress, "Evening Shade" (1991); Actress, "Harry and the Hendersons" (1991); Actress, "ABC TGIF" (1989) **AW:** Leopard Club Award, Locarno Film Festival (2019); Bambi Award, Film - International (2015); Silver Medallion Award, Telluride Film Festival (2014); Francois Truffat Award, Giffoni Film Festival (2011); Best Actress, "Amelia," Hollywood Film Awards (2009); Named Best International Actress, "P.S. I Love You," Irish Film and Television Awards (2008); Recipient, Star, Hollywood Walk of Fame (2007); Emery Award, Hetrick-Martin Institute (2006); Named Best International Actress, "Million Dollar Baby," Jupiter Awards (2006); Named Best Foreign Actress, "Million Dollar Baby," Sant Jordi Awards (2006); Academy Award for Best Performance by an Actress in a Leading Role, "Million Dollar Baby," Academy of Motion Picture Arts and Sciences (2005); Golden Globe for Best Performance by an Actress in a Motion Picture - Drama, "Million Dollar Baby," Hollywood Foreign Press Association (2005); Named Best Lead Performance, "Million Dollar Baby," Central Ohio Film Critics Association (2005); Named One of the "100 Most Influential People," TIME (2005); Golden Satellite Award, "Million Dollar Baby," Satellite Awards (2005); Named Best Actress, "Million Dollar Baby," Boston Society of Film Critics Awards (2004); Academy Award for Best Actress in a Leading Role, "Boys Don't Cry," Academy of Motion Pictures Arts and Sciences (2000); Golden Globe for Best Performance by an Actress in a Motion Picture - Drama, "Boys Don't Cry," Hollywood Foreign Press Association (2000); Best Female Lead, "Boys Don't Cry," Film Independent Spirit Awards (2000); Best Actress, "Boys Don't Cry," Broadcast Film Critics Association Awards (2000); Best Actress, "Boys Don't Cry," Chicago Film Critics Association Awards (2000); Best Actress, "Boys Don't Cry," Boston Society of Film Critics Awards (1999); Best Actress, "Boys Don't Cry," Chicago International Film Festival (1999); Best Actress, "Boys Don't Cry," Los Angeles Film Critics Association Awards (1999); Breakthrough Performance - Female, "Boys Don't Cry," National Board of Review (1999)

SWANN, FREDERICK LEWIS, T: Organist, Choral Director, Teacher **I:** Education/Educational Services **DOB:** 07/30/1931 **PB:** Lewisburg **SC:** WV/USA **PT:** Theodore Magruder Swann; Mary Fields (Davis) Swann **MS:** Single **ED:** Honorary Doctor of Music, University of Redlands (2018); Master's in Sacred Music, Union Theological Seminary (1954); MusB, Northwestern University (1952) **CT:** First Honorary FAGO Certification, American Guild of Organists (2018); Honorary FRCCO Certification, Royal Canadian College of Organists (2015) **C:** Organ Artist-in-Residence, St. Margaret's Episcopal Church, Palm Desert, CA (2001-Present); Professor of Organ and University Organist, University of Redlands (2007-2018); Organist-in-Residence, First Congregational Church, Los Angeles, CA (1998-2001); Director of Music, Organist, Crystal Cathedral, Garden Grove, CA (1982-1998); Chairman, Organ Department, Manhattan School of Music, NYC (1972-1982); Director, Music, Organist, Riverside Church, New York, NY (1958-1982) **CR:** National President, American Guild of Organists (2002-2008); Consultant, Organ Design **MIL:** U.S. Army (1956-1958) **CW:** Organ Recitalist, Numerous Performances, United States, Canada, Europe, Australia, Asia; Contributor, Articles, Professional Journals; Publisher, Numerous Choral and Organ Works; Artist, CD Recordings, Gothic Records **AW:** Award for Promotion of French Organ Music, French National Academy of Arts and Science (1972); Merit Award, Northwestern University Alumni (1970); Recipient, Numerous Prestigious Awards; Award for the Promotion of American Choral and Organ Music, American Guild of Organists **MEM:** American Guild of Organists; Hymn Society of America; Phi Beta Kappa; Phi Kappa Lambda; St. Wilfrid Club **MH:** Albert Nelson Marquis Lifetime Achievement Award **AS:** Dr. Swann attributes his success to being able to take on high profile positions consistently from an early age that remained consistent throughout his entire career. **B/I:** Dr. Swann started studying piano when he was 6 with the organist at his local church. When he was 10, the organist at his church suddenly passed away, and Dr. Swann was asked to take over the position. He has been the organist for several churches ever since; he has been active for over 70 years. **AV:** Reading; Watching movies; Seeing friends **PA:** Democrat **RE:** Episcopalian **THT:** Dr. Swann feels he has been blessed by wonderful friends around the world. He is very grateful to have been in a position to bring joy and inspiration to thousands of people through his performances. He believes giving is more important than receiving.

SWARD, ROBERT STUART MA, RETIRED, T: American Poet, Author **I:** Writing and Editing **CN:** UC Santa Cruz **DOB:** 06/23/1933 **PB:** Chicago **SC:** IL/USA **PT:** Dr. Irving Michael Sward; Gertrude (Huebsch) Sward **MS:** Widower **SPN:** Gloria K. Alford (06/19/1989, Deceased 2017) **CH:** Cheryl; Barbara; Michael; Hannah; Nicholas **ED:** Postgraduate Studies, Bristol University, England (1960-1961); Postgraduate Studies, Middlebury College, Middlbury, VT (1956-1960); MA, University of Iowa (1958); BA, University of Illinois (1956) **C:** Writer-in-Residence, Extension Program, UC Santa Cruz (1988-Present); Writer-in-Residence, Cabrillo College, Aptos, CA (1988-Present); Volunteer, Poetry in the Jail Project, Santa Cruz, CA (2016-2018); Technical Writer, Santa Cruz Operation (SCO), Santa Cruz, CA (1987-1989); Radio Broadcaster, Canadian Broadcasting Corporation, Toronto, Ontario, Canada (1979-1984); Editor, Publisher, Soft Press, Victoria (1970-1979); Assistant Professor of English, Writer-in-Residence, University of Victoria (1969-1973); Writer-in-Residence, University of Iowa (1967-1968); Writer-in-Residence, Cornell University, Ithaca, NY (1962-1964); Instructor English, Connecticut College, New London, CT (1958-1959); Volunteer, Louden Nelson Senior Community Center; Instructor, Courses in Life History, Memoir, Autobiography" **CR:** Visiting Poet, Creative Writing Program UC Santa Cruz (1992-Present); Cultural Council, Santa Cruz, CA (1984-Present); Poet Laureate of Santa Cruz County (2016-2018); Writer, Ontario Arts Council, Toronto, Canada (1979-1984); Book Reviewer, Toronto Stars and Others; Consultant to Publications **CIV:** Editor, Adviser, Jazz Press, Poet Santa Cruz Pubs. (1985-1987); Teacher, Oak Bay Senior Citizens, Victoria, British Columbia (1973-1974) **MIL:** U.S. Navy (1951-1954) **CW:** Contributing Editor, Web Del Sol (1999-Present); Author, "Love Has Made Grief Absurd, Monologue in the Voice of a SF Bay Artist Struggling with Alzheimer's" (2019); Author, "Collected Poems" (1957-2014); Author, Autobiography, "CAAS" (1991); Newsletter Editor, Writers' Union of Canada (1983-1984); Author, Poems, "New and Selected" (1983); Author, "Uncle Dog and Other Poems" (1962); Author, "Four Incarnations: New and Selected Poems, 1957-1991"; Author, Contributor, Numerous Books and Publications; Contributing Editor, Internet Library eZine **AW:** Grantee, Djerassi Foundation (1990-Present); Poet Laureate of Santa Cruz County (2016-2018); Villa Montalvo Literary Arts Award (1989-1990); Grantee, Yaddo MacDowell Colony (1959-1982); D.H. Lawrence Fellow, University of New Mexico (1966-1967); Guggenheim Fellow (1964-1965); Fulbright Grantee (1961) **MEM:** League of Canadian Poets; Writers' Union of Canada; National Writers Union **MH:** Albert Nelson Marquis Lifetime Achievement Award **AS:** Mr. Sward attributes his success to listening, perseverance, and more than 60 years of discipline. **B/I:** Mr. Sward became involved in his profession because he couldn't do anything else. He just seems to have had this inborn urge to read, write, listen, and teach. He feels privileged and incredibly grateful to have been able to carry on in this way for nearly 70 years. **AV:** Yoga; Macintosh computers; Photography; Swimming; Book design **PA:** Democrat **RE:** Jewish, Buddhist **THT:** Mr. Sward said, "Now that you know what you know... you know, I know, we know, there's no going back, that there's no 'new normal,' indeed, there may not EVER have been a 'normal'... not an old normal, not a new normal... not any kind of normal at all. My longtime colleague and friend, Santa Cruz social scientist and artist, Coeleen Kiebert, goes a step further and asks, 'Why would we even want a new normal? What exactly was wrong with the 'old normal'? It's all an illusion. Now that we know what we know, there's no denying that we live in revolutionary times. The way things were... they never WERE the way we think they were. In any case, the only constant is change. Why do we long for a normal? What would normal mean? That chaos and uncertainty would give way to a certain degree of predictability and order? Where are we now? What we are in... right now... is it possible that revolution has become normal? And why at the same time do we long for 'normal'? What are we missing... why especially at these times, do we look for something outside ourselves to root (for) to (such as a party Democrat or Republican or making us great again) that will relieve us of our terrible lack of "rootedness" and worse yet, even worse yet, offer us an idea of a new normal to brandish and parade."

SWARTZ, JAMES D., PHD, T: Professor **I:** Education/Educational Services **CN:** Miami University **DOB:** 08/13/1944 **PB:** Akron **SC:** OH/USA **PT:** Oscar Tower Swartz; Laura Ann Swartz **MS:** Married **SPN:** Dorothy (09/08/1978) **ED:** Doctor of Philosophy in Instructional Design and Technology, Ohio State University (1989); Master of Arts in Instructional Design and Technology, Ohio State University (1982); Bachelor of Arts in Speech-Telecommunications, Kent State University (1967) **C:** Professor, Miami University (2005-Present); Professor, University of Arkansas (1991-2005); Sociology Instructor, Marion Technical College, Ohio (1982-1984); Director, Media Education Services, Marion Technical College, Ohio (1982-1984) **CR:** Adjunct Assistant Professor, Ohio State University, Columbus, OH (1984-1989) **MIL:** Lieutenant, U.S. Navy (1967-1984) **CW:** 50 Publications, Artificial Intelligence; 50 Journal Articles, Artificial Intelligence; 50 Presentations, Artificial Intelligence; Chaired, 13 Doctoral Dissertations **MEM:** President, Society for Philosophy of Higher Education (2009); Chair, Special Interest Group, Media Curriculum Culture, American Education Research Association (1999); Secretary, Treasurer, Society for Philosophy of Higher Education (1997-1998); American Film Institute; Association for Education Commissions and Technology; Phi Kappa Phi; Chair, Miami University IRB Committee; Chair School of Education Technology Committee; Distinguished Lecturers Committee; Computer Activities Council; University Faculty Senate; University Faculty Senate Executive Committee; Curriculum Program Committee, University Faculty Senate; Representative to Graduate Council, College of Education and Health Professions **MH:** Albert Nelson Marquis Lifetime Achievement Award; Marquis Who's Who Top Professional **B/I:** Mr. Swartz received an undergraduate degree in radio and television, after which he became interested in the instructional design of television at Pennsylvania State University. However, he was soon drafted into the military, after which he worked in the restaurant industry as a night manager. Following this period, he pursued his education once again and became involved in higher academia. **AV:** Photography; Kayaking; Travel

SWARTZ, STEVEN R., T: President, Chief Executive Officer **I:** Media & Entertainment **CN:** Hearst Communications, Inc. **ED:** Bachelor's Degree in American Government and Politics, Harvard College (1984) **C:** President, Chief Executive Officer, Hearst Communications, Inc. (2013-Present); President, Chief Operating Officer, Hearst Com-

munications, Inc. (2012-2013); Chief Operating Officer, Hearst Communications, Inc. (2011-2012); Senior Vice President, Hearst Communications, Inc. (2009-2011); President, Hearst Newspapers (2009-2011); Executive Vice President, Hearst Newspapers (2001-2008); Chief Executive Officer, Editor-in-Chief, Hearst Newspapers (1995-2000); President, Chief Executive Officer, Editor-in-Chief, Smartmoney Magazine (1995); Editor, Smartmoney Magazine (1991-1995); Page One Editor, Wall St. Journal, Philadelphia, PA (1989-1991); Reporter, Wall Street Journal, Philadelphia, PA (1984-1989) **CR:** Board of Directors, Hearst Communications, Inc. (2009-Present) **CIV:** Investment Committee, Whitney Museum of American Art; Chairman, Board of Directors, Lincoln Center Corporate Fund, Lincoln Center for the Performing Arts; Trustee, New York-Presbyterian Hospital; Chairman, Board of Directors, Associated Press; Vice Chairman, Partnership for New York City; Board of Directors, ESPN; Business Roundtable

SWARTZEL, DENNIS D. JR., T: Engineer **I:** Information Technology and Services **CN:** Lockheed Martin Corporation **DOB:** 01/28/1963 **PB:** Wilmington **SC:** DE **PT:** Dennis; Pat **MS:** Married **SPN:** Elaine **CH:** Michelle; Sarah; Angela **ED:** Coursework in Information Systems Management, The College of the Florida Keys, Key West, FL (2006); Coursework in Data Processing, The College of the Florida Keys, Key West, FL (2005) **C:** Supervisor, Lockheed Martin Corporation (2014-Present); Engineer, Field Engineer, Lockheed Martin Corporation (1991-Present); Specialist, Cryptologic Maintenance, U.S. Air Force (1981-1990) **MIL:** Staff Sergeant, U.S. Air Force **MEM:** VFW; Phi Theta Kappa **AS:** Mr. Swartzel attributes his success to the support of his parents. He is grateful for the childhood they provided for him. **B/I:** Mr. Swartzel became involved in his profession because of his military career. He enlisted at age 18 and began his basic training just two weeks after his high school graduation. **PA:** Republican **RE:** Christian

SWEET, JULIE, T: Chief Executive Officer **I:** Technology **CN:** Accenture **PB:** Tustin **SC:** CA/USA **MS:** Married **CH:** Two daughters **ED:** JD, Columbia Law School (1992); Bachelor's Degree in International Relations, Claremont McKenna College (1989); Coursework, Taipei Language Institute, Peking University **C:** Chief Executive Officer, Accenture (2019-Present); Chief Executive Officer for North America, Accenture, Arlington, VA (2015-Present); General Counsel, Chief Compliance Officer, Corporate Secretary, Accenture, Arlington, VA (2010-2015); Partner, Cravath, Swaine & Moore LLP, New York, NY and Hong Kong (1992-2010) **CIV:** Board Member, Catalyst and TechNet Executive Council (2019-Present); Participant, New Rules Summit, The New York Times **AW:** Top CEO for Diversity, Comparably (2019); Most Powerful Women, Fortune (2016-2019)

SWEIGER, JUDITH ANN, T: Elementary and Special Education Educator **I:** Education/Educational Services **DOB:** 08/05/1946 **PB:** St. Joseph **SC:** MO/USA **PT:** Wilbert Norton Boyer; Frances Geraldine (Crouse) Boyer **MS:** Married **SPN:** Raymond J. Sweiger (12/03/1966) **CH:** Shaun Howard; Renée Daun; Stephanie Ann **ED:** BS in Elementary Education, Missouri Western State College (1989) **CT:** Certified in Special Education; Certified in Special Reading; Certified in Early Childhood; Certified in Early Childhood Special Education **C:** Tutor, St. Joseph, MO (1994); Teacher, Head Start Lead, Maysville Head Start, Missouri (1994); Director, Special Education K-12, Osborn R-O School District, Missouri (1991-1993); Painter, Weatherby, MO (1984-1986); Substitute Teacher,

DeKalb and Davies County School Districts, Missouri (1966-1994); At-home Teacher, Piano and Organ, Weatherby, MO (1966-1970); Receptionist, Thompson-Brumm-Knepper Clinic, St. Joseph, MO (1965-1966) **CIV:** Committeewoman, Representative Party, Dallas Township (1992-Present); Committee Leader, 4-H Youth, Santa Rosa, MO (1988-Present); Project Leader, 4-H Youth, Santa Rosa, MO (1988-Present); Administrative Board of Directors, Church of God Seventh Day, St. Joseph, MO (1991-1993); Leader, Brownie Division, Girl Scouts of America, Maysville, MO (1979-1981) **AW:** Named to Farm Wife Hall of Fame, Missouri Farm Bureau of Women (1982) **MEM:** Council for Exceptional Children; Missouri State Teacher Association; Automobile Club; Kappa Delta Pi **MH:** Albert Nelson Marquis Lifetime Achievement Award **B/I:** Mrs. Sweiger was inspired to become a teacher by her grandparents, who were school teachers. She enjoys watching children learn. **AV:** Crafts; Crocheting; Painting; Walking; Reading; Teaching piano to her grandchildren and hosting yearly recitals **RE:** Church of God

SWIFT, CHRISTOPHER JOHN, T: Chief Executive Officer, Chairman **I:** Financial Services **CN:** The Hartford Financial Services Group, Inc. **MS:** Married **CH:** Four Children **ED:** BS in Accounting, Marquette University (1983) **C:** Chief Executive Officer, The Hartford Financial Services Group, Inc., Hartford, CT (2014-Present); Executive Vice President, Chief Financial Officer, The Hartford Financial Services Group, Inc., Hartford, CT (2010-2014); Vice Chairman, Chief Financial Officer, American Life Insurance Co. (ALICO), American International Group, Inc. (AIG) (2009-2010); Vice President, Chief Financial Officer, Life Insurance & Retirement Services, American International Group, Inc. (AIG) (2005-2009); Executive Vice President, Chief Financial Officer, Head of Annuity Operations, AIG American General Life Companies, American International Group, Inc. (AIG) (2003-2005); Partner, KPMG LLP, Chicago, IL (1999-2003); Executive Vice President, Conning Asset Management (Conning Holdings Limited), General American Life Insurance Company (1997-1999); Head, Global Insurance Industry Practice, KPMG LLP, Chicago, IL **CR:** Chairman, Board of Directors, The Hartford Financial Services Group, Inc., Hartford, CT (2014-Present); Chairman, Board, American Insurance Association; Director, Catalyst, Inc.; Director, Insurance Information Institute, Inc.; Member, Board of Directors, American Property Casualty Insurance Association **MEM:** Council on Foreign Relations; Financial Services Roundtable; Business Roundtable; The Business Council; Chief Executives for Corporate Purpose (CECP); International Insurance Society, Inc.; The Geneva Association; Committee to Encourage Corporate Philanthropy; Federal Advisory Committee on Insurance, U.S. Department of Treasury

SWIFT, JUDY JO, T: Banker **I:** Financial Services **DOB:** 10/02/1951 **SC:** IN/USA **PT:** Clarence E.; Betty Jo Shelton **MS:** Widow **SPN:** Carl Wayne Swift (02/05/1971) **CH:** Michael Edward; Angela Elena **ED:** Coursework, University of Indianapolis (1975-1978) **C:** Branch Manager, Loan Officer, Greenfield Banking Co. (1981-Present); Assistant Vice President, Business Development, Greenfield Banking Co. (1998-2017); Branch Manager, Greenfield Banking Co. (1976-1981); Teller, Greenfield Banking Co. (1970-1976); Bookkeeping Department, Greenfield Banking Co. (1969-1970) **CIV:** Board of Directors, Treasurer, American Heart Association (1999-Present); Chairperson, American in Bloom, City of Greenfield (2004, 2006); City of Greenfield Comprehensive Plan Committee (2005); Board of Directors, Greenfield Chamber of Commerce (2003);

Chairman, American Heart Association (2002); President, Board of Directors, Leadership Hancock County (1998-2001); Relay for Life Chairperson, American Cancer Society, Hancock County, IN (1996-1997); Board of Directors, Hancock County Senior Services (1992-1995); Walk America Chairperson, March of Dimes, Hancock County, IN (1990-1991); Hancock County Heart Walk; Board of Directors, Character Council, Hancock County, IN; City of Greenfield Downtown Master Plan Committee; Hancock Economic Development Council; Hancock Regional Hospital Foundation Board; Greenfield in Bloom; Greenfield Main Street Board; Riley Festival Board; Greenfield-Central School Foundation Board; Finance Committee Chair, St. Michael Church **AW:** Business Woman of the Year (2009); Sword of Hope Award, American Cancer Society (1997) **MEM:** Finance Women International; Independent Bankers Association; Board of Directors, Greenfield Chamber of Commerce **MH:** Albert Nelson Marquis Lifetime Achievement Award **B/I:** Ms. Swift became involved in her profession after participating in a work-study program in high school. During this time, she was hired by the South Greenfield Banking Company, which introduced her to the banking industry. She was later offered a full-time position, which she accepted. Naturally, her career progressed from there. **AV:** Sewing **PA:** Republican **RE:** Catholic

SWIFT, TAYLOR ALISON, T: Musician, Singer, Songwriter **I:** Media & Entertainment **DOB:** 12/13/1989 **PB:** Reading **SC:** PA/USA **PT:** Scott Kingsley Swift; Andrea Gardner (Finlay) Swift **MS:** Single **ED:** Diploma, Aaron Academy; Student, Hendersonville High School, Wyomissing Area Junior/Senior High School **CR:** Spokesmodel, Capital One (2019-Present); Spokesmodel, AT&T (2016); Launched, Fragrances, "Wonderstruck," "Wonderstruck Enchanted," "Taylor by Taylor Swift," "Incredible Things," Elizabeth Arden; Launched, Sundress Line, l.e.i.; Spokesmodel, Sony Electronics, American Greetings, Keds, Diet Coke, CoverGirl, Verizon Wireless' Mobile Music, Jakks Pacific, National Hockey League's (NHL) Nashville Predators, Sony Electronics, Papa John's Pizza, Walgreens, Target, Diet Coke, AirAsia, Qantas, Cornetto, Subway, Xfinity, DirecTV, Fujifilm **CIV:** Donor, Tennessee Equality Project, GLAAD (2019); Donor, Regent Park School of Music (2019); Donor, March for Our Lives, Rape, Abuse & Incest National Network (2018); Collaborator, Donor, Time's Up Initiative (2018); Donor, Houston Food Bank (2017); Donor, Dolly Parton Fire Fund (2016); Donor, New York City Department of Education (2015); Donor, V Foundation for Cancer Research, Children's Hospital of Philadelphia (2014); Donor, Chegg (2012); Donor, Country Music Hall of Fame and Museum, Nashville, TN (2012); Participant, Stand Up to Cancer Telethon (2012); Donor, St. Jude Children's Research Hospital, Tennessee (2011); Donor, WSMV Telethon (2010); Recording Artist, Sound Matters (2009); Donor, American Red Cross (2008); Promoter, Every Woman Counts (2008); Launched, Campaign, Tennessee Association of Chiefs of Police (2007); Do Something Awards and the Tennessee Disaster Services; Global Youth Service Day; Performer, Sydney's Sound Relief; Donor, Numerous Organizations **CW:** Musician, "Evermore" (2020); Musician, "Folklore" (2020); Appearance, Documentary, "Miss Americana" (2020); Actress, "Cats" (2019); Musician, "Lover" (2019); Musician, "Christmas Tree Farm" (2019); Contributing Musician, "Beautiful Ghosts" (2019); Featured Musician, "Babe" (2018); Appearance, "Taylor Swift: Reputation Stadium Tour" (2018); Musician, "Reputation" (2017); Featured Musician, "Big Star (Live)" (2017); Featured Musician, "I Don't Wanna Live Forever" (2016);

Songwriter, "Better Man" (2016); Songwriter, "This is What You Came for" (2016); Appearance, "The 1989 World Tour Live" (2015); Actress, "The Giver" (2014); Musician, "1989" (2014); Contributing Musician, "Sweeter Than Fiction" (2013); Featured Musician, "Highway Don't Care" (2013); Contributing Musician, "Ronan" (2012); Voice Actress, "The Lorax" (2012); Featured Musician, "Both of Us" (2012); Contributing Musician, "Eyes Open" (2012); Musician, "Red" (2012); Musician, "Speak Now World Tour - Live" (2011); Featured Musician, "Safe & Sound" (2011); Contributor, "Hope for Haiti Now" (2010); Contributing Musician, "Today Was a Fairytale" (2010); Musician, "Speak Now" (2010); Featured Musician, "Half of My Heart" (2010); Actress, "Valentine's Day" (2010); Appearance, "Jonas Brothers: The 3D Concert Experience" (2009); Appearance, "Hannah Montana: The Movie" (2009); Featured Musician, "Two is Better Than One" (2009); Songwriter, "You'll Always Find Your Way Back Home" (2009); Songwriter, "Best Days of Your Life" (2008); Musician, "Fearless" (2008); Featured Musician, "Change" (2008); Featured Musician, "Hold On" (2007); Featured Musician, "God Bless the Children" (2006); Musician, "Taylor Swift" (2006); Musician, Numerous EPs; Appearances, Several TV Programs and Commercials **AW:** GLAAD Media Award (2020); Global Recording Artist of 2019, IFPI Global Recording Artist of the Year (2020); Best Solo Act in the World, NME Awards (2020); Artist of the Decade, Artist of the Year, Favorite Pop/Rock Female Artist, Favorite Adult Contemporary Artist, Favorite Music Video, Favorite Pop/Rock Album, American Music Awards (2019); Best International Artist, ARIA Music Awards (2019); Woman of the Decade, Billboard Women in Music (2019); Pop Award, BMI London Awards (2019); Four Award-Winning Songs, Songwriter of the Year, BMI Pop Awards (2019); Tour of the Year, Best Music Video, Titanium Award, iHeartRadio Music Awards (2019); Best 3 Albums (Western), Album of the Year (Western), Japan Gold Disc Awards (2019); Best U.S. Act, Best Video, MTV Europe Music Awards (2019); Video of the Year, Video for Good, Best Visual Effects, MTV Video Music Awards (2019); Best Female Video – International, MTV Video Music Awards Japan (2019); Favorite Global Music Star, Nickelodeon Kids' Choice Awards (2019); Album of the Year, People's Choice Awards (2019); Icon Award, Teen Choice Awards (2019); Artist of the Year, Favorite Pop/Rock Female Artist, Favorite Pop/Rock Album, Tour of the Year, American Music Awards (2018); Top Female Artist, Top Selling Album, Top U.S. Tour, Billboard Music Awards (2018); Pop Award, BMI London Awards (2018); Award-Winning Song, BMI Pop Awards (2018); Female Artist of the Year, Titanium Award, iHeartRadio Music Awards (2018); Best 3 Albums (Western), Japan Gold Disc Awards (2018); Concert Tour of the Year, People's Choice Awards (2018); Best Live Artist, Q Awards (2018); Top 50 Songs, BMI Country Awards (2017); Award-Winning Song, BMI Pop Awards (2017); International Female Artist, BreakTudo Awards (2017); Song of the Year, Country Music Association Awards (2017); Highest Annual Earnings Ever For A Female Pop Star, Guinness World Records (2017); Best Collaboration, MTV Video Music Awards (2017); Collaboration of the Year, MTV Millennial Awards (2017); Named, Ten Songs I Wish I'd Written, Nashville Songwriters Association International (2017); Favorite Artist of the Year (Western), Top Female Artist (Western), V Chart Awards (2017); Most Entertaining Celebrity, BBC Radio 1 Teen Awards (2016); Top Touring Artist, Billboard Music Awards (2016); Taylor Swift Award, Songwriter of the Year, Four Award-Winning Songs, BMI Pop Awards (2016); Bronze Award for Best Commercials, Silver Award for Best Com-

mercials, Clio Awards (2016); Album of the Year, Best Pop Vocal Album, Best Music Video, Grammy Awards (2016); Female Artist of the Year, Best Tour, Most Meme-able Moment, Album of the Year, iHeartRadio Awards (2016); Favourite International Video, Myx Music Awards (2016); Best International Solo Artist, NME Awards (2016); Favorite Female Artist, Favorite Pop Artist, People's Choice Awards (2016); Song of the Year, Best Breakup Song, Most Talked About Artist, Radio Disney Music Awards (2016); Best Singer, Shorty Awards (2016); Top Female Artist (Western), V Chart Awards (2016); 50th Anniversary Milestone Award, Academy of Country Music Awards (2015); Favorite Adult Contemporary Artist, Favorite Pop/Rock Album, Song of the Year, American Music Awards (2015); International Artist of the Year, BBC Music Awards (2015); Top Artist, Top Female Artist, Top Billboard 200 Artist, Top Hot 100 Artist, Top Digital Songs Artist, Billboard Chart Achievement Award, Top Billboard 200 Album, Top Streaming Song (Video), Billboard Music Awards (2015); Songwriter of the Year, Three Award-Winning Songs, BMI Pop Awards (2015); International Female Solo Artist, Brit Awards (2015); Woman of the Year, Elle Style Awards (2015); Named, Maxim's Hot 100 (2015); Fragrance of the Year: Women's Popular, FiFi Awards (2015); Global Recording Artist of 2014, IFPI Global Recording Artist of the Year (2015); Artist of the Year, Song of the Year, Best Lyrics, iHeartRadio Music Awards (2015); Album of the Year (Western), Best 3 Albums (Western), Japan Gold Disc Awards (2015); Best Song, Best U.S. Act, MTV Europe Music Awards (2015); Best Female Video, Best Pop Video, Video of the Year, Best Collaboration, MTV Video Music Awards (2015); Best Cover Woodie, MTVU Woodie Awards (2015); Favourite International Video, Myx Music Awards (2015); Songwriter/Artist of the Year, Ten Songs I Wish I'd Written, Nashville Songwriters Association International (2015); International Female Artist of the Year, Video of the Year, NRJ Music Awards (2015); Favorite Song, Favorite Female Artist, Favorite Pop Artist, People's Choice Awards (2015); Outstanding Creative Achievement in Interactive Media - Original Interactive Program, Primetime Emmy Awards (2015); Best Song to Dance To, Radio Disney Music Awards (2015); Best Singer, Shorty Awards (2015); Choice Summer Music Star: Female, Choice Twit, Choice Break-Up Song, Choice Music Collaboration, Teen Choice Awards (2015); Best Female Artist, Video of the Year, Telehit Awards (2015); Best Music Video of the Year, Favorite Artist of the Year (Western), Top Female Artist (Western), V Chart Awards (2015); Named, 50 Artists to Watch, YouTube Music Awards (2015); Video of the Year, Academy of Country Music Awards (2014); Dick Clark Award for Excellence, American Music Awards (2014); Woman of the Year, Billboard Women in Music (2014); Two Top 50 Songs, BMI Country Awards (2014); Two Award-Winning Songs, BMI London and Pop Awards (2014); Top Selling International Album of the Year, Country Music Awards of Australia (2014); Numerous Other Awards

SWILDENS, KARIN JOHANNA, T: Sculptor **I:** Fine Art **DOB:** 06/22/1942 **PB:** Amsterdam **SC:** Netherlands **PT:** Petrus Bernardus Swildens; Ceclia Thecla Maria Vernimmen **MS:** Married **SPN:** Claude Maurice Gaignaire (06/28/1972); Gilles Rogers Bassett (03/25/1963, Divorced 1968) **CH:** Eric Gilles Basset; Laurent Patrice Basset; Gazelle Gaignaire **ED:** Coursework, Ecole Supérieure des Arts Décoratifs, Paris, France (1963); Coursework, Art School of Rabat, Morocco; Coursework, Lycée Français of Rabat, Morocco; Coursework, Lycée Français of Tangier, Morocco **C:** Designer of Metal Wall Sculptures,

Artisan House, Los Angeles, CA (1991-2001); Designer of Scarves for Hermes, Paris, France; Art Appreciation Teacher, Charter Unified School of Brentwood, Los Angeles, CA; Illustrator for Children Magazines; Gallery Artist of Sculptures, Los Angeles, South Hampton, Laguna Beach, Long Beach, Ojai, Tujunga, Venice, CA **CIV:** Volunteer Instructor, Brentwood Unified Science Magnet School (1979-1982); Clay Horse Demonstrations, American Ceramic Society **CW:** Artist, Group Exhibition, Beatrice Wood Art Center (2019); Artist, Group Exhibition, McGroarty Arts Center, California (2012, 2013, 2016, 2018); Artist, Solo Exhibition, Napa Gallery, California State University Channel Islands (2016); Artist, Solo Exhibition, Hamilton Gallery (2015); Artist, Solo Exhibition, Del Mano Gallery (2013); Artist, Group Exhibition, Tribe and Folk Art Gallery, Studio City, CA (2012); Artist, Solo Exhibition, Les Jolis Trésors Gallery (2012); Artist, Group Exhibition, Lee and Lee Gallery, Los Angeles, CA (2012); Artist, Group Exhibition, Del Mano Gallery (2011); Artist, Exhibition, Speak Easy Gallery, Los Angeles, CA; Artist, Exhibition, Brad Cooper Gallery, Tampa, FL; Artist, Exhibition, Tops, Malibu, CA; Artist, Exhibition, Hamilton Gallery, Santa Monica, CA; Artist, Exhibition, Creative Arts Center Gallery, Burbank, CA; Artist, Exhibition, World Erotic Art Museum, Miami Beach, FL; Artist, Exhibition, Musee Erotisme, Paris, France; Author and Illustrator, "Poutou et Pitchoun"; Artist, Group Exhibition, Joel Chen Gallery, Los Angeles, CA **AW:** Best of Show at Beatrice Wood Ceramic Art Show (2019); Daumier Sculpture Award (1993) **MEM:** American Ceramic Society; Los Angeles Accueil; America Ceramic Society of Southern California **MH:** Albert Nelson Marquis Lifetime Achievement Award **AS:** Ms. Swildens attributes her success to her propensity for following her passions wherever they lead. **B/I:** Ms. Swildens became involved in her profession due to the influence of her family, which was greatly enmeshed within the arts, especially on an international level. **AV:** Teaching French; Art admiration; Reading philosophy; Writing; Drawing **PA:** Democrat

SWINDELL, ARCHIE, T: Biomedical Research **I:** Research **DOB:** 09/26/1936 **PT:** Archie Calhoun Swindell; Louise Evelyn (Ellis) Swindell **MS:** Married **SPN:** Elizabeth Brown Stevens (07/20/2014); Dolores Dyer Holland (12/28/1962, Deceased 2007) **CH:** Randy Zidick; Matthew Earl **ED:** Coursework in Statistics, Yale University (1990-1992); PhD in Biochemistry, Cornell University (1968); Master's in Nutritional Science, Cornell University (1965); BS in Chemistry, Southern Methodist University (1958) **C:** Statistical Consultant (1995-Present); Representative, Town Meeting, Groton, CT (2008-2018); Board of Education, Groton, CT (1997-2008); Town Council, Groton, CT (1993-1997); Research Science Positions in Biochemistry, Pharmacology, Statistics, Pfizer, Inc., Groton, CT (1970-1995); Postdoctoral Fellow, National Institutes of Health, Duke University Medical Center, Durham, NC (1968-1970); Biomedical Research **CR:** Operator, Quantitative Services Evaluation Consultancy (2004-Present) **CIV:** Board of Directors, LEARN (2001-2007) **MIL:** United States Army (1958-1961) **CW:** Contributor, Articles, Professional Journals (1968-2008); Patentee, Several Anti-Atherosclerosis Agents **AW:** Jacqueline B. Nixon Citizen of Year, Groton, CT **MEM:** American Association for the Advancement of Science; American Statistical Association; American Heart Association; Sigma Xi; Connecticut Botanical Society; Mathematics Association of America **MH:** Albert Nelson Marquis Lifetime Achievement Award **B/I:** Dr. Swindell was inspired to pursue his career path by his high school chemistry teacher. He was also influenced by his grandfather, John Williams Swindell, who was a physician. **AV:** Practicing nature photography; Hiking; Researching botany; Playing the banjo; Painting **PA:** Independent **THT:** Dr. Swindell is in the process of beginning and publishing an autobiography.

SWINDELL, GARY, T: Owner **I:** Law and Legal Services **CN:** Swindell & Visalli, PLLC **PB:** Woodbury **SC:** NJ/USA **MS:** Married **CH:** Two Children **ED:** JD, Georgetown University Law Center, Washington, DC (1979); BA in Philosophy and Political Science, University of Delaware, Newark, DE, Magna Cum Laude, With Distinction (1976) **C:** Owner, Swindell & Visalli, PLLC (2003-Present); Partner, McGuireWoods, Charlotte, NC (1999-2003); Founding Partner, Fennebresque, Clark, Swindell & Hay, Charlotte, NC (1993-1999); Partner, Moore & Van Allen, Charlotte, NC (1988-1993); Associate, Moore & Van Allen, Charlotte, NC (1985-1988); Vice President, General Counsel, Equity Programs Investment Corporation, EPIC Mortgage Inc., Falls Church, VA (1981-1985); Assistant General Counsel, EPIC Acceptance Corporation, Falls Church, VA (1984-1985); Associate, Repetti, Deerin, Murphy & Evans, Washington, DC (1979-1981) **CR:** Lecturer, Northwest Center for Professional Education; Lecturer, North Carolina Bar Association; Lecturer, Mecklenburg County Bar Association; Lecturer, CLE International **CIV:** Past Chairman, Former Member, Board of Directors, Carolinas Freedom Foundation; Member, Inaugural Board of Advisors, Continental Tire Bowl (Now the Meineke Car Care Bowl); Charter Steering Committee Member, Charlotte Regional Sports Commission; Charter Steering Committee Member, Fight Night for Kids Foundation; Corporate Committee, North Carolina Blumenthal Performing Arts Center; Former Member, Board of Governors, The Tower Club, ClubCorp; Past Chairman, Advisory Committee, Charlotte Regional Sports Commission; Past Chairman, United Way Campaign, Professional Division **AW:** Listee, International Who's Who of Real Estate Lawyers (2011-Present); Listee, North Carolina Super Lawyers (2006-Present); Listee, Best Real Estate Lawyers in North Carolina, Legal Elite Edition of Business North Carolina (2005-Present); Listee, Best Lawyers in America (1995-Present) **MEM:** Mecklenburg County Bar Association (1986-Present); Arlington County Bar Association (1979-1985); Mortgage Loan Opinion Subcommittee, Real Estate Section, North Carolina Bar Association; Joint Ad-Hoc Committee, Corporation Section, Real Estate Section, North Carolina Bar Association; American Bar Association **BAR:** North Carolina (1986); Supreme Court of the United States (1982); District of Columbia (1979); Virginia (1979) **MH:** Marquis Who's Who Top Professional **AS:** Mr. Swindell attributes his success to hard work and being accommodating with his clients. **B/I:** Mr. Swindell was inspired to become a lawyer after watching the television show "Perry Mason" as a child. For as long as he can remember, he wanted to be a lawyer.

SWINK, LAURENCE NIM PHD, PHD, T: Technical Consultant **I:** Consulting **DOB:** 10/24/1934 **PB:** Enid **SC:** OK/USA **PT:** Lyle Nim; Zelia Alice (Murphy) Swink Nim **MS:** Married **SPN:** Mary Ellen Beach (10/2017); Barbara Jean Trumbull, (09/1960, Divorced 1978) **CH:** Steven Marshall (Deceased, 2007) **ED:** PhD in Chemistry, Brown University (1969); MSc, Iowa State University (1959); BA in Chemistry, Witchita State University (1957) **C:** President, AZ/Tec Consulting, Enid, OK (1999-Present); President, AZ/Tec Consulting, Tempe, AZ (1989-1999); Senior Technical Consultant, Quari Electronics, Chandler, AZ (1987-1989); Senior Project Manager, Siemens Transmission Systems, Tempe, AZ (1986-1987); Technical Director, Multi-Plate Co., Inc., Dallas, TX (1982-1986); Advanced Systems Manager, Xerox Corp., Dallas, TX (1981-1982); Vice President, Research, Amorphous Materials, Inc., Garland, TX (1978-1980); Laboratory Manager, Texas Instruments, Inc., Dallas, TX (1966-1978) **CR:** United States Atomic Energy Commission; Air Craft Industry **MIL:** Captain, Nuclear Research Officer, U.S. Air Force (1960-1963) **CW:** Contributor, Articles, Professional Journals; Patentee, Numerous Patents **MEM:** American Crystallographic Association; Central Christian Church, Enid, OK **MH:** Albert Nelson Marquis Lifetime Achievement Award; Marquis Who's Who Top Professional **B/I:** Dr. Swink became involved in his profession because a lot of people needed consulting to update their quality system for the ISO9000. He always liked chemistry in high school along with the technical side of it, which inspired him to pursue the field. **AV:** Golfing **PA:** Independent **RE:** Christian, Disciples of Christ

SWINTON, TILDA, T: Actress **I:** Media & Entertainment **DOB:** 11/05/1960 **PB:** London **SC:** England **PT:** Sir John Swinton; Judith (Killen) Balfour Swinton **MS:** Partnered **SPN:** Sandro Kopp (2004-Present); John Byrne (1989, Separated 2003) **CH:** Honor Swinton Byrne; Xavier Swinton Byrne **ED:** Bachelor's Degree in Social and Political Sciences, University of Cambridge (1983) **C:** Founder, Ballerina Ballroom Cinema of Dreams (2008); Leader, Screen Academy Scotland, Edinburgh, Scotland (2006); Actress, Producer, Director, Film and Television **CR:** Member, Jury, 18th Moscow International Film Festival (1993); Member, Jury, 38th Berlin International Film Festival (1988) **CW:** Voice Actress, "Pinocchio" (2021); Actress, "The Human Voice" (2020); Actress, "Three Thousand Years of Longing" (2020); Actress, "Memoria" (2020); Actress, "The Souvenir: Part II" (2020); Actress, "The French Dispatch" (2020); Narrator, "Story and the Writer" (2020); Narrator, "Last and First Men" (2020); Executive Producer, "Memoria" (2020); Actress, "The Personal History of David Copperfield" (2019); Voice Actress, "Uncut Gems" (2019); Actress, "The Dead Don't Die" (2019); Actress, "What We Do in the Shadows" (2019); Actress, "Avengers: Endgame" (2019); Actress, "The Souvenir" (2019); Actress, "Suspiria" (2018); Voice Actress, "Isle of Dogs" (2018); Executive Producer, Documentary, "Women Make Film: A New Road Movie Through Cinema" (2018); Actress, "War Machine" (2017); Actress, "Okja" (2017); Co-Producer, "Okja" (2017); Actress, "Doctor Strange" (2016); Voice Actress, Documentary, "Letters from Baghdad" (2016); Executive Producer, Documentary, "Letters from Baghdad" (2016); Actress, "Hail, Caesar!" (2016); Executive Producer, Documentary, "The Seasons In Quincy: Four Portraits of John Berger" (2016); Director, Segment, Documentary, "The Seasons In Quincy: Four Portraits of John Berger" (2016); Actress, "A Bigger Splash" (2015); Actress, "Trainwreck" (2015); Actress, "The Grand Budapest Hotel" (2014); Narrator, "Death for a Unicorn" (2013); Actress, "The Zero Theorem" (2013); Actress, "Snowpiercer" (2013); Actress, "Only Lovers Left Alive" (2013); Actress, Music Video, "The Stars (Are Out Tonight," David Bowie (2013); Executive Producer, Documentary, "Ways of Listening" (2013); Actress, "Getting On" (2012); Actress, "Moonrise Kingdom" (2012); Actress, "We Need to Talk About Kevin" (2011); Executive Producer, "We Need to Talk About Kevin" (2011); Actress, "The Chronicles of Narnia: The Voyage of the Dawn Treader" (2010); Actress, "I Am Love" (2009); Producer, "I Am Love" (2009); Actress, "The Limits of Control" (2009); Actress, "The Curious Case of Benjamin Button" (2008); Actress, "Burn After Reading"

(2009); Actress, "The Chronicles of Narnia: Prince Caspian" (2008); Actress, "Julia" (2008); Executive Producer, "Derek" (2008); Director, Documentary, "The New Ten Commandments" (2008); Actress, "Michael Clayton" (2007); Actress, "The Man from London" (2007); Voice Actress, "Faceless" (2007); Actress, "Sleepwalkers" (2007); Narrator, "Galápagos" (2006); Actress, "Stephanie Daley" (2006); Executive Producer, "Stephanie Daley" (2006); Actress, "The Chronicles of Narnia: The Lion, the Witch and the Wardrobe" (2005); Narrator, "The Somme" (2005); Actress, "Absent Presence" (2005); Actress, "Broken Flowers" (2005); Actress, "Constantine" (2005); Actress, "Thumbsucker" (2005); Co-Executive Producer, "Thumbsucker" (2005); Actress, "The Statement" (2003); Actress, "Young Adam" (2003); Model, "One Woman Show," Vicktor & Rolf (2003); Actress, "Adaptation" (2002); Actress, "Teknolust" (2002); Actress, "Vanilla Sky" (2001); Actress, "The Deep End" (2001); Actress, "Possible Worlds" (2000); Actress, "The Beach" (2000); Actress, "The Protagonists" (1999); Actress, "The War Zone" (1999); Actress, "Love is the Devil: Study for a Portrait of Francis Bacon" (1998); Actress, "Conceiving Ada" (1997); Actress, "Female Perversions" (1996); Actress, "Remembrance of Things Fast: True Stories Visual Lies" (1994); Narrator, "Blue" (1993); Actress, "Wittgenstein" (1993); Voice Actress, "Shakespeare: The Animated Tales" (1992); Actress, "Orlando" (1992); Actress, "Man to Man" (1992); Actress, "Screenplay" (1992); Actress, "Edward II" (1991); Actress, "The Party: Nature Morte" (1991); Actress, "Your Cheatin' Heart" (1990); Actress, "The Garden" (1990); Actress, "Play Me Something" (1989); Actress, "War Requiem" (1989); Actress, "Das andere Ende der Welt" (1988); Actress, "Degrees of Clindness" (1988); Actress, "L'ispirazione" (1988); Actress, "The Last of England" (1987); Actress, "Friendship's Death" (1987); Actress, "Aria" (1987); Actress, "Caprice" (1986); Actress, "Egomania - Island Without Hope" (1986); Actress, "Zastrozzi: A Romance" (1986); Actress, "Caravaggio" (1986) **AW:** BFI Fellowship, British Film Institute (2020); Robert Altman Award, "Suspiria," Independent Spirit Awards (2018); Best Supporting Actress, "Suspiria," Fright Meter Awards (2018); Best Supporting Actress, "Doctor Strange," Saturn Awards (2017); Best Actress in a Supporting Role, "Snowpiercer," Alliance of Women Film Journalists (2014); Best Supporting Actress, "Snowpiercer," Boston Online Film Critics Association (2014); Best Actress, "Snowpiercer," Central Ohio Film Critics Association (2014); Named One of "The 100 Most Influential People in the World," Time (2012); Best Actress, "We Need to Talk About Kevin," European Film Awards (2011); Best Actress, "We Need to Talk About Kevin," Austin Film Critics Association (2011); Best Actress, "We Need to Talk About Kevin," Houston Film Critics Society (2011); Best Actress, "We Need to Talk About Kevin," National Board of Review (2011); Best Actress, "We Need to Talk About Kevin," San Francisco Film Critics Circle (2011); Best Supporting Actress, "The Curious Case of Benjamin Button," Saturn Awards (2008); Best Supporting Actress, "Michael Clayton," Academy Awards (2007); Best Actress in a Supporting Role, "Michael Clayton," British Academy of Film and Television Arts (2007); Best Supporting Actress, "Michael Clayton," Critics' Choice Movie Awards (2007); Best Supporting Actress, "Michael Clayton," Dallas-Fort Worth Film Critics Association (2007); Best Supporting Actress, "Michael Clayton," Detroit Film Critics Society (2007); Best Supporting Actress, "Michael Clayton," Kansas City Film Critics circle (2007); Best Supporting Actress, "Michael Clayton," Vancouver Film Critics Circle (2007); Best Actress in a Leading Role, "Young Adam," British Academy Scotland Awards (2003); Best Actress, "The Deep End," Boston Society of Film Critics (2001)

SYKES, RICHARD NESBITT, PHD, T: Department Chair (Retired) **I:** Education/Educational Services **DOB:** 01/11/1942 **PB:** Charlotte **SC:** NC/USA **PT:** Richard Nesbitt Sykes; Sarah Elizabeth Hovis Sykes **ED:** PhD in History, Greenwich University (2001); MA in Social Sciences, Reading Specialization, Appalachian State University (1965); BA in History and English, Southern Wesleyan University, Summa Cum Laude (1964) **CT:** Certified Educator, States of South Carolina and North Carolina **C:** Retired, Aiken Technical College, Aiken, SC (2006-Present); Department Chair, Aiken Technical College (2001-2005); History Professor, Aiken Technical College (1990-2005); Teacher, Reading Specialist, Lancaster County Schools (1979-1990); Reading Diagnostician, Chesterfield County Schools (1974-1979); Reading Specialist, Williamsburg County Schools (1973-1974); Secondary Reading Coordinator, Chester County Schools (1971-1973); History and Reading Instructor, Central Piedmont Community College, Charlotte, NC (1969-1970); Assistant Professor of History and Reading, Gardner-Webb University, Boiling Springs, NC (1967-1969); History and Political Science Instructor, Gordon State College, Barnesville, GA (1965-1967) **CIV:** Church Work; Sunday School Teacher, Reading Education **CW:** Dissertation, "Saint Anselms Life, Archbishopric, and Theology: Their Contribution to Church and Society" **AW:** Governor's Distinguished Professor Award, South Carolina Commission on Higher Education (2000); Medal, National Institute for Staff and Organizational Development (NISOD) (2000); Faculty Member of the Year, Aiken Technical College (1999); Educator of the Year, Aiken Technical College (1991-1992) **MEM:** South Carolina State Employees Association; South Carolina Technical Education Association; National Geographic Society; Smithsonian Institution **MH:** Albert Nelson Marquis Lifetime Achievement Award **AV:** Reading; Walking; Fishing **RE:** Christian

SYROPOULOS, MIKE, T: School System Supervisor (Retired) **I:** Education/Educational Services **CN:** Syropoulos Educational Consultants, Inc. **DOB:** 01/18/1934 **PB:** Kato Hora **SC:** Navpactos/Greece **PT:** Polykarpos Dimitri Syropoulos; Constantoula P. (Konstantinopoulos) Syropoulos **MS:** Widowed **SPN:** Sandra Francis Flick (01/03/1942, Deceased 2019) **CH:** Pericles; Connie; Tina **ED:** EdD, Wayne State University (1971); MEd, Wayne State University (1965); BS, Wayne State University (1960) **CT:** Certified Secondary Teacher, State of Michigan **C:** President, Research and Evaluation Specialists Inc., (Syropoulos Educational Company), Clinton Township, MI (1997-Present); Retired School Systems Supervisor (2008); Academic Achievement Consultant, Wayne RESA Instructional School District (2004-2008); Program Associate, Detroit Public Schools Community District (1976-1997); Assistant Director, Wayne County Intermediate District, MI (1974-1976); Research Assistant, Detroit Public Schools Community District (1969-1974); Supervisor, Detroit Public Schools Community District (1967-1969); Department Head, Detroit Public Schools Community District (1966-1967); Teacher, Detroit Public Schools Community District (1960-1966) **CR:** School Improvement Plans Consultant, Michigan Department of Education (2008-2017); Principal Coach, Michigan Department of Education (2006-2008); Academic Achievement Consultant, WCRESA (Now Wayne RESA) (2004-2008); Charter Schools Consultant, Central Michigan University (1997-2005); Part-time Instructor, Wayne State University (1967-1974) **CIV:** External Vice President, Hellenic Society Paedeia of Michigan (2001-2008); Board of Directors, University of Michigan Modern Greek Studies (2000-2008); Chairman, AHEPA Education Foundation, American Hellenic Educational Progressive Association (2002-2007); Appointed Chairman, Hellenic Cultural Commission, Hellenic Communication Service, LLC (2003-2005); Board of Visitors, Wayne State University College of Liberal Arts and Sciences (2003-2005); President, St. John The Baptist Greek Orthodox Church, Sterling Heights, MI (1988); Vice President, St. John The Baptist Greek Orthodox Church, Sterling Heights, MI (1987) **MIL:** With, United States Army (1956-1958) **CW:** Contributor, Articles to Educational Periodicals, Over 25 Years **AW:** Hellenic Heritage Award, from Greek Community, MI (2015); Life Achievement Award, State and Federal Projects Specialists, State of Michigan (2015); Six National/International Awards, American Educational Research Association, Over 15 Years **MEM:** Board of Directors, National Education Foundation;Chairman, National Education Foundation (2003-Present); Association for Supervision and Curriculum Development (ASCD) (1974-Present); Supreme Governor, American Hellenic Educational Progressive Association (1998-2000); Board of Directors, Michigan Association Supervision Curriculum (1994-1998); Governor, American Hellenic Educational Progressive Association (1997); Lieutenant Governor, American Hellenic Educational Progressive Association (1996); Secretary, American Hellenic Educational Progressive Association (1995); Treasurer, American Hellenic Educational Progressive Association (1994); Athletic Director, American Hellenic Educational Progressive Association (1992); National Education Foundation; Michigan Education Research Association; Michigan Association Supervision Curriculum **MH:** Albert Nelson Marquis Lifetime Achievement Award **AS:** Dr. Syropoulos was 6 years old when WWII began. Going through four years of WWII and followed by five years of civil war, he saw everything: war, death, poverty, hunger, and destruction. He prayed to God to help him live through that misery and do everything he could to make a better life for himself and his family. He attributes his success to hard work and determination. Dr. Syropoulos made up his mind that nothing was going to stop him from fulfilling his dream. **B/I:** Dr. Syropoulos came here on his own as a displaced person at the age of 17 years old. He was displaced two years from his village, which was taken over by the communists. When he came to the US, he went to Dallas, Texas, where he was sponsored by his uncle. He worked 84-hours a week for 21 dollars. He wanted to go to school to learn the English language so he went to Detroit. He worked six days a week for nine hours a day instead of 12 hours, and he went to night school. He was 18 years old in the first grade and he asked a teacher if there was any way he could speed things up. His teacher told him to go to the eighth grade and register, and if he passed language arts and math, then he would be given a certificate to go unto the ninth grade. So that's what he did and graduated. He got a job at the factory in the midnight shift; he had to go to day school and did ninth grade in summer school, followed by high school. He continued working and got a scholarship to Wayne State university and found out that if he went to the service, he could get the GI Bill so that was what he did. When he went in, it was right after the Korean war and they terminated the GI bill, which was a disappointment to him. He went to speak to his company commander and asked if there was any way he could help him. The commander told him that they could pay 75% of his tuition so he went to Tulane University and was stationed in New Orleans. He started in 1955 and graduated from Wayne State in 1960 and that was in between Tulane so he picked up a lot of work which helped him out. Now he had to decide about his future in what to major. He reflected back on his early years in his village in Greece. He didn't know anybody who had a high school education; his father had a third grade education, his mother and grandmother had none. He decided to go to teaching and help people to get an education and have a better life than he did growing up. Teaching is a noble occupation. Where would all of us would be without the teachers? **AV:** Golf; Reading **PA:** Democrat **RE:** Greek Orthodox **THT:** Dr. Syropoulos' motto is, "Know thyself first. Love your neighbor as you love yourself. Be a good person always and help your fellow human beings to the best of your ability!"

SZYMANSKI, RONALD J., ESQ., T: Lawyer (Retired) **I:** Law and Legal Services **DOB:** 06/23/1947 **PB:** Chicago **SC:** IL/USA **PT:** Joseph Szymanski; Josephine (Kosterna) Szymanski **MS:** Single **ED:** JD, John Marshall Law School, Chicago, IL (1976); BA in Criminal Justice, University of Illinois, Chicago, IL (1969) **C:** Retired Lawyer (2012); Assistant Public Defender, Cook County Public Defenders, Chicago, IL (1978-2012); Deputy Sheriff, Theft Court, Cook County Police Department, Chicago, IL **CR:** Attorney, Ronald Kitchen v. Jon Burge (2009); Specialist to Acting Sergeant, Recreation Room, United Service Organizations, South Korea **CIV:** Post-Military Service Work, Korea, Fort McCoy, Wisconsin; Precinct Captain, Democratic Party **MIL:** U.S. Army, Korea (1970-1972) **AW:** Guardian of Liberty (2008); Certificate of Appreciation, Cook County Public Defenders Office (2003); Distinguished Service Award, Cook County (1990) **MEM:** U.S. Department of Veteran Affairs **BAR:** U.S. Supreme Court (1999); Illinois (1977) **MH:** Albert Nelson Marquis Lifetime Achievement Award; Marquis Who's Who Top Professional **AS:** Mr. Szymanski attributes his success to hard work and his military experience. **B/I:** Mr. Szymanski became involved in his profession because he wanted to focus on law following his service in the U.S. Army. **AV:** Golfing **PA:** Democrat **RE:** Catholic

TABACKIN, LEWIS BARRY, T: Jazz Musician **I:** Media & Entertainment **DOB:** 03/26/1940 **PB:** Philadelphia **SC:** PA/USA **PT:** Isadore Tabackin; Sarah (Skolnick) Tabackin **MS:** Married **SPN:** Toshiko Akiyoshi (01/03/1969) **CH:** Michiru Mariano **ED:** Bachelor of Music, Philadelphia Conservatory of Music (1962) **C:** Member, Advisory Committee, Jazz Foundation of America (2002-Present); Tenor Saxophone and Flute Player (1956-Present); Principal Soloist, Toshiko Akiyoshi Jazz Orchestra featuring Lew Tabackin (1973-2003); Co-Founder, Toshiko Akiyoshi Jazz Orchestra featuring Lew Tabackin (1973) **CIV:** U.S. Army (1962-1965) **CW:** Musician, Album, "Soundscapes" (2016); Musician, Numerous Albums (1967-2016); Musician, Album, "Lew Tabackin Quartet with Randy Brecker" (1983); Musician, Album, "Tabackin" (1974); Musician, House Band, "The Tonight Show Starring Johnny Carson"; Musician, House Band, "The Dick Cavett Show"; Musician, Les and Larry Elgart Orchestra; Musician, Band, Cab Calloway; Musician, Band, Duke Pearson; Musician, Band, Thad Jones/Mel Lewis Jazz Orchestra; Musician, Band, Clark Terry; Musician, Shelly Manne Quartet **AW:** Silver Disk, "Four Seasons of Morita Village," Swing Journal (1996); Nominee, Grammy Award, Best Jazz Instrumental Performance - Big Band, "Desert Lady / Fantasy" (1994); Nominee, Grammy Award, Best Jazz Instrumental Performance - Big Band, "Carnegie Hall Concert" (1992); Nominee, Grammy Award, Best Jazz Instrumental Performance - Big Band, "March of the Tadpoles" (1985); Nominee, Grammy

Award, Best Jazz Instrumental Performance - Big Band, "Ten Gallon Shuffle" (1984); Named "Best Big Band," DownBeat Critic's Poll (1979, 1980, 1981, 1982, 1983); Named "Best Big Band," DownBeat Readers' Poll (1978, 1979, 1980, 1981, 1982); Nominee, Grammy Award, Best Jazz Instrumental Performance - Big Band, "Tanuki's Night Out" (1981); Nominee, Grammy Award, Best Jazz Instrumental Performance - Big Band, "Farewell" (1980); Nominee, Grammy Award, Best Jazz Instrumental Performance - Big Band, "Kogun" (1979); Silver Disk, Salted Gingko Nuts," Swing Journal (1979); Nominee, Grammy Award, Best Jazz Instrumental Performance - Big Band, "Insights" (1978); Jazz Album of the Year, "Insights," DownBeat Critic's Poll (1978); Nominee, Grammy Award, Best Jazz Instrumental Performance - Big Band, "Road Time" (1977); Nominee, Grammy Award, Best Jazz Instrumental Performance - Big Band, "Long Yellow Road" (1976); Gold Disk, "Insights," Swing Journal (1976); Silver Disk, "Kogun," Swing Journal (1974) **MEM:** American Federation of Musicians; National Association of Jazz Educators

TABATABAI, MAHMOOD, T: Physician (MD, PhD) **I:** Medicine & Health Care **CN:** Former Chairman, Anesthesiology Department, NPHS Hospitals, Philadelphia, PA **DOB:** 03/21/1938 **PB:** Kazeroon **SC:** Fars/Iran **PT:** Seyyed Enayatollah Tabatabai; Behjat (Sharieh) Tabatabai **CH:** Hossein-Ali; Golnar; Leila **ED:** PhD in Physiology, University of Pennsylvania, Philadelphia, PA (1969); MD, Shiraz University of Medical Sciences, Shiraz, Iran (1963) **CT:** Diplomate, American Board of Anesthesiologists **C:** Resident in Anesthesiology, Yale University, New Haven, CT (1979-1982); Intern, Hahnemann University Hospital, Philadelphia, PA (1978-1979); Chairman, Department of Physiology, Shiraz University of Medical Sciences, Shiraz, Iran (1969-1977); Former Chairman, Department of Anesthesiology, North Philadelphia Health System Hospitals, Philadelphia, PA; Former Acting Chairman, Department of Anesthesiology, VA Medical Center, Philadelphia, PA; Former Assistant, Associate, Professor, Anesthesiology, University of Pittsburgh, Pittsburgh, PA **CR:** Author, Co-Author, Over 70 Published Biomedical Research Articles, Review Articles, Book Chapters; Author, Co-Author, Over 80 Published Biomedical Abstracts **CW:** Editor-in-Chief, Iranian Journal of Medical Sciences (1972-1977) **AW:** Research Award, The Iranian Ministry of Science and Higher Education (1974, 1977); Recognition Award, The Iranian Ministry of Science and Higher Education (1963) **MEM:** American Association for the Advancement of Science; Society for Experimental Biology and Medicine; International Brain Research Organization; International Society for Heart Research; American Society of Anesthesiologists; International Anesthesia Research Society; Association of University Anesthesiologists; Educational Council, International Union of Physiological Societies **MH:** Marquis Who's Who Top Professional **AS:** Dr. Tabatabai attributes his success to his parents, teachers, family, colleagues, and hard work. **B/I:** Dr. Tabatabai's fascination with the medical field was something brought about through his own curiosity. Medicine was a calling for him. **AV:** Playing tennis; Horseback riding; Swimming; Watching movies; Attending concerts

TABBA, MOHAMMAD MYASSAR, P.E., PHD, T: Civil Engineer **I:** Engineering **CN:** TABBA Technologies International **DOB:** 01/25/1946 **PB:** Damascus **SC:** Syria **PT:** Baha-Eddin Tabba; Hayat (Arafe) Tabba **MS:** Married **SPN:** Noha Dakkak (07/24/1973) **CH:** Omar; Rima; Sheriff **ED:** PhD, McGill University (1979); Master of Engineering, McGill University (1972); BS in Engi-

neering, Damascus University (1968) **C:** Founder, President, TABBA Technologies International (2000-Present); Founder, Chief Executive Officer, Saudi Rehabilitation (1994-1999); Expert, Riyadh Development Authority (1989-1993); Director Projects, SHARACO (1985-1988); Chief Engineer, Al-Issa Consultant Engineers, Riyadh, Saudi Arabia (1983-1985); Geo-Technical Specialist, Hydro-Que, Montreal, Canada (1981-1983); Geo-Technical Project Engineer, Lavalin, Montreal, Canada (1978-1981); Project Engineer, Alcan Aluminum, Montreal, Canada (1973-1975); Structural Engineer, M. Backler & Associates, Montreal, Canada (1972-1973) **CR:** Auxiliary Professor, Department Civil Engineering, McGill University (1981-1983); Professor, Institute of Public Administration, Riyadh, Saudi Arabia **CW:** Contributor, Articles, Professional Journals **AW:** Canadian Grantee, National Research Council (1970-1972, 1975-1978) **MEM:** American Society of Civil Engineers; American Society for Testing and Materials; Chairman, Technical Activity Committee, American Concrete Institute; Quebec Order of Engineers **MH:** Albert Nelson Marquis Lifetime Achievement Award **B/I:** While living in Damascus, Syria, Dr. Tabba was inclined to pursue engineering. When he applied to university, he was admitted quickly due to his good grades. He then moved to Canada to pursue a master's degree in engineering structures. As he progressed, he decided to pursue a PhD in geotechnical engineering, which was different from structural engineering. After graduating, Dr. Tabba received a position as a consultant with Hydro-Que, the power company in Quebec, Canada. From there, his career progressed naturally.

TABOR, COREY R., T: Author, Illustrator **I:** Writing and Editing **MS:** Married **CH:** One son **CW:** Author, Illustrator, "Snail Crossing" (2020); Author, Illustrator, "Fox the Tiger" (2018); Author, Illustrator, "Fox is Late" (2018); Participant, Original Art Exhibit, Society of Illustrators (2017); Author, Illustrator, "Fox and the Bike Ride" (2017); Author, Illustrator, "Fox and the Jumping Contest" (2016); Illustrator, "A Dark, Dark Cave" (2016) **AW:** Theodor Seuss Geisel Award (2019); Cybils Easy Reader Award (2018); Grantee, Don Freeman Illustration Grant, Society of Children's Book Writers and Illustrators (2014) **MEM:** Society of Children's Book Writers and Illustrators

TAKANO, MARK ALLAN, T: U.S. Representative from California; Educator **I:** Government Administration/Government Relations/Government Services **DOB:** 12/10/1960 **PB:** Riverside **SC:** CA/USA **PT:** Williem Takano; Nancy Takano **ED:** MFA, University of California Riverside (2000); BA in Government, Harvard University (1983) **CT:** Certified Teacher, State of California **C:** Member, U.S. House of Representatives from California's 41st Congressional District, United States Congress, Washington, DC (2013-Present); Member, U.S. House Committee on Veterans' Affairs (2013-Present); Member, U.S. House Committee on Science, Space and Technology (2013-Present); Vice-Chair, House Democratic Conference (2017); Teacher, English and History, Rialto Unified School District, Riverside, CA (1988-2012); Committee on Ways and Means, United States Congress; Committee on Education and Labor, United States Congress **CR:** Board of Trustees, Riverside Community College (1990-2012) President, Riverside Community College (1992, 1997, 1998, 2005, 2006) **CIV:** Chairman, Greater Riverside Area Urban League (1989-1993); Executive Board, California Democratic Party (1988-1990) **AW:** Martin Luther King Visionaries Award **PA:** Democrat

TALBOT, JOE, T: Filmmaker **I:** Media & Entertainment **PB:** San Francisco **SC:** CA/USA **PT:** David Talbot **ED:** Coursework, Ruth Asawa San Francisco School of the Arts **C:** Co-Founder, Longshot Features (2019-Present) **CW:** Director, Producer, Writer, "The Last Black Man in San Francisco" (2019); Director, Producer, Writer, Composer, Editor, Short Film, "American Paradise" (2017)

TANNENBAUM, DEBORAH, T: Advocate **I:** Social Work **CN:** Advocates for Children and Adults **DOB:** 09/10/1964 **PB:** New York **SC:** NY/USA **PT:** Doris Choen Tannenbaum; Donald Martin Tannenbaum **MS:** Single **CH:** Aaron Horvits; Jaren Horvits **ED:** Bachelor of Arts, Adult and Continuing Education and Teaching, Framingham State College (1999); Bachelor of Science in Psychology, Boston University (1986) **CT:** Psychological Studies Certification, Recovery Learning Center (2016); Master Reiki, Shambala Training Center; Certified Advocate, Recovery Learning Center, New England; Group Facilitator Certification **C:** Life Transitions, Life Coach, Energy Therapist (2010-Present); Advocate, Advocate for Children and Adults (2009-Present); Speaker, Women's Special Needs (2012-2013); Assistant, Speaker, Special Needs Individuals (1997-2005) **CIV:** Volunteer, Various Breast Cancer Organizations; Supporter, Westborough Massachusetts Police Department; Volunteer, Various Veterans Associations; Fireman's Association; Humane Society; Rottie Nation; National Autism Association; Massachusetts Society for the Prevention of Cruelty to Animals; Head Start; Early Learning Childhood Education **AW:** Multiple Time Winner, Advocate of the Year **B/I:** Ms. Tannenbaum became involved in her profession due to her own experiences as someone living with multiple sclerosis. Throughout the course of her career, she worked closely with special needs children, particularly those with autism. Eventually, she became dedicated to serving as an advocate for those without a voice, including abused children and veterans. **AV:** Arts; Plays; Books; Traveling; Dining; Learning; Pottery

TAPPERT, TARA LEIGH, PHD, T: Art Historian, Archivist, Researcher **I:** Museums & Institutions **CN:** Tappert & Associates (D/B/A The Arts & The Military) **DOB:** 01/09/1950 **PB:** Detroit **SC:** MI/USA **PT:** Herman Henry Carl Tappert (Deceased); Carol Louise (Zannoth) (Deceased) Tappert **ED:** PhD in American Civilization, The George Washington University (1990); MLS in Library and Archives Administration, Wayne State University (1976); BA in History, Minor in Art History, Hope College (1973); Diploma (ARE) in Religious Education, Grace Bible College (1970) **C:** Curatorial Consultant and Lender, "Witness to War," Suzanne H. Arnold Art Gallery, Lebanon Valley College, Annville, PA (2018); Exhibit Facilitator, "Asclepius: Military, Medicine and Creative Forces," Virginia Tech Carilion School of Medicine, Roanoke, VA (2017); Guest Curator, "Healing Threads/Cathartic Clay: War Trauma and Art," Salina Art Center, Salina, KS (2014-2015); Exhibitions Coordinator, Combat Paper Project, Canton, NY and San Francisco, CA (2011-2015); Adjunct Faculty, Public History, University of Maryland, Baltimore County, Baltimore, MD (2013); Research Curator, "The History Factory," Washington, DC (2012-2013); Founder, Project Designer, Event Planner, "Arts, Military + Healing: A Collaborative Initiative," Seven Cultural and Medical Institutions, Washington, DC (2012); Research Associate, "The Ideal Home 1900-1920: The History of Twentieth Century American Craft," "Revivals! Diverse Traditions 1920-1945: The History of Twentieth Century American Craft," "Craft in the Machine Age 1920-1945: The History of Twentieth Century American Craft," and "Crafting Modernism: Mid-century American Art and Design," Museum of Arts and Design, New York, NY (1992-2011); Artist-in-Residence Trainer, "A History of the Arts and the Military," Smith Center for Healing and the Arts, Washington, DC (2010); Project Archivist, Nancy Patz Archives Collection, Goucher College, Baltimore, MD (2007-2008); Instructor, American Art History, Washington Semester Program, Lewis & Clark College, Portland, OR (2006); Archives and Arts Consultant, Alexander Gampietro Family, Washington, DC (2005-2006); Researcher, David R. Meschutt Family, Cornwall, NY (2005-2006); Adjunct Faculty, Master's Program in the History of Decorative Arts, Parsons School of Design and Smithsonian Associates, Washington, DC (1999-2004); Arts Consultant, Martha Tabor Arts Collection, Rising Phoenix Retreat Center, Flintstone, MD (2004); Arts Consultant, Glen Burnie Museum, Garden, and Collections, Winchester, VA (2002); Arts Consultant, Hueschen Arts Collection, Scheurer Hospital, Pigeon, MI (1999-2001); Library Consultant and Law Librarian, National Press Club, Sullivan & Cromwell, Morgan, Lewis & Bockius, District of Columbia Corporation Counsel, Washington, DC and the United States District Court of Detroit, MI (1977-1986, 1998); Docent Training, Exhibition, "American Arts from the Currier Gallery of Art" Taubman Museum of Arts, Roanoke VA (1997); Guest Curator, "Cecilia Beaux and the Arts of Portraiture," National Portrait Gallery, Smithsonian Institution, Washington, DC (1990-1995); Curatorial Researcher and Writer, Detroit Institute of Arts (1995); Guest Curator, "The Emmets: A Generation of Gifted Women," Borghi & Co., New York, NY (1990-1993); Archivist, Robert P. Fetter Family, Roanoke, VA (1991-1992); Curator of Collections and Exhibitions, Taubman Museum of Art, Roanoke, VA (1990); Curatorial Assistant, Department of Paintings and Sculpture, National Portrait Gallery, Smithsonian Institutions, Washington, DC (1987-1990); Archivist, Richard Watson Gilder Family, Tyringham, MA (1987); Fine Arts Consultant, Pennsylvania Academy Fine Arts, Philadelphia, PA (1987); Fine Arts Bibliographer, National Trust for the British Library, Cambridge, MA (1985-1986); Library Consultant, National Press Club Library Institute, Washington, DC (1984-1985) **CR:** Curator and Collections Manager, ART/Ifacts Collection, The Arts & The Military (2015-Present); Expert and Consultant to Private Collectors, Museums, Art Galleries, Auction Houses, and Cultural Institutions Interested in Artwork of American Portrait Painter Cecilia Beaux (1985-Present); Editor, Proofreader, Lecturer, Public Speaker (1985-Present); Researcher, Writer **CIV:** Advisory Board Member, Art Therapy Without Borders, Inc.; Former Board Member, Brookland Community Development Corporation; Former Advisor, DC Murals; Friends Meeting of Washington; Former House & Gardens Tour Co-Chair, Greater Brookland Garden Club; Former Board Member, Living Labyrinths for Peace, Inc.; Former Board Member, University Hall Condominium Association; Former President and Board Member, Women's Caucus for Art, DC Chapter, National Women's Caucus for Art; Member, Religious Society of Friends **CW:** Author, Exhibition Catalogue, "To Honor and to Serve: The Arts & The Military – Works of Art by United States Veterans and Civilians Interested in Issues of War" (2018); Author, Exhibition Catalogue, "War Front/Home Front: Through the Eyes of Our Military" (2018); Author, Exhibition Catalogue, "Moving Through Memories of Service and Conflict" (2017); Author, Exhibition Catalogue, "Healing Threads/Cathartic Clay: War, Trauma, and Arts" (2016); Author, Exhibition Catalogue, "Citizen. Soldier. Citizen." (2014); Author, Journal Articles, Guest Arts Editor, Journal of Military Experience (2013); Resource List Author, Exhibition Catalogue, "Crafting Modernism: Mid-Century American Art and Design" (2011); Author, E-book, "Out of the Background - Cecilia Beaux and the Art of Portraiture" (2009); Author, Journal Articles, Style 1900 (2008-2009); Author, Exhibition Catalogue, Catalogue Entry, "The Neville-Strass Collection - American Women Artists 1819-1947" (2003); Writer, Researcher, Miggs Museum of American Art (2002); Writer, Researcher, Williams College Museum of Art (2001); Author, Journal Article, Guest Co-editor, Special Issue on Cecilia Beaux, "Aimee Ernesta and Eliza Cecilia - Two Sisters, Two Choices," Pennsylvania Magazine of History and Biography (2000); Contributing Author, Exhibition Catalogue, "William Sartain and Cecilia Beaux: The Influences of a Teacher," "Pennsylvania Cultural Landscape: The Sartain Family Legacy 1830-1930" (2000); Catalogue Entries Author, "American Paintings in the Detroit Institute of Arts, Volume Two" (1997); Author, Exhibition Catalogues **AW:** Summer Institute Participant, National Endowment for the Humanities (2014, 2016); David B. Larson Fellow for Health and Spirituality, John W. Kluge Center, Library of Congress (2014-2015); Research Grantee, Center for Craft, Creativity & Design, University of North Carolina Asheville (2010); John Benjamins Award, Art Libraries Society of North America (1999); Beverly R. Robinson Doctoral Fellowship, Winterthur Museum, Garden & Library (1988); Smithsonian Pre-Doctoral Fellow, National Portrait Gallery (1986-1987); Award, Beta Chapter, Phi Delta Gamma, The George Washington University (1986-1987); Library of Congress Fellow, American Civilization Department, The George Washington University (1985-1986) **MEM:** Chapter Council, Women's Caucus for Art, Washington Chapter (2003-2005); President, Women's Caucus for Art (2002-2003); Local Arrangements, Mid-Atlantic Regional Archives Conference (1991); Student Representative, American Studies Association (1985-1987); American Alliance of Museums; American Studies Association; College Art Association of America, Inc.; Mid-Atlantic Regional Archives Conference; Women's Caucus for Art; Art Libraries Society of North America; National Coalition of Independent Scholars **MH:** Albert Nelson Marquis Lifetime Achievement Award **AS:** Dr. Tappert attributes her success to three teachers who had significant influence in her life and career. Seymour Kavesky was her high school history teacher and encouraged her interests in the arts and history. Barbara Carson was her decorative arts professor in graduate school and taught her how to do cultural work with private families and individuals. Her dissertation advisor, Dr. Lillian B. Miller, taught her how to write. She owes a tremendous debt of gratitude to all three of these gifted educators. **B/I:** Dr. Tappert's career developed in the spaces between three related professions: librarianship, archival work, and curation. Gifted with a natural ability to organize and create order, library and archival work was a good fit for those skills. She was also raised in a family with great aesthetic awareness and an interest in the arts was encouraged and supported by a maternal aunt, Dorothy Gay, who was an arts teacher at a private Quaker school in Washington, DC. She had a desire to work in cultural institutions that would allow her to do research and writing, and develop exhibitions. She has done this type of work within institutions and also independently. **AV:** Reading; Walking; Gardening **PA:** Democrat **RE:** Quaker

TAPSONY, VERONICA, T: Musician, Music Educator **I:** Media & Entertainment **CN:** Veronica Tapsony, B.M., M.M. **SC:** Hungary **PT:** Dr. John Pataky Lang; Ann Lang **MS:** Widow **ED:** MM, University of Missouri (1970); BM, University of Missouri (1968); Teacher's Diploma, Conservatory of Gyor **C:** Owner, Mozart and Beyond Piano Studio (2005-Present); Music Educator, Burlington Community College (1993-2003); Music Educator, Ocean County College, Tom's River, NJ (1987-2003); Artist in Residence, William Jewell College, Liberty, MO (1970-1979); Teacher, Conservatory of Music, University of Missouri, Kansas City, MO (1969-1977); Professor, Teacher's College, Eger, Hungary **CW:** Musician, Numerous International Performances; Featured, Salzburger Volksblatt; Featured, Salzburger Nachrichten **AW:** Franz Liszt Prize, Conservatory of Gyor, Hungary (1960) **MEM:** American Franz Liszt Society; Mu Phi Epsilon **MH:** Albert Nelson Marquis Lifetime Achievement Award **B/I:** Ms. Tapsony became involved in her profession because she had a love of music. When she was 16 years old, she decided to pursue music. **AV:** Horseback riding; Practicing gymnastics; Reading; Making art

TARANTINO, QUENTIN JEROME, T: Film Director, Screenwriter **I:** Media & Entertainment **DOB:** 03/27/1963 **PB:** Knoxville **SC:** TN/USA **PT:** Tony Tarantino; Connie (Pender) Tarantino; Curtis Zastoupil (Ex-Stepfather) **MS:** Married **SPN:** Daniella Pick (11/28/2018) **CH:** Leo **C:** Co-founder, A Band Apart Films (1991-2012); Director, Screenwriter, Producer, Actor, Films **CR:** Owner, New Beverly Cinema, Los Angeles, CA (2010-Present) **CW:** Director, Screenwriter, Producer, "Once Upon a Time... in Hollywood" (2019); Subject, Documentary, "QT8: the First Eight" (2019); Story Co-writer, "From Dusk Till Dawn: The Series" (2014-2016); Director, Screenwriter, Narrator, "The Hateful Eight" (2015); Director, Screenwriter, Actor, "Django Unchained" (2012); Director, Screenwriter, "Inglourious Basterds" (2009); Executive Producer, "Hell Ride" (2008); Executive Producer, "Hostel: Part II" (2007); Producer, "Grindhouse: Planet Terror" (2007); Director, Screenwriter, Producer, "Grindhouse: Death Proof" (2007); Executive Producer, Documentary, "Freedom's Fury" (2006); Executive Producer, "Daltry Calhoun" (2005); Executive Producer, "Hostel" (2005); Special Guest Director, "Sin City" (2005); Guest Director, Story Writer, "CSI: Crime Scene Investigation" (2005); Appearance, "The Muppets' Wizard of Oz" (2005); Director, Screenwriter, "Kill Bill: Volume 2" (2004); Executive Producer, "My Name is Modesty" (2004); Actor, "Alias" (2004, 2002); Director, Screenwriter, "Kill Bill: Volume 1" (2003); Executive Producer, "Hero" (2002); Executive Producer, TV Film, "From Dusk Till Dawn 3: The Hangman's Daughter" (1999); Executive Producer, TV Film, "From Dusk Till Dawn 2: Texas Blood Money" (1999); Executive Producer, "God Said Ha!" (1998); Director, Screenwriter, "Jackie Brown" (1997); Screenwriter, Executive Producer, "From Dusk till Dawn" (1996); Executive Producer, "Curdled" (1996); Voice Actor, Video Game, "Steven Spielberg's Director's Chair" (1996); Uncredited Co-screenwriter, "The Rock" (1996); Writer, "Crimson Tide" (1995); Guest Director, "ER" (1995); Actor, Executive Producer, "Four Rooms" (1995); Host, "Saturday Night Live" (1995); Director, Screenwriter, Actor, "Pulp Fiction" (1994); Story Writer, "Natural Born Killers" (1994); Executive Producer, "Killing Zoe" (1994); Uncredited Co-screenwriter, "It's Pat" (1994); Screenwriter, "True Romance" (1993); Director, Screenwriter, Actor, "Reservoir Dogs" (1992); Associate Producer, Uncredited Screenwriter, "Past Midnight" (1991); Director, Screenwriter, "My Best Friend's Birthday" (1987); Actor, Numerous Films and TV Series **AW:** Golden Globe for Best Screenplay - Motion Picture, "Once Upon a Time... in Hollywood," Hollywood Foreign Press Association (2020); Best Direction, "Once Upon a Time... in Hol-

lywood," AACTA International Awards (2020); Critics Choice Award, Best Original Screenplay, "Once Upon a Time... in Hollywood," Broadcast Film Critics Association Awards (2020); Best Picture, Best Original Screenplay, Critics' Choice Movie Awards (2019); Best Screenplay, "Once Upon a Time... in Hollywood," Boston Online Film Critics Association (2019); Best Screenplay, "Once Upon a Time... in Hollywood," Boston Society of Film Critics Awards (2019); Capri Movie of the Year Award, "The Hateful Eight," Capri, Hollywood (2015); Academy Award for Best Original Screenplay, "Django Unchained," Academy of Motion Picture Arts and Sciences (2013); Golden Globe for Best Screenplay - Motion Picture, "Django Unchained," Hollywood Foreign Press Association (2013); Best Original Screenplay, "Django Unchained," BAFTA Awards (2013); Best Screenplay, "Django Unchained," AACTA International Awards (2013); Saturn Award, Best Writing, "Django Unchained," Academy of Science Fiction, Fantasy and Horror Films (2013); Best Foreign Film, "Django Unchained," Association of Polish Filmmakers Critics Awards (2013); Lifetime Achievement Award, Rome Film Festival (2013); Prix Lumière, Festival Lumière (2013); Best Global Director for a Motion Picture, "Django Unchained," Huading Award (2013); Best Original Screenplay, "Django Unchained," Awards Circuit Community Awards (2012); Best Original Screenplay, "Django Unchained," Black Film Critics Circle Awards (2012); Screenwriter of the Year, "Django Unchained," Hollywood Film Awards (2012); Honorary Cesar, Academie des Arts et Techniques du Cinema (2011); Critics Choice Award, Best Original Screenplay, "Inglourious Basterds," Broadcast Film Critics Association Awards (2010); Best Original Screenplay, "Inglourious Basterds," Central Ohio Film Critics Association (2010); Order of the Merit of the Hungarian Republic (2010); Best Original Screenplay, "Inglourious Basterds," Awards Circuit Community Awards (2009); Capri Legend Award, Capri, Hollywood (2008); Filmmaker on the Edge Award, Provincetown International Film Festival (2008); Golden Eddie Filmmaker of the Year Award, American Cinema Editors (2007); Lifetime Achievement Award, Malacañan Palace (2007); Bridge Honor, Asian Excellence Awards (2006); Icon of the Decade Award, 10th Empire Awards (2005); Named, "100 Most Influential People in the World," TIME Magazine (2005); Career Achievement Award, Casting Society of America (2004); Academy Award for Best Original Screenplay, "Pulp Fiction," Academy of Motion Picture Arts and Sciences (1995); Best Original Screenplay, "Pulp Fiction," BAFTA Awards (1995); Best Foreign Film, "Pulp Fiction," Association of Polish Filmmakers Critics Awards (1995); Blue Ribbon Award, Best Foreign Language Film, "Pulp Fiction," Blue Ribbon Awards (1995); Palme d'Or, "Pulp Fiction," Cannes Film Festival (1994); Best Director, Best Screenplay, "Pulp Fiction," Film Independent Spirit Awards (1994); Best Director, "Pulp Fiction," Awards Circuit Community Awards (1994); Best Director, Best Screenplay, "Pulp Fiction," Boston Society of Film Critics Awards (1994); Named Best Original Screenplay, "Reservoir Dogs," Awards Circuit Community Awards (1992)

TARR, CHARLES EDWIN PHD, T: Physicist, Researcher **DOB:** 01/14/1940 **PB:** Johnstown **SC:** PA/USA **PT:** Charles Larned Tarr; Mary Katherine (Wright) Tarr **MS:** Married **SPN:** Gudrun Kiefer (11/18/1977); Bex Suzanne Harrell (09/04/1964, Divorced 1977) **ED:** Doctor of Philosophy, University of North Carolina, Chapel Hill, NC (1966); Bachelor of Science in Physics, University of North Carolina, Chapel Hill, NC (1961) **C:** Founder and President, PenBay Marine Instruments Inc. (2016-Present); Professor of Physics Emeritus,

Emeritus Dean of the Graduate School, University of Maine (1990-Present); Dean, Graduate School, University of Maine (1987-1997); Faculty Member, University of Maine (1968-1997); Acting Vice President of Research, University of Maine (1984-1987); Acting Dean, Graduate School, University of Maine (1981-1987); Associate Dean, College Arts and Sciences, University of Maine (1979-1981); Chairman, Physics Department, University of Maine (1977-1979); Associate Professor of Physics, University of Maine (1973-1978); Postdoctoral Fellow, University of Groningen, Netherlands (1975-1976); Research Associate, University of Pittsburgh (1966-1968); Research Associate, University of North Carolina, Chapel Hill, NC (1966) **CR:** Director, Maine Toxicology Institute (1992-Present); Member, Executive Committee, Council on Research Policy and Graduate Education, National Association of State Colleges and Land Grant Universities (1993-1997); Chairperson, Maine Toxicology Institute (1994); Co-chair, Maine Toxicology Institute (1993); Consultant in Field **CW:** Contributor, Articles to Professional Journals; Multiple Patents **AW:** Grantee, National Science Foundation (1972-1984); Grantee, National Aeronautics and Space Administration (1970-1972); Morehead Scholar, University of North Carolina (1957-1961) **MEM:** President, Northeastern Association of Graduate Schools (1990-1991); Sigma Xi; Institute of Electrical and Electronics Engineers; American Physical Society; Association of Computing Machinery **MH:** Albert Nelson Marquis Lifetime Achievement Award; Marquis Who's Who Top Professional **AV:** Sailing **RE:** Society of Friends

TATUM, CHANNING, T: Actor **I:** Media & Entertainment **DOB:** 04/26/1980 **PB:** Cullman **SC:** AL/USA **PT:** Glenn Tatum; Kay (Faust) Tatum **MS:** Divorced **SPN:** Jenna Dewan (07/11/2009, Divorced 2019) **CH:** Everly Tatum **ED:** Student, Glenville State College **C:** Founder, 33andOutProductions; Founder, Iron Horse Entertainment; Actor, Producer, Dancer **CW:** Actor, "Dog" (2021); Producer, "Dog" (2021); Director, "Dog" (2021); Screenwriter, "Dog" (2021); Voice Actor, "The Lego Movie 2: The Second Part" (2019); Producer, "Light Years" (2019); Voice Actor, "Smallfoot" (2018); Producer, "6 Balloons" (2018); Executive Producer, TV Series, "Step Up: High Water" (2018); Actor, "Kingsman: The Golden Circle" (2017); Actor, "Logan Lucky" (2017); Producer, "Logan Lucky" (2017); Actor, "Comrade Detective" (2017); Voice Actor, "The Lego Batman Movie" (2017); Voice Actor, "Comrade Detective" (2017); Executive Producer, "Comrade Detective" (2017); Actor, Music Video, "Beautiful Trauma," Pink (2017); Executive Producer, Documentary, "War Dog: A Solder's Best Friend" (2017); Actor, "Idiotsitter" (2016); Actor, "Hail, Caesar!" (2016); Himself, "Lip Sync Battle" (2016); Actor, "The Hateful Eight" (2015); Actor, "Magic Mike XXL" (2015); Producer, "Magic Mike XXL" (2015); Actor, "Jupiter Ascending" (2015); Voice Actor, Video Game, "Book of Life: Sugar Smash" (2014); Voice Actor, "The Book of Life" (2014); Actor, "22 Jump Street" (2014); Producer, "22 Jump Street" (2014); Actor, "Foxcatcher" (2014); Voice Actor, "Family Guy: The Quest for Stuff" (2014); Voice Actor, "The Lego Movie" (2014); Voice Actor, "The Simpsons" (2014); Actor, "White House Down" (2013); Executive Producer, "White House Down" (2013); Actor, "This Is the End" (2013); Actor, "G.I. Joe: Retaliation" (2013); Actor, "Side Effects" (2013); Actor, "Don Jon" (2013); Actor, "Magic Mike" (2012); Actor, "21 Jump Street" (2012); Executive Producer, "21 Jump Street" (2012); Actor, "The Vow" (2012); Host, "Saturday Night Live" (2012); Actor, "Haywire" (2011); Actor, "10 Years" (2011); Producer, "10 Years" (2011); Actor, "The Eagle" (2011); Actor, "The Son of No One" (2011); Actor, "The Dilemma"

(2011); Actor, "Morgan and Destiny's Eleventeenth Date: The Zeppelin Zoo" (2010); Actor, "Dear John" (2010); Executive Producer, Documentary, "Earth Made of Glass" (2010); Actor, "G.I. Joe: The Rise of Cobra" (2009); Actor, "Public Enemies" (2009); Actor, "Fighting" (2009); Actor, "Stop-Loss" (2008); Actor, "Step Up 2: The Streets" (2008); Actor, "The Trap" (2007); Actor, "Battle in Seattle" (2007); Actor, "Step Up" (2006); Actor, Music Video, "Get Up," Ciara Featuring Chamillionaire (2006); Dancer, Music Video, "Give It Up to Me," Sean Paul Featuring Keyshia Cole (2006); Actor, "She's the Man" (2006); Actor, "A Guide to Recognizing Your Saints" (2006); Actor, "Supercross" (2005); Actor, "Havoc" (2005); Actor, "War of the Worlds" (2005); Actor, "Coach Carter" (2005); Actor, Music Video, "Hope," Twista (2004); Actor, "CSI: Miami" (2004); Actor, Commercial, "Mountain Dew: Dew the Do" (2000); Actor, Commercial, "Pepsi: Ask for More" (2000); Dancer, Music Video, "She Bangs," Ricky Martin (2000) **AW:** Favorite Movie Actor, People's Choice Awards (2016); Special Distinction Award, "Foxcatcher," Independent Spirit Awards (2015); Best Comedic Performance, "22 Jump Street," MTV Movie & TV Awards (2015); Choice Summer Movie Star, "Magic Mike XXL," Teen Choice Awards (2015); Trailblazer Award, MTV Movie & TV Awards (2014); Choice Summer Movie Star, "22 Jump Street," Teen Choice Awards (2014); Best Actor, "Foxcatcher," International Cinephile Society Awards (2014); Best International Actor, "White House Down," Jupiter Awards (2014); Choice Movie Star, "White House Down," Teen Choice Awards (2013); Choice Movie Actor for Comedy, "21 Jump Street," Teen Choice Awards (2012); Named, "Sexiest Man Alive," People Magazine (2012); Best Actor, International Competition, "Dear John," CinEuphoria Awards (2011); Choice Movie Actor for Action Adventure, "G.I. Joe: The Rise of Cobra," Teen Choice Awards (2009); Choice Movie Actor for Drama, "Stop-Loss" (2008); Choice Movie for Dance, "Step Up," Teen Choice Awards (2007); Choice Breakout, "She's the Man," Teen Choice Awards (2006)

TAYLOR, DAVID S., T: Chief Executive Officer, President, Chairman of the Board **I:** Consumer Goods and Services **CN:** Procter & Gamble **DOB:** 04/20/1958 **PB:** Charlotte **SC:** NC/USA **MS:** Married **CH:** Three Sons **ED:** BS in Electrical Engineering, Duke University (1980) **C:** President, Chief Executive Officer, Chairman of the Board, Procter & Gamble (2015-Present); Group President, Global Beauty, Grooming, Health Care, Procter & Gamble (2015); Group President, Global Health and Grooming, Procter & Gamble (2013-2015); Group President, Global Home Care, Procter & Gamble (2005-2007); Vice President, North America Family Care, Procter & Gamble 2003-2005); Vice President, Western Europe Family Care, Procter & Gamble (2001-2003); General Manger, Vice President, Greater China Hair Care and Anti-Counterfeiting, Procter & Gamble (2001); General Manager, Greater China Hair Care and Tissues & Towels, Procter & Gamble (2000-2001); General Manager, Hong Kong and China Hair Care, Procter & Gamble (1998-2000); Marketing Director, Diaper Products, Procter & Gamble (1996-1998); Brand Manager, Pampers, Procter & Gamble (1993-1996); Assistant Brand Manager, Pampers, Procter & Gamble (1992-1993); Plant Manager, Procter & Gamble (1989-1992); Operations Manger, Procter & Gamble (1986-1989); Operations Manager, Procter & Gamble (1986-1989); Department Manager, Procter & Gamble (1983-1985); Production Manger, Procter & Gamble (1980-1983) **CR:** Member, Board of Directors, Delta Air Lines, Inc. (2019-Present); Member, Board of Directors, TRW Automotive, ZF Friedrichshafen AG (2010-2015); Board Member, HKANA Retail Association (1998-2001); Member,

Regional Development Commission (1989-1991); Board Member, U.S.-China Business Council; Board Member, Consumer Goods Forum; Board Member, Catalyst; Vice Chair, Greater China Quality Brand Protection Committee **CIV:** Chairman, Alliance to End Plastic Waste (2019-Present); Chair, 2020 Community Fundraising Campaign, United Way (2019-Present); Member, Board of Visitors, Duke University's Fuqua School of Business (2013-Present); Member, Board of Directors, Feeding America (2006-2013); Member, Board of Directors, Glad Joint Venture (2010); Chair, Board, Feeding America (2008-2010); Member, Board of Trustees, Cincinnati Scholarship Foundation (2007); Member, Greater Cincinnati Scholarship Association Advisory Committee (2007) **MEM:** Business Roundtable

TAYLOR, DOMINICA, "MINKA" STEPHENS, T: Teacher **I:** Education/Educational Services **CN:** Gold Hill Middle School **DOB:** 06/05/1965 **PB:** Richmond **SC:** VA/USA **PT:** Raphael Weller Stephens III; Anita Hening Stephens **MS:** Married **SPN:** Robert T. Taylor **CH:** Bayley E. Taylor; Kirsten A. Taylor; Zachary A. Taylor; Erik S. Taylor (Stepson) **ED:** Bachelor's Degree, Old Dominion University (1991) **CT:** Certified Middle School Teacher for Grades 6 through 8 **C:** Teacher, Gold Hill Middle School, Tega Cay, SC **CIV:** Sponsor, BBEL Academy, Uganda **AW:** Teacher of the Year (2009); Who's Who Award (1998) **MEM:** National Science Teaching Association **AS:** Ms. Taylor attributes her success to her love for children, and her mission to better herself in order to give the best to them. She also gives praise to a chemistry professor who improved her learning experience and, later, became a mentor to her. **B/I:** Initially, Ms. Taylor never thought about teaching, even though her parents and grandparents were all teachers; she preferred to study chiropractic medicine. However, a learning disability made the pursuit of science and medicine difficult in spite of her hard work, and an advisor suggested she pursue teaching science instead.

TAYLOR, HURL RICHMOND JR., T: Professor, Attorney, Military Officer (Retired) **I:** Law and Legal Services **CN:** Law Office of Hurl Taylor **DOB:** 09/20/1938 **PB:** Richmond **SC:** VA/USA **PT:** Hurl R. Taylor Sr.; Evelyn H. Taylor **MS:** Divorced **CH:** Shanda; Hurl; Michael; Rita; Terri **ED:** JD, Emory University, Atlanta, GA; PhD in Education, Georgia State University, Atlanta, GA; EdS in Education, Georgia State University, Atlanta, GA; MA in Education, Georgia State University, Atlanta, GA; BS, Hampton Institute, Hampton, VA; LLM, Emory University, Atlanta, GA; MRPL, Emory University, Atlanta, GA **CT:** Red Cross Instructor in Water Safety, First Aid, CPR, Adaptive Aquatics; Certification, FBI Citizens Academy **C:** Attorney, Private Practice; Professor, Numerous Institutions **CR:** Organizational Effectiveness Consultant **CIV:** Board of Advisors, Emory University Law School; Board of Advisors, Barton Clinic for Child Welfare; Board of Advisors, Ministry for the Incarcerated; Board of Advisors, Beulah Missionary Baptist Church **MIL:** Major, U.S. Army (1960-1980) **CW:** Speaker, Black History Month, Numerous Organizations; Host, Estate Planning Workshops for Military Veterans and Senior Citizens **AW:** Purple Heart, U.S. Army (1966) **MEM:** Disabled American Veterans; Military Order of the Purple Heart; Special Forces Association; Omega Psi Phi **BAR:** State of Georgia; U.S. Supreme Court; U.S. Court of Appeals for Veterans Claims; U.S. Court of Appeals for the Armed Forces **B/I:** Dr. Taylor became involved in his profession because he was enrolled in a partial scholarship studying biology at the Hampton Institute. He had planned

on becoming a high school science teacher. However, the U.S. Army offered him a small stipend for his last two years in college in exchange for a three-year commitment of active duty. Dr. Taylor accepted the offer in order to ease his financial challenges and entered into active duty in the U.S. Army exactly one week after his college graduation in 1960. Instead of only staying for the contracted three years, he spent a total of twenty years involved and retired in 1980. He taught biology for one year in his retirement and then embarked on a career change, that of becoming an attorney. He graduated from the Emory University School of Law in 1985, passed the bar in the same year, and has been practicing ever since. **AV:** Reading; Traveling; Watching sports in live attendance and on television **PA:** Democrat **RE:** Baptist

TAYLOR, LAWRENCE, "L.T." JULIUS, T: Sports Commentator; Former Professional Football Player **I:** Athletics **DOB:** 02/04/1959 **PB:** Williamsburg **SC:** VA/USA **PT:** Clarence Taylor; Iris Taylor **MS:** Married **SPN:** Lynette Taylor (2007); Maritza Cruz (2001, Divorced 2005); Deborah Belinda Taylor (1982, Divorced 1996) **CH:** T.J.; Tanisha; Paula; Lawrence Jr. **ED:** Coursework, University of North Carolina (1977-1980) **C:** Sports Commentator, "The Stadium Show," TNT (1994); Owner, All-Pro Products (1993); Linebacker, New York Giants, NFL (1981-1993) **CW:** Contestant, "Dancing with the Stars" (2009); Author, "Taylor" (2006); Featured, Cover, Sports Illustrated (2006); Co-author with Steve Serby, "LT: Over the Edge" (2004); Actor, "Mercy Streets" (2000); Actor, "Shaft" (2000); Appearance, "The Jamie Foxx Show" (2000); Actor, "Any Given Sunday" (1999); Actor, "The Waterboy" (1998); Actor, "Coach" (1995); Actor, "Married... with Children" (1994); Co-author with David Faulkner, "LT: Living on the Edge" (1987); Actor, Appearance, Television Shows, Video Games, Films **AW:** Named to Pro Football Hall of Fame, Canton, Ohio (1999); Named to NFL's 75th Anniversary All-time Team (1994); Winner, New York Giants, Super Bowl Championships (1986, 1990); Named National Football Conference Player of the Year, United Press International (1983, 1986); Named NFL MVP, The Associated Press (1986); Named NFL Defensive Player of the Year (1981, 1982, 1986); Humanitarian Award, National Black United Fund (1986); Bert Bell Award (1986); Named NFL All-Pro (1981-1990); Named to First-team All-Pro (1981-1990); Named to National Football Conference Pro Bowl Team (1981-1990); NFL Defensive Rookie of the Year Award (1981)

TAYLOR, NICHOLAS C., T: Lawyer **I:** Law and Legal Services **DOB:** 09/18/1937 **PB:** Washington **SC:** DC/USA **PT:** James Spear Taylor; Helen Livingston MacGregor Strauss **MS:** Married **SPN:** Elizabeth Carol Burke (07/25/2004); Catherine Blaffer (Divorced, 1999) **CH:** Nicholas Van Campen; Katherine; Christie **ED:** JD, Georgetown University (1963); AB, Harvard University (1959) **CT:** Texas (1971); New York (1966); Washington, DC (1964) **C:** Chairman, Chief Executive Officer, Mexco Energy Corp. (1983-Present); Attorney, Midland, TX (1993-Present); Chairman, State Securities Board of Texas (1995-2003); Shareholder, Stubbeman, McRae, Sealy, Laughlin & Browder, Inc., Midland, TX (1974-1993); Associate, Locke, Lord Bissell & Liddell LLP, Dallas, TX (1970-1974); Associate, Shearman & Sterling, New York, NY (1965-1970); Associate, Wilson, Woods & Villalon, Washington, DC (1964-1965) **CR:** Vice-Chairman, Texas Ethics Commission (2006-2010) **CIV:** Texas Judicial Council (1990-1995) **MIL:** Captain, U.S. Army Reserve (1959-1968); Infantry Officer, Tactics Instructor, Paratrooper, Airborne Special Forces **AW:** American Jurisprudence Prizes for Constitutional Law, Oil, and Gas Taxation, Southern Methodist University Law School **MEM:** Board of Directors, Permian Basin Petroleum Association (2002-2003, 2008-2020) **MH:** Albert Nelson Marquis Lifetime Achievement Award **B/I:** Mr. Taylor became involved in his profession because he was always interested in business, which was his primary focus in law school. He wanted to serve his community. He served in a volunteer capacity in Texas and it became his motivating factor. **RE:** Episcopalian

TAYLOR, NICHOLAS, "VAN TAYLOR" VAN CAMPEN, T: U.S. Representative from Texas; Real Estate Investment Banker **I:** Government Administration/Government Relations/Government Services **DOB:** 08/01/1972 **PB:** Dallas **SC:** TX/USA **MS:** Married **SPN:** Anne (Coolidge) Taylor (2004) **CH:** Lauren; Helen; Susie **ED:** BA in History, Harvard College (1995); MBA, Harvard Business School **C:** Member, U.S. House of Representatives from Texas' Third Congressional District, United States Congress, Washington, DC (2019-Present); Member, District Eight, Texas Senate (2015-2019); Real Estate Investment Banker, Churchill Capital Company (2002-2018); Member, District 66, Texas House of Representatives (2010-2015); Staff, Mckinsey & Company; Staff, Trammell Crow Company **MIL:** Major, United States Marine Corps Reserve; Captain, Paratrooper, Platoon Commander, Marine Corps' Company C, 4th Reconnaissance Battalion, United States Marine Corps **AW:** Decorated Navy Commendation Medal with V for Valor; Presidential Unit Citation; Combat Action Ribbon, U.S. Navy **PA:** Republican

TAYLOR, RAYMOND GEORGE, T: Professor Emeritus **I:** Education/Educational Services **CN:** North Carolina State University **DOB:** 03/02/1939 **PB:** New Brighton **SC:** PA/USA **PT:** Raymond George Taylor Sr.; Florence Lydia (Wood) Taylor **MS:** Married **SPN:** Christine Mary Morton (06/01/1959) **CH:** Raymond G. III; Leslie W. Taylor McCormick **ED:** PhD, Graduate Theological Foundation (1995); MBA, University of Southern Maine (1985); MPA, Pennsylvania State University (1976); EdD, University of Pennsylvania (1966); MS, University of Pennsylvania (1964); BS in Theology, Episcopal Theological School (1962); BS in Mathematics, Bucknell University (1959) **CT:** Superintendent of Schools, Several States **C:** Professor, North Carolina State University, Raleigh, NC (1986-Present); President, OR/Ed Laboratories, Oriental, NC (1989-1999); Superintendent, Schools, Augusta City Schools (1980-1986); Superintendent, Schools, MSAD # 54, Skowhegan, ME (1977-1980); Curriculum Director, Phoenixville School District (1974-1977); Director of Education, Vanguard Schools, Haverford, PA (1970-1974) **CW:** Contributor, Over 150 Articles, Professional Journals; Editorial Board, Several Scientific Journals **AW:** Mensa, Intellectual Benefit to Society Award (2011); Edelman Award, INFORMS (1998); Grantee, Eurasia Foundation for Work in Russia and Ukraine (1994-1996) **MH:** Albert Nelson Marquis Lifetime Achievement Award **AS:** He attributes his success to church, school and family. **B/I:** Dr. Taylor became involved in his profession because of a skilled high school mathematics teacher, Alice Richards. She exhibited a mastery both of the subject and her ability to teach it. He had a similar experience in college with professor, Gregory Wolczyn, and again in graduate schools with Merrill Tate and Bruce Andrews. **PA:** Republican **RE:** Anglican

TAYLOR, RICHARD B., CPA, T: Investment Advisor **I:** Financial Services **DOB:** 11/01/1951 **PB:** Cuthbert **SC:** GA/USA **PT:** Wilburn Bertrom Taylor; Marjorie (Hixon) Taylor **MS:** Married **SPN:** Sherrie

Lynn Lieber Taylor **ED:** BBA, University of Georgia, Athens, GA (1973); AS, Andrew College, Cum Laude (1971) **CT:** CPA, States of Georgia, Florida, Commonwealth of Pennsylvania and Arkansas **C:** Former Shareholder, HLB Gross Collins, PC, Atlanta, GA (1984-2018); Manager, HLB Gross Collins, PC, Atlanta, GA (1979-1984); Staff Accountant, Lester Witte & Co., Atlanta, GA (1973-1979); President, Owner, Avid Wealth Management Group, LLC **CR:** Executive Committee, HLB USA, Inc. (2018-Present); Former Chairman and Member, Advisory Board, Kennesaw State University School of Accountancy, Kennesaw, GA (1989-Present); Former Director and Treasurer, French American Chamber of Commerce (1998-2018) **CIV:** Board Member, The Public School Employees Retirement System, GA (2015); Board of Directors, North Cobb Christian School (1989-1990); Advisory Board, University of Georgia Athletic Association; Former Director, University of Georgia Alumni Association **CW:** Featured, TV Show, "The Great Christmas Light Fight," ABC (2019) **AW:** Inductee, Coles College of Business Hall of Fame, Kennesaw State University (2019) **MEM:** Director, Atlanta Chapter, French American Chamber of Commerce of Atlanta (2000-Present); Treasurer, Atlanta Chapter, French American Chamber of Commerce of Atlanta (2000-Present); President, Pinetree Country Club (2001-2003); Board of Directors, Pinetree Country Club (1991-1993); Treasurer, Pinetree Country Club (1991); Vice President, Pinetree Country Club (1986); Treasurer, Pinetree Country Club (1984-1985); Board of Directors, Pinetree Country Club (1983-1987); Secretary, Optimists (Optimist International) (1982-1984); American Institute of Certified Public Accountants (AICPA); The Georgia Society of CPAs (GSCPA); The Honor Society of Phi Kappa Phi; Beta Alpha Psi; Phi Theta Kappa **MH:** Albert Nelson Marquis Lifetime Achievement Award; Marquis Who's Who Top Professional; Marquis Who's Who Humanitarian Award **B/I:** Mr. Taylor became involved in his profession because he took an aptitude test in North Carolina and it narrowed his possibilities down to engineering and accounting. He was good at mathematics and trigonometry and also always liked to be around people. Mr. Taylor thought about public accounting so he could have the best of both worlds. **AV:** Gardening; Football; Travel; Golf; Dance; Christmas lights **RE:** Methodist **THT:** Over 25 years, Mr. Taylor and his wife, Sherrie, have the largest Christmas light display among residents in the state of Georgia at their home in Kennesaw, Georgia. The display features more than 600,000 lights, electronic lights, music and more than 170 trees with lights on their three-acre property. Their display takes over 1,500 hours to prepare and is visited by thousands of people each year from every age, race and national origin. The display is named "Lights of Joy" and has been featured on the Channel 2 Action News. "Lights of Joy" was a contestant on the ABC national TV series, "The Great Light Fight" in December of 2019. Mr. Taylor's other charitable activities consist of serving on boards and providing financial expertise to charitable, civic and educational institutions.

TAYLOR-HINES, REGINA, T: Owner **I:** Business Management/Business Services **CN:** Gina's Mind, Body & Balance **SC:** MA/USA **PT:** Floyd M. Taylor; Rosalie R. Taylor **MS:** Married **SPN:** Daryl **ED:** Doctoral Candidate, Capella University (2020); Degree in Holistic Massage Therapy, Cayce Reilly School of Massage (2009); MPA in Government Contracting, Troy State University (1992); BSBA in Business Information Systems, Old Dominion University, Norfolk, VA (1986) **CT:** Acupressurist, Reflexologist, Massage Therapist, VA Board of Nursing (2009); Certified Reflexologist (2009); Reiki Master

(2008); Juvenile Domestic Court Mediator, Virginia Supreme Court (2005); General Court Mediator, Virginia Supreme Court (2004); Contracting Officer Representative, U.S. Government (2001); Mediator, Virginia State Court System; Quality Assurance Officer (1988) **C:** Master Therapist, Life Coach, Owner, Gina's Mind, Body & Balance (2006-Present); Contracting Officer, Business Improvement Officer, Norfolk Naval Shipyard (2002-2006); Supply Officer, Contracting Officers, Technical Representative for D.G. 21, Naval Supply Facility, U.S. Government (2001-2002); Assistant Supply Officer, Services Officer, USS Nimitz; Food Service Officer; Sales Officer; Stock Control Officer; Disbursing Officer, U.S. Treasury Representative, Transportation Department Head, Defense Finance & Accounting Service **CR:** Regina's Root (2020); Vice President, Womens Veterans Services, Inc., Richmond, VA (2002-2003); Executive Board Member, Treasurer, Reflexology Association of Virginia **CIV:** Master Gardener, Portsmouth, VA (2005-Present); General and JD Court Mediator, Volunteer, Community Mediation Center, Norfolk, VA (2004-2006); Girl Scouts of America, Inc., Driver, VA (2004-2006) **MIL:** Retired, Lieutenant Commander, U.S. Navy (1986-2006) **CW:** Co-Creator, Norfolk Naval Shipyards Temporary Labor Program **AW:** Defense Meritorious Service Award, Navy Commendation Medal; Navy Achievement Medal; Global War on Terrorism Medal (OEF); National Defense Service Medal; Navy Sea Service Deployment Ribbon; Navy and Marine Corps Overseas Service Ribbon; Navy Unit Commendation; Navy Meritorious Unit Commendation; Navy "E" Ribbon **MEM:** National Certified Board of Therapeutic Massage & Bodywork Association; Reflexology Association of America; Associated Bodywork and Massage Professionals; Virginia Master Gardeners; Disabled American Veteran Association; Veterans of Foreign Wars Association **MH:** Albert Nelson Marquis Lifetime Achievement Award **AS:** Ms. Taylor-Hines attributes her success to God and her family. **AV:** Repairing furniture; Reading; Gardening; Traveling **PA:** Independent **RE:** Protestant

TEAGUE, A. JAMES, T: Co-chief Executive Officer **I:** Oil & Energy **CN:** Enterprise Products Partners L.P. **C:** Co-chief Executive Officer, Enterprise Products Partners L.P. (2020-Present); Director, Enterprise GP (2010-Present); Chief Executive Officer, Enterprise GP (2016-2020); Chief Operating Officer, Enterprise GP (2010-2015); Executive Vice President, Enterprise GP (2010-2013); Executive Vice President, Chief Commercial Officer, Duncan Energy Partners L.P. (2008-2011); Chief Operating Officer, Enterprise GP (2010); Director, Holdings GP (2009-2010); Director, Enterprise GP (2008-2010); Chief Commercial Officer, Enterprise GP (2008-2010); Executive Vice President, Enterprise GP (1999-2010); President, Tejas Natural Gas Liquids, LLC, Shell Oil Company (1998-1999); President, Marketing and Trading, MAPCO (1997-1998); Member, Senior Management Teams, MAPCO; Member, Senior Management Teams, Shell Oil Company; Numerous Roles, Dow Chemical Company **CR:** Member, Board, Solaris Oilfield Infrastructure, Inc. (2017-Present); Member, Board, Enterprise Products Partners L.P. (2010-Present); Member, Board of Directors, EPE Holdings, LLC (Subsidiary Dan Duncan LLC) (2009-Present) **AW:** Named Maritime Leader of the Year (2020)

TEBHA, MARK IQBAL, T: Chief Executive Officer **I:** Business Management/Business Services **CN:** Tebha, Inc. **CH:** Four Children **ED:** MBA (1971); BS in Mechanical Engineer, University of Berkley (1969) **C:** Founder, President, Chief Executive Officer, Tebha, Inc. (1983-Present) **MIL:** U.S. Army **AW:** "Number One in the Nation Vacuum Industry" **MEM:** Vacuum Trade Association of America **AS:** Mr. Tebha attributes his success to being reliable and honest, and listening to the customers needs. He also is thankful for his Muslim faith, which brings him comfort through prayer. **B/I:** Mr. Tebha became involved in his profession because when he was an engineer working for a private company, he was let go after the project was done. That is when he realized that by working for someone, he could be let go at anytime, so if he ran his own business he could control it. **THT:** Mr. Tebha helped build his local mosque so the Muslim community in his area could have a place to pray.

TEBOW, TIM, T: Baseball Player, Professional Football Player (Retired), Sports Analyst (Retired) **I:** Athletics **DOB:** 08/14/1987 **PB:** Makati **SC:** Philippines **PT:** Robert Ramsey Tebow II; Pamela Elaine Tebow **MS:** Married **SPN:** Demi-Leigh Nel-Peters (01/20/2020) **ED:** BA in Family, Youth and Community Sciences, University of Florida, Gainesville, FL (2009) **C:** Baseball Player, Outfielder, Minor League Teams, New York Mets (2016-Present); Football Player, Quarterback, Philadelphia Eagles (2015); Co-Host, "Good Morning America," ABC News (2014-2015); College Football Analyst, ESPN (2013-2014); Football Player, Quarterback, New York Jets (2012-2013); Football Player, Quarterback, Denver Broncos (2010-2012) **CIV:** Founder, Tim Tebow Foundation (2010-Present); Founder, "First and 15" for Uncle Dick's Orphanage, Philippines; Fundraiser, Pediatric Cancer Center, Shands Hospital; Volunteer, Goodwill Gators **CW:** Host, "Million Dollar Mile" (2019-Present); Co-Author, "Shaken: Fighting to Stand Strong No Matter What Comes Your Way" (2020); Executive Producer, Film, "Run the Race" (2019); Co-Author, "Shaken: Discovering Your True Identity in the Midst of Life's Storms (2018); Co-Author, "This Is the Day: Reclaim Your Dream. Ignite Your Passion. Live Your Purpose." (2018); Author, "Know Who You Are, Live Like It Matters: A Homeschooler's Interactive Guide to Discovering Your True Identity" (2017); Co-Author, "Shaken Bible Study: Discovering Your True Identity in the Midst of Life's Storms" (2016); Co-Author, "Through My Eyes" (2011); Public Speaker, Numerous Events **AW:** One of The 100 Most Influential People in the World, Time Magazine (2012); Offensive MVP, BCS Championship Game (2010); First Team All-SEC Team (2009, 2008, 2007); ESPY Award, Best Male College Athlete, ESPN (2009, 2008); William V. Campbell Trophy, National Football Foundation (2009); Second Team All-American, Associated Press (2009); Maxwell Award, Maxwell Football Club (2008, 2007); First Team All-American (2008, 2007); Manning Award, Sugar Bowl Committee (2008); Sports Spirit Award, Disney (2008); Securities and Exchange Commission Offensive MVP, The Sporting News (2008); Securities and Exchange Commission Offensive Player of the Year (2007); Chic Harley Award, Touchdown Club of Columbus (2007); James E. Sullivan Award, Amateur Athletic Union (2007); Davey O'Brien Award, Davey O'Brien Foundation (2007); Heisman Memorial Trophy, Heisman Trophy Trust (2007); Securities and Exchange Commission All-Freshman Team (2006); Nominee, Best Feature Film, "Run the Race," Christian Worldwide Film Festival **RE:** Christian

TEDESCHI, JOHN A., PHD, T: Historian, Librarian, Educator **I:** Education/Educational Services **CN:** University of Wisconsin-Madison **DOB:** 07/17/1931 **PB:** Modena **SC:** Italy **PT:** Caesar George Tedeschi; Piera (Forti) Tedeschi **MS:** Married **SPN:** Anne Wood Christian (04/12/1956) **CH:** Martha; Philip; Sara **ED:** PhD, Harvard University (1966); MA, Harvard University (1960); BA, Harvard University (1954) **C:** Curator of Rare Books and Special Collections, Memorial Library, University of Wisconsin-Madison (1984-1996); Director, Center of Renaissance Studies, Newberry Library, Chicago, IL (1979-1984); Curator of Rare Books and Manuscripts, Head of Department of Special Collections, Newberry Library, Chicago, IL (1970-1982); Bibliographer of European History and Literature, Newberry Library, Chicago, IL (1965-1984) **CR:** Honorary Fellow, Institute for Research in the Humanities, University of Wisconsin-Madison (1984-1996); Adjunct Professor, Department of History, University of Illinois, Chicago, IL (1979-1984); Visiting Professor, Department of History, University of Illinois (1972-1973); Lecturer, Department of History, University of Chicago (1969-1971) **MIL:** U.S. Army Infantry (1954-1956) **CW:** Co-Translator, "Justice Blindfolded," Adriano Prosperi (2018); Author, "Italian Jews Under Fascism, 1938-1945: A Personal and Historical Narrative" (2015); Author, "Intellettuali in Esilio, dall' Inquisizione Romana al Fascismo" (2012); Co-Translator, "Threads and Traces: True False Fictive" (2011); Co-Editor, "Dizionario storico dell'Inquisizione, Four Volumes" (2010); Co-Translator with Anne C. Tedeschi, Michele Sarfatti, "The Jews in Mussolini's Italy" (2006); Editor, "The Correspondence of Roland H. Bainton and Delio Cantimori, 1932-1966" (2002); Editor, "The Italian Reformation of the Sixteenth Century and the Diffusion of Renaissance Culture: A Bibliography of the Secondary Literature (c. 1750-1997)" (2000); Co-Translator, "The Protestant Reformation in Sixteenth-Century Italy" (1999); Co-Translator, "Books of the Body: Anatomical Ritual and Renaissance Learning" (1999); Author, "The Prosecution of Heresy: Collected Studies on the Inquisition in Early Modern Italy", (1991), Translated into Italian" (1997); Co-Translator, "Domenico Scandella Known as Menocchio: His Trials Before the Inquisition (1583-1599)" (1996); Co-Translator, "Hans Urs von Balthasar: A Theological Style" (1995); Author, "Tomasso Sassetti, Il Massacro di San Bartolomeo" (1995); Co-Translator, "Clues, Myths, and the Historical Method" (1989); Co-Editor, "The Inquisition in Early Modern Europe: Studies on Sources and Methods" (1986); Co-Translator, "The Night Battles: Witchcraft and Agrarian Cults in the Sixteenth and Seventeenth Centuries" (1983); Co-Translator, "The Cheese and the Worms, the Cosmos of a Sixteenth-Century Miller" (1980); Editor-in-Chief, "Bibliographie International de l'Humanisme et de la Renaissance" (1977-1982); Co-Editor, "Renaissance Studies in Honor of Hans Baron" (1971); Co-Editor, "Corpus Reformatorum Italicorum" (1968-1996); Editor, "Italian Reformation Studies in Honor of Laelius Socinus" (1965); Editorial Committee, "Index des Livres Interdits," Sherbrooke, Canada; Editorial Board, "Collected Works of Erasmus," Toronto, Canada; Editorial Board, "Studi e Testi per la Storia Religiosa Italiana del '500," Florence, Italy; Editorial Board, The Peter Martyr Library, Kirksville, MO; Editorial Board, Inquisizione e Società," Trieste, Italy; Contributor, Articles, Professional Journals. **AW:** Fellow, Academia Ambrosiana, Milam (2008-Present); Festschrift, L'Inquisizione romana e gli eretici, Studi in onore di John Tedeschi (2017); Fellow, Huntington Library (1984); Fellow, Institute for Research in the Humanities, University of Wisconsin-Madison (1976-1977); Old Dominion Fellowship, Harvard University Center for Italian Renaissance Studies, Villa i Tatti, Florence, Italy (1967-1968); Grantee, National Endowment for the Humanities (1967); Grantee, American Philosophical Society (1961); Honorary Counselor, Istituto Nazionale di Studi sul Rinascimento **MEM:** Elected Honorary Member, Instituto Nazionale di Studi sul Rinascimento, Florence, Italy (2009); Elected Member, Academia Ambrosiana, Milan, Italy (2008); President, Scholarly Advisory Committee, Archive of Congregation for the Doctrine of the Faith, Vatican City, Italy (1999-2002); Executive Board, Renaissance Society of America (1971-1996); President, 16th Century Studies Conference (1987); President, American Society for Reformation Research (1971); Fifty-Year Member, American Historical Association **MH:** Albert Nelson Marquis Lifetime Achievement Award **B/I:** Dr. Tedeschi's favorite subject was always history, which is what motivated him to pursue a career in the field. **PA:** Democrat

TEDESCO, PAUL, T: Humanities Educator **I:** Education/Educational Services **DOB:** 12/28/1928 **PB:** Nashua **SC:** NH/USA **PT:** Steven R. Tedesco; Ruth (Weaver) Tedesco **SPN:** Eleanor Martha Hollis (01/24/1953) **CH:** Steven Anthony; Sara Adams Tagget; James Beattie **ED:** CAGS in Administration, Northeastern University, Boston, MA (1974); PhD in History, Boston University (1970); AM in History, Boston University (1955); AB in History, Harvard College (1952) **C:** Professor, UMGC Europe, University of Maryland Global Campus (1997); Coordinator, Education, UMGC Asia, University of Maryland Global Campus (1995-1997); Team Leader, Lecturer, Joint Siberian-American Faculty, Irkutsk State University, Irkutsk Oblast, Russia (1994-1995); Lecturer, Business, History, Government, Education, UMGC Asia, University of Maryland Global Campus, Korea, Japan and Guam (1990-1994); Historian-in-Residence, City of Haverhill, Haverhill, MA (1989-1990); Fulbright Professor, History, Peking University, Beijing, China (1988-1989); Professor, Chairman, Department of Education, Northeastern University, Boston, MA (1965-1987); Chairman, Department of Social Studies, Canton High School, Canton, MA (1962-1965); Teacher, History, Great Neck North High School (Now John L. Miller Great Neck North High School), Great Neck, NY (1960-1962); Instructor, Humanities, Michigan State University, East Lansing, MI (1955-1960) **CR:** National Director, Business History and Economic Life Program, Inc., Boston, MA (1968-Present) **CIV:** Coordinator, Dover Hazardous Waste, Dover, MA (2003-2015); Commissioner, Dover Historical Communications (2001); Long-Range Planning Committee, St. Dunstan's Episcopal Church, Dover, MA (1968-1970); Finance Committee, Town of Canton, Canton, MA (1966) **MIL:** U.S. Army (1952-1954) **CW:** Co-Author, "Portable and Prefabricated Houses of the Thirties: The E.F. Hodgson Company 1935 and 1939 Catalogs: An Unabridged Reprint" (2007); Author, Editor, "Dover (Images of America Series)" (2002); Co-Author, "A New England City: Haverhill, Massachusetts" (1987); Author, "Patriotism, Protection, and Prosperity: James Moore Swank, the American Iron and Steel Association, and the Tariff, 1873-1913" (1985); Author, Editor, "The Thunder of the Mills: A New England Business and Economic History Casebook, 1690-1965" (1981); Author, "1894 Attleborough-Attleboro 1978: Hub of the Jewelry World" (1979); Author, "Teaching with Case Studies" (1978); Author, Editor, "The Creative Social Science Teacher" (1970) **AW:** National Collegiate Award, Financial Executives International (1985); George Washington Honor Medal, Economic Education, Freedoms Foundation (1984); Kidger Award, National Electronic Health Transition Authority (1975) **MEM:** President, Dover Historical Society (2000); Former President, National Electronic Health Transition Authority **MH:** Albert Nelson Marquis Lifetime Achievement Award

TEEHEE, KIMBERLY KAY, T: Advocate, Native American Lobbyist **I:** Other **DOB:** 03/02/1966 **PB:** Chicago **SC:** IL/USA **ED:** JD, College of Law, The University of Iowa (1995); BA in Political Science, Northeastern State University, Cum Laude (1991)

C: Shadow Member, Cherokee Nation, U.S. House of Representatives, Washington, DC (2019-Present); Senior Policy Adviser, Native American Affairs Domestic Policy Council, The White House, Washington, DC (2009-2012); Senior Adviser, Representative Dale Kildee, U.S. House of Representatives, Washington, DC (1998-2009); Director, Native American Outreach, President Clinton's Presidential Inauguration Committee (1997); Deputy Director, Native American Outreach, Democratic National Committee; Law Clerk, Division Law and Justice, Cherokee Nation, Oklahoma **CIV:** Supporter, Violence Against Women Act **AW:** Bureau of National Affairs Award **MEM:** Vice President, Cherokee Nation Business (2014); Tribal Member, Cherokee Nation, OK **PA:** Democrat

TELLERIA, ANTHONY F., T: Lawyer **I:** Law and Legal Services **DOB:** 06/06/1938 **PT:** Carlos E.; Melida (Amador) Telleria **MS:** Married **SPN:** Dolores A. Rockey (11/03/1962) **CH:** Matthew James Telleria; Andrea Telleria-Ruiz **ED:** Bachelor of Laws, Southwestern University (1964) **C:** Private Practice, Los Angeles, CA (1975-Present); With, Telleria & Telleria & Levy LLP (2007); With, Telleria & Telleria (2005); Senior Partner, Telleria, Townley & Doran, Los Angeles, CA (1971-1975); Private Practice, Los Angeles, CA (1964-1971) **AW:** Recognition for 50 Years of Service, State Bar of California **MEM:** Consumer Attorneys Association of Los Angeles; Los Angeles Advisory Council Accident Claims Committee, American Arbitration Association; Los Angeles County Bar Association; American Trial Lawyers Association **BAR:** California (1964) **MH:** Albert Nelson Marquis Lifetime Achievement Award **B/I:** Mr. Telleria became involved in his profession due to the influence of his father, who was a career army officer and thought that his son could do more good in the world by becoming a lawyer. **RE:** Catholic

TEMPLE, JOSEPH, "JOE" G. JR., DENG, T: Pharmaceutical Executive, Chemicals Executive **I:** Business Management/Business Services **CN:** Dow Chemical Co. **DOB:** 08/29/1929 **PB:** Brooklyn **SC:** NY/USA **PT:** Joseph George Temple; Helen Frances (Beney) Temple **MS:** Married **SPN:** Margaret Richebourg (02/26/2016); Ann Elizabeth McFerran (06/21/1952, Deceased 2003) **CH:** Linda Jo; James; John; Betsy Willett **ED:** BSChE **C:** Vice-Chairman, Marion Merrell Dow (1994-1995); Chairman, Marion Merrell Dow (1992-1994); Director, Dow, Midland, MI (1979-1994); Chairman, Chief Executive Officer, Marion Merrell Dow, Kansas City, MO (1989-1992); Chief Executive Officer, Chairman, Board of Directors, Merrell Dow, Cincinnati, OH (1988-1989); Executive Vice President, Dow (1983-1989); Dow, Midland, MI (1951-1989); Chief Executive Officer, President, Merrell Dow, Cincinnati, OH (1983-1987); Group Vice President, Human Health, Dow, Cincinnati, OH (1980-1983); President, Dow, Latin America, Coral Gables, FL (1978-1980); Vice President, Marketing, Dow, Midland, MI (1976-1978); Board of Directors, Marion Merrell Dow, Kansas City, MO **CR:** Executive Vice President, Dow (1983-1994); Chairman, Chief Executive Officer, Marion Merrell Dow (1989); President, Chief Executive Officer, Merrill Dow Pharmaceuticals (1980); President, Dow Chemical, Latin America (1978); Vice President, Sales, Dow (1977); Michigan Division, General Manager (1974); Plastics Department Manager (1969); Trustee, Committee for Economic Development; Dow Chemical Company (1951) **CIV:** President's Council, Purdue University (1978-Present); Board Fellows, Saginaw Valley State University (1987-1989) **AW:** Outstanding Chemical Engineer Award, Purdue University

(1993); Gold Knight Award, Management Association (1982); Distinguished Engineer Alumni Award, Purdue University (1978); Silver Knight Award, Management Association (1976) **MEM:** Board of Directors, Pharmaceutical Manufacturers Association (1981-1983); Board of Directors, American Institute of Chemical Engineers, Society of Plastics Industry (1980-1982); Management Association **MH:** Albert Nelson Marquis Lifetime Achievement Award; Marquis Who's Who Top Professional **AS:** Mr. Temple attributes his success to hard work, as well as his open and honest relationships with his coworkers. **B/I:** Mr. Temple became involved in his profession because he always enjoyed mathematics and chemistry. **AV:** Fishing for Blue Marlin and Sailfish; Swimming; Cheering on the Boston Celtics **RE:** Episcopalian

TENUTA, LUIGIA, T: Lawyer **I:** Law and Legal Services **CN:** Luigia Tenuta, Attorney at Law **DOB:** 06/04/1954 **PB:** Madison **SC:** WI/USA **PT:** Eugene P. Tenuta; Nancy Gardner Tenuta (Deceased) **ED:** Postgraduate Studies in Canon Law, Pontifical College Josephinum (1987-1988); JD, Capital University (1981); AB in International Studies, Miami University, with Honors, Ohio (1976) **CT:** Qualified, Appellate Counsel in Capital Cases (Ohio, Federal Criminal Justice Act Appointee) **C:** Private Law Practice, Columbus/Dublin (1981-Present); Manager, International Business Planning, Dresser Industries, Stratford, CT (1981); Analyst, Strategic Planning, Dresser Industries, Columbus, OH (1980); International Marketing Department, Dresser Industries, Columbus, OH (1976-1980) **CIV:** Former Member, Alumni Development Committee, Miami University, Ohio **AW:** Listee, Who's Who Among Students at American Colleges and Universities (1976); Inductee, Ohio Fellows Program, Miami University, Ohio (1972) **MEM:** Ohio State Bar Association; Professional Advisory Group of Catholic Foundation of Columbus; Federalist Society **BAR:** Ohio (1981); United States District Court for Southern District of Ohio; United States District Courts for the Northern District of Ohio; United States Court of Appeals for the Sixth Circuit; Supreme Court of the United States **MH:** Albert Nelson Marquis Lifetime Achievement Award **AS:** Ms. Tenuta attributes her success to her parents, as well as her entire family. She also credits wonderful friends, exceptional teachers and elders, the blessing of being an American along with divine grace and inspiration. **B/I:** Ms. Tenuta chose the law and pursued her profession, recalling an interest when John F. Kennedy was President (and he was assassinated when she was in the fourth grade). So, even in grammar school, it was an enriching profession and environment and she was encouraged to pursue law and service to others since she was very young. It was a noble profession and aspiration in those days. An interest in humanities/history furthered this course of study, happily. **RE:** Roman Catholic

TEREKHOV, YURI, PHD, T: R&D Manager **I:** Manufacturing **CN:** Laser Photonics **DOB:** 01/13/1977 **PB:** Moscow **SC:** USSR **PT:** Vyacheslav Victorovich Terekhov; Valentina Yakovlevna Terekhova **CH:** Nickolas Terehoff **ED:** PhD in Physics, University of Alabama, Birmingham (2010-2013); MS in Physics, University of Alabama, Birmingham (2006-2010); MS in Laser Physics, Moscow Engineering Physics Institute, Russia (1997-1999); BS in Physics, Moscow Engineering Physics Institute, Russia (1993-1997) **C:** R&D Manager, Laser Photonics (2015-Present); Research Associate, University of Alabama (2013-2014); Research Assistant, University of Alabama (2006-2013); Teaching Assistant, University of Alabama, Birmingham (2006-2011); Computer Technician, RM Consulting,

Calabasas, CA (2005-2006); Research Scientist, Engineer, Russian Academy of Sciences, Lebedev Physics Institute, Department of Quantum Electronics (2000-2005); Research Intern, University of Twente, Enschde, Netherlands (2000-2001); Research Intern, Moscow Engineering Physics Institute, Department of Quantum Electronics (1997); Research Intern, Russian Academy of Sciences, Lebedev Physics Institute, Department of Quantum Electronics, Moscow, Russia (1996-2000) **CW:** Developed Single Frequency Cr doped ZnS Broadly Tunable Laser with Wavelength Modulation as a Driver for the "Optical Nose" Platform; Realized Organic Molecular Trace Gas Detection in the Multi-pass Cell using Developed so called "Optical Nose" **AW:** GRSP Award, Alabama EPSCoR (2008); Huygens Grant, Nuffic Org. (2000) **MEM:** OSA (2012); SPIE (2010) **MH:** Albert Nelson Marquis Lifetime Achievement Award **AS:** Dr. Terekhov earned a Doctor of Philosophy in physics from the University of Alabama, a Master of Science in laser physics from the Moscow Engineering Physics Institute in Russia and a Bachelor of Science in physics from the aforementioned institute. He served as a research intern at the University of Twente in Enschede, the Netherlands, from 2000 to 2001 and as a research intern in the department of quantum electronics, headed by Academician and Nobel Prize winner Nikolay Basov, at the Lebedev Physical Institute of the Russian Academy of Sciences in Moscow from 1996 to 2000. In 1997, Dr. Terekhov worked as a research intern in the department of quantum electronics at the Moscow Engineering Physics Institute. He found success at the University of Alabama in various positions, including as a teaching assistant, a research assistant, and in a concluding post as a research associate in 2011. Dr. Terekhov flourished as a computer technician at RM Consulting from 2005 to 2006. Previously, he has excelled as a research scientist engineer in the department of quantum electronics at the Lebedev Physical Institute of the Russian Academy of Sciences from 2000 to 2005. **B/I:** The foundation for Dr. Terekhov's career as a research scientist was firmly set in high school. When he was presented with the choice between enrolling in a literature course or a physics mathematics course, he opted for the latter because he wanted to learn how to fix things from a technical perspective. Furthermore, Dr. Terekhov was fortunate to be taught by noted Russian scientists in mathematics and physics, in which he performed exceedingly well. When he was still in eleventh grade, he was one of only two students in his high school to pass a unique tough entrance test to a Moscow Engineering Physics Institute (MEPhI), becoming a student of the Russian university prior graduating high school. **AV:** Quantum electronics; Computers **RE:** Russian Orthodox

TERRY, ROBERT, "ROB", T: Land Surveyor, Part-Time Business Owner **I:** Other **CN:** Soltesz, Rob Terry's Landscaping **PT:** Carl A. Terry Jr.; Alicia DC Terry **CH:** Darion Atkins (Godchild); Darius Atkins (Godchild) **ED:** Jericho Christian Training College, Washington, DC; International Safety Education Institute (ISEI) American Safety Council; Jefferson Online High School, Florida **CT:** DOT New Driver Training (2014); 10-Hour OSHA Hazard Recognition Training for Construction Industry (2012) **C:** Part Time Business Owner, Rob Terry's Landscaping, Landscaping Business, (2019-Present); Land Surveyor, Instrumentman, SOLTESZ (Formerly Loiederman Soltesz Associates, Incorporated) (2001-Present); Warehouse Worker, Trak Auto, Landover, MD (1991-2001); Truck Jockey, Forklift Operator, Yellow Freight Systems, Landover, MD (1993-1998) **CR:** Survey Technician, Heritage Green, La Plata MD (2018); Survey Technician, Potomac Cove at Lexington Park, St. Mary's County, MD (2018); Survey Technician, Brevard Project, Clinton, MD (2018); Survey Technician, Andrews Air Force, Prince George's County, MD (2015); Survey Technician, Fort Meade, MD (2014); Survey Technician, Northeast-Bluegrass Quarry, Cecile County, MD (2014); Survey Technician, National Harbor, Fort Washington, MD (2001-2008); Survey Technician, Boulevard at the Capital Center, Largo, MD (2004); Survey Technician, National Harbor Fort Washington, MD; Survey Technician, Boulevard at the Capital Center, Largo, MD **CIV:** Mentor, Jericho Baptist Church, Aberdeen Proving Ground, MD **AS:** Mr. Terry attributes his success to being consistent, going to work every day, not missing any time, and being available without excuse. So, success to him really comes with being dependable and not letting any opportunity pass his way, so to speak. He has always been consistent and had a reason that he "can" opposed to a reason that he "can't." **B/I:** Mr. Terry became involved in his profession after owning a store in the 1980s. As he began to get a little older, he started to feel as if he should begin to explore other options for himself. He believed that because there were not many people who had the opportunity to go to college, he has become a great advocate for self education. He is an avid researcher. His biggest inspiration was Abraham Lincoln, who taught himself to eventually become the 16th president of the United States. While driving a tractor trailer, he was frustrated with the treatment he would receive on his job. When he discovered surveying, he enjoyed the different practices that went into the work. Within two years, he noticed that due to the physical nature of surveying, his health problems subsided and was enjoying the physical activity he received. He started the profession later in his life at around 40 years old. He bounced around company after company before landing back at Soltesz.In addition, he became involved as a part-time business owner of Rob Terry's Landscaping because everyone like his yard and would ask him what does he do. And they would ask if he could cut their grass, and then he started making money cutting everybody's grass, which lead to the business. **RE:** Baptist **THT:** Mr. Terry said, "In the United States, anything is possible. Thank God we live in America. God Bless America; it is the greatest country in the world... the land of the free and opportunity is there for those who want it... in this country, the sky is the limit..."

TESMER, NANCY S., T: Librarian (Retired) **I:** Library Management/Library Services **DOB:** 08/25/1934 **SC:** OH/USA **PT:** Ernest Lynn; Sophrona Rebecca (Pepper) Stutler **MS:** Widow **SPN:** John A. Tesmer (09/10/1980) **ED:** Bachelor of Arts, Kent State University (1956); Coursework, University of Akron (1952-1954) **C:** Retired (1990); Regional Librarian, VA Hospital, Cleveland, OH (1986-1990); Chief Librarian, VA Hospital, Cleveland, OH (1975-1981); Associate Chief Librarian, VA Hospital, Cleveland, OH (1973-1975); Chief Librarian, VA Hospital, Brecksville, OH (1965-1973); Medical Librarian, VA Hospital, Brecksville, OH (1961-1965); Hospital Librarian, VA Hospital, Northampton, MA (1959-1961); Junior Assistant Librarian, E. Branch Library, Akron, OH (1956-1959) **CR:** Chief, Regional Library Service (1986-1990) **MEM:** Northeast Ohio Medical Librarian Association; Medical Librarian Association; Zeta Tau Alpha **MH:** Albert Nelson Marquis Lifetime Achievement Award **B/I:** Ms. Tesmer became involved in her profession out of a lifelong appreciation for reading, as well as from the influence of her parents, who were well-educated in their own right. **AV:** Counter-cross-stitch; Reading

TESSIER-LAVIGNE, MARC, T: President **I:** Education/Educational Services **CN:** Stanford University **DOB:** 12/18/1959 **PB:** Trenton **SC:** Ontario/Canada **PT:** Yves Jacques Tessier-Lavigne; Sheila Christine (Midgley) Tessier-Lavigne **MS:** Married **SPN:** Mary Hynes (02/04/1989) **CH:** Christian; Kyle; Ella **ED:** Honorary Degree, University of Pavia (2006); PhD in Physiology, University College London (1986); BA in Philosophy and Physiology, University of Oxford (1982); Bachelor's Degree in Physics, McGill University (1980) **C:** President, Stanford University (2016-Present); President, Rockefeller University (2011-2016); Executive Vice President, Genentech Inc. (2009-2011); Senior Vice President, Genentech Inc. (2003-2008); Susan B. Ford Professor, School of Humanities and Sciences, Stanford University (2000-2003); Professor, University of California San Francisco (1997-2000); Associate Professor, University of California San Francisco (1995-1997); Assistant Professor, University of California San Francisco (1991-1995); Research Fellow, Center for Neurobiology, Columbia University, New York, NY (1987-1991); Research Fellow, Medical Research Council, London, England (1986-1987); Executive Director, Can. Student Pugwash Organization, Ottawa, Ontario (1982-1983) **CR:** Investigator (1997-2003); Assistant Investigator, Howard Hughes Medical Institute (1994-1997) **CW:** Contributor, Articles on Neurobiology, Professional Journals **AW:** Karl Judson Herrick Award, American Association Elected to American Philosophical Society (2017); Reeve Irvine Research Medal (2007); Robert Dow Award (2003); Wakeman Award (1998); Young Investigator Award, Society of Neuroscience (1997); Ipsen Prize for Neuronal Plasticity (1996); Ameritec Prize (1995); McKnight Investigator Award (1994); Klingenstein Fellow (1992); McKnight Scholar (1991); Searle Scholar (1991); Markey Scholar (1989); Commonwealth Scholar (1983); NY/NJ CEO Lifetime Achievement Award, Rhodes Scholar (1980); Viktor Hamburger Award, International Journal of Development and Neuroscience; Gill Distinguished Award, University of Indiana; W. Alden Spencer Award, Columbia University; Memorial Sloan-Kettering Medal; Honorary Fellow, New College; W. Maxwell Cowan Award for Outstanding Achievement in Developmental Neuroscience; Henry G. Friesen International Prize; Burke Award, The Burke Medical Research Center **MEM:** American Philosophical Society (2017-Present); Fellow, American Association for the Advancement of Science; Fellow, Royal Society of Canada; Fellow, Royal Society; Fellow, Academy of Medical Sciences; National Academy of Sciences; National Academy of Medicine

TESTER, RAYMOND, "JON" JON, T: U.S. Senator from Montana **I:** Government Administration/Government Relations/Government Services **DOB:** 08/21/1956 **PB:** Havre **SC:** MT/USA **PT:** David O. Tester; Helen Marie (Pearson) Tester **MS:** Married **SPN:** Sharla (Bitz) Tester **CH:** Chirstine; Shon **ED:** BS in Music, University of Providence, Great Falls, RI (1978) **C:** Ranking Member, Senate Committee on Veterans' Affairs (2017-Present); U.S. Senator, State of Montana (2007-Present); Chairman, Democratic Senatorial Campaign Committee (DSCC) (2015-2017); Chairman, U.S. Senate Committee on Indian Affairs (2014-2015); President, Montana State Senate (2005-2006); Member, Montana State Senate (2005-2006); Minority Leader, Montana State Senate (2003-2005); Member, District 45, Montana State Senate, Helena, MT (1998-2005); Minority Whip, Montana State Senate (2001-2003); Teacher, Big Sandy School District (1978-1980); Farmer, Organic Wheat, Barley, Lentils, Peas, Millet, Buckwheat, Alfalfa and Hay **CIV:** Chairman, Big Sandy School Board (1986-1991); Member, Big Sandy School Board (1983-1991) **AW:** Named

an Outstanding Agricultural Leader, Montana State University College of Agriculture (2005) **PA:** Democrat

THAKKAR, SWEETIE, T: Owner **I:** Apparel & Fashion **CN:** Panache Bridal & Formal **MS:** Married **SPN:** Bobby Thakkar **CH:** Miheer; Khusaal **ED:** Business Degree, India (1988) **C:** Owner, Panache Bridal & Formal **AS:** Ms. Thakkar attributes her success to the people who support her, whether it be her employees or co-workers. **B/I:** Ms. Thakkar became involved in her profession because she worked in retail for so many years. The fashion industry inspired her and she wanted to contribute to what was needed. She works in and around prom, quinceañera and bridal events. She did not envision this route. She thought she wanted to be a pharmacist but this opportunity showed itself and she fell in love. **THT:** Ms. Thakkar's motto is: "It is a blessing to do something for somebody. She wants to do something big for the needy and for a good cause."

THAKUR, NIRMALYA, T: PhD Student **I:** Sciences **CN:** University of Cincinnati **DOB:** 02/13/1995 **SC:** India **PT:** Dr. S. S. Thakur; M. Thakur **MS:** Single **ED:** MS in Computer Science, University of Cincinnati (2019); BS in Electrical Engineering, Kalinga Institute of Industrial Technology India (2017); Pursuing PhD in Computer Science, with a Specialization in Human Computer Interaction, University of Cincinnati **CT:** App Developer, Android (2015); SQL Developer, PL/SQL Developer, Oracle; Certified Java Professional, Oracle; ERP SAP ABAP, Future Career Solutions (2015); Object-Oriented Programming in Java, University of California San Diego; Python Programming Web Development, Internshala; Web Development, Internshala; Ajax, jQuery, Javascript, Internshala; Software Development using C# .Net, Kalinga Institute of Industrial Technology **C:** Graduate Assistant, Web Developer, Graduate School of Information Technology, University of Cincinnati (2019-Present); Vice President, Graduate Student Association, Department of Electrical Engineering and Computer Sciences (2018-Present); Graduate Student Researcher, Multimedia & Augmented Reality Lab, UX & Data Science Research, College of Engineering and Applied Science, University of Cincinnati (2017-Present); Graduate Assistant of Outreach and Communication, Office of Undergraduate Research (2018-2019); Full Stack Developer, Hyperloop, University of Cincinnati (2018); Graphic Designer, Hyperloop, University of Cincinnati (2018); Full Stack Web Developer, Center for Intelligent Maintenance Systems (2018); Project Coordinator, International Centre for Culture and Education (2015-2016); Project Manager, Tallenge (2015) **CW:** Contributor, 11 Research Papers in the Field of Human-Computer Interaction, Professional Journals (2018-2019); Contributor, Book Chapters (2018-2019); Reviewer, IEEE Access, Journal of Big Data and Cognitive Computing (MDPI) and Journal of Applied Sciences (MDPI) **AW:** Named, Best Campus Ambassador, Tryst (2015); First Prize, Quillorama (2015); Named, College Topper, Green Revolution Phase Two, International Centre for Culture and Education (2015); Best Ambassador Award, Indian Institute of Technology; First Prize, Quillorama, Kalinga Institute of Industrial Technology, India; Second Prize, Sherlocked, Kalinga Institute of Industrial Technology, India; Named, Best Delegate, United Nations Human Rights Council, Model United Nations Conference, Kalinga Institute of Industrial Technology; Named, Campus Ambassador, Indian Institute of Technology Tallenge, India; Named, Campus Ambassador, Indian Institute of Technology Delhi, India; Named, Campus Ambassador, Indian Institute of Technology Guwahati, India; Named, Campus Ambassador, Indian Institute of Technology Jodhpur, India; Named, Campus Ambassador, Indian Institute of Technology Indore, India; Named, Campus Ambassador, Birla Institute of Technology and Science, Pilani, India; Recipient, Internal Research Grant, University of Cincinnati; Fellowship Award, University of Cincinnati **MEM:** Association for Computing Machinery; IEEE; International Centre for Culture & Education (ICCE) **AS:** Mr. Thakur attributes his success to being able to come to the United States and work with the latest technology in the field of computer science. He is grateful for his parents who have constantly motivated him and helped him to follow his dreams of pursuing graduate studies and doing research. He also credits his friends who have always supported him. He considers himself fortunate to have always had amazing friends who have stood by him at all times. **B/I:** Mr. Thakur became involved in his profession because he originally hails from India, which is one of the developing countries of the world. Following his passion to do research for developing technology-based solutions aimed at improving the quality of life of elderly people in the future of smart homes, he came to the United States in August 2017 for the purpose of pursuing graduate studies at the University of Cincinnati. Since then, he has been involved in pursuing interdisciplinary research, specifically at the intersection of human-computer interaction, data science, Internet of things, machine learning and assistive technology. Mr. Thakur's work focuses on developing intelligent assistive systems to sustain independent living of elderly people in the future of smart homes. **AV:** Travelling; Listening to music; Watching movies **THT:** Ever since coming to the University of Cincinnati, Mr. Thakur has been one of the high achievers of his department and has been actively involved in research and development. Within the first three months of pursuing his master's degree, he published his first paper at the Annual Computing and Communication Workshop and Conference of the Institute of Electrical and Electronics Engineers in 2018. Since then, Mr. Thakur has been actively involved in doing interdisciplinary research at the intersection of human-computer interaction, data science, Internet of things, machine learning and assistive Technology. By working in these fields, he has published 11 papers including a book chapter since then. Mr. Thakur has also received a research grant, as well as a fellowship award. He is currently serving as reviewer for three journals: IEEE Access, Journal of Big Data and Cognitive Computing (MDPI) and Journal of Applied Sciences (MDPI). As a graduate assistant for the Office of Undergraduate Research at the University of Cincinnati, he played a key role in celebrating the work of numerous undergraduate researchers from as many as 34 different majors at the University of Cincinnati by highlighting them on the social media platforms of the Office of Undergraduate Research. Within a period of three months, Mr. Thakur was able to facilitate 133 connections between undergraduate and graduate students to help the former get research exposure and experience.In addition to being a PhD Student, he is currently serving as the President of the Graduate Students Association of his department. Mr. Thakur has also featured on a show in Bearcast Media, the official student-run radio broadcast and media group at the University of Cincinnati. He believes in maintaining a proper balance between work, study and enjoying life. He wishes to go on a world tour in the near future.

THAYER, BRUCE ALLEN, T: Artist **I:** Fine Art **DOB:** 02/07/1952 **PB:** Eaton Rapids **SC:** MI/USA **PT:** Alfred James; Beatrice Thayer **MS:** Married

SPN: Ilene Alice Thayer (05/26/1986) **ED:** MFA in Painting, School of the Art Institute of Chicago (1980); BFA in Painting, Central Michigan University (1975); BS, Central Michigan University (1974) **C:** Test Driver, GMC, Milford, MI (1988-Present); Art Instructor, Kresge Art Museum, Michigan State University, East Lansing, MI (1998-2001); Substitute Teacher, Lansing Schools, Michigan (1978-1979) **CR:** Speaker, Artist, Aesthetic and Ideologies Conference, Michigan State University, East Lansing, MI (1999); Visiting Artist Aquinas College, Grand Rapids, MI (1998); Visiting Artist, G.M.I. Engineering Institute, Flint, MI (1995); Cranbrook Art Museum, Bloomfield Hills, MI (1995) **CIV:** Representative, U.S. Congress, East Lansing, MI (1998, 1999); Head Juror, San Jane Venable Scholarship, Lansing, MI (1993, 1994); Juror, High School Art **CW:** Artist, 20th Biennial Regional Arts Exhibition (1999); Artist, Exhibition, 15th Biennial Michigan Arts Exhibition (1987); Artist, Exhibition, Rutgers National Works on Paper (1986); Artist, Exhibition, 5th Annual Michigan Fine Arts (1983) **AW:** Purchase Award, 20th Biennial Regional Arts Exhibition (1999); Fellow, Art Matters (1994); Purchase Award, Society of American Graphic Arts (1993); Visual Arts Fellow, Arts Midwest/NEA Regional (1990); Best of Show Award, 15th Biennial Michigan Arts Exhibition (1987); Art Grantee, Michigan Council for the Arts (1987); Purchase Award, Rutgers National Works on Paper (1986); Best of Show Award, 5th Annual Michigan Fine Arts (1983) **MEM:** Adviser, Board of Directors, Central Michigan University Art Alumni (1999-Present); Society of American Graphic Artists **MH:** Albert Nelson Marquis Lifetime Achievement Award; Marquis Who's Who Top Professional **B/I:** Mr. Thayer became involved in his profession because of the initial inspiration of his grandmother, Edna Moore, who was an elementary school teacher; he began to pursue a career as a teacher but decided to make a change. He then started working for General Motors mainly just to make money. Eventually, through hard work, he was transferred to the "proving grounds," where he would test drive cars. From this position, he discovered he had a genuine love for his career and stuck with it through the years. He eventually revisited his old initial career path as a teacher by combining his background and passion for art and became an instructor at the Kresge Art Museum.In addition, Mr. Thayer didn't choose art...it chose him. **AV:** Horticulture; Collecting arts and crafts; Pottery; Gardening

THAYER, KRISTINE, T: Pediatric Surgeon **I:** Medicine & Health Care **CN:** Kj Thayer LLC **DOB:** 05/15/1959 **PB:** Los Angeles **SC:** CA/USA **MS:** Married **ED:** Pediatric Surgery Fellowship, Nicklaus Children's Hospital (2001-2003); Internship and Residency, General Surgery, University of Medicine and Dentistry of New Jersey (1990-1995); Doctor of Medicine, New York Medical College (1990); Bachelor of Science in Medical Microbiology, Stanford University (1982) **CT:** Narcotics Certification (2014-2022); Certification, Specialty Board, American Board of Surgery (1999, 2009, 2018, 2019); Certification, General Medical Board, National Board Certified (1991); Licensure, Colorado; Licensure, Florida; Licensure, Idaho; Licensure, Illinois; Licensure, Iowa; Licensure, Maine; Licensure, Michigan; Licensure, New Jersey; Licensure, New Mexico; Licensure, New York; Licensure, Ohio; Licensure, Oklahoma; Licensure, Wisconsin **C:** Member, Temporary Staff, Pediatric Surgery, Westchester County Medical Center (2019-Present); Member, Active Staff, Pediatric Surgery, Community Medical Center (2019-Present); Assistant Professor of Surgery, University of Illinois College of Medicine Rockford (2015-Present); Private Practice, KJ Thayer LLC (2009-Present); Locums

Tenens, Pediatric Surgery, Loyola University Medical Center/Ronald McDonald Children's Hospital (2011-2012, 2017-2019); Member, Active Staff, Pediatric Surgery, Mercy Health Rockford (2015-2019); Clinical Assistant Professor of Surgery, Loyola University (2011-2018); Member, Active Staff, Pediatric Surgery, Rockford Memorial Medical Center (2013-2015); Locums Tenens, Pediatric Surgery, Albany Medical Center (2008-2013); Locums Tenens, Pediatric Surgery, Crouse Hospital (2008-2013); Locums Tenens, Pediatric Surgery, SUNY Upstate University Hospital/Golisano Children's Hospital (2008-2013); Locums Tenens, Pediatric Surgery, Presbyterian Medical Center (2012); Locums Tenens, Pediatric Surgery, Rockford Memorial Medical Center (2012); Member, Intermittent Staff, General Surgery, Togus VA Medical Center (2011); Locums Tenens, Pediatric Surgery, St. Francis Medical Center (2011); Associate Chief of Surgery, Member, Provisional Staff, General Surgery, Togus VA Medical Center (2010-2011); Member, Provisional Staff, Pediatric and Trauma Surgery, Bayfront Medical Center (2008-2009); Member, Provisional Staff, Pediatric Surgery, All Children's Hospital (2008-2009); Member, Provisional Staff, Pediatric Surgery, All Children's Hospital (2008-2009); Locums Tenens, Pediatric Surgery, All Children's Hospital (2007-2008); Member, Active Staff, Pediatric Surgery, Eastern Maine Medical Center (2005-2007); Locums Tenens, Pediatric Surgery, Eastern Maine Medical Center (2004-2005); Provisional Staff, General Surgery, Good Samaritan Hospital (2003-2005); Member, Active Staff, Pediatric & General Surgery, Northpoint Laser & Surgery Center (2004); Member, Active Staff, General Surgery, Jupiter Medical Center (1998-2001); Pediatric Surgeon, Private Practice, Ocean Surgical Specialists (1997-2001); Member, Active Staff, Pediatric Surgery, Palms West Hospital (1997-2001); Member, Active Staff, General & Pediatric Surgery, Good Samaritan Hospital (1997-2001); Member, Active Staff, General & Pediatric Surgery, St. Mary's Medical Center (1997-2001); Member, Active Staff, General Surgery, Columbia Hospital (1997-2001); Member, Active Staff, General & Pediatric Surgery, Palm Beach Gardens Medical Center (1997-2001); Member, Active Staff, Adolescent & Pediatric Surgery, United Hospital, Children's Hospital of New Jersey (1996); Member, Active Staff, General, Pediatric and Trauma Surgery, University Hospital (1995-1996); Clinical Instructor of Surgery, University of Medicine and Dentistry of New Jersey (1994-1996) **CR:** Pediatric Surgeon, University of Illinois (2012-Present); Member, OR Committee, Mercy Health (2015-2019); Pediatric Surgeon, Loyola University Medical Center (2011-2012); Pediatric Surgeon, Albany Medical Center (2008-2012); Pediatric Surgeon, All Children's Hospital (2007-2009); Member, QAQC Committee, Columbia Hospital (1999-2001); Member, Cancer Control Committee, Jupiter Medical Center (1999-2001); President, The H.O.P.E. Project, Mobile Mammography (1997-2001); Member, Board of Executives, Palm Beach County Medical Society (1998-2000); Member, Board of Executives, American Cancer Society (1998-2000); Member, Surgical QA Committee, Palm Beach Gardens Medical Center (1997-1998); Clinical Instructor of Surgery, University of Medicine and Dentistry of New Jersey (1995-1996); Clinical Instructor of Surgery, University of Medicine and Dentistry of New Jersey (1994-1995) **CIV:** American Cancer Society; Coleman Foundation **MIL:** Flight Surgeon, School of Aerospace Medicine, U.S. Air Force (2008-2009) **CW:** Contributor, Numerous Articles to Professional Journals **AW:** Army Commendation Medal for "Service in Operation Enduring Freedom" (2002, 2005); Combat Medical Badge for "Service in Operation Enduring Freedom" (2002); Advocacy for Women,

Palm Beach County Medical Society (2000); Rookie of the Year, Palm Beach County Medical Society (1998); Rookie of the Year, American Cancer Society (1998); Departmental Honors, Medical Microbiology, Stanford University (1982) **MEM:** Associate Member, American Pediatric Surgical Association (2011-Present); International Pediatric Endoscopic Group (2010-Present); Fellow, American Academy of Pediatrics (2009-Present); Society of Laparoscopic Surgeons (2007-Present); Fellow, American College of Surgeons (2000-Present); American Medical Association (1986-Present); Palm Beach County Medical Society (1997-2002) **AS:** Dr. Thayer attributes her success to resilience, perseverance and flexibility. **B/I:** Dr. Thayer became involved in her profession because her personality matched with being a surgeon on different levels. She loves being proactive. She chose neonatal surgery because she wants to help babies and their families. **THT:** Dr. Thayer's motto is, "Honesty, integrity, and service."

THERON, CHARLIZE, T: Actress, Producer **I:** Media & Entertainment **DOB:** 08/07/1975 **PB:** Benoni **SC:** South Africa **PT:** Charles Theron; Gerda Theron **CH:** Jackson (Adopted); August Theron (August) **ED:** Student of Ballet, Joffrey Ballet School, New York, NY **C:** Actress, Producer, Film, Television **CR:** Spokeswoman, J'Adore Advertisements by Christian Dior (2004-Present); Model, Print Media Advertising Campaign, Raymond Weil Watches (2005-2006) **CIV:** United Nations Messenger of Peace (2008-Present); Founder, Charlize Theron Africa Outreach Project (2007-Present); Advocate, Numerous Women's Rights Organizations; Supporter, Animal Rights; Contributor, ONE Campaign **CW:** Actress, Producer, "The Old Guard" (2020); Actress, "Bombshell" (2019); Voice Actress, Executive Producer, "The Addams Family" (2019); Executive Producer, "Hyperdrive" (2019); Executive Producer, "Murder Mystery" (2019); Producer, Actress, "Long Shot" (2019); Executive Producer, "Mindhunter" (2017-2019); Producer, "A Private War" (2018); Producer, Actress, "Gringo" (2018); Producer, "Tully" (2018); Executive Producer, "Girlboss" (2017); Producer, Actress, "Atomic Blonde" (2017); Actress, "Orville" (2017); Actress, "The Fate of the Furious" (2017); Voice Actress, "Kubo and the Two Strings" (2016); Actress, "The Last Face" (2016); Actress, "The Huntsman: Winter's War" (2016); Producer, "Brain on Fire" (2016); Actress, "Mad Max: Fury Road" (2015); Actress, Producer, "Dark Places" (2015); Actress, "A Million Ways to Die in the West" (2014); Executive Producer, "Hatfields & McCoys" (2013); Actress, "Snow White and the Huntsman" (2012); Actress, "Prometheus" (2012); Actress, Producer, "Young Adult" (2011); Voice Actress, "Astro Boy" (2009); Actress, "The Road" (2009); Actress, Executive Producer, "The Burning Plain" (2008); Actress, "Hancock" (2008); Actress, Producer, "Sleepwalking" (2008); Actress, "Battle in Seattle" (2007); Actress, "In the Valley of Elah" (2007); Voice Actress, "Robot Chicken" (2006); Producer, "East of Havana" (2006); Actress, "Arrested Development" (2005); Actress, "Aeon Flux" (2005); Actress, "North Country" (2005); Actress, "Head in the Clouds" (2004); Actress, "The Life and Death of Peter Sellers" (2004); Actress, Producer, "Monster" (2003); Actress, "The Italian Job" (2003); Actress, "Waking Up in Reno" (2002); Actress, "Trapped" (2002); Actress, "The Curse of the Jade Scorpion" (2001); Actress, "15 Minutes" (2001); Actress, "Sweet November" (2001); Actress, "The Legend of Bagger Vance" (2000); Actress, "Men of Honor" (2000); Actress, "The Yards" (2000); Actress, "Reindeer Games" (2000); Actress, "The Cider House Rules" (1999); Actress, "The Astronaut's Wife" (1999); Actress, "Mighty Joe Young" (1998); Actress, "Celebrity" (1998); Actress, "The Devil's Advocate" (1997); Actress, "Trial and Error" (1997); Actress, "Hollywood Confidential" (1997); Actress, "That Thing You Do!" (1996); Actress, "2 Days in the Valley" (1996); Actress, "Children of the Corn III: Urban Harvest" (1995) **AW:** International Star Award, "Bombshell," Palm Springs International Film Festival (2020); Honoree, Hollywood Career Achievement Award, Hollywood Film Awards (2019); Named Best Actress, "Bombshell," Nevada Film Critics Society Awards (2019); Named Best Actress, "Bombshell," North Texas Film Critics Association Awards (2019); Audience Award for Best Actress, "Atomic Blonde," CinEuphoria Awards (2018); Named Best Actress in an Action Movie, "Mad Max: Fury Road," Critics' Choice Awards (2016); Named Best Female Performance, "Mad Max: Fury Road," MTV Movie Awards (2016); Named Best Actress, "Mad Max: Fury Road," Saturn Awards (2016); Named One of the "100 Most Influential People in the World," TIME Magazine (2016); Audience Award for Best Supporting Actress, "Snow White and the Huntsman," CinEuphoria Awards (2013); Indie Impact Award, Palm Springs International Film Festival (2012); Chairman's Vanguard Award, "Young Adult," Palm Springs International Film Festival (2012); Named Best Actress of the Decade, "Monster," International Online Film Critics' Poll Awards (2010); Named Woman of the Year, Hasty Pudding Theatricals (2008); Desert Palm Achievement Award, "North Country," Palm Springs International Film Festival (2006); Hollywood Actress Award, "North Country," Hollywood Film Awards (2005); Named Best Actress, "Monster," Italian Online Movie Awards (2005); Named Best Guest Actress in a Comedy Series, "Arrested Development," Online Film and Television Association Awards (2005); Named Best Actress, "North Country," Women Film Critics Circle Awards (2005); Named Best Female Images in a Movie, "North Country," Women Film Critics Circle Awards (2005); Named Best Performance by a Female, "Aeon Flux," Spike Video Game Awards (2005); Academy Award for Best Actress, "Monster," Academy of Motion Picture Arts and Sciences (2004); Golden Globe for Best Actress in a Motion Picture - Drama, "Monster," Hollywood Foreign Press Association (2004); Named Best Female Lead, "Monster," Independent Spirit Awards (2004); Silver Bear for Best Actress, "Monster," Berlin International Film Festival (2004); Named Best Actress in a Movie, "Monster," Critics' Choice Awards (2004); Best Actress in a Motion Picture, Drama, "Monster," Satellite Awards (2004); Screen Actors Guild Award for Outstanding Performance by a Female Actor in a Leading Role in a Motion Picture, "Monster," SAG-AFTRA (2003); Named Best Actress, "Monster," Central Ohio Film Critics Association Awards (2003); Named Best Actress, "Monster," Chicago Film Critics Association Awards (2003); Named Best Actress, "Monster," Dallas-Fort Worth Film Critics Association Awards (2003); Named Best Actress, "Monster," Las Vegas Film Critics Society Awards (2003); Named Best Actress, "Monster," National Society of Film Critics Awards (2003); Named Best Actress, "Monster," New York Film Critics Online Awards (2003); Named Best Actress, "Monster," San Francisco Film Critics Circle Awards (2003); Named Best Actress, "Monster," Utah Film Critics Association Awards (2003); Named Best Actress, "Monster," Vancouver Film Critics Circle Awards (2003); Named Best Actress, "Monster," Awards Circuit Community Awards (2003); Named Best Breakthrough Performance, "Monster," National Board of Review Awards (2003) **MEM:** People for the Ethical Treatment of Animals (PETA)

THIEDA, SHIRLEY, T: Geologist **I:** Sciences **DOB:** 05/31/1943 **PB:** Chicago **SC:** IL/USA **PT:** Edward Simon Thieda; Bessie Anne (Milota) Thieda **MS:** Widowed **SPN:** Wayne Russell Skipworth (03/19/1988, Deceased 04/1998) **ED:** MST, New Mexico Institute Technology (Now New Mexico Institute of Mining and Technology) (1972); BA in Geology, Southern Illinois University (1967); Coursework, University of Illinois (1963-1966); AA, Morton Junior College (Now Morton College) (1963) **CT:** Reiki Master Level I, II, III **C:** Consulting Geologist and Landman, Albuquerque, NM (1980-Present); Senior Geologist, Cactus Resources, Phoenix, AZ (1984); Geologist, Pioneer Nuclear Incorporated, Albuquerque, NM (1974-1979); Teacher, Earth Science, Santa Rosa Middle School, NM (1972-1974); Teacher, Earth Science, Ruidoso High School, NM (1968-1971); Geologist, Illinois State Geology Survey (1964) **CR:** Reiki Master Teacher/Healer **CIV:** Fly Tying Instructor (2014-Present); Member, Rio Rancho Fishing Club (2012-Present); Volunteer Line Dance Teacher, Bernalillo Senior Center (2010-Present); Albuquerque Woodworkers Association (1994-Present); Secretary, Albuquerque Woodworkers Association (1994, 1995, 1996); Volunteer Hockey Coach, New Mexico Amateur Hockey Association (1976-1980) **CW:** Author, "Fast Ice" (1974) **AW:** Fourth Place, Line Dancing, State Senior Olympics (2018) **MEM:** President, Albuquerque Geological Society (1986); Treasurer, Albuquerque Geological Society (1984); Education Chairman, Albuquerque Landsmen's Association (1982); Secretary, Treasurer, Referee's Association Club (1978-1979); American Association of Petroleum Landmen (AAPL); American Association of Petroleum Geologists; Albuquerque Landmen's Association; Albuquerque Geological Society; Referee's Association Club **MH:** Albert Nelson Marquis Lifetime Achievement Award; Marquis Who's Who Top Professional **AS:** Ms. Thieda attributes her success to the support she received from her parents, who showed her that she could accomplish anything. Additionally, she credits her bosses at the Illinois State Geologic Survey, and Pioneer Nuclear. **B/I:** Ms. Thieda was encouraged by her parents to become whatever she wanted. As a child, they traveled a lot into the west and wherever they went, there were rocks. She was drawn to rocks and fossils; anything that was volcanic excited her. It was something she really enjoyed and loved, which is what attracted her to the field. Ms. Thieda's parents have a film of her as a young child picking up rocks; she had so many rocks in her pockets that her pants started to fall down. However, she was not getting rid of her rocks. When she went to the University of Illinois, she knew she would major in geology. She then transferred to SIU and graduated from the institution. **AV:** Gardening; Coin collecting; Hiking; Fishing; Collecting rocks **PA:** Independent **RE:** Roman Catholic **THT:** Ms. Thieda does volunteer work with a fly tying class. She also teaches line dancing twice a week at a senior center.

THIGPEN, NEAL DORSEY SYMINGTON, PHD, T: Political Science Educator **I:** Education/Educational Services **DOB:** 10/19/1939 **PB:** Baltimore **SC:** MD/USA **PT:** Guy Franklin Thigpen; Virginia (Dorsey) Thigpen **MS:** Married **SPN:** Judge Patsy S. Stone (05/21/1977) **ED:** PhD in American Government and Politics, University of Maryland, (1970); MA in Government and Politics, University of Maryland (1966); BA in American History, University of Maryland (1963) **C:** Professor, Chairman, Political Science, Francis Marion College, Florence, SC (1978-2008); Associate Professor, Political Science, Francis Marion College, Florence (1972-1978); Assistant Professor, Political Science, Francis Marion College, Florence, SC (1971-1972);

Adjunct Professor, Political Science, Western Maryland College, Westminster MD (1970-1971); Visiting Assistant Professor, Government and Politics, University of Maryland, College Park, MD (1970-1971) **CIV:** Delegate, National Republican Conventions, South Carolina (1972, 1976, 1980, 1984, 1988); Chairman, South Carolina State Election Commission, Columbia, SC (1988-1990); South Carolina State Election Commission, Columbia, SC (1978-1994); Vice Chairman, South Carolina State Republican Party (1974-1978); Chairman, Election Commission, City of Florence, SC (1973-1977) **MIL:** Corporal, U.S. Marine Corps (1963-1965) **CW:** Contributor, Articles, Monographs; Commentator, "The Presidential Contest"; Commentator, "Politics, '82"; Commentator, Primary General Elections **AW:** "Thigpen Hall", Francis Marion University, (2012); "The Neal D. Thigpen Chair in Public Affairs", Francis Marion University **MEM:** American Political Science Association; Southern Political Science Association; South Carolina Political Science Association; Pi Sigma Alpha; Omicron Delta Kappa; Pi Gamma Mu; Phi Alpha Theta **MH:** Albert Nelson Marquis Lifetime Achievement Award **B/I:** Mr. Thigpen became involved in his profession because of his interest in political science. After leaving the military, He completed his master's degree in political science. Mr. Thigpen went on to complete his PhD at Francis Marion University. He didn't expect to become a large publisher, but he knew he was a good teacher with a lot to offer. Francis Marion hired Mr. Thigpen to create their political science major. **AV:** Politics; Crabbing **PA:** Republican **RE:** Episcopalian

THIRY, KENT J., T: Chief Executive Officer **I:** Medicine & Health Care **CN:** DaVita Medical Group **ED:** MBA, Harvard University, with Honors (1983); BA in Political Science, Stanford University (1978) **C:** Chief Executive Officer, Da Vita, Inc., El Segundo, CA (1999-Present); Chairman, Da Vita Inc. (1999-2012); Chairman, Chief Executive Officer, Vivra Holdings Inc. (1997-1999); President, Chief Executive Officer, Vivra, Inc., San Francisco, CA (1992-1997); President, Chief Operating Officer, Vivra, Inc., San Francisco, CA (1991-1992); Partner, Vice President, Bain & Co., Inc. (1983-1991); Senior Consultant, Andersen Consulting (1978-1981) **CR:** Chairman, Oxford Health Plans (2002-2004); Director, Oxford Health Plans (1998-2004); Chairman, Kidney Care Partners; Member, Harvard Business School's Board of Advisors; Member, Board of Directors, Trust for Public Land **CIV:** Board of Directors, Volunteer, Center of San Mateo County **MEM:** Phi Beta Kappa

THOMAN, MARY E., PHD, I: Cosmetics **DOB:** 09/14/1949 **PB:** Kemmerer **SC:** WY/USA **PT:** William J. Thoman; Mary A. (Ferentchak) Thoman **MS:** Divorced **ED:** PhD in Vocational/Secondary Administration, Colorado State University (1981); MEd in Marketing, Colorado State University (1978); BS in Business, University of Wyoming (1972); AA, Western Wyoming Community College, Rock Springs, WY (1970) **CT:** Professional Teaching Certificate, Wyoming; Pilot License **C:** Team Manager, Mary Kay Cosmetics (2018-Present); Cattle/Sheep Rancher, Kemmerer, WY (1981-Present); Senior Sales Director, Mary Kay Cosmetics, Kemmerer, WY (1988-2018); Business and Marketing Instructor, Western Wyoming Community College , Kemmerer, WY (1983-2010); Executive Director, Montana St. Council on Vocational Education, Helena, MT (1981-1982); Assistant Director of Internship, Nevada St. Council on Vocational Education, Carson City, NV (1977); Marketing and Cooperative Educator, Green River High School, Wyoming (1975-1977); Business Education, Green River High School, Wyoming (1972-1975)

CR: Executive Committee Representing Conservation Districts (2007-Present); Wyoming Task Force on Federal Lands Policy (1998-Present); Co-Founder, Chairman (17 Years), Coalition of Local Governments (1994-Present); Elected as Supervisor to Sweetwater County Conservation District (1989-Present); Business Consultant Western Wyoming College, Rock Springs, WY (1983-Present); Wyoming State Treasurer's Special Advisory Council on State Investing (1999-2006); Executive Committee, Co-Chair, Federal Lands Policy Wyoming Woolgrowers Association (1998-2003); Two Terms as Chairman, Region VIII Regulatory Fairness Board (2002); Southwest Wyoming Collaborative Team Education Consultant Kemmerer School District (1993-1999); Wyoming Agriculture in Classroom (1992-1996); Past Chair Wyoming St. Council on Vocational Education, Cheyenne, WY (1984-1993); Founder, Cooperative Education Work Program; Educational Consultant; Chair Voc/Tech Prep, Business Curriculum Committee; Executive Committee; Wyoming Landscape Conservation Initiative **CIV:** Member, Executive Committee, Economic Study Coordinator Coalition Local Governments (2004-Present); Member, Sweetwater County Conservation District (1999-Present); Wyoming Federal Lands Task Force (1998-2000); Active Western Range Issues Testifier on Range Reform Hearings; Member, Cumberland Allotment Coordinated Resource Management Team Bureau Land Management; Supervisor, Southwest Wyoming Resource Rendezvous Steering Committee District **AW:** YWCA Professional Woman of Distinction, Sweetwater County, 1st Annual Awardee (2012); Outstanding Member, Region VIII Regulatory Fairness Board (2002); National Vocational Education Fellowships to Colorado State University (1978-1981); Educational Professional Development Act (EPDA); Graduate Leadership Professional Development Act (GLDPA) **MEM:** Board of Directors, Education Committee, Kemmerer Chamber of Commerce (1992-1999); Wyoming Woolgrowers; Wyoming Stockgrowers, Wyoming and Sweetwater County Farm Bureau; Rock Springs Chambers of Commerce **MH:** Albert Nelson Marquis Lifetime Achievement Award **B/I:** Dr. Thoman became involved in her profession because her mentor from high school was a business teacher, who gave her an interest in the field even though, at the time, he wanted to major in agriculture in order to help the Western way of life. Unfortunately, the University of Wyoming didn't accept women in the school of agriculture, so she went to her next choice of business education. She also found this as a great opportunity to be in the ranch during the summer. **AV:** Flying; Skiing; Gardening; Dance; Traveling; Reading (Romance, History) **PA:** Republican **RE:** Roman Catholic

THOMAS, CLARENCE, T: Associate Justice **I:** Law and Legal Services **CN:** Supreme Court of the United States **DOB:** 6/23/1948 **PB:** Pin Point **SC:** GA/USA **PT:** M.C. Thomas; Leola Anderson (Williams) Thomas **MS:** Married **SPN:** Virginia Lamp (05/30/1987); Kathy Grace Ambush (1971, Divorced 1984) **CH:** Jamal Adeen **ED:** Doctor of Jurisprudence, Yale Law School (1974); Bachelor of Arts in English Literature, College of the Holy Cross, Cum Laude (1971); Coursework, Conception Seminary College (1967-1968) **C:** Associate Justice, Supreme Court of the United States, Washington, DC (1991-Present); Judge, United States Court of Appeals for the District of Columbia Circuit, Washington, DC (1990-1991); Chairperson, U.S. Equal Employment Opportunity Commission, Washington, DC (1982-1990); Assistant Secretary for Civil Rights, U.S. Department of Education, Washington, DC (1981-1982); Legislative Assistant to Senator John C. Danforth, U.S. Senate, Wash-

ington, DC (1979-1981); Legal Counsel, Monsanto Company, St. Louis, MO (1977-1979); Assistant Attorney General, State of Missouri, Jefferson City, MO (1974-1977) **CR:** Member, Board of Advisors, DC Cases; Member, Board of Trustees, College of the Holy Cross **CW:** Author, "My Grandfather's Son: A Memoir" (2007) **MEM:** The International Churchill Society **BAR:** State of Missouri **PA:** Republican **RE:** Roman Catholic

THOMAS, DOROTHY J., EDD, T: Counselor **I:** Education/Educational Services **DOB:** 03/06/1931 **PB:** Lynn **SC:** MA/USA **PT:** James F. Lynch; Marion E. (White) Lynch **MS:** Widowed **CH:** Alan J.; Susan A. **ED:** EdD, Nova Southeastern University (1990); MEd, Boston University (1966); BA, Boston University (1953) **CT:** Licensed Mental Health Counselor, State of Florida; Licensed National Certified Counselor; Licensed National School Counselor **C:** Guidance Counselor, William A. Chapman Elementary School, Naranja, FL (1977-2007); Guidance Counselor, Pine Villa Elementary School, Naranja, FL (1972-1977); Fifth Grade Teacher, Naranja Elementary School, Florida (1968-1972); Fifth Grade Teacher, Waybright Elementary School, Saugus, MA (1965-1966); Third Grade Teacher, North Saugus Elementary School (1965); Eighth Grade Teacher, Saugus Junior High School (1958-1959); Teacher, Oakland Heights Elementary School, Fort Walton Beach, FL (1956-1958); Eighth Grade Teacher, Saugus Junior High School (1955-1956); Fifth Grade Teacher, Veterans Memorial School, Saugus, MA (1954-1955) **CR:** Adjunct Professor, Barry University (1993-1994); Presenter in Field **CIV:** Advisory Committee, Family Counseling Services, Miami, FL (1989-1990) **CW:** Author, "Yes, Parenting is Fun" (1994); Author, "The Guidance Clinic" (1978) **AW:** Counselor of the Year, Dade County Association for Counseling and Development (1990); Grantee, Citicorp Success Fund (1988); Career Education Award, Kiwanis Club of Miami (1980); Top Counselor of the Year, South Florida **MEM:** Fellow, American Association for Counseling and Development; Dade County Association for Counseling and Development; Florida Association for Counseling and Development; Epsilon Tau Lambda **MH:** Albert Nelson Marquis Lifetime Achievement Award **B/I:** In fifth grade, Ms. Thomas changed classes because of a negative experience with her teacher. The new teacher showed Ms. Thomas what kind of teacher she wanted to be; ever since then, she has wanted to serve as a role model for her students. **AV:** Reading; Traveling; Swimming; Biking **RE:** Congregationalist

THOMAS, DOROTHY WORTHY, PHD, T: English/French Educator **I:** Education/Educational Services **DOB:** 12/13/1940 **PB:** Charlotte **SC:** NC/USA **YOP:** 2014, Leon R. Thomas **PT:** Utah Worthy Kirkpatrick; Myrtle Lee (Harvey) Kirkpatrick **MS:** Widowed **SPN:** Leon R. Thomas (12/15/1963) **CH:** Tonya Monique; Tracy Michele; Tecla Mionne; Tasha Monette **ED:** PhD in Rhetoric and Linguistics, Indiana University of Pennsylvania (1997); Postgraduate Coursework, Indiana University of Pennsylvania (1993-Present); Certificate in Advanced Studies in Educational Administration, College of William and Mary (1982); MA in French, Hampton University (1973); BA in English and French, Bennett College (1963) **CT:** Certified Teacher, Commonwealth of Virginia **C:** Assistant Professor of English, Hampton University, VA (1991-Present); Assessment Facilitator, Department of English, Hampton University (1998-2001); Member, Catalog Committee, Hampton University (1999-2000); Chair, Hospitality Committee, Hamptons University School of Liberal Arts and Education (1995-1996); Secretary, Committee on Committees, Hampton University (1995-1996); Secretary, Faculty, Hampton University (1995-1996); Chair, Amenities Committee, English, Hampton University (1994-1996); Instructor, Staff Development Specialist, Newport News Public Schools (1988-1991); French and English Teacher, Warwick High School, Newport News Public Schools, VA (1971-1988); French and English Teacher, Huntington High School, Newport News, VA (1966-1971); English Teacher, Booker T. Washington High School, Reidsville, NC (1965-1966); French and English Teacher, Irwin Avenue Junior High School, Charlotte-Mecklenburg Schools, Charlotte, NC (1963-1965) **CR:** Executive Assistant to President William R. Harvey, Hampton University (1997-1998); Consultant, Newport News Public Schools (1988-1991) **CW:** Author, Brochure Program for Effective Teaching (1990) **MEM:** Epistoleus Member, Alpha Kappa Alpha Sorority, Incorporated (1992-Present); Reaccreditation Committee, National Council Teachers of English (NCTE) (1999-2000); Fellow, Association for Supervision and Curriculum Development (ASCD); Virginia Association Teachers of English (VATE); National Council Teachers of English (NCTE); Jack and Jill of America, Inc.; Kappa Delta Pi, International Honor Society in Education **MH:** Albert Nelson Marquis Lifetime Achievement Award; Marquis Who's Who Top Professional **AV:** Aerobics; Reading; Travel; Bowling; Tennis; Line dancing **PA:** Democrat **RE:** Presbyterian **THT:** Dr. Thomas has seven grandchildren, Howard, Leon, Alexis, Ariana, Jordan, Maia, and Matthew.

THOMAS, EARL WINTY III, T: Professional Football Player **I:** Athletics **CN:** Baltimore Ravens **DOB:** 05/07/1989 **PB:** Orange **SC:** TX/USA **MS:** Single **ED:** Coursework, University of Texas at Austin; Diploma, West Orange-Stark High School, Orange, TX **C:** Professional Football Player, Baltimore Ravens (2019-Present); Professional Football Player, Seattle Seahawks (2010-2018) **AW:** 7× Pro Bowl Champion (2011-2015, 2017, 2019); Super Bowl Champion (2014)

THOMAS, JIM G., T: MUSIC EDUCATOR **I:** EDUcation/Educational Services **DOB:** 07/10/1945 **PB:** El Paso **SC:** TX/USA **PT:** Gus Demetrios Thomopoulos; Antigone Mourgelas **MS:** Divorced **SPN:** Evi Deligianni Thomas (08/15/1970, Divorced 05/18/1998) **CH:** Gus James; Georgianna **ED:** Master of Arts, Arizona State University, Tempe, AZ (1975); Bachelor of Music in Education, Arizona State University, Tempe, AZ (1969) **C:** Music Educator, Cartwright School District, Phoenix, AZ (1979-2010); Founder, Orchestral Strings Educator, Paradise Valley District, Phoenix, AZ (1976-1979); Choral, General Music Educator, Isaac School District, Phoenix, AZ (1972-1976); Music Educator, Creighton School District, Phoenix, AZ (1970-1972) **CR:** Administrative Assistant, District Music Consultant, Cartwright School District, Phoenix, AZ (2002-Present); Music Curriculum Coordinator (1995-Present); Instructor, The Funky Fiddlers (1995-Present); Director, Educator, Summer Music Camp, Prescott, AZ (1993-2017); With, Honors String Orchestra (1979-2002) **CIV:** Volunteer, Musical Instrument Museum, Phoenix, AZ **CW:** Composer, Greek Folk Dance for Clarinet Trio, Pentozalis; Composer, 3 Greek Folk Dances for String Orchestra **AW:** O.M. Hartsell Excellence in Teaching Music Award, Arizona Music Educators Association (2002) **MEM:** Arizona Music Educators Association; American String Teachers Association; Music Educators National Conference **MH:** Albert Nelson Marquis Lifetime Achievement Award **B/I:** Mr. Thomas became involved in his profession after playing the violin in the fourth grade, which he greatly enjoyed. In high school, he drew inspiration from his orchestra teacher,

after which he became the first chair in orchestra for all four years. **AV:** Biking; Travel; Learning and performing multicultural music and instruments **PA:** Democrat **RE:** Greek Orthodox

THOMAS, LEELAMMA KOSHY, MA, BS, RN, RNC, T: Women's Health Care Nurse **I:** Medicine & Health Care **DOB:** 02/10/1936 **PB:** Kerala **SC:** Kozhencherry/India **PT:** V.T. Koshy; Kunjamma (Koruth) Koshy **MS:** Married **SPN:** C.A. Thomas (10/26/1967) **CH:** Linda Thomas Gold; Matthew; Lucie Thomas; John Thomas **ED:** MA, Karnatak University, Dharwar Karnataka, Mysore (1968); BS in Nursing, College of Nursing, Delhi, with Honors (1960) **CT:** Registered Nurse, Punjab, India, Texas; RNC **C:** Clinical Instructor, University of Texas School of Nursing, Galveston (1982-2001); Nurse Clinician IV, Women and Infants, University of Texas Medical Branch, Galveston, TX (1993); Head Nurse, University of Texas Medical Branch, Galveston, TX (1980-1992); Lecturer, Nursing, Armed Forces Medical College, Maharstra State, India (1971); PHN Operational Research, National Tuberculosis Institute, Banglore, Mysore State, India (1960-1967); Nursing Care Coordinator, OB-GYN, University of Texas Medical Branch; Nurse, Infant Special Care Unit, University Texas Medical Branch; Nurse, Labor and Delivery, University of Texas Medical Branch **CR:** Presenter in the Field; Principal Investigator of the Rocking Chair Study, Along With the Faculty Members, University of Texas Medical Branch at Galveston Texas; Rocking Activity Three Times a Day, Enabled Mothers to be Discharged Early to go Home with their Infants **CIV:** Sunday School Teacher, First Baptist Church, Galveston, TX (1982-Present) **CW:** Contributor, Articles, Professional Journals **AW:** University of Texas Medical Branch Maternal Health Council Award (1984); American Women's Scholar **MEM:** Sigma Theta Tau **MH:** Albert Nelson Marquis Lifetime Achievement Award **B/I:** Ms. Thomas became involved in her profession because while at college, she studied for two years and was thinking about what she was going to do and praying. She applied to the College of Nursing in New Delhi, and when she was accepted, what came to her was the passage from Jeremiah 32:27 "Behold I am the God of All Mankind is there anything too hard for me". It took her four days to reach the College of Nursing in 1956. It was God that planned for her to go to nursing and come to this country. Her family started a mission church. **AV:** Church Activities **RE:** Born-Again Christian

THOMAS, MICHAEL TILSON, T: Music Director **I:** Education/Educational Services **CN:** San Francisco Symphony **DOB:** 12/21/1944 **PB:** Los Angeles **SC:** CA/USA **PT:** Ted Thomas; Roberta Thomas **MS:** Married **SPN:** Joshua Mark Robison (11/02/2014) **ED:** Coursework in Piano, John Crown; Coursework in Composition, Conducting, Ingolf Dahl, University of Southern California **C:** Conductor Laureate, London Symphony Orchestra (2016-Present); Principal Guest Conductor, London Symphony Orchestra (1995-Present); Music Director, San Francisco Symphony (1995-Present); Principal Conductor, London Symphony Orchestra (1988-1995); Music Director, Ojai Music Festival (1968-1994); Founder, New World Symphony (1987); Principal Guest Conductor, Los Angeles Philharmonic Orchestra (1981-1985); Music Director, Buffalo Philharmonic Orchestra (1971-1979); Conductor, Young People's Concerts, New York Philharmonic (1971-1977); Assistant Conductor, Boston Symphony Orchestra (1969-1974); Musical Assistant, Assistant Conductor, Bayreuth Festival **CR:** President, Tomashefsky Project (2017-Present); Co-Developer, New World Center, Miami Beach, FL (2011-Present) **CW:** Con-

ductor, "Mahler: Symphony No. 8" (2010); Host, "The MTT Files" American Public Media (2007); Host, "Keeping Score," PBS (2006); Conductor, "Mahler: Symphony No. 7" (2006); Conductor, "Mahler: Symphony" (2004); Conductor, "Mahler: Symphony No. 6" (2003); Conductor, "Stravinsky: The Firebird," Peninsual Boys Choir (2000); Conductor, "The Rite of Spring," San Francisco Girls Chorus (2000); Conductor, "Persephone," San Francisco Symphony (2000); Conductor, "Prokofiev: Romeo and Juliet," San Francisco Symphony (1997); Conductor, "Orff: Carmina Burana," Cleveland Orchestra Chorus (1976) **AW:** National Medal of Arts Award, National Endowment for the Arts (2010); Decorated Chevalier Ordre des Arts et des Lettres of France; Artist of the Year, Gramophone Magazine (2005); Lifetime Achievement Award, American Symphony Orchestra League (2003); Conductor of the Year, Musical America Magazine (1995); Musician of the Year (1971); Ditson Conductor's Award, Columbia University (1993); Koussevitzky Prize, Tanglewood Music Center (1969) **MEM:** American Academy of Arts & Sciences

THOMAS, RAY, T: Singer, Musician **I:** Media & Entertainment **DOB:** 12/29/1941 **PB:** Stourport-on-Severn, Worcestershire **SC:** United Kingdom **C:** Member, The Moody Blues; Member, El Riot and the Rebels (Later Krew Cats); With, Various Groups Including The Saints and Sinners, The Ramblers; Member, Birmingham Youth Choir **CW:** Singer, Musician, with The Moody Blues, "Strange Times" (1999); Singer, Musician, with The Moody Blues, "Keys of the Kingdom" (1991); Singer, Musician, with The Moody Blues, "Sur La Mer" (1988); Singer, Musician, with The Moody Blues, "The Other Side of Life" (1986); Singer, Musician, with The Moody Blues, "The Present" (1983); Singer, Musician, with The Moody Blues, "Long Distance Voyager" (1981); Singer, Musician, with The Moody Blues, "Octave" (1978); Singer, Musician, with The Moody Blues, "Seventh Sojourn" (1972); Singer, Musician, with The Moody Blues, "Every Good Boy Deserves Favour" (1971); Singer, Musician, with The Moody Blues, "A Question of Balance" (1970); Singer, Musician, with The Moody Blues, "On the Threshold of a Dream" (1969); Singer, Musician, with The Moody Blues, "To Our Children's Children's Children" (1969); Singer, Musician, with The Moody Blues, "In Search of the Lost Chord" (1968); Singer, Musician, with The Moody Blues, "Days of Future Passed" (1967); Singer, Musician, with The Moody Blues, "The Magnificent Moodies" (1965) **AW:** Inductee, Rock and Roll Hall of Fame (2018)

THOMAS, SIDNEY RUNYAN, T: Chief Judge **I:** Law and Legal Services **CN:** United States Court of Appeals for the Ninth Circuit **DOB:** 08/14/1953 **PB:** Bozeman **SC:** MT/USA **MS:** Married **SPN:** Martha Sheehy **ED:** Honorary Doctorate, Rocky Mountain College (1998); JD, Montana State University Law School, Cum Laude (1978); BA in Speech-Communications, Montana State University (1975) **C:** Chief Judge, United States Court of Appeals for the Ninth Circuit (2014-Present); Judge, United States Court of Appeals for the Ninth Circuit, Billings, MT (1996-Present); Shareholder, Moulton, Bellingham, Longo and Mather, Professional Corporation (Now Moulton Bellingham PC), Billings, MT (1978-1996) **CR:** Adjunct Instructor, Rocky Mountain College (1982-1995) **CW:** Contributor, Articles, Professional Journals **AW:** Outstanding Faculty Award, Rocky Mountain College (1988); Governor's Award for Public Service (1978) **MEM:** American Bar Association; Yellowstone County Bar Association; State Bar of Montana **BAR:** Supreme Court of the United States (1994); United States Court of Federal Claims

(1986); United States Court of Appeals for the Ninth Circuit (1980); United States District Court for the District of Montana (1978); State of Montana (1978)

THOMPSON, ARTHUR, "ART" RAYMOND, T: Marketing Professional **I:** Corporate Communications & Public Relations **CN:** Southern Bell Telephone and Telegraph **DOB:** 05/05/1938 **PB:** Groveton **SC:** TX/USA **YOP:** 2020 **PT:** Charles Alton Thompson; Annie V. (Swor) Thompson **MS:** Married **SPN:** Alice Ann Church (09/01/1957) **CH:** John Alton; Amy Lynn; Mark Alan **ED:** AA, Florida College (1960) **C:** FEMA PA/PIO (1992-1998); Retired (1991); Manager Marketing, Southern Bell Telephone and Telegraph, Fort Lauderdale, FL (1971-1991); GOP Campaign Management (1969-1971); Reporter on Aerospace, United Press International, Cape Canaveral, FL (1963-1971) **CR:** Advisor, Radio and Television, Republican Party of Florida, Fort Lauderdale, FL (1967-1971); Vice President of Operations, Florida Broadcasting System, Fort Lauderdale, 1968-1970; chairman, board directors Rubicon Enterprises, Inc., Tampa, Florida, 1985 **CIV:** Chairman, Republican County Committee (2000-2002); Board of Directors, Truth and Freedom Ministry, Inc. (1987-1994); Coordinator, Communications for U.S. Tour of Pope John Paul II (1987); President, High School Advisory Committee Broward County, Fort Lauderdale, FL (1977-1979) **CW:** Co-author, "Theophilus and the One True Church" (1991); Author, "The Lord's Supper" (1987); Author, Republican Campaign Handbook (1968) **AW:** Named Honorary Blue Angel (1964); Honorary Member, SSBN George Washington Carver, United States Navy (1964) **MEM:** Chart Member, Cape Canaveral Space Pioneers (1962) **B/I:** In the 1960s Mr. Thompson worked as a news reporter on the Cape Canaveral "beat" for WFTV Channel 9 and WESH-TV Channel 2 in Orlando. He also did "stringer" work for outlets such as ABC and NBC. As a reporter for UPI Auadio he covered the last Mercury flight, the Gemini and Apollo programs, and three Skylab missions. He was privileged to report Neil Armstrong's first steps on the surface of the moon to an international radio audience of over 30 million, setting a record for the largest radio audience for any event up to that date. He later worked for the Republican Party of Florida, traveling the state recruiting candidates to run for office, and for various Florida candidates and legislators such as Senator Beth Johnson and Jack Eckerd. Mr. Thompson had a 20-year career at Southern Bell in Ft. Lauderdale and Miami, retiring as a Marketing Manager in 1991, and relocating to North Georgia in 1993. In retirement, he volunteered in local politics, serving as Chairman of the Walker County Republican Party, and volunteering in local campaigns in North Georgia and Tennessee, including the campaign of Chancellor Frank Brown in Chattanooga. Mr. Thompson was known for his faith in God, insatiable curiosity, his quick wit, and his love for his family. One friend aptly described him as "a Nathanael, one in whom there was no guile." **AV:** Writing **PA:** Republican **RE:** Christian

THOMPSON, BENNIE GORDON, T: U.S. Representative from Mississippi **I:** Government Administration/Government Relations/Government Services **DOB:** 01/28/1948 **PB:** Bolton **SC:** MS/USA **MS:** Married **SPN:** London Johnson (1968) **CH:** BendaLonne **ED:** BA in Political Science, Tougaloo College, MS (1968); MS in Educational Administration, Jackson State University, MS (1972); Diploma, The University of Southern Mississippi **C:** Chairman, U.S. House Committee on Homeland Security (2007-2011, 2019-Present); Member, U.S. House of Representatives from Mississippi's Second Congressional District, United States Congress, Washington, DC (1993-Present); Ranking Member, House Committee on Homeland Security (2005-2007, 2011-2019); Supervisor, Hinds County, MS (1980-1993); Mayor, City of Bolton, MS (1973-1979); Alderman, Bolton, MS (1969-1973) **CR:** Presidential Appointee, National Council on Health Planning and Development **CIV:** Board of Directors, Southern Regional Council; Board of Directors, Housing Assistance Council; Board of Trustees, Tougaloo College; Member, Hinds County Board of Supervisors; Lifetime Member, Asbury United Methodist Church, Bolton, MS **AW:** Named to the Power 150 (2008); Named One of the 100 Most Influential Black Americans, Ebony Magazine (2006) **MEM:** Founding Member, Mississippi Association of Black Supervisors; Founding Member, Mississippi Association of Black Mayors; Kappa Alpha Psi Fraternity, Inc. **PA:** Democrat **RE:** Methodist

THOMPSON, CHARLES, "MIKE" MICHAEL, T: U.S. Representative **I:** Government Administration/Government Relations/Government Services **DOB:** 01/24/1951 **PB:** St. Helena **SC:** CA/USA **PT:** Charles Thompson; Beverly (Forni) Powell **MS:** Married **SPN:** Janet Thompson (03/08/1982) **CH:** Christopher; Jon **ED:** MA in Public Administration, California State University, Chico, CA (1996); BA in Political Science, California State University, Chico, CA (1982) **C:** U.S. Representative, California's Fifth Congressional District, United States Congress, Washington, DC (2013-Present); U.S. Representative, California's First Congressional District, United States Congress, Washington, DC (1999-2013); Member, District Two, California State Senate (1991-1998); Owner, Maintenance Supervisor, Beringer Vineyards; Member, Committee on Armed Services, United States Congress; Member, Committee on Transportation and Infrastructure, United States Congress **CR:** Instructor of Public Administration and State Government, California State University, Chico and San Francisco State University; Instructor, Airborne School, U.S. Army **CIV:** Member, Blue Dog Coalition; Member, New Democratic Coalition; Co-Vice Chair, Congressional Sportsmen's Caucus; Co-Founder, Co-Chair, Congressional Wine Caucus; Chairman, House Gun Violence Prevention Task Force **MIL:** Staff Sergeant, U.S. Army, Vietnam **AW:** Outstanding Senator Award, Planned Parenthood Affiliates of California (1996); Outstanding Senator of the Year, California Professional Firefighters (1996); Outstanding Senator of the Year, California School Boards Association (1996); Senator of the Year, California Association of Homes and Services for the Aging (1995); Distinguished Service Award, APLA Health (1995); Legislative Leadership Award, California Association of Health Services at Home (1994); Legislator of the Year, Disabled in State Service (1994); Decorated Purple Heart; Legislator of the Year, PORAC; Legislator of the Year, California Association of Persons with Handicaps; Legislator of the Year, California Abortion Rights Action League; Distinguished Service Award, California Association Hospitals and Health Systems; Distinguished Service Award, California State Association of Counties **MEM:** CFA; Business & Professional Women's Association; Vietnam Veterans of America; The American Legion; Native Sons of Golden West; Order Sons and Daughters of Italy in America **PA:** Democrat **RE:** Roman Catholic

THOMPSON, DAVID MICHAEL, PHD, DD, T: Historian; Educator (Retired) **I:** Education/Educational Services **DOB:** 09/23/1942 **PB:** Leicester **SC:** United Kingdom **PT:** David Thompson; Alice (Beckett) Thompson **MS:** Married **SPN:** Margaret Clague (08/16/1969) **CH:** Andrew; Christopher; Stephen **ED:** DD, University of Cambridge; BD, University of Cambridge (1986); PhD, University of Cambridge (1969); MA, University of Cambridge (1968); BA, University of Cambridge (1964) **C:** Professor Emeritus, Modern Church History, University of Cambridge (2009-Present); President, University of Cambridge Fitzwilliam College (2009); Professor, Modern Church History, University of Cambridge (2007-2009); President, University of Cambridge Fitzwilliam College (2002-2006); Reader in Modern Church History, University of Cambridge (2001-2007); Director, Center for Advanced Religious and Theological Studies, University of Cambridge (1995-2009); University Lecturer, University of Cambridge (1970-2001); College Lecturer, History, University of Cambridge (1966-1970); Fellow, The Royal Historical Society **CIV:** President, Ecumenical Canon of Ely Cathedral (2011-Present); President, World Convention of Churches of Christ (2000-2004); Moderator, Disciples of Ecumenical Consultative Council, World Council of Churches (WCC) (1998-2004); Moderator, General Assembly, United Reformed Church (1996-1997) **CW:** Author, "Religious Life in Mid-19th-Century Cambridgeshire and Huntingdonshire" (2014); Author, "Cambridge Theology in the Nineteenth Century" (2008); Editor, "Protestant Nonconformist Texts, IV, The Twentieth Century" (2007); Author, "Baptism, Church and Society in Modern Britain" (2005); Editor, "Stating the Gospel" (1990); Author, "Let Sects and Parties Fall" (1980); Author, "Nonconformity in the Nineteenth Century" (1972); General Editor, European Section, New Oxford Dictionary of the Church **MH:** Albert Nelson Marquis Lifetime Achievement Award; Marquis Who's Who Top Professional; Marquis Who's Who Humanitarian Award **B/I:** Dr. Thompson became involved in his profession through luck. When he graduated with his PhD, he could have gone straight into history like many of his friends did. As it so happened, there was a lectureship in church history that had just opened, and he got the position. He secured a research fellowship after one year. In addition, what got him involved in his career was a passion for history, and it was something that he always wanted to specialize in. Dr. Thompson's big break was the shift from being the research fellow, where you have freedom to choose what you will research, to having a university post, where you have to relate what you research to the teaching that you have to do. But, it brought about a shift in emphasis in interest because you have to follow the curriculum. Later on, he reached the position where he could initiate changes in the curriculum himself. Hence, that is why he is particularly proud of being able to introduce World Christianity into the University of Cambridge in 2000-2001. So, that as much as anything was due to the research grants that they got for developing a particular line of study. It triggered the introduction of World Christianity, which proved itself to be very popular from a very early stage. **THT:** Both Dr. Thompson's personal and professional life revolve around the church. His research is focused on how churches work as institutions. When he was younger, the sociology of church life was considered a fringe subject, whereas now, it is a more central idea in his field. Dr. Thompson's own inspiration is to see the various churches all united. Any realistic version of this would take a long time to achieve, but if the attempt is not made, then he fears greater division could occur. He feels that religious and political divisions bring along serious consequences.

THOMPSON, DOLORES ANN, T: Special Educator (Retired) **I:** Education/Educational Services **DOB:** 01/24/1936 **PB:** Talladega **SC:** AL/USA **PT:** William Hurston Thompson; Alice Faustine

(Guest) Thompson **MS:** Single **ED:** AA, University of Alabama (1965); MA, University of Alabama (1961); BS, Samford University (1957) **CT:** Certificate in Paralegal Studies (1987) **C:** Special Education Teacher, Birmingham Board of Education (1958-2018); Special Education Teacher, Jefferson County School (1957-1958) **CR:** Freelance Writer **CW:** Author, "Training Civil Rights Workers in the Southeast"; Author, Chapter, "Employee Dress Code for Birmingham City School Employees: A Handbook," Author, "State Testing for Special Education Summary'"; Author, Lecture on Gangs as a Subculture, University of Alabama **AW:** Outstanding Young Educator, Birmingham Jaycees (1968); Fellow, U.S. Department of Education (1963-1965) **MEM:** Chaplain, Daughters of the American Revolution (1988-Present); United Daughters of the Confederacy; Alabama Symphony Orchestra; Caledonia Society; Capitol Club Member, Alabama Republican Party; The Birmingham Retired Educators Association **MH:** Albert Nelson Marquis Lifetime Achievement Award **B/I:** Ms. Thompson became involved in her profession because an adviser suggested she would do well in the field of education. **AV:** Ice skating; Designing clothes; Appearing on radio commercials **PA:** Republican **RE:** Anglican

THOMPSON, E. BRAD, MD, T: Professor Emeritus; Endocrinologist **I:** Medicine & Health Care **CN:** The University of Texas Medical Branch at Galveston; Johns Hopkins University **DOB:** 12/20/1933 **PB:** Burlington **SC:** IA/USA **PT:** Edward Bills Thompson; Lois Elizabeth (Bradbridge) Thompson **MS:** Married **SPN:** Lynn P. **CH:** Elizabeth Lynn; Edward Ernest Bradbridge **ED:** Assistant Resident, Internal Medicine, The Presbyterian Hospital (Now NewYork-Presbyterian Hospital), New York, NY (1961-1962); Intern, The Presbyterian Hospital (Now NewYork-Presbyterian Hospital), New York, NY (1960-1961); MD, Harvard University (1960); Postgraduate Coursework, University of Cambridge (1957-1958); BA, Rice University, with Distinction (1955) **C:** Professor Emeritus, The University of Texas Medical Branch at Galveston (2009-Present); Visiting Professor, Department of Biology, Johns Hopkins University (2013-2016); Senior Research Professor, Center of Nuclear Receptors & Cell Signaling, Department of Biology & Biochemistry, University of Houston (2009-2016); Professor, Department of Biochemistry & Molecular Biology, The University of Texas Medical Branch at Galveston (2003-2009); Professor of Internal Medicine, The University of Texas Medical Branch at Galveston (1984-2009); J.P. Saunders Professor, The University of Texas Medical Branch at Galveston (2006); I.H. Kempner Professor, The University of Texas Medical Branch at Galveston (1984-2005); Interim Director, Sealy Center for Molecular Science, The University of Texas Medical Branch at Galveston (1996-2003); Professor, Chairman, Department of Human Biological Chemistry and Genetics, The University of Texas Medical Branch at Galveston (1984-2003); Section Chief, Lab of Biochemistry, National Cancer Institute, National Institutes of Health, Bethesda, MD (1973-1984); Research Scientist, Lab of Biochemistry, National Cancer Institute, National Institutes of Health, Bethesda, MD (1968-1973); Research Scientist, National Institute of Arthritis and Metabolic Diseases, National Institutes of Health, Bethesda, MD (1964-1968); Research Associate, National Institute of Mental Health, National Institutes of Health, Bethesda, MD (1962-1964) **CR:** Member, Board of Scientific Overseers, Mount Desert Island Biological Laboratory (MDI Biological Laboratory) (2010-Present); Visiting Professor, Department of Biology, Johns Hopkins University (2013-2015); Co-organizer, FASEB Summer Conference (2006); Member, Education Board, American Medical and Graduate Departments of Biochemistry (1999-2003); Board of Science Overseers, Pennington Nutrition Research Center, Louisiana State University (1997-1998); Fulbright Professor, Marburg, Germany (1992-1993); Member, Council for Clinical Investigation and Research Awards, American Cancer Society, Inc. (1989-1993); Member, Advisory Committee on Biochemistry and Chemical Carcinogenesis, American Cancer Society, Inc. (1982-1986); Member, Revision Committee, Endocrinology Advisory Panel, United States Pharmacopoeial Convention, Inc. (1980-1985); Co-chairman, Gordon Research Conference (1980); Attending Physician, National Naval Medical Center (Now Walter Reed National Military Medical Center), Bethesda, MD (1978-1980); Chairman, Hormones and Cancer Task Force, National Institutes of Health, Bethesda, MD (1978-1980); United Nations Educational Visiting Expert, Institute of Genetics, Hungarian Academy of Science, Szeged, Hungary (1976); Visiting Professor, Science, Commonwealth Medical College of Pennsylvania (Now Geisinger Commonwealth School of Medicine) **CIV:** Member, External Board, Mount Desert Institute Biological Laboratory (MDI Biological Laboratory) (2010-Present); Initiator, Science Education Liaison Program, Galveston Public Schools (Now Galveston Independent School District) (1991); Member, Troop Committee, Girl Scouts of the United States of America, Rockville, MD (1970-1976); Member, PTA, Rockville, MD (1967-1977); The Wilderness Society, Washington, DC (1964-1975); Member, President's Cabinet, The University of Texas Medical Branch at Galveston **MIL:** From Officer to Medical Director, U.S. Public Health Service (1962-1984) **CW:** Member, Editorial Board, Endocrinology (2011-2015); Section Editor, "Handbook of Cell Signalling" (2004, 2005); Editor-in-chief, Endocrine Reviews (2001-2005); Member, Editorial Board, Molecular Endocrinology (1998); Member, Editorial Board, Steroids (1995); Founding Editor-in-chief, Molecular Endocrinology Journal (1985-1992); Co-editor, "Steroid Receptors and the Management of Cancer" (1979); Corresponding Editor, Journal of Steroid Biochemistry (1977-1985); Associate Editor, Cancer Research (Journal) (1976-1986); Co-editor, "Gene Expression and Carcinogenesis in Cultured Liver" (1975); Co-editor, "DNA: Protein Interactions and Gene Regulation"; Co-editor, Other Volumes in Field; Contributor, 300 Science Articles to Professional Journals **AW:** Finalist, Second Place in Age Group, Triathlon, Senior Olympics (2013); Fellow, American Association for the Advancement of Science (2005); Educator Award, Endocrine Society (2004); Honoree, Signalling Life and Death Symposium (2004); Named Distinguished Alumnus, Rice University (2001); J.G. Sinclair Award, Sigma Xi, the Scientific Research Honor Society (1997); American Cancer Society Scholar (1992-1993); Fulbright Scholar, Marburg, Germany (1992); Grantee, Walls Research, National Institute of Diabetes and Digestive and Kidney Diseases, National Cancer Institute, National Institutes of Health; **MEM:** Galveston Community Chorus; Affiliate Member, American College of Medical Genetics; Endocrine Society; American Society of Biological Chemists; American Association for Cancer Research; Bar Harbor Yacht Club; The Honor Society of Phi Kappa Phi; Alpha Omega Alpha Honor Medical Society; The Phi Beta Kappa Society; Sigma Xi, The Scientific Research Honor Society **MH:** Albert Nelson Marquis Lifetime Achievement Award; Marquis Who's Who Top Professional **AS:** Dr. Thompson attributes his success to his dedication to chosen goals and the support of family. **B/I:** Dr. Thompson became involved in his profession because his early medical school professors convinced him that in the long run he could do more for people by focusing on research. **AV:** Choral singing; Triathlons; Sailing; Gardening

THOMPSON, EMMA, T: Actress **I:** Media & Entertainment **DOB:** 04/15/1959 **PB:** Paddington **SC:** London/England **PT:** Eric Thompson; Phyllida Law **MS:** Married **SPN:** Greg Wise (07/29/2003); Kenneth Branagh (08/20/1989, Divorced 1995) **CH:** Gaia Romilly Wise; Tindyebwa Agaba Wise (Adopted Son) **ED:** Coursework in English, Newnham College and University of Cambridge **C:** Actress; Screenwriter; Activist; Author **CIV:** Supporter, London Extinction Rebellion (2019); Ambassador, Galapagos Conservation Trust; Chair, Helen Bamber Foundation for the Care of Victims of Torture; Ambassador, ActionAid; Patron, Refugee Council; Patron, Elton John AIDS Foundation; Activist, Palestinians; Supporter, Greenpeace; Active Environmentalist; Member, Footlights Troupe, Newnham College, University of Cambridge **CW:** Actress, "Cruella" (2021); Voice Actress, "Dolittle" (2020); Producer, "Last Christmas" (2019); Screenwriter, "Last Christmas" (2019); Actress, "Last Christmas" (2019); Actress, "Years and Years" (2019); Actress, "Men in Black: International" (2019); Voice Actress, "Missing Link" (2019); Actress, "How to Build a Girl" (2019); Actress, "Late Night" (2019); Executive Producer, "The Man with His Fingers in His Ears" (2019); Co-Producer, "Ponyboi" (2019); Actress, "Dear Sisters" (2018); Actress, "Johnny English Strikes Again" (2018); Narrator, "Greenpeace: There's a Rang-Tan in My Bedroom" (2018); Actress, "King Lear" (2018); Actress, "Upstart Crow" (2017); Actress, "The Children Act" (2017); Actress, "The Meyerowitz Stories" (2017); Actress, "Beauty and the Beast" (2017); Herself, "High Road" (2016); Narrator, "The Doubt Machine: Inside the Koch Brothers' War on Climate Science," The Real News Network (2016); Screenwriter, "Bridget Jones's Baby" (2016); Actress, "Bridget Jones's Baby" (2016); Actress, "Alone in Berlin" (2016); Executive Producer, "Sold" (2016); Narrator, "Sainsbury's: Mog's Christmas Calamity" (2015); Actress, "Burnt" (2015); Actress, "Barney Thomson" (2015); Actress, "Love Song" (2015); Actress, "A Walk in the Woods" (2015); Actress, "Sweeney Todd: The Demon Barber of Fleet Street - In Concert with the New York Philharmonic," "Live from Lincoln Center" (2014-2015); Screenwriter, "Effie Gray" (2014); Actress, "Effie Gray" (2014); Narrator, "Men, Women & Children" (2014); Actress, "Saving Mr. Banks" (2013); Actress, "The Love Punch" (2013); Actress, "Beautiful Creatures" (2013); Author, "The Christmas Tale of Peter Rabbit" (2013); Author, "The Further Tale of Peter Rabbit" (2012); Voice Actress, "Brave" (2012); Actress, "Walking the Dogs," "Playhouse Presents" (2012); Actress, "Men in Black 3" (2012); Actress, "Harry Potter and the Deathly Hallows: Part 2" (2011); Actress, "The Song of Lunch" (2010); Executive Producer, Screenwriter, Actress, "Nanny McPhee Returns" (2010); Executive Producer, "The Journey" (2009); Actress, "Pirate Radio" (2009); Actress, "An Education" (2009); Actress, "Last Chance Harvey" (2008); Actress, "Brideshead Revisited" (2008); Actress, "I Am Legend" (2007); Actress, "Harry Potter and the Order of the Phoenix" (2007); Actress, "Stranger Than Fiction" (2006); Screenwriter, "Nanny McPhee" (2005); Actress, "Nanny McPhee" (2005); Actress, "Harry Potter and the Prisoner of Azkaban" (2004); Actress, "Angels in America" (2003); Actress, "Love Actually" (2003); Actress, "Imagining Argentina" (2003); Voice Actress, "Treasure Planet" (2002); Actress, "Wit" (2001); Actress, "Maybe Baby" (2000); Actress, "Judas Kiss" (1998); Actress, "Primary Colors" (1998); Featured, "Ellen" (1997); Actress, "The Winter Guest" (1997); Actress,

"Hospital!" (1997); Screenwriter, "Sense and Sensibility" (1995); Actress, "Sense and Sensibility" (1995); Actress, "Carrington" (1995); Actress, "Junior" (1994); Actress, "The Blue Boy" (1994); Actress, "My Father the Hero" (1994); Actress, "In the Name of the Father" (1993); Actress, "The Remains of the Day" (1993); Actress, "Much Ado About Nothing" (1993); Actress, "Peter's Friends" (1992); Actress, "Howards End" (1992); Actress, "Cheers" (1992); Actress, "Dead Again" (1991); Actress, "Impromptu" (1991); Actress, "King Lear," Dominion Theatre, Renaissance Theatre Company (1990); Actress, "A Midsummer Night's Dream," International Tour (1990); Actress, "Look Back in Anger," Lyric Theatre, London (1989); Actress, "Henry V" (1989); Actress, "Theatre Night" (1989); Actress, "The Tall Guy" (1989); Actress, "Managing Problem People. Behavioral Skills for Leader" (1988); Actress, "Thompson" (1988); Actress, "Fortunes of War" (1987); Actress, "Tutti Frutti" (1987); Actress, "Assaulted Nuts" (1985); Actress, "Me and My Girl," Haymarket Theatre, Adelphi Theatre (1984-1985); Actress, "The Young Ones" (1984); Actress, "The Comic Strip Presents..." (1984); Performer, Playwright, "Short Vehicle," Edinburgh Festival (1984); Actress, "Alfresco" (1983-1984); Actress, "The Crystal Cube" (1983); Performer, Playwright, "Beyond the Footlights" (1982); Actress, "There's Nothing to Worry About!" (1982) **AW:** Dame Commander of the Order of the British Empire, Queen's Birthday Honours (2018); Best Actress, "Saving Mr. Banks," Empire Awards (2013); Best Actress, "Saving Mr. Banks," National Board of Review (2013); Star, Hollywood Walk of Fame (2010); European Hero for Her Work to Highlight the Plight of AIDS Sufferers in Africa, Time (2004); Best British Supporting Actress, "Love Actually," London Film Critics' Circle (2003); Outstanding Guest Actress in a Comedy Series, "Ellen," Primetime Emmy Awards (1998); Pasinetti Award, Best Actress, "The Winter Guest," Venice Film Festival (1997); Best Screenplay for a Motion Picture, "Sense and Sensibility," Golden Globes (1996); Best British Screenwriter, "Sense and Sensibility," London Film Critics' Circle (1996); Best Adapted Screenplay, "Sense and Sensibility," Academy Awards (1995); Best Screenplay, "Sense and Sensibility," Golden Globes (1995); Best Adapted Screenplay, "Sense and Sensibility," British Academy Film Awards (1995); Best Screenplay, "Sense and Sensibility," Boston Society Film Critics (1995); Best Adapted Screenplay, "Sense and Sensibility," Writers Guild of America Awards (1995); Best Screenplay, "Sense and Sensibility," Broadcast Film Critics Association (1995); Best Screenplay, "Sense and Sensibility," New York Film Critics Circle (1995); Best Actress, "Sense and Sensibility," National Board of Review (1995); Best Actress, "Howards End," Academy Awards (1993); Best Supporting Actress, "In the Name of the Father," Kansas City Film Critics Circle (1993); Best Actress, "The Remains of the Day," Kansas City Film Critics Circle (1993); Best Actress in a Leading Role, "Howards End" (1992); Best Actress, "Howards End," Boston Society Film Critics (1992); Best Actress, "Howards End," National Board of Review (1992); Best Actress, "Howards End," Kansas City Film Critics Circle (1992); Best Actress, "Howards End," Chicago Film Critics Association (1992); Best Actress, "Howards End," New York Film Critics Circle (1992); Best Actress, "Howards End," Southeastern Film Critics Association (1992); Best Actress, "Fortunes of War," "Tutti Frutti," British Academy Television Awards (1987)

THOMPSON, GLENN, "G.T." W. JR., T: U.S. Representative from Pennsylvania; Former Health Facility Administrator **I:** Government Administration/Government Relations/Government Services **DOB:** 07/27/1959 **PB:** Bellefonte **SC:** PA/USA **MS:** Married **SPN:** Penny (Ammerman) Thompson **CH:** Parker; Logan; Kale **ED:** MEd, Temple University, Philadelphia, PA (1998); BS in Therapeutic Recreation, The Pennsylvania State University (1981) **CT:** Licensed Nursing Home Administrator, Marywood University, Scranton, PA (2006) **C:** Member, U.S. House of Representatives from Pennsylvania's 15th Congressional District, United States Congress, Washington, DC (2019-Present); Member, U.S. House of Representatives from Pennsylvania's Fifth Congressional District, United States Congress, Washington, DC (2009-2019); Rehabilitation Services Manager, Susquehanna Health Systems, UPMC Susquehanna, Williamsport, PA (1995-2009); Recreational Therapist, Williamsport Hospital (UPMC Williamsport), UPMC Susquehanna, PA (1986-1995); Residential Services Aide, Hope Enterprises, Inc., Williamsport, PA (1981-1982); Residential Services Aide, Centre Crest Nursing Home, Bellefonte, PA (1977-1980); Committee on Agriculture, United States Congress; Committee on Education and the Workforce, United States Congress; Committee on Natural Resources, United States Congress **CR:** Member, International Advisory Council, Commission Accreditation Rehabilitation Facilities (CARF) (2006-2008); President, American Therapeutic Recreation Association (ATRA) (1998-2003); Board of Directors, Treasurer, American Therapeutic Recreation Association (ATRA) (1997-2000); Adjunct Faculty, Cambria County Community College, Johnstown, PA (1997-1999); Director, Pennsylvania Head Injury Foundation; Director, President, Pennsylvania Therapeutic Recreation Society **CIV:** President, Juniata Valley Council, Boy Scouts of America (2007-2009); Chair, Centre County Republican Party (2002-2008); Vice-Chair, Board of Directors, Private Industry Council Central Corridors (2000-2008); Volunteer, Howard Volunteer Fire Company (1982-2008); Scoutmaster, Howard Boy Scout Troop 353 (1981-2008); Senior Vice President, Juniata Valley Council, Boy Scouts of America (2005-2007); Alternate Delegate, Republican National Convention (2004); Board of Directors, Private Industry Council of the Central Corridor (PICCS, Inc.) (1999-2000); Bellefonte Intervalley Chamber of Commerce (1977-2000); Bald Eagle Area School Board (1990-1996) **MEM:** Pennsylvania Rural Development Council; Pennsylvania Rural Health Association; Republican Governors Club **PA:** Republican **RE:** Protestant

THOMPSON, KATHLEEN S., T: Marriage and Family Counselor **I:** Social Work **DOB:** 10/22/1945 **PB:** Bakersfield **SC:** CA/USA **PT:** Stephen W. Shambaugh; Marilyn L. Shambaugh **MS:** Married **SPN:** John W. Thompson (06/10/1967, Deceased 1971) **CH:** Stephen; Charles **ED:** MA in Counseling, University of Denver (1976); BA in English, University of Colorado (1968); Coursework, Colorado Women's College (1964) **CT:** Teaching Credential, University of Colorado (1971); Licensed Counselor, Denver, CO **C:** Marriage, Family and Child Counselor (1982-Present); Editor, Proofreader (1978-1980); Teacher, California (1978); Teacher, Denver, CO (1971-1978) **CW:** Author, "Funeral Planning, Memorial Services, and Coping with Death"; Author, "Using the Case in Professional Work"; Author, "A Journey through the Triangle of Canada, Britain, and America"; Author, "Afterlife Envision"; Author, "Creeping Greed"; Author, "Crime Awareness and Prevention, Including the Mafia"; Author, "Diary of a Drug Addict"; Author, "Eight Drama Stories: Twists and Turns"; Author, "Global Warming Causes and Solutions"; Author, "Letters to England"; Author, "Living and Traveling in the South West"; Author, "Racial Equality"; Author, "13 Science Fiction Stories: Separate Worlds"; Author, "Sex Trends in Society"; Author, "Shingles are Awful"; Author, "Stair-Temple Sites/Chilean Easter Island"; Author, "Stonehenge and Other Stone-Placement Sites"; Author, "Taking a Shower - Shower Savvy"; Author, "The Case Study-Case by Case"; Author, "The Gap Theory for Mental Assessment and Treatment"; Author, "The Outdoor Perils of Cats"; Author, Poetry Book, "Extra Poems and Short Works"; Author, Poetry Book, "Final Poems and Short Works"; Author, Poetry Book, "Spare Poems and Short Works"; Author, Children's Book, "Charlie and Mom Cat"; Author, Children's Book, "The Cygnet"; Author, Juvenile Book, "The Madame Spider"; Author, "An American Girl in Canada"; Author, "A Life Filled With Poetry"; Author, "Crime and Rehabilitation and The Gap Theory for Mental Assessment"; Author, "The Surgery Experience"; Author, "Writers and Writing"; Author, "Landscaping Any Small Lot"; Author, "The Equal Personage of the Child"; Author, "Going Through Life: Poems and Short Works"; Author, "Gina's Rehabilitation"; Author, "Brown Flowers in Gloucester"; Author, "I Care For My Cats"; Author, "Travelers"; Author, "Getting Through Life: Other Poems and Short Works"; Author, "Counseling Helps"; Author, "Next Poems and Short Work"; Author, "Stragglers Poems and Short Works"; Author, "Isolated Poems & Short Works"; Author, "A Driven Life: The Life of My Father" **AW:** International Poet Merit, International Society of Poets (2000, 2007); Listed, International Library of Poetry (2001, 2007); Listee, "One of the Best Poets of 2000" **MEM:** International Society of Poets; Delta Delta Delta **MH:** Albert Nelson Marquis Lifetime Achievement Award **B/I:** Dr. Thompson became involved in her profession because she was an editor and proofreader for a while, and that did not have much to do with her career focus at the time. She was more interested in teaching and, in time, she took extra classes that enabled her to become a licensed marriage and family counselor. She became interested in writing after a car accident. When she was younger, a group from New York was soliciting people to write and they wanted a writing sample, so she sent them a writing sample. This helped to spark her interest in starting a family and children's museum. **AV:** Rescuing; Stamp collecting; Doll collecting; Appreciating literature; Gardening **THT:** Dr. Thompson started a museum, for which she collected dolls, children's toys, and art.

THOMPSON, THOMAS M., LLB, T: Lawyer **I:** Law and Legal Services **DOB:** 01/07/1943 **PB:** Albion **SC:** PA/USA **PT:** Donald C. Thompson; Mabel Louise (Martin) Thompson **MS:** Married **SPN:** Judith E. Daucher (08/14/1965) **CH:** Reid; Chad; Matthew; Molly **ED:** JD, Harvard University, Cum Laude (1968); AB, Grove City College (1965) **C:** Of Counsel, Buchanan Ingersoll & Rooney PC, Pittsburgh, PA (2019-Present); Partner, Buchanan Ingersoll & Rooney PC, Pittsburgh, PA (1976-2018); Associate, Buchanan Ingersoll & Rooney PC, Pittsburgh, PA (1968-1976) **CR:** Adjunct Professor of Law, Past Chairman, University of Pittsburgh; Pennsylvania Lawyer Trust Accountant Board **CIV:** Past President, Board Director, Neighborhood Legal Services Association; Trustee Emeritus, Pittsburgh Public Theater **AW:** Pro Bono Award, Pennsylvania Bar Association (1989); W. Edward H. Sell Award for Business Law Lifetime Contributions; Alumni Achievement Award, Grove City College **MEM:** Chair of Business Law Section, Pennsylvania Bar Association (1989); Program Chair, Negotiated Acquisition Committee, ABA; Past President, Pittsburgh Chapter, Association for Corporation Growth (ACG); Past Chairman of Public Service Committee, Past Chairman of Business Law Council, Past Chair of PBA Legal Opinion Steering Committee, Allegheny County Bar Association; Working Group on Legal Opinions (WGLO) **BAR:** Pennsylvania Bar Association (1968) **MH:** Albert Nelson Marquis Lifetime Achievement Award **AS:** Mr. Thompson attributes his success to good teachers from high school, college, and law school. Additionally, he is grateful for the opportunities that have been provided by his law firm. **B/I:** Mr. Thompson doesn't know exactly where his interest in becoming a lawyer started, but he recalls that by his senior year of high school, he had listed in his yearbook that he had aspirations to become a corporate lawyer. Mr. Thompson knew that he wanted a career where he could rely more on his writing and people skills, and law seemed to be a perfect fit. **AV:** Travel; Tennis; Writing **PA:** Democrat

THOMPSON, TIMOTHY LEWIS, T: Lawyer, Partner **I:** Law and Legal Services **CN:** McCanliss & Early LLP **DOB:** 02/28/9148 **PB:** Stamford **SC:** CT/USA **PT:** Elbert Paul; Carol Lewis Thompson **MS:** Married **SPN:** Elizabeth Anne Wasik (1973) **CH:** Andrew Austin; Charles Erling; Nicholas James; Daniel Raymond **ED:** JD, The George Washington University (1974); BA, Columbia University (1971); Diploma, Phillips Academy, Andover, MA (1967) **C:** Lawyer/Partner, McCanliss & Early LLP (1982-Present); Associate, McCanliss & Early LLP (1974-1982) **CIV:** Director, Adirondack Explorer (2005-Present); President, Trustee, Montauk Club (2004-Present); Secretary, Trustee, Down Town Association (1996-Present); Trustee, Harding Educational and Charitable Foundation (1990-Present) **MEM:** President, Oneita Boat Club (2014-Present); New York State Bar Association; American Bar Association **BAR:** New York State Bar Association (1975) **B/I:** Mr. Thompson became involved in his profession after switching his major numerous times in college. Though he started as a music major, he ended up as a law major. **AV:** Sailing; Playing viola and violin

THOMSON, BRANDON S., ESQ., T: Attorney **I:** Law and Legal Services **CN:** The Probate Pro Law Firm **DOB:** 02/17/1984 **PB:** Dearborn **SC:** MI/USA **PT:** Scott Thomson; Karen Thomson **MS:** Married **SPN:** Laura **CH:** Brody; Brennan; Bryor; Bruce **ED:** JD, Western Michigan University Thomas M. Cooley Law School, Cum Laude; BA in History, Siena Heights University **CT:** Accredited Veterans Administration Attorney, Probate and Estate Planning Certificate; State Bar of Michigan Probate and Estate Planning Section, The Institute of Continuing Legal Education (ICLE) **C:** Probate, Estate Planning, and Elder Law Attorney, The Probate Pro Law Firm **CIV:** Boy Scouts of America; Fundraiser and Volunteer, Knights of Columbus **AW:** Named to "Top Ten Estate Planning Attorney in Michigan 2020," Attorney and Practice Magazine (2020); Named "Rising Star," Super Lawyers Magazine (2018, 2019, 2020); Named to "Top Young Rising Attorneys in Michigan Selection 2019," Crain's Detroit Business (2019); Named to "10 Best Elder Law Attorneys in Michigan 2018," American Institute of Legal Counsel (2018); Eugene Krasicky Award, Western Michigan University Cooley Law Review; Named to Top Lawyers for Dedication, Achievements, and Leadership in Probate and Estates Law **MEM:** State Bar of Michigan; Probate and Estate Planning Section, State Bar of Michigan; Elder Law Section and Disability Rights Section, State Bar of Michigan; Attorney Advisor Board Member, Henry Ford Hospital Ethics Committee; National Academy of Elder Law Attorneys (NAELA); ElderCounsel, LLC **BAR:** State of Michigan **AS:** Mr. Thomson is very inspired by his wife and four sons. He believes in working harder than any body else, and finding something you are passionate about; that way, you will never work a day

in your life and you will be successful. **B/I:** Mr. Thomson's career path to becoming an attorney was not traditional. He started off as a teacher, then a Zamboni driver at the local ice rink after school. Next, he drove a Schwan's Truck, delivering frozen food to amazing clients before and during his law school journey. While he was a "Schwan's Man," he developed a desire to advocate for the senior population. Once he learned that there was an area of law that focused on seniors, he decided that that was the area of law he wanted to practice in. He is married to his smart and beautiful wife, Laura, and they have four fantastic sons, which he describes as his pride and joy. Mr. Thomson also credits his parents, Scott and Karen Thomson for instilling in him a hard work ethic and to treat people the way you want to be treated. Mr. Thomson stated that "I have never seen my parents miss a day of work." If Brandon is not hanging around his office or with his family, you can usually catch him at the local ice rink playing Over 30 Men's league hockey. **THT:** The Probate Pro practice is focused on helping families' have confidence when faced with the legal and personal challenges presented by long life, illness, disability, or death.

THORNBERRY, WILLIAM, "MAC" MCCLELLAN, T: U.S. Representative from Texas; Lawyer **I:** Government Administration/Government Relations/Government Services **DOB:** 7/15/1958 **PB:** Clarendon **SC:** TX/USA **MS:** Married **SPN:** Sally Thornberry **CH:** Two Children **ED:** JD, The University of Texas at Austin School of Law (1983); BA in History, Texas Tech University, Summa Cum Laude (1980) **C:** Ranking Member, U.S. House Committee on Armed Services (2019-Present); Member, U.S. House of Representatives from Texas' 13th Congressional District, United States Congress, Washington, DC (1995-Present); Chairman, U.S. House Committee on Armed Services (2015-2019); Defense Attorney, Peterson, Farris, Doores & Jones, Amarillo, TX (1989-1994); Deputy Assistant Secretary for Legislative Affairs, U.S. Department of State (1988-1989); Chief of Staff to Representative Larry Combest, U.S. House of Representative (1985-1988); Legislative Counsel to Representative Tom Loeffler, U.S. House of Representatives (1983-1985) **CIV:** Council on Foreign Relations **MEM:** Texas and Southwestern Cattle Raisers Association **PA:** Republican **RE:** Presbyterian

THORNE, KIP STEPHEN, PHD, T: Physicist, Researcher **I:** Sciences **DOB:** 06/01/1940 **PB:** Logan **SC:** UT/USA **PT:** David Wynne Thorne; Alison (Comish) Thorne **MS:** Married **SPN:** Carolee Joyce Winstein (07/07/1984); Linda Jean Peterson (09/12/1960, Divorced 1977) **CH:** Kares Anne; Bret Carter **ED:** Honorary Doctor of Humane Letters, Claremont Graduate University (2002); Honorary Doctor of Science, University of Glasgow (2001); Honorary Doctor of Science, Utah State University (2000); Doctor Honoris Causa, Moscow University (1981); Honorary Doctor of Science, Illinois College (1979); Postgraduate Coursework, Princeton University (1966); Doctor of Philosophy in Physics, Princeton University (1965); Master of Arts in Physics, Princeton University (1963); Bachelor of Science in Physics, California Institute of Technology (1962) **C:** Feynman Professor of Theoretical Physics Emeritus, California Institute of Technology (2009-Present); Feynman Professor of Theoretical Physics, California Institute of Technology (1991-2009); William R. Kenan Jr. Professor, California Institute of Technology (1981-1991); Professor of Theoretical Physics, California Institute of Technology (1970-1991); Associate Professor of Theoretical Physics, California Institute of Technology (1967-1970); Research Fellow, California Institute of Technology (1966-1967); Postdoctoral Fellow

of Physics, Princeton University (1965-1966) **CR:** Member, International Committee on General Relativity and Gravitation (1971-1980, 1992-2001); Adjunct Professor, University of Utah (1971-1998); Visiting Professor, Moscow University (1969, 1975, 1978, 1982, 1983, 1986, 1988, 1990, 1998); Andrew D. White Professor-at-Large (1986-1992); Co-founder, Chair, Steering Committee, LIGO Scientific Collaboration (1984-1987); Member, Space Science Board, NASA (1980-1983); Member, Committee on U.S.-USSR Cooperative in Physics (1978-1979); Visiting Senior Research Associate, Cornell University (1977); Visiting Associate Professor, The University of Chicago (1968); Fulbright Lecturer, France (1966) **CW:** Co-author, "Black Holes and Time Warps: Einstein's Outrageous Legacy" (1994); Co-author, "Black Holes: The Membrane Paradigm" (1986); Co-author, "Gravitation" (1973); Co-author, "Gravitation Theory and Gravitational Collapse" (1965); Contributor, Articles to Professional Journals **AW:** Nobel Prize in Physics (2017); Princess of Asturias Award (2017); Named, One of the 100 Most Influential People, TIME Magazine (2016); Harvey Prize (2016); Kavli Prize (2016); Shaw Prize (2016); Gruber Prize in Cosmology (2016); Special Breakthrough Prize in Fundamental Physics (2016); Common Wealth Award in Science Invention (2005); Named, California Scientist of the Year (2004); Robinson Prize in Cosmology, University of Newcastle (2002); Herzberg Memorial Lectureship, Canadian Association of Physicists (2001); Arthur Holly Compton Memorial Lectureship, Washington University in St. Louis (2001); Charles Darwin Memorial Lectureship, Royal Astronomical Society (2000); J. Robert Oppenheimer Memorial Lectureship, University of California (1999); Karl Schwarzschild Medal, Astronomical Society of Germany (1996); Julius Edgar Lilienfeld Prize, American Physical Society (1996); P.A.M. Dirac Memorial Lectureship, University of Cambridge (1995); Science Writing Award in Physics and Astronomy, American Institute of Physics (1969, 1994); Research Fellow, Alfred P. Sloan Foundation (1966-1968); Fellow, John Simon Guggenheim Memorial Foundation (1967); Postdoctoral Fellow, National Science Foundation (1966); Fellow, National Science Foundation (1965); Fellow, Danforth Foundation (1963, 1965); Woodrow Wilson Fellow, Princeton University **MEM:** Chair, Topical Group in Gravity, American Physical Society (1997-1998); Fellow, American Physical Society; The American Philosophical Society; National Academy of Sciences; American Academy of Arts and Sciences; American Astronomical Society; International Astronomical Union, American Association for the Advancement of Science; Russian Academy of Sciences; Ligo Scientific Collaboration; Lisa International Science Team; Sigma Xi; Tau Beta Pi

THUMS, CHARLES W., T: Designer, Consultant **I:** Architecture & Construction **DOB:** 09/05/1945 **PB:** Manitowoc **SC:** WI/USA **PT:** Earl Oscar; Helen Margaret (Rusch) Thums **ED:** Bachelor of Architecture, Arizona State University (1972) **C:** Industrial Design Consultant, Tempe, AZ (2010-Present); Designer, Consultant, Design Morphology, Procedural Programming and Algorithms (1978-Present); Senior Architect of Interior Design, Infrastructure Design Standards, Salt River Project, Tempe, AZ (1986-2009); Founder, Principal, I-Squared Environmental Consultant, Tempe, AZ (1970-1978); Partner, Grafic, Tempe, AZ (1970) **CR:** Fine Arts Drawing; Watercolors; Monotypes and Prints; Photography **CW:** Co-author, with Daniel Peter Aiello, "Shelter and Culture" (1976); Co-author, with Jonathan Craig Thums, "The Rossen House" (1975);

Author, "Tombstone Planning Guide" (1974); Co-author, with Jonathan Craig Thums, "Tempe's Grand Hotel" (1973)

THUNE, JOHN RANDOLPH, T: U.S. Senator from South Dakota **I:** Government Administration/Government Relations/Government Services **DOB:** 01/07/1961 **PB:** Pierre **SC:** SD/USA **PT:** Harold Richard Thune; Yvinne Patricia (Bodine) Thune **MS:** Married **SPN:** Kimberley Jo (Weems) Thune (1984) **CH:** Brittany; Larissa **ED:** MBA, Beacom School of Business, University of South Dakota (1984); BBA, Biola University, La Mirada, CA (1983) **C:** Senate Majority Leader (2019-Present); U.S. Senator, State of South Dakota (2005-Present); Chairman, U.S. Senate Committee on Commerce, Science and Transportation (2015-2019); Chair, Senate Republican Conference (2012-2019); Member, U.S. House of Representatives from South Dakota's At-large Congressional District, United States Congress, Washington, DC (1997-2003); Executive Director, South Dakota Municipal League (1993-1996); Director, Railroad Division, State of South Dakota (1991-1993); Executive Director, South Dakota Republican Party (1989-1991); Deputy Staff Director to the Ranking Representative, U.S. Senate Committee on Small Business (1987-1989); Legislative Assistant to Senator James Abdnor, U.S. Senate (1985-1987); Founder, The Thune Group LLC **CR:** Chairman, U.S. Senate Republican Conference (2012-Present); Chairman, U.S. Senate Republican Policy Committee (RPC) (2009-2012); Vice Chairman, U.S. Senate Republican Conference (2009) **AV:** Basketball; Pheasant hunting **PA:** Republican **RE:** Protestant

TIERNEY, JENNIFER, T: Designer, Owner **I:** Apparel & Fashion **CN:** J. Tierney Designs **C:** Owner, J. Tierney Designs (2016-Present); Owner, Instructor, American Dance Center (2006-Present) **CIV:** Co-director, Costume Director, American Youth Ballet; Volunteer, Kansas City Fashion Week; Kansas City Public Television **AW:** Winner, Youth America Gran Prix (2001); 1st Place, Competition, National Society of Arts and Letters (2000) **MEM:** American Youth Ballets **AS:** Ms. Tierney attributes her success to the fact that she is not afraid to fail. She also surrounds herself with people who are experts in their own right and can contribute to her growth. **B/I:** Ms. Tierney began dancing at the age of 3, when her babysitter, a high school student, began teaching her. After enrolling in dance lessons, she struggled initially but persevered, and became a professional ballet dancer at the age of 17. **THT:** "There is no fairy godmother for life, except hard work. If you take hard work with you, everywhere you go, you dreams will come true..."

TIETJEN, JILL S., T: President and Chief Executive Officer **I:** Engineering **DOB:** 12/20/1954 **PB:** Newport News **SC:** VA/USA **PT:** Manuel Stein; Bernice Stein **MS:** Married **SPN:** David Tietjen **ED:** MBA, University of North Carolina at Charlotte, Charlotte, NC (1979); BS in Applied Mathematics, University of Virginia, Charlottesville, VA (1976) **CT:** Registered Professional Engineer, Colorado **C:** Various Titles, College of Engineering and Applied Sciences, University of Colorado at Boulder (2001-Present); President and Chief Executive Officer, Technically Speaking, Inc. (1997-Present); Chief Executive Officer, National Women's Hall of Fame (2015); Senior Engineer, McNeil Technologies (2001-2008); Senior Management Consultant, R.W. Beck (2003-2005); Director, Women in Engineering Program, University of Colorado at Boulder (1997-2000); Assistant Vice President, Stone & Webster Management Consultants, Denver, CO (1995-1997); Principal, Hagler Bailly Consulting, Inc. (Formerly RCG/Hagler Bailly), Boulder, CO (1992-1995); Assistant Vice President, Stone & Webster Management Consultants, Denver, CO (1984-1992); Planning Analyst, Mobil Corporation, Denver, CO (1981-1984); Planning Engineer, Duke Power Company, Charlotte, NC (1976-1981) **CR:** Board of Directors, Merrick & Company (2010-Present); Board of Directors, Georgia Transmission Corporation (1997-Present); Chair, Colorado State Board of Registration for Professional Engineers and Professional Land Surveyors (1996-2004); Board of Directors, Electrical Engineering Program Evaluator, ABET (Accreditation Board for Engineering and Technology, Inc.) (1998-2002); Women in the Workforce Advisory Group, Women's Foundation of Colorado (1998-2001); Board of Directors, Utility Women's Conference (1997-2000); Advisory Committee, Transformations Program, Higher Education and Advanced Technology Center (1997-1999); Executive Board and Advisory Committee, Interdisciplinary Telecommunications Program, University of Colorado at Boulder (1994-1997); External Advisory Board, Women in Engineering Program (1993-1997); Coal Market Strategies Conference Advisory Committee (1990-1993, 1997) **CIV:** Board of Directors, Mile Hi Council, Girl Scouts (1999-2007); Board of Directors, Colorado Women's Leadership Coalition, Denver, CO (2004); Board of Directors, Rocky Mountain Electrical League (1994-2002); Board of Directors, Women in Engineering Programs & Advocates Network (WEPAN) (1995-2001); President, Women's Forum of Colorado Foundation (1997-2000); Board of Directors, Arapahoe Library District (1995-2000); Steering Committee for Celebration of Women, National Academy of Engineering (1997-1999); Board of Directors, Arapahoe Library Foundation (1997-1999); Accountability Committee, Littleton Public Schools (1997-1999); Recording for the Blind and Dyslexic, Denver, CO (1997-1998); Leadership Denver Class of 1996 (1996); Violinist, Bookkeeper, Littleton Symphony Orchestra (1989-1995) **CW:** Co-Author, "Hollywood: Her Story, An Illustrated History of Women and the Movies" (2019); Co-Author, "Women in Engineering Book 9: Recognizing and Taking Advantage of Opportunities" (2016); Co-Author, "Inspiring Women of the National Women's Hall of Fame" (2015); Co-Author, "Her Story: A Timeline of the Women Who Changed America" (2008); Co-Author, "Setting the Record Straight" Series (2001, 2005); Co-Author, "Keys to Engineering Success" (2001); Co-Author, "Keys to Engineering Success" (2001); Co-Author, "She Does Math!" (1995); Contributor, Numerous Articles, Publications; Contributor, Presenter, Numerous Presentations Per Year; Contributor, Collection, The Jill Tietjen Papers, Denver Public Library, Denver, CO; Contributor, Numerous Books and Book Chapters; Co-Host, Appearances, Numerous Radio and Television Shows, YouTube Videos, and Podcasts **AW:** Colorado Authors' Hall of Fame (2019); Trailblazer Award, WorldDenver (2019); Distinguished Alumna Award, UNCC Belk College of Business (2018); General Palmer Award, ACEC-Colorado (2017); Reader's Choice Awards, Women's History, Best Introduction to Women's History, about.com (2012); Daughters of the American Revolution History Award Medal (2012); Athena Award Finalist, Colorado Women's Chamber of Commerce (2009, 2010); Distinguished Alumna Award, University of Virginia (2007); Distinguished Service Award, Western Zone, National Council of Examiners for Engineering and Surveying (2007); Distinguished Engineering Alumni Award, University of Colorado at Boulder (2005); Woman Leader of Excellence, Colorado Women's Leadership Coalition (2004); Distinguished Alumna Award, Tau Beta Pi (2004); Virginia Engineering Foundation Distinguished Alumni Award (2004); Horizon Award, Outstanding Professional, The Partnership to Advance Science, Engineering, and Technology (2003); Distinguished Service Award, SWE (2002); Presidential Citation Award, Professional Land Surveyors of Colorado (2000); Soroptimist International Women of Distinction Award (1995); John E. Daly Award for Consulting Excellence, Stone & Webster Management Consultants (1991); Certificate of Honor, Colorado Engineering Council (1990) **MEM:** Society of Women Engineers; Institute of Electrical and Electronics Engineers (IEEE); Women's Forum of Colorado; Virginia Alpha Chapter, Tau Beta Pi; Omicron Delta Kappa **MH:** Albert Nelson Marquis Lifetime Achievement Award **B/I:** Ms. Tietjen decided to pursue engineering during her time at the University of Virginia. She was determined to make it a field accessible to everyone, especially women. **AV:** Playing tennis; Practicing needlework; Traveling

TILBURY, CHARLOTTE, MBE, T: Owner, Creative Director **I:** Cosmetics **CN:** Charlotte Tilbury Beauty Ltd. **DOB:** 02/10/1973 **PB:** London **SC:** England **PT:** Lance Tilbury; Patsy Dodd **MS:** Married **SPN:** George Waud (06/2014) **CH:** Two sons **ED:** Coursework, Glauca Rossi School of Makeup **CT:** Advanced Level Certification **C:** Founder, Charlotte Tilbury Beauty Ltd. (2012-Present) **CW:** Host, YouTube Channel **AW:** Business of Fashion 500 (2013-Present); 1000 Companies to Inspire Britain, London Stock Exchange Group (2019); Best British Brand of the Year, Cosmetic Executive Women (2015-2016, 2018-2019); Order of the British Empire (2018); Nominee, Veuve Clicquot Businesswoman of the Year (2016); Best Health & Beauty eCommerce Website of the Year (2016); Walpole Award for Emerging Luxury British Brand (2014); Achiever Award, Cosmetic Executive Women (2014); Rodial Award for Best Make-up Artist (2012); Makeup Artist of the Year, Proctor & Gamble **AS:** Ms. Tilbury attributes her success to her hard work, determination and passion for her profession. **B/I:** Ms. Tilbury became involved in her profession because she always had a passion for make-up and fashion. **AV:** Spending time with her husband on holidays

TILDERS, SONNY, T: Animatronics Artist **I:** Media & Entertainment **PB:** Frankston **SC:** VIC/Australia **PT:** Dutch Tilders **C:** Creative Director, Creature Technology Company **CW:** Creature Designer, "King Kong," Broadway Theatre, New York, NY (2018); Creature Designer, "King Kong," Regent Theatre (2013); Creature Designer, "How To Train Your Dragon," Global Creatures Group, DreamWorks (2012); Team Leader, "Walking with Dinosaurs - The Arena Spectacular" (2007) **AW:** Special Tony Award, "King Kong" (2019); Outstanding Puppet Design, "King Kong," Drama Desk Awards (2019); Special Achievement Award, "King Kong," Outer Critics Circle (2019)

TILLIS, THOMAS, "THOM" ROLAND, T: U.S. Senator from North Carolina **I:** Government Administration/Government Relations/Government Services **CN:** U.S. Senate **DOB:** 8/30/1960 **PB:** Jacksonville **SC:** FL/USA **PT:** Thomas Raymond Tillis; Margie Tillis **MS:** Married **SPN:** Susan Tillis **CH:** Lindsay; Ryan **ED:** Bachelor of Science in Technology Management, University of Maryland Global Campus (1997); Coursework, Chattanooga State Community College **C:** U.S. Senator, State of North Carolina (2015-Present); Member, U.S. Senate Committee on Veterans' Affairs (2015-Present); Member, U.S. Senate Judiciary Committee (2015-Present); Member, U.S. Senate Committee on Armed Services (2015-Present); Member, U.S. Senate Committee on Agriculture, Nutrition and Forestry (2015-Present); Member, U.S. Senate Special Committee on Aging (2015-Present); Speaker, North Carolina House of Representatives (2011-2015); Member, District 98, North Carolina House of Representatives, NC (2007-2015); Commissioner, City of Cornelius, NC (2003-2005); Partner, PwC CIV: President, Parent Teacher Student Association, Hopewell High School (2005-2006) AW: Named, One of the 17 GOP Legislators to Watch, Governing Magazine (2011); Duke Power Citizenship and Service Award PA: Republican RE: Roman Catholic

TILLMAN, BARBARA BALLARD, T: Librarian I: Library Management/Library Services DOB: 08/08/1940 PB: Kingsville SC: TX/USA PT: Leslie Hallett Ballard; Lula Evelyn (Walker) Ballard MS: Divorced SPN: William Delmar Tillman (09/22/1962, Divorced 1988) CH: Andrea Clare Eakin; Kenneth Leslie Tillman ED: BA in Sociology and Psychology, Texas Christian University, Fort Worth, TX (1962) C: Library Periodicals, Midland County Public Library, Midland, TX (1978-1998); Accounts Payable Bookkeeper, Texas Christian University, Fort Worth, TX (1964-1965); Extension Department, Fort Worth Public Library, Fort Worth, TX (1962-1963) CR: Docent, Computer Entry, Peacham Historical Association, Peacham, VT (2001-2014) MH: Albert Nelson Marquis Lifetime Achievement Award B/I: Ms. Tillman became involved in her profession because she loves books and reading. She quickly found that she liked to work in a literary atmosphere and longed to work with books for the rest of her life. AV: Writing poetry and essays; Preserving land and animals

TIMBLIN, LLOYD O. JR., T: Water Resources Scientist I: Sciences DOB: 06/25/1927 PB: Denver SC: CO/USA PT: Lloyd Oswald Timblin; Winona Mary (Crosby) Timblin MS: Widowed SPN: Barbara Helen McNiel (09/06/1950) CH: Carol Lynn ED: MS in Physics, University of Denver (1967); BS in Engineering Physics, University of Colorado (1950) CT: Registered Professional Engineer, State of Colorado; Certified Corrosion Specialist C: Industrial Water Resources Consultant, Bureau of Reclamation (1992-Present); Chief, Applied Science Branch, Bureau of Reclamation (1970-1991); Chief, Chemical Engineering Branch, Bureau of Reclamation (1963-1970); Head, Special Investigations Laboratory Section, Bureau of Reclamation (1958-1963); Physicist, Bureau of Reclamation (1950-1958) CR: Committee on Environment, International Commission on Large Dams (1987-Present); Standards Committee on Thermosetting Fiberglass Reinforced Plastic Pipe (1971-1989); General Reporter, "Question 60-Reservoirs and the Environment" International Commission on Large Dams (1988); Chair, US Team, US/USSR Joint Study of Plastics in Hydrotechnical Construction (1975-1985); Chair, Technical Program, International Symposium on Geomembranes (1984); National Sanitation Foundation Joint Committee for Flexible Membrane Liners, Bureau of Reclamation (1978-1983); Colorado Advisory Council for Seminar on Environmental Arts and Sciences (1971-1974) MIL: US Navy (1944-1945) CW: Patentee in Field AW: Distinguished Service Award, U.S. Department of the Interior (1991); Merit Service Award, U.S. Department of the Interior (1977) MH: Albert Nelson Marquis Lifetime Achievement Award B/I: Mr. Timblin became involved in his profession because ever since he was in high school he was interested in science. In college, he was directed to the Bureau of Reclamation. RE: Presbyterian

TIMLIN, JAMES, T: Bishop Emeritus I: Religious DOB: 08/05/1927 PB: Scranton SC: PA/USA PT: James C. Timlin; Helen E. (Norton) Timlin ED: STB, Gregorian University, Rome, Italy (1950); AB, St. Mary's Seminary, Baltimore, MD (1948) C: Rector, Villa St. Joseph, Dunmore, PA (2004-Present); Bishop Emeritus, Diocese of Scranton (2003-Present); Administrator, St. Joseph's Church, Wilkes-Barre, PA (2004); Bishop, Diocese of Scranton (1984-2003); Pastor, Church of Nativity, Scranton, PA (1979-1984); Auxiliary Bishop, Vicar General, Diocese of Scranton (1976-1984); Chancellor, Diocese of Scranton (1971-1977); Assistant Chancellor, Secretary, Diocese of Scranton (1966-1971); Assistant Pastor, St. Peter's Cathedral, Scranton, PA (1953-1966); Assistant Pastor, St. John The Evangelist Church, Pittston, PA (1952-1953); Ordained Priest, Diocese of Scranton (1951). RE: Roman Catholic

TIMMONS, WILLIAM RICHARDSON IV, T: U.S. Representative from South Carolina; Lawyer; Entrepreneur I: Government Administration/Government Relations/Government Services DOB: 04/30/1984 PB: Greenville SC: SC/USA MS: Married SPN: Sarah (Anderson) Timmons (07/17/2019) ED: JD, University of South Carolina School of Law; MA in International Studies, University of South Carolina; BA in International Affairs and Political Science, The George Washington University Elliott School of International Affairs C: Member, U.S. House of Representatives from South Carolina's Fourth Congressional District (2019-Present); Member, District Six, South Carolina Senate (2016-2018); With, Solicitor's Office, 13th Circuit; Owner, Swamp Rabbit CrossFit; Owner, Soul Yoga; Owner, Timmons & Company, LLC CIV: Life Member, Christ Church Episcopal, Greenville, SC MIL: First Lieutenant, South Carolina Air National Guard PA: Republican RE: Episcopalian

TING, CHIN-SEN, T: Physics Professor I: Education/Educational Services DOB: 11/12/1939 PB: Shanxi SC: China MS: Married SPN: Shien S. Ting CH: One son ED: PhD in Physics, UC San Diego (1970) C: Research Associate, Physics Department, Brown University, Providence, RI (1974-1976); Postdoctoral Fellow, Physics Department, New York University, New York, NY (1970-1974) CR: Professor, Department of Physics, College of Natural Sciences and Mathematics, University of Houston (1985-Present) MEM: Fellow, American Physical Society MH: Albert Nelson Marquis Lifetime Achievement Award AS: Dr. Ting attributes his success to being persistent and hard working. B/I: Dr. Ting became involved in his profession because he found that physics was a very fascinating subject in high school and decided to make it his professional career.

TIPPETS, DENNIS W., T: Mineral Exploration Executive, State Legislator I: Mining & Metals DOB: 12/30/1938 PB: Wheatland SC: WY/USA PT: Neff H.; Elizabeth (Wilcock) T. MS: Single CH: Lynn Elizabeth; Kevin Craig; Bruce Barkley ED: Bachelor of Arts, University of Colorado Boulder (1962) CT: Administrative Law Judge (1998); Certified Real Estate Appraiser, Wyoming; National Judicial College, University of Nevada, Reno, NV C: Chairperson, Board of Directors, President, Chief Executive Officer, Minex Resources Inc., Riverton, WY (1980-Present); President, Tippets Appraisal Service, Riverton, WY (1976-1980); Vice President, Stylhomes Inc., Riverton, WY (1971-1976); Management Consultant, Roy Jorgenson Associates, Gaithersburg, MD (1967-1971); Personnel Administrator, Lamb-Grays Harbor Co. Inc., Hoquiam, Washington (1965-1967) CR: Board Director, Methanol Production Corp., Denver, CO CIV: Elected Director, Mountain View Cemetery District, Riverton, WY (2017-Present); District President, Winipeg, Manitoba, Bishoperie, High Councilman, Public Affairs Director (2010-Present); Trustee, Riverton Memorial Hospital (1993-Present); Member, Riverton Community Development Association (1993-Present); Assistant District Governor, Charter President, Rotary District 5440, Riverton, Wyoming Rotary Club (2018); Chief Tax Judge, Wyoming (1997-2000); Elected Mayor, Riverton, WY (1995); State Representative, Wyoming House of Representatives, Cheyenne, WY (1985-1993); President, Board of Directors Idea Inc., Riverton, WY (1986-1988); Member, Committee on Career Education, National School Board Association, Washington (1986-1988); Vice Chairman, Representative Caucus Chairman, Member, Riverton School Board (1975-1981); Vice President, Fremont County Republican Party, Lander, WY (1978-1980) MIL: Commanding Officer, U.S. Navy, Aberdeen, WA (1965-1968); U.S. Navy Liaison Officer, Royal Candian Air Force, Comox, BC (1963) AW: Riverton Wyoming Lifetime Service Award, Rotary International (2018); Special Award, U.S. Small Business Administration (1989); Named, Most Effective Freshman Legislator, Wyoming Capital Press Corp., Cheyenne, WY (1985) MEM: Chairperson, Science and Technology committee, Taiwan Tour Group Appraisal Institute, National Conference of State Legislatures (1989); American Mining Congress; Rocky Mountain Oil and Gas Association; Legislative Member, Energy Council; Vice Commander, Post 19, American Legion MH: Albert Nelson Marquis Lifetime Achievement Award B/I: Mr. Tippets became involved in his profession after joining his friend in the gold mining business in Nevada, after which he traveled to Wyoming to investigate opportunities in uranium mining. AV: Boating; Fishing; Tennis; Politics PA: Republican RE: The Church of Jesus Christ of Latter-day Saints

TIPSORD, MICHAEL L., T: Chairman, Chief Executive Officer I: Insurance CN: State Farm Mutual Automobile Insurance Company DOB: 06/20/1959 SPN: Conni CH: Three Children ED: JD, University of Illinois at Urbana-Champaign, Magna Cum Laude (1984); BS, Illinois Wesleyan University, Summa Cum Laude (1981) CT: Registered Attorney, State of Illinois (1984-Present); Chartered Property Casualty Underwriter (1995); Chartered Life Underwriter (1991); Certified Public Accountant C: Chairman of the Board, Chief Executive Officer, State Farm Mutual Automobile Insurance Company (2016-Present); Chief Executive Officer, State Farm Fire and Casualty Company, State Farm Mutual Automobile Insurance Company (2015-Present); President, State Farm Life Insurance Company (2014-Present); Chief Operating Officer, State Farm Mutual Automobile Insurance Company (2011-2015); Vice Chairman, State Farm Mutual Automobile Insurance Company (2005-2016); Chief Financial Officer, State Farm Mutual Automobile Insurance Company (2005-2010); Senior Vice President, State Farm Mutual Automobile Insurance Company (2002-2004); Vice President, Treasurer, State Farm Mutual Automobile Insurance Company (2001-2002); Vice President, Assistant Treasurer, State Farm Mutual Automobile Insurance Company (1998-2001); Executive Assistant, State Farm Mutual Automobile Insurance Company (1997-1998); Assistant Controller, State Farm Mutual Automobile Insurance Company (1996-1997); Director, Accounting, State Farm Mutual Automobile Insurance Company (1995-1996); Assistant Tax Counsel, State Farm Mutual Automobile Insurance Company (1988) CR: Member, Governor J.B. Pritzker's Job Creation and Economic Opportunity Committee, Illinois (2019-Present); Member, Board of Directors, Navigant Consulting, Inc. (2009-Present); Honorary Trustee, Brookings Institution; Member, Board of

Trustees, Illinois Wesleyan University; Member, Dean's Advisory Board, University of Illinois College of Law; Featured Speaker, Wharton School of Business; Trustee, State Farm Insurance Companies Savings and Thrift Plan for U.S.. Employees; Trustee, State Farm Associates' Funds Trust; Trustee, State Farm Mutual Fund Trust; Member, Board of Directors, State Farm Bank; Member, Board of Directors, Financial Stability Board; Member, Board of Directors, State Farm VP Management Corp.; Member, Board of Directors, Insurance Placement Services; Member, Board of Directors, State Farm Lloyds, Inc. **MEM:** Illinois State Bar Association; American Bar Association

TIPTON, SCOTT RANDALL, T: U.S. Representative from Colorado **I:** Government Administration/Government Relations/Government Services **DOB:** 11/09/1956 **PB:** Espanola **SC:** NM/USA **MS:** Married **SPN:** Jean Tipton **CH:** Liesl; Elizabeth **ED:** BA in Political Science, Fort Lewis College **C:** Member, U.S. House of Representatives from Colorado's Third Congressional District, United States Congress, Washington, DC (2011-Present); Member, U.S. Small Business Committee (2011-Present); Member, U.S. House Committee on Natural Resources (2011-Present); Member, U.S. House Committee on Agriculture Committee (2011-Present); Member, District 58, Colorado House of Representatives (2008-2010); Chairman, Colorado Republican Party (1997-2005); Owner, Mesa Indian Trading Co.; Co-owner, Mesa Verde Pottery; President, Tipton Properties; President, Tipton Ltd. **CR:** Chairman, McInnis for Congress (1992, 2002) **CIV:** Member, Pueblo Community College Advisory Board; Board of Trustees, Mesa Verde National Park; Board Member, Mesa Verde Foundation; Board of Trustees, Crow Canyon Archeological Center **MEM:** The 100 Club of Montezuma County **PA:** Republican

TIRUMALAI, SRIVATSAN, "DR. SRI" S., PHD, T: Professor [Emeritus] **I:** Education/Educational Services **CN:** The University of Akron **PB:** Madras (Chennai) **SC:** India **YOP:** PhD (1984) **MS:** Married **CH:** Two Children **ED:** PhD in Mechanical Engineering, Georgia Institute of Technology (1984); MS in Aerospace Engineering, Georgia Institute of Technology (1981); BS in Mechanical Engineering, Bangalore University, India (1980) **C:** Professor Emeritus, Department of Mechanical Engineering, The University of Akron, Ohio (2018-Present); Professor, Department of Mechanical Engineering, The University of Akron, Ohio (1997-2018); Associate Professor, Department of Mechanical Engineering, The University of Akron, Ohio (1992-1997); Assistant Professor, Department of Mechanical Engineering, The University of Akron, Ohio (1987-1992); Manager, Research and Development, Materials Modification, Inc., Vienna, VA (1986-1987); Research Fellow, Instructor, Georgia Tech Research Institute, Georgia Institute of Technology, Atlanta, GA (1985-1986); Research Fellow, Center for Computational Sciences, Atlanta University (Now Clark Atlanta University), Atlanta, GA (1984-1985); Graduate Research Assistant, Graduate Teaching Assistant, Georgia Institute of Technology, Atlanta, GA (1980-1984) **CR:** Collateral Faculty, Ohio Aerospace Institute, Cleveland, Ohio (1990-2005); Visiting Professor, Department of Mechanical Engineering, Indian Institute of Science, Bengaluru, India (2003-2004) **CW:** Co-editor, "High Entropy Alloys: Innovations, Advances and Applications," CRC Press, Taylor & Francis Group, Informa PLC, FL (2020); Co-editor, "Manufacturing Techniques for Materials: Engineering and Engineered," CRC Press, Taylor & Francis Group, Informa PLC, FL (2018); Co-editor, "Additive Manufacturing: Innovations, Advances, and Applications," CRC Press, Taylor &

Francis Group, Informa PLC, FL (2015); Co-editor, "Advanced Structural Materials," Taylor & Francis, Informa UK Limited, Philadelphia, PA (2006); Co-editor, "Rapid Solidification Technology: An Engineering Guide," Technomic Publishing Company Inc., PA (1993); Presented, Over 245 Technical Presentations, National and International Conferences; Author, Co-author, 365 Manuscripts to Professional International Journals; Author, Co-author, 245 Publications in Proceedings and Bound Volumes, National and International Conferences; Author, Co-author, 10 Chapters, Books; Author, Co-author, 79 Scholarly Review of Technical Books in Journals; Author, Co-author, 75 Documented Technical Reports; Author, Editor, Co-editor, 61 Books and Five Monographs **AW:** Alexander Scott Distinguished Service Award, The Minerals, Metals & Materials Society (2016); Outstanding Research Faculty, The University of Akron (2015); Louis Hill Award for Exceptional Dedication and Service, College of Engineering, The University of Akron (2006); Outstanding Research Faculty, College of Engineering, The University of Akron (1997); Outstanding Young Alumnus, Georgia Institute of Technology (1996); Award for Research, Alcoa Foundation, Aluminum Company of America (Now Alcoa Corporation) (1991); Exchange Lecturer, ASM International-IIM Co-operative Exchange Program, American Society of Materials International (ASM International) (1988); Graduate Assistantship, Research and Teaching, Georgia Institute of Technology (1980-1984); Rama Watumull Scholarship (1982-1983); Dean's List, Bangalore University, India (1975-1980) **MEM:** American Association for the Advancement of Science (2008-Present); ASM International (1982-Present); The Minerals, Metals & Materials Society (1981-Present); The American Society of Mechanical Engineers (1981-Present); Distinguished Member, European Academy of Sciences (2016); APMI International (2010-2015); Fellow, American Association for the Advancement of Science (2009); Fellow, ASM International (2002); Fellow, The American Society of Mechanical Engineers (1998) **MH:** Albert Nelson Marquis Lifetime Achievement Award **AS:** Dr. Srivatsan attributes his success to always striving to ensure that his work ethic quickly becomes infectious and beneficial to all concerned, involved and participating. While always striving for and seeking excellence, he has made all efforts to ensure that it is done by actual demonstration of his commitment to: (a) instruction (teaching), (b) execution of exemplary research, and (c) exemplary service, as opposed to simple verbal pontification. He believes that his background in education, experience through the years, relentless and ceaseless service ably coupled with professional goals have enabled him to follow a strategy that has permitted in effectiveness in execution and enhancing the efficiency while concurrently ensuring successful task accomplishment in all relevant sectors that he was involved in. This has been made possible by prudent use of his time, effort and energy in those areas having the greatest potential of achieving: (i) impact (education), (ii) visibility (research and scholarly publications), and (iii) recognition (citations), while simultaneously meeting other aspects related and relevant to needs and objectives of the mission of the academic-unit/institution in which he was associated. **B/I:** Dr. Srivatsan became involved in his profession due to both an ambition and desire to engage the individuals (the "student" at all levels of education: (a) undergraduate, (b) graduate, and (c) short courses) with the primary objective of maximizing communication and consensus building for the purpose of efficient, effective and enthusiastic imparting of education, both on- and off- the classroom setting. That would eventually

enable the "interested" individual to become not only enlightened but also empowered with knowledge that would come to his/her aid when: (i) making decisions, and (ii) either executing or performing in the professional world. His approach to education has through his years of service been both pragmatic and practical. Also, he has, during his service, exercised the role as an individual who leads by example, while concurrently being an effective manager, managing precious resources spanning both human manpower and supplies (laboratory-related). During his period in an academic institution, as a teacher (Professor), an individual chosen to educate and enlighten the students, the environment is cautiously dynamic in seeing few to several changes. His efforts and enthusiasm have enabled him to accomplish both overall development and success of the individual(s), to whom the service was rendered, (the student), coupled with an observable improvement in the nature, quality and quantity of service rendered to the education unit(s) (the department or the institution) in which he was associated.

TITUS, ALICE, "DINA" COSTANDINA, PHD, T: U.S. Representative from Nevada; Educator **I:** Government Administration/Government Relations/Government Services **DOB:** 05/23/1950 **PB:** Thomasville **SC:** GA/USA **PT:** Joe Titus **MS:** Married **SPN:** Thomas Clayton Wright **ED:** PhD in Political Science, Florida State University (1976); MA, University of Georgia (1973); AB, College of William & Mary (1970) **C:** Member, U.S. House of Representatives from Nevada's First Congressional District, United States Congress, Washington, DC (2013-Present); Member, U.S. House Committee on Veterans' Affairs (2013-Present); Member, U.S. House Committee on Transportation and Infrastructure, Washington, DC (2009-2011, 2013-Present); Commissioner, U.S. Commission on Civil Rights, Washington, DC (2011-2012); Professor, Political Science, University of Nevada, Las Vegas (1977-2009, 2011); Member, U.S. House Committee on Homeland Security, Washington, DC (2009-2011); Member, U.S. House Committee on Education and Labor, Washington, DC (2009-2011); Member, U.S. House of Representatives from Nevada's Third Congressional District, United States Congress, Washington, DC (2009-2011); Member, District Seven, Nevada State Senate (1989-2009); Minority Leader, Nevada State Senate (1993-2008); Lecturer, North Texas State University (Now University of North Texas), Denton, TX; Committee on Foreign Affairs, United States Congress **CR:** Chairman, Nevada Humanities Committee (1984-1986) **CW:** Appearance, "The American Experience: Las Vegas - An Unconventional History" (2006); Author, "Battle Born: Federal-State Relations in Nevada During the 20th Century" (1989); Author, "Bombs in the Backyard: Atomic Testing and American Politics" (1986) **AW:** Outstanding Democrat of the Year, Paradise Democratic Club of Las Vegas (2009) **MEM:** WPSA; Women's Democratic Club of Clark County; NLAPW; Aquavision; P.E.O. Sisterhood; Tortoise Group of Clark County; Nevada Test Site Historical Foundation; Nevada Women's Lobby; Women's Research Institute of Nevada, University of Nevada, Las Vegas; Nevada Commission on Participatory Democracy; Clark County Neighborhood Justice Center; Las Vegas Little Theater; Educational Commission of the States; National Wildlife Federation; The Nature Conservancy **PA:** Democrat **RE:** Greek Orthodox

TLAIB, RASHIDA, T: U.S. Representative from Michigan **I:** Government Administration/Government Relations/Government Services **DOB:** 07/24/1976 **PB:** Detroit **SC:** MI/USA **MS:** Divorced **SPN:** Fayez Tlaib (1998, Divorced 2015) **CH:** Adam;

Yousif **ED:** JD, Western Michigan University Cooley Law School (2004); BA in Political Science, Wayne State University (1998) **C:** Member, U.S. House of Representatives from Michigan's 13ᵗʰ Congressional District (2019-Present); Member, District Six, Michigan House of Representatives (2012-2014); Member, District 12, Michigan House of Representatives (2009-2012); Staff, Representative Steve Tobocman, U.S. House of Representatives (2007-2008) **CIV:** Supporter, Sugar Law Center for Economic and Social Justice **PA:** Democrat

TODD, JOHN ROBERT, T: Educational Director, Educator **I:** Education/Educational Services **DOB:** 10/29/1946 **PB:** Detroit **SC:** MI/USA **PT:** John Lyle Todd; Helen Avis (Leroy) Todd **MS:** Married **SPN:** Joyce F. Whitaker (08/25/1973) **CH:** Lacey Joy; Jessica Elizabeth **ED:** JD, Georgetown University (1979); AB, University of Michigan, Magna Cum Laude (1976); Coursework, Columbia University (1973-1974) **C:** Director, Legal Program, Michigan Christian College, Rochester, NY (1979-Present); Assistant Professor, Michigan Christian College, Rochester, NY (1979-Present); Legislative Director, Blinded Veterans Association, Washington, DC (1977-1979) **CR:** Chairman, Michigan Vietnam Veterans Leadership Program, Pontiac, MI (1983-Present) **CIV:** City Charter Commissioner, Rochester Hills, MI (1983) **MIL:** Officer, U.S. Army (1967-1970) **CW:** "Michigan Business Law for the Undergraduate" **AW:** Outstanding Disabled Veteran, Disabled American Veterans (2013); Decorated Distinguished Flying Cross, U.S. Army; Purple Heart, U.S. Army; 17 Air Medals, U.S. Army; Cross of Gallantry, Republic of Vietnam **MEM:** Spokesman, Editorialist, Freedoms Foundation (1970, 1971) **BAR:** U.S. District Court for the Eastern District of Michigan (1980); Michigan (1979) **MH:** Albert Nelson Marquis Lifetime Achievement Award **B/I:** Professor Todd became involved in his profession because he was inspired by the television show, Perry Mason. He later fell into teaching, finding that he quite enjoyed his roles at Rochester Community College. The atmosphere and faculty were wonderful, as were his students. **PA:** Republican

TOMANY, MARK ALLEN, T: State Trooper (Retired) **I:** Law and Legal Services **DOB:** 03/23/1955 **PB:** Chicago **SC:** IL/USA **PT:** Leonard W. Tomany; Joan Dolores (Schulz) Tomany **MS:** Married **SPN:** Susan D. (Poole) Tomany **CH:** Kristion Michelle; Keith Martin; Kimberly Marie **ED:** Coursework, Police Training Institute, University of Illinois at Urbana-Champaign (1977, 1978, 1988, 1989) **CT:** Certified Firefighter II and III; Arson Investigator; Communications Specialist, Communications Unit Leader (COM-L); Communications Unit Training (COM-T); Private Pilot; Amateur Radio Operator; General Radiotelephone Operator License **C:** Lead Field Technician, Aviation HF, Lake Village, IL (2015-Present); Instructor, Self-employed (2005-Present); State Trooper, Illinois State Police, Joliet, IL (1987-2010); Volunteer Firefighter, Minooka Fire Department (Minooka Fire Protection District), Minooka, IL (1987-1999); State Trooper, Illinois State Police, Crestwood, IL (1985-1987); Deputy Sheriff, Will County Sheriff's Police, Joliet, IL (1976-1985) **CR:** Lieutenant, Assistant Chief, Field Services Division, Will County Emergency Management Agency, Joliet, IL (1995-Present); Consultant, Vice President, President, Mark A. Tomany, Limited, Minooka, IL (1989-Present); Board of Directors, Illinois Knights Templar Home, Paxton, IL (2015-2018); Special Agent, Illinois Gaming Board, Chicago, IL (2006-2010); Special Agent, Medicaid Fraud Control Unit (MFCU), Chicago, IL (2004-2006); Instructor, Illinois State Police Academy (1995-2005); Special Agent, Illinois Gaming Board, Chicago, IL (1996-

2004); Engineer, Communications Officer, Lieutenant, Assistant Chief, Minooka Fire Department (Minooka Fire Protection District), IL (1987-1999) **CW:** Author, "Traffic Control for the Emergency Worker" **AW:** Department Unit Citation, Illinois State Police (2005); Department Medal of Honor, Illinois State Police (1995); Department Commendation, Illinois State Police (1995); Director's Medal of Honor, Illinois State Police (1990); Two Department Commendations, Will County Sheriff's Police (1985) **MEM:** LaMoille-Calumet Lodge #270 A.F. & A.M., Homewood, IL (2013-Present); Mystic Order of Veiled Prophets of the Enchanted Realm, Aliabad Grotto, Oak Lawn, IL (2012-Present); Allied Masonic Degrees, Illuminati Chapter #495, Addison, IL (2011-Present); Retired State Police Association of Illinois (2010-Present); Matteson Lodge #175 A.F. & A.M., Joliet, IL (2010-Present); Valley of Chicago, Bloomingdale, IL (2010-Present); Ancient Arabic Order of Nobles of the Mystic Shrine, Medinah Temple, Chicago, IL (2010-Present); Joliet York Rite Bodies, Joliet, IL (2010-Present); Executive Board, Fraternal Order Police, Illinois Trooper's Lodge #41 (1989-1994); Life Member, Illinois Trooper's Lodge #41, Fraternal Order of Police; Ancient Accepted Scottish Rite, Northern Masonic Jurisdiction **MH:** Albert Nelson Marquis Lifetime Achievement Award **B/I:** Mr. Tomany initially aspired to become an aerospace engineer, but eventually decided to leave college to explore the world. He got married, and held multiple positions at places like Pinkerton Armed Security. He had to acquire a firearms license, which led him to meet someone who told him about the auxiliary police. He went on a ride along and discovered he liked it so he pursued a career in law enforcement. Mr. Tomany also spent 19 years in fire service as assistant chief. His grandfather was a career firefighter who got him interested in fire safety. **AV:** Aviation; Amateur radio; Communications technology; Automobiles **THT:** Mr. Tomany taught "Traffic Control for the Emergency Worker," a 4-hour course of instruction for emergency workers involved in traffic control.

TOMLIN, LILY, T: Actress, Comedian, Producer **I:** Media & Entertainment **DOB:** 09/01/1939 **PB:** Detroit **SC:** MI/USA **PT:** Guy Tomlin; Lillie Mae (Ford) Tomlin **MS:** Married **SPN:** Jane Wagner (12/31/2013) **ED:** Coursework in Acting with Peggy Feury; Coursework in Mime with Paul Curtis; Coursework, Wayne State University **C:** Co-Founder, Lily Tomlin Jane Wagner Cultural Arts Center; Co-Founder, Los Angeles LGBT Center **CW:** Actress, "Grace and Frankie" (2015-2021); Executive Producer, "Grace and Frankie" (2015-2020); Actress, "The Madness Within" (2019); Voice Actress, "Spider-Man: Into the Spider-Verse" (2018); Executive Producer, "Random Girls" (2018); Voice Actress, "The Magic School Bus Rides Again" (2017-2018); Actress, "Grandma" (2015); Actress, "Web Therapy" (2011-2015); Actress, "Web Therapy" (2012-2014); Actress, "Admission" (2013); Actress, "Ctadc" (2013); Narrator, "An Apology to Elephants" (2013); Executive Producer, "An Apology to Elephants" (2013); Actress, "Malibu Country" (2012-2013); Actress, "The Procession" (2012); Actress, "Call to Action" (2012); Actress, "Walk and Talk the Vote: West Wing Reunion - Bridge Mary McCormack" (2012); Actress, "Eastbound & Down" (2012); Actress, "NCIS" (2011); Actress, "Damages" (2010); Actress, "The Pink Panther 2" (2009); Performer, "Not Playing with a Full Deck" (2009); Actress, "Desperate Housewives" (2008 -2009); Actress, "12 Miles of Bad Road" (2008); Voice Actress, "Ponyo" (2008); Actress, "The Walker" (2007); Voice Actress, "The Ant Bully" (2006); Actress, "A Prairie Home Companion" (2006); Actress, "Will & Grace" (2005, 2006); Actress,

"The West Wing" (2002-2006); Voice Actress, "The Simpsons" (2005); Actress, "I Heart Huckabees" (2004); Actress, "Orange County" (2002); Executive Producer, "Citizen Reno" (2001); Actress, "The Kid" (2000); Actress, "Tea with Mussolini" (1999); Actress, "The X-Files" (1998); Actress, "Krippendorf's Tribe" (1998); Executive Producer, "Reno Finds Her Mom" (1998); Actress, "Murphy Brown" (1996-1998); Voice Actress, "The Magic School Bus" (1994-1997); Voice Actress, "Edith Ann's Christmas (Just Say Noël)" (1996); Executive Producer, "Edith Ann's Christmas (Just Say Noël)" (1996); Actress, "Getting Away with Murder" (1996); Actress, "Flirting with Disaster" (1996); Actress, "Homicide: Life on the Street" (1996); Actress, "Blue in the Face" (1995); Co-Executive Producer, "The Celluloid Closet" (1995); Actress, "Growing Up Funny" (1994); Voice Actress, "Frasier" (1994); Voice Actress, "Edith Ann: Homeless Go Home" (1994); Voice Actress, "Edith Ann: A Few Pieces of the Puzzle" (1994); Executive Producer, "Edith Ann: A Few Pieces of the Puzzle" (1994); Creator, "Edith Ann: A Few Pieces of the Puzzle" (1994); Actress, "Sesame Street Stays Up Late!" (1993); Actress, "The Beverly Hillbillies" (1993); Actress, "And the Band Played On" (1993); Actress, "Short Cuts" (1993); Actress, "The Player" (1992); Actress, "Shadows and Fog" (1991); Actress, "The Search for Signs of Intelligent Life in the Universe" (1991); Actress, "Big Business" (1988); Performer, "The Search for Signs of Intelligent Life in the Universe" (1985); Actress, "Pryor's Place" (1984); Actress, "All of Me" (1984); Actress, "Our Time" (1983); Host, Performer, "Saturday Night Live" (1975, 1976, 1983); Actress, "The Incredible Shrinking Woman" (1981); Performer, "Lily: Sold Out" (1981); Executive Producer, "Lily: Sold Out" (1981); Actress, "9 to 5" (1980); Actress, "Moment by Moment" (1978); Performer, "The Paul Simon Special" (1977); Performer, Writer, "On Stage" (1977); Actress, "Nashville" (1975); Performer, Writer, "Modern Scream" (1975); Performer, "Lily" (1973); Performer, "The Lily Tomlin Show" (1973); Writer, "The Lily Tomlin Show" (1973); Performer, "Rowan & Martin's Laugh-In" (1970-1973); Performer, Writer, "And That's The Truth" (1972); Actress, "The Electric Company" (1972); Voice Actress, "Scarecrow in a Garden of Cucumbers" (1972); Performer, Writer, "This Is a Recording" (1971) **AW:** Lifetime Achievement Award, Screen Actors Guild Awards (2017); Honoree, Kennedy Center Honors (2014); Primetime Emmy Award for Outstanding Voice-Over Performance, "An Apology to Elephants" (2013); Honoree, 345ᵗʰ Star, Walk of Stars, Palm Springs, CA (2012); Dr. Susan M. Love Award, Fenway Health (2009); Mark Twain Prize for American Humor (2003); Lucy Award, Women in Film (2003); Inductee, Michigan Women's Hall of Fame (1998); Daytime Emmy Award for Outstanding Performance in an Animated Program, "The Magic School Bus" (1995); Women in Film Crystal Award (1992); Tony Award for Best Actress in a Play, "The Search for Signs of Intelligent Life in the Universe" (1986); Primetime Emmy Award for Outstanding Variety, Music or Comedy Series, "Lily: Sold Out" (1981); Primetime Emmy Award for Outstanding Writing in a Comedy, Variety, or Music Special, "The Paul Simon Special" (1978); Special Tony Award for Lifetime Achievement (1977); Primetime Emmy Award for Outstanding Writing in a Comedy, Variety, or Music Special, "Lily Tomlin" (1976); Primetime Emmy Award for Outstanding Writing in a Comedy, Variety, or Music Special, "Lily" (1974); Primetime Emmy Award for Outstanding Comedy-Variety, Variety or Music Special, "Lily" (1974); Grammy Award for Best Comedy Album, "This Is A Recording" (1972); Two-Time Recipient, Peabody Awards; Two-Time Recipient, Drama Desk Awards; Outer Critics Circle Award; CabeACE Award

TOMOMATSU, HIDEO, T: Physical Chemist **I:** Sciences **DOB:** 06/08/1929 **SC:** Tokyo **PT:** Shinsai Nasu Tomomatsu; Suma Tomomatsu **MS:** Married **SPN:** Yuko Ito (11/12/1967) **CH:** Tadao **ED:** PhD in Chemistry, The Ohio State University (1964); MS in Chemistry, University of the Pacific (1960); BS in Chemistry, Waseda University (1952) **CT:** Registered Professional Engineer, State of Texas; Certified U.S. Patent Agent **C:** Consultant, Y.T. Research Associates (1996- Present); Quaker Fellow, Quaker Oats Company (1972-1996); Chemist, Texaco Chemical Company (1964-1972); Chemist, Hodogaya Chemical Company (1952-1959) **CW:** Contributor, Articles, Professional Journals **MEM:** Emeritus Member, American Chemical Society **MH:** Albert Nelson Marquis Lifetime Achievement Award

TOMPSON, ANDREW F.B., PHD, T: Hydrologist, Researcher **I:** Sciences **PB:** Reno **SC:** NV/USA **PT:** Robert Tompson; Mary Tompson **MS:** Widowed **SPN:** Linda Berry (09/27/1996, Deceased 06/05/2005) **CH:** Madeline **ED:** PhD in Civil Engineering, Princeton University, NJ (1985); BS in Civil Engineering, Brown University, Providence, RI (1980) **C:** Staff Scientist, Lawrence Livermore National Laboratory, Livermore, CA (1986-Present); Postdoctoral Associate, Massachusetts Institute of Technology (MIT), Cambridge, MA (1984-1986) **CR:** Member, Editorial Board, Computational Geosciences (1994–Present); Associate Editor, Water Resources Research (2005–2011); Deputy Editor, Water Resources Research (2000–2004); Member, Editorial Board, Advances in Water Resources (1997–2016) **CW:** Contributor, More Than 35 Peer-reviewed Articles in Scientific Journals; Contributor, More Than 35 Published Scientific Conference Articles; Contributor, More Than 50 Technical Reports; More Than 80 Invited Briefings and Presentations **AW:** The Sultanate of Oman Award, The Research Council and Sultan Qaboos Higher Centre for Culture and Science (2019); "Spot" Award for Science on Saturday Presentation, "Hydrology of an Ant Farm?," Bankhead Theater, Lawrence Livermore National Laboratory, Livermore, CA (2015); Distinguished Achievement Award, Extraordinary Programmatic Contribution, Computations Directorate, Lawrence Livermore National Laboratory (1996); Co-recipient, Research and Innovations Award in Water Science **MEM:** American Geophysical Union **MH:** Albert Nelson Marquis Lifetime Achievement Award; Marquis Who's Who Top Professional **B/I:** Dr. Tompson became involved in his profession because growing up as a child in Reno, Nevada, he had aspirations to become an architect. By college, he decided he would study engineering because it would give him the necessary tools to harbor his skills as an architect and his school did not have an architectural program at the time. One day, while on break from school, Dr. Tompson and a friend went fishing at Pyramid Lake in Nevada. He was at a crossroads in his career and really began to ponder his next steps in life. Being from Nevada, he was well aware of the issues with water in the area and decided that would be a useful problem to focus on in his career. He then received an opportunity to go to Princeton University for the summer and was recruited to the graduate school program and began his studies of hydrology. **AV:** Photography; Painting; Astronomy; Travel; Hiking exploration; Gardening; History of science **THT:** Dr. Tompson is a hydrologist in the Atmospheric, Earth, and Energy Division at Lawrence Livermore National Laboratory, and served as leader of the Hydrologic Sciences Group between 2002 and 2008. His research interests include the physics of multiphase fluid flow, chemical transport, and chemical transformation in porous media and terrestrial environmental systems, applications of radiochemistry and isotope hydrology to topics in radionuclide fate and migration in terrestrial environmental systems, integrated analyses of coupled processes linking water, chemical, and energy fluxes in and between the subsurface, land surface and lower atmosphere, and coupled mathematical modeling of these processes using techniques in advanced computation, stochastic analysis, and uncertainty quantification. His work has addressed integrated groundwater supply, groundwater contamination, and reservoir engineering problems, with recent efforts in pollution of systems affected by nuclear testing, geothermal prospect evaluation, groundwater availability in arid environments, aquifer storage and recovery, and hydrologic impacts from regional climate change. He has led or been a member of numerous interdisciplinary research teams involving engineers, hydrologists, geologists, geochemists, radiochemists, applied mathematicians, computational scientists, and climate scientists. He has participated in broad based scientific and technical educational activities relating to water supply, pollution, and nuclear forensics studies in California, the American West, the Middle East, Northern Africa, and Central Asia. Dr. Tompson served on the editorial boards of Water Resources Research for 10 years and Advances in Water Resources for 18 years and continues to serve on the editorial board of Computational Geosciences. He received an ScB from Brown University in 1980, a PhD from Princeton University in 1985, both in civil engineering, and spent two years at the Massachusetts Institute of Technology as a postdoctoral associate before moving to Livermore.

TONKO, PAUL DAVID, T: U.S. Representative from New York **I:** Government Administration/Government Relations/Government Services **DOB:** 06/18/1949 **PB:** Amsterdam **SC:** NY/USA **ED:** BS in Mechanical and Industrial Engineering, Clarkson University (1971) **C:** Member, U.S. House of Representatives from New York's 20th Congressional District, United States Congress, Washington, DC (2013-Present); Member, U.S. House of Representatives from New York's 21st Congressional District, United States Congress, Washington, DC (2009-2013); President, Chief Executive Officer, New York State Research and Development Authority (Now NYSERDA), Albany, NY (2007-2008); Chairman, Energy Committee, New York State Assembly, Albany, NY (1992-2007); Member, District 105, New York State Assembly, Albany, NY (1983-2007); Chair, Montgomery County Board of Supervisors (1981-1983); Member, Montgomery County Board of Supervisors (1975-1983); Senior Valuation Engineer, New York State Department of Public Service; Engineer, New York State Department of Transportation; Member, Committee on Energy and Commerce, United States Congress; Chair, Subcommittee on Environment and Climate Change; Member, Committee on Science, Space and Technology, United States Congress; Member, Committee on Natural Resources **CIV:** Delegate, Democratic National Convention (1988); Member, Schenectady Chamber of Commerce (Now Capital Region Chamber); Member, Montgomery County Chamber of Commerce; Board of Directors, American Cancer Society, Inc., Montgomery County, NY; Board of Directors, The American National Red Cross, Montgomery County, NY **AW:** Legislative Award, New York Conference of Mayors (NYCOM) (1991) **MEM:** Kiwanis International; Elks Lodge 101; Knights of Columbus Council 209, Amsterdam, NY **PA:** Democrat **RE:** Roman Catholic

TOOMEY, PATRICK, "PAT" JOSPEH JR., T: U.S. Senator from Pennsylvania; Finance Executive **I:** Government Administration/Government Relations/Government Services **DOB:** 11/17/1961 **PB:** Providence **SC:** RI/USA **PT:** Patrick Joseph Toomey; Mary Ann (Andrews) Toomey **MS:** Married **SPN:** Kris Ann Duncan (1997) **CH:** Bridget; Patrick Jr.; Duncan **ED:** BA in Government, Harvard University, Cum Laude (1984) **C:** U.S. Senator, Commonwealth of Pennsylvania, Washington, DC (2011-Present); Member, U.S. Committee on Senate Commerce, Science and Transportation, Washington, DC (2011-Present); Member, U.S. Senate Budget Committee, Washington, DC (2011-Present); Member, U.S. Senate Committee on Banking, Housing and Urban Affairs, Washington, DC (2011-Present); Co-founder, Toomey Enterprises, Inc., Allentown, PA (1991-Present); Chairman, U.S. Senate Republican Steering Committee (2012-2015); Member, Joint Select Committee on Deficit Reduction, Washington, DC (2011); President, Chief Executive Officer, Club for Growth, Washington, DC (2004-2009); Member, U.S. House of Representatives from Pennsylvania's 15th Congressional District, United States Congress, Washington, DC (1999-2005); Financial Consultant, Hong Kong (1990-1991); Vice President, Director, U.S. Subsidiary, Morgan, Grenfell & Co. (1986-1991); Investment Banker, Chemical Bank, NY (1984-1986) **CR:** Board of Directors, Commonwealth Foundation for Public Policy Alternatives (2007-Present); Co-owner, Rookie's Restaurant, Allentown, PA (1991) **AW:** Honor Roll Award, Concord Coalition (2000); Named Man of the Year, United States Marine Corps (1999) **PA:** Republican **RE:** Roman Catholic

TORRE, JOE, T: Major League Baseball Executive, Professional Baseball Manager (Retired) **I:** Athletics **DOB:** 07/18/1940 **PB:** Brooklyn **SC:** NY/USA **PT:** Joe Torre, Sr.; Margaret Torre **MS:** Married **SPN:** Alice Wolterman (08/23/1987); Dani (1968, Divorced); Jackie Torre (1963, Divorced) **CH:** Michael; Lauren; Cristina; Andrea **ED:** Doctor of Letters (Honorary), Skidmore College (2019); Doctor of Humanities (Honorary), Rider University (2006) **C:** Chief Baseball Officer, Major League Baseball (2014-Present); Executive Vice President, Baseball Operations, Major League Baseball (2012-2014); Executive Vice President, Baseball Operations, Major League Baseball (2011-2012); Manager, Los Angeles Dodgers, Major League Baseball (2008-2010); Manager, New York Yankees, Major League Baseball (1996-2007); Manager, St. Louis Cardinals, Major League Baseball (1990-1995); Manager, Atlanta Braves, Major League Baseball (1982-1984); Manager, New York Mets, Major League Baseball (1977-1981); Professional Baseball Player, New York Mets, Major League Baseball (1975-1977); Professional Baseball Player, St. Louis Cardinals, Major League Baseball (1969-1974); Professional Baseball Player, Milwaukee/Atlanta Braves, Major League Baseball (1960-1968) **CR:** Member, Special Committee for On-Field Matters, Major League Baseball (2009-Present); Television Commentator, California Angels, NBC (1984-1989) **CIV:** Co-Founder, Joe Torre Safe at Home Foundation (2002-Present) **CW:** Himself, "The Comedians" (2015); Himself, "Castle" (2010); Co-Author, "The Yankee Years" (2009); Voice Cameo, "Everyone's Hero" (2006); Himself, "Analyze That" (2002); Co-Author, "Joe Torre's Ground Rules for Winners: 12 Keys to Managing Team Players, Tough Bosses, Setbacks, and Success" (1999); Himself, "Spin City" (1998); Co-Author, "Chasing the Dream: My Lifelong Journey to the World Series" (1997); Himself, "Taking Care of Business" (1990) **AW:** Inductee, St. Louis Cardinals Hall of Fame Museum (2016); Inductee, National Baseball Hall of Fame (2014); Willie, Mickey and the Duke Award (2011); Slocum Award (2008); Chuck Tanner Major League Baseball Manager of the Year (2007); Ranked #3, "Top 10 Coaches/Managers of the Decade," Sports Illustrated (2000-2009); Major League Baseball All-Decade Team Manager, Sports Illustrated (2000-2009); Baseball Manager of the Decade, Sporting News (2000-2009); Manager of the Year, Associated Press (1998, 1982); American League Manager of the Year Award, Sporting News (1998); BBWAA American League Manager of the Year (1998, 1996); American League Manger of the Year, Baseball Prospectus Internet Baseball Awards (1998); National League Player of the Week Award (1976); National League Player of the Month Awards (1971, 1965); Player of the Year Award, Sporting News (1971); National League Most Valuable Player Award (1971); Hutch Award (1971); Rawlings Gold Glove Award (1965)

TORRES, NORMA JUDITH, T: U.S. Representative from California **I:** Government Administration/Government Relations/Government Services **DOB:** 04/04/1965 **PB:** Escuintla **SC:** Guatemala **MS:** Married **SPN:** Louis Torres **CH:** Robert; Christopher; Matthew **ED:** BA, National Labor College; Coursework, Mt. San Antonio College; Coursework, Rio Hondo College **C:** Member, U.S. House of Representatives from California's 33rd Congressional District, United States Congress, Washington, DC (2015-Present); Member, District 61, California State Assembly (2008-2015); Mayor, City of Pomona, CA (2006-2008); Councilwoman, District Six, City of Pomona, CA (2000-2006); Member, Committee on the Judiciary; Member, Committee on Foreign Affairs; Member, Aging and Longterm Care Committee, California State Assembly; Member, Banking and Finance Committee, California State Assembly; Member, Governmental Organization Committee, California State Assembly; Member, Human Services Committee, California State Assembly; Member, Insurance Committee, California State Assembly; Member, Select Committee on Domestic Violence, California State Assembly; Chair, Housing and Community Development Committee, California State Assembly; Former 911 Dispatcher, City of Los Angeles Police Department **CR:** Treasurer, Executive Committee, National Conference of Democratic Mayors **CIV:** Volunteer, Boy Scouts of America; Volunteer, AYSO; Volunteer, Big Sisters Program, Big Brothers Big Sisters of America; Volunteer, Suicide Prevention Center; Board Member, Fairplex Blue Ribbon Committee; Board Member, Tri-City Mental Health; Board Member, Pomonoa Valley Transportation Authority; Founder, Neighbors for Pomona Committee **MEM:** American Federation of State Local 3090 **PA:** Democrat

TORRES SMALL, XOCHITL LIANA, T: U.S. Representative from New Mexico **I:** Government Administration/Government Relations/Government Services **DOB:** 11/15/1984 **PB:** Portland **SC:** OR/USA **PT:** Marcos Torres; Cynthia Torres **MS:** Married **SPN:** Nathan Small **ED:** JD, The University of New Mexico School of Law, Albuquerque; BA, Georgetown University; International Baccalaureate Diploma, Waterford Kamhlaba United World College, Mbabane, Eswatini **C:** Member, U.S. House of Representatives from New Mexico's Second Congressional District (2019-Present); Federal Law Clerk, New Mexico District (2015-2016); Field Representative, U.S. Senator Tom Udall (2009-2012); Attorney, Kemp Smith **PA:** Democratic **RE:** Lutheran

TORRES-GOMEZ, EVELYN, T: Chief Executive Officer **I:** Business Management/Business Services **CN:** Solaris Technologies Services **MS:** Married **SPN:** Miguel **CH:** Nicole; TJ **ED:** BA in Business Management, LeTourneau University, Longview, TX (1996); AA in Marketing, Mountain View College, Dallas, TX **CT:** PMI Certified (2007) **C:** Founder, Chief Executive Officer, Solaris Technologies Services, LLC, Irving, TX (2018-Present); Lead Customer Manager, North America and Latin America, Nokia Networks; Area Account Manager, Central America, Nokia Networks **CR:** Advisor, Board of Directors, University of Texas at Arlington College of Engineering, Arlington, TX **CIV:** Board of Engineering, University of Texas at Arlington **AW:** Dallas 500, Dallas Business Journal (2019); Entrepreneur of the Year, Ernst and Young (2019); STEP Award, Women Institute; Excellence in Quality Award, Dallas Hispanic Chamber; Women in Business Award, Dallas Business Journal; Outstanding Latino Business Award, DCEO **MEM:** Women in Manufacturing; The Manufacturing Institute **AS:** Ms. Torres-Gomez attributes her success to her passion. **B/I:** Ms. Torres-Gomez became involved in her profession because she wanted to be able to do something different and make a change. She has always been attracted to technology. She did not have any experience or examples growing up, however, she was the first in her family to try. It paid off for her. In addition, she got involved as a Hispanic woman in building and manufacturing towers because it was a customer need. She has always been passionate about making a difference. **AV:** Flying single-engine planes; International cooking; Traveling; Reading; Tennis

TOVAR, NICHOLAS MARIO, T: President, Chief Executive Officer **I:** Consulting **CN:** Quality Assurance Consultants, Inc. **DOB:** 01/18/1960 **PB:** Ogden **SC:** UT/USA **PT:** Gerdo Tovar; Alice (Martinez) Tovar **MS:** Married **SPN:** Suzanne Oxborrow **CH:** Ashley; Nicholas Brock; Clinton Gregory; Lance Edward; Marshall Prescott; Jarrett Stanley; Nathaniel William **ED:** BS in Mechanical Engineering and Manufacturing, National University (1990); BS in Logistics Management Engineering, Weber State University (1988) **CT:** QAC-CSSMBB, ASQ, CQM/OE, ASQ-CQA, QSM-PA, AQSM-AA, ITI-NDT-LEVEL III, FAA Repairman NDT **C:** Vice President, QSRA, Consensus Orthopedics, El Dorado Hills, CA (2019-Present); President, Chief Executive Officer, Quality Assurance Consultants, Inc., Gold River, CA (2002-Present); Program Head, Six Sigma, Cesca Therapeutics (Now ThermoGenesis Corp.), Rancho Cordova, CA (2015-2016); Director of Quality Assurance, Haemonetics Corporation, El Dorado Hills, CA (2014-2015); Executive Director of Quality Assurance, Precision Components Group - RPMI, Lincoln, CA (1998-2002); Quality Assurance Manager, Siemens Transportation Systems (Now Siemens Mobility), Sacramento, CA (1996-1998); Director of Quality Engineering, Industrial Testing International, Lincoln, CA (1994-1995); Senior Quality Engineer, BP Chemicals - Advanced Materials Division, Stockton, CA (1993-1994); Launch Support Engineer and Senior Manufacturing Engineer, Aerojet Propulsion Division, GenCorp Services, Sacramento, CA (1986-1993); Logistics Controller, Utah-Idaho Supply Co., Salt Lake City, UT (1985-1986) **CIV:** Indoor Referee, National License, USISA (2000-2019); Institutional Head, Troop 302, Boy Scouts of America (1990-1995) **MIL:** With, Civil Air Patrol, United States Air Force; With, United States Air Force Auxiliary; With, JROTC, United States Air Force **AW:** Excellence in Science Award, QAC, Inc. (2013); BP Chemicals AMD 777 Boeing Rolls Royce Team Award (1994); Total Quality Management Award, Aerojet Propulsion Division (1991); Value Engineering Award, Aerojet Propul-

sion Division (1987) **MEM:** Senior Member, American Society for Quality; The American Society for Nondestructive Testing **MH:** Albert Nelson Marquis Lifetime Achievement Award **AV:** Athletics; Wargames; History; Music **PA:** Republican **RE:** The Church of Jesus Christ of Latter-Day Saints

TOWNSEND, BEAU, T: President & Chief Executive Officer **I:** Business Management/Business Services **CN:** Beau Townsend Auto Group **C:** Owner, Beau Townsend Auto Group, OH **CIV:** Avid Philanthropist **MIL:** United States Army **AW:** Bronze Star; President's Award **MEM:** Ford Dealer Advertising Fund Committee **AS:** Unfortunately, Mr. Townsend never had an education past the 8th grade, so he knew his career options were limited. His attributes his success to the to his love for cars and people, as well as having a great reputation. **B/I:** Mr. Townsend grew up in Springfield Ohio, where his parents owned 10 car dealership showrooms. He started working in the 8th grade, and would walk five miles back and forth to work. While walking one day, he recalls passing an uncle Sam sign that said "We need you". Mr. Townsend decided to walk into the post office and spoke to a Sergeant to join the Army. Before he knew it, he was on his way to Fort Knox, Kentucky. Upon completing his basic training, Mr. Townsend was shipped to Germany where he spent two years. When he came home at age 18, his mother found him a job digging ditches. After month, he decided to look for a new job in the newspaper. He then decided he would try selling cars. His mother was against the idea but his father was all for it. His father knew that his son had a knack to be a salesman. Eventually, Mr. Townsend got the job working for Ford Motor Company. He knew he wanted to be the best salesman that they had. He worked there until about 1964, when he got married and had his first child. He landed a job at a new Ford company where he stayed for about 13 years, when he was appointed to become a sales manager. His wife, who he credits as "a big help," created a savings account for him, and saved about $95,000. There was a small dealership outside of Dayton, Ohio that he bought out. He started out the business with 25 employees that sold roughly 300 cars a year. Currently, he has 250 employees that sell about 4000 cars a year.

TOWNSHEND, PETE, T: Guitarist, Composer **I:** Fine Art **DOB:** 05/19/1945 **PB:** Chiswick **SC:** England **PT:** Cliff Townshend; Betty (Dennis) Townshend **MS:** Married **SPN:** Rachel Fuller (2016); Karen Astley (05/20/1968, Divorced 2009) **CH:** Emma; Aminta; Joseph **ED:** Honorary Doctorate, University of West London (2010); Coursework in Graphic Design, Ealing Art College (1961-1964) **C:** Guitarist, Songwriter, The Who (1964-Present); Founder, Eel Pie Publishing (1977); Founder, Eel Pie Recording Production Ltd. (1970) **CIV:** Performer, Numerous Concerts for the Teenage Cancer Trust, The Who (2000-Present); Co-Founder, Daltrey/Townshend Teen and Young Adult Cancer Program, Ronald Reagan UCLA Medical Center (2011); Performer, Five Benefit Concerts, Maryville Academy (1997-2002); Performer, Benefit Concert, Annual Bridge School Benefit (1996); Performer, Benefit Concert, Children's Health Fund (1995); Active Support, Teenage Cancer Trust; Active Supporter, Various Children's Charities **CW:** Songwriter, Guitarist, Album, "Who," The Who (2019); Author, "The Age of Anxiety" (2019); Performer, Live Album, "Live at the Fillmore East 1968," The Who (2018); Performer, Live Album, "Tommy Live at the Royal Albert Hall," The Who (2017); Performer, Live Album, "Live at the Isle of Wight Festival 2004," The Who (2017); Performer, Live Album, "Live in Hyde Park," The Who (2015); Performer, Live Album, "Quadrophenia Live in London," The

Who (2014); Performer, Live Album, "Live at Hull 1970," The Who (2012); Performer, Benefit Concert, "The Concert for Sandy Relief," The Who (2012); Author, "Who I Am" (2012); Featured, Documentary, "Amazing Journey: The Story of The Who" (2007); Songwriter, Guitarist, Album, "Endless Wire," The Who (2006); Songwriter, Guitarist, EP, "Wire & Glass," The Who (2006); Performer, Live Album, "Live from Toronto," The Who (2006); Performer, Live Album, "Live: Brixton Academy '85" (2004); Performer, Live Album, "Live at the Royal Albert Hall," The Who (2003); Performer, Live Album, "Live: Bam 1993" (2003); Performer, Benefit Concert, "The Concert for New York City," The Who (2001); Singer, Songwriter, Guitarist, EP, "O'Parvardigar" (2001); Performer, Live Album, "Blues to the Bush," The Who (2000); Executive Producer, "The Iron Giant" (1999); Performer, Live Album, "A Benefit for Maryville Academy" (1998); Performer, Live Album, "Live at the Isle of Wight Festival 1970," The Who (1996); Singer, Songwriter, Guitarist, Album, "Psychoderelict" (1993); Voice Actor, "The Secret Adventures of Tom Thumb" (1993); Singer, Songwriter, Guitarist, Album, "The Iron Man: The Musical by Pete Townshend" (1989); Performer, Live Album, "Deep End Live!" (1986); Singer, Songwriter, Guitarist, Album, "White City: A Novel" (1985); Author, "Horse's Neck" (1985); Performer, Live Album, "Who's Last," The Who (1984); Songwriter, Guitarist, Album, "It's Hard" (1982); Singer, Songwriter, Guitarist, Album, "All the Best Cowboys Have Chinese Eyes" (1982); Performer, Concert Film, "The Who Rocks America 1982" (1982); Songwriter, Guitarist, Album, "Face Dances" (1981); Performer, Benefit Concert, "Concerts for the People of Kampuchea" (1981); Singer, Songwriter, Guitarist, Album, "Empty Glass" (1980); Featured, Documentary, "The Kids Are Alright" (1979); Co-Screenwriter, Film, "Quadrophenia" (1979); Songwriter, Guitarist, Album, "Who Are You," The Who (1978); Singer, Songwriter, Guitarist, Album, "Rough Mix" (1977); Co-Author, "The Story of Tommy" (1977); Songwriter, Guitarist, Album, "The Who by Numbers," The Who (1975); Producer, Soundtrack, Film, "Tommy" (1975); Actor, Film, "Tommy" (1975); Songwriter, Guitarist, Album, "Quadrophenia," The Who (1973); Singer, Songwriter, Guitarist, Album, "Who Came First" (1972); Songwriter, Guitarist, Album, "Who's Next," The Who (1971); Performer, Live Album, "Live at Leeds," The Who (1970); Songwriter, Guitarist, Album, "Tommy," The Who (1969); Performer, Concert Film, "Woodstock," The Who (1969); Performer, Concert Film, "Monterey Pop," The Who (1968); Performer, Concert Show, "The Rolling Stones Rock and Roll Circus," The Who (1968); Producer, Bassist, Thunderclap Newman (1968); Producer, "Fire," Crazy World of Arthur Brown (1968); Songwriter, Guitarist, Album, "The Who Sell Out," The Who (1967); Songwriter, Guitarist, Album, "A Quick One," The Who (1966); Songwriter, Guitarist, Album, "The Who Sings My Generation," The Who (1965); Songwriter, "Who Are You," "Won't Get Fooled Again," "Baba O'Riley," "I Can See for Miles," "CSI: Crime Scene Investigation," "CSI: Miami," "CSI: NY," "CSI: Cyber" **AW:** George and Ira Gershwin Award for Lifetime Musical Achievement (2016); Stevie Ray Vaughn Award (2015); BMI TV Music Awards, "CSI: Crime Scene Investigation," "CSI:NY" (2013); Les Paul Award, TEC Awards (2013); Classic Album Award, "Quadrophenia," Classic Rock Roll of Honour Awards, The Roundhouse (2011); BMI TV Music Awards, "CSI: NY," "CSI: Miami," "CSI: Crime Scene Investigation" (2009); BMI TV Music Awards, "CSI: NY," "CSI: Miami" (2008); Honoree, Kennedy Center, John F. Kennedy Center for the Performing Arts (2008); Classic Songwriter, MOJO Awards (2008); Inductee, Hall of Fame, MOJO Awards (2008); South Bank Show Award (2007); Inductee, UK Music Hall of Fame (2005); BMI TV Music Awards, "CSI: Crime Scene Investigation," "CSI: Miami," "CSI: NY" (2005); BMI TV Music Awards, "CSI: Crime Scene Investigation" (2004); BMI TV Music Award, "CSI: Miami" (2004); BMI TV Music Awards, "CSI: Crime Investigation," "CSI: Miami" (2003); BMI TV Music Award, "CSI: Crime Scene Investigation" (2002); BMI TV Music Award, "CSI: Crime Scene Investigation" (2001); Lifetime Achievement Award, Ivor Novello Awards (2001); Lifetime Achievement Award, Grammy Awards (2001); Songwriter Award, Q Awards (1998); Best Musical Show Album, "The Who's Tommy," Grammy Awards (1994); Best Original Score, "The Who's Tommy," Tony Awards (1993); Living Legend Award, International Rock Awards (1991); Merit Award, Q Awards (1991); Inductee, The Who, Rock and Roll Hall of Fame (1990); Life Achievement Award, BRIT Awards (1983); Ranked #3, "Best Guitarists," The New Book of Rock Lists

TRACHTENBERG, DAVID, T: Lawyer **I:** Law and Legal Services **DOB:** 04/04/1925 **PB:** Wurtsboro **SC:** NY/USA **PT:** Jacob Trachtenberg; Frieda (Rossis) Trachtenberg **MS:** Widowed **SPN:** Selma Harris (05/27/1945, Deceased 03/17/2016) **CH:** Carl Harris; Bruce Sheldon **ED:** JD, University of Florida, With Honors (1982); EdD, New York University (1973); MA, University at Albany (1947); BA, Hartwick College, Summa Cum Laude (1944) **C:** Career Staff Attorney, Fourth District Court of Appeal (1989-1993); Senior Staff Attorney, Fourth District Court of Appeal (1986-1989); Staff Attorney, Fourth District Court of Appeal (1983-1986); Assistant Superintendent, Instructor, Enlarged City School District City of Middletown (1970-1980); Director of Instruction, Enlarged City School District City of Middletown (1968-1970); Director of Federal Programs, Enlarged City School District City of Middletown (1965-1968); Assistant Professor of Education, State University of New York at New Paltz (1964-1965); Director of School Improvement, Enlarged City School District City of Middletown (1961-1964); Guidance Counselor, Middletown High School (1959-1961); Teacher of Secondary Social Studies, Middletown High School (1949-1959); Teacher of Latin and Social Studies, Greenville Central School District (1947-1949) **CIV:** Member, Board of Directors, Regional Religious School, Lake Worth, FL (1993-Present); Vice President, Regional Religious School, Lake Worth, FL (1991-Present); Member, Board of Directors, Temple Beth Tikvah (1991-Present); Recording Secretary, Lake Worth Jewish Center (1984-1991); President, Middletown Day Nursery Association (1978-1979); Member, Board of Directors, Regional Community Action Program, Orange County, NY (1964-1967) **MIL:** European Theater of Operations, U.S. Army (1943-1946) **CW:** Research Editor, Florida Law Review (1981-1982); Co-Author, "The Nongraded School" (1965); Contributor, Articles, Professional Publications **AW:** Decorated Bronze Star with Oak Leaf Cluster; Purple Heart **MEM:** The Florida Bar; The Order of the Coif; The Honor Society of Phi Kappa Phi **BAR:** The Florida Bar (1983) **MH:** Albert Nelson Marquis Lifetime Achievement Award **B/I:** Mr. Trachtenberg became involved in his profession because at the age of 18 he entered the Army with a bachelor's degree. His original assignment in the Army was the Army Specialized Training Program, which was based on a test. If he scored highly enough, he would end up there, with the intention that he would study language or engineering at some collegiate institution. After 13 weeks of basic training, he received orders to attend the College of the Pacific, but this order was later rescinded when he was ordered into an infantry division. He moved into teaching after he left the military because his parents were immigrants and his father would say that his children would become teachers, because teachers made $25 dollars per week and, at that time, that was a lot of money. To some extent, that may have had something to do with why he became an educator. **AV:** Decorating and home carpentry; Traveling **PA:** Democrat **RE:** Conservative Judaism

TRAGEN, IRVING G., T: Legal Consultant (Retired), U.S. Foreign Service Officer **I:** Consulting **DOB:** 05/18/1922 **PB:** San Francisco **SC:** CA/USA **MS:** Widowed **SPN:** Eleanor May Dodson (08/07/1947, Deceased) **ED:** LLM, Universidad de Chile (1946); JD, University of California, Berkeley (1945); AB, University of California, Berkeley (1943) **C:** Legal Consultant (Retired)Consultant, Latin American/European Organizations on Drug Trafficking, Hanford, CA (1999-2002); Principal Adviser, Regional Central America Legal Development, San Jose, Costa Rica (1995-1997);Executive Secretary, Inter-American Drug Abuse Control Commission, Washington, DC (1984-1994); Executive Director, Inter-American Economic and Social Council, Washington, DC (1980-1984); Deputy U.S. Representative, U.S. Mission to the Organization of American States, U.S. Department State, Washington, DC (1977-1980); Director, U.S. Agency for International Development (USAID), Economic Counselor, U.S. Embassy, U.S. Agency for International Development (USAID), Panama (1975-1977); Chief, Central America Regional Office, U.S. Department State & Agency for International Development, Guatemala (1973-1975); Vice President, Inter-American Foundation, Rosslyn, VA (1971-1973); Country Director Argentina, Paraguay, Uruguay, U.S. Department of State, Washington, DC (1969-1971); Director, Agency for International Development Mission, La Paz, Bolivia (1965-1968); Director, Latin America Bureau of Institutional Development, Agency for International Development, Washington, DC (1963-1965); With, U.S. Department of State, Agency for International Development, El Salvador, Chile, Peru, Venezuela, Washington, California (1953-1963); Personnel Officer, WHO/Pan American Sanitary Bureau, Washington, DC (1950-1953); Personnel Officer, Mexican-United States Commission for the Eradication of Foot-and-Mouth Disease, Mexico (1948-1949) **CR:** Member, Board of Trustees, Museo de las Americas, Denver, CO (1999-Present); Member, Advisory Board, University of the Pacific, Stockton, CA (2000-2003) **CIV:** Trustee Emeritus, Museo de las Americas, Denver, CO (2000) **CW:** Author, "Two Lifetimes as One: Ele and Me and the Foreign Service" (2020); Member, Editorial Board, Money Laundering Alert International (2000-2001) **AW:** 2018 Global Ambassador of Peace and Public Service, International House, Berkeley (2018); 2018 Ambassador of Peace & Public Service (2018); 2010 Citation Award University of California Law School (2010); Diploma of Honor and Merit, Brazil (2005); Government of BoliviaOrder of Columbus (1994); State Department Honor Award (1980); AID Lifetime Achievement Award (1978); Order of Bolivar, International House, Berkeley, CA (1968) **MEM:** Board of Directors, Doris A. Howell Foundation for Women's Health Research **MH:** Albert Nelson Marquis Lifetime Achievement Award **AS:** Mr. Tragen attributes his success to specialized experience in inter-American relations. **B/I:** Mr. Tragen became involved in his profession because he lost his hearing at the age of 14, and essentially became a lip reader. He read lips when he went to law school and in his senior year, the dean of the Law School, Edwin Dickerson, suggested that he find a specialty or he would end up in the backroom of a law office. Shortly after that, the university offered Mr. Tragen a traveling fellowship to get an advanced degree in comparative law at the University of Chile. That was the beginning of his specialization in Latin American legal problems and his career in Latin American-U.S. relations, which is the theme that has run through since 1948. he recently wrote a book that depicts his relations with Latin America but, more importantly, showcases the important role of his wife, Eleanor (Ele) Tragen. The book was titled "Two Lifetimes as One: Ele and Me and the Foreign Service." He tried to link not only what he did in Latin America but the role that his wife played in helping him. **PA:** Independent **THT:** Mr. Tragen's book, "Two Lifetimes As One: Ele and Me and Foreign Service" was launched November 14, 2019 in Washington DC.

TRAHAN, LORI ANN, T: U.S. Representative from Massachusetts **I:** Government Administration/ Government Relations/Government Services **CN:** U.S. House of Representatives **DOB:** 10/27/1973 **PB:** Lowell **SC:** MA/USA **MS:** Married **SPN:** David Trahan **CH:** Grace; Caroline; Thomas (Stepson); Dean (Stepson); Christian (Stepson) **ED:** Bachelor of Arts in Comparative and Regional Studies in International Relations, Georgetown University **C:** Member, U.S. House of Representatives from Massachusetts' Third Congressional District (2019-Present); Chief of Staff, Campaign of Marty Meehan; Chief Executive Officer, Concire Leadership Institute; Member, House Committee on Education and Labor, United States Congress; Member, House Committee on Armed Services, United States Congress **CIV:** Member, Congressional Progressive Caucus; Member, New Democrat Coalition **PA:** Democrat

TRAMMEL, RICHARD, T: President, Sports Psychologist **I:** Professional Training & Coaching **CN:** Level 3 Sports, LLC **DOB:** 01/08/1963 **SC:** AL/USA **PT:** Judd Trammel; Linda Trammel **ED:** Coursework, MBA Studies, Auburn University (2018); EdD in Sports and Performance Psychology, University of Western States, with Distinction (2017); MS in Athletic Counseling, Springfield College (2014); BA in Interdisciplinary Studies, Sports Psychology, The University of Alabama, Summa Cum Laude (2012); AA, St. Petersburg College (2010) **CT:** Level 3 Sports Certified Trainer **C:** Sports Psychologist, Level 3 Sports, LLC (2012-Present); President, ShotSavers Golf (1996-2012); Professional Golfer, PGA of America (1989-1996); Assistant Golf Professional, Kissimmee Golf Club (1989-1996); Golf Course Operations, Dubsdread Golf Course (1984-1989) **CR:** Golf Instructor (1989-Present); With, The First Tee, MA (2012-2014); Inventor, The Wrist Firm, The Firm Knee, The Firm Arm, The Firm Grip, The Knee Strap, Dual Teaching Gloves, The Contact Sak, Swing Strap, Mist Behavin', Head Stabilizer, Stick On Reminders, The Super Mat, Trammel Golf Boot, Focus Putting Ball, and The Hit-A-Draw (1999-2007) **CIV:** Volunteer, Bryce Psychiatric Hospital, Alabama Department of Mental Health (2010) **CW:** Author, "Practitioners Use of Mindfulness Training to Reduce Harm from Self-Sabotaging Behavior" (2019); Author, "How to Improve Mental Toughness in Athletes" (2018); Author, "The POWER of Athletic Self-Talk" (2018); Author, "Make the Right Resolution" (2018); Author, "Coping with Verbal Gamesmanship in Golf: The PACE Model" (2016); Author, "Effects of Variable Grip Pressure Due to Induced Reward Anxiety and Performance on a Golf Putting Task" (2016); Author, "How To Win The US Open" (2007) **AW:** Colgan Bryan Award for Excellence in Science and Technology (2012) **MEM:** The University of Alabama Alumni Association; Phi Theta Kappa; Psi Chi, The International Honor Society in Psychology; Association for Applied Sport Psychology (AASP) **AS:** Dr. Trammel attributes his success

to God's invisible hand. Dr. Trammel is a deeply spiritual person and also credits his success to God's grace and guidance. **B/I:** Dr. Trammel played his first round of golf at the age of 21 and shot a score of 91 (a very rare feat). He was encouraged to take lessons and to continue working on his game. After seven years, he was confident enough to begin playing professional golf in Florida on various developmental mini-tours. It was during this time period when he began his teaching career in golf. Having more success as an instructor than as a player while teaching both amateur and professional players in the United States and Europe, Dr. Trammel turned his attention towards golf instruction early in his playing career due to the many requests of his playing partners during pro-am events. Through these pro-am connections on the Florida tours, he was able to begin a full-time shift from tournament play to instruction starting in 1996. Using training products to illustrate the various moves in the golf swing, Dr. Trammel decided to incorporate them into his teaching methodology. This led to the formation of his first internet company, ShotSavers Golf, Inc. in 1996, which he operated for nearly 14 years. During his tenure with ShotSavers Golf, Dr. Trammel manufactured and invented 15 golf training products, including patenting the Trammel Golf Boot (a spiked golf shoe shaped like a cowboy boot). In 2007, Dr. Trammel decided to enter college for the first time with the desire to increase his golf instruction knowledge by studying psychology. During his junior year at the University of Alabama, he was introduced to the field of sports psychology, which helped to guide his overall academic purpose. This discovery would shape the remainder of his collegiate life sending him to Springfield, Massachusetts to begin his graduate studies at Springfield College. Dr. Trammel's research primarily focused on cognitive differences between equally talented athletes and trying to determine what mental properties were present in a successful athlete that may have been absent in another and to determine if those differences could be quantified in a workable hypothesis. After many years of research, Dr. Trammel formulated a methodology entitled "The Puzzle," defined as a cognitive framework of control that can deliver successful results to virtually any athlete if they have the basic benchmarks of talent, effort, and the discipline to adhere to its principles. Since graduation, Dr. Trammel has refined "The Puzzle" working with a large variety of athletes (and professional musicians) in successfully assisting them in their career goals. **AV:** Golf **PA:** Independent **THT:** Dr. Trammel's motto is, "Life is short and hard. Might as well hit the driver." Dr. Trammel is the creator of various golf related inventions. The Wrist Firm is a wrist brace that keeps the leading wrist firm, not allowing a break down of the wrist anywhere in the swing. The Wrist Firm was featured on Golf Channel's reality show "For Inventor's Only." The Firm Knee is a padded knee brace that keeps the outside knee angle consistent. The Firm Arm is a rigid sleeve that helps to keep the left arm straight throughout the golf swing (for the right-handed player). The Firm Grip keeps the hands fastened securely on the grip throughout the swing. The Knee Strap is the same concept as the Firm Knee, except it uses straps only with no padding. Dual Teaching Gloves are a pair of gloves with lines and drawings on them that indicates the proper grip position with both hands. The Contact Sak is a vinyl bag filled with sheets or towels that squares up the clubface at impact. Swing Strap is a nylon strap that goes around the entire upper chest that promotes connectedness. Mist Behavin' is a powder mist that indicates wind direction when squeezed from a bottle. Head Stabilizer is used as

a gentle reminder to keep the head from swaying laterally on the backswing. Stick On Reminders are adhesive stickers to a golf glove or club that acts as swing triggers and was invented by Judd Trammel. The Super Mat is a dual-layered golf mat that features two surfaces, a regular turf and long turf that simulates rough. The Trammel Golf Boot is a spiked golf shoe shaped like a boot that was awarded United States Patent USD457713. The Focus Putting Ball is a regulation ball featuring lines that helps the golfer focus on the proper roll and a dot to maintain eye gaze. The Hit-A-Draw is a golf club that is specially designed to promote a right to left shot for right-handed players. It features three training aids into one golf club, each designed to help the player with different feels and positioning, promoting a draw.

TRANI, EUGENE P., PHD, T: Professor **I:** Education/Educational Services **CN:** Virginia Commonwealth University **PB:** Brooklyn **SC:** NY/USA **PT:** Frank Joseph Trani; Rose Gertrude (Kelly) Trani **MS:** Married **SPN:** Lois Elizabeth Quigley (06/02/1962) **CH:** Anne Chapman; Frank **ED:** PhD, Indiana University (1966); MA, Indiana University (1963); BA in History, University of Notre Dame, with Honors (1961) **C:** Professor, Virginia Commonwealth University (2009-Present); President, Chairman, VCU Health (2000-2009); Chairman, Virginia Biotech Research Park (1997-2009); President, Board of Directors, Virginia Biotech Research Park (1992-1997); President, Virginia Commonwealth University (1990-2009); Professor, Vice President of Academic Affairs, University of Wisconsin System (1986-1990); Professor, Vice Chancellor of Academic Affairs, University Missouri, Kansas City, MO (1980-1986); Assistant Vice President of Academic Affairs, Professor, University of Nebraska (1976-1980); Professor, Southern Illinois University, Carbondale, IL (1975-1976); Associate Professor, Southern Illinois University, Carbondale, IL (1971-1975); Assistant Professor, Southern Illinois University, Carbondale, IL (1967-1971); Instructor of History, The Ohio State University, Columbus, Ohio (1965-1967) **CR:** The Association of Public and Land-grant Universities (1980-Present); Board of Directors, Advisory Council on Graduate Studies and Research, University of Notre Dame (1994-2017); Visiting Professor, University College Dublin (2002); Board of Advisors, Institute for U.S. Studies, University of London (1993-1999); Chair, Commission on International Affairs (1993-1994); Visiting Assistant Professor, University of Wisconsin - Milwaukee (1969) **CIV:** Richmond Renaissance (1992-Present); Richmond's Future (2001-2016); Chairman, Richmond Renaissance (2001-2004); Board of Directors, Collegiate School (1998-2004); World Affairs Council of Greater Richmond (Now Richmond World Affairs Council) (1999-2003); Board of Directors, Qatar Foundation for Education Science Communications Development (2000-2002); Member, Governor's Commission, Information Technology in Virginia (1998-2000); Board of Directors, Metropolitan Business Foundation (1992-1998); Theatre Virginia (1994-1997); Board of Trustees, Virginia Historical Society (1994-1996); Member, Central Richmond Association (1992-1996); Board of Directors, Richmond Ballet (1991-1996); Board of Directors, Center for Innovative Technology (CIT), VA (1990-1996); Member, Council of Advisors, Christian Children's Fund (ChildFund) (1992-1995); Board of Directors, Science Museum of Virginia Foundation (1994); Richmond Symphony (1991-1994); National Conference of Christians and Jews, Richmond, VA (1991-1994); Permanent Member, Council on Foreign Relations, New York, NY (1979) **CW:** Co-author with Robert Holsworth, "The Indispensable University" (2010); Co-author with Donald E. Davis, "Distorted Mirrors" (2009); Co-author with Donald E. Davis, "The First Cold War" (2002); Co-author with David Wilson, "The Presidency of Warren G. Harding, Third Edition" (1989); Author "The Secretaries of the Department of the Interior, 1849-1889" (1975); Author, "The Treaty of Portsmouth: An Adventure in American Diplomacy" (1969); Author, Editor, "Concerns of a Conservative Democrat" (1968); Contributor, Articles to Professional Journals, Newspapers; Book Reviewers **MEM:** Chairman, Greater Richmond Chairman of Commission (1997-1998); Board of Directors, Greater Richmond Chairman of Commission (1991-1998); International Institute Strategic Studies; American Association for the Advancement of Slavic Studies Organization (Now Association for Slavic, East European, and Eurasian Studies (ASEEE); Organization of American Historians; The Society for Historians of American Foreign Relations; Greater Richmond Chairman of Commission; The Honor Society of Phi Kappa Phi **MH:** Albert Nelson Marquis Lifetime Achievement Award **B/I:** Dr. Trani became involved in his profession because one professor, who was his graduate advisor, Robert Ferrell, mentored him through college. **AV:** Reading; Travel; Basketball; Golf **RE:** Roman Catholic

TRAPPE, JAMES MARTIN, PHD, T: Research Mycologist **I:** Research **CN:** U. S. Forest Service, Pacific Northwest Research Station, and Oregon State University. Departments of Botany & Plant Pathology and Forest Ecosystems and Society **DOB:** 08/16/1931 **PB:** Spokane **SC:** WA/USA **PT:** Martin Carl Trappe; Esther Louise (Koss) Trappe **MS:** Divorced **SPN:** Beverly Joan Reller (12/27/1963) **CH:** Matthew; Erica; John; Angela **ED:** PhD in Forest Mycology, University of Washington (1962); MF in Silviculture, SUNY College of Environmental Science and Forestry (1955); BS in Forest Management, University of Washington (1953) **C:** Adjunct Professor, Botany-Plant Pathology and Forest Ecosystems and Society, Oregon State University (1965-2020); Principal Mycologist, Project Leader, Pacific Northwest Research Station, Corvallis, OR (1965-1985); Research Forester, Mycologist (1956-1965) **CR:** Visiting Professor of Forest Mycology, Turkish Ministry of Forestry and Mugla Sitki Kocman University, Turkey (2013-2014); Visiting Professor of Forest Mycology, Australian National University, CSIRO, Australian Capital Territory National Parks (1995-2013); Visiting Professor of Forest Mycology, Australian Council for International Agricultural Research (1994); Visiting Professor of Forest Mycology, University of Agricultural Sciences, Uppsala, Sweden (1990, 1992, 1993); Visiting Professor of Forest Mycology, CSIRO at Townesville, Australia (1988-1989); Visiting Professor of Forest Mycology, Centro Experimental Station, Agraria, Spain (1987); Visiting Professor of Forest Mycology, University of Chapingo, Mexico (1985); Visiting Professor of Forest Mycology, Indian Agricultural Research Institute (1984); Visiting Professor of Forest Mycology, Australian Commonwealth Scientific and Industrial Research Organization (CSIRO) at Perth (1982); Visiting Professor of Forest Mycology, Kuwait Scientific Research Institute (1979); Visiting Professor of Forest Mycology, Taiwan Forestry Research Institute (1978); Visiting Professor of Forest Mycology, Shiga University, Japan (1975); Visiting Professor of Forest Mycology, National Polytechnic Institute of Mexico (1972); Visiting Professor of Forest Mycology, University of Torino, Italy (1967-1968) **CIV:** Board Member, Buckner Heritage Homestead Foundation (2011-2020); Aiding Homeless or Poor Citizens, Corvallis Chapter, FISH (1975-1985); Fundraising for American Red Cross **CW:** Speaker, 10th International Conference on Mycorrhizae

(2019); Australia Annual Speaker, Terra Preta Educational Trust (2012-2018); Invited Keynote Speaker, Braidwood Truffle Festival, Australia (2015); Invited Keynote Speaker, 1st International Congress on Truffle Research, Vic, Spain (2014); Invited Keynote Speaker, Symposium on Forest Fungi, Dublin, Ireland (2013); Invited Keynote Speaker, Linnaean Society and British Mycological Society Joint Special Symposium, London, England (2013); Co-Author, Editor, "Ecology and Conservation of Truffle Fungi in Forests of the Pacific Northwest" (2009); Co-Author, Editor, "Trees, Truffles, and Beasts: How Forests Function" (2008); Co-Author, Editor, "A Field Guide to North American Truffles" (2007); Co-Author, Editor, "NATS Field Guide to Selected North American Truffles and Truffle-like Fungi" (2003); Co-Author, Editor, "From the Forest of the Sea" (1988); Special Lectureship, Salk Institute, La Jolla, CA (1976); Co-Author, Editor, "The Biology of Adler" (1968); Author, Contributor, 512 Scientific/Professional Papers; Published, Names and Descriptions of New Taxa of Fungi: One Order, Three Families, 42 Genera/Subgenera, 219 Species, 190 New Combinations **AW:** 2nd Eminent Mycologist Award, Merida, Yucatan, Mexico (2019); Gary Lincoff Award for Outstanding Service for Amateur Mycologists (2018); "Pioneer Mycorrhiza Researcher" Award (2015); McMasters Research Fellow, Australia (1999-2003); National Science Foundation awards (1971-1980, 1986-2000); Barrington Moore Memorial Award, Society of American Foresters (1995); ACLU Civil Liberties Award (1990); Weyerhauser Foundation Fellowship (1990); Visiting Scientist Award, Japan Society for Advancement of Science (1975); Sigma Xi Award (1968); Grantee, American Philosophical Society (1967-1968); Namesake, Numerous Fungal Entities In His Honor **MEM:** Co-Founder, Scientific Adviser, Honorary Life Member, North American Truffling Society (1970-Present); Honorary Life Member, Australian Truffle Growers Association (2011); Honorary Life Member, Australian Mycological Society (2001); Honorary Life Member, Japanese Mycological Society (1975); Honorary Life Member, Sociedad Mexico de Micoglia (1993); Honorary Life Member, Oregon Mycological Society (1992); Fellow, American Association for the Advancement of Science (1991); President, Northwest Scientific Association (1991); Honorary Life Member, President, Mycological Society of America (1986-1987); North American Truffling Society (1980); Honorary Life Member, Mycological Society of Japan (1975); Defenders of Wildlife; Forest Service Employees for Environmental Ethics; Nature Conservancy; North Cascades Conservation Council; National Parks Association; Wilderness Society; Smithsonian Institution **MH:** Albert Nelson Marquis Lifetime Achievement Award **AS:** Dr. Trappe attributes his success to encouraging parents, outstanding mentors, lifelong love of forest ecosystems and truffles, good friends, loving family, and strong desire to share what he has learned with family, friends, students, colleagues, and the general population. **B/I:** Dr. Trappe became involved in his profession because a good friend of his parents, Gerhardt Kempff, was a research forester with the U.S. Forest Service in Idaho. He would go with him and his family on picnics to the forest. He had a special way of explaining nature to children; he fascinated little 5-year-old Jimmy, who soaked up his stories. Because of Mr. Kempff's early influence, he loved high school biology and decided to major in forestry at the University of Washington. There, he met many positive influences, faculty and visiting researchers from around the world. They taught him how to do research. **AV:** Backpacking the Northwest mountains up to the age of 70; Nature photography; Truffle collecting; Traveling abroad;

Reading books; Classical to folk and country-western music **PA:** Democrat **THT:** Dr. Trappe said, "Life on earth has evolved over eons in the form of mutualistic symbioses between disparate organisms: that fascinates me! Darwin didn't know of it, and the concept was rejected by all but a few insightful scientists of the late 19th century. It was still challenged by some scientists into the 20th century. Now symbiosis is recognized as a fact of nearly all life on earth. It is fundamental to managing earth's resources and dealing with climate change and its effects on those resources as well as on us humans. Yet, that fundamental fact still goes largely unrecognized by most of us. Our very survival depends on symbioses with microorganisms, although generally we don't think about that!" As an early western North American researcher on mycorrhizae and sequestrate (truffle) fungi, Dr. Trappe's reputation and ability to communicate with a broad array of audiences soon led to invitations to present mycological lectures and conduct collaborative research in both the United States and abroad, e.g. as visiting Professor of Forest Mycology at numerous universities. The productivity of Dr. Trappe's research group attracted students and scientists to join the program for extended periods. They represented numerous American states, plus five continents and 24 countries. The Trappe Group customarily shared their unpublished research data, techniques, and ideas with visitors. In recognition of Dr. Trappe's contributions to knowledge of mycorrhizal fungi the following fungal entities have been named in his honor: 1. Acaulospora trappei Ames & Linderman, Mycotaxon 3:566 (1976); 2. Alpova trappei Fogel, Mycologia 69:841 (1977): 3. Trappea gen nov. Castellano, Mycotaxon 38: 3 (1990); 4. Elaphomyces trappei Galán & Moreno in G. Moreno, R. Gálan & A Montecchi, Mycotaxon 52;201-238 (1991) 5. Archaeospora trappei (Ames & Linderman) Morton & Redecker, Mycologia 93: 183 (2001) 6. Cystangium trappei T. Lebel, Aust. Syst. Bot. 16: 392-393 (2003) 7. Melanogaster trappei I.P.S. Thjnd & B. M. Sharma in Thind, Thind & Sharma, Indian Phytopath. 35: 613 (1982) 8. Trappeindia Castellano, S. L. Miller, I. Singh & Lakhanpal. Kavaka 40: 3, (2012). 9. Trappeaceae, P. M. Kirk, Index Fungorum (2008) 10. Jimtrappea M. Smith et all, IMA Fungus (2015) 11. Terfezia trappei (R. Galan & G. Moreno) A. Paz & Lavoise, Persoonia 38: 231 (2017) 12. Russula trappei (T. Lebel) T.F. Elliott, Fungal Systematics and Evolution 1:36 (2018)

TRAVAYIAKIS, SOFIA AERAKIS, T: Branch Manager **I:** Financial Services **CN:** Mortgage Network, Inc. **MS:** Married **CH:** Three Children **ED:** BS in Business, Corporate Communications (2002) **C:** Branch Manager, Mortgage Network, Inc. (2015-Present); Mortgage Banking, RMS, Residential Mortgage Services, Inc. (2013-2015); Branch Manager, Greenpark Mortgage A Division of Berkshire Bank (2008-2013); Mortgage Consultant, Countrywide Home Loans (2006-2008); Loan Officer, New York Mortgage (2004-2006); Loan Officer, Wells Fargo Home Mortgage (2002-2004); Operations and Processing, Assurance Mortgage, SLC Utah (1997-2002) **CIV:** PAA; Dance Instructor, Local Greek Community **AW:** Top Women Orginators, Scotsman Guide Media (2018); Honoring The Best in Real Estate, Boston Agent (2018); Top 1% Mortgage Originator in America (2014-2018); Who's Who, Boston Agent (2017); Expert Network Distinguished Mortgage Professional; Agents Choice Finalist **MEM:** National Association of Professional Women, Greek Collaborative Network **AS:** Ms. Travayiakis attributes her success to hard work and support. **B/I:** The mortgage industry practically fell in Ms. Travayiakis' lap. She had a small job while she was finishing her senior year in high school. After she started college, she was on the pre-education track but was really intrigued by the mortgage professionals she met when she bought her first home at age 20. She realized then that this was something she really wanted to do. She was also influenced because of an interest in real estate.

TRIANTAFILLOU, DEMOSTHENES, T: Principal **I:** Education/Educational Services **CN:** Hellenic School of the Ascension Church **SC:** Nisyros/Greece **MS:** Married **SPN:** Barbara (Halikas) (1969) **CH:** Emy Tafelski **ED:** Master of Science in School Administration and Supervision, Fordham University (2004); Master of Arts in Philosophy, New York University (1968); Bachelor of Science in Philosophy, New York University (1966); Bachelor of Arts in Biology, New York University (1965); Doctorate Coursework in Philosophy, New York University **CT:** Licensed, New York State School District Superintendent, Principal and Teacher **C:** Principal, Hellenic School of the Ascension Church (2009-Present); Assistant Principal, Summer Programs, Stuyvesant High School (2003-2008); Founder, Principal, Day School of St. Demetrios, Astoria, NY (1973-1982); Teacher, Henley College Preparatory School (1968-1972); Principal, Ascension Greek School at the Ascension Church, Fairview, NJ; Principal, Hellenic School, Greek Orthodox Church of Our Saviour, Rye, NY; Assistant Principal, High School for the Humanities; Part-time Instructor of Philosophy, Long Island University **CR:** Director, Greek schools of the Ascension Church, Fairview, NJ; Director, The Church of the Savior, Rye, NY; Research Scientist, Biochemical Department, Roosevelt Hospital, Columbia University **CIV:** President, Greek Teacher's Association Prometheus (2013-Present); Yearly Organizer, Symposium on the Life and Scientific Work of Dr. George J. Papanicolaou; Yearly Organizer, Summer Educational Trips to Greece and Greek Islands for the Study of the Greek language and Greek History **CW:** Contributor, 34 Articles to the National Herald on Greek American Schools; Author, Two Poetry Books in Greek; Contributor, Articles in Greek History and Philosophy; Author, Three Academic Papers on Clinical Nutrition **AW:** Educator of the Year, The Ethniko Kirikas (2018); Distinguished Meritorious Award, Educator of the Year, Greek American Daily (2017) **AS:** Mr. Triantafillou attributes his success to hard work, as well as an intellectual commitment to distinguish himself. Likewise, he benefited greatly from the influence of his parents, who taught him to be a good person and try to earn distinction in life. **B/I:** Mr. Triantafillou was inspired to go into his profession because of his own high school teachers. He admired language, as well as theology. He came to realize that language is the most important medium for externalizing one's thoughts and feelings, and greatly enjoyed reading the philosophical writings of Plato and Aristotle.

TRIPATHI, BRIJESH I., T: Founder, Chief Executive Officer **I:** Staffing and Recruiting **CN:** Emonics LLC **DOB:** 10/06/1987 **PB:** Mumbai **SC:** India **PT:** Ishtdeo; Mithilesh Tripathi **ED:** BA, University of Mumbai (2009) **C:** Founder, Chief Executive Officer, Emonics LLC (2016-Present); Trainee, Management, Marriott International, Inc. (2010-2011) **AW:** Forty Under 40, BridgeTower Media (2020); Listee, Inc. 5000, Mansueto Ventures (2020); Fast 50, BridgeTower Media, NJBIZ **MEM:** ALMDC; National Minority Supplier Development Council, Inc. **AS:** Mr. Tripathi attributes his success to luck and hard work, as well as the work culture he has established over the years. **B/I:** Mr. Tripathi became involved in his profession because he

was motivated to go into business for himself. He wanted to create a legacy and build something that would preserve his name and brand. **AV:** Watching documentaries; CrossFit training; Reading

TRIPLETT, ROBERT J., T: State Research Analyst (Retired) **I:** Research **DOB:** 10/28/1950 **PB:** Greenfield **SC:** MO/USA **PT:** Elizabeth Triplett **MS:** Married **SPN:** Debra Diane Belcher (09/05/2009); Dorothy LaVerne Glover (12/29/1973, Deceased 1994) **CH:** Roger L. Glover; Marcus Reynolds; LaTonya Molina; Bradley Reynolds **ED:** BS in Business Administration, Lincoln University (1974) **C:** Retired (2009), Research Analyst, Missouri House of Representatives (1977-2009); Security Professional, Missouri State Senate (1975-1976); Sales Representative, Metropolitan Life (1974-1975); Research Analyst, Missouri House of Representatives, Jefferson City, MO **CIV:** Chairman, Holts Summit Street Commission (1979-2001) **AW:** Listee, Outstanding Young Men of America (1983) **MEM:** Trustee, Board Member, Mount Vernon Missionary Baptist Church; Callaway County Democratic Central Committee **MH:** Albert Nelson Marquis Lifetime Achievement Award **B/I:** Mr. Triplett's former father-in-law told him about available job positions working for the state senate. He felt that the positions sounded interesting and decided to pursue a career in the field. **AV:** Camping; Hunting; Fishing Horseback riding; Bicycling; Motorcycle riding **PA:** Democrat **RE:** Baptist

TRONE, DAVID JOHN, T: U.S. Representative from Maryland **I:** Government Administration/Government Relations/Government Services **CN:** U.S. House of Representatives **DOB:** 09/21/1955 **PB:** Cheverly **SC:** MD/USA **PT:** Thomas Trone **MS:** Married **SPN:** June Trone **CH:** Michelle; Julie; Natalie; Rob **ED:** Master of Business Administration, The Wharton School, The University of Pennsylvania (1985); Bachelor of Arts, Furman University, Magna Cum Laude (1977) **C:** Member, U.S. House of Representatives from Maryland's Sixth Congressional District, United States Congress, Washington, DC (2019-Present); Founder, Total Wine & More (2016); President, Founder, Total Wine & More (1991-2016); Founder, Beer World, DE (1991); Founder, Beer World, PA (1984) **CIV:** Board Member, American University (2016-Present); Board Member, Montgomery County Chamber of Commerce (2016-Present); Established, Trone Family Public Policy Initiative Fund, The Wharton School, The University of Pennsylvania (2016-Present); Established, Trone Center for Justice and Equality, American Civil Liberties Union (2015-Present); Board of Trustees, Bullis School (2006-Present); Supporter, American Civil Liberties Union (1994-Present); Board of Trustees, Furman University (2010-2016); Founder, David and June Trone Family Foundation; Chair, Trone Private Sector and Education Advisory Council, Trone Center for Justice and Equality, American Civil Liberties Union **AW:** Carl F. Kohrt Distinguished Alumni Award, Furman University (2017); Achievement Award, Anti-Defamation League (2016); Entrepreneur of the Year Award, Ernst & Young, Greater Washington (2014); Distinguished Service Award, Kids Enjoy Exercise Now (2012) **MEM:** Phi Beta Kappa **PA:** Democrat

TROUT, MICHAEL NELSON, T: Professional Baseball Player **I:** Athletics **CN:** Los Angeles Angels **DOB:** 08/07/1991 **PB:** Vineland **SC:** NJ/USA **PT:** Jeff Trout; Debbie (Busonick) Trout **MS:** Married **SPN:** Jessica Cox (12/9/2017) **ED:** Diploma, Millville Senior High School, Millville, NJ (2009) **C:** Outfielder, Los Angeles Angels (2011-Present); Baseball Player, Arizona Angels, Cedar Rapids Kernels, Rancho Cucamonga Quakes, Arkansas Trav-

elers **CR:** Partner, Investor, Bodyarmor SuperDrink (2012-Present); Player, Major League Baseball Game (2012-2019); Player, Baseball America Minor League Baseball All-Star Team (2010-2011); Player, All-Star Futures Game (2010); Sponsor, Subway, SuperPretzel **AW:** Three-time Recipient, American League Most Valuable Player (2014, 2016, 2019); Hank Aaron Award (2014, 2019); Four-time Recipient, American League Player of the Week (2012, 2014-2015, 2019); Five-time Recipient, American League Player of the Month (2012, 2014-2015, 2017-2018); This Year in Baseball Award for Best Major Leaguer (2016); Five-time Recipient, Silver Slugger Award (2012-2016); ESPY Award for Best Major League Baseball Player (2015); Major League Baseball All-Star Game Most Valuable Player (2014-2015); Players Choice Award for American League Outstanding Player (2014); This Year in Baseball Hitter of the Year (2014); Baseball America Major League Player of the Year (2012-2013); Four-time Recipient, American League Rookie of the Month (2012); Fielding Bible Award (2012); Named, MLB.com Top 100 (2012); American League Rookie of the Year (2012); Players Choice Award for American League Outstanding Rookie (2012); Sporting News Rookie of the Year (2012); This Year in Baseball Award for Rookie of the Year (2012); Wilson American League Defensive Player of the Year (2012); Heart & Hustle Award (2012); Named, Baseball America Top 100 (2010-2012); Baseball America Minor League Player of the Year (2011); Named, Top 100 Prospects, ESPN's Keith Law (2011); USA Today Minor League Player of the Year (2011); J.G. Taylor Spink Award (2010); Topps Minor League Baseball All-Star (2010); Baseball America All-Star; Topps Class-A All-Star

TRUJILLO, SERGIO, T: Dancer, Stage Choreographer **I:** Media & Entertainment **PB:** Cali **SC:** Colombia **MS:** Married **SPN:** Jack Noseworthy (2011) **CH:** Lucas Alejandro Truworthy **ED:** Coursework, University of Toronto; Student, Chiropractic School **CW:** Choreographer, "Ain't Too Proud" (2019); Choreographer, "Summer: The Donna Summer Musical" (2018); Choreographer, "A Bronx Tale" (2016); Choreographer, "On Your Feet!" (2015); Musical Staging, "Hands on a Hardbody" (2013); Choreographer, "Leap of Faith" (2012); Choreographer, "The Addams Family" (2010); Choreographer, "Memphis" (2009); Musical Staging, "Next to Normal" (2009); Choreographer, "Guys and Dolls" (2009); Choreographer, "Jersey Boys" (2005); Additional Choreographer, "All Shook Up" (2005); Dancer, "Fosse" (1999); Dancer, "Guys and Dolls" (1992); Dancer, "Jerome Robbins' Broadway" (1989) **AW:** Tony Award for Best Choreography, "Ain't Too Proud" (2019); Elliot Norton Awards for Outstanding Director, Large Theater, "Arrabal" (2018); Laurence Olivier Award for Best Theatre Choreographer, "Memphis" (2015); Co-Recipient, Outer Critics Circle Award for Outstanding Choreography, "Memphis" (2010); Named, Top 100 Colombians in the World, President Juan Manuel Santos, Colombia

TRUMP, IVANKA MARIE, T: First Daughter; Senior Advisor to the President **I:** Government Administration/Government Relations/Government Services **DOB:** 10/30/1981 **PB:** Manhattan **SC:** NY/USA **PT:** Donald John Trump; Ivana Zelnickova **MS:** Married **SPN:** Jared Cory Kushner (10/25/2009) **CH:** Arabella Rose; Joseph Frederick; Theodore James **ED:** BS in Economics, The Wharton School, The University of Pennsylvania, Cum Laude (2004); Coursework, Georgetown University (2000-2002) **C:** First Daughter, Advisor to the President, United States (2017-Present); Principal, Ivanka Trump Fine Jewelry (2010-2018); Executive Vice President, Development and Acquisitions, The Trump

Organization, LLC (2007-2017); Vice President, Real Estate Development and Acquisition, The Trump Organization, LLC, New York, NY (2005-2007); Model (1997-2007); Project Manager, Retail Development Division, Forest City Enterprises (2004-2005); Launched, Ivanka Trump Lifestyle Collection **CR:** Board of Directors, 100 Women in Hedge Funds (Now 100 Women in Finance) (2011-2013); Board of Directors, Signature Bank, Inc. (2011-2013); Board of Directors, Trump Entertainment Resorts Inc. (2007-2009) **CW:** Author, "Women Who Work: Rewriting the Rules for Success" (2017); Appearance, Television Series, "Gossip Girl" (2010); Author, "The Trump Card: Playing to Win in Work and Life" (2009); Appearance, Television Series, "The Apprentice" (2006-2008); Appearance, Documentaries, "Born Rich" (2003) **AW:** Named One of the 100 Most Influential People, TIME Magazine (2017); Joseph Wharton Award for Young Leadership (2015); Named One of the 40 Under 40, Fortune Magazine (2014); Named One of the 50 Most Powerful Women in New York City, New York Post (2007, 2008)

TRUMP, MELANIA, T: First Lady of the United States **I:** Government Administration/Government Relations/Government Services **DOB:** 05/26/1970 **PB:** Novo Mesto **SC:** Slovenia **PT:** Viktor Knavs; Amalija (Ulcnik) Knavs **MS:** Married **SPN:** Donald J. Trump (01/22/2005) **CH:** Barron William **ED:** Coursework, University of Ljubljana **C:** First Lady of the United States, Washington, DC (2017-Present); Launched, Jewelry Line, Melania Timepieces (2010-2017); Model, Milan, Italy, Paris, France and NY **CIV:** Chairwoman, American Heart Association, Inc. (2010); Goodwill Ambassador, The American National Red Cross (2005-2008); Honorary Chairwoman, Martha Graham Dance Company (2005); Honorary Chairwoman, Boys' Club of New York; Participant, National Love Our Children Day and National Child Abuse Prevention Month **CW:** Model, GQ Magazine, In Style Weddings, New York Magazine, Vanity Fair and Vogue **AW:** Named Woman of the Year, Police Athletic League (2006) **PA:** Republican **RE:** Catholic

TRUNK, GARY, MD, MBA, T: Pulmonologist; Consultant **I:** Medicine & Health Care **DOB:** 07/12/1941 **PB:** Detroit **SC:** MI/USA **YOP:** 2017 **PT:** Isador Trunk; Bernice Barron Trunk **MS:** Married **SPN:** Virginia Rodriguez (01/16/1977) **ED:** MBA, Century University (1991); Fellow, United States Air Force Medical Center, Scott Air Force Base, IL (1970-1972); Resident, United States Air Force Medical Center, Keesler Air Force Base, MI (1968-1970); Intern, St. Joseph's Hospital and Medical Center, Dignity Health, Phoenix, AZ (1967-1968); MD, University of California Irvine (1967); BA, University of California Los Angeles (1963) **CT:** Diplomate, American Board of Quality Assurance and Utilization Review Physicians (ABQA-URP) **C:** With, Department of Social Services Disability Evaluation, San Diego, CA (1974-2017) **MIL:** With, United States Air Force (1968-1974); Major, United States Air Force (1970); Commissioned Second Lieutenant, United States Air Force (1968) **AW:** Fellowship, American College of Medical Quality (1987) **MEM:** Fellow, American College of Chest Physicians; American College of Physicians (ACP) **MH:** Albert Nelson Marquis Lifetime Achievement Award **B/I:** Dr. Trunk entered his profession because he dissected a frog when he was younger and was intrigued by the process. He knew in his heart then that he wanted to be a doctor.

TSALAMATA, VICKY, T: Professor **I:** Education/Educational Services **CN:** Athens School of Fine Arts **DOB:** 09/21/1948 **SC:** Athens/Greece

PT: Dimitrios Charalambos Tsalamatas; Helen Antonios Tsalamata-Triantafyllou **ED:** Research Programs on Eco-Printmaking, Edinburgh Printmakers, Scotland (2006); Research Programs on New Media, Advanced Printmaking, and Digital Imaging, Columbia College Chicago (2004); Postgraduate Coursework, London College of Printing (Now London College of Communication) (1983); Postgraduate Coursework, University College of London (1983); MA in Printmaking, Slade School of Fine Arts, University College London (1983); Diploma in Fine Arts Painting, Academy di Belle Arti, Bologna, Italy (1973); Diploma in Graphic Design, Athenian Technical Institute, Athens, Greece (1969); Postgraduate Coursework, Slade School of Fine Art; Diplôme d'études en langue française **CT:** Certificat Pratique de Langue Française, University of Paris (1966); Certificate of Knowledge of the Italian Language, Università per Stranieri di Perugia, Italy **C:** Full Professor, Athens School of Fine Arts (1998-Present); Emeritus Professor, Head of the Printmaking Department, Director of the 2nd Printmaking Studio, Athens School of Fine Arts (1998-2016); Freelance Artist (1975-1998) **CR:** Curator, Skironio Museum Polychronopoulos, Athens, Greece (2005); Invited Curator, Greek Section, Varosi Municipal Museum, Gyor, Hungary (2001); Invited Curator, Greek Section, Varosi Municipal Museum, Gyor, Hungary (1999); Curator, Athens Municipality Arts Center, Greece (1999); International Lecturer in Field; Invited Curator, International Biennial of Drawing and Graphic Arts, Varosi Municipal Museum, Hungary; Commissioner, Coordinator, Curator, Numerous Exhibition Activities **CIV:** Committee for International Relations, Administration Board, Chambers Fine Arts, Greece, Athens (1996-1997); Curator, Administration Board, Chambers Fine Arts of Greece, Athens, Greece (1992-1994); Curator of Printmaking Sector, Chamber Fine Arts of Greece, Athens, Greece (1990-1992); Juror, Chamber of Fine Arts of Greece, Athens, Greece (1986-1989); Jury Member, Numerous International Jury Committees; Participant, Numerous International Juried Exhibitions **CW:** Artist, Solo Exhibition, "Cityscapes," Teloglion Foundation of Art (2018); Artist, Solo Show, Maniatakeion Foundation, Koroni, Peloponnese, Greece (2013); Artist, Solo Show, Numismatic Museum, Athens, Greece (2012-2013); Artist, Solo Show, Contemporary Greek Art Institute, Athens, Greece (2012); Artist, Solo Show, MIET Cultural Foundation, Athens, Greece (2011); Artist, Solo Show, Evnard Exhibition Center, Cultural Foundation, National Bank of Greece (2011); Artist, Solo Show, Galerie Lucien Schweitzer, Luxembourg (2009); Artist, Solo Show, Municipal Museum of Arts, Synagogue, Gyor, Hungary (2007); Artist, Solo Show, Synagogue Museum (2007); Artist, Solo Show, Municipal Museum of Art, Gyor, Hungary (2007); Artist, Solo Show, Ninth International Biennial Drawing and Graphic Arts (2007); Artist, Solo Show, Masters Graphic Arts, Gyor, Hungary (2007); Artist, Athens School of Fine Arts, Greece (2007); Artist, Lucien Schweitzer Galerie d'Art, Luxembourg (2007); Artist, National Museum of Modern Art, Thessaloniki, Greece (2007); Artist, Group Show, Municipal Art Gallery, Greece (2004); Artist, Athens School of Fine Arts, Greece (2004); Artist, Dalarnas Museum, Falun, Sweden (2004); Artist, Group Show, Municipal Art Gallery, Chania, Greece (2003-2004); Artist, Group Show, Palace Art El Gezira, Cairo, Egypt (2003); Artist, Group Show, Museum of Fine Arts, Alexandria, Egypt (2003); Artist, Solo Show, Center Expositions et de Conference, Luxembourg (2003); Artist, National Museum of Modern Art, Thessaloniki, Greece (2003); Artist, Group Show, Municipal Art Gallery of Athens (2002); Artist, Solo Show, Bratislava City Gallery, Slovakia (2002); Artist, Solo Show, Univer-

sity of Belgrade, Yugoslavia (2001); Artist, Group Show, Municipal Museum, Sint Niklaas, Belgium (2001); Artist, Solo Show, Nadezda Petrovic Gallery, Cacak, Yugoslavia (2001); Artist, Group Show, Lalit Kala Akademi, New Delhi, India (2001); Artist, Solo Show, Museum of Fine Arts, Alexandria, Egypt (2001); Artist, Group Show, Palace Art El Gezira, Cairo, Egypt (1999); Artist, Solo Show, Terracotta Gallery (1998); Artist, Solo Show, Adam Galleries, Athens, Greece (1997); Artist, Group Show, City Gallery of Contemporary Art, Chamalières, France (1997); Artist, Group Show, City Gallery Ljubljana, Slovenia (1995); Presenter, 41 Solo Exhibitions **AW:** Printmaking Prize, 1st Print Triennial: Bridges Between the Mediterranean and the Baltic, Tressaloniki, Greece (2008); Prize of Belgrade Academy of Fine Arts, Biennial International Jury Committee, Fifth Belgrade International Printmaking Biennial (1999); Printmaking Award, 18th Alexandria Biennale, Egypt (1994); Prize Artitudes '89, International Art Competition (1989); 1st Printmaking Prize, VIII Concorso Internazionale di Pittura e Grafica, Città di Serra San Quirico, Ancona (1980); Award, XI Concours International de la Palme d'Or des Beaux-Arts, International Arts Guild (1979); Award, X Concourse International de la Palma d'Or des Beaux-Arts, International Arts Guild (1978); Award, IX Concourse Internationale de la Palme d'Or des Beaux-Arts, International Arts Guild (1977); Honorary Award, VIII Concourse International de la Palme d'Or des Beaux Arts, International Arts Guild (1976); Award, Panhellenic Graphic Art Completion, 34th Thessaloniki International Exhibition (1968) **MEM:** Founder, Administrative Committee, Union Greek Printmakers (1986-Present); Artistic Association; Federation International Culturelle Féminine; International Council of Military Museums **MH:** Albert Nelson Marquis Lifetime Achievement Award **B/I:** Ms. Tsalamata's career as a professional visual artist began early in her life; it was the consequence of an inner need to express herself. Her training in fine arts started with studies in graphic design at the Athenian Technological Institute of Athens, where she earned a degree in graphic design. Ms. Tsalamata's studies in painting and printmaking continued at the Accademia di Belle Arti di Bologna, Italy, where she received a BFA in 1973. There, she was introduced to the art of printmaking and it was love at first sight. Ms. Tsalamata was more than certain that this would be the field in which she could express herself best. She knew she could find inspiration, continuous stimulation, and creativity. The next step for her was the organization of her own printmaking studio in Athens, Greece, in 1975, where she experimented for several years in intaglio printmaking. Her career as a professional artist had already begun. But, as Ms. Tsalamata was looking for new knowledge in printmaking, she decided to continue her studies in the famous Slade School of Fine Arts of the London University College, where she earned a Master of Art in Printmaking in 1983. Many years later, in 1998, Ms. Tsalamata's academic career started in the Athens School of Fine Arts, where she taught as a professor of printmaking. She was in charge of the printmaking workshop until the end of 2015. These 16 years of teaching have been a great tenure. **AV:** Practicing photography and sports

TSANG, LINCOLN PHD, BPHARM, PHD, LLB, T: Lawyer, Pharmacist **I:** Law and Legal Services **CN:** Arnold & Porter **DOB:** 08/30/1961 **PB:** Hong Kong **PT:** Tse-kin Tsang; Shiu-man Chiu **ED:** LLB, University of London (1994); PhD, University of Aston in Birmingham (1989); BPharm, University of London (1985) **CT:** Chartered Scientist; Chartered Biologist; Chartered Chemist **C:** Partner, Arnold & Porter (Now Arnold & Porter Kaye Scholer LLP), London, England (2002-Present); Head of Biologicals and Biotechnology, Medicines Control Agency, London, England (2000-2002); Principal Pharmaceutical Officer, Medicines Control Agency, London, England (1990-2000) **CR:** Non-executive Member, Oversight Regulators Committee, Health Protection Agency (2009-Present); Governing Council Member, School of Pharmacy, University of London (2006-Present); Member, UK Ministerial Industrial Strategy Group, New Technology Group (2006-Present); Advisor, Regulatory Affairs Advisory Committee, BioIndustry Association (2002-Present); Commissioner, British Pharmacopoeia Commission (2000-Present); Vice Chair, Nomenclature Committee, British Pharmacopoeia (2000-Present); Advisor, Council of Europe (2009); Non-executive Director, National Biological Standards Board (2004-2009); Chairman, Regulatory Affairs Advisory Committee, BioIndustry Association (2003-2009); Overseas Advisor, Hong Kong Jockey Club Institute of Chinese Medicine (2002-2009); Vice Chair, Committee on Biological Materials, British Pharmacopoeia (2000-2009); Detached Expert, Biotechnology Regulation, Czech Republic Institute of Drug Control, Prague (2004-2005); Honorary Advisor, Health Sciences Authority, Singapore (2002-2003); Advisor on Biotechnology and Biologicals, European Medicines Agency (1996-2002); Member, Bioindustry Government Regulatory Advisory Group, Department of Trade and Industry, London, England (1996-2002); Advisor, World Health Organization, Geneva (1996); Chair, Education Biology, Biotechnology, British Pharmacopoeia **CIV:** Non-executive Member, Regulatory Oversight Committee, Health Protection Agency (2009-Present) **CW:** Contributor, Over 50 Papers on Legal and Regulatory Issues **AW:** International Law Office Client's Choice Award (2013); Excellent Client Care, Life Sciences and Health Care **MEM:** Fellow, Royal Pharmaceutical Society (2007); Fellow, Royal Society of Arts (2002); Fellow, Royal Society of Biology (2000); Fellow, Royal Society of Chemistry (2000) **BAR:** Hong Kong (2002); England (Inner Temple) (1995) **MH:** Albert Nelson Marquis Lifetime Achievement Award **B/I:** Dr. Tsang became involved in his profession because he worked with people who taught him whether they were family or friends. He worked with many, many talented people who guided him. His parents, Tse-kin Tsang and Shiu-man Chiu were very influential in guiding him. His siblings were very helpful and influential as well.

TSCHUMY, FREDA C., T: Artist **I:** Fine Art **CN:** Independent Studio **DOB:** 03/18/1939 **PB:** Danville **SC:** IL/USA **PT:** Frederick Winfield Coffing; Minnie Isabelle (Buck) Coffing **MS:** Married **SPN:** William Edward Tschumy Jr. (06/17/1967) **CH:** William Coffing Tschumy (1975) **ED:** MFA, University of Miami (1990); Postgraduate Coursework, Accademia di Belle Arti di Roma, Rome, Italy (1963); Postgraduate Coursework, The Art Students League, New York, NY (1961-1963); BA, Vassar College (1961) **C:** Vice President, Foundry, ArtSouth, Homestead, FL (2003-2006); Director, Foundry, University of Miami, Coral Gables, FL (1992-2003); Artist, Independent Studio; Adjunct Professor of Sculpture and Foundry, University of Miami, Coral Gables, FL (1991-2003); Instructor, Sculpture, Bass Museum School, The Bass Museum of Art, Miami Beach, FL (1989-1992); Teaching Assistant, University of Miami, Coral Gables, FL (1988-1990); Instructor, Sculpture, Metropolitan Museum School, Coral Gables, FL (1980-1989); Instructor, Painting, Barry College (Now Barry University), Miami Shores, FL (1974); Instructor, Sculpture, Continuum Gallery, Miami Beach, FL (1972-1973); Instructor, Sculpture, Upstairs Gallery, Miami Beach, FL (1971); Instructor, Ceramics, Grove House, Coconut Grove, FL (1970); Instructor, Art, Fine Arts Conservatory, Miami, FL (1968) **CR:** Founding Director, Foundry Guild, University of Miami, Coral Gables, FL (1993-2003); President, The Gallery at Mayfair, Coconut Grove, FL (1983-1984); Treasurer, The Gallery at Mayfair, Coconut Grove, FL (1982-1983); Artist in Residence, La Pietra, Hawaii School for Girls, Honolulu, HI (1987); Treasurer, Continuum Gallery, Miami Beach, FL (1975-1983); President, Founding Member, Continuum Gallery, Miami Beach, FL (1971-1975) **CIV:** National Audubon Society (2001-Present); Fairchild Tropical Botanical Garden (1999-Present); Defenders of Wildlife (1992- Present); World Wildlife Fund (1991-Present); Florida PIRG, The Public Interest Network (1986-Present); Florida Chapter, NARAL Pro-Choice America (1985-Present); The Conservation Foundation of the Gulf Coast (1978-Present); Tropical Audubon Society, Miami, FL (1975-Present) **CW:** Artist, Bronze Exterior Sculpture, "Cross & Flame," South Miami 1st Methodist Church, South Miami, FL (1999); Artist, Plexiglass & Stainless Steel Sculpture, "Light Gate," Lobby of New Main Library, Melbourne, FL (1987-1989); Artist, Cor-Ten Steel Sculpture, "Tetrahelix & Son," Miami Metrorail Rapid Transit Station, Coral Gables, FL (1980-1983); Artist, Life-Size Bronze Sculpture, "Marjory Stoneman Douglas," Biscayne Nature Center, Key Biscayne, FL (2005); On Loan to Fairchild Tropical Botanical Garden"Centennial Tree Bench," Bronze Bench, Vassar College, Poughkeepsie, NY **AW:** Fine Art Achievement Award, Binney & Smith, Inc. (Now Crayola) (1990); Grantee, Leslie T. and Frances U. Posey Foundation, Sarasota, FL (1989); Award of Excellence, Downtown Development Authority, Fort Lauderdale, FL(1972); First Prize, WCA Biennial II, All Florida Exhibition, Juror: Joyce Kozloff, artist, New York, NY (1987); "Visions Aquarius," Best in Show, Professional Artists' Guild: Juror, Eric Speyer (1978); Award of Excellence, Sculptors of Florida, Miami (1972) **MEM:** Lowe Art Museum, University of Miami (1991-Present); The International Sculpture Center (1991-Present); American Foundry Society (1991-1995); Board of Directors, Women's Caucus for Art (1980-1991); First Vice President, Local Chapter, Women's Caucus for Art (1981-1986); National Board of Directors, Women's Caucus for Art (1982-1985) **MH:** Albert Nelson Marquis Lifetime Achievement Award (2020); Who's Who in America (2000); Who's Who in the South and Southwest (1997); Who's Who in the World (1994) **AS:** Ms. Tschumy attributes her success to curiosity, hard work, perseverance, a loving family, having had some excellent, and generous teachers, having worked with some creative and original artists, and having had the opportunity to travel and experience the art of many cultures and eras. **B/I:** Ms. Tschumy became involved in her profession because she always loved to paint and draw and model small figures from clay found in the stream banks near our house. She also loved nature and science, and intended to become a doctor when she grew up. She started college following a pre-med course, but took an art history class my freshman year and realized that art can be a life's work. That changed everything. She switched my major and found that the college also offered studio courses in stone carving with Concetta Scaravaglione, a Prix de Rome winner. She was hooked. After graduating from Vassar, she continued my studies for two years at The Art Students' League in New York, and then for nine months in Rome, Italy at the Accademia di Belli Arti. **AV:** Traveling; Reading; Walking; Cooking **THT:** Ms. Tschumy said, ""Art is a vehicle of empathy. Art enables people to share experiences and is the binder that holds civilizations together. Art is culture: we grow in it. Art enables us to objectify and externalize experiences so that we can remember them, examine them, re-experience them, and share them with others. Art helps us to be human."

TSU, RAPHAEL, T: Physics and Electrical Engineering Professor **I:** Education/Educational Services **DOB:** 12/27/1932 **PB:** Shanghai **SC:** China **PT:** Adrian; Isabel Tsu **SPN:** Nancy Frost; Danusia G. Tsu **CH:** Michael; David; Maria; Melinda; Gabriel; Simone **ED:** PhD, Ohio State University (1960); BS, University Dayton, (1956) **C:** Distinguished Professor, University of North Carolina, Charlotte, NC (1988-Present); Principal Scientist, Solar Energy Research Institute DOE (1985-1987); Professor, Institute Physical and Chemistry, Sao Carlos, Brazil (1984-1985); Research Department Head, Energy Conversion Devices (1979-1984); Staff member, IBM T. J. Watson Research Center (1966-1979) **CR:** Advisory Member, Stevens Institute Tech (2010-Present); Member, Advisory Research Physics and Chemistry, University of Puerto, Humacao, Puerto Rico (2002-Present); Member, Technical Staff, Bell Telephone Lab (1960-1964) **CW:** Contributor, Articles to Professional Publications; Author, "Superlattice to Nanoelectronics", Author, "The World and I" **AW:** James C. McGroddy Prize (1985); Recipient, Senior United States Scientist Award, Alexander von Humboldt (1975); Outstanding Contribution Award, IBM Research Center (1975) **MEM:** Fellow, American Physical Society **AV:** Piano; Woodworking; Tennis; Photography; Skiing; Dance **PA:** Democrat **RE:** Roman Catholic

TUGNOLI, LORENZO, T: Photographer **I:** Media & Entertainment **SC:** Italy **C:** Freelance Photographer (2010-Present) **CW:** Co-Author, "The Little Book of Kabul" (2014); Contributor, The Washington Post; Featured, The New York Times, The Wall Street Journal, Time Magazine **AW:** Pulitzer Prize Winner in Feature Photography (2019); First Prize, General News Stories, World Press Photo (2019); Nominee, World Press Photo Story of the Year (2019)

TURNER, JEAN I., T: Musician, Educator **I:** Education/Educational Services **DOB:** 08/28/1941 **PB:** Postville **SC:** IA/USA **PT:** William Richard Belschner; Clara P. (Nelson) Belschner Blessum **MS:** Married **SPN:** James Robert Turner (05/27/1963) **CH:** Drew **ED:** BA in Music Education, University of Northern Iowa (1963) **CT:** Certified, University of Nebraska (1983); Certified, University of Nebraska (1976); Certified, Sacramento State University (1963) **C:** Private Music Teacher, Arlington, IA (1990-2015); Private Music Teacher, Bellevue (1981-1989); Teacher, Bellevue School System (1978); Substitute Teacher, Bellevue School System (1974-1977); Substitute Teacher, Beckmantown Public School (1971-1974); Sky Lark Director, Plattsburg AFB (1971-1974); Sky Lark Director, Grand Forks AFB (1969-1971); Substitute Teacher, Mills Junior High School, Rancho Cordova, CA (1963-1968) **CR:** Accompanist, Shepherds Way Baptist Church (2014-2017); Substitute Music Teacher, Starmount School, Arlington, VA (1990-1995) **CIV:** Music Director, Organist, St. John Lutheran Church, Arlington, VA (1990-2014) **CW:** Contributor, Articles, Auctions **MEM:** Vice President, Upper Iowa Music Teachers Association (1996-1997); Secretary, Upper Iowa Music Teachers Association (1995-1996) **MH:** Albert Nelson Marquis Lifetime Achievement Award; Marquis Who's Who Top Professional **B/I:** Mrs. Turner loved her childhood music teacher. In fact, she loved her so much that she decided to pursue teaching music as a career. Throughout her school years, Mrs. Turner took piano lessons and practiced solo work. All of her hard work paid off when she officially became a music teacher. **AV:** Flower show judging; Antique collecting; Listening to music; Attending church; Writing **PA:** Republican **RE:** Lutheran

TURNER, MICHAEL, "MIKE" RAY, T: U.S. Representative from Ohio **I:** Government Administration/Government Relations/Government Services **DOB:** 01/11/1960 **PB:** Dayton **SC:** OH/USA **PT:** Ray Turner; Vivian Turner **MS:** Divorced **SPN:** Majida Mourad (2015, Divorced 2018); Lori Turner (1987, Divorced 2013) **CH:** Two Daughters **ED:** MBA, University of Dayton School of Business Administration (1992); JD, Case Western Reserve University School of Law, Cleveland, Ohio (1985); BS in Political Science, Ohio Northern University, Ada, Ohio (1982) **C:** Member, U.S. House of Representatives from Ohio's 10th Congressional District, United States Congress (2013-Present); Member, U.S. House Committee on Armed Services (2003-Present); President, NATO Parliamentary Assembly (2014-2016); Member, U.S. House of Representatives from Ohio's Third Congressional District, United States Congress (2003-2013); Mayor, City of Dayton, Ohio (1994-2002); President, JMD Development; Corporate Counsel, Modern Technologies Corp., Dayton, Ohio; Member, Committee on Oversight and Government Reform, United States Congress **AW:** Restore America Hero Award, National Trust Historic Preservation/HGTV (2005); National Legislative Leadership Award, The United States Conference of Mayors (2005) **MEM:** ABA; American Corporate Counsel Association (Now Association of Corporate Counsel); Ohio State Bar Association; Dayton Bar Association **BAR:** State of Ohio (1985) **PA:** Republican **RE:** Presbyterian

TURNER, ROBERT, "BOB" L., T: State Representative (Retired) **I:** Government Administration/Government Relations/Government Services **DOB:** 09/14/1947 **PB:** Columbus **SC:** MS/USA **PT:** Roosevelt Turner; Beatrice (Hargrove) Turner **MS:** Married **SPN:** Gloria Harrell-Turner (1969) **CH:** Robert D.; Roosevelt A.; Ryan N. **ED:** BS in Business Administration, University of Wisconsin (1976) **C:** Member District 61, Wisconsin State Assembly, Madison, WI (1990-Present); Police and Fire Commissioner (2019-2023); Alderman, Racine City Council (1976-2004); Chair, State Elections Board (1990); Member, State Elections Board (1987-1990) **CIV:** Appointed, Police and Fire Commission (2019); Board of Advisors, Big Brothers/Big Sisters; State Chairman, Democrat Black Political Caucus; Board of Directors, Racine County Youth Sports Association **MIL:** Sergeant, U.S. Air Force (1967-1971) **AW:** Man of the Year, 2nd Missionary Baptist Church (1983); Decorated Commendation Medal, U.S. Army **MEM:** Veterans of Foreign Wars; National Association for the Advancement of Colored People (NAACP); American Legion; Urban League; Vietnam Veterans of America; Masons **MH:** Albert Nelson Marquis Lifetime Achievement Award **B/I:** Mr. Turner became involved in the military after he met a gentleman by the name of Leroy Willy. After he got out of service, he told Mr. Turner that he would be retiring and wanted him to take his place. After some years, Mr. Willy helped Mr. Turner become more involved in politics. He also supported him spiritually and mentally. Pastor Max C. Davis from his church also supported Mr. Turner. **AV:** Golfing; Repairing cars **PA:** Democrat **RE:** Baptist

TURNER, STACI J., T: Business Operations Manager **I:** Financial Services **CN:** JPMorgan Chase & Co. **PB:** Dayton **SC:** OH/USA **PT:** Alan; Shirley (Deceased 2019) **MS:** Single **ED:** Master of Science in Engineering in Clinical Mental Health Counseling, University of Dayton (2010); Bachelor of Arts in Psychology, Capital University (2003) **C:** Opera-

tions Analyst II, JPMorgan Chase & Co. (2015-Present); Associate, Risk Quality, JPMorgan Chase & Co. (2014-2015); Quality Analyst, Senior Underwriter, Loan Quality Review, JPMorgan Chase & Co. (2012-2014); Senior Underwriter, JPMorgan Chase & Co. (2008-2012); Manager, Business Operations, JPMorgan Chase & Co. **CIV:** Volunteer, Meals on Wheels America (2006) **MEM:** Psi Chi, The International Honor Society in Psychology; CSI; American Counseling Association **MH:** Marquis Who's Who Humanitarian Award **AS:** Ms. Turner attributes her success to her motivation, ambition and drive. **B/I:** Ms. Turner became involved in mortgage and banking gradually, and soon covered all bases of her industry. She started her career in the credit card sector and, three years later, made the transition into mortgages. Ms. Turner is thankful that her profession has given her the flexibility to attend school.

TURNER, SYLVESTER, T: Office of Turner **I:** Law and Legal Services **DOB:** 09/27/1954 **PB:** Houston **SC:** TX/USA **MS:** Married **SPN:** Cheryl Turner (1983-1991) **CH:** Ashley Paige Turner **ED:** JD, Harvard Law School, Harvard University; BA in Political Science, University of Houston, Magna Cum Laude **C:** Mayor, City of Houston, TX (2015-Present); Founder, Attorney, Barnes & Turner (Now Barry Barnes and Associates, PLLC) (1983-Present); Member, House District 139, Texas House of Representatives (1988-2014); Member, Fulbright & Jaworski LLP (Now Norton Rose Fulbright US LLP) **CR:** Adjunct Professor, Thurgood Marshall School of Law, Texas Southern University; Seminar Lecturer, South Texas College of Law; Seminar Lecturer, Continuing Legal Education Programs, University of Houston Law School; Immigration Lawyer, Houston, TX **CIV:** Member, Brookhollow Baptist Church **CW:** Featured, "60 Minutes," MSNBC, CNN, CNBC, Fox News, Wall Street Journal, Black Enterprise Magazine, Cuba Today Magazine, Ebony, New York Times, Washington Post, USA Today **AW:** Named One of the "Five Outstanding Young Texans," Texas Jaycees (2011); Named One of the "Five Outstanding Houstonians," Houston Jaycees (2010); Legislator of the Year (1995); Ohtli Award, Mexican Government; Rookie of the Year, Texas Monthly; Rising Star Award, Harris County Democratic Party **MEM:** State Bar of Texas; American Bar Association; National Bar Association; Houston Lawyers Association; Houston Bar Association; Transportation and Communications Standing Committee, U.S. Conference of Mayors; Vice Chair, National Climate Action Agenda; Advisory Board, African American Mayors Association; United Negro College Fund; American Cancer Society; Old Acres Homes Citizens Council **BAR:** Texas; Federal District Court for the Southern District Court of Texas; U.S. Court of Appeals for the Fifth Circuit **PA:** Democrat **RE:** Baptist

TURNER, TED EDWARD III, T: Media Executive, Philanthropist **I:** Media & Entertainment **DOB:** 11/19/1938 **PB:** Cincinnati **SC:** OH/USA **PT:** Robert Edward Turner II; Florence (Rooney) Turner **MS:** Divorced **SPN:** Jane Fonda (1991, Divorced 2001); Jane Shirley Smith (1965, Divorced 1988); Julia Gale Nye (1960, Divorced 1964) **CH:** Five Children **ED:** Honorary Degree, Brown University (1989); Coursework, Brown University **C:** Owner, Atlanta Braves (1976-2007); Vice Chairperson, Cable News Division, Time Warner and Turner (1996-2003); Owner, World Championship Wrestling (1988-2001); Owner, Turner Classic Movies (1994); Owner, Hanna-Barbera Productions (1991); Owner, Turner Network Television (1988); Founder, Turner Entertainment Co. (1986); Owner, MGM/UA Entertainment Co. (1986); President, Cable Network News (1982); Owner, WCNC-TV, Charlotte, NC

(1973-1979); Founder, Cable network News (1978); Owner, Turner Broadcasting Group (1978); Owner, WTBS (1978); Owner, Atlanta Hawks (1976); Owner, WTCG-TV, Atlanta, GA (1969); President, Chief Executive Officer, Turner Advertising Company (1963); General Manager, Turner Advertising Company, Macon, GA; Owner, Radio Stations **CIV:** Founder, Turner Foundation (1990-Present); Founder, Goodwill Games (1986-Present); Participant, The Giving Pledge (2010); Co-founder, The Moscow Independent Broadcasting Corporation (1993-2007); Member, Board of Directors, Time Warner (1996-2006) **MIL:** Coast Guard **CW:** Author, "Call Me Ted" (2008); Featured, "It Ain't as Easy as it Looks" (1993); Featured, "Lead, Follow or Get Out of the Way" (1981) **AW:** Lifetime Achievement - News & Documentary, Emmy Awards, Television Academy of Arts & Sciences (2015); Lifetime Achievement - Sports, Emmy Awards, Television Academy of Arts & Sciences (2014); Lone Sailor Award (2013); Inductee, National Sailing Hall of Fame (2011); Recipient, Star, Hollywood Walk of Fame (2004); Albert Schweitzer Gold Medal for Humanitarianism (2001); Edward R. Murrow Award for Lifetime Achievement in Communication (2000); Peabody Award (1997); World Series Winner, Atlanta Braves (1995); Inductee, America's Cup Hall of Fame (1993); Audubon Medal, National Audubon Society (1991); Inductee, Television Hall of Fame (1991); Named, Man of the Year, TIME Magazine (1991); Walter Cronkite Award for Excellence in Journalism (1990); Paul White Award, Radio Television Digital News Association (1989); Golden Plate Award, American Academy of Achievement (1984) **MEM:** Kappa Sigma Fraternity **AV:** Sailing

TURNER, TINA, T: Singer **I:** Media & Entertainment **DOB:** 11/26/1939 **PB:** Brownsville **SC:** TN/USA **PT:** Floyd Richard Bullock; Zelma Priscilla (Currie) Bullock **MS:** Married **SPN:** Erwin Bach (07/2013); Ike Turner (1956, Divorced 1978) **CH:** Craig; Ronnie; Ike Jr. (Adopted); Michael (Adopted) **C:** Solo Artist (1977-Present); Singer, Ike and Tina Turner Revue (1966-1975); Singer, Ike Turner and the Kings of Rhythm (1960-1965) **CW:** Author, "Happiness Becomes You: A Guide to Changing Your Life for Good" (2020); Author, "My Love Story: A Memoir" (2018); Author, "I, Tina: My Life Story" (2010); Solo Artist, "Tina Live" (2009); Solo Artist, "Tina!" (2008); Solo Artist, "All the Best" (2005); Appearance, "Ally McBeal" (2000); Solo Artist, "Twenty Four Seven" (2000); Solo Artist, "Wildest Dreams" (1996); Singer, "Collected Recordings, Sixties to Nineties" (1994); Featured, Film Based on Autobiography, "What's Love Got to Do with It?" (1993); Appearance, "Last Action Hero" (1993); Solo Artist, Film Soundtrack, "What's Love Got to Do With It?" (1993); Singer with Ike Turner, "The Ike and Tina Turner Collection" (1993); Singer with Ike Turner, "Proud Mary" (1991); Solo Artist, "Simply the Best" (1991); Singer with Ike Turner, "Greatest Hits" (1990); Singer with Ike Turner, "Ike and Tina Turner: Greatest Hits, Volumes 1, 2 and 3" (1989); Solo Artist, "Foreign Affair" (1989); Solo Artist, "Tina: Live in Europe" (1988); Solo Artist, "Break Every Rule" (1986); Appearance, "Break Every Rule" (1986); Appearance, "Mad Max Beyond Thunderdome" (1985); Performer, Song for Africa, "We are the World" (1985); Author, "I, Tina" (1985); Solo Artist, "Private Dancer" (1984); Solo Artist, "Airwaves" (1979); Solo Artist, "Rough" (1978); Appearance, "Sergeant Pepper's Lonely Hearts Club Band" (1978); Solo Artist, "Love Explosion" (1977); Solo Artist, "Acid Queen" (1975); Appearance, "Tommy" (1975); Solo Artist, "Tina Turns the Country On" (1974); Singer with Ike Turner, "Bad Dreams" (1973); Solo Artist, "Let Me Touch Your Mind" (1972); Appearance, "Soul to Soul" (1971); Performer, Japan and Africa Tour (1971); Singer with Ike Turner, "Hunter" (1970); Appearance, "Gimme Shelter" (1970); Performer, Concert Tours of Europe (1966); Singer with Ike Turner, "Ike and Tina Show" (1966); Performer, Showtime TV Concert, "Wildest Dreams"; Singer with Ike Turner, "Ike and Tina Show II"; Performer, World Tours **AW:** Featured, "Tina: The Tina Turner Musical," West End, United Kingdom (2019-Present); Featured, "Tina: The Tina Turner Musical," Hamburg, Germany (2019-2021); Named to Memphis Music Hall of Fame (2019); Grammy Lifetime Achievement Award, The Recording Academy (2018); Named (as Member of Ike & Tina Turner) to St. Louis Classic Rock Hall of Fame (2015); Named to SoulMusic Hall of Fame (2014); Named One of the 100 Greatest Artists of All Time, Rolling Stone Magazine (2010); Named One of the 100 Greatest Singers of All Time, Rolling Stone Magazine (2008); Grammy Award for Album of the Year, The Recording Academy (2008); Honoree, Kennedy Center Honors, John F. Kennedy Center for the Performing Arts (2005); Named Legion d'Honneur (1996); Legend Award, World Music Awards (1993); Chart Achievement Award, Billboard Music Awards (1993); Named (as Member of Ike & Tina Turner) to Rock and Roll Hall of Fame (1991); Named to St. Louis Walk of Fame (1991); Award for Outstanding Contribution to Music, World Music Awards (1991); Grammy Award for Best Female Rock Vocal Performance, The Recording Academy (1985, 1986, 1987, 1989); Recipient, Star, Hollywood Walk of Fame (1986); Award for Outstanding Female Actress, NAACP Image Awards (1986); Award for Singer of the Year, Billboard Music Awards (1986); Grammy Award for Record of the Year, Best Female Pop Vocal Performance, The Recording Academy (1985); Awards for Artist of the Year, Comeback of the Year, Female Vocalist of the Year, Soul/R&B Artist of the Year, Album of the Year, Billboard Music Awards (1984); Grammy Album for Best R&B Performance by a Duo or Group with Vocal, The Recording Academy (1972); Numerous Awards

TURTURRO, JOHN, T: Actor **I:** Media & Entertainment **DOB:** 02/28/1957 **PB:** Brooklyn **SC:** NY/USA **PT:** Nicholas Turturro; Katherine Florence Turturro **MS:** Married **SPN:** Katherine Borowitz (1985) **CH:** Amadeo; Diego **ED:** MFA, Yale School of Drama (1983); Degree in Theatre Arts, SUNY New Paltz (1979) **C:** Actor, Director and Producer in Films, Television and Theater **CW:** Actor, "The Batman" (2021); Actor, "The Plot Against America" (2020); Voice Actor, "Green Eggs and Ham" (2019); Director, Screenwriter, Actor, "The Jesus Rolls" (2019); Actor, "The True Adventures of Wolfboy" (2019); Executive Producer, Screenwriter, Actor, "The Name of the Rose" (2019); Actor, "Gloria Bell" (2018); Actor, "A Magical Holiday" (2017); Actor, "Difficult People" (2017); Actor, "Transformers: The Last Knight" (2017); Director, Actor, "Hair" (2017); Actor, "Landline" (2017); Actor, "The Night Of" (2016); Actor, "Hands of Stone" (2016); Actor, "The Ridiculous 6" (2015); Actor, "Mia Madre" (2015); Actor, "Partly Cloudy with Sunny Spells" (2015); Actor, "Zorba!" (2015); Actor, "Exodus: Gods and Kings" (2014); Director, Screenwriter, Segment, "Rio, I Love You" (2014); Actor, "Rio, I Love You" (2014); Actor, "God's Pocket" (2014); Actor, "Gods Behaving Badly" (2013); Director, Screenwriter, Actor, "Fading Gigolo" (2013); Actor, "The Master Builder" (2013); Editor, "Nick the Doorman" (2012); Actor, "Relatively Speaking" (2011-2012); Actor, "In the Shadows of No Towers" (2011); Narrator, "Der3k Jeter: A Yankee First" (2011); Actor, "Somewhere Tonight" (2011); Actor, "Transformers: Dark of the Moon" (2011); Voice Actor, "Cars 2" (2011); Actor, "The Cherry Orchard" (2011); Director, "Passione" (2010); Actor, "The Nutcracker in 3D" (2010); Executive Producer, "Rehearsal for a

Sicilian Tragedy" (2009); Featured, "Rehearsal for a Sicilian Tragedy" (2009); Actor, "Transformers: Revenge of the Fallen" (2009); Actor, "The Taking of Pelham 123" (2009); Executive Producer, "Beyond Wiseguys: Italian Americans & the Movies" (2008); Actor, "Miracle at St. Anna" (2008); Actor, "You Don't Mess with the Zohan" (2008); Actor, "What Just Happened" (2008); Voice Actor, "Christmas Story" (2007); Actor, "Margot at the Wedding" (2007); Actor, "The Bronx Is Burning" (2007); Actor, "Flight of the Conchords" (2007); Actor, "Transformers" (2007); Actor, "Slipstream" (2007); Actor, "A Spanish Play" (2007); Voice Actor, Audiobook, "World War Z" (2007); Actor, "The Good Shepherd" (2006); Actor, "A Few Days in September" (2006); Producer, Director, Actor, "Romance & Cigarettes" (2005); Actor, "Monk" (2004-2008); Actor, "Secret Passage" (2004); Actor, "She Hate Me" (2004); Actor, "2BPerfectlyHonest" (2004); Actor, "Secret Window" (2004); Voice Actor, "Opopomoz" (2003); Actor, "Ore 2: Calma Piatta" (2003); Actor, "Anger Management" (2003); Actor, "Fear X" (2003); Actor, "Life x 3" (2003); Voice Actor, "Frasier" (2002); Actor, "Mr. Deeds" (2002); Actor, "Collateral Damage" (2002); Actor, "Monday Night Mayhem" (2002); Narrator, "Heaven Touches Brooklyn in July" (2001); Actor, "Thirteen Conversations About One Thing" (2001); Narrator, "Hitmakers: The Teens Who Stole Pop Music," "Leiber & Stoller: Words & Music," "Biography" (2001); Voice Actor, "Monkeybone" (2001); Actor, "The Man Who Cried" (2000); Actor, "The Luzhin Defence" (2000); Actor, "Two Thousand and None" (2000); Actor, "O Brother, Where Art Thou?" (2000); Actor, "Company Man" (2000); Voice Actor, "Summer of Sam" (1999); Actor, "Cradle Will Rock" (1999); Actor, "Rounders" (1998); Producer, Director, Screenwriter, Actor, "Illuminata" (1998); Actor, "He Got Game" (1998); Actor, "O.K. Garage" (1998); Actor, "Animals with the Tollkeeper" (1998); Actor, "The Big Lebowski" (1998); Actor, "Waiting for Gofot" (1998); Actor, "Lesser Prophets" (1997); Actor, "The Truce" (1997); Actor, "Grace of My Heart" (1996); Actor, "Box of Moonlight" (1996); Actor, "Girl 6" (1996); Actor, "Sugartime" (1995); Actor, "Clockers" (1995); Actor, "Unstrung Heroes" (1995); Actor, "Search and Destroy" (1995); Actor, "The Search for One-eye Jimmy" (1994); Actor, "Quiz Show" (1994); Actor, "Being Human" (1994); Actor, "Fearless" (1993); Director, "Mac" (1992); Screenwriter, "Mac" (1992); Actor, "Mac" (1992); Actor, "Brain Donors" (1992); Actor, "Barton Fink" (1991); Actor, "Jungle Fever" (1991); Actor, "Men of Respect" (1990); Actor, "Miller's Crossing" (1990); Actor, "State of Grace" (1990); Actor, "Mo' Better Blues" (1990); Actor, "Catchfire" (1990); Actor, "Do the Right Thing" (1989); Actor, "The Fortunate Pilgrim" (1988); Actor, "The Sicilian" (1987); Actor, "Five Corners" (1987); Actor, "The Color of Money" (1986); Actor, "Off Beat" (1986); Actor, "Gung Ho" (1986); Actor, "Hannah and Her Sisters" (1986); Actor, "To Live and Die in L.A." (1985); Actor, "Desperately Seeking Susan" (1985); Actor, "Miami Vice" (1985); Actor, "The Flamingo Kid" (1984); Actor, "Exterminator 2" (1984); Actor, "Raging Bull" (1980) **AW:** Audience Award, Best Feature, "Fading Gigolo," Miami Film Festival (2014); Special Award, Cameraimage (2013); Festival President's Award, Karlovy Vary International Film Festival (2011); Award of the City of Rome, "Passione," Venice Film Festival (2010); Capri Cult Award, "Passione," Capri, Hollywood (2010); Silver Berlin Bear, "The Good Shepherd," Berlin Film Festival (2007); Chateuneuf-du-Pape Cinema Award, Avignon/New York Film Festival (2006); Guest Actor in a Comedy Series, "Monk: Mr. Monk and the Three Pies," "Monk," Primetime Emmy Awards (2004); Charles Chaplin Award, Wine Country Film Festival (2003); Independent Career Achievement Award, Video

Software Dealers Association (2001); Caméra d'Or, "Mac," Cannes Film Festival (1992); Vision Award, Sundance Film Festival (1992); Best Foreign Actor, "Barton Fink," David di Donatello Awards (1992); Best Actor, Gotham Awards (1991); Best Actor, "Barton Fink," Cannes Film Festival (1991); Actor Award, Gotham Awards

TUSCHMAN, JAMES M. ESQ., T: Lecturer, Director of Outreach and Engagement **I:** Education/Educational Services **CN:** College of Health and Human Services, University of Toledo **DOB:** 11/28/1941 **PT:** Chester Tuschman; Harriet (Harris) Tuschman **MS:** Married **SPN:** Ina S. Cheloff (09/02/1967) **CH:** Chad Michael; Jon Stephen; Sari Anne **ED:** JD, Ohio State University (1966); BS in Business, Miami University, Oxford, OH (1963) **C:** Lecturer in Legal Specialties, Director of Outreach and Engagement, College of Health and Human Services, University of Toledo (2013-Present); Of Counsel, Barkan & Robon Ltd., Maumee, OH (2002-2013); Director of Business Development, North Ohio Group, Omnisource Corp. (1999-2001); Chief Operating Officer, Ohio Ferrous Group, Omnisource Corp. (1998-1999); Co-Founder, Chairman, Operations Committee, Jacobson Maynard Tuschman & Kalur (1985-1997); Partner, Shumaker, Loop & Kendrick (1970-1984); Associate, Shumaker, Loop & Kendrick (1966-1970) **CR:** Partner, Starr Avenue Co. (1969-1986); Toledo Steel Supply Co. (1969-1986); Vice-Chairman of the Board, Kripke Tuschman Industries, Inc. (1977-1985); Chairman of the Board, Secretary, Tuschman Steel Co. (1969-1976) **CIV:** Past Trustee, Vice President, Treasurer, Temple B'nai Israel (1984-1988); Past Trustee, Chairman, Board of Trustees, University of Toledo; Past Trustee, Chairman, Finance Committee, Past Treasurer, Maumee Valley Country Day School; National Alumni Council, Ohio State University College of Law; Co-Chairman, Subcommittee on Structure, Governance, and Finance; Governor's Commission on Higher Education and Economy; Former Chairman, Board Member, Ohio Board of Regents; Chairman, Mayor's Task Force on Intermodal Transportation; Board Member, Past Chairman, Toledo Lucas County Port Authority; Past Chair, Facilities and Economic Development Committee; Chair, Government, Community, and Human Relations Committee; Board of Directors, Great Lakes Historical Society, National Museum of the Great Lakes **CW:** Author, "Practical Ethics for the Surgeon"; Author, Chapter on Medical Litigation **AW:** Listee, Top 100 Trial Lawyers, National Trial Lawyers (2013, 2014); Listee, Super Lawyers Ohio; Listee, "Best Lawyers in America" **MEM:** Fellow, International Society of Barristers; American Board of Trial Advocates; National Trial Lawyer's Association; Ohio Bar Association; Toledo Bar Association; Ohio Association of Justice; American Association of Justice; Million Dollar Advocates Forum; Zeta Beta Tau; Phi Delta Phi; Bar of the United States Supreme Court **BAR:** Ohio (1966); U.S. Court Appeals for the Sixth Circuit; U.S. Court of Appeals for the Seventh Circuit; U.S. Supreme Court **MH:** Albert Nelson Marquis Lifetime Achievement Award **AS:** Mr. Tuschman attributes his success to his parents, his educational background, and his training by the outstanding trial lawyers at his first law firm, Shumaker, Loop & Kendrick in Toledo, Ohio. **B/I:** Mr. Tuschman always wanted to be a trial lawyer. **PA:** Republican **RE:** Jewish **THT:** Mr. Tuschman's definition of success is to leave one's assignment better than one found it.

TWAIN, SHANIA, T: Singer, Musician **I:** Media & Entertainment **DOB:** 08/28/1965 **PB:** Windsor **SC:** ON/CAN **PT:** Sharon Edwards; Clarence Edwards; Jerry Twain (Stepfather) **MS:** Married

SPN: Frederic Thiebaud (01/01/2011); Robert John "Mutt" Lange (12/28/2008, Divorced 2010) **CH:** Eja **C:** Founder, Perfume, "Shania" by Stetson (2005, 2007) **CIV:** Founder, Shania Kids Can (2010) **CW:** Performer, Concert Residency, "Let's Go!" (2019-Present); Actress, "I Still Believe" (2020); Actress, "Trading Paint" (2019); Co-Presenter, Executive Producer, "Real Country" (2018); Performer, "Now Tour" (2018); Contestant, "Drop the Mic" (2018); Singer, Songwriter, Album, "Now" (2017); Featured, "Broad City" (2017); Guest Judge, "Dancing with the Stars" (2017); Performer, Live Album, "Still the One: Live from Vegas" (2015); Performer, "Rock This Country Tour" (2015); Performer, Concert Residency, "Shania: Still the One" (2012-2014); Featured, Executive Producer, "Why Not? with Shania Twain" (2011); Author, "From This Moment On" (2011); Guest Judge, "American Idol" (2009); Featured, "I Heart Huckabees" (2004); Performer, Compilation Album, "Greatest Hits" (2004); Performer, "Up! Tour" (2003-2004); Singer, Songwriter, Producer, Album, "Up!" (2002); Performer, Compilation Album, "The Complete Limelight Sessions" (2001); Performer, "Come On Over Tour" (1998-1999); Performer, Live Album, "VH1 Divas Live" (1998); Singer, Songwriter, "Come On Over" (1997); Singer, Songwriter, Album, "The Woman in Me" (1995); Singer, Songwriter, Album, "Shania Twain" (1993); Performer, Numerous Music Videos; Performer, Numerous Film Soundtracks **AW:** ARIA Award for Highest Selling International Album of the Year, "Now," CMC Music Awards (2018); Generation Award, Canadian Country Music Association (2018); Artist of a Lifetime, Country Music Association (2016); Star, Hollywood Walk of Fame (2011); Inductee, Canadian Music Hall of Fame, Juno Awards (2011); Album of the Year, "Greatest Hits," Billboard Music Awards (2005); Country Recording of the Year, "Up!", Juno Awards (2004); Top Country Album, "Up!", Billboard Music Awards (2003); Top Country Artist, Billboard Music Awards (2003); Inductee, Canada's Walk of Fame (2003); Artist of the Year, Juno Awards (2003); Country Recording of the Year, "I'm Gonna Getcha Good," Juno Awards (2003); Ranked #7, "40 Greatest Women of Country Music," Country Music Television (2002); Best Country Female Vocalist, Juno Awards (2000, 1999); Best Country Song, "Come On Over," Grammy Awards (2000); Best Female Country Vocal Performance, "Man! I Feel Like A Woman!", Grammy Awards (2000); Favorite Country Female Artist, American Music Awards (2000); Favorite Pop/Rock Female Artist, American Music Awards (2000); Best Country Song, "You're Still The One," Grammy Awards (1999); Best Female Country Vocal Performance, "You're Still The One," Grammy Awards (1999); Entertainer of the Year, Academy of Country Music (1999); Entertainer of the Year, Country Music Association (1999); Entertainer of the Year, Academy of Country Music Awards (1999); Favorite Country Album, "Come On Over," American Music Awards (1999); Favorite Country Female Artist, American Music Awards (1999); CMA International Artist Achievement, Country Music Association Awards (1999); Entertainer of the Year, Country Music Association Awards (1999); Double-Diamond Award, "The Woman In Me," "Come On Over," Academy of Country Music Awards (1998); Hot 100 Singles Artist, Billboard Music Awards (1998); Top Female Artist, Billboard Music Awards (1998); Favorite Country Female Artist, American Music Awards (1997); Numerous BMI Songwriter Awards (1996-2005); Best Country Album, "The Woman in Me," Grammy Awards (1996); Favorite Country New Artist, American Music Awards (1996); Country Album of the Year, "The Woman in Me," Billboard Music Awards (1996); Female Country Artist, Billboard Music Awards (1996); Album of the Year, "The Woman

In Me," Academy of Country Music Awards (1995); Top New Female Vocalist, Academy of Country Music Awards (1995)

TYK, BIA, T: Owner **I:** Business Management/Business Services **CN:** Tri County Investigations **DOB:** 09/17/1959 **PB:** Berwin **SC:** IL/USA **MS:** Married **CH:** Marielle Tyk **C:** Owner, Sure Find (2003-Present); Process Server, Firefly Legal (2003-Present); Process Sever, United Process Inc. (2003-Present); Private Detective, Tri County Investigations (2000-Present) **CIV:** Donor, Police Professionals; Donor, Orphanage, Nepal; Donor, Local Charities **MEM:** President, Associated Detectives and Security Agencies in Illinois; Board of Directors, ADSAI Association; Associated Detectives & Security Agencies of Illinois, Inc.; Commissioned Notary, Notary Public Association; World Association of Detectives; Worldwide Association of the Service of Process; Illinois Association of Professional Process Servers; National Council of Investigations & Security Services; National Association of Professional Process Servers **AS:** Ms. Tyk attributes her success to honesty. She works for 3,000 national attorneys; she prioritizes being ethical in her work. **B/I:** After working at her company for 12 years, Ms. Tyk bought ownership and took charge. **AV:** Spending time with grandchildren **THT:** Ms. Tyk's motto is, "Everyone has the right to their day in court."

TYKOSKI, NICK L., T: Chief Executive Officer **I:** Other **CN:** Safety Decals **MS:** Married **CH:** One Son **ED:** BS in Business and Advertising, Michigan State University (2004) **C:** Chief Executive Officer, Safety Decals (2008-Present); President, Tye's Incorporated (2000-Present); City Councilor, City of Ludington, MI (2011-2017) **CIV:** Volunteers in Community **MEM:** International Airport Equipment Manufactures Association; American Rental Association; Michigan Manufacturers Association **MH:** Marquis Who's Who Top Professional **AS:** Mr. Tykoski attributes his success to hard work and dedication to the customers. **B/I:** Mr. Tykoski became involved in his profession because grew up within the family company and started working there at the young age of 5. His grandfather came home from the war and to the Chicago Institute of Art, where he worked in neon and electric signs. His dad followed in that career, and did a lot of work with electric signs. He is now third generation in the company and took over a lot of the digital and safety decals. Mr. Tykoski merged Ty Signs and Safety Decals into what it is today. **AV:** Flying airplanes; Spending time with family **THT:** Mr. Tykoski said, "Always do what's right, and always have fun and show people you care."

TYMKOVICH, TIMOTHY MICHAEL, T: Chief Judge **I:** Law and Legal Services **CN:** United States Court of Appeals for the Tenth Circuit **DOB:** 11/02/1956 **PB:** Denver **SC:** CO/USA **MS:** Married **CH:** Two Children **ED:** JD, University of Colorado Law School (1982); BA, Colorado College (1979) **C:** Chief Judge, United States Court of Appeals for the Tenth Circuit (2015-Present); Judge, United States Court of Appeals for the Tenth Circuit (2003-2015); Partner, Hale Hackstaff Tymkovich & ErkenBrack (Now Hale Hackstaff Tymkovich Erkenbrack & Shih LLP) (1996-2003); Solicitor General, Office of Colorado Attorney General (1991-1996); Of Counsel, Bradley Campbel Carney & Madsen (1990-1991); Associate, Davis Graham & Stubbs LLP (1983-1989); Clerk, Colorado Supreme Court (1982-1983) **MEM:** American Bar Association; International Society of Barristers; Colorado Bar Foundation; The American Law Institute

TYRA, PATRICIA ANN, EDD, MS, BS, T: Mental Health Nurse, Professor Emerita **I:** Education/Educational Services **CN:** University of Massachusetts **DOB:** 02/20/1942 **PB:** Clarksburg **SC:** WV/USA **PT:** Edwin G.; Helen Shurtleff Tyra **MS:** Widowed **SPN:** Harold A. Bauld **ED:** Fellowship, Laboratory of Community Psychiatry, Harvard Medical School; EdD, Wheelock College of Education & Human Development, Boston University; BS, MS, School of Nursing, Boston University **CT:** Clinical Specialist in Adult Psychiatric Mental Health Nursing, American Nurses Credentialing Center; Certificate, University of Oslo **C:** Emergency Clinician, Martha's Vineyard Community Services (2003-2015); Professor, University of Massachusetts (1993-1996); Private Practice in Individual and Family Therapy (1977-1995); Associate Professor, University of Massachusetts (1991-1993); Assistant Professor, Associate Professor, University of Massachusetts, Lowell (1984-1991); Clinical Director, Human Resource Institute (1983-1984); Director of Consultation and Education, Metropolitan Beaverbrook Mental Health & Retardation Center (1979-1983); Volunteer Rape Counselor, Criminal Victimology Consultants (1977-1981); Assistant Professor, Boston State College (1976-1978); Instructor, Community Mental Health Nursing Specialist, Massachusetts Department of Health (1974-1976); Instructor, Lowell State College (1970-1972); Instructor, School of Nursing, Boston University (1969-1970); Instructor, McLean Hospital, Peter Bent Brigham Hospital (1967-1969); Staff Nurse, Family Care Program, Boston State Hospital (1964-1965); Staff Nurse, Boston University Hospital (1963-1964) **CR:** Presenter in Field; Several Committees, Regional Council Five, Massachusetts Nurses Association; Several Committees, American Nurses Association; President, Founding Member, Massachusetts Coalition on Consultation, Education & Prevention; Executive Committee Member, Eta Omega Chapter, Sigma Theta Tau International Honor Society of Nursing; Executive Committee Member, Society for Family Therapy & Research **CIV:** Volunteer, Martha's Vineyard Museum; Volunteer, Martha's Vineyard Community Services; Edgartown Council on Aging-Anchors; Volunteer, Citizens Observation Patrol, Broward County Sheriff's Office, FL **CW:** Contributor, Articles, Professional Journals **AW:** Research Award, Trustees' Medal, Exemplary Distinguished Public Service Award, University of Massachusetts Lowell; Awarded Professor Emerita Status, University of Massachusetts Lowell **MEM:** Cambridge Boat Club; Sigma Theta Tau International Honor Society of Nursing; American Psychiatric Nurses Association **MH:** Albert Nelson Marquis Lifetime Achievement Award; Marquis Who's Who Top Professional **AS:** Dr. Tyra attributes her success to the support of parents, friends, mentors and husband, as well as her commitment to others. **B/I:** Dr. Tyra became involved in her profession because she grew up in Martha's Vineyard, which is a fairly rural community, and decided that she wanted to be a nurse in order to help others. **AV:** Sculling; Biking; Swimming; Volunteering **PA:** Independent

TYSON, BERNARD J., T: Chief Executive Officer **I:** Medicine & Health Care **CN:** Kaiser Permanente **ED:** MBA in Health Care Administration, Golden Gate University (1985); BS in Health Services Administration, Golden Gate University (1982); Advanced Leadership Degree, Harvard University **C:** Chief Executive Officer, Kaiser Permanente (2012-Present); Chief Executive Officer, States, Kaiser Permanente (2007-Present); Senior Vice President, Health Plan and Hospital Operations, Kaiser Permanente (2006-2007); Group President, Kaiser Permanente, Regions Outside CA (1999); President, Central East Division, Kaiser Permanente, MD, Washington DC, VA and Ohio (1998); Senior Vice President, Local Market Leader, East Bay, Kaiser Permanente, CA (1996-1998); Vice President, Kaiser Permanente (1995-1996); Administrator, Hospital and Health Plan, Kaiser Permanente, Santa Rosa, CA (1992-1995); With, San Francisco Medical Center, Kaiser Permanente (1985-1992); Joined, Kaiser Permanente (1984); Executive Vice President, Health Plan and Hospital Operations, Kaiser Foundation Health Plan, Inc. and Kaiser Foundation Hospitals, National Georgia, Mid Atlantic; Chairman, Kaiser Foundation Health Plan, Mid Atlantic States, Kaiser Permanente; Senior Vice President, Brand Strategy, Kaiser Permanente; Chief Operating Officer, Kaiser Foundation Health Plan, Inc., Kaiser Permanente, Regions Outside CA; Associate Regional Manager, Kaiser Permanente, Northern CA **CIV:** Deacon Board, Refreshing Springs Church of God in Christ (Refreshing Spring COGIC); Member, United Way; Member, United Negro College Fund, Inc.; Member, The Executive Leadership Council; Member, National Association for the Advancement of Colored People (Now NAACP); Member, National Association of Health Services Executives (NAHSE); Board of Directors, Federal City Council; Board of Directors, AvMed Health Plan, Gainesville, FL; Board of Directors, Alliance for Advancing Nonprofit Health Care; Board of Directors, United Negro College Fund, Inc., San Francisco, CA; Board of Directors, Executive Leadership Council Foundation; Board of Directors, National Committee for Quality Health Care (Now National Committee for Quality Assurance); Trustee, Alliance Community Health Plans (ACHP) **AW:** Named One of the Time 100 Most Influential, TIME Magazine (2017); Named Sensitizing Corporation of America to the Talents of People of Color, NAACP Freedom Fund (2001); International Emerging Leaders in Healthcare Award (1998) **MEM:** National Managed Health Care Congress (NMHCC); Advisory Board, National Managed Health Care Congress (NMHCC); American Association of Health Plans; Board of Directors, American Association of Health Plans

TYSON, CICELY, T: Actress **I:** Media & Entertainment **DOB:** 12/19/1924 **PB:** New York **SC:** NY/USA **YOP:** 2021 **PT:** William Augustine Tyson; Theodosia Tyson **MS:** Divorced **SPN:** Miles Davis (11/26/1981, Divorced 1989) **ED:** Honorary DFA, American Film Institute; Honorary Doctorate, Clark Atlanta University; Honorary Doctorate, Columbia University; Honorary Doctorate, Howard University; Honorary Doctorate, Morehouse College; Coursework in Drama, New York University; Coursework, Vinnette Carroll, Lloyd Richards, Actors Studio **C:** Co-Founder, Dance Theatre of Harlem; Former Secretary; Former Model **CW:** Actress, "Cherish the Day" (2020); Actress, "A Fall from Grace" (2020); Actress, "Madam Secretary" (2019); Actress, "How to Get Away with Murder" (2015-2019); Actress, "Last Flag Flying" (2017); Actress, "Showing Roots" (2016); Actress, "House of Cards" (2016); Actress, "The Gin Game" (2015); Actress, "The Trip to Bountiful" (2014); Executive Producer, "The Trip to Bountiful" (2014); Actress, "The Haunting in Connecticut 2: Ghosts of Georgia" (2013); Actress, "The Trip to Bountiful" (2013); Actress, "Alex Cross" (2012); Actress, "The Help" (2011); Actress, "Why Did I Get Married Too?" (2010); Actress, "Law & Order: Special Victims Unit" (2009); Actress, "Relative Stranger" (2006); Actress, "Idlewild" (2006); Actress, "Fat Rose and Squeaky" (2006); Actress, "Madea's Family Reunion" (2006); Actress, "Diary of a Mad Black Woman" (2005); Voice Actress, "Higglytown Heroes" (2005); Actress, "Because of Winn-Dixie" (2005); Voice Actress, "The Proud Family" (2002); Actress, "The Rosa Parks Story" (2002); Actress,

"Jewel" (2001); Actress, "The Outer Limits" (2000); Actress, "Touched by an Angel" (2000); Actress, "Aftershock: Earthquake in New York" (1999); Actress, "A Lesson Before Dying" (1999); Actress, "Mama Flora's Family" (1998); Actress, "Always Outnumbered" (1998); Actress, "Ms. Scrooge" (1997); Actress, "The Road to Galveston" (1996); Actress, "Sweet Justice" (1994-1995); Actress, "Oldest Living Confederate Widow Tells All" (1994); Actress, "House of Secrets" (1993); Actress, "When No One Would Listen" (1992); Actress, "Duplicates" (1992); Actress, "Fried Green Tomatoes" (1991); Actress, "Clippers" (1991); Actress, "The Kid Who Loved Christmas" (1990); Actress, "Heat Wave" (1990); Actress, "B.L. Stryker" (1990); Actress, "The Women of Brewster Place" (1989); Actress, "Intimate Encounters" (1986); Actress, "Samaritan: The Mitch Snyder Story" (1986); Actress, "Acceptable Risks" (1986); Actress, "Playing with Fire" (1985); Actress, "The Corn Is Green" (1983); Actress, "Benny's Place" (1982); Actress, "The Marva Collins Story" (1981); Actress, "The Body Human: Becoming a Woman" (1981); Actress, "Bustin' Loose" (1981); Actress, "The Concorde... Airport '79" (1979); Host, "Love and Hate Night," Sears Radio Theater (1979); Actress, "A Woman Called Moses" (1978); Actress, "King" (1978); Actress, "A Hero Ain't Nothin' But a Sandwich" (1978); Actress, "Wilma" (1977); Actress, "Roots" (1977); Actress, "Just an Old Sweet Song" (1976); Actress, "The River Niger" (1976); Actress, "The Blue Bird" (1976); Actress, "The Autobiography of Miss Jane Pittman" (1974); Actress, "Norman Corwin Presents" (1972); Actress, "Sounder" (1972); Actress, "Wednesday Night Out" (1972); Actress, "Emergency!" (1972); Actress, "Neighbors" (1971); Actress, "Marriage: Year One" (1971); Actress, "Insight" (1971); Actress, "Gunsmoke" (1970); Actress, "Mission: Impossible" (1970); Actress, "The Billy Cosby Show" (1970); Actress, "Here Come the Brides" (1970); Actress, "The Courtship of Eddie's Father" (1969); Actress, "Medical Center" (1969); Actress, "Trumpets of the Lord" (1969); Actress, "To Be Young, Gifted and Black" (1969); Actress, "The F.B.I." (1968-1969); Actress, "The Heart Is a Lonely Hunter" (1968); Actress, "Carry Me Back to Morningside Heights" (1968); Actress, "Judd for the Defense" (1967); Actress, "Cowboy in Africa" (1967); Actress, "The Comedians" (1967); Actress, "Guiding Light" (1966); Actress, "A Man Called Adam" (1966); Performer, "A Hand Is on the Gate" (1966); Actress, "I Spy" (1965-1966); Actress, "Slattery's People" (1965); Actress, "East Side/West Side" (1963-1964); Actress, "Naked City" (1963); Actress, "Trumpets of the Lord" (1963); Actress, "The Blue Boy in Black" (1963); Actress, "The Doctors and the Nurses" (1962); Actress, "Tiger, Tiger Burning Bright" (1962); Actress, "The Blacks: A Clown Show" (1961); Actress, "CBS Repertoire Workshop" (1960); Actress, "The Cool World" (1960); Actress, "The Last Angry Man" (1959); Actress, "Odds Against Tomorrow" (1959); Actress, "Carib Gold" (1957); Actress, "Frontiers of Faith" (1951) **AW:** Inductee, Television Academy Hall of Fame (2020); Academy Honorary Award, Academy Awards (2018); Sidney Poitier Life Achievement Award, Black Reel Awards (2018); Inductee, American Theater Hall of Fame (2018); Woman of the Year, Elle Women in Hollywood Awards (2017); Presidential Medal of Freedom, The White House (2016); Lifetime Achievement Award, Gracie Allen Awards (2015); Best Performance by an Actress in a Mini-Series or Motion Picture Made for Television, "The Trip to Bountiful," Sichuan TV Festival (2015); Outstanding Actress in a Television Movie, Mini-Series or Dramatic Special, "The Trip to Bountiful," NAACP Image Awards (2015); Best Actress in a Play, "The Trip to Bountiful," Tony Awards (2013);

Special Achievement Award, African-American Film Critics Association (2012); Lifetime Achievement Award, Women Film Critics Circle Awards (2011); Spingarn Medal, National Association for the Advancement of Colored People (NAACP) (2010); Honoree, Essence Black Women in Hollywood (2010); Outstanding Supporting Actress in a Motion Picture, "Diary of a Mad Black Woman," NAACP Image Awards (2006); Best Supporting Actress - Network/Cable, "The Rosa Parks Story," Black Reel Awards (2003); Best Supporting Actress - Network/Cable, "A Less on Before Dying," Black Reel Awards (2000); Outstanding Lead Actress in a Television Movie or Mini-Series, "Mama Flora's Family," NAACP Image Awards (1999); Msue Award, New York Women in Film & Television (1999); Outstanding Lead Actress in a Television Movie or Mini-Series, "The Road to Galveston," NAACP Image Awards (1997); Star, Hollywood Motion Picture (1997); Best TV Actress, "The Road to Galveston," Lone Star Film & Television Awards (1996); Actress in a Movie in a Movie or Miniseries, "Heat Wave," CableACE Awards (1991); Oustanding Lead Actress in a Drama Series, Mini-Series or Television Movie, "Samaritan: The Mitch Snyder Story," NAACP Image Awards (1986); Best Performance by an Actress in a Dramatic Series or Miniseries or Television Movie, "The Marva Collins Story," NAACP Image Awards (1982); Outstanding Supporting Actress in a Miniseries or Special, "Oldest Living Confederate Widow Tells All," Emmy Awards (1982); Crystal Award, Women in Film Crystal Awards (1982); Outstanding Actress in a Motion Picture, "A Hero Ain't Nothin' But a Sandwich," NAACP Image Awards (1978); Outstanding Actress in a Motion Picture, "The River Niger," NAACP Image Awards (1977); Inductee, Black Filmmakers Hall of Fame (1977); Actress of the Year - Special, "The Autobiography of Miss Jane Pittman," Primetime Emmy Awards (1974); Best Lead Actress in a Drama, "The Autobiography of Miss Jane Pittman," Primetime Emmy Awards (1974); Best Actress, "Sounder," Kansas City Film Critics Circle Awards (1972); Best Actress, "Sounder," National Society of Film Critics Awards (1972); Vernon Price Award (1962) **MEM:** Delta Sigma Theta

TYSON, NEIL DEGRASSE, PHD, T: Astrophysicist, Director **I:** Sciences **CN:** Hayden Planetarium **DOB:** 10/05/1958 **PB:** New York **SC:** NY/USA **PT:** Cyril deGrasse Tyson; Sunchita Maria (Feliciano) Tyson **MS:** Married **SPN:** Alicia Young (1988) **CH:** Miranda; Travis **ED:** Honorary Doctor of Science, Yale University (2018); Honorary Doctor of Science, Baruch College (2017); Honorary Doctor of Science, University of Massachusetts-Amherst (2015); Honorary Doctor of Science, Western New England University (2012); Honorary Doctor of Science, Mount Holyoke College (2012); Honorary Doctor of Science, Gettysburg College (2011); Honorary Doctor of Science, Eastern Connecticut State University (2010); Honorary Doctor of Science, Rensselaer Polytechnic Institute (2010); Honorary Doctor of Science, University of Alabama (2010); Honorary Doctor of Science, University of Pennsylvania (2008); Honorary Doctor of Science, Worcester Polytechnic University (2007); Honorary Doctor of Science, Williams College (2007); Honorary Doctor of Science, Pace University (2006); Honorary Doctor of Science, College of Staten Island, The City University of New York (2004); Honorary Doctor of Science, Northeastern University (2003); Honorary Doctor of Science, Bloomfield College (2002); Honorary Doctor of Science, University of Richmond (2001); Honorary Doctor of Science, Dominican College (2000); Honorary Doctor of Science, Ramapo College of New Jersey (2000); Honorary Doctor of Science, The City University of New York (1997); Doctor of Philosophy in Astrophysics, Columbia University (1991); Master of Arts in Astronomy, The University of Texas at Austin (1983); Bachelor of Arts in Physics, Harvard University (1980) **C:** Frederick P. Rose Director, Hayden Planetarium, American Museum of Natural History, New York, NY (1996-Present); Research Associate, American Museum of Natural History, New York, NY (2003); Chairperson, Department of Astrophysics, American Museum of Natural History, New York, NY (1997-1999); Acting Director, Hayden Planetarium, American Museum of Natural History, New York, NY (1995-1996); Staff Scientist, Hayden Planetarium, American Museum of Natural History, New York, NY (1994-1995); Postdoctoral Research Associate, Department of Astrophysics, Princeton University, New Jersey (1991-1994) **CW:** Host, "Star Talk" (2015-Present); Host, "Cosmos: Possible Worlds" (2020); Actor, "The Last Sharknado: It's About Time" (2018); Author, "Astrophysics for People in a Hurry" (2017); Author, "Welcome to the Universe: An Astrophysical Tour" (2016); Host, "Cosmos: A Spacetime Odyssey" (2014); Author, "Space Chronicles: Facing the Ultimate Frontier" (2012); Host, "NOVA ScienceNOW," PBS (2006-2011); Author, "The Pluto Flies: The Rise and Fall of America's Favorite Planet" (2009); Author, "Death by Black Hole: And Other Cosmic Quandaries" (2007); Author, "Origins: Fourteen Billion Years of Cosmic History" (2004); Co-editor, "Cosmic Frontiers: Astronomy at the Cutting Edge" (2001); Author, "The Sky is Not the Limit: Adventures of an Urban Astrophysicist" (2000); Co-author, "One Universe: At Home in the Cosmos" (2000); Author, "Just Visiting This Planet" (1998); Author, "Universe Down to Earth" (1994); Author, "Merlin's Tour of the Universe" (1989); Contributor, Articles to Professional Journals, Chapters to Books; Appearances, Television Shows and Films **AW:** Hubbard Medal, National Geographic Society (2017); Stephen Hawking Medal for Science and Communication (2017); Grammy Award for Best Spoken Album, The Recording Academy (2017); Cosmos Award, Planetary Society (2015); Dunlap Prize (2014); Isaac Asimov Award, American Humanist Association (2009); Douglas S. Morrow Public Outreach Award, Space Foundation (2009); Named, One of the 25 Leaders Reshaping New York, Crain's New York Business (2008); Named, to the Power 150, Ebony Magazine (2007, 2008); Named to the Harvard 100: Most Influential, Harvard Alumni Magazine (2007); Klopsteg Memorial Award, American Association of Physics Teachers (2007); Award for Public Understanding of Science & Technology, American Association for the Advancement of Science (2007); Named, One of the Most Influential People in the World, TIME Magazine (2007); Distinguished Public Service Medal, NASA (2004); Named, One of the 50 Most Important African Americans in Research Science (2004); Medal of Honor, Columbia University (2001); Science Writing Award, American Institute of Physics (2001); Named, Sexiest Astrophysicist Alive, People Magazine (2000); Named, One of the 40 Under 40 (1996); Numerous Awards **MEM:** Fellow, New York Academy of Sciences; National Society Black Physicists; International Planetarium Society Inc.; Astronomical Society of the Pacific; American Physical Society; American Astronomical Society **AV:** Wine collector

UDALL, THOMAS, "TOM" STEWART, T: U.S. Senator from New Mexico; Lawyer **I:** Government Administration/Government Relations/Government Services **DOB:** 05/18/1948 **PB:** Tucson **SC:** AZ/USA **PT:** Stewart Lee Udall; Ermalee Lenora (Webb) Udall **MS:** Married **SPN:** Jill Z. Cooper **CH:** Amanda **ED:** JD, The University of New Mexico School of Law (1977); LLB in International Law, University of Cambridge, England (1975); BA in Government and Political Science, Prescott College, AZ (1970) **C:** Ranking Member, Senate Committee on Indian Affairs (2017-Present); U.S. Senator, States of New Mexico, Washington, DC (2009-Present); Member, U.S. House of Representatives from New Mexico's Third Congressional District, U.S. Congress, Washington, DC (1999-2009); Attorney General, State of New Mexico, Santa Fe, NM (1991-1999); Attorney, Miller, Stratvert, Togerson and Schlenker, P.A., Albuquerque, NM (1985-1990); Chief Counsel, New Mexico Department of Health and Environment, Santa Fe, NM (1983-1984); Private Law Practice, Santa Fe, NM (1981-1983); Assistant United States Attorney, Criminal Division, U.S. Department of Justice, Santa Fe, NM (1978-1981); Law Clerk to Chief Judge Oliver Seth, U.S. Court of Appeals for the 10th Circuit, Santa Fe, NM (1977-1978); Legislative Assistant to Senator Joe Biden, U.S. Senate, Washington, DC (1973) **CIV:** Board of Directors, Law Fund (1991-1998); Member, New Mexico Environmental Improvement Board (1986-1987); President, Rio Chama Preservation Trust; Board of Directors, Santa Fe Chamber Music Festival; Board of Directors, La Compania de Teatro de Albuquerque **AW:** Public Service Award, National Highway Traffic Safety Administration (NHTSA); Legal Impact Award, Prosecutors Section, New Mexico Bar Association; Leadership Award, National Commission Against Drunk Driving **MEM:** President, National Association of Attorneys General (1996) **BAR:** State of New Mexico (1978) **PA:** Democrat **RE:** Church of Jesus Christ of Latter-day Saints

UDELL, JON GERALD, PHD, T: Business Educator; Executive **I:** Education/Educational Services **DOB:** 06/22/1935 **PB:** Columbus **SC:** WI/USA **PT:** Roy Grant Udell; Jessie M. (Foster) Udell **MS:** Married **SPN:** Susan (Smykla) Udell (06/12/1960) **CH:** Jon G. Udell Jr.; R. Steven Udell; Susan Elizabeth Udell; Bruce F. Udell; Alan J. Udell; Keneth G. Udell **ED:** PhD, University of Wisconsin (1961); MBA, University of Wisconsin (1958); BBA, University of Wisconsin (1957) **C:** Emeritus Professor of Business, University of Wisconsin-Madison (1999-Present); Co-director, The Enterprise Center (1992-1999); Irwin Maier Professor of Business, University of Wisconsin-Madison (1975-1999); Professor of Business, University of Wisconsin-Madison (1968-1999); Associate Director, University-Industry Research Program, University of Wisconsin-Madison (1967-1977); Associate Director, Bureau of Business Research And Service (1963-1975); Instructor, Assistant Professor, Associate Professor, University of Wisconsin-Madison (1959-1968) **CR:** Board of Directors, Research Products Corporation, Madison, WI (1976-2008); Research Grants, University of Wisconsin (1960-2005); Board of Directors, Versa Technologies, Incorporated (1989-1996); Board of Directors, Wisconsin Electric Power Company, Wisconsin Energy Corporation (WEC Energy Group), Milwaukee, WI (1977-1996); Economic Consultant, Wisconsin Builders Association (1985-1990); Economic Consultant, American Newspaper Publications Association (APNA) (1964-1990); Chairman, Board of Directors, Federal Home Loan Bank of Chicago (1982-1989); Board of Directors, Wisconsin Electric Power Company (WEC Energy Group), Milwaukee, WI **CIV:** Board of Governors, Madison Children's Dyslexia Center, Inc. (2010-Present); Board Director, Wisconsin Housing and Economic Development Foundation (WHEDA) (1990-2016); Vice-chair, Director, Madison Area Concert Handbells (1997-2010); Director, Wisconsin Youth Symphony Orchestra (1991-2003); Director, Madison Opera (1976-2002); Member, Consumer Advisory Council (1990-1999); Chairman, Board, Federal Home Loan Bank of Chicago (1982-1989); Public Inter-est Director, Federal Home Loan Bank of Chicago (1982-1989); Public Interest Director, Federal Home Loan Bank of Chicago, (1973-1980); Vice President, Greater Madison Chamber of Commerce (1976); Vice President, Trustee, Greater Wisconsin Foundation (1969-1975); President, Consumer Advisory Council (1974); President, Consumer Advisory Council, WI (1973-1974); Vice President, Consumer Advisory Council (1973); Governor's Council Economic Development, WI (1967-1973); Chairman, Governor's Conference Mergers and Acquisitions (1969-1970); Elder, Deacon, Presbyterian Church **CW:** Editorial Board, Journal of Private Enterprise (1987-2006); Author, Over 125 Journal Articles and Research Monographs (1960-2004); Author, "Quality of Business Life in Wisconsin" (1991); Author, "The Future of the U.S. Economy as Envisioned by Leaders in American Industry" (1986); Author, "Reporting on Business and the Economy" (1981); Author, "Marketing in An Age of Change" (1981); Author, "The Economics of the American Newspaper" (1978); Author, "Successful Marketing Strategies in American Industry" (1972) **AW:** Governor's Citation (1969, 1971, 2019); Kent-Aronoff Service Award, The Association of Private Enterprise Education (1995); Outstanding Article Award, Journal of Private Enterprise (1991, 1995); John G. Schutz Excellence Marketing Award (1992); Presidential Award, Wisconsin Builders Association (1989); Resolutions of Appreciation Awards (1981, 1989); Paul Harris Fellowship, Rotary International (1988); Robert A. Jerred Distinguished Service Award, University of Wisconsin-Madison (1986); Freedom Award (1976); Named Marketing Man of the Year, Southern Wisconsin Chapter, American Marketing Association (1976); Named Wisconsin-ite of the Year, Wisconsin Chamber of Commerce (1973); Sidney S. Goldish Research Award, International Prom Association (1973) **MEM:** The Phi Beta Kappa Society (1958-Present); The Honor Society of Phi Kappa Phi (1954-Present); Business-Education Coordinating Council (1975-2000); Board Director, Wisconsin Alumni Association (Now Wisconsin Foundation & Alumni Association) (1984-1999); Board Director, The Association Private Enterprise Education (1978-1994); Trustee, Wisconsin Association Manufacturer and Commerce (Now Wisconsin Manufacturers & Commerce) (1981-1990); Board Director, Wisconsin Research (1979-1987); Rotary International; Chairman, Faculty, Roundtable Club (1970-1971) **AS:** Dr. Udell attributes his success to the importance of hard work and integrity, both of which were instilled in him by wonderful parents, Roy and Jessie Udell. Having a supportive wife, Susan, also was very important. She did an excellent job raising their six children while he concentrated on his work. **B/I:** During Dr. Udell's time at the University of Wisconsin, he got to know the business school staff very well. Many of his professors encouraged him to move forward with his education and pursue a master's degree. After earning a master's degree, he furthered his education again with a PhD. Though the school policy was against hiring former PhD students, Dr. Udell was hired by the University of Wisconsin. **AV:** Gardening; Fishing **PA:** Independent **RE:** Methodist

UHL, JESSICA, T: Chief Financial Officer **I:** Oil & Energy **CN:** Royal Dutch Shell **MS:** Married **SPN:** Michael Payne **CH:** Three Children **ED:** Master of Business Administration, INSEAD (1997); Bachelor of Arts in Political Economy, University of California Berkeley **C:** Chief Financial Officer, Royal Dutch Shell, The Hague, Netherlands (2017-Present); Executive Vice President of Finance, Integrated Gas, Royal Dutch Shell, The Hague, Netherlands (2016-2017); Executive Vice President of Finance, Upstream Americas, Royal Dutch Shell, Houston,

TX (2014-2015); Vice President of Finance, Unconventionals, Royal Dutch Shell, Houston, TX (2013-2014); Vice President Controller, Upstream and P&T, Royal Dutch Shell, The Hague, Netherlands (2010-2013); Vice President of Finance, Lubricants, Royal Dutch Shell, London, England (2009-2010); Head of External Reporting, Royal Dutch Shell, The Hague, Netherlands (2007-2009); Vice President of Business Development, Shell Renewables, Royal Dutch Shell, Amsterdam, Netherlands (2004-2006); Vice President of Corporate Development, Enron, Amsterdam, Netherlands (2001-2003); Director, Project Development, Enron, Panama (1998-2000); Associate, Enron (1997-1998); Associate Vice President, Commercial and Real Estate Lending, Citibank, San Francisco, CA (1990-1996) **AW:** Listed, Most Powerful International Business Women, Fortune (2019); Chancellor's Scholar, University of California Berkeley **MEM:** Phi Beta Kappa

UHLENBECK, KAREN, T: Mathematician, Educator **I:** Education/Educational Services **DOB:** 08/24/1942 **PB:** Cleveland **SC:** OH/USA **PT:** Arnold Edward Keskulla; Carolyn Elizabeth (Windeler) Keskulla **MS:** Married **SPN:** Robert F. Williams; Olke C. Uhlenbeck (1965, Divorced 1976) **ED:** PhD in Mathematics, Brandeis University, Boston, MA (1968); MA, Brandeis University, Boston, MA (1966); Graduate Coursework, Courant Institute of Mathematical Sciences, New York University (1965); BS in Mathematics, University of Michigan, Ann Arbor, MI (1964) **C:** Professor Emeritus, Sid W. Richardson Foundation Regents' Chair in Mathematics, University of Texas at Austin (1988-Present); Professor, University of Chicago (1983-1988); Associate Professor to Professor, University of Illinois at Chicago (1977-1983); Assistant Professor to Associate Professor, University of Illinois at Urbana-Champaign (1971-1976); Lecturer, University of California Berkeley (1969-1971); Instructor of Mathematics, Massachusetts Institute of Technology, Cambridge, MA (1968-1969) **CR:** Committee, Women on Science and Engineering National Research Council (1992-1994); Speaker, Plenary Address, International Congress of Mathematics (1990); Fellow, MacArthur Foundation (1983-1988); Fellow, National Science Foundation (1964-1968); Fellow, Sloan Foundation (1974-1976); Co-Founder, Steering Committee; Director, Mentoring Program for Women, Institute for Advanced Study/Park City Mathematics; Institute Co-Founder, Women and Mathematics, Princeton University; Visiting Associate, Institute for Advanced Study; Visiting Senior Research Scholar, Princeton University **CW:** Author, "Instantons and Four Manifolds" (1984); Author, Dissertation, "The Calculus of Variations and Global Analysis" (1968); Contributor, Articles, Professional Journals **AW:** Abel Prize (2019); Leroy P. Steele for Seminal Contribution to Research Award, American Mathematical Society (2007); Presidential Medal of Science (2000); Common Wealth Award for Science and Technology, PNC Bank (1995); Alumnae of the Year, Alumni Association of the University of Michigan (1984) **MEM:** Fellow, American Mathematical Society (2012); Honorary Member, London Mathematical Society (2008); American Mathematical Society; Alumni Association of the University of Michigan; Association for Women in Mathematics; Phi Beta Kappa; Fellow, American Association for the Advancement of Science; National Academy of Sciences **AV:** Gardening; Canoeing; Hiking

UICKER, JAMES LEO, T: Mechanical Engineer **I:** Engineering **DOB:** 02/05/1943 **PB:** Detroit **SC:** MI/USA **PT:** John Joseph Uicker; Elizabeth Josephine (Flint) Uicker **MS:** Married **SPN:** Suzanne Rock (10/13/1995) **CH:** James Joseph; John; Mary; William; Martha; Margaret **ED:** MS in Mechanical

Engineering, The Pennsylvania State University (1971); BSME, University of Detroit Mercy (1966) **CT:** Professional Engineer, State of Michigan **C:** Senior Engineer, Rotating Equipment, Detroit Edison (Now DTE Energy)(1979-2012); Fuel Engineer, Combustion Engineer, Great Lakes Division, National Steel Corporation (1971-1979); Graduate Assistant, The Pennsylvania State University (1969-1971) **CIV:** Treasurer, Financial Secretary, Knights of Columbus, Father Baumgartner Council #5452 (2001-2010); Board Chairman, Addison Township Fire Department (1998-2008); Vice President, Parent Group, Bloomfield Hills (1989); President, Block Club, Southfield (1989); Boy Scouts of America, Southfield, Michigan (1986) **MIL:** First Lieutenant, U.S. Army, Vietnam War (1967-1969) **MEM:** The American Society of Mechanical Engineers; National Society of Professional Engineers; The Engineering Society of Detroit; The Vibration Institute **MH:** Albert Nelson Marquis Lifetime Achievement Award; Marquis Who's Who Top Professional **B/I:** Mr. Uicker became involved in his profession because his father was a professor of engineering. **AV:** Camping; Taking photographs; Woodworking; Fishing; Studying genealogy **PA:** Republican **RE:** Roman Catholic

ULC, OTTO, PHD, T: Political Science Professor (Retired) **I:** Education/Educational Services **DOB:** 03/16/1930 **PB:** Pilsen **SC:** Czech Republic **PT:** Frantisek Ulc; Marie (Skrabkova) Ulc **MS:** Married **SPN:** Priscilla (10/09/1964) **CH:** Ota **ED:** PhD, Columbia University (1964); MA, Columbia University (1961); JD, Charles University (1953) **C:** Professor Emeritus, Binghamton University, State University of New York, Binghamton, NY (1999); Professor, Binghamton University, State University of New York, Binghamton, NY (1975-1999); Associate Professor, Binghamton University, State University of New York, Binghamton, NY (1968-1975); Assistant Professor, Binghamton University, State University of New York, Binghamton, NY (1964-1968); District Judge, Czechoslovak Judiciary, Pilsen, Czech Republic (1956-1959) **CR:** Advisor, Premier of the Cook Islands, South Pacific (1978) **CW:** Author, "Politics in Czechoslovakia" (1974); Author, "The Judge in a Communist State" (1972); Author, "Invisible Dog"; Author, 37 Books **MEM:** P.E.N. Club (Now PEN International); Czech Writers Union **B/I:** When Dr. Ulc came to the United States, he enrolled in a PhD program at Columbia University. **AV:** Foreign travel; Writing

ULLOA, ANGELA, T: Project Engineer **I:** Engineering **CN:** Advanced Drainage Systems **MS:** Married **CH:** Two Sons **ED:** Bachelor of Science in Mechanical Engineering, University of Kentucky (2014); Associate of Arts in Mechanical Engineering, College of DuPage (2011) **CT:** Engineer in Training, Kentucky State Board of Licensure for Professional Engineers and Land Surveyors (2015-2025) **C:** Project Engineer, Advanced Drainage Systems, Inc. (2019-Present); Process Improvement Engineer, Anchor Glass Container Corp. (2018-2019); Process Engineer, TSS Technologies (2017-2018); Mechanical Engineer at P&G, On Line Design Inc. (2015-2017); Habart Temporary Manufacturing Engineer, Staffmark (2015); Design Engineer, SWECO (2014-2015); Digital Measurement Engineering Specialist, Toyota (2014); Co-Op, Toyota (2012-2013) **CR:** Owner, Mechatalyst (2016-Present) **CIV:** Founder, Kentucky Chapter, Bombshell Patriots (2019); Secondary Organizer, Taylor Mill SDA YA (2016-2017); Toiletries Procurement, Taylor Mill SDA Church (2014); Gift Wrapping and Organizing, Toyota (2012); Distribution of Family Donations to Pre-Schoolers in Uzbekistan, U.S. Army (2005); Singing and Laundry Services, Osceola SDA Church (1996-2000); Food Preparation, ADRA

International (1995-1997) **MIL:** Petroleum Supply Sergeant, Army National Guard (2007-2010); Petroleum Supply Sergeant, U.S. Army (2003-2007) **AW:** Army Commendation Medal **MEM:** Pi Tau Sigma; Society for Women in Engineering **AS:** Ms. Ulloa attributes her success to her love for people, and her desire to make a difference in everything she touches. **B/I:** Ms. Ulloa became involved in her profession due to her habit of having watched how things work in her grandfather's auto body shop. She subsequently pursued an education in engineering. **THT:** If the going gets tough, get tougher.

UMPLEBY, JIM, T: Chief Executive Officer **I:** Architecture & Construction **CN:** Caterpillar Inc. **PB:** Highland **SC:** IN/USA **MS:** Married **SPN:** Katherine Umpleby **CH:** Two children **ED:** BS in Mechanical Engineering, Rose-Hulman Institute of Technology (1980) **C:** Chairman, Board of Directors, Caterpillar Inc. (2018-Present); Chief Executive Officer, Caterpillar Inc. (2017-Present); Group President of Energy and Transportation, Caterpillar Inc. (2013-2016); Vice President, Caterpillar Inc. (2010-2013); President, Solar Turbines, Caterpillar Inc. (2010-2013); Associate Engineer, Solar Turbines, Caterpillar Inc. (1980) **CR:** Member, Board of Directors, Chevron Corporation (2018-Present); Member, Board of Directors, U.S.-India Strategic Partnership Forum; Member, Board of Directors, U.S.-China Business Council; Member, Board of Directors, Peterson Institute for International Economics; Trustee, Rose-Hulman Institute of Technology **CW:** Interviewee, "Mad Money," CNBC (2019) **MEM:** Business Roundtable; Business Council; National Petroleum Council

UNDERWOOD, LAUREN ASHLEY, T: U.S. Representative from Illinois **I:** Government Administration/Government Relations/Government Services **CN:** U.S. House of Representatives **DOB:** 10/4/1986 **PB:** Naperville **SC:** IL/USA **ED:** Master of Science in Nursing, Johns Hopkins University; Master of Public Health, Johns Hopkins University; Bachelor of Science in Nursing, University of Michigan **C:** Member, U.S. House of Representatives from Illinois 14th Congressional District (2019-Present); Senior Advisor, United States Department of Health and Human Services (2016-Present); Senior Director of Strategy and Regulatory Affairs, NextLevelHealth Partners (2017); Adjunct Instructor, Georgetown University School of Nursing & Health Studies (2017); Special Assistant, President Barack Obama (2014-2016); With, Fair Housing Advisory Committee, Naperville, IL **PA:** Democrat

UNION, GABRIELLE, T: Actress **I:** Media & Entertainment **DOB:** 10/29/1972 **PB:** Omaha **SC:** NE/USA **PT:** Sylvester E. Union; Theresa (Glass) Union **MS:** Married **SPN:** Dwayne Wade (08/30/2014); Chris Howard (05/05/2001, Divorced 2006) **CH:** Kaavia James Union Wade; Three Stepchildren **ED:** Bachelor's Degree in Sociology, University of California Los Angeles, with Honors; Coursework, University of Nebraska **C:** Founder, Wine, "Vanilla Puddin"; Founder, Clothing Line, Love & Blessings; Ambassador, Creative Adviser, SensatioNail; Spokeswoman, Neutrogena **CIV:** Designer, T-Shirts, Women are Watching Campaign, Planned Parenthood Action Fund, Inc. (2014); Participant, Global Race for the Cure, Washington, DC (2012); Co-founder, Women are Watching Campaign, Planned Parenthood Action Fund, Inc. (2012); Ambassador, Circle of Promise, Susan G. Komen for the Cure; Spokesperson, Planned Parenthood Action Fund, Inc.; Advocate, Survivors of Assault **CW:** Actress, Executive Producer, "L.A.'s Finest" (2019-2020); Judge, "America's Got Talent" (2019); Actress, "Gay of Thrones" (2019); Actress, Producer, "Breaking In" (2018); Actress, "The Public"

(2018); Author, "We're Going to Need More Wine" (2017); Actress, "Sleepless" (2017); Voice Actress, "The Lion Guard" (2016-2019); Actress, Executive Producer, "Almost Christmas" (2016); Actress, "The Birth of a Nation" (2016); Actress, Executive Producer, "With This Ring" (2015); Actress, "Top Five" (2014); Actress, "Think Like a Man Too" (2014); Actress, "Being Mary Jane" (2013-2019); Executive Producer, "Being Mary Jane" (2013-2017); Actress, "The Door" (2013); Actress, "Ridin' Dirty with Officer Turner" (2013); Actress, "Miss Dial" (2013); Actress, "Think Like a Man" (2012); Actress, "In Our Nature" (2012); Actress, "Good Deeds" (2012); Actress, "Little in Common" (2011); Actress, "NTSF:SD:SUV" (2011); Featured, Music Video, "Man Down" by Rihanna (2011); Actress, "Army Wives" (2010); Actress, "Flashforward" (2009-2010); Actress, "Body Politic" (2009); Actress, "Life" (2009); Actress, "Cadillac Records" (2008); Actress, "Meet Dave" (2008); Featured, Music Video, "Miss Independent" by Ne-Yo (2008); Actress, "Football Wives" (2007); Actress, "The Perfect Holiday" (2007); Actress, "The Box" (2007); Actress, "Daddy's Little Girls" (2007); Actress, "Running with Scissors" (2006); Featured, Music Video, "I Love My Chick" by Busta Rhymes (2006); Actress, "Night Stalker" (2005-2006); Voice Actress, "Family Guy" (2005); Actress, "Say Uncle" (2005); Actress, "The Honeymooners" (2005); Actress, "Neo Ned" (2005); Actress, "Constellation" (2005); Actress, "Something the Lord Made" (2004); Actress, "Breakin' All the Rules" (2004); Actress, "The West Wing" (2004); Actress, "Ride or Die" (2003); Actress, "Bad Boys II" (2003); Actress, "Cradle 2 the Grave" (2003); Actress, "Deliver Us from Eva" (2003); Voice Actress, "The Proud Family" (2003); Featured, Music Video, "Paradise" by LL Cool J (2003); Actress, "Welcome to Collinwood" (2002); Actress, "Abandon" (2002); Actress, "Close to Home" (2001); Actress, "Two Can Play That Game" (2001); Actress, "Friends" (2001); Actress, "The Brothers" (2001); Actress, "City of Angels" (2000); Actress, "Bring It On" (2000); Actress, "Zoe, Duncan, Jack & Jane" (2000); Actress, "The Others" (2000); Actress, "Love & Basketball" (2000); Actress, "ER" (2000); Actress, "The Wonderful World of Disney" (1999); Actress, "Grown Ups" (1999); Actress, "Clueless" (1999); Actress, "10 Things I Hate About You" (1999); Actress, "She's All That" (1999); Featured, Music Video, "15 Minutes" by Marc Nelson (1999); Actress, "7th Heaven" (1996-1999); Actress, "1973" (1998); Actress, "The Steve Harvey Show" (1998); Actress, "Sister, Sister" (1997); Actress, "Star Trek: Deep Space Nine" (1997); Actress, "City Guys" (1997); Actress, "Hitz" (1997); Actress, "Dave's World" (1997); Actress, "Smart Guy" (1997); Actress, "Jungle Cubs" (1996-1997); Actress, "Goode Behavior" (1996); Actress, "Malibu Shores" (1996); Actress, "Moesha" (1996); Actress, "Saved by the Bell: The New Class" (1995-1996); Actress, "Family Matters" (1993); Feature, Debut Cover, Savoy Magazine AW: Choice TV Actress: Action, "L.A.'s Finest," Teen Choice Awards (2019); Breakthrough Producer of the Year, CinemaCon (2018); Best Book of the Year by a Black Author, "We're Going to Need More Wine," The Root (2017); Outstanding Actress in a Television Movie, Mini-Series or Dramatic Special, "Being Mary Jane," Image Awards (2014); Best Actress, "Neo Ned," Palm Beach International Film Festival (2006); Outstanding Lead Actress in a Box Office Movie, "Deliver Us from Eva," BET Comedy Awards (2004); Rising Star Award, American Black Film Festival (2003); Theatrical - Best Supporting Actress, "Bring It On," Black Reel Awards (2001); One to Watch - Female, Young Hollywood Awards (2001)

UPTON, FREDERICK, "FRED" STEPHEN, T: U.S. Representative **I:** Government Administration/Government Relations/Government Services **DOB:** 04/23/1953 **PB:** St. Joseph **SC:** MI/USA **PT:** Stephen E. Upton; Elizabeth Brooks (Vial) Upton **MS:** Married **SPN:** Amey Richmond (Rulon-Miller) Upton (11/05/1983) **CH:** Two children **ED:** BA in Journalism, University of Michigan (1975) **C:** U.S. Representative, Michigan's Sixth Congressional District (1993-Present); Chairman, House Committee on Energy and Commerce, Washington, DC (2011-2017); U.S. Representative, Michigan's Fourth Congressional District (1987-1993); Director of Legislative Affairs, Office Management and Budget, Executive Office of the President, Washington, DC (1984-1985); Deputy Director of Legislative Affairs, Office Management and Budget, Executive Office of the President, Washington, DC (1983-1984); Legislative Assistant, Office Management and Budget, Executive Office of the President, Washington, DC (1981-1983); Staff Assistant to Representative David A. Stockman, U.S. House of Representatives, Washington, DC (1976-1981); Member, Committee on Energy and Commerce, United States Congress; Member, Committee on Deficit Reduction, United States Congress **CIV:** Campaign Manager, Globensky for Congress (1981); Field Manager, Stockman for Congress, St. Joseph, MI (1975) **AW:** One of the 10 Members to Watch in the 112th Congress, Roll Call (2011); Legislator of the Year, American Ambulance Association (2000); Spirit Enterprise Award, U.S. Chamber of Commerce (1988-1993) **MEM:** SABR; Alpha Delta Phi Fraternity **PA:** Republican **RE:** Congregationalist

UPTON, THOMAS VERNON, PHD, T: Medical Educator **I:** Education/Educational Services **DOB:** 04/27/1948 **PB:** Antigo **SC:** WI/USA **PT:** Laverne Leo (Deceased); Mildred Helen (Burmeister) **MS:** Married **SPN:** Teresa Anne Ugis (06/11/1977) **CH:** Mark; Paul; Catherine; Marie **ED:** PhD, The Catholic University of America (1977); MA, The Catholic University of America (1972); BA, The Catholic University of America (1969) **C:** Retired (2015); Full Professor, Gannon University (1986-2015); Associate Professor, Gannon University (1977-1984) **CR:** Visiting Professor, The Catholic University of America (1983-1984); Consultant in Field **CW:** Author, Several Articles on Aristotle and Plato; Author, Articles, Professional Journals **AW:** Fellowship, National Endowment of the Humanities (1980, 1983, 1986, 1988); Fellowship, J.K. Ryan Foundation (1974-1977); Basselin Scholar (1968-1971) **MEM:** Board Member, American Catholic Philosophical Association (1984-1986); The American Philosophical Association **MH:** Albert Nelson Marquis Lifetime Achievement Award **B/I:** Mr. Upton became involved in his profession because he had a scholarship to a Catholic university. While taking philosophy courses, he discovered a love of the subject and never looked back. **AV:** Jogging; Fishing; Reading; Exercising; Golfing **PA:** Republican **RE:** Roman Catholic

U'REN, MARIE RITA TYLER, T: Travel Company Executive **I:** Business Management/Business Services **DOB:** 01/12/1940 **PB:** Fort Monmouth **SC:** NJ/USA **PT:** Paul Robert; Ray Rita Tyler **MS:** Married **SPN:** William Francis Henry U'Ren, Jr. (01/31/1959) **CH:** William Tyler; Christine Marie **ED:** Early Childhood Education, George Washington University, Washington, DC (1957-1958) **C:** Partner, Director, Group Sales, Custom Travel Consultants, Woodside, CA (1982-1994); Group Sales, Bulanti Travel, Redwood City, CA (1980-1982); Teacher, Calvary Lutheran Nursery School, Millbrae, CA (1967-1982) **CR:** Director, Chesapeake Film Festival (2007-2010) **CIV:** Staff Member Registrar, Reunion Committee, 1st Battalion, 7th Marines, Vietnam (1986-Present); Board of Directors, Dulaney Towers Highrise, Towson, MD (2018-2020); Volunteer, Kennedy Krieger Festival of Trees, Timonium, MD (2018-2019); Chesapeake Children's Book Festival Fundraising Committee (2016-2018); Board of Directors, United Fund of Talbot County, Easton, MD (2000-2006, 2011-2016); ACE Mentor, Program Awards Events Committee (2007-2016); Tree Decorator, Festival of Trees, Easton, MD (2006-2015); Volunteer, Duck Stamp Booth, Waterfowl Festival, Easton, MD (1996-2015); Program Book Chairman, Festival of Trees, Easton, MD (2009-2013); Board of Directors First Night Talbot (2002-2013); Costumer, Black & White Ball Committee (2012); Costumer, Avalon Foundation (2011, 2012); Co-Chairman Olde Tyme Holiday Parade, Easton, MD (1995-2012); Founding Director, Eventful Giving, a Talbot County (2011); Costumer, Eventful Giving Julie & Julia Committee (2011); Director, Easton 300th Anniversary Committee (2010); Director, Chesapeake Film Festival (2007-2010); Chairman, Promotions Committee, St. Patrick's Day Committee (2006-2010); Treasurer, Charity Antiques Show, Mental Health Association in Talbot County, Easton, MD (2004-2008); Board of Directors, The Avalon Foundation (2006); Secretary, United Fund of Talbot County, Easton, MD (2003-2006); Board of Directors, Dance Harrison St., Easton, MD (2002-2005); Chairman, Promotions Committee, Easton Main St., Inc., Easton, MD (2000-2005); Secretary, The Avalon Foundation, Easton, MD (2001-2004); Costumer, Cricket Theatre, Easton, MD (2000-2004); Christmas Wreath Co-Chairman, Main St. Easton, Easton, MD (1995-2004); Agency Review Committee, United Fund of Talbot County, Easton, MD (2000-2003); Grant Writer, Community Alliance for the Performing Arts, Easton, MD (2000-2003); House Tour Co-Chairman, Festival of Trees, Easton, MD (1999-2003); Treasurer, Talbot County American Heart Association, Easton, MD (1998-2002); Shut Down the Town Day Steering Committee, Easton Business Management Association/Main St. Easton, Easton, MD (2000-2001); Fashion Show Co-Chairman, Festival of Trees, Easton, MD (2000-2001); Chairman, Co-Chairman, Talbot County Antiques Show and Sale, Talbot County American Heart Association, Easton, MD (1997-2001); Costume Committee, Habitat for Humanity Follies, Easton, MD (1996-1999); Chair, Numerous Committees, PTAs, Belmont, CA (1972-1984); President, Bay Area Auxiliary, Myasthenia Gravis Foundation, San Mateo, CA (1976-1978) **CW:** Subject, Newspaper Article, "Giving from the Heart: One event led to another for Easton volunteer," Star Democrat (2011); Producer, "The Gin Game," Community Alliance Performing Arts (2005) **AW:** Community Service Award, General Perry Benson Chapter, Daughters of the American Revolution (2012); Easton Maryland Volunteer of the Year (2010); Nominee, Governor's Volunteer Service Award, Senate of Maryland (2008); Volunteer Recognition Award, Talbot County and State of Maryland (2002); Volunteer of Excellence, First Night Talbot (1997); Certificate of Appreciation, Talbot County American Heart Association (1996); Volunteer of the Year, Dickens of a Christmas and Easton Business Management Authority (1995); Honorary Service award, Carlmont High School Parent Teacher Student Association (PTSA) (1984); Silver Honorary Service Award, Ralson Middle School Parent Teacher Association (1980); Volunteer Service Award, Benjamin Fox Elementary School Parent Teacher Association (PTA) (1977) **MEM:** Board of Directors, Eventful Giving (2011-Present); Board of Directors, Dulaney Valley High-Rise Condo Association (2018-2020); Chesapeake Children's Book Festival Fundraising Committee (2016-2019); Board of Directors, Friends of Hospice (2002-2007, 2012-2016); Talbot County

Arts Council (2010-2016); Board of Directors, Talbot Mentors (2009-2016); Board of Directors, Wye Conservatory Music (2009-2013); Board of Directors First Night Talbot (1997-2013); Volunteer Assistant Manager, Tharpe Antiques, Talbot Historical Society (1996-2010); Chairman, Library Committee, Academy Art Museum (2002-2006); Secretary, Board of Directors, Academy Art Museum (2002-2005); Chairman, Heritage Award Committee, Talbot Historical Society (2002-2005); Secretary, Friends of Hospice (2001-2002); Staff Member, 1st Battalion 7th Marines Vietnam Association **MH:** Albert Nelson Marquis Lifetime Achievement Award **AS:** Ms. U'Ren attributes her success to the support of her family and friends, especially her husband. These individuals often gave their time and talents to support her civic projects; without these investments, she would not have found success. **B/I:** Ms. U'Ren became involved in teaching after assisting her son in the nursery school classroom. Through this experience, she found that she worked great with children and she enjoyed the process. After her children finished nursery school, she became interested in the travel industry. She slowly but surely became more familiar with the field and eventually started a career. **AV:** Reading; Crafting; Costuming **PA:** Republican **RE:** Lutheran **THT:** Ms. U'Ren believes life is what one makes it.

URQUIZA, PATRICIA, T: Chief Financial Officer **I:** Financial Services **CN:** San Dieguito Engineering, Inc. **DOB:** 05/05/1951 **ED:** MS, National University (1992); MBA in Finance, National University; BS in Computer Science **C:** Chief Financial Officer, San Dieguito Engineering, Inc. (2016-Present); Acting Chief Financial Officer, San Dieguito Engineering, Inc. (2010-2016); San Dieguito Engineering, Inc. (2003-2010) **CIV:** Volunteer, Girls Sports, Middle School, High School **CW:** Completed, IT Project **AW:** Finalist, Chief Executive Officer of the Year, San Diego Business Journal (2019) **MEM:** Accounting System, Firm **AS:** Ms. Urquiza attributes her success to one of her business mentors, who was an older gentleman who took her under his wing and taught her a lot about business, life, personality, and more. He was a friend and wrote a recommendation letter for her many years ago; he described her as having integrity, responsibility and will, which, he added, "will take her far." She will always remember these qualities as the core of herself. **B/I:** Ms. Urquiza became involved in her profession later in life. She was a single mom with two girls and needed to do something to provide for her family. She had to fulfill the basic need of caring for her children, which is what led her to pursue her career. **AV:** Traveling; Spending time with her daughters and grandchildren **THT:** Ms. Urquiza's goal is to empower kids. She embodies the values of teamwork and work-life balance.

URSPRUNG, DEBORAH LYNN, T: Special Education Educator, Counselor **I:** Education/Educational Services **DOB:** 09/10/1952 **PB:** Liberty **SC:** TX/USA **PT:** Norman Arnold Ursprung; Roberta Starr (Gay) Ursprung **MS:** Married **SPN:** Ernest Fredrick Fritzsching (07/14/1979, Divorced 12/1982); Linda **CH:** Heather; Amber **ED:** MEd, Lamar University (1999); Graduate, Sam Houston State University, Huntsville, TX (1975) **CT:** Certified, Elementary Teacher, Psychology, Special Education Teacher, State of Texas; Special Service Counselor **C:** Resource Counselor, Channelview Independent School District, Texas (2000-2014); Secondary Teacher, Special Education, Hull Daisetta Independent School District, Texas (1994-1997); Secondary Teacher, Special Education, Vidor Independent School District, Texas (1985-1993); Secondary Teacher, Special Education,

Tarkington (Texas) Independent School District (1982-1985); Elementary Teacher, Psychology, Special Education, Aldine Independent School District, Houston, TX (1976-1979) **CR:** Support Staff, Channelview Independent School District **MEM:** Secretary, Alpha Delta Kappa (1996-Present); Association for Supervision and Curriculum Development; American Association of University Women; American Counseling Association; Association Spiritual; Ethical and Religious Values in Counseling; Texas Association Classroom Teachers; Archaeology Institute America; Beta Sigma Phi **MH:** Albert Nelson Marquis Lifetime Achievement Award **B/I:** Ms. Ursprung went into education because she wanted to make the world a better place. She enjoyed working with kids because they were so exciting. Back in 1975, she worked with IDEA; there, she worked with kids who had behavioral problems. Some of them were smart kids and they had high IQs, but they were in special-ed contained rooms. One of these children eventually became her best student. Her teaching career later evolved to that of a resource counselor because she wanted to continue what she was doing. She went back to school and earned a master's degree in order to pursue the field. **AV:** Appreciating southwest art and jewelry; Making needlecrafts; Traveling; Researching archaeology; Traveling to areas in New Mexico, Arizona, and Colorado **PA:** Republican **RE:** Roman Catholic

UTZINGER, ROBERT CONDE, T: Architect; Educator, Professor Emeritus **I:** Architecture & Construction **CN:** Montana State University **DOB:** 01/09/1934 **PB:** Rock Springs **SC:** WY/USA **PT:** Robert L. Utzinger; Marguerite (Kugal) Utzinger **MS:** Married **SPN:** Karin L. Utzinger (06/17/1958) **CH:** Kirk; Jeanne; Tia **ED:** MArch, University of Michigan (1969); BS in Architectural Engineering, University of Colorado (1961); BS in Business Administration, University of Colorado (1956) **CT:** National Architecture License, United States and Canada; Licensed Architect, States of Colorado, Wyoming and Montana; Licensed Professional Engineer, States of Colorado and Wyoming **C:** Professor Emeritus, Montana State University (1995-Present); Professor of Architecture, Montana State University, Bozeman, MT (1979-1995); Dean, College of Arts & Architecture, Montana State University (1992-1994); Private Architecture Practice (1990-1992); Director, School of Architecture, Montana State University (1979-1990); Interim Dean, College of Arts & Architecture, Montana State University (1988-1989); Director of Architecture, University of Colorado (1973-1979); Associate Professor, University of Colorado (1972-1979); Assistant Professor of Architecture, University of Colorado (1969-1972); Research Associate, University of Michigan (1968-1969); Private Practice in Architecture, CO & WY (1961-1967) **CR:** Exam Committee, NCARB - National Council of Architectural Registration Boards (1983-1992); President, Member, Montana Board of Architects (1983-1992) **CIV:** Architectural Design Award Juries, States of CO, WY, and MT; President, Member, Board of Directors, Bridger Bowl Ski Area, MT; Board of Directors, Bozeman Symphony Society **MIL:** Honorable Discharge, United States Navy (1966); Lieutenant, United States Navy (1960); With, Philippines Military Defense Assistance Program, USS Duncan (DD-874), United States Navy (1956-1959); Active Duty, United States Navy **CW:** Author, "An Annotated Bibliography on Early Childhood" (1970); Author, "Some European Nursery Schools and Playgrounds" (1970) **AW:** Honorary Alumni Award, Montana State University (2018); Montana Design Award, American Institute of Architects (1996); Recipient, Travel Fellowship, Colorado American Institute of Architects (AIA)(1977); Grantee, Ford

Foundation (1969); Teaching Award, University of Colorado; Two-Time Recipient, Teaching Awards, Montana State University; Administrative Award, Mortar Board, Montana State University **MEM:** The Tau Beta Pi Association, Inc.; Sigma Tau; Chi Epsilon, Inc.; Honorary Engineering Societies **MH:** Albert Nelson Marquis Lifetime Achievement Award **B/I:** Mr. Utzinger became involved in his profession because he had a realization that he was better suited for a creative career than a career in business administration. He re-looked at his career path and felt that something creative would be a much better fit for him. His degree was in architectural engineering. Mr. Utzinger had this realization during his time in the Navy. **AV:** Drawing; Downhill skiing; Fly fishing; Traveling

VAIL, LES, T: President/Chief Executive Officer **I:** Business Management/Business Services **CN:** Gloucester County Chamber of Commerce **CH:** Two Daughters **ED:** Coursework in Accounting, Delaware County Community College **C:** President, Chief Executive Officer, Gloucester County Chamber of Commerce (2010-Present); Senior District Manager, ADP TotalSource (2004-2010); Board Chair, Gloucester County Chamber of Commerce (2007-2009); Field Sales Manager, Intuit Payroll Services (2002-2004); District Manager, InterPay (2000-2002); Auction Operations Manager, Minority Owner, Avatar Galleries (1996-2000) **CIV:** Board Member, American Cancer Society (2017-Present); Advisory Board, Columbia Bank (2017-Present); Advisory Board, Columbia Bank New Jersey (2016-Present); Board Chair, Hospitality & Tourism Board, New Jersey Department of Labor Talent Network Retail (2016-Present); Honorary Commander, Joint Base MDL (2015-Present); Board Member, Glassboro Partners Group (2014-Present); Member of Directors, Visit South Jersey (2014-Present); Executive Leadership Team, Board Member, March of Dimes (2010-Present); Board Chair, Gloucester County Workforce Development Board (2009-Present); Board Member, People for People Foundation (2008-Present); Chairman, Glassboro Planning Board (2007-Present); Board Member, Gloucester County Habitat for Humanity (2015-2017); Board Member, Entrepreneurs Forum of Southern New Jersey (2010-2016); Vice-Chair, Foundation Board, Rowan College at Gloucester County (2015); Chairman of the Board, Gloucester County Chamber of Commerce (2002-2010); Board Member, Boys and Girls Clubs of Gloucester County (2006-2009); President of the Board, Glassboro Main Street Organization (2002-2008); Chair, Glassboro Board of Education (2000-2006) **AW:** Jefferson Award for Executive Leadership (2019); Executive of the Year, South Jersey Business Magazine (2013); Distinguished Citizen Award, Boys Scouts of America; Chairman's Award, Burlington County Chamber of Commerce **AS:** Mr. Vail doesn't consider himself to be successful. Instead, he looks at every day as a day he's doing something he loves and enjoys. He loves to help people. Even when he was in corporate sales, his job every day was to help people, whether it was his sales team or his coworkers. He thrives on helping others.

VALADAO, DAVID GONCALVES, T: Former U.S. Representative **I:** Government Administration/Government Relations/Government Services **DOB:** 04/14/1977 **PB:** Hanford **SC:** CA/USA **MS:** Married **SPN:** Terra Valadao (1999) **CH:** Three children **ED:** Coursework, College of the Sequoias (1996-1998) **C:** Candidate, U.S. Representative, California's 21st Congressional District Election, United States Congress, Washington, DC (2020); U.S. Representative, California's 21st Congressional District, United States Congress, Washington, DC

(2013-2019); House Committee on Appropriations (2013-2019); Member, District 30, California State Assembly (2011-2012); Managing Partner, Valadao Dairy (1992-2018); Member, Committee on House Administration, United States Congress; Member, Committee on the Judiciary, United States Congress; Member, U.S. House of Representatives Committee on Science, Space and Technology **CR:** Chairman, Regional Leadership Council; Chairman, Land O'Lakes Inc. **AW:** Spirit of Enterprise Award, U.S. Chamber of Commerce (2014, 2016) **PA:** Republican

VALENTEKOVICH, MARIJA NIKOLETIC, PHD, **T:** Diagnostic Executive **I:** Technology **CN:** Retired **DOB:** 02/05/1932 **PB:** Dubrovnik **SC:** Croatia **PT:** Miroslav Adam Nikoletic; Vinka (Brangjolica) Nikoletic **MS:** Married **SPN:** Duro A. Valentekovich (2/3/1962) **CH:** Vladimir M.; Robert J. **ED:** PhD in Chemistry, University of Zagreb, Croatia (1963); MS in Chemical Engineering, University of Zagreb, Croatia (1957) **C:** Vice President, Operations, Careside Inc (1999-2002); Production Supervisor, Diagnostic Products Corps., Los Angeles, CA (1990-1999); Associate Director, Quality Control, Diagnostic Products Corps., Los Angeles, CA (1989-1990); Technology Director, Operations Manager, Merrel Inc., Gardena, CA (1987-1988); Vice President, Technology, Innotron-Diagnostic Co., Irvine, CA (1983-1987); Principal Chemist, Beckman Instruments Inc, Brea, CA (1979-1983); Director, Quality Assurance, Nichols Institute, San Pedro, CA (1974-1979); Head, Radiochemistry, Curtis Nuclear Co., Los Angeles, CA (1972-1974); Director, Quality Assurance, Cyclo Chemical Co., Los Angeles, CA (1968-1972); Research Associate, University of Southern California, Los Angeles, CA (1967-1968); With, University of Illinois, Urbana (1965-1967) **CW:** Presented Lecture, Free Testosterone, Clinical Chemistry Meeting in Ann Arbour, MI (1998); Presented, Research Paper on the First Generation RIA Test for Prostate Cancer (PAP), International Clinical Chemistry Congress in Vienna, Austria (1983); Visiting Lecturer, University of San Luis Potosi, Mexico (1979); Presented, PhD Dissertation, International Congress of Chemistry in Vienna, Austria (1963); Contributor, Articles, Professional Journals **MEM:** American Chemical Society; American Association of Clinical Chemistry **MH:** Albert Nelson Marquis Lifetime Achievement Award; Marquis Who's Who Top Professional **AS:** Dr. Valentekovich attributes her success to hard work and the persistence, good organizational skills. **B/I:** She became involved with her profession because of her chemistry professor in high school. **AV:** Classical music; Travel; Swimming; Photography **RE:** Roman-Catholic **THT:** Follow your dream

VALLARTA, JOSEFINA, "JOSIE" DEL MUNDO, **T:** Child Neurologist (Retired); Associate Professor of Pediatrics and Neurology Emeritus **I:** Medicine & Health Care **CN:** University of Washington **DOB:** 06/23/1935 **PB:** Manila **SC:** Philippines **PT:** Salvador Del Mundo, PhD; Josefa Gotauco Del Mundo **MS:** Married **SPN:** Leopoldo T. Vallarta, MD (05/28/1959) **CH:** Jocelyn Devita; Vivien Temperani; Maria Bransier; Paula Jurion **ED:** MSc in Neurology, McGill University, Montreal, Canada (1963); Fellow in Neuropathology, The Neuro (Montreal Neurological Institute-Hospital) (1962-1963); Resident, Fellow, Montreal Children's Hospital (1959-1962); MD, University of Santo Tomas, Manila, Philippines, Magna Cum Laude (1958); AA, University of Santo Tomas, Manila, Philippines (1953) **CT:** Diplomate, The American Board of Pediatrics; American Board of Psychiatry and Neurology, Inc. with Special Competence in Child Neurology **C:** Clinical Associate Professor Emeritus, University

of Washington (1994-Present); Retired (1994); Clinical Instructor, Clinical Associate Professor of Pediatrics and Neurology, University of Washington (1967-1994); Founder and Medical Director, Neurodevelopment Program, Mary Bridge Children's Hospital, MultiCare, Tacoma, WA (1979-1993); Child Neurologist, Mary Bridge Children's Hospital, MultiCare, Tacoma, WA (1974-1993); Child Neurologist, Neurology and Neurosurgery Associates, Tacoma, WA (1975-1990); Child Neurologist, Child Development and Mental Retardation Center (Now Center on Human Development and Disability (CHDD)), University Washington, Seattle, WA (1976-1989); President, Medical Staff, Mary Bridge Children's Hospital, MultiCare, Tacoma, WA (1980); Child Neurologist, Children's Orthopedic Hospital, Seattle, WA (1967-1975); Child Neurologist, Rainier School, Buckley, WA (1967-1975) **CR:** Washington Elks Therapy Program (1981-1993); Examiner, American Board of Neurology (Now American Board of Psychiatry and Neurology, Inc.), San Diego and Los Angeles, CA and Seattle, WA (1982, 1985, 1990, 1991); Chairman, Pediatrics, ICU Mary Bridge Children's Hospital, MultiCare (1976-1990); Member, Washington State Board of Medical Examiners (Washington Medical Commission) (1981-1986); Presenter in Field **CW:** Author, "The Thomasians: Diamond Jubliarians" (2018); Author, Editor, "The Thomasians" (2008), Author, "Golden Jubilarians" (2007); Author, "Caring for Our Special Children: Early Intervention Services" (1996); Author, Over 30 Articles in Medical Journals and Presentations **AW:** Award for Dedicated Service to the Children and Families of the Neurodevelopmental Program, Mary Bridge Children's Hospital, MultiCare (1975-1993); Named to Best Doctors of America and Doctor of the Year (1981); Named Distinguished Physician in Academic Medicine, University of Santo Tomas Faculty of Medicine & Surgery Class (1958); Winthrop Scholar (1957-1958); Full Scholarship , University of Santo Tomas Pre-med and Medical School (1951-1958); Named International Health Professional of the Year, Cambridge **MEM:** Public School Health Committee, Pierce County Medical Society (1981-1983); Ethics Committee, Pierce Country Medical Society (1980-1993); Washington State Medical Association; American Academy of Neurology; Child Neurology Society; Southwest Washington Pediatric Society; N.W. Pacific Society of Neurology and Psychiatry; Society of Developmental and Behavioral Pediatrics (SDBP); Pierce County Medical Society **MH:** Albert Nelson Marquis Lifetime Achievement Award **AS:** Dr. Vallarta attributes her success to her family, her education, core values and God given talents and blessings. **B/I:** Dr. Vallarta was 10 years old during the World War II American liberation of Manila when her father died. His sister, Dr. Fe Del Mundo, was a pediatrician who trained at Harvard. She was the founder of the first children's hospital in the Philippines. During the liberation of Manila, Dr. Vallarta and her family had to flee from the Japanese. Dr. Fe Del Mundo and American soldiers found them in the ruins in the southern part of Manila which was burned by the Japanese. Her father, Salvador Del Mundo, also influenced her, He graduated summa cum laude in chemistry from the University of the Philippines. He was a government scholar when he received his PhD in Chemistry in Berlin. Her mother graduated cum laude with a degree in pharmacy from the University of the Philippines. She became a professor of chemistry. **AV:** Travel; Jazzercise; Hiking; Dance; Quilting; Painting; Computer; Reading; Writing; Music; Studying and seminars about the neurosciences, successful aging **RE:** Roman Catholic **THT:** Dr. Vallarta published two books with essays about

her thoughts on life, pearls of wisdom, our core values, achievements, her life story, successful aging, the neurosciences and her family.

VAN DREW, JEFFERSON H., DMD, T: U.S. Representative, Dentist (Retired) **I:** Government Administration/Government Relations/Government Services **DOB:** 02/23/1953 **PB:** New York **SC:** NY/USA **MS:** Married **SPN:** Ricarda Van Drew **CH:** Two Children **ED:** DMD, Fairleigh Dickinson University; BS, Rutgers, The State University of New Jersey **C:** U.S. Representative, New Jersey's Second Congressional District, U.S. House of Representatives (2019-Present); Member, District One, New Jersey State Senate (2008-2018); Assistant Majority Leader, New Jersey General Assembly (2006-2007); Member, District One, New Jersey General Assembly (2002-2007); Mayor, Dennis Township, NJ (1994-1995, 1997-2003); Member, Board of Chosen Freeholders, Cape May County, NJ (1994-1997); Fire Commissioner, Dennis Township, NJ (1983-1986); Member, Committee on Budget and Appropriations, New Jersey State Senate; Vice Chair, Committee on Military and Veterans' Affairs, New Jersey State Senate; Chair, Committee on Community and Urban Affairs, New Jersey State Senate **MEM:** President, New Jersey Dental Association; Board Expert, New Jersey State Board of Dentistry **PA:** Democrat

VAN DYKE, DICK, T: Actor, Comedian **I:** Media & Entertainment **DOB:** 12/13/1925 **PB:** West Plains **SC:** MO/USA **PT:** Loren Wayne Van Dyke; Hazel Victoria (McCord) Van Dyke **MS:** Married **SPN:** Arlene Silver (02/29/2012); Margerie Willett (02/12/1948, Divorced 1984) **CH:** Christian; Barry; Stacey; Carrie Beth **C:** Actor, Film, Television **CR:** Owner, 1400 AM KXIV (1965-1985); Founder, Wayne Williams, Danville, IL (1946); Contributor, SIGGRAPH; Contributor, LightWave 3D **MIL:** Radio Announcer, Armed Forces Radio and Television/Armed Forces Network (AFRTS/AFN), U.S. Army Air Forces (1943-1946) **CW:** A Cappella Singer, Dick Van Dyke and the Vantastix (2000-Present); Actor, "Kidding" (2020); Actor, "Buttons, A New Musical Film" (2018); Actor, "Mary Poppins Returns" (2018); Singer, Album, "Step Back in Time" (2017); Executive Producer, "Tai Cheng with Dick Van Dyke" (2017); Author, "Keep Moving: And Other Tips and Truths About Living Well Together" (2016); Actor, "Stars in Shorts: No Ordinary Love" (2016); Voice Actor, "Trollz" (2016); Actor, "Life Is Boring" (2016); Actor, "The Middle" (2015); Actor, "Merry Xmas" (2015); Actor, "Night at the Museum: Secret of the Tomb" (2014); Voice Actor, "Mickey Mouse Clubhouse" (2014); Himself, "Alexander and the Terrible, Horrible, No Good, Very Bad Day" (2014); Author, "My Lucky Life In and Out of Show Business: A Memoir" (2011); Actor, "The Caretaker 3D" (2010); Actor, "Murder 101: New Age" (2008); Actor, "Murder 101: If Wishes Were Horses" (2007); Actor, "Murder 101: College Can Be Murder" (2007); Actor, "Night at the Museum" (2006); Voice Actor, "Curious George" (2006); Actor, "Murder 101" (2006); Voice Actor, "Batman: New Times" (2005); Actor, "The Dick Van Dyke Show Revisited" (2004); Voice Actor, "The Alan Brady Show" (2003); Actor, "The Gin Game" (2003); Actor, "Scrubs" (2003); Co-Executive Producer, "The Gin Game" (2003); Actor, "Diagnosis Murder: Without Warning" (2002); Executive Producer, "Diagnosis Murder: Without Warning" (2002); Actor, "Diagnosis Murder: Town Without Pity" (2002); Executive Producer, "Diagnosis Murder: Town Without Pity" (2002); Actor, "Sabrina the Teenage Witch" (2000); Actor, "Becker" (1999); Executive Producer, "Diagnosis Murder" (1995-2001); Actor, "Diagnosis Murder" (1993-2001); Actor, "Coach" (1993); Narrator, Voice Actor, "The Town Santa Forgot" (1993);

Actor, "Chairman's Choice" (1993); Actor, "A Twist of the Knife" (1993); Actor, "Diagnosis Murder: Diagnosis of Murder" (1992); Actor, "Jake and the Fatman" (1991); Actor, "Matlock" (1986, 1990); Actor, "Dick Tracy" (1990); Actor, "The Golden Girls" (1989); Actor, "The Van Dyke Show" (1988); Actor, "Airwolf" (1987); Actor, "Ghost of a Chance" (1987); Actor, "Highway to Heaven" (1987); Actor, "Strong Medicine" (1986); Actor, "American Playhouse" (1985); Actor, "Found Money" (1983); Voice Actor, "CBS Library" (1983); Actor, "The Country Girl" (1982); Actor, "Drop-Out Father" (1982); Actor, "Harry's Battles" (1981); Actor, "The Runner Stumbles" (1979); Actor, "Supertain" (1979); Actor, The Carol Burnett Show" (1977); Voice Actor, "Tubby the Tuba" (1975); Author, "Those Funny Kids!" (1975); Actor, "Columbo" (1974); Actor, "The Morning After" (1974); Actor, "The New Scooby-Doo Movies" (1973); Director, "Starring: Nancy Clancy" (1973); Actor, "The New Dick Van Dyke Show" (1971-1974); Actor, "Cold Turkey" (1971); Actor, "The Bill Cosby Show" (1971); Author, "Faith, Hope and Hilarity: The Child's Eye View of Religion" (1970); Actor, "The Comic" (1969); Actor, "Some Kind of a Nut" (1969); Actor, "Chitty Chitty Bang Bang" (1968); Actor, "Never a Dull Moment" (1968); Author, "Altar Egos" (1967); Actor, "Fitzwilly" (1967); Actor, "Divorce American Style" (1967); Actor, "Lt. Robin Crusoe, U.S.N." (1966); Actor, "The Art of Love" (1965); Actor, "Mary Poppins" (1964); Actor, "What a Way to Go!" (1964); Actor, "Bye Bye Birdie" (1963); Singer, Album, "Songs I Like" (1963); Actor, "The Dick Van Dyke Show" (1961-1966); Actor, "Look Up and Live" (1960); Actor, "New Comedy Showcase" (1960); Actor, "Alfred Hitchcock Presents" (1960); Actor, "The Ed Sullivan Show" (1959); Actor, "The United States Steel Hour" (1959); Actor, "True Story" (1958); Actor, "The Phil Silvers Show" (1957-1958) **AW:** Britannia Award for Excellence in Television, Britannia Awards (2017); Lifetime Achievement, Screen Actors Guild (2013); Career Achievement, Television Critics Association (2003); Lifetime Achievement Award in Comedy, American Comedy Awards (1994); Outstanding Performer in Children's Programming, "CBS Library: The Wrong Way Kid," Emmy Awards (1984); Outstanding Comedy - Variety or Music Series, "Van Dyke and Company," Emmy Awards (1977); Favorite Male Performer in a New TV Program, "Van Dyke and Company," People's Choice Awards (1976); Outstanding Continued Performance by an Actor in a Leading Role in a Comedy Series, "The Dick Van Dyke Show," Emmy Awards (1966); Outstanding Individual Achievements in Entertainment, "The Dick Van Dyke Show," Emmy Awards (1965); Outstanding Continued Performance by an Actor in a Leading Role in a Comedy Series, "The Dick Van Dyke Show," Emmy Awards (1964); Grammy Award for Best Album for Children, "Mary Poppins," Grammy Awards (1964); Best Performance by a Featured Actor in a Musical, "Bye Bye Birdie," Tony Awards (1961); Theatre World Award (1960) **MEM:** Honorary Member, Barbershop Harmony Society (1999-Present)

VAN HOLLEN, CHRISTOPHER, "CHRIS" J. JR., T: U.S. Senator from Maryland; Lawyer **I:** Government Administration/Government Relations/Government Services **DOB:** 1/10/1959 **PB:** Karachi **SC:** Pakistan **PT:** Christopher Van Hollen; Eliza (Farnsworth) Van Hollen **MS:** Married **SPN:** Katherine A. (Wilkens) Van Hollen (1987) **CH:** Anna; Nicholas; Alexander **ED:** JD, Georgetown University Law Center, Cum Laude (1990); Master of Public Policy, Harvard University (1985); BA in Philosophy, Swarthmore College, PA (1982) **C:** U.S. Senator, State of Maryland (2017-Present); Ranking Member, U.S. House Budget Committee (2011-Present); Member, U.S. House Committee on Ways and Means (2007-Present); Chairman, Democratic Senatorial Campaign Committee (2017-2019); Member, Joint Select Committee on Deficit Reduction (2011); Chairman, Democratic Congressional Campaign Committee (DCCC) (2007-2011); District, United States Congress, Washington, DC (2003-2017); Member, District 18, Maryland State Senate, Annapolis, MD (1995-2002); Associate, Arent, Fox, Kintner, Plotkin & Kahn (Now Arent Fox LLP), Washington, DC (1991-2002); Member, Maryland House of Delegates, Annapolis, MD (1991-1995); Senior Legislative Adviser to Governor William Donald Schaefer, State of Maryland, Washington, DC (1989-1991); Professional Staff Member, Committee on Foreign Relations, U.S. Senate, Washington, DC (1987-1989); Legislative Assistant for Defense and Foreign Policy to Senator Charles McCurdy Mathias Jr., U.S. Senate, MD (1985-1987); Member, U.S. House Committee on Government Reform and Oversight **AW:** Distinguished Superhero Award, National Association of Community Health Centers (2005); Named Outstanding New Member of the Year, Committee for Education Funding (2003); Leadership Award, American Cancer Society, Inc. (2002); Legislator Sponsor Award, Maryland Children's Action Network (2002); Legislator Legacy Award, Arc of Maryland (2002); Conservation Legacy Award (2002); Outstanding Legislator Award, Maryland Center Community Development (2001); Outstanding Advocacy Award, Maryland AIDS Legislative Committee (2001); Outstanding Legislator Award, Advocates for Children and Youth (2000); Environmental Leadership Award, Maryland League Conservation Voters (1992, 1994, 1996, 1998, 2000); Outstanding Service Award, Blinded American Veterans Foundation; Outstanding Leadership Award, American Lung Association **MEM:** American Bar Association; Maryland Citizens Association; Kensington Citizens Association; Atlantic Council; Montgomery Bar Association; Maryland Bar Association **BAR:** State of Maryland (1990) **PA:** Democrat **RE:** Episcopalian

VAN TASSELL, JAMES L., PHD, T: Biology Educator; Researcher **I:** Education/Educational Services **DOB:** 07/31/1945 **PB:** Amityville **SC:** NY/USA **PT:** Harry H. L.; Katherine D. (Keller) V. **MS:** Single **ED:** Research Associate-in-Residence, Department of Ichthyology, American Museum of Natural History (2000-Present); Postdoctoral Visiting Scientist, Smithsonian Tropical Research Institute (2004-2006); Research Associate-in-Residence, Biology Department, Hofstra University (2003-2010); PhD in Biology, Graduate Center, City University of New York (1998); MA in Biology, Graduate Center, City University of New York (1996); MA in Biology, Adelphi University (1975); BS in Biology, Wagner College (1969) **CT:** New York State Permanent Teaching Certificate for Biology and General Science; Scuba Certification, PADI Open Water Diver; Scuba Certification, PADI Equipment Specialist; Scuba Certification, PADI Advanced Open Water Diver; Nitrox Certified **C:** Adjunct Assistant Professor, Research Associate-in-Residence, Hofstra University (2003-2010); Field Associate, Department of Ichthyology, American Museum of Natural History (1986-1997); Adjunct Lecturer, Environmental Geology and Physical Problems of the Metropolitan Region, Adelphi University (1975-1978); Instructor, Ecology, Marine Biology, Environmental Science, Regents Biology, AP Biology, Science Research Program for Gifted and Talented Students, H. Frank Carey High School (1969-2000) **CR:** Invited Speaker, Shed Aquarium Lecture Series (1995); Invited Speaker, Earthwatch Program, American Museum of Natural History (1992); Invited Speaker, Earthwatch (1990); Presenter, Talks, Earthwatch Principal Investigators Conference (1988-1996); Adviser, H.F. Carey High School Ecology Council (1970-2000); Organizer, H.F. Carey High School Ecology Council (1970); Board of Directors, New York State Science Teachers Association (1970); Chairman, Environmental Education Committee **CW:** Co-Author, "Aspiration or expiration: hypoxia and the interpretation of fish predation in the fossil record," Palaios (2019); Co-Author, "Cryptic lineage divergence in marine environments: Genetic differentiation at multiple spatial and temporal scales in the widespread intertidal goby Gobiosoma bosc. Ecology and Evolution" (2017); Co-Author, "The Conservation Status of Marine Bony Shorefishes of the Greater Caribbean" (2017); Co-Author, "Repeated invasions into the twilight zone: Evolutionary origins of a novel assemblage of fishes from deep Caribbean reefs," Molecular Ecology (2016); Co-Author, "Molecular phylogeny, analysis of character evolution, and submersible collections enable a new classification of a diverse group of gobies (Teleostei: Gobiidae: Nes subgroup), including nine new species and four new generations.," Zoological Journal of the Linnean Society (2016); Co-Author, "Status of Gobiosoma (Teleostei: Gobiidae) from Brazil: Description of a new species, redescription of G. hemigymnum, molecular phylogeny of the genus, and key to Atlantic species," Zootaxa (2015); Co-Author, "An Annotated Checklist of Shorefishes of the Canary Islands," American Museum Novitates (1985); Author, Contributor, Editor, Three Books, Two Book Chapters, 41 Research Publications; Author, Contributor, gobynet.org **AW:** Research Fellowship, Smithsonian Tropical Research Institute (2001); Grantee, Fishery and Agricultural Funding, Canary Island Government (1994); Grantee, Canary Islands Ministry of Tourism (1989, 1988); Grantee, Earthwatch (1986-1995); Research Grantee, Sigma Xi (1982); Grantee, Marine Biology, National Science Foundation (1975-1980) **MEM:** American Society of Ichthyologists and Herpetologists; Ichthyological Society Japan; Sigma Xi **MH:** Albert Nelson Marquis Lifetime Achievement Award; Marquis Who's Who Top Professional; Marquis Who's Who Humanitarian Award **B/I:** Dr. Van Tassell became involved in his profession because he always loved teaching and inspiring young individuals. In 1976, he started working in the Canary Islands on research projects investigation the shore fish populations and kept his students involved in that research or any kind of research. **AV:** Hiking; Camping; Hiking **PA:** Democrat **RE:** Atheist **THT:** During his term, Mr. Van Tassell established a statewide conference on Environmental Education held in Binghamton, NY. While a science teacher, he started the Ecology Council at H. F. Carey High School in 1970 and was its advisor for 30 years, until his retirement. The Council started recycling in 1970 and became the largest longest lasting program in the state. By 1976, the Council took over a court yard at the school and built a forest and pond. That ecosystem attracted migratory hawks and a daily visit from a Peregrine Falcon, which feasted on the excess pigeon population.

VANDER WEIDE, VERNON JAY, T: Lawyer **I:** Law and Legal Services **DOB:** 04/03/1940 **PB:** East Grand Rapids **SC:** MI/USA **PT:** Henry Thomas Vander Weide; Della (Van Zoeren) Vander Weide **MS:** Married **SPN:** Gretchen Laurie Clemmons (09/11/1965) **CH:** Jennifer; Stephani; Vanessa **ED:** LLM, George Washington University (1971); LLB, University of Michigan (1965); BA, University of Michigan (1962); AA, Grand Rapids Junior College (1960) **CT:** United States District Court District of Minnesota (1977); Minnesota State Bar Association (1977); The District of Columbia Bar (1970);

State Bar of Michigan (1970) **C:** Of Counsel, Lockridge Grindal Nauen P.L.L.P. (2011-Present); Shareholder, Board of Directors, Head, Seifert & Vander Weide (1982-2011); Shareholder, Wiese & Cox, Minneapolis, MN (1979-1982); Branch Chief Attorney, Securities and Exchange Commission (1970-1976); Staff Attorney, Interstate Commerce Commission (1969-1970); Staff Assistant, House Republican Conference (1965-1966) **CR:** Lecturer, Continuing Legal Education Corporation (1981, 1987, 1998) **CIV:** Minnesota Futures Forum (1998-1999); Board of Deacons, Teacher, Sunday School, Westminster Presbyterian Church (1993-1999); Task Force Member, Superintendents Blue Ribbon Commission (1982); Board of Directors, Cedar-Isles-Dean Neighborhood Association **MIL:** Captain, U.S. Army (1966-1969) **CW:** Writer, Analyst, Columnist, Neighborhood Newspaper (1982-1994); Author, Opinion Pieces, "Minneapolis Star Tribune" **MEM:** American Bar Association; Minnesota State Bar Association; Hennepin County Bar Association **MH:** Albert Nelson Marquis Lifetime Achievement Award **B/I:** Mr. Vander Weide became involved in his profession because of his leadership training. After attending, he was inspired to pursue a career in law. **AV:** Sailing; Overseeing investments; Reading; Teaching; Spending time with family **PA:** Independent

VANDER ZANDEN, MARIANNE, T: Retired Paralegal/Music Educator **I:** Law and Legal Services **DOB:** 03/17/1939 **PB:** Chicago **SC:** IL/USA **PT:** Martin Sadd; Mary Sadd **MS:** Widow **CH:** Sandra; Linda; William; Mark **ED:** PhD, American Conservatory of Music (2007); MusEd, American Conservatory of Music (1993); Bachelor of Music, American Conservatory of Music (1978) **CT:** Paralegal Certificate, Roosevelt University, Chicago, IL (1985) **C:** Paralegal, Willan & Brinks (1984-2001); Private Music Educator (1960-1980) **MEM:** Gemological Institute of America; Graduate Gemologists **AS:** Dr. Vander Zanden attributes her success to working hard and staying busy. **AV:** Playing the piano and the harp **RE:** Catholic

VANDERBILT, GLORIA MORGAN, T: Artist, Actress, Fashion Designer **I:** Media & Entertainment **DOB:** 02/20/1924 **PB:** New York **SC:** NY/USA **PT:** Reginald Claypoole; Gloria (Morgan) V. **SPN:** Wyatt Emory Cooper (1963; Deceased 1978); Sidney Lumet (1956, Divorced 1963); Leopold Stokowski (1945, Divorced 1955); ?Pat DiCicco (1941, Divorced 1945) **CH:** Four Children **ED:** Personal Study, Sanford Meisner (1955); Coursework, Mary C. Wheeler, Miss Porter's Schools **CW:** Author, with Anderson Cooper, "The Rainbow Comes and Goes: A Mother and Son on Life, Love, and Loss" (2016); Author, "The Memory Book of Starr Faithful" (1994); Author, Novel, "Never Say Good-Bye" (1989); Author, "Black White, White Knight" (1987); Author, "Once Upon a Time: A True Story" (1985); Exhibited, Group Show, Hoover Gallery, San Francisco, CA (1971); Author, with Alfred Allen Lewis, "Gloria Vanderbilt Book of Collage" (1970); Exhibited, One-Woman Show, Vestart Gallery, New York, NY (1969); Exhibited, One-Woman Show, Washington Gallery of Art (1968); Exhibited, One-Woman Show, Neiman-Marcus, Dallas, TX (1968); Exhibited, One-Woman Show, Hammer Gallery, New York, NY (1966, 1968); Exhibited, Group Show, Washington Gallery of Art (1967); Exhibited, One-Woman Show, Cord Gallery, New York, NY (1966); TV Appearance, "Family Happiness on U.S. Steel Hour" (1959); TV Appearance, "Flint and Fire on U.S. Steel Hour" (1958); Stage Appearance, "Peter Pan" (1958); Stage Appearance, "The Spa" (1956); Exhibited, One-Woman Show, Juster Gallery, New York, NY (1956); Actress, "The Time of Your Life" (1955); Stage Appearance, "Picnic" (1955); TV

Appearance, "Colgate Comedy Hour" (1955); Film Appearance, "Johnny Concho" (1955); Author, Love Poems (1955); Exhibited, One-Woman Show, Bertha Shaeffer Gallery, New York, NY (1954); Exhibited, One-Woman Show, Rabun Studio, New York, NY (1948); Actress, Summer Stock Production, "The Swan"; Stage Appearance, "The Green Hat"; TV Appearance, "Tonight At 8:30"; TV Appearance, "Very Important People"; Designer, Stationary and Greeting Cards, Hallmark Co., Designer, Fabrics, Bloomcraft Co.; Designer, Bed Linens, Martex Co.; Designer, Table Linens, Peacock Co.; Exhibited, One-Woman Show, Parish Museum, Southampton, NY; Exhibited, One-Woman Show, Nantucket, MA; Exhibited, One-Woman Show, Houston, TX; Exhibited, One-Woman Show, Reading, PA; Exhibited, One-Woman Show, Monterey, CA; Exhibited, One-Woman Show, Nashville, TN; Author, with Alfred Allen Lewis, Play, "Three by Two" **AW:** Fashion Award, Neiman-Marcus (1969); Sylvania Award (1959) **MEM:** Actors' Equity Association; Screen Actors Guild; American Federation of TV and Radio Artists; Authors League of America; American Federation of Arts

VANDERHEYDEN, CAROL EVONNE, T: Elementary School Educator (Retired) **I:** Education/Educational Services **DOB:** 02/13/1946 **PB:** Delhi **SC:** NY/USA **PT:** Harlan R. Claypool; Wilda D. Claypool **MS:** Married **SPN:** Larry J. VanderHeyden (1968) **CH:** Robb; Amy **ED:** Coursework, St. Francis (1968-1969); BS in Education, Bethel College (1968) **CT:** Certified Teacher, States of Michigan, Indiana (1968) **C:** Elementary Teacher, Edwardsburg Public School, MI (1969-1999); Teacher, 7th and 8th Grade, Mathematics, Penn Harris Madison Corp (Now P-H-M School Corporation), Mishawaka, IN (1968-1969) **CW:** Author, "A Touch of Class" (2003) **AW:** Conservation Educator of the Year Award, Cass County Soil and Water Conservation District (1996); Photograph Award **MEM:** Treasurer, Solivita Travel Club (2003-2006); Retired Teachers Association, National Council on Teacher Retirement; Green Thumbs Garden Club; Book Club; Golf Club **B/I:** Mrs. VanderHeyden always loved school and her teachers; they inspired her. She had an uncle who was a principal and an aunt who was a teacher and they inspired her as well. She was raised in a family of seven children and she used to play school with them and teach them all the things she had learned in school. They had an advantage when they actually went to school because Ms. VanderHeyden already taught them to read and do math. That was the beginning of her wanting to become a teacher. She enjoyed being an elementary school teacher because it gave her a variety in what she taught. The children responded well. She was a very creative teacher. She used bulletin boards with her art work. She also assigned many projects for her students. **AV:** Boating; Painting; Flower arranging; Reading; Photography **PA:** Republican **RE:** Protestant

VANDERPOEL, JAMES ROBERT, T: Lawyer **I:** Law and Legal Services **DOB:** 09/27/1955 **PB:** Harvey **SC:** IL/USA **PT:** Waid Richard Vanderpoel; Ruth (Silberman) Vanderpoel **MS:** Married **SPN:** Dr. Alison Q. Vanderpoel (02/01/2012) **CH:** Jacqueline; Robert; Jennifer; Frederick **ED:** JD, Santa Clara University (1982); BS in Finance, Indiana University (1978) **C:** Senior Counsel, Continental Automotive Systems, Deer Park, IL (2006-Present) **CR:** Motorola, Inc. (1987-2006); Corporate Lawyer, Four-phase Systems, Inc. (1984-1987); Law Clerk, FMC Corporation **AW:** Silver Quill Award (1999); Motorola Contract Management Council Excellence Award (1996); Recipient, Company Award for Company Speakers **MEM:** Vice President, Citizens for Conservation; International Associa-

tion of Contract Management (IACCM) **BAR:** California (1982); United States District Court for the Northern District of California (1982) **MH:** Albert Nelson Marquis Lifetime Achievement Award; Marquis Who's Who Top Professional **B/I:** Mr. Vanderpoel became interested in commercial law in college. He took a required class in business law in business school that he really enjoyed, which became his inspiration. Shortly after, he took the law school admissions test to become a lawyer. He likes to read and is good at analyzing written information; he always was, even in college and high school. Reading comprehension is very important in law. **AV:** Basketball; Hiking; Golf; Snorkeling; Gardening; Fitness activities; Exercise, running, nature travel, wild land appreciation; Birding; Fishing; Involvement in our ecological reservation

VANDIVER, GERALDINE M., T: Construction Company Executive **I:** Architecture & Construction **DOB:** 06/29/1926 **PB:** Yakima **SC:** WA/USA **PT:** Iroxel Leroy Tennant; Dorothy (Strachan) Tennant **MS:** Widowed **SPN:** John H. Vandiver (07/21/1951, Deceased) **CH:** Dean H.; Roger A.; Mary D.; Mark J. **ED:** EdB, Washington State University (1949); BA in Mathematics, Washington State University (1948) **C:** Partner, John H. Vandiver Construction, Yakima, WA (1951-2015); Teacher, Franklin School, Yakima, WA (1950-1951); Dean of Women, Faculty Physical and Health Education, Yakima Valley College (1949-1950) **CIV:** Active Member, Yakima County Unit Pro-American (1976) **AW:** Winner, Yakima Valley Jr. College Girl's Singles Tennis Tournament (1946); Winner, Yakima Valley High School's Girls Single Tennis Tournament (1944); Scholarship, Yakima Valley Community College; Scholarship, Washington State University **MEM:** President, Woman's Century Club (1987-1989); President, Yakima Republican Women (1983-1984, 1987-1988); Phi Theta Kappa; Chapter CE P.E.O, Yakima, WA; Lifetime Member, American Association of University Women **MH:** Albert Nelson Marquis Lifetime Achievement Award **B/I:** Ms. Vandiver became involved in his profession because she was looking to do something to help shape young people. When she got married, her husband was a building contractor and she became very involved with construction. **AV:** Playing classical and popular piano music for groups; Gardening **PA:** Conservative **RE:** Presbyterian

VARGAS, JUAN CARLOS, T: U.S. Representative from California **I:** Government Administration/Government Relations/Government Services **DOB:** 03/07/1961 **PB:** National City **SC:** CA/USA **PT:** Tomas Vargas; Celina Vargas **MS:** Married **SPN:** Adrienne D'Ascoli (1990) **CH:** Rosa Celina; Jeanne Helena **ED:** JD, Harvard Law School (1991); MA in Humanities, Fordham University, Bronx, NY; BA in Political Science, University of San Diego, Magna Cum Laude (1983) **C:** Member, U.S. House of Representatives from California's 51st Congressional District, United States Congress, Washington, DC (2013-Present); Member, U.S. House Administration Committee (2013-Present); Member, U.S. House Committee on Foreign Affairs (2013-Present); Member, U.S. House Committee on Agriculture (2013-Present); Member, District 40, California State Senate (2010-2013); With, Insurance Company, San Deigo, CA (2007-2009); Member, District 79, California State Assembly (2001-2006); Councilman, District Eight, San Diego City Council (1993-2000); Member, Committee on the Judiciary, United States Congress; Member, Republican Study Committee, United States Congress **PA:** Democrat **RE:** Roman Catholic

VASEFF, JAMES RICHARD, T: Architect **I:** Architecture & Construction **DOB:** 01/30/1947 **PB:** Chicago **SC:** IL/USA **MS:** Married **SPN:** Heather Andrea Stilwell (05/13/1970) **CH:** Two Daughters **ED:** Loeb Fellowship for Advanced Environmental Studies (1984); Postgraduate Coursework, Harvard University (1983-1984); BArch, Boston Architectural College (1971); Coursework, Clemson University, South Carolina (1964-1967) **CT:** Registered Architect, North Carolina (1975); Registered Architect, Massachusetts (1973) **C:** Vice Chair, Member of the Board, Coperniche WEALTH Institute (2010-2015); Senior Advisor, Community and Economic Development, Manager, External Issues, Governmental Affairs, Georgia Power Company, Atlanta, GA (1982-2008); Chief, Preservation Services South East Region, National Park Service (1980-1982); Acting Chief, Historic American Engineering Record, U.S. Department of the Interior (1978-1980); Instructor of Architecture, University of North Carolina the College or Architecture, Charlotte, NC (1974-1977); Various Architectural Firms, Boston, London, North Carolina (1967-1974) **CR:** State Codes Advisory Committee (1992-2009); Member, State Planning Advisory Committee (1993-2008); Issue Management Council, Charmian, VP, Treasurer, (1992-1998); President, Georgia Downtown Development Association, Atlanta, GA (1988-1991); Chairman, Georgia National Register Review Board (1986-1989); Georgia State Planning Advisory Committee **CIV:** Docent, Porsche Experience Center (2018-Present); Vice President, Harvard Club of Georgia (1993-1995); Treasurer, Atlanta Chapter, AIA (1993-1995); Board of Directors, Atlanta Chapter, AIA (1992-1995); President, Harvard Club of Georgia (1990-1991); Board of Advisors, Atlanta Streetcar; Emeritus Member, Alumni Council, Harvard Graduate School of Design; Alumni Council, Harvard Graduate School of Design Loeb Fellowship; Alumni Council, Boston Architectural College; Board Member, Waldorf School of Atlanta; Board Member, Young Singers of Atlanta; Board Member, Treasurer, Georgia Humanities Council; President, Treasurer, Georgia Council for International Visitors; Board Member, Georgia Trust for Historic Preservation **CW:** Contributor, Articles, Professional Journals; Photography; Film **AW:** Rotarian of the Year, Atlanta Midtown Rotary (2001-2002); Howard Chase Leadership Award, Issue Management Council **MEM:** Chairman, National Regional and Urban Design Committee, American Institute of Architects (1990-1991) **MH:** Albert Nelson Marquis Lifetime Achievement Award; Marquis Who's Who Top Professional **B/I:** Mr. Vaseff always wanted to be an architect. Growing up in Chicago was inspiring. The odd thing was he never ended up working in Chicago. He worked and went to school at the same time at the Boston architectural center, it was easy to stay and work and then go on and teach. **AV:** Reading; Motorsports; Photography

VASOS, TODD J., T: Chief Executive Officer **I:** Retail/Sales **CN:** Dollar General Corporation **ED:** Bachelor's Degree in Marketing, Western Carolina University (1983) **C:** Chief Executive Officer, Dollar General Corporation (2015-Present); Chief Operating Officer, Dollar General Corporation (2013-2015); Executive Vice President, Division President, Chief Merchandising Officer, Dollar General Corporation (2008-2013); Executive Vice President, Chief Operating Officer, Longs Drug Stores Corporation (2006-2008); Executive Vice President, Chief Merchandising Officer, Longs Drug Stores Corporation (2001-2006); Senior Vice President, Chief Merchandising Officer, Phar-Mor (1994-2001); Operations, Eckerd Corporation (1983-1994) **CR:** Member, Board of Directors, Retail Industry Leaders Association **AW:** Professional Achievement Award, Western Carolina University (2017); Merchant of the Year, Mass Market Retailers (2010) **MEM:** Chief Marketing Officer Institute; Alumni Association, Western Carolina University

VAUGHN, ROBERT WEEKS, T: Health Education Specialist **I:** Education/Educational Services **DOB:** 08/08/1959 **PB:** Columbus **SC:** GA/USA **PT:** Glenn Vaughn; Nancy (Weeks) Vaughn **MS:** Married **SPN:** Janet **ED:** MS in Technical and Professional Communication, Kennesaw State University (2002); Postgraduate Coursework in Journalism, Auburn University (1983); BA in Speech Communications, Columbus State University (1982) **C:** Health Education Specialist, Centers for Disease Control and Prevention, Atlanta, GA (2016-Present); Instructional Systems Designer, Chenega Corporation, Time Solutions, LLC, Atlanta, GA (2015-2016); Instructional Media Development Manager, Georgia Department of Transportation, Atlanta, GA (2001-2015); Video Producer, Georgia Department of Transportation, Atlanta, GA (1993-2001); Video Production Specialist, Georgia Department of Transportation, Atlanta, GA (1985-1993); Staff Writer, Rome News-Tribune, Rome, GA (1983-1984); Sports Correspondent, Opelika-Auburn News, Opelika, AL (1983); News Editor, Fayette County News, Fayetteville, GA (1982) **CW:** Technical Director, Informational Video, Stone Matrix Asphalt (1996); Author, Editor, Producer, Director, Video-based Training, Precast Retaining Walls (1992); Author, Editor, Producer, Director, Video-based Training, Asphalt Plant Inspection (1991); Author, Editor, Producer, Director, Video-based Training, Erosion Control (1989) **AW:** CDC/ATSDR Honor Award (2016); James Virgil Peavy Award for Excellence in Human Capital Management (2016); Award of Excellence, The Communicator Awards "Edge Rut Repair" (2002); Award of Distinction, Videographer Awards (2000); Award of Distinction, Videographer Award "Jerry Stargel" (1998); Award of Distinction, The Communicator Awards "Stone Matrix Asphalt of Olympic Proportions" (1996); Award, American Lung Association Broadcast Commercial (PSA) Award, American Lung Association (1981) **MEM:** International Television Association **MH:** Albert Nelson Marquis Lifetime Achievement Award **AS:** Mr. Vaughn attributes his success to his family support and personal dedication to the best he can; keeping his eye on the purpose of what he is doing, customizing as needed according to the target audience. **B/I:** Mr. Vaughn became involved in his profession because he was from a newspaper family, as both his parents were publishers in Georgia. His dad started a newspaper company called Daily News and his mom started a newspaper also. His brother was an editor, so Mr. Vaughn was blessed to have come from a family in that profession, and was also able to branch out and take his profession to a higher level. **AV:** Photography; Computer repair; Coin collecting/numismatics; Hiking; Camping; Reading **PA:** Republican **RE:** Methodist

VAUGHN, THOMAS J., PROFESSOR OF EARTH SCIENCES, T: Earth Science Educator **I:** Education/Educational Services **CN:** Northeastern University **DOB:** 12/23/1944 **PB:** Lawrence **SC:** MA/USA **PT:** Thomas Wilbur Vaugn; Dorothy Agnes (Mallon) Vaughn **MS:** Married **SPN:** Priscilla Margaret Bastian (06/30/1973) **CH:** Matthew Thomas; Judith Diane **ED:** CAGS in Computers in Education, Lesley University, Cambridge, MA (1985); MEd in Secondary Educational Administration, University of Massachusetts Lowell (1977); MA in Geography, Boston University (1972); BA in History/Geography, Mount Carmel College, Niagara Falls, Ontario, Canada (1968) **CT:** Certification in Teaching; Certified General Supervisor, High School Principal, Massachusetts; Certified Online Instructor **C:** Professor, Earth Science, Thomas Edison College (2013-Present); Professor, Education, Cambridge College (2009-Present); Instructional Consultant, Class Measures-Tribal (2005-Present); Science Educator, Consultant, NASA Institute of Global Environmental Studies (2002-Present); Professor, Environmental Studies, Middlesex Community College (2004-Present); Instructor, Earth Science, Northeastern University, Boston, MA (1997-Present); Professor, Education, University of Massachusetts Lowell (2008-2014); Professor, Education, Lesley University (2006-2014); Professor, Science Education, University of Massachusetts (2005-2007); Earth Science Teacher, Lead Science Teacher, Arlington High School (1972-2004); Assistant Director, Project ESTEEM, Harvard-Smithsonian, Cambridge, MA (1993); Adult Education Instructor, Arlington Public Schools (1985-1990); Liberal Arts Professor, Bryant-Mcintosh Junior College (1971-1972); Teaching Fellow, Boston University (1969-1971); Teacher, Earth Science, Desales High School (1968-1969) **CR:** Committees for Science Education Reform, Massachusetts Department of Education (1995-Present); Science Revision Committee, Massachusetts (2009-2019); Science Mathematics Advice Council, Massachusetts Commissioner of Education (2009-2011); Telecommunications Moderator, Harvard University Science Teacher Network, Cambridge, MA (1986-1989) **CIV:** Billerica Friends of the Library (1995-Present); Lector, St. Theresa's Church, Billerica, MA (1975-Present); Trustee, Billerica Public Library (1993-2011); Board of Directors, Teacher, Leadership Academy of Massachusetts **CW:** Project IMAGE, Harvard-Smithsonian (1997); Co-Author, "Integrating Computers in Your Classroom: Middle and Secondary Science" (1994); Presenter in Field **AW:** Outstanding Adjunct Professor, National Association of Geoscience Teachers (2016); Outstanding Science Educator Award, Massachusetts Science Education Leadership Association (2007); Distinguished Alumni Award, Lesley University (2005); Sally K. Lenhardt Professional Leadership Award, Lesley University, Cambridge, MA (2005); Distinguished Alumni Award, Boston University (2002); Presidential Award for Excellence in Teaching Mathematics and Science, National Science Foundation (2000); Distinguished Alumni Award, University of Massachusetts Lowell (2000); Science Educator of the Year Award for Middlesex County, Massachusetts Association of Science Teachers (1998); Tandy Technical Scholar (1996); Inductee, Massachusetts Science Educators Hall of Fame (1992); Pathfinder Award in Techology, Massachusetts Department of Education (1991) **MEM:** Board of Directors, Independent University Alumni Association at Lowell (2005-Present); President, New England Section National Association of Geoscience Teachers (2005-2006); President, Massachusetts Association of Science Supervisors (2004-2006); National Science Teachers Association; National Geographical Society; Massachusetts Association of Science Teachers; Alpha Omega Alpha; Local President, Gamma Theta Upsilon **MH:** Albert Nelson Marquis Lifetime Achievement Award **B/I:** Mr. Vaughn's mother stressed the importance of education as he grew up. She encouraged him to continue learning for as long as he could, as academics were important. His father and grandfather were distinguished academics, both of whom inspired him to pursue a career in education. **AV:** Researching computers, telecommunications, and the internet; Reading; Walking **PA:** Democrat **RE:** Roman Catholic

VEASEY, MARC ALLISON, T: U.S. Representative from Texas **I:** Government Administration/Government Relations/Government Services **CN:** U.S. House of Representatives **DOB:** 1/3/1971 **PB:** Fort Worth **SC:** TX/USA **PT:** Joseph Veasey; Corinne Veasey **MS:** Married **SPN:** Tonya (Jackson) Veasey **CH:** Adam Clayton **ED:** Bachelor of Science in Mass Communications, Texas Wesleyan University (1995) **C:** Member, U.S. House of Representatives from Texas' 33rd Congressional District, United States Congress, Washington, DC (2013-Present); Member, U.S. House Committee on Science, Space and Technology (2013-Present); Member, U.S. House Committee on Armed Services (2013-Present); Member, District 95, Texas House of Representatives (2005-2013); Staff Member, U.S. House of Representatives; Member, U.S. Helsinki Commission; Member, Congressional Black Caucus; Member, New Democrat Coalition; Co-founder, Blue Collar Caucus **CR:** Substitute Teacher; Sportswriter; Script Writer, Advertising Agency **CIV:** Volunteer, Representative Martin Frost, U.S. House of Representatives **PA:** Democrat **RE:** Christian

VED, RAVI, T: Physician **I:** Medicine & Health Care **CN:** Allegheny Health Network **DOB:** 11/20/1986 **PB:** Cincinatti **SC:** OH/USA **MS:** Married **SPN:** Megan Boerio (08/31/2014) **CH:** Neil; Noah **ED:** MD, Lake Erie College of Osteopathic Medicine; Residency, Allegheny Health Network Medical Education Consortium **CIV:** Pittsburgh Ultimate Community **MEM:** ASSSM **AS:** Dr. Ravi attributes his success to having had great mentors during his residency. **B/I:** Dr. Ravi's biggest goal was to work with others who had a passion for their work. He played sports in high school and college, which inspired him to help athletes through their injuries. **THT:** Dr. Ravi's motto is, "We don't stop playing because we grow old, we grow old because we stop playing."

VEDDER, EDDIE, T: Singer **I:** Media & Entertainment **DOB:** 12/23/1965 **PB:** Evanston **SC:** IL/USA **PT:** Edward Louis Severson Jr.; Karen Lee Vedder **MS:** Married **SPN:** Jill McCormick (09/18/2010); Beth Liebling (06/03/1994, Divorced 2000) **CH:** Olivia; Harper **C:** Solo Artist (2007-Present); Lead Singer, Pearl Jam (1990-Present) **CW:** Singer, Album, "Gigaton," Pearl Jam (2020); Singer, Live Album, "MTV Unplugged," Pearl Jam (2019); Singer, Live Album, "Let's Play Two," Pearl Jam (2017); Actor, "Twin Peaks: The Return" (2017); Singer, Live Album, "Live at Third Man Records," Pearl Jam (2016); Himself, "Roadies" (2016); Singer, Album, "Lightning Bolt," Pearl Jam (2013); Executive Producer, "Her Aim Is True" (2013); Himself, "Jay-Z: Made in America" (2013); Himself, "Cosmic Psychos: Blokes You Can Trust" (2013); Himself, "Portlandia" (2012); Himself, "West of Memphis" (2012); Singer, Concert Film, "Water on the Road," Pearl Jam (2011); Himself, "Paradise Lost 3: Purgatory" (2011); Singer, Live Album, "9.11.2011 Toronto, Canada," Pearl Jam (2011); Singer, Live Album, "Live on Ten Legs," Pearl Jam (2011); Singer, Songwriter, Producer, "Ukulele Songs" (2011); Himself, "Conan O'Brien Can't Stop" (2011); Singer, Compilation Album, "Pearl Jam Twenty" (2011); Performer, "The People Speak" (2009); Singer, Album, "Backspacer," Pearl Jam (2009); Himself, "The People Speak" (2009); Himself, "Slacker Uprising" (2008); Himself, "Song Sung Blue" (2008); Singer, Live Album, "Live at Lollapalooza 2007," Pearl Jam (2007); Singer, Songwriter, Composer, Producer, "Into the Wild" (2007); Himself, "Amazing Journey: The Story of The Who" (2007); Himself, "Runnin' Down a Dream" (2007); Himself, "Walk Hard: The Dewey Cox Story" (2007); Singer, Live Album, "Live at the Gorge 05/06," Pearl Jam (2007); Singer, Live Album, "Live at Easy

Street," Pearl Jam (2006); Singer, Live Album, "Live in NYC 12/31/92," Pearl Jam (2006); Singer, Album, "Pearl Jam," Pearl Jam (2006); Singer, Live Album, "Live at Benaroya Hall," Pearl Jam (2004); Singer, Compilation Album, "Rearviewmirror (Greatest Hits 1991-2003)" (2004); Singer, Compilation Album, "Lost Dogs" (2003); Himself, "End of the Century: The Story of the Ramones" (2003); Singer, Album, "Riot Act," Pearl Jam (2002); Singer, Album, "Binaural," Pearl Jam (2000); Performer, "The Who & Special Guests: Live at the Royal Albert Hall" (2000); Singer, Live Album, "Live on Two Legs," Pearl Jam (1998); Singer, Album, "Yield," Pearl Jam (1998); Singer, Album, "No Code," Pearl Jam (1996); Himself, "Hype!" (1996); Singer, Album, "Vitalogy," Pearl Jam (1994); Singer, Album, "Vs.," Pearl Jam (1993); Himself, "Singles" (1992); Singer, Album, "Ten," Pearl Jam (1991) **AW:** Inductee, Rock and Roll Hall of Fame (2017); Best Recording Package, "Lightning Bolt," Pearl Jam, Grammy Awards (2015); Best Original Song, "Guarantee," "Into the Wild," Golden Globe Awards (2008); Environmentalist of the Year, SIMA Waterman's Honorees (2007); Favorite Alternative Artist, Pearl Jam, American Music Awards (1999); Favorite Heavy Metal/Hard Rock Artist, Pearl Jam, American Music Awards (1996); Favorite Alternative Artist, Peal Jam, American Music Awards (1996); Best Hard Rock Performance, "Spin the Black Circle," Pearl Jam, Grammy Awards (1996); Favorite New Heavy Metal/Hard Rock Artist, Pearl Jam, American Music Awards (1993); Favorite Pop/Rock New Artist, Pearl Jam, American Music Awards (1993); Album of the Year, "Vs.," Peal Jam, GAFFA Awards (1993); Best Direction, "Jeremy," Pearl Jam, MTV Video Music Awards (1993); Best Metal/Hard Rock Video, "Jeremy," Pearl Jam, MTV Video Music Awards (1993); Best Group Video, "Jeremy," Pearl Jam, MTV Video Music Awards (1993); Video of the Year, "Jeremy," Pearl Jam, MTV Video Music Awards (1993)

VEHLE, MIKE, T: Retired State Legislator **I:** Government Administration/Government Relations/Government Services **DOB:** 11/17/1949 **PB:** Reliance **SC:** SD/USA **PT:** Ab Vehle; Sarah Vehle **ED:** Coursework, University of South Dakota; Diploma, Chamberlain High School **C:** Vice-Chair, South Dakota Transportation Commission (2017-Present); District 20, South Dakota State Senate (2008-2016); Vice President, CorTrust Bank (1993-2010); Transportation Task Force (2008); District 20, South Dakota House of Representatives (2004-2008); President, Shanard Inc.; Legislative Aide, Congressman James Abdnor **CR:** South Dakota Agriculture and Natural Resources Committee (2009-2015); South Dakota Judiciary Committee (2009-2015); Chair, South Dakota Transportation Committee (2009-2015) **CIV:** President, Mitchell Area Chamber of Commerce; Federal Grain Inspection Service Advisory Board; Co-Chair, Council of State Government's (CSG) Transportation and Infrastructure Committee **CW:** Author, Prime Sponsor, Senate Bill 1 **AW:** Inductee, South Dakota Transportation Hall of Honor (2015) **MEM:** Founder, Chair, Mitchell Rapid City Rail Users Association **MH:** Albert Nelson Marquis Lifetime Achievement Award; Marquis Who's Who Top Professional; Distinguished Humanitarian **B/I:** When Senator Vehle graduated from college, his plan was to move to California to work in a bank. His mother suggested he call a family friend, Jim Abner, who was running for congress at the time. She thought he may be of some help. Mr. Abner said he was unable to pay him, but if he would like to help he would pay for his "sleep, eats, and travel." He traveled around the state putting up signs and meeting with people. After he won, he was looking for people, so Senator Vehle went to Washington, DC,

and became his legislative aide. He worked for him for four years. After the four years, he moved back to South Dakota and worked in the grain feed fertilizer business, at the same time keeping involved with politics to some degree. He was always active but not always political. In 2004, he was talked into running for the state house; he did that for four years. The current senator at the time was termed out, so he ran for the senate and worked there until he was termed out in 2016. The governor then wanted him to be on the transportation commission, so that is what he is doing now. **PA:** Republican

VEIGAMILTON, ANA, T: President **I:** Real Estate **CN:** José Milton Foundation **DOB:** 02/16/1966 **PB:** Havana **SC:** Cuba **PT:** Giovanni; Nora Veiga **MS:** Married **SPN:** Cecil J. Milton **CH:** Alec Milton; Eric Milton; Diana Milton **ED:** Doctor of Jurisprudence, University of Miami, Summa Cum Laude (1993); Bachelor of Science in Electrical Engineering, University of Miami, Summa Cum Laude (1987); Coursework, Master of Science in Electrical Engineering, Florida International University **C:** Member, Keys Chapter Board, American Red Cross Miami (2018-Present); Member of the Board of Trustees, University of Miami (2017-Present); Board Member, United Way of Miami-Dade (2016-Present); Miracle Society Founding Member, Big Brothers Big Sisters of Greater Miami (2014-Present); Member of the Board, Golden Angel, Guardian Angel, Jackson Health Foundation (2014-Present); Member, County Zoo Oversight Board (2013-Present); Tocqueville Society Member, Women's Leadership, United Way of Miami-Dade (2012-Present); Member of Citizens Board, University of Miami (2011-Present); President, José Milton Foundation (2012-Present); Chair, Board of Directors, Zoo Miami Foundation (2014-2016); Momentum 2 Campaign Chair, University of Miami College of Engineering (2012-2014) **CIV:** Ball Chair, American Red Cross of Greater Miami (2017-2018); University of Miami Citizens Board; Women's Committee, Big Brothers Big Sisters; Chairperson, College of Engineering Momentum 2 Campaign; With, Jackson Health Foundation; Trustee, University of Miami **AW:** Dorothy Shula Outstanding Volunteerism Award, United Way (2020); Philanthropy Volunteer of the Year, Red Cross Miami & Keys Chapter (2020); The Junior League of Miami Woman Who Makes a Difference (2020); Inductee, Hall of Fame, Miami-Dade County Public School Alumni (2019); Dean's Innovation Award, University of Miami College of Engineering (2019); Sapoznik Insurance Public School Alumni Achievement Award, Education Fund (2018); Miami Women Who Rock (2017); Inner Circle of Twelve, American Cancer Society (2013); Miracle Maker, Big Brothers Big Sisters (2011); Miami Philanthropist of the Year, Association for Fundraising Professionals; Honoree, Plaza Health Network Foundation's Women of Distinction & Caring; Mayor's Community Spirit Award, Parks Foundation; Spectrum Florida Blue Philanthropy Award for Women, American Red Cross **MEM:** Co-Chairperson, Miracle Makers Luncheon (2018); Chairperson, American Red Cross Masquerade (2018); Honorary Chairperson, Feast with the Beasts (2017, 2018); Florida Bar Association; Tau Beta Pi; Miami-Dade Community Relations Board; Zoo Miami; Chairperson, Ball of the World (2004, 2005); Emeritus Board Director, Zoo Miami Foundation Board; Chairperson, County Zoo Oversight Board; Tocqueville Society; Women United; Impact Council for Financial Stability, United Way; Engagement Chairperson, Executive Board, United Way; Secretary, Treasurer, Local Homeowners' Civic Association; Co-founder, Butterfly Scholarship; Miracle Society, Big Brothers Big Sisters; Chairperson-Elect, Executive Board, Jackson Health Foundation; President-elect, University of Miami Citizens Board; American Red Cross Tiffany Circle **BAR:** Florida **AS:** Ms. VeigaMilton attributes her success to her disciplined work ethic, her family's support, and her connections to others. **B/I:** Ms. VeigaMilton became involved in her profession after having been born in Havana, Cuba. She drew inspiration from her parents, who emphasized the power of education. **AV:** Community service; Spending time with family **THT:** Gratitude is contagious and leads to happiness.

VELA, FILEMÓN BARTOLOMÉ JR., T: U.S. Representative from Texas; Lawyer **I:** Government Administration/Government Relations/Government Services **DOB:** 02/13/1963 **PB:** Harlingen **SC:** TX/USA **PT:** Filemón Bartolomé Vela Sr.; Blanca (Sanchez) Vela **MS:** Married **SPN:** Rosa Vela **ED:** JD, The University of Texas at Austin School of Law (1987); BA, Georgetown University (1985); Intern, Representative Solomon P. Ortiz, U.S. House of Representatives, Washington, DC **C:** Member, U.S. House of Representatives from Texas' 34th Congressional District, United States Congress, Washington, DC (2013-Present); Member, U.S. House Committee on Homeland Security (2013-Present); Member, U.S. House Committee on Agriculture (2013-Present); Private Law Practice (1988-2012) **PA:** Democrat **RE:** Roman Catholic

VELÁZQUEZ, NYDIA MARGARITA, T: U.S. Representative **I:** Government Administration/Government Relations/Government Services **CN:** New York's Seventh Congressional District **DOB:** 03/28/1953 **PB:** Limones **SC:** Yabucoa/Puerto Rico **PT:** Benito Velázquez Rodriguez; Carmen Luisa (Serrano Medina) Velázquez **MS:** Divorced **SPN:** Paul Bader (2000, Divorced) **ED:** MA in Political Science, New York University (1976); BA in Political Science, University of Puerto Rico, Rio Piedras, Puerto Rico, Magna Cum Laude (1974) **C:** Chair, U.S. House Committee on Small Business (2007-2011, 2019-Present); U.S. House of Representatives from New York's Seventh Congressional District, U.S. Congress, Washington, DC (2013-Present); Ranking House Committee on Small Business (1993-Present); U.S. House of Representatives from New York's 12th Congressional District, U.S. Congress, Washington, DC (1993-2013); Director, Department of Puerto Rican Community Affairs in the U.S., Commonwealth of Puerto Rico (1989-1992); Director, Migration Division Office, Puerto Rico Department of Labor and Human Resources (1986-1989); Owner, Quick Stop Emporium (1984-1986); City Councilwoman, District 12, New York, NY (1984-1986); Special Assistant to Representative Edolphus Towns, U.S. House of Representatives (1983-1984); Adjunct Professor, Puerto Rican Studies, City University of New York Hunter College (1981-1983); Instructor, University of Puerto Rico, Humacao, Puerto Rico (1976-1981); Director, Social Science Department, University of Puerto Rico, Humacao, Puerto Rico (1977-1979); U.S. House Committee on Financial Services, U.S. Congress **CR:** Chair, Congressional Hispanic Caucus (2009-2010) **AW:** Champion of Small Business Development Award, Small Business Development Center (2005); Named, Woman of the Year, Hispanic Business Magazine (2003); HerMANA Award, MANA (2002); Small Business Beacon Award, National Small Business United (2000) **PA:** Democrat **RE:** Roman Catholic

VENERABLE, SHIRLEY M, T: Retired Educator **I:** Education/Educational Services **DOB:** 11/12/1931 **PB:** Washington **SC:** DC/USA **PT:** John Henry Washington; Jessie Josephine (Young) Washington **MS:** Married **SPN:** Wendell Grant Venerable (2/15/1958) **CH:** Angela Elizabeth Maria Venerable-Joyner; Wendell Mark **ED:** Coursework in Life Long Studies, Triton Community College, River Grove, IL (2002); Postgraduate Coursework in Education Studies, Roosevelt University (1985); MA, Roosevelt University (1976); PhB, Northwestern University (1963) **CT:** Certified in Diagnostic and Prescriptive Reading; Certified in Gifted Education; Certified in Finger Mathematics; Certified in Fine Arts **C:** Teacher, Robert Emmet School, Chicago, IL (1999-Present); Retired (2003); Self-employed, Tutorial Programs (1999-2003); Teacher, Leslie Lewis Elementary School, Chicago, IL (1988-1999); Teacher, John Hay Academy, Chicago, IL (1975-1987); Teacher, Lewis Champlin School (1963-1974) **CR:** Sponsor, Reading Marathon Club, Chicago, IL (1991-Present); Co-creator, Project SMART-Stimulating Mathematics and Reading Techniques, John Hay Academy, Chicago, IL (1987-1990); Curriculum Coordinator, John Hay Academy, Chicago, IL (1985-1987); Art Consultant, Chicago Public School (1967); Recorder, Evening Division, Northwestern University, Chicago, IL (1956-1962); Exchange Student Teacher, Conservatory School of Dance, Chicago, IL (1958-1959); Creative Dance Student, Kathryn Duham School, New York, NY (1955-1956); Creative Dance Teacher, Doris Patterson Dance School, Washington DC (1953-1955) **CIV:** Sponsor, 37th Ward Reading Association Marathon, Chicago, IL (1991-1994, 1999); Volunteer, REAC Center Programs Books, Information, Literacy and Learning (1997-1998); Active, St. Giles Council of Catholic Women (1985-1996); Solicitor, Volunteer, United Negro College Fund, Chicago, IL (1994) **CW:** Author, Primary Activities, Let's Act and Chat (1991-1994); Teacher, Black History Through Classroom Tours (1989-1990) **AW:** Cultural Pearl Inductee, Delta Sigma (2012); Diamond Achievement Award (2011); Hall of Fame Award, National Women Achievement, Inc. (2005); Eta Xi Sigma Pearl Award for Excellence in Education (1997); Meritorious Award, United Negro College Fund (1990, 1994); Recognition Award, Alderman Percy Giles, Chicago, IL (1993); ASCD Recognition of Services Award (1989) **MEM:** Associate Member, Association for Supervision and Curriculum Development; International Reading Association; Chicago Chapter, National Women of Achievement Association; National Women's History Museum; Chapter Member, Phi Delta Kappa; Eta Xi Sigma; Life Member, Sigma Gamma Rho; Graduate Chapter, Delta Sigma (1963-1993); Sigma Chapter, Delta Sigma, (1992); Eta Xi Sigma Chapter, Delta Sigma **RE:** Roman Catholic

VENINGA, ROBERT LOUIS, PHD, T: Public Health Educator **I:** Education/Educational Services **DOB:** 12/10/1941 **PB:** Milwaukee **SC:** WI/USA **PT:** Frank Veninga; Otila (Mauch) Veninga **MS:** Married **SPN:** Karen Smit Veninga (12/29/1967) **CH:** Brent Karl **ED:** PhD, University of Minnesota (1972); MA, University of Minnesota (1969); BD, North American Baptist Seminary (Now Sioux Falls Seminary) (1966); BA, University of Minnesota (1963) **C:** Professor Emeritus, University of Minnesota (2007-Present); Professor, University of Minnesota School of Public Health, Minneapolis, MN (1985-2007); Associate Professor, University of Minnesota School of Public Health, Minneapolis, MN (1976-1985); Associate Dean, University of Minnesota School of Public Health, Minneapolis, MN (1976-1980); Assistant Dean, University of Minnesota School of Public Health, Minneapolis, MN (1972-1976) **CIV:** Elected Chairman, Board of Trustees, University of Sioux Falls (2005); Active Layperson, Lutheran Church; Extensive Volunteer Service, Faith-based Organizations **CW:** Author, "Your Renaissance Years: How to Make Retirement the Best Years of Your Life" (1991); Author, "A Gift of Hope: How We Survive Our Tragedies" (1985); Author, "The Human Side of Health Administration" (1982); Co-author with James P. Spradley, "The Work Stress Connection: How to Cope with Job Burnout" (1981); Author, Over 100 Articles to Professional Literature Including Five Presentations in Vital Speechless of the Day **AW:** Cicero Award for Best Written Speech on a Health Care Topic (2012); Named Alumnus of Notable Distinction, University of Minnesota (2006); Distinguished Alumni Award, University of Sioux Falls (1999); Edgar C. Hayhow Award, American College of Hospital Administrators (American College of Healthcare Executives) (1980) **MH:** Albert Nelson Marquis Lifetime Achievement Award **RE:** Lutheran

VENTOLA, DEAN S., T: Architect, Architectural Company Executive **I:** Architecture & Construction **PB:** Montclair **SC:** NJ/USA **PT:** Nicholas Samuel Ventola; Josephine (Caputo) Ventola **MS:** Married **SPN:** Janet Ventola **CH:** Samantha Christine Ventola; Matthew St. John Ventola **ED:** BA, The University of Maryland, With Honors (1983); BArch, The University of Maryland (1982) **CT:** Registered Architect, States of New York, New Jersey, Pennsylvania, Maryland, Virginia, West Virginia, North Carolina, South Carolina, Georgia and the District of Columbia; LEED AP BD+C, U.S. Green Building Council; National Council of Architectural Registration Boards **C:** Principal, Dean Ventola Architects LLC (2016-Present); Director, DVA Architects (2014-2016); Director, JNA Architects (2008-2014); Director of Architecture, SMC Construction (2006-2008); Dean Ventola, Architect (1990-2006); Vice President, Director of Architecture, Milliner Construction (1986-1990); Project Manager, Grimm & Parker (1984-1986) **CR:** Former Equal Opportunity Employment Officer, U.S. Department of Housing and Urban Development; Former Legislative Minuteman, AIA **CIV:** Chairman, Historic District Commission, City of Gaithersburg, MD; Visiting Architect, Urbanist Juror, Carey Business School, Johns Hopkins University **CW:** Contributor, "Data Center Tips of the Trade," Data Center Journal (2018); Contributor, "Meeting Contemporary Needs," ISW Online (2008); Excellence Award Winner, Residential Design & Build Magazine (2006); Contributor, "Library Style," Chesapeake Home (2003); Featured, Interview, Chesapeake Home (2001); Contributor, "Grand Opening of Windsor Knolls Recreation Center," The Frederick News-Post (1998); Contributor, "New Bank Branch to Open," The Frederick News-Post (1997); Contributor, "On the Way Up," Warfield (1989); Featured, Regional Report Interview (1989); Author, Book Subchapter, "Commercial Building" (1989); Contributor, "New Market Center," The Frederick News-Post (1988); Featured, Cover Article, "Shopping Center to Open in June," The Mt. Airy Courier-Gazette (1988); Contributor, "Complex Planned Near New Market," The Frederick News-Post (1987) **AW:** Outstanding Employee Award, SMC Construction (2007); Who's Who of Emerging Leaders in America (1998-2002); Who's Who in the East (1994-1998); Design of Excellence Award, FCBA (1989, 1990); Thesis Award, Institute of Urban Studies (1983) **MH:** Albert Nelson Marquis Lifetime Achievement Award **B/I:** Mr. Ventola became involved in his profession because of his love of art and architecture. **AV:** Appreciating art and architecture **PA:** Republican

VENTRE, PETER, T: Chief Executive Officer **I:** Research **CN:** Research Centers of America **DOB:** 07/29/1974 **PB:** Patterson **SC:** NJ/USA **PT:** Jose Ventre; Violeta (Ramos) Ventre **MS:** Married **SPN:** Ashley (Corliss) Ventre (04/12/2013) **ED:** Resident in Internal Medicine, Mount Sinai Hospital, New York, NY (2010); Fellowship, University of Florida, Gainesville, FL (2008); Resident in Psychiatry, Icahn School of Medicine at Mount Sinai, Cabrini Medical Center, New York, NY (2005-2008); MD, Ibero-American University, Santo Domingo, Dominican Republic (2001); MS in Medical Studies, San Juan Bautista School of Medicine, Caguas, Puerto Rico (1998); BS in General Science, University of Puerto Rico, Rio Piedras, Puerto Rico (1996) **CT:** Board Certified in Psychiatry, American Board of Psychiatry and Neurology, Inc. (2010); Diplomate, American Board of Psychiatry and Neurology, Inc. (2010); Licensed Physician, State of Florida; Certified, DEA **C:** Chief Medical Officer, DreamLife Recovery Treatment Center, Donegal, PA (2019-Present); Principal Investigator, President, Research Centers of America, LLC, Hollywood, FL (2018-Present); CMO, DetoxMD, National (2017-Present); Chief, Psychiatry, Broward Health Medical Center, Fort Lauderdale, FL (2014-Present); Founder, Research Centers of America, LLC, Hollywood, FL (2011-Present); President, Psychiatrist, Ventre Medical Associates, LLC, Oakland Park, FL (2011-Present); Vice Chief, Psychiatry, University Hospital, University Pavilion Hospital, Tamarac, FL (2011-Present); Chief Executive Officer, Ventre Medical Associates, Oakland Park, FL (2010-Present); Principal Investigator, Chief Executive Officer, Research Centers of America, LLC, Oakland Park, FL (2011-2018); Principal Investigator, Behavioral Clinical Research, Inc., Lauderhill, FL (2008-2011); Principal Investigator, Sleep Disorder Solutions, Inc., Miami, FL (2008-2011); Psychiatrist, Compass Health Systems, PA (2008-2010); Sub-investigator, Fidelity Clinical Research, Psychiatrist, Compass Health Systems, PA, Miami, FL (2008-2010) **CR:** Payroll Clerk, Hospital CHC De Fajardo, Puerto Rico (1998); Payroll Clerk, Fajardo Municipal Government, Fajardo, Puerto Rico (1997-1998); Lifeguard, Professional Rescue, U.S. Navy Recreational Division, Roosevelt Roads Base, Ceiba, Puerto Rico (1996-1997) **CIV:** Volunteer, Orthopedics, Fajardo Sun-Regional Hospital, Fajardo, Puerto Rico (1995-1997); Volunteer, Unit Observer, Assistant, Rio Piedras Medical Center, San Juan, Puerto Rico (1994); Medical Advisory Committee, Artemis Pharmaceuticals; National Speaker, Janssen Pharmaceuticals **AW:** Named Most Compassionate Doctor, Vitals Consumer Services, LLC **MEM:** American Clinical Research and Psychopharmacology; American Medical Association; American Psychiatric Association; Stanford Latino Entrepreneurship Initiative, Stanford Graduate School of Business; Broward Health Medical Center; Broward Health Imperial Point; Broward Health North; Various Correctional Facilities; Good Hope Manor; Holy Cross Hospital, Holy Cross Health); John's Place; Memorial Regional Hospital, Memorial Healthcare System; Meridan Treatment Solutions; Millennium Clinic; New River Villas; Recovery First; Seminole Tribe of Florida; Serenity House Detox Florida; United States Immigration and Customs Enforcement (ICE); Windsor Place; Willow Bay **AS:** Dr. Ventre attributes his success to hard work and the example his parents set for him. He came from a very poor town; his father worked seven days a week. He got used to seeing his father work hard, which inspired Dr. Ventre to behave the same way. **B/I:** Dr. Ventre was raised in Puerto Rico since he was 4 years old after his parents went there to visit. They liked it so much they lived there for 40 years. However, he was born to parents with his dad from Argentina and his mother from Cuba. His father received a degree very late in life, around 55-years-old, to become an orthopedic doctor in a small town. Dr. Ventre became inspired to pursue medicine after being exposed to the practice through his father. Initially, he wanted to be a cardiologist or a plastic surgeon. He ended up doing very well on his board exams, which is why he went to New York to become a

cardiologist. Once he was three years into internal medicine, he began his fellowship. He recalls an incident in which someone needed a translator for a Hispanic patient who was suffering from mania. When he was asked to translate and had a chance to speak to the patient, he became fascinated by how the brain works. At the time, psychiatry was the lowest level of medicine in terms of compensation. Despite that, Dr. Ventre was fascinated by how someone could have an alternate view on reality. In addition, Dr. Ventre was the first one to go to college. His father finished sixth grade, his mother didn't finish high school in Cuba. But, what inspired him to become a doctor was that his dad, after many years of trying different things, got a job in a hospital as a technician. He was a hardworking guy who worked as an assistant to an orthopedic doctor and every time he had the opportunity, his father would bring him, so he got familiar with the hospital and doing rotations with his father. He chose the career; first it was not that popular, and he changed in 2003-2004 because a lot of people told him it didn't make sense, but he was fascinated with people having problems such as schizophrenia; they didn't have too many options in 2014 for doctors in that field. So, when the psychiatrists started getting reimbursement, then it became more popular and now it is in high demand with the salary pretty high. But, at the time it was not popular, and he saw so many people with depression and friends suffering from anxiety and he wanted to help. It is still was not well known, however, he moved to south FL where he did research to try to find answers for mental diseases because even today they don't have a cure, only treatment.

VERANO, ANTHONY FRANK, T: Banker (Retired) **I:** Financial Services **DOB:** 01/04/1931 **PB:** West Harrison **SC:** NY/USA **PT:** Frank Verano; Rose (Viscomi) Verano **MS:** Married **SPN:** Clara Cosentino (07/08/1951) **CH:** Diana Verano; Rosemarie Verano (Deceased) **ED:** Student, New Jersey Bankers Data Processing School (1966-1968); Student, Burroughs Programmers School (1965); Student, RCA Programmers School (1965); Student, Bank Administration Institute, University Wisconsin (1962-1964); Student, American Institute of Banking (1956-1960) **C:** Executive Auditor, Connecticut Bank & Trust Company (1983-Present); Executive Auditor, State National Bank of Connecticut (1979-Present); Retired, Gateway Bank, Newtown, CT (1996); Vice President, Auditor, Senior Vice President, Auditor, Gateway Bank, Newtown, CT (1987-1994); Auditor, State National Bank of Connecticut (1962-1979); Senior Auditor, County Trust Company (1960-1961); With, County Trust Company, White Plains, NY (1949-1961) **CR:** Teacher, Bank Auditing, American Institute of Banking (1976-1978) **CIV:** Member, Advisory Board, Norwalk Community College (1968) **MIL:** Served, U.S. Navy (1951-1952) **MEM:** President, BAI (Bank Administration Institute) (1971-1972); Treasurer, BAI (Bank Administration Institute) (1969-1970); Secretary, Western Connecticut Chapter, BAI (Bank Administration Institute) (1968-1969); Director, Stamford Chapter, BAI (Bank Administration Institute) (1967-1968); Certified Bank Auditor, Certified Compliance Officer, Certified Financial Services Auditor, Institute of Internal Auditors **MH:** Albert Nelson Marquis Lifetime Achievement Award **AS:** Mr. Verano attributes his success to a lot of hard work. **B/I:** Mr. Verano became involved in his profession because he always liked finance and started doing that right out of high school. **AV:** Playing golf **RE:** Roman Catholic

VERLANDER, JUSTIN BROOKS, T: Professional Baseball Player **I:** Athletics **CN:** Houston Astros **DOB:** 02/20/1983 **PB:** Manakin-Sabot **SC:** VA/USA **PT:** Richard Verlander; Kathy Verlander **MS:** Married **SPN:** Kate Upton (11/04/2017) **CH:** Genevieve **ED:** Coursework, Old Dominion University; Diploma, Goochland High School; Student, Richmond Baseball Academy **C:** Pitcher, Houston Astros (2017-Present); Pitcher, Detroit Tigers (2005-2017) **CR:** Pitcher, U.S. National Baseball Team, Pan American Games (2003); Former Pitcher, Lakeland Flying Tigers, Erie SeaWolves **CIV:** Founder, Wins for Warriors Foundation (2016); American Red Cross **CW:** Cover Athlete, "Major League Baseball 2K12" (2012) **AW:** Cy Young Award (2011, 2019); Eight-time Recipient, Major League Baseball All-Star (2007, 2009-2013, 2018-2019); Nine-time Recipient, American League Player of the Week (2006-2007, 2011-2012, 2018-2019); Five-time Recipient, American League Pitcher of the Month (2009, 2011-2012, 2016, 2018); Babe Ruth Award (2017); World Series Champion (2017); American League Championship Series Most Valuable Player (2017); Three-time Recipient, Tiger of the Year, BBWAA-Detroit Chapter (2009, 2011, 2016); American League Most Valuable Player (2011); Players Choice Award for Player of the Year (2011); Players Choice Award for AL Outstanding Pitcher (2011); Triple Crown (2011); American League Rookie of the Month (2006); American League Rookie of the Year (2006); Detroit Tigers Rookie of the Year Award, Detroit Sports Broadcasters Association (2006); Players Choice Award for AL Outstanding Rookie (2006); Male Athlete of the Year, Old Dominion University Alumni Association (2004); All-CAA Honors (2003-2004); CAA Rookie of the Year (2002)

VERNICK, JEFFREY F., T: Manager, Performance Analysis and Planning **I:** Government Administration/Government Relations/Government Services **CN:** North Jersey Transportation Planning Authority **DOB:** 06/26/1965 **PB:** Elizabeth **SC:** NJ/USA **PT:** Arnold S. Vernick (Deceased); Lynne Vernick **MS:** Single **ED:** BA Economics, McGill University, Montreal, Quebec, Canada (1988) **CT:** Licensed Planner, State of New Jersey; Certified Planner, American Institute of Certified Planners **C:** Manager, Performance Analysis and Planning, Systems Planning Division, North Jersey Transportation Planning Authority (2010-Present); Manager, Corridor Studies and Project Planning, Regional Planning Division, North Jersey Transportation Planning Authority (2007-2010); Supervising Transportation Planner, Section Head, Monmouth County Planning Board, Freehold, NJ (1998-2007); Transportation Planner, Transportation Planning Development, Parsons Brinckerhoff (Now WSP), Princeton, NJ (1994-1998); Transportation Planner, Transportation Planning Department, Raytheon Engineers & Constructors, New York, NY (1993-1994); Staff Transportation Planner, Permanent Citizens Advisory Committee to the New York Metropolitan Transportation Authority, New York, NY (1990-1993); Transportation Analyst Trainee, Bureau of Transportation and Corridor Analysis, New Jersey Department of Transportation, Trenton, NJ (1988-1990); Assistant, Corporate Planning Department, NJ Transit Corporation (1985, 1986) **CR:** Railroad Worker, New Hope and Ivyland Railroad (1998-2002); Railroad Worker, Black River and Western Railroad, New Jersey (1988-1997) **CIV:** Vice Chairman, Monmouth County Transportation Council (2008-Present); Volunteer, Medical Reserve Corps, Monmouth County Health Department (2006-Present); Restoration Volunteer, Park Ridge Railroad Station, New Jersey (1983) **CW:** Author, "Guidebook for Project Performance Measurement" (2011); Business and Travel Video

Production; Photography, Creative and Historical Research, Writing and Communication **AW:** Parsons Brinckerhoff Semi-Annual Quality Improvement Award, Development and Implementation of a Software-Based Department Level Library System with Internal Company-Wide Access and Applications (1996) **MEM:** American Planning Association; American Institute of Certified Planners; National Association of Railroad Passengers (Now Rail Passengers Association (RPA)); Rails-to-Trails Conservancy **MH:** Albert Nelson Marquis Lifetime Achievement Award; Marquis Who's Who Top Professional **AS:** Mr. Vernick attributes his success to dedication, loyalty, perseverance, building cooperative relationships, and a passionate unabated spirit of continuous improvement and seizing opportunity. **B/I:** Mr. Vernick became involved in his profession because from an early age, he has been passionate about all modes of transportation. His specific interest in the history, operations, and preservation of railroads coupled with his university education majors in economics and geography led to a career in the transportation planning profession. **AV:** Traveling; Transportation research; Industrial research; Historic preservation; Home improvement; Photography; Computers; Athletics; Bicycling; Whitewater rafting **RE:** Jewish **THT:** Mr. Vernick recognizes the importance of embracing change and encouraging continuous improvement through innovative yet practical and versatile approaches. He has embraced technology which has allowed him to create PRIME, a revolutionary new online map-based tool for dynamically incorporating, managing and correlating planning study findings across many New Jersey transportation agencies. The system's disaggregate database design, which relates records listing both problems and mutli-modal strategy solutions, is based upon Mr. Vernick's philosophy of developing broader cooperative planning relationships and scoping capabilities between planning and engineering professionals.

VERONICA, MADONNA, T: Singer, Actress, Producer **I:** Media & Entertainment **DOB:** 08/16/1958 **PB:** Bay City **SC:** MI/USA **PT:** Sylvio Anthony Ciccone; Madonna Louise (Fortin) Ciccone **SPN:** Guy Ritchie (2000, Divorced 2008); Sean Penn (1985, Divorced 1989) **CH:** Lourdes Maria (Lola) Ciccone Leon; Rocco John Ritchie; Mercy James (Adopted Son); David Banda (Adopted Son); Estere (Adopted Daughter); Stelle (Adopted Daughter) **ED:** Coursework in Dance, Martha Graham; Coursework, Dance Scholarship, University of Michigan **C:** Designer, "Material Girl" Clothing Line (2011-Present); Chief Executive Officer, Maverick (1992-Present); Founder, Maverick (1992); Dancer, Alvin Ailey Dance Theater (1979) **CIV:** Co-Founder, Raising Malawi (2006-Present); Founder, Ray of Light Foundation (1998-Present) **CW:** Singer, Producer, Songwriter, Album, "Madame X" (2019); Singer, Live Album, "Rebel Heart Tour" (2017); Singer, Producer, Songwriter, Album, "Rebel Heart" (2015); Singer, Live Album, "MDNA World Tour" (2013); Herself, "Saturday Night Live" (1986, 1991, 1992, 1993, 2009, 2013); Singer, Producer, Songwriter, Album, "MDNA" (2012); Singer, Live Album, "Sticky & Sweet Tour" (2010); Author, "The English Roses: Catch the Bouquet!" (2010); Author, "The English Roses: American Dreams" (2010); Author, "The English Roses: Ready, Set, Vote!" (2010); Singer, Compilation Album, "Celebration" (2009); Author, "The English Roses: Runway Rose" (2009); Singer, Producer, Songwriter, Album, "Hard Candy" (2008); Herself, Narrator, Producer, Screenwriter, "I Am Because We Are" (2008); Director, Executive Producer, Screenwriter, "Filth and Wisdom" (2008); Executive Producer, "Alyx" (2008); Author,

"The English Roses: A Perfect Pair" (2008); Author, "The English Roses: Hooray for the Holidays!" (2008); Author, "The English Roses: Being Binah" (2008); Singer, Live Album, "The Confessions Tour" (2007); Singer, Live Album, "I'm Going to Tell You a Secret" (2006); Voice Actress, "Arthur and the Invisibles" (2006); Author, "The English Roses: Too Good to be True" (2006); Singer, Producer, Songwriter, Album, "Confessions on a Dance Floor" (2005); Herself, Executive Producer, "I'm Going to Tell You a Secret" (2005); Author, "Lotsa de Casha" (2005); Executive Producer, "Agent Cody Banks 2: Destination London" (2004); Executive Producer, "30 Days Until I'm Famous" (2004); Author, "Yakov and the Seven Thieves" (2004); Author, "Nobody Knows Me" (2004); Author, "The Adventures of Abdi" (2004); Author, "X-Static Process" (2003); Singer, Producer, Songwriter, Album, "American Life" (2003); Singer, Compilation Album, "Remixed & Revisited" (2003); Actress, "Will & Grace" (2003); Author, "Mr. Peabody's Apples" (2003); Author, "The English Roses" (2003); Actress, "Die Another Day" (2002); Actress, "Up for Grabs" (2002); Singer, Compilation Album, "GHV2" (2001); Singer, Producer, Songwriter, Album, "Music" (2000); Actress, "The Next Best Thing" (2000); Singer, Producer, Songwriter, Album, "Ray of Light" (1998); Actress, "Evita" (1996); Actress, "Girl 6" (1996); Singer, Compilation Album, "Something to Remember" (1995); Actress, "Four Rooms" (1995); Actress, "Blue in the Face" (1995); Singer, Producer, Songwriter, Album, "Bedtime Stories" (1994); Actress, "Dangerous Game" (1993); Actress, "Body of Evidence" (1993); Singer, Producer, Songwriter, Album, "Erotica" (1992); Actress, "A League of Their Own" (1992); Author, "Sex" (1992); Actress, "Shadows and Fog" (1991); Herself, Executive Producer, "Madonna: Truth or Dare" (1991); Singer, Producer, Songwriter, Soundtrack Album, "I'm Breathless: Music from and Inspired by the Film 'Dick Tracy'" (1990); Actress, "Dick Tracy" (1990); Singer, Compilation Album, "The Immaculate Collection" (1990); Singer, Producer, Songwriter, Album, "Like a Prayer" (1989); Actress, "Speed-the-Plow" (1988); Singer, Producer, Songwriter, Soundtrack Album, "Who's That Girl: Original Motion Picture Soundtrack" (1987); Singer, Compilation Album, "You Can Dance" (1987); Actress, "Who's That Girl" (1987); Singer, Producer, Songwriter, Album, "True Blue" (1986); Actress, "Shanghai Surprise" (1986); Actress, "Goose and Tom-Tom" (1986); Actress, "Desperately Seeking Susan" (1985); Actress, "Vision Quest" (1985); Actress, "A Certain Sacrifice" (1985); Host, "Saturday Night Live" (1985); Singer, Producer, Songwriter, Album, "Like a Virgin" (1984); Singer, Producer, Songwriter, Album, "Madonna" (1983); Author, Co-Author, "The English Roses" Book Series; Author, Contributor, Numerous Articles, Professional Publications; Herself, Numerous Commercials **AW:** Woman of the Year, Billboard Women in Music (2016); No. 1 Billboard Dance Club Songs Artist, Billboard Music Awards (2016); Best Foreign Language Pop Artist, Lunas del Auditorio (2009, 2013); Best Original Song, "Masterpiece," Golden Globe Awards (2012); Named, One of "The 100 Most Powerful Women" (2010); Inductee, Rock and Roll Hall of Fame (2008); Named One of "The 100 Most Powerful Celebrities," Forbes (2008); Best Long Form Music Video, "The Confessions Tour," Grammy Awards (2008); Best Electronic/Dance Album, "Confessions on a Dance Floor," Grammy Awards (2007); Style Icon Award, Elle Style Awards (2007); Hit of the Year, "Hung Up," Echo Awards (2006); Best International Female Artist, Echo Awards (2006); International Single of the Year, "Hung Up," Amadeus Austrian Music Awards (2006); International Artist of the Year Award, American Music Awards (2003); Best International Hit,

Best International Album, "Music," Danish Music Awards (2001); Best International Female Artist, Edison Award (1999, 2001); Best Song Written for a Motion Picture, Television or Other Visual Media, "Beautiful Stranger," Grammy Awards (2000); Best Video of the Year, "Music," Billboard Music Video Awards (2000); Best Short Form Music Video, "Ray of Light," Grammy Awards (1999); Best Dance Recording, "Ray of Light," Grammy Awards (1999); Best Pop Album, "Ray of Light," Grammy Awards (1999); Best International Album, "Ray of Light," Danish Music Awards (1999); Best Actress - Motion Picture Musical or Comedy, "Evita," Golden Globe Awards (1997); Best Actress, "Evita," American Moviegoers Awards (1997); Bronze Award - Female Singer, Bravo Otto Awards (1993, 1994); Best Music Video, Long Form, "Blonde Ambition World Tour Live," Grammy Awards (1992); Silver Award - Female Singer, Bravo Otto Awards (1989, 1992); People's Choice Award, International Rock Awards (1991); Award of Courage, American Foundation for AIDS Research (1991); Favorite Dance Single, "Vogue," American Music Awards (1991); Artist of the Decade: Mega Artist, MTV (1989); Best Video, "Express Yourself," Billboard Music Video Awards (1989); Artist of the Decade, Musician Magazine (1989); Best Female Vocalist, International Rock Awards (1989); Favorite Pop/Rock Female Video Artist, American Music Awards (1987); Gold Award - Female Singer, Bravo Otto Awards (1985, 1986, 1987)

VERSACE, DONATELLA FRANCESCA, T: Fashion Designer **I:** Apparel & Fashion **DOB:** 05/02/1955 **PB:** Reggio di Calabria **SC:** Italy **PT:** Antonio Versace; Francesca Versace **MS:** Divorced **SPN:** Manuel Dallori (2004, Divorced 2005); Paul Beck (1983, Divorced 2000) **CH:** Allegra; Daniel **ED:** Degree in Literature, University of Florence, Italy **C:** Creative Director, Versace (1997-Present); Chief Executive Officer, Versace (1997-2004); Vice President, Versace (1978-1997) **CR:** Designer, Palazzo Versace Dubai (2016); Designer, Palazzo Versace Australia, Gold Coast, QLD, Australia (2000); Launched, Haute Couture Show, Hôtel Ritz Paris (1998); Designer, Advertising Campaigns, Jennifer Lopez, Madonna, Courtney Love, Christina Aguilera, Jonathan Rhys Meyers, Demi Moore, Nicki Minaj, Lady Gaga **CIV:** Board Member, Versace, Versus, Palazzo Versace Dubai; Patron, Board Director, Elton John AIDS Foundation **CW:** Exhibited, Victoria and Albert Museum, London, England (2002-2003); Appearance, "Zoolander" (2001) **AW:** Fashion Icon Award, GQ Awards Berlin (2018); Honoree, Green Carpet Fashion Awards (2018); International CFDA Award (2018); Designer of the Year, GQ Men of the Year Awards (2018); Fashion Icon of the Year, Fashion Awards, British Fashion Council (2017); Fashion Designer of the Year, Glamour (2012, 2016); Woman of the Year, Glamour (2010); Nominee, Do Something With Style Award, VH1 Do Something Awards (2010); FGI Superstar Award (2008)

VESECKY, JOHN F., T: Science Educator, Electrical Engineering Educator, Researcher **I:** Education/Educational Services **CN:** University of California Santa Cruz **DOB:** 06/20/1940 **PB:** Dallas **SC:** TX/USA **PT:** Stephen Vesecky; Mary Emily (Baum) Vesecky **MS:** Married **SPN:** Cynthia Ann Noble-Vesecky (07/17/1991); Carol Ruth Benedict (12/20/1966, Divorced 07/1990) **CH:** Stephen Vesecky (High School Math Teacher); Holly Vesecky (Floral Designer/Business Owner) **ED:** PhD in Electrical Engineering, Stanford University (1967); MS in Electrical Engineering, Stanford University (1965); BS in Electrical Engineering, Rice University (1963); BA in Electrical Engineering, Rice University (1962) **C:** Professor of Founding Chairman of Electrical Engineering, Univeristy of California Santa Cruz; Professor, Atmospheric, Oceanic and Space Science, University of Michigan, Ann Arbor, MI (1990-2000); Professor, Electrical Engineering, Stanford University (1990-1993); Senior Research Associate, Center for Radar Astronomy, STAR Laboratory, Electrical Engineering Department, Stanford University (1976-1982); Research Associate, Center for Radar Astronomy, Radioscience Laboratory, Electrical Engineering Department, Stanford University (1969-1973); Associate Professor, Astronomy, University of Leicester, England (1971-1976); Research Fellow, Astronomy, University of Leicester, England (1967-1969); Research Assistant, Radioscience Laboratory, Stanford University (1963-1967) **CR:** Consultant, Environmental Task Force, Washington DC (1992-Present); Consultant, Department of Energy Technology Oversight, Washington DC (1991-Present); Consultant, Environmental Research Institute, Michigan (1985-Present); Consultant, MITRE Corp., McLean, VA (1982-Present); Consultant, JASON, San Diego, CA (1974-Present); Research Engineer, Consultant SRI International, Menlo Park, CA (1965-Present); Consultant, SAIC, San Diego, CA (1991-1995); Participant, Aspen Global Change Institute (1990, 1991); Consultant, NAS/NRC STAR Committee, Washington DC (1989-1991); Board Visiting, Member, Technology Advisory Group for Remote Sensing, Office of Naval Research (1988-1991); Consultant, English as Second Language, Inc., Sunnyvale, CA (1985-1990); Member, National Research Council, Polar Research Board ad hoc Panel on Remote Sensing of Ice and Snow (1985-1989); Member, NASA Task Force Science Uses of Space Station (1986-1988); Member, ERS-1 Product Support Group, British National Center for Remote Sensing (1982-1987); Member, Technology Program Committee, Oceans '83 Conference, San Francisco, CA (1983); Visiting Professor, University College of London (1982-1983); Member, British National Committee, Space Research Solar Physics Working Group (1974-1976) **CIV:** Head Coach, American Youth Soccer Organization, Palo Alto, CA (1977-1987); Head Coach, Stanford Area Youth Basketball (1980-1986); Junior Warden, Calvary Episcopal Church **CW:** Author, "Radar Remote Sensing from Spacecraft" (1990); Co-author, "Long Term Impacts of Increasing Atmospheric Carbon Dioxide Levels" (1982); Co-editor, "Wave Scattering from Statistically Rough Surfaces" (1979); Contributor, Articles, Professional Journals;Contributor, Chapters, Books **AW:** Rackham Research Partners Fellow (1992-1993); NASA Fellow Stanford University (1966-1967) **MEM:** Chairman, Santa Clara Valley Section, IEEE Geoscience and Remote Sensing Society (1989-1990); Fellow, Royal Astronomical Society; IEEE; American Astronomical Society; American Geophysical Union; Oceanography Society; International Astronomical Union; International Science Radio Union; American Meteorological Society **MH:** Albert Nelson Marquis Lifetime Achievement Award **B/I:** He became involved in his profession because of amateur radio and the help and support of his parents which allowed him to grow within his profession. **AV:** Basketball; Music; Ancient astronomy **PA:** Democrat **RE:** Episcopalian

VESTBERG, HANS, T: Chief Executive Officer **I:** Telecommunications **CN:** Verizon Communications Inc. **DOB:** 06/23/1965 **PB:** Hudiksvall **SC:** Sweden **MS:** Married **SPN:** Beatrice Vestberg **CH:** Two Children **ED:** BBA, Uppsala University (1991) **C:** Chairman, Verizon Communications Inc. (2019-Present); Chief Executive Officer, Verizon Communications Inc. (2018-Present); Executive Vice President, Chief Technology Officer, Global Networks, Verizon Communications Inc. (2017-2018); Chief Executive Officer, President, Erics-

son, Telefonaktiebolaget LM Ericsson (2010-2016); Chief Financial Officer, Ericsson, Telefonaktiebolaget LM Ericsson (2007-2009); Senior Vice President, Executive Vice President, Ericsson, Telefonaktiebolaget LM Ericsson (2003-2007); President, Ericsson, Telefonaktiebolaget LM Ericsson, Mexico (2002-2003); Chief Financial Officer, Ericsson, Telefonaktiebolaget LM Ericsson, North America (2000-2002); Chief Financial Officer, Ericsson, Telefonaktiebolaget LM Ericsson, Brazil (1998-2000); Joined, Ericsson Cables (1991) **CR:** Chairman, Swedish Olympic Committee (2016-2018); Chairman, Swedish Handball Association (2011-2016); Chairman, Swedish Handball Federation (2007-2016); Former Vice Chairman, Hexagon; Founding Member, Telecommunications Union (ITU) Broadband Commission for Digital Development; Founding Member, Broadband Commission for Digital Development; Member, Board of Directors, Sony Ericsson Mobile Communications AB; Member, Board, UN Foundation; Member, Board, Whitaker Peace & Development Initiative; Member, Board, Childhood USA **CIV:** Trainer, IFK Stocksund P02 **AW:** Ranked #10, List of the "100 Most Powerful People in the Telecoms Industry," Global Telecoms Business **MEM:** Leadership Council, Sustainable Development Solution Network, United Nations

VIRMANI, SANT SINGH, T: Agronomist, Researcher, Consultant **I:** Research **PB:** Pakistan **PT:** Mani Singh; Jeewan Kaur (Muniyal) V. **MS:** Married **SPN:** Inderjeet Kaur Narula (08/10/1969) **CH:** Raminder K.; Jusmeet S. **ED:** Doctor of Philosophy in Plant Breeding, Punjab Agricultural University, Ludhiana, India (1969); Master of Science in Agricultural Botany, Vikram University, Ujjain, India (1963); Bachelor of Science in Agriculture, Vikram University, Ujjain, India (1961) **C:** Freelance Consultant, International Agricultural Research and Development, Plano, TX (2006-Present); Principal Scientist, International Rice Research Institute (2004-2005); Rice Plant Breeder, Leader, Hybrid Rice Research and Development, International Rice Research Institute (1980-2005); Deputy Head, Plant Breeding, Genetics and Biochemistry Division, International Rice Research Institute (1990-2004); Visiting Scientist, International Rice Research Institute (1979-1980); Rice Breeder, International Institute of Tropical Agriculture, Ibadan, Nigeria (1973-1979); Assistant Geneticist in Legumes, Punjab Agricultural University (1972-1973); Postdoctoral Research Fellow, International Rice Research Institute, Manila, Philippines (1970-1972); Senior Research Fellow, University Grants Commission, Punjab Agricultural University (1966-1969); Research Assistant, Pearl Millet Genetics, Punjab Agricultural University (1964-1966); Research Assistant, Sesamum Breeding, Madhya Pradesh Department of Agriculture, Pawarkheda, India (1963-1964) **CR:** Consultant, International Rice Research Institute, Manila, Philippines (2005-2006); Food and Agriculture Organization, Rome (1988, 1991, 1992, 1993) **CIV:** Member, District 5810, Rotary Club, Frisco, TX (2007-Present); Paul Harris Fellow, Frisco Rotary Club (2015); Director, International Services, Frisco Rotary Club (2013-2014); Member, District 3820, Rotary Club (1987-2005); Paul Harris Fellow, Rotary Club, Los Banos, Philippines (2003); Director, International Services, Rotary Club, Los Banos, Philippines (2003) **CW:** Editorial Board, International Journal of Plant Breeding, Euphytica (1987-Present); Contributor, Over 250 Research Papers to Science Journals and Chapters to Books; Author, Reference Book on Hybrid Rice **AW:** Padma Shri Award (2008); Pravasi Bhartiya Samman Award, President of India (2005); The Koshihikari International Rice Prize, Japan (2005); Monsanto Crop Science Distinguished Career Award (2005); Agri-

culture and Rural Development Medal, Ministry of Agriculture, Vietnam (2002); International Service in Crop Science Award, Crop Science Society of America (2002); Third World Network Science Organizations Award (2000); Commendation Letter, Government of Liberia (1977) **MEM:** Fellow, American Association for the Advancement of Science; Indian Society of Genetics and Plant Breeding; National Academy of Agricultural Sciences; American Society of Agronomy; Crop Science Society of Philippines; Crop Science Society of America; Crop Improvement Society of India; Association of Rice Research Workers in India **MH:** Albert Nelson Marquis Lifetime Achievement Award **AV:** Cricket; Tennis; Indian music; Bridge **PA:** Progressive **RE:** Sikh

VISCLOSKY, PETER, "PETE" JOHN, T: U.S. Representative, Lawyer **I:** Government Administration/Government Relations/Government Services **DOB:** 08/13/1949 **PB:** Gary **SC:** IN/USA **PT:** John Visclosky; Helen (Kauzlaric) Visclosky **MS:** Married **SPN:** Joanne Royce (2008); Anne Marie O'Keefe (Divorced) **CH:** John; Timothy **ED:** LLM in International and Comparative Law, Georgetown University (1983); JD, The Law School, University of Notre Dame (1973); BS in Accounting, Indiana University Northwest, Indianapolis, IN (1970) **C:** U.S. Representative, Indiana's First Congressional District, United States Congress, Washington, DC (1985-Present); Associate, Greco, Gouveia, Miller, Pera & Bishop, Merrillville, IN (1982-1984); Associate Staff, Budget Committee, U.S. House of Representatives, Washington, DC (1980-1982); Associate Staff, Appropriations Committee, U.S. House of Representatives, Washington, DC (1976-1980); Associate, Benjamin, Greco & Gouveia, Merrillville, IN (1973-1976); Legal Assistant, District Attorney's Office, New York, NY (1972); Member, Appropriations Committee; Member, Subcommittees on Treasury, Postal Service, General Government and Military Construction **BAR:** Indiana State Bar Association; The District of Columbia Bar; Supreme Court of the United States **PA:** Democrat **RE:** Roman Catholic

VISENTIN, JOHN, T: Chief Executive Officer **I:** Technology **CN:** Xerox Corporation **ED:** Bachelor's Degree in Commerce, Concordia University **C:** Chief Executive Officer, Vice Chairperson, Xerox Holdings Corporation (2018-Present); Senior Adviser to the Chairperson, Exela Technologies (2017-Present); Operating Partner, Advent International (2017-Present); Founder, Menda Consulting LLC (2017-Present); Consultant, Icahn Capital (2018); Chairman, Board, Presidio (2015-2017); Executive Chairperson, Chief Executive Officer, Novitex Enterprise Solutions (2013-2017); Adviser, Apollo Global Management (2013-2017); Advisory Board Member, L2 Think Tank (2013-2014); Executive Vice President, General Manger, Enterprise Services, Hewlett Packard Enterprise (2011-2012); Senior Vice President, Enterprise Services, Hewlett Packard Enterprise (2011); General Manager, Integrated Technology Services North America, IBM (2007-2011); Global Vice President, End-User Services, IBM (2006-2007); Client Advocacy Executive, Office of the Chairman, IBM (2004-2006); Vice President, Industrial Sector, East Region, IBM (2001-2004); Various Positions, IBM Canada (1984-2001)

VITERITTI, JOHN FRANK II, I: Military & Defense Services **CN:** Independent Security and Investigative Contractor **DOB:** 05/03/1959 **PB:** Glen Cove **SC:** NY/USA **YOP:** N/A **PT:** John Viteritti; Marguerite Viteritti **MS:** Single **ED:** PhD in Security Management and International Operations, Summit University (2012); MS in Security Management, Almeda University; BS in Criminal Justice, Almeda

University; AS in Architectural Design, Summit University **CT:** Certifications in Security, Investigations and Law Enforcement **C:** Security, Investigations and Crisis Response Consultant, Private Military Corporations **CIV:** New York State Rifle and Pistol Association, Inc.; Second Amendment Foundation **MIL:** Para-Military Operations, U.S. Army (2002-2010); U.S. Marines (1983) **CW:** Dissertation, Dale Systems Inc. **AW:** The Rouse School Detective Award (1992) **MEM:** DTI Association; Special Forces Association; NRA; The American Legion **AS:** Mr. Viteritti attributes his success to his education and training. **B/I:** Mr. Viteritti became involved in his profession because of my interest in space flight. **PA:** Republican **RE:** Roman Catholic **THT:** Mr. Viteritti states, "Learning is a life long experience."

VOGLER, JAMES W., PHD, T: Physicist, Consultant **I:** Sciences **DOB:** 06/04/1948 **PB:** Barrington **SC:** IL/USA **PT:** Richard D.; Shirlee (Gardner) Vogler **ED:** Doctor of Science in Theoretical Physics, Cambridge University (1997); Doctor of Philosophy in Physics, University of California Berkeley (1988); Master of Arts in Physics, University of Illinois, Chicago, IL (1978); Bachelor of Science in Physics, Massachusetts Institute of Technology (1971) **C:** Partner, Vice President R&D, Senior Scientist, Atlantis Fiberoptics, Scottsdale, AZ (1988-Present); Partner, Senior Consultant, JV Associates, Phoenix, AZ (1986-Present); Senior Partner, Mirage/KLM Communications, Morgan Hill, CA (1989-2005); Staff Engineer, Consultant, Omni Spectra Division, M/A Company, Tempe, AZ (1983-1986); Staff Engineer, Motorola, Schaumburg, IL (1976-1983); Engineer, Hewlett-Packard, Palo Alto, CA (1971-1976); Student Contributor, Harvard Project Physics, Harvard University (1965-1968) **CR:** Consultant, Teledyne, Culver City, CA (1989-Present); Consultant, Rockwell International, Cedar Rapids, IA (1987-1989); Consultant, Hughes Aircraft Company, Los Angeles, CA (1987) **CW:** Contributor, Articles to Professional Journals; Patentee in Field **AW:** John T. Chambers Memorial Award, Central States VHF Society (1991); Fellow, National Science Foundation, University of Cambridge, England (1970) **MEM:** Institute of Electrical and Electronics Engineers; American Institute of Physics **MH:** Albert Nelson Marquis Lifetime Achievement Award; Marquis Who's Who Top Professional **B/I:** Dr. Vogler became involved in his profession due to his lifelong interest in mathematics. **AV:** Amateur radio; Horseback riding; Collecting and restoring historic sports cars

VOIGHT, JON, T: Actor **I:** Media & Entertainment **DOB:** 12/29/1938 **PB:** Yonkers **SC:** NY/USA **PT:** Elmer Voight; Barbara (Camp) Voight **MS:** Married **SPN:** Marcheline Bertrand (12/12/1971, Divorced 1980); Lauri Peters (1962, Divorced 1967) **CH:** James Haven; Angelina Jolie **ED:** Trainee, Sanford Meisner, Neighborhood Playhouse; Bachelor of Arts, Catholic University of America (1960) **C:** Member, Board of Trustees, Kennedy Center (2019); Actor, Film, Television **CW:** Actor, "JL Family Ranch 2" (2020); Actor, "Ray Donovan" (2013-2020); Actor, "Orphan Horse" (2018); Actor, "Surviving the Wild" (2018); Actor, "Same Kind of Different as Me" (2017); Actor, "Fantastic Beasts and Where to Find Them" (2016); Actor, "JL Ranch" (2016); Actor, "American Wrestler: The Wizard" (2016); Actor, "Baby Geniuses and the Space Baby" (2015); Actor, "Court of Conscience" (2015); Voice Actor, "A Christmas Eve Miracle" (2015); Actor, "Woodlawn" (2015); Actor, "Deadly Lessons" (2014); Actor, "Baby Geniuses and the Treasures of Egypt" (2014); Executive Producer, "The Final Song" (2014); Actor, "Baby Geniuses Television Series" (2013); Actor, "Dracula: The Dark Prince"

(2013); Actor, "Getaway" (2013); Actor, "Baby Geniuses and the Mystery of the Crown Jewels" (2013); Actor, "Beyond" (2012); Actor, "Lone Star" (2010); Actor, "24" (2009); Voice Actor, Audio Production, "The World of Promise" (2009); Actor, "24: Redemption" (2008); Actor, "Four Christmases" (2008); Actor, "An American Carol" (2008); Actor, "Pride and Glory" (2008); Himself, "Tropic Thunder" (2008); Actor, "National Treasure: Book of Secrets" (2007); Actor, "September Dawn" (2007); Actor, "Bratz" (2007); Actor, "Transformers" (2007); Actor, "Deadly Lessons" (2006); Actor, "Glory Road" (2006); Actor, "Pope John Paul II" (2005); Actor, "The Karate Dog" (2005); Actor, "The Five People You Meet in Heaven" (2004); Actor, "National Treasure" (2004); Actor, "Superbabies: Baby Geniuses 2" (2004); Actor, "Holes" (2003); Actor, "Jasper, Texas" (2003); Actor, "Second String" (2002); Actor, "Ali" (2001); Actor, "Jack and the Beanstalk: The Real Story" (2001); Actor, "Uprising" (2001); Actor, "Zoolander" (2001); Actor, "Lara Croft: Tomb Raider" (2001); Actor, "Pearl Harbor" (2001); Executive Producer, "The Princess & the Barrio Boy" (2000); Co-Executive Producer, "Baby Geniuses" (1999); Actor, "The Prince and the Surfer" (1999); Actor, "A Dog of Flanders" (1999); Actor, "Noah's Ark" (1999); Actor, "Boys Will be Boys" (1999); Actor, "Varsity Blues" (1999); Actor, "Enemy of the State" (1998); Actor, "The General" (1998); Actor, "The Fixer" (1998); Executive Producer, "The Fixer" (1998); Actor, "The Fixer" (1998); Actor, "The Rainmaker" (1997); Actor, "Most Wanted" (1997); Actor, "U Turn" (1997); Actor, "Anaconda" (1997); Actor, "Rosewood" (1997); Actor, "Mission: Impossible" (1996); Actor, "Heat" (1995); Actor, "Convict Cowboy" (1995); Director, "The Tin Soldier" (1995); Actor, "The Tin Soldier" (1995); Actor, "Seinfeld" (1994); Actor, "Return to Lonesome Dove" (1993); Actor, "The Rainbow Warrior" (1993); Actor, "The Last of His Tribe" (1992); Actor, "Chernobyl: The Final Warning" (1991); Actor, "Eternity" (1990); Actor, "Desert Bloom" (1986); Actor, "Runaway Train" (1985); Actor, "Table for Five" (1983); Actor, "Lookin' to Get Out" (1982); Actor, "The Champ" (1979); Actor, "Coming Home" (1978); Actor, "End of the Game" (1975); Actor, "The Odessa File" (1974); Actor, "Conrack" (1974); Actor, "The All-American Boy" (1973); Actor, "Deliverance" (1972); Actor, "The Revolutionary" (1970); Actor, "Catch-22" (1970); Actor, "Midnight Cowboy" (1969); Actor, "Out of It" (1969); Actor, "Gunsmoke" (1966-1969); Actor, "Cimarron Strip" (1968); Actor, "N.Y.P.D." (1967); Actor, "Hour of the Gun" (1967); Actor, "Fearless Frank" (1967); Actor, "NET Playhouse" (1966); Actor, "Summer Fun" (1966); Actor, "The Defenders" (1963); Actor, "Naked City" (1963) **AW:** National Medal of Arts, President Donald Trump (2019); Best Ensemble Cast, "American Wrestler: The Wizard," Boston Film Festival (2016); Lifetime Achievement Diamond Award, CineRockom International Film Festival (2015); Best Performance by an Actor in a Supporting Role in a Series, Miniseries or Motion Picture Made for Television, "Ray Donovan," Golden Globes (2014); Living Legends Award, Beverly Hills Film Festival (2011); Marquee Award, CineVegas International Film Festival (2009); Grand Prix Special des Amériques, Montreal World Film Festival (2007); Career Achievement Award, National Board of Review (2001); Francois Truffaut Award, Giffoni Film Festival (1995); Actor in a Movie or Ministeries, "The Last of His Tribe," CableACE Awards (1993); Best Performance by an Actor in a Motion Picture - Drama, "Runaway Train," Golden Globes (1986); Best Actor in a Leading Role, "Coming Home," Academy Awards (1979); Best Actor in a Motion Picture - Drama, "Coming Home," Golden Globes (1979); Best Actor, "Coming Home," Cannes Film Festival

(1978); Best Actor, "Coming Home," Los Angeles Film Critics Association Awards (1978); Best Actor, "Coming Home," National Board of Review (1978); Best Actor, "Coming Home," New York Film Critics Circle Awards (1978); Most Promising Newcomer - Male, "Midnight Cowboy," Golden Globes (1970); Most Promising Newcomer to Leading Film Roles, "Midnight Cowboy," BAFTA Awards (1970); Male New Face, "Midnight Cowboy," Laurel Awards (1970); Best Actor, "Midnight Cowboy," National Society of Film Critics Awards (1970); Best Actor, "Midnight Cowboy," New York Film Critics Circle Awards (1969)

VOLANDES, STELLENE, T: Editor-in-Chief **I:** Leisure, Travel & Tourism **CN:** Town & Country **ED:** BA in English, Vassar College (1993) **C:** Editor-in-Chief, Town & Country (2016-Present); Executive Style Director, Town & Country (2014-2016) **CR:** Senior Editor, American Express; Style Editor, Departures **CW:** Author, "Jeweler: Masters and Mavericks of Modern Design"

VOLZ, PAUL ALBERT, PHD, T: Director of Mycology Laboratory (Retired) **I:** Education/Educational Services **CN:** Eastern Michigan University **PB:** Ann Arbor **SC:** MI/USA **PT:** Albert Carl Volz; Frieda Clara (Laramee) Volz **ED:** Postgraduate Coursework, University of Houston (1970-1972); PhD in Business Administration, Century University (1991); PhD in Mycology, Michigan State University (1966); MS in Botany and Plant Pathology, Michigan State University (1962); BA in Business Administration and Botany, Heidelberg College (Now Heidelberg University) (1958) **C:** Retired, Director of Mycology Laboratory, Eastern Michigan University, Ypsilanti, MI (1976-Present); Professor, Eastern Michigan University, Ypsilanti MI (1971-Present); Associate Professor, Eastern Michigan University, Ypsilanti, MI (1969-1971); Senior Postdoctoral Fellow in Biospace Technician, NASA (1969-1971); Assistant Professor, Purdue University, Indianapolis, IN (1968-1969); Postdoctoral Student in Medical Mycology, Indiana University Medical Center (1966-1968); Assistant Professor, University of Wisconsin-Milwaukee (1962-1963) **CR:** U.S. Citizen Ambassador, People-to-People in Science, China (1996); U.S. Citizen Ambassador, People-to-People in Science, Delegate to Egypt, Israel, Turkey (1995); Visiting Professor, Haifa University, Israel (1995); Science Consultant, American Standards Testing Bureau, New York, NY (1979); Visiting Professor, Wayne State University, Detroit, MI (1977); Visiting Professor, National Taiwan University, Taipei, Taiwan (1974-1976); Consultant, Medical Mycology, Numerous Hospitals (1975) **CIV:** Member, United Church of Christ **CW:** Contributor, Articles to Professional Journals and Publications with NASA **AW:** Kholodny Medal, Ukrainian Institute Botanical (Now M.G. Kholodny Institute of Botany) and Soviet Academy of Science (Now Russian Academy of Sciences) (1990); NATO Faculty Fellow (1982-1985, 1989); Fellow, NASA (1967, 1972); Fellow, NASA Langley Research Center and Virginia Commonwealth University (1968); Fellow, National Science Foundation (1962) **MEM:** Chairman, Great Lakes Chapters, The Explorers Club; American Association for the Advancement of Science; ISHAM, The International Society Human and Animal Mycology; American Institute of Biological Sciences (AIBS); The American Society for Microbiology; American Fern Society; Mycological Society of America; Michigan Academy of Science, Arts, and Letters; Association for Tropical Biology and Conservation; Atlantic Council; The New York Academy of Science; Medical Mycological Society of America; Royal Geographical Society London (Now Royal Geographical Society with IBG); Ukrainian Botanical

Journal; The Explorers Club; American Society for Engineering Education (ASEE); Sigma Xi, The Scientific Research Honor Society **MH:** Albert Nelson Marquis Lifetime Achievement Award; Marquis Who's Who Top Professional **B/I:** Dr. Volz became inspired by his undergraduate major professor, Dr. A.G McQuate, who was his mentor and professor at Heidelberg University, and a great influence. He attended Heidelberg because it was religious based. He went there with the idea of becoming a minister; although all his undergraduate friends became ministers, he decided to go the science route. Dr. McQuate was so excited about the space program and Dr. Volz tried to keep him in the loop in terms of what was being done at NASA and Cape Canaveral. Dr. McQuate explained to Dr. Volz that he should minister the space sciences instead of the ministry of the Christian religion. Shortly after, Dr. Volz switched his major and followed Dr. McQuate's suggestion. Dr. Volz made science his career, as well as teaching, and he never regretted it. **AV:** Art history; Architecture

VON BAILLOU, ASTRID, T: Executive Search Consultant **I:** Staffing and Recruiting **CN:** Kinser & Baillou **DOB:** 03/02/1944 **PB:** Neutitschein **SC:** Czech Republic **PT:** Karl Von Baillou; Angela (Stillfried) Baillou **MS:** Married **SPN:** Dennis Hallam Bigelow (10/21/1967, Divorced 10/1994) **ED:** BA in English, Sweet Briar College (1965) **C:** President, Kinser & Baillou (2005-Present); Partner, Kinser & Associates, (2000-2005); Management Director, Kinser & Associates (1994-2000); President, Baillou International (1988-1994); Senior Vice President, Ruder Finn, Inc. (1986-1987); President, Cullen & Casey (1982-1986); Vice President, Science Program Group Television (1980-1982); On-Air Reporter, Producer, London Weekend TV, PBS, BBC (1972-1980); Creative Director, Freeman Advertising (1969-1972) **MH:** Albert Nelson Marquis Lifetime Achievement Award

VON FURSTENBERG, DIANE, T: Fashion Designer **I:** Apparel & Fashion **DOB:** 12/31/1946 **PB:** Brussels **SC:** Belgium **PT:** Leon L. Halfin; Liliane L. (Nahmias) Halfin **MS:** Married **SPN:** Barry Diller (02/02/2001); Prince Egon von Furstenberg (1969, Divorced 1983) **CH:** Prince Alexander; Princess Tatiana **ED:** Honorary Doctorate, The New School (2016); Coursework in Economics, University of Geneva; Coursework, Madrid University **C:** Spokesperson, Advocating Leadership Roles for Girls, Ban Bossy Campaign (2014-Present); Founder, Chairman, Diane von Furstenberg (DVF) (Formerly Diane von Furstenberg Studio, L.P.) (1972-Present); Founder, Salvy, Paris, France (1985) **CR:** Launched Children's Collection with GapKids (2012); Launched Signature Fragrance, DIANE (2011); Launched the DVF by H. Stern Fine Jewelry Collection (2004); Launched Silk Assets Collection (1992); Project Chair, New York City Mayor Michael Bloomberg's Review of the Future of NYC's Fashion Industry, New York City Economic Development Corporation (NYCEDC); Member, Board, Vital Voices **CIV:** Director, The Diller-von Furstenberg Family Foundation; Member, Board, The Statue of Liberty-Ellis Island Foundation, Inc.; Member, Board, The Shed **CW:** Executive Producer, Documentary, "Liberty: Mother of Exiles" (2019); Executive Producer, "House of DVF" (2014-2015); Appearance, "The Fashion Fund" (2014); Author, "The Woman I Wanted to Be" (2014); Co-author, "Journey of a Dress" (2014); Author, "Diane: A Signature Life" (2013); Guest Judge, "Project Runway" (2008, 2012); Co-author, "Diego Uchitel: Polaroids" (2012); Author, "American Fashion Travel: Designers on the Go" (2011); Co-author, "In Fashion: From Runway to Retail, Everything You Need to Know to Break into the Fashion Industry" (2010); Co-author, "The

Fashion Designer Survival Guide: Start and Run Your Own Fashion Business" (2008); Author, "Be the Wonder Woman You Can Be: The Adventures of Diva, Viva and Fifa" (2008); Executive Producer, "Andy Warhol: A Documentary," "American Masters" (2006); Executive Producer, "Forty Shades of Blue" (2005); Author, "The Table" (1996); Author, "Diane von Furstenberg's Book of Beauty: How to Become a More Attractive, Confident and Sensual Woman" (1977); Featured, Cover, Newsweek (1976) **AW:** CFDA Award for Positive Change (2018); Named to "Time 100," Time Magazine (2015); Fashion Icon Award, Harper's Bazaar Women of the Year Awards (2014); Listed, 68th Most Powerful Woman in the World, Forbes (2014); Named Among the "100 Most Powerful Women," Forbes (2011-2014); Named Among the "50 Most Powerful Women in New York," Crain's New York Business (2009, 2011); Jacqueline Kennedy Onassis Medal, Municipal Arts Society (2011); Gold Medal, Queen Sofia Spanish Institute's Gold Medal Gala (2010); Gold Medal, Queen Inductee, Fashion Walk of Fame (2008); Named Among the "50 Most Powerful Women in New York City," New York Post (2007); Named Among the "100 Most Influential Women in New York City Business" (2007); Glamour Award for the Style Powerhouse (2005); Lifetime Achievement Award, Council of Fashion Designers of America (CFDA) (2005); Ellis Island Medal of Honor (1986) **MEM:** President, Council of Fashion Designers of America (CFDA) (2006-Present)

VON FURSTENBERG, GEORGE, PHD, T: Economics Professor Emeritus **I:** Education/Educational Services **DOB:** 12/03/1931 **SC:** Germany **PT:** Kaspar Freiherr von Furstenberg; Elisabeth Freifrau von Furstenberg **MS:** Widowed **SPN:** Gabrielle M. Koblitz von Willmburg (06/09/1967, Deceased 2019) **CH:** Philip G. **ED:** PhD, Princeton University, Princeton, NJ (1967); BS in Economics, Princeton University, Princeton, NJ, Magna Cum Laude (1965); Student, School of General Studies, Columbia University (1963) **C:** Economic Program Director, National Science Foundation, Arlington, VA (2006-2008); J.H. Rudy Professor of Economics, Indiana University, Bloomington, IN (2002-2006); Robert Bendheim Professor, Economic and Financial Policy, Fordham University, New York, NY (2000-2002); J.H. Rudy Professor of Economics, Indiana University, Bloomington, IN (1983-2000); Division Chief, Research Department, International Monetary Fund, Washington, DC (1978-1983); Professor of Economics, Indiana University, Bloomington, IN (1976-1978); Senior Staff Economist, Council on Economic Advisers, Washington, DC (1973-1976); Associate Professor, Indiana University, Bloomington, IN (1970-1973); Assistant Professor, Cornell University, Ithaca, NY (1966-1970) **CR:** Visiting Research Economist, Economics Department, Deutsche Bundesbank, Frankfurt, Germany (2004); Bissell-Fulbright Visiting Professor, Canada-America Relations, University of Toronto, Canada (1994-1995); Visiting Senior Economist, Planning and Analysis Staff Department State, Washington, DC (1989-1990); Senior Adviser, Brookings Institution, Washington, DC (1978-1990); Project Director, American Council of Life Insurers, Washington, DC (1976-1978) **CW:** Author, "Contingent Convertibles [Colos]: A Potent Instrument for Financial Reform" (2014); Associate Editor, "Journal Economic Asymmetries" (2004-2010); Associate Editor, Open Economics Review (1997-2007); Co-Editor, "Monetary Unions and Hard Pegs: Effects on Trade, Financial Development, and Stability" (2004); Co-Author, "Learning from the World's Best Central Bankers" (1998); Co-Author, Editor, "Regulation and Supervision of Financial Institutions in the NAFTA Countries and Beyond" (1997); Associate Editor, "Rev. Econom-

ics and Statistics" (1987-1992); Co-Author, Editor, "Acting Under Uncertainty: Multidisciplinary Conceptions" (1990); Editor, "International Money and Credit: The Policy Roles" (1983); Co-Author, Editor, "The Government and Capital Formation" (1980); Co-Author, Editor, "Capital, Efficiency and Growth" (1980); Contributor, Numerous Articles, Professional Journals; Editor, Numerous Books; Contributor, Reviews, Op-Eds, Working Papers; Researcher, Numerous Presentations **AW:** Fulbright Grantee, Poland (1991-1992) **MEM:** President, North America Economics and Financial Association (2000); American Economic Association **MH:** Albert Nelson Marquis Lifetime Achievement Award; Marquis Who's Who Top Professional; Marquis Who's Who Humanitarian Award **B/I:** Dr. von Furstenberg became involved in his profession because after becoming a United States citizen, five years after immigrating, he needed to think of something that would pay a living wage. At the same time, he had a strong commitment to social policy and economic aspects. He wanted to combine the two, and economics seemed like a natural field to pursue. In the 1960s, he was concerned with social issues, social welfare, and efficiency considerations. Richard Musgraves was very big at the time and was extremely focused on economic issues. **AV:** Playing tennis **RE:** Roman Catholic

VON SELDENECK, JUDITH, "JUDY" CROWELL, T: Interior Design Consultant (Retired) **I:** Consulting **DOB:** 02/12/1945 **PB:** New Rochelle **SC:** NY/USA **PT:** Robert Kenyon Crowell; Susan Mitchell Crowell **MS:** Married **SPN:** Roger Dean von Seldeneck (53 Years) **CH:** Jeffrey Dean von Seldeneck; Jillaine M. von Seldeneck (Daughter-in-Law); Jake (Grandson); Jaysen (Grandson) **ED:** AA, Averett Univeristy; BA, University of Richmond **CT:** Certificate (Home Study), New York School of Interior Design **CR:** Officer of Election, Office of Elections, Voter Registration of Harrisonburg, VA (13 Years, Retired 2020) **MEM:** National Society Daughters of the American Revolution (NSDAR) (1970-Present); VADAR-Massanutten Chapter District VI, National Society Daughters of the American Revolution (NSDAR); Honorary Regent, Past District VI Director; Past Organizing Secretary, VADAR; Mayflower Society; P.E.O. Sisterhood; Past Session Member, First Presbyterian Church, Harrisonburg, VA **MH:** Albert Nelson Marquis Lifetime Achievement Award **AS:** Ms. von Seldeneck attributes her success to her faith and hard work. **B/I:** Mrs. von Seldeneck became involved in her profession because her grandmother, Pearl R. Mitchell, was an American Society of Interior Designers (ASID) designer in New York City. She spent several summers with "Mama" working in the city and started her career in Lynchburg, Virginia, after completing her education at New York School of Interior Design. She worked in the field, specializing in picture groupings and furniture arrangement for her clients. While living in Baltimore, Maryland, she taught Business English & Interior Design at Patricia Stevens Career College. **AV:** Walking **PA:** Republican **RE:** Presbyterian **THT:** Ms. von Seldeneck believes in a quote from Proverbs 3: 5&6: "Trust in the Lord with all your heart, lean not on your own understanding. In all your ways acknowledge Him and He will direct your paths."

VON STAR, BRENDA LEE, BSN, FNPC, T: Primary Care Family Nurse Practitioner **I:** Medicine & Health Care **DOB:** 02/05/1948 **PB:** Lakeview **SC:** OR/USA **PT:** Leslie Darrell Denstedt; May Mabel (Hirsch) Denstedt **MS:** Divorced **SPN:** Jimmie E. Muro (8/20/1977, Divorced 1990) **CH:** Michael; Christine **ED:** BSN, Metropolitan State University, Denver, CO (1978); AS, Lane Community College,

Eugene, OR (1972) **CT:** Legal Nurse Consultant, Paralegal School of Legal Nurse Consulting, Kaplan College for Professional Studies, Boca Raton, FL (2003); Certified Family Nurse Practitioner; Advanced Cardiovascular Life Support (ACLS) **C:** Advanced Family Health, Louisville, CO (2008-2011); Family Practice Nurse Practitioner, Wheat Ridge Family Clinic (2006-2008); Front Range Clinical Research (2006-2008); Special Counsel, Wheeler, Trigg & Kennedy, Denver, CO (2005-2006); Metropolitan State University, Denver, CO (2003-2005); Family Medicine Associate, Broomfield, CO (1995-2003); Auraria Student Health, Arbor Family Medicine, Thornton, CO (1991-1995); Clinical Director of Research, Family Futures Project, Denver, CO (1990-1991); Private Collaborative Practice, Lutheran Family Practice, Arvada, CO (1985-1990); Family Pediatric Nurse Practitioner, Tri-County Health Department, Denver, CO (1982-1985); Salud Health Clinic, Ft. Lupton, CO (1980-1982); Burn Unit Nurse, University of Colorado Health Science Center, Denver, CO (1976-1980); Surgical ICU Nurse, St. Lukes Hospital, Denver, CO (1973-1976); Staff Nurse, Medical Unit, Presbyterian Intercommunity Hospital, Klamath Falls, OR (1972-1973) **CR:** Appointed, State of Colorado Medicaid Improvement Program Advisory Council (2010-2016); Chair, Colorado Nurses Association Subcommittee on Health Care Reform (2008-2011) **CIV:** U.S. Navy (1967-1970); Hospital Corp Wave **MIL:** U.S. Navy (1967-1970) **MEM:** American Academy of Nurse Practitioners; Secretary, Partners Without Partners; Colorado Nurses Association; American Association of University Women; American Association of Legal Nurse Consultants **MH:** Albert Nelson Marquis Lifetime Achievement Award **AS:** Ms. Von Star attributes her success to her grandfather's support. She additionally credits several nurses who guided her when she was first starting out in her career. Likewise, Inez Larson encouraged her to join the U.S. Navy, which provided her with an education. **B/I:** Ms. Von Star always liked to help others. She had a desire to be a nurse from childhood. While in the Navy, she witnessed independent duty corpsmen in action, which inspired her to become a nurse practitioner. **AV:** Hiking; Camping; Gardening; Researching American history; Playing tennis **PA:** Democrat

VONN, LINDSEY CAROLINE, T: Professional Skier **I:** Athletics **DOB:** 10/18/1984 **PB:** St. Paul **SC:** MN/USA **PT:** Alan Lee Kildow; Linda Anne (Krohn) Kildow **MS:** Engaged **SPN:** P.K. Subban (8/23/2019); Thomas Vonn (09/29/2007, Divorced 2013) **ED:** Diploma, University of Missouri High School **C:** Professional Alpine Skier, International Ski Federation (2000-Present); Member, U.S. Ski Team, Winter Olympic Games, Vancouver, British Columbia, Canada (2010); Member, U.S. Ski Team, Winter Olympic Games, Turin, Italy (2006); Member, U.S. Ski Team, Winter Olympic Games, Salt Lake City, UT (2002) **CW:** Author, "Rise: My Story" (2021); Herself, Documentary, "Lindsey Vonn: The Final Season" (2019); Author, "Strong Is the New Beautiful: Embrace Your Natural Beauty, Eat Clean, and Harness Your Power" (2016); Guest Appearance, "Law & Order" (2010); Featured, Cover, Glamour; Featured, Cover, Women's Health; Featured, Cover, Fitness; Featured, Cover, Sports Illustrated; Featured, Cover, ESPN; Featured, Cover, TV Guide **AW:** Princess of Asturias Award for Sports (2019); Named, 100 Most Influential People in the World, TIME Magazine (2013); Women's Combined Champion, FIS Alpine Ski World Cup (2010-2012); Women's Super G Champion, FIS Alpine Ski World Cup (2009-2012); Women's Downhill Champion (2008-2012); Women's Overall Champion (2008-2010, 2012); Best Female Athlete, ESPY Awards (2010, 2011); Kids' Choice Award for Favorite Female Athlete (2011); Laureus World Sports Award for Sportswoman of the Year (2011); Female Athlete of the Year, Associated Press (2010); Laureus Sportswoman of the Year (2010); Glamour Award for the Game Changer (2010); Gold Medal, Women's Downhill, Bronze Medal, Women's Super G, Winter Olympic Games (2010); Slieur d'Or Award (2009); Gold Medal, Downhill, Super G, FIS Alpine World Ski Championships, Val d'Isere, France (2009); Named, Athlete of the Year, Minneapolis Star Tribune (2008); Silver Medal, Downhill, Super G, FIS Alpine World Ski Championships, Are, Sweden (2007); U.S. Olympic Spirit Award (2006) **AV:** Playing tennis; Golfing; Spending time with her family and dogs

VOORHEES, STEVEN C., T: Chief Executive Officer **I:** Business Management/Business Services **CN:** WestRock **ED:** MBA, UVA Darden School of Business (1980); BA in Economics and Mathematics, Northwestern University **C:** Chief Executive Officer, President, Director, WestRock (2017-Present); Chief Executive Officer, RockTenn (2013-2015); Chief Operating Officer, President, RockTenn (2013); Chief Administrative Officer (2008-2013); Executive Vice President, Chief Financial Officer, RockTenn (2000-2013); Managing Partner, Kinetic Partners, LLC (1999-2000); Senior Vice President, Sonat Energy Services, Sonat, Inc.; Executive Vice President, Sonat Marketing Services, Sonat, Inc.; Management Positions in Electric Power Marketing, Interstate Gas Transmission, Exploration, Production and International Offshore Drilling, Senior Vice President, Sonat, Inc. **CR:** Member, Board of Directors, SunTrust Banks **CIV:** Donor, UVA Darden School of Business

VOTTO, JOSEPH DANIEL, T: Professional Baseball Player **I:** Athletics **CN:** Cincinnati Reds **DOB:** 09/10/1983 **PB:** Toronto **SC:** ON/Canada **PT:** Joseph Votto; Wendy (Howell) Votto **MS:** Single **ED:** Diploma, Richview Collegiate Institute **C:** First Baseman, Cincinnati Reds (2007-Present) **AW:** National League All-Star (2010-2013, 2017-2018); National League Player of the Week (2009, 2011, 2013, 2017-2018); Lou Gehrig Memorial Award (2017); Lou Marsh Trophy (2010, 2017); Tip O'Neill Award (2010, 2012-2013, 2015-2017); Gold Glove Award (2011); National League Most Valuable Player (2010); National League Hank Aaron Award (2010); Ernie Lombardi Award (2010); Syl Apps Athlete of the Year Award (2010); National League Rookie of the Month (2008); Several Minor League Honors

WACHTEL, ALAN R. PHD, T: Clinical Psychologist **I:** Medicine & Health Care **CN:** Alan R. Wachtel, PhD **PB:** New York **SC:** NY/USA **PT:** Nathan Wachtel; Estelle (Sollow) Wachtel **CH:** One Daughter; Two Granddaughters **ED:** PhD in Clinical Psychology, University of Montana (1973); Doctoral Dissertation, The Application of a Motivational Theory of Personality to the Study of Incidental Stimulation (1973); Clinical Psychology Internship, New York University Medical Center (1972-1973); MS in Clinical Psychology, Long Island University (1968); BA in Psychology, Pre-Med, Adelphi University (1966) **CT:** New York State Licensed Psychologist **C:** Private Practice, Clinical Psychology, Montrose, NY (1978-Present); Retired (2017); F.D.R. Department of Veterans Affairs Medical Center (1974-2017); Behavioral Specialist, Occupations Inc., Middletown, NY (1973); Teaching Assistant, University of Montana (1969-1972); Clinical psychologist; Psychology Intern Supervisor; Clinical Team Leader; Senior Member, Psychiatric and Behavioral Emergency Code Team; Consultant, Early Co-occurring Disorders Unit; Psychologist, Three Different Substance Use Disorders Units, MICA Program; Psychologist, Psychiatric Intensive Care Unit; Consultant, Other Units; Assisted by Talking a Person down from a Suicide Attempt, New York State Police, Buffalo, NY **AW:** Honorable Mention, GEICO Public Service Award (1984) **MEM:** New York State Psychological Association (NYSPA); American Psychological Association (APA) **MH:** Who's Who in the East; Albert Nelson Marquis Lifetime Achievement Award; Marquis Who's Who Top Health Care Professional **AS:** He attributes his success to learning the value of prescriptive treatment and obtaining training and experience with a large number of evidence based techniques that he could integrate for more effective treatment. This is not the case for many mental health workers who treat everybody with the few techniques that their training schools favored regardless of what the individual patient needs. In addition, he understood that proper and accurate expertise in assessment should be part of every mental health worker's training so that treatment techniques are applied based on what is wrong with the patient rather than the few techniques that the practitioner knows. **B/I:** Dr. Wachtel's parents encouraged him and his brother to pursue higher education and an education based career despite the fact that their own education was limited. Dr. Wachtel was always interested in a health related career and in human behavior. His older brother was a psychologist and Dr. Wachtel eventually concluded that it would also be an interesting career for him as well.

WADE, ROBERT PAUL, JD, T: Lawyer, General Counsel **I:** Law and Legal Services **DOB:** 08/22/1936 **PB:** Atlantic City **SC:** NJ/USA **PT:** John Joseph Wade; Irene Madeline (Saxon) Wade **MS:** Married **SPN:** Jeanne Krohn (08/05/1979) **CH:** Elliott Saxon; Kellyn Deirdre **ED:** JD, School of Law, The George Washington University (1968); BA in Philosophy, The George Washington University (1963) **C:** Partner, Robert Wade, Esq. (1994-Present); General Counsel, Executive Director, Rhythm & Blues Foundation (1986-2000); Partner, Silverberg and Wade (1986-1994); Attorney, (1984-1988); Partner, Wade & Low (1983-1986); General Counsel, National Endowment for the Arts (1972-1984); Attorney, Adviser, General Accounting Office (1970-1972); Attorney, Office of the Comptroller (1969-1972); Attorney, Private Practice (1968-1970); Associate, Denning & Wohlstetter (1968-1969) **CR:** Visiting Lecturer, Stanford University; Visiting Lecturer, New York University; Visiting Lecturer, The George Washington University **CIV:** Actor, Winchester Little Theater; Actor, Blackhearts Art Center **MIL:** Photographer, U.S. Army (1955-1958) **MEM:** Phi Sigma Tau, The International Honor Society of Philosophers **BAR:** Maryland State Bar Association (1990); DC Bar (1968) **MH:** Albert Nelson Marquis Lifetime Achievement Award **B/I:** Mr. Wade became involved in his profession because of his time as a photographer in the U.S. Army. After leaving the military, he became interested in law and philosophy. **AV:** Taking photographs

WAGNER, ANN LOUISE, T: U.S. Representative from Missouri **I:** Government Administration/Government Relations/Government Services **DOB:** 09/13/1962 **PB:** St. Louis **SC:** MO/USA **MS:** Married **SPN:** Ray Wagner **CH:** Raymond III; Stephen; Mary Ruth **ED:** BSBA, University of Missouri (1984) **C:** Member, U.S. House of Representatives from Missouri's Second Congressional District, United States Congress, Washington, DC (2013-Present); Member, U.S. House Committee on Financial Services (2013-Present); Chairwoman, Roy Blunt's Senatorial Campaign (2009-2010); U.S. Ambassador to Luxembourg, United States Department of State, Luxembourg (2005-2009); Co-chairman,

Republican National Committee, Washington, DC (2001-2005); Second Congressional District Chair, Bob Dole Presidential Campaign (1996); Advisor, Ashcroft for Senate Campaign (1994); Missouri State Executive Director, Bush/Quayle Campaign (1992); Chairman, Missouri Republican Party, Jefferson City, MO (1999-2001); Director, Missouri House and Senate Redistricting Commission, Missouri Republican Party (1991); Member, Missouri Federation of Republican Women (MoFRW); Chairman, St. Louis County Republican Central Committee, MO; Member, Committee, Lafayette Township, MO; Member, Committee on Oversight and Government Reform, United States Congress **MEM:** Committee on Arrangements, Midwestern State Chairmen's Association (2000); Delegate, Midwestern State Chairmen's Association (2000); Delegate Chairman, Midwestern State Chairmen's Association (2000); Republican National Convention; Midwestern State Chairmen's Association **PA:** Republican **RE:** Catholic

WAGNER-MANN, COLETTE CAROL, T: Adjunct Associate Teaching Professor **I:** Veterinary Care **CN:** University of Missouri College of Veterinary Medicine **DOB:** 12/03/1952 **PB:** St. Louis **SC:** MO/USA **PT:** Michael J.; Colette D. Wagner **MS:** Married **SPN:** Fred Anthony Mann **CH:** Lucas; Danielle **ED:** PhD, Texas A&M University, College Station, TX (1988); DVM, University of Missouri, Columbia, MO (1983); MA, University of Missouri, Columbia, MO (1977); BA, University of Missouri, Columbia, MO (1974) **C:** Associate Teaching Professor, University of Missouri, Columbia, MO (2011-Present); Research Assistant Professor, University of Missouri, Columbia, MO (1991-2006); Research Associate, University of Missouri, Columbia, MO (1988-1991); Director of Research, Southern Heart & Lung Institute, Opelika, AL (1988); Research Associate, Auburn University, Auburn, AL (1987-1988); Veterinary Clinical Associate, Texas A&M University, College Station, TX (1983-1986); Graduate Fellow, University of Missouri, Columbia, MO (1983) **CW:** Contributor, Articles, American Journal of Veterinary Research, International Journal Angiology **AW:** SAVMA Teaching Award for Basic Sciences (2020); VM1 Golden Aesculapius Teaching Award (2020); Young Investigator Award, Emil Bozler Symposium (1989); AH Growth Award (1983); Curators Scholar, University of Missouri (1971, 1974) **MEM:** American Veterinary Medical Association; Phi Zeta Veterinary Honor Society **MH:** Albert Nelson Marquis Lifetime Achievement Award **AS:** Dr. Wagner-Mann attributes her success to her faith in God, as well as her loving parents and supportive spouse. **B/I:** Dr. Wagner-Mann became involved in her teaching profession because she liked to interact with people. In regard to her veterinary work, she loved animals and it seemed like a good fit whereby she could work with both people and animals. **AV:** Practicing photography; Hiking; Backpacking **RE:** Roman Catholic

WAHLBERG, MARK, T: Actor, Producer, Businessman **I:** Media & Entertainment **DOB:** 06/05/1971 **PB:** Dorchester **SC:** MA/USA **PT:** Donald Edmond Wahlberg; Alma Elaine Wahlberg **MS:** Married **SPN:** Rhea Durham (08/01/2009) **CH:** Ella Rae; Grace Margaret; Michael; Brendan Joseph **C:** Co-investor, F45 Training (2019-Present); Co-partner, Bobby Layman Chevrolet (2018-Present); Co-investor, StockX (2017-Present); Co-founder, Performance Inspired (2016-Present); Co-investor, AQUAhydrate (2015-Present); Co-owner, Barbados Tridents Cricket Team (2013-Present); Co-owner, Wahlburgers (2011-Present); Actor; Producer; Rapper; Businessman **CIV:** Founder, Mark Wahlberg Youth Foundation (2001-Present); Active Supporter, Good Shepherd Center for Homeless Women and Children **CW:** Actor, "Good Joe Vell" (2020); Actor, "Infinite" (2020); Voice Actor, "Scoob!" (2020); Actor, Producer, "Spenser Confidential" (2020); Executive Producer, "McMillions" (2020); Executive Producer, "40 Days: GGG vs. Steve Rolls" (2019); Appearance, "Wahlburgers" (2014-2019); Executive Producer, "Shooter" (2016, 2018); Actor, "Instant Family" (2018); Actor, Producer, "Mile 22" (2018); Producer, "Instant Family" (2018); Executive Producer, "Ballers" (2015-2018); Actor, "All the Money in the World" (2017); Actor, Executive Producer, "Daddy's Home 2" (2017); Actor, "Transformers: The Last Knight" (2017); Actor, Producer, "Patriots Day" (2016); Actor, Producer, "Deepwater Horizon" (2016); Actor, "Daddy's Home" (2015); Actor, "Ted 2" (2015); Appearance, Producer, "Entourage" (2015); Producer, "Entourage" (2015); Actor, "Mojave" (2015); Executive Producer, "Stealing Cars" (2015); Actor, "The Gambler" (2014); Actor, "Transformers: Age of Extinction" (2014); Producer, "Breaking Boston" (2014); Producer, "The Gambler" (2014); Executive Producer, "Boardwalk Empire" (2010-2014); Actor, "Lone Survivor" (2013); Actor, "2 Guns" (2013); Actor, "Pain & Gain" (2013); Actor, "Broken City" (2013); Executive Producer, "Teamsters" (2013); Executive Producer, "The Missionary" (2013); Producer, "Lone Survivor" (2013); Executive Producer, "Prisoners" (2013); Producer, "Broken City" (2013); Actor, "Ted" (2012); Actor, Producer, "Contraband" (2012); Executive Producer, "Home Game" (2011); Executive Producer, "How to Make It in America" (2010-2011); Executive Producer, "Entourage" (2004-2011); Actor, Producer, "The Fighter" (2010); Actor, "The Other Guys" (2010); Actor, "Date Night" (2010); Executive Producer, "Untitled Ben Schwerin Project" (2010); Executive Producer, "In Treatment" (2008-2010); Actor, "The Lovely Bones" (2009); Actor, "Max Payne" (2008); Actor, "The Happening" (2008); Actor, "We Own the Night" (2007); Actor, "Shooter" (2007); Producer, "We Own the Night" (2007); Actor, "The Departed" (2006); Actor, "Invincible" (2006); Actor, "Four Brothers" (2005); Actor, "I Heart Huckabees" (2004); Executive Producer, "Juvies" (2004); Actor, "The Italian Job" (2003); Actor, "The Truth About Charlie" (2002); Actor, "Rock Star" (2001); Actor, "Planet of the Apes" (2001); Actor, "The Perfect Storm" (2000); Actor, "The Yards" (2000); Actor, "Three Kings" (1999); Actor, "The Corrupter" (1999); Actor, "The Big Hit" (1998); Actor, "Boogie Nights" (1997); Actor, "Traveller" (1997); Actor, "Fear" (1996); Rapper, Marky Mark, "Hey DJ" (1996); Rapper, Marky Mark, "No Mercy" (1995); Rapper, Prince Ital Joe Feat. Marky Mark, "Babylon" (1995); Actor, "The Basketball Diaries" (1995); Rapper, Prince Ital Joe feat. Marky Mark, "Life in the Streets" (1994); Rapper, Prince Ital Joe Feat. Marky Mark, "United" (1994); Actor, "Renaissance Man" (1994); Rapper, Prince Ital Joe Feat. Marky Mark, "Happy People" (1993); Actor, "The Substitute" (1993); Actor, "Out All Night" (1993); Actor, "The Ben Stiller Show" (1993); Rapper, Marky Mark and the Funky Bunch, "Gonna Have a Good Time" (1992); Rapper, Marky Mark and the Funky Bunch, "Make My Video" (1992); Rapper, Marky Mark and the Funky Bunch, Song, "You Gotta Believe" (1992); Rapper, Producer, Album, "You Gotta Believe" (1992); Rapper, Marky Mark and the Funky Bunch, "I Need Money" (1991); Rapper, Marky Mark and the Funky Bunch, "Wildside" (1991); Appearance, MC Hammer, "2 Legit 2 Quit" (1991); Rapper, Marky Mark and the Funky Bunch, "Good Vibrations" (1991); Rapper, Producer, Album, "Music for the People" (1991) **AW:** Generation Award, MTV Movie Awards (2014); Named Best Actor in an Action Movie, "Lone Survivor," Broadcast Film Critics Association Awards (2014); Indie Impact Award, Palm Springs International Film Festival (2011); Named One of "The 100 Most Influential People in the World," TIME (2011); Named Best Ensemble Cast, "The Fighter," Boston Society of Film Critics Awards (2010); Named Best Actor, "The Fighter," African-American Film Critics Association (AAFCA) (2010); Recipient, Star, Hollywood Walk of Fame (2010); Named Best International Programme, "Entourage," BAFTA (British Academy of Film and Television Arts) Awards (2007); Named Best Supporting Actor, "The Departed," National Society of Film Critics Awards (2007); Named Best Supporting Actor, "The Departed," Boston Society of Film Critics Awards (2006); Named Best Supporting Performance, "The Departed," Indiewire Critics' Poll (2006); Named Best Ensemble, Motion Picture, "The Departed," Satellite Awards (2006)

WALBERG, TIMOTHY, "TIM" LEE, T: U.S. Representative from Michigan; Former Pastor **I:** Government Administration/Government Relations/Government Services **DOB:** 04/12/1951 **PB:** Chicago **SC:** IL/USA **PT:** John Andrew Walberg; Alice (Wilcox) Walberg **MS:** Married **SPN:** Susan Gail Polensky (1973) **CH:** Matthew Lee; Heidi Gail; Caleb Paul **ED:** MA in Communications, Wheaton College Graduate School (1978); BS in Christian Education, Fort Wayne Bible College (Now Taylor University) (1975); Coursework, Western Illinois University (1969-1970) **CT:** Ordained Pastor **C:** Member, U.S. House of Representatives from Michigan's Seventh Congressional District, United States Congress, Washington, DC (2007-2009, 2011-Present); Member, U.S. House Committee on Oversight and Workforce, Washington, DC (2011-Present); Member, U.S. House Committee on Education and Workforce, Washington, DC (2011-Present); Member, U.S. House Committee on Homeland Security, Washington, DC (2011-Present); Division Manager, Moody Bible Institute, Chicago, IL (2001-2006); President, Warren Reuther Center for Education and Community Impact (1999-2001); Member, District 57, Michigan House of Representatives (1983-1998); Pastor, Union Gospel Church, Tipton, MI (1978-1983); Pastor, New Haven Baptist Church, IN (1973-1977); Member, U.S. Committee on Energy and Commerce; Member, Republican Study Committee **CR:** Member, Basic Human Needs Task Force, Lenawee County, MI **MEM:** Lenawee County Riding for Handicapped (Now Lenawee Therapeutic Riding); Kiwanis Club, Tecumseh, MI **PA:** Republican

WALCHER, ALAN E., T: Lawyer **I:** Law and Legal Services **DOB:** 10/02/1949 **PB:** Chicago **SC:** IL/USA **PT:** Chester R. Walcher; Dorothy E. (Kullgren) Walcher **MS:** Married **SPN:** Penny M. Walcher **CH:** Ronn; Dustin; Michael; Christopher **ED:** Doctor of Jurisprudence (1974); Bachelor of Science, University of Utah (1971) **CT:** Certified in International Relations (1971) **C:** Sole Practice (2003-Present); Partner, Epstein Becker & Green, Los Angeles, CA (1991-2003); Partner, Ford & Harrison, Los Angeles, CA (1988-1991); Judge Pro Tempore, Municipal Court, Los Angeles, CA (1986-1991); Partner, Walcher & Scheuer, Los Angeles, CA (1985-1988); Partner, Costello & Walcher, Los Angeles, CA (1979-1985); Director, Citronia Inc., Los Angeles, CA (1979-1981); Sole Practice, Salt Lake City, UT (1974-1979) **CIV:** Trial Counsel, Utah Chapter Common Cause, Salt Lake City, UT (1978-1979) **AW:** Robert Mukai Scholar, University of Utah (1971); AV Preeminent Rating, Martindale-Hubbell **MEM:** Vice President, Society of Bar & Gavel (1975-1977); American Bar Association; Owl & Key; Association of Business Trial Lawyers; Century City Bar Association, Los Angeles County Bar Association; Federal Bar Association; Phi Delta Phi **BAR:** U.S. District Court, California (1994); United

States Court of Appeals for the Ninth Circuit (1983); United States District Court for the Central District of California (1979); State of California (1979); United States Court of Appeals for the Tenth Circuit (1977); United States District Court for the District of Utah (1974); State of Utah (1974) **MH:** Albert Nelson Marquis Lifetime Achievement Award

WALDEN, DANA, T: Chief Executive Officer **I:** Media & Entertainment **DOB:** 10/13/1964 **PB:** Los Angeles **SC:** CA/USA **MS:** Married **SPN:** Matt Walden (1995) **CH:** Two Children **ED:** BA in Communications, University of Southern California **C:** Chairwoman, Walt Disney Television (2019-Present); Chairwoman, ABC Entertainment (2019-Present); Co-Chairwoman, 20ᵗʰ Century Fox Television (2007-Present); Co-Chairwoman, Co-Chief Executive Officer, Fox Television Group, 20ᵗʰ Century Fox Television (2014-2019); Executive Vice President, Drama & Comedy, 20ᵗʰ Century Fox Television (1999-2007); Programming Executive, 20ᵗʰ Century Fox Television; Public Relations, 20ᵗʰ Century Fox Television; Manager, Marketing and Communications, "The Arsenio Hall Show"; Vice President, Bender, Goldman & Helper; Assistant, Larry Goldman, Bender, Goldman & Helper **CR:** Member, Board of Directors, Live Nation Entertainment; Member, Board, Hulu **CIV:** Board Member, Los Angeles Zoo; Supporter, Chance for Bliss **CW:** Voice Actress, "Family Guy" (2016, 2019) **AW:** Named One of "The 100 Most Powerful Women in Entertainment," The Hollywood Reporter (1999-2014); Co-Recipient, Showmanship Award, Television, Publicists Guild of America (2011) **MEM:** Vice President, Hollywood Radio & TV Society (2003-Present)

WALDEN, GREGORY, "GREG" PAUL, T: U.S. Representative from Oregon **I:** Government Administration/Government Relations/Government Services **DOB:** 01/10/1957 **PB:** The Dalles **SC:** OR/USA **PT:** Paul Walden; Elizabeth (McEwen) Walden **MS:** Married **SPN:** Mylene Walden (1982) **CH:** Anthony **ED:** BS in Journalism, University of Oregon, Eugene, OR (1981) **C:** Chairman, National Republican Congressional Committee (NRCC) (2013-Present); Member, U.S. House of Representatives from Oregon's Second Congressional District, United States Congress, Washington, DC (1999-Present); Ranking Member, House Committee on Energy (2019-Present); Chairman, House Committee on Energy (2017-2019); Member, District 28, Assistant Majority Leader, Oregon State Senate (1995-1997); Majority Leader, Oregon House of Representatives (1991-1993); Member, District 56, Oregon House of Representatives (1989-1995); Owner, Columbia Gorge Broadcasters, Inc., Hood River, OR (1986-2007); Chief of Staff to Representative Denny Smith, U.S. House of Representatives (1984-1986); Press Secretary to Representative Denny Smith, U.S. House of Representatives (1981-1984) **CIV:** Honorary Member, Board of Advisors, National Student Leadership Foundation; Board of Directors, Oregon Health & Science University Foundation; Member, Executive Committee, Association of Oregon Industries; Board of Directors, Association of Oregon Industries **AW:** Named Legislator of the Year, National Republican Legislators Association (1993); Named Outstanding Young Oregonian, Oregon Jaycees (1991); Named a Friend of Farm Bureau, Oregon Farm Bureau; Named Hero of Taxpayer, Americans for Tax Reform; Named Legislator of the Year, Safari Club International; Named Legislator of the Year, Oregon Rural Electric Cooperative Association; Named Legislator of the Year, Oregon Association for Home Care; Named Legislator of the Year, National Rural Health Association; Named Legislator of the Year, National Association

Home Care & Hospice; Named Legislator of the Year, Central Oregon Visitors Association; Named Legislator of the Year, Agricultural Retailers Association; Golden Bulldog Award, Watchdog of the Treasury; Spirit of Enterprise Award, U.S. Chamber of Commerce; Senior Legislative Achievement Award, The Seniors Coalition, Inc.; Appreciation Award, Oregon Army National Guard; Wheat Advisor Award, National Association of Wheat Growers; Congressional Champion Award, National Association of Service and Conservation Corps (Now The Corps Network); Champion Award, League of Private Property Owners (Now American Land Rights Association); Distinguished Service Award, National Forest Counties and Schools Coalition; Thomas Jefferson Award, Food Distributors International; Public Service Award, American College of Nurse-Midwives; Benjamin Franklin Award, 60 Plus Association **MEM:** National Federation of Independent Business; Hood River County Chamber of Commerce; Elks Club; Rotary Club, Rotary International **PA:** Republican **RE:** Episcopalian

WALDMAN, MICHAEL, T: Charles H. Dyson Professor of Management, Professor of Economics **I:** Education/Educational Services **CN:** Cornell University **DOB:** 05/12/1955 **PB:** Paterson **SC:** NJ/USA **PT:** Henry Waldman; Nettie Waldman **MS:** Married **SPN:** Lisa Berki (07/18/1999); Karen Voris (7/09/1982, Divorced 01/1992) **CH:** David Henry Waldman; Emma Nicole Waldman **ED:** Postdoctoral Fellow, Department of Economics, University of California, Los Angeles (1982-1983); PhD in Economics, University of Pennsylvania (1982); BS in Economics, Massachusetts Institute of Technology (1977) **C:** Charles H. Dyson Professor of Management, Professor of Economics, Johnson School of Management, Cornell University (1997-Present); Professor of Economics, College of Arts and Sciences, School of Industrial and Labor Relations, Cornell University (2011-2015); Director of Institute for the Advancement of Economics, Cornell University (2008-2012); Professor of Economics, Cornell University (1991-1997); Professor of Economics, University of California Los Angeles (1991-1993); Associate Professor of Economics, University of California Los Angeles (1989-1991); Associate Professor of Economics, University of California Los Angeles (1983-1989) **CR:** Visiting Professor of Economics, Graduate School of Business, The University of Chicago (1999); John M. Olin Visiting Professor, Graduate School of Business, George J. Stigler Center for the Study of the Economy and the State, The University of Chicago (1997-1998); Visiting Professor of Economics, Yale University School of Organization and Management (1989-1990) **CW:** Editor, Journal of Labor Economics (2009-Present); Associate Editor, The Quarterly Journal of Economics (2000-2014); Co-Editor, Journal of Economic Perspectives (2000-2006); Contributor, Articles, Professional Journals; Contributor, Chapters, Books; Referee, Reviewer, Several Peer-Reviewed Journals **AW:** Winner, Reici Best Paper Award for Best Paper Published (2016); Co-Recipient, Robert F. Lanzilotti Prize for the Best Paper in Antitrust Economics, International Industrial Organization Conference (2008); Faculty Research Award, Johnson Graduate School of Management, Cornell University (2003); Warren C. Scoville Distinguished Teaching Award, Department of Economics, University of California Los Angeles (1984-1986) **MEM:** Program Committee, Industrial Organization Society (2013); Society of Labor Economists (2013); Program Committee, Industrial Organization Society (2009); American Economic Association (2004); Board Member, The Society for the Study of Autism Spectrum Disorders and Social-Communication; The Society for Research

on Copyright Issues; Royal Economic Society; The Econometric Society **MH:** Albert Nelson Marquis Lifetime Achievement Award **AV:** Racquetball

WALDT, RISA, T: Artist **I:** Fine Art **CN:** House of the RedTails Studio/Gallery **DOB:** 12/29/1951 **PB:** Tucson **SC:** AZ/USA **PT:** Carl J. Waldt; Jane D. Waldt **ED:** BA in Fine Arts, University of Arizona (1973) **CT:** EAGALA (2010); American Society Experiential Therapists (ASET) **C:** Artist, Therapist **CR:** Progressions Art and Equine Therapist, Sierra Tuscon (2007-2010); Featured, Numerous International Art Shows; Consultant in Field; Presenter in Field **CIV:** Facilitator, Numerous Job Corps, Tucson, AZ **CW:** Author, Artist, "A Story of Being" Author, Artist, "Grand Canyon"; Author, Artist, "A River Trip"; Author, Artist, Numerous Books **AW:** Recipient, Numerous Art Awards **MEM:** President, Saguaro Fellow, Southern Arizona Watercolor Guild (2003-2004); Signature Member, Women Artists of the West; Signature Member, Arizona Watercolor Association; National League of American Pen Women; National Watercolor Society; National Museum of Women in Arts; American Watercolor Society **MH:** Albert Nelson Marquis Lifetime Achievement Award; Marquis Who's Who Top Professional **AS:** Ms. Waldt attributes her success to loving light, color, and life. Likewise, she credits her parents' influence and her persistence to succeed. **B/I:** Ms. Waldt became involved in her art profession because it filled her heart and her spirit, which compelled her to paint and draw. She rode horses as a child and did some painting and drawing but only decided to pursue a career as an artist when she attended the University of Arizona. **AV:** Planting and harvesting wine grapes; Caring for horses **RE:** Episcopalian **THT:** Ms. Waldt prioritizes being kind and considerate.

WALENDOWSKI, GEORGE J., MBA, SCPM, CHE, T: Professor of Accounting and Business (Retired) **I:** Education/Educational Services **PB:** Hannoversch Münde **SC:** Germany **PT:** Stefan Walendowski (Deceased); Eugenia (Lewandowska) Walendowski **ED:** Certificate in Business Analysis, Villanova University (2007); Certificate in Finance Accounting, Villanova University (2007); Master Certificate in Organizational Leadership, Villanova University (2006); Certificate in Leadership, Cornell University (2006); MBA, Cal State LA (1972); BS, Cal State LA (1970); AA, Los Angeles City College (1968) **CT:** Certificate in Tackling the Challenges of Big Data, Massachusetts Institute of Technology (2014); Certificate in Globalization, University of Oxford (2012); Chartered Economist Certificate in Athens and Fifth Century Intellectual Revolution, University of Cambridge (2012); Certificate in Financial Planning, Control and Personnel Management, Duke University (2011); Certified Project Manager, Stanford University (2010); Certificate in Economics Measurement, National Association for Business Economics (2010); Certificate in International Financial Reporting, ACCA (2010); Certificate in Strategic Decision and Risk Management, Stanford University (2010); Certificate in New Economic Powers, University of Oxford (2008); Certified Community College Instructor in Accounting and Management, State of California; Certificate in Business Strategy Achieving Competitive Advantage, Cornell University; Certificate in Measuring and Improving Business Performance, Cornell University **C:** Retired (2012); Adjunct Associate Professor, Los Angeles City College (1995-2012); Business Analyst, Hughes Aircraft Company (1993-1995); Business Management Specialist, Hughes Aircraft Company (1986-1992); Program Controls Specialist, Hughes Aircraft Company (1984-1986); Financial Planning Specialist, Hughes

Aircraft Company (1983-1984); Senior Financial Analyst, Hughes Aircraft Company (1979-1983); Accounting Analyst, Unocal Corporation (1978-1979); Data Control Supervisor, Unocal Corporation (1976-1978); Accountant, Unocal Corporation (1972-1976) **CR:** Reviewer, Conference Papers (2011-Present); Online Tutor in Mathematics and Finance (2011-Present); Adjunct Associate Professor in Accounting, Los Angeles City College (1980-1997, 1999-2012); Adjunct Professor in Accounting, Pasadena City College (1996-2001, 2003-2007); Adjunct Professor in Accounting and Business, Pasadena City College (1996-2001, 2003-2007); Accounting Advisory Committee Member, Los Angeles City College (1984, 1987, 1989, 1999); Adjunct Associate Professor in Business Mathematics, Los Angeles City College (1976-1980); Member, Oxford Education Society; OUSSG **CW:** Editorial Board Member, Philosophical Society Annual Review (2017); Editorial Review Board Member, "Management in Practice," Society for the Advancement of Management (2007-2013); Editorial Advisory Board Member, "Strategic Finance and Management Accounting Quarterly," Institute of Management Accountants, Inc. (2002-2013); Editorial Review Board Member, "Advanced Management Journal," Society for the Advancement of Management (1999-2013); Proposal Reviewer, Delta Pi Epsilon (2005); Reviewer, "Business Policy and Strategy Division," Academy of Management (2002-2004); Reviewer, Academy of Management Learning and Education (2003); Reviewer, Teaching and Curriculum Section, American Accounting Association (1998); Reviewer, Social Issues in Management Division, Academy of Management (1991) **AW:** Fellowship, International Society for Philosophical Enquiry (2014); Certificate of Outstanding Service, Editorial Advisory Board, Institute of Management Accountants, Inc.; Outstanding Reviewer Award, Academy of Management; Superior Performance Award, Hughes Aircraft Company; Certificate of Outstanding Achievement, Hughes Aircraft Company; Robert Half Author's Award, Los Angeles Chapter, California Society of CPAs; Author Recognition Award, Los Angeles Chapter, Planning Executives Institute; Alumni Association, Cornell University; Stanford Alumni Association; Alumni Association, MIT Professional Education **MEM:** Fellow, Chartered Management Institute; Beta Gamma Sigma; Omicron Delta Epsilon; Sigma Xi, The Scientific Research Society; Kappa Delta Pi, International Honor Society in Education; Pi Lambda Theta; Alpha Iota Delta; Los Angeles Chapter, California Society of CPAs **MH:** Albert Nelson Marquis Lifetime Achievement Award; Marquis Who's Who Top Professional **B/I:** Dr. Walendowski became involved in his career simply because a friend of his mother told him there was an open position in the school and asked if he was interested. **PA:** Republican **RE:** Roman Catholic

WALES, JIMMY DONAL, T: Chief Executive Officer **I:** Information Technology and Services **DOB:** 08/07/1966 **PB:** Huntsville **SC:** AL/USA **PT:** Jimmy Wales; Doris Ann Wales **MS:** Married **SPN:** Kate Garvey (10/06/2012); Christine Rohan (1997, Divorced 2011); Pamela Green (1986, Divorced 1993) **CH:** Three Children **ED:** Doctorate Honoris Causa, Université Catholique de Louvain (2016); Doctorate Honoris Causa, Maastricht University (2015); Honorary DLitt, Glasgow Caledonian University (2014); Doctorate Honoris Causa, Faculty of Communication Sciences, Università della Svizzera italiana (2014); Honorary Degree, Knox College; Honorary Degree, Amherst College; Honorary Degree, Stevenson University; Honorary Degree, Universidad Siglo 21; Honorary Degree, MIREA University; Coursework, PhD Finance

Program, Indiana University; Coursework, PhD Finance Program, University of Alabama; MS, University of Alabama; BS in Finance, Auburn University **C:** Co-Founder, Wikia (2004-Present); Founder, Wikimedia Foundation (2003-Present); Co-Founder, Wikipedia (2001-Present); Member, Board of Trustees, Wikimedia Foundation (2001-Present); Chairman, Board of Trustees, Wikimedia Foundation (2003-2006); Founder, Nupedia (1999-2000); Co-Founder, Bomis (1996); Research Director, Chicago Options Associates (1994-2000); Instructor, Indiana University; Instructor, University of Alabama **CR:** Founder, WT: Social (2019); Founder, WikiTribune (2017); Non-Executive Director, Guardian Media Group (2016); Member, Committee on Privacy, Google (2014); Co-Chair, The People's Operator (2014); Speaker, Panel, Clinton Global Initiative University Conference, Arizona State University (2014); Former Board Member, Socialtext **CIV:** Member, Jury, Tribeca Film Festival (2011); Former Co-Chair, World Economic Forum on the Middle East (2008); Founder, Jimmy Wales Foundation for Freedom of Expression; Member, Board of Directors, Creative Commons **CW:** Co-Author, "Keep a Civil Cybertongue," The Wall Street Journal (2009); Co-Author, "Most Define User-Generated Content Too Narrowly," Advertising Age (2009); Author, "Foreword," "The Wikipedia Revolution: How a Bunch of Nobodies Created the World's Greatest Encyclopedia" (2009); Co-Author, "Foreword," "Marketing to the Social Web: How Digital Customer Communities Build Your Business" (2009); Co-Author, "Foreword," "33 Million People in the Room: How to Create, Influence, and Run a Successful Business with Social Networking" (2009); Co-Author, "Commentary: Create a tech-friendly U.S. government," CNN (2009); Co-Author, "Foreword," "Throwing Sheep in the Boardroom: How Online Social Networking Will Transform Your Life, Work and World" (2008); Co-Author, "Calling on a million minds for community annotation in WikiProteins," Genome Biology (2008); Speaker, Film, "Jimmy Wales: Vision: Wikipedia and the Future of Free Culture" (2006); Co-Author, "The Pricing of Index Options When the Underlying Assets All Follow a Lognormal Diffusion," Advances in Futures and Options Research (1994); Lecturer, Stuart Regen Visionary Series, New Museum **AW:** President's Medal of the British Academy "for facilitating the spread of information via his work creating and developing Wikipedia, the world's largest free online encyclopedia" (2017); Dan David Prize "for launching the world's largest online encyclopedia" (2015); Common Wealth Award of Distinguished Service (2015); Special Award, UK Tech4Good Awards (2014); Named One of "25 Web Superstars," The Daily Telegraph (2014); Recognized with Honour Citizenship of Esino Lario (2016); UNESCO Niels Bohr Medal, Copenhagen, Denmark (2013); Monaco Media Award (2011); Leonardo European Corporate Learning Award (2011); Pioneer Award (2011); Gottlieb Duttweiler Prize (2011); 2009 Nokia Foundation Annual Award, 7th Annual Innovation Awards and Summit, The Economist (2009); 2008 Global Brand Icon of the Year Award (2008); Named One of the "Young Global Leaders" of 2007, World Economic Forum (2007); Listed Among the "Scientists & Thinkers" Section, TIME 100 (2006); Ranked #12, "The Web Celebs 25," Forbes (2006); Pioneer Award, Electronic Frontier Foundation (2006); Inductee, Internet Hall of Fame **MEM:** Berkman Center for Internet & Society, Harvard Law School **AV:** Cooking

WALK, KATHLEEN A., T: Founder, Executive Director **I:** Nonprofit & Philanthropy **CN:** Hope International Services **CH:** Two Children **ED:** Doctor of Medicine, University of Nebraska Medical Center (1968) **C:** Founder, Executive Director, Hope International Services (1987-Present) **CW:** International Radio Program for Teaching in 180 Countries (33 Years) **AW:** Lifetime Achievement Award, International Association of Top Professionals (2018); Top Doctor of the Year, Missionary of the Year, International Association of Top Professionals (2017) **AS:** Dr. Walk attributes her success to her deep and abiding Christian faith. **B/I:** Dr. Walk became involved in her profession out of a deep desire to help people overseas, particularly in the field of medicine and healthcare.

WALKEN, CHRISTOPHER, T: Actor **I:** Media & Entertainment **DOB:** 03/31/1943 **PB:** Astoria **SC:** NY/USA **PT:** Paul Walken; Rosalie Russell Walken **MS:** Married **SPN:** Georgianne Walken (1969) **ED:** Student, Wynn Handman; Student, Washington Dance Studio; Coursework, Hofstra University **C:** Actor, Film, Television and Stage **CW:** Actor, "Wild Mountain Thyme" (2021); Actor, "The War with Grandpa" (2020); Actor, "The Jesus Rolls" (2019); Actor, "Irreplaceable You" (2018); Actor, "Father Figures" (2017); Actor, "Bai Brands: Bye Bye Bye" (2017); Actor, "Nine Lives" (2016); Voice Actor, "The Jungle Book" (2016); Narrator, "David Blaine: Beyond Magic" (2016); Actor, "Eddie the Eagle" (2015); Actor, "The Family Fang" (2015); Actor, "Joe Dirt 2: Beautiful Loser" (2015); Actor, "One More Time" (2015); Actor, "Peter Pan Live!" (2014); Actor, "Jersey Boys" (2014); Actor, "Turks & Caicos" (2014); Actor, "Gods Behaving Badly" (2013); Actor, "The Power of Few" (2013); Actor, "Stand Up Gus" (2012); Actor, "A Late Quartet" (2012); Actor, "Seven Psychopaths" (2012); Actor, "Life's a Beach" (2012); Actor, "Dark Horse" (2011); Actor, "Kill the Irishman" (2011); Actor, "A Behanding in Spokane" (2010); Himself, "30 Rock" (2009); Actor, "The Maiden Heist" (2009); Actor, "$5 a Day" (2008); Voice Actor, "Evil Calls: The Raven" (2008); Actor, "Disaster! A Major Motion Picture Ride... Starring You!" (2008); Actor, "Balls of Fury" (2007); Actor, "Hairspray" (2007); Actor, "Man of the Year" (2006); Actor, "Fade to Black" (2006); Actor, "Click" (2006); Voice Actor, "True Crime: New York City" (2005); Actor, "Domino" (2005); Actor, "Romance & Cigarettes" (2005); Actor, "Wedding Crashers" (2005); Actor, "Around the Bend" (2004); Actor, "Caesar" (2004); Actor, "The Stepford Wives" (2004); Actor, "Envy" (2004); Actor, "Man on Fire" (2004); Voice Actor, "True Crime: Streets of LA" (2003); Actor, "The Rundown" (2003); Actor, "Gigli" (2003); Actor, "Kangaroo Jack" (2003); Actor, "Catch Me If You Can" (2002); Actor, "Undertaking Betty" (2002); Actor, "Engine Trouble" (2002); Actor, "The Country Bears" (2002); Actor, "Poolhall Junkies" (2002); Actor, Dancer, "Fatboy Slim: Weapon of Choice" (2001); Actor, "The Affair of the Necklace" (2001); Actor, "America's Sweethearts" (2001); Actor, "Joe Dirt" (2001); Actor, "Scotland, Pa." (2001); Actor, "The Seagull" (2001); Actor, "The Opportunists" (2000); Actor, "The Prophecy 3: The Ascent" (2000); Actor, "James Joyce's The Dead" (2000); Actor, "Kiss Toledo Goodbye" (1999); Actor, "Sarah, Plain & Tall: Winter's End" (1999); Actor, "Sleepy Hollow" (1999); Actor, "Blast from the Past" (1999); Voice Actor, "Antz" (1998); Actor, "The Eternal" (1998); Co-Producer, "New Rose Hotel" (1998); Actor, "New Rose Hotel" (1998); Actor, "Illuminata" (1998); Actor, "The Prophecy II" (1998); Actor, "Mousehunt" (1997); Actor, "Suicide Kings" (1997); Actor, "Excess Baggage" (1997); Actor, "Touch" (1997); Voice Actor, "The Raven" by Edgar Allan Poe, "Closed on Account of Rabies" (1997); Actor, "Ripper" (1996); Actor, "Privateer 2" (1996); Actor, "Last Man Standing" (1996); Actor, "The Funeral" (1996); Actor, "Basquiat" (1996); Actor, "Celluloid" (1996); Actor, "Nick of Time" (1995); Actor, "Things to Do in Denver When You're

Dead" (1995); Actor, "Search and Destroy" (1995); Actor, "Wild Side" (1995); Actor, "The Prophecy" (1995); Actor, "The Addiction" (1995); Actor, "Him" (1995); Actor, "Pulp Fiction" (1994); Actor, "A Business Affair" (1994); Actor, "Wayne's World 2" (1993); Actor, "True Romance" (1993); Actor, "Scam" (1993); Actor, "Madonna: Bad Girl" (1993); Actor, "Skylark" (1993); Actor, "Le Grand Pardon II" (1992); Actor, "Batman Returns" (1992); Actor, "Mistress" (1992); Actor, "All-American Murder" (1991); Actor, "McBain" (1991); Actor, "Sarah, Plain and Tall" (1991); Actor, "The Comfort of Strangers" (1990); Actor, "King of New York" (1990); Actor, "Communion" (1989); Actor, "Homeboy" (1988); Actor, "Puss in Boots" (1988); Actor, "Biloxi Blues" (1988); Actor, "The Milagro Beanfield War" (1988); Actor, "Witness in the War Zone" (1987); Actor, "At Close Range" (1986); Actor, "A View to a Kill" (1985); Actor, "Guiding Light" (1984); Actor, "Hurlyburly" (1984); Actor, "The Dead Zone" (1983); Actor, "Brainstorm" (1983); Actor, "American Playhouse" (1982); Actor, "Pennies from Heaven" (1981); Actor, "The Dogs of War" (1980); Actor, "Heaven's Gate" (1980); Actor, "Last Embrace" (1979); Actor, "Shoot the Sun Down" (1978); Actor, "The Deer Hunter" (1978); Actor, "Roseland" (1977); Actor, "Annie Hall" (1977); Actor, "Kojak" (1977); Actor, "The Sentinel" (1977); Actor, "Next Stop, Greenwich Village" (1976); Actor, "Valley Forge" (1975); Actor, "Sweet Bird of Youth" (1975); Actor, "The Plough and the Stars" (1973); Actor, "The Merchant of Venice" (1973); Actor, "The Mind Snatchers" (1972); Actor, "Enemies" (1972); Actor, "The Anderson Tapes" (1971); Actor, "New York Television Theatre" (1970); Actor, "Cleopatra" (1970); Actor, "Hawaii Five-O" (1970); Actor, "NET Playhouse" (1970); Actor, "The Three Musketeers" (1969); Actor, "Me and My Brother" (1969); Actor, "A Midsummer Night's Dream" (1968); Actor, "Romeo and Juliet" (1968); Actor, "Barefoot in Athens" (1966); Actor, "The Lion in Winter" (1966); Actor, "The Rose Tattoo" (1966); Actor, "Baker Street" (1965); Actor, "High Spirits" (1964); Actor, "Naked City" (1963); Actor, "Deadline" (1960); Actor, "J.B." (1958); Actor, "The Visit" (1958); Actor, "The Boy Who Saw Through" (1956); Actor, "The Motorola Television Hour" (1954); Actor, "The Wonderful John Action" (1953); Actor, "The Climate of Eden" (1952); Host, Seven "Saturday Night Live" Episodes **AW:** Best Ensemble Cast, "Seven Psychopaths," Boston Society of Film Critics Awards (2012); Man of the Year, Hasty Pudding Theatricals (2008); Best Acting Ensemble, "Hairspray," Broadcast Film Critics Association Awards (2008); Ensemble Cast Award, "Hairspray," Palm Springs International Film Festival (2008); Best Actor in a Supporting Role, Drama, "Around the Bend," Satellite Awards (2005); Marquee Award, CineVegas International Film Festival (2005); Best Supporting Male Performance, "True Crime: New York City," Spike Video Game Awards (2005); Best Actor, "Around the Bend," Montréal World Film Festival (2004); Outstanding Performance by a Male Actor in a Supporting Role, "Catch Me If You Can," Screen Actors Guild Awards (2003); Best Performance by an Actor in a Supporting Role, "Catch Me If You Can," BAFTA Awards (2003); Best Supporting Actor, "Catch Me If You Can," National Society of Film Critics Awards (2003); Supporting Actor of the Year, ShoWest Convention (2003); Funniest Male Guest Appearance in a TV Series, "Saturday Night Live," American Comedy Awards (2001); Best Choreography in a Video, "Fatboy Slim: Weapon of Choice," MTV Video Music Awards (2001); Master Screen Artist Tribute, USA Film Festival (1998); Best Actor, "The Prophecy," Fangoria Chainsaw Awards (1996); Inductee, Fangoria Horror Hall of Fame, Fangoria Chainsaw Awards (1996); Will Award, Shakespeare Theater (1994); Best Actor, "Deadline," Shang-

hai International TV Festival (1988); Obie Award, "The Seagull" (1981); Best Actor in a Supporting Role, "The Deer Hunter," Academy Awards (1979); Best Supporting Actor, "Deer Hunter," New York Film Critics Circle Awards (1978); Obie Award, "Kid Champion" (1975); Drama Desk Award for "Outstanding Performance," "Lemon Sky" (1970); Joseph Jefferson Award, "The Night Thoreau Spent in Jail" (1970); Clarence Derwent Award, "The Lion in Winter" (1966); Theatre World Award, "The Rose Tattoo" (1966); Susan Stain Shiva Award, Joseph Papp's Public Radio Theatre

WALKER, ALICE MALSENIOR, T: Writer **I:** Writing and Editing **DOB:** 02/09/1944 **PB:** Eatonton **SC:** GA/USA **PT:** Willie Lee; Minnie (Grant) Walker **ED:** Honorary Doctor of Humane Letters, University of Massachusetts (1983); Honorary Doctor of Philosophy, Russell Sage University (1972); Bachelor of Arts, Sarah Lawrence College, Bronxville, NY (1966); Coursework, Spelman College **C:** Co-founder, Wild Trees PR, Navarro, CA (1984-1988) **CR:** Fannie Hurst Professor of Literature, Brandeis University, Waltham, MA (1982); Distinguished Writer of Afro-American Studies, University of California Berkeley (1982); Lecturer of Literature, University of Massachusetts, Boston, MA (1972-1973); Lecturer of Literature, Wellesley College, Massachusetts (1972-1973); Teacher of Black Studies, Tougaloo College, Mississippi (1970-1971); Teacher of Black Studies, Jackson State College, Mississippi (1968-1969); Consultant, Friends of the Children, Mississippi (1967) **CW:** Author, Non-Fiction, "We Are the Ones We Have Been Waiting For" (2006); Author, "Now Is The Time to Open Your Heart" (2005); Author, Collection of Poetry, "Collected Poems" (2005); Author, Collection of Poetry, "Absolute Trust in the Goodness of the Earth" (2003); Author, Collection of Poetry, "A Poem Traveled Down My Arm: Poems And Drawings" (2003); Author, Non-Fiction, "Sent By Earth: A Message from the Grandmother Spirit After the Bombing of the World Trade Center and Pentagon" (2001); Author, "The Way Forward Is with a Broken Heart" (2000); Author, Non-Fiction, "Pema Chodron and Alice Walker in Conversation" (1999); Author, "By The Light of My Father's Smile" (1998); Author, Non-Fiction, "Anything We Love Can Be Saved: A Writer's Activism" (1997); Author, Non-Fiction, "Go Girl!: The Black Woman's Book of Travel and Adventure" (1997); Author, Non-Fiction, "The Same River Twice: Honoring the Difficult" (1996); Author, "The Complete Stories" (1994); Author, Non-Fiction, "Warrior Marks" (1993); Author, "Possessing the Secret of Joy" (1992); Author, "Finding the Green Stone" (1991); Author, Collection of Poetry, "Her Blue Body Everything We Know: Earthling Poems" (1991); Author, "The Temple of My Familiar" (1989); Author, Non-Fiction, "Living by the Word" (1988); Author, "To Hell With Dying" (1988); Author, "Am I Blue?" (1986); Author, Collection of Poetry, "Horses Make a Landscape Look More Beautiful" (1985); Author, Non-Fiction, "In Search of Our Mothers' Gardens: Womanist Prose" (1983); Author, "Beauty: When the Other Dancer Is the Self" (1983); Author, Collection of Poetry, "Once" (1968); Author, "The Color Purple" (1982); Author, "You Can't Keep a Good Woman Down: Stories" (1982); Author, Collection of Poetry, "Good Night, Willie Lee, I'll See You in the Morning" (1979); Author, "Meridian" (1976); Author, "Everyday Use" (1973); Author, "In Love and Trouble: Stories of Black Women" (1973); Author, "Roselily" (1973); Author, Collection of Poetry, "Revolutionary Petunias and Other Poems" (1973); Author, "The Third Life of Grange Copeland" (1970) **AW:** Inductee, Hall of Fame, California Museum of the History of Women & Arts (2006); PEN Center USA (1990); Fred Cody Award for Life-

time Achievement, Bay Area Book Reviewers Association (1990); Nora Astorga Leadership Award (1989); O. Henry Award (1986); National Book Award, "The Color Purple" (1983); Pulitzer Prize for Fiction, "The Color Purple" (1983); Fellowship, Radcliffe Institute; Merrill Fellowship; Guggenheim Fellowship; Front Page Award for Best Magazine Criticism, Newswomen's Club of New York; Rosenthal Award, National Institute of Arts and Letters; Lillian Smith Award; Grant, National Endowment for the Arts; Freedom to Write Award

WALKER, GEORGE THEOPHILUS, T: Composer **I:** Media & Entertainment **DOB:** 07/27/1922 **PB:** Washington **SC:** DC/USA **PT:** George Theophilus Walker Sr.; Rosa (King) Walker **CH:** Gregory T.S.; Ian **ED:** Honorary DFA, Spelman College (2001); Honorary MusD, Bloomfield College (1997); Honorary DHL, Montclair State University, (1997); Honorary MusD, Curtis Institute of Music (1997); Honorary MusD, Oberlin College (1983); Honorary DFA, Lafayette College (1982); Doctor of Museum Arts, University of Rochester (1957); Artist Diploma, Curtis Institute of Music (1945); MusB, Oberlin College (1941); Coursework with Nadia Boulanger, Rudolf Serkin, and Rosario Scalero **C:** Professor Emeritus, Rutgers, The State University of New Jersey, Newark, NJ (1992-Present); Distinguished Professor, Rutgers, The State University of New Jersey, Newark, NJ (1976-1992); Associate Professor, University of Colorado, Boulder (1968-1969); Instructor to Associate Professor, Smith College, Northampton, MA (1961-1968); Instructor, The New School for Social Research, New York, NY (1961); Instructor, Dalcroze School of Music (Now Kaufman Music Center), New York, NY (1960-1961); Instructor, Dillard University, New Orleans, LA (1953-1954) **CR:** Adjunct Professor, Peabody Institute, Johns Hopkins University, Baltimore, MD (1975-1978); Distinguished Professor, University of Delaware, Newark, DE (1975-1976); Concert Pianist, Columbia Artists, New York, NY (1959-1960); Concert Pianist, National Concert of Artists, New York, NY (1950-1953) **CIV:** Member, Mary Flagler Cary Trust Commission (1998); Board of Directors, American Bach Foundation (Now American Bach Soloists) (1988) **CW:** Author, Autobiography, "Reminiscences of an American Composer and Pianist" (2009); Composer, "Concerto for Cello and Orchestra" (1982); Composer, "Sonata for Two Pianos"; Composer, "Sinfonias for Orchestra"; Composer, Numerous Sonatas, Cantatas and Concertos **AW:** Legacy Award, National Opera Association (2007); Foils for Orchestra Award, Eastman Commission (2006); A.I. duPont Award, Delaware Symphony (2001); Classical Roots Lifetime Achievement Award, Detroit Symphony (2001); Dorothy Maynor Arts Citizens' Award (2000); Inductee, American Classical Music Hall of Fame (2000); Koussevitsky Award (1988, 1998); Mary Flagler Cary Charitable Trust Award (1998); L.J. Governor's Award (1997); Pulitzer Prize (1996); Distinguished Scholar, University of Rochester (1996); Guggenheim Fellow (1969, 1988); Award, American Academy of Arts and Letter (1982); Rockefeller Fellow (1971, 1974); Harvey Gaul Prize (1963); John Hay Whitney Fellow (1958); Fulbright Fellow (1957); Grantee, Smith College, University of Colorado, Rutgers, The State University of New Jersey Research Council, National Education Association, New Jersey State Council for Arts; Commissioned, New York Philharmonic, John F. Kennedy Center for the Performing Arts; Commissioned, Cleveland Orchestra; Commissioned, Boston Symphony; Commissioned, New Jersey Symphony; Commissioned, American Guild of Organists **MEM:** ASCAP; American Academy of Arts and Letters; Member-Elect, Board of Directors, American Bach Foundation (Now American Bach Soloists); American Symphony League (Now League of American Orchestras)

WALKER, JAMES ROBERT, T: Senior Project Engineer **I:** Engineering **CN:** Laboratory Corporation of America Holdings **DOB:** 10/21/1951 **PB:** Union **SC:** SC/USA **PT:** James Robert Walker; Virginia Carolyn (Farmer) Walker **ED:** BS in Computer Science, University of South Carolina (1973) **C:** Senior Project Engineer, Laboratory Corporation of America Holdings (2001-Present); Technical Specialist, PPD Inc. (1998-2000); Trilogy Consulting Group, Inc. (1996-1998); Programmer Analyst, Hargray Communications (1993-1996); Senior Programmer, Equifax (1985-1992); Technical Specialist, Draper Corporation (1980-1985); System Software Specialist, Digital Systems, Columbia, SC (1979-1980); Programmer Analyst, Business Data (1977-1979); Senior Programmer, Advocate Lutheran General Hospital (1977); Senior Programmer, Cone Mills Corporation (1974-1977); Programmer Trainee, Spartan Mills (1973-1974) **MEM:** Chair, Stream Watch, Sierra Club (1983-1985); Pi Mu Epsilon **MH:** Albert Nelson Marquis Lifetime Achievement Award; Marquis Who's Who Top Professional **B/I:** Mr. Walker became involved in his profession because he wanted to make a difference in his field.

WALKER, KARA ELIZABETH, T: Artist **I:** Fine Art **DOB:** 11/26/1969 **PB:** Stockton **SC:** CA/USA **PT:** Larry Walker; Gwendolyn Walker **MS:** Divorced **SPN:** Klaus Bürgel (1996, Divorced 2010) **CH:** Octavia Bürgel **ED:** Master of Fine Arts, Rhode Island School of Design (1994); Bachelor of Fine Arts, Atlanta College of Art (1991) **CR:** Artist-in-Residence, American Academy in Rome (2016); U.S. Representative, 25th International São Paulo Biennial, Brazil (2002); MacArthur Fellowship (1997) **CIV:** Board of Directors, Foundation for Contemporary Arts (2011-2016) **CW:** Solo Show, "Untitled - Hyundai Commission," Tate Modern (2019); Solo Show, "Sikkema Jenkins and Co. is Compelled to Present the Most Astounding And Important Painting Show of the Fall Art Show Viewing Season!," Sikkema Jenkins & Co., New York, NY (2017); Solo Show, "The Ecstasy of St. Kara," Cleveland Museum of Art (2016); Solo Show, "A Subtlety, or the Marvelous Sugar Baby, an Homage to the unpaid and overworked Artisans who have refined our Sweet tastes from the cane fields to the Kitchens of the New World on the Occasion of the demolition of the Domino Sugar Refining Plant," Creative Time, Brooklyn, NY (2014); Co-Author, "Kara Walker: A Negress of Noteworthy Talent" (2011); Author, "Kara Walker: After the Deluge" (2007); Featured, "Salt" (2004); Permanent Collections, Minneapolis Institute of Art and the Weisman Art Museum, Minneapolis, MN, Tate Collection, London, England, Museum of Contemporary Art, Los Angeles, CA, Menil Collection, Houston, TX, Muscarelle Museum of Art, Williamsburg, VA; Co-Writer, "Suicide Demo for Kara Walker"; Featured, Numerous Articles, Professional Journals **AW:** Named, TIME Magazine's 100 Most Influential People in the World, Artists and Entertainers (2007); Larry Aldrich Award (2005); Deutsche Bank Prize **MEM:** Elected Member, American Academy of Arts and Letters (2012)

WALKER, MARK HOWARD, T: U.S. Representative from North Carolina; Pastor **I:** Government Administration/Government Relations/Government Services **DOB:** 05/20/1969 **PB:** Dothan **SC:** AL/USA **MS:** Married **SPN:** Kelly (Sears) Walker **CH:** Anna Claire; Rachel; Ryan **ED:** BA in Biblical Studies, Piedmont Baptist College (Now Piedmont International University) (1999); Coursework, Trinity Baptist College **CT:** Ordained Pastor

C: Vice Chair, House Republican Conference (2019-Present); Member, U.S. House of Representatives from North Carolina's Sixth Congressional District, United States Congress, Washington, DC (2015-Present); Chair, Republican Study Committee (2017-2019); Pastor, Worship and Music, Lawndale Baptist Church, Greensboro, NC (2008); With, Flow Automotive, NC (1991-1996); Pastor, Calvary Baptist Church, Winston-Salem, NC **CIV:** Member, War Memorial Commission, Greensboro City Council, NC (2012-Present) **PA:** Republican **RE:** Baptist

WALKER, PATRICIA BARNES, PHD, T: Educator, Theatre Producer (Retired) **I:** Writing and Editing **DOB:** 12/28/1943 **PB:** Salisbury **SC:** MD/USA **PT:** Herman Noel; Elnor Frances (Gibbons) Dykes **MS:** Married **SPN:** Kent Walker (02/27/1976); John Gordon Barnes (06/13/1961, Divorced 1976) **CH:** Carol Kimberly; Christine Kelly **ED:** Doctor of Philosophy in Urban Services, Virginia Commonwealth University (1985); Master of Education in Reading, University of Montana (1974); Bachelor of Science in Elementary Education, Salisbury University (1967) **CT:** Certified Teacher, Virginia; Wedding Officiant, Chesterfield County, VA **C:** Executive Producer Emerita, The Bifocals Theater Project, Richmond, VA (2019-Present); Executive Producer, The Bifocals Theater Project, Richmond, VA (2010-2019); President, Chamberlayne Actors Theater, Richmond, VA (2016-2018); Owner, The Aquarian Bookshop, Richmond, VA (1997-2004); With, Peopleworks Publications, Richmond, VA (1985-1995); Adjunct Faculty Member, University of Virginia, Charlottesville, VA (1986-1987); Adjunct Faculty Member, Virginia Commonwealth University, Richmond, VA (1984-1987); State Supervisor, Virginia Department Education, Richmond, VA (1981-1985); Consultant, Trainer, Allied Corp., Petersburg, VA (1984); Consultant, Trainer, Virginia Department of General Services, Richmond, VA (1984); Middle School Principal, Parksley, VA (1978-1981); Assistant Principal, Melfa, VA (1977-1978); Teacher, Accomack County Schools, Virginia (1967-1977) **CR:** Actor, Director, Producer, Playwright (2007-Present); Fabric Artist, Quilting Teacher (2002-Present); Wedding Officiant (1999-Present); Past-life Regressionist (1992-Present) **CW:** Fabric Artist; Writer, Seven One-Act Plays; Writer, Two One-Act Musicals; Writer, Three Full-Length Plays **AW:** Numerous Award-Winning Quilts **MEM:** National Association of Female Executives; Phi Kappa Phi; Phi Delta Kappa **MH:** Albert Nelson Marquis Lifetime Achievement Award **AS:** Dr. Walker attributes her success to the support she has enjoyed from her extended family and group of friends. She was taught to work hard by her parents. **B/I:** Dr. Walker became involved in her profession out of her desire to teach; meanwhile, her leadership abilities led her into positions of administration with the board of education of Accomack County, Virginia. Following this period, she transitioned to become a training consultant in leadership and supervision in business, government, education and industry.Outside of her work in education, Dr. Walker's active mind and keen curiosity led her to study metaphysics and quantum mechanics. She received training in hypnotic regression and energy healing and, for seven years, she and her husband owned and operated The Aquarian Bookshop, a metaphysical store. **AV:** Stage set design; Costume design; Fabric artist; Quilter **RE:** Spiritual

WALLACE, CHRISTOPHER, T: Broadcast Journalist **I:** Writing and Editing **DOB:** 10/12/1947 **PB:** Chicago **SC:** IL/USA **PT:** Mike Wallace; Norma (Kaphan) Wallace; Bill Leonard (Stepfather) **MS:** Married **SPN:** Lorraine Martin Smothers (1997);

Elizabeth Farrell (1973, Divorced) **CH:** Peter; Margaret; Andrew; Catherine **ED:** BA, Harvard College, Harvard University (1969) **C:** Host, "Fox News Sunday" (2003-Present); Chief Correspondent, "20/20," ABC News (1998-2003); Senior Correspondent, "Primetime Thursday," ABC News (1989-1998); Chief White House Correspondent, NBC News (1982-1989); Moderator, "Meet the Press," NBC News (1987-1988); Anchor, Sunday Edition, NBC Nightly News (1982-1984, 1986-1987); Political Correspondent, Washington Bureau, NBC News (1982); News Reader, "Today," NBC (1982); Reporter, NBC News, Washington, DC (1978-1981); Reporter, WNBC-TV, New York, NY (1975-1978); Political Reporter, Station WBBM-TV, CBS, Chicago, IL (1973-1975); National Reporter, The Boston Globe (1969-1973); Substitute Host, "Nightline," ABC News **CR:** Moderator, Third Presidential Debate, The Commission on Presidential Debates (2016); Coverage of Numerous Presidential Campaigns and Democratic and Republican Conventions (1980, 1984, 1988) **AW:** Nominee, "Outstanding Live Interview," News & Documentary Emmy Award, The National Academy of Television Arts & Sciences (2018); The Freedom of Speech Award, Media Institute (2018); "Tex" McCrary Journalism Award, Congressional Medal of Honor Society (2018); Founders Award for Excellence in Journalism, International Center for Journalists (ICFJ) (2017); Paul White Award, Radio Television Digital News Association (2013); The Sol Taishoff Award for Excellence in Broadcast Journalism, National Press Foundation (2012); National Press Foundation Award (2011); Dupont-Columbia Silver Baton for Excellence in Television Journalism (1993); George Polk Award, Long Island University (1992); Overseas Press Club of America Award (1981); Peabody Award (1978)

WALLACE, ROBERT, "BOB" L. II, T: General 7Engineer **I:** Military & Defense Services **CN:** United States Department of Defense **DOB:** 01/27/1949 **PB:** Ronceverte **SC:** WV/USA **PT:** Robert Luther Wallace; Eloise Virginia (Houck) Wallace **MS:** Married **SPN:** Lucy Alice Frazier (06/13/1981) **CH:** Sheena Rene; Lacey Christina **ED:** MS in Industrial Engineering, West Virginia University (1973); BS in Aerospace Engineering, West Virginia University (1970) **C:** Human Resource Engineer, Director of Engineering and Technology Management, Lead Plans and Programs Engineer, Headquarters, Air Force Materiel Command (1998-2010); Logistics Management Specialist, Inventory Management Division, Headquarters, Air Force Materiel Command (1997-1998); Director, Education and Training Flight, 88th Mission Support Group, Mission Support Squadron, Wright-Patterson Air Force Base (1996-1997); Chief of Operations, Education and Training Office, Mission Support Squadron, Wright-Patterson Air Force Base (1995-1996); Chief, Mission Requirements Unit, Education and Training Flight, 88th Mission Support Group, Wright-Patterson Air Force Base (1991-1995); Program Manager, Air Force Logistics Commissioned, Wright-Patterson Air Force Base (1986-1991); Logistics Management Specialist, Military Airlift Commissioned, Scott Air Force Base, IL (1984-1986); Engineering Work Leader, Air Force Logistics Command (1981-1984); Project Engineer, Air Force Logistics Command, Wright Patterson Air Force Base (1978-1981); Project Engineer, Naval Air Systems Commissioned, Washington, DC (1972-1978) **CIV:** Board of Trustees, The Ohio State University Lutheran Chapel (2005-Present); Delegate, Member, Endowment Committee, Peace Evangelical Lutheran Church, Beavercreek, Ohio (2005-Present); Board of Trustees, The Human Race Theatre Company (2004-Present); With, Leadership Dayton, Dayton Chamber (2004-Present); Assistant Lay Minister, Peace Evangelical

Lutheran Church, Beavercreek, Ohio (1987-Present); Director of Stewardship, Peace Evangelical Lutheran Church (2012-2016); Vice President of Operations, Peace Evangelical Lutheran Church, Beavercreek, Ohio (2003-2004); President, Board of Education, Beavercreek City School District (2001); Vice President, Board of Education, Beavercreek City School District (2000); Hall of Servants, Peace Evangelical Lutheran Church, Beavercreek, Ohio (1999); Member, Board of Education, Beavercreek City School District (1998-2001); Vice President, Idle Hour Swim Club, Beavercreek, Ohio (1996-1997); Vice President, Ministries, Peace Evangelical Lutheran Church, Beavercreek, Ohio (1992-1996); Trustee, Idle Hour Swim Club, Beavercreek, Ohio (1990-1998); Member, Beavercreek Schools Strategic Planning Committee, Ohio (1990); Assistant Director, Evangelism, Peace Evangelical Lutheran Church, Beavercreek, Ohio (1987-1989) **AW:** Outstanding Civilian Career Service Medal, United States Department of the Air Force (2010); Civilian Achievement Medal, United States Department of the Air Force (2006) **MEM:** Senior Member, American Institute of Aeronautics and Astronautics **MH:** Albert Nelson Marquis Lifetime Achievement Award; Marquis Who's Who Top Professional **AS:** Mr. Wallace attributes his success to an excellent education at West Virginia University. **B/I:** Mr. Wallace became involved in his profession because his initial goal was to work for NASA in the space program. Although he did not get to work for NASA, he pursued a career that was similar to his dream. He began his professional journey as a project engineer for the Naval Air Systems Command in Washington, DC, then some years later, he held the position as project engineer at the Air Force Logistics Command in Ohio. He always loved mathematics and science; it just sparked his interest. **AV:** Swimming; Sky watching; Travel; Broadway shows **PA:** Democrat **RE:** Lutheran **THT:** Mr. Wallace says, "The three most important things in life are faith, family, and friends."

WALLENBERGER, FREDERICK, T: Materials Scientist **I:** Sciences **DOB:** 08/28/1930 **PB:** St. Peter Freienstein **SC:** Austria **ED:** PhD, Fordham University (1958); MS, Fordham University (1956); ABS in Chemistry, University Graz, Austria (1954) **C:** Staff Scientist Advanced Technician, PPG Industries, Inc., Pittsburgh, PA (1995-2008); Visiting Professor, University of California Davis (1995); Research Professor, University of Illinois at Urbana-Champaign (1992-1994); Senior Research Associate, Du Pont Fibers, Wilmington, DE (1979-1992); Research Supervisor, Du Pont Fibers, Wilmington, DE (1963-1979); Research Scientist, Du Pont Fibers, Wilmington, DE (1959-1963); Research Fellow, Harvard University, Cambridge, MA (1958-1959); Lecturer In Chemistry, Fordham University (1957-1958) **CR:** Consultant in Natural, Organic and Inorganic Fibers (1992-1995); Editor-in-Chief, Akademische Nachrichten (1949-1953) **CW:** Author, "Fiberglass & Glass Technology, Energy-Friendly Composition & Applications" (2009); Author, "Natural Fibers" (2004); Author, "Advanced Reinforcing Fibers" (2002); Author, "Advanced Inorganic Fibers" (1999); Contributor, Over 269 Articles, Professional Journals **AW:** Environmental Respect Award, Du Pont (1992); Recipient, Numerous Other Awards **MEM:** Chairman, American Chemical Society (1971-1981); Fellow, American Ceramic Society; American Association Advancement of Science **MH:** Albert Nelson Marquis Lifetime Achievement Award

WALORSKI, JACQUELINE, "JACKIE" R., T: U.S. Representative from Indiana **I:** Government Administration/Government Relations/Government Services **CN:** U.S. House of Representatives

DOB: 08/17/1963 **PB:** South Bend **SC:** IN/USA **PT:** Raymond B. Walorski; Martha C. (Martin) Walorski **MS:** Married **SPN:** Dean Swihart (1995) **ED:** Bachelor of Arts in Communications and Public Administration, Taylor University (1985); Coursework, Liberty University (1981-1983) **C:** Member, U.S. House of Representatives from Indiana's Congressional District, United States Congress, Washington, DC (2013-Present); Member, U.S. House Committee on Veterans' Affairs (2013-Present); Member, U.S. House Committee on Budget (2013-Present); Member, U.S. House Committee on Armed Services (2013-Present); Member, District 21, Indiana House of Representatives (2004-2010); Director of Development, Indiana University South Bend (1997-1999); Director of Membership, South Bend Regional Chamber of Commerce (1996-1997); Director of Institutional Advancement, Ancilla College (1991-1996); Executive Director, Humane Society of St. Joseph City, IN (1989-1991); TV Reporter, WSBT-TV, Sinclair Broadcast Group (1985-1989) **CR:** Founder, Impact International (2000) **CIV:** Missionary, Romania (1999-2004); Member, South Gate Church, South Bend, IN **AW:** Named, Commander, Order of the Star of Romania (2017) **PA:** Republican **RE:** Charismatic

WALSH, CHRISTINE ANN, MD, FAAP, FACC I: Medicine & Health Care **CN:** Montefiore Medicine **DOB:** 12/31/1947 **PB:** Brooklyn **SC:** NY/USA **PT:** Martin Kull; Loretta (Lesniewski) Kull **MS:** Married **SPN:** Sean Michael Walsh (06/10/1978) **CH:** Kathleen; Sean; Stephen **ED:** MD, Yale University (1973); BS, Fordham University (1969) **CT:** Diplomate, American Board of Pediatric Cardiology; American Board of Critical Care Medicine; American Board of Pediatrics **C:** Professor Emerita of Pediatrics, Albert Einstein College of Medicine, Bronx, NY (2016-Present); Co-Director, Cardiogenetics, Montefiore Medical Center (2008-Present); Attending Pediatrician, Montefiore Medical Center, Bronx, NY (1998-Present); Director, Pediatrics Dysrhythmia Center, Montefiore Medical Center, Bronx, NY (1984-2018); Attending Pediatrician, Jacobi Medical Center, Bronx, NY (1984-2017);Attending Physician, North Central Bronx Hospital, Bronx, NY (1984-2017); Co-Chair, Admissions Committee, Albert Einstein College of Medicine, Bronx, NY (1998-2010); Chief, Division of Pediatric Cardiology, Montefiore Medical Center, Bronx, NY (2002-2007); Associate Professor, Pediatrics, Albert Einstein College of Medicine, Bronx, NY (1991-1998); Assistant Attending Pediatrician, Montefiore Medical Center, Bronx, NY (1984-1998); Assistant Professor, Albert Einstein College of Medicine, New York, NY (1984-1991); Assistant Professor, College of Physicians and Surgeons, Columbia University, New York, NY (1980-1984); Fellow, Pediatric Cardiology, Columbia University; Intern, Resident, Columbia-Presbyterian Medical Center **CR:** Postdoctorate Coursework, Cardiac Electrophysiology and Pharmacology, Columbia University College of Physicians and Surgeons, New York, NY (1978-1980); Consultant, Cranio-Facial Center, Pacemaker Center, Epilepsy Unit, Adult Arrhythmia Service, Montefiore Medical Center **CIV:** Board of Directors, Velo-Cardio-Facial Syndrome Educational Foundation, New York, NY (1995-Present) **CW:** Editor, "Adolescent Medicine," State of Art Reviews, Adolescent Cardiology; Contributor, Articles, Professional Journals **AW:** Master Teacher, Department of Pediatrics, Albert Einstein College of Medicine (2003-Present); Bronx Medical Society Peer to Peer Award (2015); Harboring Hearts Honoree (2014); Best Doctors in America, U.S. News and World Report (2012, 2013, 2014); William Obrinsky Award for Excellence in Medical Student Education, Department of Pediatrics, Albert Einstein College of Medicine (2012);

Rotary Gift of Life Humanitarian Award, Leo M. Davidoff Society of the Albert Einstein College of Medicine (2009); Distinguished Alumni Service Award, Yale School of Medicine (2008); Woman of the Year, Rachel Cooper Foundation (2007); Lewis M. Fraad Award for Excellence in Teaching, Department of Pediatrics, Albert Einstein College of Medicine (1992-1993); Inductee, Iota Sigma Pi; Edward C. Curnen, Jr. Award, Columbia-Presbyterian Medical Center; Listee, New York Magazine's Best Doctors in New York, Castle Connolly Guides; Listee, Top Doctors, New York Metro Area, America's Top Doctors; Paul Harris Fellow Award **MEM:** Fellow, American College of Cardiology; Fellow, American Academy of Pediatrics; Member, Section on Cardiology North American Society for Pacing and Electrophysiology Heart Rhythm Society; Pediatric and Congenital Electrophysiology Society; American Heart Association Council on Cardiovascular Disease in the Young Council on Basic Sciences; New York Heart Association Committee on Heart Health in the Young (1985-1993); Pediatric Cardiology Society of Greater New York Representative-at-Large (1986-1987); Treasurer, 1987-1988; Secretary (1988-1989); Vice President (1989-1990); President (1990-1991); Northeast Pediatric Cardiology Society; Eastern Society for Pediatric Research; New York Society of Pediatric Critical Care Medicine; American Chemical Society Medicinal Division; Babies Hospital Alumni Association; Fordham University Health Sciences Advisory Council (2011-Present); Fordham University Matteo Ricci Society mentor for candidates for prestigious fellowships/scholarships; Association of Yale Medical Alumni; Executive Committee (1999-Present); Secretary (2003-2006); Delegate to AYA, (2006-2009); Vice President, (2009-2011); President (2011-2013); Past President (2013-2015); Yale Alumni Association Board of Governors (2013-2016); Executive Officer of Board of Governors (2016-2018) **MH:** Albert Nelson Marquis Lifetime Achievement Award **B/I:** Dr. Walsh became involved in her profession because of her mother, who was a very progressive woman. During the depression, she worked during the day and received a free education for seven years at night from Brooklyn College. She then went to Fordham University for a Master's degree. Therefore, she was very encouraging when her daughter decided to pursue the medical profession. Dr. Walsh majored in chemistry at Fordham University and became interested in medicine while doing her thesis for the honors program. She loved chemistry, but, while spending time in the lab, realized she missed interacting with people. She then decided to go to medical school at Yale University, where she had a wonderful mentor, Dr. Marie Browne, a pediatric cardiologist who majorly influenced her career choice. Dr. Walsh and her daughter, Dr. Kathleen Walsh, are the first mother and daughter pediatric cardiologists in the United States. **AV:** Gardening; Skiing; Scuba diving; Playing piano; Camping

WALTER, KENNETH GAINES, T: Library Director (Emeritus) **I:** Library Management/Library Services **CN:** U. S. C. **DOB:** 03/14/1932 **PB:** Atlanta **SC:** GA/USA **PT:** Gaines Winningham; Freddie Lou Winningham **MS:** Married **SPN:** Eva Lou McClelland (06/10/1965) **CH:** Regina Eileen; Kevin Michael **ED:** EdD, University of Georgia (1995); MSLS, University of North Carolina at Chapel Hill (1966); Postgraduate Coursework, University of Vienna, Austria (1962); MS, Emory University (1958); BA, Emory University (1954) **C:** Director of Library Services Emeritus, Southern Connecticut State University, New Haven, CT (1997-Present); Director of Library Services, Southern Connecticut State University, New Haven, CT (1985-1997);

Director of Libraries, Georgia Southern University, Statesboro, GA (1975-1984); Assistant Director of Libraries, University of South Carolina, Columbia, SC (1968-1975); Faculty Representative, Baptist Student Union, Ohio University (1965-1968); Head of Cataloging Library, Ohio University (1965-1968); Assistant, Cataloging Library, Ohio University (1961-1965) **CR:** Faculty Advisor, Delta Tau Delta, Statesboro, GA (1976-1983); Book Reviewer, Library Journal (1970-1978); Consultant, Library Strategic Planning, Budgeting, Evaluation of Book Collections **CIV:** Emeritus Member, Connecticut Council of Academy Library Directors (1989-Present); Library Directors Committee (1985-1997); Connecticut State University Systems Library Automatic RFP Committee (1991-1993); Cataloging Board, New Haven Colony Historical Society (1987-1989); Interagency Library Planning Committee, Hartford, CT (1986-1989); Member Committee, In-State Service, Connecticut Academy of Library Directors (1985-1989); Statesboro-Georgia Southern Community Chorus (1980-1984); Chairman, Board of Supervisors, Congress of Racial Equality Credit Union, Statesboro, GA (1978-1981) **MIL:** Staff Sergeant, U.S. Army (1956-1957) **CW:** Contributor, Articles, Professional Journals **AW:** Fulbright Scholar (1961-1962); Grantee, Austrian Government (1961-1962); Scholarship, Emory University (1950-1953) **MEM:** President, Georgia Academy of Science; Georgia Association of College and Research Libraries (1983); President, Eastern Georgia Library Triangle (1976-1983); Life Member, American Library Association; Georgia Academy of Library Directors; Georgia Regents Committee (1975-1983); President, Center for Georgia Associate Libraries (1980-1982); Association of College and Research Libraries; Library Administration and Management Association; Reference and User Services Association; Southeastern Library Association; Georgia Library Association; Connecticut Library Association; Rotary; Sigma Gamma Epsilon; Beta Phi Mu; Phi Delta Kappa; Delta Tau Delta **AV:** Camping; Rock collecting; Collecting stamps; Woodworking **RE:** Baptist

WALTERS, MERCEDES, "MERCY" B., T: District Governor of Lions District 4 L-6 **I:** Nonprofit & Philanthropy **CN:** Lions Clubs International **SC:** The Philippines **PT:** Segundo A. Barnachea (Deceased) **CH:** Two Children **ED:** Baccalaureate in Nursing, University of Santo Tomas, Manila, The Philippines (1961) **CT:** Registered Nurse **C:** Retired (2003); National Director of Human Resources, Human Resource Management, Avanti Health Systems, Chicago, IL (2003); Registered Nurse (10 Years) **CIV:** Member, Legion of Mary **AW:** Leadership Medal from International President of Lions, Lions Club International; #1 Membership Growth Award, Lions Clubs International **MEM:** Society for Human Resources Management (SHRM); National Association of Recruiters (Now National Association of Executive Recruiters) **MH:** Marquis Who's Who Humanitarian Award **AS:** Ms. Walters is an overachiever. Growing up, her father challenged her. When she was in high school, she was third in her class and her father asked her, why can't she be number one? She took that as a challenge, and the following year she became number 2, eventually going on to graduate as the first in her class. Her father always made her feel that if others can do it, she can do it better. She reads about things that she wants information about and she prepares herself whenever she is tasked with something. **B/I:** Ms. Walters started school at the age of 4 in the Philippines. She was only a visitor at that age because her father did not want her to stay home during the days, so she would go to school with her older sister. While attending school with her sister in the first grade, despite being

the youngest, she had the highest grades in the class. She skipped several grades and eventually finished her bachelor's degree in Nursing at only age 19. When Ms. Walter's had been practicing as a nurse for some time, her husband was stationed at Elmendorf Air Force Base, in Anchorage, Alaska. She was unable to work as a nurse for her shift work because she had small children at home to take care of. After three years of being in Alaska, she found a job as an employment specialist with the department of labor. After doing processing claims, she felt that she needed a change and received a position as an adjudicator of unemployment insurance, where she spent five years. The position, she recalls, was very stressful. She then transferred to the placement section, where became the top employment specialist out of 36 interviewers. When she got divorced, she moved to Chicago to look for work, and that is where her career began in human resources. **THT:** Ms. Walters' motto is, "If others can do it, I can do it better..." She also says, "I don't strive for perfection, I strive for excellence..." She says, "Women have a lot of skills, knowledge and abilities that they can share."

WALTZ, CHRISTOPH, T: Actor **I:** Media & Entertainment **DOB:** 10/04/1956 **PB:** Vienna **SC:** Austria **PT:** Johannes Waltz; Elisabeth Urbancic **MS:** Married **SPN:** Judith Holste; Jackie Waltz (Divorced) **CH:** Four Children **ED:** Student, Lee Strasberg; Student, Stella Adler; Student, Singing and Opera, University of Music and Perofrming Arts Vienna; Student, Max Reinhardt Seminar **C:** Actor, Film and Television **CW:** Voice Actor, "Pinocchio" (2021); Actor, "Most Dangerous Game" (2020); Actor, "Rifkin's Festival" (2020); Actor, "No Time to Die" (2020); Actor, "The French Dispatch" (2020); Director, "Georgetown" (2019); Actor, "Georgetown" (2019); Actor, "Alita: Battle Angel" (2019); Actor, "Downsizing" (2017); Actor, "Tulip Fever" (2017); Actor, "The Legend of Tarzan" (2016); Narrator, "Clash of Clans: A Special Map Official TV Commercial" (2016); Actor, "Spectre" (2015); Actor, "Big Eyes" (2014); Actor, "Horrible Bosses 2" (2014); Actor, "Muppets Most Wanted" (2014); Host, "Saturday Night Live" (2013); Co-Producer, "The Zero Theorem" (2013); Actor, "The Zero Theorem" (2013); Voice Actor, "Epic" (2013); Actor, "Django Unchained" (2012); Actor, "Carnage" (2011); Actor, "The Three Musketeers" (2011); Actor, "Water for Elephants" (2011); Actor, "The Green Hornet" (2011); Actor, "Inglourious Basterds" (2009); Actor, "Tatort" (2008, 2006, 1987); Actor, "Das Geheimnis im Wald" (2008); Actor, "Todsünde" (2008); Actor, "Das jüngste Gericht" (2008); Actor, "Die Anwälte" (2008); Actor, "Die Zürcher Verlobung - Drehbuch zur Liebe" (2007); Actor, "Under Suspicion" (2007); Actor, "Der letzte Zeuge" (2007); Actor, "Die Verzauberung" (2007); Actor, "Der Staatsanwalt" (2007); Actor, "Franziskas Gespür für Männer" (2006); Actor, "Stolberg" (2006); Actor, "Polizeiruf 110" (2006); Actor, "Die Spezialisten: Kripo Rhein-Main" (2006); Actor, "Lapislazuli - Im Auge des Bären" (2006); Actor, "Unsolved" (2005); Actor, "Die Patriatchin" (2005); Actor, "Scheidungsopfer Mann" (2004); Actor, "Schöne Witwen küssen besser" (2004); Actor, "Mörderische Suche" (2004); Actor, "Berlin Blues" (2003); Actor, "Tigeraugen sehen besser" (2003); Actor, "Gun-shy" (2003); Actor, "Jennerwin" (2003); Actor, "Zwei Tage Hoffnung" (2003); Actor, "Pact with the Devil" (2003); Actor, "Der Fall Gehring" (2003); Actor, "Jagd auf den Flammenmann" (2003); Actor, "Angst" (2003); Actor, "Weihnachtsmann gesucht" (2002); Actor, "Dienstreise - Was für eine Nacht" (2002); Actor, "She" (2001); Actor, "Der Tanz mit dem Teufel - Die Entführung des Richard Oetker " (2001); Actor, "Riekes Liebe" (2001); Actor, "Death,

Deceit & Destiny Aboard the Orient Express" (2001); Director, "Wenn man sich traut" (2000); Writer, "Wenn man sich traut" (2000); Actor, "Engel sucht Flügel" (2001); Actor, "Queen's Messenger" (2001); Actor, "The Beast" (2000); Actor, "Falling Rocks" (2000); Actor, "Ordinary Decent Criminal" (2000); Actor, "L'histoire du samedi" (1999); Actor, "Die Braut" (1999); Actor, "Einsteins Ende" (1998); Actor, "Mörderisches Erbe - Tausch mit einer Toten" (1998); Actor, "Rache für mein totes Kind" (1998); Actor, "Love Scenes from Planet Earth" (1998); Actor, "Das Finale" (1998); Actor, "Sieben Monde" (1998); Actor, "Shock - Eine Frau in Angst" (1998); Actor, "Vickys Alptraum" (1998); Actor, "Schimanski" (1997); Actor, "Our God's Brother" (1997); Actor, "Faust" (1997); Actor, "Maître Da Costa" (1997); Actor, "Rex: A Cop's Best Friend" (1996); Actor, "Rosa Roth" (1996); Actor, "Du bist nicht allein - Die Roy Black Story" (1996); Actor, "Der Tourist" (1996); Actor, "Man(n) sucht Frau" (1995); Actor, "Prinz zu entsorgen" (1995); Actor, "The All New Alexei Sayle Show" (1995); Actor, "Die Staatsanwältin" (1995); Actor, "Ein Anfang von etwas" (1995); Actor, "Catherine the Great" (1995); Actor, "Jacob" (1994); Actor, "Tag der Abrechnung - Der Amokläufer von Euskirchen" (1994); Actor, "A King for Burning" (1993); Actor, "Die Angst wird bleiben" (1992); Actor, "5 Zimmer, Küche, Bad " (1992); Actor, "Life for Life: Maximilian Kolbe" (1991); Actor, "The Gravy Train Goes East" (1991); Actor, "St. Petri Schnee" (1991); Actor, "Napoléon et l'Europe" (1991); Actor, "The Gravy Train" (1990); Actor, "Goldeneye" (1989); Actor, "Quicker Than the Eye" (1988); Actor, "The Alien Years" (1988); Actor, "Das andere Leben" (1987); Actor, "The Old Fox" (1986-1990); Actor, "Derrick" (1986-1988); Actor, "Lenz oder die Freiheit" (1986); Actor, "Wahnfried" (1986); Actor, "Ein Fall für zwei" (1985); Actor, "Der Sandmann" (1983); Actor, "Dr. Maragarete Johnsohn" (1982); Actor, "The Mysterious Stranger" (1982); Actor, "Fire and Sword" (1982); Actor, "Die Weltmaschine" (1981); Actor, "Kopfstand" (1981); Actor, "Parole Chicago" (1979); Actor, "Feuer!" (1979); Actor, "Breakthrough" (1979); Actor, "Der Einstand" (1977); Actor, "Am Dam Des" (1977) **AW:** Outstanding European Achievement in World Cinema, European Film Awards (2015); Recipient, Star, Hollywood Walk of Fame (2014); Best Supporting Actor, "Django Unchained," Academy Awards (2012); Best Supporting Actor - Motion Picture, "Django Unchained," Golden Globe Awards (2012); Best Actor in a Supporting Role, "Django Unchained," BAFTA Awards (2012); Austrian Cross of Honour for Science and Art (2012); Best Supporting Actor, "Django Unchained," San Diego Film Critics Society Awards (2012); Best Actor, "Inglourious Basterds," Empire Awards (2010); Cinema Vanguard Award, Santa Barbara International Film Festival (2010); Favorite Actor, Romy (2010); Best Supporting Actor, "Inglourious Basterds," Denver Film Critics Society (2010); Best Supporting Actor, "Inglourious Basterds," International Online Cinema Awards (2010); Best Supporting Actor, "Inglourious Basterds," Iowa Film Critics Awards (2010); Best International Actor, "Inglourious Basterds," Jupiter Award (2010); Actor of the Year, "Inglourious Basterds," London Critics Circle Film Awards (2010); Best Supporting Actor, "Inglourious Basterds," North Texas Film Critics Association (2010); Best Performance by an Actor in a Supporting Role, "Inglourious Basterds," Phoenix Film Critics Society Awards (2009); Best Supporting Actor, "Inglourious Basterds," Dallas-Fort Worth Film Critics Association Awards (2009); Best Supporting Actor, "Inglourious Basterds," Florida Film Critics Circle Awards (2009); Best Supporting Actor, "Inglourious Basterds," Academy Awards (2009); Best Supporting Actor - Motion

Picture, "Inglourious Basterds" (2009); Best Actor in a Supporting Role, "Inglourious Basterds," BAFTA Awards (2009); Best Actor, "Inglourious Basterds," Cannes Film Festival (2009); Best Supporting Actor, "Inglourious Basterds," Critics' Choice Movie Awards (2009); Best Acting by an Ensemble, "Inglourious Basterds," Critics' Choice Movie Awards (2009); Best Supporting Actor - Motion Picture, "Inglourious Basterds," Satellite Awards (2009); Outstanding Performance by a Cast in a Motion Picture, "Inglourious Basterds," Screen Actors Guild Awards (2009); Outstanding Performance by a Male Actor in a Supporting Role, "Inglourious Basterds," Screen Actors Guild Awards (2009); Best Supporting Actor, "Inglorious Basterds," Hollywood Film Awards (2009); Best Supporting Actor, "Inglourious Basterds," Houston Film Critics Society Awards (2009); Best Supporting Actor, "Inglourious Basterds," Indiana Film Journalists Association (2009); Best Supporting Actor, "Inglourious Basterds," Las Vegas Film Critics Society Awards (2009); Best Supporting Actor, "Inglourious Basterds," Washington D.C. Area Film Critics Association Awards (2009); Best Supporting Actor, "Jagd auf den Flammenmann," German Television Awards (2003); Adolf Grimme Award, "Dienstreise – Was für eine Nacht" (2002); Adolf Grimme Award, "Der Tanz mit dem Teufel" (2001); O.E. Hasse Prize, Berlin Academy of Arts (1982)

WALTZ, MICHAEL GEORGE GLEN, T: U.S. Representative from Florida **I:** Government Administration/Government Relations/Government Services **DOB:** 01/31/1974 **PB:** Boynton Beach **SC:** FL/USA **CH:** One Daughter **ED:** BS in International Studies, Virginia Military Institute **C:** Member, U.S. House of Representatives from Florida's Sixth Congressional District (2019-Present); Director for Afghanistan Policy, Office of the Secretary of Defense; Senior Advisor on South Asia and Counter-terrorism, Vice President Dick Cheney; Co-founder, Partner, Askari Associates, LLC; President, Metis Solutions; Member, Committee on Armed Services, United States Congress; Member, Committee on Science, Space and Technology, United States Congress **MIL:** Second Lieutenant, United States Army National Guard **CW:** Author, "Warrior Diplomat: A Green Beret's Battles from Washington to Afghanistan" (2014); Contributor, FOX News, CNN, MSNBC, BBC World News and "Frontline," PBS **PA:** Republican

WALTZ, THOMAS WILLIAM, T: Economist **I:** Environmental Services **DOB:** 10/20/1940 **PB:** Youngstown **SC:** OH/USA **PT:** William Walter Edds; Viola Helena (Huhta) (Edds) (Waltz) Kask **MS:** Widowed **SPN:** Linda Estelle (Taylor) Waltz **CH:** Alexandre Nadine Beatrice Waltz **ED:** Postgraduate Coursework, University of London (1968-1969); PHD Candidate, Northwestern University (1968); BS, Massachusetts Institute of Technology (1962) **C:** President, UNICOM International Inc. and Consultant, World Bank, WA (1989-2010); Financial, Technical and Industrial Project Design and Management Oversight for the Cost-Effective Phase-out of Stratospheric Ozone Depleting Substances in Use in Developing Countries, Under the Montreal Protocol, World Bank, WA (1989-2010); Economist, National Environmental Satellite, Data and Information Service National Oceanographic and Atmospheric Administration, U.S. Department of Commerce, Washington, DC (1974-1989); Program Officer, UNICEF, Nairobi, Kenya (1972-1974); Economist, Congressional Research Service, Washington, DC (1971-1972); Economist, Howard, Needles, Tammen & Bergendoff, Alexandria, VA (1969-1971) **CR:** Directed World Bank Industry Sector-based Scientific, Technical and Financial Guidance for the Phase-out of Ozone Depleting Sub-

stances Under the Montreal Protocol in Developing Countries; Managed Implementation of All Phase-out Programs and Projects in Turkey, Ukraine, and Russia **CIV:** Economist, National Oceanic and Atmospheric Administration (NOAA) (1974-1978); UNICEF Liaison Officer, Nairobi, Kenya (1972-1974); Volunteer, University of Liberia and National Planning Agency, U.S. Peace Corps, Monrovia, Liberia (1963-1965) **CW:** Co-author with Erik Arrhenius, "The Greenhouse Effect: Implications for Economic Development," The World Bank, Discussion Paper No. 78, First Printing (1990); Author, "Ocean and Coastal Marine Resources: Implications for the World Bank, Sector and Policy Research," The World Bank (1990) **AW:** Ford Foundation Fellow (1968); Fulbright-Hays Fellow (1966-1968) **MH:** Albert Nelson Marquis Lifetime Achievement Award **AV:** Snorkeling; Archaeology; Gardening; Literature **PA:** Republican **RE:** Protestant

WALZ, ROBERT D. USA, LT. COL., T: Military Officer (Retired), Teacher (Retired) **I:** Military & Defense Services **DOB:** 05/15/1944 **PB:** Great Falls **SC:** MT/USA **PT:** Robert Chaussee Walz; Jean (DeHaven) Walz **MS:** Married **SPN:** Merrill Ann Martin (01/25/1967) **CH:** Juli Ann **ED:** MA in Government, Minor in History, University of South Dakota (1968); BA in History, and Government, University of South Dakota (1966) **C:** Instructor, Strategy, Command and General Staff College, U.S. Army, Fort Leavenworth, Kansas (1992-2007); Staff Officer, Strategy and Pacific Policy Issues, Office of Deputy Chief of Chaff for Operations and Plans, U.S. Department of the Army, Washington, DC (1989-1991); Author, Instructor (China), Command and General Staff College, U.S. Army, Fort Leavenworth, Kansas (1984-1989); Chief, New Systems Division, Target Acquisition Department, U.S. Army, Fort Sill, OK (1982-1984); Foreign Area Officer Trainee, National University of Singapore (1980-1981); Area Commander, Recruiting Area, U.S. Army, Mason City, IA (1976-1977); Staff Officer, 1st Battalion, 38th Field Artillery, U.S. Army, Camp Stanley, Korea (1974-1975); Assistant Professor of Military Science, University of Vermont, Burlington, VT (1972-1974) **MIL:** Battery Commander, Battery A, 1st Battalion, 17th Artillery, U.S. Army, Fort Sill, OK (1971-1972); Fire Support Officer, 2d Battalion, 320th Artillery, U.S. Army, Gia Le, Vietnam (1969-1970); Battery Officer, Third Battalion, 320th Artillery, U.S. Army, Fort Bragg, NC (1968-1969) **CW:** Author, Co-Author, 16 Books About the Santa Fe Railway; Contributor, Articles, Publications **AW:** Decorated Legion of Merit; Bronze Star; Meritorious Service Medal; Army Commendation Medals; Five Air Medals; Commander and General Staff College Civilian and Instructor of the Year **MEM:** Secretary, Santa Fe Railway Historical and Modeling Society (2013-2020); Board of Directors, Santa Fe Railway Historical and Modeling Society; National Railway Historical Society; Former Board of Directors, Railroad Artifacts Preservation Society **MH:** Albert Nelson Marquis Lifetime Achievement Award **B/I:** Mr. Walz became involved in his profession because he was at the University of South Dakota when ROTC was a required course from freshmen and sophomores. He did not think about a military career until that time; he was planning on becoming a lawyer. He really enjoyed ROTC. One of the courses was military history which he had always been interested in. This was during the Vietnam era and he thought it was better to serve as an officer than as an enlisted man. Especially with his education, he thought, he could make a better contribution. He signed up for the final two years and got his commission through ROTC and got in and never got out until he retired. He enjoyed what he was doing, particularly the Army because his master's

degree was in government with an emphasis on Chinese politics, so they selected him to be a specialist in China. Mr. Walz had two professors at the University of South Dakota, one of Chinese history and one of Chinese politics, and he found China fascinating so it seemed to be logical to apply for the foreign area officer program. In addition, Mr. Walz became involved in writing and focusing his creative works on the Santa Fe Railway because he started years ago building a model railway. He developed an interest in the geographical area and so he focused his first book on it. Being a history and government major at the University of South Dakota who always liked history and modeling, he thought that they kind of fit. It was also something to keep him busy and snowballed from there. **AV:** Model railroading; Photography

WALZ, TIMOTHY, "TIM" JAMES, T: Governor of Minnesota **I:** Government Administration/Government Relations/Government Services **DOB:** 04/06/1964 **PB:** West Point **SC:** NE/USA **PT:** James F. "Jim" Walz; Darlene R. Walz **MS:** Married **SPN:** Gwen Whipple (1994) **CH:** Hope; Gus **ED:** MS in Education Leadership, St. Mary's University, Winona, MN (2001); BS in Social Science Education, Chadron State College, NE (1989) **C:** Governor, State of Minnesota (2019-Present); Member, House Committee on Veterans Affairs (2007-2019); Member, Minnesota's First Congressional District, United States Congress (2007-2019); Teacher, Mankato West High School, Mankato, MN (1996-2006); Teacher, Alliance Public Schools (1991-1996); High School Teacher, People's Republic of China (1989-1990) **MIL:** Master Sergeant, United States Army National Guard (2005); Served in Operation Enduring Freedom (2005); Advanced to Command Sergeant Major, United States Army National Guard (1981-2005) **AW:** Named Minnesota Teacher of Excellence (2003); Named Mankato Teacher of the Year (2003); Minnesota Ethics in Education Award (2002); Outstanding Young Nebraskan, Nebraska Junior Chamber of Commerce (1993); Named Nebraska Citizen Soldier of the Year (1989) **PA:** Democrat **RE:** Lutheran

WANG, ALEXANDER, T: Apparel Designer **I:** Apparel & Fashion **DOB:** 12/26/1983 **PB:** San Francisco **SC:** CA/USA **PT:** Ying Wang **ED:** Coursework, Parsons School of Design **C:** Chief Executive Officer, Chairman, The Alexander Wang Brand (2016-2017); Designer, Launcher, Jewelry Line (2015); Creative Director, Balenciaga (2012-2015); Designer, H&M (2014); Owner, Alexander Wang, Soho, NY (2011); Designer, Platform Sandals (2009); Designer, Alexander Wang Women's Collection (2007); Designer, Alexander Wang (2005); Product Lines, Retailers, Barneys NYC, Neiman Marcus, Bergdorf Goodman, Dover Street Market, Browns, Otte, and Selfridges; Intern, Vogue; Intern, Teen Vogue **CIV:** Avid Supporter, LGBTQ Community **CW:** Subject, "Alexander Wang," by Sunny Chanday **AW:** Listee, "The 100 Most Influential People of 2015," Time Magazine (2015); Fashion Star, Fashion Group International (2013); Best New Menswear Designer in America, GQ (2011); Swarovski Designer of the Year Award (2010); Swiss Textiles Award (2009); 2008 Council of Fashion Designers of America/Vogue Fashion Fund Award (2008); Best Accessory Designer, Council of Fashion Designers of America

WANG, AN-MING, T: Composer **I:** Fine Art **DOB:** 11/07/1926 **PB:** Shanghai **SC:** China **PT:** Cheng Hsu Wang; Eling (Tong) Wang **MS:** Widowed **SPN:** William K. Mak (1951) **CH:** Elise; Darrell **ED:** MA in Music Education, Columbia University (1951);BA, Wesleyan Conservatory, Macon, GA (1950); BE, Central China University (1947)

C: Freelance Composer (1951) **CW:** Author, "A Child of Grace" (2019); Author, "Woodwind Octet" (2018); Author, "Ocean Medley" (2016); Author, "The Homeless Child (Ballet Suite)" (2007); Author, "Kapalua for Flute and Piano" (2005); Author, "Dazzling Jewels for High Voice and Piano" (2005); Author, "Fantasy for Solo Organ" (2001); Author, "East Wind for Flute and Piano" (1997); Composer, "Lan Ying (Opera in three Acts)" (1995); Author, "The Christmas Gift for Chorus and Keyboard/Orchestra" (1993); Composer, Gloria for Chorus and Orchestra (1991); Composer, "Piano Concerto" (1990); Composer, "The Song of Endless Sorrow" (1985); Composer, "Songs for All Seasons" (1982); Composer, "Requiem for Chorus and Orchestra/Organ" (1982) **AW:** Individual Artist Award, Maryland State Arts Council (1999); Lan Ying (Opera in Three Acts), National League of American Pen Women (1998) **MEM:** American Society of Composers; International Alliance for Women in Music; Southeastern Composers League; Society of Composers; National League of American Pen Women, Inc.; National Federation of Music Clubs; Friday Morning Music Club, Inc. (Washington); Sigma Alpha Iota **MH:** Albert Nelson Marquis Lifetime Achievement Award; Marquis Who's Who Top Professional **AS:** Ms. Wang attributes her success to hard work. **B/I:** Ms. Wang became involved in her profession because her parents were both educated in the United States, but returned to China upon graduation. When they returned to China, they also brought back western music, which is when she was first exposed to it. Additionally, her mother played the piano and she recalls hearing it and falling in love with the instrument. Although it was uncommon for women to be composers at the time, she was so in love with the piano and felt a strong desire to create; she continued to pursue her ambition to compose in secret until she moved to the United States to study music. In addition, her mother majored in music at Wellesley College. She was a pioneer woman and among the first group of Chinese Scholar women who came over to the United States to study. She won the scholarship from the University in China to come over to study. Her father also went to Yale and Princeton through the same business. That is where she got most of her inspiration from and how she got interested in western music from an early age. **PA:** Republican **RE:** Episcopalian

WANG, LIANG-GUO, T: Research Scientist **I:** Research **DOB:** 04/23/1945 **PB:** Foochow **SC:** China **PT:** Chi-hsi Wang; Yunquing Chen **MS:** Married **SPN:** Shufen Zhang (09/27/1977) **CH:** Zhijing Wang; Zhijian Wang **ED:** Doctor of Philosophy in Physics, Ohio State University (1986); Master of Science in Physics, Ohio State University (1983); Bachelor of Science in Physics, Peking University, Beijing, China (1969) **C:** Senior Scientist, Ultratech-Veeco, San Jose, CA (2013-Present); Manager, System Design, KLA-Tencor, San Jose, CA (2002-2013); Member, Technical Staff, Applied Materials, Sunnyvale, CA (1997-2002); Research Scientist, College of William and Mary, Williamsburg, VA (1989-1997); Research Assistant, University of Virginia, Charlottesville, VA (1987-1989); Research Assistant, Ohio State University, Columbus, OH (1981-1986); Research Assistant, University of Kentucky, Lexington, KY (1981); Research Assistant, Institute of Academia Sinica, Beijing, China (1978-1980); Technical Manager and Electronics Engineer, Various Companies, China (1971-1978) **CR:** Consultant, National Aeronautics and Space Administration, Langley Research Center, Hampton, VA (1989-1997) **CW:** Contributor, Articles to Professional Journals **AW:** Public Service Medal, National Aeronautics and Space Administration (1992) **MH:** Albert Nelson Marquis Lifetime Achievement

Award; Marquis Who's Who Top Professional **AS:** Dr. Wang attributes his success to the excellent education he received in the United States. **B/I:** Dr. Wang first became involved in his profession after earning his doctorate in physics. Following this accomplishment, some of his colleagues became professors, spurring him to enter into research.

WANG, LISA, T: Chief Executive Officer **I:** Business Management/Business Services **DOB:** 09/24/1988 **PB:** Madison **SC:** WI/USA **MS:** Married **ED:** Coursework in Advanced Chinese Language Study, Tsinghua University (2013); BA in American Literature, Yale University (2012) **CT:** Intermediate L2 Certification in Wines & Spirits, Wine & Spirit Education Trust (WSET) **C:** Founder, Chief Executive Owner, The Gloal League of Women (The GLOW) (2019-Present); Chief Executive Officer, Co-Founder, SheWorx (2015-2019); Founder, Fooze (2015); Hedge Fund Analyst, Wall Street; Rhythmic Gymnast, Numerous National Championships (2001-2012); Rhythmic Gymnast, Chinese National Team (2000) **CR:** Contributor, Thrive Global (2020-Present); International Keynote Speaker, Chartwell Speakers Bureau (2016-Present); Advisor, Republic (2019-Present); Contributing Writer, Forbes (2017-Present); U30 Advisory Board Member, Delta Air Lines (2019); Entrepreneur Insider, Contributor, Fortune Magazine (2017); Analyst, Balyasny Asset Management LP (2013-2014); Analyst, Events Coordination, HLD Events (2012-2013); Business Development Intern, Hong Kong Arts Festival Society, Ltd. (2011) **CIV:** Speaker, Women in Cable Telecommunications (2018); Mentor, Techstars (2018); Speaker, Global Chief Innovation Officer Summit (2017); Mentor, ESchool4Girls (2016); Teacher, Volunteer, Hope of the Future, AIESEC **CW:** Host, "The Global League of Women Podcast" **AW:** Honoree, Forbes 30 Under 30 (2017); Inductee, U.S. Gymnastics Hall of Fame (2014); Red Bull Hero of the Year; Inductee, Red Shoe Movement Hall of Fame; Listee, "100 Most Powerful Woman," Entrepreneur Magazine; Listee, CIO's Top 20 Female Entrepreneurs

WANG, LULU, T: Film Director, Writer, Producer **I:** Media & Entertainment **DOB:** 02/25/1983 **PB:** Beijing **SC:** China **PT:** Haiyan Wang; Jian Yu **MS:** Single **ED:** BA in Music and Literature, Boston College, Chestnut Hill, MA (2005); Student, New World School of Arts **CR:** Chaz and Roger Ebert Directing Fellowship, Film Independent Spirit Awards (2014); Film Independent Project Involve Directing Fellowship (2014) **CW:** Director, Producer, Writer, Web Series, "The Expatriates" (2020); Director, Writer, Producer, "The Farewell" (2019); Writer, "This American Life" (2016); Director, Writer, "Touch" (2015); Director, Writer, "Posthumous" (2014); Director, Music Video, "Still and Always Will" (2014); Director, Web Series, "Burke and Herb" (2014); Director, Music Video, "Nobody Told Me" (2011); Director, Producer, Writer, Short Film, "Can-Can" (2007); Director, Documentary Short Film, "Fishing the Gulf" (2006); Director, Producer, Writer, Short Video, "Pisces" (2005) **AW:** Best Feature, Independent Spirit Awards (2020); New Voice Award for Film, Final Draft Awards (2020); Top 10 Films, American Film Institute (2019); Directors to Watch, Palm Springs International Film Festival (2019); Best Drama, Asians on Film Festival (2015) **AV:** Playing piano

WANG, VERA, T: Fashion Designer **I:** Apparel & Fashion **DOB:** 06/27/1949 **PB:** New York **SC:** NY/USA **PT:** Cheng Ching Wang; Florence Wu **MS:** Single **SPN:** Arthur Becker (06/22/1989, Separated 2012) **CH:** Cecilia (Adopted Daughter); Josephine (Adopted Daughter) **ED:** BA in Art History, Sarah Lawrence College (1978); Student, University

of Paris **C:** Owner, Vera Wang Bridal House, Ltd. (1990-Present); Costume Designer, Nancy Kerrigan, Michelle Kwan, Evan Lysacek, Nathan Chen, Winter Olympics (1992, 1994, 1998, 2002, 2010, 2018); Design Director, Accessories, Ralph Lauren (1987-1989); Temporary Assistant, Fashion Editor, Senior Fashion Editor, Vogue (1970-1987); Owner, Vera Wang China and Crystal Collection **CR:** Designer, Ready-to-Wear Clothing, Simply Vera, Kohl's **CW:** Herself, "Scatter My Ashes at Bergdorf's" (2013); Herself, "Gossip Girl" (2012); Herself, "Keeping Up with the Kardashians" (2011); Herself, "Chelsea Lately" (2011); Herself, "The September Issue" (2009); Herself, "The Celebrity Apprentice" (2008); Herself, "Ugly Betty" (2007); Herself, "First Daughter" (2004); Author, "Vera Wang on Weddings" (2001); Costume Designer, "The Parent Trap" (1998); Costume Designer, "Sex and the City"; Costume Designer, "The Prom," "Buffy the Vampire Slayer" **AW:** Ranked #34, "America's Richest Self-Made Women 2018," Forbes (2018); Geoffrey Beene Lifetime Achievement Award, 2013 CFDA Fashion Awards (2013); Council of Fashion Designers of America Lifetime Achievement Award (2013); Leadership in Arts Award, Radcliffe-Harvard Asian American Association (2010); Inductee "for her contribution to the sport as a costume designer," U.S. Figure Skating Hall of Fame (2009); André Leon Talley Lifetime Achievement Award, Savannah College of Art and Design (2006); Council of Fashion Designers of America Womenswear Designer of the Year (2005); Woman of the Year Award, Glamour (2003); Presenter, Debutante to High Society, International Debutante Ball, Waldorf Astoria New York (1968); Featured, "Faces in the Crowd," Sports Illustrated (1968)

WANN, SHARON, T: Dentist **I:** Medicine & Health Care **CN:** Sharon Wann Family Dentist **PB:** Tulsa **SC:** OK/USA **PT:** Loyd Ray Linde; Zera Mae Linde **MS:** Married **ED:** DMD, Oral Roberts University (1985); Student, Chemistry, University of Oklahoma **C:** Dentist, Sharon Wann Family Dentist, Tulsa, OK (1985-Present) **CR:** ClearCorrect Provider **CIV:** Volunteer, "OK Mom," Oklahoma Mission of Mercy; Participant, Donating Dental Services of Tulsa **AW:** Voted One of "Tulsa's Top Dentists" **MEM:** Tulsa County Dental Society; Oklahoma Dental Association; American Dental Association; Tulsa Branch, Seattle Study Club **AS:** Dr. Wann attributes her success to being a very nurturing, caring person. She loves getting to know her patients, not rushing people. and, because of that, having three generations of families. It has been extremely rewarding to make people happy like that. Her mission has been to change people's perception of the dentist. She bought a little house to convert into an office, everything being done with patient comfort in mind. The dental equipment is all behind the patient and there are French doors so they can see out. **B/I:** Ms. Wann became involved in her profession because she has always been focused on teeth, even as a kid. She initially thought she would go to hygiene school because she had never heard of a women dentist back then. She had a counselor at the University of Oklahoma ask her if she ever thought about dental school because, with her GPA, she was sure that she could get in. That was a turning point for her, and she has loved it; it is perfect for her. **AV:** Spending time with family and friends; Reading; Motorcycling; Playing college football; Playing professional basketball

WARD, DONALD, T: Attorney **I:** Law and Legal Services **CN:** Searcy Denney Scarola Barnhart & Shipley, P.A. **MS:** Married **SPN:** Abbie Ward **ED:** JD, University of Notre Dame Law School, Cum Laude

(2011); BA in History and Religious Studies, University of Virginia, Charlottesville, VA (2008); Coursework, Study Abroad, University College, University of Oxford, Oxford, United Kingdom (2007) **C:** Associate, Searcy Denney Scarola Barnhart & Shipley, P.A., West Palm Beach, FL (2011- Present) **CW:** Author, "Is the Irreversible TRULY Unforeseeable? The Law of Suicide Prevention," Florida Justice Association Journal (2014) **AW:** Selected as a "Rising Star," Florida Super Lawyers (2013, 2014, 2015); Selected for Membership, National Trial Lawyers "Top 40 Under 40" (2014, 2015); Named to "Top 10 Personal Injury Attorneys Under 40 in South Florida," National Academy of Personal Injury Attorneys (2015) **MEM:** Order of St. Thomas More, Notre Dame Law School (2014-Present); Board of Directors, Palm Beach County Justice Association (2014-Present); The District of Columbia Bar (2012-Present); The Florida Bar (2011-Present); Florida Justice Association (2011-Present); Palm Beach County Bar Association (2011-Present); American Association for Justice (2011-Present); American Bar Association (ABA) (2011-Present); Board of Directors, Young Lawyers Section, Florida Justice Association (2012-2014); Palm Beach County Justice Association (2011); **EAGLE BAR:** United States District Court for the Southern District of Florida (2012); District of Columbia (2012); Florida (2011); United States District Court for the Northern District of Florida (2011); United States District Court for the Middle District of Florida (2011) **B/I:** Mr. Ward did not come from a family of lawyers, which is very unique in his firm; a lot of his colleagues are second and third generation lawyers. If you don't know the law or don't have an opportunity to hire someone, who has your best interest? So just the idea of being able to help his own family and friends as well as others is the driving force to be in his profession and help them navigate through a rough time through their life. **THT:** Mr. Ward lives by the golden rule. He's a firm believer that we should treat others like we would like to be treated. He holds that close to him as well as his faith.

WARD, JACQUELINE ANN, T: Nurse, Health Care Administrator, Legal Nurse Consultant **I:** Health, Wellness and Fitness **DOB:** 10/23/1945 **PB:** Somerset **SC:** PA/USA **PT:** Donald C. Beas (Adoptive); Thelma R. (Wable) Beas (Adoptive); Joseph Shurbauch (Biological); Georgie Anna Horner (Biological) **MS:** Divorced **CH:** Charles L. Ward, Jr.; Shawn M. Ward **ED:** AS in Health Services Management and Nursing Home Administration, St. Petersburg College (1997); MBA, Columbus College (Now Columbus State University) (1983); MA in Counseling and Guidance, West Virginia College of Graduate Studies (Now Marshall University) (1976); BSN, University of Pittsburgh (1966) **CT:** Legal Nurse Consultant (2007); Advanced Certified Nursing Administrator; Nursing Home Administrator Preceptor; Adult Living Facility Administrator **C:** Legal Nurse Consultant (2007-Present); Administrator, Tandem Health Care (Now Consulate Health Care of Sarasota), Sarasota, FL (2005-2007); Executive Director, Beneva Park Club (Now Beneva Lakes Healthcare and Rehabilitation Center), Sarasota, FL (2005); Administrator, Sun Terrace Rehabilitation Center, Sun City Center, FL (2002-2005); Administrator, Centers for Long Term Care, Venice, FL (2000-2001); Facilities Administrator, Long Term Care, Sarasota, FL (1999-2000); Director of Nursing, Long Term Care, Sarasota, FL (1999-2000); Adjunct, Clinical Nursing Faculty, Manatee Community College (Now State College of Florida, Manatee-Sarasota), Bradenton, FL (1998-1999); Support Services Consultant, Interim Administrator, Long Term Care (1997-1998); Director, Skilled Unit and Special Projects, Bon Secours-Venice

Hospital, Venice, FL (1995-1997); Executive Director, Vice President, Venice Memorial Hospital Life Counseling Center, Osprey, FL (1994-1995); Vice President of Operations, Venice Memorial Hospital, Venice, FL (1990-1994); Vice President of Nursing, Venice Memorial Hospital, Venice, FL (1984-1990); Director of Nursing, H.D. Cobb Memorial Hospital, Phenix City, AL (1982-1984); Staff Nurse, Memorial Division, Charleston Area Medical Center, Charleston, WV (1971-1982); Charge Nurse, Staff Nurse, Rocky Mountain Osteopathic Hospital, Denver, CO (1971); Staff Nurse, Supervisor, Bexar County Hospital, San Antonio, TX (1970); Staff Nurse, Santa Rosa Hospital, San Antonio, TX (1969); Staff Nurse, Head Nurse, Memorial Hospital, Charleston, WV (1967-1969); Staff Nurse, West Virginia University Hospital, Morgantown, WV (1966-1967); Assistant Director of Nursing, General Division, Charleston Area Medical Center; Staff Nurse, In-Service Educator, McMillan Division, Charleston Area Medical Center **CR:** Support Services Consultant, Bon Secours-Venice Hospital, Venice, FL (1996-1997); Clinical Instructor, Chattahoochee Valley Community College, Phenix City, AL (1982-1984) **CIV:** Representative, Emergency Management Committee, Sarasota County **MEM:** FADONA **MH:** Albert Nelson Marquis Lifetime Achievement Award **AS:** Ms. Ward attributes her success to her drive. She values being successful, but also strives to help others as much as she can. She believes the perfect recipe for success is hard work and good intention. Appreciate those you meet along the way toward goals and ask for their advice. Learn from them and be grateful for their suggestions. **B/I:** Ms. Ward became involved in her profession because she was inspired by her mother and her mother's friend. **AV:** Gardening; Woodworking; Doing home renovations

WARD, JO ANN, T: Chief Executive Officer (Retired) **I:** Recreational Facilities and Services **CN:** Fond du Lac Convention and Visitor's Bureau **DOB:** 10/26/1933 **PT:** Fred Hansen (Stepfather); Mildred Hansen; Ross Boettner **CH:** Cynthia Ann Ward Cusack; Darwin Cusack (Son-in-Law) **ED:** BS, University of Wisconsin, Madison, WI (1954); Coursework in Continuing Education **CT:** Real Estate Brokers License for Real Estate Development **C:** Chief Executive Officer, Fond du Lac Area Convention & Visitors Bureau, Wisconsin (1976-1999); Major Event Producer, Marketing Consultant to Board of Trustees, Illinois Masonic Medical Center, American Invesco Shopping Centers, Chances R. Systems, Rand McNally, Carson Pirie Scott and Company, Chicago, IL (1969-1976); Publicity and Special Events Director, Carson Pirie Scott & Company (1956-1969) **CR:** Major Event Producer, Vive La France, La Bella Italia, Spotlight on Scandinavia, British Fortnight (1960-1999); Instructor, Patricia Stevens Career School (1958-1959); Major Event Producer, Disney, Fiesta Bowl **CIV:** Naples Antiques Appraisal Fair Chairman of VIP Reception (2020); Ambassador, Pelican Bay Women's League Programs (2006-2020); Board Member, Spirit of America Foundation (2002-2019); Board of Directors, Latchkey League (2013-2018); Founding Committee, Vice President, Latchkey League (2016); Naples Philharmonic League (2004, 2005, 2015); Executive Committee, Tri Delta Alumni (2002-2013); Program Chairman, Pelican Bay Women's League Programs (2005-2006); Historian, Delta Delta Delta (2003-2004); Host, International Aerobatic Championships (1978-1999); Judge, Kentucky Derby Festival (1985); Developer, Lakeside Winter Celebration (1981); Developer, Breakfast With Santa (1957); Board of Directors, United Fund; President, Board of Directors, East Wisconsin Waters Region ; President and founder of Wisconsin Convention and Visitors Bureaus;

President of Service League; Trustee, First Presbyterian Church; Walleye Weekend Festival; Fond du Lac Fall Flyway, Fond du Lac Jazz Festival; Advisory Board, Windhover Center for the Arts; Photographer, Naples Press Club **CW:** Sculptures (2010-2015); Board Speaker, International Festivals and Events, Anchorage, London, Halifax, Ottowa, Disney, Fiesta Bowl (1979-1989); Speaker, Arts Award CPS (1958) **AW:** Governor's Tourism Legacy Award Nominee (2017), Fond du Lac Foundation Legacy Award for Philanthropy (2017); Ooh la la Legacy Lady Award (2016); Named, Woman of Achievement, Fond du Lac Foundation, Women's Fund (2012); Windy Center for Arts Award (2010); Eponym, Jo Ann Award, Wisconsin Festival and Events Association (2002); Paul Harris Award, Rotary International (1985-2000); Honoree, Congressional Record (1999); Lifetime Achievement Award, Upper Midwest Conference and Visitors Bureau (1999); Communications and Leadership Award, Toastmasters International (1999); Wisconsin Trailblazer Award for Lifetime Achievement,, (1999); Inductee, International Festival and Events Association Hall of Fame (1997); Named, Woman of the Year, Fond du Lac Business and Professional Women's Club (1981); President's Award, International Aerobatic Club (1981); Award for Outstanding Contributions, Wisconsin Tourism Federation; Rotarian Paul Harris Award; Corporation Award, Chicago Publicity Club; Gold Award, National Retail Merchants Association; Named, Best Special Event, United States; Life Long Achievement Award, Marian College; Lifetime Achievement Award, Association of Commerce; Experimental Aircraft Association Award, Golden Deeds Award, Exchange Club **MEM:** Thelma Center for the Arts (2013-2019); Naples Press Club; Greater Naples Panhellenic League; Pelican Bay Women's League; Shelter for Abused Women Guild; Rotary; Gulfshore Playhouse; Delta Delta Delta Alumni **MH:** Albert Nelson Marquis Lifetime Achievement Award **AS:** Ms. Ward attributes her success to her good fortune. She grew up in an amazing time and was presented with many unique opportunities, which she continues to take advantage of. **B/I:** Ms. Ward became involved in her profession because she describes herself as a "Carpe Diem person." Her motto is, "Seize the day, and do whatever you can that's good for the world, and it will all come back to you." **AV:** Sculpting; Writing; Marketing; Photography; Real estate development; Event production; Consulting **THT:** Ms. Ward said, "Walk with the dreamers, the believers, the courageous, the cheerful, the planners, the doers, the successful people with their heads in the clouds and their feet on the ground." I don't know the author is, but I think it's a great philosophy. And above all. kindness is free, so sprinkle it everywhere."

WARD, THOMAS, JD, T: President **I:** Law and Legal Services **CN:** Law Offices Of Michelizzi, Schwabacher, Ward & Ward **CH:** Four children **ED:** JD, UCLA School of Law (1967); BA in History, University of San Francisco (1964) **C:** President, Law Offices Of Michelizzi, Schwabacher, Ward & Ward (2014-Present); Associate, Partner, Law Offices Of Michelizzi, Schwabacher, Ward & Ward (1969-2014) **CR:** Attorney, Antelope Valley Transit Authority (1992-Present); City Attorney, City of Lancaster (1978-1988); Attorney, Antelope Valley Hospital Board **CIV:** Member, Financial Council, Padre Serra Council; Development Committee, Paraclete High School; Antelope Valley Hospital Foundation; Lancaster Old Town Site; Former President, Lancaster School Foundation **AW:** Schwabacher Award, Antelope Valley Bar Association **MEM:** President, Antelope Valley Bar Association (1974); The State of California Bar; American Bar Association; Local Chapter, Kiwanis International;

Lancaster Chamber of Commerce **BAR:** United States District Court Eastern District of California (1974); United States District Court Northern District of California (1974); United States District Court Southern District of California (1974); The State Bar of California (1968) **AS:** Mr. Ward attributes his success to working in a small town and working for himself. **B/I:** Mr. Ward became involved in his profession because of his interest in real estate law.

WAREHAM, RAYMOND NOBLE, T: Vice Chairman **I:** Financial Services **CN:** Rockefeller Capital Management **DOB:** 11/20/1948 **PB:** Rochester **SC:** NY/USA **PT:** Simon Harold Wareham; Barbara (Snell) Wareham **MS:** Married **SPN:** Cornelia Lee Clifford (06/28/1975) **CH:** Ellinor Park; Laura Stewart; Cornelia Ashley **ED:** Master of Business Administration, Harvard University (1975); Bachelor of Science in Industrial Engineering, Northwestern University (1970) **C:** Vice Chairman, Global Family Office, Rockefeller Capital Management (2018-Present); Managing Director, Rockefeller & Co. (2012-2017); Senior Managing Director, Sanford C. Bernstein Alliance Capital, New York, NY (2004-2012); Senior Portfolio Manager, Sanford C. Bernstein Alliance Capital, New York, NY (1999-2012); Managing Director, Corporate Financial Department, J.P. Morgan Securities, New York, NY (1992-1998); Manager Director, Head, Banking Industry Group, J.P. Morgan & Co., New York, NY (1988-1992); Executive Director, J.P. Morgan Securities Ltd., London, England (1986-1987); Head, Corporate Finance, J.P. Morgan & Co., Tokyo, Japan (1980-1985); With, J.P. Morgan & Co., New York, NY (1975-1980) **CIV:** With, Stanley Isaacs Neighborhood Center (2006-Present); Board of Trustees, Spence School, New York, NY (1993-2013), Director, 1148 Fifth Avenue Corp. (1995-2010); President (1998-2006); Juvenile Diabetes Foundation (1997-1998); Board of Directors, Brick Church Day School (1989-1992); Elder Brick Presbyterian Church, New York (1989-1992); Trustee, American School in Japan, Tokyo, Japan (1982-1985); Lieutenant, Supply Corps, U.S. Navy (1970-1973) **MIL:** Lieutenant, U.S. Navy (1970-1973) **AW:** John D Rockefeller Award for Distinguished Philanthropic Service, International House, New York **MEM:** Norleggama Junior Honorary, DERU Senior Honorary, Northwestern University; Naval Reserve Officers Training Corps Sextant Honorary Society; Naval War College Foundation; Somerset Club, Boston, MA; Boston Harvard Club; Duxbury Yacht Club, MA; Bath and Tennis Club, Palm Beach, FL; Coral Beach Club, Bermuda; Harvard Business School Century Club Honorary; Eagle Scout **MH:** Albert Nelson Marquis Lifetime Achievement Award; Marquis Who's Who Top Professional **AS:** Mr. Wareham attributes his success to hard work and good luck. **B/I:** A computer science engineer by training, Mr. Wareham attended business school after leaving the Navy, where he became interested in capital markets. Seizing the opportunity to excel in a sophisticated and globally focused career, he joined JP Morgan after graduating. **AV:** Golf; Tennis; Blue marlin deep sea fishing; Antique Japanese bronze and furniture; Natural flower gardens **PA:** Independent **RE:** Presbyterian

WARNER, MARK ROBERT, T: U.S. Senator from Virginia, Vice Chair of the Senate Intelligence Committee **I:** Government Administration/Government Relations/Government Services **CN:** U.S. Senate **DOB:** 12/15/1954 **PB:** Indianapolis **SC:** IN/USA **PT:** Robert Warner; Margaret Warner **MS:** Married **SPN:** Lisa Collis (1989) **CH:** Madison; Gillian; Eliza **ED:** Honorary Doctorate, Virginia State University (2018); Honorary Doctorate, George Mason University (2013); Honorary Doctorate, Eastern Virginia

Medical School (2007); Honorary Associate of Humane Letters, Lord Fairfax Community College (2007); Honorary Doctor of Law, Wake Forest University (2006); Honorary Doctorate of Public Service, The George Washington University (2003); Honorary LLD, College of William & Mary (2002); Doctor of Jurisprudence, Harvard Law School (1980); Bachelor of Arts, The George Washington University (1977) **C:** Vice Chair, Senate Democratic Caucus (2017-Present); Vice Chair, Senate Intelligence Committee (2017-Present); Policy Development Advisor, Democratic Policy and Communications Center (2015-Present); U.S. Senator, Commonwealth of Virginia (2009-Present); Governor, Commonwealth of Virginia, Richmond, VA (2002-2006); Founding Partner, Columbia Capital Corp., Alexandria, VA (1989) **CR:** Chairperson, National Governors Association (2004-2005); Member, Democratic National Committee (1993-1995); Chairperson, Democratic Party of Virginia (1993-1995); Chairperson, Southern Technology Council; Chairperson, Education Commission of the States **CIV:** Co-chairperson, Virginia Communities in Schools Foundation; Founder, Virginia High-Tech Partnership; Founder, TechRiders; Creator, SeniorNavigator.org; Founding Chairperson, Virginia Health Care Foundation; Member, Old Presbyterian Meeting House; Past Board of Directors, Virginia Mathematics and Science Coalition; Past Board of Directors, Virginia Foundation for Independent Colleges; Past Board of Directors, Appalachian School of Law; Past Board of Directors, The George Washington University; Past Board of Directors, Virginia Union University; Honorary Chairperson, Forward Together PAC **MEM:** First Vice Chairperson, Southern Governors Association; Recruitment Chairperson, Democratic Governors Association **PA:** Democrat **RE:** Presbyterian

WARREN, ELIZABETH ANN, T: U.S. Senator from Massachusetts; Educator **I:** Government Administration/Government Relations/Government Services **DOB:** 07/22/1949 **PB:** Oklahoma City **SC:** OK/USA **PT:** Donald Jones Herring; Pauline Louise (Reed) Herring **MS:** Married **SPN:** Bruce H. Mann (1980); Jim Warren (1968, Divorced 1978) **CH:** Amelia; Alexander **ED:** JD, Rutgers Law School, NJ (1976); BS in Speech Pathology and Audiology, University of Houston (1970); Coursework, The George Washington University (1966-1968) **C:** Vice Chair, Senate Democratic Caucus (2017-Present); U.S. Senator, Commonwealth of Massachusetts, Washington, DC (2013-Present); Member, U.S. Senate Committee on Health, Education, Labor and Pensions (2013-Present); Member, U.S. Senate Committee on Banking, Housing and Urban Affairs (2013-Present); Member, U.S. Senate Special Committee on Aging (2013-Present); Leo Gottlieb Professor of Law, Harvard Law School, Cambridge, MA (1995-Present); Candidate, Democratic Nominee, 2020 Presidential Election (2019-2020); Special Advisor to Secretary, U.S. Department of the Treasury, Washington, DC (2010-2011); Assistant to President, The White House, Washington, DC (2010-2011); Chair, Congressional Oversight Panel Overseeing Troubled Asset Relief Program (TARP), Washington, DC (2008-2010); William A. Schnader Professor of Commercial Law, University of Pennsylvania Law School, Philadelphia, PA (1990-1995); Professor of Law, University of Pennsylvania Law School, Philadelphia, PA (1987-1990); Jay H. Brown Centennial Fellow in Law, The University of Texas at Austin School of Law (1986-1987); Conoco Faculty Fellow in Law, The University of Texas at Austin School of Law (1985-1986); Professor of Law, The University of Texas at Austin School of Law (1983-1987); Research Associate, Population Research Center, The University of Texas at Austin School of Law (1983-1987); Associate Professor of Law,

University of Houston Law Center (1981-1983); Associate Dean of Academic Affairs, University of Houston Law Center (1980-1981); Assistant Professor of Law, University of Houston Law Center (1978-1980); Lecturer, Rutgers Law, Newark, NJ (1977-1978) **CR:** Editorial Advisory Board, Law School Division, Little, Brown and Company (Now Hachette Book Group) (1990-Present); Proposal Reviewer, National Science Foundation (1985-Present); Honorary Co-chairman, Massachusetts Wisconsin Victory Fund (2011-2012); Member, Executive Committee, National Bankruptcy Conference (1993-1995, 2002-2005); Committee on Judicial Education, Federal Judicial Center (1990-1999); Reporter, Consultant, Senior Advisor, National Bankruptcy Review Commission (1995-1997); Board of Trustees, The American Board of Certification (1992-1996); Advisor, German Government Task Force on Bankruptcy Reform (1993); Robert Braucher Visiting Professor of Commercial Law, Harvard University (1992-1993); Board of Editors, American Bankruptcy Law Journal (1989-1992); Visiting Professor of Law, University of Michigan (1985); Visiting Associate Professor of Law, The University of Texas at Austin School of Law (1981-1982) **CW:** Author, "This Fight is Our Fight: The Battle to Save America's Middle Class" (2017); Author, "A Fighting Chance" (2014); Co-author, "The Law of Debtors and Creditors: Text, Cases, and Problems," Sixth Edition (2008); Author, "Chapter 11: Reorganizing American Businesses" (2008); Co-Author, "Casenote Legal Briefs: Commercial Law" (2006); Co-Author, "All Your Worth: The Ultimate Lifetime Money Plan" (2005); Co-Author, "The Two-Income Trap: Why Middle-Class Mothers and Fathers are Going Broke" (2003); Co-Author, "The Fragile Middle Class: Americans in Debt" (2000); Co-Author, "Commercial Law: A Systems Approach" (1998); Co-Author, "Secured Transactions: A Systems Approach" (1995); Co-Author, "The Law of Debtors and Creditors" (1991); Co-Author, "As We Forgive Our Debtors: Consumer Credit and Bankruptcy in America" (1989) **AW:** Listee, 50 Most Influential People in Global Finance, Bloomberg Markets (2011); Listee, 100 Most Influential People in the World, TIME Magazine (2009, 2010); Listee, Decade's Most Influential Lawyers (2010); Listee, 10 Most Powerful Women in Washington, Fortune Magazine (2010); Listee, 100 Most Powerful Women, Forbes Magazine (2010); Listee, Who's Who in DC, Crain's New York Business (2009); Listee, 50 Most Powerful People in DC, GQ Magazine (2009); Bostonian of the Year, The Boston Globe (2009); Leila J. Robinson Award, Women's Bar Association & Foundation, MA (2009); Albert A. Sacks-Paul A. Freund Award for Teaching Excellence, Harvard Law School (1997, 2009); Listee, 50 Most Influential Women Lawyers in America, The National Law Journal (1998, 2007); Lawrence P. King Award, Commercial Law League of America (2002); Excellence in Education Award, National Conference of Bankruptcy Judges (2001); Champion of Consumer Rights Award, National Association of Consumer Bankruptcy Attorneys (2000); Scholarship Award, American College of Consumer Financial Services Lawyers (2000); Brown Award for Judicial Scholarship and Education, Federal Judicial Center (1998); Commendation for Service, American Board of Certification (1998); Commendation for Outstanding Public Service, American College of Bankruptcy (1998); Lindback Award for Distinguished Teaching, University of Pennsylvania (1994); Harvey Levin Award for Excellence in Teaching, University of Pennsylvania Law School (1989, 1992); Silver Gavel Award, ABA (1990); L. Hart Wright Teaching Excellence Award, University of Michigan Law School (1986); Frankel Publication Award for Outstanding Writing (1982); Outstanding Teacher Award, University of Houston Law Center (1981) **MEM:** Executive Committee Council, Transnational Insolvency Project, The American Law Institute (1998-Present); Nominating Committee, Transnational Insolvency Project, The American Law Institute (1995-Present); U.S. Adviser, Transnational Insolvency Project, The American Law Institute (1995-Present); Second Vice President Council, Transnational Insolvency Project, The American Law Institute (2000-2004); Executive Committee Council, The American Law Institute (1994-1995); Chair, Legislation Committee, Debtor-creditor Section, Association of American Law Schools (1990-1993); Chair, Debtor-creditor Section, Association of American Law Schools (1989-1990); Professional Development Committee, Association of American Law Schools (1988-1991); Planning Committee, Conference on Teaching Contract Law, Association of American Law Schools (1989); Chair, Commercial Law Workshop, Association of American Law Schools (1984); Chair, Commercial and Related Consumer Law Section, Association of American Law Schools (1983-1984); Fellow, American Association for the Advancement of Science; Fellow, American College of Bankruptcy; Women's Bar Association & Foundation, MA; Association of American Law Schools; The American Law Institute **BAR:** State of New Jersey; State of Texas **PA:** Democrat **RE:** Methodist

WARREN, RICK, T: Pastor **I:** Religious **DOB:** 01/28/1954 **PB:** San Jose **SC:** CA/USA **PT:** James Russell Warren; Dorothy Nell (Armstrong) Warren **MS:** Married **SPN:** Kay Warren (06/21/1975) **CH:** Amy Rebecca; Joshua James; Matthew David (Deceased) **ED:** DMin, Fuller Theological Seminary (1989); MDiv, Southwestern Baptist Theological Seminary (1979); BA, California Baptist College (Now California Baptist University) (1977) **C:** Founder, Senior Pastor, Saddleback Church, Lake Forest, CA (1980-Present); Assistant to President, International Evangelism Association, Fort Worth, TX (1977-1979); Associate Pastor, First Baptist Church, Norwalk, CA (1974-1976); Youth Evangelist, California Southern Baptist Convention, Fresno, CA (1970-1974); Founder, Pastors.com; Founder, Purpose Driven Network; Founder, The P.E.A.C.E. Plan **CR:** Keynote Speaker, Martin Luther King Jr. Annual Commemorative Service (2009); Host, Civil Forum on the Presidency, Lake Forest, CA (2008) **CIV:** Host, Civil Forum on the Presidency (2008); Leader, More Than 300 Community Ministries **CW:** Author, "Words to Love By" (2018); Author, "The Purpose of Christmas" (2018); Author, "God's Big Plans for Me Storybook Bible" (2017); Author, "God's Great Love for You " (2017); Author, "The Lord's Prayer: Words of Hope and Happiness" (2016); Author, "The Purpose Driven Life Devotional for Kids" (2015); Author, "The Daniel Plan 365-Day Devotional: Daily Encouragement for a Healthier Life" (2015); Author, "The Habits of Happiness Study Guide" (2015); Author, "Daring Faith, The Key to Miracles, Study Guide" (2015); Co-Author, "The Daniel Plan Cookbook: Healthy Eating for Life" (2014); Co-Author, "The Daniel Plan Jumpstart Guide: Daily Steps to a Healthier Life" (2014); Author, "The Purpose Driven Life: What on Earth Am I Here For?" (2013); Co-Author, Co-Author, "The Daniel Plan Church Campaign Kit: 40 Days to a Healthier Life" (2013); Author, "God's Answers to Life's Difficult Questions Study Guide" (2013); Author, "You Are Who God Says You Are: A Daily Hope Devotional" (2013); Author, "What On Earth Am I Here For? Study Guide" (2012); Author, "40 Days of Community Devotional: What on Earth Are We Here For?" (2012); Contributor, "Drive Your Destiny: The Secret Key to Review Your Life" (2012); Author, "40 Days in the Word: Love the Word, Learn the Word, Live the Word" (2011); Author, "Everything

is Possible with God Study Guide: Understanding the Six Phases of Faith" (2010); Author, "Better Together Study Guide: What On Earth Are We Here For?" (2010); Speaker, "Desiring God" Conference, Minneapolis, MN (2010); Author, "40 Days of Love Study Guide: We Were Made for Relationships" (2009); Author, "40 Days Of Love: We Were Made For Relationships" (2008); Co-Author, "Rev! Magazine's Bathroom Guide to Leadership" (2007); Author, "Rick Warren's Bible Study Methods" (2006); Author, "God's Answers to Life's Difficult Questions" (2006); Speaker, TED Global Set of Conferences (2006); Author, "Book of James Volume 2: Developing a Faith That Works" (2005); Author, "What on Earth Am I Here For?" (2004); Author, "Better Together: What on Earth Are We Here For?" (2004); Author, "The Purpose Driven Life Selected Thoughts and Scriptures for the Graduate" (2004); Contributor, "The Passion: The Purpose & Person of Jesus Christ" (2004); Author, "The Purpose Driven Life" (2003); Author, "The Purpose-Driven Life Deluxe Journal" (2003); Author, "Daily Inspiration for the Purpose Driven Life: Scriptures and Reflections from the 40 Days of Purpose" (2003); Author, "Meditations on the Purpose Driven Life" (2003); Author, "The Purpose-Driven Life Journal" (2002); Author, "Answers to Life's Difficult Questions" (1999); Author, "The Power To Change Your Life" (1998); Author, "The Purpose Driven Church: Growth Without Compromising Your Message and Mission" (1995); Author, "Dynamic Bible Study Methods" (1989); Invited Speaker, United Nations, World Economic Forum in Davos, African Union, Council on Foreign Relations, Harvard University's John F. Kennedy School of Government, TIME Global Health Summit, and Numerous International Congresses; Author, Contributor, Articles, Numerous Contributions **AW:** NRB Billy Graham Award for Excellence in Christian Communications (2016) **MEM:** Elected Member, Council on Foreign Relations **RE:** Baptist

WARREN, RUSSELL J., T: Managing Director **I:** Financial Services **CN:** EdgePoint Capital **DOB:** 07/28/1938 **PB:** Cleveland **SC:** OH/USA **SPN:** Doris Helen Kenyeres (06/06/1964) **ED:** MBA, Harvard University (1962); BS, Case Western Reserve University (1960) **CT:** Certified Public Accountant (CPA), State of Ohio; FINRA Series, 7, 63 & 79 **C:** Managing Director, EdgePoint Capital (2008-Present); President, The Transaction Group, Cleveland, Ohio (1987-2008); Partner-in-charge, Merger and Acquisition Services, Ernst & Whinney (Now Ernst & Young), Cleveland, Ohio (1976-1987); With, Ernst & Whinney (Now Ernst & Young), Cleveland, Ohio (1962-1987) **CR:** Board of Directors, Seneca Capital Management, Inc. (2000-2018) **CIV:** Member, Visiting Committee, Case Western Reserve University Weatherhead School of Management (1998-2004, 2007-Present); Member, Visiting Committee, Case Western Reserve University Case School of Engineering (1990-2004, 2007-Present); Chairman, City of Lyndhurst, Ohio (1980-1982, 1991-1993, 2000-2001, 2006-Present); Trustee Emeritus, Western Reserve Historical Society (2005-Present); Advisory Board, Shaker Investments (1992-Present); Board Zoning Appeals, City of Lyndhurst, Ohio (1978-Present); President, Town Hall of Cleveland, Ohio (2008); Dean's Advisory Council, Case Western Reserve University Weatherhead School of Management (2005-2007); Dean's Advisory Council, Case Western Reserve University Case School of Engineering (2005-2007); Trustee, Town Hall of Cleveland, Ohio (2005); Trustee, British American Chamber of Commerce, Great Lakes Region, Ohio (2001-2005); Chairman, Audit Committee, Case Western Reserve University (1991-2005); Trustee, Case Western Reserve University (1980-2005); Chairman, Investments Committee,

Western Reserve Historical Society (1999-2002); Trustee, Western Reserve Historical Society (1996-2002); Trustee, Cleveland Botanical Garden (1995-2002); Trustee, Cascade CDC (1992-2000); Trustee, Community Improvement Corporate Summit, Medina and Portage Counties, Ohio (1992-2000); Elder, Fairmont Presbyterian Church (1991-1993); Trustee, Fairmont Presbyterian Church (1987-1993); President, M&A International, Inc. (1992); Vice President, M&A International, Inc. (1990-1991); Director, University of Technology, Inc. (1986-1988) **CW:** Member, Editorial Board, Journal of Corporate Growth (1988); Associate Editor, Journal of Corporate Growth (1986-1987); Contributing Editor, Journal Buyouts and Acquisitions (1984-1986); Contributing Author, Venture Capital Financing Study Conducted in Five Countries for Asian Development Bank, Malaysia, Indonesia, Pakistan, Sri Lanka, Thailand (1986); Co-author, Book, "Implementing Mergers and Acquisitions in the Financial Services Industry" (1985) **MEM:** Board of Trustees, Cuyahoga Valley Scenic Railroad (2015-Present); Board of Trustees, Dunham Tavern Museum (2013-Present); Trustee Emeritus, Case Western Reserve University (2005-Present); Harvard Business School Alumni Board (2012-2015); Association for Corporate Growth (ACG); The Ohio Society Certified Public Accountants; Harvard Club of New York City; Catawba Island Club; Mayfield Sand Ridge Club; Union Club; Jesters **MH:** Albert Nelson Marquis Lifetime Achievement Award; Marquis Who's Who Humanitarian Award **B/I:** Mr. Warren became involved in his profession when the opportunity presented itself back when he was at Ernst and Young; it was an interesting field. He liked it when he began to practice in it. **AV:** Business history

WASHBURN, GLADYS RICE, T: Photographer, Writer, Filmmaker **I:** Writing and Editing **DOB:** 03/11/1927 **PB:** New York **SC:** NY/USA **PT:** Pincus; Johanna Rice **MS:** Divorced **ED:** MA in English Education, New York University (1981); BS in Communications Arts, City University of New York, Summa Cum Laude (1978) **C:** Freelance Photographer, New York, NY (1948-2007); Writing Instructor, Borough of Manhattan Community College, New York, NY (1985-2001); President, Washburn Films, New York, NY (1972-1981); Cinematographer, Picture Editor, GE-Time Life Educational Film Dynamic II, Effective Communication Arts, New York, NY (1969-1970); Photography Instructor, Germain School Photography, New York, NY (1958-1965); Photographer, Conde Nast Publications, New York, NY (1944-1948) **CR:** Writer-in-residence, Lexington for the Performing Arts, New York (1976); Featured Photographer, Anne DeCarava's A Photographer's Gallery, New York, NY (1950); Exhibiting Photographer, Baltimore Museum of Art, "Photography as Art" (1946) **CIV:** Juror, American Film Festival; Juror, CINE Conference for International Film Festival Selection **CW:** Author, Book, "Fortune's Hand" (2011); Author, Poetry Book, "Slay No Dragons" (2010); Retrospective, Washburn Photography, Bronxville Public Library, New York (2007); Designer, Editor, "Portfolio: The Photographic Vision of Pincus Rice" (1994); Contributing Writer, Hudson River Magazine (1988-1991); One-Woman Multimedia Shows, Hunter Arts Gallery, New York, NY (1976), Gallery One, Hillsdale, NY (1976), Lexington for the Performing Arts (1976); Film Production Manager, MacLaughlan-Gill Studio, New York, NY (1969); Cinematographer, Picture Editor, Producer (Short Film), "The Swing" (1964) **AW:** Museum of Modern Art Film Collection, "The Swing", (1966-Present); Diploma de participacion, Festival de Tours, Film, "The Swing" (1966); CINE Golden Eagle Award, Film, "The Swing" (1965); First and Second Prize, Photo Competition (1939)

MEM: Sierra Club **MH:** Albert Nelson Marquis Lifetime Achievement Award; Marquis Who's Who Top Professional **AS:** Ms. Washburn attributes her success to a need to have a creative project to work on. She has always been a "doer", she loves producing art and works with enthusiasm. She enjoyed working with her hands when making sculptures, she likes the perfecting process of editing her writing, and finds editing film exciting. Ms. Washburn was a professional photographer by the age of 15. She was the sole photographer for a magazine publication called "Penthouse and Terrace." As she recalls, growing up, she would take pictures with her Brownie box camera. Ms. Washburn's father was a photographer. He gave her a professional camera on her 11th birthday. When he retired, she took over his studio. In the 1960s, she made a few short art films. In the 1970s, she turned Washburn Films into a distributor of ethnographic films for educational institutions.

WASHBURN, PATRICIA, "PAT" CHEYNE, OWNER, T: Child Psychologist (Retired); Environmental Scientist; Conservationist **I:** Consulting **CN:** Children Unlimited **DOB:** 04/27/1941 **PB:** Plattsburgh **SC:** NY/USA **PT:** Gerald Kenneth Cheyne; Doris Rothermel Cheyne **MS:** Married **SPN:** Christopher Hiram Washburn (07/24/1965) **CH:** Diane Washburn Drisoll; James Stevenson Washburn **ED:** Coursework, Trained in School Counseling, Elementary and Secondary, West Chester University (1991-1993); MA in Counseling Psychology, Immaculata College (Now Immaculata University) (1991); BA in Psychology, Hartwick College (1963); Coursework, Franklin Academy, Malone, NY (1959) **CT:** Early Childhood Education, Commonwealth of Pennsylvania **C:** Planning Commissioner, North Coventry Planning (2001-Present); Chairman (2015-2018); Practice, Children Unlimited, Pottstown, PA (1991-2001); Co-founder, Coventry Land Trust (2000); Play Therapist, Consultant, Owner of Elementary School Teacher (1964-1986); New York State Juvenile Probation Officer, Oneida County, Utica, NY (1963-1964); Assistant to Dr. George Gingras, DVM, Regional Agricultural Livestock Inspector (1957-1961); Malone Central School, NY and Lower Merion School District, PA **CR:** Chester County Task Force, North Coventry Comprehensive Plan (2018-2020); Member, Art Goes to School (1978-2001); Co-founder, PA Association for Play Therapy (PA APT) (1992); Member, Governor's Task Force on Developing Curriculum for PA Public Schools on Drama, Music, and Art (1986-1988); Regional Chairman, Art Goes to School (1983-1985); Author, Volunteer Manual **CIV:** Volunteer, American Heart Association, Inc.; Volunteer, American Caner Society, Inc.; Volunteer, March of Dimes **AW:** Founder's Award, PA Association for Play Therapy (PA APT) (1993); Regional Award for DAR Citizenship Essay, Freedom Foundation (1968); Volunteer Awards for Fundraising, American Heart Association, Inc. and American Cancer Society, Inc.; Named to Chi Sigma Iota; Danforth Foundation Scholarship Award **MEM:** Charter Member, National Museum of the American Indian; Natural Lands Trust; Philadelphia Zoo; National Trust for Historic Preservation; The Nature Conservancy; Association for Play Therapy (APT); National Wildlife Federation; Macular Degeneration Society (American Macular Degeneration Foundation (AMDF)); American Cancer Society, Inc.; American Heart Association, Inc.; National Association of Planners; Pennsylvania State Townships Association (Now PA State Association of Township Supervisors (PSATS)) **MH:** Albert Nelson Marquis Lifetime Achievement Award (2020); Marquis Who's Who of American Women (2001) **AS:** Mrs. Washburn attributes her success to a deep, true and abiding love and respect for humanity,

all nature and the American way of life. She also credits sincere belief that we are led by our own individual personal choices in life, and a love and trust in a Higher Power that will lead to what is right–at the right time. **B/I:** Mrs. Washburn always wanted to work with children who had emotional problems. Coming from a rural area of New York state that was economically depressed, many children were lost in a limited system that let them be caught between the cracks. With a bit more help and guidance from schools or the courts, they could have avoided the justice system, continued their education or gotten psychological guidance that would have made them productive adults. **AV:** Gardening; Gemology; Traveling; Ancient history and anthropology; American history **PA:** Independent **RE:** Protestant **THT:** Mrs. Washburn is registered as a Republican but is a true Independent. Mrs. Washburn says, "Life has been very good to me. Having just celebrated 55 years of a wonderful marriage to a compassionate and understanding gentleman, Chris, with two very talented children in prominent careers, Diane and Jim, I am blessed. I hope I shall be remembered as a caring, non-judgemental, trusted individual who loved life to the fullest and gave my all for the betterment of the community in which I live, my beloved country, the global environment and the world in its entirety."

WASHINGTON, KERRY, T: Actress **I:** Media & Entertainment **DOB:** 01/31/1977 **PB:** The Bronx **SC:** NY/USA **PT:** Earl Washington; Valerie Washington **MS:** Married **SPN:** Nnamdi Asomugha (06/24/2013) **CH:** Isabelle Amarachi Asomugha; Caleb Kelechi Asomugha **ED:** DFA (Honorary), George Washington University (2013); BS in Anthropology and Sociology, George Washington University (1998); Student, Michael Howard Studios **C:** Actress, Film, Television, Stage **CR:** Member, President Barack Obama's Committee on Arts and Humanities (2009); Brand Ambassador, Creative Consultant, Neutrogena **CIV:** Commencement Speaker, George Washington University (2013); Speaker, Democratic National Convention (2012); Participant, 2007 Lee National Denim Day (2007); Advocate, LGBT Rights **CW:** Actress, "The Prom" (2020); Executive Producer, "Little Fires Everywhere" (2020); Actress, "Little Fires Everywhere" (2020); Producer, "The Fight" (2020); Director, Episode, "Insecure" (2020); Executive Producer, "American Son" (2019); Actress, "American Son" (2019); Actress, "Live in Front of a Studio Audience: Norman Lear's 'All in the Family' and 'The Jeffersons'" (2019); Executive Producer, "Live in Front of a Studio Audience: Norman Lear's 'All in the Family' and 'The Jeffersons'" (2019); Director, Episode, "SMILF" (2019); Executive Producer, "Man of the House" (2018); Director, Episode, "Scandal" (2018); Actress, "How to Get Away with Murder" (2018); Actress, "American Son" (2018); Producer, "Scandal" (2017-2018); Voice Actress, "Cars 3" (2017); Actress, "Confirmation" (2016); Executive Producer, "Confirmation" (2016); Host, "Saturday Night Live" (2013); Actress, "Peeples" (2013); Actress, "Scandal" (2012-2018); Actress, "Django Unchained" (2012); Actress, "A Thousand Words" (2012); Actress, "The Details" (2011); Actress, "For Colored Girls" (2010); Voice Actress, "Black Panther" (2010); Actress, "Night Catches Us" (2010); Actress, "Common: I Want You" (2009); Actress, "Mother and Child" (2009); Actress, "Life is Hot in Cracktown" (2009); Actress, "Race" (2009); Actress, "Lakeview Terrace" (2008); Actress, "Miracle at St. Anna" (2008); Actress, "Woman in Burka" (2008); Actress, "Psych" (2008); Actress, "Fantastic 4: Rise of the Silver Surfer" (2007); Actress, "Put It in a Book" (2007); Actress, "I Think I Love My Wife" (2007); Actress, "The Dead Girl" (2006); Actress, "The Last King of Scot-

land" (2006); Actress, "Little Man" (2006); Actress, "Boston Legal" (2005-2006); Actress, "Wait" (2005); Actress, "Fantastic Four" (2005); Actress, "Mr. & Mrs. Smith" (2005); Actress, "Wonderfalls" (2004); Actress, "Ray" (2004); Actress, "She Hate Me" (2004); Actress, "Sexual Life" (2004); Actress, "Strip Search" (2004); Actress, "Against the Ropes" (2004); Actress, "Sin" (2003); Actress, "The Human Stain" (2003); Actress, "The United States of Leland" (2003); Actress, "The Guardian" (2002); Actress, "Bad Company" (2002); Actress, "Take the A Train" (2002); Actress, "100 Centre Street" (2001); Actress, "Law & Order" (2001); Actress, "NYPD Blue" (2001); Actress, "Lift" (2001); Actress, "Save the Last Dance" (2001); Actress, "3D" (2000); Actress, "Our Song" (2000); Actress, "Standard Deviants" (1996); Actress, "ABC After-school Specials" (1994) **AW:** Outstanding Guest Performance in a Comedy or Drama Series, "How to Get Away with Murder," NAACP Image Awards (2019); Spotlight Award, Costume Designers Guild Awards (2018); Outstanding Actress, TV Movie or Limited Series, "Confirmation," Black Reel Awards (2017); Woman of the Year, Hasty Pudding Theatricals (2016); ACLU Bill of Rights Award (2016); GLAAD Vanguard Award, Gay & Lesbian Alliance Against Defamation, GLAAD Media Awards (2015); Vanguard Award, GLAAD Media Awards (2015); Outstanding Actress in a Drama Series, "Scandal," NAACP Image Awards (2014); Influencer Award, ACE Awards (2014); Favorite Dramatic TV Actress, SAG Foundation Awards (2014); Best Actress, "Django Unchained," BET Awards (2013); Outstanding Supporting Actress in a Motion Picture, "Django Unchained," NAACP Image Awards (2013); Best Actress, "Scandal," BET Awards (2013); President's Award, NAACP Image Awards (2013); Fan Favorite Awards, "Scandal," TV Guide Awards (2013); Outstanding Actress in a Drama Series, "Scandal," Women's Image Network Awards (2013); TV Star of the Year, TV Guide Magazine (2013); Fan Favorite Awards for Favorite Actress, TV Guide Magazine (2013); Best Actress, "Night Catches Us," Black Reel Awards (2011); Outstanding Actress in a Motion Picture, "Ray," NAACP Image Awards (2005); Breakthrough Award, Chlotrudis Awards (2004); Future of Film Award, Urbanworld Film Festival (2002); Choice Breakout Performance, "Save the Last Dance," Teen Choice Awards (2001) **MEM:** Honorary Chairperson, GLSEN Respect Awards, GLSEN; Creative Coalition; V-Day; Phi Beta Kappa

WASSERMAN SCHULTZ, DEBBIE, T: U.S. Representative **I:** Government Administration/Government Relations/Government Services **DOB:** 09/27/1966 **PB:** Forest Hills **SC:** NY/USA **PT:** Larry Wasserman; Ann Wasserman **MS:** Married **SPN:** Steve Schultz (1991) **CH:** Shelby; Jake; Rebecca **ED:** MA in Political Science, University of Florida, Gainesville, FL (1990); BA in Political Science, University of Florida, Gainesville, FL (1988) **C:** U.S. Representative, Florida's 23rd Congressional District, United States Congress, Washington, DC (2013-Present); Chief Deputy Whip (2008-Present); Member, U.S. House Committee on Appropriations (2006-Present); Chair, Democratic National Committee (2011-2016); Vice Chair, Incumbent Retention, Democratic Congressional Campaign Committee (2009-2011); Vice Chair, Democratic National Committee (2009-2011); Member, U.S. House Judiciary Committee (2005-2006, 2011); U.S. Representative, Florida's 20th Congressional District, United States Congress, Washington, DC (2005-2013); Senior Whip (2005-2006); Member, District 34, Florida State Senate (2003-2004); Member, District 32, Florida State Senate (2001-2003); Democratic Leader Pro Tempore, Florida House of Representatives (2000); Democratic Floor Leader, Florida House of Representatives

(1998-1999); Member, District 97, Florida House of Representatives (1993-2001); Legislative Aide, Office to Representative Peter Deutsch, U.S. House of Representatives, Washington, DC (1989-1992); Member, U.S. House Budget Committee, United States Congress **CR:** Chair, South Florida Democratic Caucus (1998-Present); Member, Legislative Advisory Council, Southern Regional Education Board (1995-Present); Second Vice President, Gwen Cherry Women's Political Caucus (1992-Present); Member, Gender Bias Study Implementation Commission, Florida Supreme Court (1992-Present); Honorary Chair, 50-State Program, Hillary Clinton Campaign (2016); Governor's Commission on Education (1995-1997); Florida Education Facilities Study Committee (1994); Classrooms First Task Force (1993) **CIV:** Board of Trustees, Westside Regional Medical Center, Plantation, FL (1993-Present); Board of Directors, Florida Distance Learning Network (1995-1997); Secretary, Vice President, Broward County Young Democrats (1990-1992); Secretary, Young Leadership Council, Jewish Federation of Greater Fort Lauderdale (1989-1990); Board of Directors, American Jewish Congress Southeast Region; Board of Directors, National Jewish Democratic Council; Board of Directors, South Florida Chapter, National Safety Council **AW:** Rosemary Barkett Award, Academy of Florida Trial Lawyers (Now Florida Justice Association) (1995); Quality Floridian, Florida League of Cities, Inc. (1994); Outstanding Legislator of the Year, Florida Federation Business and Professional Women (1994); Woman of the Year, AMIT (1994); One of the Six Most Unstoppable Women, South Florida Magazine (1994); Outstanding Family Advocacy Award, Florida Psychological Association, Dade County, FL (1993); Giraffe Award, Women's Advocacy of the Majority Minority (1993); Woman of Vision, Weizmann Institute of Science **MEM:** National Organization for Women; National Council of Jewish Women; Secretary, Hawkes Bluff Homeowner's Association, Inc.; Weston Florida Chamber of Commerce; Miramar Pembroke Pines Regional Chamber of Commerce; Omicron Delta Kappa **AV:** Bowling; Golfing; Staying abreast of current politics **PA:** Democrat **RE:** Jewish

WATERS, MAXINE MOORE, T: U.S. Representative from California **I:** Government Administration/Government Relations/Government Services **DOB:** 08/15/1938 **PB:** St. Louis **SC:** MO/USA **PT:** Remus Carr; Velma Lee (Moore) Carr **MS:** Married **SPN:** Sid Williams (07/23/1977); Edward Waters (1956, Divorced 1972) **CH:** Edward; Karen **ED:** Honorary Doctorate, Morgan State University; Honorary Doctorate, North Carolina Agricultural and Technical State University; Honorary Doctorate, Spelman College; BA in Sociology, California State University, Los Angeles, CA (1970) **C:** Ranking Member, House Committee on Financial Services (2012-Present); Member, U.S. House of Representatives from California's 43rd Congressional District, United States Congress, Washington, DC (2013-Present); Member, U.S. House of Representatives from California's 35th Congressional District, United States Congress, Washington, DC (1993-2013); Member, U.S. House of Representatives from California's 29th Congressional District, United States Congress, Washington, DC (1991-1993); Member, District 48, California State Assembly (1976-1991); Chief Deputy to City Councilman David S. Cunningham Jr. (1973); Volunteer Coordinator, Teacher, Head Start Program **CR:** Member, Democratic National Committee (1980-Present); Member, National Advisory Committee for Women (1978-Present); Delegate, Minority AIDS Initiative (1998); Chair, Congressional Black Caucus (1997-1998); Member, Democratic National Convention (1972-1988) **CIV:** Founder, Project Build; Founder,

Free South Africa Movement; Founder, Maxine Waters Employment Preparation Center; Member, California Peer Counseling Association; Member, National Commission for Economic Conversion and Disarmament; Member, Board, Center for the Study of Sport in Society; Member, The Women's Foundation, Los Angeles, CA **AW:** Named to the Power 150 (2008); Named One of the 100 Most Influential Black Americans, Ebony Magazine (2006); Candace Award, National Coalition of 100 Black Women (1992); Bruce F. Vento Award, NLCHP **PA:** Democrat

WATERSTON, SAM, T: Actor, Producer, Director **I:** Media & Entertainment **DOB:** 11/15/1940 **PB:** Cambridge **SC:** MA/USA **PT:** George Chychele Waterston; Alice Tucker (Atkinson) Waterston **SPN:** Lynna Louisa Woodruff (01/26/1976); Barbara Rutledge-Johns (12/28/1964, Divorced 1975) **CH:** James; Katherine Waterston; Elisabeth Waterston; Graham **ED:** BA, Yale University (1962); Student, Clinton Playhouse; Coursework, Sorbonne University **C:** Actor, Film, Television, Stage **CR:** Member, Orchestra and Chorus, Aaron Copland School of Music, Queens College **CIV:** Active Humanitarian; Board Member, Oceana; Advocate, Refugees International; Advocate, Meals on Wheels; Advocate, United Way; Advocate, The Episcopal Actors' Guild of America; Member, Advisory Committee, Lincoln Bicentennial; Donor, $25,000, Refuges International, Oceana; Spokesman, Unity 08 **CW:** Actor, "On the Basis of Sex" (2018); Actor, "Godless" (2017); Actor, "Miss Sloane" (2016); Actor, "Grace and Frankie" (2015-2021); Actress, "And It Was Good" (2015); Actor, "Anesthesia" (2015); Narrator, "Dateline: Saigon" (2015); Actor, "The Tempest" (2015); Actor, "Please Be Normal" (2014); Actor, "The Colbert Report" (2013); Narrator, "Cooper & Hemingway: The True Gen" (2013); Narrator, "The Path to Violence" (2013); Actor, "Jo" (2013); Actor, "Newsroom" (2012-2014); Actor, "King Lear" (2011); Actor, "The Old Masters" (2011); Actor, "Law & Order" (1994-2010); Actor, "Have You Seen Us?" (2009-2010); Narrator, "The Last Boat Out" (2010); Actor, "Hamlet" (2008); Host, "Mozart Dances," "Live from Lincoln Center," PBS (2007); Actor, "Masters of Science Fiction" (2007); Contestant, "Jeopardy!" (2006); Actor, "Law & Order: Trial by Jury" (2005); Actor, "Travesties" (2005); Actor, "Much Ado About Nothing" (2004); Voice Actor, Exhibit, National Constitution Center (2004); Actor, "The Commission" (2003); Actor, "The Divorce" (2003); Actor, "The Matthew Shepard Story" (2002); Actor, "Law & Order: Special Victims Unit" (2000-2018); Actor, "A House Divided" (2000); Producer, "A House Divided" (2000); Voice Actor, "Family Guy" (2000); Narrator, "Here Am I, Send Me" (1999); Narrator, "Moment of Impact: Stories of the Pulitzer Prize Photographs" (1999); Narrator, "The Unfinished Journey" (1999); Actor, "Exiled" (1998); Actor, "The Wonderful World of Disney" (1998); Actor, "Homicide: Life on the Street" (1997-1999); Actor, "Shadow Conspiracy" (1997); Actor, "Nixon" (1995); Producer, "The Journey of August King" (1995); Narrator, "Lost Civilizations" (1995); Appearance, "Saturday Night Live" (1995); Actor, "The Enemy Within" (1994); Actor, "Serial Mom" (1994); Actor, "David's Mother" (1994); Actor, "Assault at West Point: The Court-Martial of Johnson Whittaker" (1994); Actor, "A Dog Race in Alaska" (1994); Actor, "Abe Lincoln in Illinois" (1993-1994); Actor, "A Dog Race in Alaska" (1993); Actor, "I'll Fly Away: Then and Now" (1993); Actor, "Tales From the Crypt" (1993); Actor, "Warburg: A Man of Influence" (1992); Actor, "I'll Fly Away" (1991-1993); Actor, "The Man in the Moon" (1991); Actor, "The Master Builder" (1990-1991); Actor, "A Captive in the Land" (1990); Actor, "The Civil War" (1990); Actor, "Mindwalk" (1990);

Actor, "The Nightmare Years" (1989); Actor, "Crimes and Misdemeanors" (1989); Actor, "Welcome Home" (1989); Actor, "Lantern Hill" (1989); Actor, "A Walk in the Woods" (1988); Actor, "A Walk in the Woods" (1988); Narrator, "American Experience" (1988); Actor, "Lincoln" (1988); Actor, "Terrorist on Trial: The United States vs. Salim Ajami" (1988); Actor, "September" (1987); Actor, "Devil's Paradise" (1987); Actor, "The Room Upstairs" (1987); Narrator, "Nova" (1987); Actor, "Flagrant Désir" (1986); Actor, "Just Between Friends" (1986); Actor, "Amazing Stories" (1986); Actor, "The Fifth Missile" (1986); Actor, "Hannah and Her Sisters" (1986); Actor, "Benefactors" (1985-1986); Actor, "Love Lives On" (1985); Actor, "Finnegan Begin Again" (1985); Actor, "The Killing Fields" (1984); Actor, "The Boy Who Loved Trolls" (1984); Actor, "Dempsey" (1983); Actor, "Freedom to Speak" (1983); Actor, "Three Sisters" (1982-1983); Actor, "Games Mother Never Taught You" (1982); Actor, "Q.E.D." (1982); Actor, "Gardenia" (1982); Actor, "Lunch Hour" (1980-1981); Actor, "Oppenheimer" (1980); Actor, "Heaven's Gate" (1980); Actor, "Hopscotch" (1980); Actor, "Sweet William" (1980); Actor, "Eagle's Wing" (1979); Actor, "Friendly Fire" (1979); Actor, "Interiors" (1978); Actor, "Capricorn One" (1977); Actor, "Chez Nous" (1977); Actor, "Sweet Revenge" (1976); Actor, "Measure for Measure" (1976); Actor, "Hamlet" (1975-1976); Actor, "A Doll's House" (1975); Actor, "The Tempest" (1975); Actor, "Journey Into Fear" (1975); Actor, "Rancho Deluxe" (1975); Actor, "Reflections of Murder" (1974); Actor, "The Great Gatsby" (1974); Actor, "The Glass Menagerie" (1973); Actor, "Much Ado About Nothing" (1973); Actor, "Much Ado About Nothing" (1972-1973); Actor, "Hamlet" (1972); Actor, "Mahoney's Estate" (1972); Actor, "Savages" (1972); Actor, "Who Killed Mary Whats'ername?" (1971); Actor, "The Tale of Cymbeline" (1971); Actor, "NET Playhouse" (1970); Actor, "Cover Me Babe" (1970); Actor, "Hay Fever" (1970); Actor, "Indians" (1969-1970); Actor, "Three" (1969); Actor, "Generation" (1969); Actor, "Henry IV, Part 1," "Henry IV, Part 2" (1968); Actor, "Ergo" (1968); Actor, "New York Television Theatre" (1969); Actor, "Fitzwilly" (1967); Actor, "N.Y.P.D." (1967); Actor, "Halfway Up the Tree" (1967); Actor, "Posterity for Sale" (1967); Actor, "La Turista" (1967); Actor, "Hawk" (1966); Actor, "The Plastic Dome of Norma Jean" (1966); Actor, "Camera Three" (1966); Actor, "Fitz/Biscuit" (1966); Actor, "Dr. Kildare" (1965); Actor, "The Knack" (1964-1966); Actor, "Thistle in My Bed" (1963); Actor, "Oh Dad, Poor Dad, Mamma's Hung You in the Closet and I'm Feelin' So Sad" (1963); Actor, "As You Like It" (1963) **AW:** Goodermote Humanitarian Award, Bloomberg School of Public Health, Johns Hopkins University (2012); Inductee, American Theatre Hall of Fame (2012); Star, Hollywood Walk of Fame (2010); Best Performance by an Actor in a Featured Supporting Role in a Dramatic Program or Mini-Series, "The Matthew Shepard Story," Gemini Awards (2002); Outstanding Performance by a Male Actor in a Drama Series, "Law & Order," Screen Actors Guild Awards (1999); Outstanding Informational Series, "Lost Civilizations," Primetime Emmy Awards (1996); Best Performance by an Actor in a Television Series-Drama, "I'll Fly Away," Golden Globes (1993); Best Actor in a Dramatic Series, "I'll Fly Away," American Television Awards (1993) **MEM:** Actors' Equity Association; SAG-AFTRA; American Federation of Television & Radio Artists

WATFORD, DOLORES, T: Elementary School Educator **I:** Education/Educational Services **DOB:** 02/26/1951 **ED:** Professional Diploma in School Administration, Long Island University (1997); MS in Education, Long Island University (1993); MS in Special Education, Long Island University

(1990); MA in Psychological Remedial Reading, Teachers College, Columbia University (1974); BS in Education, University of Hartford (1973) C: Reading Teacher, PS 255 The Barbara Reing School (1999-2017); Reading Teacher, PS 191 Paul Robeson (1985-1999); Reading Teacher, PS 167 (1981-1985); Elementary Teacher, Public School 169 (1981-1985); Teacher, Public School, Connecticut (1976-1977); Teacher Assistant, Dalton School (1974-1976) CR: Secretary, School Leadership Team, Brooklyn (2004-2005) CIV: President, Brooklyn Reading Council (2002) AW: Recipient Service Award, Brooklyn Reading Council (2004) MEM: President, New York State Reading Association (2007-2008); Vice President, New York State Reading Association (2005-2006); International Reading Association B/I: Ms. Watford became involved in her profession because of a teacher that helped her learn to read when she was young. AV: Singing; Doing aerobics; Playing volleyball; Reading

WATKINS, STEVEN, "STEVE" CHARLES JR., T: U.S. Representative from Kansas I: Government Administration/Government Relations/Government Services DOB: 09/18/1976 PB: Lackland Air Force Base SC: TX/USA ED: MPA, Harvard University; MS, Massachusetts Institute of Technology; BS, United States Military Academy (1999) C: Member, U.S. House of Representatives from Kansas's Second Congressional District (2019-Present) MIL: With, United States Army (1999-2004) PA: Republican

WATSON, EMMA, T: Actress I: Media & Entertainment DOB: 04/15/1990 PB: Paris SC: France PT: Chris Watson; Jacqueline Luesby Watson ED: BA in English Literature, Brown University (2014); Coursework, Worcester College, Oxford (2011-2012) CT: Certified Yoga and Meditation Instructor C: Actress (2001-Present); Founder, Our Shared Shelf (2016); Model, Lancôme (2011); Model, Burberry (2009); Creative Adviser, People Tree (2009) CR: Co-Founder, Legal Advice Line for Sexual Harassment Victims, Rights of Women (2019); Speaker, Gender Equality, Numerous Venues CIV: UN Women Goodwill Ambassador (2014); Advocate, HeForShe; International Advocate, Education for Girls CW: Actress, "Little Women" (2019); Actress, "The Circle" (2017); Actress, "Beauty and the Beast" (2017); Actress, "Regression" (2015); Actress, "Colonia" (2015); Actress, "The Vicar of Dibley" (2015); Actress, "Noah" (2014); Actress, "This Is the End" (2013); Actress, "The Bling Ring" (2013); Actress, "The Perks of Being a Wallflower" (2012); Actress, "My Week with Marilyn" (2011); Actress, "Harry Potter and the Deathly Hallows: Part 2" (2011); Actress, "Harry Potter and the Deathly Hallows: Part 1" (2010); Actress, "One Night Only: Say You Don't Want It" (2010); Actress, "Harry Potter and the Half-Blood Prince" (2009); Voice Actress, "The Tale of Despereaux" (2008); Actress, "Ballet Shoes" (2007); Actress, "Harry Potter and the Order of the Phoenix" (2007); Actress, "Harry Potter and the Goblet of Fire" (2005); Actress, "Harry Potter and the Prisoner of Azkaban" (2004); Actress, "Harry Potter and the Chamber of Secrets" (2002); Actress, "Harry Potter and the Sorcerer's Stone" (2001) AW: Best Ensemble, "Little Women," Georgia Film Critics Association (2020); Woman of the Year, ELLE Style Awards (2017); Choice Movie Actress: Fantasy, "Beauty and the Beast," Teen Choice Awards (2017); Choice Movie Actress: Drama, "The Circle," Teen Choice Awards (2017); Best Actor in a Movie, "Beauty and the Beast," MTV Movie & TV Awards (2017); Acting and Activism Award, Women Film Critics Circle Awards (2016); ELLE Style Icon Award, ELLE Style Awards (2015); British Artist of the Year, BAFTA/LA Britannia Awards (2014);

British Style Icon Award, British Fashion Awards (2014); Feminist Celebrity of 2014, Ms. Foundation for Women (2014); Trailblazer Award, MTV Movie & TV Awards (2013); Favorite Dramatic Movie Actress, People's Choice Awards (2013); Choice Movie Actress: Drama, "The Perks of Being a Wallflower," Teen Choice Awards (2013); Favorite Ensemble Movie Cast, "Harry Potter and the Deathly Hallows: Part 2," People's Choice Awards (2012); Best Supporting Actress, "The Perks of Being a Wallflower," San Diego Film Critics Society Awards (2012); Best Ensemble Performance, "The Perks of Being a Wallflower," San Diego Film Critics Society Awards (2012); Capri Ensemble Cast Award, "My Week with Marilyn," Capri, Hollywood (2011); Choice Summer Movie Star: Female, "Harry Potter and the Deathly Hallows: Part 2," Teen Choice Awards (2011); Choice Movie Actress: Sci-Fi/Fantasy, "Harry Potter and the Deathly Hallows: Part 1," Teen Choice Awards (2011); Best Actress (Schauspielerin), Bravo Otto (2009); Best Actress in a Movie, "Harry Potter and the Order of the Phoenix," SyFy Portal Genre Awards (2008); Best Actress (Schauspielerin), Bravo Otto (2007); Best Performance by a Female, "Harry Potter and the Order of the Phoenix," National Movie Awards (2007); Best Actress (Schauspielerin), Bravo Otto (2006); Best Actress (Schauspielerin), Bravo Otto (2005); Best Performance by a Youth in a Leading or Supporting Role - Female, "Harry Potter and the Chamber of Secrets," Phoenix Film Critics Society Awards (2003); Best Performance in a Feature Film - Leading Young Actress, "Harry Potter and the Sorcerer's Stone," Young Artist Awards (2002)

WATSON, THOMAS STURGES, T: Professional Golfer I: Athletics DOB: 09/04/1949 PB: Kansas City PT: Raymond Etheridge Watson; Sarah Elizabeth (Ridge) Watson SPN: Linda Tova Rubin (07/08/1973, Divorced) CH: Margaret Elizabeth; Michael Barrett ED: BS, Stanford University (1971) C: Professional Golfer (1971) AW: Winner, Charles Schwab Cup (2003, 2005); Payne Stewart Award (2003); Old Tom Morris Award (1992); Hong Kong Open (1992); Inductee, Kansas Golf Hall of Fame (1991); William H. Richardson Award (1990); Named to Ryder Team Cup (1977, 1981, 1983, 1989); Elected Member, World Golf Hall of Fame, PGA of America (1988); Bob Jones Award (1987); Nabisco Championship (1987); Player of the Year, PGA of America (1977-1980, 1982, 1984); Winner, Tournament of Champions (1979-1980, 1984); Winner, Tucson Open (1978, 1984); Winner, Western Open (1974, 1977, 1984); Winner, Heritage Classic (1979, 1983); Winner, British Open (1975, 1977, 1980, 1982-1983); Los Angeles Open (1980, 1982); Winner, U.S. Open (1982); Atlantic Classic (1981); Greater New Orleans Open (1980-1981); Winner, Masters (1977, 1981); Dunlop Phoenix (1980); Byron Nelson Award (1977-1980); Winner, Andy Williams San Diego Open (1977, 1980); Winner, World Series (1975, 1980); Winner, Byron Nelson Tournament (1975, 1978-1980); Vardon Trophy (1977-1979); Winner, Memorial Tournament (1979); Winner, Colgate Hall of Fame Classic (1978, 1979); Winner, Anheuser Busch Golf Classic (1978); Winner, Bing Crosby National Pro-Am Golf Tournament (1977, 1978); Winner, El Prat (1977) MEM: United States Golf Association; The Professional Golfers' Association; GCSAA; Butler National Golf Club; Shadow Glen Golf Club; Preston Trails Golf Club; Oakwood Country Club; Par Club; Blue Hills Country Club; Kansas City Country Club; Royal and Ancient Golf Club St. Andrews

WATSON COLEMAN, BONNIE M., T: U.S. Representative from New Jersey I: Government Administration/Government Relations/Government Services DOB: 02/06/1945 PB: Camden SC: NJ/USA

MS: Married SPN: William Coleman CH: William; Jared; Troy ED: BA, Thomas Edison State College (1985); Coursework, Rutgers, The State University of New Jersey C: Member, U.S. House of Representatives from New Jersey's 12th Congressional District (2015-Present); Member, Democratic National Committee (2002-Present); Majority Leader, New Jersey General Assembly (2006-2009); Chair, New Jersey Democratic State Committee (2002-2006); Chair, Appropriations Committee, New Jersey General Assembly (2002-2005); Member, District 15, New Jersey General Assembly (1998-2015); Member, Governing Boards, New Jersey Association of State Colleges and Universities (1987-1998); Member, Ewing Township Planning Board (1996-1997); Chair, Governing Boards, New Jersey Association of State Colleges and Universities (1991-1993); President, Watson Co. Inc.; Member, Committee on Homeland Security, United States Congress; Member, Committee on Oversight and Government Reform, United States Congress CIV: Chair, Board of Trustees, Richard Stockton College (Now Stockton University), NJ (1990-1991); Member, Board of Trustees, Richard Stockton College (Now Stockton University), NJ (1981-1998) MEM: Executive Committee, Association of State Democratic Chairs (2002-Present) PA: Democrat RE: Baptist

WATTS, CHARLIE, T: Drummer I: Media & Entertainment DOB: 06/02/1941 PB: Kingsbury SC: London/England PT: Charles Richard Watts; Lillian Charlotte MS: Married SPN: Shirley Ann Shepherd (10/14/1964) CH: Seraphina Watts ED: Student, Harrow School, England C: Drummer, The Rolling Stones (1963-Present); Founder, Charlie Watts Big Band CW: Drummer, Album, "Blue & Lonesome," The Rolling Stones (2016); Drummer, "Some Girls: Live in Texas '78," The Rolling Stones (2011); Himself, Documentary, "Shine a Light," The Rolling Stones (2008); Drummer, Live Album, "Shine a Light," The Rolling Stones (2008); Drummer, Album, "A Bigger Bang," The Rolling Stones (2005); Drummer, Live Album, "Live Licks," The Rolling Stones (2004); Drummer, Album, "Watts at Scott's," The Charlie Watts Tentet (2004); Himself, "S.t.p.: A Journey Through America with the Rolling Stones" (2002); Drummer, Album, Charlie Watts Jim Keltner Project (2000); Drummer, Live Album, "No Security," The Rolling Stones (1998); Drummer, Album, "Bridges to Babylon," The Rolling Stones (1997); Drummer, Live Album, "The Rolling Stones Rock and Roll Circus," The Rolling Stones (1996); Drummer, Album, "Long Ago And Far Away," The Charlie Watts Quintet (1996); Drummer, Live Album, "Stripped," The Rolling Stones (1995); Drummer, Album, "Voodoo Lounge," The Rolling Stones (1994); Drummer, Album, "Warm and Tender," The Charlie Watts Quintet (1993); Drummer, Live Album, "Flashpoint," The Rolling Stones (1991); Drummer, Album, "Steel Wheels," The Rolling Stones (1989); Drummer, Album, "Dirty Work," The Rolling Stones (1986); Drummer, Album, "Undercover," The Rolling Stones (1983); Drummer, Live Album, "Still Life," The Rolling Stones (1982); Drummer, Documentary, "Let's Spend the Nigh Together," The Rolling Stones (1982); Drummer, Album, "Tattoo You," The Rolling Stones (1981); Drummer, Concert Video, Live Album, "Live at the Checkerboard Lounge, Chicago 1981," Muddy Waters, The Rolling Stones (1981); Drummer, Live Album, Rocket 88 (1981); Drummer, Album, "Emotional Rescue," The Rolling Stones (1980); Drummer, Album, "Some Girls," The Rolling Stones (1978); Drummer, Live Album, "Love You Live," The Rolling Stones (1977); Drummer, Album, "Black and Blue," The Rolling Stones (1976); Drummer, Album, "It's Only Rock 'n Roll," The Rolling Stones (1974); Drummer, Live Album,

"Ladies & Gentlemen: The Rolling Stones," The Rolling Stones (1974); Drummer, Album, "Goats Head Soup," The Rolling Stones (1973); Drummer, Album, "Exile on Main St.," The Rolling Stones (1972); Drummer, Album, "Sticky Fingers," The Rolling Stones (1971); Drummer, Live Album, "Get Yer Ya-Ya's Out! The Rolling Stones in Concert," The Rolling Stones (1970); Drummer, Album, "Let It Bleed," The Rolling Stones (1969); Drummer, Album, "Beggars Banquet," The Rolling Stones (1968); Drummer, Album, "Their Satanic Majesties Request," The Rolling Stones (1967); Drummer, Album, "Between the Buttons," The Rolling Stones (1967); Drummer, Album, "Aftermath," The Rolling Stones (1966); Drummer, Live Album, "Got Live if You Want It!," The Rolling Stones (1966); Drummer, Album, "December's Children (And Everybody's)," The Rolling Stones (1965); Drummer, Album, "Out of Our Heads," The Rolling Stones (1965); Drummer, Album, "The Rolling Stones, Now!," The Rolling Stones (1965); Drummer, Album, "The Rolling Stones No. 2," The Rolling Stones (1965); Drummer, Album, "12 X 5," The Rolling Stones (1964); Drummer, Album, "The Rolling Stones," The Rolling Stones (1964); Author, "Ode to a High Flying Bird" (1964) **AW:** Award for "Outstanding Contribution to Jazz," 2017 Jazz FM Awards (2017)

WEAVER, PATRICIA ELLA, T: Mathematics Educator (Retired) **I:** Education/Educational Services **DOB:** 08/29/1945 **PB:** Reading **SC:** PA/USA **PT:** Lewis Jacob Kintzer; Margie (Sherman) Kintzer **MS:** Married **SPN:** Theodore Orris Weaver (11/22/1969) **CH:** Benjamin B.; Jennifer K.; Erika L. **ED:** Postgraduate Coursework, Wilkes University (1989-1994); Master's Letter of Equivalency, Kutztown University of Pennsylvania (1992); Postgraduate Coursework, The Pennsylvania State University (1992); BS, Kutztown State College (Now Kutztown University of Pennsylvania) (1967) **CT:** Certified Teacher, Pennsylvania **C:** Advisor, Student Support Team, ELCO School District (1997-2007); Teacher, Mathematics, ELCO High School, ELCO School District, Myerstown, PA (1985-2007); Class Advisor, ELCO School District, Myerstown, PA (1991-1996); Tutor, Mathematics, Daily Subsidiary Teacher, ELCO School District, Myerstown, PA (1987-1988); Homebound Instructor, Daily Subsidiary Teacher, ELCO School District, Myerstown, PA (1979-1987); Teacher, Mathematics, Tulpehocken Area School District, Bernville, PA (1967-1973) **CR:** Lebanon County Educational Honor Society (1995-Present); Treasurer, Lebanon County Educational Honor Society (1997-1998, 2003-2004, 2009-2010, 2014-2017); Planning Committee, Tulpehocken Area School District, Bernville, PA (1971-1973); Secretary, Tulpehocken Education Association, Bernville, PA (1971-1972) **CIV:** Financial Secretary, Council, Grace United Church of Christ (2009-Present); Women's Fellow, Grace United Church of Christ (1996-Present); Secretary, Grace United Church of Christ (2006); Secretary, Girls' Basketball Boosters (1990-1993); Secretary, Girls' Hockey Boosters (1990-1992); Vice President, Council, Grace United Church of Christ (1992); Coordinator, Myerstown Girls' Summer Softball Team (1986-1992); Leader, Eastern Neighborhood Council, Girl Scouts of America, Myerstown, PA (1984-1990); Pennsylvania Dutch Council, Boy Scouts of America, Myerstown, PA (1983-1984); Band Boosters, Grace United Church of Christ; Council, Grace United Church of Christ **MEM:** President, Women's Club of Myerstown (2018-Present); Women's Club of Myerstown (2003-Present); Treasurer, Women's Club of Lebanon County (2000-2004); President, R-N Women's Club (1970-1972, 2002-2003); National Education Association; PSEA; Eastern Lebanon County EA **MH:** Albert Nelson Marquis Lifetime Achievement Award; Marquis Who's

Who Top Professional **B/I:** Mrs. Weaver became involved in her profession with inspiration from two of her high school mathematics teachers, Mr. Perry Reber and Mr. Frank Hess. She greatly admired and was influenced by the ways in which they worked with and helped their students. **AV:** Singing in the church choir; Sewing; Cultivating plants; Playing recreational ladies' softball **PA:** Republican **RE:** Protestant

WEAVER, SIGOURNEY, T: Actress **I:** Media & Entertainment **DOB:** 10/08/1949 **PB:** New York **SC:** NY/USA **PT:** Sylvester "Pat" Weaver; Elizabeth Inglis **MS:** Married **SPN:** Jim Simpson (10/01/1984) **CH:** Charlotte **ED:** MFA, Yale School of Drama, Yale University (1974); BA in English, Stanford University (1972); Coursework, Sarah Lawrence College **C:** Actress, Film, Television, Stage (1970-Present) **CIV:** Host, Trickle Up Program Annual Gala (2008); Honorary Chairwoman, Dian Fossey Gorilla Fund; Avid Environmentalist **CW:** Actress, "Avatar 5" (2027); Actress, "Avatar 4" (2025); Actress, "Avatar 3" (2023); Actress, "Avatar 2" (2021); Actress, "Ghostbusters: Afterlife" (2020); Actress, "Call My Agent!" (2020); Actress, "My Salinger Year" (2020); Voice Actress, "The Dark Crystal: Age of Resistance" (2019); Actress, "Full Frontal with Samantha Bee" (2019); Featured, "SpongeBob SquarePants" (2019); Featured, "Cleanin' Up the Town: Remembering Ghostbusters" (2019); Narrator, "Dream the Future" (2018); Actress, "The Defenders" (2017); Actress, "Rakka" (2017); Actress, "The Meyerowitz Stories" (2017); Voice Actress, "Dian Fossey: Secrets in the Mist" (2017); Herself, "Laddie: The Man Behind the Movies" (2017); Actress, "The Assignment" (2016); Actress, "A Monster Calls" (2016); Actress, "Ghostbusters" (2016); Featured, "The Beatles: Eight Days a Week" (2016); Actress, "Doc Martin" (2015-2017); Voice Actress, "Penn Zero: Part-Time Hero" (2015); Featured, "Ingrid Bergman: In Her Own Words" (2015); Actress, "Chappie" (2015); Actress, "Exodus: Gods and Kings" (2014); Voice Actress, "Alien: Isolation" (2014); Actress, "Simply Plan: Prayers for Bobby Tribute" (2014); Actress, "Vanya and Sonia and Masha and Spike" (2012-2013); Actress, "Vamps" (2012); Actress, "Political Animals" (2012); Actress, "The Cold Light of Day" (2012); Actress, "Red Lights" (2012); Actress, "Spring/Fall" (2011); Actress, "The Cabin in the Woods" (2011); Actress, "Rampart" (2011); Actress, Abduction" (2011); Actress, "Paul" (2011); Actress, "Cedar Rapids" (2011); Host, "Saturday Night Live" (2010, 1986); Actress, "You Again" (2010); Actress, "Crazy on the Outside" (2010); Actress, "Avatar" (2009); Voice Actress, "Avatar: The Game" (2009); Actress, "Prayers for Bobby" (2009); Narrator, "The Tale of Despereaux" (2008); Actress, "Eli Stone" (2008); Voice Actress, "WALL-E" (2008); Actress, "Baby Mama" (2008); Actress, "Vantage Point" (2008); Actress, "Be Kind Rewind" (2008); Actress, "Love Letters" (2007-2008); Actress, "The Girl in the Park" (2007); Voice Actress, Audiobook, "Little Bear" (2007); Actress, "Crazy Mary" (2007); Voice Actress, "Happily N'Ever After" (2006); Actress, "Infamous" (2006); Actress, "The TV Set" (2006); Actress, "Snow Cake" (2006); Narrator, "Planet Earth" (2006); Actress, "Imaginary Heroes" (2004); Actress, "The Village" (2004); Actress, "Mrs. Farnsworth" (2004); Actress, "Holes" (2003); Actress, "The Guys" (2002); Voice Actress, "Futurama" (2002); Actress, "Tadpole" (2002); Actress, "The Mercy Seat" (2002); Actress, "The Guys" (2001-2002); Voice Actress, "Big Bad Love" (2001); Actress, "Heartbreakers" (2001); Narrator, "The Roman Empire in the First Century" (2001); Actress, "Company Man" (2000); Actress, "Galaxy Quest" (1999); Actress, "A Map of the World" (1999); Narrator, "Why Dogs Smile & Chimpanzees Cry" (1999); Actress, "Alien: Resurrection" (1997); Co-Producer,

"Alien: Resurrection" (1997); Actress, "The Ice Storm" (1997); Actress, "Snow White: A Tale of Terror" (1997); Actress, "Sex and Longing" (2001-2002); Actress, "Copycat" (1995); Actress, "Jeffrey" (1995); Narrator, "The Wild Swans" (1994); Actress, "Death and the Maiden" (1994); Voice Actress, Audiobook, "Peachboy" (1994); Narrator, "Rabbit Ears: Peachboy" (1993); Actress, "Dave" (1993); Narrator, "The Snow Queen" (1992); Actress, "1492: Conquest of Paradise" (1992); Actress, Co-Producer, "Alien 3" (1992); Voice Actress, Audiobook, "The Snow Queen" (1992); Actress, "Ghostbusters II" (1989); Featured, "Helmut Newton: Frames from the Edge" (1989); Actress, "Working Girl" (1988); Actress, "Gorillas in the Mist" (1988); Actress, "The Show-Off" (1988); Actress, "The Merchant of Venice" (1986-1987); Actress, "Half Moon Street" (1986); Actress, "Aliens" (1986); Actress, "A Streetcar Named Desire" (1986); Actress, "One Woman or Two" (1985); Actress, "Hurlyburly" (1984-1985); Actress, "Ghostbusters" (1984); Actress, "Deal of the Century" (1983); Actress, "Old Times" (1983); Actress, "The Year of Living Dangerously" (1982); Actress, "Animal Kingdom" (1982); Actress, "As You Like It" (1981); Actress, "Beyond Therapy" (1981); Actress, "Das Lusitania Songspiel" (1980); Actress, "Eyewitness" (1979); Actress, "3 by Cheever" (1979); Actress, "Alien" (1979); Actress, "New Jerusalem" (1979); Actress, "Madman" (1978); Actress, "A Flea in Her Ear" (1978); Actress, "Conjuring an Event" (1978); Actress, "The Best of Families" (1977); Actress, "Marco Polo Sings a Solo" (1977); Actress, "Annie Hall" (1977); Actress, "Gemini" (1976); Actress, "Titanic" (1976); Actress, "The Constant Wife" (1975); Actress, "The Frogs" (1974); Actress, "The Nature and Purpose of the Universe" (1974); Actress, "Rise and Fall of the City of Mahagonny" (1974); Actress, "The Tempest" (1973); Actress, "The Elephant Calf" (1972); Actress, "Once in a Lifetime" (1972); Actress, "The Rat Trap" (1972); Actress, "The Resistable Rise of Arturo Ui" (1972); Actress, "Sarah B. Divine!" (1972); Actress, "Story Theatre" (1972); Actress, "Better Dead Than Sorry" (1971); Actress, "Somerset" (1970) **AW:** Voice Arts Icon Award for Arts and Humanities, Annual Voice Arts Awards, Society of Voice Arts and Sciences (SOVAS) (2018); Best Supporting Actress, "A Monster Calls," Audience Award, CinEuphoria Awards (2017); Glamour Icon, Glamour Magazine UK Women of the Year Awards (2016); Donostia Lifetime Achievement Award, San Sebastián International Film Festival (2016); Best International Actress, Golden Camera (2013); Career Audience Award, CinEuphoria Awards (2012); Best Spoken Word Album, Grammy Awards (2011); Heroine Award, Scream Awards (2010); Best Supporting Actress, "Avatar," Saturn Awards (2009); Icon Award, Elle Women in Hollywood Awards (2008); Honorary Award of the Festival, Marrakech International Film Festival (2008); Diamond Award, Edinburgh International Film Festival (2006); Lifetime Achievement Award, Empire Awards (2004); Lifetime Achievement Award, Chicago International Film Festival (2001); Star, Hollywood Walk of Fame (1999); Hasty Pudding Woman of the Year, Hasty Pudding Theatricals (1998); Icon Award, Elle Women in Hollywood Awards (1998); Best Supporting Actress, "The Ice Storm," BAFTA Awards (1997); Actor Award, Gotham Awards (1994); Best International Actress, "Gorillas in the Mist: The Story of Dian Fossey," Jupiter Award (1989); Best Supporting Actress - Motion Picture, "Working Girl," Golden Globe Awards (1988); Best Actress - Motion Picture Drama, "Gorillas in the Mist," Golden Globe Awards (1988); Female Star of the Year, Golden Apple Awards (1988); Muse Award, New York Women in Film & Television (1988); Best Actress, "Aliens," Saturn Awards (1986)

WEBB, DANIEL, "DAN" K., T: Co-Executive Chairman; Lawyer **I:** Law and Legal Services **CN:** Winston & Strawn LLP **DOB:** 09/05/1945 **PB:** Bushnell **SC:** IL/USA **MS:** Married **SPN:** Laura Webb **CH:** Five Children **ED:** Honorary LHD, Western Illinois University (2007); JD, Loyola University Chicago (1970); BA, Western Illinois University **C:** Co-Executive Chairman, Winston & Strawn LLP (2017-Present); United States Attorney, Northern District of Illinois (1981-1985); Assistant United States Attorney, Special Prosecution Division, Northern District of Illinois (1970-1975) **CR:** Co-Founder, Organized Crime Drug Enforcement Task Force; Special Counsel, Iran-Contra Affair; Special Prosecutor, Defense Counsel, Several High Profiles Cases **CW:** Participant, Mock Trial, "Twelfth Night," C-SPAN (2017) **AW:** Top Trail Group of the Year, Law360 (2018); Inductee, Lawdragon's Hall of Fame (2017); Medal of Excellence, Loyola University (2009); Person of the Year, Chicago Lawyers (2008); Lifetime Achievement Award, Illinois Association of Criminal Defense Lawyers (2006); Distinguished Service Award, Epilepsy Foundation of Greater Chicago (2006); Distinguished Public Service Award, Anti-Defamation League (1985); City of Hope Medical Center Spirit of Life Award (1983); Distinguished Service Award, Chicago Association of Commerce and Industry (1982); Number One Litigator in the United States, Euromoney's Guide to the World's Leading Lawyers; Top Litigation Expert, Guide to the World's Leading Lawyers; Number One White-Collar Criminal Defense Attorney, Corporate Crime Reporter; Listee, 100 Most Influential Lawyers in America, Best Lawyers in America; Listee, Lawdragon 500: The Legends; Recipient, Numerous Law Awards; Listee, One of the Top Attorneys in Illinois **BAR:** State of Illinois; Northern District of Illinois; United States Court of Appeals for the Sixth Circuit; United States Court of Appeals for the Seventh Circuit; United States Court of Appeals for the Eighth Circuit; Federal Circuit Court of Appeals; Supreme Court of the United States

WEBB, JASON MICHAEL, T: Composer, Lyricist, Musical Director **I:** Media & Entertainment **CW:** Composer, Arranger, Music Director, "The Rose Tattoo" (2019); Music Director, Arranger, "Choir Boy" (2019); Musical Director, Arranger/Adaptor, "Frozen: Live at the Hyperion" (2017); Associate Production Music Supervisor, "The Greatest Showman" (2017); Music Director, Conductor, Musician, "The Color Purple" (2015); Associate Conductor, Musician, "Violet" (2014); Associate Conductor, Musician, "Motown the Musical" (2013); Associate Music Director, Associate Conductor, Musician, "Leap of Faith" (2012); Associate Conductor, Musician, "Memphis" (2009-2012) **AW:** Drama Desk Award for Outstanding Music in a Play, "Choir Boy" (2019); Special Tony Award for Outstanding Arrangements, "Choir Boy" (2019)

WEBB, KAREN, T: President **I:** Education/Educational Services **CN:** Union Institute & University **MS:** Widowed **SPN:** Wallace H. Webb Jr. (Deceased 2019) **CH:** Ramona; Wallace III **ED:** PhD in Applied Linguistics, English Education, Indiana University Bloomington (1980); MS in Education, Indiana University Bloomington; BS in Spanish, Indiana University Bloomington **C:** President, Union Institute & University (2018-Present); Special Assistant, Antioch University (2016-2018); President, Midwest Campus, Antioch University (2014-2016); Provost and Vice President for Academic Affairs, Antioch University (2013-2014); Associate Provost for Engagement, Founding Dean of the Shirley M. Hufstedler School of Education, Alliant International University (2000-2013); Professor and Dean, College of Education, Southern University (1998-2000); Associate Professor and Program Director for Language Education (English, Foreign Languages, TESOL), University of Kentucky (1992-1998); Coordinator for Freshman English, Howard University (1988-1992); Assistant Professor and Assistant Director of the Learning Center, Indiana University Bloomington (1982-1987); Coordinator for Freshman Composition, Coppin State University (1973-1976); Secondary School Teacher of Foreign Languages and English as a Second Language, Alexandria, VA (1969-1972) **CR:** Consultant, Karen Schuster Webb, PhD (2010-Present) **CIV:** Executive Council, Women's Network Executive Council (WNEC), American Council on Education, Washington, DC (2018-Present); Chair-elect, Women's Network Executive Council (WNEC), American Council on Education, Washington, DC (2014-2018); Advisory Board, William V. S. Tubman University Foundation, Harper, Liberia; Board of Directors, Dayton Contemporary Dance Company; Chair, Vice Chair, ACE Northern California Women's Network; Former Member, Accrediting Commission for Schools, Western Association of Schools and Colleges (ACS WASC) and Southern Association of Colleges and Schools Commission on Colleges; Launched Workforce Development, Community Education, Outreach Initiatives, Antioch University with Dayton's Immigrant Communities; Established Midwest Campus Veterans Affairs Liaison Office, Antioch University **CW:** Speaker, Conferences, Nationally and Internationally; Published, Numerous Articles in the Areas of Urban Education, Sociolinguistics, and Language Learning **AW:** Named to Top 25 Women in Higher Education and Beyond, Diverse Issues in Higher Education Magazine (2016); Named Teacher of the Year, Doctoral Students at Alliant International University, California School of Education **AS:** Dr. Webb attributes her success to her parents in the sense that they taught her to disagree with the statement and say that everyone has a gift. She may find that something that is easy to her may be difficult for someone else and what someone else finds easy may be difficult to her. She had physical challenges with her knee early on; she was in braces for a while, and so to overcome that, you gain tenacity and you have to deal with people that don't understand your condition. That helped her to have the resilience and the desire that if she wanted to do something she could accomplish it. **B/I:** Dr. Webb was very fortunate that both of her parents were educators. Her mother was a high school teacher of business and high school counselor. Her father was in higher education and was dean of the school of business. He also helped to begin a business school in Nigeria through the United States Agency of International Development. She grew up in a household that valued education, it was very enriching. Looking at the education field was something that was all around her. First, she looked at possibly going into medicine, and later decided her calling was education. When she graduated from college, she was thinking of going into social work in Hispanic areas. She was applying for social work positions or community organizing kinds of positions in Waterbury, Connecticut, where her parents lived. It seemed there your application went into the municipal government in general, so it was all kinds of agencies that had access to the application. The first agency to call her was the school district. She wasn't an education major but over 80% of the students in the school district spoke Spanish. So they were interested if she was in traditional education an in her ability to speak Spanish. She was offered a position to teach second grade at that school district. Her first class had over 40 students in it, and they ranged in age from 7 to 13. The problem was that the older children had not been taught literacy skills in English; they had conversational skills, but in terms of standardized testing, you needed the literacy skills. So what she started to do was during recess and after school, she taught English as a second language and then teaching bilingually because the majority of her students' first language was Spanish. She would teach some days in Spanish, some days in English. Then she enrolled herself at Southern Connecticut University in an evening program to get a teaching credential. That lead later to going back to Indiana to focusing on linguistics and getting into the field of applied linguistics and English education. She feel in love with teaching there in Waterbury, Connecticut, and then she started looking at higher education as a place where she could make a larger impact as well.

WEBB, WILLIE JAMES, T: Alcohol and Drug Abuse Specialist, Minister, Instructor, Certified Clinical Supervisor **I:** Religious **CN:** Ministry **DOB:** 09/18/1935 **PB:** Tuskegee **SC:** AL/USA **YOP:** NA **MS:** Married **SPN:** Wilma S. Webb (12/20/1960) **CH:** Karen Michelle Webb **ED:** Master of Science, Georgia State University (1976); Master of Arts, Clark Atlanta University (1970); Bachelor of Arts, Morehouse College (1961); Master of Divinity, Morehouse School of Religion (1958) **CT:** Licensed, Ordained to Preach (1958); Certified, Pastoral Addiction Counselor, National Association of Forensic Counselors; Criminal Justice Specialist; Certified Clinical Chaplain; Continuing Professional Education; Certified Addiction Counselor II; CCS Certified Clinical Supervisor; Certified Pastoral Addiction Counselor; Certified Criminal Justice Specialist; Certified Public Theologian **C:** Crisis Stabilization Supervisor, Department of Human Resources, Cobb and Douglas Counties, Georgia (1988-1991); Mental Health Forensic Services Coordinator, Department of Human Resources, Cobb and Douglas Counties, Georgia (1985-1988); Mental Health, Substance Abuse Counselor, Therapist, Department of Human Resources, Cobb and Douglas Counties, Georgia (1982-1985); Psychiatric Social Worker Senior, Department of Human Resources, Marietta, GA (1977-1982); Probation, Parole Supervisor, Department of Corrections, Decatur, GA (1976-1977); Correction Specialist, Fulton County Juvenile Court, Atlanta, GA (1972-1975); Probation Officer, Supervisor, Fulton County Juvenile Court, Atlanta, GA (1968-1972); Job Corps Center, Department of Human Resources, Atlanta, GA **CR:** Founder, Christian Association of Public Theologians (2002); Founder, Christian Institute of Public Theology (2002); Founder, Foundation Baptist Church (1996); Pastoral Church Ministry; Pastoral Counseling; Mental Health Counseling; Criminal Justice; Juvenile Justice; Corrections; Theological Instruction; Community and Civic Engagement; Pastoral Addiction Counselor; Culture Crisis Theologian; Christian Author, Six Books **CIV:** Pastor, Foundation Baptist Church, Atlanta (1996-2020); Clergy Training Committee Charis Bible College, Atlanta, GA (2014-2019); Board of Directors, Alabama Bible University, Notasulga, GA (1985-1995); Interim Pastor, Wheat St. Baptist Church, Atlanta (1988-1989); President, Harwell Heights Community Association (1968-1988); Judicial Watch **CW:** Author, "Hatred Addiction Recovery" (2018); Author, "Ezekiel Saw the Wheel" (2014); Author, "New Possibilities for Juvenile Justice" (2013); Author, "The Way Out of Darkness" (2007); Author, "God's Spiritual Prescriptions" (2001); Author, "Psychotrauma Trauma: The Human Injustice Crisis" (1990) **AW:** Honorary Proclamation, Atlanta City Council (2009); Community Service Award, Governor Sonny Perdue (2009); Christian Leadership Award, Foundation Baptist Church (2002); Outstanding

Service Award, Atlanta Job Corps (2000); Pastoral Appreciation Award, Linden Short CME (1999); Employee of the Month, Atlanta Job Corps Center (1994); Community Service Award, Clark Atlanta University (1989); Service Award, Boys Club of America (1988); Outstanding Community Service Award, Wheat Street Tenants (1988); Georgia Governor's Award (1987); Outstanding Leadership Award, Wheat Street Baptist Church (1986); Ford Foundation Fellow (1973-1976); Most Outstanding Student in Religion, Morehouse College (1961); Benjamin E. Mays Debating Prize **MEM:** National Association of Addiction Counselors; Georgia Addiction Counselors Association; Georgia State University Alumni Association; Clark Atlanta University Alumni Association; Morehouse College Alumni Association; Concerned Black Clergy of Atlanta; National Association of Forensic Counselors; Christian Association of Public Theologians **MH:** Albert Nelson Marquis Lifetime Achievement Award **AS:** Reverend Webb attributes his success to a loving family, community and his Christian faith. **B/I:** After serving as a probation officer, Reverend Webb was licensed and ordained to preach. **AV:** Reading; Writing; Speaking; Counseling; Christian art; Sacred music; Sports **RE:** Baptist

WEBER, CURT M., T: Law Educator **I:** Law and Legal Services **ED:** JD, Duquesne University, Pittsburgh, PA (1982); BA, Marquette University, Milwaukee, WI (1978) **C:** Lecturer, University of Wisconsin-Whitewater (2002-Present); Adjunct instructor, Upper Iowa University, Fayette, Iowa (1994-2014); Adjunct Instructor, Concordia University Wisconsin, Mequon, WI (1996-2010); Instructor, Milwaukee Area Technical College (1982-2002) **CIV:** Director, Education Foundation of Wauwatosa (Now Tosa EFW), WI (2002-2008); President, Lutheran A. Cappella Choir of Milwaukee, WI (2003-2004); Time and Total Compensation; Representative, Whitewater Academic Staff, Governance Group, University of Wisconsin System **CW:** Contributor, Articles to Professional Journal **AW:** Hermsen Teaching Award, University of Wisconsin-Whitewater College of Business and Economics (2004) **MEM:** AICPA; Phi Alpha Delta Law Fraternity, International; International Business Law **MH:** Albert Nelson Marquis Lifetime Achievement Award **B/I:** Mr. Weber became involved in his profession because law seemed very interesting to him and no one else in the family was doing it, so he chose that profession. Mr. Weber likes to argue and found it to be profoundly interesting **AV:** Music; Bicycling; Cross country skiing; Playing his trumpet; Reading; Traveling **RE:** Christian

WEBER, JEFFREY M., MD, T: Gastroenterologist **I:** Medicine & Health Care **CN:** Cancer Treatment Centers of America **PT:** Marshall Weber, MD; Jeanette Weber **MS:** Married **SPN:** Nancy **CH:** Two Daughters; One Son **ED:** Residency in Internal Medicine, Georgetown Division, District of Columbia General Hospital, Washington, DC (1974-1977); MD, University of Wisconsin - Madison (1974); BA in English, University of Wisconsin - Madison (1970) **CT:** Diplomate, American Board of Internal Medicine; Diplomate, American Board of Gastroenterology **C:** Associate Professor of Medicine, University of Arizona College of Medicine, Phoenix Campus, AZ (2018-Present); Chairman, Board, Phoenix Cancer Support Network (2016-Present); Clinical Gastroenterologist, Cancer Treatment Centers of America (2009-2020); Owner, MDDC (1979-2009); President, Milwaukee Digestive Disease Consultants (1979-2009); Sub Investigator, Discovery Research (2006-2007); Medical Director, St. Luke's Hospital (Now Mount Sinai Morningside) (1986-1989); Medical Director, West Allis Memorial Hospital, Aurora Health Care (1986-1989)

CR: Medical Director, Aurora St. Luke's Medical Center Comprehensive Obesity Treatment Program, Aurora Health Care; Medical Director, West Allis Memorial Hospital Weight Loss Program, Aurora Health Care **CIV:** Board Member, United Nations Children's Fund (UNICEF); Board Member, Wisconsin Chapter, American Medical Association **CW:** Speaker, Colon and Esophageal Cancer Screening, Cancer Treatment Centers of America; Featured, Television Interviews **AW:** Named to The Leading Physicians of the World (2014); America's Top Physicians Award, Community Research Council of America (2003); Named Best Doctor in Milwaukee, Shepard Publications (2001) **MEM:** Milwaukee Gastroenterological Society, American Society for Gastrointestinal Endoscopy (ASGE); Fellow, American Gastroenterology Association (AGA); American Society of Parenteral and Enteral Nutrition (ASPEN); Sarcoma Foundation of America **AS:** Dr. Weber attributes his success to wife, Nancy. He would not be in gastroenterology if it wasn't for her. He always had the opportunity to go back to Wisconsin and work in the family practice with his father. His wife stated, "You like cameras, why don't you go into gastroenterology?" He applied to one fellowship, was accepted and moved forward. **B/I:** Dr. Weber's father was a family practitioner. He always felt in alliance with him. They looked like they talked a lot and it felt natural for him to go into medicine. He learned a lot about how to relate to people from his father, who was a great clinician/diagnostician. His father never encouraged him to become a physician. He actually discouraged him because the medical field was changing. But Dr. Weber followed what he felt was true and natural for him. **THT:** Dr. Weber works with an organization where they fill in the gaps in medical care that is not provided by insurance/Medicare, such as driving to and from appointments. There was a man who lost his teeth due to neck and head radiation, and they were able to give him new teeth. In 2019, they helped over 200 patients.

WEBER, JOHN B., T: Architect (Retired) **I:** Architecture & Construction **DOB:** 10/15/1930 **PB:** Evanston **SC:** IL/USA **PT:** Bertram Anton Weber; Dorothea B. Weber **MS:** Married **SPN:** Sally French Weber **CH:** Suzanne Roulston; Jane McCarthy; Patricia Blodgett; Nancy Weber **ED:** Postgraduate Coursework, Illinois Institute of Technology, Chicago, IL (1959); BArch, Princeton University, Princeton, NJ (1952) **CT:** Licensed Architect; Registered Interior Designer, State of Illinois; Energy Professional, Chicago, IL **C:** Private Practice, Winnetka, Northfield, IL (1994-2006); Private Practice, Northbrook, IL (1984-1994); Partner, Proprietor, Weber & Weber Architects, Chicago, IL (1973-1984); Architect, Bertram A. Weber Architect, Chicago, IL (1958-1973); Field Engineer, Atkinson United Construction Co., Greenup and Ashland, KY (1956-1958); Field Engineer, United Construction Co., Riverdale, ND (1952); Draftsman, Bertram A. Weber Architect, Chicago, IL (1953, 1947) **CR:** Illinois Architecture Act Revision Task Force (1982-1989); Delegate, Illinois Architects-Engineer Council (1976-1987); Chairman, Illinois Architects-Engineer Council (1981-1982) **CIV:** Active Member, Winnetka Forestry Commission (2003-2008); Active Member, Winnetka Design Review Board (2002-2008); Active Member, Winnetka Ad Hoc Zoning Committee (1995-1996); Chairman, Winnetka Zoning Board Appeals (1987-1988); Active Member, Winnetka Zoning Board Appeals (1983-1988); Chairman, Building Committee, Winnetka Community House (1977-1981); Mayor's Advisory Committee Building Codes, Chicago, IL (1975-1980); Active Member, Exmoor Country Club (1958-1978); Active Member, Winnetka Com-

munity Caucus (1974); Active Member, Winnetka Community Caucus (1965); Deacon, Elder, Winnetka Presbyterian Church **MIL:** Officer, U.S. Ship Tingey DD539, U.S. Pacific Fleet, U.S. Navy (1953-1956) **CW:** "Prestwick Country Club"; "3175 Commercial Avenue Building," Northbrook, IL; "Medical Office Building and Additions to Bi-County Hospital," Warren, MI; Contributor, Additions and Alterations, Detroit Osteopathic Hospital; Contributor, Addition, Duraclean International Building, Deerfield, IL; Contributor, Additions, The Admiral, Chicago, IL; Villa Stresov, Borovets, Bulgaria **MEM:** Board of Directors, Builders Club of Chicago (1966-Present); Board of Directors, Illinois Society of Architects (1969-1984, 1991-1999); Board of Directors, Architects Club of Chicago (1976-1986, 1994); President, Old Willow Club (1983); President, Architects Club of Chicago (1981); President, Illinois Society of Architects (1976-1978); Health Committee, American Institute of Architects (1969-1976); President, Builders Club of Chicago (1973-1974); Fellow, Association of Licensed Architects; Fellow, Illinois Society of Architects; Veterans of Foreign Wars (VFW); American Institute of Architects; National Trust for Historic Preservation; Chicago Botanic Garden; Life Member, Art Institute of Chicago; Navy League of the United States; Construction Specifications Institute; The American Legion; Dairymen's Country Club; Old Willow Club; Builders Club of Chicago; Architects Club of Chicago; Winnetka Historical Society; Winnetka Community House **MH:** Albert Nelson Marquis Lifetime Achievement Award **AS:** Mr. Weber attributes his success to his experience in hospital, residential and church work. **B/I:** Mr. Weber became involved in his profession because both his father and grandfather were architects. He studied architecture at Princeton University.

WEBER, RANDALL, "RANDY" KEITH, T: U.S. Representative from Texas; Small Business Owner **I:** Government Administration/Government Relations/Government Services **DOB:** 07/02/1953 **PB:** Pearland **SC:** TX/USA **MS:** Married **SPN:** Brenda Weber **CH:** Three Children **ED:** BA in Public Affairs, University of Houston, Clear Lake, Texas (1977); Coursework, Alvin Community College, Texas (1971-1974) **C:** Member, U.S. House of Representatives from Texas' 14th Congressional District, United States Congress, Washington, DC (2013-Present); Member, U.S. House Committee on Space, Science and Technology (2013-Present); Member, U.S. House Committee on Foreign Affairs (2013-Present); Owner, Weber's Air & Heat (1981-Present); Member, District 29, Texas House of Representatives (2009-2013); City Councilman, City of Pearland, Texas (1990-1996); Member, House Committee on Transportation & Infrastructure **PA:** Republican **RE:** Baptist

WEBSTER, ARTHUR EDWARD, T: Lawyer **I:** Law and Legal Services **DOB:** 12/02/1956 **PB:** Hartford **SC:** CT/USA **PT:** Arthur Ellsworth Webster Jr.; Carrie Mabel (Goodrich) Webster **ED:** JD, Georgetown University (1982); BA, Bradley University, Summa Cum Laude (1978) **C:** Assistant Attorney General, Office of Attorney General, State of Connecticut, Hartford, CT (1986-2017); Associate, Halloran, Sage, Phelan & Hagarty, Hartford, CT (1982-1985) **CR:** Lecturer, Complex Medical Treatment Decisions (1987-2017); Lecturer, HIV/AIDS Laws and Policy (1987-2017); Adjunct Professor of Law, School of Law, University of Connecticut (1998-2012); Medical Review Board, Connecticut Children and Families (1987-2008); Faculty, Department of Children and Families Child Welfare Training Academy (1989-2006); Co-Director, Faculty Member, Connecticut Bar Association, State of Connecticut Judicial Department Continuing Legal Education Seminars, Hartford, CT (1992-2002); Lecturer in Law, School of Law, University of Connecticut (1991-1998); Faculty Member, Trial Skills Course for Child Protection Lawyers (1996); Television Panelist on Child Abuse (1992) **CIV:** President, Middletown Branch, American Heart Association (1989-1990); Member of Steering Committee, March of Dimes, WalkAmerica (1988-1990); Vice President, Middletown Branch, American Heart Association (1987-1989) **CW:** Author, "For the Sake of a Child's Safety: The Law of Emergency Removal Proceedings" (1997); Author, "Child Protection in Connecticut Courts, Revised Edition" (1996); Author, "The Art of the Deal: A Common Sense Approach to Settlement of Child Protection Cases" (1996); Author, "Child Protection in Connecticut Courts" (1992) **AW:** Beaudry Cup Fellowship (1982); Law Fellowship, Georgetown University Law Center, Washington, DC (1981); Nyaradi Memorial Fellowship, Bradley University Institute International Studies (1978); Order of Lincoln, State of Illinois (1978) **MEM:** Board of Directors, True Colors Inc., Connecticut (2017-Present); President, Cromwell Hillside Cemetery Association (2005-Present); Juvenile Justice Committee (1983-1988); Chairman, Connecticut Bar Association **BAR:** United States District Court for the District of Connecticut (1983); Connecticut (1982) **MH:** Albert Nelson Marquis Lifetime Achievement Award; Marquis Who's Who Top Professional **B/I:** When Mr. Webster graduated from college, he was unsure of exactly what he wanted to pursue as a career. His options were to get a job in the corporate sector, government, or to attend law school. Mr. Webster recalls, while serving as student body president, that he enjoyed making changes for the better and thought law school would be the best fit.

WEBSTER, DANIEL ALAN, T: U.S. Representative from Florida; Small Business Owner **I:** Government Administration/Government Relations/Government Services **DOB:** 04/27/1949 **PB:** Charleston **SC:** WV/USA **PT:** Dennis Webster; Mildred Rada (Schoolcraft) Webster **MS:** Married **SPN:** Sandy Jordan **CH:** David Lee; Brent Alan; Jordan Daniel; Elizabeth Anne; John Elliott; Victoria Suzanna **ED:** BS in Electrical Engineering, Georgia Institute of Technology (1971) **C:** Member, House of Representatives from Florida's 11th Congressional District, United States Congress, Washington, DC (2017-Present); Member, House of Representatives from Florida's 10th Congressional District, United States Congress, Washington, DC (2013-Present); Member, U.S. House Committee on Transportation and Infrastructure (2013-Present); Member, U.S. House Rules Committee (2011-2014); Member, U.S. House of Representatives from Florida's Eighth Congressional District, United States Congress, Washington, DC (2011-2013); Majority Leader, Florida State Senate (2006-2008); Member, District Nine, Florida State Senate (2003-2008); Member, District 12, Florida State Senate (1999-2002); Speaker, Florida House of Representatives (1996-1998); Member, District 41, Florida House of Representatives (1982-1998); Republican Leader, Florida House of Representatives (1994-1996); Republican Leader Pro Tempore, Florida House of Representatives (1992-1994); Minority Whip, Florida House of Representatives (1988-1990); Vice Chairman, Minority Policy Committee, Florida House of Representatives (1985-1988); Minority Floor Leader, Florida House of Representatives (1982-1984); Owner, Webster Air Conditioning & Heating Inc. **AW:** Leadership Award, Florida Association of State Toppers (1996); Named Florida Statesman of the Year, Florida Republican Party (1995); Named Legislator of the Year, Florida Chamber of Commerce (1995); Award, Florida Banking Association (1995); Special Recognition Award, Florida Hotel & Motel Association (1995); Quality Floridian Award, Florida League of Cities (1995); Legislature Award, Florida Farm Bureau (1995); Award, Board of Regents (1995); D.I. Rainey Award, Florida Chiropractic Association, Inc. (1994); Legislature Leadership Award, Florida Medical Society (1993) **MEM:** United Community Action for Israel; American Farm Bureau Federation; West Orange County Chamber of Commerce, Winter Garden, FL; National Federation of Independent Business; Air Conditioning Contractors of America Association, Inc.; Associated Builders and Contractors; Sertoma, Inc. **PA:** Republican **RE:** Baptist

WEBSTER, LETITIA, T: Chief Sustainability Officer, Partner **I:** Financial Services **CN:** Mission Driven Capital Partners **ED:** MBA in Sustainability, Minor in Organizational Development and Change Management, Bainbridge Graduate Institute (Now Presidio Graduate School) (2008); BA in Business Communications and Environmental Policy, Bowling Green State University (1994) **C:** Chief Sustainability Officer, Partner, Mission Driven Capital Partners, New York, NY (2019-Present); Global Vice President of Corporate Sustainability, Head of Purpose, VF Corporation (2011-2018); Director of Strategic Marketing, Communications and Corporate Sustainability, The North Face (2000-2011); Director of Strategic Marketing, The North Face (2005-2009); Manager, Marketing and Communications, The North Face (2000-2005); Executive Director, Sheep Mountain Alliance, Telluride, CO (1996-1998) **CIV:** Board Director, Communities in Schools of Greater Greensboro (2015-Present); Board Director, Greensboro Montessori School (2014-Present); Board Director, Mountainfilm (2005-2008) **AW:** Lifetime VIP with Certificate, Covington (2012)

WEDEKIND, THOMAS C., MSW, T: Chief Executive Officer **I:** Health, Wellness and Fitness **CN:** Personal Enrichment Through Mental Health Services **MS:** Married **SPN:** Mary Ann **CH:** Kara; Jamie **ED:** MSW in Social Service Administration and Social Work, The University of Chicago, with Honors (1973); BA in Sociology, Colby College, with Honors (1969) **C:** Chief Executive Officer, Personal Enrichment Through Mental Health Services (2016-Present); Executive Director, Personal Enrichment Through Mental Health Services (1983-2016); Field Instructor, Case Western Reserve University; Sociology Professor, Hillsboro Community College **CR:** Consulting **CIV:** Donaldson Institute **CW:** Author, Articles on Hospital and Community Psychiatry, Professional Journals **AW:** Albion Wood Small Prize in Sociology **MEM:** National Association of Social Workers; Florida Council for Community Mental Health; Florida Association of Mental Health Administrators; American College of Healthcare Executives; NAMI **MH:** Marquis Who's Who Top Professional **THT:** Mr. Wedekind's motto is "care and crisis."

WEI, YING, T: Engineer Consultant **I:** Engineering **DOB:** 08/29/1952 **PB:** Harbin **SC:** China **PT:** Wen-Jia Wei; Su-Zhen Xu **MS:** Married **SPN:** Louis J Soule; Jian-Ming Jiang, (1/28/1981, Divorced 2/1997) **CH:** Mike (Hai-Yi) Jiang **ED:** Postdoctoral Fellow, Lamar University, Beaumont, TX (1990-1991); Postdoctoral Fellow, Agricultural and Mechanical University, College Station, TX (1989-1990); PhD, Rennes I University, France (1986); MS, Rennes I University, France (1984); BS in Chemistry, Hei Long Jiang University, China (1982) **CT:** A Water Operator License (WO0019837); A Wastewater Operator License (WW0045221; P.E. License, Texas (104851) **C:** President, WJIES; Retired (2016); City Laboratory Manager, City of Houston/Water Production (1996-2016); Laboratory Supervisor, IT Corp., Cosby, TX (1991-1995) **CR:** Environmental; Chemistry; Drinking Water Business and Wastewater Business; Engineering Consultant; Farming **CW:** Contributor, Articles, Professional Journals; Water and Wastewater Expert **MEM:** American Water Works Association **MH:** Albert Nelson Marquis Lifetime Achievement Award **B/I:** Ms. Wei became involved in her profession because in China in her generation there was a culture revolution with the Chinese government. She was waiting to go to school to study but it was hard for her to do so because she could not get the books so she studied for herself. She always wanted to do research in science and when she came to the US she did that. Each year she would go to the seminars and conferences. **AV:** Gardening; Bees (honey) business; Organic gardening; Drawing; Dancing; Singing

WEINBAUM, CHARLES H. JR., T: Insurance Company Executive **I:** Insurance **DOB:** 11/23/1926 **PB:** Beaumont **SC:** TX/USA **PT:** Charles H. Weinbaum; Eleanor (Perlstein) Weinbaum **MS:** Widower **SPN:** Gloria Wynn (08/16/1952, Deceased 2005) **CH:** Becky Hovland; Chas H. "Bo" III; Daniel A.; Jonathan; Bernard **ED:** BS in Management Engineering, Texas A&M University (1948) **CT:** Chartered Property and Casualty Underwriter **C:** Partner, Chas Weinbaum Insurance Agency, Beaumont, TX (1949) **CR:** Real Estate Developer, Shopping Center **MIL:** U.S. Air Force (1945) **MEM:** President, Rotary, Beaumont Club (1983-1984); President, Beaumont Agricultural and Mechanical Club (1958); President, Beaumont Chapter, Jaycees (1952-1953) **MH:** Albert Nelson Marquis Lifetime Achievement Award **B/I:** Mr. Weinbaum wanted to make enough money to support his wife and five children. He decided to follow in his father's footsteps and get into the building insurance industry. **AV:** Fishing; Hunting; Golfing; Playing softball **RE:** Jewish

WEINER, JOHN BARLOW, T: Associate Director for Policy, Office of Combination Products **I:** Civil Service **CN:** U.S. Food and Drug Administration **PB:** New York **SC:** NY/USA **PT:** Earl Weiner; Gina Ingoglia Weiner **MS:** Married **SPN:** Caroline Schaefer **ED:** JD, Columbia Law School, New York, NY (1996); BA in History, Princeton University, Princeton, NJ (1991) **C:** Associate Director for Policy, Office of Combination Products, U.S. Food and Drug Administration (2008-Present); Associate Chief Counsel, Office of Chief Counsel, U.S. Food and Drug Administration (2004-2008); Associate, Ropes & Gray LLP, Washington, DC (2001-2003); Associate, Beveridge & Diamond, Washington, DC (1997-2001); Law Fellow, Center for International Environmental Law, Geneva, Switzerland (1996-1997); Law Clerk, Grais & Phillips, New York, NY (1996); Summer Associate, Beveridge & Diamond, Washington, DC (1995); Pro-Bono Legal Consultant, Pueblo of Jemez, Jemez Pueblo, NM (1994-1995); Legal Intern, Office of Regional Counsel, United States Environmental Protection Agency, Boston, MA (1994); Pro-Bono Advocate, Church World Series, Haitian Refugee Asylum Project, New York, NY (1993-1996); Analyst, Organized Crime Narcotics Unit, District Attorney's Office, New York, NY (1992-1993) **CR:** Co-Chair, Committee on Combination Products, Association for the Advancement of Medical Instrumentation (2013-Present); Liaison, Section of International Law and Practice, Standing Committee on Environmental Law, American Bar Association (2003-2007); Chair, International Environmental Law Committee, Section of International Law, American Bar Association (2001-2003) **CIV:** Chair of Board, Cleveland Park Citizens Association (2019-present); Chair of Board, Food Intelligent Grids (2017-2019); Chair of Board, Gateway Georgetown Association (2007-2013); Co-Founder,

Rainforest Conservancy (1989-1992) **CW:** Author, Chapter on Regulation of Combination Products in the United States, "Handbook on Medical Device Regulatory Affairs in Asia" (2013); Author, "The Fate of Pharming," Update (2003); Author, "A Rose is a Rose is a Rose, or is it?," Hatch-Waxman Protection of Patents for Polymorphs and Hydrates, Update (2002); Co-Author, "An Introduction to the Rules of the WTO: An Environmental, Health and Safety Perspective," Trade and Environment, the WTO, and MEAs (2001); Co-Author, "Implications of China's Accession to the WTO for Environmental, Health and Safety Standards," PACE 2000: Policy Reform and the Environment in China, The World Bank (2000); Author, "Addressing Environmental Health and Safety Regulation in the 'Millennium Round' of the World Trade Organization Trade Negotiations," Environmental Law & Practice (2000); Co-Author, "The Cartagena Protocol on Biosafety: Co-Author, New Rules for International Trade in Living Modified Organisms," Georgetown International Environmental Law Review (2000); Contributor, Editor, Environmental Law, International Legal Developments in Review, The International Lawyer (1998-2003); Co-Author, Chapter on United States Law, Contaminated Property in Canada (1998); Co-Author, "A Handbook for Obtaining Documents from the World Trade Organization," International Center for Trade and Sustainable Development (1996); Co-Editor, A Jailhouse Lawyer's Manual (Fourth Ed.) (1996); Author, "Institutional Reform Consent Decrees as Conservors of Social Progress," Columbia Human Rights Law Review (1995) **AW:** Commissioners Special Citation, U.S. Food and Drug Administration **MEM:** The University Club of Washington DC (1999-present) **BAR:** The District of Columbia Bar (1998); New York State Bar Association (1998)

WEINER, LESLIE P., MD, T: Neurology Educator **I:** Education/Educational Services **CN:** Keck School of Medicine of USC **DOB:** 03/17/1936 **PB:** Brooklyn **SC:** NY/USA **PT:** Sarah (Paris) Weiner (Deceased 1991); Paul Larry Weiner (Deceased 1970) **MS:** Married **SPN:** Judith Marilyn Hoffman Weiner (12/26/1959) **CH:** Patrice Ann Weiner, MD; Allison Hope Weiner; Matthew Hoffman Weiner; Jonathan Michael Weiner, MD **ED:** Fellowship in Virology, Slow Virus Laboratory, National Institute of Neurological Disorders and Stroke, National Institutes of Health (1969); Fellowship, Johns Hopkins University (1967-1969); Residency in Neurology, Johns Hopkins Hospital (1962-1965); Residency, Baltimore City Hospital (1962-1963); Internship in Medicine, The State University of New York, Syracuse, NY (1961-1962); MD, University of Cincinnati (1961); BA, Wilkes College (1957) **CT:** Diplomate, American Board of Psychiatry and Neurology (1969) **C:** Retired (2016); Professor of Neurology and Microbiology, Richard Angus Grant Senior Chair in Neurology, Keck School of Medicine of USC (1987-2016); Chairman, Department of Neurology, Keck School of Medicine of USC (1979-2003); Associate Professor, Johns Hopkins University (1972-1975); Assistant Professor of Neurology, Johns Hopkins University (1969-1972) **CR:** Committee for the Review of Adverse Effects, National Academy of Medicine (2009-Present); Science Advisory Board Member, Hereditary Disease Foundation (1992-Present); Programs Research Advisory Committee, National Multiple Sclerosis Society (2000-2007); Chairman, Science Advisory Board, Hereditary Disease Foundation (1994-1996); Chief Neurologist, University Hospital, University of Southern California (1991-1996); Chairman, General Clinical Reserve Center, University of Southern California (1994-1995); Board of Governors, Chief Neurologist, Southern California Medical Center (1979-1994); Neuroscience Train-

ing Study Section, National Institutes of Health (1990-1993) **CIV:** Chairman, Connecticut Stem Cell Peer Review Committee (2007-Present); Board of Directors, Starbright Foundation, Inc. (1991-1999) **MIL:** Captain, Army Medical Corps, U.S. Army (1965-1967) **CW:** Editor, "Neural Stem Cells Methods and Protocols" (2007); Associate Editor, "Neurobase" (1994-1995); Contributor, 150 Articles, Professional Journals **AW:** Grantee, National Institutes of Health (1999-2016); Grantee, Teva Neuroscience (2009-2016); Grantee, Kenneth Norris Foundation (1995-2007); Grantee, Conrad Hilton Foundation (1995-1997); Grantee, Heron Foundation; Grantee, Race to Erase MS; Grantee, Oxnard Foundation **MEM:** Advisory Committee Research Program, National Multiple Sclerosis Society (2000-2007); American Association for the Advancement of Science; Fellow, American Academy of Neurology; Coalition for the Advancement of Medical Research; Association of University Professors of Neurology; Society of Scholars, Johns Hopkins University; Society for Neuroscience; American Neurological Association; American Health Assistance Foundation; Alpha Omega Alpha Honor Medical Society **MH:** Albert Nelson Marquis Lifetime Achievement Award **B/I:** Dr. Weiner became involved in his profession because of his desire to pursue research and parlay his knowledge to others. **AV:** Enjoying theater; Painting **PA:** Democrat **RE:** Jewish

WEINSHENKER, NAOMI, T: Psychiatrist **I:** Medicine & Health Care **CN:** Self-Employed **DOB:** 03/28/1961 **PB:** Ridgewood **SC:** NJ/USA **PT:** Theodore Weinshenker; Anne Betty (Jaffe) Weinshenker **MS:** Married **SPN:** Emanuel Goldman **CH:** Lila Goldman, Theodore Goldman **ED:** Resident in Adult Psychiatry, Massachusetts Mental Health Center, Harvard Medical School, Boston, MA (1990-1992); Rotating Intern, Overlook Hospital, Summit, NJ (1989-1990); MD, University of Pennsylvania (1989); BA, Yale University, Summa Cum Laude (1983) **CT:** Diplomate in Psychiatry, American Board of Psychiatry and Neurology, Inc.; Diplomate in Child and Adolescent Psychiatry, American Board of Psychiatry and Neurology, Inc. **C:** Private Practice, Psychiatry (2006-Present); Medical Reporter, Ebru TV, Somerset, NJ (2010-2012); Member, Advisory Board, New Jersey Life Health + Beauty Magazine (2010-2011); Assistant Professor, Clinical Psychiatry, NYU Grossman School of Medicine (2000-2010); Consultant, Expert Witness, Dechert LLP (2009); Medical Correspondent, Medical Missions for Children (2007-2008); Freelance Medical Reporter, News12, Norwalk, CT (2006-2007); Assistant Professor, Clinical Psychiatry, University of Medicine and Dentistry of New Jersey, Newark, NJ (1996-2000); Staff Psychiatrist, Choate Health Systems, Woburn, MA (1994-1996); Fellow in Child and Adolescent Psychiatry, Boston Children's Hospital, Harvard Medical School (1993-1994); Fellow in Child and Adolescent Psychiatry, Massachusetts Mental Health Center, Harvard Medical School, Boston, MA (1992-1993) **CR:** Member, Faculty, New York University Child Study Center (2000-2006); Director, Young Adult Inpatient Program, Tisch Hospital, NYU Langone Health (2000-2004); Assistant Director, University Hospital Psychiatric Outpatient Center (1998-2000); Staff Psychiatrist, University Behavioral HealthCare, Newark, NJ (1996-1997); Consultant, Child Outpatient Services, Tri-City Mental Health and Retardation Center, Inc., Medford, MA (1996) **CIV:** Volunteer Recruitment Coordinator, Philadelphia Adult Special Olympics (1985); Volunteer, Psychiatry Unit, Coordinator, Psychiatry Volunteers, Yale-New Haven Hospital (1979-1983) **CW:** Editorial Assistant, Emergency Medicine Magazine (1983-1984); Contributor, Articles, Pro-

fessional Journals **AW:** Elected Distinguished Fellow, American Psychiatric Association (2014); Ambassador Award In Media, Arts And Entertainment, NJ Governor's Council on Mental Health Stigma (2011) **MEM:** Co-Chair, Special Interest Group on Women (2010-Present); President-Elect, New Jersey Vice President, New Jersey Psychiatric Association (2000-2001); Secretary, New Jersey Psychiatric Association (1999-2000); Treasurer, New Jersey Psychiatric Association (1998-1999); Essex County Representative, Tri-County Chapter, New Jersey Psychiatric Association (1997-1998); American Psychiatric Association; American Academy of Child and Adolescent Psychiatry; New Jersey Council of Child and Adolescent Psychiatry; Phi Beta Kappa; Sigma Xi **MH:** Albert Nelson Marquis Lifetime Achievement Award **AV:** Theater; Nutrition; Writing; Vegetarianism **PA:** Democrat **RE:** Jewish

WEINSTEIN, MICHAEL B., T: Of Counsel **I:** Law and Legal Services **CN:** Ottosen DiNolfo Hasenbalg & Castaldo, Ltd. **PB:** Chicago **SC:** IL/USA **PT:** Bertha Kramer Karel Weinstein; Isadore Weinstein **MS:** Married **SPN:** Patricia **CH:** Paul Weinstein; Thomas Weinstein **ED:** JD, College of Law, University of Illinois, Champaign, IL (1973); BS in Political Science, University of Illinois at Chicago, Chicago, IL, With Honors (1970) **C:** Of Counsel, Ottosen DiNolfo Hasenbalg & Castaldo, Ltd., Naperville, IL (2015-Present); General Counsel, State Universities Retirement System of Illinois, Champaign, IL (2011-2015); Associate General Counsel, Illinois Municipal Retirement Fund, Oak Brook, IL (2011); Claims Counsel, Assistant Vice President, Chicago Title Insurance Co., Chicago, IL (1998-2001); Corporation Counsel, City Attorney, City of Aurora, IL (1984-1997); Assistant Attorney General, Chief of the Criminal Appeals Division, Office of the Attorney General of Illinois, State of Illinois, Chicago, IL (1973-1974, 1977-1983) **CR:** Lecturer in Legal Writing, Chicago-Kent College of Law; Lecturer in Legal Writing, Illinois Institute of Technology, Chicago, IL **CIV:** Fellow, American Bar Foundation (2019-Present); Trustee, Village of Bolingbrook, Bolingbrook, IL (1981-1983); Trustee, Fountaindale Public Library, Bolingbrook, IL (1979-1981) **MIL:** Illinois Army National Guard (1970-1976) **CW:** Contributor, "Handling Criminal Tax Cases," Illinois Institute for Continuing Legal Education (1982); Author, Articles, Section Newsletters, Illinois State Bar Association; Speaker, Pension Fund and Administrative Law Matters; Speaker, Illinois Freedom of Information and Open Meetings Acts **AW:** Listee, Outstanding Young Men in America (1983); Activities Honorary Society Initiate, University of Illinois at Chicago, Chicago, IL (1970) **MEM:** Chair, Administrative Law Section Council, Illinois State Bar Association (2020-2021); Chair, Appellate Law Section, DuPage County Bar Association (2019-2020); Vice-Chair, Administrative Law Section Council, Illinois State Bar Association (2019-2020); Secretary, Administrative Law Section Council, Illinois State Bar Association (2018-2019); Vice-Chair, Appellate Law Section, DuPage County Bar Association (2018-2019); American Bar Association; Illinois State Bar Association; Kane County Bar Association; The Chicago Bar Association; Appellate Lawyers Association; National Association of Public Pension Attorneys **BAR:** State of Illinois; United States District Court for the Northern District of Illinois; United States Court of Appeals for the Seventh Circuit; Supreme Court of the United States **MH:** Marquis Who's Who Top Professional **AS:** Mr. Weinstein attributes his success to hard work and his knack for being in the right place at the right time. **B/I:** Mr. Weinstein became involved in his profession because of his attraction to law, which was influenced by his undergraduate studies in political science. **RE:** Jewish **THT:** Mr. Weinstein's motto is taken from the Torah, "Justice, justice thou shalt pursue."

WEINTRAUB, SAM, T: Retired Reading Educator **I:** Education/Educational Services **DOB:** 04/24/1927 **PB:** St. Louis **SC:** MO/USA **PT:** Julius Weintraub; Jeannette (Swartz) Weintraub **CH:** Robert **ED:** EdD, University of Illinois (1960); MEd, The Ohio State University (1954); BS, The Ohio State University (1950); BA, The Ohio State University (1948) **C:** Professor Emeritus, University at Buffalo (1995-Present); Professor, University at Buffalo (1974-1995); Associate Professor, Indiana University, Bloomington (1968-1974); Assistant Professor, University of Chicago (1964-1968); Assistant Professor, Case Western Reserve University, Cleveland, OH (1960-1961); Teacher, Campus School Wisconsin State College, La Crosse, WI (1953-1954); Teacher, Wyandotte Public Schools, Michigan (1950-1953) **CR:** Visiting Professor, Texas Woman's University, Denton, TX (1980-1981); Consultant in Field **AW:** Legacy Builder Award, Family and Children's Service of Niagara, Inc. (2003); William S. Gray Citation of Merit, International Reading Association (1997); Special Service Award, Niagara Frontier Reading Council (1990); Named to Reading Hall of Fame (1987); Special Service Award, International Reading Association (1987) **MEM:** Vice President, Niagara Frontier Reading Council (1990-1991); President, National Conference Research in English (1978-1979); Fellow, National Conference Research in English; International Reading Association; National Council Teachers English; American Educational Research Association **MH:** Albert Nelson Marquis Lifetime Achievement Award **AV:** Reading; Travel

WEISLER, DION J, T: Former Chief Executive Officer and President **I:** Information Technology and Services **CN:** HP Inc. **DOB:** 08/01/1967 **SC:** Australia **ED:** Bachelor's Degree, Monash University **C:** President, Chief Executive Officer, HP Inc. (2015-Present); Executive Vice President of Printing, Hewlett-Packard Company (2013-2015); Senior Vice President of Printing, Hewlett-Packard Company (2012-2013) **MEM:** Board Member, Thermo Fisher Scientific Inc. (2017-Present); Board Member, HP Inc. (2015-Present)

WEISSENBORN, ANNE ADKINS, T: Esq. **I:** Law and Legal Services **DOB:** 02/15/1939 **PB:** Circleville **SC:** OH/USA **PT:** Joseph W. Adkins Jr; Eleanor Y. (Yeagley) Adkins **MS:** Widowed **SPN:** Ernest W. Weissenborn (Deceased) **CH:** Elizabeth Anne Weissenborn **ED:** JD, Catholic University, Washington, DC (1977); MEd, Harvard University, Cambridge, MA (1968); MA, Johns Hopkins School of Advanced International Studies, Washington, DC (1964); BA, Western College for Women, Oxford, OH (1961) **C:** Host, Co-Program Coordinator, Washington Study Tours, Chinese University of Hong Kong, University of Macau (2007-2013); Substitute Teacher, Secondary/Middle Schools, Montgomery County, MD (2003-2009); Retired (2003); Attorney/Senior Attorney, Acting Assistant General Counsel, Enforcement Division and Policy Division (1977-2003); Program Assistant, Federal Election Commission, Office of General Counsel, Washington, DC (1977-2003); Interim Executive Assistant to Commissioners (1986-2001); TransCentury Corporation, Washington, DC (1972-1975); Consultant, USAID-Related Positions in Africa (1972-1975); Program Assistant, Washington Office on Africa, Washington, DC (1973); Instructor, Director of Intercultural Studies, Head Resident, Western College, Oxford, OH (1969-1971); Program Assistant, International Visitors Program, African American Institute, Washington, DC (1968-1969);

Researcher/Writer, American University, Washington, DC (1967); International Student, House and the Bridge, Washington, DC; Program Assistant (1966-1967); Volunteer Teacher, School for Southern African Political Refugees (1965-1966); Program Specialist, Fulbright Program for Teachers (1963-1965); International Education Center, Dar es Salaam, Tanzania; Teacher, Exchange Section, United States Office of Education, Washington, DC **CR:** Intern, Office of Legal Counsel, U.S. Agency for International Development, Washington, DC (1976-1977) **CIV:** Christ Congregational Church, Silver Spring, MD (1978-Present); Steering Committee, Palestine/Israel Network, Central Atlantic Conference, United Church of Christ (2018-2020); Education Committee, Potomac Association, Union County College (2018-2019); Trustee, Western College Alumnae Association (1996-2016); Treasurer, Task Force on Southern Africa, Potomac Association, United Church of Christ (1974-1983, 2012-2015); Board Member, Treasurer, Board of Directors, Miami University Foundation (1991-2010); Board of Directors, The Senior Connection, Kensington, MD (1996-2004); Founding President, Board of Directors, Shaw Community Center, Washington, DC (1991-1996) **AW:** Western College Alumnae Association Service Award (2012) **MEM:** DC Bar Association; Maryland Bar Association **BAR:** Washington, DC (1980); Maryland (1977) **MH:** Albert Nelson Marquis Lifetime Achievement Award **AS:** Ms. Weissenborn feels fortunate to have known so many wonderful men in her life. Her husband and father always supported her endeavors, for which she is ever thankful. She additionally attributes her success to her writing abilities, as she is practical, readable, and not at all poetic. She learned to write in high school and college. Likewise, Ms. Weissenborn is a talented fact collector and legal researcher. **B/I:** Ms. Weissenborn's father was an attorney, and her grandfather was a common pleas judge. Likewise, she had several cousins who were also attorneys. Surrounded by many legal professionals, Ms. Weissenborn always knew she wanted to pursue a career in law. Likewise, in the late 1970s, there were limited job positions that addressed human rights law. This inspired Ms. Weissenborn to specialize in the field, and, fortunately, she has seen the field grow throughout the years. **PA:** Democrat **RE:** United Church of Christ

WEISSMAN, RICHARD, T: Chairman of the Board, Chief Executive Officer **I:** Education/Educational Services **CN:** The Learning Experience **C:** Chairman of the Board, Chief Executive Officer, The Learning Experience, Deerfield Beach, FL (2014-Present); President, The Learning Experience, Deerfield Beach, FL (2003-2014) **CR:** Partner, Tutor Time (1987) **CIV:** Chairman of the Board, Make-A-Wish Southern Florida (2020-Present) **CW:** Featured, "Small Business with Big Ideas," FOX Business **AW:** Top Personal-Service Franchises, Business of the Year Awards, Boca Raton, FL (2014)

WEITZMANN, WILLIAM HENRY, T: Education Educator, Photographer **I:** Education/Educational Services **CN:** Stroudsburg Area School District **DOB:** 04/08/1943 **PB:** Philadelphia **SC:** PA/USA **PT:** Henry P. Weitzmann; Anna H. Weitzmann **MS:** Married **SPN:** Susan L. Bower (06/25/1966) **CH:** Todd W.; Amy L. **ED:** Fellowship, Selected Photo Educators, Rochester Institute of Technology (2002); Master of Arts in Industrial Technology, Trenton State College, NJ (1972); Bachelor of Arts in Industrial Arts Education, The Pennsylvania State University, PA (1966); Photography Educators Workshops, Eastman Kodak Company, Rochester, NY; Graduate Coursework in Media Communications, East Stroudsburg University, East Stroudsburg, PA;

Postgraduate Coursework, Supervisory Certification, The Pennsylvania State University **CT:** Certified Teacher, Technology Education and Industrial Arts Education **C:** Department Head, Curriculum Coordinator, Stroudsburg Area School District, Stroudsburg, PA (1968-2012); Adjunct Professor, East Stroudsburg University, East Stroudsburg, PA (1982, 1998-2003); Small Business Owner, Operator, W H Weitzmann Commercial Photography, Stroudsburg, PA (1975-2002); Teacher, 9th-12th Grade Industrial Arts Subjects, East Stroudsburg Area School District, East Stroudsburg, PA (1966-1968) **CR:** President, Deputy President, President-Elect, Past President, Regional Vice President, Annual Conference Workshop Chairman, Technology Education Association of Pennsylvania (1993-2003) **CIV:** Chairperson, Stroudsburg Shade Tree Commission (2005-Present); President, Vice President, Secretary, NEPA Community Federal Credit Union, Stroudsburg, PA (1970-Present); Chairman of Staff, Parish Relations Committee, Stroudsburg United Methodist Church (2017-2019); Organizing Committee, Editor of Bicentennial Publication "Stroudsburg at 200," Stroudsburg Bicentennial Celebration (2015); Board of Trustees, Treasurer, Eastern Monroe Public Library (2012-2018); Scoutmaster, Boy Scouts of America (1973-2003); Member, Board of Directors, Treasurer, Eastern Monroe Public Library Foundation **CW:** Featured Photographs, Art Exhibit Curator, NEPA Community Federal Credit Union (2007-Present); Featured Photographs, One Man Show, East Stroudsburg University (1982) **AW:** Silver Service Award, Technology Education Association of Pennsylvania (2009); Good Scout Award, Minsi Trails Council Pocono District Friends of Scouting Honoree (2004); Outstanding Service Award, Technology Education Association of Pennsylvania (2003); President's Citation and Gavel, Technology Education Association of Pennsylvania (2001); Founders Award, NEPA Community Federal Credit Union (1998); Commendation, Pennsylvania Department of Education, Service on the Standards Development Task Force (1996); Outstanding Vice President Service Award, Technology Education Association of Pennsylvania (1996); Commendation, Monroe County Commissioners (1993); Commendation, The Governor's Office (1993); Commendation, The Senate of Pennsylvania (1993); Scoutmaster Award of Merit, National Eagle Scout Association (1993); Citation, The Pennsylvania House of Representatives (1990, 1993); Silver Beaver Award, Boy Scouts of America, Minsi Trails Council (1988); ITEC Microcomputer Competitive Grantee, Pennsylvania Higher Education Assistance Agency, Stroudsburg (1986); District Award of Merit, Minsi Trails Council, Pocono District (1985) **MEM:** Technology Education Association of Pennsylvania (1993-2012); National Education Association; Pennsylvania State Education Association **MH:** Albert Nelson Marquis Lifetime Achievement Award (2019) **AV:** Classic automobile restoration; Civic volunteering; Photography; Travel

WELCH, PETER FRANCIS, T: U.S. Representative, Lawyer **I:** Government Administration/Government Relations/Government Services **DOB:** 05/02/1947 **PB:** Springfield **SC:** MA/USA **PT:** Edward Welch; Mart (Tracy) Welch **MS:** Married **SPN:** Margaret Cheney (2009); Joan Smith (12/10/1986, Deceased 2004) **CH:** Three Children; Five Stepchildren **ED:** JD, UC Berkeley School of Law (1973); BA, College of the Holy Cross, Magna Cum Laude, Worcester, MA (1969) **C:** Chief Deputy Whip from Vermont, United States Congress (2011-Present); U.S. Representative, Vermont's At-Large Congressional District, United State Congress, Washington, DC (2007-Present); Member,

House Committee on Oversight and Reform (2007-Present); Member, House Committee on Energy and Commerce (2007-Present); Member, U.S. House Committee on Standards of Official Conduct (Now Committee on Ethics) (2007-2011); President Pro Tempore, Vermont State Senate (1985-1989, 2003-2007); Vermont State Senate (1981-1989, 2002-2007); Minority Leader, Vermont State Senate (1982-1984); Partner, Welch, Graham & Manby, White River Junction, VT; Attorney, Black & Planke, White River Junction, VT **CR:** Member, Rural Working Group; Member, Rural Health Care Coalition; Member, Northern Border Caucus; Member, Northeast Agricultural Caucus; Member, New England Congressional Caucus; Member, National Guard and Reserve Components Caucus; Member, House Nursing Caucus; Member, House Hunger Caucus; Member, Fire Services Caucus; Member, Congressional Progressive Caucus; Member, Congressional Arts Caucus; Member, Brain Injury Task Force **BAR:** Vermont Bar Association **PA:** Democrat **RE:** Roman Catholic

WELLMAN, STEVE, T: Owner **I:** Engineering **CN:** Wellmann Motorcycles, LLC **ED:** BS in Education, University of Oregon (1974) **CT:** Road Racing License **C:** Founder, Owner, Wellmann Motorcycles, LLC (2012-Present); Art Teacher, High School (1991-2012) **AW:** Three Race Car Trophies **AS:** Mr. Wellman attributes his success to, as a child, having an unstated idea that he knew who he was. Sir Anthony Hopkins carried around a picture of himself as a boy to remind himself that he owed his younger self a good life and Mr. Wellman did the same. **B/I:** At the age of 6, Mr. Wellman saw a race car in the drive way of a neighbor. It was being worked on by the Dad and his teenage son. The vehicle was called a "naked rolling chassis" and he was mesmerized by it.

WELLS, HUGH, "JACK" S., T: Owner **I:** Architecture & Construction **CN:** Hugh Wells Pilot Escort **DOB:** 08/01/1939 **MS:** Married **CH:** Nine Biological Children; Four Adopted Children **C:** Owner, Hugh Wells Pilot Escort (2002-Present); Maintenance, Amoco Oil (20 Years); Home Builder, Countrywide **CR:** Part-time Deputy Sheriff, FL (1967-1975) **CIV:** Travel with 16 Teenagers to Mexico, Local Church; Donor, Holiday Food/Gifts **MH:** Marquis Who's Who Top Professional **AS:** Mr. Wells attributes his success to treating people well; people know that he will not cheat them. **B/I:** Mr. Wells is inspired by the satisfaction of seeing people happy, especially the senior citizens. In the industrial world now there are so many scams out there, there are so many people who get taken advantage of. The people he has in his organization give 110% or more and that is because he treats them like human beings, and gives them the pay that they should be receiving. This is the way you get loyalty. **THT:** Mr. Wells has nine biological children and four adopted children. He has 35 grandchildren, 38 great-grandchildren and one great-great-grandson.

WELLS, MURRAY B., T: Senior Partner **I:** Law and Legal Services **CN:** Wells & Associates, PLLC **ED:** JD, University of Arkansas (1999); BFA, Westminster College (1992) **C:** Founding Partner, Wells & Associates, PLLC (2002-Present); Attorney, McCormick Barstow LLP Attorneys At Law (2000-2002) **CIV:** Scholarship Sponsor, Cecil C. Humphreys School of Law, The University of Memphis; Sponsor, Community Elementary Schools **AW:** Diversity Award, School of Law, University of Arkansas **MEM:** President, Student Bar Association; National Traveling Trial Advocacy Team; National Traveling Moot Court Team; American Bar Association; American Trail Lawyers Association (Now

American Association for Justice); Tennessee Bar Association; Memphis Bar Association **AS:** Mr. Wells attributes his success to being genuine and a little bit of luck. **B/I:** Mr. Wells became involved in his profession because he was inspired to help others. **AV:** Trekking; Exploring and climbing mountains around the globe

WELSER-MÖST, FRANZ, T: Music Director **I:** Media & Entertainment **CN:** Cleveland Orchestra **DOB:** 08/16/1960 **PB:** Linz **SC:** Austria **MS:** Married **SPN:** Angelika **ED:** Honorary LHD, Case Western Reserve University (2003); Honorary LHD, Cleveland Institute of Music; Honorary LHD, Oberlin College and Conservatory; Coursework, Balduin Sulzer **C:** Music Director, The Cleveland Orchestra (2002-Present); Generalmusikdirektor, Vienna State Opera (2010-2014); Conductor, Vienna New Year's Concert (2011, 2013); General Music Director, Zürich Opera House (2005-2008); Music Director, Zürich Opera House (1995-2000); Principal Conductor, London Philharmonic Orchestra (1990-1996); Guest Conductor, The Cleveland Orchestra (1993); Principal Conductor, Norrköping Symphony Orchestra, Sweden (1986-1991); Conductor, St. Louis Symphony Orchestra (1989); Conductor, Vienna State Opera (1987); Conductor (Debut), Salzburg Festival, Austria (1985) **CR:** Guest Conductor, Gustav Mahler Youth Orchestra (Gustav Mahler Jugendorchester); Bavarian Radio Symphony Orchestra, Vienna Philharmonic Orchestra (Wiener Philharmoniker), The Cleveland Youth Orchestra, and Berlin Philharmonic (Berliner Philharmoniker) **CW:** Recording, Beethoven's "Symphony No. 9" (2007); Recording, Franz Schmidt's "Symphony No. 4" (1996); Numerous Recordings; Appearances, Vienna Biennial, Lucerne Festival, and Carnegie Hall **AW:** Distinguished Service Award, The Cleveland Orchestra, The Musical Arts Association (2018); Academician, European Academy of Yuste (2006); Silver Medal, Region of Upper Austria (2003); Named Conductor of the Year, Musical America International Directory of the Performing Arts (2003); Gramophone Classical Musical Award for Best Orchestral Recording, Franz Schmidt's "Symphony No. 4" (1996); Outstanding Achievement Award, Western Law Center for Disability Rights (1995); Nominee, Grammy Awards, "Best Classical Album," Recording Academy **MEM:** Honorary Member, Wiener Singverein

WENDER, IRA T. JD, T: Lawyer **I:** Law and Legal Services **DOB:** 01/05/1927 **PB:** Pittsburgh **SC:** PA/USA **PT:** Louis Wedner; Luba (Kibrick) Wender **MS:** Married **SPN:** Phyllis M. Bellows (06/24/1966) **CH:** Justin B.; Sarah T; Theodore M.; Abigail A.; John B.; Matthew B. (Deceased) **ED:** LLM, New York University (1951); JD, University of Chicago (1948); Coursework, Swarthmore College (1942-1945) **C:** Of Counsel (1994-1996); Partner, Patterson, Belknap, Webb & Tyler, New York, NY (1988-1993); Of Counsel, Patterson, Belknap, Webb & Tyler, New York, NY (1986-1987); Of Counsel (1982-1986); Chairman, Chief Executive Officer, Sussex Securities Inc. (1983-1985); President, Chief Executive Officer, A. G. Becker Paribas Inc. (1978-1982); Senior Partner, Wender, Murase & White (1971-1982); Chairman, C. Brewer and Co., Ltd., Honolulu, HI (1969-1975); Founding Partner, New York, NY (1961-1971); Partner, Baker and McKenzie, Chicago, IL (1959-1961); Lecturer, New York University School of Law, New York, NY (1954-1959); Attorney, Lord, Day and Lord, New York, NY (1950-1952, 1954-1959); Assistant Director, International Program in Tax, Harvard University Law School (1952-1954) **CR:** Trustee, Putnet School (1985-Present); Chairman, Perry Ellis International, Inc., New York, NY (1994); President, Board of Managers, PARC Vendome Condominium (1990-1994); Board of Managers,

Swarthmore College (1978-1989); Trustee, Brearley School, New York, NY (1980-1985); Board of Directors, REFAC Corp., New York, NY; Dime Bancorp, New York, NY **CIV:** Director, Treasurer, Fountain House, Inc. (1998-Present); President, Millan House IMC (2007); Director, American Near East Refuge Aid, Washington, DC; Council on Foreign Relations **CW:** Co-Author, "Foreign Investment and Taxation" (1995) **MEM:** American Bar Association; New York State Bar Association; Association of Bar of City of New York **MH:** Albert Nelson Marquis Lifetime Achievement Award; Marquis Who's Who Top Professional **B/I:** In 1945, Mr. Wender enrolled in a political theory seminary. The course heavily incorporated law studies, and it was there that Mr. Wender discovered his interests in the field. **AV:** Reading

WENDT, MARILYNN SUZANN, T: Elementary School Educator, Principal **I:** Education/Educational Services **DOB:** 10/06/1939 **PB:** Bay City **SC:** MI/USA **PT:** Clarence Henry Wendt; Margaret Viola (Rugenstein) Wendt **ED:** EdD, Wayne State University (1971); MA, Central Michigan University (1964); BA, Central Michigan University (1962); AA, Bay City Junior College (1959) **CT:** Certified Elementary Administrator, Michigan **C:** Elementary Principal, Staff Development Trainer, Learning Improvement Center Supervisor, Waterford Schools (1978-2006); Teacher, Director, Elementary Education, Director, Curriculum Research, Bloomfield Hills Schools (1966-1978); Teacher, Guidance Counselor, Director, Elementary Education, Essexville-Hampton Schools (1962-1966); Teacher, Teaching Principal, Baxman School, Bay City, MI (1959-1962) **CR:** Consortium Facilitator, Michigan Department of Education Experimental & Demonstration Center, Lansing, MI (1975-1976); Part-time Faculty Member, Wayne State University, Detroit, MI (1972-1978); Mentoring of Principals **CIV:** Trustee, Peace Board of Education, Waterford, MI (2006-Present); Trustee, St. Mark's Board of Education, West Bloomfield, MI (1991-1995); Trustee, Vice President, Waterford Township Library (1990-1995) **CW:** Co-author, "Rational Basis for Planning School Accountability" (1976); Contributor, Articles, Professional Journals **AW:** Administrator of Year, Michigan Reading Association (1991); Celebrate Literacy Award, Michigan Reading Association (1989); Who's Who in American Education (1988-1989); Woman of Distinction, Delta Kappa Gamma (1982); Distinguished Service Award, Bloomfield Hills Schools (1980); Outstanding Secondary Educators of America (1974); Community Leaders of America (1970-1971); Outstanding Educator Award, U.S. Office of Education Harold Howe II (1968) **MEM:** Vice President, Delta Kappa Gamma (1990-1993); Association for Supervision and Curriculum Development; National Council of Teachers of English; International Reading Association; Michigan Reading Association; Editor, Newsletter, Conference Planner, Michigan Association for Supervision and Curriculum Development; Oakland County Reading Association; Oakland County State & Federal Program Specialists **MH:** Albert Nelson Marquis Lifetime Achievement Award; Marquis Who's Who Top Professional **B/I:** Ms. Wendt has always been passionate about learning, and she decided in the first grade to become a teacher. Her first grade teacher, John G. Weiss, was a 70 year old man, it was the last year he taught and he was an inspiration to her. He is the one who got her started on the path of education. Ms. Wendt, was the first to graduate college and the first to get her doctorate also the first to become a teacher in her family. **AV:** Reading; Swimming; Arts; Music; Theater; Loves meeting up and interacting with her friends and colleagues

WENNERSTEN, MARY AILEEN, T: Special Education Educator (Retired) **I:** Education/Educational Services **DOB:** 05/31/1962 **PB:** Edwards Air Force Base **SC:** CA/USA **PT:** John Stoakley Croswell; Beverly Anne (Leger) Croswell **SPN:** Robert Allen Wennersten (1988) **CH:** Lucas Mitchell; Sarah Aileen **ED:** MEd in Special Education, Northern Arizona University (1991); BA in Elementary Education, The University of Arizona (1985) **CT:** Certified Structured Literacy/Dyslexia Specialist; Certified K-12 Special Education Teacher, Arizona Department of Education; Certified 4-6 Elementary Education Teacher, Arizona Department of Education **C:** Teacher, Learning Disabilities, Special Education, Paradise Valley Unified School District, Scottsdale, AZ (1992-2016); Teacher, Elementary, Paradise Valley Unified School District, Scottsdale, AZ (1987-1992); Teacher, Elementary, Mammoth-San Manuel Unified School District, Arizona (1986-1987); Program Specialist, Arizona Department of Education; Director, K-5 Literacy, Arizona Department of Education **CR:** Private Consultant in Education; Structured Literacy Consultant **CIV:** Branch President, Board Member, IDA Arizona; National Board, Vice-Chair, Executive Board, Member-at-Large, International Dyslexia Association **AW:** Leadership in Literacy Award, IDA Arizona (2015); Teacher of Month Award, Parent-Teacher Association, Phoenix, AZ (1994); Special Teacher Award, Paradise Valley Unified School District (1992) **MEM:** International Dyslexia Association; Learning Disabilities Association of America; Association for Supervision and Curriculum Development **MH:** Albert Nelson Marquis Lifetime Achievement Award **B/I:** Ms. Wennersten became involved in her profession because of her own experience as a special education student; she was diagnosed with a learning disability in the fifth grade, but in spite of her specialized classes, school remained difficult for her. Ms. Wennersten would go on to graduate from high school and attend college. She grew motivated to help students who struggled with reading and mathematics, just like she did. **AV:** Hiking; Biking; Swimming; Camping

WENSTRUP, BRAD ROBERT, DPM, T: U.S. Representative, Podiatrist **I:** Government Administration/Government Relations/Government Services **DOB:** 06/17/1958 **PB:** Cincinnati **SC:** OH/USA **PT:** Frank John Wenstrup; Joan (Carletti) Wenstrup **MS:** Married **SPN:** Monica Klein (2012) **CH:** Brad, Jr.; One daughter **ED:** DPM, Dr. William M. Scholl College of Podiatric Medicine, Rosalind Franklin University of Medicine and Science (1985); BA in Psychology, University of Cincinnati, Cum Laude (1980); BS in Biology, Dr. William M. Scholl College of Podiatric Medicine, Rosalind Franklin University of Medicine and Science **C:** U.S. Representative, Ohio's Second Congressional District, United States Congress, Washington, DC (2013-Present); U.S. House Committee on Veterans' Affairs (2013-Present); U.S. House Committee on Armed Services (2013-Present); Private Podiatric Surgical Practice, Cincinnati, Ohio (1985-2012); Member, Permanent Select Committee on Intelligence, United States Congress; Member, Republican Study Committee, United States Congress **CR:** President, Thank America First Foundation **CIV:** Board Member, Boys Hope Girls Hope **MIL:** Advanced through Grades to Lieutenant Colonel, U.S. Army Reserve (1998-Present); Chief of Surgery, 344th Combat Support Hospital, Iraq (2005-2006) **AW:** Decorated Combat Action Badge; Bronze Star **MEM:** Rotary Club of Cincinnati; Sigma Alpha Epsilon Fraternity **PA:** Republican

WENTWORTH, TIMOTHY C., T: Chief Executive Officer, President **I:** Other **CN:** Express Scripts Holding Company **ED:** BS in Industrial and Labor Relations, ILR School, Cornell University (1982); AAS in Business Administration and Management, Monroe Community College (1980) **C:** President, Express Scripts Holding Company (2018-Present); President, Cigna Services (2018-Present); Chief Executive Officer, Express Scripts Holding Company (2015-2018); President, Express Scripts Holding Company (2014-2018); Senior Vice President, Head of Sales and Account Management Operation, Express Scripts Holding Company (2012-2014); Group President, Employer and Key Accounts, Medco Health Solutions Inc. (2008-2012); Chief Executive Officer, President, Accredo (2006-2008); International President, Mary Kay, Inc.; Senior Vice President of Human Resources, Mary Kay, Inc; Human Resources Manager, PepsiCo, Inc. **CR:** Member, Board of Trustees, University of Rochester (2013-Present); Co-Chair, Parents Initiative for the Meliora Challenge **CIV:** Founder, Wentworth Family Endowed Scholarship, University of Rochester (2010); Founder, Scholarship Fund for Business and Music Majors, Monroe Community College; Donor, Steinway Piano, Monroe Community College **MEM:** George Eastman Circle, University of Rochester; Parents Council, University of Rochester

WERNIMONT, NICK, T: Founder, Chief Executive Officer **I:** Food & Restaurant Services **CN:** Factor 75 **DOB:** 01/25/1978 **PB:** Lincoln **SC:** NE/USA **PT:** Dan Wernimont; Leah (Assman) Wernimont **MS:** Married **SPN:** Pamela **CH:** Leila; Aaron; Dominick; Sasha **ED:** BS in Accounting and Finance, The University of Iowa (2000) **C:** Founder and Chief Executive Officer, Chief Health, Wellness and Performance Strategist, Factor 75, IL (2012-Present); Director, Marketing, BioHorizons (2010-2012); Director, Sales, BioHorizons (2008-2010); Regional Manager, BioHorizons (2006-2008) **CIV:** Benefactor, Aaron Wernimont Inspiration Fund **AS:** Mr. Wernimont attributes his success to his drive to outwork the competition and embrace the grind. He will always do whatever it takes to win. **B/I:** Mr. Wernimont launched his company with the goal of helping people eat better in order to perform better and live longer. From his own experience, having a personal chef while he was an MMA fighter showed him the benefits of proper nutrition, including its impacts on his performance and recovery. **AV:** Skydiving; Professional boxing; Running with the bulls

WERTHEIM, MITZI, T: Professor **I:** Education/Educational Services **CN:** Cebrowski Institute **PB:** New York **SC:** NY/USA **PT:** Rudolf Mallina; Myrtle B. (McGraw) Mallina **MS:** Single **SPN:** Ronald P. Wertheim (02/25/1965, Divorced 1988) **CH:** Carter (Deceased); Tiana **ED:** BA, University of Michigan (1960) **C:** Professor, Practice Sustainability, Enterprises, and Social Networking, Naval Postgraduate School, Cebrowski Institute (2009-Present); Vice President, Enterprise Solutions, CNA Corporation (1998-2008); Vice President, Enterprise Solutions, SRA Corporation (1994-1998); Federal Sector Division, IBM (1981-1994); Deputy, Secretary, U.S. Navy (1977-1981); Executive Director, Talent Bank77 (1976); Senior Program Officer, Cafritz Foundation, Washington, DC (1970-1976); Associate Director, Peace Corps (1962-1966); Assistant Director, Division of Research, Peace Corps, Washington, DC (1961-1966) **CR:** Founder, Executive Board, Seminar on XXI Foreign Policy National Interest, Massachusetts Institute of Technology (1984); Woodrow Wilson Visiting Fellow (1979-1980) **CIV:** Board of Directors, Cebrowski Institute (2010-Present); Founder,

President, The Energy Consensus (2005-Present); Founder, Director, The Energy Conversation (2006-2009); Fellow, Maxwell School, Syracuse University (1996-1997); Board of Directors, Volunteers in Technical Service (1989-2001); Board of Directors, Youth Policy Institute (1986-1991); Visiting Committee, Massachusetts Institute of Technology (1983-1989); Board of Directors, National Coalition of Science and Technology (1983-1986) **AW:** Excellence Award, Hastings-On-Hudson High School Alumni Association (2009); Research Outstanding Contribution Award, IBM (1987); President's Award, IBM (1986); Distinguished Public Service Medal, U.S. Department of the Navy (1981); Federally Employed Women Award, U.S. Department of Defense (1980) **MEM:** IBM; Naval Studies Board; Council on Foreign Relations **MH:** Albert Nelson Marquis Lifetime Achievement Award **B/I:** Curiosity is what got Ms. Wertheim into her profession. For many years, she has been trying to get the government to put curiosity in the plans because she wants people to ask questions. **RE:** Episcopalian **THT:** Ms. Wertheim's favorite quote is, "If you do not know, ask, and we all learn together."

WESSELS, BRUCE, T: Materials Scientist, Educator **I:** Sciences **DOB:** 10/18/1946 **PB:** New York **SC:** NY/USA **MS:** Married **SPN:** Beverly T. Wessels **CH:** David; Kirsten **ED:** PhD in Materials Science, Massachusetts Institute of Technology (1973); BS in Metallurgy and Materials Science, University of Pennsylvania (1968) **C:** Walter P. Murphy Professor, Northwestern University (1998-Present); Professor, Materials Science and Engineering, Northwestern University (1984-Present);Professor by Courtesy, Electrical and Computer Engineering, Northwestern University (1987-2010); Department Chair, Electrical Engineering and Computer Science, Northwestern University (2005-2007);From Assistant Professor to Associate Professor, Northwestern University, Evanston, IL (1977-1983); Technical Staff, GE R&D Center (1972-1977); Acting Branch Manager, GE R&D Center (1976) **CR:** Member, Program Committee, International Conference on Superlattices, Microstructures, and Microdevices (1987); Visiting Scientist, Argonne National Laboratory (1978); Appointed Member, Oversight Committee of Journal of Electronic Materials **CW:** Member, Editorial Board, Journal of Electronic Materials (1982-1988, 1998-2005); Editor, "Advances in Electronic Materials" (1986); Contributor, Journal of the American Chemical Society; Contributor, The Physical Review; Contributor, Articles, Professional Journals; Patentee in Field **MEM:** Board of Trustees, American Institute of Mining (1996-1997); President, Metals and Materials Society (1996); Vice President, Metals and Materials Society (1995); Transactions of the American Institute of Mining, Metallurgical, and Petroleum Engineers Incorporated (1985-1992); Fellow, American Sports Medicine Institute; Fellow, American Physical Society; The Minerals; Electrochemical Society; Materials Research Society; Fellow, Optical Society of America; Electroceramics; Sigma Xi; Tau Beta Pi **MH:** Albert Nelson Marquis Lifetime Achievement Award; Marquis Who's Who Top Professional **B/I:** Mr. Wessels became involved in his profession as a researcher at General Electric, which was his first position after getting his doctorate. He saw an ad by general electric stating they were most interested in Tau Beta Pi engineers. So he felt inspired and felt the need to work hard while there.In addition, what attracted him to his career was Sputnik, the Russian Satellite that was launched in the 1950s.

WESSLER, MELVIN, T: Farmer, Rancher **I:** Agriculture **DOB:** 02/11/1932 **PB:** Dodge City **SC:** KS/USA **PT:** Oscar Lewis; Clara (Reiss) Wessler **MS:**

Married **SPN:** Laura Ethel Arbuthnot (8/23/1951) **CH:** Monty Dean; Charla Cay; Virgil Lewis **ED:** Graduate, High School **C:** Farmer, Rancher, Springfield, CO (1950) **CR:** Community Committee Chairman, Baca County, Agriculture Stablization and Conservation Service, Springfield (1961-1973, 1979-Present); Vice Chairman, Baca County Committee (1980-1990); President, Arkansas Valley Co-op Council, Southeast Colorado Area (1965-1987); Secretary, Colorado Co-op Council (1980-1986); President, Board, Springfield Co-op. Sales Co. (1980); Member, Committee for PROMARK, Hutchinson, KS (1978); Director, Secretary, Board, Springfield Co-op. Sales Co. (1964-1980); Vice President, Colorado Co-op Council (1974); President, Colorado Co-op Council (1969-1972); Member, Special Committee on Grain Marketing, Far-Mar-Co **CIV:** Appointed Special Committee, Farmland Industries Special Project Tomorrow (1987-Present); Chairman, Board of Directors, Springfield Cemetery Board (1985-2014); Member, Advisory Board, Denver Baptist Bible College (1984-1989) **AW:** The Colorado Cooperator Award, Colorado Cooperative Council (1990) **MEM:** Vice President, Southwest Kansas Farm Association (2007-Present); Director, Southwest Kansas Farm Association (1996-Present); Vice President, Farm Business Associate (2007-2012); Vice President, Southwest Kansas Farm Business Association (2007-2012); Big Rock Grange Master (2006-2010); Board Director, Southwest Kansas Farm Business Association (1991-2010); President, Southwest Kansas Farm Association (1999-2001); Board of Directors, Southeast Farm Business Association (1991-1995); Master, Big Rock Grange (1976-1982); Treasurer, Big Rock Grange (1964-1976); Colorado Cattlemen's Association; Colorado Wheat Growers Association; Farm Management Association of the Southwest **MH:** Albert Nelson Marquis Lifetime Achievement Award **B/I:** Mr. Wessler became involved in his profession because of his parents, Oscar Lewis and Clara (Reiss) Wessler. It was in 1950, when he started to take over and do his own farming. **PA:** Conservative Republican **RE:** Baptist Church

WEST, ALVIS H., PHD, T: Social Sciences Educator **I:** Education/Educational Services **CN:** Bakersfield College **DOB:** 03/04/1947 **PB:** Bakersfield **SC:** CA/USA **PT:** Archie Harlton West (Deceased); Verdie Bonetti (Snow) West (Deceased) **MS:** Married **SPN:** Linda L. West **CH:** Heather West; Christopher West **ED:** PhD in Theology, Trinity College of the Bible and Theological Seminary, Newburgh, IN (2003); MA in History, California State University, Bakersfield (1979); BA in History, California State University, Bakersfield (1973); AA, Bakersfield College, CA (1972) **CT:** Graduate Teacher Diploma, Evangelical Training Association (2003); Certified in Effective Teaching, Kern County Superintendent of Schools (1985); Third Degree Black Belt Certified in Karate, American Karate Do (1976); Ministerial License, First Southern Baptist Church (1967); Standard Teaching **C:** Professor of American History, Bakersfield College (2004-2010); Professor of Theology and Christian History, Summit Bible College, Bakersfield, CA (2004-2008); Junior High School and High School Teacher, Greenfield Union School District (1974-2004); Junior High School and High School Teacher, Panama-Buena Vista Union School District (1974-2004) **CIV:** Secretary, Right to Like Kern County (2007-2008); Teacher of Biblical Studies, Laurel Springs Assisted Living, Bakersfield, CA (2006-2008) **MIL:** Sergeant, Thailand (1969); Sergeant, Edwards Air Force Base, U.S. Air Force (1966-1969); Sergeant, Lackland Air Force Base, U.S. Air Force (1966) **CW:** Author, "One Life, Right to Life Story, Effort to End Abortion" (2007); Musician, CD, "Gone West, A Juxtaposition of Dying and Rising God Myths and Jesus'

Resurrection: A Paradigmatic Analysis"; Author, 11 Rock & Roll Songs, "Elvis Lives in Levi's," "It's Time," "Mighty Mississippi Blues," "I've Been Down That Road Before," "Taking the Back Way," "Send a Message to Shaila Holly," "You Forever," "Do You Remember Buddy Holly," "Brenda Go Lightly" and "My Name is Justice" **AW:** Writer of the Month, Bakersfield, CA (2008); Inductee, Teacher Hall of Fame, Kern Alliance of Business (2001); Music Award, The Arts Council of Kern (1996); Teacher of the Month, Kern Schools Federal Credit Union (1995-1996); Listed, Who's Who Among Teachers (1994); Honored Teacher, Various Times **MH:** Albert Nelson Marquis Lifetime Achievement Award **AS:** Dr. West attributes his success to his 12th grade teacher, Walt Granger. **B/I:** Dr. West became involved in his profession after hearing Chuck Berry and Buddy Holly in 1955. **AV:** Traveling **PA:** Conservative **RE:** Baptist

WEST, BEVERLY B., PHD, RN, CPN, T: Assistant Professor **I:** Education/Educational Services **DOB:** 09/06/1954 **PB:** Portland **SC:** OR/USA **PT:** Hale Henry Bockstruck; Ada Carolyn (Danielson) Bockstruck **MS:** Divorced **CH:** Kari; Heather; Allen **ED:** PhD, Capella University (2017); MSN, University of Memphis (2006); BSN, Memphis State University (1985); AA, Memphis State University (1976) **CT:** Diabetes Educator Certification (CDE), National Certification Board for Diabetes Educators (1987-2011); Pediatric Nurse Certification (CPN), Pediatric Nursing Certification Board, Inc. (2008); RN, States of Tennessee, Arkansas, Mississippi (1976) **C:** Assistant Professor, University of Memphis (2017-Present); Clinical Associate Professor, University of Memphis (2011-2017); Clinical Assistant Professor, University of Memphis (2006-2011); Coordinator, Diabetes Program, LeBonheur Children's Medical Center, Memphis, TN (1988-2006); Staff Nurse, University of Tennessee Clinical Research Center, Memphis, TN (1984-1988); Branch Manager, Home-Bound Medical Care, Somerville, TN (1980-1984); Staff Nurse, Baptist Memorial Hospital, Memphis, TN (1976-1980) **CR:** Founder, Diabetes Parent Support Group, Memphis, TN (1989-Present) **CIV:** Pediatric Asthma Management, ACEs Action Team, Urban Child Institute (2017-2019); Fetal and Infant Mortality Review (FIMR), Case Review Team, Memphis & Shelby County Health Department (2010-2012); Fetal and Infant Mortality Review (FIMR), Community Action Team, Memphis & Shelby County Health Department (2010-2012) **CW:** "West, B. B." (2017); "Special Topics in Diabetes" (2006-2007); "Poster Session: Has the Increasing Incidence of Type 2 Diabetes in Children Reached a Plateau?" (2006); "It's a Small World" (1988-2006); "Advanced Diabetes Management" (2005); "Diabetes in the School System" (2005); "Diabetes Update" (2003-2005); "The Student with Diabetes" (1988-1993); Author, "Emotional intelligence through human patient simulation: An investigation of nursing students emotional management" **AW:** Top Nurse in Memphis Award, International Nurses Association (2017); President's List, Capella University (2012-2017); Diabetes Educator Award, American Diabetes Association (2005); Celebrate Nursing Award, Tennessee Nurses Association (1991) **MEM:** International Nurses Association of Clinical Simulation and Learning (2015-Present); Tennessee Simulation Alliance (2015-Present); Society of Pediatric Nurses (2008-Present); Mid-South Chapter of Pediatric Nurses (2008-Present); National League for Nursing (2006-Present); Sigma Theta Tau International Nurses Honor Society (2004-Present); American Diabetes Association (1987-2011); American Association of Diabetes Educators (1987-2011); Board of Directors, Memphis Diabetes Association (1990-1993); Tennessee Nurses Association (1991)

B/I: Dr. West became involved in her profession because of Florence Nightingale, who served as her primary inspiration. Florence Nightingale had good hygiene and Dr. West was just like her; they believed in cleanliness. She always told her students that it was important to be clean. Her mother was a teacher and her father was a businessman with strong work ethics. She had the same values. **AV:** Scuba diving; Horseback riding; Bicycle riding **PA:** Centrist **RE:** Christian

WEST, KANYE OMARI, T: Rap Artist, Music Producer **I:** Media & Entertainment **DOB:** 06/08/1977 **PB:** Atlanta **SC:** GA/USA **PT:** Ray West; Donda West **MS:** Married **SPN:** Kim Kardashian (05/24/2014) **CH:** Saint West; Psalm West; North West; Chicago West **ED:** DFA (Honorary), School of the Art Institute of Chicago (2015); Student, Chicago State University; Student, American Academy of Art **C:** Co-Owner, Music Streaming Service, Tidal (2015-Present); Designer, DW Kanye West (2011-Present); Founder, Producer, G.O.O.D. (Getting Out Our Dreams) Music (2004-Present); Designer, Nike Air Yeezys; Designer, Adidas Yeezy Boosts; Designer, Shoe Line for Giuseppe Zanotti; Designer, Shoe Line for Louis Vitton; Owner, KW Foods LLC **CR:** Founder, Half Beast, LLC; Founder, Yeezy Home **CIV:** Founder, Kanye West Foundation (Now Donda's House, Dr. Donda West Christian) (2003-Present); Donor, $10 Million, Roden Crater (2019); Contributor, Hurricane Katrina Relief, Millions More Movement, 100 Black Men of America, Live Earth, World Water Day, Nike Runs, Hurricane Sandy Benefit Concert; Participant, Numerous Fundraisers and Benefit Concerts **CW:** Rapper, Producer, "Jesus Is King" (2019); Rapper, Producer, "Jesus Is Born" (2019); Rapper, Producer, "Ye" (2018); Rapper, Producer, "Kids See Ghosts" (2018); Rapper, Producer, "The Life of Pablo" (2016); Himself, "Saturday Night Live 40[th] Anniversary Special" (2015); Rapper, Producer, "Yeezus" (2013); Actor, "Anchorman 2: The Legend Continues" (2013); Actor, "Cruel Summer" (2012); Himself, "Keeping Up With the Kardashians" (2012); Rapper, Producer, "Watch the Throne" (2011); Himself, "The Cleveland Show" (2010-2012); Rapper, Producer, "My Beautiful Dark Twisted Fantasy" (2010); Actor, "Runaway" (2010); Author, "Glow in the Dark" (2009); Co-Author, "Through the Wire: Lyrics & Illuminations" (2009); Co-Author, "Thank You and You're Welcome" (2009); Actor, "We Were Once a Fairytale" (2009); Rapper, Producer, "808s & Heartbreak" (2008); Himself, "The Love Guru" (2008); Rapper, Producer, "Graduation" (2007); Foreword, "Raising Kanye: Life Lessons from the Mother of a Hip-Hop Superstar" (2007); Rapper, Producer, "Late Registration" (2005); Himself, "Entourage" (2007); Himself, "State Property 2" (2005); Rapper, Producer, "The College Dropout" (2004); Himself, "The College Dropout Video Anthology" (2004); Actor, "Top Buzzer" (2004); Producer, Albums, Beanie Sigel, Freeway, Cam'ron; Producer, Numerous Songs, Ludacris, Alicia Keys, Janet Jackson, Post Malone, Pusha T, Nas, Lil Pump, Christina Aguilera, Kids See Ghosts, Migos, Drake, Chance the Rapper, Sia, Travis Scott, The Weeknd, French Montana, Vic Mensa, A$AP Rocky, Wale, Madonna, Big Sean, Rihanna, Beyoncé, Chief Keef, Tyga, Rick Ross, John Legend, Game, RZA, 2 Chainz, Cassie Ventura, The World Famous Tony Williams, Consequence, Snoop Dogg, Saigon, Justin Bieber, J. Cole, B.o.B., Slim Thug, Kid Cudi, Jay-Z, Twista, Nipsy Hussle, The Game, Lil Wayne, Michael Jackson, Bone Thugs-n-Harmony, Common, Fabolous, Diddy, Lupe Fiasco, Scarface, T.I., Mashonda, Paul Wall, Syleena Johnson, Keyshia Cole, Leela James, Young Gunz, Britney Spears, Bump J, Mariah Carey, Mos Def, Mobb Deep, Shyne, Brandy, Slum

Village, Jadakiss, D12, Dead Prez, Maroon 5, Carl Thomas, Nappy Roots, Memphis Bleek, Mystic, Alicia Keys, DMX, Lil' Kim, Da Brat, Jagged Edge, The Madd Rapper, Harlem World, and Others **AW:** Pop Awards, "That Part," BMI London Awards (2017); Best Choreography, "Fade," MTV Video Music Awards (2017); Hot 100 Winning Songs, "FourFiveSeconds," ASCAP London Music Awards (2016); Best Hip-Hop Style, BET Hip Hop Awards (2016); Best Club Banger, "I Don't F— with You," BET Hip Hop Awards (2015); Michael Jackson Video Vanguard Award, MTV Video Music Awards (2015); People's Champ Award, "Blessings," BET Hip Hop Awards (2015); Best Collabo, Duo or Group, "Blessings," BET Hip Hop Awards (2015); Visionary Award, BET Honors (2015); Shoe of the Year, Adidas Yeezy Boost 350, Footwear News Achievement Awards (2015); Most Stylish Man, GQ Most Stylish Man of the Year Awards (2015); Most Stylish Man, GQ Most Stylish Man of the Year Awards (2014); Best Live Performer, BET Hip Hop Awards (2014); Best Rap/Sung Collaboration, "No Church in the Wild," Grammy Awards (2013); Best Rap Song, "Mercy," Grammy Awards (2013); Best Rap Song, "N— in Paris," Grammy Awards (2013); Best Group, "The Throne," BET Awards (2013); Best Rap Performance, "Otis," Grammy Awards (2012); Best Rap Song, "All of the Lights," Grammy Awards (2012); Best Rap/Sung Collaboration, "All of the Lights," Grammy Awards (2012); Best Rap Album, "My Beautiful Dark Twisted Fantasy," Grammy Awards (2012); Most Performed Songs, "E.T.," ASCAP Pop Music Awards (2012); Video of the Year, "N— in Paris," BET Awards (2012); Best Live Performer, "The Throne," BET Hip Hop Awards (2012); Best Club Banger, "N— in Paris," BET Hip Hop Awards (2012); Track of the Year, "N— in Paris," BET Hip Hop Awards (2012); CD of the Year, "Watch the Throne," BET Hip Hop Awards (2012); Dieline Package Design Award, "Watch the Throne," Dieline Awards (2012); Producer of the Year, BET Hip Hop Awards (2012); Best Male Hip-Hop Artist, BET Awards (2011); CD of the Year, "My Beautiful Dark Twisted Fantasy," BET Hip Hop Awards (2011); Best collaboration, "E.T.," MTV Video Music Awards (2011); Favorite Rap/Hip-Hop Album, "Graduation," American Music Awards (2011); Best Rap Song, "Run This Town," Grammy Awards (2010); Best Rap/Sung Collaboration, "Knock You Down," Grammy Awards (2010); Stylemaker Award, ACE Awards (2010); Best Commissioning Artist, Antville Music Video Awards (2010); Most Performed Songs, "Run This Town," ASCAP Pop Music Awards (2010); Most Performed Songs, "Knock You Down," ASCAP Pop Music Awards (2010); Pop Awards, "Run This Town," BMI London Awards (2010); Most Performed Songs, "Heartless," ASCAP Pop Music Awards (2010); Best Hip Hop Style, BET Hip Hop Awards (2010); Best Rap/Sung Collaboration, "American Boy," Grammy Awards (2009); Best Rap Performance by a Duo or Group, "Swagga like Us," Grammy Awards (2009); Most Performed Songs, "Good Life" (2009); Man of the Year, Glamour Awards (2009); Pop Awards, "American Boy," BMI London Awards (2009); Hype Williams Award, "Welcome to Heartbreak," Antville Music Video Awards (2009); Named One of "The 100 Agents of Change," Rolling Stone (2009); Best Rap Song, "Good Life," Grammy Awards (2008); Best Rap Performance, "Stronger," Grammy Awards (2008); Best Rap Performance by a Duo or Group, "Southside," Grammy Awards (2008); Best Rap Album, "Graduation," Grammy Awards (2008); Favorite Rap/Hip-Hop Album, "Graduation," American Music Awards (2008); Urban Awards, "Stronger," BMI London Awards (2008); Favorite Rap/Hip-Hop Male Artist, American Music Awards (2008); Best Urban Video, "Flashing Lights," Antville Music Video Awards (2008); Best Collaboration, "Good

Life," BET Awards (2008); Best Live Performer, BET Hip Hop Awards (2008); International Male Solo Artist, Brit Awards (2008); Best Hip-Hop Video, "Good Life," BET Hip Hop Awards (2008); Best Foreign Rap or Hip-Hop Album of the Year, "Graduation," Fonogram Hungarian Music Awards (2008); Best Song, "American Boy," MOBO Awards (2008); Best Video, "Stronger," MOBO Awards (2007); Best Hip-Hop Act, MOBO Awards (2007); International Man of the Year, GQ Men of the Year Awards (2007); Best Hip-Hop Video, "Stronger," BET Hip Hop Awards (2007); Named Among the "Top 25 Entertainers of Year," Entertainment Weekly (2007); Best Rap Album, "Late Registration," Grammy Awards (2006); Best Rap Solo Performance, "Gold Digger," Grammy Awards (2006); Best Rap Song, "Diamonds from Sierra Leone," Grammy Awards (2006); Best Foreign Rap or Hip-Hop Album of the Year, "Late Registration," Fonogram Hungarian Music Awards (2006); Best Male Hip-Hop Artist, BET Awards (2006); Best Collaboration, "Gold Digger," BET Awards (2006); Best Live Performance, BET Hip Hop Awards (2006); Video of the Year, "Gold Digger," BET Awards (2006); Hot Rap Track, "Gold Digger," Billboard R&B/Hip-Hop Awards (2006); Top Rap Album, "Late Registration," Billboard R&B/Hip-Hop Awards (2006); Pop Awards, "Diamonds from Sierra Leone," BMI London Awards (2006); Best International Male, Meteor Music Awards (2006); Best Solo Artist, NME Awards (2006); Best R&B Song, "You Don't Know My Name," Grammy Awards (2005); Best Rap Album, "The College Dropout," Grammy Awards (2005); Best Rap Song, "Jesus Walks," Grammy Awards (2005); Video of the Year, "Jesus Walks," BET Awards (2005); Best Album, "Late Registration," Kiss Awards (2005); Style Icon, Kiss Awards (2005); Hottest Producer, Kiss Awards (2005); Best MC, Esky Music Awards (2005); Best Visionary, Esky Music Awards (2005); Making a Difference, AEC Awards (2005); Million Man March Image Award (2005); Best Male Video, "Jesus Walks," MTV Video Music Awards (2005); Named Among the "100 Most Influential People," Time (2005); Best Male Video, "All Falls Down," MTV Video Music Awards (2004); Best New Artist, BET Awards (2004); Billboard Artist Achievement Award, Billboard Music Awards (2004); New Male Artist of the Year, Billboard Music Awards (2004); New R&B/Hip-Hop Artist of the Year, Billboard Music Awards (2004); Rap Artist of the Year, Billboard Music Awards (2004); R&B/Hip-Hop Producer of the Year, Billboard Music Awards (2004); Best Producer, MOBO Awards (2004); Video of the Year, "Through the Wire," Source Awards (2004); Album of the Year, "The College Dropout," Source Awards (2004)

WESTBROOK, RUSSELL III, T: Professional Basketball Player **I:** Athletics **CN:** Washington Wizards **DOB:** 11/12/1988 **PB:** Long Beach **SC:** CA/USA **PT:** Russell Westbrook Jr.; Shannon Horton Westbrook **MS:** Married **SPN:** Nina Earl (08/29/2015) **CH:** Noah Russell; Skye; Jordyn **ED:** Coursework, University of California Los Angeles (2006-2008); Diploma, Leuzinger High School (2006) **C:** Professional Basketball Player, Houston Rockets, NBA (2020-Present); Professional Basketball Player, Houston Rockets, NBA (2019-2020); Professional Basketball Player, Oklahoma City Thunder, NBA (2008-2019) **CR:** Endorser, Jordan Brand, Nike, Inc. (2012-Present); Global Face, Mountain Dew Kickstart, PepsiCo, Inc. (2015); Marketing Creative Director, True Religion (2015); Endorser, Kings and Jaxs Boxer Briefs (2013); U.S. National Team, Summer Olympic Games, London, England, United Kingdom (2012); FIBA World Championships, Turkey (2010) **AW:** Named, Two-time NBA Assists Leader (2018-2019); Named, Eight-time NBA All-star (2011–2013,

2015–2019); Named NBA Most Valuable Player (2017); Named, Two-time NBA Scoring Champion (2015, 2017); Named, Two-time NBA All-star Game MVP (2015-2016); Named Pac-10 Defensive Player of the Year (2008); Named, Two-time Most Valuable Player of the Bay League

WESTERMAN, BRUCE EUGENE, T: U.S. Representative from Arkansas; Engineer **I:** Government Administration/Government Relations/Government Services **DOB:** 11/18/1967 **PB:** Hot Springs **SC:** AR/USA **MS:** Married **SPN:** Sharon (French) Westerman **CH:** Eli; Asa; Amie; Ethan **ED:** MF, Yale University (2001); BS in Biological and Agricultural Engineering, University of Arkansas (1990) **C:** Member, U.S. House of Representatives from Arkansas' Fourth Congressional District (2015-Present); Member, District 30, Arkansas House of Representatives (2011-2015); Engineer, Forester, Mid-South Engineering Co. (1992-2014); Plant Engineer, Riceland Foods (1990-1992); Member, Committee on the Budget, United States Congress; Member, Committee on Natural Resources, United States Congress; Member, Committee on Science, Space and Technology, United States Congress; Member, Republican Study Committee, United States Congress **CIV:** Former Board Member, Fountain Lake School District, AR **AW:** Named Engineer of the Year, Arkansas Society of Professional Engineers (2013); Distinguished Alumni Award, University of Arkansas (2012); Outstanding Young Alumni Award, University of Arkansas (2005) **MEM:** Former President, American Society of Agricultural and Biological Engineers, Arkansas Chapter; Former Chair, Arkansas Academy of Biological and Agricultural Engineers **AV:** Hunting; Fishing **PA:** Republican **RE:** Baptist

WESTHEIMER, RUTH, "DR. RUTH", T: Sex Therapist, Media Personality **I:** Medicine & Health Care **DOB:** 06/04/1928 **PB:** Wiesenfeld **SC:** Germany **PT:** Julius Siegel; Irma (Hanauer) Siegel **MS:** Widowed **SPN:** Manfred "Fred" Westheimer (1961, Deceased 1997) **CH:** Miriam; Joel **ED:** Honorary Diploma, Bronx High School of Science (2008); Honorary Degree, Trinity College (2004); EdD, Teachers College, Columbia University (1970); MA in Sociology, The New School, New York, NY (1959) **C:** Teacher of Psychology, University of Paris (1950) **CR:** Guest Speaker, Yom HaShoah, Bronx High School of Science (2008); Postdoctoral Researcher to Adjunct Associate Professor, New York-Presbyterian Hospital; Planned Parenthood; Instructor, Lehman College, Brooklyn College, Adelphi University, Columbia University, West Point, Others **CIV:** Trustee, Museum of Jewish Heritage **CW:** Featured, Documentary, "Ask Dr. Ruth" (2019); Co-Author, "Roller Coaster Grandma: The Amazing Story of Dr. Ruth" (2018); Co-Author, "Lebe mit Lust und Liebe: Meine Ratschläge für ein erfülltes Leben" (2015); Co-Author, "The Doctor Is In: Dr. Ruth on Love, Life, and Joie de Vivre" (2015); Co-Author, "Surviving Salvation: The Ethiopian Jewish Family in Transition" (2013); Co-Author, "Dr. Ruth's Guide for the Alzheimer's Caregiver: How to Care for Your Loved One without Getting Overwhelmed... and without Doing It All Yourself" (2012); Co-Author, "Sexually Speaking: What Every Woman Needs to Know about Sexual Health" (2011); Co-Author, "Mythen der Liebe" (2010); Author, "Dr. Ruth's Guide to Teens and Sex Today" (2008); Author, Producer, Documentary, "The Olive and the Tree: The Secret Strength of the Druze" (2007); Actress, "Lipshitz Saves the World" (2007); Guest Appearances, "Between the Lions" (2001-2007); Author, "52 Lecciones para Comunicar el Amor (Superacion Personal / Personal Growth)" (2005); Author, "Dr. Ruth's Sex After 50: Revving Up the Romance, Passion & Excitement!" (2005); Author,

"Le sexe" (2004); Co-Author, "Human Sexuality: A Psychosocial Perspective" (2004); Author, "Dr. Ruth's Guide to Talking About Herpes" (2004); Author, "52 Lessons on Communicating Love: Tips, Anecdotes, and Advice for Connecting with the One You Love from America's Leading Relationship Therapist" (2004); Author, "Musically Speaking: A Life Through Song (Personal Takes)" (2003); Co-Author, "Conquering the Rapids of Life: Making the Most of Midlife Opportunities" (2003); Author, "Who Am I? Where Did I Come From?" (2001); Author, "Romance For Dummies" (2001); Author, "Rekindling Romance for Dummies -Conversation Cards" (2001); Co-Author, "Power: The Ultimate Aphrodisiac" (2001); Co-Author, "Dr. Ruth Talks about Grandparents: Advice for Kids on Making the Most of a Special Relationship" (2001); Co-Author, "Dr. Ruth: Grandma on Wheels" (2001); Author, "All in a Lifetime: An Autobiography" (2001); Author, "Sex For Dummies" (2000); Author, "Encyclopedia of Sex" (2000); Author, "Dr. Ruth's Guide to College Life: The Savvy Student's Handbook" (2000); Author, "The Art of Arousal: A Celebration of Erotic Art throughout History" (2000); Voice Actress, "The Emperor's New Clothes: An All-Star Illustrated Retelling of the Classic Fairy Tale" (1998); Co-Author, "Grandparenthood" (1998); Co-Author, "The Value of Family: A Blueprint for the 21st Century" (1997); Co-Author, "Heavenly Sex: Sexuality in the Jewish Tradition" (1996); Author, "Sex for Dummies" (1995); Author, "Dr. Ruth's Encyclopedia of Sex" (1994); Co-Host, "Min Tochnit" (1993); Author, "Dr. Ruth Talks to Kids" (1993); Author, "Dr. Ruth's Guide to Safer Sex" (1992); Co-Author, "Dr. Ruth's Guide to Erotic and Sensuous Pleasures" (1992); Host, "You're on the Air with Dr. Ruth" (1990); Producer, Host, "The Dr. Ruth Show" (1984-1990); Host, "What's Up, Dr. Ruth?" (1989); Host, "The All New Dr. Ruth Show" (1988-1989); Guest Appearances, "Hollywood Squares" (1986-1989); Co-Author, "Sex and Morality: Who Is Teaching Our Sex Standards" (1988); Author, "All in a Lifetime: An Autobiography" (1988); Co-Host, "Ask Dr. Ruth" (1987-1988); Author, "Dr. Ruth's Guide to Good Sex" (1987); Author, "Dr. Ruth's Guide for Married Lovers" (1986); Co-Author, "First Love: A Young People's Guide to Sexual Information" (1985); Actress, "Une Femme ou Deux" (1985); Host, "Good Sex! With Dr. Ruth Westheimer" (1984-1985); Actress, "Electric Dreams" (1984); Host, "Sexually Speaking," WYNY-FM (1980-1984); Author, "Dr. Ruth's Guide to Good Sex" (1983); Appearances, "The Tonight Show Starring Johnny Carson," "Late Night with David Letterman," "Quantum Leap," "This Pretty Planet," Several Commercials **AW:** 55 Most Important People in Sex from the Past 55 Years, Playboy (2009); Leo Baeck Medal (2002) **AV:** Studying different cultures and peoples **RE:** Jewish

WESTON, JANICE LEAH, T: Librarian **I:** Library Management/Library Services **DOB:** 01/03/1944 **PB:** Philadelphia **SC:** PA/USA **PT:** Robert Henry Colmer; Mildred Viola (Hale) Colmer **MS:** Married **SPN:** Leonard Charles Weston (10/28/1972); Stephen Paul Oksala (08/21/1965, Divorced 1970) **ED:** Postgraduate Coursework, Brigham Young University (1975); Postgraduate, Catholic University of America (1975); MLS, Wayne State University (1969); BA in History, University of Michigan (1966) **CT:** Certified Professional Librarian, Commonwealth of Virginia **C:** Chief Librarian, Army Ordnance Center and School, Aberdeen Proving Ground, United States Army (1972-1994); Reference Librarian, Technical Library, Aberdeen Proving Ground, United States Army, MD (1971-1972); Librarian, General Equipment Test Activity, Fort Lee, VA (1970-1971); Branch Librarian, Chester Public Library (1969-1970); Reference Librar-

ian, John Tyler Community College, Chester, VA (1969-1970); Library Clerk, Education Librarian,, University of Michigan, Ann Arbor, MI (1966-1967) **CR:** Chairman, Aberdeen Proving Ground Media Services Committee, United States Army (1978, 1983, 1988); Member, Job Analysis Task Force, Department of the Army, Washington, DC (1976) **CIV:** Friends of the Library, Cocoa Beach, FL (1996-Present); Friends of Atglen Susquehanna Trail, Inc. (1994-Present); The Humane League Friends, Lancaster, PA (1988-2004); Fulton Opera House Foundation, Lancaster, PA (1985-2004); Friends of Library Southern Lancaster County, Quarryville, PA (1985-2004); Member, James Buchanan Foundation, Lancaster, PA (1977-2004); Member, St. David's by-the-Sea Episcopal Church, Cocoa Beach, FL (1996); Fraternal Order of Eagles Auxiliary, Valrico, FL **CW:** Author, "Operating Procedures" (1988) **MEM:** Special Librarians Association; Retired Officers Association (Now Military Officers Association of America); Red Hats Club (Now The Red Hat Society, Inc.) **MH:** Albert Nelson Marquis Lifetime Achievement Award **AS:** Mrs. Weston attributes her success to the satisfaction with what she does. Its not the money, you have to love what you do. **B/I:** Mrs. Weston became involved in her profession because she went to school and got a Bachelor in History and did not want to teach, so she started as a library technician. She then went back to school to get her library science degree. **AV:** Needlecrafts; Reading; Dance; Travel; Theater; Church (St. David's By-Sea Episcopal) **RE:** Episcopalian

WESTON, RANDY EDWARD, T: Pianist, Composer **I:** Fine Art **DOB:** 04/06/1926 **PB:** New York **SC:** NY/USA **PT:** Frank Edward Weston; Vivian (Moore) Weston **MS:** Married **SPN:** Mildred Mosley (Divorced) **CH:** Cherryl; Pamela; Niles; Kim **ED:** Coursework, Parkway Music Institute, Brooklyn, NY (1950-1952) **CR:** Lecturer on African Music, United Nations **CIV:** Performer, Benefit Concerts for Anti-Apartheid Committee, African American Musicians Society, United Nations (1961) **MIL:** U.S. Army (1944-1946) **CW:** Composer, "Sound-Solo Piano" (2018); Composer, "The African Nubian Suite" (2017); Composer, "The Roots of the Blues" (2013); Composer, "The Storyteller" (2009); Composer, "Zep Tepi" (2006); Composer, "Nuit Africa" (2004); Composer, "Ancient Future" (2002); Composer, "Spirit! The Power of Music" (1999); Composer, "Khepera" (1998); Composer, "Earth Birth" (1997); Co-Composer with Vinshu Bill Wood and Lennie McBrowne, "Berkshire Blues" (1996); Composer, "Saga" (1996); Composer, "The Splendid Master Gnawa Musicians of Morocco" (1995); Performer, Monterey '66 (1994); Performer, Volcano Blues (1993); Composer, "The Spirits of Our Ancestors" (1992); Featured Guest Artist, One Hundred Years of Jazz, Amsterdam, The Netherlands (1989); Composer, "Portraits of Duke Ellington" (1989); Composer, "Portraits of Thelonious Monk" (1989); Appearance, "Randy in Tangier; Randy Weston, African Rhythms," Boston, MA (1989); Composer, "Self-Portrait of Weston" (1989); Performer, Lygano Festival of Jazz, Switzerland (1988); Performer, Jazzaldia, San Sebastian, Spain (1988); Performer, Caribbean Cultural Centers Expressions Festival, New York, NY (1988); Performer, Roots Festival, Lagos, Nigeria (1988); Performer, First Festival of Gnaoua Culture, Morocco (1987); Appearance, "Jazz Entre Amigos" (1987); Performer, International Festival of Marrahesh, Morocco (1986); Performer, Festival de Vienne, France (1985); Performer, "Portrait of Billie Holiday", Orchestra Symphonique de Lyons and Ensemble Instrumental et Big Band de Grenoble, France (1985); Performer, "African Sunrise", City of Chicago, IL (1985); Performer, Pom-

peii Jazz Festival, Italy (1985); Composer, "Blue" (1984); Performer, Tour of Brazil (1981); Commissioned Performer, "The Africans," Spoleto Festival, U.S.A. (1981); Performer, "The African Queens," Boston Pops (1981); Performer, Lecture-concerts in Europe Including Bern, Basel, and Zurich, Switzerland and Lyons, France (1975); Composer, "Blues to Africa" (1975); Performer, Kingsberg Jazz Festival, Oslo, Norway (1974); Performer, Montreux Jazz Festival, Switzerland (1974); Performer, Festival de Costa del Sol, Marbella, Spain (1974); Performer, Ahus Jazz Festival, Kristianstad, Sweden (1974); Performer, Festival at Antibes, France (1974); Composer, "Portrait of F.E. Weston" (1974); Composer, "Carnival" (1974); Performer, Carnegie Hall (1973); Performer, Philharmonic Hall, New York, NY (1973); Performer, Recital, Blue Moses (1972); Composer, "The Ganawa" (1971); Performer, Tour with Randy Weston's Sextet for State Department, North and West Africa (1967); Appearance, "Jamboree" (1966); Performer, Monterey Festival (1966); Composer, "The Last Day" (1966); Composer, "African Cook Book" (1965); Pianist, American Society of African Culture Tour, Lagos, Nigeria (1961, 1963); Composer, "Berkshire Blues" (1960); Composer, "Uhruru Africa Suite, Four Movements" (1960); Composer, "Portrait of Vivian" (1959); Performer, Newport Festival (1958); Composer, "Hi Fly" (1958); Composer, "Pam's Waltz" (1950); Composer, "Little Niles" (1950); Composer, "Nuits Americani"; Composer, "Verve"; Performer, Numerous United Nations Concerts, Billie Holiday Theatre, New York University; Performer, Major Jazz Clubs, New York, NY; Performer, European Tours, Recitals; Performer, Concerts, Radio, Television and Major U.S. Museums **AW:** World's Best Jazz Pianist, International Roots Festival, Lagos, Nigeria (1988); Grantee, French Office Nationale de Diffusion Artistique (1976); Premier Prix de l'Academie du Jazz, France (1975); Grantee, National Endowment for the Arts (1974); Pianist Most Deserving of Wider Recognition Award (1972); Broadway Award, Hollywood Advertising Club (1965); New Star Pianist Award, Down Beat International Critics Poll (1955); Recipient, Composer's Awards, ASCAP **MEM:** ASCAP; American Federation of Musicians **PA:** Sufi

WEXTON, JENNIFER LYNN, T: U.S. Representative from Virginia **I:** Government Administration/Government Relations/Government Services **DOB:** 05/27/1968 **PB:** Washington, DC **SC:** DC/USA **MS:** Married **SPN:** Andrew Wexton (2001) **CH:** Two Children **ED:** JD, William & Mary Law School (1995); BA, University of Maryland, College Park, MD (1992) **C:** Member, U.S. House of Representatives from Virginia's 10th Congressional District (2019-Present); Member, District 33, Virginia Senate (2014-2019); Assistant Commonwealth Attorney (2001-2005); Partner, Laurel Brigade Law Group; Substitute Judge, Loudoun County, VA **MEM:** The International Legal Honor Society of Phi Delta Phi **PA:** Democratic

WHAM, DAVID BUFFINGTON, T: Secondary School Educator **I:** Education/Educational Services **CN:** Chicago Public Schools **DOB:** 05/25/1937 **PB:** Evanston **SC:** IL/USA **PT:** Benjamin Wham; Virginia (Buffington) Wham **MS:** Single **SPN:** Joan Field Wilber (03/09/1968, Divorced 05/1972) **CH:** Benjamin; Rachel **ED:** MA, Southern Illinois University, Carbondale, IL (1967); BA, Harvard University, Cum Laude, Cambridge, MA (1959) **C:** Teacher, Chicago Public Schools (1994-Present); Freelance Writer, Chicago, IL (1980-1989); Legislative Assistant, U.S. Congress, Washington, DC (1969-1978); Instructor, Southern Illinois University, Carbondale, IL (1965-1967); Instructor, University of Wyoming, Powell, WY (1963-1965)

CR: Speechwriter, Dawn Netsch Gubernatorial Campaign (1994); Speechwriter, Adlai Stevenson Gubernatorial Campaign (1986) **CIV:** Interviewer, Harvard Club of Chicago (1984-Present) **MIL:** U.S. Army (1959-1962) **CW:** Author, "A Wave of Bright Boys" (1994); Author, "The Comic Genuflection" (1984); Author, "My Farewell to Bohemia" (1968); Contributor, Think-tank Publication: Bureau of Social Science Research (whose president was Robert Bower, the nephew of Ellsworth Bunker, Schomburg Center for Research in Black Culture, New York Public Library **AW:** Fiction Award, Columbia Pacific University (1994) **MEM:** Harvard Club of Chicago; Spee Club, Harvard University; Hasty Pudding Club, Harvard University **MH:** Albert Nelson Marquis Lifetime Achievement Award **PA:** Democrat **RE:** Episcopalian

WHARFF, SHERYL, I: Advertising & Marketing **CN:** Micro Focus **MS:** Married **CH:** Three Children **ED:** AS, Jackson Business University (1976) **C:** Americas Channel and Alliance Partner Marketing Leaders, Micro Focus (2017-Present); Global Product Channel Marketing, Micro Focus (2017-Present); Global Product Marketing, HPE Security-Data Security, Hewlett Packard Enterprise (2014-Present); America's Marketing Communications & Channel Marketing, Thales e-Security, Incorporated (2010-2013); Director, Channel Marketing, Kaspersky Lab (2010); Partner Enablement, Global Channels, EMC Corporation (2006-2009); Director, Channel Sales, Inmagic (2003-2005); Director, Worldwide Channel Programs, NMS Communications (2001-2002); Director, Channel Programs, Aspect Communications (2001); Director, Channels Marketing, Applix (1999-2001); Director, Marketing and Communications, GTE CyberTrust (1998-1999); Director, Communications, Digital Equipment Corporation (1981-1998); Administration to Don Brinkman, Comshare (1980-1983) **CIV:** Women in Technology; SHINE; Volunteer, Best Buddies; Volunteer, Perkins School for the Blind **AW:** Top 100 Women of the Channel Award (2013, 2019) **AS:** Ms. Wharff attributes her success to her tenacity and hard-working nature. She always does her best and makes sure to help others while doing so in order to ensure that achieving success is a collective effort. **B/I:** Ms. Wharff began her career in sales, enjoying the process of learning about her partnerships. She came into the industry for the channel and ended up sticking with it. Over the years, she has enjoyed working with other companies and helping them figure out how to be successful in their markets.

WHARTON, RALPH NATHANIEL, MD, T: Psychiatrist, Educator **I:** Medicine & Health Care **DOB:** 06/15/1932 **PB:** Boston **SC:** MA/USA **PT:** Nathaniel Philip Wharton; Deeda (Levine) Wharton **MS:** Widower **CH:** Naida Sura; Philip Matthew; Laura Beth **ED:** Degree in Psychoanalysis, Columbia University (1970); Resident, Columbia-Presbyterian Medical Center (1961-1964); Intern, Cornell Division, Bellevue Hospital, New York, NY (1957-1958); MD, Columbia University (1957); AB, Harvard University, Cum Laude (1953) **CT:** Certification in Neurology and Psychiatry (1969) **C:** Professor, College of Physicians and Surgeons (1984-Present); Attending Psychiatrist, Columbia-Presbyterian Hospital (1980-2019); Private Practice in Psychiatry/Pharmacology (1964-2019); Associate Professor, College of Physicians and Surgeons (1972-1983); Associate Attending Psychiatry, Columbia-Presbyterian Hospital (1970-1980); Assistant Professor of Clinical Psychiatry, College of Physicians and Surgeons (1969-1972); Senior Research Psychiatrist, New York State Psychiatric Institute (1964-1970); Associate of Psychiatry, College of Physicians and Surgeons (1964-1969); Senior Consultant, Supervisor, Psychiatric Service, New York-Presbyterian Hospital **CR:** Professor of Psychiatry, Columbia University Medical Center (2004-Present); Executive Director, Nathaniel Wharton Fund for Research in Brain Body and Behavior Inc. (1993-Present); Co-Director, Reiner Center for Behavioral and Psychosomatic Medicine, Columbia-Presbyterian Medical Center (1984-Present); Board Member, Medical Strollers of New York City (2015); Medical Director, Black Sea Project, Macalester College (1994-1998); Former President, Society of Practitioners (1980-1982) **CIV:** Alumni Campaign Committee, College of Physicians and Surgeons, Columbia University (2001-Present); Founding Member, Salem de Virtuoso; Founding Member, International Association for the Study of Pain **MIL:** United States Army Hospital, Orléans, France (1960-1961); Captain of Medical Corps, United States Army (1958-1960); 24th Infantry Division of Artillery, Munich, Germany (1958-1960) **CW:** Contributor, "Merritt's Textbook of Neurology" (2010); Contributor, "Merritt's Textbook of Neurology" (2008); Contributor, "Art of Aging" (2006); Contributor, "Merritt's Textbook of Neurology" (2005); Author, "Landmark Papers, Lithium Carbonate for Affective Disorders" (1966); Contributor, Numerous Papers, Publications, Professional Journals; Contributor, Chapters, Books **AW:** Obama Basin Research Award, National Institutes of Health (2008-2011); Distinguished Practitioner of the Year, Columbia University Medical Center, Society of Practitioners (2010); Distinguished Practitioner of the Year, Columbia University Medical Center, Society of Practitioners (1978); Medical Commendation Award as Chief of OPD, Medical Corp United States Army (1958-1961); Listee, One of the Best Doctors, New York Magazine **MEM:** Board of Directors, American College of Psychoanalysts (1996-Present); Founding Member, Salon de Virtuosi (1991-Present); Treasurer, Salon de Virtuosi (1991-Present); Member of Executive Committee, Society of Practitioners (1990-Present); Class Agent, Harvard Club of New York (1953-Present); Honorary Lifetime Fellow, American Psychiatric Association (2002); President, American College of Psychoanalysts (1996); Fellow, American College of Psychoanalysts; American Medical Association; Group for Advancement Psychiatry; Founding Member, International Association for the Study of Pain; Royal Society of Medicine; New York Academy of Medicine; Century Association of New York; Lotos Club; Century Association; General Affairs Committee, AHA County **MH:** Albert Nelson Marquis Lifetime Achievement Award; Marquis Who's Who Top Professional **B/I:** Dr. Wharton was influenced by a famous faculty member at Harvard University, George Wald. He won two Nobel Prizes and Dr. Wharton had the privilege of learning biochemistry from him. **AV:** Skiing; Sailing

WHEELER, ALBIN G., T: Military Officer, Educator (Retired) **I:** Education/Educational Services **DOB:** 03/16/1935 **PB:** Huntington **SC:** WV/USA **PT:** Harvey Gray; Hattie Benson (Weddle) Wheeler **MS:** Married **SPN:** Beatrice Thomas (05/17/1958) **CH:** Patrice; Michelle; Dianne **ED:** Honorary Doctor of Humane Letters, Marshall University, Huntington, WV (2004); Graduate Coursework, Professional Development Classes, Harvard University (1990); Master of Business Administration, Army War College (1976); Master of Business Administration, Pepperdine University (1975); Bachelor of Arts in English, Marshall University (1958) **C:** Retired (1996); Executive Director, Arent Fox, Washington, DC (1993-1996); Chief Executive Officer, Army and Air Force Exchange Service, Dallas, TX (1991-1993); President, Industrial College Armed Forces, Washington, DC (1985-1989); Commander, Second Support Command, VII U.S. Corps, Germany (1983-1985); Chief Executive Officer, Army & Air Force Exchange Service, Europe and the Middle East, Munich, Germany (1981-1983) **CIV:** Charter Member, Board Director, Society of Yeager Scholars, Marshall University **MIL:** Advanced through Grades to Major General, U.S. Army (1981); Commander, Division Support Command, Chief of Staff, First Infantry Division, Fort Riley, KS (1978-1980); Commissioned, Second Lieutenant, U.S. Army (1959); Enlisted, U.S. Army (1952) **AW:** Defense and Army Distinguished Service Medal; Bronze Star with Two Oak Leaf Clusters; Legion of Merit with Two Oak Leaf Clusters **MEM:** Distinguished Alumnus, Marshall University Alumni Association (1983) **B/I:** Mr. Wheeler became involved in military service shortly after joining the National Guard while attending high school. He subsequently received a commission through the ROTC at Marshall University to become a second lieutenant. **AV:** Reading; Walking; Exercise **RE:** Christian

WHEELER, ANDREW R., T: Administrator **I:** Environmental Services **CN:** Environmental Protection Agency **DOB:** 12/23/1964 **PB:** Hamilton **SC:** OH/USA **ED:** MBA, George Mason University (1998); JD, Washington University in St. Louis School of Law (1990); BA, Case Western Reserve University, Cleveland, Ohio (1987) **C:** Administrator, United States Environmental Protection Agency (2019-Present); Senior Vice President, Energy & Climate Change Practice Group, B&D Consulting, Washington, DC (2009-Present); Acting Administrator, United States Environmental Protection Agency (2018-2019); Deputy Administrator, United States Environmental Protection Agency (2018); Staff Director, Chief Counsel, United States Senate Committee on Environment and Public Works (2002-2009); Special Assistant, United States Environmental Protection Agency, Washington, DC (1991-1995); General Counsel, Representative Staff Director, United States Senate Subcommittee on Clean Air, Climate Change, Wetlands & Nuclear Safety; Legislative Counsel to Senator James Inhofe, United States Senate **CR:** John C. Stennis Congressional Staff Fellow (1999-2000); Chairmen Emeritus, National Energy Resources Organization **CIV:** Vice President, Washington Coal Club **AW:** Named a Top Congressional Staff Leader, National Journal (2005) **BAR:** The District of Columbia Bar (1991) **PA:** Republican **RE:** Presbyterian

WHEELER, WILLIAM HAROLD JR., T: Musical Director, Composer **I:** Media & Entertainment **DOB:** 07/14/1943 **PB:** St. Louis **SC:** MO/USA **MS:** Married **SPN:** Hattie Winston **ED:** Coursework, Howard University **C:** Musical Director, "Dancing with the Stars" (2005-2013) **CW:** Music Arranger, 79th Academy Awards (2007); Arranger, Conductor, "Mississippi Rising" (2005); Music Conductor, 76th Academy Awards (2004); Co-Conductor, Summer Olympics (1996); Composer, "Straight Out of Brooklyn" (1991); Composer, "The Wiz" (1978); Arranger, Producer, "Star Wars and Other Galactic Funk" (1977); Producer, Arranger, Musician, Composer, "Black Cream" (1975); Composer, "Grind" (1985); Musician, "Greetings From Asbury Park, N.J." (1973); Arranger, Conductor, Producer, "Here Comes the Sun" (1971); Sideman, "Stand by Me (Whatcha See is Whatcha Get)" (1971); Sideman, "Purdie Good!" (1971) **AW:** Special Tony Award for Lifetime Achievement in the Theater (2019); Lifetime Achievement Award, NAACP Theatre Awards (2019); Drama Desk Award for Outstanding Orchestrations, "Hairspray" (2003)

WHELAN, MELANIE, T: Former Chief Executive Officer **I:** Business Management/Business Services **CN:** SoulCycle **PB:** Baltimore **SC:** MD/USA **ED:** Degree, Engineering and Economics, Brown

University, Providence, RI (1999); Coursework, Bryn Mawr School **C:** Executive-in-Residence, Summit Partners, New York, NY (2020-Present); Chief Executive Officer, SoulCycle, New York, NY (2015-2019); Chief Operating Officer, SoulCycle, New York, NY (2012-2015); Vice President, Business Development, Equinox, New York, NY (2007-2012); Vice President, Corporate Development, Virgin USA, New York, NY (2002-2007); Corporate Development Manager, Starwood Hotels and Resorts, White Plains, NY (1999-2002) **CR:** Board of Directors, Chegg Inc. (2019-Present); Henry Crown Fellowship, The Aspen Institute (2018) **AW:** Listee, Most Creative People in Business, Fast Company (2017); Listee, 40 Under 40, Crain's New York Business (2016); Listee, 40 Under 40, Fortune (2015)

WHITACRE, ERIC, T: Composer, Conductor, Speaker **I:** Fine Art **DOB:** 01/02/1970 **PB:** Reno **SC:** NV/USA **PT:** Ross Whitacre; Roxanne Whitacre **MS:** Married **SPN:** Laurence Servaes (2019); Hila Plitmann (1998, Divorced 2017) **ED:** Master's Degree in Composition, The Juilliard School; Bachelor's Degree in Music Composition, University of Nevada **C:** Artist in Residence, Los Angeles Master Chorale, Walt Disney Concert Hall (2016-Present) **CR:** Visiting Fellow, Sidney Sussex College, Cambridge (2010) **CW:** Choir, "How to Train Your Dragon: The Hidden World" (2019); Composer, "Deep Field," Virtual Choir 5 (2018); Collaborator, "Deep Field: The Impossible Magnitude of the Universe," Kennedy Space Center (2018); Recording, "Goodnight Moon," Eric Whitacre Singers (2018); Recording, "The Star-Spangled Banner," Eric Whitacre Singers (2018); Recording, "I Carry Your Heart," Eric Whitacre Singers (2018); Recording, "Hurt," Eric Whitacre Singers (2017); Choirmaster, "Batman v Superman: Dawn of Justice" (2016); Conductor, "Kung Fu Panda 3" (2016); Recording, "The Salvage Men," Eric Whitacre Singers (2016); Recording, "iTunes Festival: London" (2015); Recording, "Enjoy the Silence," Eric Whitacre Singers (2014); Recording, "Fly to Paradise" (2013); Recording, "Water Nigh," Eric Whitacre Singers (2012); Recording, "The Chelsea Carol," Eric Whitacre Singers (2012); Co-Composer, "Pirates of the Caribbean: On Stranger Tides" (2011); Recording, "Light & Gold," Eric Whitacre Singers (2010); Choral Album, "Light & Gold," Eric Whitacre Singers (2010); Composer, "Paradise Lost: Shadows and Wings"; Choral Album, "Water Night"; Composer, "Fly to Paradise," Virtual Choir 4; Composer, "Water Night," Virtual Choir 3; Co-Presenter, Eurovision Choir of the Year; Composer, Piece, Choir of Sidney Sussex College, Cambridge; Founder, Eric Whitacre Singers; Composer, Piece, "October"; Composer, Piece, "Sleep"; Composer, Piece, "Lux Aurumque"; Composer, Piece, "Cloudburst"; Numerous Orchestral and Choral Works **AW:** Grammy Award for Best Choral Performance, "Light & Gold" (2012)

WHITAKER, FOREST STEVEN, T: Actor, Producer, Director **I:** Media & Entertainment **DOB:** 07/15/1961 **PB:** Longview **SC:** TX/USA **PT:** Forest Steven Whitaker Jr.; Laura Francis **MS:** Divorced **SPN:** Keisha Nash (1996, Divorced 2018) **CH:** Sonnet; True; Ocean Alexander; Autumn (Stepdaughter) **ED:** Honorary DFA, University of Southern California (2018); Honorary DHL, California State University, Dominguez Hills (2015); Honorary DHL, Xavier University of Louisiana (2009); BFA, Drama Conservatory, University of Southern California (1982); Coursework, Music Conservatory, University of Southern California; Coursework, California State Polytechnic University, Pomona **C:** Executive Director, Nodance Film Festival (2003-2009); Founder, Spirit Dance Entertainment **CR:** Member, President

Barack Obama's Committee on Arts and Humanities (2009); Co-chair, JuntoBox Films **CIV:** Founder, Whitaker Peace & Development Initiative (2012); Supporter, Public Advocate, Hope North **CW:** Actor, "Jingle Jangle" (2020); Actor, "Respect" (2020); Producer, "Passing" (2020); Executive Producer, Actor, "Godfather of Harlem" (2019); Voice Actor, "Star Wars Jedi: Fallen Order" (2019); Actor, "Bring Me the Horizon: In the Dark" (2019); Actor, "Finding Steve McQueen" (2019); Producer, "A Kid from Coney Island" (2019); Producer, "Devil's Pie: D'Angelo" (2019); Actor, "City of Lies" (2018); Actor, "How It Ends" (2018); Actor, "Black Panther" (2018); Actor, "Burden" (2018); Producer, Actor, "Sorry to Bother You" (2018); Actor, "Empire" (2017-2018); Actor, "The Forgiven" (2017); Executive Producer, "We Are One" (2017); Producer, "Roxanne Roxanne" (2017); Actor, "Hughie" (2016); Actor, "Rogue One: A Star Wars Story" (2016); Voice Actor, "Star Wars: Go Rogue" (2016); Actor, "Arrival" (2016); Actor, "Roots" (2016); Actor, "Southpaw" (2015); Narrator, Producer, "Dope" (2015); Producer, "Songs My Brothers Taught Me" (2015); Actor, "Taken 3" (2014); Actor, "Two Men in Town" (2014); Narrator, "Nelson Mandela" (2013); Actor, "Black Nativity" (2013); Actor, "Making a Scene" (2013); Actor, "Out of the Furnace" (2013); Actor, "Lee Daniels' The Butler" (2013); Actor, "Zulu" (2013); Actor, "Pawn" (2013); Producer, Actor, "Repentance" (2013); Actor, "The Last Stand" (2013); Producer, "Fruitvale Station" (2013); Actor, "A Dark Truth" (2012); Actor, "Freelancers" (2012); Voice Actor, "Ernest & Celestine" (2012); Executive Producer, "Rising from Ashes" (2012); Actor, "Catch .44" (2011); Actor, "Criminal Minds: Suspect Behavior" (2011); Executive Producer, "Serving Life" (2011); Executive Producer, "Monte Carlo" (2011); Executive Producer, "Brick City" (2009-2011); Actor, "Lullaby for Pi" (2010); Actor, "The Experiment" (2010); Actor, "Criminal Minds" (2010); Actor, "My Own Love Song" (2010); Actor, "Repo Men" (2010); Actor, "Our Family Wedding" (2010); Voice Actor, "Higglety Pigglety Pop! or There Must Be More to Life" (2010); Appearance, Jamie Foxx Featuring T-Pain, "Blame It" (2009); Actor, "Hurricane Season" (2009); Voice Actor, "Where the Wild Things Are" (2009); Actor, Producer, "Powder Blue" (2009); Voice Actor, "Toys in the Attic" (2009); Voice Actor, "American Dad!" (2007-2009); Actor, "Fragments" (2008); Actor, "Street Kings" (2008); Voice Actor, "Dragon Hunters" (2008); Actor, "Vantage Point" (2008); Producer, "Dewmocracy" (2008); Executive Producer, "Kassim the Dream" (2008); Actor, "The Great Debaters" (2007); Actor, Executive Producer, "Ripple Effect" (2007); Actor, "The Air I Breathe" (2007); Actor, "The Shield" (2006-2007); Voice Actor, "Everyone's Hero" (2006); Actor, "The Last King of Scotland" (2006); Actor, "The Marsh" (2006); Executive Producer, Actor, "American Gun" (2005); Actor, "A Little Trip to Heaven" (2005); Actor, "Mary" (2005); Director, Executive Producer, Narrator, "First Daughter" (2004); Appearance, "Jiminy Glick in Lalawood" (2004); Actor, "Deacons for Defense" (2003); Producer, "Chasing Papi" (2003); Consulting Producer, "The Twilight Zone" (2002-2003); Actor, "Phone Booth" (2002); Co-executive Producer, Actor, "The Feast of All Saints" (2001); Actor, "The Fourth Angel" (2001); Executive Producer, Actor, "Green Dragon" (2001); Actor, "Four Dogs Playing Poker" (2000); Actor, "Battlefield Earth" (2000); Actor, "Witness Protection" (1999); Actor, "Light It Up" (1999); Actor, "Ghost Dog: The Way of the Samurai" (1999); Director, "Hope Floats" (1998); Director, "Black Jaq" (1998); Executive Producer, "Black Jaq" (1998); Actor, "Body Count" (1998); Actor, "Rebound: The Legend of Earl 'The Goat' Manigault" (1996); Actor, "Phenomenon" (1996); Director, "Waiting to Exhale" (1995); Actor, "Mr. Hol-

land's Opus" (1995); Actor, "Species" (1995); Actor, "Smoke" (1995); Actor, "Ready to Wear" (1994); Actor, "Jason's Lyric" (1994); Actor, "The Enemy Within" (1994); Actor, "Blown Away" (1994); Director, "Strapped" (1993); Actor, "Lush Life" (1993); Actor, "Bank Robber" (1993); Actor, "Last Light" (1993); Actor, "Body Snatchers" (1993); Actor, "Consenting Adults" (1992); Actor, "The Crying Game" (1992); Actor, "Article 99" (1992); Co-producer, Actor, "A Rage in Harlem" (1991); Actor, "Diary of a Hitman" (1991); Actor, "Criminal Justice" (1990); Actor, "Downtown" (1990); Actor, "Johnny Handsome" (1989); Actor, "Bird" (1988); Actor, "Bloodsport" (1988); Actor, "Good Morning, Vietnam" (1987); Actor, "Stakeout" (1987); Actor, "Hands of a Stranger" (1987); Actor, "Platoon" (1986); Actor, "North and South, Book II" (1986); Actor, "Amazing Stories" (1986); Actor, "The Grand Baby" (1985); Actor, "North and South, Book I" (1985); Actor, "Diff'rent Strokes" (1985); Actor, "The Fall Guy" (1985); Actor, "Vision Quest" (1985); Actor, "Hill Street Blues" (1984); Actor, "Trapper John, M.D." (1984); Actor, "Cagney & Lacey" (1983); Actor, "Fast Times at Ridgemont High" (1982); Actor, "Tag: The Assassination Game" (1982); Actor, "Making the Grade" (1982) **AW:** Screen Actors Guild Award for Outstanding Performance by a Cast in a Motion Picture, "Black Panther," SAG-AFTRA (2019); Joel Siegel Award, Broadcast Film Critics Association Awards (2014); Outstanding Actor in a Motion Picture, "The Butler," NAACP Image Awards (2014); Chairman's Award, NAACP Image Awards (2014); Stanley Kramer Award, "Fruitvale Station," PGA Awards (2014); Kirk Douglas Award for Excellence in Film, Santa Barbara International Film Festival (2014); Best Actor, "The Butler," African-American Film Critics Association (2013); Tribute Award, Gotham Awards (2013); Artist Citizen of the World Award (2010); Academy Award for Best Actor, "The Last King of Scotland," Academy of Motion Picture Arts and Sciences (2007); Golden Globe Award for Best Performance by an Actor in a Motion Picture - Drama, "The Last King of Scotland," Hollywood Foreign Press Association (2007); Named Best Actor in a Leading Role, "The Last King of Scotland," BAFTA Awards, Vancouver Film Critics Circle, Black Reel Awards, and Broadcast Film Critics Association Awards (2007); Named Outstanding Actor in a Motion Picture, "The Last King of Scotland," NAACP Image Awards (2007); Screen Actors Guild Award for Outstanding Performance by a Male Actor in a Television Movie or Miniseries, "Deacons for Defense," SAG-AFTRA (2007); Named Actor of the Year, "The Last King of Scotland," London Critics Circle Film Awards (2007); Named Best Actor - Drama, "The Shield," NAMIC Vision Awards (2007); Named Best Actor, "The Last King of Scotland," National Society of Film Critics Awards, North Texas Film Critics Association, Online Film & Television Association, and Online Film Critics Society Awards (2007); Named Best Guest Actor in a Drama Series, "ER," Online Film & Television Association (2007); American Riviera Award, "The Last King of Scotland," Santa Barbara International Film Festival (2007); Recipient, Star, Hollywood Walk of Fame (2007); Named Best Actor, "The Last King of Scotland," African-American Film Critics Association, Boston Society of Film Critics Awards, Chicago Film Critics Association Awards, Dallas-Fort Worth Film Critics Association Awards, Florida Film Critics Circle Awards, Southeastern Film Critics Association Awards, St. Louis Film Critics Association, Kansas City Film Critics Circle Awards, Las Vegas Film Critics Society Awards, Los Angeles Film Critics Association Awards, National Board of Review, New York Film Critics, Oklahoma Film Critics Circle Awards, and Washington DC Area Film Critics Association Awards (2006); Capri Legend Award, Capri

Hollywood International Film Festival (2006); Named Actor of the Year, "The Last King of Scotland," Hollywood Film Awards (2006); Named Best Performance by an Actor in a Leading Role, "The Last King of Scotland," Phoenix Film Critics Society Awards (2006); Best Actor in a Motion Picture, Drama, "The Last King of Scotland," Satellite Awards (2006); Black Reel Award for Television: Best Actor, "Deacons for Defense" (2004); Primetime Emmy Award for Outstanding Made for Television Movie, "Door to Door," Television Academy (2003); Christopher Award, "Door to Door" (2003); Named Favorite Supporting Actor - Drama, "Phenomenon," Blockbuster Entertainment Awards (1997); International Critics' Award, "Strapped," Toronto International Film Festival (1993); Award for Fiction: Actor, "Criminal Justice," Biarritz International Festival of Audiovisual Programming (1992); Named Best Foreign Actor, "Bird," "Good Morning, Vietnam," Sant Jordi Awards (1989); Named Best Actor, "Bird," Cannes Film Festival (1988); Recipient, Numerous Awards AV: Yoga; Kenpo

WHITAKER, LAURA HOPE, T: Executive Director **I:** Business Management/Business Services **CN:** Extra Special People, Java Joy, Camp Hooray **MS:** Married **SPN:** Joseph **CH:** Owen Patrick; Finley Gray; Tate Alan **ED:** MEd in Adapted Curriculum Classic Autism, University of Georgia (2009); BE in Collaborative Special Education, University of Georgia (2007) **CT:** Emotional Intelligence, Leadership, Mindset Mastery (2014); Non-profit Management Consulting, NDI Certified (2013); Graduation Program, Leadership Athens (2012); Certification in Grant Writing (2010) **C:** Executive Director, Extra Special People (2005-Present); Camp Director, Extra Special People (2005-2012); Campus Ministry Intern, Alpha Omega Ministries (2004-2006); Proctor and Student Staff, Disability Services, University of Georgia, Athens, GA (2003-2006); Leadership Staff, Extra Special People (2004-2005); Executive Director, Java Joy; Executive Director, Camp Hooray **CIV:** Leadership Georgia Program Committee (2018); LEAD Athens Steering Committee, Leadership Georgia and Classic City Church; Board Member, United Way of Northwest Georgia; North Oconee Rotary, Oconee Civitan, Junior League of Athens; Organizational Development, Leadership, Fundraising, Non-Profit Consulting **CW:** Speaker, "The Dandelion Shift," TEDxUGA (2019) **AW:** Listee, 40 Under 40, The Atlanta Business Chronicle; Listee, 40 Under 40, The UGA Alumni Association; Listee, 40 Under 40, The Athens Banner-Herald; Listee, 40 Under 40, The Georgia Trend; Super Citizen Award, The Athens Banner-Herald; The Community Four-Way Test Award, Rotary Club of Oconee County; Volunteer of the Year Award, The Oconee County Chamber of Commerce; 12th Place, Top Growing Business Leaders, University of Georgia **MEM:** Leadership Georgia; Steering Committee, LEAD Athens; Prior Marketing Director, Junior League of Athens; Women's Ministry Team, Classic City Church **AS:** Ms. Whitaker attributes her success to her faith and humility. Additionally, her husband has been her greatest supporter. He has been by her side from the beginning. She has always surrounded herself with mentors who taught her what she needed to know. **B/I:** Ms. Whitaker grew up in Atlanta. Her parents served on the town board, so she constantly watched them give back to the community. They would donate money even though they were not always financially stable. In Ms. Whitaker's final year of high school, she finished many of her classes. **AV:** Thrift shop decorating; Watching children's sports and activities; Traveling; Worshipping; Spreading hope **THT:** Ms. Whitaker's motto is, "Hope is the only thing greater than fear."

WHITAKER, WILLIAM SCOTT, T: President **I:** Oil & Energy **CN:** TEXAMATION **DOB:** 11/21/1942 **PB:** New Orleans **SC:** LA/USA **PT:** Scott Turner Whitaker; Margaret Helen (Dozier) Whitaker **MS:** Married **SPN:** Merrily Ann Rush **CH:** Geoffrey; Sarah **ED:** MS in Industrial Engineering Management, University of Houston (1975); BSEE, Rice University (1967); BA in Science and Engineering, Rice University (1966) **CT:** Registered Professional Engineer, States of Texas, California and Louisiana **C:** Owner, President, TEXAMATION, Houston, Texas; Senior Technical Consultant, Emerson Electric Co., Houston, Texas; SIS Functional Safety Consultant, Emerson Electric Co., Houston, Texas; Operations Manager, Systech International, Houston, Texas; Associate, Engineering, Contech Control Services, La Porte, Texas; Manager, Control System, Litwin Engineers & Constructors, Inc. (Now Litwin Management Services, LLC), Houston, Texas; Manager, Control System, Technical Automation Service Company, La Porte, Texas; President, Engineering, Tex-A-Mation Engineering, Inc., La Porte, Texas; Manager, Engineering, Tex-A-Mation Engineering, Inc., La Porte, Texas; Engineer, Control System, Tex-A-Mation Engineering, Inc., La Porte, Texas; Engineer, Amoco Corporation (Now bp p.l.c.), Texas City, Texas **CR:** Team Member, CSE Registration Examination Review Course of Development; ISA and IEC Standards Committees **CIV:** Precinct Chair, Harris County Republican Party (1980-1986); Sunday School Teacher **CW:** Author, "Integrated Approach to Product In-Line Blending," Hydrocarbon Processing (1995); Author, "Control System Upgrade Workshop," HRI Conferences (1990); Author, "Energy Metering Audit Procedures," Industrial Energy Technology Conference (1987); Author, "Control System Evaluation Techniques," ISA Mining and Metallurgy Symposium (1985); Author, "Adapting Instrument Engineering to Meet the DCS Revolution," Texas A&M Instrumentation Symposium (1979) **AW:** Award, Eagle Scouts; Award, Mensa International **MEM:** Board of Directors, Instrument Society of America (Now International Society of Automation) (1992-1993); Board of Directors, Rice Engineering Alumni (1990-1992); US Delegate, IEC Standards Committee **MH:** Albert Nelson Marquis Lifetime Achievement Award **AS:** Mr. Whitaker attributes his success to actively listening to others without imposing any assumptions. This leads to understanding a problem and its root cause instead of just seeing the associated symptoms. **B/I:** Mr. Whitaker became involved in his profession while in high school, when he was inspired by a co-worker who attended engineering school. He felt engineering would be a great fit for him and decided to pursue it.

WHITCHURCH, ELLWOOD FALVEY, T: Certified Public Accountant, Business Executive **I:** Financial Services **DOB:** 02/02/1939 **PB:** Berwyn **SC:** IL/USA **PT:** Ellwood Falvey, Sr.; Marjorie Louise (Gilmore) Falvey **MS:** Widowed **SPN:** Vivian Ann Watson (1964) **CH:** Bradley Watson Whitchurch **ED:** BSBA, University of Arkansas (1962) **CT:** Certified Public Accountant, States of Florida and New York, Washington DC (Inactive) **C:** Co-Founder, Chief Financial Officer, Board Member, Seal Shield, LLC. (2006-2018); Financial and Business Valuation Consultant, Chief Financial Officer, Board Member, Distributed Processing Technology (1992-2006); Managing Partner, Arthur Andersen & Co. (1981-1991); Managing Partner, Arthur Andersen & Co. (1976-1980); Controller, Horizon Corporation (1972-1976); Manager, Arthur Andersen & Co. (1967-1971); Senior Accountant, PwC (1962-1966) **CR:** Board of Directors, Seal Shield, LLC. (2006-2019); Board of Advisers, Orlando Business Journal (1989-1991) **CIV:** Treasurer, Acquisition Trust, Orlando Museum of Art (1992-1994); Chairman, President, Treasurer, Junior Achievement (1981-1991); Corporate Council, Economic Development Committee, Orlando, FL (1988-1990); Board of Trustees, Orlando Science Center (1982-1984) **MIL:** Sergeant, U.S. Army Reserve (1957-1962) **AW:** Bronze Leadership Award, Junior Achievement (1988) **MEM:** Association of International Certified Professional Accountants; Florida Institute of CPAs; Orlando Regional Chamber Of Commerce; Financial Executives International; Kappa Alpha Order; Beta Alpha Psi; Omicron Delta Kappa **MH:** Albert Nelson Marquis Lifetime Achievement Award **AV:** Golfing; Playing croquet; Enjoying art; Traveling

WHITE, BETTY, T: Actress, Comedienne **I:** Media & Entertainment **DOB:** 01/17/1922 **PB:** Oak Park **SC:** IL/USA **MS:** Married **SPN:** Allen Ludden (07/14/1963, Deceased 1981); Lane Allen (1947, Divorced 1949); Dick Barker (1945, Divorced 1945) **ED:** Graduate, Beverly Hills High School **CIV:** Chair, Greater Los Angeles Zoo Association (2010-Present); Commissioner, Greater Los Angeles Zoo (1998-Present); Member, Morris Animal Foundation (1976-Present); Recognized with the Betty White Wildlife Rapid Response Fund, Morris Animal Foundation; Named "Ambassador to the Animals for the City of Los Angeles," Mayor Villaraigosa (2006); Trustee, Greater Los Angeles Zoo Association; Member, Los Angeles Zoo Commission **CW:** Voice Actress, "Forty Asks a Question" (2019); Voice Actress, "Trouble" (2019); Voice Actress, "Toy Story 4" (2019); Actress, "Young & Hungry" (2017); Actress, "Crowded" (2016); Actress, "SpongeBob SquarePants" (2016); Actress, "Fireside Chat with Esther" (2015-2018); Actress, "Bones" (2015-2017); Actress, "Hot in Cleveland" (2010-2015); Actress, "The Soul Man" (2014); Herself, "WWE Raw" (2014); Executive Producer, "Betty White's Off Their Rockers" (2012-2014); Herself, "Betty White Goes Wild" (2013); Narrator, "Letters to Jackie: Remembering President Kennedy" (2013); Voice Actress, "Mickey Mouse" (2013); Actress, "Save Me" (2013); Voice Actress, "Pound Puppies" (2010-2013); Actress, "The Client List" (2012); Voice Actress, "The Lorax" (2012); Actress, "The Lost Valentine" (2011); Herself, "Betty White: Champion for Animals" (2011); Author, "Betty & Friends: My Life at the Zoo" (2011); Author, "If You Ask Me (And of Course You Won't)" (2011); Actress, "Community" (2010); Actress, "You Again" (2010); Voice Actress, "Prep & Landing Stocking Stuffer: Operation: Secret Santa" (2010); Host, "Saturday Night Live" (2010); Actress, "You Again" (2010); Voice Actress, "Glenn Martin DDS" (2009-2010); Actress, "The Middle" (2010); Actress, "Part Two: The Warm Mission" (2009); Actress, "The Proposal" (2009); Actress, "Love N'Dancing" (2009); Herself, "30 Rock" (2009); Actress, "My Name Is Earl" (2009); Actress, "The Bold and the Beautiful" (2006-2009); Author, "Together: A Novel of Shared Vision" (2008); Voice Actress, "Ponyo" (2008); Actress, "Boston Legal" (2005-2008); Herself, "Ugly Betty" (2007); Actress, "Sea Tales" (2004-2007); Actress, "Joey" (2005); Actress, "The Third Wish" (2005); Actress, "Annie's Point" (2005); Actress, "Complete Savages" (2004-2005); Voice Actress, "Father of the Pride" (2004); Actress, "Malcolm in the Middle" (2004); Actress, "My Wife and Kids" (2004); Actress, "The Practice" (2004); Actress, "Everwood" (2003-2004); Actress, "Stealing Christmas" (2003); Herself, "I'm with Her" (2003); Voice Actress, "Gary the Rat" (2003); Voice Actress, "The Grim Adventures of Billy & Mandy" (2003); Actress, "Bringing Down the House" (2003); Actress, "That '70s Show" (2002-2003); Voice Actress, "King of the Hill" (1999, 2002); Actress, "Providence" (2002); Actress, "Yes, Dear" (2002);

Voice Actress, "Teacher's Pet" (2002); Actress, "The Ellen Show" (2001); Voice Actress, "The Wild Thornberrys: The Origin of Donnie" (2001); Actress, "The Retrievers" (2001); Actress, "Ladies Man" (1999-2001); Voice Actress, "The Wild Thornberrys" (2000); Voice Actress, "Tom Sawyer" (2000); Voice Actress, "Whispers: An Elephant's Tale" (2000); Actress, "Ally McBeal" (1999); Actress, "The Story of Us" (1999); Actress, "Lake Placid" (1999); Voice Actress, "Hercules" (1999); Actress, "L.A. Doctors" (1998); Actress, "Noddy: Anything Can Happen at Christmas" (1998); Voice Actress, "The Lionhearts" (1998); Actress, "Holy Man" (1998); Actress, "Dennis the Menace Strikes Again!" (1998); Actress, "Hard Rain" (1998); Actress, "Suddenly Susan" (1996); Actress, "A Weekend in the Country" (1996); Actress, "Maybe This Time" (1995-1996); Author, "Here We Go Again: My Life in Television" (1995); Actress, "The Naked Truth" (1995); Actress, "Diagnosis Murder" (1994); Actress, "Bob" (1993); Actress, "The Golden Palace" (1992-1993); Actress, "Empty Nest" (1989-1992); Actress, "The Golden Girls" (1985-1992); Actress, "Chance of a Lifetime" (1991); Panelist, "Match Game" (1963-1982, 1991); Author, "The Leading Lady: Dinah's Story" (1991); Actress, "Nurses" (1991); Actress, "Carol & Company" (1990); Actress, "The Earth Day Special" (1990); Actress, "Santa Barbara" (1988); Author, "Betty White in Person" (1987); Actress, "Matlock" (1987); Actress, "D.C. Follies" (1987); Actress, "Alf Loves a Mystery" (1987); Actress, "St. Elsewhere" (1985-1987); Actress, "Mama's Family" (1983-1986); Actress, "Who's the Boss?" (1985); Actress, "The Love Boat" (1980-1985); Actress, "Hotel" (1984); Author, "Betty White's Pet-Love: How Pets Take Care of Us" (1983); Actress, "Fame" (1983); Actress, "Eunice" (1982); Actress, "Love, Sidney" (1982); Actress, "Best of the West" (1981); Actress, "Stephanie" (1981); Herself, "The Gossip Columnist" (1980); Actress, "Before and After" (1979); Actress, "The Best Place to Be" (1979); Actress, "With This Ring" (1978); Actress, "The Betty White Show" (1977-1978); Actress, "The Mary Tyler Moore Show" (1973-1977); Actress, "Ellery Queen" (1975); Actress, "Lucas Tanner" (1975); Panelist, "You Don't Say!" (1963-1975); Actress, "Vanished" (1971); Actress, "Petticoat Junction" (1969); Actress, "That's Life" (1968); Actress, "Another World" (1964); Actress, "The United States Steel Hour" (1962); Actress, "Advise & Consent" (1962); Actress, "Date with the Angels" (1957-1958); Actress, "The Millionaire" (1956); Actress, "Life with Elizabeth" (1953-1955); Producer, "Life with Elizabeth" (1953); Actress, "Hollywood on Television" (1949); Actress, "Time to Kill" (1945) AW: Career - Honorary Award, CinEuphoria Awards (2019); Lifetime Achievement Award, Publicists Guild of America (2018); Lifetime Achievement Award, Daytime Emmy Awards (2015); Favorite TV Icon, People's Choice Awards (2015); Favorite TV Icon, People's Choice Awards (2015); Best Spoken Word Album, "If You Ask Me (And Of Course You Won't)," Grammy Awards (2012); Best Spoken Word Album, "If You Ask Me (And Of Course You Won't)," Grammy Awards (2012); Reality Host, "Betty White's Off Their Rockers," Gold Derby Awards (2012); Timeless Award, GALECA: The Society of LGBTQ Entertainment Critics (2012); Outstanding Performance by a Female Actor in a Comedy Series, "Hot in Cleveland," Screen Actors Guild Awards (2012); Inductee, NAB Broadcasting Hall of Fame (2012); Outstanding Performance by a Female Actor in a Comedy Series, "Hot in Cleveland," Screen Actors Guild Awards (2011); Outstanding Female Lead in a Comedy Series, "Hot in Cleveland," Gracie Allen Awards (2011); Favorite TV Icon, TV Guide Awards (2011); Outstanding Guest Actress in a Comedy Series, "Saturday Night Live," Primetime Emmy Awards (2010); Life Achievement Award, Screen Actors Guild Awards (2010); Variety Performer, "Saturday Night Live," Gold Derby Awards (2010); Best Female Performance in a Fiction Program, "Saturday Night Live," Online Film & Television Association (2010); Charlie Chaplin Britannia Award for Excellence in Comedy, Britannia Awards (2010); Choice Movie: Dance, "The Proposal," Teen Choice Awards (2010); Named as "One of the 10 Most Fascinating People of 2010," Barbara Walters Special (2010); Inductee, California Hall of Fame (2010); Entertainer of the Year, Associated Press (2010); Named Honorary Forest Ranger, U.S. Career Achievement Award, Television Critics Association Awards (2009); Disney Legend Award (2009); Lifetime Achievement Award, Gold Derby Awards (2008); Pop Culture Award, "The Golden Girls," TV Land Awards (2008); Groundbreaking Show, "The Mary Tyler Moore Show," TV Land Awards (2004); Quintessential Non-Traditional Family, "The Golden Girls," TV Land Awards (2003); Funniest Female Guest Appearance in a TV Series, "Ally McBeal," American Comedy Awards (2000); Outstanding Guest Actress in a Comedy Series, "The John Larroquette Show," Primetime Emmy Awards (1996); Inductee, Academy of Television Arts & Sciences Hall of Fame (1995); Star, Hollywood Walk of Fame (1995); Lifetime Achievement Award in Comedy, American Comedy Awards (1990); Living Legacy Award, Women's International Center (WIC) (1988); Humane Award, American Veterinary Medical Association (1987); Funniest Female Performer in a TV Series (Leading Role), Network, Cable or Syndication, "The Golden Girls," American Comedy Awards (1987); Outstanding Lead Actress in a Comedy Series, "The Golden Girls," Primetime Emmy Awards (1986); Female Star of the Year, Golden Apple Awards (1986); Outstanding Host or Hostess in a Game or Audience Participation Show, "Just Men!," Daytime Emmy Awards (1983); Outstanding Continuing Performance by a Supporting Actress in a Comedy Series, "The Mary Tyler Moore Show," Primetime Emmy Awards (1976); Golden Ike Award, Pacific Pioneer Broadcasters (1976); Genii Award, American Women in Radio and Television (1976); Outstanding Continuing Performance by a Supporting Actress in a Comedy Series, "The Mary Tyler Moore Show," Primetime Emmy Awards (1975); Recognized as a Kentucky Colonel, Commonwealth of Kentucky **MEM:** American Federation of Television and Radio Artists; American Humane; Greater Los Angeles Zoo Association

WHITE, CANDIS MARY, T: Owner **I:** Cosmetics **CN:** Crowned with Beauty **DOB:** 12/16/1985 **PB:** Manassas **SC:** VA/USA **PT:** Mark Wallace Dillon; Rebecca Hart Giles **MS:** Single **CT:** Certified Cosmetologist, Long Island Beauty School (2004) **C:** Sole Owner, Crowned with Beauty, Austin, TX (2016-Present) **CW:** Featured, Austin Women (2019) **AW:** Listee, Women to Watch, Austin Women Magazine; Leadership Award **AS:** Ms. White attributes her success to a lot of hard work, as well as her education, and her relationships with her family and God. **B/I:** Ever since Ms. White was a young girl, she loved doing hair. It quickly became a passion. In addition, she worked for other salons before starting her own. From her time in various salons, Ms. White gathered the necessary experience to start her business, Crowned with Beauty, in 2016. **AV:** Golfing; Spending time with dogs; Spending time with family **RE:** Christian **THT:** Ms. White's motto is, "Invest in your hair, it's the crown you never take off."

WHITE, DANA, T: President; Sports Association Executive **CN:** Ultimate Fighting Championship (UFC) **DOB:** 07/28/1969 **PB:** Manchester **SC:** CT/USA **PT:** Dana White; June White **MS:** Married **SPN:** Anne Stella (1996) **CH:** Dana III; Aidan; Savannah **ED:** Coursework, University of Massachusetts **C:** President, Ultimate Fighting Championship (UFC) (2000-Present); Co-owner, Zuffa LLC (2001-2016); Manager, Tito Ortiz, Chuck Liddell, Ultimate Fighting Championship (UFC) (2000); Founder, Dana White Enterprises (1992); Boxing Trainer; Group Exercise Instructor; Aerobics Instructor **CIV:** Donor, $100,000, Former High School to Fund Renovations to Their Athletic Facilities (2011); Donor, $50,000 for a Liver Transplant to Tuptim Jadnooleum (2010); Founder, Boxing Program for Inner City Children **CW:** Executive Producer, "Making it Against All Odds" (2019); Executive Producer, "UFC 25 Years in Short" (2018); Executive Producer, "UFC Embedded: Vlog Series" (2014-2018); Appearance, "It's Always Sunny in Philadelphia" (2017); Executive Producer, "Mayweather vs. McGregor Embedded" (2017); Executive Producer, "UFC Fight Flashback" (2015-2017); Executive Producer, "UFC: Road to the Octagon" (2012-2017); Executive Producer, "UFC 200 Greatest Fighters of All Time" (2016); Executive Producer, "UFC Ultimate Insider" (2012-2016); Executive Producer, "The Ultimate Fighter" (2009-2016); Appearance, "Silicon Valley" (2015); Executive Producer, "UFC: Best of 2015" (2015); Executive Producer, "The Ultimate Fighter: Brazil" (2015); Executive Producer, "UFC: Best of 2014" (2014); Executive Producer, "UFC Presents: Mana: B.J. Penn" (2014); Himself, "Ridiculousness" (2013); Actor, "The League" (2013); Executive Producer, "Forrest Griffin: The Ultimate Fighter" (2012); Executive Producer, "UFC on FOX 5: Road to the Octagon" (2012); Executive Producer, "Madso's War" (2010); Executive Producer, "UFC 110" Nogeira vs. Velasquez" (2010); Executive Producer, "UFC 105: Couture vs. Vera" (2009); Executive Producer, "Joe Rogan: Talking Monkeys in Space" (2009); Executive Producer, "UFC 95: Sanchez vs. Stevenson" (2009); Executive Producer, "UFC 87: Seek and Destroy" (2008); Executive Producer, "UFC: Silva vs. Irvin" (2008); Executive Producer, "UFC 86: Jackson vs. Griffin" (2008); Executive Producer, "UFC 85: Bedlam" (2008); Executive Producer, "UFC 84: Ill Will" (2008); Executive Producer, "UFC 83: Serra vs. St. Pierre 2" (2008); Executive Producer, "UFC Fight Night: Florian vs. Lauzon" (2008); Executive Producer, "UFC 82: Pride of a Champion" (2008); Executive Producer, "UFC 81: Breaking Point" (2008); Executive Producer, "UFC Fight Night: Swick vs Burkman" (2008); Executive Producer, "UFC 80: Rapid Fire" (2008); Executive Producer, "UFC 79: Nemesis" (2007); Executive Producer, "UFC: Best of 2007" (2007); Executive Producer, "UFC 78: Validation" (2007); Executive Producer, "UFC: Ultimate Ultimate Knockouts" (2007); Executive Producer, "UFC Hostile Territory" (2007); Executive Producer, "UFC 76: Knockout" (2007); Executive Producer, "UFC Fight Night: Thomas vs Florian" (2007); Executive Producer, "UFC 75: Champion vs. Champion" (2007); Executive Producer, "UFC 74: Respect" (2007); Executive Producer, "UFC 74: Stacked" (2007); Executive Producer, "UFC 72: Victory" (2007); Executive Producer, "UFC 71: Liddell vs. Jackson" (2007); Executive Producer, "UFC 70: Nations Collide" (2007); Executive Producer, "UFC: Fight Night 9" (2007); Executive Producer, "UFC 68: The Uprising" (2007); Executive Producer, "UFC 67: All or Nothing" (2007); Executive Producer, "UFC: Fight Night 8" (2007); Executive Producer, "UFC 66: Liddell vs. Ortiz" (2006); Executive Producer, "UFC: Fight Night 7" (2006); Executive Producer, "UFC 65: Bad Intentions" (2006); Executive Producer, "UFC

64: Unstoppable" (2006); Executive Producer, "Ortiz vs. Shamrock 3: The Final Chapter" (2006); Executive Producer, "UFC 63: Hughes vs. Penn" (2006); Executive Producer, "UFC 62: Liddell vs. Sobral" (2006); Executive Producer, "UFC 61: Bitter Rivals" (2006); Executive Producer, "UFC 59: Reality Check" (2006); Executive Producer, "UFC 57: Liddell vs. Couture 3" (2006); Executive Producer, "UFC 56: Full Force" (2005); Executive Producer, "UFC 5: Fury" (2005); Executive Producer, "UFC 53: Heavy Hitters" (2005); Producer, "UFC: Ultimate Knockouts 3" (2004); Executive Producer, "UFC 50: The War of '04" (2004); Executive Producer, Producer, "UFC 47: It's On!" (2004); Producer, "UFC 46: Supernatural" (2004); Executive Producer, "UFC 45: Revolution" (2003); Executive Producer, "UFC 43: Meltdown" (2003); Executive Producer, "UFC 42: Sudden Impact" (2003); Executive Producer, "UCF 41: Onslaught" (2003); Executive Producer, "UFC 40: Vendetta" (2002) **AW:** Named Promoter of the Year, Wrestling Observer Newsletter Awards (2005-2013, 2015-2016); Named Nevada Sportsman of the Year (2009); Named Leading Man of the Year, World MMA Awards (2008-2019); Named Among the "Most Influential People in the World of Sports," Business Week (Now Bloomberg Businessweek) (2008); Named Among the "Most Influential People in the World of Sports," SportsBusiness (2008); Patriot Award, Armed Forces Foundation

WHITE, HILARY, T: Accountant **I:** Government Administration/Government Relations/Government Services **CN:** Essex County Treasurer's Office **MS:** Married **ED:** BA in Accounting and Business Management, State University of New York Plattsburgh (2012) **C:** Accountant, Essex County Treasurer's Office (2020-Present); Chief Financial Officer, Accountant, Human Resources Manager, Housing Assistance Program of Essex County, Inc. (2016-2020); Member Service Representative, UFirst Federal Credit Union, (2015-2016); Partner, Stewart's Shops (2014-2015); Part-Time Sales Association, Dressbarn (2012-2014); District Auditor, Stewart's Shops (2013-2014); Finance Clark, Evergreen Valley Nursing Home (2012-2013); Administrative Assistant, Evergreen Valley Nursing Home (2012); Medical Records Coordinator, Evergreen Valley Nursing Home (2012); Intern, Evergreen Valley Nursing Home (2012); Lifeguard Program Instructor, American Red Cross (2007-2010) **MEM:** SHRM **AS:** Ms. White attributes her success to her failures. By learning from her failures, she has been able to grow in any position she holds. **B/I:** Ms. White became involved in her profession because she took an aptitude test during middle school that told her that her interests were relative to either being a teacher or an accountant. **THT:** Ms. White states, "You can't change what has already been done. Just be mad for a second and move forward."

WHITE, JAMES, "JIM" MACKEY, T: Management Consultant **I:** Consulting **DOB:** 01/03/1941 **PB:** Washington **SC:** DC/USA **PT:** Mackey White; Florence (Gerlich) White **MS:** Widower **SPN:** Anne Goddin White (03/28/1964) **CH:** Catherine; Eric **ED:** MBA, University of Delaware (1968); Postgraduate Coursework, University of Illinois (1963-1964); BS in Mathematics, Duke University (1963) **C:** President, International Information Tech., Inc., Evergreen, CO (1994-Present); Vice President, Technical Planning and Architecture, Charles Schwab & Co., San Francisco, CA (1992-1994); Senior Consultant, Telecom, E.I. Du Pont De Nemours & Co., Inc., Wilmington, DE (1988-1992); Manager, Remote Systems Support, E.I. Du Pont De Nemours & Co., Inc., Wilmington, DE (1982-1987); Manager, Systems Development, E.I. Du Pont De Nemours & Co., Inc., Wilmington, DE (1977-1981); Manager, European Computer Systems, E.I. Du Pont De Nemours & Co., Inc. (1972-1976); Supervisor, Telecommunications, E.I. Du Pont De Nemours & Co., Inc., Wilmington, DE (1968-1972) **CR:** Chairman, Steering Committee, Manufacturing Area Protocols **CIV:** Chairman, Save Open Lands, Vistas and Environment, Inc. (2010-Present); Committee to Elect Mauck (2010); President, Floyd Hill Area Property Owners Association (2007-2008); Committee to Elect Amick, Newark, NJ (1986-1992); President, West Chestnut Hill Resident Association, Newark, DE (1986-1988); Las Lomas High School Technical Committee; Walnut Creek School District Technical Committee **AW:** Anne Sullivan Award for Lions Club Service **MEM:** Lions Club International **AS:** Mr. White attributes his success to his experience in management and executive positions. His former experiences amount to a 30-year apprenticeship. **B/I:** Mr. White became involved in his profession through a gradual involvement. For several years, he worked at the Department of Agriculture. After attending graduate school, he realized he wanted to become a professor. However, he later got involved in computer technology. **AV:** Skiing; Learning history; Practicing civic affairs

WHITE, JAMES P., JD, T: Law Educator **I:** Law and Legal Services **DOB:** 09/29/1931 **PB:** Iowa City **SC:** IA/USA **PT:** Raymond Patrick White; Besse (Kanak) White **MS:** Widowed **SPN:** Anna R. Seim (07/02/1964) **ED:** Honorary LLD, Butler university (2016); Honorary LLD, Atlanta's John Marshall Law School (2013); Honorary LHD, Barry University (2005); LLD, Western New England College (Now Western New England University) (2002); Honorary LLD, Seattle University (2001); Honorary LLD, New England Law (2001); Honorary LLD, Roger Williams University (1999); Honorary LLD, California Western School of Law (1997); Honorary LLD, Quinnipiac University (1995); Honorary LLD, Southwestern University (1995); Honorary LLD, Campbell University (1993); Honorary JD, Whittier College (1992); Honorary LLD, Widener University (1989); Honorary LLD, University of the Pacific (1984); LLM, The George Washington University (1959); JD, The University of Iowa (1956); BA, The University of Iowa (1953) **C:** Professor Emeritus, Indiana University Robert H. McKinney School of Law, Indianapolis, IN (2002-Present); Director of Agricultural Law Research Program, Professor of Law, Indiana University Robert H. McKinney School of Law, Indianapolis, IN (1967-2002); Dean, Academy Development and Planning, Special Assistant to Chancellor, Indiana University, Indianapolis, IN (1974-1983); Director of Urban Legal Studies Program, Indiana University Robert H. McKinney School of Law, Indianapolis, IN (1971-1974); Professor, Assistant Dean, University of North Dakota School of Law (1963-1967); Associate Professor, Acting Dean, University of North Dakota School of Law (1962-1963); Assistant Professor, University of North Dakota School of Law, Grand Forks, ND (1959-1962); Teaching Fellow, GW Law (1958-1959) **CR:** Consultant Emeritus (2001); Consultant, Legal Education, American Bar Association (ABA) (1974-2001); Member, North Dakota, Commission on Uniform State Laws (Now The National Conference of Commissioners on Uniform State Laws) (1961-1966) **CIV:** Trustee, Butler University, Atlanta's John Marshall Law School, and Indianapolis Museum of Art **MIL:** First Lieutenant, United States Air Force (1956-1958); Captain, Judge Advocate General Corps **CW:** Contributor, Papers to Technology Literature **AW:** Kutak Award Medal, ABA (2001); Thomas More Award, St. Mary's University (1965); Carnegie Postdoctoral Fellow, University of Michigan Center for Study Higher Education (1964-1965); Named to Iowa City High School Hall of Fame; Distinguished Alumnus Award, University of Iowa; Sagamore of the Wabash Award, State of Indiana **MEM:** Chair, Fulbright Committee for Awards in Law, Society for Advanced Legal Studies (SALS), Institute of Advanced Legal Studies, England, United Kingdom (1989-1992); Fellow, Commissioner, China-US Commission Legal Education; Society for Advanced Legal Studies (SALS), Institute of Advanced Legal Studies, England, United Kingdom; Life Member, American Bar Foundation; Distinguished Fellow, Indianapolis Bar Foundation; American Bar Association (ABA); Indianapolis Bar Association; Life Member, American Law Institute; The Iowa State Bar Association; Indiana State Bar Association; Woodstock Club, Indianapolis, IN; Order of the Coif **BAR:** District of Columbia (1959); Supreme Court of the United States (1959); Iowa (1956) **MH:** Albert Nelson Marquis Lifetime Achievement Award; Marquis Who's Who Top Professional **B/I:** Mr. White became involved in his profession because he was interested in law from his childhood. He had relatives who were lawyers and judges. **RE:** Roman Catholic

WHITE, LAURA KATHERINE, CAPE, BAE, BA, T: Entrepreneur, Color and Image Consultant, Adapted Physical Educator **I:** Education/Educational Services **CN:** Los Angeles Unified School District **DOB:** 09/12/1959 **PB:** Glendale **SC:** CA/USA **PT:** Lawrence Russell Moss; Jane (Olsen) Edwards **MS:** Married **SPN:** Nicolas V. White **CH:** Nicole Evelyn; Katie Elaina **ED:** BA in Speech Pathology, California State University (1996); BAE, Arizona State University (1982); AA, Glendale Community College (1979) **CT:** National Certification in Adapted Physical Education (APE)(2016); Teacher Credential, Secondary English with Authorizations in Dance and Physical Education; Multi-Subject Credential with an Authorization in APE **C:** Teacher, Los Angeles Unified School District; Substitute Teacher, Glendale Unified School District **CIV:** Volunteer Special Olympics Coach; Volunteer Tutor **AW:** Recognition of Perfect Attendance, Los Angeles Unified School District; Appreciation of Years of Service, Los Angeles Unified School District **MEM:** Vice-Chair, CAPHERD; Vice-Chair, United Teachers Los Angeles; Kappa Delta Sorority Alumni **MH:** Albert Nelson Marquis Lifetime Achievement Award **AS:** Ms. White attributes her success to the exceptional professors and university lecturers she encountered, like Marci Pope from California State University. Their strong presence in the world of adapted physical education was an amazing influence. **B/I:** Ms. White feels she is a natural at teaching. She always wanted to help humanity, and she thought being a teacher would be the best way to achieve success. **AV:** Cherishing pet dogs; Creatively stitching; Playing banjo; Dancing; Studying; Reading; Swimming; Walking; Playing tennis

WHITE, MILES D., T: Chairman, Chief Executive Officer **I:** Engineering **CN:** Abbott Laboratories **DOB:** 03/10/1955 **PB:** Minneapolis **SC:** MN/USA **MS:** Married **SPN:** Kim White **ED:** MBA, Stanford University (1980); BS in Mechanical Engineering, Stanford University (1978); Student, Culver Military Academy **C:** Chairman, Chief Executive Officer, Abbott Laboratories (1999-Present); Chief Executive Officer, Abbott Laboratories (1998-1999); Executive Vice President, Abbott Laboratories (1998-1999); Senior Vice President Diagnostic Operations, Abbott Laboratories (1994-1998); Vice President Diagnostic System & Operations, Abbott Laboratories (1993-1994); Joined, Abbott Laboratories (1984); Consultant, McKinsey & Company **CR:** Member, Board of Directors, McDonald's Corporation (2009-Present); Board of Directors, Federal Reserve Bank (2002-Present); Member, Board of Directors, Abbott Laboratories (1998-Present); Motorola Inc. (2005-2009); Chairman, Federal Reserve Bank (2005-2007); The Tribune Co. (2005-2006); Federal Reserve Bank, Chicago, IL (2002-2004); Member, Board of Directors, Caterpillar Inc. **CIV:** Member, Board of Trustees, Culver Educational Foundation; Member, Board of Trustees, Joffrey Ballet, Chicago, IL; Member, Board of Trustees, Northwestern University; Chairman, Board of Trustees, Field Museum of Natural History, Chicago, IL; Stanford Advisory Council on Interdisciplinary Biosciences; Stanford Graduate School of Business Advisory Council **AW:** Executive of the Year, Scrip (2009); Listed, "America's Most Powerful People," Forbes; Recognized as "One of the World's 30 Best CEOS," Barron's (11 Consecutive Years) **MEM:** Fellow, American Academy of Arts and Sciences; Former Chairman, Pharmaceutical Research and Manufacturers of America; Former Chairman, Economic Club of Chicago; Chairman, Executives' Club of Chicago; Life Member, Kellogg School of Management; The Business Council

WHITE, SHAUN ROGER, T: Professional Snowboarder, Professional Skateboarder, Olympic Athlete **I:** Athletics **DOB:** 09/03/1986 **PB:** San Diego **SC:** CA/USA **PT:** Kathy White; Roger White **C:** Professional Skateboarder (2003-Present); Professional Snowboarder, Burton Snowboarding Team (1999-Present); Skateboarder, Tony Hawk Gigantic Skatepark Tour (2002); Founder, Shaun White Enterprises; Designer, The White Collection **CR:** Member, U.S. Snowboarding Team, Winter Olympic Games, Vancouver, Canada (2010); Member, U.S. Snowboarding Team, Winter Olympic Games, Turin, Italy (2006) **CIV:** Contributor, Make-A-Wish Foundation (2008-Present); Contributor, Fundraiser, St. Jude Children's Research Hospital, Boys & Girls Club, Target House **CW:** Cameo, "Henry Danger" (2018); Executive Producer, "Cloud 9" (2014); Cameo, "Cloud 9" (2014); Actor, "Stretch" (2014); Voice Actor, Cameo, "American Dad!" (2013); Voice Actor, "The Smurfs 2" (2013); Cameo, "Friends with Benefits" (2011); Cameo, "Extreme Makeover: Home Edition" (2011); Guest, "The Tonight Show with Jay Leno" (2010); Guest Editor, Snowboarder Magazine (2008); Cameo, "First Descent" (2005); Appeared, "The Shaun White Album" (2004); Guitarist, Bad Things; Appeared, Numerous Video Games **AW:** ESPY Award for Best Olympic Moment (2018); ESPY Award for Best Male U.S. Olympic Athlete (2010, 2018); Named Among "30 Under 30," Forbes (2016); ESPY Award for Best Male Action Sports Athlete (2010, 2011, 2012); Teen Choice Award for Choice Male Athlete (2011); "Champion of the Board," Spike TV Guys' Choice Awards (2007, 2010); Laureus World Sports Award for Action Sportsperson of the Year (2008); ESPY Award for Best U.S. Olympian (2006); ESPY Award for Best Action Sports Athlete (2003); Teen Choice Award for Choice Male Athlete (2006); Revolver Golden Gods Award for "Most Metal Athlete"; Two-Time Rider of the Year, Transworld Snowboarding

WHITE, TERESA, CFP, T: Chief Executive Officer, Owner **I:** Financial Services **DOB:** 08/11/1948 **PB:** Honesdale **SC:** PA/USA **PT:** James Bernard Jensen; LaVaughn Beatrice (Tomlinson) Nixon Jensen **MS:** Married **SPN:** Leo H. White **ED:** Coursework, San Antonio College (1966-1967); Coursework, University of the Incarnate Word (1965-1966) **CT:** Certified Financial Planner, College for Financial Planning, Denver, CO (1984-Present); Registered Investment Adviser, Securities and Exchange Commission **C:** Chief Executive Officer, Money Managers Inc. (1981-Present); Private Marketing Consultant, San Antonio, TX (1978-1980); Agent, Sales Manager, B&B Associates, San Antonio, TX

(1977-1978); Organizer, Negotiator, National Maritime Union, Galveston, TX (1973-1976); Teacher, New Age School, San Antonio, TX (1973-1976); Vice President, Outdoor Sports Center, San Antonio, TX (1968-1973) **CR:** Member, National Educational Committee, Sun American Securities Inc. (1999-2001); Adjunct Instructor, College for Financial Planning, Denver, CO (1985-1998); Adjunct Instructor, St. Mary's University, San Antonio, TX (1985-1988); Arbitrator, National Association of Securities Dealers; Expert Witness in Adviser Compliance, Legal Community **CIV:** Member, Board of Directors, Big Brother Big Sister Alamo Area, San Antonio, TX (1985); Member, Big Brother Big Sister Alamo Area, San Antonio, TX (1981); Member, Board, See the Change Educational Foundation; Member, Board of Directors, Army Residence Community **CW:** Detailed Written Policies and Procedures Manual with Turn Key System for Practice Management for Client Centric, All Referral, Independent Registered Investment Adviser and Comprehensive Financial Planning **AW:** Named Among the "25 Largest Financial Planning and Advisory Firms" (2010-2017); Five Star Wealth Adviser, Central Texas Region, Texas Monthly (2010); Business Woman of the Year for Texas, Business Advisory Council, National Republican Congressional Committee (2003, 2004); Presidential Citation, Chamber of Commerce (1982) **MEM:** State Chairperson, Institute of Certified Financial Planners (1991-Present); Financial Planners Association; Certified Financial Planner Board of Standards; Association for the Management of Innovation; Institute of Certified Financial Planners **AS:** Ms. White attributes her success to perseverance. **B/I:** Ms. White became involved in her profession because a financial planner developed a plan for her in her early work years and, shortly after, she became disabled during a serious auto accident. The comprehensive insurance and investment portfolio he designed for her allowed her to emerge with more wealth than she previously had. He saved Ms. White's financial life. **PA:** Republican **RE:** Christian

WHITEHEAD, COLSON, T: Novelist **I:** Writing and Editing **DOB:** 11/06/1969 **PB:** New York **SC:** NY/USA **MS:** Married **SPN:** Julie Barer **CH:** Two Children **ED:** Guggenheim Fellowship, John Simon Guggenheim Memorial Foundation (2013); Dorothy and Lewis B. Cullman Center for Scholars and Writers Fellowship, The New York Public Library (2007); MacArthur Fellowship, John D. and Catherine T. MacArthur Foundation (2002); BA, Harvard College, Harvard University (1991) **C:** Columnist, The New York Times Magazine (2015-Present); Author, Numerous Books, Short Stories, and Essays (1999-Present); Writer, The Village Voice (1991-1993); Writer-in-residence, Vassar College, University of Richmond, University of Wyoming; Instructor, Princeton University, New York University, University of Houston, Columbia University, Brooklyn College, Hunter College, Wesleyan University **CW:** Author, "The Nickel Boys" (2019); Author, "The Match," The New Yorker (2019); Featured, Cover, Time (2019); Author, "The Underground Railroad" (2016); Author, "The Noble Hustle: Poker, Beef Jerky & Death" (2014); Author, "Occasional Dispatches from the Republic of Anhedonia," Grantland, ESPN (2013); Author, "A Psychotronic Childhood," The New Yorker (2012); Author, "Hard Times in the Uncanny Valley," Grantland ESPN (2012); Author, "Zone One" (2011); Author, "Sag Harbor" (2009); Author, "Apex Hides the Hurt" (2006); Author, "Down in Front," Granta (2004); Author, "The Colossus of New York" (2003); Author, "John Henry Days" (2001); Author, "Lost and Found," The New York Times Magazine (2001); Author, "The Intuitionist" (1999); Author, Nonfiction, Essays, Reviews,

Numerous Publications, Including The New York Times, The New Yorker, Granta, and Harper's **AW:** International Dublin Literary Award, "The Underground Railroad" (2018); Pulitzer Prize for Fiction, "The Underground Railroad" (2017); Arthur C. Clarke Award, "The Underground Railroad" (2017); Booker Prize, "The Underground Railroad" (2017); Hurston/Wright Award for Fiction, "The Underground Railroad," Zora Neale Hurston/Richard Wright Foundation (2017); Carnegie Medal for Excellence in Fiction, "The Underground Railroad" (2017); National Book Award for Fiction, "The Underground Railroad" (2016); John Dos Passos Prize for Literature (2012); Whiting Award (2000); Finalist, Hurston-Wright Legacy Award, "Zone One"; Finalist, Hurston-Wright Legacy Award, "Sag Harbor"; Finalist, PEN/Faulkner Award for Fiction, "Sag Harbor"; PEN Oakland/Josephine Miles Literary Award, "Apex Hides the Hurt"; Finalist, Los Angeles Times Book Prize, "John Henry Days"; Finalist, National Book Critics Circle, "John Henry Days"; Finalist, Pulitzer Prize, "John Henry Days"; Anisfield-Wolf Book Award, "John Henry Days"; Young Lions Fiction Award, "John Henry Days"; Finalist, Hemingway Foundation/PEN Award, "The Intuitionist"; Quality Paperback Book Club New Voices Award, "The Intuitionist"

WHITEHOUSE, SHELDON, T: U.S. Senator, Lawyer **I:** Government Administration/Government Relations/Government Services **DOB:** 10/20/1955 **PB:** New York **SC:** NY/USA **PT:** Charles Sheldon Whitehouse; Mary Celine (Rand) Whitehouse **MS:** Married **SPN:** Sandra Christine Thornton (09/20/1986) **CH:** Two children **ED:** JD, University of Virginia School of Law (1982); BA, Yale University (1978) **C:** U.S. Senator, State of Rhode Island (2007-Present); Attorney General, State of Rhode Island, Providence, RI (1999-2003); U.S. Attorney, District of Rhode Island, The U.S. Department of Justice, Providence, RI (1994-1998); Director, Department of Business Regulation, State of Rhode Island, Providence, RI (1992-1994); Director, Governor Policy Office, State of Rhode Island, Providence, RI (1991-1992); Executive Counsel to Governor, State of Rhode Island, Providence, RI (1991); Assistant Attorney General, State of Rhode Island, Providence, RI (1989-1990); Chief Regulatory Unit, State of Rhode Island, Providence, RI (1988-1990); Special Assistant Attorney General, State of Rhode Island, Providence, RI (1985-1990); Attorney, State of Rhode Island, Providence, RI (1983-1984) **AW:** Public Achievement Award, Common Cause (1999); Secret Service Honor Award, U.S. Department of the Treasury (1998); Robert M. Goodrich Award for Outstanding Public Employee, RIPEC (1993) **BAR:** Supreme Court of the United States (1986); United States Court of Appeals for the First Circuit (1984); United States District Court District of Rhode Island (1984); Rhode Island Bar Association (1983); The West Virginia Bar Association (1982) **PA:** Democrat

WHITESIDE, HASSAN NIAM, T: Professional Basketball Player **I:** Athletics **CN:** Portland Trail Blazers **DOB:** 06/13/1989 **PB:** Gastonia **SC:** NC/USA **PT:** Hassan Arbubakrr; Debbie Whiteside **MS:** Single **ED:** Coursework, Marshall University; Diploma, The Patterson School, Lenoir, NC **C:** Basketball Player, Portland Trail Blazers (2019-Present); Basketball Player, Miami Heat (2014-2019); Basketball Player, Iowa Energy (2014); Basketball Player, Memphis Grizzlies (2014); Basketball Player, Toronto Raptors (2014); Basketball Player, Jiangsu Tongxi (2014); Basketball Player, Al Mouttahed Tripoli (2013-2014); Basketball Player, Sichuan Blue Whales (2013); Basketball Player, Rio Grande Valley Vipers (2013); Basketball Player, Sioux Falls Skyforce, NBA Development League (2012-2013);

Basketball Player, Sacramento Kings (2010-2012) **CIV:** Organizer, Nassan's Place (2012-Present) **AW:** Sporting News Second-Team All-American (2010); Conference USA Defensive Player of the Year (2010); Conference USA Freshman of the Year (2010); Conference USA Seven-Time Rookie of the Week (2010)

WHITMAN, MARGARET, T: Chief Executive Officer **I:** Technology **CN:** Quibi **DOB:** 08/04/1956 **PB:** Cold Spring Harbor **SC:** NY/USA **PT:** Hendricks Hallett Whitman Jr.; Margaret (Goodhue) Cushing **MS:** Married **SPN:** Griffith Rutherford Harsh IV (1980) **CH:** Griff; Will **ED:** Honorary Doctorate, Carnegie Mellon University (2017); MBA, Harvard Business School, Harvard University (1979); BA in Economics, Princeton University, With Honors (1977); Diploma, Cold Spring Harbor High School (1974) **C:** Chief Executive Officer, Employee, Quibi (2018-Present); Chairman, President, Chief Executive Officer, Hewlett-Packard Company, Palo Alto, CA (2014-Present); President, Chief Executive Officer, Hewlett-Packard Company, Palo Alto, CA (2011-2014); Part-Time Strategic Advisor, Kleiner Perkins Caulfield & Byers (KPCB), Menlo Park, CA (2011); Republican Nominee, Governor of California (2009-2010); Co-Chair, Republican Victory (2008); President, Chief Executive Officer, eBay, Inc., San Jose, CA (1998-2008); General Manager, Preschool Division, Hasbro Inc. (1997-1998); President, Chief Executive Officer, Florists' Transworld Delivery (FTD) (1995-1997); President, Stride Rite Division, Stride Rite Corporation (1994-1995); Executive Vice President, Keds Division, Stride Rite Corporation (1993-1994); Corporate Vice President, Strategic Planning, Stride Rite Corporation (1992-1993); Senior Vice President, Marketing & Consumer Products Division, The Walt Disney Company, Burbank, CA (1989-1992); Vice President, Bain & Company, Inc. (1982-1989); Brand Assistant, The Procter & Gamble Co. (1979-1981) **CR:** Alternate Governor of MLS Board of Governors, Minority Owner, FC Cincinnati (2019-Present); Member, Board of Directors, The Procter & Gamble Company (2011-Present, 2003-2008); Member, Board of Directors, Zaarly (2011-Present); Member, Board of Directors, Arcsight, Inc. (2011-Present); Member, Board of Directors, Hewlett-Packard Company (2011-Present); Member, Board, Immortals Gaming Club (2018); Member, Board of Directors, Zipcar, Inc. (2011-2013); Member, Board of Directors, Dreamworks Animation (SKG), Inc. (2005-2008); Member, Board of Directors, Staples Inc. (1999-2008); Member, Board of Directors, Gap Inc. (2003-2006); Member, Board of Directors, The Goldman Sachs Group Inc. (2001-2002); Member, Board of Directors, eBay, Inc. (1998-2009); Member, Board of Directors, eBay Foundation; Member, Board of Directors, Summit Public Schools **CIV:** National Board Chair, Teach for America (2020-Present); Investor, Board of Directors, Immortals Gaming Club (2018-Present); Board of Directors, The Nature Conservancy (2011-Present); Founder, Griffin R. Harsh IV and Margaret C. Whitman Charitable Foundation (2006-Present); Trustee, Princeton University **CW:** Commencement Speaker, Carnegie Mellon University (2017); Co-Author, "The Power of Many: Values for Success in Business and in Life" (2010) **AW:** Named, 50 Most Powerful Women in Business, Fortune Magazine (2011-2015, 1998-2007); Named, 100 Most Powerful Women, Forbes Magazine (2012-2014, 2010, 2005-2007); Named, 50 Most Important People on the Web, PC World (2007); Webby Lifetime Achievement Award (2007); Named, 50 Women to Watch, Wall Street Journal (2005-2006); Named, 100 Most Influential People in the World, TIME Magazine (2004-2005);

Named, Best CEO's, Worth Magazine (2002) **MEM:** Fellow, American Academy of Arts & Sciences **AV:** Fly fishing **PA:** Republican

WHITNEY, RICHARD F. II, T: Senior Managing Director **I:** Real Estate **CN:** Transwestern **MS:** Married **SPN:** Kristin **CH:** Gehrig; Gwendolyn; Graelyn; Gabriella **ED:** BArch, Virginia Polytechnic Institute and State University, VA (1999) **C:** Senior Managing Director, Transwestern (2018-Present); Managing Director, Transwestern (2015-2018); Senior Vice President, DTZ (Now Cushman & Wakefield) (2011-2015); Vice President, Jones Lang LaSalle IP, Inc. (2006-2010); Assistant Vice President, Spaulding & Slye (2000-2006) **AW:** Tenant Project of the Year, Mid-Atlantic Construction Magazine **MEM:** AIA **B/I:** Mr. Whitney became involved in his profession because he has always loved historical houses and buildings, and later based his choice of college on both the pursuit of an architecture degree and the opportunity to play soccer. When he began working as an architect, he loved the feeling of satisfaction from a finished product. **AV:** Coaching youth soccer, basketball, and baseball **THT:** Mr. Whitney was instrumental in the construction of the first TSA headquarters in the aftermath of 9/11. He was also involved in the second construction project in all of Washington, DC, and built the only rooftop basketball court in the city.

WHITSON, PEGGY ANNETTE, T: Astronaut **I:** Other **DOB:** 02/09/1960 **PB:** Mount Ayr **SC:** IA/USA **PT:** Earl Keith S.; Beth Avalee (Walters) S. **MS:** Married **SPN:** Clarence Felton Sams (05/06/1989) **ED:** Robert A. Welch Postdoctoral Fellowship, Rice University (1985-1986); PhD in Biochemistry, Rice University (1985); BS in Biology and Chemistry, Iowa Wesleyan University, Summa Cum Laude (1981) **C:** Chief, Astronaut Corps, NASA (2009-2012); Commander, Expedition 16, International Space Station, NASA (2007-2017); Chief, Station Operations Branch, Astronaut Office, NASA (2005); Deputy Chief, Astronaut Office, NASA (2003-2005); Commander, NEEMO 5 Mission, Aquarius Underwater Laboratory (2003); Flight Engineer, Endeavor on Expedition 5, Kennedy Space Center, NASA (2002); Lead, Crew Test Support Team in Russia, Johnson Space Center, NASA (1998-1999); Astronaut Candidate, Astronaut Trainee (1996-1998); Adjunct Assistant Professor, Maybee Laboratory for Biochemical and Genetic Engineering, Rice University (1997); Co-Chair, U.S.-Russian Mission Science Working Group (1995-1996); Deputy Division Chief, Medical Sciences Division, Johnson Space Center, NASA (1993-1996); Project Scientist, Shuttle-Mir Program (1992-1995); Deputy Division Chief, Medical Sciences Division, Johnson Space Center, NASA (1992-1995); Project Scientist, Shuttle-Mir Program (1992-1995); Adjunct Assistant Professor, Department of Internal Medicine, Department of Human Biological Chemistry and Genetics, University of Texas Medical Branch (1991-1997); Technical Monitor, Biomedical Operations and Research Branch, Biochemistry Research Laboratories (1991-1993); Payload Element Developer, Bone Cell Research Experiment (1991-1992); Member, U.S.-USSR Joint Working Group in Space Medicine and Biology (1991-1992); Research Biologist, Biomedical Operations and Research Branch, Johnson Space Center, NASA (1989-1993); Supervisor, Biochemistry Research Group, KRUG International, Johnson Space Center, NASA (1988-1989); National Research Council Resident Research Associate, Johnson Space Center, NASA **CR:** Chair, Astronaut Selection Board, NASA (2009); Member, Astronaut Selection Board, NASA (2004) **CW:** Contributor, Articles on Biochemistry, Journal of Biological Chemistry and Journal of Cellular Physiology

AW: Women in Space Science Award (2019); Time 100 List, Time (2018); Inductee, International Air and Space Hall of Fame (2018); Inductee, Iowa Aviation Hall of Fame (2011); BioHouston Women in Science Award (2011); Houston's 50 Most Influential Women of 2011 (2011); Medal for Merit in Space Exploration for Outstanding Contribution to the Development of International Cooperation in Manned Space Flight (2011); Texas Women on the Move Award (2010); Distinguished Alumni Award, Rice University (2010); First Lady of Iowa Award, High School Girls' Athletic Union (2010); Hero of Valor, Iowa Transportation Museum (2009); Exceptional Service Medal, NASA (1995, 2003, 2006, 2008); Space Flight Medal, NASA (2002, 2008); Lion's Club Mount Ayr Elementary Science Lab Dedication, Peggy Whitson Science Center (2008); Outstanding Leadership Medal, NASA (2006); Distinguished Alumni Award, Iowa Wesleyan University (2002); Space Act Board Award, NASA (1995, 1998); Group Achievement Award for Shuttle-Mir Program (1996); American Astronautical Society Randolph Lovelace II Award (1995); Tech Brief Award, NASA (1995); Silver Snoopy Award, NASA (1995); Certificate of Commendation, NASA (1994); Sustained Superior Performance Award, NASA (1990); Krug International Merit Award (1989); National Research Council Resident Research Associate, Johnson Space Center, NASA (1990); Krug International Merit Award (1989); Orange van Calhoun Scholarship (1980); State of Iowa Scholar (1979); President's Honor Roll (1978-1981); Academic Excellence Award (1978) **MEM:** American Society for Biochemistry and Molecular Biology; New York Academy of Sciences

WHITT, MICHAEL, "MIKE" D., T: Program Manager **I:** Engineering **DOB:** 01/27/1956 **PB:** Asheville **SC:** NC/USA **PT:** Harold Whitt; Shirley Whitt **MS:** Married **SPN:** Mary Duckett Whitt **CH:** Elliot C. Whitt **ED:** ASEE, Pellissippi State Community College, Knoxville, TN (1985) **CT:** Certified, Project Management Professional **C:** Program Manager, Mesa Associates, Incorporated (2000-Present); Design Supervisor, United Engineers and Contractors (1986-2001); Test Engineer, Pratt & Whitney (1984-1986) **MIL:** U.S.S. Inchon, LPH-12 (1981-1983); U.S.S. Puget Sound, AD-38 (1977-1981); United States Navy, IC1 (1976-1983) **CW:** Contributing Author, "A Guide to the Automation Body of Knowledge" (2018); Author, "Successful Instrumentation and Control Systems Design" (2012) **MEM:** Project Management Institute; Control Systems Integrator Association; International Society of Automation **MH:** Marquis Who's Who Top Professional **AS:** Mr. Whitt attributes his success to perseverance. When others stopped, he kept going. He additionally credits a true love for his work. It is also key that Mr. Whitt's career has spanned the computer age. When he started, instrumentation was an electro-mechanical field. The digital age has changed everything, and being there for the entire migration gives him a rare perspective. **B/I:** For Mr. Whitt, engineering was never a family avocation. On joining the Navy, he was given many choices, and selected the one field in which the person was shown working all over the ship. From the anemometers at the end of the mast to the pit sword measuring ship's speed in the keel, the instrument tech saw it all. As a young technician, learning to read prints, he had a strong desire to be the one creating the drawings that he read. After getting out of the Navy, and graduating, all of his work history was related to design and implementation, as opposed to maintenance. **AV:** Golfing; Playing Chess; Reading **PA:** Conservative **RE:** Christian **THT:** Mr. Whitt believes that focusing on the money will never get you where you need to be. Engineering is definitely a worthy profession, and he is glad he was able to contribute.

WHITTINGHAM, M. STANLEY, DPHIL, T: Distinguished Professor **I:** Research **CN:** Binghamton University **DOB:** 12/22/1941 **PB:** Nottingham **SC:** United Kingdom **PT:** William Stanley Whittingham; Dorothy Mary (Findlay) Whittingham **MS:** Married **SPN:** Georgina Judith Andai (03/23/1969) **CH:** Jennifer Judith; Michael Stanley **ED:** DPhil, University of Oxford (1968); MA, University of Oxford (1968); BA in Chemistry, University of Oxford (1964) **C:** Distinguished Professor of Chemistry, Materials Science & Engineering (1988-Present); Director, Chemical Energy Storage, Northeast Center, State University of New York (1988-2021); Honorary Fellow, University of Oxford New College, Oxford, United Kingdom (2020); Vice-chair, Board of Directors, Research Foundation (1995-2001); Vice Provost for Research, State University of New York (1994-2000); Director of Physical Sciences, Schlumberger, Ridgefield, CT (1984-1988); Manager, Chemical Engineering Technology (1980-1984); Staff Member, ExxonMobil Corporation, Linden, NJ (1972-1984); Director, Solid State Sciences (1978-1980); Group Head, Solid State Chemical Physics (1975-1978); Head, Research Associate, Solid State Electrochemistry Group, Materials Center, Stanford University (1968-1972) **CR:** Chief Scientific Officer, NAATBatt International (2017-Present); Consultant, Lecturer in Field, Japan Society for the Promotion of Science Fellow, The University of Tokyo; Vice-chair, Board of Directors, New York Battery and Energy Storage Technology Consortium; Chair, Advisory Board, Clean Energy Incubator, New York State Energy Research and Development Authority (NYSERDA), Binghamton, NY **CW:** Author, Editor, 350 Papers in Field; Author, Five Books **AW:** Nobel Prize in Chemistry (2019); David Turnbull Lectureship Award, Materials Research Society (2018); Senior Scientist Award, International Society for Solid State Ionics (ISSI) (2017); Distinguished Research Award, Binghamton Section, American Chemical Society (2015); Lois B. DeFleur Faculty Prize for Academic Achievement (2015); Lifetime Achievement Technology Award, NAATBatt International (2015); Fellowship, Materials Research Society (2013); Award for Lifetime Contributions to Chemistry, Northeast Regional Meeting, American Chemical Society (2010); Named to Top 40 Innovators for Contributions to Advancing Green Technology, Greentech Media (2010); Chancellor's Award for Excellence in Scholarship and Creative Activities, State University of New York (2007); Outstanding Research Award, Research Foundation, State University of New York (2007); Fellowship, The Electrochemical Society (2004); Battery Research Award, The Electrochemical Society (2002); Japan Society for the Promotion of Science Fellowship, Physics Department, The University of Tokyo (1993); Young Author Award, The Electrochemical Society (1971); Gas Council Scholarship, University of Oxford (1964-1967); Shipley Distinguished Lectureship Award, Clarkson University; Yeager Award for Lifetime Contributions to Battery Science **MEM:** National Academy of Engineering (2018); Fellow, Materials Research Society (2013); Chairman, Binghamton Section, American Chemical Society (1991); Chairman, Solid State Section, American Chemical Society (1987); New York Chairman, The Electrochemical Society (1980-1981); American Physical Society **MH:** Albert Nelson Marquis Lifetime Achievement Award; Marquis Who's Who Top Professional **AS:** Dr. Whittingham attributes his success to thinking outside of the box, perseverance, passion, and teaching new students. **B/I:** Dr. Whittingham was

inspired to enter his profession by his high school teachers, and then his mentor at New College, University of Oxford. **THT:** Dr. Whittingham's motto is, "Do what you like doing. Take risks. Enjoy life."

WHITTINGHAM, MICHAEL STANLEY, T: Chemist **I:** Sciences **DOB:** 12/22/1941 **PB:** Nottingham **SC:** England **PT:** William Stanley Whittingham; Dorothy Mary (Findlay) Whittingham **MS:** Married **SPN:** Dr. Georgina Judith (Andai) Whittingham **CH:** Jenniffer Judith; Michael Stanley **ED:** PhD, University of Oxford (1968); MA, University of Oxford (1967); BA in Chemistry, University of Oxford (1964); Postdoctoral Fellow, Stanford University **C:** Vice Chairman, Board of Directors, Research Foundation (1995-2001); Vice Provost for Research, State University of New York at Binghamton (1994-2000); Director, Institute for Materials Research, State University of New York at Binghamton (1988); Director, Physical Sciences, Schlumberger Limited, Ridgefield, CT (1984-1988); Manager, Chemical Engineering Technology, Stanford University (1980-1984); Director, Solid State Sciences, Stanford University (1978-1980); Group Head, Solid State Chemical Physics, Stanford University (1975-1978); Staff, Exxon Research Company, Linden, NJ (1972); Research Associate, Head, Solid State Electrochemistry Group, Materials Center, Stanford University (1968-1972) **CR:** Chief Scientific Officer, NAATBatt International (2017); Co-Chair, Chemical Energy Storage Study, Department of Education (2007); Director, Northeastern Center for Chemical Energy Storage, State University of New York at Binghamton; Consultant, Lecturer in Field; JSPS Fellow, University of Tokyo **CW:** Co-Author, "Solid-State Chemistry of Inorganic Materials IV," Materials Research Society (2003); Co-Author, "Chemistry of High Temperature Superconductors," American Chemical Society (1987); Co-Author, "Intercalation Chemistry" (1984); Co-Author, "Materials Science in Energy Technology" (1979); Co-Author, "Solid State Chemistry of Energy Conversion and Storage," American Chemical Society (1977); Editor, Papers in Field **AW:** Nobel Prize in Chemistry (2019); Turnbull Award, Materials Research Society (2018); Senior Scientist Award, International Society for Solid State Ionics (2017); Thomson Reuters Citation Laureate (2015); IBA Yeager Award for Lifetime Contribution to Lithium Battery Materials Research (2012); Top 40 Innovators for Contributions to Advancing Green Technology, Greentech Media (2010); Award for Lifetime Contributions, American Chemical Society (2010); Chancellor's Award for Excellence in Scholarship and Creative Activities, Outstanding Research Award, State University of New York at Binghamton (2007); Battery Research Award, Electrochemical Society (2003); Young Author Award, Electrochemical Society (1971); Gas Council Scholarship, Oxford University (1964-1967) **MEM:** Elected Member, National Academy of Engineering (2018-Present); Fellow, Materials Research Society (2013); Fellow, Electrochemical Society (2004); Chairman, Binghamton Section, American Chemical Society (1991); Chairman, Solid State Section, American Chemical Society (1987); New York Chairman, Electrochemical Society (1980-1981); American Physical Society; Materials Research Society

WIBLE, JAMES ORAM, T: Chairman of the Board **I:** Manufacturing **CN:** American Colors, Inc. **DOB:** 06/30/1949 **PB:** Pittsburgh **SC:** PA/USA **PT:** Lewis Alfred Wible; Wilda (Boa) Wible **MS:** Married **SPN:** Norma Joan Klaus (09/20/1975) **CH:** Judson F.; Jerald L.; Leslie K. **ED:** MBA, Xavier University (1974); BA, Allegheny College (1971) **C:** Chairman of the Board, American Colors, Inc., Sandusky, OH (2018-Present); President, American Colors,

Inc., Sandusky, OH (1975-2018); Sales Representative, PPG Industries, Cincinnati, OH (1971-1974) **CIV:** Board of Trustees, Firelands Regional Medical Center (2000-Present); Session of First Presbyterian Church (1992-Present); President, Montessori Child Enrichment Center (1989-1991); Board of Directors, Montessori Child Enrichment Center (1986-1991); President, Montessori Parents Association, Huron, OH (1986); President, Board of Trustees, First Presbyterian Church, Sandusky, OH (1981) **AW:** Pioneer Award, American Composites Manufacturers Association (2019); Distinguished Alumni Award, Fox Chapel Area School District (1989) **MEM:** Board of Trustees, Alleghany College (2014-Present); Board of Directors, American Composites Manufacturers Association (1989-1992); Plum Brook Country Club; Longue Vue Club; Sea Pines Country Club **MH:** Albert Nelson Marquis Lifetime Achievement Award; Marquis Who's Who Top Professional **AS:** Mr. Wible attributes his success to providing a lot of people with careers and potential guidance toward living good lives. He's not necessarily saying money isn't important, but it isn't more important than being ethical and moral and giving. Most of the people who have worked for American Colors have given to charities and charitable endeavors. He believes there is more to life than just "trying to make a buck." **B/I:** Mr. Wible became involved in his profession because he worked for PPG Industries right after he completed his undergraduate studies. He and some colleagues got together and started American Colors in 1975; he has been working there for more than 45 years. **AV:** Playing golf **PA:** Republican **RE:** Presbyterian

WICHMANN, DAVID S., T: Chief Executive Officer **I:** Business Management/Business Services **CN:** UnitedHealth Group **ED:** BS in Accounting, Illinois State University (1985) **C:** Chief Executive Officer, UnitedHealth Group (2017-Present); Chief Executive Officer, SCA Holdings (2017-Present); Executive Vice President, UnitedHealth Group, Minnetonka, MN (2006-Present); President, UnitedHealth Group (2014-2017); Chief Financial Officer, UnitedHealth Group (2014-2016); Chief Financial Officer, Executive Vice President, UnitedHealth Group, Minnetonka, MN (2011-2016); President of Group Operations, UnitedHealth Group, Minnetonka, MN (2008-2011); Executive Vice President, President, Commercial Markets Group, UnitedHealth Group, Minnetonka, MN (2006-2008); President, Chief Operating Officer, UnitedHealthcare, UnitedHealth Group, Minnetonka, MN (2004-2006); Chief Executive Officer, Specialized Care services (Now OptumHealth), UnitedHealth Group, Minnetonka, MN (2003-2004); Senior Vice President, Corporate Development, UnitedHealth Group, Minnetonka, MN (1998-2004); President, Chief Operating Officer, Specialized Care Services, UnitedHealth Group, Inc., Minnetonka, MN (2002-2003); Partner, Arthur Andersen LLP (1995-1998) **CIV:** Chairman, Board of Directors, YMCA of the Greater Twin Cities (2015-Present); Member, Board of Directors, Amil (2012-Present); Member, Board of Directors, Tennant Company (2009-Present); Member, Board of Directors, YMCA of the Greater Twin Cities (2008-Present); Member, Board of Directors, UnitedHealthcare Children's Foundation (2008-2016); Board Member, Minnesota Orchestra; Board Member, YMCA of Metropolitan Minneapolis

WICKER, ROGER FREDERICK, T: U.S. Senator from Mississippi; Lawyer **I:** Government Administration/Government Relations/Government Services **DOB:** 07/05/1951 **PB:** Pontotoc **SC:** MS/USA **PT:** Thomas Frederick Wicker; Wordna Glen (Threadgill) Wicker **MS:** Married **SPN:** Gayle (Long) Wicker (1975) **CH:** Margaret; Caroline; McDaniel

ED: JD, University of Mississippi School of Law (1975); BA in Political Science and Journalism, The University of Mississippi (1973) **C:** Chairman, Senate Committee on Commerce (2019-Present); U.S. Senator, State of Mississippi (2007-Present); Chairman, National Republican Senatorial Committee (NRSC) (2015-2017); Member, U.S. House Budget Committee (2003-2007); Member, U.S. House of Representatives from Mississippi's First Congressional District, United States Congress, Washington, DC (1995-2007); Member, U.S. House Appropriations Committee (1995-2007); Member, District Six, Mississippi State Senate (1988-1994); Judge Pro Tempore, Municipal Court, City of Tupelo, MS (1986-1987); Public Defender, Lee County, MS (1984-1987); Partner, Sparks, Wicker, & Colburn (1982-1994); Staff Member to Representative Trent Lott, U.S. House of Representatives, Washington, DC (1980-1982) **CIV:** Community Development Foundation; First Baptist Church, Tupelo, MS **MIL:** Advanced through Grades to Lieutenant Colonel, United States Air Force Reserve (1980-2004); Judge Advocate, Judge Advocate General's Corps, United States Air Force (1976-1980) **AW:** Award, Manufacturing Excellence, National Association of Manufacturers (2003); Capitol Dome Award, American Cancer Society, Inc. (2003); National Public Service Award, American Heart Association, Inc. (1998) **MEM:** Lions Club International **PA:** Republican **RE:** Baptist

WICKHAM, WILLIAM T., PHD, T: Management Educator and Consultant **I:** Other **DOB:** 05/28/1929 **PB:** Cleveland **SC:** OH/USA **PT:** William Terry Wickham; Rebecca Long (Dugan) Wickham **MS:** Married **SPN:** Jane Brundage (06/15/1952) **CH:** Susan Jane Walker; Mary Ellen Lemberg; W. Paul **ED:** PhD in Industrial Chemistry, Case Institute of Technology (Now Case Western Reserve University) (1956); MS, Case Institute of Technology (Now Case Western Reserve University) (1954); BA, Heidelberg University (1951) **CT:** Licensed Pilot **C:** Chairman, Department of Business Administration, Heidelberg University (1977-1999); Technical Director, Crosby Chemicals, New Orleans (1976-1977); Technical Director, Crosby Chemicals, Picayune, MS (1976-1977); Vice President of Research and Development, Dayco IP Holdings, LLC (1967-1976); Technical Manager, Celanese Corporation, Greer, SC (1964-1967); Technical Manager, Celanese Corporation, Clark, NJ (1962-1964); Adjunct Professor, University of Houston (1960-1961); Group Leader, Dow Chemical Company (1958-1962); Research Chemist, Owens-Illinois Company (1956-1958); Instructor, Case Institute of Technology (Now Case Western Reserve University (1955-1956) **CR:** Adjunct Professor, Ashland University (1988-1989); Management Consultant, National Machinery (1988-1989); Management Consultant, General Motors (1985-1987); Management Consultant, Hercules Corporation (1981-1983); Management Consultant, Dayco IP Holdings, LLC (1977-1980) **CIV:** Board of Directors, Seneca Industrial and Economic Development Corp (1983-1985) **AW:** Summer Fellow, General Electric (1981); Firestone Fellowship (1951-1952) **MEM:** President, Tiffin-Seneca County Chamber of Commerce (1984); President, Local Chapter, Rotary International (1977-1981); American Chemical Society; Honorary Member, Sigma Xi, The Scientific Research Society **MH:** Albert Nelson Marquis Lifetime Achievement Award **B/I:** Dr. Wickham became involved in his profession because of his lifelong interest in science and his innate management expertise. **PA:** Republican **RE:** United Church of Christ

WIDMAN, LORRAINE, T: Educator, Artist **I:** Education/Educational Services **DOB:** 01/11/1933 **PB:** Brooklyn **SC:** NY/USA **PT:** Martin Hirsh Balmuth; Betty (Levin) Balmuth **MS:** Married **SPN:** Harry Frederick Widman, Jr. (03/17/1956, Divorced 1987) **CH:** Matthew David; Michael Hirsh; Gabrielle Juliet **ED:** MFA, University of Oregon (1956); BFA, Cranbrook Academy of Art (1954); Coursework, Cooper Union (1951-1952); Coursework, Hunter College (1950-1951) **CT:** Certified Art Teacher, Language Arts Teacher, Oregon; Secondary Certification, Social Studies, Language Arts, and Literature **C:** Teacher, Art, English, Social Studies, Portland School District (1979-Retired); Art Instructor, Mount Hood Community College, Portland, OR (1976); Drawing Instructor, Portland State University (1975); Founder, Sculpture and Jewelry Department, Clackamas Community College, Oregon City, OR (1968-1975); Head, Art Department, Roseburg School District (1957-1960) **CR:** Scorer, National Board Certified in Art, San Francisco, CA (1996); Exhibition Coordinator, Jewish Community Center, Portland, OR (1964-1974); Presenter, Workshops in the Field of Art Education, Chairman Art Committee; Installation of Original 4'x8' Terra Cotta Relief, Mittleman Jewish Community Center, Portland, OR; Exhibitor, Public Art Work, Clackamas Community College **CIV:** Delegate, Precinct Worker, District Leader, Democratic Party, Portland, OR (1990-1997); Board of Directors, Membership Chair, Graphic Designer, Young Audiences of Portland (1972-1976); Board of Directors, Membership Chair, Vice President, Jewish Education Association, Portland, OR (1972-1976); Involved in American-Israel Relationship Organizations **CW:** Sculptor, Commemorative Menorahs Commissioned by Robison Home, Portland, OR (1992); Author, Producer, Anchorperson, TV Sculpture Course (1969-1973); Author, "Sculpture: A Studio Guide to Concepts, Methods, and Materials" (1989); Author, Art Exhibit Reviews, Manual on Sculpture; Designer, Coordinator, Major Architectural Cast Stone Reliefs, Campus, Clackamas Community College; Exhibitor, Photos, The New York Times; Exhibitor, Gimbals Department Store **AW:** Second National Scholastic Award (1950) **MEM:** Bargaining Representative, Portland Teacher's Education Association (1979-1997); Conference Delegate, Portland Teacher's Education Association (1995-1997); National Education Association; National Art Association, World Affairs Council; Oregon Art Association; Oregon Education Association; Portland Art Association; Portland City Club **MH:** Albert Nelson Marquis Lifetime Achievement Award **B/I:** Mrs. Lorraine Widman has always been interested in the arts, she attended a high school that allowed her to develop her abilities in art at the High School of Music and art in New York (The High School of Performing Arts), it was required that she take an exam for admissions. In High school Mrs. Widman created one of her first ceramic sculptures and she was featured in the New York Times with a picture of the sculpture. Shortly after she graduated high School, she attended Hunter college to take some history courses, which she was also interested in. Since Art was a strong passion, Mrs. Widman attended Cooper Union for the advancement of science and art and that added another year to her education in art. She attended school in the evening while she was working in the Garment District in New York City, Mrs. Widman also worked for Que magazine, which has become New York Magazine, in the circulation department in the evening. Mrs. Widman went on to attended Cranbrook Academy of Art in Oregon and then completed her education in Art at the University of Oregon. She became the head of the art department at Roseburg (Oregon) School district and then went on to be the founder of the sculpture and jewelry department of Clackamas Community College in Oregon. Mrs. Widman also became an art and drawing instructor for Oregon State University and Mount Hood Community College and before she retired, Mrs. Widman taught English and Social Studies in the Portland School district for almost 50 years changing many students lives. **AV:** Choral singing; Opera; Theater; Antique and artifacts collecting; Photography; Ceramics; Landscaping; Travel

WIEBENGA, WILLIAM MARTIN, PHD, T: College President **I:** Education/Educational Services **DOB:** 02/11/1938 **PB:** Burlington **SC:** WI/USA **YOP:** 2018 **PT:** Martin Peter Wiebenga; Florence (De Graaff) Wiebenga **MS:** Married **SPN:** Audrey Ella Stanton Wiebenga (06/22/1962) **CH:** Marlyse Elizabeth; Lynndelle Kristin; Gabriel Martin **ED:** PhD in Philosophy, Yale University (1966); MA, Yale University (1962); Woodrow Wilson Fellowship (1960); Danforth Graduate Fellowship (1960); BA in Philosophy and English, Calvin College (Now Calvin University) (1960) **C:** President, Professor of Philosophy, Central College, Pella, Iowa (1990); Associate Professor of Philosophy, Provost, Wittenberg University, Springfield, Ohio (1977-1990); Dean, College of Arts and Science, Associate Professor of Philosophy, Texas Christian University (1973-1977); Dean, College of Arts and Science, American University, Washington, DC (1970-1973); Associate Professor of Philosophy, American University, Washington, DC (1969-1973); Acting Dean, American University, Washington, DC (1969-1970); Associate Dean, Undergraduate Programs, College of Arts and Science, American University, Washington, DC (1969-1970); Associate Dean, Undergraduate Programs, College of Arts and Science, American University, Washington, DC (1969); Acting Chairman, Philosophy and Religion Department, American University, Washington, DC (1968-1969); Assistant Professor of Philosophy, American University, Washington, DC (1964-1969); Assistant in Instruction, Yale University, New Haven, CT (1963-1964) **CR:** Consultant, Lutheran Education Conference of North America (1986-1990); Consultant Evaluator, North Central Association (Now Higher Learning Commission), Chicago, IL (1987) **CW:** Contributor, Articles to Professional Journals **MEM:** The American Philosophical Association; Society for Values in Higher Education **MH:** Albert Nelson Marquis Lifetime Achievement Award **B/I:** Dr. Wiebenga became involved in his profession because his goal was to be a professor. He worked at American University during 1960s turmoil; student unrest caused him to get involved with administration. **PA:** Independent **RE:** Protestant

WIEDEN, DAN G., T: Co-founder **I:** Advertising & Marketing **CN:** Wieden Kennedy **PB:** Portland **SC:** OR/USA **MS:** Married **SPN:** Bonnie Wieden **ED:** BJ, University of Oregon (1967); Diploma, Ulysses S. Grant High School, Portland, OR **C:** President, Executive Creative Director, Wieden+Kennedy International (Wieden Kennedy), Portland, OR (1982-Present); With, William Cain, Portland, OR (1980-1982); McCann-Erickson (Now McCann), Portland, OR (1978-1980); Freelance Writer (1972-1978); Georgia-Pacific Corporation, Portland, OR (1967-1972) **CR:** Co-founder, Caldera Arts, Sisters, OR **CW:** Featured, Documentary, "Art & Copy" **AW:** Named to Hall of Achievement, University of Oregon School of Journalism and Communication (1999); Listed, Advertising Age 100 Ad People of the 20th Century; Named, America's 25 Most Intriguing Entrepreneurs, Inc.; Named Oregon's Professional of the Year; Named Oregon's Entrepreneur of the Year; Named One of the 50 Cyber-Elite, TIME Magazine; Named to The One Club for Creative Hall of Fame

WIEDENBACH, MAIK, T: Owner, Founder **I:** Professional Training & Coaching **CN:** Maik Wiedenbach Personal Training **ED:** BA, Fordham University, 2001; MA in Philosophy/German Literature, Ruhr University, Bochum, Germany Magna Cum Laude (2000) **CT:** NASM **C:** Owner, Founder, Maik Wiedenbach Personal Training (2009-Present); Teacher, Exercise Science, New York University **CW:** Author, "101 Fitness Myths"; Creating 500 Videos per Year **AW:** Named NYC Top Coach, Kev's Best; Musclemania Champion **MEM:** God's Love We Deliver; Phyth Cares; German National Team in Swimming; **AS:** Mr Wiedenbach attributes his success to showing up and dedicating his time. **B/I:** Mr Wiedenbach comes from an academic household. Both of his parents were professors. His parents always said it was very important to have balance. They also said to not study exercise science because you will learn that from your coaches anyway. When he was done with college, he worked on Wall Street and he was not passionate. He decided to go back to athletics. **THT:** Mr. Wiedenbach would like to prevent people from doing fad diets, and make lifestyle changes and see results.

WIETING, WILLIAM FRANK, MD, T: Internist; Consultant **I:** Medicine & Health Care **DOB:** 10/21/1938 **PB:** Boston **SC:** MA/USA **PT:** Gilbert William Wieting, BA, ThD; Katherine Nora (Peterson) Wieting, BA, MRE **MS:** Married **SPN:** Amey Verna Pepin (08/27/1960) **CH:** Geoffrey Scott Reid Wieting, BA, BMus, MMus; Carl Philip Wieting, AB, MEd **ED:** Resident in Internal Medicine, U.S. Naval Hospital, Chelsea, MA (1967-1969); Coursework, U.S. Naval Submarine Medical School, Groton, CT (1965-1966); Resident, New Britain General Hospital, CT (1964-1965); Intern, New Britain General Hospital, CT (1963-1964); MD, Boston University School of Medicine (1963); AB in German Literature, Hamilton College (1959) **CT:** Diplomate, American Board of Internal Medicine, National Board of Medical Examiners (NBME), American Board of Hyperbaric Medicine; Qualified in Submarines, Diving Medical Officer, United States Navy **C:** Consultant, Hyperbaric Medicine, U.S. Naval Regional Medical Clinic (Now Naval Medical Center Portsmouth), Portsmouth, NH (1973-2005); Practice Medicine, Specializing in Internal Medicine, Portsmouth, NH (1971-2005); Chairman, Portsmouth Regional Visiting Nurses Association (1990-2004); Chairman, Professional Advisory Committee, Portsmouth Regional Visiting Nurses Association (1975-2000); Trustee, Portsmouth Regional Hospital, C-HCA, Inc. (1979-1990); Consultant and Courtesy Staff Internist, York Hospital, Maine (1971-1990); Board of Directors, Portsmouth Regional Visiting Nurses Association (1986); Chairman, Task Force on Hyperbaric Medicine (1984); Chief of Staff, Portsmouth Regional Hospital, C-HCA, Inc. (1979-1981); Director of Electrocardiography, York Hospital, York, Maine (1971-1980); Lecturer in Diving and Hyperbaric Medicine, Incorporator, Portsmouth Regional Hospital, C-HCA, Inc. (1977-1978); Vice Chief of Staff, Portsmouth Regional Hospital, C-HCA, Inc. (1976-1978); Chief of Staff, Portsmouth Regional Hospital, C-HCA, Inc. (1975-1977); Chief of Medicine, U.S. Naval Hospital (Now Naval Medical Center Portsmouth), Portsmouth, NH (1969-1971) **CR:** Principal Investigator, Diving Program, Hyperbaric Treatment Facility (1979-1984); Clinical Instructor of Physiology and Physical Medicine, University of New Hampshire, Durham, NH (1977-1984) **CIV:** Proprietor, Portsmouth Athenaeum

(1976-Present); Member, Old York Historical Society (1976-Present); Trustee, York United Methodist Church (1977-1979, 2012-2018); Trustee, Portsmouth Athenaeum (1986-1988, 2014-2017); Trustee, Old York Historical Society (1987-1999); Board of Directors, Old York Historical Society (1988-1994); Board of Directors, Executive Vice President, Seacoast Community Concert Association (1975-1977); Chairman, York Harbor Planning Board, York Harbor, Maine (1972-1974) **MIL:** Retired Captain, Medical Corps, United States Navy (1998); Advanced Through Grades to Captain, Selected Reserve, United States Navy Ready Reserve (1973-1998); TAD Duty, Nang, Viet Nam (1969-1971); Advanced Through Grades to Lieutenant Commander, Active Duty, United States Navy (1965-1971); Submarine Medical Officer, USS Sam Houston SSBN 609(B) and USS Henry L. Stimson SSBN 655(G) (1966-1967) **CW:** Published "A Collection of Glass Paperweights" (2020); Musician, Director, Conductor, The York Singers (1973-2012); Numerous Concert Recordings, Hundreds of A Cappella Choral Works, Chiefly Classic Motets of the 16th and 17th Centuries; Published, "American Art: An Eclectic Collection," and "Contemporary Art of New England," Published "September in Ticino, Munich, and Thuringia" **AW:** American Medical Association Physician Recognition Award (1976, 1979, 1982, 1985, 1988, 1991, 1995, 2001, 2004); Awarded Combat Action Ribbon for Service, U.S. Naval Support Hospital, DaNang, Viet Nam (1971); Named to Submarine Dolphins (Medical Corps) Denoting Officer Qualification in Submarines; Diving Medical Officer Insignia; Secretary of the Navy Commendation Medal; Combat Action Ribbon; Battle Efficiency "E" Award; Navy Unit Commendation, U.S. Naval Support Hospital, DaNang, Viet Nam; National Defense Medal; Vietnam Service Medal with Star (in Country); Two-time Recipient, U.S. Naval Reserve Medal; Republic of Viet Nam Humanitarian Service Award; RVN Service Medal; Fleet Ballistic Missile Submarine Patrol Pin with Gold Star (Two Patrols of 71 and 57 Days Submerged) **MEM:** American College of Physicians; Undersea Medical Society; Association of Military Surgeons of the United States (AMSUS) President, Portsmouth Medical Society (1973-1974); New Hampshire Medical Society; Rockingham County Medical Society; Delta Phi fraternity; Director, Rotary Club of Portsmouth (1986-1987); Rotary Club of Portsmouth (1977-2005) **AS:** Dr. Wieting was blessed with intelligent, loving parents who cared at every moment of my life about his physical, emotional, and intellectual development. They saw to it that he attended an outstanding high school, and that he was able to attend Hamilton College. They facilitated his exposure to other formative experiences, such as regular attendance at church, the Boy Scout movement (yes, he was an Eagle Scout) and DeMolay, while high school and college gave him matchless opportunities to learn music, art and languages, as well as science. Dr. Wieting's parents led by example; they were thoughtful, open-minded, generous-hearted people who valued their hard-won university educations and lived by the ethical and moral codes they professed. Whatever he has done with his abilities was the product of their nature and nurture. **B/I:** Dr. Wieting was drawn to the medical profession because of the regard and deep respect his parents had for the physicians who attended their family when he was growing up. He wanted to emulate the doctors, to earn that kind of respect for himself, and, in a way, to please his parents. He can remember reading a Life magazine article around 1948 with photographs of new surgical techniques for blue babies and being fascinated. The scientific side of medicine was always of interest to him; by high school, it was clear to

Dr. Wieting that he wanted to study medicine. Because his family was of German extraction, he took two years of German in high school; at Hamilton College, he majored in German Literature, as well as carrying a full pre-med program. He was admitted to his first choice medical school at Boston University. His interest in medicine was early, but only a part of his intellectual life. **AV:** Travel; Photography; Sailing; Musical performance (choral and solo); High-quality audio recording and editing; Collecting and studying American art **PA:** Independent **RE:** Methodist **THT:** Dr. Wieting believes a liberal arts education provides an understanding of and sympathy for the human experience that profoundly enhances the effectiveness and value of any physician. A personal moral compass, based on a humanistic philosophy, is vital to carrying the responsibilities of a doctor, to making dispassionate and objective decisions, to finding creative solutions to ethical tangles, to resisting temptations and to finding the strength to put others' concerns ahead of one's own. Over the years, young residents, nurses, hospital corpsmen and brother physicians often asked him, "What do you mean when you speak of 'being professional?'" His answer, in essence, was 'consistently and reliably putting others' needs ahead of one's own; being trustworthy, objective and as selfless as possible - at every moment of one's career.' A medical professional is not just someone who has mastered an arcane craft, but someone who seeks to do good, and always strives to discern and to do the right thing. Dr. Wieting is the author of two books with two editions. This first is "American Art: An Eclectic Collection"; it is a fully illustrated study of 400 works of art by Americans dating from 1800 to 1950. The second is "Contemporary Art of New England," also a fully illustrated study of 170 works of art by artists of the northeast US done since the mid-20th century. He has published "September in Ticino, Munich, and Thuringia," a photo-illustrated travelogue of a three-week motor tour of Switzerland, Munich, and "Bach country," and "A Collection of Glass Paperweights," a fully-illustrated and annotated catalogue of a collection of over 300 paperweights from the 1840s to the present.

WIGGINS, ANDREW CHRISTIAN, T: Basketball Player **I:** Athletics **CN:** Golden State Warriors **DOB:** 02/23/1995 **PB:** Toronto **SC:** ON/CAN **PT:** Mitchell Wiggins; Marita Payne-Wiggins **MS:** Single **ED:** Coursework, University of Kansas (2013-2014); Diploma, Huntington Prep School, Huntington, WV (2013); Student, Vaughan Secondary School (2009-2011) **C:** Basketball Player, Golden State Warriors (2020-Present); Basketball Player, Minnesota Timberwolves (2014-2020); Basketball Player, Kansas Jayhawks (2013-2014) **CR:** Basketball Player, FIBA Americas Championship (2015); Canadian National Team (2015); Basketball Player, FIBA Americas Under-18 Championship (2012); Basketball Player, FIBA Under-17 World Championship (2010) **AW:** NBA Rookie of the Year (2015); NBA All-Rookie First Team (2015); Bronze Medal, FIBA AmeriCup, Mexico City, Mexico (2015); Consensus Second-Team All-American (2014); First-Team All-Big 12 (2014); Big 12 Freshman of the Year (2014); Mr. Basketball USA (2013); Gatorade National Player of the Year (2013); Naismith Prep Player of the Year (2013); McDonald's All-American (2013); First-Team Parade All-American (2013); Bronze Medal, São Sebastião do Paraíso, FIBA Americas U18 Championship (2012); Bronze Medal, FIBA World U17 Cup, Hamburg, Germany (2010)

WILCZEK, FRANK ANTHONY, T: Physics Professor **I:** Education/Educational Services **DOB:** 05/15/1951 **PB:** Mineola **SC:** NY/USA **PT:** Frank John Wilczek; Mary Rose Wilczek **MS:** Married **SPN:** Elizabeth Jordan Devine (Betsy Devine) (07/03/1973) **CH:** Amity; Mira **ED:** Honorary Doctorate, Faculty of Science and Technology, Uppsala University, Sweden (2013); Honorary Doctorate, Université de Montréal (2001); Honorary Doctorate, Ohio State University (2008); Honorary Doctorate, Clark University (2007); PhD in Physics, Princeton University (1974); MA in Mathematics, Princeton University (1972); BS in Mathematics, University of Chicago (1970) **C:** Herman Feshbach Professor of Physics, Massachusetts Institute of Technology (MIT) (2000-Present); Rudolf Peierls Visiting Professor of Physics, Oxford University (2008); Visiting Professor, Nordic Institute of Theoretical Physics (2007); Lorentz Professor, University of Leiden (1998); J. Robert Oppenheimer Professor, School of Natural Science, Institute for Advanced Study (1997-2000); Leland J. Hayworth Distinguished Scientist, Brookhaven National Laboratory (1994-1997); Professor, School of Natural Science, Institute for Advanced Study (1989-1997); Visiting Professor, Harvard University (1987-1988); Professor, Physics, University of California Santa Barbara (1980-1984); Professor, Physics, Princeton University (1980-1981); Associate Professor, Physics, Princeton University (1978-1980); Assistant Professor, Physics, Princeton University (1974-1978); Instructor, Princeton University (1974); Founding Director, T.D. Lee Institute; Chief Scientist, Wilczek Quantum Center, Shanghai Jiao Tong University; Distinguished Origins Professor, Arizona State University; Full Professor, Stockholm University **CR:** Adjunct Professor, Center for Scientific Studies, Valdivia (2002-Present); Member, Board of Trustees, Society for Science & the Public (2008-Present); Member, Science Policy Committee, European Organization for Nuclear Research (CERN) (2002-Present); Member, High Energy Physics Advisory Panel, U.S. Department of Energy (1986-1988); Member, High Energy Advisory Committee, Brookhaven National Laboratory (1978-1982); Adjunct Professor, Centro de Esudios Cienti´ficos; Lecturer, Numerous Advisory Boards, Universities and Societies; Member, Scientific Advisory Board, Future of Life Institute; Researcher in the Field **CIV:** Supporter, Campaign for the Establishment of a United Nations Parliamentary Assembly **CW:** Editor-in-Chief, Annals of Physics, Annual Reviews, Inc. (2001-Present); Author, "A Beautiful Question: Finding Nature's Deep Design" (2015); Author, "The Lightness of Being: Mass, Ether, and the Unification of Forces" (2010); Author, "Fantastic Realities: 49 Mind Journeys and a Trip to Stockholm" (2006); Guest, "Penn & Teller: Bull—!" (2005); Author, "Fractional Statistics and Anyon Superconductivity" (1990); Co-Author, "Longing for the Harmonies: Themes and Variations from Modern Physics" (1989); Author, "Geometric Phases In Physics" (1989); Contributor, Articles to Professional Journals **AW:** Co-Recipient, King Faisal International Prize for Science (2005); Co-Recipient, The Nobel Prize in Physics "for the discovery of asymptotic freedom in the theory of the strong interaction" (2004); Julius Lilienfeld Prize, American Physical Society (2003); 2003 High Energy and Particle Physics Prize, European Physical Society (2003); Michelson-Morley Prize (2002); Lorentz Medal (2002); J.J. Sakurai Prize for Theoretical Particle Physics, American Physical Society (1986); Faculty of Mathematics and Physics Commemorative Medal, Charles University, Prague **MEM:** Board of Governors, New York Academy of Sciences (2006-Present); Foreign Member, Royal Netherlands Academy of Arts and Sciences (2000); Regent's Fellow, Smithsonian Astrophysical Observatory (1986-1988); Co-Founding Member, Kosciuszko Foundation of the Collegium of Eminent Scientists of Polish Origin and Ancestry; Fellow, John D. and Catherine T. MacArthur Foundation; Fellow, American Association for the Advancement of Science; Fellow, American Philosophical Society; National Academy of Sciences; American Academy of Arts and Sciences; Scientific Advisory Committee, Perimeter Institute for Theoretical Physics **AV:** Chess; Music; Logic puzzles

WILD, SUSAN, "ELLIS" ELLIS, T: U.S. Representative from Pennsylvania; Lawyer **I:** Government Administration/Government Relations/Government Services **DOB:** 06/07/1957 **PB:** Wiesbaden Air Force Base **SC:** West Germany **PT:** Norman Leith Ellis; Susan (Stimus) Ellis **MS:** Widowed **SPN:** Kerry Acker (2003, Deceased 2019); Russell Wild (1981, Divorced 2002) **CH:** Clay; Adrienne **ED:** JD, The George Washington University Law School (1982); BA, American University (1978) **C:** Member, U.S. House of Representatives, Pennsylvania's Seventh Congressional District (2019-Present); Partner, Gross McGinley LLP (1999-Present); Member, U.S. House of Representatives from Pennsylvania's 15th Congressional District (2018-2019); Solicitor of Allentown, PA (2015-2017) **PA:** Democrat **RE:** Jewish

WILDENTHAL, CLAUD KERN, T: President Emeritus **I:** Medicine & Health Care **CN:** University of Texas Southwestern Medical Center **DOB:** 07/01/1941 **PB:** San Marcos **SC:** TX/USA **PT:** Bryan Wildenthal; Doris (Kellam) Wildenthal **MS:** Married **SPN:** Margaret Dehlinger (10/17/1964) **CH:** Pamela; Catharine **ED:** Honorary DSc, Austin College (2010); Honorary DSc, Southern Methodist University (2006); PhD, University of Cambridge, England (1970); Research Fellow, Strangeways Research Laboratory, Cambridge, England (1968-1970); Research Fellow, National Heart Institute, Bethesda, MD (1967-1968); Fellow in Cardiology, University of Texas Southwestern Medical Center, Dallas, TX (1965-1967); Resident in Medicine, Parkland Hospital, Dallas, TX (1965-1967); Intern, Bellevue Hospital, New York, NY (1964-1965); MD, The University of Texas Southwestern Medical Center, Dallas, TX (1964); BA, Sul Ross State University (1960) **C:** Past President and Consultant, Children's Medical Center Foundation (2016-PresenI); President Emeritus and Professor of Medicine Emeritus, The University of Texas Southwestern Medical Center, Dallas, TX (2013-Present); President, Children's Medical Center Foundation (2013-2016); Executive Vice President, Children's Health System of Texas (2013-2016); Professor of Internal Medicine and Physiology, The University of Texas Southwestern Medical Center, Dallas, TX (1976-2013); President, Southwestern Medical Foundation (2008-2012); President, The University of Texas Southwestern Medical Center, Dallas, TX (1986-2008); Dean, Southwestern Medical School, The University of Texas Southwestern Medical Center, Dallas, TX (1980-1986); Dean, Graduate School, The University of Texas Southwestern Medical Center, Dallas, TX (1976-1980); Assistant Professor to Professor of Internal Medicine and Physiology, The University of Texas Southwestern Medical Center, Dallas, TX (1970-1976) **CIV:** Interim Chief Executive Officer and General Director, Dallas Opera (2017-2018); Board Chair, Dallas Opera (2008-2012); Board of Directors, Dallas Opera; Board of Directors, Moncrief Cancer Foundation; Board of Directors, Hamon Foundation; Board of Directors, Reves Foundation; Board of Directors, Hoblitzelle Foundation; Board of Directors, Cambridge in America; Board of Directors, Dallas Regional Chamber of Commerce; Board of Directors, Dallas Citizen's Council; Board of Directors, Dallas Museum of Art; Board of Directors, Dallas Symphony; Board of Directors, Dallas Center for the Performing Arts; Board of Directors, Southwestern Medical Foundation **CW:** Author, "Degradative Processes in Heart and Skeletal Muscle" (1980); Author, "Regulation of Cardiac Metabolism" (1976); Contributor, Articles, Professional Journals **AW:** Dallas CEO Volunteer of the Year Award (2018); Inductee, Texas Business Hall of Fame (2008); Dallas Historical Society Achievement Award (1991); John Simon Guggenheim Memorial Foundation (1975-1976); Research Career Development Award, National Institutes of Health (1972) **MEM:** National Academy of Medicine; Association of American Physicians; American Society for Clinical Investigation; Royal Society of Medicine; American Physiological Society; Past President, American Section, International Society for Heart Research; American Federation for Clinical Research; Past Chairman, Science Policy Committee, American Heart Association; Past Chairman, Science Policy Committee, Association of Academic Health Centers **MH:** Albert Nelson Marquis Lifetime Achievement Award

WILDRICK, KENYON JONES, T: Minister Emeritus, Trustee **I:** Religious **CN:** Pilgrim Congregational Church **DOB:** 06/14/1933 **PB:** Rahway **SC:** NJ/USA **PT:** Stanley B. Wildrick; Adele (Jones) Wildrick **MS:** Married **SPN:** Nancy Ruth Mersfelder (08/23/1958) **CH:** Catherine Ruth; Margaret Jeanne; Kenyon Douglas **ED:** Honorary DD, Trinity College, CT (1985); ThM, Princeton Theological Seminary (1962); MDiv, Princeton University (1958); BA, Trinity College, Hartford, CT (1955) **CT:** Ordained to Ministry, Presbyterian Church (1958) **C:** Minister Emeritus, Community Congregational Church (1993-2008); Senior Minister, Pilgrim Congregational Church, Warren, NJ (1993-2008); Senior Minister, Community Congregational Church (1967-1993); Associate Minister, Community Congregational Church (1961-1967); Assistant Minister, Community Congregational Church, Short Hills, NJ (1958-1961) **CR:** Trustee, Investment Committee, Fellowship, Connecticut Congregational Churches (1996-Present); Trustee, Center of Theological Inquiry, Princeton, NJ (1985-Present); President, Board of Trustees, Overlook Protestant Chaplaincy Program (1973-Present); Church and Ministry Committee, New Jersey Association (1965-Present); Campus Ministry, Middle Atlantic Conference (1962-1965); Board of Directors, Milburn-Short Hills Chapter, The American National Red Cross (1963-1964) **CIV:** Trustee, Vice Chairman, Presbyterian Homes of New Jersey (1981) **MEM:** Chairman, Millburn Clergy Association (Now Millburn-Short Hills Clergy Association (1987); Director, Chatham, Millburn and Short Hills Rotary Club (1973); President, Delta Phi Epsilon **MH:** Albert Nelson Marquis Lifetime Achievement Award; Marquis Who's Who Humanitarian Award **AS:** Rev. Dr. Wildrick attributes his success to the students because they are the ones who did the work. **B/I:** Rev. Dr. Wildrick was brought up in a home where his father was the president of an advertising agency in New York City. So he was being groomed to be his successor. He went to Trinity College specifically because of an economics professor. He had no interest in religion; he went to church once in a while but nothing serious. Then he realized you couldn't graduate from Trinity College without a certain number of chapel credits. He decided that he didn't need the degree; he only came there to learn from the one professor anyway. The chaplain of the college was a good friend of his. He told him, "You're a damn fool." He said if he took one class with him, he would waive all the other credits. He then recommended him, without his knowledge, for a scholarship to go on to a seminary for people who would be good ministers that weren't brought up very religious. Rev. Dr. Wildrick didn't really want to do it but he thought he would be a better husband and father if he did, and so he went. He didn't really fit in and was the only person without a roommate. About halfway through, he decided he had enough, so he went to see the director and told him that he was about ready to leave. He told him to read everyone's report on why they wanted to be a minister, and of all of them, he felt he and three others would be truly great ministers. So Rev. Dr. Wildrick decided to stay. He stuck it out and it was two years later and time for graduation. He decided he was going to get ordained and try to sell religion. **THT:** One day after Rev. Dr. Wildrick retired, the congregational church called him to say that he was too young to retire, and requested that he start a new church. After considering the offer for a week, he declined, but some associate ministers approached him and offered to work for him for half-salary should he reconsider and start the new church. Shortly thereafter, another associate minister offered to work full-time for free. Rev. Dr. Wildrick thanked the associate ministers many times, but was still resolute in declining the offer. A few weeks later, he ran into a former parishioner, who, having heard rumors of the offer made by the congressional church, offered to donate $20,000 each year to the church for the rest of his life. Again, Rev. Dr. Wildrick thanked the man, but this time said he would think about it. Two weeks later, he received a call from the director of educator, who was asking for a letter of recommendation for another church. Taking a chance, he asked her if she would be a director of education for free at a brand new church. After taking two weeks to think about it, she accepted the offer, and he decided that he should accept his offer as well.

WILEY, JANET MAY, T: Kitchen Staff Member **I:** Food & Restaurant Services **CN:** MidAmerica Nazarene College **DOB:** 10/23/1937 **PB:** Crawfordsville **SC:** IA/USA **PT:** Thomas Julius Holmes Jr.; Julia Irene (Cassabaum) Holmes **MS:** Married **SPN:** Jack Darrell Wiley (1957) **CH:** Candice Irene; Kaylene June **ED:** Diploma, High School, Wyman, Iowa **CT:** Food Service Management, Ames Iowa College (Now Iowa State University) (1985) **C:** Director of Food Services, Vennard College, University Park, Iowa (1985-1996); Director of Food Services, Mayflower Community, Mayflower Homes, Inc., Grinnell, Iowa (1970-1984) **CR:** Employee, MidAmerica Nazarene University, Olathe, KS (1996-2007); Teacher in the Field, Food Service Director, Barclay College, Haviland, KS (1996-1997); 90-Hour Program for Food Service Supervisors (1977); Child Care Food Program Management, Vennard Daycare; Policy Writer, Mayflower Community, Mayflower Homes, Inc. and Vennard College **CIV:** Participant in School Course, "The American Character," MidAmerica Nazarene University (2001); Sunday School Teacher, Missionary President, Caravan Director, Church of the Nazarene, Inc.; Singer, Mixed Quartet, Church of the Nazarene, Inc. **AW:** "I Dare You" Leadership Award (1955) **MEM:** Banquet Leaderland Ladies Luncheon, Mayflower Community, Mayflower Homes, Inc., Vennard College and Barclay College **MH:** Albert Nelson Marquis Lifetime Achievement Award **AS:** Mrs. Wiley attributes her success to the encouragement of her grandmother, as well as her own passion for food. **B/I:** Mrs. Wiley and her sister were raised by their grandmother from the age of 9 until Mrs. Wiley graduated from high school. Her grandmother told her, "One day you will do something so big," due to Mrs. Wiley's love for food and helping others. **AV:** Crafting; Sewing;

Recipe collecting **PA:** Republican **RE:** Nazarene **THT:** Mrs. Wiley's daughter, Kaylene Wiley, wrote a poem to her about recipes: "Recipes, recipes, hundreds and more, you'll find them in the kitchen, from the ceiling to the floor. Tucked away in purses, these recipes you'll see, just anywhere my mother goes, there recipes will be. Recipes by the thousands, cookbooks by the score, if you want to make mom happy, just get her a few more. Oh, what fun she has when cooking, trying recipes that are new. 'Don't forget the parsley,' you'll hear, for plain dishes will never do."

WILEY, MYRA H., BSN, RN, CD, T: Retired Mental Health Nurse; Retired Educator **I:** Medicine & Health Care **DOB:** 01/20/1938 **PB:** Lexington **SC:** AL/USA **PT:** Joseph Aaron Haraway; Annie Lura (Putnam) Haraway **MS:** Widow **SPN:** Harold Wiley (Deceased) **CH:** Sonya; Robert; Marie **ED:** BSN, University of Alabama, Huntsville, AL (1989) **CT:** RN, Alabama; Certificate in Chemical Dependency **C:** Bradford Health Services (1997-2003); Alabama Career College (formerly Huntsville Business Institute) (1997-2000); Relief Charge Nurse for Behavioral Health, Columbia Medical Center of Huntsville (formerly Crestwood Hospital), Huntsville, AL (1995-1996); Staff Nurse Counselor, Bradford-Parkside, Madison, AL (1991-1995); Staff Nurse, Humana Hospital, Huntsville, AL (1989-1991); Nursing Assistant, North Alabama Rehabilitation Hospital, Huntsville, AL (1987-1989); Nursing Assistant, Night-Weekend Coordinator, Upjohn Health Care, Huntsville, AL (1983-1987) **MEM:** Consortium of Behavioral Health Nurses and Associates **MH:** Albert Nelson Marquis Lifetime Achievement Award **AS:** Ms. Wiley credits her husband and family as being very supportive as she continued her education, obtained her degrees, and pursued her career. For them, she is endlessly thankful. **B/I:** Ms. Wiley read nursing books when she in high school. She enjoyed reading and learning more about the profession, which led her to actively pursue a career in the field of healthcare. **RE:** Baptist

WILKIE, ROBERT LEON JR., T: United States Secretary of Veterans Affairs **I:** Government Administration/Government Relations/Government Services **DOB:** 08/06/1962 **PB:** Frankfort **SC:** West Germany **PT:** Robert Leon Wilkie; and Joy Ann (Somerville) Wilkie **MS:** Married **SPN:** Julia Cameron Bullard (05/19/1990) **CH:** Adam; Megan **ED:** Master in Strategic Studies, U.S. Army War College (2002); LLM in International Law & Legislature, Georgetown University (1992); JD, Loyola of the South (Now Loyola University New Orleans College of Law) (1988); BA, Wake Forest University, Cum Laude (1985); Diploma, College of Naval Command and Staff, U.S. Naval War College; Diploma, United States Air Force Air Command and Staff College; Diploma, Joint Forces Staff College **C:** United States Secretary of Veterans Affairs, United States Department of Veterans Affairs (2018-Present); United States Under Secretary of Defense for Personnel and Readiness, United States Department of Defense (2017-2018); Vice President, Business Development Director, CH2M Hill, Washington, DC (2010-2017); Assistant Secretary for Legislative Affairs, Untied States Department of Defense, Washington, DC (2006-2009); Acting Assistant Secretary for Legislative Affairs, United States Department of Defense, Washington, DC (2006); Principal Deputy Assistant Secretary for Legislative Affairs, United States Department of Defense, Washington, DC (2005-2006); Special Assistant to President for National Security Affairs, The White House, Washington, DC (2003-2005); Senior Director, National Security Council, Washington, DC (2003-2005); Counsel & Advisor to Senate Major-

ity Leader Trent Lott, United States Senate (1997-2003); Director, North Carolina Republican Party (1996-1997); Legislative Director to Representative David Funderburk, United States House of Representatives (1995); Legislative Counsel to Senator Jesse Helms, United States Senate, Washington, DC (1988-1995) **CR:** Member, Moot Court Board, Loyola University New Orleans College of Law (1988) **CIV:** Staff Member, Republican National Convention (1992) **MIL:** Intelligence Officer, United States Naval Reserve **CW:** Author, Newspaper Political Editorials (1990-1993); Contributor, Military Journals Including The Naval War College Review, Parameters, Armed Forces Journal International, and The Air and Space Power Journal Proceedings **AW:** Defense Distinguished Public Service Medal (2009); American Jurisprudence Awards for Excellence in Latin American Law and International Law and Legislation (1987-1988); Bustamonte Award for Outstanding Achievement in International Law, The Society of Jesus, New Orleans, LA (1987); Named Junior Intelligence Officer (Reserve) of the Year, Office of Naval Intelligence **MEM:** ABA; Republican National Lawyers Association, The Federalist Society **AV:** English history; Military history; Southern history; Literature; Distance running **PA:** Republican **RE:** Roman Catholic

WILKINSON, ROBERT SHAW JR., MD, MACP, T: Physician/Professor Emeritus of Clinical Medicine **I:** Medicine & Health Care **CN:** The George Washington University **DOB:** 07/11/1928 **PB:** Brooklyn **SC:** NY/USA **PT:** Robert Shaw Wilkinson; Melissa Ruth (Royster) Wilkinson **MS:** Married **SPN:** Carolyn Elizabeth Cobb (06/24/1951) **CH:** Amy Elizabeth; Karin Lynn; Robert Montague **ED:** Residency, Fellowship, Upstate Medical Center, Syracuse, NY (1958-1962); Internship, Kings County Hospital, Brooklyn, NY (1955-1956); MD, New York University, New York, NY (1955); BA, Dartmouth College, Hanover, NH (1950) **CT:** Re-Certified, American Board of Internal Medicine (1974); Diplomate, American Board of Internal Medicine (1965) **C:** Volunteer, Mercy Health Clinic (2007-2015); Washington Internal Medicine Group (2002-2006); Attending Physician, Courtesy Staff, Sibley Memorial Hospital (2002-2006); Attending Physician, Georgetown University Hospital (1997-2006); Attending Physician, George Washington University Hospital (1962-2006); Community Practice Network, MedStar Georgetown Medical Center (2000-2002); Community Practice Network, Georgetown University Medical Center (1996-2000); Internal Medicine Private Practice (1968-1996); Staff, Physicians Group Health Association (1962-1968) **CR:** Professor Emeritus of Clinical Medicine, George Washington University (2007-Present); Clinical Professor, George Washington University (2001-2007); Associate Professor, Georgetown University Medical Center (1998-2006); Medical Advisor, Inter-American Development Bank, Georgetown University Medical Center (1976-2006); Associate Clinical Professor, George Washington University (1974-2001); Assistant Professor of Medicine, Division of General Internal Medicine, Georgetown University Medical Center (1996-1998); Medical Advisor, World Bank and the International Monetary Fund (1968-1984); Assistant Clinical Professor of Medicine, George Washington University (1967-1974); Clinical Instructor in Medicine, George Washington University (1962-1967) **CIV:** Homemaker Health and Service, Washington, DC (1982-1985); Board of Directors, Community Federal Savings and Loans (1974-1981) **MIL:** Captain, U.S. Army Medical Corps (1956-1958) **CW:** Co-Author, "Electrocardiographic and Pathologic Features of Myocardial Infraction in Man: A Correlative Study," The

American Journal of Cardiology (1963); Co-Author, "The Relation of Precordial and Orthogonal Leads Circulation" (1963); Co-Author, "Clinical Observations with an Orthogonal Lead System Circulation" (1962); Co-Author, "On the Normalization of the Electrical Orientation of the Heart and the Representation of the Axis by Means of the Axis Map," The American Heart Journal (1961); Co-Author, "An Experimental Study of the Electrocardiographic Effects of Localized of Myocardial Lesions," American Journal of Cardiology (1961) **AW:** Leadership Award, American College of Physicians, (2019); Outstanding Volunteer Clinical Teacher Award, American College of Physicians (2016); Dr. James A. Ronan Excellence in Medical Care Award for Exemplifying the Professionalism, Dedication, and Compassion of the Mercy Health Clinic (2015); Dartmouth Class of 1950 Award (2010); AOA Volunteer Clinical Faculty Award, The George Washington University Chapter (2009); Alumni Leadership Award, New York University School of Medicine (2006); John F. Maher Memorial Laureate Award, District of Columbia Chapter, American College of Physicians (2006); Dartmouth Alumni Award (1987); Distinguished Achievement Award, American Heart Association, Nation's Capital Affiliate (1986) **MEM:** Fellow, Master, American College of Physicians (2004-Present); The Academy of Medicine (1975-Present); American Medical Association (1962-Present); Medical Society of the District of Columbia (1962-Present); Washington Society for the History of Medicine (1980-2010); Board of Directors, American Heart Association (1979-1987); American College of Physicians (1975-1977) **MH:** Albert Nelson Marquis Lifetime Achievement Award; Marquis Who's Who Top Professional **AS:** Dr. Wilkinson attributes his success to his love for medicine. Likewise, he credits his various professional relationships, all of which enabled him to grow as a doctor. **B/I:** Dr. Wilkinson was inspired by his father, a respected physician, to pursue medicine. He was a great role model. **AV:** Reading; Listening to classical music; Playing tennis; Walking **PA:** Democrat **RE:** Episcopalian **THT:** Dr. Wilkinson believes one should attempt to have a positive impact on the community and society as a whole.

WILL, FRITZ G., PHD, T: Physical Chemist, Consultant **I:** Sciences **DOB:** 01/12/1931 **PB:** Breslau **SC:** Germany **PT:** Fritz Will; Adele M. Will **MS:** Married **SPN:** Hertha M. Will (05/24/1958) **CH:** Heike; Christian; Helen **ED:** PhD in Physical Chemistry, TUM (1959); MS in Physics, TUM (1956); BS in Physics, TUM (1954) **C:** President, Owner, Battery Vision Consulting (1998-2011); Visiting Professor, National University of Singapore (1998); Manager of Electrochemical Science and Technology, Electric Power Research Institute, Inc. (1994-1998); Visiting Scientist, Electric Power Research Institute, Inc. (1993-1994); Research Professor, The University of Utah (1991-1993); Gledden Senior Fellowship, The University of Western Australia (1991); Director, Cold Fusion Institute, The University of Utah (1990-1991); Member, Research Staff, Research and Development Center, GE (1960-1990); Visiting Scientist, Murdoch University (1981); Visiting Professor, Universität Bonn (1973-1974); Visiting Professor, Universität Bonn (1973-1974); Manager of Electrochemistry, Research and Development Center, GE (1969-1973); Coordinator, Fuel Cell Program, Engineering Research and Development Laboratories, Fort Belvoir (1959-1960) **CR:** Chairman, International Advisory Panel, Institute of Materials Science and Engineering (1997) **CW:** Contributor, Articles, Professional Journals **AW:** Citation Classic Award, Information Sciences Institute (1984); Industrial Research Award, Industrial Research, Inc. (1975); Fourth

Battery Research Award (1964) **MEM:** President, The Electrochemical Society (1987-1988); Chairman, Honors and Awards Committee, The Electrochemical Society (1984-1985); Chairman, Physical Chemistry Division, The Electrochemical Society (1983-1984); Division Editor, Journal, The Electrochemical Society (1974-1984) **MH:** Albert Nelson Marquis Lifetime Achievement Award **B/I:** Dr. Will became involved in his profession because of several teachers that encouraged him along the way. **AV:** Playing tennis; Listening to opera and classical music; Taking photographs

WILLARD, JACK, T: Communications Executive **I:** Corporate Communications & Public Relations **CN:** John G. Willard Cons. **PB:** Pittsburgh **SC:** PA/USA **PT:** Cornelius Merle Willard; May E. (Hinds) Willard **MS:** Married **SPN:** Lorraine L. Franze (09/02/1978) **CH:** Mary Elizabeth; Kristen Anne; Lisa Lorraine; Jessica Kathleen **ED:** BA in Journalism, Duquesne University (1974) **C:** President, John G. Willard Consultant (1982-Present); Manager, Corporate Policy, Rockwell International Corp., Pittsburgh, PA (1981-1982); Administrator, Relocation and Corporate Personnel Procedures, Rockwell International Corp., Pittsburgh, PA (1980-1981); Administrator, Employee Benefit Administration, Rockwell International Corp., Pittsburgh, PA (1975-1980); Assistant Account Executive, Marc & Co. Advertising, Pittsburgh, PA (1975); Consultant, Communications, Better Business Bureau, Pittsburgh, PA (1974); Master Control, Technology Director, Station KDKA-TV, Pittsburgh, PA (1973); Producer, Director, Air Talent, Station WDUQ-FM, Pittsburgh, PA (1971-1973) **CW:** Contributor, Articles, Professional Journals **AW:** Kappa Tau Alpha (1974) **MEM:** Mensa; NRA **MH:** Albert Nelson Marquis Lifetime Achievement Award

WILLIAMS, BRIAN DOUGLAS, T: Newscaster **I:** Other **DOB:** 05/05/1959 **PB:** Ridgewood **SC:** NJ/USA **PT:** Gordon L. Williams; Dorothy Williams **MS:** Married **SPN:** Jane Gillan Stoddard (06/07/1986) **CH:** Allison Williams; Douglas Williams **ED:** Honorary DHL, George Washington University (2012); Honorary DHL, Fordham University (2011); Honorary LLD, University of Notre Dame (2010); Honorary DJ, Ohio State University (2008); Honorary DHL, Bates College (2005); Honorary DHL, Catholic University of America (2004); Coursework, George Washington University; Coursework, Catholic University of America; Coursework, Brookdale Community College **C:** Anchor, "The 11th Hour with Brian Williams," MSNBC (2016-Present); Chief Breaking News Anchor, MSNBC (2015-Present); Anchor, Managing Editor, "NBC Nightly News," NBC (2004-2015); Host, "Rock Center with Brian Williams," NBC (2011-2013); Anchor, "The News with Brian Williams," MSNBC (1996-2004); Weekend Anchor, "NBC Nightly News," NBC (1993-1999); White House Correspondent, NBC News (1994-1996); Correspondent, NBC News (1993-1994); Anchor, WCBS-TV (1987-1993); New Jersey Correspondent, WCAU-TV (1985-1987); Panorama Host (1985); Correspondent, WTTG-TV (1982-1986); Reporter, KOAM-TV (1981); Intern, Jimmy Carter Administration, White House (1979) **CR:** Member, Board of Directors, Congressional Medal of Honor Foundation (2006-2015) **CIV:** Former Volunteer Firefighter **CW:** Featured, "The Soup" (2013); Voice Actor, "Family Guy: (2013); Featured, "30 Rock" (2009-2012); Host, "Saturday Night Live" (2007); Guest, "Sesame Street" (2007); Guest, "The Daily Show" (2007); Guest, "Late Night with Jimmy Fallon," "Late Show with David Letterman," "Late Night with Conan O'Brien"; Author, Numerous Publications, including the New York Times and Time **AW:** One of the 100 Most Influential People in the World, Time (2007); Father of the

Year, National Father's Day Committee (1996); 11 Edward R. Murrow Awards; Four DuPont-Columbia University Awards; Walter Cronkite Award for Excellence in Journalism; George Foster Peabody Award; Numerous Emmy Awards

WILLIAMS, CONSTANCE, T: Former Senator of Pennsylvania **I:** Government Administration/Government Relations/Government Services **DOB:** 06/27/1944 **PB:** Long Branch **SC:** NJ/USA **PT:** Leon Hess; Norma (Wilentz) Hess **MS:** Married **SPN:** Sankey V. Williams **CH:** Two Children **ED:** MBA, The Wharton School, The University of Pennsylvania (1980); BA in English, Barnard College (1966) **C:** Member, Pennsylvania State Senate, Harrisburg, PA (2001-2009); Member, Pennsylvania House of Representatives, Harrisburg, PA (1996-2001) **CR:** Small Business Consultant; Staffer, U.S. Representative Marjorie Margolies-Mezvinsky **CIV:** Chair Emerita, Philadelphia Museum of Art (2016-Present); Chair, Board of Trustees, Philadelphia Museum of Art (2010-2016); Vice President, Director, Hess Foundation; Chairwoman, Democratic Committee, Lower Merion & Narberth, PA **PA:** Democrat **RE:** Jewish

WILLIAMS, ELIZABETH A., T: Financial Planner, Consultant **I:** Financial Services **DOB:** 01/16/1948 **PB:** San Francisco **SC:** CA/USA **PT:** John Williams; Myrtle Mary (Thierry) Williams **MS:** Single **CH:** Brian; Jonathan **ED:** Degree, University of California (1979); PhD in Human Services, Bryson University; MBA, University of California **C:** Retired, Chief Executive Officer, Ultimate Vacations Inc. (2015); Planning Commissioner, Pittsburgh, PA; President, EWJ & Associates Marketing Firm; President, Investments Unlimited, Oakland, CA; Consultant, Insurance and Real Estate; Patient Service Representative, Health Care Service, Oakland, CA; Manpower Coordinator, Federal Programs, U.S. Government, San Francisco, CA **CIV:** Human Relations Commissioner, Equal Employment Opportunity Commission, Contra Costa County **AW:** Public Speaking Award, Grand Juror Award, Contra Costa County; European Investment Fellow **MEM:** American Association of University Women; National Association of Female Executives; National Association for the Advancement of Colored People; National Real Estate Owners Association; National Notary Association; Order Eastern Star; Heroines Jericho; Soropotimist Inc.; Toastmistress Club; National Ritual Director, Beta Pi Sigma Society **MH:** Albert Nelson Marquis Lifetime Achievement Award; Marquis Who's Who Top Professional **B/I:** Ms. Williams became involved in her profession because she wanted to help her community. Likewise, she wanted to prove that women could succeed in business and government.

WILLIAMS, HANK JR., T: Country Music Singer, Songwriter **I:** Media & Entertainment **DOB:** 05/26/1949 **PB:** Shreveport **SC:** LA/USA **PT:** Hank Williams; Audrey Williams **MS:** Married **SPN:** Mary Jane Thomas (07/01/1990); Becky White (1977, Divorced 1983); Gwen Yeargain (1971, Divorced 1977) **CH:** Hank Williams III; Holly Williams; Katharine Diane Williams; Hilary Williams; Samuel Williams **C:** Singer-Songwriter, Musician **CW:** Featured Performer, Numerous Soundtracks (1964-2020); Singer-Songwriter, Musician, "It's About Time" (2016); Singer-Songwriter, Musician, "Old School News Rules" (2012); Singer-Songwriter, Musician, "127 Rose Avenue" (2009); Singer-Songwriter, Musician, "I'm One of You" (2003); Special Guest, "Guns & Ammo Television" (2003); Singer-Songwriter, Musician, "The Almeria Club Recordings" (2002); Voice Actor, "Tom Sawyer" (2000); Singer-Songwriter, Musician, "Stormy" (1999); Voice Actor, "The Simpsons" (1998-1999);

Singer-Songwriter, Musician, "Three Hanks: Men with Broken Hearts" (1996); Singer-Songwriter, Musician, "A.K.A. Wham Bam Sam" (1996); Singer-Songwriter, Musician, "Hog Wild" (1995); Singer-Songwriter, Musician, "Out of Left Field" (1993); Singer-Songwriter, Musician, "Maverick" (1992); Singer-Songwriter, Musician, "Pure Hank" (1991); Singer-Songwriter, Musician, "Lone Wolfe" (1990); Singer-Songwriter, Musician, "Wild Streak" (1988); Singer-Songwriter, Musician, "Born to Boogie" (1987); Singer-Songwriter, Musician, "Hank Live" (1987); Singer-Songwriter, Musician, "Montana Cafe" (1986); Singer-Songwriter, Musician, "Five-O" (1985); Singer-Songwriter, Musician, "Major Moves" (1984); Singer-Songwriter, Musician, "Man of Steel" (1983); Singer-Songwriter, Musician, "Strong Stuff" (1983); Singer-Songwriter, Musician, "High Notes" (1982); Singer-Songwriter, Musician, "The Pressure Is On" (1981); Singer-Songwriter, Musician, "Rowdy" (1981); Singer-Songwriter, Musician, "Habits Old and New" (1980); Singer-Songwriter, Musician, "Whiskey Bent and Hell Bound" (1979); Singer-Songwriter, Musician, "Family Tradition" (1979); Actor, "Willa" (1979); Actor, "Sgt. Pepper's Lonely Hearts Club Band" (1978); Singer-Songwriter, Musician, "The New South" (1977); Singer-Songwriter, Musician, "On Night Stands" (1977); Singer-Songwriter, Musician, "Hank Williams Jr. and Friends" (1975); Singer-Songwriter, Musician, "Bocephus" (1975); Singer-Songwriter, Musician, "Insights into Hank Williams in Song and Story" (1974); Singer-Songwriter, Musician, "Living Proof" (1974); Singer-Songwriter, Musician, "The Last Love Song" (1974); Singer-Songwriter, Musician, "After You, Pride's Not Hard to Swallow" (1973); Singer-Songwriter, Musician, "The Legend of Hank Williams in Song and Story" (1973); Singer-Songwriter, Musician, "Send Me Lovin' and a Whole Lotta Loving" (1972); Singer-Songwriter, Musician, "Eleven Roses" (1972); Singer-Songwriter, Musician, "I've Got a Right to Cry" (1971); Singer-Songwriter, Musician, "All for the Love of Sunshine" (1971); Singer-Songwriter, Musician, "Removing the Shadow" (1970); Singer-Songwriter, Musician, "Hank Williams Jr. Singing My Songs (Johnny Cash)" (1970); Singer-Songwriter, Musician, "Sunday Morning" (1969); Singer-Songwriter, Musician, "Live at Cobo Hall" (1969); Singer-Songwriter, Musician, "Luke the Drifter Jr. Vol. 2" (1969); Singer-Songwriter, Musician, "Song My Father Left Me" (1969); Singer-Songwriter, Musician, "Luke the Drifter Jr." (1969); Actor, "A Time to Sing" (1968); Singer-Songwriter, Musician, "A Time to Sing" (1967); Singer-Songwriter, Musician, "My Own Way" (1967); Singer-Songwriter, Musician, "Hank Williams/Hank Williams Jr. Again" (1966); Singer-Songwriter, Musician, "Country Shadows" (1966); Singer-Songwriter, Musician, "Blues My Name" (1966); Performer, "Die Drehscheibe" (1966); Singer-Songwriter, Musician, "Ballads of the Hills and Plains" (1965); Singer-Songwriter, Musician, "Father & Son" (1965); Singer-Songwriter, Musician, "Connie Francis and Hank Williams Jr. Sing Great Country Favorites" (1964); Singer-Songwriter, Musician, "Your Cheatin' Heart" (1964); Singer-Songwriter, Musician, "Hank Williams Jr. Sings the Songs of Hank Williams" (1964); Performer, "The Ed Sullivan Show" (1963) **AW:** Ranked #50, "100 Greatest Country Artists of All Time," Rolling Stone (2017); Honoree, BMI Icon for "unique and indelible influence on generations of music makers," 56th Annual BMI Country Awards (2008); Inductee, Nashville Songwriters Hall of Fame (2007); Listee, "CMT Giants," CMT (2007); Tennessean of the Year, Tennessee Sports Hall of Fame (2007); Johnny Cash Visionary Award, CMT Music Awards (2006); Ranked #20, "40 Greatest Men of Country Music," CMT (2003); Best Country Vocal Collaboration, "There's A Tear In My Beer,"

Grammy Awards (1990); Video of the Year, "There's A Tear In My Beer," TNN/Music City News (1990); Video of the Year, "There's A Tear In My Beer," Academy of Country Music (1989); Entertainer of the Year, "There's A Tear In My Beer," Academy of Country Music (1989); Music of the Year, "There's A Tear In My Beer," Country Music Association (1989); Vocal Event of the Year, "There's A Tear In My Beer," Country Music Association (1989); Entertainer of the Year, Academy of Country Music (1988); Video of the Year, "Young Country," Academy of Country Music (1988); Album of the Year, "Born to Boogie," Country Music Association (1988); Entertainer of the Year, Country Music Association (1988); Entertainer of the Year, Academy of Country Music (1987); Music Video of the Year, "My Name Is Bocephus," Country Music Association (1987); Music Video of the Year, "All My Rowdy Friends Are Coming Over Tonight," Country Music Association (1985); Music Video of the Year, "All My Rowdy Friends Are Coming Over Tonight," Academy of Country Music (1984) **RE:** Republican

WILLIAMS, HUGH A., T: Mechanical Engineer (Retired) **I:** Engineering **DOB:** 08/18/1926 **PB:** Spencer **SC:** NC/USA **PT:** Hugh Alexander Williams; Mattie Blanche (Megginson) Williams **MS:** Married **SPN:** Ruth Ann Gray (02/21/1950) **CH:** David Gray; Blanche Williams Heidengren **ED:** Postgraduate Coursework, Benedictine University (1977); MS in Diesel Engineering, NC State University (1950); BS in Mechanical Engineering, NC State University (1948) **CT:** Registered Professional Engineer, State of Illinois **C:** Staff Engineer of Advanced Mechanical Technology, Electro-Motive Division, General Motors (1986-1987); Supervisor of Product Development, Engine Design Section, Electro-Motive Division, General Motors (1963-1986); Senior Project Engineer, Electro-Motive Division, General Motors (1958-1963); Project Engineer, Electro-Motive Division, General Motors (1955-1958); Project Engineer, Baldwin-Lima Hamilton Corporation (1953-1955); Junior Engineer, Field Service Engineer, Baldwin-Lima Hamilton Corporation (1950-1952) **CIV:** Vice President, Downers Grove Sanitary District (1991-1992); Intergovernmental Task Force Committee, DuPage County (1988-1992); Trustee, Downers Grove Sanitary District (1965-1992); President, Downers Grove Sanitary District (1974-1991); Board of Directors, Illinois Association of Sanitation Districts (1977-1989); Statewide Policy Advisory Committee, Illinois Environmental Protection Agency (1977-1979); President, Illinois Association of Sanitation Districts (1976-1977); Elder, Presbyterian Church (1945) **CW:** Editor, Southern Engineer (1947-1948); Contributor, Articles, Professional Journals **AW:** Citizen's Award, Downers Grove Chapter, Kiwanis International (1991); Trustee Service Award, Illinois Association Sanitation Districts (1986); Fellowship, Norfolk Southern (1950) **MEM:** Governor, Jamestowne Society (2008-2009); President, Raleigh Chapter, National Society of the Sons of the American Revolution (2000-2001); President, Raleigh Host Lions Club (1996-1997); Honorary Member, Illinois Association of Wastewater Agencies (1992); Fellow, American Society of Mechanical Engineers; Lifetime Member, SAE International **MH:** Albert Nelson Marquis Lifetime Achievement Award **AS:** Mr. Williams attributes his work ethic to his father, Hugh Alexander. His father was a railroad worker who worked until midnight from the age of 16 until 70, only because the conductors union would not allow workers to work pass that age. **B/I:** Mr. Williams became involved in his profession because he grew up in the railway town, of Spencer, North Carolina. His father was a train conductor on the Danville division of the Southern Railway. He grad-

uated from high school in the middle of World War II. Within two weeks, he traveled down to Raleigh, and became a freshman in engineering at North Carolina State University. Mr. Williams spent a year and a half studying before enlisting in the United States Army Air Corps, one month before his 18th birthday. He was called into active duty in February of 1945. Then, he was sent to Biloxi, Mississippi, where he received his 90-day U.S. Army Air Corps training. Eighty-percent of the class failed, but Mr. Williams was among the 20-percent that did pass. **PA:** Republican **RE:** Presbyterian

WILLIAMS, JAMES R., PHD, T: Principal Ergonomist **I:** Consulting **DOB:** 04/16/1932 **PB:** Chicago **SC:** IL/USA **PT:** James Henry Williams; Margaret Lucille (Keefer) Williams **SPN:** Jonetta Rae Gilbert (12/19/59) **CH:** Janise Rebecca; Jason Richard **ED:** Doctor of Philosophy in Education, New York University (1971); Master of Science in Human Factors and Industrial Psychology, Purdue University (1960); Bachelor of Science in Psychology, Purdue University (1958) **CT:** Farm Winery License (1982) **C:** Principal Ergonomist, Synergetic Applications, Bloomsbury, NJ (2002-Present); Senior Performance Technologist, Telcordia Technologies, Piscataway, NJ (1984-2001); Technical Staff, Bell Laboratories, Piscataway, NJ (1981-1983); District Manager, AT&T, Basking Ridge, NJ (1975-1980); Supervisor, Training and Standards, Bell Laboratories, Piscataway, NJ (1969-1974); Project Manager, System Development Corporation, Paramus, NJ (1966-1969); Human Factors Engineer, Kollsman Instrument Corp., Elmhurst, NY (1964-1966); Senior Systems Consultant, System Development Corporation, Paramus, NJ (1961-1964); Technical Assistant, Science Research Associates, Chicago, IL (1960-1961) **CR:** Former Chairperson, U.S. Technical Advisory Group (1987-2017); Co-owner, Winemaker, Del Vista Vineyards (1982-1992); Consultant, New York University, New York, NY (1968) **CIV:** Volunteer, U.S. Expert to WG5 on Software Ergonomics (1986-Present); Assistant Scout Master, Boy Scouts of America (1975-1978); Cub Master, Boy Scouts of America, Watchung, NY (1973-1974) **MIL:** U.S. Air Force (1951-1955) **CW:** Author, "Developing Performance Support for Computer Systems: A Strategy for Maximizing Usability and Learnability" (2004); Author, "3D Embedded Figures Test" (1970); Editor, International Standards for Menu Dialogues, Command Dialogues and Form-fill Dialogues with Computer Systems, Human Factors Engineering of Software User Interfaces Part 3, Interaction Techniques **MEM:** Representative, Human Factors and Ergonomics Society (1986-Present); Charter Member, American Psychological Society; Delta Rho Kappa; Kappa Delta Pi **MH:** Albert Nelson Marquis Lifetime Achievement Award; Marquis Who's Who Top Professional **B/I:** Mr. Williams became involved in his profession out of a desire to be involved in the space race. He eventually began to work deeply in the field of human factors in psychology, and found himself in the private industry. **AV:** Astronomy; Body building; Wine making

WILLIAMS, JOHN, "ROGER" ROGER, T: U.S. Representative from Texas **I:** Government Administration/Government Relations/Government Services **DOB:** 09/13/1949 **PB:** Evanston **SC:** IL/USA **MS:** Married **SPN:** Patty Williams **CH:** Jaclyn; Sabrina **ED:** BA, Texas Christian University (1972) **C:** Member, U.S. House of Representatives from Texas' 25th Congressional District, United States Congress, Washington, DC (2013-Present); Member, U.S. House Committee on Transportation and Infrastructure (2013-Present); Member, U.S. House Budget Committee (2013-Present); Secretary of State, State of Texas, Austin, Texas (2004-

2007); President, Chief Executive Officer, Roger Williams Automall (1974-1995); Baseball Coach, Texas Christian University (1974-1976); Professional Baseball Player, Atlanta Braves Farm Team (1971-1974); Member, Committee on Financial Services, United States Congress; Member, Republican Study Committee, United States Congress **CR:** Chairman, Texas Republican Victory (2008); Coordinated Campaign (2007-2008); Chair, Texas Base Realignment and Closure Response Strike Force (2005); Chairman, Bush/Cheney 2004 Campaign (2004); State Finance Chair, John Cornyn for U.S. Senate (2002); Member, Republican National Committee's Eagles Program (2001); North Texas Chairman, Bush/Cheney 2000 Campaign (2000); Regional Finance Chairman, George W. Bush Gubernatorial Campaign (1994, 1998); North Texas Finance Chairman, National Grassroots Fundraising; Chair, Congressional Baseball Caucus; Chair, College Football Caucus; Coach and Manager, Republican Congressional Baseball Team **PA:** Republican **RE:** Christian

WILLIAMS, MARGARET LUWERTHA HIETT (LARY), DSCN, RN-BC, T: Registered Nurse, Midland Democratic Party County Chair **I:** Health, Wellness and Fitness **DOB:** 08/30/1938 **PB:** Midland **SC:** TX/USA **PT:** Cotter Craven Hiett; Mollie Jo (Tarter) Hiett **MS:** Widowed **SPN:** Tuck Williams (08/11/1985, Deceased); James Troy Lary (11/16/1960, Divorced 1/1963) **CH:** James Cotter Lary **ED:** Postgraduate Coursework, University of Texas (1991-1992); Postgraduate Coursework, Teachers College, New York, NY (1981); EdM, Teachers College, New York, NY (1974); MA, Teachers College, Columbia University, New York, NY (1964); BS, Texas Woman's University (1960); Certificate of Completion, University of Wisconsin, Scotland; Postgraduate, University of Wisconsin; Coursework, Trauma Nursing, Pouch Attachment Ladder System, Emergency Nursing Pediatrics, Neonatal Resuscitation, American Council of Learned Societies **CT:** Certification, Psychiatric/Mental Health Nurse, Nursing Professional Development, Clinical Nurse Specialist and Advanced Practice Nurse, American Nurses Credentialing Center **C:** Democratic Chair, Midland County (2018-2020); Nurse, Emergency Department, Midland Memorial Hospital, Midland, TX (2005-Present); Nurse, Emergency Department, Hill Regional Hospital, Hillsboro, TX (1999-Present); Owner, Margaret Hiett Williams, Registered Nurse, Clinical Nurse Specialist, Whitney, TX (1996-Present); Owner, MTW Nursing Consultation, Whitney, TX (1996-Present); Nurse, Emergency Department, Hill Regional Hospital, Hillsboro, TX (1999-2005); Clinical Development Specialist, Heritage Health Services, L.C. (1997-1999); Nurse III, Brown School, San Marcos, TX (1993-1997); Director of Nursing, Charter Healthcare Systems, Corpus Christi, TX (1992-1993); Clinical Educator, Supervisor, Glenwood, A Psychiatric Hospital, Midland, TX (1987-1992); Field Supervisor, We Care Home Health Agency, Midland, TX (1983-1987); With, Area Builders, Odessa, TX (1981-1983); Sergeant, Burns Security, Midland, TX (1979-1981); Nursing Practitioner, St. Luke's Hospital, New York, NY (1975-1979); Research Assistant, Teachers College (1973-1974); Assistant Professor, Pan American University, Edinburgh, TX (1970-1972); Director of ADNP, Laredo Junior College, Texas (1967-1970); Instructor, Odessa College, Texas (1963-1967); Nurse, Midland Memorial Hospital (1960-1963) **CR:** Content Expert, American Nurses Credentialing Center (2000-Present); Reviewer, National Council of Licensing Examiners (1999); Adjunct Professor, Southwest Texas State University (1995); Adjunct Professor, Pace University (1974-1975); Reviewer in Field **CIV:** Elected County Chair, Midland County Democratic Party (2018-2020); Midland County Election Commission (2018-2020); Member, Governor Richards' Executive Leadership Council (1991-1995); Re-election Steering Committee (1994) **AW:** Woman of Distinction Nightingale Award, Midland Memorial Hospital (2016); Achievement Award, Community Leaders of America (1989); Isabelle Hampton-Robb Award, National League for Nursing (1976); Named, Texas Woman's University Great 100 Nurses, Ladies First of Midland (1974) **MEM:** District 32, Texas Nurses Association (1970-1972); President, District 21, Texas Nurses Association (1962-1965); American Psychiatric Nurses Association; Emergency Nurses Association; Parkland Memorial Hospital Nurses Alumnae Association; Texas Woman's University Alumnae Association; Midland High School Alumni; Mensa; American Nurses Association; National Association for Female Executives; Business and Professional Women's Club; Lockhart Breakfast Lions Club **MH:** Albert Nelson Marquis Lifetime Achievement Award; Marquis Who's Who Top Professional **AS:** Good education, insatiable appetite for knowledge, Spiritual Growth, **B/I:** Ms. Williams entered her profession because when was 3 years old she used to watch the U.S. Army nurses, her mother was teaching first aid. She told her father she was going to be a nurse. From that time on, it was like she knew what she was going to do. Ms. Williams started investigating the education, where to go to school, what kinds of jobs were available and she talked to nurses. After World War II, a lot of U.S. Army nurses came to Midland, TX. As she grew, there was no shaking Ms. Williams from the notion of being a nurse. She would go to Dallas, TX, to shop and she knew where the nursing schools were and she would asked to meet someone to talk about nursing. When she was a junior in high school, a woman came to the school wanting to talk to anyone who wanted to be a nurse because she needed to hire some to be a nurse's aid in senior year, so Ms. Williams signed up. She gave bed baths, transported patients and changed beds. Most people went to hospital school and she started as a candy stripe the first year. Ms. Williams would watch the nurses and see who was the best nurses and she asked them where they went to nursing school. Some nurses told her to go to a university. Her cousin and everybody told her that she had to go to a collegiate program. It was suggested by a registered nurse that she attend Texas State College for Women and she did. **AV:** Songwriting; Public speaking; Singing; Writing **PA:** Democratic Party **RE:** Episcopalian **THT:** Get some good mentors. Attend to your spiritual growth. Follow Jesus. Trust in God, Clean House, Help Others.

WILLIAMS, MICHELLE, T: Actress **I:** Media & Entertainment **DOB:** 09/09/1980 **PB:** Kalispell **SC:** MT/USA **PT:** Larry Richard Williams; Carla (Swenson) Williams **SPN:** Phil Elverum (2018, Divorced 2019) **CH:** Matilda **C:** Actress, Film, Television **CR:** Brand Ambassador, Band of Outsiders; Brand Ambassador, Louis Vuitton **CW:** Actress, "Venom 2" (2020); Executive Producer, "Fosse/Verdon" (2019); Actress, "Fosse/Verdon" (2019); Actress, "After the Wedding" (2019); Actress, "Venom" (2018); Actress, "I feel Pretty" (2018); Actress, "The Greatest Showman" (2017); Actress, "All the Money in the World" (2017); Actress, "Wonderstruck" (2017); Actress, "Certain Women" (2016); Actress, "Blackbird" (2016); Actress, "Suite Francaise" (2014); Actress, "Cabaret" (2014); Actress, "Oz the Great and Powerful" (2013); Actress, "Cougar Town" (2013); Actress, Music Video, "Paradise" (2012); Actress, "My Week with Marilyn" (2011); Actress, "Take This Waltz" (2011); Actress, "Meek's Cutoff" (2010); Actress, "Shutter Island" (2010); Executive Producer, "Blue Valentine" (2010); Actress, "Blue Valentine" (2010); Actress, "Mammoth" (2009); Actress, "Synecdoche, New York" (2008); Actress, "Wendy and Lucy" (2008); Actress, "Deception" (2008); Actress, "Incendiary" (2008); Actress, "I'm Not There" (2007); Actress, "The Hottest State" (2006); Actress, "The Hawk Is Dying" (2006); Actress, "Brokeback Mountain" (2005); Actress, "The Baxter" (2005); Actress, "Imaginary Heroes" (2004); Actress, "Land of Plenty" (2004); Actress, "A Hole in One" (2004); Actress, "The Cherry Orchard" (2004); Actress, "The Station Agent" (2003); Actress, "The United States of Leland" (2003); Actress, "Dawson's Creek" (1998-2003); Actress, "Smelling a Rat" (2002); Actress, "Prozac Nation" (2001); Actress, "Prozac Nation" (2001); Actress, "Me Without You" (2001); Actress, "Perfume" (2001); Actress, "If These Walls Could Talk 2" (2000); Actress, "But I'm a Cheerleader" (1999); Actress, "Dick" (1999); Actress, "Killer Joe" (1999); Actress, "Halloween H20: 20 Years Later" (1998); Actress, "A Thousand Acres" (1997); Actress, "Killing Mr. Griffin" (1997); Actress, "My Son Is Innocent" (1996); Actress, "Timemaster" (1995); Actress, "Home Improvement" (1995); Actress, "Step by Step" (1994); Actress, "Lassie" (1994); Actress, "Baywatch" (1993-1994) **AW:** Best Performance by an Actress in a Limited Series or a Motion Picture Made for Television, "Fosse/Verdon," Golden Globes (2020); Outstanding Performance by a Female Actor in a Television Movie or Limited Series, "Fosse/Verdon," Screen Actors Guild Awards (2020); Best Actress in a Limited Series or Movie Made for Television, "Fosse/Verdon," Broadcast Film Critics Association Awards (2020); Outstanding Lead Actress in a Limited Series or Movie, "Fosse/Verdon," Primetime Emmy Awards (2019); Best Actress in a Motion Picture or Limited Series, "Fosse/Verdon," Online Film & Television Association (2019); Best Actress in a Miniseries & Limited Series or a Motion Picture Made for Television, "Fosse/Verdon," Satellite Awards (2019); Individual Achievement in Drama, "Fosse/Verdon," Television Critics Association Awards (2019); Best Supporting Actress, "Manchester by the Sea," Hawaii Film Critics Society (2017); Best Supporting Actress, "Manchester by the Sea," National Society of Film Critics Awards (2017); Best Supporting Actress, "Manchester by the Sea," Oklahoma Film Critics Circle Awards (2017); Cinema Vanguard Award, "Manchester by the Sea," Santa Barbara International Film Festival (2017); Best Actress in a Supporting Role, "Manchester by the Sea," Awards Circuit Community Awards (2016); Best Supporting Actress, "Manchester by the Sea," Boston Online Film Critics Association (2016); Best Supporting Actress, "Manchester by the Sea," Chicago Film Critics Association Awards (2016); Best Supporting Actress, "Manchester by the Sea," Florida Film Critics Circle Awards (2016); Best Supporting Actress, "Manchester by the Sea," New Mexico Film Critics (2016); Best Supporting Actress, "Certain Women," "Manchester by the Sea," New York Film Critics Circle Awards (2016); Best Supporting Actress, "Manchester by the Sea," North Texas Film Critics Association (2016); Best Supporting Actress, "Manchester by the Sea," Las Vegas Film Critics Society Awards (2016); Best Supporting Actress, "Manchester by the Sea," San Diego Film Critics Society Awards (2016); Best Supporting Actress, "Manchester by the Sea," Toronto Film Critics Association Awards (2016); Best Supporting Actress, "Manchester by the Sea," Vancouver Film Critics Circle (2016); Best Performance by an Actress in a Motion Picture - Comedy or Musical, "My Week with Marilyn," Golden Globes (2012); Best Female Lead, "My Week with Marilyn," Film Independent Spirit Awards (2012); Desert Palm

Achievement Award, "My Week with Marilyn," Palm Springs International Film Festival (2012); Best Actress, "Take This Waltz," San Diego Film Critics Society Awards (2012); Best Actress in a Canadian Film, "Take This Waltz," Vancouver Film Critics Circle (2012); Best Actress, "My Week with Marilyn," Boston Society of Film Critics Awards (2011); Capri Ensemble Cast Award, "My Week with Marilyn" (2011); Best Actress, "My Week with Marilyn," Chicago Film Critics Association Awards (2011); Best Actress, "My Week with Marilyn," Dallas-Forth Worth Film Critics Association Awards (2011); Best Actress, "My Week with Marilyn," Detroit Film Critics Society Awards (2011); Best Actress, "My Week with Marilyn," Florida Film Critics Circle Awards (2011); Actress of the Year, "My Week with Marilyn," Hollywood Film Awards (2011); Best Actress, "Blue Valentine," International Online Cinema Awards (2011); Best Actress, "My Week with Marilyn," Oklahoma Film Critics Circle Awards (2011); Best Actress, "My Week with Marilyn," Toronto Film Critics Association Awards (2011); Best Actress, "My Week with Marilyn," Utah Film Critics Association Awards (2011); Best Actress, "My Week with Marilyn," Washington D.C. Area Film Critics Association Awards (2011); Invisible Woman Award, "Meek's Cutoff," Women Film Critics Circle Awards (2011); Best Actress, "Blue Valentine," San Francisco Film Critics Circle (2010); Robert Altman Award, "Synecdoche, New York," Film Independent Spirit Awards (2009); Best Actress, "Wendy and Lucy," Online Film Critics Society Awards (2009); Gotham Independent Film Award, Best Ensemble Performance, "Synecdoche, New York," Gotham Awards (2008); Best Supporting Actress, "Brokeback Mountain," Broadcast Film Critics Association Awards (2006); Best Performance by an Actress in a Supporting Role, "Brokeback Mountain," Phoenix Film Critics Society Awards (2005); Lucy Award, Women in Film Lucy Awards (2000)

WILLIAMS, RICHARD L., I: Law and Legal Services **CN:** Richard L. Williams, Esq. **DOB:** 11/27/1947 **PB:** Coral Gables **SC:** FL/USA **MS:** Married **SPN:** Marta Cortina **CH:** Matthew Williams; Caroline Lewis; Christopher Williams **ED:** LLM, Harvard University (1973); JD, University of Florida, With Honors (1972); BA, Duke University (1960) **C:** Attorney, Richard L. Williams, Esq. **CR:** General Counsel, OpenMed, Inc. **AW:** Most Effective Lawyer in South Florida, Daily Business Review (2006) **MEM:** Florida Bar Association **BAR:** U.S. Supreme Court (1973); District of Columbia (1972); U.S. Court of Appeals; U.S. Court of Appeals for the Fifth Circuit; U.S. District Court; U.S. District Court for the Southern District of Florida; U.S. Court of Appeals for the Eleventh Circuit; U.S. Tax Court; Florida **AS:** Mr. Williams attributes his success to hard work. **B/I:** Mr. Williams became involved in his profession because his dad, Reginald L. Williams, was a lawyer. It was a natural progression for him.

WILLIAMS, SERENA JAMEKA, T: Professional Tennis Player **I:** Athletics **DOB:** 09/26/1981 **PB:** Saginaw **SC:** MI/USA **PT:** Richard Williams; Oracene (Price) Williams **MS:** Married **SPN:** Alexis Ohanian (11/16/2017) **CH:** Alexis Olympia, Jr. **CT:** Certified Nail Technician **C:** Chief Sporting Officer, Aston Martin (2015-Present); Professor Tennis Player, WTA Tour (1995-Present); Minority Owner, Miami Dolphins (2009); Designer, Aneres **CR:** U.S. National Team, Summer Olympic Games, London, England (2012); Launched, Signature Statement, Home Shopping Network (2009); U.S. National Team, Summer Olympic Games, Beijing, China (2008); U.S. National Team, Fed Cup (1999, 2003, 2007); Launched, Shoe Line, Nike (2004); U.S. National Team, Summer Olympic Games,

Sydney, NSW, Australia (2000); Endorser, Gatorade, Delta Air Lines, Audemars Piguet, Aston Martin, Pepsi, Beats by Dre, Mission Athletecare, Berlei, OPI Products, OnePiece, IBM, Mini, Intel, Tempur and Chase Bank; Former Designer, Puma; Numerous Other Clothing Lines **CIV:** Board of Directors, Poshmark (2019-Present); Host, Serena Williams Ultimate Fun Run, Serena Williams Fund (2014-Present); International Goodwill Ambassador, UNICEF (2011-Present); Ambassador, Allstate Foundation's Purple Purse (2017); Yetunde Price Resource Center (2016); Equal Justice Initiative (2015); Board of Directors, SurveyMonkey; Ronald McDonald House; Founder, Serena Williams Secondary School, Matooni, Kenya; Serena Williams Foundation; Serena Williams Fund; Partner, Helping Hands Jamaica; First Serve Miami; Launched, UNICEF's Schools for Asia; Williams Sisters Fund; Elton John AIDS Foundation; Great Ormond Street Hospital; Hearts of Gold; Common Ground Foundation; Small Steps Project; HollyRod Foundation; Beyond the Boroughs National Scholarship Fund; World Education; Eva Longoria Foundation; Caliber Foundation; Cure for MND Foundation **CW:** Appearance, Music Video, "Sorry" (2016); Guest Appearance, "Pixels" (2015); Guest Appearance, "Trust Us with Your Life" (2012); Guest Appearance, "Drop Dead Diva" (2012); Appearance, Documentary, "Venus and Serena" (2012); Author, "On the Line" (2009); Guest Appearance, "Avatar: The Last Airbender" (2007); Guest Appearance, "Punk'd" (2007); Appearance, Music Video, "I Want You" (2007); Co-Author, "Venus & Serena: Serving From The Hip: 10 Rules For Living, Loving and Winning" (2005); Guest Appearance, "Higglytown Heroes" (2005); Guest Appearance, "Law and Order: Special Victims Unit" (2004); Guest Appearance, "The Division" (2004); Guest Appearance, "My Wife and Kids" (2002); Guest Appearance, "The Simpsons" (2001); Guest Appearances, "Fast Cars and Superstars: The Gillette Young Guns Celebrity Race," "The Bernie Mac Show," "ER" and Others; Appearances, Commercials **AW:** Winner, Singles, Australian Open (2003, 2005, 2007, 2009-2010, 2015, 2017); Winner, Singles, Wimbledon (2002-2003, 2009-2010, 2012, 2015-2016); Winner, Doubles, Wimbledon (2000, 2002, 2008-2009, 2012, 2016); Winner, Singles, French Open (2002, 2013, 2015); Winner, Singles, U.S. Open (1999, 2002, 2008, 2012-2014); Winner, Doubles, French Open (1999, 2010); Winner, Doubles, Australian Open (2001, 2003, 2009-2010); Winner, Doubles, U.S. Open (1999, 2009); Family Circle and Prudential Financial Player Who Makes a Difference Award (2004); Celebrity Role Model Award, Avon Foundation (2003); Young Heroes Award, Big Brothers Big Sisters of Greater Los Angeles and Inland (2003); Winner, Mixed Doubles, U.S. Open (1998); Winner, Mixed Doubles, Wimbledon (1998); 35 Most Remarkable and Beautiful Black Women, Essence Magazine; President's Award, NAACP Image Awards

WILLIAMS, VANESSA L., T: Actress; Recording Artist **I:** Media & Entertainment **DOB:** 03/18/1963 **PB:** Millwood **SC:** NY/USA **PT:** Milton Augustine Williams Jr.; Helen (Tinch) Williams **MS:** Married **SPN:** Jim Skrip (2015); Rick Fox (1999, Divorced 2004); Ramon Hervey II (1987, Divorced 1997) **CH:** Sasha Gabriella Fox; Jillian Hervey; Melanie Hervey; Devin Hervey **ED:** BFA, Syracuse University (2008); Coursework in Musical Theater, Department of Drama, College of Visual and Performing Arts (Now Crous College), Syracuse University **C:** Founder, V. by Vanessa Williams for EVINE Live (2016); Actress; Singer **CR:** Spokesmodel, Proactiv Solution, The Proactiv Company Sàrl; Spokesmodel, L'Oréal Cosmetics, L'Oreal Paris **CIV:** Head Judge, Miss America 2016 Pageant (2016); Partici-

pant, "New Yorkers for Marriage Equality" (2011); Advocate, LGBT Rights and Same Sex Marriage; Partner, Dress for Success **CW:** Actress, "City of Angels" (2020); Actress, "Bad Hair" (2020); Actor, "T.O.T.S." (2019); Actress, "Miss Virginia" (2019); Actress, "The First Wives Club" (2019); Voice Actress, "Batman: Hush" (2019); Appearance, "RuPaul's Drag Race All Stars" (2018); Actress, "False Profits" (2018); Voice Actress, "The Legend of Hallowaiian" (2018); Actress, "Me, Myself and I" (2018); Voice Actress, "Suicide Squad: Hell to Play" (2018); Actress, "Milo Murphy's Law" (2016-2018); Actress, "Modern Family" (2017); Actress, "Difficult People" (2017); Actress, "Daytime Divas" (2017); Actress, "The Man from Earth: Holocene" (2017); Actress, "The Librarians" (2016-2017); Actress, "Broad City" (2016); Actress, "Fantasy Life" (2015); Actress, "The Good Wife" (2015); Actress, "Royal Pains" (2015); Actress, "The Mindy Project" (2015); Actress, "Show Boat" (2015); Actress, "Live from Lincoln Center" (1979-2015); Voice Actress, "When Marnie Was There" (2014); Actress, "The Trip to Bountiful" (2014); Actress, "After Midnight" (2014); Co-author, "You Have No Idea: A Famous Daughter, Her No-Nonsense Mother, and How They Survived Pageants, Hollywood, Love, Loss (and Each Other)" (2013); Actress, "Temptation: Confessions of a Marriage Counselor" (2013); Appearance, "He's Way More Famous Than You" (2013); Actress, "The Trip to Bountiful" (2013); Actress, "666 Park Avenue" (2012-2013); Voice Actress, "Phineas and Ferb" (2012); Voice Actress, "Delhi Safari" (2012); Actress, "Desperate Housewives" (2010-2012); Actress, "Sondheim on Sondheim" (2010); Actress, "Ugly Betty" (2006-2010); Singer, Album, "The Real Thing" (2009); Contestant, "Who Wants to Be a Millionaire" (2000, 2009); Host, "Dreams Come True: A Celebration of Disney Animation" (2009); Host, 36th Annual Daytime Emmy Awards (2009); Singer, "Just Friends" (2009); Singer, "Close to You" (2009); Singer, "Breathless" (2009); Actress, "Hannah Montana: The Movie" (2009); Actress, "Mama Mirabelle's Home Movies" (2007-2008); Host, 6th Annual TV Land Awards (2007); Executive Producer, Actress, "And Then Came Love" (2007); Narrator, Actress, "The Beautiful World of Ugly Betty" (2007); Actress, "My Brother" (2006); Actress, "South Beach" (2006); Singer, Album, "Everlasting Love" (2005); Actress, "Beck and Call" (2004); Actress, "Johnson Family Vacation" (2004); Executive Producer, "Vanessa Williams Christmas: Live by Request" (2004); Singer, Album, "Silver & Gold" (2004); Actress, "Boomtown" (2003); Actress, "The Proud Family" (2002); Actress, "Ally McBeal" (2002); Actress, "Keep the Faith, Baby" (2002); Actress, "Into the Woods" (2002); Actress, "Carmen Jones" (2002); Actress, "Lil' Romeo, Nick Cannon & 3LW: Parents Just Don't Understand" (2001); Voice Actress, "Santa Baby!" (2001); Actress, "WW 3" (2001); Executive Producer, "The Courage to Love" (2000); Actress, "A Diva's Christmas Carol" (2000); Actress, "Shaft" (2000); Actress, "Don Quixote" (2000); Actress, "The Courage to Love" (2000); Actress, "Light It Up" (1999); Actress, "The Adventures of Elmo in Grouchland" (1999); Actress, "L.A. Doctors" (1999); Host, 1998 NAACP Image Awards (1998); Actress, "Futuresport" (1998); Actress, "Dance with Me" (1998); Singer with Chayanne, "Refugio de Amor (You Are My Home)" (1998); Actress, "St. Louis Woman" (1998); Singer, Album, "Next" (1997); Singer, "Happiness" (1997); Actress, "Hoodlum" (1997); Actress, "Soul Food" (1997); Actress, "The Odyssey" (1997); Singer, "Oh How the Years Go By" (1997); Singer, Album, "Star Bright" (1996); Executive Producer, "Vanessa Williams & Friends: Christmas in New York" (1996); Actress, "Star Trek: Deep Space Nine" (1996); Singer, "Where Do We Go from Here?" (1996); Actress, "Eraser" (1996); Actress,

"Bye Bye Birdie" (1995); Actress, "Nothing Lasts Forever" (1995); Voice Actress, "Happily Ever After: Fairy Tales for Every Child" (1995); Singer, "The Way That You Love" (1995); Actress, "Various Artists: Freedom" (1995); Host, 1994 Essence Awards (1994); Singer, Album, "The Sweetest Days" (1994); Actress, "Score with Chicks" (1994); Singer, "The Sweetest Days (Romantic Version)" (1994); Singer, "The Sweetest Days (Urban Version)" (1994); Actress, "Kiss of the Spider Woman" (1994); Singer Featuring Brian McKnight, "Love Is" (1993); Singer, "What Will I Tell My Heart" (1992); Singer, "What Child Is This?" (1992); Actress, "The Fresh Prince of Bel-Air" (1992); Actress, "The Jacksons: An American Dream" (1992); Singer, "Work to Do" (1992); Singer, "Just for Tonight" (1992); Actress, "Stompin' at the Savoy" (1992); Singer, "Save the Best for Last, Holiday Version" (1992); Singer, Album, "The Comfort Zone" (1991); Singer, "Save the Best for Last" (1991); Singer, "The Comfort Zone" (1991); Singer, "Running Back to You" (1991); Actress, "Harley Davidson and the Marlboro Man" (1991); Actress, "Another You" (1991); Actress, "The Kid Who Loved Christmas" (1990); Actress, "Seriously...Phil Collins" (1990); Actress, "Perry Mason: The Case of the Silenced Singer" (1990); Singer, "Darlin' I" (1989); Actress, "Full Exposure: The Sex Tapes Scandal" (1989); Singer, Album, "The Right Stuff" (1988); Singer, "(He's Got) The Look" (1988); Singer, "Dreamin'" (1988); Singer, "The Right Stuff" (1988); Actress, "Under the Gun" (1988); Actress, "The Pick-up Artist" (1987); Actress, "The Love Boat" (1986); Actress, "T.J. Hooker" (1986); Actress, "The Red Foxx Show" (1986); Actress, "Partners in Crime" (1984) **AW:** Outstanding Supporting Actress in a Comedy Series, "Desperate Housewives," NAACP Image Awards (2013); Best Actress in a Supporting Role in a Series, Miniseries or Motion Picture Made for Television, "Desperate Housewives," Satellite Awards (2011); Mary Pickford Award, Satellite Awards (2010); Muse Award, New York Women in Film & Television (2010); Outstanding Supporting Actress in a Comedy Series, "Ugly Betty," NAACP Image Awards (2008); Outstanding Supporting Actress in a Comedy Series, "Ugly Betty," NAACP Image Awards (2007); Recipient, Star, Hollywood Walk of Fame (2007); Best Actress in a Supporting Role in a Series, Miniseries or Motion Picture Made for Television, "Ugly Betty," Satellite Awards (2007); Choice TV: Villain, "Ugly Betty," Teen Choice Awards (2007); Best Actress in a Miniseries or a Motion Picture Made for Television, "Keep the Faith, Baby," Satellite Awards (2003); Outstanding Lead Actress in a Motion Picture, "Soul Food," NAACP Image Awards (1998); Outstanding New Artist, NAACP Image Awards (1989); 11 Grammy Award Nominations **RE:** Roman Catholic

WILLIAMS, VANESSA YVONNE, T: Retired **I:** Government Administration/Government Relations/Government Services **CN:** U.S. Air Force, United States Department of Defense **DOB:** 10/02/1952 **PB:** Detroit **SC:** MI/USA **PT:** Warren Williams; Beatrice Williams **MS:** Married **SPN:** Rebecca Bartaway **CT:** Certified, Logistic Analyst; Program Management, Certified Acquisition Professional **C:** Accounting and Finance, U.S. Air Force; Airfield Management, U.S. Air Force **CIV:** Volunteer, Friends for Animals **MIL:** With, Air National Guard **AW:** Daily Point of Light Award, Friends for Animals; Meritorious Service Medal; Air Force Achievement Medal With Four Devices; Air Good Conduct Medal; Air Force Outstanding Unit; Air Reserve Forces Meritorious Service Medal With Four Devices; National Defense Medal; Air Force Longevity Service Award With Three Devices; Air Force NCO Professional Military Education Graduate; Air Force Training Ribbon; Michigan State Ribbon With Four Devices **MEM:** U.S. Air Force Association; Retired Non-Commissioned Officers Organization **AS:** Ms. Williams attributes her success to her innate passion for what she does. Likewise, she is patient, and loves to learn. **B/I:** Ms. Williams has always been drawn toward military service and, upon joining, loved it so much that she remained involved for over 35 years. **AV:** Softball; Gym; Walking her dogs **RE:** Baptist

WILLIAMS, VENUS, T: Professional Tennis Player **I:** Athletics **DOB:** 06/17/1980 **PB:** Lynwood **SC:** CA/USA **PT:** Richard Williams; Oracene Price **ED:** BSBA, Indiana University East (2015); Associate Degree in Fashion Design, Art Institute of Fort Lauderdale (2007) **C:** Founder, Designer, EleVen (2007-Present); Professional Tennis Player (1994-Present); Part-Owner, Miami Dolphins (2009); Designer, Venus Williams, Wilson's Leather; Chief Executive Officer, Design Firm, V Starr Interiors **CR:** Member, U.S. Team, Summer Olympic Games (2000, 2004, 2008, 2012, 2016) **CW:** Herself, "Venus and Serena" (2012); Co-Author, "Come to Win: Business Leaders, Artists, Doctors, and Other Visionaries on How Sports Can Help You Top Your Profession" (2010); Author, "Venus and Serena: Serving From The Hip: 10 Rules for Living, Loving, and Winning" (2005); Co-Author, "How to Play Tennis" (2004) **AW:** WTA Player of the Year, ESPN (2017); WTA Comeback Player of the Year (2015); Sportsmanship Award, U.S. Open (2015); WTA Player Service Award (2013); Star Power Award, BET Black Girls Rock! (2013); WTA Player Service Award (2012); Ranked #22, "100 Greatest Tennis Players of All Time," Tennis Channel (2012); 2012 World TeamTennis Finals Most Valuable Player (2012); Named One of the "30 Legends of Women's Tennis: Past, Present and Future," Time (2011); Jefferson Award for Outstanding Public Service in Professional Sports (2010); YWCA GLA Phenomenal Woman of the Year Award (2010); Caesars Tennis Classic Achievement Award (2010); Named #77 in the "Top 100 Most Powerful Celebrities," Forbes (2009); Anti-Defamation League Americanism Award (2008); Whirlpool 6th Sense Player of the Year Award (2008); Gitanjali Diamond Award (2007); Best Female Athlete of the Year, BET (2006); Best Female Tennis Player ESPY Award (2006); Women of the Year Award, Glamour Magazine (2005); Ranked, "25th Best Player in 40 Years," Tennis Magazine (2005); President's Award, 34th NAACP Image Awards (2003); EMMA Best Sport Personality Award (2001); Best Female Tennis Player ESPY Award (2001); Sportswoman of the Year for Team Sports, Women's Sports Foundation (2000); Extraordinary Achievement Award, Teen Choice Awards (2000); Sportswoman of the Year, Sports Illustrated for Women (2000); WTA Player of the Year (2000); Most Improved Player, Tennis Magazine (1998); Sports Image Foundation Award "for conducting tennis clinics in low-income areas" (1995) **MEM:** Players' Council, Women's Tennis Association (WTA) **AV:** Interior and fashion design **RE:** Jehovah's Witnesses

WILLIAMSON, ZION LATEEF, T: Professional Basketball Player **I:** Athletics **CN:** New Orleans Pelicans **DOB:** 07/06/2000 **PB:** Salisbury **SC:** NC/USA **PT:** Lateef Williamson; Sharonda Sampson; Lee Anderson (Stepfather) **ED:** Coursework, Duke University (2018-2019); Diploma, Spartanburg Day School, Spartanburg, SC **C:** Power Forward, Small Forward, New Orleans Pelicans (2019-Present) **CR:** Sponsor, Air Jordan (2019-Present) **AW:** Consensus National College Player of the Year (2019); Consensus First-Team All-American (2019); Wayman Tisdale Award (2019); Karl Malone Award (2019); ACC Athlete of the Year (2019); ACC Player of the Year (2019); ACC All-Freshman Team (2019); First-Team All-ACC (2019); ACC Rookie of the Year (2019); ACC Tournament MVP (2019); McDonald's All-American (2018); Jordan Brand Classic (2018); Nike Hoop Summit (2018); South Carolina Mr. Basketball (2018)

WILLIS, BRUCE, T: Actor **I:** Media & Entertainment **DOB:** 03/19/1955 **PB:** Idar-Oberstein **SC:** Germany **PT:** David Willis; Marlene Willis **MS:** Married **SPN:** Emma Heming (03/21/2009); Demi Moore (11/21/1987, Divorced 2000) **CH:** Rumer; Scout; Tallulah; Two daughters **ED:** Student, Stella Adler; Student, Drama Program, Montclair State University **C:** Co-Founder, Co-Owner, Cheyenne Enterprises (2000-2009); Co-Founder, Planet Hollywood; Owner, The Mint Bar; Owner, The Liberty Theater; Actor, Producer, Film and Television **CR:** Former Member, First Amendment Improv Troupe **CW:** Actor, "Breach" (2020); Actor, "Survive the Night" (2020); Actor, "Trauma Center" (2019); Actor, "10 Minutes Gone" (2019); Actor, "Between Two Ferns: The Movie" (2019); Actor, "Motherless Brooklyn" (2019); Voice Actor, "The Orville" (2019); Voice Actor, "The Lego Movie 2: The Second Part" (2019); Actor, "Glass" (2019); Actor, "Air Strike" (2018); Actor, "Reprisal" (2018); Actor, "Death Wish" (2018); Actor, "Acts of Violence" (2018); Actor, "First Kill" (2017); Actor, "One Upon a Time in Venice" (2017); Actor, "Split" (2016); Actor, "Marauders" (2016); Actor, "Precious Cargo" (2016); Actor, "Misery" (2015); Actor, "Extraction" (2015); Actor, "Rock the Kasbah" (2015); Actor, "Vice" (2015); Actor, "The Prince" (2014); Actor, "Sing City: A Dame to Kill For" (2014); Voice Actor, "Family Guy: The Quest for Stuff" (2014); Actor, "RED 2" (2013); Actor, "G.I. Joe: Retaliation" (2013); Actor, "A Good Day to Die Hard" (2013); Actor, "Fire with Fire" (2012); Actor, "Looper" (2012); Actor, "The Expendables 2" (2012); Actor, "Moonrise Kingdom" (2012); Actor, "The Cold Light of Day" (2012); Actor, "Lay the Favorite" (2012); Actor, "Nike: The Black Mamba" (2011); Actor, "Catch .44" (2011); Actor, "Setup" (2011); Actor, "Gorillaz Featuring Mos Def and Bobby Womack: Stylo" (2010); Actor, "RED" (2010); Actor, "The Expendables" (2010); Actor, "Cop Out" (2010); Actor, "Surrogates" (2009); Actor, "Late Show with David Letterman" (2008-2009); Actor, "What Just Happened" (2008); Actor, "Assassination of a High School President" (2008); Actor, "Planet Terror" (2007); Actor, "Nancy Drew" (2007); Actor, "Live Free or Die Hard" (2007); Actor, "Perfect Stranger" (2007); Actor, "Vanity Fair: Killers Kill, Dead Men Die" (2007); Executive Producer, "The Hip Hop Project" (2006); Voice Actor, "Hammy's Boomerang Adventure" (2006); Actor, "The Astronaut Farmer" (2006); Actor, "Fast Food Nation" (2006); Himself, "That '70s Show Special: The Final Goodbye" (2006); Voice Actor, "Over the Hedge" (2006); Actor, "16 Blocks" (2006); Actor, "Lucky Number Slevin" (2006); Actor, "Alpha Dog" (2006); Producer, "Hostage" (2005); Actor, "Hostage" (2005); Actor, "That '70s Show" (2005); Actor, "Sin City" (2005); Executive Producer, "Touching Evil" (2004); Actor, "Ocean's Twelve" (2004); Actor, "The Whole Ten Yards" (2004); Actor, "Charlie's Angels: Full Throttle" (2003); Voice Actor, "Rugrats Go Wild" (2003); Actor, "Tears of the Sun" (2003); Executive Producer, "True West" (2002); Actor, "True West" (2002); Executive Producer, "The Crocodile Hunter: Collision Course" (2002); Actor, "Grand Champion" (2002); Actor, "Hart's War" (2002); Actor, "Bandits" (2001); Actor, "Unbreakable" (2000); Actor, "The Kid" (2000); Actor, "Friends" (2000); Actor, "The Whole Nine Yards" (2000); Actor, "The Story of Us" (1999); Actor, "The Sixth Sense" (1999); Actor, "Breakfast of Champions" (1999); Actor, "Ally McBeal" (1999); Voice Actor, "Apocalypse"

(1998); Actor, "The Siege" (1998); Actor, "Armageddon" (1998); Actor, "Mercury Rising" (1998); Actor, "The Jackal" (1997); Actor, "Mad About You" (1997); Actor, "The Fifth Element" (1997); Actor, "Bruno the Kid" (1996-1997); Executive Producer, "Bruno the Kid" (1996); Voice Actor, "Bruno the Kid: The Animated Movie" (1996); Voice Actor, "Beavis and Butt-Head Do America" (1996); Actor, "Last Man Standing" (1996); Actor, "12 Monkeys" (1995); Actor, "Four Rooms" (1995); Actor, "Die Hard with a Vengeance" (1995); Actor, "Nobody's Fool" (1994); Actor, "Nobody's Fool" (1994); Actor, "Color of Night" (1994); Narrator, "North" (1994); Actor, "Pulp Fiction" (1994); Actor, "Striking Distance" (1993); Actor, "Loaded Weapon 1" (1993); Actor, "Death Becomes Her" (1992); Actor, "The Player" (1992); Actor, "The Last Boy Scout" (1991); Actor, "Billy Bathgate" (1991); Actor, "Hudson Hawk" (1991); Actor, "Mortal Thoughts" (1991); Actor, "The Bonfire of the Vanities" (1990); Voice Actor, "Look Who's Talking Too" (1990); Actor, "Die Hard 2" (1990); Voice Actor, "Look Who's Talking" (1989); Actor, "In Country" (1989); Singer, "If it Don't Kill You, It Just Makes You Stronger" (1989); Actor, "Die Hard" (1988); Actor, "Sunset" (1988); Actor, "Bruce Willis: Respect Yourself" (1987); Actor, "Blind Date" (1987); Executive Producer, "The Return of Bruno" (1987); Actor, "The Return of Bruno" (1987); Singer, "The Return of Bruno" (1987); Actor, "Seagram's: At a Bar" (1986); Actor, "Moonlighting" (1985-1989); Actor, "The Twilight Zone" (1985); Actor, "Miami Vice" (1982); Actor, "The Verdict" (1982); Actor, "Ein Guru Kommt" (1980); Actor, "The First Deadly Sin" (1980) **AW:** Best Ensemble, "Moonrise Kingdom," Central Ohio Film Critics Association (2013); Commander of the Order of Arts and Letters, Order of Arts and Letters, France (2013); Best Ensemble Acting, "Moonrise Kingdom," Phoenix Film Critics Society Awards (2012); Inductee, New Jersey Hall of Fame (2011); Star, Hollywood Walk of Fame (2006); Best International Actor, Golden Camera, Germany (2005); Man of the Year, Hasty Pudding Theatricals, USA (2002); Favorite Actor, Suspense Category, "The Sixth Sense," Blockbuster Entertainment Awards (2000); Outstanding Guest Actor in a Comedy Series, "Friends," Primetime Emmy Awards (2000); Best Guest Actor in a Comedy Series, "Friends," Online Film & Television Association (2000); Favorite Motion Picture Star in a Drama, People's Choice Awards (2000); Favorite Actor, Sci-Fi Category, "Armageddon," Blockbuster Entertainment Awards (1999); Best Cast Ensemble, "Pulp Fiction," Awards Circuit Community Awards (1994); Best Performance by an Actor in a Television Series - Comedy or Musical, "Moonlighting," Golden Globes (1987); Outstanding Lead Actor in a Drama Series, "Moonlighting," Primetime Emmy Awards (1987); Favorite Male Performer in a New TV Program, People's Choice Award (1986)

WILLIS, JOHN OSGOOD, I: Education/Educational Services **CN:** Educational Evaluator, Educator **DOB:** 07/19/1946 **PB:** Princeton **SC:** New Jersey **PT:** Raymond Smith Willis; Margaret Ellen (Osgood) Willis **MS:** Widowed **SPN:** Ursula Margaret Von Zarsk Oxley (01/03/1970) **CH:** Janet McKellar Hecht; Douglas Gordon Oxley **ED:** EdD, Vanderbilt University (1984), AB, Cornell University, Magna Cum Laude (1968) **CT:** Certified Specialist in Assessment of Intellectual Functioning; Certified Special Education Teacher, New Hampshire **C:** Consultant, Regional Service and Education (2010-Present); Assessment Specialist, Regional Services and Education Center, Amherst, NH (1974-2010); Acting Executive Director, Regional Services and Education Center, Amherst, NH (1985-1986); Director, Psychoeducational Services, Regional Services and Education Center,

Amherst, NH (1976-1986); Acting Executive Director, Crotched Mountain School, Greenfield, NH (1972-1973); Director, Student Services, Crotched Mountain School, Greenfield, NH (1972-1974); Educational Evaluator, Teacher, Crotched Mountain School, Greenfield, NH (1969-1974) **CR:** Senior Lecturer in Assessment Rivier College, Nashua, NH (1981-2017); Adjunct Faculty, Antioch/New England Graduate School, Keene, New Hampshire (1979, 1989); Adjunct Faculty, University of New Hampshire Systems, Manchester, NH (1974, 1976) **CIV:** Treasurer, Monadnock Day Care Center, Peterborough, NH (1976); Board of Directors, Monadnock Workshop, Peterborough, NH (1972-1974) **CW:** Co-author, "Essentials of Idea for Assessment Professionals," John Wiley & Sons (2011); Co-author, "Essentials of Das II Assessment," John Wiley & Sons (2009); Co-author, "Guide to Identification of Learning Disabilities, Third Edition (2002); Author, "Guide to Identification of Learning Disabilities" (1990); Contributor, Chapters, Books; Contributor, Articles, Professional Journals **AW:** Sister Mary Jane Benoit Outstanding Educator of the Year Award (2016); Named, Volunteer of Year, Victory Committee for Cerebral Palsy, Ithaca, NY (1968) **MEM:** Affiliate Member, National Association of School Psychologists; Affiliate Member, New Hampshire Association School Psychologists; Learning Disabilities Association; Psi Chi **MH:** Albert Nelson Marquis Lifetime Achievement Award **B/I:** Mr. Willis' volunteer work at a special education school when he was in High school motivated him in this field. **AV:** Fishing; Reading history

WILLIS-REICKERT, SUSAN, T: President (Retired) **I:** Fine Art **CN:** Cap Ferrat Fine Art Consultancy **MS:** Married **SPN:** Erick A. Reickert **ED:** Postgraduate Coursework, University of Oxford; Postgraduate, Cornell University; PhD, The University of Sheffield; EdM, Antioch College; BA, Briarcliff College **CT:** IDEC Corporation; American Society of Interior Designers (ASID); IBD **C:** Art Historian, Curator, Consultant to Small Private Museums and Corporate Collections; Art History, Design Professor Emerita; Founder, The Art of Peace International; Consultant, The Georgian Theater Royal, Richmond, North Yorkshire, England, United Kingdom **CR:** Lecturer, Fine Arts; Author, Painter **CIV:** Supporter, New England Home for Little Wanderers Orphanage; Supporter, Dar Tal Providenzia, Crippled Children's Home, Malta; Lady Susan Willis-Reickert Fund for British Arts and Culture, Florida Atlantic University; Georgian Theatre Royal, North Yorkshire, United Kingdom **CW:** Published Author, Books; Television Personality in Bermuda, CA, FL and Boston, MA; International Artist, Numerous Paintings in Collections in London, England, United Kingdom, Paris, France, Saint-Jean-Cap-Ferrat, France, Hong Kong, Monaco, Palm Beach and Miami, FL, NY and New England **AW:** Ford Family Lifetime Award in Philanthropy, Ford Foundation, Detroit, MI (2019); Ellis Island Medal of Honor (1999); Named Michigan Woman of the Year, Lifetime Achievement Award (1998); Knighted in Malta and Spain **MEM:** American Board of Directors, English National Opera, London, United Kingdom (2015-2020); Chairman, American Lung Association (1992); Lansdowne Club, London, United Kingdom; Retired Equestrian, Bloomfield Open Hunt Club; Circumnavigators Club, Palm Beach, FL; Oxford Union; Oxford Debating Society; Junior League of London; The Rolls Royce Club (Rolls Royce Owners' Club); Metamora Hunt Inc.; American Society for Aesthetics; Art Historians of Nineteenth Century Art (Now Association of Historians of Nineteenth-Century Art); The Paul Mellon Institute of British Art (Now Paul Mellon Centre for Studies in British

Art); Past President, Current Board Member, Women's Division, Project HOPE; Vice President, Board of Directors, St. George's Society of Palm Beach; Board Member, International Visitors Council, United States Department of State; British Lung Association; Board of Directors, Global Connections, Detroit, MI **AS:** Lady Willis-Reickert attributes her success to being a hardworking individual, having a clear vision, and never giving up. **B/I:** Lady Willis-Reickert became involved in her profession because of a natural evolution from fine arts to art history and the desire to teach her passion. She worked to become an expert and share her knowledge to assist clients. **AV:** International travel; Philanthropy; Equestrian events; Sailing **THT:** Lady Willis-Reickert's motto is, "Make every day count. Show kindness to others. Cherish the simple things and the beauty of nature.

WILSON, ADDISON, "JOE" GRAVES SR., T: U.S. Representative from South Carolina **I:** Government Administration/Government Relations/Government Services **DOB:** 07/31/1947 **PB:** Charleston **SC:** SC/USA **PT:** Hugh deVeaux Wilson; Wray Smart (Graves) Wilson **MS:** Married **SPN:** Roxanne Dusenbury McCrory Wilson (12/30/1978) **CH:** Michael Alan; Addison Graves; Julian Dusenbury; Hunter Taylor **ED:** JD, University of South Carolina School of Law, Columbia, SC (1972); BA, Washington and Lee University, Lexington, VA (1969) **C:** Member, U.S. House of Representatives from South Carolina's Second Congressional District, United States Congress, Washington, DC (2001-Present); Member, District 23, South Carolina State Senate (1985-2001); Presidential Appointee, Intergovernmental Advisory Council on Education (1990, 1991); Deputy General Counsel to Secretary Jim Edwards, U.S. Department of Energy, Washington, DC (1981, 1982); Partner, Kirkland, Wilson, Moore, Taylor & Thomas (Now Moore Taylor Law Firm), West Columbia, SC (1972-2001); Staff Member, U.S. Representative Floyd Spence, Columbia, SC (1970-1972); Staff Member, U.S. Senator Strom Thurmond, Washington, DC (1967) **CR:** Board of Directors, Bank of America Corporation, Lexington, SC **CIV:** Campaign Manager, Staff, U.S. Representative Floyd Spence, Columbia, SC (1974, 1978, 1980, 1982, 1998); Vice Chairman, South Carolina Republican Party (1972-1974); Member, First Presbyterian Church, Columbia, SC; Sheriff's Department Law Enforcement Advisory Council; Reserve Officers Association of the United States (Now Reserve Organization of America); Lexington County Historical Society (Now Lexington County Museum); County Community and Resource Development Committee; American Heart Association, Inc.; Mid-Carolina Mental Health Association; Advisory Board, NationsBank Lexington **MIL:** Advanced Through Grades to Colonel, South Carolina Army National Guard (1975-2003); With, United States Army Reserve (1972-1975) **MEM:** Rotary Club of Cayce-West Columbia; Columbia World Affairs Council; Fellowship of Christian Athletes; Woodmen of the World Life Insurance Society; Sons of Confederate Veterans; American Legislative Exchange Council; Navy League of the United States; AMVETS; Association of the United States Army; National Guard Association of the United States; Air Force Association; The American Legion; Boy Scouts of America; Sigma Nu Fraternity, Inc. **BAR:** State of South Carolina (1972) **PA:** Republican **RE:** Presbyterian

WILSON, CHARLES LEE, T: Professor Emeritus **I:** Education/Educational Services **DOB:** 06/06/1941 **PB:** Phoenix **SC:** AZ/USA **PT:** Francis Lee Wilson; Leila Frances (Harris) Wilson **MS:** Married **SPN:** Brenda (Cox) Wilson **CH:** Jennine Ward; Nicole Eriksson **ED:** PhD, State University of New York at Stony Brook (1972); MA, San Francisco State University (1967); AB, University of California Berkeley (1964) **C:** Emeritus Professor of Neurology, University of California Los Angeles Medical School (2006-Present); Research Physiologist, Sepulveda VAH (2006-2010); Professor of Neurology, University of California Los Angeles Medical School (1997-2006); Associate Professor, Department of Neurology, University of California Los Angeles Medical School (1992-1997); Assistant Professor of Neurology, University of California Los Angeles Medical School (1984-1992); Assistant Research Neurologist, University of California Los Angeles Medical School (1978-1984); Assistant Researcher, Brain Research Institute, University of California Los Angeles (1974-1978); Postdoctoral Fellow, University of California Los Angeles (1972-1974) **CR:** Committee Service, American Epilepsy Society; Grant Reviewer, National Institutes of Health **CIV:** Volunteer Teacher, High School Anatomy and Physiology **CW:** Reviewer, Over 20 Scientific Journals (1979-2016); Author, Over 200 Scientific Articles, Professional Journals; Speaker, Over 30 Invited Talks, National and Internation Science Meetings **AW:** Research Grantee in Epilepsy, National Institutes of Health, University of California Los Angeles Medical School (1984-2006); Golden Hammer Teaching Award, Department of Neurology, University of California Los Angeles Medical School (1991) **MEM:** Society for Neuroscience; American Epilepsy Society; American Society of Sleep Medicine; American Clinical Neurophysiology Society; AAA; Sierra Club **MH:** Albert Nelson Marquis Lifetime Achievement Award **AS:** Dr. Wilson attributes his success to the support and encouragement of his wife, Brenda. **B/I:** Dr. Wilson developed an interest in neuroscience while studying with Mark Rosenzweig at the University of California Berkeley in 1962, where he became interested in brain function and the physiology of the nervous system. At San Francisco State University, he continued his research and met his wife, Brenda. After a year of postgraduate research at the Palo Alto VAH, he entered the psychobiology doctoral program at Stony Brook University in New York. During that time, he attended the first meeting of the Society of Neuroscience in Washington, DC, where he heard presentations by David Hubel, Torsten Wiesel, and John Eccles, all of which inspired his doctoral work in visual physiology. In 1972, he returned to California and began post-doctoral research with Donald Lindsley at the University of California Los Angeles, covering brain stem modulation of the limbic system focusing on the hippocampus. He then worked with neurosurgeon Paul Crandall and neurologist Jerome Engel in the University of California Los Angeles' Clinical Neurophysiology Program on single neuron properties of the visual system studied in epilepsy patients implanted with diagnostic intracranial microelectrodes in the temporal lobes and hippocampus. In 1986, he joined the department of neurology, where he continued his research with funding from the National Institutes of Health for the investigation of human visual pathways using single neuron recordings from intracranial microelectrodes. His publications spanned work on visual receptive fields of human optic radiation fibers to interhemispheric connections between the temporal and frontal lobes and mechanisms of seizure generation in both patients and rodent models of epilepsy. A final major area of research involved electrophysiological recording and magnetic resonance imaging of the role of high-frequency oscillations in the generation and propagation of seizure activity in collaboration with Anatol Bragin, Richard Staba, Itzhak Fried, and Jerome Engel. He later taught courses in neuroscience, neurobiology, neuro-engineer-

ing, biomedical engineering, neuroanatomy, and neurobiology at the University of California Los Angeles Medical and Dental School. He supervised and mentored both graduate and postdoctoral students in neurology and neurobiology, as well as fellows in neurology and clinical neurophysiology. **AV:** Backpacking; Mountain climbing; Practicing viticulture **THT:** Dr. Wilson hopes more young people will be inspired to use science compassionately to not only learn about the world but also to learn how to improve the lives of all humankind.

WILSON, DIANE E., T: Music Educator, Special Education Educator **I:** Education/Educational Services **PT:** Richard Lorraine Finley; Ella Hulda Dohrmann **MS:** Married **SPN:** Wayne Everett Wilson (11/18/1950) **CH:** Matthew; Marc; Luke; Bethany **ED:** BS, Concordia College (1970); AA, Rochester Community College (1968) **CT:** Certified Middle School Teacher, State of Minnesota **C:** Teacher, Special Needs, Kenyan-Wanamingo School District (2004-Present); Teacher, Vocal Music, Grades 6-12, Stewartville Public Schools (2001-2004); Teacher, Instrumental Music, Caledonia Public Schools (1989-2001); Music Teacher, Grades K-8, St. Mary's Grade School, Caledonia, MN (1986-1989); Music Teacher, Grades K-6, Frazee Public Schools (1971-1973); Music Teacher, Grades K-12, Herman Public Schools (1970-1971) **CR:** Autism Teacher **CIV:** Community Band, Zymbrota, MN (2003); Director, Church Choir (1980-2000); Chair, Comprehensive Arts Planning Program (1992-1997) **AW:** Listee, Who's Who for Teachers **MEM:** National Education Association; Minnesota Education Association; Minnesota Music Educators Association **MH:** Albert Nelson Marquis Lifetime Achievement Award **B/I:** Ms. Wilson became involved in her profession because she was involved in music a lot in high school. She was in the honor choir and the honor band, which is how she decided to pursue music. She also wanted to be a teacher, so she took her interests and strong points, as well as the advice of a teacher who told her to become an educator, and combined that with her love of music. Later, Ms. Wilson became certified as a special needs teacher and began teaching students with autism. **AV:** Quilting; Cross stitching; Cross-country skiing **RE:** Lutheran

WILSON, EDWARD OSBORNE, T: Biologist, Researcher, Theorist **I:** Sciences **DOB:** 06/10/1929 **PB:** Birmingham **SC:** AL/USA **PT:** Edward Osborne Wilson; Inez (Freeman) Wilson **MS:** Married **SPN:** Irene Kelley (10/30/1955) **CH:** Catherine Irene **ED:** LLD, Simon Fraser University (2008); LLD, University of Mississippi Lavelle (2008); LLD, Graduate Theological Foundation (2008); Honorary LHD Williams College; Honorary LHD, Rockefeller University (2007); Honorary LHD, University of Puget Sound (2006); Honorary LHD, Albion College (2005); Honorary DSc, Clark University (2005); Honorary DSc, Harvard University (2004); DHC, University of Montreal (2004); Honorary LHD, University of South Alabama (2003); Honorary DSc, University of the South (2002); Honorary DSc, Kenyon College (2002); Honorary LHD, Connecticut College (2000); DrRerNat, University of Würzburg (2000); Honorary LHD, Yale University (1998); Honorary LHD, Muhlenburg College (1998); Honorary LHD, Bradford College (1997); Honorary DSc, University of Portland (1997); Honorary DSc, University of Guelph (1997); Honorary DSc, College of Wooster (1997); Honorary DSc, Bates College (1996); Honorary DSc, Ohio University (1996); DHC, University Madrid Complutense (1995); Honorary DSc, University of Connecticut (1995); Honorary DSc, Ripon College (1994); Honorary DSc, University of Oxford (1993); Honorary DSc, University of Massachusetts (1990); Honorary DSc, Maca-

lester College (1990); Honorary DSc, Fitchburg State College (1989); Honorary LHD, Hofstra University (1986); Honorary LHD, University of Alabama (1980); Honorary DSc, Lawrence University (1979); Honorary DSc, University of West Florida (1979); Honorary DSc, Grinnell College (1978); Honorary DSc, Duke University (1978); PhD, Harvard University (1955); MS, University of Alabama (1950); BS, University of Alabama (1949); Honorary LHD, Pennsylvania State University; DPhil, Uppsala University **C:** Lecturer, Duke University (2014-Present); Research Professor Emeritus in Entomology, Department of Organismic and Evolutionary Biology, Harvard University (2014-Present); Honorary Curator of Entomology, Society of Fellows, Harvard University (1997-Present); Professor Emeritus, Honorary Curator in Entomology, Harvard University (1996-Present); Faculty, Society of Fellows, Harvard University (1956-Present); Research Professor, Society of Fellows, Harvard University (1997-2002); Pellegrino University Professor, Society of Fellows, Harvard University (1994-1997); Curator of Entomology, Society of Fellows, Harvard University (1971-1997); Baird Professor of Science, Society of Fellows, Harvard University (1976-1994); Junior Fellow, Society of Fellows, Harvard University (1953-1956); Founder, E.O. Wilson Biodiversity Foundation, Nicholas School of the Environment, Duke University; Special Lecturer, Duke University **CR:** Board of Directors, Conservation International (1997-Present); Board of Directors, American Academy of Liberal Education (1993-2004); Board of Directors, Nature Conservancy (1994-2002); Board of Directors, American Museum of Natural History (1992-2002); Board of Directors, New York Botanical Garden (1991-1995); Board of Directors, World Wildlife Fund (1983-1994); Board of Directors, Organization for Tropical Studies (1984-1991); Selection Committee, Guggenheim Foundation (1982-1989) **CW:** Author, "Genesis: The Deep Origin of Societies" (2020); Author, "The Origins of Creativity" (2018); Author, "Homo Creator O Génio e a Perversidade da Espécie que Dominou o Mundo" (2018); Author, "Half-Earth: Our Planet's Fight for Life" (2017); Author, "The Meaning of Human Existence" (2015); Author, "Los Orígenes de la Creatividad Humana" (2015); Author, "The Social Conquest of Earth" (2015); Author, "Letters to a Young Scientist" (2014); Author, "Cartas a um Jovem Cientista" (2014); Co-Author, "The Poetic Societies: A Conversation with Edward O. Wilson and Robert Hass" (2014); Author, "The Social Conquest of Earth" (2013); Co-Author, "Ameisen: Die Entdeckung einer Faszinierenden Welt" (2013); Author, "Letters to a Young Scientist" (2013); Co-Author, "Why We Are Here: Mobile and the Spirit of a Southern City" (2012); Author, "Anthill: A Novel" (2010); Co-Author, "Kingdom of Ants: José Celestino Mutis and the Dawn of Natural History in the New World" (2010); Author, "The Creation: An Appeal to Save Life on Earth" (2007); Author, "Nature Revealed: Selected Writings, 1949-2006" (2006); Author, "The Future of Life" (2003); Author, "Pheidole in the New World: A Dominant, Hyperdiverse Ant Genius" (2003); Author, "Biological Diversity: The Oldest Human Heritage" (1999); Author, "Consilience: The Unity of Knowledge" (1998); Co-Author, "In Search of Nature" (1997); Author, "In Search of Nature" (1996); Author, "Naturalist" (1994); Author, "On Human Nature" (1994); Author, "The Diversity of Life" (1992); Author, "The Diversity of Life" (1992); Co-Author, "The Ants" (1990); Author, "Success and Dominance in Ecosystems" (1990); Author, "Biophilia" (1984); Author, "Biophilia" (1984); Author, "Promethean Fire" (1983); Co-Author, "Genes, Mind and Culture" (1981); Author, "On Human Nature" (1978); Author, "Sociology: The New Synthesis" (1975); Author, "Sociobiology:

The New Synthesis" (1975); Author, "The Insect Societies" (1974); Author, "Ecology, Evolution and Population Biology: Readings from Scientific American" (1974); Co-Author, "A Primer of Population Biology" (1971); Author, "The Insect Societies" (1971) **AW:** Kew International Medal (2014); International Cosmos Prize (2012); EarthSky Science Communicator of the Year (2010); 2010 Heartland Prize, "Anthill: A Novel" (2010); Thomas Jefferson Medal in Architecture (2010); 2010 BBVA Frontiers of Knowledge Award in the Ecology and Conservation Biology Category (2010); Explorers Club Medal (2009); Pirk Award, National PKC Association (2008); Terceuteram Silver Medal, Linnean Society (2006, 2007); TED Prize for "Positively Impacting Life on this Planet" (2007); Addison Emery Verrill Medal, Peabody Museum of Natural History (2007); Catalonia Prize, Spain (2007); Biotechnology Prize, TED (2007); George B. Stibbitz Commissioners Pioneer Award, American Computer Museum (2006); TED Prize, Sampling Foundation (2006); Prince William of Orange Medal, Leiden University (2006); Rungius Medal, American Museum of Wildlife Art (2005); Rachel Carson Award, International Society of Exotoxicology and Chemistry (2004); Distinguished Eagle Scout Award (2004); Governor's Award, Island Alliance (2004); Frances Hutchinson Medal, Chicago Botanical Garden (2004); Lowell Thomas Award, Explorers Club (2004); Silver Cross of Christopher Columbus, Dominican Republic (2003); Presidential Medal, Republic of Italy (2002); Nierenberg Prize (2001); Lewis Thomas Prize for Writing about Science (2000); Humanist of the Year, American Humanist Association (1999); Benjamin Franklin Medal for Distinguished Achievement in the Sciences, American Philosophical Society (1998); 25 Most Influential People in America, Time (1995); Audubon Medal, National Audubon Society (1995); Carl Sagan Award for Public Understanding of Science (1994); International Prize for Biology (1993); Pulitzer Prize, "The Ants" (1991); Vrafoord Prize, Royal Swedish Academy of Sciences (1990); Academy of Achievement Golden Plate Award (1988); ECI Prize, International Ecology Institute (!987); Tyler Prize for Environmental Achievement (1984); Pulitzer Prize, "On Human Nature" (1979); Leidy Award, Academy of Natural Sciences of Philadelphia (1979); National Medal of Science (1976) **MEM:** Fellow, American Philosophical Society; Fellow, American Academy of Arts and Sciences; National Academy of Sciences; Royal Society of Science; Russian Academy of Sciences; Royal Entomological Society; Finnish Academy of Sciences and Letters; Royal Society of London; Netherlands Entomological Society; Royal Society of Edinburgh; Association of Tropical Biology; Academy of Humanism; American Humanist Association; Zoological Society of London; Entomological Society of America; British Ecological Society; American Genetics Association; National Academy of Sciences; Explorers Club

WILSON, FREDERICA, T: U.S. Representative from Florida **I:** Government Administration/Government Relations/Government Services **DOB:** 11/05/1942 **PB:** Miami **SC:** FL/USA **PT:** Thirlee Smith; Beulah (Finley) Smith **MS:** Widowed **SPN:** Paul Wilson (1963, Deceased 1988) **CH:** Nicole Wilson-St. Hilaire; Lakesha Wilson-Rochelle; Paul Jr. **ED:** Honorary LHD, Florida Memorial University; MA, University of Miami, FL (1972); BS, Fisk University, TN (1963) **C:** Member, U.S. House of Representatives from Florida's 24th Congressional District, United States Congress, Washington, DC (2013-Present); Member, U.S. House Committee on Education and the Workforce (2013-Present); Member, U.S. House Committee on Space, Science and Technology (2011-Present); Founder, Exec-

utive Director, 5000 Role Models of Excellence Project (1993-Present); Member, U.S. House of Representatives from Florida's 17th Congressional District, United States Congress, Washington, DC (2011-2013); Member, U.S. House Committee on Foreign Affairs (2011-2013); Minority Whip, Florida State Senate (2008-2010); Member, District 33, Florida State Senate, Tallahassee, FL (2003-2010); Minority Leader Pro Tempore, Florida State Senate (2006-2008); Member, District 104, Florida House of Representatives, Tallahassee, FL (1998-2002); Member, Miami-Dade County School Board, FL (1992-1998); Executive Director, Office of Alternative Education and Dropout Prevention, Miami, FL **MEM:** National Alliance of Black School Educators (NABSE); The Links, Incorporated; Alpha Kappa Alpha Sorority, Incorporated **PA:** Democrat **RE:** Episcopalian

WILSON, JANET M., T: Art Educator **I:** Education/Educational Services **DOB:** 11/01/1952 **PB:** Erie **SC:** PA/USA **PT:** John Howard Wilson; Agnes M. (Jackson) Wilson **ED:** BS in Art Education, Edinboro University, Edinboro, PA (1978) **CT:** Certified Art Teacher, State of Pennsylvania **C:** Art Teacher, School District of the City of Erie, Pennsylvania (1988-2012); Substitute Contract Art Teacher, School District of the City of Erie, Pennsylvania (1987-1988); Substitute Teacher, School District of the City of Erie, Pennsylvania (1979-1986) **CR:** Assistant Director, Dr. G. Barber Center, Erie (1977); Camp Counselor (1976); Arts and Crafts Supervisor, City of Erie, Erie Youth Men's Christian Association (1973) **CIV:** Georgia O'Keeffe Museum; Smithsonian, National Gallery of Art, Washington D.C. **CW:** Group Show, The Jaye Mona Kang, Art Show (2019); Group Show, Dr. & Mrs. Robert Guelcher, Art Show, Erie, PA (2012-2017); Faculty Art Show, Harding School, Erie, PA (2008-2009); Group Show, Jury Show, Edinboro University (1977); Group Show, Printmaking Show, Edinboro University (1976) **AW:** Featured, Dutch Art in the Golden Age, National Gallery of Art, Teacher Institute, Washington, DC (2008); Listee, Who's Who in American Education (1994-1995); Recognized, Achieving Volunteers of Erie, Five Elementary Art Shows, St. Mary's Home, East Erie, PA (1991); Teacher of Year, McKinley Elementary (1989) **MEM:** National Education Association; Pennsylvania Art Education Association; National Art Education Association; Pennsylvania State Education Association; Erie Education Association; Erie Art Museum; Alumni, National Gallery of Art, Washington, DC; Georgia O'Keeffe Museum; Smithsonian; Erie Art Museum; National Art Education Association; Pennsylvania State Education Association; National Education Association **MH:** Albert Nelson Marquis Lifetime Achievement Award; Marquis Who's Who Top Professional **AS:** Ms. Wilson attributes her success to her parents. **B/I:** Ms. Wilson's mother, Agnes Wilson, was a science and English teacher who taught for 46 years. She taught Ms. Wilson dedication. Her Father, John Wilson, loved to draw and he taught her about art. Ms. Wilson was always very good at art. She had a neighbor, Don Lord, that lived next door, he was a professional artist and he gave her the inspiration to be an artist. Ms. Wilson was excited about her art and wanted to teach her students what she knew and learned. Most of all, though, she wanted to be an example. **AV:** Photography; Biking; Golf; Reading; Painting with watercolor **PA:** Democrat **RE:** Presbyterian

WILSON, JEFFREY D., T: Supervisor **I:** Government Administration/Government Relations/Government Services **CN:** City of Tullahoma **DOB:** 07/25/1992 **PB:** Norwich **SC:** NY/USA **PT:** Susan Wilson; Theodore J. Wilson **MS:** Single **ED:** Bach-

elor of Science in Economics, Emory & Henry College (2014) **C:** Animal Control Supervisor, City of Tullahoma (2019-Present); Logistics Supervisor, Volvo Trucks North America (2017-2018); Transport Coordinator, Volvo Logistics (2016-2017); Logistics Consultant, Volvo Logistics North America (2015-2016) **CIV:** With, Friends of Tullahoma Animal Shelter; With, Coffee County Humane Society; With, Coffee County Animal Welfare Coalition **CW:** Several Poems, Love_is_TruePoetry Instagram **AW:** First Place Winner, Americas Region Continuous Improvement Program, Volvo Logistics North America (2015); Pi Omicron Chapter Award, Alpha Phi Omega; Hugh & Sigrid Solomon Excellence in Service Award **MEM:** Friends of the Tullahoma Animal Shelter; Alpha Phi Omega **AS:** Mr. Wilson attributes his success to being committed to life long learning. Many people identify themselves as experts in their field, and forget to look to others for new ideas and information. Mr. Wilson utilizes the knowledge of outside experts in his field to generate innovation, and consults his team and trusted advisers in determining how to implement them. **B/I:** Mr. Wilson had a realization that, while he greatly enjoyed advancing his career and learning new skills, he was reaching a point of stress he could not sustain. He entered the field of nonprofit consultancy, and aspired to teach people how to be more effective. **PA:** Democrat

WILSON, JERRY C., T: Language Educator **I:** Education/Educational Services **DOB:** 01/01/1940 **PB:** Boise **SC:** ID/USA **PT:** Gerald Vern Wilson; Betty Lou Wilson **SPN:** Brenda Jean Urvin (06/03/1960) **CH:** Angela Sue Wilson Newburg; Stephen Jerry **ED:** MA in Spanish, UC Santa Barbara (1998); MA in Missiology, Fuller Theological Seminary, Pasadena, CA (1987); Certificate of Spanish, Institute Mexicano America, Mexico City, Mexico (1967); BA in Religion, Northwest Nazarene College (Now Northwest Nazarene University), Nampa, ID (1963) **C:** Professor of Spanish, Point Loma Nazarene University, San Diego, CA (1987-2004); Director, Study/Work Program, Church of the Nazarene, Santo Domingo, Dominican Republic (1979-1983); Seminary, Church of the Nazarene, Panama City, Panama (1976-1978); Director, Bilingual Seminary, Church of the Nazarene, Boca Cuseo Alto Morano Jungle, Peru (1973-1975); Director, Seminary, Church of the Nazarene, Chiclayo, Peru (1967-1972) **MH:** Albert Nelson Marquis Lifetime Achievement Award **B/I:** Professor Wilson became involved in his profession because his first encounter with Spanish speaking people was when he was growing up on a farm; they were farm workers who helped with the crops. He was ashamed of how the farm workers were being treated by both his parents and the other people around them, and wanted to find a way to help them. As he grew up, God led him to be a leader and a trainer in a foreign country. The workers applied at the Department of Missions for the Nazarene Church and were excepted to go to Peru. He taught for four years in Northern Peru, training pastors and layman who wanted to study. He also built a church in the jungles of Peru. **AV:** Reading; Repairing old cars; Sports

WILSON, REBECCA ANN, T: English, Special Education and Home Economics Educator (Retired) **I:** Education/Educational Services **DOB:** 02/21/1945 **PB:** Baltimore **SC:** MD/USA **PT:** Bertram Bradford Wiley; Nancy Ann (Yingling) Wiley **MS:** Married **SPN:** David Lloyd Wilson (07/29/1967) **CH:** Laura Beth Wilson; Amy Lynn Wilson Hardy **ED:** 24 Hours of Postgraduate Work with Certification in Special Education, Plus Hours in Psychology and Administration, West Virginia University (1968-1980); Bachelor of Arts in Secondary Education,

Minor in English, Shepherd College (1967); Postgraduate Coursework in Education, Psychology and Administration, West Virginia University; Nine Hours of Continuing Education in the Spectrum of Development Disabilities: Autism, Developmental Disabilities and Care of Adults with Mental Retardation through the Office of Continuing Medical Education, Johns Hopkins Medical Institutions, Baltimore, MD **CT:** Certification in Special Education, West Virginia University (1968) **C:** President, West Virginia Advisory Council for the Education of Exceptional Children (1989-1992); Appointed by the West Virginia Superintendent of Schools as a Parent Member, West Virginia Advisory Council for the Education of Exceptional Children (1986-1992); Substitute Teacher, Grades Seven Through 12, Jefferson County Schools (1975-1979); Teacher of Reading, English, Special Education and Home Economics, Jefferson County Schools (1967-1972); Governor-Appointed Member, Governor's Schools of West Virginia Advisory Board **CR:** Judge, County Fairs, Harford County and Howard County, MD (1968-Present); School Advisory Council Appointee, Jefferson County Board of Education (2001); Attendee, Three National Developmental Disability Seminars, Johns Hopkins Medical Institutions, Baltimore, MD (1997-1998); Elected Member, Jefferson County Board of Education (1994-1998); Board of Directors, Jefferson County Special Olympics (1986-1997) **CIV:** Member, Governor School Advisory Council, Charles Town, WV (2001-Present); Judge, County Fairs, Hartford County and Howard County, MD, Jefferson County Fair, WV (1968-Present); Liaison to the Eastern Panhandle Children's Summit, United Way (1995-1998); Member, Jefferson County Board Education, Charles Town, WV (1994-1998); Board of Education Liaison to Business Partner Signings (1994-1998); Past Member, Board of Directors, RESA VIII (Regional Education Service Agencies) (1994-1998); Volunteer, Jefferson County Special Olympics, Charles Town, WV (1986-1997); Chairman, West Virginia Advisory Council on Education for Exceptional Children, Charles Town, WV (1986-1992); Advisory Committee, Jefferson County Board Education, Charles Town, WV (1990); Altar Guild, Trinity Episcopal Church; Member, Board of Directors, Shepherdstown Day Care Center; Board of Directors, Potomac Center, Romney, WV; Former Member, Shepherd College Concert and Pep Bands; Past President, Home Economics Club, Shepherd College; Judge, Public School Social Studies Fairs and Science Fairs, Jefferson County, WV **MEM:** President, Eastern District of West Virginia, General Federation of Women's Clubs (2006-Present); Jefferson County Cotillion Club (1970-2011); Elected President, GFWC West Virginia Eastern District (2006-2008); President, GFWC Shepherdstown Women's Club (2000-2006); Lifetime Member, American Association of University Women; Women's Club of Martinsburg GFWC WV; Attendee Member, International Association on Jazz Education; Homemakers Club; Lifetime Member, Maryland 4-H All Stars; Charter Member, National Women's History Museum; Order of the Eastern Star #155, Shepherdstown; Jefferson County 4-H Leaders Association; Shepherd University Emeritus Club; Honorary Citizen of George Washington's Mount Vernon; Past Member, Twenty-Five-Member Citizens Advisory Committee, Jefferson County Board of Education; Past Member, Steering Committee, Jefferson County Board of Education; Creation of a TV Studio, Jefferson County Board of Education Office; Jefferson High School Vocational Advisory Council, and Board of Directors, Alliance for Technology Access; Past Member, Jefferson County High School Band Boosters; Past Member, Parent Teacher Organization, Shepherdstown Junior High School; Past Member, Shepherdstown Elementary Association; Past Member, Miller Hall Dorm Council, Shepherd College; Lifetime Member, Sigma Sigma Sigma National Sorority **MH:** Albert Nelson Marquis Lifetime Achievement Award; Marquis Who's Who Top Professional **B/I:** Ms. Wilson became involved in her profession because she was raised on a farm and became a member of the local Four-H Club at just 9 years old. She rose to positions of leadership virtually wherever she went. Ms. Wilson enjoys networking, meeting people and having conversations any time and any place. She draws great joy from providing counsel and steering people toward their goals. **AV:** Candle making; Ceramics; Clothing construction; Collecting cookbooks; Cooking; Interior decorating; Photography; Networking; Attending national conventions; Creating floor plans; Traveling; Reading; Spending time with grandchildren **PA:** Democrat **RE:** Episcopalian

WILSON, SHELLY L., T: Managing Partner **I:** Law and Legal Services **CN:** Owings, Wilson & Coleman **DOB:** 09/16/1961 **PB:** Saginaw **SC:** MI/USA **PT:** Don Harrison; Louise Harrison **MS:** Married **SPN:** Timothy R. Wilson **CH:** Two Children **ED:** JD, Stetson University College of Law, Gulfport, FL (1987); BA, Florida Southern College, Lakeland, FL, Cum Laude (1982) **C:** Managing Partner, Owings, Wilson & Coleman (2014-Present); Partner, Owings, Wilson & Coleman (2000-2014); Associate Attorney, Owings, Wilson & Coleman (1999-2000); Assistant Public Defender, State of Florida (1988-1999) **CR:** Teacher, Municipal Government Law, Lincoln Memorial University Duncan School of Law, Knoxville, TN (2019, 2020) **CIV:** General Counsel, Numerous Nonprofit Corporations in East Tennessee; Board Member, The Restoration House of East Tennessee; Zoofari Planning Committee for Zoo Knoxville; Volunteer, Remote Area Medical; Member, Volunteer, Central Baptist Church of Fountain City, Knoxville, TN; Former Board Member and Volunteer, Operation Inasmuch; Girl Scouts of the United States of America **AW:** President's Award, Knoxville Bar Association (2011) **MEM:** ABA; Antitrust Division, ABA; Tennessee Municipal Attorneys Association; Tennessee Bar Association; Knoxville Bar Association; Blount County Bar Association; Florida Bar Association; East Tennessee Lawyers' Association for Women; Former Co-chair, Committee on Continuing Legal Education, Knoxville Bar Association; Chair, Ethics Bowl CLE Program Planning Team, Knoxville Bar Association; Former Chair, Local Government Section, Tennessee Bar Association; Former Member, Board of Governors, Tennessee Bar Association; Former Officer and Member, House of Delegates, Tennessee Bar Association; Board of Governors, Knoxville Bar Association **BAR:** United States District Court for the Middle District of Florida (2015); United States Court of Appeals for the Sixth Circuit (2010); United States District Court for the Eastern District of Tennessee (1999); Tennessee (1999); Florida (1987) **MH:** Marquis Who's Who Top Professional **AS:** Mrs. Wilson attributes her success to strong work ethic and surrounding herself with people of like mind. **B/I:** Mrs. Wilson became a lawyer to be a protector of people's rights as Americans and as human beings. **AV:** Time with family, especially grandchildren; Volunteer work **RE:** Baptist **THT:** Mrs. Wilson's motto is, "I may not be able to change the world, but I can make a world of difference to some."

WILSON, THOMAS JOSEPH II, T: Chairman, President, Chief Executive Officer **I:** Insurance **CN:** The Allstate Corporation **PB:** St. Clair Shores **SC:** MI/USA **MS:** Married **SPN:** Jill Garling **CH:** Three Children **ED:** MBS, Kellogg School of Management, Northwestern University (1980); BSBA, University of Michigan **C:** President, Allstate Corporation (2005-2015, 2018-Present); Chairman, Board of Directors, Allstate Corporation (2008-Present); Chief Executive Officer, Allstate Corporation (2007-Present); President, Chief Operating Officer, Allstate Corporation (2005-2006); President, Allstate Protection (2002-2006); Chairman, President, Allstate Financial (1999-2002); Chief Financial Officer, Allstate Corporation (1995-1998); Vice President, Strategy and Analysis, Sears, Roebuck and Company (1993-1995); Managing Director, Mergers & Acquisitions, Dean Witter Reynolds (1986-1993); Numerous Financial Positions, Amoco Corporation (1980-1986) **CR:** Member, Board of Directors, State Street Corporation (2012-Present); Co-Founder, Get IN Chicago; Member, Board of Trustees, Rush University Medical Center; Board Member, Francis W. Parker School, Board Member, Property Casual Insurers Association of America; Board Member, U.s. Chamber of Commerce; Board Member, World Business Chicago; Chairman, Property and Casualty CEO Roundtable; Chairman, Financial Services Roundtable **CIV:** Civic Committee Member, Commercial Club of Chicago; Member, Board of Directors, Rush-Presbyterian-St. Luke's Medical Center; Federal Chairman, Federal Reserve Bank of Chicago **CW:** Author, Articles, New York Times, Washington Post, CNN.com; Commentator, Business and Policy Topics, National Media Outlets **MEM:** YPO (Formerly Young Presidents' Organization)

WILTON, ELISABETH STARR, PHD, T: Management Consultant (Retired); Linguistic (Retired) **I:** Professional Training & Coaching **DOB:** 04/01/1936 **PB:** Cincinnati **SC:** OH/USA **PT:** Frank Starr Wilton Jr.; Bess Virginia (Clausen) Wilton **MS:** Divorced **CH:** Bart Wilton Jenkins **ED:** PhD, University of Maryland (1978); MEd, University of Maryland (1970); BA, Lawrence University (1958) **CT:** Certified Clinical Hypnotherapist, National Board (2005) **C:** President, Consultant, Wilton Associates, Inc., McLean, VA (1999-2016); Retired, U.S. Government (1998); Psychologist (1979-1998); Linguist, Translator of French, German, Spanish, Romanian, U.S. Government, Washington, DC (1959-1979) **CR:** Training; Employee Selection **CW:** Author, Self-published, "Taking Charge: Conversations on Building Life Skills", Lulu.com (2006); Author, Poem, "Siblings" (2006); Author, Poem, "Lost Freedom" (1999); Author, Poems **AW:** Fulbright Scholar, Germany (1958-1959); American Field Service Summer Scholarship to Germany (1953) **MEM:** Secretary, Personality Assessment System Foundation (2004-2013) **MH:** Albert Nelson Marquis Lifetime Achievement Award **AS:** Dr. Wilton attributes his success to being born to good parents in a safe country with lots of opportunities. **B/I:** Dr. Wilton always liked different languages and cultures and toyed with the idea of being an anthropologist or archeologist. He did not want simply to go visit places around the world, he wanted to live there and get to know the people; the best way to do that, it seemed, was language learning. For twenty years, he worked as a translator/interpreter, which was very interesting but limited. When a visiting reading specialist suggested Dr. Wilton's son was "disturbed", he began a reading program in graduate school but soon switched to human development. The "disturbance" turned out to be culture shock, which his son quickly overcame. He came to see psychology and translation as related: both help people to understand each other. Before starting his work life, a Fulbright scholarship took him to Berlin, where he studied Russian and 15th Century Spanish. He later transferred to Hamburg and changed his major from Germanistics to pre-law, with a vague idea of going into international law. But being part of an experimental group looking at the legal responsibility of psychiatric prisoners planted the seed for his later interest in psychology. **AV:** Word derivation; Language; Puzzles; ESL teaching **THT:** To paraphrase Epictetus, Dr. Wilton says, "It's not what happens that's important, it's how you interpret it."

WINDER, CAMERON B., PHD, T: Member **I:** Business Management/Business Services **CN:** Rialto Company **DOB:** 09/02/1955 **PB:** Denver **SC:** CO/USA **PT:** W. Burch Winder; Jeanne (Wells) Winder **MS:** Married **SPN:** Valerie **ED:** BA, Pacific University (1979); PhD, University College of London **C:** Partner, Rialto Company, Denver, CO (1992-Present); Vice President, The Winder Corp., Denver, CO (1983-Present); Treasurer, Rialto Company, Denver, CO (1991-1992); Board of Directors, Denver Regional Transportation District (1989-1992); Colorado House of Representatives, Denver, CO (1988); Self-Employed Photographer, Denver, CO (1981-1983); Intern, U.S. Senate, Washington, DC (1979); Vice President, Color Card, Denver, CO **CR:** Treasurer, Denver Regional Transportation District (1991, 1992); **CIV:** Board of Directors, Regional Transportation District (1989-1992); Chairman, Public Relations Council, Denver Art Museum (1986-1988) **MH:** Albert Nelson Marquis Lifetime Achievement Award **B/I:** Dr. Winder became involved in his profession because, after he left his internship in the Senate, he became a professional model. Fortunately, one of his model colleagues decided to start a new company with him. Dr. Winder was then elected to a transit board, becoming the treasurer of the second-largest transit district in the country. In this role, he learned a lot about finance. He later traveled to London to study law with his colleague. **AV:** Practicing photography; Bicycling **PA:** Republican **RE:** Orthodox Christian

WINDERS, MONICA, T: Channel Marketing Manager **I:** Advertising & Marketing **CN:** NetApp **MS:** Married **ED:** BA in Business Administration, Azusa Pacific University **C:** WW Channels Marketing Services Manager, NetApp (2015-Present); Senior Program Manager, Consultant, Hewlett-Packard Company (HP) (2015-Present); Global Program Manager, Business Development Manager, Hewlett-Packard Company (HP) (1999-2015); Marketing Manager, SGI (1997-1999); Sales and Marketing Manager, Apple, Inc. (1997-1998) **CIV:** Director of Social Media, Porsche Racing Club (2018-Present); San Martin Planning Advisory Committee, Santa Clara County Board of Supervisors (2014-Present); Small Group Leader, Explore Coach, South Valley Community Church, Gilroy, CA (2002-Present); Mentor, Azusa Pacific University (2011-2014); Volunteer, Silicon Valley Grants, Cisco (2008-2013); Director, Take Flight for Kids Planning Committee, Valley Medical Center Foundation (2008-2013); Cisco Mentor, Business Administration and Modern Languages Departments, Azusa Pacific University (2011); Director, San Martin Neighborhood Alliance (2002-2008) **CW:** Featured, "Women of the Channel 2019: Recognizing The Unique Strengths Women Bring To The Table," The Channel (2019); Featured, "100 People You Don't Know But Should," The Channel Company (2018) **AW:** Spot Award, CMO (2017); Nineteen-Time Recipient, Achievement Awards, Cisco Systems (1999-2013); Gold Medal, Cisco Systems (2012); Honorable Mention for Excellence in Execution in Customer Success, Cisco Systems (2011) **B/I:** Ms. Winders grew up in Southern California. While she was still in college, everyone was applying for companies. She picked up a book called "Top 100 Companies to Work for in America," and she didn't know any better, so she applied to a lot of them and started

interviewing with all of them. Ms. Winders and her husband both worked at Apple, which started her love for working in high tech.

WINFREY, OPRAH GAIL, T: Broadcast Executive, Television Host, Producer, Media Executive, Actress **I:** Media & Entertainment **CN:** Harpo Productions Inc. **DOB:** 01/29/1954 **PB:** Kosciusko SC: MS/USA **PT:** Vernon Winfrey; Vernita Lee Winfrey **ED:** Honorary Doctorate, University of the Free State (2011); Honorary Doctor of Humane Letters, Duke University (2009); Bachelor of Arts in Speech Communications and Performing Arts, Tennessee State University (1987); Honorary Doctorate, Harvard University **C:** Host, "Oprah's Next Chapter," Oprah Winfrey Network, Los Angeles, CA (2011-Present); Chairperson, Chief Executive Officer, Chief Creative Officer, Oprah Winfrey Network, Los Angeles, CA (2011-Present); Owner, Producer, President, Chairperson, Chief Executive Officer, Harpo Productions Inc. (1986-Present); Chairperson, Oprah Winfrey Network, Los Angeles, CA (2011); Host, "The Oprah Winfrey Show," Harpo Productions Inc., Chicago, IL (1986-2011); Host, "Oprah After the Show," Chicago, IL (2003-2006); Host, Talk Show, "A.M. Chicago," Station WLS-TV, Chicago, IL (1983-1986); Co-host, Morning Talk Show, "People Are Talking," Station WJZ-TV, Baltimore, MD (1978-1983); News Co-anchor, Station WJZ-TV, Baltimore, MD (1977-1978); Reporter, News Anchor, Station WTVF-TV, Nashville, TN (1973-1976); News Reporter, Radio Station WVOL-AM, Nashville, TN (1971-1972) **CR:** Board of Directors, WW International Inc. (2015-Present); Founder, "Live Your Best Life" (2003-Present); Founder, O, The Oprah Magazine, South Africa (2002-Present); Host, "Oprah: After the Show," (2002-Present); Special Contributor, "60 Minutes," CBS (2017-2018); Creator, Host, "Oprah's Big Give" (2007); Creator, Oprah Radio, Sirius XM Radio Inc. (2006-2014); Founder, O at Home (2004-2008); Partner, Co-founder, Internet and Cable Television Company, Oxygen Media/Network (2002-2006); Founder, Editorial Director, "O, The Oprah Magazine," Hearst Magazines (2000); Online Leader, Oprah.com; Creator, Oprah's Book Club **CIV:** Founder, Christmas Kindness South Africa (2002-Present); Founder, Oprah Winfrey Charitable Foundation (1987-Present); Founder, Oprah's Angel Network (1997-2010); Founder, Seven Fountains Primary School, South Africa (2007); Founder, The Oprah Winfrey Leadership Academy for Girls, Henley-on-Klip, South Africa (2006); Founder, Oprah Winfrey Scholars Program **CW:** Host, "Oprah Talks COVID-19" (2020-Present); Host, "Oprah's Book Club" (2019-Present); Co-creator, Executive Producer, "Queen Sugar" (2016-Present); Executive Producer, "Greenleaf" (2016-Present); Host, "Super Soul Sunday" (2011-Present); Author, "The Path Made Clear: Discovering Your Life's Direction and Purpose" (2019); Appearance, "A Beautiful Day in the Neighborhood" (2019); Executive Producer, "Oprah Winfrey Presents: After Neverland" (2019); Executive Producer, "When They See Us" (2019); Actress, Executive Producer, "A Wrinkle in Time" (2018); Announcer, "The Handmaid's Tale" (2018); Voice Actress, "Crow: The Legend" (2018); Executive Producer, "Love Is" (2018); Host, Executive Producer, Documentary, "Oprah Presents: Master Class" (2011-2018); Executive Producer, "The Star" (2017); Executive Producer, "The Immortal Life of Henrietta Lacks" (2017); Author, "Food, Health and Happiness" (2017); Author, "The Wisdom Journal: The Companion to the Wisdom of Sundays" (2017); Author, "The Wisdom of Sundays: Life-Changing Insights from Super Soul Conversations" (2017); Host, "Oprah: Where are They Now?" (2012-2017); Co-author, "Mr. or Ms. Just Right" (2016); Host,

"Oprah Prime" (2012-2015); Author, "What I Know for Sure" (2014); Actress, Producer, "Selma" (2014); Producer, "The Hundred-Foot Journey" (2014); Host, "Oprah's Lifeclass" (2011-2014); Actress, "The Butler" (2013); Actress, "Jesus Henry Christ" (2012); Executive Producer, "Serving Life" (2011); Executive Producer, "Extraordinary Mom" (2011); Executive Producer, "Your OWN Show" (2011); Host, Supervising Producer, "The Oprah Winfrey Show" (1989-2011); Host, "The Oprah Winfrey Show" (1986-2011); Host, Executive Producer, "The Oprah Winfrey Oscar Special" (2007, 2010); Voice Actress, "The Princess and the Frog" (2009); Executive Producer, "Christmas at the White House: An Oprah Primetime Special" (2009); Executive Producer, "Precious" (2009); Executive Producer, "The Dr. Oz Show" (2009); Actress, "30 Rock" (2008); Producer, "The Great Debaters" (2007); Voice Actress, "Bee Movie" (2007); Host, Executive Producer, "Oprah's Big Give" (2007); Executive Producer, TV Films, "Oprah Winfrey Presents: Mitch Albom's For One More Day" (2007); Featured, Executive Producer, Documentary, "Building a Dream: The Oprah Winfrey Leadership Academy" (2007); Host, Executive Producer, "Legends Ball" (2006); Appearance, "Ocean's Thirteen" (2007); Voice Actress, "Charlotte's Web" (2006); Producer, Broadway, "The Color Purple" (2005); Executive Producer, "Their Eyes Were Watching God" (2005); Host, Executive Producer, "Oprah: After the Show" (2002); Executive Producer, "Amy & Isabelle" (2001); Executive Producer, "Tuesdays with Morrie" (1999); Author, "Oprah Winfrey: The Soul and Spirit of a Superstar" (2000); Appearance, "Home Improvement" (1999); Appearance, "The Hughleys" (1999); Co-author, "Make the Connection: Ten Steps to a Better Body and a Better Life" (1998); Author, "Journey to Beloved" (1998); Actress, Producer, "Beloved" (1998); Executive Producer, "The Wedding" (1998); Executive Producer, "David and Lisa" (1998); Actress, Producer, "Before Women Had Wings" (1997); Actress, "Ellen" (1997); Author, "The Uncommon Wisdom of Oprah Winfrey: A Portrait in Her Own Words" (1996); Appearance, "All American Girl" (1995); Actress, "There Are No Children Here" (1993); Executive Producer, Television Special, "Michael Jackson Talks to... Oprah Live" (1993); Producer, Television Series, "ABC Afterschool Specials" (1992-1993); Executive Producer, "Overexposed" (1992); Executive Producer, Documentary, "Nine" (1992); Appearance, "The Fresh Prince of Bel Air" (1992); Appearance, "Gabriel's Fire" (1990); Actress, Executive Producer, Television Miniseries, "The Women of Brewster Place" (1989); Appearance, "Throw Momma from the Train" (1987); Actress, "Native Son" (1986); Host, "Saturday Night Live" (1986); Actress, "The Color Purple" (1985); Host, "Dialing for Dollars"; Host, Series of Celebrity Interview Specials, "Oprah: Behind the Scenes"; Actress, Appearances, Television Shows, Films; Host, Producer, Specials, Television Shows, Films **AW:** Cecil B. DeMille Award, Golden Globe Awards, Hollywood Foreign Press Association (2018); Named, One of the 100 Most Influential People, TIME Magazine (2018); Tony Award for Best Musical Revival (2016); Daytime Emmy for Outstanding Special Class Series, Academy of Television Arts & Sciences (2014); Presidential Medal of Freedom, The White House (2013); Chairman's Award, Emmy Awards, Academy of Television Arts & Sciences (2011); Jean Hersholt Humanitarian Award, Academy of Motion Picture Arts & Sciences (2011); Honoree, Kennedy Center Honors, John F. Kennedy Center for the Performing Arts (2010); Anisfield-Wolf Book Award, (2010); Stanley Kramer Award, Producers Guild of America (2008); Inductee, NAACP Image Hall of Fame (2005); Bob

Hope Humanitarian Award, Academy of Television Arts & Sciences (2002); Primetime Emmy Award for Outstanding Made for Television Movie, Academy of Television Arts & Sciences (2000); David L. Wolper Producer of the Year Award in Long-Form, Producer Guild of America (1999); Daytime Emmy for Outstanding Talk Show Host, Academy of Television Arts & Sciences (1987, 1991, 1992, 1998); Lifetime Achievement Award, Emmy Awards, Academy of Television Arts & Sciences (1998); S. Roger Horchow Award for Greatest Public Service by a Private Citizen (1998); Daytime Emmy for Outstanding Talk Show, Academy of Television Arts & Sciences (1989, 1991, 1997); Peabody Award (1995); NAACP Image Award for Entertainer of the Year (1989); Numerous Awards, Including NAACP Image Awards, People Choice Awards

WINGROVE, PHILIP C., T: Aeronautical Engineer, Consultant **I:** Engineering **DOB:** 06/19/1930 **PB:** Portland **SC:** OR/USA **PT:** Harley Harrison Wingrove; Doris (Painton) Wingrove **MS:** Married **SPN:** Ida Elizabeth Dennis (11/25/1955) **CH:** Lelia Doris (Deceased); Elizabeth Rose; Mark Philip (Deceased); Suzanne **ED:** MS in Aeronautical Engineering, University of Washington (1954); BS in Aeronautical Engineering, University of Washington (1952) **CT:** Designated Engineering Representative for Flight Testing, Federal Aviation Administration (1971-1977); **C:** Consultant, Port Townsend, Washington (1985-Present); Flight Test Engineer, Manager, Boeing (1958-1985); Flight Test Engineer, McDonnell Aircraft Corporation (1957-1958); Pilot, United States Navy and U.S. Marine Corps **MIL:** Captain, U.S. Marine Corps (1953-1967); Cadet, U.S. Navy (1952) **CW:** Author, "Flight Test, The Total Picture," (1988) **MEM:** Flight Test Tech Committee, American Institute of Aeronautics and Astronautics (1982-1989); Charter Member, Society of Flight Test Engineers; Lifetime Member, Association of Naval Aviation **MH:** Albert Nelson Marquis Lifetime Achievement Award **B/I:** Mr. Wingrove became involved in his profession because he always liked airplanes and aviation. **AV:** Sailing; Writing; Traveling

WINKLER, HENRY FRANKLIN, T: Actor, Producer, Director **I:** Media & Entertainment **DOB:** 10/30/1945 **PB:** New York **SC:** NY/USA **PT:** Harry Irving Winkler; Ilse Anna Maria (Hadra) Winkler **MS:** Married **SPN:** Stacey Weitzman (05/05/1978) **CH:** Zoe Emily; Max Daniel; Jed Weitzman (Stepson) **ED:** Honorary DHL, Austin College (2002); Honorary DHL, Emerson College (1978); MFA, Yale School of Drama (1970); BA, Emerson College (1967) **C:** Founder, Children's Action Network; Actor, Producer, Director, Film and Television **CR:** Founder, New Haven Free Theater; Member, Yale Repertory Theater **CW:** Actor, "Barry" (2018-Present); Co-author, "Hank Zipzer" Book Series (2003-Present); Actor, "Pink Skies Ahead" (2020); Actress, "The French Dispatch" (2020); Actor, "Medical Police" (2020); Executive Producer, "MacGyver" (2016-2020); Co-author, Here's Hank: Everybody Is Somebody" (2019); Actor, "American Dad!" (2019); Voice Actor, "Guardians of the Galaxy" (2019); Co-author, "Alien Superstar (2019); Actor, "Arrested Development" (2003-2019); Actor, "Puppy Dog Pals" (2017-2018); Actor, "Sia: Santa's Coming for Us" (2017); Voice Actor, "All I Want for Christmas Is You" (2017); Voice Actor, "All Hail King Julien: Exiled" (2017); Actor, "Sandy Wexler" (2017); Actor, "All Hail King Julien" (2014-2017); Voice Actor, "Penn Zero: Part-Time Hero" (2014-2017); Actor, "You Are Nothing" (2016); Actor, "Hank Zipzer's Christmas Catastrophe" (2016); Actor, "Prism" (2016); Voice Actor, "SpongeBob SquarePants" (2016); Actor, "Donald Trump's The Art of the Deal: The Movie" (2016); Actor, "New Girl" (2016); Actor, "Hank Zipzer" (2014-2016); Actor, "Royal Pains" (2010-2016); Actor, "Childrens Hospital" (2010-2016); Voice Actor, "Uncle Grandpa" (2015); Actor, "Bob's Burgers" (2015); Actor, "Drunk History" (2015); Voice Actor, "BoJack Horseman" (2015); Actor, "Larry Gaye: Renegade Male Flight Attendant" (2015); Actor, "Comedy Bang! Bang!" (2015); Co-author, "Here's Hank: Fake Snakes and Weird Wizards" (2015); Co-author, "Here's Hank: There's a Zombie in My Bathtub" (2015); Actor, "Parks and Recreation" (2013-2015); Voice Actor, "Robot Chicken" (2012-2015); Co-author, "Here's Hank: Bookmarks Are People Too!" (2014); Co-author, "Here's Hank: A Short Tale About a Long Dog" (2014); Co-author, "Here's Hank: Stop That Frog!" (2014); Actor, "Dissonance" (2014); Actor, "The Winklers" (2014); Himself, MGMT Music Video, "Your Life Is a Lie" (2013); Author, "I've Never Met an Idiot on the River: Reflections on Family, Photography, and Fly-Fishing" (2013); Co-author, "Ghost Buddy: Always Dance with a Hairy Buffalo" (2013); Co-author, "Ghost Buddy: How to Scare the Pants Off Your Pets" (2013); Voice Actor, "Mad" (2013); Actor, "1600 Penn" (2013); Actor, "Newsreaders" (2013); Actor, "Hero Factory" (2010-2013); Executive Producer, Producer, "ESU: In the Line of Duty" (2012); Actor, "Here Comes the Boom" (2012); Co-author, "Ghost Buddy: Mind If I Read Your Mind?" (2012); Actor, "Up All Night" (2012); Co-author, "Ghost Buddy: Zero to Hero" (2012); Actor, "Handy Manny" (2012); Actor, "The Dining" (2011); Voice Actor, "Lego Hero Factory: Savage Planet" (2011); Narrator, "Adventures of Serial Buddies" (2011); Voice Actor, "Batman: The Brave and the Bold" (2011); Actor, "Running Mates" (2011); Voice Actor, "Dan vs..." (2011); Actor, "Hillers" (2010); Voice Actor, "Leg Hero Factory: Rise of the Rookies" (2010); Actor, "Group Sex" (2010); Co-author, "Hank Zipzer: A Brand-New Me!" (2010); Voice Actor, "Sit Down Shut Up" (2009); Actor, "Numb3rs" (2008-2009); Actor, "The Most Wonderful Time of the Year" (2008); Actor, "Merry Christmas, Drake & Josh" (2008); Actor, "Ron Howard's Call to Action" (2008); Actor, "You Don't Mess with the Zohan" (2008); Guest Conductor, Boston Pops by the Sea Concert, Hyannis, MA (2008); Actor, "A Plumm Summer" (2007); Actor, "Odd Job Jack" (2007); Actor, "I Could Never Be Your Woman" (2007); Co-author, "Hank Zipzer: The World's Greatest Underachiever: Who Ordered This Baby? Definitely Not Me!" (2007); Co-author, "Hank Zipzer: The Curtain Went Up, My Pants Fell Down" (2007); Co-author, "Hank Zipzer: The World's Greatest Underachiever: Barfing in the Backseat: How I Survived My Family Road Trip" (2007); Actor, "Click" (2006); Actor, "Unbeatable Harold" (2006); Actor, "The King of Central Park" (2006); Executive Producer, "Dynasty Reunion: Catfights & Caviar" (2006); Co-author, "Hank Zipzer: The World's Greatest Underachiever: My Dog's a Scaredy-Cat, A Halloween Tail" (2006); Actor, "Out of Practice" (2005-2006); Executive Producer, "Knots Landing Reunion: Together Again" (2005); Actor, "The Kid & I" (2005); Voice Actor, "Duck Dodgers" (2005); Actor, "Berkeley" (2005); Actor, "Crossing Jordan" (2005); Executive Producer, "Happy Days: 30th Anniversary Reunion" (2005); Co-author, "Hank Zipzer: The World's Greatest Underachiever: My Secret Life as a Ping Pong Wizard" (2005); Voice Actor, "Clifford's Puppy Days" (2003-2005); Executive Producer, "Biography" (2001-2005); Co-author, "Hank Zipzer: The World's Greatest Underachiever: Niagara Falls, or Does It?" (2004); Actor, "Beverly Hills S.U.V." (2004); Voice Actor, "King of the Hill" (2004); Actor, "Fronterz" (2004); Actor, "Third Watch" (2004); Co-author, "Hank Zipzer: The World's Greatest Underachiever: I Got a D in Salami" (2004); Executive Producer, "Dallas Reunion: Return to Southfork" (2004); Executive Producer, "Unexplained Mysteries" (2003-2004); Actor, "My Sister's Keeper" (2003); Actor, "Blue's Clues" (2003); Actor, "Holes" (2003); Executive Producer, "Young MacGyver" (2003); Voice Actor, "Clifford the Big Red Dog" (2003); Executive Producer, "TVography: Home Improvement - A Half Hour of Power" (2002); Executive Producer, "WinTuition" (2002); Executive Producer, "Sightings: Heartland Ghost" (2002); Voice Actor, "Ozzy & Drix" (2002); Actor, "Law & Order: Special Victims Unit" (2002); Director, Two Episodes, "Sabrina, the Teenage Witch" (2000-2002); Actor, "I Shaved My Legs for This" (2001); Actor, "The Drew Carey Show" (2001); Actor, "Big Apple" (2001); Executive Producer, "TVography: Laverne & Shirley" (2001); Executive Producer, "TVography: Happy Days" (2001); Executive Producer, "So Weird" (1999-2001); Actor, "Little Nicky" (2000); Actor, "Battery Park" (2000); Actor, "Down to You" (2000); Actor, "The Practice" (1999-2000); Actor, "Elevator Seeking" (1999); Actor, "Ugly Naked People" (1999); Voice Actor, "The Simpsons" (1999); Actor, "So Weird" (1999); Actor, "Dill Scallion" (1999); Actor, "P.U.N.K.S." (1999); Actor, "The Waterboy" (1998); Actor, "Ground Control" (1998); Voice Actor, "South Park" (1998); Executive Producer, "Hollywood Squares" (1998); Actor, "Dead Man's Gun" (1997-1998); Executive Producer, "Dead Man's Gun" (1997-1998); Director, Two Episodes, "Clueless" (1997); Actor, "Detention: The Siege at Johnson High" (1997); Actor, "Dad's Week Off" (1997); Executive Producer, "Sightings" (1991-1997); Actor, "Scream" (1996); Class Day Speaker, Yale University (1996); Actor, Producer, "A Child Is Missing" (1995); Director, "Dave's World" (1995); Director, "New York Daze" (1995); Executive Producer, "MacGyver: Trail to Doomsday" (1994); Executive Producer, "MacGyver: Lost Treasure of Atlantis" (1994); Executive Producer, "Nobody's Children" (1994); Executive Producer, "Monty" (1994); Actor, "The Larry Sanders Show" (1995); Actor, "Monty" (1994); Actor, "One Christmas" (1994); Director, "Cop & 1/2" (1993); Actor, "The Only Way Out" (1993); Executive Producer, "Sightings: Ghosts" (1992); Actor, "MC Hammer: 2 Legit 2 Quit" (1991); Actor, "Absolute Strangers" (1991); Producer, "Tim Conway's Funny America" (1990); Actor, "MacGyver" (1990); Actor, "Happy Days" (1974-1984); Actor, Numerous Plays **AW:** Best Supporting Actor in a Comedy Series, "Barry," Critic's Choice Television Awards (2019); Best Supporting Actor in a Comedy Series, "Barry," Broadcast Film Critics Association Awards (2019); Outstanding Supporting Actor in a Comedy Series, "Barry," Primetime Emmy Awards, Television Academy (2018); Named "One of the United Kingdom's Top 10 Literacy Heroes," National Literacy Trust (2013); Appointed an Honorary Officer of the Order of the British Empire "For Services to Children with Special Educational Needs and Dyslexia in the UK" (2011); Recipient, Key to the City of Winnipeg "For Contributions to Education and Literacy" (2010); Recognized with the "Bronze Fonz," Milwaukee Riverwalk (2008); The "When Bad Teens Go Good" Award, TV Land Awards (2007); Outstanding Performer in an Animated Program, "Clifford's Puppy Days," 32nd Daytime Emmy Awards, The National Academy of Television Arts & Sciences (2005); Comedy Guest Actor, "Arrested Development," Gold Derby Awards (2004); Bronze Wrangler, "Dead Man's Gun," Western Heritage Awards (1998); Humanitarian Award, Women in Film Crystal Awards (1988); Outstanding Children's Special, "All the Kids Do It," 12th Daytime Emmy Awards, The National Academy of Television Arts & Sciences (1985); Louella Parsons Award, Golden Apple Awards (1982); Recipient, Star, Hollywood Walk of Fame (1981); Best Actor -

Television Series Musical or Comedy, "Happy Days," Golden Globe Awards, Hollywood Foreign Press Association (1978); Best Actor - Television Series Musical or Comedy, "Happy Days," Golden Globe Awards, Hollywood Foreign Press Association (1977) **MEM:** American Federation of Television and Radio Artists (Now SAG-AFTRA); Screen Actors Guild (Now SAG-AFTRA); Actors' Equity Association

WINKLER, MARIA, PHD, T: Co-owner **I:** Fine Art **CN:** KW Studios **DOB:** 10/24/1945 **PB:** Krakow **SC:** Poland **PT:** Aniela Lurie Winkler; Joseph Winkler **MS:** Married **SPN:** David Komar **ED:** PhD in Art Education, The Pennsylvania State University; MFA in Drawing/Painting, The Pennsylvania State University; BA in Fine Arts, University of Pennsylvania **C:** Professor Emeritus of Art Department, California State University, Sacramento (2010-Present); Co-owner, KW Studios (1999-Present); Professor of Art, California State University, Sacramento (1977-2010); Assistant Professor of Art Education, The University of British Columbia, Vancouver, British Columbia, Canada (1975-1977); Assistant Professor of Art, Boise State University, Boise, Idaho (1973-1975); Instructor of Art, The Pennsylvania State University, University Park, PA (1972-1973) **CIV:** Creative Arts League of Sacramento; Crocker Art Museum **CW:** Artist, Group Show, "Feathers, Fins, and Fur," Archival Gallery, Sacramento, CA (2019); Artist, Group Show, "Fake It," Blue Line Arts, Roseville, CA (2019); Artist, Group Show, "Obsessed," Blue Line Arts, Roseville, CA (2019); Artist, Group Show, "Here Comes Santa," Archival Gallery, Sacramento, CA (2018); Artist, Group Show, "The Box It Came In," Group Show, Archival Gallery, Sacramento, CA (2018); Artist, Group Show, "Membership Medley," Blue Line Arts, Roseville, CA (2018); Artist, "Picture It," Photography Show, Blue Line Arts, Roseville, CA (2018); Artist, "Creative Arts League," Group Show, Blue Line Arts, Roseville, CA (2018); Artist, Group Show, "The US Show," Celebrating Diversity, Blue Line Arts, Roseville, CA (2018); Artist, Solo Exhibition, "Vintage Toys by Maria Winkler," KOH Library and Cultural Center, Sacramento, CA (2018); Artist, Solo Exhibition, "Now Playing by Maria Winkler," Pence Gallery, Davis, CA (2018); Artist, Exhibition, "Now Playing: Toys and Games," KVIE Gallery (PBS Studios), Sacramento, CA (2017); Artist, Exhibition, "Vintage Toys and Games by Maria Winkler," Roseville Chamber of Commerce, Roseville, CA (2017); Artist, Special Public Art Commissions, Utility Box Wrap: District 8, Sacramento Metropolitan Arts Commission (2017); Artist, Special Public Art Commissions, Utility Box Wrap: Alkalai Flats, Sacramento Metropolitan Arts Commission (2017); Artist, Three-Person Show," Fish, Fishing, Fish," Archival Gallery, Sacramento, CA (2017); Artist, Group Show, "The Placer Principle: Artists from Placer County," Blue Line Arts, Roseville, CA (2017) ; Artist, Group Show, "The Art of Movement," Blue Line Arts, CA (2017); Artist, Group Show, "Trump l'Oeil," Archival Gallery, Sacramento, CA (2017); Artist, Group Show, "A December to Remember," Archival Gallery, Sacramento, CA (2016); Artist, Group Show, "Mask Invitational," Kondos Gallery, Sacramento City College, Sacramento, CA (2016); Featured, "Critic's Picks: Best of Second Saturday," The Sacramento Bee (2016); Artist, Group Show, "Map It Out," Blue Line Arts, Roseville, CA (2016); Artist, Group Show, "Women's Intuition," Archival Gallery, Sacramento, CA (2016); Artist, "Forever Delta," Library Gallery, California State University, Sacramento (2016); Artist, "Forever Delta," Shimo Center for the Arts, Sacramento, CA (2015); Artist, "Forever Delta," The Old Courtland Bank, Courtland, CA (2015); Artist, "Ro Sham Bo," Archival Gallery, Sacramento, CA

(2015); Featured, "Art Preview: Gallery Art Shows in June," Inside East Sacramento, Inside Publications (2015); Featured, "Selected Blue Line Artists," Sutter Club, Sacramento, CA (2015); Artist, "Aqua Vistas," General Gomez Art Center, Auburn, CA (2015); Artist, Two-Person Exhibition, "Now Playing: Maria Winkler & David Komar," TEMP Gallery, Sacramento, CA (2014); Artist, "Sculptural Diversity...What Else?," Robert Else Gallery, California State University, Sacramento (2014); Artist, "New Paintings by Maria Winkler," Archival Gallery, Sacramento, CA (2014); Artist, "Politically Charged," Blue Line Arts, Roseville, CA (2014); Artist, "Art Preview: Gallery Art Shows in November," Inside East Sacramento, Inside Publications (2014); Artist, "The Box It Came In," Archival Gallery, Sacramento, CA (2014); Artist, "Animal Attraction," TEMP Gallery, Sacramento, CA (2014); Artist, "Mid-Century Madness," Blue Line Arts, Roseville, CA (2014); Artist, "Art You Can Feel," Blue Line Arts, Roseville, CA (2014); Artist, "Re-Purposing Wood," TEMP Gallery, Sacramento, CA (2014); Artist, "Vernal Pool Visions," Juried Show, Sacramento Splash, Mather, CA (2013); Artist, "Breaking Out," TEMP Gallery, Sacramento, CA (2013); Artist, "30/30 Anniversary Show," Archival Gallery, Sacramento, CA (2013); Artist, "Art Deco Reimagined," Blue Line Arts, Roseville, CA (2013); Artist, "The Last Collaboration of Laureen Landau," Archival Gallery, Sacramento, CA (2013); Featured, "Artists Rework Landau's Legacy," The Sacramento Bee (2013); Artist, Exhibition, "Family Game Night: Paintings by Maria Winkler, Sculpture by Eric Dahlin," Archival Gallery, Sacramento, CA (2013); Artist, Exhibition, "Maria Winkler," Shimo Center for the Arts, Sacramento, CA (2012); Artist, Juried Group Show, "Sum of the Parts," Blue Line Gallery, Roseville, CA (2012); Artist, Four-Person Show, "Celebrating Water," Capital Public Radio, Sacramento, CA (2012); Featured, "SacBee Ticket," The Sacramento Bee (2012); Artist, Four-Person Show, "Aqua-Scapes," Blue Line Gallery, Roseville, CA (2011); Artist, National Juried Show, "Celebrating Artistic Expression," William Jessup University, Rocklin, CA, (2011); Artist, Exhibition, "Maria Winkler, Landscape Paintings," KOH Library and Cultural Center, Sacramento, CA (2010); Artist, Exhibition, "Paintings and Artist Books by Maria Winkler," Robert Else Gallery, California State University, Sacramento (2010); Artist, Painting, "Water & Ice," University Union Gallery, California State University, Sacramento (2009) **AW:** First Place Award, California State University Alumni Juried Show, Sacramento Robert Else Gallery (2010); Huell Howser Award for Best Landscape **MEM:** California Art League of Sacramento **AS:** Dr. Winkler attributes her success to being encouraged by her parents from the age of 3. **B/I:** Dr. Winkler became involved in her profession because she loved art and teaching adults.

WINSLET, KATE, T: Actress **I:** Media & Entertainment **DOB:** 10/05/1975 **PB:** Reading **SC:** Berkshire/England **PT:** Roger Winslet; Sally Bridges Winslet **MS:** Married **SPN:** Edward Abel Smith (Ned Rocknroll) (2012); Sam Mendes (2003, Divorced 2011); Jim Threapleton (1998, Divorced 2001) **CH:** Mia Honey Threapleton; Joe Mendes; Bear Blaze Winslet **ED:** General Certificate of Secondary Education, United Kingdom (1991) **C:** Founder, Golden Hat Foundation (2010-Present); Designer, Watch, Longines (2017); Creator, Makeup Collection, Lancôme (2011); Brand Ambassador, Lancôme, Longines; Actress, Film and Television **CIV:** Supporter, UNICEF Campaign, World's Largest Lesson (2015); Narrator, Video, People for the Ethical Treatment of Animals (2010); Contributor, Butterfly Book (2009); Participant, Auction to Raise Funds for the Afghanistan Relief Organization

(2007); Patron, the Family Haven (2006) **CW:** Voice Actress, "Naya Legend of the Golden Dolphin" (2022); Actress, "Avatar 2" (2021); Executive Producer, "Mare of Easttown" (2020); Actress, "Mare of Easttown" (2020); Actress, "Ammonite" (2020); Voice Actress, "Black Beauty" (2020); Actress, "Moominvalley" (2019); Actress, "Blackbird" (2019); Voice Actress, "Swift" (2019); Voice Actress, "Buttons, A New Musical Film" (2018); Narrator, "Snow Bears" (2017); Narrator, "Diana: The Day Britain Cried" (2017); Actress, "Wonder Wheel" (2017); Actress, "The Mountain Between Us" (2017); Voice Actress, "Mary and the Witch's Flower" (2017); Actress, "Collateral Beauty" (2016); Voice Actress, "The Christmas Letter" (2016); Voice Actress, "Daisy Chain" (2016); Actress, "Triple 9" (2016); Actress, "The Dressmaker" (2015); Actress, "Steve Jobs" (2015); Actress, "Insurgent" (2015); Actress, "The Divergent Series: Insurgent - Shatter Reality" (2015); Narrator, "The Magic Finger" (2014); Narrator, "Matilda" (2014); Actress, "A Little Chaos" (2014); Actress, "Divergent" (2014); Actress, "Labor Day" (2014); Actress, "Movie 43" (2013); Author, "The Golden Hat: Talking Back to Autism" (2012); Narrator, "You're a Bad Man, Mr. Gum!" (2012); Narrator, "Thérèse Raquin" (2012); Actress, "Contagion" (2011); Actress, "Carnage" (2011); Actress, "Mildred Pierce" (2011); Narrator, "A Mother's Courage: Talking Back to Autism" (2009); Actress, "Revolutionary Road" (2008); Actress, "The Reader" (2008); Actress, "How to Lose Friends & Alienate People" (2008); Voice Actress, "The Fox & the Child" (2007); Actress, "Vanity Fair: Killers Kill, Dead Men Die" (2007); Narrator, "Deep Sea 3D" (2006); Actress, "The Holiday" (2006); Voice Actress, "Flushed Away" (2006); Actress, "All the King's Men" (2006); Actress, "Little Children" (2006); Actress, "Romance & Cigarettes" (2005); Actress, "Finding Neverland" (2004); Voice Actress, "Pride" (2004); Actress, "Eternal Sunshine of the Spotless Mind" (2004); Actress, "Plunge: The Movie" (2003); Actress, "The Life of David Gale" (2003); Voice Actress, "War Game" (2002); Actress, "Iris" (2001); Voice Actress, "A Christmas Carol" (2001); Actress, "Enigma" (2001); Actress, "Quills" (2000); Actress, "Holy Smoke" (1999); Voice Actress, "Faeries" (1999); Narrator, "Listen to the Storyteller" (1999); Actress, "Hideous Kinky" (1998); Actress, "Titanic" (1997); Actress, "Hamlet" (1996); Actress, "Jude" (1996); Actress, "Sense and Sensibility" (1995); Actress, "A Kid in King Arthur's Court" (1995); Actress, "Heavenly Creatures" (1994); Actress, "Casualty" (1993); Actress, "Get Back" (1992-1993); Actress, "Anglo Saxon Attitudes" (1992); Actress, "Dark Season" (1991); Actress, "Shrinks" (1991) **AW:** Dilys Powell Award, London Film Critics' Circle Awards (2017); Hollywood Actress Award, "Wonder Wheel," Hollywood Film Awards (2017); Best Actress in a Supporting Role, "Steve Jobs," British Academy Film Awards (2016); Best Supporting Actress - Motion Picture, "Steve Jobs" Golden Globe Awards (2016); Best Supporting Actress, "Steve Jobs," Iowa Film Critics Association (2016); British Icon Award, Harper's Bazaar Women of the Year Awards (2015); Best Actress, "The Dressmaker," Australian Film Critics Association (2015); Best Lead Actress, "The Dressmaker," AACTA Awards (2015); Best Actress, "The Dressmaker," Film Critics Circle of Australia (2015); Best Supporting Actress of the Year, "Steve Jobs," London Film Critics' Circle Awards (2015); Variety Award, "Steve Jobs," British Independent Film Awards (2015); Woman of the Year, Elle Women in Hollywood Awards (2015); Best Audiobook Performance, "Matilda," Odyssey Awards (2014); Best Audiobook Performance, "Matilda," Earphones Awards (2014); Recipient, Star, Hollywood Walk of Fame (2014); Appointed Commander of the Order of the British Empire "for her services to drama," 2012 Birthday Honours (2012); Best Actress in a Miniseries or Motion Picture - Television, "Mildred Pierce," Golden Globe Awards (2012); Outstanding Performance by a Female Actor in Television Movie or Miniseries, "Mildred Pierce," Screen Actors Guild Awards (2012); Honorary César, César Awards (2012); Yo Dona International Awards "for Best Humanitarian Work" (2011); Outstanding Lead Actress in a Limited Series or Television Movie, "Mildred Pierce," Emmy Awards (2011); Best Actress in a Miniseries or Motion Picture Made for Television, "Mildred Pierce," Satellite Awards (2011); Best Cast, "Carnage," Boston Society of Film Critics Awards (2011); Named One of the "100 Most Influential People in the World," Time (2009); Best Actress, "The Reader," Academy Awards (2009); Best Supporting Actress - Motion Picture, "The Reader," Golden Globe Awards (2009); Best Actress in a Motion Picture - Drama, "Revolutionary Road," Golden Globe Awards (2009); Best Actress in a Leading Role, "The Reader," British Academy Film Awards (2009); Best Actress, "The Reader," European Film Awards (2009); Outstanding Performance by a Female Actor in a Supporting Role, "The Reader," Screen Actors Guild Awards (2009); Best Supporting Actress in a Movie, "The Reader," Critics' Recognitions (2009); Best Actress - International, "The Reader," Bambi Awards (2009); Best Actress, "Revolutionary Road," Italian Online Movie Awards (2009); Best Couple on Screen, "Revolutionary Road," Gransito Movie Awards (2009); Montecito Award, "Revolutionary Road," Santa Barbara International Film Festival (2009); Best Supporting Actress, "The Reader," Chicago Film Critics Association Awards (2008); Best Actress, "Revolutionary Road," Detroit Film Critics Society Awards (2008); Best Actress of the Year, "The Reader," "Revolutionary Road," London Film Critics' Circle Awards (2008); Best Actress, "The Reader," San Diego Film Critics Society Awards (2008); Best Actress, "The Reader," "Revolutionary Road," St. Louis Gateway Film Critics Association Awards (2008); Best Actress, "The Reader," "Revolutionary Road," Vancouver Film Critics Circle Awards (2008); British Artist of the Year, Britannia Awards (2007); Desert Palm Achievement Award for Acting, "Little Children," Palm Springs International Film Festival (2007); Tribute, Gotham Awards (2006); Best British Actress, "Eternal Sunshine of the Spotless Mind," Empire Awards (2005); Best Actress, "Eternal Sunshine of the Spotless Mind," International Cinephile Society Awards (2005); Best Actress, "Eternal Sunshine of the Spotless Mind," Italian Online Movie Awards (2005); Outstanding Performance of the Year Award, "Eternal Sunshine of the Spotless Mind," "Finding Neverland," Santa Barbara International Film Festival (2005); British Actress of the Year, "Eternal Sunshine of the Spotless Mind," London Film Critics' Circle Awards (2004); Best Ensemble, "Eternal Sunshine of the Spotless Mind," Washington, DC Area Film Critics Association Awards (2004); Best Actress, "Eternal Sunshine of the Spotless Mind," Online Film Critics Society Awards (2004); Best British Actress, "Enigma," Empire Awards (2002); Jameson People's Choice Award - Best Actress, "Iris," European Film Awards (2002); Best International Actress, "Titanic," Goldene Kamera Awards (2001); Best Supporting Actress, "Iris," Los Angeles Film Critics Association Awards (2001); Best Actress, "Quills," "Enigma," "Iris," Evening Standard British Film Awards (2001); Best Spoken Word Album for Children, "Listen to the Storyteller," Grammy Awards (2000); Best British Actress, "Titanic," Empire Awards (1999); Film Actress of the Year, Variety Club of Great Britain (1999); Elvira Notari Prize, "Holy Smoke!," Venice Film Festival (1999); Best Actress, Bravo Otto (1998); Best British Actress, "Hamlet," Empire Awards (1998); Jameson People's Choice Award - Best Actress, "Titanic," European Film Awards (1998); Favorite Actress in a Drama, "Titanic," Blockbuster Entertainment Awards (1998); Best Actress in a Supporting Role, "Sense and Sensibility," British Academy Film Awards (1996); Best British Actress, "Heavenly Creatures," Empire Awards (1996); Outstanding Performance by a Female Actor in a Supporting Role, "Sense and Sensibility," Screen Actors Guild Awards (1996); Best Actress, "Sense and Sensibility," "Jude," Evening Standard British Film Awards (1996); British Actress of the Year, "Heavenly Creatures," London Film Critics' Circle Awards (1995)

WINSOR, BARBARA ANN, DOB: 07/04/1943 **PB:** Bar Harbor **SC:** ME/USA **PT:** Gordon Dow Winsor; Ruth Mary (Bennett) Winsor **ED:** Coursework in Computer Graphics, Winter Park Tech (1997-1998); BFA, Massachusetts College of Art and Design (1965) **C:** Part-Time Graphic Designer, Shadow Graphics (1995-Present); Freelance Designer, Wildlife Illustrator, Gilmanton Ironworks, NH (1991-Present); Freelance Designer, Wildlife Illustrator, Concord, NH (1987-Present); Freelance Artist (1994-1998); Substitute Teacher, Orange County (1995-1996); Senior Graphic Designer, Lehman Millet (1985-1987); Senior Artist, Walt Disney Productions (1978-1985); Art Director, Graphic Designer, Polaroid (1967-1978); Graphic Designer, The Associate Designers (1966-1967); Graphic Designer, Colorpicture (1965-1966) **CW:** Graphic Designer, Second Annual Exhibition, New Hampshire Creative Club (1990) **AW:** First Place Award, Annual Art Show, Gilmanton, NH (1991); Award, The Ad Club (1967-1978); Winner, Design Competition, Parsons Paper Company (1978); First Place Award, Insert Competition (1969)

WINSTON, JANE KUPFER, BFA, T: Secondary Education Educator; Artist **I:** Education/Educational Services **DOB:** 07/05/1947 **PB:** Omaha **SC:** NE/USA **PT:** Paul Henry Kupfer; Jean (Irwin) Kupfer **CH:** Daniel **ED:** Coursework, Midland University Lutheran College, Fremont, NE (1965-1967); BFA in Education, University of Nebraska-Lincoln (1969) **C:** Art Teacher, Skyline High School, Idaho Falls, Idaho (1987-2010); Art Teacher, Idaho Falls High School, Idaho (1975-1980); Art Teacher, Beveridge Junior High (Now Beveridge Magnet School), Omaha, NE (1969-1973) **CIV:** Member, Idaho Falls Snowfest Committee (1991) **AW:** Named Idaho Secondary Art Educator of the Year (1996); Grantee, Idaho Falls Education Foundation (1992) **MEM:** Idaho Falls Art Guild; Idaho Art Education Association; National Art Education Association; Life Member, Eagle Rock Art Guild, Inc.; Delta Kappa Gamma (DKGSI) **MH:** Albert Nelson Marquis Lifetime Achievement Award **B/I:** Ms. Winston became involved in her profession because while she was in high school, she knew she was going to college and also knew what she wanted to major in. Back then, there weren't many choices for women; the choices were either becoming a nurse, secretary or a teacher, and she chose to be a teacher. **AV:** Reading; Playing board and card games; Travel

WINTERLING, GEORGE ALFRED, T: Meteorologist, Broadcaster **I:** Sciences **DOB:** 09/01/1937 **PB:** Pine Beach **SC:** NJ/USA **PT:** Otto Gustav Winterling; Ruth (Cranmer) Winterling **MS:** Married **SPN:** Virginia Carter (06/25/1955) **CH:** George Franklin; Stephen Alan; Wendy Gale **ED:** BS in Meteorology, Florida State University, Tallahassee, FL (1957); Coursework, Jacksonville University, Jacksonville, FL (1954-1955); Coursework, Oklahoma State University, Stillwater, OK (1951-1952) **CT:** Certified Consultant, Meteorologist, American Meteorological Society (1989) **C:** Chief Meteorologist, Station WJXT-TV, Jacksonville, FL (1962-2009); Weather Forecaster, National Weather Service, Jacksonville, FL (1957-1962) **CR:** Adjunct Professor, Jacksonville University, Jacksonville, FL (1975-1994); Time-Lapse Photography; Weather Reports; Researcher, Time Lapse Radar Movements for Thunderstorms and Hurricanes **MIL:** Weather Observer, Forecaster, United States Air Force (1950-1953) **CW:** Author, "Chasing the Wind: Memories of a Pioneer TV Meteorologist" (2018) **AW:** Distinguished Alumni Award, Jacksonville University, Jacksonville, FL (1990); Award for Outstanding Service by a Broadcast Meteorologist, American Meteorological Society (1984); Distinguished Alumnus, Florida State University **MEM:** Fellow, American Meteorological Society; Golden Chief, Seminole Boosters **MH:** Albert Nelson Marquis Lifetime Achievement Award **B/I:** Mr. Winterling became involved in his profession because, since he was in high school, he was always interested in weather; he additionally enjoyed science and math. Mr. Winterling joined the United States Air Force because he had an interest in planes. His family lived near the naval air station and so they had an opportunity to watch the history of aviation evolve since the 1940s. When Mr. Winterling joined the Air Force, he was told that he would have to apply to cadet school to become a pilot. In the meantime, he had to find an occupation, so he went down the list and the word weather appealed to him. He went to a weather observer school at Chanute Air Force Base in Rantoul, Illinois. Mr. Winterling worked at weather stations in Georgia and then went to school at Oklahoma State University for a year. He then was transferred to Alaska and spent a year there, and he also traveled to Japan because he was giving weather forecasts for the planes that flew across the Pacific. That was a big effort because there were no satellites back then. When Mr. Winterling got out of the Air Force, he pursued a degree in meteorology at Florida State University. For five years, he worked with the United States Weather Bureau. After a hurricane brushed Jacksonville, Florida, Mr. Winterling went to work as a Chief Meteorologist at WJXT-TV in Jacksonville. He remained there for 47 years before he retired. Ultimately, he stayed on for five more years after that as meteorologist emeritus. **AV:** Gardening; Landscaping

WINTOUR, ANNA, DBE, T: Editor **I:** Writing and Editing **CN:** Vogue Magazine **DOB:** 11/03/1949 **PB:** Hampstead **SC:** England **PT:** Charles Wintour; Eleanor "Nonie" Trego Baker; Audrey Slaughter (Stepmother) **MS:** Married **SPN:** Shelby Bryan (2004); David Shaffer (1984, Divorced 1999) **CH:** Charles; Katherine "Bee" **ED:** Coursework, North London Collegiate School **C:** Editor, American Vogue (1988-Present); Editor, British Vogue (1985-1987); Creative Director, Vogue (1983-1985); Fashion Editor, New York (1981); Fashion Editor, Savvy (1980); Fashion Editor, Viva (1975-1978); Junior Fashion Editor, Harper's Bazaar, New York, NY (1975); Editorial Assistant, Harper's & Queen (1970); Biba (1964) **CR:** House & Garden (1987); Founder, Training Program, Harrods (1965) **CIV:** Trustee, Costume Institute, Metropolitan Museum of Art; Founder, CFDA/Vogue Fund; Fundraiser, Numerous AIDS Charities **CW:** Appearance, "The Late Late Show with James Corden" (2017); Featured, "The September Issue," Roadside Attractions (2009); Featured, "Anna Wintour, Behind the Shades," 60 Minutes, CBS News (2009); Featured, "Citizen Anna," The New York Times (2007); Featured, "Front Row: The Cool Life and Hot Times of Vogue's Editor In Chief," St. Martin's Press (2005); Featured, "The Devil Wears Prada" (2003);

Featured, "The Summer of Her Discontent" (1999) **AW:** Dame Commander of the Order of the British Empire (2017); Inductee, Hall of Fame, American Society of Magazine Editors (2010); Officer of the Order of the British Empire (2008); Editor of the Year, AdAge; Most Powerful Women in the World, Forbes **PA:** Democrat

WIRTH, MICHAEL K., T: Chairman, Chief Executive Officer **I:** Oil & Energy **CN:** Chevron Corporation **MS:** Married **SPN:** Julie Wirth **CH:** Four Children **ED:** BS in Chemical Engineering, University of Colorado (1982) **C:** Chairman, Chief Executive Officer, Chevron Corporation (2018-Present); Executive Vice President, Midstream & Development, Chevron Corporation (2016-2018); Vice Chairman, Board, Chevron Corporation (2017); Executive Vice President, Downstream & Chemicals, Chevron Corporation (2006-2015); President, Global Supply and Trading, Chevron Corporation (2003-2006); President, Marketing to Asia/Middle East/Africa, Chevron Corporation (2001-2004); President, Marketing, Caltex Corporation, Singapore (2000-2001); General Manager, Retail Marketing, Chevron Corporation (1999-2000); Senior Retail Manager, Marketing, Western Operations, Chevron Corporation (1998-1999); Design Engineer, Chevron Corporation (1982) **CR:** Member, Board of Directors, Catalyst, Inc. (2018-Present); Member, Board of Directors, Executive Committee Member, American Petroleum Institute (API) (2018-Present); Vice Chairman, Kennedy Center Corporate Fund **MEM:** International Business Council (2019-Present); National Petroleum Council (2018-Present); American Society of Corporate Executives (2018-Present); Business Roundtable (2018-Present); Business Council (2018-Present); Board Member, Caltex Australia, Ltd. (2001-2003); San Francisco 49ers Foundation; TGR Foundation

WISE, PATRICIA, T: Opera Performer, Concert Singer, Educator **I:** Media & Entertainment **PB:** Wichita **SC:** KS/USA **PT:** Melvin R. Wise; Genevieve F. (Dotson) Wise **MS:** Single **CH:** Jennifer **ED:** BS in Music Education, University of Kansas (1966) **C:** Kansas City Lyric Opera (1965-2005); Performer, Over 40 Principal Roles, Various Shows; Appearances, Numerous Leading American Opera Companies; Guest Artist, International Operas; Guest Appearances, International Shows; Bavarian Radio Orchestra; Appearances, International Orchestras **CR:** Teacher, Master Classes, Numerous Established Institutions (1995-2013); Voice Teacher, Domingo Young Artist Program, Washington Opera; Private Voice Teacher, New York, NY **AW:** Kammersaenger Vienna Staatsoper (1989); Morton Baum Award, New York City Center (1971); M.B. Rockefeller Fund Grantee (1967-1970); Sullivan Foundation Grantee (1967-1968); Dealey Memorial Award, Dallas Symphony (1966); Naftzger Young Artist Award, Wichita Symphony (1966); Midland Young Artist Award, Midland Symphony Orchestra (1966) **AV:** NATS; Opera America

WISEMAN, FRANK, T: Chemistry Professor **I:** Education/Educational Services **PT:** Barbara Wiseman; Frank Wiseman **MS:** Married **SPN:** Kay **ED:** PhD in Organic Chemistry, University of Maryland; BS in Chemistry, Bridgewater College **C:** Retired (2014); Professor Emeritus (2009); Professor, Chair, Chemistry Department, Georgetown College, Kentucky **CIV:** Commissioner on Scotl County Planning & Zoning Board; Commissioner of Scotl County Soil Conservation Board; Chairman, Lexington American Kentucky Section **AW:** U.S. Professor of the Year Award, Carnegie Foundation for Advancement of Teaching and Council for Advancement and Support of Education (2006) **MEM:** American Chemical Society (1962)

MH: Albert Nelson Marquis Lifetime Achievement Award **B/I:** Professor Wiseman became involved in his profession because of his high school chemistry teacher, Mr. Ridgeway, who made chemistry fun to learn. He also had a real chemistry kit as a kid. **AV:** Painting; Hunting; Farming (cattle/corn/hay/hops); Collecting Native American artifacts **RE:** Christian

WISSNER, ANNIE, T: Vice President of Marketing **I:** Advertising & Marketing **CN:** TraceGains, Inc. **ED:** BBA, University of Denver, CO **CT:** ITIL Certification, Information Systems Examinations Board (ISEB) (2015); Project Management Certificate, University of Washington (2005); Level 4: Pragmatic Product Marketing Certified **C:** Vice President of Marketing, TraceGains, In., CO (2018-Present); Director of Marketing, Hexagon Mining, CO (2017-Present); Director of Corporate Marketing, Cherwell Software, CO (2015-2017); Marketing Director, Software AG, CO (2014-2015);Group Marketing Manager, Microsoft, WA (2003-2014); Partner's Resource Network (PRN) Director, CA (2001-2003); Americas Customer Marketing Director, CA and IL (1996-2001) **CIV:** Librarian, Graland Country Day School, Denver, CO (2012-Present); Judge, Odyssey of the Mind (2016); Event Manager, Colorado Ballet Auxiliary (2014-2016) **AS:** Ms. Wissner's mother taught her to be strong and independent. She told her to know that she was capable, make her own money, and make her own way in life. She taught her to speak with her own voice and not to serve merely as an ornament to a man. **B/I:** Ms. Wissner was inspired to pursue her career by her mother. Her father was a highly successful chief executive officer but her mother was a great artist, who she regards as a "genius". Although Ms. Wissner's mother was highly intelligent, she played the role of the spouse to her highly successful husband. She served as great council to her father, and Ms. Wissner believes that he would not have had the success he did had it not been for her council.

WITCOFF, SHELDON W., ESQ., T: Lawyer **I:** Law and Legal Services **DOB:** 07/10/1925 **PB:** Washington, DC **SC:** DC/USA **PT:** Joseph Witcoff; Zina (Ceppos) Witcoff **MS:** Widowed **SPN:** Margot Gail Hoffner (09/06/1953, Deceased) **CH:** Lauren Jill; David Lawrence; Lisa Ann; Julie Beth **ED:** JD, The George Washington University (1953); BS in Electrical Engineering, University of Maryland (1949) **C:** Partner, Banner Witcoff Ltd., Chicago, IL (1995-Present); Partner, Allegretti & Witcoff, Ltd. (Now Banner Witcoff Ltd.), Chicago, IL (1988-1995); Partner, Allegretti, Newitt, Witcoff & McAndrews, Chicago, IL (1970-1988); Partner, Bair, Freeman & Molinare, Chicago, IL (1955-1969); Patent Lawyer, Bell Telephone Laboratories, Murray Hill, NJ (1953-1955); Patent Examiner, Patent Office, U.S. Department of Commerce (1949-1953) **CR:** Vice President, Director, Art Specialty Co., Chicago, IL (1967-1984); Vice President, Caspian Fur Trading Co., New York, NY; Co-founder, Child Abuse Unit for Studies, Education and Services, Chicago, IL **CIV:** Fire and Police Commissioner, Skokie, IL (1960-1963) **MIL:** With, United States Naval Reserve (1943-1946); U.S.S. Guam, Task Force 58 (1945) **MEM:** American Bar Association (ABA); Intellectual Property Law Association of Chicago; Order of the Coif; Tau Epsilon Phi; The International Legal Honor Society of Phi Delta Phi; B'nai B'rith International; Jewish War Veterans of the United States of America, Post 29 **BAR:** Illinois (1956); New York (1955); District of Columbia (1953); Supreme Court of the United States **MH:** Albert Nelson Marquis Lifetime Achievement Award **B/I:** Mr. Witcoff became involved in his profession after joining the Navy. Mr. Witcoff was trained as a

radar electronics technician, and wanted to continue working with electronics when he left the Navy. Wanting to work with people and technology, Mr. Witcoff decided to work at the patent office for electric computer inventions while studying law. After completing law school, Mr. Witcoff worked for Bell Laboratories, and then joined Bair, Freeman, and Molinare. **PA:** Democrat **RE:** Jewish **THT:** Mr. Witcoff is a naval veteran; his father served in World War I, and his brother fought in the Korean War. As an immigrant, Mr. Witcoff's father inspired him greatly and instilled a tremendous work effort in him. Mr. Witcoff ingrains the teachings of his father into his children and grandchildren. Patent law was so appealing to Mr. Witcoff because it's a field filled with creative people trying to improve society. Mr. Witcoff met many talented and interesting people throughout his life, including Jackie Kennedy and Albert Einstein.

WITHERSPOON, REESE, T: Actress, Producer, Entrepreneur **I:** Media & Entertainment **DOB:** 03/22/1976 **PB:** New Orleans **SC:** LA/USA **PT:** John Witherspoon; Betty Witherspoon **MS:** Married **SPN:** Jim Toth (03/26/2011); Ryan Phillippe (06/05/1999, Divorced 2007) **CH:** Ava Elizabethe Phillippe; Deacon Reese Phillippe; Tennessee James Toth **ED:** Coursework in English Literature, Stanford University **C:** Co-Founder, Hello Sunshine (2016-Present); Founder, Draper James (2015-Present); Founder, Owner, Type A Films (2000-2016); Actress, Producer, Film and Television **CR:** Spokeswoman, Global Ambassador, Avon Products, Inc. (2007-Present); Announcer, Playhouse Disney (2007-2011); Participant, CDF Project for Hurricane Katrina Victims (2006); Co-Founder, Freedom School, New Orleans, LA; Longtime Supporter, Save the Children; Member, Board, Children's Defense Fund **CW:** Voice Actress, "Sing 2" (2021); Executive Producer, "From Scratch" (2020); Producer, "Legally Blonde 3" (2020); Actress, "Legally Blonde 3" (2020); Actress, "Little Fires Everywhere" (2020); Executive Producer, "Little Fires Everywhere" (2020); Executive Producer, "The Morning Show" (2019-2020); Actress, "The Morning Show" (2019-2020); Executive Producer, "Truth Be Told" (2019-2020); Producer, "Lucy in the Sky" (2019); Author, "Whiskey in a Teacup: What Growing Up in the South Taught Me About Life, Love, and Baking Biscuits" (2018); Executive Producer, "Master the Mess" (2018); Executive Producer, "Shine On with Reese" (2018); Actress, "A Wrinkle in Time" (2018); Executive Producer, "Big Little Lies" (2017-2019); Actress, "Big Little Lies" (2017-2019); Actress, "The Mindy Project" (2017); Actress, "Home Again" (2017); Voice Actress, "Gunter Babysits" (2017); Voice Actress, "Sing" (2016); Executive Producer, "Broken" (2016); Producer, "Hot Pursuit" (2015); Voice Actress, "Nature Is Speaking" (2015); Actress, "The Muppets." (2015); Actress, "Hot Pursuit" (2015); Producer, "Gone Girl" (2014); Producer, "Wild" (2014); Actress, "9 Kisses" (2014); Actress, "Inherent Vice" (2014); Actress, "The Good Lie" (2014); Actress, "Wild" (2014); Actress, "Devil's Knot" (2013); Actress, "Mud" (2012); Actress, "This Means War" (2012); Actress, "Water for Elephants" (2011); Actress, "How Do You Know" (2010); Producer, "Legally Blondes" (2009); Voice Actress, "Monsters vs. Aliens: Mutant Pumpkins from Outer Space" (2009); Voice Actress, "Monsters vs. Aliens" (2009); Actress, "Four Christmases" (2008); Actress, "Rendition" (2007); Producer, "Penelope" (2006); Actress, "Penelope" (2006); Actress, "Just Like Heaven" (2005); Actress, "Walk the Line" (2005); Actress, "Vanity Fair" (2004); Actress, "Freedom: A History of Us" (2003); Executive Producer, "Legally Blonde 2: Red, White & Blonde" (2003); Actress, "Legally Blonde 2: Red,

White & Blonde" (2003); Actress, "Sweet Home Alabama" (2002); Actress, "The Importance of Being Earnest" (2002); Voice Actress, "The Simpsons" (2002); Host, "Saturday Night Live" (2001); Actress, "Legally Blonde" (2001); Voice Actress, "The Trumpet of the Swan" (2001); Actress, "Little Nicky" (2000); Voice Actress, "King of the Hill" (2000); Actress, "Friends" (2000); Actress, "American Psycho" (2000); Actress, "Best Laid Plans" (1999); Actress, "Election" (1999); Actress, "Cruel Intentions" (1999); Actress, "Pleasantville" (1998); Actress, "Overnight Delivery" (1998); Actress, "Twilight" (1998); Actress, "Fear" (1996); Actress, "Freeway" (1996); Actress, "S.F.W." (1994); Actress, "Return to Lonesome Dove" (1993); Actress, "Jack the Bear" (1993); Actress, "A Far Off Place" (1993); Actress, "Desperate Choices: To Save My Child" (1992); Actress, "Wildflower" (1991); Actress, "The Man in the Moon" (1991) AW: World's 100 Most Powerful Women, Forbes (2019); Best Miniseries or Television Film Producer, "Big Little Lies," Golden Globe Awards (2018); Best Television Movie or Miniseries, "Big Little Lies," Critics' Choice Awards (2018); Best Miniseries, "Big Little Lies," Satellite Awards (2017); Outstanding Limited Series, "Big Little Lies," Primetime Emmy Awards (2017); Time 100 (2015); Robert Altman Award, "Inherent Vice," Independent Spirit Awards (2015); Robert Altman Award, "Mud," Independent Spirit Awards (2014); Renaissance Award, Gene Siskel Film Center (2012); MTV Generation Award, MTV Movie Awards (2011); Star, Hollywood Walk of Fame (2010); Favorite Female Movie Star, People's Choice Awards (2009); Favorite Female Movie Star, People's Choice Awards (2008); Annual Celebrity 100 List, Forbes (2007, 2006); Favorite Leading Actress, People's Choice Awards (2006); Best Actress, "Walk the Line," Academy Awards (2006); Best Actress in a Leading Role, "Walk the Line," British Academy Film Awards (2006); Best Actress in a Motion Picture - Musical or Comedy, "Walk the Line," Golden Globe Awards (2006); Outstanding Performance by a Female Actor in a Leading Role in a Motion Picture, "Walk the Line," Screen Actors Guild Awards (2006); Choice Movie Actress: Drama, "Walk the Line," Teen Choice Awards (2006); Listed Among the Time 100 (2006); Best Actress, "Walk the Line," Boston Society of Film Critics Awards (2005); Best Actress, "Walk the Line," Florida Film Critics Circle Awards (2005); Best Actress, "Walk the Line," Kansas City Film Critics Circle Awards (2005); Best Actress, "Walk the Line," National Society of Film Critics Awards (2005); Best Performance by an Actress in a Motion Picture, Comedy or Musical, "Walk the Line" (2005); Best Actress, "Walk the Line," New York Film Critics Circle Awards (2005); Choice Movie: Liplock, "Sweet Home Alabama," Teen Choice Awards (2003); Best Line, Best Dressed, Best Comedic Performance, "Legally Blonde," MTV Movie Awards (2002); Extraordinary Achievement Award, Teen Choice Awards (2002); Best Actress, "Election," National Society of Film Critics Awards (1999); Best Breakthrough Female Performance, "Pleasantville," Young Hollywood Awards (1999); Best Youth Actress Co-Starring in a Motion Picture: Drama, "Jack the Bear," Young Artist Awards (1994); Top Accomplished Women Entertainers, CEOWorld Magazine

WITT, KATARINA, T: Professional Figure Skater (Retired) I: Athletics DOB: 12/03/1965 PB: Staaken SC: Berlin/Germany PT: Manfred Witt; Kathe Witt ED: Trainee, Jutta Müller; Coursework in Skating, Karl-Marx-Stadt Sports Club and School C: Co-founder, Business Meets Sport (2017-Present); Founder, Katarina Witt Foundation (2005-Present); Founding Member, Laureus Sport for Good, Laureus World Sports Awards Ltd. (2000-Present); Founder, With Witt Sports & Entertainment GmbH (1995-Present); Figure Skating Expert, World Championships and Olympic Games, American and German TV Channels, NBC, CBS, ABC, ZDF, ARD (1991-Present); Participant, TV-Olympic and Skating Expert, ARD, 9th Olympic Winter Games (2018); Chairwoman, 2018 Munich Olympic Bid Committee (2010-2018); Professional Figure Skater (1988-1994); Competitive Skater (1994, 1981-1988) CR: Founder, KW Arts and Entertainment, Frankfurt, Germany CW: Actress, "Der Feind in Meinem Leben (The Enemy in My Life)" (2013); Performer, "Dancing on Ice" (2012); Voice Actress, "Friends Forever" (2009); Co-author, "Only with Passion: Figure Skating's Most Winning Champion on Competition and Life" (2007); Co-actress, "Stars auf Eis" (2006); Art Director, "Divas on Ice" (2001); Actress, "V.I.P." (2000); Actress, "Nikola" (1999); Actress, "Ronin" (1998); Appearance, "Jerry Maguire" (1996); Screenwriter, Actress, "Die Eisprinzessin" (1996); Actress, "Frasier" (1996); Author, "Meine Jahre zwischen Pflicht und Kür (My Years between Compulsories and Freestyle)" (1994); Actress, "Greatest Hits on Ice" (1994); Actress, "Carmen on Ice" (1990) AW: "Le Champion des Champions de Légende" L'Équipe Awards (2013); "München Leuchtet (Munich Shines) for Her Outstanding Effort as Chair of the Munich Olympic Bid 2018" (2011); Inductee, Hall of Fame of German Sports (2010); "Golden Sportpyramide for Her Lifetime Achievements in Sports and Social Commitment" (2010); "Fair Play Mecenate" International Award (2009); "Goldenes Band," Association of Sports Journalists, Berlin-Brandenburg (2009); "German Sustainability Prize for Social Engagement," Editor, Sports Magazine "Sport Bild" (2008); Der Bild Osgar war ein Medienpreis "for an Extraordinary and Continuous Career" (2007); Recipient, Blue Heart (2006); World Business Award (2004); Award for Entertainment, "Die DDR-Show," Golden Hen Awards, Germany (2003); Named Female Athlete of the Year, American Opinion Research Institute (1999); Inductee, World Figure Skating Hall of Fame (1995); Jim Thorpe Pro Sports Award (1995); Award, Sports, Golden Camera, Germany (1994); Named Among the "50 Most Beautiful People in the World," People Magazine (1992); Primetime Emmy Award for Outstanding Performance in Classical Music/Dance Programming, "Carmen on Ice," Television Academy (1990); Jacques Favart Trophy, International Skating Union (1989); Award, International Olympic Committee (IOC) (1988); Named East German Sportswoman of the Year (1984); Voted "GDR Female Athlete of the Year," Readers of the East German Newspaper Junge Welt (1984); Named to Golden Order of Merit for the Fatherland, GDR (1984); Named "The Most Beautiful Face of Socialism," TIME Magazine PA: Socialist Unity Party of Germany

WITTER, DEBRA, T: Partner I: Law and Legal Services CN: Farrow-Gillespie Heath Witter LLP MS: Married SPN: Scott ED: JD, The University of Texas School of Law, with High Honors; BA, The University of Texas, with Highest Honors C: Partner, Farrow-Gillespie Heath Witter LLP (2013-Present); Senior Vice President, Legal, Blockbuster Inc.; Partner, Cohan, Simpson, Cowlishaw, Aranza & Wulff AW: Named Best Lawyer in America (2019); AV-Preeminent Rating, Martindale-Hubbell; Fellow, Texas Bar Foundation MEM: State Bar of Texas; Dallas Bar Association; Board of Director, The Dallas Opera; The Phi Beta Kappa Society B/I: Mrs. Witter's practice now is primarily marketing and advertising law. She was drawn to it because she gets to work with creative people and find ways for them to do what they want to do while still keeping it legal. THT: Mrs. Witter's clients value that she always has a business perspective. Her motto is, "It is often better to be kind than to be bright."

WITTMAN, ROBERT, "ROB" JOSEPH, PHD, T: U.S. Representative from Virginia I: Government Administration/Government Relations/Government Services CN: U.S. House of Representatives DOB: 02/03/1959 PB: Washington SC: DC/USA PT: Frank Joseph Wittman; Regina (Wood) Wittman MS: Married SPN: Kathryn Jane (Sisson) Wittman CH: Devon; Josh ED: Doctor of Philosophy in Public Policy and Administration, Virginia Commonwealth University (2002); Master of Public Health, The University of North Carolina at Chapel Hill (1990); Bachelor of Science in Biology, Virginia Polytechnic Institute (1981) C: Member, U.S. House of Representatives from Virginia's First District (2007-Present); Member, District 99, Virginia House of Delegates (2006-2007); Director, Division of Shellfish Sanitation, Virginia Department of Health (1992-2007); Member, Committee on Armed Services, United States Congress; Member, Committee on Natural Resources, United States Congress; Member, Republican Study Committee, United States Congress; Environmental Health Specialist, Virginia Department of Health CR: Chairperson, Westmoreland County Board of Supervisors (2003-2005); Member, Westmoreland County Board of Supervisors (1996-2005); Mayor, Town of Montross, Montross Town Council, VA (1992-1996); Councilman, Town of Montross, Montross Town Council, VA (1986-1996) CIV: Board of Visitors, United States Naval Academy (2009-Present); Member, Northern Neck Planning District Commission (2003); Chairperson, Interstate Shellfish Sanitation Conference; Chairman, Rappahannock River Basin Commission; Chairperson, Montross-Westmoreland Sewer Authority; Member, Montross Fall and Spring Festival Committee MEM: Pi Alpha Alpha; Delta Tau Delta PA: Republican RE: Episcopalian

WOELFEL, JAMES A., T: Engineering Executive, Chemist (Retired) I: Automotive DOB: 08/31/1944 PB: Fond du Lac SC: WI/USA PT: Linus Andrew; Rose Mary (Heimann) W. MS: Widowed SPN: Kathie (Deceased 03/16/2016); Arlene Marie Daun (09/10/1966) CH: Paulette; Scott; John; William ED: Master of Science in Polymer Science, University of Akron (1971); Bachelor of Science in Chemistry, Michigan Technical University (1967) C: Retired (2008); Development Engineer, Wheel Trim Lacks Wheel Trim Division (1996-2008); Manager, Paints and Finishes, Motor Wheel Corp (1991-1996); Manager, Composite Wheel Development, Motor Wheel Corporation, Lansing, MI (1984-1991); Principal Engineer, Motor Wheel Corp., Lansing, MI (1983-1984); Senior Engineer, Motor Wheel Corporation, Lansing, MI (1976-1983); Chemist, Freeman Chemical Corporation, Port Washington, WI (1975-1976); Group Leader, Goodyear Tire & Rubber Corporation, Akron, OH (1972-1975); Staff Chemist, Goodyear Tire & Rubber Corporation, Akron, OH (1967-1972) CW: Inventor in Field AW: Best Paper Award, Commercial Innovation Plastics World, Washington, DC (1990); Quality Award, American Society of Quality Control, Lansing, MI (1990); International Unique and Useful Consumer Plastics Product Award (1990); Innovation Award, Washington (1990); Grand Award, Automotive Use of Plastics Automotive Division, Society of Plastic Engineers (1989); Development Award, Society of Plastics Industry, Cincinnati (1987); Development Award, Chemical Coaters Association (1984) Outstanding Service Award, Society for the Advancement of Material and Process Engineering (1983) MEM: Society for the

Advancement of Material and Process Engineering; Society of Plastic Engineers **MH:** Albert Nelson Marquis Lifetime Achievement Award **AS:** Mr. Woelfel attributes his success on his tenacity and inventiveness. **B/I:** Mr. Woelfel became involved in his profession due to his passion and deep interest in chemistry. **AV:** Landscaping; Cooking; Remodeling; Genealogy **RE:** Roman Catholic

WOJCICKI, SUSAN DIANE, T: Media Executive **I:** Business Management/Business Services **CN:** YouTube, LLC **DOB:** 07/05/1968 **PB:** Santa Clara **SC:** CA/USA **PT:** Stanley George Wojcicki; Esther Denise (Hochman) Wojcicki **MS:** Married **SPN:** Dennis Troper (08/23/1998) **CH:** Five children **ED:** MBA in Economics, Anderson School of Management, UCLA (1998); MS in Economics, UC Santa Cruz (1993); BA in History and Literature, Harvard University, With Honors (1990) **C:** Chief Executive Officer, YouTube, LLC, Google, Inc., Mountain View, CA (2014-Present); Senior Vice President, YouTube, LLC, Google, Inc., Mountain View, CA (2014); Senior Vice President of Advertising and Commerce, Google, Inc., Mountain View, CA (2013-2014); Senior Vice President of Advertising, Google, Inc., Mountain View, CA (2011-2013); Senior Vice President of Product Management, Google, Inc., Mountain View, CA (2010-2011); Vice President of Product Management, Google, Inc., Mountain View, CA (2006-2010); Marketing Manager, Google, Inc., Mountain View, CA (1999-2006); Management Consultant, R.B. Webber & Co.; Management Consultant, Bain & Company, Inc.; Intel Corporation **CR:** Board of Directors, HomeAway.com, Inc. (2011-2012) **CIV:** Advocate, Numerous Causes, Including the Expansion of Paid Family Leave, the Plight of Syrian Refugees, Countering Gender Discrimination at Technology Companies, Getting Girls Interested in Computer Science and Prioritizing Coding in Schools **AW:** Power 100, Billboard (2019); Top 50 Best Chief Executive Officers of Large Companies, Comparably (2018); Ranked #10, Fortune's List of "Most Powerful Women" (2018); Ranked #6, Fortune's List of the "World's 100 Most Powerful Women" (2017); One of Time's 100 Most Influential People in 2015, Time Magazine (2015); 50 Most Powerful Women in Business, Fortune Magazine (2010-2015); 100 Most Powerful Women in Entertainment, Hollywood Reporter (2014); 100 Most Powerful Women, Forbes Magazine (2011-2014); Adweek 50, Adweek (2013); New Establishment, Vanity Fair (2012-2013)

WOJCIECHOWSKI, KRZYSZTOF, "KRIS" JAN, I: Consulting **DOB:** 11/19/1937 **PB:** Warsaw **SC:** Poland **PT:** Zdzislaw Jacek Wojciechowski; Irena Zygfryda Wojciechowski **ED:** DSc, National Veterinary Research Institute, Poland (1974); Doctor of Veterinary Science and Microbiology, Warsaw University of Life Sciences (1967); Degree in Veterinary Surgery, Warsaw University of Life Sciences (1961) **CT:** Honorary Diploma, The Pan African Veterinary Vaccine Centre of the African Union, Debre Zeit, Ethiopia (2003) **C:** International Consultant on Viral Disease Control and Animal Health (2000-Present); Global Consultant, Regional Technical Cooperative Program Project in Epidemiology, FAO (2001-2003); Animal Health Officer, Virology Headquarters, FAO, Rome (1982-1999); Docent, Associate Professor of Virology, Laboratory of Veterinary Hygiene, Warsaw, Poland (1974-1984); Project Manager, Animal Health Officer, FAO, Kabul, Afghanistan (1977-1981); Adviser, Ministry of Agriculture (1974-1977); Head, Virology Section, Laboratory of Veterinary Hygiene (1967-1977); Research Fellow, Veterinary Faculty Member, Warsaw University of Life Sciences (1963-1966); Microbiology, Mycologist, Polfa (1961-1962)

CR: Voluntary Custodian, Center for the History of Veterinary Medicine (2000-2007); Advisory Board Member, Veterinary Research Institute, Brno, Czech Republic (1998-2007); Founder, Co-Coordinator, Centaur Global Network (1996-2007); Adviser to Dean of the Faculty of Veterinary Medicine, Warsaw University of Life Sciences (2000-2004); Co-Initiator, Veterinary-Biotechnology Development, Poland (1991-1998); Adviser, Veterinary Department, Ministry of Agriculture, Warsaw (1973-1977); Fellow, Department of Virology, Central Veterinary Laboratory (1971-1972) **CW:** Author, "Preparation of Materials for History of Polish Society of Veterinary Sciences" (2007-2010); Author, "Mikolaj Rej Lycee in Warsaw in the Peak of Stalinism" (2006); Editor, "Flowers for Anna, Memoirs of K.M. Millak 1886-1920" (2003); Contributor, Articles, Professional Journals **AW:** Medal, Warsaw University of Life Sciences (2013); Amicus Veterinariae Medal (2011); Certificate of Appreciation, The Pan African Veterinary Vaccine Centre of the African Union (2006); George C. Poppensiek Visiting Professor in International Veterinary Medicine, Cornell University (2001); Mark of Distinction, Minister of Agriculture and Food Economy, Poland (1998); Letter of Appreciation, Government of Afghanistan (1981) **MEM:** Head, History of Veterinary Medicine Section, Polish Society of Veterinary Science (2007-2010); Chairman, Warsaw Branch, Polish Society of Veterinary Science (1975-1977); American Association for the Advancement of Science; American Society for Microbiology; Former Member, United Nations Staff Union **AV:** Studying philosophy, history and literature; Listening to jazz; Skiing **RE:** Roman Catholic

WOLBERS, HARRY LAWRENCE, PHD, T: Engineering Psychologist (Retired) **I:** Medicine & Health Care **DOB:** 01/29/1926 **PB:** Los Angeles **SC:** CA/USA **PT:** Harry Lawrence Wolbers; Edith Christine (Nordeen) Wolbers **MS:** Widower **SPN:** Mary Lou Jordan (02/18/1972, Deceased 2009) **CH:** Harry L.; Richard C.; Leslie A.; Suzanne M. **ED:** PhD in Industrial Psychology, University of Southern California, Los Angeles, CA (1955); MA, University of Southern California, Los Angeles, CA (1949); BS in Electrical Engineering, California Institute of Technology, Pasadena, CA (1946) **CT:** Licensed Psychologist, California **C:** Retired, Deputy Director, Flight Crew Systems, McDonnell Douglas Space Systems Co., Huntington Beach, CA (1985-1991); Chief Systems Engineer, Advanced Space Systems, McDonnell Douglas Astronautics Co., Huntington Beach, CA (1974-1985); Adjunct Professor, Department of Industrial and Systems Engineering, University of Southern California, Los Angeles, CA (1954-1985); Chief Program Engineer, Space Systems, Douglas Aircraft Co., Santa Monica, Huntington Beach, CA (1963-1974); Chief, Systems Research, Douglas Aircraft Co., El Segundo, CA (1954-1963); Vice President, Psychological Services, Inc., Los Angeles, CA (1948-1954) **CR:** Consultant, NASA, Washington, DC (1988-Present); U.S. Air Force Science Advisory Board, Washington, DC (1991-1996) **MIL:** U.S. Naval Service (1951); In-active Duty, U.S. Naval Reserve (1947-1951); Active Duty, U.S. Navy (1943-1947); Retired, U.S. Naval Reserve as a Naval Lieutenant **CW:** Contributor, Numerous Articles, Professional Journals **AW:** Decorated Meritorious Civilian Service Medal (1995); Engineering Merit Award, San Fernando Valley Engineers Council (1988) **MEM:** President, Orange County Chapter, Human Factors and Ergonomics Society (1989); Applied Experimental and Engineering Psychology, American Psychological Association; Society for Industrial and Organizational Psychology; Sigma Xi; Psi Chi **MH:** Albert Nelson Marquis Lifetime Achievement Award;

Marquis Who's Who Top Professional **B/I:** Dr. Wolbers became involved in his profession because the Douglas Aircraft Co. in Santa Monica and Huntington Beach had just received a contract from the office of Naval Research to examine the problems in pilots being overloaded in their work. For example, in one of the fighter air crafts, there were 145 controls, knobs, and indicators that the pilot had to know and use if under attack. It was simply overwhelming. So, the office of Naval Research and Bureau of Aeronautics wanted someone to start from scratch and not be limited by any existing concepts or aircraft instrumentation. Douglas Aircraft Co. then asked him to join their team; this was right after he had graduated from the University of Southern California. That program was the key and they found that all the information could be provided in an integrated package with just two basic displays. One was a forward-looking display and the other was a downward-looking navigational display. Furthermore, Dr. Wolbers became involved in his profession because it was interesting and he felt the work was needed. **AV:** Watching movies; Spending time with Laci (dog)

WOLBRINK, JAMES FRANCIS, T: Real Estate Investor **I:** Real Estate **DOB:** 09/08/1942 **PB:** Charles City **SC:** IA/USA **PT:** Richard William; Anna (Bult) Wolbrink **MS:** Married **SPN:** Karen Ann Dunkerly (06/18/1966) **ED:** Postgraduate Coursework, Iowa State University (1968-1972); BS in Industrial Engineering, Iowa State University (1966) **CT:** Certified Association Executive **C:** President, Wolbrink Properties (1983-Present); Commodities Broker, Clayton Brokerage (1983-1985); Managing Director, Education and Publications, American Institute of Industrial Engineers, Norcross, GA (1971-1983); Editor, Head of Engineering Publications, Engineering Research Institute, Iowa State University, Ames, Iowa (1967-1970); Technical Writer/Editor, Lawrence Radiation Laboratory, Livermore, CA (1966-1967) **CIV:** Co-chair, Chairman, Ameritas (Ameritas Mutual Holding Company) (Present); President, Friends of Caroline Hospice, Beaufort, SC (2013-2017); President, Georgia District, Optimist international **AW:** Named Outstanding Young Alumnus, Iowa State University (1977) **MEM:** Governor, Optimist International, Georgia District (1994-1995); President, Sandy Springs Optimist Club (1989-1990); Sandy Springs Optimist Club; Optimist International; The Delta Chi Fraternity **MH:** Albert Nelson Marquis Lifetime Achievement Award; Marquis Who's Who Top Professional **B/I:** Mr. Wolbrink became involved in his profession because when he graduated from college the job market was healthy. He had a choice of a number of different jobs both in technology journalism and industrial engineering. He chose the one that would be more interesting and also paid the best. **AV:** Golf **RE:** Anglican

WOLF, CHAD, T: Vice President, Power Generation and Rental Solutions **I:** Oil & Energy **CN:** Gravity Oilfield Services **PT:** Kristie Bernette **MS:** Single **CH:** Paisley **ED:** Associate of Science in Applied Science, Oklahoma State University Institute of Technology (2007) **C:** Vice President, Power Generation and Rental Solution, Gravity Oilfield Services (2017-Present); Product Manager, Natural Gas Generators (2016-2017); Region Manager, Mid-Con Energy Partners, Light Tower Rentals Inc (2016-2017); Product Manager, Natural Gas Generators, Light Tower Rentals Inc (2015-2016); With, NG Business Development, Light Tower Rentals Inc. (2013-2015); Parts and Service Sales, Warren Cat (2001-2013) **MEM:** Petroleum Equipment and Services Association; Emerging Leadership Comittee; Advisory Board, Oklahoma State Institute of Technology **THT:** Never say no and take on every opportunity to step forward.

WOLF, CHAD F., T: Acting United States Secretary **I:** Government Administration/Government Relations/Government Services **CN:** U.S. Department of Homeland Security **MS:** Married **CH:** Two Sons **ED:** BS in U.S. History, Southern Methodist University, Magna Cum Laude; Coursework, Collin College **CT:** Master Certificate in Government Contract Management, Villanova University **C:** Acting United States Secretary, U.S. Department of Homeland Security (2019-Present); Assistant Secretary, Homeland Security for Strategy, Plans, Analysis & Risk (2018-2019); Acting Under Secretary, Homeland Security for Strategy, Policy, and Plans (2018-2019); Chief of Staff, U.S. Department of Homeland Security, Washington, DC (2018); Chief of Staff, Transportation Security Administration (2017); Vice President, Senior Director, Wexler & Walker (2005-2016); Assistant Administrator, Transportation Security Policy, Transportation Security Administration (2005); With, Transportation Security Administration (2002-2005); Staff Member, U.S. Senator Chuck Hagel, U.S. Senate, Washington, DC; Staff Member, U.S. Senator Kay Bailey Hutchinson, U.S. Senate, Washington, DC; Staff Member, U.S. Senator Phil Gramm, U.S. Senate, Washington, DC

WOLF, JAMES RICHARD, T: Association Executive **I:** Business Management/Business Services **CN:** Continental Divide Trail Society **DOB:** 04/17/1930 **PB:** New York **SC:** NY/USA **PT:** Rudolf Wolf (Deceased); Janet Natalie (Selig) Wolf (Deceased) **MS:** Married **SPN:** Delray Green **ED:** JD, Yale Law School, Yale University, New Haven, CT (1956); BA, Yale University, New Haven, CT (1952) **C:** Founder, Director, Continental Divide Trail Society, Baltimore, MD (1993-Present); Founder, Director, Continental Divide Trail Society, Bethesda, MD (1978-1993); Attorney, U.S. Nuclear Regulatory Commission, Rockville, MD (1976-1993); Assistant Secretary, University Counsel, University of Pittsburgh, Pittsburgh, PA (1967-1975); Vice President, Secretary, Nuclear Science & Engineering Corporation, Pittsburgh, PA (1960-1967); Associate Director, Atomic Energy Law Research Project, University of Michigan Law School, Ann Arbor, MI (1959-1960); Attorney, U.S. Atomic Energy Commission, Washington, DC (1956-1959); Association Executive **CR:** Member, Continental Divide National Scenic Trail Advisory Council, Denver, CO (1980-1986) **CIV:** President, Audubon Society Western Pennsylvania, Pittsburgh, PA (1967-1969) **MIL:** U.S. Naval Reserves (1948-1966); Active Duty, U.S. Navy (1948-1949) **CW:** Author, Seven Book Series, with Revisions, "Guide to the Continental Divide Trail" (1976-2018); Author, "First Travelers on the Continental Divide Trail," in "The Mystery of Lost Trail Pass," Lewis and Clark Trail Heritage Foundation (2000); Author, "Essays in Annals of Wyoming: Bonneville's Foray" (1991); Author, "Essays in Annals of Wyoming: General Sheridan's Pass, 1807-1883" (1991); Author, "Essays in Annals of Wyoming: Fremont in the Wind Rivers" (1988) **AW:** Fulbright Scholarship, Austria (1952-1953); The Phi Beta Kappa Society, Alpha, CT (1952) **MEM:** Policy and Advocacy Committee, Partnership for the National Trails Systems, National Trails Association; Appalachian Trail Conservancy; Pacific Crest Trail Association; Lewis and Clark Trail Heritage Foundation (LCTHF); Oregon-California Trails Association (OCTA); The Wyoming State Historical Society; Montana Wilderness Association; National Audubon Society; The Wilderness Society; Society for the History of Discoveries; Washington Map Society; Western Environmental Law Center; Pitts-

burgh Climbers **BAR:** Pennsylvania Bar Association (1975); New York State Bar Association (1957) **MH:** Albert Nelson Marquis Lifetime Achievement Award; Marquis Who's Who Top Professional **AS:** Mr. Wolf attributes his success to the experience of the thru-hike on the Appalachian Trail; a strong belief in feasibility and value of a trail analogous to the A.T. along the Continental Divide; personal interests in natural history and cartography; law school education, as related to interactions with government agencies; feedback and encouragement from society members and others in the hiking community; and perseverance. **B/I:** Mr. Wolf became involved in his profession because he initially had an interest in maps, more so than the outdoors. As a child, his uncles would give him atlases as a present. He still loves maps; he has too many maps of the Continental Divide. In addition, Mr. Wolf was interested in atomic energy; when he got out of law school, his first job was with the Atomic Energy Commission, but afterwards, he worked with Nuclear Science and Engineering Corporation. So, between those two activities, he became interested, and reasonably knowledgeable, in both the technical and legal aspects of nuclear energy. **AV:** Backpacking; Western Americana; Natural history; Maps; Loyal fan of the Pittsburgh Pirates **RE:** Jewish

WOLF, JOAN, T: Ballet Educator **I:** Fine Art **DOB:** 07/28/1933 **PB:** Richmond **SC:** VA/USA **PT:** Simon Jacob Levin; Jean (Sturman) Levin **MS:** Widow **SPN:** Kenneth A. Weisburg (08/01/1993, Deceased 2018); Harold Lawrence Wolf (05/06/1956, Deceased) **CH:** Eric Andrew Wolf; Elizabeth Ann Wolf **ED:** Student, William & Mary (1951-1954) **C:** Entrepreneur, Joan Wolf Enterprises (1986-Present); Artistic Director, Choreographer, Joan Wolf Ballet Company, River Edge, NJ (1972-1988); Owner, Joan Wolf School of Ballet, Hillsdale, NJ (1963-1988); Owner, Joan Wolf School of Ballet, River Edge, NJ (1957-1979); Owner, Director, Joan Wolf Ballet Ensemble (1964-1972); Soloist, Richmond Ballet Company, Virginia (1949-1957); Commercial Artist, Cargill & Wilson Advertising Agency, Richmond, VA (1954-1956); Artistic Director, Choreographer, Joan Wolf Ballet Company, Hillsdale, NJ; Consultant, Artistic Adviser, Coach to Dancers and Dance Companies **CR:** "Ambassador" from World of Classical Ballet, Instructor of Classes, Moscow, Russia, Leningrad (Saint Petersburg), Russia, Paris, France, Beijing, China, Israel, and Schools in Oradell, NJ, and Hillsdale, NJ **CIV:** Board of Directors, International Dance Library of Israel (1989); Member, Bergen County Cultural Arts Commission (1977-1980); Board of Directors, Pascack Mental Health Center (1975-1977); Chairman, Bikeway Commission Woodcliff Lake (1975); Trustee, Hackensack Young Men's Hebrew Association (YMHA) (1969-1970); Consultant, Audience Developer, Florida Symphonic Pops Orchestra **CW:** Featured, Book, "There's Always a Right Job For Every Woman"; Author, "Starting on the Right Foot" **AW:** Commendation Award, Bergen County Freeholders (1981); Citation Award, New Jersey (1981); Professional Teacher Award, National Academy of Ballet (1960) **MEM:** Trustee, Chairman, Bikeway Commission, Greater Pascack Valley Chamber of Commerce (1974); President, Hillsdale Chairman of Commission (1968-1971); Greater Pascack Valley Chamber of Commerce **MH:** Albert Nelson Marquis Lifetime Achievement Award **B/I:** Ms. Wolf became involved in her profession because she grew up in Richmond, Virginia, which had its own major ballet company. Without the company in her hometown, she would have never been able to move on to the professional career aspects. She noted that the most important thing is proper ballet training, and without the proper training,

her career would not have been successful as it was. **AV:** Artist; Bicycling **THT:** Ms. Wolf owns an art studio and builds birdhouses.

WOLF, JOHN CHARLES, PHD, T: Psychologist (Retired) **I:** Social Work **DOB:** 09/29/1943 **PB:** St. Louis **SC:** MO/USA **PT:** Howard August; Wilda Lucille (French) Wolf **MS:** Married **SPN:** Carole Sue Bruce (10/21/1967) **CH:** Allan Bruce; Anne Elizabeth **ED:** Doctor of Philosophy, University of North Texas (1976); Master of Education, Stephen F. Austin State University (1969); Master of Arts, Stephen F. Austin State University (1967); Bachelor of Science, Stephen F. Austin State University (1964); Postgraduate Coursework, Texas Technical University **CT:** Certified Psychologist and Licensed Psychologist, State of Texas **C:** Consultant, Independent Practice in Psychology (2005-2013); Counseling Psychologist, U.S. Department of Veterans Affairs, Lubbock, TX (1973-2005); Counselor, VA Guidance Center, Texas Christian University, Fort Worth, TX (1970-1973); Director of Rehabilitation Services, Goodwill Industries, Fort Worth, TX (1969-1970); Instructor of Psychology, Stephen F. Austin State University (1967-1968); Staff Psychologist, Lufkin State School, Texas Department of Mental Health and Retardation (1966-1967) **CR:** Adjunct Instructor of Psychology, South Plains College, Lubbock, TX (1973-1991) **CIV:** Uniformed Services Coffee Group (2004-Present); Licensed, Eucharistic Minister and Worship Leader in Diocese of NW Texas (2000-Present); Fellowship of St. John, Society of St. John the Evangelist (2017); Member, Diocese Northwest Texas Commission Ministry (1986-1991, 2009-2011); Vestryman, St. Christopher Episcopal Church (1982-1985, 1990-1992, 1995-1998, 2003-2006); General Board Examiner, Chaplains of the Episcopal Church (1991-1997); Spiritual Development Committee, Northwest Texas Diocese (1993-1996); Board of Directors, Dixie Little League (1985-1987); Advisory Board Member, Human Services, South Plains College (1975-1987); Board of Directors, Lubbock County Committee on the Employment of the Handicapped, Lubbock Civic Chorale (1983-1985); Cantor and Bass Soloist at St. Christopher's Church, Lubbock **MIL:** U.S. Naval Reserve (1979-1983) **CW:** Contributor, Articles to Professional Journals, Books and Monographs **AW:** Outstanding Performance Award, Veterans Affairs (1978, 1982, 1984-1997, 1999-2003); Named, Outstanding Part-Time Faculty Member, South Plains College (1986-1987); Naval Reserve Meritorious Service Medal (1983) **MEM:** Westerners International, Llano Estacado Corral (2001-Present); Board of Directors, Friends of Lubbock Library (1985-Present); Lifetime Member, American Mensa; Past President, Northwest Texas VA Psychological Association; Psi Chi; Kappa Delta Pi; Lifetime Member, Naval Enlisted Reserve Association; American Legion; American Psychological Association; Member Uniformed Services Coffee Group 1, Lubbock, TX **MH:** Albert Nelson Marquis Lifetime Achievement Award **AS:** Dr. Wolf attributes his success on the influence of his mother, who cared deeply for his family after the death of his father. **B/I:** Dr. Wolf became involved in his profession due to the influence of his psychology professor, who left an indelible impression on him. **AV:** Choral singing; Golf; Hunting **RE:** Episcopalian

WOLF, LAWRENCE JOSEPH, T: 1) President Emeritus, Professor Emeritus 2) Distinguished Service Professor **I:** Engineering/Mechanical Engineering and Engineering Technology Education **CN:** 1) Oregon Institute of Technology 2) Oregon State System **DOB:** 08/10/1938 **PB:** St. Louis **SC:** MO/USA **PT:** Vincent F. Wolf; Clara A. (Holtkamp) Wolf **MS:** Married **SPN:** Barbara Ann

Bieber (8/12/1961) **CH:** Theresa; Carl; Lawrence V. **ED:** DSc, Washington University, St. Louis, MO (1971); MS, Washington University, St. Louis, MO (1962); BSME, Washington University, St. Louis, MO (1961); AA, Harris Teachers College (1959) **CT:** Professional Engineer, States of Missouri, Illinois, Indiana, Texas, Oregon, and Washington; Certified, Numerous Engineering Boards **C:** Professor, Oregon Institute of Technology, Portland, OR (1999-2017); Boeing Company, Seattle, WA (1998-1999); President, Professor, Oregon Institute of Technology (1991-1998); Dean of Technology, University of Houston (1980-1991); Department Head, Purdue University-Calumet, Hammond, IN (1978-1980); Associate Dean, St. Louis Community College-Florissant Valley (1975-1978); Dean of Instruction, Wentworth Institute, Boston, MA (1974-1975); Associate Professor, University of Petroleum and Minerals, Dhahran, Saudi Arabia (1972-1974); Instructor, Associate Professor, Department Head, St. Louis Community College-Florissant Valley (1964-1972); Design Engineer, Mcdonnell Douglas, St. Louis, MO (1963-1964); Engineer, Monsanto Corp., St. Louis, MO (1962-1963); President Emeritus, Professor Emeritus, Oregon Institute of Technology; Distinguished Service Professor, Oregon State System **CR:** Consultant, Engineer Nooter Corp., St. Louis, MO (1965-1972); Guest Scientist, Brookhaven National Laboratory, Superconducting Supercollider Laboratory; Founder, Texas Association of Schools of Engineering Technology; Board of Directors, United Way of Klamath Falls; Board of Directors, Cascades East Area Health Education Center; Consultancies, Japan, Singapore, Norway, Saudi Arabia, Iran, and Nigeria **CIV:** Houston Chairman, Sesquicentennial Cannon Committee, Houston, TX (1986); Leader Webelos, Boy Scouts of America; Board Member, Klamath County United Way; Founder, Chairman, Cascades-East Health Education Center **MIL:** U.S. Army Reserve (1956-1961); Training, Fort Leonard Wood, MO, Fort Knox, KY, Camp McCoy, WI; 705th Tank Battalion, St. Louis, MO **CW:** Editor, Journal of Engineering Technology (1985-1987); Founding Production Editor, Journal of Engineering Technology (1983-1985); Author, "Understanding Structures...A Parallel Approach to Statics and Strength of Materials"; Contributor, 60 Articles, Professional Journals **AW:** Fellow Members Award, American Society for Engineering Education (1992); James H. McGraw Award, American Society for Engineering Education (1987) **MEM:** Fellow, TAC Chairman, Accrediting Board for Engineering and Technology (ABET); American Society of Mechanical Engineers; Division Chairman, American Society for Engineering Education; Society of Manufacturing Engineers; American Association of University Professors **MH:** Albert Nelson Marquis Lifetime Achievement Award **B/I:** Mr. Wolf became involved in his profession because he was inspired by his brother, Vincent Martin Wolf, with whom he worked on various projects. They both, at different times, worked at McDonald Douglas, completing projects on airplanes. Additionally, he was inspired by a contact with and a request from his former physics professor at Harris Teachers College. **AV:** Biking; Singing; Backpacking; Dancing; Rollerblading **RE:** Catholic **THT:** From 1998 to 1999, while with the Boeing Company, Mr. Wolf spent a sabbatical year expanding OIT's BS in Manufacturing Engineering Technology Program to the Seattle sites and teaching at the new OIT facilities—a program that is still in effect.He also worked with Product Life Management software in design and manufacturing and learned CATIA, which he certainly used when he returned to OIT to teach again.

WOLF, THOMAS, "TOM" WESTERMAN, PHD, T: Governor of Pennsylvania **I:** Government Administration/Government Relations/Government Services **DOB:** 11/17/1946 **PB:** Mount Wolf **SC:** PA/USA **PT:** William Trout Wolf; Cornelia (Westerman) Rohlman **MS:** Married **SPN:** Frances (Donnelly) Wolf (1975) **CH:** Sarah; Katie **ED:** PhD in Political Science, Massachusetts Institute of Technology (1981); MPhil, University of London (1978); BA in Government, Dartmouth College, Magna Cum Laude (1972) **C:** Governor, Commonwealth of Pennsylvania, Harrisburg, PA (2015-Present); Secretary, Pennsylvania Department of Revenue, Harrisburg, PA (2007-2008); Chairman, Chief Executive Officer, Wolf Organization, Inc. (2010-2013); Co-Owner, Chief Executive Officer, Wolf Organization, Inc. (1985-2006); Forklift Operator, Wolf Organization, Inc., York, PA **CIV:** Chairman, York County Chamber of Commerce; Chairman, York College Board of Trustees; Chairman, York County Community Foundation; Chairman, United Way of York County; Volunteer, Peace Corps, India **PA:** Democrat **RE:** Episcopalian

WOLF, WALTER, T: Computer Science Educator, Dean **I:** Education/Educational Services **CN:** Golisano College of Computing and Information Sciences, Rochester Institute of Technology **DOB:** 03/09/1942 **PB:** New York **SC:** NY/USA **PT:** Theodore B. Wolf; Tasia Richman Wolf **MS:** Married **SPN:** Doris Inez (Buckley) Wolf (06/13/1964) **CH:** David (Deceased 1968); Terri-Lynn Wolf Brown; Patricia Wolf Kirk (Adopted) **ED:** Master of Science in Computer Science, Rochester Institute of Technology (1985); Doctor of Philosophy in Chemistry, Brandeis University (1967); Master of Arts, Brandeis University (1964); Bachelor of Arts, Wesleyan University (1962) **C:** Professor Emeritus, Golisano College of Computing and Information Sciences, Rochester Institute of Technology, Henrietta, NY (2012); Professor, Computer Science, Golisano College of Computing and Information Sciences, Rochester Institute of Technology, Henrietta, NY (1984-2012); Associate Professor, Eisenhower College, Seneca Falls, NY (1980-1984); Assistant Professor, Eisenhower College, Seneca Falls, NY (1977-1980); Assistant Professor, Colgate University, Hamilton, NY (1970-1977); Research Associate, Massachusetts Institute of Technology, Cambridge, MA (1967-1970) **CR:** Chair, Department of Computer Science, Golisano College of Computing and Information Sciences, Rochester Institute of Technology, Henrietta, NY; Founding Dean, Golisano College of Computing and Information Sciences, Rochester Institute of Technology, Henrietta, NY; Research Associate, New York State Agricultural Experiment Station, Cornell University, Geneva, NY **CW:** Contributor, Numerous Scientific Papers **AW:** Theatre Association of New York State Award for "Moon Over Buffalo" (1997); Community Service Award **MEM:** American Association for the Advancement of Science; Association of Computing Machinery; American Chemical Society; Sigma Xi **MH:** Albert Nelson Marquis Lifetime Achievement Award **B/I:** Dr. Wolf became involved in his profession after undertaking a summer internship at Cold Spring Harbor in the 1960s, where he performed a great deal of research on DNA analysis. **AV:** Theater; Racquetball **PA:** Liberal **RE:** Jewish

WOLFE, MARCIA JOANNE, T: President **I:** Environmental Services **CN:** M.H. Wolfe and Associates Environmental Consulting, Inc. **DOB:** 07/25/1945 **PB:** Seattle **SC:** WA/USA **PT:** Donald Woodrow Hamann; Jane Geraldine (Lind) Hamann **SPN:** Richard L. Winegar (03/15/1986, Divorced 1989); Gary John Wolfe (04/08/1972, Divorced 1979) **ED:** PhD Coursework, Colorado State University (1978-1979); MS, Washington State University (1972); BS,

University of Puget Sound, with Honors (1968) **CT:** Graduate, California Agriculture Leadership Foundation (2013); Certified Senior Ecologist, Ecological Society of America; Certified, Environmental Inspector; Certified, Environmental Consultant; Environmental Assessment Association **C:** Owner, M.H. Wolfe and Associates Environmental Consulting, Inc. (1995-Present); Senior Environmental Coordinator, ARCO Western Energy, Bakersfield, CA (1991-1994); Wildlife Management, Environmental Engineer, Bechtel Corporation, Tupman, CA (1986-1991); Habitat Restoration Specialist, EG&G Energy Measurements, Tupman, CA (1985-1986); Reclamation Engineer, Kaiser Steel Corporation, Raton, NM (1978-1985); Naturalist, Pennzoil-Vermejo Park Ranch, Raton, NM (1974-1978); Ranger, National Park Service, U.S. Department of the Interior, Longmire, WA (1970-1972); President, Certified Senior Ecologist, Ecological Society of America **CR:** Consultant, Speaker in Field; Volunteer Grade School Teacher, Science Camp **CIV:** Board Member, Kern River Parkway Foundation (2000-Present); Volunteer, Science Fair Judge, Ridgeview High School (2016-2019); Manager, Raton Little League Baseball (1983); Merit Badge Counselor, Boy Scouts of America, Bakersfield CA; Volunteer, Elementary School Science Camp **CW:** Contributor, Articles, Professional Journals; Writer, "Valley Ag Voice" **AW:** Regulation Innovators Award, Department of Pesticide Regulation, CA (1998); IDRC Award, Distinguished Service in Environmental Planning (1993); Certificate of Merit, Reclamation on the Naval Petroleum Reserves in California (1987); Certificate of Merit, Soil Science Society of America (1987); Grantee, National Science Foundation (1970) **MEM:** President, Bakersfield Business and Professional Women (1988-1989); Vice President, Bakersfield Business and Professional Women (1987); Public Committee, American Society of Surface Mining and Reclamation (1985); Treasurer, Gamma Phi Beta (1967); Public Affairs Commission, Ecological Society of America; Chair, Restoration Working Group, The Wildlife Society; Bakersfield Chamber of Commerce; Alumnae Scholarship Adviser, Gamma Phi Beta **MH:** Albert Nelson Marquis Lifetime Achievement Award; Marquis Who's Who Top Professional **B/I:** Ms. Wolfe became involved in her profession because she has always loved the outdoors. A science teacher, Art Haines, piqued her interest in biology, which encouraged her to pursue a career in the field. **AV:** Spending time with dogs; Hiking; Backpacking; Camping; Sewing; Listening to music; Bird watching; Gardening; Horseback riding **PA:** Republican **RE:** Methodist

WOLFE, SAUL A., T: Founding Member **I:** Law and Legal Services **CN:** Skoloff & Wolfe P.C. **PT:** Dan Wolfe; Bertha Wolfe **MS:** Married **SPN:** Roberta Wolfe **CH:** David Wolfe; Jonathan Wolfe; Nancy Bergman **ED:** JD, Harvard Law School (1955-1958); BA in Political Economy, Brandeis University (1955) **CT:** Certified Tax Assessor, State of New Jersey **C:** Founding Member, Skoloff & Wolfe P.C. (1961-Present) **CR:** Chair, New Jersey State Bar Association Committee on Real Property Taxation; Committee on State and Local Taxation, Real Property Section; Committee on State and Local Taxation, Taxation Section of the American Bar Association; Tax Assessor, City of Newark, New Jersey **CIV:** Former Chair, Board of the National Judicial College; Trustee, Institute for Continuing Legal Education (ICLE) **CW:** Creator, First Published Handbook, Real Estate Tax Appeals in New Jersey **AW:** Mel Narol Diversity Award, New Jersey State Bar, Minorities Section (2015); Medal of Honor for Contributions to the Advancement of the New Jersey Justice System, New Jersey State Bar Foundation **MEM:** Former President, Chair,

Administrative Law Section, Executive Committee; Taxation Section, New Jersey State Bar Association; American Bar Association; Founding Board Member, National Institute of Property Tax Attorneys; Life Fellow, American Bar Foundation; President, New Jersey State Bar Foundation; House of Delegates, American Bar Association **BAR:** State of New Jersey; Supreme Court of New Jersey **AS:** Mr. Wolfe attributes his success to a lot of hard work and luck. **B/I:** Mr. Wolfe became involved in his profession because his parents were immigrants. His father used to say, "They can take away your money and your property but the one thing nobody can take away from you is your education." Education was important to his parents, so it was important to him. **AV:** Travel; Photography

WOLFE, TOM KENNERLY JR., T: Author, Journalist **I:** Writing and Editing **DOB:** 03/02/1931 **PB:** Richmond **SC:** VA/USA **PT:** Thomas Kennerly Wolfe; Helen (Hughes) Wolfe **MS:** Married **SPN:** Sheila Berger **CH:** Alexandra; Thomas III **ED:** Honorary DLitt, University of Richmond (1993); Honorary DLitt, Johns Hopkins University (1990); Honorary DLitt, St. Andrews Presbyterian College (1990); Honorary LHD, Longwood College (1989); Honorary LHD, Manhattanville College (1988); Honorary LHD, Randolph-Macon College (1988); Honorary DFA, School of Visual Arts (1987); Honorary LHD, Southampton College, NY (1984); Honorary LHD, Virginia Commonwealth University (1983); Honorary DLitt, Washington and Lee University (1974); Honorary DFA, Minneapolis College Art and Design (1971); PhD in American Studies, Yale University (1957); AB, Washington and Lee University (1951) **C:** Writer (1965-2018); Contributing Editor, Esquire Magazine, New York, NY (1977); Contributing Editor, New York Magazine (1968-1976); Magazine Writer, New York World Journal Tribune (1966-1967); City Reporter, New York Herald Tribune (1962-1966); Reporter, Latin American Correspondent, Washington Post (1959-1962); Reporter, Springfield Union, MA (1956-1959) **CR:** Contributing Artist, Harper's Magazine, New York, NY (1978-1981); Writer, New York Sunday Magazine (1962-1966) **CW:** Author, "The Kingdom of Speech" (2016); Author, "Back to Blood" (2012); Author, "I am Charlotte Simmons" (2004); Author, "Hooking Up" (2000); Author, "A Man in Full" (1998); Author, Audio, "Ambush at Fort Bragg" (1997); Author, "The Bonfire of the Vanities" (1987); Author, "The Purple Decades: A Reader" (1982); Author, "From Bauhaus to Our House" (1981); Author, "In Our Time" (1980); Author, "The Right Stuff" (1979); Author, "Mauve Gloves and Madmen, Clutter and Vine" (1976); Author, "The Painted Word" (1975); Artist, Drawings, One-man Show, Tunnel Gallery, New York, NY (1974); Editor, Contributor, The New Journalism (1973); Author, "Radical Chic and Mau-mauing the Flak Catchers" (1970); Author, "The Electric Kool-Aid Acid Test" (1968); Author, "The Pump House Gang" (1968); Author, "The Kandy-Kolored Tangerine-Flake Streamline Baby" (1965); Artist, Drawings, One-man Show, Maynard Walker Gallery, New York, NY (1965); Contributor, Articles, Professional Journals, Including Esquire Magazine **AW:** Distinguished Contribution to American Letters (2010); Jefferson Lecture in Humanities (2006); Golden Plate Award, Academy of Achievement (2005); Award, Academy of Achievement (2005); Chicago Tribune Literary Prize for Lifetime Achievement (2003); President Award, Quinnipiac College (Now Quinnipiac University) (1993); Theodore Roosevelt Medal, Theodore Roosevelt Association (1990); Wilbur Cross Medal, Yale Graduate School Alumni Association (1990); St. Louis Literary Award (1990); Gari Melchers Medal (1986); Benjamin Pierce Cheney Medal, Eastern Washington University (1986); Washington Irving Medal, St. Nicholas Society (1986); John Dos Passos Award (1984); American Book Award (1980); Harold D. Vursell Memorial Award, American Academy and Institute of Arts and Letters (Now American Academy of Arts and Letters) (1980); Columbia Journalism Award (1980); Citation for Art History, National Sculpture Society (1980); Named Virginia Laureate for Literature (1977); Frank Luther Mott Research Award (1973); Society Magazine Writers Award for Excellence (1970); Front Page Awards for Humor and Foreign News Reporting, Washington Newspaper Guild (1961)

WOLFENBARGER, DEBORA, T: Technology Transfer Specialist **I:** Technology **CN:** Jet Propulsion Laboratory **MS:** Married **SPN:** Ken Walfenbarger **C:** Technology Transfer Specialist, Jet Propulsion Laboratory (2009-Present); Flight Operations, Voyager, Jet Propulsion Laboratory (1988-2009) **AW:** Space Flight Awareness Award (1998); NASA Group Achievement Award in Support of Flight Operations on the Voyager Neptune Encounter (1989); Multiple Westminster Kennel Club Awards **MEM:** Past President, Board of Directors, Italian Greyhound Club of America (1994-Present) **AS:** Ms. Wolfenbarger credits her success on her tenacity and propensity for making work fun, as well as her ability to get other people passionate about their work. **AV:** Shows and train dogs

WOMACK, STEPHEN, "STEVE" ALLEN, T: U.S. Representative, Former Mayor **I:** Government Administration/Government Relations/Government Services **DOB:** 02/18/1957 **PB:** Russellville **SC:** AR/USA **PT:** James Kermit Womack; Elisabeth F. (Canerday) Womack **MS:** Married **SPN:** Terri (Williams) Womack **CH:** Three children **ED:** BA, Arkansas Tech University, Russelville, AR (1979) **C:** Chairman, House Committee on the Budget (2018-Present); U.S. Representative, Arkansas' Third Congressional District, United States Congress, Washington, DC (2011-Present); Member, House Committee on Appropriations, Washington, DC (2011-Present); Mayor, City of Rogers, AR (1998-2010); Financial Consultant, Merrill Lynch, Rogers, AR (1997); Executive Officer, United States Army ROTC Program, University of Arkansas, Fayetteville, AR (1990-1996); Manager, Station KURM Radio, Rogers, AR (1979-1990) **CR:** Chairman, Northwest Arkansas Regional Planning Commission (2003-2005); Former Councilman, Rogers City Council **CIV:** Chairman, Arkansas Commission on National and Community Service (Now Arkansas Service Commission) (2001); Appointed Member, Arkansas Commission on National and Community Service (Now Arkansas Service Commission) (1999); Member, Cross Church at Pinnacle Hills, Rogers, AR; Former Member, Rogers Park Commission; Former Member, St. Mary's Hospital Foundation; Former Member, Northwest Arkansas Community College Task Force; Former President, Rogers-Lowell United Fund **MIL:** With, Arkansas Army National Guard; Retired Reservist, U.S. Army Reserve **AW:** Decorated Global War on Terrorism Expeditionary and Service Medals; Army Achievement Medal; Army Commendation Medal; Meritorious Service Medal with Oak Leaf Cluster; Legion of Merit; Citizen of the Year, March of Dimes; Paul Harris Fellow **PA:** Republican **RE:** Baptist

WONG, JEN L., T: Chief Operating Officer **I:** Internet **CN:** Reddit, Inc. **C:** Board Member, Discover Financial Services (2019-Present); Chief Operating Officer, Reddit, Inc. (2018-Present); Board Member, Marfeel, Inc. (2016-Present); President of Digital, Chief Operating Officer, Time Inc., New York, NY (2016-2018); Chief Business Officer, POPSUGAR, New York, NY (2011-2015); Senior Vice President, General Manager for AOL Media Lifestyle, Global Head of Business Operations, AOL (2010-2011); Associate Partner, McKinsey & Company (2004-2010) **CIV:** Board Member, Ad Council; Board Member, BRIC Arts Media

WONG, VICTOR, T: Faculty **I:** Education/Educational Services **CN:** Houston Community College **DOB:** 07/13/1959 **SC:** Havana/Cuba **MS:** Married **CH:** Two Children **ED:** MA in History, Texas Southern University (2009); MEd in Curriculum and Instruction, Texas Southern University (2003); Teacher Certification Program, Texas Southern University (2003); BS in Medical Technology, Texas Southern University (1986); BS in Premed/Biology, Texas Southern University (1986); AA, Blinn College (1983); EdD in Progress, Texas Southern University **C:** Instructor, George I. Sanchez Charter High School (1993-Present); Instructor, Adjunct Faculty, Houston Community College (2005-2015); Instructor, Documentarian, Instructional Supervisor, Field Supervisor, Houston Community College (1992-1998); Instructor, Catholic Charities School Systems (1992-1993) **CW:** Mentor, Science Team; Coach, Chess Team **AW:** Teacher of the Year, High School (2005, 2017-2019); Inductee, Phi Delta Kappa (2012); Inductee, Phi Alpha Theta (2009); Listee, Who's Who of America's Teachers (2002-2007); Listee, National Association of Biology Teachers **AS:** Mr. Wong believes that God gave him the grace to serve as many people as possible. Likewise, his parents and his grandfather supported him and his academia. **B/I:** Mr. Wong taught English to many of his family members. From there, he went on to teach English at the local high school and college. He has been teaching biology at the Houston Community College for over 15 years now. **RE:** Baptist

WOOD, DIANE PAMELA, T: Chief Judge **I:** Law and Legal Services **CN:** United States Court of Appeals for the Seventh Circuit **DOB:** 07/4/1950 **PB:** Plainfield **SC:** NJ/USA **PT:** Kenneth Reed Wood; Lucille (Padmore) Wood **MS:** Married **SPN:** Robert L. Sufit (2006); Dennis J. Hutchinson (1978, Divorced 1998); Steve Van (Divorced) **CH:** Kathryn Hutchinson; David Hutchinson; Jane Hutchinson; Three Stepchildren **ED:** Honorary JD, Illinois Institute of Technology (2004); Honorary JD, Georgetown University Law Center (2003); JD, The University of Texas at Austin School of Law, with High Honors (1975); BA in English, The University of Texas at Austin, with Honors (1971) **C:** Chief Judge, United States Court of Appeals for the Seventh Circuit (2013-Present); Judge, United States Court of Appeals for the Seventh Circuit (1995-Present); Senior Lecturer of Law, The University of Chicago Law School (1995-Present); Deputy Assistant Attorney General, Antitrust Division, U.S. Department of Justice (1993-1995); Harold J. & Marion F. Green Professor, International Legal Studies, The University of Chicago Law School (1990-1995); Associate Dean, The University of Chicago Law School (1989-1992); Professor of Law, The University of Chicago Law School (1988-1995); Special Consultant, Antitrust Division, International Guide, U.S. Department of Justice (1986-1987); Assistant Professor of Law, The University of Chicago Law School (1981-1988); Assistant Professor of Law, Georgetown University Law Center, Washington, DC (1980-1981); Associate, Covington & Burling LLP, Washington, DC (1978-1980); Attorney-advocate, U.S. Department of State, Washington, DC (1977-1978); Law Clerk to Justice Harry Blackmun, Supreme Court of the United States (1976-1977); Law Clerk to the Honorable Irving Goldberg, United States Court of Appeals for the Fifth Circuit (1975-1976) **CIV:** Board of Directors, Hyde Park-Kenwood

Community Health Center (1983-1985); Member, Planned Parenthood; Member, National Organization for Women **CW:** Contributor, Articles, Professional Journals; Board Editor, American Journal of International Law **AW:** Named to the Order of the Coif **MEM:** Elected Council Member, The American Law Institute (2003); Fellow, American Academy of Arts & Sciences; The American Law Institute; The American Society of International Law; Phi Alpha Delta Fraternity, International **BAR:** State of Illinois (1993); The District of Columbia (1978); State of Texas (1975) **PA:** Democrat **RE:** Protestant

WOOD, VIRGINIA ELIZABETH JONES, BS, MS, CRRN, T: Nursing Consultant (Retired) **I:** Medicine & Health Care **DOB:** 10/24/1943 **PB:** Oregon City **SC:** OR/USA **PT:** Oscar Richard Wood; Alice Marcille (Buol) Jones Wood **MS:** Widowed **SPN:** Richard C. Wood (09/13/1969, Deceased) **CH:** Edward Craig; Gregory Allen; Gloria Elizabeth **ED:** MS in Nursing Education, School of Nursing, Oregon Health & Science University (1972); BS in Nursing, School of Nursing, Oregon Health & Science University (1965) **CT:** Certificate of Training, U.S. Department of Health & Human Services (1995); Certified Rehabilitation Registered Nurse (1985-1995) **C:** Clinical Nurse Specialist in Rehabilitation, Sacred Heart Medical Center (1984-1994); Nurse Consultant, Washington State Department of Social and Health Services; Assistant Professor, Intercollegiate Center for Nursing Education, Washington State University; Nurse, St. Luke's Rehabilitation Institute; Instructor, Multnomah Hospital; Staff Nurse, Morningside Hospital; Camp Nurse, Camp Namanu; Staff Nurse, Veteran's Hospital, Portland, OR **MIL:** Active Duty Nurse, U.S. Naval Reserve (1965-1967) **AW:** U.S. Public Health Grant for Master of Science in Nursing Education, School of Nursing, Oregon Health & Science University **MEM:** Former Member, Association of Rehabilitation Nurses; Alpha Tau Delta; The Gideons International **MH:** Albert Nelson Marquis Lifetime Achievement Award **AS:** Ms. Wood attributes her success to her spirit, solid work ethic, perseverance and faith in God. **B/I:** Ms. Wood became involved in her profession because she enjoys help people and has always wanted to be a nurse. **AV:** Gardening; Watercolor painting; Traveling **PA:** Independent **RE:** Christian

WOODALL, WILLIAM, "ROB" ROBERT III, T: U.S. Representative **I:** Government Administration/Government Relations/Government Services **DOB:** 02/11/1970 **PB:** Athens **SC:** GA/USA **ED:** JD, School of Law, University of Georgia, Athens, GA (1998); BA, Furman University, Greenville, SC (1992) **C:** U.S. Representative, Georgia's Seventh Congressional District, United States Congress, Washington, DC (2011-Present); Member, House Committee on Oversight and Reform, U.S. House of Representatives (2011-Present); Member, House Committee on the Budget, Washington, DC (2011-Present); Member, House Committee on Rules (2011-Present); Chairman, Republican Study Committee (2014-2015); Chief of Staff to Representative John Linder, U.S. House of Representatives, Washington, DC (2000-2010); Legislative Correspondent, Legislative Assistant, Legislative Director, Representative John Linder, U.S. House of Representatives, Washington, DC (1994-2000); Law Clerk, Balch & Bingham LLP (1993-1994); Member, The House Committee on Transportation and Infrastructure, Washington, DC **CW:** Co-Author, "FairTax: The Truth" (2008) **PA:** Republican **RE:** Methodist

WOODARD, ALFRE, T: Actress **I:** Media & Entertainment **DOB:** 11/08/1953 **PB:** Tulsa **SC:** OK/USA **PT:** Marion H. Woodard; Constance Woodard

MS: Married **SPN:** Roderick Spencer (10/21/1983) **CH:** Mavis; Duncan **ED:** Honorary Doctorate, Boston University (2004); Diploma, Boston University (1974) **CR:** With, Committee on Arts and Humanities, President Barack Obama (2009) **CW:** Actress, "See" (2019); Voice Actress, "The Lion King" (2019); Actress, "Juanita" (2019); Actress, "Clemency" (2019); Actress, "Saint Judy" (2018); Actress, "Empire" (2018); Actress, "A Series of Unfortunate Events" (2017-2018); Actress, "Luke Cage" (2016-2018); Voice Actress, "Burning Sands" (2017); Actress, "Captain America: Civil War" (2016); Actress, "So B. It" (2016); Actress, "State of Affairs" (2014-2015); Executive Producer, Documentary, "Soft Vengeance: Albie Sachs and the New South Africa" (2014); Actress, "Annabelle" (2014); Actress, "12 Years a Slave" (2013); Actress, "Copper" (2013); Actress, "Steel Magnolias" (2012); Actress, "True Blood" (2010-2012); Actress, "Memphis Beat" (2010-2011); Actress, "Three Rivers" (2009-2010); Actress, "Maggie Hill" (2009); Actress, "The Family That Preys" (2008); Actress, "Reach for Me" (2008); Actress, "AmericanEast" (2008); Actress, "My Own Worst Enemy" (2008); Actress, "Something New" (2006); Actress, "Desperate Housewives" (2005-2006); Actress, "The Water is Wide" (2005); Actress, "Beauty Shop" (2005); Actress, "The Forgotten" (2004); Actress, "The Singing Detective" (2003); Actress, "The Core" (2003); Actress, "Radio" (2003); Actress, "A Wrinkle in Time" (2003); Voice Actress, "The Wild Thornberrys Movie" (2002); Actress, "Baby of the Family" (2002); Actress, "K-PAX" (2001); Actress, "Love and Basketball" (2000); Actress, "What's Cooking" (2000); Actress, "Holiday Heart" (2000); Actress, Off-Broadway Play, "Love and Basketball" (2000); Actress, Off-Broadway Play, "Dinosaur" (2000); Actress, Off-Broadway Play, "So Nice They Named Twice" (2000); Actress, Off-Broadway Play, "Horatio" (2000); Actress, Off-Broadway Play, "What's Cookin'" (2000); Actress, Executive Producer, "Funny Valentines" (1999); Actress, "Mumford" (1999); Actress, "Brown Sugar" (1998); Actress, "Down in the Delta" (1998); Actress, "Cadillac Desert" (1997); Actress, "Miss Evers' Boys" (1997); Actress, "Member of the Wedding" (1997); Actress, "Follow Me Home" (1996); Actress, "Star Trek: First Contact" (1996); Actress, "A Step Toward Tomorrow" (1996); Actress, "Primal Fear" (1996); Actress, "Gulliver's Travels" (1996); Actress, "Journey to Mars" (1996); Actress, "The Piano Lesson" (1995); Actress, "Wizard of Oz in Concert" (1995); Actress, "Statistically Speaking" (1995); Actress, "How to Make an American Quilt" (1995); Actress, "Race to Freedom: The Underground Railroad" (1994); Actress, "Crooklyn" (1994); Actress, "Blue Chips" (1994); Actress, "Bopha!" (1993); Actress, "Rich in Love" (1993); Actress, "Heart and Souls" (1993); Actress, "Passion Fish" (1992); Actress, "The Gun in Betty Lou's Handbag" (1992); Actress, "Grand Canyon" (1991); Actress, "Blue Bayou" (1990); Actress, "The Child Saver" (1990); Actress, "Sweet Revenge" (1990); Actress, "Miss Firecracker" (1989); Actress, Off-Broadway Play, "A Winter's Tale" (1989); Actress, "Scrooged" (1988); Actress, "L.A. Law" (1987); Actress, "Mandela" (1987); Actress, "Unnatural Causes" (1986); Actress, "The Killing Floor" (1986); Actress, "Extremities" (1986); Actress, "St. Elsewhere" (1985-1987); Actress, Off-Broadway Play, "A Map of the World" (1985); Actress, "Sara" (1985); Actress, "Hill Street Blues" (1984); Actress, "Health" (1983); Actress, "Cross Creek" (1983); Actress, "Tucker's Witch" (1982-1983); Actress, "Sophisticated Gents" (1981); Actress, "Freedom Road" (1979); Actress, "Ambush Murder" (1979); Actress, "Child Saver" (1979); Actress, "A Mother's Courage: The Mary Thomas Story" (1979); Actress, Play, "For Colored Girls Who Have Considered Suicide, When the

Rainbow is Enuf" (1977); Actress, "Remember My Name" (1976); Actress, "Trial of the Moke"; Actress, "Words by Heart"; Actress, Appearances, Plays, Television Shows and Films **AW:** Inductee, Oklahoma Hall of Fame (2019); Award for Outstanding Actress in a TV Movie, Miniseries or Dramatic Special, NAACP Image Awards (2013); Gracie Allen Award for Outstanding Supporting Actress in a Drama Series (2011); Josephine Premice Award for Sustained Excellence, Classical Theatre of Harlem (2006); Screen Actors Guild Award for Outstanding Performance by an Ensemble in a Comedy Series, Screen Actors Guild - American Federation of Television and Radio Artists (2006); Emmy Award for Guest Appearance in a Drama Series, Academy of Television Arts & Sciences (1984, 1987, 2003); Screen Actors Guild Awards for Outstanding Performance by a Female Actor in a Miniseries or Television Movie, Screen Actors Guild - American Federation of Television and Radio Artists (1996, 1998); Golden Globe Award for Best Actress in a Miniseries, Hollywood Foreign Press Association (1997); Primetime Emmy Award for Outstanding Lead Actress in a Miniseries or a Movie, Academy of Television of Arts & Sciences (1997); Awards for Outstanding Lead Actress in a Drama Series, Miniseries or Television Movie, NAACP Image Awards (1989, 1990, 1992, 1996); Numerous Awards

WOODARD, KOMOZI, PHD, T: American History Educator **I:** Education/Educational Services **DOB:** 07/07/1949 **PB:** Newark **SC:** NJ/USA **PT:** Theodore Woodard; Helen (Collier) Woodard **MS:** Married **SPN:** Joanne Carey (08/12/2019); Carmen (Divorced 2005); Lori Hunter (07/04/1992, Divorced 1994); Suzanne Woodard (06/12/1971, Divorced 1988) **CH:** Kuza; Almasi; Malik; Adimu **ED:** Postdoctoral Coursework, Northwestern University (1992); PhD, University of Pennsylvania (1991); MA in American History, University of Pennsylvania (1988); MAT, Rutgers, The State University of New Jersey (1986); BA in Sociology, Dickinson College (1971) **C:** Curator, Conversations in Black Freedom Studies, Schomburg Center for Research in Black Culture, Harlem, New York (2013-Present); Professor of American History, Sarah Lawrence College, Bronxville, New York (1989-Present); Member Faculty, The New School, New York (1992-2010); Research Associate, Northwestern University, Evanston, IL (1991); Lecturer, Saint Elizabeth University (1989); Lecturer, Rutgers, The State University of New Jersey (1988); Managing Editor, Children's Express, New York (1985-1986); Instructor, Independence High School, Newark (1984-1985); Managing Editor, Black New-Ark (1972-1978) **CR:** Program Director, National Endowment for the Humanities (2015); Adviser, Algebra Project, Chicago (1991); Research Consultant, McArthur Foundation, Philadelphia, PA (1989); Social Science Research Council (1988); Delaware Valley Community Reinvestment Fund (1988) **CIV:** Co-Founder National Black United Front (1980); African Liberation Support Committee, Washington, DC (1972); National Black Political Assembly, Gary, IN (1972) **CW:** Author, "The Strange Careers of the Jim Crow North" (2019); Co-Author, "Want to Start a Revolution?" (2009); Author, "Groundwork: Local Black Freedom Movements in America" (2005); Editor, "Freedom North: Black Freedom Struggles Outside the South, 1940-1980" (2003); Author, "A Nation Within a Nation: Amiri Baraka (LeRoi Jones) and Black Power Politics" (1999); Contributor, Articles, Professional Journals **AW:** Lipkin Teaching Award for Excellence, Sarah Lawrence College (2019); Award, National Endowment for the Humanities (2014); Hewlett-Mellon Research Award (1994-1995); Simpson Research Award (1994); Postdoctoral Fellowship, Northwestern University (1991); W.W. Smith Fellow (1989); Fontaine Fellowship

(1986-1988); Grant, New Jersey Historical Society **MEM:** African Heritage Studies Association; American Historian Association; National Council for Black Studies; Organization American Historians; Urban History Association **MH:** Albert Nelson Marquis Lifetime Achievement Award **B/I:** Dr. Woodard became involved in his industry because people in the civil rights movement were dying and he had gone to a few of the memorials. Other people told him that he should write about their history. He then started a project and got a grant for it, thus beginning his interest as a historian.

WOODBURN, CHARLES NICHOLAS, T: Chief Executive Officer **I:** Military & Defense Services **CN:** BAE Systems **ED:** PhD, Cambridge University (1995); MBA, De Erasmus Universiteit Rotterdam (EUR); Bachelor's Degree in Electrical Sciences, Cambridge University **C:** Chief Executive Officer, BAE Systems (2017-Present); Chief Operating Officer, Executive Director, BAE Systems (2016-2017); Chief Executive Officer, Expro International Group Ltd. (2010-2016); Vice President, Engineering, Manufacturing and Sustaining, Schlumberger Ltd. (2009-2010); Wireline President, Schlumberger Ltd. (2006-2009); Product Development Manager, Schlumberger Ltd. (2004-2006)

WOODS, DARREN, T: Chairman, Chief Executive Officer **I:** Business Management/Business Services **CN:** Exxon Mobil Corporation **PB:** Wichita **SC:** KS/USA **ED:** BS in Electrical Engineering, Texas A&M University; MBA, Kellogg School of Management, Northwestern University **C:** Chief Executive Officer, Chairman, Exxon Mobil Corporation (2017-Present); President, Member of the Board of Directors, Exxon Mobil Corporation (2016); Senior Vice President, Exxon Mobil Corporation (2014-2016); President, Exxon Mobil Corporation (2012-2014); Vice President, Supply and Transportation, Exxon Mobil Corporation (2010-2012); Director of Refining for Europe, Africa and the Middle East, Exxon-Mobil Refining and Supply Company, Exxon Mobil Corporation (2008-2010); Vice President, Specialty Elastomers Group Inc. (2007-2008); Manager, Joliet Refinery, Exxon Mobil Corporation (2002-2005); Manager, Investor Relations, Exxon Mobil Corporation (2001-2002); Planning Analyst, Exxon Mobil Corporation (1992) **CIV:** Public Endorser, Paris Agreement **MEM:** Chairman, American Petroleum Institute; Executive Committee, American Petroleum Institute; National Petroleum Council; Engineering Advisory Council, Texas A&M University

WOODS, TIGER, T: Professional Golfer **I:** Athletics **DOB:** 12/30/1975 **PB:** Cypress **SC:** CA/USA **PT:** Earl Dennison; Kultida Woods **SPN:** Elin Nordegren (10/05/2004, Divorced 08/23/2010) **CH:** Sam Alexis Woods; Charlie Axel Woods **ED:** Coursework, Stanford University, California (1994-1996) **C:** Professional Golfer (1996-Present) **CR:** Founder, Chairman, Tiger Woods Design (2006-Present); Ryder Cup (1997, 1999, 2002, 2004, 2006, 2010, 2012); President's Cup, U.S. Team (1998, 2000, 2003, 2005, 2007, 2009, 2011); Dunhill Cup (1998); Walker Cup Match, Porthcawl, Wales (1995); World Amateur Team Championships, Versailles, France (1994) **CIV:** Co-Founder, Tiger Woods Foundation (1996-Present) **AW:** Winner, Farmers Insurance Open (2013); Winner, WGC-Cadillac Championship (2013); Winner, The Players Championship (2001-2013); Winner, Arnold Palmer Invitational (2008-2009, 2012-2013); Player of the Year, PGA Tour (1997, 1999, 2000, 2001-2003, 2005-2007, 2009, 2013); Winner, WGC Bridgestone Invitational (2006-2007, 2009, 2013); Winner, AT&T National (2009, 2012); Winner, Memorial Tournament (1999-2001, 2009, 2012); Mark H. McCormack Award (1998-2010); One of the 40 Under 40 Rising Stars, Fortune

Magazine (2009); Athlete of the Decade, The Associated Press (2009); The World's Most Influential People, Time Magazine (2009); Inductee, Athletics Hall of Fame, Stanford University (2009); Winner, BMW Championship (2007-2009); FedEx Cup, PGA (2007, 2009); Vardon Trophy, PGA of America (1999, 2000-2003, 2005, 2007, 2009); Byron Nelson Award, PGA Tour (1999-2003, 2005-2007, 2009); Winner, Buick Open (2002-2006, 2009); Power 150, Ebony Magazine (2008); The 100 Most Powerful Celebrities, Forbes.com (2008); ESPY Award, Best Championship Performance, ESPN (2008); Winner, WGC Accenture Match Play Championship (2008); Winner, Dubai Beser Classic (2008); The Most Influential People in the World of Sports, Business Week (2007, 2008); ESPY Award, Best Golfer (2005-2008); ESPY Award, Best Male Athlete (1998, 2000-2002, 2008); Winner, U.S. Open Championship (2000, 2002, 2008); Winner, Buick Invitational (1999, 2003, 2005-2008); Charlie Barlett Award, Golf Writers Association of American (2007); Inductee, The California Hall of Fame (2007); Winner, WGC American CA Championship (2007); Winner, Target World Challenge (2007); Winner, Wachovia Championship (2007); Winner, PGA Championship (1999-2000, 2006-2007); Player of the Year, Golf Writers Association of America (2006); Winner, Deutsche Bank Championship (2006); Male Athlete of Year, The Associated Press (1997, 1999, 2000, 2006); Winner, WGC American Express Championship (1999, 2002-2003, 2005-2006); Jack Nicklaus Trophy, PGA America, Golf Writers Association of America (1997, 1999-2003, 2005-2006); Winner, Ford Championship (2005-2006); Winner, British Open Championship (2000, 2005-2006); Winner, PGA Grand Slam (1998-2002, 2005-2006); Winner, Target World Challenge (2006); Winner, WGC NEC Invitational (1999-2001, 2005); Winner, Masters Tournament (1997, 2001-2002, 2005); Winner, WGC Accenture Match Play Championship (2003-2004); Winner, Western Open (2003); Winner, Bay Hill Invitational (2000-2003); Winner, Deutsche Bank-SAP Open (1999, 2001-2002); Winner, Williams World Challenge (2001); World Champion of Champions, L'Equipe (2000); Winner, World Cup (2000); Winner, Bell Canadian Open (2000); Most Powerful Person in Sports, Sporting News (2000); Winner, AT&T Pebble Beach Pro-Am (2000); Sportsman of the Year, Reuters (2000); Winner, Johnnie Walker Classic (1998, 2000); Sportsman of the Year, Sports Illustrated (1996, 2000); Winner, Mercedes Championship (1997, 2000); World Sportsman of the Year, World Sports Academy (1999); Winner, Individual and Team Titles, World Cup (1999); Winner, Tour Championship (1999); Winner, National Car Rental Classic (1999); Winner, Motorola Western Open (1997, 1999); Winner, BellSouth Classic (1998); Winner GTE Byron Nelson Classic (1997); Winner, Asian Honda Classic (1997); Jack Nicklaus College Player of the Year (1996); Fred Haskins College Player of the Year (1996); Winner, Tri-Match Championship, Stanford University, Arizona State University, (1996); Rookie of the Year, PGA Tour (1996); Winner, Cleveland Golf Championship (1996); Winner, John A. Burns Invitational (1996); Winner, NCAA Championship (1996); Winner, Las Vegas Invitational (1996); Winner, Walt Disney World/Oldsmobile Classic (1996); Winner, NCAA West Regional (1996); Winner, Pac-10 Championship (1996); Winner, Cougar Classic (1996); First Team All-American (1995, 1996); Winner, U.S. Amateur Championship (1994-1996); Pac-10 Player of the Year (1995, 1996); Winner, Stanford Invitational (1995); Orange County League MVP (1994); Player of the Year, Orange County (1994); Winner, Jerry Pate Invitational (1994); Winner, William Tucker Invitational (1994); Winner, Pacific Northwest Amateur Championship (1994); Winner, Amateur Championship, Southern California Golf Asso-

ciation (1994); Winner, Western Amateur Championship (1994); Player of the Year, L.A. Times (1994); Player of the Year, Golf World (1993-1994); Southern California Player of the Year (1991-1993); Dial Award (1993); Winner, Southern California Junior Best Ball Championship (1993); Winner, U.S. Junior Amateur Championship (1991-1993); Winner, Pro Gear San Antonio Shootout (1992); Winner, Nabisco Mission Hills Desert Junior Championship (1992); Winner, Insurance Youth Golf Classic (1992); National Amateur of the Year, Golfweek (1991, 1992); Player of the Year, Golf Digest (1991-1992); Winner, PING/Phoenix Junior Championship (1991-1992); First Team Rolex Junior All American (1991, 1992); Player of the Year, American Junior Golf Association (1991); Winner, Orange Bowl Junior International Championship (1991); Winner, L.A. City Junior Championship (1991); Winner, Edgewood Tahoe Junior Classic (1991); Winner, CIF-Southern California HS Invitational Championship (1991); Winner, Optimist International Junior World Championship (1984-1985, 1988-1991); Winner, Insurance Youth Gold Classic (1990)

WOODWARD, JOANNE, T: Actress, Producer, Philanthropist **I:** Media & Entertainment **DOB:** 02/27/1930 **PB:** Thomasville **SC:** GA/USA **PT:** Wade Woodward; Elinor (Trimmier) Woodward **MS:** Married **SPN:** Paul Newman (01/29/1958, Deceased 2008) **CH:** Elinor Terese; Melissa Stewart; Clea Olivia **ED:** Graduate, Sarah Lawrence College (1990); Student, Drama, Louisiana State University (1947-1949); Participant, Neighborhood Playhouse School of the Theatre **C:** Artistic Director, Westport Country Playhouse (2001-2005); Co-Founder (With Paul Newman), Hole in the Wall Gang Camp (1988); Actress, Producer, Director, Film and Television **CW:** Voice Actress, Executive Producer, Film, "Lucky Them" (2013); Actress, Video Short, "Gayby" (2012); Narrator, Video Short, "All the World" (2011); Voice Actress, Song, "The Real Life" by John Cougar Mellencamp, "On the Rural Route 7609" (2010); Narrator, Film, "Change in the Wind" (2010); Actress, Television Miniseries, "Empire Falls" (2005); Executive Producer, Television Film, "Our Town" (2003); Actress, Television Series Documentary, "Freedom: A History of Us" (2003); Narrator, Film, "Even If a Hundred Ogres…" (1996); Actress, Television Film, "Breathing Lessons" (1994); Voice Actress, Television Film Documentary, "The Roots of Roe" (1993); Actress, Film, "Philadelphia" (1993); Narrator, Film, "The Age of Innocence" (1993); Actress, Co-Producer, Television Film, "Blind Spot" (1993); Actress, Television Film, "Foreign Affairs" (1993); Actress, Film, "Mr. & Mrs. Bridge" (1990); Producer, Television Series Documentary, "American Masters" (1989); Actress, Film, "The Glass Menagerie" (1987); Actress, Television Film, "Do You Remember Love" (1985); Actress, Television Film, "Passions" (1984); Actress, Film, "Harry & Son" (1984); Director, Writer, Television Series, "American Playhouse" (1982); Actress, Television Film, "Candida" (1982); Actress, Television Film, "Crisis at Central High" (1981); Actress, Television Film, "The Shadow Box" (1980); Actress, Television Film, "The Streets of L.A." (1979); Director, Television Series, "Family" (1979); Actress, Television Film, "A Christmas to Remember" (1978); Actress, Film, "The End" (1978); Actress, Television Film, "See How She Runs" (1978); Actress, Television Film, "Come Back, Little Sheba" (1977); Actress, Television Series, "NBC Special Treat" (1976); Actress, Television Miniseries, "Sybil" (1976); Actress, Television Series, "The Carol Burnett Show" (1976); Actress, Film, "The Drowning Pool" (1975); Actress, "Summer Wishes, Winter Dreams" (1973); Actress, Film, "The Effect of Gamma Rays on Man-in-the-Moon Marigolds" (1972); Actress, Television Film, "All the Way Home" (1971); Actress, Film, "They Might Be Giants" (1971); Actress, Film, "WUSA" (1970); Actress, Film, "Winning" (1969); Actress, Film, "Rachel, Rachel" (1968); Actress, Film, "A Fine Madness" (1966); Actress, Film, "A Big Hand for the Little Lady" (1966); Actress, Film, "Signpost to Murder" (1964); Actress, Film, "A New Kind of Love" (1963); Actress, Film, "The Stripper" (1963); Actress, Film, "Paris Blues" (1961); Actress, Film, "From the Terrace" (1960); Actress, Film, "The Fugitive Kind" (1960); Actress, Film, "The Sound and the Fury" (1959); Actress, Film, "Rally 'Round the Flag, Boys!" (1958); Actress, Film, "The Long, Hot Summer" (1958); Actress, Television Series, "Playhouse 90" (1958); Actress, Film, "No Down Payment" (1957); Actress, Film, "The Three Faces of Eve" (1957); Actress, Television Series, "Climax!" (1956); Actress, Television Series, "The Alcoa Hour" (1956); Actress, Television Series, "Alfred Hitchcock Presents" (1956); Actress, Film, "A Kiss Before Dying" (1956); Actress, Television Series, "General Electric Theater" (1956); Actress, Television Series, "Four Star Playhouse" (1954-1956); Actress, Television Series, "Kraft Theatre" (1955-1956); Actress, Television Series, "Studio One in Hollywood" (1954-1956); Actress, Television Series, "The United States Steel Hour" (1955); Actress, Television Series, "The 20th Century Fox-Hour" (1955); Actress, Film, "Count Three and Pray" (1955); Actress, Television Series, "The Star and the Story" (1955); Actress, Television Series, "Star Tonight" (1955); Actress, Television Series, "Ponds Theater" (1954-1955); Actress, Television Series, "Omnibus" (1952-1955); Actress, Television Series, "Armstrong Circle Theatre" (1954); Actress, Television Series, "Lux Video Theatre" (1954); Actress, Television Series, "The Elgin Hour" (1954); Actress, Television Series, "The Ford Television Theatre" (1954); Actress, Television Series, "The Web" (1954); Actress, Television Series, "You Are There" (1954); Actress, Television Series, "Danger" (1954); Actress, Television Series, "Repertory Theatre" (1953-1954); Actress, Television Series, "Robert Montgomery Presents" (1952-1954); Actress, Television Series, "Goodyear Playhouse" (1953); Actress, Television Series, "Tales of Tomorrow" (1952) **AW:** Co-Recipient, Award for Greatest Public Service Benefiting the Disadvantaged, Jefferson Awards (1994); Co-Recipient, Kennedy Center Honors for Lifetime Achievement in the Performing Arts (1992); Nominee, Academy Award for Best Actress, "Mr. and Mrs. Bridge" (1990); Emmy Award for Outstanding Lead Actress in a Miniseries or TV Movie, "Do You Remember Love?" (1985); Emmy Award for Outstanding Lead Actress in a Miniseries or TV Movie, "See How She Runs" (1978); Best Actress, "The Effect of Gamma Rays on Man-in-the-Moon Marigolds," Cannes Film Festival (1974); Nominee, Academy Award for Beset Actress in a Leading Role, "Summer Wishes, Winter Dreams" (1973); Nominee, Academy Award for Best Actress, "Rachel, Rachel" (1969); Silver Shell for Best Actress, "The Fugitive Kind," San Sebastián International Film Festival (1960); Recognized with a Star on the Hollywood Walk of Fame (1960); Academy Award for Best Actress, "The Three Faces of Eve" (1958) **PA:** Democrat **RE:** Episcopalian

WOODWARD, ROBERT, "BOB", T: Journalist, Editor **I:** Writing and Editing **CN:** The Washington Post **DOB:** 03/26/1943 **PB:** Geneva **SC:** IL/USA **PT:** Alfred Eno Woodward II; Jane (Upshur) Woodward **MS:** Married **SPN:** Elsa Walsh (11/25/1989); Frances Kuper (1974, Divorced 1979); Kathleen Middlekauff (1966, Divorced 1969) **CH:** Tali; Diana **ED:** BA in History and English Literature, Yale College, Yale University (1965); Graduate Coursework,

George Washington University **C:** Associate Editor, The Washington Post (2008-Present); Assistant Managing Editor, The Washington Post (1981-2008); Metropolitan Editor, The Washington Post (1979-1981); Reporter, The Washington Post (1971-1978); Reporter, Montgomery County Sentinel, Maryland (1970-1971) **CIV:** Founder, Woodward Walsh Foundation; Donor, Sidwell Friends School **MIL:** Discharged Lt., USS Wright, U.S. Navy (1970) **CW:** Author, "Fear: Trump in the White House" (2018); Author, "The Last of the President's Men" (2015); Author, "The Price of Politics" (2012); Author, "Obama's Wars" (2010); Author, "The War Within: A Secret White House History, 2006-2008" (2008); Lecturer, American Bankruptcy Institute, National Association of Chain Drug Stores, Mortgage Bankers Association (2008); Author, "State of Denial: Bush at War, Part III" (2006); Author, "The Secret Man: The Story of Watergate's Deep Throat" (2005); Author, "Plan of Attack" (2004); Author, "Bush at War: Inside the Bush White House" (2002); Author, "Maestro: Greenspan's Fed and the American Boom" (2000); Author, "Shadow: Five Presidents and the Legacy of Watergate, 1974-1999" (1999); Author, "The Choice: How Bill Clinton Won" (1996); Author, "The Agenda: Inside the Clinton White House" (1994); Author, "The Commanders: The Pentagon and the First Gulf War, 1989-1991" (1991); Co-Author, Miniseries, "The Nightmare Years" (1989); Author, "Veil: The Secret Wars of the CIA, 1981-1987" (1987); Co-Author, TV Film, "Under Siege" (1986); Author, "Wired: The Short Life and Fast Times of John Belushi" (1984); Co-Author, "The Brethren: Inside the Supreme Court" (1979); Co-Author, "The Final Days" (1976); Co-Author, "All the President's Men" (1974); Lecturer, Numerous Colleges and Universities **AW:** Elijah Parish Lovejoy Award "for courageous journalism as well as an honorary doctorate," Colby College (2012); #1 New York Times Bestseller, "Obama's Wars" (2010); Co-Recipient, Pulitzer Prize for National Reporting (2002); Gerald R. Ford Prize for Reporting on the Presidency (2002); Walter Cronkite Award for Excellence in Journalism (2001); William Allen White Medal (2000); Co-Recipient, Pulitzer Prize for Public Service (1973); Sigma Delta Chi Award (1973); George Polk Award (1972); Heywood Broun Award (1972); Worth Bingham Prize for Investigative Reporting (1986, 1972) **MEM:** Society of Book and Snake; Phi Gamma Delta

WOODWARD, ROGER, T: Professor **I:** Education/Educational Services **CN:** San Francisco State University **SC:** Australia **CH:** Three children **ED:** MusD, The University of Sydney (1999); Coursework in Piano, New South Wales State Conservatorium of Music (1963); Coursework, Fryderyk Chopin National Academy **C:** Professor of Classical Piano, School of Music, San Francisco State University (2002-Present); Chair of Music, University of New England (1999-2000) **CR:** Founding Director, School of Music and Dance, San Francisco State University (2002-2004) **CIV:** Founder, Director, The Sydney Spring Festival of New Music, Sydney, Australia (1990); Founding Member, Contemporary Music Series, Australia (1975); Founding Member, Contemporary Music Series, London (1972); Director, Joie et Lumiére Series; Founder, Director, The London Music Digest; Director, Chamber of Music Festival, Kotschach-Mauthen, Austria **CW:** Author, "Beyond Black and White: My Life in Music" (2014) **AW:** Honorary Fellow, Australian Academy of the Humanities (2019); National Trust, Australian National Living Treasure (1997); Companion of the Order of Australia (1992); Order of the British Empire (1980); Gloria Artis Gold Medal for Merit to Culture, Polish Government; Order of Merit, Polish Government **MEM:** National Audubon Soci-

ety; ASPCA **AS:** Mr. Woodward attributes his success to his dedication to what he does, hard work, great teachers and mentors, and his parents. **B/I:** Mr. Woodward became involved in his profession because he fell in love with music at a young age. **THT:** Mr. Woodward lives by the motto, "Beauty will save the world."

WOOTEN, RUSSELL, T: Operations Research Specialist **I:** Government Administration/Government Relations/Government Services **DOB:** 12/15/1954 **PB:** Cleveland **SC:** OH/USA **PT:** Wesley Walter Thomas Wooten, Jr.; Marie Ann Wooten **MS:** Married **SPN:** Charo D. Wooten (8/7/2002); Tatyana V. Wooten **CH:** Russell Wesley; Nicholas Rex; Jason Joseph; Jeremy Louis; Nikita A. **ED:** MBA, Cleveland State University, Cleveland, OH, Magna Cum Laude (1982); BBA, Cleveland State University, Cleveland, OH (1977) **CT:** The George Washington University Certificate, Project Management (2004); Arizona State University, Executive Certification, Managerial and Technical Leadership (1993) **C:** Retired; Manager, IT Strategy, U.S. Department of Homeland Security (DHS)/Transportation Security Administration (TSA) (2011-2016); Branch Chief, U.S. Department of Homeland Security (DHS)/Transportation Security Administration (TSA) (2008-2011); Manager, Joint Planning & Development Office for Next Generation Air Transportation System, U.S. Department of Homeland Security (DHS)/Transportation Security Administration (TSA) (2006-2008); Manager, Emerging Technologies, U.S. Department of Homeland Security (DHS)/Transportation Security Administration (TSA) (2002-2006); "C-Level" Manager, McDermott Technology, Inc.; R&D Division/Babcock & Wilcox (1989-2002); Manager, Management (Industrial) Engineering, Akron General Medical Center (1988-1989); Supervisor, Productivity Studies Department, American Greetings Corporation (1981-1988); Plant Manager, Airco Welding Products (1978-1981); Manager, Precision Winding Department, Phoenix Dye Works (1977-1978) **CR:** World Future Society, US National Capital Region (WFS) (1996-Present); Institute for Operations Research and the Management Sciences (INFORMS) (1989-Present); Institute of Industrial and Systems Engineers (IISE) (1979-Present); Professional and Volunteer Experiences, Washington Academy of Sciences (2010-2016); Washington D.C. Council of Engineering and Architectural Societies (DCEAS) (2004-2016); The Institute of Management Science (TIMS) (1989-1995) **CIV:** National Capital Chapter Director of Science and Engineering Fairs (2003-2015); Institute of Industrial and Systems Engineers (IISE); Judge, More Than 200 Science Fairs including Washington DC, Maryland, and Virginia State Finals **CW:** Conference Leadership Roles (2003-2016); Author, Numerous Professional Publications (1982-2013); Author, Professional Publication, "President's Message," National Capital Chapter Newsletter, Institute of Industrial Engineering (2005-2013); Author, Professional Publication, "President's Message," FEEDBACK, Washington, D.C. Chapter of Institute for Operations Research and the Management Sciences (2005-2009); Author, Professional Publication, "President's Message," Future Takes, National Capital Region World Future Society (2005-2007); Winter Simulation Conference (WSC); Track Chair, Emergency Response/Homeland Security IISE Solutions Conference; Track Chair, Enterprise Management (SEMS and IAB) Government IISE Research Conference (IERC); Track Chair, Homeland Security INFORMS Annual Conference; Track Chair, Homeland Security IISE Management Roundtable; Chair IISE Transformation Conference; Planning Committee **AW:** SEMS Management Award, Institute of Industrial and Systems Engineers (IISE) (2011);

INFORMS Moving Spirit Award (2009); Engineer of the Year, Washington DC Council of Engineering and Architectural Societies (DCEAS) (2007); Franz Edelman Laureate (2006); Institute for Operations Research and the Management Sciences (INFORMS) **MEM:** Beta Gamma Sigma; MENSA **MH:** Albert Nelson Marquis Lifetime Achievement Award; Marquis Who's Who Top Professional **AS:** Mr. Wooten attributes his success to belief in the power of good engineering and good management. **B/I:** Mr. Wooten became involved in his profession because upon completing college, during which he had the intention of becoming a manager, he received his first job in the industrial engineering sector and said, "I took to it like a fish in the water." In addition, he chose his profession because he didn't think that he had any choice. He blindly fell into it. Like most kids in school he had no idea what he wanted to do. He didn't get good career advisement because he was one of the smart kids that they assumed he knew everything. However, he never held a job, so he had no idea. But, he was told that he should do this and that because he was smart. So, he sort of rebelled against what he was told and took to management and be the boss. And that works out for you if you want to do it for that reason. So, his first job he fell into an industrial group being a manager in a department that he worked as an industrial engineer. He saw it as a perfect match. He picked it up and worked with it. He was focused on what was the best way to do stuff. Asking questions like, "how do I know that I am being most efficient?" "how to maximize and optimize?", stuff like that. Which was totally new to him, things that he never thought of before, but it came natural to him. That is what industrial engineering is all about and got hooked like a drug. **AV:** Chess; Reading; Watching Cleveland Indians **PA:** Conservative; Constitutionalist **RE:** Roman Catholic, Knights of Columbus 4th Degree

WORLDS, ANNIE LOIS, T: Retired Educator, Retired Assistant Chief **I:** Infrastructure **CN:** 1)Terrell County High School 2) St. Petersburg (Florida) Police Department, **DOB:** 05/16/1949 **PB:** Donalsonville **SC:** GA/USA **PT:** Allen Worlds; Edith M. (Daniels) Worlds **MS:** Single **ED:** BS in Biology, Albany State University, Georgia (1972); MPA Postgraduate Studies, University of South Florida; Graduate, 13th Command Officer's Development Course, Southern Police Institute **CT:** Certified Teacher, Georgia, Florida **C:** Retired (2001); Assistant Chief of the Administrative Bureau (1999-2001); Assistant to the Chief of Police, St. Petersburg Police Department (1997-1999); Major, District Commander Patrol Bureau, St. Petersburg Police Department (1989-1990); Lieutenant, St. Petersburg Police Department (1985-1986); Detective Sergeant, Internal Affairs, St. Petersburg Police Department (1983-1985); Sergeant, Patrol Bureau, St. Petersburg Police Department (1982-1983); Burglary Detective, Investigative Bureau, St. Petersburg Police Department (1980-1982); Training Officer, Patrol Bureau, St. Petersburg Police Department (1978-1980); Officer, St. Petersburg Police Department (1975-1978); Teacher, Terrell County High School, Dawson, GA (1972-1973); Assistant Chief, Administration Bureau, St. Petersburg Police Department; Major, Commander of Criminal Investigations, St. Petersburg Police Department **CR:** Expert Information Review Committee, St. Petersburg, FL (1987-Present); General Order Review Committee, St. Petersburg, FL (1983-1985) **CIV:** President of the Board, Board of Directors, Family Service Center, Pasco/Pinellas Alcohol, Drug Abuse and Mental Health Planning Council (1998-1999); Democratic Women of St. Petersburg (1984-1985); Junior Achievement National Forum for Black Public Administrators;

Minority Law Enforcement of Penellas County, Inc.; St. John Progressive M.B. Church, Tampa, FL **AW:** YWCA Tribute to Women (1995); Named, Outstanding Young Women of America (1985); Citizen for the Day Award, Station WPLP, St. Petersburg, FL (1983); Ned March Award (1980) **MEM:** National Organization of Black Law Enforcement Executives (1981-1983); International Association of Women Police **MH:** Albert Nelson Marquis Lifetime Achievement Award; Marquis Who's Who Top Professional **AS:** She attributes her success to God. **B/I:** Ms. Worlds became involved in her profession because in her senior year in college, she contracted meningitis and did not think she would make it, but she did. While at home with her mother recuperating she did not march with her class, but graduated in absentia, with a BS degree in Biology. All her friends had been gainfully employed and they moved on in their careers. After feeling sorry for herself for a while, she felt God speak to her and told her to get up and move. A message was sent to her that they needed a science teacher, and she went to teach there for her first year. She did not want to teach and only had a provisional certificate. What she really wanted to do was be a microbiologist. She was going to start her studies there, but had an opportunity to go to Florida to interview for the job of a microbiologist. Needless to say that at the interview, the person who had the experience for the job got it, and she needed a job and started to look for one. She saw an advertisement on TV for St. Petersburg, which she applied for, and the rest was history. **AV:** Reading; Bible study; Gospel music; Working out at the gym **PA:** Democrat **RE:** Baptist

WRAY, CHRISTOPHER ASHER, T: Director **I:** Government Administration/Government Relations/Government Services **CN:** Federal Bureau of Investigation **DOB:** 12/17/1966 **PB:** New York **SC:** NY/USA **MS:** Married **SPN:** Helen Garrison Howell (1989) **CH:** Trip; Caroline **ED:** Doctor of Jurisprudence, Yale Law School (1989); Diploma, Yale University, Cum Laude (1989) **C:** Director, Federal Bureau of Investigation, Washington, DC (2017-Present); Partner, King & Spalding LLP, Washington, DC (2005-2016); Assistant Attorney General, Criminal Division, United States Department of Justice, Washington, DC (2003-2005); Acting Assistant Attorney General, Criminal Division, United States Department of Justice, Washington, DC (2003); Principal Associate Attorney General, Criminal Division, United States Department of Justice, Washington, DC (2001-2003); Associate Deputy Attorney General, United States Department of Justice, Washington, DC (2001); Assistant U.S. Attorney, Northern District of Georgia, United States Department of Justice, Atlanta, GA (1997-2001); Associate, King & Spalding LLP, Atlanta, GA (1993-1997); Law Clerk to Honorable J. Michael Luttig, United States Court of Appeals for the Fourth Circuit (1992-1993) **CW:** Executive Editor, Yale Law Journal

WREN, JOHN D., T: Chairman and Chief Executive Officer **I:** Advertising & Marketing **CN:** Omnicom Group Inc. **DOB:** 07/22/1952 **PB:** Brooklyn **SC:** NY/USA **MS:** Married **SPN:** Diane Wren **CH:** Two Children **ED:** MBA, Adelphi University (1975); BA, Adelphi University (1975) **CT:** Certified Public Accountant (CPA) **C:** Chairman, Chief Executive Officer, Omnicom Group Inc. (2018-Present); President, Chief Executive Officer, Omnicom Group Inc., New York, NY (1997-2018); President, Omnicom Group Inc., New York, NY (1995-1997); Chairman, Chief Executive Officer, Diversified Agency Services (subsidiary Omnicom Group Inc.) (1993-1995); President, Diversified Agency Services (subsidiary Omnicom Group Inc.) (1990-1993);

Chief Financial Officer, Diversified Agency Services (subsidiary Omnicom Group Inc.) (1986-1990); Senior Vice President of Finance and Administration, DDB Needham Worldwide, Omnicom Group Inc. (1986); Controller, Norton Simon Inc. (1981-1986); Co-Founder, Manager, Olympic Deck Hockey (1980-1986); Management Consultant, Arthur Anderson & Co. (1975-1981) **CR:** Member, Board of Directors, Omnicom Group Inc. (1993-Present); Board Member, Razorfish Inc. (1996-2000); Member, International Business Council, World Economic Forum; Member, Board of Directors, Lincoln Center for the Performing Arts; Trustee, Arthur Ashe Foundation **CIV:** Advocate, Healthcare Education for Disadvantaged Communities **AW:** Ranked 48th, Best CEO of the Year (2001); Recognized as "One of the Best-Performing CEOs in the World," Harvard Business Review; Executive of the Year, Advertising Age; Best CEO, Institutional Investor; Gold Medal Award, Catholic Youth Organization; Ellis Island Medal of Honor; Numerous Accolades "for his contributions to the community" **PA:** Republican

WRIGHT, C.T., T: Chairman (Appointed) **I:** Government Administration/Government Relations/Government Services **CN:** Arizona Board of Executive Clemency **DOB:** 10/04/1942 **PB:** Social Circle **SC:** GA/USA **PT:** George Wright; Carrie Mae (Enus) Wright **MS:** Married **SPN:** Mary Stephens Wright (08/09/1974) **ED:** LHD, Mary Holmes College (2000); PhD, Boston University (1977); MA, Clark Atlanta University (1967); BS, Fort Valley State University, GA (1964) **C:** Chairman, Arizona Board of Executive Clemency, AZ Africa (2014-Present); President, AZ Africa (2004-Present); Chairman, Founder, Light of Hope Institute (2000-Present); Member, Governor's Advisory Council on Aging (2013-2019); Presidential Electoral College, AZ (2012); President, Chief Executive Officer, International for Education and Self Help (IFESH) (2001-2004); President, International Foundation and Coordinator, African American Summit (1989-2001); President, Cheyney University of Pennsylvania, Cheyney, PA (1982-1985); Vice President of Academy Affairs, Talladega College, AL (1981-1982); Program Director, Assistant Provost, Eastern Washington University, Cheney, WA (1977-1981); Adjunct Professor, Cabe Community College (1974-1977); Adjunct Faculty, Clark Atlanta University (1973-1977); Division Chairman, Morris Brown College, Atlanta, GA (1973-1977); Member, Faculty, Morris Brown College, Atlanta, GA (1967-1973); Teacher, Georgia Department of Education, Social Circle, GA (1965-1967); Vice President and Provost, Florida Memorial College (Now Florida Memorial University) **CR:** Board of Directors, Kiwanis Club of Fountain Hills (2006-Present); Chairman, Advisory Committee, AMI Consultants (2002-Present); People's Investment Fund for Africa, Leon Sullivan Trust, South Africa; International Foundation Education and Self Help, England, United Kingdom; Consultant and Lecturer in Field **CIV:** Board President, Fountain Hills School (2010-Present); Chairman Committee, World Children Relief Foundation (2002-Present); Goodwill Ambassador, State of Georgia (1997-Present); Executive Committee, Boy Scouts of America, Philadelphia, PA (1982-Present); Commissioner, Washington Public Broadcasting (Now Northwest Public Broadcasting), Olympia, WA (1980-1984) **CW:** Author, Booklet, "The History of Black Historical Mythology" (1980); Contributor, Articles to Professional Journals **AW:** Governor Howard Pyle Award (2010; Leon H. Sullivan Humanitarian Award (2009); Judge Jean Williams Award (2008; Calvin C. Goode Lifetime Achievement Award (2001); National Teaching Fellow, Boston University (1971); Human Relations Scholar (1969); Pioneer Award, Arizona State University; Established C.T. Wright Scholarship, West Campus, Arizona State University **MEM:** Committees, American Association Colleges and Universities (1982-Present); Committees, National Association for Equal Opportunity in Higher Education (NAFEO) (1982-Present); Committees, American Historical Association (1970-Present); Committees, National Education Association (1965-Present); Committees, Association for the Study of African American Life and History (ASALH) (1965-Present); Vice President, President, National Association For Equal Opportunity in Higher Education (NAFEO); Kiwanis Club; Fountain Hills; Lions Clubs International; Tuscan Club; Rotary International **MH:** Albert Nelson Marquis Lifetime Achievement Award **B/I:** Dr. Wright grew up in the southern part of the United States, in the state of Georgia, on October 4, 1942, which was a Sunday; if he had been born the day before, on October 3rd, he would have been born in a cotton field, because that's where his mother worked. Dr. Wright feels the inspiration throughout the years has been from a number of people beginning with his mother, Carrie Mae Wright, and his aunt, Victoria Smith Johnson. They were always an inspiration to him, as has his uncle, The Rev. Dr. Willie Enus. There were a number of teachers and professors who have been an inspiration to him as well. His first grade teacher, Pauline Innison, his high school inspiration came from a social studies teacher, the Rev. El Ellis, and a university professors who inspired him were Dr. Clance A. Bacote at Clark Atlanta University, Dr. John W. Blassingame from Yale University, and Dr. Robert Bruce from Foster University. In more recent years, the person who has been most influential in his life is the Rev. Theron H. Sullivan, the pastor of the nine Baptist churches in Philadelphia, Pennsylvania and the first African American to serve on a fortune 500 board of directors, which was General Motors. They worked together in creating projects in Africa which came through the International Foundation for Education and Self-Help. Such projects include building over 100 schools throughout Africa, sending 1,000 American teachers to upgrade the skills of African teachers, sending millions of books and publications to various parts of Africa, and raising over $25 million to support projects in Africa. He had the opportunity to work with over 35 African presidents and prime ministers including President Nelson Mandela. He has had the opportunity to meet seven American presidents: President Jimmy Carter, President Ronald Regan, President George H. W. Bush, President Bill Clinton, President George Bush, President Barack Obama, and President Donald Trump. He has even had the opportunity to offer prayers at several affairs with these United States presidents. **RE:** Baptist

WRIGHT, DUSTIN ARLIE, T: Founder, Director, Lead Clinician **I:** Health, Wellness and Fitness **CN:** Wright Pyschological Services PLC **MS:** Married **ED:** Specialist in Education in Community Counseling, James Madison University, Harrisonburg, VA (2008); Master of Arts in Community Counseling, James Madison University, Harrisonburg, VA (2008); Bachelor of Science in Psychology, James Madison University, Harrisonburg, VA (2005) **CT:** Master Instructor, Crisis Intervention Training, Blue Ridge Crisis Intervention Training (2010-Present); Youth Mental Health First Aid Instructor, Mental Health First Aid USA (2014-2017); Adult Mental Health Aid Instructor, Mental Health First Aid USA (2013-2017); Licensed Professional Counselor (2013) **C:** Adjunct Professor, Mary Baldwin University, Murphey Deming College of Health Sciences Master's Physician Assistant Program, Psychiatry and Behavioral Health Medicine Course (2017-Present); Director, Lead Clinician, Wright Psychological Services PLC (2015-Present); Master Instructor, Blue Ridge Crisis Intervention Training (2010-Present); Community Liaison Program Coordinator, Valley Community Services Board (2013-2017); Instructor, Mental Health First Aid (2013-2017); Co-Creator, Coordinator, My Action Plain Card Program (2013-2017); Board of Directors, President, "We Care" Augusta, National Alliance on Mental Illness (2013-2017); Board of Directors, Valley Supportive Housing (2013-2017); Creator, Coordinator, Webmaster, Valley E-Link (2008-2017); Emergency Services, Access, Outpatient Clinician, Valley Community Services Board (2008-2015); Intensive In-Home Clinician, Crossroads Counseling Center (2007-2008) **CW:** Author, Thesis, "Couples in Conflict: A Handbook for Couples Beginning Counseling" (2008); Contributor, Multiple News Coverage Stories **AW:** Behavioral Healthcare Professional of the Year Award, International Crisis Intervention Team (2018); J. Lewis Gibbs Distinguished Service Award, Mental Health America of Augusta (2018); Behavioral Health Provider of the Year Award, Virginia Crisis Intervention Team (2017); Commendation Award, Mental Health America of Augusta (2012) **MEM:** Valley Area Community Support Incorporated; National Alliance for Mental Illness; "We Care" Augusta **AS:** Mr. Wright attributes his success to his passion for positive change, as well as a persistent drive to continuously learn and surround himself with motivated, open-minded and creative colleagues, including such mentors as his father, grandfather and Dr. Lennie Echterling. **B/I:** Mr. Wright became involved in his profession due to the influence of his child psychologist, who helped him process many difficult aspects of his early youth. Years later, while attending high school, Mr. Wright decided to pursue counseling. **AV:** Skiing; Snow boarding; Family time; Watching college football

WRIGHT, KATHLEEN MARY, MA, PHD, T: Psychologist **I:** Medicine & Health Care **DOB:** 01/11/1948 **PB:** Washington, DC **SC:** DC/USA **PT:** Ferrer Bruno Picchi; Virginia Mary (Barrett) Picchi **MS:** Married **SPN:** Kevin Vallee Wright **CH:** Michelle Debra Saczynski **ED:** PhD in Psychology, Cornell University, Ithaca, NY (1983); MA in Psychology, The New School for Social Research, New York, NY (1976); MS in Administration, The George Washington University, Washington, DC (1972); BA in Psychology, College of William and Mary, Williamsburg, VA (1970) **C:** Consultant, Clinical Research Management, Inc. (2014-2017); Research Program Manager, Military Operational Medicine Research Program, United States Army Medical Research and Materiel Command, Frederick, MD (2008-2014); Director of Force Health Protection Research Program, United States Army Medical Research Unit-Europe, Walter Reed Army Institute of Research, Washington, DC (2000-2014); Research Director, Congressional Commission on Military Training and Gender-Related Issues (1998-1999); Deputy Director, Division of Neuropsychiatry, Walter Reed Army Institute of Research, Washington, DC (1997-1998); Director of Traumatic Stress Research Program, Walter Reed Army Institute of Research, Washington, DC (1989-1998); Deputy Chief, Department of Military Psychiatry, Walter Reed Army Institute of Research, Washington, DC (1994-1997); Deputy Chief for Science, Department of Military Psychiatry, Walter Reed Army Institute of Research, Washington, DC (1990-1994); Manager, Military Family Research Program, Department of Military Psychiatry, Walter Reed Army Institute of Research, Washington, DC (1985-1989); National Institute of Mental Health Postdoctoral Fellow in Clinical Psychology, Yale Psychiatric Institute, New Haven, CT (1983-1985); Clinical Psychology Associate, Veterans Affairs Medical Center, West Haven, CT (1981-1983); Research Fellow, Department of Psychology, Cornell University, Ithaca, NY (1977-1981) **CR:** United States Representative, NATO Research Group, Suicide in the Military (2008-2014); Member, Program Area Steering Committee for Defense Technical Objective Interventions to Enhance Psychological Resilience and Prevent Psychiatric Casualties (2002-2008); Member, Suicide Prevention Task Force, United States Army Europe (2000-2005); Senior Scientist, Center for the Study of Traumatic Stress, Department of Psychiatry, Uniformed Services University of the Health Sciences, Bethesda, MD (1999-2000); Adjunct Associate Professor of Psychiatry, Uniformed Services University of the Health Sciences, Bethesda, MD (1998-2014); Core Member of Headquarters, Department of the Army Family Advocacy Program Research Subcommittee (1995-2014); Member, Family Violence and Trauma Advisory Board, Center for the Study of Traumatic Stress, Department of Psychiatry, Uniformed Services University of the Health Sciences (1995-2014); Member, Program Committee for the International Society for Traumatic Stress Studies (1994); Adjunct Assistant Professor of Psychiatry, Uniformed Services University of the Health Sciences, Bethesda, MD (1988-1998) **CW:** Reviewer, Journal of Traumatic Stress, British Journal of Psychiatry, Military Medicine; Contributor, Articles, Professional Journals; Contributor, Chapters, Books **AW:** Meritorious Civilian Service Award, Department of the Army (2008-2014); Commendation, British Journal of Psychiatry (2007); Superior Civilian Service Award, Department of the Army (2000-2007); Certificate of Appreciation for Outstanding Service, Congressional Committee on Military Training and Gender-Related Issues (1999); Superior Performance Award, Walter Reed Army Institute of Research (1995-1997); Commander's Award for Exceptional Civilian Service, Walter Reed Army Institute of Research (1991-1994); Special Award, Operations Desert Shield/Desert Storm, Department of the Army (1992); Certificate of Appreciation, United States Air Force (1991); Commander's Award for Civilian Service, Department of the Army (1989-1991); Special Activity Service Award, Walter Reed Army Institute of Research (1986); Catlin Memorial Award for Clinical Research, Department of Psychology, Cornell University (1982) **MEM:** Program Committee, International Society of Traumatic Stress Studies (1991); Fellow, Inter-University Seminar on Armed Forces and Society; American Association for the Advancement of Science; American Psychological Association; The New York Academy of Sciences **MH:** Albert Nelson Marquis Lifetime Achievement Award **B/I:** Dr. Wright became involved in her profession because in her freshman year of college, she had a clinical psychology professor who influenced her decision to become a psychologist. Later, when she was completing a postdoctoral fellowship at Yale University, she interviewed at the Walter Reed Army Institute of Research with Dr. David Marlowe, who was the chief of the Department of Military Psychiatry at the time. He offered her a position conducting research on traumatic stress reactions in the military.

WRIGHT, KATIE HARPER, T: Educational Administrator; Journalist **I:** Education/Educational Services **DOB:** 10/05/1923 **PB:** Crawfordsville **SC:** AK/USA **PT:** James Hale Harper; Connie Mary (Locke) Harper **MS:** Married **SPN:** Marvin Wright (03/21/1952) **CH:** Virginia K. Jordan **ED:** EdD, St. Louis University (1979); MEd, University of Illinois (1959); BA, University of Illinois (1944) **C:** Member, System Board, United States Selective Service (2012-Present); Interim Superintendent,

East St. Louis School District 189, IL (1993-1994); Assistant Superintendent Programs, East St. Louis Public Schools, IL (1977-1979); Director of Special Education Districts 188, 189, East St. Louis Public Schools, IL (1971-1977); Director of District 189 Instructional Materials Program, East St. Louis Public Schools, IL (1965-1971); Elementary and Special Education Teacher, East St. Louis Public Schools, IL (1944-1965) **CR:** Member, Advisory Board, Southern Illinois University School of Education, Edwardsville, IL (2009-Present); Member, President's Commission on Excellence in Special Education, Interim Superintendent, District 189 Schools (1994-Present); Member of Staff, St. Louis University (1989-Present); Adjunct Professor Emeritus of Education, Harris-Stowe State College (1980) **CIV:** Board, Selective Service System (2012-Present); Member, President's Commission on Excellence in Special Education (2001-Present); East St. Louis Board of Election Commission, East St. Louis Financial Advisory Authority (1999-Present); Member, Illinois Department of Corrections School Board (1995-Present); Illinois Minority/Female Business Council (1991-Present); Board of Directors, Jackie Joyner-Kersee Youth Center Foundation (1991-Present); President, Board of Directors, St. Clair County Mental Health Center (1987-Present); Elder, First United Presbyterian Church (1981-Present); Board of Directors, River Bluff Council, Girl Scouts of the United States of America (1979-Present); Board of Directors, United Way (1979-Present); Board of Directors, Urban League (1979-Present); Provident Counseling Center (1995-1998); President, Board of Directors, St. Clair County Mental Health Centers (1987); National Board of Directors, River Bluff Council, Girl Scouts of the United States of America (1981-1984); Illinois Commission on Children (1973-1985); President, Board of Trustees, East St. Louis Public Library (1972-1977); President, Board of Directors, St. Clair County Mental Health Center (1970-1972); Member, Advisory Board, Magna Bank; Charter Member, Coalition of 100 Black Women; Member, Coordinator, Council on Ethnic Affairs, Synod of Mid-America, Presbyterian Church U.S.A.; Charter Member, Metro East Links Group; Gateway Chapter, The Links, Incorporated **CW:** National Editor, Top Ladies of Distinction (1991-Present); Feature Writer, St. Louis Argus Newspaper (1979-Present); Author, "Delta Sigma Theta/East St. Louis Chapter History" (1992); Author, "Love is Not Enough"; Contributor, Articles to Professional Journals **AW:** Lifetime Achievement Award, NAACP, East St. Louis, IL (2018); Lifetime Achievement Award, St. Louis American Foundation (2014); Lifetime Achievement Award, New Salem Baptist Association (2014); Lifetime Achievement Award, City of St. Louis, IL (2013); Lifetime Achievement Award, East St. Louis Top Ladies of Distinction (2013); Distinguished Black Alumnus Award, St. Louis University (2013); Lifetime Achievement Life Membership Award, Kappa Delta Pi, International Honor Society in Education (2012); Inspiring St. Louisan Award, NAACP (2011); Aging Award, Southwest Region Agency (2011); Racial Harmony Community Service Award (2010); Phenomenon Woman Award, Center for Racial Harmony (2009); United Way Award (2008); Ageless-Remarkable St. Louisans Award, St. Andrew's Resources for Seniors System (2007); First Place Prize, National Federation of Press Women (2007); Remarkable St. Louisianian Award (2007); Eponym, East St. Louis Elementary School (2005); Liberty Bell Award, St. Clair County Bar Associates (2005); Award, St. Clair County Bar Association (2005); Quest Award, National Federation of Press Women (2004); Merit Award, Urban League (2002); Award, Illinois Office of Education (2002); Award, Eugene B. Redmond Writers Club (2002); Tri Del Globe Award (2001);

Pioneer Award, Mosque 28B (2000); Letters Award, Delta Sigma Theta Sorority, Inc. (2000); Inductee, Senior Illinoisan Hall of Fame (1997); Named, Distinguished Alumnus, University of Illinois (1996); Named, Citizen Ambassador, South Africa (1996); Named, Black Leader of the Year, National Council of Negro Women, Inc. (1995); Dr. Martin Luther King Jr. Award, Gateway East Metropolitan Ministry (1993); Mental Health Award, St. Clair County (1992); A World of Difference Award (1992); Journalism Award, Top Ladies of Distinction (1992); Media Award, Top Ladies of Distinction (1992); SIU-E-Kimmel Award (1991); Education Award, St. Louis, YWCA (1991); Spelman College Alumni Award (1990); Recipient, A World of Difference Award (1990); Named, Hall of Fame, Vashon High School (1989); Named, National Top Lady of the Year (1988); Named, Woman of the Year in Education, St. Clair County YWCA (1987); Recipient, Service Key Award, Phi Delta Kappa (1984); Recipient, Community Service Award, Metropolitan East Bar Association (1983); Recipient, Award, National Council of Negro Women, Inc. (1983); Girl Scout Thanks Badge (1982); Citation, Delta Sigma Theta Sorority, Inc. (1979); Named, Outstanding Administrator, Southern Region III Office of Education (1975); Named, Woman of Achievement, St. Louis Globe Democrat (1974); Illinois State Citation (1974); Outstanding Working Woman Award, Downtown St. Louis, Incorporated (1967); Lamp of Learning Award, East St. Louis Junior Wednesday Club (1965); Journalist Award, Sigma Gamma Rho Sorority; Recipient, More than 300 Awards **MEM:** Regional Vice President, American Library Trustees Association (1992); President, Top Ladies of Distinction (1987-1991); Chapter President, Phi Lambda Theta (1985-1987); Chapter President, Phi Delta Kappa (PDK International) (1984-1985); National Secretary, American Library Trustees Association (1979-1980); Regional Vice President, American Library Trustees Association (1978-1979); President, East St. Louis Women's Club (1973-1975); President, Southern Illinois University Chapter, Kappa Delta Pi, International Honor Society in Education (1973-1974); Chapter President, Delta Sigma Theta Sorority, Inc. (1960-1962); Iota Phi Lambda Sorority, Inc.; Illinois Commission on Children; Mensa; President's Commission on Excellence of Special Education, Council for Exceptional Children; President, Organizer, East St. Louis Parliamentarius **MH:** Albert Nelson Marquis Lifetime Achievement Award **AV:** Fashion; Reading **PA:** Republican

WRIGHT, LETITIA MICHELLE, T: Actress **I:** Media & Entertainment **DOB:** 10/31/1993 **SC:** Georgetown/Guyana **MS:** Single **ED:** Coursework, Identity School of Acting, London, England; Coursework, Duke's Aldridge Academy **CW:** Actress, "Death on the Nile" (2020); Actress, "Guava Island" (2019); Actress, "Avengers: Endgame" (2019); Actress, "Avengers: Infinity War" (2018); Actress, "Black Panther" (2018); Actress, "Ready Player One" (2018); Actress, "The Commuter" (2018); Guest Appearance, "Black Mirror" (2017); Actress, "Humans" (2016); Guest Appearance, "Doctor Who" (2015); Actress, "Cucumber" (2015); Actress, "Banana" (2015); Actress, "Urban Hymn" (2015); Guest Appearance, "Chasing Shadows" (2014); Actress, "Glasgow Girls" (2014); Guest Appearance, "Coming Up" (2013); Actress, "My Brother the Devil" (2012); Actress, "Victim" (2011); Actress, "Top Boy" (2011); Actress, TV Movie, "Random" (2011); Guest Appearance, "Holby City" (2011); Actress, "Small Axe"; Actress, "Hold Back the Stars" **AW:** Outstanding Performance by a Cast in a Motion Picture, "Black Panther," Screen Actors Guild Awards (2019); Outstanding Breakthrough Performance in a Motion Picture, "Black Panther,"

NAACP Image Awards (2019); Rising Star Award, British Academy Film Awards (2019); Choice Sci-Fi Movie Actress, "Black Panther," Teen Choice Awards (2018) **RE:** Christian

WRIGHT, ROBIN GALE, T: Actress, Producer, Director **I:** Media & Entertainment **DOB:** 04/08/1966 **PB:** Dallas **SC:** TX/USA **PT:** Fred Wright; Gayle (Gaston) Wright **MS:** Married **SPN:** Clement Giraudet (2018); Sean Penn (1996, Divorced 2010); Dane Witherspoon (1986, Divorced 1988) **CH:** Dylan Frances; Hopper Jack **C:** Actress, Producer, Director, Film and Television **CIV:** Co-partner, Pour Les Femmes and The Sunny Lion (2014); Honorary Spokesperson, The Gordie Foundation; Activist, Human Rights, Democratic Republic of the Congo; Advocate, Stand With Congo **CW:** Appearance, Documentary, "André the Giant" (2018); Executive Producer, Television Series, "House of Cards" (2016-2018); Director, Television Series, 10 Episodes, "House of Cards" (2014-2018); Actress, Television Series, "House of Cards" (2013-2018); Actress, Film, "Justice League" (2017); Director, Executive Producer, Short Film, "The Dark of Night" (2017); Actress, Film, "Blade Runner 2049" (2017); Actress, Film, "Wonder Woman" (2017); Actress, Film, "Everest" (2015); Executive Producer, Documentary, "When Elephants Fight" (2015); Actress, Film, "Everest" (2015); Narrator, Short Film, "Until We Could" (2014); Actress, Film, "A Most Wanted Man" (2014); Actress, Film, "The Congress" (2013); Actress, Film, "Adore" (2013); Producer, Film, "The Congress" (2013); Actress, Film, "The Girl with the Dragon Tattoo" (2011); Actress, Television Series, "Enlightened" (2011); Actress, Film, "Rampart" (2011); Actress, Film, "Moneyball" (2011); Actress, Video Short, "Behind the Carol: The Full Motion-Capture Experience" (2010); Actress, Film, "The Conspirator" (2010); Actress, Film, "A Christmas Carol" (2009); Actress, Film, "State of Play" (2009); Actress, Film, "The Private Lives of Pippa Lee" (2009); Actress, Film, "New York, I Love You" (2008); Voice Actress, Video Game, "The Princess Bride Game" (2008); Actress, Film, "What Just Happened" (2008); Actress, Film, "Beowulf" (2007); Executive Producer, Actress, Film, "Hounddog" (2007); Actress, Short Video, "Room 10" (2006); Actress, Film, "Breaking and Entering" (2006); Actress, Film, "Breaking and Entering" (2006); Actress, Film, "Sorry, Haters" (2005); Actress, Television Miniseries, "Empire Falls" (2005); Actress, Short Film, "Max" (2005); Actress, Film, "Nine Lives" (2005); Actress, Film, "A Home at the End of the World" (2004); Executive Producer, Actress, Film, "Virgin" (2003); Actress, Film, "The Singing Detective" (2003); Actress, Film, "White Oleander" (2002); Actress, Film, "The Last Castle" (2001); Actress, Film, "The Pledge" (2001); Actress, Film, "Unbreakable" (2000); Actress, Film, "How to Kill Your Neighbor's Dog" (2000); Actress, Film, "Message in a Bottle" (1999); Actress, Film, "Hurlyburly" (1998); Actress, Film, "She's So Lovely" (1997); Actress, Film, "Loved" (1997); Actress, Film, "Moll Flanders" (1996); Actress, Film, "The Crossing Guard" (1995); Actress, Film, "Forrest Gump" (1994); Actress, Film, "Toys" (1992); Actress, Film, "The Playboys" (1992); Actress, Film, "State of Grace" (1990); Actress, Film, "Denial" (1990); Actress, Television Series, "A TV Dante" (1989); Actress, Television Series, "Santa Barbara" (1984-1988); Actress, Television Film, "Home" (1987); Actress, Film, "The Princess Bride" (1987); Actress, Film, "Hollywood Vice Squad" (1986); Actress, Television Series, "The Yellow Rose" (1983-1984) **AW:** Named Best Actress in a Drama Series, "House of Cards," Gold Derby Awards (2016); Golden Globe for Best Performance by an Actress in a Supporting Role in a Motion Picture, "House of Cards," Hollywood Foreign Press Association (2014); Named One of the "100 Most Influential People in the World," Time Magazine (2014); Named Best Actress - Television Series Drama, "House of Cards," Satellite Awards (2013); Named Best Actress, "Nine Lives," Locarno International Film Festival (2005); Named Outstanding Heroine: Daytime, "Santa Barbara," Soap Opera Digest Awards (1988)

WRIGHT, RONALD, "RON" JACK, T: U.S. Representative from Texas **I:** Government Administration/Government Relations/Government Services **DOB:** 04/08/1953 **PB:** Jacksonville **SC:** TX/USA **MS:** Married **SPN:** Susan Wright **CH:** Three Children **ED:** Coursework, The University of Texas at Arlington **C:** Member, U.S. House of Representatives from Texas' Sixth Congressional District, United States Congress, Washington, DC (2019-Present); Tax Assessor, Tarrant County, Texas (2011-Present); Chief of Staff to Representative Joe Narton, U.S. House of Representatives, Washington, DC (2008-Present); Mayor Pro Tempore, Arlington, Texas (2004-2008); Council Member, Arlington, Texas (2000-2008); District Manager to Representative Joe Narton, U.S. House of Representatives, Washington, DC (2000-2008)

WU, CONSTANCE, T: Actress **I:** Media & Entertainment **DOB:** 03/22/1982 **PB:** Richmond **SC:** VA/USA **PT:** Fang-Sheng Wu **ED:** BFA in Acting, Conservatory of Theatre Arts, Purchase College, State University of New York (2005); Participant, Six-Month Program, Lee Strasberg Theatre and Film Institute **C:** Actress, Film and Television (2006-Present) **CIV:** Advocate, Miry's List (2017); Founding Supporter, Time's Up; Activist, Asian Representation in the U.S. Media **CW:** Actress, Film, "Low Budget Ethnic Movie" (2020); Voice Actress, Film, "Wish Dragon" (2020); Actress, Film, "I Was a Simple Man" (2020); Actress, Film, "Hustlers" (2019); Voice Actress, Film, "Next Gen" (2018); Actress, Film, "Crazy Rich Asians" (2018); Actress, Film, "All the Creatures Were Stirring" (2018); Voice Actress, Short Film, "Crow: The Legend" (2017); Voice Actress, Film, "The Lego Ninjago Movie" (2017); Actress, Film, "The Feels" (2017); Actress, Short Film, "Nine Minutes" (2017); Actress, Television Series, "Dimension 404" (2017); Actress, Television Series, "Royal Pains" (2016); Actress, Television Series, "Fresh Off the Boat" (2015-2018); Actress, Television Series, "Children's Hospital" (2015); Actress, Film, "Parallels" (2015); Actress, Television Series, "Franklin & Bash" (2014); Actress, Television Film, "High Moon" (2014); Actress, Television Series, "Spooked" (2014); Actress, Film, "Electric Slide" (2014); Director, Writer, Executive Producer, Composer, Short Film, "My Mother Is Not a Fish" (2013); Actress, Short Film, "Taylor Manifest" (2013); Actress, Video Short, "Ties" (2013); Actress, Television Film, "Deadly Revenge" (2013); Actress, Television Series, "Covert Affairs" (2013); Actress, Television Film, "Browsers" (2013); Actress, Film, "Best Friends Forever" (2013); Actress, Television Series, "Eastsiders" (2012-2017); Actress, Television Film, "Middle Ages" (2012); Actress, Television Film, "Watching TV with the Red Chinese" (2012); Actress, Television Series, "Torchwood" (2011); Actress, Film, "Sound of My Voice" (2011); Actress, Film, "Year of the Fish" (2007); Actress, Television Series, "One Life to Live" (2007); Actress, Television Series, "Law & Order: Special Victims Unit" (2006); Actress, Film, "The Architect" (2006); Actress, Film, "Stephanie Daley" (2006) **AW:** Nominee, Best Actress in a Motion Picture, Comedy/Musical, "Hustlers," Satellite Awards (2020); Nominee, Choice Comedy Movie Actress, "Crazy Rich Asians," Teen Choice Awards (2019); Nominee, Best Actress, "Crazy Rich Asians," Dublin Film Critics' Circle (2019); Nominee, Best Acting Ensemble,

"Crazy Rich Asians," Critics' Choice Movie Awards (2019); Nominee, Best Actress in a Comedy, Critics' Choice Movie Awards (2019); Nominee, Best Ensemble, "Crazy Rich Asians," Gold Derby Awards (2019); Nominee, Best Actress in a Motion Picture - Comedy or Musical, "Crazy Rich Asians," Golden Globe Award (2019); Nominee, Outstanding Ensemble Cast in a Motion Picture, "Crazy Rich Asians," NAACP Image Awards (2019); Nominee, Outstanding Actress in a Motion Picture, "Crazy Rich Asians," NAACP Image Awards (2019); Nominee, Best Actress - Comedy or Musical, "Crazy Rich Asians," Satellite Award (2019); Best Acting by an Ensemble, "Crazy Rich Asians," National Board of Review (2019); Outstanding Achievement in Cinema, "Crazy Rich Asians," 9th The Asian Awards (2019); Breakout Ensemble Award, "Crazy Rich Asians," Hollywood Film Awards (2018); Nominee, Best Ensemble, Detroit Film Critics Society (2018); Nominee, Critics' Choice Television Award for Best Actress in a Comedy Series, "Fresh Off the Boat," Critics' Choice Television Award (2018); Best Ensemble - Drama, "EastSiders," 7th Indie Series Awards (2016); Nominee, Best Supporting Actress - Drama, "EastSiders," 7th Indie Series Awards (2016); Female Breakout Star of the Year, "Fresh Off the Boat," Unforgettable Gala - Asian American Awards (2015); Best Ensemble - Drama, "EastSiders," Indie Series Award (2014)

WURF, MILDRED KIEFER, T: Executive (Retired) **DOB:** 09/01/1926 **PB:** San Francisco **SC:** CA/USA **PT:** Nicholas Joseph Kiefer; Luise Burgh Kiefer **MS:** Widowed **SPN:** Jerry Wurf (Deceased) **CH:** Nicholas; Abigail **ED:** All But Dissertation (ABD), Columbia University; AB, University of California Berkeley **C:** Educational Director, District Council 37, AFSCME, AFL-CIO; Director of Public Policy, Girls Inc.; Labor Program Manager, Affinity Group Marketing, Washington, DC; Director, President's Council on Youth Opportunity, Washington, DC **CR:** Commission on Youth Development Programs, U.S. Department of Labor (1975-2004); Co-founder, Chair, National Collaboration for Youth, National Human Services Assembly **MEM:** Cosmos Club **MH:** Albert Nelson Marquis Lifetime Achievement Award **B/I:** Mrs. Wurf had a teacher in junior high school who talked about social justice. She had the class read the newspaper every day. They had to make clear to the teacher that they were looking out for news about social justice. She grew up in San Francisco, California, and at that time, there was a lot of union activity. When Mrs. Wurf was in high school and college, she was always active and participated in the newspaper and debate team. She was a delegate to the founding meeting of the U.S. National Student Association (NSA) in Chicago. The major issues selected for action by the assembled delegates were to end segregation in education and increase academic freedom at their own schools and communities. As one of the few women elected to the NSA Executive Committee, she also served as chair of the California-Nevada-Hawaii region. She spent the next year in Madison, WI, working with elected NSA officers to develop the national organization. **PA:** Democrat **THT:** Mrs. Wurf started asking in 1975 whether or not there was gender equity in terms of federal funding in various programs. She called the Department of Labor because she knew that girls could not attend the Job Corps program, which was residential and six weeks long. Too many young women of 15 or 16 had to care for their younger siblings and they could not leave for that amount of time. Mrs. Wurf asked the Department of Labor, other than residential programs, what was the split in terms of money spent on programs for young men and young women. The Department of Labor spokesperson said it used to be

70/30, but now it was 60/40. But Congress passed a resolution that there ought to be an equal ratio, so the department's lawyers were looking up the meaning of the word "ratio." Mrs. Wurf also raised the question of gender equity with other funding sources, such as the United Way of America and philanthropic organizations, all of which also favored young boys and men in their funding.

WYDEN, RONALD, "RON" LEE, T: U.S. Senator from Oregon **I:** Government Administration/Government Relations/Government Services **CN:** U.S. Senate **DOB:** 05/03/1949 **PB:** Wichita **SC:** KS/USA **PT:** Peter H. Wyden; Edith (Rosenow) Wyden **MS:** Married **SPN:** Nancy (Bass) Wyden (2005); Laurie Oseran (1979, Divorced 1999) **CH:** Adam David; Lilly Anne; William Peter; Ava Rose; Scarlet Willa **ED:** Doctor of Jurisprudence, University of Oregon School of Law (1974); Bachelor of Arts in Political Science, Stanford University, with Distinction (1971); Coursework, University of Santa Barbara (1969) **C:** Ranking Member, Senate Committee on Finance (2015-Present); U.S. Senator, State of Oregon (1996-Present); Chairperson, U.S. Senate Committee on Finance (2014-2015); Chairperson, U.S. Senate Committee on Energy and Natural Resources (2013-2014); Member, U.S. House of Representatives from Oregon's Third Congressional District, United States Congress, Washington, DC (1981-1996); Instructor, Gerontology, University of Portland (1980); Instructor, Gerontology, Portland State University (1979); Director, Oregon Legal Services for the Elderly (1977-1979); Instructor of Gerontology, University of Oregon (1976); Campaign Aide to Senator Wayne Morse, U.S. Senate (1972, 1974); Co-founder, Co-director, Oregon Gray Panthers (1974-1980) **CIV:** Member, Oregon Environmental Council **CW:** Contributor, Articles to Professional Journals **AW:** Named, One of the 50 Most Important People on the Web, PC World (2007); Champion of Science Award, University of Oregon/The Science Coalition (2003); Named, Legislative of the Year, Information Technology Industry Council (2000); Named, with Representative Christopher Cox, People of the Year, PC Computing Magazine (1999); Philip A. Hart Public Service Award, Consumer Federation of America (1999); Senator of the Year, National Association of Police Organizations (1997); Significant Service Award, Multnomah County Area Agency on Aging (1980); Named, Young Man of the Year, Oregon Junior Chamber of Commerce (1980); Citizen of the Year Award, Oregon Association of Social Workers (1979); Service to Oregon Consumers Award, Oregon Consumers League (1978); Inductee, Legislators Hall of Fame, American Electronics Association **MEM:** American Bar Association; Iowa State Bar Association; Oregon Bar Association **BAR:** State of Oregon (1975) **PA:** Democrat **RE:** Jewish

WYNN, AISHA CORPAS, T: President **I:** Media & Entertainment **CN:** A Wynn Wynn Production **PT:** Enrique Corpus; Beverly Barnett **MS:** Married **SPN:** Daniel Wynn **ED:** Bachelor of Arts in Film, University of California Santa Barbara, Cum Laude **C:** Executive Producer, A Wynn Wynn Production (2015-Present); Executive Producer, Snapchat (2020); Event Producer, Cartoon Network (2018-2019); Sr. Digital Producer, Disney ABC Television Group (2017); Producer, Food Network (2017); Executive Producer and Director, Pitch 5 Productions, Inc. (2016-2017); Showrunner and Co-Executive Producer, HBO (2016); Producer, Black Entertainment Television (BET) (2016); Event Producer, ITK Hollywood Experience (2015); Producer, Fox Broadcast Network (2015); Head of Production, Four Henrys Productions (2010-2014); Co-Executive Producer, VH1 (2013); Co-Executive Producer and Sr. Field Producer, A&E Television Networks (2012); Co-Executive Producer, OWN: The Oprah Winfrey Network (2011); Casting Producer, Lifetime Television (2011); Director of Development, Robyn Nash Productions (2007-2009); Development Coordinator, New Line Cinema (2003-2007) **CIV:** Los Angeles Home Building Volunteer, Habitat for Humanity International; Sponsor, SOS Children's Villages; Volunteer, Junior Board Member, After School All-stars; Reader Volunteer, Reading to Kids; Guest Speaker, Youth Business Alliance; Volunteer, Food Forward; Volunteer, My Friend's Place **CW:** Speaker, Academy of Television Arts and Science; Speaker, Walter Kaitz's Hollywood Creative Forum; Speaker, The Youth Business Alliance; Speaker, New Line Cinema Diversity in Arts; Co-Founder, The ITK Hollywood Summit **MEM:** Television Academy; Black Women Animate Organization **AS:** Ms. Wynn attributes her success to her drive, belief and faith. Being a young female of diversity, she has always upheld these values. She didn't initially realize that she was pursuing a predominantly male industry, though she noticed early on. As a result, she was encouraged to always believe in herself. Throughout her career, she had many strong mentors as well. Because of her positive experience with them, she now tries to act as a mentor to young people entering the industry. **B/I:** Ms. Wynn attended a performing arts high school, which is where she became involved with the theater department. She wanted to document everything going on behind the scenes with the school theater program. When she told her parents about this, they graciously bought her a video camera and an editor to help her produce a short film. After it was completed, her film earned overwhelmingly positive reviews from students and faculty at the school. This experience was enlightening for Ms. Wynn, as she realized what she wanted to do for the rest of her life. **AV:** Dance; Aerobics and fitness; Cooking healthy meals

WYNN, STANFORD ALAN, T: Lawyer **I:** Law and Legal Services **DOB:** 05/09/1950 **PB:** Milwaukee **SC:** WI/USA **PT:** Sherburn Wynn; Marjory (Tarrant) Wynn **MS:** Married **SPN:** Penny Wynn **ED:** LLM in Taxation, University of Miami (1976); JD, Case Western Reserve University (1975); BBA, University of Wisconsin, Milwaukee (1972) **CT:** RR (Registered Representative), National Association of Securities Dealers (Now FINRA); ChFC® (Chartered Financial Consultant®), The American College of Financial Services (1983); CLU® (Chartered Life Underwriter®), The American College of Financial Services (1981) **C:** Director, Advanced Planning, The Northwestern Mutual Life insurance Company, Milwaukee, WI (1978-2015); Associate, Walsh and Simon, Milwaukee, WI (1976-1978) **CR:** Represented, The Northwestern Mutual Life Insurance Company on the Life Insurance Management Research Association (LIMRA) Advanced Sales Committee; Represented, The Northwestern Mutual Life Insurance Company on the American Council of Life Insurance Companies(ACLI) Task Force Committee on Equity Split-dollar; National Speaker, Advanced Planning Seminars, The Northwestern Mutual Life Insurance Company; National Speaker, National Annual Meeting, American Bar Association; National Speaker, Estate Planning Councils, Various States; National Speaker, Advanced Sales Conferences, Life Insurance Management Research Association; Speaker, Conferences, Northwestern Mutual **CIV:** Board of Directors, Waukesha County Estate Planning Council (1985-1986); Board Member, Jewish National Fund for the Wisconsin Region; Board Member, Anshe Sfard Kehillat Torah, Glendale, WI; Board Member, Ovation Chai Point, Milwaukee, WI; Board Member, Ohr HaTorah Jewish Heritage Center, Glendale, WI

CW: Consulting Editor, "The Insurance Counselor-The Irrevocable Life Insurance Trust," Real Estate, Probate and Trust Law Section, American Bar Association (1995); Author, "The Insurance Counselor-Split-Dollar Insurance," Real Estate, Probate and Trust Law Section, American Bar Association (1991); Author, The Northwestern Mutual Guide to Split-Dollar (1991); Author, Numerous Articles and Pieces for Northwestern Mutual on Various Estate, Business and Personal Legal and Tax Topics **AW:** Case Western Reserve Law Review; Inductee, The Honor Society of Phi Kappa Phi; Inductee, Beta Gamma Sigma; Dean's List, University of Wisconsin-Milwaukee; Inductee, National Honor Society, John Marshall High School (Now Milwaukee Marshall High School), Milwaukee Public Schools, Milwaukee, WI; Eagle Scout, Boys Scouts of America **MEM:** State Bar of Wisconsin; The Florida Bar; American Bar Association **BAR:** States of Florida (1976); Wisconsin (1975) **MH:** Albert Nelson Marquis Lifetime Achievement Award **AS:** Mr. Wynn attributes his success to being dedicated, being competent, being honest and ethical, enjoying and being passionate in what one does, doing the right thing, enjoying working with one's associates, and striving to be better. **B/I:** At a young age, Mr. Wynn wanted to be an attorney and in particular a tax attorney. He received positive reinforcement from his parents, Sherburn and Marjory Wynn, and his grandmother, Goldie Tarrant. While he was attending the University of Wisconsin-Milwaukee, he took a tax accounting course that further sparked his interest in taxes. While in law school at Case Western Reserve, one of his professors, Leon Gabinet, inspired him and cemented his idea to pursue his interest in tax law. Mr Wynn then continued his pursuit of tax law by obtaining a LL.M in Taxation at the University of Miami School of Law.After Mr. Wynn practiced law for about two years, establishing and amending tax qualified employee benefit plans to comply under the Employee Retirement Income Security Act (ERISA) and working on other legal matters at a local Milwaukee law firm of Walsh and Simon, he then accepted an offer to be in the Advanced Planning area at the Home Office of The Northwestern Mutual Life Insurance Company located in Milwaukee, WI. That position offered him the unique opportunity to apply his tax and legal knowledge in many different types of planning areas involving business, estate, personal and employee benefit planning. He applied this knowledge when he assisted Northwestern Mutual's Financial Representatives in the sale of life, annuity disability, and long term care products as well as when he was working on various projects for or on behalf of the company. Mr. Wynn enjoyed communicating effective and practical solutions in a changing legal and tax environment by providing valuable information with creative and sound planning ideas in his role in the Advanced Planning area. He found satisfaction knowing that individuals could obtain increased financial security for their families and businesses when establishing a sound financial plan. Throughout his career at Northwestern Mutual, he found his work interesting, meaningful, challenging and rewarding. Mr. Wynn was grateful that he had the opportunity to spend 37 years of his career being apart of an outstanding, well-run, highly respected and highly financially rated company that is a leader in the financial and insurance industry. **AV:** Swimming; Walking; Reading about tax, financial, economic and legal topics; Current news events; Studying Torah; Being with friends and family **RE:** Jewish

XIE, RUI-HUA, PHD, T: Physicist, Researcher, Engineer **I:** Engineering **DOB:** 09/21/1969 **PB:** Ganxian, Jiangxi **SC:** China **PT:** Xiangan Xie;

Yuying Yang **MS:** Married **SPN:** Qin Rao **CH:** Jianing; Calvin **ED:** Postdoctoral Coursework, University of Toronto (1998); PhD, Nanjing University (1996); Master of Engineering, Wuhan University (1993); BS, Wuhan University (1991) **C:** Principal Firmware Engineer, Flowserve Co., Houston, TX (2014-Present); Principal Software/Firmware Engineer, Arbini Instruments, College Station, TX (2007-2014); Research Scientist, Texas A&M University, College Station, TX (2004-2006); Guest Researcher, National Institute of Standards and Technology (NIST), Gaithersburg, MD (2001-2004); Teaching Research Assistant, Queen's University, Ontario, Canada (2000-2001); Alexander von Humboldt Fellow, Max-Planck Institute, Gottingen, Germany (1998-2000); Researcher, University of Toronto, Ontario, Canada (1997-1998); Researcher, CCAST, Beijing, China (1996-1997); Research Assistant, Nanjing University (1993-1996); Research Assistant, Wuhan University (1991-1993) **CW:** Contributor, Articles to Professional Journals; Editor-in-chief, Journal of Computational and Theoretical Nanoscience **MEM:** American Chemical Society; American Physical Society; Sigma Xi, The Scientific Research Honor Society **MH:** Albert Nelson Marquis Lifetime Achievement Award **AV:** Stamp collecting/philately

XIONG, PAHOUA ZUAGPAAJ MOUA, T: Manager **I:** Retail/Sales **CN:** Walmart Stores, Inc. **DOB:** 09/22/1976 **PB:** Ban Vinai **SC:** Thailand **PT:** George Joua Chong Moua; Lina Phoua Kong Moua **MS:** Married **SPN:** Tousu Saydangnmvang Xiong **CH:** Chivkeeb Genesis Toupa Xiong, Naamonunas Ruth, Nujsimloob Hebrews, Nkaujzuapaaj Esther, Naomi Mayvang, Psalm Ntawvnkauj, Eve Nkaujab, Johnny Tshwmsim, Abraham Loojceeb Toupa Xiong **ED:** BS in Business Administration, California State University of Fresno, Fresno, CA (2000); Diploma, Clovis West High School, Clovis, CA (1995) **CT:** Certified in Food and Health Sanitation, Sacramento, CA (2006-Present); Certified in Life and Health Insurance, Sacramento, CA (2009-2013) **C:** Co-manager, Walmart Stores, Incorporated, Fresno, CA (2018-Present); Assistant Manager, Walmart Stores, Incorporated, CA (2012-Present); Zone Merchandise Supervisor, CA (2010-2012); Health Life Insurance Agent, Insphere Insurance Solutions (2009-2010); Store Manager, Walmart Stores, Incorporated (2007-2009); Sales Associate, Supervisor, Stockholder, Walmart Stores, Incorporated, Florida and Minnesota (1998-2006); Branch Manager, AKE Fire Safety Equipment, Incorporated, Florida (1997-1998) **CIV:** Volunteer, Community Food Bank, Fresno, CA (2018-Present); Troop Leader, Girl Scouts, Troop 5041, Naomi Xiong, Girl Scouts of Central California, Clovis, CA (2018-Present); Cheerleader Supporter, Esther Xiong, Sierra Vista Elementary, Clark Intermediate, Clovis High School, Clovis, CA (2015-Present) **CW:** Summer Mirage Arts Project, City Park, Visalia, CA (1989) **AW:** Walmart Rising Star Management Recruitment Achievement Award, Dallas, TX (2001); California Fellowship and Federal Grant Scholarship (1995-1996) **MEM:** Family Alliance Church, Fresno, CA (2006-Present); Youth Ministry, Hmong Alliance Church, Christian and Missionary Alliance, Hmong District, Visalia, CA (1980-Present) **AS:** Ms. Xiong attributes her success to her husband Tousu for support and help taking care of the children, and family for being there and supporting her. Also, she credits the many associates that she works with in her company. They are like her family away from home. There is a lot of support and team work in her work environment. **B/I:** Ms. Xiong's parents were her inspiration. Her desire to make them proud and live the American dream as immigrants to this country was her goal. Also, her children are her biggest motivation. She wants to show them to strive to always do better and help others. Ms. Xiong tried out various different jobs to see where she would fit in to make a career. When she finally moved to Florida, she received an opportunity with Walmart. Walmart was her first job in retail and she has found much success there. **AV:** Reading; Playing bass for church music band

XU, TONY, T: Co-Founder, Chief Executive Officer **I:** Business Management/Business Services **CN:** DoorDash **SC:** China **ED:** MBA, Stanford Graduate School of Business (2013); BS, Industrial Engineering and Operations Research, University of California Berkeley, With High Honors (2007) **C:** Co-Founder, Chief Executive Officer, DoorDash, Palo Alto, CA (2013-Present); Associate, Matrix Partners, Palo Alto, CA (2011-2013); Intern, International, Square, San Francisco, CA (2012); Head of Business Development, RedLaser (eBay Mobile), eBay (2011); Associate, Corporate Strategy, eBay and PayPal (2009-2011); Business Analyst, McKinsey & Company (2007-2009) **AW:** Arjay Miller Scholar, Stanford Graduate School of Business

YAMAUCHI, EDWIN M., PHD, T: History Professor Emeritus **I:** Education/Educational Services **DOB:** 02/01/1937 **PB:** Hilo **SC:** HI/USA **PT:** Shokyo Yamauchi; Haruko (Owan) Yamauchi Higa **MS:** Married **SPN:** Kimie Honda (08/31/1962) **CH:** Brian; Gail Haruko **ED:** Fellowship, Institute for Advanced Christian Studies (1974-1975); Research Fellowship, American Institute of Holy Land Studies, Jerusalem University College (1968); Fellowship, National Endowment for the Humanities (1968); Fellowship, Rutgers Research Council (1966-1965); PhD in Mediterranean Studies, Brandeis University (1964); Fellowship, National Defense for Language (1962-1964); Coursework, Summer Institute of New East Languages (1962); MA in Mediterranean Studies, Brandeis University (1962); Fellowship, Brandeis University (1961-1962); Coursework, Summer Institute of Linguistics (1961); Coursework, Summer Institute of Archaeology (1960); BA in Hebrew and Hellenistics, Shelton College (1960); Coursework, University of Hawai'i (1957-1958); Coursework, Columbia Bible College (1955-1956) **C:** Professor, Department of History, Miami University, Oxford, Ohio (1973-2005); Director of Graduate Studies, Miami University, Oxford, Ohio (1978-1982); Associate Professor, Miami University, Oxford, Ohio (1969-1973); Assistant Professor, Rutgers, The State University of New Jersey, New Brunswick, NJ (1964-1969); Graduate Assistant, Brandeis University, Waltham, MA (1962-1963); Instructor of Greek Language, Shelton College, Ringwood, NJ (1960-1961) **CR:** Director, Seminar on Archaeology, National Endowment for the Humanities (1983); Abstractor, New Testament Abstracts (1966-1970); With, Excavations at Jerusalem (1968); Abstractor, Religious and Theological Abstracts (1965-1967); Peer Reviewer, National Endowment for the Humanities; Consultant, "ABC World News" **CIV:** Monthly Speaker, Knolls Nursing Home (2008-Present); Elder, Oxford Bible Fellowship (1980-2017); Co-founder, Oxford Bible Fellowship (1970) **CW:** Editorial Board, Bulletin of the Near East Archaeological Society (1998-Present); Consulting Editor, Christianity Today (1994-Present); Editorial Board, Fides et Historia (1981-Present); Editor, "Dictionary of Daily Life in Biblical and Post-biblical Iniquity" (2017); Author, "Africa and the Bible" (2004); Editor, "Africa and Africans in Antiquity" (2001); Editorial Committee, Journal of the Evangelical Theological Society (1983-2000); Editorial Committee, Bulletin for Biblical Research (1991-1995); Editorial Board, Bulletin of the Institute for Biblical Research (1991-1995);

Senior Editor, Christianity Today (1992-1994); Author, "Persia and the Bible" (1990); Consulting Editor, Journal of the American Scientific Affiliation (1970-1983); Author, "Foes from the North Frontier" (1982); Author, "World of the First Christians" (1981); Author, "Pre-Christian Gnosticism" (1973); Papers Presented at 91 Learned Societies; Delivered 141 Lectures, Multiple Universities; Contributor, Chapters to 38 Books; Contributor, 177 Articles in 38 Reference Works; Contributor, 104 Articles in 59 Journals; Contributor, 111 Reviews in 27 Journals; Author, Books **AW:** Research and Travel Grantee, Miami University (1970-1971, 1972); Grantee, American Philosophical Society (1970) **MEM:** President, Near East Archaeological Society (2007-2013); President, The Evangelical Theological Society (2005-2006); President, Midwest Branch, American Oriental Society (2003-2004); President, Institute for Biblical Research (1987-1989); Chair, Institute for Biblical Research (1984-1986); President, American Science Affiliation (ASA) (1983); President, Conference on Faith & History (1974-1976); Chapter President, Archaeological Institute of America (1973-1974); Fellow, American Science Affiliation (ASA); American Oriental Society; Institute for Biblical Research; Conference on Faith & History; Near East Archaeological Society; Archaeological Institute of America; The Evangelical Theological Society **MH:** Albert Nelson Marquis Lifetime Achievement Award **B/I:** Dr. Yamauchi chose the "dramatic conversion to Christ" at the age of 15, which led him to study the Bible. His studies led him further to learn Greek and Hebrew language and writing. His initial goal was to become a missionary to the Japanese in Brazil. After even more intense study of the Bible, he decided that he would pursue graduate school at Brandeis University. Brandeis is a Jewish university, where Yamauchi was able to study under a world renowned biblical scholar named Cyrus Gordon. Under the direction of Mr. Gordon, Dr. Yamauchi began his career as an academic and became fully immersed in his historical studies. **RE:** Christian

YARATHA, SRIDHAR, MD, T: Psychiatrist **I:** Medicine & Health Care **CN:** RVA Recovery, LLP **SC:** Anantapur/India **MS:** Married **ED:** Resident in Internal Medicine, Psychiatry, Charleston Area Medical Center, West Virginia University, Charleston, WV (1996-2001); MD, Spartan Health Sciences University School of Medicine, Vieux Fort, St. Lucia (1995); BA in Psychology, Austin College, Sherman, Texas (1991) **CT:** Certification, American Board of Psychiatry and Neurology, Inc.; Licensed, Commonwealth of Virginia **C:** Private Practice, Part-time Outpatient Adult Psychiatry, Richmond, VA (2015-Present); Attending Psychiatrist, Outpatient Adult Psychiatry, Gateway Homes, Chesterfield, VA (2008-Present); Acting Chief of Mental Health Service, Chief of Mental Health Service Administrative Duties, Hunter Holmes McGuire VA Medical Center, Richmond, VA (2018); Assistant Chief of Mental Health Service, Assistant Chief of Mental Health Service in Administrative Duties, Hunter Holmes McGuire VA Medical Center, Richmond, VA (2018); Medical Director, Inpatient Psychiatry, Attending Psychiatrist, Hunter Holmes McGuire VA Medical Center, Richmond, VA (2016-2018); Associate Professor in Psychiatry, Virginia Commonwealth University School of Medicine, Richmond, VA (2016-2018); Forensic Psychiatrist, Central State Hospital, Petersburg, VA (2006-2016); Psychiatrist for Geriatrics Unit, Southwestern Virginia Mental Health Institute, Marion, VA (2004-2005); Contract Psychiatric Work, QTC Medical Management, Inc., Virginia Beach, VA (2004); Staff Psychiatrist, Outpatient Geriatric and Adult Psychiatry, Vera French Community Mental Health Center, Daven-

port, Iowa (2001-2003); Staff Psychiatrist, Thomas Memorial Hospital, Paycare Inc., South Charleston, WV (1999-2001) **CR:** Medical Director, Inpatient Psychiatry, Attending Physician for Inpatient Unit, Hunter Holmes McGuire VA Medical Center, Richmond, VA (2016-2018); Associate Professor in Psychiatry, Virginia Commonwealth University School of Medicine, Richmond, VA (2016-2018); Forensic Review Panel Member, Commonwealth of Virginia Appointment by Commissioner of Department of Behavioral Health and Development Services (DBHDS) (2007-2016); Staff Psychiatrist, Men's Chronic Mental Health Unit, Central State Hospital, Petersburg, VA (2006-2016); Physician for Geriatrics Unit, Southwestern Virginia Mental Health Institute, Marion, VA (2004-2005); Staff Psychiatrist, Genesis Medical Center, Davenport, Iowa (2001-2003); Staff Psychiatrist, Thomas Memorial Hospital, South Charleston, WV (1999-2001) **CIV:** Board Member, India Association of Virginia; President, Homeowner Association; Board Member, School Board **CW:** Lecturer, Numerous Seminars and Lectures (1999-2017); Author, Researcher, Numerous Publications (1992-2001) **AW:** Teaching Award, Department of Psychiatry, Virginia Commonwealth University School of Medicine Class of 2018 (2018); Teaching Award, Virginia Commonwealth University Health Systems Psychiatry Resident (2016-2017); Esther McMahon Award, Psychiatry Resident of the Year (2001); Resident of the Year Award, Pfizer, Inc. (2001); Teaching Award in Psychiatry (1999); Ranked Top Quarter of Medical School Class **MEM:** American Society of Addiction Medicine; American Psychiatric Association; American Medical Association **AS:** Dr. Yarantha attributes his success to his love of service. **B/I:** Dr. Yarantha became involved in his profession because of his love for inpatient, outpatient, and geriatric work. He likes to be someone who can take care of anyone from young to geriatric and from depression to chronic schizophrenia. He is more drawn to people struggling with substance abuse because he is in recovery himself; he has been sober for 14 and a half years and uses his strength to help others struggling to recover.

YARBOROUGH, WILLIAM CALEB, T: Race Car Driver (Retired) **I:** Athletics **DOB:** 03/27/1939 **PB:** Timmonsville **SC:** SC/USA **PT:** Julian Yarborough; Annie Yarborough **MS:** Married **SPN:** Betty Jo Thigpen (1962) **CH:** Julie; Kelley; B.J. **C:** Owner, NASCAR Winston Cup Series Team, Cale Yarborough Motorsports (1987-2000); Owner, Driver, No. 29 Oldsmobile Delta 88, Oldsmobile Cutlass Supreme, Race Hill Farm Team (Renamed Cale Yarborough Motorsports) (1987-1989); Driver, NASCAR Cup Series, Firecracker 400 (1986); Driver, NASCAR Cup Series, Daytona 500 (1984); Driver, No. 28 Hardee's Chevrolet for Ranier-Lundy, 16 Events (1983); Driver, 16 Races (1982); Driver, 18 Races, No. 27 Valvoline Buick for M.C. Anderson (1981); Driver, Junior Johnson Team, Rockingham, Bristol, MI, Texas, Atlanta, GA (1980); Driver, Junior Johnson Team, NASCAR Cup Series, Southern 500 (1978, 1974, 1973); Driver, Junior Johnson Team, NASCAR Cup Series, Daytona 500 (1977); Driver for the Wood Brothers, NASCAR Cup Series, NASCAR Winston Cup, Michigan 400, American 500 (1970); Driver, NASCAR Cup Series, Daytona 500, Atlanta 500, NASCAR Race, Michigan International Speedway, Motor State 500 (1967-1969); Driver, Vollstedt-Fords, Indianapolis 500 (1966, 1967); Driver, No. 21 Ford for the Wood Brothers (1966); Driver for Banjo Matthews (1966); Driver for Numerous Owners (1965); Driver, No. 19 Ford for Herman Beam (1963); Driver, Daytona 500 Qualifying Race (1962); Driver, NASCAR Cup Series, Southern 500 (1961); Driver, Southern States Fairgrounds (1960); Driver, No. 30 Pontiac for Bob Weatherly, NASCAR

Cup Series, Southern 500 (1957) **CR:** Owner, Cale Yarborough Honda/Mazda, Florence, SC; Owner, Goodyear Tire Distributorship; Owner, Numerous Dry Cleaning Businesses **CW:** Appearance, Television Series Documentary, "30 for 30" (2019); Appearance, Television Series Documentary, "Jim McKay: My World in My Words" (2003); Co-author, Book, "Cale: The Hazardous Life and Times of the World's Greatest Stock Car Driver" (1986); Appearance, Television Series, "Dukes of Hazzard" (1979, 1984); Actor, Film, "Stroker Ace" (1983); Appearance, Film, "Speedway" (1968); Featured, Cover Story, Sports Illustrated; Appearance, Numerous Documentaries **AW:** Inductee, South Carolina Hall of Fame (2013); Inductee, NASCAR Hall of Fame (2012); Recognition as "One of NASCAR's 50 Greatest Drivers" (1998); Inductee, Court of Legends, Charlotte Motor Speedway (1996); Inductee, Talladega Walk of Fame (1996); Inductee, National Motorsports Press Association (NMPA) Hall of Fame (1994); Inductee, Motorsports Hall of Fame of America (1994); Inductee, International Motorsports Hall of Fame (1993); Inductee, South Carolina Athletic Hall of Fame (1978); Winston Cup Champion (1976, 1977, 1978); Named the National Motorsports Press Association Driver of the Year (1976, 1977, 1978); Named American Driver of the Year (1977); Named "Most Popular Driver," Grand National Series (1967)

YARBROUGH, DAVID WYLIE, PHD, PE, T: 1) Vice President 2) Professor Emeritus **I:** Engineering **CN:** 1) R & D Services, Inc. 2) Tennessee Tech University **DOB:** 05/07/1937 **PB:** Long Beach **SC:** CA/USA **PT:** Wylie Clyde Yarbrough; Inez Beatrice (Crain) Yarbrough **MS:** Married **SPN:** Donna J. **CH:** Michael; Cynthia **ED:** PhD, Georgia Institute of Technology (1966); MS, Georgia Institute of Technology (1961); Bachelor in Chemical Engineering, Georgia Institute of Technology (1960) **CT:** Registered Professional Engineer, States of Tennessee and Florida **C:** Vice President, R & D Services, Inc. (2011-Present); Professor Emeritus, Tennessee Tech University, Cookeville, TN (1980-Present); President, R & D Services, Inc. (1994-2011); Part-time Research Staff, Oak Ridge National Laboratory, TN (1980-2011); Chairman and Professor of Chemical Engineering, Tennessee Tech University, Cookeville, TN (1987-2002); Member, Research Staff, Oak Ridge National Laboratory (1979-1980); Professor, Tennessee Tech University, Cookeville, TN (1980-1987); Associate Dean, Professor, Tennessee Tech University, Cookeville, TN (1976-1979); Associate Professor, Tennessee Tech University, Cookeville, TN (1971-1976); Assistant Professor of Chemical Engineering, Tennessee Tech University, Cookeville, TN (1968-1971) **MIL:** With, United States Army Reserve (1960-1987); Retired Lieutenant Colonel, United States Army Reserve (SIGC) **CW:** Editorial Board, Journal of Thermal Insulation and Building Envelopes (1992-Present); Editorial Board, Journal of Building Physics (1992-Present); Editor, "Thermal Conductivity 19" (1988); Contributor, Articles to Professional Journals; Contributor, 250 Publications and Presentations, Various Technical Areas **AW:** College Outstanding Faculty Award (1990); University Research Award (1987); University Sigma Xi Research Award (1983); Fellow, ASTM C16; Award of Appreciation, ASTM; Fellow, Tennessee Academy of Science; Fellow, International Thermal Conductivity Conference (ITCC); Thermal Conductivity Award, International Thermal Conductivity Conference (ITCC) **MEM:** Conference Governing Board, International Thermal Conductivity Conference (ITCC) (1988-Present); Fellow, President, Tennessee Academy of Science (1986); Chairman, Subcommittee C16.21, American Society for Testing and Materials (ASTM) (1985-1996); Fellow, Conference Governing Board, International Thermal Conductivity Conference (ITCC); Fellow, Tennessee Academy of Sciences; Fellow, American Society for Testing and Materials (ASTM); American Institute of Chemical Engineers; The Tau Beta Pi Association, Inc.; The Honor Society of Phi Kappa Phi; Pi Mu Epsilon; American Society for Heating, Refrigerating, and Air Conditioning Engineering (ASHRAE) **MH:** Marquis Lifetime Achievement Award **B/I:** Dr. Yarbrough became involved in his profession due to an early interest in science, mathematics, chemistry and chemical phenomena. **AV:** Antique automobiles **RE:** Methodist

YARBROUGH, ROSE MARIE POWERS SOMRATY, T: Geologist, Environmental Science Secondary Teacher, Software Programmer Analyst, Quality Assurance GS 12 at DoD **I:** Sciences **CN:** Geo-Technical Associates **DOB:** 08/08/1936 **PB:** Fairmont City **SC:** IL/USA **PT:** John Somraty; Gertrude Estelle (Scotchie) Powers **MS:** Widow **SPN:** Ronald E. Yarbrough (07/23/1977, Deceased 2015); James John Chiste Sr. (06/27/1957, Divorced 1974) **CH:** Fredric Michael Somraty Metzger; James John Somraty Chiste Jr; Deanna Marie Chiste; Maria Somraty Chiste (Deceased) **ED:** BA in Earth Science and Environmental Sciences, Southern Illinois University, Edwardsville, IL, Magna Cum Laude **C:** Executive Vice President, Geo-Technical Associates Inc., Collinsville, IL, (1987-Present); Cartographer, Quality Assurance Manager, Defense Mapping Agency Aerospace Center, St. Louis (1984-1987); Cartographer, Programmer Analyst, Defense Mapping Agency Aerospace Center, St. Louis (1980-1984); Teacher, Secondary Education Earth Science, Fort Zumwalt School District, O'Fallon, Missouri (1978-1980); Teacher, Secondary Education Earth Science, Ferguson Florissant School District, St. Louis (1974-1978); Supervisor, Student Union Operations, Southern Illinois University, Edwardsville (1964-1970); Bookkeeper, Secretary, Clerk for Various Companies (1955-1964); School Principal Employer, Cafeteria Service, Highland High School, Illinois (1953) **CR:** Board Member, Greater St. Louis Gateway Chapter, International Association of Quality Circles, St. Louis, MO (1984-Present); Consultant, Illinois State Office, Landfill Project, Edwardsville, IL (1973) **CIV:** Anderson Hospital, Edwardsville (1969); Board of Directors, Prelude Civic Ballet Company, Collinsville, IL (1969); School Bond Issues, Edwardsville, IL (1968); Funding Committee, Youth Men's Christian Association (YMCA) **MIL:** Department of Defense, Aerospace Center, Saint Louis, MO **CW:** Co-Author, "Association of America Geologists Field Manual," Physical Regions of the American Bottoms (1972) **AW:** Certificate of Recognition for Service (1991); National Phi Beta Kappa Award; Numerous Awards, United States Department of Defense; Inductee, Honor Society of Phi Kappa Phi **MEM:** 50th Anniversary Committee Festival (2000); American Society of Quality Control; Association of Quality & Participation; Geological Society of America; Southern Illinois Alumni Association; Southern Illinois University Geography Club; Media Club; People to People International Club; Gamma Theta Upsilon; Gamma Sigma Sigma; Advisor, Board Member, Center for Spirituality and Sustainability; St Clair County Genealogical Society **MH:** Albert Nelson Marquis Lifetime Achievement Award; Marquis Who's Who Top Professional **B/I:** Ms. Yarbrough became involved in her profession because she always thought she would become an artist or a psychologist. When she returned to school as an adult with a family, she took a geoscience course and fell in love with it. She also fell in love with bio-science, which led her to fall in love with genealogy as well. Mrs. Yarbrough began working at Southern Illinois University, as she had always loved to learn and was exposed to intellectuals that saw potential in her. A staff member recommended that she take a class. Previously, she had never considered such schooling. She then enrolled in an English class and went on to receive a four-year scholarship after applying. **AV:** Researching history and genealogy; Playing bridge; Practicing photography; Traveling; Dancing ballet; Exploring psychology; Practicing religion **PA:** Independent **RE:** Christian

YARMUTH, JOHN ALLAN, T: U.S. Representative from Kentucky; Former Newspaper Editor **I:** Government Administration/Government Relations/Government Services **DOB:** 11/04/1947 **PB:** Louisville **SC:** KY/USA **PT:** Stanley Robert Yarmuth; Edna Elaine (Klein) Yarmuth **MS:** Married **SPN:** Catherine Elizabeth (Creedon) Yarmuth (1981) **CH:** Stanley Aaron **ED:** BA in American Studies, Yale University (1969); Coursework, Georgetown University Law Center **C:** Chairman, U.S. House Committee of Budget (2019-Present); Member, U.S. House Committee on Ethics (2011-Present); Member, U.S. House of Representatives from Kentucky's Third Congressional District, United States Congress, Washington, DC (2007-Present); Ranking Democrat, U.S. House Committee of Budget (2017-2019); With, Public Relations and Marketing, Caretenders Healthcorp (1986-1990); Assistant Vice President, University Relations, University of Louisville, KY (1983-1986); Legislative Assistant to Senator Marlow Cook, U.S. Senate, Washington, DC (1971-1975); Stockbroker, Stein Brothers & Boyce, Louisville, KY (1969-1970) **CR:** Founder, President, Center for Kentucky Progress **CIV:** Board of Directors, Louisville Eccentric Observer (2003-2006); Founder, Executive Editor, Louisville Eccentric Observer (1990-2003); Board of Directors, Station WKPC-TV, Louisville, KY (1983-1988); Board of Directors, Louisville School of Art (1980-1983); Board of Regents, Northern Kentucky University, Highland Heights, KY (1980-1983); Board of Directors, Better Business Bureau, Louisville, KY (1979-1985); Board of Regents, Planned Parenthood Louisville Forum; Board of Regents, Jewish Community Center **CW:** Guest Appearance, "The Colbert Report" (2007); Guest Appearance, "Hot Button" (2004-2005); Host, Radio Talk Show, "Yarmuth & Ziegler," WAVE 3 TV (2003); Publisher, Louisville Today Magazine (1976-1982); Editor, Owner, Publication, Kentucky Golfer **AW:** Named Person of the Year, Alzheimer's Association, Louisville Chapter, KY (2004); Named to Atherton High School Hall of Fame (2002); Editorial and Column Writing Awards, Louisville Metro Journalism **MEM:** Society of Professional Journalists; Kentucky Golf Association (KGA-PGA); South Carolina Melrose Club; Valhalla Golf Club **AV:** Golf **PA:** Democrat **RE:** Jewish

YEAGER, CHUCK, T: Air Force General (Retired) **I:** Military & Defense Services **DOB:** 02/13/1923 **PB:** Myra **SC:** WV/USA **PT:** Albert Hal Yeager; Susie Mae (Sizemore) Yeager **MS:** Married **SPN:** Victoria Scott D'Angelo (2003); Glennis Dickhouse (1945, Deceased 1990) **CH:** Susan; Don; Mickey; Sharon **ED:** Doctor in Aeronautical Science, Salem College, Salem, WV (1975); Honorary DSc, Marshall University, Huntington, WV (1969); Graduate, Air War College (1961); Graduate, Air Command and Staff School (1952); Honorary DSc, West Virginia University, Morgantown, WV (1948) **C:** Director, Aerospace Safety, Norton Air Force Base, U.S. Air Force (1973-1975); Special Assistant to the Commander, Norton Air Force Base, California, U.S. Air Force (1973); Adviser, Pakistan Air Force (1971-1973); Brigadier General, Vice Commander, Seventeenth Expeditionary Air Force (17 EAF), U.S. Air Force (1969-1971); Commander, 4th Tactical Fighter Wing, Seymour Johnson Air Force Base

(1968-1969); Commander, 405th Tactical Fighter Wing, Clark Air Base (1966); First Commandant, U.S. Air Force Aerospace Research Pilot School (1962); Director, Space School, Edwards Air Force Base (1960); Fighter Pilot, Commander, F-100D Super Sabre-Equipped 1st Fighter Day Squadron (1957-1960); Fighter Pilot, Commander, F-86H Sabre-Equipped 417th Fighter-Bomber Squadron, Hahn Air Base, West Germany, Toul-Rosieres Air Base, France (1955-1957) **CR:** Leader, "Speed of Sound Tour" of Kabul and Bagram Bases in Afghanistan (2012); Honorary Chairman, Duncan Hunter Presidential Campaign (2008); Presidential Commission to Investigate Challenger Accident (1986); Consultant, Commander Test Pilot School, Edwards Air Force Base (1975-1997); Speaker in Field **CIV:** Founder, Chairman, General Yeager Foundation, California (2002-Present) **MIL:** Flight Officer, Fighter Pilot, "Ace in a Day" Pilot, Second Lieutenant, Numerous Command Assignments, U.S. Army Air Forces (1943-1962); Private, U.S. Army Air Forces (1941) **CW:** "National Memorial Day Parade" (2012); "The Legendary of Pancho Barnes and the Happy Bottom Riding Club (2009); "Thunder in the Desert" (2005); "Realizing 'The Right Stuff'" (2003); "The Real Men with 'The Right Stuff'" (2003); "Rocket Science" (2002); "Presidential Inaugural Gala" (1989); "Reaching for the Skies" (1988); "Good Morning America" (1987); "Looney Tunes 50th Anniversary" (1986); "Spaceflight" (1985-1987); Actor, "Flying Without Fear" (1985); "The Tonight Show Starring Johnny Carson" (1985); Actor, "The Right Stuff" (1983); Technical Consultant, "The Right Stuff" (1983); "Late Night with David Letterman" (1982-1985); Actor, "Smokey and the Bandit II" (1980); Subject, "The Right Stuff" by Tom Wolfe (1979); Appearence, "I Dream of Jeannie" (1964); Contestant, "What's My Line?" (1964); Uncredited Aerial Stunt Coordinator, "Jet Pilot" (1957); Appearance, "Goodyear Television Playhouse" (1953); "We, the People" (1948) **AW:** Ranked #5, "The 51 Heroes of Aviation," Flying Magazine (2013); Guest of Honor, Celebration of the 63rd Anniversary of Breaking the Sound Barrier, Sort, Spain (2010); Inductee, California Hall of Fame, California Museum (2009); Inductee, Inaugural Class, Aerospace Walk of Honor (1990); Inductee, International Space Hall of Fame (1981); Collier Trophy, Mackay Trophy, "for breaking the sound barrier for the first time" (1976); Congressional Silver Medal "for breaking the sound barrier for the first time" (1976); Silver Medal "equivalent to a noncombat Medal of Honor" for "contributing immeasurably to aerospace science by risking his life in piloting the X-1 research airplane faster than the speed of sound," U.S. Congress (1975); Air Force Distinguished Service Medal (1975); Inductee, National Aviation Hall of Fame (1973); Inductee, International Air & Space Hall of Fame (1966); Distinguished Service Medal (1954); Harmon Trophy (1953); Harmon Trophy, Citation of Honorable Mention (1940-1949); "One of the Greatest Pilots of All Time," Flying Magazine, California Hall of Fame, State of West Virginia, National Aviation Hall of Fame, U.S. Presidents, U.S. Army Air Force; Honoree, Society of Yeager Scholars; Marshall University's Highest Academic Scholarship; Silver Star with Bronze Oak Leaf Cluster; Legion of Merit with Bronze Oak Leaf Cluster; Distinguished Flying Cross; Bronze Star Medal; Purple Heart; Air Medal with Two Silver Oak Leaf Cluster; Air Force Commendation Medal; Presidential Medal of Freedom; Presidential Unit Citation with Bronze Oak Leaf Cluster; Air Force Outstanding Unit Award; American Defense Service Medal; American Campaign Medal; European-African-Middle Eastern Campaign Medal with Silver and Three Bronze Service Stars; World War II Victory Medal; Army of Occupation Medal with "Germany" Clasp; National Defense Service Medal; Armed Forces Expeditionary Medal; Vietnam Service Medal with Two Campaign Stars; Air Force Longevity Service Ribbon with One Silver and One Bronze Oak Leaf Clusters; Air Force Small Arms Expert Marksmanship Ribbon; Republic of Vietnam Campaign Medal **MEM:** Chairman, Young Eagle Program, Experimental Aircraft Association (1994-2004); Honorary Board Member, Wings of Hope

YEARWOOD, TRISHA, T: Country Music Singer, Songwriter **I:** Media & Entertainment **DOB:** 09/19/1964 **PB:** Monticello **SC:** GA/USA **PT:** Jack Howard Yearwood; Gwendolyn Yearwood **MS:** Married **SPN:** Garth Brooks (2005); Robert "Bobby" Reynolds (1994, Divorced 1999); Christopher Latham (1987, Divorced 1991) **CH:** Three Stepchildren **ED:** BBA, Belmont University (1987); Associate Degree in Business, Young Harris College; Student, University of Georgia **C:** Recording Artist, MCA Records; Demo Singer, Commercial Jingles Singer, MTM Records; Intern, MTM Records **CIV:** Participant, "National Women Build Week" (2009); Recorded "My Favorite Things" for Sears' Heroes at Home" Program (2008); Active Member, Habitat for Humanity; Assisted in the Hurricane Katrina Disaster Relief **CW:** Host, Television Series, "Trisha's Southern Kitchen" (2012-Present); Host, Television Special, "CMA Country Christmas" (2019); Singer, Album, "Every Girl" (2019); Singer, Album, "Let's Be Frank" (2019); Singer, Album, "Christmas Together" (2016); Singer, Compilation Album, "Gunslinger/Christmas Together" (2016); Actress, Television Special, "The Passion: New Orleans" (2016); Author, Book, "Trisha's Table: My Feel-Good Favorites" (2015); Herself, Television Series, "Nashville" (2014); Singer, Compilation Album, "PrizeFighter: Hit After Hit" (2014); Singer, Compilation Album, "Ballads" (2013); Musical Guest, Television Special, "Kelly Clarkson's Cautionary Christmas Music Tale" (2013); Herself, Documentary Series, "Who Do You Think You Are?" (2013); Singer, Compilation Album, "Icon: Trisha Yearwood" (2010); Author, Book, "Home Cooking with Trisha Yearwood: Stories and Recipes to Share with Family and Friends" (2010); Author, Book, "Georgia Cooking in an Oklahoma Kitchen" (2008); Singer, Compilation Album, "Love Songs" (2008); Singer, Compilation Album, "Greatest Hits" (2007); Singer, Album, "Heaven, Heartache and the Power of Love" (2007); Singer, Album, "Jasper County" (2005); Singer, Album, "Inside Out" (2001); Singer, Album, "Real Live Woman" (2000); Singer, Album, "Where Your Road Leads" (1998); Singer, Compilation Album, "Home for the Holidays" (1997); Singer, Compilation Album, "(Songbook) A Collection of Hits" (1997); Actress, Television Series, "JAG" (1997-2002); Singer, Album, "Everybody Knows" (1996); Herself, "Ellen" (1996); Singer, Album, "Thinkin' About You" (1995); Singer, Album, "The Sweetest Gift" (1994); Actress, "Dr. Quinn, Medical Woman" (1994); Singer, Album, "The Song Remembers When" (1993); Herself, "The Thing Called Love" (1993); Singer, Album, "Hearts in Armor" (1992); Singer, Album, "Trisha Yearwood" (1991) **AW:** Nominee, Outstanding Culinary Program, "Trisha's Southern Kitchen," Daytime Emmy Awards (2017); Video of the Year, "Forever Country," Academy of Country Music Awards (2016); Outstanding Culinary Program, "Trisha's Southern Kitchen," Daytime Emmy Awards (2013); Nominee, Vocal Event of the Year, "Another Try" (2008); Nominee, Top Female Vocalist, Academy of Country Music Awards (2001); Inductee, Georgia Music Hall of Fame (2000); Nominee, Best Song, "How Do I Live," Academy Awards (1998); Nominee, Top Female Vocalist, Academy of Country Music Awards (1998); Nominee, Favorite Country Album, "(Songbook) A Collection of Hits," American Music Awards (1998); Female Vocalist of the Year, Country Music Association Awards (1998); Best Female Country Vocal Performance, "How Do I Live," Grammy Awards (1997); Best Country Collaboration with Vocals, "In Another's Eyes," Grammy Awards (1997); Female Vocalist of the Year, Country Music Association Awards (1997); Nominee, Single Record of the Year, "How Do I Live," Academy of Country Music Awards (1997); Nominee, Song of the Year, "How Do I Live," Academy of Country Music Awards (1997); Top Female Vocalist, Academy of Country Music Awards (1997); Nominee, Vocal Event of the Year, "In Another's Eyes," Academy of Country Music Awards (1997); Nominee, Top Female Vocalist (1996); Album of the Year, "Common Thread: The Songs of the Eagles," Country Music Association Awards (1994); Nominee, Top Vocal Duet, with Aaron Neville, Academy of Country Music Awards (1994); Nominee, Album of the Year, "Common Thread: The Songs of the Eagles," Academy of Country Music Awards (1993); Favorite New Country Artist, American Music Awards (1992); Nominee, Favorite County Song, "She's in Love with the Boy," American Music Awards (1992); Nominee, Single Record of the Year, "She's in Love with the Boy," Academy of Country Music Awards (1991); Top New Female Vocalist, Academy of Country Music Awards (1991)

YEH, HSI-HAN, PHD, T: Senior Electronics Engineer (Retired) **I:** Engineering **CN:** Wright-Patterson Air Force Base **DOB:** 11/10/1935 **PB:** Shanghai **SC:** China **PT:** Jing-Hwa; Yu-Zhi (Lin) Ye **MS:** Married **SPN:** Lily Ye Bao (06/18/1966) **CH:** Anita Norrie; Sharon Scheitz **ED:** PhD, The Ohio State University (1967); MSc, University of New Brunswick, Canada (1963);MSc, National Chiao Tung University (1961);BSc, National Taiwan University, Taipei, Taiwan (1956) **C:** Retired (2001); Senior Electronics Engineer, Wright-Patterson Air Force Base, Ohio (1986-2001); Associate Professor, University of Kentucky, Lexington, KY (1973-1985); Assistant Professor, University of Kentucky, Lexington, KY (1967-1973) **AW:** General Foulois Award (1988); Award, Flight Dynamics Laboratory, United States Air Force **MEM:** IEEE; Sigma Xi, The Scientific Research Honor Society **MH:** Albert Nelson Marquis Lifetime Achievement Award **B/I:** Dr. Yeh became involved in his profession because he began in that field since he was in graduate school. He was inclined to do mathematics, science and engineering when he was in high school. Dr. Yeh has admired scientists and engineers ever since he was in high school. **AV:** Fishing; Hiking; Horseback riding; Scuba diving

YELICH, CHRISTIAN STEPHEN, T: Professional Baseball Player **I:** Athletics **CN:** Milwaukee Brewers **DOB:** 12/5/1991 **PB:** Thousand Oaks **SC:** CA/USA **MS:** Single **ED:** Diploma, Westlake High School, Thousand Oaks, CA **C:** Outfielder, Milwaukee Brewers (2018-Present); Outfielder, Miami Marlins (2013-2017) **CR:** U.S. National Baseball Team, World Baseball Classic (2017); All-World Baseball Classic Team (2017) **CW:** Guest Appearance, "Magnum P.I." (2019) **AW:** Major League Most Valuable Player (2018); Hank Aaron Award (2018); Batting Champion (2018); Silver Slugger Award (2016, 2018); Gold Glove Award (2014)

YERGLER, MARILYN ELAINE, T: Nurse (Retired) **I:** Medicine & Health Care **DOB:** 07/27/1949 **PB:** Fisher **SC:** AR/USA **PT:** Curtis M. Dodd; Anna Agnes (Bryant) Dodd **MS:** Married **CH:** Jason Jeffrey **ED:** MSN in Adult Health, Arkansas State University (2000); Postgraduate Studies, U.S. Army Command and General Staff College (1986-1990);

Certified, Academy of Health Sciences & Critical Care Nursing (1984); BSN, University of Arkansas (1970) **C:** Officer in Charge of Task Force Medical Training, San Antonio, TX (2006-2007); Assistant Head Nurse, Surgical ICU, Walter Reed Army Medical Center, Washington, DC (1990-1992); Charge and Staff Nurse, Lawnwood Regional Medical Center, Fort Pierce, FL (1987-1990); Staff Nurse CCU, Humana Hospital, Sebastian, FL (1987); Charge Nurse CCU, General Leonard Wood Army Hospital, Fort Leonard Wood, MO (1984-1986); Charge and Staff Nurse CCU, Brooke Army Medical Center, Fort Sam Houston, TX (1983) **CR:** Educator, VA Medical Center, Gainesville, FL (2007-2009); Courtesy Assistant Professor of Nursing, Arkansas State University, University of Florida (2004-2007); Trainer, Medics of all Branches of Deployment to Middle East, Fort Sam Houston, TX **CW:** Blogger for Church **AW:** Meritorious Service Medal (MSM), U.S. Army **MH:** Albert Nelson Marquis Lifetime Achievement Award **B/I:** Ms. Yergler became involved in her profession because her mother died early of cancer and her father was in the Army during World War II, and she enjoyed his stories about the Army hospitals he stayed in when he was wounded. **AV:** Card making; Scrapbooking; Gardening; Crafting; Spending time with grandchildren **PA:** Republican **RE:** Church of Christ

YI, XIAOBIN, MD, MBA, T: Associate Professor, Director of Pain **I:** Medicine & Health Care **CN:** Washington University Pain Center **MS:** Married **CH:** One Daughter **ED:** MBA, Washington University, St. Louis, MO (2013); Fellowship in Pain Medicine, Department of Anesthesiology, University of Virginia School of Medicine, Charlottesville, VA (2003-2004); Resident in Anesthesiology, SUNY Health Science Center, Syracuse, NY (2000-2003); Internship in Preliminary Medicine, Wayne State University Detroit Medical Center, Michigan (1999-2000); Chief Resident, Department of Medicine, Beijing Hospital, The Fifth Clinical College of Beijing University (1990-1991); MS, Chinese Academy of Medical Sciences/Peking Union Medical College (1990); Resident in Medicine, Beijing Hospital, Fifth Clinical College of Beijing University (1985-1990); MD, Southcentral University Xiangya School of Medicine, Changsha, China (1985) **CT:** Medical License, Missouri (2004-Present); Medical License, New York (2006); Diplomat, ABA Pain Medicine (2005); Diplomat, American Board of Anesthesiology (2004); Medical License, Commonwealth of Virginia (2003); USMLE/ECFMG Certificate (1999); Certificate in Pain Management and Anesthesiology **C:** Associate Professor, Department of Anesthesiology, Washington University School of Medicine, St. Louis, MO (2015-Present); Director of Pain Medicine, Missouri Baptist Medical Center, Department of Anesthesiology, Washington University School of Medicine, St. Louis, MO (2014-Present); Assistant Professor, Department of Anesthesiology, Washington University School of Medicine, St. Louis, MO (2005-2015); QI Program Director, Pain Management Center, Department of Anesthesiology, Washington University School of Medicine, St. Louis, MO (2010-2014); Instructor, Department of Anesthesiology, Washington University School of Medicine, St. Louis, MO (2004-2005); Postdoctoral Associate, Department of Molecular Physiology & Biological Physics, School of Medicine, University of Virginia (1993-1996) **CR:** Guest Professor, Institute of Functional Neurosurgery, Xianwu Hospital, Capital Medical University, Beijing, China (2014-Present); Guest Professor, National Pain Research Center, China-Japan Friendship Hospital, Beijing University (2010-Present); Guest Professor, Centralsouth University Xiangya School of Medicine (2012-2017); Visiting Professor, Capital Medical University (2013); Fel-

lowship, Anesthesiology Research, University of Virginia Health Sciences Center (1996-1999); Gastroenterology Fellow, GI Division, Department of Medicine, University of Virginia (1993); Fellowship, Gastroenterology, University of Virginia and Beijing Hospital, Fifth Clinical College of Beijing University (1992-1993); Assistant Professor, Department of Medicine Beijing Hospital, Beijing Medical University (1990-1993); Presenter in Field **CIV:** Chairman, Pain Committee, Missouri Baptist Medical Center (2014-Present); PTM Committee, Missouri Baptist Medical Center (2014-Present); QI Committee, Department of Anesthesiology, Washington University School of Medicine (2010-2014) **CW:** Editorial Board, Chinese Medical Journal; Editorial Board, Journal of Clinical Anesthesia; Editorial Board, Pain Medicine; Editorial Board, Chinese Journal of Pain Medicine; Reviewer, Pain, Clinical Interventions in Aging; Reviewer, Human Gene Therapy, Clinical Journal of Pain, Journal of Pain; Contributor, Articles, Professional Journals **AW:** Resident Scholar, ASA/FARE (2001); Young Investigator Award, Chinese Association of Gastroenterology. Dalian, China (1990) **MEM:** Chairman, International Scientific Committee, First China International Forum of Pain Medicine (2012); International Association for the Study of Pain (IASP); American Society of Anesthesiologists (ASA); American Society of Regional Anesthesia and Pain Medicine (ASRA) **AS:** Dr. Yi attributes his success to his medical training in the United States. The welcoming culture and society have helped him grow as a professional. **B/I:** Pain affects people both physically and mentally. Dr. Yi believes it is very important to help individuals who are suffering and improve their quality of life, which is why he got involved in his field. **THT:** Dr. Yi's motto is, "Work hard and help others."

YOHO, THEODORE SCOTT, DVM, T: U.S. Representative from Florida; Veterinarian **I:** Government Administration/Government Relations/Government Services **DOB:** 04/13/1955 **PB:** Minneapolis **SC:** MN/USA **MS:** Married **SPN:** Carolyn Yoho **CH:** Katie; Lauren; Tyler **ED:** DVM, University of Florida College of Veterinary Medicine (1983); BS in Animal Science, University of Florida (1979); AA, Broward College (1977) **C:** Member, U.S. House of Representatives from Florida's Third Congressional District, United States Congress, Washington, DC (2013-2020); Member, U.S. House Committee on Foreign Affairs (2013-2020); Member, U.S. House Committee on Agriculture (2013-2020); Private Veterinary Practice (1983-2010) **MEM:** National Rifle Association of America; Florida Cattlemen's Association; Florida Association of Equine Practitioners (FAEP); Florida Veterinary Medical Association; American Veterinary Medical Association **PA:** Republican **RE:** Christian

YOKEN, MEL B., T: Professor **I:** Education/Educational Services **CN:** University of Massachusetts Dartmouth (UMass Dartmouth) **DOB:** 06/25/1939 **PB:** Fall River **SC:** MA/USA **PT:** Albert Benjamin Yoken; Sylvia Sarah (White) Yoken **MS:** Married **SPN:** Cynthia Stein (06/20/1976) **CH:** Andrew Brett; David Ryan; Jonathan Barry **ED:** PhD in French Language & Literature, Five-College Cooperative Program (1972); MAT in French, Brown University, Providence, RI (1961); Coursework, NDEA French Language Institute, University of Cincinnati (1961); BA, University of Massachusetts (1960); Coursework, Middlebury College **C:** Chancellor, Professor Emeritus, French Language and Literature, University of Massachusetts Dartmouth (UMass Dartmouth) (2008); Chancellor, Professor, University of Massachusetts Dartmouth (UMass Dartmouth) (2000); Professor, University of Massachusetts Dartmouth (UMass Dartmouth)

(1981-2000); Assistant Professor, University of Massachusetts Dartmouth (UMass Dartmouth) (1976-1981); Instructor, French, University of Massachusetts Dartmouth (UMass Dartmouth) (1966-1972) **CR:** Radio Commentator (1954-Present); Translator, New Bedford Superior Court, New Bedford, MA (1985-2018); Translator, Fall Superior Court, Fall River, MA (1985-2018); Nominating Committee, Nobel Prize for Literature (1970-2016); Reader, Consultant, SAT Exams in French (1997-2012); Visiting Professor, University of Montreal, Montreal, Quebec, Canada (1981-1990); Director, French, Summer Study Program, French Institute (1981-1990); Visiting Professor, Wheaton College, Wheaton, IL (1987); Co-Host, "Jean Caya Bancroft Radio Show" **CIV:** Vice President, Friends of the University of Massachusetts Library (2009-Present); Director, Boivin Center for French Language and Culture (1999-Present); Richelieu Club (1996-Present); Vice President, American Field Service (2001-2008); President, Friends of the University of Massachusetts Library (1999-2004); Board of Directors, American Field Service (1980-2004); Vice President, Friends of the University of Massachusetts Library (1998-1999); President, American Field Service (1984-1986); President, New Bedford Public Library (1980-1982); President, Friends of the Fall River Public Library, Inc. (1972-1980); Advisory Board, The Irena Sendler Project; Elected Officer, Director, Innumerable Civic Clubs and Organizations **CW:** Columnist, Prime Times (2012-2018); Author, "Breakthrough: Essays and Vignettes in Honor of John A. Rassias" (2007); Author, "Entretiens Quebecois III" (1999); Author, "Festschrift in Honor of Stowell Goding" (1993); Author, "Letters of Robert Molloy" (1989); Author, "Entretiens Quebecois II" (1989); Author, "Entretiens Quebecois I" (1986); Author, "Speech is Plurality" (1978); Author, "Claude Tillier" (1976); Contributor, Numerous Articles, Professional Journals **AW:** French Legion of Honor (2018); Distinguished Alumni Award, University of Massachusetts Amherst (UMass Amherst) (2013); National Order of Quebec (2005); Decorated Officier, Ordre Des Palmes Académiques, Academy Française (2001); Golden Apple Award, Fall River Herald News (1998); Distinguished Alumni Award, Durfee High School (1998); Outstanding Community Service Award (1997); Medaille De Vermeil Du Rayonnement De La Langue Française, L'Académie Française (1993); Service Award, Massachusetts Foreign Language Association (1992); National Distinguished Leadership Award (1990); Grantee, Southeastern Massachusetts University (1985, 1989, 1990); Grantee, Government Of Quebec (1981-1985, 1987-1989); Governor's Citation (1986); Excellence In Teaching French Award (1984-1985); Distinguished Service Award, City Fall River, MA (1974, 1980) **MEM:** Board of Directors, Durfee High School Alumni Association (2019); Life Member, Honorary Member, UMass Dartmouth Claire T. Carney Library Associates (2010); Honorary Member, Modern Language Association (2009); Honorary Charter Member, Pi Delta Phi (2008); Life Member, Academy of American Poets (2006); Honorary Member, American Association of Teachers of French (2005); Vice President, Universal Manuscript Society (1993-1995); Coordinator, Northeast Modern Language Association (1987-1991); Board of Directors, Massachusetts Foreign Language Association (1985-1990); Life Member, American Council on the Teaching of Foreign Languages; Life Member, L'Amicale de Middlebury; Life Member, New York State Association of Foreign Language Teachers; New England Foreign Language Association; International Platform Association; Francophone Association; Association of Literary Scholars, Critics, and Writers; PEN New England; American Society of the French Academic Palms (l'Ordre des Palmes Académiques); Fall River Chamber of Commerce; Brown University Alumni Association; Richelieu International **MH:** Albert Nelson Marquis Lifetime Achievement Award **AS:** Dr. Yorken attributes his success to hard work and getting the best education possible. **B/I:** Dr. Yorken began studying French in high school at the suggestion of his father. This is how he became involved in his field. **AV:** Traveling; Learning languages; Playing baseball; Collecting postcards; Researching meteorology

YOKLEY, RICHARD CLARENCE, T: Protective Services Official **I:** Civil Service **DOB:** 12/29/1942 **PB:** San Diego **SC:** CA/USA **PT:** Clarence Ralph Yokley; Dorothy Junese (Sackman) Yokley **MS:** Married **SPN:** Jean Yokley (7/25/1964) **CH:** Richard Clarence II; Karin Denise **ED:** Coursework, Fire Service College, England (1994); Coursework, London Fire Brigade Training Academy (1994); AS, Miramar College (1975); Coursework, San Diego City College (1967) **CT:** Certified Fire Officer; Certified Fire Instructor; Certified Fire Investigator **C:** Retired, Maintenance Officer, Bonita-Sunnyside Fire Department (1993-1999); Bonita-Sunnyside Fire Department (1972-1999); Operations Chief, Bonita-Sunnyside Fire Department (1991-1993); Fire Marshal, Bonita-Sunnyside Fire Department (1981-1991); Building Engineer, Consolidated Systems, Inc., San Diego, CA (1968-1972); Disc Jockey, Station KSDS-FM, San Diego, CA (1966-1967) **CR:** Animal Care, Reid Park Zoo (2015-2019); Arizona Sonora Desert Museum, Tucson, AZ (2004-2015) Aviculture Department, Penguin Encounter, SeaWorld San Diego (2003-2004); Emergency Medical Care Committee, San Diego County, CA (2001-2004); EMT-D/C, SeaWorld San Diego (1997-2003); Council of Courage (1991-1999); Firefighter Advisory Council, San Diego Burn Institute (1989, 1999); Chairman, South Bay Emergency Medical Service (1988); Bay General Hospital (Now Scripps Hospital), Chula Vista, CA (1980-1983); Medical Technician, Hartson Ambulance, San Diego, CA (1978-1980); Volunteer Elephant Keeper **CIV:** Docent, Firehouse Museum, San Diego, CA (1990-1993); Assistant Curator, Firehouse Museum, San Diego, CA (1972-1989); Scoutmaster, Troop 874, Boy Scouts of America, Bonita, CA (1978-1979) **MIL:** U.S. Air Force (1962-1968) **CW:** Author, "First Responders of Television" (2012); Author, "Emergency Behind the Scenes" (2007); Author, "TV Firefighters" (2003); Contributor, Articles, Professional Publications **AW:** Friends of the Society Certificate, The Royal Life Saving Society, England (2004); Pioneer Award, Bonita Business & Professional Association (BBPA) (1997); Excellence Award, SeaWorld San Diego (2000); Golden Service Award, San Diego County Credit Union (1988); Heroism and Community Service Award, Firehouse Magazine, New York, NY (1987); Star News Salutes Award, Chula Vista Star-News (1987); Historian Award, Bonita Business & Professional Association (1987); Exemplary Service Award, Bonita-Sunnyside Fire Department (1984) **MEM:** Board of Directors, Bonita Historical Museum (2003-2004); Advisor, Smokey Bear Collectors Association (1998-2000); Director, Fire Mark Circle of the Americas (1994-2000); Vice President, Bonita Historical Museum (1999, 1998); Advisory Board, Bonita Historical Museum (1997); Co-Founder, Director, Smokey Bear Collectors Association (1995-1997); Deputy Director, Southern Division, California State Firefighters Association (1994-1997); Board of Directors, Bonita Business and Professional Association (1991-1993); Vice President, Sport Chalet Dive Club (1991); Co-founder, Bonita Historical Museum (1986); President, San Diego County Fire Prevention Officers (1985); Vice President, San Diego County Fire Prevention Officers

(1984); President, Local Chapter, International Association of Firefighters (1981-1982); California Fire Mechanics; South Bay Commission; Crown Firecoach Enthusiasts **MH:** Albert Nelson Marquis Lifetime Achievement Award; Marquis Who's Who Top Professional **B/I:** Mr. Yokley became involved in his profession when his neighbor told him the fire department was hiring. He passed the test and joined the fire department. **AV:** Caring for animals; Scuba diving; Visiting fire departments; Collecting fire memorabilia; Skiing; Gardening **PA:** Republican **RE:** Methodist

YORKE, THOM EDWARD, T: Singer, Songwriter **I:** Media & Entertainment **CN:** Radiohead **DOB:** 10/07/1968 **PB:** Wellingborough **SC:** Northamptonshire/United Kingdom **MS:** Widowed **SPN:** Rachel Mary Owen (05/2003, Deceased 12/18/2016) **CH:** Noah; Agnes **ED:** Coursework in English and Art, University of Exeter, England, United Kingdom (1988-1991) **C:** Singer, Songwriter, Guitarist, Radiohead (1991-Present); Singer, Songwriter, Guitarist, Atoms for Peace (2009-2013); Singer, Songwriter, Guitarist, On a Friday **CIV:** Spokesman, Friends of the Earth (2005-Present) **CW:** Musician, "Not the News Rmx EP" (2019); Musician, "Anima" (2019); Contributor, Soundtrack, "Suspiria Unreleased Material" (2019); Contributor, Soundtrack, "Motherless Brooklyn" (2019); Contributor, Soundtrack, "Suspiria" (2018); Contributor, Soundtrack, Short Film, "Time of Day" (2018); Contributor, Soundtrack, Short Film, "Why Can't We Get Along" (2018); Musician, with Radiohead, "A Moon Shaped Pool" (2016); Musician, with Radiohead, "Spectre" (2015); Musician, "Tomorrow's Modern Boxes" (2014); Musician, "Youwouldn'tlikemewhenI'mangry" (2014); Co-contributor, Soundtrack, "The UK Gold" (2013); Musician, "This" (2012); Musician, "Ego," "Mirror," "Shipwreck" (2011); Musician, with Radiohead, "The King of Limbs" (2011); Musician, with Radiohead, "TKOL RMX 1234567" (2011); Musician, with Radiohead, "The Daily Mail," "Staircase," "Supercollider," "The Butcher" (2011); Contributor, Soundtrack, "When the Dragon Swallowed the Sun" (2010); Contributor, Soundtrack, "The Twilight Saga: New Moon" (2009); Musician, with Radiohead, "These Are My Twisted Words," "Harry Patch (In Memory Of)" (2009); Featured Musician, with Björk, "Náttúra" (2008); Musician, "The Eraser Rmxs" (2008); Musician, with Radiohead, "In Rainbows" (2007); Musician, "The Eraser" (2006); Musician, "Spitting Feathers EP" (2006); Featured Musician, with Band Aid 20, "Do They Know It's Christmas?" (2004); Musician, with Radiohead, "Hail to the Thief" (2003); Musician, with Radiohead, "Amnesiac" (2001); Musician, with Radiohead, "I Might Be Wrong: Live Recordings" (2001); Featured Musician, with Björk, "I've Seen It All" (2000); Musician, with Radiohead, "Kid A" (2000); Featured Musician, with Unkle, "Rabbit in Your Headlights" (1998); Featured Musician, with Drugstore, "El President" (1998); Musician, with Radiohead, "OK Computer" (1997); Musician, with Radiohead, "The Bends" (1995); Musician, with Radiohead, "Pablo Honey" (1993); Musician, with Radiohead, "Pop is Dead" (1993); Musician, with Radiohead, Several Compilation and Video Albums, EPs **AW:** Inductee, Rock and Roll Hall of Fame (2019); Named Best Reissue, "OK Computer," NME Awards (2017); Named Best Animation, "Burn the Witch," Ibiza Music Video Festival (2016); Best Choreography, "Lotus Flower," Antville Music Video Awards (2011); Named Best Band Blog, www.radiohead.com, NME Awards (2010); Grammy Awards for Best Boxed or Special Limited Edition Package, Best Alternative Music Album, "In Rainbows," Recording Academy (2009); Named, 100 Agents of Change, Rolling Stone (2009); Named, 100 Most Influential People

in the World, TIME Magazine (2008); Named Best International Band, Meteor Music Awards (2008); John Peel Award For Musical Innovation, NME Awards (2008); Album Award, "In Rainbows," Ivor Novello Awards (2008); Named Artist of the Year, PLUG Independent Music Awards (2008); Innovation Award, MTV Asia Awards (2008); Named Best Foreign Male Act, Denmark GAFFA Awards (2007); Grammy Award for Best Engineered Album, Non-Classical, "Hail to the Thief," Recording Academy (2004); Named International Achievement in Musical Theater, Ivor Novello Awards (2004); Named Best Video for "There There," Best Album Artwork and Best Album for "Hail to the Thief," NME Awards (2004); Named Best Art Direction, "There There," MTV Video Music Awards (2003); Named Best Act in the World Today, Q Awards (2001-2003); Grammy Award for Best Recording Package, "Amnesiac," Recording Academy (2002); Named Best Alternative Video, "Knives Out," MVPA Awards (2002); Named Best Video, "Pyramid Song," NME Awards (2002); Named Best Band, NME Awards (2001); Grammy Award for Best Alternative Music Album, "Kid A," Recording Academy (2001); Named Best Foreign Live Act, Best Foreign Album for "Kid A," Best Foreign Band, Denmark GAFFA Awards (2000); Grammy Award for Best Alternative Music Album, "OK Computer," Recording Academy (1998); Named Best Song Musically and Lyrically for "Paranoid Android," Best Contemporary Song for "Karma Police," Ivor Novello Awards (1998); Named Best Album, "OK Computer," NME Awards (1998); Named Best Foreign Live Act, Best Foreign Song for "Paranoid Android," Best Foreign Album for "OK Computer," Best Foreign Band, Best Foreign Male Act, Denmark GAFFA Awards (1997); Named Best Single, "Creep," NME Awards (1994) **AV:** Yoga; Meditation

YOUNG, ALLEN MARCUS, PHD, T: Museum Curator and Administrator, Educator, Naturalist, Consultant, Writer **I:** Research **DOB:** 02/23/1942 **PB:** Ossining **SC:** NY/USA **PT:** George Marcus Young; Margaret Mary (Murphy) Young **MS:** Divorced **ED:** PhD, University of Chicago, Chicago, IL (1968); BA, State University of New York at New Paltz (1964) **C:** Curator Emeritus, Zoology, Milwaukee Public Museum (2005-Present); Vice President, Collections, Research and Public Programs, Milwaukee Public Museum (1994-Present); Vice President, Collections and Research, Milwaukee Public Museum (1994-Present); Curator, Zoology, Milwaukee Public Museum (1990-Present); Curator, Invertebrate Zoology, Milwaukee Public Museum (1975-1989); Assistant Professor, Biology, Lawrence University, Appleton, WI (1970-1975); Postdoctoral Research Associate, Organization for Tropical Studies (1968-1970) **CR:** Adjunct Professor, University of Wisconsin (1976-Present); Consultant, Chocolate Manufacturers, Hersey, PA (1980-Present); Head of Scientific Staff, Milwaukee Public Museum (1978, 1983); Chairperson, Endowment Exploration Committee, Milwaukee Public Museum (1979-1980) **CW:** Contributing Writer, Natural History Magazine (2018-Present); Project Director, National Science Foundation-funded Permanent Museum Exhibit Gallery on Biodiversity (1997-Present); Author, "Lives Intertwined: Interrelationships Between Plants and Animals" (1996); Author, "The Chocolate Tree: A Natural History of Cacao" (1994); Author, "Sarapiqui Chronicle: A Naturalist in Costa Rica" (1991); Author, "Population Biology of Tropical Insects" (1982); Contributor, Over 250 Articles, Professional Journals; Contributor, Over 100 Popular Articles, Magazines **AW:** Listee, One of 60 Most Influential Individuals and Institutions in the Development of Agriculture, Inter-American Institute for Cooperation on Agriculture (2003); American Association Museum

Award for Outstanding New Exhibit Gallery (1988); Research Grant, National Science Foundation (1972-1975) **MEM:** Ecological Society of America; Lepidopterists' Society; Association for Tropical Biology; Wisconsin Entomological Society; American Association for the Advancement of Science; International Society for Tropical Ecology; Kansas Entomological Society; New York Entomological Society **MH:** Albert Nelson Marquis Lifetime Achievement Award **AS:** Mr. Young attributes his success to his college professors. **B/I:** Mr. Young knew he wanted to work in museums after his first visit to the American Museum of Natural History. He was always interested in insects. **THT:** Mr. Young believes all life is interconnected.

YOUNG, ANDRE (DR. DRE), T: Entrepreneur, Record Producer, Rapper **I:** Media & Entertainment **DOB:** 02/18/1965 **PB:** Compton **SC:** CA/USA **PT:** Theodore Young; Verna Young **MS:** Married **SPN:** Nicole Threatt (1996) **CH:** Truice; Truly; Curtis Young; Marcel; La Tanya Danielle Young; Andre Young Jr. (Deceased) **C:** Co-founder, Beats Electronics LLC, Apple, Inc. (2006-Present); Founder, Chief Executive Officer, Aftermath Entertainment (1996-Present); Co-founder, Death Row Records (1991-1995); Rapper, N.W.A (1986-1991) **CIV:** Donor, $10 Million to the Construction of a Performing Arts Center, New Compton High School (2017); Donor, $70 Million Endowment to University of Southern California to Create the USC Jimmy Iovine and Andre Young Academy for Arts, Technology and the Business of Innovation (2013) **CW:** Featured, Documentary, "The Defiant Ones" (2017); Producer, Numerous Songs and Albums (1986-2016); Producer, Soundtrack Album, "Straight Outta Compton: Music from the Motion Picture" (2015); Rapper, Producer, Album, "Compton" (2015); Narrator, "Unity" (2015); Featured, Music Video, "I Need a Doctor" (2011); Featured, Music Video, "Kush" (2010); Rapper, Producer, Compilation Album, "Chronicles: Death Row Classics" (2006); Voice Actor, "50 Cent: Bulletproof" (2005); Producer, Songwriter, "In da Club" by 50 Cent (2003); Rapper, Producer, Compilation Album, "Chronicle: Best of the Works" (2002); Featured, Music Video, "Bad Intentions" (2002); Actor, Film, "Training Day" (2001); Producer, Soundtrack Album, "The Wash" (2001); Actor, Film, "The Wash" (2001); Featured, Music Video, "Forgot About Dre," "The Next Episode" (2000); Performer, Concert Film, "Up In Smoke Tour" (2000); Rapper, Producer, Album, "2001" (1999); Featured, Music Video, "Still D.R.E." (1999); Featured, Music Video, "Zoom" (1998); Featured, Music Video, "Been There, Done That" (1996); Actor, Film, "Set It Off" (1996); Rapper, Producer, Compilation Album, "Dr. Dre Presents the Aftermath" (1996); Rapper, Producer, Compilation Album, "Back 'n the Day" (1996); Rapper, Producer, Compilation Album, "First Round Knock Out" (1996); Featured, Music Video, "Keep Their Heads Ringin'" (1995); Featured, Music Video, "Natural Born Killaz" (1994); Rapper, Producer, Compilation Album, "Concrete Roots" (1994); Featured, Music Video, "Lil' Ghetto Boy," "Let Me Ride" (1993); Featured, Music Video, "Nuthin' but a 'G' Thang" (1992); Rapper, Producer, Album, "The Chronic" (1992); Rapper, Producer, Album, "N—4Life," N.W.A (1991); Featured, Documentary, "N—4Life: The Only Home Video" (1992); Featured, Music Video, "Deep Cover" (1991); Rapper, Producer, Album, "Straight Outta Compton," N.W.A (1988); Lead Artist, Featured Artist, Numerous Songs and Albums **AW:** Nominee, Best Compilation Soundtrack for Visual Media, "Straight Outta Compton" (2017); Echo Award for Best Hip Hop/Urban Artist, "Compton" (2016); Nominee, Best Rap Album, "Compton" (2016); Nominee, Album of the Year, "Compton,"

BET Hip Hop Awards (2016); AllMusic Best of 15, "Compton," AllMusic Year in Review (2015); Nominee, Producer of the Year (2015); Hustler of the Year, BET Hip Hop Awards (2014); Nominee, Album of the Year, "good kid, m.A.A.d city," Grammy Awards, Recording Academy (2014); Nominee, Best Rap Song, Best Rap/Sung Collaboration, "I Need a Doctor," Grammy Awards, Recording Academy (2012); Maverick Movie Award, Best Soundtrack: Feature, "Uprising: Hip Hop and the LA Riots" (2012); Nominee, Album of the Year, "Recovery," Grammy Awards, Recording Academy (2011); Founders Award, ASCAP (2010); Grammy Award for Best Rap Album, "Relapse," Recording Academy (2010); Grammy Award for Best Rap Performance by a Duo or Group, "Crack a Bottle," Recording Academy (2010); Nominee, Best Video, "Nuthin' But a 'G' Thang," MTV Video Music Awards (2009); Nominee, Best Rap Performance by a Duo or Group, "Encore," Grammy Awards, Recording Academy (2006); Nominee, Album of the Year, "Love. Angel. Music. Baby." (2006); Nominee, Best Rap Song, "In da Club," Grammy Awards, Recording Academy (2004); Nominee, Album of the Year, "The Eminem Show," Grammy Awards, Recording Academy (2003); Nominee, Best Music Video, Short Form, "Knoc," Grammy Awards, Recording Academy (2003); Grammy Award for Producer of the Year, Non-Classical, Recording Academy (2002); Grammy Award for Best Rap Album, "The Marshall Mathers LP," Recording Academy (2001); Nominee, Best Direction in a Video, "Stan," MTV Video Music Awards (2001); Grammy Award for Best Rap Performance by a Duo or Group, "Forgot About Dre," Recording Academy (2001); Best Rap Video, "Forgot About Dre," MTV Video Music Awards (2000); Best Direction in a Video, "The Real Slim Shady," MTV Video Music Awards (2000); Nominee, Breakthrough Video, "Guilty Conscience," MTV Video Music Awards (1999); Nominee, Best Direction, "My Name Is," MTV Video Music Awards (1999); Best R&B/Soul Single - Group, Band, or Duo, "No Diggity," Soul Train Awards (1997); Best Rap Video, "Keep Their Heads Ringin'," MTV Video Music Awards (1995); Grammy Award for Best Rap Solo Performance, "Let Me Ride," Recording Academy (1994)

YOUNG, ANDREW JACKSON JR., T: Consulting Firm Executive; Former Mayor; Former U.S. Representative from Georgia; Pastor **I:** Government Administration/Government Relations/Government Services **DOB:** 03/12/1932 **PB:** New Orleans **SC:** LA/USA **PT:** Andrew Jackson Young; Daisy (Fuller) Young **MS:** Married **SPN:** Carolyn McClain (1996); Jean Childs (06/07/1954, Deceased 1994) **CH:** Andrea; Lisa Dru; Paula Jean; Andrew Jackson Young III **ED:** Honorary LLD, Dartmouth University (2005); Honorary LLD, Yale University (1973); Honorary LLD, Clark College (1973); Honorary LLD, Wilberforce University (1971); Honorary DD, United Theological Seminary of the Twin Cities (1970); Honorary DD, Wesleyan University (1970); BD, Hartford Theological Seminary (Now Hartford Seminary) (1955); BS, Howard University (1951); Coursework, Dillard University (1947-1948); Numerous Other Honorary Degrees; Honorary LLD, Atlanta University (Now Clark Atlanta University); Honorary LLD, Swarthmore College **CT:** Ordained to Ministry, Congregational Church (1955) **C:** Founder, Andrew J. Young Foundation (2003-Present); Founding Principal, Co-Chairman, GoodWorks International, LLC (1996-Present); President, National Council of Churches (2000-2001); Co-Chairman, Atlanta Committee for the Olympic Games (1996); Mayor, City of Atlanta, GA (1982-1990); Permanent U.S. Representative, United Nations, New York, NY (1977-1979); Member, U.S. House of Representatives from Geor-

gia's Fifth Congressional District, United States Congress, Washington, DC (1973-1977); Executive Vice President, Southern Christian Leadership Conference (1967-1970); Executive Director, Southern Christian Leadership Conference (1964-1970); Staff, Southern Christian Leadership Conference (1961-1970); Administrator, Citizen Education Program, Southern Christian Leadership Conference (1961-1964); Associate Director, Department of Youth Work, National Council of Churches (1957-1961); Professor of Public Affairs, Georgia State University, Atlanta, GA **CR:** Chairman, National Steering Committee, Working Families for Walmart (2006); President, National Council of Churches (2000-2001) **CIV:** Co-Chairman, Summer Olympics (1996); Chairman, Atlanta Community Relations Commission (1970-1972); Pastor, Evergreen Congregational Church, Beachton, GA (1957-1959); Pastor, Bethany Congregational Church, Thomasville, GA (1955-1957); Chairman, Board, Delta Ministry of Mississippi; Board of Directors, Martin Luther King Junior Center for Social Change (Now The King Center); Board of Directors, Robert F. Kennedy Memorial Foundation; Board of Directors, Field Foundation; Board of Directors, Southern Christian Leadership Conference; Director, Drum Major Institute for Public Policy; Chairman, Board, Global Initiative for the Advancement of Nutritional Therapy; Honorary Co-Chair, World Justice Project **CW:** Author, "Walk in My Shoes: Conversations between a Civil Rights Legend and His Godson on the Journey Ahead with Kabir Sehgal" (2010); Author, "The Politician" (2010); Narrator, Documentary, "Rwanda Rising" (2007); Author, "An Easy Burden: The Civil Rights Movement and the Transformation of America" (1996); Author, "A Way Out of No Way: The Spiritual Memoirs of Andrew Young" (1994); Author, "The History of the Civil Rights Movement" (1990); Author, "Andrew Young at the United Nations" (1978); Author, "Andrew Young, Remembrance & Homage" (1978); Author, "Trespassing Ghost: A Critical Study of Andrew Young" (1978) **AW:** Ivan Allen Jr. Prize for Social Change (2018); Lifetime Achievement Emmy Award (2011); Heroes, Saints and Legends Honoree, Foundation of Wesley Woods (2010); Louisiana Legend, Louisiana Public Broadcasting, Baton Rouge, LA (2005); Eagle Award, United States Sports Academy (1995); Co-Recipient, Martin Luther King Junior Award for Public Service, Ebony Magazine (1990); French Legion of Honor Medal (1982); Presidential Medal of Freedom (1980); Pax-Christi Award, St. John's University (1970); Spingarn Medal, NAACP **MEM:** Americans for Democratic Action; Alpha Phi Alpha Fraternity, Inc. **PA:** Democrat

YOUNG, DONALD EDWIN, T: U.S. Representative from Alaska **I:** Government Administration/Government Relations/Government Services **DOB:** 06/09/1933 **PB:** Meridian **SC:** CA/USA **MS:** Married **SPN:** Anne Garland Walton (06/09/2015); Lu Fredson (1963, Deceased 08/01/2009) **CH:** Joni; Dawn **ED:** BA, California State University, Chico, CA (1958); AA, Yuba College (1952) **CT:** Mariner's License **C:** Member, U.S. House of Representatives from Alaska's At-Large Congressional District, United States Congress, Washington, DC (1973-Present); Chairman, U.S. House Committee on Transportation and Infrastructure (2001-2007); Chairman, U.S. House Committee on National Resources (1995-2001); Member, Alaska State Senate (1970-1973); Member, Alaska House of Representatives (1966-1970); Mayor, Fort Yukon City Council (1960-1968); Member, Fort Yukon City Council, Alaska (1960-1968) **CR:** Teacher, Fifth Grade, Bureau of Indian Affairs Elementary School; Captain, Tug and Barge

Operation, Yukon River, AK; Commercial Fisherman **MIL:** 41st Tank Battalion, United States Army (1955-1957) **PA:** Republican **RE:** Episcopalian

YOUNG, GARY A., T: Vocational/Economic Expert **I:** Financial Services **CN:** Young Vocational Analytics **DOB:** 02/09/1953 **PB:** Philadelphia **SC:** PA/USA **PT:** Charles Calvin Young; Henrietta Emma (Sorber) Young **MS:** Married **SPN:** Linda Witchko (05/02/1992); Shelly Lamkin (7/3/1976, Divorced 1991) **CH:** Katherine Anna; Charles Alfred Randall **ED:** MEd, Temple University (1982); BA, Eastern College, St. David's, PA (1975) **CT:** Earnings Analyst (AREA) (2012); Diplomate, American Board of Vocational Experts (2000); Certified Case Manager (1984); Certified Disability Management Specialist (1984); Certified Rehabilitation Counselor (1980) **C:** Vocational/Economic Expert, Young Vocational Analytics (1994-Present); Vocational Consultant, G.L.K. Condor, Trenton, NJ (1994-Present); Vocation Expert, Social Security Administration, Philadelphia, PA (1982-Present); Vocational Counselor, General Rehabilitation, Philadelphia, PA (1980-1982) **CR:** Continental Insurance Company, New York, NY (1990-1994) **CIV:** Committee Member, New Jersey Democratic Committee, Trenton, NJ (1994); Continental Insurance Company; Sailboat Racing Team; Board Member, Reflex Sympathetic Dystrophy Syndrome Association **MEM:** American Board of Vocational Experts; American Rehabilitation Economics Association; National Association of Forensic Economists **MH:** Albert Nelson Marquis Lifetime Achievement Award; Marquis Who's Who Top Professional **AS:** Mr. Young attributes his success to hard work, luck, intuition, and God's providence. He often was in the right place at the right time. Finding a profession that fits his personality perfectly was the key to Mr. Young's success. **B/I:** Mr. Young wanted to help people but he did not want them to have to pay for it. He got involved with the ADA (Americans with Disabilities Act) because of this desire. **AV:** Formerly singing opera

YOUNG, JOHN LEONARD MICHAEL MD, MD, T: Psychiatrist, Educator **I:** Education/Educational Services **CN:** Yale Universty School of Medicine **DOB:** 04/26/1943 **PB:** Huntington **SC:** IN/USA **PT:** Jay Alfred Young; Anne Elizabeth (Neff) Young **MS:** Single **ED:** MD, Stanford University (1977); MS, University of Notre Dame (1974); ThM, University of Notre Dame (1970); BA, Stonehill College, Magna Cum Laude (1966) **CT:** Ordained Priest, Roman Catholic Church (1971); Diplomate in Psychiatry, American Board of Forensic Psychiatry; Qualifications in Forensic Psychiatry, American Board of Forensic Psychiatry **C:** Clinical Professor, Yale University Medical School (2004-Present); Attending Psychiatrist, Whiting Forensic Division Connecticut Valley Hospital, Middletown, CT (1988-2009); Associate Clinical Professor, Yale University Medical School (1992-2004); Assistant Clinical Professor, Yale University Medical School (1989-1992); Assistant Professor, Psychiatry, Yale University Medical School (1982-1988); Postdoctoral Fellow, Yale University Medical School (1981-1982); Resident in Psychiatry, Yale University Medical School, New Haven, CT (1978-1981); Resident in Medicine, Norwalk Hospital (1977-1978) **CR:** Supervisor, Pastoral Center, New Haven, CT (1979-1986); Ethics Committee, Hospital of St. Raphael, New Haven, CT (1982-Present); Ethics Committee, Connecticut Psychiatric Society; Ethics Committee, American Academy of Psychiatry and the Law; Ethics Committee, Saint Mary's Hospital; Ethics Committee, Waterbury; Ethics Committee, Connecticut Mental Health Center; Ethics Committee, Yale-New Haven Hospital; Journal Reviewer, Psychiatric Services; Journal Reviewer, Journal of American Academy Psychiatry and the Law; Journal Reviewer, Journal of Forensic Science; Journal Reviewer, American Journal of Bioethics **CIV:** Trustee, Stonehill College, Easton, MA (1972-2001); Board of Directors, King's College, Wilkes-Barre, PA (1983-Present); Hill Health Center, New Haven, CT (1983-1985); Consultant, Law Revision Committee, Connecticut House of Representatives, Hartford, CT (1983-1985) **CW:** Contributor, Articles, Medical Journals; Contributor, Case Studies; Contributor, Chapters, Books **AW:** Howard ZonanaAlumni Award for Contributions to Forensic Psychiatry (2018); Roger Coleman Award, Connecticut Psychiatric Society (2006); President's Medal, Stonehill College (1980); Stanford University Medical Alumni Association Scholar (1976) **MEM:** Distinguished Life Member, Fellow, American Psychiatric Association; Section Chair, American Academy of Forensic Sciences; American Medical Association; American Academy of Psychiatry and the Law; 50-Year Member, American Chemical Society; American College of Psychiatrists; International Association for Forensic Psychotherapy; Society for Science Study of Religion; American Association for the Advancement of Science **MH:** Albert Nelson Marquis Lifetime Achievement Award; Marquis Who's Who Top Professional **B/I:** Dr. Young became involved in his profession because of his high school faculty, which was a major influence. They had five orders of sisters and a religious priest, all of whom led by such an incredible example. Dr. Young has tried to emulate these individuals for much of his career. **AV:** Playing piano; Swimming; Backpacking; Working out; Block printing **PA:** independent **RE:** Roman Catholic

YOUNG, NEIL, T: Singer-Songwriter, Guitarist **I:** Media & Entertainment **DOB:** 11/12/1945 **PB:** Toronto **SC:** Ontario/Canada **PT:** Scott Alexander Young; Edna Blow Ragland "Rassy" Young **MS:** Married **SPN:** Daryl Hannah (08/25/2018); Pegi Morton (08/02/1978, Divorced 2014); Susan Acevedo (1968-1970) **CH:** Ben Young; Amber Jean Young; Zeke Young **ED:** LHD (Honorary), San Francisco State University (2006); MusD (Honorary), Lakehead University (1992) **C:** Solo Artist, Singer-Songwriter, Guitarist (1969-Present); Singer, Guitarist, Crosby, Stills, Nash & Young (1969-1970, 1974-1975); Singer, Guitarist, Buffalo Springfield (1966-1968) **CIV:** Founder, Active Member of the Board of Directors, Farm Aid (1985-Present); Co-Founder, Host, Bridge School Benefit, Mountain View, CA (1986-2016); Performer, Numerous Concerts and Recordings for Activism and Charity; Advocate, Biodiesel **CW:** Singer-Songwriter, Guitarist, Album, "Colorado," Neil Young and Crazy Horse (2019); Singer-Songwriter, Guitarist, Soundtrack, "Paradox" (2018); Actor, Film, "Paradox" (2018); Singer-Songwriter, Guitarist, Album, "The Visitor" (2017); Singer-Songwriter, Guitarist, Album, "Peace Trail" (2016); Singer-Songwriter, Guitarist, Live Album, "Earth" (2016); Director, Documentary, "Muddy Track" (2015); Singer-Songwriter, Guitarist, Album, "The Monsanto Years" (2015); Singer-Songwriter, Guitarist, Album, "Storytone" (2014); Singer-Songwriter, Guitarist, Album, "A Letter Home" (2014); Featured Interviewee, Documentary, "Sound City" (2013); Singer-Songwriter, Guitarist, Album, "Psychedelic Pill," Neil Young and Crazy Horse (2012); Author, Book, "Waging Heavy Peace: A Hippie Dream" (2012); Singer-Songwriter, Guitarist, Album, "Americana," Neil Young and Crazy Horse (2010); Performer, "Long May You Run," Final Episode of "The Tonight Show with Conan O'Brien" (2010); Singer-Songwriter, Guitarist, Album, "Fork in the Road" (2009); Co-Director, Documentary, "CSNY/ Déjà Vu" (2008); Singer-Songwriter, Guitarist, Album, "Chrome Dreams II" (2007); Singer-Songwriter, Guitarist, Album, "Living with War" (2006); Singer-Songwriter, Guitarist, Album, "Prairie Wind" (2005); Singer-Songwriter, Guitarist, Compilation Album, "Greatest Hits" (2004); Singer-Songwriter, Guitarist, Album, "Greendale," Neil Young and Crazy Horse (2003); Singer-Songwriter, Guitarist, Album, "Are You Passionate?" (2002); Singer-Songwriter, Guitarist, Album, "Silver & Gold" (2000); Singer-Songwriter, Guitarist, Live Album, "Road Rock Vol. 1" (2000); Singer-Songwriter, Guitarist, Live Album, "Year of the Horse, Neil Young and Crazy Horse (1997); Singer-Songwriter, Guitarist, Album, "Broken Arrow" (1996); Singer-Songwriter, Guitarist, Soundtrack, "Dead Man" (1996); Singer-Songwriter, Guitarist, Album, "Sleeps with Angels" (1994); Singer-Songwriter, Guitarist, Soundtrack Single, "Philadelphia," "Philadelphia" (1994); Singer-Songwriter, Guitarist, Live Album, "Unplugged" (1993); Singer-Songwriter, Guitarist, Compilation Album, "Lucky Thirteen" (1993); Singer-Songwriter, Guitarist, Album, "Harvest Moon" (1992); Singer-Songwriter, Guitarist, Live Album, "Arc," Neil Young and Crazy Horse (1991); Singer-Songwriter, Guitarist, Live Album, "Weld," Neil Young and Crazy Horse (1991); Actor, "Love at Large" (1990); Singer-Songwriter, Guitarist, Album, "Ragged Glory" (1990); Singer-Songwriter, Guitarist, Album, "Freedom" (1989); Singer-Songwriter, Guitarist, EP, "Eldorado" (1989); Actor, "'68" (1988); Singer-Songwriter, Guitarist, Album, "This Note's for You" (1988); Singer-Songwriter, Guitarist, Album, "Life" (1987); Actor, "Made in Heaven," Neil Young and Crazy Horse (1987); Singer-Songwriter, Guitarist, Album, "Landing on Water" (1986); Singer-Songwriter, Guitarist, Album, "Old Ways" (1985); Singer-Songwriter, Guitarist, Album, "Everybody's Rockin'" (1983); Co-Director, Film, "Human Highway" (1982); Singer-Songwriter, Guitarist, Album, "Trans" (1982); Singer-Songwriter, Guitarist, Album, "Re·ac·tor," Neil Young and Crazy Horse (1981); Singer-Songwriter, Guitarist, Album, "Hawks & Doves" (1980); Singer-Songwriter, Guitarist, Soundtrack, "Where the Buffalo Roam" (1980); Singer-Songwriter, Guitarist, Album, "Rust Never Sleeps" (1979); Singer-Songwriter, Guitarist, Live Album, "Live Rust," Neil Young and Crazy Horse (1979); Singer-Songwriter, Guitarist, Album, "Comes a Time" (1978); Featured Performer, Documentary, "The Last Waltz" (1978); Singer-Songwriter, Guitarist, Album, "American Stars 'n Bars" (1977); Singer-Songwriter, Guitarist, Compilation Album, "Decade" (1977); Featured Performer, Numerous Documentaries (1978-2014); Singer-Songwriter, Guitarist, Album, "Long May You Run" (1976); Singer-Songwriter, Guitarist, Album, "Zuma" (1975); Singer-Songwriter, Guitarist, Album, "Tonight's the Night" (1975); Singer-Songwriter, Guitarist, Album, "On the Beach" (1974); Singer-Songwriter, Guitarist, Live Album, "Time Fades Away" (1973); Director, Documentary, "Journey Through the Past" (1973); Singer-Songwriter, Guitarist, Album, "Harvest" (1972); Singer-Songwriter, Guitarist, Soundtrack, "Journey Through the Past" (1972); Singer-Songwriter, Guitarist, Album, "After the Gold Rush" (1970); Singer-Songwriter, Guitarist, Album, "Everybody Knows This Is Nowhere, Neil Young and Crazy Horse (1969); Singer-Songwriter, Guitarist, Album, "Neil Young" (1969); Singer- Songwriter, Guitarist, "Last Time Around," Buffalo Springfield (1968); Singer-Songwriter, Guitarist, "Buffalo Springfield Again," Buffalo Springfield (1967); Singer-Songwriter, Guitarist, "Buffalo Springfield," Buffalo Springfield (1966) **AW:** Artist of the Year, Juno Awards (2011); Adult Alternative Album of the Year, Juno Awards (2011); Allan Waters Humanitarian Award, Juno Awards (2011); Best Rock Song, "Angry World," Grammy Awards (2011); Best Art Direction on a Boxed/ Special Limited Edition Package, "The Archives

Vol. 1 1963-1972," Grammy Awards (2010); Musi-Cares Person of the Year (2010); Adult Alternative Album of the Year, "Living with War" (2007); Artist of the Year, American Music Association (2006); Jack Richardson Producer of the Year, "The Painter," Juno Awards (2006); Spirit of Liberty Award, People for the American Way (2001); Best Male Artist, Juno Awards (2001); Ranked #34 in "100 Greatest Artists of All Time" List, Rolling Stone (2000); Inductee, Canada's Walk of Fame (2000); Ranked #2, "Greatest Living Songwriters" List, Paste (2000); Inductee as a Member of Buffalo Springfield, Rock and Roll Hall of Fame (1997); Inductee for his Solo Work, Rock and Roll Hall of Fame (1995); Male Vocalist of the Year, Juno Awards (1995); Nominee, Academy Award for Best Original Song, "Philadelphia," "Philadelphia" (1994); Video of the Year, "This Note's for You," MTV Video Music Awards (1989); Album of the Year, Juno Awards (1994); Inductee, Canadian Music Hall of Fame (1982)

YOUNG, SUSAN EILEEN, T: Elementary School Educator (Retired) **I:** Education/Educational Services **DOB:** 08/08/1956 **PB:** New Haven **SC:** CT/USA **PT:** James William Tobin; Rosemary Ann (Drotar) Tobin **MS:** Married **SPN:** Randy H. Young **CH:** Sarah E. Young **ED:** Postgraduate Coursework, George Mason University (1988-1991); BA, Annhurst College (1978) **CT:** Certified Teacher, State of Connecticut, Commonwealth of Virginia **C:** Retired Elementary School Educator (2004); Reading Center Paraprofessional, Ferry Farm Elementary School, Stafford, VA (2000-2004); Kindergarten Paraprofessional, Ferry Farm Elementary School, Stafford, VA (1999-2000); Preschool Special Education Paraprofessional, Ferry Farm Elementary School, Stafford, VA (1997-1999); Teacher Assistant, West Gate Elementary School, Manassas, VA (1994-1997); Teacher, Holy Spirit School, Annandale, VA (1990-1992); Teacher, St. Mary School, Branford, CT (1978-1981); Paraprofessional Reading Center, Margaret Brent School, Stafford, VA **CR:** Home Tutor, Dale City, VA, Summer (1991); Substitute Teacher, Fairfax School System (Now Fairfax County Public Schools), Prince William County Public School System, Diocese of Arlington Catholic Schools (1987-1990) **CIV:** Volunteer, Special Olympics, Denver, CO (1983) **MIL:** With, United States Navy (1983-1987); Intelligence Specialist, United States Navy **MEM:** Kappa Delta Pi, International Honor Society in Education; Phi Delta Kappa (Now PDK International) **AV:** Piano; Sports (watching basketball, softball, baseball); Crafts; Reading; Scrapbooks; Formerly playing basketball and softball **RE:** Roman Catholic

YOUNG, TODD CHRISTOPHER, T: U.S. Senator from Indiana **I:** Government Administration/Government Relations/Government Services **DOB:** 08/24/1972 **PB:** Lancaster **SC:** PA/USA **PT:** Bruce H. Young; Nancy R. (Pierce) Young **MS:** Married **SPN:** Jennifer Tucker (2005) **CH:** Tucker; Annalise; Abigail; Ava **ED:** JD, Indiana University Robert H. McKinney School of Law (2006); Diploma, HHL Leipzig Graduate School of Management (2001); MA in American Politics, University College London Institute of the Americas (2001); MBA, The University of Chicago Booth School of Business; BS in Political Science, United States Naval Academy, Cum Laude, Annapolis, MD (1995) **C:** Chairman, National Republican Senatorial Committee (2019-Present); U.S. Senator from Indiana (2017-Present); Member, U.S. House of Representatives from Indiana's Ninth Congressional District, United States Congress, Washington, DC (2011-2017); Member, U.S. House Armed Services Committee, Washington, DC (2011-2017); Member, U.S. House Budget Committee, Washington, DC

(2011-2017); Deputy Prosecutor, Orange County, IN (2007-Present); Attorney, Tucker and Tucker, P.C. Paoli, IN (2006-Present); Management Consultant, Crowe Chizek & Co. (Now Crowe LLP); Legislative Assistant, Energy Policy to U.S. Senator Richard Lugar, U.S. Senate, Washington, D.C.; Adjunct Professor, Public Affairs, Indiana University O'Neill School of Public and Environmental Affairs **CIV:** Policy Analyst, The Heritage Foundation, Washington, DC (2001); Pro Bono Mediator, Indiana Civil Rights Commission; Board Director, HVAF of Indiana; Board Director, Crisis Pregnancy Center **MIL:** Advanced to Captain, United States Marine Corps (1995-2000) **MEM:** President, Orange County Bar Association (2008); Indiana Leadership Forum **PA:** Republican **RE:** Christian

YUN, JULIANA INKYUNG, DDS, T: Periodontist **I:** Medicine & Health Care **CN:** Juliana Yun DDS PC **DOB:** 09/26/1971 **PB:** New York **SC:** NY/USA **PT:** Chongsun Tom Yun (Deceased); Jeannie Yun **MS:** Married **SPN:** Joshua Ehlin **CH:** Olivia **ED:** Postgraduate Coursework, Program in Periodontics (2006); General Practice Residency, United States Navy (1999); DDS, Stony Brook School of Dental Medicine (1998); BA in Music Performance, Violin, Stony Brook University (1994) **CT:** Diplomate, The American Board of Periodontology (2006) **C:** Periodontist, Private Practice, Juliana Yun DDS PC, Ramsey, NJ (2014-Present); Periodontist, Private Practice, Juliana Yun DDS (2006-2014); Clinical Assistant Professor, Periodontics, New York University College of Dentistry (2003-2006); Private Practice in General Dentistry, New York (1999-2005); Lecturer, HiOssen Implants LLC **MIL:** Lieutenant, U.S. Navy (1996-1999) **AW:** Bergen Magazine Top Dentist (2017-2020); New Jersey Monthly Top Dentists (2016-2020); 201 Magazine Top Dentist (2016-2020) **MEM:** Academy of Osseointegration (2009-Present); American Board of Periodontology (2003-Present); American Academy of Periodontology (2003-Present); American Dental Association (1998-Present); Northeastern Society of Periodontists (2003-2014); Stony Brook Dental Research Society (1997-1998) **AS:** Success comes with resilience, hard work, kindness, compassion, and drive. It also involves a great team of support at home and at work. **B/I:** Dr. Yun's late father was a general dentist. Growing up, her father never mentioned to his children anything about wanting them to become a dentist like him. When Dr. Yun enrolled in college, she studied violin performance as a music major. A few years into her musical studies, she realized that she would not become a professional musician, but instead find an alternate career path. She began taking courses in science and art. One day she discussed the idea of following in her father's footsteps to becoming a dentist. Because he had never mentioned the profession to his children prior, she had the notion that it wouldn't be something that he wanted for her. Instead, when she presented the idea, her father became elated, and began to share his knowledge and love of the dental profession and patient treatment. After she graduated from dental school, she completed her residency in the United States Navy, and then went into private practice with her father for several years. To announce his daughter's joining of the practice, her father proudly sent a picture of him holding the new Dr. Yun as a baby, to all of patients and friends. It was a proud moment for him. **THT:** "People will forget what you said. People will forget what you did. But people will never forget how you made them feel." She lives by this saying.

YURKO, SANDRA R., T: Technologist (Retired) **I:** Technology **CN:** University of Pittsburgh Medical Center (UPMC) **DOB:** 03/20/1938 **PB:** Pittsburgh

SC: PA/USA **PT:** Louis J. Berger; Tillie C. Berger **MS:** Widowed **SPN:** Richard M. Yurko **ED:** Associate Degree, Community College of Allegheny County (1997); Coursework, University of Pittsburgh (1970) **CT:** Registered Cardiac Sonographer, Cardiovascular Credentialing International; Diagnostic Cardiac Sonographer, American Registry for Diagnostic Medical Sonography; Diagnostic Medical Sonographer, American Registry for Diagnostic Medical Sonography **C:** Retired (2003); Cardiac Supervisor, University of Pittsburgh Medical Center (UPMC), Pittsburgh, PA (1989-2003); Senior Cardiac Sonographer, Montefiore Hospital (Now UPMC Montefiore), Pittsburgh, PA (1975-1989); Senior Cardiac Catheterization Technologist, Montefiore Hospital (Now UPMC Montefiore), Pittsburgh, PA (1965-1975); Resuscitation Response Team (1965-1975); Pulmonary Technologist, Montefiore Hospital (Now UPMC Montefiore), Pittsburgh, PA (1965-1970); Senior Allergy Technician, Montefiore Hospital (Now UPMC Montefiore), Pittsburgh, PA (1955-1965); EKG Technician, Montefiore Hospital (Now UPMC Montefiore), Pittsburgh, PA (1955) **CR:** Member, Diagnostic Medical Sonography Advisory Committee, Community College of Allegheny County (2002); Presenter in Field **CIV:** Meals on Wheels America; First Flu Shot Clinic; First Glaucoma Clinic; First Pittsburgh Disaster Drill; First Polio Shot Clinic **CW:** Knitting/Crocheting Hat/Scarf Project for Homeless, The Salvation Army USA **AW:** Echo Challenge Award, Council on Cardiac Sonography, American Society of Echocardiography (1997); Dean's List (1993-1994) **MEM:** American Registry for Diagnostic Medical Sonography, Inc.; American Institute of Ultrasound in Medicine; PIDS (Pediatric Infectious Disease Society); DHWPA; Three Rivers Birding Club; National Audubon Society **B/I:** Ms. Yurko became involved in her profession because when she was a child, she experienced World War II from afar. She remembers saying that she wanted to be a nurse and that if there was a war, she wanted to go to the war zone. That's what inspired her. She graduated and had to wait one year because she needed to be 18 to attend college, so she started working as her parents did not have money to send her to college. She had a brother four years younger, and, back then, she thought it was more important for the man to attend college. She tried to get a job. Her mother took her to the big banks in Pittsburgh and stood outside while she filled out applications. The only one that would hear her was IBM, back when they used Microfiche. She went to the local hospital and applied there; they had a position in the allergy lab. **AV:** Gardening; Traveling; Birdwatching; Volunteering; Walking; Trout fishing

ZABORSZKY, LASZLO, T: Neuroscientist, Distinguished Professor **I:** Education/Educational Services **CN:** Rutgers University **DOB:** 10/09/1944 **PB:** Budapest **SC:** Hungary **PT:** Ilona Hegedus; Geza Zaborszky **MS:** Divorced **CH:** DSc, Hungarian Academy of Sciences (1999); PhD, Hungarian Academy of Sciences, Budapest, Hungary (1981); MD, Semmelweis Medical School, Budapest, Hungary (1969) **C:** Neuroscientist, Distinguished Professor, Rutgers University (-Present); Distinguished Professor, Rutgers University - Newark (2014-Present); Faculty Chair, Rutgers University - Newark (2016-2017); Professor, Rutgers, The State University of New Jersey (2004-2014); Associate Professor, Rutgers, The State University of New Jersey (1993-2004); Associate Professor, University of Virginia, Charlottesville, VA (1981-1993) **CR:** Editor-in-Chief, Brain Structure and Function (2007-Present) **CIV:** President, Association of Hungarian-American Academicians (2018-2020); President, New York Hungarian Scientific

Society (2012-2016) **CW:** Editor, "Neuroanatomical Tract-Tracing 3: Molecules, Neurons and Systems," Springer (2006); Editor, "Neuroanatomical Tract-Tracing Methods 2," Plenum (1989); Author, "Afferent Connection of the Medial Basal Hypothalamus," Springer (1982) **AW:** Grantee, National Institutes Health/National Institute of Neurological Disorders and Stroke (1986-Present); Recipient, Board of Trustees Award for Research Excellence, Rutgers, The State University of New Jersey (2016); Recipient, Knight's Cross of Order of Merit of Hungary (2013); Foreign Member of the Hungarian Academy of Sciences (2009) **MEM:** Society for Neuroscience (1981); New York Academy of Sciences; American Association for the Advancement of Science **MH:** Albert Nelson Marquis Lifetime Achievement Award; Marquis Who's Who Top Professional **AS:** He attributes his success to steadfastness, curiosity, perseverance and sheer luck. **B/I:** Dr. Zaborszky started his medical training in Hungary. He was inspired by John Szentagothai, a world-famous scientist, then chairman of the Anatomy Department at Semmelweis Medical School in Budapest. **AV:** Classical music; New York Philharmonic; Reading biographies; Metropolitan Opera

ZAIM, SEMIH, T: Chemical Company Executive **I:** Sciences **DOB:** 03/01/1926 **PB:** Bursa **SC:** Turkey **PT:** Halil Refet Zaim; Saibe (Rustu) Zaim **MS:** Married **SPN:** Ismet Agirbas (3/9/1951) **CH:** Sina H.; Bulent R.; Beyhan **ED:** Master's Degree in Chemical Engineering, University of Istanbul (1949) **C:** Retired; President, Zaim Associates Specialty Chems., Mountain Lakes, NJ (1992-Present); President, Zaim Associates, Mountain Lakes, NJ (1993-Present); Vice President, R&D, Process Research Products Division, Chessco Industries, Trenton, NJ (1981-1992); Supervisor, R&D, Essex Chemical Company, Sayreville, NJ (1976-1981); Senior Research Chemist, Texus Research Center, Parsippany, NJ (1969-1976); Research Chemist, R&D Division, Polysar Company, Sarnia, Ontario, Canada (1962-1969); Chemical Engineer, Arge Research Laboratory, Ankara, Turkey (1949-1961) **CR:** Consultant, UN Development Program (1979, 1981) **MIL:** Served to Major, Turkish Air Force (1949-1961) **CW:** Patentee in Field **AW:** NATO Research Fellow, Carde Research Laboratory, Quebec, Canada (1961-1962) **MH:** Albert Nelson Marquis Lifetime Achievement Award; Marquis Who's Who Top Professional **B/I:** Mr. Zaim's teacher in high school back in his native country of Turkey, saw the potential in him and suggested that he pursue a career in chemistry.

ZAKARIA, FAREED RAFIQ, T: Journalist, Political Scientist, Author **I:** Media & Entertainment **DOB:** 01/20/1964 **PB:** Mumbai **SC:** India **PT:** Rafiq Ahmed Zakaria; Fatima Zakaria **MS:** Divorced **SPN:** Paula Henley Throckmorton (04/05/1997, Divorced 2018) **CH:** Omar; Lila; Sofia **ED:** Doctor of Philosophy in Government, Harvard University (1993); Bachelor of Arts, Yale University (1986); Coursework, Cathedral and John Connon School, Mumbai, India; Honorary Degrees, Harvard University, Brown University, Duke University, Johns Hopkins University, University of Miami, Oberlin College, Bates College, University of Oklahoma, Others **C:** Editor-at-Large, Columnist, TIME (2010-Present); Host, "Fareed Zakaria GPS," CNN (2008-Present); Editor, Newsweek International (2000-2010); Managing Editor, Foreign Affairs, New York, NY (1993-2000); Executive Coordinator, Changing Security Environmental Project, Olin Institute, Harvard University, Cambridge, MA (1991-1992); Reporter, Researcher, The New Republic, Washington, DC (1987); Director, Research Project on American Foreign Policy, Harvard University **CR:** Host, "Foreign Exchange with Fareed Zakaria," PBS (2005-2008); News Analyst, "This Week with George Stephanopoulos," ABC (2002-2007); Annual Orator, Philomathean Society, University of Pennsylvania (2000); Weekly Columnist, The Washington Post, Newsweek; Adjunct Professor, International Relations, Columbia University; Former Wine Columnist, Slate; Interlocutor, Annual Berggruen Prize, Berggruen Institute **CIV:** Trustee, Yale Corporation (2006-Present); Trustee, Shakespeare & Co. Inc.; Trustee, Trilateral Commission **CW:** Author, "In Defense of a Liberal Education" (2015); Producer, Consultant, Documentary Television Series, "Vice," HBO (2013); Author, "The Post-American World, Release 2.0" (2011); Author, "The Post-American World" (2008); Author, "The Future of Freedom: Illiberal Democracy at Home and Abroad" (2003); Editor, Newsweek International (2000); Author, "From Wealth to Power: The Unusual Origins of America's World Role" (1998); Co-Editor, "The American Encounter: The United States And The Making Of The Modern World: Essays From 75 Years Of Foreign Affairs" (1997); Managing Editor, Foreign Affairs (1992); Former Editor-in-Chief, Yale Political Monthly; Contributor, The New York Times, The Wall Street Journal, The New Yorker, The New Republic; Contributing Editor, Atlantic Media; Host, Primetime Specials, "Blindsided: How ISIS Shook the World," "Why Trump Won," and "Putin: The Most Powerful Man in the World," CNN Worldwide; Contributor, CNN.com; Author, Daily Digital Newsletter, "Fareed's Global Briefing" **AW:** Named, Top 10 Global Thinker of the Last 10 Years, Foreign Policy Magazine (2019); Arthur Ross Media Award, American Academy of Diplomacy (2017); Nominee, Outstanding Interview, "Fareed Zakaria GPS," Emmy Awards (2013); Peabody Award, "Fareed Zakaria GPS: Interpretation and Commentary on Iran and The GPS Primetime Special: Restoring the American Dream-Fixing Education" (2011); Padma Bhushan Award, Indian Government (2010); Named, 50 Highest-Earning Political Figures, Newsweek (2010); Person of the Year 2008, India Abroad (2009); Named, One of the 25 Most Influential Liberals in the American America, Forbes (2009); Named, Top 100 Public Intellectuals, Foreign Policy & Prospect Magazine (2007); Named, 21 Most Important People of the 21st Century, Esquire Magazine (1999); Overseas Press Club Award (1998); Five-Time Nominee, National Magazine Awards; Peabody Award **MEM:** Berggruen Institute; Board of Directors, Council on Foreign Relations; Century Association; Former Member, Yale Political Union, Scroll and Key, Party of the Right; Board of Directors, International House, Columbia University; Board of Directors, Colin Powell School for Civic and Global Leadership, City College of New York **RE:** Muslim

ZAMORA, MARIA, T: Owner **I:** Luxury Goods & Jewelry **CN:** John's Jewelers **C:** Owner, John's Jewelers, California (1998-Present); Employee, John's Jewelers, California (1991-1998) **AW:** Best Jeweler, Pajaro County **MEM:** Jewelers Board of Trade; Jewelry Industry Authority; Pajaro Valley Chamber of Commerce **AS:** Ms. Zamora attributes her success to her honesty. **B/I:** Ms. Zamora simply needed a job and was hired by John's Jewelers. After seven years of working and learning the business, she was presented with the opportunity to buy the company, which she has now owned since 1998.

ZANGER, LARRY, T: Partner **I:** Law and Legal Services **CN:** Holland & Knight LLP **DOB:** 07/10/1946 **PB:** Brooklyn **SC:** NY/USA **PT:** Mark H. Zanger; Lillian (Cohen) Zanger **MS:** Married **SPN:** Bonnie Agnes Zanger (06/08/1975) **CH:** Laura; Eric **ED:** JD, Northwestern University (1970); BSBA, Northwestern University (1967) **CT:** Certified Public Accountant, Illinois **C:** Partner, Holland & Knight's, Chicago, IL (2002-Present); Partner, McBride Baker & Coles, Chicago, IL (1990-2002); Partner, Martin, Craig, Chester & Sonnenschein, Chicago, IL (1983-1990); Partner, Zanger, Lang & Heftman, Chicago, IL (1972-1983); Adjunct Professor, University of Illinois, Chicago, IL (1972-1975); Associate, McDermott, Will & Emery, Chicago, IL (1970-1972) **CIV:** Treasurer, Elmhurst Baseball Leagues (1990-1996) **CW:** Columnist, Chicago Computer Guide (1989-Present); Columnist, VAR Business (1996-1998); Contributor, Articles, Professional Journals **AW:** The Best Lawyers in America Guide, Information Technology Law (2006-2019); Leading Lawyer, Computer & Technology Law, Leading Lawyers Magazine (2017); Elijah Watts Sells Award, American Institute of CPA's (1968); Martindale-Hubbell AV Preeminent Peer Review Rated; Chicago Law Bulletin Leading Lawyer; Who's Who in American Law; Who's Who in the Midwest; Lincoln Award Winner, Illinois Bar Journal **MEM:** Chicago Bar Association (1989-Present); Chairman, Computer Law Committee, Chicago Bar Association (1994-1995); Computer Law Association; Beta Gamma Sigma **MH:** Marquis Who's Who Top Professional **B/I:** Mr. Zanger became involved in his profession because he had a lucky break at a time in his profession when he was already in the industry, and it took off, during the time when he was a tax lawyer and was doing corporate work. He was involved with software programs and software development. However he will never forget the time when a client called him and said that they really loved him and wanted him to represent them on a piece of software to license to other people. He responded that he did not know how to do that kind of law because he was a tax and business lawyer. But, they responded to him, not to worry about it because no one else knew how to do it either. So they would figure it out together. That is how he got into the business and became an information technology lawyer. Others found out that he did the work and he did it well. So, he got a lot of clients. However, even though this fell into his lap, he chose to become an attorney because his undergraduate degree was in accounting, he enjoyed doing accounting, but he didn't want to be an accountant. So, the thing that used both tax and accounting was being a tax lawyer. So, he thought it would be fascinating. So, he went to school to become a tax lawyer.

ZAVALA, ALBERT, PHD, T: Psychologist **I:** Medicine & Health Care **DOB:** 03/10/1930 **PB:** Chicago **SC:** IL/USA **PT:** Edward Zavala; Maria Soledad (Herrejon) Zavala **SPN:** Pamela Pomeroy Zavala **CH:** Camille; Sally; Elena; Jenifer; Alexis **ED:** PhD, Kansas State University (1966); MA, Michigan State University (1961); BA, Willamette University (1959) **C:** Senior Staff Engineer, Hernandez Engineering, Inc., Santa Clara, CA (2000-2002); Bid Manager, Siemens Information and Network Communications, Inc., Santa Clara, CA (1997-2000); Senior Engineer, Nova Management Monterey, CA (1994-1997); Senior Staff Engineer, Lockheed Missiles and Space Co., Sunnyvale, CA (1985-1994); Senior Research Psychologist, SRI International, Menlo Park, CA (1980-1985); Director Projects, Inpsych, Cupertino, CA (1978-1980); Executive Director, Corp. IV, Cheektowaga, NY (1973-1977); Professor, State University of New York at Buffalo (1968-1978); Professor, Head of Life Sciences, Calspan, Buffalo, NY (1967-1973) **CIV:** Erie County Sheriff's Science Staff (1972-1978) **MIL:** U.S. Army (1955-1957) **CW:** Co-Author, "Personal Appearance Identification" (1972); Contributor, Articles, Professional Journals **AW:** Dunlap Fellow (1964); Fellow, Greater Kansas City Mental Health Foundation (1962-1963) **MEM:** American Psychological

Association; Human Factors Society; Sigma Xi; Psi Chi; Phi Kappa Phi **MH:** Albert Nelson Marquis Lifetime Achievement Award

ZEHR, ELDON IRVIN, T: Science Educator, Plant Pathologist **I:** Education/Educational Services **CN:** Clemson University **DOB:** 06/25/1935 **PB:** Manson **SC:** IA/USA **PT:** Clarence D. Zehr; Clara (Horsch) Zehr **MS:** Married **SPN:** Rosa Rebecca Waidelic (8/31/1957, Deceased) **CH:** Jeffrey; Darrell; Russell; Ann; Marie; Tammy; Judy **ED:** PhD, Cornell University (1969); MS, Cornell University (1965); BA, Goshen College (1960) **C:** Retired (1998); Professor, Emeritus Clemson University (1978-1998); Associate Professor, Clemson University (1973-1978); Assistant Professor, Clemson University (1969-1973) **CR:** Professor Emeritus (1998-Present) **CW:** Contributor, Articles, Professional Journals **AW:** Recipient Carroll R. Miller Award; Godley-Snell Award **MEM:** American Association for the Advancement of Science; American Phytopathological Society; Sigma Xi; Gamma Sigma Delta **MH:** Albert Nelson Marquis Lifetime Achievement Award **B/I:** Dr. Zehr was inspired to explore plant pathology at the suggestion of his professor, Dr. Frank Bishop. As soon as he became involved, he knew he wanted to pursue a career in the field. **AV:** Bowling; Singing; Gardening **PA:** Independent **RE:** Methodist

ZEID, BRIAN D., MBA, MOS, T: Accountant **I:** Education/Educational Services **CN:** University of Illinois at Chicago **PB:** Chicago **SC:** IL/USA **PT:** Earl I. Zeid; Lenore G. Coran-Zeid **ED:** Master of Business Administration, North Park University (1999); Bachelor of Science in Accounting, DeVry University, Summa Cum Laude (1995) **CT:** Microsoft Office Specialist (MOS) **C:** Accountant, The University of Illinois at Chicago, Chicago, IL (2000-Present); Pricing Coordinator, B.E. Atlas, Chicago, IL (1999-2000); Office Services Clerk, Kamensky Rubinstein Hochman & Delott, Lincolnwood, IL (1997-1999) **CIV:** Chancellor's Committee on Sustainability, The University of Illinois at Chicago (2013-Present); Eco-educator, Bright Beat International (2012-2019); Chicago Advocacy Committee, American Diabetes Association (2013-2014); Host Committee, Chicago Green Festival (2011-2014) **AW:** U.S. Executives Award, National Council of American Executives (2014) **MEM:** Social & Economic Justice Committee, Local 73, Service Employees International Union (2019-Present) **MH:** Lifetime Achievement Award (2018) **AS:** Mr. Zeid attributes his success to determination and persistence. **B/I:** Mr. Zeid became involved in his profession to accentuate his numerical skills in a business environment.

ZELDIN, LEE MICHAEL, T: U.S. Representative from New York; Lawyer **I:** Government Administration/Government Relations/Government Services **DOB:** 01/30/1980 **PB:** East Meadow **SC:** NY/USA **PT:** David Zeldin; Merrill (Schwartz) Zeldin **MS:** Married **SPN:** Diana Zeldin **CH:** Mikayla; Arianna **ED:** JD, Albany Law School (2003); BA in Political Science, State University of New York, Albany, Cum Laude (2001) **C:** Member, U.S. House of Representatives from New York's First Congressional District, United States Congress, Washington, DC (2015-Present); Private Practice Attorney, Smithtown, NY (2008-Present); Member, District Three, New York State Senate (2011-2015); Attorney, Raiser & Kenniff, PC, New York, NY (2007-2008); Counsel, The Port Authority of New York and New Jersey (2007); Legislative Aide, Office of Senator Kenneth P. Lavalle, NY (1998-2000); Member, Committee on Foreign Affairs; Member, Committee on Financial Services **MIL:** Captain, United States Army Reserve (2007-Present); Military Magistrate,

18th Airborne Corps, United States Army, Fort Bragg, NC (2006-2007); Judge Advocate General's Corps Attorney, Operation Iraqi Freedom, United States Army, Iraq (2006); Judge Advocate General's Corps, 82nd Airborne Division, United States Army, Fort Bragg, NC (2004-2006); Second Lieutenant, Military Intelligence Corps, United States Army, Fort Huachuca, AZ (2003-2004) **MEM:** VFW; New York State Bar Association; Jewish War Veterans of the United States of America; The American Legion **BAR:** State of New York (2004) **AV:** Piano; Tae Kwon Do; Boating **PA:** Republican **RE:** Jewish

ZETA-JONES, CATHERINE, T: Actress **I:** Media & Entertainment **DOB:** 09/25/1969 **PB:** Swansea **SC:** Wales/UK **PT:** David Jones; Patricia (Fair) Jones **MS:** Married **SPN:** Michael Douglas (11/18/2000) **CH:** Dylan Michael; Carys Zeta **ED:** Student, Three-Year Course in Musical Theatre, ArtsEd (Arts Educational Schools), Chiswick, London, England **C:** Actress, Film, Television, Stage **CR:** Founder, Casa Zeta-Jones (2017); Global Ambassador, Elizabeth Arden, Inc. (2002) **CIV:** Ambassador, National Society for the Prevention of Cruelty to Children (2005); Donor, "The Mask of Zorro" Outfit to Raise Funds for AIDS Patients in Africa (2001); Patron, Longfields Day Centre; Advocate, International Centre for Missing & Exploited Children, Noah's Ark Appeal, and Others; Founding Host, A Fine Romance, An Annual Charitable Program that Helps Raise Funds for the Motion Picture & Television Fund **CW:** Actress, Web Television Series, "Queen America" (2018-2019); Actress, Television Series, "Feud: Bette and Joan" (2017); Actress, Television Film, "Cocaine Godmother" (2017); Actress, Stage, "The Children's Monologues" (2017); Actress, Film, "Dad's Army" (2016); Actress, Film, "Red 2" (2013); Actress, Film, "Side Effects" (2013); Actress, Film, "Broken City" (2013); Actress, Film, "Playing for Keeps" (2012); Actress, Film, "Rock of Ages" (2012); Actress, Film, "Lay the Favorite" (2012); Actress, Stage, "A Little Night Music" (2009-2010); Actress, Film, "The Rebound" (2009); Actress, Film, "Death Defying Acts" (2007); Actress, Film, "No Reservations" (2007); Actress, Film, "The Legend of Zorro" (2005); Host, Television Series, "Saturday Night Live" (2005); Actress, Film, "Ocean's Twelve" (2004); Actress, Film, "The Terminal" (2004); Actress, Film, "Intolerable Cruelty" (2003); Voice Actress, Film, "Sinbad: Legend of the Seven Seas" (2003); Actress, Film, "Chicago" (2002); Actress, Film, "Traffic" (2000); Actress, Film, "High Fidelity" (2000); Actress, Film, "The Haunting" (1999); Actress, Film, "Entrapment" (1999); Actress, Film, "The Mask of Zorro" (1998); Actress, Film, "The Phantom" (1996); Actress, Television Miniseries, "Titanic" (1996); Actress, Television Film, "Catherine the Great" (1995); Actress, Film, "Blue Juice" (1995); Singer, "In the Arms of Love," Wayne's Wow! Records (1995); Actress, Television Miniseries, "The Cinder Path" (1994); Singer, Duet, "True Love Ways" (1994); Actress, Television Miniseries, "The Return of the Native" (1994); Actress, Film, "Splitting Heirs" (1993); Actress, Television Series, "The Darling Buds of May" (1991-1993); Actress, Television Series, "Out of the Blue" (1991); Actress, Film, "Christopher Columbus: The Discovery" (1992); Actress, Film, "1001 Nights" (1990); Actress, Stage, "Street Scene" (1989); Actress, Stage, "42nd Street" (1987); Actress, Stage, "The Pajama Game" (1985-1986); Actress, Stage, "Bugsy Malone" (1983); Actress, Stage, "Annie" (1981) **AW:** Nominee, Actress Made for Television Movie/Mini-Series, "Cocaine Godmother," Women's Image Awards (2019); Best Actress in a Musical, "A Little Night Music," Tony Awards (2010); Outstanding Actress in a Musical, "A Little Night Music," Drama Desk Awards (2010); Outstanding Actress in a Musical, "A Little Night

Music," Outer Critics Circle Awards (2010); Nominee, Favorite Female Action Star, "The Legend of Zorro," People's Choice Awards (2006); Woman of the Year, Hasty Pudding Theatricals (2005); Nominee, Best Acting Ensemble, "Ocean's Twelve," Critics' Choice Movie Awards (2005); Best Supporting Actress, "Chicago," Academy Awards (2003); Best Performance by an Actress in a Supporting Role, "Chicago," BAFTA Awards (2003); Best Actress in a Supporting Role, "Chicago," British Academy Film Awards (2003); Best Acting Ensemble, "Chicago," Critics' Choice Movie Awards (2003); Best Supporting Actress, "Chicago," Critics' Choice Movie Awards (2003); Best Actress, "Chicago," Evening Standard British Film Awards (2003); Outstanding Performance by a Cast in a Motion Picture, "Chicago," Screen Actors Guild (2003); Outstanding Performance by a Female Actor in a Supporting Role, "Chicago," Screen Actors Guild (2003); Best Supporting Actress, "Chicago," International Online Cinema Awards (INOCA) (2003); Best Actress in a Supporting Role, "Chicago," Phoenix Film Critics Society Awards (2003); Supporting Actress of the Year, "Chicago," ShoWest Convention, USA (2003); Nominee, Best Supporting Actress, "Chicago," Online Film Critics Society (2003); Nominee, Best Actress - Motion Picture Musical or Comedy, "Chicago," Golden Globe Awards (2003); Named "Most Beautiful Woman on the Planet," Esquire (2003); Outstanding Performance by a Cast in a Motion Picture, "Traffic," Screen Actors Guild (2001); Nominee, Best Supporting Actress - Motion Picture, "Traffic," Golden Globe Awards (2001); Nominee, Favorite Supporting Actress - Drama, "Traffic," Blockbuster Entertainment Awards (2001); Nominee, Best Supporting Actress, "Traffic," Chicago Film Critics Association (2001); Ranked #1, "Most Beautiful People," People (2000-2004, 1998); Favorite Actress - Action, "Entrapment," Blockbuster Entertainment Awards (2000); Supporting Actress of the Year, ShoWest Convention, USA (1999); Best Actress - People's Choice, "Entrapment," European Film Awards (1999); Nominee, Best Fight, "The Mask of Zorro," MTV Movie Awards (1999); Nominee, Best Breakthrough Performance, "The Mask of Zorro," MTV Movie Awards (1999); Nominee, Best Actress, "The Mask of Zorro," Saturn Awards (1999); Favorite Female Newcomer, "The Mask of Zorro," Blockbuster Entertainment Awards (1999) **MEM:** Cinema for Peace Foundation

ZHANG, XIAO-FENG, Green Energy and Smart Grid, **T:** President **I:** Nonprofit & Philanthropy **CN:** Global Green Development Alliance **DOB:** 08/08/1951 **PB:** Sichuan **SC:** People's Republic of China **PT:** Yong-Qing Zhang (Deceased 1999); Lan Li (Deceased 2016) **MS:** Married **SPN:** Paul L McEntire (06/22/1996) **CH:** John Jiang Yan; Ning Liu (Daughter-in-Law); Albert Hao Yan (Grandson); Benjamin Kang Yan (Grandson); Charles Chen Yan (Grandson) **ED:** PhD Candidate in EE, Chinese Electric Power Research Institute (EPRI), Beijing, China (1988); MS in EE, Chinese Electric Power Research Institute, Beijing, China (1983); BS in EE, Taiyuan Engineering University, Shanxi (1976) **C:** Chief Executive Officer, Silicon Valley Pacific Innovation Center, San Mateo, CA (2018-Present); Regional Marketing Director, Howard Industrial, Inc., Laurel, MS (2013-2017); Director of Marketing and Administration, JA Solar USA, Inc., San Jose, CA (2010-2013); Senior Project Manager, Senior Analysis, Pacific Gas and Electric Co (NYSE: PCG), San Francisco, CA (2002-2010); Product Manager, China Marketing Manager, ABB Systems Control (NYSE: ABB), Santa Clara, CA (1995-2001); Senior Consultant, Pacific Gas & Electrical Co., San Ramon, CA (1993-1994); Senior Engineer, Empros Systems International (SIEMENS), Plymouth, MN (1989-1993); Power System

Engineer, Systems Control (ABB), Palo Alto, CA (1988-1989); Power System Engineer, Electric Power Research Institute (EPRI), Beijing, China (1983-1988); Power Engineer, Jinzhong District Power Bureau, Shanxi, China (1976-1980); Technician in Electric Power Substation, Jinzhong District Power Bureau, Shanxi, China (1971-1973) **CR:** Executive Vice President, US-China Green Energy Council (2009-2019); Chair, US-China Green Energy Summit (2016-2018) **CIV:** Chair of BOD, Silicon Valley Women Association (SVWA) (2013-Present); Board of Directors, SVWA (2006-Present); President, SVWA (2006-2008) **CW:** Contributor, "Intelligent Voltage Regulator in Smart Grid Distribution System", 2014 China International Conference on Electricity Distribution (CICED 2014), Shenzhen, China (2014); Contributor, "Financial Benefits of Implementing Demand Response in CAISO Market", a presentation on Demand Response session at IEEE 2010 General Meeting, Minneapolis, MN (2010); Contributor, "Electricity Market Operation System," (2001); Contributor, "Two Principal Electricity Markets and Their Computer Systems," Automation of Electric Power Systems (1999); Contributor, "Distribution Short Circuit Analysis Approach Using Hybrid Compensation Method," IEEE Transactions on Power Systems, Vol. 10, No.4, (1995); Contributor, "A Decoupled Optimal Power Flow Approach Using Fletcher's Quadratic Programming Method," IFAC 9th World Congress, Vol.1, Budapest, Hungary (1984); Contributor, Articles, Professional Journals **AW:** 3rd Prize of Scientific Technology Progress Award, Chinese National Committee (1987); 2nd Prize, Ministry of Electric Power, Energy Management Systems, Beijing, China (1986); First Prize, EPRI of China (1985) **MEM:** Chair, Smart Village Committee of IEEE PES China Council (2018-Present);IEEE Senior Member, Power & Energy Society (PES) (1990-Present); IEEE Computer Society **MH:** Albert Nelson Marquis Lifetime Achievement Award (2019) **AS:** Ms. Zhang's parents are her role models. Her father was a President of Southwest Normal University, Chongqing, China. Her mother was a Top-Leader of Southwest Agricultural University, Chongqing. They dedicated their whole life to educate young teachers and train young leaders. She learned a lot from her father and mother, such as always inspiring others and learning new things, always doing good work to impact and help others.She really appreciates her husband, Dr. Paul L. McEntire, for his love and companionship in her life. He earned a PhD in Engineering-Economics at Stanford University and runs his own investment management company, Palo Alto Advisors. He always supports what she does and encourages her to do her best.She also appreciates her Professor Shuti Fu at Graduate School of Electric Power Research Institute, China, for his wisdom, knowledge, kindness and inspiration. His international view encouraged her to come to the States and start new ventures. **B/I:** Ms. Zhang believes that science and technology can bring a brighter future in the world, so she chose as her major Electrical Engineering because everyone needs electricity, especially people that live in remote areas. All areas of Science and Technology are important, however electric power gives fundamental support for all activities, and is an essential supply. Ms. Zhang loves her career and her engineering research field. She has focused for over 30 years on Smart Grids, Electricity Markets and Renewable Energy. She has worked with many global 500 leading companies, such as ABB Systems Control and Siemens. She has served as speakers at various Smart Grid and Green Energy conferences, such as in areas of "Voltage/VAR Optimization" and "Market-Based Demand Response". She is a co-author of the book "Electricity Market Operation System". She has served

as chair of various International Green Energy Summits, and organized many global conferences and seminars. **AV:** Travel; Swimming; Ping pong/table tennis; Photography

ZHAO, JIAN, "JIM", MD, PHD, MBA, FCAP, T: Physician **I:** Medicine & Health Care **DOB:** 12/26/1955 **PB:** Guangzhou **SC:** China **PT:** Minglun Zhao, MD; Shujing Shen, MD **MS:** Married **SPN:** Xiao Feng Li, MD, FAAP (04/05/1957) **CH:** Dan Zhao; Vivian Zhao **ED:** MBA, University of Central Florida, Orlando, FL (1998); Residency, Fellowship, Yale School of Medicine (1994-1996); Residency, Albert Einstein College of Medicine (1993-1994); Postdoctoral Fellowship, Rockefeller University (1988-1989); PhD, University of Oxford, England (1987); Visiting Fellowship, Brandeis University (1984-1985); MD, Guangdong Medical University, Zhanjiang, Guangdong, China (1982) **CT:** Diplomate, American Board of Pathology **C:** Professor in Health Medicine and Management, Orlando University (2005-Present); President, Orlando University (2004-Present); Courtesy Clinical Appointee, University of Central Florida, Orlando, FL (2001-Present); President, Chief Executive Officer, Oxford Diagnostics, Orlando, FL (1997-Present); Associate Professor, Guangdong Medical University (1995-Present); Professor, Nanjing Medical University (2002-2005); Director, Laboratory Diagnostic Molecular Pathology, Orlando Regional Healthcare (1998-1999) **MEM:** Lifetime Fellow, College of American Pathologists **MH:** Albert Nelson Marquis Lifetime Achievement Award; Marquis Who's Who Top Professional **B/I:** Dr. Zhao became involved in his profession because of personality issue and environment. He wanted to make a change and have an impact on people's lives. His parents, Minglun Zhao and Shujing Shen, were from the medical field and so is his wife, Xiao Feng Li. **AV:** Swimming; Reading

ZIEGERT, SUSAN H., T: Educator **I:** Education/Educational Services **PB:** Milwaukee **SC:** WI/USA **PT:** Harry Wenzel; Helen Wenzel **MS:** Married **SPN:** James W. Ziegert **CH:** Scott Ziegert; Kimberly Ziegert Bangaoil **ED:** MA in Reading Language Arts, Cardinal Stritch University, Milwaukee, WI (1990); BS in Elementary Education, University of Wisconsin-Platteville, Platteville, WI (1964) **CT:** #317 Reading Specialist License, Cardinal Stritch University, Milwaukee, WI (1991); #316 Reading Teachers License, Cardinal Stritch University, Milwaukee, WI (1988) **C:** Senior Learning Strategies Specialist, University of Wisconsin-Waukesha (1994-2011); Instructor, University of Wisconsin-Milwaukee, Milwaukee, WI (1992, 1993, 2011); Reading Specialist, Milwaukee Area Technical College, Workplace Literacy (1990-1994); Elementary Teacher, Milwaukee Public Schools (1964-1970) **CR:** Speaker, International Reading Association, College Literacy and Learning/SIG, Chicago, IL (2006); Speaker, Midwest Association of Equal Opportunity, Lake Geneva, WI (1997); Speaker,Teaching Academic Survival Skills, University of Cincinnati, Cincinnati, OH (1996), Wisconsin State Reading Association, Milwaukee, WI (1990). **CIV:** Volunteer, Milwaukee Chapter, American Diabetes Association (1979-1985) Creator, Day Camp for Children with Diabetes **CW:** Author, "Reflection: A Step Beyond the Reading of a Chapter," Journal of Reading (1994); Creator, Study Skills Website; Author, Study Skills Handbook, University of Wisconsin-Waukesha Study Skills Classes; Developer, Reading Program for Underprepared College Freshmen, University of Wisconsin-Waukesha **AW:** Volunteer of the Year for the State of Wisconsin, Milwaukee Chapter, American Diabetes Association (1982-1983) **MEM:** Wisconsin State Reading Association; International Reading Association; College of Literacy

and Learning **MH:** Albert Nelson Marquis Lifetime Achievement Award **AS:** Ms. Ziegert attributes her success to hard work and diligence. She always met her problems head-on by generating possible solutions and prioritizing them. She found success by often consulting with other professionals. All the while, she never lost sight of her goals. **B/I:** Ms. Ziegert always felt called to teaching, as she enjoyed helping others. She found meaningful, engaging, and effective methods to teach her students. Her career has brought her so much satisfaction and pleasure; it felt as though she never worked a day in her life. **AV:** Reading; Going on nature walks; Training dogs; Interior decorating; Playing Scrabble **THT:** Ms. Ziegert believes life is a journey and the road is not smooth. It's filled with uncertainties, disappointments, hardships, joys, and sorrows. Further, it is unpredictable and ever-changing.

ZIEGLER, JAMES R., T: Senior Systems Analyst **I:** Business Management/Business Services **DOB:** 10/10/1922 **PB:** Warrem **SC:** PA/USA **PT:** LeRoy Curtis Ziegler; Daisy (Gesin) Ziegler **MS:** Widowed **SPN:** Maxine Evelyn Hogue (02/10/1952, Deceased 11/1968) **CH:** Evalinde Aurelia; Charlotte Elaine; Curtis Wayman; Bruce Allan **ED:** MA in Mathematics, The Pennsylvania State University (1948); BSEE, The Pennsylvania State University (1943) **C:** Senior Consultant Analyst, San Diego Cash Register Co. (1978-1980); Senior Consultant Analyst, NCR Co., San Diego, CA (1975-1978);Advisor Director, Coast Federal Savings and Loan Association, Los Angeles, CA (1969-1974); Director, Southern Federal Savings & Loan Association, Los Angeles, CA (1968-1969); President, Turn-Key Computer Applications (1968-1975); Manager of Programming Services, Electronic Computers, NCR, Hawthorne, CA (1954-1968); Research Associate Statistician, Teachers Characteristics Study, American Council on Education (1951-1954); Instructor of Mathematics, University of California Los Angeles (1948-1954); Instructor of Mathematics, Pennsylvania State College (Now The Pennsylvania State University) (1946-1948); Researcher, UHF Wave Guide, Norden Corp., New York, NY (1943-1944) **CR:** Computer Consultant, Yemen Arab Republic National Water and Sewerage Authority (1980-1987); Psychological Research Projects, University of Southern California and The University of Utah (1956); Technology Consultant, Office of Naval Research, Study Data Processing Consultant (1955) **MIL:** With, PTO, United States Marine Corps Reserve (1944-1946) **CW:** Author: Time Sharing Data Processing Systems, 1967; contributor articles to professional journals **MEM:** Former Member, Masons; The Tau Beta Pi Association, Inc.; Sigma Tau; Eta Kappa Nu **MH:** Albert Nelson Marquis Lifetime Achievement Award **B/I:** When Mr. Ziegler worked for a group called Teachers Characteristics Studies by the American Counsel of Education and they were using hand work; he suggested to use a new computer at UCLA. He was able to use it so they changed the research project; it was enlarged from several hundred to several thousand teachers. **PA:** Republican **RE:** Methodist

ZIEGLER, JOHN A., PHD, T: Historian, Political Scientist, Educator, Short Story Writer **I:** Education/Educational Services **DOB:** 01/28/1933 **PB:** Belleville **SC:** IL/USA **PT:** John Wendell Ziegler; Georgia Elizabeth (Reppel) Ziegler **MS:** Married **SPN:** Iris Butler Scales (7/21/2012) **CH:** Nathaniel; Robin **ED:** PhD, Syracuse University (1970); Rotary Foundation Fellow, St. Andrews University, Scotland (1956-1957); MS, Southern Illinois University (1956); BS, Southern Illinois University (1955) **C:** Emeritus Professor, Hendrix College, Conway,

AR (1998-Present); Legendary Lecturer, Hendrix College, Conway, AR (1998); Harold and Lucy Cabe Distinguished Professor, History and Politics, Hendrix College, Conway, AR (1991-1998); Frequent Participant, Wilton Park Conferences (1978-1988); Professor, Hendrix College, Conway, AR (1984-1991); Associate Professor, Political Science, Hendrix College, Conway, AR (1974-1984); Lecturer, American Civilization, California State Polytechnic University, Pomona, CA (1972-1974); Assistant Professor, Political Science and Social Science, California State University, East Bay, CA (1966-1972) **CR:** Participant, Wilton Park Conferences, Wiston House International Conference Center, Sussex, England (1979-Present); Coordinator, Founder, Hendrix-Oxford Program (1979-1998); Guest Lecturer, St. Peter's College, Oxford University (1983, 1990, 1994); Guest Lecturer, Dundee University (1994); Guest Lecturer, Clare College, Cambridge University (1988, 1989); Head, Social Science Area, Hendrix-Oxford Program (1978-1982); Chairman, Department of Political Science and History, Hendrix-Oxford Program (1974-1983); Life Fellow, Westminster College, Fulton, MO **MIL:** U.S. Army (1957-1960) **CW:** Author, "Ralph Waldo Emerson on America and Britain" (2016); Author, "Experimentalism and Institutional Change" (1994, 2014); Author, "Special Relationships: Six Stories" (2012); Author, "In Search of the Special Relationship with Britain" (2001); Author, "The John Ziegler London Collection," Hendrix College Archives **MEM:** American Association of University Professors; Life Member, Friends Churchill Memorial; ACLU; Royal Oak Foundation; Life Member, South Downs Society; Dundee Curling Club, Scotland **MH:** Albert Nelson Marquis Lifetime Achievement Award; Marquis Who's Who Top Professional **AS:** He had several excellent professors- Frank Klingberg at Southern Illinois University, Nelson Blake at Syracuse University and a colleague at California State University, Charles Merrifield. **B/I:** First of all, he felt that the way to approach problems which we had and still has was through the experimentalist philosophy and he felt that the country was still very isolationist. He needed to study isolationism. **RE:** United Church of Christ

ZIGERELLI, LAWRENCE, "LARRY" J., T: President, Chief Executive Officer **I:** Business Management/Business Services **CN:** FFO Home **PT:** Attilio Zigerelli; Lois Zigerelli **MS:** Married **CH:** Three Children **ED:** BA in Administrative Science, Yale University (1980) **C:** President, Chief Executive Officer, FFO Home (2012-2019); President, Cheaper Peepers (2010-2012); President, Meijer Inc. (2005-2006); Director, Meijer Inc. (2005-2006); Executive Vice President, Meijer Inc. (2004-2005); Senior Vice President, Merchandising, Meijer Inc. (2003); Senior Vice President, Marketing, Advertising, And Corp. Development, Meijer Inc. (2002); Executive Vice President of Corporate Development, CVS Corp., Woonsocket, SC (1999-2002); Category Management, Consumer Response Specialist, Procter & Gamble (1980-1999) **CR:** President, Chief Executive Officer, Duckwall-ALCO Stores Inc. (2008-2010); Chairman of the Board, Levitz Furniture (2007-2008); New England Consulting Group, Inc.; Director, True Value Company; Retail Consultant, Prentice Capital Management, L.P. (2007) **CIV:** Board Member, University of Arkansas Business School; Board Member, BOST; Advisory Board, Arkansas College of Health Education; St. Jude Children's Research Hospital; American Heart Association **AW:** Top Performing Company, Sun Capital (2017); Marketing Leader of the Year, National Drug Store Association; Inductee, Pittsburgh Sports Hall of Fame, Beaver County, PA **MEM:** Board of Directors, Home Furnishings Association (2017-Present); Director, National Association of Chain Drug Stores

(2005) **MH:** Marquis Who's Who Top Professional **AS:** The number one thing is Mr. Zigerelli always tried to surround himself with diverse people who challenged him and are smarter than him, if possible. He was always captain of the team, president of the class, and orchestrating everything. From his sports background, he competes to win all the time; he has high standards, and is good at setting strategic direction and help motivating others to achieve it. He surrounds himself with great people. He is open and flexible to new ideas all the time. **B/I:** Mr. Zigerelli got a call from a private equity firm while living in New York; the company was in trouble, almost bankrupt, and he saw it as a big opportunity to make the company a lot bigger and to really grow it, which they have done. He has always liked consumer products and retail; he likes selling products that help people's lives. People get excited in the furniture business, and he likes helping people furnish their homes. He saw it as a huge opportunity to make the business a lot bigger. His greatest achievement was saving FFO home from bankruptcy and turned it around and made the private equity firm a lot of money. **AV:** Travel; Enjoying time with his kids

ZIL, J.S., MD, JD, T: Forensic Specialist; Psychiatrist; Educator **I:** Medicine & Health Care **PB:** Chicago **SC:** IL/USA **PT:** Stephen Vincent Zil; Marillyn Charlotte (Jackson) Zil **CH:** Charlene-Elena Zil **ED:** JD, Jefferson College, with Honors (1985); MPH, Yale University (1977); Fellow in Psychiatry, Advanced Fellow in Social, Community and Forensic Psychiatry, Yale Faculty Consultant, Connecticut State Department of Corrections (1975-1977); Intern, Resident in Psychiatry and Neurology, The University of Arizona (1973-1975); Medical Clerk, Clinica de Casa de Todos, Tijuana, Mexico (1968-1970); MD, University of California San Diego (1973); BS, University of Redlands, Magna Cum Laude (1969) **C:** Medical Director, American River Hospital (2011-2015); Director of Ethics Program, Sierra Vista Hospital, University of Southern California (2007-2015); Director of Postgraduate Training, Sierra Vista Hospital, University of Southern California (2003-2012); Medical Director, Sierra Vista Hospital, University of Southern California (2003-2007); Medical Director, American River Hospital (2003-2007); Legislative Liaison Central Office, University of California (1988-2003); Clinical Faculty, University of California Davis (1991-1999); Associate Professor of Bioengineering and Internal Medicine, University of California Berkeley, San Francisco, CA (1982-1992); Professor of Natural Science, California State University (1985-1987); Vice Chairman, Department of Psychiatry, University of California San Francisco (1983-1986); Associate Professor of Psychiatry and Internal Medicine, University of California San Francisco (1982-1986); Assistant Professor of Psychiatry, University of California San Francisco (1977-1982); Instructor of Physiology, University of Massachusetts (1976-1977); Instructor of Psychiatry, Yale University (1976-1977); Unit Chief, In-patient and Day Hospital, Connecticut Mental Health Center, Yale-New Haven Hospital (1975-1977) **CR:** Commissioner, Physician's Advisory Board, President Commission on Business, U.S. House of Representatives (2002-Present); Chief Forensic Psychiatrist, State California Department of Corrections (1986-2003); Member, Medical Advisory Committee, California State Personnel Board (1986-1995); Consultant, National Institute of Corrections (1992-1994); Appointed Councilor, California State Mental Health Plan (1988-1993); Chairman, State of California Inter-Agency Technical Advisory Committee on Mentally Ill Inmates & Parolees (1986-1992); Chief Psychiatrist, State California Department of Corrections (1986-1989);

Chairman, Department of Psychiatry and Neurology, Central San Joaquin Valley Medical Education Program and Affiliated Hospitals and Clinics (1983-1986); Invited Faculty Contributor and Editor, Resident in Training Exam, The American College of Psychiatrists (1981-1986); Principal Investigator, Sleep Research and Physiology Laboratory, University of California San Francisco (1980-1986); Chief, Psychiatry and Neurology, VA Medical Center, CA (1977-1986) **CIV:** Board of Directors, The Book Club of California, Sacramento Ballet, Others **CW:** Editor-in-chief, Corrective and Social Psychiatry Journal (2005-Present); Reviewer, Corrective and Social Psychiatry Journal (1981-Present); Referee, Corrective and Social Psychiatry Journal (1980-Present); Author, "Suicide Prevention Handbook, Eighth Edition" (2007); Co-editor, Corrective and Social Psychiatry Journal (1997-2005); Author, "Psychiatric Services in Jails and Prisons, Second Edition" (2000); Associate Editor, Corrective and Social Psychiatry Journal (1978-1997); Contributing Author, "The Measurement Mandate: On the Road to Performance Improvement in Health Care" (1993); Author, "Mentally Disordered Criminal Offenders, Second Edition" (1992); Author, "The Case of the Sleepwalking Rapist" (1992); Author, "Mentally Disordered Criminal Offenders," Five Volumes (1989); Author, "Suicide Prevention Handbook" (1987); Contributor, Articles to Professional Journals **AW:** Award, University of California (1995-1996); Campus-wide Professional Achievement Award, University of Redlands (1994); Winner, Fletcher's Severe Problem in Mathematics (1976); Kendall Award, International Symposium in Biochemistry Research (1970); Julian Lee Roberts Award, University of Redlands (1969); National Recognition Award, Bank of America Corporation (1965); National Merit Scholar (1965) **MEM:** National President, American Association of Mental Health Professionals in Corrections (2002-Present); Fellow, Distinguished Life Member, Royal Society of Health (Now Royal Society of Public Health (RSPH)), United Kingdom; American Association for Social Psychiatry; American Association of University Professors (AAUP); American Public Health Association; American Psychiatric Association; American Association of Mental Health Professionals in Corrections; National Council on Crime and Delinquency (NCCD); Past President, California Scholarship Federation; Delta Alpha; Alpha Epsilon Delta **MH:** Albert Nelson Marquis Lifetime Achievement Award **B/I:** Dr. Zil's father was a physicist, his mother was a nutritionist and also a columnist. Dr. Zil was a math major in college and early on, he decided to take the direction of being a physician. It was an opportunity he could compete for and it sounded like it would be interesting. **THT:** As director, Dr. Zil bought an ethical practice into the private practice of medicine. Dr. Zil has also done expert testimony in private practice.

ZIMMERMAN, ELAINE, T: Policy Leader and Analyst; Psychotherapist; Poet **I:** Government Administration/Government Relations/Government Services **DOB:** 06/09/1950 **PB:** Rockville Centre **SC:** NY/USA **PT:** Hal Zimmerman; Cecelia (Sachs) Zimmerman **MS:** Married **SPN:** David Plotke **CH:** Hannah Lynn; Benjamin Daniel **ED:** MSW, University of California (1976); BA, University of California Berkeley (1972); Coursework, Tufts University (1968-1970) **CT:** Licensed Marriage, Family and Child Counselor; Licensed Clinical Social Worker **C:** Regional Administrator, Administration for Children and Families, New England (2016-Present); Acting Regional Administrator, CA (2016-2019); Connecticut Commission on Children, Hartford, CT (1989-2016); Senior Consultant, Joint Select Task Force on Changing Family, California Legislature (1987-1989); Senior Consultant, Assembly Human Services Committee, California Legislature, Sacramento, CA (1985-1987); Psychotherapist, Berkeley, CA (1976-1986); Founder/Director, Women's Economic Agenda Project (1982-1985); Director, California Women USA on Gender Gap (1981-1982); Founder, Director, Demeter House for Runaway Girls, Berkeley, CA (1975-1977), Founder, Director, Berkeley Women's Center (1973-1975) **CR:** Consultant, Teacher, Author and Speaker in Field **CIV:** Founder, Board Chair, National Parent Leadership Institute, Providing Leadership Skills for Parents Across the United States to Build Change in Neighborhoods and States for Children and Youth (2016-Present); Teacher/Trainer, Eastern European Leaders in New Democracies, Jagiellonian University, Krakow, Poland (1990) **CW:** Author, "Talking to Children about Terrorism," Connecticut Commission on Children, Hartford, CT (2015); Author, ""Parent Leadership: Building a Powerful Constituency for Children, Youth and Community," Connecticut Commission on Children, Hartford, CT (2015); Author, "Two-Generational Approach, Helping Parents Work and Children Thrive," Connecticut Commission on Children, Hartford, CT (2014); Author, "A Letter to Parents and Teachers on the One Year Anniversary of the Newtown Shooting," Connecticut Commission on Children, Hartford, CT (2013); Co-author, "First Words, First Steps," Comprehensive Policy Agenda for Infants, Toddlers and Two-year-olds, Governor's Early Education Cabinet (2008); Co-author, "The Children's Stock Portfolio" (2007); Author, "Children Eclipsed by Natural and Unnatural Disaster, What They are Telling Us and What We Can Do," Connecticut Commission on Children, Hartford, CT (2006); Co-author "Parents Supporting Educational Excellence. A Curriculum for Parents on Educational Excellence," Connecticut Commission on Children and Center for School Change, Hartford, CT (2005); Author, "Parent Education of the Civic Kind," The Democracy Reader. International Debate Education Association, NY and Amsterdam, Brussels (2002); Co-author, "Brave Enough to Be Kind," Governor's Prevention Partnership and Connecticut Department of Education (2002); Author, "Parent Engagement in Child Care," Sponsored by Federal Child Care Bureau, Finance Project, Families and Work Institute and National Governor's Association (2000); Author, "Changing Our Public Policy to Make Change for Children," America's Family Support Magazine (2000); Author, "Watch Me Grow" (2000); Author, Guest Editorial, "Children's Mental Health," Connecticut Medicine, Journal of the Connecticut State Medical Society (1997); Author, "Reform for the Youngest Generation," CASD (1994); Co-author, "The Parent Leadership Training Curriculum," 20-week Curriculum of Civic Skills to Lead and Create Change for Good Child Outcomes, Connecticut Commission on Children (1993); Author, "Ready or Not - A Parent's Guide to School Readiness," Hartford Courant Magazine (1993); Author, "Introduction: The Broad Agenda of Family Supports" and "US Considerations of Paradigms for Family Supports," Family Supports Roundtable Overview, The National Center for Policy Alternatives, Washington, DC (1991); Co-author, "1-2-3-4-5 Kids Count: An Early Childhood Policy Initiative," Connecticut Legislature, Hartford, CT (1990); Co-author, "Planning a Comprehensive Family Policy for California," California Legislature, State Assembly (1989); Author, "The California Women's Economic Agenda Project," Women's Economic Justice Agenda Strategies for Legislative Success, National Center for Policy Alternatives, Washington, DC (1987); Co-author, "Family Support," America's States, National Center for Policy Alternatives Washington, DC (1986); Author, "Response to Michael Harrington on the New American Poverty," Black Law Journal, UCLA School of Law (1985); Author, "The Women's Economic Agenda," Formal Document with Policies to Reverse Family Poverty (1984); Author, "Archives-California Hearings on the Feminization of Poverty," Signs: Journal of Women in Culture and Society, University of Chicago Press, Chicago, IL (1984); Author, Guest Column, "The Odd Couple: Feminization of Poverty and the Gender Gap," California Women (1983); Author, "Empowering Parents," Child Care Action News, NY; Poet; Contributor, Numerous Journals, Newspapers and Anthologies; Author, Co-author, Essays, Curriculum, and Policy Papers **AW:** Secretary Azar Award for Meritorious Service "for Recognition of Exemplary Performance and Exceptional Leadership" (2019); CT Legislature and Bob Haller Award for Innovation and Leadership for Families (2017); Named, Speaker of the Year, People Speaking (1985); Good Housekeeping Award for Women in Government; Awards, Ford Foundation, Eagleton Institute of Politics, and Council for Excellence in Government; Recipient, Many Poetry Awards; Pushcart Nominee **MEM:** Connecticut Poetry Society (1995-Present) **MH:** Albert Nelson Marquis Lifetime Achievement Award **AS:** Outstanding mentors guided Mrs. Zimmerman to topics, new terrain and populations she could not easily access. Family and societal difficulties taught her change is possible if you understand the civic process and trust in good leaders. Listening deeply helped her sometimes create what people said they needed to excel and thrive with them. A strong commitment to democracy and what is informed by the public, anchored most of what she worked and lead on. The creative process and arts helped her speak the truth, sometimes turning from chaos. A deep commitment to diversity of all kinds brings her lessons and inspiration. **B/I:** Mrs. Zimmerman started as a change agent in the psyche as a psychotherapist. She shifted to change for the public good and came to believe in public policy as a critical source of systemic reform. **AV:** Writing; Hiking **PA:** Democrat **RE:** Jewish **THT:** Poetry helps Mrs. Zimmerman find magic and expect the unexpected in what she does. The storm becomes critical to social change, personal change and messaging. You have to walk through it, wherever and whatever it is. It is so helpful to walk through it with others. This makes a force that is remembered and used in ways that are not understood at the time.

ZIMMERMANN, MURIEL MADELINE, T: Biology Professor (Retired), Dean (Retired) **I:** Education/Educational Services **DOB:** 08/16/1942 **PB:** Sacramento **SC:** CA/USA **PT:** Max Hubertus Zimmermann; Emily Matilda Zimmermann **MS:** Married **SPN:** Vernon Richard Wheeler **CH:** Mark Dean Williams; Bret Albert Williams; Christopher William Wheeler **ED:** Advanced Coursework in Mycology and Anaerobic Bacteriology, California State Polytechnic University, Pomona (1991); Advanced Coursework in Statistics and Computer Programming, University of California, Riverside (1985); MS, California State Polytechnic University, Pomona (1977); BS, California State Polytechnic University, Pomona (1974); AA, Chaffey College, Rancho Cucamonga, CA (1971) **CT:** Certified in Hazardous Materials Management, University of California, Davis (1993) **C:** Professor Emeritus, Chaffey College, Rancho Cucamonga, CA (2004-2014); Faculty, Chaffey College, Rancho Cucamonga, CA (1974-1996, 2004-2014); Dean, Physical, Life, Health Sciences, Chaffey College, Rancho Cucamonga, CA (1996-2004); Coordinator, Environmental Hazardous Materials Technology Program, Chaffey College, Rancho Cucamonga, CA (1993-1996); Division Chairman, Physical Education, Chaffey College, Rancho Cucamonga, CA (1985-1990); Division Chairman, Life Sciences, Chaffey College, Rancho Cucamonga, CA (1981-1990); Faculty Senate Chairman, Chaffey College, Rancho Cucamonga, CA (1980-1981) **CR:** Lecturer, "The Biological Adaptiveness of Lying" **AW:** Named Alumni of Year, Chaffey College (2010); Inductee, Hall of Fame, Building Dedication Muriel M. Zimmermann (2007); Meritorious Service Award (2005-2006); Keynote Speaker, American Association of University Women Presentation: Careers in Math and Science, Fullerton College (1997); Academy Excellence, Chaffey College Student Government (1992-1995); Faculty Speaker of the Year, Chaffey College (1993); Faculty Speaker of the Year, Chaffey College, Rancho Cucamonga, CA (1992-1993); Faculty Lecturer of the Year, Chaffey College, Rancho Cucamonga, CA (1992-1993); Chaffey College Presidential Excellence Award (1991-1993); Chaffey College Nominee, NISOD Conference on Teaching Excellence (1992); Alpha Sigma Epsilon Academic Honor Society, California State Polytechnic University, Pomona (1972); Alpha Gamma Sigma California Junior College Honor Scholarship Society, Chaffey College (1972) **MEM:** American Association for the Advancement of Science; American Society for Microbiology; Alpha Gamma Sigma; Alpha Sigma Epsilon; Former Member, Sweet Adelines, Inc. **MH:** Albert Nelson Marquis Lifetime Achievement Award; Marquis Who's Who Top Professional **AS:** Ms. Zimmermann attributes her success to an excellent upbringing, a great second marriage, hard work, and supportive family and friends. **B/I:** Ms. Zimmermann became involved in her profession because she was always inquisitive; she is one of five children, with three siblings ahead of her. Many of her siblings were higher achievers but she was headed in the right direction as there were high expectations. She was always popular and was elected president of her class in eighth, ninth, and 10th grade. She dropped out in 10th grade and was out of school for a while before going back and attending Catholic school. For a moment, she lived in San Diego and came back to school and graduated a year late but managed to put her life back in perspective. She married a college graduate; after her second child was born, she decided she needed to finish her education. She attended Chaffey College, part-time at first. She finished there and transferred to Cal Poly and quickly received her master's degree and then received a position at Chaffey College. She knew she loved biology and pursued that interest. The first biology class helped her recognize that this is what she wanted to do. Although her degree was in cell biology, the school needed a microbiology teacher and she was lined up to do it. She had taken a lot of microbiology classes and even went back after teaching and took a couple more classes to get herself up to speed. She was the microbiology teacher until she became the dean. **AV:** Singing; Swimming; Playing piano **PA:** Democrat **THT:** Ms. Zimmermann said of herself: "I have had a most privileged life and recognize that more today then I ever have. I am grateful for all the opportunities that have been presented to me and for having the genetics and health to meet the challenges presented. I hope the values this country was founded upon get reestablished and we again rise to the greatness we are capable of achieving as a country."

ZIMMERMANN, ROBERT L., T: Senior Research Manager (Retired) **I:** Research **DOB:** 01/01/1932 **PB:** Minneapolis **SC:** MN/USA **PT:** Lawrence; Bertha Mabel (Foss) Zimmermann **MS:** Single **ED:** Doctor of Philosophy, University of Minnesota (1970); Master of Arts, University of Minnesota (1965); Bachelor of Arts, University of Minnesota

(1954) **C:** Senior Research Manager, Maritz Market Research, Minneapolis, MN (1984-2013); Private Consultant, Research Design and Data Analysis, Minneapolis, MN (1976-1984); Senior Scientist, Biometrics Laboratory, George Washington University, Washington, DC (1975-1976); Research Associate, Psychiatry Research Unit, University of Minnesota, Minneapolis, MN (1969-1975); Assistant Professor of Psychology, University of Winnipeg, Manitoba, Canada (1968-1969) **CR:** Adjunct Clinical Assistant Professor, Psychiatry Department, University of Minnesota, Minneapolis, MN (1976-1990); External Review Officer, Food and Drug Administration, Washington, DC (1974-1977) **CW:** Author, "Now or Never" (2017); Author, "Kendra" (2016); Author, "Prodromal: Incident in Mbandaka" (2015); Author, "Last Rites" (2015); Author (Under the Pseudonym, R. Laurenz), "The Puzzle" (2014); Contributor, Numerous Articles to Professional Journals **AW:** Fellow, National Institute of Mental Health (1958, 1961, 1969-1971); Merit Fellow, State of Minnesota **MEM:** American Association for the Advancement of Science; American Civil Liberties Union; Oxfam; Twin Cities Public Television; Minnesota Public Radio; United Nations Children's Fund; United Nations High Commissioner for Refugees **MH:** Albert Nelson Marquis Lifetime Achievement Award; Marquis Who's Who Top Professional **AV:** Writing **PA:** Democrat

ZINSMEISTER, LOUANN, PHD, RN, CNE, T: Director of Graduate Nursing Program, Professor of Nursing **I:** Medicine & Health Care **DOB:** 04/26/1956 **PB:** Lebanon **SC:** PA/USA **PT:** Joseph Albert; Lois (Hilsher) Brechbill **MS:** Married **SPN:** Robert W. Zinsmeister (06/09/1984) **CH:** Robert Joseph Zinsmeister; Kristin Zinsmeister Shaub **ED:** Doctor of Philosophy, Widener University, Chester, PA (2004); Master of Science, University of Delaware, Newark, DE (1985); Bachelor of Science in Nursing, Millersville University, Millersville, PA (1984); Diploma, Lancaster Hospital, Pennsylvania (1979) **CT:** Certified Nurse Educator (CNE); International Journal of Nursing Studies; Certificate in Church Music; Certified Geriatric Nurse Practitioner **C:** Full Professor, Messiah College, Mechanicsburg, PA (2014-Present); Director of Graduate Program in Nursing, Messiah College, Mechanicsburg, PA (2013-Present); Professor of Nursing, Messiah College, Mechanicsburg, PA (1994-Present); Associate Professor, Messiah College, Mechanicsburg, PA (2007-2014); Assistant Professor, Messiah College, Mechanicsburg, PA (2004-2007); Instructor of Nursing, Messiah College, Mechanicsburg, PA (1994-2004); Nursing Instructor, St. Joseph Hospital School Nursing, Lancaster, PA (1985-1994); Staff Nurse, Operating Room CV Surgery, Harrisburg Hospital, Harrisburg, PA (1981-1985); Staff Nurse, Critical Care, Polyclinic Medical Center, Harrisburg, PA (1979-1981) **CR:** Consultant in the Field; Presenter in the Field **CIV:** Full-time Church Organist **AW:** Traineeship, University of Delaware (1984-1985); Mary Danner Edgar Award; Florence Nightingale Award **MEM:** American Nurses Association; American Association of Critical Care Nurses; Sigma Theta Tau **MH:** Albert Nelson Marquis Lifetime Achievement Award; Marquis Who's Who Top Professional **B/I:** Dr. Zinsmeister became involved in her profession because she "felt moved" to become a nurse, despite having majored in French language studies at Pennsylvania State University and abroad. **AV:** Pianist; Crocheting; Dogs

ZJAWIONY, JORDAN KORDIAN, T: Professor **I:** Education/Educational Services **CN:** University of Mississippi **DOB:** 01/02/1943 **PB:** Czestochowa **SC:** Poland **PT:** Lucjan Zjawiony; Maria (Kornacka) Zjawiony **MS:** Widow **SPN:** Krystyna Danczak (10/16/1995, Deceased 2019); Zofia Katarzyna Grosman-Zjawiona (12/17/1970, Deceased 1993) **CH:** Agnieszka **ED:** Doctor of Philosophy in Organic Chemistry, Technical University of Lodz, Lodz, Poland (1974); Bachelor of Science and Master of Science in Pharmaceutical Chemistry & Technology, Technical University of Lodz, Lodz, Poland (1965) **C:** Professor Emeritus of Biomolecular Sciences, Division of Pharmacognosy and the Research Institute of Pharmaceutical Sciences, University of Mississippi, University, MS (2019-Present); Research Professor, Department of Pharmacognosy and the Research Institute of Pharmaceutical Sciences, University of Mississippi, University, MS (1999-Present); Visiting Professor, Bialystok University of Technology, Bialystok, Poland (2012-2018); Associate Editor, Electronic Journal, "Marine Drugs," Edited by Marine Drugs and Food Institute at the Ocean University of China (2002-2015); Partner and Scientific Advisory Board Member, Thesis Chemistry LLC, Mentor, OH (2003-2013); Partner and Scientific Advisory Board Member, Thesis Chemistry Inc., Cambridge, Ontario, Canada (2003-2013); Visiting Professor, Technical University of Lodz, Lodz, Poland (2008-2010); Consultant and Reviewer, NIH Study Section ZRG1 ICP-2, 50, International and Cooperative Projects, Fogarty International Collaboration Program, International Cooperative Biodiversity Groups (2003); Mississippi-Alabama Sea Grant Consortium Expert Reviewer (1999-2002); Director of Medical & Drug Group of International Technology Exchange Society, U.S.-Japanese Non-Profit Society (1998-2002); National Science Foundation Expert Reviewer in Organic Chemistry (1998-2000); Associate Professor and Research Associate Professor, Department of Pharmacognosy and the Research Institute of Pharmaceutical Sciences, University of Mississippi, University, MS (1991-1999); Consultant, Reviewer, NIH Study Section ZRG3-BNP-1, Bio-Organic and Natural Products Chemistry, Chemistry and Related Sciences Special Emphasis Panel (1996); Research Visiting Fulbright Scholar, Department of Pharmacognosy and the Research Institute of Pharmaceutical Sciences, University of Mississippi, University, MS (1989-1991); Guest Researcher, Gerontology Research Center, National Institute on Aging, National Institutes of Health, Baltimore, MD (1988-1989); Assistant Professor, Institute of Organic Chemistry, Technical University of Lodz, Poland (1975-1988); Postdoctoral Fellow, Macromolecular Chemistry Section of the Gerontology Research Center, National Institute on Aging, National Institutes of Health, Baltimore, MD (1978-1980); Senior Research Assistant, Institute of Organic Chemistry, Technical University of Lodz, Lodz, Poland (1968-1974); Research Assistant, Institute of Organic Chemistry, Technical University of Lodz, Lodz, Poland (1965-1968) **CR:** Member, Numerous Committees and Development Groups at the University of Mississippi (1992-Present); Scientific Consultant, Board Advisory Member, Thesis LLC (2003-2013); Scientific Consultant to ElSohy Laboratories Inc., Oxford, MS (1994-2004); Member, Scientific Committee, 36th Annual Meeting, American Society of Pharmacognosy, Oxford, MS (1995); Member, Taxol Pilot Plant Facility Planning Group, Research Institute of Pharmaceutical Sciences, University of Mississippi, Oxford, MS (1992-1994); Leader, Academic-Industrial Team for Implementation of Patents and Pilot Plant Experiments with New Technology of Manufacturing Metropolol in Pharmaceutical Company "Polfa" Rzeszow, Poland (1986-1987); Co-Founder, Research and Development Center "Ichem," Technical University of Lodz, Lodz, Poland (1986); Implementation of Developed and Patented Technologies of Ibuprofen and Naproxen in Pharmaceutical Company "Polfa" Pabianice, Poland (1974-1977); Chairman, Committee of Foreign Affairs, Polish Student Association, Technical University of Lodz, Lodz, Poland (1963-1964); Vice-President, Polish Student Association, Technical University of Lodz, Lodz, Poland **CW:** Contributor, 133 Articles to Professional Journals and 268 Abstracts to National and International Conferences; Speaker, More Than 45 Invited Lectures; Co-Author, Six Chapters to Professional Books; Speaker, Numerous Presentations **AW:** Cumberland Pharmaceuticals Faculty Research Award, School of Pharmacy, University of Mississippi (2012); Fulbright Scholarship, National Institute of Health (1988-1989); Meritorious Badge, Technical University of Lodz, Chancellor of the University (1988); Gold Cross of Merits for the 20 Years of Outstanding Work in Academic Community, State Council of Poland (1987); Medal of the 40th Anniversary of Polish People's Republic, State Council of Poland (1984); Honorable Badge of the City of Lodz, City Council of Lodz (1982); Jubilee Medal for the 35th Anniversary of the Technical University of Lodz (1980); Fogarty Fellowship, National Institutes of Health (1978-1980); Polish Government Award (1978); Polish Technical Organization Award (1977); Polish Government Award (1976); Grantee, Numerous Research Grants **MEM:** American Chemical Society; American Society of Pharmacognosy; Phytochemical Society of Europe; Polish Society of Pharmacognosy; American Heart Association; International Technology Exchange Society; Association of Polish-American Professionals; The Polish Institute of Arts & Sciences of America; Division of Organic Chemistry, Polish Chemical Society; Polish Technical Organization; The Rho Chi Society **MH:** Albert Nelson Marquis Lifetime Achievement Award; Marquis Who's Who Top Professional **AS:** Dr. Zjawiony attributes his success on the hard work of his excellent team of postdoctoral fellows and students, as well as the support of his loved ones. **B/I:** Dr. Zjawiony became involved in his profession due to the influence of his high school chemistry teacher, who inspired him to walk down the same career path. He was fascinated with the chemistry of life and everything that happens with the human body. **AV:** Good books; Movies **RE:** Catholic

ZOLL, STANLEY, "STAN" PHILIP, T: Trustee **I:** Real Estate **CN:** SRJZ Realty Trust **PB:** Boston **SC:** MA/USA **PT:** Henry Allen Zoll; Miriam Sarah (Orlick) Zoll **MS:** Married **SPN:** Robin Amy (Gamzon) Zoll **CH:** Jonathan Daniel Zoll **ED:** MS in Economic Policy & Planning, Northeastern University, Boston, MA; BA in Economics & Government, Boston University, Boston, MA **CT:** Accredited Financial Examiner; Accredited Assessor, Massachusetts **C:** Bank Examiner, Research Analyst, Massachusetts Division of Banks and Loan Agencies, Boston, MA (1971-2010); Labor Market Statistician, Mass Division Employment Security, Boston, MA (1970); Budget Analyst, Smithsonian Astrophysical Observatory, Cambridge, MA (1969); Grant, Contract Officer, Brigham and Women's Hospital, Boston, MA (1968) **CIV:** Stoughton Board of Assessors (1992-2015, 2019-2020); Treasurer, Brookline Redevelopment Authority (1977-1983); Co-Chair, Lions District Committee; Staff Officer, Coast Guard Auxiliary Division **CW:** Critique Panelist, Co-Author, "Northeast Business & Economics Association" (1986); Principal Contributor, "Ralph Nader Sponsored Small Claims Court Study Group Report" (1973) **AW:** Keeper of the Flame Award, B'nai Tikvah Brotherhood (2019); Pride in Performance Award, Division of Banks (1999); Community Service Award, Stoughton Democratic Town Committee (2009); House of Representatives Citation, Massachusetts **MH:** Albert Nelson Marquis

Lifetime Achievement Award **B/I:** Mr. Zoll became involved in his industry as a result of his skills and interests in economics and financial analysis.

ZOLOTO, JERROLD ALBERT, PHD, T: Psychologist, Consultant **I:** Medicine & Health Care **DOB:** 01/01/1944 **PB:** Chicago **SC:** IL/USA **PT:** Ben Zoloto; Marian Idele (Cohen) Zoloto **MS:** Married **SPN:** Angela Nijole Yurkus (09/29/1981) **CH:** Jill; Lydia; Alexandra **ED:** PhD, Wayne State University (1979); MS, Wayne State University (1972); BS, University of Illinois (1966) **C:** President, Anova, Inc., Chicago, IL (1985-Present); Vice President, Vici International, San Francisco, CA (1984-1985); Consultant, RHR International, Chicago, IL (1982-1984); Director, Department of Psychiatry, St. Joseph's Hospital, Chicago, IL (1981-1982); Director, DuPage Mental Health, Wheaton, IL (1973-1981) **CR:** Faculty Member, MBA Program, University of St. Francis, Joliet, IL (1997-1999); Internship Supervisor, Students at Numerous Universities (1979-1983); Faculty, College of DuPage, Glen Ellyn, IL (1974-1980); Faculty, Police Training Institute, Lisle, IL (1974-1978); Chief Executive Officer, Appleton Heart Institute **CIV:** Chairman, Board of Directors, ISM University, Vilnius, Lithuania (2011-2014); Chief Executive Officer, Chairman, Fireaway, Inc., Minneapolis, MN (2009-2012); Vice President, Breckenridge Homeowners Association, Naperville, IL (1994-1995); Chairman, Board of Directors, Mental Health Association of Illinois (1987-1989); Board of Directors, Girl Scouts of the USA, Lisle, IL (1984-1986) **CW:** Author, Inventor, 'Listen: The Leadership Information System" (1990); Inventor, Automated System for Individual and Organizational Assessment **MH:** Marquis Lifetime Achievement Award **B/I:** Mr. Zoloto became involved in his profession after he earned a doctorate degree in clinical psychology. He worked briefly in a clinical setting but eventually became more involved in mental health. He believes he is where he is today because of the opportunities he earned throughout his career. **AV:** Gardening; Swimming; Reading **THT:** Mr. Zoloto loves people and cares about what happens to them. His business is on humanizing the corporation, like corporate consulting, and tries to help leaders to find a positive work environment for everybody involved.

ZOPF, PAUL E. PHD, T: Dana Professor Emeritus **I:** Education/Educational Services **DOB:** 07/09/1931 **PB:** Bridgeport **SC:** CT/USA **PT:** Paul Edwards Zopf; Hilda Ernestine (Russell) Zopf **MS:** Married **SPN:** Evelyn Lanoel Montgomery (08/05/1956) (Deceased) **CH:** Eric; Paul **ED:** Doctor of Philosophy, University of Florida (1966); Master of Science, University of Florida (1955); Bachelor of Science, University of Connecticut (1953) **C:** Dana Professor of Sociology Emeritus, Guilford College (1993-Present); Chief College Marshal, Guilford College (1997-2005); Dana Professor of Sociology, Guilford College (1972-1993); Professor, Guilford College (1970-1972); Associate of Professor, Guilford College (1966-1970); Assistant Professor of Sociology, Guilford College, Greensboro, NC (1959-1966) **CR:** Consultant, U.S. Department of Agriculture **CW:** Author, "Mortality Patterns and Trends in the United States" (1992); Author, "Profile of Women in Greensboro" (1977, 1990); Author, "American Women in Poverty" (1989); Author, "America's Older Population" (1986); Author, "Income and Poverty Status of Women in Greensboro" (1985); Author, "Population: An Introduction to Social Demography" (1984); Author, "Cultural Accumulation in Latin America" (1980); Author, "Sociocultural Systems" (1978); Author, "Demography: Principles and Methods" (1970, 1976); Author, "Principles of Inductive Rural Sociology" (1970); Author, "North Carolina: A Demographic

Profile" (1967); Editor, Guilford College Self-Study Accreditation Report; Contributor, Articles to Professional Journals **AW:** Grantee, Guilford College (1979-1993); Grantee, Kenan Foundation (1970-1979); Teaching Excellence Award, Guilford College (1978) **MEM:** American Sociological Association; International Union Science Study Population; Southern Sociological Society; Rural Sociological Society; Population Reference Bureau **MH:** Albert Nelson Marquis Lifetime Achievement Award; Marquis Who's Who Top Professional **AV:** Cabinet making; Gardening **PA:** Democrat **RE:** Society of Friends

ZUBRETSKY, JOSEPH M., T: Chief Executive Officer, President **I:** Medicine & Health Care **CN:** Molina Healthcare, Inc. **PB:** Hartford **SC:** CT/USA **ED:** BSBA, University of Hartford **C:** President, Chief Executive Officer, Director, Molina Healthcare, Inc. (2017-Present); President, Chief Executive Officer, The Hanover Insurance Group, Inc. (2016-2017); Chief Executive Officer, Healthagen Holdings, Aetna Inc. (2015); Senior Executive Vice President, National Businesses, Aetna Inc. (2013-2014); Chief Financial Officer, Aetna Inc. (2007-2013); Senior Executive Vice President, Unum Group (2005-2007); President, Chief Executive Officer, Brera GAB Robins LLC (1999-2005); Executive Vice President of Business Development, Chief Financial Officer, MassMutual Financial Group, Massachusetts Mutual Life Insurance Company (MassMutual) (1997-1999); Partner, Coopers & Lybrand (1990-1996)

ZUCCHERO, MICHAEL, PE, CFM, LEED, T: Executive Managing Director **I:** Facility Management **CN:** Newmark Knight Frank **DOB:** 03/11/1966 **MS:** Married **SPN:** Terri (10/11/1997) **CH:** Three Children **ED:** MS, Environmental Engineering, Georgia Institute of Technology (1995); MS, Engineering Management, George Washington University (1993); BS, Civil Engineering, The Ohio State University, Cum Laude (1988) **CT:** LEED Green Associate USGBC (2013); Certified Facility Manager, International Facility Management Association (2012); Licensed Professional Engineer, Virginia (1993) **C:** Executive Managing Director, Global Head Of Facilities Management, Newmark Knight Frank (2019-Present); Facilities Management SME Consultant (2011-Present); Senior Managing Director, CBRE (2015-2019); Vice President, Jones Lang LaSalle (2011-2015); Executive Director, National Facilities Services, Hawaii Region, Kaiser Permanente (2009-2011); U.S. Navy Civil Engineer Corps Officer (1988-2009). **CIV:** IFMA Global Subject Matter Expert, International Credentials Commission **MIL:** Vice President, Facilities and Real Estate, Public Works Officer, Naval Station of Pearl Harbor, U.S. Navy (2006-2008); Assistant Operations Officer, NAVFAC, U.S. Navy, Hawaii (2005-2006); Vice President, Facilities and Real Estate, Public Works Officer, Navy Support Facility, Diego Garcia, U.S. Navy (2004-2005); Course Director, Public Works Management, Civil Engineer Corps Officer School, U.S. Navy (2004); Vice President Of Facilities And Real Estate (Public Works Officer), Naval Support Activity, U.S. Navy, Bahrain (2000-2002); Civil Engineer Corps Officer, U.S. Navy (1998-2000) **AW:** Multiple U.S. Navy Personal, Unit, and Campaign Awards **MEM:** International Facility Management Association; Former Member, American Society for Healthcare Engineering; Society of American Military Engineers; Former Member, Association of Physical Plant Administrators **MH:** Marquis Who's Who Top Professional **AS:** Mr. Zucchero attributes his success to a solid work ethic, strong integrity, humility, and selflessness. **B/I:** Service to his country in the U.S. Navy and a very successful education in engineering.

PA: Democrat **THT:** "Lead selflessly from the front and with compassion. Put forth your best effort at all times. What you put into your life will come back to you."

ZUCKER, HOWARD ALAN, MD, JD, T: Commissioner **I:** Medicine & Health Care **CN:** New York State Department of Health **DOB:** 09/06/1959 **PB:** New York **SC:** NY/USA **PT:** Saul Zucker; Phyllis (Goldblatt) Zucker **MS:** Married **SPN:** Elissa **CH:** Benjamin; Sadie **ED:** Honorary LHD, Albany College of Pharmacy and Health Sciences, Albany, NY (2017); Honorary ScD, Icahn School of Medicine at Mount Sinai, New York, NY (2017); Global Health Policy Postgraduate Diploma, London School of Hygiene & Tropical Medicine, London, England, United Kingdom (2014); LLM, Columbia University, New York, NY (2001); JD, Fordham University, Bronx, NY (2000); MD, The George Washington University, Washington, DC (1982); BS, McGill University, Montreal, Quebec, Canada (1979); Pediatric Anesthesiology Critical Care Medicine Fellow, The Children's Hospital of Philadelphia, Philadelphia, PA (1987-1988); Anesthesiology Resident, Hospital of the University of Pennsylvania, Penn Medicine, Philadelphia, PA (1985-1987); Pediatric Resident, The Johns Hopkins Hospital, Baltimore, MD (1983-1985); Pediatric Intern, The Johns Hopkins Hospital, Baltimore, MD (1982-1983) **CT:** Board Certified in Pediatric Anesthesiology (2016-Present); Board Certified in Pediatric Cardiology (2013-Present); Board Certified in Pediatric Critical Care (2012-Present); Board Certified in Anesthesia Critical Care (1991-Present); Board Certified in Anesthesiology (1990-Present); Board Certified in Pediatrics (1989-Present) **C:** Commissioner of Health, New York State (2015-Present); Professor of Public Health, University of Albany, State University of New York (2014-Present); Adjunct Professor of Clinical Anesthesiology, Albert Einstein College of Medicine, Montefiore Medical Center (2014-Present); Senior Adviser, Massachusetts General Hospital, The General Hospital Corporation (2009-Present); Presidential Leadership Scholar (2015); Acting Commissioner of Health, New York State (2014-2015); First Deputy Commissioner of Health, New York State (2013-2015); Adjunct Professor of Law, Georgetown University Law School (2011-2014); Fellow, Institute of Politics (2009); Institute of Politics Fellow, John F. Kennedy School of Government, Harvard Kennedy School (2009); Assistant Director-General, WHO, Geneva (2005-2008); Clinical Faculty, National Institutes of Health (2002-2005); Acting Deputy Assistant Secretary of Health, U.S. Department of Health & Human Services (2002-2004); Adjunct Assistant Professor of Pediatrics, Weill Cornell Medicine (2000-2005); Special Assistant to the Secretary of Health & Human Services (2001-2002); White House Fellowship, Washington, DC (2001-2002); Adjunct Assistant Professor of Pediatrics, Weill Cornell Medicine, Cornell University (2000-2001); Associate Professor of Clinical Pediatrics and Clinical Anesthesiology, Columbia University Vagelos College of Physicians & Surgeons, New York, NY (1999-2008); Director of Pediatric Transport Program, NewYork-Presbyterian Morgan Stanley Children's Hospital (1994-2001); Director of Pediatric Intensive Care Unit, NewYork-Presbyterian Morgan Stanley Children's Hospital (1992-1999); Assistant Professor of Pediatrics and Anesthesiology, Columbia University Vagelos College of Physicians and Surgeons (1992-1999); Research Affiliate, Center for Space Research, Massachusetts Institute of Technology (1990-1992); Pediatric Cardiology Fellowship, Boston Children's Hospital, Harvard Medical School (1990-1992); Clinical Fellow in Pediatrics, Harvard Medical School (1990-1992); Assistant

Professor of Anesthesiology and Pediatrics, Yale School of Medicine (1988-1990); Pediatric Anesthesiology, Critical Care Medicine Fellowship, The Children's Hospital of Philadelphia (1987-1988); Clinical Instructor in Anesthesiology, University of Pennsylvania Perelman School of Medicine (1985-1988) **CR:** Council on Foreign Relations (2003-Present); Research Affiliate, Man-vehicle Laboratory (Now Human Systems Laboratory), Massachusetts Institute of Technology (1990-1992); Affiliate, Crew Training, Space Shuttle Specialist-1 Mission, National Aeronautics and Space Administration (NASA) (1978-1980) **CIV:** Participant, Medical Missions to China, Children China Pediatrics Foundation (CCPF) (1999); Participant, Haiti Earthquake Medical Mission (1999); Chairman of the Board, Terre Verte Foundation, Inc. **CW:** TEDx Speaker, "From Einstein to Baby Shark: Relative in the Age of Virality," Cornell University (2019); Profiled, "The Message of Measles" by Nick Paumgarten, The New Yorker **AW:** "A Thousand and One Champions" Award, Apicha Community Health Center (Apicha CHC) (2018); Alpha Omega Alpha Medical Honor Society (2017); Community Advocate of the Year, Alzheimer's Association, NY (2017); Delta Omega Public Health Honor Society (2015); Named Teacher of the Year, Department of Pediatrics, Columbia University (1999-2000); Named to Woodward & White's The Best Doctor's in America (1996-2010); Named to Castle and Connelly's Best Doctor's in New York (1996-2009); Named Person of the Week, "ABC World News Tonight with Peter Jennings" (1993) **MEM:** American College of Legal Medicine; American College of Critical Care Medicine; American College of Chest Physicians; American Academy of Pediatrics; American College of Cardiology Foundation; American Medical Association; Society of Critical Care Medicine; The American National Heart Association; American Society of Anesthesiologists (ASA); Council on Foreign Relations; Council on Emerging National Security Affairs (CENSA); Medical Advisory Board, Children of China Pediatrics Foundation (CCPF); Center for the Advancement of Science in Space (CAIS); National Laboratory; Board of Directors, International Space Station, NASA **BAR:** New York State Bar Association (2019); Supreme Court of the United States (2006); New Jersey State Bar Association (2002) **MH:** Albert Nelson Marquis Lifetime Achievement Award; Marquis Who's Who Top Professional **B/I:** Dr. Zucker became involved in public health as a result of unusual twists and turns. His experience in Washington, which was originally a one-year fellowship, changed after September 11, 2001, while he worked for the Secretary of Health and Human Services. These events put him on a different path and he understood that working in public health would require him to deal with some of the issues on a national and international stage. **RE:** Jewish

ZUCKER, JEFFREY A., T: Broadcast Executive **I:** Media & Entertainment **CN:** WarnerMedia **DOB:** 04/09/1965 **PB:** Homestead **SC:** FL/USA **PT:** Matthew Zucker; Arline Zucker **MS:** Divorced **SPN:** Caryn Stephanie Nathanson (1996, Divorced 2019) **CH:** Four Children **ED:** BA in American History, Harvard University (1986); Coursework, National High School Institute Program for Journalism, Northwestern University **C:** Chairman, WarnerMedia News and Sports (2019-Present); President, CNN Worldwide (2013-Present); President, Chief Executive Officer, NBCUniversal Media, LLC (2007-2011); Chief Executive Officer, NBCUniversal Television Group (2005-2007); President, NBCUniversal Television Group (2004); President, Entertainment, News & Cable Group, NBC (2003-2005); President, NBC Entertainment (2000-2004); Executive Producer, "Today" (1992-2000); Executive Pro-

ducer, "NBC Nightly News" (1993); Field Producer, "Today," NBC News (1993); Researcher, Coverage of the 1988 Summer Olympic Games, Seoul, South Korea, NBC Sports (1986-1988) **CIV:** President, The Harvard Crimson, Harvard University (1985-1986) **CW:** Producer, "Katie," Disney-ABC Domestic Television (2012); Executive Producer, News Segment, Political Conventions (1996, 2000); Executive Producer, News Segment, Bush v. Gore Decision (2000); Executive Producer, News Segment, The Bombing of Centennial Olympic Park (1996); Executive Producer, News Segment, Presidential Inaugurations (1993, 1997); Executive Producer, ""The Brain," "Now with Tom Brokaw and Katie Couric" (1994); Executive Producer, "Tragedy in Rwanda," "Now with Tom Brokaw and Katie Couric" (1994); Executive Producer, "California Fire," "Now with Tom Brokaw and Katie Couric" (1993); Executive Producer, News Segment, Russian Coup (1991); Executive Producer, News Segment, Persian Gulf War (1991); Supervising Producer, "Senator Edward Kennedy," "Today" (1991) **AW:** Fred Dressler Leadership Award, 13th Annual Mirror Awards Ceremony (2019); Five-time Emmy Award Winner **RE:** Jewish

ZUHDI, NABIL, "BILL", JD, T: Lawyer, Litigator, Film and Concert Executive **I:** Law and Legal Services **DOB:** 06/08/1955 **PB:** New York **SC:** NY/USA **PT:** Nazih Zuhdi; Lamya Zuhdi **MS:** Married **SPN:** Darla L. Boyd (05/19/1984) **CH:** Noah **ED:** JD, The University of Oklahoma (1982); BS, University of Central Oklahoma (1979) **C:** President, catBOX Entertainment, Inc. (2007-Present); Manager, The Gap Band (1987-Present); Manager, Private Law Practice (1987-Present); Associate, Law Firm of Darrell Keith (1994); Partner, Zuhdi & Denum (1985-1987); Associate, Linn & Helms (1982-1985) **CR:** Amerisphere, Inc. (1996-Present); President, Zuhdi Entertainment Group, Inc. (1986-Present) **CIV:** Patron, Oklahoma Children's Heart Center, Oklahoma City, OK (1994-Present); Board of Directors, Friends of the Oklahoma History Center; Moderator, Continuing Legal Education Program, Literacy Summit; Criminal Justice Act Panel, United States District Court Northern District of Texas; Former Member, Death Penalty Habeas Corpus Panel, United States District Court for the Western District of Oklahoma **CW:** Featured, Radar Online, LLC (2019); Featured, New York Daily News, Inside Edition (2014); Featured, Pollstar (2013); Producer, Concerts, Frank Sinatra and Julio Iglesias; Television Producer, "Darla Z Live From Las Vegas TV Music Special"; Television Producer, "Darla Z's Christmas Round the World"; Television Producer, "Darla Z's Love Songs 'Round the World"; Promoter, "WBU World Lightweight Title Championship"; Appearances, ABC World News Tonight With Peter Jennings, Wall Street Journal, New York Times, The Oklahoman; Featured, "Trial Distortion and the End of Innocence in Federal Criminal Justice," Wake Forest University **AW:** Top 100 Trial Lawyers in America (2016-Present); Selected, Television News Archives, Vanderbilt University **MEM:** American Bar Association; Association of Trial Lawyers of America (Now American Association for Justice); State Bar of Texas; Oklahoma Bar Association; Oklahoma County Bar Association; Phi Alpha Delta; Alpha Chi Honor Society **BAR:** United States District Court Northern District of Texas (1998); U.S. Court of Appeals for the Fifth Circuit (1991); State Bar of Texas (1991); Supreme Court of the United States (1990); The United States Court of Appeals for the Tenth Circuit (1989); Oklahoma Bar Association (1982); United States District Court for the Western District of Oklahoma (1982) **MH:** Albert Nelson Marquis Lifetime Achievement Award; Marquis Who's Who Top Professional **B/I:** Mr. Zuhdi

became involved in his profession because he was inspired by the television show "Perry Mason" In regards to his entertainment career, his work in law naturally led to it. **AV:** Producing music and films; Boxing **PA:** Democrat

ZURLO, EUGENE, "GENE" JOHN, T: Founder, Chairman, Partner **I:** Technology **CN:** Plasma Technologies LLC **DOB:** 06/30/1937 **PB:** Plattsburgh **SC:** NY/USA **PT:** John Theodore Zurlo; Louise Mary (Di Gioia) Zurlo **MS:** Married **SPN:** Charlotte Rose Ahrens (08/11/1972) **CH:** Luanne Deirdre; Paul Kurt **ED:** Master of Business Administration, Long Island University (1961); Bachelor of Science in Pharmacy, Fordham University (1958) **C:** Founder, Chairman, Managing Partner, Plasma Technologies LLC (2005-Present); Chairman, Founder, Alpine Biologics Inc., Orangeburg, NY (1994-2005); Chief Operating Officer, New York Blood Center (1989-1994); Chief Operating Officer, NYPRO Inc., Clinton, MA; Senior Vice President, Millipore Inc., Bedford, MA; Various Positions, Baxter Healthcare, Northbrook, IL; Chairman, Plasma Technologies LLC **CR:** Real Estate Development, Charleston, SC **CIV:** Co-Founder, Chairman Emeritus of the Catholic Radio Association (2000-Present); Knight of the Grand Cross of the Equestrian Order of the Holy Sepulchre of Jerusalem; Co-Convener of the Charleston Meeting **AW:** Pro Ecclesia et Pontifice, Pope Benedict XVI **MEM:** Heritage Foundation; Harbor Club of Charleston **MH:** Albert Nelson Marquis Lifetime Achievement Award; Marquis Who's Who Top Professional **B/I:** Mr. Zurlo became interested in his profession out of a strong interest in science and strong parental guidance. His father was an executive and inventor, while his mother was a homemaker. **AV:** Boating; Golf; Travel; History **PA:** Republican **RE:** Roman Catholic

ZWECK, RUTH EDNA FEENEY, BSN, MS, T: Human Services Administrator, Psychiatric Nurse **I:** Medicine & Health Care **DOB:** 04/22/1935 **PB:** New York **SC:** NY/USA **PT:** Archibald Thomas; Edna Marie (Kaht) Collins **MS:** Widowed **SPN:** Robert M. Zweck (1992-2014, Deceased); Donald Feeney (1957-1983) **CH:** Donald C.; Diane C.; Scott C.; Michael C.; Thomas C. **ED:** MS in Mental Health Counseling, Long Island University (1984); BSN, Columbia University (1957) **CT:** Registered Nurse, States of New York, New Jersey and Nevada; Certified in Psychiatric and Mental Health Nursing, American Nurses Association, Diplomate, American Board of Disability Analysts **C:** Nurse Clinician, Mojave Mental Health, Las Vegas, NV (1995-2005); Clinical Nurse Coordinator, Partial Hospitalization Program, Montevista Hospital (1993-1995); Treatment Plan Coordinator, Rockland Psychiatric Center (1991-1992); Treatment Team Leader, Rockland Psychiatric Center (1985-1991); Admission and Referral Coordinator, Rockland Children's Psychiatric Center (1979-1985); Night Supervisor, Rockland Children's Psychiatric Center (1978-1979); School Nurse, Teacher, Bergen County School System (1974-1978); Psychiatric Nurse, St. Dominic's Home (1975-1976) **CR:** Member, Advisory Board, School of Nursing, Dominican College (1986-1992) **MEM:** Executive Board Member, Sigma Theta Tau International Honor Society of Nursing (1987-1989) **MH:** Albert Nelson Marquis Lifetime Achievement Award **B/I:** Ms. Zweck became involved in her profession because she wanted to be a nurse for as long as she could remember. **AV:** Playing tennis; Hiking; Sewing; Cooking; Reading

ALPHABETICAL INDEX

73rd Edition

ALPHABETICAL INDEX

73rd Edition

AAGAARD, Eva, MD — Senior Associate Dean for Education   1637

AARDE, Marjorie I. Hartog-Vander — Bureau Chief, Nursing Administrator, Educator   532

AARDE, Robert Leon Vander — Minister, Clergyman   1303

AARON, Henry, "Hank" Louis — Former Professional Baseball Player; Entrepreneur   1637

ABBOTT, David H. — Manufacturing Executive   1637

ABBOTT, Gregory, "Greg" Wayne — Governor of Texas   1637

ABDEL-LATIF, Ata A., PhD — Professor Emeritus   1637

ABDELSAMAD, Moustafa H., DBA — Finance Professor   1638

ABDUL-JABBAR, Kareem — Former Professional Basketball Player   1638

ABDULMAJID, Zara, "Iman" Mohamed — Model; Actress; Entrepreneur   1638

ABELL, Dawn — Elementary and Secondary School Educator, Administrator (Retired)   3

ABELL, Richard Bender, JD — Federal Judiciary (Retired)   4

ABELS, Zach — Head Golf Professional   1638

ABNEY, David Phillip, — Executive Chairman   1639

ABRAHAM, Katy K. — CEO, President, Owner   1639

ABRAHAM, Ralph Lee Jr., MD — U.S. Representative from Louisiana   1639

ABRAMS, Jeffrey, "J.J." Jacob — Director, Producer, Screenwriter   1639

ABRAMSON, Clarence A. — Pharmaceutical Company Executive, Lawyer   5

ABURAHMA, Ali F., MD — Professor of Surgery   6

ACCAD, Aila, MSN, RN — Nurse; Speaker; Author; Health Coach   1639

ACKER, Raymond A. — Minister, Army Chaplain (Retired)   7

ACKERMAN, Amanda — CFO   1433

ACKERMAN, Lillian, PhD — Anthropologist   8

ACKERSON, Nels John — Former Chairman/Founder, Lawyer (Retired)   9

ACKMAN, William, "Bill" Albert — Founder, CEO; Philanthropist   1640

ACOSTA, Rene, "Alex" Alexander — Former U.S. Secretary of Labor   1640

ACTON, Brian — Executive Chairman CN: Signal   1640

ADAMCZYK, Darius — Chairman and CEO   1640

ADAMO, Joseph A., PhD — Biologist, Educator, Researcher (Retired)   1640

ADAMS, Alma — U.S. Representative from North Carolina   1641

ADAMS, Claudine — Board President, CEO   1641

ADAMS, Frederick — Shareholder   1433

ADAMS, Jerome Michael, MD, MPH — U.S. Surgeon General; Vice Admiral   1434

ADAMS, Jerry L. — Owner   1641

ADAMS, John Coolidge — Composer, Conductor   1641

ADAMS, Loren — Visionary Artist, Writer, Publisher   10

ADAMS, Steven Funaki — Professional Basketball Player   1642

ADDISON REID, Barbara Jean, EdD — Management Educator, Human Resources Consultant   1642

ADDISS, Susan Silliman, MPH, MUrS — Public Health Administrator (Retired)   11

ADELSON, Sheldon Gary — Chairman, CEO   1642

ADERHOLT, Robert Brown — U.S. Representative from Alabama, Lawyer   1642

ADKERSON, Richard C. — President, Vice Chairman and CEO   1642

ADKINS, Adele Laurie Blue — Singer-Songwriter   1643

ADLER, Stephen J. — President, Editor-in-Chief   1644

ADRA, Hala, Associate Broker — Real Estate Adviser   1644

ADRI, Avi — Concept Creator   12

ADRIAN, Olivia — President   1644

AFSHAR-MOHAJER, Kambiz, DMD, MSD — Clinical Professor   1644

AGEE, Earleen Heiner — Business Owner, Sales Executive   1644

AGNEW, Janet Burnett — Secondary School Educator   1644

AGUIAR, Artur — Owner   1645

AGUILAR, Peter, "Pete" Rey — U.S. Representative from California   1645

AGUIRRE, Maria G., MD, FAAP — MD Emerita   1645

AHMED, Ali, MD   13

AHMED, S. Basheer, PhD — Research Company Executive, Educator   14

AHRENDTS, Angela Jean — Former Senior Vice President   1645

AIELLO, Francesco — Chef, Owner   1645

AIKINS, Alistine Simons, RN — Medical and Surgical Nurse   1646

AJALAT, Sol P., Esq. — Lawyer   1646

AKINS, Nicholas, "Nick" K. — President, Chairman and CEO   1646

ALAJAJIAN, Hagop Jack — Chiropractor   1646

ALBA, Jessica Marie — Actress; Co-Founder   1647

ALBERT, Elizabeth Franz — Investor, Environmentalist   15

ALBERTI, Jean M., PhD — Clinical Psychologist   16

ALBRIGHT, Cheryl — Owner/Therapist   1647

ALBRIGHT, Robert Lee — Chemist   1647

ALCON, Sonja L. — Medical Social Worker (Retired)   17

ALDER, Douglas Dexter — College President, Historian (Retired)   1647

ALEMÁN, Marthanne Payne, PhD — Environmental Scientist, Consultant   18

ALESSANDRINI, Lori — Medical Spa Owner   19

ALEXANDER, Andrew, "Lamar" Lamar Jr. — U.S. Senator   1648

ALEXANDER, Edward Harrison, PhD — Mathematician, Educator   1648

ALEXANDER, Kim D., EdD — Chancellor; President   20

ALEXANDER, Roger E. DDS — Oral and Maxillofacial Surgeon, Educator   1648

ALI, Mahershala — Actor   1649

ALI, Shamrez Esq. — Attorney   1649

ALITO, Samuel Anthony Jr. — Associate Justice   1649

ALLARD, David Henry — Judge   21

ALLARD, Edward Charles "Ed" — College Official, Industrial Education Educator   22

ALLEN, David — Owner   23

ALLEN, David, MS — Director, Officer and Principal Engineer   1649

ALLEN, Richard, "Rick" Wayne — U.S. Representative from Georgia   1650

ALLEN, Samuel R. — Chairman and CEO (Retired)   1650

ALLEN, Thomas Wesley, DO, MPH — Physician   1650

ALLEN, Woody — Filmmaker, Writer, Actor   1651

ALLER, Wayne Kendall, PhD — Psychologist, Educator, Computer Company Executive   24

ALLISON, Adrienne Amelia, MA, MPA — Senior FP/RH Consultant   1651

ALLMON, Michael, CPA — Certified Public Accountant & Financial Consultant   1652

ALLRED, Colin Zachary — U.S. Representative from Texas   1652

ALLRED, Gloria Rachel — Partner, Lawyer   1652

ALLYN, James — Retired Medical Research Scientist   1652

ALMÁNZAR, Belcalis, "Cardi B" — Rapper, Songwriter   1652

ALPERN, Robert J., MD — Medical Educator, Former Dean   1653

ALPERT, Jonathan Edward — Chair   1653

ALSOP, Marin — Music Director, Conductor, Violinist   1654

ALSTON, Alex Armstrong Jr. — Lawyer   1655

ALSTON, James — CEO   1434

ALTER, Paul R., Esq. — Real Estate Consultant, Lawyer   25

ALTMAN, Sally L. — Educator (Retired)   26

ALTON, Kevin — CEO, Founder   1655

ALVINE, Robert "Bob" — Industrialist, Entrepreneur, Board Leader   1435

AL-ZIKRY, Maad — Video Journalist   27

AMANING, K. Owusu — President; Civil Engineer   1435

AMASH, Justin — U.S. Representative from Michigan   1655

AMELIO, William, "Bill" J. — CEO   1655

AMEND, Kate — Film Editor, Educator   28

AMIRNOVIN, Ramin, MD, FAANS — Neurosurgeon   1655

AMMERMAN, Albert Jay, PhD — Research Professor, Archaeologist, Humanities Educator   29

AMODEI, Mark Eugene — U.S. Representative from Nevada 1656
AMOS, Daniel, "Dan" Paul — Chairman, President, CEO 1656
ANDERSEN, Judith Altenhein Fuller — Special Education Educator 1656
ANDERSEN, Robert A. — Federal Official (Retired) 1436
ANDERSON, Barbara Louise — County Librarian, Retired 30
ANDERSON, Belinda Childress — Academic Administrator, Dean (Retired) 1656
ANDERSON, Bill Maxwell — Owner 31
ANDERSON, Donald A. — Utilities Executive (Retired) 1656
ANDERSON, Gordon Wood — Research Physicist 32
ANDERSON, Joel D. — President, CEO 1657
ANDERSON, Julie — Editor-in-Chief 1657
ANDERSON, Lloyd PhD — Professor Emeritus, Charles F. Curtis Distinguished Professor Agriculture & Life Sciences 1657
ANDERSON, Marilyn Echols — Partner 33
ANDERSON, Merlyn D. — Lawyer 34
ANDERSON, Rhonda Valerie, RN — Registered Nurse 1657
ANDERSON, Roger C., PhD — Biology Educator 1657
ANDRETTI, Mario Gabriele — Race Car Driver (Retired) 1657
ANDREWS, Grover J., EdD — Interim Director 1658
ANDREWS, Julie — Actress 1659
ANDREWS, Mason — Associate Professor of Architecture 1659
ANDREWS, William F. — Manufacturing Company and Private Equity Firm Executive (Retired) 36
ANGEL PAYNE, Phyllis J. — Business Owner 1659
ANGEL, Dennis — Lawyer 1659
ANGELO, Peter Gregory, PhD — Professor Emeritus 37
ANGLIN, John Edson — Theatre and Television Director, Educator 1659
ANISTON, Jennifer Joanna — Actress, Producer 38
ANSARI, Mohammed R. — General and Vascular Surgery 1659
ANSARY, Cyrus — President 39
ANTALFFY, Leslie Peter — Mechanical Engineer 40
ANTHONY-SMITH, MaryAnne — Professor Emeritus of Mathematics 1660
ANTONSEN, Gregg G. — Senior Vice President, Manager 1436
ANTROBUS, John Simmons, PhD — Professor (Retired) 41
APPALARAJU, Ram V. — Executive Analyst 1660
APPLEGATE, H. Reed — Graphic Designer, Advertising Executive 1660
APPOLD, Mark Leonard — Pastor, Religion Educator 42
ARAGONESI, Nick — Owner 43
ARANDA, Jacob V. — Professor of Pediatrics, Director 1660
ARCHIBALD, Patricia A., PhD — Biology Educator, College Director 1661
ARGUIROVA, Boriana D. — Consultant; Strategic Manager/Lead Electrical Engineer 1661
ARISON, Byron Halevy, PhD — Chemist, Researcher (Retired) 44
ARISON, Micky — Chairman; Owner 1661
ARKING, Lucille Musser, RN, MSN — Nurse, Epidemiologist, Consultant 1661
ARKING, Robert, PhD — Geneticist, Gerontologist; Educator 1662
ARMOUR, David — President, CEO; Executive Producer 1662
ARMSTRONG, Daniel W., ChD — R.A. Welch Distinguished Professor 1662
ARMSTRONG, Greg L. — Chairman and CEO (Retired) 1662
ARMSTRONG, Jeanette — Realtor 1662
ARMSTRONG, Jennifer A., MD — CEO 1663
ARMSTRONG, Kelly Michael — U.S. Representative from North Dakota 1663
ARMSTRONG, Mary B. — Director, Consultant 45
ARNOLD, P A — Special Education Educator 46
ARNOLD, Robert James, SLPD, MS, CCC-SLP, BCS-S — Chief Clinical Officer 1663
ARNOLD, Sir Robert Lloyd Michael — Director 1663
ARQUETTE, Patricia — Actress, Executive Director 1663
ARRIETA, Jacob, "Jake" Joseph — Professional Baseball Player 1664
ARRINGTON, Jodey Cook — U.S. Representative from Texas 1664

ARSHT, Adrienne — Founding Chairman, Chairman Emerita, Lawyer 1664
ARTHUR, John Scripture, MD, FACS — Thoracic and Vascular Surgeon 1664
ARTZ, William Eugene — Associate Professor Emeritus 1437
ARY, Mark A. — President, CEO 47
ASENCIO, Diego C., JD — State Agency Administrator, Former Federal Commission Administrator, Consultant 1664
ASH, William James, PhD — Professor Emeritus 48
ASHE, Bernard F., Esq. — Lawyer, Arbitrator 49
ASHLEY, Kristen, "Kit" — Author 1665
ASMUS, John F. — Research Physicist 50
ASSEO, Laureen — Founder, CEO 1665
ATKINS, Gene, "Geno" Reynard Jr. — Professional Football Player 1665
ATKINS, Stephen H., PhD — Owner, Director 1437
ATKINSON, Alanna Beth — Music Educator; Church Pianist/Organist 1665
ATTIYEH, Robert S. — Biotechnology Executive (Retired) 51
ATWOOD, Margaret Eleanor, CH CC OOnt FRSC — Novelist, Poet 1665
AULL, Elizabeth Berryman — Chair, Hazardous Waste Management Commission 1666
AURICCHIO, Vincent, Esq. — Managing Partner 1438
AURNER, Robert Ray — President, CEO 1667
AUSTEN, W. Gerald, MD — Churchill Distinguished Professor, Harvard, Surgeon in Chief Emeritus 52
AUSTIN, J. Max Jr., MD — Professor Emeritus 53
AUSTIN, Neil — Lighting Designer 1667
AVALLONE, Anthony F. — Retired Lawyer 1667
AVANT, Clarence, "The Black Godfather" Alexander — Music Producer; Entrepreneur; Film Producer 1668
AVERY, Stephen — Freelance Reporter 54
AWOSIKA, Bi, MD, FACP, FHM — Associate Professor of Medicine 1438
AXNE, Cynthia, "Cindy" Lynne — U.S. Representative from Iowa 1668
AYERS, Anne Louise — Small Business Owner, Counselor, administrator 55
AYERS, Harry Brandt — Editor, Publisher, Columnist 56
AYERS, Rendall P. — Public Relations Consultant 1668
AYOUB, Elsa — Lawyer 1668
AYRES, Steven D. — Real Estate Broker; Investor 1668
AZAR, Alex Michael II — U.S. Secretary of Health and Human Services 57
AZARNOFF, Daniel L., MD — Pharmaceutical Executive 58
AZARPAY, Guitty — Education, Educator (Retired) 1669
AZIZ, Emad — Director of Cardiac Electrophysiology 1669
BAAN, Maria — Set Nurse, Actress, Author 59
BABB, E. Maurlea, LMFT, LPHA, QE — Marriage and Family Therapist 1439
BABBIN, Donald Francis Jr. — Lieutenant 1669
BABIN, Brian Philip, DDS — U.S. Representative from Texas 1669
BABROWSKI, Trissa A. — Physician 1669
BACHELDER, Joseph Elmer III — Lawyer 1669
BACON, Donald John — U.S. Representative from Nebraska 1669
BACON, Kevin Norwood — Actor 1669
BADALAMENTI, Antonino F., PhD — Adjunct Assistant Professor 60
BADALAMENTI, Fred — Artist, Educator 1670
BADAWY, Shawky Z.A., MD — Gynecologist 1670
BADDOUR, Anne Bridge — Pilot 1671
BADEN, Sheri L — Kindergarten Teacher 1671
BADER, Troy — President, CEO 1671
BADRA, Robert George — Professor 1671
BADRIYEH, Najat — Founder/CEO 61
BAEZ, Joan Chandos — Singer-songwriter; Activist 1671
BAGBY, Marvin O., LHD (Hon.) — Chemist 62
BAGWILL, John W. — Retired Pension Fund Executive 1672
BAILEY, Charles William — Management Consultant, Researcher 1672
BAILEY, F. Lee — Chairman, CEO 1672
BAILEY, Patricia P. — Lawyer; Former Government Official 63

BAILEY, Thomas Robert — President — 1439
BAILOWITZ, Anne — Pediatrician — 1672
BAINUM, Stewart William Jr. — Chairman — 1673
BAIRD, James, "Jim" Richard — U.S. Representative from Indiana — 1673
BAIRD, Scott James, PhD — English Language Educator — 1673
BAKER, Barbara Jean — Restaurant Owner — 64
BAKER, Brent H. — Foundation Executive, Blogger — 65
BAKER, Charles Duane Jr. — Governor of Massachusetts — 1673
BAKER, Earl H., PhD — Medical Psychologist, Educator, Academic Administrator — 1673
BAKER, Erica Joy — Principal Group Engineering Manager; Co-Founder — 1674
BAKER, Frank — Psychologist, Educator — 1674
BAKER, James, "Jim" Addison III — Former White House Chief of Staff; Partner — 1674
BAKER, Jill Withrow — Artist — 1674
BAKER, Kristi A., DMA — Pianist, Church Musician, Composer — 1675
BAKER, Marc — President, CEO; Head — 1675
BALDERRAMA, Celedonia, "Celia" I. — Attorney — 1675
BALDERSON, Diane K. Brown, RN — Business Owner — 1675
BALDERSON, William, "Troy" Troy — U.S. Representative from Ohio — 1675
BALDWIN, Tammy Suzanne — U.S. Senator from Wisconsin — 1676
BALDWIN, William, "Bill" Edward — Owner — 1676
BALE, Christian Charles Philip — Actor — 1676
BALL, James Dale, MD — Associate Professor Emeritus — 66
BALL, Sheri Beth — Senior Vice President — 1676
BALLARD, Robert Duane, PhD — Professer; Oceanographer — 1676
BALLINGER, Royce Eugene, PhD — Professor Emeritus, Academic Administrator, Educator — 1440
BALLMER, Steven, "Steve" Anthony — Professional Sports Team Executive — 1677
BALTHASER, Linda Irene — Faculty Academic Administrator (Retired) — 67
BANAAD-OMIOTEK, Maria Lourdes Geraldine, MD — Medical Doctor — 68
BAND, David M. — Artist, Conservator, Collector, Dealer — 1677
BANGA, Ajaypal, "Ajay" Singh — President, CEO — 1677
BANK, Richard W., MD — Portfolio Manager — 1440
BANKS, James, "Jim" Edward — U.S. Representative from Indiana — 1678
BANNON, Stephen, "Steve" Keith — Senior Counselor to the President, Media Executive, Former Investment Banker — 1678
BAPTIST, Jeremy Eduard — Allergist, Clinical Immunologist, Educator — 1678
BAQUET, Dean Paul — Executive Editor, Journalist — 1678
BARAK, Leor — Owner — 69
BARBANO, Frances Elizabeth — Writer, Photographer, Columnist — 1679
BARBE, David O., MD, MHA — Doctor; Vice President — 1679
BARBIN, Pauline C., CRNA, MEd — Academic Director — 1441
BARCELONA, Isaac G.D. — President & CEO — 1679
BARCHAS, Jack D., MD — Professor and DeWitt Wallace Distinguished Scholar (Retired) — 70
BARCUS, Robert G. — Educational Association Administrator (Ret.) — 71
BARKER, Fred, PhD — Research Geologist, Scientific Editor — 1680
BARKLEY, Charles Wade — Analyst, Professional Basketball Player (Retired) — 1680
BARKLEY, Saquon Rasul Quevis — Professional Football Player — 1680
BARNES, Harrison Bryce Jordan — Professional Basketball Player — 1680
BARNETT, Bishop Dr. Edward "Bishop" Barnett — Bishop, Mental Health (Behavior Specialist) — 72
BARNETT, Franklin Dewees, MD — Obstetrician/Gynecologist — 1680
BARNETT, George, "Bo" Rex IV — President — 1681
BARNETT, Kara Silber — Executive Director; Theater Producer — 73
BARNETT, Michele Szmania — Salon Owner, Hair Stylist — 1681
BARNETT, Sarah A. — Controller — 1681
BARNEY, Trent — CEO — 1681

BARON, Martin, "Marty" — Executive Editor — 1681
BARON, Robert Charles "Bob" — Publishing Executive — 74
BARR, Garland, "Andy" Hale IV — U.S. Representative from Kentucky — 1681
BARR, Jon-Henry — Managing Member — 1682
BARR, Marlene Joy — Volunteer — 1682
BARR, Michael — Executive Administrator, Lawyer — 1682
BARR, William Pelham — U.S. Attorney General; Lawyer — 1682
BARRA, Mary — Chair, CEO; Automotive Executive — 1683
BARRAGAN, Nanette Diaz — U.S. Representative from California — 1683
BARRAN, Linda Mari — Lawyer — 1683
BARRAN, Thomas — Emeritus Professor — 1683
BARRASSO, John Anthony — U.S. Senator from Wyoming — 1683
BARRINGTON, Martin, "Marty" Joseph — Chairman and CEO (Retired) — 1684
BARRIS, Michael Craig, PhD — Neurophysiologist — 1684
BARRON, Margaret Louise — Elementary and Music Educator — 1441
BARSNESS, Richard, "Dick" W. PhD, — Management Educator, Academic Administrator — 1684
BARSTOW, David — Professor; Journalist, Investigative Reporter (Retired) — 1684
BARTELS, Aloysia Jeanne Marie — Food Scientist, Mariculturist — 1684
BARTELS, Ann-Marie, AAP — CEO Emeritus — 1684
BARTELS, Mary Ann — Head of the Research Investment Committee and ETF — 75
BARTHEL, William Frederick Jr. — Engineer, Electronics Company Executive (Retired) — 76
BARTIROMO, Maria Sara — Anchor, Columnist, Author — 1685
BARTOL, Katherine — Mezzo Soprano, Choral Conductor, Music Educator — 77
BARTOLOMEI, Joan Marie — Elementary School Educator — 1685
BARTON, William, "Bill" Arnold — Lawyer, Educator — 1685
BARYSHNIKOV, Mikhail, "Misha" Nikolayevich — Dancer; Actor; Artistic Director — 1685
BASHSHUR, Rashid L. — Professor Emeritus of Health Management and Policy — 1686
BASINGER, Kimila, "Kim" Ann — Actress — 1686
BASQUIN, Kit Smyth, PhD — Writer, Art Historian (Retired) — 78
BASS, Karen Ruth — U.S. Representative from California — 1686
BASS, Samantha — Worldwide Top Model — 79
BASSETT, Angela Evelyn — Actress — 1686
BASSIM, Behrooz, MD — Pathologist — 1687
BASTIAN, Edward, "Ed" H. — CEO — 1687
BASTIYALI, Tarkan — Founder, President — 1687
BATEMAN, Jason Kent — Actor — 1687
BATES, Beverly B. — Lawyer — 1688
BATES, Kathleen, "Kathy" Doyle — Actress — 1688
BATES, Sharon — CEO, Founder — 1689
BATZER, John — Senior Staff Scientist (Retired) — 80
BAUER, Nancy Marshall — TV and Radio Network Executive, Retired — 1442
BAUER, Raymond G. — Sales Professional (Retired) — 1689
BAUMANN, Larry — Partner — 1689
BAUMBACH, Noah — Screenwriter; Film Director — 1689
BAYLIS, William Eric — Science Centre Director; Distinguished University Professor Emeritus — 1689
BAZZY, Najah — Founder, CEO, Interfaith Leader — 1689
BEAL, Bradley Emmanuel — Professional Basketball Player — 1690
BEARD, Chris — Former CEO — 1690
BEARD, Victoria, "Vicky" Frances — Director of Forensics, Fine Arts Chair — 1690
BEARY, Jack — Journalist; Educator; County Official; City Official — 81
BEASLEY, James W. — Attorney — 1690
BEASLEY, John S. II — University Administrator (Retired) — 1691

BEASOM, Nancy Ann — Occupational Therapist, Consultant 1442
BEATTIE, Diana Scott, PhD — Biochemistry Professor 82
BEATTY, Joyce Birdsong — U.S. Representative from Ohio 1691
BEAUFAIT, Frederick, "Fred" William, PhD — Engineering Educator
(Retired) 1691
BEAVER, Laura E. — Attorney 1692
BECCHETTI, Frederick D., PhD — Physicist, Researcher 1692
BECK, Deborah Berman — Industry Association Executive 1692
BECK, Maureen "Mo" — Sales Coordinator, Paraclimbing Athlete 83
BECKER, Boris Franz — Tennis Executive, Analyst, Coach 1692
BECKHAM, David Robert Joseph, OBE — President, Co-Owner,
Former Professional Soccer Player 84
BECKHAM, Odell Cornelious Jr. — Professional Football Player 1692
BEE, Samantha Anne — Comedian, Actress 1692
BEEBE, Abigail — Managing Partner 1692
BEEMER, John Barry, Esq. — Lawyer 85
BEFFA, Daniel Jr. — Owner 86
BEGIEBING, Robert J. — Emeritus Professor of English 87
BEGO, David A. — Owner, CEO 88
BEHLMER, Rudy H. Jr. — Director, Writer, Film Educator (Retired) 1693
BEIK, William, "Bill" Humphrey — Historian, Editor, Writer 1693
BEKEY, Ivan — Space Systems Engineer 1693
BELAFONTE, Harry George Jr. — Singer, Songwriter, Actor 1693
BELICHICK, William Stephen "Bill" — Professional Football Coach 89
BELL, Constance Conklin — Administrator (Retired) 1694
BELL, Darrin — Editorial Cartoonist 1695
BELL, James — Pastor 90
BELL, Tiffani Ashley — Founder, Executive Director 1695
BELLAS, Albert C. — Founder, Managing Director 1695
BELLE ISLE, Albert Pierre, PhD — Independent Investor 1695
BELLINGER, Cody James — Professional Baseball Player 1443
BELLO, Brook Parker, PhD — Founding CEO 1695
BELT, David Levin, LLB — Lawyer 1696
BEN-ASHER, Daniel Lawrence "Dan" — Legislative Staff Member
(Retired) 91
BENCH, Johnny Lee — Former Professional Baseball Player 1696
BENDER, Richard — Dean, Architect, Educator 1696
BENÉ, Thomas L. — Chairman, President, CEO 1696
BENING, Annette Carol — Actress 1696
BENIOFF, David — Screenwriter, Producer, Director 1697
BEN-MEIR, Marc J. — Psychologist, Substance Abuse Counselor,
Author 1697
BENN, Raymond C. "Ray", PE — Materials Engineer 92
BENNER, Dorothy Spurlock — Elementary School Educator 93
BENNET, Michael Farrand — U.S. Senator from Colorado 1697
BENNETT, Caroline, "Carol" Elise — Retired Librarian, Reporter,
Actress 1697
BENNETT, Janet — Legislative Staff Member 1698
BENNETT, John Michael, PhD — Poet; Professor; Librarian 1698
BENNETT, Robert Martin — Professor Emeritus (Medicine) 94
BENNETT, Scott L., Esq. — Lawyer 1444
BENNETT, Thomas, "Tom" Jerman, PhD — Engineer (Retired) 1698
BENNETT, Tony Dominick — Singer, Artist 1698
BENSIDOUN, Sebastien I. — Owner 95
BENTLEY, William Ross, PhD — Forestry Educator 1699
BENTZ, Gregory M. — Partner 1699
BERA, Amerish, "Ami" Babulai, MD — U.S. Representative from
California; Physician 1699
BERENBEIM, Ronald E., Senior Fellow — Business Writer, Educator 1699
BERENDT, John Lawrence — Author, Writer 1700
BERES, Milan, MD, FACS — Surgeon (Retired) 96
BERG, Christine D., MD — Radiation Oncologist; Special Volunteer 1444

BERG, Janice Carol — Elementary School Educator 1700
BERG, Janice — Elementary School Educator (Retired) 1700
BERG, Micah — CEO 97
BERGGRUEN, Nicolas — Founder, President 1700
BERGMAN, John, "Jack" Warren — U.S. Representative from Michigan;
Military Officer 1700
BERGMANSON, Diane — Director, Access & Technology Center
(Retired) 98
BERGSTEN, C. Fred, LHD, PhD — Senior Fellow, Director Emeritus 99
BERK, Carolena Adrianna van den — 1299
BERK, Paul D., MD, FACP, FAASLD, AGAF, FTOS — Internist; Research
Scientist; Educator 100
BERKLEY, Eugene Bertram "Bert", LHD — Chairman of the Board 101
BERKLEY, Robert, "Bob" John — Retired Federal Agency Professional 1701
BERLIN, Kenneth Darrell — Regents Professor, Consultant, Researcher 1701
BERLIND, Roger S. — Stage and Film Producer 1701
BERLY, Alice Anne — Financial Administrator (Retired) 1701
BERNARD, Sharon E., Esq. — Lawyer 1701
BERNHARDT, David Longly — U.S. Secretary of the Interior 1702
BERNSTEIN, Carl — Investigative Journalist; Author 1702
BERNSTEIN, Carl — Jewelry Designer; Artist 1702
BERNSTEIN, David William — Counsel 102
BERNSTEIN, Phyliss Louise, PhD — Psychologist 1702
BERRIAN, James Edwin — Field Entomologist (Retired) 103
BERRY, Dean G. — CEO 1702
BERRY, Halle Maria — Actress 1702
BERRYHILL, Mary Finley, RN, BSN — Emergency Nurse 1703
BERTINELLI, Valerie Anne — Actress; Television Personality 1703
BERTKA, Sara — Art Director, Business Analyst II 1703
BERTOLINI, Mark T. — Chairman and CEO (Retired) 1703
BERTRAM, Christopher D. — Engineer 1703
BESHEAR, Andrew, "Andy" Graham — Governor of Kentucky 1703
BETH, Richard Sprague, PhD — Retired 1703
BETZ, Adam M. — Owner 104
BEURET, Kevin Paul — Secondary School Educator 1704
BEWLEY, Brian Anthony — President, CEO 1704
BEYER, Donald, "Don" Sternoff Jr. — U.S. Representative 1704
BEYER-MEARS, Annette — Fellow of the Royal Society of Medicine 105
BEZOS, Jeff — CEO 1704
BHALLA, Vinod K. — Endocrinologist, Biochemist, Educator (Retired) 1705
BHARGAVA, Manoj — Founder, CEO 1705
BHAYANI, Nikhil K., MD, FIDSA — Physician 1445
BHOLA, Annmarie — CEO 106
BHUSRI, Aneel — Co-Founder, CEO 1705
BIALER, Martin George, MD, PhD — Geneticist 1445
BIANCHINI, Jamie — Chief Visionary Officer 1705
BIDEN, Joseph, "Joe" Robinette Jr. — President-Elect of the U.S.,
47th Vice President of the U.S., Professor 1705
BIEBER, Justin Drew — Musician 1705
BIENENSTOCK, Arthur — Physicist, Educator, Federal Official 1706
BIERNACKI, Blake — Managing Director 1446
BIGGERS, R. Lee Lee Jr. — Structural Engineer 1706
BIGGS, Andrew, "Andy" Steven — U.S. Representative from Arizona 1707
BIGGS, William C., MD, FACE — Endocrinologist, Chief Medical
Information Officer, Managing Partner 1707
BIGLER, Terri Ellen, MD — Internal Medicine and Pediatrics Doctor 1446
BIJAOUI, Nadia Judith, DHEd, PHD, MAP 107
BILES, Simone Arianne — Professional Gymnast 1447
BILIRAKIS, Gus Michael — U.S. Representative, Lawyer 1707
BINEY, Isaac Noble, MD — Physician 1707
BING, Stephen, "Steve" Leo — CEO 1707
BIPPUS, David P., — Manufacturing Financial Executive (Retired) 1707

BIRD, Larry Joe — Professional Sports Team Executive, Professional Basketball Player (Retired)   1708

BIRD, Philip, "Brad" Bradley — Film Director, Producer, Screenwriter, Animator   1708

BIRD, Wendell R., PhD, JD — Legal Historian   1708

BIRDSONG, James Charles Jr. — Founder, President & Executive Director   1708

BIRKENHEAD, Thomas Bruce, PhD — Theater Producer, Educator   1709

BIRNBAUM, Irwin Morton — Educational Consultant, Lawyer   108

BIRX, Deborah Leah — Coronavirus Response Coordinator   109

BISANZ, Annette Kay — Nurse   1709

BISHOP, Bryan Edwards, JD — Attorney   1709

BISHOP, James, "Dan" Daniel — U.S. Representative from North Carolina   1709

BISHOP, Paul Edward, PhD, MS — Microbiologist (Retired)   110

BISHOP, Robert W., Esq. — Lawyer   1709

BISHOP, Robert, "Rob" William — U.S. Representative from Utah; Ranking Member of the U.S. House Committee on Natural Resources; Former Educator   1710

BISHOP, Sanford Dixon Jr. — U.S. Representative from Georgia; Lawyer   1710

BISSELL, Michael G., MD, PhD, MPH — Professor Emeritus   111

BISTRIAN, Bruce Ryan MD, MPH, PhD — Internist, Educator   1710

BITTENBENDER, Brad James — Safety Engineer   112

BIVENS, Vicki Stiver — Public Services Librarian (Retired)   1710

BIZZI, Emilio, MD — Neuroscientist, Educator   1710

BJORKLUND, Victoria B., PhD — Chair, Lawyer   1711

BLACK, Arthur G. "Art" — Electrical Engineer   113

BLACK, Carol I. — Elementary School Educator, Principal (Retired)   1447

BLACK, Clint Patrick — Singer, Songwriter, Actor   1711

BLACK, Recca M. — Elementary School Educator   1711

BLACKBURN, Marsha — U.S. Senator from Tennessee   1711

BLACKFORD, Alan Ralph — Vocal Teacher   114

BLACKWELL, Mary Louise — Nurse   1711

BLACKWOOD, Karla Renée, APRN-NP — Nurse Practitioner   1712

BLAIR, Theresa Lucille — Records Manager, Electrical Contractor, Court Recorder   1712

BLAKELY FORBES, Joseph — Founder, President   1712

BLAKELY, Sara Treleaven — Founder, CEO   115

BLAKNEY, Michael A., CPA, CMA — Senior Level Finance Manager   116

BLAKNEY, William Gilbert Grover, MS — Associate Professor Emeritus   117

BLANK, Arthur M. — Owner, Co-Founder   118

BLANKENSHIP, James, "Jimmy" Lynn Jr., — Research Professor (Physicist)   1712

BLANKFEIN, Lloyd Craig — Senior Chairman, Investment Banker   1712

BLAYDES, Jeffrey — Attorney   1712

BLECHARCZYK, Nathan, "Nate" — Co-Founder, Chief Strategy Officer   1712

BLEDSOE, Gary L., Esq. — Owner, Attorney   1712

BLEIER, Robert, "Rocky" Patrick — Former Professional Football Player   1712

BLEWITT, Richard F. — Management Consultant   119

BLIGE, Mary J. — Singer, Songwriter, Actress   1713

BLISS, Corwin, "Corry" Albert — Political Consultant   1713

BLISS, Marian Jackson, MBA, MS — Information Systems Professional   1713

BLOCK, Stephanie Janette — Actress, Singer   1714

BLOOM, Eilene — Director   1448

BLOOMBERG, Michael, "Mike" Rubens — Financial News Services Company Executive; Publishing Executive; Former Mayor   1714

BLOOMFIELD, Suzanne L. — Artist   1714

BLOUNT, Evelyn — Executive Director/Treasurer (Retired)   120

BLUE, Monte EdD — Chairman of the Board of Regents   1715

BLUMENAUER, Earl Francis — U.S. Representative from Oregon   1715

BLUMENTHAL, Richard — U.S. Senator from Connecticut; Lawyer   1715

BLUNT, Emily Olivia Leah — Actress   1715

BLUNT, Roy Dean — U.S. Senator from Missouri   1716

BLYTH, Myrna — Senior Vice President, Editorial Director   1716

BOAL, Dean — Arts Center Administrator, Educator (Retired)   1716

BOBZIEN, David Paul Jr. — Director   1716

BOCCHINO, Robert Louis — Communications Professional; Actor; Singer; Writer   1716

BOECKMANN, Jacob Otto, MD   1717

BOEHM, Barry William, PhD, ScD — Distinguished Professor, Engineer, Researcher   121

BOELTER, Philip F. — Executive Vice President/COO   122

BOES, Lawrence William "Larry", JD — Lawyer   123

BOGER, Dan Calvin, PhD — Science Professor, Consultant   124

BOGHOSIAN, Paula der — Retired Computer Business Consultant   1478

BOGLE, Edra Charlotte, PhD — Literature Educator   125

BOGUCKI, Raymond Spencer, Attorney — Lawyer   1717

BOHANNON, Camille — National Network Radio News Correspondent   1717

BOHBOT, Alyza — Owner, CEO   1718

BOHI, Douglas Ray, PhD — Economist   1448

BOHN, Robert Herbert — Lawyer   1718

BOISVERT, Therese A., MSEd — Credentialing Compliance Coordinator   126

BOITANO, Brian Anthony — Professional Figure Skater   1718

BOLDT, Gary Dean — Farmer   127

BOLDUC, Tommy Rocky — Owner   128

BOLEN, Jean Shinoda, MD — Psychiatrist, Jungian Analyst, Author   129

BOLINO, August Constantino, PhD   130

BOLLINGER, Lee Carroll — President, Lawyer, Educator   1718

BOLTON, John Robert — Former U.S. National Security Advisor; Lawyer   1718

BOLY, Lillian — Language Educator (Retired)   1719

BON JOVI, Jon — Musician   1719

BONAMICI, Suzanne Marie — U.S. Representative from Oregon   1719

BONBON, Bernard Saturnin — Associate Professor, Researcher, Specialist in Mathematical Problems of Visual Space   131

BOND, Joseph — Retail Manager   1719

BONDS, Barry Lamar — Professional Baseball Player (Retired)   1719

BONE, Henry G., MD, MACP, FRCP, FACE — Physician, Clinical Researcher   1719

BONE, Pamela Weaver Jean — Elementary School Educator   1720

BONIN, Donna — Owner   1449

BONNETT, Aubrey W., PhD — Professor Emeritus   1720

BONOMO, Donald — Attorney, Partner   1720

BONVILLIAN, William B. — Lecturer   1720

BOOHER, Charles Forest — Business Executive   1721

BOOK, Lauren F. — Senator   132

BOOKER, Cory Anthony — U.S. Senator from New Jersey   1721

BOOMERSHINE, Donald Eugene — Municipal Official (Retired)   133

BOOTH, Carol Marie — Writer, Songwriter, Advocate   134

BOOTH, David Gilbert — Co-founder, Executive Chairman   1721

BOOTHROYD, Herbert — Insurance Company Executive (Retired)   135

BOOZMAN, John Nichols — U.S. Senator from Arkansas; Optometrist   1721

BORAS, Scott Dean — Sports Agent   1721

BORDA, Deborah — President, CEO   136

BORDEN, Richard Craig — President, CEO   1721

BORENSTEIN, Walter — Professor   137

BORER, Jeffrey Stephen, MD — Professor of Medicine   138

BORG, Björn Rune — Fashion Designer, Professional Tennis Player (Retired)   1721

BORGES, Wanda — Attorney, Owner   1722

BORN, Allen — Chairman, CEO   139

BORNSTEIN, Carl M., Esq. — Principal   1722

BORST, William Adam — Radio Personality, Educator, Writer 1722
BORUM, Rodney — Corporate Financial Executive 1722
BOS, Terry — President, CEO 140
BOSEMAN, Chadwick Aaron — Actor 1723
BOST, Michael, "Mike" Joseph — U.S. Representative from Illinois 1723
BOSTON, Bruce O., PhD — Writer, Editor, Publications Consultant 1723
BOTANA, Derrick — Vice President 1723
BOUBOULIS, Denis — MD 1449
BOUDREAUX, Gail — President, CEO 1724
BOUFFIOUX, George "Bill" — Owner, Manager 141
BOUMAN, Katherine Louise, PhD — Assistant Professor; Computer Scientist 1724
BOURLA, Albert, DVM, PhD — Chairperson and CEO 1724
BOWDEN, A. Bruce — Equity Partner 1724
BOWENS, Brenda Lee, CNOR, RN — First Assistant 142
BOWER, Maurice Donald "Bugs" — Record Company President, Producer, Composer 143
BOWER, Shelley A., Esq. — Attorney 1724
BOWIE, Mike — Owner and President 1450
BOWIE, Syretta, CCP — Vice President of Executive Compensation 1724
BOWLES, Thomas Joseph, PhD — Fellow 1450
BOWMAN, Georgianne G. — Historian 1725
BOYD, Grant C., JD — Attorney 144
BOYLE, Brendan Francis — U.S. Represetive from Pennsylvania 1725
BRAAFLADT, Arnie Rolf — Deputy Chief Counsel (Retired) 145
BRACY, Catherine — Co-Founder, Executive Director 1725
BRADEN, Everette Arnold, JD — Lawyer, Judge 146
BRADFORD, Dana G. II — Partner; Lawyer 1451
BRADLEY, David G. — Owner, Publishing Executive 147
BRADLEY, Marilynne G. — Advertising Executive, Educator 1725
BRADLEY, Roger William — Attorney 1726
BRADSHAW, Carol — Executive Director 1726
BRADSHAW, Richard Eugene — CEO 148
BRADSHER, Henry St. Amant — Journalist, Foreign Affairs Analyst 1726
BRADWAY, Robert, "Bob" A. — Chairman and CEO 1726
BRADY, Kevin Patrick — U.S. Representative from Texas 1726
BRADY, P. James "Jim", CPA — Vice Chair 149
BRADY, Thomas, "Tom" Edward Patrick Jr. — Professional Football Player 1726
BRAID, Ralph M. — Professor of Economics 1727
BRAIS, Keith S., Esq. — Attorney 1727
BRAITHWAITE, M. Christine — Elementary School Educator (Retired) 1452
BRANAGH, Kenneth Charles — Actor, Director, Producer, Writer 1727
BRANDOW, Rev. Stephen Jon, MDiv — Staff Chaplain-Alexandria VA Healthcare System/Catholic Priest 150
BRANDRISS, Michelle L. — Founder, President 1452
BRANDT, Pamela A., MAEd — Art and Art Special Education Educator 1727
BRANDYS, Paul — Computer Programmer (Retired) 1728
BRANSON, Harley Kenneth — Attorney at Law, Retired; Venture Capital, Retired 1728
BRANSON, Richard Charles Nicholas — Entrepreneur, Philanthropist 151
BRASHER, Earlene — Music Educator 1453
BRASSARD, Janice A. — Owner, Instructor, Educational Consultant 1728
BRASWELL, Jackie Boyd — State Agency Administrator 1728
BRATCHER, Carla — Obstetrician and Gynecologist 1728
BRAUN, Michael, "Mike" K. — U.S. Senator from Indiana 1729
BRAZELTON, W. Robert, PhD — Professor Emeritus 152
BREAZEALE, Helene — Arts Administrator, Educator 1729
BRECHER, Howard — Lawyer; Publishing Executive 1729
BREEDIN, B. Brent — Historian 1729
BREEN, Edward Deveaux — Executive Chairman 1729
BREES, Andrew, "Drew" Christopher — Professional Football Player 1729

BREGSTEIN, Henry — Partner 1730
BRELJE, Michael — Senior Attorney 1730
BRENNAN, Robert L. — Educational Director, Psychometrician 1730
BRENNECKE, Allen Eugene, Esq. — Attorney at Law 153
BRENT-CHESSUM, Tracey, PhD — Assistant Professor of Musical Theatre Techniques 1730
BRETSCHNEIDER, Barry — Attorney 1731
BREWER, Nevada Nancy — Teacher Supervisor 1731
BREWER, Rosalind Gates — COO, Group President 1731
BREYER, James, "Jim" William — CEO 1732
BREYER, Stephen Gerald — Associate Justice 1732
BRIDENSTINE, James, "Jim" Frederick — Administrator 1732
BRIDGES, Jeffrey, "Jeff" Leon — Actor, Musician 1732
BRIDGES, R. Barton — Medical Doctor (Retired) 1733
BRIENZA, Kristin L. — Team Leader 1733
BRIESEN, Edward Fuller von — Builder, Real Estate Developer 1319
BRIGGS-KRULL, Sharon Lee — Owner 1733
BRIGHT, Christopher Patrick — Chief 1733
BRIN, Sergey Mihailovich — Information Technology Executive, Computer Scientist 1733
BRINDISI, Anthony Joseph — U.S. Representative from New York; Lawyer 1733
BRINDLE, Lewis Carver — Arts Administrator 1733
BRINGS, Allen, DMA — Musician, Professor Emeritus 154
BRITTON, Ruth Ann — Educator 1734
BROAD, Edythe Lois — Philanthropist 1734
BROAD, Eli — Philanthropist, Entrepreneur 1734
BROADUS, Calvin, "Snoop Dogg" Cordozar Jr. — Rapper, Actor 1735
BROCAGLIA, Joyce — CEO 1735
BROCCHINI, Ronald — Architect (Retired) 1735
BROCK, D. Heyward — English Literature Educator, University Official 1736
BROCKMEIER, Norman — President (Retired) 1736
BRODERICK, Matthew John — Actor 1736
BRODSKY, Sylvia A. — Psychologist, Consultant 1453
BROG, David — Executive Director 1737
BROMMER, Gerald F., DLitt — Artist, Writer 155
BRONFMAN, Charles Rosner — Philanthropist; Former Distillery Executive 1737
BROOKS, Forest Clyde "Forrie" — Civil Engineer, Project Manager 156
BROOKS, Garth — Musician 1737
BROOKS, Morris, "Mo" Jackson Jr. — U.S. Representative, Lawyer 1738
BROOKS, Susan Lynn — U.S. Representative (Retired), Chairwoman (Retired), Lawyer 1738
BROUILLETTE, Danny, "Dan" Ray — U.S. Secretary of Energy 1738
BROUS, Thomas R. — Lawyer 1738
BROUSSARD, Bruce Dale — President and CEO 1738
BROUSSARD, Paul — Pastor 1454
BROWN, Anthony Gregory — U.S. House of Representatives from Maryland; Military Officer; Lawyer 1738
BROWN, Antonio Tavaris Sr. — Professional Football Player 1739
BROWN, B. Thomas, MD, MBA — Urologist 157
BROWN, Betty Jane — Elementary School Educator (Retired) 1739
BROWN, Brandon Scott, Master HVAC, Universal CFC Mast — Owner 158
BROWN, Carrie — Editor 1739
BROWN, David H. — Author 1739
BROWN, Dolores Connor — Medical Association Administrator 1739
BROWN, Edward L. — Cultural Arts Teacher 1740
BROWN, Ethan — President, CEO 1740
BROWN, James, "Jim" Nathaniel — Professional Football Player (Retired), Actor 1740
BROWN, Katherine, "Kate" — Governor of Oregon 1740
BROWN, KC — Executive Chef, Owner 1740

BROWN, Laura — Editor-in-chief	1454
BROWN, Lawrence, "Larry" Harvey — Professional Basketball Coach (Retired)	1740
BROWN, Lee — Chairman, CEO	159
BROWN, Millie Bobby — Actress	1740
BROWN, Omer — Lawyer	1741
BROWN, Patrick, "Pat" O'Reilly — Founder, CEO; Professor Emeritus	1741
BROWN, Sherrod Campbell — U.S. Senator from Ohio	1741
BROWN, Stephen — Superior Court Judge (Retired)	160
BROWN, Susan Elizabeth — Secondary School Educator	1741
BROWN, Timothy Charles — International Affair Specialist	161
BROWN, William Ferdinand — Artist, Writer	1741
BROWNLEY, Julia Andrews — U.S. Representative from California	1742
BRUSCH, John — Medical Director	1742
BRUSCH, John — Physician	1742
BRUTGER, James H. — Art Educator	1742
BRYAN, Justin — Partner	1455
BRYANT, Dewey, "Phil" Phillip — Governor of Mississippi	1742
BRYANT, Kobe Bean — Professional Basketball Player (Retired)	162
BRYANT, William Lloyd — Retired Air Force Officer, Classical Music Recording Engineer, Radio Broadcaster	1743
BRYANT, Yvonne — Educator (Retired)	1743
BUBLÉ, Michael Steven — Singer; Songwriter; Record Producer; Actor	1743
BUCHANAN, Elizabeth Spoon, PhD — Assistant Principal, Language Educator	163
BUCHANAN, Louise — Political Organization Worker, Consultant	1743
BUCHANAN, Vern Gale — U.S. Representative from Florida	1743
BUCHIN, Jacqueline Chase, PsyD — Research Clinician	164
BUCHIN, Stanley Ira, DBA — Marketing and Finance Educator	165
BUCK, Kenneth, "Ken" Robert — U.S. Representative	1743
BUCKLEY, Peter J. — Psychiatrist	166
BUCSHON, Larry Dean, MD — U.S. Representative, Surgeon	1744
BUCY, Erwin — Principal	1744
BUCY, Richard Snowden — Aerospace Engineering and Mathematics Educator, Consultant	1455
BUDANO, Vinny — General Manager	1744
BUDD, Patricia, "Pat" J., PhD — Psychologist	1744
BUDD, Theodore, "Ted" Paul — U.S. Representative from North Carolina	1744
BUETTNER, Russ — Investigative Reporter	1744
BUFE, Noel C., PhD — Program Director	1744
BUFF, Ernest D. — Chair, Managing Partner	167
BUFFER, Michael — Boxing Announcer; Actor	1456
BUFFETT, Warren Edward — CEO	1745
BUFORD, Delores — Education Educator, Researcher	168
BUFORD, Robert, "R.C." Canterbury — CEO	1745
BULL, Rebecca D., MEd — Music Educator, Musician	1745
BULLOCK, Sandra Annette — Actress	1745
BULLOCK, Stephen Clark — Governor of Montana	1746
BUMPAS, Stuart M. — Lawyer	1746
BUNDI, Renee — Art Director, Graphic Designer, App Designer	169
BUNN, Dorothy I. — International Conference Reporter	1746
BUOLAMWINI, Joy Adowaa — 1) Computer Scientist 2) Founder	1746
BURAKOVSKY, Leonid, PhD — Physicist, Researcher	1746
BURCHETT, Timothy, "Tim" Floyd — U.S. Representative	1747
BURCK, Joseph Russell, PhD — Medical Educator, Consultant, Minister	1747
BURGESS, Michael Clifton, MD — U.S. Representative from Texas; Physician	1747
BURGET, Jennifer A. — Owner, Hearing Instrument Specialist	1456
BURGOS-SASSCER, Ruth — Chancellor Emeritus	1747
BURGUM, Douglas, "Doug" James — Governor of North Dakota	1748
BURKE, Clement, "Clem" Anthony — Musician	1748
BURKE, David — Owner	1748
BURKE, Michael S. — Chairman and CEO	1748
BURKE, Tarana J. — Activist	1748
BURLESON, Lynn — Lawyer	1748
BURMEISTER, Paul Frederick — Owner/Farmer	170
BURNET, George V — Engineering Educator	1748
BURNETT, Mark — Television Producer; Chairman	1749
BURNS, Christine, Dr. — Program Manager, Acquisition Task Lead	1749
BURNS, Jeffrey — Founder/Partner	1749
BURNS, Lyle D. — Organic Chemist	1750
BURNS, Marian M. — Lawyer	1750
BURNS, T.D. — Small Business Owner	171
BURR, Charlene — Administrative Assistant to the Managing Director	1457
BURR, Richard Marshall — Municipal Government Administrator (Retired)	172
BURR, Richard Mauze — U.S. Senator from North Carolina	1750
BURRIS, Keith C. — Executive Editor	1750
BURROW, Deborah Jett — Class Teacher	1750
BURROW, Joseph Lee — Collegiate Football Player	1750
BURROWS, R. Anthony — Owner	173
BURSTYN, Ellen — Actress	1750
BURTON, Barbara A. — Psychotherapist	1751
BURTON, Lauren G. — Attorney	1751
BURTON, Richard Roderick, PhD — Computer Scientist	174
BURTON, Tim — Director	1751
BUSCH, Kurt Frederick — Founder, CEO	1752
BUSH, George Walker — 43rd President of the U.S.	1752
BUSH, John, "Jeb" Ellis — Governor of Florida (Retired), Consulting Firm Executive	1752
BUSH, Laura Welch — Former First Lady of the U.S.; Educator	1752
BUSH, Wesley G. — Chairman	1752
BUSH, William Read, PhD, JD — Computer Scientist	175
BUSHNELL, Roderick Paul — Owner	176
BUSQUETS, Miguel A. — Ophthalmologist	1753
BUSTOS, Cheryl, "Cheri" Lea — U.S. Representative from Illinois	1753
BUTCHER, Edward Bernie — Retired State Legislator/Business Consultant	1753
BUTKUS, Dick Marvin — Former Professional Football Player	1753
BUTLER, William L. Sr. — Business Owner (Retired)	1754
BUTNER, Robert Westbrook, MD — Ophthalmologist, Educator	1754
BUTT, Charles Clarence — Chairman, CEO	1754
BUTTERFIELD, Alexander Porter — Military Officer; Presidential Appointee; Aviation Executive	177
BUTTERFIELD, George Kenneth Jr. — U.S. Representative from North Carolina; Former State Supreme Court Justice	1754
BUTTIGIEG, Peter, "Pete" Paul Montgomery — Mayor	1754
BUTTON, Lewis A. III — Attorney	1754
BUXTON, Amity P., PhD — Founder, Educator	178
BUZASH, Michael Daniel — Professor Emeritus	1457
BYAM, Elizabeth — Chief Operating Officer	1458
BYNUM, Terrell — Distinguished Connecticut State University Professor	179
BYRD, Joseph, MusB, MA — Composer, Musician (Retired)	1754
BYRD, Lidia M. — Language Educator	1755
BYRD, Lorenda Sue, RN, BSN, MSN — Vice President of Patient Care	1755
BYRNE, Bradley Roberts — U.S. Representative from Alabama; Lawyer	1755
BYRNE, Jeffrey E., PhD — Pharmacology Researcher, Educator, Consultant	180
CABRERA, Miguel — Professional Baseball Player	1755
CACCIATORE, S. Sammy — Partner; Attorney	1458
CAFARO, Renee — U.S. Editor	1755
CAFORIO, Giovanni — Chairperson, CEO	1756

CAIN, William Howard — Private Piano Teacher, Organist, Music Educator 1756
CAINE, Edward P. — Managing Partner 1756
CAINE, Michael — Actor 1756
CAIRL, Stephan D. — Owner 1757
CALANTZOPOULOS, André — CEO 1757
CALDWELL, Billy Ray, PhD — Geologist 1757
CALDWELL, Courtney Lynn, JD, MA — Lawyer, Real Estate Consultant 181
CALHOUN, Rose Marie Taylor, RN, MEd, CPHQ, MBBLSS — Healthcare Quality Consultant 1459
CALIFANO, Joseph Anthony Jr. — Chairman Emeritus, Lawyer 1757
CALKINS, Keith G., PhD — Computational Physical Scientist 1757
CALLAHAN, Blake, CRFP, CPA, CVA, CCIFP — CFO 1459
CALLAHAN, Thomas James — Lawyer 1758
CALVERT, Kenneth, "Ken" Stanton — U.S. Representative from California 1758
CAMACHO, Catherine Bejerana — Lawyer 183
CAMERON, James Francis — Film Director, Screenwriter, Producer 1758
CAMERON, Richard Douglas "Trooper Dick", MG USA (Ret.) — Major General 184
CAMMACK, Carolyn A. — Secondary School Educator 1758
CAMPAGNA, Barbara — Bank Vice President; College Corporate Relations; Sales Marketing & Promotional Products; Community Volunteer 185
CAMPBELL, Arthur Waldron — Lawyer, Author, Educator 186
CAMPBELL, Fred — President, Owner 187
CAMPBELL, Magda, MD — Professor Emeritus; Child Psychiatrist; Researcher 1460
CAMPBELL, Samuel — Commander, General Manager 1759
CAMPOS, Leonard Peter, PhD — Clinical Psychologist 1759
CANDIDO, Kenneth David, MD — Anesthesiologist, Educator 1759
CANN, Steven J. — Political Science Professor 188
CANTWELL, Maria Elaine — U.S. Senator from Washington 1760
CAO, Youfang, PhD — Senior Scientist 1760
CAPEHART, Bonnie Mae — English Educator (Retired) 189
CAPITO, Shelley Wellons — U.S. Senator from West Virginia 1760
CAPLAN, Judith — Genealogist; Poet; Editor; Educator; Sewist 1760
CAPPELLAZZO, Amy — Chairperson, Executive Vice President 1760
CARBAJAL, Salud Ortiz — U.S. Representative from California 1760
CARBONARA, Robert Stephen, PhD — Discipline Lead, Materials Scientist 1760
CARDARELLA, C. JoAnn Foust, MSN, ARNP — Nursing Administrator 1761
CÁRDENAS, Antonio, "Tony" — U.S. Representative from California 1761
CARDIN, Benjamin Louis — U.S. Senator from Maryland 1761
CARELL, Steve John — Actor, Comedian 1761
CAREY, Mariah — Singer, Songwriter 1762
CAREY, Robert — CEO 1762
CARGILE, Kimberly — Owner 1460
CARL, Joan Strauss — Sculptor, Painter 1762
CARLINI, James MBA — Management Consultant 1762
CARLSON, Erik — CEO, President 1763
CARMEN, Ira Harris, PhD — Professor Emeritus 1461
CARMICHAEL, James V. Jr. — Library and Information Science Educator 1763
CARNES, Edward Earl — Chief Judge 1763
CARNEY, John Charles Jr. — Governor of Delaware 1763
CARNEY, Peter Mallison, MD, FAANS — Neurosurgeon 190
CARO, Dick H., MBA — Marketing and Technology Consultant 191
CARPENTER, Adelbert, "Buz" W. — Air Force Officer (Retired) 1763
CARPENTER, C. Donald Jr. — Land Surveyor, Title Researcher (Retired) 192
CARPENTER, John T., MD — Professor Emeritus 1763
CARPENTER, June Evans — Retired Educator 1764

CARPER, N. Gordon, PhD — Historian, Educator 193
CARPER, Thomas, "Tom" Richard — U.S. Senator 1764
CARR, Barry Lynn, Sr. — President, CEO 194
CARR, Eileen A. — President 1764
CARRANZA, Jovita — Administrator; Former Treasurer of the U.S. 1764
CARRERAS, José — Opera Singer 1765
CARREY, Jim Eugene — Actor; Comedian 1765
CARREYROU, John — Reporter 1461
CARRIER, Sandra L., RN, COHN/CM, ABDA, FAAOHN — President (Retired) 1765
CARRINGTON, Betty Jane Edna, EdD, FACNM — Certified Nurse-midwife, Educator 1462
CARRISON, Dale Mitchell, DO, MS, FACEP, FACOEP — Professor Emeritus 1766
CARROLL, Antionette D. — Owner 1766
CARROLL, Diahann — Actress 1767
CARROLL, Rosemary F. — Historian; Educator; Lawyer 1767
CARSON CARRUTH, Zane — President 1768
CARSON, André D. — U.S. Representative from Indiana; Marketing Specialist 1767
CARSON, Benjamin Solomon Sr. — U.S. Secretary 1768
CARSON, Tracy — CEO 195
CARTER, Annette — Former State Legislator, House of Representatives 196
CARTER, Dwayne, "Lil Wayne" Michael Jr. — Rap Artist 1768
CARTER, Earl, "Buddy" Leroy — U.S. Representative from Georgia 1769
CARTER, Eleanor, "Rosalynn" Rosalynn — Former First Lady 1769
CARTER, James, "Jimmy" Earl Jr. — 39th President of the U.S. 1769
CARTER, John L. — Lawyer 1770
CARTER, John Rice — U.S. Representative from Texas; Lawyer 1770
CARTER, Lisa — Horse Ranch Owner; AKC Yorkie Breeder 1770
CARTER, Shawn, "Jay-Z" Corey — Rapper, Music Company Executive 1770
CARTER, Thomas Allen — Engineering Executive (Retired) 197
CARTWRIGHT, Matthew Alton — U.S. Representative from Pennsylvania; Legal Services 1770
CARVEL, Robert, "Bertie" Hugh — Actor 1771
CARVER, James — Theatre Director and Consultant 1771
CARY, L. Curtis, MD — Program Director, Medical Educator 198
CASAGRANDE, Greg F. — Founder, President 1771
CASE, Edward, "Ed" Espenett — U.S. Representative from Hawaii; Lawyer 1771
CASE, Jean, — Chairman; CEO 1771
CASE, Karen A., BS, JD, LLM in Taxation — Attorney: Tax Law 1772
CASE, Stephen, "Steve" McConnell — Former Chairperson and CEO 1772
CASEY, Daniel L., EdD — School Counselor 1772
CASEY, Robert, "Bob" Patrick Jr. — U.S. Senator from Pennsylvania 1772
CASIANO, Fernando R. — Financial Analyst 1772
CASPER, Marc Nolan — CEO and President 1772
CASSAR, George, Harris, Professor Emeritus — Historian, Educator 1772
CASSIDY, DeVallo Francis — Film Manager, Writer, Consultant 1462
CASSIDY, Kevin Andrew — Engineering Company Executive (Retired) 1773
CASSIDY, William, "Bill" Morgan, MD — U.S. Senator from Louisiana 1773
CASTAN, Frederic — Executive Chef 1773
CASTANEDA, Manuel — President 1463
CASTEN, Sean Thomas — U.S. Representative from Illinois 1773
CASTLE, Lawrence Edward "Larry", Esq. 199
CASTOR, Katherine Anne — U.S. Representative from Florida 1773
CASTRO, Joaquín — U.S. Representative 1773
CASTRO, Julián — Former Secretary; Lawyer 1774
CATCHEN, Gary L., PhD — Professor Emeritus; Nuclear Engineer; Photographer 1463
CATCHINGS, Yvonne, PhD — Artist, Educator 1774
CATES, Lindley A. — Professor (Retired) 1774

CATHER, James Newton, PhD — Embryologist, Educator 200
CATTELAN, Maurizio — Artist 1775
CATURIA, Eric — Owner 1464
CATZ, Safra Ada — CEO 201
CAWLEY, Joseph, PhD — Educator Emeritus 202
CEBULKO, Warren A. — Supervisor 203
CELICO, Frank — Owner 204
CELL, Edward Charles — Philosophy Educator 1775
CERERE, Andrew — CEO, Vice Chairperson 1775
CERNY, Joseph III, PhD — Chemistry Professor, Dean, Director 205
CERVERIS, Michael — Actor 1775
CÉSPEDES, Yoenis — Professional Baseball Player 1775
CHA, Se Do, MD, FACP, FSCAI — Invasive and Interventional Cardiologist 1775
CHAKOIAN, George — Aerospace Engineer 206
CHALIF, Ronnie — 1) Co-Founder 2) Artist 1776
CHAMBERLAIN, Steven Craig, PhD — Mineralogist, Neuroanatomist, Bioengineer 1776
CHAMPAGNE, Carol Ziegler — Retired 207
CHAN, Jackie — Actor; Martial Artist 1777
CHAN, Priscilla, MD — Pediatrician; Co-founder, Co-CEO; Philanthropist 208
CHAN, Wendy — Lawyer 1777
CHANDLER, Josh — CEO, Partner 209
CHANG, Chia-Hwa Lydia Chu — Artist 1777
CHANG, Choongseok — Managing Principal Physicist 210
CHANG, Emily — Journalist 1777
CHANG, Jin Sook — Co-founder, Chief Merchandising Officer 1777
CHANG, Mona Mei-Hsuan — 1777
CHANG, William, PhD — Research Scientist 1777
CHAO, Elaine Lan — U.S. Secretary of Transportation 1777
CHAPEK, Robert "Bob" — CEO 211
CHAPEL, Harold L., MD, FACC — Physician 1464
CHAPMAN, Kenneth Maynard — Science Education Consultant 1778
CHAPMAN, Richard Alexander — Research Scientist 212
CHAPPELL, Dorothy, PhD — Biologist, Cell Biologist; Educator, Dean of Natural and Social Sciences 1778
CHAPPELLE, Dave Khari Webber — Actor, Comedian 1778
CHARTIER, Vernon Lee "Vern" — Electrical Engineer (Retired) 1465
CHARTRAND, Guy J. — President, CEO 213
CHASDI, Richard J., PhD — Professorial Lecturer 1779
CHASE, Andy — Utility Relationship Manager 1779
CHASE, Jeanette Knapp — Music Educator (Retired) 214
CHASE, William J., PhD — History Educator 1779
CHASTAIN, Jack Kessler, AA, DMD, FICD — Dentist 1780
CHATFIELD, Joan, MM — Church Administrator 215
CHATHAM, Richard Douglas — Associate Professor 216
CHATMAN, Willie Mae, BS, BA — Division Head of Business/Law 217
CHATTORAJ, Aparna — Gynecologist, Educator 1465
CHAVEZ, Javier Jr. — President 1780
CHAVKIN, Rachel — Stage Director, Artistic Director 1780
CHEADLE, Donald, "Don" Frank Jr. — Actor 1780
CHEEK, Julia Taylor — CEO and Founder 218
CHEN, Fen — Mathematician 1781
CHEN, Wen-Hsiung, PhD — Engineering Executive, Educator 219
CHENEY, Elizabeth, "Liz" Lynne — U.S. Representative from Wyoming 1781
CHENEY, Richard, "Dick" Bruce — 46th Vice President of the U.S. 1781
CHENG, Doris, Esq. — Shareholder 1781
CHENG, Theresa, MD — Neurosurgeon 220
CHENOWETH, Kristin Dawn — Actress; Singer 1782
CHERIAN, Joy, PhD — President; Former Consulting Company Executive 1782
CHERNG, Peggy, PhD — Co-CEO 1783
CHERTOW, Marian Ruth — Industrial Ecologist; Educator 1783
CHESHIRE, William Polk — Newspaper Columnist, Editor 1783
CHESNEY, Kenny Arnold — Singer, Songwriter, Musician 1783
CHIANG, Chwan-Hwa Peter — Director 221
CHIARILLI, Sara E. — Owner, Designer 222
CHICAGO, Judith, "Judy Chicago" Sylvia — Artist 1783
CHILES, Robert S. Sr. — President, CEO 1784
CHIN, Chen Oi — Scholar 1784
CHITTENDEN, Sherry Dianne — Special Education Educator 1784
CHMIELEWSKI, Dawn M. — Attorney 1785
CHO, Austina — Psychiatrist 1785
CHO, Jai H., MD — Chief Medical Officer 223
CHOI, Hyonggun, PhD — CEO, President, Owner 1785
CHOMSKY, Avram Noam, PhD — Philosopher, Political Activist, Historian 1786
CHOPRA JONAS, Priyanka — Actress 1786
CHORNEY, Michael — Musician, Music Producer 1787
CHOU, Grace I. — Assistant Controller 1787
CHOU, Richard C. — Mechanical Engineer (Retired) 1466
CHOU, Tracy — CEO; Software Engineer 224
CHOUCAIR, Bechara, MD — Senior Vice President, Chief Health Officer 1787
CHOYKE, Wolfgang Justus, PhD — Research Professor Emeritus 1787
CHRISTENSEN, Barbara Jean, RN, BS, MS — Nurse Educator, Medical and Surgical Nurse 1787
CHRISTENSEN, Raymond G., MD, FAAFP — Physician 1787
CHRISTY, James Thomas — Wealth Advisor, Lawyer 225
CHU, Jonathan Murray — Director 1788
CHU, Judy May — U.S. Representative from California 1788
CHUKWU, Chinonye — Director 1788
CICALA, Roger Stephen — Entrepreneur 1788
CICILLINE, David Nicola — U.S. Representative from Rhode Island 1788
CIFU, Douglas A. — CEO, Co-Founder 1789
CIMERA, Richard F. — Senior Director of Aerospace Engineering (Retired) 1789
CIOCHETTY, John — Protective Services Site Supervisor 1789
CIPFL, Joseph John, PhD — President, CEO Emeritus 226
CIPOLLONE, Pat — White House Counsel 1789
CIRESI, Michael V., JD — Lawyer 227
CISNEROS, Gilbert Ray Jr. — U.S. Representative 1789
CITRIN, Max — CEO, President, Owner 228
CIULLO, Rosemary Christine, PsyD — Clinical Psychologist 229
CLAIBORNE, C. Clair, PhD — Polymer Materials Scientist 230
CLANCY, Michele — Resource Room Educator 1789
CLAPTON, Eric Patrick — Guitarist, Singer 1790
CLARIDGE, David E. — Engineering Educator, Consultant 1790
CLARK, Barbara Ann — Counseling Administrator (Retired) Licensed Professional Counselor 231
CLARK, Chris Saint — Owner/Artist 1791
CLARK, Donald Lewis — Minister, Psychologist, Educator 1791
CLARK, Katherine Marlea — U.S. Representative from Massachusetts 1792
CLARK, Marcia Rachel — Lawyer 1792
CLARK, Richard L. MD — Radiologist, Educator 1792
CLARK, Sandra — Geologist 1792
CLARK, Trent L. — Owner, President, CEO 1792
CLARK, Wesley Gleason, PhD — Pharmacologist, Educator (Retired) 1792
CLARK, William N. — Lawyer, Retired Military Officer 1793
CLARKE, Benjamin King — Anesthesiologist (Retired), State Representative, State Legislator 232
CLARKE, Emilia Osobel Euphemia Rose — Actress 1793
CLARKE, Robert Reside — Biochemist, Researcher 233
CLARKE, Yvette Diane — U.S. Representative 1793

CLARKSON, Lawrence — Air Transportation Executive 1793
CLARKSON, Robert, "Bob" Noel — Commercial Photographer; Magician 1793
CLAY, Herbert — Design Engineer (Retired) 234
CLAY, William, "Lacy" Lacy Jr. — U.S. Representative from Missouri 1794
CLAYTON, Jamie, LE — President, Owner 1794
CLAYTON, William — Utilities Executive (Retired) 1794
CLEAVER, Emanuel II — U.S. Representative from Missouri; Minister 1794
CLEMENS, Roger — Retired Baseball Pitcher 1794
CLEMENT, Gilles — Interior Designer 235
CLEMENTI, Steve — Software architect 1795
CLINE, Benjamin, "Ben" Lee — U.S. Representative from Virginia 1795
CLINGER, William F. — Former U.S. Representative from Pennsylvania 1795
CLINGERMAN, Bryce — Chief Operating Officer 1795
CLINTON, Bill — 42nd President of the U.S. 1795
CLINTON, Hillary Diane — Former U.S. Secretary; Former U.S. Senator from New York; Former First Lady 236
CLINTON, Lottie D.E. — State Agency Administrator (Retired) 1795
CLONINGER, Claude Robert, MD, PhD — Psychiatrist, Epidemiologist, Educator 1796
CLOONEY, George — Actor 1796
CLOSE, Glenn — Actress 1796
CLOUD, Michael Jonathan — U.S. Representative from Texas 1797
CLOWE, Kelley A., CFP, ChFC — Certified Financial Planner, Registered Investment Adviser 1797
CLUSIN, William Thomas, — Physician, Neuroscientist, Cardiologist, Educator 1797
CLYBURN, James, "Jim" Enos — U.S. Representative from South Carolina 1797
COATES, Arthur Donwell, MA — Chemist; Consultant 1798
COATES, Ta-Nehisi — Author 1798
COATES, Wes, MBA — General Manager 237
COATS, Daniel Ray — U.S. Director of National Intelligence (Retired) 1798
COBB, Rowena Noelani — Real Estate Broker 238
COBLE, John — Partner 1798
COCHRAN, Brent Hartman — Professor 1798
COCHRAN, Rich — President, CEO 1798
COCO, Jimmy — Founder; Celebrity Tanning Expert; Visionary Inventor 1466
COELHO, Sandra Signorelli — Elementary and Secondary School Educator, Consultant 239
COEN, Ethan — Filmmaker 1799
COEN, Joel — Filmmaker 1799
COHEN, Alan — Professor of Interventional Radiology 1467
COHEN, Frederick R., PhD — Professor of Mathematics 240
COHEN, Herman Jay — Diplomat, Consultant to U.S. investors in Africa 1799
COHEN, Irving David — Science Administrator 241
COHEN, Robert Stephan — Lawyer 242
COHEN, Stephen, "Steve" Ira — U.S. Representative from Tennessee 1799
COHEN, Tim — Editor 1800
COHN, Gary David — Director (Retired) 1800
COLANDUONI, Bernadette L. Connelly RN. MEd, RN, MEd — School Nurse 1800
COLARESI, Linda Ann — Senior Industrial Engineer (Retired) 1800
COLBERT, Stephen — Talk Show Host, Comedian, Actor 1800
COLBURN, Nancy Douglas, LCSW — Social Worker; Educator 1801
COLE, Gerrit Alan — Professional Baseball Player 1801
COLE, Ransey Guy Jr. — Chief Judge 1801
COLE, Thomas, "Tom" Jeffery — U.S. Representative from Oklahoma 1801
COLE, Walter — Owner, Founder 1801
COLELLA, Alexandra — Attorney 1801
COLEMAN RADEWAGEN, Amata, "Aumua Amata" Catherine — Delegate to the U.S. House of Representatives from American Samoa 1802

COLEMAN, Carina E., CFA — Director, Pension & Trust Investments 1801
COLEMAN, D. Jackson, MD — Ophthalmologist; Professor of Ophthalmology 243
COLEMAN, Freddie Duane — Host, Commentator 1467
COLEMAN, Marshall — Psychiatrist, Psychoanalyst 1802
COLEMAN, Stephen R. — Professor of Psychology Emeritus 244
COLEMAN, Zendaya, "Zendaya" Maree Stoermer — Actress; Singer 1802
COLHOUR, Donald Bruce — Producer, Director; Clergyman, Theologian 245
COLLINS, Christopher Carl — U.S. Representative from New York (Retired) 1802
COLLINS, Dennis Glenn, PhD — Mathematics Professor (Retired) 1803
COLLINS, Douglas, "Doug" Allen — U.S. Representative from Georgia; Lawyer 1803
COLLINS, Mary Alice, PhD — Psychotherapist; Social Worker; Educator (Retired) 1468
COLLINS, Phil — Drummer 1803
COLLINS, Susan Margaret — U.S. Senator from Maine 1803
COLLINS, Suzanne — Author 1468
COLLIS, Steven H. — Chairman, CEO, and President 1803
COLLOPY, Liam Thomas — Publicist 1804
COLLUM, Lisa — CEO 1804
COLMAN, Sarah, "Olivia" Caroline Olivia — Actress 1804
COLON-NAVARRO, Fernando — Professor of Law 1805
COMANECI, Nadia — Professional Gymnast 1805
COMBS, Judi — CEO, Partner 1469
COMBS, Sean — Record Company Executive, Producer, Actor 1805
COMER, Brenda Warmee — Elementary School Educator; Real Estate Company Officer 1805
COMER, James Richardson Jr. — U.S. Representative from Kentucky 1805
COMER, Jodie Marie — Actress 1806
COMEY, James Brien Jr. — Director (Retired) 1806
COMMA, Leonard, "Lenny" A. — Chairperson, CEO 1806
COMPASS, Brandi — Teacher 246
COMSTOCK-JONES, Janis L. — Business Owner, Consultant 1469
CONAWAY, Kenneth, "Mike" Michael — U.S. Representative from Texas; Ranking Member, House Committee on Agriculture 1806
CONCOFF, Gary O. — Partner 247
CONDE, Marilyn T., MAOM, FCSP — Material Manager 1806
CONLON, James E. — Professor Emeritus 1806
CONNELY, Catherine — Associate Broker 1470
CONNERY, Sean — Actor 1806
CONNOLLY, Gerald, "Gerry" E. — U.S. Representative from Virginia 1807
CONNOLLY, Sean — CEO and President 1807
CONNOLLY-O'NEILL, Barrie Jane — Owner, Interior Designer 1807
CONRAD, Marian, "Susie" — Special Education Educator (Retired) 1807
CONRAD, T. Charles III, CPA — Partner 1808
CONSTANCE, Thomas Ernest, Esq. — Partner; Lawyer 1470
CONTINO, Richard Martin, Esq. — Lawyer, Leasing Executive, Consultant 1808
CONWAY, Beverly E. — Associate Professor of Science and Nutrition 1471
CONWAY, Kellyanne Elizabeth — Former Senior Counselor to the President 1808
CONWAY, Kevin — Actor, Director 1808
COOK, Branden C. — President 248
COOK, Ian M. — Chairman, President, and CEO 1808
COOK, Joseph V. Jr., MD — Physician and Medical Director 249
COOK, Morreece "Elaine", LCSW (Retired) — Clinical Social Work 250
COOK, Paul Jospeh Jr. — U.S. Representative from California; Military Officer (Retired) 1808
COOK, Renay — Elementary School Educator 1809
COOK, Scott David — Co-Founder 1809
COOK, Timothy, "Tim" Donald — CEO 1809

COOKE, Jessica — Founder 1809
COONEY, Patrick Louis — Writer 251
COONROD-VANNOY, Dr. Delberta "Debbie" Hollaway — Educator (Retired), Consultant 252
COONS, Christopher, "Chris" Andrew — U.S. Senator from Delaware 1809
COOPER, Anderson Hays — Broadcast Journalist, News Correspondent 1471
COOPER, Bradley — Actor 1472
COOPER, Fred W., PhD — CEO, Founder 253
COOPER, James, "Jim" Hayes Shofner — U.S. Representative from Tennessee; Lawyer 1809
COOPER, Kenneth R., PhD — Professor 1810
COOPER, Roy Asberry III — Governor of North Carolina 1810
COOPER-JONES, James — CEO 254
COOPERMAN, Leon, "Lee" G. — Former Chairperson, CEO (Retired) 1810
COPLEY, Mary Sandra "Sandy", MD — Physician 1472
COPPOLA, Francis — Film Producer, Director, Screenwriter 255
COPPOLA, Sabrina L. — Founder 1810
COPPOLA, Sofia Carmina — Film Director, Film Producer, Scriptwriter 1810
COPPOLELLA, Anthony S. — Poet, Songwriter, Author 256
COQUILLETTE, Daniel Robert — Lawyer, Educator 257
CORBAT, Michael Louis — CEO 1811
CORBIN, Richard, "Dick" H. — Business Development Consultant 1811
CORBITT, John H., Rev. Dr. — Former Pastor 1811
CORDANI, David M. — CEO and President 1811
CORDEN, James — Actor, Television Personality 1811
CORHAN, Albert — Director of Academy Operations 1811
CORLETT, Trevor — CEO, President 1812
CORMIER, Addie — Process Safety Consultant 1473
CORNELL, Brian Christian — Chairman and CEO 1812
CORNELL, Charles N., MD — Professor of Clinical Orthopedic Surgery 1473
CORNYN, John III — U.S. Senator from Texas 1812
CORREA, Jose, "Lou" Luis — U.S. Representative from California 1812
CORRIGAN, Helen Gonzalez — Cytologist (Retired) 1812
CORTEZ MASTO, Catherine Marie — U.S. Senator from Nevada 1812
CORYELL, Daniel Caroll — Minister 1813
CORZO, Juan Jr. — Vice President 1813
COSTA, James, "Jim" Manuel — U.S. Representative from California 1813
COSTA, Michael A. 1474
COSTNER, Kevin Michael — Actor 1813
COTILLARD, Marion — Actress 1813
COTTON, Thomas, "Tom" Bryant — U.S. Senator from Arkansas 1814
COUCH, James R. Jr., MD, PhD, FAAN, FANA, FAHS — Professor and Chair 258
COUCH, John Alexander, PhD — Research Biologist 1814
COUCH, Robert Barnard "Bob", MD, (Retired) — Professor Emeritus 259
COULTER, Ann Hart — Writer, Political Columnist, Lawyer 1814
COURIC, Katie Anne — Broadcast Journalist 1814
COURTNEY, Joseph, "Joe" Darren — U.S. Representative 1815
COUTINHO, Charles PhD — Managing Director 1815
COUTURE, Paul Henry, CLU, ChFC, CEP — President 260
COX, David Brummal — Accounting Firm Executive 1815
COX, Dennis, DMA — Music Educator, Conductor 261
COX, Jerome, "Jerry" Jr. — Electrical Engineer, Cybersecurity Provider 1815
COX, Jerry J. — Lawyer 262
COX, Laverne — Actress 1816
COX, Terrance, "TJ" J. — U.S. Representative from California 1816
CRAIG, Angela, "Angie" Dawn — U.S. Representative 1816
CRAIG, David R. — State Legislator (Retired) 1816
CRAIG, Ford Morris, EdD — Educational Administrator, Researcher 1816
CRAIG, Hurshel, "Gene" Eugene — Retired Agronomist 1817

CRAIG, James Hicklin — Fine Arts Consultant 1474
CRAIG, Susanne — Investigative Reporter 1817
CRAMER, Kevin John — U.S. Senator from North Dakota 1817
CRANDALL, Roger W. — Chairman, President, CEO 1817
CRANE, Christopher Mark — CEO and President 1817
CRANE, Elizabeth, "Betsy" — Professor (Retired) 1817
CRANIN, Marilyn — Landscape Designer 1818
CRANSTON, Bryan Lee — Actor 1818
CRAPO, Michael, "Mike" Dean — U.S. Senator from Idaho 1819
CRAWFORD, Eric, "Rick" Alan Rick — U.S. Representative 1819
CRAWFORD, Kate, ABR — Co-Founder, Director 1819
CRAWFORD, Katherine, "Kitty" E., RN, BSN, MSN — Pediatrics and Neonatal Nurse; Nursing Educator; Case Manager 1819
CRAWFORD, Mark H. — Analyst 1819
CRAWFORD, Richard — Musicology Educator 263
CREAMER, Jack Major — Marketing Executive 1820
CREASMAN, Carl E. Sr. 1820
CREATH, Curtis J., DMD, MS — Owner 1820
CRENN, Dominique — Chef 1820
CRENSHAW, Ben — Professional Golfer 1820
CRENSHAW, Daniel, "Dan" Reed — U.S. Representative from Texas 1820
CREWS, Mara — Writer 1821
CRIM, Loretta Grace — Music Educator 1821
CRISCUOLO, Nicole — Special Education Teacher 1821
CRISP, Polly Lenore, PhD — Psychologist (Retired) 1821
CRIST, Charles, "Charlie" Joseph Jr. — U.S. Representative from Florida, Lawyer 1821
CRIST, William Gary — Professor Emeritus 1822
CRITES, Marsha Smith, BS, MSW — Owner, Social Worker 1822
CRIVELLI, Chad — Farmer 1822
CROCKER, Charles Allan — Lawyer 1822
CROCKETT, Webb Webb — Lawyer (Retired) 1822
CROFUT, Donald Merwin, BS — Senior Buyer (Retired) 1823
CROMARTIE, Robert Samuel III, MD, FACS — Thoracic Surgeon 1823
CRONE, Patrick — Owner, President 1475
CRONIN, Robert Hillsman — Musical Instrument Manufacturer (Retired) 1823
CROSS, Clinton F. — Lawyer (Retired) 264
CROSSNEY, Joshua — CEO 265
CROSWELL, Beverly Ann — Newborn Screening Nurse, Specialty Case Manager 1823
CROW, Jason A. — U.S. Representative from Colorado 1824
CROW, June — Chief Financial Officer 266
CROW, Logan — Founder 267
CROWE, Russell — Actor 1824
CROWLEY, Mart — Playwright 268
CROYLE, Barbara Ann — Executive Director 269
CRUISE, Tom — Actor 1824
CRUZ, Judith "Judy" A. Beekman, RN, BSN, MS — Nursing Administrator 270
CRUZ, Penélope — Actress 1824
CRUZ, Rafael, "Ted" Edward — U.S. Senator from Texas; Lawyer 1824
CRUZ, Rosalina Sedillo — Marriage and Family Therapist 1475
CRUZ-ALVAREZ, Raul — CEO 1825
CRYSTAL, Billy — Actor 1825
CUBAN, Mark — Owner; Co-owner; Sports Team Executive; Entrepreneur; Television Personality; Investor 1825
CUCCINELLI, Kenneth, Thomas II — Acting Deputy Secretary of Homeland Security 271
CUDNEY, Gerald, "Jerry" Edward — Minister; Real Estate Professional 1826
CUELLAR, Henry Roberto, PhD — U.S. Representative from Texas; Lawyer 1826

CULP, Henry Lawrence Jr. — CEO, Chairman 1826
CUMBERBATCH, Benedict — Actor 1826
CUMMINGS, Anne Marie — Logistics Manager 1827
CUMMINGS, Bill — Philanthropist, Real Estate Developer 1827
CUMMINGS, Elijah Eugene — Former U.S. Representative from Maryland 272
CUMMINGS, Laureen 1827
CUMMINGS, Richard J., MD, FACS — Otologist (Retired) 1827
CUMMINGS, Rulon — Financial Counselor (Retired) 1827
CUNNINGHAM, Betty — Adult Education Educator 1828
CUNNINGHAM, George Woody, PhD — Federal Official, Nuclear Scientist (Retired) 1476
CUNNINGHAM, Joseph, "Joe" — U.S. Representative from South Carolina 1828
CUNNINGHAM, Langford Jr. — Deputy Juvenile Officer 1828
CUNNINGHAM, Sharon M., CFP — Morgan Stanley Wealth Management 1828
CUNNINGHAM, Stacey — President 1828
CUNNINGTON, Rico — Owner, Chef 1828
CUOMO, Andrew Mark — Governor of New York 1828
CUOMO, Jerome John "Jerry", PhD — Materials Scientist 273
CUPP, Darren — Entrepreneur 1828
CURIEL, Herman F. — Social Worker; Educator, Professor Emeritus 1829
CUROL, Helen Broussard, MLIS — Library Consultant 1829
CURRERI, Peter William, MD — Health Facility Administrator (Retired) 275
CURREY, Thomas Arthur, MD — Ophthalmologist (Retired) 276
CURRY, Stephen, "Steph" II — Professional Basketball Player 1830
CURTIS, David Philip — Artist, Educator 277
CURTIS, Jamie Lee — Actress 1830
CURTIS, John R. — U.S. Representative from Utah 1830
CURTIS, Thomas, "Tom" Pelham II — Artist, Small Business Owner 1830
CUSTER, John C — Portfolio Manager 1831
CUSTODIO, Brenda Kay, PhD — English Language Educator 1831
CYNAR, Sandra Jean, PhD — Electrical Engineering Educator 1831
CYRUS, Miley — Singer, Actress 1831
DABROWSKI, Edward — Television Engineering Technical Director 279
DAFOE, Willem — Actor 1831
DAGUM, Alexander, MD — Professor of Surgery and Orthopaedic Surgery, Chief of Plastic Surgery, Executive Vice Chair of Surgery 1832
DAHL, Deborah A., PhD — Principal 1832
DAHL, Per Fridtjof — Physicist 280
DAHLBERG, David J. — Forestry Technician (Prevention) 281
DAIGLE, Lauren Ashley — Singer, Songwriter 1833
DAINES, Steven, "Steve" David — U.S. Senator from Montana 1833
DALE, Adrianne Marie — Information Technology Executive, Consultant (Retired) 1833
DALEY, Sandy Dakota — Artist (Retired), Filmmaker, Photographer 1833
DALTREY, Roger — Singer 1833
DAMICO, James A. — Library Director 1834
DAMON, Matt — Actor 1834
DAMSCHEN, Elaine — President 282
DANFORTH, David N. — Associate Research Physician, Surgical Oncologist 1476
DANGERMOND, Jack — President, Co-founder 1834
DANGERMOND, Laura — Co-founder 1834
DANIEL, Arlie V., PhD — Professor Emeritus 283
DANIEL, James R. "Jim" — Vice Chairman 284
DANIELIAN, Arsen, Shareholder, Director, Officer — Attorney at Law 1835
DANIELS, Jeff — Actor 1835
DANIELS, Lee — Producer, Director 1835
DANNELS, Mark J. — Sheriff 1835
DANTZIC, Cynthia Maris — Senior Professor Emerita, Artist 1835
DARST, David Earl, BTh, BS, MEd, MBA — Finance Educator, Pastor 1836
DAS, Sumit — Product Engineer 1836

DASH, Anil — CEO 1837
DASILVA, Rodrigo — Managing Partner, Restaurateur 1837
DATCHER, Jewell A. — Mathematics Teacher (Retired) 1837
DATTA, Subhendu Kumar, Dr. — Mechanical Engineer, Educator 1837
DAUB, Hal — Senior Counsel 285
DAVENPORT, G. William — U.S. Administrative Law Judge (Retired) 1837
DAVID, Larry — Television Scriptwriter, Producer, Actor 1837
DAVIDS, Sharice Lynette — U.S. Representative from Kansas 1838
DAVIDSON, Evelyne Monique, MD — Internist; Principal Investigator 286
DAVIDSON, Thomas M. — Corporate Financial Executive 1838
DAVIDSON, Warren Earl — U.S. Representative from Ohio 1838
DAVIS III, Egbert Lawrence — Retired Partner 1841
DAVIS, Anthony Jr. — Professional Basketball Player 1838
DAVIS, C. Dean, JD — Lawyer, Consultant (Retired) 287
DAVIS, Clive Jay — Chief Creative Officer 288
DAVIS, Daniel, "Danny" K. — U.S. Representative 1838
DAVIS, Ernestine Bady — PMA Director, Nurse Educator, Administrator 1838
DAVIS, Jack C., Esq. — Lawyer 289
DAVIS, Jacquetta, "Jacque" Anderson — English Language Educator 1838
DAVIS, LeCount R. Sr., Chairman Emeritus — CFP(R) 1839
DAVIS, M. Denise — Reading Consultant, Tutor 1839
DAVIS, Paul Joseph, MD — Endocrinologist 290
DAVIS, Richard J. — Lawyer, Government Official (Retired) 1840
DAVIS, Rodney Lee — U.S. Representative 1840
DAVIS, Russ Erik, PhD — Oceanographer; Educator 1840
DAVIS, Susan Carol — U.S. Representative from California 1840
DAVIS, Viola — Actress 1840
DAVISON, Mark L., PhD — John P. Yackel and American Guidance Service Professor of Educational Assessment and Measurement 291
DAWSON, Peter J., MD — Pathologist, Educator 1841
DAY, Donald, "Donny" Gene Jr., — Owner, President, CEO 1841
DAY, Judith Elizabeth, PhD — Educator, Author, State Representative (Retired) 292
DAYANANDA, Mysore A., PhD — Professor Emeritus of Materials Engineering 1841
DAYHOFF, Nancy, EdD, RN — Managing Partner 1842
DAY-LEWIS, Daniel — Actor 1842
DE BLASIO, Bill, "Bill" — Mayor of New York City 1842
DE CASAL, Carole A. — Education Educator 1842
DE CRUZ-SÁENZ, Michèle S., PhD — Language Educator, Researcher 1843
DE JAGER, Nikkie, "NikkieTutorials" — Makeup Artist, Beauty Vlogger 1843
DE LA RENTA, Oscar — Fashion Designer 1843
DE NIRO, Robert Anthony — Actor 1843
DE SANTO, Joseph Robert — Engineering Educator 1844
DE SHIELDS, André — Actor, Singer, Choreographer 1844
DE SILVA, Deemathie, PhD — University Administrator, Educator 1844
DEALEY, Amanda Mayhew — Community Volunteer and Activist 296
DEAN, Madeleine Cunnane — U.S. Representative from Pennsylvania 1844
DEAN, Margaret Genevieve, Esq. — Lawyer; Commentator 297
DEAR, Ronald Bruce — Social Work Educator (Retired) 1845
DEBERTIN, Jay D. — CEO and President 1845
DEBEVOISE, Charles Henry — Shareholder, Lawyer 1845
DECOURCY, Colleen — Co-President, Chief Creative Officer 298
DEEB, Mohamed El Sayed Nasser El — Professor Emeritus 352
DEFAZIO, Peter Anthony — U.S. Representative 1845
DEFRANCO, Jason — President 1846
DEGETTE, Diana Louise — U.S. Representative, Lawyer 1846
DEGLER, Carl Neumann, PhD — Professor Emeritus 299
DEGNAN, John J. "Jack" III, PhD — Physicist, Technical Consultant 300
DEITCH, D. Gregory "Greg" — Meteorologist (Retired) 301
DEITRICK, George A., MD — Physician, Surgeon 1846

DEJOY, Jim — Teacher/Athletic Director	1846
DEL CONTE, LaVada Catherine, M.Spl. Education — Special Education Educator	1846
DEL ROSARIO, Nestor, MD — Physician	1846
DEL TORO, Guillermo — Film Director	1847
DELANEY, John Kevin — Former U.S. Representative	1847
DELANEY, Joseph Paul — Managing Director	302
DELAURO, Rosa Luisa — U.S. Representative from Connecticut	1847
DELBENE, Suzan Kay — U.S. Representative from Washington	1847
DELCOLLE, Michael — Owner	1847
DELGADO, Antonio Ramon — U.S. Representative from New York	1847
DELGADO, Christopher — Chef, Owner	1477
DELGADO, Manuel Eduardo — Architect, Urban Designer, Educator	1847
DELL, Michael Saul — Chairman, CEO, Founder	1848
DELONG, Bonnie — Owner, Principal	1848
DEMARK, Robin Kay — Consultant	303
DEMCHAK, William Stanton — Chairman, President, CEO	1848
DEMINGS, Valdez, "Val" Venita — U.S. Representative from Florida	1848
DEMONIC, Betty — Music Educator, Retired	1848
DEMPSEY, Mary Lu — Director of Health Insurance Benefits Administration	1848
DENCH, Judi — Actress	1849
DENEGALL, John P. Jr. — Construction Executive	1849
DENMARK-WESNER, Florence Harriet, DHL, PhD — Distinguished Research Professor	1850
DENNEHY, Brian Manion — Actor	1850
DENTON, Robert, "Pete" William — CEO	1851
DEPP, Johnny — Actor	1851
DEPRIEST, C. David — Engineering Executive, Military Officer (Retired)	304
DERISE, Nellie Louise, PhD — Nutritionist, Educator, Researcher	305
DERN, Laura Elizabeth — Actress, Director, Producer	1852
DERR, Thomas Sieger Jr., PhD — Professor Emeritus of Religion and Biblical Literature	1478
DERSHOWITZ, Alan Morton — Scholar of Constitutional Law, Lawyer	1479
DESALVA, Christopher — Attorney, Consultant, Entrepreneur	1852
DESANTIS, Ronald, "Ron" Dion — Governor of Florida	1852
DESAULNIER, Mark James — U.S. Representative from California	1852
DESJARLAIS, Scott Eugene, MD — U.S. Representative from Tennessee; Physician	1853
DESTEFANO, Johnny — Director, Office of Presidential Personnel	1853
DESYATNIKOV, Ruslan — Founder, CEO	306
DETILLION, Linda Kay — Geriatrics Rehab Nurse	1853
DETTMER, Robert G. — Beverage Company Executive (Retired)	307
DEUTCH, Theodore, "Ted" Eliot — U.S. Representative from Florida, Chair of the House Ethics Committee	1853
DEUTCH, Zoey Francis — Actress	1853
DEVALL, Richard A. — Air Force Lieutenant Colonel (Retired)	308
DEVARIS, Jeannette — Psychologist	309
DEVGAN, Onkar Dave N., PhD — Technologist, Consultant	1853
DEVITO, Danny — Actor	1854
DEVOE, Marlene Ruth, PhD — Professor Emeritus, Department of Psychology	310
DEVOS, Elisabeth, "Betsy" Dee — U.S. Secretary of Education	1854
DEWINE, Richard, "Mike" Michael — Governor of Ohio	1854
DEWITT, William O. Jr. — Managing Partner	1854
DIAMOND, Harris — Chairman, CEO	1854
DIAMOND, Jared Mason — Writer, Ecologist, Biologist	1855
DIAMOND, Lisa — CEO	1855
DIAMOND, Neil — Singer	1855
DIAMONDSTONE, Fred Alan — Lawyer	1855
DIAZ QUINONES, Juan J., MD — Chief of the General OB/GYN Division, Vice Chair of Quality and Safety	1856
DIAZ, Dalila — Principal	1856
DIAZ-BALART, Mario Rafel Caballero — U.S. Representative from Florida	1856
DIBACCO, T. Jay — Financial Planner	311
DIBRINO, Matthew D. — CEO	312
DICAPRIO, Leonardo Wilhelm — Actor; Activist	1857
DICKELMAN, Thomas S. — Founder, Senior Minister	1857
DICKERSON, Gary E. — President, CEO	1857
DICKERSON, Mattie Fry — Church of the Lord Jesus Christ, Academy of Jesus Christ	1857
DICKEY, Nancy Wilson — Professor, Physician	1857
DIDION, Joan — Writer	1857
DIENES, Timothy, "Tim" Paul — Mathematician, Educator	1858
DIESEL, Vin — Actor	1858
DIFONZO, Daniel Francis — President	313
DIGIUSTINI, Antonetta Anna — Highly Experienced, Consummate Nonprofit and Public Sector Professional; Dedicated, Accomplished Master Educator	314
DILGEN, Regina, PhD — Professor, Chairperson	1858
DILLABOUGH, Denille Lynne — Women's Health and Critical Care Nurse	1858
DILLER, Barry Charles — Chairman, Senior Executive	1858
DILLER, Elizabeth E. — Partner, Architect	1859
DILLMAN, Kristin MMus — Elementary School Educator (Retired), Musician, College Educator	1859
DILLMAN, Richard Howard, PhD — English Language Educator, Professor Emeritus of English and American Literature	1859
DILLON, Mary — CEO	315
DIMAS, Marilyn J. — Health Products Executive	1860
DIMON, Jamie — Chairman, CEO, and President	1860
DINGELL, Deborah, "Debbie" Ann — U.S. Representative, Lobbyist (Retired)	1860
DINKLAGE, Peter — Actor	1860
DION, Celine Marie Claudette — Singer	1860
DIRKS, Lee Edward — Newspaper Executive (Retired)	1861
DISKIN, Michael Edward — President, CEO & Owner Diskin Enterprises LLC	1479
DISNEY, Benjamin O. — Small Business Owner	1861
DISPENZIERE, Patricia — Professional Artist	1861
DITERESA, Michael A., MD — Physician, Internist	316
DITKOWSKY, Kenneth K. — Lawyer	1861
DIVITTORIO, Jenn — Independent Consultant	1861
DIXON, Jo-Ann C. — Management Consultant	1861
DIXSON, Judy Sue — Retired Elementary School Educator	317
DJOKOVIC, Novak — Professional Tennis Player	1862
DOELEMAN, Sheperd S. "Shep", PhD — Astrophysicist, Assistant Director	319
DOELLING, Hellmut Hans, PhD — Geologist	320
DOERR, John — Venture Capitalist	1862
DOGGETT, LLoyd Alton II — U.S. Representative from Texas	1862
DOKE, Marshall J. Jr., LLB — Partner	321
DOLCE, Philip C. — Professor of History, Chair of the Suburban Studies Group, Social Sciences	1862
DOLE, Elizabeth Alexander — Founder, Author, Former U.S. Senator	1863
DOLE, Robert, "Bob" Joseph — Former U.S. Senator from Kansas; Special Counsel	1863
DOLIM, Henry P. Jr.	1863
DOMINGUEZ, Michelle — Executive Vice President of Compliance	1863
DOMINGUEZ-WEISS, Theresa, RN — President, Director	1864
DOMKE, Gary Edward — Securities Company Executive	1864
DOMZALSKI, Callitia M. — Insurance Agent	1480
DONAHUE, Charles L. Jr. — Healthcare Consultant	322

DONALD, Aaron — Professional Football Player 1864
DONALDSON, David — Consultant Chemical Pathologist (Retired) 323
DONALDSON, John Riley — Physics Educator 1864
DONNELLY, Brian "KAWS" — Artist 324
DONNELLY, Katayoun — Attorney 1864
DONNELLY, Scott Christopher — Chairman, President, CEO 1864
DONOHUE, Joyce, PhD — Educator (Retired); Scientist; Chemical Risk Assessor 1865
DONOVAN, William Alan — Public Service Librarian (Ret.) 1480
DOOCY, Steve — Author, Television Personality 1865
DORN, Roosevelt F., JD, DD — Retired Superior Court Judge, Retired Mayor of the City of Inglewood 1865
DORNFELD, Kayla Marie — Teacher 1866
DORSEY, Jack — Internet Company Executive, Software Architect 1866
DORSEY, Robert Francis — Managing Member, President 1866
DORSEY, Sherrell — Publisher 1866
DORTCH, Clarence III, Esq. — Lawyer 1867
DOUB, Joseph Peyton, CEP, PWS — Senior Environmental Scientist 1867
DOUDNA, Jennifer Anne — Biochemist 325
DOUGHERTY, James D., — Lawyer 1867
DOUGLAS, Alexander — CEO 1867
DOUGLAS, Kirk — Actor, Film Producer, Director 326
DOUGLAS, Michael Kirk — Actor 1867
DOUGLAS, Stephen B. — Publishing Company Executive 327
DOUGLASS, H. Robert DDes, FAIA — Architect, Health Care Consultant, Educator 1868
DOVALE, Fern Louise — Civil Engineer 1868
DOWDEN, Carroll Vincent — Publishing Company Executive 1868
DOWNEY, Robert Jr. — Actor 1869
DOYLE, Michael, "Mike" F. Jr. — U.S. Representative from Pennsylvania 1869
DOYLE, Wendell E. — Band Director (Retired), Educator (Retired) 1869
DOZIER, James L. — Security Consultant (Retired); Military Officer (Retired) 328
DRANE, James Francis — Philosophy Educator 329
DRAVILLAS, Speleos G. — Vice President of Global Sales 1869
DREIER, Hannah — National Reporter 330
DRESSLER, David M., MD — Psychiatrist and Jungian Analyst 331
DREW, Clifford J., PhD — Vice President for Academic Affairs (Retired) 1481
DREYER, William MD — Professor of Pediatrics 1869
DREYFUSS, Richard — Actor 1869
DRUMMOND, Andre Jamal — Professional Basketball Player 1870
DRYFOOSE, Georgia — Retired Elementary School Educator 1870
DRYMAN, Amy, DSc — Manager 1870
DUBOSE, James Daulton, DMD — Dentist 1870
DUBOVSKY, Steven L. MD — Professor, Chair 1870
DUBUSKE, Lawrence Michael, MD — Clinical Professor of Medicine, Immunologist, Allergist 332
DUCEY, Douglas, "Doug" Anthony — Governor of Arizona 1871
DUCKWORTH, Ladda, "Tammy" Tammy — U.S. Senator from Illinois 1871
DUDZINSKI, Diane Marie, PhD — Biology Educator 1871
DUERIG, G.F., "Jill" — Interim Executive Director 1871
DUFFEY, Joseph D. — Academic Administrator 333
DUFFEY, Paul Stephen, PhD — Microbiologist 334
DUFFIELD, David A. — Co-CEO 1871
DUFFY, John — Latin Teacher, Chairman of English & Foreign Languages (Retired) 335
DUFFY, Lawrence K., PhD — Professor, Biochemist 1481
DUFFY, Sean Patrick — Senior Counsel; Former U.S. Representative from Wisconsin 1871
DUGAN, Robert M. — President 1872
DUHME, Carol McCarthy, DHL (Hon.) — Civic Leader (Retired) 336
DUKE, Phyllis Mckinney — School Administrator, Business Management 337

DULA, Arthur McKee, Esq. — Lawyer; Aerospace Transportation Executive 1482
DUNAWAY, Faye — Actress 1872
DUNCAN, Daniel W. — Labor Union Adminstrator 1872
DUNCAN, Jeffrey Darren — U.S. Representatives from South Carolina 1873
DUNCAN, Mary Ellen, PhD — President Emeritus 1482
DUNCAN, Tim — Professional Basketball Player 1873
DUNGY, Tony — NFL Coach 1873
DUNHAM, Tyrone "Ty" — Owner, Engineer and Entrepreneur 1483
DUNHAM, Wolcott Balestier Jr., Esq — Of Counsel 338
DUNLEAVY, Michael, "Mike" James — Governor of Alaska 1873
DUNN, Michael L. — Lawyer 1873
DUNN, Neal Patrick — U.S. Representative from Florida 1873
DUPERREAULT, Brian — CEO, President 1873
DURANT, Kevin Wayne — Professional Basketball Player 1873
DURBIN, Richard, "Dick" Joseph — U.S. Senator from Illinois 1874
DURFEE, Wayne King, PhD — Aquaculture Educator, Researcher, Professor 1874
DURNIN, Timothy, DC — Chiropractic Physician 1874
DUTCHER, Janice — Associate Director 1483
DUTHIE, Tracee, — Attorney 1874
DUTKOWSKY, Robert M. — CEO (Retired) 1874
DUTY, Jeff Davis Jr. — President, CEO 339
DUVALL, Robert — Actor 1874
DUVERNAY, Ava Marie — Film Director, Producer 1875
DWYER, Ann Elizabeth — Editor 1875
DWYER, Lauraine Theresa RN, MS — Ambulatory Care Administrator, Rehabilitation Nurse 1875
DWYER, Maureen E. — Of Counsel 1876
DYER-RAFFLER, Joy Ann — Special Education Diagnostician (Retired), Art Teacher (Retired), Athlete 340
DYLONG, Alexandra, RN, BSN, CNOR — Registered Nurse (Retired) 1484
DYSINGER, William MD, MPH — Emeritus Professor and Emeritus Associate Dean 1876
DZIOBA, Robert — Professor of Orthopedic Surgery 341
EAGLEHOUSE, Carolyn — Manager, President 1484
EARHARDT, Ainsley Hayden — News Correspondent 1876
EARNEST, Ola May — Historian, Genealogist 342
EASTERBROOK, Steve — CEO and President 1876
EASTWOOD, Clint — Actor, Director 1876
EATON, Douglas C., PhD — Distinguished Professor 343
EBAID, Ala — Hematology/Oncology Fellow 344
EBERHART, Robert N., PhD — Professor of Research 1877
EBERLE, Anne — Artist 1877
EBOZUE, Benson O., CPA, CGMA — Financial Analyst, Certified Public Accountant, Chartered Global Management Accountant 1877
ECKER, Harry Allen — Telecommunications Company Executive (Retired) 345
ECKSTEIN, Peter C. — Labor Union Economist (Retired) 1878
EDGERTON, Cynthia — Veterinary Corps Officer 1878
EDWARDS, Bruce George, MD — Ophthalmologist, Captain, U.S. Navy (Retired) 1878
EDWARDS, Bruce L. — Investment Company Representative 1878
EDWARDS, John Bel — Governor of Louisiana 1878
EDWARDS, John Carver, PhD — Archivist 1878
EDWARDS, Thomas S. Jr. — Senior Partner 1485
EFFRON, Marc — Founder 1879
EGAN, Charles J. Jr., LLB — Lawyer, Foundation Trustee 346
EGGERT, James E. — Educator, Writer 1879
EHLERS, William Albert — Psychiatrist 347
EHREN, Charles A. Jr., JD — Professor of Law Emeritus 348
EICHBERG, Steven J. — Attorney at Law 1879

EICHELBERGER, Ike — Broker, Owner · 1879
EICHENWALD, Derek — CEO · 1879
EICHER, David John — Editor-in-Chief · 349
EIGUREN, Roy L., JD — Managing Partner · 1879
EILISH, Billie — Singer · 1485
EIN, Daniel MD — Director · 1880
EINHORN, David A. — Lawyer · 1880
EINHORN, Michael Leonard — State Auditor · 350
EINISMAN, Myron, "Mike" Sachar · 1880
EISENBERG, Howard M. — R.K. Thompson Professor · 1880
EISENBERG, Lee — Film and Television Producer, Writer · 1881
EISGRUBER, Christopher Ludwig — President · 351
EK, Daniel — Entrepreneur, Technologist · 1881
ELBA, Idris — Actor, Singer · 1881
ELBARBARY, Dr. Ibrahim Abdel Tawab, PhD — Chemist · 353
ELEFTERAKIS, Nicholas — Founding Partner · 1486
ELGAZZAR, Andrew J. — CEO · 1881
ELIZONDO, Hector — Actor · 354
ELIZONDO, Roy J. III — Managing Attorney · 1882
ELKIN, Miriam Charlotte — Nurse · 355
ELKINS, Alfred — Insurance Company Executive (Retired) · 356
ELKINS, Lee Hand — Deputy Public Defender · 1882
ELKINS, Thomas Arthur — Chief Scientist · 1882
ELLEN-ELLIS, Jennifer — Owner · 1882
ELLIG, Bruce Robert — Human Resource Executive (Retired), Author · 357
ELLINGSEN, Mark — Professor of Church History · 1882
ELLINWOOD, Janice, MFA, BS — Professor Emerita of Fashion Design and Merchandising, Author, Artist · 358
ELLIOTT, Anne — Gifted and Talented Education Educator (Retired) · 1883
ELLIOTT, Missy — Musician · 1883
ELLIS, Anne Elizabeth — Fundraiser · 1883
ELLIS, George Fitzallen, Rear Admiral U.S. Navy (Retired) — Two Star Admiral (Retired); Corporate Vice President (Retired) · 1884
ELLIS, Trayvon — Recording Artist, Producer, Songwriter · 1884
ELLISON, Julian Jr. — Economist (Retired) · 1884
ELLISON, Keith Maurice — Attorney General from Minnesota · 1884
ELLISON, Larry — Entrepreneur · 1884
ELSE, Carolyn J. — Library Director (Retired) · 359
ELSON, David Lee — Oncologist, Educator (Retired) · 360
ELVIN-LEWIS, Memory Patience Fredrika, PhD, DSc Honoris Causa — Microbiology Educator, Researcher, Ethnobotanist · 1884
ELWOOD-AKERS, Virginia — (Retired) Librarian, Writer, Archivist, Researcher · 1885
EMANUEL, Rahm Israel — Former Mayor of Chicago; Former White House Chief of Staff · 1885
EMBLIDGE, Robert William, PhD — Principal Scientist · 1885
EMBRY, Carlos Jr. — State Legislator · 361
EMERY, Rita, "Em" — Physical Education Educator · 1886
EMMER, Thomas, "Tom" Earl Jr. — U.S. Representative from Minnesota · 1886
EMMETT, James Robert — Attorney (Retired) · 1886
EMMETT, Margaret Burke — Computer Consultant, Mathematician · 362
EMMICH, Cliff — Actor of Film, Television, and Stage · 1886
EMMONS, Diane Neal, EdM, CAS — Career Development Consultant · 1886
ENDIEVERI, Anthony — Trial Lawyer · 363
ENEYO, Ugwem I. — CEO · 1887
ENGEL, Eliot Lance — U.S. Representative from New York · 1887
ENGELBERT, Cathy — CEO · 1887
ENGELHARDT, Hermann PhD — Faculty Emeritus · 1887
ENGELHARDT, Mark Douglas — Professor of Education, Statistics and Research Methods · 1887
ENGLE, Robert Fry III — Economist, Finance Educator · 1887
ENGLERT, Roy T., JD — Lawyer · 1486

ENTI, Mazi — Owner, General Manager · 364
ENTIN, Peter — Former Vice President of Theatre Operations · 1888
ENZI, Michael, "Mike" Bradley — U.S. Senator from Wyoming · 1888
EPSTEIN, Theo Nathan — Professional Sports Team Executive · 1888
ERDOES, Mary Callahan — CEO · 182
ERGEN, Charles W. — Chairman · 1888
ERICKSON, Jeanne, RPH — Pharmacist; Real Estate Company Officer · 1888
ERICKSON, Susan Phillians — Secondary School Educator · 1888
ERICSON, David Paul, PhD — Philosophy of Education Educator · 1888
ERIVO, Cynthia Onyedinmanasu Chinasaokwu — Actress · 1889
ERLICHMAN, Stanton Roy, PhD, CEDS-S, CAP, Fiaedp — Industrial Consultant, Psychotherapist · 1889
ERNST, Joni Kay — U.S. Senator from Iowa · 1889
ERSEK, Hikmet — President, CEO · 1889
ERTZ, Julie Beth — Professional Soccer Player · 1889
ERVIN, Spencer — Lawyer · 1890
ERVING, Julius — NBA Player (Retired) · 1890
ERXLEBEN, Jorg — CEO, President, Owner · 1890
ESCOBAR, Veronica — U.S. Representative from Texas · 1890
ESHOO, Anna A. — U.S. Representative from California · 1890
ESLINGER, Kenneth Nelson — Social Sciences Educator · 1890
ESPAILLAT, Adriano de Jesus — U.S. Representative from New York · 1890
ESPER, Mark Thomas, PhD — U.S. Secretary of Defense; Former U.S. Secretary of the Army · 1891
ESPOSITO, Philip Anthony — Retired Professional Hockey Player · 1891
ESSIN, Emmett M., PhD — Professor Emeritus · 1891
ESTEFAN, Gloria Maria Milagrosa — Singer · 1891
ESTES, Kenneth William, PhD, Lt. Col. USMC (Ret.) — Military Officer; History Professor; Defense Consultant · 1892
ESTES, Ronald Gene — U.S. Representative from Kansas · 1893
ESTEVEZ, Elia F., PhD — Mathematics Educator · 1893
ETELAMAKI, Susan Louise Sheldrick, BFA — Production Potter/Owner · 1893
EVANS, David Lynn — Founder, CEO · 1893
EVANS, Dwight E. — U.S. Representative from Pennslyvania · 1894
EVANS, Gerard E., Esq. — Lobbyist · 365
EVANS, Harold Ray · 1894
EVANS, Harry L. MD — Pathologist · 1894
EVANS, Mark I., MD — Obstetrician, Geneticist · 366
EVANS, Nancy J. — Nursing Educator · 367
EVANS, Sandra "Sandee" — Director of Academic Services (Ret.) · 1487
EVATT, Parker — Commissioner, State Legislator (Retired) · 368
EVERETT, Paul — President, Owner · 1894
EVERHART, Gloria "Laiinie" — Music Educator · 1487
EVERS, Anthony, "Tony" Steven — Governor of Wisconsin · 1894
EVERT, Chris — Former Professional Tennis Player · 1894
EWING, Jack Robert — Certified Public Accountant (Retired) · 369
EYBERG, Sheila Maxine, PhD — Psychology Educator · 1894
EYO, Ikemesit, "Kem" A. — Senior Associate Attorney · 1895
EYRE, Michael J. — Attorney · 370
EYS, Jan van, MD, PhD — Retired Pediatrician, Educator, Administrator · 1300
EYSTER, John W. — Adjunct Professor · 1895
EZZO, David Albert, PhD — Nonprofit Executive; Anthropologist; Educator · 1488
FABBRI, Anne R. — Critic, Curator (Retired) · 371
FACEY, La-Toya — Franchise Owner, Entrepreneur, Instructional Facilitator · 1895
FAIR, Tasheema L., MD, FACOG — OBGYN/Health and Wellness Coach · 372
FAIRBANK, Richard D. — CEO, Chairperson · 1896
FAIRBANKS, Jonathan Leo — Emeritus Director, Senior Research Associate, Museum Executive · 373
FAIRES, O. Joe — Concert Promoter (Retired) · 374
FAKHOURY, Rami — Managing Director · 1896

FALCK, Francis, MD, PhD, MS — Eye Surgeon 1896
FALCO, Maria J., PhD — Academic Administrator, Political Scientist (Retired) 375
FALDO, Nick — Professional Golfer 1896
FALK, Diane M. — Writer, Editor, Educator Research Information Specialist 376
FALK, James Robert, PhD — President 1896
FALK, Thomas J. — Executive Chairman 1897
FALLON, Jimmy — Talk Show Host, Actor 1897
FAMA, Eugene Francis — Economics Professor 1897
FAN, Shih-fang — Professor 377
FANNING, Thomas Andrew — Chairman, President, and CEO 1897
FARBER, John PhD — Chairman of the Board 1897
FARBER, Maya M. — Artist 1898
FARBER, Robert, "Rob" J. — Senior Research Scientist 1898
FARES, Ahmad Al — Founder and CEO 1898
FARMER, Anthony Drew — Director 1898
FARNSWORTH, Brooke, JD — Lawyer 1898
FARR, David Nelson — Chairman and CEO 1898
FARR, Richard Claborn "Dick" — Corporate Executive, Private Investor 378
FARRARONS, Manu — Owner/Artist 379
FARRELL, Mark Macaulay — Bank Executive (Retired) 1898
FARRELL, Naomi, RN, MS, BS — Editor, Journalist, Medical Writer 1899
FARROW, Ronan — Television Personality, Former Federal Agency Administrator 1899
FARRUGIA, Gianrico, MD — Gastroenterologist, Researcher 1899
FARWELL, Dorothy, "Dotty" — Educator (Retired) 1899
FARWELL, Robert William, PhD — Physicist 1900
FASSBENDER, Michael — Actor 1900
FASSETT, John David "Jack" — Utility Executive (Retired), Consultant 380
FAUCI, Anthony Stephen — Director 381
FAULKNER, Judith, "Judy" R. — Co-Founder, CEO 1900
FAULKNER, William — Partner 1900
FAUPEL, Marian L. — Of Counsel 382
FAUST, Drew Gilpin — Former President, Professor of History 1900
FAUST, Marjorie Jaretta — Nursing Administrator (Retired) 1901
FAUST, Walter Luck, PhD — Physicist (Retired) 1901
FAUSTINO, Rey — CEO, Founder 1901
FAY, Thomas Fortune — Lawyer, Founder 383
FAYNZILBERG, Michael — Owner 384
FEATHERSTONE, Bruce A. — Managing Member 385
FEBRE, Alejandra — Franchise Owner 386
FEDERER, Roger — Professional Tennis Player 1901
FEDEROFF, Howard J. — Dean 1901
FEENEY, Charles, "Chuck" Francis — Founder 1901
FEINSTEIN, Dianne Emiel Berman — U.S. Senator 1901
FEINZAIG, Leslie — CEO, Founder 1902
FEIT, Michael Dennis, PhD — Physicist 387
FELICETTI, Daniel A. — Academic Administrator, Educator 388
FELIX, Allyson Michelle — Track and Field Athlete 1902
FELLERS, Paul Joseph, PhD — Research Scientist III 1488
FELSENTHAL, Steven Altus — Lawyer 1902
FELTHOUSE, Timothy Roy, ChD — Technical Fellow 389
FELVEY, Patrick — President, Owner 390
FENG, Paul 1902
FENKER, John William — Energy Company and Museum Executive 391
FENNER, William, "Bill" — Associate Manager 1903
FENTY, Robyn Rihanna — Singer 1903
FERENCZ, Robert M., PhD — Division Leader 1903
FERGUS, Gary S, JD — Lawyer 1903
FERGUSON, Anderson, "Drew" Drew IV — U.S. Representative from Georgia 1903

FERGUSON, Hugh M., MBA, CPA — Independent Management Consultant 392
FERGUSON, Jennifer Lee Berry, EdD — Retired Professor in Kinesiology, English Specialist 393
FERGUSON, Jim T. — Vice President Operations 1904
FERGUSON, Robert Watson — Attorney General of Washington 1904
FERGUSON, Roger Walter Jr. — CEO and President 1904
FERN, Joanne — Business Owner 394
FERNANDEZ, Patrick H. — Crime Lab Technician Supervisor (Retired) 1489
FERNANDEZ, Reynaldo Rey — General Manager 1579
FERNANDEZ, Waldo — Founder, Interior Designer 395
FERNGREN, Gary B. — Emeritus Professor of History 396
FERREIRA, Stacey — CEO 1904
FERRELL, Will — Actor 1904
FERRIOLA, John J. — Chairman and CEO 1904
FERRY, Kristina — Community Services Director 1904
FETTER, Trevor — Chairman (Retired) 1905
FETTERMAN, Lisa — CEO 1905
FETTERS, Thomas Torrence — Research Executive (Retired), Author 397
FEUER, Steven Z., Esq. — Lawyer 1905
FEULNER, Edwin John, PhD — Think Tank Executive (Retired) 1905
FEY, Tina — Actress, Comedian 1906
FIDOTEN, Robert Earl, PhD — Consultant, Information and Communication Educator 398
FIELD, Robert Bunten — Lawyer 1906
FIGWER, J. Jacek — Acoustics Consultant (Retired) 1906
FILYAW, Liston Nathaniel — Director of Student Activities (Retired) 1906
FINCHER, Hugh McCommon — Foreign Language Educator 1907
FINE, Jason E. — Editor 1907
FINE, Jeffrey Scott, MD — Vice Chairman of Rusk Rehabilitation 1907
FINE, Jeremy S. MD — Physician 1907
FINK, Laurence Douglas — CEO 1907
FINK, Raymond, PhD — Medical Educator 1907
FINKENAUER, Abby Lea — U.S. Representative from Iowa 1907
FINNEGAN, John Vianney, CIC — Adjunct Professor of Risk Management 1907
FINNEY, Kathryn Rebecca — Founder, CEO 1908
FINNEY, Robert, "Dr. Bob" G. PhD — Professor Emeritus 1908
FINUCANE, Anne — Vice Chair 1908
FIORATTI, Helen — Artist; Designer; Antique Dealer; Author; Lecturer 399
FIORAVANTI, Shirley J.S. — Retired Language Educator 1908
FIORI, Pamela — Publishing Executive, Writer 400
FIRE, Andrew Zachary — Biologist, Pathology Professor 1908
FIRTH, Colin Andrew — Actor 1909
FISCHER, Debra, "Deb" Lynelle — U.S. Senator 1909
FISCHMAN, Myrna Leah, PhD, CPA — Professor Emerita, Accountant, Director (Retired) 401
FISH, Daniel — Theater Director 1909
FISH, George — Writer, Poet 402
FISH, James C. Jr. — President of Waste Management 1909
FISHBURNE, Laurence — Actor 1909
FISHER, Andrew Taylor — Website Designer 1489
FISHER, Doris F. — Co-Founder 1909
FISHER, Robert J. PhD — Marketing and Corporate Executive 1910
FISHER-DALLY, Patricia A. — President, Owner 1910
FISHMAN, Lawrence Martin, MD, FACP — Professor Emeritus of Medicine 1910
FISK, Charles John — Meteorologist, Researcher, Consultant 403
FISTELL, Ira J. 404
FITCH, William C. — Professional Basketball Coach (Retired) 1910
FITHIAN, Peter Stalker — Retail Executive 1910
FITTERLING, Jim Ray — CEO 1910

FITTIPALDI, Emerson — Semi-Retired Racing Driver 1910
FITZGERALD, Oscar P. IV, PhD — Adjunct Professor 1911
FITZPATRICK, Brian Kevin — U.S. Representative from Pennsylvania 1911
FITZPATRICK, Terri L. — Chief Operating Officer, Vice President of Development 1490
FITZSIMMONS, Kimberly — President 1911
FIX WOLF, Bernice — Vice Mayor, Educator 1911
FLAHERTY, Timothy T. 1911
FLAKE, Jeffry Lane — Former U.S. Senator from Arizona 1911
FLAM, Bernard Vincent — Secondary School Educator (Retired), Actor, Author 1911
FLANAGAN, Mary Elizabeth, MLS — Elementary School Educator (Retired) 405
FLANIGAN, Mickie — Architect, Construction Executive 406
FLATTAU, Edward BA — Environmental Columnist 1912
FLAUM, Sander Allen — Founder, Principal 407
FLEISCHMANN, Charles, "Chuck" Joseph — U.S. Representative from Tennessee; Lawyer 1912
FLEISCHMANN, Roger Justice — Lawyer (Retired) 1912
FLEISS, Jennifer — Co-Founder 1912
FLEMING, Marcella — Journalist (Retired) 1912
FLEMING, Paul D. III — Professor 408
FLEMING, Peggy Gale — Former Olympic Figure Skater 1912
FLEMING, Rose Ann, PhD, JD, SNDdeN — Special Assistant to the President 1490
FLETCHER, Elizabeth, "Lizzie" Ann — U.S. Representative from Texas; Lawyer 1912
FLETCHER, John Dexter, PhD 1913
FLETCHER, Louise — Actress 1913
FLICKINGER, Joe, PhD — Professor Emeritus 409
FLOCH, Martin, MD — Professor of Gastroenterology and Nutrition 1491
FLOOD, Veronica H., MD — Associate Professor, Pediatric Hematology 1913
FLORA, Jairus D. Jr. — Statistician 1913
FLORA, Robert M., PhD — Biochemist (Retired) 1914
FLORENCE, Alfred William — Multidiscipline Systems Engineer (Retired) 1914
FLORES, William, "Bill" Hose Sr. — U.S. Representative from Texas; Former Oil Industry Executive 1914
FLOYD, George Perry Jr. 1914
FLOYD, Joseph James "Joe" — Owner 410
FLOYD, Kimberly, "Kim" Hayes — Lawyer 1914
FLOYD, Raymond — Professional Golfer 1915
FLYNN, Rev. Dr. Thomas R. — Priest, Philosopher, Educator 412
FLYNN, Robert Lopez — Author 411
FODY, Edward P. — Pathologist, Laboratory Director 1915
FOGARTY, James Vincent, EdD — CEO, Special Education Administrator, Educator 1915
FOLES, Nicholas Edward — Professional Football Player 1915
FOLEY, Harriet E. — School Librarian (Retired) 1915
FOLEY, Jonathan — Environmentalist 413
FONDA, Jane — Actress 1916
FONTAINE, Dani — Owner/Product Developer 1916
FONTANA, Santino Anthony — Actor 1916
FORD, Harrison — Actor 1916
FORD, Tom — Fashion Designer 1917
FORDE, Patricia, "Pat" Ann — Executive Director 1917
FORGIONE, Dana A., PhD — Endowed Chair of the Jessie Francis Neal Foundation & Clifton W. Coonrod Endowment, and Professor of Accounting 1917
FORMAN, Charles — Attorney 1918
FORMAN, William Harper Jr., JD — Attorney at Law 414
FORRESTER, H. Eugene, BS, BE — Agriculture Educator 1491
FORSLEFF, Louise Stewart Peterson — Psychologist, Educator 1918

FORSYTH, Eric Boyland — Electrical Engineer 1919
FORTE, Domenic J., PhD — Associate Professor 1919
FORTENBERRY, Jeffrey Lane — U.S. Representative 1919
FORTUNATO, Nancy — Artist, Educator 1492
FOSS, Eric J. — Chairman, President, CEO 1920
FOSTER, Norman — Architect 1920
FOSTER, George, "Bill" William — U.S. Representative from Illinois; Physicist 1920
FOSTER, Tim — Fastpitch Director 1920
FOSTER-RANDLE, Ellen Eugenia Dr., EdD, MA, BA — Opera and Classical Singer; Educator 1921
FOTOVICH, Ursula Ann — Nun; Archivist and Local Historian 1921
FOWLER, Vivian Delores — Insurance Company Executive 1921
FOX, Michael Andrew J. — Actor 1922
FOXX, Jamie — Actor, Comedian 1922
FOXX, Virginia Ann — U.S. Representative from North Carolina; Ranking Member of the House Committee on Education and Labor 415
FOYT, Anthony, "A.J." Joseph Jr. — Auto Racing Crew Chief, Professional Auto Racer (Retired) 1922
FRAGOMENI, James Mark, PhD — Technical Consultant, Educator, Metallurgical and Mechanical Engineer 1492
FRALINGER, Jack Bruce, MD — Surgeon 1923
FRANCAVILLA, Barbara Jean 1923
FRANCHITTI, Dario Marino — Sports Commentator, Race Car Driver (Retired) 1923
FRANCIS, Elizabeth, "Beth Ann" Ann, BHPP, BHT — Recovery Support Specialist 1923
FRANCO, James Edward — Actor, Teacher, Writer 1923
FRANCONA, Terry, "Tito" Jon — Professional Baseball Manager, Professional Baseball Player (Retired) 1924
FRANGIPANE, Ashley, "Halsey" Nicolette — Singer 1924
FRANK, Joachim, PhD — Structural Biologist; Professor; Biophysicist 1924
FRANK, John L. — Commissioner, Lawyer (Retired); Educator (Retired) 1924
FRANK, Robert Allen — Media Consultant 1925
FRANK, Stuart M., PhD — Founding Director 1925
FRANKEL, Bethenny R. — Entrepreneur 1925
FRANKEL, Lois Jane — U.S. Representative from Florida 1926
FRANKLIN, Kirk Dewayne — Singer 1926
FRANKLIN, Sylvan L. "Syl" — Commercial Bank Executive 416
FRANKS, Donald, LLC — Owner 1926
FRANKS, Herschel P. — Judge (Retired) 417
FRANKS, Stephen Field — Judge (Retired) 1493
FRANZESE, Chris J., PharmD — Principal & Clinical Leader 1926
FRASER, Jane — CEO 418
FRAZIER, Anthany V.E. — Founder, President 1927
FRAZIER, Kenneth Carelton — Chairman, President, CEO 1927
FREDERICK, James Paul — Chemical Engineer 1928
FREDERICK, William G.D., PhD — Research Scientist 1493
FREDERICKS, Margaret — Physician, Surgeon 1928
FREDRICKS, Richard — Baritone 419
FREE, Kenneth A. — Athletic Conference Commissioner 1928
FREEL, Steven — President, CEO 1928
FREEMAN, Bryant C. — Foreign Language Educator 420
FREEMAN, Morgan — Actor, Narrator 1928
FREESE, Melanie L., MLS — Associate Professor of Library Services 421
FRELING, Darryl E. — Managing Principal 1494
FRERE, Robert C. — Clinical Associate Professor 422
FREY, John Ward — Landscape Architect (Retired) 1929
FREY, Sherwood Charles Jr. — Professor Emeritus 1929
FREYD, Peter J., PhD — Professor 423
FRIDAY, Erin, CPA — President, CEO 1929

FRIEDHEIM, Stephen B. — Educational Consultant 1930
FRIEDMAN, Adena Testa — CEO 1930
FRIEDMAN, Irwin — Medical Educator 1930
FRIEDMAN, Jeffrey M. — Top Scientist 424
FRIEDMAN, Lawrence Samuel, MD — Anton R. Fried, MD, Chair; Gastroenterologist; Educator 1494
FRIEDMAN, Monroe, PhD — Professor of Psychology 1930
FRIEDMAN, Richard Charles, MD — Psychiatrist; Adjunct Research Professor of Psychology; Clinical Professor 425
FRIEDMAN, Richard I. — Public Defender (Retired) 1931
FRIEDMAN, Sonia Anne Primrose — Theater Producer 1931
FRIESEN, Oris D., PhD — Software Engineer; Historian 426
FRIMERMAN, Leslie — Senior Vice-President of Global Technologies 1495
FRITTS, Stephen J., MS 1932
FRITZ, Lance M. — Chairman, President, CEO 1932
FROILAND, Kathryn, "Kathy" G. — Oncology Clinical Educator 1932
FROMM, Erwin Fredrick — Insurance Company Executive (Retired) 1932
FRONDEVILLE, Bertrand Lambert de 293
FROST, Katherine — CEO 1495
FROST, Patricia — Chairman Emeritus 1932
FROST, Phillip — CEO 1932
FUCHS, Arnold — President 1496
FUCHS, Kenneth — Composer 427
FUDGE, Brenda — Owner 1932
FUDGE, Marcia Louise — U.S. Representative from Ohio 1933
FUJIOKA, Jo Ann Fujiko, PhD — President, Consultant 1933
FUKUYAMA, Francis, PhD — Political Scientist; Author; Director, Professor 1933
FULCHER, Russell M. — U.S. Representative from Idaho; Real Estate Broker 1934
FULFORD, Elizabeth — Director of Integrated Care Management 1934
FULKS, Robert — Computer Company Executive 1934
FULLAM, John Cronin — Clarinetist 428
FULLER, Blake — Operator 429
FULMER, Russell Francis — Librarian (Retired) 1934
FULMER, Shirley Minus Person — Art Educator 1934
FULSON, Lula M. — Educator 1934
FULTON, Gloria Jean, MLS, MA — Librarian, Educator 1496
FUNDERBURK, Eleanor Jo — Terrain Vehicle Company Executive, Realtor 1935
FURLONG, George, "Skip" Morgan 1935
FURPHY, Daniel G., ABA — Legislator; Banker (Retired) 1935
FUTTER, Ellen Victoria — President; Music Administrator 1935
GABBARD, Tulsi — U.S. Representative from Hawaii 1935
GABELLI, Mario Joseph — CEO 1936
GABELLI, Regina — Director of Institutional Marketing 1936
GABLE, Karen E., EdD — Health Sciences Educator 430
GABRIEL, Richard L. — Supreme Court Justice 1936
GADOT, Gal — Actress 1497
GADSBY, Robin Edward — Chemicals Executive 1936
GAETANO, Joyce Ann — Chemical Engineer, Business Manager (Retired) 431
GAETZ, Matthew, "Matt" Louis — U.S. Representative from Florida; Lawyer 1936
GAGLIARDI, Ugo Oscar — Application Developer 432
GAHAN, Dave — Singer 1936
GAIMAN, Neil Richard — Novelist, Comics Writer, Screenwriter 1937
GALASKO, Gail T. — Pharmacologist, Educator 433
GALATIANOS, Gus A. — Computer Company Executive, Consultant, Real Estate Developer 434
GALDA, Dwight William — Principal 1937
GALFAS, Timothy II — President, Director 435

GALISON, Peter Louis — Scientist 1937
GALKIN, Robert T. — Company Executive 1937
GALLAGHER, Diane — Nursing History and University Archivist 1938
GALLAGHER, Michael, "Mike" John, PhD — U.S. Representative from Wisconsin 1938
GALLAGHER, Thomas C. — Chairman 1938
GALLEGO, Ruben Marinelarena — U.S. Representative from Arizona 1938
GALLEHER, Gay, PhD — Clinical Psychologist, Artist 436
GALLI, Mike R., Esq. — Attorney 1938
GALLUP, Emily Bradford — Information Systems Consultant 1939
GANGAS, Lilibeth — Chief Technology Community Officer 1939
GARAMENDI, John Raymond — U.S. Representative from California 1939
GARCETTI, Eric Michael — Mayor of Los Angeles 1940
GARCIA, Isabela Amie, Esq. — Founder and Managing Attorney 437
GARCIA, Jesús, "Chuy" G. — U.S. Representative from Illinois 1940
GARCIA, Jorge — Head Band Director 1940
GARCIA, Jose Zebedeo — Political Science Educator (Retired) 1940
GARCIA, Minerva A. — Associate Director of Microbiology; General Supervisor, Microbiology Lab 438
GARCIA, Sylvia Rodriguez — U.S. Representative from Texas; Chief Judge 1940
GARD, Connie R. 1497
GARDNER, Christopher, "Chris" Paul — CEO 1940
GARDNER, Cory Scott — U.S. Senator from Colorado 1940
GARDNER, Sonia Esther — Hedge Fund Manager 1941
GARFIELD-WOODBRIDGE, Nancy — Children's Book Author 439
GARLAND, Gregory Cyril — Chairman, CEO 1941
GARLAND, Merrick Brian — Chief Judge 1941
GARMS, David John, PhD — Manager, Foreign Service Officer 1941
GARNETT, Kevin Maurice — Former Professional Basketball Player 1941
GAROFANO, Eric J. — Attorney 1498
GAROPPOLO, James, "Jimmy" Richard — Professional Football Player 1941
GARRETT, Geoffrey, PhD — Dean 1942
GARRETT, Melrose — Engineer (Retired) 1498
GARRISON, Lloyd Robert — Marketing and Sales Professional 440
GARTEN, Ina — Cookbook Author; Television Show Host 1942
GARUTTI, Randy — CEO 1942
GARVER, Mark — CEO 441
GARVIN, Charles David, PhD — Professor Emeritus; Consultant; Therapist 1942
GARY, Willie, "The Giant Killer" E. — Partner 1942
GASE, Mary Ellen — Music Teacher (Retired) 1943
GASICH, Welko Elton — Retired Aerospace Defense Executive; Management Consultant 1943
GASOL, Marc — Professional Basketball Player 1943
GASPER, Stephen E. — President 442
GATES, Bill Henry III — Entrepreneur; Software Company Executive; Philanthropist 1943
GATES, Melinda Ann — Charitable Foundation Administrator 1943
GATLIN, Larry Wayne — President 443
GATTO, Katherine Gyékényesi, PhD — Modern Languages and Literature Educator 508
GAUSAS, Roberta Elisabeth, MD — Surgeon 444
GAUTHIER, Bernard, MBBS, FRACP — Chief Emeritus 445
GAVAN, William Hutcheson — Military Officer 1944
GAVIN, Donald Glenn — Lawyer, Educator, Arbitrator, Public Speaker 1944
GAVRITY, John D. — Retired Insurance Company Executive 1944
GAW, Jerry Lewis, PhD — Historian, Minister 1944
GAY, Linda R. — Human Resources Director (Retired) 446
GAY, Norwood III — Senior Vice President, Chief Legal Officer (Retired) 1499

GAYAM, Vijay, MD — Attending Physician/Chief Hospitalist, Assistant Program Director; Clinical Assistant Professor of Medicine, Adjunct Professor of Medicine   1945
GEBBIA, Joe Jr. — Chief Product Officer   1945
GEFFEN, David Lawrence — Music Executive   447
GEHRY, Frank Owen — Architect   1945
GEIGER, Mark J. — Attorney   1946
GELB, Peter — Performing Company Executive   1946
GELDNER, Peter David, MD — Plastic Surgeon, President   448
GELLER, Margaret Joan — Astrophysicist   1499
GELWICKS, James M. — Emeritus Assistant Professor   449
GENADER, Ann Marie — Educator, Journalist, Church Musician   1946
GENNETTE, Jeffrey — Chairman, CEO   1946
GENTRY, Roger L., PhD — Research Wildlife Biologist (Retired)   450
GENTRY, Wayne — Owner   1500
GEORGE, Daniel — President   1946
GEORGE, Paul Clifton Anthony — Professional Basketball Player   1946
GEORGE, William Kyle — Partner   1946
GERARD, Redmond, "Red" — Snowboarder   1946
GERBER, Louis "Lou" — Legislative Director (Retired)   451
GERE, Richard Tiffany — Actor   1947
GERIN, John Louis, PhD — Virologist, Educator   452
GERKE, Heather D. — Owner   1947
GERKEN, Heather Kristin — Dean; Professor   1947
GERMANOTTA, Stefani (Lady Gaga) Joanne Angelina — Singer, Songwriter; Actress   1947
GERSH, Bernard J., MB, ChB, D.Phil — Professor of Medicine   1948
GERTH, Donald, "Don" R. — University President, Educator (Retired)   1948
GERVAIS, Ricky Dene — Actor; Comedian   1949
GERWIG, Greta Celeste — Actress, Director   1949
GEWITZ, Michael H. — William Russell McCurdy Physician-in-Chief   1949
GIACCHINO, Michael — Musician, Composer   1949
GIANFORTE, Gregory, "Greg" Richard — U.S. Representative, Former Information Technology Executive   1950
GIANNET, Dina — Executive Director, Activity Consultant   1950
GIARDINO, Dr. Timothy J. — Vice President of Human Resources   453
GIBBONS, Vincent Paul, MD — Pediatric Neurologist; Educator   1500
GIBBS, Betty Caldwell — Educational Administrator   1950
GIBBS, Jamie, "Terwilliger" — Principal Designer   1950
GIBBS, Joe Jackson — Professional Sports Team Executive; Former Professional Football Coach   1950
GIBBS, Robert, "Bob" Brian — U.S. Representative   1951
GIBSON, Bob — Former Professional Baseball Player   1951
GIBSON, Kevin — Professor of Medicine, Clinical, and Translational Science   1951
GIBSON, Mel Colmcille Gerard — Actor, Film Director, Producer   1951
GIDDENS, Angela — Teacher (Retired), Caretaker   1951
GIELE, Janet Zollinger — Sociologist, Educator   1951
GIER, Karan, PhD — Psychologist (Retired)   1952
GIESE, Herbert Adolph — Pediatrician   1952
GILBERT, Dan — Co-Founder   1952
GILBY, Steve W., PhD — Metallurgical Engineering Researcher   1953
GILL, George W., PhD — Anthropologist (Retired); Distinguished Professor Emeritus   1953
GILL, Gerald Lawson, MA — Professor Emeritus   1953
GILL, Vince — Singer, Songwriter   1953
GILLIBRAND, Kirsten Elizabeth — U.S. Senator from New York   1954
GILMAN, Sheldon G. — Lawyer   1954
GILMOUR, Ernest Henry "Ernie" — Professor Emeritus; Paleontology Researcher   454
GINGRICH, Newt Leroy — U.S. Representative, Writer   1954
GINSBERG, Benjamin, PhD — Political Science Educator   1955

GINSBURG, Joan "Ruth" Bader — Associate Justice   455
GINZBURG, Simon Aaron, PhD — Electrical Engineer (Retired)   456
GIRARDI, James N. — Co-Founder, Chief Operating Officer   457
GIRMA, Haben — American Disability Rights Advocate   1955
GITELSON, Susan Aurelia, PhD — President and CEO   458
GIULIANI, Rudolph, "Rudy" William Louis — Lawyer, Mayor of New York City (Retired)   1955
GLASER, Michael, "Mike" Lance, JD — Communications Law, Business Litigator   1955
GLASSMAN, Jeffrey L. — Chairman   1956
GLAUBER, Roy Jay, PhD — Theoretical Physicist, Professor   1956
GLAVINE, Tom Michael — Former Professional Baseball Player   1956
GLEASON, Stephen Michael — Former Professional Football Player   459
GLEASON, Wallace A. Jr., MD — Medical Educator and Researcher   1956
GLENN, Paul M. — U.S. Bankruptcy Judge   1501
GLICK, Richard Stephen, MD — Physician, Rheumatologist   1956
GLIMCHER, Sabrina P. R. — Chief Commercial Counsel   1957
GLOR, Jeffrey, "Jeff" Todd — News Correspondent   1957
GLOSSOP, Ronald John, PhD — Professor Emeritus   1501
GLOVER, Donald — Actor, Writer, Director   1957
GLUSKI, Andrés R. — Director, President, CEO   1957
GODARD, Jean-Luc — Film Director   1957
GODBOLD, Francis S. "Bo" — Investment Banker, Security Firm Executive   460
GODLESKI, John J., MD — Professor of Pathology Emeritus   1957
GOETZ, Jim — Venture Capitalist   1958
GOFF, Gregory J. — Executive Vice Chairperson (Retired)   1958
GOGGINS, David — Athlete   1958
GOHLKE, Lillian — School Librarian (Retired)   461
GOHMERT, Louie Buller Jr. — U.S. Representative, Judge (Retired)   1958
GOLD, Allan Philip, NCSP — District Psychologist   1958
GOLDBERG, Stanley Irwin — Real Estate Company Executive   462
GOLDBERG, Susan — Editor-in-Chief   1959
GOLDBERG, Whoopi — Actress; Comedian   1959
GOLDEN, Jared Forrest — U.S. Representative from Maine   1959
GOLDENBERG, Jean — Speech Language Pathologist   1959
GOLDENBERG, Myrna Gallant, PhD — Holocaust Educator, Professor Emerita of English Language and Literature   1960
GOLDFARB, Stanley, MD — Professor of Medicine   1960
GOLDGRABEN, Gerald Robert — Company Executive   1960
GOLDKORN, Ruthee — Owner   1502
GOLDMAN, Emanuel, PhD — Professor   1961
GOLDMAN, Laurence — Senior Attorney   1502
GOLDMAN, Lee, MD — Dean; Cardiologist; Professor   1961
GOLDS, Jeffrey A., PhD — Fellow Software Engineer   463
GOLDSMITH, Peter S. — Chairperson   1962
GOLDSTEIN, Keith S., MD, MPH, FAAFP, DABPM — Occupational Medicine Program Director; Consultant   1962
GOLDSTEIN, Ronald E., DDS — Dentist, Author, Educator, Consultant, Lecturer   1962
GOLDTHWAITE, Duncan — Petroleum Geologist, Consultant   464
GOMEZ, Jimmy — U.S. Representative from California   1963
GÓMEZ, Laura I. — Founder, Former CEO   1963
GOMEZ, Selena Marie — Actress; Singer   1963
GOMILLION-WILLIAMS, Bridgette L., PhD — Senior Silicone Chemist   465
GONZALES, Martin G. — Owner/CEO   466
GONZÁLEZ COLÓN, Jenniffer Aydin — Resident Commissioner of Puerto Rico   1964
GONZALEZ, Anthony E. — U.S. Representative from Ohio; Former Professional Football Player   1963
GONZALEZ, Erika G., MD — CEO, Physician   1963
GONZÁLEZ, Francy — Director   1964

GONZALEZ, Jesse — Founder, Chief Managing Member, Lawyer   467
GONZALEZ, Richard A. — CEO, Chairman   1963
GONZALEZ, Sarah — Chief Operating Officer   1964
GONZALEZ, Vicente Jr. — U.S. Representative from Texas, Lawyer   1964
GONZALEZ-ROMANACE, Hector R. — Bank Director and Telecommunications Executive (Retired), Private Investor   468
GOOD, Kenneth R., PhD — Anthropology Educator   1964
GOOD, Lynn Jones — Chairman, President, and CEO   1964
GOODALL, Jane — Primatologist, Anthropologist   469
GOODE, Sharon S., BS, MHA, RNC — Certified RN, Master of Science and Hospital Administration   1964
GOODELL, Roger Stokoe — Commissioner   470
GOODEN, Lance Carter — U.S. Representative from Texas   1964
GOODENOUGH, John Bannister — Scientist, Physicist, Professor   471
GOODING, Cuba Mark Jr. — Actor   1965
GOODLIN, Nick — President   1965
GOODMAN, John Stephen — Actor   1965
GOODMAN, Major M. — Botanical Sciences Educator   472
GOODMAN, Shira D. — CEO (Retired)   1965
GOODNIGHT, James Howard — Co-founder, CEO; Information Technology Executive   1966
GOODSON, J. Max, DDS, PhD — Senior Member of the Staff Emeritus   473
GOODYEAR, John L. — Artist, Professor Emeritus   474
GOODYEAR, Nancy L., EdD — Biology Educator   1966
GOOLD, Rupert, CBE — Theatre Director   1966
GOORAY, David A., MD, FACC — Cardiologist   475
GOPEZ, Evelyn V., MD — Professor of Pathology   1966
GORDER, Joe — CEO, President   1967
GORDON, Jeff Michael — Professional Stock Car Racer (Retired), Sportscaster, Sports Team Executive   1967
GORDON, Mark — Governor of Wyoming   1967
GORDON, Roy G., PhD — Chemistry Professor   1967
GORDON, Sharon Ann — Mathematics Educator (Retired)   1967
GORDON-LEVITT, Joseph Leonard — Actor   1967
GORDY, Berry III — Recording Industry Executive; Film Producer; Entrepreneur   1968
GORE, Albert, "Al" Arnold Jr. — 45th Vice President of the U.S.; Environmental Activist   1968
GORELIK, Alexander V., PhD — Associate Professor of Mass Communication   1968
GORMAN, James P. — Chairman, President, CEO   1969
GORSKY, Alex — Chairman and CEO   1969
GORSUCH, Neil McGill — Associate Justice   1969
GOSAR, Paul Anthony, DDS — U.S. Representative from Arizona; Dentist   1969
GOSCIN, Lee Alice, MD, PhD — Endocrinologist, Educator   476
GOSLING, Ryan Thomas — Actor   1969
GOSS, Robert Pike "Bob" Jr. — Assistant Professor, Assistant Dean (Retired)   477
GOSSARD, Stone Carpenter — Musician   1970
GOTO, Lori — Realtor   1970
GOTTESMAN, Noam — Co-Founder   1970
GOTTESMAN, Stephen, PhD — Professor Emeritus   1503
GOTTHEIMER, Josh — U.S. Representative from New Jersey   1970
GOTTLIEB, Daniel S. — Attorney   1970
GOULD, Harry E. Jr. — Paper Company Executive   478
GOULDING, Elena Jane "Ellie" — Singer   479
GOWER, Patricia E., PhD — Professor Emeritus (Retired)   1971
GOYER, Peter Francis Jr., MD — Medical Doctor; Researcher Teacher   480
GRACE, Daniel H. — Secretary-Treasurer   1971
GRACE, Marta — Owner, Managing Broker   1503
GRAF, Steffi — Former Professional Tennis Player   1971

GRAFF, Coty — Owner   1504
GRAFF, William Pancsovai — Architect   481
GRAFFIUS, Brenda L., RN — Manager   1971
GRAHAM, Ashley — Model   1971
GRAHAM, Aubrey, "Drake" Drake — Singer, Rapper; Actor   1971
GRAHAM, Clara Anne — Accountant, Operational Analyst   1972
GRAHAM, David Bolden — Food Products Executive   482
GRAHAM, Franklin III — President, CEO, Missionary   1972
GRAHAM, Lindsey Olin — U.S. Senator from South Carolina   1972
GRAMMER, Kelsey — Actor   1972
GRANDE, Ariana — Singer; Actress   1504
GRANGER, Norvell, "Kay" Kay — U.S. Representative from Texas; U.S. House of Representatives   1973
GRANNIS, Wayne E. — Judge   1973
GRANT, Elisabeth Franz — Elementary School Educator (Retired)   1973
GRANTS, Valdis — Engineering Manager   1973
GRASSLEY, Charles, "Chuck" Ernest — U.S. Senator from Iowa   1973
GRAUER, Douglas — Civil Engineer   1505
GRAUER, Peter — Chairman of the Board   1974
GRAVELY, William, "Will" Bernard — Professor Emeritus   1974
GRAVES, Garret Neal — U.S. Representative from Louisiana   1974
GRAVES, John William — Edgar and Margurite Henley Professor of American History   1975
GRAVES, John, "Tom" Thomas Jr. — U.S. Representative from Georgia   1974
GRAVES, Samuel Bruce Jr. — U.S. Representative from Missouri   1975
GRAVINO, Stacy — Town Clerk   1975
GRAY, Glenda Elisabeth, MBBCH — President, CEO, Physician   1975
GRAY, Judy Kay — CEO, Founder   483
GRAY, Marybeth — Senior Vice President of Health & Welfare Consulting   484
GRAY, Paul Wesley, EdD — Dean Emeritus   1505
GRAYSON, Julia — CEO   1975
GRBAC, Nicholas A. — Broadcast Engineer   1975
GRECIANO, Sandra — Voice Educator   1975
GREEN, Alexander, "Al" N. — U.S. Representative from Texas   1976
GREEN, CeeLo — Singer, Songwriter, Record Producer   1976
GREEN, John Michael — Author; Vlogger   1976
GREEN, Karen Ina — Licensed Psychologist   485
GREEN, Kirsten — Venture Capitalist   1976
GREEN, Mark Edward, MD — U.S. Representative from Tennessee; Physician   1976
GREENBAUM, Charles Hirsch, MD, FACP — Dermatologist, Educator   486
GREENBERG, Arline — Artist   1976
GREENBERG, Donna — Associate Professor of Psychiatry   1977
GREENBERG, Lillian — Elementary School Educator (Retired)   1977
GREENBERG, Philip Alan — Family Attorney, Civil Litigation   487
GREENBERG, Steven Morey — Lawyer   488
GREENE, Brian — President, CEO   1977
GREENE, Christine Elizabeth — Artist   1977
GREENE, Cynthia — Of Counsel   1977
GREENE, Edward F. — Senior Counsel   489
GREENFIELD, Sarah C., PhD — Counselor (Retired)   490
GREENGARD, Paul, — Neuroscientist, Educator   1977
GREENHALL, Charles August, PhD — Mathematician   491
GREENHOUSE, Linda Joyce — Knight Distinguished Journalist-in-residence, Joseph M. Goldstein Lecturer in Law   1977
GREENSTEIN, Scott — President, Chief Content Officer   1978
GREGG, Rosalie — Social Service Agency Administrator   1978
GREGORY, Dorothy Alice L. — Critical Care Nurse   1978
GREGORY, Jackie S., FNP — Family Nurse Practitioner   1978
GREGORY, James Paul — Lawyer   492
GREGORY, Roger Lee — Chief Judge   1978
GREGORY, Vicki L. — Library and Information   493

GREIDER, Carolyn, "Carol" Widney, PhD — Professor, Molecular Biologist 1978
GRENIER, Judson A. — History Educator 1506
GRETZKY, Wayne Douglas — Former Professional Hockey Player; Former Professional Hockey Coach 1979
GREWAL, Karan — Financial Reporting Manager 494
GRIFFEN, Agnes M., MLS — Library Administrator (Retired) 495
GRIFFIN, Blake Austin — Professional Basketball Player 1979
GRIFFIN, Joseph — CEO 1506
GRIFFITH JOYNER, Florence Delorez — Professional Track and Field Athlete (Retired) 1979
GRIFFITH, Howard, "Morgan" Morgan — U.S. Representative, Lawyer 1979
GRIFFITH, Tricia — CEO 1979
GRIGGER, Jane E. — Teacher 496
GRIJALVA, Raúl Manuel — U.S. Representative from Arizona 1980
GRILL, Richard Louis — Music Educator 497
GRIMSLEY, James Edward — Newspaper Editor, Syndicated Columnist 1980
GRINBERG, Meyer Stewart — Financial Planner 498
GRIPPANDO, Jeff — Senior Vice President, General Manager 1507
GRISCHKOWSKY, Daniel Richard, PhD — Professor Emeritus 1980
GRISHAM, Michelle Lynn — Governor of New Mexico 1980
GRISHAM, Stephanie — White House Press Secretary; White House Communications Director 1980
GRONKOWSKI, Rob James — Professional Football Player 1980
GROSS, Charles Meridith — Broadcast Executive 1980
GROSS, David Jonathan, PhD — Physicist; Professor 1981
GROSS, Mark — CEO (Retired) 1981
GROSSER, Bernard I. — Psychiatrist, Educator (Retired) 499
GROSSER, Morton — President 1981
GROSSMAN, Robert Ivin, MD — CEO; Dean; Neuroradiologist 1981
GROSSMAN, Robert, MD — Professor of Neurosurgery 500
GROSSMANN, Ignacio E. — Professor of Chemical Engineering 1982
GROTH, Edward John III — Professor 1982
GROTHMAN, Glenn S. — U.S. Representative from Wisconsin 1983
GRUBBS, Robert Howard, PhD — Professor; Chemist 1983
GRUEN, Peter H. MD — Psychiatrist, Educator 1983
GRUNINGER, Robert Martin Sr. — Civil Engineer 501
GRUZINSKA, Aleksandra, PhD, Emerita — Literature and Language Professor 1984
GU, Keqin — Mechanical Engineering Educator 1984
GUENTHER, Kenneth Allen — President, CEO (Retired) 502
GUEST, Michael Patrick — U.S. Representative from Mississippi 1984
GUFFIN, Jan Arlen — Secondary School Educator 1984
GUGLIUZZA, Kristene K., MD, FACS — Transplant and General Surgery Educator 1984
GUIDRY, Elliot — Teacher 1985
GUILHAMET, Leon Maurice, PhD — English Language Educator 1985
GULLO, Stephen Pernice, PhD — Psychologist, Corporate Executive 1985
GULNICK, Jim Reid — Vice President, Director of Operations 503
GUND, Agnes — President Emerita; Arts Patron 1507
GUND, Gordon — CEO 1985
GUPTON, Norma Jeneane — Technical Writer/Project Manager (Retired) 1985
GURNEY, Evalyn Hartung — Secondary School Educator (Retired) 504
GUSTAFSSON, Jan-Ake — Professor 505
GUSTAVSON, Mark S., Esq. — Lawyer 1986
GUTHRIE, Savannah — Broadcast Journalist 1986
GUTHRIE, Steven, "Brett" Brett — U.S. Representative from Kentucky 1986
GUTIERREZ, Alice S. — University Associate Professor 1986
GUTMANN, Amy, PhD — President 1986
GUTTMAN, Jon Sheldon — Magazine Editor, Historian 506
GUTWILER, Sharon — School System Administrator 1987

GUY, George, "Buddy" — Guitarist 1987
GWINN, Mary "Dolly", D.D.G., I.O.M., L.F.I.BA. — American Philosopher, Organizational Theorist, Business Developer 507
GWYNN, Regina — Co-Founder, CEO 1987
GYLLENHAAL, Jake Benjamin — Actor 1987
HAALAND, Debra, "Deb" Anne — U.S. Representative from New Mexico 1987
HAAS, Thomas Averill Hogan, "T. Hogan" Hogan Mr. — CEO, Executive Director 1987
HABER, Michael — Attorney 1988
HABERMAN, Maggie Lindsy — White House Correspondent 1988
HACKETT, James Patrick — CEO, President 1988
HACKMAN, Gene Allen — Actor 1988
HACKMAN, Judith — University Administrator, Researcher 1988
HACKWELL, Glenn A., PhD — Professor Emeritus of Zoology, Consultant 1989
HADDISH, Tiffany — Actress; Comedian 1989
HAFFORD, Arnold Albert — Attorney 1508
HAFKENSCHIEL, Joseph Henry — President (Retired) 1989
HAFNER, Joseph A. Jr. — Food Products Executive 1989
HAGAN, Michael P., MD — Physician 1989
HAGEDORN, James, "Jim" Lee — U.S. Representative from Minnesota 1990
HAGEN, Arthur Ainsworth, PhD — Professor, Pharmacologist (Retired) 1508
HAGLER, Tzvi Y., Esq. — Partner 1990
HAGLUND, Elaine J., PhD — Emerita Professor 1990
HAHN, Richard Wayne — Retired Hospital Administrator 1990
HAKIM, Raymond M., MD, PhD — Professor 509
HALABE, Udaya — Civil Engineering Educator, Researcher 1990
HALASA, Adel F., PhD — Chemist 510
HALASI-KUN, Adam T., LTC, USAR (Ret.) — Manager 1990
HALDON, John — Historian and Archaeologist 511
HALE, Lee L., JD — Lawyer 1990
HALEY, Nikki Randhawa — U.S. Ambassador (Retired) 1991
HALL, Alan C. — Library Director Emeritus 512
HALL, Anna Christene — Government Official (Retired) 1991
HALL, Barry G. — Evolutionary Biologist 1992
HALL, Carolyn S. — Retired Special Education Educator 1992
HALL, Edward Payson Jr., PhD — Professor Emeritus 1509
HALL, Ella Taylor, PhD — Clinical School Psychologist 1992
HALL, Geoffrey — Adjunct Professor 1992
HALL, J. Robert — CEO 513
HALL, Jean Quintero, MPA — Communication Faculty Member (Retired) 1509
HALL, Keith D., PhD — Former Director 1992
HALL, Kendra, RN, BSN, M, MSN — Nursing Administrator, Educator, Research Nurse 1992
HALL, Robert B. — Program Manager 1993
HALL, Sherry Reneé, PA-C — Physician Assistant 1510
HALL, Stanley Eckler — International Financial Consultant (Retired) 514
HALLAL, Diana — Founder, CEO 1993
HALLENGREN, Howard E. — President and Chairman 1993
HALLER, Karen S., BS in Education — Writer 1993
HALLERMANN, Gisela Elisabeth, MBA — Insurance Agent (Retired) 1994
HALLIN, David Anthony — Pilot (Retired) 1994
HALLQUIST, John O., PhD — Founder, President 515
HALVORSON, Peter L., PhD — Professor Emeritus 1510
HAM, Kay — Adjunct Faculty 1994
HAMADY, Theodore M. — Marketing Company Executive (Retired) 1994
HAMILL, Pete — Journalist 1994
HAMILTON, Arlan — Founder, Managing Partner 1994
HAMILTON, Charles J. Jr. — Attorney 516
HAMILTON, Jackie Stewart, MS Psychology — Executive Director 1995

HAMILTON, Margaret — Garden Designer 1995
HAMILTON, Matt — Reporter 1995
HAMILTON, Richard, PhD — Professor 517
HAMILTON, Susan Boyd — Assistant Professor 1995
HAMILTON, Susan Owens — Attorney; Transportation Executive (Retired) 1511
HAMLIN, Jefferson Davis — Retired Information Technology Executive 1995
HAMLIN, Winborne Leigh "Winnie" — English, Religion and Art Teacher 1511
HAMM, Jon Daniel — Actor 1995
HAMM, Mia Margaret — Professional Soccer Player 1512
HAMMERGREN, John Harvey — Chairman, CEO 1996
HAMMOND, Benjamin F., PhD, DDS — Retired Professor of Medicine 518
HAMRA, Sam F., LLB — Lawyer, Restauranter, Philanthropist 519
HANDLER, Beth Ann, EdD — Language and Learning Disabilities Specialist 1996
HANEY, Brian — Counsel 1996
HANEY, John Fredrick Brown — Psychiatrist 520
HANEY, Peter Michael, MD, PhD — Neonatologist 521
HANKS, Tom Jeffrey — Actor 1996
HANNA, Mazen, PhD — Pharmaceutical Executive, President 522
HANNA-ATTISHA, Mona, MD — Physician, Pediatric Residency Director; Assistant Professor; Public Health Advocate 1997
HANNER, Pat — Artist, Retired Nurse 1997
HANNITY, Sean Patrick — Political Commentator; Author 1997
HANSEN, Larry Lee, BS — Executive Vice President 523
HANSEN, Lars Peter, PhD — Professor; Economist 1997
HANSEN, Laurene "Laurie" — Realtor 524
HARBAUGH, Edith — CEO 1998
HARBAUGH, Jim Joseph — College Football Coach; Former Professional Football Coach; Former Professional Football Player 1998
HARBERGER, Arnold C. — Economist, Educator 525
HARDCASTLE, Brett Gene — Master Sergeant (Retired) 1512
HARDEN, James Edward Jr. — Professional Basketball Player 1998
HARDER, Joshua, "Josh" Keck — U.S. Representative 1998
HARDISH, Patrick — Librarian, Composer 1998
HARKLEROAD, Jo-Ann D. — Educational Diagnostician; Author 526
HARLING, Robert Allen — Oil 527
HARMAN, Theodore Carter "Ted", MS — Physicist, Researcher (Retired) 528
HARMENING, Jeffrey L. — Chairman, CEO 1998
HARMON, Mark — Actor 1998
HARMON, Mary L., CPA, Esq — Managing Director, Tax Counsel, Head of Tax Planning (Retired) 1998
HARNER, Stephen Glen, MD — Otolaryngologist (Retired) 1999
HAROON, Nasreen — Artist 1999
HARPER, Bryce Aron Max — Professional Baseball Player 1999
HARPER, Jacob — Co-owner 1999
HARRELSON, Woody Tracy — Actor 2000
HARRIETT, Judy A. — Medical Equipment Company Executive (Retired) 2000
HARRINGTON, Pádraig Peter — Professional Golfer 2000
HARRIS, Andy, MD — U.S. Representative from Maryland 2000
HARRIS, Ed Allen — Actor 2000
HARRIS, Jetta Ballard, MA — School Counselor (Retired) 2001
HARRIS, Kamala Devi — Vice President-Elect of the U.S. 529
HARRIS, Mark — Former U.S. Representative from North Carolina 2001
HARRIS, Neil Patrick — Actor 2001
HARRIS, Rosemary Ann — Actress 2002
HARRISON, Lonnie E., MD — CEO 2002
HARRISON-INGRAM (MCCLAFFERTY), Monica R. — President 2002
HARRY, Deborah Ann — Singer 2002
HART, Cecil W. J., MA, MB, BCh, BAO (TCD); FACS — Otolaryngologist, Surgeon 530

HART, Kevin Darnell — Actor, Comedian 2003
HART, Oliver D'Arcy, PhD — Lewis P. and Linda L. Geyser University Professor 2003
HARTER, David John de, MD — Radiation Oncologist (Retired) 294
HARTFORD, Alan C., MD, PhD, FACR — Associate Professor 531
HARTLEY, Duncan, PhD. — Owner, Duncan Hartley Fine Art Photography 1513
HARTZELL, Irene Janofsky, PhD — Educational Consultant, Psychologist, Author 533
HARTZLER, Vicky Jo — U.S. Representative from Missouri 2003
HARVEY, Deirdre Anne Shanahan — Construction Manager 1513
HARVIN, Wesley Reid — Lawyer 2003
HARYONO, Ignatius, PhD, DD — Retired Writer, Deacon 2004
HASAN, Javad K. — Founder, Chairman 534
HASHIMOTO, Tom Tsuyoshi — Engineer 2004
HASKETT, Michael L. — Founder, CEO 1514
HASLAG, Joseph — Professor and Kenneth Lay Chair in Economics 2004
HASPEL, Gina Cheri — Director 2004
HASS, Charles John William — Criminal Justice Program Coordinator 535
HASSAN, Margaret, "Maggie" C. — U.S Senator 2004
HASSETT, Kevin Allen — Chairman (Retired) 2004
HASSLER, Donald — Language Educator 2005
HASTINGS, Alcee Lamar — U.S. Representative from Florida 2005
HASTINGS, Wilmont, "Reed" Reed Jr. — CEO 2005
HATAJACK, Frank Joseph — Respiratory Therapist 2005
HATCH, Ronald R. — Engineer 1514
HATHAWAY, Anne Jacqueline — Actress 2006
HATTON, Mary Ellen, PhD — School Psychologist (Retired) 2006
HAUCK, Rachel, — Scenic Designer 2006
HAUGHT, William Dixon — Partner 2006
HAUPTFELD-DOLEJSEK, Vera, PhD, D.(ABHI), CSc — Medicine Professor, Director Histocompatibility Lab 536
HAUSER, Mary La Wayne — Elementary School Educator (Retired) 712
HAUSER, Michael George — Astronomer Emeritus 537
HAWKE, Ethan Green — Actor 2006
HAWKINS, Carl G. — President 2007
HAWKINS, Elinor Dixon — Librarian (Retired) 2007
HAWLEY, Joshua David — U.S. Senator from Missouri 2007
HAYDEN, Carla Diane — 14th Librarian 1515
HAYES, Gregory James — Chairman, President, CEO 2007
HAYES, Jahana — U.S. Representative from Connecticut 2007
HAYES, Margaret Daly, PhD — Political Scientist, Latin American Security Issues 538
HAYES, Nichelle M., MPA, MLS — Leader 2007
HAYES, Patricia Thornton — Music Educator, Director (Choral and Orchestra) 539
HAYES, Sean Patrick — Actor; Comedian 2008
HAYES, William J. III — Retired 2008
HAYMAKER, Richard Webb Riemenschneider "Dick", PhD — Emeritus Professor 540
HAYNES, Jack R., PhD — Psychology Educator 541
HAYNES, Marion E., MBA — Oil Company Executive (Retired) 2008
HAYNES, Robert V. — Professor Emeritus; Historian 2008
HAYNES, William S. Jr., MD — Internist, Cardiologist, Educator (Retired) 1515
HAYNIE, Fred Hollis — Naval Officer, Materials Engineer (Retired) 2009
HAYS, James Fred — Geologist, Educator 542
HAYS, Marilyn Patricia, JD — Lawyer, Real Estate Executive 2009
HAYTHE, Winston — Chief Counsel (Retired) 543
HAYWOOD, Betty, "BJ" Jean, MD — Anesthesiologist 2009
HAYWOOD, Kathleen, "Kathie" Marie PhD, — Professor Emerita 2009
HAZARD, John W. Jr. — Secondary School Educator (Retired) 2009

HAZELIP, Linda Ann — Musician, Small Business Owner, Senior Administrative Assistant — 544
HAZELIP, Linda Ann — Musician — 2009
HAZEN, Samuel N. — CEO — 2010
HEALY, Patricia Colleen — Social Worker, Retired — 2010
HEATH, Mark — Member — 2010
HEATH, Robert, "Bob" Thornton, PhD — Professor Emeritus — 2010
HECHTMAN, Howard R. — Financial Analyst (Retired) — 545
HECK, Denny Lynn — U.S. Representative — 2011
HECKMAN, James Joseph, PhD — Professor; Economist — 2011
HECKMANN, Richard Anderson — Zoology Educator — 2011
HEDRICK, Steven B. — Chairman, CEO — 2011
HEDVA, Beth, PhD, DABPS — Psychologist — 1516
HEEGER, Alan Jay, PhD — Physicist, Professor Emeritus — 2012
HEES, Bernardo Vieira — CEO — 2012
HEGDAL, Ruth Margaret — Accountant, Retired CPA — 2012
HEGE, Linda — Nurse (Retired) — 2012
HEGE, Mike, MRE — Realtor — 2012
HEGER, Herbert "Bert", PhD — Professor Emeritus — 546
HEIDEN, Eric Arthur, MD — Former Olympic Speed Skater; Former Professional Cyclist; Orthopedic Surgeon — 2012
HEIDUCK, Donald, "Donnie" Fred — Law Enforcement Officer, Ranger — 2013
HEILE, John David — Stockbroker — 2013
HEILICSER, Bernard Jay — Emergency Physician — 2013
HEILMANN, Flemming — Director — 2013
HEIMBURGER, Irvin LeRoy, MD — Surgeon (Retired) — 2014
HEINRICH, Martin Trevor — U.S. Senator — 2014
HEINSOHN, Thomas, "Tom" William — Professional Basketball Broadcaster; Former Professional Coach; Former Professional Player — 2014
HELBERT, Michael — Lawyer — 2014
HELIAS, Virginie — Chief Sustainability Officer — 2014
HELLER, Marielle Stiles — Actress, Director — 2015
HELMS, Bettyann S. — Principal, Designer — 2015
HEMINGER, Gary R. — CEO, Chairman — 2015
HEMINGWAY, Richard William, Esq. — Law Educator — 547
HEMPHILL, Allen Polk — Management Consultant — 548
HEMSWORTH, Chris — Actor — 2015
HENDERSON, Rickey Henley — Former Professional Baseball Player; Former Professional Baseball Coach — 2015
HENDIN, Josephine Gattuso, PhD — Language Educator, Writer — 549
HENDRICKS, Aileen Alana, PhD — Theater Educator, Scholar, Director, Actress — 2015
HENDRICKS, Diane Marie — Co-Founder, Chairperson — 2016
HENKEL, Kathy — Composer — 550
HENLEIN, Carl Arthur, Esq. — Attorney-at-Law — 551
HENLEY, Charles E. — Founding Dean — 2016
HENLEY, Darl — Librarian, Educator — 552
HENNESSEY, Jennifer, DVM, CVJ — Owner/Veterinarian — 553
HENNESY, Gerald C. — Artist — 2017
HENRY, Annie Belle — Professor Emeritus (Retired) — 554
HENRY, Mary Kay — President — 2017
HENSON, Taraji Penda — Actress — 2017
HEO, Joonghyeok, "Joon" — Assistant Professor — 2017
HERBERT, Bob — Journalist — 555
HERBERT, Gary Richard — Governor of Utah — 2018
HERCH, Frank Alan — Law Librarian, Lawyer, Lecturer — 556
HERCULES, David M., PhD — Centennial Professor Emeritus, Consultant — 557
HERD, Whitney — CEO — 2018
HERN, Kevin Ray — U.S. Representative from Oklahoma — 2018
HERNANDEZ, Enrique Jr. — Chairman, CEO — 558
HERNANDEZ, Felix, "King Felix" Abraham — Professional Baseball Player — 2018

HERNANDEZ, Myra — Owner — 2018
HERNANDEZ, Rudy — Superintendent — 1516
HERNDON, James Rodney — Instructor (Retired) — 2018
HERRERA BEUTLER, Jaime Lynn — U.S. Representative from Washington — 2019
HERRERA, Carolina — Fashion Designer — 2018
HERRICK, Robert James "Bob" — Electrical Engineering Technology Educator — 559
HERRIN, Colette M. — Owner — 2019
HERRMAN, Ernie — CEO — 2019
HERSHBERGER, Truman Verne — Retired Animal Nutritionist — 2019
HERTZ, Laura — CEO — 2019
HERZBERG-FREW, Dorothy Crews — Secondary School Educator (Retired) — 2019
HERZOG, John Orlando, PhD — Mathematics Educator, University Administrator — 2020
HERZOG, Werner — Screenwriter; Director — 2020
HERZOG, Whitey — Professional Baseball Coach (Retired), Professional Baseball Player (Retired), Executive — 2020
HESS, Steve — Chief Information Officer — 2020
HEUER, Gary, FIC — Owner/Partner — 560
HEWSON, Marillyn Adams — Chairman, President, CEO — 2021
HEWSON, Paul, "Bono" David — Singer, Songwriter, Musician — 2021
HIBBS, John D. — Computer Company Executive, Electrical Engineer, Small Business Owner — 2021
HICE, Jody Brownlow — U.S. Representative — 2021
HICKENLOOPER, George L. — Playwright, Educator — 2021
HICKEY, Benjamin M. — Curator of Exhibitions — 2022
HICKMAN, Joseph "Thomas" — Retired — 561
HIDY, George M., D.Eng — Chemical Engineer, Engineering Executive — 2022
HIEMSTRA, John E. — Reverend — 2023
HIGGINS, Brian M. — U.S. Representative from New York — 2023
HIGGINS, Glen, "Clay" Clay — U.S. Representative from Louisiana — 2023
HIGGINSON, Jerry, "Jay" Alden — President, CEO — 2023
HIGGS, Geoffrey B. — Doctor — 2023
HIGHFILL-LAGO, April — Library Director — 2024
HIGHTOWER, Glenda Phillips — Nurse — 562
HIGMAN, Francis Levi — Mathematics Educator — 2024
HILBRECHT, Norman Ty — Lawyer — 563
HILDEBRAND, Don C., PhD — Research Plant Pathologist Emeritus — 564
HILL, Faith — Singer — 2024
HILL, Gregory — President, Chief Operating Officer — 565
HILL, James, "French" French — U.S. Representative from Arkansas — 2024
HILL, Judith Margaret Deegan — Attorney — 1477
HILL, Julie — Member Outreach Manager, Board President — 566
HILL, Katherine, "Katie" Lauren — Former U.S. Representative from California — 2025
HILL, Lyda — Chairman — 2025
HILL, Montero, "Lil Nas X" Lamar — Rapper — 2025
HILL, Ronald Charles, MD, FACS — Surgeon, Educator — 567
HILLEARY, Carol Ann, MEd — Realtor; Elementary School Principal (Retired) — 1517
HILLEGAS, William J., PhD — Materials Scientist — 2025
HILLENMEYER, Henry — Restaurant Company Executive — 2025
HILLESTAD, Donna Dawn — Nurse (Retired) — 2025
HILL-WILLIAMS, Monay Francis — Nurse Practitioner — 568
HILSINGER WALLISER, Kathy Ellen — President — 2025
HILTON, Lorraine Ann, MSEd — Music Educator (Retired) — 2026
HIMES, James, "Jim" Andrew — U.S. Representative from Connecticut; Former Nonprofit Organization Executive — 2026
HINCH, Andrew, "A.J." Jay — Former Manager — 2026
HINDS, Robert James — Chemical Engineer — 2026

HINE, William Clyde — Dean Emeritus — 2026
HINES, Curtis Lee, EdD — Educational Consultant — 2026
HINOJOSA, Lynard, JD, LLB — Lawyer — 2027
HIRONO, Mazie Keiko — U.S. Senator from Hawaii — 2027
HIRSCH, Leonard S. — Financial Services Company Executive, Financial Analyst — 569
HITCHCOCK, Ken — Former Professional Hockey Coach — 2027
HITCHINS, Keith Arnold, PhD — History Professor — 2027
HITT, Danny, "Dan" Leon, — Lawyer, Retired Executive, Vice President — 2027
HLAVAC, Daniel C. — Executive Director of Development — 2028
HO, Reginald C.S. MD — Medical Educator — 2028
HOARD, John — Partner — 1517
HOBERECHT, Reynotta Jahnke — School System Administrator, Educator — 2028
HOBSON, Mellody — Co-CEO — 2028
HOCHMAN, Rod — CEO — 2028
HOCK, Hans Henrich — Professor Emeritus — 2028
HODES, Barton Lyle, MD — Ophthalmologist, Educator — 2029
HODGE, Kathleen, "Kathy" Ann — Reporting Analyst — 2029
HODGE, Rashida A. — Vice President — 2029
HODGES, George A. — Tooling, Facilites, & Production Supervisor (Retired) — 2029
HODGES, Mayme Weaver — Retired Elementary Educator — 2030
HOEHING, Kimberly — Associate — 1518
HOEN, Sheila Elizabeth Fleetwood — Artist, Lawyer (Retired) — 570
HOEVEN, John Henry III — U.S. Senator from North Dakota — 2030
HOFER, Dr. Bonnie Leah — Psychologist, Researcher, Author — 571
HOFFER, Axel, MD — Psychoanalyst — 572
HOFFMAN, Dustin Lee — Actor — 2030
HOFFMAN, James Simon — Engineering Educator (Retired) — 573
HOFFMAN, Linda — President, CEO — 1518
HOFFMAN, Michael — Associate Professor of Medicine — 2030
HOFSTADTER, Douglas Richard, PhD — Professor, Author — 2031
HOFSTETTER, Jane R., NWS — Artist, Educator, Author — 2031
HOGAN, Lawrence, "Larry" Joseph Jr. — Governor of Maryland — 2031
HOGUE, Carol Jane Rowland, PhD — Professor Emerita of Epidemiology — 574
HOLCOMB, Eric Joseph — Governor of Indiana — 2031
HOLDEN, Kris — Managing Broker/Marketing Executive — 575
HOLDEN, Matthew — President — 2031
HOLDEN, Matthew, PhD — Political Scientist; Educator; Arbitrator; Energy Consultant — 2031
HOLDER, Harold Douglas Sr. — International Entrepreneur — 576
HOLDING, George Edward Bell — U.S. Representative from North Carolina — 2032
HOLDITCH, Kenneth, PhD — Professor Emeritus — 2032
HOLDREN, John P., PhD — Educator, Physicist, Former Government Official — 2032
HOLICK, Sally Ann — Biochemist, Researcher — 2033
HOLIDAY, Jrue Randall — Professional Basketball Player — 2033
HOLLAND, Cindy — Former Vice President of Content Acquisition — 2033
HOLLAND, Nichole, MSN, CRMP — MSN, RN — 1519
HOLLAND, Woodrow Alan — Managing Member — 2033
HOLLEIN, Max — Director — 2033
HOLLEMAN, John, "Sonny" Lindsey — Priest — 2033
HOLLINGSWORTH, Joseph, "Trey" Albert III — U.S. Representative from Indiana — 2033
HOLLOWAY, Robert C. — Musician, Composer (Retired) — 2033
HOLLOWAY, Thomas M., PhD — Senior Vice President — 2034
HOLLUB, Vicki — President, CEO — 2034
HOLLY, Ramona Ann — Elementary and Secondary Education Educator — 2034
HOLM, George L. — CEO and President — 2034

HOLMES NORTON, Eleanor — Delegate to U.S. House of Representatives, Lawyer, Educator — 2035
HOLMES, Cecile S. — Associate Professor — 2034
HOLMES, Henry, Esq. — Attorney — 577
HOLMES, Richard B. — Chief Engineer — 2035
HOLOWENZAK, Stephen Paul, PhD, PFA, PFN, PGK — Professor Emeritus — 578
HOLST, Sanford — Author, International Consultant — 2035
HOLT, Lester Don Jr. — News Correspondent; Anchor — 2035
HOLTON, Gregory Allan, PhD — Environmental Engineering Consultant — 2035
HOLUTIAK-HALLICK, Stephen P. Jr. — Army Officer (Retired), Businessman, Educator — 2035
HOLZENDORF, King Jr. — City Councilman (Retired) — 2036
HONEYWELL, Leigh — CEO — 2036
HOOD, Amy Elizabeth — Executive Vice President, Chief Financial Officer — 2036
HOOPS, William James — Clergyman — 579
HOOVER, Katherine Lacy — Composer — 580
HOPKINS, Anthony — Actor — 2036
HOPKINS, Carol Sessoms, Pastor — Evangelist — 581
HOPKINS, Catherine — Music Educator — 582
HOPKINS, Linda Kay — Intellectual Property Attorney (Retired) — 2037
HOPSON, Sonya — CEO, Founder — 2037
HORN, Kendra Suzanne — U.S. Representative from Oklahoma; Lawyer — 2038
HORN, Wally Eugene — Former Senator — 2038
HORNBERGER, Walter Henry Jr. — Director of Quality Assurance (Retired) — 2038
HOROWITZ, Edward J., Esq. — Attorney — 583
HOROWITZ, Robert B.G. — Partner — 2038
HORSFORD, Steven Alexander — U.S. Representative — 2038
HOSCHEIT, Charles E. — Park District Administrator — 2039
HOSKINS, Carol, PhD — Professor Emeritus, Director, PhD Program in Nursing & Nursing Research — 1519
HOSKINS, William — Obstetrician, Educator, Gynecologist (Retired) — 584
HOSTLER, Carl E. — Attorney, Associate — 1520
HOULAHAN, Christina, "Chrissy" Marie — U.S. Representative from Pennsylvania — 2039
HOUSTON, Justin Donovan — Professional Football Player — 2039
HOWARD, Dwight David II — Professional Basketball Player — 2039
HOWARD, George, "Peter" Pratt — Airport Economist — 2039
HOWARD, Jeffrey Robert — Chief Judge — 2039
HOWARD, Melvin — Vice Chairman (Retired) — 585
HOWARD, Redemous A. — Senior Passport Specialist — 2039
HOWARD, Terrence Dashon — Actor — 2039
HOWE, John Kingman — Manufacturing, Sales and Marketing Executive — 586
HOWE, Marvine Henrietta — Newspaper Reporter — 2040
HOWELL, James B. III — Agricultural Products Company Sales Consultant (Retired) — 587
HOWELL, Rob Stuart — Costume and Set Designer — 2040
HOXIE, Chad — Vice President — 2040
HOYE, Vincent J. — Correctional Education Administrator; Consultant — 2040
HOYER, Steny Hamilton — U.S. Representative from Maryland; House Majority Leader — 2040
HOYWEGHEN, Magda Van, MD — Surgeon — 1620
HROMATKO, Wesley Vinton, D.Min. — Minister — 2041
HSU, Patrick Kuo-Heng — Language Educator (Retired); Former Librarian — 1520
HTOO, Maung S., PhD, FAIC — President — 588
HUANG, Suei-rong, PhD — Chemistry Educator — 2041
HUBBARD, Lincoln B. — Physicist — 2041
HUBBARD, Stanley, "Stub" — Broadcast Executive — 2041
HUBER, Douglas C., MD, FCAP — Pathologist (Retired) — 589

HUDLIN, Reginald Alan — Director 2041
HUDSON, Jennifer Kate — Singer, Actress 2042
HUDSON, Richard Lane Jr. — U.S. Representative 2042
HUEBNER, Walter F., PhD — Atomic Physicist, Astrophysicist, Space Scientist 590
HUFF, Norman Nelson — Computer Science Educator, International Lecturer, Engineer 2042
HUFFINGTON, Arianna — Founder, CEO, Author 2043
HUFFMAN, Jared William — U.S. Representative 2043
HUFFMAN, Steve, "Spez" — CEO 2043
HUG, Joyce E. — Founder, Director 2043
HUGHES, Kent Higgon — Economist 591
HUGHES, Larry Neal — Civil and Environmental Engineer, Educator, Consulting Engineer 2043
HUIZENGA, William, "Bill" Patrick — U.S. Representative from Michigan 2044
HULIN, Frances C. — U.S. Attorney (Retired) 2044
HULL PYLE, Joan, BSN — Director of Emergency Services (Retired) 2044
HULL, Bobby Marvin — Former Professional Hockey Player 2044
HULL, Christopher N. — State Agency Biologist, Independent Researcher, Writer 2044
HULLET, Michael Craig — Artist, Designer, Art Researcher 2044
HULT, Alex — Founder 2045
HUME, Richard T. — CEO 2045
HUNGAR, Julie Yearsley — Community College Administrator, Educator, Consultant 2045
HUNT, Johnelle Terria — Transportation Executive 2046
HUNTER, Dr. Richard C., "Butch" — Professor Emeritus of Policy, Organization, and Leadership 2046
HUNTER, Duncan Duane — U.S. Representative, Military Officer 2047
HUPPERT, Isabelle Anne Madeleine — Actress 2047
HURD, Jon R. — Nuclear Physicist 2047
HURD, Mark Vincent — Co-CEO 2047
HURD, William, "Will" Ballard — U.S. Representative of Texas 2047
HURLOCK, William Louis, Esq. — Managing Partner 592
HURNY, Beth — Executive Director 2047
HURST, Kimberly Ann — Co-Owner 593
HURT, William McChord — Actor 2048
HUSAIN, Nadeem — Medical Director 2048
HUSSAIN, Faisal Roomi — President, CEO 2048
HUTCHINSON, Lawrence — Veterinarian 2048
HUTCHINSON, Peter A. — Artist 2049
HUTCHINSON, Scott W. — Director of Tennis 2049
HUTCHINSON, William, "Asa" Asa II — Governor of Arkansas 2049
HUTCHINSON, Y-Vonne — Founder, CEO 2049
HUTCHISON, Jane Campbell, PhD — Professor Emerita of Art History 594
HUTNER, Martin Wolff — Interior Designer 2049
HUYSMAN, Frederick J. — Newspaper Editor 2049
HYDE, John Michael — History Educator Emeritus 595
HYDE-SMITH, Cindy — U.S. Senator 2050
HYMAN, Jennifer — Co-founder, CEO 2050
HYTKEN, Franklin Harris — Lawyer 2050
IACOCCA, Lee — Former Automobile Executive 2050
IBOS, Brandy — Owner 596
IBRAHIM, Nuhad Khalil — Oncologist 2050
ICAHN, Carl Celian — Investment Company Executive, Special Adviser to the President (Retired) 2050
IDLE, Jeffrey, "Jeff" Robert, PhD, FRSC, FRSB, FBPhS — Director of Systems Pharmacology and Pharmcogenomic, Endowed Professor 2051
IFEDIORA, Okechukwu Chigozie — Nephrologist; Educator 2051
IGE, David Yutaka — Governor of Hawaii 2051
IGE, Kolapo Akanfe — Professor, The Provost 597

IGER, Bob — CEO 598
ILES, Lawrence Irvine — Liberal Arts Educator, Historian 599
ILITCH, Marian — Co-Founder 2051
ILLIAN-MASQUELETTE, Alice Fontaine — Owner, CEO, Founder 2051
IMAI, Dorothy K., PhD — Psychotherapist (Retired) 2052
IMBIMBO, Rich — Owner 600
IMMEL, Barbara Kay — Management Consultant 601
IMMEL, Joseph Herbert Jr., PhD — Scientist, Biologist, Physiologist, Anatomist 602
IMMEL, Judy Ann — Educator (Retired) 603
IMMOOS, Marilyn Sue, PhD — Senior Psychologist Specialist 604
INFANTINO, Gianni Vicenzo — President; Sports Association Executive 2052
INGMIRE, Jennifer Joan — Aerospace/Mechanical Engineer 605
INHOFE, James, "Jim" Mountain — U.S. Senator 2052
INSALACO-DE NIGRIS, Anna Maria Theresa — Middle School Educator 2052
INSERRA, Ben Anthony — Construction Management Company Executive, Consultant 2053
INSLEE, Jay Robert — Governor of Washington 2053
IONESCU, Sabrina Elaine — Professional Basketball Player 606
IRESON, Roger William, Ordained Minister/General Secretary — General Secretary of Higher Education and Ministry 2053
IRVING, Donald J. — University Dean 2053
IRVING, Kyrie Andrew — Professional Basketball Player 2053
IRWIN, Lindy, PMA — Studio Owner 2054
IRWIN, Stormy 607
ISAACSON, Walter — Professor of American History, Journalist, Historian 2054
ISAKSON, John, "Johnny" Hardy — U.S. Senator from Georgia (Retired) 2054
ISERBYT, Charlotte Thomson — Researcher, Writer, Educational Consultant 1521
ISRAEL, Lesley Lowe — Political Consultant (Retired) 608
IVANKOVICH, Anthony D., MD — Anesthesiologist 609
IVEY, Kay Ellen — Governor of Alabama 2054
IZZO, Thomas — College Basketball Coach 2054
JACKLIN, Kathleen B. — Archivist 2055
JACKMAN, Hugh Michael — Actor 2055
JACKOBOICE, Sandra Kay — Artist 2055
JACKSON LEE, Sheila — U.S. Representative from Texas 2057
JACKSON, Barbara Garvey, BM, MM, PhD — Music Educator; Publisher (Retired) 610
JACKSON, Chris — Publisher, Editor-in-Chief 2055
JACKSON, Curtis, "50 Cent" James III — Rap Artist; Actor; Entrepreneur 2055
JACKSON, Henry Woodrow "Woody", PhD — Physicist, Researcher 1521
JACKSON, Jesse Louis — Civil Rights Activist; Clergyman 2056
JACKSON, Lamar Demeatrice Jr. — Professional Football Player 611
JACKSON, Michael J. — Chairperson, CEO 2056
JACKSON, Mona, EdD — Educational Administrator, Assistant Principal 612
JACKSON, O'Shea, "Ice Cube" — Rap Artist; Actor 2056
JACKSON, Phil Douglas — Former Professional Basketball Coach; Former Professional Basketball Player; Sports Team Executive 2056
JACKSON, Rosa, MEd — Elementary School Educator 2056
JACKSON, Samuel Leroy — Actor 2057
JACKSON, William Richard, PhD, DSc — Founder, Chairman of the Board 613
JACKSON-LOWMAN, Huberta — Professor 2057
JACOBI, Peter P. — Journalism Educator, Writer 2058
JACOBS, Darleen M. — Lawyer 614
JACOBS, Diane Margaret, PhD — Professor Emerita 615
JACOBS, Marc — Fashion Designer 2058
JACOBS, Patricia, "Trish" Louise, CNA — Geriatrics Nurse Assistant 2058
JACOBSON, Michael S. — Doctor 616

JACOBSZ ROSIER, Rene, "Ducky" Marcel, Founder — President 2058
JAGGER, Mick Phillip — Singer 2058
JAMALUDDIN, Abu Saeed, PhD — Advisor, Combustion & Heat Transfer Engineering (Retired) 2059
JAMBECK, Jenna — Professor 2059
JAMES, Annette L. — Kinleiner 617
JAMES, Ashley — Curator 2060
JAMES, LeBron Raymone — Professional Basketball Player 2060
JAMES, R. Aileen, DMA — Concert Pianist, Educator 618
JAMES, Ray Allan — Songwriter; Author; Singer; Insurance Adjuster 2060
JAMISON, Thomas H. — Principal; Of Counsel 619
JAMSHIDI, Mohammad — Electrical Engineer 2060
JAN, Conchita Tseng — Music Educator 2061
JANAK, Robert — Foreign Language Educator 2061
JANOS, James, "Jesse Ventura" George — Former Governor of Minnesota; Professional Wrestler (Retired) 2061
JANSON, Barbara Jean — President 620
JAO, Tze-Chi, PhD — Research and Development Scientist (Retired) 1522
JARVIK, Robert Koffler, MD — Founder, President, CEO; Biomedical Research Scientist 2062
JASWAL, Tony — Principal 2062
JATTAN-CUNNINGHAM, Lynette S., MD, FAAP — Pediatrician 2062
JAVOREK, Richard Alan — History Educator (Retired), Lafayette Township Zoning Chairman, Consultant 2062
JAYAPAL, Pramila — U.S. Representative 2062
JAZVIC, Beryl Jacqueline — Professional Artist, Art Teacher 1522
JEDLICKA, Gerald Frank — Business/Accounting Educator 2062
JEFFERSON, Melissa Viviane "Lizzo" — Singer, Rapper, Songwriter 1523
JEFFRIES, Hakeem Sekou — U.S. Representative from New York; Lawyer 2063
JELINEK, Walter Craig — CEO, President 2063
JENKINS, Gaye Ranck, BHS, MEd — Adult Educator, Academic Specialist, Sociology Professor 2063
JENKINS, Jo Ann — CEO 2063
JENNE, Arthur Kirk — Secondary School Educator 1523
JENNER, Kendall Nicole — Media Personality, Model 2063
JENNER, Kylie Kristen — Media Personality, Founder, Owner 621
JENSEN, Mona Dickson, PhD, MBA — Biochemist (Retired) 622
JERVIS-WHITE, Gwendolyn T. — Mental Health Services Professional 2064
JETER, Derek Sanderson — CEO, Co-owner; Former Professional Baseball Player 2064
JEWELL, Sarah, "Sally" Margaret — Former U.S. Secretary of the Interior; Former Outdoor Apparel Company Executive 2064
JEWELL, Sheila S. Stiles, PhD — Research Geneticist, Marine Biologist 1225
JEYNES, William H. — Education Educator; Religious Organization Administrator; Minister 623
JHA, Kulanand — Professor, Geotechnical Engineer 624
JIMENEZ, Harlyn, LMT, NST, NMT — Founder, CEO 2064
JINKERSON, Maxine Louise — Facilitator for Gifted and Talented Education 2064
JITOMIRSKAYA, Svetlana — Scientist 2064
JOB, Raymond Franklin "Soames", PhD — Global Lead for Road Safety 1524
JOBS, Laurene — Educational Association Administrator; Philanthropist 2065
JOEL, Billy Martin — Singer, Songwriter, Musician 2065
JOERGENSEN, John — Senior Associate Dean 2065
JOERGER, Jay Herman — Psychologist; Entrepreneur 2065
JOHAL, Jugjit S. — Principal 625
JOHANSON, Robert Gail, PhD — Acting Quality Manager, Senior Applications Engineer 626
JOHANSSON, Scarlett Ingrid — Actress 627
JOHLFS, Craig S. — Certified Financial Planner 2065
JOHN, Daymond Garfield — Entrepreneur; Television Personality; Author, Motivational Speaker 2066

JOHN, Elton Hercules — Singer, Songwriter, Musician 2066
JOHNS, Jasper — Artist 2066
JOHNSEN, Eugene Carlyle, Research & Consulting — Mathematician, Mathematical Social Scientist 2067
JOHNSON, Abigail Pierrepont — CEO, President 628
JOHNSON, Carl — Marriage and Family Therapist 629
JOHNSON, David G., PhD — Chinese History Educator 2067
JOHNSON, David S. — Civil Engineer 1524
JOHNSON, Dustin, "Dusty" M. — U.S. Representative from South Dakota 2067
JOHNSON, Dwayne, "The Rock" Douglas — Founder; Actor, Former Professional Wrestler 2068
JOHNSON, Earvin, "Magic" Jr. — Chairperson, CEO, Professional Basketball Player (Retired) 2068
JOHNSON, Eddie Bernice — U.S. Representative 2068
JOHNSON, Gerald A. — Health Facility Executive (Retired) 2068
JOHNSON, Gregory H., Col. (Ret.), USAF — Aerospace Space/Consultant 630
JOHNSON, Henry, "Hank" Calvin Jr. — U.S. Representative from Georgia, Lawyer 2069
JOHNSON, Howard A. Jr. — Corporate Executive, Operations Analyst, Financial Officer 2069
JOHNSON, James, "Mike" Michael — U.S. Representative from Louisiana 2069
JOHNSON, Jeffrey Mark — Music Director 2069
JOHNSON, Jeffry Lynn — Projectionist 2069
JOHNSON, Jimmie Kenneth — Professional Stock Car Racer 2069
JOHNSON, Jimmy William — Sports Commentator; Former Football Coach 2070
JOHNSON, John Henry — Film Director, Producer, Photographer; Educator 2070
JOHNSON, Joseph, "J.J." — Chef 2070
JOHNSON, Josephine Powell — District Manager (Retired) 2071
JOHNSON, Judy Dianne — Retired Elementary School Educator 2071
JOHNSON, Keith Liddell — Chemical Executive, Management Consultant (Retired) 631
JOHNSON, Kevin — CEO, President 2071
JOHNSON, Lawrence Tufts — Pilot (Retired) 2071
JOHNSON, Leo Francis, PhD — Physicist 632
JOHNSON, Michael Duane — Professional Sprinter (Retired) 2071
JOHNSON, Randy, "The Big Unit" David — Former Professional Baseball Player 2071
JOHNSON, Richard Darrell — Management Consultant 2071
JOHNSON, Richard N, PhD — President 2072
JOHNSON, Richard Turner — Television Producer, Consultant 2072
JOHNSON, Ronald, "Ron" Harold — U.S. Senator 2072
JOHNSON, William, "Bill" Leslie — U.S. Representative from Ohio 2072
JOHNSON, Yvonne — Elementary School Educator 633
JOHNSON-VELAZCO, Nancy Ruth — Marketing Professional 634
JOHNSTON, John Phillips "Phil" Little, JD, MBA — Founder/Chief Legal Officer 635
JOHNSTON, Virgil LLoyd — Utility Consultant; Corrosion Engineer (Retired) 636
JOHNSTONE, C. Bruce — Investment Company Executive 2073
JOLIE, Angelina — Actress 2073
JOLLY, Daniel E., DDS — Dental Educator and Consultant 637
JOLY, Hubert Bernard — Former CEO, Executive Chairman 2073
JONAS, Jeff — Director, CEO 2073
JONES, Barbara Ewer — Teacher, School Psychologist, Occupational Therapist 2074
JONES, Brenda Gail — School District Administrator (Retired) 1525
JONES, Charles E. — CEO 2074
JONES, Charles Hill — President, Treasurer 638

JONES, Christopher Arlen, EdD — Educator (Retired)	2074
JONES, Claris Eugene Jr. — Botanist, Educator	2074
JONES, Donald Kelly — Head (Retired), Investment Promotion	2074
JONES, Edwin Channing Jr., BSEE, PhD — University Professor Emeritus	1525
JONES, Franklin — CEO/President/Owner	2075
JONES, Gordon, "Doug" Douglas — U.S. Senator, Lawyer	2075
JONES, Hannah — Apparel Executive	2075
JONES, James Earl, — Actor	2075
JONES, Jerral, "Jerry" Wayne — Professional Sports Team Owner	2075
JONES, Jerry Frank — Attorney	2076
JONES, K. C. — Former Professional Basketball Coach; Former Professional Basketball Player	2076
JONES, Kent — Director	2076
JONES, Kimberly, "Lil' Kim" Denise — Rap Artist	2076
JONES, Mildred Pauline — Apparel Executive, Consultant	2076
JONES, Radhika — Editor-in-Chief	2077
JONES, Roger C., Esq. — Construction Lawyer	639
JONES, Starlet "Star" Marie — Attorney, Advocate, Media Personality	640
JONES, Todd — CEO	2077
JONES, Tommy Lee — Actor	2077
JORDAN, Bob — Partner	2077
JORDAN, James, "Jim" Daniel — U.S. Representative from Ohio	2077
JORDAN, Joseph — Owner	641
JORDAN, Michael Bakari — Actor	2077
JORDAN, Michael Jeffrey — Professional Sports Team Executive, Retired Professional Basketball Player	2078
JORDAN, Noel Chase — President	2078
JOSEPHS, Bonnie P. — Lawyer	2078
JOYCE, David Patrick — U.S. Representative from Ohio, Lawyer	2078
JOYCE, John Patrick, MD — U.S. Representative from Pennsylvania; Dermatologist	2078
JOYCE, Thomas P. Jr. — CEO and President	2078
JOYCE-BRADY, Martin Francis — Clinical Professor of Medicine	2078
JOYNER-KERSEE, Jackie — Former Track and Field Athlete	2079
JUDGE, Aaron James — Professional Baseball Player	2079
JUDICE, Marc Wayne — Lawyer	642
JULIANO, John L. — Trial Lawyer	643
JULY, Lisa, — Vice President of Data Intelligence	2079
JUMPER, Roy Davis, PhD — Writer, Educator	644
JUNE, Carl Howard — Immunologist	2079
JUSTICE, Barbara J., MD, ABPN, ABFP — Forensic Psychiatrist	645
JUSTICE, James Conley II — Governor of West Virginia	2079
KACHURIN, Anatoly, PhD — Director of Innovative Methods	2079
KADAMANI, Esteban — Owner, Managing Director	2080
KADISH, Richard L. — Chairman, Founder	646
KAELIN, William George Jr., MD — Professor of Medicine; Researcher	647
KAEPERNICK, Colin Rand — Professional Football Player	2080
KAGAN, Elena — Associate Justice; Professor	2080
KAHLE, Lynn R., PhD — Professor Emeritus	648
KAHN, Gordon Jacques — Principal, Owner	2080
KAHNEMAN, Daniel, PhD — Professor Emeritus	2080
KAHRL, Robert, JD, LPCC — Lawyer	2080
KAINE, Leonard Paul "Len" — Founder, President	649
KAINE, Timothy, "Tim" Michael — U.S. Senator from Virginia; Lawyer	2081
KAISER, Walter Christian Jr., PhD — President Emeritus, Academic Administrator	650
KAISER-BOTSAI, Sharon — Primary School Educator (Retired)	1526
KALINA, Jon — CEO	651
KALING, Mindy — Actress; Writer, Television Producer	2081
KALLAKIS, Achilleas M.	2081
KALLAY, Thomas, "Tom" — Managing Attorney, 2nd Appellate District	2081
KALLEN, Elliot H. — CEO, Financial Planner, Wealth Manager	2082
KALOGJERA, Ikar J., MD, DFAPA, DFAACP — Psychiatrist, Educator	652
KALTENEGGER, Lisa — Astronomer	2082
KAMERSCHEN, Robert Kam — Senior Business Executive, Private Investor, Consultant	653
KAMILLI, Robert, "Bob" J., PhD — Scientist Emeritus	2082
KANDARIAN, Steven A. — Chairman, President, CEO	2082
KANDEL, Eric Richard, MD — Neuroscientist; Professor	2082
KANE, David Lawrence — Attorney	2083
KANE, Sara Wyn — Partner	2083
KANIA, Alan J.	2083
KANNAN, Sandra Jean — Elementary School Educator, Retired Teaching Assistant Principal	2083
KANNANGARA, Don Walter, MD, MSc, PhD, DTM&H, MRCP — Infectious Disease Consultant	2084
KANODE, Carolyn — School Nurse Practitioner, Pediatrics Nurse	654
KANT, Ravi, MD — Endocrinologist	655
KAO, Min H. — Co-Founder	2084
KAO, Tzu-Min, MD — Physiatrist	656
KAPLAN, Virginia, "Gini" Lee — Landscape Design & Plant Care	2084
KAPPES, Philip Spangler — Lawyer	657
KAPTUR, Marcia, "Marcy" Carolyn — U.S. Representative from Ohio	2084
KARAVITE, Carlene M. — Psychologist, Coach, Real Estate Property Manager	658
KARDASHIAN WEST, Kim Noel — Media Personality; Fashion Executive; Model	2084
KARNEI, Robert Frederick Jr., MD — Physician	659
KARP, David — Founder; Internet Company Executive; Web Developer	2084
KARPEL, Craig — Journalist, Editor	2084
KASBAR, Michael J. — President, CEO	660
KATKO, John Michael — U.S. Representative, Lawyer	2084
KATZ, Dr. Jane — Professor of Health and Physical Education	661
KATZ, Joel Abraham — Entertainment Attorney	2085
KATZ, Joel — Information and Graphic Designer	2085
KATZMANN, Robert Allen — Chief Judge; Professor	2085
KAUFMAN, Stephen E., Esq. — President, Attorney	662
KAUFMANN, Charles A., MD — Psychiatrist, Neuroscientist, Educator	2086
KAUFMANN, Michael C. — CEO	2086
KAVANAGH, Sean P. — Partner	1526
KAVANAUGH, Brett Michael — Associate Justice	663
KAVASERRY, Ramakrishnan, DPT CDN — Director, Physical Therapist	2086
KAWAMOTO, Kensaku — Associate Chief Medical Information Officer	2086
KAY, David Blair, PhD — Principal Optical Scientist (Retired)	1527
KAYMAKCALAN, M. Orhan, MD, FACS — Doctor	664
KAZMIER, W. Jan, MD, PhD — President	2086
KEANE, Margaret — CEO, President	2087
KEARFOTT, Ralph Baker, PhD — Professor, Mathematician, Researcher	2087
KEARNS, Martha Mary — Professor, Humanities Educator, Author, Critic	2087
KEATING, Christopher Patrick — Capitol Bureau Chief, Reporter	2087
KEATING, William, "Bill" Richard — U.S. Representative from Massachusetts; Former Prosecutor	2087
KEATON, Diane — Actress	2087
KECK, Trish Harris — Artist	2088
KEEHN, Neil F. — President, CEO	2088
KEEHNER, Michael A.M. — Owner and Managing Director	2088
KEELER, Roger Norris — Physicist	665
KEENAN-BOLGER, Celia — Actress, Singer	666
KEENE, Lonnie S., Esq.	2088
KEHOE, Peter, PhD — President	1527
KEIDEL, Robert W., PhD — Management Consultant, Writer, Educator	2088
KEITH, Toby — Singer, Songwriter	2089
KELLER, Thomas A. — Chef; Restaurateur; Author	2089

KELLEY, Dale Russell — Mayor 667
KELLEY, David Edward — Executive Producer, Writer 2089
KELLMAN, Barnet — Professor, Robin Williams Endowed Chair in Comedy 2089
KELLY, Alfred F. Jr. — CEO 2090
KELLY, Colleen A., PhD — Secondary School Educator 2090
KELLY, Daniel John, MD — Consolidated Pathology Consultant (Retired) 668
KELLY, Edward A. Jr., MD — Physician 669
KELLY, Gary Clayton — Chairman, CEO 2090
KELLY, George, "Mike" Joseph Jr. — U.S. Representative from Pennsylvania 2090
KELLY, John, "Trent" Trent — U.S. Representative from Mississippi 2091
KELLY, Laura — Governor of Kansas 2091
KELLY, Megyn Marie — News Anchor; Journalist 2091
KELLY, Robin Lynne — U.S. Representative from Illinois 2091
KELLY, Thomas Michael — Partner 2091
KEMBLE, Brian C. — Director 2091
KEMMERLING, Lisa — Owner, Entrepreneur 2091
KEMP, Brian Porter — Governor of Georgia 2092
KEMP, Roger L., PhD — Career City Manager 670
KENDALL, Richard Parker — Principal Consultant 2092
KENDE, Christopher Burgess, JD — Lawyer, Educator 2092
KENNEDY, Anthony McLeod — Associate Justice (Retired) 2092
KENNEDY, David Stewart — Chief U.S. Bankruptcy Judge 1528
KENNEDY, John Neely — U.S. Senator from Louisiana 2092
KENNEDY, Joseph, "Joe" Patrick III — U.S. Representative from Massachusetts 2092
KENNEDY, Kathleen — President; Film Producer 2092
KENNEDY, Lesa Dawn — Vice Chairperson; CEO 2093
KENNEDY, Susan O., PhD — Physical Education Educator, Consultant, Sports Official 671
KENNEDY, Thomas A. — Chairperson, CEO 2093
KENNEDY, Timothy, "Tim" Fred — MMA Fighter 2093
KENNEDY, X.J. — Writer, Poet 672
KENNEY, James A. III — Senior Judge 1528
KENNEY, James, "Jim" Francis — Mayor of the City of Philadelphia 2093
KENT, Jeanne Yvonne — Artist, Poet 2093
KERCHER, David M. — Mechanical Engineer (Retired) 673
KERN, Charles William, PhD — Professor of Chemistry, Emeritus 674
KERNS, Christian Randolph — Chemist (Retired) 1529
KERR, Donald MacLean, PhD — Physicist, Federal Official 2094
KERR, Valerie Ann — Public Health Nurse 2094
KERRY, John Forbes — U.S. Secretary of State (Retired) 2094
KERSHAW, Clayton Edward — Professional Baseball Player 2095
KESHISHYAN, Gary — Realtor 675
KESSLER, Michael William, MD — Associate Professor 2095
KETTLESON, David Noel — Retired Orthopaedic Surgeon, Timber Manager 2095
KETTLEWELL, Gail B. — Global Development Education Professional 2096
KEULEGAN, Emma — Retired Special Education Educator 676
KEYS, Alicia — Singer, Songwriter, Musician 2096
KEYWELL, Brad — Founder, CEO 2096
KHAN, Badrul — Information Technology Educator 2097
KHAN, Shahid, "Shad" — CEO, Manufacturing Executive, Professional Sports Team Executive 2097
KHANNA, Rohit, "Ro" — U.S. Representative from California; Lawyer 2097
KHOSROWSHAHI, Dara — CEO 2097
KICKLIGHTER, Alma Louise — Communicable Diseases Specialist, Nurse, County Administrator 2097
KIDD, Michel — Environmental Health and Safety Specialist 2097
KIELER, Mary — Nurse 1529
KIEST, Alan S. — Senior Vice President, Co-Founder 2097

KILANOWSKI, Dana Marcotte — Historian, Writer, Filmmaker, Archaeologist 2097
KILDEE, Daniel, "Dan" Timothy — U.S. Representative 2098
KILGORE, Brad — Chef-Owner 677
KILLEBREW, Ellen Jane, MD — Cardiologist, Educator 1530
KILMEADE, Brian — Television and Radio Personality 2098
KILMER, Derek Christian — U.S. Representative from Washington 2098
KIM, Andrew, "Andy" N. — U.S. Representative from New Jersey 2098
KIM, Chris — Coordinator 1530
KIM, Donghwan — Online Marketer 2098
KIM, Unsup, MD, FACS — University Director, Educator 678
KIM, YJ — Master Instructor 2098
KIMBALL, Donald Robert — Director of Regulatory Affairs (Retired) 679
KIMBALL, Toby — Founder, President 1531
KIME, Milford, "Mil" Burton PhD — Applied Physicist 2099
KIMMEL, Jimmy Christian, — Television Personality 2099
KIND, Ronald, "Ron" James — U.S. Representative from Wisconsin; Lawyer 2099
KING, Angus Stanley Jr. — U.S. Senator 2099
KING, Billie Jean — Former Professional Tennis Player 2099
KING, Bradley — Theatrical Lighting Designer 2100
KING, Carole Joan — Singer, Songwriter 2100
KING, Frances — Education Educator (Retired) 2100
KING, Gayle — Journalist 2101
KING, Howard Pickett — Circuit Court Judge, Of Counsel 2101
KING, Joy Kerler — Professor Emerita 680
KING, Peter Thomas — U.S. Representative, Lawyer 2101
KING, Regina Rene — Actress 681
KING, Steven, "Steve" Arnold — U.S. Representative from Iowa 2101
KING, William Richard "Bill", PhD — Business Educator, Writer, Consultant 682
KINGSLEY, Ben — Actor 2101
KINKELAAR, Shawn — Pointing Dog Trainer 683
KINNE, Frances Bartlett, PhD — Chancellor Emerita and Past President 2102
KINNEAR, John Kenyon Jr. — Architect 2102
KINNEY, Jeffrey, "Jeff" Patrick — Author; Cartoonist 2103
KINS, Gloria Starr — President of Public Relations Firm, Photojournalist, Writer 2103
KINSELLA, Kathleen E. — Managing Director, Head Fixed Income, Money Market and Global Emerging Market Sales 2103
KINSMAN, Robert Preston, MBA — Biomedical Plastics Engineer 684
KINZINGER, Adam Daniel — U.S. Representative 2103
KIRBY, Harry Scott — Priest in Charge 2104
KIRK, Wiley Price — Professor of Physics, Materials Science and Electrical Engineering; Business Owner and President of Research and Development Company 685
KIRKENDOLL, Tommie — Education 1531
KIRKPATRICK, Ann Leila — U.S. Representative 2104
KIRKPATRICK, Anne Saunders — Systems Analyst 686
KIRSCH, Donald — Financial Consultant 2104
KISSINGER, Henry Alfred — International Consulting Company Executive; Former U.S. Secretary of State 2105
KITCHENS, Clarence, "Wes" Wesley Jr. — Consultant 2105
KLARMAN, Seth Andrew — Hedge Fund Manager 2105
KLECKNER, Kelli — Office Manager 2105
KLEE, Margaret Ann — Software Engineer 687
KLEGERMAN, Melvin Earl, PhD — Biochemist, Biomedical Engineer 2105
KLEID, Wallace — Lawyer 2106
KLEIN, Benjamin Endsley — Theatre Director 2106
KLEIN, Calvin Richard — Fashion Designer 2106
KLEIN, Gordon Leslie, MD — Senior Scientist, Adjunct Professor 688
KLEIN, Naomi — Journalist, Author 2106

KLEIN, Peter — Theatrical Producer 689
KLEIN, Renny D., PhD — Psychotherapist, Writer, Columnist 690
KLEINER, Heather Smith — Academic Administrator (Retired) 2107
KLEINSCHNITZ, Barbara Joy — Oil Company Executive, Consultant 2107
KLINE, Kevin Delaney — Actor 2107
KLINGER, Eric, PhD — Psychologist, Educator 691
KLOBUCHAR, Amy Jean — U.S. Senator from Minnesota 2107
KLOSS, Karlie Elizabeth — Model 2108
KLOTMAN, Mary E. — Dean 2108
KLOTTER, James Christopher — State Historian, Educator 692
KLUBER, Corey Scott — Professional Baseball Player 2108
KLUM, Heidi — Model 2108
KNIGHT, Constance N. Dodge, PhD — Independent Geologist 318
KNIGHT, Philip Hampson "Phil" — Retail Company Executive 693
KNIGHT, Stephen, "Steve" Thomas — U.S. Representative (Retired) 2108
KNOSPE, William H., MD — Medical Educator 2108
KNOTT, Stephen F., PhD — Professor 2108
KNOWLES-CARTER, Beyoncé Giselle — Singer; Actress 2109
KNOWLTON, John "Jack", CPBD, GMB, CAPS — President 1532
KNUTH, Donald Ervin, PhD — Computer Sciences Educator 2109
KOBILKA, Brian Kent, MD — Professor; Molecular Biologist 2110
KOBRINE, Arthur I., MD, PhD — Neurosurgeon 694
KOCH, Charles — Chemical Engineer 2110
KOCH, Christina — Astronaut, Engineer 695
KOCH, David Hamilton — Businessman, Philanthropist 696
KOCH, Jill L. — Owner 1532
KOCH, Randall G., MPA — Hospital Administrator 697
KOCHARIAN, Armen N. DSc/PhD/Prof. — Professor in Physics; Senior Research Scientist 2110
KOCSIS, Joan B., — Elementary School Educator 2111
KOEHNKE, Donna R. — Secretary 2111
KOENIG, Harold Paul — Management Consultant 2111
KOENIG, Robert August, PhD — Minister, Educator 2112
KOENINGER, Jimmy G., PhD — Executive Director 2112
KOEPKA, Brooks — Professional Golfer 698
KOEPPE, Patsy Poduska, MD — Internist, Medical Educator 2112
KOHLHEPP, Edward John Sr. — Founder, CEO 2112
KOHNEN, Michael Phillip 2113
KOIRALA, Navaneet — Principal 2113
KOK, Hans — Consulting Engineer 699
KOKKINOS, Spiro John — Owner 700
KOLB, James J., PhD — Drama Educator 701
KOLKEY, Daniel M. — Former Judge, Lawyer 2113
KOMARAVOLU, V.C. Rao — Engineering Educator 2114
KONKOL, Richard J., MD, PhD — Pediatric Neurologist 2114
KOOLHAAS, Remment Lucas — Architect; Professor 2114
KOONTZ, Dean Ray — Author 2115
KOPEL, Robert Frank — Anesthesiologist 2115
KOPROSKI, Alexander R., Knight of Malta — Real Estate Company Executive 2115
KORDESTANI, Omid R. — Executive Chairman 2116
KOREN, Edward Franz Jr. — Chairperson Emeritus 2116
KORN, David G., PhD — Computer Scientist, Researcher 1533
KORNBERG, Roger David, PhD — Professor in Medicine; Biochemist 2117
KORNER, Russell B. Jr. — Lawyer 1533
KOSHY, Elizabeth, "Liza" Shaila — Actress, Television Host, Comedian, YouTuber 2117
KOTB, Hoda — News Correspondent; Television Personality 2117
KOTCH, Mary — Global Chief Information Officer 2117
KOTTHA, Jagannadham — CEO 1534
KOUDELKA, George — Retired Music Educator 2117

KOUDOU, Ahile Nicolas — Professor of Business Administration 2118
KOUFAX, Sandy — Professional Baseball Player (Retired) 2118
KOUM, Jan Boris — Co-Founder, CEO, Entrepreneur 2118
KRAFKA, Mary Baird JD, — Lawyer 2118
KRAFT, Robert Kenneth — Principal Owner, Chairman, CEO; Professional Sports Team Executive 2118
KRAMER, Carl Edward, PhD — Historian, Urban Planner 2118
KRAMER, George M. — U.S. Senior Master Chess Player 702
KRAMER, Rebecca Ann — Artist 2119
KRAMER, Richard J. — Chairman, President, CEO 2119
KRANZ, Peter Lewis, PhD — Professor 2119
KRASINSKI, John Burke — Director, Actor 2120
KRAUS, John Walter — Aerospace Engineering Company Executive (Retired) 703
KRAVITZ, Zoë Isabella — Actress 2120
KRAWCZYK, Jon — Owner 704
KREIMER, Herbert Frederick — Professor Emeritus 2120
KREINES, Joseph — Conductor 705
KREITZER, Lois M. — Investor 2120
KREMENSKY, Kenneth — Fire Chief 2121
KRENZLER, Brandon — CEO, Founder, Journalist 2121
KRICK, Edwin H., MPH, MD — Emeritus Associate Professor of Medicine 706
KRIEGEL, Charlie — Founder, CEO, Owner 2121
KRISHNAMOORTHI, Subramanian, "Raja" Raja — U.S. Representative from Illinois 2121
KRITCHEVSKY, Evelyn Sholtes, PhD — President 707
KRITZER, David S. — Founding Partner 708
KROEMER, Herbert, PhD — Professor Emeritus 709
KROENKE, Stanley — Professional Sports Team Owner 2121
KRONCHER, Allan E., PhD — Economist (Retired) 710
KRONEN, Jerilyn — Psychologist 2121
KRUGMAN, Paul Robin, PhD — Professor; Columnist 2121
KRUSZYNSKI, Timothy Edward — Protective Services Official, Poet (Retired) 2122
KRZYZEWSKI, Mike — College Basketball Coach 2122
KUDLOW, Lawrence Alan — Director, Former Financial News Correspondent, Economist 2122
KUHN, James E., JD — Judge 2123
KULENOVIC, Mustafa PhD — Mathematics Professor 2123
KULIK, Dolores, "Dee" Michael — Research Geologist, Geophysicist (Retired) 711
KULIK, Tom A., JD — Partner 2123
KUMAR, Tobi J. — Photographer; Poet (Retired) 2123
KUNDERA, Milan — Author 2123
KURFEHS, Harold, "Hal" Charles — Vice President 2123
KURZMAN, Stephen — Lawyer, Government Official (Retired) 2124
KUSHAR, Kent — Information Technology Executive; Executive Coach; Business Advisor 2124
KUSHNER, Eva — Academic Administrator, Educator; Author 2124
KUSHNER, Jared Corey — Senior Advisor to the President; Director; Real Estate Executive 2125
KUSHNER, Tony Robert — Playwright, Scriptwriter 2125
KUSTER, Ann L. — U.S. Representative from New Hampshire; Lobbyist 2126
KUSTOFF, David Frank — U.S. Representative from Tennessee; Lawyer 2126
L'HEUREUX, Richard Joseph — Volunteer Advocate 2153
LA BARGE, William Joseph — Tutor, Researcher 2126
LA ROSA, Francisco G., MD — Pathologist, Researcher, Educator 2126
LA RUSSA, Tony Jr. — Senior Advisor of Baseball Operations; Former Professional Baseball Manager; Former Professional Baseball Player 2127
LABUZA, Theodore P. — Researcher, Educator 713
LACEY, John W. "Jack" III, MD — Chief Medical Officer Emeritus 1534

LACHER, Miriam Browner, PhD — Clinical Neuropsychologist (Retired) 2127
LACKLAND, Theodore H., Esq. — Lawyer 714
LADD, Culver S., PhD, MA — Secondary School Educator 2127
LADENHEIM, Jules — Neurosurgeon 2127
LADMAN, Jerry R., PhD 2128
LAENUI, Poka — Human Rights Advocate/Lawyer 2128
LAFITTE, Jacqueline — Youth Mentor 2129
LAFLEUR, Guy — Retired Professional Hockey Player 2129
LAGASSE, Emeril John III — Chef; Restaurateur; Television Show Host 2129
LAGOW, Richard J. "Dick", PhD — Chemistry Professor 715
LAHAM, Michel, MD — Physician 2130
LAHEY, Bonita Louise — Business and Market Development Projects Consultant 2130
LAHOOD, Darin McKay — U.S. Representative from Illinois; Lawyer 2130
LAMALFA, Douglas Lee — U.S. Representative from California; Farmer 2130
LAMANDA, Al — Author 2130
LAMB, Conor James — U.S. Representative from Pennsylvania 2131
LAMB, Robert — Diplomat (Retired); Professional Society Administrator 2131
LAMB, Tommy — President 2131
LAMBERT, Miranda Leigh — Singer, Songwriter 2131
LAMBERT, Rene — Executive Director 2131
LAMBORN, Douglas, "Doug" Lawrence — U.S. Representative from Colorado; Lawyer 2132
LAMONT, Edward, "Ned" Miner Jr. — Governor of Connecticut 2132
LAMPE, David Elwood — Professor of English Emeritus 2132
LAMPERT, Eddie — CEO (Retired) 2132
LAMPHERE, Louise, PhD — Anthropologist 1535
LAMUNIÈRE, Carolyn P. — Artist 716
LANCE, Ryan Michael — Chairperson, CEO 2132
LANDMAN, Jonathan I. — Managing Editor 2132
LANE, Cristy — Country Singer 717
LANE, Edward "Beau" — Breeder, Trainer, Owner, Horseman 718
LANE, Harris — President, CEO 719
LANE, Joseph M., MD — Professor of Orthopaedic Surgery 720
LANE, Nathan — Actor 2132
LANG, Barbara — CEO 1535
LANG, George Russell Jr. — Oil Company Executive (Retired) 2133
LANGE, Jessica Phyllis — Actress 2133
LANGE, Nicholas Theodore, PhD — Biostatistician, Educator 2134
LANGENBACH, Randolph — Sole Practitioner 2134
LANGER, Dennis H. — Pharmaceutical Company Executive, Board of Directors 721
LANGERMAN, Duane Lee — Construction Executive 2134
LANGEVIN, James, "Jim" R. — U.S. Representative from Rhode Island 2135
LANGFORD, Roland Everett — Owner 2135
LANGLEY, Lester D., PhD — Historian, Author 2135
LANKFORD, James Paul — U.S. Senator from Oklahoma 2135
LANNIE, Paul Anthony — Executive Vice President, General Counsel 722
LAPIERRE, Wayne R. Jr. — CEO 2135
LAQUATRA, Joseph Jr., PhD — Professor Emeritus 1536
LAQUERCIA, Thomas Michael — Trial Lawyer for Personal Injury Cases 2136
LARKIN, Michael — Choral and Orchestral Conductor, Composer, Educator 2136
LARRIMORE, Judith, "Judy" Rutledge, RN — Administrative Nursing 2136
LARSEN, Kimbert E. — Journalist 2136
LARSEN, Richard, "Rick" Ray — U.S. Representative from Washington 2137
LARSON, Brie — Actress 2137
LARSON, David, "Dave" Royal PhD, Mathematics Department — Mathematics Educator, Researcher 2137
LARSON, John Barry — U.S. Representative from Connecticut; Insurance Company Executive 2137
LARSON, Marilyn J. — Music Educator (Retired) 2137

LASKIN, Emma Jane — Medical Doctor 723
LASORDA, Tommy Charles — Former Professional Baseball Manager 2138
LATHROP, Kaye D., PhD — Nuclear Scientist, Educator 724
LATTA, George H. III, MD, MBA, FAAP, FACHE, CPE — Physician 2138
LATTA, Robert, "Bob" Edward — U.S. Representative from Ohio 2138
LATTIMORE, Steven, PhD — Classicist (Retired) 725
LAU, Vincent W., JD — Immigration Attorney 726
LAUDADIO, Fred, EdD — Executive Director of Learning Services and Technology 2138
LAUPER, Cyndi Ann Stephanie — Singer; Actress 2138
LAUREN, Ralph — Fashion Designer, Fashion Company Executive 2139
LAURENCE, Peter, "Pete" A., Broker Emeritus — Real Estate Broker 2139
LAURENCE, Richard Robert — History Educator 727
LAUTER, Richard S., JD — Partner 728
LAVIGNE, Robert James, PhD — Entomologist, Educator, Researcher 1536
LAWER, Betsy — Banker; Small Business Owner; Vintner; Director 729
LAWRENCE, Brenda Lulenar — U.S. Representative, Former Mayor 2139
LAWRENCE, Jennifer Schrader — Actress 2139
LAWRENCE, Lu — Photographer, Educator 2140
LAWRENCE, Merloyd — Editor 2140
LAWSON, Alfred, "Al" James Jr. — U.S. Representative from Florida Insurance Company Executive 2140
LAWSON, H. Blaine Jr., PhD — Mathematician, Educator 2140
LAWSON, Jack W. 2141
LAWSON, Pat, ND, CNHP, CCN, CRR — President 730
LAYTON, Donald Harvey — CEO 2141
LAZARUS, Sean, DPM — Podiatrist 1537
LAZERWITZ, Miles, DDS — Owner, Principal 2141
LAZO, Waleuska — President 2141
LE GRAND, Charles Heyward Sr., CIA, CISA — CEO 2141
LE GUIN, Ursula Kroeber — Author 2141
LE VINE, Duane Gilbert — Petroleum Company Executive 2142
LEAF, Dan — CEO 2142
LEAHY, Patrick Joseph — U.S. Senator from Vermont 2142
LEAMAN, Jack E., FASLA, FAICP — Landscape Architect, Community and Regional Planner 731
LEAR, Norman Milton — Producer, Writer, Director 2142
LEAVITT, Randy T, Attorney — Owner 2143
LEBLANG, Paul, PhD — Marketing Professional 732
LECISTON, David J. — Computer Engineer, Computer Scientist 733
LECLAIR, Susan J., PhD, CLS (NCA) — Chancellor Professor Emerita 734
LEE, Anne Lim — Chief, Cyber Architecture & Multi-Domain Command and Control Operations Lead 735
LEE, Barbara Jean — U.S. Representative from California 2143
LEE, Helen — Music Educator 2143
LEE, Jung-Lim, PhD — Associate Professor 736
LEE, Margaret — Music Educator 2143
LEE, Michael, "Mike" Shumway — U.S. Senator from Utah; Lawyer 2144
LEE, Richard, "Rich" Hoyt — Microscopist; Analyst (Retired) 2144
LEE, Ruth Davidson — Tax Collector (Retired) 2144
LEE, Spike — Film Producer, Director, Screenwriter 2144
LEE, Suzanne Marie — U.S. Representative from Nevada 2145
LEE, William Lamborn, PhD — Literature Educator 737
LEE, William, "Bill" Byron — Governor of Tennessee 2145
LEECH, Michael J. — Principal Lawyer 2145
LEFKOWITZ, Robert Joseph, MD — Physician; Professor 2145
LEGGETT, Anthony, "Tony" James — Professor Emeritus; Physics Researcher 2145
LEGRANGE, Ulyesse J., CPA — Oil Company Executive 2146
LEHAN, Richard D. — English Language Educator, Writer 2146
LEHRER, Jim Charles "Dean of Moderators" — Former News Anchor; Journalist 738

LEHTO, Alison Ragna — Middle School Educator 739
LEIBOVITZ, Anna-Lou, "Annie" — Photographer 2146
LEITE, Eduardo — Chairman Emeritus, Senior Partner 1537
LELAND, Harry V., PhD — Aquatic Ecologist (Retired) 740
LEMAHIEU, David, "D.J." John — Professional Baseball Player 2146
LEMANN, Thomas B. — Retired Lawyer 2146
LEMMA, Mulatu, "Mulle", PhD — Distinguished Professor of Mathematics 2147
LEMOINE, Frank Eugene — Judge, Lawyer 741
LEMOND, Sharon J. — President 742
LENARD, Mary Jane — Accounting Educator 2147
LENDARIS, George Gregory — Professor Emeritus of Systems Science and of Electrical & Computer Engineering 2147
LENG, Douglas Ellis, PhD — Research Fellow 743
LENK, Carla — President 2147
LENO, Jay Douglas Muir — Comedian; Former Television Personality 2148
LENT, John Anthony, PhD — Researcher, Educator, Author 744
LENTZ, Jacek — Asset Forfeiture Attorney 2148
LEON, Rigo — Artist 2148
LEONARD, Annie Louise — Executive Director 745
LEONARD, Ethan G. — Chief Medical Officer; Professor of Pediatrics 2148
LEONARD, Gilbert Stanley, BS, MS — Oil Company Executive 2149
LEONARD, Kawhi Anthony — Professional Basketball Player 2149
LEONE, Douglas M. — Global Managing Partner 2149
LEONE, Stephen Joseph — Deputy Secretary of Education, Commissioner for Libraries (Retired) 746
LEPKOWSKI, Matt J. — President/Business Automation Expert 747
LEPKOWSKI, Wilbert Charles "Wil" — Journalist 748
LEPOW, Martha, MD — Professor Emeritus of Pediatrics, Director of Division of Pediatric Infectious Disease 1538
LERMAN, Cathy Jackson — Lawyer 2149
LERNER, Leon Maurice, PhD — Professor Emeritus of Biochemistry 749
LERNER, Norman Conrad PhD, PE — Professor, President 2149
LESKO, Debra, "Debbie" Kay — U.S. Representative from Arizona 2150
LESLIE, W. Bruce, PhD — Distinguished Service History Professor 2150
LESTER, Gillian L.L. — Dean, Professor 2150
LESTER, Jonathan Tyler — Professional Baseball Player 2150
LETTERMAN, David Michael — Talk Show Host (Retired); Producer; Comedian; Writer 2150
LEUNG, Patrick — Doctor of Medicine 750
LEVENDOGLU-TUGAL, Oya — Professor, Medical Director 2151
LEVI-FALK, Natane W. — Orthopedist 751
LEVIN, Andrew, "Andy" Saul — U.S. Representative from Michigan 2151
LEVIN, Fredric Gerson — Lawyer 752
LEVIN, Michael, "Mike" Ted — U.S. Representative from California 2151
LEVINE, Adam Noah — Singer, Musician 2151
LEVINE, Alan Hillel — CEO 2151
LEVINE, Leonard — Attorney at Law 1538
LEVINESS, Thomas R. — President 1539
LEVITT, Stephan Hillyer — Anthropologist, Indologist 2151
LEVKOVA-LAMM, Innessa — Art Critic, Writer, Curator 2152
LEWIN, Sharyn — Director of Gynecologic Oncology 2152
LEWIS, Billie Jean — Retired Library Director 2152
LEWIS, Carl — Track and Field Athlete (Retired), Assistant Coach 2152
LEWIS, David Carleton, MD — Professor Emeritus, Donald G. Millar Distinguished Professor of Alcohol and Addiction Studies 1539
LEWIS, Gerald J. — Justice 753
LEWIS, John Robert — Georgia Congressman 754
LEWIS, Jonathan Joseph, MD, PhD — Surgeon, Biomedical Researcher, Oncologist 755
LEWIS, Paul Howard — Professor Emeritus 756
LEWIS, Perry — Investment Banker 2152

LEWITT, Miles — Engineer, Patented Inventor & Vice President 2153
LI, Ke, PhD — Professor 757
LI, ShinHwa, PhD, ME, MS — Product Manager 2153
LICK, Dale Wesley, PhD — Chairperson 2154
LICKONA, Thomas, PhD — Director, Professor Emeritus 2154
LIEBERMAN, Douglas Lionel — Instructional Designer, Screenwriter, Playwright 2154
LIEBMANN, George — Lawyer 2154
LIEN, Eric Jungchi, PhD — Professor Emeritus, Pharmacy 2155
LIENHART, David Arthur — Forensic Engineering Geologist 1540
LIESCH, Barry W., PhD — Music Educator 2155
LIEU, Ted W. — U.S. Representative from California 2155
LIGGINS-ROGERS, Sharron E., EdD — Founder, CEO; Consulting Executive Director 2155
LIGHT, Judith Ellen — Actress 2156
LIGHTHIZER, Robert Emmet — U.S. Trade Representative 2156
LIGHTNER, James Edward, PhD — Mathematics Educator 2157
LIGON, Marilyn, MD, FAAFP — Physician 758
LILIEN, Elliot — Secondary School Educator 2157
LILLIS, Patricia Prophit, DSN, PhD — Professor Emeritus 2157
LIM, Henry Chol — Biochemical Engineering Educator, Researcher 2157
LIMBAUGH, Rush Hudson III — Radio Talk Show Host 2157
LIN, Jenny — Chief Operating Officer, Board Director 2158
LIN, Kenneth C. — CEO 2158
LINCECUM, Tim Leroy — Professional Baseball Player (Retired) 2158
LINDBLAD, Richard Arthur, DrPH — Public Health Officer 2158
LINDHOLM, William Charles — Clergyman 759
LINDNER, Cynthia Ms. — Certified Hypnotherapist 2158
LINDSAY, Ray A. — Colonel (Retired); Executive 760
LINDSEY, Seth Mark — Lawyer (Retired) 2158
LINNEY, Laura Leggett — Actress 2159
LINNINGTON, Michael S. — CEO 2159
LINZEY, Verna May — Reverend 761
LIPINSKI, Daniel William, PhD — U.S. Representative from Illinois 2159
LIPINSKI, Tara Kristen — Professional Figure Skater (Retired), Sportscaster 2159
LIPSKY, Lester — Professor Emeritus 2159
LIPTON, James — Television Personality; Dean Emeritus; Actor; Author 762
LISSKA, Anthony Joseph, PhD — Maria Theresa Barney Chair in Philosophy, Professor 2159
LISTON, Jefferson — Lawyer 2160
LITCHFIELD, Jean Anne — Nurse 763
LITCHFIELD, John H., PhD — Adjunct Professor 764
LITHGOW, John Arthur — Actor 2160
LITTLE, Bradley, "Brad" Jay — Governor of Idaho 2161
LITTLE, R. Donald — Real Estate Entrepreneur 765
LITTLE, R. John John, PhD — President, Botanist 2161
LITTLEFIELD, Christina — Attorney 2161
LITTMAN, Baruch S. — Corporate Vice President of Development (Retired) 766
LITVAK, Marvin Mark, PhD — Physicist 2161
LIU, Elizabeth, MD, PhD — President 767
LIU, Paul Y. — Plastic Surgeon, Educator 2161
LOCKHART, Verdree Sr., PhD — Professional Counselor (Retired) 768
LOCKWOOD, Frances Mann PhD — Clinical Psychologist 2162
LODI, Umbreen S. — Assistant Professor 2162
LOEBSACK, David, "Dave" Wayne, PhD — U.S. Representative from Iowa; Former Political Science Professor 2162
LOEWEN, Heidi — Artist, Gallery Owner, Teacher 769
LOEWENHARDT, Pauline Maria, MSN — Community Nursing Coordinator 2162
LOFGREN, Susan, "Zoe" Ellen — U.S. Representative from California 2163

LOGAN, Thomas — Computer Scientist, Consultant 2163
LOMBARDI, Frederick — Lawyer 2163
LONCHYNA-LISOWSKY, Maria, MMus, Music Educator, Pianist — Music Educator 2164
LONG, David H. — Chairman, President, and CEO 2164
LONG, Donlin Martin, PhD — Surgeon; Researcher; Educator 2164
LONG, Michael J. — Chairman, President, and CEO 2165
LONG, Thad Gladden — Lawyer 2165
LONG, William B. — Administrator 2165
LONG, William, "Billy" Hollis II — U.S. Representative from Missouri 2165
LOOMIS, James Cook — Mathematician; Cyberneticist; Writer; Educator; Navigator 2165
LOPER, Kathryn — Director of Special Events & International Tours 1540
LOPEZ, Jennifer, "J.Lo." Lynn — Actress, Singer, Dancer 2165
LOREN, Sophia — Actress 2166
LORENZEN, Robert Frederick, MD — Ophthalmologist 2166
LORING, John — Design Director Emeritus; Artist; Author 2166
LORNE, Simon M. — Vice Chairman, Chief Legal Officer 2167
LOSH, Samuel Johnston — President 770
LOTT, Dolores M., EdD — School System Administrator (Retired) 2167
LOTT, Marjorie — Accountant 771
LOUDERMILK, Barry Dean — U.S. Representative from Georgia 2167
LOUGANIS, Greg Efthimios — Former Professional Diver 2168
LOUIS-DREYFUS, Julia Scarlett Elizabeth — Actress; Comedian 2168
LOUNSBERRY, Gary Richard, PhD, MPH, ACSW — Professor Emeritus, Public Health Official (Retired) 772
LOVATO, Demi Devonne — Singer, Actress 2168
LOVELACE, Byron Keith, PhD, JD — Lawyer, Management Consultant 773
LOVELL, James Arthur Jr. — Astronaut (Retired) 2168
LOW, Gilbert Irvine — Lawyer 2169
LOWENTHAL, Alan Stuart — U.S. Representative from California 2169
LOWEY, Nita Sue — U.S. Representative from New York; Chair of the House Committee on Appropriations 2169
LOWRIE, Yvonne — Artist, Educator, Volunteer 2169
LOWRY, Eugene L. — Theological Educator 2170
LOWRY, Glenn David — Director 2170
LU, Mi, PhD — Professor; Computer Engineer 1541
LUA, Oscar — Partner; Former Professional Football Player 1541
LUBETZKY, Daniel — Founder, CEO; Philanthropist 774
LUCAS, Frank Dean — U.S. Representative from Oklahoma 2170
LUCAS, George Walton Jr. — Film Director, Producer, Screenwriter 775
LUCAS, Lenell Jr., Owner — Accountant (Retired); Inventor 2170
LUCAS, Robert Emerson Jr., PhD — Economist; Professor Emeritus 2171
LUCAS, Robert J. — Founder, Owner 776
LUCERO, Chelsea R., LPCC, LADAC, NCC — Behavioral Health Manager 2171
LUCIANO, Juan Ricardo — Chairman, President, CEO 2171
LUDWIG, Logan T., PhD, FMLA — Former Deputy Supreme Knight, Assoc. Provost, Consultant 777
LUETKEMEYER, William, "Blaine" Blaine — U.S. Representative 2171
LUJAN, Ben Ray Jr. — U.S. Representative from New Mexico; Assistant Speaker of the U.S. House of Representatives 2171
LUJÁN, Ben Ray Sr. — Former U.S. Representative from New Mexico 2171
LUNA, Rene Immanuel, MD, FACOG — Director Robotics, OB/GYN 778
LUND, Lisa — Owner/Broker 779
LUNSETH, John B. II — Shareholder 780
LUNSFORD, Rachel — Partner 2171
LUO, Yixiao — Professor, Researcher 781
LUPONE, Patti Ann — Actress; Singer 2172
LURIA, Elaine — U.S. Representative from Virginia 2172
LUTHER, David B. — Management Consultant (Retired) 2172
LUTTRELL, Cynthia, "Cyndi" R.F. — IT Specialist 2173

LY, Leanne — Managing Director 782
LYMAN, David, Esq. — Chairman, Chief Values Officer 783
LYNCH, Bob David — Retired Business Agent 2173
LYNCH, David Keith — Film Producer; Director; Screenwriter 2173
LYNCH, Stephen Francis — U.S. Representative from Massachusetts 2173
LYNCH, Stephen — Editor-in-Chief 2173
LYND, Melody — Plastic Surgeon 784
LYNE, Stephen R., PhD — Ambassador, Professor 785
LYNN, Kenny E. — Owner 786
LYNN, Loretta Webb — Singer 2173
LYTLE, Michael A. — Forensic Criminologist, Consultant 2174
LYYTINEN, Kalle J. — Iris S. Wolstein Professor of Management Design 787
MA, Alan W. C. JD, MBA — Lawyer 2174
MA, Shan-lyn — CEO 2174
MABRY, Cathy Darlene — Retired Elementary School Administrator 788
MACARTHUR, Thomas, "Tom" Charles — Former U.S. Representative 2174
MACCRACKEN, Thomas Gregg, PhD — Musicologist, Independent Scholar 2175
MACDIARMID, Alan Graham, PhD — Chemist; Professor 2175
MACDONALD, Karen — Occupational Therapist, Geriatrics Services Professional 2175
MACDOUGALL, Priscilla Ruth — Lawyer 789
MACHANN, Clinton J. — English Educator 2175
MACK, Khalil Delshon — Professional Football Player 2175
MACKEY, Aaron K., MEd — Superintendent (Retired) 2175
MACKEY, John P. — CEO 2175
MACKEY, William Arthur Godfrey — Director of Finance & Administration 2175
MACKIEWICZ, John Stanley, PhD — Distinguished Teaching Professor Emeritus 1542
MACLAINE, Shirley — Actress 2176
MACLEOD, John — Lawyer (Retired) 1542
MACLIN, Arlene Paige — Program Director 2176
MACNEIL, Robert, "Robin" Breckenridge Ware — Journalist, Writer (Retired) 2177
MACQUEEN, Cherie K. — Radio & TV Broadcaster; Interior Designer 790
MACY, William Hall Jr. — Actor 2177
MADDEN, John Earl — Former Sportscaster; Former Professional Football Coach 2178
MADDEN, John — Lawyer 2177
MADDON, Joe John Jr. — Professional Baseball Manager 2178
MADDOW, Rachel Anne — Television and Radio Personality; Political Commentator 1543
MADDREY, Willis Crocker, MD, MACP, FRCP — Professor of Internal Medicine 791
MADDUX, Greg Alan — Professional Sports Team Executive; Professional Baseball Player (Retired) 2178
MADERO, Blanche Vergobbi — Retired Nurse, Administrator 2178
MADIRAJU, Durga, Senior Software Engineer — Senior Software Engineer 2178
MAESAKA, John Kazuaki, MD — Nephrologist, Professor of Medicine 792
MAGILL, Mary, "M." Elizabeth — Executive Vice President, Provost, Professor of Law 2179
MAGSIG, Judith A — Retired Primary School Educator 2179
MAGUIRE, Joseph — Acting Director of National Intelligence; Director of the National Counterterrorism Center 2179
MAGUIRE, Robert Wyman — Publisher 793
MAGUIRE, Tobey Vincent — Actor 2179
MAHAN, Mary Hoyle, EdD — Physical Educator, Athletics Administrator (Retired) 1543
MAHER, Bill — Political Commentator; Television Personality; Comedian 2179
MAHMUD, Shireen D. — Photographer/Photojournalist 2180

MAHOMES, Patrick Lavon II — Professional Football Player   2180

MAIN, Amanda M., PhD — Associate Professor of Management and Academic Program Coordinator for Social Entrepreneurship, Social Innovation and Business Administration   2180

MAITLAND, Gary — Partner   2181

MAKRICOSTAS, Dean George — Lawyer   794

MAKRIDES, Lydia, MCSP, BPT, MSc, PhD — President, Blogger; Global Wellness Head   2181

MALAIHOLLO, Natasia — Head of Business Development; Co-founder, Former CEO   2181

MALASPINA, Alex, PhD — Soft Drink Company Executive   2181

MALEK, Marlene — Foundation Administrator   2181

MALHOTRA, Deepak, MD, PhD — Nephrologist   795

MALININ, Theodore — Professor Emeritus of Orthopaedics   2181

MALINOWSKI, Tomasz, "Tom" P. — U.S. Representative from New Jersey   2182

MALKOVICH, John Gavin — Actor   2182

MALONE, John D., MD, MPH — Infectious Diseases Physician Scientist   2182

MALONE, Karl Anthony — Professional Basketball Coach; Former Professional Basketball Player   2182

MALONEY, Carolyn Jane — U.S. Representative from New York   2182

MALONEY, Sean Patrick — U.S. Representative from New York; Lawyer   2183

MANAKTALA, Alka — Vice President   796

MANCHIN, Joseph, "Joe" III — U.S. Senator from West Virginia; Former Governor of West Virginia   2183

MANDERSCHEID, Ronald, PhD — Executive Director   797

MANFRED, Robert D. Jr. — Commissioner   798

MANGUS, Carl William — Technical Safety and Standards Consultant, Engineer   799

MANHOLD, John H. — Dental Educator, Consultant   2183

MANILLA, Jack — Author, Contractor, Entrepreneur, Educator   2183

MANIMTIM, Winston Mendoza, MD, FAAP — Neonatologist   800

MANLEY, Edward, "Ed" Harry Jr. — Owner, Food Safety and Management Trainer; Professional Association Administrator; Veteran's Charity Founder   2184

MANN, Frank Bert — Artist, Educator, Writer   801

MANN, Noel R., PhD — Professor   2184

MANNICK, John, MD — Surgeon   2185

MANNING, John F. — Dean; Professor   2185

MANNING, Peyton Williams — Former Professional Football Player   2185

MANOUGIAN, Edward — Physician (Retired)   802

MANSELL, Kevin B. — Chairman, President, and CEO   2185

MANSFIELD, William A. — Lawyer   2185

MANSOLILLO, Charles Ronald, Esq. — Lawyer   2186

MANTEL, Linda Habas, PhD   2186

MANTERFIELD, Eric A. — Banker; Law Educator; Lawyer (Retired)   2186

MARANO, Lori A. — Partner   803

MARCHANT, Kenny Ewell — U.S. Representative   2187

MARCHETTA, Justin — Partner   1544

MARCU, Len — Owner   2187

MARCUS, Craig Brian — Lawyer   804

MARGO, Rod David, DCL, LLB — Lawyer (Retired)   805

MARGULIES, Julianna Luisa — Actress   2187

MARGULIES, Stanley Ira — Radiologist   2187

MARINO, Thomas, "Tom" Anthony — Former U.S. Representative from Pennsylvania; Former Federal Prosecutor   2187

MARK, Arthur — Emeritus Professor of Teacher Education   2188

MARK, Marion, EdD — Writing Educator   806

MARKEY, Edward, "Ed" John — U.S. Senator from Massachusetts   2188

MARKLEY, Lynn McMaster — Rubber and Plastics Company Executive   807

MARONE, Richard Anthony, Esq. — Partner   2188

MARQUARDT, Michele C. — Founding Member   808

MARQUIS, Barbara S., RN, BS — Maternal and Women's Health Nurse   2188

MARREN, Howard Leslie — Composer   1544

MARROW, Tracy, "Ice-T" Lauren — Rap Artist; Actor   2188

MARS, Bruno, — Singer, Songwriter, Music Producer   2189

MARSH, Robert Buford — Chemical Engineer, Consultant   2189

MARSHALL, C. Travis — Telecommunications Executive, Government Relations Specialist   809

MARSHALL, Elizabeth Eileen — Cultural Organization Administrator, Teacher   810

MARSHALL, Jo Taylor, MSW, LCSW, ACSW — Social Worker   811

MARSHALL, Roger Wayne, MD — U.S. Representative from Kansas   2189

MARSHALL, Sheila, LLB — Lawyer   812

MARSHALL, Vincent dePaul, PhD — Microbiologist   2189

MARTER, Joan M., PhD — Distiguished Professor Emerita, Art Critic and Curator   2190

MARTIN, Calia Marsai — Producer, Actress   2190

MARTIN, Dan Merrill, PhD — Foundation Executive (Retired)   1545

MARTIN, Dennis Charles, DDS — Dentist   813

MARTIN, George Raymond Richard — Author   2190

MARTIN, Hulbert, "Hugh" — Author, Educator, Investment Advisor, Life Guide   2191

MARTIN, Jerry Wayne — Family Physician (Retired)   2191

MARTIN, Joseph Leonard — Business, Real Estate Investor, Educator   2192

MARTIN, Mirta Maruri — President   2192

MARTIN, Paula J. — Executive Director   2193

MARTIN, Steve Glenn — Actor; Comedian; Musician   2193

MARTIN, Thomas J., MD — Pediatrician   2193

MARTIN, William C. Sr. — Hospital Administrator (Retired)   814

MARTIN-DAVIS, Juanita V. — Retired Elementary School Educator   815

MARTINEZ, Bonita — Attorney-at-Law   1545

MARTINEZ, Dave — Manager   2194

MARTINEZ, Jerry   816

MARTINEZ, Pedro Jaime — Sportscaster; Former Professional Baseball Player   2194

MARTINEZ, Roman IV — Investment Banker, Board Member (Retired)   2194

MARTINSON, Doris Ann — Archivist, Manger   2194

MARTY, Sandra Joy Del Corso — Nursing Administrator   2194

MARUOKA, JoAnn Elizabeth — Retired Information Systems Manager   817

MARVIN, Karen — Owner   2195

MARX, Anthony William "Tony" — President and CEO; Former Academic Administrator   1546

MASKIN, Eric Stark, PhD — Professor of Economics and Mathematics   2195

MASLAND, Lynne — University Official (Retired)   2195

MASOTTI, Louis Henry, PhD — Professor Emeritus   818

MASSIE, Thomas Harold — U.S. Representative from Kentucky; Farmer   2195

MAST, Brian Jeffery — U.S. Representative from Florida   2195

MATERNA, Joseph Anthony, Esq — Attorney   819

MATHAS, Theodore A. — Chairman, President, CEO   2195

MATHAVAN, Sudershan Kumar "Matt" — Principal Engineer   820

MATHER, John Cromwell, PhD — Senior Scientist; Astrophysicist   2196

MATHERNE, Ray, "Doc" Joseph — Educational Administrator; Real Estate Developer   2196

MATHERS, Marshall (Eminem) — Rap Artist, Producer   2196

MATHES, Edward C. — Chairman   2196

MATHEWSON, Christopher C., PE, PG — Engineer; Geologist; Educator   821

MATSUI, Doris Kazue — U.S. Representative   2197

MATSUMURA, Molleen — Educational Organization Executive   822

MATTHEW, Thomas Lewis, MD — Director   2197

MATTHEWS, Chris John — Former Political Commentator; Author   2197

MATTHIAS, John, Emeritus Professor, American Poet — English Literature Educator   2197

MATTONE, Joseph Michael — Real Estate Developer, Attorney   823

MATTOS, Dana Jon — Owner, Manager   2198
MATTSON, Janet Marie — Contracting Officer, Microbiologist   2198
MATTSON, Maureen, "Mo" — Physical Education Teacher   2198
MATTY, Vera Anna — Public Speaker in Washington Senate   2198
MAURER, Frank W., PhD — Land Trust Administrator   2199
MAXWELL, Richard A. — Retail Executive   1546
MAY, Joseph, "Jack" L. — Lawyer, Manufacturer of Socks   2199
MAY, Rebecca, "Becky" Shrum, NCTM, ACM — Piano Educator   2199
MAYER, Daniella — Partner   2199
MAYER, Marion Sidney, PhD — Research Entomologist   2199
MAYES, Glenn Howard, LCSW, ACSW, QCSW, DCSW, BCD, CPHQ, —
    Licensed Clinical Social Worker   2200
MAYNE, Thom — Principal; Architect   2200
MAYOPOULOS, Timothy J. — CEO, President   2201
MAYOR, Michel Gustave Edouard, PhD — Professor Emeritus;
    Astrophysicist   1547
MAYS, Willie Howard Jr. — Former Professional Baseball Player   2201
MAYTHAM, Thomas — Art and Museum Consultant   2201
MAZIE, Deonka — Coordinator   2201
MAZO, Robert Marc — Professor Emeritus   2201
MAZUR, Sherri — Attorney   2201
MCADAM, Lowell Clayton — Chairman and CEO (Retired)   2202
MCADAMS, Benjamin, "Ben" Michael — U.S. Representative from Utah   2202
MCAULIFFE, Rosemary, Esq — Lawyer   824
MCBATH, Lucia, "Lucy" Kay — U.S. Representative from Georgia   2202
MCBRIDE, Joanne, ABR, GRI — Realtor   1547
MCBRIDE, Martina Mariea — Singer, Songwriter   2202
MCBRIDE, William Leon, PhD — Philosopher   825
MCCANN, Lawrence A. "Larry" — Music Educator, Church Musician   826
MCCARTHY, Kevin Bart — Lawyer   2202
MCCARTHY, Kevin Owen — U.S. Representative from California, House
    Minority Leader   2202
MCCARTHY, Melissa Ann — Actress   2202
MCCARTHY, Robert — Physics Professor, Researcher   1548
MCCARTNEY, James Robert, MD — Psychiatrist   2203
MCCARTNEY, Paul — Singer, Songwriter, Musician   827
MCCAUL, Michael Thomas Sr. — U.S. Representative from Texas; Lawyer   2203
MCCLANAHAN, Judy Carol — County Administrator   2203
MCCLANAHAN, Preston Moore III — Artist, Educator   828
MCCLEARY, Monica Jean, RN, CNM, MSN — Certified Nurse Midwife
    (Retired)   2203
MCCLINTOCK, Thomas, "Tom" Miller II — U.S. Representative from
    California   2203
MCCLURE, Alvin Bruce — President   2203
MCCOLLOUGH, Bill — President, CEO   829
MCCOLLOUGH, Carol Keeney — Academic Administrator   2204
MCCOLLUM, Betty Louise — U.S. Representative from Minnesota   2204
MCCOLLUM, Bill — Lawyer; Former State Attorney General;
    Former United States Representative from Florida   830
MCCONATHY, Walter James, PhD — Biochemist   2204
MCCONAUGHEY, Matthew David — Actor   2204
MCCONKIE, George Wilson, PhD — Professor Emeritus   2205
MCCONNELL, Addison "Mitch" Jr. — U.S. Senator from Kentucky;
    Lawyer   831
MCCORD, Don Lewis — Surgeon (Retired)   832
MCCORMICK, William Frederick, MD — Forensic Pathologist,
    Neuropathologist   833
MCCOURT, Peter J. II, Deacon — President, CEO   2205
MCCOY, William James, PE — Electrical Engineer; Consultant   1548
MCCRACKEN, Robert Dale — Anthropologist, Writer   2205
MCCRAY, Mark — Vice President of Programming and Operations   2205
MCCULLAGH, Grant Gibson Sr. — Managing Director   2206

MCCULLAR, Caia Kent — Professor of Music, Program Director of
    Music Education   834
MCCURDY, Robert Layton, MD — Dean Emeritus   2206
MCCURRY, Margaret I., FAIA, FIIDA — Architect, Furniture & Interior
    Designer; Educator   2206
MCCUTCHEON, Steven C., PhD — Ecological and Environmental
    Engineer, Hydrologist   2207
MCDANIEL, Ronna — Chair   2207
MCDONALD, Jane A., EdD — Associate Professor   835
MCDONALD, Malcolm W. — Real Estate Company Executive (Retired)   836
MCDONALD, Sharon Holliday — Special Education Educator (Retired)   837
MCDONOUGH, John R. — Retired Cardiologist   2207
MCDORMAND, Frances Louise — Actress   2207
MCEACHERN, William D., JD, LLM — Novelist   838
MCEACHIN, Aston, "Donald" Donald — U.S. Representative from
    Virginia   2207
MCELVEEN, Joseph James Jr. — Journalist, Writer, Newscaster,
    Educator   2208
MCENROE, John Patrick Jr. — Former Professional Tennis Player   2208
MCENTIRE, Reba Nell — Singer; Musician; Actress   2208
MCEWIN, Aaron — Director of Sustainability   2209
MCFADDEN, Daniel Little, PhD — Professor Emeritus; Professor of
    Economics   2209
MCGARRY, Michael — Chairman, CEO   2209
MCGEACHIN, Robert Bruce — Academic Librarian, Educator   2209
MCGEE, John P. Jr., Esq. — Lawyer   839
MCGEE, Sue, RN, MSN — Pediatrics Nurse, Educator,
    Administrator (Retired)   840
MCGINNIS, Richard Provis, PhD — Chemical Educator   2209
MCGOVERN, Alicia — Financial Adviser   2210
MCGOVERN, Gail J. — President, CEO   2210
MCGOVERN, James, "Jim" Patrick — U.S. Representative from
    Massachusetts   2210
MCGOWAN, Jon G., PhD — Mechanical Engineer, Educator   2210
MCGRAW, Tim — Musician; Actor   2210
MCGREGOR, Conor Anthony — Professional Boxer,
    Former Professional Mixed Martial Artist   2211
MCGREGOR, Ewan Gordon — Actor   2211
MCGREGOR, John M., MD — Associate Professor   2211
MCGUFFIE, Linda Marie — Chief Operating Officer   1549
MCGUIRE, John — Partner   1549
MCGUIRE, Megan, Esq. — Attorney; Associate Attorney   1550
MCHARGUE, Carl J., PhD — Educator   2211
MCHENRY, Debra Colleen — Ironworker   2212
MCHENRY, Patrick Timothy — U.S. Representative from North Carolina   2212
MCHUGH, Peter Chadwick, Academic/Research Consortium —
    Director, FAA and Aeronautics Programs   2212
MCILROY, Rory, MBE — Professional Golfer   2212
MCINTOSH, Carolyn — Librarian (Retired)   2212
MCINTURFF, Alfred Don — Physicist   1550
MCINTYRE, J. Lawrence — Lawyer   841
MCKECHNIE, C. Logan — Lawyer   2213
MCKEE, Ann — Chief Neuropathologist   842
MCKENNA, Andrew J. — Wholesale Distribution, Printing Company
    Executive   843
MCKENZIE, Kevin Patrick — Artistic Director   2213
MCKINLEY, David Bennett — U.S. Representative, Civil Engineer   2213
MCKISSICK, Michael Landon — Transportation Consultant (Retired)   2213
MCKNIGHT, John Lacy — Professor Emeritus of Physics   844
MCLARTY, Greg — Drama Instructor   2213
MCLAUGHLIN, Clara — Owner, Publisher   845

MCLEAN, Cari — Dance Studio Owner, Competition Judge, Master Teacher 2213

MCLELLAN, John Sidney — Judge 2214

MCLEOD, James — Minister; Author; Teacher 846

MCLEOD, James R. — Language Educator (Retired) 2214

MCLEOD, Walton James III — Lawyer, Former State Legislator, Businessman 847/2214

MCMAHON, Linda Marie — Administrator (Retired) 2214

MCMAKIN, Joseph Hamilton "Joe" — Chemical 848

MCMANUS, John William — Associate Professor 2215

MCMANUS, Michael — Vice Chairman 1551

MCMANUS, Richard P. — Lawyer, Agricultural Products Executive 2215

MCMASTER, Henry Dargan — Governor of South Carolina 2215

MCMASTER, Herbert, "H.R." Raymond — U.S. National Security Adviser (Retired) 2216

MCMILLAN, Mae Frances, MD — Child Psychiatrist 1551

MCMILLAN, Robert Walker, PhD — Physicist; Consultant 2216

MCMILLON, Carl, "Doug" Douglas — Retail Company Executive 2216

MCMORRIS RODGERS, Cathy Anne — U.S. Representative from Washington 2216

MCMULLEN, Rodney — Chairman, CEO 849

MCNAB, Brian K., PhD — Professor Emeritus 2216

MCNAIR, Robert, "Bob" C. — Chairman, CEO, Owner 2216

MCNEALL, Peter Ian — Systems Engineer (Retired) 2217

MCNERNEY, Gerald, "Jerry" Mark — U.S. Representative from California; Engineer 2217

MCNULTY, Kathleen A., PhD — Clinical Psychologist, Teacher, Mentor 2217

MCPARTLAND, Thomas Joseph, PhD — Director (Retired) 850

MCPHAIL, Lawrence "Larry" — Executive Director 851

MCPHERSON, Alice R. — Ophthalmology Department 852

MCQUARRIE, Irvine G. "Irv", MD, PhD — Associate Professor; Neurosurgeon; Financier 1552

MCREYNOLDS, John W. — President 2217

MCSALLY, Martha Elizabeth — U.S. Senator from Arizona 2217

MCSHANE, Lawrence Edward 2217

MCWHORTER, Sharon Louise — President 853

MEADOR, Jo — Author; Teacher; Speaker 2218

MEADOWS, Grady Millidge — President 2218

MEADOWS, Mark Randall — U.S. Representative from North Carolina 2218

MEARS, Rick Ravon — Professional Race Car Driver (Retired) 2218

MEAUX, Alan — Facilities Technician, Artist, Bronze Sculptor 2219

MECIAS-MURPHY, Annie — Co-Owner, President 854

MEDIN, Julia A., PhD — Mathematics Professor, Researcher 2219

MEDVECKY, Robert S., Esq. — Lawyer 2219

MEEKS, Donna M. — Professor and Chair 2219

MEEKS, Gregory Weldon — U.S. Representative from New York 2219

MEIER, Deborah 2219

MEIR, Jessica Ulrika — Astronaut 1552

MEISELS, Gerhard George, PhD — Academic Administrator, Chemist, Educator 2220

MELIN, Arthur, "Art" Walden, Income Maintenance Specialist — Auditor, Income Maintenance Specialist 2220

MELLINGER, Regina G. — President, CEO 1553

MELTON, Jean Edith — Retired Elementary Education Educator 855

MELTZER, David Sumo — Owner 1242

MENDE, Howard Shigeharu — Mechanical Engineer 856

MENDELSON, Michael Drew — Writer, Novelist 857

MENDES, Shawn Peter Raul — Singer 2220

MENDIOLA, Patricia — Associate Professor in Practice 2220

MENEAR, Craig Albert — CEO and President 2220

MENEFEE, Samuel P., JD — Lawyer, Academic 2220

MENENDEZ, Robert, "Bob" — U.S. Senator from New Jersey; Lawyer 2221

MENG, Grace — U.S. Representative from New York; Lawyer 2221

MENZIES, Carl S., PhD — Agriculturist, Researcher, Nutritionist 2222

MERANI, Peter C., Esq. — Principal Partner 858

MERCER, Evelyn Lois Robinson — Counseling Administrator 2222

MERCER, Rebekah — Foundation Director 2222

MERCHANT, Carolyn, PhD — Professor Emerita 859

MEREDITH, Keith E., PhD — Academic Administrator, Educator (Retired) 860

MERKLEY, Jeffrey, "Jeff" Alan — U.S. Senator from Oregon 2222

MERLO, Larry J. — CEO and President 2222

MERRELL, Richard G. — Electronics Systems Engineer (Retired) 2222

MERRILL, Frank Harrison — Contract Developer; Software Developer 1553

MERRITT, Marytherese — Geologist; Industry Analyst 2223

MERRY, Tony C. — Owner 861

MERSHON, Jerry L. — Retired Judge 2223

MERTON, Robert Cox, PhD — Economist, Professor 2223

MESSENGER, Tony — Columnist 2224

MESSIER, Mark Douglas — Retired Professional Hockey Player 2224

MESSINA, Maggie Cole — 1) Owner, Master Instructor 2) Founder 862

MESSING, Debra Lynn — Actress 2224

METAFERIA, Getachew, PhD — Political Science Educator 2224

METCALF, Laurie Elizabeth — Actress 2224

METER, Karen — Music Educator (Retired); Veterans Advocate 2225

METZGER, James Borchard — Partner 2225

MEUSER, Daniel, "Dan" P. — U.S. Representative from Pennsylvania 2225

MEYER, Benny Lee — Systems Engineer, Manager 2225

MEYER, Danny — Founder, CEO, Restaurateur 2225

MEYER, Darla A., CPA — Accountant 2226

MEYER, Edmond, PhD — Professor Emeritus of Chemistry; Academic Administrator 2226

MEYER, Frances Anthony, PhD, CHES — Executive Director 863

MEYER, Jack E., MD — Radiologist, Educator 2226

MEYER, Mara — Educational Consultant 2226

MEYER, Paul J. — Owner 2227

MEYER, Robert Eugene — Owner 864

MEYER, Steven John — Development and Investments Officer 2227

MEYERS, David W. — Lawyer, Writer, Educator 2228

MEYERS, Mark — Executive Director 2228

MEYERS, Seth Adam — Television Host; Actor; Writer, Television Producer; Comedian 2228

MICHAEL, George C — Advertising and Public Relations Executive 2228

MICHAEL, Maggie — Journalist 2228

MICHAELIS, Karen L., PhD, JD — Law Educator 2228

MICHAELS, Kevin Richard — Attorney 865

MICHAELS, Lorne — Television Producer 2229

MICHALSKI, Patty — Executive Editor 2229

MICHELETTI, Gildo A. — Dermatologist 866

MICHELSON, Louis — Attorney 2229

MICHROWSKI, Eric — President, CEO 867

MICKEL, Emanuel John, PhD — Professor Emeritus 2229

MICKEL, Ronald Eldon, PhD — Historian, Educator 868

MICKLOS, Janet Mae — County Agency Administrator (Retired); Human Services Director 869

MIDDLETON, Reece MA — Addictions Treatment Executive, Retired 2229

MIDLER, Bette — Singer, Actress 2230

MIDYETT, Sarah Overstreet, Owner — Author (Retired) 2230

MIERA, Lucille Catherine — Artist, Educator, Engineering Draftsman 870

MIGNONE, Madeline — Biology Professor 2230

MIHALIK, Colin, DDS, MS — Board-Certified Orthodontist 2231

MIKES, Judith Pauline, MEd — Director 2231

MIKKELSON, Ruth Lynn, PhD — Mathematics Educator (Retired) 2232

MILES, Bradley Robert — Rancher, Construction and Design Consultant 2232
MILES, Joanna — Actress 871
MILLER, Aaron L. — Owner & Manager 872
MILLER, Andrew Pickens — Attorney (Retired) 873
MILLER, Beverly, RN, MSN, GNP-C, APRN, BC — Geriatric Nurse Practitioner (Retired) 874
MILLER, Carol — U.S. Representative from West Virginia 2232
MILLER, Carolyn A. — Nurse Midwife, Educator 875
MILLER, Charles E., MD — Gynecologist 876
MILLER, DeAnna — Superintendent 2232
MILLER, Dwight Merrick — Senior Archivist, Historian 2232
MILLER, E. Joan, PhD — Geography Educator 2232
MILLER, Jeff — Chairman, President, and CEO 2233
MILLER, Linda B., PhD — Political Scientist 2233
MILLER, Linda Ellen — Museum Administrator; Education Expert 2233
MILLER, Linda Karen, EdD — Educator (Retired) 877
MILLER, Lori — Humanities Educator 1554
MILLER, Melody Jean — Senior Aide, Kennedy Family Spokesperson (Retired) 2233
MILLER, Michael G. — Purchasing Management 2233
MILLER, Philip Nicholson — Engineering and Technology Educator; Consultant 2233
MILLER, Pringl Lee, MD, FACS — General Surgeon, Hospice and Palliative Medicine Specialist, Clinical Medical Ethicist 2234
MILLER, Robert G. — CEO 2234
MILLER, Ronald H., PhD — President 878
MILLER, Sarabeth — Secondary School Educator (Retired) 2234
MILLER, Stephen Ralph, JD — Lawyer 879
MILLER, Stephen — Senior Adviser to the President 2235
MILLER, Vel — Artist 2235
MILLHAM, Charles Blanchard, PhD — Mathematician, Environmental Scientist, Educator 880
MILLIGAN, Tara L. — Assistant Clinical Professor 1554
MILLS, David L., PhD — Electrical Engineer 2235
MILLS, Elizabeth "Betsy" — Art Educator 1555
MILLS, Janet Trafton — Governor of Maine 2235
MILNER, Charles, "Monty" Fremont Jr. — Manufacturing Executive 2235
MILONAS, Herodotos Minos, MFA — Artist, Poet 2235
MINAJ, Nicki — Rap Artist 2236
MINARD, James "Jim", PhD — Psychologist, Associate Professor, Research Chief 1555
MINGE, Joan A. — Senior Project Manager 2236
MINKEL, Herbert P. Jr. — Lawyer 2236
MINNELLI, Liza May — Singer; Actress 2236
MINOR, John David — Physician 881
MINOR, Robert Lynn — Lawyer, Military Officer, Court Executive 2237
MINSHEW, Kathryn — Founder, CEO 2237
MINTER, Alan Huntress, JD — Lawyer 882
MINYARD, Blair — Mechanical Engineer 2237
MIRAMS, William C. — Construction Executive 883
MIRANDA, Lin-Manuel — Composer, Actor, Producer, Playwright 2237
MIRIPOL, Jerilyn — Poet, Writer, Writing Therapist; Pianist 2237
MIRREN, Helen Lydia — Actress 1556
MIRZA, Leona Lousin, EdD — Mathematics Statistics Professor 884
MISIEK, Dale J., DMD — Professor 2238
MISTRETTA, Dawn T., JD — Partner 1556
MITCHELL, David Vokes 885
MITCHELL, Jere Holloway, MD — Cardiovascular and Exercise Physiologist 886
MITCHELL, Paul III — U.S. Representative from Michigan 2238
MITCHELL, Robert — Founder 2238

MITTY, Harold A. MD — Radiologist 2238
MIXSON, Imogene Mathison, PhD — Academic Dean (Retired) 887
MIYAMOTO, Richard T., MD — Otolaryngologist 2239
MNUCHIN, Steven Terner — U.S. Secretary of the Treasury 888
MOBLEY, Jonniepat, PhD — Theater Director, Professor 2239
MOCHAN, Karen — Secondary School Educator 889
MOCK, Robert Claude — Architect 2239
MODICA, Ippolito — Site Director of Anatomic Pathology 2239
MOESSNER, David P., Dr.theol — A.A. Bradford Chair of Religion 2239
MOGUL, Harriette Rosen, BA, MD, MPH — Endocrinologist; Author 2240
MOHAMMED WOODS, Mario, — Founder, CEO 2240
MOHEN, Jacqueline C. — Research Fellow 890
MOIR, Ralph Wayne — Physicist 2240
MOKULIS, Paula — Director, Visual Information Directorate 891
MOLIÈRE, John — Chairman 2240
MOLINA, Mario Jose, PhD — Founder; Physical Chemist; Professor 1557
MOLLIGAN, Peter Nicholas — Lawyer 2241
MOLNAR, Robyn L. — Registered Nurse 2241
MOLTON, Peter M., PhD, — Waste Conversion Researcher, Consultant 2241
MOMJIAN, Mark Albert — Lawyer 2241
MOMOA, Joseph Jason — Actor 2241
MONDALE, Walter, "Fritz" Frederick — Former Vice President of the U.S.; Lawyer 2241
MONDELLO, Mark T. — CEO 2242
MONTANA, Joe Clifford Jr. — Former Professional Football Player 2242
MONTGOMERY, Denise Karen RN, RN — Nurse, Office Administration 2242
MONTGOMERY, J. Paul — Foundation Administrator 892
MONTGOMERY, John Richard, MD — Pediatrician 893
MONTGOMERY, Will — CEO 894
MONTOOTH, Minerva Houston — Coordinator of Social Events 1557
MOOK, Sarah — Chemist (Retired) 2242
MOOLENAAR, John Robert — U.S. Representative from Michigan 2242
MOON, Peter S. — Librarian (Retired) 2243
MOONEY, Alexander, "Alex" Xavier — U.S. Representative from West Virginia 2243
MOORE, Alecia, "Pink" Beth — Singer 2243
MOORE, Carissa Kainani — Professional Surfer 895
MOORE, David Lowell — Dental Professor (Retired) 2243
MOORE, Gordon Earle, PhD — Co-founder, Chairperson Emeritus 2243
MOORE, Gwendolynne, "Gwen" Sophia — U.S. Representative from Wisconsin 2244
MOORE, James D., JD — Lawyer 2244
MOORE, James R. — Lawyer 2244
MOORE, Julianne — Actress 2244
MOORE, Nancy M., EdD — Secondary School Educator 2245
MOORE, Pamela R. — Master of Specific Learning Disabilities 2245
MOORE, Samuel David — Vocalist 2245
MOORMAN, Rose — County Administrator, Systems Analyst 896
MORA, Antonio "Tony" Valdovinos De La — CEO, Founder 1296
MORA, Juanita — MD, CEO 2245
MORALES, Jesus — Chef, Owner 2245
MORAN, Gerald, "Jerry" Wesley — U.S. Senator from Kansas; Lawyer 2245
MORAN, Jason — Jazz Pianist, Composer, Educator 2245
MORAVA, Alice J. — Corporate Executive 2246
MORAYTIS, Louis J., JD — Lawyer 2246
MORDY, James Calvin, JD, BA — Lawyer 897
MOREHOUSE, Kristi Kay — Elementary School Educator (Retired) 2246
MOREL, Marilyn Anne — Dietitian (Retired) 2246
MORELLE, Joseph D. — U.S. Representative from New York 2246
MORELLO, Daniel C. MD — Plastic Surgeon 2246
MORENO, Pedro — Professor, Director of Quality Assurance and Promotions 2247

MORENO, Rita — Actress 2247
MORÉTEAU, Olivier, PhD — Law Educator 2247
MORGAN, Alfred V. — Management Consulting Company Executive 1558
MORGAN, Dennis Brent — Minister, Psychologist, Psychoanalyst 2248
MORGAN, Jeffrey — Chief Financing Officer, Treasurer 1558
MORGAN, Jennifer — Co-CEO 2248
MORGAN, Mendell D. Jr. — Director 1559
MORGANROTH, Mayer — Attorney 898
MORIARTY, Richard Graham — City Retirement System Manager 2248
MORITZ, Michael Jonathan — Chairman; Venture Capitalist 2248
MORITZ, Milton, "Mick" E., CPP — Security Consultant 2249
MORNINGSTAR, Robert D. — Computer Company Executive 2249
MORRICAL, Art — Quality Manager (Retired) 1559
MORRIS WINSTON, Alyce A. — Founder, CEO 2250
MORRIS, Dolores O., PhD, ABPP — Psychologist, Psychoanalyst 2249
MORRIS, Gordon J., President — Emeritus Financial Company Executive, Consultant, Investor 2249
MORRIS, J.W. Jr. — Materials Science Educator; Consultant 2250
MORRIS, James Malachy, Attorney at Law — Executive Assistant, Counsel to the Chairman 2250
MORRIS, John Selwyn, PhD, DLitt, LLD, MA — Philosopher, Educator, Academic Administrator (Retired) 899
MORRISETT, Lloyd N., PhD — Retired Foundation Executive 2250
MORRISON, Frederick Foster — Mathematician, Writer, Editor 2251
MORRISON, Jaydene — Education Counseling Firm Executive 900
MORRISON, Toni — Literature and Language Professor (Retired), Writer, Educator 2251
MORRIS-SMITH, Tim — Finance Company Executive 2251
MORS, Matthew — President 2252
MORTENSEN, Gordon Louis — Artist, Printmaker 2252
MORTIMER, Wendell R. — Judge 901
MORTON, Audrey Farrar — Public Administrator 1560
MOSCHINI, Silvina — Co-founder, President 2252
MOSER, Jeffery Richard — English Literature Educator; Writer; Political Advocate; Party Leader 2252
MOSES, Ronald Elliot — Toiletries Products Executive (Retired), Chemist 2253
MOSKOVITZ, Dustin Aaron — Co-founder; Entrepreneur; Social Networking Company Executive 2253
MOSLEY, Clint Jr. — Professional Football Player 2253
MOSS, Bill Ralph — Lawyer 2253
MOSS, Elisabeth Singleton — Actress 2253
MOSSINGHOFF, Gerald Joseph — Lawyer, Educator 2254
MOSTOFI, Hormoz — Owner 2254
MOTT, Peggy Laverne, PhD — Instructor of Sociology (Retired) 2254
MOTTA, Dick — Former Professional Basketball Coach 2254
MOUDE, Denise Ann Da, MA — Passport Clerk (Retired) 278
MOULTON, Seth Wilbur — U.S. Representative from Massachusetts 2254
MOUSER, Barbara Christine, RNC, MSN — Family Nurse Practitioner 2254
MOYER, Nancy Jan, PhD — Professor Emerita of Art 2254
MOYERS, Bill Don — White House Press Secretary (Retired), Journalist, Writer 2255
MOYLAN, Susan Nelis — Business and Industry Center Director 2255
MOYNIHAN, Brian Thomas — Chairman, President, CEO 2255
MUCARSEL-POWELL, Debbie Jessika — U.S. Representative from Florida 2255
MUCEDOLA, Michael S. — Department Chair 2255
MUCHA, John III, JD — Attorney 2256
MUDD, Douglas A. — Curator/Museum Director 2256
MUEGGE, G. Paul — State Legislator, Farmer (Retired) 2257
MUEHLBAUER, James H. — Manufacturing and Distribution Executive 2257
MUELLER, Robert Swan III — Special Counsel; Lawyer 2257

MUENCH, Karl H. — Professor of Medicine 902
MUHAMMAD, Ibtihaj — Fencer 2258
MUILENBURG, Dennis A. — Chairman, President, and CEO 2258
MUIR, David Jason — News Correspondent; Anchor 2258
MULLALLY, Megan — Actress 2258
MULLEN, Elaine H. — Research Scientist 2258
MULLENDORE, Walter Edward, PhD — Economist (Retired) 903
MULLER, Richard, "Dick" Louis Sr. — Retired Government Executive 2258
MULLIGAN, Maxine — Secondary School Educator (Retired) 1560
MULLIN, Markwayne — U.S. Representative from Oklahoma; Plumber; Rancher 2259
MULLIS, Kary Banks, PhD — Biochemist 2259
MULVANEY, John, "Mick" Michael — Acting White House Chief of Staff 2259
MULZOFF, Paul — Project Manager 1561
MUNDEY, Paul Eston — Minister 2259
MUNDT, Barry M. — Management Consultant 2260
MUNOZ, Oscar — CEO and President 904
MUNSINGER, Harry, JD, PhD — Owner 905
MUNSON, Virginia A. — Interior Designer, Decorator 2260
MUNYON, Marvin L. — Cultural Organization Administrator 2260
MURADYAN, Lilit — CEO 906
MURAI, Kevin M. — Director, President, CEO 2260
MURAKAMI, Haruki — Author, Professor 2260
MURDOCH, James — Chairman (Retired) 2260
MURDOCH, Robert W., ESO, FSA SCOT — Lawyer 2261
MURDOCH, Rupert — Broadcast Executive 2261
MURKOWSKI, Lisa Ann — U.S. Senator for Alaska; Lawyer 2261
MURPHY, Bobby Cornelius — Co-founder 2262
MURPHY, Christopher, "Chris" Scott — U.S. Senator from Connecticut; Lawyer 2262
MURPHY, Eddie Regan — Actor; Comedian 2262
MURPHY, Gregory, "Greg" Francis, MD — U.S. Representative from North Carolina; Physician 2262
MURPHY, Pearl Marie, RNC — Medical and Surgical Nurse 1561
MURPHY, Philip, "Phil" Dunton — Governor of New Jersey 2262
MURPHY, Ryan Patrick — Screenwriter, Director, Producer 2262
MURPHY, Stephanie — U.S. Representative from Florida 2263
MURRAY, Bill James — Actor, Writer 2263
MURRAY, Fred F. — Attorney 2263
MURRAY, James Michael, Esq. — Retired Law Librarian, Lawyer 907
MURRAY, John E. — Vice President of Commercial Lending 908
MURRAY, Kathleen Paula — Client Advocate, Claims Specialist 2264
MURRAY, Matt — Deputy Editor-in-chief 909
MURRAY, Michael W. — Owner 2264
MURRAY, Patricia, "Patty" Lynn — U.S. Senator from Washington 2264
MURRAY, Thomas Veatch — Lawyer 2264
MURRELL, Denise, PhD — Curator 910
MURREN, James Joseph — CEO 2264
MURTHY, Vanukuri Krishna, PhD, PE, MASCE — Civil Engineer 911
MUSGRAVES, Kacey Lee — Musician 2265
MUSIHIN, Konstantin K. — Senior Engineer, Electrical Engineer (Retired) 2265
MUSK, Elon Reeve — Founder, CEO; Technology Entrepreneur; Engineer 2265
MUZINICH, Justin George — U.S. Deputy Secretary of the Treasury 2265
MYERS, Gregory E. — Aerospace Engineer 2265
MYHRE, Janet — Doctor, Professor Emerita 912
MYTELKA, Arnold K. — Lawyer 2266
N. (NESRALLAH) TANNIS, Winston, "W.G." George, Esq. — Founding Executive Chair, Author-Artist, Publisher/Producer-Financier 2266
NADAL, Rafael, "Rafa" — Professional Tennis Player 2267
NADEAU, Michael J. "Mike" — Staff Assistant (Retired), Purchasing Agent (Retired) 913

NADER, Ralph — Advocate; Lawyer; Author — 2267
NADLE, Marlene Ms. — Reporter — 2267
NADLER, Jerrold, "Jerry" Lewis — U.S. Representative, Lawyer — 2267
NAFZIGER, Ralph H., PhD — Research Chemist, Research Supervisor — 2267
NAGI, Catherine Raseh — Retired Community School Superintendent; Financial Planner — 914
NAKAMURA, Shuji — Professor of Engineering — 2268
NAKATSUKASA, Walter Mitsuo, PhD — Microbiologist — 1562
NAPOLI, Marie, Esq. — Partner — 1562
NAPOLITANO, Graciela, "Grace" Flores — U.S. Representative from California — 2268
NAPOLITANO, Theresa — Attorney — 915
NAROUZE, Samer, MD, PhD, DABPM, FIPP — Founder, President; Clinical Professor; Physician — 1563
NARVAEZ, Bernice Marie — Principal Systems Engineer — 2268
NASH, Donald R., PhD — Immunologist, Bacteriologist (Retired) — 2268
NASH, Seymour C., MD, FACS — Urological Surgeon — 2269
NASH, William D. — CEO, President — 2269
NASHIF, Taysir N. — Researcher, Writer — 2269
NASSETTA, Christopher J. — President, CEO — 2269
NATALICIO, Diana Siedhoff, PhD — President Emeritus — 2269
NATHANSON, S. David, MD, FRCS, FACS — Oncologist, Surgeon, Educator — 916
NATION, David — Computer Scientist (Retired), Sculptor — 2270
NAUGLE, Ronald Clinton, PhD — Historian, Professor Emeritus — 917
NAVRATILOVA, Martina — Former Professional Tennis Player — 2270
NAYLOR-WELLS, Nicole, DDS — Dentist — 1563
NAZAIRE, Michel Harry — Surgeon — 2270
NAZIRI, Kourosh "Cyrus" — General Manager — 918
NEAL, Gail, PT — President/Owner (Retired) — 919
NEAL, Richard Edmund — U.S. Representatives — 2270
NEECE, Olivia H. — Investment Company Executive, Consultant — 2270
NEEDELMAN, Martin Seidel — Attorney — 2271
NEESON, Liam John — Actor — 2271
NEGISHI, Ei-ichi, PhD — Chemistry Professor — 2271
NEGUSE, Joseph, "Joe" D. — U.S. Representative from Colorado — 2272
NEIDORFF, Michael F. — Chairperson, President, CEO — 2272
NEJEDLO, Derek K. — Senior Applications Consultant — 2272
NEJMAN, Aleksandra — President/CEO/CFO — 920
NELSON, Jeffrey — Neurosurgeon — 2272
NELSON, Jerry R., PhD, SM(AAM) — Microbiologist, Educator, Inventor — 2272
NELSON, W. John — Geologist — 2272
NELSON, Warren B. — Commodity Trader (Retired) — 2272
NELSON, Willie Hugh — Musician — 2272
NEMANICK, Richard C. "Rich" Sr., JD, LLM — Business Executive (Retired) — 921
NERUD, Anthony Francis — Lawyer — 2273
NESTLER, Eric J., MD, PhD — Neuroscientist, Medical Educator — 922
NEUKOM, William, "Bill" Horlick — Founder and CEO; Professional Sports Team Executive (Retired); Lawyer — 2273
NEUMANN, Charles H. — Professor Emeritus — 923
NEUWIRTH, Stephen R. — Lawyer — 2274
NEVILLE, Nancy Marie — Aerospace Engineer — 2274
NEWCOM, Samuel Ralph, MD — Professor of Medicine (Emeritus) — 924
NEWELL, Roger Austin, PhD — Geologist, Mining Executive, Consultant — 925
NEWHOUSE, Daniel, "Dan" Milton — U.S. Representative, Farmer — 2274
NEWMAN, Louis I. — Attorney, Managing Partner — 1564
NEWSOM, Gavin Christopher — Governor of California — 2274
NEWSOME, Patricia H., MEd — Elementary School Educator (Retired) — 926
NEWTON, Elizabeth Deane — Elementary Music Teacher (Retired) — 2274
NEWTON, George Durfee Jr., LLB — Lawyer (Retired) — 927
NÉZET-SÉGUIN, Yannick — Music Director — 2274

NIBLOCK, Robert A. — Chairman, President, CEO (Retired) — 2275
NICHOLAS, Samuel John Jr. — Arbitrator and Mediator — 928
NICHOLLS, Richard Allen, MA — Educator (Retired) — 929
NICHOLLS, Robert Lee, PhD — Civil Engineer, Educator — 1564
NICHOLS, Carol J., EdS — Retired Nurse Educator — 930
NICHOLS, Cathrene — Administrator — 1565
NICHOLS, Jan Hildreth — Elementary School Educator, Childbirth and Parenting Educator (Retired) — 931
NICHOLS, John D., CPCU, LUTCF, ARE — Insurance Agent, Insurance Broker, Business Owner — 2275
NICHOLS, Nancy — Business Executive, Financial Consultant — 2275
NICHOLSON, Jack — Actor — 2275
NICHOLSON, William J. — Energy and Environmental Consultant (Retired) — 932
NICKS, Stevie Lynn — Singer, Songwriter — 1565
NIECESTRO, Robert M. — Managing Director — 933
NIELSEN, Kirstjen Michele — Former U.S. Secretary of Homeland Security, Lawyer — 2276
NITZSCHKE, Dale Frederick, PhD — Chancellor (Retired) — 934
NIXON, Cynthia Ellen — Actress — 2276
NOAH, Trevor — Television Personality, Comedian — 2276
NOBLE, Tal D. — Founder, Director — 2276
NODEEN, Janey Price — President — 2276
NODINE, Martha, "Marti" Lockhart — Writer, Educator — 2277
NOEL, Don O. — Editor, Author, Columnist (Retired) — 2277
NOEM, Kristi Lynn — Governor of South Dakota — 2277
NOHRIA, Nitin, PhD — Dean — 2277
NOLAN, Christopher Edward — Film Director, Producer, Writer — 2278
NOLAN, George Harry, MD — Obstetrician/Gynecologist — 935
NOLAN, Janiece Simmons, PhD — Retired Health System CEO, Scientist and Board Director — 936
NOLAND, Wayland Evan, PhD — Professor Emeritus — 1566
NORBACK, Judith, PhD — Academic Faculty & Director of Workplace & Academic Communication — 1566
NORCROSS, Donald W. — U.S. Representative from New Jersey — 2278
NOREEN, Terry Gene Sr. — — 2278
NORIEGA, Norman J. — Minister — 2278
NORMAN, Ralph Warren Jr. — U.S. Representative from South Carolina; Real Estate Executive — 2278
NORMAN, Tyler — CEO — 937
NORTHAM, Ralph Shearer — Governor of Virginia — 2278
NORTHCUTT, Kayla — Teacher — 1567
NORTON, Edward Harrison — Actor — 2278
NOSEFF, Justin — President — 1567
NOSEK, Frank — Senior Attorney — 938
NOVAK, Joseph — Professor Emeritus of Plant Biology and Science Education — 2279
NOVAKOVIC, Phebe N. — Chairman, CEO — 2279
NOVÁNYÓN IDIZOL, Angélá — Olori Erelu Gro Mambo/Head of Religious Order, Writer — 2279
NOVETZKE, Sally Johnson — Former Ambassador — 939
NOWIERSKI, Robert M., PhD — Entomologist, National Program Leader for Bio-Based Pest Management — 2279
NOYES, Deanna Kuiper, PhD — Professor — 940
NUMBERE, Aroloye — Lecturer — 2280
NUNES, Devin Gerald — U.S. Congressman from California — 2280
NUSBAUM, Geoffrey D., PhD — Psychotherapist — 941
NUSBAUM, Jesse A. — Bronze Sculptor — 942
NUSSBAUM, Ronald A., PhD — Professor Emeritus of Ecology and Evolutionary Biology, Curator Emeritus of Herpetology — 943
NUTTER, David — Director — 2280
NYQUIST, Corinne, PhD — Librarian — 2281

NZEWI, Ugochukwu-Smooth C., PhD — Artist, Curator 2281
O'BRIEN, Conan Christopher — Talk Show Host; Writer 2283
O'BRIEN, Joan Susan — Lawyer, Educator 2283
O'BRIEN, Mary — Commissioner, Acting President 945
O'BRIEN, Robert Charles — U.S. National Security Advisor 2283
O'CONNELL, Finneas — Singer, Songwriter, Record Producer 2284
O'CONNELL, Mark — Auxiliary Bishop 1569
O'CONNOR, John Arthur — Artist, Educator, Director 2284
O'CONNOR, Mallory — Curator, Art Historian, Author 2284
O'CONNOR, Marilyn — Paralegal 2285
O'CONNOR, Otis — Lawyer, Director (Retired) 2285
O'CONNOR, Sandra — Chancellor (Retired),
    Associate Justice of the Supreme Court (Retired) 2285
O'DONNELL, Brendan James — Captain (Retired) 2286
O'GRADY, Tommy — President 953
O'HALLERAN, Thomas, "Tom" Charles — U.S. Representative from
    Arizona 2287
O'HAMILL, Richard P. — CEO 954
O'MALLEY, Michelle, DSChemE — Associate Professor 2291
O'MALLEY, Sean Patrick, PhD — Cardinal; Archbishop of Boston 2291
O'NEAL, Shaquille, "Shaq" Rashaun — Sportscaster, Professional
    Basketball Player (Retired) 2291
O'NEILL, Edward Leonard — Actor 2291
O'ROURKE, James — Attorney 2294
O'ROURKE, Robert, "Beto" Francis — Former U.S. Representative 2294
OAKES, Andra Nan — Lawyer 2281
OATES, John Alexander III, MD, MACP — Physician, Medical Educator
    and Biomedical Scientist 2281
OATES, Joyce Carol — Author; Professor Emerita 2282
OBAMA, Barack Hussein II — 44th President of the U.S. 2282
OBAMA, Michelle LaVaughn — Former First Lady of the U.S.; Lawyer;
    University Administrator 1568
OBERBILLIG, Molly — Founding Sponsor 944
OBST, Norman P., PhD — Economist; Educator 2284
OCASEK, Ric — Rock Vocalist, Songwriter, Guitar Player, Producer 2284
OCASIO-CORTEZ, Alexandria — U.S. Representative from New York 1568
OCCHIATO, Michael 946
ODEGARD, Mark E. — Chief Geoscientist; CTO and Director 2286
ODELL, Wendy — President, CEO 947
ODELL, William D., MD, PhD, MACP — Physician, Educator, Research
    Scientist 948
OELMAN, Bradford Coolidge — Senior Vice President of Government
    and Public Affairs, Retired 2286
OERTER, Al Adolph Jr. — Former Professional Discus Throw Athlete 2287
OGBURN, Joyce Lanier — Professor of Practice 949
OGBURN-STOKES, Heather 950
OGDEN, Maureen B. — State Legislator for Environmental Issues
    (Retired) 951
OGILVIE, Lloyd John, DD — Clergyman 952
OH, Sandra Miju — Actress 2287
OHMER, Steven Russell — Judge 2287
OHNO, Apolo Anton — Former Olympic Speed Skater 2287
OHOTNICKY, Stephen Thaddeus — Engineering Executive 2288
OKAFOR, Tochukwu — CEO 2288
OKAMOTO, Jeffrey K. MD — Developmental-Behavioral Pediatrician 2288
OKINAKA, Alton M. PhD, PhD — Associate Professor 2288
OLAJUWON, Hakeem Abdul — Former Professional Basketball Player 2288
OLALDE, Josh — Photographer 2289
OLDKNOW, Antony — English Educator; Writer; Publisher; Visual Artist 955
OLDMAN, Gary Leonard — Actor 2289
OLESEN, Michael D. — Owner 2289

OLIPHANT, Thomas J. — Executive Vice President, President,
    Entrepreneur 2289
OLIVER, David Burdette — Communications Company Executive
    (Retired) 2289
OLIVER, John William — Comedian; Television Host 2290
OLNEY, Nancy Helen — Secondary School Educator (Retired) 956
OLSEN, M. Kent, Esq. — Lawyer, Educator 1569
OLSHAKER, Mark Bruce — Author, Filmmaker 2290
OLSON, Donald B., PhD — Professor 2290
OLSON, Keith Waldemar — Historian 957
OLSON, Lois Ruth, MEd — Mathematics Teacher; Learning Disability &
    Emotionally Disturbed Professional 958
OLSON, Peter, "Pete" Graham — U.S. Representative 2290
OLSON, Walter J. Jr. — Sole Proprietor 2290
OMAR, Ilhan Abdullahi — U.S. Representative from Minnesota 2291
OMIDYAR, Pierre M. — Internet Company Executive; Film Company
    Executive 2291
ONISHI, Lisa — Chemical Engineer, Senior Process Enigineer 959
OPDAHL, Viola Elizabeth — Secondary School Educator 2292
OPFER, Neil David, PhD — Construction Educator; Consultant 2292
OPLINGER, Kathryn — President, CEO 2292
OPP, Chris — Owner, Operator 2292
OPPERMAN, Kim — President, Founder 960
OPRE, Thomas — President, CEO (Retired) 1570
ORDÓÑEZ, Andrés — Chief Creative Officer 2293
ORLEANS, Carole Tracy — Senior Scientist 2293
ORMAN, Suze Lynn — Financial Consultant; Writer; Columnist 2293
OROSZ, Joel J., PhD — Philanthropist, Educator 2293
ORSAK, Pamela D., JD — Attorney 961
ORSINI, Paul V. Jr. — Music Educator 2294
ORTEGA PERRIER, Ricardo — Entrepreneur 2294
ORTH, Charles D., PhD — Physicist 962
ORTIZ TAYLOR, Sandra — Artist, Educator 2294
OSAKA, Naomi — Professional Tennis Player 2295
OSBORNE, Thomas — Oral and Maxillofacial Surgery 2295
OSMAN, Henry P. — President, CEO 2295
OSTDAHL, Roger Harold — Neurological Surgeon 963
OSTEEN, Joel Scott — Minister 2295
OSTERBERG, James Newell Jr. — Composer, Singer, Musician 2295
OSTRIKER, Jeremiah Paul, PhD — Astrophysicist; Professor 2295
OSTROW, Alec Paul — Lawyer 2296
OSTROY, Joan Patsy — Lawyer, Mediator 2296
OSWALD, James Marlin, EdD — Educator, Researcher, Agriculturalist 2296
OTTO, Marie — Educational Administrator, Educational Consulting
    Company Executive 964
OUBOU, Iman — Founder, CEO 2297
OWEN, Wendy — Lead Designer, Owner 2297
OWENS, Cynthia Denise, DO — Physician 2297
OWENS, Dana, "Queen Latifah" — Rapper, Singer, Songwriter, Actress,
    Producer 2297
OWENS, John Arthur, Esq. — Senior Partner 965
OWEN-TOWLE, Carolyn Sheets — Minister (Retired) 966
OWSLEY, David T. — Art Consultant, Appraiser, Lecturer, Author 967
OXLEY, Margaret Stewart — Elementary School Educator 2298
OYUELA, Fredy — Installation Manager 1570
PACE, R. Wayne, PhD — Professor Emeritus 968
PACELLA-SAMS, Mary Ann — Educational Administrator (Retired);
    Corporate Executive 969
PACIFICO, Joseph C. — Counselor (Retired) 2298
PACIFICO, Larry — CEO, President, Owner 2298
PACINO, Al James — Actor 2298

PACKARD, Martin Everett, PhD — Electronics Company Executive (Retired) — 970
PACKER, Douglas L., MD — Cardiologist — 971
PACKER, Nancy Huddleston — Educator, Writer, Professor Emerita — 972
PACKWOOD, J.D. Jr., JD, MA — Owner, Solo Practitioner — 1571
PAGE, Jimmy Patrick — Singer, Musician — 2299
PAGE, Lawrence, "Larry" Edward — Information Technology Officer — 2299
PAGELS, Elaine Hiesey, PhD — Professor; Author — 2299
PAI, Ajit Varadaraj — Chairman; Lawyer — 2300
PAISLEY, Brad Douglas — Singer, Songwriter, Musician — 2300
PALADINO, Constance — President — 2300
PALAZZO, Steven McCarty — U.S. Representative from Mississippi — 2300
PALAZZOLO, Angie — Managing Broker, Owner — 2300
PALLONE, Frank Joseph Jr. — U.S. Representative from New Jersey; Ranking Member of Committee on Energy and Commerce; Lawyer — 2300
PALMER, Gary James — U.S. Representative from Alabama; Public Policy Research and Education Executive — 2301
PALMER, James Joseph — Arbitrator and Mediator, Labor/Employee Relations Consultant — 973
PALTROW, Gwyneth Kate — Actress — 2301
PANDEY, Ramesh C., PhD — Chemist, Educator, Entrepreneur — 974
PANETTA, James, "Jimmy" Varni — U.S. Representative from California; Lawyer — 2301
PANZA, David R., CEBS, RHU — AVP, Underwriting Consultant — 1571
PAO, Ellen Kangru — Investor, Activist, Co-Founder — 2301
PAPPAS, Christopher, "Chris" Charles — U.S. Representative from New Hampshire — 2301
PAPPONI, Paula LuMetta — Superintendent — 2301
PARCAK, Sarah Helen — Egyptologist — 2302
PARCELLS, Bill — Professional Sports Executive; Sportscaster; Former Professional Football Coach — 2302
PARENT, Mary Campbell — Film Producer, Studio Executive — 2302
PARÉS-MATOS, Elsie I. — Professor — 2302
PARIS, Bernard J., PhD — Emeritus Professor of English — 975
PARK, Chui Suh, "Chris", BS, MS, RPh — Pharmacist (Retired) — 2302
PARKER, Barry R. — Physics Educator (Ret.) — 976
PARKER, Doug — CEO — 2302
PARKER, Mark G. — Chairman, President, CEO — 977
PARKER, Sarah Jessica — Actress; Producer — 2303
PARKER, Sean — Venture Capitalist, Entrepreneur — 2303
PARKER, Stuart Blain — CEO — 2303
PARKER-CONRAD, Jane E., RN, PhD — Nursing Consultant — 2303
PARKS, Arva Moore — President; Historian; Author — 1572
PARMLEY, William Watts, MD — Doctor (Retired), Professor Emeritus — 978
PARONE, Anthony Daniel, Esq. — Attorney at Law — 979
PARRELLA, Susan Irene, EdD — Superintendent of Schools, Special Educator, Adjunct Professor — 2303
PARRISH, Carmelita Beal, MA, MED, BSED, AA — Secondary School Educator, Language Educator (Retired) — 980
PARRON-RAGLAND, Delores L., PhD — Federal Agency Administrator (Retired) — 981
PARROTT, Billy James — Film Director, Communications Executive — 2304
PARSON, Michael L. — Governor of Missouri — 2304
PARSONS, David Stanley, MD, FAAP, FACS — Otolaryngologist, Pediatrician (Retired); Professor; Missionary — 2304
PARSONS, Jim Joseph — Actor — 2304
PARSONS, Lorraine Leighton — Nurse; Pre-school Administrator — 2305
PARTON STANARD, Susan Lorane, MA — Director of Choral Ensembles and Vocal Studies — 2305
PARTON, Dolly Rebecca, — Singer, Songwriter; Actress — 2305
PASCHAL, James Alphonso — College Professor; Family Counseling Center Director (Retired) — 982
PASCHAL, Saundra — Mathematics Teacher — 983

PASCRELL, William, "Bill" James Jr. — U.S. Representative — 2306
PASIK-DUNCAN, Bozenna, PhD, DSc — Mathematics Professor, Researcher — 2306
PASTIAN, Alan D. — Pastor — 2306
PATE, J'Nell Laverne — History and Government Educator (Retired), Writer — 2306
PATRICK, Carlianne — Assistant Professor — 2307
PATTERSON, James Brendan — Author; Former Advertising Executive — 984
PATTERSON, William Brown — Professor Emeritus of History, Dean (Retired) — 985
PATTON, Fitz — Sound Designer — 2307
PAUL, Chris Emmanuel — Professional Basketball Player — 2307
PAUL, M. Lee EdD — Professor of Psychology, Psychotherapist — 2307
PAUL, Randal, "Rand" Howard, MD — U.S. Senator from Kentucky; Ophthalmologist — 2307
PAUL, Ronald, "Ron" Earnest, MD — Former U.S. Representative from Texas; Physician — 2307
PAULEY, Bruce — Professor Emeritus — 2308
PAULEY, Jane — Newscaster; Journalist — 2308
PAULSEN, Lisa — Chief Nursing Officer — 2308
PAULSON, Sarah Catharine — Actress — 2308
PAULUS, Basil Mantas, MD — Physician, Medical Director — 986
PAVELKA, Elaine B., PhD — Emeritus Mathematics Professor — 2309
PAYNE, Donald Milford Jr. — U.S. Representative from New Jersey — 2309
PAYNE, Donald Milford — Former U.S. Representative from New Jersey — 2309
PAYNE, Mary Libby, JD, LLD (Hon.) — Emerita Dean, Professor, Judge (Retired) — 987
PAYNE, Philip H. — Founder, CEO — 2309
PAZ, Jessica — Sound Designer — 2309
PAZ, R. Samuel — CEO, Civil Rights Lawyer — 988
PEACE, H.W. II — Small Business Owner, Retired Oil Industry Executive — 2309
PEARSON, Robert Lawrence — Executive Recruiter — 989
PEASE, Donald E., PhD — Humanities Educator — 2310
PECK, Art — CEO — 2310
PEDIGO, Paul F., BA, BEChE, JD — Managing Attorney — 990
PEELE, Jordan Haworth — Actor, Comedian, Director, Producer — 2310
PEGG, Stuart P., AM, MD — Emeritus Professor — 991
PEGULA, Terry Michael — Professional Sports Team Executive; Former Gas Industry Executive — 2310
PEI, I.M. — Architect — 2310
PELLETIER, Nancy A. — Obstetrical and Gynecological Nurse; Educator (Retired) — 2311
PELLETIER, Paul — Scottsdale Boxing Club — 2311
PELLI, Cesar — Architect — 2311
PELOSI, Nancy Patricia — Speaker of the House — 2312
PELTON, Joseph Neal, PhD — Executive Board — 2312
PEMBERTON, Charles Edward, BS, MS — CEO, Primary Instructor — 2313
PENCE, Gregory, "Greg" Joseph — U.S. Representative from Indiana — 2313
PENCE, Karen Sue — Second Lady of the U.S.; Teacher — 992
PENCE, Michael, "Mike" Richard — Vice President of the U.S. — 2313
PENDERGRASS, Ewell Dean "Bub" — Communications Executive (Retired) — 993
PENN, Sean — Actor, Director — 2313
PENSKE, Roger S. Jr. — Chairman, CEO — 994
PEPE, Frank A. — Cell and Developmental Biology Educator — 995
PÉPIN, Jacques — Chef, Television Personality — 2313
PERA, Robert J. — Communications Company Executive, Professional Sports Team Owner — 2314
PERDUE, David Alfred Jr. — U.S. Senator from Georgia; Management Consultant — 2314
PERDUE, Sonny III — U.S. Secretary of Agriculture — 2314
PEREDNEY, Christine — Social Worker, Educator, Community Volunteer — 2314

PEREIRA, Armando M. — Principal, Designer — 2314
PERETZ, David, MD — Staff Member — 2314
PEREZ, Jorge Luis — Manufacturing Executive — 2315
PEREZ, Thomas Edward — Chairman — 2315
PERILSTEIN, Fred M. — Electrical Engineering Consultant — 996
PERKIN, Ronald Murray — Pediatrician, Educator — 2315
PERKINS, Edward Joseph, PhD — U.S. Ambassador (Retired) — 2315
PERKINS, Marian E. — Judge — 2316
PERKINS, Matthew — CEO — 2316
PERLMAN, Itzhak — Violinist — 2316
PERLMUTTER, Edwin, "Ed" George — U.S. Representative from Colorado; Lawyer — 2317
PERLOFF, Jean — Property Manager, Lawyer (Retired) — 2317
PEROT, Ross — Data Processing Executive, Real Estate Company, Investment Company — 2317
PERRONE, Thomas J., JD — Systems Analyst, Consultant — 997
PERRY, James, "Rick" Richard — Former U.S. Secretary of Energy — 2317
PERRY, Katy — Singer — 2317
PERRY, Reginald — President, CEO — 2318
PERRY, Scott Gordon — U.S. Representative from Pennsylvania — 2318
PERRY, Tyler A. — Playwright, Actor, Film Director, Producer — 2318
PERRY, William A. III — Health Care Sales Executive — 1572
PESCI, Joe — Actor — 2319
PESSINA, Stefano — Vice Chairperson, CEO — 2319
PETERS, Bernadette — Actress — 2319
PETERS, Gary Charles Sr. — U.S. Senator from Michigan; Lawyer — 2319
PETERS, Scott Harvey — U.S. Representative from California; Lawyer — 2320
PETERSON, Adrian — Professional Football Player — 2320
PETERSON, Collin Clark — U.S. Representative from Minnesota — 2320
PETERSON, Douglas L. — CEO — 2320
PETERSON, Jeremy — CEO — 2320
PETERSON, John — Civil Engineering Educator — 2320
PETERSON, Sophia PhD — Political Scientist, Educator — 2320
PETESCH, Natalie L.M., PhD — Author — 998
PETITTI, Tony — President of Sports and Entertainment; Former Chief Operating Officer — 2320
PETREQUIN, Harry Joseph Jr. — Senior Foreign Service Officer (Retired) — 2321
PETRICK, Joseph Anthony — Management Professor (Retired), Business Ethics Consultant, American Philosopher — 2321
PETROLA, Renee Danette — Retired Teacher, Author — 999
PETRONE, John R. — Music Educator, Composer (Retired) — 2321
PETTIT, Christy — Owner — 1000
PETTY, Bob — News Reporter, Anchor — 2322
PEW, Robert — Real Estate and Equipment Leasing Corporation Officer (Retired) — 2322
PFEIFFER, Mary Louise, "Mary Lou" — Artist, Educator — 2322
PFEIFFER, Michelle Marie — Actress — 2322
PFLAUM, Steven Forbes — Partner, Co-Chair of Litigation Department, Chair of Pro Bono Committee — 2322
PHELPS, Wayne Howe, PhD — Director of Planning and Educational Research (Retired) — 1001
PHILBIN, Gary M. — CEO, President — 2323
PHILBRICK, Delaney — Real Estate Agent — 1573
PHILIPP, Karla Ann — Musician, Educator, Conductor — 2323
PHILIPSON, Tomas, PhD — Acting Chairman, Vice Chair; Professor — 2323
PHILLIPS, Dean Benson — U.S. Representative from Minnesota — 2323
PHILLIPS, Kenneth W. — President and CEO — 2323
PHILLIPS, Laramie — IT Manager — 1573
PHILLIPS, Todd — Director — 2323
PHIPPS, Benjamin K. — Lawyer — 2324
PHOENIX, Joaquin Raphael — Actor — 1574

PIASECKI, Bruce — President, Founder — 1574
PICHAI, Sundar — CEO, Engineer — 2324
PICK, James B. — Business Professor, Writer — 2324
PIEGARI, James — Psychologist — 2324
PIERCE, Frederick, "Fred" Watson IV — President, CEO — 2325
PIERCE, John G., JD — Attorney (Retired) — 1002
PIERCE, Roger A. II — Pharmacist, Director — 2325
PIERCE, Stacia — Owner — 1003
PIERINO, Thomas Michael, EdD — School Psychologist, Vocational Evaluator, Counselor — 2326
PILKERTON, Christopher Michael — Acting Administrator, Genreal Counsel — 2326
PILLAI, A.K.B. — Chair — 2326
PINEDA, Arnel — Singer — 2327
PINEDA, Ramiro — 2327
PINGREE, Chellie Marie — U.S. Representative from Maine — 2327
PINKETT SMITH, Jada — Actress — 2327
PINNA, William Peter — Lawyer — 1004
PINSKY, Robert Neal — Poet, Educator — 2328
PINSON, William Meredith Jr., ThD — 2328
PIRCHER, Leo — Lawyer, Director — 2328
PIRKLE, George Emory — Photographer, Instructional Media Producer — 2328
PIRLOT, Diane Elaine — Special Education Educator — 1005
PISACANO, Don Arlie — Attorney — 2329
PISANI, Anthony Michael — Architect — 1006
PITKIN, Roy Macbeth — Retired Obstetrician, Educator — 2329
PITMAN, Kathryn Annette, PhD — Mental Health Counseling Executive (Retired), Consultant (Retired) — 2329
PITT, Brad — Actor, Film Producer — 1007
PIZZO, Joseph Francis, PhD — Physics Educator — 2330
PLANT, Robert Anthony — Singer; Musician — 2330
PLASKETT, Stacey E. — U.S. Representative from the Virgin Islands; Lawyer — 2330
PLATT, Nicholas — Consultant, Ambassador (Retired); President Emeritus — 1008
PLODZIEN, Carol Anna — Retired Physical Education Teacher — 2330
PLOWDEN, David — Photographer; Writer — 2331
PLUMLEY, Geraldine Virgil — Health Services Director, Training Coordinator — 2331
PLUMLEY, Michael, "Mike" A. — Rubber Manufacturing Company Executive, Consultant to Industry — 2331
PLUMMER, Stephen Ray — IT Project Manager — 2332
PLUNKETT, Melba Kathleen — Manufacturing Company Executive — 2332
POCAN, Mark William — U.S. Representative from Wisconsin — 2332
PODESTA, Anthony, "Tony" Thomas — Lobbyist (Retired) — 2332
POE, Lenora Madison — Psychotherapist, Author — 2332
POEHLER, Amy — Comedienne, Actress — 2333
POITIER, Sidney — Actor — 2333
POLAN, David R. — Public Administration & Finance Executive (Retired) — 2334
POLIS, Jared Schutz — Governor of Colorado — 2334
POLISI, Joseph William — President Emeritus — 2334
POLIZZI, Joseph — Social Scientist, Cultural Historian, Professor Emeritus — 2334
POLLACK, Marsha — Secondary School Educator — 2335
POLLARD, Herschel Newton, PhD — Artist, Psychologist — 2335
POLLIHAN, Thomas H. — Corporate Lawyer — 1575
POMPEO, Michael, "Mike" Richard — U.S. Secretary of State — 2335
PORAT, Ruth M. — Senior Vice President, Chief Financial Officer — 2335
PORTER, Dennis D., BA, MA, PhD — Professor of French and Comparative Literary Studies (Retired) — 1009
PORTER, Jeanne S. — Civic Worker — 1010

PORTER, Katherine, "Katie" — U.S. Representative from California; Educator 2336
PORTER, Otto Jr. — Professional Basketball Player 2336
PORTMAN, Natalie — Actress 2336
PORTMAN, Robert, "Rob" Jones — U.S. Senator from Ohio; Lawyer 2336
PORTMAN, Robin — President, CEO 1011
POSEN, Zac — Apparel Designer 1012
POSEY, William, "Bill" Joseph — U.S. Representative from Florida; Real Estate Executive 2336
POSNANSKY, Merrick, PhD — History and Archaeology Educator 2337
POST, Austin, "Post Malone" Richard, — Rap Artist 2337
POSTON, Rebekah J. — Senior Partner 2337
POTTENGER, Mark McClelland — Computer Programmer 2337
POWELL, Colin Luther — Former U.S. Secretary of State; Strategic Advisor 2337
POWELL, Heidi — Fitness Trainer; Co-founder; Co-host 2338
POWELL, Jerome Hayden "Jay" — Chair 1013
POWELL, Melissa — President, Chief Operating Officer 1575
POWELL, Robert Eugene — Computer Operator 2338
POWER, Samantha Jane — Former U.S. Ambassador; Public Policy Educator 2338
POWERS, Kirsten Anne — Author, Columnist, Political Analyst 2338
POYDASHEFF, Robert Stephen — Lawyer 2338
PRATA, Enrico Alfonso — Educational Administrator 2339
PRATHER, Elbert Charlton Sr., MD — State Health Officer 1014
PRATT, Chris — Actor 2339
PRATTE, Paul Alfred — Journalist 2339
PRAY, Merle Evelyn, RN, APN, MS — Nurse Psychotherapist, Educator (Retired) 2339
PREGGER, Fred Titus, EdD — Professor Emeritus 1576
PRESSLEY, Ayanna Soyini — U.S. Representative from Massachusetts 2340
PRESSLY, Laurence — Executive Vice President 1015
PRESTON, Dean Laverne — Theoretical Physicist 2340
PRESTON, Steven C. — President, CEO 2340
PREUSS, Harry George, MD, MACN, CNS — Internist, Nephrologist, Nutritionist 2340
PRICE, David Eugene, PhD — U.S. Representative, Professor 2341
PRICE, Morton L. — Lawyer, Partner 2341
PRIEBUS, Reinhold, "Reince" Richard — Former White House Chief of Staff; Lawyer 2341
PRINCE, Anna — Composer, Music Publisher; Construction Executive 2341
PRINGLE, Paul — Staff Writer 2342
PRIOLEAU, Darwin — Dance Educator, Choreographer 2342
PRITCHETT-HILTON, Shirley — 21st Century Foundational Hematologist, Oncologist, Neurologist 1016
PRITZKER, Jay, "J.B." Robert — Governor of Illinois 2342
PROCTOR, Mark Alan — Consultant; Elected Official; Real Estate Executive; Television Panelist; Commentator 2342
PROST, Mary Jane — School Nurse 2343
PROVENZANO, Dominic — Information Specialist 2343
PRYCE, Jonathan, CBE — Actor 2343
PUCK, Wolfgang — Chef 2344
PUCKETT, Dale, — Owner 2344
PUERTA, José Ramón "José Andrés" Andrés — Chef; Founder 35
PUGH, Florence — Actress 2344
PUIG, Dora — Owner, Founder 1017
PULIDO, Mauricio — CEO 2344
PULIPAKA, Ganapathi, PhD — Chief Data Scientist 1018
PUMA, Grace M. — Executive Vice President of Global Operations 2344
PURVIN FOX, Ronnie Ilaine — Volunteer Educator 2344
PUST, August B., PhD — Multicultural and International Relations Specialist (Retired); Artist 1576

PUT, Dirk Van de — Chairman, CEO 1298
PUTH, Charlie Otto Jr. — Singer 2345
QUARNE, Tracey J. — Superintendent 2345
QUAYLE, James, "Dan" Danforth — Former Vice President of the U.S.; Investment Company Executive 2345
QUESADA, George — Partner 2345
QUIAMBAO STEVENSON, Dalisay Lelay — Dietitian; Consultant; Surveyor 2345
QUIGLEY, Michael, "Mike" Bruce — U.S. Representative from Illinois 2346
QUINCEY, James Robert B. — CEO, President 2346
QUINN, John Michael — Physicist, Geophysicist 1019
QUINN, Virginia Lynn — Paramedic 2346
QUINTERO, Yamile — District Family Facilitator/Homeless Liaison 2346
RABOVITSER, Iosif (Joseph) K. — Director of R&D of Combustion Systems 2346
RACICH, David — President, CEO 1577
RACINE, Nathalie — Portfolio Manager 1020
RACOMA, Fawn — Owner/Chef/Entrepreneur 2347
RADASHAW, Sharon Lee — Music Educator(Retired), Entertainer 1021
RADEFELD, Matthew, Esq. — Partner 2347
RADIL, Gary W. — Of Counsel 2347
RAE, Issa — Actress, Writer, Director 2347
RAFFA, Jean — Author; Educator 2347
RAGATZ, Thomas — Lawyer 2348
RAGGETTE, Nathaniel Joseph — Chairman, CEO 1022
RAGLAND, Terry Eugene "Gene", MD — Emergency Physician 1023
RAGUTHU, Manjula, MD — Physician, Director 1024
RAIMONDO, Gina Marie — Governor of Rhode Island 2348
RAJAGOPAL, Keshava, MD, PhD — Associate Professor, Cardiothoracic/Vascular Surgery 1025
RAJAKUMAR, Charles, PhD — Mechanical Engineer 2348
RALES, Mitchell P. — Co-founder 2348
RAMÍREZ-RIVERA, José, MD, FCCP, MACP — Professor Emeritus, Professor of Medicine, Physician (Retired) 1026
RAMOS, Jesus, "Jess" G. — Sheriff 2348
RAMOS, Jorge — Newscaster 2349
RAMSAY, Tammy — Realtor 1027
RAMSEY, Ocean — Shark Conservationist, Marine Biologist, Model 2349
RAMSTEIN, William Louis, MBA, CPA — Retired Manufacturing Executive 1028
RANALLI, George — Architect, Educator 1029
RANCK, James Byrne Jr., MD — Neuroscience Researcher, Educator 1030
RANDALL, Kay Temple, — Accountant (Retired); Real Estate Agent 2349
RANDOLPH, Richard Rutherford III — Real Estate Executive 2349
RANGASWAMI, Arun A. — Associate Professor of Pediatrics 1031
RANSOM, Clifton Louis — Lawyer, Real Estate Investor 2349
RANSONE, Robin Key — Proposals Consultant 2349
RAPINO, Michael — Music Company Executive 2350
RAPINOE, Megan Anna — Professional Soccer Player 1032
RAPPACH, Norma Jeanne — Nurse, Health Occupations Educator 2350
RASKIN, Jamin, "Jamie" Ben — U.S. Representative from Maryland 2350
RASMUSSEN, Robert — CEO 2350
RASMUSSEN, Stephen Scott — CEO and President 2350
RASMUSSON, Bobby — Group Product Manager, Head of Core Consumer 2351
RASSEL, Richard E. — Chairman 2351
RATCLIFFE, John Lee — U.S. Representative, Lawyer 2351
RAUEN, Laurian — CEO 1033
RAWIE-ROOK, Judith — Co-Founder, President, Producer/Writer 1034
RAY, Rachael Domenica — Cookbook Author, Television Personality 2351
RAYMOND, Susan Grant — Sculptor 2351

RAYNOR, Patricia Herbert — Special Education Educator, K-12 Mild/ Moderate Disabilities 2352

REA, Roger — Chemistry Educator, Consultant 2352

READ, Robert R., PhD — Mathematical Statistics Educator (Retired) 1035

REASONER, Harry M. — Lawyer 1036

REAVES, Charles D. — Investment Company Executive, Lawyer 2352

RECKFORD, Jonathan Thomas More — Nonprofit Organization Administrator 2352

REDFIELD, Robert Ray Jr., MD — Director; Virologist 1037

REDFORD (CHARLES ROBERT REDFORD), Robert — Actor, Film Director, Producer 2352

REDMAN, Ann — President 2353

REDSTONE, Shari Ellin — Chairwoman 1038

REED, Bernard T. — President 1577

REED, David George — Entrepreneur 2353

REED, Emily Ann — Criminal Justice Analyst, Systems and Database Administrator, Adjunct Professor 1578

REED, George Elliott, DVM, MD — Scholar, Surgeon and Healer 1039

REED, Jeffrey, "Jeff" Garth, PhD — Organizational Psychologist (Retired); Educator (Retired) 2354

REED, John, "Jack" Francis — U.S. Senator 2354

REED, Jonathan — Founder, CEO 2354

REED, Thomas, "Tom" W. II — U.S. Representative, Lawyer 2355

REED, William Piper Jr., MD, FACS — Emeritus Professor 1040

REES, Terry Dalton "Tiger", DDS, MSD — Professor Emeritus 1041

REEVES, Keanu Charles — Actor 2355

REGENBOGEN, Adam Esq. — Judge 2355

REICH, Rose Marie, MA — Art Educator (Retired) 1578

REICH, Steve — Composer 2355

REID, John Reynolds Jr., PhD — Geologist, Geomorphologist, Educator 2356

REIF, L. Rafael — President 2356

REILLY, Joy Harriman, PhD — Associate Professor Emeritus 1042

REIMANN, Katalin, MA — President 1043

REINKE, William John — Lawyer (Retired) 1044

REINLEITNER, Katherine M., PhD — Psychologist; Foundation Administrator 2356

REINTGEN, Douglas Scott MD — Professor of Surgery 2356

REINTJES, John F., PhD — Senior Research Physicist 1045

REIS, Peggy D. — Township Official 2357

REITMEISTER, Noel, PhD — Certified Financial Planner 1046

REMNICK, David Jay — Editor 2357

REN, Dingkun, DEng — Development Engineer 2357

RENO, Joseph David — Protective Services Official, Researcher, Writer 2357

RENSALIER, Dolores M. Van — CEO, President, Founder 1301

RENSE, William Childs, PhD — Geography Educator (Retired) 1047

RENUART, Ronald, "Doc" Joseph Sr., DO, FACP — Osteopathic Physician 2358

REPICCI, John A., DDS/MD — Doctor (Retired) 1048

REPP, Michael — Public Relations, Community Outreach, Patron Liaison 2359

RESCHENTHALER, Guy Lorin — U.S. Representative from Pennsylvania; Lawyer 2359

RESIO, Donald T., PhD — Director 2359

RESMINI, Adam J. — Attorney 1579

RESNICK, Lynda Rae — Businesswoman 2359

RESNICK, Stewart Allen — Chairperson, President 2359

RESTIVO, Todd — Attorney 2359

RETZ, Linda J., JD, Esq. — Proprietor 2359

REVELEY, W. Taylor III — President Emeritus 2360

REVERDIN, Bernard J. — Lawyer 2360

REW, Robert 2360

REYES, Arianne — Assistant Chief of Airport Operations 2360

REYNOLDS, Albert Barnett — Nuclear Engineer, Educator 2360

REYNOLDS, Glenn Franklin — Medicinal Research Scientist (Retired) 2360

REYNOLDS, Kim Kay — Governor of Iowa 2361

REYNOLDS, Robert Joel — Principal Emeritus, Economist; Consultant 1580

REYNOLDS, Ryan — Actor, Producer 2361

RHAMES, Ving — Actor 2361

RHEI, Esther — Medical Director 2362

RHETT, William Paterson Jr. — The Reverend Doctor 2362

RHIMES, Shonda — Television Producer, Director, Writer 2362

RHOTEN, Juliana T. — Principal (Retired) 1049

RHYNE, James Jennings "Jim", PhD — Research Physicist (Retired) 1580

RIBLEY-BORCK, Joan, BSN, RN — Medical/Surgical Rehabilitation Nurse 1581

RICCA, Michael H. — Member 1581

RICE, Anne — Writer 2362

RICE, Condoleezza — Political Science Professor, Former U.S. Secretary of State 2363

RICE, Denis Timlin, JD — Senior Counsel 1050

RICE, Hugh, "Tom" Thompson Jr. — U.S. Representative from South Carolina; Lawyer 2363

RICE, Jerry Lee Sr. — Former Professional Football Player 2363

RICE, Joan S. — Pediatric Nurse, Author, Parent Educator 2364

RICE, Joy Katharine, PhD — Psychologist, Educator 2364

RICE, Kathleen Maura — U.S. Representative, Former Prosecutor 2364

RICE, Mary E., PhD — Senior Research Scientist Emeritus; Biologist 1582

RICH, Robert F., PhD — Law Educator 2364

RICHARDS, Keith — Guitarist 2365

RICHARDS, Norma Jane, RN, BSN, MS — Medical/Surgical Nurse, Educator (Retired) 1582

RICHARDS, Thomas Edward — Executive Chairman, President (Retired), CEO (Retired) 2365

RICHARDSON, Camala — Attorney 1051

RICHARDSON, Elisha Roscoe — Dentist, Educator 1052

RICHARDSON, Ernest Ray — Housing Program Supervisor (Retired) 2365

RICHERSON, David W. — Ceramic Engineer, Educator 1053

RICHESON, Jack Wayne — Realtor 1054

RICHIE, Lionel B. Jr. — Singer, Lyricist, Theater Producer 2365

RICHMOND, Cedric Levon — U.S. Representative from Louisiana 2366

RICHMOND, Nancy T. — State Agency Administrator (Retired) 1055

RICHMOND, Rocsan — Television Producer 2366

RICHMOND, William Frederick — Lawyer 1056

RICHTER, Janell — Principal, Minister 2366

RICHTER, Peter C. — Lawyer 2366

RICKELS, Karl, MD — Psychiatrist 1057

RICKETTS, John, "Pete" Peter — Governor of Nebraska 2366

RICKLEFS, Karen Lee — Quality Assurance Consultant 2367

RICKS, John Addison III — Professor Emeritus 1058

RIDDLE, Douglas S., MMUS — Music Educator, Choral Director 2367

RIDENHOUR, Carlton, "Chuck D." Douglas — Rap Musician 2367

RIEGER, Terry, Custom Designed Jewelry — Owner, Jeweler 2367

RIESS, George F., Esq. — Lawyer, Educator 1059

RIGALI, Justin Francis — Cardinal 2368

RIGGLEMAN, Denver Lee III, — U.S. Representative from Virginia 2368

RIGGS, Robert Dale, PhD — Plant Pathology and Nematology Educator, Researcher 1060

RIGNEY, Florence Mae "See See" — Nurse 1583

RIKON, Michael "Mike", CRE — Partner 1061

RILEY, Patrick James — Professional Sports Team Executive 2368

RINGER, Merikay PhD — Professor Emeritus, Psychologist 2368

RINK, Lawrence D. — Cardiologist, Director of Cardiac Rehabilitation 2368

RIORDAN, Rick — Writer 2368

RIPA, Kelly Maria — Television Personality, Actress 2369

RIPOLL, Shakira Isabel — Singer 2369

RISCH, James, "Jim" Elroy — U.S. Senator from Idaho; Lawyer 2370
RISS, Richard Michael, PhD — Associate Dean of Traditional
Undergraduate Studies, Professor of History and Biblical Studies 2370
RITCHEY, Kenneth William — Human Services Administrator/Trainer 1583
RITCHIE, Albert — Lawyer 2370
RITCHIE, James, "Jim" Bowers III — Attorney-At-Law Esquire,
Preeminent Attorney, Emeritus Attorney; Protestant Army Chaplain
(Captain) 2370
RITCHIE, Robert (Kid Rock) — Singer 2372
RIVERA, Chita — Actress, Singer, Dancer 2372
RIVERA, Geraldo — Attorney, Reporter, Author 2372
RIVERA, Mariano — Professional Baseball Player (Retired) 2372
RIVERS, Doc — Professional Basketball Coach 2373
RIVLIN, Lewis Allen — Entrepreneur, Former Lawyer 1584
ROBBIE, Margot — Actress, Producer 2373
ROBBINS, Chuck — CEO 2373
ROBBINS, Frances E. — Educational Administrator 2373
ROBBINS, Tim — Actor, Film Director, Screenwriter 2373
ROBE, Thurlow Richard — Dean Emeritus, Cruse W. Moss Professor
Emeritus 1062
ROBERSON, Robert S. — Investment Company Executive 1063
ROBERTS, Bill — Fire Chief (Retired) 1064
ROBERTS, Brian L. — Chairman, CEO 1584
ROBERTS, Carter S. — President, CEO 2374
ROBERTS, Charles, "Pat" Patrick — U.S. Senator 2374
ROBERTS, Delmar, "Del" Lee — Managing Editor Emeritus 2374
ROBERTS, Joan — English Language Professor 1065
ROBERTS, John Glover Jr. — Chief Justice 2374
ROBERTS, Julia — Actress 2375
ROBERTS, Michele A. — Lawyer, Union Leader 2375
ROBERTS, Nora — Writer 2375
ROBERTS, Ricky Elias, PhD, ThD — Linguist, Educator 2376
ROBERTS, Robin René — Co-anchor 2376
ROBERTSON, Arthur K. Jr. — Entrepreneur; Minister;
Communications Specialist 2376
ROBERTSON, Edwin David — Lawyer 1066
ROBERTSON, Julian Hart Jr. — Hedge Fund Manager 2377
ROBERTSON, Patricia R. — Language Professional, Assistant Professor
of English 2377
ROBINOWITZ, Joe Reece — Media Executive 2377
ROBINSON, Ann — State Representative 2377
ROBINSON, Barbara S. — Cultural Organization Consultant 1067
ROBINSON, David Maurice — Former NBA Player 2378
ROBINSON, David — Drummer 2377
ROBINSON, Duncan — Army School Instructor 2378
ROBINSON, James Sidney — Public Health Service Officer 2378
ROBINSON, Kassie — Sales and Marketing Manager 2378
ROBINSON, Marilynne — Writer 2378
ROBINSON, Michael A., Esq. — Founder/Owner 1585
ROBINSON, Nicole — Senior Vice President – Global Government 1068
ROBINSON, Richard Gary — President 2378
ROBINSON, Ruth Freddie Carleson — Secondary School Educator
(Retired) 1069
ROBINSON, Sir James L. "Jackrabbit", OSJ — Architect Planner/
Developer 1070
ROBITSHEK, Heidrun S. — Artistic Director 1071
ROBLES, Rosalie — Elementary School Educator 1585
ROBO, James L. — Chairman, CEO 2379
ROBSON, John Edward — Nursing Administrator 2379
ROBY, Martha Kehres — U.S. Representative, Lawyer 2379
ROBY, Pamela Ann, PhD — Sociologist, Educator 2379

ROCHELLE, Lugenia NMN DPD — Assistant Professor of English,
Director, QEP 2380
ROCHESTER, Lisa LaTrelle Blunt — U.S. Representative from Delaware 2381
ROCK, Chris — Comedian 2381
ROCKEFELLER, Sharon Lee — Former First Lady 2381
ROCKWELL, S. Kay, PhD — Educator 1072
ROCKWELL, Sam — Actor 2381
ROCQUE, Vincent, "Vin" Joseph — Attorney at Law 2382
RODENBAUGH, Marcia Wimer — Retired Elementary School Educator 2382
RODGERS, Aaron Charles — Professional Football Player 2382
RODGERS, Wilma Louise, PhD — Mathematics Educator (Retired) 2382
RODNEY, Paul Frederick, PhD — Physicist 2383
RODRIGUEZ, Alex — Former Professional Baseball Player 2383
RODRIGUEZ, Ernesto A. — Passenger Service Representative, Artist,
Researcher 2383
RODRIGUEZ, Gina — Actress 2383
RODRIGUEZ, Javier J. — CEO 2384
ROE, Charles P. — Aeronautical Information Specialist 2384
ROE, David, "Phil" Phillip, MD — U.S. Representative from Tennessee;
Physician 2384
ROEHL, Jerrald J. — Attorney 2384
ROEMER, David, PhD — Educator (Retired) 1586
ROESSNER, Karl A. — CEO (Retired) 2385
ROETHLISBERGER, Ben, "Big Ben" Todd Sr. — Professional Football
Player 2385
ROFF, Hugh Jr. — Energy Executive 1073
ROGAN, John Francis — Private Practice Consultant 1074
ROGERS, Ailene — Retired Secondary School Educator 2385
ROGERS, Alan Ernest Exel — Research Scientist 1075
ROGERS, Harold, "Hal" Dallas — U.S. Representative 2385
ROGERS, Jon M., PhD, ChFC, MRFC, CKA — Chairman, CEO 1076
ROGERS, Kenneth, "Kenny" Ray — Country Singer 2385
ROGERS, Lee Frank, MD — Professor Emeritus of Radiology 1077
ROGERS, Mike, "Mike" Dennis — U.S. Representative from Alabama 2386
ROGERS, Susan Haley, EdD — Secondary School Educator 1586
ROGINSKI, Raymond Stephen, MD, PhD — Medical Educator, Staff
Anesthesiologist 1078
ROJAS, Carmen, PhD — Founder, CEO 2386
ROKUSEK, Cecilia F., EdD, MSc, RDN — President, CEO 2386
ROLLINS, Sonny — Composer, Musician 2387
ROMAN, Michael F. — Chairperson, CEO 2387
ROMETTY, Ginni — Executive Chairman 2387
ROMNEY, Willard, "Mitt" Mitt — U.S. Senator from Utah 2388
RONAN, Saoirse — Actress 2388
RONSON, Mark Daniel — Music Producer 2388
RONSTADT, Linda Marie — Singer 2389
ROONEY, Laurence, "Francis" Francis — U.S. Representative from
Florida; Construction Executive 2389
ROOTH, Barry — Owner 1587
ROPCHAN, Jim R., PhD — Research Scientist 1079
RORSCHACH, Richard Gordon — Lawyer 2389
RORTY, Mary Varney, PhD — Philosopher, Bioethicist 2390
ROSA, Lucille Marie — Supervisory Librarian (Retired) 2390
ROSE, Daniel — Chairman 1080
ROSE, John Williams — U.S. Representative from Tennessee; Farmer 2390
ROSE, Max N. — U.S. Representative from New York 2390
ROSE, Peter Edward — Professional Baseball Player (Retired),
Professional Baseball Coach (Retired) 2390
ROSE, Richard Loomis Richard — Attorney (Retired) 2390
ROSE, Susan Porter, LHD (Hon.) — Former Chief of Staff to
Barbara Bush 1081
ROSEMAN, Charles S. — Lawyer 2390

ROSEN, Jacklyn, "Jacky" Sheryl — U.S. Senator from Nevada 2391
ROSEN, Jeffrey Adam — U.S. Deputy Attorney General 2391
ROSEN, Nathan Aaron JD, MLS — Law Librarian, Lawyer, Consultant 2391
ROSENBERG, Howard — Founder, CEO 2391
ROSENSTEIN, Robert A., PhD — Scientific Consultant 2391
ROSENSTEIN, Rod Jay — Former U.S. Deputy Attorney General; Lawyer 2391
ROSENZWEIG, Rachel Zoe — Fashion Stylist 2392
ROSOFF, William A. — Counsel 1082
ROSS, Diana — Singer; Actress; Entertainer; Fashion Designer 2392
ROSS, Hugh Courtney — Electrical Engineer 1083
ROSS, Ivy E. — Apparel Executive, Artist 2392
ROSS, Stephen Michael — Real Estate Company Executive, Professional Sports Team Owner 2392
ROSS, Wilbur Louis Jr. — U.S. Secretary of Commerce 2392
ROTCH, James — Attorney/Shareholder 2393
ROTH, Georgia Ann Middlebrooks — Accounting and Business Law Educator (Retired) 2393
ROTH, Philip Milton — Author; Professor 2393
ROTH, Veronica — Author 2394
ROTHBLATT, Martine Aliana — President, CEO 2394
ROTHENBERG, Robert Philip — Public Relations Counselor 2394
ROTHSCHILD, Jeff — Vice President of Infrastructure Software 2394
ROTI, Thomas David — Judge 1084
ROTROFF JACOBS, Linda Rotroff — Elementary School Educator 2394
ROUDA, Harley Edwin Jr. — U.S. Representative from California; Lawyer; Real Estate Executive 2395
ROUNDS, Linnea K. — Library Administrator (Retired) 1085
ROUNDS, Marion Michael "Mike" — U.S. Senator from South Dakota; Former Governor of South Dakota 1086
ROUNICK, Jack — Lawyer 1087
ROUNSLEY, Robert Richard, PhD — Chemical Engineer, Educator (Retired) 1088
ROUSE, Leo E. — Professor and Dean Emeritus, ADEA Consultant 2395
ROUZE, Jeffrey Allen — President; Real Estate Executive 1587
ROUZER, David Cheston — U.S. Representative from North Carolina 2395
ROWE, Donald Eugene — Professional Director (Retired) 2395
ROWE, Larry Jordan — Lawyer 2395
ROWE, Larry Jordan — Partner 2396
ROWLAND, Pleasant — Founder 2396
ROWLING, J.K. — Writer 2396
ROWSON, Richard Cavanagh — Foreign Affairs Publishing 2396
ROY, Charles, "Chip" Eugene — U.S. Representative from Texas; Lawyer 2396
ROYBAL-ALLARD, Lucille Elsa — U.S. Representative from California 2397
ROYCE, Edward, "Ed" Randall — Former U.S. Representative from California 2397
ROYER, Thomas Jerome "Jerry", RFC — CEO 1089
ROYSTON, Donald C. "Don" — Former President 1090
RUBEN, Alan Miles, JD — Advisory Professor; Emeritus Professor of Law 1091
RUBENSTEIN, David Mark — Co-Founder, Co-Executive Chairman, Private Equity Firm Executive 2397
RUBIN, Gretchen Anne — Author, Blogger 2397
RUBINO, Michael C. — Of Counsel 2397
RUBINSON, Evan A. — CEO, President 1092
RUBIO, Marco Antonio — U.S. Senator from Florida 2397
RUDDY, Christopher — News Media Executive 2398
RUDMAN, Kal Solomon, EdM — Humanitarian, Philanthropist, Media Executive 1093
RUDOLF, John "Jan", MS, PE — Chief Structural Engineer 1094
RUEDA, Alfonso, PhD — Physics Researcher; Professor Emeritus 1588
RUGGERA, Paul S., MS — Special Product Engineer 2398

RUHLE, Stephanie Leigh — Anchor, Senior Business Correspondent 2398
RUIZ, Brunilda "Brunie" — Dancer, Dance Instructor, Choreographer 1095
RUIZ, Raul, MD — U.S. Representative from California; Physician 2398
RUMER, Darin L. — Partner 1588
RUMMEL, Raymond, "Butch" Howard, EdS, MEd — Mathematics Educator (Retired) 2398
RUMSFELD, Donald Henry — Former U.S. Secretary of Defense 2398
RUNYON, Chuck — CEO 2399
RUPPERSBERGER, Charles, "Dutch" Albert III — U.S. Representative from Maryland 2399
RUSEV, Rusen — Managing Broker 1096
RUSH, Bobby Lee — U.S. Representative 2399
RUSHDIE, Salman — Writer 2399
RUSHTON, Gerard, PhD — Professor Emeritus, Researcher 1097
RUSSEL, Richard A., DCS, AeE — Space Systems Engineer (Retired) 1098
RUSSELL, Steven, "Steve" Dane — Former U.S. Representative from Oklahoma 2400
RUSSIN, Jonathan — Lawyer, Consultant 2400
RUSSO, Danny — Creative Director of Design 1099
RUST, Robert W. — Lawyer (Retired), Colonel (Retired), U.S. Marine Corps Forces Reserve 1100
RUTHERFORD, John Henry — U.S. Representative from Florida; Former Sheriff 2400
RUTHERFORD, William D. — Investment Executive 2401
RUTLEDGE, Thomas M. — Chairman, CEO 2401
RUTNER, Stephen M., PhD — Brigadier General; Professor 2401
RYAN, Clayton — Manager 2402
RYAN, Diane Phyllis "Di", PhD, AGPCNP-BC, FNP-BC — Nurse 1101
RYAN, Earl Martin — Public Affairs Analyst 2402
RYAN, Elizabeth Ellen — Chief Executive Director, Film Director 2402
RYAN, Harriet — Reporter 2402
RYAN, Matt Thomas — Professional Football Player 2402
RYAN, Nolan — Professional Baseball Team Executive, Former Professional Baseball Player 2402
RYAN, Paul Davis — Former Speaker of the House 2402
RYAN, Tara — President/Owner 1589
RYAN, Timothy, "Tim" John — U.S. Representative from Ohio 2403
RYANS, Lisa — Director of Communications 2403
RYU, Dewey Doo-Young, PhD — Professor Emeritus 1102
RZUCIDLO, Eva Marie, MD — Director and Chief of Vascular Surgery 1589
SABAN, Nick — College Football Coach, Former Professional Football Coach 2403
SABANAYAGAM, Muthukrishna, MD — Neuropsychiatrist 1103
SABLAN, Gregorio Kilili Camacho — Delegate to the U.S. House of Representatives from the Northern Mariana Islands 2403
SABO, Ronald William, Esq. — Lawyer, Financial Consultant 1104
SABOL, Steve Douglas — Filmmaker 2403
SABRINA, Danielle — Founder, CEO 2404
SABU, Sneha — Coordinator, Corporate Planning and Reporting 1105
SAENZ, Jeremy — Founder, Owner 1106
SAGER, Lawrence C., PhD, PMP — Human Systems Integration Consultant; Psychologist 1590
SAGERMAN, Robert Howard, MD, FACR — Professor Emeritus 1107
SAKALL, Dan, MPA, BTh — Educator, Chaplain, Cognitive Behavioral Therapist 2404
SALAMANCA, Maria — Investor 2404
SALAS, Angela M. — Small Business Management; Tax Consultant 2404
SALAZAR, Angelique — Vice President 1590
SALAZAR, Edward J. — 1) Respiratory Therapist 2) Vice President 2404
SALERNO, Alexandra, MS, NCC, LPC — Behavioral Health Therapist 2404
SALGO, Ivan S., MD — Cardiothoracic Anesthesiologist 1108
SALISBURY, Frank Boyer, PhD — Professor Emeritus; Botanist; Author 1451

SALITERMAN, Richard Arlen — President 1109
SALKE, Jennifer — Head 2405
SALL, John — Co-Founder 2405
SALLUS, Marc — Partner 1110
SALMOIRAGHI, Gian Carlo — Physiologist, Educator 2405
SALT, Alfred L., Rev. — Priest 1111
SAMPAS, Dorothy Myers, PhD — Government Official (Retired) 1112
SAMPRAS, Pete — Professional Tennis Player (Retired) 2405
SAMPSON, J. Frank — Professor Emeritus; Artist 1591
SAMUELI, Henry — Chief Technology Officer 2405
SAN NICOLAS, Michael Franklin Quitugua — Delegate to the U.S. House
    of Representatives from Guam 2405
SÁNCHEZ, Linda Teresa — U.S. Representative from California 2406
SANCHEZ, Nicole — Founder, Managing Partner 2406
SAND, Shara, PsyD — Psychologist 2406
SANDBERG, Sheryl Kara — Executive, Chief Operating Officer 1113
SANDERS, Bernard "Bernie" — U.S. Senator from Vermont 1114
SANDERS, Sarah Elizabeth — Former White House Press Secretary 2406
SANDHU, Daljit Singh — Retired 1115
SANDHU, M. Akram — Co-Owner, Chemist, Business Executive 1116
SANFORD, Thomas Denny — Founder, CEO, Philanthropist 2406
SANTANA, Carlos — Guitarist, Musician 2406
SANTER, Richard Arthur — Geography Educator (Retired) 2407
SANTI, Ernest Scott — CEO, Chairperson 2407
SANTILLI, Arthur Attilio, PhD — Senior Research Fellow, Chemist
    (Retired) 2407
SARANDON, Susan — Actress 2407
SARBANES, John Peter Spyros — U.S. Representative, Lawyer 2408
SARGENT, Walter Harriman II — Lawyer, President of Law Firm
    Handling State and Federal Civil Appeals 2408
SARKAR, Chitto Priyo, DO, PhD — Family Medicine Physician,
    Research Scientist 1117
SARRATT, Janet Platt — Librarian 2408
SARSOUR, Linda — Political Activist; Former Executive Director 2409
SASAHARA, Arthur Asao, MD — Senior Physician 2409
SASSE, Benjamin, "Ben" Eric, PhD — U.S. Senator from Nebraska 2409
SASSER, Charles W. — Journalist, Educator, Writer 1591
SATINSKY, David, MD — Medical Doctor (Retired) 1118
SATRIANO, Pietro — Chairperson, President, CEO 2410
SATTERLEE, Warren S. II — Retail Management Professional, Writer 1119
SAUNDERS, Benjamin — Attorney 1120
SAUNDERS, Martha A. — Professor of English Emerita 2410
SAVAGE, Robert Charles — Insurance and Finance Company Executive 2410
SAVOY, Chyrl Lenore — Artist, Educator 2410
SAWARDEKER, Jawahar Sazro, PhD — Group Quality Worldwide
    (Retired) 2410
SAWYER, Diane — Broadcast Journalist 1121
SAWYER, Hugh 2411
SAWYER, Robert L., MD — Physician 1592
SAXENA, Subhash Chandra, PhD — Mathematics Professor,
    Researcher, Academic Administrator 1592
SAYEGH, Monet Nasser, MD — General Surgery/Medical Senior
    Consultant 2411
SAYLOR, Nancy Lee, BS — Teacher (Retired) 1122
SCAFFIDI, Roy F. — Senior Member 2411
SCALES, James L. Jr., MS, MD — Physician 2411
SCALIA, Eugene — U.S. Secretary of Labor 2412
SCALING, Sam, "Chipper , Chip" Tilden, MD — Founder, President
    (Retired); Obstetrician, Gynecologist 2412
SCALISE, Stephen, "Steve" Joseph — U.S. Representative from
    Louisiana 2412
SCAPPLE, Sharon, "Shari" M., PhD — Professor Emeritus 2412

SCARAMUCCI, Anthony, "The Mooch" — Former White House Director
    of Communication; Finance Executive 2413
SCARBOROUGH, Joe — Talk Show Host 2413
SCARBROUGH, Dorothy Ray, RNC, BSN, MSN — Nursing Educator;
    Consultant 1123
SCARBROUGH, Glenda Judith — Elementary School Educator 2413
SCHAFER, Joyce — Investment Broker 1124
SCHAFFER, Mark A. — President, Owner 1125
SCHAFFNER, J., "Skip" Luray, Artist — Vice President 2413
SCHAFFNER, John Albert — Retail Merchandising Executive, Designer 2414
SCHAKOWSKY, Janice, "Jan" — U.S. Representative from Illinois 2414
SCHALK, Willi Georg — Founder 1126
SCHALL, Susan O., DEng — Founder & Lead Consultant 1127
SCHARF, Charles W. — CEO, President 2414
SCHARFF, Andrea — Owner 2414
SCHATZ, Brian Emanuel — U.S. Senator from Hawaii 2414
SCHEIER, Mindy — President, Founder 2414
SCHELLING, Thomas Crombie, PhD — Distinguished Professor
    Emeritus; Economist 2414
SCHEMMEL, Robert A. — Electronics Engineering Technician 1593
SCHIFF, Adam Bennett — U.S. Representative from California; Lawyer 2415
SCHIFF, Craig M. — President, CEO 2415
SCHIFF, David T. — Investment Banker 1128
SCHIFF, Marlene Sandler — Entrepreneur 1129
SCHILLER, Justin Galland — Antiquarian Bookseller, Researcher, Editor 2415
SCHILLING, Brittany — Biology Teacher 2415
SCHILLING-NORDAL, Geraldine A. — Secondary School Educator
    (Retired) 2415
SCHIMKE, Clyde V. — Owner, Inventor 2416
SCHIMMELFENNIG, Ladona Beth — Special Education Educator,
    Management Consultant, School System Administrator 2416
SCHIPPERS, Dave A., ScD, CISSP — Assistant Professor; Professional
    Cyber Investigator 2416
SCHIZER, David Michael — Dean, Law Educator, Economics Professor 2417
SCHLAERTH, Katherine R. — Physician 1130
SCHLESINGER, Tim — Attorney 2417
SCHLIFSKE, John E. — Chairman, CEO 2417
SCHLITT, W. Joseph "Joe" III, PhD, PE — Metallurgical Engineer 1593
SCHLOSSBERG, Dan — Writer, Author, Broadcaster 2417
SCHMALTZ, Lawrence, "Larry" G. — Engineer, Consultant,
    General Contractor 2418
SCHMIDT, Eric Emerson — Chairman 2418
SCHMIDT, James Robert — Facilities Engineer 2418
SCHMIDT, Valerie A. — Marketing Director 2418
SCHMIDTMAN, Andrew A. Jr., CPA — Accountant 2419
SCHMITT, George Frederick Jr., FSAMPE, MBA — Director of
    International Programs 2419
SCHMITTLEIN, David C. — Dean 2419
SCHMITZ, John — Writer, Educator 2419
SCHMITZ, Matthew — Physician 2420
SCHNEIDER, Alexander W. Jr., PE, F-IEEE — Reliability Engineer
    (Retired) 1594
SCHNEIDER, Bradley, "Brad" Scott — U.S. Representative from Illinois 2420
SCHNEIDER, Carol, PhD — Attendant and Clinical Professor Emerita;
    Psychologist 1131
SCHNEIDER, Frederick R. — Professor of Law Emeritus 1132
SCHNEIDER, Valerie Lois, PhD — Professor of Speech Communication
    (Retired) 1133
SCHNEPS, Jacob "Jack", PhD — Emeritus Professor of Physics,
    Department Chairman 1134
SCHNITZER, Alan D. — CEO and Chairman CN: The Travelers
    Companies Inc. 2420
SCHOCH, Michael P. A. — CEO 1135

SCHOCHOR, Jonathan, JD — Lawyer; Law Educator 1136

SCHOPPER, Sue — Maternal, Women's Health and Medical/Surgical Nurse 2420

SCHORNACK, John J. — Vice Chairman, Retired 1137

SCHRADER, Walter, "Kurt" Kurt, DVM — U.S. Representative from Oregon; Veterinarian 2420

SCHRAM, Geraldine Phyllis — Security Administrator 2421

SCHRANK, Shirley Ann, — Artist 2421

SCHRIER, Kimberly, "Kim" Merle, MD — U.S. Representative from Washington; Physician 2421

SCHRODER, Mitch J. — Owner 1138

SCHROEDER, Donna, OSB, PhD — Professor Emeritus of Biology 2421

SCHROEDER, Marsha, MA, LPC, PLLC — Therapist, Licensed Professional Counselor 2421

SCHROER-LAMONT, Anne Christine, PhD — University Administrator; Psychologist 2421

SCHUCKMAN, Nancy Lee — Principal (Retired) 2422

SCHULER, John — CEO 2422

SCHULMAN, Daniel H. — President, CEO 2422

SCHUMER, Amy — Comedienne, Actress 2422

SCHUMER, Charles Ellis "Chuck" — U.S. Senator from New York 1139

SCHURZ, Scott C. — Chairman of the Board 1140

SCHWARTZ, Bart M. — Chairman 2423

SCHWARTZ, Donald Ray — Communications Educator, College Official, Associate Professor 2423

SCHWARTZ, Walter Richard, MD, FACOG — Obstetrician/Gynecologist (Retired) 1141

SCHWARZ, Michael — Lawyer 2423

SCHWARZE, Martin W., DO — Cardiologist 2423

SCHWARZNEGGER, Arnold Alois — Actor, Former Politician 2424

SCHWEIGHARDT, Frank K., PhD — Chemist 2424

SCHWEIKERT, David S. — U.S. Representative from Arizona; Real Estate Executive 2425

SCHWERY, Luetta, RN, BSN — Community Health Nurse 2425

SCORSESE, Martin — Film Director, Film Producer 1142

SCOTT, Barbara Ann, PhD — Sociology Professor, Peace Activist 2425

SCOTT, David Albert — U.S. Representative from Georgia; Advertising Company Executive 2425

SCOTT, Freida — Parent Educator Coordinator 1143

SCOTT, James, "Austin" Austin — U.S. Representative from Georgia; Insurance Company Executive 2425

SCOTT, Jane — Artist 2426

SCOTT, Lisa — Owner, Founder 2426

SCOTT, Philip, "Phil" Brian — Governor of Vermont 2426

SCOTT, Richard, "Rick" Lynn — U.S. Senator from Florida; Healthcare Executive 2426

SCOTT, Robert, "Bobby" Cortez — U.S. Representative, Lawyer 2426

SCOTT, Suzanne — CEO 1594

SCOTT, Timothy, "Tim" Eugene — Junior U.S. Senator from South Carolina; Insurance Company Executive 2426

SCOULAR, Robert F. — Lawyer 2426

SCREMIN, Anthony James — Lawyer, Head Trial Attorney 2427

SCROGGS, Larry K. — Lawyer, State Legislator 2427

SCUDDER, Thayer — Anthropologist 2427

SCULLY, Vincent Edward — Sports Broadcaster 2427

SEACREST, Ryan John — Television and Radio Personality, Entrepreneur 2428

SEAGLE, Edgar Franklin, Dr. P.H., P.E. — Environmental Engineer, Consultant 2428

SEAGO, James L. — Biologist, Educator 2428

SEALE, James Lawrence Jr., PhD — Agricultural Studies Educator 2429

SEARLE, Robert Ferguson, BS, MDiv, DMin, MA — Minister 2429

SEATON, David T. — Chairman, CEO 2429

SEAVER, Tom — Professional Baseball Player (Retired) 2429

SEBERT, Kesha Rose — Singer 2429

SECCHIAROLI, Lawrence Nazzareth — Mechanical Design Engineer (Retired) 2429

SECUNDA, Thomas, "Tom" — Financial Services Executive 2430

SEDLER, Robert A. — Distinguished Professor of Law 1144

SEEMAN, Linda — Counselor 2430

SEGAL, Rena — Artist 1145

SEGER, Bob — Musician 2430

SEGUROLA, Romualdo Jr., MD — Chief of Cardiac Surgery 1146

SEIDLER, Petra — Team Leader 1147

SEIFERT, Karl E., PhD — Geology Educator 1148

SEINFELD, Jerry — Comedian, Actor, Television Producer, Writer 2430

SEITZ, Carole J., BME, MME — Associate Professor Emerita, Coordinator of Music Division 2430

SEIZER, Fern Victor, — Health Services Administrator 2431

SELBY, Jerome M. — Municipal and Business Consultant 1149

SELDEN, Lynde — General Counsel 2431

SELES, Monica — Professional Tennis Player (Retired) 2431

SELF, Bill — College Basketball Coach 2431

SELLECK, Tom — Actor 2431

SELLMAN, Wayne Steven, PhD — Vice President for Strategic Planning (Retired) 1150

SEMENZA, Gregg Leonard, MD, PhD — Professor of Genetic Medicine; Director of Vascular Program 1151

SENDEL, Barry — Founder & CEO 1152

SENSENBRENNER, Frank, "Jim" James Jr. — U.S. Representative 2432

SEPPI, Edward Joseph — Physicist (Retired) 1153

SERKIS, Andy Clement — Actor 2432

SERRANO, José Enrique — U.S. Representative from New York 2432

SESSA, David Joseph — Chemist, Biochemist 1154

SETH, Akhil K. — Doctor 1595

SEVAYEGA, Dina Maria, EdD — Associate in Education (Retired) 1595

SEVENICH, David Mark PhD — Senior Scientist 2432

SEWELL, Terrycina, "Terri" Andrea — U.S. Representative, Lawyer 2433

SEYMOUR, Lesley Jane — Editor, Author, Entrepreneur 2433

SEYMOUR, Richard Burt — President, CEO; Author; Health Educator (Retired) 1155

SHABAKER, Liz — CEO 2433

SHAEFFER, Charlie Willard, MD — Cardiologist, Lipidologist 2433

SHAEVSKY, Mark — Lawyer 2433

SHAH, Gulzar H. — Professor & Department Chair of Health Policy and Management 2434

SHAH, Harshad — Founder 1596

SHAH, Rishi U. — Co-Founder 2434

SHAH, Vinod P. PhD, President — Pharmaceutical Consultant 2434

SHAHEEN, Cynthia, "Jeanne" Jeanne — U.S. Senator 2434

SHAHEEN, David R., Esq. — Trial Attorney 1156

SHAHIDI, Freydoon, PhD — Mathematician, Mathematics Educator, Distinguished Professor of Mathematics 2435

SHAINMAN, Jack — Co-Founder 2435

SHALALA, Donna Edna, PhD — U.S. Representative from Florida; Educator 2435

SHANAHAN, Patrick Michael — Former Acting U.S. Secretary of Defense 2435

SHAO, Zhenhua — Electrical Engineer, Consultant 1596

SHAPIRO, Robert Leslie — Attorney 1157

SHARFMAN, William L. — Author, Writer, Interviewer, Consulting Strategist 2435

SHARMA, Pankaj, MD, PhD, FRCP — Neurologist, Researcher, Scientist 2436

SHARP, David H., PhD — Physicist 2436

SHARP, Gary Duane, PhD — Marine Biologist 2436

SHARP, George Richard — Aerospace Engineer 2437

SHARP, James Franklin, PhD — Finance Educator, Portfolio Manager 2437

SHARPLES, Edward, PhD — Academic Administrator, English Professor 2437
SHARPLESS, Karl — Chemist, Educator 2437
SHATNER, William — Actor 2437
SHAW, Alan Roger — Market Analyst, Stock Brokerage Company Executive (Retired) 1158
SHAW, Roderick, DDS — General Dentistry 2438
SHEA, James L. — Chairman Emeritus, Attorney 2438
SHEA-STONUM, Marilyn — Federal Bankruptcy Judge (Retired) 2439
SHEEN, Martin — Actor 2439
SHEERAN, Ed — Musician 2440
SHEFFIELD, Dewey — Retired 2440
SHEINDLIN, Judith Susan "Judge Judy" — Television Personality; Judge 1597
SHELBY, Richard Craig — U.S. Senator from Alabama; Lawyer 2440
SHELLENBERGER, Jeffrey — President, CEO 2440
SHELLEY, E. Dorinda, MD — Dermatologist, Author 1159
SHELTON, Blake Tolison — Musician 2440
SHEMS, Estherina, MD — Child Psychiatrist (Retired) 1160
SHENEFELT, Philip D — Dermatologist 2440
SHENKMAN, Mark R. — Founder and President 1161
SHEPHERD, Deborah Gulick — Elementary School Educator (Retired) 2440
SHEPHERD, Kikuko T. — Artist 1162
SHEPPARD, Naomi Kate — Nursing Educator (Retired) 2441
SHERMAN, Bradley James — U.S. Representative from California 2441
SHERMAN, Cindy — Artist, Photographer 2441
SHERMAN, Danya — CEO, Founder 2441
SHERRILL, Rebecca, "Mikie" Michelle — U.S. Representative from New Jersey; Lawyer 2442
SHEWARD, Clarence W. — Gaseous Diffusion Company Executive 2442
SHIFFRIN, Mikaela Pauline — Alpine Skier 1163
SHIH, Hong — Fellow 1164
SHIH, Sheng Yun — Church Deacon 2442
SHILLADY, Donald, "Don" Douglas, PhD — Professor Emeritus of Chemistry 2442
SHIMKUS, John Mondy — U.S. Representative from Illinois 2442
SHINE, William, "Bill" — Senior Adviser, White House Director of Communications (Retired) 2443
SHIRLEY, Frank Connard — Forester, Consultant 2443
SHIRLEY, Jon Hardy — Physicist 1597
SHIRLEY, Otis Allen — Criminal Justice Educator; Management Consultant 2443
SHOAF, Bruce Allen — Instrument Engineer (Retired) 2443
SHOEMAKER, Frances — Sculptor 2443
SHORE, Kirk — Senior Vice President of Integrated Product Team 2443
SHORT, Martin — Actor 2444
SHOTWELL, Gwynne — President, COO 2444
SHPILBERG, Victor J. — Physician 2444
SHUCK, L. Zane, PhD, PE — Distinguished Research Scientist; Founder, President 1165
SHULMAN, Abraham, MD, FACS — Otolaryngology Educator; Hospital Administrator 1166
SHULMISTER, M. Ross — Attorney 1167
SHURTLEFF, William Roy, Author, Founder, SoyInfo Center — Author, Publishing Executive 2445
SHUVAL, Joshua — Director of Operations and Risk Management 1598
SIARNY, William D. — Librarian, Archivist 2445
SIBILLO, Agostino, "Ago", PhD — CEO, Computer Scientist 2445
SIBLET, Jean-Philippe — Museum Director 1168
SIBLEY, Charlotte Elaine — Independent Director 2445
SICKAFOOSE, Todd — Jazz Musician, Composer, Producer 2446
SIDEBOTTOM, Charles B. — Engineering Executive (Retired) 2446
SIDER, E. Morris — Professor Emeritus of History and English Literature 2446

SIDERIS, Rhonda Cannada — President, Founder 2446
SIDMAN, Richard Leon "Dick", MD — Neuroscientist, Educator 1169
SIDWELL, Robert William, PhD — Virologist, Educator (Retired) 2447
SIEBEL, Thomas M. — CEO 2447
SIEGEL, Stuart, "Stu" E., MD — Pediatric Hematologist-Oncologist; Educator (Retired) 2447
SIEGELMAN, Stanley S., MD — Radiologist, Educator 1598
SIEKIERSKI, Kamilla Malgorzata CDT — Dental Laboratory Technologist 2448
SIGMOND, Carol Ann — Attorney, Chair; Construction Law Team 1599
SIGNORILE, Vincent — Lawyer 2448
SILBERMANN, Ben — Co-Founder, CEO 2448
SILLIMAN, Thomas Boughton, PE — Electrical Engineer 2448
SILLIN JOHNSON, Julie E. — Educator (Retired) 2449
SILVER, Adam — Commissioner 1599
SILVER, Leon Theodore, PhD — W.M. Keck Foundation Professor for Resource Geology, Emeritus 2449
SILVERIO, Nick E. — Founder 2449
SILVERMAN, Arthur Charles, Esq. — Building Construction Lawyer 1170
SILVERMAN, Sarah — Comedian, Actress 2449
SILVERSHEIN, Joel Michael, Esq. — Assistant State Attorney 2450
SILVERSTEIN, Herbert, MSc, MD, FACS — President 2450
SIMMONDS, Robert Maurer — Educator, Web Developer, Operations Research Analyst (Retired) 1171
SIMMONS, Adele, PhD — Foundation Administrator 1172
SIMMONS, Betty Jo — Civil Engineer, Draftsman 2450
SIMMONS, Lee Guyton Jr., DVM — Chairman of the Board 1173
SIMON, John G. — Augustus Lines Professor Emeritus of Law 1174
SIMONDS, John E. — Newspaper Editor (Retired) 2451
SIMONS, Nathaniel, "Nat" — Co-Founder 2451
SIMPKINS, Lucille Angelique — Personnel Administrator, Ecumenical Minister 2451
SIMPSON, Harold Yazzie — Founder, Owner 1175
SIMPSON, Michael — Retired Metals Service Center Executive 1176
SIMPSON, Michael, "Mike" Keith, DDS — U.S. Representative from Idaho 2451
SIMPSON, Raymond W., PhD — Electronics Engineer 2451
SIMS, Lowery Stokes — Curator, Art Historian; Writer; Educator 2451
SIMS, Marsha Lois, — Archaeologist (Retired) 2452
SINAI, Allen L., PhD — Chief Global Economist/Strategist & President 1177
SINCLAIR-SMITH, Susanne, "Susie" — CEO 2452
SINEMA, Kyrsten Lea, PhD — U.S. Senator from Arizona; Lawyer 2453
SINGER, Frederick Raphael, MD — Medical Researcher 1178
SINGH, Bhawandeep — Researcher, Lecturer, Independent Consultant 2453
SINGH, Jag Jeet, PhD — Research Physicist 1179
SINGH, Lilly — YouTuber, Comedian, Talk Show Host 2453
SINGH, Nitin Kumar — Scientist 2453
SINGH, Yesh P., PhD — Professor Emeritus 2453
SINNING, Allan — Interim Chair/Professor 2453
SIPOS, John Francis Jr. — Historian for Village of Cassadaga, and Town of Stockton, NY 1180
SIPRESS, Morton — Political Scientist, Professor Emeritus 1181
SIRES, Albio B. — U.S. Representative from New Jersey 2453
SIRIANNI, Joyce Elaine, PhD — Anthropologist, Educator 2454
SIRIANO, Christian — Fashion Designer 2454
SISOLAK, Stephen, "Steve" F. — Governor of Nevada 2454
SKALER, Robert Morris — Forensic Architect, Architect; Educator 1600
SKARSGÅRD, Alexander — Actor 2454
SKEEN, Vicki — Director of Delivery and Customer Enablement 1182
SKERRITT, Elizabeth — Prof. Librarian, Information Scientist 2455
SKIDMORE WILSON, Joyce Fox Thorum Jacobsen — Public Relations and Communication Executive 2455

SKIRNICK, Robert, "Bob" Andrew Esq. — Lawyer 2455
SKOLNICK, Lawrence, MD, MPH — Director of Neonatology (Retired) 2456
SLADE, Michael — Playwright, Librettist, Author, Writer 2456
SLATER, Christian — Actor 2456
SLATKIN, Leonard Edward — Composer 2457
SLAVITT, Ben, JD — Lawyer 2457
SLAYTON, Thomas Kennedy — Editor, Writer 2457
SLEDGE, William Hurt, MD — Deputy Chair of Psychiatry for Clinical Services (Retired) 2458
SLOAN, Andrew E., MD, FACS — Professor, Vice Chair of Neurosurgery 1183
SLOAN, Frank — Economist, Educator Emeritus 2458
SLOAN, Mary, "Mary Love" Stringfield — Hospital Interior Designer 2459
SLOAN, Phillip Reid, PhD — Liberal Studies Educator, Historian of Science, Philosopher of Life Science 2459
SLOAN, Timothy J. — CEO 2460
SLOANE ROEMER, Elaine — Real Estate Broker 2460
SLOBIN, Kathleen Overin, PhD — Professor Emerita, Consultant 1184
SLOTKIN, Elissa Blair — U.S. Representative from Michigan 2460
SMALL, James William — Occupational and Public Health Physician (Retired) 2460
SMILEY, Marilynn Jean, PhD — Professor Emerita 1185
SMITH, Adam D. — Managing Attorney 1600
SMITH, Adrian Michael — U.S. Representative from Nebraska; Real Estate Agent 2461
SMITH, Allie Maitland, PhD — Engineering Educator (Retired) 1186
SMITH, Barry H., MD, PhD — President, CEO 2461
SMITH, Bill, "Deacon Bill" Richard — Deacon 2461
SMITH, Charles W., MD — Professor, Family Medicine 2462
SMITH, Christine, "Tina" Elizabeth — U.S. Senator 2462
SMITH, Christopher, "Chris" — U.S. Representative 2462
SMITH, Daisy Mullett — Publisher 2462
SMITH, Daniel Owen — Consultant,Thermal Engineer 1187
SMITH, David W. — Reverend Doctor 2463
SMITH, David, "Adam" Adam — U.S. Representative from Washington 2462
SMITH, David, "D. Brooks Smith" Brookman — Chief Judge 2462
SMITH, Dawn E. — Owner, CEO 1188
SMITH, Fred — Chairman, President, CEO 2463
SMITH, G. Louis — Senior Research Scientist 1189
SMITH, Harriet G., Educator — Secondary School Educator, Writer 2463
SMITH, James (LL Cool J), — Rap Artist, Actor 2464
SMITH, James E. II, MSW, PhD., LSCSW — Professor/Licensed Specialist Clinical Social Worker 1190
SMITH, James Edward II — Microbiologist, Chemist 2463
SMITH, James Howell, PhD — Historian, Educator (Retired) 2463
SMITH, James Marshall — Author, Physicist 1601
SMITH, James Randolph Jr. — Attorney 2464
SMITH, Jason Thomas — U.S. Representative 2464
SMITH, Joan — Elementary Education Educator, Principal 2464
SMITH, Joseph Lee — Diplomat, Academic Administrator 2464
SMITH, Karla — Executive Vice President 1601
SMITH, Laurie — Professor of Sociology, Dean 2465
SMITH, Lavenski, "Vence" Roy — Chief Judge 2465
SMITH, Madison H. — Senior Vice President 1602
SMITH, Maggie — Actress 2465
SMITH, Margaret — Owner 1602
SMITH, Patricia J. (Goering) — Photographer, Writer, Political Scientist 2466
SMITH, Robert John — Chair 2466
SMITH, Robert, "Bob" Bruce, PhD — 2466
SMITH, Sally J. — President, Former CEO 2466
SMITH, Sheila Robertson — Hematology Technician (Retired) 1603
SMITH, Shepard — Journalist 2466

SMITH, Tracy K. — Poet, Educator 2467
SMITH, Wayne Thomas — Chairman, President, CEO 2467
SMITH, Will Carroll Jr. — Actor; Rap Artist 1603
SMITHIES, Oliver — Geneticist; Professor 2467
SMOOT, George Fitzgerald III — Astrophysicist 2467
SMOTHERMAN, Kenneth — Owner, Operator 2467
SMUCKER, Lloyd Kenneth — U.S. Representative from California 2468
SMYTH, Adrienne Charlene — Program Executive 1604
SMYTH, Glen Miller — Management Consultant, Human Resources Executive 1191
SNELLING, Diane B. — Chair 2468
SNETSINGER, Kenneth, "Ken" G. PhD — Retired Mineralogist 2468
SNIPES, Wesley — Actor, Producer 2468
SNYDER, Jean — Lawyer 1192
SNYDER, John G. — Managing Director, General Counsel 2468
SNYDER, Ned IV, MD — President/Plastic Surgeon 1193
SNYDER, Travis — Owner 2468
SNYDER-ELLINGSON, Lynsi Lavelle — President 2468
SOBIESKI, Jaroslaw — Aerospace Engineer 2469
SODERBERGH, Steven Andrew — Film Producer, Director, Screenwriter 2469
SODOLSKI, John — President (Retired) 1194
SOENNICHSEN, Jean, "Betty" Elizabeth, MA — Senior Advocate 2469
SOLAK, Marek Krzysztof, PhD — Senior Manager 2469
SOLER, Arturo — Real Estate Investor, Entreprenuer 1195
SOLOMON, David Michael — CEO, Chairman 1196
SOMERS, Ryan P. — Owner 1197
SOMERS, Willard C. — CEO/Manufacturing Executive 2470
SONG, Moon K., PhD — Biomedical Research Scientist 2470
SONNEK, Bonnie, PhD — Education Educator 2470
SOPER, Richard G. — CEO, Medical Director 1604
SORA, Sebastian Antony, DPS, PMC — Business Machines Manufacturing Executive, Educator 2470
SORENSON, Arne — CEO, President 2470
SORKIN, Aaron — Writer 2471
SOROS, George — Hedge Fund Manager; Entrepreneur; Philanthropist 2471
SOSSAMAN, Scott — Lieutenant Colonel (R), U.S. Army 2471
SOTO, Darren Michael — U.S. Representative from Florida 2471
SOTOMAYOR, Sonia Maria — Associate Justice 1605
SOUTER, David Hackett — Associate Justice (Retired) 2472
SOUTHREY, Melissa Anne — Registered Diabetes Educator, Certified Diabertes Educator, Aqua Instructor 2472
SOVERN, Douglas — Author, Journalist; Musician 2472
SOVERS, Ojars Juris, PhD — Research Physicist 1198
SOWERS, Amy B. — Speech-Language Pathologist 1199
SOWERS, Katie — Offensive Assistant Coach 2472
SOX, Harold, "Hal" Carleton — Director of Peer Review 2472
SPACEK, Sissy — Actress 2473
SPADA, Jessica Marie — Director/Owner 2473
SPADER, James — Actor 2473
SPAIN, Jack Holland Jr. — Senior Counsel 2474
SPALDING, Catherine, Esq — Family Court Attorney, Guardian Ad Litem 1200
SPANBERGER, Abigail Anne — U.S. Representative from Virginia 2474
SPANO, Vincent, "Ross" Ross — U.S. Representative from Florida 2474
SPARKS, Barbara L., MBA — Pharmaceutical Manager (Retired) 1201
SPARKS, Lisa D. — Owner 1605
SPARKS, Nicholas Charles — Author; Screenwriter 1606
SPEARS, Britney — Singer 2474
SPEELMAN, Dale Arthur — Proprietor 1202
SPEER, Richard — Senior Security Analyst 1203
SPEIER, Karen, "Jackie" Lorraine Jacqueline — U.S. Representative from California 2474
SPEIGHT, Joseph B. Sr. — CEO, Agent 2474

SPELBRING, Ralph Eugene — Chemist (Retired) 1204
SPENCE, Gerry — Lawyer, Writer 2475
SPENCER, Octavia — Actress, Producer, Author 2475
SPIEGEL, Evan Thomas — Entrepreneur, Application Developer 2475
SPIELBERG, Steven Allan — Film Director, Producer 1205
SPIETH, Jordan Alexander — Professional Golfer 2475
SPILKER, James Julius Jr., DEng — Engineer; Consulting Professor 2476
SPINA, Anthony Ferdinand, Esq., — Lawyer 2476
SPITZNAGEL, John K., MD, FACP — Microbiologist, Immunologist, Physician (Retired) 1206
SPIVEY, Bruce E., MD, MS, MEd — Ophthalmologist; Educator; Organizational Creator & Leader 2476
SPOLTER, Pari Dokht, PhD — Science Writer 2477
SPRENKLE, Case PhD — Economist, Educator 2477
SPRINGMAN, Clark Alton BS — Marketing Professional 2477
SQUERI, Stephen J. — CEO 2477
ST. ANTOINE, Theodore, "Ted" Joseph — Law Educator, Arbitrator (Retired) 2478
STABENOW, Ann, "Debbie" — U.S. Senator from Michigan 2478
STAEHLE, Alan W. — Retired County Police and Public Safety Official, Elected Official, Emergency Manager 2478
STALEY, James, "Jes" Edward — Bank Executive 2479
STALLONE, Sylvester Gardenzio — Actor, Film Director, Screenwriter, Producer 2479
STALLWORTH, Terresa, MD — Clinical Director 2479
STANDLEY, John T. — Chairperson, CEO 2479
STANISLAWSKI, Barbara — Curator, Secondary School Educator 1207
STANKEY, John T. — CEO 2480
STANLEY, Ronald Alwin, PhD — Environmental Scientist 2480
STANLEY, Steven Mitchell, PhD — 1) Paleontologist 2) Professor 1208
STANTON, Giancarlo Cruz Michael — Professional Baseball Player 2480
STANTON, Gregory, "Greg" John — U.S. Representative from Arizona 2480
STANTON, M. Duncan, PhD — Professor Emeritus 1209
STANTON, Roger D. — Attorney 1210
STANTON, Sylvia Doucet — Artist, Gallery Owner, Author 1211
STAPLES, Brent, PhD — Writer, Reporter 2480
STARKEBAUM, Gordon Alan, MD, MACR — Emeritus Professor, Staff Rheumatologist 2480
STARR, Ringo, — Drummer 2481
STASACK, Edward — Artist, Professor Emeritus 2481
STATLER, Irving C., PhD — Associate Emeritus 1212
STAUBER, Peter, "Pete" Allen — U.S. Representative from Minnesota 2482
STAUFFER, Sharon T. — Executive Director 2482
STECHMAN, John Vance — Rangeland Management Educator, Owner 1213
STECKBAUER, James, "Jim" J. — Quality Assurance Specialist (Retired) 2482
STECKLER, Jessica A. — Owner/Consultant 2482
STEEL, Danielle — Author 2482
STEELE, Jack, PhD — Professor Emeritus of Chemistry 1214
STEFANI, Gwen Renée — Singer 2483
STEFANIK, Elise Marie — U.S. Representative from New York 2484
STEHR, Justin — Estimating and Business Development Manager 2484
STEIL, Bryan George — U.S. Representative from Wisconsin; Lawyer 2484
STEIN, Ellen G. — Information Technology Executive (Retired) 2484
STEIN, Michael A., MD — Vice President; Cardiologist; Medical Educator; Medical Researcher 1606
STEIN, Robert, "Robin" M. Jr., MCP — Special Assistant to the Mayor 2484
STEINBERG, Nevin — Sound Designer 2484
STEINBERG, Robin Faith — Ophthalmologist 1215
STEINFELD, Hailee — Actress, Singer 2484
STEINHORN, Irwin Harry, JD — Lawyer, Corporate Financial Executive; Educator 2485
STEININGER, Jeffrey Lynn Jr. — Makeup Artist 2485

STEINWACHS, Donald M., PhD — Public Health Educator, Academic Administrator 1216
STEITZ, Thomas Arthur, PhD — Biophysicist, Professor 2485
STEPHANOPOULOS, George Robert — News Anchor, Political Correspondent 1607
STEPHENS, Deborah Lynn — Founder, Chairman, CEO 2485
STEPHENS, H. Jeannette Jeannette, BS, MS, PhD — Mathematics Educator 2485
STEPHENSON, Randall L. — Chairman, CEO, President 2485
STERN, Matthew B., MD — Professor Emeritus of Neurology 2486
STERN, Michael D., DDS — Dentist 2486
STERN, Walter W. III — Consultant, Senior Emeritus Attorney 1217
STETZ, Sylvia Ann — Small Business Owner 1607
STEUBE, William, "Greg" Gregory — U.S. Representative from Florida; Lawyer 2487
STEUCKE, Paul Theodore Sr. — Professional Association Administrator; Artist 2487
STEVENS, Haley Maria — U.S. Representative from Michigan 2487
STEVENS, John Paul — Associate Justice (Retired) 2487
STEVENS, Leonard — Education Consultant 2487
STEVENS, Lizbeth Jane Curme, PhD, CCC-SLP — Speech-Language Pathologist, Special Education Educator, Researcher 274
STEVENS, Sandra G., CLU, CFC — Financial Services Representative 1218
STEVOS, Joyce Louise, PhD — Adjunct Professor 1219
STEWART, Carl E. — Former Chief Judge 2488
STEWART, Christopher, "Chris" Douglas — U.S. Representative; Author 2488
STEWART, David James — Cardiologist 1220
STEWART, David Wayne, PhD — President's Professor of Marketing and Business Law 1221
STEWART, James H. — President/Managing Director 1222
STEWART, Jon — Television Personality, Comedian 2488
STEWART, LaTanya — Payroll Manager, Owner 1608
STEWART, Michael Glenn, MD, MPH — Vice Dean, Professor, Chairman 1223
STEWART, Patrick — Actor, Producer 2488
STIFLER, Venetia — Artistic and Executive Director 1224
STIGLITZ, Joseph — Economist 2489
STINGILY, Diamond — Artist, Poet 2490
STINSON, Robert Wayne — Meat Company Executive 1226
STITT, John, "Kevin" Kevin — Governor of Oklahoma 2490
STIVERS, Steven, "Steve" Ernst — U.S. Representative 2490
STOCKTON, Beverly Ann — Physiology and Pharmacology Educator 2490
STODDARD-HAYES, Marlana K. — Artist, Educator 1608
STOLL, Neal Richard — Retired Partner 1227
STOLTMAN, James Bernard — Professor Emeritus, Anthropology 1228
STONE, Chris, PE, FNSPE, FASCE, LEED AP — CEO, Senior Principal, Engineer 2490
STONE, David — Theatre Producer 2490
STONE, Donald G. — Attorney 2491
STONE, Emma — Actress 2491
STONE, Howard L., C.P.A., C.F.E., J.D. — Partner 1229
STONE, Kipp Franklin — Investment Professional 2491
STONEMARK, Ray — Operating Partner 2491
STOREY, Jeffrey K. — CEO 2491
STORK, Donald Arthur — Advertsing Executive (Retired) 1609
STOSS, Frederick W. MLS — Librarian, Educator 2492
STOUT, Krista — Digital Sales Manager 2492
STRAFACE, Paul "Paulie" — Service Manager/Technician 1230
STRAIT, George — Musician 2492
STRANGFELD, John R. Jr. — Chairman, President, CEO 2492
STRASBURG, Stephen James — Professional Baseball Player 2493
STRATHMAN, John Henry — Electrical Engineer (Retired) 1231
STREEP, Meryl — Actress 2493

STREET, Robert Anderson Jr. — Professor of Computer Information Systems 2493
STRESEN-REUTER, Jared James — CEO 2494
STRINGER, Howard, PhD — Electronics Executive 1232
STRODE, Joseph Arlin — Lawyer 2494
STRODE, Scott Kreider — Communications Educator (Retired) 2494
STROH, Guy Weston, PhD — Philosophy Educator 2494
STROKER, Ali — Actress, Singer 2494
STRONG, Carolyn Ray — Information Designer (Retired) 1233
STRONG, Christina Cordaire — Writer, Artist 2494
STROUCE, Richard Arnold — Management Consultant 2495
STRUCK, Norma — Artist 2495
STRUMPF, David — Vice President of Research and Development 2495
STRUNK, Betsy Ann Whitenight, MEd — Retired Education Educator 1367
STRUNK, Harold Kenneth — Insurance Company Executive, Naval Officer (Retired) 2495
STRUYK, Jack — President, Partner 2495
STUART, Rose — Owner 2496
STUBBS, Donald C. — Secondary School Educator (Retired) 1234
STUEMPFLE, Arthur, "Art" Karl — Research Scientist 2496
STUMPFF, Robert Thomas "Bob" — Director of Public Works (Retired) 1235
STUPPARD, Charles L., PhD — CEO, Founder, Owner 1236
STYCOS, Maria Nowakowska, PhD — Senior Lecturer (Retired) 2496
SUAREZ ELLER, Alicia — Retired Educator and Children's Music Director 2496
SUAREZ-RESNICK, Dulce — Vice President 1609
SUBRAMANIAN, Mani, Adjunct Professor 2497
SUBRAMANIAN, Siva, MD, FAAP — Professor, Neonatologist 1237
SUHR, John Nicholas Jr. — Partner 2497
SUHR, Paul Augustine, Esq. — Managing Member 1238
SUHRE, Walter Anthony — Lawyer, Brewery Executive (Retired) 2497
SULC, Jean Luena Mestres — Lobbyist, Consultant (Retired) 1239
SULLIVAN, Cornelius Wayne — Marine Biology Educator, University Research Foundation and Government Agency Administrator 1240
SULLIVAN, Daniel, "Dan" Scott — U.S. Senator from Alaska; Lawyer 2497
SULLIVAN, James Gerald — Small Business Owner 1241
SULLIVAN, John Joseph — U.S. Deputy Secretary of State 2497
SULLIVAN, Neil Samuel, PhD — Physicist, Researcher, Educator, Former Dean 2497
SULLIVAN, Warren Gerald — Lawyer, Consultant 2498
SUMMERS, Charles PhD — Entomologist, Educator 2498
SUMNER, Gordon, "Sting" Matthew Thomas — Musician 2498
SUNDQUIST, Don — Former Governor 1243
SUNUNU, Christopher, "Chris" T. — Governor of New Hampshire 2498
SUOZZI, Thomas, "Tom" Richard — U.S. Representative from New York 2499
SURPLUS, Robert W. — Music Educator (Retired) 1244
SUSSMAN, Gary Mark — Assistant Treasurer 1245
SUTHERLAND, Alexander, "Alec" Charles — Professor Emeritus of English (Retired) 2499
SUTHERLAND, Kiefer — Actor 2499
SUTTON, Jennifer — Partner, President 1610
SUTTON, Mark Stephan — Chairman, CEO 2499
SUWANAKUL, Sontachai — Economist, Educator 2499
SVOBODA, Angela Mae "Angel Mae" — Coordinator, Business Education Department Chair (Retired) 1610
SVOBODA, Janice J., RN, BSN, HNB-BC — Nurse 2500
SWAGEL, Phillip, "Phil" Lee, PhD — Director; Professor of Economics 2500
SWAIM, John, "Frank" Franklin, MD, ABFP, AAFP — Physician, Healthcare Executive 2500
SWALWELL, Eric Michael Jr. — U.S. Representative from California 2500
SWAN, Anna Rose, RN, BSN — School Nurse 2500
SWAN, Robert Holmes — CEO 2500

SWANK, Hilary — Actress, Producer 2501
SWANN, Frederick Lewis — Organist, Choral Director, Teacher 2501
SWANSON, Martha B. "Marti" — Secondary Educator (Retired), Consultant 1246
SWARD, Robert Stuart MA, Retired — American Poet, Author 2501
SWARTZ, James D., PhD — Professor 2502
SWARTZ, Steven R. — President, CEO 2502
SWARTZEL, Dennis D. Jr. — Engineer 2502
SWEENER, Bernard Francis "Bernie" — Clinician-Licensed Master Social Worker 1611
SWEET, Julie — CEO 2502
SWEIGER, Judith Ann — Elementary and Special Education Educator 2502
SWETMAN, Margot — Self Development and Executive Leadership Life Coach 1611
SWIFT, Christopher John — CEO, Chairman 2502
SWIFT, Judy Jo — Banker 2502
SWIFT, Taylor Alison — Musician, Singer, Songwriter 2503
SWIGAR, Mary Eva, MD — Neuro-Psychiatry Educator; Chair 1247
SWILDENS, Karin Johanna — Sculptor 2503
SWINDELL, Archie — Biomedical Research 2504
SWINDELL, Gary — Owner 2504
SWINFORD, Carol — Manager 1248
SWINK, Laurence Nim, PhD — Technical Consultant 2504
SWINTON, Tilda — Actress 2504
SWISHER, Debora Taylor, BSN, RN-BC — Registered Nurse, Complex Care Manager 1612
SYKES, Richard Nesbitt, PhD — Department Chair (Retired) 2505
SYROPOULOS, Mike — School System Supervisor (Retired) 2505
SZYMANSKI, Ronald J., Esq. — Lawyer (Retired) 2506
TABACKIN, Lewis Barry — Jazz Musician 2506
TABATABAI, Mahmood — Physician (MD, PhD) 2506
TABBA, Mohammad Myassar, P.E., PhD — Civil Engineer 2506
TABOR, Corey R. — Author, Illustrator 2506
TAFOLLA, Carmen — Professor Emerita, President 1612
TAHIRAJ, Desi — Business Consultant; Life Coach 1613
TAKANO, Mark Allan — U.S. Representative from California; Educator 2506
TALBOT, Joe — Filmmaker 2507
TALBOT, Lee Merriam, PhD — Professor 1249
TALVI, Ilkka — Concert Violinist 1250
TAMEZ, Raquel — CEO 1251
TANENBAUM, Jay Harvey — Lawyer 1252
TANNENBAUM, Deborah — Advocate 2507
TAO, Rongjia, PhD — Professor 1613
TAPPER, Jake — News Correspondent, Journalist 1614
TAPPERT, Tara Leigh, PhD — Art Historian, Archivist, Researcher 2507
TAPSONY, Veronica — Musician, Music Educator 2507
TARANTINO, Quentin Jerome — Film Director, Screenwriter 2508
TARR, Charles Edwin PhD — Physicist, Researcher 2508
TATUM, Channing — Actor 2508
TAUTFEST, Eric S. — Lawyer 1253
TAYLOR, David L. — President 1254
TAYLOR, David S. — CEO, President, Chairman of the Board 2509
TAYLOR, Dominica, "Minka" Stephens — Teacher 2509
TAYLOR, Hurl Richmond Jr. — Professor, Attorney, Military Officer (Retired) 2509
TAYLOR, Lawrence, "L.T." Julius — Sports Commentator; Former Professional Football Player 2509
TAYLOR, Nell Cochrane — Nonprofit Association Executive (Retired) 1614
TAYLOR, Nicholas C. — Lawyer 2509
TAYLOR, Nicholas, "Van Taylor" Van Campen — U.S. Representative from Texas; Real Estate Investment Banker 2510

TAYLOR, Raymond George — Professor Emeritus 2510
TAYLOR, Richard B., CPA — Investment Advisor 2510
TAYLOR-HINES, Regina — Owner 2510
TCHOBANOGLOUS, George, PhD — Professor Emeritus 1255
TEAGUE, A. James — Co-CEO 2510
TEBHA, Mark Iqbal — CEO 2510
TEBOW, Tim — Baseball Player, Professional Football Player (Retired), Sports Analyst (Retired) 2511
TEDESCHI, John A., PhD — Historian, Librarian, Educator 2511
TEDESCO, Paul — Humanities Educator 2511
TEEHEE, Kimberly Kay — Advocate, Native American Lobbyist 2511
TELLERIA, Anthony F. — Lawyer 2512
TELLO, Donna — Tax Strategist; Practitioner; Writer 1256
TEMPLE, Joseph, "Joe" G. Jr., DEng — Pharmaceutical Executive, Chemicals Executive 2512
TENORE, Jean — Real Estate Professional 1257
TENUTA, Luigia — Lawyer 2512
TEREKHOV, Yuri, PhD — R&D Manager 2512
TERRY, Robert, "Rob" — Land Surveyor, Part-Time Business Owner 2512
TERRY, Ward Edgar Jr. — Lawyer 1258
TESAR, Patricia Marie, PhD — Special Education Administrator 1615
TESMER, Nancy S. — Librarian (Retired) 2513
TESSIER-LAVIGNE, Marc — President 2513
TESTER, Raymond, "Jon" Jon — U.S. Senator from Montana 2513
THAKKAR, Sweetie — Owner 2513
THAKUR, Nirmalya — PhD Student 2513
THANGAVELAUTHAM, Jekan — Assistant Professor 1259
THARP, Larry Alan — Chemical Engineer 1260
THAYER, Bruce Allen — Artist 2514
THAYER, Kristine — Pediatric Surgeon 2514
THEILEN, Gordon Henry, DVM, DACVIM — Veterinary Surgery Scientist Educator 1261
THERON, Charlize — Actress, Producer 2515
THIEDA, Shirley — Geologist 2515
THIESSEN, Brian David — Lawyer 1262
THIGPEN, James Tate, MD — Oncologist 1263
THIGPEN, Neal Dorsey Symington, PhD — Political Science Educator 2515
THIRY, Kent J. — CEO 2516
THOMAN, Mary E., PhD 2516
THOMAS, Clarence — Associate Justice 2516
THOMAS, D. Russell D. — Owner/President 1264
THOMAS, Dorothy J., EdD — Counselor 2516
THOMAS, Dorothy Worthy, PhD — English/French Educator 2516
THOMAS, Earl Winty III — Professional Football Player 2517
THOMAS, Jim G. — Music Educator 2517
THOMAS, Leelamma Koshy, MA, BS, RN, RNC, — Women's Health Care Nurse 2517
THOMAS, Michael Tilson — Music Director 2517
THOMAS, Ray — Singer, Musician 2517
THOMAS, Sidney Runyan — Chief Judge 2517
THOMPSON, Arthur, "Art" Raymond — Marketing Professional 2518
THOMPSON, Bennie Gordon — U.S. Representative from Mississippi 2518
THOMPSON, Billy — President/CEO 1265
THOMPSON, Charles, "Mike" Michael — U.S. Representative 2518
THOMPSON, David Michael, PhD, DD — Historian; Educator (Retired) 2518
THOMPSON, Dolores Ann — Special Educator (Retired) 2518
THOMPSON, E. Brad, MD — Professor Emeritus; Endocrinologist 2519
THOMPSON, Emma — Actress 2519
THOMPSON, Glenn, "G.T." W. Jr. — U.S. Representative from Pennsylvania; Former Health Facility Administrator 2520
THOMPSON, Kathleen S. — Marriage and Family Counselor 2520
THOMPSON, Thomas M., LLB — Lawyer 2520

THOMPSON, Timothy Lewis — Lawyer, Partner 2521
THOMSON, Brandon S., Esq. — Attorney 2521
THORNBERRY, William, "Mac" McClellan — U.S. Representative from Texas; Lawyer 2521
THORNE, Kip Stephen, PhD — Physicist, Researcher 2521
THORNTON, Ival Crandall "Val" — Interior Architect 1266
THUMS, Charles W. — Designer, Consultant 2522
THUNBERG, Greta Tintin Eleonora — Climate Activist 1267
THUNE, John Randolph — U.S. Senator from South Dakota 2522
THUNE, Ronald L. — Professor 1615
TIERNEY, Jennifer — Designer, Owner 2522
TIETJEN, Jill S. — President and CEO 2522
TIGUE, Virginia Beth "Ginny" — Community Volunteer 1268
TILBURY, Charlotte, MBE — Owner, Creative Director 2522
TILDERS, Sonny — Animatronics Artist 2522
TILLIS, Thomas, "Thom" Roland — U.S. Senator from North Carolina 2522
TILLMAN, Barbara Ballard — Librarian 2523
TILLMAN, Burton L., Esq. — Founder & Attorney 1616
TIMBLIN, Lloyd O. Jr. — Water Resources Scientist 2523
TIMLIN, James — Bishop Emeritus 2523
TIMMERMAN, Robert Wilson, PE, CEM, LEED AP — Engineering Executive, Researcher 1616
TIMMONS, William Richardson IV — U.S. Representative from South Carolina; Lawyer; Entrepreneur 2523
TING, Chin-Sen — Physics Professor 2523
TIPPETS, Dennis W. — Mineral Exploration Executive, State Legislator 2523
TIPSORD, Michael L. — Chairman, CEO 2523
TIPTON, Scott Randall — U.S. Representative from Colorado 2524
TIRUMALAI, Srivatsan, "Dr. SRI" S., PhD — Professor [Emeritus] 2524
TITUS, Alice, "Dina" Costandina, PhD — U.S. Representative from Nevada; Educator 2524
TLAIB, Rashida — U.S. Representative from Michigan 2524
TOBIN, Joseph William — Archbishop 1269
TODD, John Robert — Educational Director, Educator 2525
TOMANY, Mark Allen — State Trooper (Retired) 2525
TOMKIES, Michael — Partner 1617
TOMLIN, Lily — Actress, Comedian, Producer 2525
TOMOMATSU, Hideo — Physical Chemist 2526
TOMPKINS, Joseph B. Jr. — Lawyer 1270
TOMPSON, Andrew F.B., PhD — Hydrologist, Researcher 2526
TONIETTI, Marco E., PhD — Professor Emeritus 1271
TONK, Hampton Scott — President 1272
TONKO, Paul David — U.S. Representative from New York 2526
TOOMEY, Patrick, "Pat" Jospeh Jr. — U.S. Senator from Pennsylvania; Finance Executive 2526
TORRE, Joe — Major League Baseball Executive, Professional Baseball Manager (Retired) 2526
TORRES SMALL, Xochitl Liana — U.S. Representative from New Mexico 2527
TORRES, Norma Judith — U.S. Representative from California 2527
TORRES-GOMEZ, Evelyn — CEO 2527
TOVAR, Nicholas Mario — President, CEO 2527
TOVEY, Craig Aaron, PhD — Engineering Educator 1273
TOWLE, Margaret Beggs — Senior Vice President, Financial Advisor 1443
TOWNSEND, Beau — President & CEO 2527
TOWNSHEND, Pete — Guitarist, Composer 2527
TOWSNER, Cynthia Merle "Cindy" — Academic Administrator, Educator 1274
TRACHTENBERG, David — Lawyer 2528
TRACHTENBERG, Matthew J., Esq. — Chairman, President, CEO 1275
TRAGEN, Irving G. — Legal Consultant (Retired), U.S. Foreign Service Officer 2528
TRAGESER, Raymond Mattern — Insurance Executive 1276

TRAHAN, Lori Ann — U.S. Representative from Massachusetts 2529
TRAMMEL, Richard — President, Sports Psychologist 2529
TRANI, Eugene P., PhD — Professor 2529
TRAPPE, James Martin, PhD — Research Mycologist 2530
TRAUB, Stephen I. — Senior Partner (Retired) 1277
TRAVAYIAKIS, Sofia Aerakis — Branch Manager 2530
TRAYANOVA, Natalia Alexandrova, PhD — Biomedical Engineering Educator 1278
TREBEK, Alex — Television Personality, Game Show Host 1279
TRENT, James Alfred — Founder/President 1280
TREVISANI, Thomas P. — Chief Surgeon 1281
TRIANTAFILLOU, Demosthenes — Principal 2531
TRIMBLE, Robert Bogue, PhD — Research Scientist (Retired) 1282
TRIPATHI, Brijesh I. — Founder, CEO 2531
TRIPLETT, Robert J. — State Research Analyst (Retired) 2531
TRIPP, Russell W. — Real Estate Company Officer 1283
TRIVELPIECE, Alvin W., PhD — Scientist (Retired) 1284
TRONE, David John — U.S. Representative from Maryland 2531
TROUT, Michael Nelson — Professional Baseball Player 2531
TROUT, Monroe Eugene, MD, JD — Health Facility Administrator 1285
TRUJILLO, Sergio — Dancer, Stage Choreographer 2531
TRUMP, Donald John — 45th President of the U.S.; Real Estate Developer 1286
TRUMP, Ivanka Marie — First Daughter; Senior Advisor to the President 2531
TRUMP, Melania — First Lady of the U.S. 2532
TRUNK, Gary, MD, MBA — Pulmonologist; Consultant 2532
TSALAMATA, Vicky — Professor 2532
TSANG, Lincoln PhD, BPharm, PhD, LLB — Lawyer, Pharmacist 2532
TSCHUMY, Freda C. — Artist 2533
TSU, Raphael — Physics and Electrical Engineering Professor 2533
TUCH, Gayle S. — Attorney, Certified Mediator 1617
TUGNOLI, Lorenzo — Photographer 2533
TULLOCH, Edwin Fred, PhD — Minister, Chaplain, Psychotherapist 1287
TURCO, Lewis Putnam "Turk" — Professor Emeritus 1288
TURINO, Gerard Michael — John H. Keating Sr. Professor of Medicine Emeritus 1289
TURNER, Elvin Leroy — School System Administrator (Retired) 1618
TURNER, Jean I. — Musician, Educator 2533
TURNER, Michael, "Mike" Ray — U.S. Representative from Ohio 2534
TURNER, Natalie Ann — Consultant (Retired) 1290
TURNER, Robert, "Bob" L. — State Representative (Retired) 2534
TURNER, Staci J. — Business Operations Manager 2534
TURNER, Sylvester — Office of Turner 2534
TURNER, Ted Edward III — Media Executive, Philanthropist 2534
TURNER, Tina — Singer 2534
TURTURRO, John — Actor 2535
TUSCHMAN, James M. Esq. — Lecturer, Director of Outreach and Engagement 2535
TWAIN, Shania — Singer, Musician 2535
TYK, Bia — Owner 2536
TYKOSKI, Nick L. — CEO 2536
TYMKOVICH, Timothy Michael — Chief Judge 2536
TYRA, Patricia Ann, EdD, MS, BS — Mental Health Nurse, Professor Emerita 2536
TYRRELL, James E. Jr., Esq. — Member 1618
TYSON, Bernard J. — CEO 2536
TYSON, Cicely — Actress 2537
TYSON, Neil deGrasse, PhD — Astrophysicist, Director 2537
U'REN, Marie Rita Tyler — Travel Company Executive 2540
UDALL, Thomas, "Tom" Stewart — U.S. Senator from New Mexico; Lawyer 2538
UDELL, Jon Gerald, PhD — Business Educator; Executive 2538

UHL, Jessica — Chief Financial Officer 2538
UHLENBECK, Karen — Mathematician, Educator 2539
UICKER, James Leo — Mechanical Engineer 2539
ULC, Otto, PhD — Political Science Professor (Retired) 2539
ULLOA, Angela — Project Engineer 2539
UMANA, Ufot Frank Sr. — Counselor Educator 1619
UMANZOR, Juan A. Jr. — Realtor 1291
UMPLEBY, Jim — CEO 2539
UNDERWOOD, Carrie Marie — Singer 1292
UNDERWOOD, Lauren Ashley — U.S. Representative from Illinois 2539
UNION, Gabrielle — Actress 2539
UNTERBERG, Susan — Photographer, Philanthropist 1619
UPTON, Frederick, "Fred" Stephen — U.S. Representative 2540
UPTON, Thomas Vernon, PhD — Medical Educator 2540
URBINA, Manuel II, PhD, JD — Founder, Curator 1293
URQUIDEZ, Benny "The Jet" — Kickboxer, Martial Arts Choreographer, Actor 1294
URQUIZA, Patricia — Chief Financial Officer 2541
URSPRUNG, Deborah Lynn — Special Education Educator, Counselor 2541
UTZINGER, Robert Conde — Architect; Educator, Professor Emeritus 2541
UY, Kathleen W., MD — Medical Director, Fresenius Medical Care Lakeshore Unit, Medical Director 1295
VAIL, Les — President/CEO 2541
VALADAO, David Goncalves — Former U.S. Representative 2541
VALENTEKOVICH, Marija Nikoletic, PhD — Diagnostic Executive 2542
VALLARTA, Josefina, "Josie" Del Mundo — Child Neurologist (Retired); Associate Professor of Pediatrics and Neurology Emeritus 2542
VAMOS, Ivan P., AICP — State Agency Administrator (Retired) 1297
VAN DREW, Jefferson H., DMD — U.S. Representative, Dentist (Retired) 2542
VAN DYKE, Dick — Actor, Comedian 2542
VAN HOLLEN, Christopher, "Chris" J. Jr. — U.S. Senator from Maryland; Lawyer 2543
VAN TASSELL, James L., PhD — Biology Educator; Researcher 2543
VANDER WEIDE, Vernon Jay — Lawyer 2543
VANDER ZANDEN, Marianne — Retired Paralegal/Music Educator 2544
VANDERBILT, Gloria Morgan — Artist, Actress, Fashion Designer 2544
VANDERHEYDEN, Carol Evonne — Elementary School Educator (Retired) 2544
VANDERPOEL, James Robert — Lawyer 2544
VANDERWALKER, Diane Mary, PhD — Materials Research Engineer (Retired) 1304
VANDIVER, Geraldine M. — Construction Company Executive 2544
VANHAECKE, Erwin, PhD — Pharmaceutical Executive 1305
VARGAS, Juan Carlos — U.S. Representative from California 2544
VASEFF, James Richard — Architect 2545
VASOS, Todd J. — CEO 2545
VATTILANA, Joseph William — Chief State Safety Inspector (Retired) 1306
VAUGHN, Robert Weeks — Health Education Specialist 2545
VAUGHN, Thomas J., Professor of Earth Sciences — Earth Science Educator 2545
VAZIRANI-FALES, Heea, JD — Legislative Staff Member(Retired), Lawyer (Retired) 1307
VEASEY, Marc Allison — U.S. Representative from Texas 2546
VECELLIO, Leo A. Jr. — Construction, Mining and Petroleum Company Executive 1308
VED, Ravi — Physician 2546
VEDDER, Eddie — Singer 2546
VEHLE, Mike — Retired State Legislator 2546
VEIGAMILTON, Ana — President 2546
VELA, Filemón Bartolomé Jr. — U.S. Representative from Texas; Lawyer 2547
VELASQUEZ, Antonio — Owner 1620
VELÁZQUEZ, Nydia Margarita — U.S. Representative 2547

VELICER-GEIGER, Janet Frances "Jan" — Elementary School Educator (Retired) 1309

VENERABLE, Grant Delbert II, PhD — Artist, Teacher, Chemical Scientist 1310

VENERABLE, Shirley M — Retired Educator 2547

VENINGA, Robert Louis, PhD — Public Health Educator 2547

VENKATARAMAN, Krish — Chief Financial Officer 1311

VENTOLA, Dean S. — Architect, Architectural Company Executive 2547

VENTRE, Peter — CEO 2547

VERANO, Anthony Frank — Banker (Retired) 2548

VERLANDER, Justin Brooks — Professional Baseball Player 2548

VERMA, Seema — Administrator 1621

VERNICK, Jeffrey F. — Manager, Performance Analysis and Planning 2548

VERONICA, Madonna — Singer, Actress, Producer 2549

VERSACE, Donatella Francesca — Fashion Designer 2549

VESECKY, John F. — Science Educator, Electrical Engineering Educator, Researcher 2549

VESTBERG, Hans — CEO 2550

VIE, Richard Carl — Chairman Emeritus 1312

VIEIRA, Linda Marie — Chief Financial Officer, Secretary 1313

VILLA, Valentine Marie, PhD — Professor 1621

VILLANUEVA, Miguel — Administrator 1314

VILLONE, Maryann, RN — Nursing Consultant 1315

VIRMANI, Sant Singh — Agronomist, Researcher, Consultant 2550

VISCLOSKY, Peter, "Pete" John — U.S. Representative, Lawyer 2550

VISENTIN, John — CEO 2550

VITE, Frank — Realtor 1316

VITERITTI, John Frank II 2550

VNOUKOV, Roman — Principal Designer 1317

VOCE, Mary F., Esq. — Former Chair of the Cross Border Tax Planning Practice 1622

VOGEL, Cedric Wakelee, Esq. — Lawyer 1318

VOGLER, James W., PhD — Physicist, Consultant 2551

VOIGHT, Jon — Actor 2551

VOLANDES, Stellene — Editor-in-Chief 2551

VOLZ, Paul Albert, PhD — Director of Mycology Laboratory (Retired) 2551

VON BAILLOU, Astrid — Executive Search Consultant 2552

VON FURSTENBERG, Diane — Fashion Designer 2552

VON FURSTENBERG, George, PhD — Economics Professor Emeritus 2552

VON SELDENECK, Judith, "Judy" Crowell — Interior Design Consultant (Retired) 2552

VON STAR, Brenda Lee, BSN, FNPC — Primary Care Family Nurse Practitioner 2552

VONN, Lindsey Caroline — Professional Skier 2553

VOORHEES, Steven C. — CEO 2553

VOTTO, Joseph Daniel — Professional Baseball Player 2553

VRANISH, John — Electrical Engineer, Researcher 1622

VULAKH, Leonid Ya, PhD — Mathematics Educator (Retired) 1320

WACHTEL, Alan R. PhD — Clinical Psychologist 2553

WADE, Robert Paul, JD — Lawyer, General Counsel 2553

WADHWANI, Romesh — Application Developer 1321

WAGNER, Ann Louise — U.S. Representative from Missouri 2553

WAGNER, Charolette Jo — State Legislator (Retired) 1322

WAGNER, Jack Andrew, Jr. — Electrical Engineer (Retired) 1323

WAGNER-MANN, Colette Carol — Adjunct Associate Teaching Professor 2554

WAHLBERG, Mark — Actor, Producer, Businessman 2554

WALBERG, Timothy, "Tim" Lee — U.S. Representative from Michigan; Former Pastor 2554

WALCHER, Alan E. — Lawyer 2554

WALDEN, Dana — CEO 2555

WALDEN, Gregory, "Greg" Paul — U.S. Representative from Oregon 2555

WALDMAN, Michael — Charles H. Dyson Professor of Management, Professor of Economics 2555

WALDT, Risa — Artist 2555

WALENDOWSKI, George J., MBA, SCPM, ChE — Professor of Accounting and Business (Retired) 2555

WALES, C.L. — Assistant Project Manager 1324

WALES, Jimmy Donal — CEO 2556

WALK, Kathleen A. — Founder, Executive Director 2556

WALKEN, Christopher — Actor 2556

WALKER, Alice Malsenior — Writer 2557

WALKER, Darren — Foundation Administrator 1325

WALKER, George Theophilus — Composer 2557

WALKER, James Robert — Senior Project Engineer 2558

WALKER, Kara Elizabeth — Artist 2558

WALKER, Mark Howard — U.S. Representative from North Carolina; Pastor 2558

WALKER, Patricia Barnes, PhD — Educator, Theatre Producer (Retired) 2558

WALKER, William — Investment Banker 1326

WALLACE, Christopher — Broadcast Journalist 2558

WALLACE, Robert, "Bob" L. II — General 7Engineer 2558

WALLEN, Sharon Rose — Elementary School Teacher 1623

WALLENBERGER, Frederick — Materials Scientist 2559

WALORSKI, Jacqueline, "Jackie" R. — U.S. Representative from Indiana 2559

WALSH, Christine Ann, MD, FAAP, FACC — 2559

WALSH, Gerald T. — Roman Catholic Priest, Bishop 1327

WALSH, R. Lynette "Lyn", OTR — Occupational Therapist (Retired) 1328

WALSH-MCGEHEE, Martha Bosse — Ornithologist 1329

WALTER, Kenneth Gaines — Library Director (Emeritus) 2559

WALTERS, Mercedes, "Mercy" B. — District Governor of Lions District 4 L-6 2560

WALTON, James Carr "Jim" — Retail Company Executive; Bank Executive 1330

WALTZ, Christoph, — Actor 2560

WALTZ, Michael George Glen — U.S. Representative from Florida 2561

WALTZ, Thomas William — Economist 2561

WALZ, Robert D. USA, Lt. Col. — Military Officer (Retired), Teacher (Retired) 2561

WALZ, Timothy, "Tim" James — Governor of Minnesota 2561

WANEBO, Harold Joseph, MD, FACS — Cancer Surgeon, Investigator 1331

WANG, Alexander — Apparel Designer 2561

WANG, An-Ming — Composer 2561

WANG, James Chung Fang — Mechanical Engineer (Retired) 1332

WANG, Liang-Guo — Research Scientist 2562

WANG, Lisa — CEO 2562

WANG, Lulu — Film Director, Writer, Producer 2562

WANG, Vera — Fashion Designer 2562

WANG, Xingwu, PhD — Professor of Electrical Engineering 1333

WANN, Sharon — Dentist 2562

WARD, Donald — Attorney 2562

WARD, Jacqueline Ann — Nurse, Health Care Administrator, Legal Nurse Consultant 2563

WARD, Jo Ann — CEO (Retired) 2563

WARD, Nicholas Donnell — Lawyer 1334

WARD, Thomas, JD — President 2563

WARDEN, Kathy J. — President, CEO 1335

WAREHAM, Raymond Noble — Vice Chairman 2564

WARNER, Mark Robert — U.S. Senator from Virginia, Vice Chair of the Senate Intelligence Committee 2564

WARNER, Neari F., PhD — Visiting Clinical Professor; Former Acting University President 1336

WARREN, Diane Eve — Songwriter 1623

WARREN, Elizabeth Ann — U.S. Senator from Massachusetts; Educator 2564

WARREN, Rick — Pastor   2565
WARREN, Russell J. — Managing Director   2565
WASFIE, Tarik, MD, FACS, FICS — Surgeon, Educator   1337
WASHBURN, Gladys Rice — Photographer, Writer, Filmmaker   2565
WASHBURN, John Rosser "Jack" — Entrepreneur   1338
WASHBURN, Patricia, "Pat" Cheyne, Owner — Child Psychologist (Retired); Environmental Scientist; Conservationist   2566
WASHINGTON, Kerry — Actress   2566
WASSERMAN SCHULTZ, Debbie — U.S. Representative   2566
WASSERMAN, Leonard M., Esq. — Consultant; Adjunct Professor   1339
WATERS, Maxine Moore — U.S. Representative from California   2567
WATERSTON, Sam — Actor, Producer, Director   2567
WATFORD, Dolores — Elementary School Educator   2567
WATKINS, Steven, "Steve" Charles Jr. — U.S. Representative from Kansas   2568
WATSON COLEMAN, Bonnie M. — U.S. Representative from New Jersey   2568
WATSON, Denton L. — Professor   1340
WATSON, Emma — Actress   2568
WATSON, George Elder III — Ornithologist   1341
WATSON, Raymond Coke, PhD, PE — Lead Consultant   1342
WATSON, Thomas Sturges — Professional Golfer   2568
WATTS, Charlie — Drummer   2568
WEATHERS, Leroy Edward — Retired   1343
WEAVER, Patricia Ella — Mathematics Educator (Retired)   2569
WEAVER, Sigourney — Actress   2569
WEBB, Daniel, "Dan" K. — Co-Executive Chairman; Lawyer   2570
WEBB, Jason Michael — Composer, Lyricist, Musical Director   2570
WEBB, Karen — President   2570
WEBB, Willie James — Alcohol and Drug Abuse Specialist, Minister, Instructor   2570
WEBER, Curt M. — Law Educator   2571
WEBER, Jeffrey M., MD — Gastroenterologist   2571
WEBER, John B. — Architect (Retired)   2571
WEBER, Randall, "Randy" Keith — U.S. Representative from Texas; Small Business Owner   2571
WEBER, Robert, EdD — Adapted Physical Education Educator, Academic Administrator   1344
WEBSTER, Arthur Edward — Lawyer   2571
WEBSTER, Daniel Alan — U.S. Representative from Florida; Small Business Owner   2572
WEBSTER, Letitia — Chief Sustainability Officer, Partner   2572
WEDEKIND, Thomas C., MSW — CEO   2572
WEEMS, Robert E. Jr. — Willard W. Garvey Distinguished Professor of Business History   1345
WEGMILLER, Donald Charles "Don", MHA, FACHE — Chairman, CEO   1346
WEI, Ying — Engineer Consultant   2572
WEICHMAN, Douglas John — Fleet Manager of County Government   1347
WEICKERT, Wanda Opal — Child Welfare and Attendance Counselor, Psychotherapist, Educator (Retired)   1348
WEINBAUM, Charles H. Jr. — Insurance Company Executive   2572
WEINBERG, Florence May, PhD — Modern Language and Literature Educator (Retired)   1349
WEINER, John Barlow — Associate Director for Policy, Office of Combination Products   2572
WEINER, Leslie P., MD — Neurology Educator   2573
WEINSHENKER, Naomi — Psychiatrist   2573
WEINSTEIN, Michael B. — Of Counsel   2573
WEINTRAUB, Sam — Retired Reading Educator   2574
WEISLER, Dion J — Former CEO and President   2574
WEISS, Daniel H., PhD — President, CEO, Art Historian   1624
WEISS, Gerson, MD — Reproductive Endocrinologist, Educator (Retired)   1350
WEISSENBORN, Anne Adkins — Esq.   2574

WEISSMAN, Richard — Chairman of the Board, CEO   2574
WEISSMUELLER, Ryan J., CPA — President   1624
WEITZENHOFFER, Aaron Max — Theatrical Producer   1351
WEITZMANN, William Henry — Education Educator, Photographer   2574
WELCH, Arthur Stellhorn — Association Executive (Retired); Consultant   1625
WELCH, John Francis "Jack" Jr., PhD — Former Chairman, CEO   1352
WELCH, Peter Francis — U.S. Representative, Lawyer   2574
WELLING, Charles L.   1625
WELLMAN, Steve — Owner   2575
WELLON, Robert G. — Lawyer   1626
WELLS, Hugh, "Jack" S. — Owner   2575
WELLS, Murray B. — Senior Partner   2575
WELSER-MÖST, Franz — Music Director   2575
WEMLINGER, John V. — Author   1626
WENDER, Ira T. JD — Lawyer   2575
WENDT, Marilynn Suzann — Elementary School Educator, Principal   2575
WENDT, Vernon E., MD — Internist, Cardiologist   1353
WENNERSTEN, Mary Aileen — Special Education Educator (Retired)   2576
WENSTRUP, Brad Robert, DPM — U.S. Representative, Podiatrist   2576
WENTWORTH, Timothy C. — CEO, President   2576
WERNER, Mark H., MD — Neurologist, Researcher   1354
WERNIMONT, Nick — Founder, CEO   2576
WERT, Jacqueline Irene, MSW, LCSW — Private Practice/ Licensed Clinical Social Worker   1355
WERTHEIM, Mitzi — Professor   2576
WESSELS, Bruce — Materials Scientist, Educator   2576
WESSLER, Melvin — Farmer, Rancher   2576
WEST, Alvis H., PhD — Social Sciences Educator   2577
WEST, Beverly B., PhD, RN, CPN — Assistant Professor   2577
WEST, Douglas Xavier, PhD — Professor of Chemistry   1356
WEST, Kanye Omari — Rap Artist, Music Producer   2577
WESTBROOK, Russell III — Professional Basketball Player   2578
WESTERMAN, Bruce Eugene — U.S. Representative from Arkansas; Engineer   2578
WESTHEIMER, Ruth, "Dr. Ruth" — Sex Therapist, Media Personality   2578
WESTON, Janice Leah — Librarian   2579
WESTON, Randy Edward — Pianist, Composer   2579
WETTERBERG, Gary Bernard — International Forestry Support Program Manager (Retired)   1627
WETTSTEIN, Shannon — Experimental Classical Pianist   1357
WEXTON, Jennifer Lynn — U.S. Representative from Virginia   2579
WHAM, David Buffington — Secondary School Educator   2579
WHARFF, Sheryl   2580
WHARTON, Ralph Nathaniel, MD — Psychiatrist, Educator   2580
WHEALEY, Lois Deimel — Citizen Activist   1358
WHEALEY, Robert Howard, PhD — Historian   1359
WHEELER, Albin G. — Military Officer, Educator (Retired)   2580
WHEELER, Andrew R. — Administrator   2580
WHEELER, William Harold Jr. — Musical Director, Composer   2580
WHELAN, Melanie — Former CEO   2580
WHELESS, James W., BScPharm, MD, FAAP, FACP, FAAN, FAES — Neurologist   1360
WHITACRE, Eric — Composer, Conductor, Speaker   2581
WHITAKER, Forest Steven — Actor, Producer, Director   2582
WHITAKER, Laura Hope — Executive Director   2582
WHITAKER, Lori J. — President   1361
WHITAKER, William Scott — President   2582
WHITCHURCH, Ellwood Falvey — Certified Public Accountant, Business Executive   2582
WHITE, Betty — Actress, Comedienne   2582
WHITE, Candis Mary — Owner   2583

WHITE, Dana — President; Sports Association Executive 2583
WHITE, Hilary — Accountant 2584
WHITE, James P., JD — Law Educator 2584
WHITE, James, "Jim" Mackey — Management Consultant 2584
WHITE, Laura Katherine, CAPE, BAE, BA — Entrepreneur, Color and Image Consultant, Adapted Physical Educator 2584
WHITE, Miles D. — Chairman, CEO 2584
WHITE, Noel W. — President, CEO 1362
WHITE, Shaun Roger — Professional Snowboarder, Professional Skateboarder, Olympic Athlete 2585
WHITE, Stephen Halley — Biophysicist, Educator 1363
WHITE, Teresa, CFP — CEO, Owner 2585
WHITEHEAD, Colson — Novelist 2585
WHITEHEAD, Michael Anthony, DSc, PhD — Professor Emeritus 1364
WHITEHOUSE, C. Barton, EdD — Avionics & Aviation History instructor 1365
WHITEHOUSE, Sheldon — U.S. Senator, Lawyer 2585
WHITELAW, Dolores T. — Artist 1366
WHITESIDE, Hassan Niam — Professional Basketball Player 2585
WHITMAN, Margaret — CEO 2586
WHITMER, Gretchen Esther — Governor of Michigan 1368
WHITNEY, Ralph Roy Jr. — Partner; Director; Owner 1369
WHITNEY, Richard F. II — Senior Managing Director 2586
WHITSON, Peggy Annette — Astronaut 2586
WHITT, Michael, "Mike" D. — Program Manager 2586
WHITTEMORE, Anthony D., MD — Chief Medical Officer (Emeritus) 1370
WHITTEMORE, Ronald Clarence "Ron" — Senior Olympian; Computer Program Analyst 1371
WHITTINGHAM, M. Stanley, DPhil — Distinguished Professor 2587
WHITTINGHAM, Michael Stanley — Chemist 2587
WIBLE, James Oram — Chairman of the Board 2587
WICHMANN, David S. — CEO 2587
WICKER, Roger Frederick — U.S. Senator from Mississippi; Lawyer 2587
WICKHAM, William T., PhD — Management Educator and Consultant 2588
WIDMAN, Lorraine — Educator, Artist 2588
WIEBENGA, William Martin, PhD — College President 2588
WIEDEBUSCH, Mary Kathryne — Dancer 1372
WIEDEN, Dan G. — Co-founder 2588
WIEDENBACH, Maik — Owner, Founder 2589
WIEDLE, Gary Eugene — Real Estate Broker 1627
WIETING, William Frank, MD — Internist; Consultant 2589
WIGGINS, Andrew Christian — Basketball Player 2589
WILCOX, Dale Lee — Executive Director, General Counsel 1373
WILCOX, David Eric, MS, PE — Electrical Engineer, Educator, Consultant 1374
WILCOX, Roger — Psychologist, Researcher 1375
WILCZEK, Frank Anthony — Physics Professor 2590
WILD, Susan, "Ellis" Ellis — U.S. Representative from Pennsylvania; Lawyer 2590
WILDCRAFT, Marjory — CEO, President, Owner 1376
WILDENTHAL, Claud Kern — President Emeritus 2590
WILDER, Donny — Editor, Publisher, Owner 1377
WILDER, Raymond Leigh — Statistician; Consultant 1378
WILDRICK, Kenyon Jones — Minister Emeritus, Trustee 2590
WILEY, Janet May — Kitchen Staff Member 2591
WILEY, Myra H., BSN, RN, CD — Retired Mental Health Nurse; Retired Educator 2591
WILHELMY, Thomas — Attorney, Vice President 1379
WILKIE, Robert Leon Jr. — U.S. Secretary of Veterans Affairs 2591
WILKINSON, Edward Starsmeare Jr. — Retired 1628
WILKINSON, Robert Shaw Jr., MD, MACP — Physician/Professor Emeritus of Clinical Medicine 2591

WILL, Fritz G., PhD — Physical Chemist, Consultant 2592
WILLARD, Jack — Communications Executive 2592
WILLIAMS, Alfred B., PhD — Management Educator (Retired) 1380
WILLIAMS, Brian Douglas — Newscaster 2592
WILLIAMS, Constance — Former Senator of Pennsylvania 2592
WILLIAMS, Cory — CEO, Entrepreneur 1381
WILLIAMS, DeWayne A. — Artist 1382
WILLIAMS, Ebb Harry III — Lawyer 1383
WILLIAMS, Elizabeth A. — Financial Planner, Consultant 2592
WILLIAMS, Hank Jr. — Country Music Singer, Songwriter 2592
WILLIAMS, Hugh A. — Mechanical Engineer (Retired) 2593
WILLIAMS, James R., PhD — Principal Ergonomist 2593
WILLIAMS, John, "Roger" Roger — U.S. Representative from Texas 2593
WILLIAMS, Margaret LuWertha Hiett (Lary), DScN, RN-BC — Registered Nurse, Midland Democratic Party County Chair 2594
WILLIAMS, Michelle — Actress 2594
WILLIAMS, Richard L. 2595
WILLIAMS, Serena Jameka — Professional Tennis Player 2595
WILLIAMS, Terry — President 1628
WILLIAMS, Tonda — Entrepreneur, Consultant 1384
WILLIAMS, Vanessa L. — Actress; Recording Artist 2595
WILLIAMS, Vanessa Yvonne — Retired 2596
WILLIAMS, Venus — Professional Tennis Player 2596
WILLIAMSON, Zion Lateef — Professional Basketball Player 2596
WILLIS, Bruce — Actor 2596
WILLIS, John Osgood 2597
WILLIS-REICKERT, Susan — President (Retired) 2597
WILSON, Addison, "Joe" Graves Sr. — U.S. Representative from South Carolina 2597
WILSON, Bertina Iolia — Elementary Educator, School Administrator (Retired) 1629
WILSON, Bobby L., PhD — L. Lloyd Woods Distinguished Professor of Chemistry and Shell Oil Endowed Chaired Professor of Environmental Toxicology 1385
WILSON, Charles Lee — Professor Emeritus 2597
WILSON, Diane E. — Music Educator, Special Education Educator 2598
WILSON, Edward Osborne — Biologist, Researcher, Theorist 2598
WILSON, Frederica — U.S. Representative from Florida 2599
WILSON, Janet M. — Art Educator 2599
WILSON, Janice Crabtree, PhD — Vice President 1386
WILSON, Jeffrey D. — Supervisor 2599
WILSON, Jerry C. — Language Educator 2599
WILSON, John David — Founder, Chairman 1387
WILSON, Lorraine McCarty, PhD, RN — Professor Emerita 1388
WILSON, Paula J., DNM — President, Owner, Doctor 1389
WILSON, R. Marshall, PhD — Research Professor 1390
WILSON, Rebecca Ann — English, Special Education and Home Economics Educator (Retired) 2599
WILSON, Shelly L. — Managing Partner 2600
WILSON, Thomas Joseph II — Chairman, President, CEO 2600
WILSON, Thomas Matthew III — Of Counsel (Retired) 1391
WILT, Jeffrey L., MD — Pulmonary and Critical Care Physician, Educator 1392
WILTON, Elisabeth Starr, PhD — Management Consultant (Retired); Linguistic (Retired) 2600
WINDER, Cameron B., PhD — Member 2601
WINDERS, Monica — Channel Marketing Manager 2601
WINE, Jeff — CEO 1393
WINFREY, Oprah Gail — Broadcast Executive, Television Host, Producer 2601
WINGROVE, Philip C. — Aeronautical Engineer, Consultant 2602
WINKEL, Raymond Norman — Aerospace 1394

WINKLER, Dolores Eugenia — Health Facility Administrator 1395
WINKLER, Henry Franklin — Actor, Producer, Director 2602
WINKLER, Maria, PhD — Co-owner 2603
WINSLET, Kate — Actress 2603
WINSOR, Barbara Ann 2604
WINSTANLEY, Derek — Chief Emeritus, Illinois State Water Survey 1396
WINSTEAD, Daniel — Professor (Retired) 1629
WINSTON, Jane Kupfer, BFA — Secondary Education Educator; Artist 2604
WINTERLING, George Alfred — Meteorologist, Broadcaster 2604
WINTOUR, Anna, DBE — Editor 2604
WIRSCHING, Norbert Rolf — Electronics Company Executive (Retired) 1630
WIRTH, Michael K. — Chairman, CEO 2605
WISE, Joseph Stephen — Secondary Education Educator, Artist 1397
WISE, Patricia — Opera Performer, Concert Singer, Educator 2605
WISEMAN, Frank — Chemistry Professor 2605
WISHENGRAD, Marcia H. — Lawyer 1630
WISSNER, Annie — Vice President of Marketing 2605
WITCOFF, Sheldon W., Esq. — Lawyer 2605
WITHERSPOON, Reese — Actress, Producer, Entrepreneur 2605
WITMER, Aaron C. — Chief Operating Officer 1631
WITT, Katarina — Professional Figure Skater (Retired) 2606
WITTER, Debra — Partner 2606
WITTMAN, Robert, "Rob" Joseph, PhD — U.S. Representative from
    Virginia 2606
WITZEL, Maryalice, RN, BSN, MA — Paramedic Educator, Emergency
    Trauma Nurse 1631
WOELFEL, James A. — Engineering Executive, Chemist (Retired) 2606
WOJCICKI, Anne E. — Co-Founder,
    Genomics and Biotechnology Company Executive 1398
WOJCICKI, Susan Diane — Media Executive 2607
WOJCIECHOWSKI, Krzysztof, "Kris" Jan 2607
WOLBERS, Harry Lawrence, PhD — Engineering Psychologist (Retired) 2607
WOLBRINK, James Francis — Real Estate Investor 2607
WOLF, Chad F. — Acting U.S. Secretary 2608
WOLF, Chad — Vice President, Power Generation and Rental Solutions 2607
WOLF, Dale Edward, PhD — Former Governor of Delaware 1632
WOLF, James Richard — Association Executive 2608
WOLF, Joan — Ballet Educator 2608
WOLF, John Charles, PhD — Psychologist (Retired) 2608
WOLF, Lawrence Joseph — President Emeritus, Professor Emeritus;
    Distinguished Service Professor 2608
WOLF, Thomas, "Tom" Westerman, PhD — Governor of Pennsylvania 2609
WOLF, Walter — Computer Science Educator, Dean 2609
WOLFE, Julia — Composer 1399
WOLFE, Marcia Joanne — President 2609
WOLFE, Saul A. — Founding Member 2609
WOLFE, Tom Kennerly Jr. — Author, Journalist 2610
WOLFENBARGER, Debora — Technology Transfer Specialist 2610
WOLFF, Manfred P. "Fred", PhD — Geologist, Educator,
    Environmental Scientist 1400
WOLF-WILETS, Vivian C., PhD, RN — Clinical Nursing Educator 1401
WOMACK, Stephen, "Steve" Allen, — U.S. Representative,
    Former Mayor 2610
WONG, Chorng-Huey, PhD — Former Deputy Director of IMF Institute,
    International Monetary Fund 1402
WONG, Jen L. — Chief Operating Officer 2610
WONG, Sun Yet — Engineer, Consultant (Retired) 1403
WONG, Victor — Faculty 2610
WONHAM, Frederick S. — Trust Bank Executive, Investment Banking
    Executive 1404
WOO, Peng-Yung "吴本荣" — Electrical Engineering Educator and
    Researcher 1405

WOOD, Diane Pamela — Chief Judge 2610
WOOD, Virginia Elizabeth Jones, BS, MS, CRRN — Nursing Consultant
    (Retired) 2611
WOODALL, William, "Rob" Robert III — U.S. Representative 2611
WOODARD, Alfre — Actress 2611
WOODARD, Komozi, PhD — American History Educator 2611
WOODBURN, Charles Nicholas — CEO 2612
WOODS, Darren — Chairman, CEO 2612
WOODS, Tiger — Professional Golfer 2612
WOODWARD, Joanne — Actress, Producer, Philanthropist 2612
WOODWARD, Robert, "Bob" — Journalist, Editor 2613
WOODWARD, Roger — Professor 2613
WOOLRIDGE, Kay Ellen — Music Educator 1406
WOOTEN, Russell — Operations Research Specialist 2613
WORLDS, Annie Lois — Retired Educator, Retired Assistant Chief 2614
WORLEY, Lynn — IT Director, Licensed Practical Nurse 1632
WRAY, Christopher Asher — Director 2614
WREN, John D. — Chairman and CEO 2614
WREN, Robert James — Aerospace Engineering Manager 1407
WRIGHT, C.T. — Chairman (Appointed) 2615
WRIGHT, Dustin Arlie — Founder, Director, Lead Clinician 2615
WRIGHT, Kathleen Mary, MA, PhD — Psychologist 2615
WRIGHT, Katie Harper — Educational Administrator; Journalist 2615
WRIGHT, Letitia Michelle — Actress 2616
WRIGHT, Robin Gale — Actress, Producer, Director 2616
WRIGHT, Ronald, "Ron" Jack — U.S. Representative from Texas 2617
WRUCK, Erich-Oskar, PhD — Foreign Language Educator,
    Administrator (Retired) 1408
WU, Constance — Actress 2617
WURF, Mildred Kiefer — Executive (Retired) 2617
WURTH, Lynn Ruth — Advertising Executive 1409
WYDEN, Ronald, "Ron" Lee — U.S. Senator from Oregon 2617
WYNN, Aisha Corpas — President 2617
WYNN, Stanford Alan — Lawyer 2618
WYSS, Halina — Associate Professor 1633
XIE, Rui-Hua, PhD — Physicist, Researcher, Engineer 2618
XIONG, Pahoua Zuagpaaj Moua — Manager 2618
XU, Tony — Co-Founder, CEO 2619
YAKATAN, Gerald Joseph, PhD — Chairman, CEO 1410
YAMAUCHI, Edwin M., PhD — History Professor Emeritus 2619
YANCEY, Richard Charles — Investment Banker (Retired) 1411
YANG, Andrew — Entrepreneur, Philanthropist; Lawyer 1412
YANGA, Ismael Duran — Surgeon, Primary Care Physician 1413
YARATHA, Sridhar, MD — Psychiatrist 2619
YARBOROUGH, William Caleb — Race Car Driver (Retired) 2619
YARBROUGH, David Wylie, PhD, PE — Vice President; Professor
    Emeritus 2620
YARBROUGH, Rose Marie Powers Somraty — Geologist, Environmental
    Science Secondary Teacher, Software Programmer Analyst 2620
YARMUTH, John Allan — U.S. Representative from Kentucky; Former
    Newspaper Editor 2620
YEAGER, Chuck — Air Force General (Retired) 2620
YEARWOOD, Trisha — Country Music Singer, Songwriter 2621
YEH, Hsi-Han, PhD — Senior Electronics Engineer (Retired) 2621
YELICH, Christian Stephen — Professional Baseball Player 2621
YERGLER, Marilyn Elaine — Nurse (Retired) 2621
YI, Xiaobin, MD, MBA — Associate Professor, Director of Pain 2622
YOHO, Theodore Scott, DVM — U.S. Representative from Florida;
    Veterinarian 2622
YOKEN, Mel B. — Professor 2622
YOKLEY, Richard Clarence — Protective Services Official 2623
YONTS, Brent — State Legislator 1414

YORK, Jonathon C. — Professor of Government — 1415
YORKE, Thom Edward — Singer, Songwriter — 2623
YOST, Richard — Founder, CEO — 1416
YOUNG, Allen Marcus, PhD — Museum Curator and Administrator, Educator, Naturalist — 2623
YOUNG, Andre (Dr. Dre) — Entrepreneur, Record Producer, Rapper — 2624
YOUNG, Andrew Jackson Jr. — Consulting Firm Executive; Former Mayor; Former U.S. Representative from Georgia; Pastor — 2624
YOUNG, Donald Edwin — U.S. Representative from Alaska — 2624
YOUNG, Gary A. — Vocational/Economic Expert — 2625
YOUNG, John Leonard Michael, MD — Psychiatrist, Educator — 2625
YOUNG, Neil — Singer-Songwriter, Guitarist — 2625
YOUNG, Sara — OB/GYN Clinical Nurse Specialist/IBCLC — 1417
YOUNG, Stuart — Allergist, Immunologist, Medical Legal Consultant — 1633
YOUNG, Susan Eileen — Elementary School Educator (Retired) — 2626
YOUNG, Todd Christopher — U.S. Senator from Indiana — 2626
YOUNG, Virgil M., EdD — Education Educator — 1418
YUN, Juliana Inkyung, DDS — Periodontist — 2626
YURKO, Sandra R. — Technologist (Retired) — 2626
ZABORSZKY, Laszlo — Neuroscientist, Distinguished Professor — 2626
ZAIM, Semih — Chemical Company Executive — 2627
ZAKARIA, Fareed Rafiq — Journalist, Political Scientist, Author — 2627
ZAMORA, Maria — Owner — 2627
ZANGER, Larry — Partner — 2627
ZATAR, Wael — Dean, J. H. Distinguished Engineering Chair, Interim Chair — 1419
ZAVALA, Albert, PhD — Psychologist — 2627
ZEEUW, Christine Elizabeth De — Electrical Engineer — 295
ZEHR, Eldon Irvin — Science Educator, Plant Pathologist — 2628
ZEID, Brian D., MBA, MOS — Accountant — 2628
ZELDIN, Lee Michael — U.S. Representative from New York; Lawyer — 2628
ZELLWEGER, Renée — Actress, Producer — 1420
ZEMIALKOWSKI, Walter Jr. — Airport Consultant — 1421
ZES, Tikey A. — Music Minister — 1422
ZETA-JONES, Catherine — Actress — 2628
ZHANG, Xiao-Feng, — President — 2628
ZHAO, Jian, "Jim", MD, PhD, MBA, FCAP — Physician — 2629
ZICCARDI, Anthony — Founder — 1634
ZIEGERT, Susan H. — Educator — 2629
ZIEGLER, Henry Steinway, Esq. — Partner — 1423
ZIEGLER, James R. — Senior Systems Analyst — 2629
ZIEGLER, John A., PhD — Historian, Political Scientist, Educator — 2629
ZIGERELLI, Lawrence, "Larry" J. — President, CEO — 2630
ZIL, J.S., MD, JD — Forensic Specialist; Psychiatrist; Educator — 2630
ZIMMERMAN, Elaine — Policy Leader and Analyst; Psychotherapist; Poet — 2630
ZIMMERMANN, Muriel Madeline — Biology Professor (Retired), Dean (Retired) — 2631
ZIMMERMANN, Robert L. — Senior Research Manager (Retired) — 2631
ZIMMERMANN, Thomas Callander Price, PhD — Historian, Educator (Retired) — 1424
ZINSMEISTER, Louann, PhD, RN, CNE — Director of Graduate Nursing Program, Professor of Nursing — 2632
ZJAWIONY, Jordan Kordian — Professor — 2632
ZLATOFF-MIRSKY, Everett Igor — Violinist — 1425
ZOLL, Stanley, "Stan" Philip — Trustee — 2632
ZOLOTO, Jerrold Albert, PhD — Psychologist, Consultant — 2633
ZOPF, Paul E. PhD — Dana Professor Emeritus — 2633
ZUBCEVIC, Irena, OISC/DESA — Chief of Branch DESA — 1426
ZUBRETSKY, Joseph M. — CEO, President — 2633
ZUCCHERO, Michael, PE, CFM, LEED — Executive Managing Director — 2633
ZUCKER, Howard Alan, MD, JD — Commissioner — 2633

ZUCKER, Jeffrey A. — Broadcast Executive — 2634
ZUCKERBERG, Mark Elliot — Co-Founder, Chairman, CEO — 1427
ZUCKERMAN, Gordon Nathaniel — President — 1428
ZUHDI, Nabil, "Bill", JD — Lawyer, Litigator, Film and Concert Executive — 2634
ZURLO, Eugene, "Gene" John — Founder, Chairman, Partner — 2634
ZWECK, Ruth Edna Feeney, BSN, MS — Human Services Administrator, Psychiatric Nurse — 2634
ZWEDEN, Jaap van — Music Director — 1302
ZWEIDLER, Alfred — Doctor of Natural Philosophy, Biomedical Scientist, Educator (Retired) — 1429